# Hoover's Handbook of

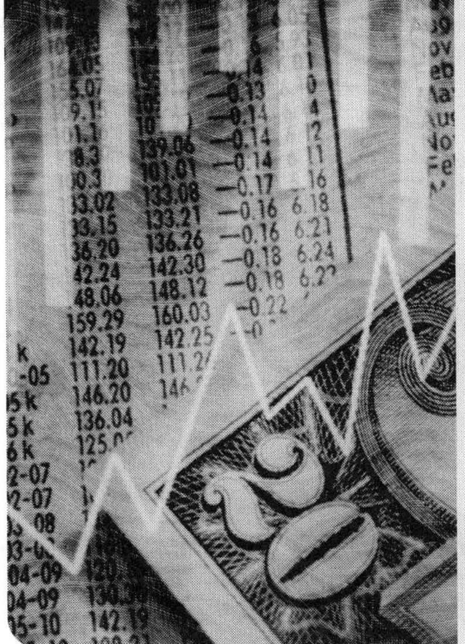

# American Business 2008

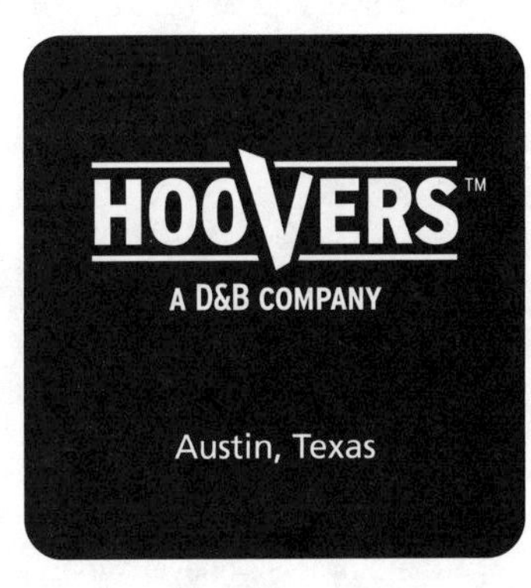

The financial data (Historical Financials sections) in this book are from a variety of sources. EDGAR Online provided selected data for the Historical Financials sections of publicly traded companies. For private companies and for historical information on public companies prior to their becoming public, we obtained information directly from the companies or from trade sources deemed to be reliable. Hoover's, Inc., is solely responsible for the presentation of all data.

10 9 8 7 6 5 4 3 2 1

Publishers Cataloging-in-Publication Data

Hoover's Handbook of American Business 2008

Includes indexes.

ISBN: 978-1-57311-120-1

ISSN 1055-7202

1. Business enterprises — Directories. 2. Corporations — Directories.

HF3010 338.7

Hoover's Company Information is also available on the Internet at Hoover's Online (www.hoovers.com). A catalog of Hoover's products is available on the Internet at www.hooversbooks.com.

The Hoover's Handbook series is produced for Hoover's Business Press by:

Sycamore Productions, Inc.
5808 Balcones Drive, Suite 205
Austin, Texas 78731
info@syprod.com

Cover design is by John Baker. Electronic prepress and printing are by R.R. Donnelley, Owensville, Missouri.

**U.S. AND WORLD BOOK SALES**

Hoover's, Inc.
5800 Airport Blvd.
Austin, TX 78752
Phone: 512-374-4500
Fax: 512-374-4538
e-mail: orders@hoovers.com
Web: www.hooversbooks.com

**EUROPEAN BOOK SALES**

William Snyder Publishing Associates
5 Five Mile Drive
Oxford OX2 8HT
England
Phone & fax: +44-186-551-3186
e-mail: snyderpub@aol.com

### ABOUT HOOVER'S, INC. – THE BUSINESS INFORMATION AUTHORITY℠

Hoover's, a D&B company, gives its customers a competitive edge with insightful information about industries, companies, and key decision makers. Hoover's provides this updated information for sales, marketing, business development, and other professionals who need intelligence on U.S. and global companies, industries, and the people who lead them. This information, along with powerful tools to search, sort, download, and integrate the content, is available through Hoover's (www.hoovers.com), the company's premier online service. Hoover's business information is also available through corporate intranets and distribution agreements with licensees, as well as via Hoover's books. The company is headquartered in Austin, Texas.

# Abbreviations

**AFL-CIO** – American Federation of Labor and Congress of Industrial Organizations
**AMA** – American Medical Association
**AMEX** – American Stock Exchange
**ARM** – adjustable-rate mortgage
**ASP** – application services provider
**ATM** – asynchronous transfer mode
**ATM** – automated teller machine
**CAD/CAM** – computer-aided design/ computer-aided manufacturing
**CD-ROM** – compact disc – read-only memory
**CD-R** – CD-recordable
**CEO** – chief executive officer
**CFO** – chief financial officer
**CMOS** – complimentary metal oxide silicon
**COO** – chief operating officer
**DAT** – digital audiotape
**DOD** – Department of Defense
**DOE** – Department of Energy
**DOS** – disk operating system
**DOT** – Department of Transportation
**DRAM** – dynamic random-access memory
**DSL** – digital subscriber line
**DVD** – digital versatile disc/digital video disc
**DVD-R** – DVD-recordable
**EPA** – Environmental Protection Agency
**EPROM** – erasable programmable read-only memory
**EPS** – earnings per share
**ESOP** – employee stock ownership plan
**EU** – European Union
**EVP** – executive vice president
**FCC** – Federal Communications Commission
**FDA** – Food and Drug Administration
**FDIC** – Federal Deposit Insurance Corporation
**FTC** – Federal Trade Commission
**FTP** – file transfer protocol
**GATT** – General Agreement on Tariffs and Trade
**GDP** – gross domestic product
**HMO** – health maintenance organization
**HR** – human resources
**HTML** – hypertext markup language
**ICC** – Interstate Commerce Commission
**IPO** – initial public offering
**IRS** – Internal Revenue Service
**ISP** – Internet service provider
**kWh** – kilowatt-hour
**LAN** – local-area network
**LBO** – leveraged buyout
**LCD** – liquid crystal display
**LNG** – liquefied natural gas
**LP** – limited partnership
**Ltd.** – limited
**mips** – millions of instructions per second
**MW** – megawatt
**NAFTA** – North American Free Trade Agreement
**NASA** – National Aeronautics and Space Administration
**NASDAQ** – National Association of Securities Dealers Automated Quotations
**NATO** – North Atlantic Treaty Organization
**NYSE** – New York Stock Exchange
**OCR** – optical character recognition
**OECD** – Organization for Economic Cooperation and Development
**OEM** – original equipment manufacturer
**OPEC** – Organization of Petroleum Exporting Countries
**OS** – operating system
**OSHA** – Occupational Safety and Health Administration
**OTC** – over-the-counter
**PBX** – private branch exchange
**PCMCIA** – Personal Computer Memory Card International Association
**P/E** – price to earnings ratio
**RAID** – redundant array of independent disks
**RAM** – random-access memory
**R&D** – research and development
**RBOC** – regional Bell operating company
**RISC** – reduced instruction set computer
**REIT** – real estate investment trust
**ROA** – return on assets
**ROE** – return on equity
**ROI** – return on investment
**ROM** – read-only memory
**S&L** – savings and loan
**SCSI** – Small Computer System Interface
**SEC** – Securities and Exchange Commission
**SEVP** – senior executive vice president
**SIC** – Standard Industrial Classification
**SOC** – system on a chip
**SVP** – senior vice president
**USB** – universal serial bus
**VAR** – value-added reseller
**VAT** – value-added tax
**VC** – venture capitalist
**VoIP** – Voice over Internet Protocol
**VP** – vice president
**WAN** – wide-area network
**WWW** – World Wide Web

## Contents

# List of Lists

## HOOVER'S RANKINGS



## THE BIGGEST AND THE RICHEST



## MEDIA



## RETAIL



## LEGAL, BUSINESS, AND FINANCIAL SERVICES



## THE WORKPLACE

# Companies Profiled

## Companies Profiled (continued)

## Companies Profiled (continued)

## Companies Profiled (continued)

# About Hoover's Handbook of American Business 2008

Things aren't always what they seem, or so the events in the world appear to suggest; as a result, fact-finding and digging for information have become incredibly valuable skills. When it's information about companies you need, we believe that Hoover's Business Press is the place to turn. For our Hoover's Handbooks series of guides to businesses, we've done the sorting and sifting of information, leaving you with the facts you need to make the important decisions you face.

This 18th edition of *Hoover's Handbook of American Business,* as it has throughout its history, stands as one of America's premier sources of business information, packed with the information you need.

*Hoover's Handbook of American Business* is the first of our four-title series of handbooks that covers, literally, the world of business. The series is available as an indexed set, and also includes *Hoover's Handbook of World Business, Hoover's Handbook of Private Companies,* and *Hoover's Handbook of Emerging Companies*. This series brings you information on the biggest, fastest-growing, and most influential enterprises in the world.

**HOOVER'S ONLINE FOR BUSINESS NEEDS**

In addition to the 2,550 companies featured in our handbooks, comprehensive coverage of more than 40,000 business enterprises is available in electronic format on our Web site, Hoover's Online (www.hoovers.com). Our goal is to provide one site that offers authoritative, updated intelligence on US and global companies, industries, and the people who shape them. Hoover's has partnered with other prestigious business information and service providers to bring you all the right business information, services, and links in one place.

We welcome the recognition we have received as the premier provider of high-quality company information — online, electronically, and in print — and continue to look for ways to make our products more available and more useful to you.

We believe that anyone who buys from, sells to, invests in, lends to, competes with, interviews with, or works for a company should know all there is to know about that enterprise. Taken together, this book and the other Hoover's products and resources represent the most complete source of basic corporate information readily available to the general public.

This latest version of *Hoover's Handbook of American Business* contains, as always, profiles of the largest and most influential companies in the United States. Each of the companies profiled here was chosen because of its important role in American business. For more details on how these companies were selected, see the section titled "Using Hoover's Handbooks."

**HOW TO USE THIS BOOK**

This book has four sections:

1. "Using Hoover's Handbooks" describes the contents of our profiles and explains the ways in which we gather and compile our data.
2. "A List-Lover's Compendium" contains lists of the largest, smallest, best, most, and other superlatives related to companies involved in American business.
3. The company profiles section makes up the largest and most important part of the book — 750 profiles of major US enterprises.
4. Three indexes complete the book. The first sorts companies by industry groups, the second by headquarters location. The third index is a list of all the executives found in the Executives section of each company profile.

As always, we hope you find our books useful. We invite your comments via phone (512-374-4500), fax (512-374-4538), mail (5800 Airport Boulevard, Austin, Texas 78752), or e-mail (custsupport@hoovers.com).

The Editors,
Austin, Texas,
October 2007

# Using Hoover's Handbooks

## SELECTION OF THE COMPANIES PROFILED

The 750 enterprises profiled in this book include the largest and most influential companies in America. Among them are:

- more than 680 publicly held companies, from 3M to Zale
- more than 40 large private companies (such as Cargill and Mars)
- several mutual and cooperative organizations (such as USAA and Ace Hardware)
- a selection of other enterprises (such as Kaiser Foundation Health Plan, the United States Postal Service, and the TVA) that we believe are sufficiently large and influential enough to warrant inclusion.

In selecting these companies, our foremost question was "What companies will our readers be most interested in?" Our goal was to answer as many questions as we could in one book — in effect, trying to anticipate your curiosity. This approach resulted in four general selection criteria for including companies in the book:

**1. Size.** The 500 or so largest American companies, measured by sales and by number of employees, are included in the book. In general, these companies have sales in excess of $2 billion, and they are the ones you will have heard of and the ones you will want to know about. These are the companies at the top of the *FORTUNE*, *Forbes*, and *Business Week* lists. We have made sure to include the top private companies in this number.

**2. Growth.** We believe that relatively few readers will be going to work for, or investing in, the railroad industry. Therefore, only a few railroads are in the book. On the other hand, we have included a number of technology firms, as well as companies that provide medical products and services — pharmaceutical and biotech companies, health care insurers, and medical device makers.

**3. Visibility.** Most readers will have heard of the Hilton Hotels and Wm. Wrigley companies. Their service or consumer natures make them household names, even though they are not among the corporate giants in terms of sales and employment.

**4. Breadth of coverage.** To show the diversity of economic activity, we've included, among others, a professional sports team, one ranch, the Big Four accounting firms, and one of the largest law firms in the US. We feel that these businesses are important enough to enjoy at least "token" representation. While we might not emphasize certain industries, the industry leaders are present.

## ORGANIZATION

The profiles are presented in alphabetical order. This alphabetization is generally word by word, which means that Legg Mason precedes Leggett & Platt. You will find the commonly used name of the enterprise at the beginning of the profile; the full, legal name is found in the Locations section. If a company name is also a person's name, like Walt Disney, it will be alphabetized under the first name; if the company name starts with initials, like J. C. Penney or H.J. Heinz, look for it under the combined initials (in the above examples, JC and HJ, respectively). Basic financial data is listed under the heading Historical Financials; also included is the exchange on which the company's stock is traded if it is public, the ticker symbol used by the stock exchange, and the company's fiscal year-end.

The annual financial information contained in the profiles is current through fiscal year-ends occurring as late as May 2007. We have included certain nonfinancial developments, such as officer changes, through September 2007.

## OVERVIEW

In the first section of the profile, we have tried to give a thumbnail description of the company and what it does. The description will usually include information on the company's strategy, reputation, and ownership. We recommend that you read this section first.

## HISTORY

This extended section reflects our belief that every enterprise is the sum of its history and that you have to know where you came from in order to know where you are going. While some companies have limited historical awareness and were unable to help us much and other companies are just plain boring, we think the vast majority of the enterprises in this book have colorful backgrounds. We have tried to focus on the people who made the enterprises what they are today. We have found these histories to be full of twists and ironies; they make fascinating reading.

## EXECUTIVES

Here we list the names of the people who run the company, insofar as space allows. In the case of public companies, we have shown the ages and pay of key officers. In some cases the published data is for the previous year although the company has announced promotions or retirements since year-end. The pay represents cash compensation, including bonuses, but excludes stock options.

Although companies are free to structure their management titles any way they please, most modern corporations follow standard practices. The ultimate power in any corporation lies with the shareholders, who elect a board of directors, usually including officers or "insiders" as well as individuals from outside the company. The chief officer, the person on whose desk the buck stops, is usually called the chief executive officer (CEO). Often, he or she is also the chairman of the board.

As corporate management has become more complex, it is common for the CEO to have a "right-hand person" who oversees the day-to-day operations of the company, allowing the CEO plenty of time to focus on strategy and long-term issues. This right-hand person is usually designated the chief operating officer (COO) and is often the president of the company. In other cases one person is both chairman and president.

A multitude of other titles exists, including chief financial officer (CFO), chief administrative officer, and vice chairman. We have always tried to include the CFO, the chief legal officer, and the chief human resources or personnel officer. Our best advice is that officers' pay levels are clear indicators of who the board of directors thinks are the most important members of the management team.

The people named in the Executives section are indexed at the back of the book.

The Executives section also includes the name of the company's auditing (accounting) firm, where available.

#### LOCATIONS

Here we include the company's full legal name and its headquarters, street address, telephone and fax numbers, and Web site, as available. The back of the book includes an index of companies by headquarters locations.

In some cases we have also included information on the geographic distribution of the company's business, including sales and profit data. Note that these profit numbers, like those in the Products/Operations section below, are usually operating or pretax profits rather than net profits. Operating profits are generally those before financing costs (interest income and payments) and before taxes, which are considered costs attributable to the whole company rather than to one division or part of the world. For this reason the net income figures (in the Historical Financials section) are usually much lower, since they are after interest and taxes. Pretax profits are after interest but before taxes.

Headquarters for companies that are incorporated in Bermuda, but whose operational headquarters are in the US, are listed under their US address.

#### PRODUCTS/OPERATIONS

This section lists as many of the company's products, services, brand names, divisions, subsidiaries, and joint ventures as we could fit. We have tried to include all its major lines and all familiar brand names. The nature of this section varies by company and the amount of information available. If the company publishes sales and profit information by type of business, we have included it.

#### COMPETITORS

In this section we have listed companies that compete with the profiled company. This feature is included as a quick way to locate similar companies and compare them. The universe of competitors includes all public companies and all private companies with sales in excess of $500 million. In a few instances we have identified smaller private companies as key competitors.

#### HISTORICAL FINANCIALS

Here we have tried to present as much data about each enterprise's financial performance as we could compile in the allocated space. The information varies somewhat from industry to industry and is less complete in the case of private companies that do not release data (although we have always tried to provide annual sales and employment). There are a few industries, venture capital and investment banking, for example, for which revenue numbers are unavailable as a rule.

The following information is generally present.

A 5-year table, with relevant annualized compound growth rates, covers:

- Sales — fiscal year sales (year-end assets for most financial companies)
- Net income — fiscal year net income (before accounting changes)
- Net profit margin — fiscal year net income as a percent of sales (as a percent of assets for most financial firms)
- Employees — fiscal year-end or average number of employees
- Stock price — the fiscal year close
- P/E — high and low price/earnings ratio
- Earnings per share — fiscal year earnings per share (EPS)
- Dividends per share — fiscal year dividends per share
- Book value per share — fiscal year-end book value (common shareholders' equity per share)

The information on the number of employees is intended to aid the reader interested in knowing whether a company has a long-term trend of increasing or decreasing employment. As far as we know, we are the only company that publishes this information in print format.

The numbers on the left in each row of the Historical Financials section give the month and the year in which the company's fiscal year actually ends. Thus, a company with a March 31, 2007, year-end is shown as 3/07.

In addition, we have provided in graph form a stock price history for most public companies. The graphs, covering up to 5 years, show the range of trading between the high and the low price, as well as the closing price for each fiscal year. Generally, for private companies, we have graphed net income, or, if that is unavailable, sales.

Key year-end statistics in this section generally show the financial strength of the enterprise, including:

- Debt ratio (long-term debt as a percent of shareholders' equity)
- Return on equity (net income divided by the average of beginning and ending common shareholders' equity)
- Cash and cash equivalents
- Current ratio (ratio of current assets to current liabilities)
- Total long-term debt (including capital lease obligations)
- Number of shares of common stock outstanding
- Dividend yield (fiscal year dividends per share divided by the fiscal year-end closing stock price)
- Dividend payout (fiscal year dividends divided by fiscal year EPS)
- Market value at fiscal year-end (fiscal year-end closing stock price multiplied by fiscal year-end number of shares outstanding)

Per share data has been adjusted for stock splits. The data for public companies has been provided to us by EDGAR Online. Other public company information was compiled by Hoover's, which takes full responsibility for the content of this section.

In the case of private companies that do not publicly disclose financial information, we usually did not have access to such standardized data. We have gathered estimates of sales and other statistics from numerous sources.

# Hoover's Handbook of

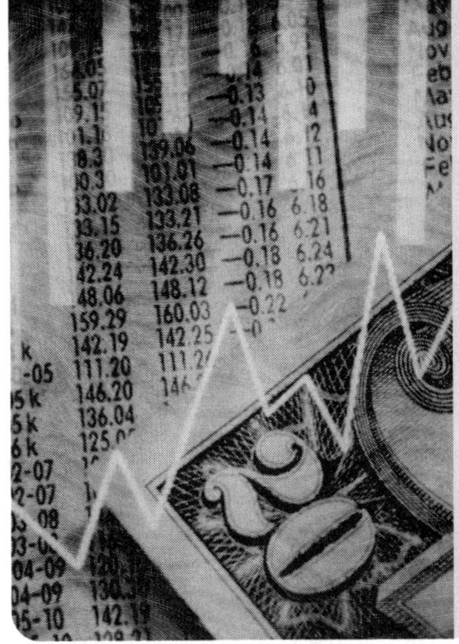

# American Business

## A List-Lover's Compendium

## The 300 Largest Companies by Sales in *Hoover's Handbook of American Business 2008*

| Rank | Company | Sales ($ mil.) |
|---|---|---|
| 1 | Exxon Mobil | 377,635 |
| 2 | Wal-Mart Stores | 348,650 |
| 3 | Chevron Corporation | 210,118 |
| 4 | General Motors | 207,349 |
| 5 | ConocoPhillips | 188,523 |
| 6 | General Electric | 163,391 |
| 7 | Ford Motor | 160,123 |
| 8 | Citigroup | 146,558 |
| 9 | Bank of America | 117,017 |
| 10 | American International Group | 113,194 |
| 11 | Altria Group | 101,407 |
| 12 | JPMorgan Chase | 99,845 |
| 13 | Berkshire Hathaway | 98,539 |
| 14 | McKesson Corporation | 92,977 |
| 15 | Valero Energy | 91,833 |
| 16 | Hewlett-Packard | 91,658 |
| 17 | International Business Machines | 91,424 |
| 18 | Home Depot | 90,837 |
| 19 | Koch Industries | 90,000 |
| 20 | Verizon Communications | 88,144 |
| 21 | Cardinal Health | 81,364 |
| 22 | Morgan Stanley | 76,551 |
| 23 | Procter & Gamble | 76,476 |
| 24 | Cargill, Incorporated | 75,208 |
| 25 | United States Postal Service | 72,650 |
| 26 | UnitedHealth Group | 71,542 |
| 27 | Merrill Lynch | 70,591 |
| 28 | Goldman Sachs | 69,353 |
| 29 | The Kroger Co. | 66,111 |
| 30 | Marathon Oil | 65,449 |
| 31 | AT&T Inc. | 63,055 |
| 32 | The Boeing Company | 61,530 |
| 33 | AmerisourceBergen | 61,203 |
| 34 | State Farm Mutual | 60,500 |
| 35 | Costco Wholesale | 60,151 |
| 36 | Target Corporation | 59,490 |
| 37 | Chrysler LLC | 58,622 |
| 38 | WellPoint, Inc. | 56,953 |
| 39 | Dell Inc. | 55,908 |
| 40 | Johnson & Johnson | 53,324 |
| 41 | Microsoft Corporation | 51,122 |
| 42 | Fannie Mae | 50,149 |
| 43 | Dow Chemical | 49,124 |
| 44 | MetLife, Inc. | 48,396 |
| 45 | Pfizer Inc. | 48,371 |
| 46 | Wells Fargo | 47,998 |
| 47 | United Technologies | 47,829 |
| 48 | United Parcel Service | 47,547 |
| 49 | Walgreen Co. | 47,409 |
| 50 | Lowe's Companies | 46,927 |
| 51 | Wachovia Corporation | 46,810 |
| 52 | Lehman Brothers Holdings | 46,709 |
| 53 | Time Warner | 44,224 |
| 54 | CVS/Caremark | 43,814 |
| 55 | Freddie Mac | 43,087 |
| 56 | Motorola, Inc. | 42,879 |
| 57 | Medco Health Solutions | 42,544 |
| 58 | Caterpillar Inc. | 41,517 |
| 59 | Sprint Nextel | 41,028 |
| 60 | Safeway Inc. | 40,185 |
| 61 | Lockheed Martin | 39,620 |
| 62 | Sunoco, Inc. | 38,715 |
| 63 | SUPERVALU INC. | 37,406 |
| 64 | Archer Daniels Midland | 36,596 |
| 65 | Best Buy | 35,934 |
| 66 | Allstate Corporation | 35,796 |
| 67 | Intel Corporation | 35,382 |
| 68 | FedEx Corporation | 35,214 |
| 69 | PepsiCo | 35,137 |
| 70 | SYSCO Corporation | 35,042 |
| 71 | Kaiser Foundation Health Plan | 34,400 |
| 72 | Kraft Foods | 34,356 |
| 73 | Walt Disney | 34,285 |
| 74 | Prudential Financial | 32,488 |
| 75 | Johnson Controls | 32,235 |
| 76 | Honeywell International | 31,367 |
| 77 | Ingram Micro | 31,358 |
| 78 | Alcoa Inc. | 30,379 |
| 79 | Northrop Grumman | 30,148 |
| 80 | Sears, Roebuck | 30,030 |
| 81 | E. I. duPont de Nemours | 28,982 |
| 82 | Hess Corporation | 28,720 |
| 83 | Cisco Systems | 28,484 |
| 84 | American Express | 27,136 |
| 85 | Macy's, Inc. | 26,970 |
| 86 | Hartford Financial Services Group | 26,500 |
| 87 | Washington Mutual | 26,454 |
| 88 | Delphi Corporation | 26,392 |
| 89 | Tyson Foods | 25,559 |
| 90 | HCA Inc. | 25,477 |
| 91 | News Corporation | 25,327 |
| 92 | Aetna Inc. | 25,146 |
| 93 | The Travelers Companies | 25,090 |
| 94 | Comcast Corporation | 24,966 |
| 95 | Countrywide Financial | 24,877 |
| 96 | Coca-Cola | 24,088 |
| 97 | General Dynamics | 24,063 |
| 98 | Liberty Mutual | 23,520 |
| 99 | 3M Company | 22,923 |
| 100 | Merck | 22,636 |
| 101 | Halliburton Company | 22,576 |
| 102 | AMR Corporation | 22,563 |
| 103 | Abbott Laboratories | 22,476 |
| 104 | Plains All American Pipeline | 22,444 |
| 105 | Nationwide Mutual Insurance | 22,253 |
| 106 | Deere & Company | 22,148 |
| 107 | International Paper | 21,995 |
| 108 | PricewaterhouseCoopers | 21,986 |
| 109 | Weyerhaeuser Company | 21,896 |
| 110 | Publix Super Markets | 21,820 |
| 111 | McDonald's | 21,586 |
| 112 | Tech Data | 21,440 |
| 113 | Humana Inc. | 21,417 |
| 114 | Electronic Data Systems | 21,268 |
| 115 | Mars, Incorporated | 21,000 |
| 116 | New York Life Insurance | 20,980 |
| 117 | Carlson Wagonlit Travel | 20,500 |
| 118 | Bechtel Group | 20,500 |
| 119 | Wyeth | 20,351 |
| 120 | Raytheon Company | 20,291 |
| 121 | Goodyear Tire & Rubber | 20,258 |
| 122 | Emerson Electric | 20,133 |
| 123 | Deloitte Touche Tohmatsu | 20,000 |
| 124 | J. C. Penney | 19,903 |
| 125 | Coca-Cola Enterprises | 19,804 |
| 126 | Northwestern Mutual Life Insurance | 19,733 |
| 127 | UAL Corporation | 19,340 |
| 128 | Apple Inc. | 19,315 |
| 129 | Constellation Energy Group | 19,285 |
| 130 | Schlumberger Limited | 19,231 |
| 131 | U.S. Bancorp | 19,109 |
| 132 | AutoNation | 18,989 |
| 133 | Kmart Corporation | 18,647 |
| 134 | Ernst & Young International | 18,400 |
| 135 | Accenture Ltd | 18,228 |
| 136 | Staples, Inc. | 18,161 |
| 137 | Occidental Petroleum | 18,160 |
| 138 | Tesoro Corporation | 18,104 |
| 139 | Whirlpool Corporation | 18,080 |
| 140 | Massachusetts Mutual Life Insurance | 18,020 |
| 141 | Oracle Corporation | 17,996 |
| 142 | Bristol-Myers Squibb | 17,914 |
| 143 | Loews Corporation | 17,911 |
| 144 | Lear Corporation | 17,839 |
| 145 | Express Scripts | 17,660 |
| 146 | Manpower Inc. | 17,563 |
| 147 | Rite Aid | 17,508 |
| 148 | TJX Companies | 17,405 |
| 149 | Delta Air Lines | 17,171 |
| 150 | KPMG International | 16,880 |

SOURCE: HOOVER'S, INC., DATABASE, AUGUST 2007

## The 300 Largest Companies by Sales in *Hoover's Handbook of American Business 2008* (continued)

| Rank | Company | Sales ($ mil.) |
|---|---|---|
| 151 | Kimberly-Clark | 16,747 |
| 152 | Bear Stearns | 16,551 |
| 153 | CIGNA Corporation | 16,547 |
| 154 | Dominion Resources | 16,482 |
| 155 | PACCAR Inc | 16,454 |
| 156 | NIKE, Inc. | 16,326 |
| 157 | Lennar Corporation | 16,267 |
| 158 | The Gap Inc. | 15,943 |
| 159 | Xerox Corporation | 15,895 |
| 160 | Anheuser-Busch | 15,717 |
| 161 | United States Steel | 15,715 |
| 162 | FPL Group | 15,710 |
| 163 | Eli Lilly | 15,691 |
| 164 | Exelon Corporation | 15,655 |
| 165 | Union Pacific | 15,578 |
| 166 | Kohl's Corporation | 15,544 |
| 167 | Capital One Financial | 15,191 |
| 168 | Duke Energy | 15,184 |
| 169 | D.R. Horton | 15,051 |
| 170 | Office Depot | 15,011 |
| 171 | Burlington Northern Santa Fe | 14,985 |
| 172 | Computer Sciences | 14,857 |
| 173 | The Progressive Corporation | 14,786 |
| 174 | The DIRECTV Group | 14,756 |
| 175 | Nucor Corporation | 14,751 |
| 176 | ABC, Inc. | 14,638 |
| 177 | Aflac Incorporated | 14,616 |
| 178 | CHS Inc. | 14,384 |
| 179 | Southern Company | 14,356 |
| 180 | CBS Corporation | 14,320 |
| 181 | Pulte Homes | 14,274 |
| 182 | Amgen Inc. | 14,268 |
| 183 | Texas Instruments | 14,255 |
| 184 | Avnet, Inc. | 14,254 |
| 185 | Fluor Corporation | 14,079 |
| 186 | Illinois Tool Works | 14,055 |
| 187 | The Chubb Corporation | 14,003 |
| 188 | Qwest Communications | 13,923 |
| 189 | Sun Microsystems | 13,873 |
| 190 | Arrow Electronics | 13,577 |
| 191 | USAA | 13,416 |
| 192 | Waste Management | 13,363 |
| 193 | SunTrust Banks | 13,311 |
| 194 | Eastman Kodak | 13,274 |
| 195 | Cox Enterprises | 13,200 |
| 196 | Continental Airlines | 13,128 |
| 197 | National City | 12,953 |
| 198 | Health Net | 12,908 |
| 199 | Masco Corporation | 12,778 |
| 200 | Pepsi Bottling Group | 12,730 |

| Rank | Company | Sales ($ mil.) |
|---|---|---|
| 201 | Edison International | 12,622 |
| 202 | American Electric Power | 12,622 |
| 203 | Northwest Airlines | 12,568 |
| 204 | PG&E Corporation | 12,539 |
| 205 | L-3 Communications | 12,477 |
| 206 | General Mills | 12,442 |
| 207 | Circuit City Stores | 12,430 |
| 208 | TIAA-CREF | 12,378 |
| 209 | Eaton Corporation | 12,370 |
| 210 | AES Corporation | 12,299 |
| 211 | Medtronic, Inc. | 12,299 |
| 212 | Sara Lee | 12,278 |
| 213 | Colgate-Palmolive | 12,238 |
| 214 | Fox Entertainment Group | 12,175 |
| 215 | Public Service Enterprise Group | 12,164 |
| 216 | Marriott International | 12,160 |
| 217 | Consolidated Edison | 12,137 |
| 218 | ConAgra Foods | 12,028 |
| 219 | Centex Corporation | 12,015 |
| 220 | Marsh & McLennan | 11,921 |
| 221 | Smithfield Foods | 11,911 |
| 222 | ONEOK, Inc. | 11,896 |
| 223 | Carnival Corporation | 11,839 |
| 224 | Williams Companies | 11,813 |
| 225 | Sempra Energy | 11,761 |
| 226 | ARAMARK Corporation | 11,621 |
| 227 | US Airways Group | 11,557 |
| 228 | FirstEnergy Corp. | 11,501 |
| 229 | Textron Inc. | 11,490 |
| 230 | Ingersoll-Rand | 11,409 |
| 231 | Omnicom Group | 11,377 |
| 232 | Cummins, Inc. | 11,362 |
| 233 | Seagate Technology | 11,360 |
| 234 | American Standard | 11,208 |
| 235 | EMC Corporation | 11,155 |
| 236 | PNC Financial Services Group | 11,146 |
| 237 | Highmark Inc. | 11,084 |
| 238 | PPG Industries | 11,037 |
| 239 | KB Home | 11,004 |
| 240 | Sanmina-SCI | 10,955 |
| 241 | Entergy Corporation | 10,932 |
| 242 | Kellogg Company | 10,907 |
| 243 | World Fuel Services | 10,785 |
| 244 | Parker Hannifin | 10,718 |
| 245 | Amazon.com | 10,711 |
| 246 | Limited Brands | 10,671 |
| 247 | Google Inc. | 10,605 |
| 248 | Schering-Plough | 10,594 |
| 249 | Devon Energy | 10,578 |
| 250 | Unum Group | 10,535 |

| Rank | Company | Sales ($ mil.) |
|---|---|---|
| 251 | Genuine Parts | 10,458 |
| 252 | Trump Organization | 10,400 |
| 253 | Baxter International | 10,378 |
| 254 | CNA Financial | 10,376 |
| 255 | Jabil Circuit | 10,266 |
| 256 | Anadarko Petroleum | 10,187 |
| 257 | Dean Foods | 10,099 |
| 258 | YRC Worldwide | 9,919 |
| 259 | Principal Financial Group | 9,871 |
| 260 | Xcel Energy | 9,840 |
| 261 | EchoStar Communications | 9,819 |
| 262 | Danaher Corporation | 9,596 |
| 263 | Progress Energy | 9,570 |
| 264 | CSX Corporation | 9,566 |
| 265 | YUM! Brands | 9,561 |
| 266 | State Street | 9,525 |
| 267 | BB&T Corporation | 9,487 |
| 268 | Norfolk Southern | 9,407 |
| 269 | CenterPoint Energy | 9,319 |
| 270 | R. R. Donnelley & Sons | 9,317 |
| 271 | Genentech, Inc. | 9,284 |
| 272 | FMR Corp. | 9,200 |
| 273 | ArvinMeritor | 9,195 |
| 274 | Tennessee Valley Authority | 9,185 |
| 275 | Applied Materials | 9,167 |
| 276 | Southwest Airlines | 9,086 |
| 277 | Lincoln National | 9,063 |
| 278 | Bank of New York Mellon | 9,062 |
| 279 | Baker Hughes | 9,027 |
| 280 | DTE Energy | 9,022 |
| 281 | H. J. Heinz | 9,002 |
| 282 | OfficeMax | 8,966 |
| 283 | Aon Corporation | 8,954 |
| 284 | Automatic Data Processing | 8,882 |
| 285 | Air Products and Chemicals | 8,850 |
| 286 | Fortune Brands | 8,769 |
| 287 | Avon Products | 8,764 |
| 288 | Tenet Healthcare | 8,701 |
| 289 | Liberty Media | 8,613 |
| 290 | Nordstrom, Inc. | 8,561 |
| 291 | Reynolds American | 8,510 |
| 292 | First American | 8,499 |
| 293 | BJ's Wholesale Club | 8,480 |
| 294 | Fifth Third Bancorp | 8,472 |
| 295 | Praxair, Inc. | 8,324 |
| 296 | SAIC, Inc. | 8,294 |
| 297 | Apache Corporation | 8,289 |
| 298 | Rohm and Haas | 8,230 |
| 299 | Hilton Hotels | 8,162 |
| 300 | Hertz Global Holdings | 8,058 |

## The 300 Most Profitable Companies in *Hoover's Handbook of American Business 2008*

| Rank | Company | Net Income ($ mil.) |
|---|---|---|
| 1 | Exxon Mobil | 39,500 |
| 2 | Citigroup | 21,538 |
| 3 | Bank of America | 21,133 |
| 4 | General Electric | 20,829 |
| 5 | Pfizer Inc. | 19,337 |
| 6 | Chevron Corporation | 17,138 |
| 7 | ConocoPhillips | 15,550 |
| 8 | JPMorgan Chase | 14,444 |
| 9 | Microsoft Corporation | 14,065 |
| 10 | American International Group | 14,048 |
| 11 | Altria Group | 12,022 |
| 12 | Wal-Mart Stores | 11,284 |
| 13 | Johnson & Johnson | 11,053 |
| 14 | Berkshire Hathaway | 11,015 |
| 15 | Procter & Gamble | 10,340 |
| 16 | Goldman Sachs | 9,537 |
| 17 | International Business Machines | 9,492 |
| 18 | Wells Fargo | 8,482 |
| 19 | Wachovia Corporation | 7,791 |
| 20 | Merrill Lynch | 7,499 |
| 21 | Morgan Stanley | 7,472 |
| 22 | AT&T Inc. | 7,356 |
| 23 | Time Warner | 6,552 |
| 24 | Fannie Mae | 6,347 |
| 25 | MetLife, Inc. | 6,293 |
| 26 | Hewlett-Packard | 6,198 |
| 27 | Verizon Communications | 6,197 |
| 28 | Home Depot | 5,761 |
| 29 | PepsiCo | 5,642 |
| 30 | Cisco Systems | 5,580 |
| 31 | Valero Energy | 5,463 |
| 32 | Marathon Oil | 5,234 |
| 33 | Coca-Cola | 5,080 |
| 34 | Intel Corporation | 5,044 |
| 35 | Allstate Corporation | 4,993 |
| 36 | Anadarko Petroleum | 4,854 |
| 37 | U.S. Bancorp | 4,751 |
| 38 | Merck | 4,434 |
| 39 | Texas Instruments | 4,341 |
| 40 | Oracle Corporation | 4,274 |
| 41 | The Travelers Companies | 4,208 |
| 42 | United Parcel Service | 4,202 |
| 43 | Wyeth | 4,197 |
| 44 | Occidental Petroleum | 4,182 |
| 45 | UnitedHealth Group | 4,159 |
| 46 | Lehman Brothers Holdings | 4,007 |
| 47 | 3M Company | 3,851 |
| 48 | United Technologies | 3,732 |
| 49 | Dow Chemical | 3,724 |
| 50 | Schlumberger Limited | 3,710 |
| 51 | American Express | 3,707 |
| 52 | Motorola, Inc. | 3,661 |
| 53 | Dell Inc. | 3,572 |
| 54 | Washington Mutual | 3,558 |
| 55 | McDonald's | 3,544 |
| 56 | Caterpillar Inc. | 3,537 |
| 57 | TIAA-CREF | 3,453 |
| 58 | Prudential Financial | 3,428 |
| 59 | Walt Disney | 3,374 |
| 60 | Agilent Technologies | 3,307 |
| 61 | E. I. duPont de Nemours | 3,148 |
| 62 | Lowe's Companies | 3,105 |
| 63 | WellPoint, Inc. | 3,095 |
| 64 | Google Inc. | 3,077 |
| 65 | Kraft Foods | 3,060 |
| 66 | Bank of New York Mellon | 3,011 |
| 67 | Amgen Inc. | 2,950 |
| 68 | Devon Energy | 2,846 |
| 69 | Chrysler LLC | 2,805 |
| 70 | Medtronic, Inc. | 2,802 |
| 71 | Target Corporation | 2,787 |
| 72 | Hartford Financial Services Group | 2,745 |
| 73 | Countrywide Financial | 2,675 |
| 74 | Eli Lilly | 2,663 |
| 75 | PNC Financial Services Group | 2,595 |
| 76 | Apache Corporation | 2,552 |
| 77 | Comcast Corporation | 2,533 |
| 78 | Lockheed Martin | 2,529 |
| 79 | The Chubb Corporation | 2,528 |
| 80 | Loews Corporation | 2,491 |
| 81 | QUALCOMM Incorporated | 2,470 |
| 82 | Baker Hughes | 2,419 |
| 83 | Capital One Financial | 2,415 |
| 84 | Halliburton Company | 2,348 |
| 85 | USAA | 2,330 |
| 86 | News Corporation | 2,314 |
| 87 | National City | 2,300 |
| 88 | New York Life Insurance | 2,298 |
| 89 | Carnival Corporation | 2,279 |
| 90 | Alcoa Inc. | 2,248 |
| 91 | The Boeing Company | 2,215 |
| 92 | Freddie Mac | 2,211 |
| 93 | SunTrust Banks | 2,118 |
| 94 | Nationwide Mutual Insurance | 2,113 |
| 95 | Genentech, Inc. | 2,113 |
| 96 | Honeywell International | 2,083 |
| 97 | Bear Stearns | 2,054 |
| 98 | FedEx Corporation | 2,016 |
| 99 | Chesapeake Energy | 2,003 |
| 100 | Apple Inc. | 1,989 |
| 101 | Anheuser-Busch | 1,965 |
| 102 | Hess Corporation | 1,916 |
| 103 | Burlington Northern Santa Fe | 1,887 |
| 104 | Duke Energy | 1,863 |
| 105 | General Dynamics | 1,856 |
| 106 | Corning Incorporated | 1,855 |
| 107 | Emerson Electric | 1,845 |
| 108 | Nucor Corporation | 1,758 |
| 109 | Walgreen Co. | 1,751 |
| 110 | Illinois Tool Works | 1,718 |
| 111 | Abbott Laboratories | 1,717 |
| 112 | Aetna Inc. | 1,702 |
| 113 | Deere & Company | 1,694 |
| 114 | CBS Corporation | 1,661 |
| 115 | The Progressive Corporation | 1,648 |
| 116 | Liberty Mutual | 1,626 |
| 117 | Union Pacific | 1,606 |
| 118 | Exelon Corporation | 1,592 |
| 119 | Bristol-Myers Squibb | 1,585 |
| 120 | Southern Company | 1,573 |
| 121 | Automatic Data Processing | 1,554 |
| 122 | Northrop Grumman | 1,542 |
| 123 | Cargill, Incorporated | 1,537 |
| 124 | BB&T Corporation | 1,528 |
| 125 | Applied Materials | 1,517 |
| 126 | Kimberly-Clark | 1,500 |
| 127 | PACCAR Inc | 1,496 |
| 128 | NIKE, Inc. | 1,492 |
| 129 | Aflac Incorporated | 1,483 |
| 130 | Norfolk Southern | 1,481 |
| 131 | Freeport-McMoRan Copper & Gold | 1,457 |
| 132 | The DIRECTV Group | 1,420 |
| 133 | Sempra Energy | 1,406 |
| 134 | Baxter International | 1,397 |
| 135 | Transocean Inc. | 1,385 |
| 136 | Dominion Resources | 1,380 |
| 137 | Best Buy | 1,377 |
| 138 | United States Steel | 1,374 |
| 139 | CVS/Caremark | 1,369 |
| 140 | Colgate-Palmolive | 1,353 |
| 141 | Regions Financial | 1,353 |
| 142 | Fox Entertainment Group | 1,353 |
| 143 | Sprint Nextel | 1,329 |
| 144 | Lincoln National | 1,316 |
| 145 | Archer Daniels Midland | 1,312 |
| 146 | CSX Corporation | 1,310 |
| 147 | EOG Resources | 1,300 |
| 148 | Raytheon Company | 1,283 |
| 149 | FPL Group | 1,281 |
| 150 | Franklin Resources | 1,268 |

SOURCE: HOOVER'S, INC., DATABASE, AUGUST 2007

## The 300 Most Profitable Companies in *Hoover's Handbook of American Business 2008* (continued)

| Rank | Company | Net Income ($ mil.) |
|---|---|---|
| 151 | FirstEnergy Corp. | 1,254 |
| 152 | D.R. Horton | 1,233 |
| 153 | Charles Schwab | 1,227 |
| 154 | EMC Corporation | 1,224 |
| 155 | Reynolds American | 1,210 |
| 156 | Xerox Corporation | 1,210 |
| 157 | Fifth Third Bancorp | 1,188 |
| 158 | Edison International | 1,181 |
| 159 | Gannett Co. | 1,161 |
| 160 | CIGNA Corporation | 1,155 |
| 161 | J. C. Penney | 1,153 |
| 162 | Waste Management | 1,149 |
| 163 | General Mills | 1,144 |
| 164 | Schering-Plough | 1,143 |
| 165 | Entergy Corporation | 1,133 |
| 166 | eBay Inc. | 1,126 |
| 167 | Danaher Corporation | 1,122 |
| 168 | The Kroger Co. | 1,115 |
| 169 | KKR & Co. | 1,113 |
| 170 | Kohl's Corporation | 1,109 |
| 171 | CNA Financial | 1,108 |
| 172 | State Street | 1,106 |
| 173 | Costco Wholesale | 1,103 |
| 174 | Publix Super Markets | 1,097 |
| 175 | Principal Financial Group | 1,064 |
| 176 | KeyCorp | 1,055 |
| 177 | International Paper | 1,050 |
| 178 | CIT Group | 1,046 |
| 179 | Harley-Davidson | 1,043 |
| 180 | Starwood Hotels & Resorts | 1,043 |
| 181 | HCA Inc. | 1,036 |
| 182 | Ingersoll-Rand | 1,033 |
| 183 | Johnson Controls | 1,028 |
| 184 | Kellogg Company | 1,004 |
| 185 | American Electric Power | 1,002 |
| 186 | SYSCO Corporation | 1,001 |
| 187 | Cardinal Health | 1,000 |
| 188 | Macy's, Inc. | 995 |
| 189 | PG&E Corporation | 991 |
| 190 | Marsh & McLennan | 990 |
| 191 | Praxair, Inc. | 988 |
| 192 | Sunoco, Inc. | 979 |
| 193 | Staples, Inc. | 974 |
| 194 | Accenture Ltd | 973 |
| 195 | Eaton Corporation | 950 |
| 196 | Constellation Energy Group | 936 |
| 197 | Cincinnati Financial | 930 |
| 198 | Seagate Technology | 913 |
| 199 | McKesson Corporation | 913 |
| 200 | FMR Corp. | 908 |
| 201 | Weatherford International | 896 |
| 202 | Comerica Incorporated | 893 |
| 203 | McGraw-Hill | 882 |
| 204 | Safeco Corporation | 880 |
| 205 | Ambac Financial Group | 876 |
| 206 | Safeway Inc. | 871 |
| 207 | PPL Corporation | 865 |
| 208 | Omnicom Group | 864 |
| 209 | Liberty Media | 840 |
| 210 | Fortune Brands | 830 |
| 211 | Parker Hannifin | 830 |
| 212 | Northwestern Mutual Life Insurance | 829 |
| 213 | YUM! Brands | 824 |
| 214 | MBIA Inc. | 819 |
| 215 | Massachusetts Mutual Life Insurance | 810 |
| 216 | BJ Services | 805 |
| 217 | Tesoro Corporation | 801 |
| 218 | Newmont Mining | 791 |
| 219 | H. J. Heinz | 786 |
| 220 | The Gap Inc. | 778 |
| 221 | ENSCO International | 770 |
| 222 | Campbell Soup | 766 |
| 223 | ConAgra Foods | 765 |
| 224 | Becton, Dickinson | 752 |
| 225 | Yahoo! Inc. | 751 |
| 226 | Pioneer Natural Resources | 740 |
| 227 | Public Service Enterprise Group | 739 |
| 228 | TJX Companies | 738 |
| 229 | Consolidated Edison | 737 |
| 230 | Rohm and Haas | 735 |
| 231 | Noble Corporation | 732 |
| 232 | Air Products and Chemicals | 723 |
| 233 | Aon Corporation | 720 |
| 234 | Cummins, Inc. | 715 |
| 235 | PPG Industries | 711 |
| 236 | Diamond Offshore Drilling | 707 |
| 237 | Monsanto Company | 689 |
| 238 | Pulte Homes | 688 |
| 239 | Toll Brothers | 687 |
| 240 | Nordstrom, Inc. | 678 |
| 241 | Limited Brands | 676 |
| 242 | Northern Trust | 665 |
| 243 | MGM MIRAGE | 648 |
| 244 | Legg Mason | 647 |
| 245 | Royal Caribbean Cruises | 634 |
| 246 | Precision Castparts | 633 |
| 247 | Medco Health Solutions | 630 |
| 248 | E*TRADE Financial | 629 |
| 249 | Synovus Financial | 617 |
| 250 | EchoStar Communications | 608 |
| 251 | Marriott International | 608 |
| 252 | Rockwell Automation | 607 |
| 253 | Textron Inc. | 601 |
| 254 | Bed Bath & Beyond | 594 |
| 255 | Lennar Corporation | 594 |
| 256 | Qwest Communications | 593 |
| 257 | Mattel, Inc. | 593 |
| 258 | NVR, Inc. | 587 |
| 259 | The Brink's Company | 587 |
| 260 | Quest Diagnostics | 586 |
| 261 | Zions Bancorporation | 583 |
| 262 | ITT Corporation | 581 |
| 263 | Sherwin-Williams | 576 |
| 264 | Hilton Hotels | 572 |
| 265 | Allegheny Technologies | 572 |
| 266 | Xcel Energy | 572 |
| 267 | Progress Energy | 571 |
| 268 | AutoZone | 569 |
| 269 | Starbucks | 564 |
| 270 | Western Digital | 564 |
| 271 | Simon Property Group | 564 |
| 272 | Dover Corporation | 562 |
| 273 | The Hershey Company | 559 |
| 274 | Analog Devices | 550 |
| 275 | St. Jude Medical | 548 |
| 276 | Ameren Corporation | 547 |
| 277 | American Standard | 541 |
| 278 | VF Corporation | 534 |
| 279 | T. Rowe Price Group | 530 |
| 280 | Wm. Wrigley Jr. | 529 |
| 281 | KLA-Tencor | 528 |
| 282 | TD Ameritrade | 527 |
| 283 | L-3 Communications | 526 |
| 284 | Pepsi Bottling Group | 522 |
| 285 | Torchmark Corporation | 519 |
| 286 | Office Depot | 516 |
| 287 | Paychex, Inc. | 516 |
| 288 | UST Inc. | 506 |
| 289 | Adobe Systems | 506 |
| 290 | Sara Lee | 504 |
| 291 | Southwest Airlines | 499 |
| 292 | CHS Inc. | 490 |
| 293 | Masco Corporation | 488 |
| 294 | Humana Inc. | 487 |
| 295 | Black & Decker | 486 |
| 296 | KB Home | 482 |
| 297 | Goodrich Corporation | 482 |
| 298 | Harris Corporation | 480 |
| 299 | Avon Products | 478 |
| 300 | Genuine Parts | 475 |

## The 300 Most Valuable Public Companies in *Hoover's Handbook of American Business 2008*

| Rank | Company | Market Value* ($ mil.) |
|---|---|---|
| 1 | Exxon Mobil | 439,013 |
| 2 | General Electric | 382,421 |
| 3 | Microsoft Corporation | 276,429 |
| 4 | Citigroup | 273,598 |
| 5 | Bank of America | 238,021 |
| 6 | AT&T Inc. | 223,035 |
| 7 | Wal-Mart Stores | 197,007 |
| 8 | Procter & Gamble | 191,641 |
| 9 | Johnson & Johnson | 191,011 |
| 10 | American International Group | 186,402 |
| 11 | Pfizer Inc. | 184,512 |
| 12 | JPMorgan Chase | 167,199 |
| 13 | Chevron Corporation | 159,160 |
| 14 | International Business Machines | 146,355 |
| 15 | Altria Group | 137,587 |
| 16 | Berkshire Hathaway | 122,922 |
| 17 | ConocoPhillips | 121,627 |
| 18 | Wells Fargo | 120,091 |
| 19 | Intel Corporation | 116,762 |
| 20 | Coca-Cola | 111,844 |
| 21 | Cisco Systems | 110,198 |
| 22 | Wachovia Corporation | 108,433 |
| 23 | Verizon Communications | 108,424 |
| 24 | Hewlett-Packard | 105,839 |
| 25 | Google Inc. | 104,837 |
| 26 | PepsiCo | 102,457 |
| 27 | Oracle Corporation | 98,974 |
| 28 | Merck | 94,515 |
| 29 | The Boeing Company | 89,929 |
| 30 | Genentech, Inc. | 85,430 |
| 31 | Time Warner | 84,158 |
| 32 | Goldman Sachs | 83,193 |
| 33 | Merrill Lynch | 80,502 |
| 34 | Amgen Inc. | 79,649 |
| 35 | Home Depot | 78,682 |
| 36 | Abbott Laboratories | 74,879 |
| 37 | Schlumberger Limited | 74,396 |
| 38 | American Express | 72,743 |
| 39 | UnitedHealth Group | 72,267 |
| 40 | Wyeth | 68,500 |
| 41 | Dell Inc. | 68,176 |
| 42 | Morgan Stanley | 67,559 |
| 43 | Apple Inc. | 65,838 |
| 44 | U.S. Bancorp | 63,865 |
| 45 | Walt Disney | 63,685 |
| 46 | QUALCOMM Incorporated | 62,545 |
| 47 | United Technologies | 62,251 |
| 48 | Medtronic, Inc. | 61,287 |
| 49 | Eli Lilly | 58,960 |
| 50 | Comcast Corporation | 58,143 |
| 51 | 3M Company | 57,229 |
| 52 | Sprint Nextel | 54,724 |
| 53 | Publix Super Markets | 53,784 |
| 54 | McDonald's | 53,360 |
| 55 | Target Corporation | 53,332 |
| 56 | Lowe's Companies | 52,079 |
| 57 | Bristol-Myers Squibb | 51,640 |
| 58 | United Parcel Service | 50,162 |
| 59 | Walgreen Co. | 49,849 |
| 60 | Motorola, Inc. | 49,291 |
| 61 | WellPoint, Inc. | 48,434 |
| 62 | Fannie Mae | 47,372 |
| 63 | E. I. duPont de Nemours | 44,914 |
| 64 | MetLife, Inc. | 44,375 |
| 65 | Washington Mutual | 42,964 |
| 66 | Occidental Petroleum | 42,515 |
| 67 | Texas Instruments | 41,761 |
| 68 | News Corporation | 41,605 |
| 69 | Exelon Corporation | 41,466 |
| 70 | eBay Inc. | 41,151 |
| 71 | Allstate Corporation | 40,498 |
| 72 | Prudential Financial | 40,449 |
| 73 | Caterpillar Inc. | 39,607 |
| 74 | Lehman Brothers Holdings | 39,293 |
| 75 | Lockheed Martin | 38,761 |
| 76 | Dow Chemical | 38,226 |
| 77 | Anheuser-Busch | 37,534 |
| 78 | The Travelers Companies | 36,418 |
| 79 | Honeywell International | 36,219 |
| 80 | Schering-Plough | 35,153 |
| 81 | Yahoo! Inc. | 34,741 |
| 82 | FedEx Corporation | 34,379 |
| 83 | Colgate-Palmolive | 33,446 |
| 84 | Capital One Financial | 31,490 |
| 85 | Halliburton Company | 30,988 |
| 86 | Kimberly-Clark | 30,958 |
| 87 | Valero Energy | 30,889 |
| 88 | The DIRECTV Group | 30,589 |
| 89 | Carnival Corporation | 30,521 |
| 90 | Baxter International | 30,176 |
| 91 | General Dynamics | 30,171 |
| 92 | Hartford Financial Services Group | 30,169 |
| 93 | Aflac Incorporated | 30,163 |
| 94 | SunTrust Banks | 29,972 |
| 95 | Devon Energy | 29,785 |
| 96 | Corning Incorporated | 29,281 |
| 97 | Dominion Resources | 29,260 |
| 98 | EMC Corporation | 28,015 |
| 99 | Southern Company | 27,512 |
| 100 | Regions Financial | 27,305 |
| 101 | Archer Daniels Midland | 27,067 |
| 102 | Franklin Resources | 26,781 |
| 103 | Cardinal Health | 26,427 |
| 104 | Burlington Northern Santa Fe | 26,415 |
| 105 | Alcoa Inc. | 26,095 |
| 106 | Illinois Tool Works | 25,812 |
| 107 | Monsanto Company | 25,768 |
| 108 | Starbucks | 25,703 |
| 109 | CVS/Caremark | 25,524 |
| 110 | Boston Scientific | 25,335 |
| 111 | Duke Energy | 25,142 |
| 112 | Union Pacific | 24,861 |
| 113 | Countrywide Financial | 24,841 |
| 114 | Charles Schwab | 24,469 |
| 115 | McGraw-Hill | 24,076 |
| 116 | Applied Materials | 24,021 |
| 117 | Baker Hughes | 23,884 |
| 118 | BB&T Corporation | 23,787 |
| 119 | Transocean Inc. | 23,657 |
| 120 | Adobe Systems | 23,643 |
| 121 | Raytheon Company | 23,542 |
| 122 | Kohl's Corporation | 23,480 |
| 123 | Northrop Grumman | 23,419 |
| 124 | Automatic Data Processing | 23,198 |
| 125 | National City | 23,120 |
| 126 | Simon Property Group | 22,871 |
| 127 | Fifth Third Bancorp | 22,767 |
| 128 | Loews Corporation | 22,568 |
| 129 | State Street | 22,420 |
| 130 | Danaher Corporation | 22,329 |
| 131 | Aetna Inc. | 22,281 |
| 132 | Best Buy | 22,278 |
| 133 | CBS Corporation | 22,041 |
| 134 | FPL Group | 22,040 |
| 135 | Apache Corporation | 21,997 |
| 136 | Costco Wholesale | 21,889 |
| 137 | NIKE, Inc. | 21,798 |
| 138 | The Chubb Corporation | 21,761 |
| 139 | PNC Financial Services Group | 21,694 |
| 140 | Freeport-McMoRan Copper & Gold | 21,226 |
| 141 | General Mills | 20,451 |
| 142 | Anadarko Petroleum | 20,324 |
| 143 | SYSCO Corporation | 20,185 |
| 144 | Safeway Inc. | 20,131 |
| 145 | Fortune Brands | 20,058 |
| 146 | Norfolk Southern | 19,986 |
| 147 | Kellogg Company | 19,909 |
| 148 | Waste Management | 19,624 |
| 149 | Reynolds American | 19,355 |
| 150 | Deere & Company | 19,344 |

*Market value at the latest available fiscal year-end

SOURCE: HOOVER'S, INC., DATABASE, AUGUST 2007

## The 300 Most Valuable Public Companies in *Hoover's Handbook of American Business 2008* (continued)

| Rank | Company | Market Value ($ mil.) |
|---|---|---|
| 151 | FirstEnergy Corp. | 19,248 |
| 152 | Newmont Mining | 19,087 |
| 153 | Praxair, Inc. | 19,037 |
| 154 | Staples, Inc. | 19,010 |
| 155 | Sun Microsystems | 18,947 |
| 156 | Thermo Fisher Scientific | 18,868 |
| 157 | Entergy Corporation | 18,710 |
| 158 | Marriott International | 18,587 |
| 159 | Lincoln National | 18,310 |
| 160 | Allergan, Inc. | 18,233 |
| 161 | The Kroger Co. | 18,224 |
| 162 | Harley-Davidson | 18,185 |
| 163 | The Progressive Corporation | 18,117 |
| 164 | Bear Stearns | 17,903 |
| 165 | PG&E Corporation | 17,645 |
| 166 | General Motors | 17,377 |
| 167 | Becton, Dickinson | 17,347 |
| 168 | McKesson Corporation | 17,269 |
| 169 | Accenture Ltd | 17,220 |
| 170 | Marsh & McLennan | 16,922 |
| 171 | American Electric Power | 16,890 |
| 172 | Emerson Electric | 16,870 |
| 173 | Public Service Enterprise Group | 16,771 |
| 174 | Weyerhaeuser Company | 16,723 |
| 175 | Nucor Corporation | 16,450 |
| 176 | Forest Laboratories | 16,438 |
| 177 | Amazon.com | 16,336 |
| 178 | MGM MIRAGE | 16,282 |
| 179 | Kraft Foods | 16,278 |
| 180 | Office Depot | 16,267 |
| 181 | Genzyme Corporation | 16,197 |
| 182 | PACCAR Inc | 16,128 |
| 183 | Marathon Oil | 16,084 |
| 184 | Xerox Corporation | 16,038 |
| 185 | Qwest Communications | 15,908 |
| 186 | The Gap Inc. | 15,846 |
| 187 | Principal Financial Group | 15,755 |
| 188 | Electronic Arts | 15,662 |
| 189 | Hess Corporation | 15,615 |
| 190 | Williams Companies | 15,596 |
| 191 | Symantec Corporation | 15,560 |
| 192 | International Paper | 15,464 |
| 193 | Paychex, Inc. | 15,439 |
| 194 | Medco Health Solutions | 15,415 |
| 195 | Broadcom Corporation | 15,300 |
| 196 | EOG Resources | 15,221 |
| 197 | NYSE Euronext | 15,195 |
| 198 | KeyCorp | 15,180 |
| 199 | CSX Corporation | 15,072 |
| 200 | H. J. Heinz | 14,998 |
| 201 | Gilead Sciences | 14,970 |
| 202 | Edison International | 14,818 |
| 203 | Campbell Soup | 14,782 |
| 204 | Sempra Energy | 14,682 |
| 205 | AES Corporation | 14,659 |
| 206 | Nordstrom, Inc. | 14,585 |
| 207 | Avon Products | 14,581 |
| 208 | Air Products and Chemicals | 14,419 |
| 209 | Precision Castparts | 14,277 |
| 210 | Weatherford International | 14,200 |
| 211 | Gannett Co. | 14,193 |
| 212 | Electronic Data Systems | 14,169 |
| 213 | Johnson Controls | 14,045 |
| 214 | Network Appliance | 13,877 |
| 215 | International Game Technology | 13,869 |
| 216 | Agilent Technologies | 13,831 |
| 217 | PPL Corporation | 13,798 |
| 218 | Ford Motor | 13,796 |
| 219 | CA, Inc. | 13,607 |
| 220 | Hilton Hotels | 13,506 |
| 221 | TJX Companies | 13,383 |
| 222 | Starwood Hotels & Resorts | 13,343 |
| 223 | Chesapeake Energy | 13,288 |
| 224 | Northern Trust | 13,273 |
| 225 | Liberty Media | 13,179 |
| 226 | Micron Technology | 12,950 |
| 227 | St. Jude Medical | 12,940 |
| 228 | Sara Lee | 12,605 |
| 229 | ConAgra Foods | 12,568 |
| 230 | Progress Energy | 12,564 |
| 231 | Vulcan Materials | 12,555 |
| 232 | Constellation Energy Group | 12,432 |
| 233 | Legg Mason | 12,220 |
| 234 | Ingersoll-Rand | 12,004 |
| 235 | Southwest Airlines | 12,000 |
| 236 | Textron Inc. | 11,777 |
| 237 | Seagate Technology | 11,647 |
| 238 | T. Rowe Price Group | 11,597 |
| 239 | Masco Corporation | 11,467 |
| 240 | TD Ameritrade | 11,454 |
| 241 | Parker Hannifin | 11,373 |
| 242 | Limited Brands | 11,367 |
| 243 | Ecolab Inc. | 11,360 |
| 244 | NVIDIA Corporation | 11,360 |
| 245 | Consolidated Edison | 11,260 |
| 246 | Rohm and Haas | 11,187 |
| 247 | Wm. Wrigley Jr. | 11,135 |
| 248 | Advanced Micro Devices | 11,131 |
| 249 | Ameren Corporation | 11,101 |
| 250 | CIT Group | 11,059 |
| 251 | Eaton Corporation | 10,985 |
| 252 | Bed Bath & Beyond | 10,958 |
| 253 | CNA Financial | 10,931 |
| 254 | El Paso Corporation | 10,652 |
| 255 | Analog Devices | 10,646 |
| 256 | Intuit Inc. | 10,625 |
| 257 | Aon Corporation | 10,545 |
| 258 | PPG Industries | 10,536 |
| 259 | KLA-Tencor | 10,515 |
| 260 | ITT Corporation | 10,399 |
| 261 | Diamond Offshore Drilling | 10,330 |
| 262 | Quest Diagnostics | 10,279 |
| 263 | Noble Corporation | 10,249 |
| 264 | L-3 Communications | 10,242 |
| 265 | Pitney Bowes | 10,190 |
| 266 | Autodesk, Inc. | 10,104 |
| 267 | Synovus Financial | 10,069 |
| 268 | Dover Corporation | 10,016 |
| 269 | IAC/InterActiveCorp | 9,930 |
| 270 | Rockwell Automation | 9,923 |
| 271 | H&R Block | 9,853 |
| 272 | MBIA Inc. | 9,851 |
| 273 | Coca-Cola Enterprises | 9,795 |
| 274 | SanDisk Corporation | 9,747 |
| 275 | Ambac Financial Group | 9,726 |
| 276 | E*TRADE Financial | 9,558 |
| 277 | Xcel Energy | 9,392 |
| 278 | UST Inc. | 9,347 |
| 279 | Comerica Incorporated | 9,246 |
| 280 | The Clorox Company | 9,225 |
| 281 | Humana Inc. | 9,217 |
| 282 | VF Corporation | 9,208 |
| 283 | Allegheny Technologies | 9,177 |
| 284 | Computer Sciences | 9,035 |
| 285 | Fiserv, Inc. | 8,969 |
| 286 | AmerisourceBergen | 8,875 |
| 287 | BJ Services | 8,834 |
| 288 | Zions Bancorporation | 8,798 |
| 289 | Omnicom Group | 8,797 |
| 290 | Royal Caribbean Cruises | 8,752 |
| 291 | Mattel, Inc. | 8,708 |
| 292 | United States Steel | 8,670 |
| 293 | Apollo Group | 8,664 |
| 294 | Expeditors International | 8,630 |
| 295 | DTE Energy | 8,575 |
| 296 | C. R. Bard | 8,559 |
| 297 | Sherwin-Williams | 8,492 |
| 298 | Pulte Homes | 8,456 |
| 299 | The Hershey Company | 8,438 |
| 300 | Newell Rubbermaid | 8,424 |

## The 300 Largest Employers in *Hoover's Handbook of American Business 2008*

| Rank | Company | Employees |
|---|---|---|
| 1 | Manpower | 4,030,000 |
| 2 | Wal-Mart Stores | 1,900,000 |
| 3 | Kelly Services | 750,000 |
| 4 | United States Postal Service | 696,138 |
| 5 | McDonald's | 465,000 |
| 6 | United Parcel Service | 428,000 |
| 7 | Home Depot | 364,000 |
| 8 | International Business Machines | 355,766 |
| 9 | Target Corporation | 352,000 |
| 10 | Citigroup | 337,000 |
| 11 | General Electric | 319,000 |
| 12 | The Kroger Co. | 310,000 |
| 13 | AT&T Inc. | 302,000 |
| 14 | Ford Motor | 283,000 |
| 15 | YUM! Brands | 280,000 |
| 16 | General Motors | 280,000 |
| 17 | Spherion Corporation | 273,000 |
| 18 | Verizon Communications | 242,000 |
| 19 | Berkshire Hathaway | 217,000 |
| 20 | United Technologies | 214,500 |
| 21 | Lowe's Companies | 210,000 |
| 22 | Safeway Inc. | 207,000 |
| 23 | Bank of America | 203,425 |
| 24 | Walgreen Co. | 195,000 |
| 25 | SUPERVALU INC. | 191,400 |
| 26 | Macy's, Inc. | 188,000 |
| 27 | HCA Inc. | 186,000 |
| 28 | CVS/Caremark | 176,000 |
| 29 | Altria Group | 175,000 |
| 30 | JPMorgan Chase | 174,360 |
| 31 | Delphi Corporation | 171,400 |
| 32 | PepsiCo | 168,000 |
| 33 | Wells Fargo | 158,000 |
| 34 | Kaiser Foundation Health Plan | 156,000 |
| 35 | Hewlett-Packard | 156,000 |
| 36 | J. C. Penney | 155,000 |
| 37 | The Gap Inc. | 154,000 |
| 38 | The Boeing Company | 154,000 |
| 39 | Marriott International | 150,600 |
| 40 | Cargill, Incorporated | 149,000 |
| 41 | Starbucks | 145,800 |
| 42 | Starwood Hotels & Resorts | 145,000 |
| 43 | PricewaterhouseCoopers | 142,162 |
| 44 | Best Buy | 140,000 |
| 45 | Lockheed Martin | 140,000 |
| 46 | Accenture Ltd | 140,000 |
| 47 | Publix Super Markets | 140,000 |
| 48 | Johnson Controls | 136,000 |
| 49 | Deloitte Touche Tohmatsu | 135,000 |
| 50 | Walt Disney | 133,000 |
| 51 | Electronic Data Systems | 131,000 |
| 52 | Emerson Electric | 127,800 |
| 53 | Costco Wholesale | 127,000 |
| 54 | Limited Brands | 125,500 |
| 55 | TJX Companies | 125,000 |
| 56 | Alcoa Inc. | 123,000 |
| 57 | Johnson & Johnson | 122,200 |
| 58 | Northrop Grumman | 122,200 |
| 59 | Chrysler LLC | 121,000 |
| 60 | Honeywell International | 118,000 |
| 61 | Ernst & Young International | 114,000 |
| 62 | Kohl's Corporation | 114,000 |
| 63 | KPMG International | 113,000 |
| 64 | Brinker International | 110,800 |
| 65 | Wachovia Corporation | 108,238 |
| 66 | Tyson Foods | 107,000 |
| 67 | American International Group | 106,000 |
| 68 | Hilton Hotels | 105,000 |
| 69 | Halliburton Company | 104,000 |
| 70 | Lear Corporation | 104,000 |
| 71 | Sprint Nextel | 103,483 |
| 72 | Pfizer Inc. | 98,000 |
| 73 | Caterpillar Inc. | 94,593 |
| 74 | Intel Corporation | 94,100 |
| 75 | Time Warner | 92,700 |
| 76 | Kraft Foods | 90,000 |
| 77 | Comcast Corporation | 90,000 |
| 78 | Global Hyatt | 88,647 |
| 79 | AMR Corporation | 86,600 |
| 80 | Abercrombie & Fitch | 86,400 |
| 81 | Exxon Mobil | 82,100 |
| 82 | General Dynamics | 81,000 |
| 83 | Cox Enterprises | 80,000 |
| 84 | Koch Industries | 80,000 |
| 85 | Raytheon Company | 80,000 |
| 86 | Computer Sciences | 79,000 |
| 87 | Goodyear Tire & Rubber | 77,000 |
| 88 | 3M Company | 75,333 |
| 89 | ABM Industries | 75,000 |
| 90 | Carnival Corporation | 74,700 |
| 91 | CBRL Group | 74,031 |
| 92 | Jabil Circuit | 74,000 |
| 93 | Coca-Cola Enterprises | 74,000 |
| 94 | Staples, Inc. | 73,646 |
| 95 | Whirlpool Corporation | 73,000 |
| 96 | Coca-Cola | 71,000 |
| 97 | Pepsi Bottling Group | 70,400 |
| 98 | MGM MIRAGE | 70,000 |
| 99 | Schlumberger Limited | 70,000 |
| 100 | Rite Aid | 69,700 |
| 101 | Tenet Healthcare | 68,952 |
| 102 | State Farm Mutual | 68,000 |
| 103 | Blockbuster Inc. | 67,300 |
| 104 | Abbott Laboratories | 66,663 |
| 105 | Dell Inc. | 66,100 |
| 106 | Omnicom Group | 66,000 |
| 107 | Motorola, Inc. | 66,000 |
| 108 | YRC Worldwide | 66,000 |
| 109 | American Express | 65,400 |
| 110 | L-3 Communications | 63,700 |
| 111 | Chevron Corporation | 62,500 |
| 112 | American Standard | 62,200 |
| 113 | International Paper | 60,600 |
| 114 | Merck | 60,000 |
| 115 | Eaton Corporation | 60,000 |
| 116 | Manor Care | 59,500 |
| 117 | E. I. duPont de Nemours | 59,000 |
| 118 | UnitedHealth Group | 58,000 |
| 119 | Affiliated Computer Services | 58,000 |
| 120 | Nordstrom, Inc. | 57,400 |
| 121 | Masco Corporation | 57,000 |
| 122 | Merrill Lynch | 56,200 |
| 123 | Morgan Stanley | 55,310 |
| 124 | Marsh & McLennan | 55,200 |
| 125 | UAL Corporation | 55,000 |
| 126 | Kindred Healthcare | 55,000 |
| 127 | Kimberly-Clark | 55,000 |
| 128 | Cardinal Health | 55,000 |
| 129 | Illinois Tool Works | 55,000 |
| 130 | Countrywide Financial | 54,655 |
| 131 | Sanmina-SCI | 54,397 |
| 132 | Xerox Corporation | 53,700 |
| 133 | AutoZone | 53,000 |
| 134 | R. R. Donnelley & Sons | 53,000 |
| 135 | Office Depot | 52,000 |
| 136 | Dillard's, Inc. | 51,385 |
| 137 | Delta Air Lines | 51,300 |
| 138 | Bob Evans Farms | 51,092 |
| 139 | Union Pacific | 50,739 |
| 140 | Wyeth | 50,060 |
| 141 | U.S. Bancorp | 50,000 |
| 142 | Wakefern Food | 50,000 |
| 143 | Cisco Systems | 49,926 |
| 144 | Washington Mutual | 49,824 |
| 145 | Gannett Co. | 49,675 |
| 146 | The Brink's Company | 48,700 |
| 147 | Baxter International | 48,000 |
| 148 | Waste Management | 48,000 |
| 149 | News Corporation | 47,300 |
| 150 | Dole Food | 47,000 |

SOURCE: HOOVER'S, INC., DATABASE, AUGUST 2007

## The 300 Largest Employers in *Hoover's Handbook of American Business 2008* (continued)

| Rank | Company | Employees |
|---|---|---|
| 151 | MetLife, Inc. | 47,000 |
| 152 | Weyerhaeuser Company | 46,700 |
| 153 | Deere & Company | 46,500 |
| 154 | Automatic Data Processing | 46,000 |
| 155 | Wendy's International | 46,000 |
| 156 | Volt Information Sciences | 46,000 |
| 157 | Foot Locker | 45,406 |
| 158 | VF Corporation | 45,000 |
| 159 | Danaher Corporation | 45,000 |
| 160 | Jack in the Box | 44,300 |
| 161 | SAIC, Inc. | 44,100 |
| 162 | Family Dollar Stores | 44,000 |
| 163 | MacAndrews & Forbes | 44,000 |
| 164 | United States Steel | 44,000 |
| 165 | Continental Airlines | 43,770 |
| 166 | Aon Corporation | 43,100 |
| 167 | Circuit City Stores | 43,011 |
| 168 | Bristol-Myers Squibb | 43,000 |
| 169 | Ingersoll-Rand | 43,000 |
| 170 | Royal Caribbean Cruises | 42,958 |
| 171 | Dow Chemical | 42,578 |
| 172 | Interpublic Group | 42,000 |
| 173 | WellPoint, Inc. | 42,000 |
| 174 | Eli Lilly | 41,500 |
| 175 | Movie Gallery | 41,400 |
| 176 | Quest Diagnostics | 41,000 |
| 177 | Burlington Northern Santa Fe | 41,000 |
| 178 | Eastman Kodak | 40,900 |
| 179 | Avon Products | 40,300 |
| 180 | RadioShack | 40,000 |
| 181 | Textron Inc. | 40,000 |
| 182 | Mars, Incorporated | 40,000 |
| 183 | Bechtel Group | 40,000 |
| 184 | Pilgrim's Pride | 39,900 |
| 185 | Prudential Financial | 39,814 |
| 186 | First American | 39,670 |
| 187 | Whole Foods Market | 39,500 |
| 188 | Liberty Mutual | 39,000 |
| 189 | Barnes & Noble | 39,000 |
| 190 | Williams-Sonoma | 38,800 |
| 191 | Big Lots | 38,738 |
| 192 | ConocoPhillips | 38,400 |
| 193 | PetSmart | 38,400 |
| 194 | Qwest Communications | 38,000 |
| 195 | Medtronic, Inc. | 38,000 |
| 196 | A&P | 38,000 |
| 197 | Allstate Corporation | 37,900 |
| 198 | Fluor Corporation | 37,560 |
| 199 | ITT Corporation | 37,500 |
| 200 | Mohawk Industries | 37,100 |
| 201 | Burger King Holdings | 37,000 |
| 202 | US Airways Group | 37,000 |
| 203 | Apollo Group | 36,416 |
| 204 | Fortune Brands | 36,251 |
| 205 | Nationwide Mutual Insurance | 36,000 |
| 206 | CSX Corporation | 36,000 |
| 207 | OfficeMax | 36,000 |
| 208 | Regions Financial | 35,900 |
| 209 | Ross Stores | 35,800 |
| 210 | Bed Bath & Beyond | 35,000 |
| 211 | Colgate-Palmolive | 34,700 |
| 212 | Baker Hughes | 34,600 |
| 213 | Cummins, Inc. | 34,600 |
| 214 | Health Management Associates | 34,500 |
| 215 | Pitney Bowes | 34,454 |
| 216 | Borders Group | 33,600 |
| 217 | SunTrust Banks | 33,599 |
| 218 | Schering-Plough | 33,500 |
| 219 | Molex Incorporated | 33,200 |
| 220 | H. J. Heinz | 33,000 |
| 221 | The Bon-Ton Stores | 33,000 |
| 222 | Dover Corporation | 33,000 |
| 223 | HealthSouth | 33,000 |
| 224 | Weatherford International | 33,000 |
| 225 | Leggett & Platt | 32,828 |
| 226 | The Travelers Companies | 32,800 |
| 227 | Southwest Airlines | 32,664 |
| 228 | PPG Industries | 32,200 |
| 229 | AES Corporation | 32,000 |
| 230 | Mattel, Inc. | 32,000 |
| 231 | GameStop Corp. | 32,000 |
| 232 | Genuine Parts | 32,000 |
| 233 | Capital One Financial | 31,800 |
| 234 | McKesson Corporation | 31,800 |
| 235 | Unisys Corporation | 31,500 |
| 236 | Hertz Global Holdings | 31,500 |
| 237 | National City | 31,270 |
| 238 | EMC Corporation | 31,100 |
| 239 | Hartford Financial Services Group | 31,000 |
| 240 | Texas Instruments | 30,986 |
| 241 | Sherwin-Williams | 30,767 |
| 242 | Cooper Industries | 30,561 |
| 243 | Norfolk Southern | 30,541 |
| 244 | Thermo Fisher Scientific | 30,500 |
| 245 | Anheuser-Busch | 30,183 |
| 246 | Charming Shoppes | 30,000 |
| 247 | Northwest Airlines | 30,000 |
| 248 | Avis Budget Group | 30,000 |
| 249 | Advance Publications | 30,000 |
| 250 | Aetna Inc. | 30,000 |
| 251 | Manpower Inc. | 30,000 |
| 252 | FMR Corp. | 29,424 |
| 253 | BB&T Corporation | 29,300 |
| 254 | URS Corporation | 29,300 |
| 255 | NCR Corporation | 28,900 |
| 256 | DaVita Inc. | 28,900 |
| 257 | Boston Scientific | 28,600 |
| 258 | Ryder System | 28,600 |
| 259 | Estée Lauder | 28,500 |
| 260 | Marathon Oil | 28,195 |
| 261 | Brunswick Corporation | 28,000 |
| 262 | Owens-Illinois | 28,000 |
| 263 | McDermott International | 27,800 |
| 264 | The Progressive Corporation | 27,778 |
| 265 | American Eagle Outfitters | 27,600 |
| 266 | ArvinMeritor | 27,500 |
| 267 | CIGNA Corporation | 27,100 |
| 268 | Payless ShoeSource | 27,100 |
| 269 | Praxair, Inc. | 27,042 |
| 270 | Denny's Corporation | 27,000 |
| 271 | Vishay Intertechnology | 27,000 |
| 272 | EMCOR Group | 27,000 |
| 273 | Becton, Dickinson | 26,990 |
| 274 | Archer Daniels Midland | 26,800 |
| 275 | Goldman Sachs | 26,467 |
| 276 | Dean Foods | 26,348 |
| 277 | Southern Company | 26,091 |
| 278 | Kellogg Company | 26,000 |
| 279 | AutoNation | 26,000 |
| 280 | Lehman Brothers Holdings | 25,900 |
| 281 | Duke Energy | 25,600 |
| 282 | Black & Decker | 25,500 |
| 283 | Jones Lang LaSalle | 25,500 |
| 284 | The Timken Company | 25,418 |
| 285 | Smurfit-Stone Container | 25,200 |
| 286 | IKON Office Solutions | 25,000 |
| 287 | Chiquita Brands International | 25,000 |
| 288 | Washington Group International | 25,000 |
| 289 | Universal Corporation | 25,000 |
| 290 | Corning Incorporated | 24,500 |
| 291 | Triarc Companies | 24,372 |
| 292 | Allied Waste Industries | 24,200 |
| 293 | MeadWestvaco Corporation | 24,000 |
| 294 | Campbell Soup | 24,000 |
| 295 | Freescale Semiconductor | 24,000 |
| 296 | Hewitt Associates | 24,000 |
| 297 | CB Richard Ellis Group | 24,000 |
| 298 | PNC Financial Services Group | 23,783 |
| 299 | CBS Corporation | 23,654 |
| 300 | Micron Technology | 23,500 |

## The 100 Fastest-Growing Companies by Sales Growth in *Hoover's Handbook of American Business 2008*

| Rank | Company | Annual % Change* |
|---|---|---|
| 1 | Google Inc. | 121.6% |
| 2 | Triarc Companies | 88.3% |
| 3 | Carlson Wagonlit Travel | 78.3% |
| 4 | Chesapeake Energy | 77.5% |
| 5 | World Fuel Services | 62.5% |
| 6 | Yahoo! Inc. | 61.1% |
| 7 | Gilead Sciences | 59.6% |
| 8 | SanDisk Corporation | 56.6% |
| 9 | ONEOK, Inc. | 54.2% |
| 10 | CIT Group | 54.2% |
| 11 | Schnitzer Steel Industries | 49.6% |
| 12 | eBay Inc. | 48.9% |
| 13 | TD Ameritrade | 48.2% |
| 14 | The Bon-Ton Stores | 48.2% |
| 15 | Movie Gallery | 48.1% |
| 16 | Holly Corporation | 45.9% |
| 17 | Spectrum Brands | 45.3% |
| 18 | WellPoint, Inc. | 43.9% |
| 19 | DRS Technologies | 42.9% |
| 20 | Countrywide Financial | 42.8% |
| 21 | Constellation Energy Group | 42.3% |
| 22 | SkyWest, Inc. | 41.6% |
| 23 | GameStop Corp. | 40.8% |
| 24 | YRC Worldwide | 39.4% |
| 25 | Liberty Media | 38.7% |
| 26 | Symantec Corporation | 38.7% |
| 27 | Cephalon, Inc. | 36.6% |
| 28 | CB Richard Ellis Group | 36.2% |
| 29 | EOG Resources | 35.9% |
| 30 | Genentech, Inc. | 35.9% |
| 31 | Superior Essex | 35.9% |
| 32 | Valero Energy | 35.8% |
| 33 | Broadcom Corporation | 35.7% |
| 34 | Apple Inc. | 35.4% |
| 35 | Quiksilver, Inc. | 35.3% |

| Rank | Company | Annual % Change |
|---|---|---|
| 36 | ConocoPhillips | 34.7% |
| 37 | Apache Corporation | 34.1% |
| 38 | Network Appliance | 33.2% |
| 39 | Cleveland-Cliffs | 33.0% |
| 40 | L-3 Communications | 32.8% |
| 41 | Commercial Metals | 32.6% |
| 42 | Nucor Corporation | 32.4% |
| 43 | Goldman Sachs | 32.0% |
| 44 | Freeport-McMoRan Copper & Gold | 31.9% |
| 45 | Jabil Circuit | 30.4% |
| 46 | UnitedHealth Group | 30.0% |
| 47 | Weatherford International | 29.6% |
| 48 | Ryerson, Inc. | 29.6% |
| 49 | The Travelers Companies | 29.5% |
| 50 | Lehman Brothers Holdings | 29.2% |
| 51 | Terex Corporation | 28.6% |
| 52 | Diamond Offshore Drilling | 28.5% |
| 53 | Amazon.com | 28.5% |
| 54 | Carnival Corporation | 28.3% |
| 55 | Sunoco, Inc. | 28.1% |
| 56 | Legg Mason | 28.1% |
| 57 | Boston Scientific | 27.9% |
| 58 | Plains All American Pipeline | 27.9% |
| 59 | Anadarko Petroleum | 27.5% |
| 60 | DaVita Inc. | 27.4% |
| 61 | Toll Brothers | 27.3% |
| 62 | USEC Inc. | 27.1% |
| 63 | Jefferies Group | 27.0% |
| 64 | ENSCO International | 27.0% |
| 65 | Allegheny Technologies | 26.8% |
| 66 | Amgen Inc. | 26.8% |
| 67 | AirTran Holdings | 26.8% |
| 68 | CACI International | 26.7% |
| 69 | Bank of America | 26.3% |
| 70 | Tesoro Corporation | 26.3% |

| Rank | Company | Annual % Change |
|---|---|---|
| 71 | Precision Castparts | 26.1% |
| 72 | General Cable | 26.0% |
| 73 | Merrill Lynch | 25.7% |
| 74 | QUALCOMM Incorporated | 25.4% |
| 75 | Cytec Industries | 25.4% |
| 76 | Omnicare, Inc. | 25.3% |
| 77 | Thor Industries | 25.3% |
| 78 | Apollo Group | 25.2% |
| 79 | Devon Energy | 25.1% |
| 80 | Occidental Petroleum | 24.8% |
| 81 | Olin Corporation | 24.8% |
| 82 | Hovnanian Enterprises | 24.6% |
| 83 | Bear Stearns | 24.5% |
| 84 | Genzyme Corporation | 24.4% |
| 85 | Jones Lang LaSalle | 24.4% |
| 86 | The Pantry, Inc. | 24.3% |
| 87 | Hess Corporation | 24.1% |
| 88 | Starbucks | 24.0% |
| 89 | Morgan Stanley | 23.9% |
| 90 | UGI Corporation | 23.9% |
| 91 | McDermott International | 23.9% |
| 92 | BJ Services | 23.7% |
| 93 | Berkshire Hathaway | 23.5% |
| 94 | PACCAR Inc | 22.9% |
| 95 | Pioneer Natural Resources | 22.8% |
| 96 | JPMorgan Chase | 22.7% |
| 97 | Chiquita Brands International | 22.6% |
| 98 | Koch Industries | 22.5% |
| 99 | D.R. Horton | 22.2% |
| 100 | Autodesk, Inc. | 22.2% |

*These rates are compounded annualized increases, and may have resulted from acquisitions or one time gains. If less than 5 years of data are available, growth is for the years available.

SOURCE: HOOVER'S, INC., DATABASE, AUGUST 2007

## The 100 Fastest-Growing Companies by Employment Growth in *Hoover's Handbook of American Business 2008*

| Rank | Company | Annual % Change* |
|---|---|---|
| 1 | Google Inc. | 88.0% |
| 2 | Chesapeake Energy | 54.2% |
| 3 | Triarc Companies | 48.4% |
| 4 | Koch Industries | 47.3% |
| 5 | SanDisk Corporation | 42.4% |
| 6 | Symantec Corporation | 41.2% |
| 7 | Abercrombie & Fitch | 40.8% |
| 8 | The Bon-Ton Stores | 40.0% |
| 9 | Jabil Circuit | 38.7% |
| 10 | Schnitzer Steel Industries | 35.9% |
| 11 | Quiksilver, Inc. | 35.9% |
| 12 | Spectrum Brands | 35.7% |
| 13 | The Travelers Companies | 35.6% |
| 14 | SUPERVALU INC. | 35.1% |
| 15 | eBay Inc. | 34.8% |
| 16 | Kaiser Foundation Health Plan | 34.8% |
| 17 | Yahoo! Inc. | 33.4% |
| 18 | CB Richard Ellis Group | 33.3% |
| 19 | YRC Worldwide | 30.2% |
| 20 | Movie Gallery | 30.0% |
| 21 | Thermo Fisher Scientific | 29.3% |
| 22 | Western Digital | 29.1% |
| 23 | Network Appliance | 28.5% |
| 24 | NVIDIA Corporation | 28.2% |
| 25 | Hovnanian Enterprises | 27.4% |
| 26 | DRS Technologies | 26.8% |
| 27 | Global Hyatt | 24.7% |
| 28 | Plains All American Pipeline | 24.7% |
| 29 | GameStop Corp. | 24.1% |
| 30 | L-3 Communications | 23.9% |
| 31 | Starbucks | 23.8% |
| 32 | Perot Systems | 23.5% |
| 33 | Regions Financial | 23.0% |
| 34 | Cephalon, Inc. | 22.9% |
| 35 | Burger King Holdings | 22.1% |

| Rank | Company | Annual % Change |
|---|---|---|
| 36 | DaVita Inc. | 22.1% |
| 37 | WellPoint, Inc. | 21.1% |
| 38 | Weatherford International | 20.4% |
| 39 | Lehman Brothers Holdings | 20.4% |
| 40 | Boston Scientific | 19.8% |
| 41 | Broadcom Corporation | 19.2% |
| 42 | Tupperware Brands | 19.2% |
| 43 | Gilead Sciences | 19.1% |
| 44 | World Fuel Services | 19.0% |
| 45 | Carnival Corporation | 19.0% |
| 46 | Genentech, Inc. | 19.0% |
| 47 | Amgen Inc. | 18.8% |
| 48 | Electronic Arts | 18.5% |
| 49 | Molex Incorporated | 17.7% |
| 50 | Dell Inc. | 17.6% |
| 51 | CDW Corporation | 17.4% |
| 52 | CACI International | 17.1% |
| 53 | Toll Brothers | 17.0% |
| 54 | Countrywide Financial | 16.9% |
| 55 | Accenture Ltd | 16.9% |
| 56 | Amazon.com | 16.7% |
| 57 | JPMorgan Chase | 16.6% |
| 58 | Lincoln National | 16.5% |
| 59 | TD Ameritrade | 16.4% |
| 60 | St. Jude Medical | 16.2% |
| 61 | Adobe Systems | 16.2% |
| 62 | UnitedHealth Group | 16.0% |
| 63 | Brightpoint, Inc. | 16.0% |
| 64 | Omnicare, Inc. | 15.8% |
| 65 | The McClatchy Company | 15.8% |
| 66 | EMC Corporation | 15.6% |
| 67 | C.H. Robinson Worldwide | 15.4% |
| 68 | R. R. Donnelley & Sons | 15.3% |
| 69 | American Eagle Outfitters | 15.1% |
| 70 | Apple Inc. | 14.9% |

| Rank | Company | Annual % Change |
|---|---|---|
| 71 | Thor Industries | 14.8% |
| 72 | SkyWest, Inc. | 14.7% |
| 73 | AT&T Inc. | 14.5% |
| 74 | Technical Olympic USA | 14.3% |
| 75 | Capital One Financial | 14.1% |
| 76 | Highmark Inc. | 13.9% |
| 77 | Scotts Miracle-Gro | 13.8% |
| 78 | CVS/Caremark | 13.8% |
| 79 | Precision Castparts | 13.6% |
| 80 | Macy's, Inc. | 13.6% |
| 81 | Jefferies Group | 13.5% |
| 82 | Pioneer Natural Resources | 13.5% |
| 83 | Humana Inc. | 13.4% |
| 84 | Hewitt Associates | 13.2% |
| 85 | Church & Dwight Co. | 13.2% |
| 86 | Whole Foods Market | 13.1% |
| 87 | PetSmart | 13.1% |
| 88 | MGM MIRAGE | 13.0% |
| 89 | AnnTaylor Stores | 12.9% |
| 90 | HNI Corporation | 12.7% |
| 91 | Pilgrim's Pride | 12.6% |
| 92 | Apache Corporation | 12.6% |
| 93 | Genzyme Corporation | 12.6% |
| 94 | Affiliated Computer Services | 12.5% |
| 95 | Noble Corporation | 12.5% |
| 96 | Henry Schein | 12.4% |
| 97 | First American | 12.4% |
| 98 | Ross Stores | 12.3% |
| 99 | Ryerson, Inc. | 12.2% |
| 100 | Procter & Gamble | 12.1% |

*These rates are compounded annualized increases, and may have resulted from acquisitions or one time gains. If less than 5 years of data are available, growth is for the years available.

SOURCE: HOOVER'S, INC., DATABASE, AUGUST 2007

## 50 Shrinking Companies by Sales Growth in *Hoover's Handbook of American Business 2008*

| Rank | Company | Annual % Change* |
|---|---|---|
| 1 | Safeguard Scientifics | (41.4%) |
| 2 | El Paso Corporation | (23.0%) |
| 3 | Silicon Graphics | (22.8%) |
| 4 | Dynegy Inc. | (22.2%) |
| 5 | Winn-Dixie Stores | (21.9%) |
| 6 | Avis Budget Group | (20.3%) |
| 7 | Merck | (18.7%) |
| 8 | ContiGroup Companies | (17.0%) |
| 9 | Saks Incorporated | (16.0%) |
| 10 | Viad Corp | (14.7%) |
| 11 | PRIMEDIA Inc. | (14.5%) |
| 12 | Gemstar-TV Guide | (13.1%) |
| 13 | CBS Corporation | (12.7%) |
| 14 | Global Crossing | (12.0%) |
| 15 | Nicor Inc. | (11.8%) |
| 16 | Kmart Corporation | (11.8%) |
| 17 | ConAgra Foods | (11.8%) |
| 18 | J. C. Penney | (11.4%) |
| 19 | A&P | (10.7%) |
| 20 | Sara Lee | (9.5%) |
| 21 | TIAA-CREF | (8.8%) |
| 22 | Texas Industries | (7.6%) |
| 23 | The Brink's Company | (6.9%) |
| 24 | Nationwide Mutual Insurance | (6.7%) |
| 25 | HealthSouth | (6.7%) |
| 26 | Citizens Communications | (6.7%) |
| 27 | Universal Corporation | (6.6%) |
| 28 | La-Z-Boy | (6.5%) |
| 29 | Service Corporation | (6.4%) |
| 30 | CMS Energy | (5.6%) |
| 31 | Hanover Insurance Group | (5.5%) |
| 32 | Cooper Tire & Rubber | (5.3%) |
| 33 | Agilent Technologies | (4.6%) |
| 34 | Newell Rubbermaid | (4.5%) |
| 35 | CNA Financial | (4.1%) |
| 36 | Novell, Inc. | (3.9%) |
| 37 | CIGNA Corporation | (3.8%) |
| 38 | Fleetwood Enterprises | (3.5%) |
| 39 | American Electric Power | (3.5%) |
| 40 | American Greetings | (3.3%) |
| 41 | IKON Office Solutions | (3.3%) |
| 42 | International Paper | (3.1%) |
| 43 | Con-way Inc. | (3.0%) |
| 44 | Safeco Corporation | (2.9%) |
| 45 | SPX Corporation | (2.8%) |
| 46 | Wendy's International | (2.6%) |
| 47 | MeadWestvaco Corporation | (2.6%) |
| 48 | Qwest Communications | (2.5%) |
| 49 | Westar Energy | (2.4%) |
| 50 | Visa International | (2.3%) |

*These rates are compounded and annualized and may have resulted from divestitures. If less than 5 years of data are available, rates are for the years available.

SOURCE: HOOVER'S, INC., DATABASE, AUGUST 2007

## 50 Shrinking Companies by Employment Growth in *Hoover's Handbook of American Business 2008*

| Rank | Company | Annual % Change* |
|---|---|---|
| 1 | Raymond James Financial | (44.9%) |
| 2 | Gateway, Inc. | (38.0%) |
| 3 | CBS Corporation | (33.5%) |
| 4 | Alberto-Culver | (31.1%) |
| 5 | Safeguard Scientifics | (27.6%) |
| 6 | American Greetings | (26.7%) |
| 7 | Dynegy Inc. | (26.7%) |
| 8 | Saks Incorporated | (25.5%) |
| 9 | Avis Budget Group | (22.9%) |
| 10 | Sara Lee | (22.6%) |
| 11 | J.B. Hunt Transport | (22.3%) |
| 12 | Xcel Energy | (22.0%) |
| 13 | Kmart Corporation | (20.8%) |
| 14 | Westar Energy | (20.3%) |
| 15 | ConAgra Foods | (19.4%) |
| 16 | El Paso Corporation | (19.2%) |
| 17 | Silicon Graphics | (19.1%) |
| 18 | EarthLink, Inc. | (18.9%) |
| 19 | Williams Companies | (18.6%) |
| 20 | Brown-Forman | (17.6%) |
| 21 | Public Service Enterprise Group | (16.9%) |
| 22 | A&P | (16.7%) |
| 23 | Ashland Inc. | (16.7%) |
| 24 | Newell Rubbermaid | (15.9%) |
| 25 | Agilent Technologies | (15.1%) |
| 26 | Winn-Dixie Stores | (14.9%) |
| 27 | Texas Industries | (14.1%) |
| 28 | PRIMEDIA Inc. | (13.9%) |
| 29 | Cooper Tire & Rubber | (12.7%) |
| 30 | Eastman Kodak | (12.6%) |
| 31 | Furniture Brands International | (12.6%) |
| 32 | SPX Corporation | (12.3%) |
| 33 | Tenet Healthcare | (12.0%) |
| 34 | Safeco Corporation | (12.0%) |
| 35 | NACCO Industries | (11.7%) |
| 36 | National Fuel Gas | (11.0%) |
| 37 | CNA Financial | (10.8%) |
| 38 | HealthSouth | (10.3%) |
| 39 | Centex Corporation | (10.2%) |
| 40 | Smurfit-Stone Container | (10.1%) |
| 41 | Viad Corp | (10.0%) |
| 42 | CIGNA Corporation | (9.9%) |
| 43 | International Paper | (9.7%) |
| 44 | Dun & Bradstreet | (9.6%) |
| 45 | ConocoPhillips | (9.4%) |
| 46 | Northwest Airlines | (9.3%) |
| 47 | AK Steel Holding | (9.2%) |
| 48 | J. C. Penney | (9.2%) |
| 49 | Motorola, Inc. | (9.2%) |
| 50 | Exelon Corporation | (9.1%) |

*These rates are compounded and annualized and may have resulted from divestitures. If less than 5 years of data are available, rates are for the years available.

SOURCE: HOOVER'S, INC., DATABASE, AUGUST 2007

## The *FORTUNE* 500 Largest US Corporations

| Rank | Company | Sales ($ mil.) |
|---|---|---|
| 1 | Wal-Mart Stores | 351,139.0 |
| 2 | Exxon Mobil | 347,254.0 |
| 3 | General Motors | 207,349.0 |
| 4 | Chevron | 200,567.0 |
| 5 | ConocoPhillips | 172,451.0 |
| 6 | General Electric | 168,307.0 |
| 7 | Ford Motor | 160,126.0 |
| 8 | Citigroup | 146,777.0 |
| 9 | Bank of America Corp. | 117,017.0 |
| 10 | American International Group | 113,194.0 |
| 11 | J.P. Morgan Chase & Co. | 99,973.0 |
| 12 | Berkshire Hathaway | 98,539.0 |
| 13 | Verizon Communications | 93,221.0 |
| 14 | Hewlett-Packard | 91,658.0 |
| 15 | IBM | 91,424.0 |
| 16 | Valero Energy | 91,051.0 |
| 17 | Home Depot | 90,837.0 |
| 18 | McKesson | 88,050.0 |
| 19 | Cardinal Health | 81,895.1 |
| 20 | Morgan Stanley | 76,688.0 |
| 21 | UnitedHealth Group | 71,542.0 |
| 22 | Merrill Lynch | 70,591.0 |
| 23 | Altria Group | 70,324.0 |
| 24 | Goldman Sachs Group | 69,353.0 |
| 25 | Procter & Gamble | 68,222.0 |
| 26 | Kroger | 66,111.2 |
| 27 | AT&T | 63,055.0 |
| 28 | Boeing | 61,530.0 |
| 29 | AmerisourceBergen | 61,203.1 |
| 30 | Marathon Oil | 60,643.0 |
| 31 | State Farm Insurance Cos. | 60,528.0 |
| 32 | Costco Wholesale | 60,151.2 |
| 33 | Target | 59,490.0 |
| 34 | Dell | 57,095.0 |
| 35 | Wellpoint | 56,953.0 |
| 36 | Johnson & Johnson | 53,324.0 |
| 37 | MetLife | 53,275.0 |
| 38 | Sears Holdings | 53,012.0 |
| 39 | Pfizer | 52,415.0 |
| 40 | Dow Chemical | 49,124.0 |
| 41 | Wells Fargo | 47,979.0 |
| 42 | United Technologies | 47,829.0 |
| 43 | United Parcel Service | 47,547.0 |
| 44 | Walgreen | 47,409.0 |
| 45 | Lowe's | 46,927.0 |
| 46 | Wachovia Corp. | 46,810.0 |
| 47 | Lehman Brothers Holdings | 46,709.0 |
| 48 | Time Warner | 44,788.0 |
| 49 | Microsoft | 44,282.0 |
| 50 | Freddie Mac | 44,002.0 |

| Rank | Company | Sales ($ mil.) |
|---|---|---|
| 51 | CVS/Caremark | 43,813.8 |
| 52 | Motorola | 43,739.0 |
| 53 | Sprint Nextel | 43,531.0 |
| 54 | Medco Health Solutions | 42,543.7 |
| 55 | Caterpillar | 41,517.0 |
| 56 | Safeway | 40,185.0 |
| 57 | Lockheed Martin | 39,620.0 |
| 58 | Caremark Rx | 36,750.2 |
| 59 | Archer Daniels Midland | 36,596.1 |
| 60 | Sunoco | 36,081.0 |
| 61 | Allstate | 35,796.0 |
| 62 | Intel | 35,382.0 |
| 63 | PepsiCo | 35,137.0 |
| 64 | Walt Disney | 34,285.0 |
| 65 | Sysco | 32,628.4 |
| 66 | Prudential Financial | 32,488.0 |
| 67 | Johnson Controls | 32,413.0 |
| 68 | FedEx | 32,294.0 |
| 69 | Honeywell International | 31,367.0 |
| 70 | Ingram Micro | 31,357.5 |
| 71 | Alcoa | 30,896.0 |
| 72 | Best Buy | 30,848.0 |
| 73 | Northrop Grumman | 30,304.0 |
| 74 | DuPont | 28,982.0 |
| 75 | Hess | 28,720.0 |
| 76 | Federated Department Stores | 28,711.0 |
| 77 | Cisco Systems | 28,484.0 |
| 78 | New York Life Insurance | 28,365.1 |
| 79 | American Express | 27,145.0 |
| 80 | TIAA-CREF | 26,756.8 |
| 81 | Washington Mutual | 26,561.0 |
| 82 | Hartford Financial Services | 26,500.0 |
| 83 | Delphi | 26,392.0 |
| 84 | Comcast | 25,700.0 |
| 85 | Aetna | 25,568.6 |
| 86 | Tyson Foods | 25,559.0 |
| 87 | HCA | 25,477.0 |
| 88 | News Corp. | 25,327.0 |
| 89 | Travelers Cos. | 25,090.0 |
| 90 | Massachusetts Mutual Life Insurance | 24,863.4 |
| 91 | Countrywide Financial | 24,444.6 |
| 92 | General Dynamics | 24,212.0 |
| 93 | International Paper | 24,186.0 |
| 94 | Coca-Cola | 24,088.0 |
| 95 | Liberty Mutual Insurance Group | 23,520.0 |
| 96 | Raytheon | 23,274.0 |
| 97 | 3M | 22,923.0 |
| 98 | Deere | 22,768.9 |
| 99 | Merck | 22,636.0 |
| 100 | Halliburton | 22,576.0 |

| Rank | Company | Sales ($ mil.) |
|---|---|---|
| 101 | AMR | 22,563.0 |
| 102 | Abbott Laboratories | 22,476.3 |
| 103 | Plains All American Pipeline | 22,444.4 |
| 104 | Nationwide | 22,253.0 |
| 105 | Weyerhaeuser | 22,250.0 |
| 106 | Lyondell Chemical | 22,228.0 |
| 107 | Publix Super Markets | 21,819.7 |
| 108 | McDonald's | 21,586.4 |
| 109 | Tech Data | 21,446.1 |
| 110 | Humana | 21,416.5 |
| 111 | Electronic Data Systems | 21,337.0 |
| 112 | Northwestern Mutual | 20,726.2 |
| 113 | Wyeth | 20,350.7 |
| 114 | Goodyear Tire & Rubber | 20,258.0 |
| 115 | Emerson Electric | 20,133.0 |
| 116 | J.C. Penney | 19,903.0 |
| 117 | Supervalu | 19,863.6 |
| 118 | Coca-Cola Enterprises | 19,804.0 |
| 119 | Constellation Energy | 19,446.1 |
| 120 | UAL | 19,340.0 |
| 121 | Apple | 19,315.0 |
| 122 | AutoNation | 19,314.4 |
| 123 | U.S. Bancorp | 19,109.0 |
| 124 | Occidental Petroleum | 19,029.0 |
| 125 | Sara Lee | 18,539.0 |
| 126 | Staples | 18,160.8 |
| 127 | Whirlpool | 18,080.0 |
| 128 | Tesoro | 18,002.0 |
| 129 | Bristol-Myers Squibb | 17,914.0 |
| 130 | Lear | 17,838.9 |
| 131 | Manpower | 17,786.5 |
| 132 | Express Scripts | 17,660.0 |
| 133 | TJX | 17,516.4 |
| 134 | Rite Aid | 17,271.0 |
| 135 | Loews | 17,227.6 |
| 136 | Delta Air Lines | 17,171.0 |
| 137 | Kimberly-Clark | 16,746.9 |
| 138 | Bear Stearns | 16,551.4 |
| 139 | Cigna | 16,547.0 |
| 140 | Dominion Resources | 16,524.0 |
| 141 | Paccar | 16,454.1 |
| 142 | Lennar | 16,266.7 |
| 143 | Duke Energy | 15,967.0 |
| 144 | Gap | 15,943.0 |
| 145 | Xerox | 15,895.0 |
| 146 | Anheuser-Busch | 15,717.1 |
| 147 | United States Steel | 15,715.0 |
| 148 | FPL Group | 15,710.0 |
| 149 | Eli Lilly | 15,691.0 |
| 150 | Exelon | 15,654.0 |

SOURCE: *FORTUNE*, APRIL 30, 2007

# The *FORTUNE* 500 Largest US Corporations (continued)

| Rank | Company | Sales ($ mil.) |
|---|---|---|
| 151 | Union Pacific | 15,578.0 |
| 152 | Kohl's | 15,544.2 |
| 153 | Centex | 15,465.1 |
| 154 | Capital One Financial | 15,191.0 |
| 155 | D.R. Horton | 15,051.3 |
| 156 | Office Depot | 15,010.8 |
| 157 | Burlington Northern Santa Fe | 14,985.0 |
| 158 | Nike | 14,954.9 |
| 159 | Progressive | 14,786.4 |
| 160 | DIRECTV Group | 14,755.5 |
| 161 | Nucor | 14,751.3 |
| 162 | Texas Instruments | 14,630.0 |
| 163 | Computer Sciences | 14,623.6 |
| 164 | AFLAC | 14,616.0 |
| 165 | CBS | 14,479.1 |
| 166 | CHS | 14,383.8 |
| 167 | Oracle | 14,380.0 |
| 168 | Southern | 14,356.0 |
| 169 | Murphy Oil | 14,307.4 |
| 170 | Pulte Homes | 14,274.4 |
| 171 | Amgen | 14,268.0 |
| 172 | Avnet | 14,253.6 |
| 173 | ConAgra Foods | 14,171.9 |
| 174 | Fluor | 14,078.5 |
| 175 | Illinois Tool Works | 14,055.0 |
| 176 | Chubb | 14,003.0 |
| 177 | Enterprise GP Holdings | 13,991.0 |
| 178 | Qwest Communications | 13,923.0 |
| 179 | Arrow Electronics | 13,577.1 |
| 180 | USAA | 13,416.4 |
| 181 | Waste Management | 13,363.0 |
| 182 | Eastman Kodak | 13,274.0 |
| 183 | SunTrust Banks | 13,260.4 |
| 184 | Huntsman | 13,148.2 |
| 185 | TRW Automotive Holdings | 13,144.0 |
| 186 | Continental Airlines | 13,128.0 |
| 187 | Sun Microsystems | 13,068.0 |
| 188 | National City Corp. | 12,952.7 |
| 189 | Health Net | 12,908.4 |
| 190 | Masco | 12,833.0 |
| 191 | Pepsi Bottling | 12,730.0 |
| 192 | American Electric Power | 12,622.0 |
| 192 | Edison International | 12,622.0 |
| 194 | Textron | 12,591.0 |
| 195 | Northwest Airlines | 12,568.0 |
| 196 | PG&E Corp. | 12,539.0 |
| 197 | L-3 Communications | 12,476.9 |
| 198 | Eaton | 12,370.0 |
| 199 | Public Service Enterprise Group | 12,288.0 |
| 200 | Colgate-Palmolive | 12,237.7 |
| 201 | Kinder Morgan | 12,208.0 |
| 202 | Toys "R" Us | 12,206.0 |
| 203 | Marriott International | 12,160.0 |
| 204 | Consolidated Edison | 12,137.0 |
| 205 | United Auto Group | 12,109.9 |
| 206 | Phelps Dodge | 12,090.2 |
| 207 | Marsh & McLennan | 12,069.0 |
| 208 | ONEOK | 11,906.8 |
| 209 | Bank of New York Co. | 11,891.0 |
| 210 | Sempra Energy | 11,850.0 |
| 211 | Williams | 11,812.9 |
| 212 | FirstEnergy | 11,726.0 |
| 213 | General Mills | 11,640.0 |
| 214 | Aramark | 11,621.2 |
| 215 | Circuit City Stores | 11,597.7 |
| 216 | US Airways Group | 11,557.0 |
| 217 | Smithfield Foods | 11,506.8 |
| 218 | Viacom | 11,466.5 |
| 219 | Visteon | 11,418.0 |
| 220 | Omnicom Group | 11,376.9 |
| 221 | Cummins | 11,362.0 |
| 222 | Medtronic | 11,292.0 |
| 223 | American Standard | 11,208.2 |
| 224 | EMC | 11,155.1 |
| 225 | Entergy | 11,066.6 |
| 226 | PPG Industries | 11,037.0 |
| 227 | Genworth Financial | 11,029.0 |
| 228 | KB Home | 11,003.8 |
| 229 | Reliant Energy | 10,985.4 |
| 230 | Sanmina-SCI | 10,955.4 |
| 231 | PNC Financial Services Group | 10,939.0 |
| 232 | Kellogg | 10,906.7 |
| 233 | Anadarko Petroleum | 10,904.0 |
| 234 | TXU | 10,856.0 |
| 235 | World Fuel Services | 10,785.1 |
| 236 | Unum Group | 10,718.8 |
| 237 | Amazon.com | 10,711.0 |
| 238 | Progress Energy | 10,702.0 |
| 239 | Devon Energy | 10,696.0 |
| 240 | Limited Brands | 10,670.6 |
| 241 | Google | 10,604.9 |
| 242 | Schering-Plough | 10,594.0 |
| 243 | Solectron | 10,560.7 |
| 244 | Genuine Parts | 10,457.9 |
| 245 | Baxter International | 10,378.0 |
| 246 | Dean Foods | 10,339.0 |
| 247 | Aon | 10,311.0 |
| 248 | Ashland | 10,007.0 |
| 249 | YRC Worldwide | 9,918.7 |
| 250 | Principal Financial | 9,870.0 |
| 251 | Xcel Energy | 9,847.8 |
| 252 | Echostar Communications | 9,818.5 |
| 253 | ArvinMeritor | 9,810.0 |
| 254 | Harrah's Entertainment | 9,780.7 |
| 255 | Dana | 9,724.0 |
| 256 | Alltel | 9,723.3 |
| 257 | Guardian Life of America | 9,693.7 |
| 258 | Tenet Healthcare | 9,622.0 |
| 259 | TEPPCO Partners | 9,612.2 |
| 260 | Danaher | 9,596.4 |
| 261 | CSX | 9,566.0 |
| 262 | Yum Brands | 9,561.0 |
| 263 | State Street Corp. | 9,525.0 |
| 264 | Fidelity National Financial | 9,436.1 |
| 265 | BB&T Corp. | 9,414.8 |
| 266 | Parker Hannifin | 9,407.6 |
| 267 | Norfolk Southern | 9,407.0 |
| 268 | S&C Holdco | 9,350.0 |
| 269 | H.J. Heinz | 9,331.4 |
| 270 | CenterPoint Energy | 9,319.0 |
| 271 | R.R. Donnelley & Sons | 9,316.6 |
| 272 | Automatic Data Processing | 9,263.2 |
| 273 | Dollar General | 9,169.8 |
| 274 | Applied Materials | 9,167.0 |
| 275 | Air Products & Chemicals | 9,158.8 |
| 276 | Southwest Airlines | 9,086.0 |
| 277 | Lincoln National | 9,062.9 |
| 278 | Baker Hughes | 9,034.1 |
| 279 | DTE Energy | 9,024.0 |
| 280 | OfficeMax | 8,965.7 |
| 281 | Liberty Media | 8,948.0 |
| 282 | Lucent Technologies | 8,796.0 |
| 283 | Avon Products | 8,763.9 |
| 284 | SLM | 8,751.2 |
| 285 | Sonic Automotive | 8,706.4 |
| 286 | Nordstrom | 8,560.7 |
| 287 | BJ's Wholesale Club | 8,524.2 |
| 288 | Reynolds American | 8,510.0 |
| 289 | First American Corp. | 8,499.1 |
| 290 | Pepco Holdings | 8,362.9 |
| 291 | Praxair | 8,324.0 |
| 292 | Rohm & Haas | 8,308.0 |
| 293 | Apache | 8,288.8 |
| 294 | Fortune Brands | 8,255.0 |
| 295 | ITT | 8,185.9 |
| 296 | Hilton Hotels | 8,162.0 |
| 297 | Ameriprise Financial | 8,140.0 |
| 298 | SAIC | 8,127.0 |
| 299 | Fifth Third Bancorp | 8,108.0 |
| 300 | Assurant | 8,070.6 |

## The *FORTUNE* 500 Largest US Corporations (continued)

| Rank | Company | Sales ($ mil.) |
|---|---|---|
| 301 | Hertz Global Holdings | 8,058.4 |
| 302 | Gannett | 8,033.4 |
| 303 | Smurfit-Stone Container | 7,944.0 |
| 304 | Mohawk Industries | 7,905.8 |
| 305 | Winn-Dixie Stores | 7,878.2 |
| 306 | Energy Transfer Equity | 7,859.1 |
| 307 | Dillard's | 7,849.4 |
| 308 | Boston Scientific | 7,821.0 |
| 309 | Sherwin-Williams | 7,809.8 |
| 310 | Starbucks | 7,786.9 |
| 311 | Campbell Soup | 7,778.0 |
| 312 | Regions Financial | 7,756.4 |
| 313 | Coventry Health Care | 7,733.8 |
| 314 | Terex | 7,647.6 |
| 315 | MGM Mirage | 7,588.0 |
| 316 | Commercial Metals | 7,555.9 |
| 317 | Qualcomm | 7,526.0 |
| 318 | Owens-Illinois | 7,523.5 |
| 319 | KeyCorp | 7,507.0 |
| 320 | NiSource | 7,495.9 |
| 321 | Eastman Chemical | 7,450.0 |
| 322 | Jacobs Engineering Group | 7,421.3 |
| 323 | Monsanto | 7,344.0 |
| 324 | Smith International | 7,333.6 |
| 325 | Chesapeake Energy | 7,325.6 |
| 326 | KeySpan | 7,181.6 |
| 327 | Dover | 7,179.6 |
| 328 | Crown Holdings | 7,140.0 |
| 329 | Land O'Lakes | 7,102.3 |
| 330 | Clear Channel Communications | 7,099.4 |
| 331 | First Data | 7,076.4 |
| 332 | VF | 7,033.5 |
| 333 | National Oilwell Varco | 7,025.8 |
| 334 | Integrys Energy Group | 6,979.2 |
| 335 | CIT Group | 6,927.7 |
| 336 | PPL | 6,904.0 |
| 337 | Northeast Utilities | 6,897.4 |
| 338 | American Family Insurance Group | 6,893.1 |
| 339 | Ameren | 6,880.0 |
| 340 | Liberty Global | 6,812.9 |
| 341 | CMS Energy | 6,810.0 |
| 342 | CDW | 6,785.5 |
| 343 | Newell Rubbermaid | 6,709.5 |
| 344 | Calpine | 6,705.8 |
| 345 | IAC/InterActiveCorp | 6,684.2 |
| 346 | Celanese | 6,668.0 |
| 347 | Virgin Media | 6,637.4 |
| 348 | Ball | 6,621.5 |
| 349 | C.H. Robinson Worldwide | 6,556.2 |
| 350 | MeadWestvaco | 6,530.0 |

| Rank | Company | Sales ($ mil.) |
|---|---|---|
| 351 | Enbridge Energy Partners | 6,509.0 |
| 352 | Estée Lauder | 6,508.9 |
| 353 | Omnicare | 6,493.0 |
| 354 | Realogy | 6,492.0 |
| 355 | Owens Corning | 6,461.0 |
| 356 | Black & Decker | 6,447.3 |
| 357 | Yahoo! | 6,425.7 |
| 358 | Mellon Financial Corp. | 6,395.0 |
| 359 | Family Dollar Stores | 6,394.8 |
| 360 | Synnex | 6,343.5 |
| 361 | Federal-Mogul | 6,326.4 |
| 362 | Ryder System | 6,306.6 |
| 363 | Safeco | 6,289.9 |
| 364 | Quest Diagnostics | 6,272.3 |
| 365 | CarMax | 6,260.0 |
| 366 | McGraw-Hill | 6,255.1 |
| 367 | Dole Food | 6,219.3 |
| 368 | Interpublic Group | 6,190.8 |
| 369 | Harley-Davidson | 6,185.6 |
| 370 | Thrivent Financial for Lutherans | 6,164.6 |
| 371 | NVR | 6,156.8 |
| 372 | Atmos Energy | 6,152.4 |
| 373 | Hovnanian Enterprises | 6,148.2 |
| 374 | NCR | 6,142.0 |
| 375 | Toll Brothers | 6,123.5 |
| 376 | Autoliv | 6,118.0 |
| 377 | Group 1 Automotive | 6,083.5 |
| 378 | AK Steel Holding | 6,069.0 |
| 379 | Allied Waste Industries | 6,028.8 |
| 380 | Cablevision Systems | 6,006.7 |
| 381 | Starwood Hotels & Resorts | 5,979.0 |
| 382 | Brunswick | 5,971.3 |
| 383 | eBay | 5,969.7 |
| 384 | AutoZone | 5,948.4 |
| 385 | Ryerson | 5,908.9 |
| 386 | Molson Coors Brewing | 5,902.8 |
| 387 | Agilent Technologies | 5,891.0 |
| 388 | W.W. Grainger | 5,883.7 |
| 389 | Charles Schwab | 5,880.0 |
| 390 | Goodrich | 5,878.3 |
| 391 | Asbury Automotive Group | 5,863.1 |
| 392 | Becton Dickinson | 5,834.8 |
| 393 | Performance Food Group | 5,826.7 |
| 394 | NRG Energy | 5,812.0 |
| 395 | Pitney Bowes | 5,811.2 |
| 396 | USG | 5,810.0 |
| 397 | Bed Bath & Beyond | 5,809.6 |
| 398 | Freeport-McMoRan Copper & Gold | 5,790.5 |
| 399 | Boise Cascade Holdings | 5,779.9 |
| 400 | Unisys | 5,757.2 |

| Rank | Company | Sales ($ mil.) |
|---|---|---|
| 401 | Foot Locker | 5,750.0 |
| 402 | Reliance Steel & Aluminum | 5,748.4 |
| 403 | Hormel Foods | 5,745.5 |
| 404 | Darden Restaurants | 5,720.6 |
| 405 | Avis Budget Group | 5,689.0 |
| 406 | Mattel | 5,650.2 |
| 407 | Advanced Micro Devices | 5,649.0 |
| 408 | Kelly Services | 5,639.0 |
| 409 | Charter Communications | 5,613.0 |
| 410 | Blockbuster | 5,611.3 |
| 411 | Whole Foods Market | 5,607.4 |
| 412 | Avery Dennison | 5,583.1 |
| 413 | Tribune | 5,582.6 |
| 414 | Temple-Inland | 5,581.0 |
| 415 | Ross Stores | 5,570.2 |
| 416 | Rockwell Automation | 5,561.4 |
| 417 | Triad Hospitals | 5,537.9 |
| 418 | Owens & Minor | 5,533.7 |
| 419 | Leggett & Platt | 5,505.4 |
| 420 | Beazer Homes USA | 5,462.0 |
| 421 | AGCO | 5,435.0 |
| 422 | Stryker | 5,405.6 |
| 423 | W.R. Berkley | 5,394.8 |
| 424 | Affiliated Computer Services | 5,353.7 |
| 425 | Wesco International | 5,320.6 |
| 426 | GameStop | 5,318.9 |
| 427 | Mosaic | 5,305.8 |
| 428 | Timken | 5,301.5 |
| 429 | Micron Technology | 5,272.0 |
| 430 | Barnes & Noble | 5,261.3 |
| 431 | Peabody Energy | 5,256.3 |
| 432 | Pilgrim's Pride | 5,235.6 |
| 433 | Hexion Specialty Chemicals | 5,233.0 |
| 434 | Energy East | 5,230.7 |
| 435 | UGI | 5,221.0 |
| 436 | Pantry | 5,211.2 |
| 437 | Pacific Life | 5,201.9 |
| 438 | Henry Schein | 5,191.0 |
| 439 | Corning | 5,174.0 |
| 440 | Avaya | 5,148.0 |
| 441 | Marshall & Ilsley Corp. | 5,127.9 |
| 442 | Lexmark International | 5,108.1 |
| 443 | Longs Drug Stores | 5,097.1 |
| 444 | Auto-Owners Insurance | 5,090.1 |
| 445 | Franklin Resources | 5,050.7 |
| 446 | Peter Kiewit Sons' | 5,049.0 |
| 447 | Newmont Mining | 5,039.0 |
| 448 | Emcor Group | 5,021.0 |
| 449 | El Paso | 5,011.0 |
| 450 | Graybar Electric | 5,009.1 |

## The *FORTUNE* 500 Largest US Corporations (continued)

| Rank | Company | Sales ($ mil.) |
|---|---|---|
| 451 | Liz Claiborne | 4,994.3 |
| 452 | Host Hotels & Resorts | 4,958.0 |
| 453 | Hershey | 4,944.2 |
| 454 | Anixter International | 4,938.6 |
| 455 | Allegheny Technologies | 4,936.6 |
| 456 | BlueLinx Holdings | 4,899.4 |
| 457 | Ecolab | 4,895.8 |
| 458 | DaVita | 4,880.7 |
| 459 | H&R Block | 4,872.8 |
| 460 | Western & Southern Financial | 4,838.1 |
| 461 | MDC Holdings | 4,801.7 |
| 462 | Frontier Oil | 4,796.0 |
| 463 | Erie Insurance Group | 4,785.5 |
| 464 | Shaw Group | 4,781.4 |
| 465 | Level 3 Communications | 4,778.0 |
| 466 | RadioShack | 4,777.5 |
| 467 | Ryland Group | 4,757.2 |
| 468 | Aleris International | 4,748.8 |
| 469 | Big Lots | 4,743.0 |
| 470 | Jones Apparel Group | 4,742.8 |
| 471 | SPX | 4,723.0 |
| 472 | Wm. Wrigley Jr. | 4,686.0 |
| 473 | Tenneco | 4,685.0 |
| 474 | Mirant | 4,684.0 |
| 475 | Clorox | 4,660.0 |
| 476 | Nash-Finch | 4,631.6 |
| 477 | Expeditors International | 4,626.0 |
| 478 | Advance Auto Parts | 4,616.5 |
| 479 | Sovereign Bancorp | 4,612.0 |
| 480 | Constellation Brands | 4,603.4 |
| 481 | BorgWarner | 4,585.4 |
| 482 | XTO Energy | 4,576.0 |
| 483 | SCANA | 4,563.0 |
| 484 | Cincinnati Financial | 4,550.0 |
| 485 | United Stationers | 4,546.9 |
| 486 | Fiserv | 4,544.2 |
| 487 | Comerica | 4,539.0 |
| 488 | Chiquita Brands International | 4,499.1 |
| 489 | Mutual of Omaha Insurance | 4,497.6 |
| 490 | Northern Trust Corp. | 4,473.0 |
| 491 | Global Partners | 4,472.4 |
| 492 | Western Union | 4,470.2 |
| 493 | Conseco | 4,467.4 |
| 494 | Community Health Systems | 4,369.9 |
| 495 | BJ Services | 4,367.9 |
| 496 | M&T Bank Corp. | 4,359.9 |
| 497 | Kindred Healthcare | 4,355.9 |
| 498 | Western Digital | 4,341.3 |
| 499 | Sealed Air | 4,327.9 |
| 500 | SunGard Data Systems | 4,323.0 |

## The *Forbes* Largest Private Companies in the US

| Rank | Company | Sales ($ mil.) |
|---|---|---|
| 1 | Koch Industries | 90,000 |
| 2 | Cargill | 69,902 |
| 3 | PricewaterhouseCoopers | 21,300 |
| 4 | Publix Super Markets | 20,745 |
| 5 | SemGroup | 20,174 |
| 6 | Mars | 20,000 |
| 7 | C&S Wholesale Grocers | 19,936 |
| 8 | Ernst & Young | 18,400 |
| 9 | Bechtel | 18,100 |
| 10 | Meijer | 13,200 |
| 11 | H.E. Butt Grocery | 12,400 |
| 12 | Cox Enterprises | 11,596 |
| 13 | Toys "R" Us | 11,275 |
| 14 | Fidelity Investments | 11,130 |
| 15 | TransMontaigne | 10,475 |
| 16 | Tenaska Energy | 10,000 |
| 17 | Flying J | 9,454 |
| 18 | JM Family Enterprises | 9,400 |
| 19 | Swift & Co. | 9,350 |
| 20 | Capital Group Cos. | 9,246 |
| 21 | Enterprise Rent-A-Car | 9,040 |
| 22 | Platinum Equity | 8,000 |
| 23 | Hertz Global Holdings | 7,469 |
| 24 | Menard | 7,400 |
| 25 | Reyes Holdings | 7,400 |
| 26 | Advance Publications | 7,315 |
| 27 | Alticor | 7,290 |
| 28 | QuikTrip | 7,157 |
| 29 | S.C. Johnson & Son | 7,000 |
| 30 | Murdock Holding Company | 6,988 |
| 31 | Southern Wine & Spirits | 6,500 |
| 32 | Giant Eagle | 6,061 |
| 33 | Transammonia | 6,059 |
| 34 | Unisource Worldwide | 6,000 |
| 35 | Marmon Group | 5,919 |
| 36 | Boise Cascade | 5,907 |
| 37 | Pro-Build Holdings | 5,700 |
| 38 | Sinclair Oil | 5,600 |
| 39 | Gulf Oil | 5,400 |
| 40 | Hy-Vee | 5,140 |
| 41 | Guardian Industries | 5,000 |
| 42 | RaceTrac Petroleum | 4,969 |
| 43 | MBM | 4,964 |
| 44 | Carlson Cos. | 4,933 |
| 45 | Gulf States Toyota | 4,600 |
| 46 | Hearst | 4,550 |
| 47 | Colonial Group | 4,500 |
| 48 | Hexion Specialty Chemicals | 4,470 |
| 49 | Allegis Group | 4,400 |
| 50 | Graybar Electric | 4,288 |
| 51 | Kohler | 4,200 |
| 52 | Peter Kiewit Sons' | 4,145 |
| 53 | Levi Strauss & Co. | 4,125 |
| 54 | Neiman Marcus Group | 4,106 |
| 55 | Bloomberg | 4,100 |
| 56 | Hallmark Cards | 4,003 |
| 57 | SunGard Data Systems | 4,002 |
| 58 | Kinray | 4,000 |
| 59 | OSI Group | 4,000 |
| 60 | TravelCenters of America | 4,000 |
| 61 | 84 Lumber | 3,920 |
| 62 | Gordon Food Service | 3,915 |
| 63 | Wawa | 3,905 |
| 64 | Love's Travel Stops | 3,807 |
| 65 | McKinsey & Co. | 3,800 |
| 66 | Wegmans Food Markets | 3,800 |
| 67 | Booz Allen Hamilton | 3,700 |
| 68 | Roundy's Supermarkets | 3,700 |
| 69 | Bi-Lo Holdings | 3,600 |
| 70 | HT Hackney | 3,550 |
| 71 | InterTech Group | 3,500 |
| 72 | Schneider National | 3,500 |
| 73 | Burlington Coat Factory Warehouse | 3,449 |
| 74 | JF Shea | 3,429 |
| 75 | Perdue Farms | 3,400 |
| 76 | Stater Bros. Markets | 3,400 |
| 77 | Schwan Food | 3,375 |
| 78 | Raley's | 3,370 |
| 79 | Sheetz | 3,320 |
| 80 | JohnsonDiversey | 3,310 |
| 81 | Milliken & Co. | 3,301 |
| 82 | Aecom Technology | 3,300 |
| 83 | Cumberland Farms | 3,300 |
| 84 | Red Apple Group | 3,300 |
| 85 | J.R. Simplot | 3,300 |
| 86 | Eby-Brown | 3,200 |
| 87 | Global Hyatt | 3,200 |
| 88 | Southwire | 3,200 |
| 89 | Edward Jones | 3,190 |
| 90 | CH2M Hill Cos. | 3,152 |
| 91 | VWR International | 3,138 |
| 92 | Keystone Foods | 3,119 |
| 93 | Whiting-Turner Contracting | 3,066 |
| 94 | Andersen | 3,000 |
| 95 | Ergon | 3,000 |
| 96 | Golub | 3,000 |
| 97 | Kingston Technology | 3,000 |
| 98 | Schreiber Foods | 3,000 |
| 99 | Belk | 2,969 |
| 100 | Charmer Sunbelt Group | 2,900 |
| 101 | Glazer's Wholesale Drug | 2,900 |
| 102 | Jeld-Wen | 2,900 |
| 103 | Vanguard Car Rental Group | 2,891 |
| 104 | Vistar | 2,850 |
| 105 | WinCo Foods | 2,850 |
| 106 | Clark Enterprises | 2,844 |
| 107 | International Data Group | 2,840 |
| 108 | Gilbane | 2,832 |
| 109 | Consolidated Elec. Distributors | 2,800 |
| 110 | Grant Thornton International | 2,740 |
| 111 | Parsons | 2,729 |
| 112 | E&J Gallo Winery | 2,700 |
| 113 | Anderson Cos. | 2,696 |
| 114 | Linens 'n Things | 2,695 |
| 115 | Vanguard Health Systems | 2,653 |
| 116 | Alex Lee | 2,600 |
| 117 | ABC Supply | 2,597 |
| 118 | Structure Tone | 2,592 |
| 119 | Ashley Furniture Industries | 2,550 |
| 120 | Ingram Industries | 2,539 |
| 121 | Grocers Supply | 2,531 |
| 122 | US Oncology | 2,519 |
| 123 | Amsted Industries | 2,512 |
| 124 | Sports Authority | 2,509 |
| 125 | Bashas' | 2,500 |
| 126 | Save Mart Supermarkets | 2,500 |
| 127 | Services Group of America | 2,500 |
| 128 | Graham Packaging Holdings | 2,473 |
| 129 | Tishman Construction | 2,458 |
| 130 | DeBruce Grain | 2,437 |
| 131 | Mervyns | 2,433 |
| 132 | Solo Cup | 2,432 |
| 133 | Travelport | 2,429 |
| 134 | Sammons Enterprises | 2,400 |
| 135 | Quintiles Transnational | 2,399 |
| 136 | AMC Entertainment | 2,388 |
| 137 | Golden State Foods | 2,375 |
| 138 | Asplundh Tree Expert | 2,366 |
| 139 | JE Dunn Construction Group | 2,364 |
| 140 | Houchens Industries | 2,360 |
| 141 | Walsh Group | 2,350 |
| 142 | Fry's Electronics | 2,340 |
| 143 | Central National-Gottesman | 2,300 |
| 144 | Heico Cos. | 2,300 |
| 145 | HP Hood | 2,300 |
| 146 | JM Huber | 2,300 |
| 147 | Hunt Consolidated/Hunt Oil | 2,300 |
| 148 | Schnuck Markets | 2,300 |
| 149 | Leprino Foods | 2,285 |
| 150 | NewPage | 2,280 |

SOURCE: *FORBES*, NOVEMBER 27, 2006

## The *Forbes* Largest Private Companies in the US (continued)

| Rank | Company | Sales ($ mil.) |
|---|---|---|
| 151 | Brightstar | 2,252 |
| 152 | General Parts | 2,250 |
| 153 | Mary Kay | 2,200 |
| 154 | Petters Group Worldwide | 2,200 |
| 155 | Quality King Distributors | 2,200 |
| 156 | ShopKo Operating | 2,200 |
| 157 | UniGroup | 2,200 |
| 158 | Altivity Packaging | 2,186 |
| 159 | Follett | 2,184 |
| 160 | Dot Foods | 2,164 |
| 161 | Medline Industries | 2,160 |
| 162 | Affinia Group | 2,132 |
| 163 | HealthMarkets | 2,121 |
| 164 | Brookshire Grocery | 2,100 |
| 165 | Mansfield Oil | 2,100 |
| 166 | WinWholesale | 2,100 |
| 167 | Software House Intl. | 2,051 |
| 168 | Rosen's Diversified | 2,000 |
| 169 | Delaware North Cos. | 2,000 |
| 170 | Demoulas Super Markets | 2,000 |
| 171 | Ebsco Industries | 2,000 |
| 172 | Ben E. Keith | 2,000 |
| 173 | Rich Products | 2,000 |
| 174 | Scoular | 2,000 |
| 175 | Truman Arnold Cos. | 2,000 |
| 176 | Petco Animal Supplies | 1,996 |
| 177 | McCarthy Building Cos. | 1,987 |
| 178 | W.L. Gore & Associates | 1,983 |
| 179 | Covalence Specialty Materials | 1,970 |
| 180 | NTK Holdings | 1,959 |
| 181 | Life Care Centers of America | 1,957 |
| 182 | G-I Holdings | 1,956 |
| 183 | Maines Paper & Food Service | 1,950 |
| 184 | Quad/Graphics | 1,950 |
| 185 | Frank Consolidated Enterprises | 1,918 |
| 186 | Bass Pro Shops | 1,915 |
| 187 | ContiGroup Cos. | 1,900 |
| 188 | Metaldyne | 1,887 |
| 189 | Select Medical | 1,858 |
| 190 | Discount Tire | 1,856 |
| 191 | William Lyon Homes | 1,856 |
| 192 | World Wide Technology | 1,852 |
| 193 | Swinerton | 1,830 |
| 194 | Cooper-Standard Automotive | 1,827 |
| 195 | National Distributing | 1,825 |

| Rank | Company | Sales ($ mil.) |
|---|---|---|
| 196 | Bose | 1,800 |
| 197 | Foster Farms | 1,800 |
| 198 | Drummond | 1,798 |
| 199 | Yates Cos. | 1,761 |
| 200 | Bradco Supply | 1,760 |
| 201 | McWane | 1,753 |
| 202 | AG Spanos Cos. | 1,750 |
| 203 | Marsh Supermarkets | 1,744 |
| 204 | Holiday Cos. | 1,742 |
| 205 | Ardent Health Services | 1,731 |
| 206 | Hensel Phelps Construction | 1,728 |
| 207 | Landmark Communications | 1,719 |
| 208 | Renco Group | 1,710 |
| 209 | Taylor | 1,706 |
| 210 | Dunavant Enterprises | 1,704 |
| 211 | Baker & Taylor | 1,700 |
| 212 | Dresser | 1,700 |
| 213 | Hunt Construction Group | 1,700 |
| 214 | National Gypsum | 1,700 |
| 215 | Young's Market | 1,700 |
| 216 | Warren Equities | 1,690 |
| 217 | SAS Institute | 1,680 |
| 218 | CC Industries | 1,660 |
| 219 | Knowledge Learning | 1,654 |
| 220 | Brasfield & Gorrie | 1,645 |
| 221 | Iasis Healthcare | 1,644 |
| 222 | Metals USA | 1,639 |
| 223 | SSA Marine | 1,634 |
| 224 | Wilbur-Ellis | 1,632 |
| 225 | Berwind Group | 1,629 |
| 226 | Skadden, Arps | 1,610 |
| 227 | O'Neal Steel | 1,605 |
| 228 | Black & Veatch | 1,600 |
| 229 | FHC Health Systems | 1,600 |
| 230 | Parsons Brinckerhoff | 1,600 |
| 231 | Republic Beverage | 1,600 |
| 232 | Rooms To Go | 1,600 |
| 233 | Verso Paper | 1,600 |
| 234 | J. M. Smith | 1,596 |
| 235 | Duane Reade | 1,589 |
| 236 | Red Chamber Group | 1,580 |
| 237 | Golden Living | 1,570 |
| 238 | Sierra Pacific Industries | 1,570 |
| 239 | Arctic Slope Regional | 1,567 |
| 240 | Shamrock Foods | 1,566 |

| Rank | Company | Sales ($ mil.) |
|---|---|---|
| 241 | Petro Stopping Centers | 1,548 |
| 242 | Metro-Goldwyn-Mayer | 1,536 |
| 243 | West Corp. | 1,524 |
| 244 | Vertis | 1,510 |
| 245 | American Tire Distributors | 1,505 |
| 246 | Academy Sports & Outdoors | 1,501 |
| 247 | Bellco Health | 1,500 |
| 248 | Boston Consulting Group | 1,500 |
| 249 | Guthy-Renker | 1,500 |
| 250 | Reynolds and Reynolds | 1,500 |
| 251 | Soave Enterprises | 1,500 |
| 252 | Tang Industries | 1,500 |
| 253 | Visant | 1,498 |
| 254 | Conair | 1,488 |
| 255 | Merit Energy | 1,487 |
| 256 | Pinnacle Foods | 1,486 |
| 257 | Lucasfilm | 1,483 |
| 258 | Roll International | 1,479 |
| 259 | L.L. Bean | 1,470 |
| 260 | Crown Equipment | 1,466 |
| 261 | D&H Distributing | 1,465 |
| 262 | Hobby Lobby Stores | 1,465 |
| 263 | Carpenter | 1,456 |
| 264 | McJunkin | 1,446 |
| 265 | MediaNews Group | 1,436 |
| 266 | US Oil | 1,431 |
| 267 | Kum & Go | 1,428 |
| 268 | Barnes & Noble College Booksellers | 1,415 |
| 269 | K-VA-T Food Stores | 1,414 |
| 270 | Latham & Watkins | 1,413 |
| 271 | Towers Perrin | 1,413 |
| 272 | Camac International | 1,400 |
| 273 | Haworth | 1,400 |
| 274 | Koch Foods | 1,400 |
| 275 | Estes Express Lines | 1,394 |
| 276 | Dart Container | 1,388 |
| 277 | Great Lakes Cheese | 1,375 |
| 278 | International Specialty Products | 1,360 |
| 279 | Austin Industries | 1,359 |
| 280 | Sigma Plastics Group | 1,350 |
| 281 | ICC Industries | 1,342 |
| 282 | BE&K | 1,339 |
| 283 | Berry Plastics | 1,338 |
| 284 | GNC | 1,318 |
| 285 | Day & Zimmermann | 1,300 |

## The *Forbes* Largest Private Companies in the US (continued)

| Rank | Company | Sales ($ mil.) |
|---|---|---|
| 286 | Hampton Affiliates | 1,300 |
| 287 | LPL Financial Services | 1,300 |
| 288 | New Balance Athletic Shoe | 1,300 |
| 289 | Oxbow | 1,300 |
| 290 | Pella | 1,300 |
| 291 | Washington Cos. | 1,300 |
| 292 | Vought Aircraft Industries | 1,297 |
| 293 | Jones Day | 1,285 |
| 294 | Houghton Mifflin | 1,282 |
| 295 | Goody's Family Clothing | 1,275 |
| 296 | David Weekley Homes | 1,272 |
| 297 | Maritz | 1,270 |
| 298 | Peerless Importers | 1,270 |
| 299 | Printpack | 1,268 |
| 300 | Newegg.com | 1,260 |
| 301 | Plastipak Packaging | 1,258 |
| 302 | Beall's | 1,256 |
| 303 | Big Y Foods | 1,250 |
| 304 | Chemcentral | 1,250 |
| 305 | Michael Foods | 1,242 |
| 306 | Gould Paper | 1,240 |
| 307 | Red Man Pipe & Supply | 1,239 |
| 308 | North Pacific Group | 1,232 |
| 309 | Remy International | 1,229 |
| 310 | TIC Holdings | 1,224 |
| 311 | Interactive Brokers Group | 1,217 |
| 312 | Foodarama Supermarkets | 1,215 |
| 313 | Honickman Affiliates | 1,215 |
| 314 | Topa Equities | 1,202 |
| 315 | Advanced Drainage Systems | 1,200 |
| 316 | Ilitch Holdings | 1,200 |
| 317 | MA Laboratories | 1,200 |
| 318 | Les Schwab Tire Centers | 1,200 |
| 319 | Suffolk Construction | 1,200 |
| 320 | ViewSonic | 1,200 |
| 321 | Affinion Group | 1,199 |
| 322 | Crowley Maritime | 1,191 |
| 323 | Long & Foster Cos. | 1,190 |
| 324 | Ritz Camera Centers | 1,185 |
| 325 | Drees Co. | 1,183 |
| 326 | Wirtz | 1,180 |
| 327 | Zachry Construction | 1,175 |
| 328 | Associated Materials | 1,174 |
| 329 | GSC Enterprises | 1,174 |
| 330 | Freeman Cos. | 1,173 |
| 331 | Education Management | 1,170 |
| 332 | Gate Petroleum | 1,170 |
| 333 | Alsco | 1,169 |
| 334 | Roseburg Forest Products | 1,162 |
| 335 | ATA Airlines | 1,160 |
| 336 | SavaSeniorCare | 1,160 |
| 337 | M. A. Mortenson | 1,157 |
| 338 | Concentra Operating | 1,155 |
| 339 | UGS | 1,155 |
| 340 | Forever Living Products Intl. | 1,150 |
| 341 | PC Richard & Son | 1,150 |
| 342 | MTD Products | 1,131 |
| 343 | Bain & Co. | 1,130 |
| 344 | Sidley Austin | 1,124 |
| 345 | Tube City IMS | 1,123 |
| 346 | Weitz | 1,111 |
| 347 | ASI | 1,110 |
| 348 | Dawn Food Products | 1,110 |
| 349 | United Components | 1,107 |
| 350 | Williamson-Dickie Mfg. | 1,102 |
| 351 | Beaulieu of America Group | 1,100 |
| 352 | Connell Limited Partnership | 1,100 |
| 353 | Genmar Holdings | 1,100 |
| 354 | Goss International | 1,100 |
| 355 | Goya Foods | 1,100 |
| 356 | Key Safety Systems | 1,100 |
| 357 | Kimball Hill Homes | 1,100 |
| 358 | Rooney Holdings | 1,100 |
| 359 | Sutherland Lumber | 1,100 |
| 360 | Greatwide Logistics Services | 1,087 |
| 361 | McKee Foods | 1,085 |
| 362 | Micro Electronics | 1,083 |
| 363 | Rexnord | 1,081 |
| 364 | Barton Malow | 1,080 |
| 365 | Bozzuto's | 1,080 |
| 366 | Pacific Coast Building Products | 1,077 |
| 367 | 24 Hour Fitness Worldwide | 1,077 |
| 368 | Pliant | 1,073 |
| 369 | Boscov's Department Store | 1,072 |
| 370 | Lifetouch | 1,070 |
| 371 | Plastech Engineered Products | 1,069 |
| 372 | Euramax International | 1,068 |
| 373 | Columbia Forest Products | 1,050 |
| 374 | Appleton Papers | 1,047 |
| 375 | White & Case | 1,046 |
| 376 | Alberici | 1,033 |
| 377 | Inserra Supermarkets | 1,030 |
| 378 | Electro-Motive Diesel | 1,029 |
| 379 | ClubCorp | 1,028 |
| 380 | Holiday Retirement | 1,027 |
| 381 | Nypro | 1,023 |
| 382 | Stewart's Shops | 1,023 |
| 383 | Cinemark USA | 1,021 |
| 384 | Apex Oil | 1,020 |
| 385 | Thorntons | 1,018 |
| 386 | Weil Gotshal & Manges | 1,017 |
| 387 | Team Health | 1,015 |
| 388 | TriMas | 1,001 |
| 389 | Bartlett & Co. | 1,000 |
| 390 | Esselte | 1,000 |
| 391 | M. Fabrikant & Sons | 1,000 |
| 392 | The Kraft Group | 1,000 |
| 393 | Purity Wholesale Grocers | 1,000 |
| 394 | Swagelok | 1,000 |

## Top 20 in CEO Compensation

| Rank | Name | Company | Total Pay* ($ mil.) |
|---|---|---|---|
| 1 | Steven P. Jobs | Apple | 646.6 |
| 2 | Ray R. Irani | Occidental Petroleum | 321.6 |
| 3 | Barry Diller | IAC/InterActiveCorp | 295.1 |
| 4 | William P. Foley II | Fidelity National Finl. | 179.6 |
| 5 | Terry S. Semel | Yahoo! | 174.2 |
| 6 | Michael S. Dell | Dell | 153.2 |
| 7 | Angelo R. Mozilo | Countrywide Financial | 142.0 |
| 8 | Michael S. Jeffries | Abercrombie & Fitch | 114.6 |
| 9 | Kenneth D. Lewis | Bank of America | 99.8 |
| 10 | Henry C. Duques | First Data | 98.2 |
| 11 | Harold M. Messmer Jr. | Robert Half Intl. | 74.3 |
| 12 | Lawrence J. Ellison | Oracle | 72.4 |
| 13 | Bob R. Simpson | XTO Energy | 72.3 |
| 14 | Richard M. Kovacevich | Wells Fargo | 72.0 |
| 15 | John T. Chambers | Cisco Systems | 71.3 |
| 16 | Gregg L. Engles | Dean Foods | 66.1 |
| 17 | Lew Frankfort | Coach | 65.9 |
| 18 | Joseph H. Moglia | TD AMERITRADE Holding | 62.2 |
| 19 | James Dimon | JPMorgan Chase | 57.2 |
| 20 | William R. Berkley | W. R. Berkley | 54.6 |

*Includes salary, bonus, and long-term compensation

SOURCE: *FORBES*, MAY 3, 2007

## Top 20 Most Powerful Women in Business

| Rank | Name | Position |
|---|---|---|
| 1 | Indra Nooyi | CEO, PepsiCo |
| 2 | Anne Mulcahy | Chairman and CEO, Xerox |
| 3 | Meg Whitman | CEO and President, eBay |
| 4 | Pat Woertz | CEO and President, Archer Daniels Midland |
| 5 | Irene Rosenfeld | CEO, Kraft Foods |
| 6 | Brenda Barnes | Chairman and CEO, Sara Lee |
| 7 | Andrea Jung | Chairman and CEO, Avon |
| 8 | Oprah Winfrey | Chairman, Harpo Inc. |
| 9 | Sallie Krawcheck | CFO, Head of Strategy, Citigroup |
| 10 | Susan Arnold | Vice Chair, Beauty and Health, Procter & Gamble |
| 11 | Christine Poon | Vice Chairman, Johnson & Johnson |
| 12 | Judy McGrath | Chairman and CEO, MTV Networks, Viacom |
| 13 | Anne Sweeney | Co-Chair, Disney Media Networks; President, Disney-ABC Television |
| 14 | Ann Livermore | EVP, Technology Solutions Group, Hewlett-Packard |
| 15 | Ann Moore | Chairman and CEO, Time Inc. |
| 16 | Ginni Rometty | SVP, Global Business Services, IBM |
| 17 | Susan Desmond-Hellmann | President, Product Development, Genentech |
| 18 | Abigail Johnson | President, Fidelity Employer Services, Fidelity |
| 19 | Zoe Cruz | Co-President, Morgan Stanley |
| 20 | Susan Ivey | Chairman and CEO, R.J. Reynolds Tobacco |

SOURCE: *FORTUNE*, OCTOBER 16, 2006

## *Forbes* 20 Greatest US Fortunes

| Rank | Name | Age | Net Worth ($ bil.) | Source |
|---|---|---|---|---|
| 1 | William Gates III | 51 | 59.0 | Microsoft |
| 2 | Warren Buffett | 77 | 52.0 | Berkshire Hathaway |
| 3 | Sheldon Adelson | 74 | 28.0 | Casinos, hotels |
| 4 | Lawrence Ellison | 63 | 26.0 | Oracle |
| 5 | Sergey Brin | 34 | 18.5 | Google |
| 5 | Larry Page | 34 | 18.5 | Google |
| 7 | Kirk Kerkorian | 90 | 18.0 | Investments, casinos |
| 8 | Michael Dell | 42 | 17.2 | Dell |
| 9 | Charles Koch | 71 | 17.0 | Oil, commodities |
| 9 | David Koch | 67 | 17.0 | Oil, commodities |
| 11 | Paul Allen | 54 | 16.8 | Microsoft, investments |
| 12 | Christy Walton & family | 52 | 16.3 | Wal-Mart inheritance |
| 12 | Jim Walton | 59 | 16.3 | Wal-Mart |
| 12 | S. Robson Walton | 63 | 16.3 | Wal-Mart |
| 15 | Alice Walton | 58 | 16.1 | Wal-Mart |
| 16 | Steven Ballmer | 51 | 15.2 | Microsoft |
| 17 | Abigail Johnson | 45 | 15.0 | Fidelity |
| 18 | Carl Icahn | 71 | 14.5 | Leveraged buyouts |
| 19 | Forrest Mars Jr. | 76 | 14.0 | Candy, pet food |
| 19 | Jacqueline Mars | 67 | 14.0 | Candy, pet food |
| 19 | John Mars | 71 | 14.0 | Candy, pet food |
| 19 | Jack Taylor & family | 85 | 14.0 | Enterprise Rent-A-Car |

SOURCE: *FORBES*, OCTOBER 8, 2007

## *Forbes* 20 Most Powerful Celebrities

| Rank | Name | Earnings ($ mil.) |
|---|---|---|
| 1 | Oprah Winfrey | 260 |
| 2 | Tiger Woods | 100 |
| 3 | Madonna | 72 |
| 4 | Rolling Stones | 88 |
| 5 | Brad Pitt | 35 |
| 6 | Johnny Depp | 92 |
| 7 | Elton John | 53 |
| 8 | Tom Cruise | 31 |
| 9 | Jay-Z | 83 |
| 10 | Steven Spielberg | 110 |
| 11 | Tom Hanks | 74 |
| 12 | Cast of *Grey's Anatomy* | 33 |
| 13 | Howard Stern | 70 |
| 14 | Angelina Jolie | 20 |
| 15 | David Beckham | 33 |
| 16 | Phil Mickelson | 42 |
| 17 | David Letterman | 40 |
| 18 | Bon Jovi | 67 |
| 19 | Donald Trump | 32 |
| 20 | Celine Dion | 45 |

*Forbes*' rankings are based on income and media recognition (Web prominence, magazine covers, radio/TV and newspaper coverage)

SOURCE: *FORBES*, JUNE 14, 2007

## *Advertising Age's* Top 50 Media Companies by Revenue

| Rank | Company | Headquarters | 2006 Media Revenue ($ mil.) |
|---|---|---|---|
| 1 | Time Warner | New York | 33,993 |
| 2 | Comcast Corp. | Philadelphia | 27,392 |
| 3 | Walt Disney Co. | Burbank, CA | 16,838 |
| 4 | News Corp. | New York | 14,091 |
| 5 | DIRECTV Group | El Segundo, CA | 13,744 |
| 6 | NBC Universal (General Electric) | New York | 13,240 |
| 7 | CBS Corp. | New York | 12,183 |
| 8 | Cox Enterprises | Atlanta | 10,385 |
| 9 | EchoStar Communications Corp. | Englewood, CO | 9,456 |
| 10 | Viacom | New York | 8,444 |
| 11 | Advance Publications | New York | 7,837 |
| 12 | Gannett Co. | McLean, VA | 6,332 |
| 13 | AT&T | San Antonio | 5,684 |
| 14 | Charter Communications | St. Louis | 5,504 |
| 15 | Cablevision Systems Corp. | Bethpage, NY | 5,410 |
| 16 | Clear Channel Communications | San Antonio | 5,267 |
| 17 | Tribune Co. | Chicago | 5,262 |
| 18 | Hearst Corp. | New York | 4,523 |
| 19 | Google | Mountain View, CA | 4,095 |
| 20 | Sony Corp. | New York/Tokyo | 4,091 |
| 21 | Yahoo! | Sunnyvale, CA | 3,422 |
| 22 | The New York Times Co. | New York | 3,290 |
| 23 | Idearc | DFW Airport, TX | 3,221 |
| 24 | R.H. Donnelley Corp. | Cary, NC | 2,685 |
| 25 | McClatchy Co. | Sacramento, CA | 2,455 |
| 26 | E.W. Scripps Co. | Cincinnati | 2,362 |
| 27 | Valassis Communications | Livonia, MI | 2,317 |
| 28 | The Washington Post Co. | Washington | 2,221 |
| 29 | Univision Communications | Los Angeles | 2,026 |
| 30 | Yellow Book USA (Yell Group) | Uniondale, NY/Reading, UK | 1,858 |
| 31 | Discovery Communications | Silver Spring, MD | 1,752 |
| 32 | Belo Corp. | Dallas | 1,588 |
| 33 | MediaNews Group | Denver | 1,441 |
| 34 | Meredith Corp. | Des Moines | 1,317 |
| 35 | Dow Jones & Co. | New York | 1,299 |
| 36 | Insight Communications Co. | New York | 1,263 |
| 37 | Liberty Media Corp. | Englewood, CO | 1,259 |
| 38 | Mediacom Communications Corp. | Middletown, NY | 1,210 |
| 39 | A&E Television Networks | New York | 1,189 |
| 40 | Lee Enterprises | Davenport, IA | 1,129 |
| 41 | Microsoft Corp. | Redmond, WA | 1,128 |
| 42 | Lamar Advertising Co. | Baton Rouge, LA | 1,120 |
| 43 | Media General | Richmond, VA | 1,034 |
| 44 | International Data Group | Boston | 990 |
| 45 | Citadel Broadcasting Corp. | Las Vegas | 986 |
| 46 | McGraw-Hill Cos. | New York | 985 |
| 47 | Reader's Digest Association | Pleasantville, NY | 968 |
| 48 | Lifetime Entertainment Services | New York | 920 |
| 49 | XM Satellite Radio Holdings | Washington | 877 |
| 50 | Metro-Goldwyn-Mayer | Los Angeles | 875 |

SOURCE: *ADVERTISING AGE*, OCTOBER 1, 2007

## *Chain Store Age's* Top 20 US Retailers

| Rank | Company | Headquarters | 2006 Revenue ($ mil.) |
|---|---|---|---|
| 1 | Wal-Mart Stores Inc. | Bentonville, AR | 344,992.0 |
| 2 | The Home Depot | Atlanta | 90,837.0 |
| 3 | The Kroger Co. | Cincinnati | 66,111.0 |
| 4 | Target Corp. | Minneapolis | 59,490.0 |
| 5 | Costco | Issaquah, WA | 58,963.2 |
| 6 | Sears Holdings | Hoffman Estates, IL | 53,012.0 |
| 7 | Walgreen Co. | Deerfield, IL | 47,409.0 |
| 8 | Lowe's Cos. | Mooreville, NC | 46,927.0 |
| 9 | CVS Caremark Corp. | Woonsocket, RI | 43,813.8 |
| 10 | Safeway | Pleasanton, CA | 40,185.0 |
| 11 | Best Buy | Richfield, MN | 35,934.0 |
| 12 | Supervalu | Eden Prairie, MN | 28,016.0 |
| 13 | Macy's | Cincinnati | 26,970.0 |
| 14 | Ahold USA | Chantilly, VA | 22,437.0 |
| 15 | Publix Super Markets | Lakeland, FL | 21,654.8 |
| 16 | J.C. Penney | Plano, TX | 19,903.0 |
| 17 | Staples | Framingham, MA | 18,160.8 |
| 18 | Rite Aid | Camp Hill, PA | 17,507.7 |
| 19 | TJX Cos. | Framingham, MA | 17,404.6 |
| 20 | Delhaize America | Salisbury, NC | 17,289.2 |

SOURCE: *CHAIN STORE AGE*, AUGUST 2007

## *Supermarket News'* Top 20 Supermarket Companies

| Rank | Company | Headquarters | 2006 Revenue ($ mil.) |
|---|---|---|---|
| 1 | Wal-Mart Stores | Bentonville, AR | 232.9 |
| 2 | Kroger Co. | Cincinnati | 66.1 |
| 3 | Costco Wholesale Corp. | Issaquah, WA | 59.0 |
| 4 | Safeway | Pleasanton, CA | 40.5 |
| 5 | Supervalu | Minneapolis | 37.4 |
| 6 | Loblaw Cos. | Toronto | 26.5 |
| 7 | Ahold USA Retail | Quincy, MA | 24.0 |
| 8 | Publix Super Markets | Lakeland, FL | 21.7 |
| 9 | C&S Wholesale Grocers | Keene, NH | 19.4 |
| 10 | Delhaize America | Salisbury, NC | 17.3 |
| 11 | 7-Eleven | Dallas | 15.0 |
| 12 | Meijer | Grand Rapids, MI | 13.2 |
| 13 | Sobeys | Stellarton, Nova Scotia | 12.5 |
| 14 | H.E. Butt Grocery Co. | San Antonio | 12.4 |
| 15 | Metro | Montreal | 9.6 |
| 16 | Wakefern Food Corp. | Elizabeth, NJ | 9.5 |
| 17 | Dollar General Corp. | Goodlettsville, TN | 9.2 |
| 18 | BJ's Wholesale Club | Natick, MA | 8.6 |
| 19 | Albertsons LLC | Boise, ID | 8.0 |
| 20 | Winn-Dixie Stores | Jacksonville, FL | 7.5 |

SOURCE: *SUPERMARKET NEWS*, JANUARY 22, 2007

## Top 20 Bank Holding Companies

| Rank | Company | Headquarters | 2006 Total Assets ($ mil.) |
|---|---|---|---|
| 1 | Citigroup Inc. | New York | 2,220,866.0 |
| 2 | Bank of America | Charlotte, NC | 1,535,684.3 |
| 3 | J.P. Morgan Chase & Co. | New York | 1,458,042.0 |
| 4 | Wachovia Corporation | Charlotte, NC | 719,922.0 |
| 5 | Taunus Corporation | New York | 579,062.0 |
| 6 | Wells Fargo & Company | San Francisco | 539,865.0 |
| 7 | HSBC North America | Prospect Heights, IL | 483,630.1 |
| 8 | U.S. Bancorp | Minneapolis | 222,530.0 |
| 9 | Suntrust Banks | Atlanta | 180,314.4 |
| 10 | ABN AMRO North America | Chicago | 160,342.0 |
| 11 | Citizens Financial Group | Providence, RI | 159,392.7 |
| 12 | Capital One | McLean, VA | 145,938.0 |
| 13 | National City Corporation | Cleveland | 140,648.2 |
| 14 | Regions Financial | Birmingham, AL | 137,624.2 |
| 15 | BB&T Corporation | Winston-Salem, NC | 127,577.1 |
| 16 | Bank Of New York | New York | 126,457.0 |
| 17 | PNC Financial Services | Pittsburgh | 125,736.7 |
| 18 | State Street Corporation | Boston | 112,345.8 |
| 19 | Fifth Third Bancorp | Cincinnati | 101,389.7 |
| 20 | Keycorp | Cleveland | 93,490.9 |

SOURCE: FEDERAL RESERVE SYSTEM, JUNE 30, 2007

## Top 20 US Law Firms

| Rank | Law Firm | 2006 Gross Revenue ($ mil.) |
|---|---|---|
| 1 | Skadden, Arps, Slate, Meagher & Flom | 1,850.0 |
| 2 | Latham & Watkins | 1,624.0 |
| 3 | Baker & McKenzie | 1,522.0 |
| 4 | Jones Day | 1,310.0 |
| 5 | Sidley Austin Brown & Wood | 1,246.5 |
| 6 | White & Case | 1,185.0 |
| 7 | Kirkland & Ellis | 1,145.0 |
| 8 | Mayer, Brown, Rowe & Maw | 1,084.0 |
| 9 | Weil, Gotshal & Manges | 1,050.0 |
| 10 | Greenberg Traurig | 1,040.5 |
| 11 | DLA Piper US | 1,016.0 |
| 12 | Morgan, Lewis | 922.0 |
| 13 | Sullivan & Cromwell | 900.0 |
| 14 | Wilmer Cutler | 897.0 |
| 15 | O'Melveny & Myers | 869.0 |
| 16 | McDermott Will & Emery | 860.0 |
| 17 | Shearman & Sterling | 842.0 |
| 18 | Paul, Hastings | 813.5 |
| 19 | Cleary, Gottlieb, Steen & Hamilton | 813.0 |
| 20 | Gibson, Dunn & Crutcher | 809.0 |

SOURCE: *AMERICAN LAWYER*, MAY 2007

## Top 20 Money Managers

| Rank | Company | Headquarters | 2006 Total Assets ($ mil.) |
|---|---|---|---|
| 1 | Barclays Global Investors | San Francisco | 1,813,820 |
| 2 | State Street Global Advisors | Boston | 1,743,517 |
| 3 | Capital Group Cos. | Los Angeles | 1,403,053 |
| 4 | Fidelity Investments | Boston | 1,384,328 |
| 5 | BlackRock | New York | 1,124,627 |
| 6 | JPMorgan Asset Mgmt. | New York | 1,012,700 |
| 7 | Legg Mason | Baltimore, MD | 957,558 |
| 8 | AXA Group | Paris/New York | 915,148 |
| 9 | Mellon Financial Corp. | Pittsburgh | 879,658 |
| 10 | Vanguard Group | Valley Forge, PA | 832,394 |
| 11 | Allianz Global Investors of America | Newport Beach, CA | 764,975 |
| 12 | Northern Trust Global Investments | Chicago | 697,166 |
| 13 | Goldman Sachs Group | New York | 657,193 |
| 14 | Morgan Stanley Investment Mgmt. | New York | 586,346 |
| 15 | Wellington Mgmt Co. | Boston | 575,492 |
| 16 | Franklin Resources | San Mateo, CA | 552,905 |
| 17 | Prudential Financial | Newark, NJ | 520,022 |
| 18 | Columbia Mgmt. and Affiliates | Boston | 518,800 |
| 19 | TIAA-CREF | New York | 405,647 |
| 20 | MassMutual Financial Group | Springfield, MA | 368,219 |

SOURCE: *INSTITUTIONAL INVESTOR*, JULY 2007

## Top 20 Tax & Accounting Firms by US Revenue

| Rank | Firm | Headquarters | 2006 US Revenue ($ mil.) |
|---|---|---|---|
| 1 | Deloitte & Touche | New York | 8,769.0 |
| 2 | PricewaterhouseCoopers | New York | 6,922.4 |
| 3 | Ernst & Young | New York | 6,890.0 |
| 4 | KPMG | New York | 4,801.0 |
| 5 | RSM/McGladrey & Pullen | Bloomington, MN | 1,322.2 |
| 6 | Grant Thornton | Chicago | 939.6 |
| 7 | BDO Seidman | Chicago | 558.0 |
| 8 | CBiz/Mayer Hoffman McCann | Cleveland | 466.8 |
| 9 | Crowe Group | South Bend, IN | 423.0 |
| 10 | BKD | Springfield, MO | 287.0 |
| 11 | Moss Adams | Seattle | 271.0 |
| 12 | Plante & Moran | Southfield, MI | 242.6 |
| 13 | UHY Advisors | Chicago | 241.6 |
| 14 | Clifton Gunderson | Peoria, IL | 198.0 |
| 15 | Virchow, Krause & Co. | Madison, WI | 182.2 |
| 16 | J.H. Cohn | Roseland, NJ | 175.0 |
| 17 | Dixon Hughes | High Point, NC | 155.0 |
| 18 | LarsonAllen | Minneapolis | 140.0 |
| 19 | Reznick Group | Bethesda, MD | 136.6 |
| 20 | Weiser | New York | 110.0 |

SOURCE: *ACCOUNTING TODAY*, FEBRUARY 2007

## *FORTUNE*'s 100 Best Companies to Work for in America

| Rank | Company | US Employees |
|---|---|---|
| 1 | Google | 6,500 |
| 2 | Genentech | 9,979 |
| 3 | Wegmans Food Markets | 33,737 |
| 4 | Container Store | 2,866 |
| 5 | Whole Foods Market | 37,806 |
| 6 | Network Appliance | 3,553 |
| 7 | S.C. Johnson & Son | 3,400 |
| 8 | Boston Consulting Group | 1,434 |
| 9 | Methodist Hospital System | 9,424 |
| 10 | W.L. Gore & Associates | 4,945 |
| 11 | Cisco Systems | 27,493 |
| 12 | David Weekley Homes | 1,622 |
| 13 | Nugget Market | 1,099 |
| 14 | Qualcomm | 8,860 |
| 15 | American Century Investments | 1,783 |
| 16 | Starbucks Coffee | 109,873 |
| 17 | Quicken Loans | 3,512 |
| 18 | Station Casinos | 13,957 |
| 19 | Alston & Bird | 1,598 |
| 20 | QuikTrip | 7,833 |
| 21 | Griffin Hospital | 1,098 |
| 22 | Valero Energy | 18,730 |
| 23 | Vision Service Plan | 1,968 |
| 24 | Nordstrom | 48,374 |
| 25 | Ernst & Young | 24,995 |
| 26 | Arnold & Porter | 1,292 |
| 27 | Recreational Equipment (REI) | 8,522 |
| 28 | Kimley-Horn & Associates | 2,173 |
| 29 | Edward Jones | 30,326 |
| 30 | Russell Investment Group | 1,206 |
| 31 | Adobe Systems | 3,604 |
| 32 | Plante & Moran | 1,501 |
| 33 | Intuit | 6,889 |
| 34 | Umpqua Bank | 1,435 |
| 35 | Children's Healthcare of Atlanta | 5,256 |
| 36 | Goldman Sachs | 12,542 |
| 37 | Northwest Community Hospital | 3,299 |
| 38 | Robert W. Baird | 2,080 |
| 39 | J.M. Smucker | 2,853 |
| 40 | Amgen | 13,554 |
| 41 | JM Family Enterprises | 4,452 |
| 42 | PCL Construction | 3,020 |
| 43 | Genzyme | 5,920 |
| 44 | Yahoo | 6,840 |
| 45 | Bain & Co. | 1,370 |
| 46 | First Horizon National | 12,491 |
| 47 | American Fidelity Assurance | 1,358 |
| 48 | SAS Institute | 5,239 |
| 49 | Nixon Peabody | 1,511 |
| 50 | Microsoft | 44,298 |
| 51 | Stew Leonard's | 1,899 |
| 52 | OhioHealth | 10,836 |
| 53 | Four Seasons Hotels | 11,584 |
| 54 | Baptist Health Care | 4,095 |
| 55 | Dow Corning | 4,052 |
| 56 | Granite Construction | 4,662 |
| 57 | Publix Super Markets | 136,863 |
| 58 | PricewaterhouseCoopers | 28,463 |
| 59 | Pella | 9,331 |
| 60 | MITRE | 5,759 |
| 61 | SRA International | 4,861 |
| 62 | Mayo Clinic | 39,457 |
| 63 | Booz Allen Hamilton | 16,691 |
| 64 | Perkins Coie | 1,519 |
| 65 | Alcon Laboratories | 6,460 |
| 66 | Jones Lang LaSalle | 7,812 |
| 67 | HomeBanc Mortgage | 1,312 |
| 68 | Procter & Gamble | 34,142 |
| 69 | Nike | 13,664 |
| 70 | Paychex | 10,911 |
| 71 | AstraZeneca | 12,263 |
| 72 | Medtronic | 21,648 |
| 73 | Aflac | 4,326 |
| 74 | American Express | 29,145 |
| 75 | Quad/Graphics | 10,099 |
| 76 | Deloitte & Touche USA | 34,011 |
| 77 | Principal Financial Group | 13,075 |
| 78 | Timberland | 2,016 |
| 79 | TDIndustries | 1,345 |
| 80 | Lehigh Valley Hospital & Health Network | 7,838 |
| 81 | Baptist Health S. Florida | 9,446 |
| 82 | CDW | 4,293 |
| 83 | EOG Resources | 1,181 |
| 84 | Capital One Financial | 19,047 |
| 85 | Standard Pacific | 2,856 |
| 86 | National Instruments | 2,294 |
| 87 | Texas Instruments | 15,274 |
| 88 | CarMax | 12,553 |
| 89 | Marriott International | 124,350 |
| 90 | Men's Wearhouse | 11,508 |
| 91 | Memorial Health | 4,685 |
| 92 | Bright Horizons | 14,164 |
| 93 | Milliken | 9,500 |
| 94 | Bingham McCutchen | 1,618 |
| 95 | Vanguard | 11,410 |
| 96 | IKEA North America | 11,157 |
| 97 | KPMG | 21,042 |
| 98 | Synovus | 12,474 |
| 99 | A.G. Edwards | 15,794 |
| 100 | Stanley | 2,309 |

SOURCE: *FORTUNE*, JANUARY 22, 2007

## *FORTUNE*'s 10 Most Admired Companies

| Rank | Company | CEO | 2006 Revenue ($ mil.) |
|---|---|---|---|
| 1 | General Electric | Jeffrey R. Immelt | 163,391.0 |
| 2 | Starbucks | James L. Donald | 7,786.9 |
| 3 | Toyota Motor | Yukitoshi Funo | 179,083.0 |
| 4 | Berkshire Hathaway | Warren E. Buffett | 98,539.0 |
| 5 | Southwest Airlines | Herbert D. Kelleher | 9,086.0 |
| 6 | FedEx | Frederick W. Smith | 32,294.0 |
| 7 | Apple | Steven P. Jobs | 19,315.0 |
| 8 | Google | Eric E. Schmidt | 10,604.9 |
| 9 | Johnson & Johnson | William C. Weldon | 53,324.0 |
| 10 | Procter & Gamble | Alan G. Lafley | 68,222.0 |

SOURCE: *FORTUNE*, MARCH 19, 2007

## Top 20 Black-Owned Businesses*

| Rank | Company | 2006 Revenue ($ mil.) |
|---|---|---|
| 1 | World Wide Technology Inc. | 2,100.0 |
| 2 | CAMAC International Corp. | 1,599.0 |
| 3 | ACT-1 Group | 800.0 |
| 4 | Bridgewater Interiors L.L.C. | 751.0 |
| 5 | Philadelphia Coca-Cola Bottling Co. | 530.0 |
| 6 | Barden Cos. Inc. | 501.0 |
| 7 | Johnson Publishing Co. | 472.2 |
| 8 | RLJ Development L.L.C. | 460.0 |
| 9 | Converge | 447.5 |
| 10 | MV Transportation Inc. | 430.5 |
| 11 | Radio One Inc. | 413.2 |
| 12 | TAG Holdings L.L.C. | 404.0 |
| 13 | The Peebles Corp. | 403.4 |
| 14 | ZeroChaos | 366.8 |
| 15 | H. J. Russell and Co. | 364.4 |
| 16 | RS Information Systems Inc. (RSIS) | 328.0 |
| 17 | Harpo Inc. | 325.0 |
| 18 | Global Automotive Alliance L.L.C. | 287.4 |
| 19 | Manna Inc. | 276.0 |
| 20 | MIG-Visteon Automotive Systems | 259.4 |

*Industrial and service companies only

SOURCE: *BLACK ENTERPRISE*, JUNE 2007

## Top 20 Hispanic-Owned Businesses

| Rank | Company | 2006 Revenue ($ mil.) |
|---|---|---|
| 1 | Brightstar Corp. | 3,600.0 |
| 2 | The Burt Automotive Network | 2,065.2 |
| 3 | Molina Healthcare Inc. | 2,000.0 |
| 4 | The Related Group of Florida | 1,409.0 |
| 5 | Prestige Builders Partners LLC | 1,000.0 |
| 6 | MasTec Inc. | 946.0 |
| 7 | International Bancshares Corp. | 786.0 |
| 8 | Ancira Enterprises Inc. | 628.7 |
| 9 | The Diez Group | 513.0 |
| 10 | Lopez Foods Inc. | 465.0 |
| 11 | Quirch Foods Co. | 453.0 |
| 12 | Greenway Ford Inc. | 451.8 |
| 13 | General Real Estate Corp. | 441.6 |
| 14 | Sedano's Supermarkets and Pharmacies | 437.1 |
| 15 | Lou Sobh Automotive | 420.0 |
| 16 | Urbieta Oil Inc. | 420.0 |
| 17 | Crossland Construction Co. Inc. | 412.8 |
| 18 | Ruiz Food Products Inc. | 383.0 |
| 19 | General Tobacco | 300.0 |
| 20 | Gonzales Automotive Group Inc. | 296.2 |

SOURCE: *HISPANIC BUSINESS*, MAY 2007

## Top 10 Companies for Female Executives

| Rank | Company | % Women Senior Managers | % Women Board Directors |
|---|---|---|---|
| 1 | Aetna Inc. | 35 | 31 |
| 2 | Allstate Insurance Company | 35 | 18 |
| 3 | Colgate-Palmolive Company | 33 | 22 |
| 4 | Gannett Co., Inc. | 36 | 38 |
| 5 | General Mills | 34 | 31 |
| 6 | IBM Corporation | 25 | 23 |
| 7 | Liz Claiborne, Inc. | 65 | 27 |
| 8 | Marriott International, Inc. | 38 | 18 |
| 9 | MetLife, Inc. | 39 | 21 |
| 10 | Patagonia, Inc. | 46 | 38 |

SOURCE: NATIONAL ASSOCIATION OF FEMALE EXECUTIVES, MARCH 2007

Hoover's Handbook of

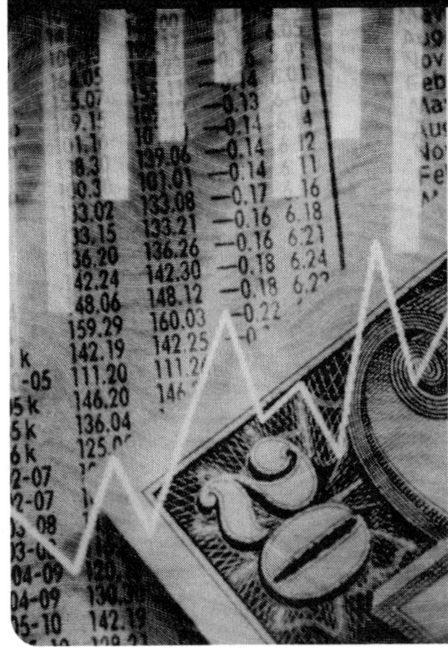

# American Business

## The Companies

# 3M Company

Loath to be stuck on one thing, 3M makes everything from masking tape to asthma inhalers. The company has six operating segments: display and graphics (specialty film, traffic control materials); health care (dental and medical supplies, and health IT); safety, security, and protection (commercial care, occupational health and safety products); electro and communications (connecting, splicing, and insulating products); industrial and transportation (specialty materials, tapes, and adhesives); and consumer and office. Well-known brands include Scotchgard fabric protectors, Post-it Notes, Scotch-Brite scouring products, and Scotch tapes. Sales outside the US account for about two-thirds of 3M's sales.

Former Brunswick Corporation CEO George Buckley took over as chairman and CEO in late 2005 after Jim McNerney resigned from 3M to take the same positions at Boeing.

After a relatively slow period of M&A activity, 3M has been actively looking for acquisition targets since 2005. And the company delivered on those expectations in mid-2005 with the $1.35 billion acquisition of liquid filtration producer CUNO. 3M's own filtration products business — primarily air filters — amounted to more than $1 billion in annual sales before the deal, and the deal added nearly half a billion to that. CUNO's filtration products are used in the health care, potable water, and fluid processing markets. Nearly half of its business is generated outside the US, and it's that international water filtration business that had 3M most excited. Like many others — GE, for instance, with its acquisition of Ionics — 3M expects the provision of clean water to become a huge growth industry as the developing world continues to industrialize.

In 2006 3M bought dental supplies maker OMNII Oral Pharmaceuticals and followed that up with another acquisition, this one for the General Industrial Diamond Company, a maker of superabrasive grinding wheels, dressing tools, and machines. Later in 2006 the company agreed to buy SCC Products and JJ Converting. The former makes flexible static control packaging and the latter makes the films that are used to make that packaging. 3M then acquired Credence Technologies, which, too, makes static control products, and Biotrace International, a UK company that manufactures microbiology products used by the food and beverage, defense, and pharmaceutical industries.

The company signaled a new strategic direction in 2006 when it put its pharmaceutical unit under review, looking into a possible sale of the business. 3M decided that it had brought the branded pharmaceuticals business as far as it could and that the unit can progress further under the wing of a dedicated pharmaceuticals company. Late in the year 3M announced it had broken up the unit along geographic lines and sold it in pieces. The North and South American business was sold to Graceway Pharmaceuticals, the European unit to Meda AB, and the Asia/Pacific division to Australian private equity firms Ironbridge Capital and Archer Capital. In total 3M got $2.1 billion for the sale of its pharmaceutical operations.

In 2007 the company acquired Innovative Paper Technologies LLC, Powell LLC, and Diamond Productions Inc.

## HISTORY

Five businessmen in Two Harbors, Minnesota, founded Minnesota Mining and Manufacturing (3M) in 1902 to sell corundum to grinding-wheel manufacturers. The company soon needed to raise working capital. Co-founder John Dwan offered his friend Edgar Ober 60% of 3M's stock. Ober persuaded Lucius Ordway, VP of a plumbing business, to help underwrite 3M. In 1905 the two took over the company and moved it to Duluth.

In 1907 future CEO William McKnight joined 3M as a bookkeeper. Three years later the plant moved to St. Paul. The board of directors declared a dividend to shareholders in the last quarter of 1916, and 3M hasn't missed a dividend since. The next two products 3M developed — Scotch-brand masking tape (1925) and Scotch-brand cellophane tape (1930) — assured its future.

McKnight introduced one of the first employee pension plans in 1931, and in the late 1940s he implemented a vertical management structure. 3M introduced the first commercially viable magnetic recording tape in 1947.

In 1950, after a decade of work and $1 million in development costs, 3M employee Carl Miller completed the Thermo-Fax copying machine, which was the foundation of 3M's duplicating division.

Products in the 1960s included 3M's dry-silver microfilm, photographic products, carbonless papers, overhead projection systems, and medical and dental products. The company moved into pharmaceuticals, radiology, energy control, and office markets in the 1970s and 1980s.

A 3M scientist developed Post-it Notes (1980) because he wanted to attach page markers to his church hymnal. Recalling that a colleague had developed an adhesive that wasn't very sticky, he brushed some on paper and began a product line that now generates hundreds of millions of dollars each year.

In 1990 the company bought sponge maker O-Cel-O. But not all of its inventions have brought 3M good news. In 1995, along with fellow silicone breast-implant makers Baxter International and Bristol-Myers Squibb, it agreed to settle thousands of personal-injury claims related to implants. The companies paid an average $26,000 per claim.

3M spun off its low-profit imaging and data-storage businesses in 1996 as Imation Corp. and closed its audiotape and videotape businesses. The next year 3M sold its National Advertising billboard business to Infinity Outdoor for $1 billion and its Media Network unit (a printer of advertising inserts) to Time Warner.

The company created the 3M Nexcare brand for its line of first-aid and home health products in 1998. To regain earnings growth, 3M closed about 10% of its plants in the US and abroad and cut 6% of its workforce by the end of 1999. It also discontinued unprofitable product lines. The next year 3M sold its heart-surgery-equipment health care unit to Japan's Terumo and its Eastern Heights Bank subsidiary to Norwest Bank of Minnesota. It also bought out Hoechst AG's 46% stake in Dyneon LLC, a fluorine elastomer joint venture between the two companies.

3M bought Polaroid's Technical Polarizer and Display Films business and a controlling stake in Germany-based Quante AG (telecom systems) in 2000. In addition, 3M decided to stop making many of its Scotchgard-brand repellant products due to research revealing that one of the compounds (perfluorooctane sulfonate) used in the manufacturing process is "persistent and pervasive" in the environment and in people's bloodstreams. As 2000 drew to a close, 3M named GE executive James McNerney to succeed L. D. DeSimone as its chairman and CEO. With the sale of Eastern Heights and several health care businesses (including its cardiovascular systems unit), 3M was rewarded with its second-best financial performance in 14 years.

3M then bought Robinson Nugent (electronic connectors) and MicroTouch Systems (touch screens) in 2001. It also announced plans to cut 6,000 jobs and authorized a stock buy-back program of up to $2.5 billion. 3M said in 2002 that it would cut another 2,500 jobs.

The company changed its legal name from Minnesota Mining and Manufacturing Company to 3M Company that year. Also in 2002 3M restructured its business segments around end uses rather than products or raw materials. So the Health Care segment encompassed everything from transdermal skin patches to software for hospital coding and classification. Similarly, the Consumer and Office Business unit became responsible for Post-its, O-Cel-O sponges, wood-finishing materials, and air conditioner filters.

By the end of that year the company had cut more than 8,500 jobs, 11% of its total workforce.

Nevertheless, a strong year in 2003 emboldened the company to look to expand. 3M closed a deal to buy fellow Minnesota resident HighJump Software, a maker of supply chain software for businesses, in February 2004. That year 3M closed a deal to purchase Swedish protective equipment manufacturer Hornell International.

McNerney left 3M in 2005 to join Boeing in the same capacity and was replaced by George Buckley, formerly of the Brunswick Corporation.

## EXECUTIVES

**Chairman, President, and CEO:** George W. Buckley, age 59, $327,287 pay
**EVP, Consumer and Office Business:** Moe S. Nozari, age 65, $1,025,805 pay
**EVP, Enterprise Services:** James B. Stake, age 54
**EVP, Electro and Communications Business:** Joe E. Harlan, age 48
**EVP, Research and Development and CTO:** Frederick J. Palensky, age 57
**EVP, Health Care Business:** Brad T. Sauer, age 48
**EVP, Industrial and Transportation Business:** Hak Cheol (H.C.) Shin, age 49
**EVP, International Operations:** Inge G. Thulin, age 53
**EVP, Safety, Security, and Protection Services Business:** Jean Lobey, age 55
**SVP and CFO:** Patrick D. (Pat) Campbell, age 55, $1,113,519 pay
**SVP, Asia Pacific:** Jay V. Ihlenfeld, age 55
**SVP, Corporate Supply Chain Operations:** John K. Woodworth
**SVP, Human Resources:** Angela S. Lalor, age 40
**SVP, Legal Affairs and General Counsel:** Marschall I. Smith, age 62
**SVP, Marketing and Sales:** Robert D. MacDonald, age 56
**VP, Europe, Middle East, and Africa:** Herman E. Nauwelaerts
**VP, Latin America and Canada:** William G. Allen
**VP and Treasurer:** Janet L. Yeomans
**Secretary:** Gregg M. Larson
**General Auditor:** David G. Werpy
**Director, Investor Relations:** Matt Ginter
**Public Relations and Corporate Communications:** Dan E. Gahlon
**President, CUNO:** Mark G. Kachur, age 64
**Auditors:** PricewaterhouseCoopers LLP

## LOCATIONS

**HQ:** 3M Company
3M Center, St. Paul, MN 55144
**Phone:** 651-733-1110 **Fax:** 651-733-9973
**Web:** www.mmm.com

3M Company has manufacturing operations worldwide.

### 2006 Sales

| | $ mil. | % of total |
|---|---|---|
| US | 8,853 | 39 |
| Asia/Pacific | 6,251 | 27 |
| Europe/Africa/Middle East | 5,726 | 25 |
| Latin America/Canada | 2,080 | 9 |
| Other regions | 13 | — |
| **Total** | **22,923** | **100** |

## PRODUCTS/OPERATIONS

### 2006 Sales

| | $ mil. | % of total |
|---|---|---|
| Industrial & Transportation | 6,754 | 30 |
| Health Care | 4,011 | 18 |
| Display & Graphics | 3,765 | 16 |
| Consumer & Office | 3,238 | 14 |
| Safety, Security & Protection Services | 2,621 | 11 |
| Electro & Communications | 2,483 | 11 |
| Corporate | 51 | — |
| **Total** | **22,923** | **100** |

### Selected Segments and Products

Industrial and Transportation
- Aerospace and defense products
- Automotive aftermarket products
- Automotive products
- Closures for disposable diapers
- Commercial vehicle products
- Coated and nonwoven abrasives
- Marine trades products
- Specialty adhesives
- Tapes

Health Care
- Dental products
- Drug delivery systems
- Health information systems
- Infection prevention
- Medical and surgical supplies
- Microbiology products
- Skin health products

Display and Graphics
- Commercial graphics products
- Optical systems
- Specialty film and media products
- Traffic control materials

Consumer and Office
- Carpet and fabric protectors
- Commercial cleaning products
- Energy control products
- Fabric protectors (Scotchgard)
- Floor matting
- High-performance cloth (Scotch-Brite)
- Home-improvement products
- Repositionable notes (Post-it)
- Scour pads (Scotch-Brite)
- Sponges (O-Cel-O)
- Tape (Scotch)

Safety, Security, and Protection
- Commercial care products
- Consumer safety products
- Corrosion protection products
- Industrial mineral products
- Occupational health and safety products
- Safety and security products

Electro and Communications
- Insulating and splicing products for electronics, telecommunications, and electrical industries
- Packaging and interconnection devices

## COMPETITORS

ACCO Brands
Avery Dennison
BASF AG
Bayer
Beiersdorf
Bostik
Corning
DuPont
Eastman Kodak
GE
H.B. Fuller
Henkel
Honeywell International
Illinois Tool Works
Imperial Chemical
International Paper
International Specialty Products
Intertape Polymer
Johnson & Johnson
Kimberly-Clark
PPG
Ricoh
RPM
S.C. Johnson
Sealed Air Corporation
Solutia
Tyco
UCB
USG

## HISTORICAL FINANCIALS

Company Type: Public

### Income Statement

FYE: December 31

| | REVENUE ($ mil.) | NET INCOME ($ mil.) | NET PROFIT MARGIN | EMPLOYEES |
|---|---|---|---|---|
| **12/06** | 22,923 | 3,851 | 16.8% | 75,333 |
| **12/05** | 21,167 | 3,199 | 15.1% | 69,315 |
| **12/04** | 20,011 | 2,990 | 14.9% | 67,071 |
| **12/03** | 18,232 | 2,403 | 13.2% | 67,072 |
| **12/02** | 16,332 | 1,974 | 12.1% | 68,774 |
| **Annual Growth** | 8.8% | 18.2% | — | 2.3% |

### 2006 Year-End Financials

Debt ratio: 11.2%
Return on equity: 38.4%
Cash ($ mil.): 1,918
Current ratio: 1.22
Long-term debt ($ mil.): 1,112
No. of shares (mil.): 734
Dividends
Yield: 2.4%
Payout: 36.4%
Market value ($ mil.): 57,229

### Stock History

NYSE: MMM

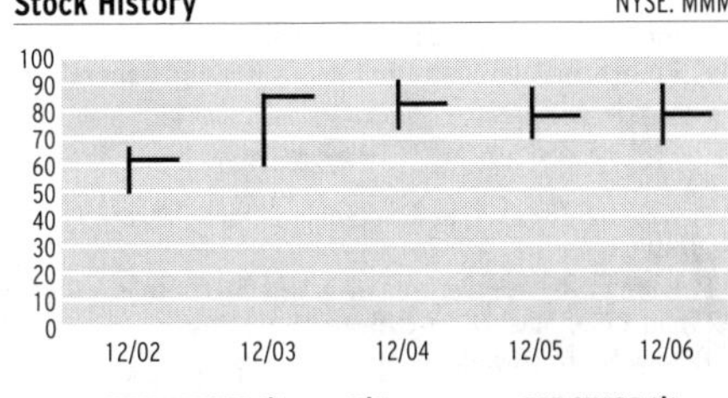


| | STOCK PRICE ($) FY Close | P/E High | P/E Low | PER SHARE ($) Earnings | Dividends | Book Value |
|---|---|---|---|---|---|---|
| **12/06** | 77.93 | 17 | 13 | 5.06 | 1.84 | 13.56 |
| **12/05** | 77.50 | 21 | 17 | 4.12 | 1.68 | 13.39 |
| **12/04** | 82.07 | 24 | 20 | 3.75 | 1.44 | 13.42 |
| **12/03** | 85.03 | 28 | 20 | 3.02 | 0.99 | 10.06 |
| **12/02** | 61.65 | 26 | 20 | 2.49 | 1.55 | 15.36 |
| **Annual Growth** | 6.0% | — | — | 19.4% | 4.4% | (3.1%) |

# 7-Eleven, Inc.

"If convenience stores are open 24 hours, why the locks on their doors?" If anyone knows, it's 7-Eleven. The North American subsidiary of Seven-Eleven Japan, 7-Eleven operates more than 6,000 stores in the US and Canada under the 7-Eleven name. (An additional 460 US stores are operated by licensees.) 7-Eleven also has an interest in nearly 600 stores in Mexico. Overall, the company's Japanese parent operates, franchises, or licenses about 31,000 stores worldwide.

The US's leading convenience store chain was taken private in late 2005 by its largest shareholder, the Japanese conglomerate Seven & I Holdings, the holding company for Seven-Eleven Japan, Ito-Yokado, Denny's restaurants, and other businesses.

Seven & I is Japan's largest retailer, by sales, ahead of AEON CO.

The company is growing through acquisitions, most recently, through the purchase of the White Hen Pantry chain, an operator of more than 200 convenience stores, mainly in the metro Chicago area. The White Hen purchase was 7-Eleven's largest acquisition in more than 20 years and the first since it was taken private.

7-Eleven stores range from 2,400 to 3,000 sq. ft. and sell about 2,800 items. Merchandise (including Slurpees, beer, perishables, phone cards, and tobacco items) accounts for about 60% of sales. Gasoline is offered at about 2,100 stores — less than half of its total number of stores — but accounts for about 40% of overall sales.

Ending a 20-year relationship with CITGO Petroleum Corporation, 7-Eleven dropped the gasoline supplier in late 2006 — looking, instead, to distributors Tower Energy Group (California), Sinclair Oil Corporation (Utah), and Frontier Oil Corporation (Texas) for fuel.

About 80% of 7-Eleven's North American stores provide fresh foods, mainly Big Eats Bakery goods and Big Eats Deli sandwiches, but also more innovative fare in Southern California, such as six-packs of sushi rolls. 7-Eleven is upgrading and expanding its fresh foods offerings, including proprietary items such as Dreammm Doughnuts and its own brands of beer (Santiago) and wine (Regions). The company recently launched its own brand of pre-paid wireless cell phone service, called "7-Eleven Speaks Out," in Dallas/Fort Worth.

In a deal valued at $135 million in cash, 7-Eleven agreed to sell its ATMs and Vcom kiosks to Houston's Cardtronics. In recent years 7-Eleven had installed some 5,500 ATMs and about 1,000 Vcom kiosks, which provide its customers with financial and other services in all its stores. Among the services offered through the kiosks are auto insurance sign-up and bill payment. As part of the deal, Cardtronics will have exclusive rights to operate all 7-Eleven ATMs and Vcom kiosks across the US, including new locations 7-Eleven opens, for 10 years.

The company plans to trim investment costs by building smaller stores, which have been successful in Asia. South of the border, the convenience store chain plans to double its presence from 600 outlets to 1,000 shops over the next several years.

The company is in the process of turning most of its US stores into franchises, a plan which it would like to complete within five years.

## HISTORY

Claude Dawley formed the Southland Ice Company in Dallas in 1927 when ice was a precious necessity during Texas summers for storing and transporting food. Dawley bought four other Texas ice plant operations with backing from Chicago utility magnate Martin Insull. The purchases included Consumers Ice, where Joe Thompson had increased profits by selling chilled watermelons off the truck docks.

After the Dawley enterprise was underway, a dock manager in Dallas began stocking a few food items for customers. (Ice docks were exempt from Texas' blue laws and could operate even on Sundays.) He relayed the idea to Thompson, then running the ice operations, who adopted it at all company locations.

Thompson promoted the grocery operations by calling them Tote'm Stores and erecting totem poles by the docks. In 1928 he added gas stations to some store locations.

Insull bought out Dawley in 1930, and Thompson became president. He expanded Southland's operations even as the company operated briefly under the direction of bankruptcy court (1932-34). Having become the largest dairy retailer in the Dallas/Fort Worth area, in 1936 the company began its own dairy, Oak Farms, to supply some of its milk (sold in 1988). Ten years later the company changed its name to The Southland Corporation and adopted the store name 7-Eleven, a reference to the stores' hours of operation at the time.

After Thompson died in 1961, his eldest son, John, became president. John opened stores in Colorado, New Jersey, and Arizona in 1962 and in Utah, California, and Missouri in 1963. The company introduced the Slurpee, a fizzy slush drink, in 1965. Southland franchised the 7-Eleven format in the UK (1971) and in Japan (1973).

To supply its gas pumps, in 1983 the company purchased Citgo, a gasoline refining and marketing business with about 300 gas stations. It soon sold a 50% interest of the business to the Venezuelan government-owned oil company Petróleos de Venezuela (PDVSA) in 1986.

In 1988 John and his two brothers borrowed heavily to buy 70% of Southland's stock in an LBO. Stymied by debt, the company sold its remaining 50% stake in Citgo to PDVSA in 1990. However, Southland defaulted on $1.8 billion in publicly traded debt later that year and filed for bankruptcy protection. The company then persuaded bondholders to restructure its debt and take 25% of its stock, clearing the way for the purchase of 70% of Southland in 1991 by its Japanese partner, Ito-Yokado. Company veteran Clark Matthews was named CEO that year.

From 1991 to 1993 sales declined as Southland closed stores, renovated others, and upgraded its merchandise. In 1998 Southland began testing in-store electronic banking kiosks, which allow users to cash checks, pay bills, and transfer funds. New store openings and acquisitions (Christy's in New England, red D marts in Indiana) added 299 more units that year.

Southland changed its name to 7-Eleven in 1999 to better reflect the lone business of the company. In early 2000 Ito-Yokado raised its stake in 7-Eleven to nearly 73%. (Ito-Yokado and its licensee Seven-Eleven Japan were acquired in late-2005 by Japanese conglomerate Seven & I Holdings.) COO Jim Keyes (a 15-year veteran who began managing 7-Eleven's Citgo gasoline business) replaced Matthews as CEO in April 2000.

In honor of its 75th anniversary, among other reasons, 7-Eleven launched the most extensive advertising campaign in its history in May 2002. The company cancelled plans in November 2002 to open a flagship store in New York City's Times Square. Also in 2002 the company closed 133 underperforming stores and opened 127 new locations in North America. Overseas licensees opened a net 1,792 stores.

In 2003 chairman Ito retired from the board of directors along with co-vice chairman Matthews.

A year later 7-Eleven sold its 42-story Cityplace Center headquarters building in downtown Dallas to Prentiss Properties for approximately $125 million. In October the California Attorney General's Office fined 7-Eleven $5 million in damages and required the chain to make $10 million in improvements to its gasoline storage tanks for violating environmental and safety regulations at 232 stores in California.

Seven-Eleven Japan completed a tender offer for the remainder of 7-Eleven, Inc. in late 2005. As a result 7-Eleven became a subsidiary of Seven-Eleven Japan, which is in turn a subsidiary of holding company Seven & I Holdings, Japan's largest retailer by sales.

In August 2006 7-Eleven acquired WHP Holdings Corp., the holding company for the White Hen Pantry and Pantry Select chains of convenience stores. White Hen Pantry operates 206 stores, mainly in the metro Chicago area, and about 55 licensed stores in and around Boston. The terms of the deal were not disclosed.

The next year, 7-Eleven sold 500 ATMs and financial-services kiosks, or Vcoms, to Cardtronics for about $135 million. The company said it will use the proceeds to invest in its convenience stores.

## EXECUTIVES

**Chairman:** Toshifumi Suzuki, age 71
**President and CEO:** Joseph M. (Joe) DePinto, age 44
**EVP, COO, and Director:** Masaaki Asakura, age 62
**SVP and CFO:** Stanley W. Reynolds, age 41
**SVP, Franchising:** Jeffrey A. (Jeff) Schenck
**SVP, Merchandising:** Cynthia L. Davis
**SVP, Merchandising and Logistics:** Kevin Elliott, age 39
**SVP, Store Operations:** John W. Harris
**VP, Business Development:** Rick Updyke
**VP and CIO:** Sharon Stufflebeme
**VP, Construction and Maintenance:** Steve Hall
**VP and Controller:** Sylvester (Sly) Johnson
**VP, Corporate Planning:** Carole Davidson
**VP, Field Merchandising:** Alan Beach
**VP, Franchise Administration and Assistant General Counsel:** Mike Davis
**VP, Fresh Foods Merchandising:** Joanne DeLorenzo, age 46
**VP, General Counsel, and Secretary:** Dave Fenton, age 42
**VP, Human Resources:** Donald E. (Don) Thomas
**VP and Chief Marketing Officer:** Doug Foster
**VP, New Store Development:** Mark Wise
**VP and Treasurer:** Shiro Ozeki
**President and CEO, White Hen Pantry:** Nancy A. Smith
**Press Contact:** Margaret Chabris
**Auditors:** PricewaterhouseCoopers LLP

## LOCATIONS

**HQ:** 7-Eleven, Inc.
2711 N. Haskell, Dallas, TX 75204
**Phone:** 972-828-7011 **Fax:** 972-828-7848
**Web:** www.7-eleven.com

### 2007 Company-Owned Stores

| | No. |
|---|---|
| US | 5,581 |
| Canada | 469 |
| **Total** | **6,050** |

## PRODUCTS/OPERATIONS

### 2007 Stores

| | No. |
|---|---|
| Company-owned | 6,050 |
| Licensed | 460 |
| **Total** | **6,510** |

### 2007 Sales

| | % of total |
|---|---|
| Merchandise | 60 |
| Gasoline | 40 |
| **Total** | **100** |

## COMPETITORS

Allsup's
Casey's General Stores
Chevron
Couche-Tard
Cumberland Farms
Exxon Mobil
Gate Petroleum
H-E-B
Holiday Companies
Krause Gentle
Kroger
Loblaw
Marathon Oil
Minyard Group
Murphy Oil
The Pantry
Pilot Corporation
QuikTrip
Racetrac Petroleum
Royal Dutch Shell
Sheetz
Shell
Uni-Marts
Walgreen
Wawa, Inc.

## HISTORICAL FINANCIALS

Company Type: Subsidiary

### Income Statement

FYE: February 28*

| | REVENUE ($ mil.) | NET INCOME ($ mil.) | NET PROFIT MARGIN | EMPLOYEES |
|---|---|---|---|---|
| **12/04†** | 12,246 | — | — | 31,622 |
| **12/03** | 10,827 | — | — | 31,622 |
| **12/02** | 9,831 | — | — | 31,000 |
| **Annual Growth** | 11.6% | — | — | 1.0% |

*Fiscal year change †Most recent year available

### Revenue History

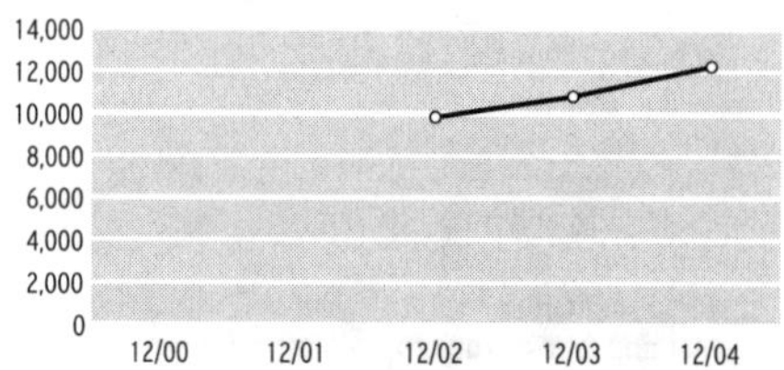


# A&P

Once the biggest bagger of groceries in the US, The Great Atlantic & Pacific Tea Company (A&P) has been reduced to a handful of regional grocery chains. The company runs 400-plus supermarkets in nine states and the District of Columbia. A&P sold it Canadian division to METRO INC. in 2005. In addition to its mainstay A&P chain, it operates seven others, including Farmer Jack in Michigan; Super Fresh along the East Coast from New Jersey to Virginia; Waldbaum in New York and New Jersey; and Sav-A-Center in the South. A&P has agreed to acquire its rival in the Northeast, Pathmark Stores, for about $1.3 billion. Germany's Tengelmann Group owns 57% of A&P.

Reversing years of decline, in March 2007 A&P agreed to acquire Pathmark in a deal that will create a 550-store chain with stores in the New York, New Jersey, Philadelphia, and Baltimore-Washington, DC metropolitan areas. The transaction is expected to close in fall 2007.

A&P believes Pathmark's success in urban settings will be a strong asset, since A&P has mostly focused on suburban locations. When the deal closes, 86% of the combined company will be held by A&P sharesholders and 14% will be held by former Pathmark investors. The Tengelmann Group, A&P's majority shareholder, will remain the largest shareholder.

A&P's chairman and former CEO Christian Haub and his family own Tengelmann. In mid-August 2005 Haub became executive chairman, handing his CEO title to Eric Claus, who previously headed A&P Canada. The management changes resulted from the sale of its 236-store Canadian division to rival Montreal supermarket chain METRO.

A&P Canada had out-performed its US counterpart, and its hefty sales price — about $1.5 billion — should help A&P ease its substantial debt load and reinvest in its aging US stores. A&P Canada operated supermarkets under the banners A&P, Dominion, Ultra Food & Drug stores, Food Basics, and The Barn.

Superstores and discounters have eaten into the sales of A&P's outdated outlets. The company, in response, announced its second major restructuring effort in three years, which resulted in the A&P Canada sale and the anticipated divestment of its Midwest retail operations to concentrate on its core business in the northeastern and mid-Atlantic US markets. To that end, A&P has put its Detroit-based Farmer Jack and Food Basics chains up for sale. On the wholesale side, A&P has outsourced its distribution operations to New England's largest food wholesaler, C&S Wholesale Grocers, as part of the restructuring. The move eliminated about 300 jobs at warehouses in Edison, New Jersey and the Bronx, New York, which were shut down.

A&P is seeking a buyer for its 21 Sav-A-Center stores in Louisiana, in order to focus more resources on its Northeast operations.

A&P recently launched an online grocery buying service for Food Emporium customers in the outer boroughs of New York City and on Long Island in an effort to win back sales lost to e-tailers FreshDirect and Peapod. With customer retention rates well above the 50-60% average, A&P is working to differentiate itself from the competition. In 2006 it debuted a weight-management grocery list developed by Long Island doctors.

## HISTORY

George Gilman and George Hartford of Augusta, Maine, set up shop in 1859 on New York City's docks to sell tea at a 50% discount by eliminating middlemen. The Great American Tea Company advertised by drawing a red wagon through the city's streets. By 1869 the company, renamed The Great Atlantic & Pacific Tea Company (A&P), had 11 stores offering discounted items. Gilman retired in 1878, and Hartford brought in his sons George and John. In 1912, when the company had 400 stores, John opened a store on a low-price, cash-and-carry format, without customer credit or premiums, which proved popular. When the company passed to the sons four years later, A&P had more than 1,000 cash-and-carry stores.

The company expanded at a phenomenal pace during the 1920s and 1930s, growing to 15,900 stores by the mid-1930s; however, a movement by small retailers to restrict chain stores tarnished the country's view of A&P in particular. To improve A&P's image, John initiated innovative marketing and customer service policies.

A&P grew in the 1940s by converting its stores to supermarkets, but an antitrust suit in 1949 and the company's reluctance to carry more non-food items pushed it into decline. Management shut stores in California and Washington to shore up its northeastern business.

In 1975, after a long period of poor sales and failed discount format attempts, the board named former Albertson's president Jonathan Scott as CEO. (He eventually left A&P to become CEO of American Stores.) Scott closed stores and reduced the workforce, but the company's sales increases failed to keep ahead of inflation, and A&P lost $52 million in 1978.

A year later the Hartford Foundation sold its A&P holdings to the German Tengelmann Group (owned by the Haub family), which in 1980 appointed English-born James Wood as CEO. A&P made several acquisitions, including Super Fresh (1982), Kohl's (1983), Ontario's Miracle Food Mart (1990), and Atlanta's Big Star (1992).

Rivals' superior supermarkets stripped away market share in New York City, Long Island, and Detroit in the early 1990s. In response, A&P closed hundreds of old stores, remodeled several hundred more, and planned openings of larger stores.

Christian Haub replaced Wood as CEO in 1998 (and became chairman in mid-2001), and A&P stepped up its modernization efforts. Following the discovery in May 2002 of accounting irregularities related to the timing for recognition of vendor allowances and inventory accounting, in July A&P restated — and improved — its financial results for 1999 and 2000 and adjusted its 2001 results. In October Brian Piwek was named president and CEO of A&P US; Eric Claus, formerly of Co-op Atlantic, joined the grocery chain as president and CEO of A&P Canada.

In October 2004 A&P settled a class action lawsuit with 29 franchisees of its Food Basics chain in Ontario, Canada. The retailer agreed to pay $32 million to purchase stores from the franchisees involved in the dispute. In November the company elevated Piwek to president and COO.

In August 2005 A&P sold its 236-store Canadian division, A&P Canada, to rival METRO INC. for approximately $1.5 billion.

In November 2006 A&P acquired six former Clemens Family Markets locations from C&S, which had recently purchased them from Clemens. The stores, all in the Philadelphia area, reopened as Super Fresh stores.

## EXECUTIVES

**Executive Chairman:** Christian W. E. Haub, age 43, $772,346 pay
**President and CEO:** Eric Claus, age 50, $698,077 pay
**SVP and CFO:** Brenda M. Galgano, age 38, $385,000 pay
**SVP Human Resources, Labor Relations, and Legal Services:** Allan Richards, age 43, $385,000 pay
**SVP Marketing and Communications:** Jennifer MacLeod, age 46
**SVP Merchandising and Supply and Logistics:** Rebecca Philbert, age 45
**SVP Operations:** Paul Wiseman, age 46, $385,000 pay
**VP and Corporate Controller:** Melissa Sungela, age 41
**VP and Treasurer:** William J. Moss, age 59
**VP Own Brands:** Douglas Palmer
**VP Marketing:** Robert (Bob) James
**President Sav-A-Center:** Glenn Dickson
**Executive Managing Director Strategy and Corporate Development, and Director:** Andreas Guldin, age 45
**Senior Director Corporate Affairs:** Richard P. (Rick) De Santa
**Director of Ethnic Merchandising:** Kevin O'Brien
**Director of Communication:** Robert Carson
**Auditors:** PricewaterhouseCoopers LLP

## LOCATIONS

**HQ:** The Great Atlantic & Pacific Tea Company, Inc.
2 Paragon Dr., Montvale, NJ 07645
**Phone:** 201-573-9700 **Fax:** 201-571-8667
**Web:** www.aptea.com

The Great Atlantic & Pacific Tea Company operates supermarkets in nine New England, mid-Atlantic, Midwestern, and southern states, and the District of Columbia.

**2007 Stores**

| | No. |
|---|---|
| New York | 128 |
| New Jersey | 92 |
| Michigan | 66 |
| Pennsylvania | 31 |
| Maryland | 30 |
| Connecticut | 26 |
| Louisiana | 21 |
| Delaware | 9 |
| Mississippi | 2 |
| District of Columbia | 1 |
| **Total** | **406** |

## PRODUCTS/OPERATIONS

**Selected Store Names**

A&P
Farmer Jack
Food Basics
Food Emporium
Sav-A-Center
Super Foodmart
Super Fresh
Waldbaum

**Selected Private-Label Brands**

America's Choice
Body Basics
Basics for Less
Equality
Master Choice
Health Pride
Savings Plus

## COMPETITORS

Acme Markets
Delhaize America
Duane Reade
Foodarama Supermarkets
Genuardi's
Giant Food
King Kullen Grocery
Kings Super Markets
Kroger
Meijer
Pathmark
Penn Traffic
Red Apple Group
Rite Aid
Safeway
Shaw's
Stew Leonard's
Stop & Shop
SUPERVALU
Village Super Market
Wakefern Food
Walgreen
Wal-Mart
Wegmans
Western Beef

## HISTORICAL FINANCIALS

Company Type: Public

**Income Statement** FYE: Last Saturday in February

| | REVENUE ($ mil.) | NET INCOME ($ mil.) | NET PROFIT MARGIN | EMPLOYEES |
|---|---|---|---|---|
| **2/07** | 6,850 | 27 | 0.4% | 38,000 |
| **2/06** | 8,740 | 393 | 4.5% | 38,000 |
| **2/05** | 10,855 | (188) | — | 73,000 |
| **2/04** | 10,813 | (147) | — | 74,000 |
| **2/03** | 10,794 | (194) | — | 79,000 |
| **Annual Growth** | (10.7%) | — | — | (16.7%) |

**2007 Year-End Financials**

Debt ratio: 72.9%
Return on equity: 4.9%
Cash ($ mil.): 158
Current ratio: 1.34
Long-term debt ($ mil.): 314
No. of shares (mil.): 42
Dividends
Yield: 23.3%
Payout: 1,132.8%
Market value ($ mil.): 1,292

**Stock History** NYSE: GAP

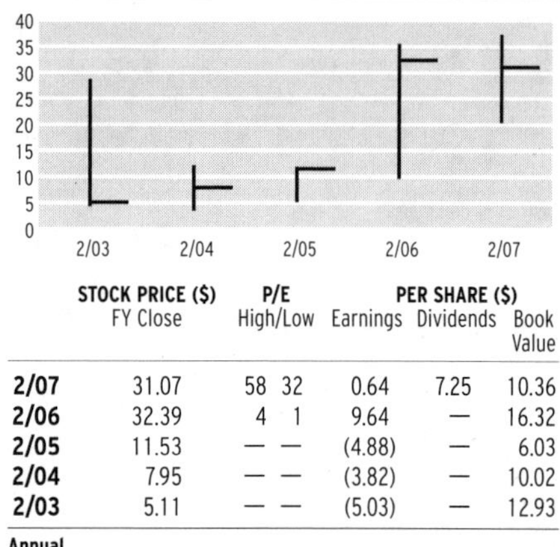


| | STOCK PRICE ($) FY Close | P/E High/Low | PER SHARE ($) Earnings | Dividends | Book Value |
|---|---|---|---|---|---|
| **2/07** | 31.07 | 58 32 | 0.64 | 7.25 | 10.36 |
| **2/06** | 32.39 | 4 1 | 9.64 | — | 16.32 |
| **2/05** | 11.53 | — — | (4.88) | — | 6.03 |
| **2/04** | 7.95 | — — | (3.82) | — | 10.02 |
| **2/03** | 5.11 | — — | (5.03) | — | 12.93 |
| **Annual Growth** | 57.0% | — — | — | — | (5.4%) |

# Abbott Laboratories

Don't be lulled by Abbott Laboratories' innocuous name: It is one of the US's top health care products makers. The company's pharmaceuticals include HIV treatment Norvir, rheumatoid arthritis therapy HUMIRA, and obesity drug Meridia. Its nutritional products division makes such well-known brands as Similac infant formula and the Ensure line of nutrition supplements. TAP Pharmaceutical Products, the company's joint venture with Takeda Pharmaceutical, markets best-selling acid reflux remedy Prevacid. Abbott Labs also makes laboratory diagnostic systems and devices to treat vascular disease. The company sells its products in more than 130 countries through affiliates and distributors.

Abbott's pharmaceuticals division — which focuses on the therapeutic areas of immunology, oncology, neuroscience, metabolic disorders, and infectious disease — brings in more than half of sales. The launch of HUMIRA in 2004 proved a big hit for the division and considerable R&D and marketing money is dedicated to maximizing sales for the drug. The division had co-promoted several products for Boehringer Ingelheim, but terminated that partnership early in 2006. The pharmaceuticals unit grew that year, however, with the purchase of Kos Pharmaceuticals, whose Niaspan and Advicor complement Abbott's portfolio of lipid-management products.

Abbott has made a number of acquisitions and strategic alliances in other parts of its business as well. It strengthened its diagnostics unit with purchases of genomic testing company Vysis and diabetes test maker TheraSense, and it has forged an alliance with Celera to add to its portfolio of molecular diagnostics. The company has also expanded its nutritionals division (also known as Ross Products) with the acquisition of Zone Perfect and its vascular unit with Guidant's vascular product line, which includes stents and coronary guidewires. Since buying the Guidant business, Abbott has launched drug-coated stent Xience in Europe and is seeking US approval for the device.

Though diagnostics (including lab tests for HIV, cancer, and pregnancy) were once the core of Abbott's product line, acquisitions have shifted the company's focus towards pharmaceuticals. That shift would have become even more pronounced if its 2007 plans to sell much of its diagnostics business to GE Healthcare had gone through. GE had agreed to pay about $8 billion for Abbott's point-of-care and in vitro diagnostics operations before the deal collapsed.

Like its druggernaut brethren, the company knows the pains of patent expiration. Since 2004, the company's Synthroid, Biaxin, and Sevorane have begun to face generic competition; key patents protecting Omnicef and Prevacid from generic rivals expire in 2007 and 2009, respectively. Abbott is hoping new candidates in its R&D pipeline, as well as expanded indications for drugs like HUMIRA, will make up for any resulting losses.

## HISTORY

Dr. Wallace Abbott started making his dosimetric granule (a pill that supplied uniform quantities of drugs) at his home outside Chicago in 1888. Aggressive marketing earned Abbott the American Medical Association's criticism, though much of the medical profession supported him.

During WWI, Abbott scientists synthesized anesthetics previously available only from Germany. Abbott improved its research capacity in 1922 by buying Dermatological Research Laboratories; in 1928 it bought John T. Milliken and its well-trained sales force. Abbott went public in 1929.

Salesman DeWitt Clough became president in 1933. International operations began in the mid-1930s with branches in Argentina, Brazil, Cuba, Mexico, and the UK.

Abbott was integral to the WWII effort; the US made only 28 pounds of penicillin in 1943 before the company began to ratchet up production. Consumer, infant, and nutritional products (such as Selsun Blue shampoo, Murine eye drops, and Similac formula) joined the roster in the 1960s. The FDA banned Abbott's artificial sweetener Sucaryl in 1970, saying it might be carcinogenic, and in 1971 millions of intravenous solutions were recalled following contamination deaths.

Robert Schoellhorn became CEO in 1979; profits increased but research and development was cut. In the 1980s Abbott began selling Japanese-developed pharmaceuticals in the US.

Duane Burnham became CEO in 1989; under his conservative management the company received FDA approvals to market insomnia treatment ProSom (1990), hypertension drug for enlarged prostates Hytrin (1994), and ulcer treatment Prevacid and central nervous system disorder treatment Depakote (1995).

In 1996 Abbott paid $32.5 million to settle claims by 17 states of infant formula price-fixing. In 1997 FTC action prompted Abbott to stop claiming that doctors recommended its Ensure nutritional supplement for healthy adults. That year the FDA allowed Abbott to use Norvir to treat HIV and AIDS in children, after approving its use in adults in a record 72 days in 1996.

In 1999 the FDA fined the company $100 million and pulled 125 of its medical diagnostic kits off the market, citing quality assurance problems. That year the FDA approved Gengraf, a drug that fights organ transplant rejection, and Kaletra, a promising protease inhibitor designed to combat AIDS.

Insider Miles White was named chairman and CEO in 2001. That same year Abbott bought Knoll Pharmaceuticals, a pharmaceutical unit of German chemicals giant BASF, and also purchased Vysis, thereby acquiring that company's worldwide distribution network and adding its products for the evaluation and management of cancer, prenatal disorders, and other genetic diseases to its portfolio of diagnostics.

In 2002 the FDA thwarted the company's launch of new diagnostic products by declaring that Abbott's Chicago manufacturing plant was not up to snuff. Attempting to move forward in the test market despite the setback, the company licensed a patent to OraSure Technologies and made plans to jointly distribute OraSure's rapid HIV diagnostic test. That same year, the FDA approved the company's Synthroid thyroid treatment, which had already been on the market for nearly 50 years.

Abbot ceased selling attention deficit drug Cylert in early 2005, citing declining sales, concurrent with a consumer advocacy group's complaint that the drug caused over 20 cases of liver failure. The FDA withdrew approval for the drug later that year.

## EXECUTIVES

**Chairman and CEO:** Miles D. White, age 51, $1,661,973 pay
**President, COO, and Director:** Richard A. (Rick) Gonzalez, age 53, $973,931 pay
**EVP, Corporate Development:** Richard W. Ashley, age 64
**EVP, Diagnostic and Animal Health Divisions:** Joseph M. Nemmers Jr., age 52
**EVP, Finance and CFO:** Thomas C. (Tom) Freyman, age 52, $812,884 pay
**EVP, Global Nutrition:** Holger Liepmann, age 55, $625,962 pay
**EVP, Secretary and General Counsel:** Laura J. Schumacher, age 43
**SVP, Abbott and Executive Vice President, TAP:** Edward J. (Ed) Fiorentino, age 48
**SVP, Abbott Vascular:** John M. Capek, age 44
**SVP, Diabetes Care Operations:** Robert B. (Chip) Hance
**SVP, Diagnostic Operations and President, Abbott Diagnostics:** Jeffrey R. Binder, age 43
**SVP, Human Resources:** Stephen R. (Steve) Fussell, age 49
**SVP, International Operations:** Olivier Bohuon, age 48
**SVP, Manufacturing Supply, Global Pharmaceutical Operations:** John C. Landgraf, age 55
**SVP, Nutrition International Operations:** Thomas F. Chen, age 57
**SVP, Pharmaceutical Operations:** William G. Dempsey, age 55, $630,583 pay
**SVP, Pharmaceutical Operations:** James L. Tyree, age 53
**VP and Treasurer:** Robert E. Funck, age 44
**VP, Corporate Marketing:** Susan M. Widner, age 50
**VP, Investor Relations:** John Thomas
**VP, Public Affairs:** Catherine V. Babington, age 54
**Auditors:** Deloitte & Touche LLP

## LOCATIONS

**HQ:** Abbott Laboratories
100 Abbott Park Rd., Abbott Park, IL 60064
**Phone:** 847-937-6100 **Fax:** 847-937-9555
**Web:** www.abbott.com

### 2006 Sales

| | % of total |
|---|---|
| US | 53 |
| The Netherlands | 5 |
| Japan | 5 |
| Germany | 4 |
| Italy | 4 |
| Canada | 3 |
| France | 3 |
| Spain | 3 |
| UK | 2 |
| Other | 18 |
| **Total** | **100** |

## PRODUCTS/OPERATIONS

### 2006 Sales

| | % of total |
|---|---|
| Pharmaceuticals | 55 |
| Nutritionals | 19 |
| Diagnostics | 18 |
| Vascular | 5 |
| Other | 3 |
| **Total** | **100** |

### Selected Products

Pharmaceutical
- Biaxin (anti-infective)
- Depakote (epileptic seizures, bipolar disorder, migraines)
- HUMIRA (rheumatoid arthritis)
- Isoptin (hypertension)
- Kaletra (HIV)
- Lupron/Lucrin (advanced prostate cancer, endometriosis, through TAP Pharmaceutical Products)
- Mavik (hypertension)
- Meridia (obesity)
- Niaspan (high cholesterol)
- Norvir (HIV and AIDS)
- Ogastro/Prevacid (ulcers, erosive esophagitis, through TAP Pharmaceutical Products)
- Omnicef (antibiotic)
- Reductil (obesity)
- Synthroid (hyperthyroidism)
- Tarka (hypertension)
- TriCor (dyslipidemia)
- Ultane (anesthesia)
- Zemplar (hyperparathyroidism)

Diagnostic
- Abbott PRISM (high-volume blood-screening system)
- Aeroset (clinical chemistry system)
- ARCHITECT c8000 (clinical chemistry system)
- AxSYM (immunoassay system)
- Cell-Dyn (hematology systems and reagents)
- FreeStyle (glucose monitoring meters, test strips, data management software, and accessories)
- i-STAT (point-of-care diagnostics, blood analysis)
- PathVysion (breast cancer diagnostic test)
- UroVysion (bladder cancer)

Nutritional
- Alimentum (infant formula)
- Ensure (adult nutrition)
- Glucerna (nutritional beverage for diabetics)
- Isomil (soy-based infant formula)
- Jevity (liquid food)
- Pedialyte (electrolyte solution for infants)
- PediaSure (children's nutrition)
- Similac (infant formula)
- Survanta (infant respiratory distress syndrome)
- Zone Perfect (nutritional bars)

Vascular
- Acculink/Accunet (carotid stent)
- Asahi (coronary guidewire)
- BMW (coronary guidewire)
- Multi-Link Vision (coronary metallic stent)
- StarClose (vessel closure)
- Xience V (drug-eluting stent)
- Voyager (balloon dilation products)

## COMPETITORS

Amgen
AstraZeneca
Barr Pharmaceuticals
Baxter
Bayer
BD
Boston Scientific
Bristol-Myers Squibb
C. R. Bard
Cordis
Eli Lilly
Genentech
GlaxoSmithKline
Johnson & Johnson
Mallinckrodt
Medtronic CardioVascular
Merck
Mylan Labs
Nestlé
Novartis
Numico
Pfizer
Roche
Sandoz International GmbH
Sanofi-Aventis
Schering-Plough
Solvay
Teva Pharmaceuticals
Watson Pharmaceuticals
Wyeth

## HISTORICAL FINANCIALS

Company Type: Public

### Income Statement

FYE: December 31

| | REVENUE ($ mil.) | NET INCOME ($ mil.) | NET PROFIT MARGIN | EMPLOYEES |
|---|---|---|---|---|
| **12/06** | 22,476 | 1,717 | 7.6% | 66,663 |
| **12/05** | 22,338 | 3,372 | 15.1% | 59,735 |
| **12/04** | 19,680 | 3,236 | 16.4% | 60,600 |
| **12/03** | 19,681 | 2,753 | 14.0% | 72,200 |
| **12/02** | 17,685 | 2,794 | 15.8% | 71,819 |
| **Annual Growth** | 6.2% | (11.5%) | — | (1.8%) |

### 2006 Year-End Financials

Debt ratio: 49.9%
Return on equity: 12.1%
Cash ($ mil.): 1,373
Current ratio: 0.94
Long-term debt ($ mil.): 7,010
No. of shares (mil.): 1,537
Dividends
Yield: 2.4%
Payout: 103.6%
Market value ($ mil.): 74,879

### Stock History

NYSE: ABT

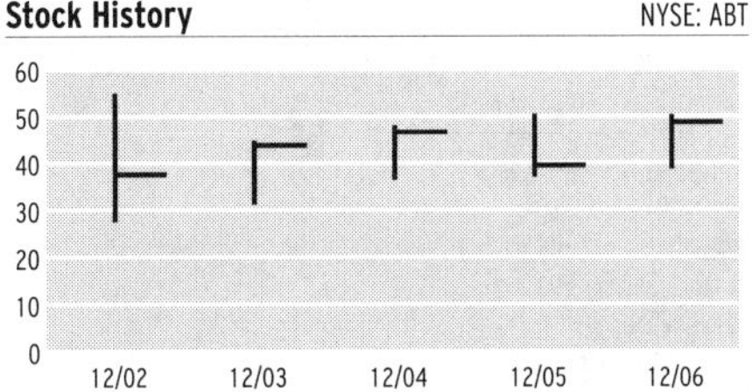


| | STOCK PRICE ($) FY Close | P/E High | P/E Low | PER SHARE ($) Earnings | Dividends | Book Value |
|---|---|---|---|---|---|---|
| **12/06** | 48.71 | 45 | 35 | 1.12 | 1.16 | 9.14 |
| **12/05** | 39.43 | 23 | 17 | 2.16 | 1.09 | 9.37 |
| **12/04** | 46.65 | 23 | 18 | 2.06 | 1.02 | 9.18 |
| **12/03** | 43.79 | 25 | 18 | 1.75 | 0.97 | 8.36 |
| **12/02** | 37.59 | 31 | 16 | 1.78 | 0.92 | 6.82 |
| **Annual Growth** | 6.7% | — | — | (10.9%) | 6.0% | 7.6% |

# ABC, Inc.

Some *Desperate Housewives,* a group of *Lost* plane crash survivors, and doctors schooled in *Grey's Anatomy* call this network home. ABC operates the #3 television network in the US (behind CBS and FOX), with 225 affiliates (including 10 corporate-owned stations). ABC also owns ESPN, a leader in cable sports broadcasting with a stable of channels including ESPN2, ESPN Classic, and ESPN News, as well as its flagship channel. In addition, the company operates mass market publisher Hyperion. ABC is the cornerstone of Disney-ABC Television Group, the TV division of parent Walt Disney.

ABC suffered a dip in viewership during the 2006-07 season and slipped from second to third place in the ratings race. The decline came in part due to a long winter hiatus for hit show *Lost*, as well as the loss of former ratings stalwart *Monday Night Football*, which was picked up for the 2006 NFL season by ESPN.

Despite its troubles, ABC is still performing much better than it was earlier in the decade when the network was mired in third-place due to a lack of program development and over-reliance on the once red-hot *Who Wants to Be a Millionaire* quiz show. It has a sizable and loyal fan base for both *Grey's Anatomy* and *Desperate Housewives*, and it may have found a new breakout hit with the critically acclaimed *Ugly Betty*. ABC is sticking with what it knows best — dramas — in 2007. The company has announced plans to include five new dramas in its Fall lineup, including the *Grey's Anatomy* spin-off *Private Practice*.

Disney in 2007 spun off its radio broadcasting operations, including ABC Radio Networks, which merged with Citadel Broadcasting. It hopes by shedding the radio stations it can focus ABC's efforts on television. The $2.7 billion deal left Disney shareholders owning 57% of the combined company. ESPN Radio and Radio Disney were not part of the spinoff and merger.

The company is also developing alternative channels for revenue, including online broadcasting and downloadable TV episodes. It struck a deal with Apple to make episodes of *Lost* and *Desperate Housewives*, among others, available for new iPods that can play video. ABC also sells archived news clips through Apple's iTunes store. (Apple head honcho Steve Jobs is the largest shareholder in Disney, with a 7% stake.) In addition, ABC offers some of its popular programs on the Internet for free the day after they air. Viewers have to watch the commercials on the Web broadcasts and cannot skip through them.

## HISTORY

ABC was launched in 1927 as the Blue Network by RCA. A sister network to NBC (now owned by General Electric), Blue Network was sold to Life Savers candy magnate Edward J. Noble in 1943 after an FCC ruling that prohibited ownership of more than one network. Renamed the American Broadcasting Company three years later, ABC struggled with just 100 radio stations in its network and no big stars. By 1953 the company had expanded into television with 14 affiliates. That year United Paramount Theatres, led by Leonard Goldenson, bought ABC for $25 million.

To compete with CBS and NBC, Goldenson turned to Hollywood. He signed a $40 million deal with Walt Disney in 1953 that gave ABC access to the Disney film library and an exclusive programming alliance. The network turned to other studios for programming such as *77 Sunset Strip* and *Maverick*. During the 1960s ABC fended off takeover attempts by ITT and Howard Hughes, and in the 1970s it pioneered the long-form mini-series with *Roots* and *Rich Man, Poor Man*. Hit shows, including *Happy Days* and *Charlie's Angels*, helped put the network on top during the 1976 season. In 1984 the company bought cable sports channel ESPN. (It sold 20% of ESPN to Hearst in 1991.) The next year ABC was sold to Capital Cities Communications for $3.5 billion.

Founded by Frank Smith as Hudson Valley Broadcasting, Capital Cities had started out as a bankrupt TV station in Albany, New York. In 1957 it acquired a second station in Raleigh, North Carolina, changed its name, and went public in 1964. Smith died in 1966, and Thomas Murphy took over as chairman and CEO. The company bought magazine publisher Fairchild Publications in 1968 and newspapers such as the *Fort Worth Star-Telegram* and *Kansas City Star* in the 1970s. By the 1980s Capital Cities had revenues of more than $1 billion.

During the early 1990s Capital Cities/ABC saw ratings soar with hits, including *Roseanne* and *Home Improvement*. Robert Iger was appointed president in 1994. Two years later Disney bought the company for $19 billion, selling off its newspapers for $1.65 billion. In 1998 ABC agreed to pay $9.2 billion for National Football League broadcast rights through 2005. In addition, Patricia Fili-Krushel was named president of ABC Television, making her the first woman to head a major broadcast network. Iger was named chairman of ABC in 1999, and ESPN chief Steven Bornstein took over as president.

In 1999 Disney sold ABC's Fairchild magazine unit to Advance Publications for about $650 million. Bornstein left late that year to head Disney's GO.com (now Walt Disney Internet Group). In early 2000 Iger was named president and COO of Disney, leaving broadcast president Robert Callahan in charge. Fili-Krushel later resigned. (Iger became CEO of Disney in 2005.) Negotiations over rebroadcast rights between Disney and Time Warner Cable went south that year and ABC broadcasts were briefly suspended for about 3.5 million viewers. (Time Warner Cable was later admonished by the FCC for dropping the stations during sweeps periods.) Despite the interruption, ABC finished #1 in the ratings for the first time in five years. That success was short-lived, however, as the network's audience share eroded the next season and ABC fell to #2.

Callahan resigned from ABC in 2001, and Bornstein returned from Disney Internet to become broadcast group president that year. Later Disney bought the Fox Family Channel, renamed ABC Family, and the international assets of the Fox Kids Network (later rebranded as JETIX) from News Corp. and Haim Saban for $5.2 billion (including debt).

Bornstein resigned as president in mid-2002. ABC reshuffled management again in 2004, with Anne Sweeny taking over management of all Disney's television operations, and Stephen McPherson taking over ABC's primetime entertainment duties.

In 2007 Disney spun off the radio broadcasting operations of ABC, including ABC Radio Networks, which merged with Citadel Broadcasting. The $2.7 billion merger left Disney shareholders owning 57% of the combined company.

## EXECUTIVES

**Co-Chairman, Disney Media Networks; President, Disney-ABC Television Group:** Anne M. Sweeney
**EVP and CFO, ABC and Touchstone Television:** James L. (Jim) Hedges
**EVP ABC Entertainment:** Jeffrey D. (Jeff) Bader
**EVP ABC Entertainment Television Group; President, Touchstone Television:** Mark Pedowitz
**SVP Deputy General Counsel:** T. Scott Fain
**SVP Human Resources:** Jeffrey S. Rosen
**SVP Labor Relations:** Jeffrey Ruthizer
**SVP Movies and Mini-Series:** Lance B. Taylor
**SVP Motion Pictures for Television and Mini-Series:** Quinn Taylor
**VP Broadcasting Legal and Business Affairs:** Jane B. Stewart
**VP Communications:** Heather Rim
**VP Corporate Projects:** Julie Hoover
**VP Human Resources:** Susan Dumond
**VP Corporate Initiatives:** Brad Jamison
**VP Human Resources Operations:** Sandy Hooper
**President, ABC-Owned Television Stations:** Walter C. Liss Jr.
**President, ABC Primetime Entertainment:** Stephen McPherson
**President, Sales and Marketing, ABC Television Network:** Mike Shaw
**Auditors:** PricewaterhouseCoopers LLP

## LOCATIONS

**HQ:** ABC, Inc.
77 W. 66th St., 3rd Fl., New York, NY 10023
**Phone:** 212-456-7777 **Fax:** 212-456-1424
**Web:** abc.go.com

## PRODUCTS/OPERATIONS

### Selected Network Shows

*20/20*
*According to Jim*
*America's Funniest Home Videos*
*Boston Legal*
*Brothers & Sisters*
*Dancing With the Stars*
*Desperate Housewives*
*Extreme Makeover: Home Edition*
*George Lopez*
*Grey's Anatomy*
*Lost*
*Men in Trees*
*Notes from the Underbelly*
*Supernanny*
*Ugly Betty*
*Wife Swap*

### Television Stations

KABC (Los Angeles)
KFSN (Fresno, CA)
KGO (San Francisco)
KTRK (Houston)
WABC (New York City)
WJRT (Flint, MI)
WLS (Chicago)
WPVI (Philadelphia)
WTVD (Raleigh-Durham, NC)
WTVG (Toledo, OH)

## COMPETITORS

CBS
The CW
Discovery Communications
Fox Entertainment
MyNetworkTV
NBC
Turner Broadcasting
Univision

## HISTORICAL FINANCIALS

Company Type: Subsidiary

**Income Statement** FYE: September 30

| | REVENUE ($ mil.) | NET INCOME ($ mil.) | NET PROFIT MARGIN | EMPLOYEES |
|---|---|---|---|---|
| **9/06** | 14,638 | — | — | — |
| **9/05** | 13,207 | — | — | — |
| **9/04** | 11,778 | — | — | — |
| **9/03** | 10,941 | — | — | — |
| **9/02** | 9,733 | — | — | — |
| **Annual Growth** | 10.7% | — | — | — |

**Revenue History**

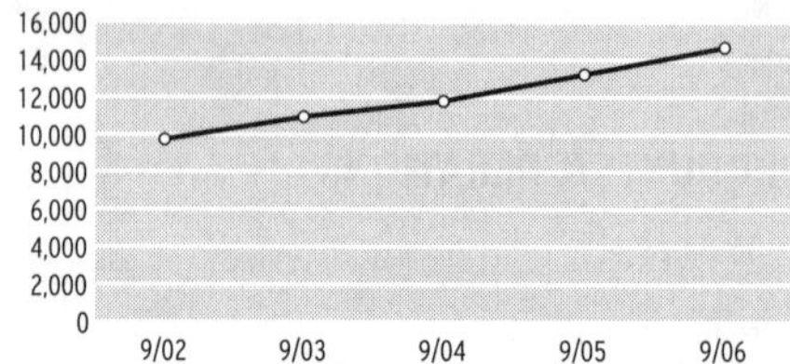


# Abercrombie & Fitch

Trading on its century-old name, Abercrombie & Fitch (A&F) sells upscale men's, women's, and kids' casual clothes and accessories — quite a change from when the company outfitted Ernest Hemingway and Teddy Roosevelt for safaris. A&F has about 950 stores in North America (mostly in malls) and also sells via its catalog and online. A&F targets college students, and has come under fire for some of its advertising campaigns, as well as for some of its short-run products. The company also runs a fast-growing chain of teen stores called Hollister Co., and a chain targeted at boys and girls ages seven to 14 called abercrombie. Its newest format, RUEHL, is a Greenwich Village-inspired concept for the post-college set.

A&F's carefully selected college-age sales staff and photos of twenty-something models adorning the walls imbue its main stores with an upscale fraternity house feel. Its image as the clothier for a preppy social elite has, in some circles, earned its clientele the nickname "Aber-Snobbies."

Although the company has ceased publication of its magazine and toned down its product lines, A&F has not overtly stopped antagonizing conservatives.

In 2004, A&F launched a new brand aimed at its customers who have grown older — a relative term for A&F. The brand, called RUEHL, runs more than a dozen stores in major shopping centers in Honolulu, San Francisco, Las Vegas, and Garden City, New York. The stores target customers aged 22 to 30, traditionally J. Crew and Banana Republic customers, offering hip styles at lower prices. Hollister stores, launched in 2000, outnumbered Abercrombie & Fitch stores for the first time in 2006.

Adidas America, subsidiary of the German sporting goods giant adidas, has filed suit against A&F to protect its trademark three-stripe logo, which it argues the company copied for its latest line of casual apparel.

In response to healthy international Internet sales, A&F opened a half-dozen stores in Canada in 2005 and its first European store in London in

March 2007. A&F has announced plans for further expansion in Europe, including Italy, France, Germany, Spain, Denmark, and Sweden.

A&F is searching for a new president and COO following the resignation of Robert Singer, after only 15 months with the company. Singer's abrupt departure was due to a disagreement over the company's international expansion strategy.

The SEC has launched an investigation concerning trading in A&F's common shares.

## HISTORY

Scotsman David Abercrombie began selling camping equipment in lower Manhattan in 1892. Joined by lawyer Ezra Fitch, Abercrombie & Fitch (A&F) soon established itself as the purveyor of outdoors equipment for the very rich. A&F supplied Theodore Roosevelt and Ernest Hemingway for safaris and provided gear for Charles Lindbergh and polar explorer Richard Byrd. In 1917 the company moved into a 12-story edifice in Manhattan that included a log cabin (which Fitch lived in) and a casting pool.

A&F thrived through the 1960s. Mounted animal heads adorned its New York store, which offered 15,000 types of lures and 700 different shotguns. However, by the 1970s A&F's core customers were as extinct or endangered as the animals they had hunted, and the company struggled to find new markets. In 1977 A&F filed for bankruptcy. A year later sports retailer Oshman's (now The Sports Authority) bought the company and expanded the number of stores while providing an eclectic assortment of goods. In 1988 clothing retailer The Limited bought A&F, then with about 25 stores, and shifted the company's emphasis to apparel.

Michael Jeffries took over in 1992 and transformed the still money-losing chain into an outfitter for college students. The new *jefe* micromanaged, issuing a 29-page book on everything from how A&F salespeople (who earned around $6 an hour) must look to exactly how many sweaters can be placed in a stack. Draconian perhaps, but the strategy worked, and A&F returned to profitability in fiscal 1995. The company went public in 1996 with more than 110 stores.

In 1998 The Limited spun off its remaining 84% stake. Also that year A&F sued rival American Eagle Outfitters, claiming it illegally copied A&F's clothing and approach (the suit was dismissed in 1999), and it raised the hackles of Mothers Against Drunk Driving with a catalog article entitled "Drinking 101." The company got attention of a different sort in 1999 when the SEC launched an investigation after A&F leaked sales figures to an analyst before they were made available to the public. In 2000 A&F launched its new teen store concept called Hollister Co.

A&F continued to push the envelope with its A&F Quarterly in summer 2001. Under the theme "Let Summer Begin," the catalog featured naked and half-naked models having "wet 'n' wild summer fun" and T-shirts logos that read "I Have a Big One" and "Get on the Stick."

The company pushed a little further in Spring 2002 with a line of T-shirts portraying Asian caricatures. Vocal protests from Asian groups forced A&F to pull the T-shirts from its shelves and issue an apology. Later that spring, A&F may have pushed a little too hard. A line of children's-sized thong underwear bearing sexually suggestive messages caused a furor among family-advocacy groups.

In December 2003, Abercrombie & Fitch toned down further with the discontinuation of its popular and racy A&F Quarterly magazine. Using half-nude models, the publication targeted consumers aged 18-24. In September 2004 it launched a young professionals' brand called RUEHL.

In May 2005 A&F established a Japanese subsidiary company called ANF. In November the company opened its first Ruehl Accessories store, a tiny (600 square feet) shop on Manhattan's Bleecker Street. Also in November the company opened its first off-mall, flagship store on New York's Fifth Avenue at 56th Street.

## EXECUTIVES

**Chairman and CEO:** Michael S. (Mike) Jeffries, age 62, $1,494,231 pay
**EVP and CFO:** Michael W. Kramer, age 42, $586,538 pay
**EVP, Planning and Allocation:** Leslee K. Herro, age 46, $826,058 pay
**SVP and General Manager:** Beverly House
**SVP and General Manager, Hollister:** Charles F. Kessler
**SVP, Allocation:** Rebecca F. Lee
**SVP, Real Estate:** Jeffrey Sinkley
**SVP, Stores Human Relations:** David L. Leino, age 41
**VP, Hollister:** Chad Kessler
**Senior Director of Brand Protection:** Shane Berry
**Director of Brand Protection:** John Carriero
**VP, Corporate Communications:** Thomas D. (Tom) Lennox
**Auditors:** PricewaterhouseCoopers LLP

## LOCATIONS

**HQ:** Abercrombie & Fitch Co.
6301 Fitch Path, New Albany, OH 43054
**Phone:** 614-283-6500 **Fax:** 614-283-6710
**Web:** www.abercrombie.com

### 2007 Stores

| | No. |
|---|---|
| California | 120 |
| Texas | 76 |
| Florida | 59 |
| New York | 44 |
| Illinois | 43 |
| Pennsylvania | 43 |
| Ohio | 40 |
| Michigan | 34 |
| New Jersey | 31 |
| North Carolina | 29 |
| Georgia | 27 |
| Virginia | 26 |
| Indiana | 25 |
| Massachusetts | 25 |
| Tennessee | 21 |
| Washington | 21 |
| Missouri | 20 |
| Connecticut | 18 |
| Minnesota | 18 |
| Arizona | 16 |
| Alabama | 15 |
| Kentucky | 15 |
| Louisiana | 15 |
| Maryland | 15 |
| Wisconsin | 15 |
| South Carolina | 13 |
| Oregon | 13 |
| Oklahoma | 10 |
| Other states | 96 |
| Canada | 6 |
| UK | 1 |
| **Total** | **950** |

## PRODUCTS/OPERATIONS

### 2007 Sales

| | $ mil. | % of total |
|---|---|---|
| Abercrombie & Fitch | 1,515.1 | 46 |
| Hollister | 1,363.2 | 41 |
| abercrombie | 405.8 | 12 |
| RUEHL | 34.0 | 1 |
| **Total** | **3,318.1** | **100** |

### Selected Products

Backpacks
Belts
Caps
Footwear
Fragrances
Hats
Jackets
Jeans
Outerwear
Pants
Shirts
Shorts
Skirts
Sweaters
Swimwear
Tank tops
Underwear

## COMPETITORS

Aéropostale
American Eagle Outfitters
Benetton
Buckle
Dillard's
Eddie Bauer
Express
Gap
Guess
H&M
J. Crew
Lands' End
Levi Strauss
Limited Brands
L.L. Bean
Macy's
Macy's Northwest
Mossimo
Nordstrom
Pacific Sunwear
Polo Ralph Lauren
Quiksilver
Target
Tommy Hilfiger
Urban Outfitters
Wet Seal

## HISTORICAL FINANCIALS

Company Type: Public

### Income Statement

FYE: Saturday nearest January 31

| | REVENUE ($ mil.) | NET INCOME ($ mil.) | NET PROFIT MARGIN | EMPLOYEES |
|---|---|---|---|---|
| **1/07** | 3,318 | 422 | 12.7% | 86,400 |
| **1/06** | 2,785 | 334 | 12.0% | 76,100 |
| **1/05** | 2,021 | 216 | 10.7% | 62,140 |
| **1/04** | 1,708 | 205 | 12.0% | 30,200 |
| **1/03** | 1,596 | 195 | 12.2% | 22,000 |
| **Annual Growth** | 20.1% | 21.3% | — | 40.8% |

### 2007 Year-End Financials

Debt ratio: —
Return on equity: 35.2%
Cash ($ mil.): 530
Current ratio: 2.14
Long-term debt ($ mil.): —
No. of shares (mil.): 88
Dividends
Yield: 0.9%
Payout: 15.3%
Market value ($ mil.): 7,132

### Stock History

NYSE: ANF

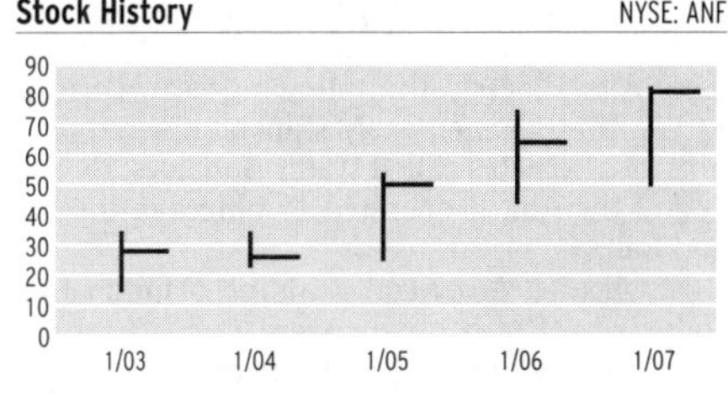


| | STOCK PRICE ($) FY Close | P/E High/Low | | PER SHARE ($) Earnings | Dividends | Book Value |
|---|---|---|---|---|---|---|
| **1/07** | 80.77 | 18 | 11 | 4.59 | 0.70 | 15.92 |
| **1/06** | 64.06 | 20 | 12 | 3.66 | 0.60 | 11.34 |
| **1/05** | 49.93 | 23 | 11 | 2.28 | 0.50 | 7.78 |
| **1/04** | 25.90 | 16 | 11 | 2.06 | — | 9.07 |
| **1/03** | 27.84 | 17 | 8 | 1.94 | — | 7.71 |
| **Annual Growth** | 30.5% | — | — | 24.0% | 18.3% | 19.9% |

# ABM Industries

ABM Industries makes a clean sweep of things. The company is one of the nation's largest facility services contractors, providing cleaning, engineering, and maintenance services to owners and operators of office parks and buildings, hospitals, manufacturing plants, schools, and transportation centers throughout the US. Its Ampco System Parking unit operates about 1,600 parking lots and garages primarily at airports in some 30 states, while its American Commercial Security Services (ACSS) subsidiary offers electronic safety monitoring, investigative services, and security consulting services. ABM Industries' largest division, however, remains its ABM Janitorial segment.

Like other conglomerates in the business services sector, the company has grown mainly by acquiring local and regional operating companies and their client rosters. ABM can then generate cost savings by centralizing many business functions, such as marketing, sales, and accounting. This strategy also allows ABM to increase sales by leveraging its diverse portfolio of service offerings.

Janitorial services currently account for about 55% of the company's sales, but segments such as parking and security have been growing at a rapid pace.

## HISTORY

Morris Rosenberg invested $4.50 in a bucket and cleaning tools and began cleaning San Francisco storefront windows in 1909. Later that year he purchased Chicago Window Cleaning for $300 and, armed with new supplies and a Ford Model T, began offering annual cleaning contracts. He changed the company's name to American Building Maintenance in 1913 to emphasize its broadening services. By 1920 the company had established three west coast offices, and it became the first contractor to clean a major college campus when it signed an agreement with Stanford University in 1921.

The company added cleaning supplies to its offerings in 1927 with the acquisition of Easterday Janitorial Supply Company and continued to grow, even during the Great Depression, by providing cleaning services cheaper than its clients could provide for themselves. ABM expanded to the East Coast in 1932. Morris Rosenberg died in 1935, leaving the company to his oldest son Theodore, who bought electrical services company Alta Electric the following year. During WWII ABM cleaned Navy ships and wired amphibious vehicles called Water Buffaloes. By the end of the war, it operated 17 offices in the US and Canada.

Now called American Building Maintenance Industries, the company went public in 1962 with Theodore serving as chairman and younger brother Sydney as CEO. To diversify its services, ABM Industries stepped up its acquisition pace in the late 1960s, buying Ampco Auto Parks (1967, parking facilities), Commercial Air Conditioning (1968, equipment maintenance), and General Elevator Corporation (1969, elevator maintenance and repair).

ABM Industries continued to expand its business into diverse services and regions through a three-decade buying spree. In 1981 the company combined its air-conditioning, elevator, lighting, and energy services into American Technical Services Company (Amtech) to better focus on the high-growth tech and energy businesses. A management-led buyout of the company failed in 1990 on opposition from the Rosenberg brothers. Although ABM Industries' president stepped down and several lawsuits were filed following the aborted LBO, the company continued to post impressive sales and profit numbers.

The company shortened its name to ABM Industries in 1994, the same year William Steele was named CEO. Sydney Rosenberg retired as chairman in 1997, marking the end of family control. The following year the company formed a Facility Services division to provide one-stop shopping for all of its services. It moved into landscaping services in 1999 with the purchase of Commercial Landscape Systems. The following year Steele stepped down as CEO and Henrik Slipsager, a former executive of Dutch services giant ISS, was tapped as the company's new chief.

In 2001 ABM sold off its Easterday Janitorial Supply subsidiary to AmSan West. ABM acquired six companies in 2001 and 2002, including Lakeside Building Maintenance, a large Midwestern janitorial contractor. In 2003 the company sold its Amtech Elevator Services to Otis Elevator Company for $112 million. Two years later, the company sold its CommAir Mechanical Services unit to Carrier Corp.

In 2005 ABM sold the last of its mechanical operations, divesting its water treatment business to San Joaquin Chemicals.

## EXECUTIVES

**Chairman:** Maryellen C. Herringer, age 63
**President, CEO, and Director:** Henrik C. Slipsager, age 51, $1,312,500 pay
**EVP and CFO:** George B. Sundby, age 55, $620,000 pay
**EVP; President, ABM Facility Services and President, Amtech Lighting:** Steven M. Zaccagnini, age 45, $620,000 pay
**EVP; President, ABM Janitorial Services:** James P. (Jim) McClure, age 50, $729,238 pay
**EVP:** James S. Lusk, age 48
**SVP, Director of Business Development, and Chief Marketing Officer:** Gary R. Wallace, age 56
**SVP, Chief of Staff, and Treasurer:** David L. Farwell, age 45
**SVP, Human Resources:** Erin M. Andre, age 47
**SVP, General Counsel, and Secretary:** Linda S. Auwers, age 59, $459,904 pay
**VP, Controller, and Chief Accounting Officer:** Maria de Martini, age 47
**VP and Deputy General Counsel:** Glenn M. Hammond, age 34
**President and CEO, American Commercial Security Services:** John Moore II
**President, American Commercial Security Services and Security Services of America:** Larry T. Smith
**President, Ampco System Parking:** Rich Kindorf
**President, ABM Engineering Services:** Mike Latham
**Auditors:** KPMG LLP

## LOCATIONS

**HQ:** ABM Industries Incorporated
160 Pacific Ave., Ste. 222, San Francisco, CA 94111
**Phone:** 415-733-4000 **Fax:** 415-733-7333
**Web:** www.abm.com

## PRODUCTS/OPERATIONS

### 2006 Sales

| | $ mil. | % of total |
|---|---|---|
| Janitorial | 1,563.8 | 56 |
| Parking | 440.0 | 16 |
| Security | 307.9 | 11 |
| Engineering | 285.2 | 10 |
| Lighting | 113.0 | 4 |
| Other | 82.8 | 3 |
| **Total** | **2,792.7** | **100** |

### Selected Operations

ABM Engineering Services
ABM Facility Services
ABM Janitorial Services
ABM Security Services
American Commercial Security Services (ACSS)
Ampco System Parking
Amtech Lighting Services

## COMPETITORS

Allied Security
ARAMARK
Central Parking
Comfort Systems USA
Guardsmark
Healthcare Services
Impark
OneSource Management
ServiceMaster
Sodexho
Standard Parking
Temco Service Industries
UNICCO Service

## HISTORICAL FINANCIALS

Company Type: Public

### Income Statement

FYE: October 31

| | REVENUE ($ mil.) | NET INCOME ($ mil.) | NET PROFIT MARGIN | EMPLOYEES |
|---|---|---|---|---|
| **10/06** | 2,793 | 93 | 3.3% | 75,000 |
| **10/05** | 2,588 | 58 | 2.2% | 73,000 |
| **10/04** | 2,416 | 31 | 1.3% | 70,000 |
| **10/03** | 2,263 | 91 | 4.0% | 64,000 |
| **10/02** | 2,192 | 47 | 2.1% | 62,000 |
| **Annual Growth** | 6.2% | 18.9% | — | 4.9% |

### 2006 Year-End Financials

Debt ratio: —
Return on equity: 18.3%
Cash ($ mil.): 134
Current ratio: 1.98
Long-term debt ($ mil.): —
No. of shares (mil.): 49
Dividends
Yield: 2.2%
Payout: 23.4%
Market value ($ mil.): 966

### Stock History

NYSE: ABM

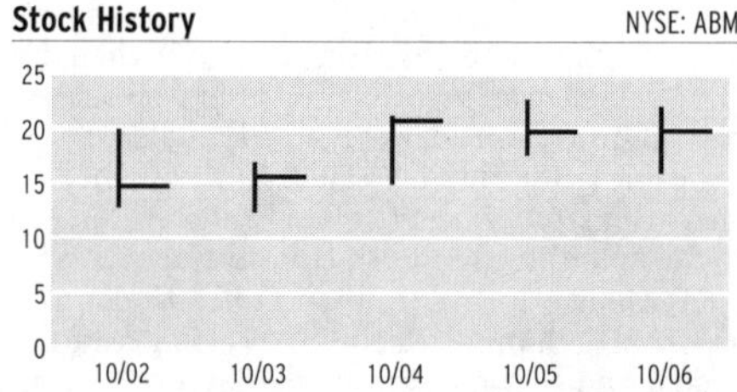


| | STOCK PRICE ($) FY Close | P/E High | P/E Low | PER SHARE ($) Earnings | PER SHARE ($) Dividends | PER SHARE ($) Book Value |
|---|---|---|---|---|---|---|
| **10/06** | 19.86 | 12 | 9 | 1.88 | 0.44 | 11.13 |
| **10/05** | 19.78 | 20 | 16 | 1.15 | 0.42 | 9.70 |
| **10/04** | 20.75 | 34 | 25 | 0.61 | 0.40 | 9.08 |
| **10/03** | 15.56 | 9 | 7 | 1.81 | 0.38 | 9.18 |
| **10/02** | 14.69 | 21 | 14 | 0.92 | 0.36 | 7.89 |
| **Annual Growth** | 7.8% | — | — | 19.6% | 5.1% | 9.0% |

# Accenture Ltd

For Accenture, the accent is on trying to help businesses improve their performance. The world's largest consulting firm, Accenture offers management consulting, information technology and systems integration, and business process outsourcing (BPO) services to customers around the globe. The company divides its practices into five main operating groups — communications and high technology, financial services, government, products, and resources — that encompass more than 15 industries. Accenture, which is domiciled in Bermuda but headquartered in New York, operates from more than 150 locations in about 50 countries.

Traditional business consulting remains a core function for Accenture, but systems integration and outsourcing have become key growth sectors. In 2006 Accenture expanded its outsourcing operations by buying NaviSys, a leading provider of software for the life insurance industry, along with key assets of Savista. The next year it added to its marketing sciences offerings in the Asia Pacific when it acquired Mediasenz, a media auditor based in Australia. In addition, Accenture is investing in staff development initiatives designed to more closely integrate the firm's IT-related and strategy-related consulting offerings.

Accenture disperses its advice widely — no single operating group accounts for more than a quarter of the firm's sales. Similarly, Accenture has diversified its operations geographically. Revenue from outside the US makes up a majority of its sales mix. However, as with the rest of the outsourcing services industry, the company is looking to India as its key area for major expansion: In early 2007, Accenture announced it was expanding its staff in the country by 30%. It also has its eye on China and Brazil.

## HISTORY

Accenture traces its history back to the storied accounting firm of Arthur Andersen & Co. Founded by Northwestern University professor and accounting legend Arthur Andersen in 1913, the firm's expanding scope of operations led it into forensic accounting and advising clients on financial reporting processes, forming the basis for a management consulting arm. Arthur Andersen led the firm until his death in 1947. His successor, Leonard Spacek, split off the consulting operations as a separate unit in 1954.

The consulting business grew quickly during the 1970s and 1980s, thanks in part to an orgy of US corporate re-engineering. By 1988 consulting accounted for 40% of Andersen's sales. Chafing at sharing profits with the auditors (who faced growing price pressures and a rising tide of legal action due to the accounting irregularities of their clients), the consultants sought more power within the firm. The result was a 1989 restructuring that established Andersen Worldwide (later Andersen) as the parent of two independent units, Arthur Andersen and Andersen Consulting (AC). The growing revenue imbalance between the operations remained unresolved, however, and a year later Arthur Andersen poured gas on the flames by establishing its own business consultancy.

Meanwhile, AC continued to expand during the 1990s by forming practices focused on manufacturing, finance, and government. It addressed the shift from mainframes to PCs by forming alliances with technology heavyweights Hewlett-Packard, Sun Microsystems, and Microsoft. In 1996 AC teamed up with Internet service provider BBN (acquired by GTE in 1997) to form ServiceNet, a joint venture to develop Internet commerce and other systems.

The Andersen family feud took a turn for the worse in 1997 with the retirement of CEO Lawrence Weinbach. A deadlocked vote for a new leader led the board to appoint accounting partner W. Robert Grafton as CEO, angering the consulting partners. Later that year AC asked the International Chamber of Commerce to negotiate a breakup of Andersen Worldwide. George Shaheen, to whom many attributed the heightened tensions between the units, resigned as CEO of AC in 1999 and was replaced by Joe Forehand.

While the separation dispute dragged on, the consulting business grew and diversified amid increasing consolidation in the industry. In 1999 the company moved into e-commerce venture funding with the formation of Andersen Consulting Ventures, and in 2000 it inked partnership deals with Microsoft (Microsoft system implementation services), Sun Microsystems (for B2B Internet office supply sales), and BT (Internet-based human resources services).

That year an international arbitrator finally approved AC's separation from its parent, ruling that the consultancy must change its name and pay Andersen Worldwide $1 billion (far less than the $15 billion demanded by the accounting partners). Renamed Accenture, the company went public in 2001. While the new name (a made-up word) might have struck some as a marketing challenge, having an identity distinct from that of its former parent proved to be a stroke of luck for Accenture. Andersen broke apart in 2002 after becoming embroiled in the accounting scandals of energy giant Enron.

In 2004 Accenture successfully bid on a $10 billion, 10-year contract to create a system to identify visitors and immigrants coming into the country. Dubbed US-VISIT (United States Visitor and Immigrant Status Indicator Technology), the system was to be employed by the Department of Homeland Security to prevent terrorists from entering the US. However, Accenture's bid nearly ran afoul of congressional critics who tried to pass spending amendments barring firms headquartered outside the US from winning security-related business.

Forehand stepped down as CEO of Accenture in 2004 and was replaced by company veteran William Green. Forehand remained chairman until he retired in 2006, when Green was named to that post, as well.

Accenture acquired Capgemini's North American health practice in 2005 for $175 million in order to strengthen its offerings to hospitals and health care systems.

## EXECUTIVES

**Chairman and CEO:** William D. (Bill) Green, age 53, $2,612,000 pay
**International Chairman:** Michael G. (Mike) McGrath, age 60, $3,239,527 pay
**International Chairman:** Diego Visconti, age 56, $2,162,334 pay
**COO:** Stephen J. (Steve) Rohleder, age 49
**CFO:** Pamela J. Craig, age 49
**CTO:** Donald J. (Don) Rippert
**Chief Diversity Officer and Managing Director, US:** Kedrick Adkins
**Chief Human Resources Officer:** Jill B. Smart
**Chief Quality and Risk Officer:** Robert N. Frerichs
**Chief Strategy and Corporate Development Officer:** R. Timothy S. (Tim) Breene, age 57
**Group Chief Executive, Financial Services:** Adrian J. Lajtha, age 49
**Group Chief Executive, Communications and High Tech:** Martin I. (Marty) Cole, age 50
**Group Chief Executive, Business Consulting and Integrated Markets:** Mark Foster, age 46, $2,497,898 pay
**Group Chief Executive, Products:** Gianfranco Casati, age 47
**Group Chief Executive, Resources:** Sander van 't Noordende, age 43
**Group Chief Executive, Systems Integration, Technology, and Delivery:** Karl-Heinz Flöther, age 54, $3,967,655 pay
**Chief Marketing and Communications Officer:** Roxanne Taylor
**General Counsel and Secretary:** Douglas G. (Doug) Scrivner, age 55
**Principal Accounting Officer and Controller:** Anthony G. Coughlan, age 49
**Executive Director, Office of the CEO:** Lori L. Lovelace
**Senior Director, Investor Relations:** David Straube
**Auditors:** KPMG LLP

## LOCATIONS

**HQ:** Accenture Ltd
1345 Avenue of the Americas, New York, NY 10105
**Phone:** 917-452-4400 **Fax:** 917-527-9915
**Web:** www.accenture.com

### 2006 Sales

| | % of total |
|---|---|
| Americas | 46 |
| Europe, Middle East & Africa | 46 |
| Asia/Pacific | 8 |
| **Total** | **100** |

## PRODUCTS/OPERATIONS

### 2006 Sales

| | % of total |
|---|---|
| Communications & high technology | 25 |
| Products | 24 |
| Financial services | 22 |
| Resources | 16 |
| Government | 13 |
| **Total** | **100** |

### Selected Practice Areas

Communications and high technology
- Communications
- Electronics and high technology
- Media and entertainment

Products
- Automotive
- Consumer goods and services
- Health and life sciences
- Industrial equipment
- Retail
- Transportation and travel services

Financial services
- Banking
- Capital markets
- Insurance

Resources
- Chemicals
- Energy
- Natural resources
- Utilities

Government

### Selected Services

Business consulting
- Customer relationship management
- Finance and performance management
- Human performance
- Strategy
- Supply chain management

Outsourcing
- Application outsourcing
- Business process outsourcing (BPO)
  - Customer contact
  - Finance and accounting
  - Human resources
  - Learning
  - Procurement
- Infrastructure outsourcing

Systems integration and technology
- Enterprise architecture
- Information management
- Infrastructure consulting
- Intellectual property
- Research and development

## COMPETITORS

Bain & Company
BearingPoint
Booz Allen
Boston Consulting
Capgemini
Capgemini US
Charteris
Computer Sciences Corp.
Deloitte Consulting
EDS
IBM
McKinsey & Company
Perot Systems
Siemens AG
Towers Perrin
Unisys

## HISTORICAL FINANCIALS

Company Type: Public

### Income Statement

FYE: August 31

| | REVENUE ($ mil.) | NET INCOME ($ mil.) | NET PROFIT MARGIN | EMPLOYEES |
|---|---|---|---|---|
| **8/06** | 18,228 | 973 | 5.3% | 140,000 |
| **8/05** | 17,094 | 941 | 5.5% | 123,000 |
| **8/04** | 15,114 | 691 | 4.6% | 100,000 |
| **8/03** | 13,397 | 498 | 3.7% | 83,000 |
| **8/02** | 13,105 | 245 | 1.9% | 75,000 |
| **Annual Growth** | 8.6% | 41.2% | — | 16.9% |

### 2006 Year-End Financials

Debt ratio: 1.4%
Return on equity: 54.2%
Cash ($ mil.): 3,420
Current ratio: 1.26
Long-term debt ($ mil.): 27
No. of shares (mil.): 581
Dividends
Yield: 1.0%
Payout: 18.9%
Market value ($ mil.): 17,220

### Stock History

NYSE: ACN

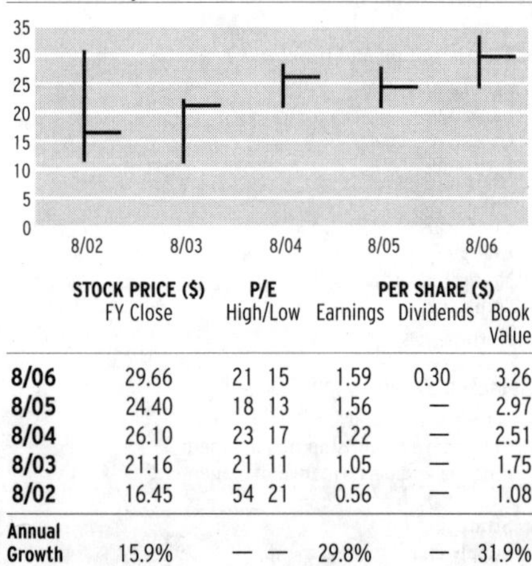


| | STOCK PRICE ($) FY Close | P/E High | P/E Low | PER SHARE ($) Earnings | Dividends | Book Value |
|---|---|---|---|---|---|---|
| **8/06** | 29.66 | 21 | 15 | 1.59 | 0.30 | 3.26 |
| **8/05** | 24.40 | 18 | 13 | 1.56 | — | 2.97 |
| **8/04** | 26.10 | 23 | 17 | 1.22 | — | 2.51 |
| **8/03** | 21.16 | 21 | 11 | 1.05 | — | 1.75 |
| **8/02** | 16.45 | 54 | 21 | 0.56 | — | 1.08 |
| **Annual Growth** | 15.9% | — | — | 29.8% | — | 31.9% |

# Ace Hardware

Luckily, Ace has John Madden up its sleeve. Despite the growth of warehouse-style competitors, Ace Hardware has remained a household name, thanks to ads featuring Madden, a former Oakland Raiders football coach and TV commentator. By sales the company is the #1 hardware cooperative in the US, ahead of Do It Best. Ace dealer-owners operate more than 4,600 Ace Hardware stores, home centers, and lumber and building materials locations in all 50 US states and about 70 other countries. From about 15 warehouses Ace distributes such products as electrical and plumbing supplies, garden equipment, hand tools, housewares, and power tools. Ace's paint division is the 12th largest paint manufacturer in the US.

It also makes its own brand of paint and offers thousands of other Ace-brand products. In addition to its own-brand paints, Ace began offering Benjamin Moore products in its stores in 2006.

Ace additionally provides training programs and advertising campaigns for its dealers. Ace dealers own the company and receive dividends from Ace's profits.

Challenged by big-box chains such as The Home Depot and Lowe's, Ace has unveiled its Next Generation store concept, which calls for signage with detailed product descriptions and different flooring to set off departments, among other features. The company is also focusing on opening smaller neighborhood stores to entice customers who would rather not drive to edge-of-town big-box chains. In its most ambitious expansion plan to date, Ace Hardware will add 150 to 200 stores. Up to 40 stores are planned for the Detroit, Ann Arbor, and Flint, Michigan markets in 2007.

The company is also increasing the size of its stores. The average store is 10,000 sq. ft., but newer stores are about 14,000 sq. ft. To support store growth in the West, Ace is expanding its distribution center in Prescott Valley, Arizona.

In mid-2007 CEO Ray Griffith sent a letter to its retailers, saying the company was considering changing from a cooperative to a traditional corporation. The change is being considered to become more competitive and to better fuel growth.

Shortly after, the company announced a $154 million accounting shortfall uncovered while Ace prepared to convert formats. It has called off the conversion as it researches the error and said it may not be able to make the normal profit payout to store owners this year due to the problem.

## HISTORY

A group of Chicago-area hardware dealers — William Stauber, Richard Hesse, Gern Lindquist, and Oscar Fisher — decided in 1924 to pool their hardware buying and promotional costs. In 1928 the group incorporated as Ace Stores, named in honor of the superior WWI fliers dubbed aces. Hesse became president the following year, retaining that position for the next 44 years. The company also opened its first warehouse in 1929, and by 1933 it had 38 dealers.

The organization had 133 dealers in seven states by 1949. In 1953 Ace began to allow dealers to buy stock in the company through the Ace Perpetuation Plan. During the 1960s Ace expanded into the South and West, and by 1969 it had opened distribution centers in Georgia and California — its first such facilities outside Chicago. In 1968 it opened its first international store in Guam.

By the early 1970s the do-it-yourself market began to surge as inflation pushed up plumber and electrician fees. As the market grew, large home center chains gobbled up market share from independent dealers such as those franchised through Ace. In response, Ace and its dealers became a part of a growing trend in the hardware industry — cooperatives.

Hesse sold the company to its dealers in 1973 for $6 million (less than half its book value), and the following year Ace began operating as a cooperative. Hesse stepped down in 1973. In 1976 the dealers took full control when the company's first Board of Dealer-Directors was elected.

After signing up a number of dealers in the eastern US, Ace had dealers in all 50 states by 1979. The co-op opened a plant to make paint in Matteson, Illinois, in 1984. By 1985 Ace had reached $1 billion in sales and had initiated its Store of the Future Program, allowing dealers to borrow up to $200,000 to upgrade their stores and conduct market analyses. Former head coach John Madden of the National Football League's Oakland Raiders signed on as Ace's mouthpiece in 1988.

A year later the co-op began to test ACENET, a computer network that allowed Ace dealers to check inventory, send and receive e-mail, make special purchase requests, and keep up with prices on commodity items such as lumber. In 1990 Ace established an International Division to handle its overseas stores. (It had been exporting products since 1975.) EVP and COO David Hodnik became president in 1995. That year the co-op added a net of 67 stores, including a three-store chain in Russia. Expanding further internationally, Ace signed a five-year joint-supply agreement in 1996 with Canadian lumber and hardware retailer Beaver Lumber. Hodnik added CEO to his title in 1996.

Ace fell further behind its old rival, True Value, in 1997 when ServiStar Coast to Coast and True Value merged to form TruServ (renamed True Value in 2005), a hardware giant that operated more than 10,000 outlets at the completion of the merger.

Late in 1997 Ace launched an expansion program in Canada. (The co-op already operated distribution centers in Ontario and Calgary.) In 1999 Ace merged its lumber and building materials division with Builder Marts of America to form a dealer-owned buying group to supply about 2,700 retailers. In 2000, Ace gained 208 member outlet stores, but saw 279 member outlets terminated. The next year it gained 220, but lost 255.

Sodisco-Howden bought all the shares of Ace Hardware Canada in February 2003. To better serve international members, Ace opened its first international buying office, in Hong Kong, in April 2004.

The company added 131 new stores in 2005. That year, after 33 years with the company, David F. Hodnik retired as president and CEO of Ace Hardware. He was succeeded by COO Ray A. Griffith.

## EXECUTIVES

**Chairman:** J. Thomas (Tom) Glenn
**President and CEO:** Ray A. Griffith, age 53
**SVP, General Counsel, and Secretary:** Arthur J. (Art) McGivern
**SVP, International and Paint:** David F. (Dave) Myer

**VP, Business Development:** John Venhuizen, age 36
**VP, Information Technology:** Michael G. (Mike) Elmore
**VP, Retail Operations:** Kenneth L. (Ken) Nichols
**VP, Merchandising, Marketing, and Advertising:** Lori L. Bossmann
**VP, Retail Development, New Business, and Company Stores:** Michael A. (Mike) Zipser
**VP, Finance:** Ronald J. (Ron) Knutson
**VP, Human Resources:** Jimmy Alexander
**VP, Retail Support:** William J. (Bill) Bauman
**VP, Supply Chain:** Daniel C. (Dan) Prochaska
**Manager, Advertising:** Frank Rothing
**Director, Advertising and Brand Development:** Paula K. Erickson
**Manager, New Business:** Bill Jablonowski
**Director, Global Retail Operations:** Angel L. Garcia
**Specialty Business Manager:** Russ Goerlitz
**Auditors:** KPMG LLP

## LOCATIONS

**HQ:** Ace Hardware Corporation
2200 Kensington Ct., Oak Brook, IL 60523
**Phone:** 630-990-6600 **Fax:** 630-990-6838
**Web:** www.acehardware.com

## COMPETITORS

84 Lumber
Akzo Nobel
Benjamin Moore
Building Materials Holding
Costco Wholesale
Do it Best
Fastenal
Grossman's
Handy Hardware Wholesale
Home Depot
ICI American
Kmart
Lowe's
McCoy
Menard
Northern Tool
Orgill
Reno-Depot
Sears
Sherwin-Williams
Stock Building Supply
Sutherland Lumber
True Value
United Hardware Distributing
Wal-Mart

## HISTORICAL FINANCIALS

Company Type: Cooperative

### Income Statement

FYE: Saturday nearest December 31

| | REVENUE ($ mil.) | NET INCOME ($ mil.) | NET PROFIT MARGIN | EMPLOYEES |
|---|---|---|---|---|
| **12/06** | 3,770 | 107 | 2.8% | 5,000 |
| **12/05** | 3,466 | 100 | 2.9% | 4,976 |
| **12/04** | 3,289 | 102 | 3.1% | 5,000 |
| **12/03** | 3,159 | 101 | 3.2% | 5,100 |
| **12/02** | 3,029 | 82 | 2.7% | 5,268 |
| **Annual Growth** | 5.6% | 6.9% | — | (1.3%) |

### Net Income History

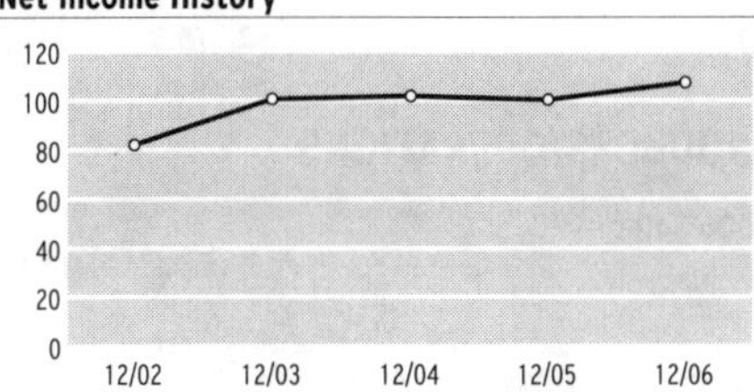


# Adams Resources & Energy

Bud Adams may have moved his football team to Tennessee, but his Adams Resources & Energy remains a Houston oiler. Subsidiary Gulfmark Energy buys crude oil at the wellhead for transport to refiners and other customers, and the company's Ada Resources subsidiary markets refined petroleum products such as gasoline and diesel fuel. With exploration and production mainly in Texas and Louisiana, Adams Resources boasts proved reserves of 8.3 billion cu. ft. of natural gas and 396,000 barrels of oil. Chairman and CEO Adams, owner of the NFL's Tennessee Titans, controls 49.3% of the company.

Adams Resources & Energy also owns and operates Service Transport, a trucking firm that delivers petroleum products and liquid chemicals throughout the continental US and Canada.

The company expanded its operations in 1999 by setting up Adams Resources Marketing as a wholesale purchaser, distributor, and marketer of natural gas. In 2000 it ramped up operations in the US Northeast by forming a regional retail marketing group to sell natural gas and other energy products.

Unusually warm winter weather and charges related to its Enron contracts (Enron had been a major customer) depressed the company's results in 2001. However, Adams Resources & Energy is focusing on niche markets where the company has a strong track record, in order to boost profitability and to reduce the level of price risks associated with its operations. After 2002 results were still below expectations, the company bounced back in 2003.

## HISTORY

Bud Adams founded Ada Oil in 1947 to explore for and produce oil and gas. These operations, with some real estate holdings, formed the core of what became Adams Resources when the company went public in 1974. An investment in coal in Illinois and Kentucky led to $65 million in losses in 1981 and the closure of those operations. In 1992 Adams Resources bought GulfMark Energy, a crude oil trading company that specialized in oil transport and the marketing of specialty grades of crude.

When intrastate trucking was deregulated in 1995, Adams Resources faced new competition in Texas, where it made 40% of its trucking sales. The company had to cut prices that year, and transportation earnings fell 30%. Adams Resources enjoyed greater production from a series of successful gas wells in the Austin Chalk region in 1996, and the company and partner Nuevo Energy added three wells in Austin Chalk the next year.

Adams Resources completed a 7.5-mile offshore Louisiana crude oil pipeline in 1998, which boosted the company's Gulf of Mexico crude oil throughput by more than 15,000 barrels per day.

## EXECUTIVES

**Chairman and CEO:** K. S. (Bud) Adams Jr., age 84, $225,000 pay
**President, COO, and Director:** Frank T. (Chip) Webster, age 58, $378,440 pay
**VP and CFO:** Richard B. (Rick) Abshire, age 54, $220,000 pay (prior to title change)
**President, Service Transport Company:** Claude H. Lewis, age 63
**President, Adams Resources Marketing:** Tony A. Gant, age 54
**President, Adams Resources Exploration:** James Brock Moore III, age 64
**VP, Gulfmark Energy:** Juanita G. Simmons, age 49, $224,000 pay
**Secretary:** David B. Hurst, age 53
**President, Gulfmark Energy:** Geoffrey L. (Geoff) Griffith
**President, Ada Resources:** James L. Smith
**Auditors:** Deloitte & Touche LLP

## LOCATIONS

**HQ:** Adams Resources & Energy, Inc.
4400 Post Oak Pkwy., Ste. 2700, Houston, TX 77027
**Phone:** 713-881-3600 **Fax:** 713-881-3491
**Web:** www.adamsresources.com

Adams Resources produces oil and gas in Texas and Louisiana; markets oil and gas products on the Gulf Coast and in New England; and provides energy transportation services throughout the US and Canada.

## PRODUCTS/OPERATIONS

### 2006 Sales

| | $ mil. | % of total |
|---|---|---|
| Marketing | 2,167.5 | 96 |
| Transportation | 62.2 | 3 |
| Oil & gas | 16.9 | 1 |
| **Total** | **2,246.6** | **100** |

### Selected Subsidiaries

Ada Crude Oil Company
Ada Mining Corporation
Ada Resources, Inc. (petroleum products marketing)
Ada Resources Marketing, Inc. (wholesale natural gas marketing)
Adams Resources Exploration Corporation
Adams Resources Marketing, Ltd. (natural gas marketing)
Bayou City Pipelines, Inc.
Buckley Mining Corporation
CJC Leasing, Inc.
Classic Coal Corporation
Gulfmark Energy, Inc. (crude oil marketing)
Service Transport Company (liquid chemicals and petroleum products transport)

## COMPETITORS

Abraxas Petroleum
Anadarko Petroleum
Apache
BP
Cabot Oil & Gas
Chevron
EOG
Exxon Mobil
Pioneer Natural Resources
Pogo Producing
Royal Dutch Shell

## HISTORICAL FINANCIALS

Company Type: Public

### Income Statement

FYE: December 31

| | REVENUE ($ mil.) | NET INCOME ($ mil.) | NET PROFIT MARGIN | EMPLOYEES |
|---|---|---|---|---|
| **12/06** | 2,247 | 11 | 0.5% | 748 |
| **12/05** | 2,365 | 18 | 0.7% | 745 |
| **12/04** | 2,070 | 9 | 0.4% | 672 |
| **12/03** | 1,722 | 3 | 0.2% | 634 |
| **12/02** | 2,323 | 2 | 0.1% | 646 |
| **Annual Growth** | (0.8%) | 62.7% | — | 3.7% |

**2006 Year-End Financials**

Debt ratio: 4.0%
Return on equity: 15.0%
Cash ($ mil.): 21
Current ratio: 1.17
Long-term debt ($ mil.): 3
No. of shares (mil.): 4
Dividends
 Yield: 1.4%
 Payout: 16.9%
Market value ($ mil.): 127

**Stock History** AMEX: AE

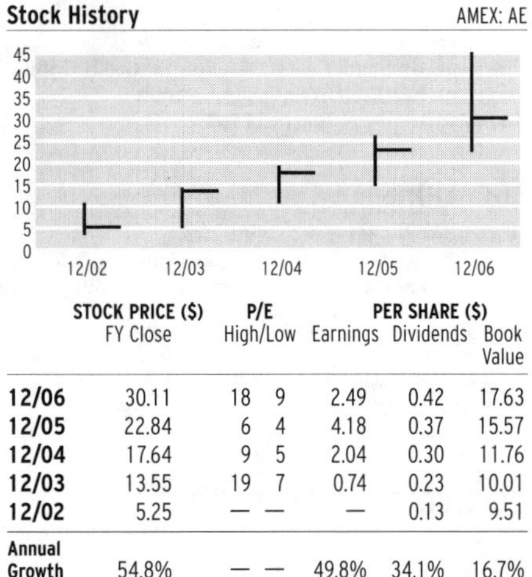


| | STOCK PRICE ($) FY Close | P/E High | P/E Low | PER SHARE ($) Earnings | Dividends | Book Value |
|---|---|---|---|---|---|---|
| **12/06** | 30.11 | 18 | 9 | 2.49 | 0.42 | 17.63 |
| **12/05** | 22.84 | 6 | 4 | 4.18 | 0.37 | 15.57 |
| **12/04** | 17.64 | 9 | 5 | 2.04 | 0.30 | 11.76 |
| **12/03** | 13.55 | 19 | 7 | 0.74 | 0.23 | 10.01 |
| **12/02** | 5.25 | — | — | — | 0.13 | 9.51 |
| **Annual Growth** | 54.8% | — | — | 49.8% | 34.1% | 16.7% |

# Adobe Systems

Adobe Systems' role as a leading desktop publishing software provider is well documented. The company offers the ubiquitous Acrobat Reader (distributed free of charge), a tool that displays portable document format (PDF) files on the Internet. The company's Web and print publishing products include Photoshop, Illustrator, and PageMaker. Adobe's offerings also include print technology geared toward manufacturers, as well as Web design (GoLive) and electronic book publishing software. Its InDesign publishing package provides professional layout and design applications. Adobe's Professional Services group offers implementation, training, and support.

Adobe acquired rival Macromedia for approximately $3.4 billion in stock late in 2005. Macromedia's popular Web site design and animation tools include Dreamweaver and Flash. Adobe agreed to acquire publishing software provider Scene7 in 2007.

Graphics and Web designers, technical writers, photographers, and other publishing professionals use Adobe's products to create online and print-based documents. The company's largest product segment, creative solutions, accounts for more than half of Adobe's revenues; products in the segment include InDesign, a professional page layout product that competes primarily against Quark's XPress product, as well as its popular Photoshop image editor.

Adobe sells directly and through distributors and resellers. Ingram Micro and Tech Data together accounted for about a third of the company's sales in fiscal 2006.

Though Adobe generates the majority of its sales through Web and print products, the company's activities aren't limited to developing its own software. In addition to direct investments in a handful of high-tech companies, it operates four venture partnerships with Granite Ventures. Adobe has investments in more than 30 companies (including Convio and PSS Systems) whose products and services complement its own.

## HISTORY

When Charles Geschke hired John Warnock as chief scientist for Xerox's new graphics and imaging lab, he set the stage for one of the world's largest software makers. While at the Xerox lab, the pair developed the PostScript computer language, which tells printers how to reproduce digitized images on paper. When Xerox refused to market it, the duo left that company and started Adobe (named after a creek near their homes in San Jose, California) in 1982.

Their original plan was to produce an electronic document processing system based on PostScript, but the company changed direction when Apple whiz Steve Jobs hired it to co-design the software for his company's LaserWriter printer. A year later Adobe went public. Meanwhile, PostScript was pioneering the desktop publishing industry by enabling users to laser print nearly anything they created on a computer.

In 1987 the company branched into the European market with the establishment of subsidiary Adobe Systems Europe. It also entered the PC market by adapting PostScript for IBM's operating system. Two years later the company began marketing its products in Asia.

Adobe grew throughout the 1990s by acquiring other software firms, including OCR Systems and Nonlinear Technologies (1992), and AH Software and Science & Art (1993). In 1993 the company began licensing its PostScript software to printer manufacturers; it also started marketing its Acrobat software.

Adobe bought Aldus (1994), whose PageMaker software had been instrumental in establishing the desktop publishing market. (PageMaker's success depended on the font software that Adobe made and the two companies had a history of cooperation.) Next the company bought Frame Technology (FrameMaker publishing software, 1995), but that acquisition proved disastrous. Frame sales plummeted, partly the result of Adobe's move to eliminate Frame's technical support operations. Adobe's purchase of Web toolmaker Ceneca Communications that year was more fruitful.

In 1996 Adobe spun off its pre-press applications operations as Luminous. That year its licensing sales suffered a blow when one of its largest customers, Hewlett-Packard, introduced a clone version of PostScript. Also in 1997, for the first time, Adobe's revenues from Windows-based software exceeded those of its once-dominant Macintosh-based software.

In 1998 a takeover bid by competitor Quark proved unsuccessful. Drooping sales that year, which Adobe blamed on the Asian crisis (but some analysts blamed on its product strategy), prompted the company to shed a layer of executives, 10% of its workforce, and its Adobe Enterprise Publishing Services and Image Club Graphics units. Its 1999 acquisition of GoLive Systems expanded its Web publishing product line. That year Adobe released professional page layout application InDesign, which immediately spurred the biggest backlog in the company's history.

In December 2000 CEO Warnock passed the helm to president Bruce Chizen. Warnock remained co-chairman along with Geschke. The company boosted its electronic book offerings by acquiring software maker Glassbook. In 2002, in a move to expand its ePaper division, Adobe purchased electronic forms provider Accelio for $72 million.

In early 2003 the company restructured its divisions, creating its Creative Professional segment to replace the Cross-media Publishing division, and its Digital Imaging and Video unit to replace its former Graphics division. This realignment was a part of Adobe's plan to focus on its core market of creative professionals. In order to expand its digital video offerings, the company also acquired the assets of digital audio tools-maker Syntrillium Software that year.

In 2004, the company acquired OKYZ, a Paris-based maker of 3D collaboration software; the acquisition added 3D technology to Adobe's Intelligent Document Platform. Adobe acquired Trade and Technologies France (TTF), a developer of CAD data interoperability software, in 2006.

## EXECUTIVES

**Co-Chairman:** Charles M. (Chuck) Geschke, age 67
**Co-Chairman:** John E. Warnock, age 66
**CEO and Director:** Bruce R. Chizen, age 51
**President and COO:** Shantanu Narayen, age 43, $951,925 pay
**EVP and CFO:** Mark S. Garrett, age 49
**SVP and Chief Software Architect, Platform Business Unit:** Kevin M. Lynch
**SVP, General Counsel, and Secretary:** Karen O. Cottle, age 58, $558,700 pay
**SVP Platform Business Unit:** John D. Brennan
**SVP, Corporate Marketing and Communications:** Ann Lewnes
**SVP, Worldwide Human Resources:** Margaret B. (Peg) Wynn, age 55, $386,533 pay
**SVP, Print and Classic Publishing Solutions Business Unit; Managing Director, India Research and Development:** Naresh Gupta
**SVP and Chief Software Architect, Advanced Technology Labs:** Tom Malloy
**SVP Corporate Development:** Robert M. (Rob) Tarkoff, age 38
**SVP and CIO:** Gerri Martin-Flickinger
**VP, Corporate Controller, and Principle Accounting Officer:** Richard T. Rowley, age 51
**President, Adobe Japan:** Garrett J. Ilg
**Manager, Corporate Public Relations:** Autumn Blatchford
**Auditors:** KPMG LLP

## LOCATIONS

**HQ:** Adobe Systems Incorporated
345 Park Ave., San Jose, CA 95110
**Phone:** 408-536-6000 **Fax:** 408-537-6000
**Web:** www.adobe.com

**2006 Sales**

| | $ mil. | % of total |
|---|---|---|
| Americas | 1,266.7 | 49 |
| Europe, Middle East & Africa | 770.1 | 30 |
| Asia | 538.5 | 21 |
| **Total** | **2,575.3** | **100** |

## PRODUCTS/OPERATIONS

**2006 Sales**

| | $ mil. | % of total |
|---|---|---|
| Products | 2,484.7 | 96 |
| Services | 90.6 | 4 |
| **Total** | **2,575.3** | **100** |

### 2006 Sales

| | $ mil. | % of total |
|---|---|---|
| Creative solutions | 1,424.9 | 55 |
| Knowledge worker solutions | 671.0 | 26 |
| Enterprise & developer solutions | 189.2 | 7 |
| Mobile & device solutions | 37.7 | 2 |
| Other | 252.5 | 10 |
| **Total** | **2,575.3** | **100** |

## COMPETITORS

ACD Systems
Apple
ArcSoft
Autodesk
Avid Technology
Bare Bones Software
Canon
Canopus
Corel
Dell
FormScape
Google
Hewlett-Packard
IBM
Metastorm
Microsoft
Monotype
Nikon
Nuance
Pinnacle Systems
Quark
Sonic Solutions
Sony

## HISTORICAL FINANCIALS

Company Type: Public

### Income Statement

FYE: Friday nearest November 30

| | REVENUE ($ mil.) | NET INCOME ($ mil.) | NET PROFIT MARGIN | EMPLOYEES |
|---|---|---|---|---|
| 11/06 | 2,575 | 506 | 19.6% | 6,082 |
| 11/05 | 1,966 | 603 | 30.7% | 5,734 |
| 11/04 | 1,667 | 450 | 27.0% | 3,142 |
| 11/03 | 1,295 | 266 | 20.6% | 3,507 |
| 11/02 | 1,165 | 191 | 16.4% | 3,341 |
| Annual Growth | 21.9% | 27.5% | — | 16.2% |

### 2006 Year-End Financials

Debt ratio: —
Return on equity: 14.4%
Cash ($ mil.): 2,281
Current ratio: 4.26
Long-term debt ($ mil.): —
No. of shares (mil.): 601
Dividends
Yield: —
Payout: —
Market value ($ mil.): 23,643

### Stock History

NASDAQ (GS): ADBE

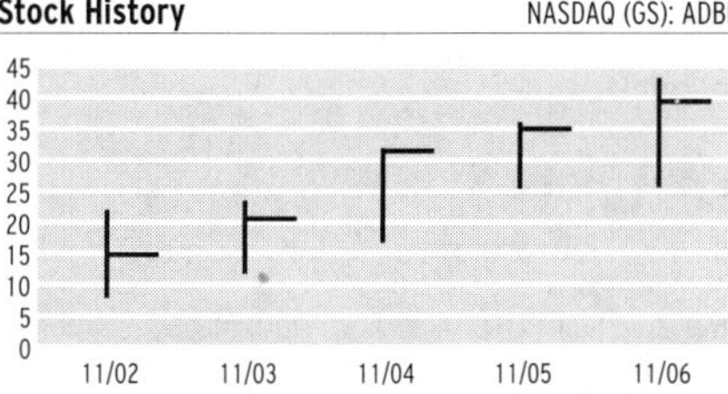

| | STOCK PRICE ($) FY Close | P/E High | P/E Low | PER SHARE ($) Earnings | Dividends | Book Value |
|---|---|---|---|---|---|---|
| 11/06 | 39.35 | 52 | 31 | 0.83 | — | 8.57 |
| 11/05 | 34.97 | 30 | 22 | 1.19 | 0.01 | 3.15 |
| 11/04 | 31.48 | 35 | 19 | 0.91 | 0.03 | 4.81 |
| 11/03 | 20.66 | 42 | 22 | 0.55 | 0.03 | 4.62 |
| 11/02 | 14.77 | 55 | 21 | 0.40 | 0.03 | 2.92 |
| Annual Growth | 27.8% | — | — | 20.0% | (30.7%) | 30.9% |

# Advance Publications

Advance Publications gets its marching orders from the printed page. A leading US newspaper publisher, Advance owns some 25 daily newspapers around the country, including *The Star-Ledger* (New Jersey), *The Cleveland Plain Dealer,* and its namesake *Staten Island Advance.* It also owns American City Business Journals (more than 40 weekly papers) and Parade Publications (*Parade Magazine* Sunday insert). The company is a top magazine publisher through its Condé Nast unit. Aside from print publishing, Advance is a major online publisher with 10 regional news Web sites, and owns television assets. Samuel "Si" Newhouse Jr. and his brother, Donald, own the company.

In addition to its print publications, Advance has a healthy online presence with such Internet properties as Epicurious (food and dining) and Concierge (travel). The company also has interests in cable television through affiliate Advance/Newhouse Communications, which has an economic interest in some Florida cable systems through a partnership with Time Warner Cable, as well as a 33% stake in cable broadcaster Discovery Communications.

The company's Condé Nast unit publishes such popular titles as *Allure, Glamour,* and *Vanity Fair*. Trade journal publisher Fairchild Publications (*Women's Wear Daily*) is a division of Condé Nast.

## HISTORY

Solomon Neuhaus (later Samuel I. Newhouse) got started in the newspaper business after dropping out of school at age 13. He went to work at the *Bayonne Times* in New Jersey and was put in charge of the failing newspaper in 1911; he managed to turn the paper around within a year. In 1922 he bought the *Staten Island Advance* (founded in 1886) and formed the Staten Island Advance Company in 1924. After buying up more papers, he changed the name of the company to Advance Publications in 1949. By the 1950s the company had local papers in New York, New Jersey, and Alabama.

In 1959 Newhouse bought magazine publisher Condé Nast as an anniversary gift for his wife. (He joked that she had asked for a fashion magazine, so he bought her *Vogue.*) His publishing empire continued to grow with the addition of the *Times-Picayune* (New Orleans) in 1962 and *The Cleveland Plain Dealer* in 1967. In 1976 the company paid more than $300 million for Booth Newspapers, publisher of eight Michigan papers and *Parade Magazine.*

Newhouse died in 1979, leaving his sons Si and Donald to run the company, which encompassed more than 30 newspapers, a half-dozen magazines, and 15 cable systems. The next year Advance bought book publishing giant Random House from RCA. Si resurrected the Roaring Twenties standard *Vanity Fair* in 1983 and added *The New Yorker* under the Condé Nast banner in 1985. The Newhouses scored a victory over the IRS in 1990 after a long-running court battle involving inheritance taxes. Condé Nast bought Knapp Publications (*Architectural Digest*) in 1993 and Advance later acquired American City Business Journals in 1995.

In 1998 the company sold the increasingly unprofitable Random House to Bertelsmann for about $1.2 billion. It later bought hallmark Internet magazine *Wired* (though it passed on Wired Ventures' Internet operations). That year revered *New Yorker* editor Tina Brown, credited with jazzing up the publication's content and increasing its circulation, left the magazine; staff writer and Pulitzer Prize winner David Remnick was named as Brown's replacement.

In 1999 Advance joined Donrey Media Group (now called Stephens Media Group), E.W. Scripps, Hearst Corporation, and MediaNews Group to purchase the online classified advertising network AdOne (later named PowerOne Media). It also bought Walt Disney's trade publishing unit, Fairchild Publications, for $650 million. In 2000 the company shifted *Details* from Condé Nast to Fairchild and relaunched the magazine as a fashion publication. Later that year the company announced it would begin creating Web versions of its popular magazine titles.

In 2001 Condé Nast bought a majority stake in Miami-based Ideas Publishing Group (Spanish language versions of US magazines; its name was later changed to Condé Nast Americas). Also that year Advance bought four golf magazines, including *Golf Digest,* from the New York Times Company for $430 million. Condé Nast picked up *Modern Bride* magazine from PRIMEDIA in 2002 for $52 million.

Richard Diamond, a Newhouse relative who'd been publisher of the *Staten Island Advance* since 1979, died in 2004.

## EXECUTIVES

**Chairman and CEO; Chairman, Condé Nast Publications:** Samuel I. (Si) Newhouse Jr., age 76
**President:** Donald E. Newhouse, age 72
**COO; CEO, Condé Nast:** Charles H. (Chuck) Townsend, age 61
**Chairman and CEO, American City Business Journals:** Ray Shaw
**Chairman, CEO, and Publisher, Parade Publications:** Walter Anderson
**President, Advance Internet:** Peter Weinberger
**President, CondéNet:** Sarah Chubb
**SVP Consumer Marketing; SVP Circulation, Condé Nast Publications:** Peter A. Armour
**Publisher, Staten Island Advance:** Caroline Harrison

## LOCATIONS

**HQ:** Advance Publications, Inc.
950 Fingerboard Rd., Staten Island, NY 10305
**Phone:** 212-286-2860 **Fax:** 718-981-1456
**Web:** www.advance.net

## PRODUCTS/OPERATIONS

### Selected Operations

Broadcasting and Communications
- Cartoonbank.com (database of cartoons from *The New Yorker*)
- Discovery Communications (33%, cable TV channel)
- Newhouse News Service
- Religion News Service

Magazine Publishing
- Conde Nast Publications
- Fairchild Publications

Newspaper Publishing
  American City Business Journals (41 weekly titles in 22 states)
    *Sporting News*
    Street & Smith's Sports Business Group
  Newhouse Newspapers (25 papers across the US)
    *The Birmingham News* (Alabama)
    *The Oregonian* (Portland)
    *The Plain Dealer* (Cleveland)
    *The Star-Ledger* (Newark, NJ)
    *Staten Island Advance* (New York)
    *The Times-Picayune* (New Orleans)
  Parade Publications
Online Publishing
  Advance Internet
    al.com (Alabama)
    cleveland.com
    MassLive.com (Massachusetts)
    MLive (Michigan)
    NJ.com (New Jersey)
    NOLA.com (New Orleans)
    OregonLive.com
    PennLive.com (Pennsylvania)
    SILive (New York)
    Syracuse.com (New York)
  CondéNet
    Concierge (travel information)
    Epicurious (recipes and fine dining)
    STYLE.com (fashion and beauty)

## COMPETITORS

American Express
American Media
Crain Communications
Dow Jones
E. W. Scripps
Essence Communications
F+W Publications
Forbes
Freedom Communications
Gannett
Gruner + Jahr
Hearst
Johnson Publishing
Lagardère Active Media
Martha Stewart Living
McClatchy Company
Meredith
New York Times
News Corp.
Newsweek
North Jersey Media
PRIMEDIA
Reader's Digest
Reed Elsevier Group
Rodale
Time
Tribune
Washington Post
Wenner Media

## HISTORICAL FINANCIALS

Company Type: Private

**Income Statement** FYE: December 31

| | ESTIMATED REVENUE ($ mil.) | NET INCOME ($ mil.) | NET PROFIT MARGIN | EMPLOYEES |
|---|---|---|---|---|
| 12/05 | 7,315 | — | — | 30,000 |

# Advanced Micro Devices

Advanced Micro Devices (AMD) has made some advances in its battle against Intel. AMD ranks #2 in PC and server microprocessors, far behind its archrival. Though Intel commands about three-quarters of the world processor market, AMD has at times eroded that market share thanks to the popularity of its Athlon and Opteron chip families. AMD is also a top maker — in rivalry with Intel, Samsung Electronics, Toshiba, and others — of flash memory chips, which are key components of electronic devices such as cellular phones. AMD also makes embedded processors and other chips for communications and networking applications. Hewlett-Packard accounts for 23% of sales.

AMD and Intel have engaged in extended processor pricing wars that have depressed the sales figures of both companies. Their intense competition has led many of the biggest computer manufacturers to embrace the processor lines of both companies in their products, keeping each chip maker on its toes.

After posting a net loss of $611 million on lower sales in the first quarter of 2007, partly due to price cutting, AMD laid off 430 employees, nearly 3% of its global workforce.

In 2006 AMD acquired ATI Technologies for about $5.4 billion in cash and stock. Buying ATI, a leading supplier of graphics processors, gives the company a broader product portfolio to better compete against Intel. AMD exchanged around $4.3 billion in cash and 58 million shares of its common stock for ATI's shares and stock options. The company will meld the central processing unit and the graphics processing unit of a computer into a new processor design code-named "Fusion." AMD expects to start rolling out Fusion processors for consumer electronics, desktop and laptop computers, servers, and workstations in late 2008 or early 2009.

Leading the charge for AMD is industry veteran Hector Ruiz, who headed Motorola's chip operations (now spun off as Freescale) before joining AMD.

AMD has attacked Intel's dominant market share with a lineup of microprocessors led by the high-performance Athlon. In its battle with Intel, AMD has sometimes been its own worst enemy. Design flaws and other manufacturing problems, including lack of production capacity, plagued the company over the years, contributing to losses and testing the market's patience. The company's eighth-generation products, 64-bit processors code-named Hammer, were launched (after repeated delays) in 2003. One of the first releases, formally called Opteron, competes with Intel's Itanium chip in the server market.

AMD plans to spend some $2.5 billion over three years to upgrade its fabs in Dresden. The changes will enable the company to boost output from the Dresden fabs to 45,000 300mm wafers a month by the end of 2008. The company will also build a new fab in Malta, New York. AMD expects to spend more than $5 billion over five years on the project. New York State will provide about $1 billion in incentives for the project.

Capital Research and Management owns about 10% of AMD. OppenheimerFunds holds nearly 8% of the company. AXA has an equity stake of around 5%.

## HISTORY

Silicon Valley powerhouse Fairchild Camera & Instrument axed marketing whiz Jerry Sanders, reportedly for wearing a pink shirt on a sales call to IBM. In 1969 Sanders and seven friends started a semiconductor company (just as his former boss, Intel co-founder Robert Noyce, had done a year earlier) based on chip designs licensed from other companies.

Advanced Micro Devices (AMD) went public in 1972. Siemens, eager to enter the US semiconductor market, paid $30 million for nearly 20% of AMD in 1977. (Siemens had sold off its stake by 1991). In 1982 AMD inked a deal with Intel that let AMD make exact copies of Intel's iAPX86 microprocessors, used in IBM and compatible PCs.

By the mid-1980s the company was developing its own chips. In 1987 AMD sued Intel for breaking the 1982 agreement that allowed AMD to second-source Intel's new 386 chips. Intel countersued for copyright infringement when AMD introduced versions of Intel's 287 math coprocessor (1990), 386 chip (1991), and 486 chip (1993).

AMD acquired Monolithic Memories in 1987, broadening its portfolio of memory devices. The company began work on its Submicron Development Center at headquarters in Sunnyvale, California, where crucial work on future products would be done.

In 1993 AMD formed a joint venture with Fujitsu to make flash memory devices. After a federal jury decided in AMD's favor in the 287 math coprocessor case in 1994, AMD and Intel settled their legal differences in 1995. Each agreed to pay damages, and AMD won a perpetual license to the microcode of Intel's 386 and 486 chips. AMD's K5 microprocessor (a rival of Intel's Pentium) hit the market in 1996 — more than a year late.

In 1996 AMD bought microprocessor developer NexGen and its technology for use in the K6 chip. AMD unveiled its K6 microprocessor the next year, but had trouble increasing production to meet demand. The company debuted its Athlon (K7) chip in 1999 to positive reviews and soon won Compaq and IBM as customers.

Early in 2000 AMD named Hector Ruiz (former head of Motorola's semiconductor operations) president and COO — and thus heir apparent — to Sanders.

Improved manufacturing processes, increased sales of high-end Athlons, and a worldwide shortage of flash memory helped AMD turn a profit (and a big one) in 2000, its first since 1995. In the face of a dismal slump in the global chip business, though, AMD cut costs in 2001 by closing two chip plants in Texas and by cutting about 2,300 jobs — 15% of its total workforce — there and in Malaysia.

In 2002 Sanders handed over the CEO reins to Ruiz. In 2003 AMD joined long-time joint-venture partner Fujitsu in forming a new company, called FASL (later renamed Spansion), to pool the two chip makers' flash memory operations. In 2004 Ruiz succeeded Sanders as chairman as well; Sanders remains a director. The following year AMD filed an antitrust suit against Intel, alleging that the chip giant has used improper subsidies and coercion to secure sales.

The European Commission, the antitrust regulator for the European Union nations, brought formal charges against Intel on behalf of AMD in 2007.

## EXECUTIVES

**Chairman and CEO:** Hector de J. Ruiz, age 61, $1,046,358 pay
**President and COO:** Derrick R. (Dirk) Meyer, age 45, $631,759 pay
**EVP and CFO:** Robert J. (Bob) Rivet Sr., age 52, $564,252 pay
**EVP, Chief Administrative Officer and Legal Affairs:** Thomas M. (Tom) McCoy, age 56, $541,404 pay
**EVP, Sales and Marketing Officer:** Henri Richard, age 49, $567,234 pay
**EVP, Computing Products Group:** Mario Rivas, age 52
**SVP and Chief Innovation Officer:** William T. (Billy) Edwards, age 50
**SVP, Technology Development, Manufacturing and Supply Chain:** Douglas (Doug) Grose

**Corporate VP and CTO:** Phil D. Hester
**Corporate VP; Commercial Business and Performance Computing, Microprocessor Solutions Sector (MSS):** Marty Seyer
**VP, Human Resources:** Reid Linney
**Secretary:** Hollis O'Brien
**President, EMEA:** Guiliano Meroni
**Senior Fellow and Chief Platform Architect:** Steve Polzin
**Manager, Investor Relations:** Ruth Cotter
**Public Relations:** Eric DeRitis
**Auditors:** Ernst & Young LLP

## LOCATIONS

**HQ:** Advanced Micro Devices, Inc.
1 AMD Place, Sunnyvale, CA 94088
**Phone:** 408-749-4000 **Fax:** 408-982-6164
**Web:** www.amd.com

Advanced Micro Devices has manufacturing operations in China, Germany, Malaysia, Singapore, and the US. The company has sales offices worldwide.

### 2006 Sales

| | $ mil. | % of total |
|---|---|---|
| China | 1,478 | 26 |
| US | 1,399 | 25 |
| Europe | 1,345 | 24 |
| Japan | 116 | 2 |
| Other countries | 1,311 | 23 |
| **Total** | **5,649** | **100** |

## PRODUCTS/OPERATIONS

### 2006 Sales

| | $ mil. | % of total |
|---|---|---|
| Computation Products | 5,104 | 90 |
| Graphics & Chipsets | 278 | 5 |
| Embedded Products | 149 | 3 |
| Consumer Electronics | 120 | 2 |
| Adjustment | (2) | — |
| **Total** | **5,649** | **100** |

### Selected Products

Computation
- Microprocessors (Athlon and Opteron lines)
- Motherboard reference design kits and chipsets

Personal connectivity
- Embedded processors (Geode line)
- Networking chips
  - Ethernet controllers
  - Physical layer devices

## COMPETITORS

Analog Devices
Atmel
Broadcom
Epson
Fairchild Semiconductor
Freescale Semiconductor
Genesis Microchip
Hitachi
IBM Microelectronics
Infineon Technologies
Intel
LG Electronics
LSI Corp.
Marvell Technology
Matrox Electronic Systems
MediaTek
MIPS Technologies
NEC Electronics
NVIDIA
NXP
Panasonic
QUALCOMM
Renesas
Samsung Electronics
SANYO
Silicon Integrated Systems
STMicroelectronics
Sun Microsystems
Texas Instruments
Toshiba
Transmeta
Trident Microsystems
VIA Technologies
Zoran

## HISTORICAL FINANCIALS

Company Type: Public

### Income Statement

FYE: Last Sunday in December

| | REVENUE ($ mil.) | NET INCOME ($ mil.) | NET PROFIT MARGIN | EMPLOYEES |
|---|---|---|---|---|
| **12/06** | 5,649 | (166) | — | 16,500 |
| **12/05** | 5,848 | 166 | 2.8% | 9,860 |
| **12/04** | 5,001 | 91 | 1.8% | 15,900 |
| **12/03** | 3,519 | (275) | — | 14,300 |
| **12/02** | 2,697 | (1,303) | — | 12,146 |
| **Annual Growth** | 20.3% | — | — | 8.0% |

### 2006 Year-End Financials

Debt ratio: 63.5%
Return on equity: —
Cash ($ mil.): 1,541
Current ratio: 1.39
Long-term debt ($ mil.): 3,672
No. of shares (mil.): 547
Dividends
Yield: —
Payout: —
Market value ($ mil.): 11,131

### Stock History

NYSE: AMD

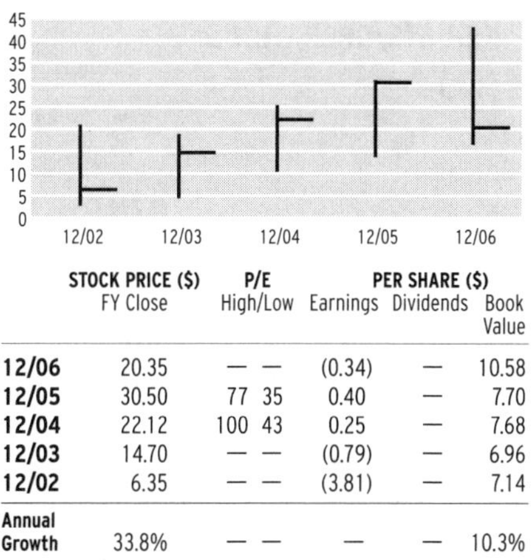


| | STOCK PRICE ($) FY Close | P/E High | P/E Low | PER SHARE ($) Earnings | Dividends | Book Value |
|---|---|---|---|---|---|---|
| **12/06** | 20.35 | — | — | (0.34) | — | 10.58 |
| **12/05** | 30.50 | 77 | 35 | 0.40 | — | 7.70 |
| **12/04** | 22.12 | 100 | 43 | 0.25 | — | 7.68 |
| **12/03** | 14.70 | — | — | (0.79) | — | 6.96 |
| **12/02** | 6.35 | — | — | (3.81) | — | 7.14 |
| **Annual Growth** | 33.8% | — | — | — | — | 10.3% |

# AES Corporation

The right place at the right time — is it kismet? No, it's AES, one of the world's leading independent power producers. The company has interests in more than 120 generation facilities in 26 countries in the Americas, Europe, Asia, Africa, and the Caribbean that give it a combined net generating capacity of 35 gigawatts of power (primarily fossil-fueled). AES sells electricity to utilities and other energy marketers through wholesale contracts or on the spot market. AES also sells power directly to customers worldwide through its interests in distribution utilities, mainly in Latin America. In 2006 the company announced plans to expand its alternative energy business.

AES has announced plans to build a $1.2 billion coal-fired power plant in India through its AES India Private Ltd. unit. The company plans to sell a minority stake in its Indiana utility IPALCO. The company is abandoning its Dominican Republic distribution utility and its telecommunications operations.

While it is expanding its alternative energy operations by acquiring stakes in wind power generation firms, AES is still fond of older methods of power generation: coal powered plants. AES has earmarked $150 million to build a coal-fueled power plant in El Salvador. The 250 MW plant, estimated to be operational by 2009, will be the first of its kind in the Latin American country. Owning four of the five electricity distribution companies in El Salvador, AES controls nearly 80% of the country's electric distribution utility.

AES is facing controversy in Brazil, where an unstable power market has caused the company to default on debts incurred from its purchases of stakes in local utilities (as well as bankrupt telecom firm Eletronet) in recent years. To restructure its debt with Banco Nacional de Desenvolvimento Economico e Social (BNDES), AES has completed a deal in which the firm's interests in AES Eletropaulo, AES Uruguaiana, AES Tiete, and AES Sul have been placed into a new holding company (Brasiliana Energia). AES owns 50.1% of the new company, while BNDES holds 49.9%.

In 2007 the company acquired two 230 MW petroleum coke-fired power generation facilities in Tamuin, Mexico for $611 million. It also bought a 51% stake in Turkish power generator IC ICTAS Energy Group.

## HISTORY

Applied Energy Services (AES) was founded in 1981, three years after passage of the Public Utilities Regulation Policies Act, which enabled small power firms to enter electric generation markets formerly dominated by utility monopolies. Co-founders Roger Sant and Dennis Bakke, who had served in President Nixon's Federal Energy Administration, saw that an independent power producer (IPP) could make money by generating cheap power in large volumes to sell to large power consumers and utilities.

AES set about building massive cogeneration plants (producing both steam and electricity) in 1983. The first plant, Deepwater, went into operation near Houston in 1986. By 1989 AES had three plants on line, and it then opened plants in Connecticut and Oklahoma. In 1991 the company, formally renamed AES, went public, but one plant's falsified emissions reports caused AES's stock to plummet in 1992.

Facing environmental groups' opposition to new power plant construction and an overall glut in the US power market, AES bought interests in two Northern Ireland plants in 1992 and began expanding into Latin America in 1993. Also in 1993 AES set up a separately traded subsidiary, AES China Generating Co., to focus on Chinese development projects. AES won a plant development contract with the Puerto Rico Electric Power Authority (1994) and a bid to privatize an Argentine hydrothermal company (1995).

In 1996 AES began adding stakes in electric utility and distribution companies to its portfolio, including interests in formerly state-owned Brazilian electric utilities Light-Servicos de Eletricidade (1996) and CEMIG (1997); one Brazilian and two Argentine distribution companies (1997); and a distribution company in El Salvador (1998).

AES almost doubled its revenues after buying Destec Energy's international operations from NGC (now Dynegy) in 1997. By the next year, prospects in international markets were dimming, so AES turned to the US market again. It bought three California plants from Edison International and arranged for The Williams Companies to supply natural gas to the facilities and market the electricity generated. AES also won a bid to buy six plants from New York State Electric & Gas (now Energy East) affiliate NGE.

Also in 1998, despite black days in many world markets, AES bought 90% of Argentine electric distribution company Edelap and a 45% stake in state-owned Orissa Power Generation in India. Its moves paid off: AES posted a 70% gain in sales that year.

It bought CILCORP, an Illinois utility holding company, in an $886 million deal in 1999. Boosting its presence in the UK, AES bought the Drax power station, a 3,960-MW coal-fired plant, from National Power. It also bought a majority stake in Brazilian data transmission company Eletronet from Brazil's government-owned utility ELETROBRÁS. In 2000 AES increased its interests in Brazilian power distributors. It also gained a 73% stake (later expanded to 87%) in Venezuelan electric utility Grupo EDC in a $1.5 billion hostile takeover.

The next year AES bought IPALCO, the parent of Indianapolis Power & Light, in a $3 billion deal. Also in 2001 AES acquired the outstanding shares of Chilean generation company Gener, in which it previously held a 60% stake.

That year AES moved to take control of CANTV, Venezuela's #1 telecom company. Through Grupo EDC, which already owned 6.9% of CANTV, AES offered to buy 43.2% of the company. But AES withdrew the offer after the CANTV board rejected it. (AES sold Grupo EDC's stake in CANTV the following year.) AES also sold some generation assets in Argentina to TOTAL FINA ELF (now TOTAL) for about $370 million.

In 2002 AES sold its 24% interest in Light Serviços de Eletricidade (Light) to Electricité de France (EDF) in exchange for a 20% stake in Brazilian utility Eletropaulo (increasing its stake in Eletropaulo to 70%). In that same year the company sold its retail energy marketing unit (AES NewEnergy) to Constellation Energy Group for $240 million, and its CILCORP subsidiary, which holds utility Central Illinois Light, to Ameren.

## EXECUTIVES

**President, CEO, and Director:** Paul T. Hanrahan, age 48
**EVP and CFO:** Victoria D. Harker, age 40
**EVP:** Robert F. Hemphill Jr., age 64
**EVP, Business Excellence and Chief Human Resources Officer:** Jay L. Kloosterboer, age 45
**EVP, Business Development and Strategy:** William R. Luraschi, age 42
**EVP, Business Development:** Shahzad S. Qasim
**EVP, General Counsel and Secretary:** Brian A. Miller, age 40
**EVP, Regional President, Europe and Africa:** John McLaren, age 44
**SVP, Development:** Sarah Slusser
**Regional President, North America Group:** David S. Gee, age 51
**EVP and COO:** Andrés R. Gluski
**Regional President, Asia and Middle East:** Haresh Jaisinghani, age 38
**VP, Communications:** Robin Pence
**VP and CIO:** George Coulter
**VP, Internal Audit:** Richard A. Bulger
**VP and Chief Compliance Officer:** John Giraudo
**VP and Treasurer:** Chip Hoagland
**VP, Global Business Transformation:** Andrew Vesey
**VP, Investor Relations:** Scott S. Cunningham
**VP Investor Relations:** Ahmed Pasha
**VP and Controller:** Mary E. Wood, age 52
**Auditors:** Deloitte & Touche LLP

## LOCATIONS

**HQ:** The AES Corporation
4300 Wilson Blvd., 11th Fl., Arlington, VA 22203
**Phone:** 703-522-1315 **Fax:** 703-528-4510
**Web:** www.aes.com

AES has operations in Argentina, Brazil, Cameroon, Canada, Chile, China, Colombia, the Czech Republic, the Dominican Republic, El Salvador, Hungary, India, Italy, Kazakhstan, Mexico, the Netherlands, Nigeria, Oman, Pakistan, Panama, Qatar, Spain, Sri Lanka, the Ukraine, the UK, the US, and Venezuela.

### 2006 Sales

| | $ mil. | % of total |
|---|---|---|
| Brazil | 4,161 | 34 |
| US | 2,554 | 21 |
| Venezuela | 652 | 5 |
| Chile | 595 | 5 |
| Argentina | 542 | 4 |
| El Salvador | 437 | 4 |
| Other countries | 3,358 | 27 |
| **Total** | **12,299** | **100** |

## PRODUCTS/OPERATIONS

### 2006 Sales

| | $ mil. | % of total |
|---|---|---|
| Regulated | 6,849 | 56 |
| Non-regulated | 5,450 | 44 |
| **Total** | **12,299** | **100** |

### Selected Electric Utilities and Distribution Companies

AES CLESA (64%, electric utility, El Salvador)
AES Edelap (60%, electric utility, Argentina)
AES Eden (60%, electric utility, Argentina)
AES Edes (60%, electric utility, Argentina)
AES Gener (electric generation, Chile)
AES India Private Ltd.
AES SeaWest, Inc.
AES Telasi (75%, electric utility, Georgia)
Brasiliana Energia (50.1%)
- AES Sul Distribuidora Gaucha de Energia SA (AES Sul, electric utility, Brazil)
- AES Tiete (power generation, Brazil)
- AES Uruguaiana (power generation, Brazil)
- Eletropaulo Metropolitana Eletricidade de São Paulo S.A. (AES Electropaulo, 70%, electric distribution, Brazil)

CAESS (75%, electric utility, El Salvador)
DEUSEM (74%, electric utility, El Salvador)
Companhia Energética de Minas Gerais (CEMIG, 21%, Brazil)
EEO (89%, electric utility, El Salvador)
Grupo La Electricidad de Caracas (EDC, 87%, electric generation and distribution, Venezuela)
IC ICTAS Energy Group (51%, power generation, Turkey)
IPALCO Enterprises, Inc. (holding company)
- Illinois Power & Light Company (IPL, electric utility)

## COMPETITORS

Alliant Energy
Bonneville Power
Calpine
CenterPoint Energy
CMS Energy
CPFL Energia
Duke Energy
Dynegy
Edison International
El Paso
Endesa S.A.
Energias de Portugal
Enersis
Entergy
E.ON UK
Exelon
FPL Group
Huadian Power
IBERDROLA
Indeck Energy
International Power
MidAmerican Energy
Mirant
Nicor
NRG Energy
PG&E
PSEG
Reliant Energy
Sempra Energy
Siemens AG
SUEZ-TRACTEBEL
TXU
Xcel Energy

## HISTORICAL FINANCIALS

Company Type: Public

### Income Statement

FYE: December 31

| | REVENUE ($ mil.) | NET INCOME ($ mil.) | NET PROFIT MARGIN | EMPLOYEES |
|---|---|---|---|---|
| **12/06** | 12,299 | 261 | 2.1% | 32,000 |
| **12/05** | 11,086 | 630 | 5.7% | 30,000 |
| **12/04** | 9,463 | 292 | 3.1% | 30,000 |
| **12/03** | 8,415 | (403) | — | 30,000 |
| **12/02** | 8,632 | (3,509) | — | 36,000 |
| **Annual Growth** | 9.3% | — | — | (2.9%) |

### 2006 Year-End Financials

Debt ratio: 490.5%
Return on equity: 11.1%
Cash ($ mil.): 2,763
Current ratio: 1.31
Long-term debt ($ mil.): 14,892
No. of shares (mil.): 665
Dividends
Yield: —
Payout: —
Market value ($ mil.): 14,659

### Stock History

NYSE: AES

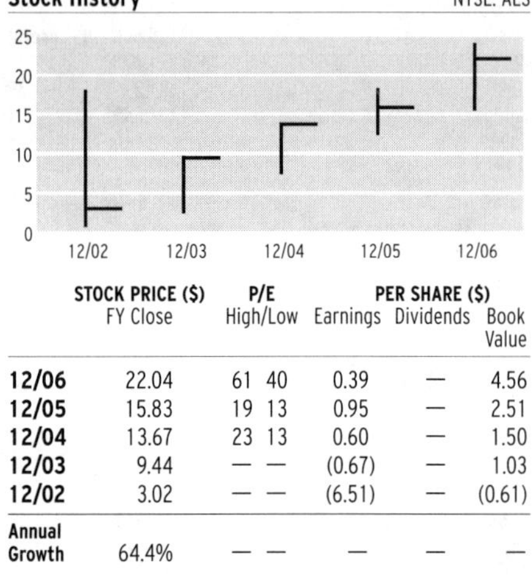

| | STOCK PRICE ($) FY Close | P/E High | P/E Low | PER SHARE ($) Earnings | PER SHARE ($) Dividends | PER SHARE ($) Book Value |
|---|---|---|---|---|---|---|
| **12/06** | 22.04 | 61 | 40 | 0.39 | — | 4.56 |
| **12/05** | 15.83 | 19 | 13 | 0.95 | — | 2.51 |
| **12/04** | 13.67 | 23 | 13 | 0.60 | — | 1.50 |
| **12/03** | 9.44 | — | — | (0.67) | — | 1.03 |
| **12/02** | 3.02 | — | — | (6.51) | — | (0.61) |
| **Annual Growth** | 64.4% | — | — | — | — | — |

# Aetna Inc.

Mount Etna is Europe's most active volcano; Aetna is one of the most active health insurance companies in the US. The company operates in three segments. Its Health Care division offers HMOs, PPOs, point-of-service (POS) plans, health savings accounts, and traditional indemnity coverage, along with dental, vision, behavioral health, and Medicare plans. Aetna covers more than 15 million individuals under its health plans, some 13 million dental plan members, and 10 million pharmacy members. Its Group Insurance segment sells life, disability, and long-term care insurance, covering about 15 million people. The Large Case Pensions segment offers pensions, annuities, and other retirement savings products.

The company is always looking to expand its health plan offerings, particularly in ways that mitigate rising health care costs and that shift responsibility for decisions onto consumers. Its Aetna HealthFund consumer-directed plans combine traditional deductible-based coverage with medical expense funds that accrue money each year. It has also introduced Web-based access to personal health records, giving members the ability to view their medical histories and giving them tools to make health care decisions.

Additionally, subsidiary ActiveHealth (acquired in 2005) uses technology and data analytics to provide disease management programs, clinical decision support, and other services that identify at-risk plan members and help get the right care to patients before they need hospitalization or other expensive procedures.

Aetna looks for acquisitions that help it expand its services and geographic presence. Besides ActiveHealth, it made a number of other acquisitions in 2005 and 2006, including Strategic Resource Company, which administers benefits for hourly workers and HMS Healthcare, a regional health care network in Michigan and Colorado. In 2006 it bought Broadspire, a disability and leave management company.

The insurance game isn't just about visits to doctors and hospitals any more, and Aetna is looking to maximize its opportunities. It has been expanding its pharmacy services through purchases and other means; its Aetna Specialty Pharmacy, formerly a joint venture with Curascript, serves patients with chronic illnesses. Aetna bought out Curascript's share in the joint venture before that company's merger with Express Scripts.

In 2007 it acquired Schaller Anderson, which manages state Medicaid plans, as well as commercial and self-funded plans, in eight states.

## HISTORY

Hartford, Connecticut, businessman and judge Eliphalet Bulkeley started Connecticut Mutual Life Insurance in 1846. Agents gained control of the firm the following year. Undeterred, Bulkeley and a group of Hartford businessmen founded Aetna Life Insurance in 1853 as a spinoff of Aetna Fire Insurance. Among its offerings was coverage for slaves, a practice for which the company apologized in 2000.

A nationwide agency network fueled early growth at Aetna, which expanded in the 1860s by offering a participating life policy, returning dividends to policyholders based on investment earnings. (This let Aetna compete with mutual life insurers.) In 1868 Aetna became the first firm to offer renewable term life policies.

Eliphalet's son, Morgan, became president in 1879. Aetna moved into accident (1891), health (1899), workers' compensation (1902), and auto and other property insurance (1907) during his 43-year tenure. He served as Hartford mayor, Connecticut governor, and US senator, all the while leading Aetna.

By 1920 the company sold marine insurance, and by 1922 it was the US's largest multiline insurer. Aetna overexpanded its nonlife lines (particularly autos) during the 1920s, threatening its solvency. It survived the Depression by restricting underwriting and rebuilding reserves. After WWII the firm expanded into group life, health, and accident insurance. In 1967 it reorganized into holding company Aetna Life and Casualty.

The 1960s, 1970s, and 1980s were go-go years: The company added lines and bought and sold everything from an oil services firm to commercial real estate. The boom period led to a bust and a 1991 reorganization in which Aetna eliminated 8,000 jobs, withdrew from such lines as auto insurance, and sold its profitable American Reinsurance.

To take advantage of the boom in retirement savings, in 1995 it got permission to set up bank AE Trust to act as a pension trustee.

With its health care business accounting for some 60% of sales by 1995, the company restructured in the late 1990s. Aetna sold its property/casualty, behavioral managed care (1997), and individual life insurance (1998) businesses. It then expanded overseas and bought U.S. Healthcare and New York Life's NYLCare managed health business (1998).

Controversy marred 1998. Contract terms — including a "gag" clause against discussing uncovered treatments — prompted 400 Texas doctors to leave its system; defections followed in Kentucky and West Virginia. Consumers balked over Aetna's refusal to cover some treatments, including experimental procedures and advanced fertility treatments. One group sued for false advertising.

The American Medical Association that year decried Aetna's plan to buy Prudential's health care unit as anticompetitive; in 1999 the government required Aetna to sell operations, including NYLCare, to gain approval. Also in 1999 Aetna became the second insurer (after Humana) to be sued for misleading clients about treatment decisions; it reached a settlement the next year with the State of Texas over capitation, physician incentives, and other matters.

In 2000 Aetna restated earnings for seven previous quarters at the behest of the SEC. Flagging earnings prompted CEO Richard Huber to resign; William Donaldson, one of the founders of Donaldson, Lufkin & Jenrette, now Credit Suisse First Boston (USA), took his place. Also in 2000 Aetna went through major restructuring and sold its financial services and international divisions to Netherlands-based ING Groep.

John "Jack" Rowe took over the helm as CEO in 2001 and announced that Aetna may require two years to recover from turbulent changes and rising medical costs. In 2002 the company returned to operating profitability after reducing its workforce, raising premiums, and restructuring critical operations.

The following year it bought a mail-order pharmacy facility from Eckerd Health Services. Ronald Williams succeeded Jack Rowe as CEO in 2006.

## EXECUTIVES

**Chairman, President, and CEO:** Ronald A. Williams, age 56, $1,073,077 pay
**President:** Mark T. Bertolini, age 51
**EVP, Finance and CFO:** Joseph M. Zubretsky, age 50
**SVP and CIO:** Margaret (Meg) McCarthy
**SVP, Chief Investment Officer, and Chief Enterprise Risk Officer:** Timothy A. Holt, age 53, $468,269 pay
**SVP, General Counsel, and Corporate Secretary:** William J. Casazza, age 51
**SVP and Chief Medical Officer:** Troyen A. Brennan, age 52
**SVP and Deputy General Counsel, Health:** Charles H. Klippel
**SVP, Communications:** Roger Bolton
**SVP, Human Resources:** Elease E. Wright
**SVP, Aetna Dental:** Patricia A. (Pat) Farrell
**SVP, Network and Provider Services:** Andrew Allocco
**SVP, Strategic Marketing and Consumer Insights:** J. David (Dave) Mahder
**SVP, Strategic Marketing and Communications:** Robert E. Mead
**SVP, Strategic Planning and Business Development:** Craig R. Callen, age 51, $611,923 pay
**Chief of Staff, Office of the CEO and President:** Kim A. Keck
**VP, CTO, and Deputy CIO:** Michael J. Connolly
**VP, Business Communications:** Jill Griffiths
**VP and Controller:** Ronald M. Olejniczak
**VP, Counsel and Chief Compliance Officer:** Thomas C. Strohmenger
**VP, Investor Relations:** David W. Entrekin
**VP, Finance and Treasurer:** Alfred P. Quirk Jr.
**Director, Investor Relations:** Jeffrey Chaffkin
**Auditors:** KPMG LLP

## LOCATIONS

**HQ:** Aetna Inc.
151 Farmington Ave., Hartford, CT 06156
**Phone:** 860-273-0123 **Fax:** 860-273-3971
**Web:** www.aetna.com

Aetna sells its Health Care products and services in all 50 states and Washington, DC. Its Group Insurance products are available in 49 states (not New Mexico) and the District of Columbia, as well as in Canada, Guam, Puerto Rico, and the US Virgin Islands.

## PRODUCTS/OPERATIONS

### 2006 Sales

| | $ mil. | % of total |
|---|---|---|
| Healthcare | | |
| Premiums | | |
| Commercial risk | 17,356.5 | 69 |
| Medicare | 1,787.7 | 7 |
| Medicaid | 9.3 | — |
| Fees & other revenue | 2,743.7 | 11 |
| Net investment income | 334.2 | 1 |
| Net realized capital gains | 9.1 | — |
| Group insurance | | |
| Premiums | | |
| Life | 1,257.6 | 5 |
| Disability | 401.5 | 2 |
| Long-term care | 102.8 | 1 |
| Net investment income | 294.1 | 1 |
| Fees & other revenue | 84.6 | — |
| Net realized capital gains | 11.5 | — |
| Large case pensions | | |
| Net investment income | 536.4 | 2 |
| Premiums | 194.1 | 1 |
| Net realized capital gains | 11.6 | — |
| Other | 11.0 | — |
| **Total** | **25,145.7** | **100** |

### Selected Subsidiaries

Active Health Management, Inc.
Aelan Inc.
Aetna Life & Casualty (Bermuda) Limited
Aetna Health Holdings, LLC
AET Health Care Plan, Inc.
Aetna Dental Inc.
Aetna Health Management, LLC
Aetna RX Home Delivery, LLC
Chickering Benefit Planning Insurance Agency, Inc.
Chickering Claims Administrators, Inc.
NYLCare Health Plans, Inc.
Sanus of New York and New Jersey, Inc.
Aetna Criterion Communications, Inc.
Aetna Financial Holdings, LLC
Aetna Behavioral Health, LLC
Aetna Health Information Solutions, Inc.
Aetna Integrated Informatics, Inc.
Aetna InteliHealth Inc.
Integrated Pharmacy Solutions, Inc.
Managed Care Coordinators, Inc.
Aetna Life Insurance Company
Aetna Government Health Plans, LLC
Aetna Health Administrators, LLC
Aetna Health and Life Insurance Company
Aetna Health Insurance Company of New York
Aetna Risk Indemnity Company Limited (Bermuda)
Aetna Specialty Pharmacy, LLC (40%)
ASI Wings, L.L.C.
Corporate Health Insurance Company
Luettgens Limited

## COMPETITORS

| | |
|---|---|
| AMERIGROUP | Kaiser Foundation |
| Blue Cross | Medco Health Solutions |
| Caremark | MetLife |
| Centene | Molina Healthcare |
| CIGNA | Oxford Health |
| Coventry Health Care | PacifiCare |
| DeCare | Principal Financial |
| Delta Dental Plans | Prudential |
| Express Scripts | Sierra Health |
| Guardian Life | UnitedHealth Group |
| Health Net | USAA |
| Humana | WellPoint |

## HISTORICAL FINANCIALS

Company Type: Public

**Income Statement** FYE: December 31

| | REVENUE ($ mil.) | NET INCOME ($ mil.) | NET PROFIT MARGIN | EMPLOYEES |
|---|---|---|---|---|
| **12/06** | 25,146 | 1,702 | 6.8% | 30,000 |
| **12/05** | 22,492 | 1,635 | 7.3% | 28,200 |
| **12/04** | 19,904 | 2,245 | 11.3% | 26,700 |
| **12/03** | 17,976 | 934 | 5.2% | 27,600 |
| **12/02** | 19,879 | (2,523) | — | 28,000 |
| **Annual Growth** | 6.1% | — | — | 1.7% |

**2006 Year-End Financials**

| | |
|---|---|
| Debt ratio: 26.7% | No. of shares (mil.): 516 |
| Return on equity: 17.7% | Dividends |
| Cash ($ mil.): 16,783 | Yield: 0.1% |
| Current ratio: 2.58 | Payout: 1.3% |
| Long-term debt ($ mil.): 2,442 | Market value ($ mil.): 22,281 |

**Stock History** NYSE: AET

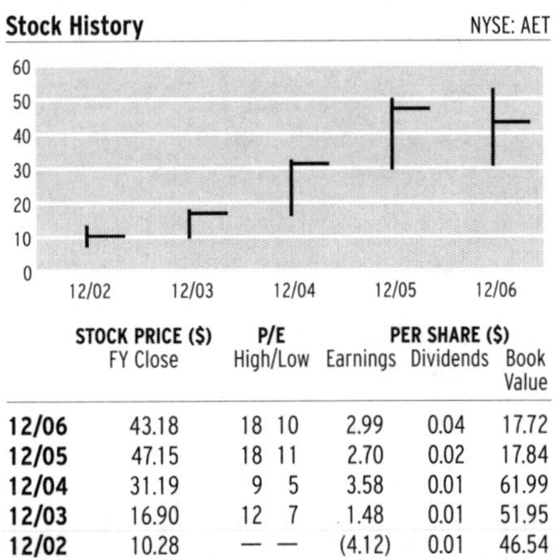


| | STOCK PRICE ($) FY Close | P/E High/Low | PER SHARE ($) Earnings | Dividends | Book Value |
|---|---|---|---|---|---|
| **12/06** | 43.18 | 18 10 | 2.99 | 0.04 | 17.72 |
| **12/05** | 47.15 | 18 11 | 2.70 | 0.02 | 17.84 |
| **12/04** | 31.19 | 9 5 | 3.58 | 0.01 | 61.99 |
| **12/03** | 16.90 | 12 7 | 1.48 | 0.01 | 51.95 |
| **12/02** | 10.28 | — — | (4.12) | 0.01 | 46.54 |
| **Annual Growth** | 43.2% | — — | — | 41.4% | (21.4%) |

# Affiliated Computer Services

Affiliated Computer Services (ACS) handles jobs its clients would rather hand off. The company provides business process outsourcing and technology-related services for commercial enterprises and government agencies. As an outsourcer, ACS handles functions such as administration, including health care claims processing; finance and accounting; human resources; payment processing; sales, marketing, and customer care call centers; and supply chain management. Business process outsourcing accounts for about 75% of sales. ACS also provides information technology and systems integration services. Founder and chairman Darwin Deason, who controls a 41% voting stake in the company, has placed ACS on the selling block.

In mid-2007, Deason placed a $6.2 billion bid (backed by investment firm Cerberus Capital Management) on the company, but he eventually dropped the proposal in hopes of luring higher competing bids to the table.

The move to take ACS private comes in the wake of an SEC investigation of the company's stock options practices. ACS is among more than 100 companies that have drawn attention for their stock option grants — typically for issuing options with effective dates in the past, when share prices were lower. CEO Mark King and CFO Warren Edwards resigned in 2006 when an internal inquiry concluded that they violated the company's rules regarding the granting of stock options. EVP and COO Lynn Blodgett was chosen to replace King as CEO.

Under Blodgett, ACS operates from a network of about 290 offices in the US and some 80 offices in more than 25 other countries. US-based clients account for about 95% of sales.

Along with other business process outsourcing companies, ACS has benefited from a cost-conscious mindset at both businesses and government agencies. It draws commercial clients from a wide variety of industries, and its government arm serves federal, state, and local agencies. The US Department of Education, for which ACS provides student loan processing services, is the company's biggest customer, accounting for about 5% of sales.

ACS hopes to grow by gaining new clients and by selling new services to existing clients; in addition, it will continue to pursue acquisitions in hopes of augmenting existing business lines. In 2007 ACS paid about $26 million for key assets of Albion, a Cambridge Solutions unit that makes software used by health and human services agencies. Still focusing on software, ACS bought CDR Associates, LLC — a maker of auditing and accounting services software geared towards the health care industry — later that year.

## HISTORY

In 1967 Darwin Deason took over a company called Affiliated Computer Systems (ACS). Eight years later he sold that company to Dallas-based MTech, but stayed on as its president. Under Deason, MTech became the largest provider of financial data processing in the US. When MTech was bought by General Motors subsidiary Electronic Data Systems in 1988, Deason left to start an entirely new ACS, this one called Affiliated Computer Services.

The new company was created as a financial computer services provider, focused on processing bank transactions. Its 1992 acquisition of Dataplex ushered the company into business process outsourcing, and ACS went public two years later. ACS' 1995 acquisition of The Systems Group extended the company's offerings to include professional services.

The company continued its rapid rate of growth throughout the late 1990s, building a string of acquisitions that included Intelligent Solutions (1997), Computer Data Systems (1997), Betac International (1998), and Canmax's retail systems subsidiary (1998). In 1998 ACS bought the Unclaimed Property Services Division of State Street Corporation. Early the following year it acquired IT services company BRC Holdings. Deason stepped down as CEO (he remained chairman), passing the reins to president Jeffrey Rich, a former Citibank investment banker. Later in 1999 ACS bought Consultec, a provider of IT services for state health programs, from GenAmerica's General American Life subsidiary in a $105 million deal.

In 2000 the company sold its ATM business for about $180 million. It also boosted its government outsourcing capabilities with the acquisition of Intellisource Group. The next year ACS acquired Lockheed Martin's IMS subsidiary, a provider of outsourcing services to municipal and state governments, for $825 million.

In 2002 the company acquired FleetBoston Financial's education services subsidiary, AFSA Data, for about $410 million, and with it a student loan portfolio worth about $85 billion. Also that year COO Mark King assumed the president post from Rich, who remained CEO.

In 2003, moving away from its federal government services business and extending its commercial reach, ACS sold most of its federal government IT services business to Lockheed Martin and bought Lockheed's commercial IT business. The following year the company sold the defense support services portion of its federal government business to ManTech International.

Rich resigned from the company in 2005 and was replaced by King. Also that year ACS moved to expand its business process outsourcing operations through acquisitions. The company bought health care technology services provider Superior Consultant Holdings for about $106 million and formed a new division, ACS Healthcare Solutions. ACS paid about $400 million for Mellon Financial's human resources outsourcing operations (renamed Buck Consultants). The company also bought LiveBridge (customer care and call center services).

In 2006, however, ACS came under SEC investigation. Later that year, King and CFO Warren Edwards resigned when it was ruled they violated the company's ethics code regarding stock options practices.

Also in 2006 ACS bought INTELLINEX, a provider of outsourced training services, from Ernst & Young. Later in the year, ACS acquired Primax Recoveries, a services provider catering to the health care sector.

## EXECUTIVES

**Chairman:** Darwin Deason, age 67, $845,447 pay
**President, CEO, and Director:** Lynn R. Blodgett, age 52, $554,998 pay (prior to promotion)
**EVP and COO:** Tom Burlin, age 49
**EVP, CFO, and Director:** John H. Rexford, age 49
**EVP, General Counsel, and Corporate Secretary:** William L. (Bill) Deckelman Jr., age 49
**EVP and Chief People Officer:** Lora Villarreal
**EVP Sales, ACS Government Solutions:** Harvey V. Braswell, age 61
**SVP and Chief Marketing Officer:** Lesley Pool
**SVP and Managing Director, Federal Solutions, Government Solutions Group:** Timothy C. (Tim) Conway
**SVP, Corporate Controller, and Interim Chief Accounting Officer:** Laura Rossi
**SVP Strategy and Product Development:** Will Saunders
**SVP and Chief Information Security Officer:** Christopher Leach
**SVP, Workplace Resources:** David Jarrett

**Managing Director, Application Management Services:** Russ Malz
**Managing Director, ACS Healthcare Solutions:** Charles O. Bracken, age 57
**President and CEO, LiveBridge:** R. Patrick (Pat) Hanlin
**President, ACS Education Solutions Group:** Brad Martin
**COO, Commercial Solutions Group:** Ann Vezina, age 43
**Auditors:** PricewaterhouseCoopers LLP

## LOCATIONS

**HQ:** Affiliated Computer Services, Inc.
2828 N. Haskell, Dallas, TX 75204
**Phone:** 214-841-6111 **Fax:** 214-821-8315
**Web:** www.acs-inc.com

## PRODUCTS/OPERATIONS

### 2006 Sales

| | $ mil. | % of total |
|---|---|---|
| Commercial | 3,167.6 | 59 |
| Government | 2,186.1 | 41 |
| **Total** | **5,353.7** | **100** |

### 2006 Sales

| | $ mil. | % of total |
|---|---|---|
| Business process outsourcing | 3,996.6 | 75 |
| Information technology services | 971.8 | 18 |
| Systems integration services | 385.3 | 7 |
| **Total** | **5,353.7** | **100** |

### Selected Services

Business process outsourcing
- Administration
- Finance and accounting
- Human resources
- Payment services
- Sales, marketing, and customer care
- Supply chain management

Information technology
- Consulting
- Data center operations
- Data security services
- Desktop and seat management
- Hardware and software procurement
- Help desk
- Imaging
- Information assurance
- Mainframes, midranges, and client/server services
- Network management
- Scanning
- Storage solutions
- Training

Systems integration
- Application support
- Consulting
- Systems design and development
- Systems integration
- Training

## COMPETITORS

Accenture
ADP
Capgemini US
CGI Group
CIBER
Computer Sciences Corp.
Convergys
Coventry Health Care
EDS
Hewitt Associates
IBM Global Services
Infosys
Keane
ManTech
MAXIMUS
Northrop Grumman
Perot Systems
Unisys
Wipro Technologies

## HISTORICAL FINANCIALS

Company Type: Public

### Income Statement

FYE: June 30

| | REVENUE ($ mil.) | NET INCOME ($ mil.) | NET PROFIT MARGIN | EMPLOYEES |
|---|---|---|---|---|
| **6/06** | 5,354 | 359 | 6.7% | 58,000 |
| **6/05** | 4,351 | 416 | 9.6% | 52,000 |
| **6/04** | 4,106 | 530 | 12.9% | 43,000 |
| **6/03** | 3,787 | 307 | 8.1% | 40,000 |
| **6/02** | 3,063 | 230 | 7.5% | 36,200 |
| **Annual Growth** | 15.0% | 11.8% | — | 12.5% |

### 2006 Year-End Financials

Debt ratio: 65.7%
Return on equity: 13.6%
Cash ($ mil.): 101
Current ratio: 1.85
Long-term debt ($ mil.): 1,614
No. of shares (mil.): 107
Dividends
Yield: —
Payout: —
Market value ($ mil.): 5,500

### Stock History

NYSE: ACS

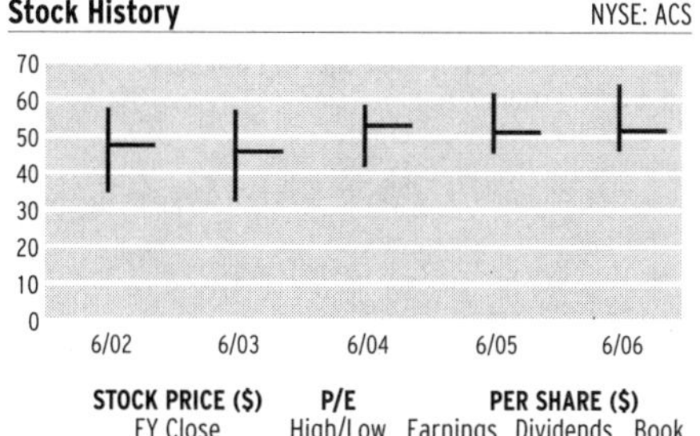


| | STOCK PRICE ($) FY Close | P/E High | P/E Low | PER SHARE ($) Earnings | Dividends | Book Value |
|---|---|---|---|---|---|---|
| **6/06** | 51.61 | 22 | 16 | 2.87 | — | 23.05 |
| **6/05** | 51.10 | 19 | 14 | 3.19 | — | 23.93 |
| **6/04** | 52.94 | 15 | 11 | 3.83 | — | 19.05 |
| **6/03** | 45.73 | 26 | 15 | 2.20 | — | 19.19 |
| **6/02** | 47.48 | 32 | 20 | 1.76 | — | 16.71 |
| **Annual Growth** | 2.1% | — | — | 13.0% | — | 8.4% |

# Aflac Incorporated

Aflac's clients may not welcome accidents and illness any more than a visit from Gilbert Gottfried, but at least they won't have to suffer financial ruin because of it. Aflac (whose popular ads feature a valiant duck voiced by comedian Gottfried) sells supplemental health and life insurance policies that cover special conditions, primarily cancer. It is one of the largest sellers of supplemental insurance in the US and is an industry leader in Japan's cancer insurance market. Aflac, which is marketed through and is an acronym for American Family Life Assurance Company, sells policies that pay cash benefits for hospital confinement, emergency treatment, and medical appliances.

Aflac also offers accident, intensive care, and on- and off-the-job disability insurance.

Despite its US roots, Aflac makes most of its insurance sales in Japan (more than 70%), where its policies fill in gaps not covered by the national health insurance system. Its reliance on Japan has a downside: The company is vulnerable to currency fluctuations between the dollar and the yen. It also faces increased competition because of deregulation of Japan's insurance industry.

In Japan, Aflac primarily sells through an agency system in which a corporation forms a subsidiary to sell Aflac insurance to its employees. The company also has a marketing alliance with Dai-ichi Mutual Life, Japan's second-largest life insurer. The company's US approach is similar in that Aflac sells primarily through the workplace, with employers deducting premiums from paychecks.

The company's strategy for growth consists of expanding its sales force and product offerings. Building on its strong brand recognition, Aflac is now hoping to grow its US business by adding more sales associates.

## HISTORY

American Family Life Assurance Company (AFLAC) was founded in Columbus, Georgia, in 1955 by brothers John, Paul, and William Amos to sell life, health, and accident insurance. Competition was fierce, and the little company did poorly.

With AFLAC nearing bankruptcy, the brothers looked for a niche.

The polio scares of the 1940s and 1950s had spawned insurance coverage written especially against that disease; the Amos brothers (whose father was a cancer victim) took a cue from that concept and decided to sell cancer insurance. In 1958 they introduced the world's first cancer-expense policy. It was a hit, and by 1959 the company had written nearly a million dollars in premiums and expanded across state lines.

The enterprise grew quickly during the 1960s, especially after developing its cluster-selling approach in the workplace, where employers were usually willing to make payroll deductions for premiums. By 1971 the company was operating in 42 states.

While visiting the World's Fair in Osaka in 1970, John Amos decided to market supplemental cancer coverage to the Japanese, whose national health care plan left them exposed to considerable expense from cancer treatment. After four years the company finally won approval to sell in Japan because the policies did not threaten existing markets and because the Amoses found notable backers in the insurance and medical industries. AFLAC became one of the first US insurance companies to enter the Japanese market, and it enjoyed an eight-year monopoly on the cancer market. In 1973 AFLAC organized a holding company and began buying television stations in the South and Midwest.

The 1980s were marked by US and state government inquiries into dread disease insurance. Critics said such policies were a poor value because they were relatively expensive and covered only one disease. However, the inquiries led nowhere and demand for such insurance increased, bringing new competition. In the 1980s, AFLAC's scales tilted: US growth slowed, while business grew in Japan, which soon accounted for most of the company's sales.

In 1990 John Amos died of cancer and was replaced as CEO by his nephew Dan. Two years later the company officially renamed itself AFLAC (partly because Dan planned to increase the company's US profile and so many US companies already used the name "American").

AFLAC has sought to supplement its cancer insurance by introducing new products and improving old ones to encourage policyholders to add on or trade up. Its Japanese "living benefit" product, which includes lump sum payments for heart attacks and strokes, struck a chord with the aging population.

Connecticut in 1997 repealed its ban on specified-disease insurance; New York followed suit. Also in 1997 AFLAC sold its seven TV stations to Raycom Media to focus on insurance.

The company boosted its name recognition in the US from 2% in 1990 to more than 56%, primarily through advertising, including slots during the 1998 Olympic Winter Games and NASCAR races. In 1999 the company signed a three-year cross-selling agreement for its supplemental insurance with what is now HR Logic, a human resources outsourcing firm.

Accident/disability premiums surpassed cancer premiums in the US for the first time in the company's history in 2000. Also, facing up to Japan's deregulated life insurance industry, AFLAC formed a marketing alliance with one of Japan's biggest life insurers, Dai-ichi Mutual Life.

The Aflac duck made its first appearance in a 2001 Japanese commercial for accident insurance. Shortly thereafter it debuted in the US where it quickly achieved advertising icon status.

## EXECUTIVES

**Chairman and CEO:** Daniel P. (Dan) Amos, age 55, $1,242,000 pay
**President, CFO, and Director:** Kriss Cloninger III, age 59, $796,000 pay
**EVP, General Counsel, and Corporate Secretary:** Joey M. Loudermilk, age 53
**EVP and Chief Administrative Officer:** Rebecca C. (Becky) Davis, age 56
**SVP and Chief Marketing Officer:** Jeffrey M. (Jeff) Herbert
**SVP and Corporate Actuary:** Susan R. Blanck, age 40
**SVP, Account Implementation and Management:** Bob Ottman
**SVP, Community Relations:** Angela S. Hart
**SVP, Financial Services Accounting Officer:** Ralph A. Rogers Jr., age 58
**SVP, Corporate Finance:** Martin A. Durant III, age 56
**SVP and Director of Sales, Aflac US:** Ronald E. (Ron) Kirkland, age 62, $600,000 pay
**SVP, Governmental Relations:** Phillip J. (Jack) Friou
**SVP, Investor Relations:** Kenneth S. (Ken) Janke Jr., age 48
**SVP and Deputy Chief Administrative Officer:** Teresa White
**SVP, Client Services:** Janet Baker
**SVP, Information Technology, and CIO:** Gerald Shields
**2nd VP, Corporate Communications:** Laura Kane
**2nd VP, Human Resources and Diversity:** Brenda Mullins
**Chairman, Aflac Japan:** Akitoshi Kan, age 59
**Vice Chairman, Aflac, Japan:** Charles D. Lake II, age 45
**President; COO, Aflac US:** Paul S. Amos II, age 31
**Media Relations Manager:** Mechell Clark
**President and CEO, Communicorp:** James C. Woodall
**President and COO, Aflac Japan:** Tohru Tonoike
**Auditors:** KPMG LLP

## LOCATIONS

**HQ:** Aflac Incorporated
1932 Wynnton Rd., Columbus, GA 31999
**Phone:** 706-323-3431 **Fax:** 706-324-6330
**Web:** www.aflac.com

### 2006 Sales

| | $ mil. | % of total |
|---|---|---|
| Aflac Japan | 10,475 | 71 |
| Aflac US | 4,027 | 27 |
| Other business | 42 | — |
| Realized investment gains | 79 | 1 |
| Corporate | 87 | 1 |
| Adjustments | (94) | — |
| **Total** | **14,616** | **100** |

## PRODUCTS/OPERATIONS

### 2006 Sales

| | $ mil. | % of total |
|---|---|---|
| Premiums | 12,314 | 84 |
| Net investment income | 2,171 | 15 |
| Realized investment gains | 79 | 1 |
| Other revenues | 52 | — |
| **Total** | **14,616** | **100** |

### Selected Subsidiaries

Aflac Counsel, Limited
Aflac Information Technology, Incorporated
Aflac Insurance Services Company, Limited
Aflac International, Incorporated
Aflac Payment Service, Limited
aflacdirect.com, Limited (78%)
American Family Life Assurance Company of Columbus (Aflac)
American Family Life Assurance Company of New York
Communicorp, Incorporated
ITSUMO, Limited

## COMPETITORS

AIG
Allianz
American Fidelity Assurance Company
American National Insurance
Aon
Asahi Mutual Life
Conseco
Daido Life
Hartford Life
MetLife
Nationwide Financial Network
Sony
Taiyo Life
Torchmark
UnitedHealth Group
Unum Group

## HISTORICAL FINANCIALS

Company Type: Public

### Income Statement

FYE: December 31

| | ASSETS ($ mil.) | NET INCOME ($ mil.) | INCOME AS % OF ASSETS | EMPLOYEES |
|---|---|---|---|---|
| **12/06** | 59,805 | 1,483 | 2.5% | 7,411 |
| **12/05** | 56,361 | 1,483 | 2.6% | 6,970 |
| **12/04** | 59,326 | 1,299 | 2.2% | 6,531 |
| **12/03** | 50,964 | 795 | 1.6% | 6,186 |
| **12/02** | 45,058 | 821 | 1.8% | 5,797 |
| **Annual Growth** | 7.3% | 15.9% | — | 6.3% |

### 2006 Year-End Financials

Equity as % of assets: 13.9%
Return on assets: 2.6%
Return on equity: 18.2%
Long-term debt ($ mil.): 1,426
No. of shares (mil.): 656
Dividends
Yield: 1.2%
Payout: 18.6%
Market value ($ mil.): 30,163
Sales ($ mil.): 14,616

### Stock History

NYSE: AFL

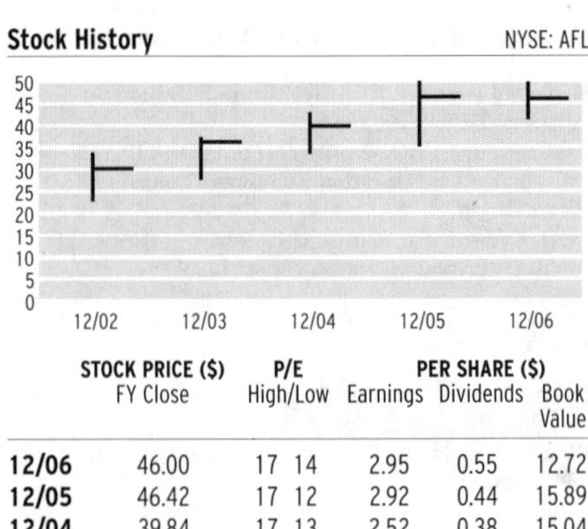


| | STOCK PRICE ($) FY Close | P/E High/Low | | PER SHARE ($) Earnings | Dividends | Book Value |
|---|---|---|---|---|---|---|
| **12/06** | 46.00 | 17 | 14 | 2.95 | 0.55 | 12.72 |
| **12/05** | 46.42 | 17 | 12 | 2.92 | 0.44 | 15.89 |
| **12/04** | 39.84 | 17 | 13 | 2.52 | 0.38 | 15.04 |
| **12/03** | 36.18 | 24 | 18 | 1.52 | 0.30 | 13.03 |
| **12/02** | 30.12 | 21 | 15 | 1.57 | 0.23 | 12.43 |
| **Annual Growth** | 11.2% | — | — | 17.1% | 24.4% | 0.6% |

# AGCO Corporation

AGCO's annual harvests might be smaller than those of larger rivals John Deere (#1) and CNH Global (#2), but it's still able to reap profits worldwide. AGCO sells its tractors, combines, hay tools, sprayers, forage equipment, and replacement parts through a global network of more than 3,200 independent dealers and distributors. Brand names include Massey Ferguson, Gleaner, and Fendt. The company also offers financing services to some customers and dealers through a joint venture with Netherlands-based Rabobank. It has acquired Caterpillar's high-tech MT series tractor line as part of its strategy to expand its product line.

Late in 2006 AGCO announced a new growth initiative dubbed "Always Growing." The strategy makes some basic assumptions about the trends emerging in global agriculture. They include: the increase in mega-farms, exponential growth in certain developing countries, increased demand for biofuels in developed nations, and increasingly advanced technology.

AGCO plans to position its products and brands to take advantage of these trends by improving its dealer networks and by emphasizing the importance of service and support programs.

AGCO's traditional markets in South America — namely Brazil and Argentina — aim to guard their market share while exploring targeted growth in surrounding nations.

The company plans to expand its operations in areas where it has less market penetration, such as Central and Eastern Europe, the far East, and China.

The company sells its products in more than 140 countries; more than 80% of sales come from outside the US.

## HISTORY

In 1861 American Edward Allis purchased the bankrupt Reliance Works, a leading Milwaukee-based manufacturer of sawmills and flour-milling equipment. Under shrewd management, The Reliance Works of Edward P. Allis & Co. weathered financial troubles — bankruptcy in the Panic of 1873 — but managed to renegotiate its debt and recover. By the time Allis died in 1889, Reliance Works employed some 1,500 workers.

The company branched into different areas of manufacturing in the late 19th century, and by the 20th century the Edward P. Allis Co. (as it was then known) was the world leader in steam engines. In 1901 the company merged with another manufacturing giant, Fraser & Chalmers, to form the Allis-Chalmers Company. In the 1920s and 1930s, Allis-Chalmers entered the farm equipment market.

Although overshadowed by John Deere and International Harvester (IH), Allis-Chalmers made key contributions to the industry — the first rubber-tired tractor (1932) and the All-Crop harvester. Allis-Chalmers spun off its farm equipment business in the 1950s, and phased out several unrelated products. The company, with its orange-colored tractors, expanded and prospered from the 1940s through the early 1970s. Then the chaffing farm economy of the late 1970s and early 1980s hurt Allis-Chalmers' sales.

After layoffs and a plant shutdown in 1984, the company was purchased in 1985 by German machinery maker Klockner-Humbolt-Deutz (KHD), who moved the company (renamed Deutz-Allis) to Georgia. In the mid-1980s low food prices hurt farmers and low demand hurt the equipment market. KHD was never able to bring profits up to a satisfactory level, and in 1990 the German firm sold the unit to the US management in a buyout led by Robert Ratliff. Ratliff believed the company could succeed by acquiring belly-up equipment makers, turning them around, and competing on price.

Renamed AGCO, the company launched a buying spree in 1991 that included Fiat's Hesston (1991), White Tractor (1991), the North American distribution rights for Massey Ferguson (1993), and White-New Idea (1993). The bumper crop of product growth enabled AGCO to slice into competitors Deere and Case's market share. AGCO went public in 1992. Its 1994 purchase of the remainder of Massey Ferguson (with 20% of the world market) vaulted AGCO among the world's leading farm equipment makers.

In 1996 AGCO launched a five-year plan for European growth. In 1997 the company acquired German farm equipment makers Fendt and Dronniberg. It also picked up Deutz Argentina, a supplier of agricultural equipment, engines, and vehicles, as part of an effort to expand into Latin and South America.

AGCO entered the agricultural sprayer market in 1998 by acquiring the Spra-Coupe line from Ingersoll-Rand and the Willmar line from Cargill. A worldwide drop in farm equipment sales caused AGCO to cut about 10% of its workforce.

To further overcome stalled sales and slumping profits, in 1999 the company announced it was permanently closing an Ohio plant and would cease production at a Texas plant. The next year AGCO closed its Missouri plant and trimmed its workforce by about 5%.

In 2001 AGCO acquired fertilizer equipment manufacturer Ag-Chem Equipment, and the next year it completed the purchase of certain assets relating to the design, assembly, and marketing of the MT 700 and MT 800 series of Caterpillar's Challenger rubber-tracked farm tractors.

AGCO added to its harvesting equipment segment in 2002 by purchasing Beloit-based Sunflower Manufacturing for an undisclosed price. That year AGCO suffered a tragic loss when president and CEO John Shumejda and SVP Ed Swingle were killed in an airplane accident in the UK.

In early 2004 AGCO added Valtra, a global tractor and off-road engine maker, to its fold for about $750 million. In 2004 chairman Robert Ratliff handed Martin Richenhagen the president and CEO titles he had taken on after the death of Shumejda.

## EXECUTIVES

**Chairman, President, and CEO:** Martin H. Richenhagen, age 54, $921,125 pay
**SVP, Strategy and Integration, and General Manager Engines:** Hubertus Muehlhaeuser, age 37, $373,565 pay
**SVP and CFO:** Andrew H. (Andy) Beck, age 43, $312,417 pay
**SVP, Global Sales and Marketing:** Randall G. (Randy) Hoffman, age 55
**SVP, Materials Management Worldwide:** David L. Caplan, age 59
**SVP and General Manager, EAME and EAPAC:** Gary L. Collar, age 50, $251,348 pay
**SVP and General Manager, North America:** Robert B. Crain, age 47
**SVP and General Manager, South America:** Andre M. Carioba, age 55
**SVP, Corporate Development and General Counsel:** Stephen D. Lupton, age 62, $354,667 pay
**SVP, Human Relations:** Norman L. (Norm) Boyd, age 63
**SVP, Engineering:** Garry L. Ball, age 59
**SVP, Manufacturing Technologies and Quality:** Frank N. Lukacs, age 47
**CIO:** Kevin Lilly
**VP, Corporate Relations:** Molly Dye
**VP, Customer Support North America Parts Division:** Gretchen DeCoster
**Manager, Corporate Public Relations:** Cheryl Thompson
**Auditors:** KPMG LLP

## LOCATIONS

**HQ:** AGCO Corporation
4205 River Green Pkwy., Duluth, GA 30096
**Phone:** 770-813-9200 **Fax:** 770-813-6118
**Web:** www.agcocorp.com

AGCO Corporation has facilities in Argentina, Australia, Brazil, Denmark, Finland, France, Germany, the UK, and the US.

### 2006 Sales

| | $ mil. | % of total |
|---|---|---|
| Europe, Africa & Middle East | 3,334.4 | 61 |
| North America | 1,283.8 | 24 |
| South America | 657.2 | 12 |
| Asia/Pacific | 159.6 | 3 |
| **Total** | **5,435.0** | **100** |

### 2006 Sales

| | $ mil. | % of total |
|---|---|---|
| Europe | | |
| Finland & Scandinavia | 657.5 | 12 |
| Germany | 627.0 | 11 |
| France | 624.8 | 11 |
| UK | 322.6 | 6 |
| Other countries | 857.6 | 16 |
| US | 1,008.0 | 18 |
| South America | 644.0 | 12 |
| Canada | 200.2 | 4 |
| Middle East | 151.2 | 3 |
| Australia | 101.0 | 2 |
| Mexico, Central America & Caribbean | 88.7 | 2 |
| Asia | 58.6 | 1 |
| Africa | 93.8 | 2 |
| **Total** | **5,435.0** | **100** |

## PRODUCTS/OPERATIONS

### 2006 Sales

| | $ mil. | % of total |
|---|---|---|
| Tractors | 3,634.7 | 67 |
| Replacement parts | 752.8 | 14 |
| Application equipment | 266.8 | 5 |
| Combines | 214.0 | 4 |
| Other machinery | 566.7 | 10 |
| **Total** | **5,435.0** | **100** |

### Selected Brand Names

AGCO
Challenger
Farmhand
Fendt
Gleaner
Glencoe
Heston
LOR'AL
Massey Ferguson
New Idea
RoGator
Spra-Coupe
Sunflower
TerraGator
Tye
White
Willmar

## COMPETITORS

Caterpillar
CNH
Deere
Hitachi Construction Machinery
Kubota
Steyr-Daimler-Puch Aktiengesellschaft
Volvo

## HISTORICAL FINANCIALS

Company Type: Public

### Income Statement

FYE: December 31

| | REVENUE ($ mil.) | NET INCOME ($ mil.) | NET PROFIT MARGIN | EMPLOYEES |
|---|---|---|---|---|
| **12/06** | 5,435 | (65) | — | 12,800 |
| **12/05** | 5,450 | 32 | 0.6% | 13,000 |
| **12/04** | 5,273 | 159 | 3.0% | 14,300 |
| **12/03** | 3,495 | 74 | 2.1% | 11,300 |
| **12/02** | 2,923 | (84) | — | 11,555 |
| **Annual Growth** | 16.8% | — | — | 2.6% |

### 2006 Year-End Financials

Debt ratio: 38.7%
Return on equity: —
Cash ($ mil.): 401
Current ratio: 1.42
Long-term debt ($ mil.): 577
No. of shares (mil.): 91
Dividends
Yield: —
Payout: —
Market value ($ mil.): 2,821

### Stock History

NYSE: AG

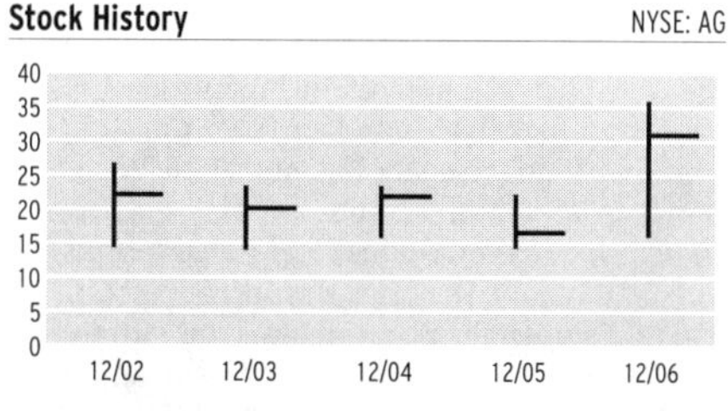


| | STOCK PRICE ($) FY Close | P/E High | P/E Low | PER SHARE ($) Earnings | Dividends | Book Value |
|---|---|---|---|---|---|---|
| **12/06** | 30.94 | — | — | (0.71) | — | 16.38 |
| **12/05** | 16.57 | 63 | 42 | 0.35 | — | 15.64 |
| **12/04** | 21.89 | 14 | 9 | 1.71 | — | 15.74 |
| **12/03** | 20.14 | 24 | 15 | 0.98 | — | 12.02 |
| **12/02** | 22.10 | — | — | (1.14) | — | 9.54 |
| **Annual Growth** | 8.8% | — | — | — | — | 14.5% |

# Agilent Technologies

Agilent Technologies keeps scientists on their toes. A leading manufacturer of scientific instruments and analysis equipment, Agilent is the #1 supplier of electronic test and measurement products, including data generators, multimeters, and oscilloscopes. Its life sciences and chemical analysis unit manufactures laboratory equipment and other scientific instruments. Agilent's customers include global giants such as Cisco, Dow Chemical, GlaxoSmithKline, Intel, Merck, and Samsung. Agilent has acquired Stratagene, a developer of life science research and diagnostic products, for about $250 million in cash.

In one of the largest acquisitions Agilent has made in its short history as a stand-alone company, the instrument maker will bolster its product offerings in life sciences for genomics and proteomics with the Stratagene portfolio, particularly among academic and government research customers. Agilent's substantial sales organization is expected to pay benefits for Stratagene, as well.

In 2005 Agilent announced a divestiture plan designed to help it focus on its measurement products. The company sold its semiconductor operations — which produce such products as application-specific integrated circuits (ASICs), optoelectronic components, and RF chipsets — late in 2005. The semiconductor operations, now called Avago Technologies, were acquired by two buyout firms — Kohlberg Kravis Roberts & Co. and Silver Lake Partners — for approximately $2.7 billion. Agilent sold its stake in Lumileds Lighting (LEDs) to Royal Philips Electronics for $950 million. It also spun off its memory and system-on-chip (SoC) test system operations with an IPO in 2006; the new company is called Verigy.

Agilent's test and measurement unit offers a wide range of services, such as consulting on hardware purchases, equipment repair and calibration, and professional engineering. That Agilent is a leader in the test and measurement equipment industry should come as no surprise — it is the original business started by technology pioneers William Hewlett and David Packard. Hewlett-Packard spun off the business in 1999 so that it could focus on its computer products operations. Being a leader has not spared the company from tough times in the electronics industry, however. Agilent has made serious job cuts and reduced salaries to control costs.

The company is also outsourcing more of its production, and moving manufacturing operations to Asia, in an effort to further lower costs.

In an effort to strengthen its offerings in informatics, Agilent acquired privately held Silicon Genetics, a maker of genomics data analysis and management software for the life sciences market, in 2004. Agilent entered the flat-panel display (FPD) test arena with the introduction of new LCD and OLED test product lines, as well as the acquisition of IBM's thin-film transistor (TFT) array test and charge test product line assets. The company acquired Scientific Software, a developer of chromatography data systems and content and business process management applications. It also acquired Molecular Imaging, a maker of measurement tools used by nanotechnology researchers.

## HISTORY

Agilent Technologies was formed in 1999 when Hewlett-Packard (HP) split off its measurement business. But Agilent's roots run as deep as HP's — Agilent's core products served as the original business of Stanford-trained electrical engineers William Hewlett and David Packard. The friends started HP in 1939 as a test and measurement equipment maker. Their first product, developed in Packard's garage (Hewlett was living in a rented cottage behind Packard's house) was an audio oscillator for testing sound equipment; Walt Disney Studios bought eight to help make the animation classic *Fantasia*.

Demand for electronic test equipment during WWII pushed sales from $34,000 in 1940 (when HP had three employees and eight products) to nearly $1 million three years later. The company entered the microwave field in 1943, creating signal generators for the Naval Research Laboratory. Its postwar line of microwave test products made it a market leader for signal generation equipment.

Expanding beyond the US in the late 1950s, HP established a plant in West Germany. The company went public in 1957. It entered the medical field in 1961 with the purchase of Sanborn, and the analytical instrumentation business in 1965 with the purchase of F&M Scientific. In the 1970s president Hewlett and chairman Packard began shifting HP's focus toward the computer market. Late in that decade they stepped back from day-to-day management (they would retire in 1987 and 1992, respectively).

Sales hit $3 billion in 1980. In 1991 HP broadened its communications component offerings when it bought Avantek. HP moved into the DNA analysis field in 1994 with pharmaceutical research and health care products. David Packard died in 1996. In 1997 HP bought Heartstream, maker of an automatic external defibrillator.

In 1999 HP formed Agilent as a separate company for its test and measurement and other non-computer operations, which by then accounted for 16% of sales. Edward Barnholt, a 30-year HP veteran, was named CEO of the new company. In a move to energize its computer business, HP spun off 15% of Agilent to the public in November 1999. The remainder was distributed to HP shareholders in mid-2000.

In 2000 Philips Electronics agreed to buy Agilent's Healthcare Solutions unit for $1.7 billion. (After lengthy scrutiny from US and European regulators, the deal was completed in mid-2001.)

In a move to bolster its networking business, Agilent completed its $665 million acquisition of network management software maker Objective Systems Integrators in early 2001. The company also implemented cost-cutting measures such as temporary pay cuts. Later that year, in the face of harsh market conditions, Agilent announced two separate layoffs of 4,000 employees each, representing a total staff reduction of about 18%. The company sold its health care business (patient monitoring and other clinical measurement and diagnostic equipment) to Philips Electronics. William Hewlett died that same year.

In 2002 the company announced plans to consolidate the operations of three older California fabs (wafer fabrication plants) into a new facility in Colorado; the new fab is to specialize in chips made from high-performance indium phosphide (InP) rather than silicon.

Barnholt retired early in 2005; Agilent's COO, Bill Sullivan, was tapped to replace him as president and CEO.

## EXECUTIVES

**Chairman:** James G. Cullen, age 64
**President, CEO, and Director:** William P. (Bill) Sullivan, age 56, $2,046,200 pay
**EVP, Finance and Administration and CFO:** Adrian T. Dillon, age 53, $1,275,682 pay
**SVP, General Counsel, and Secretary:** D. Craig Nordlund, age 57, $672,632 pay
**SVP; President and CEO, Verigy:** Jack P. Trautman, age 55
**SVP; President, Life Sciences and Chemical Analysis:** Chris van Ingen, age 60, $665,339 pay
**SVP, Human Resources:** Jean M. Halloran, age 54
**VP and CIO:** Rick Burdsall
**VP and CTO, Agilent Laboratories:** Darlene J. Solomon
**VP and General Manager, System Products Division:** Scott Sampl
**VP and General Manager, Computing and Networking Solutions:** Werner Huettemann
**VP and General Manager, Consumables and Service Solutions, Life Sciences and Chemical Analysis Group:** May Van
**VP and General Manager, Design Validation Division:** David S. Churchill, age 50
**VP and General Manager, Digital Verification Solutions Division:** Siegfried (Sigi) Gross
**VP and General Manager, Hachioji Semiconductor Test Division:** Minoru Ebihara
**VP and General Manager, Network Systems Test Division:** Steve Witt
**VP and General Manager, Technology and Services:** Mark Pierpoint
**VP, Corporate Relations:** Cynthia Johnson
**VP and Treasurer:** Hilliard Terry
**Director, Investor Relations:** Rodney Gonsalves, age 41
**Public Relations Manager:** Amy Flores
**Auditors:** PricewaterhouseCoopers LLP

## LOCATIONS

**HQ:** Agilent Technologies, Inc.
5301 Stevens Creek Blvd., Santa Clara, CA 95051
**Phone:** 408-345-8886 **Fax:** 408-345-8474
**Web:** www.agilent.com

Agilent Technologies has manufacturing and R&D facilities in Australia, Canada, China, Germany, Japan, Malaysia, Singapore, South Korea, the UK, and the US, with marketing centers and sales offices throughout the world.

### 2006 Sales

| | $ mil. | % of total |
|---|---|---|
| US | 1,698 | 34 |
| Japan | 657 | 13 |
| Other countries | 2,618 | 53 |
| **Total** | **4,973** | **100** |

## PRODUCTS/OPERATIONS

### 2006 Sales

| | $ mil. | % of total |
|---|---|---|
| Electronic measurement | 3,419 | 69 |
| Bio-analytical measurement | 1,554 | 31 |
| **Total** | **4,973** | **100** |

### 2006 Sales by Revenue Type

| | $ mil. | % of total |
|---|---|---|
| Products | 4,125 | 83 |
| Services & other | 848 | 17 |
| **Total** | **4,973** | **100** |

**Selected Products**

Test and Measurement
- Automated test equipment
- Electronic component test equipment
- Electronic design automation software
- Fiber-optic test equipment
- General-purpose test equipment
- In-circuit testing equipment
- Network monitoring systems and test equipment
- Optical inspection equipment
- Oscilloscopes
- Precision distance measurement and calibration instruments
- Telecom network test equipment
- Wireless communications instruments and systems

Life Sciences and Chemical Analysis
- Bioanalyzers
- Bioinformatic software
- Chromatograph columns, analytical reagents, and other consumables
- Gas chromatography systems
- Liquid chromatography systems
- Microarrays

## COMPETITORS

Advantest
Aeroflex
Affymetrix
Anritsu
Ansoft
Applied Biosystems
Applied Materials
Applied Wave Research
EXFO
Fluke
GE Healthcare
IBM Software
Invitrogen
Ixia
JDS Uniphase
Keithley Instruments
LeCroy
McAfee
National Instruments
PerkinElmer
Photon Dynamics
Rohde & Schwarz
Shimadzu
Spirent
Tektronix
telent
Teradyne
Thermo Fisher Scientific
Varian
Waters

## HISTORICAL FINANCIALS

Company Type: Public

**Income Statement** FYE: October 31

| | REVENUE ($ mil.) | NET INCOME ($ mil.) | NET PROFIT MARGIN | EMPLOYEES |
|---|---|---|---|---|
| **10/06** | 4,973 | 3,307 | 66.5% | 18,700 |
| **10/05** | 5,139 | 327 | 6.4% | 21,000 |
| **10/04** | 7,181 | 349 | 4.9% | 28,000 |
| **10/03** | 6,056 | (2,058) | — | 29,000 |
| **10/02** | 6,010 | (1,032) | — | 36,000 |
| **Annual Growth** | (4.6%) | — | — | (15.1%) |

**2006 Year-End Financials**

| | |
|---|---|
| Debt ratio: 41.1% | No. of shares (mil.): 408 |
| Return on equity: 85.6% | Dividends |
| Cash ($ mil.): 2,262 | Yield: — |
| Current ratio: 2.57 | Payout: — |
| Long-term debt ($ mil.): 1,500 | Market value ($ mil.): 13,831 |

**Stock History** NYSE: A

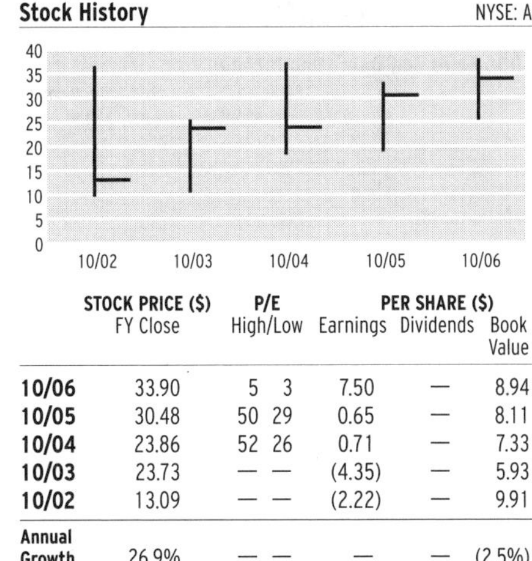


| | STOCK PRICE ($) FY Close | P/E High | P/E Low | PER SHARE ($) Earnings | Dividends | Book Value |
|---|---|---|---|---|---|---|
| **10/06** | 33.90 | 5 | 3 | 7.50 | — | 8.94 |
| **10/05** | 30.48 | 50 | 29 | 0.65 | — | 8.11 |
| **10/04** | 23.86 | 52 | 26 | 0.71 | — | 7.33 |
| **10/03** | 23.73 | — | — | (4.35) | — | 5.93 |
| **10/02** | 13.09 | — | — | (2.22) | — | 9.91 |
| **Annual Growth** | 26.9% | — | — | — | — | (2.5%) |

# Air Products and Chemicals

Much like Jumpin' Jack Flash, business at Air Products and Chemicals is a gas gas gas. The company provides gases such as argon, hydrogen, nitrogen, and oxygen to manufacturers, health care facilities, and other industries. Not all is light and airy, however. It also produces chemicals, including catalysts, surfactants, and intermediates used to make polyurethane and emulsions derived from vinyl acetate monomer (VAM). Air Products also makes gas containers and equipment that separates air, purifies hydrogen, and liquefies gas. The company distributes industrial gases by building on-site plants (a strategy nearly as old as the company itself) or by truck for companies with less extensive needs.

It created its Air Products Healthcare unit in 1999 and expanded it greatly three years later when it bought the company American Homecare Supply. The company added to the division again with the 2005 acquisition of Nightingale Medical, a homecare supply company that serves a portion of the American Midwest. Air Products Healthcare consists of a number of regional providers of respiratory and rehabilitative products and services. It covers much of the eastern half of the US.

In 2006 Air Products sold its amines business to chemical company Taminco for $210 million. The company also announced that it would sell its polymers operations, which is run through a joint venture with Wacker-Chemie called Air Products Polymers. Around the same time the company bought Tomah3 Products for $115 million. That company makes surfactants and processing aids used by the industrial and institutional cleaning, mining, and oil field industries.

Early the next year Air Products made a small but strategic move into Eastern Europe. The company took advantage of Linde's sell-off of some BOC assets after the German company bought BOC in 2006. Air Products agreed to acquire the Polish Gazy SP for just under $500 million with the hopes of moving into the Central and Eastern European markets to take advantage of the migration of manufacturing to the region.

## HISTORY

In the early 1900s Leonard Pool, the son of a boilermaker, began selling oxygen to industrial users. By the time he was 30, he was district manager for Compressed Industrial Gases. In the late 1930s Pool hired engineer Frank Pavlis to help him design a cheaper, more-efficient oxygen generator. In 1940 they had the design, and Pool established Air Products in Detroit (initially sharing space with the cadavers collected by his brother, who was starting a mortuary science college). The company was based on a simple, breakthrough concept: the provision of on-site gases. Instead of delivering oxygen in cylinders, Pool proposed to build oxygen-generating facilities near large-volume gas users and then lease them, reducing distribution costs.

Although industrialists encouraged Pool to pursue his ideas, few orders were forthcoming, and the company faced financial crisis. The outbreak of WWII got the company out of difficulty, as the US military became a major customer. During the war the company moved to Chattanooga, Tennessee, for the available labor.

The end of the war brought with it another downturn as demand dried up. By waiting at the Weirton Steel plant until a contract was signed, Pool won a contract for three on-site generators. Weirton was nearly the company's only customer. Pool relocated the company to Allentown, Pennsylvania, to be closer to the Northeast's industrial market, where he could secure more contracts with steel companies.

The Cold War and the launching of the Sputnik satellite in 1957 propelled the company's growth. Convinced that Soviet rockets were powered by liquid hydrogen, the US government asked Air Products to supply it with the volatile fuel. The company entered the overseas market that year through a joint venture with Butterley (UK), to which it licensed its cryogenic processes and equipment. The company went public in 1961 and formed a subsidiary in Belgium in 1964.

Air Products diversified into chemicals when it bought Houdry Process (chemicals and chemical-plant maintenance, 1962) and Airco's chemicals and plastics operations in the 1970s. The company continued to diversify in the mid-1980s, building large-scale plants for its environmental- and energy-systems business and adding Anchor Chemical and the industrial chemicals unit of Abbott Labs.

In 1995 and 1996 Air Products expanded into China and other countries by winning 20 contracts with semiconductor makers. It bought Carburos Metalicos, Spain's #1 industrial gas supplier, in 1996. To focus on its core gas and chemical lines, the company shed most of its environmental- and energy-systems business.

Expanding further in Europe, Air Products bought the methylamines and derivatives unit of UK-based Imperial Chemical Industries (ICI) in 1997. The company sold its remaining interest in American Ref-Fuel (a waste-to-energy US operation). In 1998 Air Products bought Solkatronic Chemicals and opened a methylamines plant in Florida to complement its ICI purchase. To further target semiconductor makers, it formed Air Products Electronic Chemicals and allied with AlliedSignal Chemical (now part of Honeywell International).

The next year Air Products and France's L'Air Liquide agreed to buy and break up BOC Group. European Union regulators initially approved the deal, but in 2000 the companies shelved the plan when other regulatory issues arose. Also in 2000 Air Products sold its polyvinyl alcohol business to Celanese for about $326 million. The company boosted its European presence in 2001 with the acquisition of Messer Griesheim's (Germany) respiratory home-care business and 50% of AGA's Netherlands industrial gases operations.

Air Products was hurt by the slowdown in manufacturing, primarily in the electronics and steel industries, which are major customers for gases. Its chemical revenues also were hurt by pressure on pricing. To improve profits, the company initiated cost cuts, including job cuts (about 10% of its employees) and divestitures such as its US packaged gas business.

The company broadened its health care operations in late 2002 by acquiring American Homecare Supply (now called Air Products Healthcare), which serves the home health care industry with medical gases and related equipment.

## EXECUTIVES

**Chairman and CEO:** John P. Jones III, age 56
**President, COO, and Director; CEO-Elect:** John F. McGlade, age 52
**Group VP, Development and Technology:** Arthur T. Katsaros, age 58
**VP and CFO:** Paul E. Huck, age 55, $855,000 pay
**VP, General Counsel, and Secretary:** W. Douglas Brown, age 59, $855,000 pay
**VP and Treasurer:** George G. Bitto
**VP and Controller, Tonnage Gases, Equipment and Energy Division:** Laurie K. Stewart, age 45
**VP and Director, Corporate Audit:** Joe H. Folger
**VP and General Manager, Healthcare:** John W. Marsland
**VP and Chief Risk Officer:** Diane L. Sheridan
**VP, Chief Technology Officer:** Montgomery (Monty) Alger
**VP and Corporate Development Officer:** Jeffrey Kramer
**VP, Energy and Materials:** Patricia A. Mattimore
**VP, Environmental Health, Safety, and Quality:** Larry W. Allen
**VP, Global Customer Engagement:** Norma J. Curby
**VP, Human Resources:** Lynn C. Minella, age 47
**VP Enterprise Operations and CIO:** Glenn E. Beck
**VP North American Gases:** Thomas J. Ward
**VP, Taxes:** Kenneth R. Petrini
**President, Air Products Asia:** Wilbur W. Mok
**President, Air Products Europe:** Bernard Guerini
**President, Air Products Japan:** Tetsushi Kuse
**Director, Investor Relations:** Nelson Squires
**Media Contact:** Beth Mentesana
**Auditors:** KPMG LLP

## LOCATIONS

**HQ:** Air Products and Chemicals, Inc.
7201 Hamilton Blvd., Allentown, PA 18195
**Phone:** 610-481-4911 **Fax:** 610-481-5900
**Web:** www.airproducts.com

Air Products and Chemicals has operations in just over 30 countries on all continents except Australia and Antarctica.

### 2006 Sales

| | $ mil. | % of total |
|---|---|---|
| US | 4,986.9 | 57 |
| Europe | 2,509.9 | 28 |
| Asia | 1,124.7 | 13 |
| Latin America | 120.9 | 1 |
| Canada | 108.0 | 1 |
| **Total** | **8,850.4** | **100** |

## PRODUCTS/OPERATIONS

### 2006 Sales and Operating Income

| | Sales | | Operating Income | |
|---|---|---|---|---|
| | $ mil. | % of total | $ mil. | % of total |
| Merchant Gases | 2,712.8 | 31 | 470.0 | 41 |
| Tonnage Gases | 2,224.1 | 25 | 341.3 | 30 |
| Electronics & Performance Materials | 1,898.6 | 22 | 195.3 | 17 |
| Chemicals | 907.6 | 10 | 64.0 | 5 |
| Healthcare | 570.8 | 6 | 8.4 | 1 |
| Equipment & Energy | 536.5 | 6 | 68.9 | 6 |
| **Total** | **8,850.4** | **100** | **1,147.9** | **100** |

### Selected Products and Services

Industrial Gases
- Argon
- Carbon dioxide
- Carbon monoxide
- Helium
- Hydrogen
- Nitrogen
- Oxygen
- Synthesis gas

Chemicals
- Epoxy additives
- Polymer emulsions
- Polyurethane chemicals and intermediates
- Process chemicals (fluorine chemicals, hydrogen chloride, ethyl chloride)
- Resins
- Specialty additives
- Surfactants
- Ultrapure chemicals for semiconductors

Equipment and Services
- Air-pollution control systems
- Air-separation equipment
- Hydrogen-purification equipment
- Natural gas-liquefaction equipment

## COMPETITORS

Airgas
BASF AG
CHEMCENTRAL
Dow Chemical
Honeywell Specialty Materials
Imperial Chemical
L'Air Liquide
Linde
Messer Group
Praxair
Rohm and Haas Electronic Materials
Taiyo Nippon Sanso

## HISTORICAL FINANCIALS

Company Type: Public

### Income Statement

FYE: September 30

| | REVENUE ($ mil.) | NET INCOME ($ mil.) | NET PROFIT MARGIN | EMPLOYEES |
|---|---|---|---|---|
| **9/06** | 8,850 | 723 | 8.2% | 20,700 |
| **9/05** | 8,144 | 712 | 8.7% | 19,500 |
| **9/04** | 7,411 | 604 | 8.2% | 19,900 |
| **9/03** | 6,297 | 397 | 6.3% | 18,500 |
| **9/02** | 5,401 | 525 | 9.7% | 17,200 |
| **Annual Growth** | 13.1% | 8.3% | — | 4.7% |

### 2006 Year-End Financials

Debt ratio: 46.3%
Return on equity: 15.2%
Cash ($ mil.): 35
Current ratio: 1.12
Long-term debt ($ mil.): 2,280
No. of shares (mil.): 217
Dividends
Yield: 2.0%
Payout: 42.1%
Market value ($ mil.): 14,419

### Stock History

NYSE: APD

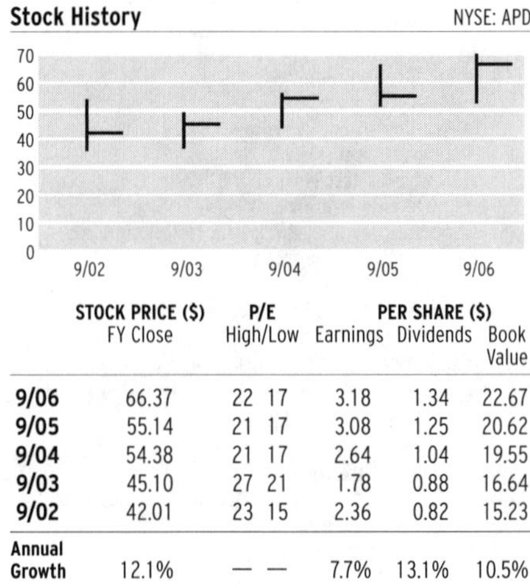


| | STOCK PRICE ($) FY Close | P/E High | P/E Low | PER SHARE ($) Earnings | Dividends | Book Value |
|---|---|---|---|---|---|---|
| **9/06** | 66.37 | 22 | 17 | 3.18 | 1.34 | 22.67 |
| **9/05** | 55.14 | 21 | 17 | 3.08 | 1.25 | 20.62 |
| **9/04** | 54.38 | 21 | 17 | 2.64 | 1.04 | 19.55 |
| **9/03** | 45.10 | 27 | 21 | 1.78 | 0.88 | 16.64 |
| **9/02** | 42.01 | 23 | 15 | 2.36 | 0.82 | 15.23 |
| **Annual Growth** | 12.1% | — | — | 7.7% | 13.1% | 10.5% |

# Airgas, Inc.

Airgas has floated to the top of the industrial gas distribution industry by buying up more than 350 companies since its founding in 1986. The company's extensive North American network of more than 1,000 locations includes retail stores, gas fill plants, specialty gas labs, production facilities, and distribution centers. Airgas distributes argon, helium, hydrogen, nitrogen, oxygen, welding gases, and a variety of medical and specialty gases, as well as dry ice and protective equipment (hard hats, goggles). Its Merchant Gases unit operates air-separation plants that produce oxygen, nitrogen, and argon. It also sells welding machines, rents industrial gas tanks, and produces acetylene and nitrous oxide.

Around 80% of the company's sales come from distributing small bulk gases (nitrogen, oxygen, argon, helium), gas cylinders, and welding equipment. Airgas also distributes dry ice. The manufacturing industry accounts for about a third of the company's sales; customers primarily make fabricated metal products, industrial transportation and equipment, chemical products, and primary metal products. Other industries served include medical and health services, agriculture, mining, construction, and wholesale trade.

The company continually strives to grow its business through acquisitions. In 2004 and 2005 it bought units from giants like Air Products and Chemicals, BOC, and LaRoche Industries. In 2006 Airgas continued to build with the purchase of 10 businesses, including Union Industrial Gas, which supplies Texas and much of the Southwest, and then Linde's US bulk gas business for $495 million early the next year. Linde, in the process of integrating its 2006 acquisition of BOC, then sold to Airgas a portion of its US packaged gas business for $310 million.

In 2007 the company acquired Lehner & Martin, Inc.

Founder and CEO Peter McCausland and his family control a 10% stake in Airgas.

## HISTORY

In the early 1980s Peter McCausland was a corporate attorney involved in mergers and acquisitions for Messer Griesheim, a large German industrial gas producer. When the German firm declined McCausland's recommendation in 1982 to buy Connecticut Oxygen, he raised money from private sources and bought it himself. He acquired other distributors and then left Messer Griesheim in 1987 to run Airgas full-time.

Airgas began buying mostly small local and regional gas distributors in the US. By 1994 strategy shifted to purchasing larger "superregional" distributors such as Jimmie Jones Co. and Post Welding Supply of Alabama, which added about $70 million combined to the company's revenues.

Airgas then began "rolling up" additional similar businesses. In 1995 it bought more than 25 companies, and two years later it added more than 20 gas distributors. Also in 1997 Airgas expanded its manufacturing capabilities by building five plants that could fast-fill whole pallets of gas cylinders (the old, manual system rolls cylinders two at a time). By 2000 the company had about 100 cylinder fill plants.

Struggling to integrate acquisitions while dealing with softening markets, Airgas began a companywide realignment in 1998. To that end, it sold its calcium carbide and carbon products operations to former partner Elkem ASA later that year; the company also consolidated 34 hubs into 16 regional companies and sold its operations in Poland and Thailand to Germany-based Linde in 1999.

In 2000 Airgas acquired distributor Mallinckrodt's Puritan-Bennett division (gas products for medical uses) with 36 locations in the US and Canada. The company also acquired the majority of Air Products' US packaged gas business, excluding its electronic gases and magnetic resonance imaging-related helium operations, in 2002.

Airgas acquired BOC's US packaged gas business in 2004; the deal was worth about $200 million. Early in 2006 Airgas bought Pennsylvania-based West Point Supply Co., Inc. and its Polar Ice Co., West Point Cryogenics Inc., and West Point Ice Co. Inc. affiliates.

## EXECUTIVES

**Chairman, President and CEO:** Peter McCausland, age 56, $1,600,000 pay
**EVP and COO:** Michael L. Molinini, age 55, $524,790 pay
**SVP and CIO:** Robert A. Dougherty, age 48
**SVP and CFO:** Robert M. McLaughlin, age 49
**SVP, Corporate Development:** Leslie J. Graff
**SVP, Distribution Operations:** Michael E. (Mike) Rohde
**SVP, Human Resources:** Dwight T. Wilson, age 49
**SVP, Sales:** Patrick M. Visintainer, age 41
**VP, Controller, and Chief Accounting Officer:** Thomas M. (Tom) Smyth
**VP, Communications:** James S. (Jim) Ely
**VP, General Counsel, and Secretary:** Dean A. Bertolino, age 37
**VP, Treasurer:** Joseph C. Sullivan
**President, Airgas Dry Ice/Carbonic:** Jim Filer
**President, Airgas East:** Jim Muller
**President and CFO, Airgas South:** L. Jay Sullivan
**Division President, East:** B. Shaun Powers, age 54
**Division President, West:** Max Hooper
**Division President, Gas Operations:** Ted R. Schulte, age 55, $439,297 pay
**President, Airgas Gaspro:** Jeff Finch
**Director, Investor Relations:** Jay Worley
**Auditors:** KPMG LLP

## LOCATIONS

**HQ:** Airgas, Inc.
259 N. Radnor-Chester Rd., Ste. 100,
Radnor, PA 19087
**Phone:** 610-687-5253 **Fax:** 610-225-3271
**Web:** www.airgas.com

Airgas distributes industrial and medical gases, safety products, and dry ice from more than 1,000 locations throughout the US and in Canada and Mexico.

## PRODUCTS/OPERATIONS

**2007 Sales**

| | $ mil. | % of total |
|---|---|---|
| Distribution | 2,691.8 | 82 |
| Other operations | 579.7 | 18 |
| Adjustments | (66.4) | — |
| **Total** | **3,205.1** | **100** |

**2007 Sales**

| | $ mil. | % of total |
|---|---|---|
| Gas & rentals | 1,823.5 | 57 |
| Hardgoods | 1,381.6 | 43 |
| **Total** | **3,205.1** | **100** |

**Selected Products and Services**

Products
- Carbon dioxide
- Dry ice
- Industrial gases
- Argon
- Carbon dioxide
- Helium
- Hydrogen
- Liquid oxygen
- Nitrogen
- Nitrous oxide
- Oxygen
- Safety equipment
- Specialty gases

Services
- Container rental
- Welding equipment rental

## COMPETITORS

Air Liquide America
Air Products
L'Air Liquide
Lincoln Electric
Matheson Tri-Gas
Praxair Distribution
Valley National Gases
W.W. Grainger

## HISTORICAL FINANCIALS

Company Type: Public

**Income Statement** FYE: March 31

| | REVENUE ($ mil.) | NET INCOME ($ mil.) | NET PROFIT MARGIN | EMPLOYEES |
|---|---|---|---|---|
| **3/07** | 3,205 | 154 | 4.8% | 11,500 |
| **3/06** | 2,830 | 124 | 4.4% | 10,300 |
| **3/05** | 2,411 | 92 | 3.8% | 11,000 |
| **3/04** | 1,896 | 80 | 4.2% | 9,700 |
| **3/03** | 1,787 | 68 | 3.8% | 8,500 |
| **Annual Growth** | 15.7% | 22.7% | — | 7.8% |

**2007 Year-End Financials**

Debt ratio: 116.4%
Return on equity: 14.9%
Cash ($ mil.): 26
Current ratio: 1.28
Long-term debt ($ mil.): 1,310
No. of shares (mil.): 79
Dividends
Yield: 0.7%
Payout: 14.6%
Market value ($ mil.): 3,316

**Stock History** NYSE: ARG

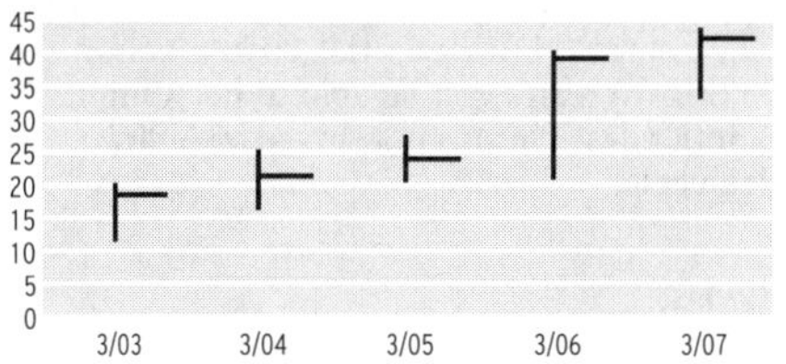

| | STOCK PRICE ($) FY Close | P/E High | P/E Low | PER SHARE ($) Earnings | PER SHARE ($) Dividends | PER SHARE ($) Book Value |
|---|---|---|---|---|---|---|
| **3/07** | 42.15 | 23 | 17 | 1.92 | 0.28 | 14.31 |
| **3/06** | 39.09 | 25 | 13 | 1.57 | 0.24 | 12.26 |
| **3/05** | 23.89 | 23 | 17 | 1.20 | 0.22 | 10.70 |
| **3/04** | 21.30 | 23 | 15 | 1.07 | 0.16 | 9.14 |
| **3/03** | 18.51 | 21 | 13 | 0.94 | — | 7.87 |
| **Annual Growth** | 22.8% | — | — | 19.5% | 20.5% | 16.1% |

# AirTran Holdings

The Atlanta airport is one of the world's busiest, and AirTran Holdings is partly responsible. Through its main subsidiary, AirTran Airways, the company offers low-fare passenger transportation, primarily from its Atlanta hub. AirTran Airways flies to more than 50 cities, mainly in the eastern US. The airline operates a fleet of about 130 Boeing aircraft, including the 717-200 and the 737-700. It is a leading carrier in the Atlanta market, behind Delta, which handles the largest share of the traffic at Hartsfield-Jackson International Airport. In an effort to expand, AirTran Holdings tried to buy smaller rival Midwest Air Group during the first half of 2007.

AirTran Holdings in December 2006 proposed to buy Midwest Air Group for $290 million in cash and stock, but Midwest's board promptly rejected the offer. AirTran Holdings raised its bid to about $345 million in January 2007 and was again turned down. In April 2007, AirTran Holdings increased its offer to $389 million but again failed to gain the blessing of Midwest directors. Shortly after, AirTran Holdings nominated three director candidates who won approval at Midwest's annual meeting in June 2007. All this proved fruitless, however, as an investment group led by TPG Capital, and which included Northwest Airlines, placed a $450 million winning bid for Midwest a month later.

With the deal being thwarted, AirTran Airways has continued to expand its operations out of Atlanta. The carrier also is adding departures from other cities, such as Orlando and Baltimore, and it has introduced service to western US markets. Outside the US, AirTran Airways offers service to the Bahamas.

The carrier successfully blends a couple of industry models. It often offers lower fares than Delta, but unlike low-fare leader Southwest Airlines, AirTran Airways provides reserved seats and business-class service. In addition, it relies on its Atlanta hub more than Southwest relies on any single airport.

In a move touted as a first among low-fare carriers, AirTran Airways and Frontier Airlines in 2006 announced a marketing partnership in which the carriers will refer passengers to each other and credit miles from one another's frequent-flyer programs. The deal stops short of code-sharing, but potential customers on the AirTran Web site will be able to book flights to Frontier destinations not served by AirTran, and vice-versa.

## HISTORY

What became AirTran Holdings began in 1992 when airline veterans Robert Priddy, Maurice Gallagher, and Timothy Flynn founded ValuJet, basing it in Atlanta. By year's end the company operated six aircraft on 34 daily flights to Fort Lauderdale, Jacksonville, Orlando, and Tampa, Florida. By late 1994 it flew 22 jets between 16 cities, mainly in the Southeast. ValuJet continued to expand, linking Washington, DC, to Chicago and Montreal in 1995 and to New York in 1996.

In May 1996 a ValuJet DC-9 crashed in the Florida Everglades, killing all 110 people aboard. The FAA reviewed the company's safety and maintenance procedures after the crash, forcing the airline to shut down for 15 weeks. ValuJet resumed flights in September, offering $19 one-way flights to lure back passengers. Turnaround specialist Joseph Corr, formerly of TWA and Continental Airlines, came aboard in November as CEO to help ValuJet change its course.

To recover passenger bookings, the airline joined the SABRE computer reservation system in 1997, sparking a 60% increase in SABRE bookings. That year ValuJet acquired AirTran Airways through its purchase of Airways Corporation, rebranded itself as AirTran Airlines, kicked off an advertising campaign to overhaul its image, and moved to Orlando. In 1999 Joseph Leonard, a former Eastern Airlines executive, succeeded Corr as CEO. That year AirTran began to replace aging aircraft by taking delivery of new Boeing 717 regional jets, becoming the first airline to use that new aircraft model.

AirTran made an effort to acquire ailing industry giant TWA in 2000, but talks between the two airlines ended shortly after they began. Also that year, AirTran transferred to the American Stock Exchange from the Nasdaq.

In 2001 AirTran retired the last of its Boeing 737s as it continued to update its fleet with smaller Boeing 717 jets. The carrier added four destinations in 2003, including Reagan National Airport in Washington, DC.

An effort to acquire Chicago landing slots from bankrupt ATA fell short in 2004, as rival Southwest Airlines outbid AirTran to gain additional space at Midway Airport.

## EXECUTIVES

**Chairman and CEO:** Joseph B. (Joe) Leonard, age 63, $956,250 pay
**President, COO, and Director:** Robert L. Fornaro, age 54, $789,538 pay
**SVP, General Counsel, and Secretary:** Richard P. Magurno, age 63, $358,010 pay
**SVP, Finance and CFO:** Stanley J. (Stan) Gadek, age 55, $370,481 pay
**SVP, Customer Service, AirTran Airways:** Alfred J. (Jack) Smith III, age 55
**SVP, Operations, AirTran Airways:** Stephen J. Kolski, age 66, $394,231 pay
**VP and Chief Accounting Officer, AirTran Airways:** Mark W. Osterberg, age 54
**VP and CIO, AirTran Airways:** Rocky Wiggins
**VP, Finance and Treasurer, AirTran Airways:** Arne Haak
**VP, Flight Operations, AirTran Airways:** Klaus Goersch
**VP, Human Resources, AirTran Airways:** Loral Blinde
**VP, Inflight Service, AirTran Airways:** Susan Manfredi
**VP, Maintenance and Engineering, AirTran Airways:** Kirk Thornburg
**VP, Marketing and Sales, AirTran Airways:** Tad Hutcheson
**VP, Operations, AirTran Airways:** Jim Tabor
**VP, Planning, AirTran Airways:** Kevin P. Healy
**Director, Corporate Safety, AirTran Airways:** Jean-Pierre (J. P.) Dagon
**Auditors:** Ernst & Young LLP

## LOCATIONS

**HQ:** AirTran Holdings, Inc.
9955 AirTran Blvd., Orlando, FL 32827
**Phone:** 407-318-5600 **Fax:** 407-318-5900
**Web:** www.airtran.com

## PRODUCTS/OPERATIONS

**2006 Sales**

| | $ mil. | % of total |
|---|---|---|
| Passenger | 1,816.2 | 96 |
| Cargo | 3.9 | — |
| Other | 73.3 | 4 |
| **Total** | **1,893.4** | **100** |

## COMPETITORS

AMR Corp.
Continental Airlines
Delta Air
JetBlue
Northwest Airlines
Southwest Airlines
UAL
US Airways

## HISTORICAL FINANCIALS

Company Type: Public

**Income Statement** FYE: December 31

| | REVENUE ($ mil.) | NET INCOME ($ mil.) | NET PROFIT MARGIN | EMPLOYEES |
|---|---|---|---|---|
| **12/06** | 1,893 | 16 | 0.8% | 7,700 |
| **12/05** | 1,451 | 8 | 0.6% | 6,900 |
| **12/04** | 1,041 | 12 | 1.2% | 6,100 |
| **12/03** | 918 | 101 | 10.9% | 5,500 |
| **12/02** | 733 | 11 | 1.5% | 5,000 |
| **Annual Growth** | 26.8% | 9.7% | — | 11.4% |

**2006 Year-End Financials**

Debt ratio: 189.2%
Return on equity: 4.2%
Cash ($ mil.): 335
Current ratio: 1.06
Long-term debt ($ mil.): 724
No. of shares (mil.): 91
Dividends
Yield: —
Payout: —
Market value ($ mil.): 1,070

**Stock History** NYSE: AAI

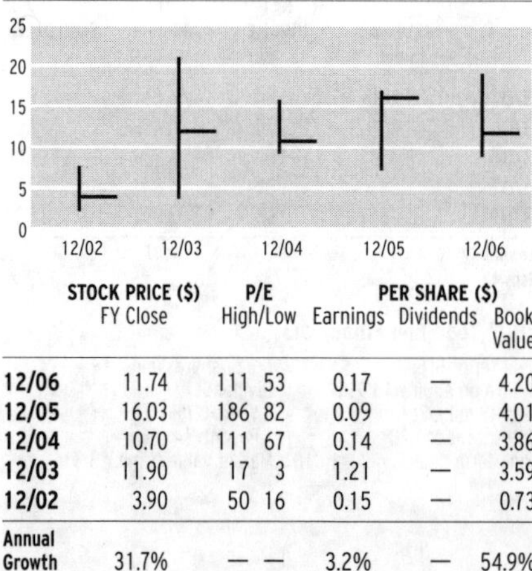


| | STOCK PRICE ($) FY Close | P/E High | P/E Low | PER SHARE ($) Earnings | Dividends | Book Value |
|---|---|---|---|---|---|---|
| **12/06** | 11.74 | 111 | 53 | 0.17 | — | 4.20 |
| **12/05** | 16.03 | 186 | 82 | 0.09 | — | 4.01 |
| **12/04** | 10.70 | 111 | 67 | 0.14 | — | 3.86 |
| **12/03** | 11.90 | 17 | 3 | 1.21 | — | 3.59 |
| **12/02** | 3.90 | 50 | 16 | 0.15 | — | 0.73 |
| **Annual Growth** | 31.7% | — | — | 3.2% | — | 54.9% |

# AK Steel Holding

Automobile sales help AK Steel's business keep rolling. The company manufactures carbon, stainless, and electrical steel. It sells hot- and cold-rolled carbon steel to construction companies, steel distributors and service centers, and automotive and industrial machinery producers. AK Steel also sells cold-rolled and aluminum-coated stainless steel to automakers. The company produces electrical steels (iron-silicon alloys with unique magnetic properties) for makers of power transmission and distribution equipment. In addition, it makes carbon and stainless steel tubular products through AK Tube. Sales to automakers make up nearly half of AK Steel's business; GM is its largest customer, generating 10% of sales.

The steel industry has been consolidating for years as troubled companies have been snapped up by market leaders. AK Steel was outbid in a couple of major acquisition efforts early in the decade, and analysts have since speculated that the company itself may be an acquisition candidate. AK Steel has maintained its independence, however, in part because of its status as a leading supplier of some high-grade niche products, such as components of stainless steel exhaust systems, for carmakers.

In 2006 the company announced plans to increase production capacity at many of its facilities. Total investments have been about $70 million and should improve AK Steel's electrical and tubular steel output. The company's sales to automobile makers has declined as a percentage of total sales due primarily to its ability to raise prices for its other products, boosting revenue for those other segments. These capacity increases should only help that trend continue.

## HISTORY

George Verity, who was in the roofing business in Cincinnati around the turn of the century, often had trouble getting sheet metal, so in 1900 he founded his own steel company, American Rolling Mill. His first plant, in Middletown, Ohio, was followed by a second production facility 11 years later in Ashland, Kentucky. Plant superintendent John Tytus, whose family was in paper milling, applied those rolling techniques to make American Rolling Mill's steel more uniform in thickness.

In 1926 Columbia Steel developed a process to overcome several production problems inherent in the Tytus method, and in 1930 American Rolling Mill bought Columbia Steel. The company changed its name to Armco Steel in 1948.

Armco began diversifying in the 1950s and continued diversifying until the early 1980s. Subsidiaries were involved in coal, oil, and gas-drilling equipment and insurance and financial services, among other things. In 1978 the company changed its name to Armco Inc.

Armco began shedding subsidiaries in the early 1980s. Sales and market share increased as the company approached the billion-dollar mark at the end of the decade. In 1989 Armco formed Armco Steel Company with Japan's Kawasaki Steel Corporation.

Armco's sales reached $1.3 billion in 1991, though the high operating expenses in the steel industry of the 1990s kept profits low. Armco began looking outside the company for help, and in 1992 it persuaded retired steel executive Tom Graham to head the company. Graham brought with him another industry veteran, Richard Wardrop, who would succeed Graham as CEO in 1995. After evaluating the company's holdings, the two divested more than 10 subsidiaries and divisions. Armco also worked on improving quality and customer service, with special emphasis placed on timely delivery.

In 1994 Armco's limited partnership with Kawasaki was altered and AK Steel Holding Corporation was formed, with AK Steel Corporation as its main subsidiary and the Middletown and Ashland plants as its production base. The holding company went public the same year, raising more than $650 million, enabling the company to pay off its debt.

AK Steel Holding moved its headquarters to Middletown, Ohio, in 1995. Despite many naysayers, Graham then pushed a plan to build a state-of-the-art $1.1 billion steel production facility. Many doubted the wisdom of going into long-term debt so soon after coming out of the hole — especially when a similar facility had produced lackluster results for Inland Steel. Graham stuck by his plant, and in 1997 ground was broken on the facility in Spencer County near Rockport, Indiana (Rockport Works). Graham retired that year, and Wardrop took over as chairman.

In 1998 the company opened its Rockport Works cold-rolling mill and began operating a hot-dip galvanizing and galvannealing line. The next year AK Steel bought former parent Armco for $842 million. AK Steel acquired welded steel tubing maker Alpha Tube Corporation (renamed AK Tube LLC) in 2001. In late 2001 the company took a charge of $194 million for losses in its pension fund, which had been battered by a weak stock market and lowered interest rates.

AK Steel sold its Sawhill Tubular Division to John Maneely Company (Collingswood, NJ) for roughly $50 million in 2002.

AK Steel offered to purchase National Steel, which was operating under Chapter 11 bankruptcy protection. However, AK Steel's bid was trumped in 2003 by one from U.S. Steel that included a ratified labor agreement with the United Steelworkers of America. AK Steel also lost out in an effort to acquire Rouge Industries (later Severstal North America).

Chairman and CEO Wardrop and president John Hritz left their posts in September 2003. CFO James Wainscott was named president and CEO, and Robert Jenkins became chairman. (Wainscott succeeded Jenkins as chairman in January 2006.)

In an effort to reduce its debt, AK Steel in 2004 sold its Douglas Dynamics unit, a maker of snow and ice removal equipment, for $260 million, and its Greens Port Industrial Park, a 600-acre development in Houston, for $75 million.

## EXECUTIVES

**SVP, General Counsel, and Secretary:** David C. Horn, age 55
**Chairman, President, and CEO:** James L. Wainscott, age 50, $900,000 pay
**SVP Operations:** John F. Kaloski, age 57, $435,000 pay
**VP Finance and CFO:** Albert E. Ferrara Jr., age 58, $390,000 pay
**VP Government and Public Relations:** Alan H. McCoy, age 55
**VP Human Resources:** Lawrence F. Zizzo Jr., age 58
**General Manager, Manufacturing Planning:** Bill Cross
**Chief Accounting Officer and Controller:** Roger K. Newport
**VP Sales and Customer Service:** Douglas W. Gant, age 48, $330,000 pay
**Chief Compliance Officer and Assistant General Counsel:** John J. Kuzman, age 51
**Director Safety:** F. R. (Dick) Smith
**Manager Finance:** Linda Pleiman
**Director Purchasing:** Jess A. Elger
**Manager Public Relations:** Barry Racey
**Auditors:** Deloitte & Touche LLP

## LOCATIONS

**HQ:** AK Steel Holding Corporation
703 Curtis St., Middletown, OH 45043
**Phone:** 513-425-5000 **Fax:** 513-425-2676
**Web:** www.aksteel.com

AK Steel operates manufacturing facilities in Indiana, Kentucky, Ohio, and Pennsylvania.

**2006 Sales**

| | $ mil. | % of total |
|---|---|---|
| US | 5,379.7 | 89 |
| Other countries | 689.3 | 11 |
| **Total** | **6,069.0** | **100** |

## PRODUCTS/OPERATIONS

**2006 Sales**

| | $ mil. | % of total |
|---|---|---|
| Carbon steel | 3,356.9 | 55 |
| Stainless & electrical steel | 2,476.5 | 41 |
| Tubular steel | 235.6 | 4 |
| **Total** | **6,069.0** | **100** |

**2006 Sales**

| | % of total |
|---|---|
| Automotive | 41 |
| Distributors, service centers & converters | 30 |
| Appliance, industrial machinery/equipment & construction | 29 |
| **Total** | **100** |

## COMPETITORS

Dofasco
Nucor
Steel Dynamics
United States Steel
Worthington Industries

## HISTORICAL FINANCIALS

Company Type: Public

**Income Statement** FYE: December 31

| | REVENUE ($ mil.) | NET INCOME ($ mil.) | NET PROFIT MARGIN | EMPLOYEES |
|---|---|---|---|---|
| **12/06** | 6,069 | 12 | 0.2% | 7,000 |
| **12/05** | 5,647 | (2) | — | 8,000 |
| **12/04** | 5,217 | 238 | 4.6% | 8,400 |
| **12/03** | 4,042 | (560) | — | 9,000 |
| **12/02** | 4,289 | (502) | — | 10,300 |
| **Annual Growth** | 9.1% | — | — | (9.2%) |

**2006 Year-End Financials**

Debt ratio: 267.4%
Return on equity: 3.8%
Cash ($ mil.): 519
Current ratio: 2.73
Long-term debt ($ mil.): 1,115
No. of shares (mil.): 110
Dividends
Yield: —
Payout: —
Market value ($ mil.): 1,864

**Stock History** NYSE: AKS

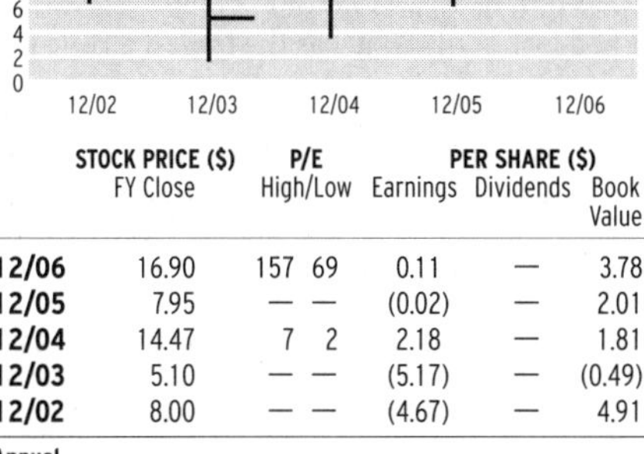

| | STOCK PRICE ($) FY Close | P/E High/Low | | PER SHARE ($) Earnings | Dividends | Book Value |
|---|---|---|---|---|---|---|
| **12/06** | 16.90 | 157 | 69 | 0.11 | — | 3.78 |
| **12/05** | 7.95 | — | — | (0.02) | — | 2.01 |
| **12/04** | 14.47 | 7 | 2 | 2.18 | — | 1.81 |
| **12/03** | 5.10 | — | — | (5.17) | — | (0.49) |
| **12/02** | 8.00 | — | — | (4.67) | — | 4.91 |
| **Annual Growth** | 20.6% | — | — | — | — | (6.3%) |

# Alaska Air Group

Whether you want to capture a Kodiak moment or down a daiquiri by the Sea of Cortez, an Alaska Air Group unit can fly you there. The company serves as holding company for Alaska Airlines and Horizon Air Industries. Alaska Airlines serves some 40 cities in Alaska, other western states, and western Canada; it also flies to selected major cities elsewhere in the US and about 10 cities in Mexico. It has a fleet of some 115 jets (Boeing 737s and MD-80s). Alaska Airlines operates from hubs in Anchorage, Alaska; Portland, Oregon; Los Angeles; and Seattle. Regional carrier Horizon Air flies to another 40 cities in the western US and Canada with a fleet of some 20 jets and 50 turboprops.

Alaska Airlines' leadership in the Alaska air travel market and strong presence on the West Coast have made it an attractive code-sharing partner for airlines such as Air France, American, Continental, KLM, and Northwest.

Alaska Airlines hopes to grow mainly by increasing the frequency of flights within its existing route structure, but also by adding service to new markets as demand warrants.

Like other major US airlines, however, Alaska Airlines is working to keep a lid on costs in the face of increased competition from low-fare carriers. As part of its cost-control program, the carrier is retiring its older, less fuel-efficient MD-80s in favor of new 737 models. It plans to transition into an all-737 fleet by the end of 2008.

## HISTORY

Pilot Mac McGee started McGee Airways in 1932 to fly cargo between Anchorage and Bristol Bay, Alaska. He joined other local operators in 1937 to form Star Air Lines, which began airmail service between Fairbanks and Bethel in 1938. In 1944, a year after buying three small airlines, Star adopted the name Alaska Airlines.

The company expanded to include freight service to Africa and Australia in 1950. This expansion, coupled with the seasonal nature of the airline's business, caused losses in the early 1970s. Developer Bruce Kennedy gained control of the board, turning the firm around by the end of 1973. But the Civil Aeronautics Board forced the carrier to drop service to northwestern Alaska in 1975, and by 1978 it served only 10 Alaskan cities and Seattle.

Kennedy became CEO the next year. The 1978 Airline Deregulation Act allowed Alaska Air to move into new areas as well as regain the routes it had lost. By 1982 it was the largest airline flying between Alaska and the lower 48 states.

In 1985 the airline reorganized, forming Alaska Air Group as its holding company. The next year Alaska Air Group bought Jet America Airlines (expanding its routes eastward to Chicago, St. Louis, and Dallas) and Seattle-based Horizon Air Industries (which served 30 Northwest cities). When competition in the East and Midwest cut profits in 1987, Kennedy shut down Jet America to focus on West Coast operations.

To counterbalance summer traffic to Alaska, the airline began service to two Mexican resorts in 1988. Fuel prices and sluggish traffic hurt 1990 earnings, but Alaska Air Group stayed in the black, unlike many other carriers. Kennedy retired as chairman and CEO in 1991.

That year the airline began service to Canada and seasonal flights to two Russian cities. Neil Bergt's MarkAir airline declared war, cutting fares and horning in on Alaska Air Group's territory. Alaska Air Group's profits were slashed, and MarkAir went into bankruptcy.

Alaska Air extended Russian flights to year-round in 1994. The airline began service to Vancouver in 1996. That year it became the first major US carrier to use the GPS satellite navigation system. In 1997 it added service to more than a dozen new cities but halted service to Russia because of that country's economic woes in 1998.

Alaska Air Group and Dutch airline KLM agreed to a marketing alliance in 1998 that included reciprocal frequent-flier programs and code-sharing, and in 1999 it added code-sharing agreements with several major airlines, including American and Continental. Alaska Airlines developed an online check-in system, a first among US carriers.

In 2000 an Alaska Airlines MD-83 crashed into the Pacific Ocean near Los Angeles, killing all 88 people on board. A federal investigation of Alaska Airlines' maintenance practices found deficiencies, but the FAA eventually accepted the airline's plan to tighten safety standards.

Like most carriers in the latter part of 2001, Alaska Airlines cut back its flights as a result of reduced demand after the September 11 terrorist attacks. As demand slowly returned in 2002, Alaska Airlines began to add new destinations and increase the number of flights on some established routes.

In 2005 Alaska Airlines announced plans to buy 35 Boeing 737-800s between 2006 and 2011.

## EXECUTIVES

**Chairman, President, and CEO; Chairman, President, and CEO, Alaska Airlines:** William S. (Bill) Ayer, age 52, $360,000 pay
**President and CEO, Horizon Air Industries:** Jeffrey D. Pinneo, age 50, $357,923 pay
**EVP, Finance and Planning and CFO; EVP, Finance and Planning and CFO, Alaska Airlines:** Bradley D. (Brad) Tilden, age 46
**VP, Finance and Controller; VP, Finance and Controller, Alaska Airlines:** Brandon S. Pedersen, age 40
**VP, Legal and Corporate Affairs, General Counsel, and Corporate Secretary; VP, Legal and Corporate Affairs, General Counsel, and Corporate Secretary, Alaska Airlines:** Keith Loveless, age 50
**EVP, Flight and Marketing, Alaska Airlines:** Gregg A. Saretsky, age 47
**EVP, Strategic Projects and Interim VP, Flight Operations, Alaska Airlines:** Kevin P. Finan, age 59
**EVP, Aiport Services, Maintenance, and Engineering, Alaska Airlines:** Glenn S. Johnson, age 48
**SVP, Alaska, Alaska Airlines:** William L. (Bill) MacKay
**SVP, Customer Services, Horizon Air:** Andrea L. Schneider
**SVP, Information and Communication Services, Alaska Airlines:** Robert M. Reeder
**SVP, Operations, Horizon Air:** Thomas M. Gerharter
**VP, Employee Resources, Horizon Air:** Marne K. McCluskey
**VP, Employee Services, Alaska Airlines:** Dennis J. Hamel
**VP, Finance and Treasurer, Horizon Air:** Rudi H. Schmidt
**VP, Flight Operations, Alaska Airlines:** Benjamin F. Forrest Jr.
**VP, Flight Operations, Horizon Air:** Eugene C. Hahn
**VP Strategy and Corporate Development:** Donald S. Garvett
**VP, Safety and Security, Alaska Airlines:** Chris R. Glaeser
**VP, Sales and Customer Experience, Alaska Airlines:** Stephen B. Jarvis
**VP Human Resources Strategy and Culture, Alaska Airlines:** Kelley J. Dobbs
**Staff VP, Finance and Treasurer; Staff VP, Finance and Treasurer, Alaska Airlines:** John F. Schaefer Jr.
**Auditors:** KPMG LLP

## LOCATIONS

**HQ:** Alaska Air Group, Inc.
19300 International Blvd., Seattle, WA 98188
**Phone:** 206-392-5040 **Fax:** 206-392-2804
**Web:** www.alaskaair.com

## PRODUCTS/OPERATIONS

**2006 Sales**

| | $ mil. | % of total |
|---|---|---|
| Alaska Airlines | 2,692.5 | 81 |
| Horizon Airlines | 644.0 | 19 |
| Other | 1.1 | — |
| Adjustments | (3.2) | — |
| **Total** | **3,334.4** | **100** |

## COMPETITORS

ACE Aviation
Aeromexico
AMR Corp.
Continental Airlines
Delta Air
MAIR Holdings
Mesa Air
Northwest Airlines
SkyWest
Southwest Airlines
UAL
US Airways
WestJet

## HISTORICAL FINANCIALS

Company Type: Public

**Income Statement** FYE: December 31

| | REVENUE ($ mil.) | NET INCOME ($ mil.) | NET PROFIT MARGIN | EMPLOYEES |
|---|---|---|---|---|
| **12/06** | 3,334 | (53) | — | 14,485 |
| **12/05** | 2,975 | (6) | — | 13,768 |
| **12/04** | 2,724 | (15) | — | 14,584 |
| **12/03** | 2,445 | 14 | 0.6% | 14,738 |
| **12/02** | 2,224 | (119) | — | 14,943 |
| **Annual Growth** | 10.7% | — | — | (0.8%) |

**2006 Year-End Financials**

Debt ratio: 116.5%
Return on equity: —
Cash ($ mil.): 1,125
Current ratio: 1.27
Long-term debt ($ mil.): 1,032
No. of shares (mil.): 40
Dividends
Yield: —
Payout: —
Market value ($ mil.): 1,592

**Stock History** NYSE: ALK

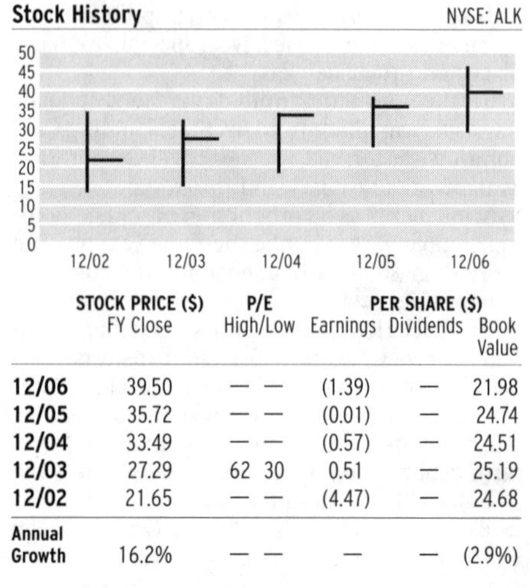


| | STOCK PRICE ($) FY Close | P/E High/Low | PER SHARE ($) Earnings | Dividends | Book Value |
|---|---|---|---|---|---|
| **12/06** | 39.50 | — — | (1.39) | — | 21.98 |
| **12/05** | 35.72 | — — | (0.01) | — | 24.74 |
| **12/04** | 33.49 | — — | (0.57) | — | 24.51 |
| **12/03** | 27.29 | 62 30 | 0.51 | — | 25.19 |
| **12/02** | 21.65 | — — | (4.47) | — | 24.68 |
| **Annual Growth** | 16.2% | — — | — | — | (2.9%) |

# Alberto-Culver

From the bath to the kitchen, Alberto-Culver has it covered. It makes products for hair care (Alberto VO5, Nexxus, TRESemmé, Consort, Motions), skin care (St. Ives Swiss Formula), and personal care (FDS); sweeteners and seasonings (Molly McButter, Mrs. Dash, SugarTwin, Baker's Joy); and laundry-care items (Static Guard). Its Cederroth International segment serves Nordic countries. A plan to sell the business to Regis Corporation fell through in early 2006. In November of that year, however, Alberto-Culver parted ways with its Sally Beauty unit, the world's #1 beauty supply retailer and distributor to professionals and consumers. The move included a split with its Beauty Systems Group, as well.

Having cut off its retail arm, Alberto-Culver now concentrates solely on making and marketing its portfolio of personal care, food, and household products in the US (about 75% of sales ) and internationally. It also consolidated its marketing units and outsourced certain international services after the spin-off to purge its operations that supported Sally Beauty. Its Pro-Line International segment is one of the world's top manufacturers of ethnic hair care items under the Motions and Soft & Beautiful brand names.

The company's international markets include Africa, Asia, the Caribbean, Europe and the UK, Latin America, and Argentina, Australia, Canada, Chile, and Mexico.

Although dwarfed by consumer products and beauty care giants, such as Procter & Gamble, Alberto-Culver has increased sales by boosting marketing efforts and updating core products.

The Lavin and Bernick families run Alberto-Culver and control about 13% of the voting rights of the newly reorganized company.

## HISTORY

Alberto VO5 Conditioning Hairdressing (featuring five vital oils in a water-free base) was developed in the early 1950s by a chemist named Alberto to rejuvenate the coiffures of Hollywood's movie stars from the damage of harsh studio lights. In 1955 36-year-old entrepreneur Leonard Lavin and his wife, Bernice, borrowed $400,000, bought the Los Angeles-based firm that made VO5 from Blaine Culver, and relocated it to Chicago. That year Alberto-Culver implemented a key component of its corporate strategy — aggressive marketing — by running the first television commercial for VO5. Within three years Alberto VO5 led its category. In 1959 the company expanded its product line by buying TRESemmé Hair Color.

Lavin built a new plant and headquarters in Melrose Park, Illinois, in 1960, took the company public in 1961, and formed an international marketing division. A series of product innovations included Alberto VO5 Hair Spray (1961), New Dawn Hair Color (the first shampoo-in, permanent hair color; 1963), Consort Hair Spray for Men (1965), and FDS (1966). Acquisitions in 1969 included low-calorie sugar substitute SugarTwin and 10-store beauty supply chain Sally Beauty Supply.

Alberto-Culver restyled TV advertising in 1972 by putting two 30-second ads in a 60-second spot (it later pioneered the "split 30," back-to-back 15-second ads for two different products). It launched TCB (an ethnic hair care line) in 1975 and Static Guard antistatic spray in 1976.

The firm developed a series of food-substitute products in the 1980s, including Mrs. Dash (1983) and Molly McButter (1987). It also expanded the fast-growing Sally chain to the UK (1987). Lavin's son-in-law Howard Bernick succeeded him as president and COO in 1988.

By 1990 the Sally chain had about 800 stores, many added through the purchases of smaller chains. It bought the bankrupt Milo Beauty & Barber Supply chain (about 90 stores) in 1991. That year Alberto-Culver also bought Cederroth International, a Swedish maker of health and hygiene goods. Bernick became CEO in 1994, though Lavin stayed on as chairman.

In 1995 the firm acquired the toiletries division of Swedish beauty and cleaning products maker Molnlycke, combining it with Cederroth to form one of Scandinavia's largest consumer packaged goods marketers. Also that year Lavin's daughter, Carol Bernick, became head of Alberto-Culver USA and led the division to more than $300 million in sales.

The 1,500-store Sally chain opened its first 10 outlets in Japan through a joint venture in 1995 and acquired a small chain in Germany the next year. Also in 1996 Alberto-Culver made its largest acquisition ever, paying $110 million for St. Ives Laboratories, maker of St. Ives Swiss Formula hair and skin care products.

In 1997 the consumer products division cut nearly 25% of its product line to focus on its best-sellers. In 1998 Sally entered Canada by acquiring two beauty supply companies specializing in salon lines. In 1999 the company bought Argentina-based La Farmaco, a personal care products company, and professional products distributor Heil Beauty Supply.

As of November 5, 2003, the company had only one class of common stock outstanding. Previously, it had two publicly traded classes of common stock since 1986. The change was intended to encourage greater trading of the company's shares by institutions and it reduced the voting power of the Lavin and Bernick families to 21% from 27%. In December Alberto-Culver completed its acquisition of West Coast Beauty Supply Co., a distributor of beauty aids with more than 120 stores in 14 western states.

In October 2004 founder and chairman Leonard Lavin stepped down after 49 years as chairman, passing his title to his daughter, Carol Lavin Bernick. Leonard Lavin became chairman emeritus and director of the firm. A director since 1955, Bernice Lavin retired from the board in late January 2005.

Alberto-Culver bought California's Nexxus Products Company in May 2005 and spun off its entire retail operations business, including Sally Beauty and Beauty Systems Group, into a separately traded company in late 2006. As part of the deal, Alberto-Culver spun off its beauty supply business into a standalone company renamed Sally Beauty Holdings, Inc., and paid shareholders a one-time dividend of $25 per share upon completion. Private-equity firm Clayton, Dubilier & Rice bought a 47.5% stake in Sally Beauty for at least $575 million. Alberto-Culver shareholders own the rest. When the transaction closed Sally Beauty began trading on the New York Stock Exchange under the SBH symbol.

## EXECUTIVES

**Chairman Emeritus:** Leonard H. Lavin, age 87
**Chairman:** Carol Lavin Bernick, age 54, $1,260,000 pay
**President, CEO, and Director:** V. James Marino, age 56, $1,141,250 pay
**SVP, General Counsel, and Secretary:** Gary P. Schmidt, age 55, $667,750 pay
**SVP and CFO:** Ralph J. Nicoletti, age 49
**Group VP, Global Research and Development:** John R. Berschied Jr., age 63, $633,500 pay
**VP Worldwide Operations:** Richard Mewborn, age 47
**Media Relations:** Doug Craney
**Auditors:** KPMG LLP

## LOCATIONS

**HQ:** Alberto-Culver Company
2525 Armitage Ave., Melrose Park, IL 60160
**Phone:** 708-450-3000 **Fax:** 708-450-3409
**Web:** www.alberto.com

### 2006 Sales

| | $ mil. | % of total |
|---|---|---|
| US | 2,864.2 | 76 |
| International | 917.8 | 24 |
| Adjustments | (10.0) | — |
| **Total** | **3,772.0** | **100** |

## PRODUCTS/OPERATIONS

### 2006 Sales

| | $ mil. | % of total |
|---|---|---|
| Global Consumer Products | 1,428.9 | 38 |
| Beauty Supply Distribution | | |
| Sally Beauty Supply | 1,419.3 | 37 |
| Beauty Systems Group | 953.8 | 25 |
| Adjustments | (30.0) | — |
| **Total** | **3,772.0** | **100** |

### Selected Brands

Alberto VO5 (hair care products)
Baker's Joy (cooking spray)
Bliw (liquid hand soap, Europe)
Consort (hair care products)
Farmaco (soap, Latin America)
FDS (feminine deodorant spray)
Grumme Tvattsapa (detergent, Europe)
Jordan (toothbrushes, Europe)
Just For Me (ethnic personal care products)
L300 (skin care products, Europe)
Molly McButter (butter-flavored sprinkles)
Motions (ethnic hair care products)
Mrs. Dash (salt-free seasoning)
Nexxus (hair care)
St. Ives Swiss Formula (hair care and skin care products)
Salveqvik (adhesive bandages, Europe)
Samarin (antacids, Europe)
Seltin (salt substitute, Europe)
Soft & Beautiful (ethnic personal care products)
Static Guard (antistatic spray)
SugarTwin (sugar substitute)
Suketter (sugar substitute, Europe)
TCB (ethnic hair care products)
TRESemmé (hair care products)
Veritas (soap, Latin America)

### Subsidiaries

Alberto-Culver Holdings (Australia) Pty. Ltd.
Alberto-Culver Canada, Inc.
Alberto-Culver Company (U.K.), Limited
Alberto-Culver International, Inc.
Alberto-Culver de Mexico, S.A. de C.V.
Alberto-Culver (P.R.), Inc.
Alberto-Culver USA, Inc.
BDM Grange, Ltd. (New Zealand)
Cederroth International AB (Sweden)
CIFCO, Inc.
Nexxus Products Company

## COMPETITORS

Alticor
Avlon Industries
Avon
Bristol-Myers Squibb
Colgate-Palmolive
Combe
Cumberland Packing
Del Labs
Dial
Estée Lauder
Gillette
Helen of Troy
Johnson & Johnson
Johnson Publishing
L'Oréal
Mary Kay
McCormick
Nu Skin
Orly International
Procter & Gamble
Regis
Revlon
Schwarzkopf & Henkel
Shiseido
Unilever

## HISTORICAL FINANCIALS

Company Type: Public

### Income Statement

FYE: September 30

| | REVENUE ($ mil.) | NET INCOME ($ mil.) | NET PROFIT MARGIN | EMPLOYEES |
|---|---|---|---|---|
| **9/06** | 3,772 | 205 | 5.4% | 3,800 |
| **9/05** | 3,531 | 211 | 6.0% | 19,000 |
| **9/04** | 3,258 | 142 | 4.4% | 18,300 |
| **9/03** | 2,891 | 162 | 5.6% | 17,000 |
| **9/02** | 2,651 | 138 | 5.2% | 16,900 |
| **Annual Growth** | 9.2% | 10.5% | — | (31.1%) |

### 2006 Year-End Financials

Debt ratio: 7.1%
Return on equity: 12.6%
Cash ($ mil.): —
Current ratio: —
Long-term debt ($ mil.): 122

**Net Income History** NYSE: ACV

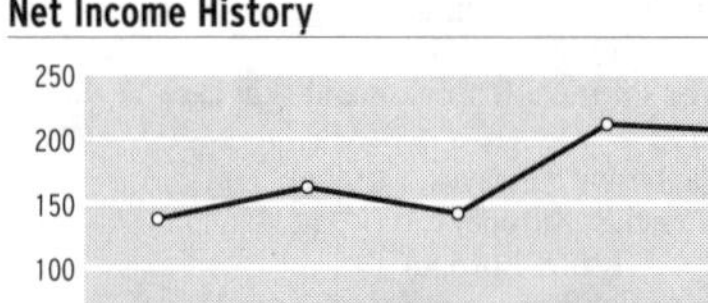


# Alcoa Inc.

Alcoa is among the world's top producers of alumina (aluminum's principal ingredient, processed from bauxite) and aluminum. Its vertically integrated operations include bauxite mining, alumina refining, and aluminum smelting; primary products include alumina and its chemicals, automotive components, and sheet aluminum for beverage cans. The company's non-aluminum products include consumer products, fiber-optic cables, food service and flexible packaging products, and plastic closures. Major markets include the aerospace, automotive, construction, and packaging industries. In mid-2007 Alcoa offered to buy the world's #3 aluminum producer, Alcan, for $33 billion but was trumped by Rio Tinto's $38 billion offer.

Alcoa has gained presence in China's aluminum market by forming a strategic alliance with Aluminum Corporation of China (Chalco). Its 8% stake in Chalco enables Alcoa to partake in China's aluminum market, the fastest-growing in the world. In 2005 Alcoa bought two fabricating facilities in Russia for more than $250 million. The company hopes the new plants provide a gateway not only into Russia but into the rest of Eastern Europe and Asia as well.

As part of its divestment strategy, in early 2004 Alcoa sold its automotive fastener unit to privately held Kaminski Holdings for an undisclosed price. That same year, the company sold its specialty chemicals unit for $342 million to Rhone Capital LLC and Teachers' Merchant Bank.

Alcoa and Fujikura Ltd. had shared a joint venture called Alcoa Fujikura. The two JV partners disbanded Alcoa Fujikura in 2005 though, splitting it evenly between the parents. Alcoa acquired the automotive cable operations based in Detroit, and Fujikura kept the telecommunications unit that is based in Nashville. In 2006 the company sold its Home Exteriors unit to Ply Gem Industries; it also sold its aerospace service business to ThyssenKrupp.

The 2007 merger of Russian aluminum giants RUSAL and Sual (along with Glencore's aluminum operations) created the world's largest aluminum company, pushing Alcoa and Alcan down a notch each. Should the Alcan/Rio Tinto combination go forward, RUSAL would step down a notch and become the #2 aluminum producer.

That year Alcoa formed a soft-alloy extrusion joint venture with Sapa Group (part of Orkla) called Sapa AB. It is the world's largest aluminum shaper.

## HISTORY

In 1886 two chemists, one in France and one in the US, simultaneously discovered an inexpensive process for aluminum production. The American, Charles Hall, pursued commercial applications. Two years later, with an investor group led by Captain Alfred Hunt, Hall formed the Pittsburgh Reduction Company. Its first salesman, Arthur Davis, secured an initial order for 2,000 cooking pots.

In 1889 the Mellon Bank loaned the company $4,000. In 1891 the firm recapitalized with the Mellon family holding 12% of the stock.

Davis led the business after Hunt died in 1899 and stayed on until 1957 (he died in 1962 at age 95). The company introduced aluminum foil (1910) and found applications for aluminum in newly developing products such as airplanes and cars. It became the Aluminum Company of America in 1907.

By the end of WWI, Alcoa had integrated backward into bauxite mining and forward into end-use production. By the 1920s the Mellons had raised their stake to 33%.

The government and Alcoa had debated antitrust issues in court for years since the smelting patent expired in 1912. Finally a 1946 federal ruling forced the company to sell many operations built during WWII, as well as its Canadian subsidiary (Alcan).

In the competitive aluminum industry of the 1960s, Alcoa's lower-cost production helped it seize market share, especially in beverage cans. In the 1970s Alcoa began offering engineered products such as aerospace components, and in the 1980s it invested in research, acquisitions, and plant modernization.

Paul O'Neill (former president of International Paper) arrived as CEO in 1987 and shifted the company's focus back to aluminum. Sales and earnings set records the next two years but plunged afterward, reflecting a weak global economy and record-low aluminum prices. Then the fall of the Soviet Union in the early 1990s led to a worldwide glut as Russian exports soared.

The company expanded in Europe in 1996, acquiring Italy's state-run aluminum business, followed by the purchase of Inespal, Spain's state-run aluminum operations, in 1998. Alcoa also bought #3 US aluminum producer Alumax for $3.8 billion in 1998, but only after divesting its cast-plate operations.

Known by the nickname "Alcoa" since the late 1920s, the company adopted that as its official name in 1999. O'Neill retired as CEO in 1999; COO Alain Belda succeeded him.

In 2000 Alcoa paid $4.5 billion for Reynolds Metals after agreeing to divest some assets — including all of Reynolds' alumina refineries — to satisfy regulators. Late in 2000 President-elect George W. Bush named Alcoa's chairman Paul O'Neill to be treasury secretary. (O'Neill subsequently resigned the post in December 2002.)

Alcoa sold its majority stake in the Worsley alumina refinery (Australia) to BHP Billiton in 2001 for about $1.5 billion as part of its refinery divestments.

Late in the year Alcoa agreed to buy an 8% stake in Aluminium Corporation of China (Chalco). The deal gave Alcoa a seat on the board and 27% of Chalco's initial public offering.

Early in 2002 Alcoa made a bid to acquire Elkem, a Norway-based metals producer; Elkem spurned the offer. Later that year Alcoa bought Elkem shares in the open market, increasing its ownership to around 46%. Alcoa also purchased Ivex Packaging (Chicago-based industrial packaging group), which excluded Ivex's 48% stake in Packaging Dynamics for an estimated $790 million.

The acquisitions kept apace into the next year. In 2003 Alcoa acquired Camargo Correa Group's 41% stake in the South American businesses of Alcoa, including its largest subsidiary in the group — Alcoa Aluminio S.A. (Brazil) — and operations in Argentina, Chile, Colombia, Peru, Uruguay, and Venezuela.

Faced with lower aluminum prices, Alcoa decided to divest under-performing businesses primarily in its automotive, packaging, and specialty chemicals units. Alcoa also cut its workforce by 6% (largely from its Mexican auto parts plants).

## EXECUTIVES

**Chairman and CEO:** Alain J. P. Belda, age 63, $1,401,442 pay
**EVP, General Counsel, and Chief Compliance Officer:** Lawrence R. (Larry) Purtell, age 60
**EVP; President, Engineered Products and Solutions:** William F. (Bill) Christopher, age 53, $535,096 pay
**EVP; President, Global Primary Products:** Bernt Reitan, age 59, $550,000 pay
**EVP, Market Strategy, Technology, and Quality:** Mohammad A. Zaidi, age 54
**EVP; President, Global Rolled Products, Hard Alloy Extrusions, and Asia:** Helmut Wieser, age 53
**EVP, Corporate Development:** Barbara S. Jeremiah, age 55
**EVP; President, Packaging and Consumer Products:** Paul D. Thomas, age 50, $560,577 pay
**VP and Corporate Controller:** Joseph R. (Joe) Lucot, age 43
**VP and CFO:** Charles D. (Chuck) McLane Jr., age 53
**VP and Treasurer:** Peter Hong, age 48
**VP, Environment, Health, and Safety, Global Communications, and Public Strategy:** Richard L. (Jake) Siewert, age 43
**VP, Government Affairs:** Russell C. Wisor
**VP, Pension Fund Investments and Analysis:** Robert G. Wennemer
**VP, Tax:** Ronald D. Dickel
**VP, Audit:** Julie A. Caponi
**VP, Human Resources:** Regina M. Hitchery, age 58
**VP; President, Alcoa Russia:** William J. (Bill) O'Rourke Jr., age 57
**Secretary and Corporate Governance Counsel:** Donna C. Dabney, age 56
**Director, Investor Relations:** Tony Thene
**President, Asia/Pacific Region:** Jinya Chen
**Auditors:** PricewaterhouseCoopers LLP

## LOCATIONS

**HQ:** Alcoa Inc.
390 Park Ave., New York, NY 10022
**Phone:** 412-553-4545 **Fax:** 412-553-4498
**Web:** www.alcoa.com

Alcoa has more than 350 operating locations in more than 40 countries.

**2006 Sales**

| | $ mil. | % of total |
|---|---|---|
| US | 17,141 | 56 |
| Australia | 3,160 | 10 |
| Spain | 1,813 | 6 |
| Hungary | 1,148 | 4 |
| Brazil | 1,093 | 4 |
| UK | 956 | 3 |
| Germany | 768 | 3 |
| Other countries | 4,284 | 14 |
| Corporate | 16 | — |
| **Total** | **30,379** | **100** |

## PRODUCTS/OPERATIONS

### 2006 Sales

| | $ mil. | % of total |
|---|---|---|
| Flat-rolled Products | 8,297 | 27 |
| Primary Metals | 6,171 | 20 |
| Engineered Solutions | 5,456 | 18 |
| Extruded & End Products | 4,419 | 15 |
| Packaging & Consumer | 3,235 | 11 |
| Alumina | 2,785 | 9 |
| Corporate | 16 | — |
| **Total** | **30,379** | **100** |

### Selected Products

Engineered products (aluminum extrusions, forgings, castings, investment castings, fasteners)
Flat-rolled products (light gauge sheet products, such as rigid container sheet and foil, for the packaging market; sheet and plate mill products for the transportation, building, and construction markets)
Primary aluminum (smelted from alumina, which is derived from bauxite)
Packaging and consumer (foil and plastic consumer packaging, closures, packaging equipment)
Alumina and chemicals (bauxite, alumina, alumina-based chemicals, transportation services for bauxite and alumina)

### Selected Operations

Alcoa Automotive Castings
Alcoa Closure Systems Japan, Ltd.
Alcoa Aluminum Deutschland, Inc.
Alcoa Europe S.A.
Alcoa Latin American Holdings Corporation
Alcoa Packaging Equipment
Alcoa (Shanghai) Aluminum Products Ltd.
Alcoa World Alumina — Atlantic
Alcoa World Alumina and Chemicals — Australia
Cordant Technologies Holding Company
Halco (Mining) Inc. (45%)
Howmet International Inc.
Kawneer Company
Reynolds Metals Company

## COMPETITORS

Alcan
Aluminum Corporation of China
BHP Billiton
Boeing
Corus Group
Crown Holdings
Hayes Lemmerz
Hydro Aluminium
Nippon Light Metal
Ormet
Quanex Corporation
Rio Tinto
RUSAL
Showa Denko
Superior Industries

## HISTORICAL FINANCIALS

Company Type: Public

### Income Statement

FYE: December 31

| | REVENUE ($ mil.) | NET INCOME ($ mil.) | NET PROFIT MARGIN | EMPLOYEES |
|---|---|---|---|---|
| **12/06** | 30,379 | 2,248 | 7.4% | 123,000 |
| **12/05** | 26,159 | 1,233 | 4.7% | 129,000 |
| **12/04** | 23,478 | 1,310 | 5.6% | 119,000 |
| **12/03** | 21,504 | 938 | 4.4% | 120,000 |
| **12/02** | 20,263 | 420 | 2.1% | 127,000 |
| **Annual Growth** | 10.7% | 52.1% | — | (0.8%) |

### 2006 Year-End Financials

Debt ratio: 40.5%
Return on equity: 16.1%
Cash ($ mil.): 801
Current ratio: 1.26
Long-term debt ($ mil.): 5,910
No. of shares (mil.): 870
Dividends
Yield: 2.0%
Payout: 23.3%
Market value ($ mil.): 26,095

### Stock History

NYSE: AA

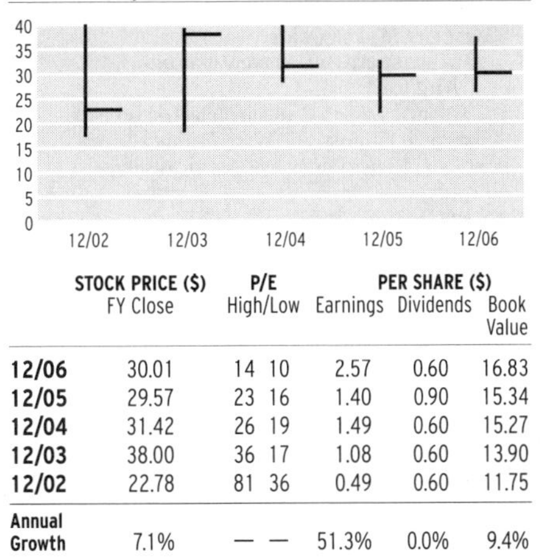


| | STOCK PRICE ($) FY Close | P/E High | P/E Low | PER SHARE ($) Earnings | Dividends | Book Value |
|---|---|---|---|---|---|---|
| **12/06** | 30.01 | 14 | 10 | 2.57 | 0.60 | 16.83 |
| **12/05** | 29.57 | 23 | 16 | 1.40 | 0.90 | 15.34 |
| **12/04** | 31.42 | 26 | 19 | 1.49 | 0.60 | 15.27 |
| **12/03** | 38.00 | 36 | 17 | 1.08 | 0.60 | 13.90 |
| **12/02** | 22.78 | 81 | 36 | 0.49 | 0.60 | 11.75 |
| **Annual Growth** | 7.1% | — | — | 51.3% | 0.0% | 9.4% |

# Allegheny Energy

Even when the Allegheny Moon isn't shining, Allegheny Energy (AE) can provide plenty of light. The company's Allegheny Power unit provides electricity to some 1.5 million customers in Maryland, Pennsylvania, West Virginia, and Virginia through regulated utilities Monongahela Power, Potomac Edison, and West Penn Power. Subsidiary Allegheny Energy Supply provides power to AE's utilities and sells electricity to wholesale and retail customers. Subsidiary Allegheny Ventures controls Allegheny Communications Connect (telecommunications) and Allegheny Energy Solutions (energy consulting).

AE is reducing its wholesale power trading operations due to a downturn in the industry, which was brought on by #1 energy trader Enron's collapse in 2001. Prior to the downturn, AE had been focused on expanding its nonregulated generation and marketing businesses; however, it now plans to focus on its core energy delivery operations. Allegheny Energy Supply has exited the western US wholesale energy market; it sold its power supply contract with the California Department of Water Resources to a division of The Goldman Sachs Group in 2003.

To further improve its precarious financial situation, AE has been selling noncore assets, including some real estate and power generation holdings. The company has sold Monongahela Power's West Virginia natural gas operations for a reported $217 million. AE also has canceled several power plant developments, and it has postponed plans to spin off up to 18% of a new holding company that would own Allegheny Energy Supply.

In 2005 Allegheny sold a 512-MW generating station to The Cincinnati Gas & Electric and PSI Energy for $100 million.

## HISTORY

American Water Works & Electric Company was one of many utility holding companies created by financiers as the US power industry consolidated in the 1880s. It bought many electric plants and water facilities in the Northeast and united 53 Pennsylvania power companies to form West Penn Power in 1916. It also formed The Potomac Edison Company in 1923, a similar amalgamation of small utilities that supplied power to western Maryland. The next year American Water Works formed Washington County Light & Power Company (later Monongahela Power) to serve customers in West Virginia and Ohio.

In 1925 West Penn Electric Company was born when American Water Works began integrating the systems' power plants, transformers, and lines under that name. The 1929 stock market crash brought the octopus-like holding companies under scrutiny, and in 1935 the Public Utility Holding Company Act restricted utilities' ownership to contiguous regions. American Water Works was dissolved in 1948, and the newly independent West Penn Electric became the owner of the three geographically linked utilities.

The steel industry — which accounted for the largest share of the company's sales — began exiting the region in the 1950s. West Penn was saved because its location was in the middle of one of the richest coal regions in the country. The company divested its nonutility interests, and in 1960 it was renamed Allegheny Power System.

In 1981 Allegheny formed Allegheny Generating Company (AGC), which held 40% of a Virginia hydroelectric station it bought that year. Passage of the Clean Air Act of 1990, which set limits on sulfur dioxide emissions, cost coal-dependent Allegheny an estimated $2 billion.

The Energy Policy Act of 1992 opened the door for deregulation of the energy industry, and Allegheny formed a nonutility holding company (AYP Capital) in 1994. Two years later Pennsylvania approved deregulation legislation, and AYP Capital took over two new subsidiaries: AYP Energy (wholesale power) and Allegheny Communications Connect (telecommunications). In 1997 the company was renamed Allegheny Energy (AE), and it formed Allegheny Energy Solutions to market energy services to Pennsylvania retail customers. It also agreed to buy Pennsylvania utility DQE (now Duquesne Light Holdings), but DQE later backed out.

In 1998 AE entered Pennsylvania's deregulation pilot program. Full competition arrived in Pennsylvania's electricity markets in 1999, and AE formed Allegheny Energy Supply to hold its generation assets, including those of AYP Energy. AYP Capital became Allegheny Ventures, which took charge of AE's telecom unit and Allegheny Energy Solutions.

Expanding its West Virginia operations, the company purchased the West Virginia Power unit of UtiliCorp United (now Aquila) for $75 million, and in 2000 bought natural gas distributor Mountaineer Gas (200,000 customers). AE also entered a communications venture with five other companies; the venture, America's Fiber Network (now AFN Communications), operates a 13-state fiber-optic network.

Moving to expand Allegheny Energy Supply's power trading operations, AE in 2001 bought Merrill Lynch's Global Energy Markets unit for $490 million and a 2% stake in Allegheny Energy Supply. The company purchased three gas-fired merchant plants (1,700 MW of capacity) in Illinois, Indiana, and Tennessee from Enron for $1 billion that year. AE also purchased two energy services firms (Fellon-McCord & Associates and Alliance Energy Services Partnership), which it sold to Constellation Energy Group the following year.

The company reversed its expansion strategy in 2002 as it began facing financial difficulties due to a downturn in the electricity market; that year the company restructured its management and reduced its workforce by about 10%. Allegheny Energy Supply sold 150,000 retail customer accounts in Pennsylvania and Ohio to Dominion Resources' retail marketing unit that year.

Also in 2002, regional transmission organization (RTO) PJM Interconnection began managing AE's regulated transmission assets.

## EXECUTIVES

**Chairman, President and Chief Executive Officer:** Paul J. Evanson, $2,440,900 pay
**Senior Vice President and Chief Financial Officer:** Philip L. Goulding
**VP and Treasurer:** Suzanne C. Lewis
**VP, Controller, Chief Accounting Officer and Chief Information Officer:** Thomas R. Gardner
**VP and General Counsel:** David M. Feinberg
**VP, Environment, Health and Safety:** David C. Cannon Jr.
**VP Human Resources and Security:** Edward (Ed) Dudzinski
**VP Quality:** J. Michael (Mike) Adams
**VP Generation Operations; Allegheny Energy Supply and Allegheny Generating:** Leo C. Rajter
**Chief Risk Officer:** Raymond L. Bummer
**VP Transmission Allegheny Power:** James R. Haney
**VP Distribution Allegheny Power:** David Flitman
**VP, Chief Accounting Officer and Controller:** William F. Wahl III, age 46
**VP and Treasurer:** Barry E. Pakenham
**VP Chief Information Officer:** James Kauffman
**Executive Director, Investor Relations and Corporate Communications:** Max Kuniansky
**Director, Employee Relations and Organizational Development:** Debra J. West
**Director, Finance, Allegheny Energy Supply:** Patricia Shanahan
**Director Supply Chain and Chief Procurement Officer:** James R. Wright
**Director System Security:** Scott Webber
**Manager Communications:** Janice D. Lantz
**Media Contact Corporate Communications:** Allen Staggers
**Auditors:** PricewaterhouseCoopers LLP

## LOCATIONS

**HQ:** Allegheny Energy, Inc.
800 Cabin Hill Dr., Greensburg, PA 15601
**Phone:** 724-837-3000 **Fax:** 724-830-5284
**Web:** www.alleghenyenergy.com

Allegheny Energy's utilities deliver electricity in Maryland, Ohio, Pennsylvania, Virginia, and West Virginia and natural gas in West Virginia.

## PRODUCTS/OPERATIONS

### 2006 Sales

| | $ mil. | % of total |
|---|---|---|
| Delivery & services | 2,717.7 | 60 |
| Generation & marketing | 1,834.4 | 40 |
| Adjustments | (1,430.6) | — |
| **Total** | **3,121.5** | **100** |

### Selected Subsidiaries and Divisions

Allegheny Energy Service Corporation (support services)
Allegheny Energy Supply Company, LLC (AE Supply, electricity generation and energy trading and marketing)
Allegheny Energy Supply — Marketing and Trading Division (formerly Allegheny Energy Global Markets)
Allegheny Generating Company (59% owned by AE Supply, 41% owned by Monongahela Power)
Allegheny Power (energy delivery division)
Monongahela Power Company (electric and gas utility, West Virginia and Ohio)
Mountaineer Gas Company (gas utility, West Virginia)
The Potomac Edison Company (electric utility; Maryland, Virginia, and West Virginia)
West Penn Power Company (electric utility, Pennsylvania)
Allegheny Ventures, Inc.
Allegheny Communications Connect, Inc. (telecommunications)
AFN, LLC (formerly America's Fiber Network, venture with five energy and telecommunications companies)
Allegheny Energy Solutions, Inc. (energy consulting services, on-site generation)

## COMPETITORS

AEP
Avista
CMS Energy
Constellation Energy
Delmarva Power
Dominion Peoples
Dominion Resources
DPL
Duke Energy
Duquesne Light Holdings
Exelon
FirstEnergy
National Fuel Gas
NiSource
Pepco Holdings
PPL
PSEG Energy Holdings
TVA
Vectren
WGL Holdings

## HISTORICAL FINANCIALS

Company Type: Public

### Income Statement

FYE: December 31

| | REVENUE ($ mil.) | NET INCOME ($ mil.) | NET PROFIT MARGIN | EMPLOYEES |
|---|---|---|---|---|
| **12/06** | 3,122 | 319 | 10.2% | 4,362 |
| **12/05** | 3,038 | 63 | 2.1% | 4,460 |
| **12/04** | 2,756 | (311) | — | 5,100 |
| **12/03** | 2,472 | (355) | — | 5,148 |
| **12/02** | 2,989 | (633) | — | 5,300 |
| **Annual Growth** | 1.1% | — | — | (4.8%) |

### 2006 Year-End Financials

Debt ratio: 163.9%
Return on equity: 16.9%
Cash ($ mil.): 154
Current ratio: 1.11
Long-term debt ($ mil.): 3,410
No. of shares (mil.): 165
Dividends
Yield: —
Payout: —
Market value ($ mil.): 7,592

### Stock History

NYSE: AYE

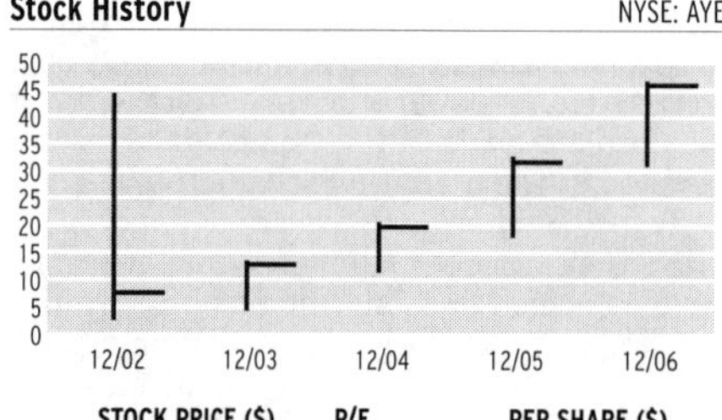


| | STOCK PRICE ($) FY Close | P/E High/Low | PER SHARE ($) Earnings | Dividends | Book Value |
|---|---|---|---|---|---|
| **12/06** | 45.91 | 24 17 | 1.89 | — | 12.58 |
| **12/05** | 31.65 | 81 46 | 0.40 | — | 10.55 |
| **12/04** | 19.71 | — — | (1.93) | — | 9.85 |
| **12/03** | 12.76 | — — | (2.80) | — | 11.94 |
| **12/02** | 7.56 | — — | (5.04) | 1.29 | 15.26 |
| **Annual Growth** | 57.0% | — — | — | — | (4.7%) |

# Allegheny Technologies

Well, isn't that special? Allegheny Technologies, Inc. (ATI) manufactures stainless and specialty steels, nickel- and cobalt-based alloys and superalloys, titanium and titanium alloys, tungsten materials, and such exotic alloys as niobium and zirconium. The company's flat-rolled products (sheet, strip, and plate) account for a great majority of its sales. Its high-performance metals unit produces metal bar, coil, foil, ingot, plate, rod, and wire. Allegheny Technologies' largest markets include aerospace, the chemical process, and oil and gas industries. Three-fourths of its sales are in the US. ATI was formed from the 1996 merger of Teledyne and stainless-steel producer Allegheny Ludlum.

To offset rapidly rising costs in raw materials, energy, health care, and transportation costs, the company has increased prices on several of its metal grades. Those price increases helped ATI achieve record sales in 2006. The demand in the aerospace and oil and gas industries hasn't subsided and has led to the strong performance.

## HISTORY

Allegheny Ludlum Steel began in 1938 when Allegheny Steel Company (founded in Pennsylvania in 1898) and Ludlum Steel Company (founded in New Jersey in 1854) merged. Allegheny Steel veteran W. F. Detwiler became Allegheny Ludlum Steel's first chairman. During WWII the company developed heat-resisting alloys for aircraft turbine engines.

After the war the focus was on stainless steel and flat-rolled silicon electrical steel used to make electrical transformers. In 1956 the company doubled its capacity for making specialty alloys and installed the industry's first semi-automated system for working hot steel. It expanded outside the US by opening a plant in Belgium in the 1960s.

The company adopted the name Allegheny Ludlum Industries in 1970 and, after diversifying, sold its specialty steel division in a management-led buyout that formed Allegheny Ludlum Steel (1980). In 1986 it became Allegheny Ludlum Corp. It went public in 1987.

Henry Singleton and George Kozmetsky, former Litton Industries executives, invested $225,000 each in 1960 to found Teledyne to make electronic aircraft components. First year sales of $4.5 million grew to nearly $90 million by 1964. Kozmetsky left the firm in 1966.

Under Singleton, Teledyne bought more than 100 successful manufacturing and technology firms in defense-related areas such as engines, unmanned aircraft, specialty metals, and computers. Teledyne also moved into offshore oil-drilling equipment, insurance and finance, and the Water Pik line of oral-care products.

Teledyne spun off its Argonaut Insurance unit in 1986 and left the insurance business entirely with its 1990 spinoff of Unitrin. Its defense businesses were caught in a 1989 fraud probe, and the company paid $4.4 million in restitution. In 1991 Teledyne consolidated its 130 operations into 21 companies. It paid a $13 million fine in 1995 on charges of knowingly selling zirconium to a Chilean arms manufacturer for use in cluster bombs sold to Iraq.

Despite Teledyne's rebuff of holding company WHX's 1994 takeover offer, in 1996 WHX came back with a new proposal that led to the $3.2 billion merger of Teledyne and Allegheny Ludlum in 1997. Also in 1997 CEO William Rutledge was succeeded by former Allegheny Ludlum CEO Richard Simmons. Allegheny and Bethlehem Steel entered into a bidding war for steelmaker Lukens. Bethlehem won but in 1998 granted exclusive access to or sold most of Lukens' stainless-steel operations to Allegheny. The company also bought UK-based Sheffield Forgemaster's Group's aerospace division and titanium producer Oregon Metallurgical.

Allegheny restructured to focus on specialty metals in 1999, changing its name to Allegheny Technologies. The company sold Ryan Aeronautical (aerial drones) to Northrop Grumman, its mining equipment business to Astec Industries, and its lift-truck making business to Terex. It spun off its consumer oral-hygiene business as Water Pik Technologies and its remaining aerospace businesses as Teledyne Technologies. Lockheed Martin executive Thomas Corcoran became president and CEO in 1999 but abruptly resigned in late 2000. That same year the company bought Baker Hughes' tungsten carbide products unit. VC Robert Bozzone served as chairman and CEO until insider James Murdy was named CEO in 2001.

In order to cut costs, in 2001 Allegheny Technologies closed a plant in Pennsylvania, made workforce cuts, and sold its North American titanium distribution operations to management.

In 2002 the company had another round of workforce cuts (around 275 employees), mostly in its flat-rolled product unit. The following year, Allegheny Technologies formed a joint venture with Russian-based VSMPO AVISMA to make a range of commercially pure titanium products.

Allegheny Technologies purchased J&L Specialty Steel, one of its competitors, for an undisclosed price in 2004. Other buys that year included two plants in Pennsylvania and Ohio from Arcelor. Still it initiated cost-cutting efforts aimed at saving $200 million a year, announcing in 2004 cuts of more than 950 jobs at Allegheny Ludlum. The plants acquired from Arcelor lost more than 300 of their workforce.

## EXECUTIVES

**Chairman, President, and CEO:** L. Patrick (Pat) Hassey, age 62, $2,187,584 pay

**EVP, Corporate Planning and International Business Development:** Douglas A. (Doug) Kittenbrink, age 51, $530,912 pay

**EVP, Corporate Development and Chief Technical Officer:** Jack W. Shilling, age 63, $530,912 pay

**EVP, Finance and CFO:** Richard J. (Rich) Harshman, age 50, $530,912 pay

**EVP, Human Resources, Chief Legal and Compliance Officer, General Counsel, and Secretary:** Jon D. Walton, age 64, $530,912 pay

**VP, Treasurer, Controller, and Chief Accounting Officer:** Dale G. Reid, age 51

**Auditors:** Ernst & Young LLP

## LOCATIONS

**HQ:** Allegheny Technologies Incorporated
1000 Six PPG Place, Pittsburgh, PA 15222

**Phone:** 412-394-2800 **Fax:** 412-394-3034

**Web:** www.alleghenytechnologies.com

Allegheny Technologies has operations throughout the US and in China, France, Germany, Switzerland, and the UK.

### 2006 Sales

| | $ mil. | % of total |
|---|---|---|
| US | 3,765.9 | 76 |
| UK | 218.1 | 4 |
| China | 178.6 | 4 |
| Germany | 146.5 | 3 |
| France | 137.8 | 3 |
| Canada | 133.9 | 3 |
| Mexico | 51.3 | 1 |
| Japan | 41.5 | 1 |
| Other countries | 263.0 | 5 |
| **Total** | **4,936.6** | **100** |

## PRODUCTS/OPERATIONS

### 2006 Sales and Operating Income

| | Sales $ mil. | Sales % of total | Operating Income $ mil. | Operating Income % of total |
|---|---|---|---|---|
| Flat-Rolled Products | 2,697.3 | 55 | 344.3 | 33 |
| High-Performance Metals | 1,806.6 | 36 | 657.5 | 62 |
| Engineered Products | 432.7 | 9 | 56.7 | 5 |
| **Total** | **4,936.6** | **100** | **1,058.5** | **100** |

### Selected Operations and Products

Flat-Rolled Products
- Allegheny Ludlum (stainless steel, nickel-based alloys, titanium, silicon electrical steels, tool steels, high-tech alloy and titanium plate)
- Allegheny Rodney (stainless steel strip)
- Shanghai STAL Precision Stainless Steel Company Ltd. (60%, precision-rolled strip stainless steel, with Baosteel Group)
- Uniti LLC (50%, industrial titanium maker, owned jointly with the Russian metals maker VSMPO-AVISMA)

High-Performance Metals
- Allvac (nickel-based alloys and superalloys, cobalt-based alloys and superalloys, titanium and titanium-based alloys, specialty steel)
- Allvac Ltd. (UK) (nickel-based alloys and superalloys, cobalt-based alloys and superalloys, specialty steel)
- Wah Chang/Oremet (zirconium, zirconium chemicals, hafnium, niobium, tantalum, titanium and titanium-based alloys)

Engineered Products
- Casting Service (large gray iron castings, large ductile iron castings)
- Metalworking Products (cutting tools and tungsten carbide products)
- Portland Forge (carbon forgings, alloy steel forgings, nonferrous forgings)
- Rome Metals (processor of titanium, zirconium, nickel alloy, and other specialty metals)

## COMPETITORS

A. M. Castle
AK Steel
Carpenter Technology
Eramet
Kennametal
Metallurg
Nippon Steel
Nucor
Olympic Steel
Ryerson
Special Metals
Timken
Titanium Metals
United States Steel
WHX

## HISTORICAL FINANCIALS

Company Type: Public

### Income Statement

FYE: December 31

| | REVENUE ($ mil.) | NET INCOME ($ mil.) | NET PROFIT MARGIN | EMPLOYEES |
|---|---|---|---|---|
| **12/06** | 4,937 | 572 | 11.6% | 9,500 |
| **12/05** | 3,540 | 360 | 10.2% | 9,300 |
| **12/04** | 2,733 | 20 | 0.7% | 9,000 |
| **12/03** | 1,937 | (315) | — | 8,800 |
| **12/02** | 1,908 | (66) | — | 9,650 |
| **Annual Growth** | 26.8% | — | — | (0.4%) |

### 2006 Year-End Financials

Debt ratio: 35.5%
Return on equity: 49.9%
Cash ($ mil.): 502
Current ratio: 3.08
Long-term debt ($ mil.): 530
No. of shares (mil.): 101
Dividends
Yield: 0.5%
Payout: 7.7%
Market value ($ mil.): 9,177

### Stock History

NYSE: ATI

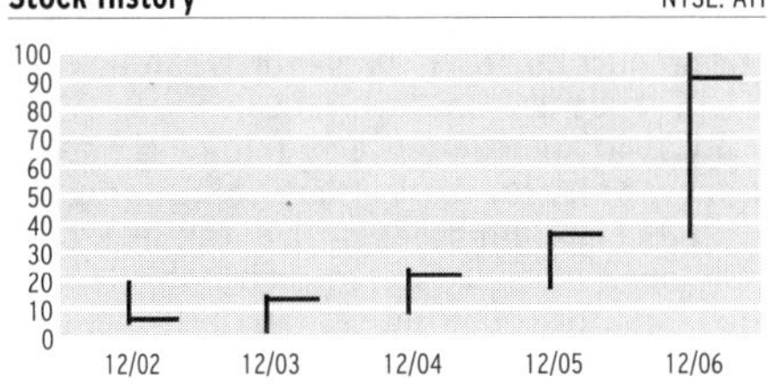

| | STOCK PRICE ($) FY Close | P/E High | P/E Low | PER SHARE ($) Earnings | PER SHARE ($) Dividends | PER SHARE ($) Book Value |
|---|---|---|---|---|---|---|
| **12/06** | 90.68 | 18 | 6 | 5.59 | 0.43 | 14.75 |
| **12/05** | 36.08 | 10 | 5 | 3.57 | 0.28 | 8.15 |
| **12/04** | 21.67 | 107 | 39 | 0.22 | 0.24 | 4.45 |
| **12/03** | 13.22 | — | — | (3.89) | 0.24 | 2.17 |
| **12/02** | 6.23 | — | — | (0.82) | 0.66 | 5.57 |
| **Annual Growth** | 95.3% | — | — | — | (10.2%) | 27.6% |

# Allergan, Inc.

Don't let the name fool you, Allergan can't help you with that runny nose. Instead, the company is a leading maker of eye care and skin care products; it also produces best-selling pharmaceutical Botox. Botox was originally used to treat muscle spasms (as well as eye spasms and misalignment) but has found a more popular application: diminishing facial wrinkles. Allergan's eye care products include medications for cataracts, glaucoma, and pink eye, as well as eye and contact lens moisturizers. The company's skin care products include treatments for acne and psoriasis. Allergan's Inamed subsidiary sells implants used in breast augmentation and weight-loss surgery; other products include dermatological gels.

Allergan is focusing on acquiring and developing new niche pharmaceuticals, as well as new uses for its existing ones. The company is eyeing other Botox uses, including treatments for migraine, lower back pain, and excessive sweating.

Allergan is also looking to develop new drugs to expand its market share and replace older products nearing patent expiration. In addition to expanding existing product lines, the company is also researching vitamin A derivatives (retinoids) for possible diabetes, cancer, and bone disease treatments.

The company began adding surgical products to its product line in 2006 with the acquisition of implant maker Inamed for $3.2 billion. Inamed, which operates as a subsidiary of the Allergan Medical division, is the maker of the Lap-Band treatment for obesity; it also sells silicon breast implants. In 2007 Allergan spent $97 million on obesity implant maker EndoArt.

Customers Cardinal Healthcare and McKesson each account for 13% of sales. The company does more than two thirds of its business in the US.

## HISTORY

In 1950 Gavin Herbert set up a small ophthalmic business above one of his drugstores in Los Angeles. Chemist Stanley Bly invented the company's first product, antihistamine eye drops called Allergan. The company adopted the name of the eye drops and expanded the business and the product range. Herbert's son Gavin Jr., then a USC student, helped with the business.

By 1960 Allergan was a $1 million company; it moved into the contact lens solution market with its Liquifilm product that year. In 1964 it developed its first foreign distributorship, in Iraq, and the following year it started its first foreign subsidiary, in Canada. International expansion and limited competition for hard contact lens care products sustained sales growth around 20% throughout the 1960s.

Allergan went public in 1971. During the 1970s the company became Bausch & Lomb's contractual supplier of Hydrocare lens solution and enzymatic cleaner for soft contact lenses. By 1975 Allergan had about a third of the hard contact lens care market. When Gavin Sr. died in 1978, Gavin Jr. succeeded him as president and CEO and also became chairman. By 1979 revenues topped $62 million.

SmithKline bought Allergan in 1980 just as the soft contact lens market boomed. In 1984 SmithKline acquired International Hydron, the #2 soft contact lens maker behind Bausch & Lomb; International Hydron became part of Allergan in 1987.

The next year the company acquired the rights to a botulinum toxin product called Oculinum, which would later evolve into Botox.

In 1989 SmithKline merged with Beecham and spun off Allergan.

By the early 1990s the contact lens and lens care markets had begun to mature, leading to a company restructuring and a new focus on specialty pharmaceuticals. In 1992 Allergan sold its North and South American contact lens businesses; the rest of its contact lens businesses were sold in 1993.

The company boosted its presence in the intraocular lens market with the 1994 purchase of Ioptex Research. Also in 1994 Allergan and joint venture partner Ligand Pharmaceuticals made their enterprise an independently operating company, Allergan Ligand Retinoid Therapeutics (ALRT). The next year Allergan recalled about 400,000 bottles of contact lens solution because of potential eye irritation.

In 1995 Allergan acquired cataract surgery equipment maker Optical Micro Systems and the contact lens care business of Pilkington Barnes Hind. That year the government probed the company for exporting the botulism toxin in Botox — it feared the product's use in biological weapons — but did not press charges. The company's 1995 income was hurt by a $50 million contribution to ALRT; its 1996 income was the result of a $70 million write-off for restructuring. In 1996 it was discovered that Allergan's Botox could be used to lessen facial wrinkles.

In 1997 Allergan received approval for a handful of new products, including its multifocus eye lens for cataract patients; acne and psoriasis treatment Tazorac; and glaucoma treatment Alphagan. That year Allergan and Ligand acquired the assets of ALRT and formed subsidiary Allergan Specialty Therapeutics to research and develop new drugs. The unit was spun off in 1998, but Allergan bought it back again in 2001.

In 1998 the company restructured, cutting jobs and closing about half of its manufacturing plants. In 2000 Botox was approved by the FDA to treat cervical dystonia.

In 2003, Allergan bought ophthalmic drug company Oculex Pharmaceuticals, which makes the Posurdex implanted drug delivery device, and Bardeen Sciences, which had a complimentary drug pipeline.

Subsidiary Advanced Medical Optics was spun off in 2004.

## EXECUTIVES

**Chairman and CEO:** David E. I. Pyott, age 53, $1,233,769 pay
**Vice Chairman:** Herbert W. Boyer, age 70
**President:** F. Michael (Mike) Ball, age 52, $593,613 pay
**EVP, Finance and Business Development and CFO:** Jeffrey L. Edwards, age 46, $432,262 pay
**EVP, Chief Administration Officer, General Counsel, and Secretary:** Douglas S. Ingram, age 46, $453,141 pay
**EVP, Global Technical Operations:** Raymond (Ray) Diradoorian, age 49
**EVP, Research and Development:** Scott M. Whitcup, age 47, $470,714 pay
**VP; President, Allergan Medical:** Robert E. Grant, age 36
**VP and Corporate Controller:** James F. Barlow, age 48
**Investor Relations:** Jim Hindman
**Investor Relations:** Joann Bradley
**Media Contact:** Heather Katt
**Media Contact:** Caroline Van Hove
**Auditors:** Ernst & Young LLP

## LOCATIONS

**HQ:** Allergan, Inc.
2525 Dupont Dr., Irvine, CA 92612
**Phone:** 714-246-4500 **Fax:** 714-246-4971
**Web:** www.allergan.com

Allergan has facilities in Australia, Brazil, Canada, France, Germany, Hong Kong, Ireland, Italy, Spain, the UK, and the US.

### 2006 Sales

| | % of total |
|---|---|
| US | 67 |
| Europe | 18 |
| Latin America | 6 |
| Asia/Pacific | 5 |
| Other | 4 |
| **Total** | **100** |

## PRODUCTS/OPERATIONS

### 2006 Sales

| | % of total |
|---|---|
| Specialty pharmaceuticals | |
| Eye care | 51 |
| Botox/Neuromodulator | 33 |
| Skin care products | 4 |
| Medical devices | |
| Breast aesthetics | 6 |
| Obesity intervention | 5 |
| Facial aesthetics | 1 |
| **Total** | **100** |

### Selected Products

Eye Care
- Acular (allergic conjunctivitis)
- Alphagan (glaucoma)
- Combigan (glaucoma, ocular hypertension)
- Elestat (allergic conjunctivitis)
- Exocin (ophthalmic anti-infective)
- Lumigan (glaucoma)
- Ocuflox (ophthalmic anti-infective)
- Oflox (ophthalmic anti-infective)
- Restatis (chronic dry eye disease)
- Zymar (bacterial conjunctivitis)

Skin Care
- Avage (skin wrinkles or discoloration)
- Azelex (acne treatment)
- Finacea (rosacea)
- M.D. Forte (line of alpha hydroxy acid products)
- Tazorac (treatment for acne and psoriasis)

Other
- Botox (neuromuscular disorder treatment)
- Botox Cosmetic (wrinkle reduction)
- Pred Forte (topical steroid)

## COMPETITORS

Alcon
Bausch & Lomb
Bristol-Myers Squibb
CIBA Vision
Connetics
Cooper Companies
Dermik Laboratories
Elan
GlaxoSmithKline
Hoffmann-La Roche
Johnson & Johnson
L'Oréal
Medicis Pharmaceutical
Mentor Corporation
Merck
Nestlé
Novartis
NutraMax
Pfizer
Sanofi-Aventis
Schering-Plough
Thermage

## HISTORICAL FINANCIALS

Company Type: Public

### Income Statement

FYE: December 31

| | REVENUE ($ mil.) | NET INCOME ($ mil.) | NET PROFIT MARGIN | EMPLOYEES |
|---|---|---|---|---|
| **12/06** | 3,063 | (127) | — | 6,772 |
| **12/05** | 2,319 | 404 | 17.4% | 5,055 |
| **12/04** | 2,046 | 377 | 18.4% | 5,030 |
| **12/03** | 1,771 | (53) | — | 4,930 |
| **12/02** | 1,425 | 75 | 5.3% | 4,900 |
| **Annual Growth** | 21.1% | — | — | 8.4% |

### 2006 Year-End Financials

Debt ratio: 51.1%
Return on equity: —
Cash ($ mil.): 1,369
Current ratio: 3.24
Long-term debt ($ mil.): 1,606
No. of shares (mil.): 152
Dividends
Yield: 0.3%
Payout: —
Market value ($ mil.): 18,233

### Stock History

NYSE: AGN

| | STOCK PRICE ($) FY Close | P/E High | P/E Low | PER SHARE ($) Earnings | Dividends | Book Value |
|---|---|---|---|---|---|---|
| **12/06** | 119.74 | — | — | (0.87) | 0.40 | 20.64 |
| **12/05** | 107.96 | 37 | 23 | 3.01 | 0.40 | 11.80 |
| **12/04** | 81.07 | 33 | 24 | 2.82 | 0.36 | 8.49 |
| **12/03** | 76.81 | — | — | (0.40) | 0.36 | 5.52 |
| **12/02** | 57.62 | 129 | 86 | 0.57 | 0.36 | 6.24 |
| **Annual Growth** | 20.1% | — | — | — | 2.7% | 34.9% |

# Alliance One International

Alliance One International keeps one eye on the world's tobacco farmers and the other eye on the cigarette makers. The company is a leading global leaf-tobacco merchant, behind slightly larger rival Universal Corporation. Alliance One buys leaf tobacco directly from growers in more than 45 countries. It also processes flue-cured, burley, and oriental tobaccos and sells them to large, multi-national cigarette and cigar manufacturers, such as Altria Group, in some 90 countries. Alliance One was formed through the mid-2005 merger of tobacco processor DIMON and Standard Commercial.

Altria and Japan Tobacco, two of Alliance One's largest customers, accounted for nearly 35% and 20%, respectively, of the company's 2007 revenue.

To provide its customers with a less-expensive leaf tobacco, Alliance One has expanded internationally. (Prices in the US are artificially supported by the government, which has driven away foreign buyers.)

Like Universal Corporation, Alliance One has also seen its revenue hurt by the latest trends in tobacco purchasing. While demand for tobacco in the US drops with the decrease in the number of smokers, more cigarette companies are choosing to buy their tobacco directly from farmers or from merchants overseas rather than through domestic auctions.

Alliance One (then DIMON) joined other major cigarette manufacturers in settling a class-action lawsuit from tobacco farmers who alleged the company and others conspired to keep tobacco prices artificially low. The firm made no admission of guilt but agreed to pay $6 million as its share of the $200 million settlement.

In 2007 Brian Harker, chairman, resigned. CEO Robert Harrison was named to replace him.

## HISTORY

DIMON was formed with the 1995 merger of Dibrell Brothers and Monk-Austin, two of the US's leading leaf-tobacco dealers. Founded in 1873 by Alphonso and Richard Dibrell, Dibrell Brothers bought and processed tobacco in the South and sold it in North America, expanding overseas during the 1920s. Early sales were for traditional uses such as chewing tobacco and cigars, and the company began doing business with large US cigarette makers in the early 1930s.

Publicly traded by the end of WWII, Dibrell Brothers diversified in the 1960s and 1970s, adding makers of ice-cream freezers (Richmond Cedar Works) and wooden lamps (Dunning Industries) and a chain of steakhouses (Kentucky Rib-Eye) but exited those businesses by 1990. Throughout the 1970s Dibrell Brothers established operations in Latin America, the Far East, India, and Italy. It moved into Zimbabwe in 1980 and the next year acquired B.V. Tabak Export & Import Compagnie, a Dutch tobacco firm with holdings in Brazil, the Dominican Republic, West Germany, and Zimbabwe.

In another diversification effort, Dibrell Brothers acquired 54% of Florimex Worldwide in 1987 (buying the rest during the next three years). The flower distributor helped boost sales in 1988. In the 1990s the firm's tobacco fortunes picked up with the growing demand for American-blend tobacco from countries in areas such as Eastern Europe, which previously only had access to high-tar cigarettes.

In 1995 Dibrell Brothers reached an agreement to combine with Monk-Austin, the product of a 1990 merger between tobacco firms A.C. Monk and the Austin Company. Founded by A. C. Monk in 1907, A.C. Monk & Company had interests in North Carolina tobacco plants. Subsequent members of the Monk family expanded its operations. It acquired rival Austin Company in 1990 and went public two years later. In 1993 Monk-Austin acquired tobacco trader T.S. Ragsdale; beefed up its operations in Brazil, Malawi, and Zimbabwe; and began building a tobacco processing plant in China. The company won a contract from R.J. Reynolds Tobacco in 1994 to supply all the domestic leaf tobacco that Reynolds requires.

Upon completion of the 1995 merger of Dibrell Brothers and Monk-Austin, Dibrell Brothers CEO Claude Owen became CEO of the newly formed company, DIMON Inc. Also that year the company acquired tobacco operations in Bulgaria, Greece, Italy, and Turkey and reached an agreement to buy and process leaf tobacco for Lorillard Tobacco. DIMON recorded a $30 million loss for the year, largely because of restructuring costs.

The company acquired #4 tobacco merchant Intabex Holdings Worldwide in 1997 for about $246 million. That year the firm extended its relationship with R.J. Reynolds, agreeing to process all of its tobacco. In 1998 DIMON sold Florimex to U.S.A. Floral Products for $90 million, in part to finance debt from the purchase of Intabex. Sales were slowed that year and in 1999 by a worldwide glut of leaf tobacco.

In 1999 DIMON settled a lawsuit it had filed against Intabex's owners and management for allegedly misrepresenting its value; the purchase price was reduced by $50 million. In 2000 the company acquired Greece-based facility operator Austro-Hellenique to expand its operations in that country.

DIMON's sales decreased somewhat in 2001 as the company transitioned to direct contract buying (as opposed to buying tobacco at auction). In 2005 DIMON and Standard Commercial merged and became Alliance One International.

## EXECUTIVES

**Chairman, President, and CEO:** Robert E. (Pete) Harrison, age 52
**EVP and CFO:** James A. (Jim) Cooley, age 55, $283,390 pay
**SVP and CIO:** William D. Pappas, age 53
**SVP, Chief Legal Officer, and Secretary:** Henry C. Babb, age 61
**SVP Human Resources:** Michael K. McDaniel, age 56
**VP and Controller:** Thomas G. Reynolds
**VP and Treasurer:** Joel L. Thomas
**VP Tax:** Gregory T. Bryant
**VP Compensation and Benefits:** Laura D. Jones
**VP International Risk:** Dennis A. Paren
**VP and CTO:** Tracey Purvis
**VP Corporate Audit Services:** B. Holt Ward
**Assistant Treasurer:** B. Lynne Finney
**Assistant General Counsel and Assistant Secretary:** William L. O'Quinn Jr.
**Assistant Controller:** Hampton R. Poole Jr.
**Auditors:** Deloitte & Touche LLP

## LOCATIONS

**HQ:** Alliance One International, Inc.
8001 Aerial Center Pkwy., Morrisville, NC 27560
**Phone:** 919-379-4300 **Fax:** 919-379-4346
**Web:** www.aointl.com

### 2007 Sales

| | $ mil. | % of total |
|---|---|---|
| Belgium | 357.4 | 18 |
| US | 340.8 | 17 |
| Germany | 169.4 | 9 |
| Netherlands | 150.5 | 8 |
| Other | 961.0 | 48 |
| **Total** | **1,979.1** | **100** |

## PRODUCTS/OPERATIONS

### Selected Subsidiaries

Alliance One Brasil Exportadora de Tabacos Ltda.
DIMON Hellas Tobacco S.A.
DIMON International Kyrgyzstan
DIMON Leaf (Thailand) Ltd.
Intabex Netherlands BV
Leaf Trading Company Ltd.
Standard Commercial Tobacco Company (UK) Ltd.
Werkhof GmbH

## COMPETITORS

Altadis
British American Tobacco
Japan Tobacco
Universal Corporation

## HISTORICAL FINANCIALS

Company Type: Public

### Income Statement

FYE: March 31

| | REVENUE ($ mil.) | NET INCOME ($ mil.) | NET PROFIT MARGIN | EMPLOYEES |
|---|---|---|---|---|
| **3/07** | 1,979 | (22) | — | 4,700 |
| **3/06** | 2,113 | (448) | — | 5,400 |
| **3/05** | 1,311 | 13 | 1.0% | 4,200 |
| **3/04*** | 817 | (33) | — | 4,100 |
| **6/03** | 1,272 | 28 | 2.2% | 3,700 |
| **Annual Growth** | 11.7% | — | — | 6.2% |

*Fiscal year change

### 2007 Year-End Financials

Debt ratio: 322.2%
Return on equity: —
Cash ($ mil.): 80
Current ratio: 1.89
Long-term debt ($ mil.): 727
No. of shares (mil.): 96
Dividends
Yield: —
Payout: —
Market value ($ mil.): 890

### Stock History

NYSE: AOI

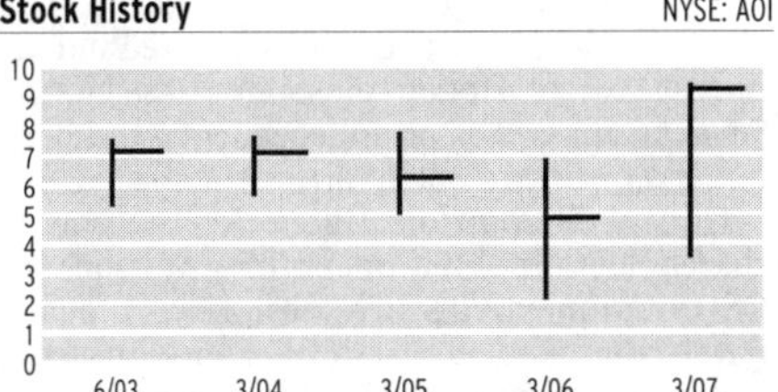

| | STOCK PRICE ($) FY Close | P/E High | P/E Low | PER SHARE ($) Earnings | Dividends | Book Value |
|---|---|---|---|---|---|---|
| **3/07** | 9.23 | — | — | (0.25) | — | 2.34 |
| **3/06** | 4.86 | — | — | (5.51) | 0.10 | 2.26 |
| **3/05** | 6.25 | 27 | 17 | 0.29 | — | 9.13 |
| **3/04*** | 7.10 | — | — | (0.73) | — | 9.19 |
| **6/03** | 7.16 | 12 | 9 | 0.62 | — | 10.16 |
| **Annual Growth** | 6.6% | — | — | — | — | (30.7%) |

*Fiscal year change

# Alliant Techsystems

You wouldn't want to hold a candle to Alliant Techsystems (ATK), maker of ammunition, smart bombs, and rocket propulsion systems. A leader in the production of solid propulsion rocket motors, ATK builds motors for space launch vehicles such as the Trident II and the Delta II. ATK is also one of the top suppliers of ammunition — from small-caliber rounds to tank ammunition — to the US and its allies. Additional lethal offerings include anti-tank mines, aircraft weapons systems, and high-tech weapons components. The US government and its prime contractors account for nearly 80% of sales.

In the wake of a bevy of acquisitions, ATK has realigned its business operations — again. The company's operations are now aligned along three business groups: Ammunition Systems (military and commercial ammunition); Mission Systems (advanced weapons, space systems and sensors, propulsion and control systems, tactical systems, aircraft sensor integration services); and Launch Systems (solid rocket motor systems, strategic missiles, missile defense interceptors)

ATK got another acquisition in its crosshairs in 2007 when it purchased Swales Aerospace, a provider of satellite components and small spacecraft. Swales' customers include NASA and the US DoD, as well as commercial satellite customers. The addition of Swales has also bolstered ATK's engineering capability.

## HISTORY

Alliant Techsystems (ATK) was formed in 1990 when Honeywell spun off its defense-related businesses to shareholders. Honeywell's roots in the defense business go back to 1941, when it was known as Honeywell-Minnesota. A maker of consumer electronics products such as switches, buttons, and appliances, Honeywell joined the war effort and began producing tank periscopes, turbo engine regulators, automatic ammunition firing control devices, and automatic bomb-release systems.

After WWII Honeywell-Minnesota found that the Cold War provided a reliable and profitable income stream for defense contractors. By 1964 the company had focused on electronics systems. Provisions for the Vietnam War boosted sales, but the fall of Saigon led to downsizing.

When the Iron Curtain fell in the late 1980s, Honeywell's defense operations misfired and ran up huge losses. Honeywell sought to sell its defense businesses as an independent subsidiary, but was unable to obtain an acceptable bid.

Honeywell spun off Alliant Techsystems to shareholders in 1990 under Toby Warson, the CEO of Honeywell's UK subsidiary. A former naval commander, Warson began with about 8,300 employees and lots of bureaucratic layers; he quickly cut about 800 administrative jobs.

Although the Soviet Union and its Eastern Bloc allies had collapsed, a new threat raised its head: Iraq. Cutbacks in the defense budget meant that advanced high-dollar systems were put on the back burner while cheaper alternatives, such as improved ammunition, were moved to the front. During the Gulf War, ATK's ordnance contributions included 120mm uranium-tipped anti-tank shells, 25mm shells for the Bradley Fighting Vehicle, and the 30mm bullets used by Apache helicopters and A-10 Warthog anti-tank planes.

Warson cut another 800 jobs after the Gulf War and reduced the number of management layers from 14 to seven. ATK divested its only non-munitions unit, Metrum Information Storage (data recording and storage devices), in 1992. Metrum had incurred setbacks that caused the company to write off millions of dollars. The next year ATK acquired three companies: Accudyne Corporation (electronic and mechanical assemblies, fuses), Kilgore (sold in 2001), and Ferrulmatic (metal parts). ATK expanded into additional aerospace markets and achieved vertical integration in propellant production in 1995 with the purchase of the aerospace division of Hercules Incorporated, a maker of space rocket motors, strategic and tactical weapons systems, and ordnance. In 1996 ATK withdrew from demilitarization ventures in the former Soviet republics of Belarus and Ukraine.

ATK refocused on its core operations in 1997 and jettisoned its marine systems group (torpedoes, underwater surveillance systems). The next year the company was awarded a $1 billion contract to make components for Boeing's Delta IV rockets. In 1999 chairman and CEO Dick Schwartz retired from the company and was replaced by retired Navy admiral Paul David Miller.

Miller consolidated plants, improved manufacturing processes, and bought back more than 1.3 million shares of ATK's stock in 2000. While the conventional munitions segment posted slight sales declines that year, primarily due to reduced sales of tactical tank ammunition as the US Army transitioned into the next-generation tank round, Miller's efforts led to greater company profitability. In 2001 ATK acquired Thiokol Propulsion Corp. for about $700 million. In September Alliant bought the defense unit of Safety Components International that makes metallic belt links for ammunition. In December the company added another acquisition to the mix with the purchase of the ammunitions unit of Blount International for about $250 million in stock.

In 2002 ATK announced a broad restructuring and bought a small ordnance unit from Boeing. The company restructured from two units (Aerospace and Defense) to three units (Aerospace, Precision Systems, and Ammunition) in 2003. That year Dan Murphy became CEO, with Miller remaining as chairman. (Miller retired in 2005 and Murphy assumed that role, as well.)

Acquisitions in 2004 included national security specialist Mission Research Corporation (now ATK Mission Research), and PSI Group, a maker of propellant systems and satellite parts.

In 2006 Alliant sold its lithium battery business to EnerSys for an undisclosed sum.

## EXECUTIVES

**Chairman, President and CEO:** Daniel J. (Dan) Murphy, age 58, $1,713,462 pay
**CFO and President, ATK Tactical Systems:** John L. Shroyer, age 43
**EVP, Mission Systems Group:** Blake E. Larson
**SVP, General Counsel, and Corporate Secretary:** Keith D. Ross, age 50
**SVP; President, Mission Systems Group:** John J. (Jack) Cronin, age 50
**SVP Human Resources and Administrative Services:** Paula J. Patineau, age 53
**SVP and CIO:** Karen Kirwan
**SVP Ammunition Systems Group:** Mark W. DeYoung, age 48, $584,000 pay
**SVP Launch Systems Group:** Ronald D. Dittemore, age 55, $465,500 pay (prior to title change)
**SVP Corporate Strategy and Business Development:** Mark L. Mele, age 50
**SVP Tidewater Operations:** Thomas R. Wilson, $480,000 pay (prior to title change)
**SVP Washington DC Operations:** Steven Cortese, age 45
**VP and Controller:** John S. Picek, age 51
**VP and Treasurer:** Robert J. McReavy, age 47
**VP, Treasurer and Investor Relations:** Steve Wold
**VP Corporate Development:** Michael B. Dolby, age 47
**VP Communications:** Bryce Hallowell
**Auditors:** Deloitte & Touche LLP

## LOCATIONS

**HQ:** Alliant Techsystems Inc.
5050 Lincoln Dr., Edina, MN 55436
**Phone:** 952-351-3000 **Fax:** 952-351-3025
**Web:** www.atk.com

## PRODUCTS/OPERATIONS

### 2007 Sales

| | $ mil. | % of total |
|---|---|---|
| Ammunition systems group | 1,276.2 | 36 |
| Mission systems group | 1,210.5 | 34 |
| Launch systems group | 1,078.2 | 30 |
| **Total** | **3,564.9** | **100** |

### 2007 Sales by Customer

| | % of total |
|---|---|
| US Government | |
| US Army | 29 |
| US Air Force | 17 |
| NASA | 15 |
| US Navy | 13 |
| Other | 5 |
| Commercial & foreign customers | 21 |
| **Total** | **100** |

### Selected Operations and Products

Ammunition Systems Group
- Civil ammunition and accessories
- Military ammunition and gun systems
- Propellant and energetic material

Mission Systems Group
- Aerospace systems
  - Electronic warfare and aircraft integration programs
  - High-temperature engine components
  - High-performance radomes and apertures
  - Precision engineered, low-observable structural components
- Space systems
  - Antennas
  - Optical support structures
  - Propulsion motors for expendable launch vehicles
  - Solar arrays
  - Solar panel substrates
  - Titanium propellant tanks
- Technical services
  - Contract research and development services
  - Scientific, engineering, and technical assistance
  - Specialized testing
- Weapon systems
  - Barrier systems
  - Large-caliber ammunition
  - Missile systems
  - Precision-guided munitions
  - Soldier weapon systems
  - Speed-of-light weapons

Launch Systems Group
- Cargo Space Launch Vehicles
  - Commercial and government rocket motor systems
- Conventional and Strategic Missiles
  - Solid rocket motors for Minuteman and Trident missiles
- Human space launch vehicles
  - Solid rocket motors for the Space Shuttles
- Missile defense interceptors
  - Orion rocket motor systems

## COMPETITORS

| | |
|---|---|
| Aerojet | GIAT |
| Allied Defense Group | ITT Corp. |
| BAE Systems Inc. | Kaman Aerospace |
| Boeing | Lockheed Martin |
| E'Prime Aerospace | Lockheed Martin Missiles |
| Expro Chemical Products | Northrop Grumman |
| GenCorp | Olin |
| General Dynamics | Raytheon |

## HISTORICAL FINANCIALS

Company Type: Public

### Income Statement

FYE: March 31

| | REVENUE ($ mil.) | NET INCOME ($ mil.) | NET PROFIT MARGIN | EMPLOYEES |
|---|---|---|---|---|
| **3/07** | 3,565 | 184 | 5.2% | 16,000 |
| **3/06** | 3,217 | 154 | 4.8% | 15,200 |
| **3/05** | 2,801 | 154 | 5.5% | 14,000 |
| **3/04** | 2,366 | 162 | 6.9% | 13,100 |
| **3/03** | 2,172 | 124 | 5.7% | 12,000 |
| **Annual Growth** | 13.2% | 10.3% | — | 7.5% |

### 2007 Year-End Financials

| | |
|---|---|
| Debt ratio: 260.8% | No. of shares (mil.): 33 |
| Return on equity: 31.0% | Dividends |
| Cash ($ mil.): 16 | Yield: — |
| Current ratio: 2.04 | Payout: — |
| Long-term debt ($ mil.): 1,455 | Market value ($ mil.): 2,908 |

### Stock History

NYSE: ATK

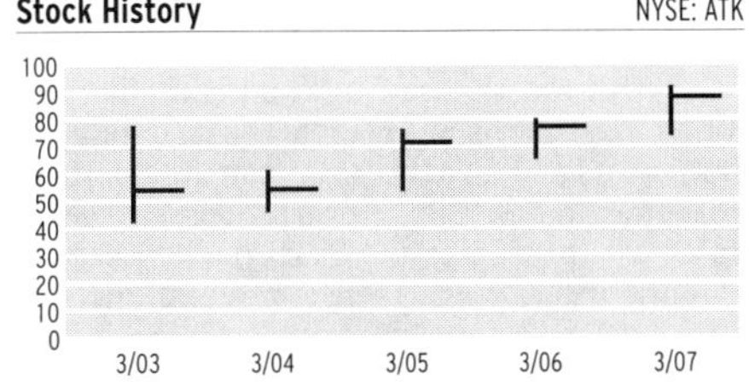


| | STOCK PRICE ($) FY Close | P/E High | P/E Low | PER SHARE ($) Earnings | Dividends | Book Value |
|---|---|---|---|---|---|---|
| **3/07** | 87.92 | 17 | 14 | 5.32 | — | 16.87 |
| **3/06** | 77.17 | 19 | 16 | 4.11 | — | 17.85 |
| **3/05** | 71.45 | 19 | 13 | 4.03 | — | 18.43 |
| **3/04** | 54.40 | 15 | 11 | 4.14 | — | 15.07 |
| **3/03** | 54.01 | 24 | 14 | 3.16 | — | 12.42 |
| **Annual Growth** | 13.0% | — | — | 13.9% | — | 8.0% |

# Allied Waste Industries

Allied Waste Industries proves every day that one person's trash is another person's treasure. The company is the US's second-largest waste-hauler, behind only Waste Management, Inc. Allied Waste picks up the garbage of about 10 million residential, commercial, and industrial customers throughout the US. Its vast collection, recycling, and landfill operations include a network of 304 collection companies, 161 transfer stations, 168 active landfills, and 57 recycling facilities in 37 states. Residential, commercial, and roll-off (dumpsters) collection accounts for about two-thirds of sales. Officers and directors control about 36% of the company.

Allied Waste has worked hard to consolidate the operations of Browning-Ferris Industries, which it acquired in 1999. After major job cuts and closings of overlapping facilities, the company focused on internal growth. Allied Waste structured its operations into four geographic areas of the US (eastern, southern, central, and western) and 12 regions in order to create smaller, more manageable segments.

By the end of 2004, however, Allied Waste had dropped its four geographic areas, reduced its regions from 12 to nine, and realigned some districts. It is also working to increase vertical integration — controlling the waste stream from collection to transfer station to landfill — in all of its markets. The company operates facilities in about 110 major markets across the US.

Although Allied Waste has been paring down operations and paying down its debt load, it could not pass up the chance to buy a Texas-based municipal and industrial landfill from American Ecology, which is focusing on hazardous and radioactive waste. Allied Waste believes its diverse asset base will help it survive the US economic downturn and maintain its position within the industry as the economy recovers.

That said, the company restructured its $7.8 billion debt with $3.425 billion in new financing in 2005 as it increased its level of capital spending. Allied Waste also restructured its operating structure in 2005, reducing its number of operating regions from nine to five. Helped by organic growth, operating income more than tripled in 2005, from $58 million in 2004 to $194 million in 2005.

## HISTORY

In 1987 entrepreneur Bruce Lessey looked around Houston at all the garbage trucks his Quick Wrench firm was servicing and saw an opportunity. He changed his company's name to Allied Waste, went public, and started buying waste companies. Two years later Allied Waste was in trouble. In stepped Roger Ramsey, cofounder of Browning-Ferris Industries (BFI), who left BFI in 1976. He was a partner in an investment company that owned part of Allied Waste. Ramsey joined the board (becoming CEO in 1989), and Lessey stepped down. Over the next seven years, the company acquired 30 waste haulers in seven states.

One of them (acquired in 1992) was R.18, an Illinois firm owned by Arizona native Thomas Van Weelden. Ramsey, the money man, and Van Weelden, a nonconformist whose entire family was in the garbage business, struck up a close partnership. Van Weelden became Allied Waste's president (and CEO in 1997), and the two moved the company to Scottsdale, Arizona, in 1993 to get away from Houston-based heavyweight (and future partner) BFI.

The two men implemented a rapid growth strategy through the loose consolidation of vertically integrated, locally managed operations. In 1996 Allied Waste bought a rich prize, Laidlaw, for $1.6 billion, which tripled the company's revenues in 1997. It sold Laidlaw's Canadian operation to pay down debt.

Allied Waste acquired 54 other operators in 1998, including Seattle-based Rabanco Cos., which gave it a foothold in the Pacific Northwest. It also paid $1.1 billion for American Disposal Services. Late that year Van Weelden succeeded Ramsey as chairman, and merger negotiations with big boy BFI got serious.

Between 1992 and the time Allied Waste made its biggest deal, it had collected more than 200 companies. In 1999 it bought its largest company yet, BFI, a $4.7 billion operation. The $9.4 billion acquisition sent Allied Waste's customer base soaring from 2.6 million to 9.9 million. At the time of its acquisition, BFI operated in 46 US states, Canada, and Puerto Rico.

Founded in 1967, BFI had been on the buyout trail for decades. During its first six years it acquired 157 waste-disposal companies and expanded overseas. In the 1980s it bought more than 500 firms and gained another 100 in the early 1990s.

All was not well at BFI, however. The company had slipped in the late 1980s, when price-fixing charges and environmental violations cost it more than $5 million and resulted in a lot of bad press. By 1998 BFI was bloated and revenues were stagnant. It sold all operations outside North America to Suez Lyonnaise, in exchange for $1 billion and a 20% stake in SITA, Europe's #1 waste company. The rest of BFI's holdings went to Allied in 1999 in a deal valued at about $9 billion.

To raise about $1.6 billion and gain regulatory clearance for the BFI acquisition, Allied in 1999 and 2000 sold a number of assets that it gained from BFI. Besides selling selected US solid-waste operations to eliminate overlap, Allied sold all of BFI's operations in Canada, its medical waste business, and its stake in SITA. In integrating BFI's operations with its own, Allied Waste cut 2,900 jobs and closed 51 facilities within a year of the BFI acquisition. Allied continued to trim excess operations in 2001 with the sale of commercial routes in Florida, Georgia, Tennessee, and Virginia.

Still cleaning up debt in 2002, Allied Waste sold its Tennessee collection and transfer operations in Knoxville and Cleveland to rival Waste Connections for $50 million. However, the next year the group paid American Ecology $10 million for an industrial landfill near Corpus Christi, Texas. In 2003 the company sold its Norfolk, Virginia, and Clarkesville, Tennessee, operations to Waste Industries USA; it acquired Waste Industries' operations in Charlotte, North Carolina; Sumter, South Carolina; Mobile, Alabama; and Biloxi, Mississippi.

By early 2004, Allied Waste had completed its $300 million in divestitures slated for 2003, which included its northern and central Florida operations, as well as some of its operations in Idaho, Virginia, and Wyoming.

In 2005 Allied Waste obtained $3.425 billion of financing to cut costs and improve its capital structure.

## EXECUTIVES

**Chairman and CEO:** John J. Zillmer, age 51, $869,125 pay
**President and COO:** Donald W. (Don) Slager, age 45, $766,875 pay
**EVP and CFO:** Peter S. Hathaway, age 50, $593,050 pay
**EVP and Chief Personnel Officer:** Edward A. Evans, age 54, $429,450 pay
**EVP General Counsel and Secretary:** Timothy R. (Tim) Donovan, age 51
**EVP Human Resources:** Ed Evans
**SVP and Treasurer:** Michael S. Burnett, age 44
**SVP Public Affairs, Communications, and Investor Relations:** James P. (Jim) Zeumer
**VP, Deputy General Counsel, and Assistant Corporate Secretary:** Jo Lynn White
**VP Financial Analysis and Planning:** John S. Quinn, age 44
**VP Tax:** Dale L. Parker, age 44
**VP and Deputy General Counsel:** Catharine D. Ellingsen
**Auditors:** PricewaterhouseCoopers LLP

## LOCATIONS

**HQ:** Allied Waste Industries, Inc.
18500 N. Allied Way, Phoenix, AZ 85054
**Phone:** 480-627-2700 **Fax:** 480-627-2701
**Web:** www.alliedwaste.com

Allied Waste Industries has operations in 128 major markets in 37 states.

### 2006 Sales

| | $ mil. | % of total |
|---|---|---|
| West | 1,351.2 | 22 |
| Northeast | 1,256.6 | 21 |
| Midwest | 1,236.4 | 20 |
| Southeast | 1,059.7 | 18 |
| Southwest | 991.6 | 17 |
| Other | 133.3 | 2 |
| **Total** | **6,028.8** | **100** |

## PRODUCTS/OPERATIONS

### 2006 Sales

| | $ mil. | % of total |
|---|---|---|
| Collection | | |
| Commercial | 1,502.0 | 25 |
| Roll-off | 1,333.3 | 22 |
| Residential | 1,205.2 | 20 |
| Recycling | 202.4 | 3 |
| Disposal | | |
| Landfill | 850.7 | 14 |
| Transfer | 424.4 | 7 |
| Recycling — Commodity | 217.5 | 4 |
| Other | 293.3 | 5 |
| **Total** | **6,028.8** | **100** |

### Selected Operations

BFI Energy Systems of Boston, Inc.
BFI Energy Systems of Plymouth, Inc.
BFI Services Group, Inc.
BFI Trans River (LP), Inc.
Browning-Ferris Industries Asia Pacific, Inc.
Browning-Ferris Industries Europe, Inc.
Consolidated Processing, Inc.

## COMPETITORS

Casella Waste Systems
IESI
Republic Services
Veolia ES Solid Waste
Waste Connections
Waste Industries USA
Waste Management

## HISTORICAL FINANCIALS

Company Type: Public

### Income Statement

FYE: December 31

| | REVENUE ($ mil.) | NET INCOME ($ mil.) | NET PROFIT MARGIN | EMPLOYEES |
|---|---|---|---|---|
| **12/06** | 6,029 | 161 | 2.7% | 24,200 |
| **12/05** | 5,735 | 204 | 3.6% | 26,000 |
| **12/04** | 5,362 | 49 | 0.9% | 26,000 |
| **12/03** | 5,248 | 129 | 2.5% | 26,000 |
| **12/02** | 5,517 | 215 | 3.9% | 29,000 |
| **Annual Growth** | 2.2% | (7.0%) | — | (4.4%) |

### 2006 Year-End Financials

Debt ratio: 221.1%
Return on equity: 5.8%
Cash ($ mil.): 94
Current ratio: 0.68
Long-term debt ($ mil.): 6,674
No. of shares (mil.): 368
Dividends
Yield: —
Payout: —
Market value ($ mil.): 4,521

### Stock History

NYSE: AW

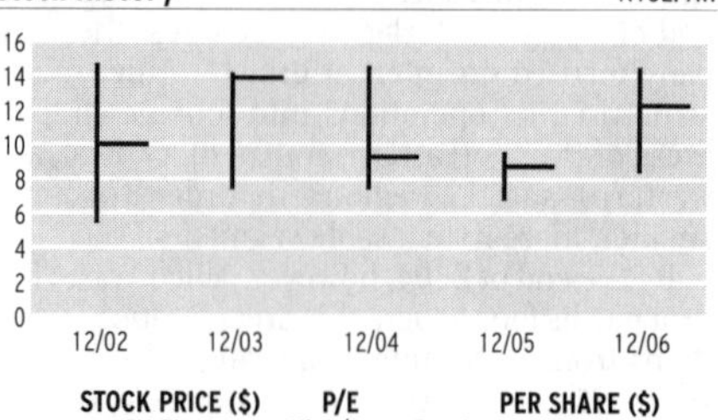


| | STOCK PRICE ($) FY Close | P/E High | P/E Low | PER SHARE ($) Earnings | PER SHARE ($) Dividends | PER SHARE ($) Book Value |
|---|---|---|---|---|---|---|
| **12/06** | 12.29 | 44 | 26 | 0.33 | — | 9.78 |
| **12/05** | 8.74 | 21 | 15 | 0.46 | — | 10.38 |
| **12/04** | 9.28 | 160 | 83 | 0.09 | — | 8.20 |
| **12/03** | 13.88 | — | — | (2.42) | — | 7.87 |
| **12/02** | 10.00 | 20 | 8 | 0.71 | — | 3.51 |
| **Annual Growth** | 5.3% | — | — | (17.4%) | — | 29.2% |

# Allstate Corporation

Ya gotta hand it to Allstate. The "good hands" company is the second-largest US personal lines insurer, behind rival State Farm. The company sells auto, homeowners, property/casualty, and life insurance products in Canada and the US. The company's life insurance subsidiaries include Allstate Life, American Heritage Life, and Lincoln Benefit Life. Allstate Financial provides life insurance and investment products, targeting affluent and middle-income consumers. Allstate Motor Club provides emergency road service, and adding to its repertoire, the company launched the nationwide Allstate Bank.

Allstate maintains a network of exclusive agencies which sell its Allstate-branded insurance products. Independent agencies sell the company's Deerbrook and Encompass-branded products as well as its Allstate lines. Consumers can also purchase some products by telephone and over the Internet. Its financial products are sold through its exclusive agencies, independent agents, banks, and broker dealers.

The company has disposed of the majority of its operations outside North America (including Allstate Investments in Japan and the direct auto business in Germany and Italy), focusing on its core markets in Canada and the US.

Streamlining its operations further, the company has rolled together all of its property/casualty operations to form Allstate Protection. Selling primarily private passenger auto and homeowners insurance, Allstate Protection accounts for some 90% of total premiums. California, Florida, New York, and Texas make up more than 40% of Allstate Protection's sales.

The 2005 hurricane season with Katrina, Rita, and Wilma combined to account for $5.67 billion in catastrophe losses for Allstate. However with the quiet 2006 season its catastrophe losses amounted to only $810 million.

To brace itself for future hurricane seasons, the company has upped its reinsurance and has stopped writing new homeowners policies for properties along the Gulf Coast, Connecticut, Delaware, and New Jersey. The company has also stopped renewing certain types of policies for coastal parts of New York and has increased its premium rates in Florida. To address the many Allstate Floridian customers whose homeowner policies won't be renewed, the company has struck an agreement with newly formed Royal Palm Insurance Company. Royal Palm will offer property policies, which will be sold through Allstate agencies.

Customers in earthquake-prone areas will have to look elsewhere for new optional earthquake coverage. Allstate no longer offers it, and is considering doing away with it from its renewable policies as well. In California the company has made changes to its homeowners underwriting requirements in order to reduce its exposure to claims for fires following earthquakes.

## HISTORY

Allstate traces its origins to a friendly game of bridge played in 1930 on a Chicago-area commuter train by Sears president Robert Wood and a friend, insurance broker Carl Odell. The insurance man suggested Sears sell auto insurance through the mail. Wood liked the idea, financed the company, and in 1931 put Odell in charge (that hand of bridge must have shown Wood that Odell was no dummy). The company was named Allstate, after one of Sears' tire brands. Allstate was born just as Sears was beginning its push into retailing, and Allstate went with it, selling insurance out of all the new Sears stores.

Growth was slow during the Depression and WWII, but the postwar boom was a gold mine for both Sears and Allstate. Suburban development made cars a necessity; 1950s prudence necessitated car insurance; and Sears made it easy to buy the insurance at their stores and, increasingly, at freestanding agencies.

In the late 1950s Allstate added home and other property/casualty insurance lines. It also went into life insurance — in-force policies zoomed from zero to $1 billion in six years, the industry's fastest growth ever.

Sears formed Allstate Enterprises in 1960 as an umbrella for all its noninsurance operations. In 1970 that firm bought its first savings and loan (S&L). The insurer continued to acquire other S&Ls and to add subsidiaries throughout the 1970s and 1980s.

This strategy dovetailed with Sears' strategy, which was to become a diversified financial services company. In 1985 Sears introduced the Discover Card through Allstate's Greenwood Trust Company. However, by the late 1980s it was obvious Sears would never be a financial services giant. Moreover, it was losing so much in retailing that by 1987 Allstate was the major contributor to corporate net income. Sears began to dismantle its financial empire in the 1990s.

Allstate also suffered from a backlash against high insurance rates. When Massachusetts instituted no-fault insurance in 1989, Allstate stopped writing new auto insurance there. Later the company had to refund $110 million to customers to settle a suit with California over rate rollbacks required by 1988's Proposition 103.

Allstate went public in 1993, when Sears sold about 20% of its stake. That year it began reducing its operations in Florida to protect itself against high losses from hurricanes. Two years later the retailer sold its remaining interest to its shareholders. Also in 1995 Allstate sold 70% of PMI, its mortgage insurance unit, to the public.

In 1996 Allstate worked to reduce its exposure to hurricane and earthquake losses. (Together, Hurricane Andrew and the Northridge quake helped account for almost $4 billion in casualty losses.) It created a Florida-only subsidiary that would buy reinsurance to protect against losses in case of another major hurricane. That year Allstate sold its Northbrook property/casualty business and Allstate Reinsurance to St. Paul and SCOR, respectively.

In 1998 Allstate sold its real estate portfolio for nearly $1 billion; chairman and CEO Jerry Choate retired and was succeeded by president and COO Edward Liddy; and Allstate opened a savings bank. In 2000 Allstate restructured and added online and telephone distributions to increase its sales and bought Provident National Assurance Co. from UNUMProvident. Reducing expenses, Allstate cut some 10% of its staff (some 4,000 jobs) that year and turned its agents into independent contractors. With its purchase of Sterling Collision Centers, Allstate entered the car repair business in 2001.

## EXECUTIVES

**Chairman:** Edward M. Liddy, age 61
**President and CEO:** Thomas J. Wilson II, age 49
**VP and CFO:** Danny L. (Dan) Hale, age 62, $732,713 pay
**VP and General Counsel:** Michael J. (Mick) McCabe, age 61
**President and CEO, Allstate Financial:** James E. (Jim) Hohmann, age 51
**President, Allstate Investments:** Eric A. Simonson, age 61, $1,206,966 pay
**President, Allstate Protection, Allstate Insurance Company:** George E. Ruebenson, age 58
**President, Deerbrook Insurance Company:** Gregory A. Meyer
**President, Encompass Insurance Company:** Cynthia Hardy Young
**SVP and CTO, Allstate Insurance Company:** Catherine S. Brune, age 53
**SVP, Allstate Property-Casualty Claim Service, Allstate Insurance Company:** Michael J. Roche, age 55
**SVP Human Resources, Allstate Insurance Company:** Joan M. Crockett, age 56
**SVP, Allstate Protection Product Distribution, Allstate Insurance Company:** Ronald D. McNeil, age 54, $1,381,014 pay
**Interim Chief Marketing Officer and SVP Corporate Relations, Allstate Insurance Company:** Joan H. Walker, age 59
**VP Corporate Relations:** Sari L. Macrie
**VP Auditing:** Kathleen Swain, age 47
**Auditors:** Deloitte & Touche LLP

## LOCATIONS

**HQ:** The Allstate Corporation
2775 Sanders Rd., Northbrook, IL 60062
**Phone:** 847-402-5000 **Fax:** 847-326-7519
**Web:** www.allstate.com

Allstate operates in Canada and the US.

## PRODUCTS/OPERATIONS

### 2006 Sales

| | $ mil. | % of total |
|---|---|---|
| Property/liability insurance premiums | 27,369 | 77 |
| Net investment income | 6,177 | 17 |
| Life & annuity premiums & contract charges | 1,964 | 5 |
| Realized capital gains & losses | 286 | 1 |
| **Total** | **35,796** | **100** |

### Selected Subsidiaries

Allstate Bank
Allstate Distributors, L.L.C.
Allstate Insurance Company
  Allstate Insurance Company of Canada
  Allstate Life Insurance Company
  Ivantage Group, LLC
    Northbrook Indemnity Company
      Deerbrook Insurance Company
      Encompass Insurance Company
Allstate International Insurance Holdings, Inc.
  Allstate Reinsurance Ltd. (Bermuda)
  Pembridge America Inc.
Allstate Non-Insurance Holdings, Inc.
American Heritage Life Investment Corporation
Kennett Capital, Inc.

## COMPETITORS

AIG
Farmers Group
GEICO
Hanover Insurance
MetLife
Nationwide
Progressive Corporation
Prudential
State Farm
Travelers Companies
USAA

## HISTORICAL FINANCIALS

Company Type: Public

### Income Statement

FYE: December 31

| | ASSETS ($ mil.) | NET INCOME ($ mil.) | INCOME AS % OF ASSETS | EMPLOYEES |
|---|---|---|---|---|
| **12/06** | 157,554 | 4,993 | 3.2% | 37,900 |
| **12/05** | 156,072 | 1,765 | 1.1% | 38,300 |
| **12/04** | 149,725 | 3,181 | 2.1% | 39,400 |
| **12/03** | 134,142 | 2,705 | 2.0% | 39,631 |
| **12/02** | 117,426 | 1,134 | 1.0% | 40,320 |
| **Annual Growth** | 7.6% | 44.9% | — | (1.5%) |

### 2006 Year-End Financials

Equity as % of assets: 13.9%
Return on assets: 3.2%
Return on equity: 23.8%
Long-term debt ($ mil.): 4,650
No. of shares (mil.): 622
Dividends
Yield: 2.2%
Payout: 17.9%
Market value ($ mil.): 40,498
Sales ($ mil.): 35,796

### Stock History

NYSE: ALL

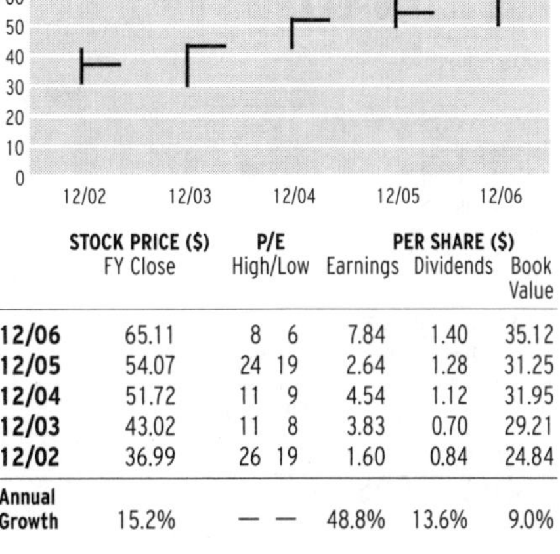


| | STOCK PRICE ($) FY Close | P/E High | P/E Low | PER SHARE ($) Earnings | Dividends | Book Value |
|---|---|---|---|---|---|---|
| **12/06** | 65.11 | 8 | 6 | 7.84 | 1.40 | 35.12 |
| **12/05** | 54.07 | 24 | 19 | 2.64 | 1.28 | 31.25 |
| **12/04** | 51.72 | 11 | 9 | 4.54 | 1.12 | 31.95 |
| **12/03** | 43.02 | 11 | 8 | 3.83 | 0.70 | 29.21 |
| **12/02** | 36.99 | 26 | 19 | 1.60 | 0.84 | 24.84 |
| **Annual Growth** | 15.2% | — | — | 48.8% | 13.6% | 9.0% |

# Altria Group

The house the Marlboro Man built, Altria Group (formerly Philip Morris Companies), is the world's largest tobacco firm. Altria operates its cigarette business through subsidiaries Philip Morris USA and Philip Morris International, which sell Marlboro — the world's best-selling cigarette brand since 1972. (Altria plans to spin off its international arm.) The firm, which controls about half of the US tobacco market, also makes and markets Parliament, Virginia Slims, and Basic cigarette brands. Altria owns some 29% of brewer SABMiller plc. The tobacco giant's long-awaited spinoff of its Kraft Foods division (Jell-O, Kool-Aid, Maxwell House) to shareholders was completed in March 2007.

Altria had been pondering spinning off Kraft since 2005. The move gives the slow-growing food maker room to breathe and separates Kraft from tobacco litigation under Altria. The company gets nearly 75% of its sales and an even bigger chunk of its profits from tobacco.

Altria plans to spin off Philip Morris International into a separate company in a bid to separate its fast-growing international business from Philip Morris USA, its declining US unit. The details of the deal will be decided at a board meeting in early 2008. Altria's CEO Louis Camilleri will take over as the new head of the international unit.

To boost its customer base abroad, Altria has been busy in recent years extending its reach into foreign markets through its Philip Morris International unit. It's vying for a profitable piece of Pakistan's rich smoking market. It inked a deal in early 2007 to acquire a majority stake in Lakson Tobacco Company, which is Pakistan's second-largest tobacco firm with a cigarette volume of nearly 30 billion units annually.

A given in an industry that peddles potentially dangerous products, Altria is in a haze over lawsuits. Altria and its Big Tobacco rivals continue to try to resolve lawsuits over smoking-related illnesses. The industry has reached settlements with US states amounting to nearly $250 billion, and a number of civil suits are pending. However, US courts can't touch revenues from international tobacco markets that bring in more than 45% of Altria's sales.

In July 2006 the Florida Supreme Court upheld a lower court's ruling that had overturned a $145 billion award for punitive damages against Big Tobacco defendants, among them Altria's Philip Morris. While the ruling upheld findings, such as smoking cigarettes causes diseases and that nicotine is addictive, it signaled to some investors that the threat of tobacco-related class action lawsuits was lessening.

In 2007 Altria received more good court news when the federal Supreme Court threw out a nearly $80 million award against the company stemming from a case where an Oregon wife sued after her husband, a smoker, died. The court said the defendants should not be punished for those who aren't named in a lawsuit.

## HISTORY

Philip Morris opened his London tobacco store in 1847 and by 1854 was making his own cigarettes. Morris died in 1873, and his heirs sold the firm to William Thomson just before the turn of the century. Thomson introduced his company's cigarettes to the US in 1902. American investors bought the rights to leading Philip Morris brands in 1919, and in 1925 the new company, Philip Morris & Co., introduced Marlboro, which targeted women smokers and produced modest sales.

When the firm's larger competitors raised their prices in 1930, Philip Morris Companies countered by introducing inexpensive cigarettes that caught on with Depression-weary consumers. By 1936 it was the fourth-biggest cigarette maker.

The firm acquired Benson & Hedges in 1954. It signed ad agency Leo Burnett, which promptly initiated the Marlboro Man campaign. Under Joseph Cullman (who became president in 1957), Philip Morris experienced tremendous growth overseas. After dipping to sixth place among US tobacco companies in 1960, it rebounded at home, thanks to Marlboro's growing popularity among men (Marlboro became the #1 cigarette brand in the world in 1972).

In 1970 Philip Morris bought the nation's seventh-largest brewer, Miller Brewing, and with aggressive marketing it vaulted to #2 among US beer makers by 1980. To protect itself against a shrinking US tobacco market, in 1985 Philip Morris paid $5.6 billion for General Foods (Kool-Aid, Post, Stove Top). In 1988 it bought Kraft (Miracle Whip, Velveeta). The next year Philip Morris joined Kraft with General Foods.

In 1994 Australian Geoffrey Bible became CEO. By late 1998 the company and its rivals had settled tobacco litigation with most states, agreeing to pay about $250 billion over 25 years to receive protection from further state suits.

In 1999 Philip Morris bought three cigarette brands (L&M, Chesterfield, and Lark) from the Brooke Group. The US government filed a massive lawsuit against Big Tobacco, and Philip Morris admitted that smoking increases the risk of getting cancer and other illnesses.

In 2000 Philip Morris vowed to appeal after a state court awarded $74 billion in punitive damages to Florida smokers. The court later ruled that Philip Morris, Lorillard, and the Liggett Group would pay at least $709 million in the case regardless of the outcome, but would not have to pay damages until after the appeals are resolved.

In December 2000 Philip Morris completed its purchase of Nabisco Holdings for $18.9 billion. In June 2001 Philip Morris spun off Kraft Foods in what was the second-largest IPO in US history; it retained an 84% stake in the company and 97% of the voting rights.

In April 2002 CFO Louis Camilleri succeeded Bible as CEO; in September Camilleri became chairman upon Bible's retirement. In July 2002, Philip Morris sold Miller Brewing to South African Breweries for $5.6 billion ($3.6 billion in SAB stock and the assumption of $2 billion in Miller debt) in July 2002.

In the ongoing saga of tobacco-related litigation, Philip Morris said it would appeal an October 2002 verdict by a California jury that ordered the company to pay $28 billion in punitive damages, the most ever in an individual tobacco liability lawsuit (later reduced to $28 million). In January 2003 Philip Morris changed its name to Altria Group in an effort to distance itself from its tobacco litigation. In March 2003 Philip Morris USA lost an Illinois lawsuit, which claimed the company's use of the word "light" was misleading and violated Illinois consumer fraud laws. The judge ordered Philip Morris USA to pay damages of $10 billion and post a $12 billion bond. The Illinois Supreme Court has lowered the bond to $7 billion and agreed to hear Philip Morris USA's appeal of the original verdict.

In 2005 Altria purchased a $4.8 billion stake in Indonesia's third-largest tobacco firm, PT Hanjaya Mandala Sampoerna, which makes kreteks, or clove cigarettes. Also in 2005 the company formed a long-term alliance with China National Tobacco Corp.

In mid-2006 Altria unseated Roger Deromedi from Kraft's top spot and appointed Irene Rosenfeld, former chairman and CEO of Frito-Lay, to head the company. The executive realignment was part of Altria's plan to spin off Kraft.

In March 2007 Altria completed the spinoff of Kraft Foods to Altria shareholders.

## EXECUTIVES

**Chairman and CEO:** Louis C. Camilleri, age 52, $1,750,000 pay
**SVP and CFO:** Dinyar S. Devitre, age 60, $769,615 pay
**SVP and Chief Compliance Officer:** David I. Greenberg, age 52
**SVP and General Counsel:** Charles R. Wall, age 61, $1,010,808 pay
**SVP, Corporate Affairs:** Steven C. Parrish, age 56, $969,615 pay
**SVP, Mergers and Acquisitions:** Nancy J. De Lisi, age 56
**VP and Associate General Counsel:** Stephen Krigbaum
**VP and Associate General Counsel:** William Ohlemeyer
**VP, Associate General Counsel, and Corporate Secretary:** G. Penn Holsenbeck, age 60
**VP and Controller:** Joseph A. Tiesi, age 48
**VP and Treasurer:** Amy J. Engel, age 50
**VP, Government Affairs Policy and Outreach, Altria Corporate Services:** A. Shuanise Washington
**CEO, Kraft Foods:** Irene B. Rosenfeld, age 53
**Chairman and CEO, Philip Morris USA:** Michael E. Szymanczyk, age 58, $1,152,000 pay
**President and CEO, Philip Morris International:** André Calantzopoulos, age 50
**Manager, Media Affairs, Altria Corporate Services:** Lisa Gonzalez
**President and CEO, Philip Morris Capital Corporation:** John Mulligan
**Auditors:** PricewaterhouseCoopers LLP

## LOCATIONS

**HQ:** Altria Group, Inc.
120 Park Ave., New York, NY 10017
**Phone:** 917-663-4000 **Fax:** 917-663-2167
**Web:** www.altria.com

## PRODUCTS/OPERATIONS

### 2006 Sales

| | % of total |
|---|---|
| International tobacco | 47 |
| Domestic tobacco | 26 |
| North American food | 21 |
| International food | 5 |
| Financial services | 1 |
| **Total** | **100** |

### Selected Subsidiaries

Philip Morris Capital Corp. (100% owned)
Philip Morris International Inc. (100% owned)
Philip Morris USA Inc. (100% owned)

## COMPETITORS

3M
Altadis
Anheuser-Busch
British American Tobacco
Coca-Cola
Grupo Modelo
Heineken
InBev
Japan Tobacco
Loews
Molson Coors
PepsiCo
Reynolds American

## HISTORICAL FINANCIALS

Company Type: Public

### Income Statement

FYE: December 31

| | REVENUE ($ mil.) | NET INCOME ($ mil.) | NET PROFIT MARGIN | EMPLOYEES |
|---|---|---|---|---|
| **12/06** | 101,407 | 12,022 | 11.9% | 175,000 |
| **12/05** | 97,854 | 10,435 | 10.7% | 199,000 |
| **12/04** | 89,610 | 9,416 | 10.5% | 156,000 |
| **12/03** | 81,832 | 9,204 | 11.2% | 165,000 |
| **12/02** | 80,408 | 11,102 | 13.8% | 166,000 |
| **Annual Growth** | 6.0% | 2.0% | — | 1.3% |

### 2006 Year-End Financials

Debt ratio: 36.6%
Return on equity: 31.9%
Cash ($ mil.): 5,020
Current ratio: 1.03
Long-term debt ($ mil.): 14,498
No. of shares (mil.): 2,097
Dividends
Yield: 5.1%
Payout: 58.1%
Market value ($ mil.): 137,587

### Stock History

NYSE: MO

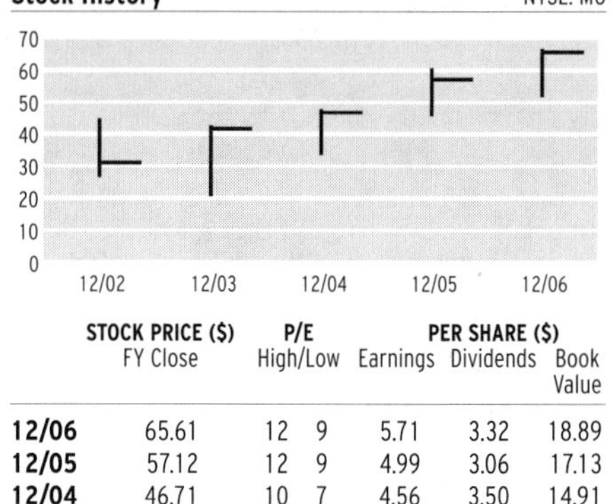

| | STOCK PRICE ($) FY Close | P/E High | P/E Low | PER SHARE ($) Earnings | Dividends | Book Value |
|---|---|---|---|---|---|---|
| **12/06** | 65.61 | 12 | 9 | 5.71 | 3.32 | 18.89 |
| **12/05** | 57.12 | 12 | 9 | 4.99 | 3.06 | 17.13 |
| **12/04** | 46.71 | 10 | 7 | 4.56 | 3.50 | 14.91 |
| **12/03** | 41.60 | 9 | 5 | 4.52 | 2.64 | 12.31 |
| **12/02** | 30.99 | 8 | 5 | 5.21 | 0.64 | 9.55 |
| **Annual Growth** | 20.6% | — | — | 2.3% | 50.9% | 18.6% |

# Amazon.com

What started as Earth's biggest bookstore has rapidly become Earth's biggest anything store. Expansion has propelled Amazon.com in innumerable directions. The firm's main Web site offers millions of books, CDs, DVDs, and videos (which still account for the majority, 65%, of the firm's sales), not to mention auto parts, toys, tools, electronics, home furnishings, apparel, health and beauty goods, prescription drugs, groceries, and services including film processing. Long a model for Internet companies that put market share ahead of profits, Amazon.com also made acquisitions funded by meteoric market capitalization and is now focused on profits. Founder Jeff Bezos owns more than 24% of the firm.

Although it still goes toe-to-toe with competitor Barnes & Noble and others in the book business, Amazon.com has competition on many fronts. The company debuted clothing sales in 2002, and it continues to invest in that area, most recently its 2006 purchase of Shopbop.com. Hundreds of retailers, including The Gap, Nordstrom, and Lands' End, own and deliver the merchandise, but customers are able to purchase it all in one place.

The company has linked its virtual stores to the bricks-and-mortar players, such as its operation of rival bookseller Borders' Web presence. It also relaunched CDNOW's music retailing Web site; Amazon handles all Web site operations including inventory management, customer service, and shipping. Additional syndicated store programs include Virgin Group's virginmega.com and the UK's HMV Group's Waterstones Web site.

In October 2006 IBM filed a pair of patent infringement lawsuits alleging that Amazon.com has been violating at least five of its patents — including technologies that govern how the online retailer handles product recommendations and displays advertising — for about four years. IBM, the world's leading patent holder, is seeking unspecified damages.

In 2004 Amazon.com launched A9.com, a start-up company aimed at developing commercial search engines for both Amazon.com and other e-commerce Web sites. It also purchased Joyo.com, which operates the top online retail Web sites in China for books, videos, music, and a variety of other items. The deal was valued at about $75 million. The site has become Amazon's fastest-growing business and was renamed Joyo Amazon in 2007.

Amazon.com began testing the online grocery waters in 2007. Its pilot program in a neighborhood in Seattle provides next-day delivery of fresh groceries.

Amazon.com struck a deal with TiVo in early 2007, announcing they would partner to bring Web content to the television through Amazon's Unbox digital video download service. Unbox debuted in 2006; the TiVo service launched in spring 2007. Also in 2007 Amazon.com announced it will begin selling digital music free of copyright restrictions that can be played on any digital music player, including Apple's iPod.

Returning to its books roots, the company agreed to buy audio book publisher Brilliance Audio in 2007. Amazon.com plans to use the purchase to make the audio format available to more authors and publishers.

## HISTORY

Jeff Bezos was researching the Internet in the early 1990s for hedge fund D.E. Shaw. He realized that book sales would be a perfect fit with e-commerce because book distributors already kept meticulous electronic lists. Bezos, who as a teen had dreamed of entrepreneurship in outer space, took the idea to Shaw. The company passed on the idea, but Bezos ran with it, trekking cross country to Seattle (close to a facility owned by major book distributor Ingram) and typing up a business plan along the way.

Bezos founded Amazon.com in 1994. After months of preparation, he launched a Web site in July 1995 (Douglas Hofstadter's *Fluid Concepts and Creative Analogies* was its first sale); it had sales of $20,000 a week by September. Bezos and his team kept working with the site, pioneering features that now seem mundane, such as one-click shopping, customer reviews, and e-mail order verification.

Amazon.com went public in 1997. Moves to cement the Amazon.com brand included becoming the sole book retailer on AOL's Web site and Netscape's commercial channel.

In 1998 the company launched its online music and video stores, and it began to sell toys and electronics. Amazon.com also expanded its European reach with the purchases of online booksellers in the UK and Germany, and it acquired the Internet Movie Database.

By midyear Amazon.com had attracted so much attention that its market capitalization equaled the combined values of profitable bricks-and-mortar rivals Barnes & Noble and Borders Group, even though their combined sales were far greater than the upstart's. Late that year Amazon.com formed a promotional link with Hoover's, publisher of this profile.

After raising $1.25 billion in a 1999 bond offering, Amazon.com began a spending spree, buying all or part of several dot-coms. However, some have since been sold (HomeGrocer.com) and others have gone out of business or bankrupt — Pets.com, living.com (furniture).

Amazon.com began conducting online auctions in early 1999 and partnered with venerable auction house Sotheby's. In 2000 Amazon.com inked a 10-year deal with Toysrus.com to set up a co-branded toy and video game store. (The partnership came to a bitter end in 2006 after Toys "R" Us sued Amazon.com when it began selling toys from other companies.) Also that year Amazon.com added foreign-language sites for France and Japan.

In 2001 Amazon.com cut 15% of its workforce as part of a restructuring plan that also forced a $150 million charge. As part of a deal to expand their marketing partnership, AOL invested $100 million in Amazon.com in 2001.

The next year Amazon.com introduced clothing sales, featuring hundreds of retailers including names such as The Gap, Nordstrom, and Lands' End. The company received accreditation from ICANN (the Internet Corporation for Assigned Names and Numbers) as an Internet domain name registrar, becoming one of about 160 entities permitted to register Internet addresses.

Amazon.com expanded into China in 2004 with the purchase of Joyo.com. The company acquired shopping site Shopbop.com in 2006, boosting its apparel offerings, and in May 2007 it acquired London-based digital camera review site Dpreview.com for an undisclosed amount.

## EXECUTIVES

**Chairman, President, and CEO:** Jeffrey P. (Jeff) Bezos, age 43, $81,840 pay
**SVP and CFO:** Thomas J. (Tom) Szkutak, age 46, $600,000 pay
**SVP, General Counsel, and Secretary:** L. Michelle Wilson, age 44
**SVP and CIO:** Richard L. (Rick) Dalzell, age 49
**SVP, Worldwide Hardlines Retail:** Kal Raman, age 37, $508,333 pay
**SVP, North America Retail:** Jeffrey A. (Jeff) Wilke, age 40, $155,000 pay
**SVP, Ecommerce Platform:** H. Brian Valentine, age 47
**SVP, Web Services:** Andrew Jassy, age 39
**SVP, Business Development:** Jeffrey Blackburn, age 37
**SVP, Worldwide Digital Media:** Steven Kessel, age 41
**SVP, Worldwide Operations:** Marc Onetto, age 56
**VP, Amazon Services Europe:** Eric Broussard
**VP, Global Public Policy:** Paul Misener
**VP, Investor Relations:** Tim Halladay
**VP, Software Development:** Neil Roseman
**VP, Services:** G. Charles (Cayce) Roy III, age 41
**CEO, A9.com:** David L. Tennenhouse
**General Manager, Amazon.com in Theaters and IMDb.com:** Satbir Khanuja
**Director of North American Music, DVD, and Computer and Video Games:** Greg Hart
**Senior Manager, Amazon.com in Theaters and IMDb.com:** Bob Hogan
**Business Development Manager:** Toni Reid-Thomelin
**Auditors:** Ernst & Young LLP

## LOCATIONS

**HQ:** Amazon.com, Inc.
1200 12th Ave. South, Ste. 1200, Seattle, WA 98144
**Phone:** 206-266-1000
**Web:** www.amazon.com

### 2006 Sales

| | $ mil. | % of total |
|---|---|---|
| North America | 5,869 | 55 |
| Other countries | 4,842 | 45 |
| **Total** | **10,711** | **100** |

## PRODUCTS/OPERATIONS

### 2006 Sales

| | $ mil. | % of total |
|---|---|---|
| Media | 7,067 | 66 |
| Electronics & other general merchandise | 3,361 | 31 |
| Other | 283 | 3 |
| **Total** | **10,711** | **100** |

### Selected Partners

Fidelity Investments
Shutterfly
Target.com
Tire Rack
Weight Watchers

### Selected Departments

Apparel
Auctions
- Art and antiques
- Books
- Cars and transportation
- Coins and stamps
- Collectibles
- Comics, cards, and sci-fi
- Computers and software
- Electronics and photography
- Jewelry, gems, and watches
- Movies and video
- Music
- Sports
- Toys and games

Books
Cameras and photo items
- Accessories (photo albums, frames, scrapbooks)
- Binoculars
- Cameras
- Film
- Film processing
- Projectors
- Telescopes and microscopes

Cars
Computer and video games
DVDs
Electronics
- Cabling
- Calculators
- Computers
- Handheld items
- Printers
- Scanners

Gourmet food
Health and beauty items
- Baby and toddler items
- Bath and spa products
- Personal care products (shampoos, deodorants, oral care products, soaps and bodywash)
- Prescription drugs
- Vitamins and supplements
- Weight management (scales, heart rate monitor, weight loss supplements)

Kitchen and houseware items

Music
- Audiocassettes
- CDs
- Downloads
- Music accessories
- Musical and multimedia editing software
- Musical instruments
- Portable audio players
- Records

Non-perishable grocery items
Outdoor living items
- Grills
- Lawn care products
- Patio items

Outlet (discount merchandise)
Seasonal
- Birthday items
- Holiday items
- University curricular and extracurricular products

Software
Sporting goods
Tools and hardware
Vacuums
Toys and games
Videos
Wireless phones

## COMPETITORS

Autobytel
AutoNation
AutoZone
Barnes & Noble
barnesandnoble.com
Best Buy
Blockbuster
Bluefly
Books-A-Million
Borders
Buy.com
Circuit City
Columbia House
eBay
GSI Commerce
Hastings Entertainment
Hollywood Media
Home Depot
HSN
Indigo Books & Music
Lowe's
Netflix
Overstock.com
PPR
RedEnvelope
Sears
Tower Records
Wal-Mart
Yahoo!

## HISTORICAL FINANCIALS

Company Type: Public

**Income Statement** FYE: December 31

| | REVENUE ($ mil.) | NET INCOME ($ mil.) | NET PROFIT MARGIN | EMPLOYEES |
|---|---|---|---|---|
| **12/06** | 10,711 | 190 | 1.8% | 13,900 |
| **12/05** | 8,490 | 359 | 4.2% | 12,000 |
| **12/04** | 6,921 | 589 | 8.5% | 9,000 |
| **12/03** | 5,264 | 35 | 0.7% | 7,800 |
| **12/02** | 3,933 | (149) | — | 7,500 |
| **Annual Growth** | 28.5% | — | — | 16.7% |

**2006 Year-End Financials**

Debt ratio: 294.0%
Return on equity: 56.1%
Cash ($ mil.): 2,019
Current ratio: 1.33
Long-term debt ($ mil.): 1,267
No. of shares (mil.): 414
Dividends
Yield: —
Payout: —
Market value ($ mil.): 16,336

**Stock History** NASDAQ (GS): AMZN

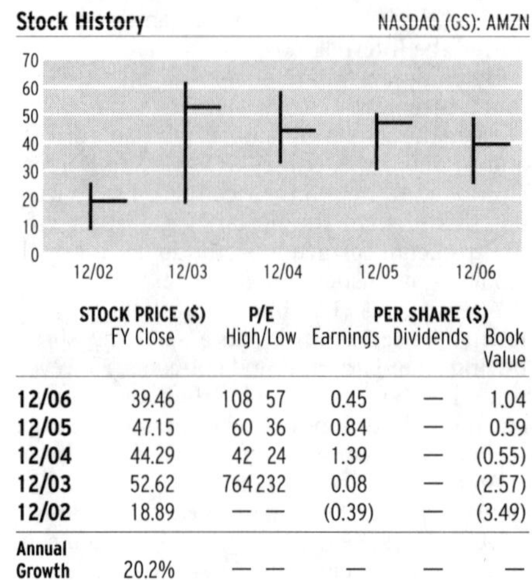


| | STOCK PRICE ($) FY Close | P/E High/Low | PER SHARE ($) Earnings | Dividends | Book Value |
|---|---|---|---|---|---|
| **12/06** | 39.46 | 108 57 | 0.45 | — | 1.04 |
| **12/05** | 47.15 | 60 36 | 0.84 | — | 0.59 |
| **12/04** | 44.29 | 42 24 | 1.39 | — | (0.55) |
| **12/03** | 52.62 | 764 232 | 0.08 | — | (2.57) |
| **12/02** | 18.89 | — — | (0.39) | — | (3.49) |
| **Annual Growth** | 20.2% | — — | — | — | — |

# Ambac Financial Group

Ambac Financial Group gives an A+ to those school bonds. Ambac Assurance, the holding company's primary subsidiary, sells financial guarantee insurance and other credit enhancement products for municipal bonds, and asset- and mortgage-backed securities in the US market. In the international market the company insures high-quality infrastructure, structured finance, and utility finance transactions. Ambac's financial services segment, through Ambac Financial Services, offers investment contracts, interest rate swaps, and investment management primarily to states and municipal authorities in connection with their bond financing.

As the US market matures, Ambac Financial is looking overseas for growth. Spurred by an increase in public/private partnerships in the UK and Western Europe, the company has broadened its presence there. Most recently, Ambac Assurance UK opened a Milan office in 2005. While the Japanese market is still slow, an alliance with Sompo Japan will give Ambac access to it as it expands.

International markets accounted for 25% of Ambac's 2005 net premiums earned.

FMR owns 12.5% and J.P. Morgan Chase owns about 10% of Ambac Financial.

## HISTORY

Mortgage Guaranty Insurance Corporation (MGIC) in 1971 founded American Municipal Bond Assurance Corporation (Ambac Indemnity) in Milwaukee. That year Ambac wrote the very first municipal bond insurance policy for a bond to fund a medical building and a sewage treatment facility in Juneau, Alaska. New York City's 1975 moratorium on debt payments helped make the new product more attractive. The company wrote the first insurance policies for mutual funds (1977) and secondary market municipal bonds (1983). In 1981 Ambac moved to New York; four years later it became a Citibank subsidiary. It went public in 1991.

In 1995 Ambac and rival MBIA allied to offer bond insurance overseas. Two years later the company formed a UK subsidiary to serve Europe. In recognition of the growing market, the joint venture was amended in 2000 to provide for individual operations by the two partners in Europe, though they continue to reinsure each other there and to work jointly in Japan. Ambac went on a buying spree in 1996 and 1997, buying the investment advisory and broker dealer operations of Cadre and Construction Loan Insurance (renamed Connie Lee Holdings), a guarantor of college bonds and hospital infrastructure bonds.

In 1998 as Ambac lost share in the US municipal bond market because it declined to cut premiums, the company began concentrating on asset-backed securities and international bonds. Two years later, Ambac entered the Japanese market through a joint venture with Yasuda Fire & Marine.

The company sold its Cadre Financial Services and Ambac Securities divisions in 2004.

International expansion served Ambac well: It went on to become one of the world's top guarantors by 2005.

## EXECUTIVES

**Chairman:** Phillip B. Lassiter, age 63, $250,000 pay
**President, CEO, and Director:** Robert J. Genader, age 60, $1,475,000 pay
**EVP, ABS, MBS, Conduits, Global Utilities, Emerging Markets, Structured Insurance and Leasing & Asset Finance:** John W. Uhlein III, age 50, $918,750 pay
**SVP and CFO:** Sean T. Leonard, age 42, $824,231 pay
**SVP, Chief Administrative Officer and Employment Counsel:** Gregg L. Bienstock, age 42
**SVP and General Counsel:** Kevin J. Doyle, age 50
**Senior Managing Director, Capital Markets and Structured Credit:** Thomas J. Gandolfo, age 46
**Senior Managing Director; Chairman, Ambac Assurance UK:** Douglas C. Renfield-Miller, age 53, $808,750 pay
**Senior Managing Director, Portfolio and Market Risk Management:** David W. Wallis, age 47, $993,957 pay
**Senior Managing Director and Chief Risk Officer:** William T. McKinnon, age 57, $895,000 pay
**Senior Managing Director Public Finance:** Robert G. Shoback, age 47
**Managing Director and CIO:** Kenneth S. Plotzker
**Managing Director and Corporate Secretary:** Anne Gill Kelly
**Managing Director and Director of Tax:** Wes Kirchhoff
**Managing Director and Corporate Controller:** Robert B. Eisman
**Managing Director, Investor Relations:** Peter R. Poillon
**Managing Director, Legal:** David N. Abramowitz
**Managing Director, Marketing:** Susan Oehrig
**Managing Director and Chief Investment Officer:** Rodney D. Kumasaki
**Treasurer:** David Trick
**Auditors:** KPMG LLP

## LOCATIONS

**HQ:** Ambac Financial Group, Inc.
1 State Street Plaza, New York, NY 10004
**Phone:** 212-668-0340 **Fax:** 212-509-9190
**Web:** www.ambac.com

Ambac Financial Group has offices in Australia, Italy, Japan, the UK, and the US.

## PRODUCTS/OPERATIONS

**Selected Subsidiaries**

Ambac Assurance Corporation (bond insurance)
Ambac Assurance UK Limited
Ambac Capital Corporation (investment agreements)
Ambac Capital Funding, Inc. (investment agreements)
Ambac Capital Services, LLC
Ambac Credit Products, LLC (structured credit derivatives)
Ambac Financial Services, LLC
Ambac Investments, Inc.

## COMPETITORS

Alleghany
Assured Guaranty
Everest Re
FGIC
Financial Security Assurance
Kingsway
MBIA
MGIC Investment
Radian Asset Assurance
Radian Group
XL Capital

## HISTORICAL FINANCIALS

Company Type: Public

**Income Statement** FYE: December 31

| | ASSETS ($ mil.) | NET INCOME ($ mil.) | INCOME AS % OF ASSETS | EMPLOYEES |
|---|---|---|---|---|
| **12/06** | 20,268 | 876 | 4.3% | 359 |
| **12/05** | 19,725 | 751 | 3.8% | 354 |
| **12/04** | 18,585 | 725 | 3.9% | 360 |
| **12/03** | 16,747 | 619 | 3.7% | 407 |
| **12/02** | 15,356 | 433 | 2.8% | 391 |
| **Annual Growth** | 7.2% | 19.3% | — | (2.1%) |

**2006 Year-End Financials**

Equity as % of assets: 30.5%
Return on assets: 4.4%
Return on equity: 15.2%
Long-term debt ($ mil.): 1,659
No. of shares (mil.): 109
Dividends
Yield: 0.9%
Payout: 10.3%
Market value ($ mil.): 9,726
Sales ($ mil.): 1,834

**Stock History** NYSE: ABK

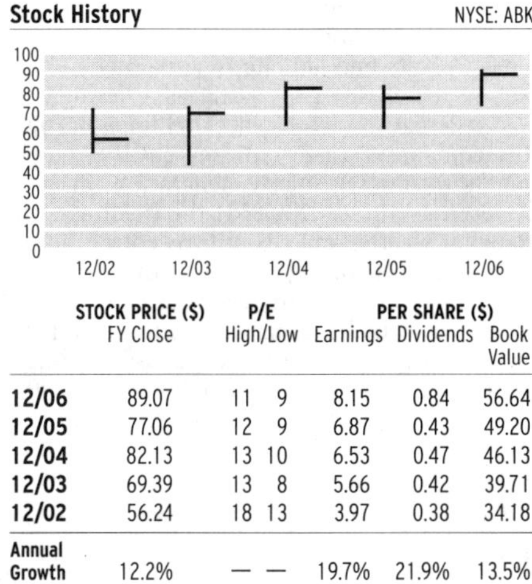


| | STOCK PRICE ($) FY Close | P/E High/Low | | PER SHARE ($) Earnings | Dividends | Book Value |
|---|---|---|---|---|---|---|
| **12/06** | 89.07 | 11 | 9 | 8.15 | 0.84 | 56.64 |
| **12/05** | 77.06 | 12 | 9 | 6.87 | 0.43 | 49.20 |
| **12/04** | 82.13 | 13 | 10 | 6.53 | 0.47 | 46.13 |
| **12/03** | 69.39 | 13 | 8 | 5.66 | 0.42 | 39.71 |
| **12/02** | 56.24 | 18 | 13 | 3.97 | 0.38 | 34.18 |
| **Annual Growth** | 12.2% | — | — | 19.7% | 21.9% | 13.5% |

# AMERCO

U-Haul, u-work, u-strain, u-hurt . . . u-sure you don't want to spend the extra money for movers? If not, there's AMERCO, whose principal operation, U-Haul International, rents trucks, trailers, and vehicle tow devices and sells packing supplies to do-it-yourself movers through some 14,000 independent dealers and about 1,450 company-owned centers in the US and Canada. In addition, U-Haul is a leading operator of self-storage facilities. It maintains more than 1,000 storage locations in the US and Canada, consisting of some 378,000 rooms with about 33 million sq. ft. of space. Members of the founding Shoen family, led by chairman and president Edward "Joe" Shoen, own about 40% of AMERCO.

The U-Haul rental fleet consists of about 93,000 trucks, 80,700 trailers, and 33,500 tow devices. To help customers get on the road, many locations sell and install towing systems and hitches, and the company's eMove Web site connects customers with independent moving and self-storage companies that provide services such as packing, loading, and unloading. In addition, nearly 1,000 U-Haul centers sell propane.

U-Haul accounts for about 90% of AMERCO's sales. Other businesses include two insurance companies: Republic Western provides claims management services and offers property and casualty insurance to U-Haul customers, and Oxford Life reinsures and originates single and group life insurance, disability coverage, and annuities. AMERCO's SAC Holding unit owns self-storage facilities that are managed by U-Haul.

Already the leader in the do-it-yourself moving industry, AMERCO hopes to grow by expanding U-Haul's equipment rental fleet and self-storage facilities and by adding dealers to the company's network.

## HISTORY

Leonard Samuel (L.S.) Shoen earned his nickname, "Slick," as a poor kid trying to make a buck during the Depression. In 1945, as a Navy veteran, he started U-Haul International in Ridgefield, Washington, to serve long-distance do-it-yourself movers who could not return a truck to its origin. Shoen bought used equipment and hit the road, convincing gas station owners to act as agents.

Shoen and his first wife, Anna Mary, who died in 1957, had six children. In 1958 Shoen remarried and with his second wife, Suzanne, had five children. Shoen bestowed stock on all his offspring but neglected to keep a controlling interest. In the 1960s Shoen brought his sons into the company.

U-Haul moved to Phoenix in 1967. Two years later it bought Oxford Life Insurance Co. Shoen formed AMERCO in 1971 as U-Haul's parent. The oil crunch of the 1970s caused U-Haul's network to shrink as gas stations closed, so the company opened its own agencies. New competitors entered the market, and the company's share of business dropped to below 50%. Shoen took AMERCO into debt to diversify into general consumer rentals. The company also established real estate and insurance subsidiaries.

Shoen's second wife divorced him after the out-of-wedlock birth of his 12th child in 1977. His brief marriage to the mother ended in divorce, and he remarried again (and, later, yet again). Meanwhile, Shoen tapped his eldest son Sam for help in pursuing the diversification strategy. In 1979 sons Edward "Joe" and Mark left the company in dispute. Sam became president.

In 1986 Joe and Mark gained the support of enough siblings to constitute a voting majority and ousted their father and brother. L. S. and Sam almost regained control two years later but were outmaneuvered by Joe, who as chairman issued enough stock to a few loyal employees to shift the balance. Then the outside faction sued the people who had been directors in 1988 over issuance of the stock.

Joe refocused on the self-moving business and began upgrading the fleet, reducing the average age of the equipment from 11 to 5 years. In 1993 AMERCO preferred stock began trading on the NYSE, and the next year its common stock was listed on Nasdaq.

The lawsuit moved glacially through the courts. In 1994 the 1988 directors were found to have wrongfully excluded dissenting family members from the board. An initial award of $1.47 billion was later reduced to $462 million, due from the 1988 directors individually. However, they declared bankruptcy, and AMERCO indemnified them for the award. So in 1996 the company issued new stock and sold (and leased back) tens of thousands of vehicles and trailers to fulfill the judgment. In return, the dissenting family faction (including founder L. S.) gave up their 48% stake in AMERCO.

In 1997 AMERCO held its first stockholders' meeting since 1993. The next year Joe lost an appeal to overturn a ruling that he had acted with malice in dealing with family members in the 1988 stock transaction; he was ordered to pay $7 million in punitive damages to relatives, exclusive of the $462 million previously awarded.

In 1999 founder L.S. died at age 83 in a one-car accident believed to be suicide. In 2001 the company debuted its online storage reservation system. AMERCO denied reports published in August 2002 by the Financial Times that the Securities and Exchange Commission was investigating AMERCO's accounts and probing why it dismissed its auditor of 24 years, PricewaterhouseCoopers. The company failed to make a $100 million debt principal payment in October 2002.

AMERCO announced in March 2003 that it had obtained a four-year $865.8 million credit facility. The following month the company filed suit against PricewaterhouseCoopers, alleging negligence and fraud in its audit work. AMERCO disclosed in May that federal securities regulators were investigating its financial statements. (The investigation ended in 2006 with no action being taken against the company.)

Amid its financial difficulties, the company filed for Chapter 11 bankruptcy protection in June 2003. Nine months later, in March 2004, AMERCO emerged from bankruptcy.

## EXECUTIVES

**Chairman and President:** Edward J. (Joe) Shoen, age 58, $755,034 pay
**EVP U-Haul Field Operations:** Ronald C. Frank, age 66
**Principal Accounting Officer:** Jason A. Berg, age 34
**VP U-Haul Business Consultants and Director:** James P. Shoen, age 47, $615,962 pay
**President, Amerco Real Estate:** Carlos Vizcarra, age 60
**President, Oxford Life Insurance:** Mark A. Haydukovich, age 51
**President, Republic Western Insurance:** Richard M. Amoroso, age 48
**VP, U-Haul Business Consultants:** Mark V. Shoen, age 56, $623,077 pay
**Treasurer; Assistant Treasurer, U-Haul:** Gary B. Horton, age 63, $761,878 pay
**Assistant Treasurer:** Rocky D. Wardrip, age 49
**General Counsel:** Laurence J. (Larry) De Respino, age 46
**Controller, U-Haul:** Robert T. Peterson, age 56
**President, U-Haul Company of Northwestern Ohio:** Ali Gillentine
**EVP, U-Haul Field Operations:** Robert R. Wilson, age 56
**President, U-Haul Company North Philadelphia:** Joe Thomas
**President, U-Haul Company of San Fernando Valley:** Jim George
**President, U-Haul Company of Dallas:** Scott Graydon
**Auditors:** BDO Seidman, LLP

## LOCATIONS

**HQ:** AMERCO
1325 Airmotive Way, Ste. 100, Reno, NV 89502
**Phone:** 775-688-6300 **Fax:** 775-688-6338
**Web:** www.amerco.com

**2007 Sales**

| | $ mil. | % of total |
|---|---|---|
| US | 1,994.5 | 96 |
| Canada | 91.1 | 4 |
| **Total** | **2,085.6** | **100** |

## PRODUCTS/OPERATIONS

**2007 Sales**

| | $ mil. | % of total |
|---|---|---|
| Moving & storage | 1,875.9 | 89 |
| Life insurance | 148.8 | 7 |
| SAC Holdings | 46.6 | 2 |
| Property & casualty insurance | 38.5 | 2 |
| Adjustments | (24.2) | — |
| **Total** | **2,085.6** | **100** |

**Selected Operating Units**

Oxford Life Insurance Company
Republic Western Insurance Company (property and casualty insurance)
SAC Holding II Corporation (owns self-storage properties managed by U-Haul)
U-Haul International, Inc. (self-moving truck and trailer rental, self-storage unit rental, sales of packing supplies)

## COMPETITORS

AIG
Allstate
Atlas World Group
Budget Rent A Car
Extra Space
The Hartford
MetLife
Penske Truck Leasing
Prudential
Public Storage
SIRVA
Sovran
UniGroup

## HISTORICAL FINANCIALS

Company Type: Public

**Income Statement** FYE: March 31

| | REVENUE ($ mil.) | NET INCOME ($ mil.) | NET PROFIT MARGIN | EMPLOYEES |
|---|---|---|---|---|
| **3/07** | 2,086 | 91 | 4.3% | 18,000 |
| **3/06** | 2,107 | 121 | 5.8% | 17,500 |
| **3/05** | 2,008 | 89 | 4.5% | 18,300 |
| **3/04** | 2,168 | (3) | — | 17,230 |
| **Annual Growth** | (1.3%) | — | — | 1.5% |

**2007 Year-End Financials**

Debt ratio: —
Return on equity: 12.8%
Cash ($ mil.): 77
Current ratio: 0.14
Long-term debt ($ mil.): —
No. of shares (mil.): 21
Dividends
Yield: —
Payout: —
Market value ($ mil.): 1,438

**Stock History** NASDAQ (GS): UHAL

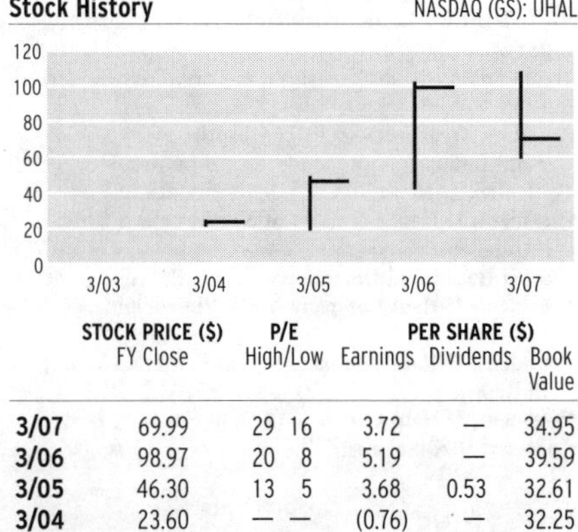


| | STOCK PRICE ($) FY Close | P/E High | P/E Low | PER SHARE ($) Earnings | Dividends | Book Value |
|---|---|---|---|---|---|---|
| **3/07** | 69.99 | 29 | 16 | 3.72 | — | 34.95 |
| **3/06** | 98.97 | 20 | 8 | 5.19 | — | 39.59 |
| **3/05** | 46.30 | 13 | 5 | 3.68 | 0.53 | 32.61 |
| **3/04** | 23.60 | — | — | (0.76) | — | 32.25 |
| **Annual Growth** | 43.7% | — | — | — | — | 2.7% |

# Ameren Corporation

Ameren might be considered amorous when it comes to courting and acquiring midwestern utility companies. The holding company, which has been focused on growing its core energy operations, distributes electricity to 2.4 million customers and natural gas to more than 960,000 in Missouri and Illinois through its utility subsidiaries AmerenUE, AmerenIP, AmerenCIPS, and AmerenCILCO.

Ameren has a generating capacity of more than 16,200 MW (primarily coal-fired), most of which is controlled by utility AmerenUE and nonregulated subsidiary AmerenEnergy Resources. Other nonutility operations include energy marketing and trading and management and consulting services.

In addition to operating power plants, AmerenEnergy Resources procures natural gas for its affiliated companies, builds new power plants, and provides long-term energy supply contracts. Another subsidiary, AmerenEnergy, markets and trades electricity to wholesale and retail customers and provides risk management and other energy-related services.

To comply with FERC requirements, Ameren has transferred control of AmerenCIPS and AmerenUE's transmission assets to the Midwest Independent Transmission System Operator (Midwest ISO) through an agreement with independent company GridAmerica. AmerenCILCO and AmerenIP were already members of the Midwest ISO.

## HISTORY

More than 30 St. Louis companies had built a chaotic grid of generators and power lines throughout the city by 1900. Two years later many of them merged into the Union Company, which attracted national notice when it lit the St. Louis World's Fair in the first broad demonstration of electricity's power. In 1913 the company, by then named Union Electric (UE), began buying electricity from an Iowa dam 150 miles away — the greatest distance power had ever been transmitted in such quantity.

UE pushed into rural Missouri and began buying and building fossil-fuel plants. Despite a slowdown during the Depression, UE built Bagnell Dam on Missouri's Osage River in the early 1930s to gather power for a hydroelectric plant. At the onset of WWII, construction began on new plants with larger generators and lower production costs; however, demand for electricity lagged. In the late 1940s UE compensated by joining a "power pool," a system of utilities with interconnected transmission lines that shared electricity.

Growth in the 1950s came from acquisitions, including Missouri Power & Light (1950) and Missouri Edison (1954). In the 1960s and 1970s, UE built five new plants, including the Labadie plant (2,300 MW), one of the largest coal-fired plants in the US.

UE began producing nuclear energy in 1984 at its Callaway nuke. High costs and the expenses of a scrapped second plant caused UE to battle the Missouri Public Service Commission throughout the 1980s for rate increases.

Charles Mueller became president in 1993 and CEO one year later. He oversaw continued staff reductions and cost cutting through the 1990s in an increasingly competitive market. In 1997 UE expanded into Illinois through its purchase of CIPSCO, which owned utility Central Illinois Public Service Company (CIPS).

CIPS began as a Mattoon, Illinois, streetcar company in the early 1900s. The firm bought Mattoon's electric power plant in 1904 and began growing its power business, buying small electric companies in the 1920s and 1930s. CIPS built five generating units in the 1940s and 1950s and became part-owner (along with UE) of Electric Energy Inc., which built a power plant on the Ohio River. The company bought Illinois Electric and Gas Company in the 1960s and the state's Gas Utilities in the 1980s. To prepare for competition under deregulation, CIPS created holding company CIPSCO in the 1990s to diversify.

UE's purchase of CIPSCO expanded its geographic scope, and the new company was named Ameren in 1997 to reflect its American energy focus. The next year the company committed to adding generating capacity through several natural gas-fired combustion turbines. It joined nine other utilities to form the Midwest Independent System Operator to manage their transmission needs.

In 1999 Ameren bought a 245-mile railroad line between St. Louis and Kansas City to help the area's economic development. Looking for new opportunities in deregulated energy markets, the company purchased Data & Metering Specialties.

In 2000 Ameren created subsidiary AmerenEnergy Generating to operate its nonregulated power plants and affiliate AmerenEnergy Marketing to sell the generating facilities' power. When deregulation took effect in Illinois in 2002, the company transferred AmerenCIPS' power plants to AmerenEnergy Generating. In 2003 Ameren acquired CILCORP, the holding company for electric and gas utility Central Illinois Light (now operating as AmerenCILCO), from independent power producer AES in a $1.4 billion deal. To further expand its utility operations, Ameren acquired power and gas utility Illinois Power from Dynegy in a $2.3 billion deal in 2004. As part of the agreement, Ameren gained Dynegy's 20% stake in power generator Electric Energy, in which Ameren already held a 60% stake.

## EXECUTIVES

**Chairman, President, and CEO:** Gary L. Rainwater, age 60, $900,000 pay
**EVP and COO; President and CEO, Ameren UE; SVP, UE, CIPS, Ameren Services, CILCORP, CILCO, and IP:** Thomas R. Voss, age 59, $440,000 pay (prior to title change)
**EVP and CFO; President, CEO and CFO, CIPS, UE, Ameren Services, AEG, CILCORP, CILCO, and IP:** Warner L. Baxter, age 45, $500,000 pay (prior to title change)
**SVP, General Counsel, and Secretary:** Steven R. Sullivan, age 46, $380,000 pay
**SVP and Chief Nuclear Officer, UE:** Charles D. Naslund, age 54, $335,000 pay
**SVP, CILCO, CIPS, CILCORP, Genco, IP, and UE:** Daniel F. Cole, age 53
**SVP, Generation; President and CEO, AmerenEnergy Resources:** R. Alan Kelley, age 54
**SVP and Chief Human Resources Officer, Ameren Services:** Donna K. Martin, age 59
**VP and Treasurer; VP and Treasurer, Ameren Services, CIPS, CILCORP, CILCO, UE, and Resources:** Jerre E. Birdsong, age 52
**VP and Controller; VP and Controller, UE, CIPS, Genco, AERG, AFS, Medina Valley, CILCORP, CILCO, Ameren Services, and IP:** Martin J. Lyons, age 40
**VP, Corporate Planning, Ameren Services; VP, AmerenCIPS:** Craig D. Nelson, age 51
**VP, Gas Operations and Support, Ameren Services:** Jim L. Davis, age 57

**VP, Energy Delivery Distribution Services, Ameren Services and AmerenUE:** Ronald C. Zdellar, age 60
**VP, Energy Delivery Technical Services, Ameren Services:** David J. Schepers, age 51
**VP, Power Operations, AmerenUE:** Mark C. Birk, age 40
**VP, Environmental, Safety, and Health, Ameren Services:** Michael L. Menne, age 50
**VP, Generation Technical Services, Ameren Services; President, Electric Energy:** Robert L. (Bob) Powers, age 56
**VP, Information Technology, Ameren Services:** Charles A. Bremer, age 60
**VP, Transmission, Ameren Services:** Maureen A. Borkowski, age 48
**VP, UE, Ameren Services:** Dennis W. Weisenborn, age 50
**Chairman, President, and CEO, CILCO, CIPS, and IP:** Scott A. Cisel, age 53
**President, AFS:** Michael G. Mueller, age 43
**President, Ameren Energy Marketing Company:** Andrew M. Serri, age 45
**Auditors:** PricewaterhouseCoopers LLP

## LOCATIONS

**HQ:** Ameren Corporation
1901 Chouteau Ave., St. Louis, MO 63103
**Phone:** 314-621-3222 **Fax:** 314-554-3801
**Web:** www.ameren.com

Ameren distributes electricity and natural gas throughout most of Missouri and Illinois.

## PRODUCTS/OPERATIONS

### 2006 Sales

| | $ mil. | % of total |
|---|---|---|
| Electric | 5,585 | 81 |
| Gas | 1,295 | 19 |
| **Total** | **6,880** | **100** |

### 2006 Fuel Mix

| | % of total |
|---|---|
| Coal | 65 |
| Nuclear | 10 |
| Hydro | 1 |
| Natural gas | 1 |
| Oil | 1 |
| Purchased & interchanged fuels | 22 |
| **Total** | **100** |

### Selected Subsidiaries

AmerenEnergy, Inc. (power marketing and trading, risk management, and energy services)
AmerenEnergy Resources Company (holding company)
- AmerenEnergy Development Company (power plant development)
  - AmerenEnergy Generating Company (nonregulated power generation)
- AmerenEnergy Fuels and Services Company (natural gas procurement)
- AmerenEnergy Marketing Company (retail and wholesale energy marketing, long-term power supply contracts)

Ameren Services Company (provides support services for Ameren and subsidiaries)
Central Illinois Public Service Company (AmerenCIPS, electric and gas utility)
CILCORP Incorporated (holding company)
- Central Illinois Light Company (AmerenCILCO, electric and gas utility)
  - AmerenEnergy Resources Generating Company (formerly Central Illinois Generation, nonregulated power generation)

Illinois Power Company (AmerenIP, electric and gas utility)
Union Electric Company (AmerenUE, electric and gas utility)

## COMPETITORS

AES
AmerenIP
Aquila
Atmos Energy
CenterPoint Energy
Empire District Electric
Exelon
Great Plains Energy
Laclede Group
MidAmerican Energy
Midwest Generation
Nicor
Southern Union
Westar Energy

## HISTORICAL FINANCIALS

Company Type: Public

### Income Statement

FYE: December 31

| | REVENUE ($ mil.) | NET INCOME ($ mil.) | NET PROFIT MARGIN | EMPLOYEES |
|---|---|---|---|---|
| **12/06** | 6,880 | 547 | 8.0% | 8,988 |
| **12/05** | 6,780 | 606 | 8.9% | 9,136 |
| **12/04** | 5,160 | 530 | 10.3% | 9,388 |
| **12/03** | 4,593 | 524 | 11.4% | 7,650 |
| **12/02** | 3,841 | 382 | 9.9% | 7,422 |
| **Annual Growth** | 15.7% | 9.4% | — | 4.9% |

### 2006 Year-End Financials

Debt ratio: 80.3%
Return on equity: 8.4%
Cash ($ mil.): 137
Current ratio: 0.85
Long-term debt ($ mil.): 5,285
No. of shares (mil.): 207
Dividends
Yield: 4.7%
Payout: 95.5%
Market value ($ mil.): 11,101

### Stock History

NYSE: AEE

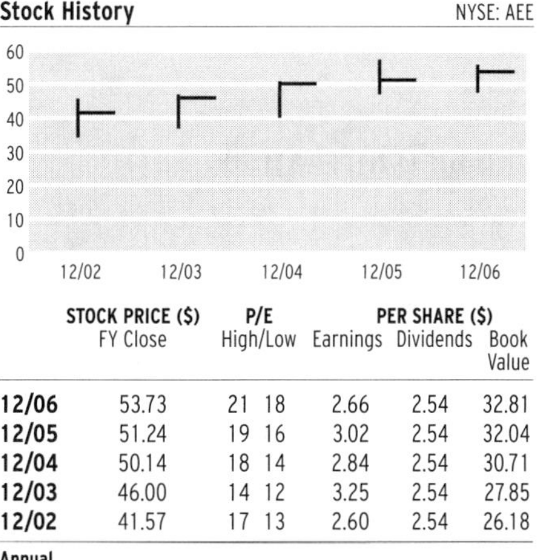


| | STOCK PRICE ($) FY Close | P/E High | P/E Low | PER SHARE ($) Earnings | Dividends | Book Value |
|---|---|---|---|---|---|---|
| **12/06** | 53.73 | 21 | 18 | 2.66 | 2.54 | 32.81 |
| **12/05** | 51.24 | 19 | 16 | 3.02 | 2.54 | 32.04 |
| **12/04** | 50.14 | 18 | 14 | 2.84 | 2.54 | 30.71 |
| **12/03** | 46.00 | 14 | 12 | 3.25 | 2.54 | 27.85 |
| **12/02** | 41.57 | 17 | 13 | 2.60 | 2.54 | 26.18 |
| **Annual Growth** | 6.6% | — | — | 0.6% | 0.0% | 5.8% |

# American Eagle Outfitters

It was once a purveyor of outdoor gear, but American Eagle Outfitters now feathers its nest with polos and khakis. The mall-based retailer sells casual apparel and accessories (shirts, jeans, shorts, sweaters, skirts, footwear, belts, bags) aimed at men and women ages 15-25. Virtually all of the company's products bear its private-label brand names: American Eagle Outfitters and AE. It operates more than 900 American Eagle stores in the US and Canada and plans to open more. Direct sales come from the company's Web site and its AE Magazine, a lifestyle magazine which doubles as a catalog. The Schottenstein family (which has interests in Value City department and furniture stores) owns 13% of American Eagle.

American Eagle boasts lower prices than its archrival in the 'tween market, Abercrombie & Fitch. Recently the retailer has introduced new store formats and brands.

A new casual sportswear concept targeting 25- to 40-year-old women and men — called MARTIN + OSA — debuted in September 2006 and currently operates five stores. (About a dozen new MARTIN + OSA stores are slated to open in 2007.) Also, a new intimate apparel sub brand called "aerie by American Eagle" launched in September 2006. At least 15 stand-alone aerie stores are slated to open this year. The new line includes bras, panties, and personal care products targeted at the 15-to-25 set. Aerie is available in several stand-alone aerie by American Eagle stores as well as within AE stores. (The company plans to rename its seven American Eagle intimates shops in the US and Canada aerie by American Eagle.) The apparel retailer also entered the fragrance game with a pair of scents for men and women, under the American Eagle Real banner, that debuted in AE stores in October 2006.

Taking flight for the first time beyond North America, American Eagle plans to open stores in Japan in 2007. (Japan is the top market for the retailer's direct selling business.) In all, about 100 stores are planned for the Japanese market and other parts of Asia.

The retailer plans to relocate its corporate headquarters from Warrendale to a building it has agreed to purchase for about $21 million in the SouthSide Works along the Pittsburgh waterfront. The move is expected to take place in 2007.

## HISTORY

Retail Ventures, an operator of specialty clothing stores owned by the Silverman family, founded the first American Eagle Outfitters (AE) store in 1977. Another retailing clan, the Schottenstein family (led by Jerome, who died in 1992), bought a 50% stake in Retail Ventures when the Silvermans encountered financial difficulties in 1980. The Schottenstein family had built a retail empire by buying and revamping dying retail chains (holdings include Value City Department and Furniture stores). The retailer returned to financial health and expanded rapidly in the late 1980s.

In 1991 the Schottensteins acquired the remainder of Retail Ventures, and with it, 153 American Eagle Outfitters stores. The company had been running up substantial losses, so the Schottensteins brought in new management and took the company public in 1994 as American Eagle Outfitters, with about 170 stores. AE opened more than 80 stores the following year.

Former president and CEO Sam Forman bought the company's 32-store outlet division in 1995 and attained a license to continue to operate the stores under the American Eagle Outlets name. Two years later AE acquired New York-based Prophecy, an apparel-sourcing firm (the Schottenstein family was Prophecy's majority owner).

In recent years, AE has toned down its rugged, value-conscious image in favor of a collegiate look. One result: In 1998 across-the-mall nemesis Abercrombie & Fitch sued the company claiming AE copied product designs as well as the look of its stores; the suit wound its way up through the courts and was dismissed three times in four years.

In late 2000 the company crossed the border into Canada with the purchase of 160 Thrifty/Bluenotes and Braemar stores and distribution facilities from Canada's Dylex Limited, all for about $74 million. In 2001 the Braemer stores were converted to American Eagle Outfitters. American Eagle Outfitters opened 81 new US stores in 2001, and it introduced the American Eagle brand to Canada with 46 new stores there.

In November 2003, Jim O'Donnell was named CEO and Roger S. Markfield became vice chairman and president. Previously, the duo had been co-CEOs of the company. Late 2004 saw the company divest of its struggling Bluenotes chain in Canada.

In December 2004 American Eagle Outfitters sold its Bluenotes apparel chain in Canada to Stitches owner Michael Gold.

In 2005 the company expanded into all 50 states with the opening of a pair of stores in Alaska. In September 2005 EVP and CFO Laura A. Weil resigned to join Ann Taylor Stores as its new COO. She was replaced in April 2006 by Joan Hilson, formerly SVP of finance for the company.

## EXECUTIVES

**Chairman:** Jay L. Schottenstein, age 52
**Vice Chairman:** Roger S. Markfield, age 65
**CEO and Director:** James V. (Jim) O'Donnell, age 66, $3,865,600 pay
**President and Chief Merchandising Officer:** Susan P. McGalla, age 42
**EVP and CFO, American Eagle Brand:** Joan Holstein Hilson
**EVP and Chief Design Officer:** LeAnn Nealz, age 50, $2,070,100 pay
**EVP and Chief Marketing Officer:** Katherine J. (Kathy) Savitt, age 43
**EVP Store Operations and Real Estate:** Joseph E. Kerin, age 61
**EVP E-Commerce and AE International:** Fredrick W. Grover
**EVP Human Resources:** Thomas (Tom) DiDonato, age 48
**EVP Production and Sourcing, Martin + Osa:** Howard Landon
**EVP and COO, New York Design Center:** Dennis R. Parodi, age 55
**EVP, Customs Compliance Officer:** Guy Bradford
**EVP Blue Star Imports:** Hank Shechtman
**SVP and COO, MARTIN + OSA:** Chuck Chupein
**SVP New Concept Development:** Christopher Fiore
**SVP Technology, Logistics, and Imports, and Chief Supply Chain Officer:** Michael Rempell
**SVP and Senior Merchandising Officer, AE Brand:** Henry Stafford
**SVP and Chief Merchandising Officer, aerie:** Betsy Schumacher
**VP and CIO:** Rick Milazzo
**VP, General Counsel, and Secretary:** Neil Bulman Jr.
**VP Investor Relations:** Judy Meehan
**VP Public Relations and Corporate Communications:** Jani Strand
**Auditors:** Ernst & Young LLP

## LOCATIONS

**HQ:** American Eagle Outfitters, Inc.
150 Thorn Hill Dr., Warrendale, PA 15086
**Phone:** 724-776-4857 **Fax:** 724-779-5776
**Web:** www.ae.com

### 2007 Stores

| | No. |
|---|---|
| US | |
| California | 79 |
| Texas | 62 |
| Pennsylvania | 49 |
| Florida | 46 |
| New York | 41 |
| Ohio | 37 |
| Michigan | 30 |
| Illinois | 29 |
| Virginia | 28 |
| Massachusetts | 27 |
| Georgia | 26 |
| North Carolina | 24 |
| New Jersey | 22 |
| Tennessee | 20 |
| Alabama | 18 |
| Indiana | 18 |
| Maryland | 18 |
| Washington | 18 |
| Missouri | 17 |
| Minnesota | 16 |
| Wisconsin | 15 |
| Colorado | 14 |
| Arizona | 13 |
| Louisiana | 13 |
| South Carolina | 13 |
| Iowa | 12 |
| Oklahoma | 12 |
| Kentucky | 11 |
| Connecticut | 10 |
| Utah | 10 |
| Oregon | 9 |
| Kansas | 8 |
| Other states | 74 |
| Canada | 72 |
| **Total** | **911** |

## PRODUCTS/OPERATIONS

### 2007 Sales

| | % of total |
|---|---|
| Women's apparel & accessories | 60 |
| Men's apparel & accessories | 35 |
| Footwear — men's & women's | 5 |
| **Total** | **100** |

### Selected Products

Accessories
Cargo pants
Footwear
Graphic T-shirts
Khakis
Outerwear
Polo shirts
Rugby shirts
Swimwear

## COMPETITORS

Abercrombie & Fitch
Aéropostale
Benetton
Buckle
Calvin Klein
Columbia Sportswear
Dillard's
Eddie Bauer
Fossil
Gap
Guess
Hot Topic
Hudson's Bay
J. C. Penney
J. Crew
Lands' End
Levi Strauss
Limited Brands
Liz Claiborne
L.L. Bean
Macy's
Nautica Enterprises
Nordstrom
Pacific Sunwear
Polo Ralph Lauren
Reitmans
Target
Tommy Hilfiger
Urban Outfitters
VF

## HISTORICAL FINANCIALS

Company Type: Public

### Income Statement

FYE: Saturday nearest January 31

| | REVENUE ($ mil.) | NET INCOME ($ mil.) | NET PROFIT MARGIN | EMPLOYEES |
|---|---|---|---|---|
| **1/07** | 2,794 | 387 | 13.9% | 27,600 |
| **1/06** | 2,309 | 294 | 12.7% | 23,000 |
| **1/05** | 1,881 | 213 | 11.3% | 20,600 |
| **1/04** | 1,520 | 60 | 3.9% | 17,400 |
| **1/03** | 1,463 | 89 | 6.1% | 15,720 |
| **Annual Growth** | 17.6% | 44.6% | — | 15.1% |

### 2007 Year-End Financials

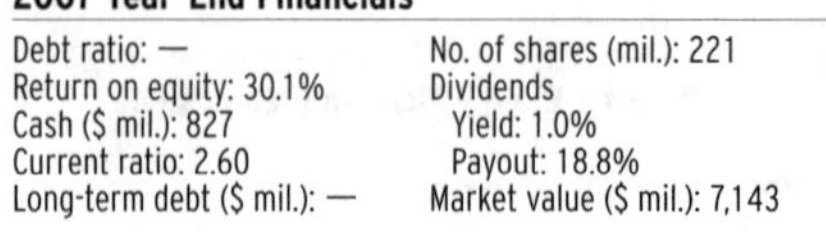

Debt ratio: —
Return on equity: 30.1%
Cash ($ mil.): 827
Current ratio: 2.60
Long-term debt ($ mil.): —
No. of shares (mil.): 221
Dividends
Yield: 1.0%
Payout: 18.8%
Market value ($ mil.): 7,143

### Stock History

NYSE: AEO

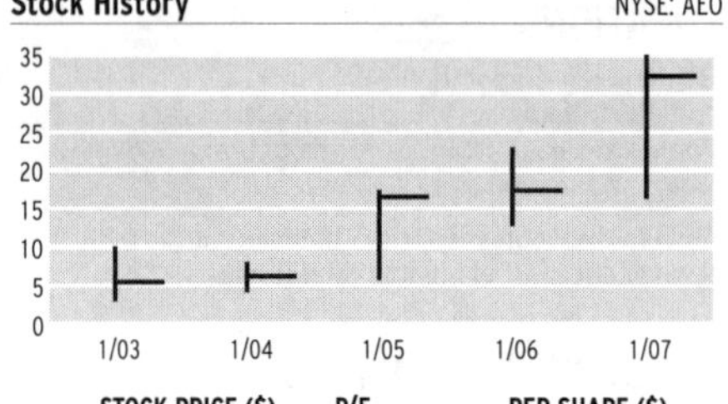


| | STOCK PRICE ($) FY Close | P/E High | P/E Low | PER SHARE ($) Earnings | Dividends | Book Value |
|---|---|---|---|---|---|---|
| **1/07** | 32.28 | 20 | 10 | 1.70 | 0.32 | 6.40 |
| **1/06** | 17.36 | 18 | 10 | 1.26 | 0.18 | 7.81 |
| **1/05** | 16.50 | 18 | 6 | 0.95 | 0.04 | 6.45 |
| **1/04** | 6.21 | 28 | 16 | 0.28 | — | 9.04 |
| **1/03** | 5.47 | 24 | 8 | 0.41 | — | 8.13 |
| **Annual Growth** | 55.9% | — | — | 42.7% | 182.8% | (5.8%) |

# American Electric Power

American Electric Power (AEP) takes its slice of the US power pie out of Middle America. The holding company is one of the largest power generators and distributors in the US: AEP owns the nation's largest electricity transmission system, a network of nearly 39,000 miles. Its electric utilities serve more than 5 million customers in 11 states and have more than 36,000 MW of largely coal-fired generating capacity. AEP is a top wholesale energy company; it markets and trades electricity, natural gas, and other commodities and has interests in independent power plants. Other operations include natural gas transportation, storage, and processing; barge transportation; and telecommunications infrastructure services.

The company will attempt to keep its debt-to-capitalization ratio below 60% and focus its efforts on regulatory activities in Texas. AEP has earmarked $3.7 billion through 2010 for upgrades at its coal-fired generating plants, and an additional $1.5 billion through 2020.

In response to deregulation, AEP had been expanding its merchant energy activities; however, due to the collapse of the energy trading industry (spurred by Enron's collapse and the ensuing financial scrutiny of other top marketers), AEP is scaling back its nonregulated operations. The firm has shut down or sold its European trading operations, but it continues to participate in wholesale energy transactions in regions of the US where it owns assets. It is also selling its independent power production operations.

In 2006 AEP agreed to form a joint venture company with MidAmerican Energy Holdings to build and own new electric transmission assets within the Electric Reliability Council of Texas.

## HISTORY

In 1906 Richard Breed, Sidney Mitchell, and Henry Doherty set up American Gas & Electric (AG&E) in New York to buy 23 utilities from Philadelphia's Electric Company of America. With properties in seven northeastern US states, AG&E began acquiring and merging small electric properties, creating the predecessors of Ohio Power (1911), Kentucky Power (1919), and Appalachian Power (1926). AG&E also bought the predecessor of Indiana Michigan Power (1925).

By 1926 the company was operating in Indiana, Kentucky, Michigan, Ohio, Virginia, and West Virginia. In 1935 AG&E engineer Philip Sporn, later known as the Henry Ford of power, introduced his high-voltage, high-velocity circuit breaker. AG&E picked up Kingsport Power in 1938.

Becoming president in 1947, Sporn began an ambitious building program that continued through the 1960s. Plants designed by AG&E (renamed American Electric Power in 1958) were among the world's most efficient, and electric rates stayed 25% to 38% below the national average.

AEP bought Michigan Power in 1967, six years after Donald Cook succeeded Sporn as president. Cook, who refused to attach scrubbers to the smokestacks of coal-fired plants, was criticized in the early 1970s by environmental protesters. AEP's first nuclear plant, named in Cook's honor, went on line in Michigan in 1975. He retired in 1976.

The firm moved from New York to Columbus, Ohio, in 1980 after buying what is now Columbus Southern Power (formed in 1883). It set up AEP Generating in 1982 to provide power to its electric utilities.

AEP began converting its second nuke, Zimmer, to coal in 1984. In 1992 AEP finally began installing scrubbers at its coal-fired Gavin plant in Ohio after being ordered to comply with the Clean Air Act. It also cleaned up its image by planting millions of trees in 1996.

After Congress passed the Telecommunications Act of 1996, the company formed AEP Communications. The next year AEP jumped into the UK's deregulated electric market; AEP and New Century Energies (now Xcel Energy) bought Yorkshire Electricity (later Yorkshire Power Group) for $2.8 billion. However, a $109 million UK windfall tax on the transaction — and increased wholesale competition — hurt AEP's bottom line.

As the normally staid electric industry succumbed to merger mania, AEP agreed in 1997 to buy Central and South West (CSW) of Texas in a $6.6 billion deal. AEP's sales would nearly double, and CSW was to bring its own UK utility, SEEBOARD, and other overseas holdings.

In 1998 AEP bought a 20% stake in Pacific Hydro, an Australian power producer, and CitiPower, an Australian electric distribution company. AEP also bought Equitable Resources' Louisiana natural gas midstream operations, including an intrastate pipeline. In 1999 China's Pushan Power Plant (70%-owned by AEP) began operations. Environmental concerns resurfaced that year when the EPA sued the utility, alleging its old coal-powered plants, which had been grandfathered from the Clean Air Act, had been quietly upgraded to extend their lives.

In 2000 regulators approved the company's acquisition of CSW, but AEP had to agree to relinquish control of its 22,000 miles of transmission lines to an independent operator. The CSW deal closed later that year. (However, the SEC's approval of the deal was challenged by a federal appeals court in 2002.)

AEP sold its 50% stake in Yorkshire Power Group to Innogy (now RWE npower) in 2001. AEP became one of the largest US barge operators that year when it bought MEMCO Barge Line from Progress Energy. It also purchased two UK coal-fired power plants (4,000 MW) from Edison Mission Energy, a subsidiary of Edison International, in a $960 million deal.

In 2002 AEP sold its UK utility, SEEBOARD, to Electricité de France in a $2.2 billion deal; it also sold its Australian utility, CitiPower, to a consortium led by Cheung Kong Infrastructure and Hongkong Electric for $855 million. The following year, the company sold two of its competitive Texas retail electric providers (WTU Retail Energy and CPL Retail Energy) to UK utility Centrica. It also divested its power plant development subsidiary, AEP Pro Serv, and its stakes in telecom firms C3 Communications and AFN.

The company sold two UK power plants to Scottish and Southern Energy for $456 million in 2004, and it sold a 50% stake in a third UK plant to Scottish Power in a $210 million deal. AEP has also sold four independent power plants in Florida and Colorado to Bear Stearns for $156 million.

## EXECUTIVES

**Chairman, President, and CEO; Chairman, President, and CEO, American Electric Power Service Corporation:** Michael G. (Mike) Morris, age 60
**EVP and CFO; EVP and CFO, American Electric Power Service Corporation:** Holly K. Koeppel, age 48
**EVP; EVP, AEP Utilities East; Director, American Electric Power Service Corporation:** Robert P. (Bob) Powers, age 52
**EVP; EVP AEP Utilities West; Director, American Electric Power Service Corporation:** Thomas M. (Tom) Hagan, age 62, $904,183 pay
**EVP; EVP Generation and Director, American Electric Power Service Corporation:** Nicholas K. (Nick) Akins, age 46
**EVP; EVP and Director, Shared Services, American Electric Power Service Corporation:** Susan Tomasky, age 53
**SVP, Chief Accounting Officer, and Controller:** Joseph M. Buonaiuto
**SVP and Treasurer:** Stephen P. Smith, age 45
**SVP, General Counsel, Chief Compliance Officer, and Secretary; SVP, General Counsel, and Director, American Electric Power Service Corporation:** John B. (Jack) Keane, age 60
**President, AEP Utilities; Director, American Electric Power Service Corporation:** Carl L. English, age 60
**President and COO, Columbus Southern Power and Ohio Power Company:** Kevin E. Walker, age 43
**President and COO, AEP Texas:** Charles R. Patton
**President and COO, Appalachian Power and Kingsport Power Company:** Dana E. Waldo, age 55
**President and COO, Kentucky Power:** Timothy C. (Tim) Mosher
**President and COO, Public Service Company of Oklahoma:** J. Stuart Solomon
**President and COO, Southwestern Electric Power Co.:** Venita McCellon-Allen, age 46
**President and COO, Indiana Michigan Power Company:** Helen J. Murray
**Managing Director Investor Relations:** Bette Jo Rozsa
**Director Corporate Media Relations:** Pat D. Hemlepp
**Auditors:** Deloitte & Touche LLP

## LOCATIONS

**HQ:** American Electric Power Company, Inc.
1 Riverside Plaza, Columbus, OH 43215
**Phone:** 614-716-1000 **Fax:** 614-716-1823
**Web:** www.aep.com

American Electric Power distributes electricity in Arkansas, Indiana, Kentucky, Louisiana, Michigan, Ohio, Oklahoma, Tennessee, Texas, Virginia, and West Virginia. It has natural gas pipeline interests in Louisiana and Texas. The company also markets energy in North America and has independent power plant interests in Texas, as well as in Australia and Mexico.

## PRODUCTS/OPERATIONS

### 2006 Sales

| | $ mil. | % of total |
|---|---|---|
| Electric utility | | |
| Retail | 9,050 | 72 |
| Wholesale | 2,624 | 21 |
| Gas investments | 463 | 3 |
| Other | 485 | 4 |
| **Total** | **12,622** | **100** |

### Selected Subsidiaries

AEP Energy Services, Inc. (energy marketing and trading)
AEP Generating Co. (electricity generator, marketer)
AEP Retail Energy (retail energy marketing in deregulated territories)
AEP Texas Central Company (formerly Central Power and Light, electric utility)
AEP Texas North Company (formerly West Texas Utilities, electric utility)
AEP Towers (wireless communications towers)
Appalachian Power Company (electric utility)
Columbus Southern Power Company (electric utility)
Indiana Michigan Power Company (electric utility)
Kentucky Power Company (electric utility)
Kingsport Power Company (electric utility)
Ohio Power Company (electric utility)
Public Service Company of Oklahoma (electric utility)
Southwestern Electric Power Company (electric utility)
Wheeling Power Company (electric utility)

### Utility Distribution/Customer Service Divisions

AEP Ohio (handles distribution, customer service, and external affairs functions for Columbus Southern Power Company, Ohio Power Company, and Wheeling Power Company)
AEP Texas (handles distribution, customer service, and external affairs functions for AEP Texas Central Company and AEP Texas North Company)
Appalachian Power (handles distribution, customer service, and external affairs functions for Appalachian Power Company and Kingsport Power Company)
Indiana Michigan Power (handles distribution, customer service, and external affairs functions for Indiana Michigan Power Company)
Kentucky Power (handles distribution, customer service, and external affairs functions for Kentucky Power Company)
Public Service Company of Oklahoma (handles distribution, customer service, and external affairs functions for Public Service Company of Oklahoma)
Southwestern Electric Power Company (handles distribution, customer service, and external affairs functions for Southwestern Electric Power Company)

## COMPETITORS

Allegheny Energy
Aquila
BP
Calpine
CenterPoint Energy
CMS Energy
Constellation Energy Group
Delmarva Power
Dominion Resources
DTE
Duke Energy
Dynegy
El Paso
Entergy
Exelon
FirstEnergy
Koch
Mirant
NiSource
PG&E
Reliant Energy
Sempra Energy
Southern Company
TVA
TXU
UTC Power
Xcel Energy

## HISTORICAL FINANCIALS

Company Type: Public

**Income Statement** FYE: December 31

| | REVENUE ($ mil.) | NET INCOME ($ mil.) | NET PROFIT MARGIN | EMPLOYEES |
|---|---|---|---|---|
| **12/06** | 12,622 | 1,002 | 7.9% | 20,442 |
| **12/05** | 12,111 | 814 | 6.7% | 19,630 |
| **12/04** | 14,057 | 1,089 | 7.7% | 19,893 |
| **12/03** | 14,545 | 110 | 0.8% | 22,075 |
| **12/02** | 14,536 | (519) | — | 22,083 |
| **Annual Growth** | (3.5%) | — | — | (1.9%) |

**2006 Year-End Financials**

Debt ratio: 132.1%
Return on equity: 10.8%
Cash ($ mil.): 846
Current ratio: 0.66
Long-term debt ($ mil.): 12,429
No. of shares (mil.): 397
Dividends
Yield: 4.4%
Payout: 74.7%
Market value ($ mil.): 16,890

**Stock History** NYSE: AEP

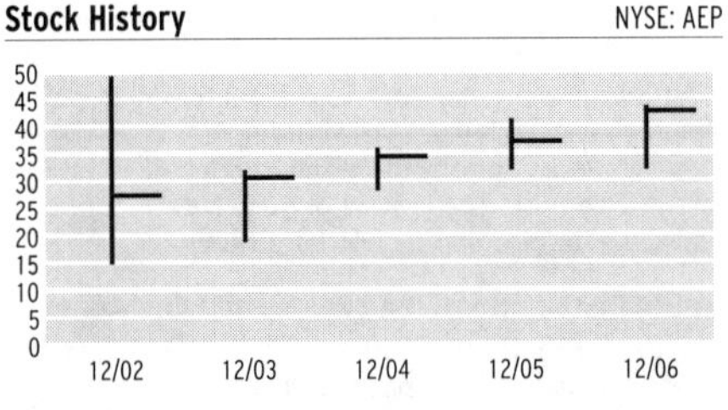


| | STOCK PRICE ($) FY Close | P/E High | P/E Low | PER SHARE ($) Earnings | Dividends | Book Value |
|---|---|---|---|---|---|---|
| **12/06** | 42.58 | 17 | 13 | 2.53 | 1.89 | 23.88 |
| **12/05** | 37.09 | 20 | 16 | 2.08 | 1.42 | 23.24 |
| **12/04** | 34.34 | 13 | 10 | 2.75 | 1.40 | 21.66 |
| **12/03** | 30.51 | 109 | 66 | 0.29 | 1.65 | 20.09 |
| **12/02** | 27.33 | — | — | (1.57) | 2.40 | 20.85 |
| **Annual Growth** | 11.7% | — | — | — | (5.8%) | 3.5% |

# American Express

American Express makes money even if you do leave home without it. The company is one of the world's largest travel agencies, but it is equally as well known for its charge cards and revolving credit cards. Oh yes, the company still issues traveler's checks and publishes such magazines as *Food & Wine* and *Travel & Leisure* through its American Express Publishing unit, while its travel agency operations have more than 2,200 locations worldwide and its Travelers Cheque Group is the world's largest issuer of traveler's checks (it also issues gift cards). But the company's charge and credit cards are its bread and butter, and they've diversified along with the rest of the firm.

American Express offers several levels of charge cards, including the standard green card, Gold, Platinum, and super-premium Centurion card. The company has worked to expand the number and types of merchants who accept the card, which is the company's primary source of revenue. It also offers revolving credit though its Blue cards; the Blue card is one of several issued by the company that has an embedded smart chip.

American Express has been aggressively trying to open its merchant network and card product portfolio to third-party issuers around the world. Citigroup and Bank of America, two of the largest card issuers in the world, now distribute American Express-branded credit cards. In 2004 the company announced a milestone agreement with Industrial and Commercial Bank of China (ICBC), one of the biggest banks in China, to issue the first American Express-branded credit cards in that country.

To focus on its travel and credit card operations, the company in 2005 spun off Ameriprise Financial (formerly American Express Financial Advisors), which provides insurance, mutual funds, investment advice, and brokerage and asset management services.

In separate transactions toward that same end, American Express sold its Tax and Business Services division to H&R Block and its UK-based American Express Financial Services Europe to TD Waterhouse (now part of TD AMERITRADE). In 2005, the company sold its equipment leasing business to Key Equipment Finance.

In 2007 the company's business travel division bought the rest of Farrington American Express Travel Services Limited it didn't already own. The travel management company had been a joint venture with Farrington Travel. The move is part of American Express's global expansion push, especially in the Asia-Pacific region.

Warren Buffett's Berkshire Hathaway owns about 13% of American Express.

## HISTORY

In 1850 Henry Wells and his two main competitors combined their delivery services to form American Express. When directors refused to expand to California in 1852, Wells and VP William Fargo formed Wells Fargo while remaining at American Express.

American Express merged with Merchants Union Express in 1868 and developed a money order to compete with the government's postal money order. Fargo's difficulty in cashing letters of credit in Europe led to the offering of Travelers Cheques in 1891.

In WWI the US government nationalized and consolidated all express delivery services, compensating the owners. After the war, American Express incorporated as an overseas freight and financial services and exchange provider (its freight operation was sold in 1970). In 1958 the company introduced the American Express charge card. It bought Fireman's Fund American Insurance (sold gradually between 1985 and 1989) and Equitable Securities in 1968.

James Robinson, CEO from 1977 to 1993, hoped to turn American Express into a financial services supermarket. The company bought brokerage Shearson Loeb Rhoades in 1981 and investment banker Lehman Brothers in 1984, among others. In 1987 it introduced Optima, a revolving credit card, to compete with MasterCard and Visa; it had no experience in underwriting credit cards and was badly burned by losses.

Most of the financial units were combined as Shearson Lehman Brothers. But the financial services supermarket never came to fruition, and losses in this area brought a steep drop in earnings in the early 1990s. Harvey Golub was brought in as CEO in 1993 to restore stability.

The company sold its brokerage operations as Shearson (to Travelers, now Citigroup) and spun off investment banking as Lehman Brothers in 1994. In late 1996 it teamed with Advanta Corp. to allow Advanta Visa and MasterCard holders to earn points in the American Express Membership Rewards program. The move sparked a lawsuit from Visa and MasterCard, which prohibit their member banks from doing business with American Express. This move set off a spate of lawsuits culminating in the US Justice Department filing an antitrust suit against Visa and MasterCard. A federal judge sided with the Justice Department in 2001, but Visa and MasterCard appealed.

In 1997 Kenneth Chenault became president and COO, putting him in line to succeed Golub.

Online banking service Membership B@nking was launched in 1999. That year American Express invested in Ticketmaster Online-CitySearch (now Ticketmaster). In 2000 the company established a headquarters in Beijing to develop business in China.

In 2001 Chenault replaced Golub as chairman and CEO. American Express was hit hard that year by bad investments in below-investment grade bonds by its money-management unit, which shaved about $1 billion from earnings. Adding to its woes, the company's employees at its New York City headquarters, across the street from the World Trade Center, were displaced by the 2001 terrorist attacks; its headquarters reopened in May 2002.

To grow its corporate travel management business, Amex acquired Rosenbluth International, a leading global travel management company with corporate travel operations in 15 countries, in 2003. When Rosenbluth became fully integrated into the organization in mid-2004, American Express announced a relaunch of its corporate travel organization, renamed American Express Business Travel.

American Express underwent a mild shakedown in late 2004 when it cut 2.5% of its workforce in a restructuring that included its business travel operations. The move also included the sale of the company's banking operations in Bangladesh, Egypt, Luxembourg, and Pakistan and the relocation of some finance operations.

## EXECUTIVES

**Chairman and CEO:** Kenneth I. Chenault, age 55, $7,100,000 pay
**Vice Chairman:** Edward P. (Ed) Gilligan, age 47
**President:** Alfred F. (Al) Kelly Jr., age 48
**EVP and Acting CFO:** Dan Henry
**EVP and CIO:** Stephen (Steve) Squeri, age 47
**EVP Corporate Affairs and Communications:** Thomas Schick, age 60
**EVP and General Counsel:** Louise M. Parent, age 55, $1,644,923 pay
**EVP Global Advertising and Brand Management and Chief Marketing Officer:** John D. Hayes, age 51
**EVP Human Resources and Quality:** L. Kevin Cox, age 43
**SVP and Treasurer:** David L. Yowan
**SVP Investor Relations:** Ron Stovall
**SVP and Comptroller:** Joan C. Amble, age 53
**Corporate Governance Officer and Secretary:** Stephen P. Norman
**President, Global Establishment Services Group:** William H. (Bill) Glenn
**Head of Establishment Services, Japan, Asia Pacific, and Australia, Global Establishment Services:** Mark Gamble
**Head of Establishment Services, Europe, Middle East, and Africa, Global Establishment Services:** David Herrick
**Head of Global Network Services:** Peter Godfrey
**President, Global Travelers Cheque and Prepaid Services, U.S. Card Services:** Valerie (Val) Soranno-Keating
**President and CEO, US Consumer Business:** Judson C. (Jud) Linville
**President, Risk, Information Management, and Banking; Chief Risk Officer:** Ash Gupta
**President, Global Commercial Card:** Anre Williams
**President, International Consumer Business:** Douglas E. Buckminster
**Auditors:** PricewaterhouseCoopers LLP

## LOCATIONS

**HQ:** American Express Company
World Financial Center, 200 Vesey St.,
New York, NY 10285
**Phone:** 212-640-2000 **Fax:** 212-640-2458
**Web:** www.americanexpress.com

### 2006 Sales

| | $ mil. | % of total |
|---|---|---|
| US | 18,376 | 68 |
| Europe | 3,564 | 13 |
| Asia/Pacific | 2,482 | 9 |
| Other regions | 2,714 | 10 |
| **Total** | **27,136** | **100** |

## PRODUCTS/OPERATIONS

### 2006 Sales

| | $ mil. | % of total |
|---|---|---|
| Discount revenue | 12,978 | 48 |
| Cardholder lending net finance charge revenue | 3,457 | 13 |
| Net card fees | 1,994 | 7 |
| Travel commissions & fees | 1,778 | 7 |
| Other commissions & fees | 2,555 | 9 |
| Net securitization income | 1,489 | 5 |
| Other investment & interest income, net | 1,078 | 4 |
| Other | 1,807 | 7 |
| **Total** | **27,136** | **100** |

### 2006 Sales By Segment

| | $ mil. | % of total |
|---|---|---|
| US Card Services | 13,955 | 51 |
| International Card & Global Commercial Services | 9,464 | 35 |
| Global Network & Merchant Services | 3,161 | 12 |
| Corporate & other | 556 | 2 |
| **Total** | **27,136** | **100** |

## COMPETITORS

Advance Publications
Allstate
Bank of America
Barclays
BCD Travel
Capital One
Carlson Wagonlit
Citigroup
Discover
Expedia
FMR
John Hancock
JPMorgan Chase
JTB
MasterCard
Merrill Lynch
MetLife
Morgan Stanley
Ovation Travel Group
Prudential
Visa
Western Union

## HISTORICAL FINANCIALS

Company Type: Public

### Income Statement

FYE: December 31

| | ASSETS ($ mil.) | NET INCOME ($ mil.) | INCOME AS % OF ASSETS | EMPLOYEES |
|---|---|---|---|---|
| **12/06** | 127,853 | 3,707 | 2.9% | 65,400 |
| **12/05** | 113,960 | 3,734 | 3.3% | 65,800 |
| **12/04** | 192,638 | 3,445 | 1.8% | 77,500 |
| **12/03** | 175,001 | 2,987 | 1.7% | 78,200 |
| **12/02** | 157,253 | 2,671 | 1.7% | 75,500 |
| **Annual Growth** | (5.0%) | 8.5% | — | (3.5%) |

### 2006 Year-End Financials

Equity as % of assets: 8.2%
Return on assets: 3.1%
Return on equity: 35.2%
Long-term debt ($ mil.): 42,747
No. of shares (mil.): 1,199
Dividends
Yield: 0.9%
Payout: 18.1%
Market value ($ mil.): 72,743
Sales ($ mil.): 27,136

### Stock History

NYSE: AXP

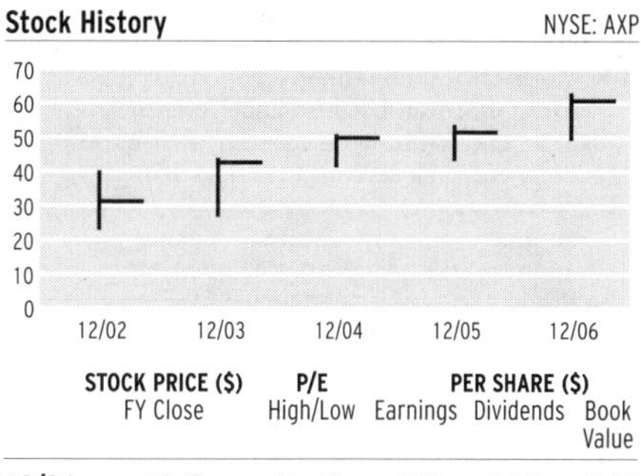


| | STOCK PRICE ($) FY Close | P/E High | P/E Low | PER SHARE ($) Earnings | Dividends | Book Value |
|---|---|---|---|---|---|---|
| **12/06** | 60.67 | 21 | 17 | 2.99 | 0.54 | 8.77 |
| **12/05** | 51.46 | 18 | 15 | 2.97 | 13.92 | 8.50 |
| **12/04** | 49.80 | 19 | 16 | 2.68 | 0.28 | 12.83 |
| **12/03** | 42.61 | 19 | 12 | 2.30 | 0.34 | 11.93 |
| **12/02** | 31.23 | 20 | 12 | 2.01 | 0.35 | 10.62 |
| **Annual Growth** | 18.1% | — | — | 10.4% | 11.5% | (4.7%) |

# American Financial Group

American Financial Group (AFG) insures throughout the world. Through the Great American Insurance Group of companies and its flagship Great American Insurance Company, AFG offers property/casualty insurance focused on specialty commercial lines such as workers' compensation, professional liability, ocean and inland marine, and multiperil crop insurance. AFG also provides car insurance, especially nonstandard (read: high-risk) motorist insurance. The growing retirement-savings market plays a big role in AFG's product mix — especially flexible and single-premium deferred annuities sold through its Great American Financial Resources (GAFRI) subsidiary. Chairman Carl Lindner and his sons own more than 30% of AFG.

AFG holds only 81% of GAFRI, but has made an offer to purchase the remaining 19%.

While the company writes some reinsurance for its own companies, and others, it chooses to limit its exposure by purchasing catastrophe reinsurance from other providers.

The company has shed some commercial lines to concentrate on property/casualty and life and annuities businesses. To further refine its mix, AFG transferred Atlanta Casualty Company, Infinity Insurance Company, Leader Insurance Company, and Windsor Insurance Company into 40%-owned Infinity Property and Casualty, which went public in 2003. In 2004 the company exchanged its stake in Provident Financial Group for a holding in National City Corporation.

The company is engaged in non-insurance operations, primarily commercial real estate holdings in Cincinnati, as well as in Charleston, South Carolina; Chesapeake Bay; New Orleans; Palm Beach, Florida; and elsewhere.

Lindner, who is also part owner of the Cincinnati Reds, retired as CEO in 2005 and was succeeded by two of his sons, Carl Lindner III and Craig Lindner, who share the CEO job.

## HISTORY

When his father became ill in the mid-1930s, Carl Lindner dropped out of high school to take over his family's dairy business. He built it into a large ice-cream store chain called United Dairy Farmers (now run by his brother Robert). Lindner branched out in 1955 with Henthy Realty, and in 1959 he bought three savings and loans. The next year Lindner changed the company's name to American Financial Corp. (AFC). He took it public in 1961, using the proceeds to buy United Liberty Life Insurance (1963) and Provident Bank (1966).

Lindner also formed the American Financial Leasing & Services Company in 1968 to lease airplanes, computers, and other equipment. In 1969 the company acquired Phoenix developer Rubenstein Construction and renamed it American Continental. AFC bought several life, casualty, and mortgage insurance firms in the 1970s, including National General, parent of Great American Insurance Group, later the core of AFC's insurance segment. The company also moved into publishing by buying 95% of the *Cincinnati Enquirer,* paperback publisher Bantam Books, and hardback publisher Grosset & Dunlap.

But the publishing interests soon went back on the block, as Lindner concentrated on insurance, which was then suffering from an industrywide slowdown. In addition to selling the *Enquirer,* AFC spun off American Continental in 1976. American Continental's president was Charles Keating, who had joined AFC in 1972 and whose brother published the *Enquirer.* Keating (who was later jailed, released, then eventually pleaded guilty in connection with the failure of Lincoln Savings) underwent an SEC investigation during part of his time at AFC for alleged improprieties at Provident Bank. The bank was spun off in 1980.

Lindner took AFC private in 1981. That year, following a strategy of bottom-feeding, the company began building its interest in the nonrailroad assets of Penn Central, the former railroad that had emerged from bankruptcy as an industrial manufacturer. Later that decade AFC increased its ownership in United Brands (later renamed Chiquita Brands International) from 29% to 45%. Lindner installed himself as CEO and reversed that company's losses. In 1987 AFC acquired a TV company, Taft Communications (renamed Great American Communications), entailing a heavy debt load. To reduce its debt, AFC trimmed its holdings, including Circle K, Hunter S&L, and an interest in Scripps Howard Broadcasting.

Great American Communications went bankrupt in 1992 and emerged the next year as Citicasters Inc. (sold 1996). In 1995 Lindner created American Financial Group to effect the merger of AFC and Premier Underwriters, of which he owned 42%. The result was American Financial Group (AFG).

Lindner's bipartisan political donations gained publicity when it became known that his gifts to Republicans had brought support in a dispute with the EU over the banana trade. The next year AFG sold some noncore units, including software consultancy Millennium Dynamics and its commercial insurance operations. In 1999 AFG bought direct-response auto insurer Worldwide Insurance Company as part of its efforts to build depth in the highly commodified auto insurance market.

In 2000 American Financial Group agreed to pay $75 million over the next 30 years to get its name on the Cincinnati Reds' new stadium, known as the Great American Ball Park. In 2001 AFG sold its Japanese property and casualty division to Japanese insurer Mitsui Marine & Fire (now Mitsui Sumitomo Insurance).

AFG's results in the 1990s were uneven, and typically did not make an underwriting profit. In 2003, the company kept operating expenses down (partly by merging two of its holding company subsidiaries into AFG) and swung to a profit even though premium revenue was down.

## EXECUTIVES

**Chairman:** Carl H. Lindner, age 86, $130,000 pay
**Co-President, Co-CEO, and Director:** S. Craig Lindner, age 51, $2,915,000 pay
**Co-President, Co-CEO, and Director:** Carl H. Lindner III, age 52, $2,915,000 pay
**SVP:** Keith A. Jensen, age 55, $1,125,000 pay
**Senior Vice President and General Counsel:** James E. Evans, age 60, $1,990,000 pay
**SVP Taxes:** Thomas E. Mischell, age 58, $951,500 pay
**VP and CIO:** Piyush K. Singh
**VP, Secretary, and Deputy General Counsel:** James C. Kennedy
**VP and Controller:** Robert H. Ruffing
**VP and Treasurer:** David J. Witzgall
**VP and Assistant General Counsel:** Karl J. Grafe
**VP Human Resources:** Scott Beeken
**VP Investor Relations:** Anne N. Watson
**VP Taxation:** Kathleen J. Brown
**Auditors:** Ernst & Young LLP

## LOCATIONS

**HQ:** American Financial Group, Inc.
1 E. 4th St., Cincinnati, OH 45202
**Phone:** 513-579-2121 **Fax:** 513-579-2113
**Web:** www.amfnl.com

American Financial Group operates primarily in the US, but also in Canada, Europe, and Mexico.

## PRODUCTS/OPERATIONS

### 2006 Sales

| | $ mil. | % of total |
|---|---|---|
| Premiums | | |
| Property/casualty | 2,563.1 | 60 |
| Life, accident & health | 354.7 | 8 |
| Investment income | 939.1 | 22 |
| Realized gains on securities | 29.0 | 1 |
| Realized losses on subsidiaries | (0.5) | — |
| Other income | 364.7 | 9 |
| **Total** | **4,250.1** | **100** |

### Selected Subsidiaries

American Money Management Corporation
APU Holding Company
- American Premier Underwriters, Inc.
- Premier Lease & Loan Services Insurance Agency, Inc.
- Premier Lease & Loan Services of Canada, Inc.
- Republic Indemnity Company of America
  - Republic Indemnity Company of California

Great American Holding, Inc.
- American Empire Surplus Lines Insurance Company
  - American Empire Insurance Company
- Mid-Continent Casualty Company
  - Mid-Continent Insurance Company
  - Oklahoma Surety Company

Great American Insurance Company
- Brothers Property Corporation (80%)
- GAI Warranty Company
  - GAI Warranty Company of Florida
- Great American Alliance Insurance Company
- Great American Assurance Company
- Great American Custom Insurance Services, Inc.
  - Professional Risk Brokers, Inc.
- Great American E&S Insurance Company
- Great American Fidelity Insurance Company
- Great American Financial Resources, Inc. (81%)
  - AAG Holding Company, Inc.
    - American Annuity Group Capital Trust II
    - Great American Life Insurance Company
- Great American Insurance Company of New York
- Great American Management Services, Inc.
- Great American Protection Insurance Company
- Great American Security Insurance Company
- Great American Spirit Insurance Company
- National Interstate Corporation (53%)
  - National Interstate Insurance Company
    - National Interstate Insurance Company of Hawaii, Inc.
  - National Interstate Capital Trust I
- Worldwide Casualty Insurance Company

## COMPETITORS

ACE Limited
AIG
Allianz Life
Arch Capital
Bankers Life and Casualty
Chubb Corp
Cincinnati Financial
CNA Financial
The Hartford
HCC Insurance
ING
LSW
Markel
Midland National Life
Mutual of Omaha
Ohio Casualty
OM Financial
Philadelphia Consolidated
Travelers Companies
W. R. Berkley
XL Capital
Zenith National

## HISTORICAL FINANCIALS

Company Type: Public

### Income Statement

FYE: December 31

| | ASSETS ($ mil.) | NET INCOME ($ mil.) | INCOME AS % OF ASSETS | EMPLOYEES |
|---|---|---|---|---|
| **12/06** | 25,101 | 453 | 1.8% | 5,200 |
| **12/05** | 22,816 | 207 | 0.9% | 6,100 |
| **12/04** | 22,560 | 360 | 1.6% | 6,800 |
| **12/03** | 20,197 | 294 | 1.5% | 6,600 |
| **12/02** | 19,505 | 85 | 0.4% | 7,100 |
| **Annual Growth** | 6.5% | 52.2% | — | (7.5%) |

### 2006 Year-End Financials

Equity as % of assets: 11.7%
Return on assets: 1.9%
Return on equity: 16.8%
Long-term debt ($ mil.): 921
No. of shares (mil.): 119
Dividends
Yield: 1.0%
Payout: 9.9%
Market value ($ mil.): 4,284
Sales ($ mil.): 4,250

### Stock History

NYSE: AFG

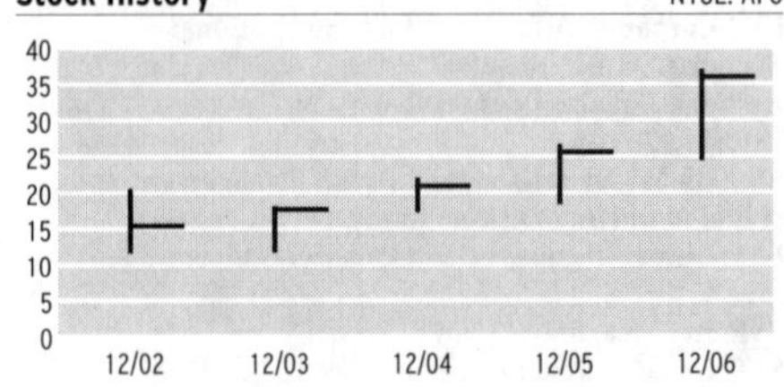


| | STOCK PRICE ($) FY Close | P/E High | P/E Low | PER SHARE ($) Earnings | PER SHARE ($) Dividends | PER SHARE ($) Book Value |
|---|---|---|---|---|---|---|
| **12/06** | 35.91 | 10 | 7 | 3.75 | 0.37 | 24.55 |
| **12/05** | 25.54 | 15 | 11 | 1.75 | 0.33 | 31.48 |
| **12/04** | 20.87 | 7 | 5 | 3.21 | 0.33 | 31.72 |
| **12/03** | 17.64 | 6 | 4 | 2.75 | 0.33 | 28.42 |
| **12/02** | 15.38 | 25 | 15 | 0.81 | 0.33 | 24.82 |
| **Annual Growth** | 23.6% | — | — | 46.7% | 2.9% | (0.3%) |

# American Greetings

American Greetings has been building its sturdy house of cards for more than a century. The #2 US maker of greeting cards (behind Hallmark), the company makes American Greetings, Carlton Cards, and Gibson Greetings brand missives. While greeting cards make up more than half of its sales, the company also produces DesignWare party goods, Plus Mark gift wrap, and DateWorks calendars. The company also operates about 440 retail outlets in North America, while its AG Interactive subsidiary operates the AmericanGreetings.com e-card site. American Greetings' products are sold in 125,000 retail stores worldwide.

To bring a smile to investors' faces, the company has been focused on cost controls and streamlining operations in order to improve margins. American Greetings has also trimmed away some non-core businesses, selling its GuildHouse candle line and subsidiary education publisher Learning Horizons in 2007. The company also closed about 60 underperforming retail stores during 2006.

Meanwhile, American Greetings has been investing in its digital media products, such as e-cards, ringtones, and mobile phone wallpapers, in response to the growing popularity of e-mail and online messaging. Its AG Interactive unit boasts more than 2.5 million subscribers and attracts more than 30 million visitors each month to its sites, which also include BlueMountain.com and Egreetings.com.

Chairman Morry Weiss and his family control about 25% of American Greetings' voting power. Weiss stepped down as CEO in 2003, but remains on the board. His sons, Zev and Jeff, took on the roles of CEO and president, respectively.

## HISTORY

In 1906 Polish immigrant Jacob Sapirstein founded Sapirstein Greeting Card Company and began selling postcards from a horse-drawn wagon. The outbreak of WWI and the resulting separation of families helped spur demand for the company's products. The impact of the war also helped shape the company's future: After an embargo was imposed on cards produced in Germany, Sapirstein decided to begin manufacturing his own cards.

Sapirstein's sons eventually joined the burgeoning company and, in 1940, after adopting the American Greetings Publishers name, the company's sales topped $1 million. The company incorporated as American Greetings in 1944 and went public in 1952. It introduced Hi Brows, a line of funny studio cards, in 1956 and broke ground on a 1.5 million-sq.-ft. headquarters building the same year.

In 1960 Sapirstein's son, Irving Stone (all three Sapirstein sons changed their surname to Stone, a derivative of Sapirstein) was appointed president, and Jacob Sapirstein became chairman. The ubiquitous Holly Hobbie made her first appearance on greeting cards in 1967 (within a decade, she had become the world's most popular licensed female character). In 1968 American Greetings' sales exceeded $100 million.

American Greetings introduced the Ziggy character in 1972 and launched Plus Mark, a maker of seasonal wrapping paper, boxed cards, and accessories six years later. Irving Stone succeeded his father as chairman and CEO in 1978, and Morry Weiss, Irving Stone's son-in-law, was appointed president.

The success of Holly Hobbie licensing prompted American Greetings to create its own licensing division in 1980. In 1982 it introduced the Care Bears, licensed characters that appeared in animated films. Following the death of Jacob Sapirstein in 1987 (at age 102), Morry Weiss became chairman and CEO, and Irving Stone became founder-chairman.

The company bought Magnivision (nonprescription reading glasses) in 1993. It ventured onto the Internet two years later, when it began offering online greeting cards. Its 1996 attempt to acquire #3 card maker Gibson Greetings proved unsuccessful. The company branched into supplemental educational products the following year when it unveiled its Learning Horizons product line.

Acquisitions of greeting card companies Camden Graphics and Hanson White in 1998 helped American Greetings double its presence in the UK. As part of an international restructuring, in 1999 it shuttered a Canadian plant, eliminating 650 jobs. Later that year, in an expansion of its existing agreement with America Online (now part of Time Warner), AmericanGreetings.com became AOL's exclusive provider of electronic greetings. The company subsequently filed to take its online unit public, intending to retain a majority of the company. (It withdrew its filing the following year when the Internet market went sour.)

Founder-chairman Irving Stone died in early 2000 at the age of 90. Also that year American Greetings paid $175 million for smaller rival Gibson Greetings, along with Gibson's stake in Egreetings Network. The company later expanded its profile in the gift wrap market through its acquisition of CPS Corporation, a supplier of gift wrap and packaging. In 2001 the company bought the remaining shares of Egreetings Network and folded the business into its online business, and later that year did the same with ExciteHome's BlueMountain.com e-mail cards unit.

In 2003 CEO Morry Weiss and president James Spira resigned from the management of the company. Weiss retained his chairman title and Spira remained on the board. Morry's sons, Zev and Jeffrey, became CEO and president, respectively. The next year the company changed the name of its digital unit to AG Interactive to better encompass its activities.

Later that year, the company sold its Magnivision unit to AAi.FosterGrant. In late 2004 the company closed one of its plants in Tennessee and laid off 450 people. The company also purchased a stake in Hatchery LLC, a family entertainment production company (sold in 2007).

In 2007 the company sold its educational products unit Learning Horizons to a portfolio company of Evolution Capital Partners.

## EXECUTIVES

**Chairman:** Morry Weiss, age 67
**CEO and Director:** Zev Weiss, age 40, $790,000 pay
**President, COO, and Director:** Jeffrey M. (Jeff) Weiss, age 43, $638,750 pay
**SVP and CFO:** Stephen J. Smith, age 43, $248,208 pay
**SVP and Executive Supply Chain Officer:** Michael L. Goulder, age 47, $429,880 pay
**SVP Creative and Merchandising; President, Carlton Cards Retail:** Thomas H. Johnston, age 59
**SVP and Executive Sales and Marketing Officer:** Steven S. Willensky, age 52, $428,141 pay
**SVP, General Counsel, and Secretary:** Catherine M. Kilbane, age 44
**SVP International:** John S.N. Charlton, age 61
**SVP Specialty Business:** Erwin Weiss, age 58, $765,000 pay
**SVP Wal-Mart Team:** William R. Mason, age 62
**SVP Human Resources:** Brian T. McGrath, age 56
**VP and Corporate Controller:** Joseph B. Cipollone, age 48
**VP Information Services:** Douglas W. (Doug) Rommel, age 51
**Director Investor Relations and Treasurer:** Gregory M. Steinberg
**Media Relations:** Megan Ferington
**Media Relations:** Frank Cirillo
**Auditors:** Ernst & Young LLP

## LOCATIONS

**HQ:** American Greetings Corporation
1 American Rd., Cleveland, OH 44144
**Phone:** 216-252-7300 **Fax:** 216-252-6778
**Web:** corporate.americangreetings.com

American Greetings has operations in Australia, Canada, Mexico, the UK, and the US.

### 2007 Sales

| | $ mil. | % of total |
|---|---|---|
| US | 1,288.4 | 74 |
| UK | 227.3 | 13 |
| Other countries | 228.9 | 13 |
| **Total** | **1,744.6** | **100** |

## PRODUCTS/OPERATIONS

### 2007 Sales

| | $ mil. | % of total |
|---|---|---|
| Everyday greeting cards | 656.9 | 38 |
| Seasonal greeting cards | 363.8 | 21 |
| Gift packaging | 278.1 | 16 |
| Other | 445.8 | 25 |
| **Total** | **1,744.6** | **100** |

### 2007 Sales

| | $ mil. | % of total |
|---|---|---|
| Social expression products | 1,425.8 | 82 |
| Retail operations | 207.2 | 12 |
| AG Interactive | 85.4 | 5 |
| Other | 26.2 | 1 |
| **Total** | **1,744.6** | **100** |

## COMPETITORS

1-800-FLOWERS.COM
Clinton Cards
CSS Industries
Eos International
FTD Group
Hallmark
International Greetings
SPS Studios
Taylor Corporation

## HISTORICAL FINANCIALS

Company Type: Public

### Income Statement

FYE: Last day in February

| | REVENUE ($ mil.) | NET INCOME ($ mil.) | NET PROFIT MARGIN | EMPLOYEES |
|---|---|---|---|---|
| **2/07** | 1,745 | 42 | 2.4% | 9,400 |
| **2/06** | 1,886 | 84 | 4.5% | 29,500 |
| **2/05** | 1,903 | 95 | 5.0% | 26,900 |
| **2/04** | 2,009 | 105 | 5.2% | 30,800 |
| **2/03** | 1,996 | 121 | 6.1% | 32,600 |
| **Annual Growth** | (3.3%) | (23.1%) | — | (26.7%) |

### 2007 Year-End Financials

Debt ratio: 22.1%
Return on equity: 3.8%
Cash ($ mil.): 145
Current ratio: 2.14
Long-term debt ($ mil.): 224
No. of shares (mil.): 51
Dividends
Yield: 1.4%
Payout: 45.1%
Market value ($ mil.): 1,189

### Stock History

NYSE: AM

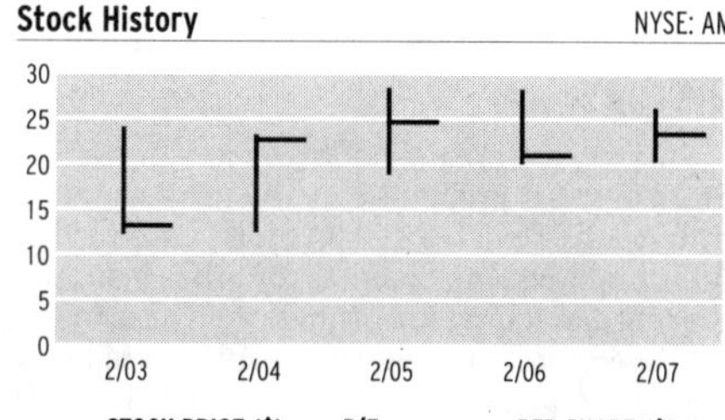


| | STOCK PRICE ($) FY Close | P/E High | P/E Low | PER SHARE ($) Earnings | Dividends | Book Value |
|---|---|---|---|---|---|---|
| **2/07** | 23.38 | 37 | 29 | 0.71 | 0.32 | 19.92 |
| **2/06** | 20.98 | 24 | 18 | 1.16 | 0.32 | 21.74 |
| **2/05** | 24.63 | 23 | 15 | 1.25 | 0.12 | 21.38 |
| **2/04** | 22.67 | 16 | 9 | 1.40 | — | 20.16 |
| **2/03** | 13.12 | 15 | 8 | 1.63 | — | 17.58 |
| **Annual Growth** | 15.5% | — | — | (18.8%) | 63.3% | 3.2% |

# American International Group

American International Group (AIG) is one of the world's largest insurance firms. Domestically the company is known as a leading provider of property/casualty, life, and specialty insurance to commercial, institutional, and individual customers. Internationally, AIG provides reinsurance, life insurance and retirement services, asset management, and financial services (including aircraft leasing) in more than 130 countries. Acquisitions have brought in leading annuities firm AIG SunAmerica, insurer AIG American General, and other companies specializing in retail financial markets.

Additional operations include auto insurance (through 21st Century Insurance) and residential mortgage guaranty (through United Guaranty).

The company, which has a long history of insurance operations in Asia, has supported China's accession to the World Trade Organization. AIG's growth plans include expanding its operations in China and India.

Seizing a moment, in early 2007 AIG's Global Investment Group snapped up the US port operations from Dubai-based DP World. DP World bought the operations in 2006, only to find that the deal attracted too much attention from US lawmakers fearful that such ownership might compromise US security. From that acquisition, AIG apparently developed a taste for ports and shortly thereafter announced agreements to purchase North American port operation companies AMPORTS and MTC Holdings. MTC brought with it operations at 32 US ports, primarily based on the west coast.

The dust is slowly settling for AIG, which was at the center of two investigations by state and federal regulators over accounting irregularities, fraud, and its use of offshore reinsurers. In addition to it agreeing to pay $1.6 billion, the company has retained an independent consultant to review its internal controls as part of its 2006 settlement.

## HISTORY

Former ice cream parlor owner Cornelius Starr founded property/casualty insurer American Asiatic Underwriters in Shanghai in 1919. After underwriting business for other insurers, Starr began selling life insurance policies to the Chinese in 1921 (foreign companies were loath to do so despite the longevity of the Chinese). In 1926 he opened a New York office specializing in foreign risks incurred by American companies. As WWII loomed, Starr moved his base to the US; when the war cut off business in Europe, he focused on Latin America. After a brief postwar return to China, the company was kicked out by the communist government.

In the 1950s the company began providing disability, health, and life insurance and pension plans for employees who moved from country to country. Starr chose his successor, Maurice "Hank" Greenberg, in 1967 and died the next year. Greenberg, who had come aboard in 1960 to develop overseas operations, took over the newly formed American International Group, a holding company for Starr's worldwide collection of insurance concerns. Greenberg's policy of achieving underwriting profits forced the company to use tight fiscal discipline. AIG went public in 1969.

By 1975 AIG was the largest foreign life insurer in much of Asia and the only insurer with global sales and support facilities. AIG's underwriting policies saved it when price wars from 1979 to 1984 brought heavy losses to most insurers. In 1987 AIG became the second US-owned insurer (after Chubb) to enter the traditionally closed South Korean market.

The 1980s saw AIG begin investment operations in Asia, increase its presence in health care, and form a financial services group. It bought International Lease Finance Corporation, which leases and remarkets jets to airlines, in 1990. AIG soon moved into parts of Eastern Europe.

The company resumed its Chinese operations in 1993 after triumphing over stiff opposition from state-owned monopolies.

In 1995 the company formed the Asian Infrastructure Fund, a mutual fund for individual investors. The following year AIG acquired SPC Credit, a consumer and commercial finance company with offices in the Philippines, Taiwan, and Thailand.

In 1998 AIG bought SunAmerica for $18.3 billion, giving the company access to a sales-driven distribution network and greater flexibility in the consolidating financial services industry.

In 2001 AIG agreed to be the business sponsor for the troubled Chiyoda Mutual Life Insurance Company (now AIG Star Life Insurance); it also bought American General, wooing the insurer away from rival suitor Prudential plc to bolster AIG's share of the lucrative US retirement-planning market.

The insurer paid out about $800 million in claims related to the attacks on the World Trade Center. Even though rate increases helped AIG's premium revenues grow, capital losses and the weak stock market dragged the company's net result down in 2002.

Legal settlements forced the company to take a $1.8 billion charge in 2003 in a move that surprised analysts and sent shock waves throughout the industry, causing other large insurance stocks to plummet. The company said the charge would be used to bolster reserves used for paying claims.

Legal woes continued to befall AIG in 2004, when two company executives pleaded guilty to charges of involvement in an alleged price-fixing scheme that also involved insurance broker Marsh and insurer ACE. AIG also reached a $126 million settlement with federal regulators in 2004 over allegations the insurer sold products and services used to help customers improve their financial appearance.

In 2004 AIG came under investigation by the Office of the Attorney General for the State of New York, the New York Insurance Department, and the SEC into possible accounting irregularities and the company's use of offshore reinsurers. In early 2005 Hank Greenberg was forced to step down as CEO. Former vice chairman and co-COO Martin Sullivan was named to succeed him. Soon after, Greenberg — the man most associated with the company — was forced to give up his chairman's seat. He stepped down from the board later that year.

As a result of the allegations, which included accounting irregularities, fraud, and bid-rigging, and along with acknowledging some wrongdoing, in 2006 the company agreed to pay a $1.6 billion settlement to the three agencies.

## EXECUTIVES

**Chairman:** Robert B. (Bob) Willumstad, age 61
**President, CEO, and Director:** Martin J. Sullivan, age 51, $7,750,337 pay
**Senior Vice Chairman, Life Insurance; Director:** Edmund S.W. Tse, age 69, $2,374,942 pay
**Vice Chairman, Global Economic Strategies:** Jacob A. Frenkel, age 64
**Vice Chairman, External Affairs:** Frank G. Wisner, age 68
**EVP and CFO:** Steven J. (Steve) Bensinger, age 52
**EVP and Chief Investment Officer; Chairman and CEO, Global Investment Group:** Win J. Neuger, age 57, $2,050,000 pay
**EVP and COO Life Insurance:** Rodney O. (Rod) Martin Jr., age 53
**EVP, General Counsel, and Senior Regulatory and Compliance Officer:** Anastasia D. (Stasia) Kelly, age 57
**EVP, Domestic General Insurance:** Kristian P. Moor, age 47, $1,865,673 pay
**EVP, Domestic Personal Lines:** Robert M. Sandler, age 64
**EVP, Foreign General Insurance; President and CEO, American International Underwriters:** Nicholas C. (Nick) Walsh, age 55
**EVP, Retirement Services; President and CEO, SunAmerica:** Jay S. Wintrob, age 48, $2,276,000 pay
**SVP and Secretary:** Kathleen E. Shannon, age 57
**SVP and Comptroller:** David L. Herzog, age 47
**SVP, Domestic General Insurance; Chairman and CEO, Lexington Insurance:** Kevin H. Kelley
**SVP, Investments:** Richard W. Scott, age 53, $1,672,212 pay
**SVP and Chief Human Resources Officer:** Andrew J. Kaslow, age 53
**VP and Director, Investor Relations:** Charlene M. Hamrah
**Chairman, AIG Companies in China:** Olin L. Wethington
**President, AIG Global Risk Management, Inc.:** Louis P. Iglesias
**President and CEO, AIG American General Life Companies:** Matthew E. Winter, age 49
**President and COO, American Life Insurance Company:** Joyce A. Phillips
**President Consumer Finance Group:** Rick Pfeiffer
**Auditors:** PricewaterhouseCoopers LLP

## LOCATIONS

**HQ:** American International Group, Inc.
70 Pine St., New York, NY 10270
**Phone:** 212-770-7000 **Fax:** 212-509-9705
**Web:** www.aigcorporate.com

### 2006 Sales

| | $ mil. | % of total |
|---|---|---|
| North America | 57,986 | 51 |
| Asia | 33,795 | 30 |
| Other regions | 21,413 | 19 |
| **Total** | **113,194** | **100** |

## PRODUCTS/OPERATIONS

### 2006 Sales

| | $ mil. | % of total |
|---|---|---|
| Premiums & other considerations | 74,083 | 66 |
| Net investment income | 25,292 | 22 |
| Other revenues | 13,713 | 12 |
| Realized capital gains | 106 | — |
| **Total** | **113,194** | **100** |

**2006 Sales**

| | $ mil. | % of total |
|---|---|---|
| Life insurance & retirement services | 50,163 | 44 |
| General insurance | 49,206 | 44 |
| Financial services | 8,010 | 7 |
| Asset management | 5,814 | 5 |
| Other | 1 | — |
| **Total** | **113,194** | **100** |

### Selected Subsidiaries

Asset Management
- AIG SunAmerica Asset Management Corp. (SAAMCo)
- AIG Global Asset Management Holdings Corp. (AIGGIG)

Financial Services
- International Lease Finance Corporation
- American General Finance, Inc. (AGF)
- AIG Consumer Fnance Group, Inc. (AIGCFG)
- Imperial A.I. Credit Companies

General Insurance
- 21st Century Group (62%)
- American Home Assurance Company (American Home)
- American International Underwriters Overseas, Ltd. (AIUO)
- The Hartford Steam Boiler Inspection and Insurance Company (HSB)
- Lexington Insurance Company (Lexington)
- National Union Fire Insurance Company of Pittsburgh, Pa. (National Union)
- New Hampshire Insurance Company (New Hampshire)
- Transatlantic Reinsurance Company
- United Guaranty Residential Insurance Company

Life Insurance & Retirement Services
- AIG Annuity Insurance Company (AIG Annuity)
- AIG SunAmerica Life Assurance Company
- American General Life Insurance Company (AIG American General)
- American General Life and Accident Insurance Company (AGLA)
- SunAmerica Life Insurance Company
- The United States Life Insurance Company in the City of New York (USLIFE)
- The Variable Annuity Life Insurance Company (VALIC)

## COMPETITORS

| | |
|---|---|
| ACE Limited | Lloyd's |
| AEGON | Manulife Financial |
| Allianz | MassMutual |
| Allstate | Meiji Yasuda Life |
| American Family | MetLife |
| Aon | MGIC Investment |
| AXA | Millea Holdings |
| Berkshire Hathaway | Nationwide |
| Chubb Corp | New York Life |
| CIGNA | Northwestern Mutual |
| CNA Financial | Prudential |
| COUNTRY Insurance | Prudential plc |
| GE | Safeco |
| GEICO | Skandia |
| General Re | Software Performance Systems |
| Hanover Insurance | State Farm |
| The Hartford | Sun Life |
| ING | TIAA-CREF |
| John Hancock | Travelers Companies |
| Legal & General Group | Zurich Financial Services |
| Liberty Mutual | |

## HISTORICAL FINANCIALS

Company Type: Public

**Income Statement** FYE: December 31

| | ASSETS ($ mil.) | NET INCOME ($ mil.) | INCOME AS % OF ASSETS | EMPLOYEES |
|---|---|---|---|---|
| **12/06** | 979,414 | 14,048 | 1.4% | 106,000 |
| **12/05** | 853,370 | 10,477 | 1.2% | 97,000 |
| **12/04** | 801,145 | 9,839 | 1.2% | 92,000 |
| **12/03** | 678,346 | 9,274 | 1.4% | 86,000 |
| **12/02** | 561,229 | 5,519 | 1.0% | 80,000 |
| **Annual Growth** | 14.9% | 26.3% | — | 7.3% |

**2006 Year-End Financials**

Equity as % of assets: 10.4%
Return on assets: 1.5%
Return on equity: 14.9%
Long-term debt ($ mil.): 134,210
No. of shares (mil.): 2,601
Dividends
Yield: 0.9%
Payout: 11.8%
Market value ($ mil.): 186,402
Sales ($ mil.): 113,194

**Stock History** NYSE: AIG

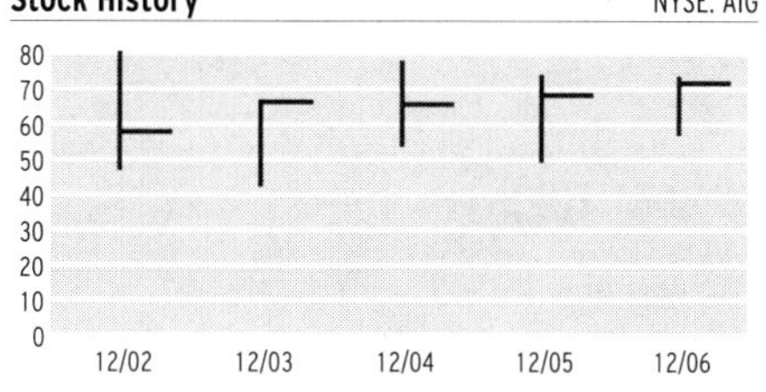


| | STOCK PRICE ($) FY Close | P/E High | P/E Low | PER SHARE ($) Earnings | Dividends | Book Value |
|---|---|---|---|---|---|---|
| **12/06** | 71.66 | 14 | 11 | 5.36 | 0.63 | 39.09 |
| **12/05** | 68.23 | 18 | 13 | 3.99 | 0.55 | 33.24 |
| **12/04** | 65.67 | 21 | 15 | 3.73 | 0.28 | 30.69 |
| **12/03** | 66.28 | 19 | 12 | 3.53 | 0.22 | 27.39 |
| **12/02** | 57.85 | 38 | 23 | 2.10 | 0.14 | 22.65 |
| **Annual Growth** | 5.5% | — | — | 26.4% | 45.6% | 14.6% |

# American Standard

Air conditioning, hot and cold running water, and cars. Ain't civilization grand? American Standard Companies is a leading maker of air-conditioning systems, plumbing products, and automotive braking systems. Its air-conditioning division makes consumer and commercial systems under the Trane and American Standard brand names. Its kitchen and bath segment makes plumbing fixtures (toilets, tubs, sinks, and faucets) under such names as American Standard, Ideal Standard, JADO, and Porcher. American Standard makes vehicle braking systems through subsidiary WABCO. The company is restructuring, spinning off WABCO and selling its kitchen and bath division to Bain Capital for more than $1.75 billion.

The moves come after the company realized that maybe combining three such disparate businesses under one name could be confusing as well as self-defeating. It hopes that three separate companies will better be able to compete in their individual markets.

Once the transactions are complete, American Standard will rename itself Trane, after its best-selling brand.

## HISTORY

In 1881 American Radiator began making steam and water-heating equipment in Buffalo, New York. J. P. Morgan acquired the company, along with almost every other US heating-equipment firm, and consolidated them as American Radiator in 1899. That year Ahrens & Ott joined with Standard Manufacturing to create Standard Sanitary, which produced enameled cast-iron plumbing fixtures.

Both American Radiator and Standard Sanitary grew through acquisitions early in the 20th century. In 1929 the companies merged to form American Radiator & Standard Sanitary, expanding operations across the Americas and into Europe. By the 1960s the company was the world's #1 manufacturer of plumbing fixtures.

The firm became American Standard in 1967 and began diversifying through acquisitions. In 1968 it bought Westinghouse Air Brake (WABCO), which made railway brakes and, later, automotive products. (WABCO traces its history to Union Switch and Signal, founded in 1882.) During the 1970s and 1980s the firm consolidated operations and sold numerous businesses. It bought Trane (air conditioners) in 1984.

American Standard fought off a hostile takeover by Black & Decker in 1988 and then agreed to be purchased by ASI Holding (formed by LBO firm Kelso & Company) and taken private. The transaction left the firm deeply in debt. To raise cash, it sold its Manhattan headquarters, its railway signal business, its Steelcraft division, and its pneumatic-controls business in 1988.

The company suffered throughout the 1990s from slow sales growth and poor earnings, prompting the company to streamline operations, shake up management in several areas, and institute a just-in-time manufacturing system to help pare inventory. American Standard sold its railway brake operations in 1990 and its Tyler Refrigeration unit in 1991, losing $22 million in the deal. In 1994 the company acquired 70% of Deutsche Perrot-Bremsen's automotive brake business in a joint venture. American Standard went public again in 1995 and bought the 67% of Etablissements Porcher Paris (bathroom fixtures) that it did not already own. Late in 1996 American Standard fought off a takeover bid by Tyco. The next year Horst Hinrichs (SVP at WABCO) was appointed vice chairman of the corporation to provide management succession.

In 1999 the company bought the bathroom-fixtures business of Blue Circle (UK) for $417 million to boost its sales in Europe. American Standard also hired AlliedSignal's president, Frederic Poses, to replace Emanuel Kampouris as chairman and CEO and began seeking a buyer for its medical diagnostics operations that year. (The company's medical systems group, which began operating in 1989, made low-cost analyzers and diagnostic supplies for use in doctors' offices.) American Standard sold its medical unit in 2000. Later that year the company sold its Calorex water heater business.

A sputtering economy adversely affected 2001 sales, especially for braking systems. Poses dealt with the company's heavy debt and sluggish profit margins by improving employee performance and cutting jobs. To reduce costs, American Standard laid off about 8% of its workforce in 2001. Also that year the company's air-conditioning subsidiary, Trane, announced plans for a global alliance with a Japanese air-conditioning manufacturer, Daikin, to cross-market and sell each other's products beginning in 2002.

In early 2003 American Standard acquired Spain's second-largest manufacturer of porcelain sanitary-ware, Uralita's Sangra business, to strengthen its position in Europe. The company announced in 2004 that it was extending Poses' contract through December 2007.

## EXECUTIVES

**Chairman and CEO:** Frederic M. (Fred) Poses, age 64, $1,000,000 pay
**SVP and CFO:** G. Peter D'Aloia, age 62, $600,000 pay
**SVP, General Counsel, and Secretary:** Mary Elizabeth Gustafsson, age 47
**SVP Human Resources:** Lawrence B. (Larry) Costello, age 59, $414,658 pay
**SVP; President, Bath and Kitchen:** Dale F. Elliott, age 52
**SVP; President, Trane Commercial Systems:** W. Craig Kissel, age 55, $525,000 pay
**VP; President, Residential Systems:** David R. (Dave) Pannier, age 56
**VP and CFO, Bath and Kitchen:** Richard S. (Rich) Paradise, age 45
**VP and General Tax Counsel:** Nicholas A. (Nick) Anthony
**VP and CFO, Residential Systems:** R. Scott Massengill, age 44
**VP Government and Public Affairs:** David (Dave) Modi
**VP and Chief Communications Officer:** Shelly J. London
**VP and Chief Marketing Officer:** Sally Genster Robling
**VP Strategic Planning and Investor Relations:** R. Bruce Fisher
**VP and Treasurer:** David S. Kuhl, age 46
**VP and General Auditor:** Edward Schlesinger, age 39
**VP, Marketing, Strategy, and Investor Relations, WABCO:** Mike Thompson
**Auditors:** Ernst & Young LLP

## LOCATIONS

**HQ:** American Standard Companies Inc.
One Centennial Ave., Piscataway, NJ 08855
**Phone:** 732-980-6000 **Fax:** 732-980-3340
**Web:** www.americanstandard.com

### 2006 Sales

| | $ mil. | % of total |
|---|---|---|
| US | 5,944 | 53 |
| Europe | | |
| Germany | 990 | 9 |
| UK | 562 | 5 |
| Italy | 462 | 4 |
| France | 379 | 4 |
| Other Europe | 1,170 | 10 |
| Other countries | 1,701 | 15 |
| **Total** | **11,208** | **100** |

## PRODUCTS/OPERATIONS

### 2006 Sales

| | $ mil. | % of total |
|---|---|---|
| Air-conditioning systems & services | 6,758 | 60 |
| Bath & kitchen | 2,435 | 22 |
| Vehicle control systems | 2,015 | 18 |
| **Total** | **11,208** | **100** |

### Selected Products

Air Conditioning
- Commercial applied systems (chillers, air handlers, variable air volume units, and fan coils)

Light and large commercial unitary systems
Split-system and packaged residential systems
- (condensing units, furnaces, air handlers, heat pumps, coils, and air filtration devices)

Thermostats
Bath and Kitchen
- Bathroom and kitchen fittings and fixtures
- Bathroom and kitchen faucets
- Bathtubs

Vehicle Control Systems
- ABS braking systems
- EBS braking systems
- Pneumatic braking control systems

### Selected Trademarks

American Standard
Armitage Shanks
Dolomite
Ideal Standard
Jado
Porcher
Standard
Trane
WABCO

## COMPETITORS

A. O. Smith Water Products
ArvinMeritor
Black & Decker
BorgWarner
Carrier
Daikin
Dana
Eaton
Electrolux
Geberit
Gerber Plumbing Fixtures
Goodman Global
Goodman Manufacturing
Grohe
Jacuzzi Brands
Johnson Controls
Knorr-Bremse
Kohler
Lennox
Masco
Moen
Mueller Industries
Nordyne
Robert Bosch
Tecumseh Products
TOTO
United Electric Company
United Technologies
Villeroy & Boch
Watsco
Whirlpool
Yazaki Energy Systems

## HISTORICAL FINANCIALS

Company Type: Public

### Income Statement — FYE: December 31

| | REVENUE ($ mil.) | NET INCOME ($ mil.) | NET PROFIT MARGIN | EMPLOYEES |
|---|---|---|---|---|
| **12/06** | 11,208 | 541 | 4.8% | 62,200 |
| **12/05** | 10,264 | 556 | 5.4% | 27,100 |
| **12/04** | 9,509 | 313 | 3.3% | 61,500 |
| **12/03** | 8,568 | 405 | 4.7% | 60,000 |
| **12/02** | 7,795 | 371 | 4.8% | 60,000 |
| **Annual Growth** | 9.5% | 9.9% | — | 0.9% |

### 2006 Year-End Financials

Debt ratio: 173.3%
Return on equity: 58.6%
Cash ($ mil.): 294
Current ratio: 1.34
Long-term debt ($ mil.): 1,601
No. of shares (mil.): 200
Dividends
Yield: 2.2%
Payout: 27.5%
Market value ($ mil.): 6,571

### Stock History — NYSE: ASD

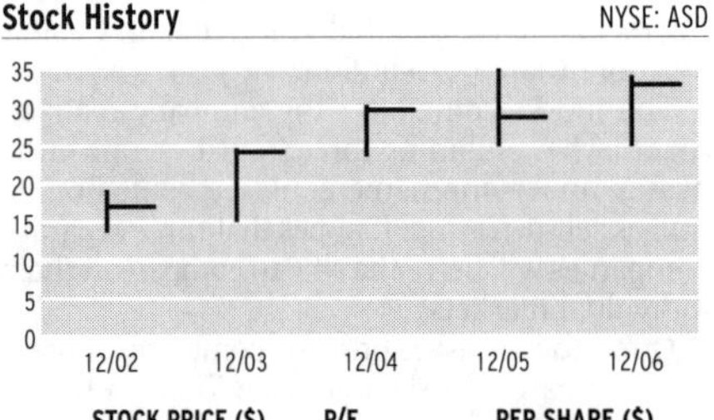

| | STOCK PRICE ($) FY Close | P/E High | P/E Low | PER SHARE ($) Earnings | Dividends | Book Value |
|---|---|---|---|---|---|---|
| **12/06** | 32.87 | 13 | 10 | 2.62 | 0.72 | 4.62 |
| **12/05** | 28.64 | 14 | 10 | 2.56 | 0.60 | 4.46 |
| **12/04** | 29.62 | 21 | 17 | 1.42 | — | 4.34 |
| **12/03** | 24.07 | 13 | 8 | 1.83 | — | 9.83 |
| **12/02** | 17.00 | 11 | 8 | 1.68 | — | 3.16 |
| **Annual Growth** | 17.9% | — | — | 11.8% | 20.0% | 9.9% |

# AmeriCredit Corp.

Bad credit is a good risk, according to AmeriCredit. The company purchases loans made by more than 17,000 franchised and select independent auto dealers to shoppers with credit limitations or past credit trouble. It typically finances low-mileage, late-model used cars, and the occasional new automobile. Loans made through franchised dealers make up some 95% of AmeriCredit's loan portfolio. The company securitizes and sells most of its loans, retains the servicing, and reinvests the proceeds in new loans. The lender has more than 1 million customers and some $12 billion in managed auto receivables. It operates about 80 branches in nearly 35 states.

At the beginning of 2007 the company's AmeriCredit Financial Services subsidiary bought indirect subprime auto lender Long Beach Acceptance from ACC Capital for some $283 million. AmeriCredit also purchased auto lending company Bay View Acceptance Corporation (BVAC) from what is now Great Lakes Bancorp for about $62 million in 2006.

In 2005 Dan Berce succeeded Clifton Morris, Jr. as CEO of AmeriCredit. Morris retained his position as chairman, a position he has held at the company since it was founded.

## HISTORY

AmeriCredit began in 1986 as UrCarco — used car lots offering both sales and financing to customers with poor credit. It was the inspiration of Cash America pawnshop executives Jack Daugherty and Clifton Morris, who financed UrCarco with four other investors and created the nation's first chain of used car lots. The company's 1989 IPO met with great success, but the excitement was short-lived; after quadrupling in size to 20 lots, UrCarco became mired in huge losses from poor underwriting and bad loans on top of declining car sales. In 1991 the company began reinventing itself, completely restructuring after receiving $10 million from Rainwater Management.

In 1992 UrCarco changed its name to AmeriCredit, liquidated its used car business, and expanded its indirect lending services. The company improved its underwriting by adopting a credit-risk scorecard in 1994 (with assistance from credit-scoring industry leader Fair Isaac Corporation). In 1996 AmeriCredit acquired California-based Rancho Vista Mortgage (it became AmeriCredit Corporation of California) and established a home equity lending operation, making and acquiring loans through a network of mortgage brokers.

The late 1990s provided their challenges. AmeriCredit survived the subprime market meltdown of 1997 and faced continuing criticism for its accounting practices. In 1999 it formed an alliance with Chase Manhattan (now JPMorgan Chase) to provide subprime financing to auto dealers who do business with Chase. That year it discontinued its mortgage operations and began liquidating its AmeriCredit Corporation of California subsidiary to focus on its auto lending.

In 2001 it teamed with JPMorgan Chase, Wells Fargo, and other finance companies to launch DealerTrack, an online system that allows dealers to submit loan applications electronically to various lenders, and receive faster responses.

In 2002 AmeriCredit began closing branches, scaling back on originations, downsizing its workforce, and closing its Canadian lending activities.

## EXECUTIVES

**Chairman:** Clifton H. Morris Jr., age 71, $2,465,959 pay
**President, CEO, and Director:** Daniel E. (Dan) Berce, age 53, $2,594,418 pay
**EVP and COO, Originations:** Preston A. Miller, age 42, $1,034,735 pay
**EVP and COO, Servicing:** S. Mark Floyd, age 53, $1,034,735 pay
**EVP, CFO, and Treasurer:** Chris A. Choate, age 43, $919,110 pay
**EVP, Chief Credit and Risk Officer:** Steven P. Bowman, age 39
**SVP, Human Resources:** Nancy Smart
**SVP Dealer Services, Canada:** Howard Cobham
**VP, Investor Relations:** Caitlin DeYoung
**VP, Public Relations and Communication:** John Hoffman
**Manager, Public Relations:** Amy Allen
**Auditors:** Deloitte & Touche LLP

## LOCATIONS

**HQ:** AmeriCredit Corp.
801 Cherry St., Ste. 3900, Fort Worth, TX 76102
**Phone:** 817-302-7000 **Fax:** 817-302-7101
**Web:** www.americredit.com

## PRODUCTS/OPERATIONS

### 2006 Sales

| | $ mil. | % of total |
|---|---|---|
| Finance charges | 1,641.1 | 91 |
| Servicing fees | 75.2 | 4 |
| Other | 95.0 | 5 |
| **Total** | **1,811.3** | **100** |

## COMPETITORS

The Aegis Consumer Funding Group, Inc.
Capital One
Consumer Portfolio
Credit Acceptance
First Investors Financial Services
HSBC Finance
iDNA

## HISTORICAL FINANCIALS

Company Type: Public

### Income Statement

FYE: June 30

| | ASSETS ($ mil.) | NET INCOME ($ mil.) | INCOME AS % OF ASSETS | EMPLOYEES |
|---|---|---|---|---|
| **6/06** | 13,068 | 306 | 2.3% | 4,025 |
| **6/05** | 10,947 | 286 | 2.6% | 3,653 |
| **6/04** | 8,825 | 227 | 2.6% | 3,535 |
| **6/03** | 8,108 | 21 | 0.3% | 3,639 |
| **6/02** | 4,225 | 348 | 8.2% | 5,250 |
| **Annual Growth** | 32.6% | (3.1%) | — | (6.4%) |

### 2006 Year-End Financials

Equity as % of assets: 15.4%
Return on assets: 2.6%
Return on equity: 14.8%
Long-term debt ($ mil.): 10,880
No. of shares (mil.): 127
Dividends
Yield: —
Payout: —
Market value ($ mil.): 3,555
Sales ($ mil.): 1,811

### Stock History

NYSE: ACF

| | STOCK PRICE ($) FY Close | P/E High | P/E Low | PER SHARE ($) Earnings | Dividends | Book Value |
|---|---|---|---|---|---|---|
| **6/06** | 27.92 | 15 | 10 | 2.08 | — | 15.78 |
| **6/05** | 25.50 | 15 | 10 | 1.73 | — | 14.57 |
| **6/04** | 19.53 | 14 | 4 | 1.42 | — | 13.48 |
| **6/03** | 8.55 | 189 | 10 | 0.15 | — | 12.02 |
| **6/02** | 28.05 | 17 | 4 | 3.87 | — | 16.69 |
| **Annual Growth** | (0.1%) | — | — | (14.4%) | — | (1.4%) |

# AmeriGas Partners

America has a gas with AmeriGas Partners. Purveying propane has propelled the company to its position as one of the top two US retail propane marketers (rivaling Ferrellgas for the #1 slot). It serves 1.3 million residential, commercial, industrial, agricultural, motor fuel, and wholesale customers from about 600 locations in 46 states. AmeriGas also sells propane-related supplies and equipment and exchanges prefilled portable tanks for empty ones. The company stores propane in Arizona, California, and Virginia and distributes its products through an interstate carrier structure that runs through 48 states in the US and in Canada. Utility holding company UGI owns 44% of AmeriGas.

In a consolidating industry, the fuel supplier has pursued a strategy of growth through acquisition, and has purchased more than 75 local and regional propane marketers. AmeriGas Partners boosted its market share by buying the Columbia Energy Group propane businesses from NiSource. It has purchased the propane distribution assets of Active Propane, Rocky Mountain LP, and Noreika Gas; as well as three propane distribution outlets from Suburban Propane Partners. In 2003 AmeriGas also purchased the retail propane distribution assets of Horizon Propane.

AmeriGas plans to grow internally through the expansion of its prefilled propane business (PPX) located at about 22,000 retail locations in the US.

In 2007 the company acquired Royal Dutch Shell's US retail propane operations.

## HISTORY

The forerunner of AmeriGas Partners was set up in 1959, when UGI subsidiary Ugite Gas entered the liquefied petroleum gas market in Maryland and Pennsylvania. By the early 1970s the company had expanded into eight states, and in 1977 AmeriGas was formed to replace Ugite Gas.

In the 1980s UGI began to focus more on propane. AmeriGas became one of the industry's leading players when it acquired Cal Gas in 1987, and three years later UGI merged AmeriGas with AP Propane. In 1993 UGI acquired a stake in propane marketer Petrolane, and the next year it formed AmeriGas Partners to acquire AmeriGas Propane, AmeriGas Propane-2 (another UGI unit), and Petrolane.

In 1995 UGI sold 42% of AmeriGas Partners to the public. AmeriGas Partners acquired Hawaii's Oahu Gas Service, Pur-Gas Service in Florida, and Enderby Gas in Texas the next year. In 1997 it acquired 14 firms in Florida, Georgia, Illinois, Louisiana, Mississippi, and South Carolina. The next year it bought 10 more companies and expanded its prefilled propane tank operations by more than 4,000 locations.

AmeriGas gained retail propane operations in five western states from All Star Gas in 2000. The next year the company paid $202 million for NiSource's Columbia Energy Group propane businesses. In 2003 AmeriGas purchased the propane distribution assets of Active Propane, Rocky Mountain LP, and Noreika Gas; as well as three propane distribution outlets from Suburban Propane Partners. Later that year, the company purchased the retail propane distribution business of Horizon Propane.

## EXECUTIVES

**Chairman; Chairman and CEO, UGI:** Lon R. Greenberg, age 56, $2,508,565 pay
**Vice Chairman:** John L. Walsh, age 51, $666,717 pay
**President, CEO, and Director:** Eugene V. N. Bissell, age 53, $705,442 pay
**VP Finance and CFO, AmeriGas Propane:** Jerry E. Sheridan, age 40
**VP, Secretary, and General Counsel:** Robert H. Knauss, age 53, $516,109 pay
**VP Human Resources:** William D. Katz, age 52, $318,123 pay
**VP Sales and Marketing:** Carey M. Monaghan, age 54
**VP Supply and Logistics:** David L. Lugar, age 48
**VP Finance and CFO, UGI:** Michael J. Cuzzolina, age 61
**CIO:** R. W. Fabrizio
**Chief Accounting Officer and Controller:** William J. Stanczak, age 50
**Investor Relations:** Robert W. Krick
**Media Relations:** Brenda Blake
**Auditors:** PricewaterhouseCoopers LLP

## LOCATIONS

**HQ:** AmeriGas Partners, L.P.
460 N. Gulph Rd., King of Prussia, PA 19406
**Phone:** 610-337-7000 **Fax:** 610-992-3259
**Web:** www.amerigas.com

AmeriGas Partners operates in 46 states in the US.

## PRODUCTS/OPERATIONS

### 2006 Sales

| | $ mil. | % of total |
|---|---|---|
| Propane | | |
| Retail | 1,816.0 | 86 |
| Wholesale | 137.7 | 6 |
| Other | 165.6 | 8 |
| **Total** | **2,119.3** | **100** |

### Selected Subsidiaries

AmeriGas Eagle Finance Corp.
AmeriGas Finance Corp.
AmeriGas Propane, L.P. (99%)
AmeriGas Eagle Propane, L.P. (99%)
AmeriGas Eagle Parts & Service, Inc.
AmeriGas Propane Parts & Service, Inc.
AmeriGas Eagle Propane, Inc.
AmeriGas Eagle Holdings, Inc.
Active Propane of Wisconsin LLC
AP Eagle Finance Corp.

## COMPETITORS

All Star Gas
Energy Transfer
Ferrellgas Partners
Piedmont Natural Gas
Southern States
Star Gas Partners
Suburban Propane

## HISTORICAL FINANCIALS

Company Type: Public

**Income Statement** FYE: September 30

| | REVENUE ($ mil.) | NET INCOME ($ mil.) | NET PROFIT MARGIN | EMPLOYEES |
|---|---|---|---|---|
| **9/06** | 2,119 | 91 | 4.3% | 5,900 |
| **9/05** | 1,963 | 61 | 3.1% | 6,000 |
| **9/04** | 1,776 | 92 | 5.2% | 6,100 |
| **9/03** | 1,628 | 72 | 4.4% | 6,200 |
| **9/02** | 1,308 | 55 | 4.2% | 6,300 |
| **Annual Growth** | 12.8% | 13.3% | — | (1.6%) |

**2006 Year-End Financials**

Debt ratio: 420.7%
Return on equity: 32.6%
Cash ($ mil.): 85
Current ratio: 0.97
Long-term debt ($ mil.): 932
No. of shares (mil.): 57
Dividends
Yield: 7.4%
Payout: 143.4%
Market value ($ mil.): 1,753

**Stock History** NYSE: APU

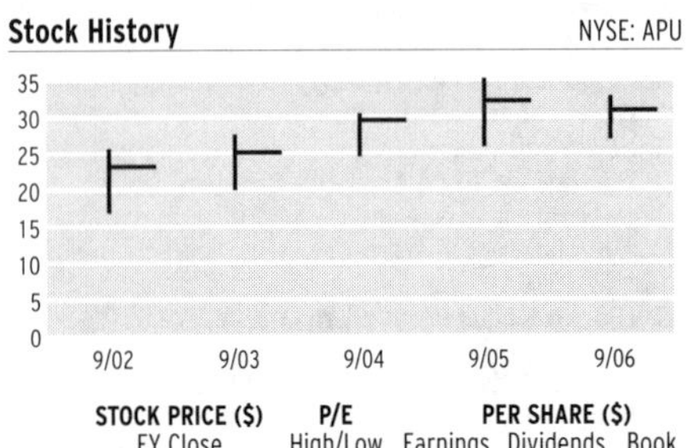


| | STOCK PRICE ($) FY Close | P/E High | P/E Low | PER SHARE ($) Earnings | Dividends | Book Value |
|---|---|---|---|---|---|---|
| **9/06** | 30.86 | 20 | 17 | 1.59 | 2.28 | 3.90 |
| **9/05** | 32.18 | 32 | 24 | 1.10 | 2.22 | 5.94 |
| **9/04** | 29.53 | 18 | 15 | 1.71 | 1.65 | 5.31 |
| **9/03** | 25.10 | 19 | 14 | 1.42 | 2.20 | 4.85 |
| **9/02** | 23.16 | 23 | 15 | 1.12 | 2.20 | 5.78 |
| **Annual Growth** | 7.4% | — | — | 9.2% | 0.9% | (9.4%) |

# AmerisourceBergen

AmerisourceBergen is *the* source for many of North America's pharmacies and retailers. The company provides pharmaceutical distribution and other services to hospitals, community drugstores, nursing homes, clinics, prescription benefits managers, mass merchandisers, and other clients from more than 25 distribution centers throughout the US and Canada. The company primarily distributes generic, branded, and OTC pharmaceuticals, but offers toiletries, sundries, and medical supplies as well. In 2007 the company spun off its PharMerica subsidiary, which delivers pharmaceuticals and provides services through its institutional pharmacies.

AmerisourceBergen spun off PharMerica's long-term care business and merged it with Kindred Healthcare's institutional pharmacy unit. The mutual venture became the second-largest institutional pharmacy (i.e., preparing and distributing drugs and other pharmaceuticals to institutions such as hospices, hospitals, and nursing homes) in the US, right out of the running gate.

The Pharmaceutical Division includes its key whole drug distribution business, as well as the AmerisourceBergen Specialty Group, which distributes drugs and supplies for specific disease targets (i.e., oncology) to health care providers specializing in those areas of medicine. Other members of this division are AmerisourceBergen Packaging Group and AmerisourceBergen Technology Group, which sells automated pharmacy dispensing cabinets and other products to help customers better control their supplies and to help reduce medical errors. Institutional clients (health care providers and facilities and mail-order pharmacies) account for about 60% of the Pharmaceutical Division's sales, while retailers (chain drugstores, independent pharmacies, and supermarket and mass merchandiser pharmacies) make up the rest.

AmerisourceBergen's top client is Medco Health Solutions, which accounted for 7% of the company's 2006 operating revenue. Two group purchasing organizations — Novation and Premier Purchasing Partners — together accounted for 8% of operating revenue in 2006.

AmerisourceBergen has been expanding through acquisitions, primarily looking to grow its services for pharmaceutical manufacturers and expand its geographic reach. Acquisitions have made AmerisourceBergen Canada the second largest pharmaceutical distributor in Canada. In addition, the company is streamlining its existing operations by expanding some distribution facilities while closing others. Since 2001, the firm has closed nearly 30 facilities and built six.

## HISTORY

In 1977 Cleveland millionaire and horse racing enthusiast Tinkham Veale went into the drug wholesaling business. His company, Alco Standard (now IKON Office Solutions), already owned chemical, electrical, metallurgical, and mining companies, but by the late 1970s the company was pursuing a strategy of zeroing in on various types of distribution businesses.

Alco's first drug wholesaler purchase was The Drug House (Delaware and Pennsylvania); next was Duff Brothers (Tennessee). The company then bought further wholesalers in the South, East, and Midwest. Its modus operandi was to buy small, well-run companies for cash and Alco stock and leave the incumbent management in charge.

By the early 1980s Alco was the US's third-largest wholesale drug distributor and growing quickly (28% between 1983 and 1988) at a time of mass consolidation in the industry (the number of wholesalers dropped by half between 1980 and 1992). In 1985 Alco Standard spun off its drug distribution operations as Alco Health Services, retaining 60% ownership.

Alco Health boosted its sales above $1 billion mostly via acquisitions and expanded product lines. The company offered marketing and promotional help to its independent pharmacy customers (which were beleaguered by the growth of national discounters) and also targeted hospitals, nursing homes, and clinics.

The US was in the midst of its LBO frenzy in 1988, but an Alco management group failed in its attempt. Rival McKesson then tried to acquire Alco Health, but that deal fell through for antitrust reasons. Later in 1988 management turned for backing to Citicorp Venture Capital in another buyout attempt. This time the move succeeded, and a new holding company, Alco Health Distribution, was formed.

In 1993 Alco Health was named as a defendant in suits by independent pharmacies charging discriminatory pricing policies; a ruling the next year limited its liability. To move away from a reliance on independent drugstores, Alco Health began targeting government entities and others.

Alco Health went public as AmeriSource Health in 1995. Throughout the next year, AmeriSource made a series of acquisitions to move into related areas, including inventory management technology, drugstore pharmaceutical supplies, and disease-management services for pharmacies.

In 1997 AmeriSource acquired Alabama-based Walker Drug, adding 1,500 independent and chain drugstores in the Southeast to its customer list. That same year, McKesson once again made an offer to buy AmeriSource, this time for $2.4 billion, while two other major wholesale distributors, Cardinal Health and Bergen Brunswig, reached a similar pact. The deals were scrapped in 1998 when the Federal Trade Commission voted against both pacts, and a federal judge supported that decision.

In 2001 AmeriSource bought Bergen Brunswig, and the combined company renamed itself AmerisourceBergen.

In 2005, the company acquired Trent Drugs (Wholesale), a Canadian pharmaceutical wholesaler, and renamed it AmerisourceBergen Canada. The following year, it acquired Canadian pharmaceutical distributors Asenda Pharmaceutical Supplies (Western Canada), and Rep-Pharm (Central and Eastern Canada).

AmerisourceBergen was highly acquisitive throughout 2006. That year it acquired I.G.G. of America, a specialty pharmacy specialized in blood derivative IVIG. It also purchased medical education and analytical research firm Network for Medical Communications & Research, LLC (NMCR); NMCR became part of AmerisourceBergen's manufacturer services business. In March of that year, AmerisourceBergen acquired UK-based pharmaceutical packaging manufacturer Brecon Pharmaceuticals. It also purchased Florida-based Health Advocates, which provides cost containment services to insurance payors.

## EXECUTIVES

**Chairman:** Richard C. Gozon, age 68
**CEO and Director:** R. David (Dave) Yost, age 60, $2,667,197 pay
**President, COO, and Director:** Kurt J. Hilzinger, age 46, $1,516,556 pay
**EVP and CFO:** Michael D. DiCandilo, age 45, $1,157,631 pay
**SVP; President, AmerisourceBergen Specialty Group:** Steven H. Collis, age 45, $933,441 pay
**SVP, Supply Chain Management:** Leonardo (Len) DeCandia
**SVP, Human Resources:** Jeanne B. Fisher
**SVP; President, AmerisourceBergen Drug:** Terrance P. (Terry) Haas, age 41, $757,116 pay
**SVP and CIO:** Thomas H. Murphy
**SVP, Retail Sales and Marketing:** David W. (Dave) Neu
**SVP, Health Systems Solutions:** John Palumbo
**SVP and General Counsel:** William D. (Bill) Sprague

**VP, Deputy General Counsel, and Secretary:** John G. Chou
**VP and Corporate Controller:** Tim G. Guttman
**VP, Corporate and Investor Relations:** Michael N. Kilpatric
**VP and Corporate Treasurer:** J. F. (Jack) Quinn
**VP, Strategy and Corporate Development:** David M. Senior
**Director, Corporate and Investor Relations:** Barbara A. Brungess
**Auditors:** Ernst & Young LLP

## LOCATIONS

**HQ:** AmerisourceBergen Corporation
1300 Morris Dr., Ste. 100, Chesterbrook, PA 19087
**Phone:** 610-727-7000 **Fax:** 610-727-3600
**Web:** www.amerisourcebergen.com

AmerisourceBergen has facilities in 22 US states, as well as in Puerto Rico; it operates facilities in six Canadian provinces.

## PRODUCTS/OPERATIONS

**2006 Sales**

| | $ mil. | % of total |
|---|---|---|
| Pharmaceutical distribution | 55,907.5 | 90 |
| Bulk deliveries to customer warehouses | 4,530.2 | 7 |
| PharMerica | 1,668.3 | 3 |
| Adjustments | (902.9) | — |
| **Total** | **61,203.1** | **100** |

**Selected Subsidiaries**

American Health Packaging
AmerisourceBergen Services Corporation
ASD Healthcare
AutoMed
Choice Systems, Inc.
MedSelect

## COMPETITORS

Cardinal Health
Covance
FFF Enterprises
Henry Schein
Kinray
McKesson
Owens & Minor
PSS World Medical
Quality King
UPS Logistics Technologies
US Oncology

## HISTORICAL FINANCIALS

Company Type: Public

**Income Statement** FYE: September 30

| | REVENUE ($ mil.) | NET INCOME ($ mil.) | NET PROFIT MARGIN | EMPLOYEES |
|---|---|---|---|---|
| **9/06** | 61,203 | 468 | 0.8% | 14,700 |
| **9/05** | 54,577 | 265 | 0.5% | 13,400 |
| **9/04** | 53,179 | 468 | 0.9% | 14,100 |
| **9/03** | 49,657 | 441 | 0.9% | 14,800 |
| **9/02** | 45,235 | 345 | 0.8% | 13,700 |
| **Annual Growth** | 7.9% | 7.9% | — | 1.8% |

**2006 Year-End Financials**

Debt ratio: 26.4%
Return on equity: 11.1%
Cash ($ mil.): 1,329
Current ratio: 1.23
Long-term debt ($ mil.): 1,094
No. of shares (mil.): 196
Dividends
Yield: 0.2%
Payout: 3.6%
Market value ($ mil.): 8,875

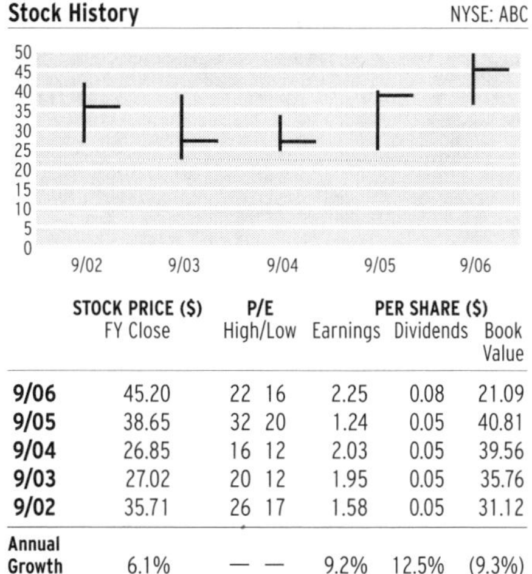


| | STOCK PRICE ($) FY Close | P/E High | P/E Low | PER SHARE ($) Earnings | Dividends | Book Value |
|---|---|---|---|---|---|---|
| **9/06** | 45.20 | 22 | 16 | 2.25 | 0.08 | 21.09 |
| **9/05** | 38.65 | 32 | 20 | 1.24 | 0.05 | 40.81 |
| **9/04** | 26.85 | 16 | 12 | 2.03 | 0.05 | 39.56 |
| **9/03** | 27.02 | 20 | 12 | 1.95 | 0.05 | 35.76 |
| **9/02** | 35.71 | 26 | 17 | 1.58 | 0.05 | 31.12 |
| **Annual Growth** | 6.1% | — | — | 9.2% | 12.5% | (9.3%) |

# Amgen Inc.

Amgen is among the biggest of the biotech big'uns. And it's determined to get even bigger. The company uses cellular biology and medicinal chemistry to target cancer, nephrology, inflammatory disorders, and metabolic and neurodegenerative diseases. Anti-anemia drugs Epogen and Aranesp account for about half of its sales. Enbrel, another leading drug, treats rheumatoid arthritis and is one of the best-selling drugs in this multi-billion-dollar market. The company has a promising drug pipeline and marketing alliances with Hoffmann-La Roche, Japanese brewer and drugmaker Kirin, and other pharmas. Amgen's top customers are wholesale distributors like AmerisourceBergen.

Amgen's newer drugs account for more of its sales. The worldwide sales of both Aranesp and Neulasta (30% and 28% respectively) have surpassed that of the company's former top seller Epogen (18%). Enbrel (21%) has also enjoyed growing popularity.

In 2007 anemia treatment Aranesp took a significant hit in the world marketplace following damaging reports of adverse effects of the drug on the heart. As a result, Medicare capped its use by chemotherapy patients. The anticipated loss of revenue forced Amgen to announce a restructuring of the company, including a reduction of nearly $2 billion in planned capital expenditures. Amgen said it would lay off some 2,600 workers to help counter the loss of revenues from the sale of Aranesp.

The biotech is also a key player in the rheumatoid arthritis market. Enbrel not only treats rheumatoid arthritis but also a form of psoriasis and another related condition. Enbrel's sales are poised to climb even higher as the FDA approves the drug to be used for larger patient populations. Centocor's Remicade is Amgen's top rival for this market.

Vectibix, the company's treatment for colorectal cancer (which the company acquired when it bought Abgenix), was approved by the FDA in 2006; however, it was rejected by the EU in 2007, a decision the company plans to appeal. In the pipeline are drug candidates for bone loss associated with hormone therapy in breast and prostate cancer patients, as well as osteoporosis in postmenopausal women.

The company has entered a licensing agreement with Yeda Research and Development for ImClone's ERBITUX colorectal cancer treatment; ImClone had been licensing the technology from Sanofi-Aventis, which lost its patent rights to Yeda in 2006. Opening the 2007 year, Amgen acquired the options to a heart failure treatment in development by Cytokinetics.

Amgen has filed a patent-infringement suit against Roche, stating that Roche's anemia treatment, Cera, infringes on Aranesp and Epogen.

In 2006 Amgen acquired Abgenix, a company that manufactures human therapeutic antibodies, and Avidia, Inc., a developer of treatments for inflammation and autoimmune diseases. Continuing in its acquisitive phase, a pair of privately held buys came midway through 2007: Ilypsa, a biotech working in renal disease care, and Alantos, which has been working on therapies for rheumatoid arthritis and for Type II Diabetes.

## HISTORY

Amgen was formed as Applied Molecular Genetics in 1980 by a group of scientists and venture capitalists to develop health care products based on molecular biology. George Rathmann, a VP at Abbott Laboratories and researcher at UCLA, became the company's CEO and first employee. Rathmann decided to develop a few potentially profitable products rather than conduct research. The company initially raised $19 million.

Amgen operated close to bankruptcy until 1983, when company scientist Fu-Kuen Lin cloned the human protein erythropoietin (EPO), which stimulates the body's red blood cell production. Amgen went public that year. It formed a joint venture with Kirin Brewery in 1984 to develop and market EPO. The two firms also collaborated on recombinant human granulocyte colony stimulating factor (G-CSF, later called Neupogen), a protein that stimulates the immune system.

Amgen joined Johnson & Johnson subsidiary Ortho Pharmaceutical (now Ortho-McNeil Pharmaceutical) in a marketing alliance in 1985 and created a tie with Roche in 1988. Fortunes soared in 1989 when the FDA approved Epogen (the brand name of EPO) for anemia. (It is most commonly used to counter side effects of kidney dialysis.)

In 1991 Amgen received approval to market Neupogen to chemotherapy patients. A federal court ruling also gave it a US monopoly for EPO. The following year Amgen won another dispute, forcing a competitor to renounce its US patents for G-CSF.

In 1993 Amgen became the first American biotech to gain a foothold in China through an agreement with Kirin Pharmaceuticals to sell Neupogen (under the name Gran) and Epogen there. The purchase of Synergen in 1994 added another research facility, accelerating the pace of and increasing the number of products in research and clinical trials.

Although Amgen had two proven sellers in Epogen and Neupogen, its growth lay in its pipeline. Its new drug Stemgen for breast cancer patients undergoing chemotherapy was recommended for approval by an FDA advisory committee in 1998.

Amgen had to swallow a couple of tough legal pills in 1998. First, a dispute with J&J over Amgen's 1985 licensing agreement with Ortho

Pharmaceutical ended when an arbiter ordered Amgen to pay about $200 million. Later that year, however, Amgen won a legal battle with J&J over the rights to a promising anemia drug.

In 2002 it won EU and US approval for Aranesp, an updated version of Epogen; Amgen in 2002 teamed with former J&J marketing partner Fresenius to sell ARANESP in Germany and take some market share away from J&J. Meanwhile, an arbitration committee found J&J had breached its contract with Amgen when it sold Procrit to the dialysis market, which Amgen had reserved for itself in their 1985 licensing deal.

In 2003 the company bought leukemia and rheumatoid arthritis drugs maker Immunex. As part of the FTC's blessing on the $10.3 billion union, Amgen and Immunex licensed some technologies to encourage competition. Merck Serono gained access to Enbrel data, and Regeneron Pharmaceuticals licensed some interleukin inhibitor rights.

In 2004 Amgen spent $1.3 billion to purchase the remaining 79% of cancer treatment technology maker Tularik that it did not already own.

## EXECUTIVES

**Chairman, President, and CEO:** Kevin W. Sharer, age 59, $14,286,992 pay
**EVP and CFO:** Robert (Bob) Bradway, age 44
**EVP, Global Commercial Operations:** George J. Morrow, age 54, $928,596 pay
**EVP, Research and Development:** Roger M. Perlmutter, age 54, $883,769 pay
**EVP Operations:** Fabrizio Bonanni, age 60
**SVP and CIO:** Thomas (Tom) Flanagan
**SVP, Global Government Affairs:** David W. Beier, age 58
**SVP, International Chief Medical Officer:** Willard Dere
**SVP, International Operations:** Rolf K. Hoffmann
**SVP, North America Commercial Operations:** Jim Daly
**SVP Head of Research:** David L. Lacey
**SVP, Human Resources:** Brian M. McNamee, age 50
**SVP, Research and Development:** Joseph P. Miletich, age 55
**SVP, General Counsel, and Secretary:** David J. Scott, age 54
**VP, Global Marketing:** Craig L. Brooks
**VP, Corporate Planning and Control and Chief Accounting Officer:** Michael Kelly
**VP, Corporate Communications and Philanthropy:** Phyllis J. Piano
**VP, International Medical Affairs:** William P. (Bill) Sheridan
**VP, Investor Relations:** Arvind K. Sood
**VP, Project Management Research and Development:** Nahed Ahmed
**VP, Finance:** Steven J. Schoch
**Auditors:** Ernst & Young LLP

## LOCATIONS

**HQ:** Amgen Inc.
1 Amgen Center Dr., Thousand Oaks, CA 91320
**Phone:** 805-447-1000 **Fax:** 805-447-1010
**Web:** www.amgen.com

Amgen has facilities in Asia and the Pacific Rim, Europe, and North America.

**2006 Sales**

| | % of total |
|---|---|
| US | 83 |
| Other countries | 17 |
| **Total** | **100** |

## PRODUCTS/OPERATIONS

**2006 Sales**

| | % of total |
|---|---|
| Aranesp | 30 |
| Neulasta/NEUPROGEN | 28 |
| ENBREL | 21 |
| EPOGEN | 18 |
| Sensipar | 2 |
| Other | 1 |
| **Total** | **100** |

**Products**

Aranesp (sustained duration Epogen)
Enbrel (rheumatoid arthritis)
Epogen (anemia)
Infergen (hepatitis C, licensed to InterMune)
Kepivance (chemotherapy-induced oral mucositis)
Kineret (rheumatoid arthritis)
Neulasta (chemotherapy-induced neutropenia)
Neupogen/Granulokine (immune system stimulation)
Sensipar (chronic kidney disease)
Stemgen (stem cell transplantation stimulator)

## COMPETITORS

Abbott Labs
Affymax
ALZA
Astellas
AstraZeneca
Baxter
Bayer
Bayer HealthCare Pharmaceuticals
Bayer Schering Pharma
Biogen Idec
Bristol-Myers Squibb
Centocor
Cephalon
Chugai
Degussa
Eli Lilly
Genentech
GlaxoSmithKline
Human Genome Sciences
Johnson & Johnson
Kosan Biosciences
Kyowa Hakko Kogyo
MedImmune
Merck
Merck KGaA
Millennium Pharmaceuticals
Novartis
Ortho Biotech
Pfizer
QLT USA
Regeneron Pharmaceuticals
Roche
Sanofi-Aventis
Schering-Plough
Shire
TAP Pharmaceutical Products
Vertex Pharmaceuticals
Wyeth

## HISTORICAL FINANCIALS

Company Type: Public

**Income Statement** FYE: December 31

| | REVENUE ($ mil.) | NET INCOME ($ mil.) | NET PROFIT MARGIN | EMPLOYEES |
|---|---|---|---|---|
| **12/06** | 14,268 | 2,950 | 20.7% | 20,100 |
| **12/05** | 12,430 | 3,674 | 29.6% | 16,500 |
| **12/04** | 10,550 | 2,363 | 22.4% | 14,400 |
| **12/03** | 8,356 | 2,260 | 27.0% | 12,900 |
| **12/02** | 5,523 | (1,392) | — | 10,100 |
| **Annual Growth** | 26.8% | — | — | 18.8% |

**2006 Year-End Financials**

Debt ratio: 37.6%
Return on equity: 15.0%
Cash ($ mil.): 6,277
Current ratio: 1.67
Long-term debt ($ mil.): 7,134
No. of shares (mil.): 1,166
Dividends
Yield: —
Payout: —
Market value ($ mil.): 79,649

**Stock History** NASDAQ (GS): AMGN

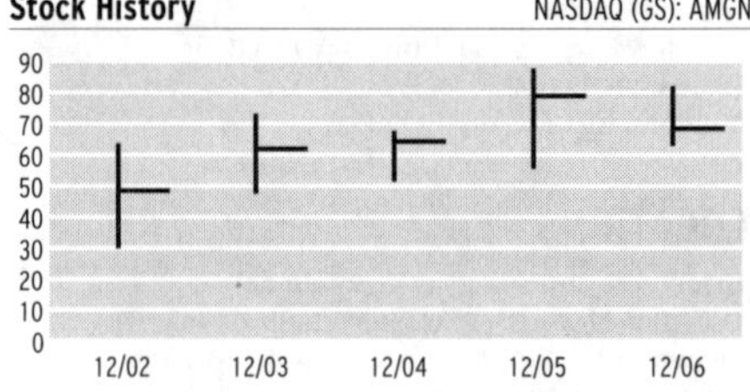


| | STOCK PRICE ($) FY Close | P/E High | P/E Low | PER SHARE ($) Earnings | Dividends | Book Value |
|---|---|---|---|---|---|---|
| **12/06** | 68.31 | 33 | 26 | 2.48 | — | 16.26 |
| **12/05** | 78.86 | 30 | 19 | 2.93 | — | 16.71 |
| **12/04** | 64.15 | 37 | 29 | 1.81 | — | 15.64 |
| **12/03** | 61.79 | 43 | 28 | 1.69 | — | 15.10 |
| **12/02** | 48.34 | — | — | (1.21) | — | 14.19 |
| **Annual Growth** | 9.0% | — | — | — | — | 3.5% |

# Amkor Technology

Amkor Technology is more than amicable about lending a hand with chip packaging. Amkor is a top provider of semiconductor packaging and test services. Packaging includes dicing semiconductor wafers into separate chips, die bonding, wire bonding, and encapsulating chips in protective plastic. Amkor's testing procedures verify function, current, timing, and voltage. Amkor has hundreds of customers worldwide, including such industry leaders as Altera, Atmel, Conexant Systems, Freescale Semiconductor, Intel, IBM, Samsung Electronics, STMicroelectronics, Texas Instruments, and Toshiba. Founder and CEO James Kim and his family own nearly 46% of Amkor.

Struggling for years to make money in a highly competitive market, Amkor cut its workforce by about 5% (1,300 positions) in 2006 and posted net income of $170 million for the year, its best annual profit since 2000. The company continued to cut jobs in 2007, eliminating 125 jobs at its manufacturing facility in Morrisville, North Carolina — its last remaining plant in the US — and redirecting production to Asian facilities. The Morrisville plant was picked up in the company's 2004 acquisition of Unitive Inc.

Amkor was originally the US marketing arm of South Korean manufacturer Anam Industrial Co., a company that was started by Kim's father. After purchasing Anam's four packaging plants in 1999 and 2000, Amkor retained exclusive rights to the output of Anam's remaining semiconductor wafer foundry. In 2002, though, Amkor sold almost half of its formerly controlling stake in Anam to Korean foundry operator Dongbu; early in 2003, it completed its divestment of Anam and exited the wafer fabrication business. The foundry business is now known as DongbuAnam Semiconductor.

FMR (Fidelity Investments) owns nearly 13% of Amkor.

## HISTORY

Kim Joo-Jin (James Kim), the oldest of seven children, came to the US from South Korea in 1955 to study business. A year later his father started electronics firm Anam Industrial, and in 1968 James Kim (chairman and CEO) founded Amkor (short for "American-Korean") Electronics as its US marketing agent.

To lessen its dependence on the volatile semiconductor market, Anam Industrial began diversifying in 1975, first into watchmaking, and eventually into banking, construction, environmental services, and electronics. (James Kim's wife, Agnes, began selling electronic watches and calculators from a kiosk near the family home in Pennsylvania; the business grew into the Electronics Boutique chain, now part of GameStop.)

James Kim joined the board of California semiconductor maker VLSI Technology (now part of NXP, formerly Philips Semiconductors) in 1982, leading the company into the application-specific integrated circuit market. Anam Industrial, meanwhile, continued to grow along with the semiconductor industry. By 1990 it had 50% of the world's semiconductor package assembly business, and was only one unit of South Korean *chaebol* (family-run, non-legal conglomerate) Anam Group. That year the group took over a plant in Manila from Advanced Micro Devices and established Amkor/Anam Pilipinas on that site. It also acquired Scotland-based ITEQ Europe Ltd., Europe's leading semiconductor assembly contractor.

During the early 1990s Anam Industrial developed the tape-automated bonding manufacturing process. When the senior Kim retired in 1992, James Kim also became head of the Anam Group.

In 1993 Amkor licensed ball-grid array (BGA) packaging technology from Motorola. At the time BGA — in which tiny balls of solder are used for connections, instead of fragile lead wires — was still an emerging standard. By 1995 Amkor had become a leader in BGA packaging. That year the company announced that it would build the US's first independent BGA facility, in Arizona (it opened in 1999).

Anam Industrial began building its fourth semiconductor assembly plant in 1996, this one in the Philippines, with a production goal of 50 million chips per month. In 1997 Amkor opened its complementary metal oxide semiconductor wafer (CMOS) plant near Seoul, using Texas Instruments' technology, as part of a 10-year cooperative agreement. It also created Amkor Industries to consolidate the various Amkor companies. Also that year Amkor/Anam formed an agreement with Acer and Taiwan Semiconductor Manufacturing to build a semiconductor assembly and test facility in Taiwan.

Amkor went public in 1998. That year Anam Industrial changed its name to Anam Semiconductor and announced plans to divest its non-core businesses to focus on chip packaging. In 1999 Amkor opened a support center in France and bought a packaging plant in South Korea from Anam Semiconductor. In 2000 Amkor bought three more plants from Anam Semiconductor — which was still restructuring as its chaebol broke up — and upped its stake in Anam to 42%.

In 2002 Amkor acquired the Japan-based chip assembly business of Citizen Watch. The company also announced the formation of a chip packaging joint venture with Fujitsu in 2002, but the deal was later scrapped. In late 2002 and early 2003 Amkor exited the foundry business when it sold its stake in Anam to Korean conglomerate (and foundry operator) Dongbu.

Early in 2004, Amkor expanded its capacity by acquiring an assembly and test plant from Taiwan-based FICTA Technology. Later that year, it struck a major agreement with IBM under which Amkor acquired IBM properties in China and Singapore, and will supply the computing giant with assembly and test services.

The US Securities and Exchange Commission in 2004 opened an informal inquiry into stock trading by certain Amkor insiders and other people, covering a period from June 2003 to July 2004. In 2005 the SEC probe was upgraded to a formal inquiry. The former general counsel of the company, who resigned in early 2005, has been indicted in Pennsylvania for alleged violations of securities laws.

In mid-2006 Amkor's board created a special committee to review the company's historical practices in granting stock options from May 1998. The committee found, as has been the practice at many other high-tech firms, that the grant dates of certain stock options differed from the recorded dates of the grants and the actual dates of the grants. The company restated eight years of financial results as a result.

The SEC inquiry has widened to include the stock-option granting practices.

## EXECUTIVES

**Chairman and CEO:** James J. Kim, age 71, $830,000 pay
**EVP and COO:** Oleg Khaykin, age 42, $270,000 pay
**EVP and CFO:** Kenneth T. Joyce, age 60, $295,000 pay
**EVP, Corporate Strategy:** JooHo Kim, age 53, $270,000 pay
**SVP Human Resources:** Michael Gentry
**VP Worldwide Sales:** Michael J. (Mike) Lamble, age 50
**Director Investor Relations:** Greg Peterson
**Secretary:** Joanne Solomon
**Manager Brand Communications:** Phil Jones
**Manager Corporate Public Relations:** Cheryl Thompson
**Corporate VP and General Counsel:** Gil C. Tilly, age 53
**President, Korea:** KyuHyun Kim, age 58
**VP Wire Bond Products:** James (Jim) Fusaro, age 44
**VP and Assistant General Counsel:** Jerry Allison
**Auditors:** PricewaterhouseCoopers LLP

## LOCATIONS

**HQ:** Amkor Technology, Inc.
1900 S. Price Rd., Chandler, AZ 85248
**Phone:** 480-821-5000 **Fax:** 480-821-8276
**Web:** www.amkor.com

Amkor Technology has manufacturing facilities in China, Japan, the Philippines, Singapore, South Korea, Taiwan, and the US; it has sales and service offices in China, France, Japan, the Philippines, Singapore, South Korea, Taiwan, the UK, and the US.

### 2006 Sales

| | $ mil. | % of total |
|---|---|---|
| US | 992.9 | 36 |
| Singapore | 573.1 | 21 |
| Japan | 262.1 | 10 |
| Taiwan | 208.0 | 8 |
| South Korea | 149.4 | 5 |
| China & Hong Kong | 138.2 | 5 |
| Other countries | 404.9 | 15 |
| **Total** | **2,728.6** | **100** |

## PRODUCTS/OPERATIONS

### 2006 Sales

| | $ mil. | % of total |
|---|---|---|
| Packaging services | | |
| Laminate | 1,312.4 | 48 |
| Leadframe | 1,015.1 | 37 |
| Other | 120.1 | 5 |
| Testing services | 281.0 | 10 |
| **Total** | **2,728.6** | **100** |

### Products and Services

Chip Packaging
- Advanced leadframe (plastic mold with thermal, electrical characteristics)
- Laminate (plastic or tape rather than leadframe substrate)
- Traditional leadframe (plastic mold with metal leads)

Test Services (analog, digital logic, and mixed-signal chips)

## COMPETITORS

Advanced Semiconductor Engineering
ASAT Holdings
ASE Test
ChipMOS
Kingston Technology
PSi Technologies
Siliconware Precision Industries
STATS ChipPAC
Tessera
UTAC

## HISTORICAL FINANCIALS

Company Type: Public

### Income Statement

FYE: December 31

| | REVENUE ($ mil.) | NET INCOME ($ mil.) | NET PROFIT MARGIN | EMPLOYEES |
|---|---|---|---|---|
| **12/06** | 2,729 | 170 | 6.2% | 22,700 |
| **12/05** | 2,100 | (137) | — | 24,000 |
| **12/04** | 1,901 | (38) | — | 22,033 |
| **12/03** | 1,604 | 2 | 0.1% | 20,261 |
| **12/02** | 1,406 | (827) | — | 20,276 |
| **Annual Growth** | 18.0% | — | — | 2.9% |

### 2006 Year-End Financials

Debt ratio: 468.2%
Return on equity: 55.1%
Cash ($ mil.): 247
Current ratio: 1.35
Long-term debt ($ mil.): 1,844
No. of shares (mil.): 179
Dividends
Yield: —
Payout: —
Market value ($ mil.): 1,676

### Stock History

NASDAQ (GS): AMKR

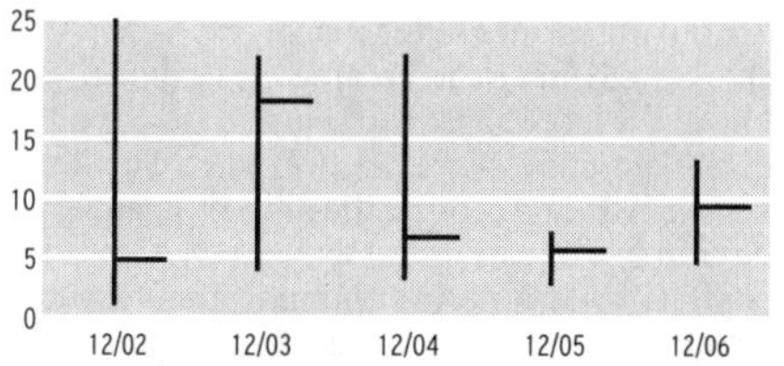

| | STOCK PRICE ($) FY Close | P/E High | P/E Low | PER SHARE ($) Earnings | PER SHARE ($) Dividends | PER SHARE ($) Book Value |
|---|---|---|---|---|---|---|
| **12/06** | 9.34 | 15 | 5 | 0.90 | — | 2.20 |
| **12/05** | 5.60 | — | — | (0.78) | — | 1.27 |
| **12/04** | 6.68 | — | — | (0.21) | — | 2.10 |
| **12/03** | 18.14 | 2,173 | 404 | 0.01 | — | 2.30 |
| **12/02** | 4.76 | — | — | (5.04) | — | 1.40 |
| **Annual Growth** | 18.4% | — | — | — | — | 11.9% |

# AMR Corporation

AMR knows America's spacious skies — and lots of others. Its main subsidiary is American Airlines, the #1 airline in the US (UAL's United is #2) and one of the largest in the world. Together with sister company American Eagle and its network of regional carriers, American Airlines serves some 250 destinations in about 40 countries in the Americas, Europe, and the Asia/Pacific region. The overall fleet exceeds 1,000 aircraft; American Airlines operates about 675 jets. The carrier extends its geographic reach through code-sharing arrangements. It is part of the Oneworld global marketing alliance, along with British Airways, Cathay Pacific, Qantas, and other airlines.

Unlike peers such as UAL, Delta, Northwest, and US Airways, AMR was able to navigate the airline industry downturn that followed the September 11, 2001, terrorist attacks without making a stop in bankruptcy court. American Airlines reduced its capacity, its fleet, and its workforce and won concessions from its unions; in the meantime, the parent company lost money for five straight years — and piled up debt — before posting a profit in 2006.

Cost control continues to be a focus for AMR. At the same time, American Airlines hopes to gain revenue by expanding its services to destinations in the Asia/Pacific region, particularly in China, where the number of direct flights from the US is limited by law. The carrier began nonstop service from Chicago to Shanghai in April 2006. Its bid to launch service from Dallas/Fort Worth to Beijing was rejected in 2007, however, in favor of a competing proposal from United for service between Washington, DC, and Beijing. (American Airlines offers service to Beijing and other cities in China through code-sharing with partners such as China Eastern Airlines.)

## HISTORY

In 1929 Sherman Fairchild created a New York City holding company called the Aviation Corporation (AVCO), combining some 85 small airlines in 1930 to create American Airways. In 1934 the company had its first dose of financial trouble after the government suspended private airmail for months. Corporate raider E. L. Cord took over and named the company American Airlines.

Cord put former AVCO manager C. R. Smith in charge, and American became the leading US airline in the late 1930s. The Douglas DC-3, built to Smith's specifications, was introduced by American in 1936 and became the first commercial airliner to pay its way on passenger revenues alone.

After WWII American bought Amex Airlines, which flew to northern Europe, but another financial crisis prompted Amex's sale in 1950. The airline introduced Sabre, the first automated reservations system, in 1964. Smith left American four years later to serve as secretary of commerce in the Johnson administration.

In 1979, the year after airline industry deregulation, American moved to Dallas/Fort Worth. Former CFO Bob Crandall became president in 1980 (and later, CEO). Using Sabre to track mileage, he introduced the industry's first frequent-flier program (AAdvantage). In 1982 American created AMR as its holding company. After acquiring commuter airline Nashville Eagle in 1987, AMR established American Eagle.

After ducking a 1989 takeover bid by Donald Trump, AMR bought routes to Japan, Latin America, and London from other carriers. American's 1994 attempt to simplify pricing led to a fare war that hurt industry profits. Tragedy struck American Eagle that year — two crashes resulted in 83 deaths. The next year American's 16-year fatality-free flying record ended when an airliner crashed into a mountain near Cali, Colombia, killing 160.

In 1996 AMR spun off nearly 20% of Sabre and announced plans for a code-sharing pact with British Airways (BA) that sparked a wave of alliances, including Oneworld, which took effect in 1999. American's code-sharing deal with BA, however, ran into opposition from regulators, who were concerned about the airlines' dominance of landing slots at London's Heathrow airport.

Crandall retired in 1998 (after a major airline strike was averted only by President Clinton's intervention) and was replaced by Donald Carty. American also bought Reno Air, and concerns about integrating the smaller airline (completed in 1999) culminated in American pilots calling in sick for a week in 1999. The union was later ordered to pay almost $46 million in compensation.

In 1999 nine people died when an American jet tried to land in Arkansas during a storm and slid off the runway. The Justice Department dealt another blow in 2000 when it filed a suit accusing American of predatory pricing to fend off low-fare startups. (A federal judge dismissed the case in 2001, however.) Also in 2000 AMR spun off the rest of Sabre.

In 2001 AMR moved to become a stronger competitor to UAL by buying the assets of troubled rival TWA for $742 million. Later that year American and BA revived plans to seek regulatory clearance for a code-sharing deal.

Also in 2001 American Airlines lost two aircraft that were used in the September 11 terrorist attacks on the World Trade Center in New York and the Pentagon in Washington, DC. In anticipation of reduced demand for air travel, AMR announced a 20% reduction in flights and layoffs of at least 20,000 employees. Later that year another American Airlines jet crashed in New York, killing all 260 passengers.

American Airlines' planned partnership with BA, which the airlines had been negotiating since 1996, received conditional approval from the US Department of Transportation (DOT) in 2002, only to be abandoned by the airlines. The DOT wanted the airlines to give up 224 slots at London's Heathrow airport, something they were not willing to do.

In August 2002 the carrier set about reducing its capacity by 9% and reducing its workforce by some 7,000 employees.

Carty resigned in 2003 after rankling union leaders by failing to disclose executive compensation perquisites during labor negotiations aimed at keeping the airline giant out of bankruptcy. Carty was replaced as CEO by former president and COO Gerard Arpey. Director Edward Brennan, a former chairman and CEO of Sears, Roebuck & Co., was named non-executive chairman. Brennan relinquished the chairman role to Arpey in 2004, but remained a director.

## EXECUTIVES

**Chairman, President, and CEO, AMR and American Airlines:** Gerard J. Arpey, age 49, $526,620 pay
**EVP, Finance and Planning and CFO, AMR and American Airlines:** Thomas W. Horton, age 45
**EVP, Marketing, AMR and American Airlines:** Daniel P. Garton, age 50, $479,349 pay
**SVP, Customer Service, American Airlines:** Ralph L. Richardi
**SVP, Customer Relationship Marketing and Reservations, American Airlines:** Isabella D. (Bella) Goren
**SVP, General Counsel, and Chief Compliance Officer:** Gary F. Kennedy, age 52, $427,700 pay
**SVP, Global Sales, American Airlines:** C. David Cush, age 43
**SVP, Government Affairs, AMR and American Airlines:** William K. (Will) Ris Jr.
**SVP, Human Resources, American Airlines:** Jeffery J. Brundage, age 53
**SVP, International, American Airlines:** Craig S. Kreeger, age 44
**SVP, Information Technology and CIO, American Airlines:** Monte E. Ford, age 47
**SVP, Miami, Caribbean, and Latin America, American Airlines:** Peter J. Dolara, age 69
**SVP, Planning, American Airlines:** Henry C. Joyner, age 53
**SVP, Technical Operations, American Airlines:** Robert W. (Bob) Reding, age 57, $431,850 pay
**VP and Controller, American Airlines:** Brian McMenamy
**VP, Corporate Communications and Advertising, American Airlines:** Roger Frizzell
**President, American Eagle:** Peter M. Bowler, age 52
**Corporate Secretary:** Kenneth W. Wimberly
**Auditors:** Ernst & Young LLP

## LOCATIONS

**HQ:** AMR Corporation
4333 Amon Carter Blvd., Fort Worth, TX 76155
**Phone:** 817-963-1234 **Fax:** 817-967-9641
**Web:** www.aa.com

### 2006 Sales

| | $ mil. | % of total |
|---|---|---|
| US | 14,159 | 63 |
| Latin America | 4,024 | 18 |
| Atlantic | 3,409 | 15 |
| Pacific | 971 | 4 |
| **Total** | **22,563** | **100** |

### American Airlines Hub Locations

Chicago (O'Hare)
Dallas/Fort Worth
Los Angeles
Miami
San Juan, Puerto Rico

## PRODUCTS/OPERATIONS

### 2006 Sales

| | $ mil. | % of total |
|---|---|---|
| Passenger | | |
| American Airlines | 17,862 | 79 |
| Regional affiliates | 2,502 | 11 |
| Cargo | 827 | 4 |
| Other | 1,372 | 6 |
| **Total** | **22,563** | **100** |

### Selected Subsidiaries

American Airlines, Inc.
American Beacon Advisors, Inc. (investment management)
Americas Ground Services Inc. (ground handling)
AMR Eagle Holding Corporation (regional services)
American Eagle Airlines, Inc.
AMR Leasing Corporation
Executive Airlines, Inc.

## COMPETITORS

Air France-KLM
AirTran Holdings
Alaska Air
China Southern Airlines
Continental Airlines
Delta Air
FedEx
Frontier Airlines
Greyhound
JetBlue
Mesa Air
Northwest Airlines
Pinnacle Airlines
SkyWest
Southwest Airlines
UAL
UPS
US Airways
Virgin Atlantic Airways

## HISTORICAL FINANCIALS

Company Type: Public

**Income Statement** FYE: December 31

| | REVENUE ($ mil.) | NET INCOME ($ mil.) | NET PROFIT MARGIN | EMPLOYEES |
|---|---|---|---|---|
| **12/06** | 22,563 | 231 | 1.0% | 86,600 |
| **12/05** | 20,712 | (861) | — | 88,400 |
| **12/04** | 18,645 | (761) | — | 92,100 |
| **12/03** | 17,440 | (1,228) | — | 96,400 |
| **12/02** | 17,299 | (3,511) | — | 109,600 |
| **Annual Growth** | 6.9% | — | — | (5.7%) |

**2006 Year-End Financials**

Debt ratio: —
Return on equity: —
Cash ($ mil.): 5,183
Current ratio: 0.81
Long-term debt ($ mil.): 12,041
No. of shares (mil.): 222
Dividends
Yield: —
Payout: —
Market value ($ mil.): 6,718

**Stock History** NYSE: AMR

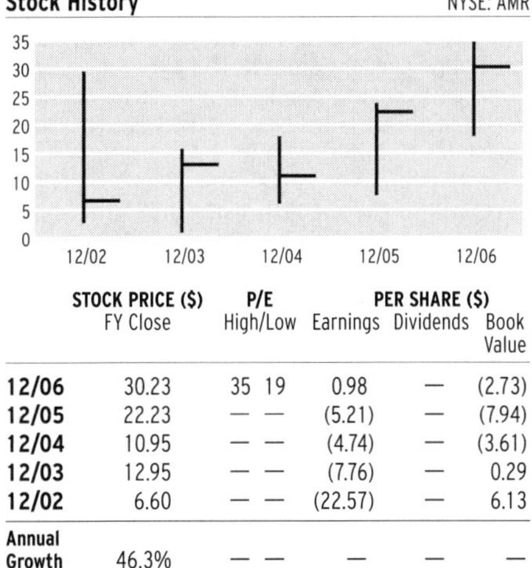


| | STOCK PRICE ($) FY Close | P/E High/Low | | PER SHARE ($) Earnings | Dividends | Book Value |
|---|---|---|---|---|---|---|
| **12/06** | 30.23 | 35 | 19 | 0.98 | — | (2.73) |
| **12/05** | 22.23 | — | — | (5.21) | — | (7.94) |
| **12/04** | 10.95 | — | — | (4.74) | — | (3.61) |
| **12/03** | 12.95 | — | — | (7.76) | — | 0.29 |
| **12/02** | 6.60 | — | — | (22.57) | — | 6.13 |
| **Annual Growth** | 46.3% | — | — | — | — | — |

# Anadarko Petroleum

Anadarko Petroleum has ventured beyond its original area of operation — the Anadarko Basin — to explore for, develop, produce, and market oil, natural gas, natural gas liquids, and related products worldwide. The large independent company has proved reserves of 1.5 billion barrels of crude oil and 10.5 trillion cu. ft. of natural gas, more than half of which are in the US (Alaska, Louisiana, Texas, the midcontinent and Rocky Mountain regions, and the Gulf of Mexico). Other activities include coal, trona, and mineral mining.

In 2006 the company acquired Kerr McGee for $16.4 billion and Western Gas Resources for $4.7 billion. That year it sold its Gulf of Mexico shelf subsidiary to W&T Offshore for $1 billion. Anadarko has set aside as much as $100 million to develop four deep-water oil and gas projects in the Gulf of Mexico operated by Chevron.

Anadarko has a daily production of about 520,000 barrels of oil equivalent. It also operates seven gas-gathering systems (more than 3,250 miles of pipeline) in the mid-continent. Internationally, the company has substantial oil and gas interests in Algeria's Sahara Desert, Venezuela, and western Canada. It gained a stake in the Middle East by purchasing Gulfstream Resources Canada, which has operations in Oman and Qatar.

In 2006 the company sold its Anadarko Canada Corp. business to Canadian Natural Resources for $4.2 billion. It also agreed to sell offshore assets in the Gulf of Mexico to Statoil for $901 million, and the Genghis Khan discovery in the Gulf of Mexico to owners of the nearby Shenzi field for $1.35 billion.

In early 2007 Anadarko sold its Louisiana gas fields to EXCO Resources, Inc. for $1.6 billion. The company also agreed to sell its stakes in the Elk Basin and Gooseberry oil fields in Wyoming to Encore Acquisition for $400 million.

In a move to futher cut debt, in 2007 Anadarko agreed to sell its interests in 28 crude oil fields in West Texas to Apache Corp. for about $1 billion. It subsequently sold oil and gas assets in the Mid-Continent and Gulf Coast areas of Oklahoma and Texas to EXCO Resources for $860 million. The company also agreed to sell a portion of its stake in the K2 Unit in the Gulf of Mexico to two undisclosed parties for about $1.2 billion. It also agreed to sell its operations in Qatar.

## HISTORY

In 1959 the Panhandle Eastern Pipe Line Company set up Anadarko (named after the Anadarko Basin) to carry out its gas exploration and production activities. The new company was also formed to take advantage of a ruling by the Federal Power Commission (now the Federal Energy Regulatory Commission) to set lower price ceilings for producing properties owned by pipeline companies.

The company grew rapidly during the early 1960s, largely because of its gas-rich namesake. It bought Ambassador Oil of Fort Worth, Texas, in 1965 — adding interests in 19 states in the US and Canada. The firm also relocated from Kansas to Fort Worth.

Anadarko began offshore exploration in the Gulf of Mexico in 1970 and focused there early in the decade. After moving to Houston in 1974, Anadarko increased its oil exploration activities when the energy crisis led to higher gas prices. A deal with Amoco (now part of BP) led to major finds on Matagorda Island, off the Texas coast, in the early 1980s.

To realize shareholder value, Panhandle spun off Anadarko in 1986 — separating transmission from production. At the time more than 90% of Anadarko's reserves were natural gas. The next year Anadarko made new discoveries in Canada.

Low domestic natural gas prices led Anadarko overseas. It signed a production-sharing agreement with Algeria's national oil and gas firm, SONATRACH, in 1989. The deal covered 5.1 million acres in the Sahara. Two years later Anadarko began operating in the South China Sea and in Alaska's North Slope.

Back home, the company spent $190 million in 1992 for properties in West Texas, and in 1993 Anadarko began divesting noncore assets. Along with some of its partners, the company also discovered oil in the Mahogany Field offshore Louisiana. Production from Mahogany began in 1996.

In 1997 Anadarko added exploration acreage in the North Atlantic and Tunisia. The next year it made two major oil and gas discoveries in the Gulf of Mexico. Anadarko decided to sell some of its noncore Algerian assets in 1999 and teamed up with Texaco (later acquired by Chevron) in a joint exploration program in the Gulf of Mexico, offshore Louisiana. The next year the company acquired Union Pacific Resources in a $5.7 billion stock swap.

Anadarko expanded its presence in western Canada in 2001 by buying Berkley Petroleum for more than $1 billion in cash and assumed debt; a smaller purchase that year, Gulfstream Resources Canada, landed Anadarko in the Persian Gulf and added 70 million barrels of oil equivalent to its reserves.

## EXECUTIVES

**Chairman Emeritus:** Robert J. Allison Jr., age 67
**Chairman, President, and CEO:** James T. (Jim) Hackett, age 53
**SVP Finance and CFO:** R. A. (Al) Walker, age 50
**SVP, General Counsel, and Chief Administrative Officer:** Robert K. (Bobby) Reeves, age 50
**SVP Worldwide Exploration:** Robert P. (Bob) Daniels, age 48
**SVP Worldwide Operations:** Charles A. (Chuck) Meloy, age 47
**COO:** Karl F. Kurz, age 46
**VP and Chief Accounting Officer:** Bruce W. Busmire, age 48
**VP Finance and Treasurer:** Robert G. Gwin, age 44
**Controller:** Allyn R. Skelton
**VP Corporate Development:** Albert L. (Al) Richey, age 56
**VP, Corporate Services:** Donald R. (Don) Willis, age 56
**VP Government Relations:** Gregory M. (Greg) Pensabene, age 57
**VP Human Resources:** Preston H. Johnson Jr., age 52
**VP Information Technology Services and CIO:** Mario M. Coll III, age 45
**VP:** Charlene A. Ripley, age 43
**VP Canada; President, Anadarko Canada Corporation (ACC):** Michael O. (Mike) Bridges
**Investor Contact:** Stewart Lawrence
**Media Contact:** Susan Richardson
**Media Contact:** Teresa Wong
**Auditors:** KPMG LLP

## LOCATIONS

**HQ:** Anadarko Petroleum Corporation
1201 Lake Robbins Dr., The Woodlands, TX 77380
**Phone:** 832-636-1000 **Fax:** 832-636-8220
**Web:** www.anadarko.com

Anadarko Petroleum has US operations in Alaska, the Gulf of Mexico, Louisiana, the midcontinent, the Rocky Mountain region, and Texas. Internationally, it has major operations in Algeria, Qatar, and Venezuela.

**2006 Sales**

| | $ mil. | % of total |
|---|---|---|
| US | 7,491 | 80 |
| Algeria | 1,526 | 16 |
| Other countries | 368 | 4 |
| Adjustments | 802 | — |
| **Total** | **10,187** | **100** |

## PRODUCTS/OPERATIONS

**2006 Sales**

| | $ mil. | % of total |
|---|---|---|
| Oil & condensate | 4,601 | 45 |
| Gas | 4,186 | 41 |
| Gathering, processing & marketing | 718 | 7 |
| Natural gas liquids | 594 | 6 |
| Other | 88 | 1 |
| **Total** | **10,187** | **100** |

**2006 Sales**

| | $ mil. | % of total |
|---|---|---|
| Oil & gas exploration & production | 9,284 | 91 |
| Gathering, processing & marketing | 815 | 8 |
| Minerals | 59 | 1 |
| Adjustments | 29 | — |
| **Total** | **10,187** | **100** |

**Selected Subsidiaries**

Anadarko Algeria Company, LLC
Kerr-McGee Corporation
Western Gas Resources, Inc.

## COMPETITORS

Adams Resources
Apache
BP
Cabot Oil & Gas
Chesapeake Energy
Chevron
Cimarex
ConocoPhillips
Devon Energy
EOG
Exxon Mobil
Hunt Consolidated
Key Energy
National Fuel Gas
Noble Energy
Pioneer Natural Resources
Pogo Producing
Royal Dutch Shell

## HISTORICAL FINANCIALS

Company Type: Public

**Income Statement** FYE: December 31

| | REVENUE ($ mil.) | NET INCOME ($ mil.) | NET PROFIT MARGIN | EMPLOYEES |
|---|---|---|---|---|
| **12/06** | 10,187 | 4,854 | 47.6% | 5,200 |
| **12/05** | 7,100 | 2,471 | 34.8% | 3,300 |
| **12/04** | 6,067 | 1,606 | 26.5% | 3,300 |
| **12/03** | 5,122 | 1,292 | 25.2% | 3,500 |
| **12/02** | 3,860 | 831 | 21.5% | 3,800 |
| **Annual Growth** | 27.5% | 55.5% | — | 8.2% |

**2006 Year-End Financials**

Debt ratio: 77.5%
Return on equity: 37.6%
Cash ($ mil.): 491
Current ratio: 0.28
Long-term debt ($ mil.): 11,520
No. of shares (mil.): 467
Dividends
Yield: 0.6%
Payout: 2.6%
Market value ($ mil.): 20,324

**Stock History** NYSE: APC

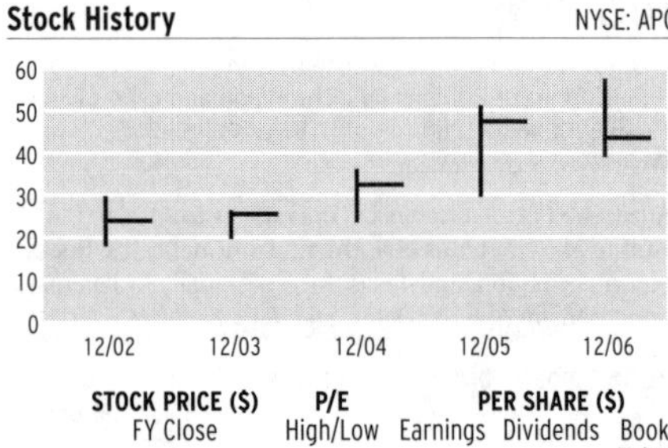

| | STOCK PRICE ($) FY Close | P/E High | P/E Low | PER SHARE ($) Earnings | Dividends | Book Value |
|---|---|---|---|---|---|---|
| **12/06** | 43.52 | 5 | 4 | 10.46 | 0.27 | 31.93 |
| **12/05** | 47.38 | 10 | 6 | 5.20 | 0.36 | 47.65 |
| **12/04** | 32.40 | 11 | 8 | 3.18 | 0.28 | 38.74 |
| **12/03** | 25.50 | 10 | 8 | 2.55 | 0.22 | 33.72 |
| **12/02** | 23.95 | 18 | 11 | 1.61 | 0.16 | 27.73 |
| **Annual Growth** | 16.1% | — | — | 59.7% | 14.0% | 3.6% |

# Analog Devices

Analog Devices, Inc. (ADI) is fluent in both analog and digital. The company is a leading maker of analog (linear and mixed-signal) and digital integrated circuits (ICs), including digital signal processors (DSPs). Its linear ICs translate real-world phenomena such as pressure, temperature, and sound into digital signals. ADI's thousands of chip designs are used in industrial applications, medical and scientific instrumentation, communications equipment, computers, and consumer electronics devices. ADI's chips are used in high-tech goods from companies such as Alcatel-Lucent, Dell, Ericsson, Philips, Siemens, and Sony. Ford and Volkswagen use the company's products for air bag deployment.

Throughout a brutal years-long market downturn that affected all parts of the semiconductor industry in the early 21st century, ADI continued to keep R&D spending high to promote new product development. The company is among the most consistently profitable ventures in the semiconductor industry.

ADI leveraged its early analog know-how by integrating mixed-signal technology onto DSPs in time to catch the Internet tidal wave. At the same time, the company widened its focus, pioneering tiny silicon devices called micromachines, primarily accelerometers used in air bags.

Customers outside North America account for three-quarters of ADI's sales.

Capital Research and Management owns more than 10% of Analog Devices. T. Rowe Price holds nearly 9% of the company. FMR (Fidelity Investments) has an equity stake of 7%.

## HISTORY

Ray Stata, an MIT graduate and Hewlett-Packard veteran, and Matthew Lorber founded Analog Devices, Inc. (ADI) in 1965 to make amplifiers for strengthening electrical signals. The company soon expanded into converters used to control machinery and take measurements, and went public in 1968. Lorber left the company that year and went on to found several startups, including Printer Technology, Torque Systems, and Copley Controls.

In 1969 ADI began manufacturing semiconductors. Stata become chairman and CEO in 1973. In 1977 he launched the influential Massachusetts High Technology Council to fight taxes that he felt were restricting the growth of high-tech firms.

During the early 1980s ADI acquired stakes in several technology firms, including Charles River Data Systems (microcomputer hardware and software), Jupiter Systems (color graphics computers), Photodyne (fiber optics test instruments), and Tau-Tron (high-speed digital instrumentation). In the mid-1980s ADI's profits declined as Japanese competitors acquired market share.

In 1990 the company acquired Precision Monolithics, a maker of passive electronic components. The next year ADI introduced the world's first commercial micromachine, an automotive air-bag trigger.

In 1992 ADI formed a joint venture with Hewlett-Packard to develop mixed-signal chips. The company extended its global reach in 1996 by acquiring Mosaic Microsystems, a UK radio-frequency design company. It also formed Washington State-based chip producer WaferTech with Taiwan Semiconductor and others. Also in 1996 company veteran Jerald Fishman became ADI's president and CEO; Stata remained chairman.

In 1998 ADI acquired MediaLight, a Toronto-based developer of digital subscriber line software. ADI also sold its disk drive integrated circuit business to Adaptec for about $27 million. The next year the company bought White Mountain DSP (development software for DSPs) and Edinburgh Portable Compilers (software compilers for embedded applications).

In 2000 and early 2001 ADI completed a string of acquisitions, headlined by the purchases of Ireland-based BCO Technologies ($163 million; wafers for optical components) and Chiplogic ($68 million; broadband networking chips for voice and video). ADI sold its 4% stake in WaferTech to joint venture partner Taiwan Semiconductor in 2000.

Ray Stata garnered the chip industry's highest honor in 2001 when he received the Semiconductor Industry Association's Robert N. Noyce Award, which is named after the late industry titan who co-founded Intel and co-invented the integrated circuit.

The Stata Center for Computer, Information, and Intelligence Sciences was opened at MIT in 2004. The distinctive building, designed by Gehry Partners, was built on the site of the institute's legendary "Building 20," a structure built during WWII that was intended to be temporary but went on to house various programs for 55 years.

The company marked its 40th anniversary in 2005. In late 2005 ADI and CEO Jerry Fishman reached a settlement with the US Securities and Exchange Commission on the company's practices in granting stock options from 1998 to 2001. Without admitting or denying the commission's findings from its year-long investigation, the company agreed to pay a civil penalty of $3 million, while Fishman paid $1 million.

Early in 2006 ADI sold its network processor business to Ikanos Communications for $30 million in cash. The product line accounted for about 2% of ADI's sales.

The SEC stock-options probe led to the company receiving a subpoena in 2006 from a federal grand jury in New York investigating backdating and other options abuses. ADI promised to cooperate with the investigation, which targeted numerous other publicly held companies, as well.

Later that year ADI acquired Integrant Technologies, a Korean company specializing in high-performance analog circuits for reconfigurable radio-frequency signal processing, for about $127 million in cash. Integrant's low-power radio tuners allow computers, consumer electronics devices, and mobile handsets to receive digital TV and digital radio broadcasts. Integrant's shareholders may receive up to $33 million in additional compensation, depending on performance milestones.

## EXECUTIVES

**Chairman:** Ray Stata, age 72
**President, CEO, and Director:** Jerald G. (Jerry) Fishman, age 61
**VP, DSP and Systems Products Group:** Brian P. McAloon, age 56
**VP, Finance and CFO:** Joseph E. McDonough, age 59
**VP, General Counsel, and Secretary:** Margaret K. Seif
**VP; General Manager, Analog Semiconductor Components:** Robert McAdam, age 56

**VP; General Manager, Micromachined Products:** William N. (Bill) Giudice, age 52
**VP, Research and Development:** Samuel H. Fuller, age 60
**VP, Worldwide Manufacturing:** Robert R. (Rob) Marshall, age 52
**VP, Worldwide Sales:** Vincent Roche, age 46
**VP, Human Resources:** William (Bill) Matson, age 47
**VP, Power Management Products:** Peter Henry
**Treasurer:** William A. Martin, age 47
**Director, Corporate Communications:** Maria Tagliaferro
**Auditors:** Ernst & Young LLP

## LOCATIONS

**HQ:** Analog Devices, Inc.
1 Technology Way, Norwood, MA 02062
**Phone:** 781-329-4700 **Fax:** 781-461-3638
**Web:** www.analog.com

Analog Devices has facilities in Austria, Belgium, China, Denmark, Finland, France, Germany, Hong Kong, India, Ireland, Israel, Italy, Japan, the Netherlands, the Philippines, Singapore, South Korea, Sweden, Taiwan, the UK, and the US.

### 2006 Sales

| | $ mil. | % of total |
|---|---|---|
| Asia/Pacific | | |
| Japan | 487 | 19 |
| China | 335 | 13 |
| Other countries | 525 | 21 |
| North America | 653 | 25 |
| Europe | 573 | 22 |
| **Total** | **2,573** | **100** |

## PRODUCTS/OPERATIONS

### 2006 Sales

| | $ mil. | % of total |
|---|---|---|
| Industrial | 1,084 | 42 |
| Communications | 748 | 29 |
| Consumer | 442 | 17 |
| Computer | 299 | 12 |
| **Total** | **2,573** | **100** |

### Selected Products

Integrated Circuits (ICs)
- Analog
  - Amplifiers
  - Analog signal processing devices
  - Comparators
  - Data converters
  - Interface circuits
  - Power management ICs
  - Voltage references
- Digital signal processing (DSP) devices
- Multifunction mixed-signal devices

Assembled Products
- Hybrid products (mounted and packaged chips and discrete components)
- Multi-chip modules
- Printed circuit board modules

Micromachined Products
- Accelerometers

## COMPETITORS

Analogic
Broadcom
Cirrus Logic
Conexant Systems
CST
DENSO
DSP Group
Fairchild Semiconductor
Freescale Semiconductor
Infineon Technologies
Intel
International Rectifier
Intersil
Linear Technology
Marvell Technology
Maxim Integrated Products
Micrel
Microsemi
National Semiconductor
NXP
ON Semiconductor
Panasonic
Robert Bosch
ROHM
Semtech
SigmaTel
Silicon Image
Silicon Laboratories
Siliconix
Standard Microsystems
STMicroelectronics
Texas Instruments

## HISTORICAL FINANCIALS

Company Type: Public

### Income Statement

FYE: Saturday nearest October 31

| | REVENUE ($ mil.) | NET INCOME ($ mil.) | NET PROFIT MARGIN | EMPLOYEES |
|---|---|---|---|---|
| **10/06** | 2,573 | 550 | 21.4% | 9,800 |
| **10/05** | 2,389 | 415 | 17.4% | 8,800 |
| **10/04** | 2,634 | 571 | 21.7% | 8,900 |
| **10/03** | 2,047 | 298 | 14.6% | 8,400 |
| **10/02** | 1,708 | 105 | 6.2% | 8,600 |
| **Annual Growth** | 10.8% | 51.1% | — | 3.3% |

### 2006 Year-End Financials

Debt ratio: —
Return on equity: 15.4%
Cash ($ mil.): 2,128
Current ratio: 6.13
Long-term debt ($ mil.): —
No. of shares (mil.): 342
Dividends
Yield: 1.4%
Payout: 29.7%
Market value ($ mil.): 10,646

### Stock History

NYSE: ADI

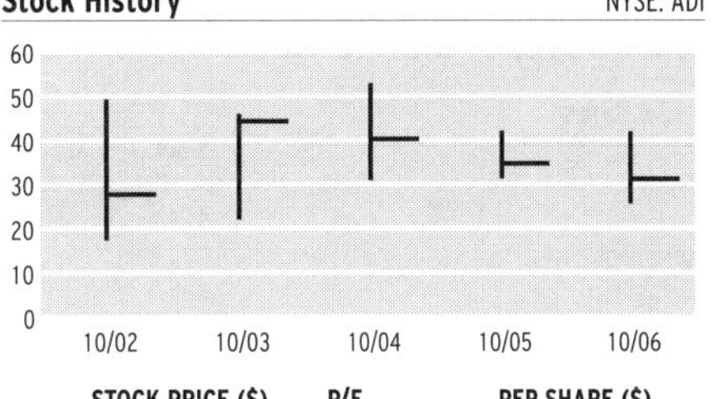


| | STOCK PRICE ($) FY Close | P/E High | P/E Low | PER SHARE ($) Earnings | Dividends | Book Value |
|---|---|---|---|---|---|---|
| **10/06** | 31.13 | 28 | 18 | 1.48 | 0.44 | 10.05 |
| **10/05** | 34.61 | 39 | 29 | 1.08 | 0.32 | 10.06 |
| **10/04** | 40.26 | 36 | 22 | 1.45 | 0.20 | 10.11 |
| **10/03** | 44.33 | 58 | 29 | 0.78 | — | 8.88 |
| **10/02** | 27.69 | 174 | 64 | 0.28 | — | 7.98 |
| **Annual Growth** | 3.0% | — | — | 51.6% | 48.3% | 5.9% |

# Anheuser-Busch

Anheuser-Busch Companies (A-B) wants to be the life of every party, whether with its brews or its theme parks. One of the world's largest brewers (at 157 million barrels of brew for 2006), the company is best known for Budweiser and Bud Light, as well as such labels as Busch and Michelob. Its beers lead the US with a market share of some 48%. A-B also owns a 35% stake in Mexico's top brewer, Grupo Modelo, maker of Corona and Negra Modelo. In addition to beer, Anheuser-Busch produces energy drinks and non-alcoholic malt beverages. A-B has several operations outside of brewing as well, including its Busch Entertainment theme-park business.

A-B owns the Metal Container Corporation, an aluminum-can-manufacturing business. It also operates in the real-estate development sector through its Busch Properties (resorts and conference centers) subsidiary and owns and operates Manufacturers Railway. It owns and operates 12 breweries, all located in the US.

But beer is A-B's major operation. To tap the premium and specialty beer sector, A-B owns several malt and specialty brews (Tequiza, ZiegenBock Amber) and has minority stakes in various small breweries, including a 33% stake in Redhook Ale Brewery and 40% in Widmer Brothers Brewing. The company also has a licensing agreement with Japanese brewer Kirin Brewery to brew its beers in the US.

The company's market share outside the US, however, is somewhat anemic, even though it sells its products in more than 60 countries. A-B has its sights set on Latin America and Asia to improve international growth. The firm is also seeking to increase its sales through investments in top brewers. In China, the world's largest beer market, the company owns 27% of that country's leading brewer Tsingtao, as well as Harbin Brewery Group.

Vying for female beer drinkers, in 2005 the company introduced Bud Select, a low-carb and low-calorie beer. With the leveling off of beer sales, A-B began moving into the spirits market, with the creation of a wholly owned subsidiary, Long Tail Libations in 2005. Long Tail is test marketing a liqueur called Jekyll & Hyde. That year A-B also created a new division to market specifically to Hispanics.

In 2006 the company began test marketing Peel, a fruit juice and alcohol beverage, aimed at women. It acquired the Rolling Rock brands from InBev USA for $82 million and agreed to distribute Hansen's energy drinks, including Monster Energy, Lost Energy, and Rumba.

A-B launched a new energy drink in 2006 called 180 Blue, featuring the acai berry as an ingredient. The company sells the drinks in bars as well as convenience and grocery stores.

August A. Busch IV took over as president and CEO in 2006, replacing Patrick Stokes, who moved to the role of chairman. Busch IV, great great grandchild of company co-founder Adolphus Busch, is the fifth generation of the family to run the company.

In 2007 the company made its first foray into India, forming a 50-50 joint venture with Crown Beers India to make and sell A-B products in the country.

Warren Buffet's Berkshire Hathaway owns more than 5% of the company, as does Barclay's Global Investors.

## HISTORY

George Schneider founded the Bavarian Brewery in St. Louis in 1852. Eight years later he sold the unprofitable brewery to Eberhard Anheuser. Anheuser's son-in-law, Adolphus Busch, joined the company in 1864 and in 1876 assisted restaurateur Carl Conrad in creating Budweiser, a light beer like those brewed in Bohemia. The brewery's rapid growth was based in part on the popularity of Budweiser over heavier, darker beers.

When Adolphus died in 1913, his son August took over the company, which was renamed Anheuser-Busch Companies in 1919. During Prohibition (1920-33), August saved the company by selling yeast, refrigeration units, truck bodies, syrup, and soft drinks. When repeal came in 1933, August quickly resumed brewing; he delivered a case of Budweiser to Franklin Roosevelt in a carriage drawn by Clydesdale horses, which became Anheuser-Busch's symbol.

Anheuser-Busch acquired the St. Louis Cardinals baseball team in 1953. Four years later the brewer knocked Schlitz out of first place among US brewers. In 1959 the company established its Busch Entertainment theme park division.

August Busch III was named CEO in 1975, beginning a reign that would last 27 years. The company bought Campbell Taggart (baked goods) and created its Eagle snack foods unit in 1982. Budweiser was introduced in England and

Japan in 1984 through licensing. In 1989 Anheuser-Busch acquired SeaWorld from Harcourt Brace Jovanovich.

Anheuser-Busch formed a joint venture with Kirin Brewery in 1993 to distribute Budweiser in Japan. In 1999 the arrangement became a licensing agreement.

Anheuser-Busch sold the Cardinals baseball team and stadium for $150 million and spun off its Campbell Taggart baking unit in 1996. The company then closed its Eagle Snacks unit, completing its exit from the food business.

To increase its presence internationally, Anheuser-Busch acquired interests in brewers in China (Budweiser Wuhan International Brewing) in 1995 and Argentina (Compañía Cervecerías). In 1998 the company increased its holding in Grupo Modelo from 18% (acquired in 1993) to about 50%.

Early in 2001 the company purchased nearly 20% of top Chilean brewer Compañía Cervecerías to further develop its business in Latin America. In February of that year the company sold its SeaWorld Cleveland theme park to Six Flags, Inc.

Company veteran Patrick Stokes became the first nonfamily member to lead Anheuser-Busch when he succeeded Busch III (who remained chairman) as president and CEO in 2002.

Capitalizing on the success of Bacardi Silver — a flavored drink in the "malternative" segment ruled by Diageo's Smirnoff Ice — Anheuser-Busch introduced orange-flavored Bacardi Silver O(3) and raspberry-flavored Bacardi Raz in 2003.

In 2005 Busch introduced BE, a new flavored brew containing caffeine, guarana, and ginseng. It is largely seen as a brand to compete in bars where energy drinks and flavored spirits have seen growing popularity. That year the company lost its NFL sponsorship to Molson Coors. (The Molson Coors deal runs through the 2010 football season.) A-B remained the exclusive beer advertiser for the Super Bowl.

A-B became the exclusive US importer of Grolsch brand beers.

## EXECUTIVES

**Chairman; Chairman and CEO, Anheuser-Busch, Inc.; Chairman, Anheuser-Busch International:** Patrick T. (Pat) Stokes, age 64, $4,399,516 pay
**President, CEO, and Director; President, Anheuser-Busch, Inc.:** August A. Busch IV, age 42, $2,172,917 pay
**Group VP and Chief Legal Officer:** Mark T. Bobak, age 47, $1,177,600 pay
**Group VP, Brewing Operations and Technology, Anheuser-Busch, Inc.:** Douglas J. Muhleman, age 52, $1,099,750 pay
**VP and CFO:** W. Randolph Baker, age 60, $1,215,000 pay
**VP and Controller:** John F. Kelly, age 50
**VP and General Counsel:** Lisa A. Joley
**VP and Secretary:** JoBeth G. Brown
**VP and Treasurer:** William J. Kimmins Jr.
**VP, Consumer Affairs:** John Kaestner
**VP, Corporate Communications and Consumer Affairs:** Francine I. Katz, age 48
**VP, Corporate Development; President and CEO, Anheuser-Busch International:** Thomas W. (Tom) Santel, age 48
**VP and CIO:** Joseph P. (Joe) Castellano, age 53
**VP, Corporate Human Resources:** John T. (Tim) Farrell
**VP, Investor Relations:** David C. Sauerhoff
**VP, Public Communications:** Teresa H. Vogt
**VP, Marketing, Anheuser-Busch, Inc.:** Michael J. Owens, age 52, $1,000,000 pay
**VP and Tax Controller:** Dennis Gelner
**President and CEO, Asia Pacific Operations:** Stephen J. (Steve) Burrows, age 55
**Chairman and President, Busch Entertainment Corporation:** Keith M. Kasen, age 63
**Chief Creative Officer:** Robert C. (Bob) Lachky, age 53
**President and CEO, Manufacturers Railroad; St. Louis Refrigerator Car:** Kurt R. Andrew
**Auditors:** PricewaterhouseCoopers LLP

## LOCATIONS

**HQ:** Anheuser-Busch Companies, Inc.
1 Busch Place, St. Louis, MO 63118
**Phone:** 314-577-2000 **Fax:** 314-577-2900
**Web:** www.anheuser-busch.com

### 2006 Worldwide Beer Volume

| | Millions of barrels |
|---|---|
| A-B brands — domestic | 102 |
| Equity partner brands — international | 32 |
| A-B brands — international | 23 |
| **Total** | **157** |

## PRODUCTS/OPERATIONS

### 2006 Sales

| | $ mil. | % of total |
|---|---|---|
| Beer | | |
| US | 11,388.2 | 73 |
| Other countries | 998.2 | 6 |
| Packaging | 1,665.9 | 11 |
| Entertainment | 1,178.5 | 7 |
| Other | 486.3 | 3 |
| **Total** | **15,717.1** | **100** |

### Selected Brands

A-B Beers
- American Red
- Anheuser World Lager
- Bare Knuckle Stout
- Bud Extra (formerly known as BE)
- Busch
- Busch Light
- Land Shark Lager
- Natty Up
- Natural Ice
- Natural Light
- Redbridge
- Rock Green Light
- Rolling Rock
- Stone Mill Pale
- Wild Hop Lager
- ZiegenBock Amber

A-B Energy Drinks
- 180

A-B Malt Liquors
- Hurricane High Gravity
- Hurricane Ice
- Hurricane Malt
- King Cobra

A-B Nonalcohol Brews
- Busch NA
- O'Doul's
- O'Doul's Amber

A-B Specialty Malt Beverages
- BACARDI Silver
- BACARDI Silver Big Apple
- BACARDI Silver O3
- BACARDI Silver Peach
- BACARDI Silver Raz
- BACARDI Silver Strawberry
- BACARDI Silver Watermelon

Alliance Partner Products
- Goose Island
- Kona
- Redhook Ale
- Widmer Brothers

Imported Products
- Bass Pale Ale
- Beck's
- Czechvar Premium Czech Lager
- Grolsch Amber
- Grolsch Blonde
- Grolsch Lager
- Grolsch Light
- Hoegaarden
- Kingsbrucke
- Leffe
- Stella Artois
- Tiger Lager

Joint Venture Products
- Kirin
- Kirin-Ichiban
- Kirin Light

## COMPETITORS

Alcan
Alcoa
American Rice
Anchor Hocking
Asahi Breweries
Ball Corporation
Boston Beer
Burlington Northern Santa Fe
Carlsberg A/S
Cedar Fair
Danone
Diageo
Disney Parks & Resorts
FEMSA
Foster's
Gambrinus
Grolsch
Heineken
Heineken USA
InBev
InBev USA
Kirin Holdings
Labatt
Libbey
Molson Coors
Pabst
Producers Rice Mill
Rexam Beverage Can
Rexam Europe & Asia
Riceland Foods
Riviana Foods
SABMiller
Scottish & Newcastle
Sims
Six Flags
Suntory Ltd.
Union Pacific Railroad
Universal Parks
Waste Management
WM Recycle America

## HISTORICAL FINANCIALS

Company Type: Public

### Income Statement

FYE: December 31

| | REVENUE ($ mil.) | NET INCOME ($ mil.) | NET PROFIT MARGIN | EMPLOYEES |
|---|---|---|---|---|
| **12/06** | 15,717 | 1,965 | 12.5% | 30,183 |
| **12/05** | 15,036 | 1,839 | 12.2% | 31,485 |
| **12/04** | 14,934 | 2,240 | 15.0% | 31,435 |
| **12/03** | 14,147 | 2,076 | 14.7% | 23,316 |
| **12/02** | 13,566 | 1,934 | 14.3% | 23,176 |
| **Annual Growth** | 3.7% | 0.4% | — | 6.8% |

### 2006 Year-End Financials

Debt ratio: 194.3%
Return on equity: 54.0%
Cash ($ mil.): 219
Current ratio: 0.81
Long-term debt ($ mil.): 7,654
No. of shares (mil.): 763
Dividends
Yield: 2.3%
Payout: 44.7%
Market value ($ mil.): 37,534

**Stock History** NYSE: BUD

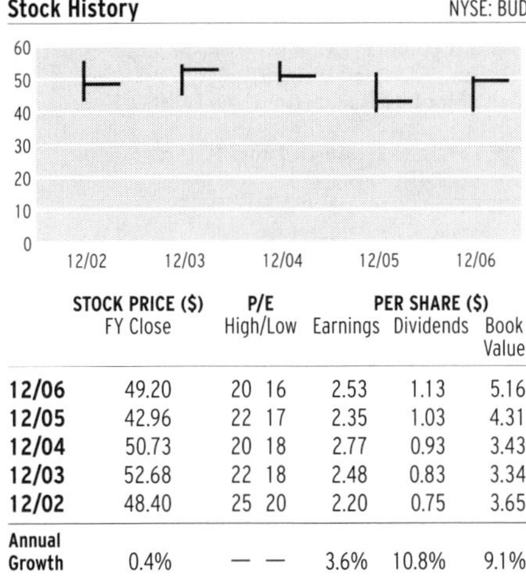


| | STOCK PRICE ($) FY Close | P/E High | P/E Low | PER SHARE ($) Earnings | Dividends | Book Value |
|---|---|---|---|---|---|---|
| **12/06** | 49.20 | 20 | 16 | 2.53 | 1.13 | 5.16 |
| **12/05** | 42.96 | 22 | 17 | 2.35 | 1.03 | 4.31 |
| **12/04** | 50.73 | 20 | 18 | 2.77 | 0.93 | 3.43 |
| **12/03** | 52.68 | 22 | 18 | 2.48 | 0.83 | 3.34 |
| **12/02** | 48.40 | 25 | 20 | 2.20 | 0.75 | 3.65 |
| **Annual Growth** | 0.4% | — | — | 3.6% | 10.8% | 9.1% |

# Anixter International

Psssst — need wiring products? Anixter International has got connections. The company is a major global distributor of wiring systems, networking products, and fasteners. Anixter sells more than 350,000 different items — including copper and fiber-optic transmission cable, electrical wiring systems, and security system components — through a worldwide network of sales and distribution centers. The company obtains products from more than 5,000 suppliers and sells worldwide to more than 95,000 active customers, including resellers such as contractors, installers, engineers, and wholesale distributors.

Anixter maintains strong relationships with its suppliers and participates in product planning and technical support activities. It gets nearly three-quarters of sales from North America.

The company regularly resorts to acquisitions (and occasionally to divestitures) in shaping its businesses. In 2006 Anixter bought IMS, Inc. for $28.5 million in cash. IMS is a cable and wire distributor, primarily operating in the northeastern US and the mid-Atlantic states. Later that year the company paid about $61 million in cash and assumed nearly $6 million in debt to acquire MFU Holding S.p.A., a fastener distributor that does most of its business in Italy.

Anixter's chairman, billionaire financier Samuel Zell, owns about 14% of the company.

## HISTORY

Two San Francisco businessmen, Gary Friedman and Peter Redfield, founded SSI Computer in 1967 to lease computer systems. The company bought $90 million worth of IBM computers and leased them at rates lower than IBM's.

In 1968 SSI entered the intermodal container and railcar leasing business when it purchased SSI Container Corp. The next year it bought Management Data Processing Corp., and in 1970 the company renamed itself Itel.

During the 1970s the company diversified into aircraft leasing (Itel Air) and capital goods (Itel Capital). By the mid-1970s Itel's computer-leasing business was starting to falter. In 1979 Itel left the computer business, handing most of its sales and service over to National Semiconductor. After both Friedman and Redfield were dismissed, CEO James Maloon focused Itel on transportation services, but by 1981 the company was $1.3 billion in debt and had filed Chapter 11.

When reorganization failed to resurrect the debt-strapped company, Samuel Zell, a Chicago financier, began buying Itel stock. In 1984 he earned a seat on the board and the next year became chairman.

Zell and vice chairman Rod Dammeyer, former Household International CFO, acquired Great Lakes International (marine dredging, 1986), Anixter Bros. (wire and cable, 1986), Pullman (railcars, 1988), and a minority stake in Santa Fe Southern Pacific (railroad, 1988). Other acquisitions included Flexi-Van Leasing (1987), the assets of Evans Asset Holding (railcars, 1987), and B.C. Hydro (rail freight line, 1988). By 1988 Itel was North America's leading railcar leasing company.

In the 1990s Itel repositioned itself, selling its container-leasing business (1990) and its Itel Distribution Systems and Great Lakes Dredge & Deck Co. (1991). When the smoke cleared, Anixter was the company's core operation. Anixter spun off its cable television products subsidiary ANTEC in 1993. Also that year Dammeyer replaced Zell as Itel's CEO.

Itel's focus became developing new markets in the burgeoning global communications industry. The company sold its remaining rail-leasing interests in 1994. The next year Itel sold its stake in Santa Fe Energy Resources and changed its name to Anixter.

When an ANTEC subsidiary merged with cable TV equipment firm TSX Corp. in 1997, Anixter's ownership in ANTEC was reduced to 19%. That year the company joined with security software maker Check Point Software Technologies to provide network-security products in Europe.

Anixter sold its ANTEC holdings in 1998 to finance the repurchase of its common stock, and bought Pacer Electronics, an electrical and data cabling distributor. Also that year, company veteran Robert Grubbs became CEO.

The next year Anixter sold its European network integration business to Persetel Q Data Holdings of South Africa and its data-network design and consulting unit to Ameritech for $200 million in cash. It also sold North America Integration and Asia Pacific Integration, completing the dissolution of its integration segment by the close of 1999.

In 2000 Anixter formed a consortium with Panduit, Rockwell Automation, and Siemens for the production of industrially hardened Ethernet connectors. Anixter signed an agreement to distribute network cabling products for IBM in 2001.

In 2002 Anixter was named as a *Forbes* "Platinum 400" company, chosen by the magazine's editors as one of America's "best-performing" corporations by industry. Later in that same year it acquired Pentacon (now Anixter Pentacon), a fastener distribution company.

Early in 2003 Anixter sold its cable testing program to Underwriters Laboratories. Increasing its fastener holdings, Anixter acquired Walters Hexagon Group, a UK-based fastener distribution company, later in the year.

The company acquired fastener distributor Infast Group for approximately $72 million in 2005.

## EXECUTIVES

**Chairman:** Samuel (Sam) Zell, age 65
**President, CEO, and Director:** Robert W. Grubbs Jr., age 50, $900,000 pay
**SVP, Finance and CFO; EVP and CFO, Anixter Inc.:** Dennis J. Letham, age 55, $400,000 pay
**VP and Controller:** Terrance A. Faber, age 55, $227,500 pay
**VP and Treasurer, Anixter International and Anixter Inc.:** Rodney A. Shoemaker, age 49, $189,000 pay
**VP, General Counsel, and Secretary; General Counsel and Secretary, Anixter Inc.:** John A. Dul, age 45, $245,000 pay
**VP, Taxes:** Philip F. Meno, age 47
**VP, Human Resources:** Rodney A. Smith, age 49
**Auditors:** Ernst & Young LLP

## LOCATIONS

**HQ:** Anixter International Inc.
2301 Patriot Blvd., Glenview, IL 60026
**Phone:** 224-521-8000 **Fax:** 224-521-8100
**Web:** www.anixter.com

Anixter International operates about 200 warehouses in more than 45 countries.

### 2006 Sales

| | $ mil. | % of total |
|---|---|---|
| North America | | |
| US | 3,055.1 | 62 |
| Canada | 556.6 | 11 |
| Europe | 980.4 | 20 |
| Other regions | 346.5 | 7 |
| **Total** | **4,938.6** | **100** |

## PRODUCTS/OPERATIONS

### Selected Products

Copper and fiber-optic cable
Electrical wiring systems
Fasteners and connectors
Mainframe peripheral equipment
Video surveillance equipment

## COMPETITORS

Border States Electric
Communications Systems
Consolidated Electrical
Crescent Electric Supply
Gexpro
Graybar Electric
Kirby Risk
Labinal
Precision Industries
Premier Farnell
Rexel
Sonepar USA
Southwire
Superior Essex
TESSCO
WESCO International

## HISTORICAL FINANCIALS

Company Type: Public

**Income Statement** FYE: Friday nearest December 31

| | REVENUE ($ mil.) | NET INCOME ($ mil.) | NET PROFIT MARGIN | EMPLOYEES |
|---|---|---|---|---|
| **12/06** | 4,939 | 209 | 4.2% | 7,500 |
| **12/05** | 3,847 | 90 | 2.3% | 6,800 |
| **12/04** | 3,275 | 78 | 2.4% | 5,600 |
| **12/03** | 2,625 | 42 | 1.6% | 5,000 |
| **12/02** | 2,520 | 43 | 1.7% | 5,000 |
| **Annual Growth** | 18.3% | 48.4% | — | 10.7% |

**2006 Year-End Financials**

Debt ratio: 62.1%
Return on equity: 25.1%
Cash ($ mil.): 51
Current ratio: 2.19
Long-term debt ($ mil.): 597
No. of shares (mil.): 40
Dividends
Yield: —
Payout: —
Market value ($ mil.): 2,145

**Stock History** NYSE: AXE

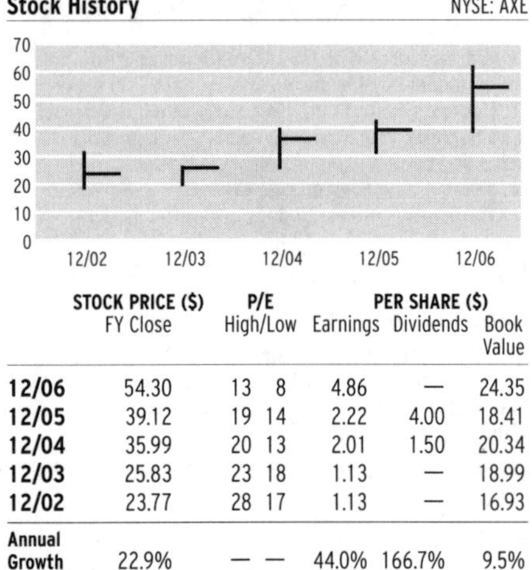


| | STOCK PRICE ($) FY Close | P/E High | P/E Low | PER SHARE ($) Earnings | Dividends | Book Value |
|---|---|---|---|---|---|---|
| **12/06** | 54.30 | 13 | 8 | 4.86 | — | 24.35 |
| **12/05** | 39.12 | 19 | 14 | 2.22 | 4.00 | 18.41 |
| **12/04** | 35.99 | 20 | 13 | 2.01 | 1.50 | 20.34 |
| **12/03** | 25.83 | 23 | 18 | 1.13 | — | 18.99 |
| **12/02** | 23.77 | 28 | 17 | 1.13 | — | 16.93 |
| **Annual Growth** | 22.9% | — | — | 44.0% | 166.7% | 9.5% |

# AnnTaylor Stores

At AnnTaylor, basic black is as appreciated by its customers as its classic styles. The company (named for a fictional person) is a national retailer of upscale women's clothing designed exclusively for its stores. Its AnnTaylor and AnnTaylor LOFT shops offer apparel, shoes, and accessories. Targeting fashion-conscious professional women, AnnTaylor operates about 870 stores in 46 states across the nation, as well as the District of Columbia and Puerto Rico. Most are located in malls or upscale retail centers. Ann Taylor LOFT stores offer their own label of mid-priced apparel, while AnnTaylor Factory Stores sell clearance merchandise. AnnTaylor also has its own e-commerce Web site.

Launched in 1999, the fast-growing AnnTaylor LOFT format overtook its more mature sister chain in 2005 in terms of the number of outlets. The company added about 50 new LOFT stores last year; five times the number of new AnnTaylor stores added. As many as 60 new LOFT stores, 10 to 15 AnnTaylor stores, and 10 factory outlets are slated to open in 2007.

With this expansion momentum and success, AnnTaylor can't afford a lull in activity or demand for its LOFT brand. LOFT's same-stores sales growth, which had been outpacing AnnTaylor's same-store sales, now trail its sister chain. Holiday sales in 2006 suffered as well, which spurred AnnTaylor to quickly purge LOFT executive Donna Noce from its payroll and appoint CEO Kay Krill to oversee the division's operations. A couple factors, such as LOFT pushing heavy sweaters during warm weather and fashion misses, have been cited as reasons for the brand's sales dip. After a six-month search for a new president to lead LOFT failed, the retailer instead appointed Diane Holtz as top merchant at LOFT in June 2007. Holtz will report to Krill.

AnnTaylor stores are on average 5,200 sq. ft., Loft stores are about 5,900 sq. ft., and the factory stores are around 8,400 sq. ft. About 75% of its core AnnTaylor stores are located in shopping malls and upscale retail centers. The company's three flagship stores are located in Chicago, New York City, and San Francisco. AnnTaylor's products are made in more than 20 countries with about 40% originating in China and Hong Kong.

## HISTORY

AnnTaylor Stores started out in 1954 as a shop on Chapel Street in New Haven, Connecticut. Founder Robert Liebskind targeted women who would later be called "preppie," using the conservative (and fictitious) Ann Taylor name. The stores proliferated in New England. In 1977 Liebskind sold out to Garfinckel, Brooks Brothers, Miller & Rhodes, which in 1981 was bought by Allied Stores. Under Allied, AnnTaylor was the top performer, thanks in large part to the merchandising savvy of Sally Frame Kasaks, who was president from 1983 to 1985.

Campeau Corporation made a hostile takeover of Allied in 1985. Heavily in debt, and with ill-fated designs on the bigger prize of Federated Department Stores, Campeau mined AnnTaylor for cash and then sold it in 1988 for $420 million to private investors and the division's management. AnnTaylor had suffered from image drift under Campeau, and its new management continued to ignore the company's target career-woman customer; in addition, the chain was slow to see the trend toward more casual career dressing.

In 1991 AnnTaylor went public, but it continued to founder under high debt load and a fuzzy fashion image. Kasaks returned as CEO that year and transformed the store name into a brand name with original designs. She also added shoe stores and a lower-priced apparel concept (Ann Taylor LOFT). The company's fashion sense became a problem again — cropped T-shirts didn't fit in with the workplace attire its customers sought — and AnnTaylor suffered a loss in fiscal 1996. Kasaks was ousted that year.

New CEO Patrick Spainhour and new president Patricia DeRosa quickly led AnnTaylor to another turnaround. They closed the shoe stores in 1997 and refocused the company's designs. The company opened 29 Ann Taylor LOFT stores in 1999 in pursuit of younger, more cost-conscious consumers. In early 2001 DeRosa left the company.

AnnTaylor attempted a short-lived cosmetic line in 2000, which it discontinued in 2001.

In 2004 the company opened five new Ann Taylor stores and 75 Ann Taylor LOFT stores.

In June 2005 the company completed its move to its new headquarters in Times Square Tower in New York City. In August the New York retailer announced it had entered into a trademark licensing agreement with China's Guangzhou Pan Yu San Yuet Fashion Manufactory Ltd. that owns rights to use the Ann Taylor name in China. In September chairman and CEO J. Patrick Spainhour retired and was succeeded as CEO by the company's president Kay Krill. Ronald W. Hovsepian, a director of the company since 1998, became chairman.

In May 2006 COO Laura Weil resigned after less than a year with the company. (Weil had joined AnnTaylor Stores from American Eagle Outfitters in 2005.)

## EXECUTIVES

**Chairman:** Ronald W. (Ron) Hovsepian, age 46
**President, CEO, and Director; Interim President, AnnTaylor LOFT:** Katherine (Kay) Lawther Krill, age 51
**EVP, CFO, and Treasurer:** James M. (Jim) Smith, age 45, $391,000 pay
**EVP, General Counsel, and Secretary:** Barbara K. Eisenberg, age 61
**EVP, Human Resources:** Mark Morrison
**EVP, Planning and Allocation, Ann Taylor Loft and Ann Taylor Factory:** Debra Berit
**SVP, Finance and Assistant Treasurer:** Linda M. Siluk, age 49
**SVP, General Merchandise Manager, Ann Taylor Stores:** Sonya Lee
**SVP, Marketing, Ann Taylor Stores:** Elizabeth O'Neill
**SVP, Design, Ann Taylor Stores:** Michael Smaldone
**SVP, Global Sourcing, Ann Taylor Stores:** Liisa Pierce Fiedelholtz
**SVP, Sourcing, Ann Taylor LOFT Stores and Ann Taylor Factory Stores:** Jeanne Varvaro
**SVP, Sourcing Operations and Strategy:** Barbara Fevelo-Hoad
**VP, Product Development:** Philippa Abeles
**CIO:** Michael Kingston
**President, AnnTaylor Stores:** Adrienne Lazarus-Marlazzi, age 39, $670,017 pay
**President, Ann Taylor Factory Stores:** Brian Lynch, age 49, $532,898 pay
**Auditors:** Deloitte & Touche LLP

## LOCATIONS

**HQ:** AnnTaylor Stores Corporation
7 Times Square, 15th Fl., New York, NY 10036
**Phone:** 212-541-3300 **Fax:** 212-541-3379
**Web:** www.anntaylor.com

## PRODUCTS/OPERATIONS

**2007 Stores**

| | No. |
|---|---|
| Ann Taylor LOFT | 464 |
| Ann Taylor | 348 |
| Ann Taylor Factory | 57 |
| **Total** | **869** |

**2007 Sales**

| | $ mil. | % of total |
|---|---|---|
| Ann Taylor LOFT | 1,146.5 | 49 |
| Ann Taylor | 912.7 | 39 |
| Other | 283.7 | 12 |
| **Total** | **2,342.9** | **100** |

**Store Formats**

Ann Taylor (upscale specialty stores selling women's apparel)
Ann Taylor Factory Store (clearance stores for Ann Taylor and Ann Taylor LOFT merchandise)
Ann Taylor LOFT (mid-priced specialty stores selling women's apparel)

## COMPETITORS

Banana Republic
Benetton
Bernard Chaus
Bill Blass
Brooks Brothers
Caché
Calvin Klein
Dillard's
Donna Karan
Ellen Tracy
Gap
J. Crew
J. Jill Group
Jones Apparel
Lands' End
Laura Ashley
Limited Brands
Liz Claiborne
Macy's
Macy's North
New York & Company
Nordstrom
Polo Ralph Lauren
Retail Brand Alliance
Saks Inc.
St. John Knits
Talbots

## HISTORICAL FINANCIALS

Company Type: Public

### Income Statement

FYE: Saturday nearest January 31

| | REVENUE ($ mil.) | NET INCOME ($ mil.) | NET PROFIT MARGIN | EMPLOYEES |
|---|---|---|---|---|
| **1/07** | 2,343 | 143 | 6.1% | 17,700 |
| **1/06** | 2,073 | 82 | 4.0% | 16,900 |
| **1/05** | 1,854 | 63 | 3.4% | 14,900 |
| **1/04** | 1,588 | 101 | 6.4% | 13,000 |
| **1/03** | 1,381 | 80 | 5.8% | 10,900 |
| **Annual Growth** | 14.1% | 15.6% | — | 12.9% |

### 2007 Year-End Financials

| | |
|---|---|
| Debt ratio: — | No. of shares (mil.): 69 |
| Return on equity: 13.7% | Dividends |
| Cash ($ mil.): 361 | Yield: — |
| Current ratio: 2.31 | Payout: — |
| Long-term debt ($ mil.): — | Market value ($ mil.): 2,451 |

### Stock History

NYSE: ANN

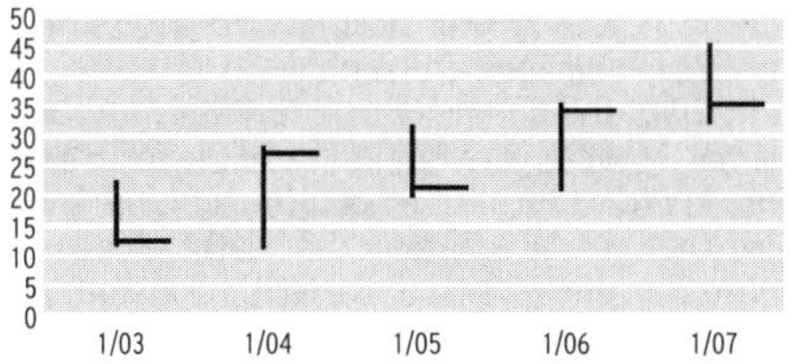

| | STOCK PRICE ($) FY Close | P/E High | P/E Low | PER SHARE ($) Earnings | Dividends | Book Value |
|---|---|---|---|---|---|---|
| **1/07** | 35.33 | 23 | 16 | 1.98 | — | 15.13 |
| **1/06** | 34.24 | 31 | 19 | 1.13 | — | 14.27 |
| **1/05** | 21.31 | 36 | 23 | 0.88 | — | 13.12 |
| **1/04** | 27.00 | 20 | 8 | 1.42 | — | 18.30 |
| **1/03** | 12.41 | 19 | 10 | 1.15 | — | 15.92 |
| **Annual Growth** | 29.9% | — | — | 14.5% | — | (1.3%) |

# A. O. Smith

Aerosmith has a lot of fans — A. O. Smith has a lot of fan motors. The company makes electric motors and water heaters. Its Electrical Products segment makes pump motors for home water systems, swimming pools, and hot tubs; fan motors for furnaces and air conditioners; and hermetic motors for compressors and commercial refrigeration units. The company's Water Products segment makes residential gas and electric water heaters and commercial water-heating systems. A. O. Smith customers include York International and Sears. Members of the founding Smith family control the company.

A. O. Smith's sales were roughly split between electrical products and water systems prior to the GSW acquisition in 2006, which tilted the balance to water systems. It sells most of its electrical products to equipment manufacturers, but it also has some aftermarket and distribution sales. Its water systems are sold through wholesale distributors and retail channels. Customers in the US account for 80% of A. O. Smith's sales.

T. Rowe Price owns about 10% of A. O. Smith's common shares outstanding. Holding equity stakes of about 5% each are Franklin Resources, The Vanguard Group, Goldman Sachs Asset Management, and Dimensional Fund Advisors.

## HISTORY

Charles Jeremiah Smith founded a machine shop in 1874 to make parts for baby carriages. The business expanded into making bicycles, and by 1895 it was a global leader in bicycle parts. The Smith family sold the firm in 1899. Charles' eldest son, Arthur, began tinkering with car frames, and by 1902 he had a breakthrough design. Arthur bought the company back in 1904 to make car frames and incorporated it as A. O. Smith.

A huge 1906 contract from Ford spurred Arthur to retool the factory, increasing production tenfold. In 1921 A. O. Smith unveiled the first automated assembly line for car frames. Dubbed the Mechanical Marvel, it could produce a frame every eight seconds and did so for the next 40 years.

The firm began production of the first glass-lined residential water heaters in 1939. Acquisitions over the next decade allowed A. O. Smith to enter the electric motor market, and in 1959 it established a plastics unit for its fiberglass pipe.

In 1986 A. O. Smith expanded its electric motor business when it bought Westinghouse's small-motor division. The company doubled the size of its tank business by buying Peabody TecTank (dry storage tanks) the next year. Company veteran Robert O'Toole was named CEO in 1989.

A. O. Smith sold its auto business in 1997 and bought private motor producer UPPCO. The company became the #1 North American maker of compressor motors for the air-conditioning industry with its 1998 purchase of a General Electric motor unit. The next year it bought the electric-motor unit of Magnetek, doubling the size of its pump motor business.

In 2000 the company sold its fluid handling (fiberglass pipe) business to Varco International (Texas). The next year A. O. Smith sold its storage products business to CST Industries (Kansas).

A. O. Smith elected to sell some 3.5 million shares of its common stock in early 2002, with the intention of repaying a portion of its debt. To expand its manufacturing capabilities, the company acquired an electric motor maker in China from the Changheng Group (air-moving motors for the Chinese air-conditioning market). A. O. Smith also pumped up its water systems by acquiring privately held State Industries (water heaters), which contributed about $313 million to its annual net sales. The same year A. O. Smith bought the assets of the Athens Products division of Electrolux.

In 2003 A. O. Smith again expanded its global motor manufacturing business, buying the assets of Taicang Special Motor Co., Ltd., a maker of hermetic electric motors based in China.

In 2005 the company bought another Chinese motor manufacturer, Yueyang Special Electrical Machinery.

O'Toole retired at the end of 2005 and company president Paul Jones was named CEO.

In 2006 A. O. Smith acquired GSW, a Canadian supplier of water heaters, for about $320 million in cash. The acquisition gave A. O. Smith entree as a supplier to home improvement giant Lowe's.

In late 2006 the company sold GSW Building Products, a manufacturer of vinyl rain ware systems, to Euramax International. GSW Building Products employs about 100 people in Barrie, Ontario, and posted 2005 sales of $30 million. A. O. Smith received net proceeds of about $11.3 million from the sale.

## EXECUTIVES

**Chairman and CEO:** Paul W. Jones, age 58, $807,000 pay
**EVP, Corporate Technology and Global Supply Chain:** Ronald E. (Ron) Massa, age 57, $339,875 pay
**EVP and CFO:** Terry M. Murphy, age 58, $500,000 pay
**EVP; President, Electrical Products:** Christopher L. (Chris) Mapes, age 45, $386,667 pay
**EVP; President, Water Products:** Ajita G. Rajendra, age 55, $410,250 pay
**EVP, General Counsel, and Secretary:** James F. Stern
**SVP, Asia:** Michael J. Cole, age 62
**SVP, Corporate Development:** Steve W. Rettler, age 52
**SVP, Human Resources and Public Affairs:** Mark A. Petrarca, age 43
**SVP, Information Technology:** Randall S. (Randy) Bednar, age 54
**SVP, Treasurer, and Controller:** John J. Kita, age 51
**Auditors:** Ernst & Young LLP

## LOCATIONS

**HQ:** A. O. Smith Corporation
11270 W. Park Place, Milwaukee, WI 53224
**Phone:** 414-359-4000 **Fax:** 414-359-4064
**Web:** www.aosmith.com

A. O. Smith has manufacturing facilities in Canada, China, Hungary, Mexico, the Netherlands, the UK, and the US.

### 2006 Sales

| | $ mil. | % of total |
|---|---|---|
| US | 1,720.9 | 80 |
| China | 154.2 | 7 |
| Canada | 137.3 | 6 |
| Other countries | 148.9 | 7 |
| **Total** | **2,161.3** | **100** |

## PRODUCTS/OPERATIONS

### 2006 Sales

| | $ mil. | % of total |
|---|---|---|
| Water Products | 1,260.8 | 58 |
| Electrical Products | 905.9 | 42 |
| Adjustments | (5.4) | — |
| **Total** | **2,161.3** | **100** |

### Divisions and Products

Electric Products
- Fractional horsepower electric motors
- Hermetic electric motors
- Integral horsepower A/C and D/C electric motors

Water Products
- Commercial water heaters
- Copper tube boilers
- Residential water heaters

## COMPETITORS

AMETEK
AMTROL
Baldor Electric
Bradford White
Emerson Electric
EXX
Franklin Electric
GE
Haier Group
Hayward Industries
Indesit
Jakel
Kinetek
Lindeteves-Jacoberg
Lochinvar
Paloma
Pentair
RBS Global
Regal-Beloit
Tecumseh Products
Water Pik Technologies
WEG

## HISTORICAL FINANCIALS

Company Type: Public

**Income Statement** FYE: December 31

| | REVENUE ($ mil.) | NET INCOME ($ mil.) | NET PROFIT MARGIN | EMPLOYEES |
|---|---|---|---|---|
| **12/06** | 2,161 | 77 | 3.5% | 18,000 |
| **12/05** | 1,689 | 47 | 2.8% | 17,650 |
| **12/04** | 1,653 | 35 | 2.1% | 16,600 |
| **12/03** | 1,531 | 52 | 3.4% | 17,000 |
| **12/02** | 1,469 | 51 | 3.5% | 16,200 |
| **Annual Growth** | 10.1% | 10.5% | — | 2.7% |

**2006 Year-End Financials**

Debt ratio: 63.1%
Return on equity: 11.8%
Cash ($ mil.): 26
Current ratio: 1.74
Long-term debt ($ mil.): 432
No. of shares (mil.): 22
Dividends
Yield: 1.8%
Payout: 26.7%
Market value ($ mil.): 842

**Stock History** NYSE: AOS

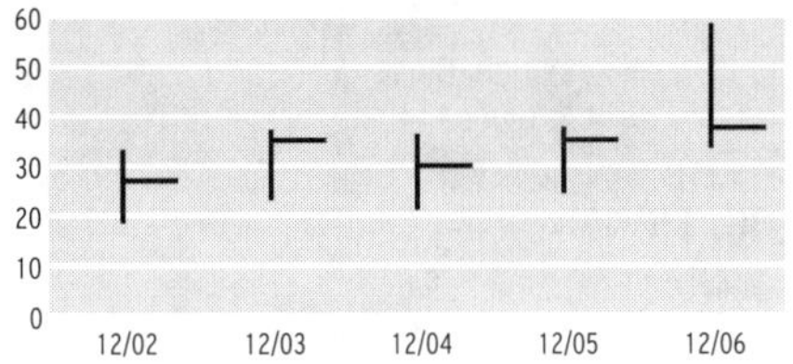

| | STOCK PRICE ($) FY Close | P/E High | P/E Low | PER SHARE ($) Earnings | Dividends | Book Value |
|---|---|---|---|---|---|---|
| **12/06** | 37.56 | 24 | 14 | 2.47 | 0.66 | 30.55 |
| **12/05** | 35.10 | 24 | 16 | 1.54 | 0.64 | 25.49 |
| **12/04** | 29.94 | 30 | 18 | 1.18 | 0.62 | 27.89 |
| **12/03** | 35.05 | 21 | 13 | 1.76 | 0.58 | 23.99 |
| **12/02** | 27.01 | 18 | 10 | 1.86 | 0.54 | 21.33 |
| **Annual Growth** | 8.6% | — | — | 7.3% | 5.1% | 9.4% |

# Aon Corporation

Aon (the name means "oneness" in Gaelic) is the world's #2 insurance brokerage (Marsh & McLennan is #1 based on total revenue) and the leading reinsurance broker. The company operates in three major segments: commercial brokerage, consulting services, and consumer insurance underwriting. The company's brokerage operations include retail and wholesale insurance for groups and businesses. Its consulting business specializes in employee benefits administration. Its London General Insurance subsidiary offers extended service plans to large manufacturers, distributors, and retailers of retail goods, as well as home buyers/sellers and other products.

Aon's older but smaller insurance underwriting segment (including founder W. Clement Stone's original insurance underwriting business, Combined Insurance) offers supplementary health, accident, and life insurance and extended warranties for consumer goods.

As part of a restructuring effort that followed on the coattails of an investigation into the company's payment practices, the company began to pare down its operations in late 2005. Begun in 2004, the investigation resulted in $190 million in fines for Aon and a shakeup of top managment.

The company sold its wholesale brokerage operations, Swett & Crawford (the largest in the US), to a group of investors led by Hicks, Muse, Tate & Furst (now HM Capital Partners). Aon also shed its credit, warranty, and property and casualty underwriting operations; it sold its Aon Warranty Group division (including Virginia Surety) to Onex for $710 million in late 2006. The company concurrently sold off its Construction Program Group, which was part of its property and casualty operations, to Old Republic Insurance for $85 million.

## HISTORY

Aon's story begins with the birth of W. Clement Stone around the turn of the 20th century. At age six he started working as a paperboy in Chicago. The young Stone devoured the optimistic messages of the 19th-century Horatio Alger novels, which detailed the successes of plucky, enterprising heroes.

Stone's mother bought a small Detroit insurance agency and in 1918 brought her son into the business. Young Stone sold low-cost, low-benefit accident insurance, underwriting and issuing policies on-site. The next year he founded his own agency, the Combined Registry Co. While selling up to 122 policies per day, he recruited a nationwide force of agents.

As the Depression took hold, Stone reduced his workforce and improved training. Forced by his son's respiratory illness to winter in the South, Stone followed the sun to Arkansas and Texas. In 1939 he bought American Casualty Insurance Co. of Dallas. It was consolidated with other purchases as the Combined Insurance Co. of America in 1947.

The company grew through the 1950s and 1960s, continuing to sell health and accident policies. In the 1970s Combined expanded overseas despite being hit hard by the recession.

In 1982, after 10 years of stagnant growth under Clement Stone Jr., the elder Stone (then 79) resumed control until the completion of a merger with Ryan Insurance Co. allowed him to transfer power to Patrick Ryan.

Ryan, the son of a Wisconsin Ford dealer, had started his company as an auto credit insurer in 1964. In 1976 the company bought the insurance brokerage units of the Esmark conglomerate. Ryan's less-personal management style differed radically from Stone's rah-rah boosterism, but the men's shared interest in philanthropy helped seal the deal.

Ryan focused on insurance brokering and added more upscale insurance products. He also trimmed staff and took other cost-cutting measures, and in 1987 he changed Combined's name to Aon. In 1995 the company sold its remaining direct life insurance holdings to focus on consulting. The following year it began offering hostile takeover insurance policies to small and midsized companies.

In 1997 Aon bought The Minet Group, as well as troubled insurance brokerage Alexander & Alexander Services in a deal that made Aon (temporarily) the largest insurance broker worldwide. The firm made no US buys in 1998, but doubled its employee base with purchases including Spain's largest retail insurance broker, Gil y Carvajal, and the formation of Aon Korea, the first non-Korean firm of its kind to be licensed there.

In 1999 it bought Nikols Sedgwick Group, an Italian insurance firm, and formed RiskAttack (with Zurich US), a risk analysis and financial management concern aimed at technology companies. The cost of integrating its numerous purchases, however, hammered profits in 1999.

Despite its troubles, in 2000 Aon bought Reliance Group's accident and health insurance business, as well as Actuarial Sciences Associates, a compensation and employee benefits consulting company. Later in that year, however, the company decided to cut 6% of its workforce as part of a restructuring effort.

Aon was hit hard by the attacks on the World Trade Center (where it was headquartered) in 2001; the company lost some 175 employees.

Aon teamed up with the Giuliani Group, former New York mayor Rudolph Giuliani's consulting firm, to provide business risk assessment and crisis management services in 2002.

In 2003 the company saw revenues increase primarily because of rate hikes in the insurance industry (meaning higher commissions for Aon). Also that year Endurance Specialty, the company's Bermuda-based underwriting operations, went public. The next year Aon sold most of its holdings in Endurance.

Two years later, following an investigation into its compensation practices resulting in a $190 million settlement with regulators in three states, Ryan stepped down as CEO. Ryan retained his position as executive chairman, but was replaced as CEO by McKinsey executive Gregory Case.

In 2004-2005 Aon, along with Marsh & McLennan and Willis Group Holdings, fell under regulatory investigation. At issue was the practice of insurance companies' payments to brokers (known as contingent commissions). The payments are thought to bring a conflict of interest, swaying broker decisions on behalf of carriers, rather than customers. Eliot Spitzer, who launched the investigation, emphasized that brokers are supposed to represent the interests of insurance buyers, not insurers, and that such practices skewed the relationship and resulted in bid rigging.

## EXECUTIVES

**Executive Chairman:** Patrick G. (Pat) Ryan, age 68, $2,745,000 pay
**President and CEO:** Gregory C. (Greg) Case, age 43, $3,920,192 pay (partial-year salary)
**SEVP and Executive Chairman, Aon Re Global:** Michael D. O'Halleran, age 56, $1,960,000 pay
**EVP and General Counsel:** D. Cameron Findlay, age 46
**EVP; CEO, Aon Re Global:** Ted T. Devine, age 42
**EVP and National Sales Leader, Global Large Corporate:** Matthew Horwitch
**SVP and Senior Investment Officer:** Michael A. Conway, age 58
**SVP and Controller:** Daniel F. Hunger, age 54
**SVP and Head of Human Resources:** Jeremy G.O. Farmer, age 56
**SVP, Corporate Communications:** Gary Sullivan
**SVP Corporate Secretary and Chief Governance Officer:** Kevann M. Cooke
**SVP Aon Financial Services Group:** Michael S. Flanagan
**SVP Global Real Estate:** Roy Keller
**SVP Chief Risk Officer and Treasurer:** Diane M. Aigotti, age 41
**VP and Head Investor Relations:** Scott Malchow

**Chairman and CEO, Aon Risk Services International:** Dirk P. M. Verbeek, age 56, $2,099,104 pay
**Chairman, President, and CEO, Combined Insurance Company of America:** Richard M. Ravin, age 63
**CEO, Aon Consulting Worldwide:** Andrew M. Appel, age 41
**Chairman and CEO, Aon Warranty Group and Virginia Surety Company:** David L. Cole
**Chairman, Aon Risk Services Americas:** Michael D. Rice, age 63
**Global Chief Marketing and Communications Officer:** Philip Clement
**Global CIO:** Baljit (Bal) Dail
**Global VP Public Relations:** David P. Prosperi
**Auditors:** Ernst & Young LLP

## LOCATIONS

**HQ:** Aon Corporation
Aon Center, 200 E. Randolph St., Chicago, IL 60601
**Phone:** 312-381-1000 **Fax:** 312-381-6032
**Web:** www.aon.com

Aon Corporation operates in some 130 countries around the world.

### 2006 Sales

| | $ mil. | % of total |
|---|---|---|
| Americas | | |
| US | 4,185 | 48 |
| Other countries | 940 | 10 |
| Europe, Middle East & Africa | | |
| UK | 1,384 | 15 |
| Other countries | 1,787 | 20 |
| Asia Pacific | 658 | 7 |
| **Total** | **8,954** | **100** |

## PRODUCTS/OPERATIONS

### 2006 Sales

| | $ mil. | % of total |
|---|---|---|
| Risk & insurance brokerage services | 5,628 | 63 |
| Insurance underwriting | 2,046 | 23 |
| Consulting | 1,282 | 14 |
| Adjustments | (2) | — |
| **Total** | **8,954** | **100** |

### Selected Subsidiaries

Consulting
Aon Consulting Worldwide, Inc.

Insurance Brokerage
Aon Group, Inc.
Aon Holdings International BV
Aon Limited (UK)
Aon Re Global, Inc.
Aon Risk Services Companies, Inc.
Aon Services Group, Inc.
Cananwill, Inc.
Premier Auto Finance, Inc.

Insurance Underwriting
Aon Warranty Group, Inc.
Combined Insurance Company of America
Combined Life Insurance Company of New York
London General Insurance Company Limited (UK)
Sterling Life Insurance Company
Virginia Surety Company, Inc.

## COMPETITORS

Aflac
AIG
AIG American General
Arthur Gallagher
Benfield Group
Chubb Corp
CIGNA
Citigroup
General Re
HCSC
Heath
Marsh & McLennan
MetLife
StanCorp Financial Group
Torchmark
Unum Group
Willis Group

## HISTORICAL FINANCIALS

Company Type: Public

### Income Statement

FYE: December 31

| | REVENUE ($ mil.) | NET INCOME ($ mil.) | NET PROFIT MARGIN | EMPLOYEES |
|---|---|---|---|---|
| **12/06** | 8,954 | 720 | 8.0% | 43,100 |
| **12/05** | 9,837 | 737 | 7.5% | 46,600 |
| **12/04** | 10,172 | 546 | 5.4% | 48,000 |
| **12/03** | 9,810 | 628 | 6.4% | 54,000 |
| **12/02** | 8,822 | 466 | 5.3% | 55,000 |
| **Annual Growth** | 0.4% | 11.5% | — | (5.9%) |

### 2006 Year-End Financials

Debt ratio: 43.0%
Return on equity: 13.7%
Cash ($ mil.): 4,604
Current ratio: —
Long-term debt ($ mil.): 2,243
No. of shares (mil.): 298
Dividends
Yield: 1.7%
Payout: 28.2%
Market value ($ mil.): 10,545

### Stock History

NYSE: AOC

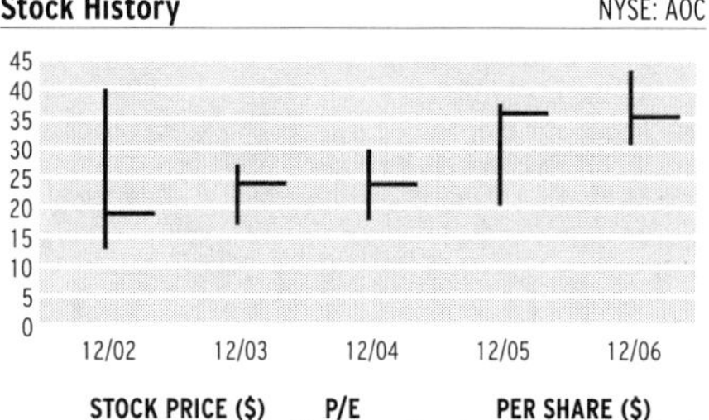


| | STOCK PRICE ($) FY Close | P/E High/Low | | PER SHARE ($) Earnings | Dividends | Book Value |
|---|---|---|---|---|---|---|
| **12/06** | 35.34 | 20 | 15 | 2.13 | 0.60 | 17.49 |
| **12/05** | 35.95 | 17 | 10 | 2.17 | 0.60 | 16.51 |
| **12/04** | 23.86 | 18 | 11 | 1.63 | 0.60 | 16.07 |
| **12/03** | 23.94 | 14 | 9 | 1.97 | 0.60 | 14.29 |
| **12/02** | 18.89 | 24 | 8 | 1.64 | 0.82 | 12.50 |
| **Annual Growth** | 17.0% | — | — | 6.8% | (7.5%) | 8.7% |

# Apache Corporation

There's more than a patch of oil in Apache's portfolio. Apache is an oil and gas exploration and production company with onshore and offshore operations in North America and in Argentina, Australia, Egypt, and the UK. The company has estimated proved reserves of 2.3 billion barrels of oil equivalent, mostly from five North American regions: the Gulf of Mexico, the Gulf Coast of Texas and Louisiana, the Permian Basin in West Texas, the Anadarko Basin in Oklahoma, and Canada's Western Sedimentary Basin. The company sold its China oil and gas assets in 2006. In 2007 Anadarko Petroleum agreed to sell its interests in 28 crude oil fields in West Texas to Apache for about $1 billion.

Although Apache has been dumping nonstrategic properties, including its Ivory Coast operations, it hasn't stopped buying. It has expanded its Gulf of Mexico operations with the acquisition of Occidental Petroleum's continental shelf properties, and its Canadian operations have been augmented with purchases from Fletcher Challenge Energy and Phillips Petroleum (later ConocoPhillips).

Late in 2002 in a move aimed at boosting its natural gas production by more than 10%, Apache acquired 234,000 net acres of land in southern Louisiana, for $260 million. That year the company also announced three oil discoveries in the Carnarvon Basin offshore Western Australia.

In 2003 Apache acquired UK and US oil and gas assets from BP for $1.3 billion. The main prize was the Forties field, one of the North Sea's oldest discoveries (dating back to the early 1970s), and its largest.

In 2004 it acquired more than two dozen mature US and Canadian fields from Exxon Mobil for $347 million and Gulf of Mexico properties from Anadarko Petroleum for $525 million. In 2005 Hurricane Katrina destroyed eight of its 241 Gulf rigs.

In 2006 Apache sold its 55% stake in Egypt's West Mediterranean Concession to Hess for $413 million, in return for buying Amerada Hess' stakes in eight fields in the Permian Basin for $404 million.

That year the company acquired Pioneer Natural Resources' Argentine operations for $675 million. It also bought BP's remaining producing properties on the Outer Continental Shelf of the Gulf of Mexico for $845 million.

## HISTORY

Originally, Raymond Plank wanted to start a magazine. Then it was an accounting and tax-assistance service. Plank and his co-founding partner, Truman Anderson, had no experience in any of these occupations, but their accounting business succeeded. In the early 1950s Plank and Anderson branched out again, founding APA, a partnership to invest in new ventures, including oil and gas exploration. The partnership founded Apache Oil in Minnesota in 1954. Investors put up the money, and Apache managed the drilling, spreading the risk over several projects.

As problems with government regulations in the oil industry mounted during the 1960s, Apache diversified into real estate. The real estate operations were pivotal in driving a wedge between Plank and Anderson. In 1963 Anderson called a board meeting to ask the directors to fire Plank. Instead, Anderson resigned, and Plank took over.

Apache's holdings soon encompassed 24 firms, including engineering, electronics, farming, and water-supply subsidiaries. Understanding that its fortunes were tied to varying oil and gas prices, the company reassessed its diversified structure in the 1970s. When the energy crisis rocketed oil prices skyward, Apache sold its non-energy operations, which would have been hurt by the price increases.

Apache formed Apache Petroleum in 1981 as an investment vehicle to take advantage of tax laws favoring limited partnerships. Initially the strategy was a success, but it fell victim in the mid-1980s to a one-two punch: Oil prices sank like a rock, and Congress put an end to the tax advantage. After suffering its first loss in 1986, Apache reorganized into a conventional exploration and production company.

Still under Plank's leadership, the company began steadily buying oil and gas properties and companies in 1991. That year it purchased oil and gas sites with more than 100 million barrels of reserves from Amoco and put the wells back into production. By buying Hadson Energy Resources, which operated fields in western Australia, Apache gained entry into the relatively unexplored region in 1993.

In 1995 Apache merged with Calgary, Canada-based DEKALB Energy (later renamed DEK Energy) and continued picking up properties. It bought $600 million worth of US reserves from Texaco (acquired by Chevron in 2001) that year. In 1996 it expanded its Chinese operations and bought Phoenix Resource Companies, which operated solely in Egypt. A 1998 agreement with Texaco expanded its Chinese acreage thirtyfold. Apache also bought oil and gas properties and production facilities in waters off western Australia from a Mobil unit.

Apache joined with FX Energy and Polish Oil & Gas in 1998 to begin exploratory drilling in Poland. It also worked with XCL and China National Oil & Gas Exploration & Development in Bohai Bay, though the project was slowed by a dispute between Apache and XCL over costs. In 1999 Apache bought Gulf of Mexico assets from a unit of Royal Dutch Shell and acquired oil and gas properties in western Canada from Shell Canada. That year Apache sold its Ivory Coast oil and gas holdings for $46 million.

Still shopping, however, Apache agreed in 2000 to buy assets in western Canada and Argentina with proved reserves of more than 700 billion cu. ft. of natural gas equivalent from New Zealand's Fletcher Challenge Energy. To help pay for the $600 million acquisition, which closed in 2001, Apache sold $100 million in stock to Shell, which acquired other Fletcher Challenge Energy assets. Apache bought the Canadian assets of Phillips Petroleum (later ConocoPhillips) for $490 million in 2000 and acquired the Egyptian assets of Repsol YPF for $410 million in 2001.

## EXECUTIVES

**Chairman:** Raymond Plank, age 84, $1,331,250 pay
**President, CEO, COO, and Director:** G. Steven (Steve) Farris, age 59, $1,331,250 pay
**EVP and CFO:** Roger B. Plank, age 50, $490,625 pay
**EVP Eurasia, Latin America, and New Ventures:** Floyd R. Price, age 57
**EVP Apache North Sea:** John A. Crum, age 54, $366,042 pay
**EVP Exploration and Production Technology:** Michael S. (Mike) Bahorich, age 50
**EVP; VP and General Manager, Egyptian Operations:** Rodney J. Eichler, age 57, $341,459 pay
**SVP Policy and Governance:** Sarah Ball Teslik, age 53
**SVP and General Counsel:** P. Anthony Lannie, age 52
**SVP Gulf Coast Region:** Jon A. Jeppesen, age 59
**VP and Controller:** Rebecca (Becky) Hoyt, age 42
**VP Human Resources:** Jeffrey M. Bender, age 55
**VP Security:** Michael J. Benson, age 54
**VP Corporate Planning:** Thomas P. (Tom) Chambers, age 51
**VP Business Development:** John J. Christmann IV, age 40
**VP and Treasurer:** Matthew W. (Matt) Dundrea, age 53
**VP Investor Relations:** Robert J. Dye, age 51
**VP Public and International Affairs:** Anthony R. (Tony) Lentini Jr., age 57
**VP Oil and Gas Marketing:** Janine J. McArdle, age 46
**VP Corporate Reservoir Engineering:** W. Kregg Olson, age 53
**VP and Managing Director, Australia:** Eve Howell
**VP Tax:** Jon W. Sauer, age 46
**Corporate Secretary:** Cheri L. Peper, age 53
**Auditors:** Ernst & Young LLP

## LOCATIONS

**HQ:** Apache Corporation
2000 Post Oak Blvd., Ste. 100, Houston, TX 77056
**Phone:** 713-296-6000 **Fax:** 713-296-6496
**Web:** www.apachecorp.com

Apache has onshore holdings in Alaska, Arkansas, Colorado, Illinois, Kansas, Louisiana, Michigan, New Mexico, Oklahoma, Pennsylvania, Texas, Utah, and Wyoming and offshore holdings in the Gulf of Mexico. It also owns exploration or production properties in Argentina, Australia, Canada, Egypt, and the UK.

**2006 Sales**

| | $ mil. | % of total |
|---|---|---|
| US | 3,027.2 | 38 |
| Egypt | 1,664.1 | 20 |
| Canada | 1,379.6 | 17 |
| UK (North Sea) | 1,355.1 | 17 |
| Australia | 408.5 | 5 |
| Argentina | 167.2 | 2 |
| Other countries | 72.5 | 1 |
| Adjustments | 214.6 | — |
| **Total** | **8,288.8** | **100** |

## PRODUCTS/OPERATIONS

**2006 Sales**

| | $ mil. | % of total |
|---|---|---|
| Oil | 4,911.9 | 59 |
| Natural gas | 3,001.3 | 36 |
| Gain on sale of China assets | 173.5 | 2 |
| Natural gas liquids | 161.1 | 2 |
| Adjustments | 41.0 | 1 |
| **Total** | **8,288.8** | **100** |

**Selected Subsidiaries**

Apache Canada Ltd.
Apache Energy Limited
Apache International, Inc.
Apache North Sea Limited
Apache Overseas, Inc.
DEK Energy Company

## COMPETITORS

Adams Resources
Anadarko Petroleum
BP
Chesapeake Energy
Chevron
Devon Energy
El Paso
EOG
Exxon Mobil
Forest Oil
Helmerich & Payne
Hess
National Onshore
Pioneer Natural Resources
Royal Dutch Shell
Santos
Shell
XTO Energy

## HISTORICAL FINANCIALS

Company Type: Public

**Income Statement** FYE: December 31

| | REVENUE ($ mil.) | NET INCOME ($ mil.) | NET PROFIT MARGIN | EMPLOYEES |
|---|---|---|---|---|
| **12/06** | 8,289 | 2,552 | 30.8% | 3,150 |
| **12/05** | 7,584 | 2,624 | 34.6% | 2,805 |
| **12/04** | 5,333 | 1,669 | 31.3% | 2,642 |
| **12/03** | 4,190 | 1,122 | 26.8% | 2,353 |
| **12/02** | 2,560 | 554 | 21.7% | 1,958 |
| **Annual Growth** | 34.1% | 46.5% | — | 12.6% |

**2006 Year-End Financials**

Debt ratio: 15.4%
Return on equity: 21.7%
Cash ($ mil.): 280
Current ratio: 0.65
Long-term debt ($ mil.): 2,020
No. of shares (mil.): 331
Dividends
Yield: 0.7%
Payout: 5.9%
Market value ($ mil.): 21,997

**Stock History** NYSE: APA

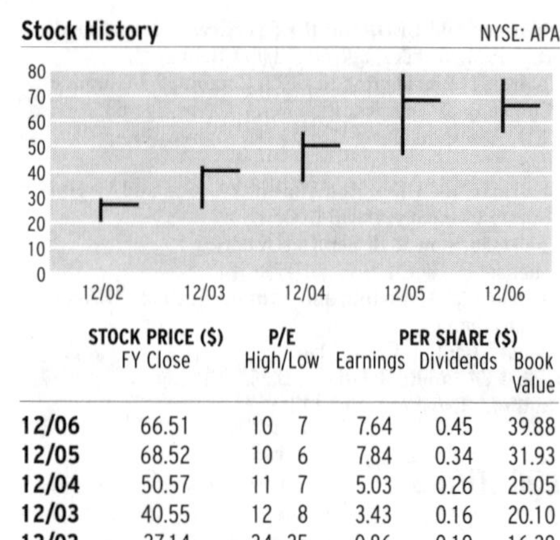


| | STOCK PRICE ($) FY Close | P/E High | P/E Low | PER SHARE ($) Earnings | Dividends | Book Value |
|---|---|---|---|---|---|---|
| **12/06** | 66.51 | 10 | 7 | 7.64 | 0.45 | 39.88 |
| **12/05** | 68.52 | 10 | 6 | 7.84 | 0.34 | 31.93 |
| **12/04** | 50.57 | 11 | 7 | 5.03 | 0.26 | 25.05 |
| **12/03** | 40.55 | 12 | 8 | 3.43 | 0.16 | 20.10 |
| **12/02** | 27.14 | 34 | 25 | 0.86 | 0.19 | 16.28 |
| **Annual Growth** | 25.1% | — | — | 72.6% | 24.1% | 25.1% |

# Apollo Group

Even the sun god needs a college degree these days. Apollo Group is a for-profit education company that provides programs tailored to working adults. Its University of Phoenix, with more than 300,000 students at some 160 learning centers and 100 campuses (including an online campus), is the US's largest private university. The university offers undergraduate and graduate degrees in such areas as business, education, nursing, and information technology. Apollo provides consulting services to private colleges developing their own adult education programs through the Institute for Professional Development. Founder John Sperling and his son Peter (SVP and board member) together own about 50% of Apollo.

Apollo operates two additional higher-learning institutions — Western International University and the College for Financial Planning. The company plans to add seven to nine new University of Phoenix campuses per year. It also plans to expand internationally, particularly in China and India.

Chairman, CEO, and president Todd Nelson resigned in early 2006. Nineteen-year company veteran and president of Apollo's subsidiary, the University of Phoenix, Brian Mueller replaced him as president. Sperling was appointed interim chairman. The company also acquired Insight Schools in 2006, adding operations and expertise in online education for grades K-12.

## HISTORY

The son of Missouri sharecroppers, John Sperling's first interest in higher education was his own. Following WWII he attended Reed College on the GI Bill and eventually received a PhD in economic history from Cambridge. He started the Institute for Professional Development in 1973 to offer nontraditional programs designed for working adults. Sperling's program was rejected by San Jose State University, where he was a tenured professor, so he took his idea to the University of San Francisco. There he designed a curriculum program for firefighters, police officers, and other workers. Within two years, the program had 2,500 students, but the regional accrediting board accused him of running a diploma mill and yanked his accreditation.

Sperling moved to Arizona (which falls under a different accrediting board), where he founded the University of Phoenix (UOP) in 1976. UOP received accreditation in 1978; its first graduating class had eight students. UOP expanded into new states through the 1980s, and in 1989 it added distance learning to its services using its own dial-up computer network. The company went public as Apollo Group in 1994.

To further expand its reach, Apollo bought Western International University (founded in 1978) in 1995 and the College for Financial Planning from National Endowment of Financial Education in 1997. That year it formed Apollo Learning Group to offer hi-tech training programs. UOP received approval to offer its first doctoral program in 1998, a doctor of management degree. The next year Apollo made its first entry into the northeast US when it was approved by the state of Pennsylvania. It also expanded and upgraded its online operations that year, centralizing its operations in Phoenix.

In 2001 UOP introduced FlexNet, courses that combined classroom and online instruction. The weakening economy in 2001 and 2002 benefited Apollo — as jobs became more scarce, many professionals sought further education as a competitive advantage. In 2003 UOP received state approval to offer courses in New Jersey.

Although it denied the claims, in 2004 Apollo agreed to pay almost $10 million in fines after a US Department of Education inquiry claimed that University of Phoenix recruiters had used unethical or illegal tactics to enroll unqualified students.

## EXECUTIVES

**President, CEO, and Director:** Brian Mueller
**SVP, Secretary, and Treasurer:** Peter V. Sperling, age 46
**SVP and Chief Communication Officer:** Terri Bishop
**Chief Human Resources Officer:** Diane Thompson
**President, University of Phoenix:** William (Bill) Pepicello
**VP International Controller:** Carlos L. Rojas
**CFO:** Joseph L. D'Amico
**Chief Administrative Officer:** John Kline
**VP, Finance:** Larry Fleischer
**SVP Finance and Chief Accounting Officer:** Brian Swartz
**EVP Global Strategy and Director:** Gregory Cappelli, age 39
**VP Taxes:** Scott St. Clair
**VP and Controller:** Gregory J. Iverson
**Corporate Treasurer:** Junette C. West
**Auditors:** Deloitte & Touche LLP

## LOCATIONS

**HQ:** Apollo Group, Inc.
4615 E. Elwood St., Phoenix, AZ 85040
**Phone:** 480-966-5394 **Fax:** 480-379-3503
**Web:** www.apollogrp.edu

Apollo Group has campuses and learning centers across the continental US, as well as in Puerto Rico, and Alberta and British Columbia, Canada.

## PRODUCTS/OPERATIONS

### 2006 Sales

| | $ mil. | % of total |
|---|---|---|
| Tuition | 2,304.3 | 93 |
| Online course material review | 138.7 | 6 |
| IPD services | 74.4 | 3 |
| Application & related fees | 33.8 | 1 |
| Other | 31.7 | 1 |
| Adjustments | (105.4) | — |
| **Total** | **2,477.5** | **100** |

### 2006 Enrollment by Degree Program

| | % of total |
|---|---|
| Bachelor's | 50 |
| Associate's | 26 |
| Master's | 22 |
| Doctoral | 2 |
| **Total** | **100** |

### 2006 Enrollment by Age

| | % of total |
|---|---|
| 23 to 29 | 33 |
| 30 to 39 | 33 |
| 40 to 49 | 19 |
| 22 and under | 8 |
| 50 and over | 7 |
| **Total** | **100** |

### Selected Programs

College for Financial Planning
- Master of Science
  - Finance
  - Financial Analysis
  - Financial Planning
- Non-degree programs
  - Accredited Asset Management Specialist
  - Chartered Retirement Planning Counselor
  - Chartered Retirement Plans Specialist

Institute for Professional Development
- Associate of Arts
  - Business
  - Leadership Studies
  - Liberal Arts, Business Emphasis
- Associate of Science
  - Business
- Bachelor of Arts
  - Business
  - Management
- Bachelor of Business Administration
- Bachelor of Science
  - Accounting
  - Business Administration
  - Business Information Systems
  - Management
  - Management Information Systems
  - Nursing
- Master of Business Administration
- Master of Science
  - Management
  - Nursing

University of Phoenix
- Associate of Arts in General Studies
- Bachelor of Science
  - Business
  - Business Administration
  - Health Care Services
  - Human Services
  - Information Technology
  - Management
  - Nursing
- Doctor of Management
- Master of Arts
  - Education
  - Organizational Management
- Master of Business Administration
- Master of Counseling
- Master of Science
  - Computer Information Systems
  - Nursing

Western International University
- Associate of Arts
- Bachelor of Arts
  - Administration of Justice
  - Behavioral Science
- Bachelor of Science
  - Accounting
  - Business Administration
  - Finance
  - Information Technology
  - International Business
  - Management
  - Marketing
- Master of Business Administration
  - Finance
  - Information Technology
  - International Business
  - Management
  - Marketing
- Master of Public Administration
- Master of Science
  - Information Technology
  - Information Systems Engineering

## COMPETITORS

Canterbury Consulting
Career Education
Concorde Colleges
Corinthian Colleges
DeVry
Education Management
INVESTools
ITT Educational
Kaplan
Laureate Education
Lincoln Educational Services
Strayer Education
Universal Technical
VCampus

## HISTORICAL FINANCIALS

Company Type: Public

### Income Statement

FYE: August 31

| | REVENUE ($ mil.) | NET INCOME ($ mil.) | NET PROFIT MARGIN | EMPLOYEES |
|---|---|---|---|---|
| **8/06** | 2,478 | 415 | 16.7% | 36,416 |
| **8/05** | 2,252 | 445 | 19.8% | 32,666 |
| **8/04** | 1,798 | 278 | 15.4% | — |
| **8/03** | 1,340 | 247 | 18.4% | 25,572 |
| **8/02** | 1,010 | 161 | 16.0% | 23,577 |
| **Annual Growth** | 25.2% | 26.7% | — | 11.5% |

### 2006 Year-End Financials

Debt ratio: —
Return on equity: 63.3%
Cash ($ mil.): 593
Current ratio: 1.35
Long-term debt ($ mil.): —
No. of shares (mil.): 173
Dividends
Yield: —
Payout: —
Market value ($ mil.): 8,664

### Stock History

NASDAQ (GS): APOL

100 90 80 70 60 50 40 30 20 10 0
8/02 8/03 8/04 8/05 8/06

| | STOCK PRICE ($) FY Close | P/E High | P/E Low | PER SHARE ($) Earnings | PER SHARE ($) Dividends | PER SHARE ($) Book Value |
|---|---|---|---|---|---|---|
| **8/06** | 50.21 | 34 | 18 | 2.35 | — | 3.50 |
| **8/05** | 78.66 | 37 | 26 | 2.39 | — | 3.94 |
| **8/04** | 78.00 | 127 | 79 | 0.77 | — | 5.10 |
| **8/03** | 64.07 | 52 | 29 | 1.30 | — | 5.86 |
| **8/02** | 41.83 | 50 | 25 | 0.87 | — | 4.04 |
| **Annual Growth** | 4.7% | — | — | 28.2% | — | (3.5%) |

# Apple Inc.

Computers are still an important part of its mix, but these days music-related products are at the top of Apple's playlist. The company scored a runaway hit with its digital music players (iPod) and online music store (iTunes). Apple's desktop and laptop computers — all of which feature its OS X operating system — include its Mac mini, iMac, and MacBook for the consumer and education markets, and more powerful Power Mac and MacBook Pro for high-end consumers and professionals involved in design and publishing. Other products include mobile phones (iPhone), servers (Xserve), wireless networking equipment (Airport), and publishing and multimedia software. Its FileMaker subsidiary makes database software.

Only co-founder, CEO, and Apple crusader Steve Jobs may have expected the level of success the company's music-related products have enjoyed. Since debuting the iPod in 2001, Apple has provided regular updates to the line, including color displays and flash memory-based models. In 2003 Apple announced the launch of an online music service called the iTunes Music Store that lets computer users purchase and download songs for 99 cents each. Apple has since expanded the offerings to include music videos, audiobooks, television shows, and other content. Early in 2006 it began offering select television content on a subscription basis with a service called Multi-Pass. Later that year the company launched an online movie service, and previewed a device called iTV for watching downloaded content on televisions. Apple announced availability of its television device, redubbed Apple TV, early the following year.

Early in 2007 the company finally unveiled a long-rumored Apple mobile phone — the iPhone — that combines features of a high-end handset with those of an iPod.

Once the world's top PC maker, Apple has been relegated to niche status in a market dominated by "Wintel" machines (computers using Microsoft Windows software and Intel processors). Macintosh computers run Apple's own UNIX-based operating system.

In addition to its proprietary operating system, a traditional differentiator for Apple had been its use of IBM's PowerPC processors (manufactured by IBM and Freescale). However, in 2005 Apple announced it would begin incorporating Intel chips into its PC lines. Apple debuted its first Intel-based computers early in 2006, and it completed the transition across its entire line later that year. The company also released software that allows its Intel-based computers to run Microsoft's XP operating system.

In an effort to boost its appeal among consumers, the company has opened more than 100 Apple retail stores across the US; it also has stores in Canada, Japan, and the UK.

## HISTORY

College dropouts Steve Jobs and Steve Wozniak founded Apple in 1976 in California's Santa Clara Valley. After Jobs' first sales call brought an order for 50 units, the duo built the Apple I in his garage and sold it without a monitor, keyboard, or casing. Demand convinced Jobs there was a distinct market for small computers, and the company's name (a reference to Jobs' stint on an Oregon farm) and the computer's user-friendly look and feel set it apart from others.

By 1977 Wozniak added a keyboard, color monitor, and eight peripheral device slots (which gave the machine considerable versatility and inspired numerous third-party add-on devices and software). Sales jumped from $7.8 million in 1978 to $117 million in 1980, the year Apple went public. In 1983 Wozniak left the firm and Jobs hired PepsiCo's John Sculley as president. Apple rebounded from failed product introductions that year by unveiling the Macintosh in 1984. After tumultuous struggles with Sculley, Jobs left in 1985 and founded NeXT Software, a designer of applications for developing software. That year Sculley ignored Microsoft founder Bill Gates' appeal for Apple to license its products and make the Microsoft platform an industry standard.

In 1986 Apple blazed the desktop publishing trail with its Mac Plus and LaserWriter printers. The following year it formed the software firm that later became Claris. The late 1980s brought new competition from Microsoft, whose Windows operating system (OS) featured a graphical interface akin to Apple's. Apple sued but lost its claim to copyright protection in 1992.

In 1993 earnings fell drastically, so the company trimmed its workforce. (Sculley was among the departed.) In 1996 it hired Gilbert Amelio, formerly of National Semiconductor, as CEO, but sales kept dropping and it subsequently cut about 30% of its workforce, canceled projects, and trimmed research costs. Meanwhile Apple's board ousted Amelio and Jobs took the position back on an interim basis.

In early 2000, after two-and-a-half years as the semipermanent executive in charge, Jobs took the "interim" out of his title. Apple introduced a digital music player called the iPod in 2001.

In 2002 Apple introduced a new look for its iMac line; featuring a half-dome base and a flat-panel display supported by a pivoting arm, the redesign was the first departure from the original (and, at the time, radical) all-in-one design since iMac's debut in 1998. It continued its new product push that year with the announcement that it would begin offering a rack-mount server called Xserve. In 2004, Apple debuted a streamlined iMac design powered by its G5 processor.

Apple announced it would begin incorporating Intel chips into its PC lines in 2005; the transition was completed the following year. Late in 2005 Apple, Motorola, and Cingular Wireless (now AT&T Mobility) announced the debut of a mobile phone with iTunes functionality. Apple also unveiled the iPod nano, an updated (and even smaller) version of its miniature iPod model, as well as an iPod capable of playing video. In 2006 Apple reached a settlement in a dispute with Creative Technology over technology used in digital music players; Apple agreed to pay the company $100 million in exchange for a license to use Creative's patent related to navigation and organization. Late in 2006 Apple acquired UK-based Proximity, a developer of software used to manage digital audio and video assets.

Apple unveiled a mobile phone offering called the iPhone early in 2007. To reflect the growing breadth of its product portfolio, the company announced it would change its name from Apple Computer to simply Apple.

## EXECUTIVES

**CEO and Director:** Steven P. (Steve) Jobs, age 52, $1 pay
**COO:** Timothy D. (Tim) Cook, age 46, $1,221,880 pay
**SVP and CFO:** Peter Oppenheimer, age 44, $1,065,006 pay
**SVP and General Counsel:** Donald J. Rosenberg, age 56
**SVP Applications:** Sina Tamaddon, age 49
**SVP Industrial Design:** Jonathan Ive
**SVP iPod:** Anthony (Tony) Fadell, age 38
**SVP Software Engineering:** Bertrand Serlet, age 46
**SVP Worldwide Product Marketing:** Philip W. Schiller, age 46, $869,942 pay
**VP Applications Product Marketing:** Rob Schoeben
**VP iPod Product Marketing:** Greg Joswiak
**VP Worldwide Mac Product Marketing:** David Moody
**VP Worldwide Corporate Communications:** Katie Cotton
**General Manager Hong Kong:** Simon Hong
**Director Product Marketing iTunes:** Chris Bell
**General Manager UK:** Mark Rogers
**Senior Director Marketing Consumer Applications:** Peter Lowe
**Senior Manager Investor Relations:** Joan Hoover
**Auditors:** KPMG LLP

## LOCATIONS

**HQ:** Apple Inc.
1 Infinite Loop, Cupertino, CA 95014
**Phone:** 408-996-1010 **Fax:** 408-974-2113
**Web:** www.apple.com

### 2006 Sales

| | $ mil. | % of total |
|---|---|---|
| US | 11,486 | 59 |
| Japan | 1,327 | 7 |
| Other countries | 6,502 | 34 |
| **Total** | **19,315** | **100** |

### 2006 Sales by Operating Segment

| | $ mil. | % of total |
|---|---|---|
| Americas | 9,307 | 48 |
| Europe | 4,094 | 21 |
| Retail | 3,359 | 18 |
| Asia/Pacific & Filemaker | 1,347 | 7 |
| Japan | 1,208 | 6 |
| **Total** | **19,315** | **100** |

## PRODUCTS/OPERATIONS

### 2006 Sales

| | $ mil. | % of total |
|---|---|---|
| Music-related products | | |
| iPod | 7,676 | 40 |
| iTunes Music Store & other | 1,885 | 10 |
| Computers | | |
| Portable | 4,056 | 21 |
| Desktop & server | 3,319 | 17 |
| Peripherals & other hardware | 1,100 | 6 |
| Software, services & other | 1,279 | 6 |
| **Total** | **19,315** | **100** |

### Selected Products

Hardware
- Desktop computers (iMac, Mac mini, Power Macintosh)
- Portable computers (MacBook, MacBook Pro)
- Displays (Cinema, Studio)
- Keyboards
- Mice (Mighty Mouse)
- Mobile phones (iPhone)
- Portable digital music player (iPod, iPod nano, iPod shuffle)
- Rack-mount servers (Xserve)
- Stereo systems (iPod Hi-Fi)
- Storage systems (Xserve RAID)
- Web cams (iSight)
- Wireless networking systems (AirPort)

Software
- Multimedia (DVD Studio Pro, FinalCut, GarageBand, iDVD, iLife suite, iMovie, iPhoto, iTunes, Quicktime, Soundtrack)
- Networking (Apple Remote Desktop, AppleShare IP)
- Operating system (OS X)
- Personal productivity (AppleWorks, FileMaker, iWork, Keynote, Pages)
- Server (Mac OS X Server)
- Storage area network (SAN) file system (Xsan)
- Web browser (Safari)

Online Services
- .Mac
- Electronic greeting cards (iCard)
- E-mail (Webmail)
- Personal Web page creation (HomePage)
- Remote network storage (iDisk)
- Software (anti-virus, backup)
- Technical support
- iTunes Music Store

## COMPETITORS

Acer
Amazon.com
Archos
Best Buy
Bose
Cisco Systems
Creative Technology
Dell
eMachines
EMusic.com
Ericsson
Fujitsu Siemens
Gateway
Hewlett-Packard
IBM
Kyocera
Lenovo
Matsushita Electric
Microsoft
Motorola, Inc.
MTV Networks
MusicNet
Napster
NEC
Nokia
Palm
Philips Electronics
RealNetworks
Red Hat
Reigncom
Samsung Electronics
Samsung Group
SanDisk
SANYO
SGI
Sharp Electronics
Sony
Sony Ericsson Mobile
Sun Microsystems
Target
Toshiba
Wal-Mart
Yahoo!

## HISTORICAL FINANCIALS

Company Type: Public

**Income Statement** FYE: Last Friday in September

| | REVENUE ($ mil.) | NET INCOME ($ mil.) | NET PROFIT MARGIN | EMPLOYEES |
|---|---|---|---|---|
| **9/06** | 19,315 | 1,989 | 10.3% | 17,787 |
| **9/05** | 13,931 | 1,335 | 9.6% | 16,820 |
| **9/04** | 8,279 | 276 | 3.3% | 13,426 |
| **9/03** | 6,207 | 69 | 1.1% | 10,912 |
| **9/02** | 5,742 | 65 | 1.1% | 10,211 |
| **Annual Growth** | 35.4% | 135.2% | — | 14.9% |

**2006 Year-End Financials**

Debt ratio: —
Return on equity: 22.8%
Cash ($ mil.): 10,110
Current ratio: 2.24
Long-term debt ($ mil.): —
No. of shares (mil.): 855
Dividends
Yield: —
Payout: —
Market value ($ mil.): 65,838

**Stock History** NASDAQ (GS): AAPL

| | STOCK PRICE ($) FY Close | P/E High | P/E Low | PER SHARE ($) Earnings | Dividends | Book Value |
|---|---|---|---|---|---|---|
| **9/06** | 76.98 | 38 | 21 | 2.27 | — | 11.67 |
| **9/05** | 53.20 | 34 | 12 | 1.56 | — | 8.94 |
| **9/04** | 18.65 | 55 | 27 | 0.35 | — | 12.97 |
| **9/03** | 10.35 | 123 | 67 | 0.09 | — | 11.52 |
| **9/02** | 7.36 | 145 | 77 | 0.09 | — | 11.41 |
| **Annual Growth** | 79.8% | — | — | 124.1% | — | 0.6% |

# Applied Biosystems Group

Applied Biosystems Group, a tracking-stock unit of Applera, makes the big machines for life scientists to peer into the details of DNA and proteins and chart the future of medicine. Its product line includes thermal cyclers and systems to detect the polymerase chain reactions used to identify DNA sequences. It also provides gene expression assays for various species, specialized enzymes called reagents, and disposable plastic devices to hold DNA samples. Its customers include biotech firms and research institutes studying how drugs interact with the body's systems (pharmacokinetics) and genetic makeup (pharmacogenomics), testing food and the environment for contaminants, and performing DNA-based identification.

The firm also oversees licensing of sister company and key client Celera Group's genome databases as that company tries to focus on drug development.

Other products include mass spectrometry systems and biochromatography media products used in studying proteins, peptides, and small molecules. The company also offers software products to help labs manage their information and make sense of what they've discovered. Through acquisition the company has added products to assist in the research of RNA.

While the company's customers are using Applied Biosystem's equipment to make the next generation of drugs, fertilizers, diagnostics, and other "modern miracles," Applied Biosystems itself is busy developing the products that will help bring the next revolution in life sciences. As researchers are just beginning to understand the role of proteins in developing, curing, and even preventing disease, developers at the firm's Proteomics Research Center are creating tools to bring that understanding into sharper focus and using that information to yield the *next* next generation of life science products.

At the same time, Applied Biosystems has set up a division to apply its products and software to more here-and-now uses such as biosecurity, food and drug testing, and forensic analysis and human identification.

## HISTORY

Hewlett-Packard veteran Dr. Sam Eletr and a group of scientists (many California Institute of Technology alumni) founded Applied Biosystems in 1981. After market leader Beckman Instruments (now Beckman Coulter) spurned the university over development-time concerns, Caltech offered the fledgling firm the rights to commercially develop a revolutionary DNA synthesizer. The company launched the model 470 A protein sequencer a year later and sold units to Du Pont, Eli Lilly, Hoffmann-La Roche, and others. The profitable biotech (a rarity) went public in 1983.

The following year the firm teamed with Becton, Dickinson to develop research and clinical diagnostic products; Becton took a 10% stake in its partner. In 1986 Applied Biosystems and Caltech launched another breakthrough product that could sequence the four chemical bases (represented by the letters A, C, G, and T) for the first time.

In 1987, however, product delays and a drop in European sales stunted the company's growth. That year Eletr stepped down as chairman for health reasons; co-founder and president Andre Marion succeeded him, while Irvin Smith, who'd worked at the analytical systems division of Abbott Labs, came on board as EVP and COO. Sales rebounded in 1988, largely from an influx of orders from Japan. Applied Biosystems teamed with future parent Perkin-Elmer to develop molecular biology instruments and reagents. The firm closed the decade in turmoil, though Smith, who'd become president and CEO, was forced to resign as sales again slumped due to increased competition and decreased demand. The start of an international effort to map the human genome that year promised another boom, so the company ramped up product development.

Sales were mixed in 1991, but they took off in 1992, when Applied Biosystems claimed to have some 70% of the automated sequencer market. That year it formed and spun off Lynx Therapeutics to develop drugs based on its growing genomics expertise; Eletr returned to head up the venture. By year's end Perkin-Elmer announced plans to buy the firm. The deal closed in early 1993, and Applied Biosystems became a division of its new parent, absorbing Perkin-Elmer's life science instruments operations. Perkin-Elmer's 1993 sales were more than $1 billion; however, its analytical instruments division was a drag on earnings throughout the 1990s.

A management shakeup in 1995 was followed by a refocus: New CEO Tony White began building the Applied Biosystems division through a series of acquisitions that included genetic analysis system maker PerSeptive BioSystems in 1998. That year Perkin-Elmer formed Celera Genomics with prominent gene research Dr. Craig Venter.

Perkin-Elmer in 1999 reorganized to capitalize on the growth in genomics. It sold its analytical systems unit to EG&G (now PerkinElmer), made Celera and Applied Biosystems (known briefly as PE Biosystems) its operating companies, issued tracking stocks for them, and took the name PE Corp. In 2000 Celera finished mapping the human genome with the help of its sister's equipment. For better brand recognition,

PE Corp. became Applera, a blend of its two units' names. When the sector focus began shifting from mapping to drug development in 2001, Applied Biosystems and its family followed. They announced plans to research and develop drugs based on the smallest form of genetic variations (SNPs), as well as to work with The SNP Consortium to map these variations. The mapping efforts were completed in 2002.

The company spent $279 million to acquire Ambion's research products unit, which specializes in RNA analysis, in early 2006. That same year, Applied Biosystems also plunked down $120 million to buy up Agencourt Personal Genomics from Agencourt Bioscience Corporation. Agencourt Personal Genomics' operations and DNA analysis technology were placed under Applied Biosystems' Molecular and Cell Biology division.

## EXECUTIVES

**Interim President:** Tony L. White, age 60
**VP, Finance and Controller:** Sandeep Nayyar, age 46
**VP, Global Operations:** Claude Crawford
**VP, Research and Chief Scientific Officer:** Dennis A. Gilbert, age 47
**VP, Quality and Regulatory Compliance:** John D'Angelo
**VP, Strategic Planning and Business Development:** Paul D. Grossman
**VP and General Manager, Genetic Analysis:** Kevin Corcoran
**VP and General Manager, Real-Time PCR Systems and Microarrays:** Carl W. Hull
**President, Applied Biosystems Europe:** Lars Holmkvist, age 45
**President, Applied Biosystems Japan:** Masahide Habu, age 57
**President, Asia Pacific:** TLV Kumar, age 51
**Director, Investor Relations:** Linda M. Greub
**Auditors:** PricewaterhouseCoopers LLP

## LOCATIONS

**HQ:** Applied Biosystems Group
850 Lincoln Centre Dr., Foster City, CA 94404
**Phone:** 650-570-6667 **Fax:** 650-572-2743
**Web:** www.appliedbiosystems.com

Applied Biosystems Group has facilities in Japan, Singapore, the UK, and the US.

### 2006 Sales

| | % of total |
|---|---|
| US | 45 |
| Europe | 33 |
| Asia Pacific | 18 |
| Latin America and other | 4 |
| **Total** | **100** |

## PRODUCTS/OPERATIONS

### 2006 Sales

| | % of total |
|---|---|
| Real time PCR & applied genomics | 31 |
| DNA sequencing products | 29 |
| Mass spectrometry | 24 |
| Core PCR & DNA synthesis | 10 |
| Other products | 6 |
| **Total** | **100** |

## COMPETITORS

Affymetrix
Beckman Coulter
Bio-Rad Labs
Dionex
Enzo Biochem
Medallion Foods
PerkinElmer
Sigma-Aldrich
Stratagene
TECHNE
Waters

## HISTORICAL FINANCIALS

Company Type: Public

### Income Statement

FYE: June 30

| | REVENUE ($ mil.) | NET INCOME ($ mil.) | NET PROFIT MARGIN | EMPLOYEES |
|---|---|---|---|---|
| **6/06** | 1,911 | 275 | 14.4% | 4,570 |
| **6/05** | 1,787 | 237 | 13.3% | 4,030 |
| **6/04** | 1,741 | 172 | 9.9% | 4,400 |
| **6/03** | 1,683 | 200 | 11.9% | 4,540 |
| **6/02** | 1,604 | 169 | 10.5% | 4,790 |
| **Annual Growth** | 4.5% | 13.0% | — | (1.2%) |

### Net Income History

NYSE: ABI

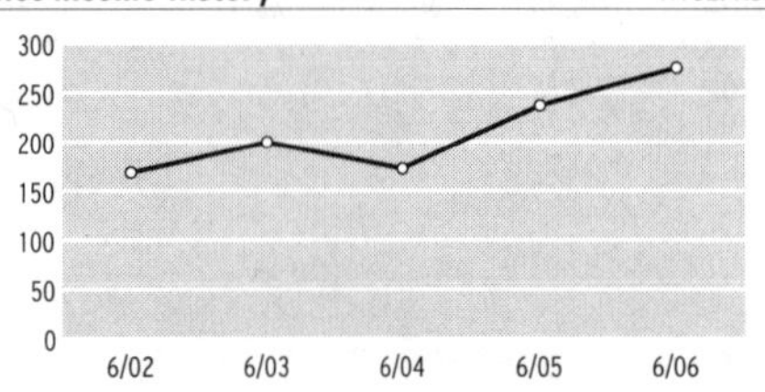


# Applied Industrial Technologies

Just imagine getting lost in *that* warehouse. Applied Industrial Technologies distributes literally millions of parts made by thousands of manufacturers. The short list of products includes bearings, power transmission components, hydraulic and pneumatic components, fabricated rubber products, and linear motion systems. It primarily sells these items through about 450 service centers throughout the US (including Puerto Rico), Canada, and Mexico. Customers include both the maintenance repair operations (MRO) and original equipment manufacturing (OEM) markets. Applied also operates regional mechanical, rubber, and fluid power shops that perform services such as engineering design and conveyor belt repair.

Applied has spent the 2000s expanding the reach of its distribution and service networks through purchases, especially in Canada and Mexico. In 2006 Applied bought Minnesota Bearing Company, which distributes bearings and power transmission products.

The company relies on a local presence to deliver much of its business. Those 450 service locations are located in 48 states, five Canadian provinces, and six Mexican states.

## HISTORY

In 1928 founder Joseph Bruening bought the Cleveland office of Detroit Ball Bearing and incorporated his own company as Ohio Ball Bearing. His company acquired a reputation for aggressive acquisitions and maintaining a large inventory. In 1952 the firm bought bearings makers in three other states and changed its name to Bearings Specialists and then to Bearings. By 1973 the company had operations in 25 states. After a serious sales slump in the mid-1980s, former Diamond Shamrock executive John Dannemiller was hired as COO in 1988. He became CEO four years later.

Dannemiller revitalized the company by diversifying its product line, primarily through acquisitions. By 1995 nonbearings technologies accounted for 55% of the company's revenues, up from 35% in 1989. After expanding the company's product lines to include drive systems, rubber products, and fluid power components, it started competing in a broader $21 billion market, rather than the $1.7 billion market for bearings alone.

The company adopted the Applied Industrial Technologies name in 1997. That year it made its largest acquisition to date with the purchase of Invetech, a Detroit distributor with 88 branches in 19 states. It also bought Midwest Rubber and Supply of Denver. Applied broadened its product lines in 1998 by acquiring specialized distributors of bearings and mechanical- and electrical-drive systems. The company closed out the century by shutting down 28 underperforming facilities.

To streamline its businesses, in 2000 Applied reorganized its field sales and service organizations into two product platforms — industrial products and fluid power. It also acquired 21 bearing and power transmission service centers, three rubber fabrication centers, and 15 fluid power facilities from Canada's Dynavest Corp. In 2001 Applied added four facilities in Mexico with its purchase of Baleros Industriales, SA de CV (BISA), a distributor of bearings and power transmission products.

Late in 2002 Applied acquired Canadian industrial parts distributor Industrial Equipment Co., Ltd. Mexico-based Rodamientos y Bandas de la Laguna (industrial product distribution) was acquired the following year for a reported $2.8 million.

## EXECUTIVES

**Chairman and CEO:** David L. Pugh, age 58, $818,000 pay
**President:** Bill L. Purser, age 63
**EVP and COO:** Ben J. Mondics, age 48
**VP, CFO, and Treasurer:** Mark O. Eisele, age 50, $357,500 pay
**VP and CIO:** James T. Hopper, age 63
**VP, Communications and Learning:** Richard C. Shaw, age 58
**VP, Acquisitions and Global Business Development:** Todd A. Barlett, age 51
**VP, Chief Administrative Officer and Government Business:** Michael L. Coticchia, age 44
**VP, General Counsel, and Secretary:** Fred D. Bauer, age 41, $283,000 pay
**VP, Marketing and Supply Chain Management:** Jeffrey A. Ramras, age 52, $280,000 pay
**VP, Strategic Planning and Development:** Maryann R. Correnti
**VP North Atlantic Area:** John Leyo
**Corporate Controller:** Daniel T. (Dan) Brezovec, age 45
**Media Relations:** Julie Kho
**Auditors:** Deloitte & Touche LLP

## LOCATIONS

**HQ:** Applied Industrial Technologies, Inc.
1 Applied Plaza, Cleveland, OH 44115
**Phone:** 216-426-4000 **Fax:** 216-426-4845
**Web:** www.appliedindustrial.com

Applied Industrial Technologies operates more than 450 facilities in 48 US states, five Canadian provinces, six Mexican states, and in Puerto Rico.

## 2006 Sales

| | $ mil. | % of total |
|---|---|---|
| US | 1,686.1 | 89 |
| Canada | 194.6 | 10 |
| Other countries | 20.1 | 1 |
| **Total** | **1,900.8** | **100** |

## PRODUCTS/OPERATIONS

### 2006 Sales

| | $ mil. | % of total |
|---|---|---|
| Industrial products | 1,554.6 | 82 |
| Fluid power products | 346.2 | 18 |
| **Total** | **1,900.8** | **100** |

### Selected Products

Bearings
- Plane bearings
- Rolling element bearings
  - Ball bearings
  - Mounted and unmounted bearings
  - Roller bearings

Drive Components and Systems
- Electrical components
  - Electric motors (AC, DC)
  - Motor starters
  - Photoelectrics, encoders, sensors
  - Variable speed controllers (AC, DC)
  - Servo motion controllers
- Mechanical components
  - Belt drive components
  - Chain drive components
  - Clutch/brake mechanicals
  - Coupling and U joints
  - Material handling products
  - Open gears
  - Speed reducers and gear motors

Fluid Power
- Accessories (gauges, ball valves, accumulators, subplates, manifold, hose and fittings, hydraulic oil)
- Cylinders
- Filters
- Motors
- Power supplies
- Pumps
- Valves

Linear Technologies
- Bellows
- Cable and hose carriers
- Controls
- Gearheads
- Linear motors
- Precision balls
- Precision mechanical components
- Steps and servo motors

Rubber Products
- Belt drive components
- Conveyor belting and accessories
- Hydraulic hose, fittings, and equipment
- Industrial hose and fittings
- Power transmission belts
- Rubber shop services

Specialty Products
- Analytical tools
- Chemicals (adhesives, lubricants, paints, sealants)
- Fluid sealing products (seals, gaskets)
- General mill supplies
- Maintenance tools
- Precision mechanical components

Shop Services
- Cylinder repair and manufacturing
- Fluid cleanliness consulting
- Hydraulic pump and motor repair
- Hydraulic servo and proportional valve services
- Mechanical repair and maintenance services
- Pneumatic circuit services
- Rubber shop services

## COMPETITORS

Commercial Solutions
Dana
DXP Enterprises
Fastenal
Fenner
General Parts
Genuine Parts
Hillman Companies
HORIZON Solutions
Ingersoll Rand
Kaman
Kaydon
Mark IV
McMaster-Carr
Motion Industries
MSC Industrial Direct
NN Inc.
Parker Hannifin
Premier Farnell
SKF
Tomkins
Tuthill
W.W. Grainger

## HISTORICAL FINANCIALS

Company Type: Public

### Income Statement

FYE: June 30

| | REVENUE ($ mil.) | NET INCOME ($ mil.) | NET PROFIT MARGIN | EMPLOYEES |
|---|---|---|---|---|
| **6/06** | 1,901 | 72 | 3.8% | 4,683 |
| **6/05** | 1,717 | 55 | 3.2% | 4,415 |
| **6/04** | 1,517 | 32 | 2.1% | 4,312 |
| **6/03** | 1,464 | 20 | 1.4% | 4,355 |
| **6/02** | 1,447 | 3 | 0.2% | 4,508 |
| **Annual Growth** | 7.1% | 127.5% | — | 1.0% |

### 2006 Year-End Financials

Debt ratio: 18.4%
Return on equity: 17.9%
Cash ($ mil.): 106
Current ratio: 2.96
Long-term debt ($ mil.): 76
No. of shares (mil.): 44
Dividends
Yield: 1.6%
Payout: 25.5%
Market value ($ mil.): 1,071

### Stock History

NYSE: AIT

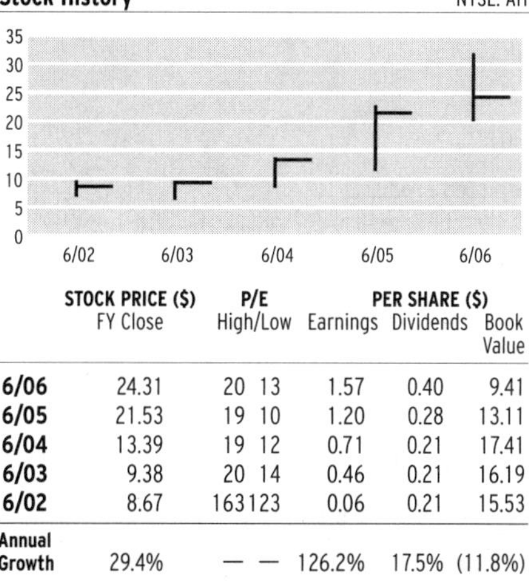


| | STOCK PRICE ($) FY Close | P/E High | P/E Low | PER SHARE ($) Earnings | Dividends | Book Value |
|---|---|---|---|---|---|---|
| **6/06** | 24.31 | 20 | 13 | 1.57 | 0.40 | 9.41 |
| **6/05** | 21.53 | 19 | 10 | 1.20 | 0.28 | 13.11 |
| **6/04** | 13.39 | 19 | 12 | 0.71 | 0.21 | 17.41 |
| **6/03** | 9.38 | 20 | 14 | 0.46 | 0.21 | 16.19 |
| **6/02** | 8.67 | 163 | 123 | 0.06 | 0.21 | 15.53 |
| **Annual Growth** | 29.4% | — | — | 126.2% | 17.5% | (11.8%) |

# Applied Materials

Today, semiconductor manufacturing; tomorrow, the world — of alternative energy sources. Applied Materials is, by far, the world's largest maker of semiconductor production equipment. With its 2006 acquisition of Applied Films, the company moved into the market for equipment used in making solar power cells. Applied's machines vie for supremacy in many segments of the chip-making process, including deposition (layering film on wafers), etching (removing portions of chip material to allow precise construction of circuits), and semiconductor metrology and inspection equipment.

Applied acquired Applied Films, a supplier of thin-film deposition equipment, for around $464 million in cash. Following the acquisition of Applied Films, the company created a new product segment, Adjacent Technologies, that covers equipment used to fabricate solar photovoltaic cells, flexible electronics, and energy-efficient glass. Applied sees the solar photovoltaic production equipment market increasing from $1 billion in 2006 to more than $3 billion in 2010.

The company is delving further into the solar energy market by acquiring HCT Shaping Systems for 583 million Swiss francs (approximately $475 million). HCT supplies equipment for making the crystalline silicon wafers that go into producing solar cells. Applied expects the proposed acquisition to help reduce the cost of manufacturing photovoltaic cells. The transaction is scheduled to close by the end of October 2007.

Applied Ventures, the venture-capital arm of the company, has invested $3 million in Soliacx, a supplier of single-crystal silicon wafers for the solar photovoltaic industry.

The company has acquired the Brooks Software division of competitor Brooks Automation for $125 million in cash. The transaction broadened Applied's portfolio of factory control software for the wafer fabrication plant. Brooks Software became part of the Applied Global Services organization.

As semiconductors are incorporated into more and more products, demand for ever-smaller and more complex chips grows. Just as quickly, chip-making machinery becomes obsolete — which is good news for Applied's sales. To keep up with the chip industry's constant drive toward smaller circuits, larger wafers, and new technologies such as copper interconnects, Applied relies on heavy R&D efforts.

The company has also used a combination of acquisitions and internal development to bolster its moves into the few areas of chip manufacturing — such as atomic layer deposition equipment — where it wasn't already a major player. Applied has partnered with specialized construction firms to offer services to speed installation of chip equipment in new plants.

Capital Research and Management owns nearly 12% of Applied Materials. Capital Group International holds about 7% of the company.

## HISTORY

Applied Materials was founded in 1967 in Mountain View, California, as a maker of chemical vapor deposition systems for fabricating semiconductors. After years of rapid growth, the company went public in 1972. Two years later it purchased wafer maker Galamar Industries.

In 1975 Applied Materials suffered a 45% drop in sales as the semiconductor industry (and the US economy) contracted. Financial and managerial problems plagued the company following the recession, so in 1976 James Morgan, a former division manager for conglomerate Textron, was chosen to replace founder Michael McNeilly as CEO. Two years later Morgan also became chairman.

After selling Galamar (1977) and other noncore units and extending the company's line of credit, Morgan announced a plan to move into Japan. The company's first joint venture, Applied Materials Japan, was set up in 1979.

Morgan's hunch that Japan would become a semiconductor hub paid off. His early arrival, plus his attention to Japanese ways of doing business, put Applied way ahead of its American competitors. Morgan wrote *Cracking the Japanese Market* about his experiences doing business in Japan, which came to account for one-sixth of the company's sales.

When another slump hit the chip industry in 1985, Morgan revved up research and development. With two separate manufacturing technologies poised to compete, Morgan essentially bet on the fast but unproven one-at-a-time, multiple-chamber method (as opposed to the existing batch process system). The resulting Precision 5000 series machines revolutionized the industry and catapulted Applied Materials to the top of it. Applied's sales passed the $1 billion mark for the first time in 1993.

Shaking off an industry slump, in 1996 Applied acquired two Israeli companies, Opal (scanning electronic microscopes used in wafer inspection) and Orbot Instruments (wafer and photomask inspection systems), to grab nearly 5% of the crowded chip inspection tools market.

In early 2000 Applied began its move into photolithography — one of the few industry segments in which it didn't operate — by acquiring Etec Systems, a leading maker of semiconductor mask pattern generation equipment, for nearly $2 billion.

A sharp global downturn in the chip industry led the company in early 2001 to take a variety of cost-cutting measures (including executive pay cuts, a voluntary separation plan, and temporary plant shutdowns) that stopped short of layoffs. Later that year, though, Applied let go about 2,000 employees — about 10% of its workforce — in response to continuing poor conditions in the chip market. Late that year the company enacted another 10% layoff, this one affecting 1,700 workers. It repeated the move late in 2002 as the chip industry's worst-ever slump stretched across two full years.

In 2003 longtime Intel executive Michael Splinter succeeded Morgan as CEO; Morgan remains chairman.

In mid-2005 Applied filed to create a holding company in China to coordinate its efforts in the giant economy. Marketing semiconductor equipment in China since 1984, the company had more than 300 employees at five locations in the People's Republic, and it set plans to establish a Global Development Capability center in China.

In early 2006 the company set plans to sell or shut down facilities it no longer needed in California (the former Etec Systems plant), Massachusetts, and Oregon, and also overseas in Japan and South Korea. It took asset impairment and restructuring charges of about $212 million, including $122 million in asset writeoffs, as a result.

## EXECUTIVES

**Chairman:** James C. (Jim) Morgan, age 68
**President, CEO, and Director:**
Michael R. (Mike) Splinter, age 56, $945,000 pay
**EVP, Sales and Marketing:** Franz Janker, age 57, $339,926 pay
**SVP and CTO; General Manager, New Business and New Products Group:** Mark R. Pinto, age 47, $500,000 pay
**SVP and CFO:** George S. Davis, age 49, $466,575 pay
**SVP; General Manager, Applied Global Services:**
Manfred Kerschbaum, age 52
**SVP; General Manager, Silicon Systems Group:**
Thomas (Tom) St. Dennis, age 54
**SVP, General Counsel, and Corporate Secretary:**
Joseph J. Sweeney, age 58
**Group VP and CIO:** Ron Kifer, age 55
**Group VP and Chief of Staff:** Menachem Erad
**Group VP, Global Operations:**
Christopher P. (Chris) Belden
**Group VP; General Manager, Process Diagnostics and Control Product Business Group:** Gilad Almogy, age 41
**Group VP, Global Human Resources:**
Jeannette Liebman
**VP and Controller:** Yvonne Weatherford, age 55
**VP, Corporate Strategy:** John McClure
**Auditors:** KPMG LLP

## LOCATIONS

**HQ:** Applied Materials, Inc.
3050 Bowers Ave., Santa Clara, CA 95054
**Phone:** 408-727-5555 **Fax:** 408-748-9943
**Web:** www.appliedmaterials.com

Applied Materials has more than 100 facilities in China, France, Germany, India, Israel, Italy, Japan, Malaysia, the Netherlands, Singapore, South Korea, Taiwan, the UK, and the US.

### 2006 Sales

| | $ mil. | % of total |
|---|---|---|
| Asia/Pacific | | |
| Taiwan | 2,079 | 23 |
| South Korea | 1,699 | 18 |
| Japan | 1,518 | 16 |
| China & other countries | 1,157 | 13 |
| North America | 1,708 | 19 |
| Europe | 1,006 | 11 |
| **Total** | **9,167** | **100** |

## PRODUCTS/OPERATIONS

### 2006 Sales

| | $ mil. | % of total |
|---|---|---|
| Silicon | 5,971 | 65 |
| Fab Solutions | 2,210 | 24 |
| Display | 966 | 11 |
| Adjacent Technologies | 20 | — |
| **Total** | **9,167** | **100** |

### Selected Products

Chemical mechanical polishing/planarization systems (wafer polishing)
Deposition systems (deposit layers of conducting and insulating material on wafers)
- Dielectric deposition (chemical vapor deposition, or CVD)
- Metal (CVD, electroplating, or physical vapor deposition)
- Silicon and thermal deposition
- Sputtering (physical vapor deposition) for solar cells
- Thin-film silicon solar cells
- Web coating for flexible solar cells

Etch systems (remove portions of a wafer surface for circuit construction)
Inspection systems (defect review for reticles — patterned plates which hold precise images of chip circuit patterns — and wafers)
Ion implant systems (implant ions into wafer surface to change conductive properties)
Manufacturing process optimization software
Metrology systems
- CD-SEM (scanning electron microscope system)

Optical monitoring systems (for glass or web coating systems)
Rapid thermal processing systems (heat wafers to change electrical characteristics)

## COMPETITORS

AIXTRON
ASM International
ASML
Aviza Technology
Axcelis Technologies
Canon
Dainippon Screen
Ebara
Electroglas
Fab Solutions
FEI
FSI International
HamaTech
Hitachi
Ibis Technology
KLA-Tencor
Lam Research
Mattson Technology
Micronic Laser Systems
Nanometrics
Nikon
Novellus
Semitool
SEZ Group
Spire
Sumitomo Heavy Industries
Sumitomo Metal Industries
Tegal
Tokyo Electron
Toshiba
ULVAC
Varian Semiconductor
Veeco Instruments
Zygo

## HISTORICAL FINANCIALS

Company Type: Public

### Income Statement

FYE: Last Sunday in October

| | REVENUE ($ mil.) | NET INCOME ($ mil.) | NET PROFIT MARGIN | EMPLOYEES |
|---|---|---|---|---|
| **10/06** | 9,167 | 1,517 | 16.5% | 14,072 |
| **10/05** | 6,992 | 1,210 | 17.3% | 12,576 |
| **10/04** | 8,013 | 1,351 | 16.9% | 12,960 |
| **10/03** | 4,477 | (149) | — | 12,050 |
| **10/02** | 5,062 | 269 | 5.3% | 16,077 |
| **Annual Growth** | 16.0% | 54.1% | — | (3.3%) |

### 2006 Year-End Financials

Debt ratio: 3.1%
Return on equity: 19.5%
Cash ($ mil.): 1,897
Current ratio: 2.50
Long-term debt ($ mil.): 205
No. of shares (mil.): 1,392
Dividends
Yield: 0.9%
Payout: 16.5%
Market value ($ mil.): 24,021

### Stock History

NASDAQ (GS): AMAT

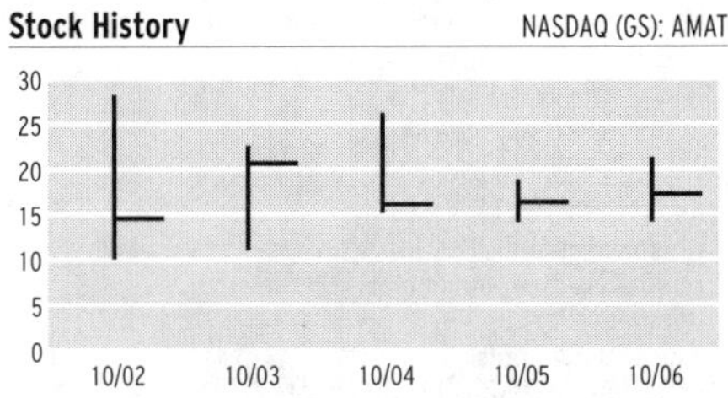


| | STOCK PRICE ($) FY Close | P/E High | P/E Low | PER SHARE ($) Earnings | Dividends | Book Value |
|---|---|---|---|---|---|---|
| **10/06** | 17.26 | 22 | 15 | 0.97 | 0.16 | 4.78 |
| **10/05** | 16.36 | 25 | 20 | 0.73 | 0.06 | 5.56 |
| **10/04** | 16.10 | 33 | 20 | 0.78 | — | 5.51 |
| **10/03** | 20.65 | — | — | (0.09) | — | 4.81 |
| **10/02** | 14.51 | 175 | 64 | 0.16 | — | 4.87 |
| **Annual Growth** | 4.4% | — | — | 56.9% | 166.7% | (0.4%) |

# ARAMARK Corporation

Keeping employees fed and clothed is one mark of this company. ARAMARK is the world's #3 foodservice provider (behind Compass Group and Sodexho Alliance) and the #2 uniform supplier in the US (behind Cintas). It offers corporate dining services and operates concessions at many sports arenas, concert halls, and other entertainment venues. It also offers facilities management and maintenance services. Its ARAMARK Refreshment Services is a leading provider of vending and beverage services. In addition, the company provides professional uniforms through ARAMARK Uniform and Career Apparel. Founded in 1959, ARAMARK is owned by an investment group led by chairman and CEO Joseph Neubauer.

With backing from such investment firms as CCMP Capital, Thomas H. Lee Partners, and Warburg Pincus, Neubauer took the company private for $8.3 billion, including the assumption of $2 billion in debt, in 2007. (The executive already owned 40% of ARAMARK.) The deal marked the second such transaction for the company, having been taken private by Neubauer and a management group in the 1980s.

Already a leader in its industry, the company continues to look for opportunities to expand not only its client base, but also to expand the number of services it supplies for its existing customers. For new business, ARAMARK is targeting such industry segments as correctional facilities and health care operators.

It is also keen on international expansion with a focus on Europe and Japan, as well as the burgeoning market in China. Already operating in the country through subsidiary Bright China Service, ARAMARK in 2006 acquired Beijing-based food services outfit Golden Collar. The following year, the company was selected to provide foodservices for the 2008 Olympics in Beijing.

## HISTORY

Davre Davidson began his career in foodservice by selling peanuts from the backseat of his car in the 1930s. He landed his first vending contract with Douglas Aircraft (later McDonnell Douglas, now part of Boeing) in 1935. Through that relationship, Davidson met William Fishman of Chicago, who had vending operations in the Midwest. Davidson and Fishman merged their companies in 1959 to form Automatic Retailers of America (ARA). Davidson became chairman and CEO of the new company; Fishman served as president.

Focusing on candy, beverage, and cigarette machines, ARA became the leading vending machine company in the US by 1961, with operations in 38 states. Despite slimmer profit margins, ARA moved into food vending in the early 1960s. It acquired 150 foodservice businesses between 1959-1963, quickly becoming a leader in the operation of cafeterias at colleges, hospitals, and work sites. The company (which changed its name to ARA Services in 1966) grew so rapidly that the FTC stepped in; ARA agreed to restrict future food vending acquisitions.

ARA provided foodservices at the 1968 Summer Olympics in Mexico City, beginning a long-term relationship with the amateur sports event. The company also diversified into publication distribution that year, and in 1970 it expanded into janitorial and maintenance services. A foray into residential care for the elderly began in 1973 (and ended in 1993 with the sale of the subsidiary). ARA also entered into emergency room staffing services (sold 1997). The company expanded into child care (National Child Care Centers) in 1980.

CFO Joseph Neubauer became CEO in 1983 and was named chairman in 1984. To avoid a hostile takeover shortly thereafter, he led a $1.2 billion leveraged buyout. After the buyout, ARA began refining its core operations. It acquired Szabo (correctional foodservices) in 1986, Children's World Learning Centers in 1987, and Coordinated Health Services (medical billing services) in 1993.

ARA changed its name to ARAMARK in 1994 as part of an effort to raise its profile with its ultimate customers, the public. The company's concession operations suffered from long work stoppages in baseball (1994) and hockey (1995). ARAMARK acquired Galls (North America's #1 supplier of public safety equipment) in 1996, and in 1997 announced plans to become 100% employee-owned. In 2000 the company was on hand to supply foodservices to the Olympic Games in Sydney.

With the new millennium the company was focused on expansion, buying the food and beverage concessions business of conglomerate Ogden Corp. for $236 million. The company penned a 10-year deal with Boeing in 2000 to supply foodservices to about 100 locations, one of the biggest foodservice contracts ever. It also bought Wackenhut's Correctional Foodservice Management division.

ARAMARK continued its expansion with the purchase of ServiceMaster's management services division in 2001 for about $800 million — opening doors in non-food management, grounds keeping, and custodial services. However, the company lost a bid to cater the 2002 Olympic Games in Salt Lake City to rival Compass Group. In late 2001 ARAMARK went public.

In 2002 the company bought Hilton's 14 Harrison Conference Centers and university lodgings for about $49 million. Also it paid $100 million for Premier, Inc.'s Clinical Technology Services, which maintains and repairs clinical equipment in about 170 hospitals and health care facilities in the US. ARAMARK also completed its acquisition of Fine Host Corporation, which added approximately 900 client locations.

In 2003 ARAMARK exited the child care business when it sold its Educational Resources unit (operator of Children's World Learning Centers) to Michael Milken's Knowledge Learning Corporation for $225 million. Longtime executive Bill Leonard was named president and CEO that year, with Neubauer taking on the title of executive chairman.

Expanding its Canadian presence in cleanroom services in 2004, ARAMARK acquired Toronto-based Cleanroom Garments, a supplier of apparel and accessories for Canadian manufacturers in pharmaceutical, aerospace, and automotive industries. That same year, ARAMARK made its first foray into China by acquiring a 90% stake in Bright China Service Industries, a facilities services firm. After a brief reign, Leonard resigned that year and Neubauer returned to being CEO of the company.

In 2007 Neubauer, with the backing of such investment firms as CCMP Capital, Thomas H. Lee Partners, and Warburg Pincus, took ARAMARK private for $8.3 billion, including the assumption of $2 billion in debt.

## EXECUTIVES

**Chairman and CEO:** Joseph (Joe) Neubauer, age 65, $2,750,000 pay
**EVP, Corporate Affairs:** Timothy P. (Tim) Cost, age 47, $823,750 pay
**EVP, General Counsel, and Secretary:** Bart J. Colli, age 58, $942,800 pay
**EVP, Human Resources:** Lynn B. McKee, age 51, $917,800 pay
**EVP and CFO:** L. Frederick Sutherland, age 54, $1,042,800 pay
**EVP, ARAMARK Business and Industry Facility Services:** Joseph J. Tinney Jr.
**EVP; President Domestic Food, Hospitality, and Facilities:** Andrew C. Kerin, age 43, $975,850 pay
**EVP; President ARAMARK International:** Ravi K. Saligram, age 50, $917,800 pay
**EVP; President ARAMARK Uniform and Career Apparel:** Thomas J. (Tom) Vozzo, age 44, $893,750 pay
**SVP Human Resources, Aramark Domestic Food, Hospitality and Facility Services:** Tangee Gibson
**SVP, ARAMARK and President, ARAMARK Business, Sports, and Entertainment:** John R. (Jack) Donovan Jr., age 47
**SVP, ARAMARK Marketing:** Chris Malone
**SVP, Controller and Chief Accounting Officer:** John M. Lafferty, age 62
**SVP and CIO:** David S. Kaufman
**SVP and Treasurer:** Christopher S. (Chris) Holland, age 40
**VP, Strategic Marketing:** Oscar Budejen
**VP Culinary Development, ARAMARK Innovative Dining Solutions:** R. Douglas (Doug) Martinides
**VP, Human Resources:** David Kahn
**VP, Taxes:** Michael J. O'Hara
**Auditors:** KPMG LLP

## LOCATIONS

**HQ:** ARAMARK Corporation
ARAMARK Tower, 1101 Market St., Philadelphia, PA 19107
**Phone:** 215-238-3000 **Fax:** 215-238-3333
**Web:** www.aramark.com

ARAMARK has operations in the US and 19 other countries.

## PRODUCTS/OPERATIONS

### 2006 Sales

| | $ mil. | % of total |
|---|---|---|
| Food & support services | | |
| US | 7,454 | 64 |
| International | 2,547 | 22 |
| Uniform & career apparel | | |
| Rental | 1,202 | 10 |
| Direct marketing | 418 | 4 |
| **Total** | **11,621** | **100** |

### Selected Operations

Food and support services
- ARAMARK Convention Centers
- ARAMARK Education
- ARAMARK Facility Services
- ARAMARK Harrison Lodging (conference centers)
- ARAMARK Healthcare
- ARAMARK Higher Education
- ARAMARK Parks & Resorts
- ARAMARK Refreshment Services (vending services)
- ARAMARK Sports and Entertainment

Uniform and career apparel
- ARAMARK Work Apparel & Uniform Services
- Galls (tactical equipment and apparel)

## COMPETITORS

ABM Industries
Centerplate
Cintas
Compass Group
Crothall Services
Delaware North
Elior
G&K Services
Healthcare Services
HMSHost
ISS A/S
ServiceMaster
Sodexho Alliance
Thompson Hospitality
UNICCO Service
UniFirst

## HISTORICAL FINANCIALS

Company Type: Private

**Income Statement** FYE: Friday nearest September 30

| | REVENUE ($ mil.) | NET INCOME ($ mil.) | NET PROFIT MARGIN | EMPLOYEES |
|---|---|---|---|---|
| **9/06** | 11,621 | 261 | 2.2% | 240,000 |
| **9/05** | 10,963 | 289 | 2.6% | 240,000 |
| **9/04** | 10,192 | 263 | 2.6% | 242,500 |
| **9/03** | 9,448 | 301 | 3.2% | 200,000 |
| **9/02** | 8,770 | 270 | 3.1% | 200,000 |
| **Annual Growth** | 7.3% | (0.8%) | — | 4.7% |

**2006 Year-End Financials**

Debt ratio: 115.9%
Return on equity: 18.3%
Cash ($ mil.): 48
Current ratio: 0.96
Long-term debt ($ mil.): 1,763

**Net Income History**

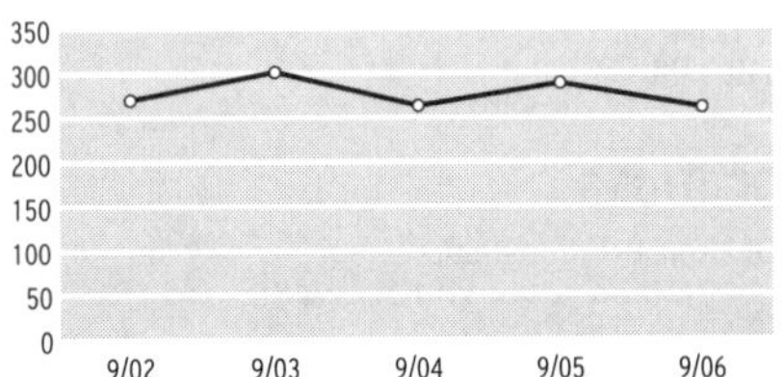


# Arch Coal

What powers your power company? Perhaps Arch Coal. About half of the electricity generated in the US comes from coal, and Arch Coal is one of the country's largest coal producers, behind industry leader Peabody Energy. Arch Coal produces about 130 million tons of coal a year from nearly two dozen mines in the western US and Central Appalachia; the company has proved and probable reserves of 2.9 billion tons. Steam coal — low-ash coal used by electric utilities to produce steam in boilers — accounts for the vast majority of the company's sales. To store and ship its Appalachian coal, the company operates the Arch Coal Terminal near the Ohio River.

In 2005 Arch Coal sold four of its mining operations in southern West Virginia to Magnum Coal, a company backed by affiliates of investment firm ArcLight Capital. Previously, Arch Coal had planned to contribute the assets to Magnum in exchange for a stake in the company.

The asset sale was part of Arch Coal's strategy of focusing on its core areas, the Central Appalachian Basin and the Powder River Basin. In 2004 the company acquired Triton Coal and its mines in the Powder River Basin for $364 million. Conversely, Arch Coal dipped its toe into the increasingly important Illinois Basin region with the acquisition of a one-third interest in Knight Hawk Coal.

The company sells its coal primarily to utilities in the US, but foreign sales did account for nearly 7% of total sales in 2005 and 2006. That figure was up from just 3% two years prior.

## HISTORY

Raised in the Oklahoma oil patch, J. Fred Miles founded the Swiss Drilling Company in 1910 and started wildcatting oil wells. Unable to compete against the low prices offered by Standard Oil, Miles moved his company in 1916 to eastern Kentucky and acquired control of 200,000 acres of oil land. With powerful backers such as the Armours of Chicago, Swiss Oil Company soon became one of the leading oil companies in Kentucky.

In the early 1920s the company's oil wells started to play out during a postwar depression. Miles fought back by expanding into refining, buying Tri-State Refining in 1930. The company changed its name in 1936 to Ashland Oil and Refining Company, a business that turned a profit even during the darkest days of the Depression. Miles didn't survive the transition, however. By 1926 Ashland was outperforming its parent, and investors eased Miles out the corporate door.

Pearl Harbor only brought more success to a business the American war machine needed to fuel its ships, planes, and tanks. Although peace brought the inevitable recession, America's postwar love affair with the automobile helped Ashland continue to thrive.

During the 1950s, Ashland's refineries ran at near capacity. In 1969 Merle Kelce and Guy Heckman, along with help from Ashland, formed Arch Mineral. Ashland had decided that it needed to diversify and lessen its dependence on oil refining. The Hunt family of Dallas, Texas, put their money into the venture in 1971, and in the following years the company bought Southwestern Illinois Coal Corporation, USX's Lynch Properties, Diamond Shamrock Coal, and Lawson-Hamilton Properties. By the end of 1996, the company owned some 1.5 billion tons of recoverable coal reserves.

Ashland struck out on its own in the coal business in 1975, forming Ashland Coal. Ashland Coal then began a series of acquisitions lasting 15 years. The company bought Addington Brothers Mining (1976), Hobet Mining and Construction (1977), Saarbergwerke (1981), Coal-Mac (1989), Mingo Logan (1990), and Dal-Tex Coal (1992). Growing through that binge of acquisitions, the company went public in 1988.

In 1997 Arch Mineral and Ashland Coal merged into Arch Coal, an entity that consolidated Ashland's coal assets. Ashland kept a 58% stake. In 1998 Arch Coal purchased Atlantic Richfield's (ARCO) US coal operations for $1.14 billion, making itself the second-largest coal producer in the US. That year Arch Coal also created Arch Western Resources, a joint venture in which Arch Coal owns 99% and ARCO owns 1%.

Regulatory pressures and low coal prices in 1999 forced the company to close three mines — the Dal-Tex in West Virginia and two surface mines in Kentucky.

Arch Coal recorded a $346 million loss in 1999. To recover from the profit plunge and benefit from increased demand as utilities complied with Clean Air Act mandates, the company boosted production at its low-sulfur coal Black Thunder mine in Wyoming. In 2000 Ashland reduced its stake in Arch Coal to 12%; it sold the remainder of its stock the next year.

In 2002 Arch Coal and WPP Group formed a partnership, Natural Resource Partners, which went public that October. The next year Arch Coal sold a portion of its stake back to Natural Resource's management for $115 million, and by 2004 Arch Coal had divested its remaining holdings in the partnership.

## EXECUTIVES

**Chairman and CEO:** Steven F. Leer, age 54, $750,000 pay
**President, COO, and Director:** John W. Eaves, age 49, $450,000 pay
**SVP and CFO:** Robert J. Messey, age 61, $335,000 pay
**SVP, Strategic Development; President, Arch Energy Resources:** C. Henry Besten Jr., age 58, $265,000 pay
**SVP Operations:** Paul A. Lang, age 46
**VP and CIO:** Michael T. Abbene
**VP, Analysis and Strategy:** Lawrence (Larry) Metzroth
**VP Business Development:** David B. Peugh, age 52
**VP, Human Resources:** Sheila B. Feldman, age 51
**VP Investor Relations and Public Affairs:** Deck S. Slone, age 43
**VP, Law, General Counsel, and Secretary:** Robert G. Jones, age 50, $300,000 pay
**VP Marketing and Trading:** David N. Warnecke, age 51
**VP, Sales, Market Research:** Andy Blumenfeld
**VP, Accounting and Finance:** John Drexler
**President, Arch Energy Resources:** Jennifer J. Johnson
**President, Western Bituminous Region Operations:** Gene DiClaudio
**Treasurer:** James E. Florczak
**Controller:** John W. Lorson
**Director, Corporate Safety:** Doug Conaway
**President, Arch Coal Sales:** John Ziegler Jr.
**Auditors:** Ernst & Young LLP

## LOCATIONS

**HQ:** Arch Coal, Inc.
1 CityPlace Dr., Ste. 300, St. Louis, MO 63141
**Phone:** 314-994-2700 **Fax:** 314-994-2878
**Web:** www.archcoal.com

**2006 Sales and Operating Income**

| | Sales $ mil. | Sales % of total | Operating Income $ mil. | Operating Income % of total |
|---|---|---|---|---|
| Powder River Basin | 1,043.4 | 42 | 215.7 | 54 |
| Central Appalachia | 998.1 | 40 | 58.8 | 15 |
| Western Bituminous | 458.9 | 18 | 126.4 | 31 |
| Adjustments | — | — | (64.2) | — |
| **Total** | **2,500.4** | **100** | **336.7** | **100** |

## PRODUCTS/OPERATIONS

**Selected Operations**

Central Appalachia
- Coal-Mac (West Virginia)
- Lone Mountain (Kentucky)

Western United States
- Arch of Wyoming (Wyoming)
- Black Thunder (Wyoming)
- Coal Creek (Wyoming)
- Dugout Canyon (Utah)
- Skyline (Utah)
- SUFCO (Utah)
- West Elk (Colorado)

**Selected Subsidiaries and Affiliates**

Arch Coal Terminal
Arch Western Resources, LLC (99%)
- Arch of Wyoming, LLC
- Canyon Fuel Co., LLC
- Mountain Coal Company, LLC
  - West Elk mine (Colorado)
- Thunder Basin Coal Company, LLC
  - Black Thunder mine ( Wyoming)

Dominion Terminal Associates (17.5%, coal loading facility in Newport News, Virginia)
Los Angeles Export Terminal (9%)

## COMPETITORS

Alliance Resource
Alpha Natural Resources
CONSOL Energy
Drummond
Foundation Coal
International Coal Group
James River Coal
Massey Energy
Peabody Energy

## HISTORICAL FINANCIALS

Company Type: Public

### Income Statement

FYE: December 31

| | REVENUE ($ mil.) | NET INCOME ($ mil.) | NET PROFIT MARGIN | EMPLOYEES |
|---|---|---|---|---|
| **12/06** | 2,500 | 261 | 10.4% | 4,050 |
| **12/05** | 2,509 | 38 | 1.5% | 3,700 |
| **12/04** | 1,907 | 114 | 6.0% | 4,150 |
| **12/03** | 1,558 | 17 | 1.1% | 3,650 |
| **12/02** | 1,534 | (3) | — | 3,750 |
| **Annual Growth** | 13.0% | — | — | 1.9% |

### 2006 Year-End Financials

Debt ratio: 82.2%
Return on equity: 20.5%
Cash ($ mil.): 3
Current ratio: 1.11
Long-term debt ($ mil.): 1,123
No. of shares (mil.): 142
Dividends
Yield: 0.7%
Payout: 12.2%
Market value ($ mil.): 4,270

### Stock History

NYSE: ACI

60
50
40
30
20
10
0
12/02 12/03 12/04 12/05 12/06

| | STOCK PRICE ($) FY Close | P/E High/Low | | PER SHARE ($) Earnings | Dividends | Book Value |
|---|---|---|---|---|---|---|
| **12/06** | 30.03 | 31 | 14 | 1.80 | 0.22 | 9.60 |
| **12/05** | 39.75 | 235 | 95 | 0.17 | 0.16 | 16.61 |
| **12/04** | 17.77 | 22 | 15 | 0.89 | 0.15 | 17.38 |
| **12/03** | 15.59 | 169 | 85 | 0.09 | 0.14 | 12.93 |
| **12/02** | 10.80 | — | — | (0.03) | 0.12 | 10.20 |
| **Annual Growth** | 29.1% | — | — | — | 16.4% | (1.5%) |

# Archer Daniels Midland

Archer Daniels Midland (ADM) knows how to grind and squeeze a fortune out of humble plants. It is one of the world's largest processors of oilseeds, corn, and wheat. Its main offerings include soybean, peanut, and other oilseed products. From corn, it produces syrups, sweeteners, citric and lactic acids, and ethanol, among other items. ADM also produces wheat and durum flour for bakeries and pasta makers. It processes cocoa beans and has a variety of other business interests, ranging from fish farming to banking and insurance. Archer Daniels Midland has interests in food processors in Asia, Canada, Europe, South America, and the US.

With more than 240 plants, ADM processes the three largest crops in the US: corn, soybeans, and wheat for sale to food, beverage, and chemical industries. About one-third of the company's sales come from its oilseed products, including vegetable oils, animal feeds, and emulsifiers. Its 50% joint venture with Golden Peanut Company is a major domestic and foreign supplier of peanuts. ADM also makes vitamin E, textured vegetable protein, and cotton cellulose pulp (for making paper).

ADM increased its production of liquid sorbitol by 60% due to the increased demand for sugar-free products in the marketplace. Sorbitol is used in the manufacture of items such as toothpaste and chewing gum. It has also increased production of ethanol, which can be used as an alternative fuel for automobiles. It has announced the building of two new ethanol plants, both with a 275-million gallon annual capacity, bringing ADM's total annual capacity to 550 million gallons.

The company continues to introduce value-added products. A line of trans-free fats and oils, NovaLipid, allows the production of margarines, shortenings, and other products with near zero levels of trans-fatty acids. It also makes cholesterol-lowering CardioAid plant steroids, which can be added to such food as sauces, pasta, beverages, and cereals.

In 2007 long-time chairman G. Allen Andreas stepped down and was replaced by company CEO and president, Patricia Woertz. That year ADM formed a 50-50 joint venture with Metabolix (called Telles) to produce and commercialize Mirel, a biobased and biodegradable plastic.

Barclays Global Investors, N.A., owns almost 10% of the company; State Farm Mutual Automobile Insurance Company owns about 9%.

## HISTORY

John Daniels began crushing flaxseed to make linseed oil in 1878, and in 1902 he formed Daniels Linseed Company in Minneapolis. George Archer, another flaxseed crusher, joined the company the following year. In 1923 the company bought Midland Linseed Products and became Archer Daniels Midland (ADM). ADM kept buying oil processing companies in the Midwest during the 1920s. It also started to research the chemical composition of linseed oil.

ADM entered the flour milling business in 1930 when it bought Commander-Larabee (then the #3 flour miller in the US). In the 1930s the company discovered a method for extracting lecithin (an emulsifier food additive used in candy and other products) from soybean oil, significantly lowering its price.

The enterprise grew rapidly following WWII. By 1949 it was the leading processor of linseed oil and soybeans in the US and was fourth in flour milling. During the early 1950s ADM began foreign expansion in earnest.

In 1966 the company's leadership passed to Dwayne Andreas, a former Cargill executive who had purchased a block of Archer family stock. Andreas focused ADM on soybeans, including the production of textured vegetable protein, a cheap soybean by-product used in foodstuffs.

Andreas' restructuring paved the way for productivity and expansion. In 1971 the company acquired Corn Sweeteners (glutens, high-fructose syrups). Other acquisitions included Tabor (grain, 1975) and Colombian Peanut (1981). ADM formed a grain-marketing joint venture with GROWMARK in 1985.

In 1995 the FBI — aided by ADM executive-turned-informer Mark Whitacre — joined a federal investigation of lysine and citric acid price-fixing by the company. The next year ADM agreed to plead guilty to two criminal charges of price-fixing and paid $100 million in penalties, a record at that time for a US criminal antitrust case. Whitacre later lost his immunity when convicted of defrauding ADM out of $9 million. He and two other ADM executives, including one-time ADM heir apparent Michael Andreas, were tried and convicted in 1998 and sentenced to prison in 1999.

Meanwhile, ADM continued to grow. In 1997 it acquired W. R. Grace's cocoa business and, after naming Allen Andreas (Dwayne's nephew) as CEO, bought 42% of Canada-based United Grain Growers. Dwayne turned over the chairman post to Allen in early 1999. In 2000 ADM was again cited for involvement in the price-fixing of lysine and was fined $45 million by the European Commission.

In 2002 ADM acquired Minnesota Corn Processors (MCP). MCP was the company's chief competitor in the ethanol market and the addition of MCP increased ADM's ethanol production such that it controls almost half of the US market.

In 2003 ADM reached a settlement with the US government regarding violations of the Clean Air Act and agreed to pay approximately $340 million to clean up air pollution at 52 of its Midwestern food-processing plants. ADM announced a joint research agreement with Volkswagen AG in 2004 in order to develop next-generation, clean, renewable biodiesel fuels for the auto industry.

In mid-2004 ADM agreed to shell out $400 million to settle a class-action anti-trust lawsuit claiming the company conspired to fix the price of high fructose corn syrup between the years of 1991 and 1995. Syrup customers involved in the suit included Coca-Cola and PepsiCo. Faced with potential damage awards of nearly $5 billion, the company chose to settle before going to trial.

President and COO Paul Mulhollem retired from the company in 2005. Chairman and CEO G. Allen Andreas assumed Mulhollem's duties until a replacement was found. In 2006 the company named Patricia Woertz as president, CEO, and director. With her appointment, ADM became the largest publicly traded US company to be headed by a woman.

In 2006 ADM (along with two Dutch companies, Akso Nobel and Avebe) was found guilty of price fixing in the cleaning agent sodium gluconate sector by an EU court. ADM was fined almost $13 million.

## EXECUTIVES

**Chairman Emeritus:** Dwayne O. Andreas, age 87
**Chairman, President, and CEO:** Patricia A. (Pat) Woertz, age 54, $950,000 pay
**EVP, Global Marketing and Risk Management:** John D. Rice, age 52, $841,067 pay
**EVP, Global Processing:** William H. Camp, age 57, $841,067 pay
**EVP, Secretary, and General Counsel:** David J. Smith, age 51, $856,311 pay
**SVP and CFO:** Douglas J. Schmalz, age 61, $735,360 pay
**SVP, Agricultural Services, President ADM/GROWMARK River System:** Lewis W. Batchelder, age 61
**SVP, Strategic Planning:** Steven R. Mills, age 51
**SVP, Ethanol Sales and Marketing, ADM Corn Processing:** Martin A. Lyons
**SVP, Corn and Specialty Food and Feed:** Edward A. Harjehausen, age 56
**SVP, Human Resources:** Michael (Mike) D'Ambrose

**VP, Corporate Marketing:** Graham P. Keen
**VP, Investor Relations:** Dwight E. Grimestad
**VP, Public Relations:** Karla M. Miller
**VP and Controller:** John Stott
**VP and Treasurer:** Vikram Luthar, age 39
**VP, Corporate Communications:** Victoria Podesta
**CTO:** Michael A. Pacheco
**Auditors:** Ernst & Young LLP

## LOCATIONS

**HQ:** Archer Daniels Midland Company
4666 Faries Pkwy., Decatur, IL 62525
**Phone:** 217-424-5200 **Fax:** 217-424-6196
**Web:** www.admworld.com

**2006 Sales**

| | $ mil. | % of total |
|---|---|---|
| US | 20,358.1 | 56 |
| Germany | 5,396.2 | 15 |
| Other countries | 10,841.8 | 29 |
| **Total** | **36,596.1** | **100** |

## PRODUCTS/OPERATIONS

**2006 Sales**

| | $ mil. | % of total |
|---|---|---|
| Agricultural services | 16,647.0 | 43 |
| Oilseeds processing | 12,017.9 | 31 |
| Corn processing | 5,227.6 | 14 |
| Other | 4,544.6 | 12 |
| Eliminations | (1,841.0) | — |
| **Total** | **36,596.1** | **100** |

**Selected Consumer Brands**
Enova (Trans-fat-free edible oil)
NutriSoy (Soy protein powder)
Soy7 (Soy pasta)

**Selected Manufacturer Brands**
Ambrosia (Chocolate)
Arcon (Soy protein concentrate)
Beakin (Lecithin)
Capsulec (Lecithin)
Clintose (Maltodextrin)
CornSweet (Fructose crystals and syrup)
De Zaan (Cocoa powder)
Merckens (Chocolate)
NovaLipid (Fats and oils)
NovaSoy (Isoflavones)
NovaXan (Xanthan gum)
NuSun (Sunflower oil)
NutriSoy (Soy protein powder)
NutriSoy Next (Soy-based meat substitute)
OptiXan (Xanthan gum)
Panalite 90 (Monoglycerides)
Paniplex (Dough conditioner)
PFL (Soy protein)
Pro-Fam (Soy proteins)
Superb (Vegetable oil and shortening)
Thermolec (Lecithin)
Ultralec (Lecithin)
Yelkin (Fluid lecithin)

**Selected Products**
Acids (citric, feed-grade amino, lactic)
Corn
Corn germ and gluten feed
Distillers grains
Ethyl alcohol (ethanol)
Feed-grade vitamins
Food emulsifiers
Grits
Lactates
Sorbitol
Sugars (dextrose, glucose, high fructose, starch, syrup)
Xanthan gum

**Selected Oilseed Products**
Cotton cellulose pulp
Crude vegetable oil (used in margarine, oil, salad dressing, shortening)
Diacylglycerol oil (Enova, used in margarine, oil, salad dressing, shortening)
Distilled monoglycerides (an emulsifier)
Natural vitamin E
Oilseed meals (used in livestock and poultry feed)
Partially refined oil (used in chemicals and paints)
Soy products — additives (lecithin, Novasoy, Isoflavones, Nutrisoy, soybean meal, textured vegetable protein)
Soy products — edible (soy-based milk, soy flour, soy protein meat substitute)
Vegetable oils and meals (canola, corn, soybeans, sunflowers)

**Selected Wheat and Other Milled Products**
Bulgur
Durum flour
Milo
Wheat flour

## COMPETITORS

Abengoa Bioenergy
Ag Processing
AGRI Industries
Ajinomoto
Andersons
ASAlliances
Badger State Ethanol
Barry Callebaut
Bartlett and Company
Brenntag North America
Buckeye Technologies
Bunge Limited
Bunge Milling
C P Kelco US
Cargill
CHS
Corn Products International
CP Kelco
Crop Production Services
Danisco
Danisco A/S
Green Plains
Hain Celestial
Hershey
Intrepid Technology & Resources
King Arthur Flour
Koch
Liberty Vegetable Oil
Little Sioux Corn Processors
Malt Products Corporation
Mars & Co.
MGP Ingredients
Nestlé
Nisshin Oillio
Riceland Foods
Südzucker
Scoular
Tate & Lyle
US BioEnergy
VeraSun

## HISTORICAL FINANCIALS

Company Type: Public

**Income Statement** FYE: June 30

| | REVENUE ($ mil.) | NET INCOME ($ mil.) | NET PROFIT MARGIN | EMPLOYEES |
|---|---|---|---|---|
| **6/06** | 36,596 | 1,312 | 3.6% | 26,800 |
| **6/05** | 35,944 | 1,044 | 2.9% | 25,641 |
| **6/04** | 36,151 | 495 | 1.4% | 26,317 |
| **6/03** | 30,708 | 451 | 1.5% | 26,197 |
| **6/02** | 23,454 | 511 | 2.2% | 24,746 |
| **Annual Growth** | 11.8% | 26.6% | — | 2.0% |

**2006 Year-End Financials**

Debt ratio: 41.3%
Return on equity: 14.4%
Cash ($ mil.): 2,334
Current ratio: 1.92
Long-term debt ($ mil.): 4,050
No. of shares (mil.): 656
Dividends
Yield: 0.9%
Payout: 18.5%
Market value ($ mil.): 27,067

**Stock History** NYSE: ADM

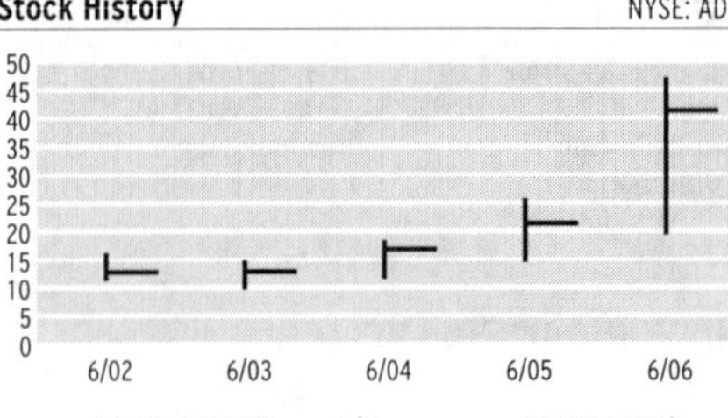

| | STOCK PRICE ($) FY Close | P/E High | P/E Low | PER SHARE ($) Earnings | Dividends | Book Value |
|---|---|---|---|---|---|---|
| **6/06** | 41.28 | 23 | 10 | 2.00 | 0.37 | 14.96 |
| **6/05** | 21.38 | 16 | 9 | 1.59 | 0.32 | 12.97 |
| **6/04** | 16.78 | 24 | 16 | 0.76 | 0.27 | 11.83 |
| **6/03** | 12.87 | 21 | 14 | 0.70 | 0.24 | 10.96 |
| **6/02** | 12.79 | 20 | 15 | 0.78 | 0.15 | 10.60 |
| **Annual Growth** | 34.0% | — | — | 26.5% | 25.3% | 9.0% |

# Arrow Electronics

Arrow Electronics knows its target market. The company is one of the world's largest distributors of electronic components and computer products, alongside rival Avnet. Arrow sells semiconductors, computer peripherals, passive components, and interconnect products from about 600 suppliers to more than 140,000 computer manufacturers and commercial customers worldwide. The company distributes products made by such manufacturers as 3Com, CA, Hitachi, Intel, Motorola, and Texas Instruments. Arrow also provides value-added services, such as component design, inventory management, and contract manufacturing. The company has bought the computer distribution business of Agilysys for $485 million in cash.

Arrow acquired the assets and operations of the Agilysys KeyLink Systems Group, and signed a long-term procurement agreement with the Agilysys Enterprise Solutions Group, the company's value-added reseller business. KeyLink is a distributor of computer servers, data storage products, and software in Canada and the US. The business carries products made by Hewlett-Packard, IBM, and other vendors. KeyLink employs about 500 people and had 2006 sales of around $1.6 billion. Arrow previously acquired the electronic components distribution business of Agilysys, in 2003.

The KeyLink acquisition is the latest in a series of purchases made by Arrow Electronics targeted at serving value-added resellers, the smaller firms that actually hit the street to sell and service IT products. KeyLink funnels computer hardware and software to more than 800 resellers.

FMR (Fidelity Investments) owns nearly 15% of Arrow Electronics. Wellington Management holds about 12% of the company. AXA has an equity stake of around 8%. Barclays Global Investors owns almost 6%.

## HISTORY

Arrow Radio began in 1935 in New York City as an outlet for used radio equipment. In the mid-1960s the company was selling various home entertainment products and wholesaling electronic parts. In 1968 three Harvard Business School graduates got Arrow in their sights. Duke Glenn, Roger Green, and John Waddell led a group of investors that acquired the company for $1 million in borrowed money. The three also bought a company that reclaimed lead from used car batteries.

With the money they made in the lead reclamation business, the trio enlarged Arrow's wholesale electronics distribution inventory. The company expanded rapidly during the 1970s, primarily through internal growth, and by 1977 it had become the US's fourth largest electronics distributor. In 1979 Arrow bought the #2 US distributor, Cramer Electronics. Although the purchase of West Coast-based Cramer was financed with junk bonds and left Arrow deeply in debt, revenues doubled. Arrow went public in 1979.

One year later a hotel fire killed 13 members of Arrow's senior management, including Glenn and Green. Waddell, who had remained at company headquarters to answer questions about a stock split announced that day, was named acting CEO. Company stock fell 19% the first day it traded after the fire and another 14% before the end of the month. Adding to the company's woes, a slump hit the electronics industry in 1981. That year Arrow's board lured Alfred Stein to leave Motorola and to lead the company's new management team as president and CEO; Waddell remained chairman.

Stein did not mesh with Arrow, and in early 1982 the board fired him and put Waddell in charge again. By 1983 the industry slump was over, and Arrow was temporarily back in the black. However, another industry downturn led to significant losses between 1985 and 1987.

In the mid-1980s Arrow began a major global expansion, acquiring in 1985 a 40% interest in Germany's largest electronics distributor, Spoerle Electronic (Arrow owned the company by 2000). President Stephen Kaufman, a former McKinsey & Company consultant, was named CEO in 1986 (Waddell remained VC). Arrow bought Kierulff Electronics, the fourth largest US distributor, in 1988, and Lex Electronics, the third largest, three years later.

Arrow expanded into Asia in 1993 with the acquisition of Hong Kong-based Components Agents and New Zealand's Components+Instrumentation in 1995. The next year Italian subsidiary Silverstar acquired Eurelettronica, one of Italy's biggest semiconductor distributors.

In 1999 Arrow acquired passive components distributor Richey Electronics and the Electronics Distribution Group of Bell Industries. Kaufman stepped down from the CEO post in 2000; company president Francis Scricco was named to the position. Later in 2000 Arrow purchased Wyle Components and Wyle Systems (both North American computer products distributors) from German utility giant E.ON.

Facing a broad downturn in the electronics industry, the company in 2001 laid off 1,500 employees. The next year Arrow sold its Gates/Arrow unit (distribution of PC peripherals and software to North American resellers) to SYNNEX Information Technologies (now just SYNNEX). Also in 2002 Scricco resigned as CEO; Kaufman left his post as chairman to take the reins once again as CEO and director Daniel Duval stepped in as chairman. Later that year Kaufman retired and Duval was named CEO.

Early in 2003 former Solectron executive Bill Mitchell took over as president and CEO; Duval remained chairman. The same year, the company purchased the industrial electronics components division of Agilysys (formerly Pioneer-Standard Electronics) for about $240 million.

Late in 2005 Arrow purchased DNSint.com, a German computer distributor, for about $157 million.

Also in 2006 Arrow acquired Alternative Technology, a distributor of networking and security products, for about $80 million, including assumed debt. The company has about 150 employees in Canada and the US; it supports value-added resellers in North America.

That same year Arrow acquired the assets of the Specialist Distribution division of InTechnology for £41 million (about $80 million) in cash. InTechnology Distribution specializes in security and data storage products for value-added resellers in the UK. It employs about 200 people and had 2006 sales of nearly $400 million.

Mitchell added chairman to his title in 2006 when Duval stepped down from that post (but remained a director).

## EXECUTIVES

**Chairman, President, and CEO:** William E. (Bill) Mitchell, age 63, $1,370,880 pay
**Vice Chairman:** John C. Waddell, age 69
**SVP, Supplier Marketing and Asset Management, Arrow Global Components:** Bhawnesh C. Mathur, age 48
**SVP and CFO:** Paul J. Reilly, age 50, $496,287 pay
**SVP, General Counsel, and Secretary:** Peter S. Brown, age 56
**SVP; President, Arrow Global Components:** Michael J. (Mike) Long, age 48, $460,000 pay
**SVP; President, Arrow Enterprise Computing Solutions:** M. Catherine Morris, age 48
**SVP; President, Arrow Enterprise Computing Solutions:** Kevin J. Gilroy, age 51
**SVP, Human Resources:** John P. McMahon, age 48
**VP, Legal Affairs, and Chief Compliance Officer:** Wayne Brody
**VP Global Marketing, Arrow Global Components:** Albert G. (Skip) Streber
**VP and CIO:** Vincent P. (Vin) Melvin, age 43
**VP; President, Global Alliance and Supply Chain, Arrow Global Components:** Brian P. McNally, age 47
**VP; President, Arrow Asia/Pacific:** Peter T. Kong, $361,200 pay
**VP; SVP, Global Sales Excellence, Arrow Global Components:** Vincent (Vinnie) Vellucci
**VP; EVP, Arrow Europe, Middle East, Africa, and South America:** Jan M. Salsgiver, age 50
**VP; Chairman, Arrow Europe, Middle East, Africa and South America:** Germano Fanelli, age 58, $494,158 pay
**VP; President, Arrow Europe, Middle East, Africa, and South America:** Philippe Combes, age 52
**Director, Marketing:** Ed Burke
**Director, Retail Services Enterprise Computing Solutions IBM:** Lance Sedlak
**Auditors:** Ernst & Young LLP

## LOCATIONS

**HQ:** Arrow Electronics, Inc.
50 Marcus Dr., Melville, NY 11747
**Phone:** 631-847-2000 **Fax:** 631-847-2222
**Web:** www.arrow.com

Arrow Electronics has nearly 300 locations around the world.

**2006 Sales**

| | $ mil. | % of total |
|---|---|---|
| North America | 6,846.5 | 50 |
| Europe, Middle East, Africa & South America | 4,348.5 | 32 |
| Asia/Pacific | 2,382.1 | 18 |
| **Total** | **13,577.1** | **100** |

## PRODUCTS/OPERATIONS

**2006 Sales**

| | $ mil. | % of total |
|---|---|---|
| Electronic components | 10,818.4 | 80 |
| Computer products | 2,758.7 | 20 |
| **Total** | **13,577.1** | **100** |

**Selected Products and Services**

Computer Products
- Communication control equipment
- Controllers
- Design systems
- Desktop computers
- Flat panel displays
- Microcomputer boards and systems
- Monitors
- Printers
- Servers
- Software
- Storage products
- System chassis and enclosures
- Workstations

Electronic Components
- Capacitors
- Connectors
- Potentiometers
- Power supplies
- Relays
- Resistors
- Switches

Services
- Analysis, implementation, and support
- Component design
- Contract manufacturing
- Forecast and order management
- Inventory management

## COMPETITORS

All American Semiconductor
Avnet
Bell Microproducts
Digi-Key
ePlus
Future Electronics
Heilind Electronics
Ingram Micro
Newark InOne
N.F. Smith
Nu Horizons Electronics
Premier Farnell
Richardson Electronics
Sager Electrical
SED International
SYNNEX
Tech Data
TTI Inc.

## HISTORICAL FINANCIALS

Company Type: Public

**Income Statement** FYE: December 31

| | REVENUE ($ mil.) | NET INCOME ($ mil.) | NET PROFIT MARGIN | EMPLOYEES |
|---|---|---|---|---|
| **12/06** | 13,577 | 388 | 2.9% | 12,000 |
| **12/05** | 11,164 | 254 | 2.3% | 11,400 |
| **12/04** | 10,646 | 208 | 1.9% | 11,500 |
| **12/03** | 8,679 | 26 | 0.3% | 11,200 |
| **12/02** | 7,390 | (611) | — | 11,700 |
| **Annual Growth** | 16.4% | — | — | 0.6% |

**2006 Year-End Financials**

Debt ratio: 32.6%
Return on equity: 14.5%
Cash ($ mil.): 338
Current ratio: 1.96
Long-term debt ($ mil.): 977
No. of shares (mil.): 122
Dividends
Yield: —
Payout: —
Market value ($ mil.): 3,862

**Stock History** NYSE: ARW

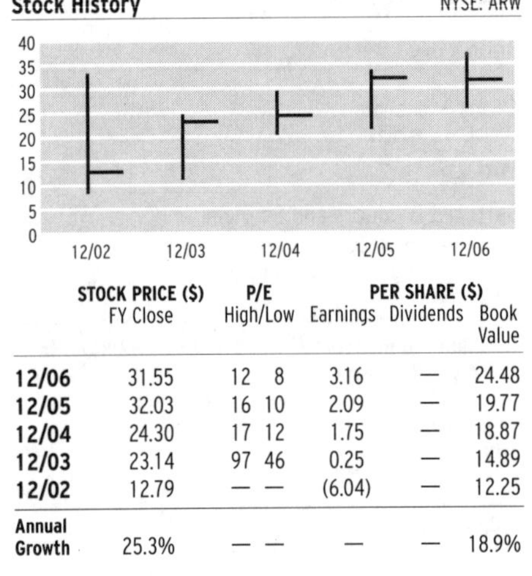


| | STOCK PRICE ($) FY Close | P/E High/Low | | PER SHARE ($) Earnings | Dividends | Book Value |
|---|---|---|---|---|---|---|
| **12/06** | 31.55 | 12 | 8 | 3.16 | — | 24.48 |
| **12/05** | 32.03 | 16 | 10 | 2.09 | — | 19.77 |
| **12/04** | 24.30 | 17 | 12 | 1.75 | — | 18.87 |
| **12/03** | 23.14 | 97 | 46 | 0.25 | — | 14.89 |
| **12/02** | 12.79 | — | — | (6.04) | — | 12.25 |
| **Annual Growth** | 25.3% | — | — | — | — | 18.9% |

# ArvinMeritor

Whether it's building axles for big rigs or steel wheels for passenger cars, ArvinMeritor's actions are always meritorious. Once known as Meritor Automotive, ArvinMeritor was formed when Meritor acquired Arvin Industries. The company makes components for commercial vehicles (axles, transmissions, and clutches) as well as for light vehicles (door, roof, wheels, and suspension systems). ArvinMeritor is divesting its light vehicle aftermarket product businesses on a piecemeal basis. It has already sold its aftermarket exhaust (North America), filters, and motion control operations. Volkswagen accounts for 11% of sales; General Motors and Ford each account for 10%.

In the face of worldwide automotive overcapacity and high costs for fuel and steel, ArvinMeritor is looking for ways to tighten its belt in order to remain competitive. To that end it has announced it will lay off about 1,850 workers and close or consolidate 11 of its plants.

ArvinMeritor has also decided to exit the automotive aftermarket in order to focus on meeting the needs of its OEM automotive and heavy-duty truck customer base. The company has also sold its off-highway brake parts business to Carlisle Companies for about $39 million. In early 2006 ArvinMeritor agreed to sell its light vehicle aftermarket Purolator filters business to Robert Bosch and MANN+HUMMEL (the deal closed later in 2006). Soon afterward the company sold its North American light vehicle aftermarket exhaust business to IMCO (International Muffler Company). The company has also sold its light vehicle aftermarket motion control business to AVM Industries LLC. In 2007 the company sold its emissions technologies business to One Equity Partners, an affiliate of JPMorgan Chase, for about $310 million. Later in 2007 ArvinMeritor sold its light vehicle aftermarket European exhaust division to Klarius Group of the UK. The move marked ArvinMeritor's complete exit of the light vehicle aftermarket.

ArvinMeritor plans to use the proceeds of the divestitures to pay down debt and invest in its core business.

Geographic expansion is also a part of ArvinMeritor's strategic goals. The company has formed a joint venture in China to build sunroofs for Chinese-built Volkswagens, and has established two more joint ventures in France to provide AB Volvo with commercial vehicle drive axles.

Asia is a big part of ArvinMeritor's growth scheme. The company hopes that Asia will eventually account for one-third of sales. In 2007 ArvinMeritor moved forward on its Asian strategy when it announced the formation of a joint venture with China's Chery Automobile.

## HISTORY

ArvinMeritor's earliest progenitor was the Wisconsin Parts Company, a small axle plant Willard Rockwell bought in 1919 to build a truck axle he had designed himself. In 1953 Rockwell merged Wisconsin Parts with Standard Steel and Spring and Timken-Detroit Axle to form Rockwell Spring and Axle Company. Timken-Detroit was a 1909 spinoff of the Timken Roller Bearing Axle Company, whose buggy springs predated the invention of the automobile.

Rockwell Spring and Axle changed its name in 1958 to Rockwell-Standard Corp. In 1967 Rockwell-Standard took over North American Aviation. North American Aviation needed to improve its public image by burrowing into a reputable company after the Apollo space capsule it had built ignited during a ground test, killing all three astronauts aboard. The new company, called North American Rockwell, was headed by Willard.

North American Rockwell made car and truck parts, tools, printing presses, industrial sewing machines, and electronic flight and navigation instruments. In 1973 North American Rockwell bought Willard Rockwell Jr.'s Rockwell Manufacturing and changed its name once again, to Rockwell International (now Rockwell Automation).

Under Willard Jr.'s leadership, Rockwell bought a number of high-risk businesses. During one period in the early 1970s, the company was losing a million dollars a day. Willard Jr. retired in 1979, and Robert Anderson, who had come to Rockwell in 1968 from Chrysler Corporation, became chairman. Anderson moved the company away from the high-profile consumer market that Willard Jr. had been so keen on. He also required all company divisions to submit profit goals. Under Anderson's management, Rockwell's debt fell dramatically.

In 1986 Rockwell brought out a new line of single-speed and two-speed drive axles for heavy vehicles, and in 1989 it introduced a family of nine- and 13-speed on-highway transmissions. The next year the company's Meritor WABCO unit (a joint venture with American Standard Companies) began supplying antilock brakes for trailers and tractors.

In the 1990s Rockwell's automotive division began growing through acquisitions and overseas expansion. It bought Czech auto parts maker Skoda Miada Boleslav in 1993 and Dura Automotive Systems' window-regulator business in 1995. The next year the division entered into a joint venture with China's Xuzhou Construction Machinery Axle and Case Co. It also introduced the Engine Synchro Shift transmission system, designed to shift gears easily.

Rockwell spun off Meritor Automotive in 1997 as an independent, publicly traded company. The new company derived its name from the Latin word "meritum," meaning service, worth, and benefit. In 1999 Meritor bought UK-based LucasVarity's heavy vehicle braking system division; Volvo's heavy-duty truck axle unit; and Euclid Industries, which makes replacement parts for medium- and heavy-duty trucks.

In 2000 Meritor acquired Arvin Industries. Renamed ArvinMeritor, the combined companies formed an automotive systems titan with $7.5 billion in sales. Later that year ArvinMeritor announced that it would reduce its worldwide workforce by about 4% (1,500) because of a slump in the heavy truck industry.

In 2003 ArvinMeritor announced that it intended to acquire Dana Corporation for $15 per share or about $2.2 billion. The deal later disintegrated when ArvinMeritor's sweetened offer of $2.67 million was rejected by Dana's board.

In 2004 the company announced plans to exit the aftermarket business in order to focus on the needs of its OEM customers. That year ArvinMeritor sold its coil coating operations.

## EXECUTIVES

**Chairman, President, and CEO:** Charles G. (Chip) McClure Jr., age 53, $2,015,441 pay
**SVP and CFO:** James D. Donlon III, age 60, $1,043,524 pay
**SVP and General Counsel:** Vernon G. Baker II, age 53, $693,958 pay
**SVP, Communications:** Linda M. (Lin) Cummins
**SVP, Human Resources:** Robert Ostrov, age 57
**SVP and President, Commercial Vehicle Systems:** Carsten Reinhardt, age 39
**SVP and President, Light Vehicle Systems:** Philip R. Martens, age 46
**VP and Secretary:** Bonnie Wilkinson, age 56, $428,928 pay
**VP and Treasurer:** Mary Lehmann, age 47
**VP and Controller:** Jeffrey A. (Jay) Craig, age 46
**VP, Information Technology, Commercial Vehicle Systems:** Jay McLean
**Senior Director, Corporate Communications and Media Relations:** Krista McClure
**Director, Investor Relations:** Terry Huch
**CIO:** Kevin Haskew
**Auditors:** Deloitte & Touche LLP

## LOCATIONS

**HQ:** ArvinMeritor, Inc.
2135 W. Maple Rd., Troy, MI 48084
**Phone:** 248-435-1000 **Fax:** 248-435-1393
**Web:** www.arvinmeritor.com

ArvinMeritor operates 112 manufacturing plants in the Americas, Australia, Europe, the Far East, and South Africa.

**2006 Sales**

| | $ mil. | % of total |
|---|---|---|
| North America | 4,609.0 | 50 |
| Europe | 3,499.0 | 38 |
| Asia & other | 1,087.0 | 12 |
| **Total** | **9,195.0** | **100** |

## PRODUCTS/OPERATIONS

**2006 Sales**

| | $ mil. | % of total |
|---|---|---|
| Light vehicle systems | 4,905.0 | 53 |
| Commercial vehicle systems | 4,290.0 | 47 |
| **Total** | **9,195.0** | **100** |

**Selected Products**

Light Vehicle Systems
- Access-control systems
- Door systems
- Roof systems
- Suspension systems
- Wheel products

Commercial Vehicle Systems
- Axles
- Brakes
- Clutches
- Drivelines
- Exhaust products
- Ride control products
- Suspension systems
- Trailer products (including axles and air suspension products)

## COMPETITORS

Accuride
AISIN World Corp.
American Axle & Manufacturing
American Standard
ASC
Benteler Automotive
Boler
BorgWarner
Borla Performance Industries
Carlisle Companies
Dana
Delphi
Eaton
Faurecia
Federal-Mogul
Haldex
Hayes Lemmerz
Inalfa Roof Systems
Intier
Knorr-Bremse
Metaldyne
NHK Spring
Robert Bosch
SOGEFI
Tenneco
ThyssenKrupp Automotive
Titan International
Topy
Tower Automotive
TRW Automotive
Valeo
Visteon
Webasto Sunroofs
Williams Controls
ZF Friedrichshafen

## HISTORICAL FINANCIALS

Company Type: Public

### Income Statement

FYE: September 30

| | REVENUE ($ mil.) | NET INCOME ($ mil.) | NET PROFIT MARGIN | EMPLOYEES |
|---|---|---|---|---|
| **9/06** | 9,195 | (175) | — | 27,500 |
| **9/05** | 8,903 | 12 | 0.1% | 29,000 |
| **9/04** | 8,033 | (42) | — | 31,000 |
| **9/03** | 7,788 | 136 | 1.7% | 32,000 |
| **9/02** | 6,882 | 107 | 1.6% | 32,000 |
| **Annual Growth** | 7.5% | — | — | (3.7%) |

### 2006 Year-End Financials

Debt ratio: 132.2%
Return on equity: —
Cash ($ mil.): 350
Current ratio: 1.21
Long-term debt ($ mil.): 1,248
No. of shares (mil.): 71
Dividends
Yield: 2.8%
Payout: —
Market value ($ mil.): 1,005

### Stock History

NYSE: ARM

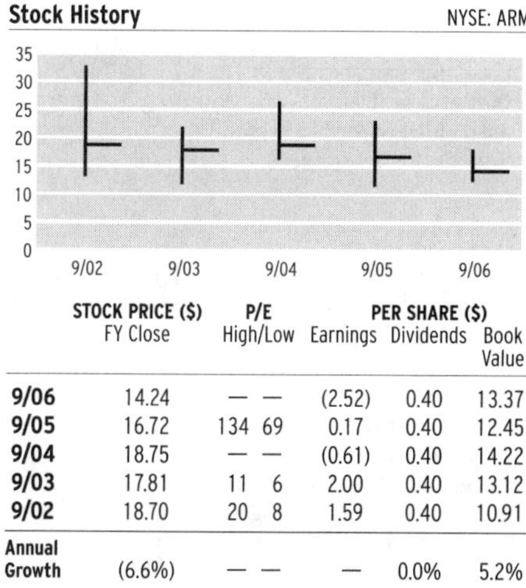


| | STOCK PRICE ($) FY Close | P/E High/Low | | PER SHARE ($) Earnings | Dividends | Book Value |
|---|---|---|---|---|---|---|
| **9/06** | 14.24 | — | — | (2.52) | 0.40 | 13.37 |
| **9/05** | 16.72 | 134 | 69 | 0.17 | 0.40 | 12.45 |
| **9/04** | 18.75 | — | — | (0.61) | 0.40 | 14.22 |
| **9/03** | 17.81 | 11 | 6 | 2.00 | 0.40 | 13.12 |
| **9/02** | 18.70 | 20 | 8 | 1.59 | 0.40 | 10.91 |
| **Annual Growth** | (6.6%) | — | — | — | 0.0% | 5.2% |

# Ashland Inc.

Ashland is built on chemicals and cars. The company consists of four business units. Ashland Distribution buys chemicals and plastics and then blends and repackages them for distribution in Europe and North America. Ashland Performance Materials makes specialty resins, polymers, and adhesives. Ashland Water Technologies provides both chemical and non-chemical products for commercial, industrial, and municipal water treatment facilities. The company's Valvoline unit operates an oil-change chain and markets Valvoline motor oil and Zerex antifreeze. Ashland sold construction unit APAC (which supplies highway materials, builds bridges, and paves streets) in 2006 to Oldcastle Materials for $1.3 billion.

Ashland also had been involved in petroleum refining through a joint venture with Marathon Oil but sold its interest in the JV. Marathon Petroleum Company (formerly Marathon Ashland Petroleum, or MAP) has a refinery and distribution network and retail gas stations, and it is a leading asphalt producer in the US. After more than a year and a half of negotiations and bargaining, Marathon paid Ashland about $3.7 billion for its interest in the company. The transaction finally closed in the middle of 2005. Ashland ended up with about $1 billion in cash on hand after payment of its debt obligations.

In mid-2005 Valvoline bought car cleaning products maker Car Brite for an undisclosed sum. And the next year Ashland used some more of that cash to purchase Degussa's water treatment business (operating as Stockhausen) for about $155 million.

In 2006 the company acquired adhesives and coatings company Northwest Coatings, which makes coatings that use ultraviolet and electron beam polymerisation technologies, for about $75 million.

Also that year Ashland decided to sell APAC to Oldcastle, the US division of Irish construction company CRH. The move, coming as it did on the heels of the divestiture of MAP, transforms Ashland into solely a chemicals company with four units: Distribution, Performance Materials, Water Technologies, and Valvoline.

## HISTORY

After moving to Kentucky in 1917, Fred Miles formed the Swiss Oil Company. In 1924 Swiss Oil bought a refinery in Catlettsburg, a rough town near sedate Ashland, and created a unit called Ashland Refining. Miles battled Swiss Oil directors for control, lost, and resigned in 1927.

Swiss Oil bought Tri-State Refining in 1930 and Cumberland Pipeline's eastern Kentucky pipe network in 1931. Swiss Oil changed its name to Ashland Oil and Refining in 1936. After WWII it bought small independent oil firms, acquiring the Valvoline name in 1950 by buying Freedom-Valvoline.

The firm formed Ashland Chemical in 1967 after buying Anderson-Prichard Oil (1958), United Carbon (1963), and ADM Chemical (1967). Ashland Chemical changed its name to Ashland Oil. It added the SuperAmerica convenience store chain (1970) and started exploring for oil in Nigeria after OPEC nations raised oil prices.

Scandal hit in 1975, the year Ashland Coal was formed. CEO Orin Atkins admitted to ordering Ashland executives to make illegal contributions to the 1972 Nixon presidential campaign. Atkins was deposed in 1981 after the company made questionable payments to highly placed "consultants" with connections to oil-rich Middle Eastern governments. In 1988 Atkins was arrested for trying to fence purloined documents regarding litigation between Ashland and the National Iranian Oil Company (NIOC). Ashland, which launched the federal investigation that led to Atkins' arrest, settled with NIOC in 1989. Atkins pleaded guilty and received probation.

Ashland went on a shopping spree in the 1990s. The company bought Permian (crude oil gathering and marketing) in 1991 and merged it into Scurlock Oil. In 1992 Ashland Chemical bought most of Unocal's chemical distribution business, and two years later it bought two companies that produce chemicals for the semiconductor industry. Also in 1994 Ashland made a promising oil discovery in Nigeria.

The company, by then named Ashland Inc., spent $368 million on 14 acquisitions to expand its energy and chemical divisions in 1995. It received a $75 million settlement with Columbia Gas System (now Columbia Energy Group) for abrogated natural gas contracts resulting from Columbia's bankruptcy.

In 1996 president Paul Chellgren became CEO and, with the company under shareholder fire, began a major reorganization. The next year Arch Mineral and Ashland Coal combined to form Arch Coal, with Ashland owning 58%. Also that year Ashland made more than a dozen acquisitions to bolster its chemical and construction businesses. Its exploration unit, renamed Blazer Energy, was sold to Norway's Statoil for $566 million.

Ashland joined USX-Marathon (now Marathon Oil) in 1998 to create Marathon Ashland Petroleum (now called Marathon Petroleum). It bought 20 companies, including Eagle One Industries, a maker of car-care products, and Masters-Jackson, a group of highway construction companies. Ashland reduced its holdings in Arch Coal from 58% to 12% in 2000; it sold the remainder in early 2001.

In 2002 the company was jolted when Chellgren was forced to retire after violating a company policy prohibiting romantic office relationships. James O'Brien replaced Chellgren.

Ashland had a record year in 2001 but was hampered in 2002 by smaller profits from MAP, which was hurt by reduced demand for petroleum products and tighter margins. Ashland Distribution also hurt the bottom line, which led Ashland to reorganize that unit's management and sales teams.

After that record year Ashland came back to earth with much smaller profits in 2002 and the next year; APAC, particularly, was hit hard in 2003. The construction division swung from $120 million in profits in 2002 to a loss of more than $40 million in 2003; the company attributes the decline to unusual weather conditions, which can greatly affect the construction business more than others. (The pendulum swung back into the black in 2004 with more than $100 million in operating income.)

The company sold its interest in Marathon Petroleum to Marathon in the middle of 2005.

## EXECUTIVES

**Chairman and CEO:** James J. (Jim) O'Brien Jr., age 52
**SVP and CFO:** J. Marvin Quin, age 59
**SVP, General Counsel and Corporate Secretary:** David L. Hausrath, age 54
**VP; President, Ashland Water Technologies and Ashland Performance Materials:** Frank L. (Hank) Waters, age 46
**VP; President, Ashland Consumer Markets:** Samuel J. (Sam) Mitchell Jr., age 45
**VP; President, Ashland Distribution:** Theodore L. (Ted) Harris, age 41
**VP; President, Ashland Supply Chain:** Michael J. Shannon, age 46
**VP; President, Ashland China:** Dale M. MacDonald
**VP; President, Ashland Europe:** Peter H. Rijneveldshoek, age 54
**VP and Controller:** Lamar M. Chambers, age 51
**VP and CIO:** Roger B. Craycraft
**VP and Chief Growth Officer:** Walter H. Solomon
**VP, Business Integration:** Larry L. Detjen
**VP, Business Process Redesign:** Rick E. Music
**VP, Communications and Corporate Affairs:** Martha C. Johnson
**VP, Human Resources and Communications:** Susan B. Esler, age 44
**Treasurer:** J. Kevin Willis
**Assistant General Counsel and Corporate Secretary:** Linda L. Foss
**General Auditor:** John F. Guldig
**Auditors:** Ernst & Young LLP

## LOCATIONS

**HQ:** Ashland Inc.
50 E. RiverCenter Blvd., Covington, KY 41012
**Phone:** 859-815-3333 **Fax:** 859-815-5053
**Web:** www.ashland.com

Ashland has worldwide operations with primary US offices in Georgia, Kentucky, and Ohio.

### 2006

| | $ mil. | % of total |
|---|---|---|
| US | 5,321 | 73 |
| Other countries | 1,956 | 27 |
| **Total** | **7,277** | **100** |

## PRODUCTS/OPERATIONS

### 2006 Sales and Operating Income

| | Sales | | Operating Income | |
|---|---|---|---|---|
| | $ mil. | % of total | $ mil. | % of total |
| Distribution | 4,070 | 55 | 120 | 49 |
| Performance Materials | 1,425 | 19 | 112 | 45 |
| Valvoline | 1,409 | 19 | (21) | — |
| Water Technologies | 502 | 7 | 14 | 6 |
| Adjustments | (129) | — | (55) | — |
| **Total** | **7,277** | **100** | **170** | **100** |

## COMPETITORS

Arkema
BASF AG
BP Lubricants USA
Brenntag North America
CHEMCENTRAL
Chemtura
DuPont
GE Plastics
Harcros Chemicals
HELM U.S.
Hexion
Hydrite
Jiffy Lube
Lyondell Chemical
Univar USA

## HISTORICAL FINANCIALS

Company Type: Public

### Income Statement

FYE: September 30

| | REVENUE ($ mil.) | NET INCOME ($ mil.) | NET PROFIT MARGIN | EMPLOYEES |
|---|---|---|---|---|
| **9/06** | 7,277 | 407 | 5.6% | 11,700 |
| **9/05** | 9,860 | 2,004 | 20.3% | 20,900 |
| **9/04** | 8,781 | 378 | 4.3% | 21,200 |
| **9/03** | 7,865 | 75 | 1.0% | 22,500 |
| **9/02** | 7,792 | 117 | 1.5% | 24,300 |
| **Annual Growth** | (1.7%) | 36.6% | — | (16.7%) |

### 2006 Year-End Financials

Debt ratio: 2.3%
Return on equity: 11.9%
Cash ($ mil.): 2,169
Current ratio: 2.08
Long-term debt ($ mil.): 70
No. of shares (mil.): 67
Dividends
Yield: 1.7%
Payout: 19.5%
Market value ($ mil.): 4,273

### Stock History

NYSE: ASH

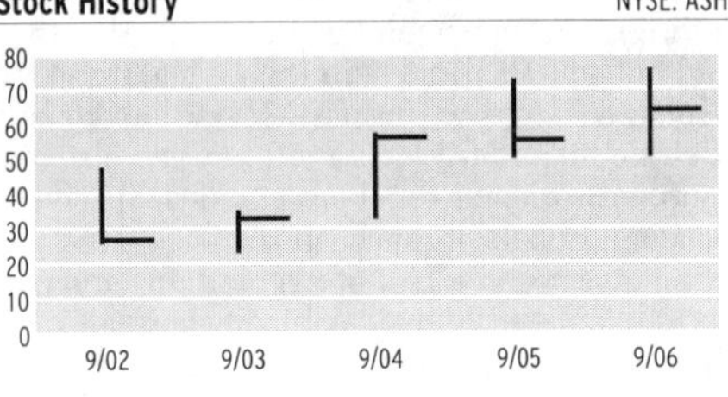


| | STOCK PRICE ($) FY Close | P/E High | P/E Low | PER SHARE ($) Earnings | PER SHARE ($) Dividends | PER SHARE ($) Book Value |
|---|---|---|---|---|---|---|
| **9/06** | 63.78 | 13 | 9 | 5.64 | 1.10 | 46.21 |
| **9/05** | 55.24 | 3 | 2 | 26.85 | 0.55 | 52.57 |
| **9/04** | 56.08 | 11 | 6 | 5.31 | — | 37.58 |
| **9/03** | 32.85 | 31 | 21 | 1.10 | — | 32.84 |
| **9/02** | 26.79 | 28 | 16 | 1.67 | — | 31.84 |
| **Annual Growth** | 24.2% | — | — | 35.6% | 100.0% | 9.8% |

# AT&T Inc.

Is it Ma Bell's revenge? AT&T, the matronly telecom icon broken apart in 1984 after a landmark antitrust case, is reuniting the Bell family. AT&T Inc. (formerly SBC Communications) was formed in 2005 when former Baby Bell SBC bought AT&T Corp. for some $16 billion, creating the largest telecom outfit in the US. After the merger, SBC adopted the globally familiar AT&T moniker. In 2006 AT&T purchased southern Baby Bell BellSouth in the largest telecommunications takeover in US history, valued at $86 billion. AT&T now has more than 68 million access lines in service. AT&T Mobility (formerly Cingular Wireless), singularly controlled by AT&T, is the nation's leading wireless carrier.

Once the smallest of the Baby Bells, Ma Bell's offspring from the Lone Star State, SBC, became King of the Hill with the purchase of its former parent (sound Shakespearean?). The cash and stock deal added valuable enterprise customers to the company's strong repertoire of consumer offerings. The former AT&T's industry-leading voice, IP-voice, video, and data communications network spans the globe reaching every country and metro area that matters. Its customers include all of the *FORTUNE* 1000, a client list that SBC had trouble making inroads into with its little-known brand (outside its local operating areas, that is).

COO Randall Stephenson officially took over AT&T's reins as chairman and CEO from former SBC chairman and CEO Ed Whitacre in 2007; former AT&T chairman and CEO David Dorman had previously served as the combined company's president briefly before walking off into the sunset with a severance package worth nearly $20 million.

With the $86 billion BellSouth deal, AT&T now serves an additional 14 million consumer lines and 6 million business lines. Prior to the merger, AT&T had 27 million consumer lines and 17 million business lines, as well as 5 million wholesale lines. AT&T expects to reap total cost savings of $18 billion from the BellSouth acquisition. The former BellSouth (which is expected to incur 10,000 job cuts as a result of the takeover) will operate under the AT&T Southeast name and retain its headquarters in Atlanta.

The BellSouth deal also gave AT&T complete control of mobile phone service provider Cingular Wireless, formerly a joint venture between the two companies. In 2004 Cingular Wireless acquired AT&T Wireless in a cash deal valued at $41 billion, creating the #1 US wireless operator, toppling former market leader Verizon Wireless. In 2007 Cingular Wireless LLC became AT&T Mobility LLC. AT&T is gradually transitioning Cingular's products and services over to the AT&T brand. The Cingular brand is expected to be phased out by mid-year. Going forward, AT&T plans to push its wireless services (consolidating the ownership and management of AT&T Mobility and Internet search site Yellowpages.com), as well as putting an emphasis on its advertising efforts.

In addition to its major markets (California, Illinois, and Texas accounted for 60% of its lines prior to the BellSouth merger), AT&T's realm of well-known regional affiliates includes the former Nevada Bell (now AT&T Nevada) and Southern New England Telecommunications (AT&T East). With the addition of BellSouth, AT&T provides telephone service to 22 US states. Looking to grow its base in rural areas, the company agreed to purchase Dobson Communications for $2.8 billion in mid-2007.

The company is further expanding its realm with a $4.4 billion initiative to deploy fiber-to-the-home (FTTH), also known as fiber-to-the-premises (FTTP). The project plans to reach 18 million households in 13 states by the end of 2008 and will enable the company to offer IP-based video (called U-Verse TV), expanded broadband, and VoIP services.

## HISTORY

In 1878 a dozen customers signed up for the first telephone exchange in St. Louis (later Bell Telephone Company of Missouri). That exchange and the Missouri and Kansas Telephone Company later merged into Southwestern Bell, which became a regional arm of the AT&T monopoly in 1917.

The old AT&T was broken up in 1984, and Southwestern Bell emerged as a regional Bell operating company (RBOC) with local phone service rights in five states, a cellular company, a directory business, and a stake in R&D arm Bellcore (now Telcordia). In 1987 the company bought paging and cellular franchises from Metromedia.

Edward Whitacre, a Texan who had worked his way from measuring phone wire to an executive spot at Southwestern Bell, became CEO in 1990.

That year the RBOC joined with France Telecom and Mexican conglomerate Grupo Carso to purchase 20% of Teléfonos de México (Telmex), the former state monopoly.

The company was renamed SBC Communications in 1994. The federal Telecommunications Act passed in 1996 and in early 1997 SBC acquired Pacific Telesis, the parent of Pacific Bell and Nevada Bell.

SBC bought Southern New England Telecommunications (SNET) in 1998, gaining a foothold on the East Coast. The next year the company took a minority stake in Williams Communications Group (now WilTel Communications) — the first significant investment in a long-distance carrier by a Baby Bell.

SBC completed the $62 billion purchase of Ameritech in 1999. The acquisition extended SBC's local access dominance into five Midwestern states, but about half of Ameritech's wireless business was sold as a condition of the deal. SBC agreed to provide competitive local phone service in 30 cities outside its home territory by 2002 to win regulatory approval. Also in 1999 the company announced plans to spend $6 billion over three years to make its networks capable of delivering high-speed digital subscriber line (DSL) Internet access to 80% of its customers.

In 2000 SBC combined its US wireless operations with those of BellSouth to form Cingular Wireless, a carrier with operations in 38 states. Also in 2000 the FCC approved SBC's application to sell long-distance service in Texas, and the company racked up more than a million long-distance customers in less than six months.

In 2001 SBC won approval to offer long-distance in Arkansas, Kansas, Missouri, and Oklahoma, but was fined by the FCC — it paid $69 million between December 2000 and August 2001 — for failing to meet standards for opening its local networks to competitors. The company expanded its long-distance network to include Texas and Connecticut, and entered the lucrative California market, after receiving regulatory approval on a 3-1 vote by the FCC in late 2002.

It sold its 16% stake in Bell Canada to BCE in a deal valued at $3.2 billion. It also sold stakes in international holdings, including TDC (for about $2.1 billion), and South African carrier Telkom SA. In 2004 the company sold its interest in a directory publishing partnership in Illinois and Indiana to partner R. H. Donnelley in a cash deal valued at about $1.45 billion.

SBC acquired AT&T Corp. in 2005 and took that company's more well-known name — AT&T Inc. Whitacre handed over the chief executive reins to COO Randall Stephenson in 2007.

## EXECUTIVES

**Chairman and CEO:** Randall L. Stephenson, age 47
**SEVP and CFO:** Richard G. (Rick) Lindner, age 52, $977,833 pay
**Group President, Operations Support:** John T. Stankey, age 44
**SEVP Executive Operations:** James W. (Jim) Callaway, age 60
**SEVP, External and Legislative Affairs:** James W. (Jim) Cicconi, age 54
**SEVP, IP Operations and Services:** Lea Ann Champion, age 46
**SEVP and General Counsel:** Wayne Watts, age 53
**SEVP Human Resources:** William A. (Bill) Blase Jr., age 52
**SEVP and Global Marketing Officer:** Catherine M. (Cathy) Coughlin, age 49
**EVP, Programming:** Dan York
**EVP, AT&T Entertainment Services:** Scott C. Helbing
**SVP and Secretary:** Ann Effinger Meuleman
**SVP, AT&T Worldwide Customer Service:** Chris Rooney
**SVP, Enterprise Systems and Software Engineering:** Michele M. Macauda
**SVP and Controller:** John J. Stephens, age 45
**SVP and Treasurer:** Jonathan P. Klug, age 49
**SVP, Network Integration:** Francis J. (Frank) Jules, age 50
**SVP, Network Services:** Kirk R. Brannock
**VP, Investor Relations:** Richard C. (Rich) Dietz, age 58
**President, State Legislative and Regulatory Affairs:** Robert E. Ferguson, age 45
**Group President, Global Business Services:** Richard A. (Dick) Anderson, age 47
**Group President, Regional Telecommunications and Entertainment:** Ralph de la Vega, age 55
**Group President, Corporate Strategy and Development:** Forrest E. Miller, age 54
**Group President, Diversified Businesses:** Rayford (Ray) Wilkins Jr., age 55
**Group President, Global Business Services:** Ron Spears, age 59
**Auditors:** Ernst & Young LLP

## LOCATIONS

**HQ:** AT&T Inc.
175 E. Houston, San Antonio, TX 78205
**Phone:** 210-821-4105 **Fax:** 210-351-2071
**Web:** www.att.com

## PRODUCTS/OPERATIONS

### Selected Subsidiaries and Affiliates

Illinois Bell Telephone Company (AT&T Illinois)
Indiana Bell Telephone Company, Incorporated (AT&T Indiana)
Michigan Bell Telephone Company (AT&T Michigan)
Nevada Bell Telephone Company (AT&T Nevada)
Pacific Bell Telephone Company (AT&T California)
Pacific Telesis Group (AT&T West)
Southern New England Telecommunications Corporation (AT&T East)
Southwestern Bell Telephone, L. P. (AT&T Arkansas, AT&T Kansas, AT&T Missouri, AT&T Oklahoma, AT&T Texas, AT&T Southwest)
Southwestern Bell Yellow Pages, Inc.
Sterling Commerce, Inc.
The Ohio Bell Telephone Company (AT&T Ohio)
The Southern New England Telephone Company (AT&T Connecticut)
The Woodbury Telephone Company (AT&T Woodbury)
Wisconsin Bell, Inc. (AT&T Wisconsin)

## COMPETITORS

ALLTEL
Birch
Cable & Wireless
CenturyTel
Consolidated Communications
EarthLink
Global Crossing
McLeodUSA
Qwest
Sprint Nextel
TDS Metrocom
Telephone & Data Systems
Time Warner Telecom
U.S. Cellular
Verizon

## HISTORICAL FINANCIALS

Company Type: Public

### Income Statement

FYE: December 31

| | REVENUE ($ mil.) | NET INCOME ($ mil.) | NET PROFIT MARGIN | EMPLOYEES |
|---|---|---|---|---|
| **12/06** | 63,055 | 7,356 | 11.7% | 302,000 |
| **12/05** | 43,862 | 4,786 | 10.9% | 189,000 |
| **12/04** | 40,787 | 5,887 | 14.4% | 162,000 |
| **12/03** | 40,843 | 8,505 | 20.8% | 168,000 |
| **12/02** | 43,138 | 5,653 | 13.1% | 175,400 |
| **Annual Growth** | 10.0% | 6.8% | — | 14.5% |

### 2006 Year-End Financials

Debt ratio: 43.3%
Return on equity: 8.6%
Cash ($ mil.): 2,418
Current ratio: 0.63
Long-term debt ($ mil.): 50,063
No. of shares (mil.): 6,239
Dividends
Yield: 3.7%
Payout: 70.4%
Market value ($ mil.): 223,035

### Stock History

NYSE: T

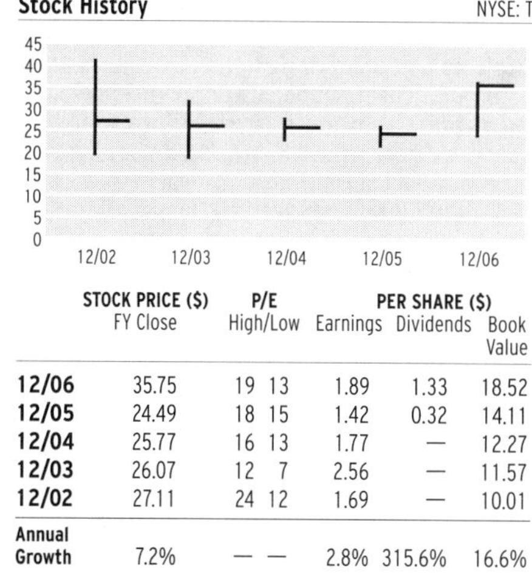


| | STOCK PRICE ($) FY Close | P/E High/Low | | PER SHARE ($) Earnings | Dividends | Book Value |
|---|---|---|---|---|---|---|
| **12/06** | 35.75 | 19 | 13 | 1.89 | 1.33 | 18.52 |
| **12/05** | 24.49 | 18 | 15 | 1.42 | 0.32 | 14.11 |
| **12/04** | 25.77 | 16 | 13 | 1.77 | — | 12.27 |
| **12/03** | 26.07 | 12 | 7 | 2.56 | — | 11.57 |
| **12/02** | 27.11 | 24 | 12 | 1.69 | — | 10.01 |
| **Annual Growth** | 7.2% | — | — | 2.8% | 315.6% | 16.6% |

# Autodesk, Inc.

Autodesk has creative designs on moving past the desks of architects. The company is a provider of computer-aided design (CAD) software. Its flagship AutoCAD product is used primarily by architects and engineers to design, draft, and model products and buildings. Autodesk's other products include geographic information systems (GIS) packages for mapping and precision drawing software for drafting. The company also develops multimedia tools for digital content creation, including applications for animation, film editing, and creating special effects. In addition, Autodesk offers professional consulting and training services.

Autodesk's customers come from such industries as manufacturing, utilities, civil engineering, and media and entertainment.

In 2005 Autodesk acquired COMPASS Systems, a data management software provider based in Germany, and Colorfront, a color correction technology developer based in Hungary. It also purchased Solid Dynamics, a France-based developer of motion simulation and analysis technology.

Autodesk completed its acquisition of 3D graphics software developer Alias Systems for $197 million in cash early in 2006. Later that year the company also purchased construction and facility project management software developer Constructware for $46 million.

## HISTORY

John Walker founded Autodesk in 1982 as a diversified PC software supplier, and when he bought the software rights to AutoCAD from inventor Michael Riddle, Autodesk took off. While competitors went after more complex computer systems, Autodesk focused on PC software. When PC sales boomed in the early 1980s, the firm was there to take advantage of a growing market. Autodesk went public in 1985.

The company established a multimedia unit and released its first animation tool, 3D Studio, in 1990. Carol Bartz, a former Sun Microsystems executive, took over as CEO in 1992. She sold off and terminated online information, advanced database networking, and other noncore projects and operations to focus on design automation. The upgraded CAD modules and complementary software fueled a return to strong sales growth. In 1993 Autodesk acquired 3D graphics specialist Ithaca Software. Walker resigned in 1994. That year Autodesk lost a trade secret lawsuit to Vermont Microsystems and was ordered to pay $25.5 million; the fine was later lowered to $7.8 million.

In 1996 the company spun off its multimedia unit as Kinetix, geared toward 3-D PC and Web applications. Continuing its acquisition drive, Autodesk bought interior decorating software developer Creative Imaging Technologies in 1996 and rival CAD software developer Softdesk in 1997.

In an effort to expand its presence in the entertainment software realm, the company bought digital video effects and editing tools maker Discreet Logic for $520 million in 1999. Later that year Autodesk bolstered its geographic information systems division by acquiring Canadian mapping software company VISION*Solutions from WorldCom for $26 million. Product delays helped prompt Autodesk that year to reorganize into four divisions, and cut 350 jobs — about 10% of its workforce.

Late in 1999 the company spun off Buzzsaw.com, an Internet portal aimed at the design and construction industry. The next year Autodesk spun off its second portal, RedSpark, targeting the manufacturing industry.

In 2001 the company re-acquired the 60% stake in Buzzsaw.com it had previously spun off. The next year Autodesk acquired architectural software provider Revit Technology for about $130 million. As part of a larger restructuring, the company also discontinued its RedSpark portal operations.

Autodesk continues to focus on leveraging its products online, targeting the manufacturing and construction industries. In 2002 the company acquired privately held CAiCE Software. With the purchase, Autodesk formed a Transportation Group to develop applications for designing highways, airports, and railroads.

The company made two small acquisitions in early 2003, both of which were absorbed within Autodesk's Manufacturing Solutions Division. Linius Technologies developed software allowing wire harness designers to develop three-dimensional prototypes. VIA Development provided electrical schematics, wire diagram, and controls engineering automation software.

## EXECUTIVES

**Chairman:** Carol A. Bartz, age 59, $1,111,667 pay (prior to title change)
**President, CEO, and Director:** Carl Bass, age 50, $1,220,833 pay (prior to promotion)
**EVP Worldwide Sales and Services:** George M. (Ken) Bado, age 53, $417,500 pay
**SVP and CFO:** Alfred J. (Al) Castino, age 55, $695,833 pay
**SVP Human Resources and Corporate Real Estate:** Jan Becker, age 54
**SVP, General Counsel, and Secretary:** Pascal W. Di Fronzo, age 43
**SVP Worldwide Marketing:** Chris Bradshaw, age 45
**SVP Manufacturing Solutions Division:** Robert (Buzz) Kross, age 53
**SVP Strategic Planning and Operations:** Moonhie K. Chin, age 49
**SVP Media and Entertainment:** Marc Petit, age 43
**SVP Platform Solutions and Emerging Business:** Amar Hanspal, age 44
**VP, Investor Relations:** Sue Pirri
**VP, Worldwide Marketing:** Tracey Stout
**CIO:** Billy Hinners
**Senior Director, Product Marketing:** Mark Strassman
**Director, Government Affairs, and Corporate Counsel:** David Crane
**Director Corporate Communications:** Caroline Kawashima
**Auditors:** Ernst & Young LLP

## LOCATIONS

**HQ:** Autodesk, Inc.
111 McInnis Pkwy., San Rafael, CA 94903
**Phone:** 415-507-5000 **Fax:** 415-507-5100
**Web:** usa.autodesk.com

Autodesk has offices in more than 30 countries.

### 2007 Sales

| | $ mil. | % of total |
|---|---|---|
| Americas | 735 | 40 |
| Europe, Middle East & Africa | 687 | 37 |
| Asia/Pacific | 418 | 23 |
| **Total** | **1,840** | **100** |

## PRODUCTS/OPERATIONS

### 2007 Sales

| | $ mil. | % of total |
|---|---|---|
| Maintenance | 424 | 23 |
| License & other | 1,416 | 77 |
| **Total** | **1,840** | **100** |

### Selected Products

Software
- Design Solutions
  - 2-D and 3-D mechanical design (Mechanical Desktop)
  - Architectural design tools (AutoCAD Architectural Desktop)
  - Computer-aided design tool (AutoCAD)
  - Geographic data analysis (Autodesk World)
  - Low-cost 2-D CAD tool (AutoCAD LT)
  - Mapmaking and engineering-based analysis (AutoCAD Map)
  - Precision drawing tool (AutoSketch)
- Discreet Products
  - 3-D modeling and animation (3ds max)
  - Digital editing (fire)
  - Online digital image processing system (inferno)
  - Online, nonlinear editing and finishing (smoke)
  - Production application for broadcast market (frost)
  - Real-time, nonlinear, digital image processing system (flame)

## COMPETITORS

Adobe
Advanced Visual Systems
Analytical Surveys
ANSYS
Apple
Avid Technology
Bentley Systems
BPO Management Services
Broadcaster
Cimatron
Dassault
Delcam
Eagle Point Software
ENOVIA MatrixOne
ESRI
Graphisoft
Intergraph
Lectra
Mentor Graphics
Moldflow
MSC.Software
NAVTEQ
Nemetschek North America
ObjectFX
Parametric Technology
Pitney Bowes MapInfo
PlanGraphics
Rand A Technology
SofTech
SolidWorks
Tele Atlas
think3
UGS Corp.
Vero International Software
Vizrt

## HISTORICAL FINANCIALS

Company Type: Public

### Income Statement

FYE: January 31

| | REVENUE ($ mil.) | NET INCOME ($ mil.) | NET PROFIT MARGIN | EMPLOYEES |
|---|---|---|---|---|
| **1/07** | 1,840 | 290 | 15.7% | 5,169 |
| **1/06** | 1,523 | 329 | 21.6% | 4,813 |
| **1/05** | 1,234 | 222 | 18.0% | 3,477 |
| **1/04** | 952 | 120 | 12.6% | 3,493 |
| **1/03** | 825 | 32 | 3.9% | 3,498 |
| **Annual Growth** | 22.2% | 73.6% | — | 10.3% |

### 2007 Year-End Financials

Debt ratio: —
Return on equity: 30.4%
Cash ($ mil.): 778
Current ratio: 2.07
Long-term debt ($ mil.): —
No. of shares (mil.): 231
Dividends
Yield: —
Payout: —
Market value ($ mil.): 10,104

### Stock History

NASDAQ (GS): ADSK

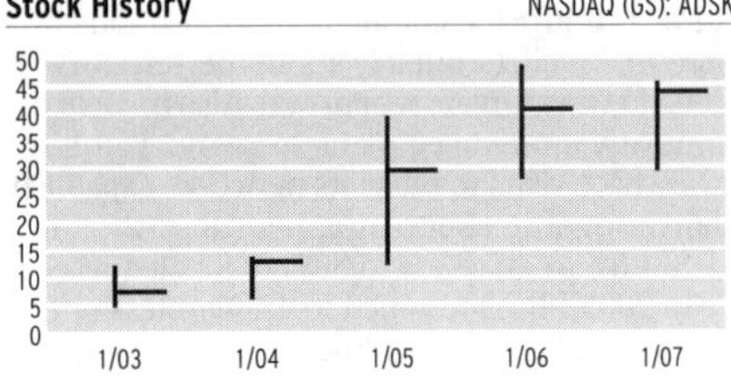


| | STOCK PRICE ($) FY Close | P/E High | P/E Low | PER SHARE ($) Earnings | Dividends | Book Value |
|---|---|---|---|---|---|---|
| **1/07** | 43.72 | 38 | 25 | 1.19 | — | 4.82 |
| **1/06** | 40.59 | 36 | 21 | 1.33 | 0.01 | 3.45 |
| **1/05** | 29.37 | 43 | 14 | 0.90 | 0.05 | 2.85 |
| **1/04** | 12.85 | 223 | 107 | 0.06 | 0.06 | 5.56 |
| **1/03** | 7.47 | 85 | 36 | 0.14 | 0.05 | 5.02 |
| **Annual Growth** | 55.5% | — | — | 70.7% | (41.5%) | (1.0%) |

# Automatic Data Processing

The original outsourcer, Automatic Data Processing (ADP) has still got it. ADP is one of the world's largest payroll and tax filing processors, serving more than 570,000 clients. Employer services account for the majority of the company's sales; ADP also provides inventory and other computing and data services to more than 25,000 auto and truck dealers. Other offerings include accounting, auto collision estimates for insurers, employment background checks, desktop applications support, and business development training services. In 2007 ADP spun off its brokerage services division (investor communications and securities transaction processing) to shareholders as Broadridge Financial Solutions.

The data processing giant's employer services segment has proven somewhat resilient in economic hard times as clients outsource more human resource functions.

ADP is expanding internationally and extending its services through acquisitions (it has purchased about three dozen established providers around the globe since 1998). ADP continues to boost its Web-based offerings and small-business services.

In 2006 the company sold its Claims Services Group (CSG) to Solera and GTCR Golder Rauner for $975 million. Later in the year, one of ADP's divisions bought Employease, a provider of Web-based human resources and benefits management software. Maintaining this software expansion strategy, in October 2006, ADP snatched up VirtualEdge, a software designer specializing in recruitment, or pre-employment, screening tools and services. The next year, ADP acquired the outsourced payroll operations of finance software provider Intuit. The deal augments ADP's customer base by 25,000.

ADP has also been concentrating on boosting its tax compliances services capabilities. In late 2006, it bought Taxware, LP (from First Data Corp.) and Mintax; both are businesses used to assist with tax calculations and related services.

## HISTORY

In 1949, 22-year-old Henry Taub started Automatic Payrolls, a manual payroll preparation service in Paterson, New Jersey. Taub's eight accounts created gross revenue of around $2,000 that year. In 1952 his brother Joe joined the company, and a childhood friend, Frank Lautenberg, took a pay cut to become its first salesman.

Automatic Payrolls grew steadily during the 1950s. In 1961 the company went public and changed its name to Automatic Data Processing (ADP). The next year it offered back-office services to brokerage houses and bought its first computer. The company's sales reached $1 million in 1962.

During the 1970s ADP bought more than 30 companies in Brazil, the UK, and the US — all involved in data and payroll processing or financial services. Its stock began trading on the NYSE in 1970. By 1971 revenue had reached $50 million. Lautenberg became CEO in 1975.

ADP bought more than 25 businesses during the 1980s in Canada, Germany, and the US. Its purchases of stock information provider GTE Telenet (1983) and Bunker Ramo's information system business (1986) brought the company 45,000 stock quote terminals in brokerages such as E.F. Hutton, Dean Witter, and Prudential-Bache. When Lautenberg resigned to become one of New Jersey's US senators in 1983, Josh Weston, who had joined the company as a VP in 1970, replaced him.

By 1985 ADP sales had climbed to $1 billion. That year Taub retired. The company installed 15,000 computer workstations at brokerages in 1986; it began installing more than 38,000 new integrated workstations at Merrill Lynch and Shearson Lehman three years later. ADP shed units, including its Canadian stock quote and Brazilian businesses, in 1989 and 1990.

After being deterred from major acquisitions by the inflated prices of the late 1980s, the company bought BankAmerica's 17,000-client Business Services division (1992) and Industry Software's back-office and international equities business (1993).

In 1994 the company purchased Peachtree Software (accounting and payroll software for small companies), National Bio Systems (medical bill auditing), and V-Crest (auto dealership management systems). ADP acquired chief rival AutoInfo and its network of 3,000 salvage yards the next year, and further expanded into Western Europe with its purchase of Paris-based computing services firm GSI.

The buying binge continued in 1996 with acquisitions including Global Proxy Services (proxy processing services), Health Benefits America (benefits management), and Merrin Financial (automated securities trade order management). Former Deloitte & Touche partner Arthur Weinbach, an ADP executive since 1980, was named CEO that year. ADP was ordered in an antitrust settlement in 1997 to help re-create AutoInfo as a viable competitor to its salvage yard business.

Among its dozen acquisitions in 1998 was Swiss Reinsurance's European collision estimates business. The company also sold its money-losing stock quote business that year to financial information provider Bridge Information Systems. Weston retired in 1998; Weinbach was named chairman. The company also filed to spin off Peachtree to the public, but in early 1999 it sold the unit to UK-based software firm The Sage Group. The buying spree continued that year; ADP's largest purchase was The Vincam Group, an employment management contractor, for about $295 million.

In 2000 the company acquired Cunningham Graphics, a provider of printing services to the financial services industry, and Traver Technologies, which offers consulting and training services to automobile dealers in the US. The following year it acquired Avert, a provider of employment screening services, and the output services business of IBM Global Services, specializing in printing and distributing communications for the financial services industry. In 2003 the company bought ProBusiness Services, a payroll and human resource processing service provider, for about $500 million. The next year ADP purchased EDS's Automotive Retail Group, a provider of dealer management systems, as well as ProQuest Business Solutions' DMS business.

In August 2006, Weinbach retired as chairman and CEO, and former president and COO Gary Butler was elevated to top executive at that time. The same year, ADP sold its Claims Services Group (CSG) to Solera and GTCR Golder Rauner for $975 million.

## EXECUTIVES

**Chairman:** Arthur F. Weinbach, age 63, $3,497,500 pay (prior to title change)
**President, CEO, and Director:** Gary C. Butler, age 60, $1,596,254 pay (prior to promotion)
**CFO:** Christopher R. (Chris) Reidy, age 49
**EVP and Group President, Brokerage Services, Securities Clearing & Outsourcing Services, Dealer Services, and Claims Services:** James D. (Jim) Aramanda, age 54
**VP and Treasurer:** Raymond L. Colotti, age 60
**VP, General Counsel, and Secretary:** James B. Benson, age 61
**VP, Strategic Development:** Jan Siegmund, age 42
**Group President, ADP Brokerage Services:** John P. Hogan, age 58, $725,553 pay
**Group President, ADP Brokerage Services:** Richard J. Daly, age 53, $710,753 pay
**Group President, Employer Services:** S. Michael Martone, age 58, $954,672 pay
**President, ADP TotalSource Group:** Carlos A. Rodriguez
**President, Claims Solutions Group:** Janice M. Colby, age 51
**President, Clearing & Outsourcing Services:** Joe Barra
**President, Dealer Services:** Steven J. Anenen, age 53
**President, Employer Services, International:** George I. Stoeckert, age 58
**President, National Accounts:** Regina Lee
**President, Tax, Retirement and Pre-Employment Services:** Campbell B. Langdon, age 45
**Managing Director of Global Relationship Management, ADP Brokerage Services:** Jeffrey H. Smith
**Public Relations:** Terry Corallo
**Corporate Controller and Principal Accounting Officer:** Alan Sheiness, age 49
**Auditors:** Deloitte & Touche LLP

## LOCATIONS

**HQ:** Automatic Data Processing, Inc.
1 ADP Blvd., Roseland, NJ 07068
**Phone:** 973-974-5000 **Fax:** 973-974-3334
**Web:** www.adp.com

Automatic Data Processing has locations in Asia, Australia, Canada, Europe, South America, and the US.

### 2006 Sales

| | $ mil. | % of total |
|---|---|---|
| US | 7,437.7 | 84 |
| Europe | 844.6 | 10 |
| Canada | 477.1 | 5 |
| Other | 122.1 | 1 |
| **Total** | **8,881.5** | **100** |

## PRODUCTS/OPERATIONS

### 2006 Sales

| | $ mil. | % of total |
|---|---|---|
| Employer services | 5,763.4 | 65 |
| Brokerage services | 1,852.8 | 21 |
| Dealer services | 1,132.4 | 13 |
| Securities Clearing & Outsourcing Services | 80.6 | — |
| Other | 109.1 | 1 |
| Adjustment | (56.8) | — |
| **Total** | **8,881.5** | **100** |

### Selected Services

Dealer Services
- Business management
- Computer systems sales
- Employee productivity training
- Hardware maintenance
- Manufacturer and dealer data communications networks
- Software licensing and support
- Vehicle registration services

Employer Services
- 401(k) record keeping and reporting
- Benefits administration and outsourcing
- Employment screening and background checks
- Human resource record keeping and reporting
- Payroll processing
- Tax filing
- Unemployment compensation management

## COMPETITORS

Administaff
CBIZ
Ceridian
Computer Sciences Corp.
DST
EDS
First Data
Fiserv
Gevity HR
Hewitt Associates
Intuit
Paychex
Reynolds and Reynolds
SunGard
Total System Services

## HISTORICAL FINANCIALS

Company Type: Public

### Income Statement

FYE: June 30

| | REVENUE ($ mil.) | NET INCOME ($ mil.) | NET PROFIT MARGIN | EMPLOYEES |
|---|---|---|---|---|
| **6/06** | 8,882 | 1,554 | 17.5% | 46,000 |
| **6/05** | 8,499 | 1,055 | 12.4% | 44,000 |
| **6/04** | 7,755 | 936 | 12.1% | 42,000 |
| **6/03** | 7,147 | 1,018 | 14.2% | 41,000 |
| **6/02** | 7,004 | 1,101 | 15.7% | 40,000 |
| **Annual Growth** | 6.1% | 9.0% | — | 3.6% |

### 2006 Year-End Financials

Debt ratio: 297.1%
Return on equity: 26.3%
Cash ($ mil.): 2,269
Current ratio: 1.84
Long-term debt ($ mil.): 17,862
No. of shares (mil.): 561
Dividends
Yield: 1.7%
Payout: 26.5%
Market value ($ mil.): 23,198

### Stock History

NYSE: ADP

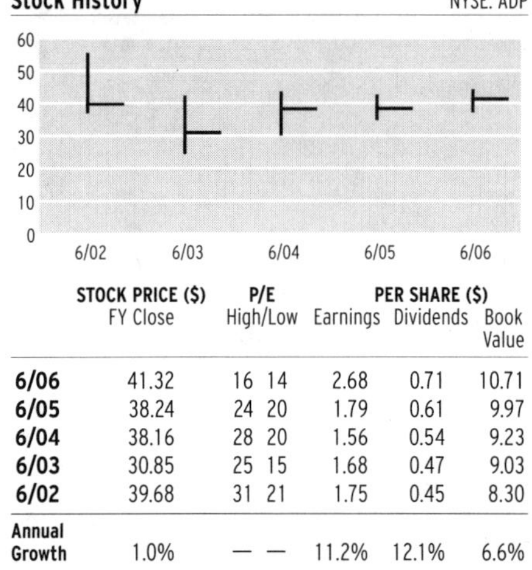


| | STOCK PRICE ($) FY Close | P/E High/Low | | PER SHARE ($) Earnings | Dividends | Book Value |
|---|---|---|---|---|---|---|
| **6/06** | 41.32 | 16 | 14 | 2.68 | 0.71 | 10.71 |
| **6/05** | 38.24 | 24 | 20 | 1.79 | 0.61 | 9.97 |
| **6/04** | 38.16 | 28 | 20 | 1.56 | 0.54 | 9.23 |
| **6/03** | 30.85 | 25 | 15 | 1.68 | 0.47 | 9.03 |
| **6/02** | 39.68 | 31 | 21 | 1.75 | 0.45 | 8.30 |
| **Annual Growth** | 1.0% | — | — | 11.2% | 12.1% | 6.6% |

# AutoNation

AutoNation wants to instill patriotic fervor in the fickle car-buying public. Brainchild of entrepreneur and former chairman Wayne Huizenga (Waste Management, Blockbuster Video), AutoNation is the largest car dealer in the US. It owns about 330 new vehicle franchises in more than 15 states and offers no-haggle sales policies and online sales through AutoNation.com and individual dealer Web sites.

In addition to auto sales, AutoNation (formerly known as Republic Industries) provides maintenance and repair services, sells auto parts, and finances and insures vehicles. ESL Investments, whose CEO, Edward Lampert, and president, William Crowley, are AutoNation directors, owns more than 29% of the company.

AutoNation has been a driving force in the consolidation of the US car-sales business. It clusters dealerships within markets so that they can share inventory, cross-sell to customers, and reduce marketing costs — basically cutting and combining costs in an attempt to become the auto industry's Wal-Mart.

AutoNation had been in the acquisition fast lane, but it has slowed down and is shedding more stores than it is buying. It hasn't stepped off the gas, however, on the AutoNation.com Web site, which lists tens of thousands of cars at any given time. Regionally, the company has developed brand loyalty by uniting its bricks-and-mortar operations under local brand names as it has done with the John Elway AutoNation group in Denver and the AutoWay dealerships in Tampa Bay.

## HISTORY

AutoNation started in 1980 as Republic Resources, which brokered petroleum leases, did exploration and production, and blended lubricants. In 1989, after oil prices crashed and a stockholder group tried to force Republic into liquidation, Browning-Ferris Industries (BFI) founder Thomas Fatjo gained control of the company and refocused it on a field he knew well — solid waste. He renamed the firm Republic Waste.

Michael DeGroote, founder of BFI rival Laidlaw, bought into Republic in 1990. (Fatjo left the next year.) DeGroote's investment funded more acquisitions. Republic moved into hazardous waste in 1992, just before the industry nosedived due to stringent new environmental rules. In 1994 Republic spun off its hazardous-waste operations as Republic Environmental Systems, and Republic's stock began rising immediately.

That attracted the attention of Wayne Huizenga, who had founded Waste Management and Blockbuster Video. To him, Republic was not merely a midsized solid-waste firm. No, Huizenga saw Republic as a publicly traded vehicle that could allow him to tap into the stock market to fund his latest project: an integrated, nationwide auto dealer — a first for the highly fragmented and localized industry.

In 1995 Republic bought Hudson Management, a trash business owned by Huizenga's brother-in-law, and Huizenga bought a large interest in Republic. As a result, Huizenga took control of Republic's board. The firm became Republic Industries, and DeGroote stepped back from active management.

Huizenga's investment helped Republic acquire more waste businesses, and his name brought a flood of new investors. The firm diversified with electronic security acquisitions, but growth in this field faltered with a failed bid to buy market leader ADT in 1996. (Republic sold its security division to Ameritech in 1997.)

By 1996 Huizenga's still-separate auto concept, AutoNation, was operational, with 55 automobile franchises and seven used-car stores. Republic bought Alamo Rent A Car and National Car Rental System, and in 1997 AutoNation was bought by Republic. The combined company continued buying dealerships and car rental firms at a sizzling rate.

Republic spun off its solid-waste operations to the public in 1998 as Republic Services. That year Republic bought or agreed to buy 181 new-car franchises, opened nine AutoNation USA dealerships, and opened 62 CarTemps USA insurance-replacement locations.

Republic became AutoNation in 1999 and announced plans to spin off its rental division. In September 1999 Mike Jackson, the former president and CEO of Mercedes-Benz USA, was named CEO of AutoNation. In December the company closed most of its poorly performing used-car superstores and laid off about 1,800 employees.

In May 2000 AutoNation acquired AutoVantage, an online car-buying service linking over 900 dealerships, and inked a deal to be America Online's (now a division of Time Warner) exclusive auto retailer. Later the company completed its spinoff of ANC Rental (Alamo, National, and CarTemps, with more than 3,400 rental car locations worldwide), making AutoNation a pure-play auto retailer.

Due to guarantees related to the spinoff, AutoNation took a $20 million charge after ANC Rental filed for Chapter 11 bankruptcy protection in 2001. Also that year AutoNation closed its auto-loan unit to further focus on car sales. Huizenga retired as chairman of the company at the end of 2002. Jackson assumed the chairmanship while continuing in his role as CEO.

In March 2003 AutoNation agreed to pay the IRS about $470 million in relation to the tax treatment of some 1997-1999 transactions. It bought a dealership that accounts for some 10% of Mercedes-Benz USA sales, Glauser Mercedes-Benz in Sarasota, Florida, in May 2004. The dealership is now called Mercedes-Benz of Sarasota.

## EXECUTIVES

**Chairman and CEO:** Michael J. (Mike) Jackson, age 58, $1,150,000 pay
**President, COO, and Director:** Michael E. (Mike) Maroone, age 53, $1,000,000 pay
**EVP and CFO:** Michael J. (Mike) Short, age 45
**EVP, Secretary, and General Counsel:** Jonathan P. Ferrando, age 41, $561,000 pay
**SVP, Corporate Development:** Alan T. Haig
**SVP, eCommerce:** Gary Marcotte
**SVP, Sales:** Kevin P. Westfall, age 51, $450,000 pay
**SVP, Corporate Communications:** Marc Cannon
**SVP, Regional Operations and Industry Relations:** Donna Parlapiano
**VP, Human Resources:** Julie Staub
**VP, Investor Relations:** John M. Zimmerman
**VP, IT:** Joyce Vonada
**VP, Media Services:** Ed Cicale
**VP and Treasurer:** James J. Teufel
**VP and Corporate Controller:** Michael J. Stephan, age 44
**President, California Region:** Jerry Heuer
**President, East Central Region:** Hank Phillips
**President, Florida Region:** James (Jim) Bender
**President, Texas Region:** Dan Agnew
**President, West Central Region:** Todd Maul
**Auditors:** KPMG LLP

## LOCATIONS

**HQ:** AutoNation, Inc.
110 SE 6th St., Fort Lauderdale, FL 33301
**Phone:** 954-769-6000 **Fax:** 954-769-6537
**Web:** corp.autonation.com

AutoNation has about 330 new-car franchises in Alabama, Arizona, California, Colorado, Florida, Georgia, Illinois, Maryland, Minnesota, North Carolina, Nevada, New York, Ohio, Tennessee, Texas, Virginia, Washington.

## PRODUCTS/OPERATIONS

### 2006 Sales

| | $ mil. | % of total |
|---|---|---|
| New vehicle | 11,163 | 59 |
| Used vehicle | 4,518.1 | 24 |
| Parts and service | 2,600.4 | 14 |
| Finance & insurance | 634.3 | 3 |
| Other | 72.8 | — |
| **Total** | **18,988.6** | **100** |

### Primary Operations

AutoNation.com (Internet sales)
Franchised vehicle dealerships

## COMPETITORS

| | |
|---|---|
| Asbury Automotive | JM Family Enterprises |
| Bill Heard | Morse Operations |
| Brown Automotive | Penske Automotive |
| Burt Automotive | Potamkin Automotive |
| CarMax | Sixt |
| Group 1 Automotive | Sonic Automotive |
| Hendrick Automotive | United Auto Group |
| Holman Enterprises | VT Inc. |

## HISTORICAL FINANCIALS

Company Type: Public

**Income Statement** FYE: December 31

| | REVENUE ($ mil.) | NET INCOME ($ mil.) | NET PROFIT MARGIN | EMPLOYEES |
|---|---|---|---|---|
| **12/06** | 18,989 | 317 | 1.7% | 26,000 |
| **12/05** | 19,253 | 497 | 2.6% | 27,000 |
| **12/04** | 19,425 | 434 | 2.2% | 27,000 |
| **12/03** | 19,381 | 479 | 2.5% | 28,000 |
| **12/02** | 19,479 | 382 | 2.0% | 28,500 |
| **Annual Growth** | (0.6%) | (4.5%) | — | (2.3%) |

**2006 Year-End Financials**

| | |
|---|---|
| Debt ratio: 42.0% | No. of shares (mil.): 207 |
| Return on equity: 7.6% | Dividends |
| Cash ($ mil.): 52 | Yield: — |
| Current ratio: 1.12 | Payout: — |
| Long-term debt ($ mil.): 1,558 | Market value ($ mil.): 4,408 |

**Stock History** NYSE: AN

| | STOCK PRICE ($) FY Close | P/E High | P/E Low | PER SHARE ($) Earnings | Dividends | Book Value |
|---|---|---|---|---|---|---|
| **12/06** | 21.32 | 17 | 14 | 1.38 | — | 17.96 |
| **12/05** | 21.73 | 12 | 10 | 1.85 | — | 17.81 |
| **12/04** | 19.21 | 12 | 9 | 1.59 | — | 16.13 |
| **12/03** | 18.37 | 11 | 7 | 1.67 | — | 14.64 |
| **12/02** | 12.56 | 16 | 8 | 1.19 | — | 13.12 |
| **Annual Growth** | 14.1% | — | — | 3.8% | — | 8.2% |

# AutoZone

Imagine that you are in your garage making some weekend car repairs. The wheel cylinders are leaking . . . the brake shoe adjuster nut is rusted solid . . . you're about to enter . . . the AutoZone. With some 4,000 stores in the US, AutoZone is the nation's #1 auto parts chain and has made inroads abroad with about 100 stores are located in Mexico and Puerto Rico. AutoZone stores sell hard parts (alternators, engines, batteries), maintenance items (oil, antifreeze), accessories (car stereos, floor mats), and other merchandise under brand names as well as under private labels, including Duralast and Valucraft. It also loans tools. ESL Partners, controlled by Edward S. Lampert, owns nearly 33% of the company.

In December 2006, Lampert stepped down from AutoZone's board sparking speculation that ESL might sell its stake in the company. However, Lampert has said that ESL plans to remain a significant shareholder in AutoZone for the foreseeable future. Minority shareholders in the company include investment firms Pzena Investment Management and D.E. Shaw & Co.

In addition to auto parts, AutoZone stores also offer diagnostic testing for starters, alternators, and batteries. They do not sell tires or perform general auto repairs. More than 60% of AutoZone's stores serve professional auto repair shops. AutoZone's ALLDATA unit sells automotive diagnostic and repair software.

AutoZone has grown quickly through a series of acquisitions over the past several years but now is focused on internal growth and development. Among the factors AutoZone considers when opening new stores — at a rate of 150 to 200 per year — is how many cars in an area are OKVs or "our kind of vehicle," that is, cars older than seven years and no longer under their manufacturers' warranty. AutoZone is also growing in Mexico, where cars are even older — and in need of more repairs — than in the US.

## HISTORY

Joseph "Pitt" Hyde took over the family grocery wholesale business, Malone & Hyde (established 1907) in 1968. He expanded into specialty retailing, opening drugstores, sporting goods stores, and supermarkets, but his fortunes began to race on Independence Day 1979, when he opened his first Auto Shack auto parts store in Forrest City, Arkansas.

Using retailing behemoth Wal-Mart as a model, Hyde concentrated on smaller markets in the South and Southeast, emphasizing everyday low prices and centralized distribution operations. He stressed customer service to provide his do-it-yourself customers with expert advice on choosing parts. While a number of retailers have tried to copy Wal-Mart's successful model, Hyde had an inside track: Before starting Auto Shack he served on Wal-Mart's board for seven years.

Auto Shack had expanded into seven states by 1980, and by 1983 it had 129 stores in 10 states. The next year Malone & Hyde's senior management, with investment firm Kohlberg Kravis Roberts (KKR), took the company private in an LBO. Auto Shack continued to expand, reaching 192 stores in 1984.

A year later Auto Shack introduced its Express Parts Service, the first service in the industry to offer a toll-free number and overnight delivery of parts. The following year it introduced another first: a limited lifetime warranty on its merchandise. Also in 1986 Auto Shack introduced its own Duralast line of auto products.

The company was spun off to Malone & Hyde's shareholders in 1987, and Malone & Hyde's other operations were sold. Auto Shack brought its electronic parts catalog online that year. The company changed its name to AutoZone in 1987, in part to settle a lawsuit with RadioShack. By this time it had 390 stores in 15 states.

The company went public in 1991. By the end of that year, it had nearly 600 stores and five distribution centers. The company topped $1 billion in sales in 1992. The next year it opened new distribution centers in Illinois and Tennessee and closed its Memphis operation.

AutoZone began selling to commercial customers such as service stations and repair shops in 1996. It also acquired auto diagnostic software company ALLDATA. Hyde stepped down as CEO that year and as chairman in 1997 and was replaced by COO Johnston (John) Adams.

The company made several key purchases in 1998. It acquired Chief Auto Parts for $280 million, adding 560 stores (most in California) that were converted to AutoZones in 1999. It also purchased Adap and its 112 Auto Palace stores in the Northeast, heavy-duty truck parts distributor TruckPro, and (from Pep Boys) 100 Express stores. Also in 1998 AutoZone opened its first store in Mexico (Nuevo Laredo).

Hyde sold much of his stake by early 1999. Late that year AutoZone expanded its board of directors to 10 members, making room for increasingly active longtime shareholder Edward Lampert.

In January 2001 Steve Odland, formerly COO at supermarket retailer Ahold USA, succeeded Adams as chairman and CEO. In December 2001 AutoZone sold its TruckPro subsidiary to an investor group led by Paratus Capital Management of Boston and New York.

Odland resigned in 2005 to become CEO of Office Depot. He was replaced by Bill Rhodes, AutoZone's former EVP for store operations.

## EXECUTIVES

**Chairman, President, and CEO:** William C. (Bill) Rhodes III, age 41
**EVP Information Technology and Store Development, CFO, and Treasurer:** William T. (Bill) Giles, age 47
**EVP Merchandising, Marketing, and Supply Chain:** James (Jim) Shea, age 61
**EVP Retail Operations, Commercial Operations, and Mexico:** Robert D. (Bob) Olsen, age 53
**EVP, Secretary, and General Counsel:** Harry L. Goldsmith, age 55, $539,476 pay
**SVP Human Resources:** Timothy W. Briggs, age 45
**SVP Marketing:** Lisa R. Kranc, age 53
**SVP Supply Chain:** William W. Graves, age 46
**SVP and Controller:** Charlie Pleas III, age 41
**SVP Store Operations:** Thomas B. Newbern
**SVP Commercial:** Larry Roesel
**VP, Assistant General Counsel, and Assistant Secretary:** Rebecca W. Ballou
**VP and Chief Information Officer:** Kenneth L. Brame
**VP, Assistant General Counsel, and Assistant Secretary:** Diana H. Hull
**VP Goverment and Community Relations:** Raymond A. Pohlman
**VP Information Technology:** Jon A. Bascom
**VP Investor Relations and Tax:** Brian L. Campbell
**VP Marketing:** Jose E. Marrero
**VP Marketing:** Brett L. Shanaman
**Auditors:** Ernst & Young LLP

## LOCATIONS

**HQ:** AutoZone, Inc.
123 S. Front St., Memphis, TN 38103
**Phone:** 901-495-6500 **Fax:** 901-495-8300
**Web:** www.autozone.com

**2006 Stores**

| | No. |
|---|---|
| US | |
| Texas | 457 |
| California | 418 |
| Ohio | 203 |
| Illinois | 180 |
| Florida | 170 |
| Georgia | 149 |
| Tennessee | 138 |
| North Carolina | 136 |
| Michigan | 132 |
| Indiana | 120 |
| New York | 111 |
| Arizona | 105 |
| Pennsylvania | 93 |
| Alabama | 88 |
| Missouri | 88 |
| Louisiana | 86 |
| Virginia | 78 |
| Mississippi | 76 |
| Kentucky | 71 |
| Massachusetts | 66 |
| Oklahoma | 66 |
| South Carolina | 61 |
| Arkansas | 55 |
| Colorado | 54 |
| New Mexico | 52 |
| New Jersey | 50 |
| Wisconsin | 48 |
| Nevada | 40 |
| Washington | 39 |
| Kansas | 37 |
| Maryland | 37 |
| Utah | 34 |
| Connecticut | 29 |
| Oregon | 25 |
| Other states | 179 |
| Mexico | 100 |
| **Total** | **3,871** |

## PRODUCTS/OPERATIONS

**Selected Merchandise**

Accessories
- Car stereos
- Floor mats
- Lights
- Mirrors

Hard Parts
- Alternators
- Batteries
- Brake shoes and pads
- Carburetors
- Clutches
- Engines
- Spark plugs
- Starters
- Struts
- Water pumps

Maintenance Items
- Antifreeze
- Brake fluid
- Engine additives
- Oil
- Power steering fluid
- Transmission fluid
- Waxes
- Windshield wipers

Other
- Air fresheners
- Dent filler
- Hand cleaner
- Paint
- Repair manuals
- Tools

**Selected Brands**

AutoZone
Duralast
Duralast Gold
Valucraft

## COMPETITORS

Advance Auto Parts
CARQUEST
Costco Wholesale
CSK Auto
Fisher Auto Parts
Genuine Parts
Goodyear
Kmart
O'Reilly Automotive
Pep Boys
Sears
Target
Wal-Mart

## HISTORICAL FINANCIALS

Company Type: Public

**Income Statement** FYE: Last Saturday in August

| | REVENUE ($ mil.) | NET INCOME ($ mil.) | NET PROFIT MARGIN | EMPLOYEES |
|---|---|---|---|---|
| **8/06** | 5,948 | 569 | 9.6% | 53,000 |
| **8/05** | 5,711 | 571 | 10.0% | 52,000 |
| **8/04** | 5,637 | 566 | 10.0% | 49,000 |
| **8/03** | 5,457 | 518 | 9.5% | 47,727 |
| **8/02** | 5,326 | 428 | 8.0% | 44,179 |
| **Annual Growth** | 2.8% | 7.4% | — | 4.7% |

**2006 Year-End Financials**

Debt ratio: 395.5%
Return on equity: 132.3%
Cash ($ mil.): 92
Current ratio: 1.03
Long-term debt ($ mil.): 1,857
No. of shares (mil.): 71
Dividends
Yield: —
Payout: —
Market value ($ mil.): 6,199

**Stock History** NYSE: AZO

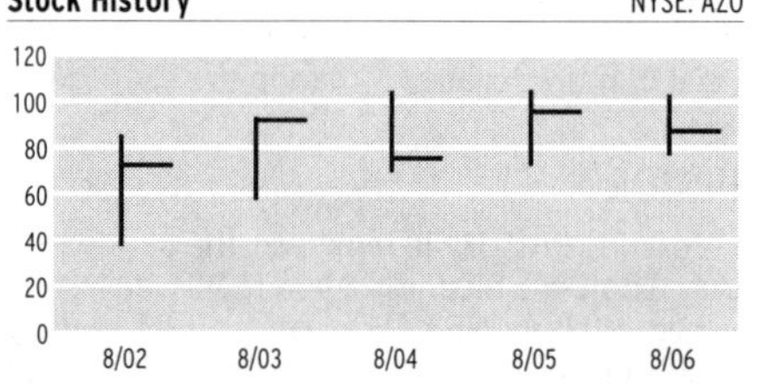


| | STOCK PRICE ($) FY Close | P/E High/Low | PER SHARE ($) Earnings | Dividends | Book Value |
|---|---|---|---|---|---|
| **8/06** | 87.21 | 14 10 | 7.50 | — | 6.61 |
| **8/05** | 95.45 | 14 10 | 7.18 | — | 5.10 |
| **8/04** | 75.36 | 16 11 | 6.56 | — | 2.15 |
| **8/03** | 91.80 | 17 11 | 5.34 | — | 4.21 |
| **8/02** | 72.35 | 21 10 | 4.00 | — | 6.94 |
| **Annual Growth** | 4.8% | — — | 17.0% | — | (1.2%) |

# Avery Dennison

Avery Dennison is easy to label: It's a global leader in the making of adhesive labels used on packaging, mailers, and other items. Pressure-sensitive adhesives and materials account for more than half of the company's sales. Under the Avery Dennison and Fasson brands, the company makes papers, films, and foils coated with adhesive and sold in rolls to printers. The company also makes school and office products (Avery, Marks-A-Lot, HI-LITER) such as notebooks, three-ring binders, markers, fasteners, business forms, tickets, tags, and imprinting equipment. Perhaps its most widely used products are the self-adhesive stamps used by the US Postal Service since 1974.

The company, which operates manufacturing facilities and sales offices around the world, has been expanding its international operations through acquisitions, especially into China. The expansion has benefitted the company to such an extent that Avery Dennison's international sales exceeded its sales in the US each of the past three years.

The company has partnered with Microsoft to co-brand Avery Digital Photo Paper with Microsoft's Picture It! software — the package combines software and photo-quality printing paper products.

In 2007 the company made a major move to expand its Retail Information Services unit, which offers products and services to retailers designing and producing labels and tags as well as supply-chain management services. Avery Dennison bought Paxar, whose strength in the European market greatly enhances Avery Dennison's own, mostly US business, for $1.3 billion.

## HISTORY

Avery Dennison was created in 1990 by the merger of Avery International and Dennison Manufacturing. In 1935 Stanton Avery founded Kum-Kleen Products, which would become Avery International. After a fire destroyed the plant's equipment in 1938, Avery, who had renamed the company Avery Adhesives, improved the machinery used in making the labels.

During and after WWII, Avery Adhesives shifted toward the industrial market for self-adhesives. The company incorporated in 1946. At that time Avery Adhesives sold 80% of its production, consisting of industrial labels, to manufacturers that labeled their own products.

The company lost its patent rights for self-adhesive labels in 1952, transforming the firm and the entire industry. As a result, a new division was created — the Avery Paper Company (later renamed Fasson) — to produce and market self-adhesive base materials.

Avery Adhesives went public in 1961. Three years later it had four divisions: label products, base materials, Rotex (hand-operated embossing machines), and Metal-Cal (anodized and etched aluminum foil for nameplates). Renamed Avery International in 1976, the company closed some manufacturing facilities and cut 8% of its workforce in the late 1980s.

In 1990 Avery International merged with Dennison Manufacturing. Dennison was started in 1844 by the father-and-son team of Andrew and Aaron Dennison to produce jewelry boxes. By 1849 Aaron's younger brother, Eliphalet Whorf (E. W.), was running the business and expanding it into tags, labels, and tissue paper. Dennison was incorporated in 1878 with $150,000 in capital.

By 1911 Dennison sold tags, gummed labels, paper boxes, greeting cards, sealing wax, and tissue paper, and it had stores in Boston, Chicago, New York City, Philadelphia, St. Louis, and London. Henry Dennison, E. W.'s grandson, was president from 1917 to 1952.

From the 1960s to the 1980s, Dennison spent heavily on research and development and helped to develop such products as electronic printers and pregnancy test supplies. In the mid-1980s the firm reorganized its operations, selling seven businesses, closing four others, and focusing on stationery, systems, and packaging.

In addition to office products and product identification and control systems, the 1990 merger combined Dennison's office products operations in France (Doret and Cheval Ordex) with Avery International's sizable self-adhesive base materials business.

Avery Dennison sold its 50% interest in a Japanese label converting company, Toppan, in 1996, clearing the way to develop its own businesses in Asia. In 1997 an alliance with Taiwanese rival Four Pillars turned sour when Avery Dennison accused the company of stealing trade secrets. (Two executives at Four Pillars were convicted of espionage in 1999.)

President and COO Philip Neal was promoted to CEO in 1998. (He became chairman in 2000.) In 1999, adhering to its goal of global expansion, Avery Dennison formed office products joint ventures in Germany with Zweckform Buro-Produkte and in Japan with Hitachi Maxell. Record 1998 sales and earnings were dampened by the news of slowing growth, and in 1999 Avery Dennison closed five plants and began laying off workers. Later that year the company bought Stimsonite, a maker of reflective highway safety products.

In early 2000 Avery Dennison began a $40 million expansion of its Chinese manufacturing operations while eliminating 1,500 jobs worldwide. Later in the year the company agreed to jointly package instant imaging and labeling products with Polaroid. Several acquisitions in 2001 included CD Stomper (CD and DVD labels and software). Avery Dennison continued its acquisitive ways in 2002, acquiring Jackstadt (German maker of pressure-sensitive adhesive materials), RVL Packaging (maker of woven and printed labels and other tags for the apparel and retail industries), and L&E Packaging (key supplier and printer for RVL).

In 2003 the company sold its European package label converting business (including plants in Denmark and France) to label and packaging company CCL Industries. As part of the deal, Avery Dennison began to supply pressure-sensitive base materials to CCL Industries. The divestiture was part of the company's strategy to concentrate its efforts in adhesive materials, office products, and retail information services.

Phillip Neal retired as chairman and CEO in 2005 and was replaced by director Kent Kresa as chairman and by Dean Scarborough as president and CEO.

## EXECUTIVES

**Chairman:** Kent Kresa, age 70
**President, CEO, and Director:** Dean A. Scarborough, age 51, $1,971,000 pay
**EVP, General Counsel and Secretary:** Robert G. van Schoonenberg, age 60, $1,072,683 pay
**EVP Finance and CFO:** Daniel R. O'Bryant, age 49, $1,025,067 pay
**SVP Corporate Strategy and Technology:** Robert M. Malchione, age 49, $857,992 pay
**SVP Worldwide Communications and Advertising:** Diane B. Dixon, age 55
**SVP Human Resources:** J. Terry Schuler
**SVP and Chief Human Resources Officer:** Anne Hill, age 45
**Group VP Roll Materials Worldwide:** Christian A. Simcic, $819,675 pay
**VP and CIO:** Kenneth A. Wolinsky
**VP and CTO:** David N. Edwards
**VP and Treasurer:** Karyn E. Rodriguez, age 47
**VP Global Operations:** Stephen A. Mynott
**VP Internal Audit and Tax:** Ahmed Rubaie
**VP and General Counsel:** Susan C. Miller
**Media Relations:** Laurence J. Dwyer
**Investor Relations:** Cynthia S. Guenther
**Auditors:** PricewaterhouseCoopers LLP

## LOCATIONS

**HQ:** Avery Dennison Corporation
150 N. Orange Grove Blvd., Pasadena, CA 91103
**Phone:** 626-304-2000 **Fax:** 626-792-7312
**Web:** www.averydennison.com

Avery Dennison operates about 120 manufacturing and distribution facilities in more than 40 countries; it sells its products in more than 85 countries.

### 2006 Sales

| | $ mil. | % of total |
|---|---|---|
| US | 2,333.8 | 42 |
| Europe | 1,798.8 | 32 |
| Asia | 748.7 | 13 |
| Latin America | 332.4 | 6 |
| Other regions | 362.2 | 7 |
| **Total** | **5,575.9** | **100** |

## PRODUCTS/OPERATIONS

### 2006 Sales and Operating Income

| | Sales $ mil. | Sales % of total | Operating Income $ mil. | Operating Income % of total |
|---|---|---|---|---|
| Pressure-sensitive Materials | 3,236.3 | 58 | 301.2 | 56 |
| Office & Consumer Products | 1,072.0 | 19 | 179.0 | 33 |
| Retail Information Services | 667.7 | 12 | 45.0 | 8 |
| Other specialty converting businesses | 599.9 | 11 | 17.2 | 3 |
| Adjustments | — | — | (116.8) | — |
| **Total** | **5,575.9** | **100** | **425.6** | **100** |

### Selected Products

Pressure-Sensitive Adhesives and Materials
- Base materials
  - Paper and film materials
  - Pressure-sensitive coated papers, films, and foils
  - Proprietary film face materials
- Graphic products
  - Durable cast and reflective films
  - Metallic dispersion products
  - Proprietary woodgrain film laminates
  - Specialty print-receptive films
- Performance polymers products
  - Solvent- and emulsion-based acrylic polymer adhesives, top coats, protective coatings
- Specialty tape products
  - Single- and double-coated tapes and transfer adhesives

Consumer and Converted Products
- Binder and presentation dividers
- Computer software
- Custom label products (pressure-sensitive and heat-seal labels)
- Ink-jet and laser print card and index products
- Label machines (imprinting, dispensing, attaching)
- Labels (copier, data processing, ink-jet, and laser printer)
- Markers and highlighters
- Presentation and organizing systems
- Self-adhesive battery labels and postage stamps
- Sheet protectors
- Tags (graphic and bar-coded tags)
- Three-ring binders

### Selected Brands

Avery
Avery Dennison
Fasson
HI-LITER
Index Maker
Marks-A-Lot
Stabilo
Zweckform

## COMPETITORS

3M
Bemis
Bostik
Brady
Esselte
Fortune Brands
H.B. Fuller
Newell Rubbermaid
Standard Register
UPM-Kymmene

## HISTORICAL FINANCIALS

Company Type: Public

### Income Statement

FYE: Saturday nearest December 31

| | REVENUE ($ mil.) | NET INCOME ($ mil.) | NET PROFIT MARGIN | EMPLOYEES |
|---|---|---|---|---|
| **12/06** | 5,576 | 367 | 6.6% | 22,700 |
| **12/05** | 5,474 | 226 | 4.1% | 22,600 |
| **12/04** | 5,341 | 280 | 5.2% | 21,400 |
| **12/03** | 4,763 | 268 | 5.6% | 20,300 |
| **12/02** | 4,207 | 257 | 6.1% | 20,500 |
| **Annual Growth** | 7.3% | 9.3% | — | 2.6% |

### 2006 Year-End Financials

Debt ratio: 29.8%
Return on equity: 23.0%
Cash ($ mil.): 59
Current ratio: 0.97
Long-term debt ($ mil.): 502
No. of shares (mil.): 98
Dividends
Yield: 2.3%
Payout: 42.9%
Market value ($ mil.): 6,678

### Stock History

NYSE: AVY

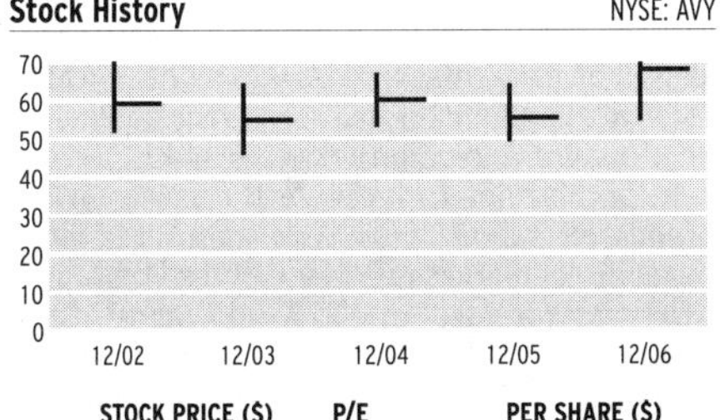


| | STOCK PRICE ($) FY Close | P/E High | P/E Low | PER SHARE ($) Earnings | PER SHARE ($) Dividends | PER SHARE ($) Book Value |
|---|---|---|---|---|---|---|
| **12/06** | 67.93 | 19 | 15 | 3.66 | 1.57 | 17.09 |
| **12/05** | 55.27 | 28 | 22 | 2.25 | 1.53 | 15.16 |
| **12/04** | 59.97 | 24 | 19 | 2.78 | 1.49 | 15.47 |
| **12/03** | 54.71 | 24 | 17 | 2.68 | 1.45 | 13.24 |
| **12/02** | 59.05 | 27 | 20 | 2.59 | 1.35 | 10.64 |
| **Annual Growth** | 3.6% | — | — | 9.0% | 3.8% | 12.6% |

# Avis Budget Group

Whether you're a business traveler on an expense account or you're on a family vacation and you're counting every penny, Avis Budget Group has a car rental brand for you. The company's Avis Rent A Car unit, which targets corporate and leisure travelers at the high end of the market, has 2,100 locations in the Americas and the Asia/Pacific region. Budget Rent A Car, marketed to those who watch costs closely, rents cars from 1,900 locations in the same regions and trucks from 2,700 facilities in the US. Avis Budget Group, formerly known as Cendant, changed its name in 2006 after spinning off its hotel operations (Wyndham Worldwide) and its real estate division (Realogy) and selling its travel unit (Travelport).

The new Avis Budget Group and its former corporate brethren have signed marketing agreements intended to take advantage of cross-selling opportunities between car rental, hotel, and travel booking businesses. Avis Budget Group stands on its own, though, with its well-known car and truck rental brands. The company has formed numerous marketing alliances with hotels and travel agents outside the former Cendant family.

Although Avis and Budget maintain separate brand identities, the companies share a vehicle fleet and an administrative infrastructure. Like several of their rivals, Avis and Budget are working to open more facilities outside airports to compete in the insurance replacement and general use markets, where Enterprise has gained a leadership position.

An unrelated company, Avis Europe, holds rights to the Avis and Budget brands in Europe, Africa, the Middle East, and parts of Asia.

## HISTORY

Cendant began life through the 1997 merger of CUC International and HFS. A giant in hospitality, HFS was cobbled together as Hospitality Franchise Systems by LBO specialist Blackstone Group in 1992. With brands including Days Inn, Ramada, and Howard Johnson, HFS went public that year. In 1995 HFS bought real estate firm Century 21. The next year it added Electronic Realty Associates (ERA) and Coldwell Banker. Also in 1996, HFS acquired the Super 8 Motels brand as well as car-rental firm Avis. The next year it sold 75% of Avis' #1 franchisee to the public and later bought relocation service firm PHH.

In an attempt to leverage the power of his brands, HFS CEO Henry Silverman began looking at direct marketing giant CUC International. CUC was founded in 1973 as Comp-U-Card America by Walter Forbes and other investors envisioning a computer-based home shopping network. During the 1980s CUC developed as a discount direct marketer and catalog-based shopping club. It went public in 1983 with 100,000 members. CUC saw explosive growth as it signed up 7.6 million members between 1989 and 1993. In 1996 CUC acquired Rent Net, an online apartment rental service, and later bought entertainment software publishers Davidson & Associates and Sierra On-Line. In 1997 CUC bought software maker Knowledge Adventure and launched online shopping site NetMarket.

CUC and HFS completed their $14.1 billion merger in December 1997 with Silverman as CEO and Forbes as chairman. While the name Cendant was derived from "ascendant," the marriage quickly headed in the opposite direction. Accounting irregularities from before the merger that had inflated CUC's revenue and pretax profit by about $500 million were revealed in 1998. Cendant's stock price tumbled, taking a $14 billion hit in one day. Forbes resigned that summer. Silverman quickly took action and began to sell off operations. Cendant Software, National Leisure Group, National Library of Poetry, and Match.Com all were sold that year for a total of about $1.4 billion. The company also acquired Jackson Hewitt, the US's #2 tax-preparation firm, and UK-based National Parking.

Through 1999 the company continued to sell assets. Cendant sold its fleet business — including PHH Vehicle Management Services — to Avis Rent A Car for $5 billion and sold its Entertainment Publications unit, the world's largest coupon book marketer and publisher, to The Carlyle Group. Cendant later paid $2.8 billion in one of the largest shareholder class action lawsuit settlements. (Accounting firm Ernst & Young also settled with Cendant shareholders for $335 million.)

In 2001 Cendant sought to expand its travel holdings with a slew of acquisitions. Its purchases included timeshare resort firm Fairfield Communities; travel services firm Galileo International; online travel reservation service Cheap Tickets. In late 2001 Cendant cut some 6,000 jobs to improve its bottom line and announced that during the next year or so it would cut an additional 10,000 jobs and eliminate about 7% of its franchised hotels.

In 2002 Cendant purchased car-rental company Budget Rent A Car for about $110 million, then slashed costs by closing facilities and laying off more than 450 employees.

In 2004 Cendant's Jackson Hewitt subsidiary filed for its IPO. Also that year, former chairman Walter Forbes and former vice chairman E. Kirk Shelton went to trial on federal fraud and conspiracy charges stemming from pre-merger accounting irregularities that were discovered in 1998. (Shelton was found guilty of multiple counts of fraud in early 2005.)

In 2004 Cendant acquired online travel firm Orbitz in a deal valued at about $1.25 billion. As 2004 wound to a close Cendant completed the acquisition of the Ramada International Hotels & Resorts brand and franchising operations from Marriott International.

Cendant in 2005 spun off its mortgage operations, PHH Mortgage (formerly Cendant Mortgage), and fleet management (PHH Arval) businesses under the PHH Corporation umbrella. Also that year Cendant spun off Wright Express (payment processing and information services for fleet management) in an IPO and sold its marketing services division to Apollo Management for about $1.8 billion.

The divestitures that began in 2005 culminated in the unwinding of the Cendant conglomerate the next year. The company spun off its hotel and real estate operations and sold its travel services division in 2006, reconfiguring itself around its rental car businesses and renaming itself Avis Budget Group. Silverman became chairman and CEO of the company's real estate business, Realogy, and Nelson took over as chairman and CEO of the slimmed-down Avis Budget Group, which took on its new name in September 2006.

## EXECUTIVES

**Chairman and CEO:** Ronald L. (Ron) Nelson, age 54, $818,511 pay (partial-year salary)
**President, COO, and Director:** F. Robert (Bob) Salerno, age 55, $626,589 pay (partial-year salary)
**EVP, CFO, and Treasurer:** David B. Wyshner, $467,788 pay (partial-year salary)
**EVP and General Counsel:** Karen Sclafani
**EVP and Chief Human Resources Officer:** Mark J. Servodidio, $320,418 pay (partial-year salary)
**EVP Operations:** Larry De Shon
**EVP Strategy:** Scott Deaver
**EVP International Operations:** Patric Siniscalchi
**SVP and CIO:** Mary LeBlanc
**SVP Commercial Sales:** Bob Lambert
**SVP Fleet Services:** Edward Gitlitz
**SVP Marketing:** Becky Alseth
**VP Corporate Communications and Public Affairs:** John Barrows
**Chief Accounting Officer:** Brett D. Weinblatt, age 38
**Auditors:** Deloitte & Touche LLP

## LOCATIONS

**HQ:** Avis Budget Group, Inc.
6 Sylvan Way, Parsippany, NJ 07054
**Phone:** 973-496-3500 **Fax:** 888-304-2315
**Web:** www.avisbudgetgroup.com

### 2006 Sales

| | $ mil. | % of total |
|---|---|---|
| US | 4,928 | 87 |
| Other countries | 761 | 13 |
| **Total** | **5,689** | **100** |

## PRODUCTS/OPERATIONS

### 2006 Sales

| | $ mil. | % of total |
|---|---|---|
| Domestic car rental | 4,395 | 77 |
| International car rental | 761 | 14 |
| Truck rental | 472 | 8 |
| Corporate & other | 61 | 1 |
| **Total** | **5,689** | **100** |

## COMPETITORS

AMERCO
Dollar Thrifty Automotive
Enterprise Rent-A-Car
Hertz
Penske Truck Leasing
Vanguard Car Rental

## HISTORICAL FINANCIALS

Company Type: Public

### Income Statement

FYE: December 31

| | REVENUE ($ mil.) | NET INCOME ($ mil.) | NET PROFIT MARGIN | EMPLOYEES |
|---|---|---|---|---|
| **12/06** | 5,689 | (1,994) | — | 30,000 |
| **12/05** | 18,236 | 1,341 | 7.4% | 84,800 |
| **12/04** | 19,785 | 2,082 | 10.5% | 87,000 |
| **12/03** | 18,192 | 1,172 | 6.4% | 87,000 |
| **12/02** | 14,088 | 846 | 6.0% | 85,000 |
| **Annual Growth** | (20.3%) | — | — | (22.9%) |

### 2006 Year-End Financials

Debt ratio: 105.3%
Return on equity: —
Cash ($ mil.): 172
Current ratio: 0.96
Long-term debt ($ mil.): 2,572
No. of shares (mil.): 101
Dividends
Yield: —
Payout: —
Market value ($ mil.): 2,195

### Stock History

NYSE: CAR

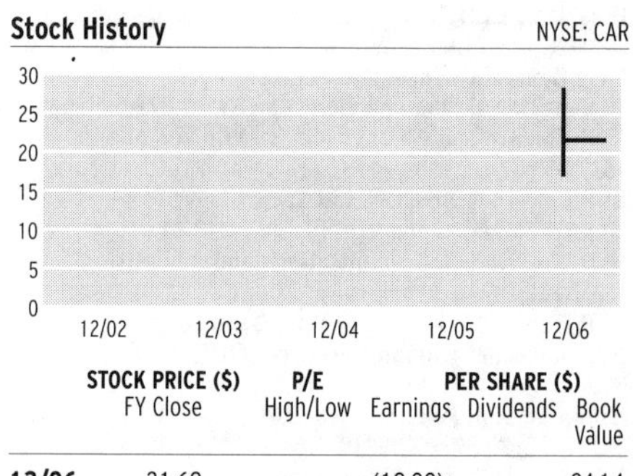


| | STOCK PRICE ($) FY Close | P/E High | P/E Low | PER SHARE ($) Earnings | PER SHARE ($) Dividends | PER SHARE ($) Book Value |
|---|---|---|---|---|---|---|
| **12/06** | 21.69 | — | — | (19.82) | — | 24.14 |

# Avnet, Inc.

If you're after an electronic component, Avnet probably has it. The company is one of the world's largest distributors of electronic components and computer products, alongside rival Arrow Electronics. Avnet's suppliers include 300-plus component and systems makers; the company distributes these suppliers' products to more than 100,000 manufacturers and resellers. Avnet Electronics Marketing handles semiconductors and other components. Its Computer Marketing Group (computer products and services for resellers and large end-users) and its Applied Computing Group (system-level components, such as motherboards) were combined to form Avnet Technology Solutions.

Avnet has acquired Access Distribution, the computer products distribution business of General Electric, for about $410 million in cash. Access Distribution, which specializes in computer hardware made by Sun Microsystems, will be integrated into Avnet Technology Solutions.

In 2007 the company agreed to acquire the European Enterprise Infrastructure Division of Magirus Group. The European Enterprise Infrastructure Division, which generates about $500 million in annual sales, will be integrated into the European operations of Avnet Technology Solutions, the company's IT distribution division.

About two-thirds of Avnet's sales come from its Electronics Marketing unit, which targets industrial, commercial, and military customers. The company distributes products in some 70 countries; customers located in the Americas account for about half of sales.

IBM-made products account for around 16% of sales, while Avnet derives about 10% of sales from semiconductor products of Xilinx, the programmable logic device company.

FMR (Fidelity Investments) owns 15% of Avnet. AXA Financial holds about 9% of the company. First Pacific Advisors has an equity stake of nearly 6%.

## HISTORY

In 1921, before the advent of commercial battery-operated radios, Charles Avnet started a small ham radio replacement parts distributorship in Manhattan, selling parts to designers, inventors, and ship-to-shore radio users on docked ships. The stock market crash in 1929 left the business strapped; it went bankrupt in 1931. A few years later Avnet founded another company, making car radio kits and antennas. But competition got the best of him, and that company also went bankrupt.

During WWII Charles, joined by his sons Lester and Robert, founded Avnet Electronic Supply to sell parts to government and defense contractors. After the war the company bought and sold surplus electrical and electronic parts. A contract from Bendix Aviation spurred company growth, and Avnet opened a West Coast warehouse. In 1955 the company incorporated as Avnet Electronics Supply, with Robert as chairman and CEO and Lester as president. Sales reached $1 million that year, although the company lost $17,000. It changed its name to Avnet Electronics in 1959.

In 1960 Avnet made its first acquisition, British Industries, and went public. Acquisitions continued throughout the 1960s with Hamilton Electro (1962), Fairmount Motor Products (1963), Carol Wire & Cable (1968), and Time Electronic Sales (1968).

To acknowledge its diversification into motors and other products, the company again changed its name, to Avnet, Inc., in 1964. Robert Avnet died the next year and Lester took over as chairman; Lester died in 1970.

In 1973 Intel, which had introduced the microprocessor, signed Avnet as a distributor, and by 1979 Avnet's sales had topped $1 billion. A soft 1982 market caused price declines that led Avnet to sell its wire and cable business. The company consolidated many of its operations to its Arizona headquarters in 1987.

During 1991 and 1992 Avnet spent more than $100 million for acquisitions strategic to the European market. In 1993 the company outbid Wyle Laboratories for Hall-Mark Electronics, the US's third-largest distributor; it also acquired Penstock, the top US distributor of microwave radio-frequency products, in 1994. Thanks to its purchases, Avnet was Europe's #2 electronics distributor by 1994, despite having had almost no European operations prior to 1990.

The company continued to expand globally in 1995, acquiring Hong Kong distributor WKK Semiconductor, among others. Also that year it began selling its non-electronics operations.

In 1998 the company reorganized around separate global computer and electronics businesses. Also that year, president and COO Roy Vallee became chairman and CEO. As part of its restructuring, the company sold its Allied Electronics subsidiary to UK-based components distributor Electrocomponents in 1999 for $380 million. That year Avnet acquired rival Marshall Industries in a deal valued at about $760 million.

In 2000 Avnet acquired IBM midrange server distributor Savoir Technology Group in a $140 million deal, making Avnet the leading distributor of IBM midrange products. Later that year the company acquired a part of Germany-based EBV Group (semiconductor distribution) and RKE (computer products and services), both from German utility giant E.ON, in a cash deal worth about $740 million.

In 2001 Avnet acquired smaller rival Kent Electronics for about $600 million. Also that year the company bought Chinese competitor Sunrise Technology.

In an effort to reduce costs during a global downturn in the electronics industry, Avnet reduced its headcount by about 1,100 people in 2003 and 2004. Also in 2004 the company launched Avnet Logistics (later renamed Avnet Supply Chain Services) as a separate business unit to provide assembly, asset management, distribution, programming, and warehousing services to its customers.

Avnet acquired semiconductor distributor Memec Group Holdings for approximately $663 million in 2005. Also that year it sold the assets of its radio-frequency and microwave components business to Teledyne Technologies. To focus the operations of Avnet Technology Solutions on distribution, Avnet sold its Hewlett-Packard end-user business to Logicalis. It sold its Avnet Enterprise Solutions business to networking firm Calence. Both transactions closed in early 2006.

## EXECUTIVES

**Chairman and CEO:** Roy A. Vallee, age 54, $1,475,464 pay
**SVP and COO:** Richard (Rick) Hamada, $729,440 pay (prior to title change)
**SVP, CFO, and Assistant Secretary:** Raymond (Ray) Sadowski, age 52, $552,937 pay
**EVP; Supply Chain Services Worldwide:** Gregory A. (Greg) Frazier
**SVP and CIO:** Steve Phillips, age 43
**SVP and Chief Operational Excellence Officer:** Edward B. (Ed) Kamins, age 58
**SVP and Director, Administrative Services:** Patrick Jewett
**SVP, Secretary and General Counsel:** David R. Birk, age 59, $555,644 pay
**SVP and Chief Human Resources Development Officer:** Steven C. (Steve) Church
**SVP, Business Operations and Operational Excellence:** David (Dave) Rapier
**SVP and Deputy General Counsel:** R. Neil Taylor
**SVP; President, Electronics Marketing Global:** Harley M. Feldberg, $560,105 pay
**SVP; President, Cilicon:** Jeffrey (Jeff) Ittel
**SVP, Sales and Marketing, Logistics Services:** James K. Commiskey
**VP and Chief Communications Officer:** Allen W. (Al) Maag
**VP and Director, Investor Relations:** Vince Keenan
**VP, Public Relations:** Jan Jurcy
**Auditors:** KPMG LLP

## LOCATIONS

**HQ:** Avnet, Inc.
2211 S. 47th St., Phoenix, AZ 85034
**Phone:** 480-643-2000 **Fax:** 480-643-7370
**Web:** www.avnet.com

Avnet has more than 250 locations worldwide.

### 2006 Sales

| | $ mil. | % of total |
|---|---|---|
| Americas | 7,224 | 51 |
| Europe, Middle East & Africa | 4,374 | 31 |
| Asia/Pacific | 2,656 | 18 |
| **Total** | **14,254** | **100** |

## PRODUCTS/OPERATIONS

### 2006 Sales

| | $ mil. | % of total |
|---|---|---|
| Avnet Electronics Marketing | 9,263 | 65 |
| Avnet Technology Solutions | 4,991 | 35 |
| **Total** | **14,254** | **100** |

### 2006 Sales

| | $ mil. | % of total |
|---|---|---|
| Semiconductors | 8,896 | 62 |
| Computer products | 4,237 | 30 |
| Connectors | 548 | 4 |
| Passives, electromechanical & other | 573 | 4 |
| **Total** | **14,254** | **100** |

### Selected Operations

- Avnet Electronics Marketing (component distribution)
  - Avnet Cilicon (semiconductors)
    - Analog
    - Communications
    - Digital Signal Processors (DSPs)
    - Discrete
    - Memory
    - Microprocessors and microcontrollers
    - Optoelectronics
    - Programmable logic
    - Standard logic
  - Avnet IP&E (interconnect, passive, and electromechanical devices)
  - Design Chain Services (integrated circuit and systems-level design services)

Supply Chain Services
  - Asset management
  - Demand planning
  - Information services
  - Logistics
  - Order management
  - Warehousing
- Production Supplies & Test (electronics production supplies and test equipment)

Avnet Technology Solutions (computer distribution and information technology services)
- Avnet Hall-Mark (computers, software, storage, and services to resellers)
- Avnet Applied Computing
  - Products
    - Displays
    - Memory devices
    - Motherboards
    - Networking equipment
    - Peripherals
    - Point-of-sale
    - Processors
    - Software
    - Storage
    - Wireless
  - Supply chain services
    - Financing
    - Integration
    - Logistics
    - Materials management
    - Technical service
- Avnet Computing Components (microprocessors for systems integrators)

## COMPETITORS

Agilysys
All American Semiconductor
Arrow Electronics
Bell Microproducts
Digi-Key
Future Electronics
Heilind Electronics
Ingram Micro
N.F. Smith
Nu Horizons Electronics
Premier Farnell
Richardson Electronics
Sager Electrical
SYNNEX
Tech Data
TTI Inc.
WPG Holdings

## HISTORICAL FINANCIALS

Company Type: Public

**Income Statement** — FYE: Friday nearest June 30

| | REVENUE ($ mil.) | NET INCOME ($ mil.) | NET PROFIT MARGIN | EMPLOYEES |
|---|---|---|---|---|
| **6/06** | 14,254 | 205 | 1.4% | 10,900 |
| **6/05** | 11,067 | 168 | 1.5% | 9,800 |
| **6/04** | 10,245 | 73 | 0.7% | 9,900 |
| **6/03** | 9,048 | (46) | — | 10,100 |
| **6/02** | 8,920 | (665) | — | 11,000 |
| **Annual Growth** | 12.4% | — | — | (0.2%) |

**2006 Year-End Financials**

Debt ratio: 32.5%
Return on equity: 8.3%
Cash ($ mil.): 277
Current ratio: 1.83
Long-term debt ($ mil.): 919
No. of shares (mil.): 147
Dividends
Yield: —
Payout: —
Market value ($ mil.): 2,936

**Stock History** — NYSE: AVT

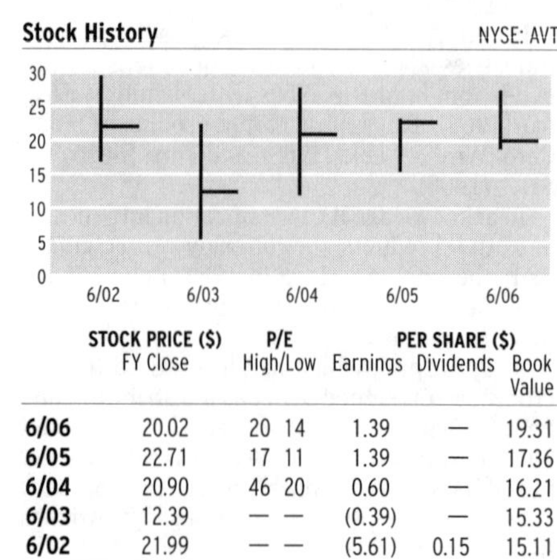


| | STOCK PRICE ($) FY Close | P/E High/Low | PER SHARE ($) Earnings | Dividends | Book Value |
|---|---|---|---|---|---|
| **6/06** | 20.02 | 20 14 | 1.39 | — | 19.31 |
| **6/05** | 22.71 | 17 11 | 1.39 | — | 17.36 |
| **6/04** | 20.90 | 46 20 | 0.60 | — | 16.21 |
| **6/03** | 12.39 | — — | (0.39) | — | 15.33 |
| **6/02** | 21.99 | — — | (5.61) | 0.15 | 15.11 |
| **Annual Growth** | (2.3%) | — — | — | — | 6.3% |

# Avon Products

"Avon calling" — calling for a younger crowd and improved global operational efficiencies. Avon Products, the world's largest direct seller of cosmetics and beauty-related items, is busy building a global brand and enticing younger customers (while retaining its core base of middle-aged buyers). Direct selling remains the firm's *modus operandi*, but sales also come from catalogs, mall kiosks, a day spa (Avon Salon and Spa in New York), and a Web site. Its products include cosmetics, fragrances, toiletries, jewelry, apparel, and home furnishings. Avon has signed approximately 5.3 million independent representatives. It launched a multiyear, four-part restructuring in late 2005.

Avon's makeover involves purging staff, streamlining global manufacturing, and adjusting its supply chain with regard to procurement and distribution. The beauty company also plans to outsource transactional and other services where necessary and to navigate toward countries that offer lower operating costs. Avon is funneling funds into advertising (actually doubling its ad spending by 2008), consumer research, market intelligence, and product innovation. The cost of the reorganization is estimated at $700 million a year. But Avon says that once the restructuring is completed, it expects to save $300 million each year.

As part of the restructuring Avon during 2006 laid off 1,300 of its employees to "remove layers of the organization," as well as purged unprofitable operations. Also, in early 2007 Avon rolled out its plans to restructure its US distribution operations. The plan will result in more than 600 lost positions.

With growth fairly stagnant at home, the company has shed product lines in favor of developing global brands. The company has said it wants to become the Coca-Cola of the beauty industry. Avon also is promoting its image as "The Company for Women" by providing business opportunities for women in countries where women have fewer choices. Avon products are available in more than 110 countries worldwide through sales and distribution.

Despite resistance from China for years, Avon has been trying to get its foot in the country's door. In 1998 China banned direct selling because consumers there found it difficult to distinguish between companies that direct sell and those that have pyramid schemes. The beauty firm sees China as an untapped goldmine and as of April 2005 was given approval from the country's government to test its direct-selling in parts of China, specifically the cities of Beijing and Tianjin and the province of Guangdong.

Avon anticipates driving additional growth based on fragrances (Today, Tomorrow, Always) and skin care (Anew anti-aging) sales.

Catering to the testosterone set, Avon launched its first men's catalog, M — The Men's Catalog, which showcases the company's men's treatment lines.

## HISTORY

In the 1880s book salesman David McConnell gave small bottles of perfume to New York housewives who listened to his sales pitch. The perfume was more popular than the books, so in 1886 McConnell created the California Perfume Company and hired women to sell door-to-door. (He renamed the company Avon Products in 1939 after being impressed by the beauty of Stratford-upon-Avon in England.) Through the 1950s these women, mostly housewives seeking extra income, made Avon a major force in the cosmetics industry.

From the 1960s until the mid-1980s, Avon was the world's largest cosmetics company, known for its appeal to middle-class homemakers. But the company hit hard times in 1974 — the recession made many of its products too pricey for blue-collar customers, and women were leaving home for the workforce. Discovering that Avon's traditional products had little appeal for younger women, Avon began an overhaul of its product line, introducing the Colorworks line for teenagers with the slogan, "It's not your mother's makeup."

Avon acquired prestigious jeweler Tiffany & Co. in 1979 (sold 1984) to help improve the company's image. To boost profits, it entered the retail prestige fragrance business by launching a joint venture with Liz Claiborne (1985) and buying Giorgio Armani (1987, the Giorgio Beverly Hills retail operations were sold in 1994). But Liz Claiborne dissolved the joint venture when Avon bought competitor Parfums Stern in 1987 (sold 1990). It sold 40% of Avon Japan (started 1969) to the Japanese public that year.

Avon Color cosmetics were introduced in 1988, and sleepwear, preschool toys, and videos followed in 1989. The company introduced apparel in 1994 and the next year worked with designer Diane Von Furstenberg to launch a line of clothing.

Mattel and Avon joined forces in 1996 to sell toys — Winter Velvet Barbie became Avon's most successful product introduction ever. In 1997 the company launched a new home furnishings catalog and bought direct seller Discovery Toys (sold in early 1999).

Passing over several high-ranking female executives (the company felt they weren't ready), Avon made Charles Perrin its CEO in mid-1998. Andrea Jung, the brain behind the makeover, became president. Avon also began selling makeup in 1998 at mall kiosks and through a catalog.

In 1999 Jung became Avon's first female CEO by replacing the retiring Perrin. Former Goodyear and Rubbermaid CEO Stanley Gault was elected chairman of the board. In March 2000 Avon announced an alliance with Swiss pharmaceutical group Roche to develop a line of women's vitamins and nutritional products (its first) launched in 2001.

In September 2001 Jung was elected chairman of the board. In 2002, as part of a move to improve operating efficiencies, Avon closed its jewelry manufacturing plant in San Sebastian, Puerto Rico. The closure marked Avon's exit from jewelry manufacturing. It now outsources its full jewelry line by purchasing finished goods from Asia. In another cost-cutting move, Avon laid off 3,500 employees, or 8% of its workforce, in March 2002, saying that the economic recession in Argentina, which accounts for about 5% of Avon's sales, made the layoffs necessary.

As part of its focus on the younger market, in 2003 Avon launched a new cosmetics line called "mark." — targeted to the 16 to 24 age group. Named for young women making their mark on the world, the line includes 300 products, such as cosmetics, skin care, fragrance, accessories, jewelry, and handbags.

In 2004 Avon agreed to pay some $50 million for a 20% stake in its two Chinese joint ventures with Masson Group.

## EXECUTIVES

**Chairman and CEO:** Andrea Jung, age 48, $1,375,000 pay
**EVP, Finance and Technology and CFO:** Charles W. (Chuck) Cramb, age 60, $700,000 pay
**EVP, North America and Global Marketing:** Elizabeth A. (Liz) Smith, age 44, $650,000 pay
**EVP, Global Sales:** Brian C. Connolly, age 51, $494,178 pay
**SVP and COO, North America:** Gina R. Boswell, age 44
**SVP and Global Brand President:** Geralyn R. Breig
**SVP and CIO:** Harriet Edelman, age 51
**SVP, Global Communications:** Nancy Glaser
**SVP, Human Resources:** Lucien Alziari, age 47
**SVP and President, Global Marketing:** William F. (Bill) Susetka, age 48
**SVP, WEMEA and China:** Bennett R. (Ben) Gallina, age 52
**SVP, Global Supply Chain:** John F. Owen, age 49
**SVP, Latin America:** Charles M. Herington, age 47
**SVP, Central and Eastern Europe:** John Philip Higson, age 48
**SVP, Asia Pacific:** James C. Wei, age 49
**SVP, Corporate Strategy and Global Business Development:** Pauline J. Brown
**SVP and General Counsel:** Gilbert L. Klemann II, age 56, $504,301 pay
**Group VP and Corporate Controller:** Richard S. Foggio, age 47
**Director of Investor Relations:** Robert (Rob) Foresti
**Corporate Media Relations:** Victor Beaudet
**Auditors:** PricewaterhouseCoopers LLP

## LOCATIONS

**HQ:** Avon Products, Inc.
1345 Avenue of the Americas, New York, NY 10105
**Phone:** 212-282-5000 **Fax:** 212-282-6049
**Web:** www.avoncompany.com

Avon Products has operations in the US and 63 other countries. Its products are available in more than 110 countries.

### 2006 Sales

| | $ mil. | % of total |
|---|---|---|
| Latin America | 2,743.4 | 31 |
| North America | 2,554.0 | 29 |
| Western Europe, Middle East & Africa | 1,320.2 | 15 |
| Central & Eastern Europe | 1,123.7 | 13 |
| Asia Pacific | 810.8 | 9 |
| China | 211.8 | 3 |
| **Total** | **8,763.9** | **100** |

## PRODUCTS/OPERATIONS

### 2006 Sales

| | $ mil. | % of total |
|---|---|---|
| Beauty (cosmetics, fragrances, skin care & toiletries) | 6,028.8 | 69 |
| Beauty Plus (fashion jewelry, watches, apparel & accessories) | 1,676.6 | 19 |
| Beyond Beauty (home products & gift & decorative products) | 971.9 | 11 |
| Other revenue | 86.6 | 1 |
| **Total** | **8,763.9** | **100** |

### Selected Brands

Avon Color
Beyond Color
Color Trend
Hydra Finish
mark.
Perfect Wear

### Selected Products

Fragrances
- Dolce Aura
- Far Away
- Imari Eau de Cologne
- Incandescence
- Little Black Dress
- mark.blu
- Perceive
- Women of Earth

Hair Care
- Advance Techniques
- Herbal Care

Health and Wellness
- Avon Wellness
- Body and Mind
- VitAdvance
- VitaTonics

Skin Care, Bath, and Body
- Anew
- Aromatherapy
- Avon Bubble Bath
- Avon Skin Care
- Clearskin
- foot works
- Milk Made
- Moisture Therapy
- Naturals
- Skin-So-Soft

## COMPETITORS

Alberto-Culver
Alticor
Amway China
Bath & Body Works
BeautiControl
Beiersdorf
Body Shop
Chanel
Clarins
Colgate-Palmolive
Coty Inc.
Dana Classic Fragrances
Dillard's
DLI Holding
Elizabeth Arden Inc
Enesco
Estée Lauder
Forever Living
Hanover Direct
Intimate Brands
J. C. Penney
Johnson & Johnson
Johnson Publishing
Kanebo
L'Oréal
LVMH
Macy's
Mary Kay
Murad, Inc.
Nu Skin
Perrigo
Prestige Cosmetics
Procter & Gamble
Revlon
Sara Lee
Shaklee
Shiseido
Target
Tupperware
Unilever
Wal-Mart

## HISTORICAL FINANCIALS

Company Type: Public

### Income Statement

FYE: December 31

| | REVENUE ($ mil.) | NET INCOME ($ mil.) | NET PROFIT MARGIN | EMPLOYEES |
|---|---|---|---|---|
| **12/06** | 8,764 | 478 | 5.4% | 40,300 |
| **12/05** | 8,150 | 848 | 10.4% | 49,000 |
| **12/04** | 7,748 | 846 | 10.9% | 47,700 |
| **12/03** | 6,876 | 665 | 9.7% | 45,900 |
| **12/02** | 6,228 | 535 | 8.6% | 45,000 |
| **Annual Growth** | 8.9% | (2.8%) | — | (2.7%) |

### 2006 Year-End Financials

Debt ratio: 148.1%
Return on equity: 60.3%
Cash ($ mil.): 1,199
Current ratio: 1.31
Long-term debt ($ mil.): 1,171
No. of shares (mil.): 441
Dividends
Yield: 2.1%
Payout: 66.0%
Market value ($ mil.): 14,581

### Stock History

NYSE: AVP

| | STOCK PRICE ($) FY Close | P/E High | P/E Low | PER SHARE ($) Earnings | Dividends | Book Value |
|---|---|---|---|---|---|---|
| **12/06** | 33.04 | 32 | 25 | 1.06 | 0.70 | 1.79 |
| **12/05** | 28.55 | 25 | 13 | 1.81 | 0.66 | 1.76 |
| **12/04** | 38.70 | 26 | 17 | 1.77 | 0.28 | 2.02 |
| **12/03** | 33.74 | 25 | 18 | 1.39 | 0.42 | 1.58 |
| **12/02** | 26.93 | 26 | 20 | 1.11 | 0.40 | (0.54) |
| **Annual Growth** | 5.2% | — | — | (1.1%) | 15.0% | — |

# Baker & McKenzie

Baker & McKenzie believes big is good and bigger is better. One of the world's largest law firms, it has about 3,400 attorneys practicing from some 70 offices — from Bangkok to Berlin to Buenos Aires — in almost 40 countries. It offers expertise in a wide range of practice areas, including antitrust, intellectual property, international trade, mergers and acquisitions, project finance, and tax law. Baker & McKenzie's client list includes big companies from numerous industries, including banking and finance, construction, and technology, as well as smaller enterprises. The firm was founded in 1949.

Baker & McKenzie is known for the geographic scope of its practice — some 80% of the firm's attorneys work outside the US. The firm touts its widespread network of offices as an advantage for clients with multinational interests.

The vast scale of Baker & McKenzie's operations increases the firm's exposure to liability, however, and that concern led Baker & McKenzie to reorganize itself as a Swiss Verein in 2004. Under the new structure, which is used by accounting firms such as Deloitte Touche Tohmatsu, Baker & McKenzie's member firms operate as separate entities, insulating the parent firm from liability. Baker & McKenzie was the first international law firm to organize itself under a Verein structure.

## HISTORY

Russell Baker traveled from his native New Mexico to Chicago on a railroad freight car to attend law school. Upon graduation in 1925 he started practicing law with his classmate Dana Simpson under the name Simpson & Baker. Inspired by Chicago's role as a manufacturing and agricultural center for the world and influenced by the international focus of his alma mater, the University of Chicago, Baker dreamed of creating an international law practice. He began developing an expertise in international law, and in 1934 Abbott Laboratories retained him to handle its worldwide legal affairs. Baker was on his way to fulfilling his dream.

Baker joined forces with Chicago litigator John McKenzie in 1949, forming Baker & McKenzie. In 1955 the firm opened its first foreign office in Caracas, Venezuela, to meet the needs of its expanding US client base. Over the next 10 years it branched out into Asia, Australia, and Europe, with offices in London, Manila, Paris, and Tokyo. Baker's death in 1979 neither slowed the firm's growth nor changed its international character. The next year it expanded into the Middle East and opened its 30th office in 1982 (Melbourne). To manage the sprawling law firm, Baker & McKenzie created the position of chairman of the executive committee in 1984.

In late 1991 the firm dropped the Church of Scientology as a client, losing an estimated $2 million in business. It was speculated that pressure from client Eli Lilly (maker of the drug Prozac, which Scientologists actively oppose) influenced the decision. In 1992 Baker & McKenzie was ordered to pay $1 million for wrongfully firing an employee who later died of AIDS. (The case became the basis for the 1993 film *Philadelphia.*) The firm fought the verdict but eventually settled for an undisclosed amount in 1995.

In 1994 Baker & McKenzie closed its Los Angeles office (the former MacDonald, Halsted & Laybourne; acquired 1988) amid considerable rancor. Also that year a former secretary at the firm received a $7.1 million judgment for sexual harassment by a partner. (A San Francisco Superior Court judge later reduced the award to $3.5 million.)

John Klotsche, a senior partner from the firm's Palo Alto, California, office was appointed chairman in 1995. The following year the firm began a major expansion into California's Silicon Valley as part of an initiative to serve technology companies around the world. It also expanded its Warsaw, Poland, office through a merger with the Warsaw office of Dickinson, Wright, Moon, Van Dusen & Freman.

In 1998 Baker & McKenzie formed a special unit in Singapore to deal with business generated by the financial troubles in Asia. The opening of offices in Taiwan and Azerbaijan in 1998 brought the firm's total number of offices to 59. Klotsche stepped down in 1999 as the firm celebrated its 50th anniversary; Christine Lagarde replaced him. In early 2001 Baker & McKenzie created a joint venture practice with Singapore-based associate firm Wong & Leow. Also that year it merged with Madrid-based Briones Alonso y Martin to create the largest independent law firm in Spain.

Lagarde stepped down as executive chairman in 2004, and John Conroy was chosen to lead the firm.

## EXECUTIVES

**Chairman of the Executive Committee:** John J. Conroy Jr.
**COO:** Craig Courter
**CFO:** Robert S. Spencer, age 59
**CTO:** Sue Hall
**Chief Global Press Officer:** Judith Green
**General Counsel:** Edward J. Zulkey
**Senior Operating Officer, Global Client Services:** Bill Wood
**Regional Operating Officer, Asia Pacific:** Paul Malliate
**Regional Operating Officer, Europe, Middle East and Central Asia:** Kate Stonestreet
**Regional Operating Officer, Latin America:** Leon J. Sacks
**Regional Operating Officer, North America:** Joseph Plack
**Partner, Chicago and Executive Committee Member:** David P. Hackett
**Partner, Hong Kong and Executive Committee Member:** Poh Lee Tan
**Partner, London and Executive Committee Member:** Russell M. E. Lewin
**Partner, Monterrey and Executive Committee Member:** Andrés Ochoa-Bünsow
**Partner, Paris and Executive Committee Member:** Eric M. Lasry
**Partner, Sydney and Executive Committee Member:** David Jacobs
**Partner, Washington DC and Executive Committee Member:** Nicholas F. Coward
**Director of Marketing:** David Tabolt
**Director of Professional Responsibility, Of Counsel:** William J. Linklater
**Director of Strategy Implementation:** Hilda Soo
**Senior Manager, Press:** Doug MacDonald
**Senior Public Relations Coordinator:** Jessica Benzon

## LOCATIONS

**HQ:** Baker & McKenzie
130 E. Randolph Dr., Ste. 2500, Chicago, IL 60601
**Phone:** 312-861-8800 **Fax:** 312-861-8823
**Web:** www.bakernet.com

Baker & McKenzie has offices in the Asia/Pacific region; Europe, the Middle East, and Central Asia; Latin America; and North America.

## PRODUCTS/OPERATIONS

### Selected Practice Areas

Antitrust and trade
Banking and finance
Corporate
Dispute resolution
Employment
Insurance
Intellectual property
International/commercial
IT/communications
Major projects and project finance
Pharmaceuticals and health care
Real estate, construction, environment, and tourism
Tax

## COMPETITORS

Clifford Chance
Jones Day
Kirkland & Ellis
Latham & Watkins
Mayer, Brown, Rowe & Maw
McDermott Will & Emery
Shearman & Sterling
Sidley Austin
Skadden, Arps
Sullivan & Cromwell
Weil, Gotshal
White & Case

## HISTORICAL FINANCIALS

Company Type: Partnership

**Income Statement** FYE: June 30

| | REVENUE ($ mil.) | NET INCOME ($ mil.) | NET PROFIT MARGIN | EMPLOYEES |
|---|---|---|---|---|
| 6/06 | 1,522 | — | — | 9,503 |
| 6/05 | 1,352 | — | — | 8,500 |
| 6/04 | 1,228 | — | — | 8,400 |
| 6/03 | 1,134 | — | — | 8,401 |
| 6/02 | 1,060 | — | — | 8,000 |
| Annual Growth | 9.5% | — | — | 4.4% |

**Revenue History**

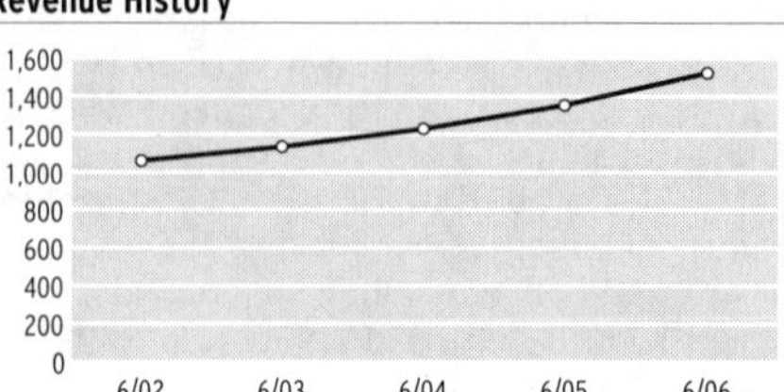


# Baker Hughes

Baker Hughes cooks up a baker's dozen of products and services for the global petroleum market. Through its Drilling and Evaluation segment, Baker Hughes makes products and services used to drill oil and natural gas wells. Through its Completion and Production segment, the company provides equipment and services used from the completion phase through the productive life of oil and natural gas wells. The company tests potential well sites and drills and operates the wells; it also makes bits and drilling fluids, makes submersible pumps, and provides equipment and services to maintain oil and gas wells. In 2006 Baker Hughes sold its 30% stake in WesternGeco to joint-venture partner Schlumberger.

The Drilling and Evaluation segment consists of Baker Hughes Drilling Fluids (drilling fluids), Hughes Christensen (drill bits), INTEQ (directional drilling, measurement-while-drilling and logging-while-drilling) and Baker Atlas (downhole well logging and services).

Baker Hughes' Completion and Production segment consists of Baker Oil Tools (completion, workover and fishing equipment), Baker Petrolite (oilfield specialty chemicals such as drilling fluids and stimulation additives) and Centrilift (electric submersible and progressing cavity pumps).

The company formed its major segment, Baker Hughes Drilling Fluids, by separating its INTEQ business from its Oilfield segment in 2004. Baker Hughes has sold its discontinued Baker Hughes Mining Tools unit, which formerly operated under its Hughes Christensen division, to Atlas Copco North America.

Baker Hughes has made a comeback with the increasing price of oil. With its rig counts at a 10-year high, the company is hoping for a renewed gusher of cash as the increase in per-barrel prices prompts oil companies to reinvest in exploration and production. The company also has been helped by the rising price of natural gas.

The company expanded its pipeline inspection business with the acquisition of Cornerstone

Pipeline Inspection Group. Unable to sell it in whole, Baker Hughes split its Process division (waste-separation equipment) into pieces, selling each of the division's subsidiaries one by one.

Through its Baker Atlas subsidiary, Baker Hughes acquired the borehead seismic data acquisition business of Compagnie Générale de Géophysique-Veritas (CGV). After the acquisition, Baker Hughes and CVG joined forces to create a new joint venture company, VSFusion. Baker Hughes has also formed a joint venture company, named QuantX, with Expro International.

## HISTORY

Howard Hughes Sr. developed the first oil well drill bit for rock in 1909. Hughes and partner Walter Sharp opened a plant in Houston, and their company, Sharp & Hughes, soon had a near monopoly on rock bits. When Sharp died in 1912, Hughes bought his partner's half of the company, incorporating as Hughes Tool. Hughes held 73 patents when he died in 1924; the company passed to Howard Hughes Jr.

It is estimated that between 1924 and 1972 Hughes Tool provided Hughes Jr. with $745 million in pretax profits, which he used to diversify into movies (RKO), airlines (TWA), and Las Vegas casinos. In 1972 he sold the company to the public for $150 million. After 1972 the company expanded into tools for aboveground oil production. In 1974, under the new leadership of chairman James Leach, Hughes bought the oil field equipment business of Borg-Warner.

In 1913 drilling contractor Carl Baker organized the Baker Casing Shoe Company in California to collect royalties on his three oil tool inventions. The firm began to make its own products in 1918, and during the 1920s it expanded nationally, opened global trade, and formed Baker Oil Tools (1928). The company grew in the late 1940s and the 1950s as oil drilling boomed.

During the 1960s Baker prospered, despite fewer US well completions. Foreign sales increased. From 1963 to 1975 Baker bought oil-related companies Kobe, Galigher, Ramsey Engineering, and Reed Tool.

US expenditures for oil services fell between 1982 and 1986 from $40 billion to $9 billion. In 1987 both Baker and Hughes faced falling revenues. The two companies merged to form Baker Hughes. By closing plants and combining operations, the venture became profitable by the end of 1988. The company bought Eastman Christensen (the world leader in directional and horizontal drilling equipment) and acquired the instrumentation unit of Tracor Holdings in 1990.

Baker Hughes spun off BJ Services (pumping services) to the public in 1991 and sold the Eastern Hemisphere operations of Baker Hughes Tubular Services (BHTS) to Tuboscope. It sold the Western Hemisphere operations of BHTS to ICO the following year.

Also in 1992 Baker Hughes bought Teleco Oilfield Services, a pioneer in directional drilling techniques, from Sonat. In 1996 company veteran Max Lukens became CEO. He replaced James Woods as chairman the next year.

In a move to boost its oil field chemicals business the company bought Petrolite in 1997 and rival Western Atlas for $3.3 billion in 1998, strengthening its land-based seismic data business (#1 in that market) and testing business. A downturn in the Asian economy, disruptions from tropical storms, and slumping oil prices caused oil companies to reduce demand for Baker Hughes' products. The company suffered a big loss in 1998 and in response trimmed its workforce by about 15% in 1999.

In 2000 Lukens stepped down after accounting blunders caused the company to restate earnings. Company director and Newfield Exploration Company CEO Joe Foster replaced him as acting CEO until Michael Wiley was named to that office.

In 2002 Cornerstone Pipeline Management was acquired in an effort to expand the pipeline inspection services provided by its Baker Petrolite division. In 2004 Baker Hughes exited its Process division when it completed the sale of its Bird Machine subsidiary to Austrian-based machinery manufacturer Andritz. Michael Wiley retired from his position as chairman and CEO of Baker Hughes. Chad Deaton, formerly president and CEO of Hanover Compressor, was named chairman and CEO to replace him.

In 2005 the company acquired Scotland-based Zeroth Technologies, a company than manufactures expandable metal sealing elements. In 2006 Baker Hughes acquired Nova Technology, a Louisiana-based company that supplies monitoring and chemical injection systems for use in offshore gas and oil well operations.

## EXECUTIVES

**Chairman and CEO:** Chad C. Deaton, age 54, $1,001,923 pay
**President and COO:** James R. (Rod) Clark, age 56, $696,600 pay
**SVP and CFO:** Peter A. Ragauss, age 49, $339,231 pay (partial-year salary)
**SVP and General Counsel:** Alan R. Crain Jr., age 55
**Group President, Baker Hughes Completion and Production:** David H. Barr, age 57
**Group President, Baker Hughes Drilling and Evaluation:** Martin S. Craighead, age 47
**VP; President, Baker Oil Tools:** Christopher P. (Chris) Beaver, age 49
**VP; President, Baker Petrolite Corporation:** John A. O'Donnell, age 58
**VP; President, Centrilift:** Charles S. (Charlie) Wolley, age 52
**VP, Corporate Development:** David E. Emerson
**VP, Tax:** John H. Lohman Jr.
**VP; President, INTEQ:** Paul S. Butero, age 50
**VP; President, Baker Atlas:** Stephen K. Ellison
**VP; President, Baker Hughes Drilling Fluids:** Richard L. Williams, age 51
**VP; President, Baker Hughes Russia:** Frank M. (Mike) Davis, age 52
**VP; President, Hughes Christensen:** Gary G. Rich, age 48
**VP Enterprise Marketing:** William P. (Wil) Faubel, age 52
**VP, Chief Compliance Officer, and Senior Deputy General Counsel:** Jay G. Martin, age 55
**VP and Treasurer:** Douglas C. Doty
**VP and Controller:** Alan J. Keifer, age 52
**VP Human Resources:** Didier Charreton, age 43
**Director, Investor Relations:** Gary R. Flaharty
**Corporate Secretary:** Sandra E. Alford
**Auditors:** Deloitte & Touche LLP

## LOCATIONS

**HQ:** Baker Hughes Incorporated
2929 Allen Pkwy., Ste. 2100, Houston, TX 77019
**Phone:** 713-439-8600 **Fax:** 713-439-8699
**Web:** www.bakerhughes.com

Baker Hughes operates 46 manufacturing plants worldwide.

### 2006 Sales

| | $ mil. | % of total |
|---|---|---|
| US | 3,392.5 | 38 |
| Canada | 607.1 | 7 |
| UK | 514.8 | 6 |
| Norway | 438.4 | 5 |
| Saudi Arabia | 391.3 | 4 |
| China | 212.0 | 2 |
| Venezuela | 190.1 | 2 |
| Other countries | 3,281.2 | 36 |
| **Total** | **9,027.4** | **100** |

## PRODUCTS/OPERATIONS

### 2006 Sales

| | $ mil. | % of total |
|---|---|---|
| Drilling & evaluation | 4,660.8 | 52 |
| Completion & production | 4,366.6 | 48 |
| **Total** | **9,027.4** | **100** |

### Selected Operations

Baker Atlas (downhole data acquisition, processing and analysis; pipe recovery)
Baker Oil Tools (completion, workover, and fishing technologies and services)
Baker Petrolite (specialty chemicals for petroleum, transportation, and refining)
Centrilift (electric submersible pumps and downhole oil/water separation)
Hughes Christensen (oil well drill bits)
ITEQ (conventional and rotary directional drilling, measurement-while-drilling and logging-while-drilling)

## COMPETITORS

Aker Kværner
BJ Services
CGGVeritas
FMC
Grant Prideco
Halliburton
John Wood Group
Nabors Industries
Nalco
Petroleum Geo-Services
Precision Drilling
Schlumberger
Smith International
Technip
Weatherford International

## HISTORICAL FINANCIALS

Company Type: Public

### Income Statement

FYE: December 31

| | REVENUE ($ mil.) | NET INCOME ($ mil.) | NET PROFIT MARGIN | EMPLOYEES |
|---|---|---|---|---|
| **12/06** | 9,027 | 2,419 | 26.8% | 34,600 |
| **12/05** | 7,186 | 878 | 12.2% | 29,100 |
| **12/04** | 6,104 | 529 | 8.7% | 26,900 |
| **12/03** | 5,293 | 129 | 2.4% | 26,650 |
| **12/02** | 5,020 | 169 | 3.4% | 26,500 |
| **Annual Growth** | 15.8% | 94.5% | — | 6.9% |

### 2006 Year-End Financials

| | |
|---|---|
| Debt ratio: 20.5% | No. of shares (mil.): 320 |
| Return on equity: 48.7% | Dividends |
| Cash ($ mil.): 1,104 | Yield: 0.7% |
| Current ratio: 3.06 | Payout: 7.2% |
| Long-term debt ($ mil.): 1,074 | Market value ($ mil.): 23,884 |

**Stock History** NYSE: BHI

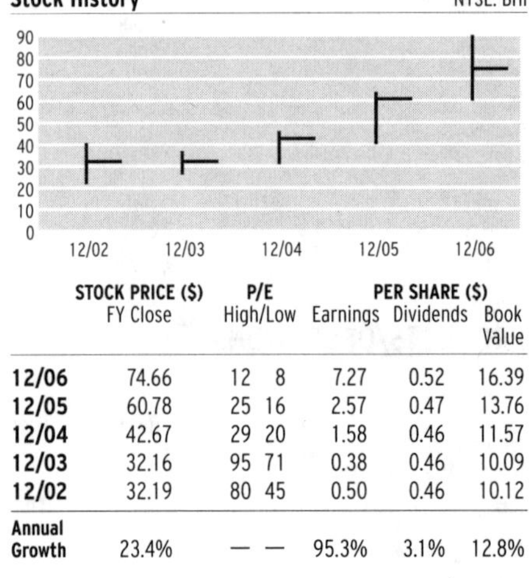


| | STOCK PRICE ($) FY Close | P/E High | P/E Low | PER SHARE ($) Earnings | Dividends | Book Value |
|---|---|---|---|---|---|---|
| **12/06** | 74.66 | 12 | 8 | 7.27 | 0.52 | 16.39 |
| **12/05** | 60.78 | 25 | 16 | 2.57 | 0.47 | 13.76 |
| **12/04** | 42.67 | 29 | 20 | 1.58 | 0.46 | 11.57 |
| **12/03** | 32.16 | 95 | 71 | 0.38 | 0.46 | 10.09 |
| **12/02** | 32.19 | 80 | 45 | 0.50 | 0.46 | 10.12 |
| **Annual Growth** | 23.4% | — | — | 95.3% | 3.1% | 12.8% |

# Ball Corporation

The well-rounded Ball Corporation makes cans and containers for the food and beverage industries as well as products for the space and defense industries. Ball's food and beverage packaging products include aluminum, steel, and polyethylene terephthalate (PET) plastic containers. The company's high-tech operations are handled through its Ball Aerospace & Technologies subsidiary, which makes imaging, communications, and information components (antennas, sensors), and offers engineering and manufacturing services. As a result of Ball's mixed operations, its primary customers include PepsiCo, Coca-Cola Enterprises, SABMiller plc (brewer), Pepsi and Coke bottlers, and aerospace and defense contractors.

Ball is divided into five business segments: Its North American operations (metal beverage packaging, metal food packaging, and plastic packaging) account for two-thirds of sales; international packaging operations account for nearly a quarter of sales; and aerospace and technologies account for the remainder.

Ball owes much to the thirsty public: In 2006 brewer SABMiller plc accounted for 11% of sales; PepsiCo accounted for 9%; and Coke and Pepsi bottlers accounted for 29% of sales.

Ball has expanded into key markets through acquisitions. The company has also closed and consolidated some operations in order to reduce excess capacity and inventory. Early in 2006 Ball acquired U.S. Can's US and Argentinean operations for about $550 million and 1.1 million stock shares. The deal, which included ten US plants and two Argentinean plants, made Ball the US's largest maker of aerosol cans. The acquired operations have annual sales of about $600 million. Around the same time Ball added to its plastic bottle manufacturing operations, buying three facilities from Alcan for about $180 million.

Ball closed two factories in December 2006 to consolidate its manufacturing footprint in the wake of acquisitions. One made plastic pails in Ohio, the other made metal food cans in Ontario.

Ball Packaging Europe is part of Ball's international packaging segment and Ball reckons that the company has become Europe's second largest maker of metal beverage containers. In mid-2006 Ball announced that it would invest more than $110 million to expand one German plant and to rebuild another that had been damaged by fire. Elsewhere, the company's Ball Asia Pacific Limited is one of China's largest makers of drink cans.

## HISTORY

The Ball Corporation began in 1880 when Frank Ball and his four brothers started making wood-jacket tin cans to store and transport kerosene and other materials. In 1884 the company switched to tin-jacketed glass containers for kerosene lamps. The lamps, however, were soon displaced by Thomas Edison's electric light bulb.

The Ball brothers then learned that the patent to the original sealed-glass storage container (the Mason jar) had expired. By 1886 the brothers had entered the sealed-jar business and imprinted their jars with the Ball name. In their first year, they made 12,500 jars and sparked a patent war with the two reigning jar producers, who asserted that they controlled the correct patents and threatened to sue. The Ball lawyers proved that the patents had expired, and the jar remained Ball's mainstay for many years.

The company began diversifying, but a 1947 antitrust ruling prohibited it from buying additional glass subsidiaries. Ball decided to take advantage of the space race by buying Control Cells (aerospace science research) in 1957; that operation became Ball Brothers Research Corporation (later Ball Aerospace Systems Division). The Soviets launched Sputnik that year, igniting a massive US scientific effort in 1958, and Ball won federal contracts to make equipment for the US space program.

Ball established its metal beverage-container business in 1969 when it bought Jeffco Manufacturing of Colorado. The operation soon won contracts to supply two-piece cans to Budweiser, Coca-Cola, Dr Pepper, Pepsi, and Stroh's Beer.

John Fisher became president and CEO in 1971. The last company president who was a member of the Ball family, Fisher wanted Ball to diversify. He took the company public in 1972 to fund his efforts. That year he acquired a Singapore-based petroleum equipment company. Next he led Ball into agricultural irrigation systems and prefabricated housing. In 1974 Ball acquired a small California computer firm, which formed the basis of its telecommunications division.

Fisher retired in 1981. Ball's metal-container business suffered in the late 1980s from overcapacity and price wars in its industry. In 1989 the company's aerospace division was hard hit by $10 million in losses on an Air Force contract and by cuts in defense spending.

Ball spun off its Alltrista canning supplies subsidiary to shareholders in 1993 and purchased Heekin Can, a manufacturer for the food, pet food, and aerosol markets. That year Ball's $50 million mirror system corrected the Hubble Space Telescope's blurred vision. The company entered the polyethylene terephthalate (PET) container business in 1995 and placed its glass-container business into a newly formed company, Ball-Foster Glass Container, and the next year sold its stake to its partner, French materials company Saint-Gobain Group.

Ball sold its aerosol-can business to BWAY Corp in 1996. It acquired M.C. Packaging of Hong Kong in 1997. Ball popped the top on another big deal in 1998 when it bought Reynolds Metals' aluminum-can business (Reynolds is now owned by Alcoa). In 1999 and 2000 the company closed four can plants in an effort to improve an imbalance in supply and demand.

In 2001 Ball and ConAgra Grocery Products formed a joint venture, Ball Western Can Company, to make metal food containers. Also that year subsidiary Ball Aerospace & Technologies landed a $260 million contract with the US Air Force, and Ball's president and COO, David Hoover, was named CEO. That November, Ball entered into a joint venture with Coors Brewing Co. called Rocky Mountain Metal Container to operate Coors' can facilities, making 4.5 billion cans per year. The company also acquired Wis-Pak Plastics, Inc., adding to its plastic container operations.

In 2003, Ball finalized its purchase of German can maker Schmalbach-Lubeca (renamed Ball Packaging Europe) for about $890 million. The deal made Ball the second-largest can maker in Europe.

## EXECUTIVES

**Chairman, President, and CEO:** R. David Hoover, age 61, $1,000,000 pay
**SVP and COO, North American Packaging:** John R. Friedery, age 50, $414,000 pay
**EVP and CFO:** Raymond J. Seabrook, age 55, $420,096 pay
**EVP, Administration and Corporate Secretary:** David A. Westerlund, age 56, $380,615 pay
**VP and Controller:** Douglas K. Bradford, age 49
**VP and Treasurer:** Scott C. Morrison, age 44
**VP, Corporate Relations:** Harold L. Sohn, age 60
**VP; President, Packaging Europe:** John A. Hayes, age 41, $323,000 pay
**Chairman and CEO, Ball Asia Pacific Limited:** Terence P. Voce, age 57
**President, Ball Metal Food and Household Products Packaging Division, Americas:** Michael W. Feldser, age 56
**President and CEO, Ball Aerospace & Technologies:** David L. (Dave) Taylor, age 54
**President, Metal Beverage Container Operations:** Michael D. Herdman, age 57
**President, Metal Food Container Operations:** Brian M. Cardno, age 61
**President, Plastic Container Operations:** Larry J. Green, age 59
**VP, General Counsel and Corporate Secretary:** Charles E. Baker, age 49
**Investor Relations:** Ann Scott
**Media Relations and General Information:** Scott McCarty
**SVP, Sales and Marketing, Metal Food Containers:** Tom Hale
**Auditors:** PricewaterhouseCoopers LLP

## LOCATIONS

**HQ:** Ball Corporation
10 Longs Peak Dr., Broomfield, CO 80021
**Phone:** 303-469-3131 **Fax:** 303-460-2127
**Web:** www.ball.com

Ball Corporation has manufacturing facilities in Argentina, China, North America (Arkansas, British Columbia, California, Colorado, Florida, Georgia, Hawaii, Indiana, Illinois, Iowa, Maryland, Missouri, New Jersey, New York, North Carolina, Ohio, Ontario, Pennsylvania, Puerto Rico, Tennessee, Texas, Virginia, Washington, West Virginia, and Wisconsin), and Europe (France, Germany, The Netherlands, Poland, Serbia, and the UK).

**2006 Sales**

| | $ mil. | % of total |
|---|---|---|
| US | 4,868.6 | 74 |
| Other countries | 1,752.9 | 26 |
| **Total** | **6,621.5** | **100** |

## PRODUCTS/OPERATIONS

### 2006 Sales

| | $ mil. | % of total |
|---|---|---|
| Americas metal beverage packaging | 2,604.4 | 39 |
| Europe/Asia metal beverage packaging | 1,512.5 | 23 |
| Americas metal food/household products packaging | 1,186.9 | 18 |
| Aerospace & technologies | 672.3 | 10 |
| Americas plastic packaging | 645.4 | 10 |
| **Total** | **6,621.5** | **100** |

### Selected Products

Packaging
- Metal
  - Two- and three-piece metal food containers
  - Two-piece metal beverage containers
- Plastic
  - PET plastic food and beverage containers
  - Polypropylene food and beverage containers

Aerospace and Technologies
- Products
  - Antennas
  - Cryogenics
  - Laser communications
  - Lubrication
  - Mirrors
  - Pointing and tracking
  - Sensors
  - Remote sensing
  - Video products
  - Wireless communications
- Services
  - Commercial products and technologies manufacturing
  - Global communications and video solutions
  - Systems engineering

## COMPETITORS

Alcan
Alcoa
Amcor
Anchor Glass
Boeing
BWAY
CLARCOR
Consolidated Container
Constar International
Crown Holdings
Orbital Sciences
Owens-Illinois
PLM AB
Rexam
Rockwell Collins
Saint-Gobain Containers
Sequa
Silgan
Teledyne Technologies
Tetra Laval

## HISTORICAL FINANCIALS

Company Type: Public

### Income Statement

FYE: December 31

| | REVENUE ($ mil.) | NET INCOME ($ mil.) | NET PROFIT MARGIN | EMPLOYEES |
|---|---|---|---|---|
| **12/06** | 6,622 | 330 | 5.0% | 15,500 |
| **12/05** | 5,751 | 262 | 4.5% | 13,100 |
| **12/04** | 5,440 | 296 | 5.4% | 13,200 |
| **12/03** | 4,977 | 230 | 4.6% | 12,700 |
| **12/02** | 3,859 | 156 | 4.0% | 12,500 |
| **Annual Growth** | 14.5% | 20.5% | — | 5.5% |

### 2006 Year-End Financials

Debt ratio: 194.8%
Return on equity: 32.9%
Cash ($ mil.): 152
Current ratio: 1.21
Long-term debt ($ mil.): 2,270

No. of shares (mil.): 104
Dividends
Yield: 0.9%
Payout: 12.7%
Market value ($ mil.): 4,540

### Stock History

NYSE: BLL

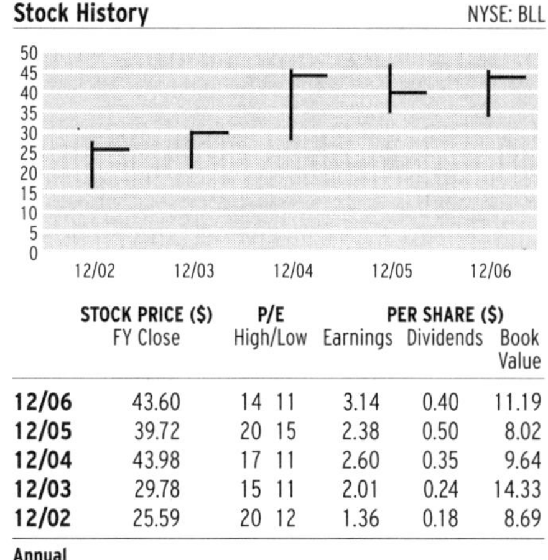


| | STOCK PRICE ($) FY Close | P/E High | P/E Low | PER SHARE ($) Earnings | Dividends | Book Value |
|---|---|---|---|---|---|---|
| **12/06** | 43.60 | 14 | 11 | 3.14 | 0.40 | 11.19 |
| **12/05** | 39.72 | 20 | 15 | 2.38 | 0.50 | 8.02 |
| **12/04** | 43.98 | 17 | 11 | 2.60 | 0.35 | 9.64 |
| **12/03** | 29.78 | 15 | 11 | 2.01 | 0.24 | 14.33 |
| **12/02** | 25.59 | 20 | 12 | 1.36 | 0.18 | 8.69 |
| **Annual Growth** | 14.2% | — | — | 23.3% | 22.1% | 6.5% |

# Bank of America

Welcome to the machine. The second-largest bank in the US by assets (behind Citigroup), Bank of America boasts the country's most extensive branch network, with more than 5,700 locations covering some 30 states from coast to coast. Its core services include consumer and small business banking, credit cards, investment banking and brokerage, and asset management. Bank of America fattened up by purchasing northeastern banking behemoth FleetBoston for some $50 billion in 2004 and credit card giant MBNA in early 2006. It later bought U.S. Trust from Charles Schwab for more than $3 billion and arranged to acquire Chicago-based LaSalle Bank for some $21 billion from Netherlands-based ABN AMRO.

There is one small hitch in the latter deal. ABN AMRO has agreed to be acquired by Barclays in one of the largest bank mergers ever, but is also being courted by a consortium led by Royal Bank of Scotland and Banco Santander Central Hispano that would retain LaSalle Bank.

Following the 2007 acquisition of U.S. Trust, Bank of America merged the asset manager with its private banking and wealth management business to form U.S. Trust, Bank of America Private Wealth Management.

Bank of America's purchase of MBNA, worth approximately $35 billion in cash and stock, roughly doubled the bank's credit card customer base (as well as its income from credit card fees) and gives the bank access to some 5,000 organizations and institutions with which MBNA had affinity marketing relationships.

Global Consumer and Small Business Banking, which includes credit cards, is Bank of America's largest segment. The bank claims market share leadership in such key (and far-flung) markets as California, Florida, Massachusetts, New Jersey, and Washington State.

Federal law prohibits banks from surpassing 10% of domestic deposits through acquisitions, and the MBNA deal caused Bank of America to approach that threshold, as did the FleetBoston purchase. As a result, the bank has not been aggressively bidding for corporate deposits and has taken the unusual tack of lowering interest rates on deposit and savings accounts in California, perhaps to discourage new or existing customers. The only bank near the 10% cap, Bank of America holds about 9.7% of all domestic deposits.

Abroad, Bank of America has offices in about 40 countries. It owns about a quarter of one of Mexico's largest banks, Grupo Financiero Santander Serfin, a subsidiary of Santander Central Hispano (SCH), augmenting Bank of America's domestic campaign to attract Hispanic customers. In Asia, Bank of America acquired a 9% stake in China Construction Bank in 2006. As part of the deal, it later sold its operations in Hong Kong and Macau to the Chinese bank.

Bank of America bought a 5% stake in General Motors from Kirk Kerkorian's Tracinda Corporation in 2006.

## HISTORY

Bank of America predecessor NationsBank was formed as the Commercial National Bank in 1874 by citizens of Charlotte, North Carolina. In 1901 George Stephens and Word Wood formed what became American Trust Co. The banks merged in 1957 to become American Commercial Bank, which in 1960 merged with Security National to form North Carolina National Bank.

In 1968 the bank formed holding company NCNB, which by 1980 was the largest bank in North Carolina. Under the leadership of Hugh McColl, who became chairman in 1983, NCNB became the first southern bank to span six states.

NCNB profited from the savings and loan crisis of the late 1980s by managing assets and buying defunct thrifts at fire-sale prices. The company nearly doubled its assets in 1988, when the FDIC chose it to manage the shuttered First Republicbank, then Texas' largest bank. The company renamed itself NationsBank in 1991.

A 1993 joint venture with Dean Witter and Discover to open securities brokerages in banks led to complaints that customers were not fully informed of the risks of some investments and that brokers were paying rebates to banking personnel for customer referrals. Dean Witter withdrew from the arrangement in 1994, and SEC investigations and a class-action lawsuit ensued. NationsBank settled the lawsuit for about $30 million the next year. (The company agreed to pay nearly $7 million to settle similar charges in 1998.)

Enter BankAmerica. Founded in 1904 as Bank of Italy, BankAmerica had once been the US's largest bank but had fallen behind as competitors consolidated. The company's board of directors was pondering ways to become more competitive and in 1998 decided a merger was the best way, and NationsBank obliged.

After the merger, the combined firm announced it would write down a billion-dollar bad loan to D.E. Shaw & Co., which followed the same Russian-investment-paved path of descent as Long-Term Capital Management. David Coulter (head of the old BankAmerica, which made the loan) took the fall for the loss, resigning as president; the balance of power shifted to the NationsBank side in 1999 when Kenneth Lewis took the post. The bank changed its name to Bank of America that year.

EVP Frank Gentry, who crafted the NationsBank/BankAmerica deal, retired in 2000. McColl retired as chairman in 2001.

In 2003 Bank of America's mutual fund chief Robert Gordon was among several employees who left the firm amidst a New York attorney general's investigation into hedge fund client

Canary Capital Partners, which allegedly had access to Bank of America's trading platform to make illegal after-hours trades of the company's erstwhile Nations Funds. Bank of America also paid $10 million for failing to provide documents to the SEC during its investigation of the scandal, the largest-ever fine levied by the regulatory body for such an infraction.

In early 2005 the company struck a deal with regulators to implement tighter controls, cut fees charged to investors, exit the mutual fund clearing business, and pay more than $500 million in fines, including $140 million to settle complaints against FleetBoston. Also that year, Bank of America remitted about another $460 million to settle investor claims that it did not adequately conduct due diligence when underwriting bonds of doomed telecom firm WorldCom in 2001 and 2002. (The claim involved 17 other investment banks as well; Citigroup paid more than $2.2 billion to clear itself of similar charges in late 2004.)

The company sold its securities clearing and broker/dealer services units to ADP in 2004.

## EXECUTIVES

**Chairman, President, and CEO:** Kenneth D. (Ken) Lewis, age 60, $7,150,000 pay
**Vice Chairman and President, Global Corporate and Investment Banking:** R. Eugene (Gene) Taylor, age 56, $3,841,667 pay
**COO for the Office of the CFO:** Milton H. Jones Jr.
**CFO:** Joe Price, age 45
**President, Bank of America Card Services:** Bruce L. Hammonds, age 56
**President, Global Consumer and Small Business Banking:** Liam E. McGee, age 50, $3,776,667 pay (prior to title change)
**President, Global Wealth and Investment Management:** Brian T. Moynihan, age 46, $3,676,667 pay
**EVP and Brand Marketing Executive:** Rick Parsons
**Global Risk Executive:** Amy W. Brinkley, age 49, $3,850,000 pay
**EVP and General Counsel:** Timothy (Tim) Mayopoulos, age 44
**SVP and Securities Regulation and Conflicts Management Executive:** Cynthia (Cindy) Fornelli
**SVP and Sports Sponsorship Executive:** Ray Bednar
**SVP, Brand and Advertising, Corporate Marketing Communications:** Kevin Anderson
**SVP and Strategic Marketing Executive, NASCAR Programs:** Jill Gregory
**SVP and Chief Accounting Officer:** Neil A. Cotty
**Global Technology, Service, and Fulfillment Executive:** Barbara J. Desoer, age 51, $3,776,667 pay
**Consumer Sales and Service Executive:** Susan Faulkner
**Corporate Personnel Executive:** J. Steele Alphin
**Corporate Communications and Public Relations Executive:** Michael F. (Mike) Clement
**Chief Marketing Officer:** Anne M. Finucane, age 53
**Global Treasury Services Executive:** Catherine P. (Cathy) Bessant
**President, Bank of America California:** Janet Lamkin
**Principal Compliance Executive:** Charles Bowman
**Corporate Secretary and Deputy General Counsel:** William J. Mostyn III
**CTO:** Don Obert
**Treasurer:** J. Chandler (Chan) Martin
**Head, Corporate Security:** Chris Swecker, age 51
**Chief Investment Officer:** Walter J. Muller
**Investor Relations Executive:** Kevin Stitt
**Auditors:** PricewaterhouseCoopers LLP

## LOCATIONS

**HQ:** Bank of America Corporation
100 N. Tryon St., Bank of America Corporate Ctr., Charlotte, NC 28255
**Phone:** 704-386-5681 **Fax:** 704-386-6699
**Web:** www.bankofamerica.com

Bank of America has US branches in Arizona, Arkansas, California, Connecticut, the District of Columbia, Florida, Georgia, Idaho, Illinois, Iowa, Kansas, Maine, Maryland, Massachusetts, Missouri, Nevada, New Hampshire, New Jersey, New Mexico, New York, North Carolina, Oklahoma, Oregon, Pennsylvania, Rhode Island, South Carolina, Tennessee, Texas, Virginia, and Washington.

## PRODUCTS/OPERATIONS

**2006 Sales**

| | $ mil. | % of total |
|---|---|---|
| Interest | | |
| Loans & leases, including fees | 48,274 | 41 |
| Securities, including dividends | 11,655 | 10 |
| Federal funds sold & securities purchased under resale agreements | 7,823 | 7 |
| Trading account assets | 7,232 | 6 |
| Other | 3,601 | 3 |
| Noninterest | | |
| Card income | 14,293 | 12 |
| Service charges | 8,224 | 7 |
| Investment & brokerage services | 4,456 | 4 |
| Equity investment gains | 3,189 | 3 |
| Trading account profits | 3,166 | 3 |
| Investment banking income | 2,317 | 2 |
| Other | 2,787 | 2 |
| **Total** | **117,017** | **100** |

**2006 Assets**

| | $ mil. | % of total |
|---|---|---|
| Cash & equivalents | 185,859 | 13 |
| Trading account | 153,052 | 10 |
| Derivative assets | 23,439 | 2 |
| Mortgage-backed securities | 156,893 | 11 |
| Other securities | 35,953 | 2 |
| Net loans & leases | 697,474 | 48 |
| Other | 207,067 | 14 |
| **Total** | **1,459,737** | **100** |

## COMPETITORS

American Express
BB&T
Citigroup
Citizens Financial Group
Countrywide Financial
HSBC Holdings
HSBC USA
JPMorgan Chase
KeyCorp
RBC Financial Group
SunTrust
TD Banknorth
UnionBanCal
U.S. Bancorp
Wachovia
Washington Mutual
Wells Fargo

## HISTORICAL FINANCIALS

Company Type: Public

**Income Statement** FYE: December 31

| | ASSETS ($ mil.) | NET INCOME ($ mil.) | INCOME AS % OF ASSETS | EMPLOYEES |
|---|---|---|---|---|
| **12/06** | 1,459,737 | 21,133 | 1.4% | 203,425 |
| **12/05** | 1,291,803 | 16,465 | 1.3% | 176,638 |
| **12/04** | 1,110,457 | 14,143 | 1.3% | 175,742 |
| **12/03** | 736,445 | 10,810 | 1.5% | 133,549 |
| **12/02** | 660,458 | 9,249 | 1.4% | 133,944 |
| **Annual Growth** | 21.9% | 22.9% | — | 11.0% |

**2006 Year-End Financials**

Equity as % of assets: 9.1%
Return on assets: 1.5%
Return on equity: 18.1%
Long-term debt ($ mil.): 230,009
No. of shares (mil.): 4,458
Dividends
Yield: 4.0%
Payout: 46.2%
Market value ($ mil.): 238,021
Sales ($ mil.): 117,017

**Stock History** NYSE: BAC

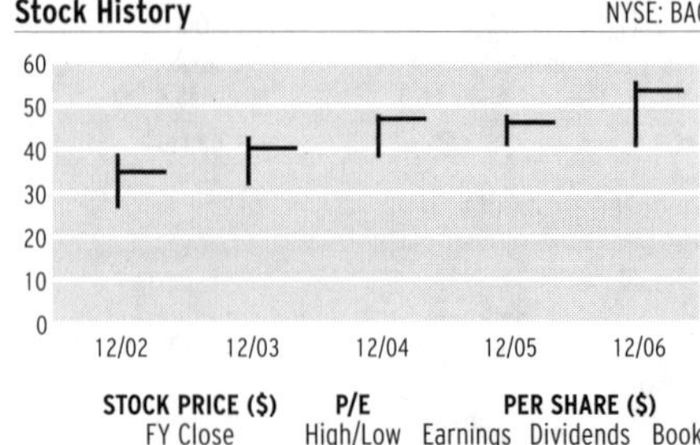


| | STOCK PRICE ($) FY Close | P/E High | P/E Low | PER SHARE ($) Earnings | Dividends | Book Value |
|---|---|---|---|---|---|---|
| **12/06** | 53.39 | 12 | 9 | 4.59 | 2.12 | 30.34 |
| **12/05** | 46.15 | 12 | 10 | 4.04 | 1.90 | 25.39 |
| **12/04** | 46.99 | 13 | 10 | 3.69 | 1.70 | 24.62 |
| **12/03** | 40.22 | 12 | 9 | 3.57 | 1.44 | 33.29 |
| **12/02** | 34.78 | 13 | 9 | 2.95 | 1.22 | 33.53 |
| **Annual Growth** | 11.3% | — | — | 11.7% | 14.8% | (2.5%) |

# Bank of New York Mellon

Big Apple, meet Iron City. The Bank of New York cemented its status as one of the world's largest asset administration firms with the 2007 acquisition of Pittsburgh-based Mellon Financial. The merger also fits in with the company's other areas of focus, asset management and corporate trust services. It was The Bank of New York's third attempt to acquire Mellon. Now known as The Bank of New York Mellon (BNY Mellon), the firm has about $20 trillion in assets under custody and more than $1 trillion of assets under management. The company has a presence in over 35 countries, including more than 80 wealth management offices in the US and the UK. Its Pershing subsidiary is a leading securities clearing firm.

The Bank of New York has jettisoned much of its traditional banking services for more lucrative fee-based securities and financial services; it swapped its retail branch network for JPMorgan Chase's trust business in 2006. In the deal, the bank swapped virtually its entire branch network in metropolitan New York for JPMorgan Chase's corporate trust business. Both units were valued at more than $2 billion each, and JPMorgan Chase paid an additional $150 million in cash to make up the difference.

By cutting loose its retail banking operations, The Bank of New York eliminated a stable source of reliable income but apparently feels the trade-off is worth it. The Mellon deal is part of a string of acquisitions through which the company is building its fee-based operations. The strategy has pushed the firm to the top of the heap of corporate trust providers, and its acquisition of TD Banknorth's bond administration operations gave it 350 bond trusteeships.

Subsidiaries BNY Capital Markets and Mellon Financial Markets offer investment banking services; BNY Mellon Asset Management serves institutions, while BNY Wealth Management courts well-to-do individual investors. Other services include brokerage, treasury management, and asset servicing.

The bank streamlined its order execution operations in a leveraged buyout deal that merged its trading businesses with Eze Castle Software. The deal created a new company called BNY ConvergEx. BNY owns more than 35%; GTCR Golden Rauner holds the same stake. Other insiders own the rest.

## HISTORY

In 1784 Alexander Hamilton (at 27, already a Revolutionary War hero and economic theorist) and a group of New York merchants and lawyers founded New York City's first bank, The Bank of New York (BNY). Hamilton saw a need for a credit system to finance the nation's growth and to establish credibility for the new nation's chaotic monetary system.

Hamilton became US secretary of the treasury in 1789 and soon negotiated the new US government's first loan — for $200,000 — from BNY. The bank later helped finance the War of 1812 by raising $16 million and the Civil War by loaning the government $150 million. In 1878 BNY became a US Treasury depository for the sale of government bonds.

The bank's conservative fiscal policies and emphasis on commercial banking enabled it to weather economic turbulence in the 19th century. In 1922 it merged with New York Life Insurance and Trust (formed in 1830 by many of BNY's directors) to form Bank of New York and Trust. The bank survived the crash of 1929 and remained profitable, paying dividends throughout the Depression. In 1938 it reclaimed its Bank of New York name.

During the mid-20th century, BNY expanded its operations and its reach through acquisitions, including Fifth Avenue Bank (trust services, 1948) and Empire Trust (serving developing industries, 1966). In 1968 the bank created holding company The Bank of New York Company to expand statewide with purchases such as Empire National Bank (1980).

BNY relaxed its lending policies in the 1980s and began to build its fee-for-service side, boosting its American Depositary Receipts business by directly soliciting European companies and seeking government securities business. The bank bought New York rival Irving Trust in a 1989 hostile takeover and in 1990 began buying other banks' credit card portfolios.

As the economy cooled in the early 1990s, BNY's book of highly leveraged transactions and nonperforming loans suffered, so the company sold many of those loans.

In the mid-1990s BNY bought processing and trust businesses and continued to build its retail business in the suburbs. It pared noncore operations, selling its mortgage banking unit (and in 1998 moved its remaining mortgage operations into a joint venture with Alliance Mortgage); credit card business (1998); and factoring and asset-based lending operations (1999). In late 1997 and again in 1998, the bank tried to woo Mellon Bank (now Mellon Financial) into a merger but was rejected: it had better luck in 2006.

The growth of the firm's custody services accelerated in the late 1990s. In 1997 BNY bought operations from Wells Fargo, Signet Bank (now part of First Union), and NationsBank (now Bank of America). In 2000 it acquired the trust operations of Royal Bank of Scotland and Barclays Bank. During this period BNY also built its other operations, largely through purchases. It bought the Bank of Montreal's UK-based fiscal agency business (1998) and Eastbrook Capital Management, which manages assets for businesses and wealthy individuals (1999).

Scandal rocked the firm in 1999 when the US began investigating the possible flow of money related to Russian organized crime; the following year a former bank executive admitted to having laundered about $7 billion through BNY.

In 2000 BNY bought the corporate trust business of Dai-Ichi Kangyo Bank (now part of Mizuho Financial) and Harris Trust and Savings Bank. It also purchased a trio of securities clearing and processing firms, in addition to hedge fund manager Ivy Asset Management.

BNY's purchases in 2002 included equity research firm Jaywalk, institutional trader Francis P. Maglio & Co., and a pair of Boston-area asset managers for high-net-worth individuals, Gannet Welsh & Kotler and Beacon Fiduciary Advisors. BNY bought Pershing from Credit Suisse First Boston in 2003.

Fallout from the money laundering scandal lingered. In 2006 the Federal Reserve accused the bank of not tightening its own controls to prevent a recurrence of illegal activity.

## EXECUTIVES

**Executive Chairman:** Thomas A. Renyi, age 61, $2,592,000 pay
**Vice Chairman and General Counsel:** John M. Liftin, age 63
**Vice Chairman; Co-Head, Integration:** Donald R. (Don) Monks, age 57, $1,618,000 pay
**Senior Vice Chairman; Co-Head, Integration:** Steven G. Elliott, age 60
**CEO and Director:** Robert P. (Bob) Kelly, age 52
**President and Director:** Gerald L. Hassell, age 55, $1,875,000 pay
**CFO:** Bruce W. Van Saun, age 50, $1,681,000 pay
**Chief Risk Officer:** Thomas P. (Todd) Gibbons, age 49, $1,791,000 pay (prior to title change)
**CEO, Pershing:** Richard F. (Rich) Brueckner
**Vice Chairman, Gannett Welsh & Kotler:** Benjamin H. Gannett
**CEO, Gannett Welsh & Kotler:** Harold G. Kotler
**Co-President, Gannett Welsh & Kotler:** Thomas F.X. (Tom) Powers
**Co-President, Gannett Welsh & Kotler:** T. Williams (Bill) Roberts III
**CEO, Issuer and Treasury Services:** Brian G. Rogan, $2,160,000 pay
**CEO, The Bank of New York Mellon Corporate Trust:** Karen B. Peetz
**CEO, BNY Mellon Wealth Management:** David F. (Dave) Lamere, age 46
**CEO, BNY Mellon Asset Management:** Ronald P. (Ron) O'Hanley, age 50
**Co-CEO, BNY Mellon Asset Servicing:** James P. (Jim) Palermo, age 50
**Co-CEO, BNY Mellon Asset Servicing:** Timothy F. (Tim) Keaney
**Head of Corporate Consulting:** Kevin C. Piccoli, age 48
**Head, Product Development and Risk Management Group, The Private Bank and BNY Asset Management:** Joseph F. Murphy
**Managing Director and Head, Investor Services, Asia-Pacific, The Bank of New York:** Chong Jin Leow
**Chief Client Management Officer:** Torry Berntsen
**CIO:** Kurt D. Woetzel
**Chairman, Mellon Global Investments and Dreyfus:** Jonathan M. (Jon) Little
**Managing Director and Head, Investor Relations:** Kenneth A. (Ken) Brause
**Chief Human Resources Officer:** Lisa B. Peters
**General Counsel:** Carl Krasik
**Auditors:** Ernst & Young LLP

## LOCATIONS

**HQ:** The Bank of New York Mellon Corporation
1 Wall St., 10th Fl., New York, NY 10286
**Phone:** 212-495-1784 **Fax:** 212-809-9528
**Web:** www.bnymellon.com

## PRODUCTS/OPERATIONS

### 2006 Sales

| | $ mil. | % of total |
|---|---|---|
| Interest | | |
| Loans | 1,779 | 20 |
| Securities | 1,130 | 12 |
| Bank deposits | 538 | 6 |
| Other | 293 | 3 |
| Noninterest income | | |
| Securities servicing fees | 3,537 | 39 |
| Private banking & asset management fees | 569 | 6 |
| Foreign exchange & other trading activity | 425 | 5 |
| Global payment services | 252 | 3 |
| Other service charges & fees | 207 | 2 |
| Other | 332 | 4 |
| **Total** | **9,062** | **100** |

### 2006 Assets

| | $ mil. | % of total |
|---|---|---|
| Cash & equivalents | 16,012 | 16 |
| Trading assets | 5,544 | 5 |
| Securities | 21,106 | 21 |
| Net loans | 37,506 | 36 |
| Other | 23,202 | 22 |
| **Total** | **103,370** | **100** |

## COMPETITORS

Bank of America
Brown Brothers Harriman
CIBC
Citigroup
Credit Suisse (USA)
Deutsche Bank
HSBC Holdings
ING
JPMorgan Chase
KeyCorp
Mizuho Financial
Northern Trust
State Street
UBS
Wachovia

## HISTORICAL FINANCIALS

Company Type: Public

### Income Statement

FYE: December 31

| | ASSETS ($ mil.) | NET INCOME ($ mil.) | INCOME AS % OF ASSETS | EMPLOYEES |
|---|---|---|---|---|
| **12/06** | 103,370 | 3,011 | 2.9% | 22,961 |
| **12/05** | 102,074 | 1,571 | 1.5% | 23,451 |
| **12/04** | 94,529 | 1,440 | 1.5% | 23,363 |
| **12/03** | 92,397 | 1,157 | 1.3% | 22,901 |
| **12/02** | 77,564 | 902 | 1.2% | 19,435 |
| **Annual Growth** | 7.4% | 35.2% | — | 4.3% |

### 2006 Year-End Financials

Equity as % of assets: 11.2%
Return on assets: 2.9%
Return on equity: 28.0%
Long-term debt ($ mil.): 10,398
Sales ($ mil.): 9,062

### Net Income History

NYSE: BK

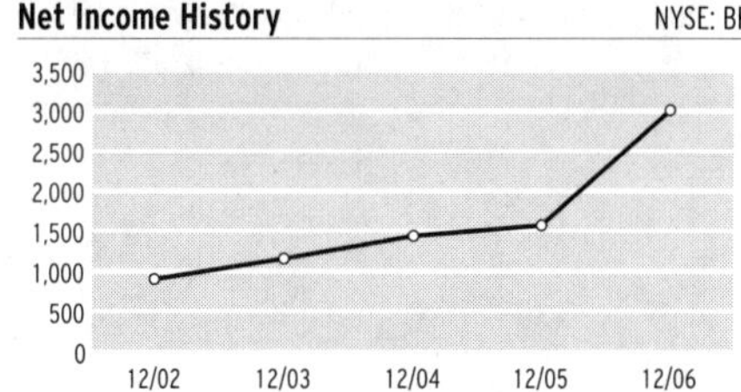

# Barnes & Noble

Barnes & Noble does business — big business — by the book. As the #1 bookseller in the US, it operates some 700 Barnes & Noble superstores throughout all 50 US states and the District of Columbia. It also owns almost 100 mostly mall-based B. Dalton bookstores. In cyberspace, the firm conducts sales through barnesandnoble.com (accounting for about 10% of total sales). Barnes & Noble's remaining businesses include general trade book publisher Sterling Publishing Co., and a 74% interest in seasonal kiosk retailer Calendar Club. The company exited the video game retailing business in 2004 when it spun off its GameStop subsidiary — the #1 US video game retailer.

Barnes & Noble stores are typically 10,000 to 60,000 sq. ft. and stock between 60,000 to 200,000 book titles. Many locations contain Starbucks cafes, as well as music departments carrying over 40,000 music titles. The company intends to open about 35 to 40 Barnes & Noble locations in fiscal 2007. B. Dalton locations are about 2,000 to 6,000 sq. ft., with more than 90% of those locations in enclosed shopping malls. B. Dalton has largely been an underperforming business unit, and Barnes & Noble is gradually shutting down those stores (it closed more than 20 B. Daltons in 2006). All told, the company controls about 17% of the consumer book market.

Not the most comfortable of bedfellows to begin with, Barnes & Noble further aggravated mainstream publishers when it purchased Sterling Publishing in 2003. Barnes & Noble expects its publishing business to grow to 10% of its revenues before 2010. In addition to the how-to books, Barnes & Noble courts self-published authors through a 22% stake in publishing portal iUniverse.

Chairman Leonard Riggio controls about 20% of the company.

## HISTORY

Barnes & Noble dates back to 1873 when Charles Barnes went into the used-book business in Wheaton, Illinois. By the turn of the century, he was operating a thriving bookselling operation in Chicago. His son William took over as president in 1902. William sold his share in the firm in 1917 (to C. W. Follett, who built Follett Corp.) and moved to New York City, where he bought an interest in established textbook wholesalers Noble & Noble. The company was soon renamed Barnes & Noble. It first sold mainly to colleges and libraries, providing textbooks and opening a large Fifth Avenue shop. Over the next three decades, Barnes & Noble became one of the leading booksellers in the New York region.

Enter Leonard Riggio, who worked at a New York University bookstore to help pay for night school. He studied engineering but got the itch for bookselling. In 1965, at age 24, he borrowed $5,000 and opened Student Book Exchange NYC, a college bookstore. Beginning in the late 1960s, he expanded by buying other college bookstores.

In 1971 Riggio paid $1.2 million for the Barnes & Noble store on Fifth Avenue. He soon expanded the store, and in 1974 he began offering jaw-dropping, competitor-maddening discounts of up to 40% for best-sellers. Acquiring Marboro Books five years later, the company entered the mail-order and publishing business.

By 1986 Barnes & Noble had grown to about 180 outlets (including 142 college bookstores). Along with Dutch retailer Vendex, that year it bought Dayton Hudson's B. Dalton mall bookstore chain (about 800 stores), forming BDB Holding Corp. (Vendex had sold its shares by 1997.) In 1989 the company acquired the Scribner's Bookstores trade name and the Bookstop/Bookstar superstore chain. BDB began its shift to superstore format and streamlined its operations to integrate Bookstop and Doubleday (acquired in 1990) into its business.

BDB changed its name to Barnes & Noble in 1991. With superstore sales booming, the retailer went public in 1993 (the college stores remained private). It bought 20% of Canadian bookseller Chapters (now Indigo Books) in 1996 (then sold in 1999).

The bookseller went online in 1997, and in 1998 sold a 50% stake in its Web operation subsidiary to Bertelsmann (which it re-purchased in 2003) in an attempt to strengthen both companies in the battle against online rival Amazon.com.

Also in 1998 Barnes & Noble agreed to buy #1 US book distributor Ingram Book Group, but the deal was called off in 1999 because of antitrust concerns. Also in 1999 barnesandnoble.com went public and Barnes & Noble bought small book publisher J.B. Fairfax International USA, which included coffee-table book publisher Michael Friedman Publishing Group. Later that year the company bought a 49% stake in book publishing portal iUniverse.com (later reduced to 22%). It also bought Riggio's financially struggling Babbage's Etc., a chain of about 500 Babbage's, Software Etc., and GameStop stores, for $215 million.

The company's Babbage's Etc. subsidiary (renamed GameStop, Inc.) acquired video game retailer Funco for $161.5 million in 2000. In 2001 Barnes & Noble joined barnesandnoble.com in acquiring a majority stake in magazine subscription seller enews.com.

In 2002 the company completed an IPO of its GameStop unit, reducing its ownership interest to about 63%. Leonard also handed over the CEO title to his brother, Steve Riggio. Another development during that busy year included shutting down enews.com due to repeated quarterly losses.

In 2003, the company beefed up its self-publishing efforts with the purchase of Sterling Publishing, a specialist in how-to and craft books. In addition, Barnes & Noble's half-owned *BOOK* magazine shut down. The next year saw Barnes & Noble exit the video game retailing business when it spun off its remaining shares in GameStop.

## EXECUTIVES

**Chairman:** Leonard S. Riggio, age 66, $500,000 pay
**Vice Chairman and CEO:** Stephen (Steve) Riggio, age 52, $786,538 pay
**COO:** Mitchell S. Klipper, age 49, $786,538 pay
**CFO:** Joseph J. Lombardi, age 45, $830,385 pay
**EVP Distribution and Logistics:** William F. Duffy, age 51, $417,115 pay
**SVP, Corporate Communications and Public Affairs:** Mary Ellen Keating, age 50
**VP and Director of Stores:** Mark Bottini, age 46
**VP Author Relations:** Brenda Marsh
**VP Barnes & Noble Development:** David S. Deason, age 48
**VP Human Resources:** Michelle Smith, age 54
**President, Barnes & Noble Publishing Group:** J. Alan Kahn, age 60, $990,000 pay
**CEO, barnesandnoble.com:** Marie J. Toulantis, age 53, $1,636,538 pay
**VP and CIO:** Christopher (Chris) Grady-Troia, age 55
**Director of Corporate Communications:** Carolyn Brown
**Manager of Investor Relations:** Andy Milevoj
**Auditors:** BDO Seidman, LLP

## LOCATIONS

**HQ:** Barnes & Noble, Inc.
122 5th Ave., New York, NY 10011
**Phone:** 212-633-3300 **Fax:** 212-675-0413
**Web:** www.barnesandnobleinc.com

Barnes & Noble has bookstores in all 50 US states and Washington, DC.

**2007 Stores**

| | No. |
|---|---|
| Barnes & Noble | 695 |
| B. Dalton | 98 |
| **Total** | **793** |

## PRODUCTS/OPERATIONS

**2007 Sales**

| | $ mil. | % of total |
|---|---|---|
| Barnes & Noble stores | 4,534 | 86 |
| barnesandnoble.com | 433 | 8 |
| B. Dalton stores | 102 | 2 |
| Other | 192 | 4 |
| **Total** | **5,261** | **100** |

## COMPETITORS

Amazon.com
Best Buy
Book-of-the-Month Club
Books-A-Million
Borders
Buy.com
Circuit City
Costco Wholesale
Half Price Books
Hastings Entertainment
HMV
Wal-Mart

## HISTORICAL FINANCIALS

Company Type: Public

**Income Statement** FYE: Saturday nearest January 31

| | REVENUE ($ mil.) | NET INCOME ($ mil.) | NET PROFIT MARGIN | EMPLOYEES |
|---|---|---|---|---|
| **1/07** | 5,261 | 151 | 2.9% | 39,000 |
| **1/06** | 5,103 | 147 | 2.9% | 39,000 |
| **1/05** | 4,874 | 143 | 2.9% | 42,000 |
| **1/04** | 5,951 | 152 | 2.6% | 43,000 |
| **1/03** | 5,269 | 100 | 1.9% | 39,000 |
| **Annual Growth** | (0.0%) | 10.8% | — | 0.0% |

**2007 Year-End Financials**

Debt ratio: —
Return on equity: 13.2%
Cash ($ mil.): 349
Current ratio: 1.28
Long-term debt ($ mil.): —
No. of shares (mil.): 65
Dividends
Yield: 1.5%
Payout: 27.6%
Market value ($ mil.): 2,632

**Stock History** NYSE: BKS

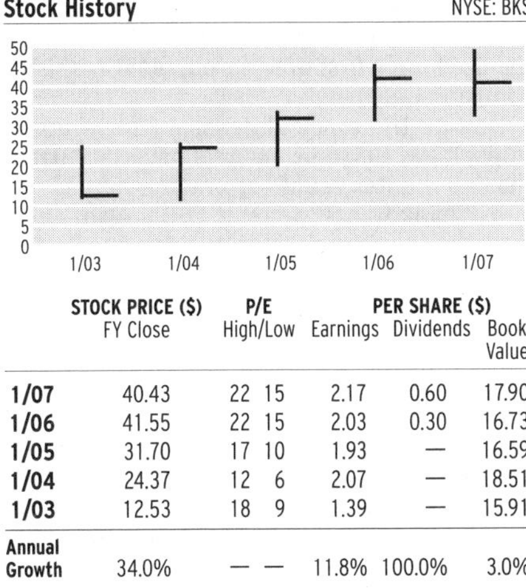


| | STOCK PRICE ($) FY Close | P/E High/Low | | PER SHARE ($) Earnings | Dividends | Book Value |
|---|---|---|---|---|---|---|
| **1/07** | 40.43 | 22 | 15 | 2.17 | 0.60 | 17.90 |
| **1/06** | 41.55 | 22 | 15 | 2.03 | 0.30 | 16.73 |
| **1/05** | 31.70 | 17 | 10 | 1.93 | — | 16.59 |
| **1/04** | 24.37 | 12 | 6 | 2.07 | — | 18.51 |
| **1/03** | 12.53 | 18 | 9 | 1.39 | — | 15.91 |
| **Annual Growth** | 34.0% | — | — | 11.8% | 100.0% | 3.0% |

# Baxter International

Baxter International wants to treat you right. The company makes treatments for those who suffer from cancer, kidney disease, immune deficiencies, and other diseases. It is a leading maker of intravenous (IV) supplies and systems via its Medication Delivery segment. Baxter's BioScience segment makes equipment to collect and separate blood and blood components and also develops plasma protein therapies for such blood-related disorders as hemophilia. Baxter's Renal segment markets products for the treatment of end-stage renal disease (ESRD). Baxter has been selling off underperforming units and cutting jobs in an effort to better the bottom line.

Baxter has divested the majority of the services portion of its Renal division. The company has also sold off some of its dialysis clinics, especially clinics located in Latin America and Europe. It has also sold its Transfusion Therapies business, which makes blood-collection and storage products, to Texas Pacific Group.

Baxter bought Fusion Medical in 2002 to expand its BioScience unit. The BioScience segment, which develops products such as recombinants and plasma proteins used in the treatment of blood disorders like hemophilia, accounts for more than 40% of sales. The company's Avate product is the only Factor VIII treatment for hemophilia that does not utilize human or animal proteins in the production process. As a result, treatments are shifting from plasma-based products to recombinants, leading to a decline in sales from the former.

The BioScience unit also makes vaccines for infectious diseases such as meningitis C and smallpox. It is developing products for SARS, Lyme disease, and influenza. In 2007 the company inked a deal with the British government to supply the flu vaccine in case of pandemic.

Baxter's Medication Delivery unit accounts for nearly 40% of sales. The division manufactures IV drug delivery systems, infusion systems, and anesthesia products. One recent product development in this area is a wireless drug delivery system that links the Colleague CX infusion pump with its barcode tracking and patient management software products.

Along with dialyzers — dialysis equipment used primarily in hospitals or outpatient environments — Baxter is also a leading maker of a self-administered renal dialysis treatment used in the home known as peritoneal dialysis.

## HISTORY

Idaho surgeon Ralph Falk, his brother Harry, and California physician Donald Baxter formed Don Baxter Intravenous Products in 1931 to distribute the IV solutions Baxter made in Los Angeles. Two years later the company opened its first plant, located outside Chicago. Ralph Falk bought Baxter's interest in 1935 and began R&D efforts leading to the first sterilized vacuum-type blood collection device (1939), which could store blood for weeks instead of hours. Product demand during WWII spurred sales above $1.5 million by 1945.

In 1949 the company created Travenol Laboratories to make and sell drugs. Baxter went public in 1951 and began an acquisition program the next year. In 1953 failing health caused both Falks to give control to William Graham, a manager since 1945. Under Graham's leadership, Baxter absorbed Wallerstein (1957); Fenwal Labs (1959); Flint, Eaton (1959); and Dayton Flexible Products (1967).

In 1975 Baxter's headquarters moved to Deerfield, Illinois. In 1978 the company debuted the first portable dialysis machine and had $1 billion in sales. Vernon Loucks Jr. became CEO two years later. Baxter claimed the title of the world's leading hospital supplier in 1985 when it bought American Hospital Supply (a Baxter distributor from 1932 to 1962). Offering more than 120,000 products and an electronic system that connected customers with some 1,500 vendors, Baxter captured nearly 25% of the US hospital supply market in 1988. That year it became Baxter International.

In 1992 Baxter spun off Caremark (home infusion therapy and mail-order drugs) but kept a division that controlled 75% of the world's dialysis machine market.

In 1993 Baxter pleaded guilty (and was temporarily suspended from selling to the Veterans Administration) to bribing Syria to remove Baxter from a blacklist for trading in Israel.

The company entered the US cardiovascular perfusion services market in 1995 with the purchases of PSICOR and SETA. Baxter, along with two other silicone breast-implant makers, agreed to settle thousands of claims (at an average of $26,000 each) from women suffering side-effects from the implants. The next year Baxter spun off its cost management and hospital supply business as Allegiance (sold to Cardinal Health in 1999). Buys in 1997 boosted Baxter's presence in Europe and its share of the open-heart-surgery devices market. That year it agreed to pay about 20% of a $670 million legal settlement in a suit relating to hemophiliacs infected with HIV from blood products.

In response to concerns posed by shareholders, Baxter in 1999 said it would phase out the use of PVC (polyvinyl chloride) in some products by 2010. In 2000 the firm spun off its underperforming cardiovascular unit as Edwards Lifesciences. To strengthen core operations, it lined up a number of purchases, including North American Vaccine.

Purchases in 2001 included the cancer treatment unit of chemicals firm Degussa. Also that year Baxter withdrew dialysis equipment from Spain and Croatia after patients who used its products died. It also ended production of two types of dialyzers that were sold there. As the number of deaths mounted to more than 50 in seven countries, Baxter began facing lawsuits; it later settled with the families of many of the patients. In September 2002, the FDA issued a warning when several patients died after using Baxter's Meridian dialysis machines.

Robert L. Parkinson, Jr. took over as chairman and CEO in April 2004. Parkinson succeeded Harry M. Jansen Kraemer, Jr. William Graham, who remained on the Baxter board of directors as honorary chairman emeritus after his official retirement in 1996, died in 2006.

In 2005 the FDA seized Baxter's existing inventories of previously recalled 6,000 Colleague Volumetric Infusion Pumps and nearly 1,000 Syndeo PCA Syringe Pumps; the federal agency resorted to these measures after the company did not fix production and design problems with the pumps in a suitable amount of time; the initial recalls had taken place in July of that year. The pumps have been blamed for three deaths and six serious injuries.

## EXECUTIVES

**Chairman and CEO:** Robert L. Parkinson Jr., age 56, $1,190,769 pay
**Corporate VP and CFO:** Robert M. Davis, age 40, $359,331 pay
**Corporate VP; President, Baxter Europe:** Peter Nicklin
**Corporate VP and President, BioScience:** Joy A. Amundson, age 52, $508,053 pay
**Corporate VP and President, International:** John J. Greisch, age 51, $564,000 pay
**Corporate VP and President, Medication Delivery:** Peter J. Arduini, age 42, $477,077 pay
**Corporate VP; President, Renal:** Bruce McGillivray, age 51
**Corporate VP, Global Manufacturing Operations:** James Michael Gatling, age 57
**Corporate VP, Human Resources:** Jeanne K. Mason, age 51
**Corporate VP and General Counsel:** Susan R. Lichtenstein, age 50
**Corporate VP and Chief Scientific Officer:** Norbert G. Riedel, age 49
**Corporate VP and CIO:** Karenann K. Terrell, age 45
**Corporate VP, Integration and Strategy:** James R. Hurley, age 55
**Corporate VP, Quality:** Cheryl L. White, age 53
**Corporate VP; President, Asia Pacific:** Gerald Lema, age 46
**Corporate VP, Associate General Counsel, and Corporate Secretary:** David P. Scharf, age 39
**Corporate VP and Treasurer:** Robert J. Hombach, age 40
**VP, Global Regulatory Affairs and Medical Vigilance:** Steven Caffe
**VP, Investor Relations:** Mary Kay Ladone
**VP, Corporate Communications:** Thomas Kline
**VP, Research and Development, Medical Devices:** Robert H. Armstrong
**President, Baxter Latin America:** Carlos Alonso
**Corporate Controller:** Michael J. Baughman, age 42
**Director, External Communications:** Deborah Spak
**Auditors:** PricewaterhouseCoopers LLP

## LOCATIONS

**HQ:** Baxter International Inc.
1 Baxter Pkwy., Deerfield, IL 60015
**Phone:** 847-948-2000 **Fax:** 847-948-2016
**Web:** www.baxter.com

Baxter International has facilities in Australia, Austria, Belgium, Brazil, Canada, Chile, China, Colombia, Costa Rica, the Dominican Republic, France, Germany, Ireland, Italy, Japan, Malta, Mexico, New Zealand, the Philippines, Poland, Puerto Rico, Singapore, Spain, Switzerland, Tunisia, Turkey, the UK, and the US.

## PRODUCTS/OPERATIONS

### Selected Subsidiaries

Baxter AG (Austria)
Baxter BioScience Manufacturing Sarl (Switzerland)
Baxter Corporation (Canada)
Baxter Deutschland Holding GmbH (Germany)
Baxter Deutschland GmbH (Germany)
Baxter Export Corporation
Baxter Global Holdings Inc.
Baxter Handel GmbH
Baxter Healthcare (Asia) Pte. Ltd. (Singapore)
Baxter Healthcare (Holdings) Limited (UK)
Baxter Healthcare Corporation
Baxter Healthcare Corporation of Puerto Rico
Baxter Healthcare Limited (UK)
Baxter Healthcare Pty Ltd (Australia)
Baxter Healthcare S.A. (Switzerland)
Baxter Holdings Limited (Japan)
Baxter Holding Mexico S. de R.L. de C.V. (Mexico)
Baxter Hospitalar Ltda. (Brazil)
Baxter International, Inc.
Laboratorios Baxter S.A.
Baxter Manufacturing S.p.A. (Italy)
Baxter Plasma Services L.P.
Baxter Pharmaceutical Solutions LLC
Baxter S.A. (Belgium)
Baxter S.A. de C.V. (Mexico)
Baxter S.A.S. (France)
Baxter Services Corporation
Baxter Trading GmbH (Austria)
Baxter Trading GmbH (Switzerland)
Baxter Travenol S.A.S (France)
Baxter World Trade Corporation
Baxter World Trade S.A. (Belgium)
Bieffe Medital S.p.A. (Italy)

## COMPETITORS

Abbott Labs
Abraxis BioScience
Amgen
Bayer
BD
Boston Scientific
C. R. Bard
Covidien
CSL Behring
Eli Lilly
Fresenius Medical Care
Gambro AB
Genentech
Hospira
Johnson & Johnson
Medtronic
Merck
Novartis
Novo Nordisk
Pfizer
Roche
Sanofi-Aventis
Spectrum Laboratories
United States Surgical
Wyeth

## HISTORICAL FINANCIALS

Company Type: Public

**Income Statement** FYE: December 31

| | REVENUE ($ mil.) | NET INCOME ($ mil.) | NET PROFIT MARGIN | EMPLOYEES |
|---|---|---|---|---|
| **12/06** | 10,378 | 1,397 | 13.5% | 48,000 |
| **12/05** | 9,849 | 956 | 9.7% | 47,000 |
| **12/04** | 9,509 | 388 | 4.1% | 48,000 |
| **12/03** | 8,904 | 866 | 9.7% | 51,300 |
| **12/02** | 8,110 | 778 | 9.6% | 54,600 |
| **Annual Growth** | 6.4% | 15.8% | — | (3.2%) |

**2006 Year-End Financials**

Debt ratio: 40.9%
Return on equity: 26.4%
Cash ($ mil.): 2,485
Current ratio: 1.93
Long-term debt ($ mil.): 2,567
No. of shares (mil.): 650
Dividends
Yield: 1.3%
Payout: 27.2%
Market value ($ mil.): 30,176

**Stock History** NYSE: BAX

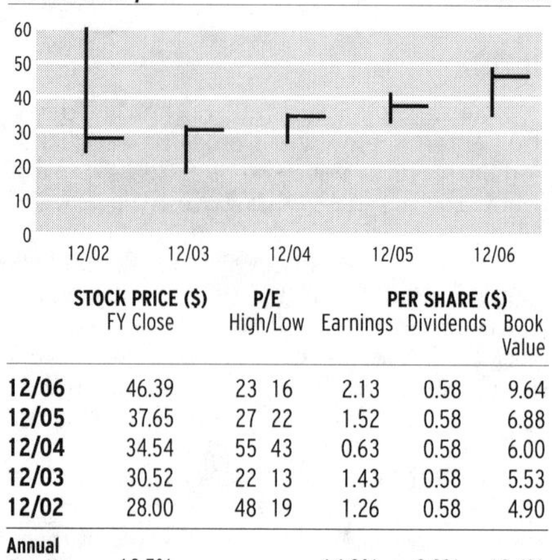


| | STOCK PRICE ($) FY Close | P/E High | P/E Low | PER SHARE ($) Earnings | PER SHARE ($) Dividends | PER SHARE ($) Book Value |
|---|---|---|---|---|---|---|
| **12/06** | 46.39 | 23 | 16 | 2.13 | 0.58 | 9.64 |
| **12/05** | 37.65 | 27 | 22 | 1.52 | 0.58 | 6.88 |
| **12/04** | 34.54 | 55 | 43 | 0.63 | 0.58 | 6.00 |
| **12/03** | 30.52 | 22 | 13 | 1.43 | 0.58 | 5.53 |
| **12/02** | 28.00 | 48 | 19 | 1.26 | 0.58 | 4.90 |
| **Annual Growth** | 13.5% | — | — | 14.0% | 0.0% | 18.4% |

# BB&T Corporation

Big, Bold & Temerarious? That might be an apt description of BB&T, the wildly acquisitive banking company that's been spreading across the Southeast like kudzu. The company serves consumers, small to midsized businesses, and government entities through more than 1,400 branches. Its flagship subsidiary, Branch Banking and Trust (aka BB&T), is one of North Carolina's oldest banks and a leading originator of residential mortgages in the Southeast. In addition to deposit accounts and loans, the company offers insurance, mutual funds, discount brokerage, wealth management, and financial planning services. Business services include leasing, factoring, and investment banking (through Scott & Stringfellow).

The company's ravenous expansion is all about creating cross-selling opportunities. By snatching up small insurance agencies (nearly 80 acquired since 1990), asset managers, and banks throughout the Southeast, the company has the ability to be a one-stop financial products shop. BB&T's bulk allows it to trump smaller competitors, yet the company has a community bank feel. Indeed, BB&T maintains decentralized regional management of its banks, and virtually all of its senior executives have been with the firm for two to three decades.

After snapping up several banks in 2003 and 2004 (including First Virginia Banks, one of BB&T's largest deals to date), the company took a breather in 2005 in order to assimilate its holdings. The buying began again in 2006, with deals for banks in Georgia (Main Street Banks), Tennessee (First Citizens Bancorp), and South Carolina (Coastal Financial).

BB&T also continued its strategy of purchasing niche companies with products that can be sold throughout the company. The purchase of AFCO Credit boosted the insurance premium financing operations of BB&T's specialized lending segment; it also expanded BB&T's reach into Canada for the first time, through AFCO's sister company CAFO.

Despite the renewed penchant for acquisitions, however, some analysts have speculated that the hunter could become the hunted if a larger bank wants to buy BB&T to gain entry into, or fortify a position in, the growing Southeast market. For its own part, BB&T has said it will probably need to forge a merger-of-equals deal during the coming years to survive.

## HISTORY

The predecessor to Branch Banking and Trust (BB&T) was founded in 1872 by Alpheus Branch, son of a wealthy planter, who founded Branch and Company, a mercantile business, in Wilson, North Carolina. He and Thomas Jefferson Hadley, who was organizing a public school system, created the Branch and Hadley bank. They helped rebuild farms and small businesses after the Civil War.

In 1887 Branch bought out Hadley and changed the bank's name to Branch and Company, Bankers. Two years later Branch secured a state trust charter for the Wilson Banking and Trust Company. He never got the business running, however, and died in 1893. The trust charter was amended to change the name to Branch Banking and Company, and Branch and Company, Bankers, was folded into it in 1900.

In 1907 the bank finally got its trust operations running and began calling itself Branch Banking and Trust Company. In 1922 it opened its first insurance department; the next year it started its mortgage loan activities.

BB&T survived the 1929 stock market crash with the help of the Post Office. Nervous customers withdrew their funds from BB&T and other banks and deposited them in postal savings accounts, unaware that BB&T was the local Post Office's bank and the withdrawn funds went right back to the bank. BB&T opened six more branches between 1929 and 1933.

After WWII consumerism skyrocketed, resulting in more car loans and mortgages. During the 1960s and 1970s the bank embarked on a series of mergers and acquisitions, forming the thin end of a buying wedge that would widen significantly in the coming decades.

By 1994 BB&T was the fourth-largest bank in North Carolina. In 1995 it merged with North Carolina's fifth-largest bank, Southern National Corp., founded in 1897.

With banking regulations loosening to allow different types of operations, BB&T in 1997 made several acquisitions, including banks, thrifts, and securities brokerage Craigie.

BB&T's 1998 activities included three bank acquisitions that pushed it into metro Washington, DC. The company also increased holdings in fields such as insurance sales, venture capital for Southern businesses, and investment banking (through its acquisition of Scott & Stringfellow Financial, the South's oldest NYSE member).

In 1999 Craigie was melded into Scott & Stringfellow. That year BB&T bought several insurance companies and small banks. The company continued its march through the South the following year, buying several Georgia banks and Tennessee's BankFirst. In 2001 BB&T purchased South Carolina's FirstSpartan Financial, multibank holding company Century South Banks, Maryland-based FCNB Corporation, and western Georgia's Community First Banking Company. To bolster its presence in the Washington, DC, market, it bought Virginia Capital Bancshares and F&M National.

BB&T purchased Alabama-based Cooney, Rikard & Curtin, a wholesale insurance broker active in 45 states, in 2002. Also that year it added about 100 branches in Kentucky after buying MidAmerica Bancorp and AREA Bancshares, and entered the coveted Florida market following its purchase of Regional Financial, the privately held parent of First South Bank.

## EXECUTIVES

**Chairman and CEO, BB&T and Branch Banking and Trust Company:** John A. Allison IV, age 59, $1,881,000 pay
**COO:** Kelly S. King, age 58, $1,201,750 pay
**SEVP and Chief Credit Officer:** W. Kendall (Ken) Chalk, age 61, $824,591 pay
**SEVP and Manager, Administrative Services; President, Branch Banking and Trust Company:** Robert E. Greene, age 57, $715,641 pay
**SEVP and CFO:** Christopher L. (Chris) Henson, age 46
**SEVP and Chief Marketing Officer:** Steven B. (Steve) Wiggs, age 49
**SEVP and Operations Division Manager:** C. Leon Wilson III, age 52, $692,922 pay
**SEVP and Operations Division Manager:** Leon Wilson
**EVP and Corporate Controller:** Edward D. (Ed) Vest
**SVP, Executive Communications and Corporate Communications:** Robert A. Denham
**SVP, Investor Relations:** Tamera Gjesdal, age 43
**Manager, Advertising and Public Relations:** Ron Denny
**Financial Services:** Robert L. (Lee) Youngblood, age 60
**President and CEO, Scott & Stringfellow:** Walter S. Robertson III
**President, BB&T Investment Services:** John D. Vaughan Jr.
**President, AFCO Credit and CAFO:** Daryl Zupan
**President, Commercial Finance:** J. Tol Broome Jr.
**Media Relations Manager:** A.C. McGraw
**Auditors:** PricewaterhouseCoopers LLP

## LOCATIONS

**HQ:** BB&T Corporation
200 W. 2nd St., Winston-Salem, NC 27101
**Phone:** 336-733-2000 **Fax:** 336-733-2470
**Web:** www.bbt.com

### 2006 Branches

| | No. |
|---|---|
| Virginia | 399 |
| North Carolina | 341 |
| Georgia | 150 |
| Maryland | 126 |
| Florida | 101 |
| South Carolina | 101 |
| Kentucky | 91 |
| West Virginia | 78 |
| Tennessee | 58 |
| Washington, DC | 10 |
| **Total** | **1,455** |

## PRODUCTS/OPERATIONS

### 2006 Sales

| | $ mil. | % of total |
|---|---|---|
| Interest income | | |
| Loans | 5,941 | 63 |
| Dividends, securities & other | 952 | 10 |
| Insurance commissions | 813 | 8 |
| Service charges on deposits | 548 | 6 |
| Investment banking & brokerage fees & commissions | 317 | 3 |
| Other nondeposit fees & commissions | 167 | 2 |
| Checkcard fees | 155 | 2 |
| Trust income | 154 | 2 |
| Bankcard fees & merchant discounts | 122 | 1 |
| Mortgage banking income | 108 | 1 |
| Income from bank-owned life insurance | 93 | 1 |
| Other | 117 | 1 |
| **Total** | **9,487** | **100** |

### 2006 Assets

| | $ mil. | % of total |
|---|---|---|
| Cash & equivalents | 2,865 | 2 |
| Trading securities | 2,147 | 2 |
| Securities available for sale | 20,721 | 17 |
| Net loans & leases | 82,023 | 68 |
| Other | 13,595 | 11 |
| **Total** | **121,351** | **100** |

### Selected Subsidiaries and Affiliates

BB&T Asset Management, Inc. (mutual funds)
BB&T Bankcard Corporation (revolving credit products)
BB&T Equipment Finance Corporation (lease financing)
BB&T Insurance Services, Inc. (insurance products)
BB&T Investment Services, Inc. (brokerage services)
Branch Banking and Trust Company (retail banking)
CRC Insurance Services, Inc. (wholesale insurance brokerage)
Laureate Capital, LLC (commercial mortgage lending)
Lendmark Financial Services, Inc. (subprime consumer and mortgage loans)
McGriff, Seibels & Williams, Inc. (insurance products)
MidAmerica Gift Certificate Company (retail gift certificates and gift cards)
Prime Rate Premium Finance Corporation, Inc. (insurance premium financing)
Regional Acceptance Corporation (indirect financing for consumer auto loans)
Scott & Stringfellow, Inc. (investment banking and brokerage)
Sheffield Financial LLC (consumer and commercial lending for outdoor power equipment)
Stanley, Hunt, DuPree & Rhine, Inc. (employee benefit plans and related consulting)

## COMPETITORS

Bank of America
First Charter
First Citizens BancShares
First Horizon
RBC Centura Banks
Regions Financial
SunTrust
Synovus
United Bankshares
Wachovia

## HISTORICAL FINANCIALS

Company Type: Public

### Income Statement

FYE: December 31

| | ASSETS ($ mil.) | NET INCOME ($ mil.) | INCOME AS % OF ASSETS | EMPLOYEES |
|---|---|---|---|---|
| **12/06** | 121,351 | 1,528 | 1.3% | 29,300 |
| **12/05** | 109,170 | 1,654 | 1.5% | 27,700 |
| **12/04** | 100,509 | 1,558 | 1.6% | 26,100 |
| **12/03** | 90,467 | 1,065 | 1.2% | 26,300 |
| **12/02** | 80,217 | 1,303 | 1.6% | 22,500 |
| **Annual Growth** | 10.9% | 4.1% | — | 6.8% |

### 2006 Year-End Financials

Equity as % of assets: 9.7%
Return on assets: 1.3%
Return on equity: 13.4%
Long-term debt ($ mil.): 15,904
No. of shares (mil.): 541
Dividends
Yield: 3.6%
Payout: 56.9%
Market value ($ mil.): 23,787
Sales ($ mil.): 9,487

### Stock History

NYSE: BBT

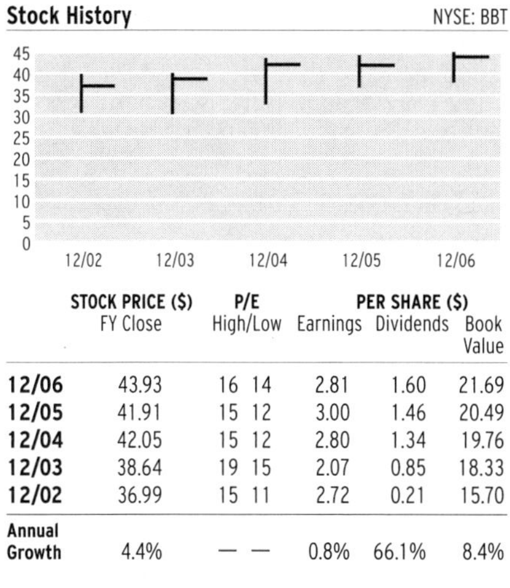


| | STOCK PRICE ($) FY Close | P/E High/Low | | PER SHARE ($) Earnings | Dividends | Book Value |
|---|---|---|---|---|---|---|
| **12/06** | 43.93 | 16 | 14 | 2.81 | 1.60 | 21.69 |
| **12/05** | 41.91 | 15 | 12 | 3.00 | 1.46 | 20.49 |
| **12/04** | 42.05 | 15 | 12 | 2.80 | 1.34 | 19.76 |
| **12/03** | 38.64 | 19 | 15 | 2.07 | 0.85 | 18.33 |
| **12/02** | 36.99 | 15 | 11 | 2.72 | 0.21 | 15.70 |
| **Annual Growth** | 4.4% | — | — | 0.8% | 66.1% | 8.4% |

# Bear Stearns

This bear never hibernates. One of the top investment banking, clearing, and brokerage firms in the US, The Bear Stearns Companies serves a worldwide clientele of corporations, institutional investors, governments, and well-to-do individuals. The company, through several subsidiaries, provides asset management, clearing and custody, securities lending, trust, and mergers and acquisitions advisory services. It is also a leading market-maker for NYSE-listed securities (through Bear Wagner Specialists), as well as for OTC shares, corporate and government bonds, and derivative products. Founded in 1923, Bear Stearns boasts more than 80 consecutive years of turning a profit.

Subsidiary Bear Energy, its energy industry trading unit, is acquiring the power trading assets of The Williams Companies.

Bear Stearns operates through three divisions: Capital Markets, Global Clearing Services, and Wealth Management. Capital Markets, the largest part of the firm's business, serves institutional and corporate clients and offers securities underwriting and trading, strategic advice to businesses, and merchant banking services. Global Clearing Services offers prime brokerage and clearing services, including margin lending and securities borrowing. Wealth Management encompasses Bear Stearns' private client and asset management business, which manages some $52 billion in assets for clients.

The company is increasing focus on middle-markets business, targeting banks, municipalities, and other institutions with less than $10 billion in assets. In 2007 it bought the subprime mortgage operations of ECC Capital Corporation. Through its Bear Growth Capital Partners subsidiary, it increased its retail investments with swimwear chain Just Add Water, which it added to its existing holdings in Everything But Water.

The company formed a joint venture with a consortium of Saudi businessmen called Bear Stearns Arabia Asset Management.

In 2007 Bear Stearns had to bail out two hedge funds that had invested heavily in subprime mortgages. The risky bet failed during a subprime market plunge, after many borrowers defaulted because of rising interest rates.

## HISTORY

Joseph Bear, Robert Stearns, and Harold Mayer formed Bear, Stearns & Co. in 1923 with $500,000 in capital. The firm weathered 1929's crash with no layoffs; during the Depression, Bear Stearns aggressively promoted government bonds.

Its first Chicago branch opened in 1940; it created an international department in 1948 and opened an Amsterdam office in 1955. Branches followed in Geneva (1963), San Francisco (1965), Paris (1967), and Los Angeles (1968).

Formerly a runner at Salomon Brothers, trader Salim "Cy" Lewis guided Bear Stearns in the 1950s and 1960s. He worked his way up to chairman, becoming a Wall Street legend as the driven, Scotch-drinking taskmaster of "The Bear" (and driving out Jerome Kohlberg, Henry Kravis, and George Roberts).

In 1973 Bear Stearns pulled profit out of unused space by giving independent brokers free rent in return for their use of the company for stock trade clearing. The practice became a major contributor to the firm's bottom line.

When Lewis died in 1978, Alan Greenberg became CEO; he surpassed Lewis' reputation for aggressive trading. Kansas-born, Oklahoma-reared Greenberg had worked his way up from clerk to the risk arbitrage desk at age 25.

Under Greenberg's colorful leadership the firm formed departments for government securities (1979) and mortgage-backed securities (1981) and also formed New Jersey bank and trust company Bear Stearns Asset Management and Custodial Trust (1984).

Bear Stearns went public in 1985 as The Bear Stearns Companies Inc. It moved into investment banking in the late 1980s and became the leading underwriter in the Latin American market in 1991. The firm also formed Bear Stearns Securities Corp. to handle clearing.

With success and a high profile came difficulties. The firm's underwriting volume prompted a deluge of lawsuits relating to junk bonds, hot IPOs that fizzled, point-of-sale and in-store advertising, and diet planner Jenny Craig.

The 1994 bond market crash mauled Bear Stearns. Because its fiscal year did not align with the calendar year, decreased earnings resulting from the crash were not posted until mid-1995, when most of its competitors had recovered. Lower earnings brought reduced bonuses, which prompted several high-level bond executives to leave.

In 1997 Bear Stearns joined forces with the National Mortgage Bank of Greece to introduce mortgage/asset securitization to that country; it also opened an office in Ireland to provide access to the unifying European market. That year the firm began investing in high-tech, communications, and media businesses.

Legal woes resurfaced in 1998 when the firm suffered adverse judgments over actions initiated in the late 1980s. One jury award ($108 million, reduced to $30 million by 2000) related to now-defunct Daisy Systems' purchase of Cadnetix; another award to bond underwriting for Weintraub Entertainment Group may eventually cost more than $120 million. In 1999 Bear Stearns agreed to pay $42 million to settle SEC charges relating to the firm's relationship with defunct brokerage A. R. Baron Company, which was accused of defrauding customers. The SEC also charged Richard Harriton, president of Bear Stearns' clearing unit, with fraud in connection with the case.

In 2001, the firm bought NYSE specialist Wagner Stott Mercator and merged it with its market-making joint venture with Hunter Partners; the unit was renamed Wagner Stott Bear Specialists (and later, Bear Wagner Specialists). In the same year, CEO James Cayne assumed the helm when Greenberg stepped down after more than 50 years with the company.

## EXECUTIVES

**Chairman and CEO, Bear Stearns Companies and Bear Stearns & Co.:** James E. (Jimmy) Cayne, age 72
**COO and CFO, Bear Stearns Companies and Bear, Stearns & Co.:** Samuel L. (Sam) Molinaro Jr., age 49
**Chairman of the Executive Committee:** Alan C. (Ace) Greenberg, age 79
**CIO, Co-Head of Equity Analytics and Systematic Trading, and Head of Operations and Technology:** Peter D. Cherasia
**President, Bear Stearns Companies and Bear, Stearns & Co.:** Alan D. Schwartz, age 56
**Senior Managing Director and Chief Risk Officer:** Michael Alix
**SVP Finance; Controller, Bear Stearns Companies and Bear Stearns & Co.:** Jeffrey M. Farber, age 42
**Treasurer, Bear Stearns Companies and Bear Stearns & Co.:** Michael (Mike) Minikes, age 63
**General Counsel, Bear Stearns Companies and Bear Stearns & Co.:** Michael S. Solender, age 42
**Senior Managing Director and Global Head of Human Resources:** Pamela O. Kimmet
**Senior Managing Director; Vice Chairman, Bear Stearns & Co.:** Fares D. Noujaim
**Vice Chairman, Bear Stearns & Co.:** E. John Rosenwald Jr., age 73
**Chairman, European Investment Banking:** Paul Abecassis, age 57
**CEO, Bear Stearns International:** Michel Peretie
**Chairman and CEO, Bear Stearns Asset Management (BSAM):** Jeffrey B. (Jeff) Lane
**Media Relations:** Russell Sherman
**Director of Investor Relations:** Elizabeth Ventura
**Auditors:** Deloitte & Touche LLP

## LOCATIONS

**HQ:** The Bear Stearns Companies Inc.
383 Madison Ave., New York, NY 10179
**Phone:** 212-272-2000 **Fax:** 212-272-4785
**Web:** www.bearstearns.com

The Bear Stearns Companies has US offices in Atlanta, Boston, Chicago, Dallas, Denver, Los Angeles, New York, San Francisco, and Scottsdale, Arizona. It also has offices in Beijing; Dublin, Ireland; Hong Kong; London; Lugano, Switzerland; Milan; San Juan, Puerto Rico; São Paulo; Seoul; Shanghai; Singapore; and Tokyo.

## PRODUCTS/OPERATIONS

### 2006 Sales

| | $ mil. | % of total |
|---|---|---|
| Interest & dividends | 8,536.0 | 52 |
| Principal transactions | 4,995.0 | 30 |
| Investment banking | 1,333.8 | 8 |
| Commissions | 1,162.7 | 7 |
| Asset management & other | 523.9 | 3 |
| **Total** | **16,551.4** | **100** |

### Selected Subsidiaries

Bear, Stearns & Co. Inc.
Bear Stearns Bank plc (Ireland)
Bear Stearns Capital Markets Inc.
Bear Stearns Commercial Mortgage, Inc.
Bear Stearns Credit Products Inc.
Bear Stearns Financial Products Inc.
Bear Stearns Forex Inc.
Bear Stearns Global Lending Limited (Cayman Islands)
Bear, Stearns International Trading Limited (UK)
Custodial Trust Company
EMC Mortgage Corporation

## COMPETITORS

AIG
AXA Financial
Banc of America Securities
Barclays
Brown Brothers Harriman
Charles Schwab
CIBC World Markets
Citigroup
Citigroup Global Markets
Credit Suisse
Deutsche Bank
Deutsche Bank Alex. Brown
Edward Jones
FMR
Goldman Sachs
HSBC Holdings
ING
INVESCO
JPMorgan Chase
Lehman Brothers
Merrill Lynch
Mitsubishi UFJ Financial Group
Morgan Stanley
National Financial Partners
Nomura Securities
Prudential
UBS
UBS Financial Services
UBS Investment Bank

## HISTORICAL FINANCIALS

Company Type: Public

### Income Statement

FYE: November 30

| | REVENUE ($ mil.) | NET INCOME ($ mil.) | NET PROFIT MARGIN | EMPLOYEES |
|---|---|---|---|---|
| 11/06 | 16,551 | 2,054 | 12.4% | 13,566 |
| 11/05 | 11,553 | 1,462 | 12.7% | 11,843 |
| 11/04 | 8,422 | 1,345 | 16.0% | 10,961 |
| 11/03 | 7,395 | 1,156 | 15.6% | 10,532 |
| 11/02 | 6,891 | 878 | 12.7% | 10,574 |
| Annual Growth | 24.5% | 23.7% | — | 6.4% |

### 2006 Year-End Financials

Debt ratio: 727.8%
Return on equity: 18.5%
Cash ($ mil.): 71,885
Current ratio: —
Long-term debt ($ mil.): 85,669
No. of shares (mil.): 117
Dividends
Yield: 0.7%
Payout: 7.8%
Market value ($ mil.): 17,903

### Stock History

NYSE: BSC

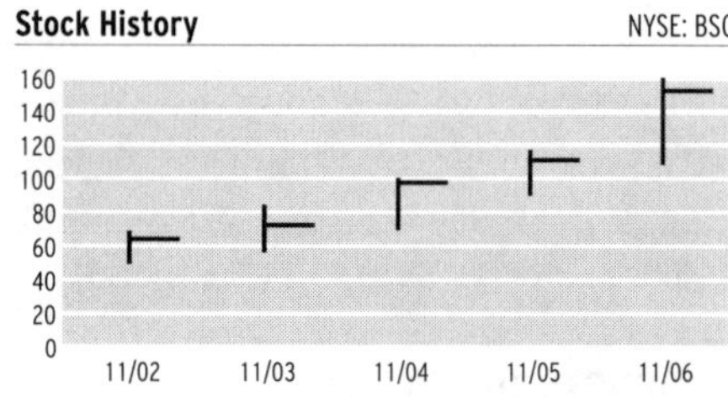


| | STOCK PRICE ($) FY Close | P/E High | P/E Low | PER SHARE ($) Earnings | PER SHARE ($) Dividends | PER SHARE ($) Book Value |
|---|---|---|---|---|---|---|
| 11/06 | 152.48 | 11 | 8 | 14.27 | 1.12 | 103.31 |
| 11/05 | 110.99 | 11 | 9 | 10.31 | 1.00 | 94.77 |
| 11/04 | 97.58 | 10 | 7 | 9.76 | 0.85 | 86.63 |
| 11/03 | 72.46 | 10 | 7 | 8.52 | 0.74 | 72.83 |
| 11/02 | 64.00 | 10 | 8 | 6.47 | 0.62 | 63.81 |
| Annual Growth | 24.2% | — | — | 21.9% | 15.9% | 12.8% |

# Beazer Homes USA

Beazer Homes USA builds for the middle-class buyer who's ready to make the move into the white-picket-fence scene. Beazer builds nearly 19,000 single-family homes a year — at an average price of about $287,000 — for entry-level and move-up buyers. The company operates in high-growth regions in more than 20 states. Its Beazer Mortgage subsidiary originates mortgages for its homebuyers; another unit provides title insurance services in selected Beazer markets. Company-operated design centers offer homebuyers customization regarding such features as appliances, cabinetry, flooring, fixtures, and wall coverings. Like most large homebuilders, Beazer subcontracts to build its homes.

While Beazer Homes USA primarily builds in the eastern and western regions of the US — along with Texas in the middle — it would like to cover the country like the dew. To achieve geographic expansion, the company has absorbed other builders (as it did with its Crossman Communities acquisition), extending its reach into the Southeast and Midwest.

Beazer is working to leverage its brand across the markets it serves in order to build recognition and address customer needs as one company, in an industry that is rapidly consolidating. Roughly 55% of the company's staff serve in sales, marketing, or executive roles.

In 2005 Beazer announced it would take a goodwill impairment charge related to its operations in Indiana, Kentucky, North Carolina, and Ohio. It concluded that operations in those areas suffered from relatively weak economies and strong price competition in the entry-level price range. The same year, Beazer began operations in new markets in California, Florida, Georgia, Indiana, New Mexico, and New York.

Although new construction had been going gangbusters for most of 2005, the housing bubble eventually began to leak, if not actually burst. Beazer and its competitors reported a decline in orders and a general contraction of the market in 2006. The company was investigated by federal regulators regarding its subprime mortgage lending practices. The company responded by reorganizing its overhead structure, cutting about 25% of its employees, and exiting some of its land options, as well as markets in Indiana and Tennessee. Beazer in 2006 teamed with The St. Joe Company in an agreement for Beazer to build single-family homes in several Florida communities developed by St. Joe.

## HISTORY

Beazer Homes USA traces its roots to a construction business started in the late 1950s in Bath, England, by the Beazer family. The company's operations grew to include homebuilding, quarrying, contracting, and real estate. In 1985 Beazer moved into the US and expanded throughout the Southeast in a series of acquisitions.

In 1988 the company bought US aggregates company Koppers in a deal that gave Beazer a presence in US building materials but also left it deep in debt. That debt, plus a recession, had Beazer struggling by 1991, when it was acquired by UK-based Hanson PLC. Hanson spun off the US homebuilding portion of Beazer in 1994 as Beazer Homes USA, which has continued to expand geographically through acquisitions in growth markets. In 1995 it bought Bramalea Homes Texas.

Beazer continued its march across the Sunbelt in 1996, buying homebuilders in Arizona, Florida, and Texas, and it established Beazer Mortgage. During that year Beazer ran into trouble in Nevada, where cost overruns dragged down the company's 1997 results. That year Beazer acquired Florida homebuilder Calton and formed a joint venture with Mexico's Corporacion GEO to build affordable housing; however, the venture was closed in 2000. The next year it bought Snow Construction of Florida and entered the Mid-Atlantic market by buying Kvaerner's US homebuilding arm, Trafalgar House.

In 2001 the company moved into Colorado by buying Denver-based builder Sanford Homes. The next year Beazer acquired Crossman Communities in a $500 million cash and stock deal, which contributed to a 2% increase in new orders for fiscal 2003. Overall, new orders were up 20% that year, breaking the company's record. The company also had a record 7,426 homes (valued at $1.6 billion) in its backlog. Beazer continued to break its own record through 2004 with annual revenues nearing the $4 billion mark, along with a 36.5% increase in annual earnings. Its backlog that year exceeded 8,400 homes.

In 2005 Beazer entered new markets in California (Fresno), Florida (Sarasota), Georgia (Savannah), Indiana (Ft. Wayne), New Mexico (Albuquerque), and New York (Orange County) and closed on more than 18,100 homes. It ended the year with more than 9,200 homes (worth more than $2.7 billion) in backlog.

## EXECUTIVES

**Chairman:** Brian C. Beazer, age 72
**President, CEO, and Director:** Ian J. McCarthy, age 53, $8,333,653 pay
**EVP and COO:** Michael H. (Mike) Furlow, age 56, $4,000,844 pay
**EVP and CFO:** Allan P. Merrill, age 40
**SVP Corporate Strategy and Innovation:** Jonathan P. Smoke, age 36
**SVP Financial Services and Treasurer:** Cory J. Boydston, age 47
**SVP, Forward Planning:** John Skelton, age 57
**SVP, Human Resources:** Fred Fratto, age 51
**SVP and General Counsel, Real Estate:** C. Lowell Ball, age 48
**VP Audit and Controls:** John D. Maggard
**VP Construction Quality and Workplace Safety:** Edmond G. Snider Jr.
**VP Investor Relations and Corporate Communications:** Leslie H. Kratcoski
**VP National Brand:** Joseph C. Thompson
**VP Planning and Design:** Gonzolo Romero
**VP Risk Management:** W. Mark Berry
**VP Sales and Marketing:** Marilyn Gardner
**President, Beazer Mortgage Corporation:** Ron J. Kuhn
**CIO:** Cindy B. Tierney
**Auditors:** Deloitte & Touche LLP

## LOCATIONS

**HQ:** Beazer Homes USA, Inc.
1000 Abernathy Rd., Ste. 1200, Atlanta, GA 30328
**Phone:** 770-829-3700 **Fax:** 770-481-2808
**Web:** www.beazer.com

Beazer Homes USA operates in Arizona, California, Colorado, Delaware, Florida, Georgia, Indiana, Kentucky, Maryland, Nevada, New Jersey, New Mexico, New York, North Carolina, Ohio, Pennsylvania, South Carolina, Tennessee, Texas, Virginia, and West Virginia.

### 2006 Homes Closed

| | No. |
|---|---|
| Southeast | |
| Florida | 2,274 |
| Other states | 4,289 |
| West | 5,035 |
| Mid-Atlantic | 2,086 |
| Other | 4,985 |
| **Total** | **18,669** |

## PRODUCTS/OPERATIONS

### 2006 Sales

| | $ mil. | % of total |
|---|---|---|
| Homebuilding | 5,325.6 | 97 |
| Land & lot sales | 90.2 | 2 |
| Mortgage origination | 65.8 | 1 |
| Adjustments | (19.6) | — |
| **Total** | **5,462.0** | **100** |

## COMPETITORS

C. P. Morgan
Centex
D.R. Horton
Hovnanian Enterprises
KB Home
Lennar
M.D.C.
Meritage Homes
NVR
Pulte Homes
Ryland
Standard Pacific
Toll Brothers
William Lyon Homes

## HISTORICAL FINANCIALS

Company Type: Public

### Income Statement

FYE: September 30

| | REVENUE ($ mil.) | NET INCOME ($ mil.) | NET PROFIT MARGIN | EMPLOYEES |
|---|---|---|---|---|
| **9/06** | 5,462 | 389 | 7.1% | 4,234 |
| **9/05** | 4,995 | 263 | 5.3% | 4,578 |
| **9/04** | 3,907 | 236 | 6.0% | 3,428 |
| **9/03** | 3,177 | 173 | 5.4% | 2,986 |
| **9/02** | 2,641 | 123 | 4.6% | 2,890 |
| **Annual Growth** | 19.9% | 33.4% | — | 10.0% |

### 2006 Year-End Financials

Debt ratio: 108.0%
Return on equity: 24.2%
Cash ($ mil.): 172
Current ratio: 28.53
Long-term debt ($ mil.): 1,839
No. of shares (mil.): 39
Dividends
Yield: 1.0%
Payout: 4.5%
Market value ($ mil.): 1,518

### Stock History

NYSE: BZH

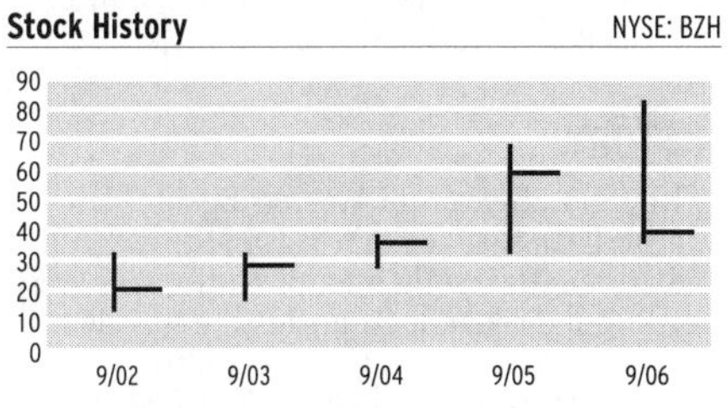


| | STOCK PRICE ($) FY Close | P/E High | P/E Low | PER SHARE ($) Earnings | Dividends | Book Value |
|---|---|---|---|---|---|---|
| **9/06** | 39.04 | 9 | 4 | 8.89 | 0.40 | 43.76 |
| **9/05** | 58.67 | 11 | 6 | 5.87 | 0.33 | 36.08 |
| **9/04** | 35.63 | 7 | 5 | 5.70 | 0.13 | 89.74 |
| **9/03** | 28.13 | 7 | 4 | 4.26 | — | 73.37 |
| **9/02** | 20.35 | 9 | 4 | 3.58 | — | 62.00 |
| **Annual Growth** | 17.7% | — | — | 25.5% | 75.4% | (8.3%) |

# Bechtel Group

Whether the job is raising an entire city or razing a nuclear power plant, you can bet the Bechtel Group will be there to bid on the business. The firm is the US's #1 contractor (ahead of Fluor) per *Engineering News-Record*. The engineering, construction, and project management firm operates worldwide and has participated in such notable projects as the construction of Hoover Dam and the cleanup of the Chernobyl nuclear plant. Bechtel's Oil, Gas & Chemical business unit and Bechtel National, its government contracts group, are its leading revenue producers. The group is in its fourth generation of leadership by the Bechtel family, with chairman and CEO Riley Bechtel at the helm.

Bechtel has made a name for itself by participating in mega-projects. In addition to providing its core project management and design services, it offers such services as environmental restoration and remediation, telecommunications infrastructure (installing cable-optic networks and constructing data centers), and project financing through Bechtel Enterprises.

Bechtel National is the prime contractor for design and construction of the Hanford Waste Treatment Plant in Washington State, one of the DOE's most complex cleanup projects. The project's aim is to treat 53 million gallons of high-level radioactive waste stored at the Hanford site.

Among Bechtel's more traditional (perhaps notorious) infrastructure projects has been its involvement in the "Big Dig," Boston's Central Artery/Tunnel project. Bechtel, in a joint venture with Parsons Brinckerhoff, has served as lead contractor on the $14.6 billion project, which has been the subject of much dispute over cost overruns and safety issues. After a death occurred in which the ceiling collapsed on a motorist, the National Transportation Safety Board said that Bechtel was partially at fault.

In Europe it is expanding its rail business by participating in the construction of the Channel Tunnel Rail Link, the UK's first major new railroad project in a century. It is also managing the upgrade of the UK's West Coast main line and has joined a consortium to renovate part of London's 140-year-old subway. The group provides telecommunications services to US government entities through its Bechtel Federal Telecoms unit.

Bechtel was one of the companies that received contracts to help rebuild Iraq's infrastructure beginning in 2003. It exited the country in 2006 as its contracts expired.

## HISTORY

In 1898 25-year-old Warren Bechtel left his Kansas farm to grade railroads in the Oklahoma Indian territories, then followed the rails west. Settling in Oakland, California, he founded his own contracting firm. Foreseeing the importance of roads, oil, and power, he won big projects such as the Northern California Highway and the Bowman Dam. By 1925, when he incorporated his company as W.A. Bechtel & Co., it ranked as the West's largest construction company. In 1931 Bechtel helped found the consortium that built Hoover Dam.

Under the leadership of Steve Bechtel (president after his father's death in 1933), the company obtained contracts for large infrastructure projects such as the San Francisco-Oakland Bay Bridge. Noted for his friendships with influential people, including Dwight Eisenhower, Adlai Stevenson, and Saudi Arabia's King Faisal, Steve developed projects that spanned nations and industries, such as pipelines in Saudi Arabia and numerous power projects. By 1960, when Steve Bechtel Jr. took over, the company was operating on six continents.

In the next two decades, Bechtel worked on transportation projects — such as San Francisco's Bay Area Rapid Transit (BART) system and the Washington, DC, subway system — and power projects, including nuclear plants. After the 1979 Three Mile Island accident, Bechtel tried its hand at nuclear cleanup. With nuclear power no longer in vogue, it focused on other markets, such as mining in New Guinea (gold and copper, 1981-84) and China (coal, 1984). Bechtel's Jubail project in Saudi Arabia, begun in 1976, raised an entire industrial port city on the Persian Gulf.

The US recession and rising developing-world debt of the early 1980s sent Bechtel reeling. It cut its workforce by 22,000 and stemmed losses by piling up small projects.

Riley Bechtel, great-grandson of Warren, became CEO in 1990. After the 1991 Gulf War, Bechtel extinguished Kuwait's flaming oil wells and worked on the oil-spill cleanup. During the decade it also worked on such projects as the Channel tunnel (Chunnel) between England and France, the new Hong Kong airport, and pipelines in the former Soviet Union.

Bechtel was part of the consortium contracted in 1996 to build a high-speed passenger rail line between London and the Chunnel. International Generating (InterGen), Bechtel's joint venture with Pacific Gas and Electric (PG&E), was chosen to help build Mexico's first private power plant. In 1996 Bechtel bought PG&E's share of InterGen, then sold a 50% stake in InterGen to a unit of Royal Dutch Shell in early 1997.

In 1998 Bechtel joined Battelle and Electricité de France in project management of a long-term plan to stabilize the damaged reactor of the Chernobyl nuclear plant in Ukraine.

The next year Bechtel was hired to decommission the Connecticut Yankee nuclear plant. It also won contracts with Internet companies, including failed online grocer Webvan, to build a series of 26 automated grocery warehouses in the US in a deal worth nearly $1 billion. However, only four were completed before Webvan fizzled in mid-2001.

Bechtel expanded its telecommunications operations in 2001 to provide turnkey network implementation services in Europe, the Middle East, and Asia. In 2002 Bechtel was once again called on to work on the UK's rail system, taking over management of the upgrade of the West Coast main line from financially troubled Railtrack. As part of a consortium with UK facilities management giants Jarvis and Amey, Bechtel began work that year on a 30-year project to modernize part of London's aging subway system.

In 2005 Bechtel and joint venture partner Shell Oil sold InterGen, its power production joint venture, to AIG Highstar Capital for about $1.75 billion.

## EXECUTIVES

**Chairman Emeritus:** Stephen D. (Steve) Bechtel Jr., age 82
**Chairman and CEO:** Riley P. Bechtel, age 54
**President, COO, and Director:** Adrian Zaccaria
**EVP, Deputy COO, and Director:** Jude Laspa
**EVP and Director; Chairman, Bechtel National, Inc.; President, Bechtel Systems and Infrastructure:** Thomas F. (Tom) Hash
**EVP and Director; President, Oil, Gas & Chemicals:** Bill Dudley
**EVP and Director; President, Telecommunications:** Tim Statton
**EVP, Engineering, Procurement & Construction Functions:** Carl Rau
**EVP Strategy, Marketing, and Business Development, Bechtel Systems and Infrastructure:** Craig Weaver
**EVP, Houston Operations:** Jim Jackson
**SVP, CFO, and Director:** Peter Dawson
**SVP, General Counsel, and Director; Manager, Legal and Internal Audit:** Judith Miller
**SVP and Director; President, Power Global Business Unit:** Scott Ogilvie
**SVP and Manager, Upstream Market Sector, Oil, Gas and Chemicals:** Jim Illich
**SVP and Manager, Human Resources:** Mary Moreton
**Secretary and Director:** Foster Wollen
**Manager, External Affairs and Communications:** James (Jim) Lamble
**Auditors:** PricewaterhouseCoopers LLP

## LOCATIONS

**HQ:** Bechtel Group, Inc.
50 Beale St., San Francisco, CA 94105
**Phone:** 415-768-1234 **Fax:** 415-768-9038
**Web:** www.bechtel.com

Bechtel Group operates worldwide from offices in a dozen states in the US, along with international offices in Australia, Brazil, Canada, Chile, Greater China, Egypt, France, India, Indonesia, Japan, Korea, Malaysia, Mexico, Peru, Philippines, Qatar, Russia, Saudi Arabia, Singapore, Thailand, Turkey, United Arab Emirates, and the UK.

## PRODUCTS/OPERATIONS

### Selected Services

Construction
Engineering
Financing and development
Procurement
Project management
Safety
Technology

### Selected Markets

Civil infrastructure (airports, rail, highways, heavy civil)
Communications (wireless and other telecommunications)
Mining and metals
Oil, gas, and chemicals (Design and construction for chemical, petrochemical, LNG and natural gas plants, and pipelines)
Power electrical (gas, oil, coal, and nuclear power plants)
U.S. Government Services (defense, space, demilitarization, security, nuclear, and environmental restoration and remediation services)

## COMPETITORS

ABB Lummus Global
Aker Kværner
AMEC
Balfour Construction
Black & Veatch
Bouygues
CH2M HILL
Chiyoda Corp.
EIFFAGE
Fluor
Foster Wheeler
Halliburton
HOCHTIEF
Hyundai Engineering
ITOCHU
Jacobs Engineering
Kajima
Marelich Mechanical
Parsons
Perini
Peter Kiewit Sons'
RWE
Schneider Electric
Shaw Group
Siemens AG
Skanska
SNEF
Technip
URS
VINCI
Washington Group
Weston
WFI Government Services

## HISTORICAL FINANCIALS

Company Type: Private

**Income Statement** FYE: December 31

| | REVENUE ($ mil.) | NET INCOME ($ mil.) | NET PROFIT MARGIN | EMPLOYEES |
|---|---|---|---|---|
| **12/06** | 20,500 | — | — | 40,000 |
| **12/05** | 18,100 | — | — | 40,000 |
| **12/04** | 17,378 | — | — | 40,000 |
| **12/03** | 16,337 | — | — | 44,000 |
| **12/02** | 11,622 | — | — | 47,000 |
| **Annual Growth** | 15.2% | — | — | (4.0%) |

**Revenue History**

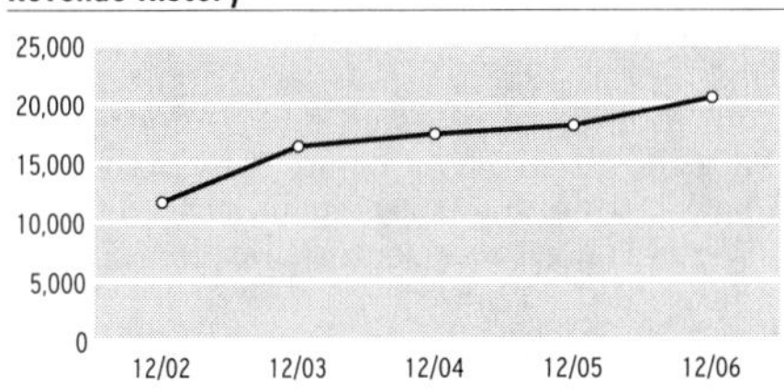


# Beckman Coulter

Like the nerdiest kid in school, Beckman Coulter never saw a test it didn't love. The company makes all kinds of diagnostic testing systems, from simple blood tests to complicated genetic diagnostic tools used by hospital-based and other clinical laboratories to suss out diseases and monitor their progression. Its clinical products include immunoassay, clinical chemistry, and hematology systems, as well as products in the growing field of molecular diagnostics. In addition to its systems for diagnosing patients, Beckman Coulter makes products used by life sciences researchers, including those at academic research centers and drug companies, to understand disease and develop new therapies.

Beckman Coulter has installed more than 200,000 of its systems around the world. Along with instruments, it sells reagents and supplies that provide recurring revenue over the life of a system.

The company counts on developing improved and new systems that cost-effectively perform high volumes of tests for its health care and life sciences clients. In 2006 it introduced a new parathyroid hormone immunoassay and a new large hematology system, among other products. It also announced plans to develop a fully automated molecular diagnostics system for clinical laboratories.

The company has gained new technologies and products through acquisitions as well. In 2005 it bought Diagnostic Systems Laboratories, a maker of specialty diagnostics in the areas of reproductive endocrinology and cardiovascular risk assessment. The following year it acquired Lumigen, whose proprietary chemiluminescent chemistry is the same detection technology used in Beckman Coulter's Access line of immunoassay systems.

The company announced in 2007 an agreement to acquire Biosite, a maker of immunoassay tests, in an effort to strengthen Beckman's immunoassay capabilities. A rival offer from Inverness Medical Innovations, however, sparked a bidding war over Biosite, and Beckman eventually decided to bow out of the fight.

In addition to new product development, Beckman Coulter's growth strategy focuses on committing resources to developing markets such as China and India and creating new reagents and other consumables that will strengthen its recurring revenue stream.

The company has taken several measures to streamline its operations and better use its resources, including restructuring in 2005 into one reporting segment (it had formerly operated in two divisions: clinical diagnostics and biomedical research). As part of the restructuring, the firm reduced its workforce and exited some development projects, including tests for mad cow disease and sepsis. It is also streamlining its supply chain operations and has announced plans to close its Palo Alto, California, manufacturing facility.

## HISTORY

Arnold Beckman created his first chemistry lab as a child in a shed his blacksmith father had built for him. Beckman studied chemical engineering, worked at Bell Labs (now part of Lucent Technologies), and then earned his doctorate in photochemistry in 1928 from the California Institute of Technology. In 1935, while teaching at CalTech and working as a consultant, Beckman created a special ink for the National Postage Meter Company. He formed the National Inking Appliance Company (later National Technical Laboratories), which was 90% owned by National Postage Meter and 10% owned by Beckman.

In 1935 Beckman also created a device for a Southern California citrus processor that measured lemon juice acidity. Beckman's acidity, or pH, meter soon became a standard tool in chemical laboratories. In 1941 he debuted a wavelength spectrum analysis system, a forerunner of today's analytical precision and chemical analysis instruments. That year the company's sales topped $250,000.

The company became Beckman Instruments in 1950 and went public two years later. During that period the company created products for aerospace, military, and industrial markets. However, it increasingly focused on the medical and research niches, and during the 1960s it introduced glucose analyzers and protein peptide sequencers. By 1975 Beckman Instruments' annual sales neared $230 million.

An 82-year-old Beckman sold his company to SmithKline in 1982, creating SmithKline Beckman. In 1988 Louis Rosso, who as president had guided Beckman's move into life sciences and diagnostics, was named CEO. SmithKline Beckman in 1989 merged with UK pharmaceuticals pioneer Beecham Group, becoming SmithKline Beecham. (That company merged with Glaxo Wellcome to become GlaxoSmithKline plc in 2000.) Beckman, operating as a unit within SmithKline Beecham, suffered financially as a result of cuts in health care spending. SmithKline Beecham spun the company off that year as a medical and research market instrument maker.

New products and cost controls returned Beckman Instruments to health. The company restructured in 1993 (taking write-offs in 1993 and 1994), then launched a buying spree. It acquired Genomyx, a maker of DNA sequencing products, in 1996. In late 1997 the company acquired Coulter, which served the same hospitals and medical offices as Beckman — only with hematology products — for $1.2 billion.

Wallace Coulter in 1948 discovered a new technology for blood cell analysis, dubbed the Coulter Principle. With brother Joe, an electrical engineer, Wallace (who died in 1998) began producing the Coulter Counter cell and particle analyzer. The brothers formed Coulter Electronics in 1958. Over the years the private company made tests to detect everything from colon cancer to strep throat, but it became best known for blood cell analysis diagnostic systems.

Beckman Instruments' purchase of Coulter, which led to job cuts (13% of its workforce), caused losses for 1997. The next year the company changed its name to Beckman Coulter. John Wareham, an executive with Beckman since the early 1980s, replaced Rosso as CEO.

The addition of the Coulter product lines enabled the company to win 1999 contracts from several regional health care networks and large purchasing organizations. In 2000 the company initiated some restructuring by closing plants in Argentina, Brazil, and Hong Kong.

## EXECUTIVES

**Chairman:** Betty Woods, age 68
**President, CEO, and Director:** Scott Garrett, age 57, $730,366 pay
**EVP, Worldwide Commercial Operations:** Robert W. (Bob) Kleinert Jr., age 55, $331,894 pay
**SVP and Chief Scientific Officer:** G. Russell (Russ) Bell, age 61
**SVP and CFO:** Charles P. (Charlie) Slacik, age 52, $112,692 pay (partial-year salary)
**SVP, General Counsel, and Secretary:** Arnold A. Pinkston, age 48, $380,000 pay
**SVP, Human Resources and Communications:** J. Robert Hurley, age 57
**SVP, Quality and Regulatory Affairs:** Robert (Bob) Boghosian, age 61
**SVP, Strategy and Business Development:** Paul Glyer, age 50
**Corporate VP, Asia Pacific and Latin America Commercial Operations:** James F. (Jim) Widergren
**Group VP, Lab Systems and Routine Testing, Diagnostics Division:** Jeff McHugh
**VP, Controller, and Principal Accounting Officer:** Carolyn D. Beaver, age 48, $221,952 pay
**VP and Treasurer:** Roger B. Plotkin
**Director, Investor Relations:** Robert H. Raynor
**Corporate Communications:** Mary F. Luthy
**Auditors:** KPMG LLP

## LOCATIONS

**HQ:** Beckman Coulter, Inc.
4300 N. Harbor Blvd., Fullerton, CA 92834
**Phone:** 714-871-4848 **Fax:** 714-773-8283
**Web:** www.beckmancoulter.com

Beckman Coulter has facilities in Australia, Austria, China, France, Germany, India, Ireland, Switzerland, and the US.

### 2006 Sales

| | $ mil. | % of total |
|---|---|---|
| US | 1,330.0 | 53 |
| Other countries | 1,198.5 | 47 |
| **Total** | **2,528.5** | **100** |

## PRODUCTS/OPERATIONS

### 2006 Sales

| | $ mil. | % of total |
|---|---|---|
| Cellular systems | 806.3 | 32 |
| Chemistry systems | 677.1 | 27 |
| Discovery & automation systems | 560.7 | 22 |
| Immunoassay systems | 484.4 | 19 |
| **Total** | **2,528.5** | **100** |

### Selected Products

Cellular systems
- Flow cytometry systems (COULTER EPICS ALTRA HyPerSort Cell Sorting System, Cytomics FC 500)
- Hematology systems (COULTER LH, COULTER Ac-T)
- Hemostasis systems (ACL, Hemoliance)

Chemistry systems
- Electrophoresis systems (Paragon)
- Routine chemistry systems (UniCel DxC 600, UnicEl DxC 800 SYNCHRON)
- Point-of-care testing (Hemoccult, Gastrocult, FlexSure HP)

Discovery and automation systems
- Biomarker discovery (ProteomeLab)
- Centrifugation (Microfuge, Allegra, Avanti)
- Clinical laboratory automation (Power Processor System, AutoMate 800)
- Genetic analysis systems (CEQ, GenomeLab)
- Life sciences automation (Biomek)
- Molecular diagnostics (Vidiera)
- Particle characterization products (Vi-CELL)

Immunoassay systems (Access)

## COMPETITORS

Abbott Labs
Agilent Technologies
Applied Biosystems
BD Biosciences
Bio-Rad Labs
Caliper Life Sciences
Dade Behring
Dako
GE Healthcare
GE Healthcare Bio-Sciences
Harvard Bioscience
Hitachi High-Technologies
Kendro Laboratory Products
Luminex
Ortho-Clinical Diagnostics
PerkinElmer
Roche Diagnostics
Shimadzu
Siemens Medical Solutions Diagnostics
Sysmex Amer
Thermo Fisher Scientific
Ventana Medical
Vysis
Waters Corporation

## HISTORICAL FINANCIALS

Company Type: Public

### Income Statement

FYE: December 31

| | REVENUE ($ mil.) | NET INCOME ($ mil.) | NET PROFIT MARGIN | EMPLOYEES |
|---|---|---|---|---|
| **12/06** | 2,529 | 187 | 7.4% | 10,340 |
| **12/05** | 2,444 | 151 | 6.2% | 10,416 |
| **12/04** | 2,408 | 211 | 8.8% | 10,200 |
| **12/03** | 2,193 | 207 | 9.5% | 9,900 |
| **12/02** | 2,059 | 136 | 6.6% | 10,000 |
| **Annual Growth** | 5.3% | 8.4% | — | 0.8% |

### 2006 Year-End Financials

Debt ratio: 82.5%
Return on equity: 15.9%
Cash ($ mil.): 75
Current ratio: 1.88
Long-term debt ($ mil.): 952
No. of shares (mil.): 61
Dividends
Yield: 1.0%
Payout: 20.5%
Market value ($ mil.): 3,648

### Stock History

NYSE: BEC

| | STOCK PRICE ($) FY Close | P/E High | P/E Low | Earnings | Dividends | Book Value |
|---|---|---|---|---|---|---|
| **12/06** | 59.80 | 21 | 17 | 2.92 | 0.60 | 18.92 |
| **12/05** | 56.90 | 32 | 21 | 2.32 | 0.56 | 18.93 |
| **12/04** | 66.99 | 21 | 15 | 3.21 | 0.48 | 17.76 |
| **12/03** | 50.83 | 16 | 9 | 3.21 | 0.40 | 14.48 |
| **12/02** | 29.52 | 25 | 12 | 2.08 | 0.35 | 9.71 |
| **Annual Growth** | 19.3% | — | — | 8.9% | 14.4% | 18.2% |

(PER SHARE ($): Earnings, Dividends, Book Value)

# Becton, Dickinson

Don't worry, you'll only feel a slight prick if Becton, Dickinson (BD) is at work. The company's BD Medical segment is one of the top manufacturers of syringes and other injection and infusion devices in the world. BD Medical also makes pre-fillable drug delivery systems, sharp disposal units, surgical blades, and ACE brand elastic bandages. Once the needle has done its work, BD's Diagnostics segment offers specimen management systems, data capture systems, test kits, and diagnostic assays. Finally, to help researchers get a closer look at specimens, BD Biosciences segment makes cellular analysis systems, labware, and growth media. BD's customers include blood banks, hospitals, pharmacies, and research labs.

Now that it has reorganized into three units under the BD brand, the company can focus on expanding its market overseas, where nearly half of its sales are already generated. BD also continues to cash in on regulations that require safer needle devices — it already had several of such products in the works before the passage of the Needlestick Safety and Prevention Act. BD plans to develop additional versions of its products that are safer and less painful.

Earlier efforts to build up its diabetes-care products line have had mixed results and in late 2006 the company announced it would discontinue distributing blood glucose monitors and test strips.

## HISTORY

Maxwell Becton and Fairleigh Dickinson established a medical supply firm in New York in 1897. In 1907 the company moved to New Jersey and became one of the first US firms to make hypodermic needles.

During WWI, Becton, Dickinson (BD) made all-glass syringes and introduced the cotton elastic bandage. After the war, its researchers designed an improved stethoscope and created specialized hypodermic needles. The company supplied medical equipment to the armed forces during WWII. Becton and Dickinson helped establish Fairleigh Dickinson Junior College (now Fairleigh Dickinson University) in 1942. The company continued to develop products such as the Vacutainer blood-collection apparatus, its first medical laboratory aid.

After the deaths of Dickinson (1948) and Becton (1951), their respective sons, Fairleigh Jr. and Henry, took over. The company introduced disposable hypodermic syringes in 1961. BD went public in 1963 to raise money for new expansion. In the 1960s the company opened plants in Brazil, Canada, France, and Ireland and climbed aboard the conglomeration bandwagon by diversifying into such businesses as industrial gloves (Edmont, 1966) and computer systems (Spear, 1968). BD also went on a major acquisition spree in its core fields during the 1960s and 1970s, buying more than 25 medical supply, testing, and lab companies by 1980.

Wesley Howe, successor to Fairleigh Dickinson Jr., expanded foreign sales in the 1970s. Howe thwarted a takeover by the diversifying oil giant Sun Company (now Sunoco) in 1978 and began to sell BD's nonmedical businesses in 1983, ending with the 1989 sale of Edmont. Acquisitions, including Deseret Medical (IV catheters, surgical gloves and masks; 1986), sharpened BD's focus on medical and surgical supplies.

In the 1990s BD formed a number of alliances and ventures, including a 1991 agreement to make and market Baxter International's InterLink needleless injection system, which reduces the risk of accidental needle sticks, and a 1993 joint venture with NeXagen (now part of Gilead Sciences) to make and market in vitro diagnostics. As tuberculosis reemerged in the US as a serious health threat, the firm improved its TB-detection and drug-resistance test systems, which cut testing time from as much as seven weeks to less than two.

In 1996 BD introduced GlucoWatch (a glucose monitoring device developed by Cygnus), and acquired the diagnostic business and brand name of MicroProbe (now Epoch Pharmaceuticals).

Previously known on Wall Street as a homely company that focused on cutting costs, BD changed its image with a string of acquisitions beginning in 1997. The firm acquired PharMingen (biomedical research reagents) and Difco Laboratories (microbiology media), which broadened its product lines. BD also collaborated with Nanogen on diagnosis products for infectious disease.

In 1998 BD bought The BOC Group's medical devices business. The company also settled a lawsuit by a health care worker claiming that BD continued selling conventional syringes that could spread disease through accidental needle sticks instead of promoting safer technology. BD still faced several lawsuits from health workers who had sustained needle sticks. In 1999 the firm joined forces with Millennium Pharmaceuticals to develop cancer tests and treatments; it also bought genetic test maker Clontech Laboratories. In a cost-cutting effort, BD made plans in 2000 to cut its workforce by 1,000 (about 4%).

BD sold its Clontech division (part of BD Biosciences) to Takara Bio, part of Takara Holdings, in 2005.

During 2006 the company acquired GeneOhm Sciences which develops molecular diagnostic testing systems specifically for the rapid detection of bacterial organisms that cause health care-associated infections in hospitalized patients, including MRSA (methicillin resistant *Staphylococcus aureus*) and Group B Strep (rapid testing for bacteria). That same year the company also acquired the 93% of TriPath Imaging that it didn't already own for $350 million. TriPath brought with it a line of cancer management products.

## EXECUTIVES

**Chairman, President, and CEO:** Edward J. Ludwig, age 55, $2,170,915 pay
**SEVP and CFO:** John R. Considine, age 56, $1,120,693 pay
**SVP and CTO:** Scott P. Bruder
**SVP, Corporate Regulatory and External Affairs:** Patricia B. Shrader, age 56
**SVP, Human Resources:** Donna M. Boles, age 53
**SVP and General Counsel:** Jeffrey S. Sherman, age 51
**VP and Treasurer:** Richard K. Berman
**VP, Taxes:** Mark H. Borofsky
**VP, Corporate Secretary and Public Policy:** Dean J. Paranicas
**VP and Controller:** William A. Tozzi
**VP, Chief Intellectual Property Counsel, and Assistant Secretary:** David W. Highet
**President, Asia Pacific:** Helen Cunniff
**President, BD Japan:** Rex C. Valentine
**President, North Latin America:** Laureen Higgins
**President, South Latin America:** Geraldo Q. Barbosa
**Director, Corporate Communications:** Colleen White
**Communications Manager:** Marion Plumley
**Director Sales and Business Development, BD.id Preanalytical Systems:** Jefferey Lee
**Auditors:** Ernst & Young LLP

## LOCATIONS

**HQ:** Becton, Dickinson and Company
1 Becton Dr., Franklin Lakes, NJ 07417
**Phone:** 201-847-6800 **Fax:** 201-847-6475
**Web:** www.bd.com

Becton, Dickinson has offices in some 50 countries in Africa, Asia Pacific, Europe, the Middle East, North America, and South America.

### 2006 Sales

| | $ mil. | % of total |
|---|---|---|
| US | 2,828.0 | 49 |
| Europe | 1,764.6 | 30 |
| Other | 1,242.2 | 21 |
| **Total** | **5,834.8** | **100** |

## PRODUCTS/OPERATIONS

### 2006 Sales

| | $ mil. | % of total |
|---|---|---|
| BD Medical | | |
| Medical surgical systems | 1,748.7 | 30 |
| Diabetes care | 753.3 | 13 |
| Pharmaceutical systems | 639.7 | 11 |
| Ophthalmic systems | 61.7 | 1 |
| BD Diagnostics | | |
| Preanalytical systems | 927.8 | 16 |
| Diagnostic systems | 827.1 | 14 |
| BD Biosciences | | |
| Immunocytometry systems | 502.8 | 8 |
| Discovery Labware | 216.4 | 4 |
| Pharmingen | 157.3 | 3 |
| **Total** | **5,834.8** | **100** |

### Selected Products

Medical
- Anesthesia needles
- Critical care systems
- Elastic support products
- Hypodermic needles and syringes
- Infusion therapy devices
- Ophthalmic surgery devices
- Prefillable drug-delivery systems
- Surgical blades and scalpels
- Thermometers

Diagnostics
- Bar-code systems for patient identification and data capture
- Consulting services
- Hematology instruments
- Immunodiagnostic test kits
- Microbiology products
- Sample collection products
- Specimen management systems

Biosciences
- Cell growth and screening products
- Cellular analysis systems
- Labware
- Molecular biology reagents (for study of genes)
- Monoclonal antibodies (for biomedical research)

## COMPETITORS

Abbott Labs
Accelr8
Apogent Technologies inc.
Baxter
Boston Scientific
Covidien
Harvard Bioscience
Hospira
Johnson & Johnson
Terumo
Trinity Biotech
United States Surgical

## HISTORICAL FINANCIALS

Company Type: Public

### Income Statement

FYE: September 30

| | REVENUE ($ mil.) | NET INCOME ($ mil.) | NET PROFIT MARGIN | EMPLOYEES |
|---|---|---|---|---|
| **9/06** | 5,835 | 752 | 12.9% | 26,990 |
| **9/05** | 5,415 | 722 | 13.3% | 25,571 |
| **9/04** | 4,935 | 467 | 9.5% | 25,005 |
| **9/03** | 4,528 | 547 | 12.1% | 24,783 |
| **9/02** | 4,033 | 480 | 11.9% | 25,249 |
| **Annual Growth** | 9.7% | 11.9% | — | 1.7% |

### 2006 Year-End Financials

| | |
|---|---|
| Debt ratio: 24.9% | No. of shares (mil.): 245 |
| Return on equity: 21.1% | Dividends |
| Cash ($ mil.): 1,107 | Yield: 1.2% |
| Current ratio: 2.02 | Payout: 29.4% |
| Long-term debt ($ mil.): 957 | Market value ($ mil.): 17,347 |

### Stock History

NYSE: BDX

| | STOCK PRICE ($) FY Close | P/E High | P/E Low | PER SHARE ($) Earnings | Dividends | Book Value |
|---|---|---|---|---|---|---|
| **9/06** | 70.67 | 24 | 17 | 2.93 | 0.86 | 15.63 |
| **9/05** | 52.43 | 22 | 18 | 2.77 | 0.72 | 13.26 |
| **9/04** | 51.70 | 31 | 20 | 1.77 | 0.60 | 12.30 |
| **9/03** | 36.12 | 20 | 14 | 2.07 | 0.40 | 11.54 |
| **9/02** | 28.40 | 22 | 14 | 1.79 | 0.39 | 9.74 |
| **Annual Growth** | 25.6% | — | — | 13.1% | 21.9% | 12.6% |

# Bed Bath & Beyond

Bed Bath & Beyond (BBB) has everything you need to play "house" for real. It's the #1 superstore domestics retailer in the US (ahead of Linens 'n Things), with some 815 BBB stores in 46 states and Puerto Rico. The stores' floor-to-ceiling shelves stock better-quality (brand-name and private-label) goods in two main categories: domestics (bed linens, bathroom and kitchen items) and home furnishings (cookware and cutlery, small household appliances, picture frames, and more). Everyday low prices eliminate the need for sales. BBB relies exclusively on circulars, mailings, and word-of-mouth for advertising. New superstore openings — 70 or more per year — account for much of the firm's growth.

The retailer's decentralized structure allows store managers to have more control than their peers at other retailers (and the company has less manager turnover). The company cuts costs by locating its stores in strip shopping centers, freestanding buildings, and off-price malls, rather than in pricier regional malls. To cut costs further, BBB's vendors ship merchandise directly to the stores, eliminating the expense of a central distribution center and reducing warehousing costs. With the acquisitions of Harmon Stores (2002) and Christmas Tree Shops (2003) under its belt, the company is keeping an eye out for new acquisitions.

In addition to its 815 Bed Bath & Beyond stores, the company's Christmas Tree Shops sells giftware and household items from more than 30 stores in eight states, while health-and-beauty retailer Harmon Stores operates about 40 shops in three states.

In 2007 the company broadened its offerings with its acquisition of retailer buybuy BABY, which operates eight stores on the Eastern coast, for $67 million. buybuy BABY is run by Richard and Jeffrey Feinstein, the sons of Bed Bath & Beyond's co-chairman.

Founders Warren Eisenberg and Leonard Feinstein (co-chairmen who operate from separate locations) have slowly reduced their holdings in Bed Bath & Beyond to about 2% of the company's shares each.

## HISTORY

Warren Eisenberg and Leonard Feinstein, both employed by a discounter called Arlan's, brainstormed an idea in 1971 for a chain of stores offering only home goods. They were betting that customers were, in Feinstein's words, interested in a "designer approach to linens and housewares." The two men started two small linens stores (about 2,000 sq. ft.) named bed n bath, one in New York and one in New Jersey.

Expansion came at a fairly slow pace as the company moved only into California and Connecticut by 1985. By then the time was right for such a specialty retailer: Department stores were cutting back on their houseware lines to focus on the more profitable apparel segment, and baby boomers were spending more leisure time at their homes (and more money on spiffing them up). Eisenberg and Feinstein opened a 20,000-sq.-ft. superstore in 1985 that offered a full line of home furnishings. The firm changed its name to Bed Bath & Beyond two years later in order to reflect its new offerings.

With the successful superstore format, the company built all new stores in the larger design. Bed Bath & Beyond grew rapidly; square footage quadrupled between 1992 and 1996. The company went public in 1992. That year it eclipsed the size of its previous stores when it opened a 50,000-sq.-ft. store in Manhattan. (It later enlarged this store to 80,000 sq. ft.; the company's stores now average 42,000 sq. ft.)

Bed Bath & Beyond's management has attributed its success, in part, to the leeway it gives its store managers, who monitor inventory and have the freedom to try new products and layouts. One example often cited by the company is the case of a manager who decided to sell glasses by the piece instead of in sets. Sales increased 30%, and the whole chain incorporated the practice.

The retailer opened 28 new stores in fiscal 1997, 33 in fiscal 1998 (its first-ever billion dollar sales year), and 45 in fiscal 1999.

In 1999 the company dipped a toe into the waters of e-commerce by agreeing to buy a stake in Internet Gift Registries, which operates the WeddingNetwork Web site. The company later began offering online sales and bridal registry services. Keeping up its rapid expansion pace, the company opened 70 stores in fiscal 2000, 85 in fiscal 2001, and 95 in fiscal 2002.

In March 2002 Bed Bath & Beyond acquired Harmon Stores Inc., a health and beauty aid retailer with 29 stores in three states. Several months later (June 2003) Bed Bath & Beyond acquired Christmas Tree Shops, a giftware and household items retailer with 23 stores in six US states, for $200 million.

## EXECUTIVES

**Co-Chairman:** Warren Eisenberg, age 76, $1,100,000 pay
**Co-Chairman:** Leonard (Lenny) Feinstein, age 70, $1,100,000 pay
**CEO and Director:** Steven H. (Steve) Temares, age 48, $1,230,769 pay
**President and Chief Merchandising Officer:** Arthur (Art) Stark, age 52, $821,154 pay
**SVP Investor Relations:** Ronald (Ron) Curwin, age 73
**SVP Stores:** Matthew Fiorilli, age 50, $686,000 pay
**CFO and Treasurer:** Eugene A. (Gene) Castagna, age 41
**VP, CIO:** Kevin R. Murphy
**VP, Finance:** Susan E. Lattmann
**VP and Corporate Counsel:** Michael J. Callahan
**VP and General Merchandise Manager, Hardlines:** Nancy J. Katz
**VP and General Merchandise Manager, Planning and Allocation:** Scott Hames
**VP Construction and Store Development:** Jim Brendle
**VP, Corporate Development; President, Harmon Stores:** G. William Waltzinger Jr.
**VP, Corporate Operations and Chief Strategy Officer:** Richard C. (Rich) McMahon
**VP, Legal and General Counsel:** Allan N. Rauch
**VP, Marketing:** Rita Little
**VP, Tax:** Hal R. Shapiro
**VP, Human Resources:** Concetta Van Dyke
**Investor Relations:** Paula J. Marbach
**CEO, Christmas Tree Shops, Inc.:** Charles (Chuck) Bilezikian
**President, Buy Buy Baby, Inc.:** Richard S. Feinstein
**Auditors:** KPMG LLP

## LOCATIONS

**HQ:** Bed Bath & Beyond Inc.
650 Liberty Ave., Union, NJ 07083
**Phone:** 908-688-0888 **Fax:** 908-688-6483
**Web:** www.bedbathandbeyond.com

### 2007 Locations

| | No. |
|---|---|
| California | 95 |
| Texas | 67 |
| Florida | 60 |
| New York | 51 |
| Illinois | 34 |
| New Jersey | 34 |
| Ohio | 34 |
| Michigan | 30 |
| Pennsylvania | 27 |
| North Carolina | 24 |
| Colorado | 23 |
| Georgia | 23 |
| Virginia | 23 |
| Massachusetts | 22 |
| Washington | 20 |
| Arizona | 18 |
| Indiana | 17 |
| Maryland | 16 |
| Tennessee | 16 |
| Connecticut | 13 |
| South Carolina | 13 |
| Missouri | 12 |
| Utah | 11 |
| Alabama | 10 |
| Louisiana | 10 |
| Wisconsin | 10 |
| Minnesota | 9 |
| Oregon | 9 |
| Kansas | 7 |
| Kentucky | 7 |
| Nevada | 7 |
| Other states | 63 |
| **Total** | **815** |

### 2007 Christmas Tree Shops Stores

| | No. |
|---|---|
| Massachusetts | 15 |
| New York | 6 |
| New Jersey | 3 |
| Connecticut | 3 |
| New Hampshire | 2 |
| Rhode Island | 2 |
| Maine | 2 |
| Vermont | 1 |
| **Total** | **34** |

### 2007 Harmon Stores

| | No. |
|---|---|
| New Jersey | 28 |
| New York | 9 |
| Connecticut | 2 |
| **Total** | **39** |

## PRODUCTS/OPERATIONS

### Selected Merchandise

- Domestics
  - Bath accessories
    - Hampers
    - Shower curtains
    - Towels
  - Bed linens
    - Bedspreads
    - Pillows
    - Sheets
  - Kitchen textiles
    - Cloth napkins
    - Dish towels
    - Placemats
    - Tablecloths
  - Window treatments
- Home Furnishings
  - Basic housewares
    - Accessories (lamps, chairs, accent rugs)
    - General housewares (brooms, ironing boards)
    - Small appliances (blenders, coffeemakers, vacuums)
    - Storage items (hangers, organizers, shoe racks)
  - General home furnishings
    - Artificial plants and flowers
    - Candles
    - Gift wrap
    - Picture frames
    - Seasonal merchandise
    - Wall art
  - Kitchen and tabletop items
    - Cookware
    - Cutlery
    - Flatware
    - Gadgets
    - Glassware
    - Serveware

## COMPETITORS

Anna's Linens
Bombay Company
Burlington Coat Factory
Container Store
Cost Plus
Dillard's
Euromarket Designs
Garden Ridge
IKEA
J. C. Penney
Kmart
Lillian Vernon
Linens 'n Things
Macy's
Pier 1 Imports
Ross Stores
Saks Inc.
Sears
Target
TJX Companies
Tuesday Morning
Wal-Mart
Williams-Sonoma

## HISTORICAL FINANCIALS

Company Type: Public

### Income Statement

FYE: Saturday nearest February 28

| | REVENUE ($ mil.) | NET INCOME ($ mil.) | NET PROFIT MARGIN | EMPLOYEES |
|---|---|---|---|---|
| **2/07** | 6,617 | 594 | 9.0% | 35,000 |
| **2/06** | 5,810 | 573 | 9.9% | 33,000 |
| **2/05** | 5,148 | 505 | 9.8% | 31,000 |
| **2/04** | 4,478 | 400 | 8.9% | 29,000 |
| **2/03** | 3,665 | 302 | 8.2% | 23,000 |
| **Annual Growth** | 15.9% | 18.4% | — | 11.1% |

### 2007 Year-End Financials

Debt ratio: —
Return on equity: 24.2%
Cash ($ mil.): 988
Current ratio: 2.36
Long-term debt ($ mil.): —
No. of shares (mil.): 277
Dividends
Yield: —
Payout: —
Market value ($ mil.): 10,958

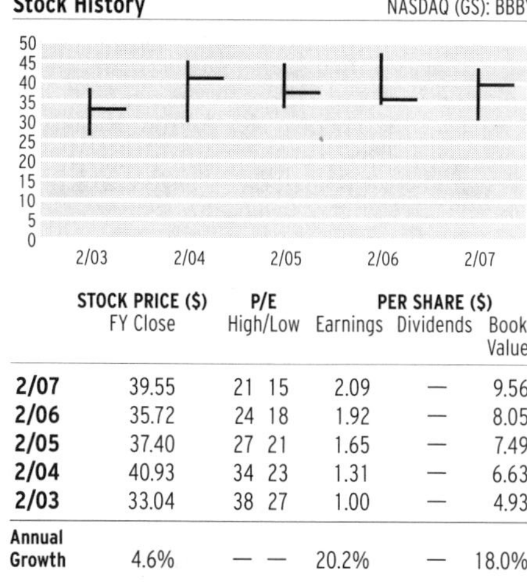


| | STOCK PRICE ($) FY Close | P/E High | P/E Low | PER SHARE ($) Earnings | Dividends | Book Value |
|---|---|---|---|---|---|---|
| **2/07** | 39.55 | 21 | 15 | 2.09 | — | 9.56 |
| **2/06** | 35.72 | 24 | 18 | 1.92 | — | 8.05 |
| **2/05** | 37.40 | 27 | 21 | 1.65 | — | 7.49 |
| **2/04** | 40.93 | 34 | 23 | 1.31 | — | 6.63 |
| **2/03** | 33.04 | 38 | 27 | 1.00 | — | 4.93 |
| **Annual Growth** | 4.6% | — | — | 20.2% | — | 18.0% |

# Bell Microproducts

Bell Microproducts aims to be ahead of the curve in its industry. The company distributes network storage, semiconductor, and other computer products, primarily to computer makers and resellers. It sells products from more than 150 suppliers, including Advanced Micro Devices, EMC, IBM, NEC, Quantum, Seagate Technology, Sony, and Toshiba. Bell Micro offers storage-focused services such as subsystems integration and kitting (providing materials in kit form, ready for assembly). The company also manufactures and sells storage devices under its own brand, while reselling and supporting storage products from Brocade Communications, HP, Hitachi, Intransa, Iomega, LeftHand Networks, and StorageTek, among others.

Joining in its industry's rapid consolidation, Bell Micro has used acquisitions to expand product lines and distribution facilities.

To increase its business in Latin America, Bell Micro in July 2005 bought Brazil-based Net Storage Computers, a distributor of storage products and peripherals. In December 2005 Bell Micro bought the assets of MCE, a leading European distributor of disk drives and components, including IBM products. The company acquired assets of ProSys Information Systems for $41 million in cash and stock in 2006.

## HISTORY

Don Bell had worked for several electronics distributors before leading the group that founded Bell Microproducts in 1987. The company primarily sold semiconductors until 1990, when demand slumped and profits sank. Bell Micro began to diversify its product line and in 1991 created its services division. It acquired contract manufacturers Quadrus and Adlar Turnkey in 1993 and was selected as an authorized distributor for IBM Microelectronics. The company went public in 1993.

The next year Bell Micro acquired semiconductor distributor Vantage Components and some assets of UNIX reseller UNIX Central. In 1995 the company added a center to custom design programmable semiconductors. A write-down for unsold dynamic random-access memory chips contributed to a drop in profits that year.

Bell Micro added Harris Semiconductor to its supplier list in 1996 and Diamond Multimedia (now S3) in 1997. That year Quadrus moved to a new facility, doubling its manufacturing space. A stalled disk drive was partly to blame for a 1997 income drop.

In 1998 Bell Micro began focusing on distribution. It bought Canadian storage products distributor Tenex Data, and acquired the computer products unit of Almo Corp. The company sold its Quadrus contract manufacturing division the next year. Also in 1999 it acquired Future Tech International, a computer components distributor serving Latin America.

In 2000 Bell Micro made its first step into the European market when it acquired Rorke Data, a storage systems provider with operations in the Netherlands. The company also bought UK-based distributor Ideal Hardware. Bell Micro bought another storage systems integrator, Total Tec, in 2001.

Although North American sales had accounted for about 50% of sales in 2001 and 2002, the company extended its operations into Europe and Latin America in response to the sluggish distribution climate in the US. Latin American sales squeaked past North American sales for the first time in 2003. Its October 2003 purchase of EBM Mayorista, based in Mexico, helped fuel Bell Micro's Latin American expansion.

In June 2004, Bell Micro acquired Manchester, UK-based OpenPSL Holdings, a distributor of enterprise, storage, and security products and related professional services to VARs, system integrators, and software companies in the UK and Ireland. The acquisition was made for approximately $36 million; it fit into Bell Microproducts' strategy of expanding its business in the UK and across Europe.

## EXECUTIVES

**Chairman, President, and CEO:** W. Donald (Don) Bell, age 68, $1,041,672 pay
**COO; President, The Americas:** James E. (Jim) Illson, age 50, $586,400 pay (prior to promotion)
**EVP and CFO:** William E. (Bill) Meyer, age 45
**EVP, Enterprise Distribution:** Philip M. (Phil) Roussey, age 61
**EVP, OEM:** Walter Tobin
**SVP, Human Resources:** Richard J. (Dick) Jacquet, age 66, $322,800 pay
**VP, Global Software Distribution:** Alex Tatham
**VP, Information Technology and CIO:** Robert J. (Bob) Sturgeon, age 50, $318,929 pay
**VP and General Manager, Continental Europe:** Jens Hartmann
**VP, Marketing, Rorke Data:** Joe Rorke
**VP, Sales, Rorke Data:** Bob Herzan
**VP, Services and Technical Support, North America:** Paul Collins
**Director, Technical Support, Rorke Data:** Pam Moeller
**Manager, Group Credit Services, Bell Microproducts Europe:** Eddie Pacey
**Broadcast Product Manager, Rorke Data:** Christopher (Chris) Stone
**European Product Manager:** Tom Ellis
**Investor Relations Representative:** Rob Damron
**General Counsel and Secretary:** Andrew S. Hughes
**President, Bell Microproducts Latin America:** Lou Leonardo
**President, Europe:** Graeme A. Watt, age 44, $493,155 pay
**President, North American Distribution:** Jerry Kagele
**CEO, Empresas Berny Mayoreo S.A. de C.V.:** Federico Berny
**Auditors:** PricewaterhouseCoopers LLP

## LOCATIONS

**HQ:** Bell Microproducts Inc.
1941 Ringwood Ave., San Jose, CA 95131
**Phone:** 408-451-9400 **Fax:** 408-451-1600
**Web:** www.bellmicro.com

### 2005 Sales

| | $ mil. | % of total |
|---|---|---|
| North America | 1,410.1 | 44 |
| Europe | 1,374.6 | 43 |
| Latin America | 409.1 | 13 |
| **Total** | **3,193.8** | **100** |

## PRODUCTS/OPERATIONS

### Products

Computers
- Data storage
  - Hard, floppy, and optical disk drives
  - Redundant array of independent disk (RAID) systems
  - Tape drives
- Monitors
- Motherboards
- Networking systems

Semiconductors
- Logic devices
- Memory devices
- Microprocessors
- Peripheral components
- Specialty components

### Services

Disk and tape data storage subsystems and RAID systems (Bellstor brand)
Kitting (custom kit-form assembly)
Private-label PCs and servers (Trademark brand)
Software loading
Subsystem modifications
Systems integration

## COMPETITORS

Agilysys
All American Semiconductor
Arrow Electronics
Avnet
Azlan Group
Black Box
CompuCom
Digi-Key
Electrocomponents
Future Electronics
Ingram Micro
Jaco Electronics
MA Laboratories
Merisel
New Age Electronics
N.F. Smith
Nu Horizons Electronics
Pomeroy IT
Premier Farnell
Richardson Electronics
Softmart
Software House
Supercom
SYNNEX
Tech Data

## HISTORICAL FINANCIALS

Company Type: Public

### Income Statement

FYE: December 31

| | REVENUE ($ mil.) | NET INCOME ($ mil.) | NET PROFIT MARGIN | EMPLOYEES |
|---|---|---|---|---|
| **12/05*** | 3,194 | 1 | 0.0% | 1,827 |
| **12/04** | 2,828 | 11 | 0.4% | 1,480 |
| **12/03** | 2,230 | (5) | — | 1,294 |
| **12/02** | 2,105 | (7) | — | 1,344 |
| **12/01** | 2,007 | (22) | — | 1,476 |
| **Annual Growth** | 12.3% | — | — | 5.5% |

*Most recent year available

### 2005 Year-End Financials

Debt ratio: 115.8%
Return on equity: 0.2%
Cash ($ mil.): 30
Current ratio: 1.77
Long-term debt ($ mil.): 255
No. of shares (mil.): 30
Dividends
Yield: —
Payout: —
Market value ($ mil.): 230

**Stock History** NASDAQ (GM): BELM

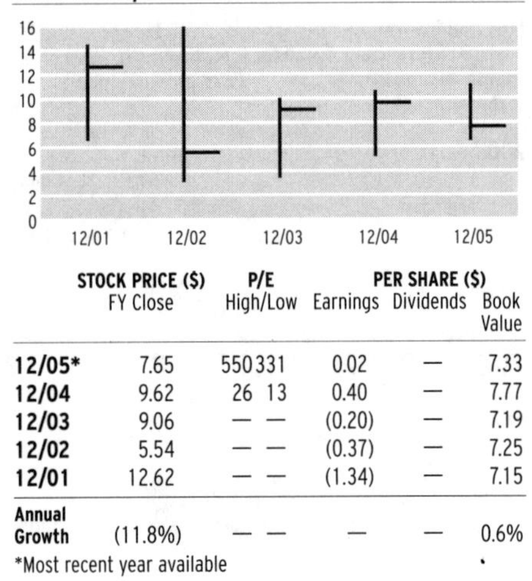


| | STOCK PRICE ($) FY Close | P/E High | P/E Low | PER SHARE ($) Earnings | Dividends | Book Value |
|---|---|---|---|---|---|---|
| **12/05*** | 7.65 | 550 | 331 | 0.02 | — | 7.33 |
| **12/04** | 9.62 | 26 | 13 | 0.40 | — | 7.77 |
| **12/03** | 9.06 | — | — | (0.20) | — | 7.19 |
| **12/02** | 5.54 | — | — | (0.37) | — | 7.25 |
| **12/01** | 12.62 | — | — | (1.34) | — | 7.15 |
| **Annual Growth** | (11.8%) | — | — | — | — | 0.6% |

*Most recent year available

# Bemis Company

Thanks to companies like Bemis, modern delectables such as potato chips and snack cakes have longer shelf lives than most marriages. Bemis makes a broad line of flexible packaging materials, including polymer films, barrier laminates, and paper-bag packaging that customers in the food industry use to package all manner of edibles. In addition to bags, Bemis also produces pressure-sensitive products ranging from label paper and graphic films to thin-film adhesives. Although Bemis' primary market is the food industry, the company also sells to the agricultural, chemical, medical, personal care, and printing industries. The US accounts for about two-thirds of sales.

Bemis' Flexible Packaging segment accounted for 82% of sales in 2006; the food industry typically accounts for about 60% of sales. Bemis has grown significantly through acquisitions, especially in Europe.

Intent on strengthening its market presence in South America, Bemis bought a majority stake in Brazil-based Dixie Toga in 2005, one of the country's largest packaging companies. Bemis had originally purchased a one-third interest in Dixie Toga as far back as 1998.

Bemis restructured its operations to reduce costs during 2006; the move primarily consisted of manufacturing facility consolidations that resulted in seven plant closings.

## HISTORY

Judson Moss Bemis founded J. M. Bemis and Company, Bag Manufacturers, in St. Louis in 1858. The 25-year-old received advice and equipment from cousin Simeon Farwell, who owned an established bag-making factory. St. Louis' role as a trading center supported by major railroads and the Mississippi River helped Bemis' business. The company introduced preprinted and machine-sewn flour sacks to the city's millers, and by the end of its first year it was making about 4,000 sacks a day. In its second year Edward Brown, a relative of Farwell's, became Bemis' partner, and the company was renamed Bemis and Brown.

During the Civil War, Brown opened an office in Boston to make the most of fluctuating exchange rates. Bemis also began trading in raw cotton (priced sky-high because of the war), and it started recycling burlap shipping bags into gunnysacks. The company soon began producing its own burlap sacks from imported jute.

Stephen Bemis, Judson's brother, became a partner in the firm in 1870 and took over its St. Louis operations. Judson joined Brown in Boston, where he could be involved in commodity purchases and financial operations. Soon after, he bought out Brown's share of the firm for an amount considered extravagant at the time — $300,000.

By the early 1880s Bemis Bros. and Co. was the US's #2 bag maker. It opened a second factory in 1881 in Minneapolis, which was home to such companies as General Mills and Pillsbury. During the late 1800s and the early 1900s, Bemis opened plants throughout the US.

Judson retired in 1909, but the company continued to be run by Bemis family members. In 1914 the company entered the emerging industry of paper milling and paper-bag making, but it continued to focus on textile packaging until WWII, when shortages of cotton and jute expanded the role of paper packaging and led to development of polyethylene packaging. By the 1950s Bemis' core products were paper and plastic packaging. In 1959 the company opened its own R&D facility. During the late 1950s and 1960s Bemis made several important acquisitions, including Curwood (packaging for medical products) and MACtac (pressure-sensitive materials). The company was renamed Bemis Company in 1965.

Bemis sold more than $100 million of noncore businesses during the 1970s and 1980s. In its effort to become an industry leader, the company began a major capital expansion program. Bemis' sales topped $1 billion in 1988.

Bemis bought candy-packaging producer Milprint, Inc., in 1990; Princeton Packaging's bakery-packaging business in 1993; and Banner Packaging in 1995. In 1996 Bemis introduced the on-battery tester, developed with Eveready. Bemis' medical packaging segment was rejuvenated that year with the purchase of Malaysia-based Perfecseal. The company sold its packaging-equipment business in 1997 and began closing plants and consolidating operations.

In 1998 Bemis purchased a one-third interest in Brazil-based Dixie Toga's flexible-packaging operations. That year it also acquired Belgium's Techy International, which became Bemis' base for sales and distribution in Europe.

Bemis invested more than $100 million to modernize its packaging manufacturing and printing operations in 1999. The next year it acquired Arrow Industries' flexible packaging operations, Viskase's plastic-films business, and Kanzaki Specialty Papers' pressure sensitive materials business. Bemis acquired plastic film maker Duralam in 2001.

The company opened its pocketbook again in 2002, purchasing the Clysar shrink film business of DuPont (with operations in both the US and Europe) for more than $140 million. The purchase gave Bemis a worldwide reach for its shrink bags, film, and heat-set packaging products. Later that year, Bemis acquired the Walki Films business of UPM-Kymmene for about $69 million.

In 2003 Bemis expanded its operations in Europe through the acquisition of Multi-Fix's pressure sensitive materials business for about $11 million. The next year Bemis acquired flexible packaging assets in Mexico from Masterpak S.A. de C.V. The company also restructured its Pressure Sensitive Materials division, which included the closing of two facilities.

## EXECUTIVES

**Chairman and CEO:** Jeffrey H. (Jeff) Curler, age 56, $1,261,600 pay
**President and COO:** Henry J. Theisen, age 53, $1,010,000 pay
**SVP, CFO, and Director:** Gene C. Wulf, age 56, $478,000 pay
**VP and Controller:** Stanley A. Jaffy, age 58
**VP and Treasurer, Director of Investor Relations:** Melanie E. R. Miller, age 43
**VP, General Counsel, and Secretary:** James J. Seifert, age 50
**VP, Human Resources:** Eugene H. (Gene) Seashore Jr., age 57, $372,000 pay
**VP Operations:** Robert F. Hawthorne
**VP Operations; President and CEO, Pressure Sensitive Materials; President, MACtac Americas:** William F. Austen, age 48, $399,000 pay
**VP Operations:** James W. (Jim) Ransom
**President, Bemis Graphics:** David F. Birkett
**President, Bemis Flexible Packaging Europe:** Marc Dussart
**President, MACtac Americas:** Peter R. (Pete) Mathias
**President, MACtac Europe:** Guido Alvino
**President, MACtac Mexico:** Jose Martin Alba
**President, Milprint/Banner:** Donald E. Nimis
**President, Perfecseal:** Paul R. Verbeten
**President, Paper Packaging:** Gary V. Stone
**President, Polyethylene Packaging:** James A. (Jim) Russler
**President and CEO, Dixie Toga:** Walter Schalka
**Director Global Sourcing:** Jeffrey E. Lammers
**Auditors:** PricewaterhouseCoopers LLP

## LOCATIONS

**HQ:** Bemis Company, Inc.
1 Neenah Center, 4th Fl., Neenah, WI 54957
**Phone:** 920-727-4100 **Fax:** 920-527-7600
**Web:** www.bemis.com

Bemis Company has operations in the Americas, the Asia Pacific, and Europe.

### 2006 Sales

| | $ mil. | % of total |
|---|---|---|
| North America | | |
| US | 2,400.5 | 66 |
| Canada | 64.8 | 2 |
| Europe | 595.9 | 16 |
| South America | 491.3 | 14 |
| Other regions | 86.9 | 2 |
| **Total** | **3,639.4** | **100** |

## PRODUCTS/OPERATIONS

### 2006 Sales

| | $ mil. | % of total |
|---|---|---|
| Flexible packaging | 3,000.6 | 82 |
| Pressure sensitive materials | 643.3 | 18 |
| Adjustments | (4.5) | — |
| **Total** | **3,639.4** | **100** |

### Selected Products

Flexible Packaging
- Blown and cast stretchfilm
- Carton sealing tape
- Coated and laminated polymer film
- Industrial and consumer paper-bag packaging
- Polyethylene packaging
- Thermoformed plastic packaging

Pressure-Sensitive Materials
- Graphic films
- Medical adhesives
- Narrow web roll label products
- Technical thin-film adhesives

### Selected Subsidiaries

Bemis Clysar, Inc.
Bemis Deutschland Holdings GmbH
Bemis Europe Holdings, SA (Belgium)
  Bemis Monceau S.A. (Belgium)
Bemis France Holdings S.A.S.
  Bemis Packaging France S.A.S.
  Bemis Le Trait S.A.S. (France)
  Bemis Epernon S.A.S. (France)
Bolsas Bemis S.A. de C.V. (Mexico)
Curwood, Inc.
  Curwood Packaging (Canada) Limited
  Bemis Packaging (Ireland) Limited
  Bemis Swansea Limited (UK)
  Perfecseal, Inc.
Dixie Toga S.A. (Brazil)
Hayco Liquidation Company
MacKay, Inc.
Milprint, Inc.
Morgan Adhesives Company
Pervel Industries, Inc.

## COMPETITORS

3M
Alcan
Amcor
Avery Dennison
Cantex
Constar International
Curwood
Dow Chemical
DuPont
Exopack
Flexcon Company
Green Bay Packaging
Hood Packaging
International Paper
Intertape Polymer
Koç
Pactiv
Pliant
Printpack
Rexam
Ricoh Corporation
Sealed Air Corporation
Smurfit-Stone Container
Sonoco Products
Southern Film Extruders
UPM-Kymmene
Wausau Paper

## HISTORICAL FINANCIALS

Company Type: Public

### Income Statement

FYE: December 31

| | REVENUE ($ mil.) | NET INCOME ($ mil.) | NET PROFIT MARGIN | EMPLOYEES |
|---|---|---|---|---|
| **12/06** | 3,639 | 176 | 4.8% | 15,700 |
| **12/05** | 3,474 | 163 | 4.7% | 15,900 |
| **12/04** | 2,834 | 180 | 6.4% | 11,907 |
| **12/03** | 2,635 | 147 | 5.6% | 11,500 |
| **12/02** | 2,369 | 166 | 7.0% | 11,800 |
| **Annual Growth** | 11.3% | 1.6% | — | 7.4% |

### 2006 Year-End Financials

Debt ratio: 49.1%
Return on equity: 12.5%
Cash ($ mil.): 112
Current ratio: 1.97
Long-term debt ($ mil.): 722
No. of shares (mil.): 105
Dividends
  Yield: 2.2%
  Payout: 46.1%
Market value ($ mil.): 3,563

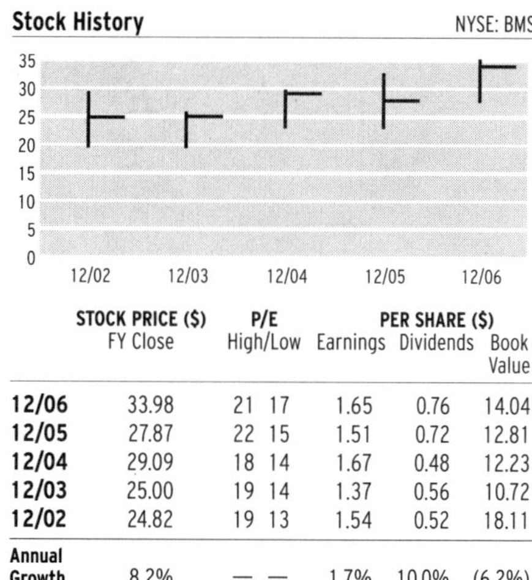


| | STOCK PRICE ($) FY Close | P/E High/Low | | PER SHARE ($) Earnings | Dividends | Book Value |
|---|---|---|---|---|---|---|
| **12/06** | 33.98 | 21 | 17 | 1.65 | 0.76 | 14.04 |
| **12/05** | 27.87 | 22 | 15 | 1.51 | 0.72 | 12.81 |
| **12/04** | 29.09 | 18 | 14 | 1.67 | 0.48 | 12.23 |
| **12/03** | 25.00 | 19 | 14 | 1.37 | 0.56 | 10.72 |
| **12/02** | 24.82 | 19 | 13 | 1.54 | 0.52 | 18.11 |
| **Annual Growth** | 8.2% | — | — | 1.7% | 10.0% | (6.2%) |

# Benchmark Electronics

Benchmark Electronics is setting a benchmark for electronics manufacturing services (EMS). The company, which provides contract manufacturing services to electronics makers, produces complex printed circuit boards and related electronics systems and subsystems. Its customers include manufacturers of computers, medical devices, telecommunications and industrial control equipment, and test instruments. Benchmark also offers design, engineering, materials management, testing, distribution, and other services. Sun Microsystems (39% of sales) is the company's biggest customer.

Benchmark benefits from the continuing push toward outsourced manufacturing, which helps major electronics firms cut costs. In order to expand globally in the competitive and rapidly consolidating EMS market — where giants such as Solectron and Flextronics dominate — the company has acquired several smaller businesses and added manufacturing facilities and engineering design teams in Asia and Latin America, where it can operate less expensively. Benchmark now has some 24 facilities worldwide and ranks among the top dozen EMS providers.

Helping along the EMS consolidation trend, Benchmark in early 2007 acquired PEMSTAR, an EMS provider that counts IBM and Motorola among its largest customers. The company exchanged stock and assumed debt in a transaction valued at around $300 million.

Earnest Partners owns around 6% of Benchmark, while Wellington Management holds nearly 6% of the company. FMR (Fidelity Investments) has an equity stake of more than 5% and Royce & Associates owns around 5%.

## HISTORY

Benchmark Electronics was formed in 1979 as Electronics, Inc., to produce patient monitoring equipment. It was incorporated in 1981 as a wholly owned subsidiary of medical implant maker Intermedics, which pioneered surface-mount technology in pacemakers. In 1986 Intermedics sold 90% of Benchmark's stock to Electronic Investors Corp. (EIC), a company formed by Intermedics executives Donald Nigbor, Steven Barton, and Cary Fu. (Nigbor began serving as president.) In 1988 EIC became Benchmark, and Mason & Hangar (engineering and construction) bought 60% of the company. Benchmark went public in 1990.

In 1994 the company moved its headquarters from Clute, Texas, to a larger plant in nearby Angleton. Benchmark made its first acquisition — electronics contract manufacturer EMD Technologies — in 1996. In 1998 the company acquired Hudson, New Hampshire-based electronics firm Lockheed Commercial Electronics (which later became Benchmark's Hudson Division). That year, despite a prolonged slump in the electronics industry and turmoil in Asian markets, Benchmark's sales grew more than 50%.

The company acquired Stratus Computer Ireland, a Dublin, Ireland-based subsidiary of Ascend Communications, in 1999. (Lucent Technologies bought Ascend later that year.) The deal included a three-year contract to supply systems integration services to Ascend. Later that year Benchmark acquired J.M. Huber's AVEX Electronics subsidiary, then sued Huber for misrepresenting AVEX's operations.

In 2000 Benchmark sold a manufacturing plant in Sweden that it inherited from its AVEX acquisition. Early in 2001 John Custer stepped aside as chairman, and CEO Nigbor took his place. Fu, who had been an EVP, became president and COO of the company. Also that year Benchmark opened a systems integration facility in Singapore, expanding its geographic reach and its service capabilities.

In 2002 Benchmark acquired the UK and Thailand operations of ACT Manufacturing for $46 million.

In 2004 Benchmark split the roles of chairman and CEO in an effort to improve corporate governance. Nigbor remained chairman, and Fu was promoted to CEO.

The company opened its third manufacturing site in Thailand, a systems integration facility, in 2005.

## EXECUTIVES

**Chairman:** Donald E. (Don) Nigbor, age 59, $250,000 pay
**CEO and Director:** Cary T. Fu, age 58, $603,604 pay
**President:** Gayla J. Delly, age 47, $422,577 pay
**CFO:** Donald F. Adam, age 43, $179,856 pay
**EVP and Director:** Steven A. Barton, age 58, $250,000 pay
**Group President:** Jon J. King
**Group President, Ireland Operations:** John E. Culliney
**VP, Asia Operations:** Doug Hebard
**Singapore Operations:** Charlie Goh
**Director, Singapore, and Asia IPO:** Vincent Ong
**Auditors:** KPMG LLP

## LOCATIONS

**HQ:** Benchmark Electronics, Inc.
3000 Technology Dr., Angleton, TX 77515
**Phone:** 979-849-6550 **Fax:** 979-848-5270
**Web:** www.bench.com

Benchmark Electronics has about 24 manufacturing plants in Brazil, China, Ireland, Mexico, the Netherlands, Romania, Singapore, Thailand, and the US.

### 2006 Sales by Origin

| | $ mil. | % of total |
|---|---|---|
| Americas | 2,514.5 | 67 |
| Asia | 896.0 | 24 |
| Europe | 358.3 | 9 |
| Adjustments | (861.5) | — |
| **Total** | **2,907.3** | **100** |

### 2006 Sales by Destination

| | $ mil. | % of total |
|---|---|---|
| US | 2,221.4 | 76 |
| Europe | | |
| The Netherlands | 319.7 | 11 |
| Other countries | 230.1 | 8 |
| Asia | 112.1 | 4 |
| Other regions | 24.0 | 1 |
| **Total** | **2,907.3** | **100** |

## PRODUCTS/OPERATIONS

### 2006 Sales

| | $ mil. | % of total |
|---|---|---|
| Printed circuit boards | 2,080.2 | 72 |
| Systems integration & box build | 827.1 | 28 |
| **Total** | **2,907.3** | **100** |

### 2006 Sales by Market

| | % of total |
|---|---|
| Computers & related products | 58 |
| Medical devices | 13 |
| Telecommunication equipment | 12 |
| Industrial control equipment | 11 |
| Testing & instrumentation products | 6 |
| **Total** | **100** |

**Services**

Circuit assembly, box build, and depot repair
Design
Distribution
Engineering
Materials procurement and management
Packaging
Prototyping
Quality analysis
Systems integration
Testing
TIME (secure Web-based information system for customers)

## COMPETITORS

Celestica
Cofidur
DDi Corp.
Flash Electronics
Flextronics
Hon Hai
Jabil
Merix
Nam Tai
NatSteel
Plexus
Sanmina-SCI
Saturn Electronics
SigmaTron
SMTC
Solectron
Sparton
Suntron
SYNNEX
TTM Technologies
Viasystems

## HISTORICAL FINANCIALS

Company Type: Public

**Income Statement** — FYE: December 31

| | REVENUE ($ mil.) | NET INCOME ($ mil.) | NET PROFIT MARGIN | EMPLOYEES |
|---|---|---|---|---|
| **12/06** | 2,907 | 112 | 3.8% | 9,548 |
| **12/05** | 2,257 | 81 | 3.6% | 8,972 |
| **12/04** | 2,001 | 71 | 3.5% | 7,393 |
| **12/03** | 1,840 | 55 | 3.0% | 6,274 |
| **12/02** | 1,630 | 36 | 2.2% | 6,380 |
| **Annual Growth** | 15.6% | 32.8% | — | 10.6% |

### 2006 Year-End Financials

Debt ratio: —
Return on equity: 12.2%
Cash ($ mil.): 224
Current ratio: 2.86
Long-term debt ($ mil.): —
No. of shares (mil.): 65
Dividends
Yield: —
Payout: —
Market value ($ mil.): 1,577

**Stock History** — NYSE: BHE

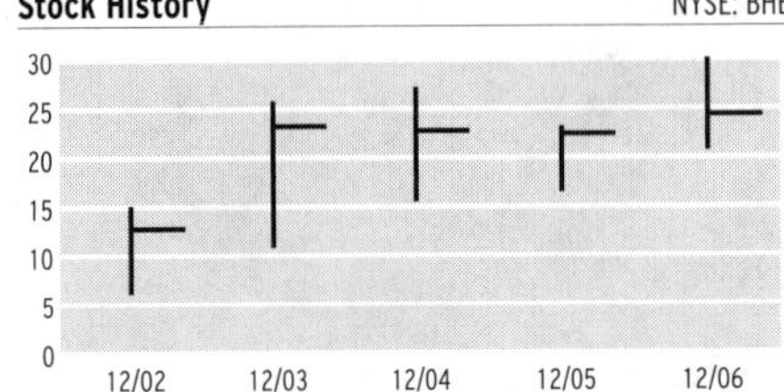


| | STOCK PRICE ($) FY Close | P/E High | P/E Low | PER SHARE ($) Earnings | Dividends | Book Value |
|---|---|---|---|---|---|---|
| **12/06** | 24.36 | 17 | 12 | 1.71 | — | 15.21 |
| **12/05** | 22.42 | 18 | 13 | 1.25 | — | 20.07 |
| **12/04** | 22.73 | 24 | 14 | 1.11 | — | 18.06 |
| **12/03** | 23.21 | 28 | 12 | 0.93 | — | 16.24 |
| **12/02** | 12.74 | 22 | 9 | 0.67 | — | 20.49 |
| **Annual Growth** | 17.6% | — | — | 26.4% | — | (7.2%) |

# Berkshire Hathaway

Berkshire Hathaway is where Warren Buffett, the world's second richest man (behind Bill Gates), spreads his risk by investing in a variety of companies, from insurance and building materials to apparel and furniture retailers. Insurance subsidiaries include National Indemnity, GEICO Corporation, and reinsurance giant General Re. The company also owns McLane Company, Dairy Queen, Clayton Homes, and MidAmerican Energy Holdings. Buffett owns about a third of Berkshire Hathaway.

Buffett sidestepped the stock market's "Great Bubble" of the late 1990s and consequently missed the "Dot-com Meltdown," only to have profits hit by losses in the reinsurance industry in the aftermath of the September 11 attacks. Berkshire's long-term health looks just fine, however, and that's exactly the way Buffett wants it. He ignores the vicissitudes of the market to focus on long-term value creation. To that end, he's refused to split the company's shares, or buy back any, and Berkshire Hathaway is by far the most expensive stock in the US. (It became the first ever to breach the $100,000 per-share price in 2006. Keeps the day traders away.)

Berkshire Hathaway's attachment to safe-but-boring industries ensures the company maintains a relatively steady course. Under the guidance of the plainspoken Buffett, who pens his annual shareholder's letter in the first person and dubbed his company's annual meeting a "Woodstock for Capitalists," the firm proudly eschews get-rich-quick financial swashbuckling in favor of a measured, no-frills approach to growth. He seeks out large companies with consistent earnings and easy-to-understand business models. Most acquisitions are made with cash, and most firms retain their management after the transaction.

The firm now owns more than 70 companies. Its plain-vanilla investments include building products maker Johns Manville, carpet maker Shaw Industries, and Acme Brick. Berkshire also owns stakes in gems (Helzberg Diamonds), candy (See's), pilot training (FlightSafety International), footwear (H.H. Brown and Justin), and apparel (Fruit of the Loom and Garan).

Subsidiary MidAmerican Energy Holdings has been picking up bargains in the post-Enron energy industry. In 2006, it acquired electric utility PacifiCorp, which serves some 1.6 million customers in six western states.

Berkshire Hathaway also holds a sizeable portion of the ubiquitous Coca-Cola, which it plans to hold "forever." Stakes in companies such as American Express, Anheuser-Busch, Moody's, USG, The Washington Post Company, and Wells Fargo help round out the company's holdings.

Investors are becoming increasingly speculative about the future leadership of Berkshire Hathaway. The septuagenarian Buffett acknowledged his mortality by announcing in 2006 that his successor had been chosen; Berkshire's new CEO will come from one of its portfolio companies, though Buffett did not reveal him other than saying that it will indeed be a man.

Also in 2006 Buffett announced he will donate 85% of his Berkshire Hathaway stock (worth some $44 billion) to five charitable organizations, with the Bill & Melinda Gates Foundation, led by his close friends, getting the largest portion by far.

## HISTORY

Warren Buffett bought his first stock — three shares of Cities Service — at age 11. In the 1950s he studied at Columbia University under famed investor Benjamin Graham. Graham's axioms: Use quantitative analysis to discover companies whose intrinsic worth exceeds their stock prices; popularity is irrelevant; the market will vindicate the patient investor.

In 1956 Buffett, then 25, founded Buffett Partnership. Its $105,000 in initial assets multiplied as the company bought Berkshire Hathaway (textiles, 1965) and National Indemnity (insurance, 1967). When Buffett nixed the partnership in 1969 because he believed stocks were overvalued, value per share had risen 30-fold.

Buffett continued investing under the Berkshire Hathaway name, looking for solid businesses, such as See's Candies (1972), advertising agencies (Interpublic, Ogilvy & Mather), newspapers (*Washington Post, Boston Globe,* and *Buffalo News*), and television (Capital Cities/ABC, 1985).

Buffett bought Nebraska Furniture Mart (1983) and Scott Fetzer (*World Book* encyclopedias and Kirby vacuum cleaners, 1986). The scale of investments grew as the company bought stakes in Salomon Brothers (investment banking, 1987), Gillette (1989), American Express (1991), Coca-Cola (1988-89), and Wells Fargo (1989-91).

Buffett increased Berkshire Hathaway's insurance holdings, including an 82% stake in Central States Indemnity (credit insurance, 1992) and a total buyout of GEICO (1996).

In 1996, as the company's share price soared toward $35,000 — easily the highest per-share priced security in the US, outsiders threatened to start a mutual fund to invest in Berkshire Hathaway stock. In response, Buffett created a class B stock that is 1/30 the price of the class A.

Continuing to invest in what he knew, Buffett bought General Re, and time-share private jets through NetJets (called Executive Jet in 1998).

In 2000 purchases included furniture rental company CORT Business Services; boot maker Justin Industries; paint maker Benjamin Moore and Co.; and more than 80% of Shaw Industries, the world's largest carpet maker. The next year Buffett did a little housekeeping: He dumped 80% of his Disney stock after Mickey's earnings slipped, and sold most of the firm's holdings in Fannie Mae and Freddie Mac.

Berkshire's insurance and reinsurance businesses — especially General Re — took a hard hit from the September 11 terrorist attacks. In a mea culpa that's rare for modern CEOs but not for him, Buffett said in his annual letter to shareholders that he had considered the risk of terrorism but hadn't adequately acted upon it.

Berkshire went on to acquire Albecca, Fruit of the Loom (pulling the company out of chapter 11), Garan, The Pampered Chef, and CTB during 2002.

In an interesting and contrary (and, it turns out, profitable) move, Berkshire Hathaway began investing in foreign currencies in 2002 as a result of the US's trade deficit and the weak value of the dollar. It expanded this position in 2003, encompassing some $12 billion in exchange contracts. Berkshire bought grocery distributor McLane Company from Wal-Mart for $1.5 billion the same year.

Buffett's wife, Susan, died in 2004. She had been a member of the board of directors and owned about 3% of the company.

## EXECUTIVES

**Chairman and CEO:** Warren E. Buffett, age 76, $100,000 pay
**Vice Chairman; Chairman, President, and CEO, Wesco Financial:** Charles T. (Charlie) Munger, age 83, $100,000 pay
**VP, CFO, and Treasurer:** Marc D. Hamburg, $662,500 pay
**Secretary:** Forrest N. Krutter
**Controller:** Daniel J. Jaksich
**Director of Financial Assets:** Mark D. Millard
**Director of Internal Auditing:** Rebecca K. Amick
**Director of Taxes:** Jo Ellen Rieck
**Auditors:** Deloitte & Touche LLP

## LOCATIONS

**HQ:** Berkshire Hathaway Inc.
1440 Kiewit Plaza, Omaha, NE 68131
**Phone:** 402-346-1400 **Fax:** 402-346-3375
**Web:** www.berkshirehathaway.com

## PRODUCTS/OPERATIONS

### 2006 Sales

| | $ mil. | % of total |
|---|---|---|
| Insurance sales & service revenues | 51,803 | 53 |
| Insurance premiums earned | 23,964 | 24 |
| Utilities & energy | 10,644 | 11 |
| Finance & financial products | 6,049 | 6 |
| Other insurance revenue | 6,079 | 6 |
| **Total** | **98,539** | **100** |

### Major Equity Investments

American Express (12.6%)
Anheuser-Busch Companies, Inc. (5%)
Coca-Cola (8.6%)
M&T Bank Corporation (6%)
Moody's Corp. (17%)
USG Corp. (19%)
Washington Post Co. (18%)
Wells Fargo & Co. (6.5%)
White Mountains Insurance Group (16%)

### Subsidiaries and Selected Holdings

Acme Brick Company
Acme Building Brands, Inc. (face brick and other building materials)
Albecca Inc. (custom picture framing products)
Aurafin LLC (gold jewelry manufacturing)
Bel-Oro International (gold jewelry manufacturing)
Ben Bridge Jeweler, Inc. (retailing fine jewelry)
Benjamin Moore & Co. (architectural and industrial paint)
Berkshire Hathaway Credit Corporation
Berkshire Hathaway Finance Corporation
Berkshire Hathaway International Insurance Ltd. (UK)
Berkshire Hathaway Life Insurance Company of Nebraska
BHG Life Insurance Company
BH Finance LLC (proprietary investment strategies)
Borsheim Jewelry Company, Inc. (retailing fine jewelry)
Business Wire (news service)
California Insurance Company
Central States Indemnity Co. of Omaha (credit and disability insurance)
Clayton Homes, Inc. (manufactured housing and financing)
CMH Homes, Inc.
CMH Manufacturing, Inc.
Cologne Reinsurance Company Ltd.
Columbia Insurance Company
Continental Divide Insurance Company
Cornhusker Casualty Company
CORT Business Services Corporation (provider of rental furniture, accessories, and related services)
CTB International Corp. (manufacturer of equipment and systems for poultry, hog, and egg production)
Cypress Insurance Company
Dexter Shoe Company (dress, casual, and athletic shoes)
Fairfield Insurance Company
Faraday Reinsurance Company Ltd.
The Fechheimer Brothers Company (uniforms and accessories)
FlightSafety International, Inc. (high technology training to operators of aircraft and ships)
Forest River, Inc. (recreational vehicles)
Fruit of the Loom, Inc. (apparel)
Garan, Incorporated (apparel)
GEICO Casualty Company
GEICO Corporation (property/casualty insurance)
GEICO General Insurance Company
General Re Corporation (property/casualty reinsurance)
General Re Life Corporation
General Reinsurance Corporation
General Star National Insurance Company
Government Employees Insurance Company
H. H. Brown Shoe Company, Inc. (work shoes, boots, and casual footwear)
Helzberg's Diamond Shops, Inc. (retailing fine jewelry)
HomeServices of America, Inc. (residential real estate brokerage)
International Dairy Queen, Inc. (licensing and servicing Dairy Queen Stores)
Johns Manville (building and equipment insulation)
Jordan's Furniture, Inc. (retailing home furnishings)
Justin Brands, Inc. (western footwear and apparel)
Lowell Shoe, Inc. (women's and nurses' shoes)
McLane Company, Inc. (wholesale distribution of groceries and non-food items)
The Medical Protective Company (Med Pro; professional liability insurer)
MidAmerican Energy Holdings Company
MiTek, Inc. (connector products, software)
National Indemnity Company
National Re Company
National Reinsurance Company
Nebraska Furniture Mart, Inc. (retailing home furnishings)
NetJets Inc. (fractional ownership programs for general aviation aircraft)
PacifiCorp (utility)
Pier One Imports (home furnishings retail)
The Pampered Chef, Ltd. (kitchenware and housewares)
Precision Steel Warehouse, Inc. (steel service center)
R.C. Willey Home Furnishings (retailing home furnishings)
Scott Fetzer Company (manufacture and distribution of diversified industrial products)
See's Candies (boxed chocolates and other confectionery products)
Shaw Industries Group, Inc. (carpets and rugs)
Star Furniture Company (retailing home furnishings)
Wesco Financial Corporation
XTRA Corporation (transportation equipment)

## COMPETITORS

AEA Holdings
AIG
Allstate
AXA Financial
Blackstone Group
Chubb Corp
CIGNA
Citigroup
CNA Financial
The Hartford
HM Capital Partners
KKR
Leucadia National
Lincoln Financial Group
Loews
MacAndrews & Forbes
Moscow CableCom
Munich Re
Onex
Progressive Corporation
Prudential
State Farm
Swiss Re

## HISTORICAL FINANCIALS

Company Type: Public

### Income Statement

FYE: December 31

| | REVENUE ($ mil.) | NET INCOME ($ mil.) | NET PROFIT MARGIN | EMPLOYEES |
|---|---|---|---|---|
| **12/06** | 98,539 | 11,015 | 11.2% | 217,000 |
| **12/05** | 82,451 | 8,528 | 10.3% | 192,000 |
| **12/04** | 74,382 | 7,308 | 9.8% | 180,000 |
| **12/03** | 63,859 | 8,151 | 12.8% | 172,700 |
| **12/02** | 42,353 | 4,286 | 10.1% | 147,000 |
| **Annual Growth** | 23.5% | 26.6% | — | 10.2% |

### 2006 Year-End Financials

Debt ratio: 33.7%
Return on equity: 11.0%
Cash ($ mil.): 43,743
Current ratio: —
Long-term debt ($ mil.): 36,488
No. of shares (mil.): 1
Dividends
Yield: —
Payout: —
Market value ($ mil.): 122,922

### Stock History

NYSE: BRK.A

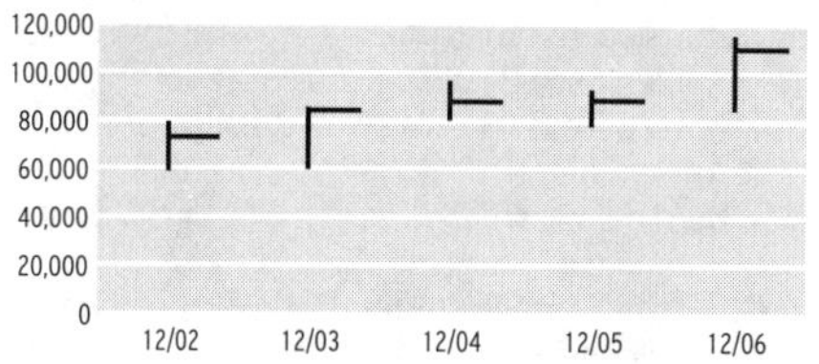

| | STOCK PRICE ($) FY Close | P/E High/Low | PER SHARE ($) Earnings | Dividends | Book Value |
|---|---|---|---|---|---|
| **12/06** | 109,990 | — — | — | — | 97,013 |
| **12/05** | 88,620 | — — | — | — | 72,553 |
| **12/04** | 87,900 | — — | — | — | 67,703 |
| **12/03** | 84,250 | — — | — | — | 60,696 |
| **12/02** | 72,750 | — — | — | — | 48,839 |
| **Annual Growth** | 10.9% | — — | — | — | 18.7% |

# Best Buy

The biggest consumer electronics outlet in the US is also the best — Best Buy, that is. The company operates a chain of more than 1,170 stores in the US, Canada, and now China offering a wide variety of electronic gadgets, movies, music, computers, and appliances. In addition to selling products, the stores offer installation and maintenance services, technical support, and subscriptions for cell phone and Internet services. Covering an average of about 42,000 sq. ft., the big box stores are located in 49 states and five Canadian provinces. In addition to the Best Buy brand, the company operates under the names Magnolia Audio Video (20 stores in the US) and Future Shop (about 120 locations in Canada).

To enhance its technology product offering for small businesses, Best Buy in early 2007 inked a deal to acquire Seattle-based Speakeasy, a provider of broadband voice, data, and IT services. Best Buy has expanded its relationship with Apple Inc. and will begin selling Apple computers in some stores by the end of 2007.

The company has chosen China for its first foray into overseas expansion. Best Buy, in partnership with Jiangsu Five Star Appliance Co., opened its first store in China in early 2007. To facilitate that strategy, Best Buy paid $180 for a minority stake in Jiangsu Five in May 2006. The Chinese appliance and electronics retailer has more than 135 stores in eight China provinces.

To reach into new markets at home, Best Buy has started developing smaller concept stores in selected markets designed to target specific consumer segments, such as women or hip, urban youngsters. It is also expanding its Geek Squad business, which offers residential and commercial technical support. Most Geek Squads are located within existing Best Buy locations, but the company plans to open more stand-alone Geek Squads. In 2006 the chain acquired home appliance and remodeling retailer Pacific Sales Kitchen and Bath Centers for about $410 million.

While business at its stores has been strong, Best Buy has hit a couple of bumps in the road over the past year. Philip Schoonover, a top executive in charge of customer segments, defected to rival Circuit City in 2004. Best Buy also dismissed Ernst & Young as its independent auditor after a former board member disclosed personal business dealings with the firm.

In 2007 the attorney general in Connecticut filed a lawsuit against the company, alleging it overcharged its customers by deceiving them. The suit accused Best Buy employees of showing in-store customers a Web site used internally that looked like Best Buy's main Web shopping site, but the internal site had higher prices. Best Buy denied the charges.

Chairman and founder Dick Schulze owns about 15% of Best Buy.

## HISTORY

Tired of working for a father who ignored his ideas on how to improve the business (electronics distribution), Dick Schulze quit. In 1966, with a partner, he founded Sound of Music, a Minnesota home/car stereo store. Schulze bought out his partner in 1971 and began to expand the chain. While chairing a school board, Schulze saw declining enrollment and realized his target customer group, 15- to 18-year-old males, was shrinking. In the early 1980s he broadened his product line and targeted older, more affluent customers by offering appliances and VCRs.

After a 1981 tornado destroyed his best store (but not its inventory), Schulze spent his entire marketing budget to advertise a huge parking-lot sale. The successful sale taught him the benefits of strong advertising and wide selection combined with low prices. In 1983 Schulze changed the company's name to Best Buy and began to open larger superstores. The firm went public two years later.

Buoyed by the format change and the fast-rising popularity of the VCR, Best Buy grew rapidly. Between 1984 and 1987 it expanded from eight stores to 24, and sales jumped from $29 million to $240 million. The next year another 16 stores opened and sales jumped by 84%. But Best Buy began to butt heads with many expanding consumer electronics retailers, and profits took a beating.

To set Best Buy apart from its competitors, in 1989 Schulze introduced the Concept II warehouse-like store format. Thinking that customers could buy products without much help, Schulze cut payroll by taking sales staff off commission and reducing the number of employees per store by about a third. The concept proved to be such a hit in the company's home territory, Minneapolis/St. Paul, that it drove major competitor Highland Appliance to bankruptcy. Customers were happy, but many of Best Buy's suppliers, believing sales help was needed to sell products, pulled their products from Best Buy stores. The losses didn't seem to hurt Best Buy; it took on Sears and Montgomery Ward in the Chicago market in 1989 and continued expanding.

In 1994 the company debuted Concept III, an even larger store format. Best Buy opened 47 new stores in 1995 but found itself swimming in debt. Earnings plummeted in fiscal 1997, partly due to a huge PC inventory made obsolete by Intel's newer product. Best Buy started selling CDs on its Web site in 1997. That year it realized it had overextended itself with its expansion, super-sized stores, and financing promotions. Best Buy underwent a speedy, massive makeover by scaling back expansion and doing away with its policy of "no money down, no monthly payments, no interest" (and next-to-no profits).

In 1999 Best Buy began to enter new markets (including New England) and introduced its Concept IV stores, which highlighted digital products and featured stations for computer software and DVD demonstrations.

In early 2001 Best Buy bought The Musicland Group (at the time, operator of more than 1,300 Sam Goody, Suncoast, On Cue, and Media Play music stores) for about $425 million. The company began its international expansion in November 2002 with its $377 million acquisition of Future Shop, Canada's leading consumer electronics retailer.

In June 2002 Schulze turned over his responsibilities as CEO to vice chairman Brad Anderson; Schulze remained as chairman of the board. Best Buy acquired Geek Squad, a computer support provider, for $3 million the same year.

Best Buy shut down more than 100 Musicland stores (90 Sam Goody music stores and 20 Suncoast video stores) and laid off about 700 employees in January 2003; in June it sold the entire Musicland subsidiary (then about 1,100 stores) to an affiliate of investment firm Sun Capital Partners.

## EXECUTIVES

**Chairman:** Richard M. (Dick) Schulze, age 66, $1,000,000 pay
**Vice Chairman:** Allen U. (Al) Lenzmeier, age 63, $1,927,445 pay
**Vice Chairman and CEO:** Bradbury H. (Brad) Anderson, age 57, $1,172,995 pay
**President and COO:** Brian J. Dunn, age 46, $746,309 pay
**EVP, Best Buy For Business:** Thomas C. Healy, age 45
**EVP Finance and CFO:** Darren R. Jackson, age 42, $597,643 pay
**EVP Entertainment, Multichannel, and Human Capital:** Shari L. Ballard, age 40
**EVP Retail Sales:** Timothy D. (Tim) McGeehan, age 40
**EVP Strategy and International:** Kalendu (Kal) Patel, age 43
**EVP Enterprise Transformation:** Greg Thorson, age 52
**SVP and Chief Communications Officer:** Susan S. Hoff, age 41
**SVP, General Counsel, and Assistant Secretary:** Joseph M. Joyce, age 55
**SVP Advertising and Promotional Marketing:** Ruby Anik, age 49
**SVP Merchandising:** Michael (Mike) Vitelli
**SVP and CFO, Best Buy U.S.:** James L. (Jim) Muehlbauer, age 45
**SVP and CFO; New Growth Platforms:** Ryan D. Robinson, age 41
**SVP International Merchandising:** Tasso Koken
**SVP Retail Support and Operations:** Tamara A. (Tami) Kozikowski
**SVP Entertainment:** Julie Owen, age 42
**SVP Retail Support and Operations:** Ben Moore
**SVP Merchandising:** David J. (Dave) Morrish
**CEO, Best Buy International:** Robert A. Willett, age 60, $622,962 pay
**Senior Director Investor Relations:** Charles Marentette
**Director of Corporate Public Relations:** Susan Busch
**Secretary and Director:** Elliot S. Kaplan, age 70
**Auditors:** Deloitte & Touche

## LOCATIONS

**HQ:** Best Buy Co., Inc.
7601 Penn Ave. South, Richfield, MN 55423
**Phone:** 612-291-1000 **Fax:** 612-292-4001
**Web:** www.bestbuy.com

Best Buy has distribution centers in Ardmore, Oklahoma; Bloomington, Minnesota; Dinuba and Whittier, California; Dublin, Georgia; Findlay, Ohio; Franklin, Indiana; Nichols, New York; and Staunton, Virginia; and in Burnaby, British Columbia; and Brampton, Ontario.

### 2007 Sales

| | $ mil. | % of total |
|---|---|---|
| US | 31,031 | 86 |
| International | 4,903 | 14 |
| **Total** | **35,934** | **100** |

### 2007 Locations

| | No. |
|---|---|
| US | |
| Best Buy | 822 |
| Magnolia Audio Video | 20 |
| Pacific Sales | 14 |
| US Geek Squad | 12 |
| International | |
| Future Shop Canada | 121 |
| Best Buy Canada | 47 |
| Five Star/Best Buy China | 136 |
| **Total** | **1,172** |

**2007 Best Buy Locations**

| | No. |
|---|---|
| California | 91 |
| Texas | 81 |
| Illinois | 49 |
| Florida | 46 |
| New York | 40 |
| Ohio | 34 |
| Michigan | 30 |
| Georgia | 26 |
| Pennsylvania | 26 |
| North Carolina | 25 |
| Virginia | 24 |
| Minnesota | 21 |
| Maryland | 20 |
| Massachusetts | 20 |
| Wisconsin | 20 |
| Indiana | 19 |
| New Jersey | 19 |
| Washington | 19 |
| Arizona | 18 |
| Missouri | 18 |
| Colorado | 14 |
| Iowa | 12 |
| Tennessee | 12 |
| South Carolina | 11 |
| Alabama | 10 |
| Connecticut | 10 |
| Louisiana | 10 |
| Kansas | 8 |
| Kentucky | 8 |
| Utah | 8 |
| Nevada | 7 |
| Oklahoma | 7 |
| Oregon | 7 |
| Other states | 42 |
| **Total** | **822** |

**2007 Magnolia Audio Video Locations**

| | No. |
|---|---|
| California | 11 |
| Washington | 7 |
| Oregon | 2 |
| **Total** | **20** |

## PRODUCTS/OPERATIONS

**2007 US Sales**

| | % of total |
|---|---|
| Consumer electronics | 45 |
| Home office | 29 |
| Entertainment software | 19 |
| Appliances | 7 |
| **Total** | **100** |

**2007 International Sales**

| | % of total |
|---|---|
| Consumer electronics | 45 |
| Home office | 33 |
| Entertainment software | 12 |
| Appliances | 10 |
| **Total** | **100** |

**Selected Products**

Consumer Electronics
- Audio
  - Car stereos
  - Home theater audio systems
  - MP3 players
  - Satellite radio systems
- Video
  - Digital cameras and camcorders
  - DVD players
  - Televisions

Home Office
- Computers
- Networking equipment
- Office furniture
- Printers
- Scanners
- Supplies
- Telephones

Entertainment Software
- CDs
- Computer software
- DVDs
- Subscription plans
- Video game hardware and software

Appliances
- Dishwashers
- Microwave ovens
- Refrigerators
- Stoves and ranges
- Vacuum cleaners
- Washers and dryers

## COMPETITORS

Amazon.com
Apple
Barnes & Noble
Borders
Circuit City
CompUSA
Costco Wholesale
Dell
Fry's Electronics
Gateway
Hastings Entertainment
Office Depot
OfficeMax
RadioShack
Sears Holdings
Staples
Systemax
Target
Tower Records
Trans World Entertainment
Wal-Mart

## HISTORICAL FINANCIALS

Company Type: Public

**Income Statement** FYE: Sat. nearest last day in Feb.

| | REVENUE ($ mil.) | NET INCOME ($ mil.) | NET PROFIT MARGIN | EMPLOYEES |
|---|---|---|---|---|
| **2/07** | 35,934 | 1,377 | 3.8% | 140,000 |
| **2/06** | 30,848 | 1,140 | 3.7% | 128,000 |
| **2/05** | 27,433 | 984 | 3.6% | 109,000 |
| **2/04** | 24,547 | 705 | 2.9% | 100,000 |
| **2/03** | 20,946 | 99 | 0.5% | 98,000 |
| **Annual Growth** | 14.4% | 93.1% | — | 9.3% |

**2007 Year-End Financials**

Debt ratio: 9.5%
Return on equity: 24.0%
Cash ($ mil.): 3,793
Current ratio: 1.44
Long-term debt ($ mil.): 590
No. of shares (mil.): 481
Dividends
Yield: 0.8%
Payout: 12.9%
Market value ($ mil.): 22,278

**Stock History** NYSE: BBY

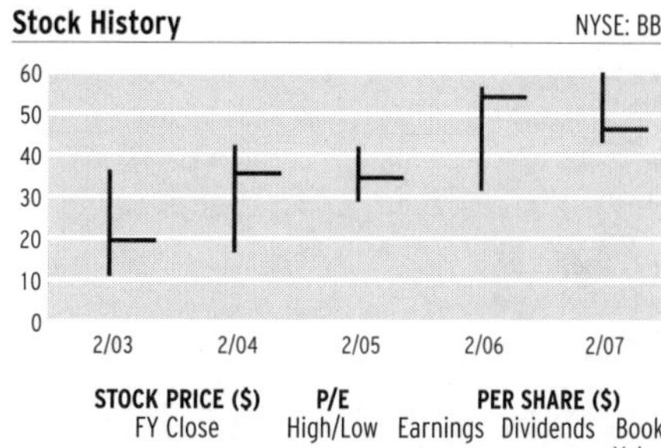


| | STOCK PRICE ($) FY Close | P/E High | P/E Low | PER SHARE ($) Earnings | Dividends | Book Value |
|---|---|---|---|---|---|---|
| **2/07** | 46.35 | 21 | 16 | 2.79 | 0.36 | 12.90 |
| **2/06** | 54.04 | 25 | 14 | 2.27 | 0.31 | 10.84 |
| **2/05** | 34.46 | 21 | 15 | 1.96 | 0.28 | 13.55 |
| **2/04** | 35.50 | 29 | 12 | 1.43 | 0.07 | 10.54 |
| **2/03** | 19.38 | 179 | 57 | 0.20 | — | 8.48 |
| **Annual Growth** | 24.4% | — | — | 93.3% | 72.6% | 11.1% |

# Big Lots

Big Lots believes that a product's shelf life depends solely on which shelf it's on. The company is the nation's #1 closeout retailer, with some 1,375 Big Lots stores (down from a high of 1,500 in 2005) in 47 states. (More than one-third of its stores are located in California, Florida, Ohio, and Texas.) It sells a variety of brand-name products that have been overproduced or discontinued, typically at 20% to 40% below discounters' prices, as well as private-label items. Big Lots closed 43 Big Lots Furniture stores in 2005. It sold its KB Toys unit (about 1,300 stores in 50 states, Guam, and Puerto Rico, and one of the top toy retailers in the US) in 2002 to a group led by its management team and Bain Capital.

Big Lots also operates a wholesale division (Big Lots Wholesale), which sells its discounted merchandise to a variety of retailers, manufacturers, distributors, and other wholesalers.

Big Lots has struggled in recent years as it lost sales to dollar and discount stores. In 2005 it hired a new CEO in the hope of reviving its sagging sales. In addition to closing poorly performing stores, the company is testing a new store format — with a racetrack-style center aisle — designed to highlight brand-name products selling for closeout prices. The new prototype is an effort to improve product visibility in Big Lots' often cluttered stores and enhance the shopping experience for its customers.

Its merchandise mix includes name-brand and private-label housewares, electronics, foods, toiletries, tools, toys, and clothing. To stock the shelves of its stores, Big Lots buys truckloads of orphaned bric-a-brac (discontinued, overproduced, and outdated items) at steep discounts from stores and manufacturers.

In August 2002 the company finished converting a confusing mix of formats and names — Odd Lots, Mac Frugal's, and Pic 'N' Save, among others — to the Big Lots banner. The name change is part of a larger initiative to broaden the appeal of closeout retailing and to build a national brand. Big Lots is spending $60 million to spruce up many poorly maintained stores and boost its TV advertising in an effort to appeal to higher-income shoppers. It is also adding international foods sections and furniture departments to its stores. (Nearly 95% of Big Lots stores sell furniture.)

## HISTORY

As a kid growing up in Columbus, Ohio, Russian-born Sol Shenk (pronounced "Shank") couldn't stand to pay full price for anything. His frugality blossomed into a knack for buying low and wholesaling. After a failed effort to make auto parts, Shenk began the precursor to Consolidated Stores in 1967, backed by brothers Alvin, Saul, and Jerome Schottenstein.

The company started by wholesaling closeout auto parts and buying retailers' closeout items to sell to other retailers. By 1971 Shenk had branched into retailing, selling closeout auto parts through a small chain, Corvair Auto Stores.

One of Shenk's sons suggested they devote space in the Corvair stores to closeout merchandise other than car parts. Sales surged, and Shenk decided to sell the Corvair outlets and focus on closeout stores. The first Odd Lots opened in 1982. Consolidated grew more than 100% annually for the next three years. By 1986, the year after it went public, the company was opening two stores a week in midsized markets around the Midwest.

Shenk found that people would buy anything as long as the price was right. Two years after the mania for Rubik's Cubes ended, Odd Lots bought 6 million of the puzzles (once priced at $8) at 8 cents apiece, marked them up 500%, and sold them all.

By 1987 the company had nearly 300 Odd Lots/Big Lots stores. But runaway growth had created massive inventory shortages and losses as disappointed customers stopped browsing the company's sparsely stocked shelves. The woes coincided with a falling-out with the Schottensteins. Shenk retired in 1989.

Apparel and electronics retail executive William Kelley was named chairman and CEO the next year. Kelley returned Consolidated to its closeout roots and increased sales through acquisitions and creating new discount chains.

Consolidated doubled its size in 1996 with the $315 million purchase of more than 1,000 struggling Kay-Bee Toys (now KB Toys) stores from Melville Corp. The expansion continued with the 1998 purchase of top closeout competitor Mac Frugal's Bargains — Closeouts. (Mac Frugal's had nearly bought Consolidated in 1989 before Consolidated board members vetoed the deal.) The $1 billion acquisition of Mac Frugal's gave Consolidated another 326 western stores under the Pic 'N' Save and Mac Frugal's names.

In 1999 Consolidated combined its online toy sales operations with those of BrainPlay.com to form KBkids.com. In mid-2000 Kelley was ousted as CEO, handing the title over to CFO Michael Potter.

In December 2000 the company sold KB Toys (including KBkids.com) to a group led by KB management and global private equity firm Bain Capital for about $300 million. In mid-2001 the company changed its name to Big Lots and began converting all stores to that name to establish a national brand. Big Lots bought the inventory of bankrupt Internet home furnishings giant Living.com in June.

In 2002 the company completed converting 434 stores to the Big Lots banner, including 380 stores previously operating under the names of Odd Lots, Mac Frugal's, and Pic 'N' Save. During the year Big Lots opened 87 new stores and closed 42 others.

Potter stepped down in July 2005. He was succeeded by Steven S. Fishman who became the company's chairman, CEO, and president. Fishman is a veteran of the Pamida, Frank's Nursery & Crafts, and Rhodes Furniture retail chains. Also that year, Kelley unsuccessfully sought to join the Big Lots' board by asking large shareholders to elect him. Overall, the company shuttered 174 stores in 2005. Store closures continued in 2006 with a net loss of 25 locations.

In late 2006 the company reached tentative settlements of two employee-related class actions suits, including one by some 1,400 Big Lots employees in Louisiana and Texas who alleged that they were wrongly classified as managers so that they could be denied overtime pay. The settlements amounted to nearly $10 million. (In February 2004 Big Lots settled a similar suit brought by more than 1,000 California employees by agreeing to pay $10 million.)

## EXECUTIVES

**Chairman, President, and CEO:** Steven S. (Steve) Fishman, age 56, $960,000 pay
**EVP, Human Resources, Loss Prevention, Real Estate, and Risk Management:** Brad A. Waite, age 49, $516,978 pay
**EVP, Merchandising:** John C. Martin, age 56, $473,475 pay
**EVP, Store Operations:** Donald A. Mierzwa, age 57
**SVP and CFO:** Joe R. Cooper, age 49, $371,209 pay
**SVP, Marketing:** Robert C. Claxton, age 52
**SVP, Special Projects:** Kent A.W. Larsson, age 61
**SVP and CIO:** John M. Zavada, age 40
**SVP, General Counsel, and Secretary:** Charles W. Haubiel II, age 41
**SVP, General Merchandise Manager:** Norman J. (Norm) Rankin, age 50
**SVP, Merchandise Planning and Allocation and CIO:** Lisa M. Bachmann, age 45, $396,195 pay
**VP, Wholesale Merchandise Manager:** Armen J. Bahadurian, age 59
**VP, Real Estate:** Kevin R. Day
**VP, Strategic Planning and Investor Relations:** Timothy A. (Tim) Johnson, age 39
**VP, Marketing and Merchandise Presentation:** Richard J. Marsan Jr.
**VP, Store Operations:** Steven B. Page
**VP, Divisional Merchandise Manager:** Judith A. Panoff
**VP, Human Resources Services:** Jo L. Roney
**Director, Public Relations:** Keriake (Keri) Lucas
**Auditors:** Deloitte & Touche LLP

## LOCATIONS

**HQ:** Big Lots, Inc.
300 Phillipi Rd., Columbus, OH 43228
**Phone:** 614-278-6800 **Fax:** 614-278-6676
**Web:** www.biglots.com

Big Lots operates about 1,375 stores in 47 US states.

### 2007 Stores

| | No. |
|---|---|
| California | 188 |
| Texas | 112 |
| Ohio | 107 |
| Florida | 104 |
| Pennsylvania | 61 |
| North Carolina | 60 |
| Georgia | 57 |
| New York | 45 |
| Indiana | 44 |
| Michigan | 42 |
| Tennessee | 42 |
| Kentucky | 40 |
| Virginia | 36 |
| Illinois | 35 |
| Arizona | 34 |
| Alabama | 29 |
| South Carolina | 29 |
| Missouri | 25 |
| Louisiana | 24 |
| Colorado | 22 |
| Washington | 19 |
| West Virginia | 18 |
| Oklahoma | 17 |
| Mississippi | 15 |
| Wisconsin | 15 |
| Massachusetts | 14 |
| Nevada | 14 |
| New Jersey | 13 |
| New Mexico | 13 |
| Oregon | 13 |
| Maryland | 12 |
| Arkansas | 10 |
| Kansas | 10 |
| Utah | 10 |
| Other states | 46 |
| **Total** | **1,375** |

## PRODUCTS/OPERATIONS

### 2007 Sales

| | $ mil. | % of total |
|---|---|---|
| Home | 1,473.0 | 31 |
| Consumables | 1,369.6 | 29 |
| Seasonal & toys | 840.4 | 18 |
| Other | 1,060.0 | 22 |
| **Total** | **4,743.0** | **100** |

## COMPETITORS

99 Cents Only
Amazon.com
Bill's Dollar Stores
BJ's Wholesale Club
Costco Wholesale
Dollar General
Dollar Tree
Family Dollar Stores
Fred's
Goodwill
J. C. Penney
Kmart
Liquidation World
Quality King
Retail Ventures
Ross Stores
Salvation Army
Sears
Simply Amazing
Target
TJX Companies
Tuesday Morning
Variety Wholesalers
Walgreen
Wal-Mart

## HISTORICAL FINANCIALS

Company Type: Public

### Income Statement

FYE: Saturday nearest January 31

| | REVENUE ($ mil.) | NET INCOME ($ mil.) | NET PROFIT MARGIN | EMPLOYEES |
|---|---|---|---|---|
| **1/07** | 4,743 | 124 | 2.6% | 38,738 |
| **1/06** | 4,430 | (10) | — | 43,985 |
| **1/05** | 4,375 | 24 | 0.5% | 46,241 |
| **1/04** | 4,174 | 81 | 1.9% | 47,249 |
| **1/03** | 3,869 | 77 | 2.0% | 44,451 |
| **Annual Growth** | 5.2% | 12.8% | — | (3.4%) |

### 2007 Year-End Financials

Debt ratio: —
Return on equity: 11.2%
Cash ($ mil.): 282
Current ratio: 2.42
Long-term debt ($ mil.): —
No. of shares (mil.): 110
Dividends
Yield: —
Payout: —
Market value ($ mil.): 2,850

### Stock History

NYSE: BIG

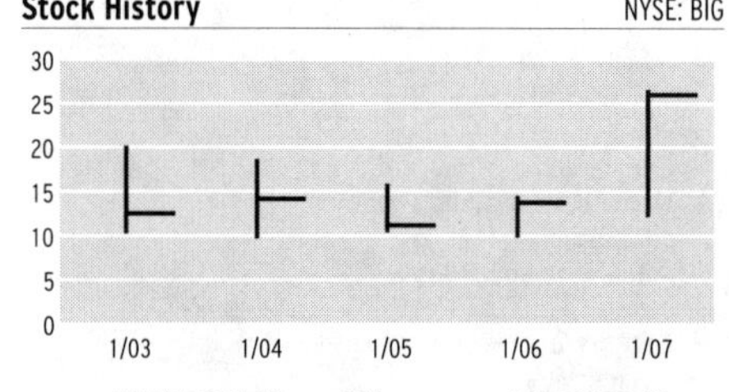


| | STOCK PRICE ($) FY Close | P/E High | P/E Low | PER SHARE ($) Earnings | Dividends | Book Value |
|---|---|---|---|---|---|---|
| **1/07** | 26.00 | 24 | 11 | 1.11 | — | 10.30 |
| **1/06** | 13.74 | — | — | (0.09) | — | — |
| **1/05** | 11.16 | 74 | 51 | 0.21 | — | — |
| **1/04** | 14.13 | 27 | 14 | 0.69 | — | — |
| **1/03** | 12.50 | 30 | 16 | 0.66 | — | — |
| **Annual Growth** | 20.1% | — | — | 13.9% | — | — |

# BJ Services

BJ Services keeps the pressure on oil production. Along with Halliburton and Schlumberger, the company is one of the top providers of pressure-pumping services used to protect the oil formation. BJ Services stimulates production through acidizing, cementing, coiled tubing, fracturing, and sand control. Its oilfield services include casing and tubular services, process and pipeline services, production chemicals, completion tools, and completion fluids services. The company operates onshore and offshore in most of the world's major oil and gas producing regions.

The bulk of BJ Services' revenues come from pressure pumping, which consists of cementing and stimulation services used during new oil and gas well completion. Its oilfield services include tubular services (installing casing and tubing to protect the wellbore), pipe connection inspection, and specialty chemical treatments to reduce corrosion and other problems. Through its BJ Chemical Services subsidiary (formerly BJ Unichem), the company provides chemicals used for oil and gas applications such as corrosion and scale inhibitors, emulsion breakers, desalting solutions, microbiocides, and refinery chemicals.

Although BJ Services generates the majority of its revenue from the US and Canada, it also serves the international market through its foreign subsidiaries and joint venture companies. The company has grown internationally by expanding its operations into Central America, Southeast Africa, New Zealand, and Turkey.

## HISTORY

BJ Services was founded in 1872 as Byron Jackson Company, a pump and equipment maker for the farming and mining industries. The company owned 50% of oil field service firm International Cementers and adopted the Cementers name in 1940. It pioneered practical air-powered drilling and, later, high-pressure power cementing.

In 1951 the company bought out its partners and changed its name to BJ Services. Acquired in 1974 by Hughes Tool, it became BJ-Hughes in 1975. Ten years later, Dresser Industries, BJ-Hughes, and Hughes Tool formed a partnership, BJ-Titan Services, which lasted until 1989. The next year the company went public as BJ Services.

Hughes Tool veteran J. W. Stewart was appointed CEO of BJ Services in 1990. Acquisitions were key to BJ Services' growth that decade. In 1995 the company acquired rival Western Company of North America, the #4 pressure-pumping company in the US, and the next year it bought Nowsco Well Service, Canada's #1 pressure-pumping firm.

BJ Services bought Louisiana-based oil field equipment company Top Tool in 1998. The next year it bought another Canadian oil well services company, Fracmaster, and combined it with Nowsco to create Nowsco-Fracmaster, to handle the company's Canadian operations.

In 2001 BJ Services won a major offshore contract to service two North Sea oil fields for global oil giant TOTAL FINA ELF. The following year the company acquired OSCA, a major provider of oil and gas well completion fluids, services, and tools, from Great Lakes Chemical (now Chemtura).

## EXECUTIVES

**Chairman, President, and CEO:** James W. Stewart, age 62, $2,256,105 pay
**VP, Finance and CFO:** Jeffrey E. (Jeff) Smith, age 44
**VP; President, International Division:** David D. Dunlap, age 45, $793,612 pay
**VP; President, US /Mexico Division:** Kenneth A. Williams, age 56, $869,865 pay
**VP and General Counsel:** Margaret B. Shannon, age 57, $673,537 pay
**VP International Pressure Pumping Operations:** Alasdair I. Buchanan, age 46
**Treasurer and Chief Tax Officer:** D. Bret Wells, age 41
**Controller:** Brian T. McCole, age 47
**Director, Human Resources:** Susan E. Douget, age 46
**CIO:** Paul F. Yust, age 53
**VP Technology and Logistics:** Jeff Hibbeler
**Auditors:** Deloitte & Touche LLP

## LOCATIONS

**HQ:** BJ Services Company
4601 Westway Park Blvd., Houston, TX 77092
**Phone:** 713-462-4239 **Fax:** 713-895-5851
**Web:** www.bjservices.com

BJ Services operates in most of the major oil and natural gas producing regions of Africa, Asia, Europe, Latin America, the Middle East, North America, and Russia.

### 2006 Sales

| | $ mil. | % of total |
|---|---|---|
| US | 2,600.9 | 60 |
| Canada | 526.6 | 12 |
| Other countries | 1,240.4 | 28 |
| **Total** | **4,367.9** | **100** |

## PRODUCTS/OPERATIONS

### 2006 Sales

| | $ mil. | % of total |
|---|---|---|
| Pressure pumping | 3,719.9 | 85 |
| Other oilfield services | 648.0 | 15 |
| **Total** | **4,367.9** | **100** |

### Selected Operations

Acidizing
Casing and tubular services
Cementing
Coiled tubing services
Downhole tools
Fracturing
Nitrogen services
Pipeline testing and commissioning services
Process and pipeline services
Sand control
Specialty chemical services

## COMPETITORS

Baker Hughes
Grey Wolf
Halliburton
M-I Swaco
Nabors Industries
Nabors Well Services
Pride International
Schlumberger
Smith International
TETRA Technologies
Tidewater
Weatherford International

## HISTORICAL FINANCIALS

Company Type: Public

### Income Statement

FYE: September 30

| | REVENUE ($ mil.) | NET INCOME ($ mil.) | NET PROFIT MARGIN | EMPLOYEES |
|---|---|---|---|---|
| **9/06** | 4,368 | 805 | 18.4% | 16,000 |
| **9/05** | 3,243 | 453 | 14.0% | 13,600 |
| **9/04** | 2,601 | 361 | 13.9% | 12,825 |
| **9/03** | 2,143 | 188 | 8.8% | 11,990 |
| **9/02** | 1,866 | 167 | 8.9% | 11,130 |
| **Annual Growth** | 23.7% | 48.3% | — | 9.5% |

### 2006 Year-End Financials

Debt ratio: 23.3%
Return on equity: 34.8%
Cash ($ mil.): 92
Current ratio: 1.54
Long-term debt ($ mil.): 500
No. of shares (mil.): 293
Dividends
Yield: 0.7%
Payout: 7.9%
Market value ($ mil.): 8,834

### Stock History

NYSE: BJS

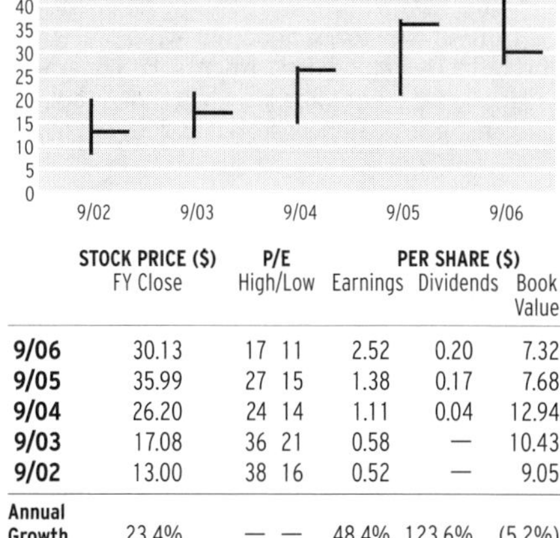


| | STOCK PRICE ($) FY Close | P/E High | P/E Low | PER SHARE ($) Earnings | Dividends | Book Value |
|---|---|---|---|---|---|---|
| **9/06** | 30.13 | 17 | 11 | 2.52 | 0.20 | 7.32 |
| **9/05** | 35.99 | 27 | 15 | 1.38 | 0.17 | 7.68 |
| **9/04** | 26.20 | 24 | 14 | 1.11 | 0.04 | 12.94 |
| **9/03** | 17.08 | 36 | 21 | 0.58 | — | 10.43 |
| **9/02** | 13.00 | 38 | 16 | 0.52 | — | 9.05 |
| **Annual Growth** | 23.4% | — | — | 48.4% | 123.6% | (5.2%) |

# BJ's Wholesale Club

"Exclusive membership" has never been as common as it is at BJ's Wholesale Club. The firm is the nation's #3 membership warehouse club (behind leaders Costco and SAM'S CLUB) and #1 in New England, with more than 8.5 million members and about 170 locations in 16 states, mostly in the Northeast. BJ's stores sell some 7,500 products, including canned, fresh, and frozen foods (food accounts for nearly 60% of sales). It also sells general merchandise, including apparel, housewares, office equipment, small appliances, and gas. Unlike its major rivals, BJ's targets individual retail customers rather than small businesses. Half of BJ's stores sell discounted gas to members.

Slumping sales at BJ's has led to management changes and a reevaluation of the chain's merchandising and pricing strategies. Chairman Herb Zarkin, who led BJ's in the 1990s, returned to the chief executive's office in March. Zarkin plans to trim the number of brands and sizes BJ's carries to free up shelf space for a wider assortment of new products and more luxury items. Fierce price competition between Costco and SAM'S CLUB has forced BJ's to cut its prices. Overall, the struggling chain plans to dramatically change its sales mix.

In early 2007 BJ's closed its two ProFoods Restaurant Supply clubs in the Bronx and Queens, New York, and shut down its in-store pharmacies in order to focus on its core warehouse club operation.

While BJ's focuses on store sales, it is keeping an eye on other strategies and in late 2006 it launched its online offensive against its rivals by selling some of its products online at BJs.com.

Like Costco and SAM'S CLUB, BJ's requires membership and offers a limited selection of items in warehouses that span, on average, 113,000 sq. ft. (although it does operate some smaller warehouses that cover a mere 71,000 sq.

ft. in small cities). To distinguish itself, BJ's employs a liberal membership policy and has added other consumer-minded accoutrements, such as brake and muffler service, food courts with brand-name fast-food restaurants, one-hour photo service, and optical stores.

It is also upgrading many of its clubs. Planned improvements include upgrading decor, moving expanded health and beauty aids departments to the front of the stores, and improving presentation in its fresh food departments. BJ's operates about 80 gas stations and is adding more. It plans to open eight to 10 new stores in 2007.

## HISTORY

In 1984, with Price Club (now part of Costco) thriving and Wal-Mart Stores' SAM'S CLUB beginning to dot the horizon, Zayre Corp. opened BJ's Wholesale Club, New England's first warehouse club. Zayre, a Massachusetts-based chain of discount department stores, placed the first store in Medford, Massachusetts, and named the operation after top executive Mervin Weich's wife, Barbara Jane. In return for an annual membership fee, customers could buy a mix of goods priced at around 8%-10% above what they cost BJ's.

Zayre's bought the California-based HomeClub chain of home improvement warehouses in 1986 and combined HomeClub with BJ's to form Zayre's warehouse division. Weich was replaced by John Levy the next year.

By mid-1987 BJ's had 15 stores and more than half a billion dollars in annual sales. Over the next few years, the chain expanded into 11 states in the Northeast and Midwest, including stores in the Chicago area. Despite the chain's rapid growth — or because of it — BJ's failed to post profits.

A debt-burdened Zayre began shifting its focus to its moderate-priced chains (including T.J. Maxx and Hit or Miss) during the late 1980s. In 1989 it spun off its warehouse division to shareholders and renamed it Waban (after a nearby Massachusetts town). Zayre was renamed TJX Companies.

Waban cracked the $1 billion sales mark in 1990. During the early 1990s the company moved into the midwestern US, but its stores failed to thrive. In 1991 it closed one of its four Chicago stores and in 1992 turned the other three into HomeBase stores.

Also during those years, BJ's added fresh meats, bakery items, optical departments, and travel agents to its stores. In 1993 Herbert Zarkin, BJ's president, replaced Levy as CEO. That year BJ's had 52 stores and 2.6 million members; its sales reached $2 billion. A new inventory scanning system implemented by the company helped cut costs.

Once again, however, strong sales didn't add up to big profits. In 1993 BJ's per-store profits were far below those of its competitors, primarily due to intense competition and a regional recession. Two years later it became the first warehouse club to accept MasterCard and issued its own store-brand version of that card. BJ's added nine stores in 1995, 10 the next year, and four in 1997.

Meanwhile, Waban was struggling with HomeBase, which was still failing to show a profit due to restructuring charges. In 1997 Waban spun off BJ's Wholesale Club — its star performer — to keep it from being undervalued; Waban then changed its name to HomeBase. Also in 1997 John Nugent was named BJ's CEO.

In September 2002 CEO Nugent resigned and was replaced by Michael T. Wedge, formerly an executive vice president of the company. In November two clubs in Columbus, Ohio, and a third in Florida shut down. BJ's entered the Atlanta market in 2002 with four clubs there.

In June 2005 BJ's agreed to settle charges brought by the Federal Trade Commission alleging the company failed to protect information on thousands of its customers. Without admitting guilt the company agreed to implement new security procedures and to periodic audits of those procedures. In 2005, the warehouse club operator opened eight new outlets, all in existing markets.

BJ's opened about a dozen new clubs in 2006. In September 2006 BJ's replaced its distribution center in Franklin, Massachusetts with a new 618,000-sq.-ft. facility in Uxbridge. The Uxbridge warehouse serves 65 clubs throughout Massachusetts, Maine, New Hampshire, Connecticut, Rhode Island, New York, and Ohio and has the capacity to support up to 86 clubs as the company expands. In November Mike Wedge resigned as CEO after 4 years in that position. He was succeeded, on an interim basis, by chairman Herb Zarkin. (Zarkin was permanently reappointed to the job in March 2007.) In February 2007 BJ's closed its two Pro Foods Restaurant Supply stores and discontinued in-store phamacy sales.

## EXECUTIVES

**Chairman, President, and CEO:**
Herbert J. (Herb) Zarkin, age 68
**EVP and CFO:** Frank D. Forward, age 52
**EVP, Merchandising and Logistics:** Laura J. Sen, age 50
**EVP, Store Operations:** Thomas F. Gallagher, age 55
**SVP, General Merchandise Manager, General Merchandise:** Richard E. Wilson
**SVP, Director of Human Resources:** Thomas Davis III
**SVP, Director of Sales Operations:** Kenneth A. Hayes
**SVP and CIO:** John A. Polizzi
**SVP and Controller:** Christina M. Neppl
**SVP, Director of ProFoods:** Henry G. Ragin, age 46
**SVP, General Merchandise Manager, Perishables and DSD:** Brian E. Riccio
**SVP, Director of Member Insight:** Deirdre Evens
**SVP, Divisional Merchandise Manager:** Bruce L. Graham
**SVP, Marketing and Membership:**
Edward F. (Ed) Gillooly, age 57
**SVP, Director of Logistics:** Ray R. Sareeram
**SVP, General Counsel, and Secretary:** Lon F. Povich, age 47
**SVP and Treasurer:** Arthur T. Silk Jr.
**VP; Manager, Financial Reporting:** John A. Brent
**VP, Manager of Operations and Sales:** David A. Evans
**VP, Assistant General Counsel and Corporate Secretary:**
Arlene C. Feldman
**VP; Manager, Investor Relations:**
Cathleen M. (Cathy) Maloney
**Auditors:** PricewaterhouseCoopers LLP

## LOCATIONS

**HQ:** BJ's Wholesale Club, Inc.
1 Mercer Rd., Natick, MA 01760
**Phone:** 508-651-7400 **Fax:** 508-651-6114
**Web:** www.bjswholesale.com

**2007 Locations**

| | No. |
|---|---|
| New York | 33 |
| Florida | 27 |
| Massachusetts | 18 |
| New Jersey | 18 |
| Pennsylvania | 13 |
| Connecticut | 9 |
| Maryland | 9 |
| Virginia | 9 |
| Georgia | 8 |
| North Carolina | 8 |
| New Hampshire | 6 |
| Ohio | 6 |
| Rhode Island | 3 |
| Maine | 2 |
| Delaware | 2 |
| South Carolina | 1 |
| **Total** | **172** |

## PRODUCTS/OPERATIONS

**2007 Sales**

| | % of total |
|---|---|
| Food | 60 |
| General merchandise | 40 |
| **Total** | **100** |

**2007 Sales**

| | $ mil. | % of total |
|---|---|---|
| Merchandise & services | 8,303.5 | 98 |
| Membership fees & other | 176.8 | 2 |
| **Total** | **8,480.3** | **100** |

**Selected Merchandise**

Food
- Baked goods
- Canned goods
- Dairy products
- Dry grocery items
- Fresh produce
- Frozen foods
- Meat and fish

General Merchandise
- Apparel
- Auto accessories
- Books
- Computer software
- Consumer electronics
- Greeting cards
- Hardware
- Health and beauty aids
- Household paper products and cleaning supplies
- Housewares
- Jewelry
- Office equipment
- Office supplies
- Seasonal items
- Small appliances
- Tires
- Toys

## COMPETITORS

Aurora Wholesalers
Best Buy
Big Lots
Costco Wholesale
Family Dollar Stores
Hannaford Bros.
IGA
J. C. Penney
Kmart
Office Depot
Pathmark
Penn Traffic
SAM'S CLUB
Sears
Shaw's
Staples
Stop & Shop
Target
Wal-Mart
Weis Markets

## HISTORICAL FINANCIALS

Company Type: Public

**Income Statement** FYE: Saturday closest to January 31

| | REVENUE ($ mil.) | NET INCOME ($ mil.) | NET PROFIT MARGIN | EMPLOYEES |
|---|---|---|---|---|
| **1/07** | 8,480 | 72 | 0.8% | 21,200 |
| **1/06** | 7,950 | 129 | 1.6% | 20,300 |
| **1/05** | 7,375 | 114 | 1.6% | 19,600 |
| **1/04** | 6,724 | 103 | 1.5% | 18,500 |
| **1/03** | 5,860 | 131 | 2.2% | 17,000 |
| **Annual Growth** | 9.7% | (13.9%) | — | 5.7% |

**2007 Year-End Financials**

Debt ratio: 1.7%
Return on equity: 7.1%
Cash ($ mil.): 56
Current ratio: 1.23
Long-term debt ($ mil.): 17
No. of shares (mil.): 65
Dividends
Yield: —
Payout: —
Market value ($ mil.): 2,031

**Stock History** NYSE: BJ

| | STOCK PRICE ($) FY Close | P/E High | P/E Low | PER SHARE ($) Earnings | Dividends | Book Value |
|---|---|---|---|---|---|---|
| **1/07** | 31.35 | 31 | 23 | 1.08 | — | 15.74 |
| **1/06** | 32.01 | 19 | 14 | 1.87 | — | 15.08 |
| **1/05** | 27.78 | 20 | 12 | 1.63 | — | 13.59 |
| **1/04** | 21.65 | 18 | 6 | 1.49 | — | 12.21 |
| **1/03** | 15.40 | 26 | 8 | 1.84 | — | 10.69 |
| **Annual Growth** | 19.4% | — | — | (12.5%) | — | 10.2% |

# Black & Decker

Other toolmakers would like to borrow the power tools, hardware, and home improvement products that Black & Decker has in its shed. Black & Decker is the nation's #1 maker of power tools and accessories, mainly under the DEWALT and Black & Decker names. It also makes electric lawn and garden tools, plumbing products (Price Pfister), specialty fastening and assembly systems, security hardware (Kwikset), and cleaning and lighting products (Dustbuster, SnakeLight, Scumbuster). Its largest customers include Home Depot and Lowe's, which together account for more than 10% of sales. It purchased power products maker Vector Products in 2006 for $160 million.

In 2005 Black & Decker began licensing its name to Vector to design and market power inverters, rechargeable spotlights, jump-starters, and vehicle battery chargers. Its 2006 acquisition of the company gives it more control of operations. Black & Decker has sorted its business units, more or less, by products and services. It operates three business segments: Power Tools and Accessories, Hardware and Home Improvement, and Fastening and Assembly Systems.

## HISTORY

When Duncan Black and Alonzo Decker opened The Black & Decker Manufacturing Company in Baltimore in 1910 with a $1,200 investment, they began a partnership that would last more than 40 years. Starting with milk-bottle-cap machines and candy dippers, the partners introduced their first major tool in 1916 — a portable half-inch electric drill with patented pistol grip and trigger switch, now on display at the Smithsonian Institution.

In 1917 the company built its first manufacturing plant, which would become its headquarters, in rural Towson, Maryland. Sales passed $1 million in 1919, and the company added a 20,000-sq.-ft. factory. Black & Decker quickly established itself in international markets with sales representatives in Australia, Japan, and Russia that year, and it built a manufacturing plant in England in 1939.

The founders led Black & Decker until they died — Black in 1951 (a year before the company went public) and Decker in 1956; family members took control of operations until the 1970s. Alonzo Decker Jr., the co-founder's only son, was president from 1960 to 1972, chief executive from 1964 to 1975, and chairman from 1968 to 1979, remaining on the board of directors until 2001. (It was Decker Jr. who introduced power tools for home use, and he designed the first cordless drill in the 1960s. He died in March 2002.)

The company acquired the General Electric (GE) housewares operations in 1984, replacing GE's trademark with the Black & Decker hexagonal trademark on such items as toaster ovens, can openers, and irons. Nolan Archibald became Black & Decker's CEO in 1986 and began a major restructuring. Renamed The Black & Decker Corporation, it closed five plants, streamlined distribution systems, consolidated overseas facilities, and cut payroll 10%. Earnings doubled in 1987.

Two years later Black & Decker acquired megaconglomerate Emhart (formerly American Hardware), but the purchase caused earnings to fall. To service its debt, the firm sold off pieces of its acquisition, including Emhart's Bostik adhesives, True Temper Hardware, and North American Mallory Controls.

Black & Decker expanded its international presence in 1995, beginning joint operations in India and China and introducing DEWALT power tools to Europe and Latin America.

The company sold its sluggish household products operations in the US and Latin America (except Brazil) to small-appliance maker Windmere-Durable Holdings (now Applica Incorporated) in 1998. (It kept the more profitable lighting and cleaning lines.) Black & Decker also sold True Temper Sports to Cornerstone Equity Investors and sold Emhart Glass to Bucher Holdings of Switzerland. The sales and restructuring eliminated about 5,000 jobs and allowed the company to focus on its DEWALT brand. The company posted a loss in 1998 due to restructuring and $900 million in goodwill charges.

In 1999 heir apparent and EVP Joseph Galli left; GE veteran Paul McBride replaced him. The company announced in 2002 that it would undergo restructuring that includes cutting 2,400 jobs, closing several plants, and transferring some operations from the US and the UK to Mexico, China, and Central Europe.

Also in 2002 the company entered into a cooperative agreement with Tokyo-based Hitachi Koki in their power tools business. That year Home Depot decided to stop selling Black & Decker's plumbing products east of the Rockies.

In 2003 Black & Decker acquired the Baldwin Hardware and Weiser Lock businesses from Masco for about $275 million. Also that year the company closed its plant in Easton, Maryland, eliminating 1,300 jobs there, and leaving the company with virtually no manufacturing presence in its home state.

Black & Decker sold Nemef, a Dutch maker of locks and cylinders, and Corbin, an Italian distributor of cylinders, locks, and padlocks, to ASSA ABLOY in January 2004.

The toolmaker acquired Pentair's Tools Group, which includes Delta, DeVilbiss Air Power, FLEX, Oldham Saw, and Porter-Cable, in 2004. The purchased entity was folded into Black & Decker's Power Tools and Accessories segment. FLEX, the major European component of the Porter-Cable and Delta Tools Group, was sold in November 2005.

## EXECUTIVES

**Chairman, President, and CEO:** Nolan D. Archibald, age 63
**EVP; President, Fastening and Assembly Systems Group:** Paul A. Gustafson, age 63, $765,000 pay
**SVP and CFO:** Michael D. Mangan, age 50, $1,011,000 pay
**SVP and General Counsel:** Charles E. Fenton, age 58, $956,167 pay
**SVP, Human Resources and Corporate Initiatives:** Paul F. McBride, age 51, $1,110,000 pay
**SVP, Public Affairs and Corporate Secretary:** Barbara B. Lucas, age 60
**Group VP; President, Industrial Products Group, Power Tools and Accessories:** John W. Schiech, age 48, $761,462 pay
**VP; President, Asia Pacific, Power Tools and Accessories:** Bhupinder S. (Ben) Sihota, age 48
**Group VP; President, Consumer Products Group, Power Tools and Accessories:** Bruce W. Brooks, age 42
**Group VP; President, Hardware and Home Improvement:** James T. (Jim) Caudill, age 39
**VP; President, Power Tools and Accessories, Consumer Products Group, Power Tools and Accessories:** Robert I. Rowan, age 46
**VP and Controller:** Christina M. McMullen, age 51
**VP, Investor Relations and Treasurer:** Mark M. Rothleitner, age 48
**VP; President, Commercial Operations, North and South America, Power Tools and Accessories:** Edward J. Scanlon, age 52
**VP; President, Europe/Middle East/Africa Power Tools and Accessories:** Les H. Ireland, age 42
**VP; VP, Global Finance, Power Tools, and Accessories:** Stephen F. Reeves, age 47
**VP, IT, Power Tools Division:** Jeffrey L. Comer
**Director, Brand Communications and Consumer Insights:** Kirsten Smith
**Director, Supply Chain Systems:** Bruce Twery
**VP; President, Fastening and Assembly Systems:** Michael A. (Mike) Tyll, age 50
**VP and Corporate Secretary:** Natalie A. Shields, age 50
**VP; VP, Business Development:** James R. Raskin, age 46
**Auditors:** Ernst & Young LLP

## LOCATIONS

**HQ:** The Black & Decker Corporation
701 E. Joppa Rd., Towson, MD 21286
**Phone:** 410-716-3900 **Fax:** 410-716-2933
**Web:** www.bdk.com

**2006 Sales**

| | $ mil. | % of total |
|---|---|---|
| US | 4,149.9 | 64 |
| Europe | 1,357.1 | 21 |
| Canada | 356.5 | 6 |
| Other regions | 583.8 | 9 |
| **Total** | **6,447.3** | **100** |

## PRODUCTS/OPERATIONS

### 2006 Sales

| | $ mil. | % of total |
|---|---|---|
| Power tools & accessories | 4,735.6 | 73 |
| Hardware & home improvement | 1,003.4 | 16 |
| Fastening & assembly systems | 666.5 | 10 |
| Adjustment | 41.8 | 1 |
| **Total** | **6,447.3** | **100** |

## COMPETITORS

American Standard
ASSA ABLOY
Atlas Copco
Cooper Industries
Danaher
Eaton
Electrolux
Emerson Electric
Energizer Holdings
Exmark Manufacturing
Fortune Brands
Hitachi
Illinois Tool Works
Ingersoll-Rand
Jacuzzi Brands
Kohler
Makita
Masco
Matsushita Electric
Robert Bosch LLC
Royal Appliance
Snap-on
Stanley Works
Textron
Toro

## HISTORICAL FINANCIALS

Company Type: Public

### Income Statement

FYE: December 31

| | REVENUE ($ mil.) | NET INCOME ($ mil.) | NET PROFIT MARGIN | EMPLOYEES |
|---|---|---|---|---|
| **12/06** | 6,447 | 486 | 7.5% | 25,500 |
| **12/05** | 6,524 | 544 | 8.3% | 27,200 |
| **12/04** | 5,398 | 456 | 8.4% | 26,200 |
| **12/03** | 4,483 | 293 | 6.5% | 22,100 |
| **12/02** | 4,394 | 230 | 5.2% | 22,300 |
| **Annual Growth** | 10.1% | 20.6% | — | 3.4% |

### 2006 Year-End Financials

| | |
|---|---|
| Debt ratio: 100.6% | No. of shares (mil.): 67 |
| Return on equity: 36.2% | Dividends |
| Cash ($ mil.): 233 | Yield: 1.9% |
| Current ratio: 1.52 | Payout: 23.2% |
| Long-term debt ($ mil.): 1,170 | Market value ($ mil.): 5,337 |

### Stock History

NYSE: BDK

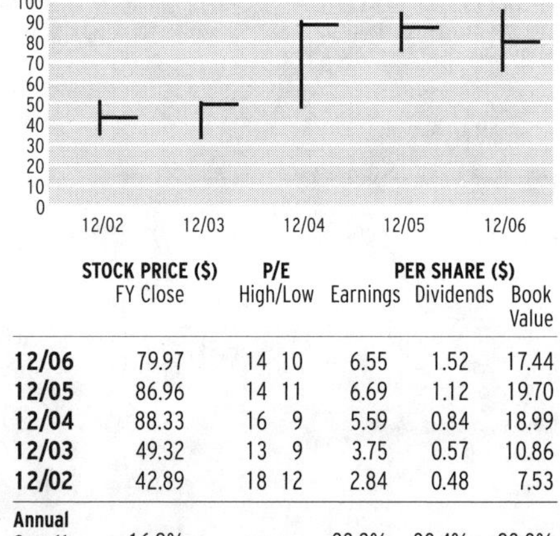


| | STOCK PRICE ($) FY Close | P/E High | P/E Low | PER SHARE ($) Earnings | Dividends | Book Value |
|---|---|---|---|---|---|---|
| **12/06** | 79.97 | 14 | 10 | 6.55 | 1.52 | 17.44 |
| **12/05** | 86.96 | 14 | 11 | 6.69 | 1.12 | 19.70 |
| **12/04** | 88.33 | 16 | 9 | 5.59 | 0.84 | 18.99 |
| **12/03** | 49.32 | 13 | 9 | 3.75 | 0.57 | 10.86 |
| **12/02** | 42.89 | 18 | 12 | 2.84 | 0.48 | 7.53 |
| **Annual Growth** | 16.9% | — | — | 23.2% | 33.4% | 23.3% |

# Blockbuster Inc.

When it comes to renting movies, this company is a Blockbuster. Blockbuster is the world's largest video rental chain, with more than 8,300 company-owned or franchised stores in more than 20 countries (about 60% are in the US). The chain rents more than 1 billion videos, DVDs, and video games at its Blockbuster Video outlets each year. Customers can also make rentals through its Web site, Blockbuster Online, which has taken on a more prominent role as the company attempts to fend off competitors such as Netflix. The company is closing struggling stores and has announced plans to divest its foreign operations and focus on its business in North America.

Blockbuster has a new chairman and CEO: 7-Eleven veteran James Keyes. (Keyes spent more than 20 years in various capacities at 7-Eleven before retiring in late 2005.) He succeeds John Antioco, who in March agreed to leave the company after a public battle over his hefty $51.6 million compensation package with Blockbuster's board.

The company is retrenching to focus on its business in North America. To that end, in early 2007 it agreed to sell its Australian subsidiary and grant master franchise rights to Video Ezy, an Australia-based video rental store operator. Other recent divestments include the sale of the company's Brazilian franchisee and its Taiwan subsidiary, closing its stores in Spain, and selling its US-based 72-store RhinoVideo Game chain to GameStop and its Game Station Ltd. business to The GAME Group plc.

In 2007 Blockbuster announced it would close another 280 struggling stores in the US, in part to focus more on its online business. The company closed about 300 stores in 2006. On the plus side, Blockbuster acquired Movielink, an online movie-downloading company owned by major Hollywood studios, in August 2007.

In response to the growing popularity of Netflix, Blockbuster launched its Blockbuster Online service where members can rent unlimited DVDs online and have them delivered via postal mail for a monthly fee. (Netflix filed suit against Blockbuster in 2006, claiming the video giant's online service violates Netflix's patent on such a video rental system. The two settled their differences in a confidential deal in 2007.)

The company has also added a monthly in-store subscription service called Blockbuster Movie Pass, which allows members to keep two or three movies at a time (depending on the plan selected) with no late fees. In addition, Blockbuster eliminated late fees on all of its traditional, in-store rentals in the US and Canada. It heavily marketed the plan, and lost more than $500 million in late fee revenues in 2005. In addition, Blockbuster took heat over the program's fine print, which states that rentals still have standard due dates, and if customers keep the movies or games for too long (seven days after the due date) the rental is converted into a sale and the customer is charged the difference.

Angering other movie rental companies who call it anti-competitive and unfair, Blockbuster struck an exclusive four-year deal in 2006 with The Weinstein Company, which provides Blockbuster exclusive US rental rights to all of Weinstein's movie releases.

Director and activist investor Carl Icahn owns about 9% of Blockbuster.

## HISTORY

After selling his computing services company, David Cook turned to operating flashy, computerized video rental stores, opening his first in 1985 and adopting the moniker Blockbuster Entertainment in 1986. Entrepreneur Wayne Huizenga took over in 1987, injecting $18 million into Blockbuster and buying the company outright by the end of the year. Huizenga's acquisitions rapidly expanded the number of Blockbuster stores to 130. Other acquisitions (including Major Video, a 175-store chain, and Erol's, the US's third-largest video chain) increased the number of stores to 1,500 by 1990.

Blockbuster became the largest video renter in the UK in 1992 through the purchase of 875-unit Cityvision. It also branched into music retailing that year when it bought the Sound Warehouse and Music Plus chains and created Blockbuster Music. The following year it acquired a majority stake in Spelling Entertainment, then was itself acquired in 1994 by Viacom for $8.4 billion. Viacom took Spelling Entertainment under its wing and formed a division for its new chain of video stores called Blockbuster Entertainment Group. Following the deal, Huizenga left the company.

Over the next few years, Blockbuster experienced a rash of poor business decisions and executive departures, starting with Steven Berrard (CEO after Viacom's 1994 takeover), who resigned in 1996 to head Huizenga's used-car operations. Wal-Mart veteran Bill Fields replaced him and started promoting the retailer as a "neighborhood entertainment center," selling videotapes (instead of renting them), books, CDs, gift items, and music. After closing 50 music outlets in 1996, the company moved its headquarters from Florida to Dallas in 1997, a move many employees refused to make.

Fields resigned later that year and John Antioco replaced him as chairman and CEO. Antioco's reign began with Viacom taking a $300 million charge related to the turmoil at Blockbuster. He immediately started unraveling many of Fields' efforts, especially his focus on non-rental operations. Antioco also set the video rental industry on its ear in 1997 by forcing the movie studios into a revenue-sharing agreement that replaced the standard practice of buying rental copies for as much as $120 each. It not only saved money, it allowed Blockbuster to stock more copies for less. The company finished returning to its rental roots by selling Blockbuster Music in 1998. By 1999 Viacom spun off a minority stake in Blockbuster.

In 2004 Blockbuster acquired American Satellite and Video, operator of some 40 southeastern Rhino Video Games stores that buy, sell, and trade video games. Later that year the company launched a $700 million takeover bid for rival Hollywood Entertainment. Hollywood refused to consider the offer and eventually agreed to a purchase by its smaller rival, Movie Gallery, in 2005. In response, Blockbuster launched a hostile bid for Hollywood, raising its offer to $1.3 billion. Hollywood's directors rejected the Blockbuster offer and urged their shareholders to do the same. Blockbuster later abandoned the takeover effort. Movie Gallery completed its purchase of Hollywood later that year, creating a strong #2 in the industry.

In July 2007 James Keyes, formerly president and CEO of convenience store operator 7-Eleven, joined Blockbuster as chairman and chief executive. He succeeded John Antioco.

## EXECUTIVES

**EVP, CFO, and Chief Administrative Officer:** Larry J. Zine, age 52, $640,000 pay
**SEVP and COO:** Nicholas P. (Nick) Shepherd, age 48
**SVP, Business Development:** Dean M. Wilson, age 44
**SVP and Chief of Marketing:** Curt Andrews
**SVP and General Manager, Blockbuster Online:** Shane Evangelist
**SVP, Rental Film:** Joyce Woodward
**SVP, Corporate Communications:** Karen Raskopf
**SVP, Human Resources and Administration:** Dan Satterthwaite
**SVP, Finance and Accounting and Treasurer:** Mary Bell
**SVP and General Merchandise Manager:** Matthew Smith
**SVP, Internal Audit:** Stephen Shelton
**Senior Director, Corporate Communications:** Randy Hargrove
**Director, Investor Relations:** Angelika Torres
**SVP, U.S. Operations:** Bryan Bevin
**SVP and U.S. Controller:** Thomas Kurrikoff
**SVP, Franchise and Development:** Steve Krumholz
**Managing Director, Blockbuster Entertainment Limited:** Martin Higgins
**SVP; President and Managing Director, Blockbuster Canada:** Miguel A. Foegal
**SVP and General Manager Supply Chain:** John Butler
**SVP and Controller:** James Howell
**SVP, Worldwide IT:** Debra Moody
**SVP, Tax and Treasury and Assistant Treasurer:** Bruce Lewis
**Chairman and CEO:** James W. (Jim) Keyes, age 48
**Auditors:** PricewaterhouseCoopers LLP

## LOCATIONS

**HQ:** Blockbuster Inc.
1201 Elm St., Dallas, TX 75270
**Phone:** 214-854-3000 **Fax:** 214-254-3677
**Web:** www.blockbuster.com

Blockbuster has 8,360 stores; some 3,166 are located outside of the US.

### 2006 US Locations

| | No. |
|---|---|
| California | 620 |
| Texas | 458 |
| Florida | 425 |
| New York | 224 |
| Illinois | 219 |
| Georgia | 188 |
| Ohio | 175 |
| Pennsylvania | 175 |
| New Jersey | 153 |
| Michigan | 152 |
| North Carolina | 141 |
| Arizona | 131 |
| Virginia | 129 |
| Washington | 123 |
| Massachusetts | 120 |
| Maryland | 120 |
| Indiana | 117 |
| Colorado | 114 |
| Tennessee | 109 |
| Missouri | 98 |
| Louisiana | 88 |
| Oregon | 88 |
| Kentucky | 82 |
| South Carolina | 78 |
| Alabama | 75 |
| Wisconsin | 70 |
| Oklahoma | 67 |
| Connecticut | 61 |
| Minnesota | 57 |
| Kansas | 56 |
| Utah | 51 |
| Other states | 425 |
| Guam | 3 |
| Virgin Islands | 2 |
| **Total** | **5,194** |

### 2006 International Locations

| | No. |
|---|---|
| Great Britain | 892 |
| Canada | 449 |
| Australia | 375 |
| Mexico | 319 |
| Italy | 246 |
| Ireland (Republic) and Northern Ireland | 196 |
| Brazil | 141 |
| Taiwan | 129 |
| Argentina | 84 |
| Chile | 78 |
| Denmark | 71 |
| New Zealand | 40 |
| Portugal | 27 |
| Thailand | 22 |
| Colombia | 22 |
| Venezuela | 20 |
| Panama | 16 |
| Israel | 15 |
| Guatemala | 8 |
| Spain | 8 |
| El Salvador | 5 |
| Uruguay | 3 |
| **Total** | **3,166** |

## PRODUCTS/OPERATIONS

### 2006 Sales

| | $ mil. | % of total |
|---|---|---|
| Rental revenues | 4,030.1 | 73 |
| Merchandise sales | 1,432.2 | 26 |
| Other revenues | 61.2 | 1 |
| **Total** | **5,523.5** | **100** |

## COMPETITORS

Amazon.com
Barnes & Noble
Best Buy
Borders
CinemaNow
Circuit City
Comcast
DIRECTV
EchoStar Communications
GameStop
Hastings Entertainment
iN DEMAND
Kroger
Movie Gallery
Netflix
Redbox
Starz Entertainment
Target
Time Warner Cable
Tower Records
Trans World Entertainment
Wal-Mart

## HISTORICAL FINANCIALS

Company Type: Public

### Income Statement

FYE: December 31

| | REVENUE ($ mil.) | NET INCOME ($ mil.) | NET PROFIT MARGIN | EMPLOYEES |
|---|---|---|---|---|
| **12/06** | 5,524 | 55 | 1.0% | 67,300 |
| **12/05** | 5,864 | (588) | — | 72,600 |
| **12/04** | 6,053 | (1,249) | — | 84,300 |
| **12/03** | 5,912 | (984) | — | 81,350 |
| **12/02** | 5,566 | (1,628) | — | 85,200 |
| **Annual Growth** | (0.2%) | — | — | (5.7%) |

### 2006 Year-End Financials

Debt ratio: 151.8%
Return on equity: 10.2%
Cash ($ mil.): 395
Current ratio: 1.12
Long-term debt ($ mil.): 900
No. of shares (mil.): 117
Dividends
Yield: —
Payout: —
Market value ($ mil.): 621

### Stock History

NYSE: BBI

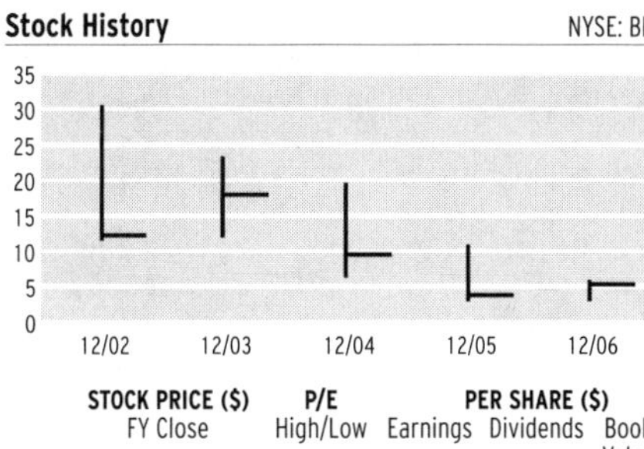

| | STOCK PRICE ($) FY Close | P/E High | P/E Low | PER SHARE ($) Earnings | Dividends | Book Value |
|---|---|---|---|---|---|---|
| **12/06** | 5.29 | 24 | 14 | 0.23 | — | 6.33 |
| **12/05** | 3.75 | — | — | (3.20) | 0.04 | 5.51 |
| **12/04** | 9.54 | — | — | (6.89) | 5.08 | 9.52 |
| **12/03** | 17.95 | — | — | (5.46) | 0.08 | 88.06 |
| **12/02** | 12.25 | — | — | (8.96) | 0.08 | 117.05 |
| **Annual Growth** | (18.9%) | — | — | — | (20.6%) | (51.8%) |

# Bob Evans Farms

Bob Evans Farms brings home the bacon and serves it at the table. The company is well-known for its meat and pork products served at about 580 family-style restaurants in about 20 states. Popular for its breakfast menu, the chain also serves traditional American fare for lunch and dinner. The company sells its Bob Evans and Owens Country Sausage brand meat products through grocery stores, along with Bob Evans branded frozen dinners. In addition to its core brands, Bob Evans owns SWH Corporation, which operates Mimi's Café, a chain of about 115 full-service restaurants offering American-style dishes served with a New Orleans twist.

Bob Evans has slowed the pace of expansion of its flagship restaurant chain to focus on improving sales and margins at its outlets. The company opened just 10 new locations during 2006 (down from 20 the year before) and plans to reduce that number further during 2007 and 2008. At the same time, it closed almost 20 underperforming locations during 2006.

The company's chain of Mimi's Café eateries, however, is accelerating growth, opening more than a dozen new units during 2006-07. It plans to add about 15 Mimi's locations during 2007 and 2008. Adding to the challenge, Mimi's CEO Russell Bendel has announced plans to resign from the company; Mimi's will be led by COO Daniel Dillon until a permanent replacement is found. The Mimi's chain, acquired in 2004, has helped diversify Bob Evans' revenue stream away from its aging core concept.

To help re-invigorate its core brand, the company hired Steven Davis as CEO in 2006. He previously worked for fast-food giant YUM! Brands as president of its Long John Silver's and A&W chains. (Stewart Owens, whose family started Bob Evans, resigned in 2005.) High on his priority list is marketing the Bob Evans chain to a younger clientele and increasing its share of the lunch and dinner crowd.

Bob Evans continues to develop food products for grocery store shelves, introducing such items as microwaveable Brunch Bowls and new frozen potato products. It also launched a new version of its popular Brown 'n' Serve link sausage under the name Bob Evans Express.

In its first foray outside the US, in 2007 the company has agreed to sell its sausage and some of its other breakfast food products in supermarkets and other retail food outlets in Canada. The outlets include the upscale grocery chain, Longo's, as well as some 250 Wal-Mart stores in Alberta, Manitoba, Ontario, and Quebec. Food product sales account for almost 20% of sales.

The company prides itself on the fact that it has never franchised its restaurant operations and that it maintains its own fleet of trucks to distribute food products from its processing plants.

Founder Bob Evans died in 2007. He was 89 years old.

## HISTORY

In 1946 Bob Evans opened the Bob Evans Steak House in Gallipolis, Ohio. The trucker's diner featured sausage made from hogs raised on Evans' own farm. In 1953 he and some friends and family members established the company as Bob Evans Farm Sales. By 1957, 14 trucks were delivering Bob Evans Farms sausage to southern and central Ohio customers overnight. When it went public in 1963, the company covered all of Ohio. Dan Evans, Bob's cousin, took over as CEO in 1971, when the business had just five restaurants. Dan oversaw much of the company's growth (more than 300 units by 1994), but a dispute between the cousins in 1986 led to Bob's resignation as president.

In 1987 the company acquired Texas-based Owens Country Sausage for $16 million. Stewart Owens, whose family had started the business in 1928, continued to run the subsidiary as its president and COO. Bob Evans diversified in 1991 by acquiring salad maker Mrs. Giles Country Kitchens. A year later it bought Hickory Specialties (charcoal products; sold in 2001) and launched a new restaurant line, Cantina del Rio, to compete in the growing Mexican-food market. In 1995 Owens became president and COO of the company.

With high pork prices and consumer preferences for lower-fat foods putting pressure on restaurant sales, the company closed its Cantina del Rio chain in 1996. (It also reduced the fat content of its sausage from 40% to 25%-30%.) The next year Bob Evans Farms slowed down its expansion to focus on improving existing locations and revising menus to feature homier items. These changes, combined with declining hog prices, returned Bob Evans to steady growth in 1998.

Stewart Owens took over as CEO in 2000, becoming the first person outside the Evans family to lead the company. (He was named chairman the next year.) That same year the company rebuffed shareholders (and founder Bob Evans) who, angry that the company's stock hadn't moved since 1985, called for the firm's sale. The following year Bob Evans Farms opened 30 new restaurants. Bob Evans' daughter Deborrah Donskoy again called for the sale of the company and again shareholders voted down the proposal.

Bob Evans opened its 500th restaurant in 2002 as expansion began to accelerate during the company's 50th year in business. In 2004 the company acquired SWH Corporation, owner of the Mimi's Café casual-dining chain, for $182 million. It also opened about 40 new Bob Evans restaurants.

Owens resigned from the company in 2005; he was replaced as chairman by Robert Rabold. Longtime executive Larry Corbin was called out of retirement to serve as interim president and CEO until the company brought in Steven Davis as a permanent replacement for Owens in 2006. Davis previously served as president of the Long John Silver's and A&W chains for fast-food giant YUM! Brands. Rabold died of a heart attack later that year and Davis took on the added responsibility of chairman.

Founder Bob Evans died in 2007 at age 89.

## EXECUTIVES

**Chairman and CEO:** Steven A. (Steve) Davis, age 47
**CFO, Treasurer, and Secretary:** Donald J. Radkoski, age 52, $493,301 pay
**EVP Food Products:** J. Michael (Mike) Townsley
**EVP Restaurant Operations:** Randall L. (Randy) Hicks, age 47, $354,627 pay
**SVP Facilities, Restaurant Division:** John F. Curry
**SVP Finance, Controller, Assistant Treasurer, and Assistant Secretary:** Tod P. Spornhauer, age 41
**SVP IS, Finance Group:** Larry Beckwith
**SVP Restaurant Marketing:** Mary L. Cusick, age 51
**SVP Food Products Production:** R. Earl Beery
**SVP Restaurant Operations:** Joe L. Gillen, age 56
**SVP Restaurant Operations:** James S. Merchant Jr., age 53
**SVP Restaurant Purchasing and Technical Services:** L. Merl Beery
**SVP and Director of Real Estate:** Stephen A. Warehime
**SVP Sales Food Products:** Anton G. (Skip) Larson Jr.
**VP, General Counsel, and Assistant Secretary:** Mary L. Garceau, age 34
**VP Human Resources, Mimi's:** Matthew Kimble, age 54
**Director Corporate Communications:** Tammy Roberts Myers
**Senior Manager Marketing:** Peter Keiser
**Executive Development Chef:** Chad Congrove
**President, Bob Evans Restaurants:** Roger D. Williams, age 56
**President and CEO, Mimi's Café:** Russell W. (Russ) Bendel, age 52, $516,170 pay
**Auditors:** Ernst & Young LLP

## LOCATIONS

**HQ:** Bob Evans Farms, Inc.
3776 S. High St., Columbus, OH 43207
**Phone:** 614-491-2225 **Fax:** 614-492-4949
**Web:** www.bobevans.com

In addition to its restaurants, Bob Evans Farms has seven meat processing plants in Bidwell, Springfield, and Xenia, Ohio; Galva, Illinois; Hillsdale, Michigan; and Richardson and Sulphur Springs, Texas. It also runs a distribution center in Springfield, Ohio.

### 2007 Locations

| | No. |
|---|---|
| Ohio | 199 |
| Indiana | 60 |
| Florida | 59 |
| California | 53 |
| Michigan | 52 |
| Pennsylvania | 39 |
| West Virginia | 30 |
| Maryland | 28 |
| Missouri | 25 |
| Kentucky | 24 |
| Illinois | 17 |
| Virginia | 17 |
| North Carolina | 15 |
| Arizona | 10 |
| Other states | 66 |
| **Total** | **694** |

## PRODUCTS/OPERATIONS

### 2007 Sales

| | $ mil. | % of total |
|---|---|---|
| Restaurants | 1,385.8 | 82 |
| Food products | 304.7 | 18 |
| Adjustments | (36) | — |
| **Total** | **1,654.5** | **100** |

### 2007 Locations

| | No. |
|---|---|
| Bob Evans | |
| Bob Evans Restaurant | 572 |
| Bob Evans Restaurant & General Store | 7 |
| Mimi's Café | 115 |
| **Total** | **694** |

### Selected Food Product Brands

Bob Evans
Country Creek Farm
Owens Country Sausage

## COMPETITORS

Applebee's
Big Boy Restaurants
Brinker
Buffets Holdings
Carlson Restaurants
CBRL Group
Country Kitchen
Darden
Denny's
Fresh Enterprises
Frisch's
Garden Fresh Restaurants
Golden Corral
Hormel
Houlihan's
Huddle House
IHOP
Perkins & Marie Callender's
P.F. Chang's
Ruby Tuesday
Shoney's
Smithfield Foods
Tyson Fresh Meats
VICORP Restaurants
Waffle House

## HISTORICAL FINANCIALS

Company Type: Public

### Income Statement

FYE: Last Friday in April

| | REVENUE ($ mil.) | NET INCOME ($ mil.) | NET PROFIT MARGIN | EMPLOYEES |
|---|---|---|---|---|
| **4/07** | 1,655 | 61 | 3.7% | 51,092 |
| **4/06** | 1,585 | 55 | 3.5% | 50,810 |
| **4/05** | 1,460 | 37 | 2.5% | 52,558 |
| **4/04** | 1,198 | 72 | 6.0% | 42,035 |
| **4/03** | 1,091 | 75 | 6.9% | 40,446 |
| **Annual Growth** | 11.0% | (5.3%) | — | 6.0% |

### 2007 Year-End Financials

Debt ratio: 24.4%
Return on equity: 8.6%
Cash ($ mil.): 29
Current ratio: 0.51
Long-term debt ($ mil.): 172
No. of shares (mil.): 35
Dividends
Yield: 1.5%
Payout: 32.5%
Market value ($ mil.): 1,304

**Stock History** NASDAQ (GS): BOBE

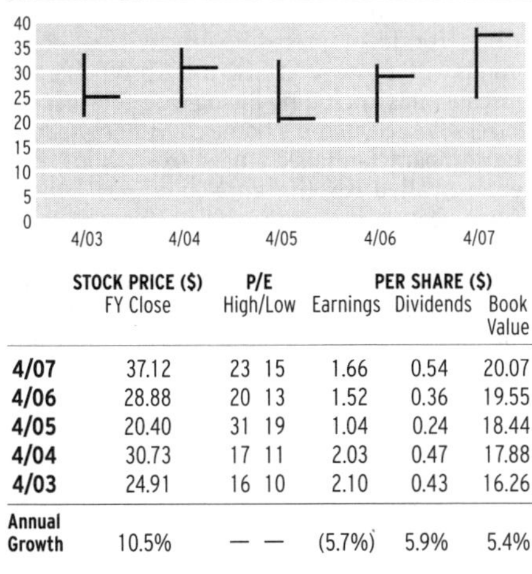


| | STOCK PRICE ($) FY Close | P/E High/Low | | PER SHARE ($) Earnings | Dividends | Book Value |
|---|---|---|---|---|---|---|
| **4/07** | 37.12 | 23 | 15 | 1.66 | 0.54 | 20.07 |
| **4/06** | 28.88 | 20 | 13 | 1.52 | 0.36 | 19.55 |
| **4/05** | 20.40 | 31 | 19 | 1.04 | 0.24 | 18.44 |
| **4/04** | 30.73 | 17 | 11 | 2.03 | 0.47 | 17.88 |
| **4/03** | 24.91 | 16 | 10 | 2.10 | 0.43 | 16.26 |
| **Annual Growth** | 10.5% | — | — | (5.7%) | 5.9% | 5.4% |

# The Boeing Company

Boeing is the 800-pound gorilla of US aerospace. The world's largest aerospace company, Boeing is the #2 maker of large commercial jets (behind its troubled rival Airbus) and the #2 defense contractor behind Lockheed Martin. Boeing has two major segments: Commercial Airplanes and Integrated Defense Systems. Boeing's commercial aircraft include the 787 Dreamliner (due in 2008), 767, 747, and the next-generation 737; military aircraft include the F/A-18 Hornet, the F-15 Eagle, the C-17 Globemaster III transport, and the AH-64D Apache helicopter. Boeing's space operations include communications satellites, missiles, the International Space Station, and the Space Shuttle (with Lockheed).

Following a post-9/11 slump, Boeing and Airbus both enjoyed a massive resurgence in orders in 2005: Boeing notched a record 1,002 orders — just behind Airbus' 1,055. Airbus outstripped Boeing in deliveries in 2006 (434 vs. Boeing's 398), but 2007 will likely belong to Boeing. The company racked up a record 1,004 plane orders in 2006, besting Airbus' anemic 790.

To compensate for the 2001-2004 downturn in commercial plane orders, Boeing cut costs, combined operations, and laid off thousands. It also focused on a super-efficient, long-range (7,000-8,000 miles), mid-sized (200-250 seat) plane — the Boeing 787 Dreamliner.

Dreamliner orders slowed, however, when rumors surfaced that Airbus was building an A330-derived plane to compete head-to-head with the Dreamliner. Airbus announced in December of 2004 that it was going ahead with plans to build the A350, a mid-sized, long-range plane that it expects to deliver in 2010. While all this was going on, Boeing also stepped up its campaign against Airbus' 1992 government loans deal, contending more strenuously than ever that it amounts to unfair subsidies.

Given its problems in the commercial aircraft market early in the decade, the Boeing restructured in 2002 to place more emphasis on its military and space operations, combining its Military Aircraft and Missile Systems and Space and Communications units to create Boeing Integrated Defense Systems (IDS). IDS has benefitted from the military buildup and spending related to homeland security and the conflicts in Iraq and Afghanistan. IDS also scored a major win in 2006 when it landed a $2 billion contract from the US Department of Homeland Security to build the Secure Border Initiative, which is intended to secure the land borders that the US shares with Canada and Mexico.

## HISTORY

Bill Boeing, who had already made his fortune in Washington real estate, built his first airplane in 1916 with naval officer Conrad Westervelt. His Seattle company, Pacific Aero Products, changed its name to Boeing Airplane Company the next year.

During WWI Boeing built training planes for the US Navy and began the first international airmail service (between Seattle and Victoria, British Columbia). The company added a Chicago-San Francisco route in 1927 and established an airline subsidiary, Boeing Air Transport. The airline's success was aided by Boeing's Model 40A, the first plane to use Frederick Rentschler's new air-cooled engine.

Rentschler and Boeing combined their companies as United Aircraft and Transport in 1929 and introduced the all-metal airliner in 1933. The next year new antitrust rules forced United to sell portions of its operations as United Air Lines and United Aircraft (later United Technologies). This left Boeing Airplane (as it was known until 1961) with the manufacturing concerns.

During WWII Boeing produced such planes as the B-17 "Flying Fortress" and B-29 bombers. At one point the company was producing 362 planes per month for the war effort.

Between 1935 and 1965 Boeing's commercial planes included the Model 314 Clipper, the Model 307 Stratoliner (with the first pressurized cabin), and the 707 (the first successful jetliner) and 727. In the 1960s it built the rockets used in the Apollo space program. The company delivered the first 737 in 1967. The 747 (the first jumbo jet) also went into production in the late 1960s.

Boeing expanded its information services and aerospace capabilities by establishing Boeing Computer Services in 1970. World fuel shortages and concern over aircraft noise prompted Boeing to design the efficient 757 and 767 models in the late 1970s.

Boeing bought Rockwell's aerospace and defense operations in 1996. The next year it purchased rival and leading military aircraft maker McDonnell Douglas for $16 billion.

Boeing acquired Hughes Electronics' (now The DIRECTV Group) satellite-making unit in a $3.85 billion deal in 2000. Boeing officially moved its corporate headquarters from Seattle to Chicago in September 2001. The airline industry was rocked on the 11th of that month, when terrorists crashed hijacked commercial jets in New York City, near Washington, DC, and in rural Pennsylvania. As airlines reduced their flight schedules in the aftermath, Boeing announced that it would lay off 25,000-30,000 people (about 30% of its commercial aviation workforce) by the end of 2002 (12,000 by the end of 2001 and 8,000 more by mid-2002).

Boeing was found to have obtained a 1998 launch contract with the help of confidential Lockheed Martin documents, and in 2003 was barred from bidding on launch contracts for almost two years. Even higher-profile was the scandal in which Boeing recruited Darleen Druyun — then the Air Force's #2 procurement officer — for a high-level position with Boeing, thus violating conflict of interest laws. She reportedly shared inside information with Boeing and helped the company land a contract for 100 767 refueling tankers. Michael Sears, Boeing's former CFO, was sentenced to four months in prison for his role in the incident; Druyun received nine months. CEO Phil Condit resigned in the wake of the scandals and was replaced by Harry Stonecipher in December of 2003.

CEO Stonecipher announced in 2004 that he would step down in 2006 at age 70, but was forced to resign in March of 2005 when an internal investigation revealed that he had been having an extra-marital relationship with another Boeing executive. CFO James A. Bell served as interim president and CEO until W. James McNerney, Jr., former head of 3M, was named chairman, president, and CEO.

In September of 2005 more than 18,000 Boeing machinists went on strike, bringing commercial aircraft production to a halt, but a sweetened deal brought machinists back in less than a month.

Later that year Boeing bought aviation services and parts distributor Aviall Inc. for $1.7 billion. Aviall became a wholly owned subsidiary of Boeing within the aerospace giant's commercial aviation services division.

## EXECUTIVES

**Chairman, President, and CEO:**
W. James (Jim) McNerney Jr., age 57, $1,750,000 pay
**EVP and CFO:** James A. Bell, age 58, $690,769 pay
**EVP; President and CEO, Integrated Defense Systems:**
James F. (Jim) Albaugh, age 56, $865,769 pay
**SVP; President, Connexion by Boeing:**
Laurette T. Koellner, age 52, $612,115 pay
**EVP; COO, Integrated Defense Systems:**
David O. Swain, age 65, $823,254 pay
**SVP, Business Development and Strategy:**
Shepard W. (Shep) Hill, age 54
**SVP and General Counsel:** J. Michael Luttig, age 52
**SVP; President, Boeing Capital Corporation:**
Walter E. (Walt) Skowronski, age 59
**SVP, Public Policy and Communications:** Tod R. Hullin, age 63
**SVP, Communications:** Thomas J. (Tom) Downey, age 42
**SVP, Corporate Secretary and Assistant General Counsel:** James C. Johnson, age 54
**SVP, Human Resources and Administration:**
Richard D. (Rick) Stephens, age 54, $486,308 pay
**SVP, International Relations:**
Thomas R. (Tom) Pickering
**SVP, Shared Services:** Richard D. Stevens, age 53
**SVP and CFO, Commercial Airplanes:**
Robert J. (Rob) Pasterick, age 51
**SVP, Missile Defense Systems, Integrated Defense Systems:** James W. (Jim) Evatt, age 66
**SVP, Engineering, Operations and Technology:**
John J. Tracy, age 52
**SVP, Office of Internal Governance:**
Wanda Denson-Low, age 50
**VP, Investor Relations:** R. Paul Kinscherff
**Auditors:** Deloitte & Touche LLP

## LOCATIONS

**HQ:** The Boeing Company
100 N. Riverside Plaza, Chicago, IL 60606
**Phone:** 312-544-2000 **Fax:** 312-544-2082
**Web:** www.boeing.com

Boeing's principal operations are in Australia, Canada, and the US.

**2006 Sales**

| | $ mil. | % of total |
|---|---|---|
| US | 38,499 | 63 |
| Asia | | |
| China | 2,659 | 4 |
| Other countries | 10,663 | 17 |
| Europe | 5,445 | 9 |
| Oceania | 1,206 | 2 |
| Africa | 967 | 2 |
| Canada | 660 | 1 |
| Latin America, Caribbean & other regions | 1,431 | 2 |
| **Total** | **61,530** | **100** |

## PRODUCTS/OPERATIONS

**2006 Sales**

| | $ mil. | % of total |
|---|---|---|
| Commercial airplanes | 28,465 | 46 |
| Integrated defense systems | | |
| Precision engagement & mobility systems | 14,350 | 23 |
| Network & space systems | 11,980 | 19 |
| Support systems | 6,109 | 10 |
| Boeing Capital Corporation | 1,025 | 2 |
| Other | 299 | — |
| Eliminations | (698) | — |
| **Total** | **61,530** | **100** |

**Selected Operations**

Commercial airplanes
- 737 Next Generation (short-to-medium-range two-engine jet)
- 747 (long-range four-engine jet)
- 767 (medium-to-long-range two-engine jet)
- 777 (long-range two-engine jet)
- 787 (long-range, super-efficient, 200-250 passenger capacity; due in 2008)

Military aircraft and missile systems
- AH-64D Apache helicopter
- AV-8B Harrier II
- C-17 Globemaster III
- C-40 Clipper
- CH-47 Chinook
- F/A-15 Eagle
- F/A-18E/F Super Hornet
- Harpoon Missile
- T-45 Flight Training System
- V-22 Osprey tilt-rotor aircraft
- Various classified projects
- X-45 (Unmanned Combat Air Vehicle — the UCAV is an advanced technology demonstrator)

Space and communications
- 737 AEW&C (Airborne Early Warning and Control)
- Global Positioning System satellites (GPS)
- International Space Station (contractor to NASA)
- National Missile Defense Lead Systems Integrator (NMDD LSI)
- Space Shuttle
- Various classified projects

## COMPETITORS

AgustaWestland
Airbus
BAE SYSTEMS
BAE Systems Inc.
Bombardier
Cessna
Daimler
Dassault Aviation
EADS
EADS North America
Eurocopter
GE Aviation
Goodrich
Kaman
L-3 Vertex
Lockheed Martin
MBDA
Northrop Grumman
Panasonic Avionics Corporation
Raytheon
Sextant Avionique
Textron
United Technologies

## HISTORICAL FINANCIALS

Company Type: Public

**Income Statement** — FYE: December 31

| | REVENUE ($ mil.) | NET INCOME ($ mil.) | NET PROFIT MARGIN | EMPLOYEES |
|---|---|---|---|---|
| **12/06** | 61,530 | 2,215 | 3.6% | 154,000 |
| **12/05** | 54,845 | 2,572 | 4.7% | 153,000 |
| **12/04** | 52,457 | 1,872 | 3.6% | 159,000 |
| **12/03** | 50,485 | 718 | 1.4% | 157,000 |
| **12/02** | 54,069 | 492 | 0.9% | 166,000 |
| **Annual Growth** | 3.3% | 45.7% | — | (1.9%) |

**2006 Year-End Financials**

Debt ratio: 172.1%
Return on equity: 28.0%
Cash ($ mil.): 6,386
Current ratio: 0.77
Long-term debt ($ mil.): 8,157
No. of shares (mil.): 1,012
Dividends
Yield: 1.4%
Payout: 42.1%
Market value ($ mil.): 89,929

**Stock History** — NYSE: BA

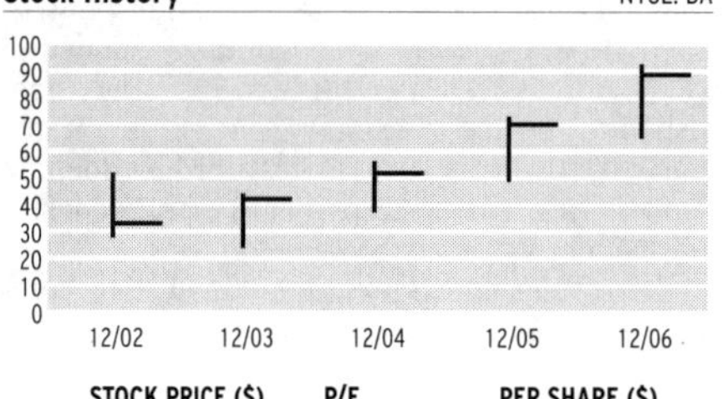


| | STOCK PRICE ($) FY Close | P/E High | P/E Low | PER SHARE ($) Earnings | Dividends | Book Value |
|---|---|---|---|---|---|---|
| **12/06** | 88.84 | 32 | 23 | 2.85 | 1.20 | 4.68 |
| **12/05** | 70.24 | 23 | 15 | 3.20 | 1.00 | 13.82 |
| **12/04** | 51.77 | 24 | 17 | 2.30 | 0.77 | 13.56 |
| **12/03** | 42.14 | 49 | 28 | 0.89 | 0.68 | 10.16 |
| **12/02** | 32.99 | 84 | 47 | 0.61 | 0.68 | 9.16 |
| **Annual Growth** | 28.1% | — | — | 47.0% | 15.3% | (15.5%) |

# The Bon-Ton Stores

Fashion hounds lost in the wilds from Maine to Montana can take refuge in The Bon-Ton Stores. The company operates about 280 department stores under eight nameplates, including the Bon-Ton, Elder-Beerman, and Carson Pirie Scott banners, in almost 25 states. The stores sell branded (Calvin Klein, Estée Lauder, Liz Claiborne, Nautica, and Waterford) and private-label women's, children's, and men's clothing; accessories; cosmetics; and home furnishings. The Bon-Ton Stores acquired the 142-store Northern Department Store Group from Saks in 2006, doubling its store count. The firm also operates two furniture stores. The Grumbacher family, who founded The Bon-Ton Stores in 1898, owns abut 37% of the company's stock.

Bon-Ton Stores paid about $1.05 billion to Saks for its Northern Department Store Group (NDSG), which included more than 140 stores under such brands as Carson Pirie Scott, Bergner's, Boston Store, Herberger's and Younkers, all located throughout more than 10 Midwestern and Great Plains states. The acquisition landed Bon-Ton Stores in second place among regional department store operators (behind Dillard's).

Bon-Ton has replaced its private label home brands with those of NDSG's more profitable and upscale lines, including Living Quarters and the actress Jane Seymour's home collection. In 2007 the company launched a new luxury home collection called KN (Karen Neuburger) Luxury Home, featuring items such as 610-count sheet sets. Since the acquisition from Saks, Bon-Ton Stores reshuffled the executive seats. It promoted Stephen Byers to head the firm's stores, operations, private brand, merchandise planning and allocation, and Internet merchandising divisions as vice chairman.

Continuing to make acquisitions, Bon-Ton Stores in October 2006 purchased four Parisian department stores from Belk, which had acquired the chain from Saks.

The retailer also offers harder-to-find customer services such as free gift wrap and special ordering. Women's clothing accounts for about a quarter of sales.

## HISTORY

The Bon-Ton began in York, Pennsylvania, in 1898 when Sam Grumbacher and his son Max opened a one-room millinery and dry goods store, naming it for the French term for good taste. Max's son Tom joined the company — S. Grumbacher & Son — in 1931, assisted his mother and brother in guiding the business through the Depression, and took charge in the early 1940s. A second store opened in 1946, and the company expanded gradually over the next four decades, entering Maryland, New York, and West Virginia.

Tom's son Tim became CEO in 1985. S. Grumbacher & Son bought Pomeroy's, an 11-store Pennsylvania chain, from Allied Stores two years later. With 33 stores and eager to fund further expansion, the company went public in 1991 as The Bon-Ton Stores. It doubled in size in 1994 by buying 35 stores — including 20 Hess stores in Georgia, New Jersey, New York, and Pennsylvania from Crown Holding and 10-store Buffalo, New York-based Adam, Meldrum & Anderson — for about $106 million.

Growing fast but losing money in the process, the chain hired May Department Stores executive Heywood Wilansky as CEO — the first from outside the family — in 1995. To get The Bon-Ton back on track, Wilansky closed 10 stores and began upgrading merchandise and using fewer vendors. In 1997 he reaffirmed the company's commitment to stick to smaller markets as it opens new stores.

To celebrate its centennial in 1998, The Bon-Ton opened a store in Westfield, Massachusetts, its first location in New England. The Bon-Ton opened seven stores in New England and New Jersey the next year.

In 2000, following a management restructuring, Tim Grumbacher reassumed the position of CEO when Wilansky retired.

The Bon-Ton Stores has been steadily increasing its sales of private-label merchandise from 9.8% in 2000 to nearly 11% in fiscal 2003. In 2003 Bon-Ton bought The Elder-Beerman Stores (67 department stores and two furniture stores in nine US states) for $92.8 million.

In July 2005 the company sold its private-label credit card business to HSBC Retail Services for about $316 million (less $226 million in accounts receivable), closed its corporate credit department, and eliminated about 85 jobs. Under the terms of the deal, HSBC will administer the credit card business and pay Bon-Ton Stores a portion of the revenue generated from future credit card sales.

In March 2006 The Bon-Ton Stores completed the acquisition of Saks Incorporated's Northern Department Store Group (NDSG). As a result, Bon-Ton Stores operated 279 department stores with some $3.4 billion in annual sales. In October the company purchased four Parisian department stores from Belk, which had acquired the chain from Saks.

## EXECUTIVES

**Chairman:** M. Thomas (Tim) Grumbacher, age 67, $675,000 pay
**President, CEO, and Director:** Byron L. (Bud) Bergren, age 60, $971,154 pay
**Vice Chairman, President, Merchandising:** Anthony J. (Tony) Buccina, age 56, $995,105 pay
**Vice Chairman, Private Brands, Planning and Allocation, and Internet Marketing:** David B. Zant, age 50, $519,231 pay
**Vice Chairman, Stores, Operations, Private Brand, Merchandise Planning and Allocation, and Internet Merchandising:** Stephen R. (Steve) Byers, age 53
**EVP, CFO, and Chief Accounting Officer:** Keith E. Plowman, age 49, $380,769 pay
**EVP Stores and Visual Merchandising:** James M. (Jim) Zamberlan, age 60
**EVP Human Resources:** Dennis R. Clouser, age 54
**EVP, Sales Promotion and Marketing:** Edward P. Carroll Jr., age 60
**SVP, Planning and Allocation:** Barbara Schrantz
**SVP, General Merchandise Manager:** Therese Callahan
**SVP, Marketing and Administrative Services:** Michael J. Hayes, age 41
**SVP, Planning and Allocation:** Robert A. Geisenberger, age 44
**SVP and CIO:** James (Jim) Lance, age 56
**SVP, Operations, Corporate Communications, and Community Services:** Ryan J. Sattler, age 60
**VP, Corporate Credit:** John J. Gleason, age 62
**VP, General Counsel, and Secretary:** Robert E. Stern, age 57
**VP, Controller:** Jeff Miller
**VP, Public and Investor Relations:** Mary Kerr
**VP, Procurement:** Teresa Arnold
**Auditors:** KPMG LLP

## LOCATIONS

**HQ:** The Bon-Ton Stores, Inc.
2801 E. Market St., York, PA 17402
**Phone:** 717-757-7660 **Fax:** 717-751-3108
**Web:** www.bonton.com

The Bon-Ton Stores operates 279 department stores in 23 US states.

## PRODUCTS/OPERATIONS

### 2007 Sales

| | % of total |
|---|---|
| Women's apparel | 27 |
| Home | 18 |
| Men's apparel | 13 |
| Cosmetics | 12 |
| Accessories | 8 |
| Shoes | 8 |
| Children's apparel | 6 |
| Intimate apparel | 4 |
| Juniors' apparel | 4 |
| **Total** | **100** |

### 2007 Stores

| | No. |
|---|---|
| Bon-Ton | 71 |
| Elder-Beerman | 66 |
| Younkers | 46 |
| Herberger's | 40 |
| Carson Pirie Scott | 31 |
| Bergner's | 13 |
| Boston Store | 10 |
| Parisian | 2 |
| **Total** | **279** |

### Selected Private Labels

Breckenridge
Consensus
Cuddle Bear
Karen Neuberger Home
Laura Ashley
Living Quarters
Pursuits, Ltd.
Relativity
Ruff Hewn
Statements
Studio Works

## COMPETITORS

Belk
Boscov's
Dillard's
Gap
J. C. Penney
J. Crew
J. Jill Group
Kohl's
Lands' End
Limited Brands
Loehmann's
Macy's
Sears
Target
Wal-Mart
Williams-Sonoma

## HISTORICAL FINANCIALS

Company Type: Public

### Income Statement

FYE: Saturday nearest January 31

| | REVENUE ($ mil.) | NET INCOME ($ mil.) | NET PROFIT MARGIN | EMPLOYEES |
|---|---|---|---|---|
| **1/07** | 3,456 | 47 | 1.4% | 33,000 |
| **1/06** | 1,308 | 26 | 2.0% | 33,500 |
| **1/05** | 1,320 | 20 | 1.5% | 12,600 |
| **1/04** | 930 | 21 | 2.2% | 13,500 |
| **1/03** | 716 | 10 | 1.3% | 8,600 |
| **Annual Growth** | 48.2% | 48.7% | — | 40.0% |

### 2007 Year-End Financials

Debt ratio: 343.4%
Return on equity: 14.7%
Cash ($ mil.): 25
Current ratio: 1.79
Long-term debt ($ mil.): 1,190
No. of shares (mil.): 14
Dividends
Yield: 0.3%
Payout: 3.6%
Market value ($ mil.): 540

### Stock History

NASDAQ (GS): BONT

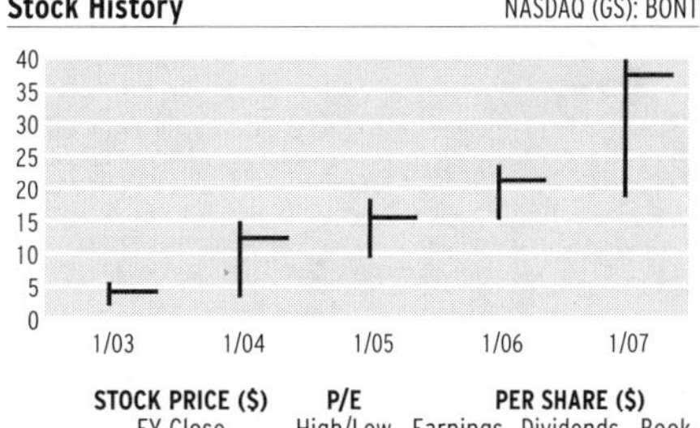

| | STOCK PRICE ($) FY Close | P/E High | P/E Low | PER SHARE ($) Earnings | Dividends | Book Value |
|---|---|---|---|---|---|---|
| **1/07** | 37.32 | 14 | 7 | 2.78 | 0.10 | 23.94 |
| **1/06** | 21.18 | 15 | 10 | 1.57 | 0.10 | 21.08 |
| **1/05** | 15.45 | 14 | 8 | 1.24 | 0.10 | 19.84 |
| **1/04** | 12.34 | 11 | 3 | 1.33 | 0.08 | 18.83 |
| **1/03** | 4.14 | 9 | 4 | 0.62 | — | 17.41 |
| **Annual Growth** | 73.3% | — | — | 45.5% | 7.7% | 8.3% |

# Borders Group

If you want John Updike or Janet Jackson to go with your java, Borders is for you. The #2 bookstore operator in the US (after Barnes & Noble), Borders Group has stores in 50 states, as well as in the UK, Australia, New Zealand, Puerto Rico, and Singapore. (The company plans to sell or franchise its international stores.) Its more than 1,200 retail stores include about 570 Borders superstores, about 560 mall-based Waldenbooks stores, and 30 UK-based Books etc. shops. To lure customers, the superstores host literary events and promote an environment with comfortable seats and cafes; they also sell music, videos, and DVDs.

Borders strives to reflect local tastes and interests in its superstores, even employing community relations representatives. Literary and community events include author signings, lectures, and local musician showcases.

Borders superstores carry on average 94,500 book titles, 14,000 music titles, and 7,400 movie titles; and average about 25,000 sq. ft. Its Waldenbooks stores are an average size of 3,800 sq. ft. and Books etc. stores, located mainly in London and in airports around the UK, average about 4,600 sq. ft. There are about 70 international Borders-brand superstores.

Spurred by the competitive pressures of the industry, the company announced a change in strategy in early 2007: to focus on its core domestic business and establish its own proprietary Web site. Previously, Border's Web operations were operated through an agreement with rival Amazon.com. The company is ending its relationship with Amazon and will debut its new stand-alone e-commerce site in 2008.

As part of the announced strategy change, Borders plans to sell or franchise its international stores. It also continues to reduce the number of its Waldenbooks locations, expecting to have only 300 by the end of 2008.

The company wants to grow by opening new stores and drastically remodeling existing locations. It generally averages almost 50 new international and domestic superstores per year, and remodels about 100 stores. Borders is putting its remodeling on hold as it develops a new store prototype that incorporates "digital centers" for customers to interact with various digital products such as e-books and MP3 players. Borders also plans to make more exclusive book deals to drive more people into the stores.

In addition to bookstores, Borders operates Paperchase Products (97%-owned) — a UK stationery and gift items retailer with about 100 locations. The company has expanded that business to the US by opening about 250 Paperchase shops inside select Borders superstores. Borders Group has a licensing agreement with Seattle's Best Coffee (SBC), a subsidiary of coffee house giant Starbucks, under which almost all domestic Borders have SBC-branded cafes.

## HISTORY

Brothers Louis and Tom Borders founded their first bookstore in 1971 in Ann Arbor, Michigan. The store originally sold used books but soon added new books. As titles were added, Louis developed tracking systems for the growing inventory. It's been said that the former MIT student stumbled upon the system while trying to create a software program to predict horse race winners. In the mid-1970s the brothers formed Book Inventory Systems to market the system to other independent bookstores.

Through the late 1970s and early 1980s, the brothers focused on building the service part of their business, but by the mid-1980s they were having trouble finding enough large, independent bookstore customers. Refocusing on retail, they opened their second store (Birmingham, Michigan) in 1985.

They had five stores by 1988 and hired Robert DiRomualdo (president of cheese log chain Hickory Farms) to run Borders and mount a national expansion. Discount retailer Kmart bought Book Inventory Systems (including 19 Borders bookstores) in 1992.

Kmart already owned Waldenbooks, which had been founded in 1933 and named for the Massachusetts pond that inspired Thoreau. Started by Larry Hoyt as a book rental library, Waldenbooks had 250 outlets by 1948. In 1968 the bookseller opened its first all-retail bookstore in Pittsburgh.

By placing stores in the growing number of US shopping malls, Waldenbooks expanded rapidly during the 1970s. In 1979 the company hired former Procter & Gamble executive Harry Hoffman to run the company. Hoffman drew the ire of traditionalists in the book retailing industry because he focused on best sellers instead of literary works. Hoffman also added nonbook items such as greeting cards to the stores' merchandise mix.

In 1981 Waldenbooks became the first bookseller to operate in all 50 states. Kmart acquired the chain three years later. As part of a plan to revive its discount business, in 1995 Kmart spun off Borders Group (which by this time included Waldenbooks, Borders, and part of Planet Music, formerly CD Superstore) to the public. Borders consolidated its three divisions under one roof and bought the rest of Planet Music (closed in 1997). With mall traffic slowing nationally, Borders CEO DiRomualdo steered the company away from Waldenbooks and toward superstores.

Philip Pfeffer, a former top executive with publisher Random House and book distributor Ingram (part of Ingram Industries) who succeeded DiRomualdo as CEO in late 1998, was forced out five months later, in part for being slow to address the company's lagging efforts online.

In November 1999 Greg Josefowicz, the former president of Albertson's Jewel-Osco division, was named CEO. In 2001 Borders laid off its entire borders.com workforce and struck a deal to have the online unit run by rival Amazon.com. In 2002 DiRomualdo stepped down as chairman, and Josefowicz assumed the role.

As a result of the ongoing saga in digital music distribution, Borders became a member of Echo; a joint venture founded in January 2003 by Best Buy, Hastings Entertainment, Tower Records, Trans World Entertainment, Virgin Entertainment, and Wherehouse Music. The consortium's goal is to devise a technology and licensing platform for the delivery of digital music to its retail members.

International expansion continued in 2005 when Borders boosted its stake in Paperchase Products to 97%. The following year, Josefowicz announced that he planned to retire from the company by the end of 2007. When George Jones was hired in mid-2006 to lead the company, Josefowicz stepped down.

## EXECUTIVES

**Chairman:** Lawrence I. (Larry) Pollock, age 59
**President, CEO, and Director:** George L. Jones, age 56, $432,212 pay (partial-year salary)
**EVP, Merchandising and Marketing:** Robert P. (Rob) Gruen, age 57
**EVP, U.S. Stores:** Kenneth H. Armstrong, age 57
**SVP and CFO:** Edward W. (Ed) Wilhelm, age 48, $353,654 pay
**SVP, General Counsel, and Secretary:** Thomas D. Carney, age 60, $273,654 pay
**SVP, Borders Group Operations:** Steve Davis
**SVP, Borders Stores:** Anne Kubek
**SVP, Merchandise Operations and Supply Chain:** Mark Palmucci
**SVP, Human Resources:** Daniel T. (Dan) Smith, age 42, $260,385 pay
**SVP and Chief Marketing Officer:** Michael A. Tam
**SVP, Trade Books:** Bill Nasshan
**SVP, Children's, Periodicals, Calendars, and Multimedia:** Linda Jones
**VP, Seasonal Business, Airports and Outlets:** Susan Zewicke
**VP, Cafe Operations:** Chris Nichols
**VP, Information Technology:** Dan Shull
**VP, Strategic Marketing and Entertainment Alliances:** Myles Romero
**Public Relations:** Anne Roman
**CIO:** Susan Harwood
**Auditors:** Ernst & Young LLP

## LOCATIONS

**HQ:** Borders Group, Inc.
100 Phoenix Dr., Ann Arbor, MI 48108
**Phone:** 734-477-1100 **Fax:** 734-477-1285
**Web:** www.bordersgroupinc.com

Borders Group has US distribution centers in California, Indiana, Ohio, Pennsylvania, and Tennessee, with additional international centers in Australia, Malaysia, New Zealand, Puerto Rico, Singapore, and the UK.

**2007 Borders Domestic Locations**

| | No. |
|---|---|
| California | 80 |
| Illinois | 35 |
| New York | 29 |
| Florida | 24 |
| Pennsylvania | 23 |
| Texas | 22 |
| Ohio | 19 |
| Michigan | 17 |
| New Jersey | 17 |
| Georgia | 15 |
| Virginia | 15 |
| Colorado | 14 |
| Massachusetts | 13 |
| Arizona | 12 |
| Indiana | 12 |
| Maryland | 12 |
| Washington | 12 |
| Connecticut | 10 |
| Missouri | 10 |
| North Carolina | 10 |
| Minnesota | 8 |
| Hawaii | 7 |
| Kansas | 7 |
| Oregon | 7 |
| Tennessee | 7 |
| Nevada | 6 |
| Wisconsin | 6 |
| Other states | 50 |
| **Total** | **499** |

## PRODUCTS/OPERATIONS

**2007 Sales**

| | $ mil. | % of total |
|---|---|---|
| Borders | 2,750.0 | 67 |
| Waldenbooks | 663.9 | 16 |
| International | 650.0 | 16 |
| Other | 51.9 | 1 |
| Adjustment | (2.3) | — |
| **Total** | **4,113.5** | **100** |

## COMPETITORS

Amazon.com
Barnes & Noble
barnesandnoble.com
Best Buy
Blockbuster
Book-of-the-Month Club
Books-A-Million
CDNOW
Columbia House
Half Price Books
Hastings Entertainment
HMV
Movie Gallery
Tower Records
Wal-Mart
WHSmith

## HISTORICAL FINANCIALS

Company Type: Public

**Income Statement** FYE: Saturday nearest January 31

| | REVENUE ($ mil.) | NET INCOME ($ mil.) | NET PROFIT MARGIN | EMPLOYEES |
|---|---|---|---|---|
| **1/07** | 4,114 | (151) | — | 33,600 |
| **1/06** | 4,079 | 101 | 2.5% | 35,500 |
| **1/05** | 3,903 | 132 | 3.4% | 32,700 |
| **1/04** | 3,731 | 120 | 3.2% | 32,300 |
| **1/03** | 3,513 | 112 | 3.2% | 32,700 |
| **Annual Growth** | 4.0% | — | — | 0.7% |

**2007 Year-End Financials**

Debt ratio: 0.8%
Return on equity: —
Cash ($ mil.): 120
Current ratio: 1.08
Long-term debt ($ mil.): 5
No. of shares (mil.): 58
Dividends
Yield: 1.9%
Payout: —
Market value ($ mil.): 1,248

**Stock History** NYSE: BGP

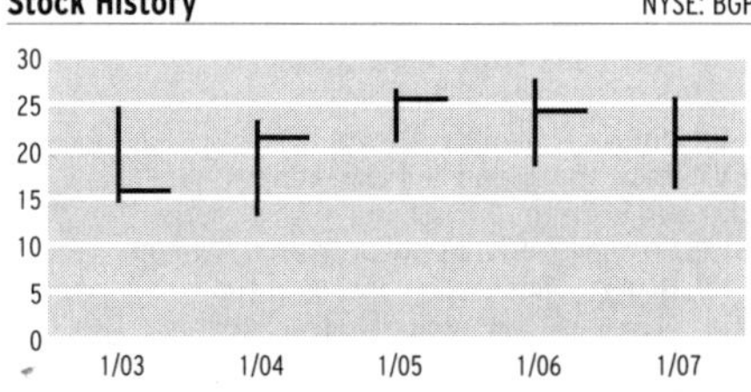


| | STOCK PRICE ($) FY Close | P/E High | P/E Low | PER SHARE ($) Earnings | Dividends | Book Value |
|---|---|---|---|---|---|---|
| **1/07** | 21.35 | — | — | (2.44) | 0.41 | 10.98 |
| **1/06** | 24.28 | 19 | 13 | 1.42 | 0.37 | 14.46 |
| **1/05** | 25.57 | 16 | 13 | 1.69 | 0.33 | 14.74 |
| **1/04** | 21.45 | 15 | 9 | 1.52 | 0.08 | 14.73 |
| **1/03** | 15.78 | 18 | 11 | 1.39 | — | 13.09 |
| **Annual Growth** | 7.9% | — | — | — | 72.4% | (4.3%) |

# BorgWarner Inc.

If suburbanites need four-wheel-drive vehicles to make it up their steep driveways, that's OK with BorgWarner (formerly Borg-Warner Automotive), a leading maker of power train products for the world's major automakers. Its largest customers include Ford (13% of sales), Volkswagen (13%), General Motors (9%), and Daimler and Chrysler, which together make up 11%. Its power train products include four-wheel-drive and all-wheel-drive transfer cases (primarily for light trucks and sport utility vehicles), as well as automatic transmission and timing-chain systems. BorgWarner operates more than 50 manufacturing facilities worldwide.

BorgWarner is in high gear. The company is growing profits while many of its peers do well to break even.

BorgWarner has been savvy about winning new business from customers outside the US such as Honda, Hyundai and Kia, and Volkswagen and AUDI. The company's strategy is to follow market share as it shifts increasingly away from Detroit and toward Asia and Europe. In 2006 60% of sales came from companies building cars outside the US (although many are later imported to the US). BorgWarner now generates more business from Volkswagen than it does from General Motors or DaimlerChrysler.

A part of BorgWarner's global growth strategy is to situate manufacturing operations where its customers reside. The company has steadily increased its presence in South Korea (Hyundai and Kia) and has expanded operations in China as Western automotive companies scramble to grab market share in that emerging market.

Although it attempted to insulate itself from Detroit's woes, few could have predicted the massive 2006 production cuts at Ford, GM, and Chrysler. To adjust, late in 2006 BorgWarner said it would cut about 800 jobs at 19 facilities in the US, Canada, and Mexico — or about 13% of its total North American workforce.

Soon after the job cut announcement, BorgWarner acquired Eaton's European Transmission and Engine Controls product lines. Products include high-pressure control solenoids for automated transmissions, as well as for rail diesel and gasoline engines. Terms of the deal were not disclosed.

## HISTORY

BorgWarner traces its roots to the 1928 merger of major Chicago auto parts companies Borg & Beck (clutches), Warner Gear (transmissions), Mechanics Universal Joint, and Marvel Carburetor. The newly named Borg-Warner Corporation quickly began buying other companies, including Ingersoll Steel & Disc (agricultural blades and discs) and Norge (refrigerators).

The company survived the Depression largely through the contributions of its Norge and Ingersoll divisions. In the latter 1930s, the company purchased Calumet Steel (1935) and US Pressed Steel (1937), along with several other companies.

During the early 1940s Borg-Warner made parts for planes, trucks, and tanks. Between 1942 and 1945 it produced more than 1.6 million automotive transmissions and gained the experience and manufacturing capacity to handle the postwar car boom. Its 1948 contract with Ford to build half of its transmissions resulted in massive growth.

Roy Ingersoll, president of the Ingersoll Steel & Disc division, took leadership of Borg-Warner in 1950 and embarked on a major diversification program. Borg-Warner's 1956 purchases included York, Humphreys Manufacturing, Industrial Crane & Hoist, Dittmer Gear, and the Chemical Process Company, among others. James Bert became president in 1968 and continued diversification.

Borg-Warner entered the security business in 1978 by buying Baker Industries (armored transport under the Wells Fargo name). In 1980 Borg-Warner sold its Ingersoll Products division. It acquired Burns International Security Services in 1982 and spun off York to its shareholders in 1986.

In the face of a 1987 takeover attempt, Merrill Lynch Capital Partners organized an LBO and took the company private, assuming $4.5 billion in debt. Borg-Warner then sold everything but its automotive and security units, including its chemical group to General Electric for $2.3 billion (1988) and its credit unit, Chilton, to TRW for $330 million (1989).

The company went public again in 1993 as Borg-Warner Security; it spun off Borg-Warner Automotive to its shareholders. (Borg-Warner Security changed its name to Burns International Services in 1999.) In 1995 Borg-Warner Automotive purchased the precision-forged products division of US-based Federal-Mogul.

To expand its air- and fluid-control business, the company acquired Holley Automotive, Coltec Automotive, and Performance Friction Products from component maker Coltec Industries in 1996. The following year Borg-Warner Automotive sold its money-losing manual-transmission business to Transmisiones y Equipos Mecanicos of Mexico.

Reduced production of Ford trucks, a weak Asian economy, and a strike at GM hurt 1998 sales. The next year the company bought diesel-engine component maker Kuhlman and then sold Kuhlman's electrical transformer and wire/cable businesses. Borg-Warner Automotive also sold its interests in joint ventures Warner-Ishi and Warner-Ishi Europe to partner Ishikawajima-Harima Heavy Industries.

In 1999 Borg-Warner Automotive bought the Fluid Power Division (automotive cooling systems) of Eaton Corporation for $130 million. The company changed its name to BorgWarner in 2000. Early the next year BorgWarner sold its fuel systems interests to private equity group TMB Industries.

In 2004 BorgWarner agreed to purchase a controlling 60% stake in Germany's BERU AG. The deal was completed in the first week of 2005 at a price of about $290 million.

## EXECUTIVES

**Chairman and CEO:** Timothy M. Manganello, age 57, $900,000 pay
**EVP, CFO, Chief Administration Officer and Director:** Robin J. Adams, age 53, $466,000 pay
**VP and CIO:** Jamal M. Farhat, age 47
**VP and Controller:** Jeffrey L. Obermayer, age 51
**VP and Treasurer:** Anthony D. Hensel, age 48
**VP, Business Development and M&A:** Christopher H. Vance, age 47
**VP, General Counsel, and Secretary:** John J. Gasparovic, age 49
**VP, Global Supply Chain:** John J. McGill, age 52
**VP, Investor Relations and Corporate Communications:** Mary E. Brevard, age 60
**VP, Advanced Product Technology:** Mark A. Perlick, age 60, $257,500 pay
**President, BorgWarner Morse TEC and BorgWarner Thermal Systems:** Alfred O. Weber, $375,000 pay
**VP; President, BorgWarner TorqTransfer Systems:** Cynthia A. Niekamp, age 47, $450,000 pay
**VP; President, BorgWarner Turbo Systems and Borg Warner Emissions Systems:** Roger J. Wood, age 44, $395,000 pay
**VP; President and General Manager, BorgWarner Transmission Systems:** Bernd W. Matthes, age 46
**Chief Compliance Officer and Assistant Secretary:** Laurene H. Horiszny, age 51
**Auditors:** Deloitte & Touche LLP

## LOCATIONS

**HQ:** BorgWarner Inc.
3850 Hamlin Rd., Auburn Hills, MI 48326
**Phone:** 248-754-9200 **Fax:** 248-754-9397
**Web:** www.bwauto.com

BorgWarner Inc. operates 64 manufacturing, assembly, and technical facilities worldwide.

### 2006 Sales

| | $ mil. | % of total |
|---|---|---|
| US | 1,819.4 | 40 |
| Europe | | |
| Germany | 1,567.0 | 34 |
| Hungary | 230.7 | 5 |
| UK | 200.8 | 4 |
| Other countries | 253.4 | 6 |
| South Korea | 224.3 | 5 |
| Other regions | 289.8 | 6 |
| **Total** | **4,585.4** | **100** |

## PRODUCTS/OPERATIONS

### 2006 Sales

| | $ mil. | % of total |
|---|---|---|
| Engine | 3,154.9 | 68 |
| Drivetrain | 1,461.4 | 32 |
| Adjustments | (30.9) | — |
| **Total** | **4,585.4** | **100** |

### Selected Products

Engine Group
- Air-control valves
- Chain tensioners and snubbers
- Complete engine induction systems
- Complex solenoids and multi-function modules
- Crankshaft and camshaft sprockets
- Electric air pumps
- Engine hydraulic pumps
- Exhaust gas-recirculation valves
- Fan clutches
- Front-wheel and four-wheel-drive chain and timing-chain systems
- Intake manifolds
- On-off fan drives
- Single-function solenoids
- Throttle bodies
- Throttle position sensors
- Turbochargers

Drivetrain Group
- Four-wheel-drive and all-wheel-drive transfer cases
- Friction plates
- One-way clutches
- Torque converter lock-up clutches
- Transmission bands

Joint Ventures
- BorgWarner Transmission Systems Korea, Inc. (60%)
- Borg-Warner Shenglong (Ningbo) Co. Ltd. (70%, China)
- Divgi-Warner Limited (60%, India)
- NSK-Warner KK (50%, Japan)

## COMPETITORS

Dana
Delphi
Eaton
Honeywell
JTEKT
Kolbenschmidt Pierburg
MAGNA Powertrain
Mitsubishi
NGK SPARK PLUG
Renold
Robert Bosch
Valeo

## HISTORICAL FINANCIALS

Company Type: Public

### Income Statement

FYE: December 31

| | REVENUE ($ mil.) | NET INCOME ($ mil.) | NET PROFIT MARGIN | EMPLOYEES |
|---|---|---|---|---|
| **12/06** | 4,585 | 212 | 4.6% | 17,400 |
| **12/05** | 4,294 | 240 | 5.6% | 17,400 |
| **12/04** | 3,525 | 218 | 6.2% | 14,500 |
| **12/03** | 3,069 | 175 | 5.7% | 14,300 |
| **12/02** | 2,731 | (119) | — | 14,000 |
| **Annual Growth** | 13.8% | — | — | 5.6% |

## 2006 Year-End Financials

Debt ratio: 30.4%
Return on equity: 12.0%
Cash ($ mil.): 182
Current ratio: 1.39
Long-term debt ($ mil.): 569
No. of shares (mil.): 58
Dividends
Yield: 1.1%
Payout: 17.5%
Market value ($ mil.): 3,405

## Stock History

NYSE: BWA

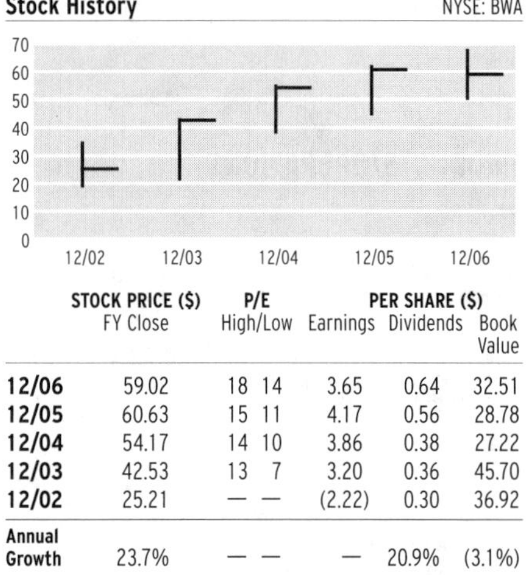


| | STOCK PRICE ($) FY Close | P/E High/Low | | PER SHARE ($) Earnings | Dividends | Book Value |
|---|---|---|---|---|---|---|
| 12/06 | 59.02 | 18 | 14 | 3.65 | 0.64 | 32.51 |
| 12/05 | 60.63 | 15 | 11 | 4.17 | 0.56 | 28.78 |
| 12/04 | 54.17 | 14 | 10 | 3.86 | 0.38 | 27.22 |
| 12/03 | 42.53 | 13 | 7 | 3.20 | 0.36 | 45.70 |
| 12/02 | 25.21 | — | — | (2.22) | 0.30 | 36.92 |
| Annual Growth | 23.7% | — | — | — | 20.9% | (3.1%) |

# Boston Scientific

Boston Scientific operates under the threat of minimal invasion. The company makes medical supplies used in minimally invasive surgical procedures. Its products are used to diagnose and treat conditions in a variety of medical fields, including cardiology, gynecology, oncology, radiology, urology, and vascular surgery. Products include catheters, surgical grafts, coronary and ureteral stents, polypectomy snares, and lithotripsy devices. Boston Scientific markets in some 70 countries worldwide, primarily through its own direct sales staff. After a long struggle with rival Johnson & Johnson to acquire Guidant, Boston Scientific emerged the winner; the deal is valued at $27 billion and was completed in 2006.

The company allied itself with equity investor Abbott Laboratories to gain the upper hand in the Guidant acquisition negotiations; Abbott snatched up Guidant's vascular device business as a part of Boston Scientific's victory. As a result, however, Abbott Laboratories was required by the FTC to divest of its equity in Boston Scientific.

As part of the deal, Boston Scientific was forced to pay a $700 million breakup fee to Johnson & Johnson. Johnson & Johnson subsequently sued Boston Scientific and Abbott Laboratories, seeking $5.5 billion in damages and claiming that Guidant leaked confidential information to Abbott. At the same time, within months of the acquisition Boston Scientific realized some 550 lawsuits over Guidant's ICD devices, including more than 70 class-action suits.

The medical community has raised concerns about drug-coated stents raising the risk of blood clots, which has caused a decrease in sales. The company has committed to financing additional studies on the effects of drug-coated stents but maintains that these stents are as safe as and more effective than bare-metal stents.

In early 2007, Boston Scientific acquired stent maker EndoTex Interventional Systems. The purchase came on the heels of FDA approval of EndoTex's NexStent Carotid Stent System, which was studied along with the Boston Scientific FilterWire EZ Embolic Protection System.

Cardiovascular products, which are used in procedures that affect the heart and systems carrying blood, account for about 80% of sales. The Endosurgery product line is responsible for almost all the rest, addressing the areas of oncology, vascular surgery, endoscopy, urology, and gynecology. The company's newest segment, neuromodulation devices (for the treatment of deafness and chronic pain), accounts for a small percentage of revenues.

Boston Scientific has approval in the US and Europe to sell its coronary stent system, Taxus. Nearly one third of Boston Scientific's revenues come from the sale of the Taxus Express 2 stent and have been integral to the company's increased revenues over the past few years.

Co-founders John Abele and Peter Nicholas (with their families) together control more than 20% of the company.

## HISTORY

Many medical companies start near a hospital, but Boston Scientific's roots sprouted at a children's soccer game where two dads found common ground. John Abele and Peter Nicholas had complementary interests: Wharton MBA Nichols wanted to run his own company; philosophy and physics graduate Abele wanted a job that would help people.

In 1979 the two men founded Boston Scientific to buy medical device maker Medi-Tech. Abele and Nichols had to borrow half a million dollars from a bank and raise an additional $300,000. Medi-Tech's primary product was a steerable catheter, a soft-tipped device that could be maneuvered within the body. The catheter revolutionized gallstone operations in the early 1970s, and Boston Scientific expanded on the success of the product. The company adapted it for a slew of new procedures for the heart, lungs, intestines, and other organs.

Boston Scientific's sales were healthy in 1983, but the firm still lacked funds. It eagerly accepted $21 million from Abbott Laboratories in exchange for a 20% stake. New FDA regulations slowed product introduction and put a crimp in the company's growth. Boston Scientific found a legal loophole in the late 1980s to avoid lengthy delays: The company described its products in the vaguest possible terms so upgraded devices were considered similar enough to predecessors to escape the in-depth scrutiny of the new approval process. Still, Abele and Nicholas had to mortgage their personal properties to stay afloat before this linguistic legerdemain helped to clear government red tape. Boston Scientific returned to profitability in 1991 and went public the next year, buying back Abbott Laboratories' interest in the company as well.

Boston Scientific acquired a bevy of medical device companies in 1995, doubling its sales. Among them were SCIMED Life Systems, which specialized in cardiology products; Heart Technology, a maker of systems to treat coronary atherosclerosis; and Meadox Medicals, which made arterial grafts.

Late in 1998, news came out that Boston Scientific's Japanese subsidiary had inflated sales over several years by as much as $90 million. Restated earnings subsequently revealed a loss, compounding the company's assimilation and recall problems.

The 1998 purchase of stent maker Schneider Worldwide fattened Boston Scientific's pipeline and payroll; the company in 1999 cut 14% of workers. That year a federal judge ruled that the company's Bandit PTCA catheter infringed on a Guidant patent. In 2000 the company settled with Guidant and the two companies agreed to license products to each other.

In spite of ongoing patent infringement suits (including a particularly ugly one recently settled with stent-supplier Medinol), Boston Scientific continues to develop new products and acquire smaller companies. The firm bought Advanced Stent Technologies, which develops stents for bifurcated heart vessels (a condition caused by the branching of one vessel into two). It has also acquired CryoVascular Systems. That company produces an angioplasty device used to treat atherosclerotic disease that was distributed by Boston Scientific. The acquisition of Rubicon Medical brings non-invasive stent delivery systems and other less invasive endovascular devices to the company's product portfolio. Boston Scientific acquired a portfolio of endoscopic (throat and esophageal) stents from Teleflex subsidiary Willy Rusch GmbH in 2005.

## EXECUTIVES

**Chairman:** Peter M. (Pete) Nicholas, age 65
**President, CEO, and Director:** James R. (Jim) Tobin, age 62, $922,576 pay
**COO:** Paul A. LaViolette, age 49, $660,000 pay
**EVP, Finance and Information Systems and CFO:** Sam R. Leno, age 61
**EVP and CTO:** Fredericus A. (Fred) Colen, age 54, $488,341 pay
**EVP, Human Resources:** Lucia L. Quinn, age 54
**EVP, Secretary, and General Counsel:** Paul W. Sandman, age 59, $460,027 pay
**EVP and President, International:** Jeffrey H. (Jeff) Goodman, age 59
**SVP:** James (Jim) Gilbert, age 49
**SVP and Group President, Endosurgery:** Stephen F. (Steve) Moreci, age 55
**SVP, Corporate Communications:** Paul Donovan, age 51
**SVP, Operations:** Kenneth J. (Ken) Pucel, age 40
**SVP and Group President, Interventional Cardiology:** William H. (Hank) Kucheman
**SVP, Administration, Cardiac Rhythm Management:** William F. (Bill) McConnell Jr., age 57
**SVP, Global Sales and Marketing, Cardiac Rhythm Management:** Mark C. Bartell, age 46
**SVP, Chief Medical and Scientific Officer:** Donald S. Baim
**VP, Global Government Affairs:** Brenda Becker
**VP, Investor Relations:** Daniel J. Brennan
**VP and Treasurer:** Milan Kofol
**Auditors:** Ernst & Young LLP

## LOCATIONS

**HQ:** Boston Scientific Corporation
1 Boston Scientific Place, Natick, MA 01760
**Phone:** 508-650-8000 **Fax:** 508-647-2393
**Web:** www.bostonscientific.com

Boston Scientific has facilities in France, Ireland, Japan, the Netherlands, Singapore, and the US.

### 2006 Sales

| | $ mil. | % of total |
|---|---|---|
| US | 4,840 | 62 |
| Europe | 1,529 | 20 |
| Japan | 630 | 8 |
| Other regions | 782 | 10 |
| Adjustment | 39 | — |
| **Total** | **7,821** | **100** |

## PRODUCTS/OPERATIONS

### 2006 Sales

| | $ mil. | % of total |
|---|---|---|
| Cardiovascular | 6,241 | 80 |
| Endosurgery | 1,346 | 17 |
| Neuromodulation | 234 | 3 |
| **Total** | **7,821** | **100** |

## COMPETITORS

Arrow International
Baxter
BD
C. R. Bard
Cook Group
Covidien
Datascope
Johnson & Johnson
Kimberly-Clark Health
Medtronic
St. Jude Medical
United States Surgical

## HISTORICAL FINANCIALS

Company Type: Public

### Income Statement

FYE: December 31

| | REVENUE ($ mil.) | NET INCOME ($ mil.) | NET PROFIT MARGIN | EMPLOYEES |
|---|---|---|---|---|
| **12/06** | 7,821 | (3,577) | — | 28,600 |
| **12/05** | 6,283 | 628 | 10.0% | 19,800 |
| **12/04** | 5,624 | 1,062 | 18.9% | 17,500 |
| **12/03** | 3,476 | 472 | 13.6% | 15,000 |
| **12/02** | 2,919 | 373 | 12.8% | 13,900 |
| **Annual Growth** | 27.9% | — | — | 19.8% |

### 2006 Year-End Financials

Debt ratio: 58.1%
Return on equity: —
Cash ($ mil.): 1,668
Current ratio: 1.86
Long-term debt ($ mil.): 8,895
No. of shares (mil.): 1,475
Dividends
Yield: —
Payout: —
Market value ($ mil.): 25,335

### Stock History

NYSE: BSX

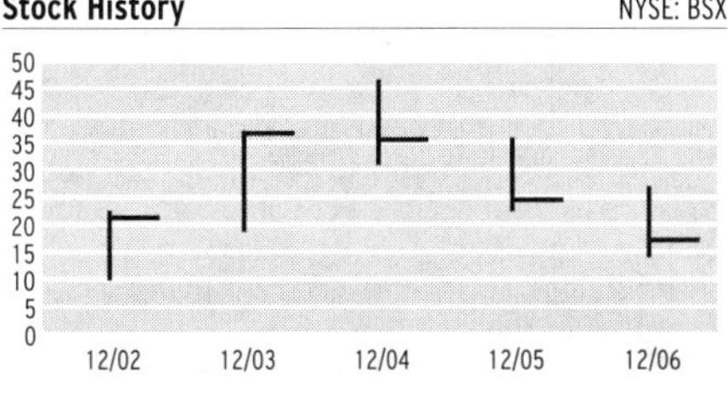


| | STOCK PRICE ($) FY Close | P/E High/Low | | PER SHARE ($) Earnings | Dividends | Book Value |
|---|---|---|---|---|---|---|
| **12/06** | 17.18 | — | — | (2.81) | — | 10.37 |
| **12/05** | 24.49 | 47 | 30 | 0.75 | — | 5.22 |
| **12/04** | 35.55 | 37 | 25 | 1.24 | — | 4.82 |
| **12/03** | 36.76 | 66 | 34 | 0.56 | — | 3.46 |
| **12/02** | 21.26 | 49 | 23 | 0.45 | — | 6.00 |
| **Annual Growth** | (5.2%) | — | — | — | — | 14.7% |

# Boyd Gaming

A key ingredient for Boyd Gaming's success is — or was — stardust. One of the country's leading casino operators, Boyd demolished the iconic Stardust Resort and Casino on the Las Vegas Strip in 2007 to make way for a new development, Echelon Place, which is set to open in 2010. The company's 16 properties include locations in Las Vegas, Florida, Indiana, Illinois, Louisiana, and Mississippi, and together have some 23,000 slot machines and 500 table games; the casinos typically feature multiple restaurants, lounges, and showrooms. Boyd also owns Coast Casino, as well as 50% of Atlantic City's Borgata Hotel Casino with MGM MIRAGE. Chairman and CEO William S. Boyd and his family own 36% of Boyd Gaming.

Boyd's properties outside of Nevada, including Sam's Town Hotel and Gambling Hall in Mississippi, Sam's Town Hotel and Casino in Louisiana, and the Par-A-Dice Hotel and Casino in Illinois, are riverboat operations. Boyd and MGM Mirage debuted a $200 million expansion of their Borgata Hotel Casino in 2006.

Boyd's $1.3 billion purchase of Coast Casinos created the fifth-largest gaming company in the US. (Boyd ditched Coast's South Coast Casino due to underperformance.) The company expanded into Florida with the 2007 purchase of Dania Jai Alai. The $152.5 million deal includes about 50 acres of related land.

Its $4 billion Echelon Place is planned to be a megacasino, spanning more than 60 acres.

## HISTORY

Boyd Gaming patriarch Sam Boyd may have caught the gambling bug early in life: His grandfather reportedly played poker with the outlaw Jesse James. After a stint working on gambling ships during the 1930s, Boyd arrived in Las Vegas in 1941 with less than $100 in his pockets and started running a penny roulette wheel. After years of saving half of what he made, Boyd invested $10,000 for an interest in the Sahara Hotel in 1952. He and his son William purchased the Eldorado Club in Henderson, Nevada, ten years later. Together, they founded Boyd Gaming in 1974 and opened the California Hotel in downtown Vegas the following year. In 1979 they opened Sam's Town on Las Vegas' Boulder Strip.

In 1985 the Boyds bought the Stardust (then a mob-tainted casino on the Las Vegas Strip) and acquired the Fremont Hotel and Casino near their California Hotel. Boyd Gaming was incorporated in 1988 as a holding company, and William was appointed chairman and CEO. Sam Boyd died in 1993, the same year that Boyd Gaming went public.

The company opened three casinos in Mississippi and Louisiana in 1994. That year it began managing the Treasure Chest Casino, a riverboat casino in Louisiana (it also owned a 15% stake). Two years later it acquired the Par-A-Dice Gaming riverboat casino in East Peoria, Illinois. When a federal investigation of Louisiana governor Edwin Edwards pointed toward Robert Guidry, a principal in the Treasure Chest operation, Boyd bought the remaining 85% it didn't already own. (Guidry pleaded guilty in 1998 to making payoffs to Edwards.)

In 1999 the company spent $23 million to renovate the aging Stardust, which later signed Vegas icon Wayne Newton to a 10-year engagement (a contract reportedly worth about $250 million). Boyd Gaming also gained its first foothold in Atlantic City that year when it formed a joint venture with Mirage Resorts (now owned by MGM MIRAGE) to build The Borgata (Italian for "village"), a 2,000-room, $1 billion casino resort. Renovation work at its Sam's Town casinos during 2000 ended Boyd's streak of earnings growth. The next year the company bought the Delta Downs racetrack near Lake Charles, Louisiana. The renamed Delta Downs Racetrack and Casino opened its casino in 2002. That year the company also purchased Isle of Capri's Tunica, Mississippi, property, adjacent to Sam's Town, for $7.5 million.

In 2004 Boyd acquired Coast Casinos for $1.3 billion. Several Boyd properties in Louisiana were temporarily closed in the wake of Hurricane Katrina, which hit the Gulf Coast in August 2005.

## EXECUTIVES

**Chairman and CEO:** William S. (Bill) Boyd, age 75, $1,750,000 pay
**Vice Chairman and SVP:** Marianne Boyd Johnson, age 48, $220,000 pay
**President, COO, and Director:** Keith E. Smith, age 47, $750,000 pay
**EVP, CFO, and Treasurer:** Paul J. Chakmak, age 42, $439,583 pay (partial-year salary)
**SVP, General Counsel, and Secretary:** Brian A. Larson, age 51
**SVP Administration:** William J. (Bill) Noonan
**SVP Operations:** Christopher R. Gibase
**SVP Operations, Central Regions:** Hector Mon, age 54
**VP and Director:** William R. Boyd, age 47
**VP and Controller:** Jeffrey G. Santoro, age 45
**VP and Assistant General Counsel:** Thomas F. Twesme
**VP Corporate Communications:** Robert D. (Rob) Stillwell
**VP Design:** Ralph E. Weise
**VP Development:** Blake Cumbers
**VP Information Systems:** Dennis J. (Denny) Frey
**VP Internal Audit:** Paula Eylar, age 44
**VP Strategic Procurement:** Richard A. (Rick) Darnold
**VP Marketing, Borgata:** Dave Coskey
**VP and General Manager, The Water Club, Borgata:** Drew Schlesinger
**VP Human Resources:** Robert Gerst
**Director; President and CEO, Echelon Resorts:** Robert L. (Bob) Boughner, age 54, $1,000,000 pay
**Auditors:** Deloitte & Touche LLP

## LOCATIONS

**HQ:** Boyd Gaming Corporation
2950 Industrial Rd., Las Vegas, NV 89109
**Phone:** 702-792-7200 **Fax:** 702-792-7313
**Web:** www.boydgaming.com

### Selected Operations and Locations

Boulder Strip (Las Vegas)
- Eldorado Casino
- Jokers Wild Casino
- Sam's Town Las Vegas

Downtown Las Vegas
- Barbary Coast
- California Hotel and Casino
- Fremont Hotel and Casino
- Gold Coast
- Main Street Station Casino, Brewery and Hotel
- The Orleans
- Suncoast

Central US
- Blue Chip Hotel & Casino (riverboat casino; Michigan City, IN)
- Par-A-Dice Hotel and Casino (East Peoria, IL)
- Sam's Town Hotel and Gambling Hall (Tunica, MI)
- Treasure Chest Casino (riverboat casino; Kenner, LA)

Other operations
- Delta Downs (horse racing track; Lake Charles, LA)
- Orleans Arena (Las Vegas)
- Vacations Hawaii (charter flights from Hawaii to Las Vegas)

## PRODUCTS/OPERATIONS

**2006 Sales**

| | % of total |
|---|---|
| Gaming | 74 |
| Food & beverage | 13 |
| Room | 7 |
| Other | 6 |
| **Total** | **100** |

## COMPETITORS

Ameristar Casinos
Argosy Gaming
Aztar
Harrah's Entertainment
Isle of Capri Casinos
Las Vegas Sands
MGM MIRAGE
Pinnacle Entertainment
Rio All-Suite Hotel & Casino
Station Casinos

## HISTORICAL FINANCIALS

Company Type: Public

**Income Statement** FYE: December 31

| | REVENUE ($ mil.) | NET INCOME ($ mil.) | NET PROFIT MARGIN | EMPLOYEES |
|---|---|---|---|---|
| **12/06** | 2,279 | 117 | 5.1% | 18,300 |
| **12/05** | 2,223 | 145 | 6.5% | 23,400 |
| **12/04** | 1,734 | 111 | 6.4% | 19,293 |
| **12/03** | 1,253 | 41 | 3.3% | 13,835 |
| **12/02** | 1,357 | 40 | 2.9% | 14,225 |
| **Annual Growth** | 13.8% | 30.7% | — | 6.5% |

**2006 Year-End Financials**

Debt ratio: 192.2%
Return on equity: 10.6%
Cash ($ mil.): 182
Current ratio: 1.13
Long-term debt ($ mil.): 2,133
No. of shares (mil.): 87
Dividends
Yield: 1.5%
Payout: 51.5%
Market value ($ mil.): 3,947

**Stock History** NYSE: BYD

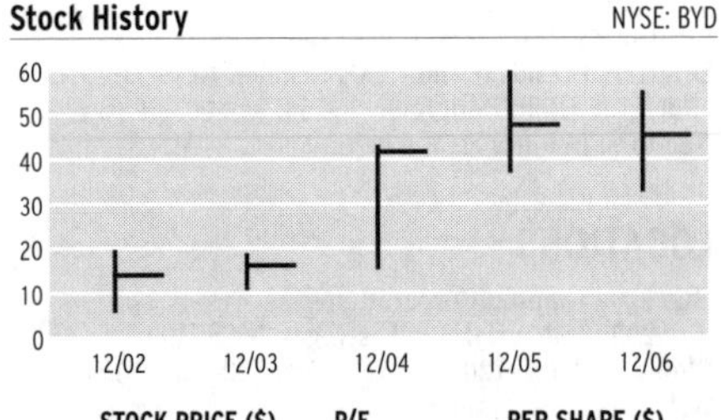


| | STOCK PRICE ($) FY Close | P/E High/Low | | PER SHARE ($) Earnings | Dividends | Book Value |
|---|---|---|---|---|---|---|
| **12/06** | 45.31 | 42 | 25 | 1.30 | 0.67 | 12.74 |
| **12/05** | 47.66 | 37 | 23 | 1.60 | 0.46 | 12.30 |
| **12/04** | 41.65 | 30 | 11 | 1.42 | 0.32 | 10.78 |
| **12/03** | 16.14 | 30 | 18 | 0.62 | 0.15 | 6.79 |
| **12/02** | 14.05 | 31 | 10 | 0.61 | — | 6.31 |
| **Annual Growth** | 34.0% | — | — | 20.8% | 64.7% | 19.2% |

# Briggs & Stratton

Briggs & Stratton doesn't mind getting yanked around. The company is the world's largest manufacturer of air-cooled gas engines (ranging from 3-to-31 horsepower) for use in lawn mowers and garden tillers. Through its chief subsidiary, Briggs & Stratton Power Products Group, the company also manufactures portable generators, pressure washers, switches, welders, and other related products. Lawn and garden equipment manufacturers are its biggest customers, with generator, pressure washer, and pump manufacturers following. Engine products include the Classic, I/C, Sprint, Quattro, Quantum, INTEK, and Vanguard brands. The engines are made in the US and are sold worldwide through its own sales and service centers.

Lawn and garden equipment accounts for more than three-quarters of sales. OEMs Global Garden Products, Husqvarna Outdoor Products (a unit of AB Electrolux), and MTD Products are the company's largest customers.

As worldwide emissions standards become more stringent, the company is expanding its product line to serve markets that have been traditionally dominated by two-cycle engine makers.

The vast majority of Briggs & Stratton's sales (more than 75%) are to the US market. And the vast majority of those sales (more than 80%) are made through big-box retailers like Wal-Mart, Home Depot, Sears, and Lowe's. Pricing pressure from those companies certainly reaches down and affects Briggs & Stratton's business. In fact, the company is beginning to experience the same effects in its industrial and other consumer products businesses.

In early 2007 Briggs & Stratton decided to close its engine manufacturing plant in Rolla, Missouri, and to transfer production to facilities in China and elsewhere in the US. Later that year the company elected to shutter its factory in Port Washington, Wisconsin, a facility that was picked up in the 2004 acquisition of Simplicity Manufacturing. Production at Port Washington, where outdoor power equipment is made, will be transferred to other facilities.

The company is best known for its small engines that go into lawn mowers and other gear, but Briggs & Stratton is also a big supplier of racing engines for dragsters, sprint cars, and junior stock cars. The company's Motorsports division markets a variety of engines under such brand names as Animal, Blockzilla, and Raptor.

FMR (Fidelity Investments) owns nearly 12% of Briggs & Stratton.

## HISTORY

In 1909 inventor Stephen Foster Briggs and grain merchant Harold Stratton gathered $25,000 and founded Briggs & Stratton to produce a six-cylinder, two-cycle engine that Briggs had developed while in college. However, the engine proved too expensive for mass production. A brief foray into the auto assembly business also failed as the company skirted bankruptcy. But in 1910 Briggs received a patent for a single-spark gas engine igniter. It wasn't a runaway success, but the company had found its niche making automotive electrical components. By 1920 Briggs & Stratton was the largest US producer of specialty lights, ignitions, regulators, and starting switches. These specialties accounted for two-thirds of the firm's total business through the mid-1930s.

The company acquired the A. O. Smith Motor Wheel (a gasoline-driven wheel designed to be attached to bicycles) and the Flyer (a two-passenger vehicle similar to a buckboard) in 1919. Neither product was successful and both were soon sold, but the company gained crucial knowledge and experience. In 1923 Briggs & Stratton introduced a stationary version of the Motor Wheel designed to power washing machines, garden tractors, and lawn mowers. The company continued to diversify, moving into the auto lock business in 1924. Its die-cast cylinder lock outsold competitors' brass models, and by the end of the decade, Briggs & Stratton had the lion's share of the market. The company formed BASCO to make auto body hardware. Briggs & Stratton bought Evinrude Outboard Motor Company in 1928, but sold the business within a year.

As with many other industrial manufacturers, Briggs & Stratton benefited by the onset of WWII: The war triggered an insatiable need for the company's products. Its wartime contributions included airplane ignition switches, artillery ammunition, and engines for generators, pumps, compressors, fans, repair shops, emergency hospitals, and mobile kitchens.

After the war Briggs & Stratton focused on small engines for lawn and garden equipment, and soon it dominated the market. In 1953 the company introduced an aluminum die-cast engine that was lighter than competing models and could withstand greater operating temperatures and pressures. Baby boomers' parents fueled sales, and the small market attracted little competition; Briggs & Stratton thrived making air-cooled engines and automobile components, such as locks and switches.

By the end of the 1970s sales had risen to about $590 million and, as the low-cost producer in the industry, the company was without a rival. During the early 1980s, however, Japanese companies (including Honda, Kawasaki, Mitsubishi, and Suzuki) entered the market after motorcycle sales crested. As a result of the strong dollar, these new competitors were able to provide engines to equipment makers at less expense than could Briggs & Stratton; the company suffered a decline in the late 1980s.

The company experienced a resurgence during the early 1990s. Frederick Stratton Jr., grandson of the co-founder, took over as president in 1992, and Briggs & Stratton benefited from a dollar that was weak relative to the yen.

In mid-2001 Stratton Jr. stepped down as president (he remained chairman until 2003) and COO John Shiely became president and CEO. Shiely succeeded Stratton as chairman in 2003.

Briggs & Stratton acquired outdoor power equipment manufacturer Simplicity Manufacturing for about $227 million in 2004. Briggs & Stratton acquired the assets of Murray Inc. in early 2005. Murray had once been one of Briggs & Stratton's biggest customers; however, in late 2004 the OEM filed for bankruptcy. Murray operations ceased that summer, but Briggs & Stratton continues to make Murray-branded products.

The company sold the assets of Briggs & Stratton Canada in 2004 to Power Source Canada Ltd. (PSC), a new company set up for the transaction. PSC took over distribution of Briggs & Stratton products in the Great White North.

## EXECUTIVES

**Chairman, President, and CEO:** John S. Shiely, age 54, $881,000 pay
**EVP and COO:** Todd J. Teske, age 41, $417,122 pay
**SVP and CFO:** James E. (Jim) Brenn, age 58, $345,138 pay
**SVP, Administration:** Thomas R. Savage, age 58, $345,740 pay
**SVP and President, Engine Power Products Group:** Paul M. Neylon, age 58, $301,140 pay
**SVP and President, International Power Products Group:** Michael D. Schoen, age 46
**SVP and President, Yard Power Products Group:** Vincent R. Shiely Jr., age 47
**SVP and President, Engine Power Products Group:** Joseph C. Wright, age 46
**VP and President, Home Power Products Group:** Harold L. Redman, age 42
**VP, General Counsel, and Secretary:** Robert F. Heath, age 57
**VP, Consumer Sales:** Michael M. Miller
**VP, Corporate Communications and Community Relations:** George R. Thompson III, age 58
**VP, Engineering Design:** Peter Hotz
**VP, Human Resources:** Jeffrey G. Mahloch
**Treasurer:** Carita R. Twinem, age 51
**Controller:** Ricky T. Dillon, age 35
**Auditors:** PricewaterhouseCoopers LLP

## LOCATIONS

**HQ:** Briggs & Stratton Corporation
12301 W. Wirth St., Wauwatosa, WI 53222
**Phone:** 414-259-5333 **Fax:** 414-259-5773
**Web:** www.briggsandstratton.com

Briggs & Stratton has manufacturing facilities in the US in Alabama, Georgia, Kentucky, Missouri, and Wisconsin, and through joint ventures in China, India, and Japan.

### 2006 Sales

| | $ mil. | % of total |
|---|---|---|
| US | 2,353 | 93 |
| Other countries | 189 | 7 |
| **Total** | **2,542** | **100** |

## PRODUCTS/OPERATIONS

### 2006 Sales

| | $ mil. | % of total |
|---|---|---|
| Engines | 1,648 | 58 |
| Power Products | 1,186 | 42 |
| Adjustments | (292) | — |
| **Total** | **2,542** | **100** |

### Selected Brands and Products

Brands
- Classic
- I/C
- Industrial Plus
- INTEK
- Murray
- Quantum
- Quattro
- Snapper
- Sprint
- Vanguard

Products
- Garden tillers
- Generators
- Lawn mowers (riding and walking)
- Outboard motors (gas and electric)
- Pressure washers
- Pumps
- Snow throwers
- Yard care products

## COMPETITORS

Aura Systems
Campbell Hausfeld
Coleman
DeVilbiss
Graco Inc.
Honda
Kawasaki Heavy Industries
Kohler
Kubota Engine America
Suzuki Motor
Tecumseh Products
Toro

## HISTORICAL FINANCIALS

Company Type: Public

### Income Statement

FYE: Sunday nearest June 30

| | REVENUE ($ mil.) | NET INCOME ($ mil.) | NET PROFIT MARGIN | EMPLOYEES |
|---|---|---|---|---|
| **6/06** | 2,542 | 102 | 4.0% | 8,701 |
| **6/05** | 2,655 | 137 | 5.1% | 9,169 |
| **6/04** | 1,947 | 136 | 7.0% | 7,732 |
| **6/03** | 1,658 | 81 | 4.9% | 7,249 |
| **6/02** | 1,529 | 53 | 3.5% | 6,971 |
| **Annual Growth** | 13.5% | 17.8% | — | 5.7% |

### 2006 Year-End Financials

Debt ratio: 38.8%
Return on equity: 10.9%
Cash ($ mil.): 95
Current ratio: 3.01
Long-term debt ($ mil.): 383
No. of shares (mil.): 51
Dividends
Yield: 2.8%
Payout: 44.4%
Market value ($ mil.): 1,593

### Stock History

NYSE: BGG

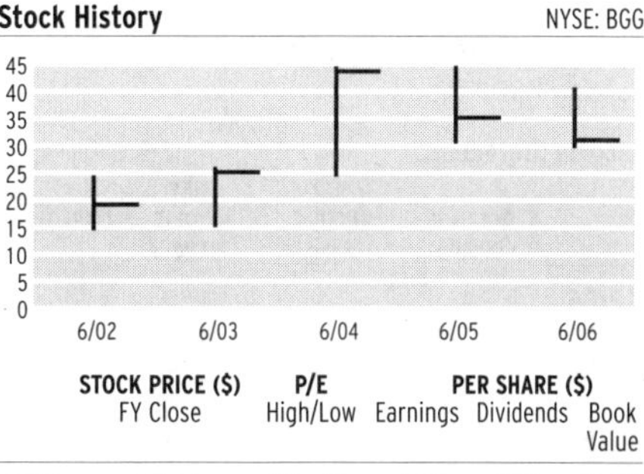


| | STOCK PRICE ($) FY Close | P/E High | P/E Low | PER SHARE ($) Earnings | Dividends | Book Value |
|---|---|---|---|---|---|---|
| **6/06** | 31.11 | 20 | 15 | 1.98 | 0.88 | 19.28 |
| **6/05** | 35.18 | 17 | 12 | 2.63 | 0.85 | 17.19 |
| **6/04** | 43.70 | 16 | 9 | 2.77 | 0.66 | 32.01 |
| **6/03** | 25.13 | 15 | 9 | 1.75 | 0.64 | 23.64 |
| **6/02** | 19.17 | 21 | 13 | 1.18 | 0.63 | 20.78 |
| **Annual Growth** | 12.9% | — | — | 13.8% | 8.7% | (1.9%) |

# Brightpoint, Inc.

Brightpoint makes money moving mobiles. The company is a top global distributor of mobile phones and other wireless products, acting as a middleman between manufacturers and wireless service providers. It ships the equipment to companies that sell mobile phones and accessories, including wireless carriers, dealers, and retailers; customers include Vodafone, Best Buy, and Sprint Nextel. Brightpoint also offers a range of services that includes warehousing, product fulfillment, purchasing, contract manufacturing, call center outsourcing, customized packaging, activation, and Web marketing.

About half of Brightpoint's revenue in fiscal 2006 came from the sale of cell phones made by Nokia. Other brands sold by the company include Sony Ericsson, Motorola, Kyocera, and LG Electronics.

The company continues to broaden its selection of services by forming new alliances with telecom and computing equipment makers. Brightpoint has also grown through acquisitions. In 2006 it purchased fellow wireless product distributor Trio Industries. The company acquired the assets of CellStar's operations serving the US and Latin America for approximately $62 million in cash in 2007. It also purchased Dangaard Telecom, a Danish mobile phone distributor with subsidiaries in 14 countries, for about $385 million in stock.

## HISTORY

Robert Laikin started in the portable phone business in 1985, when he established Century Car Phones (later renamed Century Cellular Network). The company grew rapidly but demand grew faster, and by 1989 Laikin's business was having trouble keeping up. That year he and Daniel Koerselman, a salesman for a car phone accessory company, started Wholesale Cellular to supply Century and others with phones. Laikin stepped down as president of Century in 1993. Wholesale Cellular went public a year later and changed its name to Brightpoint in 1995.

That year Brightpoint moved into the foreign market by forming partnerships with UK and India technology companies. It improved its distribution capabilities in North and South America by merging with Philadelphia-based Allied Communications in 1996. The next year Brightpoint further augmented its international operations by acquiring businesses in Hong Kong, Sweden, and Venezuela. It also bought the remaining 20% minority interests of its joint ventures in China, the UK, and Australia. Brightpoint continued its focus on international markets in 1998 with the acquisitions of distributors in the Netherlands and Taiwan.

Facing continuing pressures from resellers, the company in 1999 announced a restructuring plan that curtailed the global expansion, and divested its operations in Argentina, Poland, and the UK; its joint ventures in China; its accessories company in Hong Kong; and its distribution center in the Netherlands. A shareholder lawsuit was filed that summer, charging that Brightpoint withheld news of its mounting troubles in Asia and Latin America from shareholders and institutional investors (the suit was dismissed in 2001).

Despite an extension of the company's US distribution agreement with Nokia, the restructuring helped cause annual losses for Brightpoint in 1999. By 2000 the company had added new pacts and contract extensions on five continents. That year Brightpoint was awarded a patent for its wireless fulfillment system; the company promptly filed a patent infringement suit against chief rival Cellstar.

Late in 2001 Brightpoint announced a joint venture with Hong Kong-based wireless communications company Chinatron; the venture, called Brightpoint China, was established to distribute wireless phones to customers in China. The deal was finalized early in 2002. Within months, however, Brightpoint sold its 50% stake to its joint-venture partner in return for a minority stake in Chinatron. In 2004 Brightpoint sold its operations in Ireland to Celtic Telecom.

## EXECUTIVES

**Chairman and CEO:** Robert J. Laikin, age 43, $750,000 pay
**President, Brightpoint and Brightpoint Americas:** J. Mark Howell, age 42, $455,000 pay
**EVP, CFO, and Treasurer:** Anthony W. Boor, age 44, $350,000 pay
**EVP, General Counsel, and Secretary:** Steven E. Fivel, age 46, $360,000 pay
**SVP Global Strategy, Investor, and Public Relations:** Anurag Gupta
**SVP Human Resources:** Annette Cyr
**SVP and CIO:** Dan Taylor
**VP, Chief Accounting Officer, and Controller:** Vincent Donargo, age 46, $82,308 pay (partial-year salary)
**VP and Controller:** Gregory L. Wiles
**VP Human Resources:** John B. Williams
**VP Internal Audit:** Anthony Mackle
**VP Marketing:** Lee Kimball
**VP Taxation, Global Credit, and Risk Management:** David P. O'Connell
**President, International Operations:** R. Bruce Thomlinson, $465,905 pay
**President, Brightpoint Europe:** Magnus Coxner
**President, Emerging Markets:** John Alexander Du Plessis (Jac) Currie, age 42, $400,000 pay
**General Director, Brightpoint Russia:** Endre Kadas
**Director, Finance and Operations:** Tomi Maarni
**Auditors:** Ernst & Young LLP

## LOCATIONS

**HQ:** Brightpoint, Inc.
2601 Metropolis Pkwy., Ste. 210,
Plainfield, IN 46168
**Phone:** 317-707-2355 **Fax:** 317-707-2512
**Web:** www.brightpoint.com

### 2006 Sales

| | $ mil. | % of total |
|---|---|---|
| Asia/Pacific | 1,115.7 | 46 |
| Americas | 814.6 | 34 |
| Europe | 495.1 | 20 |
| **Total** | **2,425.4** | **100** |

## PRODUCTS/OPERATIONS

### 2006 Sales

| | $ mil. | % of total |
|---|---|---|
| Product distribution | 2,097.5 | 86 |
| Logistics services | 327.9 | 14 |
| **Total** | **2,425.4** | **100** |

### Suppliers

Audiovox
Kyocera
LG Electronics
Logitech
Motorola
Nokia
Novatel Wireless
Palm
Plantronics
Samsung
SanDisk
Sanyo
Sierra Wireless
Sony Ericsson
UTStarcom

### Services

Channel development
- Outbound sales
- Product marketing
- Field training and support
- Merchandising
- Credit determination
- Co-op funds disbursement/tracking
- Commissions management
- Sales incentive programs
- VAR programs

Logistics services
- Inventory management
- Kitting and packaging
- Device programming
- Bulk and end user order processing
- Returns management and processing
- Receivables management
- Credit services

Subscriber services
- Customer contact center
- E-business solutions
- Outbound marketing
- Fulfillment services

## COMPETITORS

Aftermarket Technology
Avenir Telecom
BearCom
Bertelsmann
Brightstar Corp.
Caterpillar Logistics Services
CLST
Ericsson
Euronet
European Telecom
Hello Direct
InfoSonics
Ingram Micro
Kuehne + Nagel
Kyocera
Motorola, Inc.
Nokia
Panasonic Mobile Communications
PFSweb
Quality Distributors, LLC
SED International
Siemens AG
Sony
Tech Data
TESSCO
UPS Supply Chain Solutions

## HISTORICAL FINANCIALS

Company Type: Public

### Income Statement

FYE: December 31

| | REVENUE ($ mil.) | NET INCOME ($ mil.) | NET PROFIT MARGIN | EMPLOYEES |
|---|---|---|---|---|
| **12/06** | 2,425 | 36 | 1.5% | 2,112 |
| **12/05** | 2,140 | 10 | 0.5% | 1,683 |
| **12/04** | 1,859 | 14 | 0.7% | 1,264 |
| **12/03** | 1,800 | 12 | 0.6% | 1,153 |
| **12/02** | 1,276 | (42) | — | 1,168 |
| **Annual Growth** | 17.4% | — | — | 16.0% |

### 2006 Year-End Financials

Debt ratio: 1.9%
Return on equity: 20.7%
Cash ($ mil.): 54
Current ratio: 1.28
Long-term debt ($ mil.): 4
No. of shares (mil.): 51
Dividends
Yield: —
Payout: —
Market value ($ mil.): 684

### Stock History

NASDAQ (GS): CELL

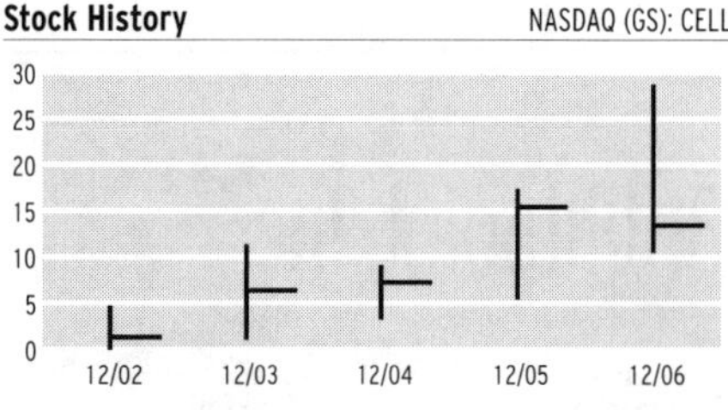


| | STOCK PRICE ($) FY Close | P/E High | P/E Low | PER SHARE ($) Earnings | Dividends | Book Value |
|---|---|---|---|---|---|---|
| **12/06** | 13.45 | 41 | 15 | 0.70 | — | 3.83 |
| **12/05** | 15.41 | 82 | 27 | 0.21 | — | 3.59 |
| **12/04** | 7.24 | 33 | 13 | 0.27 | — | 8.42 |
| **12/03** | 6.39 | 48 | 6 | 0.23 | — | 7.66 |
| **12/02** | 1.30 | — | — | (1.96) | — | 14.17 |
| **Annual Growth** | 79.3% | — | — | — | — | (27.9%) |

# Brinker International

This company is one hot player in the restaurant industry. Brinker International is the world's #2 casual-dining restaurant operator in terms of revenue (behind Darden Restaurants), with more than 1,600 restaurant locations in some 20 countries. Its flagship Chili's Grill & Bar chain boasts about 1,200 restaurants and trails only Applebee's as the largest full-service restaurant chain. Specializing in southwestern-style dishes, Chili's menu features fajitas, margarita grilled chicken, and its popular baby back ribs. Brinker also operates the Italian-themed Romano's Macaroni Grill, with more than 240 locations, as well as such smaller chains as On The Border Mexican Grill & Cantina and Maggiano's Little Italy.

Named after founder and casual-dining pioneer Norman Brinker, the company has successfully capitalized on America's love of ethnic and regional foods, and it continues to create eateries based around unified themes in which the menu matches the surroundings. Brinker's flagship Chili's and Macaroni Grill chains continue to enjoy loyal followings thanks in part to aggressive spending on advertising in an effort to stay ahead of the competition. The company has pursued a modest expansion strategy, with plans to add about 140 Chili's locations, including about a dozen franchised units. Brinker also intends to introduce new menu selections and more efficient service at Chili's to stay attractive to its customer base.

To achieve its expansion goals, Brinker is looking beyond its core markets in metropolitan areas and opening new restaurants in smaller towns — taking a page out of Applebee's playbook — as well as in non-traditional locations, such as shopping malls and airports.

In line with its strategy to expand both domestic and overseas franchise ownership of its brands, in 2007 Brinker sold 95 company-owned Chili's restaurants to Pepper Dining, an affiliate of private investment firm Olympus Partners. Priced at $155 million, it is the largest franchise transaction in Brinker history.

The outlook has not been quite as rosy, however, for Brinker's fledgling brands. In 2006 the company sold its Corner Bakery chain to Italian restaurant and bakery operation Il Fornaio, and later that year it sold its 43% stake in emerging seafood concept Rockfish Seafood Grill back to the chain's founders. Brinker hopes the divestitures will help it focus on Chili's and its other core restaurant brands.

## HISTORY

Norman Brinker opened his first Steak & Ale in Dallas in 1966, ushering in the so-called "casual-dining" segment. In 1971 he took the company public and watched it grow to more than 100 locations by 1976 when Pillsbury bought the chain. After serving as president of Pillsbury Restaurant Group (which included Burger King, Poppin' Fresh Restaurants, and Steak & Ale), Brinker left in 1983 to take over Chili's, a chain of southwestern-styled eateries founded by Larry Lavine in 1975. With plans to develop the company into a major chain, Brinker took Chili's public in 1984.

The company began recruiting joint venture and franchise partners. It also expanded the

Chili's menu to include items such as fajitas, staking the company's growth on aging baby boomers who were looking for something more than fast food. Stymied in attempts to regain control of his former S&A Restaurant (later acquired by Metromedia) and to acquire such fast-food chains as Taco Cabana and Flyer's Island Express, Brinker decided to focus on the casual, low-priced restaurant market. In 1989 Chili's acquired Knoxville, Tennessee-based Grady's Goodtimes and Romano's Macaroni Grill, a small Italian chain founded by Texas restaurateur Phil Romano in 1988. Reflecting the expansion of its restaurant offerings, the company changed its name to Brinker International in 1990.

Brinker introduced Spageddies (a casual, lower-priced pasta restaurant) in 1992. With two Italian-cuisine chains in his network, the entrepreneur began to take on rival Olive Garden. Brinker suffered a major head injury in 1993 while playing polo, leaving him comatose for two weeks. Despite the traumatic event and poor early prognosis, he made a rapid recovery and returned to running the company. In 1994 Brinker International expanded to cash in on the popularity of Mexican food. It acquired Cozymel's Coastal Mexican Grill that year and bought the $50 million, 21-unit On The Border Mexican-food chain in 1995.

That year Brinker retired as CEO and was replaced by Ronald McDougall. McDougall sold Grady's and Spageddies to Quality Dining, since they no longer fit the company's overall strategy, and acquired two restaurant concepts (Corner Bakery and Maggiano's Little Italy) from Rich Melman's Lettuce Entertain You Enterprises. With Romano in 1996, the company opened a test location (in Dallas) of eatZi's Market & Bakery, a takeout concept to capitalize on the public's increasing desire not to cook.

The company began a major overhaul of Chili's menu in 1997, led by Brian Kolodziej, a 34-year-old former chef at Dallas' ritzy Mansion on Turtle Creek hotel. Two years later Brinker began expanding into Guatemala, Saudi Arabia, and Mexico. McDougall was named vice chairman in 1999 and eventually replaced Brinker as chairman the following year.

In 2001 the company gained complete control of Big Bowl and bought a 40% stake in Rockfish Seafood Grill. With an emphasis on company-owned restaurants, Brinker purchased 47 Chili's and On The Border restaurants from New England Restaurant Co. and 39 Chili's restaurants from Sydran Services in 2001. The following year the company sold its chain of eatZi's Market & Bakery to Romano and investment group Castanea Partners.

In 2003 Brinker sold Cozymel's Coastal Mexican Grill to a group that included restaurateur Jack Baum, former Electronic Data Systems president Morton H. Meyerson, and their investment firm 2M Companies. McDougall stepped down from the executive ranks in early 2004, with company president Doug Brooks taking the reins as CEO. (McDougall also retired from the board later that year.)

In 2005 Brinker reached an historic milestone when it opened its 1,000th Chili's location. Company president Wilson Craft resigned that year after only 20 months on the job. The company also began shedding some of its emerging concepts to focus on its core brands, selling Big Bowl Asian Kitchen to Lettuce Entertain You in 2005 and shedding Corner Bakery the following year in a deal with upscale Italian operator Il Fornaio. Also in 2006, Brinker sold its stake in Rockfish Seafood Grill back to that chain's founders.

## EXECUTIVES

**Chairman Emeritus:** Norman E. Brinker, age 76
**Chairman, President, and CEO:** Douglas H. (Doug) Brooks, age 54, $2,250,000 pay
**EVP and CFO:** Charles M. (Chuck) Sonsteby, age 53, $1,255,990 pay
**EVP, Chief Administrative Officer, Secretary, and General Counsel:** Roger F. Thomson, age 57, $929,697 pay
**EVP and President, Chili's Bar and Grill:** Todd E. Diener, age 49, $1,087,754 pay
**EVP Brand Solutions:** Michael B. (Happy) Webberman, age 46, $373,452 pay
**EVP Marketing and Chief Marketing and Brand Officer:** Rebeca (Becky) Johnson, age 50
**SVP and Controller:** David R. Doyle
**SVP, Deputy General Counsel, and Assistant Secretary:** Jay L. Tobin
**SVP and President, Global Business Development:** Gregory Louis (Greg) Walther, age 52
**SVP and President, Maggiano's Little Italy:** Wyman T. Roberts, age 47
**SVP and President, On The Border:** David M. Orenstein, age 48
**SVP and President, Romano's Macaroni Grill:** Jean M. Birch, age 46, $476,107 pay
**SVP and COO, Chili's Grill & Bar:** Michael D. (Mike) Dzura
**SVP Information Solutions:** Michael L. Furlow
**VP and COO Global Markets:** George E. Michel
**VP Corporate Accounting and Assistant Controller:** Marie L. Perry
**VP Corporate Affairs:** Joseph G. (Joe) Taylor
**VP Investor Relations and Treasurer:** Lynn S. Schweinfurth
**Chief PeopleWorks Officer:** Valerie L. Davisson, age 45
**Director Corporate Communications:** Suzanne Keen
**Auditors:** KPMG LLP

## LOCATIONS

**HQ:** Brinker International, Inc.
6820 LBJ Fwy., Ste. 200, Dallas, TX 75240
**Phone:** 972-980-9917 **Fax:** 972-770-9593
**Web:** www.brinker.com

### 2007 Locations

| | No. |
|---|---|
| US | 1,649 |
| Other countries | 152 |
| **Total** | **1,801** |

## PRODUCTS/OPERATIONS

### 2007 Locations

| | No. |
|---|---|
| Chili's Grill & Bar | 1,361 |
| Romano's Macaroni Grill | 241 |
| On the Border Mexican Grill & Cantina | 158 |
| Maggiano's Little Italy | 41 |
| **Total** | **1,801** |

### 2007 Locations

| | No. |
|---|---|
| Company-owned | 1,312 |
| Franchised | 489 |
| **Total** | **1,801** |

## COMPETITORS

Applebee's
Bob Evans
Carlson Restaurants
CBRL Group
Cheesecake Factory
Darden
Hooters
Landry's
Lone Star Steakhouse
Metromedia Restaurant Group
OSI Restaurant Partners
P.F. Chang's
RARE Hospitality
Ruby Tuesday

## HISTORICAL FINANCIALS

Company Type: Public

### Income Statement

FYE: Last Wednesday in June

| | REVENUE ($ mil.) | NET INCOME ($ mil.) | NET PROFIT MARGIN | EMPLOYEES |
|---|---|---|---|---|
| **6/07** | 4,377 | 230 | 5.3% | 113,900 |
| **6/06** | 4,151 | 212 | 5.1% | 110,800 |
| **6/05** | 3,913 | 160 | 4.1% | 108,500 |
| **6/04** | 3,708 | 151 | 4.1% | — |
| **6/03** | 3,285 | 169 | 5.1% | — |
| **Annual Growth** | 7.4% | 8.1% | — | 2.5% |

### 2007 Year-End Financials

Debt ratio: 102.7%
Return on equity: 24.5%
Cash ($ mil.): 85
Current ratio: 0.69
Long-term debt ($ mil.): 827
No. of shares (mil.): 110
Dividends
Yield: 1.0%
Payout: 16.8%
Market value ($ mil.): 3,226

### Stock History

NYSE: EAT

| | STOCK PRICE ($) FY Close | P/E High | P/E Low | PER SHARE ($) Earnings | Dividends | Book Value |
|---|---|---|---|---|---|---|
| **6/07** | 29.29 | 19 | 11 | 1.85 | 0.31 | 7.31 |
| **6/06** | 23.61 | 18 | 14 | 1.62 | 0.20 | 12.88 |
| **6/05** | 26.55 | 25 | 17 | 1.15 | — | 12.34 |
| **6/04** | 22.75 | 26 | 18 | 1.03 | — | 11.15 |
| **6/03** | 23.99 | 22 | 14 | 1.13 | — | 11.65 |
| **Annual Growth** | 5.1% | — | — | 13.1% | 55.0% | (11.0%) |

# The Brink's Company

The Brink's Company's (formerly The Pittston Company) businesses once moved your goods by airplane or armored vehicle, but its travel plans have now been grounded. In 2006 the company sold its BAX Global unit, which arranges for the delivery of overnight and second-day freight from business to business in more than 120 countries, to Deutsche Bahn for $1.1 billion. The Brink's Company then sold Air Transport International, formerly a part of BAX Global, to Cargo Holdings International. The company's Brink's, Inc. unit is a leading operator of armored cars that transport cash for banks and retailers (85% of sales), and Brink's Home Security (BHS) installs and monitors alarm systems (15% of sales).

More than 90% of the company's employees work at Brink's, Inc; the remainder are at BHS. The company plans to expand its offerings through acquisitions of companies in different sectors of the security industry.

Once a major coal miner, the company began moving to leave that business in 2000, and by the end of 2002 it had sold or closed its remaining mines. But Brink's retains liabilities associated with its former coal operations, including employees' pensions and health care costs and environmental reclamation obligations.

## HISTORY

The Brink's Company was originally the Pennsylvania Coal Company, founded in 1838 in Pittston, Pennsylvania. In 1901 it was acquired by the Erie Railroad, which itself was purchased by the Alleghany Corp. in 1916.

In the late 1920s intense competition in the coal industry and antitrust concerns prevented Alleghany's expansion. Alleghany created the Pittston Company in 1930 and offered Pittston stock to Alleghany stockholders while retaining a controlling interest. At its founding, Pittston acquired United States Distributing Corp., which owned a trucking firm, warehouses, a wholesale coal distributor, and a Wyoming mining company.

But coal consumption was falling. In 1944 the company began mining bituminous coal (which was increasingly used by industry and utilities), and in the 1950s it entered the fuel oil market. Its trucking and warehousing businesses also expanded, accounting for 43% of net income by 1954. Pittston gained its independence that year: Alleghany purchased a railroad, which raised antitrust concerns and forced the company to sell its 50% stake in Pittston.

Seeking other revenue sources, in 1956 Pittston acquired a 22% stake in (and subsequently control of) the world's largest armored car company, Chicago-based Brink's. Brink's had begun as a delivery company in 1859 and started making payroll deliveries in 1891. Pittston acquired the entire company in 1962.

By the early 1970s Pittston was the #1 exporter of metallurgical coal, used in steel manufacturing. The OPEC oil embargo and the energy crisis of the 1970s increased demand for coal; in 1976 some 90% of company profits were coal-related. However, by the late 1970s labor disputes and a steel industry slump decreased profits dramatically.

Meanwhile, Brink's suffered from rising costs and increased competition in the 1970s. In 1976 a federal grand jury investigated possible antitrust violations in the armored car business. Brink's paid nearly $6 million the following year to settle antitrust charges.

The company diversified further in the 1980s, setting up Brink's Home Security (1984) after the sale of its warehousing operations. Pittston also entered the highly competitive airfreight express business by purchasing Burlington Air Express (1982).

Pittston began trading as two tracking stocks in 1993: Pittston Services Group (security and transportation) and Pittston Minerals Group (mining). In 1996, to further rationalize its business structure, Pittston split its security and transportation unit into two distinct businesses, each with its own tracking stock: Pittston Brink's Group and Pittston Burlington Group (later BAX Global).

Expanding globally, Brink's formed a transportation venture in 1997 with Switzerland's Zurcher Freilager, a freight-handling company. It also bought out affiliates in the Netherlands and Hong Kong in 1997 and in France and Germany in 1998. In 1999 BHS formed Brink's Mobile Security to provide wireless tracking systems for vehicles.

With its Pittston Minerals unit beset by a growing number of worker-injury lawsuits (black lung and other claims), The Pittston Company in 2000 made plans to exit the coal mining business to minimize future liability. Also that year the company abandoned its tracking stock structure.

In 2002 the company sold some of its coal assets to Braxton-Clay Land & Mineral and Massey Energy, and by the end of the year Pittston had ceased active involvement in the coal business. By 2004 Pittston had sold its remaining natural resources interests, which included natural gas and timber operations.

Also in 2003, the company changed its name to The Brink's Company to reflect the shift in its core businesses. It sold BAX Global and Air Transport International in 2006.

## EXECUTIVES

**Chairman, President, and CEO; CEO, Brink's, Incorporated:** Michael T. Dan, age 56, $2,377,846 pay
**VP and CFO:** Robert T. Ritter, age 55, $836,750 pay
**VP and Chief Administrative Officer:** Frank T. Lennon, age 65, $620,096 pay
**VP, General Counsel, and Secretary:** Austin F. Reed, age 55, $721,692 pay
**VP Corporate Finance and Treasurer:** James B. Hartough, age 59, $394,311 pay
**VP Risk Management and Insurance:** Arthur E. Wheatley, age 64
**President, Brink's Home Security:** Robert B. (Bob) Allen, age 53
**Controller:** Matthew A. P. Schumacher, age 48
**Auditors:** KPMG LLP

## LOCATIONS

**HQ:** The Brink's Company
1801 Bayberry Ct., Richmond, VA 23226
**Phone:** 804-289-9600 **Fax:** 804-289-9770
**Web:** www.brinkscompany.com

## PRODUCTS/OPERATIONS

**2006 Sales**

| | $ mil. | % of total |
|---|---|---|
| US | 1,146.4 | 41 |
| France | 546.5 | 19 |
| Venzuela | 171.7 | 6 |
| Other regions | 973.0 | 34 |
| **Total** | **2,837.6** | **100** |

**2006 Sales**

| | $ mil. | % of total |
|---|---|---|
| Brink's | 2,398.6 | 85 |
| Brink's Home Security | 439.0 | 15 |
| **Total** | **2,837.6** | **100** |

## COMPETITORS

AT Systems
ATI Systems
Cam-Dex Security
Dunbar Armored
G4S
Prosegur
Protection One
PSBTECH
Rochester Armored Car
Securitas
Tyco Fire & Security

## HISTORICAL FINANCIALS

Company Type: Public

**Income Statement** FYE: December 31

| | REVENUE ($ mil.) | NET INCOME ($ mil.) | NET PROFIT MARGIN | EMPLOYEES |
|---|---|---|---|---|
| **12/06** | 2,838 | 587 | 20.7% | 48,700 |
| **12/05** | 2,549 | 142 | 5.6% | 45,800 |
| **12/04** | 4,718 | 122 | 2.6% | 54,000 |
| **12/03** | 3,999 | 29 | 0.7% | 36,000 |
| **12/02** | 3,777 | 26 | 0.7% | 37,500 |
| **Annual Growth** | (6.9%) | 117.8% | — | 6.8% |

**2006 Year-End Financials**

Debt ratio: 16.8%
Return on equity: 73.8%
Cash ($ mil.): 137
Current ratio: 1.24
Long-term debt ($ mil.): 126
No. of shares (mil.): 49
Dividends
Yield: 0.3%
Payout: 1.8%
Market value ($ mil.): 3,100

**Stock History** NYSE: BCO

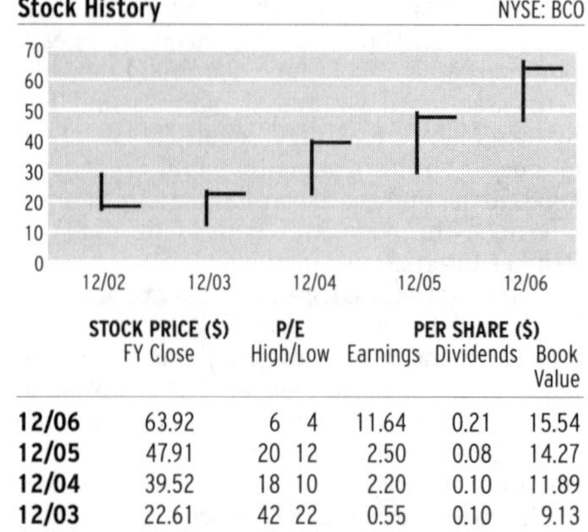


| | STOCK PRICE ($) FY Close | P/E High | P/E Low | PER SHARE ($) Earnings | Dividends | Book Value |
|---|---|---|---|---|---|---|
| **12/06** | 63.92 | 6 | 4 | 11.64 | 0.21 | 15.54 |
| **12/05** | 47.91 | 20 | 12 | 2.50 | 0.08 | 14.27 |
| **12/04** | 39.52 | 18 | 10 | 2.20 | 0.10 | 11.89 |
| **12/03** | 22.61 | 42 | 22 | 0.55 | 0.10 | 9.13 |
| **12/02** | 18.48 | 60 | 36 | 0.48 | 0.08 | — |
| **Annual Growth** | 36.4% | — | — | 121.9% | 27.3% | 19.4% |

# Bristol-Myers Squibb

Pharmaceutical giant Bristol-Myers Squibb (BMS) makes big bucks on matters of the heart. The company's blockbuster cardiovascular lineup includes heart disease drug Plavix, as well as Pravachol (which lowers cholesterol) and Avapro (for hypertension). BMS also makes antipsychotic medication Abilify and drugs in a number of other therapeutic categories, particularly oncology, virology (including HIV), and autoimmune disease. Through its Mead Johnson subsidiary, BMS makes Enfamil infant formula and other nutritional products for children. Its ConvaTec business produces ostomy supplies and wound-cleansing products.

Additionally, the company's Medical Imaging unit produces radiopharmaceutical agents used to enhance visibility during medical imaging procedures such as radiography and ultrasound.

As is the case for many of its druggernaut brethren, BMS has struggled with aging products losing patent protection (and thus market exclusivity). The company has begun to face generic competition for Pravachol and anti-infective Cefzil and will lose patent protection on Zerit in 2008.

Patents on blockbuster Plavix don't expire until 2011. In mid-2006, however, Canadian generics maker Apotex managed to flood the market with a generic version of Plavix for several weeks. The release of the drug followed bungled attempts by BMS to negotiate a deal with Apotex that would have kept it off the market. The debacle led to federal investigations into whether that deal violated anti-trust laws (among other things) and also resulted in the ouster of CEO Peter Dolan. Though a judge put a halt to the manufacturing of the generic until the courts could straighten the whole thing out (the dispute is ongoing), the short-term generic competition hurt Plavix sales to the tune of more than $1 billion.

BMS is pinning its hopes on compounds in development and on its newly approved drugs to replace products going off-patent. Lead candidates include apixaban for blood clots, saxagliptin for diabetes, and tumor fighter Ixabepilone. The company won FDA approval for rheumatoid arthritis drug Orencia in 2005 (it was launched commercially the following year) and cancer drug Sprycel in 2006. Also in 2006, it began marketing Emsam, a treatment for major depressive disorder developed with Somerset Pharmaceuticals (a joint venture between Mylan Laboratories and Watson Pharmaceuticals).

Additionally, in 2006, BMS and joint venture partner Gilead Sciences began marketing Atripla, an HIV therapy that combines BMS's Sustiva with Gilead's Truvada.

## HISTORY

Bristol-Myers Squibb is the product of a merger of rivals.

Squibb was founded by Dr. Edward Squibb in New York City in 1858. He developed techniques for making pure ether and chloroform; he turned the business over to his sons in 1891.

Sales of $414,000 in 1904 grew to $13 million by 1928. The company supplied penicillin and morphine during WWII. In 1952 it was bought by Mathieson Chemical, which in turn was bought by Olin Industries in 1953, forming Olin Mathieson Chemical. Squibb maintained its separate identity.

From 1968 to 1971 Olin Mathieson went through repeated reorganizations and adopted the Squibb name. Capoten and Corgard, two major cardiovascular drugs, were introduced in the late 1970s. Capoten was the first drug engineered to attack a specific disease-causing mechanism. Squibb formed a joint venture with Denmark's Novo (now Novo Nordisk) in 1982 to sell insulin.

William Bristol and John Myers founded Clinton Pharmaceutical in Clinton, New York, in 1887 (renamed Bristol-Myers in 1900) to sell bulk pharmaceuticals. The firm made antibiotics after the 1943 purchase of Cheplin Biological Labs. It began expanding overseas in the 1950s and eventually bought Clairol (1959); Mead Johnson (drugs, infant and nutritional formula; 1967); and Zimmer (orthopedic implants, 1972). Bristol-Myers launched new drugs to treat cancer (Platinol, 1978) and anxiety (BuSpar, 1986). That year it acquired biotech companies Oncogen and Genetic Systems.

The firm bought Squibb in 1989. In 1990 the new company bought arthroscopy products and implant business lines and joined Eastman Kodak and Elf Aquitaine to develop new heart drugs in 1993. Despite these initiatives, earnings slipped. In 1994 company veteran Charles Heimbold became CEO and moved to increase profits. BMS in 1995 bought wound and skin care products firm Calgon Vestal Laboratories. Also that year the company, along with fellow silicone breast implant makers 3M and Baxter International, agreed to settle thousands of personal injury claims at an average of $26,000 per claim.

Facing an antitrust suit filed by independent drugstores, BMS and other major drugmakers agreed in 1996 to charge pharmacies the same prices as managed care groups for medications.

As the company entered the 21st century, it began streamlining. It sold its Sea Breeze skin care brand (1999); Matrix Essentials hair care products unit (2000); and Clairol hair and personal care products business (2001).

The firm bought a 20% stake in ImClone in 2002 to collaborate on the development of cancer drug Erbitux and to stay on top of the cancer drug market. Instead, BMS found itself embroiled in the controversy over insider information and stock deals surrounding the biotech. Persistence paid off, however; Erbitux was approved by the FDA in 2004.

During 2005, the company cleaned out parts of its medicine cabinet. Analgesics Excedrin and Bufferin had made the company a household name, but in 2005 the company sold its US and Canadian consumer products operations to Novartis. The deal also meant saying goodbye to such brands as Comtrex (cold medications), Choice (blood sugar monitoring supplies), and Keri (lotions, skin care).

That same year, BMS sold Oncology Therapeutics Network, which distributes cancer drugs to oncology doctors, to private equity firm One Equity Partners.

As part of an agreement with the New Jersey US Attorney's office in 2005 to settle an investigation into inventory control and accounting practices, the company split the role of chairman and CEO into two separate offices. Long-time BMS director James Robinson III was elected the company's new chairman at that time.

In early 2006, BMS sold off its psoriasis treatment Dovonex to Warner Chilcott.

## EXECUTIVES

**Chairman:** James D. Robinson III, age 71
**CEO and Director:** James M. Cornelius, age 62
**EVP and President, Worldwide Pharmaceuticals:** Lamberto Andreotti, age 56, $1,553,507 pay
**EVP and CFO:** Andrew R. J. Bonfield, age 44
**EVP and Chief Scientific Officer; President, Pharmaceutical Research Institute:** Elliott Sigal, age 55
**SVP and General Counsel:** Sandra Leung, age 46
**SVP, Corporate Affairs:** Robert T. Zito, age 53
**SVP, Human Resources:** Stephen E. Bear, age 56
**SVP, Strategy and Medical and External Affairs:** Andrew G. Bodnar, age 59
**VP, Alliance Management:** Michael Levy
**VP, Business Development:** Graham R. Brazier
**VP, Business Development, Japan/Asia:** Mark Dennish
**VP, Business Development, Japan/International:** James E. (Jim) Foley
**VP, Corporate Development:** Charles H. Simmons
**VP, External Science, Technology, and Licensing:** Jack Geltosky
**VP, Investor Relations:** John Elicker
**VP and Controller:** Joseph Caldarella, age 51
**VP and Treasurer:** Edward M. Dwyer, age 50
**CIO and VP, Global Shared Services:** Susan O'Day
**Chief Marketing Officer and President, Global Marketing:** Wendy L. Dixon, age 51
**President, Bristol-Myers Squibb Medical Imaging:** Tim Ravenscroft
**President, US Pharmaceuticals:** Anthony C. Hooper, age 52
**Auditors:** Deloitte & Touche LLP; PricewaterhouseCoopers LLP

## LOCATIONS

**HQ:** Bristol-Myers Squibb Company
345 Park Ave., New York, NY 10154
**Phone:** 212-546-4000 **Fax:** 212-546-4020
**Web:** www.bms.com

Bristol-Myers Squibb has nearly 40 manufacturing plants worldwide.

**2006 Sales**

| | $ mil. | % of total |
|---|---|---|
| US | 9,729 | 55 |
| Europe, Middle East & Africa | 4,544 | 25 |
| Pacific | 2,026 | 11 |
| Other Western Hemisphere | 1,615 | 9 |
| **Total** | **17,914** | **100** |

## PRODUCTS/OPERATIONS

**2006 Sales**

| | $ mil. | % of total |
|---|---|---|
| Pharmaceuticals | | |
| Cardiovascular | | |
| Plavix | 3,257 | 18 |
| Pravachol | 1,197 | 7 |
| Avapro/Avalide | 1,097 | 6 |
| Coumadin | 220 | 1 |
| Monopril | 159 | 1 |
| Virology | | |
| Reyataz | 931 | 5 |
| Sustiva franchise | 791 | 4 |
| Zerit | 155 | 1 |
| Baraclude | 83 | — |
| Other infectious diseases | | |
| Cefzil | 87 | 1 |
| Oncology | | |
| Erbitux | 652 | 4 |
| Taxol | 563 | 3 |
| Sprycel | 25 | — |
| Psychiatric disorders | | |
| Abilify | 1,282 | 7 |
| Emsam | 18 | — |
| Immunoscience | | |
| Orencia | 89 | 1 |
| Other pharmaceuticals | | |
| Efferalgan | 266 | 1 |
| Other | 2,989 | 17 |
| Nutritionals | 2,347 | 13 |
| Other health care | 1,706 | 10 |
| **Total** | **17,914** | **100** |

### Selected Products

Pharmaceuticals
- Abilify (schizophrenia)
- Avapro/Avalide (hypertension)
- Baraclude (hepatitis B)
- BuSpar (anxiety)
- Cefzil (antibiotic)
- Coumadin (anticoagulant)
- Efferalgan (effervescent tablet formulation of acetaminophen)
- Emsam (major depressive disorder)
- Erbitux (colorectal cancer, with ImClone Systems)
- Glucophage (diabetes)
- Monopril (hypertension)
- Orencia (rheumatoid arthritis)
- Paraplatin (ovarian cancer)
- Plavix (platelet inhibitor)
- Pravachol (cholesterol)
- Reyataz (HIV)
- Serzone (depression)
- Sprycel (leukemia)
- Sustiva (HIV)
- Taxol (cancer)
- Tequin (respiratory infections)
- Videx/Videx EC (HIV)
- Zerit (HIV)

Nutritionals (Mead Johnson)
- Enfamil infant formulas

Other health care
- AQUACEL (wound care)
- Cardiolite (medical imaging)
- DuoDERM (wound care)
- Esteem (ostomy care)
- Sur-Fit (ostomy care)
- Versiva (wound care)

## Selected Subsidiaries

Allard Laboratories, Inc.
AMCARE Limited
Apothecon, Inc.
ConvaTec Limited
Lawrence Laboratories
Linson Pharma Co.
Mead Johnson & Company
NOVACARE Limited
Princeton Pharmaceutical Products, Inc.
Von Heyden Pharma G.m.b.H.

## COMPETITORS

Abbott Labs
Amgen
Apotex
AstraZeneca
Barr Pharmaceuticals
Bayer
Biogen Idec
Biomet
Boehringer Ingelheim
Eli Lilly
Forest Labs
Genentech
Gilead Sciences
GlaxoSmithKline
Johnson & Johnson
Merck
Mylan Labs
Novartis
Pfizer
Ranbaxy
Roche
Sandoz
Sanofi-Aventis
Schering-Plough
Teva Pharmaceuticals
Watson Pharmaceuticals
Wyeth

## HISTORICAL FINANCIALS

Company Type: Public

### Income Statement

FYE: December 31

| | REVENUE ($ mil.) | NET INCOME ($ mil.) | NET PROFIT MARGIN | EMPLOYEES |
|---|---|---|---|---|
| **12/06** | 17,914 | 1,585 | 8.8% | 43,000 |
| **12/05** | 19,207 | 3,000 | 15.6% | 43,000 |
| **12/04** | 19,380 | 2,388 | 12.3% | 43,000 |
| **12/03** | 20,894 | 3,106 | 14.9% | 44,000 |
| **12/02** | 18,119 | 2,066 | 11.4% | 44,000 |
| **Annual Growth** | (0.3%) | (6.4%) | — | (0.6%) |

### 2006 Year-End Financials

Debt ratio: 72.5%
Return on equity: 15.0%
Cash ($ mil.): 4,013
Current ratio: 1.59
Long-term debt ($ mil.): 7,248
No. of shares (mil.): 1,962
Dividends
Yield: 4.3%
Payout: 138.3%
Market value ($ mil.): 51,640

### Stock History

NYSE: BMY

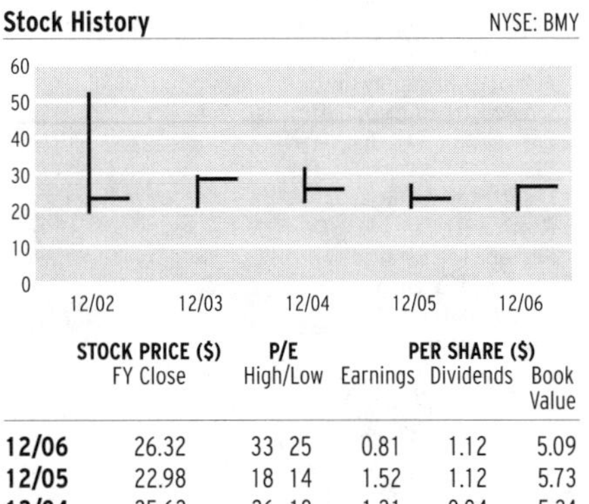


| | STOCK PRICE ($) FY Close | P/E High/Low | | PER SHARE ($) Earnings | Dividends | Book Value |
|---|---|---|---|---|---|---|
| **12/06** | 26.32 | 33 | 25 | 0.81 | 1.12 | 5.09 |
| **12/05** | 22.98 | 18 | 14 | 1.52 | 1.12 | 5.73 |
| **12/04** | 25.62 | 26 | 18 | 1.21 | 0.84 | 5.24 |
| **12/03** | 28.60 | 18 | 13 | 1.59 | 1.12 | 5.04 |
| **12/02** | 23.15 | 49 | 18 | 1.07 | 3.40 | 4.63 |
| **Annual Growth** | 3.3% | — | — | (6.7%) | (24.2%) | 2.4% |

# Broadcom Corporation

Broadcom harbors broad ambitions for its chips' impact on broadband communications: it wants them to drive every part of the high-speed networks of the future. The core applications for its integrated circuits (ICs) are digital set-top boxes, cable modems, servers, and local-area and home networking gear. Broadcom also makes ICs for digital subscriber line (DSL), carrier access, and wireless communications equipment. Co-founders Henry Samueli (chairman and CTO) and Henry Nicholas each control about 30% of the voting power in the fabless semiconductor company.

Looking to diversify its product portfolio, Broadcom has stoked its acquisition program. The company has paid about $143 million in cash to buy Global Locate, a developer of Global Positioning System (GPS) and assisted GPS semiconductors and software. Global Locate's products are used in wireless handsets and in personal navigation devices made by TomTom, a leading GPS product vendor. The company will set aside up to $80 million in potential earnout payments to Global Locate shareholders.

The GPS chip market is projected to grow to more than $1 billion by 2012 — a healthily growing market that Broadcom wants to tap. Broadcom plans to combine GPS chips with its Bluetooth, Wi-Fi, and FM radio semiconductors to provide handset manufacturers with increased functionality for their products. Aiming to widen its offerings for the cable-based home networking market, Broadcom has also acquired Octalica, a fabless semiconductor startup.

In mid-2006 the company announced that an internal investigation had revealed potential problems with the backdating of stock options during 2000; the company said that it would likely take a $750 million charge and would need to restate five years' worth of financial statements.

Broadcom later doubled the size of the estimated non-cash charge it would need to take, to $1.5 billion, and finally disclosed in early 2007 that the charge would total around $2.2 billion. The company's CFO decided to move up his retirement. The internal investigation later revealed backdating problems existed from June 1998 to May 2003. In addition, an informal inquiry by the SEC has been upgraded to a formal investigation, and the company has been cooperating with federal prosecutors, as well.

Later in 2007, Broadcom disclosed that chairman/CTO Henry Samueli and David Dull, SVP and general counsel, received Wells notices from the staff of the SEC, a notification that the securities regulators may seek civil charges against the company and the executives, related to past practices in granting stock options. Dull has headed up Broadcom's highly successful patent litigation against competitor QUALCOMM.

The AXA Group owns more than 12% of Broadcom's Class A common shares. FMR (Fidelity Investments) holds nearly 10% of those shares. Sands Capital Management has an equity stake of about 5%, as does Wellington Management.

## HISTORY

Henry Samueli and Henry Nicholas began their partnership at UCLA as professor and student, respectively, although the two had earlier worked together as product designers for technology specialist TRW's military integrated circuit operation. In 1988 Samueli helped found copper line-based data transmission firm PairGain Technologies (now part of ADC Telecommunications). Though only in his 20s, Nicholas was PairGain's director of microelectronics.

Convinced that the fastest microchip would own the market for devices combining computers, televisions, and phones, Samueli and Nicholas left PairGain in 1991 to found Broadcom. The duo accepted no venture capital; they wanted to be able to offer heady stock options to potential employees.

Broadcom's pioneering chip efforts soon attracted the attention of larger companies. In 1993 Broadcom introduced an advanced chip for cable boxes that was chosen by Scientific-Atlanta for use in its pioneering interactive cable television trials for Time Warner. The company began shipping production quantities of its chips in 1994. Other early customers included Analog Devices, Intel, Rockwell, and the US Air Force.

Intel invested $5 million in Broadcom in 1994, and Broadcom formed chip development alliances with Hewlett-Packard in 1995 and with Northern Telecom (now Nortel Networks) in 1996.

In 1997 Broadcom unveiled chipsets that enabled different manufacturers' cable modem equipment to work together; the chips soon became the industry standard. The company went public in 1998 in an IPO that made more than 200 of its employees millionaires (and made Samueli and Nicholas billionaires).

Flush with IPO cash, in 1999 Broadcom began beefing up its technology through acquisitions. The spree continued through 2000 and into 2001, as the company spent almost $10 billion to round out its product offerings and acquire new engineering talent.

In 2002, though, the company acquired Mobilink Telecom, a maker of chipsets for wireless devices. Late that year, the company laid off about 500 workers — a sixth of its staff — in the face of brutal industry conditions.

In 2003 the intensely driven and energetic Nicholas resigned as president and CEO, citing his wish to stave off divorce. (Nicholas retired from the company's board in mid-2003.) Board member and interim COO Alan Ross succeeded Nicholas as president and CEO.

When the market picked up by 2004, Broadcom picked up the pace of its acquisitions. It bought RAIDCore, a privately held company that produces software for RAID (redundant array of independent disks) storage applications, for $16 million; Sand Video, which designs video compression chips, for $80 million; WIDCOMM for nearly $50 million; Zyray Wireless, which designs baseband co-processor chips, for $80 million; and Alphamosaic, which designs multimedia processors, for $120 million. Early in 2005 it acquired wireless chip designer Zeevo for $32 million in cash and stock. It then purchased Siliquent Technologies, a developer of processors used in network interface controllers, for about $76 million in cash. It also acquired Athena Semiconductors for about $21 million.

Outgoing Philips Semiconductors (now NXP) chief Scott McGregor succeeded Ross as president and CEO at the beginning of 2005.

Early in 2006 Broadcom purchased Sandburst, a designer of networking chipsets.

## EXECUTIVES

**Chairman and CTO:** Henry Samueli, age 52, $1 pay
**President, CEO, and Director:** Scott A. McGregor, age 50, $840,000 pay
**SVP and CFO:** Eric K. Brandt, age 44
**SVP and CIO:** Kenneth E. (Ken) Venner, age 44
**SVP and General Manager, Broadband Communications Group:** Daniel A. (Dan) Marotta, age 46
**SVP and General Manager, Mobile Platforms Group:** Yossi Cohen, age 42
**SVP, Worldwide Sales:** Thomas F. (Tom) Lagatta, age 49, $367,346 pay
**SVP and General Manager, Wireless Connectivity Group:** Robert A. (Bob) Rango, age 49
**SVP and General Manager, Enterprise Networking Group:** Ford G. Tamer, age 45
**SVP, Business Affairs, General Counsel, and Secretary:** David A. Dull, age 58, $375,712 pay
**SVP, Central Engineering:** Neil Y. Kim, age 48
**SVP, Global Human Resources:** Dianne Dyer-Bruggeman, age 57
**SVP, Global Manufacturing Operations:** Vahid Manian, age 46, $375,712 pay
**SVP and General Manager, Enterprise Networking Group:** Nariman Yousefi
**VP, Research and Development:** Edward H. (Ed) Frank, age 50
**VP, Investor Relations:** T. Peter Andrew, age 40
**Corporate Media Relations:** Bill Blanning
**Auditors:** Ernst & Young LLP

## LOCATIONS

**HQ:** Broadcom Corporation
5300 California Ave., Irvine, CA 92617
**Phone:** 949-926-5000 **Fax:** 949-926-5203
**Web:** www.broadcom.com

Broadcom has offices in Belgium, Canada, China, France, Greece, India, Israel, Japan, the Netherlands, Singapore, South Korea, Taiwan, the UK, and the US.

### 2006 Sales

| | % of total |
|---|---|
| US | 72 |
| Asia/Pacific | 19 |
| Europe & other regions | 9 |
| **Total** | **100** |

## PRODUCTS/OPERATIONS

### Selected Markets and Products

Broadband processors (processors for broadband networking equipment)
Cable modems (high-speed data transmission and media access control devices)
Cable set-top boxes (graphics and video decoders, modulators and demodulators, and single-chip set-top box ICs)
Carrier access (voice over Internet protocol, or VoIP, broadband telephony chips)
Digital subscriber lines (DSLs; broadband transceivers and loop emulators)
Enterprise networking (Ethernet controllers, security processors, repeaters, switches, transceivers, and matching software for LANs)
Home networking (iLine controllers and chipsets)
Optical networking (wide-area and metropolitan-area network products — including amplifiers, framer/mappers, receivers, and transceivers — addressing various Ethernet and SONET/SDH protocols)
Servers (ServerWorks ICs that speed the input/output functions of servers, storage platforms, network appliances, and workstations)
Software (OpenVoIP Product Suite used in networking gateways, cable modems, ADSL modems, LAN PBXs, and computer telephony systems)
Wireless communications (Bluetooth chipsets and digital broadcast satellite, terrestrial digital broadcast, and broadband fixed wireless television receivers)

## COMPETITORS

AMD
Analog Devices
Applied Micro Circuits
Cirrus Logic
Conexant Systems
Cypress Semiconductor
Freescale Semiconductor
Fujitsu
IBM Microelectronics
Infineon Technologies
Intel
LSI Corp.
Marvell Technology
National Semiconductor
NEC Electronics
NXP
Oki Semiconductor
PMC-Sierra
QUALCOMM
Renesas
RF Micro Devices
Samsung Electronics
STMicroelectronics
Texas Instruments
Toshiba
Zarlink

## HISTORICAL FINANCIALS

Company Type: Public

### Income Statement

FYE: December 31

| | REVENUE ($ mil.) | NET INCOME ($ mil.) | NET PROFIT MARGIN | EMPLOYEES |
|---|---|---|---|---|
| **12/06** | 3,668 | 379 | 10.3% | 5,233 |
| **12/05** | 2,671 | 367 | 13.7% | 4,287 |
| **12/04** | 2,401 | 219 | 9.1% | 3,373 |
| **12/03** | 1,610 | (960) | — | 2,833 |
| **12/02** | 1,083 | (2,237) | — | 2,589 |
| **Annual Growth** | 35.7% | — | — | 19.2% |

### 2006 Year-End Financials

Debt ratio: —
Return on equity: 10.3%
Cash ($ mil.): 2,680
Current ratio: 4.94
Long-term debt ($ mil.): —
No. of shares (mil.): 474
Dividends
Yield: —
Payout: —
Market value ($ mil.): 15,300

### Stock History

NASDAQ (GS): BRCM

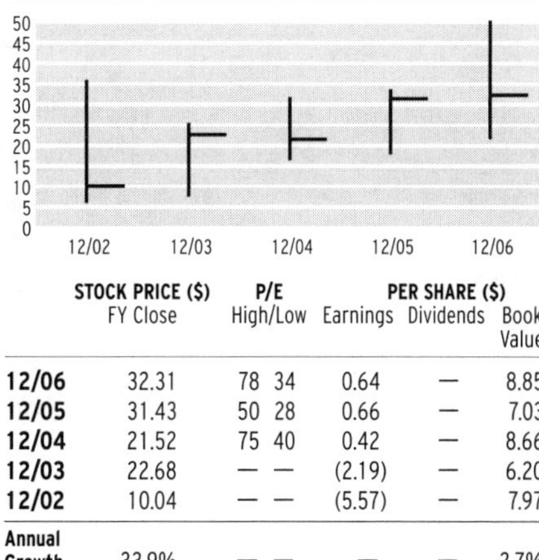

| | STOCK PRICE ($) FY Close | P/E High/Low | PER SHARE ($) Earnings | Dividends | Book Value |
|---|---|---|---|---|---|
| **12/06** | 32.31 | 78 34 | 0.64 | — | 8.85 |
| **12/05** | 31.43 | 50 28 | 0.66 | — | 7.03 |
| **12/04** | 21.52 | 75 40 | 0.42 | — | 8.66 |
| **12/03** | 22.68 | — — | (2.19) | — | 6.20 |
| **12/02** | 10.04 | — — | (5.57) | — | 7.97 |
| **Annual Growth** | 33.9% | — — | — | — | 2.7% |

# Brown Shoe Company

There's no business like shoe business for Brown Shoe Company (formerly Brown Group). Brown Shoe owns about 1,000 Famous Footwear stores in the US, about 275 Naturalizer stores in the US and Canada, and 16 F.X. LaSalle stores around Montreal, Canada. Besides its venerable Buster Brown line, its brands include Airstep, Connie, LifeStride, and Nickels; it also sells Dr. Scholl's, Power Rangers, and Disney licensed footwear. It distributes footwear worldwide through more than 2,000 retailers, including independent, chain (DSW), and department stores (Sears). Brown Shoe is opening new stores, closing underperforming ones, and updating styles to appeal to youth. In 2005 it acquired Bennett Footwear Group.

Brown Shoe is courting more well-heeled customers with its purchase of Bennett's better footwear brands, which include Via Spiga, Etienne Aigner, and Nickels. The Bennett Footwear purchase also added eight Via Spiga retail stores to Brown Shoe's store operations. However, in late 2006 the company began closing the Via Spiga stores, citing disappointing sales.

The company's value-priced Famous Footwear retail stores account for about half of its sales. (Famous Footwear also operates stores under the Factory Brand Shoes, Supermarket of Shoes, and Warehouse Shoes names.) Brown Shoe has been expanding its Famous Footwear business and introducing new styles, including a line designed by musician Carlos Santana, to appeal to younger customers. However, beginning in 2005 the company began closing more than 100 underperforming Naturalizer stores in North America to improve profitability.

Brown Shoe made plans to open 65 Famous Footwear shops in 2007, with the Naturalizer store count declining slightly. The company announced later that year that it would open more than 30 Naturalizer shoe stores in Japan in the next couple of years, through a deal with Japan-based footwear retailer Regal Corp. In more Asian news, Brown Shoe formed a joint venture with Hongguo International Holdings Limited in 2007 with plans to open some 400 stores and department store shops in China over the next five years to sell its Naturalizer and Via Spiga brands.

Its Brown Shoe Wholesale Division distributed more than 90 million pairs of shoes last year to department stores (Federated, Nordstrom, and Dillard's), mass merchandisers (Wal-Mart and Target), and independent retailers, primarily in the US and Canada.

The company's online shops include Shoes.com (purchased in 2000), FamousFootwear.com, and Naturalizer.com. Brown Shoe also sells private-label products and licensed brands such as Barbie, Dr. Scholl's, That's So Raven, *Star Wars, Bob the Builder*, and Power Rangers. It has added a number of licensed Disney characters to its Buster Brown division, including Mickey and Minnie Mouse, Winnie the Pooh, Bambi, and others.

Nearly 90% of the company's shoes are made in China.

## HISTORY

Salesman George Brown began mass-producing women's shoes in St. Louis in 1878, unusual at a time when the shoe industry was firmly entrenched in New England. With the financial backing of partners Alvin Bryan and

Jerome Desnoyers, Brown hired five shoemakers and opened Bryan, Brown and Company. The firm's fashionable first shoes were a pleasant contrast to the staid, black shoes typical of New England and were an instant success. The enterprise grew rapidly, and in 1893 Brown, by then the sole remaining partner, renamed the operation Brown Shoe Company. By 1900 sales had reached $4 million.

Company executive John Bush introduced cartoonist Richard Outcault's Buster Brown comic strip character in 1902 at the St. Louis World's Fair as a trademark for Brown's children's shoes. Bush failed to purchase the exclusive rights, and Buster Brown became the trademark for scores of products, even cigars and whiskey.

Brown Shoe became a public company in 1913 and introduced its second brand, Naturalizer, in 1927. During the Great Depression, company VP Clark Gamble developed the concept, later commonplace, of having salesmen sell only specific branded shoe lines instead of traveling with samples of all the company's shoes. Brown Shoe modernized its operations and entered the retailing business during the 1950s by purchasing Wohl Shoe, Regal Shoe, and G. R. Kinney (sold in 1963 to Woolworth because of antitrust litigation). The first Naturalizer store opened in Jamaica, New York, in 1954.

Diversifying, Brown Shoe bought Cloth World stores (1970), Eagle Rubber (toys and sporting goods, 1971), Hedstrom (bicycles and equipment, 1971), Meis Brothers (department stores, 1972), and Outdoor Sports Industries (1979), among others. It became the Brown Group in 1972.

The company acquired the 32-store Famous Footwear chain in 1981 and expanded it rapidly (especially from 1990 to 1995, when it added more than 500 stores, reaching a total of about 815). In 1985 the company sold its recreational products segment and in 1989 shed all of its specialty retailers except Cloth World.

As the US shoe manufacturing industry fell prey to cheaper foreign imports, Brown Group in 1991 and 1992 closed nine US shoe factories, cutting capacity in half. It discontinued its Wohl Leased Shoe Department business in 1994 and, still facing declining sales and profits, closed five shoe factories and discontinued its Connie and Regal footwear chains. Brown Group also sold its Cloth World chain and discontinued its Maryland Square catalog business.

Brown Group continued its restructuring in 1995, closing its last five plants in the US (it still has two in Canada).

In 2000 the company opened 92 new Famous Footwear stores and added another 26 stores to that chain through its purchase of the Mil-Mar chain and bought a majority interest in e-tailer Shoes.com. The company opened another 100 mostly large-format Famous Footwear stores in 2001 and closed 100 smaller stores.

In 2003 the company gained licensure of the Bass label from Phillips-Van Heusen. A year later Brown Shoe consolidated its wholesale operations under one division — Brown Show Wholesale — and launched Specialty Retail, which will manage the company's Naturalizer and FX LaSalle brands.

In April 2005 Brown Shoe acquired Boston-based Bennett Footwear Holdings for about $205 million. The company has closed more than 100 Naturalizer stores since early 2005. In late 2006 the shoe store operator closed all but one of its Via Spiga stores.

## EXECUTIVES

**Chairman and CEO:** Ronald A. (Ron) Fromm, age 56, $862,980 pay
**President and COO and Director:** Diane M. Sullivan, age 51, $718,462 pay
**SVP and CFO:** Mark E. Hood, age 54, $96,923 pay
**SVP and Chief Talent Officer:** Doug Koch, age 55
**SVP, General Counsel, and Secretary:** Michael I. Oberlander, age 38
**SVP and Chief Accounting Officer:** Richard C. Schumacher, age 59
**SVP Marketing:** Scott Cooper
**SVP Strategic Planning:** Paul M. Malutinok
**SVP Product and Sourcing:** Daniel R. (Dan) Friedman
**SVP Information Systems and Technology:** Richard T. Price
**SVP Brown Shoe International:** Timothy R. Heard
**SVP and General Manager, Children's Division:** Paul M. Shapiro
**SVP and General Manager, Naturalizer Retail, Naturalizer Div.:** W. Bradley Adams
**SVP Brown Shoe International Sales and Licensing; Pacific Rim and Europe:** Howard B. Herman
**SVP Specialty Retail:** John R. Mazurk
**SVP and Chief Marketing Officer:** Sheri Wilson-Gray
**SVP Finance and Corporate Development:** Thomas H. Lucas
**President, Brown Shoe St. Louis Wholesale:** Gary M. Rich, age 56, $507,462 pay
**President, Worldwide Sourcing:** Charles C. Gillman
**President, Brown Shoe Retail and Famous Footwear:** Joseph W. (Joe) Wood, age 59, $529,885 pay
**President, Brown Shoe New York Wholesale:** Richard M. (Rick) Ausick, age 53
**Auditors:** Ernst & Young LLP

## LOCATIONS

**HQ:** Brown Shoe Company, Inc.
8300 Maryland Ave., St. Louis, MO 63105
**Phone:** 314-854-4000 **Fax:** 314-854-4274
**Web:** www.brownshoe.com

Brown Shoe Company has about 1,290 retail stores in the US and Canada. It also sells shoes wholesale to more than 2,000 retailers in Canada and the US.

**2007 Sales**

| | $ mil. | % of total |
|---|---|---|
| US | 1,996.7 | 81 |
| East Asia | 384.7 | 15 |
| Canada | 89.9 | 4 |
| Adjustments | (.4) | — |
| **Total** | **2,470.9** | **100** |

**2007 Country of Origin**

| | Mil. of pairs | % of total |
|---|---|---|
| China | 81.1 | 89 |
| Brazil | 9.5 | 10 |
| Other countries | 0.9 | 1 |
| **Total** | **91.5** | **100** |

## PRODUCTS/OPERATIONS

**2007 Sales**

| | % of total |
|---|---|
| Women's | 65 |
| Men's | 24 |
| Children's | 11 |
| **Total** | **100** |

**2007 Stores**

| | No. |
|---|---|
| Famous Footwear | 999 |
| Naturalizer | 273 |
| F.X. LaSalle | 16 |
| Via Spiga | 1 |
| **Total** | **1,289** |

**Selected Products**

Children's Shoes
- Airborne
- Barbie (licensed)
- Bass
- Bob the Builder (licensed)
- Buster Brown
- Chill Chasers by Buster Brown
- Disney Standard Characters (licensed)
- Kim Possible (licensed)
- Mary-Kate and Ashley (licensed)
- Power Rangers (licensed)
- Red Goose
- Star Wars (licensed)
- That's So Reven (licensed)
- Winnie The Pooh (licensed)
- Zoey 101 (licensed)

Men's Shoes
- Bass
- Basswood
- Big Country
- Brown Shoe
- Dr. Scholl's (licensed)
- FX
- Francois Xavier Collection
- Natural Soul
- Regal
- TX Traction
- Via Spiga

Women's Shoes
- AirStep
- Bass
- Basswood
- Carlos by Carlos Santana (licensed)
- Connie
- Dr. Scholl's (licensed)
- Eurosole
- Fanfares
- F.X. LaSalle
- Francois Xavier Collection
- Hot Kiss (licensed)
- LifeStride
- LS Studio
- Maserati
- Naturalizer
- Nickels
- Original Dr. Scholl's (licensed)
- TX Traction
- Vision Comfort
- VS by Via Spiga
- Zodiac

## COMPETITORS

Berkshire Hathaway
Dillard's
DSW
Footstar
Genesco
Iconix Brand Group
J. C. Penney
Kenneth Cole
Kmart
Macy's
Nine West
Nordstrom
Payless ShoeSource
Phillips-Van Heusen
Rack Room Shoes
Reebok
Ross Stores
Saks Inc.
Sears
Shoe Carnival
Stride Rite
Target
TJX Companies
Wal-Mart

## HISTORICAL FINANCIALS

Company Type: Public

**Income Statement** FYE: Saturday nearest January 31

| | REVENUE ($ mil.) | NET INCOME ($ mil.) | NET PROFIT MARGIN | EMPLOYEES |
|---|---|---|---|---|
| **1/07** | 2,471 | 66 | 2.7% | 12,700 |
| **1/06** | 2,292 | 41 | 1.8% | 12,800 |
| **1/05** | 1,942 | 43 | 2.2% | 12,000 |
| **1/04** | 1,832 | 47 | 2.6% | 11,600 |
| **1/03** | 1,841 | 45 | 2.5% | 12,000 |
| **Annual Growth** | 7.6% | 9.8% | — | 1.4% |

## 2007 Year-End Financials

Debt ratio: 28.6%
Return on equity: 13.7%
Cash ($ mil.): 54
Current ratio: 1.91
Long-term debt ($ mil.): 150
No. of shares (mil.): 43
Dividends
Yield: 0.6%
Payout: 13.9%
Market value ($ mil.): 1,560

## Stock History

NYSE: BWS

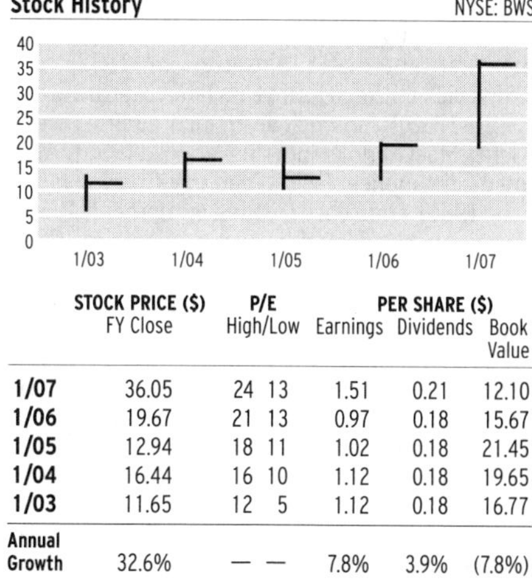


| | STOCK PRICE ($) FY Close | P/E High/Low | | PER SHARE ($) Earnings | Dividends | Book Value |
|---|---|---|---|---|---|---|
| **1/07** | 36.05 | 24 | 13 | 1.51 | 0.21 | 12.10 |
| **1/06** | 19.67 | 21 | 13 | 0.97 | 0.18 | 15.67 |
| **1/05** | 12.94 | 18 | 11 | 1.02 | 0.18 | 21.45 |
| **1/04** | 16.44 | 16 | 10 | 1.12 | 0.18 | 19.65 |
| **1/03** | 11.65 | 12 | 5 | 1.12 | 0.18 | 16.77 |
| **Annual Growth** | 32.6% | — | — | 7.8% | 3.9% | (7.8%) |

# Brown-Forman

Don't blame Brown-Forman (B-F) employees if the company Christmas party gets out of control; they have lots to drink on hand. B-F's products include such well-known spirits as Jack Daniel's, Canadian Mist, Early Times, Korbel, Southern Comfort, Old Forester, Finlandia, Gentleman Jack, and Pepe Lopez. Its wine labels include Bolla, Fetzer, Bel Arbor, Five Rivers, Little Black Dress, and Michel Picard. Offering more than 35 brands of wine and spirits, the company's products are available in more than 135 countries. The founding Brown family, including current chairman Owen Brown II, owns more than 70% of Brown-Forman's voting shares.

Headquartered in Louisville, Kentucky, Brown-Forman has found global success by introducing Jack Daniels into new markets overseas (it has become the leading US whiskey sold worldwide). And while it is an international company, about two-thirds of its sales are generated in the US.

Due to a difficult competitive market in the US tabletop and giftware industries, Brown-Forman sold its Lenox subsidiary in 2005 to Department 56 for about $190 million in cash.

In 2006 the company purchased Chambord Liqueur (a black raspberry liqueur) from Charles Jacquin et Cie for $255 million in cash and it also acquired Australian spirits and winemaker Swift + Moore. Boosting its presence in the tequila market, Brown-Forman announced it would acquire Mexican company Grupo Industrial Herradura SA, which makes several leading higher-priced tequila brands, for $876 million in cash.

The company snapped its suitcase shut with the 2007 sale of its Hartmann luggage subsidiary to investment firm Clarion Capital Partners. Brown-Forman also sold its other non-liquor business, gift unit Brooks & Bentley. Terms of the deals were not disclosed.

## HISTORY

George Brown and John Forman opened the Brown-Forman Distillery in Louisville, Kentucky, in 1870 to produce Old Forester-brand bourbon. Old Forester sold well through the end of the century, in part because of the company's innovative packaging (safety seals and quality guarantees on the bottles). When Forman died in 1901, Brown bought his interest in the company.

Old Forester continued to be successful under the Brown family. Brown-Forman obtained government approval to produce alcohol for medicinal purposes during Prohibition. In 1923 it made its first acquisition, Early Times, but stored its whiskey in a government warehouse (removed only by permit). The firm went public in 1933 and re-established the Old Forester image as an alcoholic beverage after the repeal of Prohibition.

During WWII the government greatly curtailed alcoholic beverage production (alcohol was needed for the war effort). The company compensated by providing alcohol for wartime rubber and gunpowder production. In 1941 Brown-Forman correctly predicted that the war would be over by the end of 1945 and started the four-year aging process for its bourbon. As a result, Early Times dominated the whiskey market after the war.

In 1956 Brown-Forman expanded beyond Old Forester by purchasing Lynchburg, Tennessee-based Jack Daniel's (sour mash whiskey). The company retained the simple, black Jack Daniel's label and promoted the image of a small Tennessee distillery for the brand.

Brown-Forman continued to expand its alcohol line during the 1960s and 1970s, acquiring Korbel (champagne and brandy, 1965), Quality Importers (Ambassador Scotch, Ambassador Gin, and Old Bushmills Irish Whisky; 1967), Bolla and Cella (wines, 1968), and Canadian Mist (blended whiskey, 1971). In 1979 it purchased Southern Comfort (a top-selling liqueur).

Nonbeverage acquisitions included Lenox (a leading US maker of fine china, crystal, gifts, and Hartmann luggage; 1983), Kirk Stieff (silver and pewter, 1990), and Dansk International Designs (china, crystal, silver, and the high-quality Gorham line; 1991). Brown-Forman launched Gentleman Jack Rare Tennessee Whiskey in 1988, its first new whiskey from its Jack Daniels distillery in more than 100 years.

The company acquired Jekel Vineyards in 1991 and the next year bought Fetzer Vineyards. In 1993 Owsley Brown II succeeded his brother Lee as CEO. A year later Moore County, Tennessee, voters approved a referendum that allowed whiskey sales in Lynchburg (home of Jack Daniel's) for the first time since Prohibition. Also in 1995 Brown-Forman formed a joint venture with Jagatjit Industries, India's third-largest spirits producer.

A 1997 licensing agreement with Carlson, whose T.G.I. Friday's restaurants came out with a Jack Daniel's line of meat dishes, stealthily slipped the brand into national television advertising. Brown-Forman bought an 80% stake in Sonoma-Cutrer Vineyards in 1999 (and later bought the rest).

In 2000 Brown-Forman bought 45% of Finlandia Vodka Worldwide for $83 million; Altia (owned by the Finnish government) owns 55%. That year the company lost the bidding battle for the alcoholic drinks business of Seagram (Glenlivet, Sterling Vineyards, Martell Cognac) to rival pair Diageo and Pernod Ricard. Brown-Forman became a majority owner of Finlandia Vodka in 2004.

The company stirred up fans of Jack Daniel's in 2004 when it announced that it had reduced the alcohol content of Jack Daniel's Black Label whiskey from 90 proof to 80 proof. Brown-Forman also announced in that year plans to close its Dansk outlet stores over a two-year period.

The company switched its Canadian distribution partner from Bacardi to Charton-Hobbs in 2005. In conjunction with British billionaire Richard Branson, Brown-Forman introduced the wine label Virgin Vines. Also that year, Paul Varga succeeded Owsley Brown as CEO. Brown remained as chairman.

## EXECUTIVES

**Vice Chairman, Secretary, and General Counsel:** Michael B. Crutcher, age 63, $900,777 pay
**Vice Chairman, Strategy and Human Resources:** James S. Welch Jr., age 48
**Chairman, President and CEO:** Paul C. Varga, age 43, $1,931,134 pay
**SVP and Chief of Staff:** Philip A. (Phil) Lichtenfels
**Vice Chairman and CFO:** Phoebe A. Wood, age 54
**EVP and COO:** James L. (Jim) Bareuther, age 61, $916,045 pay
**EVP and Chief Brand Officer:** Mark I. McCallum
**SVP Global Production; President, Brown-Forman Distillery:** James B. Chiles
**SVP and Deputy General Counsel:** William A. Blodgett Jr.
**SVP Corporate Communications and Corporate Services:** Lois A. Mateus
**VP and Controller:** Jane C. Morreau, age 48
**VP and Treasurer:** Meredith M. Parente
**VP and Director HR Employee Services:** Bruce Cote
**Assistant VP and Director Investor Relations:** T.J. Graven
**President and COO, Brown-Forman Wines:** David C. M. Dearie
**President, Brown-Forman Spirits Americas:** Donald C. Berg
**President, Brown-Forman Spirits Asia/Pacific:** Stuart Beck
**Auditors:** PricewaterhouseCoopers LLP

## LOCATIONS

**HQ:** Brown-Forman Corporation
850 Dixie Hwy., Louisville, KY 40210
**Phone:** 502-585-1100 **Fax:** 502-774-7876
**Web:** www.brown-forman.com

### 2007 Sales

| | $ mil. | % of total |
|---|---|---|
| US | 1,498 | 53 |
| Europe | 816 | 29 |
| Other countries | 492 | 18 |
| **Total** | **2,806** | **100** |

## PRODUCTS/OPERATIONS

### 2007 Sales

| | $ mil. | % of total |
|---|---|---|
| Spirits | 2,425 | 86 |
| Wines | 381 | 14 |
| **Total** | **2,806** | **100** |

### Selected Brands

Spirits
- Canadian Mist (whiskey)
- Don Eduardo (tequila)
- Early Times (whiskey)
- Finlandia (vodka)
- Gentleman Jack (whiskey)
- Jack Daniel's (whiskey)
- Jack Daniel's Country Cocktails (low-alcohol freezer cocktails)
- Old Forester (bourbon)
- Pepe Lopez (tequila)
- Southern Comfort (liqueur)
- Woodford Reserve (whiskey)

Wines
- Bel Arbor
- Bolla
- Bonterra Vineyards
- Chateau Tahblik Australian wines
- Fetzer
- Five Rivers
- Fontana Candida
- Korbel (champagnes and wines)
- Mariah
- Michel Picard (marketed in the US)
- One.6 Chardonnay (low-carb)
- One.9 Merlot (low-carb)
- Sonoma-Cutrer Vineyards
- Virgin Vines

## COMPETITORS

Anheuser-Busch
Bacardi USA
Barton Inc.
Beam Global Spirits & Wine
Blavod Extreme Spirits
Constellation Brands
Diageo
Fortune Brands
Foster's Americas
Gallo
Heaven Hill Distilleries
Jose Cuervo
Kendall-Jackson
Paramount Distillers
Pernod Ricard
Skyy
Taittinger
V&S
VRANKEN

## HISTORICAL FINANCIALS

Company Type: Public

**Income Statement** — FYE: April 30

| | REVENUE ($ mil.) | NET INCOME ($ mil.) | NET PROFIT MARGIN | EMPLOYEES |
|---|---|---|---|---|
| **4/07** | 2,806 | 389 | 13.9% | 4,400 |
| **4/06** | 2,444 | 320 | 13.1% | 3,750 |
| **4/05** | 2,729 | 308 | 11.3% | 6,100 |
| **4/04** | 2,577 | 258 | 10.0% | 6,400 |
| **4/03** | 2,378 | 245 | 10.3% | 6,700 |
| **Annual Growth** | 4.2% | 12.3% | — | (10.0%) |

**2007 Year-End Financials**

Debt ratio: 26.8%
Return on equity: 24.8%
Cash ($ mil.): 369
Current ratio: 1.21
Long-term debt ($ mil.): 422
No. of shares (mil.): 66
Dividends
Yield: 1.3%
Payout: —
Market value ($ mil.): 4,243

**Stock History** — NYSE: BFB

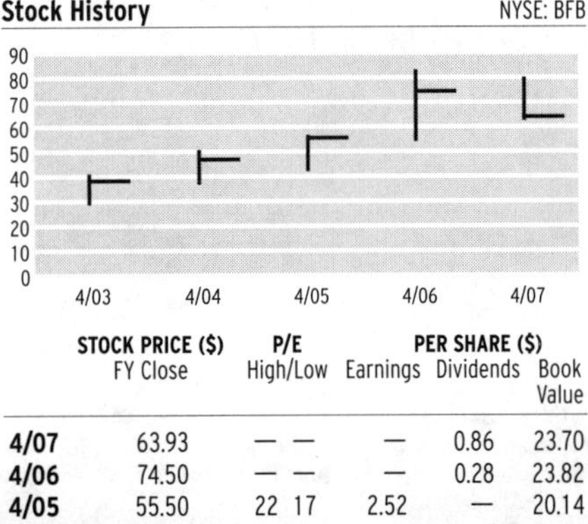


| | STOCK PRICE ($) FY Close | P/E High/Low | | PER SHARE ($) Earnings | Dividends | Book Value |
|---|---|---|---|---|---|---|
| **4/07** | 63.93 | — | — | — | 0.86 | 23.70 |
| **4/06** | 74.50 | — | — | — | 0.28 | 23.82 |
| **4/05** | 55.50 | 22 | 17 | 2.52 | — | 20.14 |
| **4/04** | 46.86 | 24 | 18 | 2.11 | — | 16.76 |
| **4/03** | 38.27 | 22 | 16 | 1.82 | 0.54 | 26.60 |
| **Annual Growth** | 13.7% | — | — | 17.7% | 12.3% | (2.8%) |

# Brunswick Corporation

Brunswick's business is everyone else's free time. A global leader in the leisure products industry, the company's Brunswick Boat Group's pleasure boat brands include Sea Ray, Bayliner, Boston Whaler, Lund, and Hatteras, just to name a few. The company also makes marine engines ranging from 40 to 300 horsepower under nameplates including Mercury and Mariner. It also makes Brunswick bowling and billiards products, as well as fitness equipment (Life Fitness, ParaBody, and Hammer Strength). Brunswick owns or franchises 107 fun centers throughout Canada, Europe, and the US that feature bowling, billiards, restaurants, and "Cosmic (glow-in-the-dark) Bowling."

A longtime kingpin of bowling and billiards equipment, Brunswick has shifted its focus to marine engines and boats (more than 80% of sales).

The company has developed a new line of high-horsepower, high-torque, four-stroke engines that it feels will set a new industry standard. The company also has formed a new joint venture, Cummins MerCruiser Diesel Marine LLC, with Cummins Marine (a division of Cummins, Inc.) to offer integrated diesel marine propulsion units to the global market.

Brunswick is aiming at creating a company that is modeled more after the car industry than its peers in the boating industry. The company feels the boat industry could learn a lot from the automobile industry's dealer organizations, warranty policies, customer service, and the integration of cutting-edge technologies into its products. Brunswick thinks that by letting high consumer expectations drive innovation, the competition will be left in its wake.

Late in 2006, in anticipation of reduced production volumes in 2007, Brunswick announced some cost-reduction measures. The company's strategy had been to acquire enough boat brands to establish a presence in almost every possible segment of the market. Having largely accomplished this goal, Brunswick decided it was time for some house cleaning.

In mid-2007 the company announced it would close its plant in Salisbury, Maryland, in 2008, eliminating 180 jobs. Brunswick has also decided to sell off its Brunswick New Technologies business on a piecemeal basis. New Technologies' marine electronics operations were sold in 2007 to Navico International. Soon after the Navico deal, Brunswick sold New Technologies' portable navigation device operations to MiTAC International Corporation. In mid-2007 Brunwick said New Technologies' fleet management business was being sold to Navman Wireless Holdings.

## HISTORY

Swiss immigrant woodworker John Brunswick built his first billiard table in 1845 in Cincinnati. In 1874 he formed a partnership with Julius Balke, and a decade later they teamed with H. W. Collender to form Brunswick-Balke-Collender Company.

Following Brunswick's death, son-in-law Moses Bensinger became president. The company diversified into bowling equipment during the 1880s. Bensinger's son, B. E., followed as president (1904) and led the company into wood and rubber products, phonographs, and records. (Al Jolson recorded "Sonny Boy" on the Brunswick label.) Brunswick went public after WWI.

By 1930 Brunswick focused on bowling and billiards, sports that had seedy reputations during the 1920s and 1930s. When B. E. died in 1935, his son Bob became CEO and launched a massive promotional campaign to make his meal tickets respectable.

Bob's brother Ted succeeded him as CEO in 1954. Bowling equipment rival AMF introduced the first automatic pinsetter in 1952, and Brunswick followed four years later, capturing the lead by 1958. Brunswick diversified, adding Owens Yacht, MacGregor (sporting goods, 1958), Aloe (medical supplies, 1959), Mercury (marine products, 1961), and Zebco (fishing equipment, 1961). The company adopted its present name in 1960.

Bowling sales plummeted in the 1960s, and Brunswick cut costs by selling unprofitable units and focusing on new products such as an automatic scorer. Acquisitions in the 1970s brought Brunswick into the medical diagnostics and energy and transportation markets. CEO Jack Reichert, a former pin boy who became chairman in 1983, cut corporate staff in half and promoted the marine business.

Brunswick sparked an industrywide consolidation trend in 1986 by buying Bayliner and Ray Industries (boats), followed by Kiekhaefer Aeromarine (marine propulsion engines, 1990) and Martin Reel Company (fly reels, 1991). In 1992 Brunswick and Tracker Marine formed a partnership to build boats and marine equipment. Also that year Brunswick bought the Browning line of rods and reels.

In 1993 Brunswick began selling its businesses in the automotive, electronics, and defense industries. Brunswick expanded its outdoor recreation business in 1996 by purchasing Nelson/Weather Rite (camping equipment) from Roadmaster Industries (later named the RDM Sports Group) along with Roadmaster's bicycle business. Also that year Brunswick acquired the Boston Whaler line of saltwater boats from Meridian Sports.

The company lost antitrust lawsuits in 1999 that totaled nearly $300 million. However, all but two cases (with judgments of $65 million) were overturned on appeal.

In early 2001 Brunswick cut some jobs and rolled its bicycle business over to Pacific Cycle. Stung by the US's economic slowdown, the company announced 500 more job cuts in its powerboat division, even as it acquired Princecraft Boats from Outboard Marine. Then Brunswick completed the acquisition of Hatteras Yachts from Genmar Industries.

Early in 2002 Brunswick closed the sale of its European fishing business to Zebco Sports Europe Ltd., a company newly formed by the operation's management. As 2002 came to a close, Brunswick completed the purchase of marine navigation electronics maker Northstar Technologies, Inc, and propeller maker Teignbridge Propellers. Brunswick acquired the Crestliner, Lowe, and Lund lines of aluminum boats from Genmar Holdings for a reported $191 million.

In 2005 Brunswick's Mercury Marine division expanded its offering of offshore sportfishing products with the acquisition of Albemarle Sportfishing Boats Inc. It also acquired Triton Boat Company, a maker of fiberglass bass and saltwater and aluminum fishing boats.

Brunswick's marina of boat brands continued to grow in early 2006 with the purchase of Cabo Yachts of Adelanto, California.

## EXECUTIVES

**Chairman and CEO:** Dustan E. (Dusty) McCoy, age 57, $800,000 pay
**SVP and CFO:** Peter G. Leemputte, age 49, $443,262 pay
**EVP; COO, Marine and President, Mercury Marine Group:** Patrick C. (Pat) Mackey, age 60, $499,615 pay
**VP; President, Brunswick New Technologies:** Tzau J. (T.J.) Chung, age 43
**VP; President, Life Fitness Division:** John E. Stransky, age 55
**VP; President, US Marine Division:** Stephen M. Wolpert, age 52
**VP and Chief Human Resources Officer:** B. Russell (Russ) Lockridge, age 57
**VP and CIO:** William L. Avery
**VP and Controller:** Alan L. Lowe, age 55
**VP and Treasurer:** William L. Metzger, age 46
**VP, Corporate and Investor Relations:** Kathryn J. Chieger, age 58
**VP, Strategy and Corporate Development, Bowling and Billiards:** Dale B. Tompkins, age 45
**VP, Supply Chain Management; President, Latin America Group:** William J. Gress, age 52
**VP, Tax:** Judith P. Zelisko, age 56
**VP, General Counsel, and Secretary:** Lloyd C. Chatfield II, age 39
**Director, Public and Financial Relations:** Daniel (Dan) Kubera
**Auditors:** Ernst & Young LLP

## LOCATIONS

**HQ:** Brunswick Corporation
1 N. Field Ct., Lake Forest, IL 60045
**Phone:** 847-735-4700 **Fax:** 847-735-4765
**Web:** www.brunswick.com

### 2006 Sales

| | $ mil. | % of total |
|---|---|---|
| US | 3,863 | 68 |
| Other countries | 1,802 | 32 |
| **Total** | **5,665** | **100** |

## PRODUCTS/OPERATIONS

### 2006 Sales

| | $ mil. | % of total |
|---|---|---|
| Marine | | |
| Boat | 2,865 | 47 |
| Marine engine | 2,271 | 37 |
| Fitness | 593 | 9 |
| Bowling & billiards | 458 | 7 |
| Adjustments | (522) | — |
| **Total** | **5,665** | **100** |

### Selected Brands and Products

Boats
- Albermarle
- Aquador
- Arvor
- Baja
- Bayliner
- Boston Whaler
- Cabo Yachts
- Crestliner
- Hatteras yachts
- Lowe
- Lund
- Maxum
- Mercury
- Meridian
- Palmetto
- Princecraft
- Sea Boss
- Sea Pro
- Sea Ray
- Sealine
- Triton
- Trophy

Marine engines
- Mariner
- MerCruiser
- Mercury
- MotoTron
- Quicksilver
- Teignbridge propellers

Fitness
- Hammer Strength
- Life Fitness
- ParaBody

Recreation centers
- Brunswick Zones

Sporting goods
- Brunswick Billiards
- Tornado (foosball tables)
- Brunswick Bowling

## COMPETITORS

AMF Bowling
Bowl America
Carver Yachts
Dave & Buster's
Fountain Powerboat
Genmar Holdings
Giant Manufacturing
Honda
Marine Products
Soloflex
Yamaha

## HISTORICAL FINANCIALS

Company Type: Public

### Income Statement

FYE: December 31

| | REVENUE ($ mil.) | NET INCOME ($ mil.) | NET PROFIT MARGIN | EMPLOYEES |
|---|---|---|---|---|
| **12/06** | 5,665 | 134 | 2.4% | 28,000 |
| **12/05** | 5,924 | 385 | 6.5% | 27,500 |
| **12/04** | 5,229 | 270 | 5.2% | 25,600 |
| **12/03** | 4,129 | 135 | 3.3% | 23,225 |
| **12/02** | 3,712 | 78 | 2.1% | 21,015 |
| **Annual Growth** | 11.1% | 14.3% | — | 7.4% |

### 2006 Year-End Financials

Debt ratio: 38.8%
Return on equity: 7.0%
Cash ($ mil.): 283
Current ratio: 1.61
Long-term debt ($ mil.): 726
No. of shares (mil.): 91
Dividends
Yield: 1.9%
Payout: 42.6%
Market value ($ mil.): 2,899

### Stock History

NYSE: BC

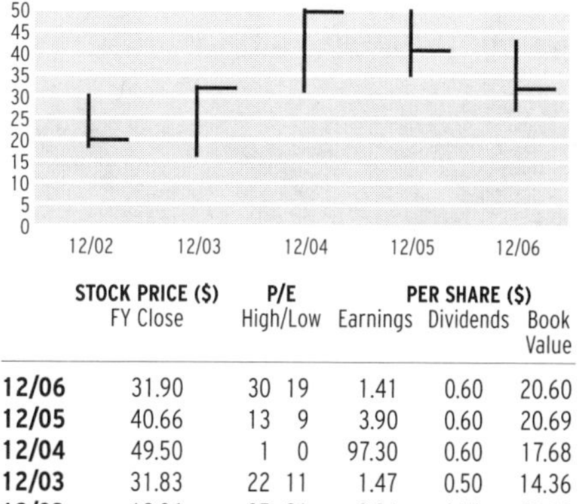


| | STOCK PRICE ($) FY Close | P/E High | P/E Low | PER SHARE ($) Earnings | Dividends | Book Value |
|---|---|---|---|---|---|---|
| **12/06** | 31.90 | 30 | 19 | 1.41 | 0.60 | 20.60 |
| **12/05** | 40.66 | 13 | 9 | 3.90 | 0.60 | 20.69 |
| **12/04** | 49.50 | 1 | 0 | 97.30 | 0.60 | 17.68 |
| **12/03** | 31.83 | 22 | 11 | 1.47 | 0.50 | 14.36 |
| **12/02** | 19.86 | 35 | 21 | 0.86 | 0.50 | 12.22 |
| **Annual Growth** | 12.6% | — | — | 13.2% | 4.7% | 13.9% |

# Burger King Holdings

This king rules a whopper of a fast-food empire. Burger King Holdings operates the world's #2 hamburger chain (behind McDonald's) with more than 11,100 restaurants in the US and about 65 other countries. In addition to its popular Whopper sandwich, the chain offers a variety of burgers, chicken sandwiches, salads, and breakfast items. More than 1,200 BK locations are company-owned, while the rest are owned and operated by franchisees. Burger King was founded by James McLamore and David Edgerton in 1954. Investment firms TPG Capital, Bain Capital, and Goldman Sachs each own about 25% of the company.

The company, which has suffered its share of trials and tribulations in the past, has managed to put itself on a trajectory of slow and steady growth thanks in large part to the efforts of turnaround specialist Greg Brenneman. Coming in as CEO in 2004, he led the burger baron to introduce a $1 value menu and focused the company's marketing efforts on 18- to 34-year-old men — so-called superfans — with new menu items and off-kilter ads featuring boxing chickens and a slightly askew BK mascot. Brenneman left Burger King ahead of its 2006 IPO, however, and it will be up to new CEO John Chidsey, who formerly served as president and CFO, to continue building the business. Burger King hopes to open about 450 new locations during 2006-07, with the lion's share of that expansion coming in overseas markets. In 2007 the company announced the start of operations in Indonesia.

In addition to fighting rivals such as McDonald's, Wendy's, and YUM! Brands for market share, Chidsey also has the task of maintaining good relations with BK's famously cantankerous franchise association. Franchisees have been vocal in the past about the chain's marketing efforts — they claimed it was turning off women and families — and the two sides parted ways briefly after a power struggle erupted at the annual franchise meeting in 2005. The company and its franchisees have made progress in mending fences, but Chidsey will have to continue to build on that goodwill as Burger King continues to pursue its target superfan market.

Despite the potential pitfalls facing the business, Burger King is still in a much better position than it has been in the past. Its IPO marked the end of a long and difficult period for the chain, which largely treaded water for several years as a subsidiary of food and beverage giant Diageo. TPG, then known as Texas Pacific Group, acquired the business for $1.5 billion in 2002, but multiple attempts to revive the business resulted mostly in a revolving door at the top of the executive ranks.

## HISTORY

In 1954 restaurant veterans James McLamore and David Edgerton opened the first Burger King in Miami. Three years later, the company added the Whopper sandwich (which then sold for 37 cents) to its menu of hamburgers, shakes, and sodas. Burger King used television to help advertise the Whopper (its first TV commercial appeared in 1958). During its infancy, Burger King was the first chain to offer dining rooms.

In order to expand nationwide, Burger King turned to franchising in 1959. McLamore and Edgerton took a hands-off approach, allowing franchises to buy large territories and operate with autonomy. Although their technique spurred growth, it also created large service inconsistencies among Burger Kings across the US; this gaffe would haunt the company for years. Having grown to 274 stores in the US and abroad, Burger King was sold to Pillsbury in 1967.

During the early 1970s Burger King continued to add locations. The company did well during this time, launching its successful "Have It Your Way" campaign in 1974 and introducing drive-through service a year later. Yet parent Pillsbury had to fight to rein in large franchisees who argued they could run their Burger Kings better than a packaged-goods company could. In 1977 Pillsbury handed control of Burger King to Donald Smith, a McDonald's veteran, who soon silenced the insurrection. Smith tightened franchising regulations, created 10 regional management offices, and instituted annual visits.

Smith left for Pizza Hut in 1980, and by 1982 Burger King had reached the #2 hamburger chain plateau, trailing only McDonald's. The company struggled through the rest of the 1980s, hurt by high management turnover and a string of unsuccessful ad campaigns (such as the ill-fated 1986 NFL Super Bowl "Herb the Nerd" concept). Pillsbury became the target of a hostile takeover by UK-based Grand Metropolitan, and in 1988 Grand Met acquired Pillsbury along with its 5,500 Burger King restaurants.

Grand Met bolstered Burger King's foreign operations in 1990 by converting about 200 recently acquired UK-based Wimpy hamburger stores into Burger Kings. International expansion increased with new restaurants in Mexico (1991), Saudi Arabia (1993), and Paraguay (1995).

In 1997 Grand Met and Guinness combined their operations to form Diageo, making Burger King a subsidiary. That year Dennis Malamatinas left Grand Met's Asian beverage division to become Burger King's CEO.

In 2000 Diageo announced plans to spin off Burger King, but the burger chain's slow sales delayed action. Malamatinas resigned as CEO and was replaced in 2001 by John Dasburg, former CEO of Northwest Airlines.

An investment group led by Texas Pacific Group (now TPG Capital) acquired Burger King for $1.5 billion in 2002. Earlier that year, Texas Pacific had agreed to pay $2.26 billion but renegotiated amid falling sales and a downturn in the burger market. Shortly after the purchase, Dasburg was ousted and Brad Blum, vice chairman of Darden Restaurants, was named as his replacement.

After just 18 months on the job, Blum resigned his post as CEO in 2004, citing differences with the company's board. He was replaced by Greg Brenneman.

Burger King had consistent sales growth in 2004, and Brenneman's presence was a boost for the company. In addition, that year the company signed a deal (with rancher Luiz Eduardo Batalha) to develop about 50 restaurants in Brazil over a five-year period.

In 2006 the company ran advertising during the Super Bowl for the first time in 11 years. Brenneman resigned that year shortly before Burger King went public; the company tapped president and CFO John Chidsey as his replacement.

## EXECUTIVES

**Chairman:** Brian Thomas Swette, age 52
**CEO and Director:** John W. Chidsey, age 44, $7,953,737 pay
**EVP and Chief Global Operations Officer:** James F. (Jim) Hyatt, age 50, $1,887,764 pay
**EVP and CFO:** Ben K. Wells, age 53
**SVP, Company Operations:** Dave Gagnon, age 59
**SVP, Franchise Operations and Marketing EMEA:** Martin Brok, age 39
**SVP, Global Communications and External Affairs:** Clyde Rucker, age 43
**SVP, Investor Relations:** Amy E. Wagner, age 41
**SVP, Development and Franchising:** Jonathan (John) Fitzpatrick
**SVP, Global Business Intelligence and Strategy:** Michael (Mike) Kappitt
**SVP, Global Operations Research and Development:** John Reckert
**SVP, Finance:** Christopher M. Anderson, age 39
**VP, Marketing Field North America:** Robert Levite
**VP, Marketing Impact:** Brian Gies
**VP, Audit and Risk Management:** Betty Ann Blandon
**VP, Food Safety, Quality Assurance, and Regulatory Compliance:** Steven F. (Steve) Grover
**General Counsel and Secretary:** Anne Chwat, age 47, $1,768,923 pay
**President, North America:** Charles M. (Chuck) Fallon Jr., age 44
**President, Asia Pacific:** Peter Tan, age 51
**President, EMEA:** Peter B. Robinson
**President, Latin America:** Julio Ramirez, age 52
**Chief Human Resources Officer:** Peter C. (Pete) Smith, age 50, $2,323,644 pay
**President, Global Marketing Strategy and Innovation:** Russell B. (Russ) Klein, age 49, $1,992,127 pay
**Auditors:** KPMG LLP

## LOCATIONS

**HQ:** Burger King Holdings, Inc.
5505 Blue Lagoon Dr., Miami, FL 33126
**Phone:** 305-378-3000 **Fax:** 305-378-7262
**Web:** www.burgerking.com

**2006 Sales Company-owned Restaurants**

| | $ mil. | % of total |
|---|---|---|
| US & Canada | 1,032 | 68 |
| Europe, the Middle East, Africa & Asia Pacific | 428 | 28 |
| Latin America | 56 | 4 |
| **Total** | **1,516** | **100** |

**2006 Locations**

| | No. |
|---|---|
| US & Canada | 7,534 |
| Europe, the Middle East, Africa & Asia Pacific | 2,787 |
| Latin America | 808 |
| **Total** | **11,129** |

## PRODUCTS/OPERATIONS

**2006 Sales**

| | $ mil. | % of total |
|---|---|---|
| Restaurants | 1,516 | 74 |
| Franchising | 420 | 21 |
| Property | 112 | 5 |
| **Total** | **2,048** | **100** |

**2006 Locations**

| | No. |
|---|---|
| Franchised | 9,889 |
| Company-owned | 1,240 |
| **Total** | **11,129** |

## COMPETITORS

AFC Enterprises
Arby's
Chick-fil-A
CKE Restaurants
Dairy Queen
Domino's
Jack in the Box
Little Caesar's
McDonald's
Papa John's
Quiznos
Subway
Wendy's
YUM!

## HISTORICAL FINANCIALS

Company Type: Public

**Income Statement** FYE: June 30

| | REVENUE ($ mil.) | NET INCOME ($ mil.) | NET PROFIT MARGIN | EMPLOYEES |
|---|---|---|---|---|
| **6/06** | 2,048 | 27 | 1.3% | 37,000 |
| **6/05** | 1,940 | 47 | 2.4% | 30,300 |
| **6/04** | 1,754 | 5 | 0.3% | — |
| **Annual Growth** | 8.1% | 132.4% | — | 22.1% |

**2006 Year-End Financials**

Debt ratio: 186.9%
Return on equity: 5.2%
Cash ($ mil.): 259
Current ratio: 0.92
Long-term debt ($ mil.): 1,060
No. of shares (mil.): 133
Dividends
Yield: —
Payout: —
Market value ($ mil.): 2,096

**Stock History** NYSE: BKC

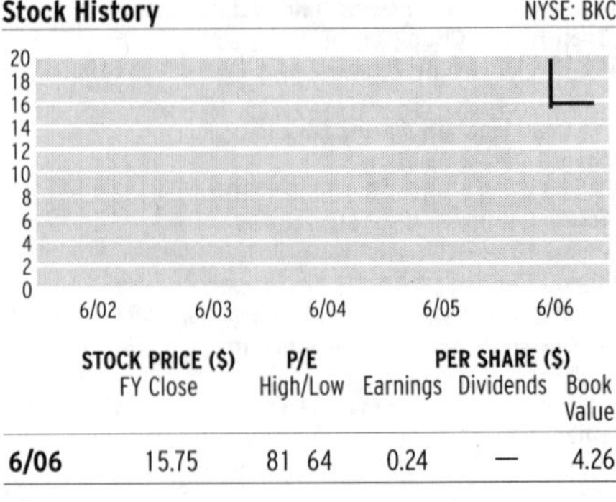


| | STOCK PRICE ($) FY Close | P/E High | P/E Low | PER SHARE ($) Earnings | PER SHARE ($) Dividends | PER SHARE ($) Book Value |
|---|---|---|---|---|---|---|
| **6/06** | 15.75 | 81 | 64 | 0.24 | — | 4.26 |

# Burlington Northern Santa Fe

Over the years the number of major US railroads has dwindled, but Burlington Northern Santa Fe (BNSF) thrives as one of the survivors. Through its primary subsidiary, BNSF Railway, the company is the second-largest railroad operator in the US, behind Union Pacific. BNSF makes tracks through 28 states in the West, Midwest, and Sunbelt regions of the US and in two Canadian provinces. The company operates its trains over a system of about 32,000 route miles, consisting of 23,000 route miles owned by BNSF and 9,000 route miles of trackage rights, which allow BNSF to use tracks owned by other railroads.

BNSF's largest revenue source is its consumer products business, which handles containerized freight and automotive products. The railroad's industrial products business transports building and construction products, chemicals and plastics, food and beverages, and petroleum products.

The company plans to continue to invest in its fast-growing intermodal operations, which involve the movement of freight by multiple methods, such as train and truck. It operates major intermodal freight transfer facilities in Chicago and Southern California. Increased trade with China is fueling much of the growth of BNSF's international intermodal business.

To improve the efficiency of its network, BNSF is adding track along its busiest routes. Double- and triple-track projects have increased the railroad's capacity in its coal-hauling territory in Wyoming and Nebraska and along its main transcontinental line, between Chicago and Los Angeles.

Warren Buffett's Berkshire Hathaway owns about 12% of BNSF.

## HISTORY

Burlington Northern (BN) was largely created by James Hill, who bought the St. Paul & Pacific Railroad in Minnesota in 1878. By 1893 Hill had completed the Great Northern Railway, extending from St. Paul to Seattle. The next year he gained control of Northern Pacific (chartered in 1864), which had been built between Minnesota and Washington. In 1901, with J.P. Morgan's help, Hill acquired the Chicago, Burlington & Quincy (Burlington), whose routes included Chicago-St. Paul and Billings, Montana-Denver-Fort Worth, Texas-Houston. The Spokane, Portland & Seattle Railway (SP&S), completed in 1908, gave Great Northern an entrance to Oregon.

Hill intended to merge Great Northern, Northern Pacific, SP&S, and Burlington under his Morgan-backed Northern Securities Company, but in 1904 the Supreme Court found that Northern Securities had violated the Sherman Antitrust Act. The holding company was dissolved, but Hill controlled the individual railroads until he died in 1916. Hill's railroads produced well-known passenger trains: Great Northern's Empire Builder began service in 1929, and in 1934 Burlington Zephyr was the nation's first streamlined passenger diesel.

After years of deliberation, the Interstate Commerce Commission allowed Great Northern and Northern Pacific to merge in 1970, along with jointly owned subsidiaries Burlington and SP&S. The new company, Burlington Northern (BN), acquired the St. Louis-San Francisco Railway in 1980, adding more than 4,650 miles to its rail network.

The company formed Burlington Motor Carriers (BMC) in 1985 to manage five trucking companies it had acquired. But to focus on its rail operations, BN sold BMC in 1988 and spun off Burlington Resources, a holding company for its other nonrailroad businesses.

A fiery collision between a BN freight train and one operated by Union Pacific in 1995 propelled the rivals to begin joint testing of global positioning satellites for guiding trains. Besides improving safety, the two hoped to end rail bottlenecks.

That year BN and Santa Fe Pacific (SFP), founded in 1859, formed Burlington Northern Santa Fe in a $4 billion merger. BN's strength lay in transporting manufacturing, agricultural, and natural resource commodities, and SFP specialized in intermodal shipping (combining train, truck, and ship). SFP (originally the Atchison, Topeka & Santa Fe) had taken the name Santa Fe Pacific in 1989 after its forced sale of Southern Pacific.

The new BNSF acquired Washington Central Railroad in 1996, adding a third connection between central Washington and the Pacific Coast. In 1997 customers protested when BNSF couldn't come up with enough cars and locomotives for grain shipping. A year later UP was in trouble with clogged rail lines: BNSF opened a joint dispatching center in Houston with UP to help unsnarl traffic. The effort proved successful, and in 1999 BNSF and UP began to combine dispatching in Southern California; the Kansas City, Missouri, area; and Wyoming's Powder River Basin.

In 1999 BNSF announced a $2.5 billion capital improvement program, but later decided to trim spending to $2.28 billion and cut 1,400 jobs.

Later that year BNSF agreed to merge with Canadian National Railway. The companies terminated the deal in 2000, however, after a US moratorium on rail mergers was upheld on appeal. Also in 2000 BNSF began offering intermodal service between the US and Monterrey, Queretaro, and Mexico City, Mexico, its first such US-Mexico service.

In 2001 BNSF became the first US railroad to use the Internet to purchase fuel (via the American Petroleum Exchange). Another milestone followed, albeit a more dubious one: To settle the first federal lawsuit against workplace genetic testing, BNSF agreed to drop its testing program. Without their knowledge, employees who had been diagnosed with carpal tunnel syndrome were tested for genetic defects.

Also in 2001 BNSF announced plans to join with a group of chemical and plastics companies to build a rail-spur southeast of Houston in order to compete with Union Pacific for petrochemical shipping business.

In 2002 BNSF completed the construction of its BNSF Logistics Park in Chicago, designed to integrate direct rail, truck, intermodal, transload services, distribution, and warehousing in a single location.

## EXECUTIVES

**Chairman, President, and CEO; Chairman, President, and CEO, BNSF Railway:** Matthew K. (Matt) Rose, age 47, $1,100,000 pay
**EVP and COO:** Carl R. Ice, age 50, $533,650 pay
**EVP and CFO:** Thomas N. Hund, age 53, $485,925 pay
**EVP and Chief Marketing Officer:** John P. Lanigan Jr., age 51, $513,125 pay
**EVP, Law and Secretary:** Roger Nober, age 42
**VP and Chief Sourcing Officer:** Dennis R. Johnson, age 43
**VP and General Counsel:** Paul R. Hoferer
**VP and Corporate General Counsel:** James H. (Jim) Gallegos
**VP and General Tax Counsel:** Shelley J. Venick
**VP and General Manager, BNSF Logistics:** Eric Wolfe
**VP and Senior Regulatory Counsel:** Richard E. (Rick) Weicher
**VP, Corporate Audit Services:** David W. Stropes
**VP, Human Resources and Medical:** Jeanne E. Michalski
**VP, Investor Relations:** Marsha K. Morgan
**VP, Network Development:** Peter J. Rickershauser, age 58
**VP, Technology Services and CIO:** Jeffrey J. Campbell
**VP and Controller:** Paul W. Bischler
**Treasurer:** Linda J. Hurt
**General Director, Corporate Communications:** Patrick (Pat) Hiatte
**Director, Investor Relations:** Mark Bracker
**Auditors:** PricewaterhouseCoopers LLP

## LOCATIONS

**HQ:** Burlington Northern Santa Fe Corporation
2650 Lou Menk Dr., Fort Worth, TX 76131
**Phone:** 800-795-2673 **Fax:** 817-352-7171
**Web:** www.bnsf.com

## PRODUCTS/OPERATIONS

**2006 Sales**

| | $ mil. | % of total |
|---|---|---|
| Freight | | |
| Consumer products | 5,613 | 37 |
| Industrial products | 3,589 | 24 |
| Coal | 2,916 | 20 |
| Agricultural products | 2,427 | 16 |
| Other | 440 | 3 |
| **Total** | **14,985** | **100** |

## COMPETITORS

American Commercial Lines
APL Logistics
Canadian National Railway
Canadian Pacific Railway
CSX
Hub Group
Ingram Industries
J.B. Hunt
Kansas City Southern
Kirby
Landstar System
Norfolk Southern
Pacer International
Schneider National
Union Pacific
Werner Enterprises

## HISTORICAL FINANCIALS

Company Type: Public

**Income Statement** FYE: December 31

| | REVENUE ($ mil.) | NET INCOME ($ mil.) | NET PROFIT MARGIN | EMPLOYEES |
|---|---|---|---|---|
| **12/06** | 14,985 | 1,887 | 12.6% | 41,000 |
| **12/05** | 12,987 | 1,531 | 11.8% | 40,000 |
| **12/04** | 10,946 | 791 | 7.2% | 38,000 |
| **12/03** | 9,413 | 816 | 8.7% | 36,500 |
| **12/02** | 8,979 | 760 | 8.5% | 36,000 |
| **Annual Growth** | 13.7% | 25.5% | — | 3.3% |

**2006 Year-End Financials**

Debt ratio: 66.5%
Return on equity: 19.0%
Cash ($ mil.): 375
Current ratio: 0.66
Long-term debt ($ mil.): 6,912
No. of shares (mil.): 358
Dividends
Yield: 1.2%
Payout: 17.6%
Market value ($ mil.): 26,415

**Stock History** NYSE: BNI

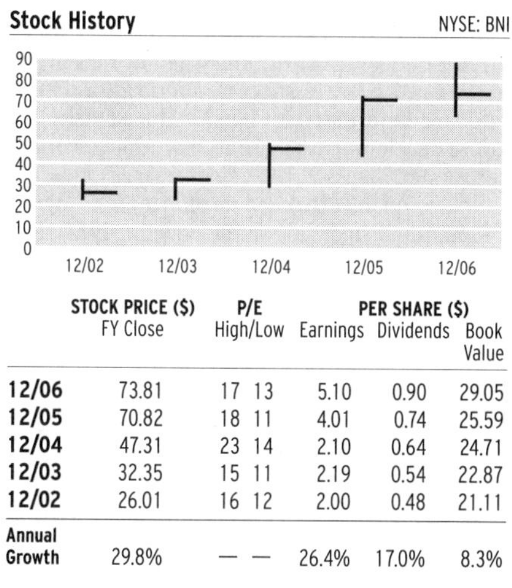


| | STOCK PRICE ($) FY Close | P/E High | P/E Low | PER SHARE ($) Earnings | Dividends | Book Value |
|---|---|---|---|---|---|---|
| **12/06** | 73.81 | 17 | 13 | 5.10 | 0.90 | 29.05 |
| **12/05** | 70.82 | 18 | 11 | 4.01 | 0.74 | 25.59 |
| **12/04** | 47.31 | 23 | 14 | 2.10 | 0.64 | 24.71 |
| **12/03** | 32.35 | 15 | 11 | 2.19 | 0.54 | 22.87 |
| **12/02** | 26.01 | 16 | 12 | 2.00 | 0.48 | 21.11 |
| **Annual Growth** | 29.8% | — | — | 26.4% | 17.0% | 8.3% |

# CA, Inc.

CA wants to put your information technology under new management. One of the world's largest software companies, CA provides tools for managing networks, databases, applications, storage, security, and other systems. The company's Unicenter enterprise management software is designed to give customers centralized control over network infrastructure. Its applications work across both mainframes and distributed computing environments. The company also offers consulting, implementation, and training services. It markets worldwide to businesses, government agencies, and schools.

CA sells directly and through various resale channels. Software subscriptions account for the majority of the company's revenues. It generates roughly half of its sales outside the US.

A highly acquisitive company throughout its history, CA continues to expand its application portfolio with strategic purchases. In 2005 it acquired network management specialist Concord Communications for about $330 million. CA also acquired firewall developer Tiny Software, IT management software maker Niku, and document security software provider iLumin Software Services that year. The company purchased application management specialist Wily Technology for $375 million early in 2006. It then acquired job scheduling software developer Cybermation for $75 million in cash, enterprise records management software maker MDY, and data recovery specialist XOsoft.

Swiss billionaire Walter Haefner owns about a quarter of the company.

## HISTORY

Born in Shanghai, Charles Wang fled Communist China with his family in 1952 and grew up in Queens, New York. After working in sales for software developer Standard Data, Wang started a joint venture in 1976 with Swiss-owned Computer Associates (CA) to sell software in the US. He started with four employees and one product, a file organizer for IBM storage systems. It was a great success, and in 1980 Wang bought out his Swiss partners. CA went public in 1981.

Wang realized that a far-flung distribution and service network (continuously fed by new products) was the key to success. Acquiring existing software (and its customers) reduced risky in-house development and moved products to market sooner.

The company expanded its offerings by buying the popular SuperCalc spreadsheet in 1984. The 1987 purchase of chief utilities rival UCCEL gave investor Walter Haefner what remains the largest individual stake in CA.

CA's purchases of mostly struggling software firms made it, in 1989, the first independent software company to reach $1 billion in sales. The $300 million acquisition of Cullinet that year added database and banking applications to CA's product line.

By the early 1990s, CA's acquisition methods had developed a reputation that were seen by some as ruthless — swoop in, gobble up, cut costs, and get rid of employees. As a new owner, CA strongly defended its licensing contracts — often in court.

In 1994 CA promoted EVP of operations Sanjay Kumar to president. Kumar's shift away from older systems to focus on network software was reflected by the acquisitions of ASK Group (1994), Legent (1995), and network management expert Cheyenne Software (1996). CA continued its practice of buying in cash to avoid diluting stock.

Acquisition-related charges caused losses for fiscal 1996. With its lack of a major service operation taking a bite out of potential business, CA made a $9.8 billion hostile takeover offer for consulting firm Computer Sciences Corp. (CSC) in 1998. CA soon dropped its bid in the face of CSC's fierce opposition and later acquired smaller computer service specialist Realogic.

The acquisitions helped cause a drop in profits for fiscal 1999. Later that year CA bought database management software company PLATINUM technology for about $3.5 billion.

In 2000 CA acquired business software specialist Sterling Software in a deal valued at nearly $4 billion. Later that year the company began spinning off some of its promising software businesses; Wang stepped down as CEO to focus on new opportunities for CA as chairman. He handed the CEO reins to Kumar.

Alleging corporate mismanagement, in 2001 Sam Wyly (co-founder of Sterling Software) initiated a proxy fight designed to elect a new board of directors. Wyly's bid failed, however, as it was voted down by shareholders. He initiated a second proxy fight in 2002, but abandoned it after reaching a settlement with the company, which included a $10 million payment. Later in 2002, the board elected Kumar chairman after Wang retired.

An SEC investigation into the company's accounting practices led to the resignation of CA's CFO late in 2003. The investigation continued into 2004, resulting in additional executive resignations. Late in 2004 CA agreed to pay $225 million to shareholders in order to avoid criminal prosecution by the SEC and US Justice Department for fraudulently recording and reporting revenues. Shortly after the settlement was announced former CEO Sanjay Kumar and former EVP Stephen Richards were indicted on charges of securities fraud, conspiracy, and obstruction of justice. Kumar resigned as chairman, president, and CEO that year (he left the company entirely after a brief stint as chief software architect). IBM veteran John Swainson was named CEO.

Also in 2004 the company expanded its desktop management product line through the purchase of Miramar Systems, and it bulked up its security software portfolio with the purchases of eSecurity Online, Silent Runner, and Netegrity. It sold its ACCPAC subsidiary to Sage Group for about $110 million in 2004.

Early in 2006 Computer Associates International officially changed its name to CA.

## EXECUTIVES

**Chairman:** William E. (Bill) McCracken, age 64
**President, CEO, and Director:** John A. Swainson, age 53, $1,337,565 pay
**EVP and COO:** Michael J. (Mike) Christenson, age 47
**EVP and CFO:** Nancy E. Cooper, age 53
**Chief Administrative Officer:** James E. Bryant, age 62
**EVP and Chief Marketing Officer:** Donald R. (Don) Friedman, age 61
**EVP and General Counsel:** Amy Fliegelman Olli
**EVP Global Risk & Compliance and Corporate Secretary:** Kenneth V. (Ken) Handal, age 58
**EVP Worldwide Human Resources:** Andrew (Andy) Goodman, age 48
**EVP Products:** Russell M. Artzt, age 60, $952,543 pay
**EVP and General Manager Governance and Service Management:** Jacob Lamm
**EVP and General Manager Management and Security:** Ajei S. Gopal
**EVP and CTO:** Alan F. Nugent, age 52
**SVP and Corporate Controller:** Robert G. Cirabisi, age 42
**SVP and Chief Learning Officer:** Bradley J. (Brad) Samargya
**SVP and Treasurer:** Mary Stravinskas, age 46
**SVP Worldwide Sales Operations:** John Ruthven
**SVP, Finance:** William H. Hogan
**SVP Worldwide Public Relations:** Dan Kaferle, age 55
**SVP Worldwide Home/Small Office Sales:** George Kafkarkou
**SVP, Worldwide Sales Finance:** Claude Pumilia, age 38
**SVP, Worldwide Partner Sales:** James Hanley
**SVP Corporate Communications:** Bill Hughes
**VP, Investor Relations:** Olivia Bellingham
**Corporate Communications:** Michael Kornspan
**Auditors:** KPMG LLP

## LOCATIONS

**HQ:** CA, Inc.
1 CA Plaza, Islandia, NY 11749
**Phone:** 631-342-6000 **Fax:** 631-342-4854
**Web:** www.ca.com

### 2007 Sales

| | $ mil. | % of total |
|---|---|---|
| US | 2,131 | 54 |
| Europe | 1,131 | 29 |
| Other regions | 681 | 17 |
| **Total** | **3,943** | **100** |

## PRODUCTS/OPERATIONS

### 2007 Sales

| | $ mil. | % of total |
|---|---|---|
| Subscription | 3,067 | 78 |
| Maintenance | 391 | 10 |
| Professional services | 351 | 9 |
| Financing fees | 26 | — |
| Software fees & other | 108 | 3 |
| **Total** | **3,943** | **100** |

### Selected Product Groups

Application development and databases
Application performance management
Database management
Infrastructure and operations management
IT service and asset management
Mainframe
Project, portfolio, and financial management
Security management
Storage and information governance

## COMPETITORS

BEA Systems
BMC Software
Check Point Software
Cognos
Compuware
EMC
Hewlett-Packard
IBM
McAfee
Microsoft
Novell
Oracle
RSA Security
SAP
Sun Microsystems
Sybase
Symantec

## HISTORICAL FINANCIALS

Company Type: Public

### Income Statement

FYE: March 31

| | REVENUE ($ mil.) | NET INCOME ($ mil.) | NET PROFIT MARGIN | EMPLOYEES |
|---|---|---|---|---|
| **3/07** | 3,943 | 118 | 3.0% | 14,500 |
| **3/06** | 3,796 | 159 | 4.2% | 16,000 |
| **3/05** | 3,560 | (4) | — | 15,300 |
| **3/04** | 3,276 | 25 | 0.8% | 15,300 |
| **3/03** | 3,116 | (267) | — | 16,000 |
| **Annual Growth** | 6.1% | — | — | (2.4%) |

### 2007 Year-End Financials

Debt ratio: 70.8%
Return on equity: 2.8%
Cash ($ mil.): 2,280
Current ratio: 0.83
Long-term debt ($ mil.): 2,611
No. of shares (mil.): 525
Dividends
Yield: 0.6%
Payout: 72.7%
Market value ($ mil.): 13,607

### Stock History

NYSE: CA

| | STOCK PRICE ($) FY Close | P/E High/Low | PER SHARE ($) Earnings | Dividends | Book Value |
|---|---|---|---|---|---|
| **3/07** | 25.91 | 125 86 | 0.22 | 0.16 | 7.03 |
| **3/06** | 27.21 | 110 96 | 0.27 | 0.16 | 8.19 |
| **3/05** | 27.10 | — — | (0.01) | 0.08 | 8.42 |
| **3/04** | 26.86 | 740 333 | 0.04 | 0.08 | 8.10 |
| **3/03** | 13.66 | — — | (0.46) | 0.08 | 7.57 |
| **Annual Growth** | 17.4% | — — | — | 18.9% | (1.8%) |

# Cabot Corporation

Even if it lost money, Cabot still would be in the black. The company is the world's #1 producer of carbon black, a reinforcing and pigmenting agent used in tires, inks, cables, and coatings. It has about 25% of the world market for carbon black. Cabot also holds its own as a maker of fumed metal oxides such as fumed silica and fumed alumina, which are used as anti-caking, thickening, and reinforcing agents in adhesives and coatings. Other products include tantalum (used to make capacitors used in electronics) and specialty fluids for gas and oil drilling.

The company is among a small group of carbon black producers with a global presence. Columbian Chemicals and Degussa also operate worldwide. Much of its carbon black business is done with the top automobile tire makers with Goodyear Tire & Rubber being its largest customer, accounting for about 15% of its entire business.

Asset management company State Street controls approximately 15% of Cabot.

## HISTORY

A descendant of two old-line Boston merchant families, Godfrey Lowell Cabot graduated from Harvard in 1882. His brother had a paint business in Pennsylvania that used coal tars to make black pigment, and the two decided that carbon black — an abundant waste product of the oil fields — would be their business. The brothers built a carbon black plant in Pennsylvania in 1882; five years later Godfrey bought his brother's share in the company. A carbon black glut and the increasing use of natural gas led Godfrey to drill his first gas well in 1888. He took advantage of the glut by buying distressed carbon black factories.

As the Pennsylvania oil fields dried up near the turn of the century, Godfrey moved operations to West Virginia, where he added to his gas holdings and, in 1914, built a natural gas extraction plant. Meanwhile, products such as high-speed printing presses increased the demand for carbon black. The reinforcing and stabilizing properties of the compound became widely known after its use in tires during WWI. The company was incorporated in 1922 as Godfrey L. Cabot, Inc.

The production of carbon black soon moved west, and by 1930 Cabot had eight plants in Texas and one in Oklahoma. Early that decade the company developed dustless carbon black pellets, which, along with gas profits, got Cabot through the Depression. In 1935 Cabot began drilling for oil and gas and processing natural gas in Texas. Soon natural gas accounted for more than half of sales.

WWII led to rubber shortages and temporary government control over the industry. It also led to the construction and improvement (with government assistance) of Cabot plants in Louisiana, Oklahoma, and Texas. The company was the #1 producer of carbon black in 1950 and began its fumed silica operations in 1952. The postwar economic boom allowed Cabot to open carbon black plants in Canada, France, Italy, and the UK by the end of the decade.

In 1960 the company's businesses were united under the Cabot Corporation name. During the 1960s expansion continued into Argentina, Colombia, Germany, and Spain. Godfrey Cabot died in 1962. The next year the company started producing titanium, sold a 12% stake in a public offering, and began experimenting with plastic polymers.

CEO Robert Sharpie used the cash derived from Cabot's chemical businesses during the 1970s for acquisitions — including Kawecki Berylco Industries (tantalum, 1978) and TUCO, Inc. (gas processing and pipeline, 1979) — while its chemical plants deteriorated. The oil crisis early in the decade resulted in the rapid growth of Cabot's energy business. However, when gas prices fell in the 1980s, Cabot's revenue base shrank and its liabilities didn't.

The Cabot family, which owned 30% of the company, replaced Sharpie with Samuel Bodman as CEO in 1987. Bodman invested in the plants and divested many of Cabot's noncore assets, including ceramics, metal manufacturing, and semiconductors. He also exited the energy production and exploration businesses.

In 1996 Cabot formed divisions to make pigment-based inks (inkjet colorants) and drilling fluids (Cabot Specialty Fluids) and sold TUCO. Two years later the company began field testing a drilling fluid (cesium formate) that would half the drilling time in high-temperature, high-pressure wells. Cabot opened a slurry plant (for semiconductor manufacturing) in Japan in 1999 and completed the second phase of its carbon black plant in China, a joint venture with a Chinese firm. It also spun off 15% of its microelectronics materials business and sold Cabot LNG to Tractebel for around $680 million.

Cabot spun off its remaining stake (about 80%) in Cabot Microelectronics in 2000. The next year Kennett Burnes was named CEO and chairman after Bodman stepped down to become Deputy Treasury Secretary. (President Bush nominated Bodman to become Secretary of Energy for his second term, and Bodman was confirmed in early 2005.)

In 2002 Cabot purchased the remainder of Showa Cabot Supermetals (tantalum) from its joint venture partner, Showa Denko, for about $100 million and another $100 million in debt. However, the company experienced lower sales volumes of tantalum because of contract disagreements with some of its customers, including KEMET and AVX.

Cabot continued to develop and expand its newer businesses, including its growing ink jet colorants unit. In late 2002 Cabot launched its new aerogels business (Nanogel), which produces materials for thermal and sound insulating purposes. Cabot sold its 40% stake in Aearo Corporation (maker of safety products like eyewear; formerly called Cabot Safety Holding Corporation) in 2004.

The following year, Cabot purchased Showa Denko's interest in another joint venture, Showa Cabot K.K., which marketed carbon black products in Japan.

## EXECUTIVES

**Chairman, President, and CEO:** Kennett F. Burnes, age 63, $1,490,000 pay
**EVP and CFO:** Jonathan P. Mason, age 48, $531,731 pay
**EVP and General Manager, Carbon Black:** William J. Brady, age 45, $450,000 pay
**EVP, General Manager, Europe, and Director:** Dirk L. Blevi, age 58, $517,359 pay
**VP and General Manager, Asia Pacific:** Nicholas P. Ballas
**VP and General Manager, Cabot Supermetals:** Eduardo E. Cordeiro, age 39, $382,307 pay
**VP and General Manager, Performance Products:** Sean Keohane
**VP; President, Cabot Supermetals, KK:** Yasuto Komatsu
**VP and General Manager, South America:** Chang Loo Sih
**VP and General Manager, Metal Oxides Business:** Ravijit Paintal, age 45
**VP and General Manager, Inkjet Colorants:** Friedrich von Gottberg
**VP and General Manager, China:** Xinsheng Zhang
**VP, Corporate Planning:** Paul J. Gormisky, age 52
**VP and General Counsel:** Brian A. Berube, age 44, $443,750 pay
**VP, Strategic Development:** Ho-il Kim
**VP, Human Resources:** Robby D. Sisco
**VP and Treasurer:** Irene Sudac
**Director, Global Sales:** Jose Olivares
**Director, Investor Relations:** Susannah Robinson
**Secretary:** Jane A. Bell
**Auditors:** PricewaterhouseCoopers LLP

## LOCATIONS

**HQ:** Cabot Corporation
2 Seaport Ln., Ste. 1300, Boston, MA 02210
**Phone:** 617-345-0100 **Fax:** 617-342-6103
**Web:** www.cabot-corp.com

Cabot operates manufacturing facilities in more than 20 countries.

### 2006 Sales

| | $ mil. | % of total |
|---|---|---|
| US | 790 | 31 |
| Japan | 351 | 14 |
| Other | 1,402 | 55 |
| **Total** | **2,543** | **100** |

## PRODUCTS/OPERATIONS

### 2006 Sales

| | $ mil. | % of total |
|---|---|---|
| Carbon black | | |
| Rubber blacks | 1,378 | 54 |
| Performance products | 488 | 19 |
| Inkjet colorants & other | 51 | 2 |
| Supermetals | 292 | 12 |
| Metal oxides | 254 | 10 |
| Specialty fluids | 44 | 2 |
| Other | 36 | 1 |
| **Total** | **2,543** | **100** |

### Selected Products

Carbon black
- Rubber blacks (for tires and industrial products)
- Performance products (for electronics, inks, coatings, and plastics)
- Inkjet colorants
- Superior MicroPowders (business development)

Supermetals
- Niobium
- Tantalum

Metal oxides
- Fumed alumina
- Fumed silica
- Nanogel (insulative aerogel materials)

Specialty fluids (cesium formate drilling fluids)

## COMPETITORS

Aditya Birla Nuvo
Akzo Nobel
Allegheny Technologies
BASF AG
Clariant
Columbian Chemicals
Degussa
Dow Chemical
Flint Group
GE Plastics
J.M. Huber
MacDermid
Mitsubishi Chemical
Tokai Carbon
Wacker Chemie

## HISTORICAL FINANCIALS

Company Type: Public

**Income Statement** FYE: September 30

| | REVENUE ($ mil.) | NET INCOME ($ mil.) | NET PROFIT MARGIN | EMPLOYEES |
|---|---|---|---|---|
| **9/06** | 2,543 | 88 | 3.5% | 4,300 |
| **9/05** | 2,125 | (48) | — | 4,400 |
| **9/04** | 1,934 | 124 | 6.4% | 4,300 |
| **9/03** | 1,795 | 80 | 4.5% | 4,400 |
| **9/02** | 1,557 | 106 | 6.8% | 4,500 |
| **Annual Growth** | 13.0% | (4.5%) | — | (1.1%) |

**2006 Year-End Financials**

Debt ratio: 40.3%
Return on equity: 8.1%
Cash ($ mil.): 190
Current ratio: 2.49
Long-term debt ($ mil.): 459
No. of shares (mil.): 63
Dividends
Yield: 1.7%
Payout: 50.0%
Market value ($ mil.): 2,354

**Stock History** NYSE: CBT

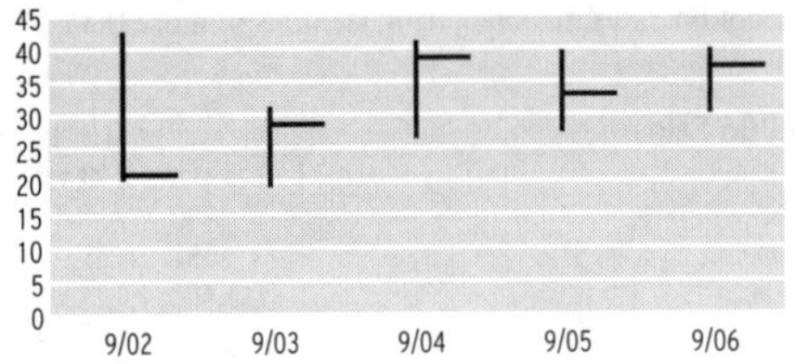

| | STOCK PRICE ($) FY Close | P/E High | P/E Low | PER SHARE ($) Earnings | Dividends | Book Value |
|---|---|---|---|---|---|---|
| **9/06** | 37.20 | 31 | 24 | 1.28 | 0.64 | 18.90 |
| **9/05** | 33.01 | — | — | (0.84) | 0.64 | 17.45 |
| **9/04** | 38.57 | 22 | 15 | 1.82 | 0.60 | 18.89 |
| **9/03** | 28.51 | 27 | 17 | 1.14 | 0.54 | 17.34 |
| **9/02** | 21.00 | 28 | 14 | 1.50 | 0.52 | 15.86 |
| **Annual Growth** | 15.4% | — | — | (3.9%) | 5.3% | 4.5% |

# CACI International

CACI International doesn't need a lot of clients — just a few with deep pockets. Deriving more than 70% of its revenues from the US Department of Defense and nearly 95% from the US government, CACI is one of the largest government information technology (IT) contractors. The company, which also serves commercial clients, provides a wide range of technology services including systems integration, network management, knowledge management, and engineering and simulation. CACI also develops marketing software and databases for sales tracking, demographics reporting, and other market analysis applications, and it provides debt management and litigation support services.

CACI is focusing its efforts on serving large clients such as the Department of Defense, which is increasingly trying to do business with a smaller number of large contractors.

Two of the company's main clients are already part of the Department of Defense: the Defense Information Systems Agency (DISA) and the US Army's Communications-Electronics Command (CECOM). CACI also holds a significant GENESIS II contract with the United States Army Intelligence and Security Command (INSCOM). In addition, civilian agencies such as the Department of Justice (CACI staffs its litigation support services and maintains an automated debt management system), the Department of Veterans Affairs, the Securities and Exchange Commission, the Space and Naval Warfare Systems Command's Naval Tactical Command Support System, and the US Customs Services drive a large portion of CACI's revenues.

CACI in 2006 acquired Falls Church, Virginia-based IT firm AlphaInsight. The deal expands CACI's business with civilian agencies of the federal government including the state and justice department and provides additional contract opportunities with the Department of Homeland Security and the defense department. CACI also acquired Information Systems Support (ISS), a government systems integrator specializing in communications, IT, and logistics. The transaction was completed in early 2006. ISS has approximately 1,100 employees in 10 states and around $200 million in revenues for 2005.

In 2007 CACI announced plans to purchase the Institute for Quality Management, a performance management consultancy and provider of operational support servicers to the intelligence and homeland security community. It additionally plans to acquire government consulting firm Wexford Group.

## HISTORY

In 1962 Harry Markowitz (winner of the 1990 Nobel Memorial Prize in Economic Sciences) and Herb Karr formed California Analysis Center, which provided services related to the SIMSCRIPT programming language. The company went public in 1968 and four years later moved from Santa Monica, California, to the Washington, DC, area. Its name was changed to CACI in the late 1970s. J.P. London, a 12-year company veteran, became CEO in 1984.

Through the 1980s and early 1990s, CACI's dependence on a struggling military sector hurt operations. The company got a big boost in 1991, however, when it won a US Justice Department contract for litigation support services worth $130 million over five years. Profits were revived by 1995. The next year it won a $66 million subcontract to provide information processing support to VGS, a software integration firm charged with building a federal information processing program.

In 1997 CACI gained a foothold in the government and commercial communications services segments when it acquired Infonet Services' Government Systems subsidiary. Also that year it bought AnaData (now CACI Ltd.), a UK-based database marketing software firm. In 1998 the company acquired QuesTech (now CACI Technologies), a computer services contractor to the military and national security segment; CACI began bundling products and services for availability over Internet-based networks.

In 2000 CACI acquired government services specialist XEN Corporation (systems engineering and IT services) and CENTECH (network services and e-commerce) as well as the network services and related assets (Federal Services Business) of net.com.

As part of its growth strategy, in October 2003 CACI acquired C-CUBED Corporation, which provides specialized support services known as C4ISR (Command, Control, Communications, Computers, Intelligence, Surveillance, and Reconnaissance) to clients in the Department of Defense, federal, and intelligence communities.

CACI also acquired intelligence contractor Premier Technology Group (PTG) for an undisclosed amount in mid-2003. Prior to PTG, CACI purchased IT service providers Acton Burnell and Digital Systems International, the Government Solutions Division of Condor Technology Solutions, and Applied Technology Solutions of Northern VA.

The company also purchased CMS Information Services, Inc. (CMS) in 2004. That year it also bought American Management Systems' (AMS) Defense Intelligence Group, which performs work for the Department of Defense and government intelligence agencies. The deal, valued at $415 million, happened in 2004 when CGI Group acquired the entirety of AMS, and then sold part of it to CACI.

In 2007 US operations president Paul Cofoni was named the company's new CEO, replacing London, who retained the title of chairman.

## EXECUTIVES

**Chairman:** J. P. (Jack) London, age 69, $1,560,052 pay
**CEO, CACI Limited and President, Information Solutions Group:** Gregory R. Bradford, age 57, $771,999 pay
**President and CEO:** Paul M. Cofoni, age 58, $980,365 pay
**President, US Operations:** William M. Fairl, age 57, $781,330 pay
**COO, US Operations:** Randall C. (Randy) Fuerst, age 51
**EVP, CFO, and Treasurer:** Thomas A. (Tom) Mutryn, age 52
**EVP Business Development:** Dale Luddeke
**EVP and Chief Human Resources Officer:** H. Robert (Bob) Boehm
**EVP and CTO:** Deborah B. Dunie
**EVP and Director, Corporate Business Development:** Robert V. (Bob) Donovan
**EVP, National Solutions Business Group:** Gail E. Phipps
**EVP, Corporate Strategic Business Development:** Ronald A. (Ron) Schneider
**EVP, Transformation Solutions Business Group:** Gilbert B. (Gil) Guarino
**EVP, Government Business Operations:** Steven H. Weiss
**EVP, Public Relations and Business Communications:** Jody A. Brown
**EVP, Mission Systems Business Group:** Joseph (Keith) Kellogg Jr., age 57
**EVP, Strategic Intelligence Opportunities, National Solutions Group:** Lowell (Jake) Jacoby
**SVP, Acting Director, Legal Division, and Assistant Secretary:** Arnold D. Morse
**SVP, Corporate Controller, and Chief Accounting Officer:** Carol P. Hanna, age 44
**SVP, Financial Accounting:** S. Mark Monticelli
**SVP, Investor Relations:** David Dragics
**Auditors:** Ernst & Young LLP

## LOCATIONS

**HQ:** CACI International Inc
1100 N. Glebe Rd., Ste. 200, Arlington, VA 22201
**Phone:** 703-841-7800 **Fax:** 703-841-7882
**Web:** www.caci.com

CACI International has more than 100 offices in the UK and the US.

**2006 Sales**

| | $ mil. | % of total |
|---|---|---|
| US | 1,692.5 | 96 |
| Other countries | 62.8 | 4 |
| **Total** | **1,755.3** | **100** |

## PRODUCTS/OPERATIONS

### 2006 Sales

| | $ mil. | % of total |
|---|---|---|
| Department of Defense | 1,282.6 | 73 |
| Federal civilian agencies | 374.5 | 21 |
| Commercial | 73.6 | 4 |
| State & local government | 24.6 | 2 |
| **Total** | **1,755.3** | **100** |

### Selected Services

Asset management
Automated procurement
Customer database management integration
Electronic commerce
Engineering support
Information management development
Intelligent document management integration
Knowledge management
Litigation support
Logistics support
Marketing and customer database management development
Networking support
Product data and supply-chain management integration
Records management development
Simulation and modeling languages
Software development
Systems integration and reengineering
Weapons systems/equipment configuration management integration

### Selected Products

Automated bid/contracting systems (QuickBid)
Automated contracting system (SACONS)
Automated procurement systems (Comprizon)
Demographic information software and reports (SITE)
Demographic information systems (ACORN)
Document imaging software (ADIIS)
Electronic mapping software (Map Data)
Internet user demographic information systems (eTypes)
Marketing and demographic information systems (InSite)
Object-based analytical simulation software (SIMPROCESS)
Simulation programming language (SIMSCRIPT)

## COMPETITORS

Affiliated Computer Services
Alion
Apptis
BAE SYSTEMS
Boeing
Booz Allen
Computer Sciences Corp.
EDS
General Dynamics Information Technology
GTSI
IBM
Jacobs Engineering
L-3 Communications
Lockheed Martin
ManTech
Northrop Grumman
Raytheon
SAIC
SRA International
Unisys

## HISTORICAL FINANCIALS

Company Type: Public

### Income Statement

FYE: June 30

| | REVENUE ($ mil.) | NET INCOME ($ mil.) | NET PROFIT MARGIN | EMPLOYEES |
|---|---|---|---|---|
| **6/06** | 1,755 | 85 | 4.8% | 10,400 |
| **6/05** | 1,623 | 85 | 5.3% | 9,600 |
| **6/04** | 1,146 | 64 | 5.6% | 9,300 |
| **6/03** | 843 | 45 | 5.3% | 6,300 |
| **6/02** | 682 | 31 | 4.5% | 5,524 |
| **Annual Growth** | 26.7% | 29.1% | — | 17.1% |

### 2006 Year-End Financials

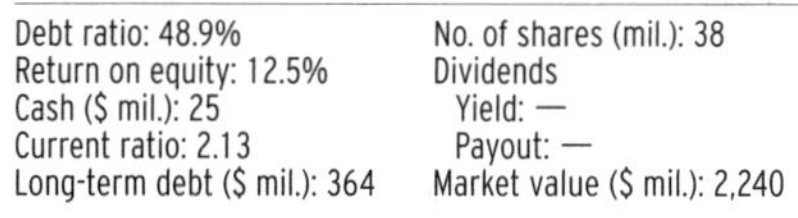

Debt ratio: 48.9%
Return on equity: 12.5%
Cash ($ mil.): 25
Current ratio: 2.13
Long-term debt ($ mil.): 364
No. of shares (mil.): 38
Dividends
Yield: —
Payout: —
Market value ($ mil.): 2,240

### Stock History

NYSE: CAI

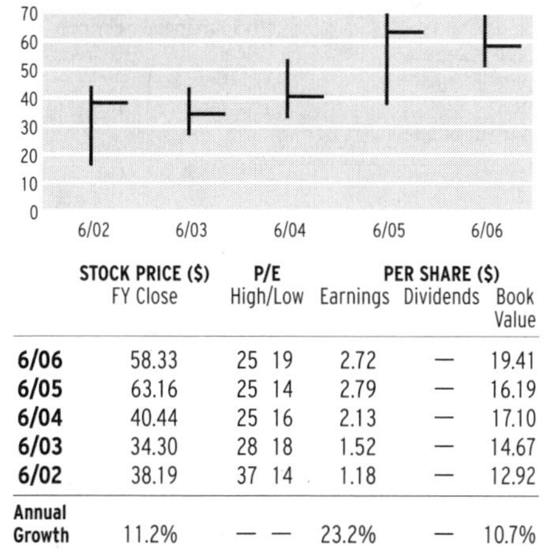


| | STOCK PRICE ($) FY Close | P/E High/Low | | PER SHARE ($) Earnings | Dividends | Book Value |
|---|---|---|---|---|---|---|
| **6/06** | 58.33 | 25 | 19 | 2.72 | — | 19.41 |
| **6/05** | 63.16 | 25 | 14 | 2.79 | — | 16.19 |
| **6/04** | 40.44 | 25 | 16 | 2.13 | — | 17.10 |
| **6/03** | 34.30 | 28 | 18 | 1.52 | — | 14.67 |
| **6/02** | 38.19 | 37 | 14 | 1.18 | — | 12.92 |
| **Annual Growth** | 11.2% | — | — | 23.2% | — | 10.7% |

# CalPERS

California's public-sector retirees already have a place in the sun; CalPERS gives them the money to enjoy it. CalPERS is the California Public Employees' Retirement System, one of the largest public pension systems in the US. It manages retirement and health plans for more than 1.4 million beneficiaries (employees, retirees, and their dependents) from more than 2,500 government agencies and school districts. Even though the system's beneficiaries are current or former employees of the Golden State, CalPERS brings its influence to bear in all 50 states and beyond.

With more than $240 billion in assets in its investment funds, CalPERS uses its clout to sway such corporate governance issues as company performance, executive compensation, and even social policy. In the absence of a strong federal effort to purge corporations of corruption, CalPERS has often acted as a force for reform, urging companies to remove conflicts of interest and make themselves more accountable to shareholders, employees, and the public. CalPERS is also a powerful negotiator for such services as insurance; rates established by the system serve as benchmarks for employers throughout the nation.

Most of CalPERS' revenue comes from its enormous investment program: It has interests in US and foreign securities, real estate development and investment, and even hedge funds and venture capital activities. CalPERS has steadily increased its investments in private equity, looking to take ownership stakes in more firms.

During the coming years CalPERS may be forced to sell assets, as it is expected to be hit with a wave of early retirements by middle-aged workers. In the meantime it is eyeing more short-term investments with higher returns.

CalPERS' board consists of six elected, three appointed, and four designated members (the director of the state's Department of Personnel Administration, the state controller, the state treasurer, and a member of the State Personnel Board). The board has seen its share of disputes, on issues ranging from staff salaries to how to invest assets. The public and sometimes nasty donnybrooks have led to the exodus of several key personnel. In 2004 the president of CalPERS' board, Sean Harrigan, was ousted when the State Personnel Board voted to remove him as its representative. Harrigan had drawn the ire of the business community because of his labor ties and because, under his leadership, the board had withheld votes for directors of most of the companies in which CalPERS invests.

## HISTORY

The state of California founded CalPERS in 1931 to administer a pension fund for state employees. By the 1940s the system was serving other public agencies and educational institutions on a contract basis.

When the Public Employees' Medical and Hospital Care Act was passed in 1962, CalPERS added health coverage. The fund was conservatively managed in-house, with little exposure to stocks. Despite slow growth, the state used the system's funds to meet its own cash shortfalls.

CalPERS became involved in corporate governance issues in the mid-1980s, when California treasurer Jesse Unruh became outraged by corporate greenmail schemes. In 1987 he hired as CEO Wisconsin pension board veteran Dale Hanson, who led the movement for corporate accountability to institutional investors.

In the late 1980s CalPERS moved into real estate and Japanese stocks. When both crashed around 1990, Hanson came under pressure. CalPERS was twice forced to take major write-downs for its real estate holdings and turned to expensive outside fund managers, but its investment performance deteriorated and member services suffered.

Legislation in 1990 enabled CalPERS to offer long-term health insurance. Governor Pete Wilson's 1991 attempt to use $1.6 billion from CalPERS to help meet a state budget shortfall resulted in legislation banning future raids. CalPERS made its first direct investment in 1993, an energy-related infrastructure partnership with Enron.

CalPERS suffered in the 1994 bond crash. That year Hanson resigned amid criticism that his focus on corporate governance had depressed fund performance. The system moved to an indexing strategy.

CalPERS eased its corporate relations stance, creating a separate office to handle investor issues and launching an International Corporate Governance Program. However, the next year CalPERS was uninvited from a KKR investment pool because of criticism of its fund management and fee structure.

In 1996 the system teamed with the Asian Development Bank to invest in the Asia/Pacific region; it took a major hit in the Asian financial crisis the next year, but used the downturn as an opportunity to expand its position there in undervalued stocks. In 1998 CalPERS pressured foreign firms to adopt more transparent financial reporting methods.

In 2000 the system raised health care premiums almost 10% to keep up with rising care costs. It also moved into real estate development, buying Genstar Land Co. with Newland Communities. CalPERS said that year it would sell off more than $500 million in tobacco holdings.

In 2001 California state controller and CalPERS board member Kathleen Connell successfully sued the system for not following state-sanctioned rules regarding pay increases. CalPERS was forced to cut salaries for investment managers, a move that prompted chief investment officer Daniel Szente to resign.

In 2003 CalPERS agreed to a record $250 million settlement relating to an age-discrimination suit brought by the Equal Employment Opportunity Commission. Also that year CalPERS clamored for (and got) the resignation of New York Stock Exchange (NYSE) chairman Richard Grasso. CalPERS and others claimed Grasso's pay of $140 million a year made it impossible for him to effectively monitor the exchange's member companies for corruption.

In another row, CalPERS in 2003 sued the NYSE and several specialist firms, including Bear Wagner Specialists, Fleet Specialist, LaBranche & Co, and Van der Moolen Holding's Van Der Moolen Specialists USA. The pension fund's suit accused the exchange and the specialists of using the trading system for their own gain at the expense of investors. CalPERS found itself on the receiving end of a corporate governance issue in 2004 when a media group sued, demanding CalPERS make public the fees it pays to venture capital firms and hedge funds. CalPERS settled the suit by disclosing the fees.

## EXECUTIVES

**President, Board:** Rob Feckner
**CEO:** Fred R. Buenrostro Jr., age 54
**Deputy Executive Officer, Operations:** Gloria Moore Andrews
**Deputy Executive Officer, Benefits Administration:** Jarvio A. Grevious
**Assistant Executive Officer, Public Affairs:** Patricia K. Macht
**Assistant Executive Officer, Administrative Services:** John Hiber
**Assistant Executive Officer, Information Technology Services:** Ronald E. (Gene) Reich
**Assistant Executive Officer, Investment Operations:** Anne Stausboll
**Assistant Executive Officer, Actuarial and Employer Services Branch:** Kenneth W. Marzion
**Assistant Executive Officer, Member and Benefit Services Branch:** Kathie Vaughn
**Assistant Executive Officer, Health Benefits:** Terri Westbrook
**Assistant Division Chief, Public Affairs:** Brad W. Pacheco
**Chief Actuary:** Ronald L. (Ron) Seeling
**Chief Compliance Officer:** Sherry Johnstone
**Chief Investment Officer:** Russell Read
**Chief, Benefit Services Division:** Donna Lum
**Chief, Customer Service and Education Division:** Ron Kraft
**Chief, Fiscal Services Division:** Russ Fong
**Chief, Innovation Services Division:** Terry Bridges
**Chief, Member Services:** Darryl Watson
**Interim Chief, Office of Governmental Affairs:** Danny Brown
**Chief, Policy & Program Development:** Ken Nitschke
**General Counsel:** Peter H. Mixon
**Auditors:** Macias, Gini & Company LLP

## LOCATIONS

**HQ:** California Public Employees' Retirement System
Lincoln Plaza, 400 Q St., Sacramento, CA 95814
**Phone:** 916-795-3829 **Fax:** 916-795-4001
**Web:** www.calpers.ca.gov

## COMPETITORS

A.G. Edwards
AllianceBernstein
AXA Financial
Charles Schwab
Citigroup Global Markets
FMR
Franklin Resources
Janus Capital
Legg Mason
Merrill Lynch
MFS
Morgan Stanley
Nationwide Financial
Principal Financial
Putnam
Raymond James Financial
State Street
T. Rowe Price
TIAA-CREF
UBS Financial Services
USAA
VALIC
The Vanguard Group

## HISTORICAL FINANCIALS

Company Type: Government-owned

**Income Statement** FYE: June 30

| | ASSETS ($ mil.) | NET INCOME ($ mil.) | INCOME AS % OF ASSETS | EMPLOYEES |
|---|---|---|---|---|
| **6/06** | 254,763 | — | — | 1,924 |
| **6/05** | 235,759 | — | — | 1,924 |
| **6/04** | 198,633 | — | — | 1,687 |
| **6/03** | 173,333 | — | — | 1,687 |
| **6/02** | 162,167 | — | — | 1,614 |
| **Annual Growth** | 12.0% | — | — | 4.5% |

**Asset History**

300,000
250,000
200,000
150,000
100,000
50,000
0
6/02 6/03 6/04 6/05 6/06

# Campbell Soup

Soup means *M'm! M'm! Money!* for the Campbell Soup Company. The company is the world's biggest soup maker; its almost 70% share in the US is led by Campbell's chicken noodle, tomato, and cream of mushroom soups. The company also makes meal kits, Franco-American sauces and canned pasta, Godiva chocolates, Pace picante sauce, Pepperidge Farm baked goods (yes, the goldfish crackers you sneak at midnight), and V8 beverages. Its Australian division produces snack food and its popular "down-under" Arnott's biscuit brand. Descendants of John Dorrance, who invented condensed soup, own approximately 43% of Campbell.

Campbell is striving to heat up lukewarm sales as consumers seek more convenience in the kitchen and competitors slurp into its market share. The company offers meal-kits, ready-to-serve soups in pop-top, resealable, and microwaveable containers.

Challenged on quality and in sales by General Mills' Progresso brand, Campbell has tried boosting the taste of its products — adding more veggies to its vegetable soup, and making its cream soups creamier. The company's Away From Home unit is following customers out of the kitchen, selling soup and buns to cafeterias, fast-food restaurants, and harried consumers via the supermarket. It has also added microwaveable versions of its Chunky and Select soups.

Soup is not the company's only sustenance: Campbell also operates Godiva chocolate boutiques around the world. But a change of menu is in the offing at Campbell. In an effort to concentrate on its soup and snacks businesses, the company put Godiva up for sale in 2007.

## HISTORY

Campbell Soup Company began in Camden, New Jersey, in 1869 as a canning and preserving business founded by icebox maker Abram Anderson and fruit merchant Joseph Campbell. Anderson left in 1876 and Arthur Dorrance took his place. The Dorrance family assumed control after Campbell retired in 1894.

Arthur's nephew, John Dorrance, joined Campbell in 1897. The young chemist soon found a way to condense soup by eliminating most of its water. Without the heavy bulk of water-filled cans, distribution was cheaper; Campbell products quickly spread.

In 1904 the firm introduced the Campbell Kids characters. Entering the California market in 1911, Campbell became one of the first US companies to achieve national distribution of a food brand. It bought Franco-American, the first American soup maker, in 1915.

The company's ubiquity in American kitchens made its soup can an American icon (consider Andy Warhol's celebrated 1960 print) and brought great wealth to the Dorrance family.

With a reputation for conservative management, Campbell began to diversify, acquiring V8 juice (1948), Swanson (1955), Pepperidge Farm (1961), Godiva Chocolatier (33% in 1966, full ownership in 1974), Vlasic pickles (1978), and Mrs. Paul's seafood (1982). It introduced Prego spaghetti sauce and LeMenu frozen dinners in the early 1980s.

Much of Campbell's sales growth in the 1990s came not from unit sales but from increasing its prices. In 1993 it took a $300 million restructuring charge, and over the next two years it sold poor performers at home and abroad. John Sr.'s grandson, Bennett Dorrance, took up the role of vice chairman in 1993, becoming the first family member to take a senior executive position in 10 years.

In 1995 Campbell paid $1.1 billion for Pace Foods (picante sauce) and acquired Fresh Start Bakeries (buns and muffins for McDonald's) and Homepride (popular cooking sauce in the UK).

As part of its international expansion, in 1996 the firm acquired Erasco, a top German soup maker, and Cheong Chan, a food manufacturer in Malaysia. However, back at home it sold Mrs. Paul's. In 1997 Campbell sold its Marie's salad dressing unit and bought Groupe Danone's Liebig (France's leading wet-soup brand). Also that year Dale Morrison, a relative newcomer to the firm, succeeded David Johnson as president and CEO. To reduce costs and focus on other core segments, in 1998 Campbell spun off Swanson frozen foods and Vlasic pickles into Vlasic Foods International. (Vlasic later filed bankruptcy and was snapped up in a leveraged buyout.) In 1999 Campbell redesigned its soup can labels, altering an American icon.

Morrison resigned abruptly as president and CEO in 2000; Johnson returned to the helm during the search for a permanent chief. In early 2001 Douglas Conant, previously of Nabisco Foods, joined Campbell as president and CEO. A fresh plan was introduced to spend up to

$600 million on marketing, product development, and quality upgrades (at the expense of shareholder dividends). In 2001 Campbell also bought the Batchelors, Royco, and Heisse Tasse brands of soup, as well as the Oxo brand of stock cubes, from Unilever for about $900 million. The deal made Campbell the leading soup maker in Europe. In 2003 Campbell bought Snack Foods Limited, a leading snack food maker in Australia, and Irish dry soup maker Erin Foods from Greencore.

Campbell reorganized its North American business in 2004 into the following units: US Soup, Sauces, and Beverages; Campbell Away From Home, and Canada, Mexico, and Latin America; Pepperidge Farm; and Godiva Worldwide. (In response to dietary trends, the company announced that year that it was removing all transfatty acids from its Pepperidge Farm breads.) The company retired the Franco-American brand in 2004; products which carried the brand (most notably SpaghettiOs) now bear the Campbell brand. Also that year company chairman George M. Sherman retired and was replaced by Harvey Golub.

In 2006 Campbell sold its UK and Irish businesses to Premier Foods for about $870 million. Brands involved in the sale included Homepride sauces, OXO stock cubes, and Batchelors, McDonnells, and Erin soups.

## EXECUTIVES

**Chairman:** Harvey Golub, age 67
**President, CEO, and Director:** Douglas R. Conant, age 56, $3,577,500 pay
**EVP and President, Campbell North America:** Mark A. Sarvary, age 47, $1,467,132 pay
**SVP and CFO:** Robert A. Schiffner, age 56, $1,058,250 pay
**SVP, Chief Human Resources and Communications Officer:** Nancy A. Reardon, age 54
**SVP and CIO:** Doreen A. Wright, age 50
**SVP and Chief Strategy Officer:** M. Carl Johnson III, age 58
**SVP, Global Research and Development and Quality:** Arthur B. Anderson
**SVP, Global Supply Chain:** David R. White, age 51
**SVP, Law and Government Affairs:** Ellen Oran Kaden, age 55, $1,135,457 pay
**SVP; President, Campbell International:** Larry S. McWilliams, age 50, $1,055,000 pay
**SVP; President, US Soup, Sauces, and Beverages:** Denise M. Morrison, age 53
**SVP, Public Affairs:** Jerry S. Buckley
**SVP, Sales US:** Mike Salzberg
**VP, Taxes:** Richard J. Landers
**VP and Controller:** Anthony P. DiSilvestro, age 47
**VP and Corporate Secretary:** John J. Furey
**VP and Treasurer:** William J. O'Shea
**Auditors:** PricewaterhouseCoopers LLP

## LOCATIONS

**HQ:** Campbell Soup Company
1 Campbell Place, Camden, NJ 08103
**Phone:** 856-342-4800 **Fax:** 856-342-3878
**Web:** www.campbellsoup.com

Campbell Soup Company has principal manufacturing facilities in Australia, Belgium, Canada, France, Germany, Indonesia, Malaysia, Mexico, the Netherlands, Sweden, and the US. Its products are available worldwide.

### 2006 Sales

| | $ mil. | % of total |
|---|---|---|
| US | 5,120 | 70 |
| Australia/Asia Pacific | 988 | 13 |
| Europe | 660 | 9 |
| Other countries | 575 | 8 |
| **Total** | **7,343** | **100** |

## PRODUCTS/OPERATIONS

### 2006 Sales

| | $ mil. | % of total |
|---|---|---|
| US soup, sauces & beverages | 3,257 | 44 |
| Baking & snacking | 1,747 | 24 |
| International soup & sauces | 1,255 | 17 |
| Other | 1,084 | 15 |
| **Total** | **7,343** | **100** |

### Selected Brand Names

Domestic
- Campbell's (soups)
- Godiva (chocolates, ice cream, and liqueur)
- Pace (Mexican sauces)
- Pepperidge Farm (cookies and crackers)
- Prego (pasta sauces)
- Stockpot (foodservice soups)
- Swanson (broths)
- V8 and V8 Splash (vegetable and fruit juices)

International
- Arnott's (biscuits, crackers, and potato chips; Australia)
- Erasco (soups, Germany)
- Godiva (chocolate)
- Heisse Tasse (soups, Germany)
- Lesieur (sauces, France)
- Royco (soups, Belgium and France)
- V8 Splash (beverages)

## COMPETITORS

Bush Brothers
Cadbury Schweppes
Canyon Creek Food Company
ConAgra
Del Monte Foods
Ferrero
Frito-Lay
General Mills
Harry's Fresh Foods
Heinz
Hershey
Hormel
Kellogg Snacks
Kellogg USA
Kraft Foods
Kraft International Commercial
Kraft North America Commercial
Lindt & Sprüngli
Mars
Mott's
Nestlé
Nestlé USA
Ocean Spray
PepsiCo
Reily Foods
Unilever
Unilever Foodsolutions

## HISTORICAL FINANCIALS

Company Type: Public

### Income Statement

FYE: Sunday nearest July 31

| | REVENUE ($ mil.) | NET INCOME ($ mil.) | NET PROFIT MARGIN | EMPLOYEES |
|---|---|---|---|---|
| **7/06** | 7,343 | 766 | 10.4% | 24,000 |
| **7/05** | 7,548 | 707 | 9.4% | 24,000 |
| **7/04** | 7,109 | 647 | 9.1% | 24,000 |
| **7/03** | 6,678 | 595 | 8.9% | 25,000 |
| **7/02** | 6,133 | 525 | 8.6% | 25,000 |
| **Annual Growth** | 4.6% | 9.9% | — | (1.0%) |

### 2006 Year-End Financials

Debt ratio: 123.6%
Return on equity: 50.4%
Cash ($ mil.): 657
Current ratio: 0.71
Long-term debt ($ mil.): 2,186
No. of shares (mil.): 402
Dividends
Yield: 2.0%
Payout: 38.9%
Market value ($ mil.): 14,782

### Stock History

NYSE: CPB

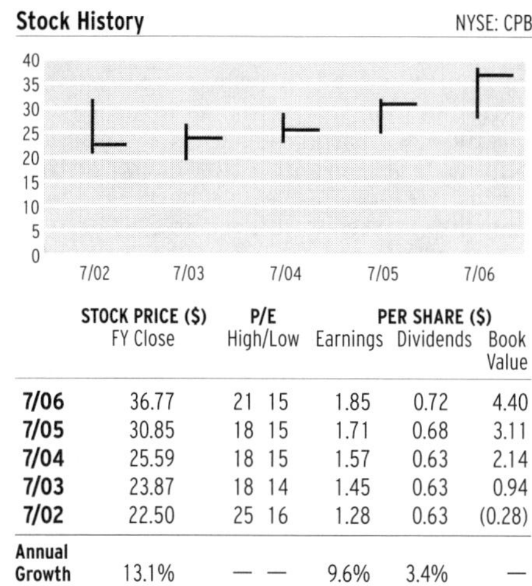

| | STOCK PRICE ($) FY Close | P/E High | P/E Low | PER SHARE ($) Earnings | Dividends | Book Value |
|---|---|---|---|---|---|---|
| **7/06** | 36.77 | 21 | 15 | 1.85 | 0.72 | 4.40 |
| **7/05** | 30.85 | 18 | 15 | 1.71 | 0.68 | 3.11 |
| **7/04** | 25.59 | 18 | 15 | 1.57 | 0.63 | 2.14 |
| **7/03** | 23.87 | 18 | 14 | 1.45 | 0.63 | 0.94 |
| **7/02** | 22.50 | 25 | 16 | 1.28 | 0.63 | (0.28) |
| **Annual Growth** | 13.1% | — | — | 9.6% | 3.4% | — |

# Capital One Financial

Capital One isn't #1, but it's pretty darn close. One of the top credit card issuers in the US, the company offers Visa and MasterCard plastic with a variety of annual percentage rates, credit limits, finance charges, and fees. Products range from platinum and gold cards for preferred customers to secured and unsecured cards for customers with poor or limited credit histories. The company, which boasts nearly 50 million customer accounts, also provides mortgage services, auto financing, credit insurance, and other consumer lending products. Immersing itself in the banking business, Capital One bought regional bank holding company North Fork Bancorporation in 2006.

The $13.2 billion stock-and-cash deal gives the company more than 250 bank branches in New York, New Jersey, and Connecticut. It comes on the heels of the 2005 purchase of another regional bank, New Orleans-based Hibernia, in a stock and cash transaction valued at some $5 billion, about 9% less than the originally agreed-upon price. The transaction was delayed, then renegotiated, after Hurricane Katrina devastated Hibernia's home city. Hibernia, which relocated to Houston, adopted the Capital One moniker. The bank is opening new branches in Texas as well.

Prior to the acquisitions, Capital One Financial's bank subsidiaries basically offered only consumer loans, credit cards, and deposit products. The company hopes the Hibernia and North Fork deals will expand its customer base, strengthen its balance sheet, and lower its cost of borrowing. The transactions also built Capital One into one of the 15 largest banks in the US in less than two years.

Continuing to diversify its operations, Capital One expanded its auto financing business with the purchases of Onyx Acceptance, as well as KeyCorp's non-prime auto loan portfolio, in 2005, to go along with previously existing subsidiary Capital One Auto Finance. The deals augment the company's dealer relationships, market penetration, and product offerings among prime borrowers.

Capital One works hard to keep the *custom* in customer. Its cards are decked in themes ranging from kittens to pro wrestlers; card terms run the gamut from secured cards with annual fees (for those with spotty credit) to a low annual percentage rate, no-fee card that offers cash back (for affluent "superprime" customers). The company also markets to college and high school students. All told, the firm manages almost $150 billion in consumer debt.

Capital One Financial also pursues mammon through its mammoth database. When customers call Capital One to check balances or make payments, chances are they'll be offered goods or services that match their profiles from the company's colossal database. Under this information-based strategy, Capital One pitches such customized products as affinity cards, home mortgages, car insurance, and shopping catalogs to incoming callers.

The UK is Capital One's largest international market. To broaden its presence there, Capital One bought home equity loan broker Hfs Group in 2005. Capital One is also active in Canada.

Institutional investors Dodge & Cox (more than 7%) and Wellington Management (5%) are Capital One's largest shareholders.

## HISTORY

Capital One Financial is a descendant of the Bank of Virginia, which was formed in 1945. The company began issuing products similar to credit cards in 1953 and was MasterCard issuer #001. Acquisitions and mergers brought some 30 banks and several finance and mortgage companies under the bank's umbrella between 1962 and 1986, when Bank of Virginia became Signet Banking.

Signet's credit card operations had reached a million customers in 1988, when the bank hired consultants Richard Fairbank and Nigel Morris (eventually the top two officers at Capital One) to implement their "Information-Based Strategy." Under the duo's leadership, the bank began using sophisticated data-collection methods to gather massive amounts of information on existing or prospective customers; it then used the information to design and mass-market customized products to the customer.

In 1991 — after creating an enormous database and developing sophisticated screening processes and direct-mail marketing tactics — Signet escalated the credit card wars, luring customers from its rivals with its innovative balance-transfer credit card. The card let customers of other companies transfer what they owed on higher-interest cards to a Signet card with a lower introductory rate.

The new card immediately drew imitators (by 1997 balance-transfer cards accounted for 85% of credit card solicitations). After skimming off the least risky customers, Fairbank and Morris began going after less desirable credit customers who could be charged higher rates. The result was what they call second-generation products — secured and unsecured cards with lower credit lines and higher annual percentage rates and fees for higher-risk customers.

The credit card business had grown to 5 million customers by 1994, but at a high cost to Signet, which had devoted most of its resources to finding and servicing credit card holders. That year Signet spun off its credit card business as Capital One to focus on banking. (Signet was later acquired by First Union.)

The company expanded into Florida and Texas in 1995 and into Canada and the UK in 1996; that year it established its savings bank, mainly to offer products and services to its cardholders. In 1997 the company used this unit to move into deposit accounts, buying a deposit portfolio from J. C. Penney. In 1998 the company began marketing its products to such clients as immigrants and high school students (whose parents must co-sign for the card). The company also expanded in terms of products and geography, acquiring auto lender Summit Acceptance and opening a new office in Nottingham, England.

In 1999 the firm's growth continued. The company stepped up its marketing efforts and was rewarded with significant boosts to its noninterest income and customer base. The next year the company launched The Capital One Place, an Internet shopping site. In 2001 the company acquired AmeriFee, which provides loans for elective medical and dental surgery; and PeopleFirst, Inc., the nation's largest online provider of direct motor vehicle loans.

In response to industry-wide concern over subprime lending, Capital One agreed in 2002 to beef up reserves on its subprime portfolio. Also in 2002, the company's UK operations proved profitable for the first time.

## EXECUTIVES

**Chairman, President, and CEO:** Richard D. (Rich) Fairbank, age 56
**EVP and CFO:** Gary L. Perlin, age 55, $1,601,666 pay
**EVP and CIO:** Gregor S. Bailar, age 43
**EVP and Chief Credit Officer:** Peter A. Schnall, age 43
**EVP and Chief Commercial Credit Risk Officer:** Suzanne Hammett, age 52
**EVP and Chief Human Resources Officer:** Matthew W. (Matt) Schuyler, age 41
**EVP and Head of U.S. Card Business:** Jory Berson, age 37
**EVP; President, Banking:** J. Herbert (Herb) Boydstun, age 60
**EVP; President and CEO, Capital One Auto Finance:** David R. (Dave) Lawson, age 59, $1,302,083 pay
**EVP, Corporate Reputation and Governance, General Counsel, and Corporate Secretary:** John G. Finneran Jr., age 57, $1,402,083 pay
**EVP, Global Financial Services:** Larry A. Klane, age 46, $865,327 pay
**EVP, Enterprise Customer Management:** Robert M. Alexander
**SVP and Chief Internal Auditor:** Thomas E. Emerson
**Treasurer:** Steve Linehan
**Director, Corporate Media:** Tatiana Stead
**President, Banking:** Lynn Pike
**Investor Relations:** Jeff Norris
**Public Relations:** Diana Don
**SVP Corporate Affairs:** Richard Woods
**Auditors:** Ernst & Young LLP

## LOCATIONS

**HQ:** Capital One Financial Corporation
1680 Capital One Dr., McLean, VA 22102
**Phone:** 703-720-1000 **Fax:** 804-284-5728
**Web:** www.capitalone.com

## PRODUCTS/OPERATIONS

**2006 Sales**

| | $ mil. | % of total |
|---|---|---|
| Interest | | |
| Loans | 7,117.5 | 47 |
| Securities available for sale | 676.7 | 4 |
| Other | 400.0 | 3 |
| Noninterest | | |
| Servicing & securitizations | 4,209.6 | 28 |
| Service charges & other customer fees | 1,770.4 | 11 |
| Interchange | 549.1 | 4 |
| Mortgage banking | 173.3 | 1 |
| Other | 294.4 | 2 |
| **Total** | **15,191.0** | **100** |

## COMPETITORS

American Express
AmeriCredit
Bank of America
CIT Group
Citigroup
Credit Acceptance
Discover
HSBC Finance
JPMorgan Chase
Wells Fargo

## HISTORICAL FINANCIALS

Company Type: Public

**Income Statement** FYE: December 31

| | ASSETS ($ mil.) | NET INCOME ($ mil.) | INCOME AS % OF ASSETS | EMPLOYEES |
|---|---|---|---|---|
| **12/06** | 149,739 | 2,415 | 1.6% | 31,800 |
| **12/05** | 88,701 | 1,809 | 2.0% | 21,000 |
| **12/04** | 53,747 | 1,544 | 2.9% | 14,481 |
| **12/03** | 46,284 | 1,136 | 2.5% | 17,760 |
| **12/02** | 37,382 | 900 | 2.4% | 18,757 |
| **Annual Growth** | 41.5% | 28.0% | — | 14.1% |

**2006 Year-End Financials**

Equity as % of assets: 16.9%
Return on assets: 2.0%
Return on equity: 12.3%
Long-term debt ($ mil.): 33,982
No. of shares (mil.): 410
Dividends
Yield: 0.2%
Payout: 1.7%
Market value ($ mil.): 31,490
Sales ($ mil.): 15,191

**Stock History** NYSE: COF

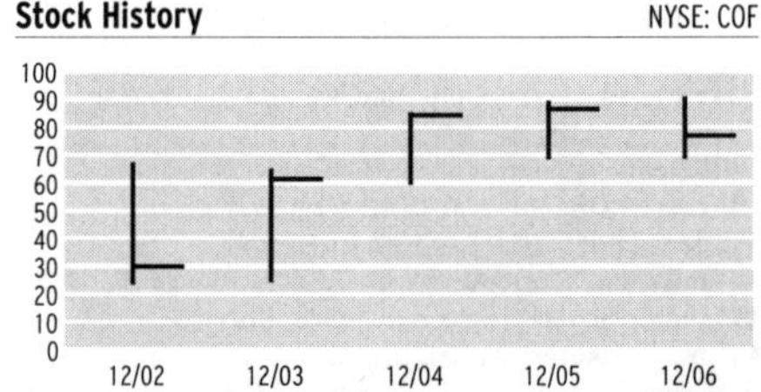

| | STOCK PRICE ($) FY Close | P/E High | P/E Low | PER SHARE ($) Earnings | Dividends | Book Value |
|---|---|---|---|---|---|---|
| **12/06** | 76.82 | 12 | 9 | 7.62 | 0.13 | 61.56 |
| **12/05** | 86.40 | 13 | 10 | 6.73 | 0.11 | 46.92 |
| **12/04** | 84.21 | 14 | 10 | 6.21 | 0.11 | 33.94 |
| **12/03** | 61.29 | 13 | 5 | 4.85 | 0.11 | 25.75 |
| **12/02** | 29.72 | 17 | 6 | 3.93 | 0.11 | 20.44 |
| **Annual Growth** | 26.8% | — | — | 18.0% | 4.3% | 31.7% |

# Cardinal Health

Cardinal Health seeks to deliver medicine to all points of the compass. The company is the second-largest distributor of pharmaceuticals and other medical supplies and equipment in the US; McKesson is #1. The largest of the company's business segments is health care supply chain services, which includes the company's medical product distribution and nuclear pharmacy services divisions and accounts for about 60% of the firm's revenues. Cardinal Health's other business segments include medical products manufacturing, generic intravenous medicines, pharmaceutical regulatory consulting, and clinical technologies and services.

Cardinal Health's medical and surgical products segment manufactures and distributes surgical supplies, instruments, and apparel to hospitals and other medical facilities. The company also offers drug delivery systems, packaging services, and development services through its pharmaceutical technologies and services unit. Its clinical technologies and services segment offers automated pharmacy equipment and clinical information system services.

Cardinal reorganized its business in 2005, combining its three distribution lines (pharmaceutical, medical products, and nuclear pharmacy services) into one division in order to streamline its logistical operations. Its reportable segments now fall under three categories: pharmaceutical distribution and provider services; medical products and services; and clinical technologies and services.

Cardinal Health has expanded through acquisitions of companies and products within those four segments. Since 1980, Cardinal Health has acquired more than 40 companies, including medical products company Alaris Medical Systems, gelcap maker R.P. Scherer, drug distributors Medicine Shoppe International and Bindley Western, medical and surgical supplies distributor Allegiance Healthcare (now known as Cardinal Medical Products and Services), radiopharmaceutical maker Syncor International, and generic drug distributor ParMed Pharmaceuticals.

In 2007 Cardinal dropped about $1.5 billion on medical equipment manufacturer Viasys Healthcare. Viasys develops and produces specialized equipment like ventilators, feeding tubes, patient monitoring systems, orthopedic implants, and medical imaging components for the neuroscience, orthopedic, respiratory care, critical care, and surgical care markets.

On the paring side, the company unloaded its health care marketing services unit; it has also announced plans to shutter its small drug division, which traded excess inventories on the secondary drug market with other wholesalers. Even more significantly, in 2007 Cardinal sold its pharmaceutical technologies and services division to The Blackstone Group for $3.3 billion. As part of the deal, Cardinal will hang onto two businesses which complement its generic pharmaceutical operations.

With CEO Kerry Clark taking charge in April 2006, Cardinal plunges ahead: it joined the "bird flu crew" by signing a collaborative agreement with Roche Diagnostics for the production and distribution of avian flu treatment Tamiflu; later it acquired data miner MedMined, which tracks adverse health events such as the occurrence of deadly infections in hospitals.

## HISTORY

Cardinal Health harks back to Cardinal Foods, a food wholesaler named for Ohio's state bird. In 1971 Robert Walter, then 26 and with the ink still fresh on his Harvard MBA, acquired Cardinal in a leveraged buyout. He hoped to grow Cardinal by acquisitions but was frustrated when he found that the food distribution industry was already highly consolidated.

In 1980 Cardinal moved into pharmaceuticals distribution with the acquisition of Zanesville. It went public in 1983 as Cardinal Distribution and Walter began looking for more acquisitions. Cardinal soon expanded nationwide by swallowing other distributors. During the 1980s these purchases included two pharmaceuticals distributors headquartered in New York and a Massachusetts-based pharmaceuticals and food distributor. In 1988 Cardinal sold its food group, including Midland Grocery Co. and Mr. Moneysworth Inc., to Roundy's and narrowed its focus to pharmaceuticals.

Drug distributors joined the rest of the pharmaceutical industry in its rush toward consolidation during the 1990s. Cardinal's acquisitions in those years included Ohio Valley-Clarksburg (1990, the Mid-Atlantic), Chapman Drug Co. (1991, Tennessee), PRN Services (1993, Michigan), Solomons Co. (1993, Georgia), Humiston-Keeling (1994, Illinois), and Behrens (1994, Texas).

One of Cardinal's most important acquisitions during this period was its cash purchase of Whitmire Distribution in 1994. Formerly Amfac Health Care, Whitmire had been a subsidiary of Amfac, one of Hawaii's "Big Five" landholders. When Amfac Health Care was spun off in 1988, its president, Melburn Whitmire, led a management group that acquired a majority interest. When Cardinal bought it, Whitmire was the US's #6 drug wholesaler; the purchase bumped Cardinal up to #3. At that time the company changed its name to Cardinal Health and Melburn Whitmire became Cardinal's vice chairman.

In 1995 Cardinal made its biggest acquisition yet when it purchased St. Louis-based Medicine Shoppe International, the US's largest franchisor of independent retail pharmacies. Founded by two St. Louis obstetricians in 1970, the Medicine Shoppe had 987 US outlets and 107 abroad at the time of its purchase by Cardinal (for $348 million in stock).

Since that time, Cardinal has continued to grow through acquisitions, including automatic drug dispensing system maker Pyxis, pharmaceutical packaging company PCI Services, and pharmacy management services company Owen Healthcare.

In 1998, however, plans to acquire Bergen Brunswig were blocked by the Federal Trade Commission, along with rival McKesson's bid to buy AmeriSource Health. This did not deter the company from its strategy, which acquired surgical equipment company Alliance about a year later.

## EXECUTIVES

**Chairman:** Robert D. (Bob) Walter, age 61, $3,976,643 pay
**President, CEO, and Director:** R. Kerry Clark, age 54, $756,428 pay
**EVP and CFO:** Jeffrey Henderson, age 41, $437,537 pay
**EVP and Chief Ethics and Compliance Officer:** Daniel J. Walsh, age 51
**EVP, Human Resources:** Carole S. Watkins, age 46
**EVP, Quality and Regulatory Affairs:** Gary D. Dolch, age 59
**EVP, Communications:** Shelley Bird
**EVP Strategy and Corporate Development:** Vivek Jain, age 35
**EVP and Controller:** Jim Hinrichs, age 39
**Chief Legal Officer and Secretary:** Ivan K. Fong, age 45
**Chief Medical Officer:** Stephen R. Lewis
**VP, Marketing:** Eric Timm
**Chairman and CEO, Clinical Technologies and Services; CEO, Pharmaceutical Technologies and Services and Medical Products Manufacturing:** David L. (Dave) Schlotterbeck, age 59, $1,356,810 pay
**CEO, Healthcare Supply Chain Services:** Mark W. Parrish, age 51
**Chairman and CEO, Pharmaceutical Technologies and Services:** Joseph C. Papa, age 51
**Group President, Medical Products Manufacturing:** Michael Lynch
**Group President, Healthcare Supply Chain Services Medical Segment:** Michael C. Kaufmann, age 45
**Group President, Healthcare Supply Chain Services-Pharmaceutical:** Scott A. Storrer, age 40
**Auditors:** Ernst & Young LLP

## LOCATIONS

**HQ:** Cardinal Health, Inc.
7000 Cardinal Place, Dublin, OH 43017
**Phone:** 614-757-5000 **Fax:** 614-757-8871
**Web:** www.cardinal.com

Cardinal Health operates manufacturing and distribution facilities in 44 US states and Puerto Rico; it also has international facilities in Argentina, Australia, Belgium, Brazil, Canada, the Dominican Republic, France, Germany, Ireland, Italy, Japan, Malaysia, Malta, Mexico, the Netherlands, Thailand, and the UK.

## PRODUCTS/OPERATIONS

### 2006 Sales

| | $ mil. | % of total |
|---|---|---|
| Pharmaceutical distribution & provider services | 67,100.7 | 81 |
| Medical products & services | 10,013.8 | 12 |
| Pharmaceutical technologies & services | 2,826.4 | 4 |
| Clinical technologies & services | 2,430.3 | 3 |
| Other | (1,007.6) | — |
| **Total** | **81,363.6** | **100** |

### Selected Subsidiaries

Allegiance Corporation
Armand Scott, LLC
C. International, Inc.
Cardinal Health 303, Inc. (formerly ALARIS Medical Systems, Inc.)
Cardinal Health 409, Inc. (formerly R.P. Scherer Corporation)
Cardinal Health Systems, Inc.
Cardinal Health Technologies, LLC
Centricity, LLC
CMI Net, Inc.
Diagnostic Purchasing Group, Inc.
Dover Communications, LLC
Ellipticare, LLC
Leader Drugstores, Inc.
Medicine Shoppe International, Inc.
OnPointe Medical Communications, LLC

## COMPETITORS

AmerisourceBergen
B. Braun Medical
Baxter
Henry Schein
Hospira
Johnson & Johnson
McKesson
Moore Medical
Omnicell
Owens & Minor
PSS World Medical

## HISTORICAL FINANCIALS

Company Type: Public

### Income Statement

FYE: June 30

| | REVENUE ($ mil.) | NET INCOME ($ mil.) | NET PROFIT MARGIN | EMPLOYEES |
|---|---|---|---|---|
| **6/06** | 81,364 | 1,000 | 1.2% | 55,000 |
| **6/05** | 74,911 | 1,051 | 1.4% | 55,000 |
| **6/04** | 65,054 | 1,475 | 2.3% | 55,000 |
| **6/03** | 56,737 | 1,406 | 2.5% | 50,000 |
| **6/02** | 51,136 | 1,056 | 2.1% | 50,000 |
| **Annual Growth** | 12.3% | (1.4%) | — | 2.4% |

### 2006 Year-End Financials

| | |
|---|---|
| Debt ratio: 30.6% | No. of shares (mil.): 411 |
| Return on equity: 11.7% | Dividends |
| Cash ($ mil.): 2,109 | Yield: 0.4% |
| Current ratio: 1.30 | Payout: 11.6% |
| Long-term debt ($ mil.): 2,600 | Market value ($ mil.): 26,427 |

### Stock History

NYSE: CAH

| | STOCK PRICE ($) FY Close | P/E High | P/E Low | PER SHARE ($) Earnings | Dividends | Book Value |
|---|---|---|---|---|---|---|
| **6/06** | 64.33 | 33 | 24 | 2.33 | 0.27 | 20.67 |
| **6/05** | 57.58 | 25 | 15 | 2.41 | 0.15 | 20.07 |
| **6/04** | 70.05 | 23 | 16 | 3.35 | 0.12 | 18.51 |
| **6/03** | 64.30 | 23 | 15 | 3.10 | 0.10 | 17.30 |
| **6/02** | 61.41 | 33 | 26 | 2.30 | 0.10 | 14.24 |
| **Annual Growth** | 1.2% | — | — | 0.3% | 28.2% | 9.8% |

# Cargill, Incorporated

Cargill may be private, but it's highly visible. The US's second largest private corporation (after Koch Industries), Cargill's diversified operations include grain, cotton, sugar, and petroleum trading; financial trading; food processing; futures brokering; and agricultural services including animal feed and fertilizer production. The company is the leading grain producer in the US, and its Excel unit is one of the top US meatpackers. Cargill's brands include Diamond Crystal (salt), Gerkens (cocoa), Honeysuckle White (poultry), and Sterling Silver (fresh meats).

Being private doesn't mean Cargill is cut off from the world. The agribusiness giant has operations in 63 countries throughout the world. Along with its grain and meatpacking businesses, Cargill is a commodity trader and a producer of animal feed and crop fertilizers. It is also a global supplier of oils, syrups, flour, and other products used in food processing.

Long the largest private company in the US, it lost that title in 2005 when conglomerate Koch Industries acquired forest products maker Georgia-Pacific Corp. However, Cargill is still a powerhouse. It is involved in petroleum trading, financial trading, futures brokering, and shipping. To focus on processing, Cargill sold its seed operations and coffee trading business and is selling part of its steel business. It formed a joint venture with Hormel Foods to market fresh beef, along with pork, under the Always Tender brand. Cargill is also a major US supplier for McDonald's, providing the burger behemoth with eggs, oils, sauces, and beef products.

Diving into the US's health care morass, in 2006 Cargill announced the formation of Harvest Health, a Cargill-funded health care plan for grain farmers. The company contributes up to $5,450 per family or $2,700 per individual per year in exchange for which the farmer contributes up to 25% of his or her annual corn or soybean crop. Cargill said it set up the program because it kept hearing from farmers that health care costs were squeezing their profits and because it guarantees a more predictable grain supply for the company.

The company acquired a 100% ownership of Chinese xanthan gum operation Zibo Cargill Huanghelong Bioengineering (ZCHB) in 2006 by buying out its joint venture partner in ZCHB, Shandong Huanghelong Group. Xanthan gum is used in cosmetics and food products as a viscosity modifier.

Long-time CEO Warren Staley retired in 2007. Cargill's board chose 33-year company veteran and president and COO, Gregory Page, as his replacement. Page stated that he hopes to make Cargill, an historically tight-lipped company, more visible.

## HISTORY

William W. Cargill founded Cargill in 1865 when he bought his first grain elevator in Conover, Iowa. He and his brother Sam bought grain elevators all along the Southern Minnesota Railroad in 1870, just as Minnesota was becoming an important shipping route. Sam and a third brother, James, expanded the elevator operations while William worked with the railroads to monopolize transport of grain to markets and coal to farmers.

Around the turn of the century, William's son William S. invested in a number of ill-fated projects. William W. found that his name had been used to finance the projects; shortly afterward, he died of pneumonia. Cargill's creditors pressed for repayment, which threatened to bankrupt the company. John MacMillan, William W.'s son-in-law, took control and rebuilt Cargill. It had recovered by 1916 but lost its holdings in Mexico and Canada. MacMillan opened offices in New York (1922) and Argentina (1929), expanding grain trading and transport operations.

In 1945 Cargill bought Nutrena Mills (animal feed) and entered soybean processing; corn processing began soon after and grew with the demand for corn sweeteners. In 1954 Cargill benefited when the US began making loans to help developing countries buy American grain. Subsidiary Tradax, established in 1955, became one of the largest grain traders in Europe. A decade later, Cargill began trading sugar by purchasing sugar and molasses in the Philippines and selling them abroad.

Cargill made its finances public in 1973 (as a requirement for its unsuccessful takeover bid of Missouri Portland Cement), revealing it to be one of the US's largest companies, with $5.2 billion in sales. In the 1970s it expanded into coal, steel, and waste disposal and became a major force in metals processing, beef, and salt production.

To placate family heirs who wanted to take Cargill public, CEO Whitney MacMillan, grandson of John, created an employee stock plan in 1991 that allowed shareholders to cash in their shares. He also boosted dividends and reorganized the board, reducing the family's control. MacMillan retired in 1995 and non-family member Ernest Micek became CEO and chairman.

The firm bought Akzo Nobel's North American salt operations in 1997, becoming the #2 US salt company. Micek resigned as CEO in 1999 and was replaced by Warren Staley. Also in 1999 Cargill fessed up to misappropriating some genetic seed material from rival Pioneer Hi-Bred, killing the $650 million sale of its North American seed assets to Germany's AgrEvo.

In order to expand its sweetener segment, in 2002 Cargill formed a marketing alliance with Southern Minnesota Beet Sugar Cooperative and in 2003 it formed another such agreement with Wyoming Sugar. Later in 2003 the company formed a joint venture with Hain Celestial to develop healthy functional foods and beverages using Cargill's isoflavones, inulin, and chondroitin products. In 2004 the company announced the discovery of genetic markers in cattle that predict whether or not a specific steer will produce good-tasting meat.

In 2004 Cargill combined its crop-nutrition segment with phosphate fertilizer maker IMC Global to form a new, publicly traded company called Mosaic. Cargill owns about 66% of the company. This is the first time privately held Cargill has ventured into the public sector.

In 2005 Cargill acquired The Dow Chemical Company's interest in the two companies' 50-50 plastics business joint venture, Cargill Dow LLC, and renamed it NatureWorks. It also broke ground for its first oil refinery in Russia.

That year it also sold its subsidiary Cargill Investor Services (CIS) financial-services to the now bankrupt company REFCO for $208 million cash and future cash payments of between $67 million and $192 million, contingent on CIS's performance. (Prior to REFCO's bankruptcy, CIS — renamed Refco Investment Services — was acquired by the Man Group.)

## EXECUTIVES

**Chairman:** Warren R. Staley, age 63
**Vice Chairman:** F. Guillaume (Bassy) Bastiaens, age 63
**Vice Chairman and Executive Supervisor, Cargill Asia:** David W. Raisbeck, age 57
**President and CEO:** Gregory R. (Greg) Page, age 55
**SVP and CFO:** William W. Veazey
**SVP and Director, Corporate Affairs:** Robbin S. Johnson Sr.
**Corporate VP:** Jerry R. Rose
**Corporate VP and Treasurer:** Jayme D. Olson
**Corporate VP, Information Technology, and CIO:** Rita J. Heise
**Corporate VP, Procurement:** James T. (Jim) Prokopanko, age 53
**Corporate VP, Public Affairs:** Bonnie E. Raquet
**Corporate VP, Transportation and Product Assurance:** Frank L. Sims, age 56
**Corporate VP, Research and Development:** Christopher P. (Chris) Mallett
**Corporate VP and President, Animal Nutrition:** Richard D. Frasch
**Corporate VP and President, Cargill Food System Design:** Robert R. Parmelee
**Corporate VP and President, Juice:** Martin G. Dudley
**Corporate VP and President, Petroleum:** David W. Maclennan

**Corporate VP, General Counsel, and Corporate Secretary:** Steven C. Euller
**Corporate VP and CTO:** Ronald L. Christenson
**Corporate VP and Controller:** Galen G. Johnson
**Corporate VP Human Resources:** Peter Vrijsen, age 52
**Director, Stakeholder and Investor Relations:** Lisa Clemens
**Director, Government Relations and Public Affairs:** Jennifer Engh
**Auditors:** KPMG LLP

## LOCATIONS

**HQ:** Cargill, Incorporated
15407 McGinty Rd. West, Wayzata, MN 55391
**Phone:** 952-742-7575 **Fax:** 952-742-7393
**Web:** www.cargill.com

Cargill has operations in some 60 countries worldwide.

## PRODUCTS/OPERATIONS

### Selected Divisions

Agriculture Services
- Cargill AgHorizons Canada
- Cargill AgHorizons United States
- Cargill Animal Nutrition
- Frontier Agriculture

Food Ingredients and Applications
- Food Ingredients Europe
- Food Ingredients Latin America
- Food Ingredients North America
- Food System Design
- Meat Solutions
- Retail Foodservice Solutions

Industrial
- Agricultural Feedstocks
- Fertilizer
- Salt
- Steel and Ferrous Raw Materials

Origination and Processing
- Cargill Cotton
- Cargill Grain & Oilseed Supply Chain
- Cargill Sugar

Risk Management and Financial
- Black River Asset Management
- Cargill Coal
- Cargill Ferrous International
- Cargill Petroleum
- Cargill Power & Gas Markets
- Cargill Risk Management
- Cargill Trade & Structured Finance
- CarVal Investors
- Cargill Ventures

### Selected Joint Ventures

Banks Cargill Agriculture
Horizon Milling
Progressive Baker
PLGA-1
Renessen Feed & Processing
The Mosaic Company

## COMPETITORS

ADM
Ag Processing
BASF AG
Bunge Limited
CHS
COFCO
ContiGroup
Corn Products International
Dow Chemical
DuPont
General Mills
Hormel
King Arthur Flour
Koch
Land O'Lakes Purina Feed
Morton Salt
Nippon Steel
Nucor
Perdue
Rohm and Haas
Saskatchewan Wheat Pool
Smithfield Foods
Tate & Lyle
Tyson Foods
Tyson Fresh Meats
United States Steel

## HISTORICAL FINANCIALS

Company Type: Private

**Income Statement** FYE: May 31

| | REVENUE ($ mil.) | NET INCOME ($ mil.) | NET PROFIT MARGIN | EMPLOYEES |
|---|---|---|---|---|
| **5/06** | 75,208 | 1,537 | 2.0% | 149,000 |
| **5/05** | 71,066 | 2,103 | 3.0% | 124,000 |
| **5/04** | 62,907 | 1,331 | 2.1% | 101,000 |
| **5/03** | 54,390 | 1,290 | 2.4% | 98,000 |
| **5/02** | 50,398 | 798 | 1.6% | 97,000 |
| **Annual Growth** | 10.5% | 17.8% | — | 11.3% |

**Net Income History**

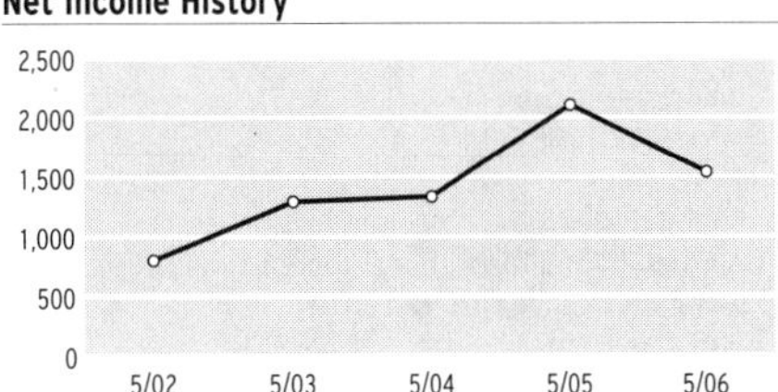


# Carlisle Companies

The theme song for Carlisle Companies could be "Stop, in the name of trucks." The company is a leading maker of heavy-duty truck brakes and brakes for off-highway equipment. Nothing if not diverse, Carlisle also makes industrial components (tensioners, tires, and wheels), construction and roofing materials (rubber, plastic, and FleeceBACK sheeting), food service equipment (dishes, light equipment, and tableware), and aerospace wire and cable assemblies and interconnects. In 2005 the company sold Carlisle Engineered Products (now Creative Engineered Polymer Products) to the Reserve Group.

Carlisle continues to grow through acquisitions and joint ventures (more than 50 since 1990). The company typically focuses on niche markets where it can gain a leading market share, and is constantly tweaking its mix of businesses to optimize value.

It also looks out for bolt-on acquisitions that bolster its existing activities. To that end Carlisle bought the off-highway brake business of competitor ArvinMeritor for just under $40 million late in 2005.

That same year Carlisle announced plans to sell its Carlisle Systems & Equipment operations. The businesses include Carlisle Process Systems (cheese-making and food processing equipment) and the Walker Group (industrial stainless steel storage vessels and trailers). The move is similar to the decision to sell off the former Carlisle Engineered Products business, as the company is looking to strengthen its higher margin businesses. Late in 2006 Carlisle found a buyer for Carlisle Process Systems, and the sale to Tetra Laval subsidiary Tetra Pak was completed later that year. The Walker Group, including Walker Transport, was sold to private investment firm Insight Equity, also in 2006.

As 2006 wound to a close, Carlisle expanded the reach of its tire and wheel business with the agreement to purchase China's Meiyan Tire Group. The move enhances Carlisle Tire & Wheel's capabilities in large tires used in the construction and agriculture industries.

In 2007 Carlisle purchased Insulfoam from privately held Premier Industries for about $160 million. Insulfoam, a maker of block molded polystyrene insulation products for the construction industry, now operates as part of the company's Construction Materials division.

Carlisle has announced plans to exit the food-service business in order to focus on its core, higher margin operations.

The company has also reorganized into five segments from three. The new organization is comprised of: Construction Materials, Industrial Components, Transportation Products, Specialty Products, and General Industry.

## HISTORY

Charles Moomy founded Carlisle Tire and Rubber Company in Carlisle, Pennsylvania, in 1917 to make rubber inner tubes for auto tires. The company debuted its full-molded inner tube in 1926. Success followed until the stock market crash of 1929.

Carlisle limped through the Depression with help from the New Deal's Industrial Loan Act. However, Moomy was forced to turn his stock over to the Federal Reserve Bank of Philadelphia, which became Carlisle's biggest shareholder. Pharis Tire and Rubber Company acquired Carlisle from the Federal Reserve Bank in 1943. Upon Pharis' liquidation in 1949, Carlisle stock was distributed to Pharis stockholders and company officials. Carlisle Corporation was formed, and it bought Dart Truck (mining and construction trucks).

Carlisle continued to diversify. During the 1960s it added jar sealant rings, roofing materials, automotive accessories, and tires for recreational vehicles. It moved to Cincinnati in the 1970s and acquired food service product and computer peripherals companies.

In the 1980s, unable to compete with the big car tire makers, Carlisle focused on tires for smaller vehicles (motorcycles and snowblowers), and it sold car tires to the auto aftermarket. The company restructured as Carlisle Companies Incorporated in 1986 and moved to Syracuse, New York, the next year.

Carlisle bought Brookpark Plastics (plastic compression molding) and Off-Highway Braking Systems (from B.F. Goodrich Aerospace) in 1990, gaining factories in Europe and South America. After taking a hit in the early 1990s recession, Carlisle consolidated operations and sold its communications and electronics industries. With its 1993 purchase of Goodyear's roofing products business, Carlisle became the US's top maker of nonresidential roofing products.

Since the mid-1990s Carlisle increased its acquisitions, buying Sparta Brush (specialty brushes and cleaning tools), Trial King Industries (specialized low-bed trailers), Ti-Brook (trailers and dump bodies), Walker Stainless (trailers and in-plant processing equipment), Intero (steel and aluminum wheel rims), and Unique Wheel (steel wheels). The company also bought the engineered plastics unit of Johnson Controls and Hartstone (ceramic tableware, cookware, and decorative products).

Carlisle stopped making refrigerated marine shipping containers in 1999, and its Carlisle Tire & Wheel Company subsidiary sold its surfacing products division. Carlisle bought privately owned Johnson Truck Bodies that year to boost its production of insulated dairy trucks. It also bought Innovative Engineering (cheese-making system supplier, New Zealand) and Marko International (table coverings and accessories for the food service market).

In 2000 Carlisle bought Red River Manufacturing (custom trailers and paving equipment) and Damrow Denmark and Damrow USA (cheese-making equipment). It also bought Titan International's consumer tire and wheel business and Process Controls Engineering, a control systems designer that serves the food and dairy industries.

The deal-making continued apace in early 2001 with the acquisitions of Wincanton Engineering (food- and beverage-processing equipment) and EcoStar (roofing). Carlisle also bought Mark IV Industries' Dayco industrial power transmission business for about $150 million. Carlisle acquired the MiraDri division (waterproofing) from Nicolon Corporation in late 2002. In early 2003 the company sold its European-based power transmission belt operations to Italy-based Megadyne and closed its Erie-Bundy Park, Pennsylvania, manufacturing facility (plastic automotive parts). In that same year Carlisle added Flo-Pac, a broom and cleaning tool manufacturer, to its General Industry segment. Specialty tire and wheel manufacturer Trintex was acquired by Carlisle in 2004 for $32.5 million.

## EXECUTIVES

**Chairman, President, and CEO:** David A. Roberts, age 59
**Director:** Stephen P. Munn, age 64
**Director:** Richmond D. (Rick) McKinnish, age 57, $2,700,000 pay
**Group President, Construction Materials:** John W. Altmeyer, age 48, $1,200,000 pay
**Group President, Diversified Components:** Michael D. (Mike) Popielec, age 45, $815,000 pay
**Group President, Industrial Components:** Barry Littrell, $775,000 pay
**President, Asia/Pacific:** Kevin G. Forster, age 53, $410,000 pay
**President, Carlisle Process Systems and President, Scherping Systems:** Tim High
**President, Carlisle FoodService Products:** David (Dave) Shannon
**President, Carlisle Motion Control; President, Carlisle Industrial Brake & Friction:** Michael A. Brammer
**President, Trail King:** Jerry N. Thomsen
**President, Tensolite:** John E. Berlin
**VP, Corporate Development:** Scott C. Selbach, age 46
**VP and CFO:** Carol P. Lowe, $625,000 pay
**VP, Secretary, and General Counsel:** Steven J. Ford, age 47, $395,000 pay
**VP, Kenro:** Joe Rellick
**VP, Walker Transportation Products:** Denny Tenhoff
**VP and General Manager, Carlisle Coatings & Waterproofing:** Bob Stout
**Manager, Human Resources:** Beverly Sharp
**Auditors:** Ernst & Young LLP

## LOCATIONS

**HQ:** Carlisle Companies Incorporated
13925 Ballantyne Corporate Place, Ste. 400, Charlotte, NC 28277
**Phone:** 704-501-1100 **Fax:** 704-501-1190
**Web:** www.carlisle.com

Carlisle Companies operates more than 60 manufacturing facilities in China, Europe, and North America.

## PRODUCTS/OPERATIONS

### 2006 Sales

| | $ mil. | % of total |
|---|---|---|
| Construction materials | 1,111.2 | 43 |
| Industrial components | 764.5 | 30 |
| General industry | 326.2 | 13 |
| Specialty products | 187.6 | 7 |
| Transportation products | 183.0 | 7 |
| **Total** | **2,572.5** | **100** |

### Selected Products

Construction Materials
- Roofing accessories (coatings, fasteners, flashings, sealing tapes, and waterproofings)
- Roofing systems (FleeceBack, plastic, and rubber)

Industrial Components
- Pulleys
- Small bias-ply tires
- Stamped and roll-formed wheels
- Tensioners

General Industry
- Commercial and institutional foodservice equipment
- High-performance wire and cable
- Refrigerated truck bodies

Specialty Products
- On- and off-highway motion control systems

Transportation products
- Specialty trailers

### Selected Subsidiaries

Carlisle Asia Pacific Limited (Hong Kong)
Carlisle Engineered Products, Inc.
Carlisle Europe Off-Highway BV (The Netherlands)
Carlisle Flight Services, Inc.
Carlisle FoodService Products Incorporated
Carlisle Roofing Systems, Inc.
Carlisle SynTec Incorporated
Carlisle Tire & Wheel Company
Johnson Truck Bodies, Inc.
Kenro Incorporated
Motion Control Industries, Inc.

## COMPETITORS

ArvinMeritor
Bridgestone
CertainTeed
Dana
Dover
Evergreen Marine
General Cable
G-I Holdings
Johns Manville
Michelin
Owens Corning Sales
Pirelli & C.
Raytech
Southwire
Sumitomo Electric
Superior Essex
Wabash National

## HISTORICAL FINANCIALS

Company Type: Public

### Income Statement

FYE: December 31

| | REVENUE ($ mil.) | NET INCOME ($ mil.) | NET PROFIT MARGIN | EMPLOYEES |
|---|---|---|---|---|
| **12/06** | 2,573 | 216 | 8.4% | 11,000 |
| **12/05** | 2,210 | 106 | 4.8% | 11,000 |
| **12/04** | 2,228 | 80 | 3.6% | 13,677 |
| **12/03** | 2,108 | 89 | 4.2% | 11,434 |
| **12/02** | 1,971 | 29 | 1.5% | 11,631 |
| **Annual Growth** | 6.9% | 65.7% | — | (1.4%) |

### 2006 Year-End Financials

Debt ratio: 29.2%
Return on equity: 25.8%
Cash ($ mil.): 144
Current ratio: 2.10
Long-term debt ($ mil.): 275
No. of shares (mil.): 31
Dividends
Yield: 1.3%
Payout: 15.0%
Market value ($ mil.): 1,210

### Stock History

NYSE: CSL

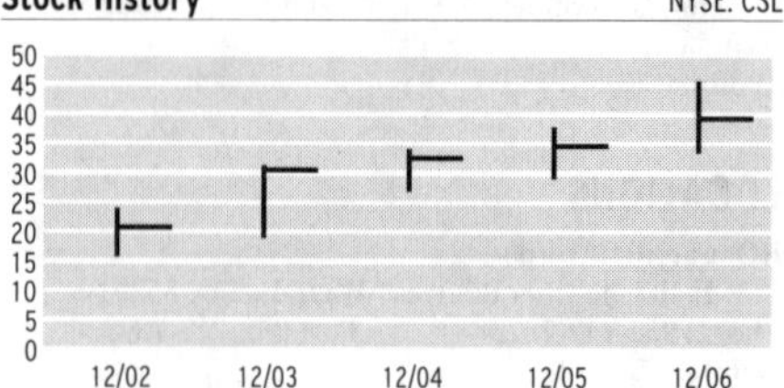


| | STOCK PRICE ($) FY Close | P/E High | P/E Low | PER SHARE ($) Earnings | Dividends | Book Value |
|---|---|---|---|---|---|---|
| **12/06** | 39.25 | 13 | 10 | 3.46 | 0.52 | 30.55 |
| **12/05** | 34.58 | 22 | 17 | 1.71 | 0.48 | 24.05 |
| **12/04** | 32.46 | 26 | 21 | 1.27 | 0.45 | 22.61 |
| **12/03** | 30.43 | 21 | 13 | 1.44 | 0.44 | 20.39 |
| **12/02** | 20.69 | 50 | 34 | 0.47 | 0.43 | 18.08 |
| **Annual Growth** | 17.4% | — | — | 64.7% | 4.9% | 14.0% |

# Carlson Wagonlit Travel

Descending from Europe's Wagons-Lits (literally, sleeping cars) company and from the US's oldest travel agency chain (Ask Mr. Foster), Carlson Wagonlit Travel (CWT) manages business travel from more than 3,000 travel offices in 145 countries. The company is the #2 travel firm in the world behind American Express and is co-owned by the US firm Carlson Companies (whose US leisure and franchise operations also fall under the Carlson Wagonlit brand) and JP Morgan affiliate One Equity Partners. In a big move for the travel industry, CWT acquired leading business travel firm Navigant International in August 2006.

The Navigant acquisition (valued at $510 million) doubles CWT's size in North America, and adds to its presence in other key regions such as Australia and New Zealand.

Carlson Companies is a service conglomerate with nonbusiness travel operations such as hospitality (it franchises Radisson Hotels, T.G.I. Friday's and Italianni's restaurants, and luxury cruise lines) and marketing services (motivational and incentive programs for businesses). France's Accor, who used to own 50% of CWT, reaped the benefits of training the company's travel agents in booking Accor hotel rooms. Both Carlson Companies and Accor invested $100 million to get Carlson Wagonlit online with business-to-consumer and business-to-business sites.

However, Accor sold its stake in Carlson Wagonlit in August 2006. As a result, Carlson Companies now owns 55% and JP Morgan affiliate One Equity Partners owns the remaining 45%.

The company's joint venture project with China Air Service (51% owned by CAS; 49% Carlson Wagonlit) opened offices in Shanghai and Guangzhou in 2004, further strengthening its position as China's leading corporate travel management company.

## HISTORY

Belgian inventor Georges Nagelmackers' first enterprise was adding sleeping compartments to European trains in 1872. Nagelmackers later created the Orient Express. Over the years his Wagons-Lits company expanded its mission to become Wagonlit Travel.

While Nagelmackers was establishing his business in Europe, Ward G. Foster was giving out steamship and train schedules from his gift shop facing the stately Ponce de Leon Hotel in St. Augustine, Florida. As legend has it, hotel patrons with travel questions were directed to Foster's shop with: "Ask Mr. Foster. He'll know." In 1888 he founded Ask Mr. Foster Travel (it became the oldest travel agency in the US). By 1913 the company had offices located in pricey department stores and in the lobbies of upscale hotels and resorts throughout the country. After 50 years at the helm, Foster sold his business in 1937, three years before his death.

After suffering hard times during WWII and into the 1950s, the company changed hands again in 1957 when Donald Fisher and Thomas Orr, two Ask Mr. Foster shareholders, bought controlling interests for $157,000. In 1972 Peter Ueberroth (future Major League Baseball commissioner and Los Angeles Olympic Organizing Committee president) bought the company, then sold it in 1979 to Carlson Companies. In 1990 Ask Mr. Foster became Carlson Travel Network. Also that year Carlson Companies acquired the UK's A.T. Mays, the Travel Agents — a leading UK seller of vacation and tour packages. By 1992 Carlson Companies, besides adding a travel agency a day to the 2,000-plus it already owned, was adding a new hotel every 10 days.

In 1994 Carlson Companies joined with French hotelier Accor to form the joint venture Carlson Wagonlit Travel. (Accor had acquired a majority stake in Wagonlit Travel in 1990.) Under a dual-president ownership, the parent companies owned operations in specific world regions. The two companies began developing new business technology and expanded into new global business markets. Carlson Wagonlit acquired Germany's Brune Reiseburo travel agency and opened a branch office in Moscow. Through 1995 and 1996 acquisitions targeted the Asia/Pacific region, including Hong Kong's and Japan's Dodwell Travel and the corporate travel business of Singapore's Jetset Travel. The joint venture also formed a partnership with Traveland, an Australian travel agency.

In 1997 Carlson and Accor finalized the integration of their travel businesses and named Carlson Travel veteran Travis Tanner global CEO. The following year the new company acquired Florida's Travel Agents International, with more than 300 franchised operations and $600 million in annual sales. Also in 1998 Jon Madonna, formerly KPMG International chairman, was named CEO of Carlson Wagonlit. In 1999 three travel agencies in eastern Canada consolidated under the Carlson Wagonlit Travel brand, creating the largest travel network in that region. That same year Carlson Companies founder and Carlson Wagonlit Travel chairman Curtis Carlson died.

In 2000 Madonna was replaced as CEO by former European operations chief Herve Gourio. The following year Carlson Wagonlit joined with Japan Travel Bureau (now JTB Corp.) to form JTB Business Travel Solutions, a Japan-based travel management joint venture. The arrangement increased Carlson Wagonlit's presence in Asia while increasing the number of JTB locations in North America. In 2001 Carlson Wagonlit cut jobs because of a slowdown in business travel.

In 2003 the company formed a joint venture with China Air Service, creating China's leading corporate travel management company. In 2004 the joint venture project opened offices in Shanghai and Guangzhou. That same year, Gourio stepped down as CEO and was replaced by former Vivendi Universal executive Hubert Joly.

The year 2006 brought about much change for Carlson Wagonlit. During the middle of the year, Accor sold its 50% stake in the company, and by August, Carlson Wagonlit became a joint venture owned by Carlson Companies (55%) and JP affiliate One Equity Partners (45%). In a stunning move, the company also acquired leading travel management firm Navigant International for $510 million that same month. The Navigant acquisition doubled Carlson Wagonlit's size in North America and significantly added to its presence in the Asia Pacific.

## EXECUTIVES

**President and CEO:** Hubert Joly, age 48
**EVP and CFO:** Tim Hennessy
**COO, Asia Pacific:** Berthold Trenkel
**COO, EMEA and Hotels:** Richard Lovell
**COO, North America:** Jack O'Neill
**President, Latin America and Partners Network:** Geoffrey Marshall
**EVP Global Accounts and Solutions:** Martin Warner
**EVP Human Resources:** Philippe Vinay
**EVP Technology and Product Management; and CIO:** Loren Brown
**EVP and General Manager, Canada:** Bill McLean
**EVP Mediterranean:** M. Faccini
**EVP North Europe:** Jan Willem Dekker
**EVP Account Management, EMEA:** Jim Tweedie
**EVP and CFO, EMEA:** Nicholas Francou
**EVP Operations, EMEA:** T. Hopwood
**EVP Strategic Development, EMEA:** Len Blackwood
**VP Corporate and Marketing Communications:** Isabelle Koch
**Global Public Relations:** Kim Derderian

## LOCATIONS

**HQ:** Carlson Wagonlit Travel, Inc.
31 rue du Colonel Pierre Avia, 75904 Paris, France
**Phone:** +33-1-41-33-65-00 **Fax:** +33-1-41-33-65-81
**US HQ:** 701 Carlson Pkwy., Minneapolis, MN 55459
**US Phone:** 763-212-2197 **US Fax:** 763-212-2409
**Web:** www.carlsonwagonlit.com

## COMPETITORS

American Express
BCD Travel
JTB
Kuoni Travel
Ovation Travel Group
Thomas Cook
TUI
Tzell Travel Group

## HISTORICAL FINANCIALS

Company Type: Subsidiary

**Income Statement** FYE: December 31

| | REVENUE ($ mil.) | NET INCOME ($ mil.) | NET PROFIT MARGIN | EMPLOYEES |
|---|---|---|---|---|
| 12/06 | 20,500 | — | — | 22,000 |
| 12/05 | 11,500 | — | — | 22,000 |
| Annual Growth | 78.3% | — | — | 0.0% |

**Revenue History**

# CarMax, Inc.

To the greatest extent possible, CarMax helps drivers find inexpensive autos. The nation's largest specialty used-car retailer buys, reconditions, and sells cars and light trucks at about 80 retail units in more than 20 states, mainly in the Southeast and Midwest; CarMax also operates seven new-car franchises (all integrated or co-located with the used-car dealers). CarMax sells cars that are generally under six years old with less than 60,000 miles. CarMax also sells used cars through its ValuMax program. ValuMax cars are older than six years or have more than 60,000 miles. The company's Web site lets customers search CarMax outlets nationwide for a particular model.

Following the same road to success that made Circuit City Stores a category killer (Circuit City spun off the company in 2002), CarMax targets populous and growing areas and offers large inventories.

CarMax plans to open about a dozen new superstores this year in new and existing markets. The company will focus this growth on mid-sized markets initially, but will later move into larger markets. To make room for more used-car sales, which drive most of the company's business, CarMax has divested half of its new-car franchises and may sell more.

CarMax's new CEO, Thomas Folliard, is a 13-year company veteran and former EVP.

## HISTORY

Looking for new retailing channels to conquer, in 1993 Circuit City Stores began test-driving the used-car concept when it opened its first CarMax outlet in Richmond, Virginia. Richard Sharp, who was named Circuit City's CEO in 1986, became the chairman and CEO for CarMax Group as well.

A pioneer in the car industry, CarMax offered computerized shopping, play areas for children, and no-haggle pricing. Competing car dealers criticized CarMax's TV ads, which tarred rivals with a stereotype of sleaze and greed. Some dealers disputed CarMax's low-price claims.

The company extended its geographical reach into North Carolina, Georgia, and Florida in 1995 and 1996. In 1996 CarMax began selling new cars at an Atlanta store.

No longer riding it as a test-drive, Circuit City spun off about 25% of CarMax to the public in 1997. The following year it moved into Illinois.

Also in 1998 CarMax bought a new-car Toyota dealership in Maryland and the multi-make Mauro Auto Mall of Wisconsin. It entered South Carolina that year and added a Georgia Mitsubishi dealership in early 1999. The company acquired two new-car franchises in the competitive Los Angeles market in mid-1999.

In mid-2001 Circuit City reduced its share in CarMax from 75% to about 65%, having sold some stock to help remodel the company's electronics stores. Circuit City then spun off CarMax as an independent company in October 2002. President Austin Ligon took the CEO title at that time (Sharp remained chairman).

CarMax opened five superstores, but sold four new-car dealerships in 2003.

Ligon retired as CEO in June 2006. He was succeeded by EVP Thomas J. Folliard who was named president, CEO, and a director of the company.

## EXECUTIVES

**Chairman:** William R. Tiefel, age 73
**President, CEO, and Director:**
Thomas J. (Tom) Folliard, age 42, $645,602 pay
**EVP, CFO, Corporate Secretary and Director:**
Keith D. Browning, age 54, $554,933 pay
**EVP and Chief Administrative Officer:**
Michael K. (Mike) Dolan, age 57, $499,511 pay
**SVP and CIO:** Richard M. Smith, age 49, $229,585 pay
**SVP, Marketing and Strategy:** Joseph S. Kunkel, age 44, $493,274 pay
**VP, CarMax Auto Finance:** Angela Schwarz Chattin
**VP and Controller:** Kim D. Orcutt
**VP, Human Resources:** Scott A. Rivas
**VP, Management Information Systems:** David D. Banks
**VP, Management Information Systems:**
Barbara B. Harvill
**VP, Auction Services:** William D. (Bill) Nash
**VP, Strategy:** Anu Agarwal
**VP, CarMax Auto Finance Credit:** Todd House
**VP, Real Estate:** K. Douglass Moyers
**VP, Service Operations:** Edwin J. (Ed) Hill
**VP, Store Administration:** Fred S. Wilson
**VP and Treasurer:** Thomas W. (Tom) Reedy Jr.
**Assistant VP, Field Human Resources:** Edward Fabritiis
**Assistant VP, Investor Relations:** Dandy Barrett
**Assistant VP, Public Affairs:** Lisa Van Riper
**Auditors:** KPMG LLP

## LOCATIONS

**HQ:** CarMax, Inc.
12800 Tuckahoe Creek Parkway,
Richmond, VA 23238
**Phone:** 804-747-0422 **Fax:** 804-217-6819
**Web:** www.carmax.com

### 2007 Stores

| | No |
|---|---|
| Florida | 11 |
| Texas | 11 |
| California | 9 |
| Illinois | 6 |
| North Carolina | 6 |
| Virginia | 6 |
| Georgia | 4 |
| Maryland | 4 |
| Tennessee | 4 |
| Connecticut | 2 |
| Indiana | 2 |
| Kansas | 2 |
| Nevada | 2 |
| Ohio | 2 |
| South Carolina | 2 |
| Wisconsin | 2 |
| Alabama | 1 |
| Kentucky | 1 |
| Missouri | 1 |
| New Mexico | 1 |
| Oklahoma | 1 |
| Utah | 1 |
| **Total** | **81** |

## PRODUCTS/OPERATIONS

### 2007 Sales

| | $ mil. | % of total |
|---|---|---|
| Used vehicles | 5,872.8 | 79 |
| Wholesale vehicles | 918.4 | 12 |
| New vehicles | 445.1 | 6 |
| Other | 229.3 | 3 |
| **Total** | **7,465.6** | **100** |

## COMPETITORS

Asbury Automotive
AutoNation
Bill Heard
Brown Automotive
DriveTime
Ed Morse Auto
Group 1 Automotive
Hendrick Automotive
Holman Enterprises
JM Family Enterprises
Penske Automotive Group
Red McCombs Automotive Group
Serra Automotive
Sonic Automotive
VT Inc.

## HISTORICAL FINANCIALS

Company Type: Public

### Income Statement

FYE: February 28

| | REVENUE ($ mil.) | NET INCOME ($ mil.) | NET PROFIT MARGIN | EMPLOYEES |
|---|---|---|---|---|
| **2/07** | 7,466 | 199 | 2.7% | 13,736 |
| **2/06** | 6,364 | 148 | 2.3% | 12,061 |
| **2/05** | 5,260 | 113 | 2.1% | 11,175 |
| **2/04** | 4,598 | 116 | 2.5% | 9,722 |
| **2/03** | 4,067 | 95 | 2.3% | 8,756 |
| **Annual Growth** | 16.4% | 20.3% | — | 11.9% |

### 2007 Year-End Financials

Debt ratio: 2.7%
Return on equity: 18.0%
Cash ($ mil.): 26
Current ratio: 2.25
Long-term debt ($ mil.): 34
No. of shares (mil.): 216
Dividends
Yield: —
Payout: —
Market value ($ mil.): 5,692

### Stock History

NYSE: KMX

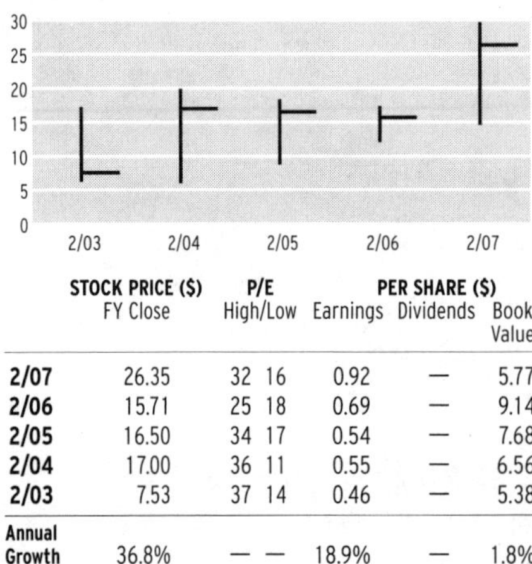


| | STOCK PRICE ($) FY Close | P/E High | P/E Low | PER SHARE ($) Earnings | Dividends | Book Value |
|---|---|---|---|---|---|---|
| **2/07** | 26.35 | 32 | 16 | 0.92 | — | 5.77 |
| **2/06** | 15.71 | 25 | 18 | 0.69 | — | 9.14 |
| **2/05** | 16.50 | 34 | 17 | 0.54 | — | 7.68 |
| **2/04** | 17.00 | 36 | 11 | 0.55 | — | 6.56 |
| **2/03** | 7.53 | 37 | 14 | 0.46 | — | 5.38 |
| **Annual Growth** | 36.8% | — | — | 18.9% | — | 1.8% |

# Carnival Corporation

Carnival offers a boatload of fun. The company is the world's #1 cruise operator, with 12 cruise lines and almost 80 ships carrying 7 million passengers. Carnival operates in North America primarily through its Princess Cruise Line, Holland America, and Seabourn luxury cruise brand, as well as its flagship Carnival Cruise Lines unit. Brands such as AIDA, P&O Cruises, and Costa Cruises offer services to passengers in Europe while the Cunard Line operates the ocean liners *Queen Mary 2* and *Queen Elizabeth 2*. Carnival operates as a dual listed company with UK-based Carnival plc, forming a single enterprise under a unified executive team. CEO Micky Arison and his family own 30% of the company.

Carnival maintains its top position in the industry by leveraging its cruise lines to penetrate a number of different markets. Carnival Cruises, a leading brand in the US, and Princess both target families, retirees, and other upper middle class customers with competitively priced cruise packages to popular destinations in the Caribbean, along the Mexican Riviera, and in Alaska. P&O Cruises targets similar markets in the UK with trips to the Mediterranean and Scandinavia. (P&O also operates out of Australia and New Zealand.) Holland America is known for its scenic getaways in New England, Canada, and along the Pacific coast. In 2006 the company began offering trips to the Asian market through Costa Cruises.

Carnival's Seabourn brand offers luxury cruises targeting upscale travelers with fine food, personalized service, and exotic destinations around the world. Similarly, its Swan Hellenic brand offers premium cruises throughout Europe and in Asia. Of course, luxury is the name of the game for venerable Cunard, offering ocean voyages and round-the-world cruises on its two ocean liners. In June 2007, the company agreed to sell one of Cunard's ships (*Queen Elizabeth 2*) to Dubai-based Istithmar for $100 million.

Despite fears over terrorism and war, the company has been growing at full steam since its $5.4 billion acquisition of UK-based rival P&O Princess in 2003. The mega deal increased Carnival's presence in the UK and throughout Europe and put it leagues ahead of #2 cruising company Royal Caribbean. Fueled by optimism for the future, Carnival has orders in place to build more than 15 additional cruise ships, which it will integrate into its fleet between early 2006 and late 2009. Carnival has also ordered a new $470 million ocean liner, to be christened *Queen Victoria*, for its Cunard Line. It is scheduled to begin service by the end of 2007.

To fill its expanding inventory of passenger berths, Carnival continues to spend heavily on marketing its cruises, especially to consumers who have never taken to the high seas (about 85% of the population in the US). The company has also expanded the number of ports its ships operate from to put cruising possibilities closer to customers.

Carnival became a dual listed company after its acquisition of P&O Princess, with P&O being recast as Carnival plc. The deal gives Carnival increased access to capital markets in the US and the UK.

Arison, one of the wealthiest people in Miami, also owns the Miami Heat basketball team.

## HISTORY

Israeli emigrant Ted Arison got into the cruise business in the mid-1960s, forming Norwegian Caribbean Lines with shipping magnate Knut Kloster. After their partnership ended in 1971, Arison persuaded old friend Meshulam Riklis to bankroll his $6.5 million purchase of the *Empress of Canada* in 1972. Riklis owned (among other things) the Boston-based American International Travel Service (AITS). Arison set up Carnival Cruise Lines as an AITS subsidiary and renamed his ship the *Mardi Gras*. Unfortunately, she ran aground on her maiden voyage, sending Carnival into red ink for three years.

Arison bought out Riklis in 1974 for $1 and assumed Carnival's $5 million debt. He envisioned a cruise line that would offer affordable vacation packages to young, middle-class consumers, and invented a new type of cruise ship featuring live music, gambling, and other entertainment on board. Carnival was profitable within a month, and by the end of the following year, Arison had paid off Carnival's debt and bought its second ship. Arison's son, Micky, became CEO in 1979. Despite the rising costs of shipbuilding and fuel prices, Carnival continued to add to its fleet. The company grew to become the world's #1 cruise operator, and the Arisons took Carnival public in 1987.

The company acquired luxury cruise business Holland America Line in 1989 and formed a joint venture with Seabourn Cruise Lines in 1992. Carnival changed its name to Carnival Corporation in 1994 to reflect its diversifying operations, and it took a 50% stake in Seabourn the following year. Carnival stepped up its European expansion in 1996 by buying a stake in UK-based Airtours.

Carnival signed a deal with two shipyards in 1998 to build twelve more ships for the company by 2004 (six each for its Carnival and Holland America lines). It also bought a majority interest in the prestigious Cunard Line (*Queen Elizabeth 2*) that year, merged it with Seabourn, and bought the remainder of the two cruise lines in 1999. An ugly lawsuit reared its head that year after a woman claimed to have been sexually assaulted while on a Carnival ship. Carnival acknowledged that it had received more than 100 similar complaints against its cruise employees dating back to 1995. (The suit was settled later that year.)

In 2000 Carnival acquired the remaining 50% of Costa Crociere from Airtours. The next year, Carnival sold its 25% stake in Airtours (now known as MyTravel Group).

In 2001 the company countered competitor Royal Caribbean's agreement to merge with P&O Princess Cruises with its own offer of £2.15 billion. P&O shareholders snubbed the offer but later softened and said it would consider a revised offer, leaving the door open for a bidding war between Carnival and Royal Caribbean. That same year, the company pleaded guilty to charges of polluting the ocean and falsifying oil-contaminated discharge records. It agreed to pay $18 million in fines and environmental costs, hire overseers to monitor its ships, and hire an environmental standards officer.

In 2003 Carnival succeeded in wooing P&O away from Royal Caribbean and the two corporations merged operations via a dual-listed company structure. Consequently, P&O changed its name to Carnival plc.

## EXECUTIVES

**Chairman and CEO:** Micky Arison, age 57, $3,450,000 pay
**Vice Chairman and COO:** Howard S. Frank, age 65, $3,250,000 pay
**President and CEO, Carnival Cruise Lines:** Gerald R. (Gerry) Cahill, age 56
**SVP, General Counsel, and Secretary:** Arnaldo Perez, age 46
**SVP International:** Ian J. Gaunt, age 54
**SVP and CFO:** David Bernstein, age 49
**VP Employee Services:** Susan Herrmann
**VP Public Affairs:** Tom Dow
**VP and CIO:** Rafael Sanchez
**VP Investor Relations:** Beth Roberts
**Director; Chairman and CEO, Costa Crociere:** Pier Luigi Foschi, age 60, $2,385,743 pay
**President and CEO, Holland America Line:** Stein Kruse, age 48
**President and Managing Director, Cunard Line:** Carol Marlow
**President and CEO, Seabourn Cruise Line:** Pamela C. Conover, age 49
**Director; CEO, P&O Princess Cruises International:** Peter G. Ratcliffe, age 58, $2,084,500 pay
**President and CEO Princess Cruises:** Alan B. Buckelew, age 57
**President, AIDA Cruises:** Michael Thamm, age 43
**President, Costa Crociere:** Gianni Onorato
**CEO Carnival UK:** David K. Dingle, age 49
**CEO, Carnival Australia:** Ann C. Sherry, age 51
**Auditors:** PricewaterhouseCoopers LLP

## LOCATIONS

**HQ:** Carnival Corporation
3655 NW 87th Ave., Miami, FL 33178
**Phone:** 305-599-2600 **Fax:** 305-406-4700
**Web:** www.carnivalcorp.com

**2006 Sales**

| | % of total |
|---|---|
| North America | 65 |
| Europe | 29 |
| Other | 6 |
| **Total** | **100** |

## PRODUCTS/OPERATIONS

**2006 Sales**

| | % of total |
|---|---|
| Cruises | 96 |
| Other | 4 |
| **Total** | **100** |

**Selected Cruise Ships**

AIDA
- *AIDAaura* (launched in 2003; 1,266 passengers)
- *AIDAblu* (1990; 1,666)
- *AIDAcara* (1996; 1,180)
- *AIDAvita* (2002; 1,266)

Carnival Cruise Lines
- *Carnival Conquest* (2002; 2,966)
- *Carnival Destiny* (1996; 2,634)
- *Carnival Glory* (2003; 2,968)
- *Carnival Legend* (2002; 2,120)
- *Carnival Liberty* (2005; 2,966)
- *Carnival Miracle* (2004; 2,120)
- *Carnival Pride* (2001; 2,120)
- *Carnival Spirit* (2001; 2,122)
- *Carnival Triumph* (1999; 2,750)
- *Carnival Valor* (2004; 2,966)
- *Carnival Victory* (2000; 2,750)
- *Celebration* (1987; 1,484)
- *Ecstasy* (1991; 2,050)
- *Elation* (1998; 2,050)
- *Fantasy* (1990; 2,054)
- *Fascination* (1994; 2,050)
- *Holiday* (1985; 1,450)
- *Imagination* (1995; 2,050)
- *Inspiration* (1996; 2,050)
- *Paradise* (1998; 2,048)
- *Sensation* (1993; 2,050)

Costa Cruises
- *Costa Allegra* (1992; 784)
- *Costa Atlantica* (2000; 2,114)
- *Costa Classica* (1991; 1,302)
- *Costa Concordia* (2006; 2,978)
- *Costa Europa* (1986; 1,488)
- *Costa Fortuna* (2003; 2,702)
- *Costa Magica* (2004; 2,702)
- *Costa Marina* (1990; 762)
- *Costa Mediterranea* (2003; 2,114)
- *Costa Romantica* (1993; 1,344)
- *Costa Victoria* (1996; 1,928)

Cunard Line
- *Queen Elizabeth 2* (1969; 1,788)
- *Queen Mary 2* (2003; 2,592)

Holland America Line
- *Amsterdam* (2000; 1,380)
- *Maasdam* (1993; 1,258)
- *Noordam* (2006; 1,918)
- *Oosterdam* (2003; 1,848)
- *Prinsendam* (1988; 794)
- *Rotterdam* (1997; 1,316)
- *Ryndam* (1994; 1,258)
- *Statendam* (1993; 1,258)
- *Veendam* (1996; 1,258)
- *Volendam* (1999; 1,432)
- *Westerdam* (2004; 1,848)
- *Zaandam* (2000; 1,432)
- *Zuiderdam* (2002; 1,848)

Ocean Village
- *Ocean Village* (1989; 1,578)

P&O Cruises
- *Arcadia* (2005; 1,948)
- *Artemis* (1984; 1,188)
- *Aurora* (2000; 1,870)
- *Oceana* (2000; 2,016)
- *Oriana* (1995; 1,818)

P&O Cruises Australia
- *Pacific Star* (1982; 994)
- *Pacific Sun* (1986; 1,480)

Princess Cruise Lines
- *Caribbean Princess* (2004; 3,100)
- *Coral Princess* (2002; 1,974)
- *Crown Princess* (2006; 3,080)
- *Dawn Princess* (1997; 1,998)
- *Diamond Princess* (2004; 2,674)
- *Golden Princess* (2001; 2,598)
- *Grand Princess* (1998; 2,592)
- *Island Princess* (2003; 1,974)
- *Pacific Princess* (1999, 668)
- *Regal Princess* (1991; 1,596)
- *Sapphire Princess* (2004; 2,674)
- *Sea Princess* (1998; 2,016)
- *Star Princess* (2002; 2,598)
- *Sun Princess* (1995; 2,022)
- *Tahitian Princess* (2000; 668)

Seabourn
- *Seabourn Legend* (1992; 208)
- *Seabourn Pride* (1988; 208)
- *Seabourn Spirit* (1989; 208)

Swan Hellenic
- *Minerva II* (2001; 678)

## COMPETITORS

Carlson
Club Med
Disney
NCL
NYK Line
Royal Caribbean Cruises
Saga Group
Star Cruises
TUI

## HISTORICAL FINANCIALS

Company Type: Public

### Income Statement

FYE: November 30

| | REVENUE ($ mil.) | NET INCOME ($ mil.) | NET PROFIT MARGIN | EMPLOYEES |
|---|---|---|---|---|
| **11/06** | 11,839 | 2,279 | 19.2% | 74,700 |
| **11/05** | 11,087 | 2,257 | 20.4% | 71,200 |
| **11/04** | 9,727 | 1,854 | 19.1% | 69,500 |
| **11/03** | 6,718 | 1,194 | 17.8% | 66,000 |
| **11/02** | 4,368 | 1,016 | 23.3% | 37,200 |
| **Annual Growth** | 28.3% | 22.4% | — | 19.0% |

### 2006 Year-End Financials

| | |
|---|---|
| Debt ratio: 34.9% | No. of shares (mil.): 623 |
| Return on equity: 13.0% | Dividends |
| Cash ($ mil.): 1,163 | Yield: 2.1% |
| Current ratio: 0.37 | Payout: 36.8% |
| Long-term debt ($ mil.): 6,355 | Market value ($ mil.): 30,521 |

### Stock History

NYSE: CCL

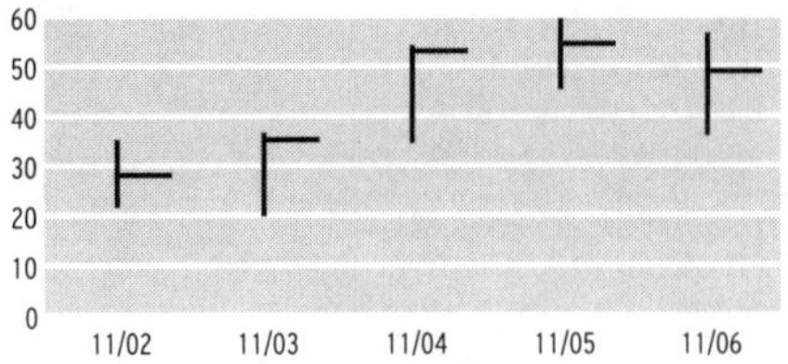

| | STOCK PRICE ($) FY Close | P/E High | P/E Low | PER SHARE ($) Earnings | Dividends | Book Value |
|---|---|---|---|---|---|---|
| **11/06** | 48.99 | 20 | 13 | 2.77 | 1.02 | 29.23 |
| **11/05** | 54.49 | 22 | 17 | 2.70 | 0.80 | 26.64 |
| **11/04** | 53.01 | 24 | 16 | 2.24 | 0.52 | 24.86 |
| **11/03** | 35.19 | 22 | 12 | 1.66 | 0.44 | 21.89 |
| **11/02** | 28.05 | 20 | 13 | 1.73 | 0.42 | 12.64 |
| **Annual Growth** | 15.0% | — | — | 12.5% | 24.8% | 23.3% |

# Casey's General Stores

Casey's General Stores makes sure that small towns in the Midwest get their fill of convenient shopping. The company operates or franchises more than 1,450 convenience stores, mostly in Illinois, Iowa, and Missouri, but also in Indiana, Kansas, Minnesota, Nebraska, South Dakota, and Wisconsin, all within about 500 miles of the company's headquarters and distribution center. Casey's stores sell beverages, gasoline, groceries, and fresh prepared foods, such as donuts, pizza, and sandwiches. Casey's also sells tobacco products, automotive products, and other nonfood items, including ammunition, housewares, and photo supplies.

Gasoline or gasohol, sold at every Casey's store, accounts for about 70% of the company's sales. Towns with 5,000 people or fewer, where the rent is low and the competition scarce, host about 60% of Casey's stores.

Nearly all Casey's stores sell donuts (as well as cookies, brownies, Danishes, cinnamon rolls, and muffins) and pizza prepared on the premises.

Casey's has been growing in existing markets by acquiring other Midwestern chains. In 2006 the company bought 33 HandiMart convenience stores in Iowa from Nordstrom Oil and another 50 convenience stores in Nebraska from Gas 'N Shop Inc. This year the company plans to acquire about 50 stores and build 10 others.

T. Rowe Price Associates owns about 6% of the company's common stock. Co-founder and former chairman Donald Lamberti owns nearly 5%.

## HISTORY

Donald Lamberti, who had run his family's grocery store, founded Casey's General Stores with Kurvin C. "K. C." Fish. The men converted a gas station into the first Casey's convenience store in 1968. To expand and build brand recognition, the company began franchising outlets two years later. By focusing on small towns, the company avoided competition and expensive building and property costs. A significant growth spurt in 1979 took Casey's from 119 stores to 226. Fish retired the following year.

The company went public in 1983 and began to curtail its franchising efforts in favor of more profitable company-owned stores (at the time there were about 190 company-owned stores and about 215 franchised outlets; today only about 130 are franchised). Casey's introduced carry-out pizza in 1984 and sandwiches two years later. Fueled by another stock offering in 1985, the company continued to grow quickly. It opened its 500th store that year and by 1990 had stores in eight states.

By 1996 Casey's had 1,000 stores, and it continued to add about 70 stores a year. After 30 years at the helm, in 1998 Lamberti retired as CEO; president Ronald Lamb took his place. In 2000 Casey's continued to expand at a rate of about 85 stores per year.

The company was accused of charging up to $5 a gallon for gas at 25 Casey's stores in Illinois on September 11, 2001, the day of terrorist attacks in New York City and Washington, DC. Casey's agreed the next month to pay $25,000 to the Red Cross and $5,000 to the state of Illinois. It also agreed to refund customers who were overcharged for gas. In fiscal 2002 the company opened more than 50 company-owned stores.

In fiscal 2003 the company built 15 new stores and purchased another. In April 2003 co-founder Lamberti retired from the company and Ronald Lamb added chairman to his title in May.

In early 2006 the company acquired 51 convenience stores in Nebraska from Gas 'N Shop for about $29 million. In June COO Robert Myers was named CEO of Casey's, succeeding Ronald Lamb, who held onto the chairman's title. In October the company acquired 33 HandiMart convenience stores in Iowa from Nordstrom Oil for about $63 million.

In the fiscal year ended April 2007, the company acquired about 50 stores and built nearly 10 others.

## EXECUTIVES

**Chairman:** Ronald M. (Ron) Lamb, age 70
**President, CEO, and Director:** Robert J. (Bob) Myers, age 59
**COO:** Terry W. Handley, age 46, $411,750 pay
**SVP and CFO:** William J. (Bill) Walljasper, age 41, $310,500 pay
**SVP and Secretary:** John G. Harmon, age 52, $285,000 pay
**SVP, Transportation and Support Operations:** Sam J. Billmeyer, age 49
**VP and Corporate Counsel:** Eli J. Wirtz
**VP and Treasurer:** Russell D. Sukut
**VP, Human Resources:** Julie L. Jackowski
**VP, Information Systems:** Bradley G. (Brad) Heyer
**VP, Marketing:** Michael R. (Mike) Richardson
**VP, Real Estate and Store Development:** Cleo R. Kuhns
**VP, Store Operations:** Robert C. Ford, age 48
**VP, Support Services:** Hal D. Brown
**Auditors:** KPMG LLP

## LOCATIONS

**HQ:** Casey's General Stores, Inc.
1 Convenience Blvd., Ankeny, IA 50021
**Phone:** 515-965-6100 **Fax:** 515-965-6160
**Web:** www.caseys.com

## PRODUCTS/OPERATIONS

### 2007 Sales

| | $ mil. | % of total |
|---|---|---|
| Gasoline | 2,881.0 | 72 |
| Grocery & other merchandise | 852.8 | 21 |
| Prepared food & fountain | 267.3 | 7 |
| Other | 22.2 | — |
| Franchise | 0.7 | — |
| **Total** | **4,024.0** | **100** |

### 2007 Stores

| | No. |
|---|---|
| Company owned | 1,448 |
| Franchises | 15 |
| **Total** | **1,463** |

### Selected Merchandise

Ammunition
Automotive products
Beverages
Food
Gasoline (self-service)
Health and beauty aids
Housewares
Pet products
Photo supplies
School supplies
Tobacco products

### Subsidiaries

Casey's Marketing Co. (operation of company-owned stores in Missouri, Indiana, Iowa, and Wisconsin; operation of wholesale business)
Casey's Services Co. (construction and transportation services)

## COMPETITORS

7-Eleven
Chevron
CVS/Caremark
Exxon Mobil
Holiday Companies
Hy-Vee
IGA
Krause Gentle
Kroger
Kwik Trip
Martin & Bayley
QuikTrip
Royal Dutch Shell
Walgreen

## HISTORICAL FINANCIALS

Company Type: Public

### Income Statement

FYE: April 30

| | REVENUE ($ mil.) | NET INCOME ($ mil.) | NET PROFIT MARGIN | EMPLOYEES |
|---|---|---|---|---|
| **4/07** | 4,024 | 62 | 1.5% | 17,136 |
| **4/06** | 3,515 | 61 | 1.7% | 15,692 |
| **4/05** | 2,811 | 37 | 1.3% | 14,440 |
| **4/04** | 2,369 | 37 | 1.5% | 14,574 |
| **4/03** | 2,158 | 40 | 1.8% | 14,388 |
| **Annual Growth** | 16.9% | 11.6% | — | 4.5% |

### 2007 Year-End Financials

| | |
|---|---|
| Debt ratio: 34.9% | No. of shares (mil.): 51 |
| Return on equity: 11.3% | Dividends |
| Cash ($ mil.): 107 | Yield: 0.6% |
| Current ratio: 1.03 | Payout: 12.3% |
| Long-term debt ($ mil.): 200 | Market value ($ mil.): 1,272 |

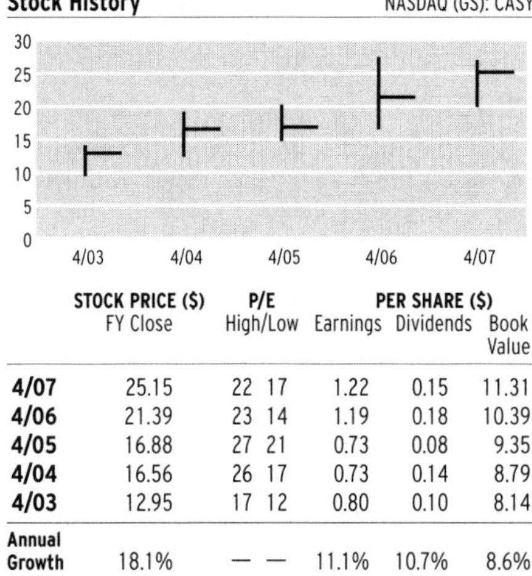


| | STOCK PRICE ($) FY Close | P/E High/Low | | PER SHARE ($) Earnings | Dividends | Book Value |
|---|---|---|---|---|---|---|
| **4/07** | 25.15 | 22 | 17 | 1.22 | 0.15 | 11.31 |
| **4/06** | 21.39 | 23 | 14 | 1.19 | 0.18 | 10.39 |
| **4/05** | 16.88 | 27 | 21 | 0.73 | 0.08 | 9.35 |
| **4/04** | 16.56 | 26 | 17 | 0.73 | 0.14 | 8.79 |
| **4/03** | 12.95 | 17 | 12 | 0.80 | 0.10 | 8.14 |
| **Annual Growth** | 18.1% | — | — | 11.1% | 10.7% | 8.6% |

# Caterpillar Inc.

Building more than cocoons, Caterpillar is the world's #1 maker of earthmoving machinery and a leading supplier of agricultural equipment. The company makes construction, mining, and logging machinery; diesel and natural gas engines; industrial gas turbines; and electrical power-generation systems. Caterpillar has plants worldwide and sells its equipment globally via a network of 3,500 locations in 180 countries. Caterpillar offers rental services through more than 1,600 outlets worldwide and it provides financing and insurance for its dealers and customers. Cat Power Ventures invests in power projects that use Caterpillar power generation equipment. Caterpillar Logistics Services offers supply chain solutions.

Nearly half of Caterpillar's sales are generated in the US. Engines account for about a third of sales. Like other manufacturers in the industry, Caterpillar is taking steps to reduce costs. The company is facing increased retiree pension, health care, and related benefits costs, but plans to offset most of the expenses through improved operations.

In 2004 Caterpillar expanded its remanufacturing services (Cat Reman) to include new automotive and industrial OEMs and the defense industry. The following year the unit acquired the French company Eurenov, which greatly enhanced Cat Reman's reach into the European market.

Those moves were just a precursor, though. The company decided to raise the profile of Cat Reman even more later in 2005. Formerly a unit within Caterpillar's Product Support division, Cat Reman became its own division at the end of the year, marking it as a company focus in the coming years. The unit grew again early in 2006 when Caterpillar agreed to acquire the rail and non-Cat engine component remanufacturing business of O.E.M. Remanufacturing Company, a subsidiary of Caterpillar distributor Finning. Caterpillar and OEM Reman already have an agreement whereby the latter performs remanufacturing services on Caterpillar branded equipment in Canada.

## HISTORY

In 1904 in Stockton, California, combine maker Benjamin Holt modified the farming tractor by substituting a gas engine for steam and replacing iron wheels with crawler tracks. This improved the tractor's mobility over dirt.

The British adapted the "caterpillar" (Holt's nickname for the tractor) design to the armored tank in 1915. Following WWI, the US Army donated tanks to local governments for construction work. The caterpillar's efficiency spurred the development of earthmoving and construction equipment.

Holt merged with Best Tractor in 1925. The company, renamed Caterpillar (Cat), moved to Peoria, Illinois, in 1928. Cat expanded into foreign markets in the 1930s and phased out combine production to focus on construction and road-building equipment.

Sales volume more than tripled during WWII when Cat supplied the military with earthmoving equipment. Returning GIs touted Cat durability and quality, and high demand continued. Cat held a solid first place in the industry, far ahead of #2 International Harvester.

Moving beyond US borders, Cat established its first overseas plant in the UK (1951). In 1963 it entered a joint venture with Japanese industrial titan Mitsubishi. Cat bought Solar Turbines (gas turbine engines) in 1981. Fifty consecutive years of profits ended, however, when Cat ran up $953 million in losses between 1982 and 1984 as equipment demand fell and foreign competition intensified. Cat doubled its product line between 1984 and 1989 and shifted production toward smaller equipment.

In 1990 CEO Donald Fites reorganized Cat along product lines. The next year the company clashed with the UAW (United Auto Workers) over wage and health benefits. A strike resulted, and Cat reported its first annual loss since 1984. Most of the striking workers returned to work without a contract by mid-1992.

The firm completed a six-year, $1.8 billion modernization program in 1993 that automated many of its plants. That investment benefited the company when almost two-thirds of Cat's UAW employees at eight plants in Colorado, Illinois, and Pennsylvania went on strike in 1994. Company management hired replacement workers and used its foreign factories to help fill orders. In 1995, after two years of record earnings at Cat, the UAW called off the strike. Cat set up a holding company, Caterpillar China Investment Co. Ltd., in 1996 for joint ventures in China.

In 1998 Cat and the UAW (with federal mediation) hammered out their first contract agreement in more than six years. That year Cat paid $1.33 billion for LucasVarity's UK-based Perkins Engines, expanding its capacity to produce small and midsize diesel engines.

Fites retired in 1999; vice chairman Glen Barton succeeded him. Cat cut back its workforce and production after slowdowns in the agricultural, mining, and oil exploration industries reduced machinery orders. In 2001 Caterpillar announced a restructuring that involved facility consolidation, the retirement of several executives, and the sale of the high-tech MT series tractor line to AGCO Corp. A deal to sell the company's rubber-belted track component business to Canada-based Camoplast was completed in late 2002.

In January 2003 Caterpillar received certification by the US Environmental Protection Agency for its ACERT-equipped engine (Advanced Combustion Emission Reduction Technology, a technology that provides long-term emissions solutions) for the North American trucking, bus, construction, and mining industries; the technology also positions Caterpillar to meet future emissions regulations for both on- and off-highway engines.

Also in 2003 the company inked a deal with diversified global resources company BHP Billiton to supply an estimated $1.5 billion in equipment and support to its operations.

In 2004 Caterpillar acquired Swiss industrial gas turbine packager Turbomach S.A. In the same year recreation vehicle manufacturer Fleetwood Enterprises announced that it would equip all of its diesel-powered vehicles with Caterpillar engines by the end of 2005. Williams Technology, a transmission remanufacturing company, was acquired by Caterpillar from Remy International in late 2004.

In 2006 Caterpillar bought Progress Rail from One Equity Partners for about $1 billion in cash, Caterpillar stock, and the assumption of long-term debt.

## EXECUTIVES

**Chairman and CEO:** James W. (Jim) Owens, age 61, $1,650,003 pay
**Group President:** Gérard R. Vittecoq, age 58, $868,851 pay
**Group President:** Stuart L. Levenick, age 53, $761,253 pay
**Group President:** Douglas R. (Doug) Oberhelman, age 53, $904,248 pay
**Group President:** Gerald L. (Gerry) Shaheen, age 62, $856,248 pay
**Group President:** Steven H. Wunning, age 55, $787,747 pay
**VP and CFO:** David B. Burritt, age 51, $445,750 pay
**VP and CIO:** John S. Heller, age 51
**VP Corporate Auditing and Compliance:** Ali M. Bahaj, age 52
**VP; President, Caterpillar Financial Services:** Kent M. Adams, age 51
**VP; President, Global Mining:** Christopher C. Curfman, age 53
**VP, General Counsel, and Secretary:** James B. (Jim) Buda, age 58
**VP Human Services Division:** Sidney C. (Sid) Banwart, age 60
**VP, Operations, Asia Pacific Division:** Richard P. Lavin, age 53
**VP Marketing and Product Support Division:** William F. (Bill) Springer, age 54
**VP and President, Solar Turbines:** Stephen A. (Steve) Gosselin, age 48
**VP, Marketing, Europe, Middle East, Africa:** Paolo Fellin, age 51
**VP; President and CEO, Progress Rail Services:** William P. (Billy) Ainsworth, age 50
**Director Investor Relations:** Mike DeWalt
**Auditors:** PricewaterhouseCoopers LLP

## LOCATIONS

**HQ:** Caterpillar Inc.
100 NE Adams St., Peoria, IL 61629
**Phone:** 309-675-1000 **Fax:** 309-675-1182
**Web:** www.cat.com

**2006 Sales**

| | $ mil. | % of total |
|---|---|---|
| US | 19,636 | 47 |
| Other countries | 21,881 | 53 |
| **Total** | **41,517** | **100** |

## PRODUCTS/OPERATIONS

### 2006 Sales

| | $ mil. | % of total |
|---|---|---|
| Machinery | 26,062 | 63 |
| Engines | 12,807 | 31 |
| Financing & insurance services | 2,648 | 6 |
| **Total** | **41,517** | **100** |

### Selected Products

Machinery
- Articulated trucks
- Backhoe loaders
- Log loaders
- Log skidders
- Mining shovels
- Motor graders
- Off-highway trucks
- Paving products
- Pipelayers
- Related parts
- Skid steer loaders
- Telescopic handlers
- Track and wheel excavators
- Track and wheel loaders
- Track and wheel tractors
- Wheel tractor-scrapers

Engines
- Engines for Caterpillar machinery
- Engines for electric power generation systems
- Engines for marine, petroleum, construction, industrial, and agricultural applications
- Engines for on-highway trucks and locomotives

Financial and Insurance Services
- Financing to customers and dealers
- Insurance to customers and dealers

### Selected Brands

Cat
Caterpillar
F.G. Wilson
MaK
Olympian
Perkins
Solar Turbines

## COMPETITORS

AGCO
Bamford Excavators
CAMECO Industries
Charles Machine
CIT Group
Citibank
CNH
Cummins
Daimler
Deere
DHL
Dresser
GE
GENCO Distribution System
Hitachi Construction Machinery
Hyundai Heavy Industries
Ingersoll-Rand
Isuzu
Komatsu
Menlo Worldwide
Multiquip
Sandvik
Sumitomo Heavy Industries
Terex
Toyota
UPS Supply Chain Solutions
Volvo
Woods Equipment Company

## HISTORICAL FINANCIALS

Company Type: Public

### Income Statement

FYE: December 31

| | REVENUE ($ mil.) | NET INCOME ($ mil.) | NET PROFIT MARGIN | EMPLOYEES |
|---|---|---|---|---|
| **12/06** | 41,517 | 3,537 | 8.5% | 94,593 |
| **12/05** | 36,339 | 2,854 | 7.9% | 85,116 |
| **12/04** | 30,251 | 2,035 | 6.7% | 76,920 |
| **12/03** | 22,763 | 1,099 | 4.8% | 69,139 |
| **12/02** | 20,152 | 798 | 4.0% | 68,990 |
| **Annual Growth** | 19.8% | 45.1% | — | 8.2% |

### 2006 Year-End Financials

Debt ratio: 257.8%
Return on equity: 46.3%
Cash ($ mil.): 779
Current ratio: 1.20
Long-term debt ($ mil.): 17,680
No. of shares (mil.): 646
Dividends
Yield: 1.8%
Payout: 21.3%
Market value ($ mil.): 39,607

### Stock History

NYSE: CAT

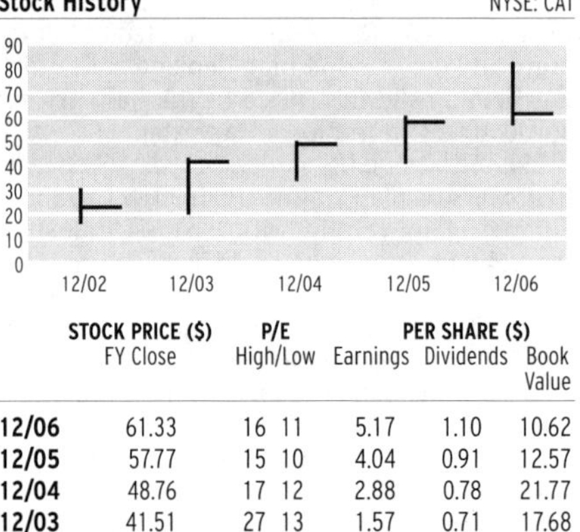


| | STOCK PRICE ($) FY Close | P/E High | P/E Low | PER SHARE ($) Earnings | Dividends | Book Value |
|---|---|---|---|---|---|---|
| **12/06** | 61.33 | 16 | 11 | 5.17 | 1.10 | 10.62 |
| **12/05** | 57.77 | 15 | 10 | 4.04 | 0.91 | 12.57 |
| **12/04** | 48.76 | 17 | 12 | 2.88 | 0.78 | 21.77 |
| **12/03** | 41.51 | 27 | 13 | 1.57 | 0.71 | 17.68 |
| **12/02** | 22.86 | 26 | 15 | 1.15 | 0.70 | 15.90 |
| **Annual Growth** | 28.0% | — | — | 45.6% | 12.0% | (9.6%) |

# CB Richard Ellis Group

CB Richard Ellis Group (CBRE) is all about location, location, location — not to mention *ubicación, l'emplacement, posizione,* and *Standort.* The world's largest commercial real estate services company and an international powerhouse, CBRE has operations in nearly 35 countries. Through subsidiaries Insignia Financial, whose acquisition made CBRE the largest commercial-property manager in the world, and Trammell Crow, CBRE oversees real estate management, investment, property development, and related operations for top corporations that outsource their real estate requirements. It manages more than 1.7 billion sq. ft. Other offerings include asset and investment management and brokerage services.

CBRE has expanded to about 300 offices; its three geographic segments are the Americas; Europe, the Middle East, and Africa (EMEA); and Asia-Pacific. The Americas division accounts for 62% of the firm's sales.

CB Richard Ellis makes no bones about its acquisition strategy — now that it has acquired firms Insignia Financial and Trammell Crow (acquired in 2006 for $2.2 billion) it looks for fill-in acquisitions that complement or expand existing operations.

Richard Blum maintains a nearly 11% stake in CBRE through Blum Capital Partners.

## HISTORY

Colbert Coldwell and Albert Tucker started real estate brokerage Tucker, Lynch, & Coldwell in 1906 in San Francisco. In 1922 the company expanded to Los Angeles, where it began developing real estate in 1933 with a 60-acre subdivision in the burgeoning city.

Having profited from California's rapid growth in the 1950s and 1960s, the firm expanded out of state. The partnership incorporated in 1962 as Coldwell Banker, which went public in 1968. Sears, Roebuck & Co. bought the company in 1981 for 80% above its market price. But by 1991 Sears had abandoned aims to become a financial services giant and sold Coldwell Banker's commercial operations to The Carlyle Group as CB Commercial Real Estate Services Group.

Free of Sears but $56 million in the red, the company didn't return to profitability until 1993. Two years later it embarked on a shopping spree in real estate services, buying tenant representatives Langon Rieder and Westmark Realty. In 1996 the company went public and bought mortgage banker L. J. Melody & Company; it purchased Koll Real Estate Services in 1997.

In 1998 the company widened its global scope with the acquisition of REI Limited, the non-UK operations of Richard Ellis; it was renamed CB Richard Ellis Services. CB Richard Ellis also bought Hillier Parker May & Rowden (now operating in the UK as CB Hillier), a London-based provider of commercial property services.

CB Richard Ellis experienced a revenue crunch in 1999 and responded by restructuring its North American operations into three divisions (transaction, financial, and management services) and cutting management ranks by 30%. Growth continued in 1999 with the purchase of Pittsburgh-based Gold & Co., the addition of an office in Venezuela, and a fat contract to manage more than 1,100 locations for Prudential.

In 2000 the company committed significant resources to the Internet, inking a deal to offer the lease management services of MyContracts.com and investing in Canadian real estate transaction tracker RealNet Canada.

A group of investors including then-CEO Ray Wirta, chairman Richard Blum (and his BLUM Capital Partners), and Freeman Spogli took the company private in 2001. Blum Capital Partners bought the 60% of publicly traded CBRE that it did not already own, forming CBRE Holding. Three years later the company went public once again.

In 2003 CBRE merged with top commercial real estate broker and property manager Insignia Financial. The next year the company changed its name to CB Richard Ellis Group and went public. It bought rival Trammell Crow in 2006, as well as a dozen or so other companies as it sought to fill in its holdings.

## EXECUTIVES

**Vice Chairman & Partner Investment Properties:** Darcy A. Stacom
**Vice Chairman Investment Properties:** Jack C. Fraker
**Vice Chairman Brokerage Services:** Michael Geoghegan, age 47
**Vice Chairman, Global Corporate Services:** John G. Nugent, age 45
**Vice Chairman Investment Properties:** William M. (Bill) Shanahan, age 50
**Vice Chairman, Global Corporate Services:** William F. (Bill) Concannon, age 51

**President, CEO and Director:** W. Brett White, age 47, $2,577,363 pay
**SEVP and President, Americas:** Calvin W. (Cal) Frese Jr., age 50, $1,262,000 pay
**CFO:** Kenneth J. (Ken) Kay, age 51, $1,042,200 pay
**EVP and Global Controller:** Gil Borok, age 39
**EVP, General Counsel, Chief Compliance Officer, and Secretary:** Laurence H. Midler, age 41, $539,700 pay
**EVP Litigation and General Counsel:** Ellis (D.) Reiter Jr.
**SVP, Corporate Human Resources:** Jack Van Berkel, age 46
**Chairman, Global Brokerage Services:** Stephen B. Siegel, age 62
**President, EMEA:** Michael (Mike) Strong
**President, CB Richard Ellis Investors:** Robert H. (Bob) Zerbst
**Senior Director, Corporate Communications:** Robert W. McGrath
**Director, Investor Relations:** Shelley Young
**Auditors:** Deloitte & Touche LLP

## LOCATIONS

**HQ:** CB Richard Ellis Group, Inc.
100 N. Sepulveda Blvd., Ste. 1050,
El Segundo, CA 90245
**Phone:** 310-606-4700 **Fax:** 949-809-4357
**Web:** www.cbre.com

### 2006 Sales

| | $ mil. | % of total |
|---|---|---|
| Americas | 2,506.9 | 62 |
| EMEA | 933.5 | 23 |
| Asia Pacific | 354.8 | 9 |
| Global investment management | 228.0 | 6 |
| Development services (Trammell Crow) | 8.8 | — |
| **Total** | **4,032.0** | **100** |

## PRODUCTS/OPERATIONS

### Selected Subsidiaries

CB Richard Ellis, Inc.
CB Richard Ellis Limited (UK)
CB Richard Ellis Real Estate Services, LLC
CB Richard Ellis Services, Inc
CBRE Melody & Company
CBRE Melody of Texas, L.P.
CBRE Real Estate Services, Inc.
Insignia Financial Group, LLC
Relam Amsterdam Holdings B.V. (The Netherlands)
Trammell Crow Company

## COMPETITORS

CarrAmerica
Colliers International
Cushman & Wakefield
DTZ
FirstService
Forest City Enterprises
Grubb & Ellis
Hines
Inland Group
JMB Realty
Jones Lang LaSalle
Lend Lease
Lincoln Property
Mitsui Fudosan
Realogy
Shorenstein
Staubach
Studley
Tishman

## HISTORICAL FINANCIALS

Company Type: Public

### Income Statement

FYE: December 31

| | REVENUE ($ mil.) | NET INCOME ($ mil.) | NET PROFIT MARGIN | EMPLOYEES |
|---|---|---|---|---|
| **12/06** | 4,032 | 319 | 7.9% | 24,000 |
| **12/05** | 2,911 | 217 | 7.5% | 14,500 |
| **12/04** | 2,365 | 65 | 2.7% | 13,500 |
| **12/03** | 1,630 | (35) | — | — |
| **12/02** | 1,170 | 19 | 1.6% | — |
| **Annual Growth** | 36.2% | 103.2% | — | 33.3% |

### 2006 Year-End Financials

Debt ratio: 189.0%
Return on equity: 32.3%
Cash ($ mil.): 813
Current ratio: 1.16
Long-term debt ($ mil.): 2,233
No. of shares (mil.): 227
Dividends
Yield: —
Payout: —
Market value ($ mil.): 7,552

### Stock History

NYSE: CBG

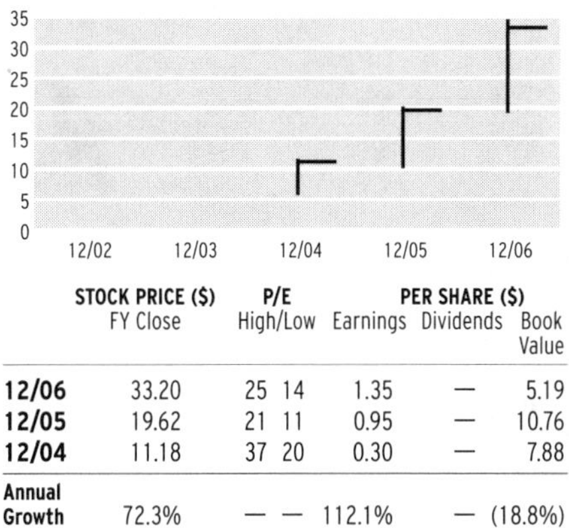


| | STOCK PRICE ($) FY Close | P/E High | P/E Low | PER SHARE ($) Earnings | Dividends | Book Value |
|---|---|---|---|---|---|---|
| **12/06** | 33.20 | 25 | 14 | 1.35 | — | 5.19 |
| **12/05** | 19.62 | 21 | 11 | 0.95 | — | 10.76 |
| **12/04** | 11.18 | 37 | 20 | 0.30 | — | 7.88 |
| **Annual Growth** | 72.3% | — | — | 112.1% | — | (18.8%) |

# CBRL Group

CBRL Group has gotten ahead in the restaurant business by holding on to a bit of the past. The company operates more than 540 Cracker Barrel Old Country Store restaurants in about 40 states, which are known for their country kitsch, rustic decor, and down-home cooking. The eateries offer mostly standard American fare, such as chicken, ham, and roast beef dishes but are most popular as breakfast spots. Each Cracker Barrel location features a retail area where patrons can buy hand-blown glassware, cast iron cookware, and woodcrafts, as well as jellies and old-fashioned candies.

CBRL's Cracker Barrel chain gained initial attention and success by building most of its restaurants along interstate freeways and continues to focus on the traveling public with new units located near tourist destinations. That strategy has come back to haunt the chain, though, as rising gasoline prices have led many Americans to travel less.

Looking to cash out its investment in the steakhouse segment, CBRL announced planned in 2006 to spin off its Logan's Roadhouse business through an IPO. Later that year, however, it sold the chain to a group of private investment firms including Bruckmann, Rosser, Sherrill & Co., Canyon Capital Advisors, and Black Canyon Capital for about $486 million. The move allows CBRL to focus solely on its flagship chain. Prior to sale, company veteran and Cracker Barrel president Cyril Taylor retired from CBRL; CEO Michael Woodhouse later took charge of the Cracker Barrel operation.

While CBRL's restaurants are popular, its policies and practices have made the company the focus of controversy and lawsuits. Its Cracker Barrel chain drew criticism for its openly anti-gay hiring practices in the early 1990s (the policy was later rescinded) and it has been the target of several racial discrimination lawsuits. (CBRL has never been found guilty of any discrimination, however.)

## HISTORY

Dan Evins opened the first Cracker Barrel Old Country Store in Lebanon, Tennessee, in 1969. As a sales representative for Shell Oil, Evins believed he could sell more gas if he combined gas stations with restaurants. He also envisioned placing his new concept along what was then a relatively new enterprise — the interstate highway system. The company was incorporated in 1970.

Four years later Evins resigned from his job at Shell Oil to give full attention to his burgeoning restaurant chain, which had grown to a dozen locations. The oil embargo of the mid-1970s prompted the company to back away from the sale of gas, and it completely did away with gas pumps by the mid-1980s. Cracker Barrel went public in 1981.

Company sales slumped in 1985, when a plan to force its smaller stores to squeeze out large-store scale revenue failed. The company rebounded by remodeling the smaller stores to the dimensions of the larger stores and by creating middle management positions to oversee real estate purchasing, gift shop merchandising, and human resource training. It also introduced an incentive program to reward store managers for curbing costs and increasing sales. Between 1980 and 1990, the company added 84 new restaurants to its rapidly expanding chain.

Controversy struck the company during the 1990s when its old country values clashed with present day reality. In 1991 the company issued a statement declaring that it would no longer employ "individuals whose sexual preferences fail to demonstrate normal heterosexual values." Believing that the sexual orientation of such individuals was not in line with the values of its customer base, the company fired more than a dozen employees. Cracker Barrel later rescinded the policy, but the incident deeply scarred the company's image and continued to haunt it throughout the decade. The controversy also spurred changes in SEC regulations — a protest by Cracker Barrel stockholders who opposed the policy eventually led to a 1998 decision permitting stockholders to propose resolutions on employment matters.

Cracker Barrel acquired Carmine's Prime Meats (later Carmine Giardini's Gourmet Market), a chain of gourmet food stores, in 1998. With addition of a second chain of stores, the company restructured into a holding company called CBRL Group the following year and later acquired the Logan's Roadhouse steakhouse chain (founded in 1991) for about $180 million. A group of African-American employees filed a lawsuit against the company in 1999, claiming racial discrimination.

All Cracker Barrel units were company-owned until 2000, when CBRL executed a sale-leaseback deal for 65 of these restaurants. Evins resigned his post as CEO in 2001 and was replaced by company veteran Michael Woodhouse.

Even as the 1999 racial discrimination suit was pending, the company was hit by a class action discrimination suit by 21 customers claiming that African-Americans were seated in segregated areas, denied service, and served food taken from the garbage. In 2002 a federal court in Georgia ruled against the plaintiffs, claiming that they'd failed to prove that a set of discriminatory circumstances existed to warrant a national class action suit.

That same year the US Justice Department began an investigation into the public accommodations policies of CBRL's Cracker Barrel division. As part of a 2004 settlement with the department, Cracker Barrel agreed to hire an independent auditor to monitor its race-bias policies. New allegations were brought against the company in 2004 when 10 employees at three Illinois restaurants filed federal charges of sexual harassment and racial discrimination. Later that year CBRL settled a handful of lawsuits at once (while denying any wrongdoing), paying a total of $8.7 million in a variety of southern US courts.

The following year the company dealt with a lawsuit brought on by donations made to a political group called Texans for a Republican Majority, a political action group connected to former congressman Tom DeLay that was alleged to be involved in illegal campaign contributions. CBRL settled their involvement in the case by agreeing to donate money to fund a nonpartisan information program at the University of Texas' LBJ School of Public Affairs.

Looking to focus on its flagship restaurant chain, the company announced plans to spin off Logan's through an IPO in 2006. Before the offering, though, it sold the steakhouse business to a group of private equity firms.

## EXECUTIVES

**Chairman, President, and CEO; President, Cracker Barrel Old Country Store:** Michael A. (Mike) Woodhouse, age 61, $937,500 pay
**SVP Finance and CFO:** Lawrence E. White, age 56, $425,000 pay
**SVP, Secretary, and General Counsel:** N.B. Forrest Shoaf, age 57, $309,000 pay
**SVP Corporate Affairs:** Diana S. Wynne, age 51
**SVP Marketing and Innovation and Chief Marketing Officer:** Simon A. Turner, age 51
**SVP Strategic Initiatives:** Edward A. Greene, age 51
**SVP Human Resources, Cracker Barrel Old Country Store:** Robert J. Harig
**SVP Restaurant Operations, Cracker Barrel Old Country Store:** Douglas E. (Doug) Barber
**SVP Retail Operations, Cracker Barrel Old Country Store:** Terry A. Maxwell
**VP Accounting and Tax and Chief Accounting Officer:** Patrick A. Scruggs, age 42
**VP Financial Planning and Analysis:** Brian R. Eytchison
**VP Internal Audit and Loss Prevention:** Brently G. Baxter
**VP, General Counsel, and Secretary, Cracker Barrel Old Country Store:** Michael J. Zylstra
**VP Finance, Cracker Barrel Old Country Store:** P. Doug Couvillion
**VP Information Services, Cracker Barrel Old Country Store:** Timothy W. (Tim) Mullen
**VP Management Training and Development, Cracker Barrel Old Country Store:** Thomas R. Pate
**VP Product Development and Quality Assurance, Cracker Barrel Old Country Store:** Robert F. (Bob) Doyle
**Director Corporate Communications:** Julie K. Davis
**Auditors:** Deloitte & Touche LLP

## LOCATIONS

**HQ:** CBRL Group, Inc.
305 Hartmann Dr., Lebanon, TN 37088
**Phone:** 615-444-5533 **Fax:** 615-443-9476
**Web:** www.cbrlgroup.com

### 2006 Locations of Company-Owned Stores

| | No. |
|---|---|
| Tennessee | 65 |
| Florida | 63 |
| Texas | 57 |
| Georgia | 48 |
| Alabama | 39 |
| Indiana | 38 |
| Kentucky | 36 |
| Ohio | 35 |
| Michigan | 31 |
| Virginia | 31 |
| North Carolina | 30 |
| Illinois | 22 |
| Pennsylvania | 22 |
| Missouri | 20 |
| South Carolina | 19 |
| Mississippi | 17 |
| Louisiana | 14 |
| West Virginia | 13 |
| Arkansas | 12 |
| Arizona | 9 |
| New York | 8 |
| Oklahoma | 8 |
| New Jersey | 6 |
| Wisconsin | 5 |
| Colorado | 4 |
| Kansas | 4 |
| Maryland | 4 |
| Massachusetts | 4 |
| Utah | 4 |
| Other states | 19 |
| **Total** | **687** |

## PRODUCTS/OPERATIONS

### 2006 Sales

| | $ mil. | % of total |
|---|---|---|
| Restaurant services | 2,169 | 82 |
| Retail | 471 | 18 |
| Franchising | 3 | — |
| **Total** | **2,643** | **100** |

### 2006 Locations

| | No. |
|---|---|
| Company-owned | 687 |
| Franchised | 25 |
| **Total** | **712** |

### 2006 Locations

| | No. |
|---|---|
| Cracker Barrel | 544 |
| Logan's Roadhouse | 168 |
| **Total** | **712** |

## COMPETITORS

Applebee's
Bob Evans
Brinker
Buffets Holdings
Carlson Restaurants
Cheesecake Factory
Darden
Denny's
Golden Corral
Hooters
Houlihan's
Huddle House
IHOP
Landry's
Lone Star Steakhouse
Metromedia Restaurant Group
O'Charley's
OSI Restaurant Partners
Perkins & Marie Callender's
RARE Hospitality
Roadhouse Grill
Romacorp
Ruby Tuesday
Shoney's
Texas Roadhouse
VICORP Restaurants
Waffle House

## HISTORICAL FINANCIALS

Company Type: Public

### Income Statement

FYE: Friday nearest July 31

| | REVENUE ($ mil.) | NET INCOME ($ mil.) | NET PROFIT MARGIN | EMPLOYEES |
|---|---|---|---|---|
| **7/06** | 2,643 | 116 | 4.4% | 74,031 |
| **7/05** | 2,568 | 127 | 4.9% | 75,029 |
| **7/04** | 2,381 | 112 | 4.7% | 69,230 |
| **7/03** | 2,198 | 107 | 4.8% | 65,192 |
| **7/02** | 2,067 | 92 | 4.4% | 60,897 |
| **Annual Growth** | 6.3% | 6.1% | — | 5.0% |

### 2006 Year-End Financials

Debt ratio: 323.7%
Return on equity: 19.8%
Cash ($ mil.): 90
Current ratio: 0.91
Long-term debt ($ mil.): 978
No. of shares (mil.): 31
Dividends
Yield: 1.6%
Payout: 20.8%
Market value ($ mil.): 1,002

### Stock History

NASDAQ (GS): CBRL

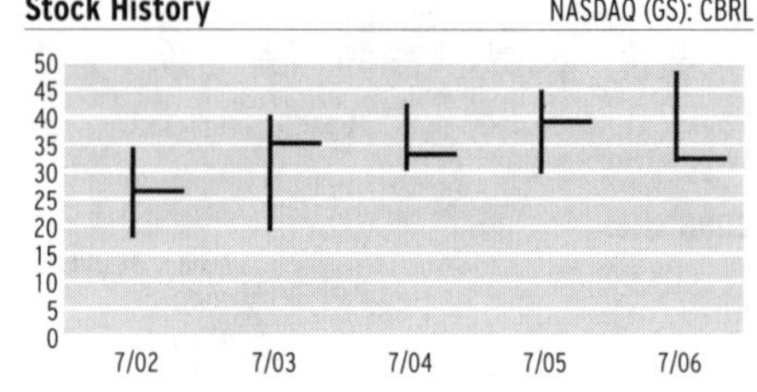


| | STOCK PRICE ($) FY Close | P/E High/Low | | PER SHARE ($) Earnings | Dividends | Book Value |
|---|---|---|---|---|---|---|
| **7/06** | 32.41 | 19 | 13 | 2.50 | 0.52 | 9.77 |
| **7/05** | 39.17 | 18 | 12 | 2.45 | 0.71 | 18.66 |
| **7/04** | 33.22 | 19 | 14 | 2.23 | 0.33 | 17.91 |
| **7/03** | 35.19 | 19 | 9 | 2.09 | 0.02 | 16.60 |
| **7/02** | 26.39 | 21 | 11 | 1.64 | 0.02 | 15.57 |
| **Annual Growth** | 5.3% | — | — | 11.1% | 125.8% | (11.0%) |

# CBS Corporation

This media conglomerate has its eye focused on the TV. CBS Corporation is one of the leading television broadcasting and production companies in the world, operating the #1 TV network in the US, CBS. It also operates about 40 TV stations around the country and owns 50% of The CW Network. On cable, CBS owns movie channel Showtime and sports channel CSTV. It creates and distributes programming through CBS Television Distribution Group and CBS Paramount Network Television. In addition to TV, the company owns CBS Radio, CBS Outdoor, and book publisher Simon & Schuster. Chairman Sumner Redstone has more than 70% voting control over CBS Corp. through his National Amusements cinema chain.

CBS was once part of the Viacom conglomeration of TV, cable, and film companies, but in late 2005 the media behemoth split into two separate, publicly traded companies: The "new" Viacom and CBS Corporation. Viacom, under the leadership of Tom Freston (who resigned in 2006), took over the cable and film assets, including Paramount Pictures and MTV Networks, while CBS took on the primarily advertising supported media assets (television, radio, and Internet operations). Les Moonves, formerly the head of the CBS network, was appointed to lead CBS Corp.

While the "old" Viacom possessed an impressive array of blue-chip media assets, its volatile movie studio tended to overshadow the better performing parts of the company, namely its cable and broadcast television operations. The decision was made, therefore, to split up the company in the hope that shareholders would value the parts more than the whole.

In 2006, CBS Corp. made waves in the television broadcasting industry when it announced it would merge netlet UPN with its rival The WB to form The CW Network. CBS Corp. operates the new network with Warner Bros. Entertainment as a 50-50 joint venture. The CW launched in the fall of 2006 with a select mix of programming pulled from UPN and The WB, as well as some original shows.

Late that same year, the company entered the music business by launching CBS Records. It plans to use its broadcasting operations to help promote its artists by integrating their songs into various TV programs. CBS is also expanding its new media operations to both sell advertising and generate interest for its TV operations. It is streaming episodes of such shows as *CSI* and *Survivor* through its Web site with some commercials, and it is simulcasting its Evening News program online, with new anchor Katie Couric, in an attempt to reach a broader audience. Its CSTV unit is also broadcasting sporting events through an online subscription service.

To streamline its production and distribution operations, the company formed CBS Television Distribution Group in 2006 to oversee production unit King World, as well as its domestic and international distribution networks. The reorganization should help the company leverage its library of TV shows (consisting of about 3,000 titles — 77,000 hours of programming) and take advantage of new digital distribution capabilities. The new division boasts such hit syndicated programs as *Wheel of Fortune*, the Oprah Winfrey show, and the new talk show hosted by Rachel Ray.

## HISTORY

The company that would eventually become CBS Corporation began as Viacom in 1970. Viacom is the result of mergers and acquisitions dating back nearly 90 years, combining everything from a movie studio to a company that made car bumpers. CBS launched Viacom after the FCC ruled that TV networks could not own cable systems and TV stations in the same market. Viacom took over CBS's program syndication division and bought TV and radio stations in the late 1970s and early 1980s. In 1978 it cofounded pay-TV network Showtime. Viacom became full owner in 1982 and combined Showtime with The Movie Channel the following year to form Showtime Networks. Viacom also began producing TV series and bought MTV Networks in 1986.

After a bidding war with renowned financier Carl Icahn and a Viacom management group, Sumner Redstone's National Amusements bought 83% of Viacom in 1987. Viacom bought King's Entertainment (theme parks) shortly thereafter and followed that with two mega-deals in 1994: it bought Paramount Communications for about $10 billion (which included Simon & Schuster) and Blockbuster for $8.4 billion (which included Spelling Entertainment). The next year, along with Chris-Craft, Viacom launched UPN (United Paramount Network), the fifth broadcast TV network in the US.

Chiseling away at a mountain of debt, Viacom dumped its radio stations and sold its share in USA Networks (now named IAC/InterActiveCorp) to Universal for $1.7 billion in 1997. In 1998 it sold the reference and education publishing divisions of Simon & Schuster to Pearson for $4.6 billion and unloaded the unprofitable Blockbuster Music chain to Wherehouse Entertainment for $115 million.

Viacom created an Internet division (MTV Networks Online) in 1999 to house its MTV, VH1, and Nickelodeon Web sites (later decentralized into The MTVi Group and Nickelodeon Online). Later that year it sold 18% of Blockbuster in an IPO and sold 10% of MTVi to TCI Music (now Liberty Digital) in exchange for the SonicNet Web sites.

Viacom bought Chris-Craft's 50%-stake in the struggling UPN Network for a paltry $5 million in 2000 by exercising a buy-sell clause in the contract. BHC Communications (Chris-Craft's 80%-owned subsidiary that actually owned the stake in UPN) filed suit to block Viacom's merger with CBS claiming that it violated a non-compete clause in the contract, but the New York Supreme Court ruled in Viacom's favor. Its $45 billion merger with CBS went through (reuniting two companies split apart by the government 30 years ago), and Viacom was given one year to sell UPN. However, a federal law prohibiting ownership of more than one TV network was overturned in 2001 allowing Viacom to keep the network.

In 2001, Viacom bought the rest of Infinity Broadcasting that it didn't already own, as well as BET Holdings (the media company targeting African-Americans) for $3 billion.

In 2004 Viacom finally sold its majority stake in Blockbuster, which never really fit in with Viacom's other media properties.

Shortly after its 2005 split from Viacom, CBS Corp. sold Paramount Parks to Cedar Fair for $1.2 billion. A newly formed network called The CW, a combination of UPN and The WB, debuted in 2006.

## EXECUTIVES

**Executive Chairman:** Sumner M. Redstone, age 84
**Vice Chairman:** Shari E. Redstone, age 53
**President, CEO, and Director:** Leslie (Les) Moonves, age 57
**EVP and CFO:** Frederic G. Reynolds, age 56
**EVP and General Counsel:** Louis J. Briskman, age 58
**EVP and Chief Communications Officer:** Gil Schwartz, age 55
**EVP Human Resources and Administration:** Anthony G. Ambrosio, age 46
**EVP Investor Relations:** Martin M. Shea, age 63
**EVP Office of the Chairman:** Carl D. Folta, age 49
**EVP Planning, Policy, and Government Relations:** Martin D. Franks, age 56
**SVP and CIO:** Amy Berkowitz
**SVP Finance and Treasurer:** Joseph R. Ianniello, age 39
**SVP, Controller, and Chief Accounting Officer:** Susan C. Gordon, age 53
**SVP, Deputy General Counsel, and Secretary:** Angeline C. Straka, age 61
**SVP and General Tax Counsel:** Richard M. Jones, age 41
**President and CEO, CBS Television Stations:** Tom Kane
**President, CBS Entertainment:** Nina Tassler
**President, CBS News and CBS Sports:** Sean McManus
**President, CBS Paramount Network Television Entertainment Group:** Nancy Tellem, age 53
**President, CBS Paramount International Television:** Armando Nuñez Jr.
**President, CBS Paramount Network Television:** David Stapf
**President, The CW:** Dawn Ostroff
**President, Creative Affairs and Development, King World and CBS Paramount Domestic Television:** Terry Wood
**Auditors:** PricewaterhouseCoopers LLP

## LOCATIONS

**HQ:** CBS Corporation
51 W. 52nd St., New York, NY 10019
**Phone:** 212-975-4321 **Fax:** 212-975-4516
**Web:** www.cbscorporation.com

### 2006 Sales

| | $ mil. | % of total |
|---|---|---|
| US | 12,739.9 | 89 |
| Europe | | |
| UK | 484.5 | 3 |
| Other countries | 548.5 | 4 |
| Canada | 276.5 | 2 |
| Other regions | 270.8 | 2 |
| **Total** | **14,320.2** | **100** |

## PRODUCTS/OPERATIONS

### 2006 Sales

| | $ mil. | % of total |
|---|---|---|
| Television | 9,487.1 | 66 |
| Outdoor advertising | 2,103.4 | 15 |
| Radio | 1,959.9 | 14 |
| Publishing | 807.0 | 5 |
| Adjustments | (37.2) | — |
| **Total** | **14,320.2** | **100** |

### 2006 Sales

| | $ mil. | % of total |
|---|---|---|
| Advertising | 10,373.1 | 72 |
| TV license fees | 1,606.8 | 11 |
| Affiliate fees | 1,069.6 | 7 |
| Publishing | 807.0 | 6 |
| Home entertainment | 83.4 | 1 |
| Other | 380.3 | 3 |
| **Total** | **14,320.2** | **100** |

### Selected Operations

Television
- CBS Broadcasting
- CBS Paramount Network Television (production and distribution)
- CBS Television Distribution Group
  - CBS Paramount Domestic Television (TV syndication)
  - CBS Paramount International Television (international distribution)
  - King World Productions (TV production and distribution)
- CBS Television Stations (21 CBS, 18 UPN, and one independent TV stations)
- CSTV Networks, Inc. (college sports)
  - MaxPreps, Inc. (high school sports)
- The CW TV Network (50%)
- Showtime Networks
  - FLIX
  - The Movie Channel
  - Showtime
  - Sundance Channel

Outdoor advertising
- CBS Outdoor (outdoor advertising)

Radio
- CBS Radio
- CBS Radio Network
- Spanish Broadcasting System (15%)
- Westwood One (19%)

Publishing
- Simon & Schuster
  - The Free Press
  - Pocket Books
  - Scribner
  - Simon & Schuster Audio (audio books)
  - Simon & Schuster Interactive (CD-ROMs)
  - Simon & Schuster Online (SimonSays.com)

Other
- CBS Consumer Products
- CBS Interactive
  - CBS.com
  - CBSNews.com
  - CBS SportsLine.com
  - Last.fm
  - Wallstrip.com

## COMPETITORS

Citadel Broadcasting
Clear Channel
Cumulus Media
Disney
JCDecaux
Lamar Advertising
NBC Universal
News Corp.
Penguin Group
Random House
Sony Pictures Television
Time Warner

## HISTORICAL FINANCIALS

Company Type: Public

**Income Statement** FYE: December 31

| | REVENUE ($ mil.) | NET INCOME ($ mil.) | NET PROFIT MARGIN | EMPLOYEES |
|---|---|---|---|---|
| **12/06** | 14,320 | 1,661 | 11.6% | 23,654 |
| **12/05** | 14,536 | (7,089) | — | 32,160 |
| **12/04** | 22,526 | (17,462) | — | 38,350 |
| **12/03** | 26,585 | 1,417 | 5.3% | 117,750 |
| **12/02** | 24,606 | 726 | 2.9% | 120,630 |
| **Annual Growth** | (12.7%) | 23.0% | — | (33.5%) |

**2006 Year-End Financials**

Debt ratio: 29.9%
Return on equity: 7.3%
Cash ($ mil.): 3,075
Current ratio: 1.85
Long-term debt ($ mil.): 7,027
No. of shares (mil.): 707
Dividends
Yield: 2.4%
Payout: —
Market value ($ mil.): 22,041

**Stock History** NYSE: CBS

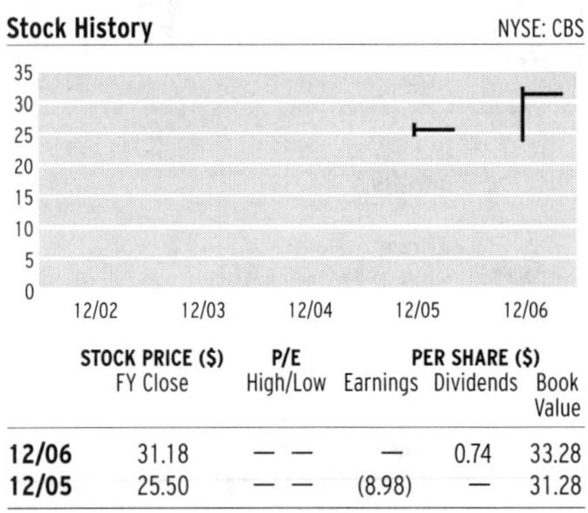


| | STOCK PRICE ($) FY Close | P/E High/Low | PER SHARE ($) Earnings | Dividends | Book Value |
|---|---|---|---|---|---|
| **12/06** | 31.18 | — — | — | 0.74 | 33.28 |
| **12/05** | 25.50 | — — | (8.98) | — | 31.28 |
| **Annual Growth** | 22.3% | — — | — | — | 6.4% |

# CDW Corporation

CDW Corporation takes more orders than Beetle Bailey. The firm offers some 100,000 computer products, mostly through catalogs, telesales, and the company's Internet and extranet Web sites. Brands include Adobe, Apple, Cisco, Lenovo, Samsung, ViewSonic, and others. In addition to computers, CDW also sells items such as printers, software, accessories, and networking products from companies including Hewlett-Packard, IBM, Microsoft, Sony, and Toshiba. Almost all of CDW's sales come from private business and public sector customers. Founder and chairman emeritus Michael Krasny owns nearly 22% of CDW.

The firm acquired IT solution provider Berbee Information Networks in late 2006 in a bid to enhance its advanced technology products and services offerings. The purchase brought with it several large enterprise customers within the corporate, health care, education, and state and local government sectors.

CDW continues to expand its public sector business, which accounted for some 32% of 2006 sales, through its CDW Government subsidiary. The division sells exclusively to government (federal, state, and local) and education customers.

In May 2007 the company announced that it agreed to be acquired by private equity firm Madison Dearborn Partners for about $7 billion.

## HISTORY

Michael Krasny started Computer Discount Warehouse at his kitchen table in 1984. Weary of selling used cars at his father's Chicago lot (though he did like using his programming skills to computerize the dealership), Krasny quit and had to sell his own computer to raise cash. A classified ad in the *Chicago Tribune* generated phenomenal response, and Krasny sold his computer almost immediately.

When the calls kept coming in, he bought more computers and sold them to people responding to the original ad, and his mail-order business was under way. Krasny chose new, stripped-down IBM clones, packaged them with monitors and printers, and advertised them as used computer systems. Because PCs were still in their infancy and because customers were lost in the technology, computer setup and repair became a large part of the early business.

CDW launched its first catalog in 1987. Figuring that some buyers would shy away from purchasing costly PC systems by mail, Krasny in 1990 opened his first retail showroom (one of two) in Chicago.

The company went public in 1993 after changing the name to CDW Computer Centers. By then it had intensified its push into the corporate market, which featured bulk purchases and solid repeat business. Sales that year nearly doubled from 1992.

CDW launched an Internet site in 1995. The next year it expanded its telemarketing-based sales strategy and began taking online orders. In 1996 CDW enlarged its Chicago showrooms.

Intense marketing and low prices boosted sales in 1997 with multimedia products, data storage devices, PCs, software, and video products as the fastest sellers. That year the company relocated its offices (and one of its showrooms) to a larger facility in Vernon Hills, Illinois. CDW pushed past the $1 billion mark for the first time in 1997, logging sales of nearly $1.3 billion. The following year the company formed CDW Government, a subsidiary set up to focus on sales to government and education institutions.

In May 2001 Krasny assumed the role of chairman emeritus; CEO John Edwardson added chairman to his duties. In May 2003 shareholders approved a decision to change the company name to CDW Corporation.

In October 2006 CDW completed the acquisition of privately held Berbee Information Networks for $184 million.

## EXECUTIVES

**Chairman and CEO:** John A. Edwardson, age 57, $760,629 pay
**EVP Sales; President CDW Government:** James R. (Jim) Shanks, age 42, $320,639 pay
**EVP Marketing, Purchasing, and Business Development:** Harry J. Harczak Jr., age 50, $320,639 pay
**SVP and CFO:** Barbara A. Klein, age 52, $282,999 pay
**SVP Operations, Logistics, and Customer Services:** Douglas E. (Doug) Eckrote, age 42, $260,639 pay
**SVP, General Counsel, and Corporate Secretary; Secretary, CDW Government:** Christine A. Leahy, age 42
**SVP, Coworker Services and Chief Coworker Services Officer:** Dennis G. Berger, age 42
**SVP and CIO:** Jonathan J. (Jon) Stevens, age 37
**VP, Treasurer, and Assistant Secretary; Treasurer and Assistant Secretary, CDW Government:** Robert J. Welyki
**VP Business Development:** Anne B. Ireland
**VP Sales:** Steven M. (Steve) Schuldt
**VP Investor Relations:** Cindy T. Klimstra
**VP Marketing:** Mark Gambill, age 47
**VP Purchasing:** Matthew A. Troka
**VP Services:** James J. (Norm) Lillis
**VP Small Business:** Maria M. Sullivan
**Director of Information Technology:** K. C. Tomsheck
**Media Relations Manager:** Gary Ross
**Auditors:** PricewaterhouseCoopers LLP

## LOCATIONS

**HQ:** CDW Corporation
300 N. Milwaukee Ave., Vernon Hills, IL 60061
**Phone:** 847-465-6000
**Web:** www.cdw.com

## PRODUCTS/OPERATIONS

**2006 Sales**

| | $ mil. | % of total |
|---|---|---|
| Corporate sector | 4,514.1 | 66 |
| Public sector | 2,162.4 | 32 |
| Berbee | 109.0 | 2 |
| **Total** | **6,785.5** | **100** |

## COMPETITORS

Amazon.com
Apple
ASAP Software
AT&T
Best Buy
Buy.com
Circuit City
CompuCom
CompUSA
Costco Wholesale
Dell
EDS
Fry's Electronics
Gateway
GTSI
Hewlett-Packard
IBM
Insight Enterprises
Micro Electronics
Newegg
Office Depot
OfficeMax
PC Connection
PC Mall
PC Warehouse
Pomeroy IT
Softchoice
Software House
Staples
SunGard Higher Education
Systemax
VeriCenter
Verizon
Wal-Mart
Zones

## HISTORICAL FINANCIALS

Company Type: Public

### Income Statement

FYE: December 31

| | REVENUE ($ mil.) | NET INCOME ($ mil.) | NET PROFIT MARGIN | EMPLOYEES |
|---|---|---|---|---|
| **12/06** | 6,786 | 266 | 3.9% | 5,500 |
| **12/05** | 6,292 | 272 | 4.3% | 4,300 |
| **12/04** | 5,738 | 241 | 4.2% | 3,800 |
| **12/03** | 4,665 | 175 | 3.8% | 3,700 |
| **12/02** | 4,265 | 185 | 4.3% | 2,900 |
| **Annual Growth** | 12.3% | 9.5% | — | 17.4% |

### 2006 Year-End Financials

| | |
|---|---|
| Debt ratio: — | No. of shares (mil.): 79 |
| Return on equity: 20.1% | Dividends |
| Cash ($ mil.): 352 | Yield: 0.7% |
| Current ratio: 2.93 | Payout: 15.8% |
| Long-term debt ($ mil.): — | Market value ($ mil.): 5,539 |

### Stock History

NASDAQ (GS): CDWC

80 70 60 50 40 30 20 10 0

12/02 12/03 12/04 12/05 12/06

| | STOCK PRICE ($) FY Close | P/E High | P/E Low | PER SHARE ($) Earnings | Dividends | Book Value |
|---|---|---|---|---|---|---|
| **12/06** | 70.32 | 22 | 15 | 3.30 | 0.52 | 17.61 |
| **12/05** | 57.58 | 21 | 16 | 3.26 | 0.43 | 15.81 |
| **12/04** | 66.35 | 27 | 20 | 2.79 | 0.36 | 14.91 |
| **12/03** | 57.76 | 31 | 18 | 2.03 | 0.30 | 12.73 |
| **12/02** | 43.85 | 29 | 19 | 2.10 | — | 11.01 |
| **Annual Growth** | 12.5% | — | — | 12.0% | 20.1% | 12.5% |

# CenterPoint Energy

CenterPoint Energy (formerly Reliant Energy) has made a complete pivot around its core operations. The company, which had evolved from a local utility into a global power provider, has spun off most of its nonregulated operations and has returned to its roots. CenterPoint Energy's regulated utilities distribute natural gas and electricity to more than 5 million customers in six states, primarily in the southern US. CenterPoint Energy also operates 7,900 miles of gas pipeline, and it has gas gathering and storage operations. The company's main stomping ground is Texas, where it has regulated power distribution operations through subsidiary CenterPoint Energy Houston Electric.

The company's natural gas distribution subsidiaries serve about 3 million customers in Arkansas, Louisiana, Minnesota, Mississippi, Oklahoma, and Texas. CenterPoint Energy also markets natural gas to large retail customers and provides HVAC and other energy-related services through its gas division.

CenterPoint Energy changed its name in 2002 in preparation for the spin off of its 83% stake in Reliant Resources (now Reliant Energy), a global independent power producer and energy marketer; the spin off was completed later that year. (Reliant Resources changed its name to Reliant Energy in 2004.) CenterPoint Energy transferred its nonregulated Texas retail power supply business to Reliant Resources before spinning off the unit.

As part of its corporate reorganization, and in response to Texas' electricity deregulation (which took effect in 2002), CenterPoint Energy has separated its Texas power generation and distribution operations and will work toward exiting the electric generation business. The company spun off 19% of its Texas Genco unit to shareholders in 2003. CenterPoint Energy has agreed to sell Texas Genco to GC Power Acquisition (owned by investment firms The Blackstone Group, Hellman & Friedman, Kohlberg Kravis Roberts, and Texas Pacific Group) for $3.65 billion, following the buyback of Texas Genco's publicly held shares.

The company has also divested all of its international assets, including its Latin American utility interests. To further its focus on core operations, CenterPoint Energy has sold its Energy Management Services division to Entergy.

In 2005 CenterPoint Energy sold its majority stake in Texas Genco (now NRG Texas), which owns power plants with 14,000 MW of generating capacity.

## HISTORY

CenterPoint Energy's earliest predecessor, Houston Electric Lighting and Power, was formed in 1882 by a group including Emanuel Raphael, cashier at Houston Savings Bank, and Mayor William Baker. In 1901 General Electric's financial arm, United Electric Securities Company, took control of the utility, which became Houston Lighting & Power (HL&P). United Electric sold HL&P five years later; by 1922 HL&P ended up in the arms of National Power & Light Company (NP&L), a subsidiary of Electric Bond & Share (a public utility holding company that had been spun off by General Electric).

In 1942 NP&L was forced to sell HL&P in order to comply with the 1935 Public Utility Holding Company Act. As the oil industry boomed in Houston after WWII, so did HL&P.

HL&P became the managing partner in a venture to build a nuclear plant on the Texas Gulf Coast in 1973. Construction on the South Texas Project, with partners Central Power and Light and the cities of Austin and San Antonio, began in 1975. In 1976 Houston Industries (HI) was formed as the holding company for HL&P.

By 1980 the nuke was four years behind schedule and over budget. HL&P and its partners sued construction firm Brown & Root in 1982 and received a $700 million settlement in 1985. (The City of Austin also sued HL&P for damages but lost.) The nuke was finally brought online in 1988, with the final cost estimated at $5.8 billion.

Meanwhile, HI diversified into cable TV in 1986 by creating Enrcom (later Paragon Communications) through a venture with Time Inc. Two years later it bought the US cable interests of Canada's Rogers Communications. HI left the cable business in 1995, selling out to Time Warner.

Developing Latin fever, HI joined a consortium that bought 51% of Argentinean electric company EDELAP in 1992. (However, in 1998 HI sold its stake to AES.) On a roll, HI acquired 90% of Argentina's electric utility EDESE (1995); joined a consortium that won a controlling stake in Light, a Brazilian electric utility (1996); bought a stake in Colombian electric utility EPSA (1997); and bought interests in three electric utilities in El Salvador (1998).

Back in the US, HI acquired gas dealer NorAm for $2.5 billion in 1997. The next year it bought five generating plants in California from Edison International and laid plans to build merchant plants in Arizona (near Phoenix), Illinois, Nevada (near Las Vegas, in partnership with Sempra Energy), and Rhode Island. Overseas, HI finished a power plant in India in 1998.

In 1999 HI became Reliant Energy and HL&P became Reliant Energy HL&P. That year the company bought a 52% stake in Dutch power generation firm UNA; it bought the remaining 48% the next year. Also in 2000 Reliant Energy paid Sithe Energies (now a part of Dynegy) $2.1 billion for 21 power plants in the mid-Atlantic states. It transferred all of its nonregulated operations to subsidiary Reliant Resources.

Reliant Energy netted about $1.7 billion in 2001 from the sale to the public of nearly 20% of Reliant Resources. Later that year Reliant Resources announced that it would acquire US independent power producer Orion Power Holdings in a $4.7 billion deal; the deal was completed in 2002. Deregulation took effect in Texas that year, and Reliant Energy transferred its retail power supply business to Reliant Resources.

As the finances of wholesale energy companies came under scrutiny in 2002, the SEC issued a formal investigation into "round-trip" energy trades completed by Reliant Resources. These activities artificially inflated the company's trading volumes and led it to restate its 1999, 2000, and 2001 financial results; it also reduced its energy marketing and trading workforce by about 35%.

Reliant Energy announced plans in 2001 to form a new holding company (CenterPoint Energy) for itself and Reliant Resources; it completed the name change in 2002. CenterPoint Energy spun off its remaining 83% stake in Reliant Resources to shareholders later that year. Reliant Resources changed its name to Reliant Energy in 2004.

## EXECUTIVES

**Chairman:** Milton Carroll, age 56
**President, CEO, and Director:** David M. McClanahan, age 57, $1,956,500 pay
**EVP and CFO:** Gary L. Whitlock, age 57, $658,750 pay
**EVP, General Counsel, and Corporate Secretary:** Scott E. Rozzell, age 56, $687,843 pay
**SVP and Chief Accounting Officer, CenterPoint Energy, CenterPoint Energy Houston Electric, and Texas Genco Holdings:** James S. Brian, age 59
**SVP and Group President, CenterPoint Energy Pipeline and Field Services:** Byron R. Kelley, age 57, $599,000 pay
**SVP and Group President, Regulated Operations:** Thomas R. (Tom) Standish, age 57, $549,500 pay
**VP and Treasurer:** Marc Kilbride, age 53
**VP and Controller:** Walter L. Fitzgerald, age 48
**VP Corporate Communications:** Floyd J. LeBlanc, age 46
**Division President and COO, CenterPoint Energy Houston Electric:** Georgianna E. Nichols, age 57
**Division President and COO, CenterPoint Energy Minnesota Gas:** Gary M. Cerny, age 50
**Division President, CenterPoint Energy Services:** Wayne D. Stinnett, age 55
**Division President and COO, CenterPoint Energy Southern Gas Operations:** Constantine S. (Dean) Liollio, age 48
**Division SVP and COO, CenterPoint Energy Pipelines:** Cyril J. Zebot, age 56
**Division SVP and COO, CenterPoint Energy Field Services:** Hugh G. Maddox, age 59
**Division SVP, CenterPoint Energy Pipeline Services:** Walter L. Ferguson, age 49
**Division SVP Finance, Regulated Operations:** Joseph B. McGoldrick, age 52
**Auditors:** Deloitte & Touche LLP

## LOCATIONS

**HQ:** CenterPoint Energy, Inc.
1111 Louisiana St., Houston, TX 77002
**Phone:** 713-207-1111 **Fax:** 713-207-3169
**Web:** www.centerpointenergy.com

CenterPoint Energy has regulated energy distribution operations in Arkansas, Louisiana, Minnesota, Mississippi, Oklahoma, and Texas, and it has other energy-related operations in those states plus Alabama, Colorado, Illinois, Iowa, Kansas, Missouri, New Mexico, Pennsylvania, Wisconsin, and Wyoming.

## PRODUCTS/OPERATIONS

**2006 Sales**

| | $ mil. | % of total |
|---|---|---|
| Retail gas | 4,546 | 49 |
| Wholesale gas | 2,331 | 25 |
| Electric delivery | 1,781 | 19 |
| Gas transport | 550 | 6 |
| Energy products & services | 111 | 1 |
| **Total** | **9,319** | **100** |

## COMPETITORS

AEP
AEP Texas Central
AEP Texas North
Ameren
Aquila
Avista
Cleco
CMS Energy
Constellation Energy
Dominion Resources
Duke Energy
El Paso
Entergy
Exelon
Koch
Mirant
Mississippi Power
OGE Energy
ONEOK
Progress Energy
Southern Company
Southwestern Electric Power
Southwestern Energy
TXU
Williams Companies
Xcel Energy

## HISTORICAL FINANCIALS

Company Type: Public

**Income Statement** FYE: December 31

| | REVENUE ($ mil.) | NET INCOME ($ mil.) | NET PROFIT MARGIN | EMPLOYEES |
|---|---|---|---|---|
| **12/06** | 9,319 | 432 | 4.6% | 8,623 |
| **12/05** | 9,722 | 252 | 2.6% | 9,001 |
| **12/04** | 8,000 | (905) | — | 9,093 |
| **12/03** | 9,760 | 484 | 5.0% | 11,046 |
| **12/02** | 7,923 | (3,920) | — | 12,019 |
| **Annual Growth** | 4.1% | — | — | (8.0%) |

**2006 Year-End Financials**

Debt ratio: 506.6%
Return on equity: 30.3%
Cash ($ mil.): 696
Current ratio: 0.71
Long-term debt ($ mil.): 7,882
No. of shares (mil.): 314
Dividends
Yield: 3.6%
Payout: 45.1%
Market value ($ mil.): 5,206

**Stock History** NYSE: CNP

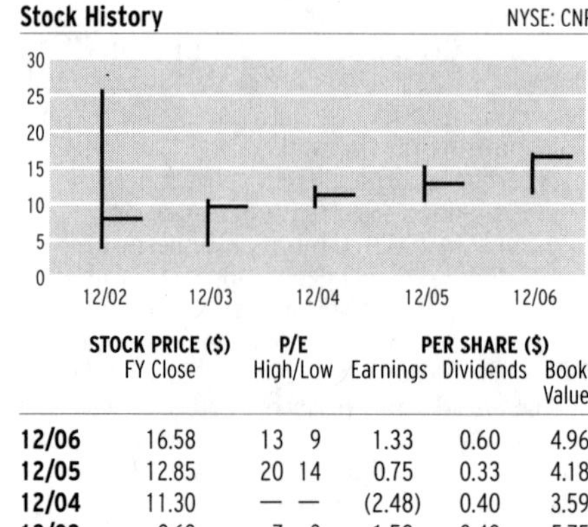


| | STOCK PRICE ($) FY Close | P/E High | P/E Low | PER SHARE ($) Earnings | Dividends | Book Value |
|---|---|---|---|---|---|---|
| **12/06** | 16.58 | 13 | 9 | 1.33 | 0.60 | 4.96 |
| **12/05** | 12.85 | 20 | 14 | 0.75 | 0.33 | 4.18 |
| **12/04** | 11.30 | — | — | (2.48) | 0.40 | 3.59 |
| **12/03** | 9.69 | 7 | 3 | 1.58 | 0.40 | 5.75 |
| **12/02** | 8.00 | — | — | (13.08) | 0.65 | 4.66 |
| **Annual Growth** | 20.0% | — | — | — | (2.0%) | 1.5% |

# Centex Corporation

Centex has built its way to the top: Its Centex Homes business is a top US homebuilder, behind only D.R. Horton, Lennar, and Pulte Homes by units. Centex Homes operates in nearly 700 neighborhoods in the US, and in fiscal 2007 it sold some 36,000 homes (average price about $307,000) to first-time and move-up buyers. Subsidiary Centex HomeTeam Services offers pest-control and security-monitoring services. Centex also offers commercial contracting services and has interests in land development, mortgage banking, and commercial real estate.

Preparing for the housing market slowdown, Centex has cut the number of corporate owned lots by 50% and reduced its workforce. With the exception of Texas, revenues from all of its markets decreased when compared to 2006.

The company has been paring away at its holdings over the last several years to focus on its home building operations. It has sold its manufactured homes, construction products, lawn care, and subprime mortgage holdings. In 2007 it sold its construction division to Balfour Beatty plc.

CTX Mortgage operates some 200 offices across the US. It makes loans to about 70% of its parent's homebuyers. The firm's Centex HomeTeam Services subsidiary provides pest control and security monitoring services.

Its Centex Destination Properties division primarily sells homes in resort areas, whereas its Fox & Jacobs unit targets first-time homeowners.

## HISTORY

Tom Lively and Ira Rupley, who built their first large subdivision near Dallas in 1949, founded homebuilder Centex the next year. Centex's first out-of-Texas project was a development of 7,000 houses near Chicago.

By 1960 it had built 25,000 houses. Branching out from homebuilding, Centex built its first cement plant in 1963 and established four more over the next 25 years. Centex expanded into commercial construction with the 1966 purchase of Dallas contractor J. W. Bateson (founded in 1936). In the 1970s it picked up other general contractors, moving into Florida, California, and Washington, DC. To combine homebuilding with home financing, Centex began mortgage banking in 1973, and when oil prices soared during the 1970s, the enterprising company formed subsidiary Cenergy to go digging for petroleum (spun off in 1984).

Centex increasingly built outside its Southwest territory — from 28% of all new homes in 1979 to 45% in 1984. Larry Hirsch, a New York-reared lawyer who had headed a Houston cement and energy company, became COO in 1985 (and CEO in 1988). The early 1980s were a boom time for Texas real estate as deregulation spurred S&Ls to make loans — any loans. The market became overbuilt, and when oil prices collapsed in 1986 and 1987, credit dried up. With the spectacular failure of several Texas S&Ls, the Texas real estate market crashed. Centex was pinched, but it survived on sales from less-depressed areas of the US.

Centex Development was established in 1987 as a custodian for land the company could not develop during the bust. Centex created Centex Rodgers that year to focus on construction of medical facilities. In 1994 the company took its construction products division public and sold off its S&Ls.

In 1995 Centex entered ventures to build luxury houses in the UK and living centers for sufferers of Alzheimer's disease and memory disorders. The next year Centex purchased parts of security firm Advanced Protection Systems and pest-control company Environmental Safety Systems — both are now part of Centex HomeTeam.

The company was selected by *Builder* and *Home* magazines in 1997 to build the Home of the Future, showcasing cutting-edge products and design. On the other end of the housing spectrum, Centex acquired 80% of manufactured-home maker Cavco Industries (it bought the rest in 2000 and spun off the unit in 2003). The next year Cavco bought AAA Homes, which had about 260 manufactured-home retail outlets in 12 states, Canada, and Japan. Also in 1998 Centex entered Ohio and New Jersey by acquiring Wayne Homes and Calton Homes, respectively.

In 2000 Centex joined other leading homebuilders to form HomebuildersXchange, a supply chain services Web site, but the project soon collapsed. Centex expanded in the Midwest by acquiring Detroit homebuilder Selective Group in 2001. It also acquired CityHomes, a Dallas-based builder of upscale townhomes and condos. In 2002 the company's Centex HomeTeam Services subsidiary sold its chemical lawn care operations, including 12 branches in Florida, Georgia, and Texas, to The Scotts Company.

Subsidiary Centex Homes acquired the St. Louis- and Indianapolis-area homebuilding operations of The Jones Company early in 2003. The St. Louis operations became a new St. Louis division that markets under The Jones Company brand, while the Indianapolis operations sell Centex Homes-branded housing.

In 2003 Centex board members approved the spinoff of Cavco, its principal manufactured housing business and the largest manufactured homebuilder in Arizona, to Centex stockholders in a tax-free exchange that was made final in June. Also that year Centex Homes gained recognition as the only company to rank within the top 10 US homebuilders for each of the past 35 years, according to *Professional Builder* magazine.

The company spun off Centex Construction Products, Inc. (which became Eagle Materials Inc.) to shareholders in early 2004. It also completed its acquisition of 3333 Holding Corp. and Centex Development Company, L.P., ending the tandem trading relationship of its common stock with the securities of the acquired companies. Centex Home Equity Company (now Nationstar Mortgage), the company's sub-prime home lending unit, was sold to Fortress Investment Group in 2006.

## EXECUTIVES

**Chairman, President, and CEO:** Timothy R. (Tim) Eller, age 57, $11,533,500 pay
**EVP and CFO:** Catherine R. (Cathy) Smith, age 43
**SVP Human Resources:** Joseph A. (Joe) Bosch, age 49
**SVP Strategy and Corporate Development:** Robert S. Stewart, age 52, $1,812,000 pay
**SVP, Chief Legal Officer, General Counsel, and Assistant Secretary:** Brian J. Woram, age 45
**SVP Administration:** Michael S. Albright
**SVP Finance:** Lawrence Angelilli
**SVP and Controller:** Mark D. Kemp, age 44
**VP Communications and Public Affairs:** Neil J. Devroy
**VP and CIO:** Lisa R. Hoffman
**VP, Corporate Counsel, and Assistant Secretary:** Paul M. Johnston
**VP Internal Audit:** Steven L. McDowell, age 42
**VP Investor Relations:** Matthew G. (Matt) Moyer
**VP and Treasurer:** Gail M. Peck
**VP, Deputy General Counsel, and Secretary:** James R. Peacock III
**VP Talent Management:** Kirk K. Thor
**Director Communications and Public Affairs:** Ken Smalling
**Co-President and Co-COO, Centex Real Estate Corporation, East Operating Region:** Andrew J. Hannigan, age 54, $8,907,785 pay
**Co-President and Co-COO, Centex Real Estate Corporation, West Operating Region:** David L. Barclay, age 53
**Chairman, CTX Mortgage Company:** John L. Matthews, age 59
**Chairman, President, and CEO, CTX Mortgage Company:** Timothy M. (Tim) Bartosh
**VP Human Resources, Centex Construction Group; Centex Rooney Construction Co., Inc.; and Southeast Division, Centex Construction Company:** Jack Carr
**Auditors:** Ernst & Young LLP

## LOCATIONS

**HQ:** Centex Corporation
2728 N. Harwood, Dallas, TX 75201
**Phone:** 214-981-5000 **Fax:** 214-981-6859
**Web:** www.centex.com

### 2007 Closings

| | No. units | % of total |
|---|---|---|
| Texas | 7,083 | 20 |
| East | 6,720 | 19 |
| Southwest | 6,209 | 17 |
| Southeast | 5,374 | 15 |
| Central | 4,789 | 13 |
| Northwest | 4,709 | 13 |
| Other | 901 | 3 |
| **Total** | **35,785** | **100** |

## PRODUCTS/OPERATIONS

### 2007 Sales

| | $ mil. | % of total |
|---|---|---|
| Home Building | 11,414.8 | 95 |
| Financial Services | 468.0 | 4 |
| Other | 131.8 | 1 |
| **Total** | **12,014.6** | **100** |

### 2007 Sales

| | $ mil. | % of total |
|---|---|---|
| Home Building | | |
| Southwest | 2,730.4 | 23 |
| East | 2,255.7 | 19 |
| Northwest | 2,121.7 | 18 |
| Southeast | 1,686.0 | 14 |
| Texas | 1,154.7 | 9 |
| Central | 1,048.9 | 9 |
| Other homebuilding | 417.5 | 3 |
| Financial Services | 468.0 | 4 |
| Corporate & Other | 131.7 | 1 |
| **Total** | **12,014.6** | **100** |

## COMPETITORS

AT&T
Barratt Developments
Beazer Homes
C.F. Jordan
Clayton Homes
Countrywide Financial
David Weekley Homes
D.R. Horton
Fluor
Foster Wheeler
Gehan Homes
Hovnanian Enterprises
Imperial Construction
KB Home
Kimball Hill inc
Lennar
M.D.C.
Meritage Homes
MGIC Investment
M/I Homes
Morrison Homes
NVR
Pardee Homes
Peter Kiewit Sons'
PMI Group
Pulte Homes
Rollins
Ryland
Standard Pacific
Taylor Wimpey
Thos. S. Byrne
Toll Brothers
Turner Corporation
Tyco
Walter Industries
Weyerhaeuser Real Estate
Whiting-Turner

## HISTORICAL FINANCIALS

Company Type: Public

### Income Statement

FYE: March 31

| | REVENUE ($ mil.) | NET INCOME ($ mil.) | NET PROFIT MARGIN | EMPLOYEES |
|---|---|---|---|---|
| **3/07** | 12,015 | 268 | 2.2% | 11,418 |
| **3/06** | 14,400 | 1,289 | 9.0% | 18,544 |
| **3/05** | 12,860 | 1,011 | 7.9% | 17,134 |
| **3/04** | 10,363 | 828 | 8.0% | 16,532 |
| **3/03** | 9,117 | 556 | 6.1% | 17,540 |
| **Annual Growth** | 7.1% | (16.6%) | — | (10.2%) |

### 2007 Year-End Financials

Debt ratio: 108.9%
Return on equity: 5.3%
Cash ($ mil.): 1,029
Current ratio: 4.35
Long-term debt ($ mil.): 5,567
No. of shares (mil.): 120
Dividends
Yield: 0.4%
Payout: 7.2%
Market value ($ mil.): 5,012

### Stock History

NYSE: CTX

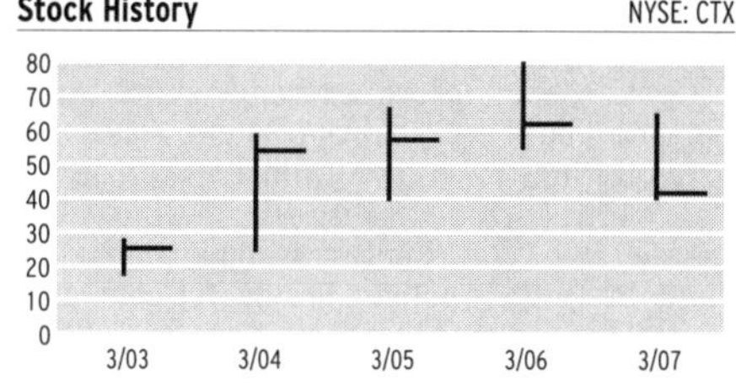


| | STOCK PRICE ($) FY Close | P/E High/Low | | PER SHARE ($) Earnings | Dividends | Book Value |
|---|---|---|---|---|---|---|
| **3/07** | 41.78 | 29 | 18 | 2.23 | 0.16 | 42.61 |
| **3/06** | 61.99 | 8 | 6 | 9.71 | 0.16 | 41.04 |
| **3/05** | 57.27 | 9 | 5 | 7.64 | 0.16 | 33.51 |
| **3/04** | 54.06 | 9 | 4 | 6.40 | 3.10 | 24.87 |
| **3/03** | 25.24 | 6 | 4 | 4.41 | 0.08 | 43.69 |
| **Annual Growth** | 13.4% | — | — | (15.7%) | 18.9% | (0.6%) |

# CenturyTel, Inc.

Bright lights and big cities are *not* for CenturyTel. The integrated communications company provides local exchange services, long-distance, Internet access, and broadband services. Its rural local-exchange carrier (RLEC) subsidiaries operate in the suburbs and small towns of 25 states scattered throughout the US, from Arizona to Minnesota, and from Washington to Tennessee. The local-exchange units maintain about 2.1 million local access lines. They do about 70% of their business in Alabama, Arkansas, Missouri, Washington, and Wisconsin. CenturyTel's offerings also include cable TV and business data services.

The company has teamed up with EchoStar to provide DISH satellite TV service to CenturyTel customers. CenturyTel also offers security monitoring services in some markets.

After exiting the wireless communications business by selling those assets in 2002 to ALLTEL, the company has expanded its wireline network operations through acquisitions that include the regional fiber-optic business of bankrupt wholesale transport services provider Digital Teleport and fiber-optic assets and customers from KMC Telecom. It also bought switched phone lines from Verizon Communications in Alabama and Missouri. CenturyTel acquired metro fiber networks in 16 markets from KMC for $65 million in cash.

In 2007 CenturyTel purchased Madison River Communications for $830 million. To re-enter the wireless business, CenturyTel agreed to offer services through a reseller agreement with Cingular Wireless (now AT&T Mobility).

## HISTORY

Today's CenturyTel began in 1930 when Marie and William Clarke Williams bought the Oak Ridge Telephone Company in Oak Ridge, Louisiana. In 1946 they gave the 75-line company as a wedding present to their son, Clarke, who launched a course of growth by acquisition, buying the Marion, Louisiana, telephone exchange in 1950 (Clarke Williams remained active in the company until his death in 2002). The company was renamed Century Telephone Enterprises in 1971; it went public in 1978.

Century bought local-exchange and cellular networks, building regional clusters. States targeted during the early to mid-1990s included Louisiana, Michigan, Mississippi, Ohio, Tennessee, and Texas. Century's biggest purchase came in 1997: It bought Pacific Telecom, Inc. (PTI) from electric utility PacifiCorp for $2.2 billion. Century gained operations in 12 western and Midwestern states and in Alaska, more than doubling its telephone customer base.

Also in 1997 Century merged its Metro Access Networks (MAN) subsidiary into Brooks Fiber and became Brooks' largest shareholder. Brooks' shares rose when WorldCom agreed to buy it, and Century sold 85% of its interest in Brooks.

The company rolled out the CenturyTel brand name in 1998 and bought Ameritech's local-exchange and directory operations in 21 Wisconsin communities. To help pay for the acquisition, the carrier sold its Alaska operations in 1999 to Alaska Communications Systems Holdings, a firm headed by former PTI executives. It also bought the Montana ISP DigiSys.

CenturyTel purchased nearly 500,000 access lines from GTE (now Verizon) in Arkansas, Missouri, and Wisconsin in 2000 and the next year sold its PCS licenses to Leap Wireless.

ALLTEL offered to buy CenturyTel in 2001 for $6.1 billion in cash and stock and $3.3 billion in assumed debt. ALLTEL announced the offer to the public after being told by CenturyTel that the company was not for sale. CenturyTel subsequently sued ALLTEL for releasing information about the company's plans. Tensions eased, however, and in 2002 the two companies reached the agreement that sent CenturyTel's wireless operations, which served more than 800,000 customers in six states, to ALLTEL. The $1.6 billion cash deal enabled the company to expand its fixed-line business, including the acquisition that year of 675,000 switched phone lines in Alabama and Missouri from Verizon for about $2.2 billion.

In 2003 CenturyTel acquired the regional fiber-optic business of bankrupt wholesale transport services provider Digital Teleport in a deal valued at $38 million. It also acquired fiber transport assets in Arkansas, Missouri, and Illinois, from Level 3 Communications in a deal valued at about $16 million.

The company further expanded its network operations with the 2005 acquisition of the fiber-optic network and customer base of KMC Telecom's operations in Monroe and Shreveport, Louisiana, as well as metro fiber networks in 16 additional markets for $65 million in cash.

## EXECUTIVES

**Chairman and CEO:** Glen F. Post III, age 54, $1,768,019 pay
**Vice Chairman:** Harvey P. Perry, age 61
**President and COO:** Karen A. Puckett, age 47, $957,315 pay
**EVP and CFO:** R. Stewart Ewing Jr., age 55, $797,738 pay
**SVP and CIO:** Michael E. (Mike) Maslowski, age 59
**SVP Operations Support:** David D. Cole, age 49, $574,500 pay
**SVP, General Counsel, and Secretary:** Stacey W. Goff, age 41, $518,358 pay
**VP and Controller:** Neil A. Sweasy
**VP Investor Relations:** Tony Davis
**VP Corporate Communication:** Patricia Cameron
**External Communication Manager:** Annmarie Sartor
**Auditors:** KPMG LLP

## LOCATIONS

**HQ:** CenturyTel, Inc.
100 CenturyTel Dr., Monroe, LA 71203
**Phone:** 318-388-9000 **Fax:** 318-388-9064
**Web:** www.centurytel.com

CenturyTel has operations in Alabama, Arizona, Arkansas, Colorado, Idaho, Indiana, Iowa, Louisiana, Michigan, Minnesota, Mississippi, Missouri, Montana, Nevada, New Mexico, Ohio, Oregon, Tennessee, Texas, Washington, Wisconsin, and Wyoming.

## PRODUCTS/OPERATIONS

### 2006 Sales

| | % of total |
|---|---|
| Voice | 35 |
| Network access | 36 |
| Data | 14 |
| Fiber transport & CLEC | 6 |
| Other | 9 |
| **Total** | **100** |

### Selected Services

Audiotext services
Cable TV
Cellular phone service
Competitive local-exchange services
Internet access
Long-distance
Printing, database management, and direct mail services
Security monitoring

## COMPETITORS

ALLTEL
AT&T
BellSouth
Birch
McLeodUSA
NTELOS
Sprint Nextel
Verizon

## HISTORICAL FINANCIALS

Company Type: Public

### Income Statement

FYE: December 31

| | REVENUE ($ mil.) | NET INCOME ($ mil.) | NET PROFIT MARGIN | EMPLOYEES |
|---|---|---|---|---|
| **12/06** | 2,448 | 370 | 15.1% | 6,400 |
| **12/05** | 2,479 | 335 | 13.5% | 6,900 |
| **12/04** | 2,407 | 337 | 14.0% | 6,800 |
| **12/03** | 2,381 | 345 | 14.5% | 6,720 |
| **12/02** | 1,972 | 802 | 40.6% | 6,960 |
| **Annual Growth** | 5.6% | (17.6%) | — | (2.1%) |

### 2006 Year-End Financials

Debt ratio: 75.8%
Return on equity: 10.9%
Cash ($ mil.): 26
Current ratio: 0.47
Long-term debt ($ mil.): 2,413
No. of shares (mil.): 113
Dividends
Yield: 0.6%
Payout: 8.1%
Market value ($ mil.): 4,945

### Stock History

NYSE: CTL

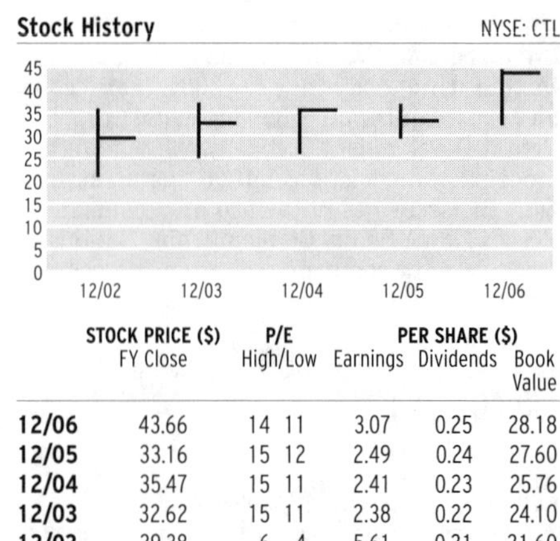


| | STOCK PRICE ($) FY Close | P/E High | P/E Low | PER SHARE ($) Earnings | Dividends | Book Value |
|---|---|---|---|---|---|---|
| **12/06** | 43.66 | 14 | 11 | 3.07 | 0.25 | 28.18 |
| **12/05** | 33.16 | 15 | 12 | 2.49 | 0.24 | 27.60 |
| **12/04** | 35.47 | 15 | 11 | 2.41 | 0.23 | 25.76 |
| **12/03** | 32.62 | 15 | 11 | 2.38 | 0.22 | 24.10 |
| **12/02** | 29.38 | 6 | 4 | 5.61 | 0.21 | 21.60 |
| **Annual Growth** | 10.4% | — | — | (14.0%) | 4.5% | 6.9% |

# Cephalon, Inc.

Cephalon isn't asleep at the wheel. The company sells PROVIGIL, a treatment for the sleep disorder narcolepsy, in the US and select countries around the world. The company's other top sellers are epilepsy treatment GABITRIL (licensed from Abbott Labs and Novo Nordisk) and cancer pain medication ACTIQ. It sells five products in the US and has more than 25 approved drugs on the market in Europe. Cephalon's drug development activities focus on central nervous system disorders, including Parkinson's and Alzheimer's diseases, as well as cancer, addiction, and pain.

Cephalon's three top sellers — PROVIGIL, ACTIQ, and GABITRIL — bring in nearly three-quarters of the company's product revenues. Distributors Cardinal Health, McKesson, and AmerisourceBergen are the company's chief customers. Collectively the three account for over 70% of sales.

In 2006 the FDA rejected a variation of PROVIGIL (named SPARLON) as a treatment for attention deficit hyperactivity disorder (ADHD) in children. Also that year, Cephalon received approval for lead drug candidate FENTORA, which could help cancer patients in pain who aren't helped by other pain medications.

Another narcotic approved in 2006 to help cancer patients conquer insurmountable pain is the novel lollipop ACTIQ. The drug was not approved for uses in any other context, but the company has been investigated by the Connecticut Attorney General Richard Blumenthal for pushing the drug for off-label uses (e.g., for use against migraines). ACTIQ is 80 times stronger than morphine, is highly addictive, and accounted for nearly a half-billion dollars in sales during the first nine months of 2006. Oncologists and pain management specialists accounted for less than five percent of prescriptions in the first six months of 2006.

The company's research and development focus is on developing therapies for neurological disorders and cancer. It is developing kinase inhibitors to potentially treat hematological cancers, solid tumors (with Sanofi-Aventis), and Parkinson's.

## HISTORY

A senior research biologist with DuPont, Dr. Frank Baldino formed Cephalon in 1987 to research neural degeneration. The company raised $500 million in venture capital and went public in 1991.

Cephalon in 1990 teamed with Schering-Plough to research Alzheimer's disease. By 1992 it had developed Myotrophin to treat amyotrophic lateral sclerosis (ALS, or Lou Gehrig's disease).

With optimism running high for Myotrophin, Cephalon in 1992 bought a drug plant (sold 1996). The next year it joined with SmithKline Beecham (now GlaxoSmithKline) to research neurodegenerative diseases. In 1995 the firm established a sales force. Word of promising Myotrophin trial results sent the stock soaring, but criticism of the trial brought it crashing back. A 1996 shareholder suit charging that Cephalon hid poor results was settled for $17 million in 1999.

Meanwhile, it bought rights to PROVIGIL from Group Lafon and shepherded it through the FDA approval process.

In 1997 the FDA rejected Myotrophin; Cephalon's research agreements with Schering-Plough and SmithKline Beecham ended too. The next year the FDA ruled Myotrophin "potentially approvable" and required more expensive trials. Better news came from Ireland and the UK, where PROVIGIL was approved for sale.

In 1999 Cephalon won a research contract with Dutch drug maker H Lundbeck to research neurodegenerative diseases. Later that year Cephalon threw in the towel on Myotrophin, disappointing ALS victims who had been taking the drug in trials.

In 2000 PROVIGIL failed to treat attention deficit hyperactivity disorder in trials. Cephalon bounced back by boosting its pipeline with the purchase of pain drugmaker Anesta. The following year it bought Group Lafon to gain full control of PROVIGIL's marketing rights. Spooked by the on-the-sly partnerships that helped bring down Enron, Cephalon also acquired control of two joint ventures it had set up to market PROVIGIL and GABITRIL to avoid arousing suspicion among investors. It also bought back European rights to ACTIQ from Elan.

Cephalon received approval from the FDA in 2004 to market PROVIGIL as a therapy for other sleep disorders such as obstructive sleep apnea.

The company's 2004 purchase of CIMA allowed Cephalon to develop new versions of its existing drugs using CIMA's delivery technologies. But the acquisition didn't come without costs — in addition to the $515 million it paid for CIMA, Cephalon agreed to give Barr Pharmaceuticals the right to license a generic version of ACTIQ to gain FDA approval.

Cephalon acquired drug maker Zeneus Pharma in late 2005. Zeneus added nearly 15 products to the company's portfolio, but more importantly Zeneus' 15 European operations will greatly expand Cephalon's presence across the pond. Also that year the company expanded its cancer pipeline with its purchases of Salmedix and of the TRISENOX franchise from Cell Therapeutics.

## EXECUTIVES

**Chairman and CEO:** Frank Baldino Jr., age 52, $2,279,100 pay
**EVP; President, Research and Development Division:** Jeffry L. Vaught, age 56
**EVP and Chief Administrative Officer:** Carl A. Savini, age 57
**EVP, Pharmaceutical Operations:** Robert P. Roche Jr., age 51, $674,700 pay
**EVP, Worldwide Technical Operations:** Peter E. Grebow, age 60
**SVP and CFO:** J. Kevin Buchi, age 51, $725,700 pay
**SVP, General Counsel, and Secretary:** John E. Osborn, age 49, $861,000 pay
**SVP, Worldwide Medical and Regulatory Operations:** Lesley Russell
**VP, Business Development:** Natalie Barndt
**VP, Marketing:** Lynne M. Brooks
**VP, Public Affairs:** Robert W. Grupp
**VP, Regulatory Affairs, Europe:** Susan F. Sullman
**VP, Risk Management:** Stephen J. Burns
**VP, Sales:** Roy Craig
**VP, Worldwide Drug Development:** Joseph S. Turi
**VP, Worldwide Export Business:** John M. Farah Jr., age 54
**VP, Worldwide Quality Control:** Ernest Kelly, age 57
**Senior Director, Corporate Affairs:** Fritz Bittenbender, age 34
**Senior Director, Human Resources, Technical Operations:** Daniel P. Lawlor
**Senior Director, Investor Relations:** Robert S. (Chip) Merritt
**Senior Director, Public Relations:** Sheryl L. Williams
**Auditors:** PricewaterhouseCoopers LLP

## LOCATIONS

**HQ:** Cephalon, Inc.
41 Moores Rd., Frazer, PA 19355
**Phone:** 610-344-0200 **Fax:** 610-738-6590
**Web:** www.cephalon.com

Cephalon has office or manufacturing facilities in Denmark, France, Germany, Italy, the Netherlands, Poland, Spain, Switzerland, the UK, and the US.

### 2006 Sales

| | $ mil. | % of total |
|---|---|---|
| US | 1,473.0 | 84 |
| Europe | 291.0 | 16 |
| **Total** | **1,764.0** | **100** |

## PRODUCTS/OPERATIONS

### 2006 Sales

| | $ mil. | % of total |
|---|---|---|
| Products | | |
| PROVIGIL | 734.8 | 42 |
| ACTIQ | 577.6 | 33 |
| GABITRIL | 59.3 | 3 |
| Generic OTFC | 54.8 | 3 |
| FENTORA | 29.3 | 2 |
| Other products | 264.3 | 15 |
| Other | 43.9 | 2 |
| **Total** | **1,764.0** | **100** |

### Selected Products

US
- ACTIQ (cancer pain)
- GABITRIL (epilepsy)
- PROVIGIL (narcolepsy, obstructive sleep apnea, shift work sleep disorder)
- TRISENOX (promyelocytic leukemia)
- VIVITROL (alcohol dependence)

Europe
- ACTIQ
- FONZYLANE (vascular disorders)
- NAXY (antibiotic)
- PROVIGIL
- SPASFON (bowel and urinary tract ailments)

## COMPETITORS

Allergan
Amgen
Athena Neurosciences
Biogen Idec
Ceregene
Cortex Pharmaceuticals
DRAXIS
Eli Lilly
Genentech
GlaxoSmithKline
Johnson & Johnson
McNeil
Millennium Pharmaceuticals
Neurocrine Biosciences
Novartis
Pfizer
Sanofi-Aventis
Shire

## HISTORICAL FINANCIALS

Company Type: Public

### Income Statement

FYE: December 31

| | REVENUE ($ mil.) | NET INCOME ($ mil.) | NET PROFIT MARGIN | EMPLOYEES |
|---|---|---|---|---|
| **12/06** | 1,764 | 145 | 8.2% | 2,895 |
| **12/05** | 1,212 | (175) | — | 2,895 |
| **12/04** | 1,015 | (74) | — | 2,173 |
| **12/03** | 715 | 84 | 11.7% | 1,646 |
| **12/02** | 507 | 172 | 33.8% | 1,271 |
| **Annual Growth** | 36.6% | (4.1%) | — | 22.9% |

### 2006 Year-End Financials

Debt ratio: 17.2%
Return on equity: 15.1%
Cash ($ mil.): 522
Current ratio: 0.87
Long-term debt ($ mil.): 225
No. of shares (mil.): 66
Dividends
Yield: —
Payout: —
Market value ($ mil.): 4,619

### Stock History

NASDAQ (GS): CEPH

| | STOCK PRICE ($) FY Close | P/E High | P/E Low | PER SHARE ($) Earnings | Dividends | Book Value |
|---|---|---|---|---|---|---|
| **12/06** | 70.41 | 40 | 25 | 2.08 | — | 19.96 |
| **12/05** | 64.74 | — | — | (3.01) | — | 10.54 |
| **12/04** | 50.88 | — | — | (1.31) | — | 14.40 |
| **12/03** | 48.41 | 38 | 26 | 1.44 | — | 13.87 |
| **12/02** | 48.67 | 28 | 13 | 2.79 | — | 11.65 |
| **Annual Growth** | 9.7% | — | — | (7.1%) | — | 14.4% |

# C.H. Robinson Worldwide

C.H. Robinson Worldwide (CHRW) keeps merchandise moving. One of the largest third-party logistics providers in North America, CHRW arranges freight transportation using trucks, trains, ships, and airplanes belonging to other companies. It contracts with some 45,000 carriers. CHRW handles more than 5 million shipments per year for its 25,000-plus customers, which include companies in the food and beverage, manufacturing, and retail industries. CHRW also offers supply chain management services. In addition, the company buys, sells, and transports fresh produce throughout the US, and its T-Chek unit provides fuel purchasing management services for motor carriers.

Truckload services are CHRW's primary transportation offering, but the company is endeavoring to diversify by providing more less-than-truckload and freight consolidation services. The company also hopes to sell more supply chain management services to its transportation customers.

Although CHRW does most of its business in the US, the company also has branch offices elsewhere in the Americas and in Europe and Asia. It has about 215 offices altogether. The company has been working to expand — especially outside North America — both through organic growth and through acquisitions. In 2006 CHRW bought US-based freight broker Payne, Lynch & Associates, as well as an India-based freight forwarder, Triune.

In addition, CHRW hopes to expand its wholesale produce business by promoting its own brand, "The Fresh 1."

## HISTORY

In the early 1900s Charles H. Robinson began a produce brokerage in Grand Forks, North Dakota. Robinson entered a partnership in 1905 with Nash Brothers, the leading wholesaler in North Dakota, and the company C.H. Robinson was born.

Robinson became president but soon relinquished control under mysterious circumstances (rumor had it he ran off with Annie Oakley). H. B. Finch took charge, and by 1913 a new company, Nash Finch, became C.H. Robinson's sole owner.

As a subsidiary, C.H. Robinson primarily procured produce for Nash Finch, which helped it expand into Illinois, Minnesota, Texas, and Wisconsin. To avoid FTC scrutiny over preferential treatment, Nash Finch split CHR into two companies: C.H. Robinson Co., owned by C.H. Robinson employees, which sold produce to Nash Finch warehouses; and C.H. Robinson, Inc., owned by Nash Finch.

After WWII the interstate highway system and refrigerated trucks changed the industry. No longer dependent on railroads, C.H. Robinson began charging for truck brokerage of perishables. The two companies formed by the 1940s split reunited under the C.H. Robinson name in the mid-1960s; Nash Finch kept a 25% stake in the company and sold the rest to employees. Not surprisingly, Nash Finch wanted to divert C.H. Robinson profits to its other businesses, so in 1976 C.H. Robinson employees bought out Nash Finch.

The next year D. R. "Sid" Verdoorn was named president and Looe Baker became chairman. They focused on increasing C.H. Robinson's data-processing capability and adding branch offices. In 1980 the Motor Carrier Act deregulated the transportation industry, and C.H. Robinson entered the freight-contracting business, acting as a middleman for all types of goods. The company grew rapidly, from about 30 offices in 1980 to more than 60 in 1990.

As part of its overall effort to become a full-service provider, C.H. Robinson formed its Intermodal Division (more than one mode of transport) in 1988. It also established an information services division (1991) and bought fruit juice concentrate distributor Daystar International (1993). By this time the company was working with more than 14,000 shippers and moving more than 500,000 shipments a year.

Meanwhile, C.H. Robinson had ventured overseas with the launch of its international division in 1989. It entered Mexico in 1990 and added airfreight operations and international freight forwarding through the 1992 purchase of C.S. Green International. In 1993 C.H. Robinson picked up a 30% stake in French motor carrier Transeco (acquiring the rest later) and opened offices in Mexico City, Chile, and Venezuela.

In 1997 the company went public and became C.H. Robinson Worldwide; the next year Verdoorn, who was CEO, assumed the additional role of chairman.

The company acquired Argentina's Comexter transportation group in 1998 to gain market share in South America, and it expanded its European operation in 1999 through the purchase of Norminter, a French third-party logistics provider. Much closer to home, CHRW bought Eden Prairie-based Preferred Translocation Systems, a logistics provider to less-than-truckload carriers, and Chicago-based transportation provider American Backhaulers.

In 2000 the company partnered with PaperExchange.com, Inc., the global e-business marketplace for the pulp and paper industry, to provide an exclusive logistics service to PaperExchange.com members.

CHRW continued to expand in 2002 with the purchase of Miami-based Smith Terminal Transportation Services. Verdoorn stepped down as CEO that year, and company president John Wiehoff was promoted to replace him.

The company acquired three US-based produce sourcing and marketing companies, FoodSource, Inc., FoodSource Procurement, and Epic Roots, in 2004 for a reported $270 million. Also that year, CHRW added seven offices in China by acquiring a Dalian-based freight forwarder, and in 2005 it gained operations in Germany, Italy, and the US by buying two freight forwarding companies, Hirdes Group Worldwide and Bussini Transport.

Verdoorn retired at the end of 2006, and Wiehoff was named his successor.

## EXECUTIVES

**Chairman, President, and CEO:** John P. Wiehoff, age 45, $400,000 pay
**President, T-Chek:** Bryan D. Foe
**VP and CFO:** Chad M. Lindbloom, age 42, $260,000 pay
**VP, General Counsel, and Secretary:** Linda U. Feuss, age 50
**VP, Human Resources:** Laura Gillund
**VP, International Forwarding:** Jeffrey Scovill
**Treasurer and Assistant Secretary:** Troy A. Renner
**VP and CIO:** Thomas K. (Tom) Mahlke, age 35
**Director, Investor Relations:** Angela K. (Angie) Freeman
**Auditors:** Deloitte & Touche LLP

## LOCATIONS

**HQ:** C.H. Robinson Worldwide, Inc.
8100 Mitchell Rd., Eden Prairie, MN 55344
**Phone:** 952-937-8500 **Fax:** 952-937-6714
**Web:** www.chrobinson.com

**2006 Sales**

| | $ mil. | % of total |
|---|---|---|
| US | 6,066 | 93 |
| Other countries | 490 | 7 |
| **Total** | **6,556** | **100** |

## PRODUCTS/OPERATIONS

**2006 Sales**

| | $ mil. | % of total |
|---|---|---|
| Transportation | 5,322 | 81 |
| Sourcing | 1,192 | 18 |
| Information services | 42 | 1 |
| **Total** | **6,556** | **100** |

**Selected Services**

Transportation (truck, rail, intermodal, ocean, and air transportation of freight through third parties)
Sourcing (fresh produce sourcing and distribution to wholesalers, grocery chains, and food service companies)
Information services (fuel purchase contracts, fuel tax reporting, online access to customized reports)

## COMPETITORS

APL Logistics
Cass Information Systems
CEVA Logistics
Comdata
DB Logistics
DHL
EGL Eagle Global Logistics
Exel Transportation Services
Expeditors
FedEx Trade Networks
GeoLogistics
Greatwide Logistics
Hub Group
Kuehne + Nagel
Menlo Worldwide
Pacer Global Logistics
Panalpina
Penske Truck Leasing
Ryder
Schneider Logistics
Transplace
UPS Supply Chain Solutions
YRC Logistics

## HISTORICAL FINANCIALS

Company Type: Public

**Income Statement** FYE: December 31

| | REVENUE ($ mil.) | NET INCOME ($ mil.) | NET PROFIT MARGIN | EMPLOYEES |
|---|---|---|---|---|
| **12/06** | 6,556 | 267 | 4.1% | 6,768 |
| **12/05** | 5,689 | 203 | 3.6% | 5,776 |
| **12/04** | 4,342 | 137 | 3.2% | 4,806 |
| **12/03** | 3,614 | 114 | 3.2% | 4,112 |
| **12/02** | 3,295 | 96 | 2.9% | 3,814 |
| **Annual Growth** | 18.8% | 29.0% | — | 15.4% |

**2006 Year-End Financials**

Debt ratio: —
Return on equity: 31.0%
Cash ($ mil.): 473
Current ratio: 1.83
Long-term debt ($ mil.): —
No. of shares (mil.): 173
Dividends
Yield: 1.4%
Payout: 37.3%
Market value ($ mil.): 7,060

**Stock History** NASDAQ (GS): CHRW

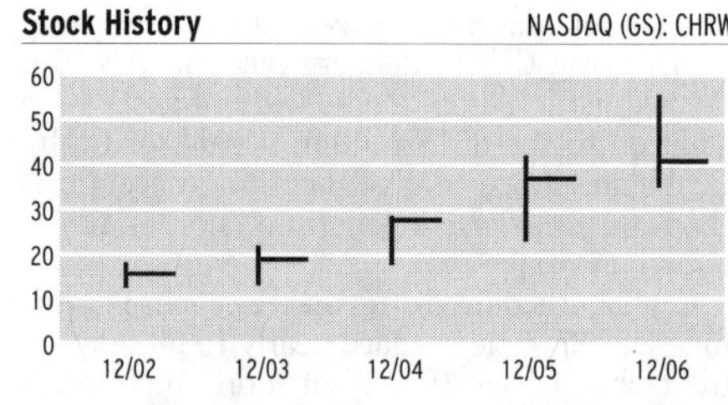


| | STOCK PRICE ($) FY Close | P/E High | P/E Low | PER SHARE ($) Earnings | Dividends | Book Value |
|---|---|---|---|---|---|---|
| **12/06** | 40.89 | 36 | 23 | 1.53 | 0.57 | 5.47 |
| **12/05** | 37.03 | 36 | 20 | 1.16 | 0.13 | 4.51 |
| **12/04** | 27.76 | 35 | 23 | 0.80 | — | 7.28 |
| **12/03** | 18.95 | 32 | 20 | 0.67 | — | 6.06 |
| **12/02** | 15.60 | 32 | 23 | 0.56 | — | 5.04 |
| **Annual Growth** | 27.2% | — | — | 28.6% | 338.5% | 2.1% |

# Champion Enterprises

Champion Enterprises is back on top as the #1 builder of manufactured homes in the US, ahead of rival Palm Harbor. The company sells about 21,000 homes annually. Champion mainly produces multi-section ranch-style homes, but it also makes one-and-a-half story homes, two-story homes, single-section homes, and multi-family units; sizes range from 400 sq. ft. to more than 4,000 sq. ft. Retail prices range from $25,000 to more than $200,000 (averaging $185,000). Champion operates around 30 plants in 16 states and Canada, and markets its homes through 20 company-owned sales centers and through about 2,700 independent retailers, including 900 Champion Home Centers.

Champion spent much of the first half of the decade closing and consolidating plants and retail facilities. Its only remaining retail locations are 16 "non-traditional" (homes in manufactured housing communities) locations in California.

Once it pared down, it began buying. The company bolstered its operations in 2005 by acquiring New Era Building Systems and its Castle Housing of Pennsylvania and Carolina Building Solutions affiliates. The companies manufacture modular housing in Pennsylvania and North Carolina.

In early 2006 the company acquired the UK manufacturer Calsafe Group, which operates through Caledonian Building Systems. The transaction, valued at $110 million, gives Champion three manufacturing facilities that make steel-framed modular buildings used as prisons, military buildings, and multi-story hotels and residences.

## HISTORY

Champion Home Builders started in 1953, just in time to take advantage of the burgeoning postwar American economy and the passage of a 1956 law allowing mobile homes to be up to 10 feet wide. The increase made mobile homes increasingly popular — by 1960 a majority were "10-wides." The change shifted the main benefit of mobile homes from mobility to affordability. Champion prospered, and it went public in 1962. By the mid-1960s it was one of the leaders in its market.

Part of Champion's success could be attributed to its vertically integrated manufacturing process. Champion made and installed all the components in a home, from plumbing to drapes. This policy increased efficiency, and productivity was twice that of most of its rivals. Despite these advantages, the mid-1970s recession hit the company hard. Industry sales fell about a third from their 1972 peak. Champion felt the recession's brunt in its mobile-home sales, but sales of recreational vehicles (RVs) and low-priced motor homes helped temper the losses. The increase of prices for site-built housing helped Champion and other mobile-home makers out of the slump.

At the start of the 1980s, Champion recovered briefly, but by the mid-1980s the company was again struggling. By 1990 the firm had lost $30 million over the previous five years and was considering bankruptcy proceedings. Walter Young took over that year and quickly revamped the company. To stave off bankruptcy, Young sold some businesses (RV making and component manufacturing) for much-needed cash. Young also gutted the central office and eliminated 248 of 260 jobs.

In 1993 Champion settled on a growth strategy involving both internal sales and acquisitions. The company soon acted on its plan by purchasing Dutch Housing in 1994 and Chandeleur Homes and Crest Ridge Homes a year later. The company opened a plant to make midsize buses in 1995.

The company seemed to experience its greatest growth in 1996. Champion acquired Redman Industries, the #3 US manufactured-housing builder at the time (Champion was #2). The acquisition pushed Champion to the top spot in terms of sales that year. In addition, Champion opened five new plants that combined with the Redman purchase increased the number of plants Champion operated from 23 to 50.

In 1998 Champion sold its midsize-bus business to narrow its focus on housing. That year the company bought manufactured-housing seller The ICA Group, operator of 23 retail outlets. In 1999 Champion bought Care Free Homes (Utah), Central Mississippi Manufactured Housing, Homes of Merit (Florida), and Heartland Homes (Texas).

Although sales increased, Champion's profits nearly halved in 1999 because of bad inventory control, excess retail sites, and tighter consumer financing requirements. In response, the company closed or consolidated eight manufacturing plants and streamlined and upgraded inventory-control processes. Slowing demand and increased competition forced the company to close more than 60 retail outlets and seven of its factories in 2000. The company idled two additional factories and 30 more retail centers in 2001.

The next year Champion closed 12 manufacturing facilities and 126 of its retail sales centers, with a reduction of jobs estimated at 1,500, or 15% of its total workforce. Champion acquired the manufactured housing consumer loan origination business of CIT Group/Sales Financing, Inc., to operate as HomePride Finance Corp.; it also formed a joint venture, in which it held a 49% stake, with loan originator National City Mortgage Co. to provide real estate financing under the name HomePride Mortgage, LP. Champion discontinued the loan origination operations in 2003.

Champion closed five manufacturing plants (in Arizona, Georgia, Kentucky, North Carolina, and Texas) in 2003 and moved production at a facility in Alabama to an idle plant. The company cut its workforce by 13% (about 1,000 jobs) and shuttered 35 retail centers.

The next year Champion sold its western retail region, which included eight retail sales operations in Colorado, Idaho, Nevada, Utah, and Washington, to Blaser Holding, Inc., for about $4 million. Champion also sold three retail sales centers in Kentucky and one in Texas in 2004.

Champion completed the sale of its traditional retail locations in 2005. The same year, in the aftermath of Hurricane Katrina, Champion received a $60 million order from the Federal Emergency Management Agency (FEMA) to build some 2,000 homes for displaced storm victims. Late in the year Champion acquired New Era Building Systems and its Castle Housing of Pennsylvania and Carolina Building Solutions affiliates. The companies manufacture modular housing in Pennsylvania and North Carolina.

Still on the acquisition track, Champion acquired modular builder Highland Manufacturing for $23 million early in 2006.

## EXECUTIVES

**Chairman, President, and CEO:** William C. (Bill) Griffiths, age 55, $675,000 pay
**EVP, CFO, and Treasurer:** Phyllis A. Knight, age 44, $364,000 pay
**SVP Sales and Marketing:** Roger D. Lasater
**VP and Controller:** Richard P. (Rick) Hevelhorst, age 59
**VP, Human Resources:** Jeffrey L. Nugent, age 60, $208,000 pay
**VP, Investor Relations:** Lisa D. Lettieri
**VP, Operations:** Bobby J. (B.J.) Williams, age 60, $273,000 pay
**President, Canadian Operations:** Don DeHart
**President, Central Retail Region:** Edward B. Lasater
**President, Eastern Region:** Richard Egger
**President, Iseman Corporation:** R. James Scoular
**President, Midwestern Region:** Pat Cross
**President, Midwestern Retail Region:** Christopher L. Richter
**President, Retail Operations:** M. Mark Cole, age 41, $379,800 pay
**President, San Jose Advantage Homes:** Glenn Gilliam
**President, Southern Region:** Paul Jarvis
**President, Southern Retail:** Richard A. Brugge
**President, Southern Showcase:** Gary L. Good
**President, Western Region:** Richard Barrett
**President, Western Retail Region:** Robert S. Bagwell
**President, Highland Manufacturing Co.:** Greg DeGroot
**Auditors:** Ernst & Young

## LOCATIONS

**HQ:** Champion Enterprises, Inc.
2701 Cambridge Ct., Ste. 300,
Auburn Hills, MI 48326
**Phone:** 248-340-9090 **Fax:** 248-340-9345
**Web:** www.championhomes.net

Champion Enterprises manufactures homes at 30 plants in 16 US states and western Canada. It also owns and operates 16 retail locations in California.

## PRODUCTS/OPERATIONS

### 2006 Sales

| | $ mil. | % of total |
|---|---|---|
| Manufacturing | 1,195.8 | 85 |
| Retail | 117.4 | 8 |
| International | 90.7 | 7 |
| Adjustments | (39.3) | — |
| **Total** | **1,364.6** | **100** |

### Selected Subsidiaries

CBS Monaco Limited
Calsafe Group
Champion Enterprises Management Co.
Champion Homes of Boaz, Inc.
Dutch Housing, Inc.
Star Fleet, Inc.
Highland Acquisition Corp.
Highland Manufacturing Company, LLC
Homes of Merit, Inc.
Moduline International, Inc.
Moduline Industries (Canada) Ltd.
New Era Building Systems, Inc.
North American Housing Corp.
Redman Industries, Inc.

## COMPETITORS

American Homestar
Cavalier Homes
Cavco
Clayton Homes
Coachmen
Dynamic Homes
Fairmont Homes
Fleetwood Enterprises
Four Seasons Housing
General Housing
Horton Industries
Liberty Homes
Nobility Homes
Origen Financial
Palm Harbor Homes
Patriot Homes
Skyline
Southern Energy Homes
Sunshine Homes
TRIGANO

## HISTORICAL FINANCIALS

Company Type: Public

**Income Statement** FYE: Saturday nearest December 31

| | REVENUE ($ mil.) | NET INCOME ($ mil.) | NET PROFIT MARGIN | EMPLOYEES |
|---|---|---|---|---|
| **12/06** | 1,365 | 138 | 10.1% | 7,000 |
| **12/05** | 1,273 | 38 | 3.0% | 7,400 |
| **12/04** | 1,150 | 17 | 1.5% | 6,800 |
| **12/03** | 1,141 | (103) | — | 6,800 |
| **12/02** | 1,372 | (256) | — | 8,000 |
| **Annual Growth** | (0.1%) | — | — | (3.3%) |

**2006 Year-End Financials**

Debt ratio: 83.7%
Return on equity: 61.6%
Cash ($ mil.): 70
Current ratio: 1.30
Long-term debt ($ mil.): 252
No. of shares (mil.): 76
Dividends
Yield: —
Payout: —
Market value ($ mil.): 716

**Stock History** NYSE: CHB

| | STOCK PRICE ($) FY Close | P/E High | P/E Low | PER SHARE ($) Earnings | Dividends | Book Value |
|---|---|---|---|---|---|---|
| **12/06** | 9.36 | 9 | 3 | 1.78 | — | 3.95 |
| **12/05** | 13.62 | 32 | 17 | 0.48 | — | 1.94 |
| **12/04** | 11.82 | 58 | 30 | 0.21 | — | 1.07 |
| **12/03** | 7.01 | — | — | (1.86) | — | 0.23 |
| **12/02** | 2.91 | — | — | (5.22) | — | 0.71 |
| **Annual Growth** | 33.9% | — | — | — | — | 53.6% |

# Charles Schwab

The once-rebellious Charles Schwab is all grown up. The discount broker now offers the same traditional brokerage services it shunned some three decades ago. Schwab manages approximately $1.3 trillion for more than 7 million individual and institutional clients. Traders can access its services via telephone, wireless device, the Internet, and through more than 300 US offices. Besides discount brokerage, the firm offers private banking, bond trading, annuities, and proprietary Schwab and Laudus mutual funds, as well as mortgages, CDs, and other banking products through its Charles Schwab Bank. Schwab sold U.S. Trust to Bank of America for some $3.3 billion in cash in 2007.

Schwab's primary business remains making trades for investors who make their own decisions. The company's services include futures and commodities trading, access to IPOs, and investment educational material. Schwab's OneSource service offers investors access to more than 2,000 no-load funds. The company also provides access to nearly 21,000 bonds, bond funds, and other fixed-income investment products.

With the launch of Charles Schwab Bank, the company remains in step with the industry-wide movement toward one-stop shopping for financial services. Schwab has also reduced its minimum investment requirement in its brokerage accounts and savings accounts, and instituted a simpler, less expensive trading fee structure that recalls the company's discount roots.

The company has said it is looking to grow its service offerings through acquisitions; a first step in that strategy is Schwab's 2007 acquisition of The 401(k) Companies from Nationwide Financial Services. The addition compliments the company's existing Charles Schwab Trust subsidiary, which serves as a trustee for employee benefit plans.

Schwab plans to shut down CyberTrader by the end of 2007 and will merge the direct-access brokerage's business with its own.

Charles Schwab owns nearly 20% of his namesake firm.

## HISTORY

During the 1960s Stanford graduate Charles Schwab founded First Commander Corp., which managed investments and published a newsletter. But he failed to properly register with the SEC, and after a hiatus, he returned to the business under the name Charles Schwab & Co. in 1971. Initially a full-service broker, Schwab moved into discount brokerage after the SEC outlawed fixed commissions in 1975. While most brokers defiantly raised commissions, Schwab cut its rates steeply.

From 1977 to 1983 Schwab's client list increased thirtyfold, and revenues grew from $4.6 million to $126.5 million, enabling the firm to automate its operations and develop cash-management account systems. To gain capital, Charles sold the company to BankAmerica (now Bank of America) in 1983. Schwab grew, but federal regulations prevented expansion into such services as mutual funds and telephone trading. Charles bought his company back in 1987 and took it public. When the stock market crashed later that year, trading volume fell by nearly half, from 17,900 per day. Stung, Schwab diversified further, offering new fee-based services. Commission revenues fell from 64% of sales in 1987 to 39% in 1990, but by 1995 the long bull market had pushed commissions to more than 50%.

In 1989 Schwab introduced TeleBroker, a 24-hour Touch-Tone telephone trading service available in English, Spanish, Mandarin, or Cantonese.

Schwab continued to diversify, courting independent financial advisors. Other buys included Mayer & Schweitzer (1991, now Schwab Capital Markets), an OTC market maker that accounted for about 7% of all NASDAQ trades. In 1993 the firm opened its first overseas office in London, but traded only in dollar-denominated stocks until it bought Share-Link (later Charles Schwab Europe), the UK's largest discount brokerage, in 1995. It subsequently sold the British pound sterling brokerage business to Barclays PLC, although it has maintained its US dollar business in the UK.

During the next year Schwab made a concerted effort to build its retirement services by creating a 401(k) administration and investment services unit. In 1997 Schwab allied with J.P. Morgan, Hambrecht & Quist (now J.P. Morgan H&Q), and Credit Suisse First Boston (CSFB) to give its customers access to IPOs; the next year the relationship with CSFB deepened to give Schwab access to debt offerings. In late 1997 and early 1998, Schwab reorganized to reflect its new business lines. The firm also began recruiting talent rather than promoting from within.

Expansion was key at the turn of the century. In 1999 Schwab moved toward more broker-advised investing: It inked a deal (geared toward its retirement products customers) with online financial advice firm Financial Engines, and introduced Velocity, a desktop system designed to make trading easier for fiscally endowed investors. In 2000 Schwab bought online broker CyBerCorp (now CyberTrader), as well as U.S. Trust, which markets to affluent clients.

While Schwab's World Trade Center offices were destroyed by the September 11 terrorist attacks, the company did not lose any of its New York staff.

To pare expenses, Schwab reduced its workforce by about 35% between 2000 and 2003.

Founder and chairman Charles Schwab relinquished his role of co-CEO in early 2003, only to move back into the driver's seat in mid-2004 when former CEO David Pottruck was asked to step down by the company's board.

One of Schwab's first orders of business was to reexamine the company's 2004 acquisition of SoundView Technology Group, which was combined with its Capital Markets operations to form Schwab SoundView Capital Markets. While the purchase was intended to help the company beef up its services for institutional investors, Schwab said that SoundView lacked "synergy" with the company's tradition of supporting the individual investor and sold the business to Swiss bank UBS.

## EXECUTIVES

**Chairman and CEO:** Charles R. (Chuck) Schwab, age 69, $900,000 pay
**President and COO:** Walter W. (Walt) Bettinger II, age 46
**CFO:** Joseph Martinetto, age 45
**EVP and CIO:** Gideon Sasson, age 51
**EVP; President, Schwab Financial Products:** Randall W. Merk, age 52
**EVP and Chief Marketing Officer:** Rebecca (Becky) Saeger, age 51
**EVP, Corporate Oversight, General Counsel, and Secretary:** Carrie E. Dwyer, age 56, $490,000 pay
**EVP, Human Resources:** Jan Hier-King, age 52
**EVP, Risk and Credit Management:** Bryce R. Lensing
**EVP, Operations:** Maurisa Sommerfield
**EVP, Client Experience, Schwab Investor Services:** John S. Clendening, age 44
**EVP, Internal Audit:** Robert J. Almeida
**President and CEO, Charles Schwab Investment Management:** Evelyn S. Dilsaver
**EVP; Head of Schwab Institutional:** Charles G. Goldman, age 45
**EVP; COO, U.S. Trust:** James L. Bailey
**SVP and Head of Corporate Public Relations:** Greg Gable
**SVP, Investor Relations:** Richard G. Fowler
**Chief Investment Strategist:** Elizabeth A. (Liz Ann) Sonders
**President and CEO, U.S. Trust Corporation:** Frances Aldrich Sevilla-Sacasa
**Auditors:** Deloitte & Touche LLP

## LOCATIONS

**HQ:** The Charles Schwab Corporation
101 Montgomery St., San Francisco, CA 94104
**Phone:** 415-636-7000 **Fax:** 415-636-9820
**Web:** www.schwab.com

## PRODUCTS/OPERATIONS

### 2006 Sales

| | $ mil. | % of total |
|---|---|---|
| Interest | 2,113 | 42 |
| Asset management & administration fees | 1,945 | 39 |
| Trading revenue | 785 | 16 |
| Other | 145 | 3 |
| **Total** | **4,988** | **100** |

### Selected Subsidiaries

Charles Schwab Bank, National Association
Charles Schwab Investment Management, Inc. (mutual fund investment adviser)
Schwab Holdings, Inc.
Charles Schwab & Co., Inc. (securities broker-dealer)

## COMPETITORS

A.G. Edwards
Ameriprise
Citigroup
E*TRADE Financial
Edward Jones
FMR
John Hancock Financial Services
Morgan Stanley
Prudential
Raymond James Financial
Scottrade
ShareBuilder
TD Ameritrade
UBS Financial Services
Wells Fargo

## HISTORICAL FINANCIALS

Company Type: Public

### Income Statement

FYE: December 31

| | REVENUE ($ mil.) | NET INCOME ($ mil.) | NET PROFIT MARGIN | EMPLOYEES |
|---|---|---|---|---|
| **12/06** | 4,988 | 1,227 | 24.6% | 12,400 |
| **12/05** | 5,151 | 725 | 14.1% | 14,000 |
| **12/04** | 4,479 | 286 | 6.4% | 14,200 |
| **12/03** | 4,328 | 472 | 10.9% | 16,300 |
| **12/02** | 4,480 | 109 | 2.4% | 16,700 |
| **Annual Growth** | 2.7% | 83.2% | — | (7.2%) |

### 2006 Year-End Financials

Debt ratio: 7.7%
Return on equity: 25.9%
Cash ($ mil.): 15,369
Current ratio: —
Long-term debt ($ mil.): 388

No. of shares (mil.): 1,265
Dividends
Yield: 0.7%
Payout: 14.7%
Market value ($ mil.): 24,469

### Stock History

NASDAQ (GS): SCHW

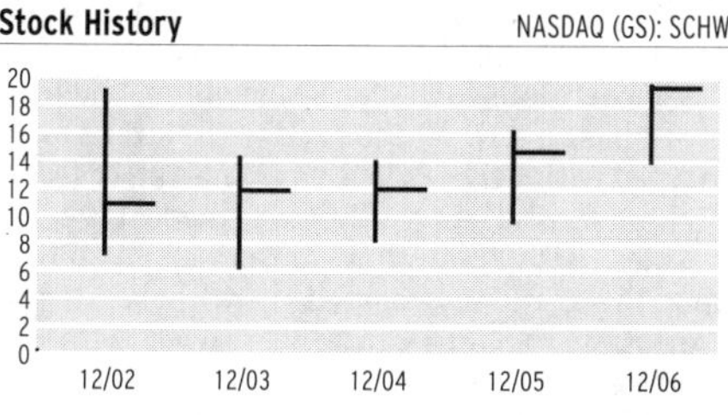


| | STOCK PRICE ($) FY Close | P/E High | P/E Low | PER SHARE ($) Earnings | Dividends | Book Value |
|---|---|---|---|---|---|---|
| **12/06** | 19.34 | 21 | 15 | 0.95 | 0.14 | 3.96 |
| **12/05** | 14.67 | 29 | 18 | 0.55 | 0.09 | 3.45 |
| **12/04** | 11.96 | 66 | 39 | 0.21 | 0.07 | 3.30 |
| **12/03** | 11.84 | 41 | 18 | 0.35 | 0.05 | 3.29 |
| **12/02** | 10.85 | 238 | 90 | 0.08 | 0.04 | 2.98 |
| **Annual Growth** | 15.5% | — | — | 85.6% | 36.8% | 7.3% |

# Charming Shoppes

Charming Shoppes wants its shoppers to be mesmerizing. The company runs about 2,375 stores in 48 US states at three apparel chains that cater to plus-size women: 1,000-plus Fashion Bug stores that sell moderately priced apparel and accessories in girls, juniors, misses, and plus sizes; about 465 Catherines Plus Size stores; and 860 Lane Bryant and Lane Bryant Outlet stores. Across the US, Charming Shoppes serves low- to middle-income women and teens who follow fashion styles rather than set them. The company's purchase of Lane Bryant from Limited Brands in 2001 elevated Charming Shoppes to #1 in the plus-size market. The company also owns Crosstown Traders, a direct marketer of women's apparel.

To expand its direct-to-consumer business (catalogs and Internet sales) Charming Shoppes in mid-2005 acquired Crosstown Traders, which sells women's apparel, shoes, and accessories through about a dozen catalogs and corresponding Web sites, from JPMorgan Partners for about $218 million (plus debt). Charming Shoppes operates Crosstown Traders as a separate entity based in Tucson, Arizona. Currently, the company's direct-to-consumer business accounts for about 15% of sales. Charming Shoppes also plans to launch its own catalog for the Lane Bryant brand in October 2007.

About half of American women wear size 14 or larger and Americans continue to gain weight, presenting Charming Shoppes with a growth market. To reach that market, Charming Shoppes' *Figure* magazine, launched in 2003, caters to plus-sized readers and promotes the company's brands, as well as providing information about lifestyle; circulation hovers around 440,000.

At the opposite end of the spectrum Charming Shoppes, which acquired the Petite Sophisticate brand from Retail Brand Alliance (RBA) in 2006 when it assumed the leases of Casual Corner stores, has opened 45 Petite Sophisticate shops next to its Lane Bryant stores. The retailer is betting that the women's petite market is anything but: estimating its size at $10 billion.

To further expand its Lane Bryant retail channel, Charming Shoppes assumed the leases of 75 Casual Corner outlet stores from RBA. RBA sold the Casual Corner chain in 2005 to liquidator Gordon Brothers, which then shut it down. The stores reopened under the Lane Bryant Outlet banner in mid-2006. The company is also opening Lane Bryant stores in outlet malls. Overall, the company plans to grow its Lane Bryant chain to 1,000 stores.

## HISTORY

Morris and Arthur Sidewater opened their first women's apparel store, called Charm Shoppes, in Philadelphia in 1940. Morris, a buyer with apparel company Associated Merchandising, and Arthur, who performed as a dancer on tour with Red Skelton, were challenged from the start: Legal notice came during their first week that the "Charm" name was already taken. The brothers responded by changing the name of the store to Charming Shoppes.

By the end of the 1940s, the brothers began taking on partners to add new stores, with the new partners becoming store managers of the outlets they opened. In 1951 the brothers formed what would become the most significant of their partnerships with a friend of Arthur's, David Wachs, and David's brother Ellis. That year the Sidewater and Wachs brothers opened a store in Norristown, Pennsylvania; later they added another store in Woodbury, New Jersey.

During the 1960s the pairs of brothers moved to follow the steady flight of consumers to malls and large shopping centers, opening new stores in those areas under the Fashion Bug name and renaming old stores. By 1971, the year the company went public, Charming Shoppes operated 21 stores and had a total of 18 partners. As rent at the mall climbed in the mid-1970s, the company began expanding into cheaper strip malls, where rents were less than half those in enclosed malls.

As it entered the 1980s, Charming Shoppes operated nearly 160 stores. That decade marked a period of rapid expansion for the company. Charming Shoppes began opening Fashion Bug Plus stores (and departments within existing stores), featuring sizes for larger women. By 1985 it had more than 500 stores (about 65% of which were located in strip malls). That year the company expanded its product line by adding fashions for preteens.

During the last half of the decade, Charming Shoppes began changing its selection from name brands to private brands. In 1988 David became CEO, replacing Morris, who had served as CEO since the company went public. Although sales had increased unabated for two decades, shrinking profits led the company to curtail expansion, but only slightly. By the end of 1989, it operated more than 900 outlets.

Charming Shoppes continued to grow and increase sales, adding menswear in the early 1990s. With more than 1,400 stores in 1995, the company named Dorrit Bern, a former group VP of apparel and home merchandise at Sears, as CEO.

That year Charming Shoppes reported its biggest loss of $139 million. Bern promptly laid off a third of the company's workforce. She closed nearly 300 poorly performing stores and revamped Charming Shoppes' merchandising strategy, stemming losses in 1996 and bringing the company back to profitability the next year.

In 1998 Charming Shoppes closed another 65 poorly performing stores, replacing them with about 65 new sites. Restructuring charges contributed to a loss for fiscal 1999. Charming Shoppes bought plus-sized chain Modern Woman and integrated the stores with its acquisition of 436-store Catherines Plus Size chain.

Charming Shoppes positioned itself as a leader in plus-size women's apparel in 2001 with the $335 million purchase of plus-size apparel chain Lane Bryant (with more than 650 stores) from retailer The Limited.

In a move to cut out its biggest drains on capital, the company closed its 80-store Added Dimensions and The Answer plus-size chains, closed 130 Fashion Bug stores, and converted about 45 of its Fashion Bug stores to the more successful Lane Bryant format in 2002.

In June 2005 the plus-size chain acquired catalog retailer Crosstown Traders, which sells women's apparel, shoes, and accessories, from JPMorgan Partners for about $218 million (plus debt). Crosstown Traders sells women's apparel through its Old Pueblo Traders, Bedford Fair Lifestyles, Bedford Fair Shoestyles, Willow Ridge, Lew Magram, Brownstone Studio, Regalia, Intimate Appeal, Monterey Bay Clothing Company, and Coward Shoe catalog titles.

## EXECUTIVES

**Chairman, President, and CEO:** Dorrit J. Bern, age 57, $5,312,002 pay
**EVP and COO:** Joseph M. Baron, age 59, $559,081 pay
**EVP and CFO:** Eric M. Specter, age 49, $852,146 pay
**EVP, E-Commerce and President, Charming Interactive:** Gary L. Breitbart
**EVP, Corporate and Labor Relations, and Business Ethics:** Anthony A. DeSabato, age 58, $580,258 pay
**EVP, General Counsel, and Secretary:** Colin D. Stern, age 58, $689,193 pay
**EVP Human Resources:** Gale H. Varma, age 56
**EVP Sourcing:** Michel Bourlon, age 47
**EVP, Supply Chain Management, Information Technology, and Shared Business Services:** James G. (Jim) Bloise, age 63
**EVP, Quality Assurance, Control and Technical Design:** Erna Zint, age 61
**SVP and CIO:** Denis F. Gingue
**SVP Corporate Marketing:** Tim White
**SVP, Finance, Treasury, and Business Development:** Steven R. Wishner, age 55
**SVP and Corporate Controller:** John J. Sullivan, age 60
**VP, Corporate Human Resources:** Robert M. (Bob) Chessen
**President, Fashion Bug:** Diane M. Paccione
**Group Divisional President, Lane Bryant and Cacique Brands:** LuAnn Via
**Director Investor Relations:** Gayle M. Coolick
**Auditors:** Ernst & Young LLP

## LOCATIONS

**HQ:** Charming Shoppes, Inc.
450 Winks Ln., Bensalem, PA 19020
**Phone:** 215-245-9100 **Fax:** 215-633-4640
**Web:** www.charmingshoppes.com

Charming Shoppes operates about 2,375 stores in 48 states.

## PRODUCTS/OPERATIONS

**2007 Stores**

| | No. |
|---|---|
| Fashion Bug | 1,009 |
| Lane Bryant | 859 |
| Catherines Plus Sizes | 465 |
| Other | 45 |
| **Total** | **2,378** |

**2007 Sales**

| | $ mil. | % of total |
|---|---|---|
| Retail | | |
| Lane Bryant | 1,202.3 | 39 |
| Fashion Bug | 1,058.3 | 35 |
| Catherines Plus Sizes | 367.7 | 12 |
| Direct-to-consumer | | |
| Crosstown Traders | 427.8 | 14 |
| Other | 11.4 | — |
| **Total** | **3,067.5** | **100** |

**Store Names**
Catherines Plus Sizes
Fashion Bug
Lane Bryant

## COMPETITORS

Burlington Coat Factory
Cato
Charlotte Russe Holding
Chico's FAS
Claire's Stores
Coldwater Creek
Deb Shops
dELiA*s
Dress Barn
Eddie Bauer Holdings
Foot Locker
Gap
Goody's Family Clothing
Hot Topic
J. C. Penney
Kmart
Kohl's
Limited Brands
Ross Stores
Sears
Stage Stores
Stein Mart
Talbots
Target
TJX Companies
Tween Brands
United Retail
Wal-Mart

## HISTORICAL FINANCIALS

Company Type: Public

**Income Statement** FYE: Saturday nearest January 31

| | REVENUE ($ mil.) | NET INCOME ($ mil.) | NET PROFIT MARGIN | EMPLOYEES |
|---|---|---|---|---|
| **1/07** | 3,068 | 109 | 3.6% | 30,000 |
| **1/06** | 2,756 | 99 | 3.6% | 28,000 |
| **1/05** | 2,332 | 65 | 2.8% | 27,000 |
| **1/04** | 2,286 | 41 | 1.8% | 25,000 |
| **1/03** | 2,412 | (3) | — | 24,000 |
| **Annual Growth** | 6.2% | — | — | 5.7% |

**2007 Year-End Financials**

Debt ratio: 19.1%
Return on equity: 12.4%
Cash ($ mil.): 206
Current ratio: 2.11
Long-term debt ($ mil.): 181
No. of shares (mil.): 123
Dividends
Yield: —
Payout: —
Market value ($ mil.): 1,636

**Stock History** NASDAQ (GS): CHRS

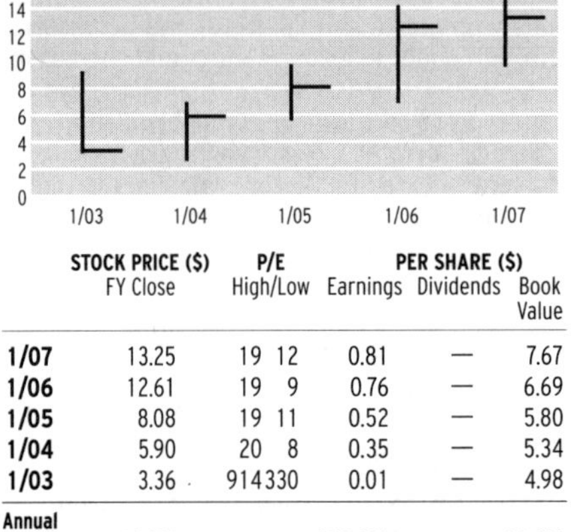


| | STOCK PRICE ($) FY Close | P/E High/Low | PER SHARE ($) Earnings | Dividends | Book Value |
|---|---|---|---|---|---|
| **1/07** | 13.25 | 19 12 | 0.81 | — | 7.67 |
| **1/06** | 12.61 | 19 9 | 0.76 | — | 6.69 |
| **1/05** | 8.08 | 19 11 | 0.52 | — | 5.80 |
| **1/04** | 5.90 | 20 8 | 0.35 | — | 5.34 |
| **1/03** | 3.36 | 914330 | 0.01 | — | 4.98 |
| **Annual Growth** | 40.9% | — — | 200.0% | — | 11.4% |

# Charter Communications

Charter Communications is contracted to direct traffic on the information superhighway. The cable TV system operator serves nearly 6 million subscribers in 40 US states, making it the #4 cable company, behind Comcast, Time Warner Cable, and Cox Communications. Not just a leading cable TV player, Charter Communications embarked on a $3.5 billion system upgrade to be able to offer broadband services. Its new products include HDTV capabilities and digital telephone services (it has almost half a million phone customers). Charter has agreements with Digeo and OpenTV to provide interactive TV services. Microsoft co-founder and company chairman Paul Allen controls about 90% of Charter's voting power.

Driven by dreams of creating a "wired world," Allen has poured more than $7 billion into Charter since 1998, and the billionaire has seen most of that investment evaporate. After purchasing a slew of small-town cable assets that needed extensive upgrades, Charter has been mired with subscriber losses and a tremendous debt load (about $19 billion). Former CEO Carl Vogel was never able to turn things around during his four years in charge of Charter (he resigned in early 2005 and was replaced later that year by former AOL executive Neil Smit). Throw in several other executive departures and a securities investigation that led to convictions against former COO Dave Barford (sentenced to one year in prison) and former CFO Kent Kalkwarf (14 months in prison), and you've got a very unhealthy company.

Charter, though, is still pursuing the "wired world" strategy. It offers an interactive TV service that allows viewers to instantly access Web information related to programming, and works with partners to develop personalized interactive TV services. The company touts its ability to provide voice, Internet access, and other data services as a complete package. Charter is particularly focused on growing subscribers to its cable telephony service, which now stands at about 120,000 customers.

The company struck a deal in 2006 to sell nearly $900 million in assets. It sold systems in Illinois and Kentucky to New Wave Communications and systems in West Virginia and Virginia to Cebridge Connections. Shedding more assets, Charter agreed to sell cable TV systems serving nearly 70,000 customers in the Western US to subsidiaries of Orange Broadband Holding Company.

## HISTORY

Crown Media bought St. Louis-based Cencom Cable in 1992. Rather than relocate to Crown's Dallas home, Cencom CEO Howard Wood joined with fellow executives Barry Babcock and Jerry Kent to form Charter Communications as a cable acquisition and management company in St. Louis. With an investment from Crown, owned by Hallmark Cards, the trio partnered with LEB Communications in 1994 to manage Charter's growth. And grow it did.

In 1994 Charter paid about $900 million for a majority stake in Crown. Charter spent $3 billion on 15 cable acquisitions in its first four years. It had more than 1 million subscribers by early 1997 and began offering high-speed cable Internet access and paging services in some of its markets.

Charter went into acquisition overdrive in 1998 when Microsoft co-founder Paul Allen took control with his $4.5 billion investment. The deal closely followed Allen's $2.8 billion takeover of Dallas-based Marcus Cable; Marcus was merged with Charter. The new Charter, based in St. Louis with Kent as CEO, was the #7 US cable business with 2.5 million subscribers. Also that year the company teamed up with Wink and WorldGate to offer TV Internet services with set-top boxes.

Before the ink was dry on the merger papers, Allen was at it again. The company's 1999 acquisitions included Falcon Communications (1 million cable subscribers) and Fanch Cablevision (more than 500,000); it also bought cable systems from Helicon, InterMedia Partners, Avalon Cable, InterLink Communications, Renaissance Media, and Rifkin. Charter said it would spend $3.5 billion upgrading its systems over three years after raising that amount in a major junk bond sale. Months later the company raised $3.2 billion in its IPO.

In 2000 Charter completed its purchase of Bresnan Communications (700,000 subscribers) and bought a system from Cablevision to form a major cluster in Michigan, Minnesota, and Wisconsin. The next year the company gained 554,000 subscribers by swapping noncore cable systems and $1.8 billion in cash to AT&T Broadband in exchange for systems serving the St. Louis area, parts of Alabama, and the Reno area of Nevada and California. Also in 2001 Kent resigned from the company and its board of directors and was replaced as CEO by former Liberty Media executive Carl Vogel. Vogel stayed on the job until early 2005, at which point he also retired. Former AOL executive Neil Smit replaced Vogel later that year.

## EXECUTIVES

**Chairman:** Paul G. Allen, age 54
**President, CEO, and Director:** Neil Smit, age 48, $1,200,000 pay
**EVP and COO:** Michael J. Lovett, age 45
**EVP and CFO:** Jeffrey T. (J.T.) Fisher, age 44, $542,308 pay
**EVP and CTO:** Marwan Fawaz, age 44
**EVP and Chief Marketing Officer:** Robert A. Quigley, age 63, $650,000 pay
**EVP, General Counsel, and Corporate Secretary:** Grier C. Raclin, age 54, $443,269 pay
**SVP Business Development:** Gregory S. Rigdon
**SVP Acquisition and Retention Marketing:** Barbara Hedges
**SVP Strategic Planning:** Eloise E. Schmitz
**SVP Human Resources:** Lynne F. Ramsey, age 49
**SVP Advertising Sales:** James (Jim) Heneghan
**SVP and General Manager Telephone:** Ted Schremp
**SVP Technical Operations:** Saconna Blair
**Corporate VP High-Speed Internet Product Management:** Himesh Bhise
**VP and Chief Accounting Officer:** Kevin D. Howard, age 37
**VP Investor Relations and Communications:** Mary Jo Moehle
**Auditors:** KPMG LLP

## LOCATIONS

**HQ:** Charter Communications, Inc.
12405 Powerscourt Dr., Ste. 100,
St. Louis, MO 63131
**Phone:** 314-965-0555 **Fax:** 314-965-9745
**Web:** www.charter.com

## PRODUCTS/OPERATIONS

### 2006 Sales

| | % of total |
|---|---|
| Video | 61 |
| High-speed Internet | 19 |
| Telephone | 2 |
| Advertising sales | 6 |
| Commercial | 6 |
| Other | 6 |
| **Total** | **100** |

### Selected Services

Broadband Internet access via cable modems
Cable TV
Digital TV
High-definition TV
Interactive video programming
Pay-per-view
Telephony
Video-on-demand

## COMPETITORS

AOL
AT&T
Cablevision Systems
Comcast
Cox Communications
DIRECTV
EarthLink
EchoStar Communications
Insight Communications
Mediacom
Pegasus Communications
Road Runner
Suddenlink
Time Warner Cable
Verizon

## HISTORICAL FINANCIALS

Company Type: Public

### Income Statement

FYE: December 31

| | REVENUE ($ mil.) | NET INCOME ($ mil.) | NET PROFIT MARGIN | EMPLOYEES |
|---|---|---|---|---|
| **12/06** | 5,504 | (1,370) | — | 15,500 |
| **12/05** | 5,254 | (967) | — | 17,200 |
| **12/04** | 4,977 | (4,341) | — | 15,500 |
| **12/03** | 4,819 | (238) | — | 15,500 |
| **12/02** | 4,566 | (2,514) | — | 18,600 |
| **Annual Growth** | 4.8% | — | — | (4.5%) |

### 2006 Year-End Financials

Debt ratio: —
Return on equity: —
Cash ($ mil.): 60
Current ratio: 0.26
Long-term debt ($ mil.): 19,119
No. of shares (mil.): 408
Dividends
Yield: —
Payout: —
Market value ($ mil.): 1,248

### Stock History

NASDAQ (GM): CHTR

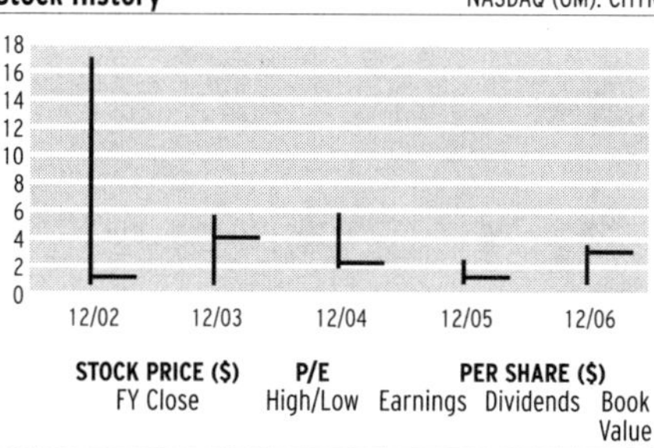


| | STOCK PRICE ($) FY Close | P/E High/Low | | PER SHARE ($) Earnings | Dividends | Book Value |
|---|---|---|---|---|---|---|
| **12/06** | 3.06 | — | — | (4.13) | — | (15.24) |
| **12/05** | 1.22 | — | — | (3.13) | — | (11.82) |
| **12/04** | 2.24 | — | — | (14.47) | — | (14.44) |
| **12/03** | 4.02 | — | — | (0.82) | — | (0.59) |
| **12/02** | 1.18 | — | — | (8.55) | — | 0.14 |
| **Annual Growth** | 26.9% | — | — | — | — | — |

# Chesapeake Energy

Chesapeake Energy knows the peaks and valleys of the oil and gas business. The independent exploration and production company concentrates on building natural gas reserves through acquisitions in the US midcontinent region. This region accounts for the vast majority of the company's estimated proved reserves of 9 trillion cu. ft. of natural gas equivalent, but Chesapeake also has assets along the Gulf Coast, in the Permian Basin, and in the Ark-La-Tex region. In 2005, in a major move, the company acquired Columbia Natural Resources for $2.2 billion.

Once an aggressive national leader in deep vertical and horizontal drilling, Chesapeake (which was named after the childhood Chesapeake Bay haunts of one of its founders) is concentrating on growing its proved reserves through acquisitions.

Chesapeake claims to be the sixth-most-active driller of natural gas wells in the US, with drilling projects in Arkansas, Kansas, Louisiana, New Mexico, Oklahoma, and Texas.

Buoyed by rising oil and gas prices, the company expanded with the acquisition of midcontinent natural gas producer Gothic Energy in 2001. The next year Chesapeake bought Canaan Energy and bought additional midcontinent natural gas assets. In 2003 the company acquired 25% of Pioneer Drilling. In 2004 Chesapeake bought privately owned Concho Resources for $420 million. The next year the company acquired privately held BRG Petroleum, which held assets of more than 450 wells with proved reserves of more than 275 billion cu. ft. of natural gas, for $325 million.

In 2005 Chesapeake acquired 20% of Gastar Exploration (reduced to 15% by 2007).

In 2006 the company acquired oil and natural gas assets located in the Barnett Shale, South Texas, Permian Basin, Midcontinent, and East Texas regions for $796 million. It also bought 13 drilling rigs and related assets from Martex Drilling for $150 million.

Chesapeake co-founders Tom Ward (former president) and Aubrey McClendon (current CEO) own 6.4% and 5.8% of the company, respectively. Ward resigned from the company in 2006.

## HISTORY

Aubrey McClendon (who grew up near Chesapeake Bay, Maryland) and Tom Ward had been nonoperating partners in about 600 wells in Oklahoma before forming their own company in 1989 to develop new fields in Texas and Oklahoma during the 1990s. The firm went public in 1993. In 1995 the company acquired oil and gas acreage in Louisiana, as well as Princeton Natural Gas, an Oklahoma City-based gas marketing firm.

Oil finds in Louisiana and strong production from its Texas and Oklahoma wells helped lift Chesapeake's sales in 1996. That year it acquired Amerada Hess' (later renamed Hess) half of their joint operations in two Oklahoma fields. In 1997 chairman McClendon and president Ward acquired control of Chesapeake.

The company's success was based on its "growth through the drillbit" strategy — developing new wells. But after a 1997 loss, Chesapeake modified its strategy and sought to grow by acquiring other companies. That year it bought energy company AnSon Production. Chesapeake subsequently bought oil and gas explorer-producer Hugoton Energy and energy company DLB Oil & Gas.

In 1998 the company acquired a 40% stake in Canadian oil producer Ranger Oil and paid Occidental Petroleum $105 million for natural gas reserves in the Texas Panhandle. Chesapeake then began to transform itself from a hotshot driller to an acquirer of natural gas properties, almost tripling its proved reserves. The company suffered a huge loss that year, in part from the acquisitions and continuing lower gas prices.

With gas prices soaring again, the company continued its buying spree into 2000, when it agreed to buy midcontinent natural gas producer Gothic Energy for $345 million in stock and assumed debt. The deal closed in 2001. The company also sold its Canadian assets that year, in order to focus on its core US properties.

In 2002 Chesapeake acquired oil and gas producer Canaan Energy for about $118 million.

Later that year the company announced plans to sell or trade its Permian basin assets.

In 2003 Chesapeake acquired a 25% stake in Pioneer Drilling (which it subsequently sold). In 2004 the company acquired Barnett Shale assets from Hallwood Energy for $292 million.

## EXECUTIVES

**Chairman and CEO:** Aubrey K. McClendon, age 47, $2,251,000 pay
**EVP Operations and COO:** Steven C. Dixon, age 48
**EVP Finance and CFO:** Marcus C. Rowland, age 54, $1,311,000 pay
**EVP Acquisitions and Divestitures:** Douglas J. Jacobson, age 53
**EVP Exploration:** J. Mark Lester, age 54
**SVP Accounting, Chief Accounting Officer, and Controller:** Michael A. Johnson, age 41, $631,000 pay
**SVP Drilling:** Stephen W. Miller, age 50
**SVP Human Resources and Treasurer:** Martha A. Burger, age 54, $978,500 pay
**SVP Information Technology and CIO:** Cathlyn L. Tompkins, age 45
**SVP Information Technologies and CIO:** Thomas L. Winton, age 60
**SVP Corporate Development:** Thomas S. Price Jr., age 55
**SVP Investor Relations and Research:** Jeffrey L. Mobley, age 38
**SVP Land and Legal and General Counsel:** Henry J. Hood, age 46
**SVP Production:** Jeffrey A. Fisher, age 47
**VP Secretary, and Assistant Treasurer:** Jennifer M. Grigsby, age 38
**Director, Media Relations:** Jim Gipson
**Auditors:** PricewaterhouseCoopers LLP

## LOCATIONS

**HQ:** Chesapeake Energy Corporation
6100 N. Western Ave., Oklahoma City, OK 73118
**Phone:** 405-848-8000 **Fax:** 405-843-0573
**Web:** www.chkenergy.com

Chesapeake Energy has oil and gas assets in Arkansas, Colorado, Kansas, Kentucky, Louisiana, Maryland, Michigan, Montana, New Mexico, New York, North Dakota, Ohio, Pennsylvania, Texas, Virginia, and West Virginia.

### 2006 Proved Reserves

| | % of total |
|---|---|
| Midcontinent | 47 |
| Appalachia | 17 |
| Fort Worth Barnett Shale | 13 |
| Permian & Delaware Basins | 8 |
| Ark-La-Tex | 8 |
| South Texas & Texas Gulf Coast | 7 |
| **Total** | **100** |

## PRODUCTS/OPERATIONS

### 2006 Sales

| | $ mil. | % of total |
|---|---|---|
| Exploration & production | 5,618.9 | 56 |
| Marketing | 4,134.5 | 41 |
| Other | 324.8 | 3 |
| Adjustments | (2,752.6) | — |
| **Total** | **7,325.6** | **100** |

## COMPETITORS

Adams Resources
Anadarko Petroleum
Apache
Ashland
Basic Earth Science Systems
BP
Cabot Oil & Gas
Chevron
ConocoPhillips
Devon Energy
Exxon Mobil
Koch
Noble Energy
Occidental Petroleum
Pioneer Natural Resources
Royal Dutch Shell

## HISTORICAL FINANCIALS

Company Type: Public

### Income Statement

FYE: December 31

| | REVENUE ($ mil.) | NET INCOME ($ mil.) | NET PROFIT MARGIN | EMPLOYEES |
|---|---|---|---|---|
| **12/06** | 7,326 | 2,003 | 27.3% | 4,900 |
| **12/05** | 4,665 | 948 | 20.3% | 2,885 |
| **12/04** | 2,709 | 515 | 19.0% | 1,718 |
| **12/03** | 1,717 | 313 | 18.2% | 1,192 |
| **12/02** | 739 | 40 | 5.5% | 866 |
| **Annual Growth** | 77.5% | 165.5% | — | 54.2% |

### 2006 Year-End Financials

Debt ratio: 81.1%
Return on equity: 28.8%
Cash ($ mil.): 228
Current ratio: 0.61
Long-term debt ($ mil.): 7,536
No. of shares (mil.): 457
Dividends
Yield: 0.8%
Payout: 5.3%
Market value ($ mil.): 13,288

### Stock History

NYSE: CHK

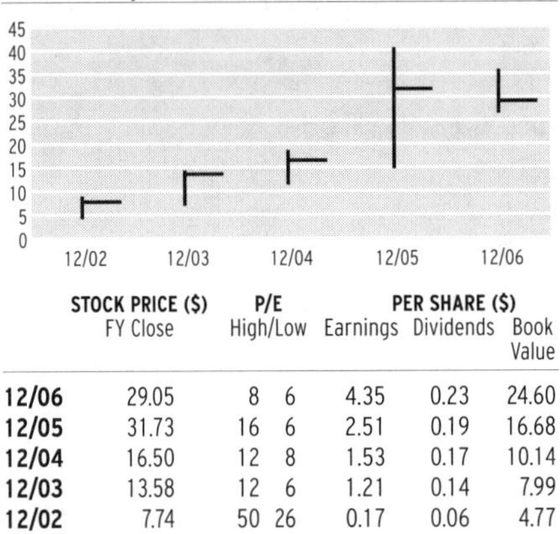


| | STOCK PRICE ($) FY Close | P/E High | P/E Low | PER SHARE ($) Earnings | Dividends | Book Value |
|---|---|---|---|---|---|---|
| **12/06** | 29.05 | 8 | 6 | 4.35 | 0.23 | 24.60 |
| **12/05** | 31.73 | 16 | 6 | 2.51 | 0.19 | 16.68 |
| **12/04** | 16.50 | 12 | 8 | 1.53 | 0.17 | 10.14 |
| **12/03** | 13.58 | 12 | 6 | 1.21 | 0.14 | 7.99 |
| **12/02** | 7.74 | 50 | 26 | 0.17 | 0.06 | 4.77 |
| **Annual Growth** | 39.2% | — | — | 124.9% | 39.9% | 50.7% |

# Chevron Corporation

Having added Texaco's star (and, more recently, Unocal's authority) to its stripes, Chevron (formerly ChevronTexaco) can pull rank on its rivals. The second-largest US integrated oil company (behind Exxon Mobil) expanded dramatically through its 2001 acquisition of Texaco. It has proved reserves of 11.6 billion barrels of oil equivalent and daily production of 2.6 million barrels of oil equivalent, and it owns interests in chemicals, pipelines, and power production businesses. The company, which is restructuring its refinery and retail businesses, owns or has stakes in 25,800 gas stations operating under the Chevron, Texaco, and Caltex brands. In 2005 Chevron acquired Unocal for $16.4 billion.

The acquisition of Unocal increased Chevron's proved reserves by about 15%. The company aproduction was about 3 million barrels per day at the end of 2006. Equally attractive is the location of Unocal's operations; at a time when industries are trying to get a foothold in China, the reserves in Southeast Asia can easily be transported not only to China, but to a surging India as well. Unocal's other operations can easily supply the US (from the Gulf of Mexico) and Europe (Caspian Sea) with gas and oil. Chevron owns stakes in chemicals producer Chevron Phillips Chemical and power producer and marketer Dynegy.

Part of the 2001 deal to acquire Texaco required Chevron to sell exclusive rights to the Texaco brand for a period of three years. A division of Royal Dutch Shell owned rights to the Texaco brand until 2004 and changed the name of the service stations to Shell. Once Chevron regained the rights to the Texaco name, it revitalized the brand name by adding about 400 Texaco stations in the western US.

The company has followed the path blazed by the cost-saving mergers of other oil giants (Exxon and Mobil, BP and Amoco). To obtain US government approval for the deal, Chevron sold its stakes in its Equilon and Motiva refining and marketing joint ventures. Shell bought Chevron's 44% interest in Equilon, which operates in the West and Midwest as Shell Oil Products US. Chevron's 35% stake in Motiva, which operates along the Gulf Coast and the Eastern Seaboard, was sold to partners Shell and Saudi Aramco. The company also sold its interest in the Discovery Pipeline, its stakes in the Enterprise Fractionator (near Houston), and Dixie Pipeline.

In 2006 Chevron agreed to buy a 5% stake in Indian refiner Reliance Petroleum for about $300 million. That year a company-led group of exploration firms announced a new successful oil strike in the Gulf of Mexico.

In 2007 BP agreed to buy Chevron's 31% stake in a Netherlands-based refinery and other assets for $900 million. That year it also sold its fuels marketing business in Belgium, the Netherlands, and Luxembourg to Delek Petroleum for $515 million.

## HISTORY

Thirty years after the California gold rush, a small firm began digging for a new product — oil. The crude came from wildcatter Frederick Taylor's well located north of Los Angeles. In 1879 Taylor and other oilmen formed Pacific Coast Oil, attracting the attention of John D. Rockefeller's Standard Oil. The two competed fiercely until Standard took over Pacific Coast in 1900.

When Standard Oil was broken up in 1911, its West Coast operations became the stand-alone Standard Oil Company (California), which was nicknamed Socal and sold Chevron-brand products. After winning drilling concessions in Bahrain and Saudi Arabia in the 1930s, Socal summoned Texaco to help, and they formed Caltex (California-Texas Oil Company) as equal partners. In 1948 Socony (later Mobil) and Jersey Standard (later Exxon) bought 40% of Caltex's Saudi operations, and the Saudi arm became Aramco (Arabian American Oil Company).

Socal exploration pushed into Louisiana and the Gulf of Mexico in the 1940s. In 1961 it bought Standard Oil Company of Kentucky (Kyso). The 1970s brought setbacks: Caltex holdings were nationalized during the OPEC-spawned upheaval, and the Saudi Arabian government claimed Aramco in 1980.

In 1984 Socal was renamed Chevron and doubled its reserves with its $13 billion purchase of Gulf Corp., which had origins in the 1901 Spindletop gusher in Texas. Gulf became an oil power by developing Kuwaiti concessions but was hobbled when those assets were nationalized in 1975. After Gulf was rocked by disclosures that it had an illegal political slush fund, Socal stepped in. The deal loaded the new company with debt, and it cut 20,000 jobs and sold billions in assets.

Chevron bought Tenneco's Gulf of Mexico properties in 1988 and in 1992 swapped fields valued at $1.1 billion for 15.7 million shares of Chevron stock owned by Pennzoil. It also moved into the North Sea in 1994.

In the 1990s Chevron gave its retailing units a tuneup. It allied with McDonald's (1995) to combine burger stands and gas stations in 12 western states. In addition, the company sold 450 UK gas stations and a refinery to Shell (1997). Meanwhile, Chevron sold its natural gas operation in 1996 for a stake in Houston-based NGC (later Dynegy), and it signed an onshore exploration contract in China the next year.

Poor economic conditions in Asia and slumping oil prices in 1998 forced Chevron to shed some US holdings. Chevron trimmed about 10% of its workforce in 1999 and 2000 in an effort to cut costs. As the rest of the industry consolidated, Chevron discussed merging with Texaco, but the talks collapsed in 1999. Later that year CEO Ken Derr retired, and vice chairman Dave O'Reilly replaced him.

In 2000 Chevron formed a joint venture with Phillips Petroleum (later ConocoPhillips) that combined the companies' chemicals businesses as Chevron Phillips Chemical. That year talks with Texaco were revived and Chevron agreed to acquire its Caltex partner for about $35 billion in stock and about $8 billion in assumed debt. The deal, completed in 2001, formed ChevronTexaco.

In 2002 ChevronTexaco divested its stakes in US downstream joint ventures Equilon (to Shell) and Motiva (to Shell and Saudi Aramco). It also sold part of a Gulf of Mexico pipeline and two natural gas plants in Louisiana to Duke Energy, and its 12.5% stake in a natural gas liquids fractionator to Enterprise Products Partners. In 2004 ChevronTexaco sold 150 US natural gas and oil properties to XTO Energy for $912 million. The company changed its name to Chevron Corporation in 2005. Later that year Chevron acquired Unocal for $16.4 billion.

## EXECUTIVES

**Chairman and CEO:** David J. (Dave) O'Reilly, age 60, $1,620,833 pay
**Vice Chairman and Office of the Chairman:** Peter J. Robertson, age 60, $935,417 pay
**EVP Global Downstream:** Michael K. (Mike) Wirth, age 46
**EVP Technology and Services:** John E. Bethancourt, age 55
**EVP Upstream and Gas:** George L. Kirkland, age 56, $679,583 pay
**VP Finance and CFO:** Stephen J. (Steve) Crowe, age 59, $553,125 pay
**VP and CTO:** Donald L. (Don) Paul, age 61
**VP and Controller:** Mark A. Humphrey, age 55
**VP and General Counsel:** Charles A. James, age 53
**VP and General Manager Government Affairs:** Lisa Barry
**VP Business Development:** Jay R. Pryor, age 48
**VP Human Resources:** Alan R. Preston, age 55
**VP Policy, Government, and Public Affairs:** Rhonda I. Zygocki, age 50
**VP and Treasurer:** Patricia E. (Pat) Yarrington, age 51
**VP Strategic Planning:** John W. McDonald, age 55
**VP; President, Chevron Global Gas:** John D. Gass, age 55
**President, Chevron North America Exploration and Production:** Gary P. Luquette, age 51
**EVP Strategy and Development:** John S. Watson, age 50, $685,417 pay
**Corporate Secretary:** Lydia I. Beebe, age 54
**General Manager Public Affairs:** David Samson
**Manager Investor Relations:** Randy Richards
**Auditors:** PricewaterhouseCoopers LLP

## LOCATIONS

**HQ:** Chevron Corporation
6001 Bollinger Canyon Rd., San Ramon, CA 94583
**Phone:** 925-842-1000 **Fax:** 925-842-3530
**Web:** www.chevron.com

Chevron Corporation has operations in more than 180 countries.

### 2006 Sales

| | $ mil. | % of total |
|---|---|---|
| US | 107,713 | 46 |
| Other countries | 128,967 | 54 |
| Adjustments | (26,562) | — |
| **Total** | **210,118** | **100** |

## PRODUCTS/OPERATIONS

### 2006 Sales

| | $ mil. | % of total |
|---|---|---|
| Refining, marketing & transportation | 170,748 | 71 |
| Exploration & production | 59,829 | 25 |
| Chemicals | 1,799 | 1 |
| Other | 6,530 | 3 |
| Adjustments | (28,788) | — |
| **Total** | **210,118** | **100** |

## COMPETITORS

Anadarko Petroleum
BP
ConocoPhillips
Devon Energy
Eni
Exxon Mobil
Hess
Imperial Oil
Koch
PDVSA
PEMEX
PETROBRAS
Repsol YPF
Royal Dutch Shell
Shell Aviation
Shell Hong Kong
TOTAL

## HISTORICAL FINANCIALS

Company Type: Public

### Income Statement

FYE: December 31

| | REVENUE ($ mil.) | NET INCOME ($ mil.) | NET PROFIT MARGIN | EMPLOYEES |
|---|---|---|---|---|
| **12/06** | 210,118 | 17,138 | 8.2% | 62,500 |
| **12/05** | 198,200 | 14,099 | 7.1% | 59,000 |
| **12/04** | 155,300 | 13,328 | 8.6% | 56,000 |
| **12/03** | 121,761 | 7,230 | 5.9% | 50,582 |
| **12/02** | 99,049 | 1,132 | 1.1% | 53,014 |
| **Annual Growth** | 20.7% | 97.3% | — | 4.2% |

### 2006 Year-End Financials

Debt ratio: 11.1%
Return on equity: 26.0%
Cash ($ mil.): 11,446
Current ratio: 1.28
Long-term debt ($ mil.): 7,679
No. of shares (mil.): 2,165
Dividends
Yield: 2.7%
Payout: 25.8%
Market value ($ mil.): 159,160

### Stock History

NYSE: CVX

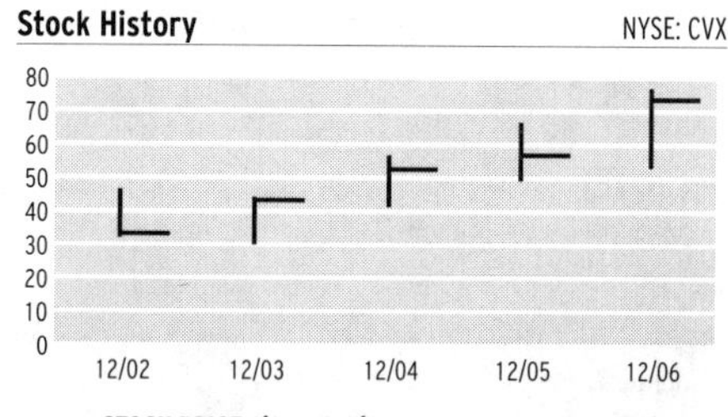


| | STOCK PRICE ($) FY Close | P/E High | P/E Low | PER SHARE ($) Earnings | Dividends | Book Value |
|---|---|---|---|---|---|---|
| **12/06** | 73.53 | 10 | 7 | 7.80 | 2.01 | 31.85 |
| **12/05** | 56.77 | 10 | 8 | 6.54 | 1.30 | 28.07 |
| **12/04** | 52.51 | 9 | 7 | 6.28 | 1.53 | 21.47 |
| **12/03** | 43.19 | 12 | 9 | 3.48 | 1.43 | 33.95 |
| **12/02** | 33.24 | 86 | 61 | 0.54 | 1.05 | 29.59 |
| **Annual Growth** | 22.0% | — | — | 95.0% | 17.6% | 1.9% |

# Chiquita Brands International

As one of the world's top banana producers, Chiquita Brands International deals in big bunches. The company grows, procures, markets, and distributes bananas and other fresh fruits and vegetables under the premium Chiquita brand. Its products are sold in some 80 countries worldwide. Bananas account for approximately 43% of Chiquita's total sales; other products include whole citrus fruits, melons, grapes, apples, and tomatoes, as well as fresh-cut items and processed fruit ingredients. Chiquita's Fresh Express unit is the leading seller of packaged salads in North America, controlling 48% of the retail market share in that sector.

To pursue growth in new product areas, Chiquita acquired Performance Food Group's Fresh Express unit for $855 million in 2005. The unit serves the retail grocery and food service industries. The Fresh Express acquisition supports Chiquita's strategy of providing more convenient, healthy food options in order to meet consumers' needs and also makes the company less susceptible to unfavorable EU import regulations.

After Chiquita voluntarily revealed in 2004 that one of its Colombian banana subsidiaries had made protection payments from 1997 though 2004 to terrorist groups, the Justice Department began a criminal investigation, examining the role and conduct of Chiquita and some of its officers in the criminal activity. Chiquita sold the subsidiary in 2004 but owned it at the time of the payments, admitting the payments were improper but that it was trying to ensure the safety of its employees. In 2007 Chiquita agreed to pay $25 million to settle the case.

That year it sold its fleet of 12 refrigerated cargo ships to Eastwind Maritime for $227 million. Chiquita immediately leased the ships from the alliance between Eastwind and NYKLauritzenCool that was formed as a result of the sale.

FMR Corp. owns almost 15% of Chiquita, Dimensional Fund Advisors owns about 7%, and Wells Fargo about 6%.

## HISTORY

Lorenzo Baker sailed into Jersey City, New Jersey, in 1870 with 160 bunches of Jamaican bananas. Baker arranged to sell bananas through Boston produce agent Andrew Preston and, with the support of Preston's partners, the two formed the Boston Fruit Company in 1885. In 1899 Boston Fruit merged with three other banana importers and incorporated as United Fruit Company. Soon the company was importing bananas from numerous Central American plantations for expanded distribution in the US.

United Fruit entered the Cuban sugar trade with the purchase of Nipe Bay (1907) and Saetia Sugar (1912). It bought Samuel Zemurray's Cuyamel Fruit Company in 1930, leaving Zemurray as the largest shareholder. Zemurray, who had masterminded the overthrow of the Honduran regime in 1905 to establish one favorable to his business, forcibly established himself as United Fruit's president in 1933.

In 1954, when Guatemalan president Jacobo Arbenz threatened to seize United Fruit's holdings, the company claimed he was a communist threat and provided ships to transport CIA-backed troops and ammunition for his overthrow.

Diversifying in the 1960s, United Fruit purchased A&W (restaurants and root beer, 1966) and Baskin-Robbins (ice cream, 1967). Eli Black, founder of AMK (which included the Morrell meat company), bought United Fruit in 1970 and changed its name to United Brands. Through American Financial Group, Carl Lindner began acquiring large amounts of United Brands' stock in 1973; he became chairman of the company in 1984. During the 1970s and 1980s, United Brands sold many of its holdings, including Baskin-Robbins (1973) and A&W (restaurants, 1982; soft drinks, 1987).

The firm became Chiquita Brands International in 1990. Chiquita acquired Friday Canning two years later. It then began divesting its meat operations, and all were sold by 1995.

In 1993 the European Union (EU) set up trade barriers against banana imports from Latin America, favoring banana-producing former European colonies in the Caribbean. The preference system angered Chiquita, whose bananas come from non-favored countries, although it retained more than 20% of the European market. In 1997 the WTO ruled the EU's trade policy illegal; the battle continued, however, over just how open the market should be.

Chiquita bought vegetable canners Owatonna Canning (1997), American Fine Foods (1997), and Stokely USA (1998) and merged them with Friday Canning in 1998. In 2000 the company announced cost-cutting efforts that included job cuts and a reorganization of some divisions.

Beset by a weakened European currency and a banana glut, the company announced in January 2001 that it was unable to pay its public debt. Chiquita also sued the European Commission, demanding $525 million in damages, due to the EU banana trade policy. The EU and the US later reached an agreement modifying quotas and tariffs until 2006, when all such restrictions are set to end. In November 2001 Chiquita filed a debt-restructuring plan under Chapter 11 seeking approval for an agreement the company made with bondholders to change more than $700 million of debt into equity. The plan was approved and the reorganization went into effect in mid-March of 2002 and the company began trading again on the NYSE. That same month, Chiquita announced the resignation of Steve Warshaw as the company president, CEO, and director. Cyrus Freidheim Jr. was named new chairman and CEO.

The company sold its Los Angeles-based Progressive Produce to Progressive's management for about $7 million in 2003. Also that year Chiquita acquired Atlanta AG, one of Germany's leading fresh fruit and vegetable distributors.

In a move to further concentrate on its fresh produce business, in 2003 the company sold its subsidiary, Chiquita Processed Foods (vegetable canning), to Seneca Foods for $110 million in cash, as well as stock, and debt assumption. Also that year Chiquita sold its unprofitable Pacific division, located in Panama (Puerto Armuelles Fruit Co.) to a cooperative of banana workers. It sold its interest in a joint venture with The Packers of Indian River, a grapefruit grower and packer, to its joint venture partner. Fernando Aguirre took over the roles of chairman, president, and CEO during 2004.

## EXECUTIVES

**Chairman, President, and CEO:** Fernando Aguirre, age 49, $2,603,337 pay
**SVP and CFO:** Jeffrey M. Zalla, age 41, $551,452 pay (partial-year salary)
**SVP, General Counsel, Secretary, and Chief Compliance Officer:** James E. Thompson, age 46
**SVP, Government and International Affairs and Corporate Responsibility Officer:** Manuel Rodriguez, age 57
**SVP, Human Resources:** Kevin R. Holland, age 45
**SVP, Global Suppy Chain and Procurement:** Waheed Zaman, age 46
**VP, Controller, and Chief Accounting Officer:** Brian W. Kocher, age 35
**VP, Finance, and Treasurer:** William A. Tsacalis, age 60
**VP, Global Strategies, Bananas:** Jeff E. Filliater, age 43
**VP, Global Quality and Food Safety:** Mark Smith
**President, Chiquita Fresh North America:** Richard M. Continelli
**President, Atlanta AG:** Peter Jung, age 45
**President, Chiquita Fresh Group - Asia-Pacific & Middle East:** Peter F. Smit
**President, Fresh Group-Europe:** Michel Loeb, age 46
**President, Fresh Express:** Tanios Viviani, age 45, $644,900 pay
**President, TransFresh:** Jim Lugg
**President and COO, Chiquita Fresh:** Robert F. (Bob) Kistinger, age 54, $1,271,606 pay
**President and COO, Fresh Group Far and Middle East/Australia Region:** Craig A. Stephen
**Director, Corporate Communications:** Michael (Mike) Mitchell
**Auditors:** Ernst & Young LLP

## LOCATIONS

**HQ:** Chiquita Brands International, Inc.
250 E. 5th St., Cincinnati, OH 45202
**Phone:** 513-784-8000 **Fax:** 513-784-8030
**Web:** www.chiquita.com

### 2006 Sales

| | $ mil. | % of total |
|---|---|---|
| US | 1,864.4 | 41 |
| Germany | 1,188.0 | 26 |
| Italy | 218.6 | 6 |
| Other countries | 1,228.1 | 27 |
| **Total** | **4,499.1** | **100** |

## PRODUCTS/OPERATIONS

### 2006 Sales

| | $ mil. | % of total |
|---|---|---|
| Bananas | 1,933.9 | 43 |
| Fresh select | 1,356.0 | 30 |
| Fresh cut | 1,139.1 | 25 |
| Other | 70.1 | 2 |
| **Total** | **4,499.1** | **100** |

### Selected Products

Bananas

Fresh select (whole fresh fruits and vegetables)
- Apples
- Citrus fruit
- Grapes
- Kiwi
- Melons
- Pineapples
- Stonefruit
- Tomatoes

Fresh cut (packaged salads and fresh-cut fruits, including Fresh Express products)

## COMPETITORS

Agrial
Bonduelle
Coca-Cola
Del Monte Foods
Dole Food
Fresh Del Monte Produce
Frugi Venta
Fyffes
Giumarra Companies
Global Berry Farms
Goya
Grimmway Enterprises
Hanover Foods
Jamaica Producers Group
J.G. Boswell Co.
Lykes Bros.
Maui Land & Pineapple
Moonlight Packing Corporation
National Grape Cooperative
Ocean Spray
Pacific Coast Producers
Pictsweet
Ready Pac
River Ranch Fresh Foods
Seneca Foods
Smucker
Sunkist
Tanimura & Antle
Tropicana
Village Farms

## HISTORICAL FINANCIALS

Company Type: Public

### Income Statement

FYE: December 31

| | REVENUE ($ mil.) | NET INCOME ($ mil.) | NET PROFIT MARGIN | EMPLOYEES |
|---|---|---|---|---|
| **12/06** | 4,499 | (96) | — | 25,000 |
| **12/05** | 3,904 | 131 | 3.4% | 25,000 |
| **12/04** | 3,072 | 55 | 1.8% | 21,000 |
| **12/03** | 2,614 | 99 | 3.8% | 24,000 |
| **12/02** | 1,990 | (385) | — | 28,000 |
| **Annual Growth** | 22.6% | — | — | (2.8%) |

### 2006 Year-End Financials

Debt ratio: 109.2%
Return on equity: —
Cash ($ mil.): 65
Current ratio: 1.39
Long-term debt ($ mil.): 951
No. of shares (mil.): 42
Dividends
Yield: 1.3%
Payout: —
Market value ($ mil.): 673

### Stock History

NYSE: CQB

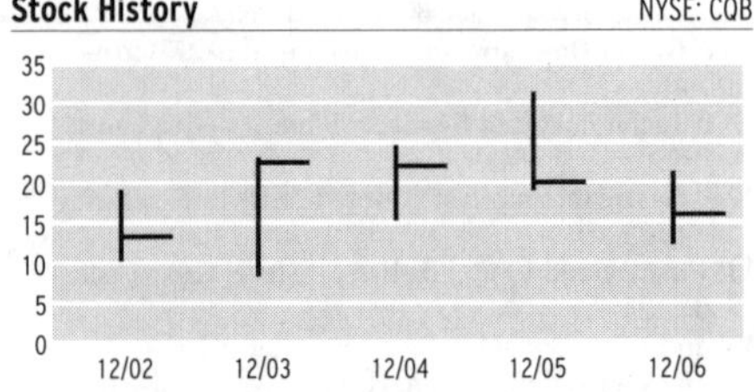


| | STOCK PRICE ($) FY Close | P/E High | P/E Low | PER SHARE ($) Earnings | Dividends | Book Value |
|---|---|---|---|---|---|---|
| **12/06** | 15.97 | — | — | (2.28) | 0.20 | 20.66 |
| **12/05** | 20.01 | 11 | 7 | 2.92 | 0.40 | 23.69 |
| **12/04** | 22.06 | 18 | 12 | 1.33 | 0.10 | 20.72 |
| **12/03** | 22.53 | 9 | 3 | 2.46 | — | 18.92 |
| **12/02** | 13.26 | — | — | (4.75) | — | 15.79 |
| **Annual Growth** | 4.8% | — | — | — | 41.4% | 6.9% |

# Chrysler LLC

The divorce is final: Daimler got the Mercedes and Chrysler got the minivan. After almost a decade of trying to make the most audacious merger in automotive history work, DaimlerChrysler is now Daimler and Chrysler. In 2007 private equity concern Cerberus Capital Management bought Chrysler for about $7.4 billion — or about one-fifth of the $37 billion Daimler paid in 1998. In addition to its eponymous Chrysler brand, the company also controls the Dodge and Jeep marquees. Specific models include Chrysler 300, Dodge Ram pickups, and Jeep Grand Cherokee. The company offers financing to both consumers and dealers through Chrysler Financial Services LLC.

It looked good on paper. The plan had been to leverage Chrysler's mass market expertise with Daimler's engineering prowess and quality. But none of that ever came to fruition. Throughout their tumultuous relationship, Daimler and Chrysler were never simultaneously healthy, and in 2007 the cries of angry DaimlerChrysler investors became impossible to ignore any longer.

That year Daimler agreed to sell the company to Cerberus after months of speculation and haggling with labor forces, primarily the United Auto Workers (UAW).

Cerberus inherits Chrysler's labor contracts and pension liabilities. Chrysler lost $1.5 billion in 2006, and Cerberus has to find a way to stop the bleeding. This will be hard, as much of the carnage is being caused by something that can't be fixed quickly — a lack of small cars. The Caliber is the smallest car Chrysler makes, and it's not very small.

As fuel prices climb ever higher, drivers flock away from large, American-made trucks and SUVs and into smaller, usually Japanese, cars. To address this issue Chrysler is doing what no one in the North American car industry wants to do — including Chrysler itself: it will be the first company to import cars from China into the US market. In 2006 Chrysler struck a deal with Chery Automobile of China for the building of small cars. Profit margins for small cars are so razor thin, it's almost impossible to make money building them with US labor. Chery will build a small car based on modifications to one of its domestic models, and it will be branded as a Dodge, Chrysler, or Jeep.

Cerberus has tapped someone the business world had largely given up on. Cerberus didn't own Chrysler for long before naming Robert Nardelli as the new CEO. The former GE executive, who left The Home Depot under a cloud in early 2007 (with an extremely generous severance package), succeeded Thomas LaSorda as CEO of Chrysler; LaSorda was named vice chairman and president.

As chairman and CEO of Chrysler, Nardelli effectively will have to answer to only one big shareholder, Cerberus. He becomes the second CEO among the Detroit Three to come from outside of the automotive industry, along with Ford Motor's Alan Mulally, who previously served as the boss of Boeing Commercial Airplanes.

Cerberus owns about 80% of Chrysler; Daimler retains about a 20% stake.

## HISTORY

When the Maxwell Motor Car Company entered receivership in 1920, a bankers' syndicate hired Walter Chrysler, former Buick president and General Motors (GM) VP, to reorganize it. Chrysler became president in 1923 and in 1924 introduced his own car, the Chrysler, which borrowed from WWI aircraft in the design of its six-cylinder engine. The next year Chrysler took over Maxwell and renamed it after himself.

In 1928 the company acquired Dodge and introduced the low-priced Plymouth and the more luxurious DeSoto. Its research and development budget never decreased during the Depression, and innovations included overdrive and a three-point engine suspension on rubber mountings. In 1933 Chrysler's sales surpassed Ford's, and two years later Walter retired.

To minimize costs, Chrysler kept the same car models from 1942 until 1953, while other makers were adding yearly style modifications. The company lost market share and slipped to third place by 1950. Chrysler misjudged customer demands in the 1960s, when it introduced small cars, and in the 1970s, when it maintained production of large cars, resulting in massive losses. Facing the prospect of bankruptcy, Chrysler negotiated $1.5 billion in loan guarantees from the federal government and brought in Lee Iacocca, former Ford president (and the man behind the Ford Mustang), as CEO in 1978.

Iacocca became one of the most visible CEOs ever, appearing in TV commercials, publishing his autobiography, and making an issue of Japanese trading practices. Chrysler reorganized, closed several plants, and cut its workforce; by 1983 it had repaid all guaranteed loans, seven years ahead of schedule. The next year it introduced the first minivan.

The company diversified, buying Gulfstream Aerospace (corporate jets, sold 1990), E.F. Hutton Credit, and Finance America for a total of $1.2 billion. In 1986 Chrysler created a joint venture with Mitsubishi (Diamond-Star, sold 1993) to sell Mitsubishi cars in the US, and the following year it purchased American Motors. Between 1989 and 1991 Chrysler bought Thrifty, Snappy, Dollar, and General car rental agencies.

Corporate raider Kirk Kerkorian bought about 10% of Chrysler in 1990. An economic downturn in 1992 forced the carmaker to sell nonautomotive assets. Iacocca stepped down as chairman late that year and was replaced by GM's head of European operations, Robert Eaton.

Making progress on its pledge to shed some noncore businesses, Chrysler in 1996 sold most of its aerospace and defense holdings to Raytheon for $475 million. In 1997 the automaker sold its electronics unit, Pentastar Electronics, to investment group PEI Acquisition and spun off the Dollar Thrifty Group, which operates Dollar Rent A Car and Thrifty Rent-A-Car.

The next year Daimler-Benz agreed to acquire Chrysler in a deal worth an estimated $37 billion. The purchase marked the largest takeover of a US firm by a foreign buyer to that time. The deal brought a windfall for Chrysler execs; for instance, chairman Robert Eaton got an estimated $70 million in stock and cash.

## EXECUTIVES

**Chairman and CEO:** Robert L. (Bob) Nardelli, age 57
**Vice Chairman and President:**
Thomas W. (Tom) LaSorda, age 53
**EVP Manufacturing:** Frank J. Ewasyshyn, age 54
**SVP and CIO:** Jan A. Bertsch, age 49
**SVP Global Service and Parts:**
Christine K. (Chris) Cortez, age 52
**VP Powertrain Manufacturing:** Richard A. Chow-Wah
**EVP Procurement and Supply:** Simon Boag, age 40
**EVP Product Development:** Frank O. Klegon, age 54
**EVP North America, Sales and Marketing, Service and Parts:** Steven J. (Steve) Landry, age 48
**EVP International Sales, Marketing, and Business Development:** Michael Manley, age 43
**SVP Employee Relations:** John S. Franciosi, age 51
**SVP Global External Affairs and Public Policy:**
Robert G. Liberatore
**SVP Human Resources:** Nancy A. Rae, age 50
**SVP and CFO:** Ronald E. Kolka, age 47
**Executive Director, Corporate Diversity Office:**
Monica E. Emerson
**Director International Marketing and Communications:**
Judith K. Wheeler

## LOCATIONS

**HQ:** Chrysler LLC
1000 Chrysler Dr., Auburn Hills, MI 48326
**Phone:** 248-576-5741 **Fax:** 248-512-2912
**Web:** www.chryslerllc.com

Chrysler sells its cars, minivans, and trucks in more than 140 countries, though North America accounts for the majority of sales.

## PRODUCTS/OPERATIONS

### Selected Products

Chrysler
- Cirrus
- Concorde
- Sebring
- Town & Country

Dodge
- Caravan
- Neon
- Ram
- Stratus
- Viper

Eagle
- Talon

Jeep
- Grand Cherokee
- Jamboree

Plymouth
- Breeze
- Grand Voyager
- Neon
- Voyager

### Selected Subsidiaries and Affiliates

Chrysler do Brasil Ltda.
Chrysler Financial Corp. (loans and leasing plans)
Chrysler Japan Sales Limited
Chrysler Motors de Venezuela, SA
Chrysler Realty Corp.
Chrysler Sales & Services (Thailand) Ltd.
New Venture Gear Inc. (64%, auto parts)

## COMPETITORS

BMW
Daimler
Fiat
Ford
Fuji Heavy Industries
General Motors
Honda
Isuzu
Kia Motors
Mazda
Nissan
Peugeot
Peugeot Motors of America, Inc.
Renault
Saab Automobile
Saab Automobile USA
Suzuki Motor
Toyota
Volkswagen

# CHS Inc.

CHS Inc. goes with the grain. As one of the largest US cooperative marketers of grain and oilseed, CHS represents local cooperatives from the Great Lakes to the Pacific Northwest and from the Canadian border to Texas. CHS trades grain and sells supplies to members through its stores. It also processes soybeans for use in food and animal feeds, and markets petroleum. In addition, CHS grinds wheat into flour used in pastas and bread; subsidiary Sparta Foods makes tortillas. The co-op has joint ventures which sell crop nutrient and protection products, and market grain.

CHS's grain trading activities include buying, selling, and arranging for transport. The co-op operates wheat mills to produce flour for pasta and bread, and it provides farm supplies to its approximately 800 Cenex/Ampride stores; CHS also processes soybeans for use in margarine, salad dressings, and animal feed. Extending its reach beyond the US, the company formed a joint venture (Multigrain S.A.) with Brazilian agricultural commodities company Multigrain Comercio.

The company's energy division operates oil refineries, and the Country Energy subsidiary sells wholesale propane and other petroleum products. Joint ventures with United Grain Corporation (United Harvest) and Cargill (TEMPCO) operate grain terminals and export grain. CHS also provides ethanol-blended fuel products, supplying 500 million gallons annually.

In a move away from commodities, in 2006 CHS formed a joint venture with drive-through coffee kiosk company Mountain Mudd Espresso. Mountain Mudd has operations in 22 states. Adding to its lubricants offerings, in 2007 the company acquired two Minnesota companies: Nor-Lakes Services Midwest and The Farm-Oyl Company.

CHS and Land O'Lakes realigned the businesses of their 50-50 joint venture Agriliance in 2007, with CHS acquiring its crop-nutrients wholesale-products business and Land O'Lakes acquiring the crop-protection products business. The two companies are looking for a buyer for the one remaining Agriliance operation, retail agronomy.

## HISTORY

To help farmers through the Great Depression, the Farmers Union Terminal Association (a grain marketing association formed in 1926) created the Farmers Union Grain Terminal Association (GTA) in 1938. With loans from the Farmers Union Central Exchange (later known as CENEX) and the Farm Credit Association, the organization operated a grain elevator in St. Paul, Minnesota. By 1939 GTA had 250 grain-producing associations as members.

GTA leased terminals in Minneapolis and Washington and built others in Wisconsin and Montana in the early 1940s. It then took over a Minnesota flour mill and created Amber Milling. GTA also began managing farming insurance provider Terminal Agency. In 1958 the association bought 57 elevators and feed plants from the McCabe Company.

Adding to its operations in 1960, GTA bought the Honeymead soybean plant. The next year the co-op acquired Minnesota Linseed Oil. In 1977 it acquired Jewett & Sherman (later Holsum Foods), which helped transform the company into a provider of jams, jellies, salad dressings, and syrups.

In 1983 GTA combined with North Pacific Grain Growers, a Pacific Northwest co-op incorporated in 1929, to form Harvest States Cooperatives. Harvest States grew in the early and mid-1990s by acquiring salad dressing makers Albert's Foods, Great American Foods, and Saffola Quality Foods; soup stock producer Private Brands; and margarine and dressings manufacturer and distributor Gregg Foods.

The company started a joint venture to operate the Ag States Agency agricultural insurance company in 1995. The next year the co-op's Holsum Foods division and Mitsui & Co.'s edible oils unit, Wilsey Foods, merged to form Ventura Foods, a distributor of margarines, oils, spreads, and other food products.

Harvest States merged in 1998 with Minnesota-based CENEX, a 16-state agricultural supply co-op that had been founded in 1931 as Farmers Union Central Exchange. (Among CENEX's major operations was a farm inputs, services, marketing, and processing joint venture with dairy cooperative Land O'Lakes formed in 1987.) CENEX CEO Noel Estenson took the helm of the resulting co-op, Cenex Harvest States Cooperatives, which soon formed a petroleum joint venture called Country Energy with Farmland Industries.

CHS members rejected a proposed merger with Farmland Industries in 1999. Also that year Cenex/Land O'Lakes Agronomy (it became Agriliance in 2000 when Farmland Industries joined the joint venture) bought Terra Industries' $1.7 billion distribution business (400 farm supply stores, seed and chemical distribution operations, partial ownership of two chemical plants).

CHS bought the wholesale propane marketing operations of Williams Companies in 2000, and the co-op paid $14 million for tortilla and tortilla chip maker Sparta Foods. Additionally Estenson retired that year and company president John Johnson took over as CEO. CHS launched an agricultural e-commerce site (Rooster.com) in conjunction with Cargill and DuPont in 2000. The site was shut down the next year, however, because of a lack of funds. Also in 2001 the cooperative became the full owner of Country Energy by purchasing Farmland Industries' share.

In 2002 CHS acquired Agway's Grandin, North Dakota-based sunflower business and formed a wheat-milling joint venture (Horizon Milling) with Cargill. In 2003 the company changed its name from Cenex Harvest States Cooperatives to CHS Inc. and began trading on the Nasdaq. It used the proceeds from the stock offering to repay its short-term debts.

In 2004 CHS purchased all of bankrupt Farmland Industries' ownership of Agriliance, thus giving CHS a 50% ownership of Agriliance (with Land O'Lakes owning the other 50%). With an eye to this growing energy sector, CHS acquired a 28% ownership of ethanol-production and marketing company, US BioEnergy Corporation, in 2005. Also that year it sold off its Mexican foods business and sold 81% of its 20% ownership of crop-nutrient manufacturer CF Industries in an initial public offering. It now owns about 4% of CF.

## EXECUTIVES

**President and CEO:** John D. Johnson, age 58, $2,700,000 pay
**EVP and COO, Ag Business:** Mark Palmquist, age 49, $1,253,520 pay
**EVP and COO, Energy:** Leon E. Westbrock, age 59, $1,303,680 pay
**EVP and COO, Processing:** Jay D. Debertin, age 46, $946,080 pay
**EVP and CFO:** John Schmitz, age 56, $1,159,680 pay
**EVP, Business Solutions:** Thomas D. (Tom) Larson, age 58, $814,800 pay
**EVP, Corporate Administration:** Patrick Kluempke, age 58, $814,800 pay
**SVP, Grain Marketing:** Rick Browne
**SVP and General Counsel:** David (Dave) Kastelic
**SVP, Oilseed Processing:** Dennis Wendland
**Director, Business Development and Sales Western Region:** Jerry Jueneman
**Director, Bulk Distribution Services:** Darin Hunoff
**Director, Business Development and Sales Feed Operations Western Region:** Dick Wark
**Director, Corporate Communications:** Lani Jordan
**Director, Governmental Affairs:** Jim Bareksten
**Auditors:** PricewaterhouseCoopers LLP

## LOCATIONS

**HQ:** CHS Inc.
5500 Cenex Dr., Inver Grove Heights, MN 55077
**Phone:** 651-355-6000
**Web:** www.chsinc.com

## PRODUCTS/OPERATIONS

### 2006 Sales

| | % of total |
|---|---|
| Energy | 51 |
| Ag business | 45 |
| Processing | 4 |
| **Total** | **100** |

### Selected Operations

Convenience stores (Cenex)
Farm financing (Fin-Ag, Inc.)
Farm supplies (Agri-Service Centers)
- Crop-protection products
- Fertilizer
- Grain purchasing
- Seeds

Feed manufacturing
Futures and option services (Country Hedging, Inc.)
Grain merchandising (grain purchasing, transportation, and sales)
Petroleum marketing (Country Energy, LLC)
Soybean crushing (soybean conversion into animal feed and crude soybean oil)
Soybean refining (soybean oil conversion into margarine, salad dressings, and baked goods)
Wheat milling (semolina and durum wheat milling for flour)

## COMPETITORS

ADM
Ag Processing
AmeriGas Partners
Andersons
Bartlett and Company
Bunge Limited
Bunge Milling
Bunge North America
Cargill
Central Soya
ContiGroup
Dakota Growers
Ferrellgas Partners
GROWMARK
Kraft Foods
Land O'Lakes
Land O'Lakes Purina Feed
Louis Dreyfus
Riceland Foods
Scoular
Shell Oil Products
Smucker
Unilever NV
Wilbur-Ellis

## HISTORICAL FINANCIALS

Company Type: Public

### Income Statement

FYE: August 31

| | REVENUE ($ mil.) | NET INCOME ($ mil.) | NET PROFIT MARGIN | EMPLOYEES |
|---|---|---|---|---|
| **8/06** | 14,384 | 490 | 3.4% | 6,540 |
| **8/05** | 11,941 | 250 | 2.1% | 6,370 |
| **8/04** | 11,051 | 221 | 2.0% | 6,800 |
| **8/03** | 9,399 | 124 | 1.3% | 6,820 |
| **8/02** | 7,270 | 126 | 1.7% | 6,750 |
| **Annual Growth** | 18.6% | 40.4% | — | (0.8%) |

### 2006 Year-End Financials

Debt ratio: 36.6%
Return on equity: 27.1%
Cash ($ mil.): 113
Current ratio: 1.46
Long-term debt ($ mil.): 684

No. of shares (mil.): 6
Dividends
Yield: 7.6%
Payout: —
Market value ($ mil.): 154

### Stock History

NASDAQ (GS): CHSCP

| | STOCK PRICE ($) FY Close | P/E High/Low | PER SHARE ($) Earnings | Dividends | Book Value |
|---|---|---|---|---|---|
| **8/06** | 26.30 | — — | — | 2.00 | 344.02 |
| **8/05** | 26.80 | — — | — | 2.00 | 355.03 |
| **8/04** | 27.39 | — — | — | 2.00 | 328.81 |
| **8/03** | 27.54 | — — | — | 0.50 | 350.50 |
| **Annual Growth** | (1.5%) | — — | — | 58.7% | (0.0%) |

# The Chubb Corporation

Here's the skinny on Chubb: The insurer is best known for comprehensive homeowners insurance for the demographic that owns yachts (the company insures those, too). Chubb also offers property/casualty insurance to companies. The company's specialty commercial insurance includes the lucrative executive risk business that offers professional liability policies to executives. Other specialty commercial insurance includes policies written for marine, surety, and financial institutions. Although the US accounts for more than three-fourths of Chubb's direct business, developing its presence in foreign markets is an element in the company's growth strategy.

Chubb is now squarely focused on property/casualty insurance and has been carefully pruning away any non-core operations. In 2005 it sold its reinsurance unit to Harbor Point, taking a 16% stake in the company, and sold its Personal Lines Insurance Brokerage subsidiary to Hub International.

The company has moved other operations into run-off, including its real estate group, which had been involved in developing commercial and residential properties in Florida and New Jersey, and its financial solutions business.

## HISTORY

Thomas C. Chubb and his son Percy formed Chubb & Son in New York in 1882 to underwrite cargo and ship insurance. The company soon became the US manager for Sea Insurance Co. of England and co-founded New York Marine Underwriters (NYMU). In 1901 NYMU became Chubb's chief property/casualty affiliate, Federal Insurance Co.

Chubb expanded in the 1920s, opening a Chicago office (1923) and, just before the 1929 crash, organizing Associated Aviation Underwriters. Growth slowed during the Depression, but Chubb recovered enough by 1939 to buy Vigilant Insurance Co.

The company bought Colonial Life in 1959 and Pacific Indemnity in 1967. That year Chubb Corporation was formed as a holding company, with Chubb & Son designated the manager of the property/casualty insurance businesses. A 1969 takeover attempt by First National City Corp. (predecessor of Citigroup) was foiled by federal regulators.

Chubb acquired Bellemead Development in 1970 to expand its real estate portfolio. Following a strategy of offering specialized insurance, Chubb in the 1970s launched insurance packages for the entertainment industry, including films and Broadway shows. After the Tylenol poisonings of 1982, Chubb developed insurance against product tampering (which it no longer offers). During the 1980s Chubb focused on specialized property/casualty insurance lines; in 1985 it retreated from medical malpractice insurance.

The company combined three subsidiaries into Chubb Life Insurance Co. of America in 1991. The next year Chubb subsidiary Pacific Indemnity settled a suit over Fibreboard Corporation's asbestos liability (Fibreboard was later bought by Owens Corning); the company ultimately paid some $675 million in asbestos-related settlements.

Financial difficulties at Lloyd's of London caused that market to rethink and subsequently relax its rules about doing business with corporate insurance companies. Chubb took advantage of the opportunity and opened an office at Lloyd's in 1993. The next year Chubb's acquisitions included the personal lines business of Alexander & Alexander (now part of Aon Corporation).

Since the 1880s, Chubb had maintained an alliance with UK-based Royal & Sun Alliance Insurance Group and its predecessors. Royal & Sun Alliance owned about 5% of Chubb, and Chubb held about 3% of Royal & Sun Alliance. In 1993 the US insurer formed a new joint venture with the British company, with the purpose of extending to the UK Chubb's insurance products targeting the affluent. But in 1996, a major client of Royal & Sun Alliance Insurance Group defected and Chubb ended the agreement.

To focus on the property/casualty market, Chubb in 1997 sold its life and health insurance operations to Jefferson Pilot and parts of its Bellemead real estate business to Paine Webber and Morgan Stanley Dean Witter. (Chubb blamed the real estate market for its lower 1996 earnings.) The next year the commercial lines market tanked and was followed by a drop in Chubb's earnings.

With losses dragging down its otherwise profitable property/casualty segment, Chubb vowed to get tough — raising rates and getting out of unprofitable businesses. It also forged ahead with its overseas plans, buying Venezuelan insurer Italseguros Internacional and creating Chubb Re to offer international reinsurance. In 1999 Chubb bought corporate officer insurer Executive Risk (now with a Chubb prefix) to beef up its executive protection and financial services lines. The next year UK aviation insurer British Aviation Group bought Chubb's Associated Aviation Underwriters.

Severely affected by terrorist strikes on September 11, 2001, and the collapse of Enron, Chubb paid out almost $900 million in claims. In 2002 Chubb took a $700 million charge related to asbestos and toxic waste. The company's property/casualty lines (primarily the commercial segment) had a strong year in 2003, primarily thanks to higher pricing, but this was negatively impacted by large asbestos-related charges.

In 2004 the company sold its post-secondary educational subsidiary, The Chubb Institute.

## EXECUTIVES

**Chairman, President, and CEO:** John D. Finnegan, age 58, $1,275,000 pay
**Vice Chairman and COO:** Thomas F. Motamed, age 58, $715,001 pay
**Vice Chairman and CFO:** Michael O'Reilly, age 63, $661,251 pay
**Vice Chairman and Chief Administrative Officer:** John J. Degnan, age 62, $636,250 pay
**EVP:** Ned I. Gerstman
**EVP; COO, Chubb Commercial Insurance; EVP, Chubb & Son:** Paul J. Krump, $432,875 pay
**EVP and General Counsel:** Maureen A. Brundage,, age 50
**EVP and Managing Director, Chubb & Son; COO, Chubb Personal Insurance:** Andrew A. McElwee Jr., age 52
**EVP, Chubb & Son; COO, Chubb Specialty Insurance:** Robert C. Cox, age 48
**SVP and Chief Accounting Officer:** Henry B. Schram, age 60
**VP and Secretary:** W. Andrew Macan
**VP and Treasurer:** Douglas A. Nordstrom
**Manager, Public Relations:** Mark Schussel
**VP IT, Chubb & Son:** Owen E. Williams
**Auditors:** Ernst & Young LLP

## LOCATIONS

**HQ:** The Chubb Corporation
15 Mountain View Rd., Warren, NJ 07061
**Phone:** 908-903-2000 **Fax:** 908-903-2027
**Web:** www.chubb.com

Chubb has operations in the Americas, Asia, Australia, and Europe.

## PRODUCTS/OPERATIONS

### 2006 Sales

| | $ mil. | % of total |
|---|---|---|
| Premiums earned | 11,958 | 85 |
| Investment income | 1,485 | 11 |
| Realized investment gains | 245 | 2 |
| Other revenues | 315 | 2 |
| **Total** | **14,003** | **100** |

### Selected Subsidiaries

Bellemead Development Corporation
Chubb Atlantic Indemnity Ltd.
- DHC Corporation
  - Chubb do Brasil Companhia de Seguros (99%, Brazil)

Federal Insurance Company
- Executive Risk Indemnity Inc.
  - Executive Risk Specialty Insurance Company
- Great Northern Insurance Company
- Pacific Indemnity Company
  - Northwestern Pacific Indemnity Company
  - Texas Pacific Indemnity Company
- Vigilant Insurance Company

## COMPETITORS

AIG
Allianz
Allstate
Aviva
AXA
Berkshire Hathaway
CIGNA
Citigroup
CNA Financial
General Re
The Hartford
Liberty Mutual
Loews
Millea Holdings
Travelers Companies

## HISTORICAL FINANCIALS

Company Type: Public

**Income Statement** FYE: December 31

| | ASSETS ($ mil.) | NET INCOME ($ mil.) | INCOME AS % OF ASSETS | EMPLOYEES |
|---|---|---|---|---|
| **12/06** | 50,277 | 2,528 | 5.0% | 10,800 |
| **12/05** | 48,061 | 1,826 | 3.8% | 10,800 |
| **12/04** | 44,260 | 1,548 | 3.5% | 11,800 |
| **12/03** | 38,361 | 809 | 2.1% | 12,300 |
| **12/02** | 34,114 | 223 | 0.7% | 13,300 |
| **Annual Growth** | 10.2% | 83.5% | — | (5.1%) |

**2006 Year-End Financials**

Equity as % of assets: 27.6%
Return on assets: 5.1%
Return on equity: 19.2%
Long-term debt ($ mil.): 2,466
No. of shares (mil.): 411
Dividends
Yield: 1.9%
Payout: 16.7%
Market value ($ mil.): 21,761
Sales ($ mil.): 14,003

**Stock History** NYSE: CB

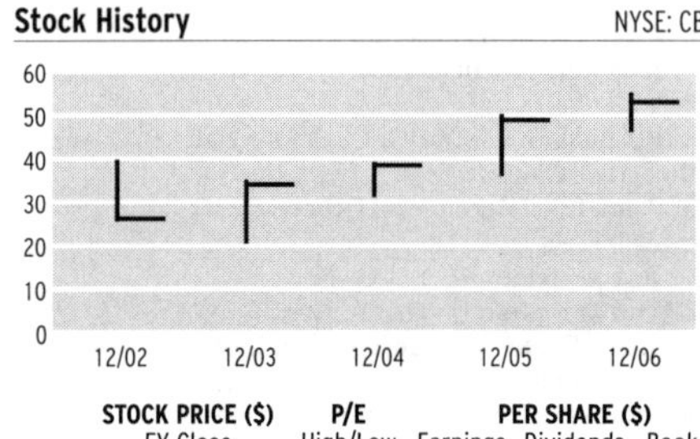

| | STOCK PRICE ($) FY Close | P/E High | P/E Low | PER SHARE ($) Earnings | Dividends | Book Value |
|---|---|---|---|---|---|---|
| **12/06** | 52.91 | 9 | 8 | 5.98 | 1.00 | 33.71 |
| **12/05** | 48.83 | 11 | 8 | 4.47 | 0.86 | 59.35 |
| **12/04** | 38.45 | 10 | 8 | 4.01 | 0.78 | 52.56 |
| **12/03** | 34.05 | 16 | 9 | 2.23 | 0.72 | 45.34 |
| **12/02** | 26.10 | 61 | 40 | 0.64 | 0.70 | 40.07 |
| **Annual Growth** | 19.3% | — | — | 74.8% | 9.3% | (4.2%) |

# Church & Dwight Co.

Whether you call it saleratus (aerated salt), sodium bicarbonate, or plain old baking soda, Church & Dwight is the world's #1 maker of the powder. Church & Dwight's ARM & HAMMER baking soda is used as a deodorizer, a cleaner, a swimming pool pH stabilizer, and as leavening. The firm makes laundry detergent, bathroom cleaners, cat litter, carpet deodorizer, air fresheners, toothpaste, and antiperspirants. Church & Dwight also makes Brillo scouring pads, Trojan condoms, and industrial-grade carbonates. Its purchase of Carter-Wallace's consumer products units (alongside Kelso & Company) gave it Arrid antiperspirant and Lambert Kay brands. It also bought Procter & Gamble's SpinBrush unit for $75 million.

Church & Dwight's consumer products accounted for 89% of its 2006 sales. The company sells three-fourths of its consumer products domestically. Church & Dwight combined its laundry detergents business with USA Detergents (Xtra, Nice 'N Fluffy) to cut costs, but it eventually ended up buying USA Detergents. Church & Dwight also has a specialty products division, which logged some 11% in 2006 sales, that makes antacid feed additives for cattle, industrial- and medical-grade sodium bicarbonate (used in kidney dialysis), ammonium bicarbonate, potassium carbonate (used in video monitor glass), and industrial cleaning products.

The siren song of overseas consumer markets has fallen on deaf ears at Church & Dwight, which has stayed focused on building its brands within the US and Canada and expanding through domestic acquisitions (Brillo, Clean Shower). To that end, the company acquired Orange Glo for $325 million in August 2006. Church & Dwight quickly began to leverage Orange Glo's savvy in infomercials and other direct-to-consumer marketing as a way to launch new products more quickly.

A small subsidiary in the UK produces specialty chemicals for European markets.

Church & Dwight purchased Unilever's oral care brands in the US and Canada in 2003. Products included in the deal are Mentadent toothpaste and toothbrushes, Pepsodent and Aim toothpaste, and exclusive licensing rights to Close-Up toothpaste. It expanded its oral care brand portfolio by buying Procter & Gamble's SpinBrush for $75 million plus up to $30 million for performance-related payments. SpinBrush logged sales of $110 million for the fiscal year ended June 30, 2005. About 80% of the brand's revenue was generated in the US and Canada.

To tap into new target markets with existing products, Church & Dwight, in 2005, developed a line of Trojan condoms called Elexa to be marketed to women and available on aisles where feminine hygiene products are sold.

Having been appointed president and CEO in mid-2004, James Craigie added the title of chairman in May 2007, when Robert Davies announced he would retire as chairman but remain on the board.

## HISTORY

Chemistry enthusiast Dr. Austin Church and his marketing-driven brother-in-law, John Dwight, founded a company to make bicarbonate of soda for baking in 1846. The ARM & HAMMER trademark — representing Vulcan, the Roman god of fire, and originally used by Church's son James, owner of the Vulcan Spice Mills — was adopted in 1867.

After Church's retirement, his sons ran a separate company until 1896, when they formed Church & Dwight. The company became known for direct marketing and distinctive packaging. Church & Dwight began preaching alternative uses for baking soda in the 1920s and accelerated the effort after WWII as home baking declined.

Dwight Minton, great-great-grandson of Church, was named CEO in 1968. Under his direction the company began appealing to "green" sentiments with new products such as nonphosphate laundry detergent (1970). Church & Dwight went public in 1977.

The Statue of Liberty's inner walls were cleaned with ARM & HAMMER baking soda in 1986 in preparation for its 100th anniversary. New product introductions intensified in the late 1980s and into the 1990s; offerings included toothpaste (1988), carpet deodorizer (1988), and deodorant and other products (1994). The product introductions were badly handled, and a large earnings drop ensued. Minton resigned in 1995 and was replaced by former marketing VP Robert Davies, the first CEO without ties to the founding family.

Broadening its household cleaning products base, the company bought the Brillo soap pad and five other brands from Dial in 1997 and folded Dial's Toss 'N Soft fabric softener business into its laundry basket in 1998. In 1999 it bought the Clean Shower brand (from Clean Shower L.P.) and the Scrub Free and Delicare brands (from Reckitt Benckiser), doubling its household cleaner business.

In 2000 Church & Dwight agreed to combine its laundry detergent business with value-brand cleaning products company USA Detergents. The two companies formed a joint venture, Armkel LLC, before Church & Dwight decided to buy all of USA Detergents in 2001.

Also in 2001 the company acquired Carter-Wallace's consumer products business (Arrid, Trojan, Nair) for $739 million. It bought the US antiperspirant and pet care businesses outright, but the larger part of the deal was made in partnership with private equity firm Kelso & Company. In early 2004 Church & Dwight bought the balance of Kelso & Company's stake for more than $250 million.

In July 2004 chairman and CEO Davies stepped down as CEO, retaining his title as chairman. Former president and CEO of Spalding Sports, James Craigie, took over as president, CEO, and director of the company.

## EXECUTIVES

**Chairman Emeritus:** Dwight C. Minton
**Director:** Robert A. (Bob) Davies III, age 71
**Chairman, President, and CEO; Interim President, Domestic Personal Care:** James R. (Jim) Craigie, age 53, $772,500 pay
**Director; President, ARAMARK International; EVP, ARAMARK:** Ravi K. Saligram, age 50
**VP, Corporate Development:** James L. Rogula
**VP, Domestic Consumer Sales:** Louis H. (Lou) Tursi, age 46, $324,600 pay
**VP Finance and Treasurer:** Gary P. Halker, age 56
**VP, Finance and CFO:** Matthew T. Farrell, age 50, $528,077 pay
**VP, General Counsel, and Secretary:** Susan E. Goldy, age 53
**VP, Global Operations:** Mark G. Conish, age 54
**VP, Global Research and Development:** Paul A. Siracusa, age 50
**VP, Human Resources:** Jacquelin J. (Jackie) Brova, age 53
**VP, Research and Development:** Raymond L. Bendure
**VP, Global New Products Innovation:** Steven P. Cugine, age 44, $521,200 pay
**VP; President and COO, Specialty Products Division:** Joseph A. Sipia Jr., age 58, $296,800 pay
**VP; President, International Consumer Products:** Adrian J. Huns, age 59, $722,750 pay
**VP and Chief Marketing Officer:** Bruce F. Fleming, age 49
**Media Relations:** Andrew C. Forsell
**Investor Relations:** Judy Schenk
**Auditors:** Deloitte & Touche LLP

## LOCATIONS

**HQ:** Church & Dwight Co., Inc.
469 N. Harrison St., Princeton, NJ 08543
**Phone:** 609-683-5900 **Fax:** 609-497-7269
**Web:** www.churchdwight.com

## PRODUCTS/OPERATIONS

### 2006 Sales

| | $ mil. | % of total |
|---|---|---|
| Consumer products | 1,725.3 | 89 |
| Specialty products | 220.3 | 11 |
| **Total** | **1,945.6** | **100** |

### Consumer Products

Aim toothpaste
ARM & HAMMER Advance White toothpaste
ARM & HAMMER baking soda
ARM & HAMMER carpet & room deodorizer
ARM & HAMMER cat litter deodorizer
ARM & HAMMER Dental Care gum
ARM & HAMMER Dental Care toothpaste
ARM & HAMMER deodorant/antiperspirant
ARM & HAMMER deodorizing air freshener
ARM & HAMMER Enamel Care toothpaste
ARM & HAMMER Fresh 'n Soft dryer sheets
ARM & HAMMER Fridge-n-Freezer
ARM & HAMMER laundry detergent
ARM & HAMMER PeroxiCare toothpaste
ARM & HAMMER Super Scoop clumping litter
ARM & HAMMER Super washing soda
Arrid antiperspirants
Brillo soap pads
Cameo metal cleaner
Clean Shower bathroom cleaner
Close-Up (exclusive licensing rights)
Delicare liquid detergent
First Response pregnancy test kits
Lambert Kay pet care products
Mentadent
Nair depilatories
Nice 'N Fluffy
Orange Clean cleanser and degreaser,
Orange Glo wood polish and cleaner
OxiClean laundry additive
Parsons' ammonia
Pepsodent
Scrub Free household cleaner
Sno Bol toilet bowl cleaner
SpinBrush
Trojan condoms
Trojan Elexa condoms
Xtra

### Specialty Products

Armakleen aqueous cleaner
Armicarb fungicide
ARM & HAMMER ammonium bicarbonate
ARM & HAMMER feed-grade sodium bicarbonate
ARM & HAMMER sodium bicarbonate
Armand potassium carbonate
Armex blast media
Bio-Chlor
Fermenten
MEGALAC rumen bypass fat (animal feed supplement)
SQ-810 rumen buffer (animal feed supplement)

## COMPETITORS

Alticor
Clorox
Colgate-Palmolive
Dial
Dr. Bronner's
FMC
Henkel Corp.
Inverness Medical Innovations
Johnson & Johnson
Nestlé Purina PetCare
Oil-Dri
Procter & Gamble
Reckitt Benckiser
Sara Lee Household
S.C. Johnson
SSL International
Unilever

## HISTORICAL FINANCIALS

Company Type: Public

### Income Statement

FYE: December 31

| | REVENUE ($ mil.) | NET INCOME ($ mil.) | NET PROFIT MARGIN | EMPLOYEES |
|---|---|---|---|---|
| **12/06** | 1,946 | 139 | 7.1% | 3,700 |
| **12/05** | 1,737 | 123 | 7.1% | 3,700 |
| **12/04** | 1,462 | 89 | 6.1% | 3,800 |
| **12/03** | 1,057 | 81 | 7.7% | 2,266 |
| **12/02** | 1,047 | 67 | 6.4% | 2,256 |
| **Annual Growth** | 16.8% | 20.1% | — | 13.2% |

### 2006 Year-End Financials

Debt ratio: 91.8%
Return on equity: 17.8%
Cash ($ mil.): 110
Current ratio: 1.25
Long-term debt ($ mil.): 793
No. of shares (mil.): 65
Dividends
Yield: 0.6%
Payout: 12.6%
Market value ($ mil.): 2,788

### Stock History

NYSE: CHD

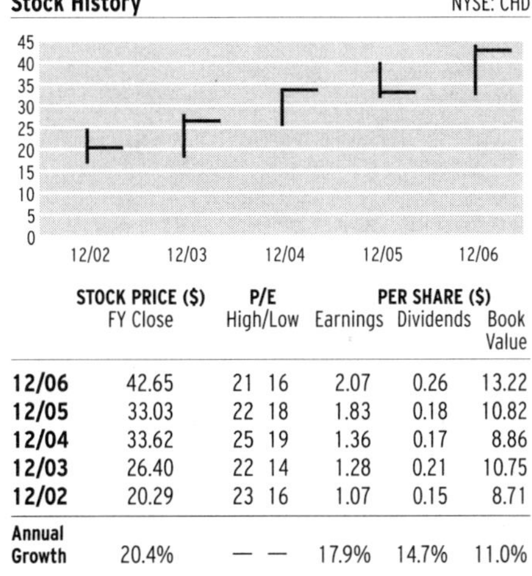


| | STOCK PRICE ($) FY Close | P/E High/Low | | PER SHARE ($) Earnings | Dividends | Book Value |
|---|---|---|---|---|---|---|
| **12/06** | 42.65 | 21 | 16 | 2.07 | 0.26 | 13.22 |
| **12/05** | 33.03 | 22 | 18 | 1.83 | 0.18 | 10.82 |
| **12/04** | 33.62 | 25 | 19 | 1.36 | 0.17 | 8.86 |
| **12/03** | 26.40 | 22 | 14 | 1.28 | 0.21 | 10.75 |
| **12/02** | 20.29 | 23 | 16 | 1.07 | 0.15 | 8.71 |
| **Annual Growth** | 20.4% | — | — | 17.9% | 14.7% | 11.0% |

# CIGNA Corporation

One of the top US health insurers, CIGNA covers more than 9 million people with its various medical plans, which include PPO, HMO, point-of-service (POS), indemnity, and consumer-directed products. CIGNA also offers other health coverage in the form of dental, vision, pharmacy, and behavioral health plans; and it sells group accident, life, and disability insurance. Its customers include employers, government entities, unions, Medicare recipients, and other individuals in the US and Canada. Internationally, the company sells life, accident, and supplemental health insurance in parts of Asia, the European Union, and Chile and provides health coverage to expatriate employees of multi-national companies.

CIGNA is trying to grow its health care segment by offering new and innovative products, particularly trendy consumer-directed programs such as health savings accounts (through its CIGNA Choice Fund line), health risk assessments, and online tools for comparing coverage options and making sound health care decisions. To that end, the company in 2006 bought UK-based vielife, which provides online health management and coaching services. Additionally, CIGNA has jumped on the Medicare Part D bandwagon, offering a Medicare prescription drug benefit program jointly with NationsHealth .

The company's health care operations (accounting for nearly 70% of revenue) manage care for its members through a network of some 5,000 hospitals and 518,000 providers. CIGNA continually works to strengthen that network of providers, partially through strategic alliances with regional managed care organizations; it has agreements with MVP Health Plan and HealthPartners, among others.

CIGNA does much of its business with large employers, but it plans to expand its customer base to include more small and midsized businesses, seniors, government entities, and individuals. As part of this strategy, it acquired Star-HRG, a voluntary health coverage business offering low-cost plans to hourly and part-time workers. Other elements of the company's strategy include mitigating rising health care costs through more favorable reimbursement contracts with providers and enhancing operating and administrative efficiencies.

CIGNA's disability and life insurance operations, which account for about 15% of sales, offer long- and short-term disability insurance, workers' compensation case management, group life insurance, and accident insurance, among other products. The company sells the policies to employers and employees and to professional associations through brokers and consultants. It covers nearly 6 million lives with its group life insurance policies.

## HISTORY

The Insurance Company of North America (INA) was founded in 1792 by Philadelphia businessmen. INA was the US's first stock insurance company and its first marine insurer. It later issued life insurance, fire insurance, and coverage for the contents of buildings. In 1808 it began using agents outside Pennsylvania. INA grew internationally in the late 1800s, appointing agents in Canada as well as in London and Vienna in Europe. It was the first US company to write insurance in China, beginning in Shanghai in 1897.

In 1942 INA provided both accident and health insurance for men working on the Manhattan Project, which developed the atomic bomb. It introduced the first widely available homeowner coverage in 1950. In 1978 INA bought HMO International, which was then the largest publicly owned health maintenance organization in the US. INA merged with Connecticut General in 1982 to form CIGNA.

Connecticut General began selling life insurance in 1865 and health insurance in 1912. It wrote its first group insurance (for the *Hartford Courant* newspaper) in 1913 and the first individual accident coverage for airline passengers in 1926. In the late 1930s Connecticut General was a leader in developing group medical coverage. The company offered the first group medical coverage for general use in 1952 and in 1964 added group dental insurance.

After the merger, CIGNA bought Crusader Insurance (UK, 1983; sold 1991) and AFIA (1984). To begin positioning itself as a provider of managed health care, the company sold its individual insurance products division to InterContinental Life in 1988 and its Horace Mann Cos. (individual financial services) to an investor group in 1989. To further its goal, in 1990 CIGNA bought

EQUICOR, an HMO started by Hospital Corporation of America (now part of HCA Inc.) and what is now AXA Equitable Life Insurance.

In the early 1990s it began to withdraw from the personal property/casualty business to focus on small and midsized commercial clients in the US, cutting sales overseas and combining them with life and health operations. It also exited such areas as airline insurance and surety bonds.

CIGNA expanded internationally in the mid-1990s, opening a Beijing office in 1993, 43 years after its departure from China. The next year the company bought 60% of an Indonesian insurance company. It also acquired 45% of Mediplan, a managed health care organization in Mexico.

Reeling from unforeseen environmental liabilities (chiefly related to asbestos), CIGNA in 1995 split its remaining property/casualty business between a healthy segment that continued to write new policies and one for run-off business. Four years later it finally sold these operations (including Cigna Insurance Co. of Europe) to ACE Limited in order to fund internal growth and acquisitions.

In the late 1990s, the company continued to cultivate its health care segment, acquiring managed care provider Healthsource in 1997. The company expanded its group benefits operations to India, Brazil, and Poland; at home, it cut its payroll by 1,300 in the US to counter rising costs. The company sold its domestic individual life insurance and annuity business in 1998 but began offering investment and pension products in Japan in 1999. In 2000 CIGNA settled a federal lawsuit over Medicare billing fraud. It also sold its reinsurance businesses that year to a subsidiary of Swiss Reinsurance Company.

In 2002 CIGNA formed a joint venture with SDZ, an affiliate of China Merchants Group, to sell life insurance in China.

CIGNA sold its retirement division to Prudential in early 2004. Later that year, the company also sold its TimesSquare Capital Management unit to Bear Stearns.

## EXECUTIVES

**Chairman and CEO:** H. Edward Hanway, age 55, $1,110,000 pay
**EVP and CFO:** Michael W. Bell, age 43, $575,000 pay
**EVP and General Counsel:** Carol Ann Petren, age 53
**EVP, Human Resources and Services:** John M. Murabito, age 48, $535,000 pay
**SVP, Public Affairs and Associate General Counsel:** John Cannon III
**SVP, Sales and Distribution:** Craig Guiffre
**VP and Chief Accounting Officer:** Annmarie T. Hagan
**VP and Chief Counsel, Corporate and Financial Law:** Pauline A. Candaux
**VP and Treasurer:** Mordecai Schwartz
**VP, Brand Strategy and Integration:** Edward A. Faruolo
**VP, Corporate Communications:** Wendell Potter
**VP, Corporate Equal Employment Opportunity/People Diversity:** Curtis Mathews Jr.
**VP, Employee Benefits and Health Management:** Gerald T. Meyn
**VP, Finance:** Tom McCarthy
**VP, Human Resources:** William Kraus
**VP, Investor Relations:** Edwin J. (Ted) Detrick
**VP, Leadership Development:** Pamela C. (Pam) Lawless
**VP Sales, Small Group:** James Saad
**VP, Operational Planning:** Frank LaMay
**President, CIGNA Healthcare:** David M. (Dave) Cordani, age 41, $535,000 pay
**Corporate Marketing:** Ewa Whiteside
**Auditors:** PricewaterhouseCoopers LLP

## LOCATIONS

**HQ:** CIGNA Corporation
2 Liberty Place, Philadelphia, PA 19192
**Phone:** 215-761-1000 **Fax:** 215-761-5515
**Web:** www.cigna.com

CIGNA operates in Asia and the Pacific Rim, Europe, and North and South America.

## PRODUCTS/OPERATIONS

**2006 Sales**

| | $ mil. | % of total |
|---|---|---|
| Health Care | | |
| Medical premiums | | |
| Commercial HMO | 2,744 | 16 |
| Experience-rated | 1,760 | 11 |
| Dental | 776 | 5 |
| Medicare & Medicaid | 321 | 2 |
| Medicare Part D | 215 | 1 |
| Other | 1,947 | 12 |
| Life & other non-medical premiums | 305 | 2 |
| Fees | 1,762 | 11 |
| Net investment income | 261 | 2 |
| Other | 1,371 | 8 |
| Disability & Life | | |
| Premiums & fees | 2,108 | 13 |
| Net investment income | 256 | 2 |
| Other | 161 | 1 |
| International | | |
| Premiums & fees | 1,526 | 9 |
| Net investment income | 79 | — |
| Other | 2 | — |
| Run-Off Retirement | | |
| Premiums & fees | 2 | — |
| Net investment income | 32 | — |
| Other | 18 | — |
| Run-Off Reinsurance | | |
| Premiums & fees | 64 | — |
| Net investment income | 95 | — |
| Other | (97) | — |
| Other Operations | | |
| Premiums & fees | 111 | 1 |
| Net investment income | 435 | 3 |
| Other | 84 | — |
| Corporate | | |
| Other & eliminatons | (48) | — |
| Net investment income | 37 | — |
| Realized investement gains | 220 | 1 |
| **Total** | **16,547** | **100** |

## COMPETITORS

AEGON
Aetna
AIG
Allianz
Allstate
Aon
AXA
Blue Cross
Caremark Pharmacy Services
CNA Financial
COUNTRY Insurance
Coventry Health Care
Express Scripts
The Hartford
Health Net
Highmark
Humana
ING
John Hancock Financial Services
Kaiser Foundation Health Plan
MassMutual
Medco Health Solutions
MetLife
New York Life
Northwestern Mutual
Oxford Health
Principal Financial
Prudential
Sierra Health
TIAA-CREF
UnitedHealth Group
WellPoint

## HISTORICAL FINANCIALS

Company Type: Public

**Income Statement** FYE: December 31

| | REVENUE ($ mil.) | NET INCOME ($ mil.) | NET PROFIT MARGIN | EMPLOYEES |
|---|---|---|---|---|
| **12/06** | 16,547 | 1,155 | 7.0% | 27,100 |
| **12/05** | 16,684 | 1,625 | 9.7% | 32,700 |
| **12/04** | 18,176 | 1,438 | 7.9% | 28,600 |
| **12/03** | 18,808 | 650 | 3.5% | 32,700 |
| **12/02** | 19,348 | (398) | — | 41,200 |
| **Annual Growth** | (3.8%) | — | — | (9.9%) |

**2006 Year-End Financials**

Debt ratio: 29.9%
Return on equity: 23.8%
Cash ($ mil.): 1,481
Current ratio: —
Long-term debt ($ mil.): 1,294
No. of shares (mil.): 99
Dividends
Yield: 0.1%
Payout: 0.9%
Market value ($ mil.): 4,327

**Stock History** NYSE: CI

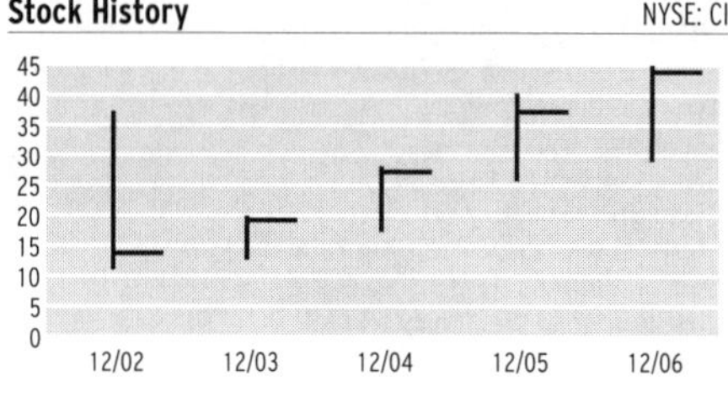

| | STOCK PRICE ($) FY Close | P/E High | P/E Low | PER SHARE ($) Earnings | Dividends | Book Value |
|---|---|---|---|---|---|---|
| **12/06** | 43.86 | 13 | 9 | 3.43 | 0.03 | 43.89 |
| **12/05** | 37.23 | 10 | 6 | 4.17 | 0.03 | 44.23 |
| **12/04** | 27.19 | 7 | 5 | 3.81 | 0.14 | 39.41 |
| **12/03** | 19.17 | 13 | 8 | 1.54 | 0.44 | 16.57 |
| **12/02** | 13.71 | — | — | (0.94) | 0.44 | 27.75 |
| **Annual Growth** | 33.7% | — | — | — | (48.9%) | 12.1% |

# Cincinnati Financial

Ohio has no clichés or tired jokes, but it does have a solid insurance company: Cincinnati Financial Corporation (CFC). Its flagship Cincinnati Insurance (with subsidiaries Cincinnati Casualty and Cincinnati Indemnity) sells commercial property, liability, auto, bond, and fire insurance; personal lines include homeowners and liability products. Cincinnati Life sells life, disability income, and annuities. The company's CFC Investment subsidiary provides financing, leasing, and real estate services, and its CinFin Capital Management leverages the company's in-house asset management expertise.

CFC has also made its investment operations a key part of the mix — it owns about 13% of Fifth Third Bancorp.

Cincinnati Financial markets its policies in 32 states through more than 1,000 independent agencies. The company writes nearly 25% of its business in Ohio, and is strong in Illinois, Indiana, and Pennsylvania. Cincinnati Financial's commercial lines segment targets primarily small to midsized businesses. The company has tied its growth to expanding the territories it markets in, and increasing the number of new agencies it strikes relationships with.

The founding Schiff family owns 12% of Cincinnati Financial.

## HISTORY

Jack Schiff spent three years with the Travelers Company before he joined the Navy in WWII. He returned to Cincinnati to start his own independent insurance agency in 1946 and was joined by his younger brother Robert; both were Ohio State graduates whose affection for the Buckeyes led them in later years to close company banquets with the school fight song. The brothers incorporated Cincinnati Insurance with $200,000 from investors.

Under Harry Turner, the company's first president, the company offered property/casualty insurance to small businesses and homeowners through its network of agents. By 1956 the company had spread into neighboring Kentucky and Indiana. During the next decade Cincinnati Insurance expanded its products and network, adding auto, burglary, and commercial all-risk lines and enlisting agents throughout the Midwest.

In 1963 Turner took the chairman's seat and Jack Schiff became president, introducing a more aggressive leadership style. In 1969 the company reorganized and went public, forming Cincinnati Financial Corporation as a holding company for the insurance operation. CFC used the money to pay off debts and buy new businesses, forming two subsidiaries: CFC Investment Company, in 1970, to deal in commercial real estate and financing; and Queen City Indemnity (later named The Cincinnati Casualty Company), in 1972, to offer direct-bill personal policies.

By 1973 operations included The Life Insurance Company of Cincinnati, Queen City Indemnity, and fellow Cincinnati giant Inter-Ocean Insurance Company. That year Jack Schiff added CEO to his title.

CFC continued to grow throughout the 1970s with a new emphasis on independent investments. In 1982 Cincinnati Financial veteran Robert Morgan became president and CEO. The company's conservative roots and investment base helped it shake off the early-1980s recession and a string of natural disasters that left many other insurers dangling in the wind.

Also during the 1980s, the company started to shift its focus from personal to commercial lines. In 1988 it reorganized its life insurance subsidiaries under the Cincinnati Life banner and formed The Cincinnati Indemnity Company to offer workers' compensation and personal insurance. In 1998 a string of storms (reminiscent of others earlier in the decade) dampened the company's earnings.

Also that year the company — a laggard in the industrywide move into financial services — created CinFin Capital Management. The unit offers the company's in-house asset management skills to corporations, institutions, and wealthy individuals.

In 1999 Jack Schiff Jr. succeeded Morgan as president and CEO. The next year, 96-year-old Harry Turner died. After a 1999 decision by the Ohio Supreme Court that increased exposure on auto policies, CFC set up $110 million in reserves for uninsured motorists claims that year and the following year; the decision was overturned in 2003.

## EXECUTIVES

**Chairman and CEO:** John J. Schiff Jr., age 63
**Vice Chairman, President, COO, and Chief Insurance Officer; President, Cincinnati Insurance Company and Cincinnati Indemnity Company:** James E. Benoski, age 68
**EVP, CFO, Secretary, and Treasurer; EVP, CFO, Secretary, The Cincinnati Insurance Company:** Kenneth W. Stecher, age 60
**President and CEO, The Cincinnati Life Insurance Company:** David H. Popplewell, age 61
**President, The Cincinnati Casualty Company; SVP, The Cincinnati Insurance Company and Cincinnati Indemnity Company:** Larry R. Plum, age 60
**SVP, Investments and Chief Investment Officer, The Cincinnati Insurance Company:** Kenneth S. Miller, age 51
**SVP, Corporate Accounting, The Cincinnati Insurance Company:** Eric N. Mathews, age 51
**SVP, Chief Underwriter, The Cincinnati Life Insurance Company:** Brad E. Behringer
**SVP, Bond and Executive Risk, The Cincinnati Insurance Company:** Daniel T. McCurdy, age 72
**SVP, Corporate Communications, The Cincinnati Insurance Company:** Joan O. Shevchik, age 56
**SVP, Information Technology, The Cincinnati Insurance Company:** Craig W. Forrester, age 48
**SVP, Operations, The Cincinnati Insurance Company:** Timothy L. Timmel, age 58
**SVP, Sales and Marketing, The Cincinnati Insurance Company:** Jacob F. Scherer Jr., age 54
**SVP Strategic Planning, Property Casualty Insurance Subsidiaries:** Donald J. Doyle Jr.
**VP, Investor Relations, Property Casualty Insurance Subsidiaries:** Heather J. Wietzel
**VP, Investments, Cincinatti Financial and Cincinnati Life Insurance:** Michael Abrams
**Auditors:** Deloitte & Touche LLP

## LOCATIONS

**HQ:** Cincinnati Financial Corporation
6200 S. Gilmore Rd., Fairfield, OH 45014
**Phone:** 513-870-2000 **Fax:** 513-870-2911
**Web:** www.cinfin.com

Cincinnati Financial operates in some 30 states, primarily in the East and Midwest.

## PRODUCTS/OPERATIONS

### 2006 Sales

| | $ mil. | % of total |
|---|---|---|
| Premiums | | |
| Property & casualty | 3,163 | 70 |
| Life | 115 | 3 |
| Investment income | 570 | 12 |
| Realized investment gains | 684 | 15 |
| Other | 18 | — |
| **Total** | **4,550** | **100** |

### Selected Subsidiaries

CFC Investment Company (leasing, financing, real estate services)
The Cincinnati Insurance Company
The Cincinnati Casualty Company
The Cincinnati Indemnity Company
The Cincinnati Life Insurance Company
CinFin Capital Management Company (asset management)

## COMPETITORS

ALLIED Group
CNA Financial
Erie Indemnity
Farmers Group
Great American Insurance
The Hartford
Indiana Insurance
metLife
Ohio Casualty
OneBeacon
Progressive Corporation
Selective Insurance
Travelers Companies
Westfield Group
Zurich American

## HISTORICAL FINANCIALS

Company Type: Public

### Income Statement

FYE: December 31

| | ASSETS ($ mil.) | NET INCOME ($ mil.) | INCOME AS % OF ASSETS | EMPLOYEES |
|---|---|---|---|---|
| **12/06** | 17,222 | 930 | 5.4% | 4,048 |
| **12/05** | 16,003 | 602 | 3.8% | 3,983 |
| **12/04** | 16,107 | 584 | 3.6% | 3,884 |
| **12/03** | 15,509 | 374 | 2.4% | 3,720 |
| **12/02** | 14,059 | 238 | 1.7% | 3,511 |
| **Annual Growth** | 5.2% | 40.6% | — | 3.6% |

### 2006 Year-End Financials

Equity as % of assets: 39.5%
Return on assets: 5.6%
Return on equity: 14.4%
Long-term debt ($ mil.): 840
No. of shares (mil.): 173
Dividends
Yield: 3.0%
Payout: 25.3%
Market value ($ mil.): 7,839
Sales ($ mil.): 4,550

### Stock History

NASDAQ (GS): CINF

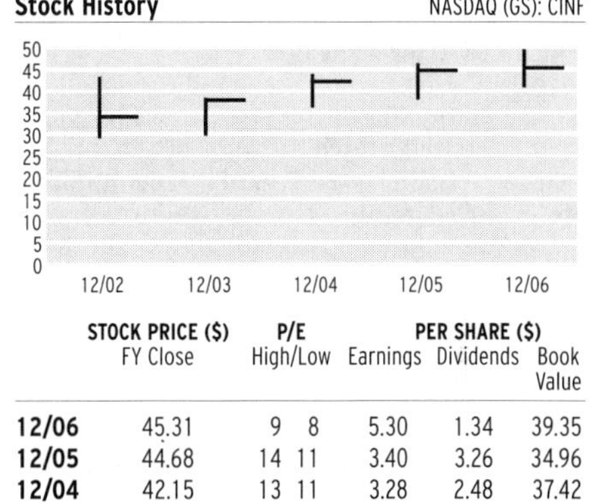


| | STOCK PRICE ($) FY Close | P/E High/Low | | PER SHARE ($) Earnings | Dividends | Book Value |
|---|---|---|---|---|---|---|
| **12/06** | 45.31 | 9 | 8 | 5.30 | 1.34 | 39.35 |
| **12/05** | 44.68 | 14 | 11 | 3.40 | 3.26 | 34.96 |
| **12/04** | 42.15 | 13 | 11 | 3.28 | 2.48 | 37.42 |
| **12/03** | 37.87 | 18 | 14 | 2.10 | 0.91 | 38.78 |
| **12/02** | 34.06 | 32 | 22 | 1.32 | 0.81 | 34.56 |
| **Annual Growth** | 7.4% | — | — | 41.6% | 13.4% | 3.3% |

# Cintas Corporation

If Cintas had its way, you'd never agonize over what to wear to work. The #1 uniform supplier in the US, the company has more than 700,000 clients (Delta Air Lines, DHL), and some 5 million people wear its garb each day. Cintas, which sells, leases, and rents uniforms, has more than 410 facilities across the US and Canada. In addition to offering shirts, jackets, slacks, and footwear, the company provides cleanroom apparel and flame resistant clothing. Other products offered by Cintas include uniform cleaning, first aid and safety products, document handling/storage, and cleanroom supplies. Cintas chairman and founder Richard T. Farmer owns nearly 14% of the company. His son Scott runs the business.

Uniform rentals generate 75% of Cintas' sales. The remainder of the company's revenue comes from uniform sales and its array of other products and services. Despite its position as the country's leading renter of corporate uniforms, the company still sees growth potential in the uniform rental market. However, Cintas is also looking to expand its non-uniform operations and in 2004 replaced its corporate slogan "The Uniform People" with a new logo — "The Service

Professionals" — to reflect the expanded focus of the company.

Cintas employees must wear a Cintas uniform or business suit to work. The company, which was established in 1968, was named among the nation's "Most Admired Companies" by *Fortune* magazine for the fifth consecutive year in 2005.

## HISTORY

In 1929 onetime animal trainer, boxer, and blacksmith Richard "Doc" Farmer started a business of salvaging old rags, cleaning them, and then selling them to factories. Farmer later began renting the rags to his customers. He would pick up the dirty rags, clean them, and return them to the factory. By 1936 the Acme Overall & Rag Laundry had established itself in Cincinnati with plans to convert an old bathhouse into a laundry. Farmer, along with his adopted son Herschell, suffered a setback from flood damage in 1937, but the family rebuilt and continued to grow the business.

In 1952 Doc Farmer died, and Herschell assumed command of the company. Five years later Herschell turned the reins over to his 23-year-old son, Richard. Richard Farmer immediately moved Acme into the uniform rental market, and the company blossomed. Throughout the 1960s the company grew enormously, aided by Richard's innovative leadership. (The company was the first to use a polyester-cotton blend that lasted twice as long as normal cotton work uniforms.) Through a holding company, Richard established a string of uniform plants in the Midwest, starting with a factory in Cleveland in 1968. Four years later the company changed its name to Cintas.

At this time the company began tapping into the new corporate identity market, pushing the idea that uniforms convey a sense of professionalism and present a cleaner, safer image. The company began to custom design the uniforms, adding logos and distinctive colors. This aspect of the business compelled Cintas to expand to help accommodate its national clients; by 1972 the company had offices throughout Ohio and in Chicago, Detroit, and Washington, DC. By 1975 Cintas was operating in 13 states.

The company went public in 1983. For the rest of the 1980s, Cintas rode the wave of consolidation in the uniform rental industry, making a slew of acquisitions. The company also expanded from its blue-collar base into the service industry and began to supply uniforms to hotels, restaurants, and banks. By the early 1990s Cintas was a presence in most major US cities, and its share of the US market had climbed to about 10%. Farmer turned over the title of CEO to president Robert Kohlhepp in 1995. That year the company acquired Cadet Uniform Services, a Toronto uniform rental business, for $41 million.

Scott Farmer, Richard's 38-year-old son, was named president and COO in 1997. That year Cintas made a number of acquisitions, including Micron-Clean Uniform Service and Canadian firms Act One Uniform Rentals and DW King Services. The company also moved into the first aid supplies industry with its purchase of American First Aid, and added clean-room garments to its expanding list of uniform rentals. In 1998 Cintas acquired uniform rental company Apparelmaster, as well as Chicago-based Uniforms To You, a $150 million design and manufacturing company. In an effort to expand its corporate uniform business, the company acquired rival Unitog in 1999 for about $460 million.

As part of the integration of Unitog, in 2000 Cintas closed several of Unitog's uniform rental operations, distribution centers, and manufacturing plants. The company also established first aid supplies and safety equipment unit Xpect. In 2002 Cintas purchased Omni Services, marking its largest acquisition to date.

## EXECUTIVES

**Chairman:** Richard T. (Dick) Farmer, age 71, $250,000 pay
**Vice Chairman:** Robert J. (Bob) Kohlhepp, age 63, $500,000 pay
**President, CEO, and Director:** Scott D. Farmer, age 47, $866,000 pay
**SVP and CFO:** William C. Gale, age 52, $475,000 pay
**VP and CIO:** G. Thomas Thornley
**VP and Treasurer:** Michael L. Thompson
**VP, Secretary, and General Counsel:** Thomas E. Frooman, age 37, $455,000 pay
**VP and Deputy General Counsel, Labor and Employment:** Michael A. Womack
**VP Business Strategy:** John E. Myers
**VP Corporate Communications:** Pamela J. (Pam) Lowe
**VP Corporate Development:** Michael P. (Mike) Gaburo
**VP Garment Business Strategy:** Rodger V. Reed
**VP Logistics and Manufacturing:** Glenn W. Larsen
**VP Marketing and Merchandising:** Jay Bruscato
**Director, Marketing:** Kirk Kirssin
**Corporate Communications Manager:** Mike Wallner
**President and COO, First Aid and Safety Division:** David Pollak Jr.
**President and COO, National Account Sales Division:** William L. Cronin
**President and COO, Rental Division East:** John W. Milligan
**Auditors:** Ernst & Young LLP

## LOCATIONS

**HQ:** Cintas Corporation
6800 Cintas Blvd., Cincinnati, OH 45262
**Phone:** 513-459-1200 **Fax:** 513-573-4130
**Web:** www.cintas-corp.com

Cintas has operations in 280 cities in the US and Canada.

## PRODUCTS/OPERATIONS

### 2007 Sales

| | $ mil. | % of total |
|---|---|---|
| Rentals | 2,734.6 | 74 |
| Other services | 972.3 | 26 |
| **Total** | **3,706.9** | **100** |

### Selected Products and Services

Cleanroom supplies
Document shredding and storage
Entrance mats
Fender covers
Fire protection
First aid and safety products and services
Linen products
Mops
Restroom supplies
Towels
Uniform cleaning
Uniform rental and sales

## COMPETITORS

Alsco
Angelica
ARAMARK
G&K Services
Iron Mountain
NCH
Superior Uniform Group
UniFirst

## HISTORICAL FINANCIALS

Company Type: Public

### Income Statement

FYE: May 31

| | REVENUE ($ mil.) | NET INCOME ($ mil.) | NET PROFIT MARGIN | EMPLOYEES |
|---|---|---|---|---|
| **5/07** | 3,707 | 335 | 9.0% | 34,000 |
| **5/06** | 3,404 | 327 | 9.6% | 32,000 |
| **5/05** | 3,067 | 301 | 9.8% | 30,000 |
| **5/04** | 2,814 | 272 | 9.7% | 28,300 |
| **5/03** | 2,687 | 249 | 9.3% | 27,700 |
| **Annual Growth** | 8.4% | 7.6% | — | 5.3% |

### 2007 Year-End Financials

Debt ratio: 40.5%
Return on equity: 15.7%
Cash ($ mil.): 155
Current ratio: 2.87
Long-term debt ($ mil.): 877
No. of shares (mil.): 159
Dividends
Yield: 1.0%
Payout: 18.7%
Market value ($ mil.): 6,087

### Stock History

NASDAQ (GS): CTAS

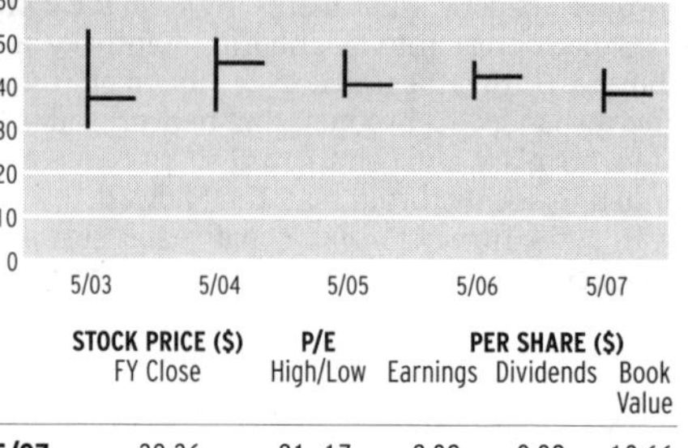


| | STOCK PRICE ($) FY Close | P/E High | P/E Low | PER SHARE ($) Earnings | Dividends | Book Value |
|---|---|---|---|---|---|---|
| **5/07** | 38.36 | 21 | 17 | 2.09 | 0.39 | 13.66 |
| **5/06** | 42.36 | 23 | 19 | 1.94 | 0.35 | 12.80 |
| **5/05** | 40.37 | 28 | 22 | 1.74 | 0.32 | 12.33 |
| **5/04** | 45.33 | 32 | 22 | 1.58 | 0.29 | 11.02 |
| **5/03** | 37.02 | 36 | 21 | 1.45 | 0.27 | 9.65 |
| **Annual Growth** | 0.9% | — | — | 9.6% | 9.6% | 9.1% |

# Circuit City Stores

A short circuit in this city might leave a lot of electronic gadgets on the shelves. Circuit City Stores is a top consumer electronics retailer in the US (along with Best Buy and Wal Mart), with more than 650 superstores in about 45 states. The big box outlets offer a wide array of televisions, DVD players, and audio systems, as well as CDs and DVDs. Circuit City also sells personal computers and peripherals, mobile computing devices, telephones, and video games. In addition to its retail stores, the company sells products through its Web site. Circuit City's international operations are conducted by Canadian subsidiary InterTAN, which operates more than 800 locations in that country.

Trying to make up ground against its bigger rival, the company has been remodeling and relocating some of its stores to attract more customer traffic. At the same time, Circuit City has closed some underperforming locations as well as a distribution center to cut costs.

In 2007 the company announced it would close more than 60 stores in Canada, in addition to a distribution center and seven superstores in the US, after intense competition in the flat panel TV arena. It also reorganized its management structure to improve channel alignment and accountability. It is letting go another 3,500 employees who were paid above the market rate and will hire new employees compensated at "the current market range." Later that year CEO Philip Schoonover said he planned to cut another 800 jobs, mostly management jobs and positions at headquarters.

However, its efforts have generally been undercut by aggressive pricing by Best Buy and other chains and by declining sales in some product categories (such as DVD players). In another bid to emulate its bigger rival, in fall 2006 Circuit City launched a home installation and support service — called Firedog — modeled after Best Buy's successful Geek Squad. In addition to in-home tech help, Firedog offers home theater installation and support service for other home entertainment media.

Circuit City has also used acquisitions to expand into new markets. It gained a foothold in Canada when it bought InterTAN for about $280 million in 2004. InterTAN operates more than 800 stores under the name Battery Plus, as well as more than 500 company-owned locations that formerly operated under the RadioShack name. However, a dispute with the US retail chain over advertising fees ended the licensing deal and InterTAN rebranded most of its stores under the banner The Source By Circuit City. In 2007 the company said it would explore selling its InterTAN unit.

The company jumped into a new avenue for growth in 2007. It announced that it had formed a new digital music service with Napster called Circuit City + Napster, which gives subscribers access to its library of music for a monthly fee, as well as the ability to download songs for an additional 99 cents.

Veteran CEO Alan McCollough retired in 2006, handing the reigns to Schoonover, who was lured away from Best Buy.

## HISTORY

While on vacation in Richmond, Virginia, in 1949, Samuel Wurtzel learned from a local barber that the first TV station in the South was about to go on the air. Wurtzel decided to launch a southern TV retailing operation and founded Wards Company (an acronym for family names Wurtzel, Alan, Ruth, David, and Samuel) in Richmond that year, gradually diversifying into small appliances. Wards went public in 1961. Throughout the 1960s and early 1970s, Wards expanded by acquiring several appliance retailers. Samuel's son Alan joined the business in 1966, when the company was focused on selling stereos. Predicting the end of the stereo boom, Alan converted the stores into full-line electronics specialty retailers.

Wards took a bold step in 1975, when it spent half of its net worth to open an electronics superstore in Richmond. It was an immediate success, and in 1981 it branched into the New York City market with the purchase of Lafayette Radio Electronics. The company found itself unable to compete with exuberant competitors in New York, such as Crazy Eddie (which went out of business), and abandoned the market. From its New York experience, Wards developed a strategy of blitzing single markets in the South and the West with a high number of stores. In 1984 the company changed its name to Circuit City Stores.

Two years later Alan stepped down as CEO, and company leadership passed to Richard Sharp, a former computer consultant who had designed Circuit City's computerized sales system. Sharp made it a priority to maintain an efficient distribution and records system. Earnings slipped in 1990 as consumer spending dropped and the industry was slow to introduce new products. During this time, Circuit City started opening mall stores named Impulse and introduced the Circuit City credit card.

Circuit City began selling recorded music in its superstores in 1992. The next year it entered Chicago with 18 stores and renamed its Impulse stores Circuit City Express. Also in 1993 Circuit City opened its first used-car-retailing venture, a CarMax dealership in Richmond.

Rival Best Buy surpassed Circuit City's sales in fiscal year 1996, partly due to Best Buy's aggressive expansion.

In an effort to compete with online computer retailers, in 1999 the company began offering $400 rebates to customers who signed up with Internet service provider CompuServe. In 2000 president and COO Alan McCollough replaced Sharp as CEO. (McCollough became chairman two years later.) The following month Circuit City began a $1 billion remodeling plan for its superstores that would phase out major appliances in favor of high-profit consumer electronics and home office products.

In 2002 Circuit City Stores spun off its CarMax unit as an independent entity. Late the next year the company sold its credit card operations to FleetBoston Financial (now Bank of America), a move intended to allow the retailer to focus on its store improvement plans.

In 2004 Circuit City acquired Canadian electronics retailer InterTAN, which had operated more than 500 stores under the licensed RadioShack name. However, a dispute with RadioShack over unpaid advertising fees ended the relationship and InterTAN rebranded its stores The Source By Circuit City the next year. McCollough retired as chairman and CEO in 2006, handing the reigns to former Best Buy executive Philip Schoonover.

## EXECUTIVES

**Chairman, President, and CEO:** Philip J. Schoonover, age 47, $894,615 pay
**EVP, Multi-Channel Sales; President, Retail Stores:** George D. (Danny) Clark Jr., age 47, $523,462 pay
**EVP and CFO:** Bruce H. Besanko, age 48
**SVP and CIO:** William E. McCorey Jr., age 49
**SVP and Chief Marketing Officer:** Peter Weedfald, age 53
**EVP, Merchandising, Services, and Marketing:** David L. Mathews, age 47
**SVP, General Counsel, and Secretary:** Reginald D. (Reggie) Hedgebeth, age 39, $337,115 pay
**SVP and General Manager, Services:** Marc J. Sieger, age 38
**SVP and General Merchandise Manager:** Randall W. (Randy) Wick, age 46
**SVP and General Merchandise Manager, Entertainment:** Irynne V. MacKay, age 37
**SVP Retail Operations:** Marshall J. Whaling, age 52
**SVP, Treasurer, and Controller:** Philip J. Dunn, age 54
**SVP Human Resources:** Eric A. Jonas Jr., age 52, $370,192 pay
**SVP; President, Small Stores:** Steven P. Pappas, age 43
**SVP Supply Chain and Inventory Management:** Ronald G. (Ron) Cuthbertson, age 50
**Director of Corporate Communications:** Bill Cimino
**Auditors:** KPMG LLP

## LOCATIONS

**HQ:** Circuit City Stores, Inc.
9950 Mayland Dr., Richmond, VA 23233
**Phone:** 804-486-4000 **Fax:** 804-527-4164
**Web:** www.circuitcity.com

### 2007 Sales

| | $ mil. | % of total |
|---|---|---|
| US | 11,859.6 | 95 |
| Other countries | 570.2 | 5 |
| **Total** | **12,429.8** | **100** |

### 2007 Locations

| | No. |
|---|---|
| California | 89 |
| Texas | 54 |
| Florida | 49 |
| New York | 33 |
| Illinois | 31 |
| Pennsylvania | 30 |
| Ohio | 26 |
| Virginia | 24 |
| Georgia | 22 |
| Michigan | 22 |
| North Carolina | 21 |
| New Jersey | 19 |
| Massachusetts | 19 |
| Maryland | 17 |
| Colorado | 16 |
| Arizona | 14 |
| Indiana | 13 |
| Washington | 13 |
| Tennessee | 12 |
| Missouri | 11 |
| Connecticut | 10 |
| Louisiana | 9 |
| Minnesota | 9 |
| South Carolina | 9 |
| Alabama | 8 |
| Wisconsin | 8 |
| Kentucky | 7 |
| Oregon | 7 |
| Nevada | 6 |
| New Hampshire | 6 |
| Mississippi | 5 |
| Oklahoma | 5 |
| Utah | 5 |
| Other states | 25 |
| **Total** | **654** |

## PRODUCTS/OPERATIONS

### 2007 Domestic Sales

| | % of total |
|---|---|
| Video | 42 |
| Information technology | 25 |
| Audio | 15 |
| Entertainment | 11 |
| Warranty, services, and other | 7 |
| **Total** | **100** |

### 2007 Domestic Locations

| | No. |
|---|---|
| Superstores | 642 |
| Other | 12 |
| **Total** | **654** |

### 2007 International Stores

| | No. |
|---|---|
| Company-owned stores | 509 |
| Dealer outlets | 296 |
| Battery Plus | 1 |
| **Total** | **806** |

### Selected Products

Video
- Camcorders
- Digital cameras
- Digital video recorders
- DVD players
- Satellite television receivers
- Televisions

Information Technology
- Computers
- Mobile devices
- Monitors
- Networking equipment
- Printers
- Scanners
- Telephones

Audio
- Car audio systems
- CD players
- Home theater audio systems
- MP3 players
- Satellite radio systems
- Stereo receivers and speakers

Entertainment
- CDs
- Computer software
- DVDs
- Music downloads
- Toys
- Video game systems and software

## COMPETITORS

Amazon.com
Apple
Best Buy
CompUSA
Dell
Fry's Electronics
Hastings Entertainment
Office Depot
OfficeMax
PC Mall
RadioShack
Staples
Systemax
Tower Records
Trans World Entertainment
Wal-Mart

## HISTORICAL FINANCIALS

Company Type: Public

**Income Statement** FYE: Last day of February

| | REVENUE ($ mil.) | NET INCOME ($ mil.) | NET PROFIT MARGIN | EMPLOYEES |
|---|---|---|---|---|
| **2/07** | 12,430 | (8) | — | 43,011 |
| **2/06** | 11,598 | 140 | 1.2% | 46,007 |
| **2/05** | 10,472 | 62 | 0.6% | 45,946 |
| **2/04** | 9,745 | (89) | — | 42,258 |
| **2/03** | 9,954 | 106 | 1.1% | 39,432 |
| **Annual Growth** | 5.7% | — | — | 2.2% |

**2007 Year-End Financials**

Debt ratio: 2.8%
Return on equity: —
Cash ($ mil.): 739
Current ratio: 1.68
Long-term debt ($ mil.): 50
No. of shares (mil.): 171
Dividends
Yield: 0.6%
Payout: —
Market value ($ mil.): 3,243

**Stock History** NYSE: CC

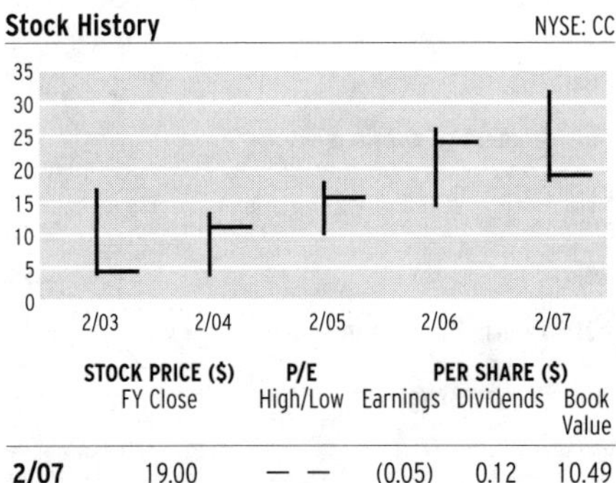


| | STOCK PRICE ($) FY Close | P/E High/Low | | PER SHARE ($) Earnings | Dividends | Book Value |
|---|---|---|---|---|---|---|
| **2/07** | 19.00 | — | — | (0.05) | 0.12 | 10.49 |
| **2/06** | 24.03 | 34 | 19 | 0.77 | 0.08 | 11.18 |
| **2/05** | 15.63 | 58 | 33 | 0.31 | 0.07 | 11.09 |
| **2/04** | 11.18 | — | — | (0.43) | 0.07 | 10.91 |
| **2/03** | 4.42 | 42 | 10 | 0.40 | 0.06 | 11.15 |
| **Annual Growth** | 44.0% | — | — | — | 18.9% | (1.5%) |

# Cisco Systems

The ruler of routers, the sultan of switches, Cisco Systems continues to dominate the market for equipment used to link networks and power the Internet. The company's bread and butter products are routers and switches; Cisco's switch line includes equipment based on Ethernet, Gigabit Ethernet, and ATM technologies. Other products include remote access servers, IP telephony equipment used to transmit data and voice communications over the same network, optical networking components, and network service and security systems. It sells its products primarily to large enterprises and telecommunications service providers, but it also has products designed for small businesses and consumers.

Cisco has used acquisitions — more than 100 since 1993 — to broaden its product lines and secure engineering talent in the highly competitive networking sector. The company acquired WebEx Communications for approximately $3.2 billion in 2007. WebEx is a leading provider of Internet conferencing systems.

The company acquired cable set-top box leader Scientific-Atlanta for approximately $6.9 billion. The deal, which closed early in 2006, was the second largest purchase in its history. (Cisco paid $7 billion for optical networking equipment maker Cerent in 1999.) Cisco has long been an advocate of the convergence of technology behind data, voice, and television networks, and the acquisition of Scientific-Atlanta made it one of the leading providers of the set-top boxes that cable service providers use to deliver advanced features such as movies-on-demand.

Though dominant in its sector, Cisco has not been immune to market rigors. The company's heavy investment in Internet Protocol-based telecommunications equipment proved costly when an industry wide downturn slowed spending among telecom service providers in 2001. CEO John Chambers guided Cisco through significant rebuilding measures, including job cuts and a reorganization that aligned its operations around core technologies rather than customer segments.

The company continues to branch into new markets across the enterprise, consumer, and telecom sectors. It quickly became a major player in the market for Fibre Channel switches used in enterprise storage networks. The company made a move to increase its presence in the home networking sector, acquiring Linksys for $500 million in stock in 2003. It acquired conferencing systems specialist Latitude Communications for approximately $80 million in cash the following year, and wireless networking equipment maker Airespace for approximately $450 million in stock early in 2005. Cisco acquired network and e-mail security software developer IronPort Systems for $830 million in 2007. Soon after it set its sights on the social networking sector, acquiring software platform developer Five Across, as well as assets of Utah Street Networks, the operator of the Tribe.net online communities.

Late in 2006 Cisco's advanced technologies unit launched a video messaging product called the Cisco Digital Media System. The system, which includes video encoders, management software, and a Web portal, lets companies distribute video messages to employees and customers.

## HISTORY

Cisco Systems was founded by Stanford University husband-and-wife team Leonard Bosack and Sandra Lerner and three colleagues in 1984. Bosack developed technology to link his computer lab's network with his wife's network in the graduate business school. Anticipating a market for networking devices, Bosack and Lerner mortgaged their house, bought a used mainframe, put it in their garage, and got friends and relatives to work for deferred pay. They sold their first network router in 1986. Originally targeting universities, the aerospace industry, and the government, the company in 1988 expanded its marketing to include large corporations. Short of cash, Cisco turned to venture capitalist Donald Valentine of Sequoia Capital, who bought a controlling stake and became chairman. He hired John Morgridge of laptop maker GRiD Systems as president and CEO.

Cisco, whose products had a proven track record, had a head start as the market for network routers opened up in the late 1980s. Sales leapt from $1.5 million in 1987 to $28 million in 1989.

The company went public in 1990. That year Morgridge fired Lerner, with whom he had clashed, and Bosack quit. The couple sold their stock for about $200 million, giving most to favorite causes, including animal charities and a Harvard professor looking for extraterrestrials.

With competition increasing, Cisco began expanding through acquisitions. Purchases included networking company Crescendo Communications (1993) and Ethernet switch maker Kalpana (1994). Cisco also surpassed the $1 billion revenue mark in 1994. In 1995 EVP John Chambers succeeded Morgridge as president and CEO; Morgridge became chairman (and Valentine vice chairman).

Cisco entered the service provider market in 1996, when it introduced a line of customer premises equipment (CPE) products. The following year the company broke into the *FORTUNE* 500.

Cisco acquired several niche players in 1998, such as Precept Software (video transmission software) and American Internet Corporation (software for set-top boxes and cable modems). That year Cisco's market capitalization passed the $100 billion milestone, a landmark accomplishment for a company its age.

In 1999 Cisco launched a new business line aimed at bringing high-speed Internet access to the consumer market. In its largest acquisition to date, Cisco bought Cerent (fiber-optic network equipment) for $7 billion.

The company continued its acquisitive ways in 2000, snatching up more than 20 companies, including wireless network equipment maker Aironet. With a market capitalization exceeding $500 billion, Cisco also enjoyed a turn as the world's most valuable company that year.

Hard hit by an economic slump that affected companies across the technology sector, in 2001 Cisco reorganized and cut 15% of its workforce. To save a few jobs, Chambers voluntarily cut his salary to $1. Entering yet another new market, Cisco acquired storage networking switch maker Andiamo Systems in 2002 (the deal closed in 2004).

Key acquisitions over the next few years included home networking specialist Linksys (2003), conferencing systems provider Latitude Communications (2004), and wireless networking vendor Airespace (2005).

## EXECUTIVES

**Chairman Emeritus:** John P. Morgridge, age 72
**Chairman and CEO:** John T. Chambers, age 57, $1,650,000 pay
**SVP and CFO:** Dennis D. Powell, age 58, $1,470,855 pay
**SVP and Chief Development Officer; President, Cisco-Linksys:** Charles H. (Charlie) Giancarlo, age 48, $1,567,149 pay
**SVP, Worldwide Government Affairs and Chief Marketing Officer:** Susan L. (Sue) Bostrom, age 46
**SVP Global Government Solutions Group and Corporate Security Programs:** Bradford J. (Brad) Boston, age 53
**SVP and CTO, Global Government Solutions:** Gregory (Greg) Akers
**SVP and General Manager, Cisco Media Solutions Group:** Daniel (Dan) Scheinman
**SVP, Corporate Business Development:** Ned Hooper
**SVP, Commercial Business:** James G. Richardson, age 49
**SVP, Office of the President and Director:** Larry R. Carter, age 63
**SVP Research and Advanced Development:** Joel Bion
**SVP, Internet Business Solutions Group:** Gary Bridge
**SVP, Network Management Technology Group:** Clifford Meltzer
**SVP, New England Executive Sponser:** Carl Redfield, age 60
**SVP, Office of the President:** Howard S. Charney
**SVP, Operations, Processes, and Systems:** Randy Pond, age 52, $1,417,149 pay
**SVP, Legal Services, General Counsel, and Secretary:** Mark Chandler, age 50
**SVP Human Resources:** Brian (Skip) Schipper
**SVP Strategy and Planning, Worldwide Operations:** Inder Sidhu, age 47
**SVP Finance:** Frank Calderoni, age 45
**VP, Controller, and Principal Accounting Officer:** Jonathan Chadwick, age 40
**VP Corporate Communications:** Blair Christie
**Auditors:** PricewaterhouseCoopers LLP

## LOCATIONS

**HQ:** Cisco Systems, Inc.
170 W. Tasman Dr., Bldg. 10, San Jose, CA 95134
**Phone:** 408-526-4000 **Fax:** 408-526-4100
**Web:** www.cisco.com

### 2006 Sales

| | $ mil. | % of total |
|---|---|---|
| US & Canada | 15,785 | 55 |
| Europe | 6,079 | 21 |
| Asia/Pacific | | |
| Japan | 1,291 | 5 |
| Other countries | 2,853 | 10 |
| Emerging markets | 2,476 | 9 |
| **Total** | **28,484** | **100** |

## PRODUCTS/OPERATIONS

### 2006 Sales

| | $ mil. | % of total |
|---|---|---|
| Products | | |
| Switches | 10,833 | 38 |
| Advanced technologies | 6,228 | 22 |
| Routers | 6,005 | 21 |
| Other | 851 | 3 |
| Services | 4,567 | 16 |
| **Total** | **28,484** | **100** |

### Selected Products

Access servers
Cable modems
Cables and cords
Content delivery devices
Customer contact software
Digital video recorders
Ethernet concentrators, hubs, and transceivers
Interfaces and adapters
Network management software
Networked applications software
Optical platforms
Power supplies
Routers
Security components
Switches
Telephony access systems
Television set-top boxes
Video networking
Virtual private network (VPN) systems
Voice integration applications
Wireless networking

## COMPETITORS

3Com
Alcatel-Lucent
ARRIS
Avaya
Avici Systems
Belkin
Brocade Communications
Check Point Software
Ciena
Dell
D-Link
ECI Telecom
Enterasys
Ericsson
Extreme Networks
F5 Networks
Force10
Foundry Networks
Fujitsu
Harris Corp.
Hewlett-Packard
Huawei Technologies
Internet Security Systems
Juniper Networks
Motorola, Inc.
MRV Communications
NEC
NETGEAR
Nokia Siemens Networks
Nortel Networks
Novell
Pace Micro
Polycom
Redback Networks
Sycamore Networks
Symantec
Tellabs
THOMSON
UTStarcom
ZTE

## HISTORICAL FINANCIALS

Company Type: Public

### Income Statement

FYE: Last Sunday in July

| | REVENUE ($ mil.) | NET INCOME ($ mil.) | NET PROFIT MARGIN | EMPLOYEES |
|---|---|---|---|---|
| **7/06** | 28,484 | 5,580 | 19.6% | 49,926 |
| **7/05** | 24,801 | 5,741 | 23.1% | 38,413 |
| **7/04** | 22,045 | 4,401 | 20.0% | 34,000 |
| **7/03** | 18,878 | 3,578 | 19.0% | 34,000 |
| **7/02** | 18,915 | 1,893 | 10.0% | 36,000 |
| **Annual Growth** | 10.8% | 31.0% | — | 8.5% |

### 2006 Year-End Financials

Debt ratio: 26.5%
Return on equity: 23.7%
Cash ($ mil.): 17,814
Current ratio: 2.27
Long-term debt ($ mil.): 6,332
No. of shares (mil.): 6,095
Dividends
Yield: —
Payout: —
Market value ($ mil.): 110,198

### Stock History

NASDAQ (GS): CSCO

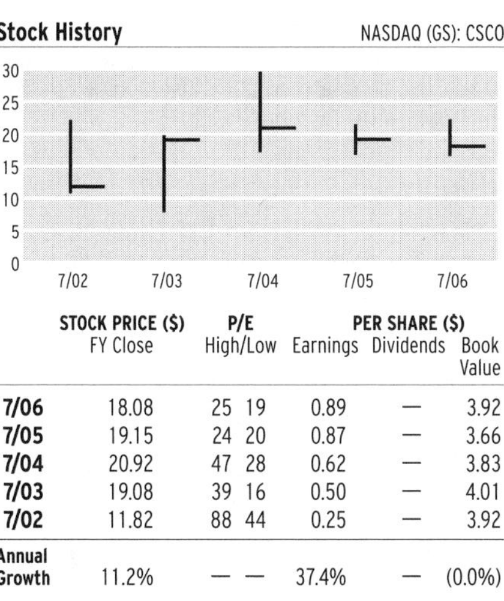


| | STOCK PRICE ($) FY Close | P/E High | P/E Low | PER SHARE ($) Earnings | Dividends | Book Value |
|---|---|---|---|---|---|---|
| **7/06** | 18.08 | 25 | 19 | 0.89 | — | 3.92 |
| **7/05** | 19.15 | 24 | 20 | 0.87 | — | 3.66 |
| **7/04** | 20.92 | 47 | 28 | 0.62 | — | 3.83 |
| **7/03** | 19.08 | 39 | 16 | 0.50 | — | 4.01 |
| **7/02** | 11.82 | 88 | 44 | 0.25 | — | 3.92 |
| **Annual Growth** | 11.2% | — | — | 37.4% | — | (0.0%) |

# CIT Group

If you haven't heard of CIT Group, then you're O-U-T of the proverbial loop. On the big business landscape for about a century, CIT Group is a commercial and consumer finance firm offering finance and lease products, as well as advisory services, to clients ranging from single borrowers to some 80% of the *FORTUNE* 1000. CIT Group offers companies such products as vendor, equipment, operating, aircraft, rail car, and locomotive financing, as well as factoring, Small Business Administration loans, asset-based lending, and structured financing. The company is active in some 50 countries around the world.

CIT Group has nearly $75 billion in managed assets and serves clients across some 30 industries, with a focus on manufacturing and retail; it has added lending units targeting the health care, media, entertainment, and education financing sectors.

Traditionally known for conservative management, CIT Group has passed through several hands in recent decades, including RCA, Dai-Ichi Kangyo Bank (now part of Mizuho Financial Group), and Tyco International. Jeff Peek took the reins of the company from longtime chairman and CEO Al Gamper in 2004.

The company has increasingly looked overseas for growth, taking such steps as obtaining a UK banking license, a move that allows CIT Group to make loans throughout the European Union and moves the company closer to its goal of doubling the size of its non-US business by the end of the decade. It has also continued to acquire assets, portfolios, and businesses that mesh with its strategy, including its 2007 purchases of M&A advisory firm Edgeview Partners and a portion of Barclays' vendor finance businesses in Germany and the UK.

CIT Group's Education Lending unit was one of several companies in the student-lending industry that came under investigation for business practices in 2007.

To free up capital for for use in higher-growth business areas, CIT Group in 2007 agreed to sell its CIT Construction unit to Wells Fargo; the unit provides financing to construction firms and to dealers of construction equipment. Amid losses, the company in 2007 also decided to exit the home mortgage business.

## HISTORY

Henry Ittleson founded CIT Group as Commercial Credit and Investment Trust in St. Louis in 1908. Initially financing horse-drawn carriages, it moved to New York in 1915 as Commercial Investment Trust (CIT) to participate in one of the milestones of modern consumer debt: Its auto financing program, launched in collaboration with Studebaker, was the first of its kind.

CIT diversified into industrial financing during the 1920s and went public in 1924 on the NYSE. Cars remained a strong focus, though: When Ford Motor Co. ran into difficulties in 1933, it sold financing division Universal Credit Corp. to CIT. CIT continued to expand into industrial financing, incorporating its industrial business as CIT Financial Corp. in 1942.

During the post-WWII boom, CIT began financing manufactured home sales and offering small loans. In 1964 it consolidated factoring operations into Meinhard-Commercial Corp. By the end of the 1960s, the firm started to retreat from auto financing, focusing instead on industrial leasing, factoring, and equipment financing.

In 1980 RCA bought CIT, seeking to buy financing to develop its other businesses. RCA found the debt from the purchase unwieldy, however, and sold CIT to Manufacturers Hanover Bank (Manny Hanny) in 1984. The bank bought CIT to expand outside its home state of New York: Though it could not open banks out of state, Manny Hanny could still offer financial services through CIT, which became The CIT Group in 1986.

Manny Hanny executives tried to bring aggressive management to staid, top-heavy CIT. CIT sold its Inventory Finance division in 1987, divested the consumer loan business in 1988, and consolidated the Meinhard-Commercial and Manufacturers Hanover factoring units in 1989. By then Manny Hanny was cash-strapped over losses incurred from foreign loans, so it sold a 60% stake in CIT to The Dai-Ichi Kangyo Bank of Japan.

CIT gave Dai-Ichi entrée into the US financial services market, and it began expanding CIT's range of services again, including equity investment (1990), credit finance (from its purchase of Fidelcor Business Credit in 1991), and venture capital (1992). CIT also reentered the consumer loan market (including home equity lending) with a new Consumer Finance group (1992).

In 1995 Chemical Bank (Manny Hanny's successor; now part of J.P. Morgan Chase & Co.) sold an additional 20% share to Dai-Ichi, bumping the Japanese bank's holdings to 80% and arranging to sell its remaining shares to Dai-Ichi. In 1997, instead of Dai-Ichi buying the rest of Chase's shares, CIT bought them and spun them off to the public. In 1998 Dai-Ichi reduced its stake.

In 1999 CIT bought Newcourt Credit Group, North America's #2 equipment finance and leasing firm; it also bought Heller Financial's commercial services unit. In 2000 the firm worked on integrating Newcourt and sold its Hong Kong consumer finance unit.

Tyco International bought CIT in 2001, renaming the new subsidiary Tyco Capital. Under Tyco's umbrella, it sold its manufactured home loan portfolio to Lehman Brothers and recreational vehicle portfolio to Salomon Smith Barney in an effort to exit noncore businesses. Tyco, however, expanded too far too fast, and the next year announced an about-face on its financial services subsidiary, deciding to spin off the division and return it to its CIT identity.

## EXECUTIVES

**Chairman and CEO:** Jeffrey M. (Jeff) Peek, age 59, $800,000 pay
**Vice Chairman and CFO:** Joseph M. Leone, age 53, $500,000 pay
**Vice Chairman and Chief Credit Officer:** Lawrence A. Marsiello, age 56, $500,000 pay
**Vice Chairman, Specialty Finance:** Thomas B. Hallman, age 54, $500,000 pay
**EVP and Global Head of Human Resources:** James J. (Jim) Duffy
**EVP, Controller, and Principal Accounting Officer:** William J. Taylor, age 55
**EVP, General Counsel, and Secretary:** Robert J. (Bob) Ingato, age 46
**EVP and Global CIO:** Michael Baresich
**EVP, Marketing and Corporate Communications:** Kelley J. Gipson
**VP, Investor Relations:** Steve Klimas
**President, CIT Corporate Finance:** Walter J. Owens, age 46
**President, CIT Canada and CIT Group Securities (Canada):** J. Daryl MacLellan
**President and Founder, CIT Healthcare Financial:** Flint D. Besecker
**President, CIT Small Business Lending:** Christine (Chris) Reilly
**President, Global Insurance Services:** Paul G. Petrylak
**Director of External Communications and Media Relations:** C. Curtis (Curt) Ritter
**Senior Managing Director and Group Head, Investment Banking Services, CIT Mergers and Acquisitions:** Gregg H. Smith, age 43
**Chief Marketing Officer, CIT Healthcare:** Jeremy P. Miller
**Auditors:** PricewaterhouseCoopers LLP

## LOCATIONS

**HQ:** CIT Group Inc.
505 5th Ave., New York, NY 10017
**Phone:** 212-771-0505
**Web:** www.cit.com

**2006 Finance and Leasing Assets**

| | % of total |
|---|---|
| US | |
| Northeast | 19 |
| West | 18 |
| Midwest | 18 |
| Southeast | 15 |
| Southwest | 10 |
| Canada | 5 |
| Other countries | 15 |
| **Total** | **100** |

## PRODUCTS/OPERATIONS

**2006 Sales**

| | % of total |
|---|---|
| Finance income | 82 |
| Gain on receivable sales & syndication fees | 4 |
| Factoring commissions | 3 |
| Gain on sales of equipment | 2 |
| Fees & other income | 9 |
| **Total** | **100** |

**2006 Industry Financing**

| | % of total |
|---|---|
| Consumer-based lending | |
| Home mortgages | 15 |
| Student lending | 13 |
| Non-real estate lending | 2 |
| Manufacturing | 12 |
| Commercial airlines (excluding regional airlines) | 11 |
| Retail | 10 |
| Service industries | 6 |
| Health care | 5 |
| Transportation | 4 |
| Wholesaling | 4 |
| Other | 18 |
| **Total** | **100** |

**2006 Managed Assets By Segment**

| | % of total |
|---|---|
| Commercial Finance | |
| Corporate finance | 29 |
| Transportation finance | 16 |
| Trade finance | 9 |
| Specialty Finance | |
| Consumer & small business lending | 29 |
| Vendor finance | 17 |
| **Total** | **100** |

## COMPETITORS

Advanta
AXA Financial
Citigroup
Conseco
Deutsche Bank
FINOVA
GE Commercial Aviation
GECF
HSBC Finance
ILFC
JPMorgan Chase
Lehman Brothers
Merrill Lynch
National City
ORIX

## HISTORICAL FINANCIALS

Company Type: Public

**Income Statement** FYE: December 31

| | ASSETS ($ mil.) | NET INCOME ($ mil.) | INCOME AS % OF ASSETS | EMPLOYEES |
|---|---|---|---|---|
| **12/06** | 77,068 | 1,046 | 1.4% | 7,345 |
| **12/05** | 63,387 | 949 | 1.5% | 6,340 |
| **12/04** | 51,111 | 754 | 1.5% | 5,860 |
| **12/03** | 46,343 | 567 | 1.2% | 5,800 |
| **12/02** | 41,932 | 141 | 0.3% | — |
| **Annual Growth** | 16.4% | 64.9% | — | 8.2% |

**2006 Year-End Financials**

Equity as % of assets: 9.4%
Return on assets: 1.5%
Return on equity: 15.3%
Long-term debt ($ mil.): 58,305
No. of shares (mil.): 198
Dividends
Yield: 1.4%
Payout: 16.0%
Market value ($ mil.): 11,059
Sales ($ mil.): 6,943

**Stock History** NYSE: CIT

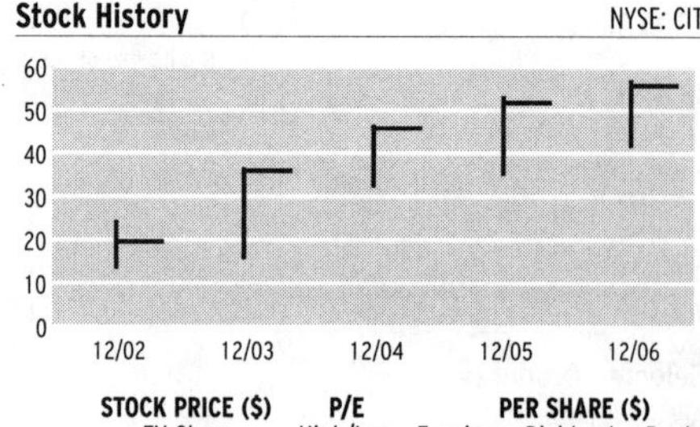


| | STOCK PRICE ($) FY Close | P/E High | P/E Low | PER SHARE ($) Earnings | Dividends | Book Value |
|---|---|---|---|---|---|---|
| **12/06** | 55.77 | 11 | 8 | 5.00 | 0.80 | 39.09 |
| **12/05** | 51.78 | 12 | 8 | 4.44 | 0.61 | 34.97 |
| **12/04** | 45.82 | 13 | 9 | 3.50 | 0.52 | 28.72 |
| **12/03** | 35.95 | 14 | 6 | 2.66 | 0.48 | 25.47 |
| **12/02** | 19.60 | 36 | 21 | 0.67 | 0.12 | 23.02 |
| **Annual Growth** | 29.9% | — | — | 65.3% | 60.7% | 14.2% |

# Citigroup

Citigroup has its eyes set on the world. One of the largest financial services firms on the planet, the company has more than 3,000 bank branches and consumer finance offices in the US and Canada, plus more than an additional 2,000 locations in about 100 other countries. The first US bank with more than $1 trillion in assets, Citigroup and its myriad subsidiaries offer deposits and loans (mainly through Citibank), credit cards, investment banking, brokerage, and a host of other retail and corporate financial services. Chairman Sandy Weill, who built Citigroup through several high-profile acquisitions, retired in 2006. The company continues to grow by acquisitions, particularly overseas.

Weill's successor, CEO Chuck Prince, has been recasting Citigroup by shedding some core businesses while beefing up its retail operations.

Few other banks, domestic or foreign, can equal Citigroup's global reach. The company owns stakes in regional banks in several countries (notably, Shinhan Bank and KorAm Bank in South Korea, and one of Mexico's largest banks, Banamex) in addition to its own offices.

A healthy chunk of Citigroup's growth comes from abroad, particularly Asia. It is part of a consortium that is acquiring a controlling stake in Guangdong Development Bank; once the deal is complete, Citigroup will own about 20% of the southern China-based bank. It is one of the first foreign banks to issue credit cards in that country.

Citigroup has added more heft to its credit card and mortgage businesses by buying the credit card portfolios of Sears, Roebuck and Co.; Federated Department Stores; Principal Financial Group's mortgage banking business; and Hibernia's residential mortgage servicing portfolio.

In Japan, where Citigroup is one of the leading foreign banks, regulators pulled the plug on the company's private banking operations in 2004 after determining that Citigroup misled customers regarding the sale of certain structured bonds. The closures led to the forced resignation of three top executives in the company's asset management and private banking units about a month later. Citigroup maintains retail banking operations in the country.

Citigroup hopes to save more than $10 billion through 2009 by cutting some 17,000 jobs, including some layers of management, and by moving other duties to less-expensive locations overseas, particularly India and Poland.

## HISTORY

Empire builder Sanford "Sandy" Weill, who helped build brokerage firm Shearson Loeb Rhoades, sold the company to American Express (AmEx) in 1981. Forced out of AmEx in 1985, Weill bounced back in 1986, buying Control Data's Commercial Credit unit.

Primerica caught Weill's eye next. Its predecessor, American Can, was founded in 1901 as a New Jersey canning company; it eventually expanded into the paper and retail industries before turning to financial services in 1986. The firm was renamed Primerica in 1987 and bought brokerage Smith Barney, Harris Upham & Co.

Weill's Commercial Credit bought Primerica in 1988. In 1993 Primerica bought Shearson from AmEx, as well as Travelers, taking its name and logo.

Weill set about trimming Travelers. He sold life subsidiaries and bought Aetna's property/casualty business in 1995. In 1996 he consolidated all property/casualty operations to form Travelers Property Casualty and took it public. The next year Travelers bought investment bank Salomon Brothers.

Weill sold Citicorp chairman and CEO John Reed on the idea of a merger in 1998, in advance of the Gramm-Leach-Bliley act, which deregulated the financial services industry in the US. By the time the merger went through, a slowed US economy and foreign-market turmoil brought significant losses to both sides. The renamed Citigroup consolidated in 1998 and 1999, laying off more than 10,000 employees. So many executives (including co-chairmen and co-CEOs Weill and Reed) were paired through "co" titling that the company was dubbed "the ark."

In 1999 former Treasury Secretary Robert Rubin joined Citigroup as a co-chairman. In 2000 Citigroup bought subprime lender Associates First Capital (now part of CitiFinancial) for approximately $27 billion to expand its consumer product lines and its international presence. In 2002 Citigroup paid some $215 million to settle federal allegations that Associates First Capital made customers unwittingly purchase credit insurance by automatically billing for the service. The agreement was one of the largest consumer-protection settlements ever.

The company also became embroiled in the Enron mess as regulators scrutinized short-term loans that Citigroup floated to the energy trader and were possibly used by Enron in transactions with offshore entities to mask debt and inflate cash flow figures. Citigroup neither confirmed nor denied allegations that it helped fudge Enron's books, but in 2003 remitted more than $100 million earmarked to pay victims who lost money because of Enron's malfeasance.

A landmark ruling by the SEC in 2003 implied that Citigroup issued favorable stock ratings to companies in exchange for investment banking contracts. As part of the ruling, erstwhile star analyst Jack Grubman agreed to pay some $15 million in fines for his overly rosy stock reports and accepted a lifetime ban from working in the securities industry. Citigroup forked over $400 million in fines, the largest portion of a total of some $1.4 billion levied against 10 brokerage firms regarding conflicts of interest between analysts and investment bankers.

Amid the investigations, Citigroup separated its stock-picking and corporate advisory businesses, creating a retail brokerage and equity research unit called Smith Barney. In the SEC's 2003 ruling such a "Chinese Wall" between bankers and analysts was later made mandatory at all firms.

In 2004 the company — while admitting no wrongdoing — paid $2.65 billion to investors who were burned when WorldCom went bankrupt amid an accounting scandal. (Citigroup was one of the lead underwriters of WorldCom stocks and bonds.) The settlement was one of the largest ever for alleged securities fraud, and compelled Citigroup to set aside an additional $5 billion to cover legal fees for this case and others involving Enron and spinning. The company eventually paid $2 billion in mid-2005 to investors who lost money on publicly traded Enron stocks and bonds, again settling the matter while denying it broke any laws. Enron shareholders had argued that Citigroup helped Enron to set up offshore companies and shady partnerships to exaggerate the energy trader's cash flow.

Weill ended years of speculation in 2003 by anointing corporate and investment bank head Chuck Prince as his successor. Weill retired as chairman in 2006 and Prince assumed that title as well.

## EXECUTIVES

**Chairman and CEO:** Charles O. (Chuck) Prince III, age 57, $14,200,000 pay (prior to title change)
**Chairman of the Executive Committee and Director:** Robert E. Rubin, age 68, $9,400,000 pay
**Vice Chairman and Senior International Officer; Chairman, President and Chief Executive Officer, Citibank N.A.; Chairman, President and Chief Executive Officer, Citicorp Holdings Inc.:** William R. (Bill) Rhodes, age 71
**Vice Chairman and Chief Administrative Officer:** Lewis B. (Lew) Kaden, age 64
**Vice Chairman:** Stephen R. Volk, age 71, $5,870,000 pay
**COO:** Robert (Bob) Druskin, age 59
**CFO:** Gary L. Crittenden, age 53
**Chairman and CEO, Global Consumer Group, International:** Ajay Banga, age 47
**Chairman and CEO, Global Consumer Group, North America:** Steven J. Freiberg, age 49
**Chairman and CEO, Citi Global Wealth Management:** Sallie L. Krawcheck, age 42
**Chief Operations and Technology Officer:** Kevin M. Kessinger
**President, International Franchise Management:** Michael Schlein
**SVP, Global Government Affairs:** Nicholas E. (Nick) Calio
**Chief Auditor:** Bonnie Howard
**Chief Tax Officer:** Saul M. Rosen
**Chief Compliance Officer:** Martin J. Wong
**General Counsel and Corporate Secretary:** Michael S. Helfer, age 61
**Controller and Chief Accounting Officer:** John Gerspach, age 53
**Director, Investor Relations:** Arthur H. (Art) Tildesley Jr.
**Senior Human Resources Officer:** Edith Ginsburg
**Auditors:** KPMG LLP

## LOCATIONS

**HQ:** Citigroup Inc.
399 Park Ave., New York, NY 10043
**Phone:** 212-559-1000 **Fax:** 212-793-3946
**Web:** www.citigroup.com

## PRODUCTS/OPERATIONS

**2006 Sales**

| | $ mil. | % of total |
|---|---|---|
| Interest | | |
| Loans, including fees | 55,022 | 38 |
| Federal funds sold & securities purchased under resale agreements | 14,199 | 10 |
| Trading account assets | 11,865 | 8 |
| Investments, including dividends | 10,399 | 7 |
| Deposits with banks | 2,289 | 2 |
| Other | 2,657 | 2 |
| Noninterest | | |
| Commissions & fees | 19,535 | 13 |
| Principal transactions | 7,708 | 5 |
| Asset management & other fiduciary fees | 6,934 | 5 |
| Insurance premiums | 3,202 | 2 |
| Realized gains from sales of investments | 1,791 | 1 |
| Other | 10,957 | 7 |
| **Total** | **146,558** | **100** |

**2006 Assets**

| | $ mil. | % of total |
|---|---|---|
| Cash & equivalents | 351,853 | 19 |
| Trading account | 393,925 | 21 |
| Treasury & agency securities | 24,531 | 1 |
| Mortgage-backed securities | 82,413 | 4 |
| Foreign government securities | 73,783 | 4 |
| US corporate bonds | 32,455 | 2 |
| Other securities | 60,409 | 3 |
| Loans | | |
| Consumer | 512,921 | 27 |
| Corporate | 166,271 | 9 |
| Allowance for loan losses | (8,940) | — |
| Other | 194,697 | 10 |
| **Total** | **1,884,318** | **100** |

## COMPETITORS

American Express
AXA Financial
Bank of America
Bank of New York Mellon
Bear Stearns
Capital One
Deutsche Bank
FMR
GE
Goldman Sachs
HSBC Holdings
JPMorgan Chase
Lehman Brothers
Merrill Lynch
Mizuho Financial
Morgan Stanley
UBS
UBS Financial Services
USAA
Wachovia
Wells Fargo

## HISTORICAL FINANCIALS

Company Type: Public

**Income Statement** FYE: December 31

| | ASSETS ($ mil.) | NET INCOME ($ mil.) | INCOME AS % OF ASSETS | EMPLOYEES |
|---|---|---|---|---|
| **12/06** | 1,884,318 | 21,538 | 1.1% | 337,000 |
| **12/05** | 1,494,037 | 24,589 | 1.6% | 307,000 |
| **12/04** | 1,484,101 | 17,046 | 1.1% | 294,000 |
| **12/03** | 1,264,032 | 17,853 | 1.4% | 259,000 |
| **12/02** | 1,097,190 | 15,276 | 1.4% | 255,000 |
| **Annual Growth** | 14.5% | 9.0% | — | 7.2% |

**2006 Year-End Financials**

Equity as % of assets: 6.3%
Return on assets: 1.3%
Return on equity: 18.7%
Long-term debt ($ mil.): 288,494
No. of shares (mil.): 4,912
Dividends
Yield: 3.5%
Payout: 45.5%
Market value ($ mil.): 273,598
Sales ($ mil.): 146,558

**Stock History** NYSE: C

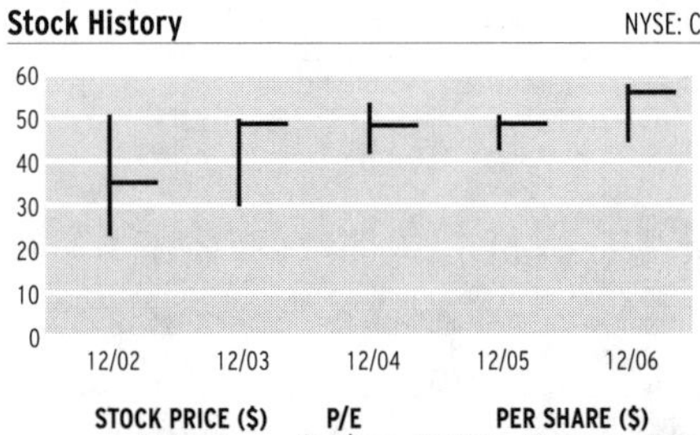

| | STOCK PRICE ($) FY Close | P/E High | P/E Low | PER SHARE ($) Earnings | Dividends | Book Value |
|---|---|---|---|---|---|---|
| **12/06** | 55.70 | 13 | 10 | 4.31 | 1.96 | 24.39 |
| **12/05** | 48.53 | 11 | 9 | 4.75 | 1.76 | 22.60 |
| **12/04** | 48.18 | 16 | 13 | 3.26 | 1.20 | 21.04 |
| **12/03** | 48.54 | 14 | 9 | 3.42 | 1.10 | 19.01 |
| **12/02** | 35.19 | 17 | 8 | 2.94 | 0.68 | 16.87 |
| **Annual Growth** | 12.2% | — | — | 10.0% | 30.3% | 9.7% |

# Citizens Communications

Serving city dwellers and country folk alike, Citizens Communications (operating as Frontier Communications) provides phone, TV, and Internet services to more than 2.5 million access lines in parts of 23 states, primarily in rural and suburban markets, where it is the incumbent local-exchange carrier (ILEC) operating under the Frontier Communications brand. Citizens has added TV to its platter of services by teaming up with EchoStar's DISH Network. The company had put itself up for sale and drew interest from buyout firms Kohlberg Kravis, Blackstone Group, and rural carrier CenturyTel. Potential deals fell through after concerns arose about the company's asking price versus the perceived value of its wirelines.

To focus on telecommunications, Citizens sold its electric utility operations, completing the sale of its last utility holding (its Vermont electric utility division) in 2004. Citizens acquired Commonwealth Telephone in 2007, expanding its access to the Pennsylvania market. It additionally inked a $62 million deal to acquire Global Valley Networks, a California provider of telephone and Internet services.

States in which Citizens Communications provides local telephone service include Arizona, California, Illinois, Minnesota, Montana, Nebraska, Nevada, New Mexico, New York, North Dakota, Oregon, Pennsylvania, Tennessee, Utah, West Virginia, and Wisconsin.

## HISTORY

Citizens Utilities Company was formed in 1935 to acquire Public Utilities Consolidated Corporation, a Minneapolis-based company with interests in electric, gas, water, and telephone utilities throughout the US. From 1950 to 1970 the company bought utilities in rural and suburban areas of Arizona, California, Hawaii, Illinois, Indiana, Ohio, and Pennsylvania. A major acquisition was Hawaii's Kauai Electric Company, in 1969. By the mid-1970s, electric power brought in 40% of the company's revenues.

Leonard Tow, head of Century Communications, was brought on board in 1989 and elected chairman the next year, remaining in that position until 2004. Expanding Citizens through more electric, water, and natural gas acquisitions, he tripled the company's revenues in less than 10 years.

In 1993 Citizens acquired a majority stake in Electric Lightwave, the first competitive local-exchange carrier (CLEC) west of the Mississippi River. Citizens started its long-distance telephone service in 1994. It also acquired 500,000 local access lines in nine states from GTE, quadrupling the size of its operations. By 1995 the telecom group was the fastest-growing segment of the company.

After the Telecommunications Act was passed in 1996, Citizens acquired another 110,000 local access lines and cable systems with more than 7,000 customers from ALLTEL and bought three Southern California cable systems with Century Communications. Citizens aggressively marketed local phone service in neighboring areas to its service territories, but the company didn't see the return it expected and by 1997 had to cut its workforce and tighten cost controls. In light of the cutbacks, bookkeeping troubles, and 1996 threats from Vermont to revoke Citizens' license there for accounting and permit problems, the board voted Tow a pay cut.

The company sold a minority stake in Electric Lightwave to the public in 1997 (Citizens reacquired the stake in 2002 and Electric Lightwave became a wholly owned subsidiary). Citizens continued its buying spree with telecom and gas firms in New York and Hawaii, and a local phone company in Pennsylvania, in 1998.

The next year, Citizens began turning itself into a pure telecom company through a series of transactions. It agreed to pay about $2.8 billion for 900,000 local phone lines owned by U S WEST and GTE. It also sold its cable TV interests and agreed to sell its water and wastewater operations (for $835 million).

Citizens bought more than 1 million local phone lines in 2001 from Global Crossing for about $3.5 billion. Later that year the company canceled its pending acquisition agreements with Qwest, U S WEST's successor, amid a dispute over how much revenue the local lines were producing. The terminated deals, valued at $1.7 billion, would have given Citizens another 540,000 local lines. It later pulled out of a deal to buy an additional 63,000 access lines in Arizona and California from Verizon Communications.

The company also sold part of its natural gas business for $375 million in 2001, the same year it changed its name to Citizens Communications. Although an earlier deal to sell its electric properties fell through, the company completed the sale of its Kauai Electric division in 2002 for $215 million to the Kauai Island Utility Cooperative. That year it also reached an agreement to sell its Hawaiian gas division in a deal valued at $115 million and completed the following year.

In November 2002 two executives of the company's public utilities division were dismissed after an SEC investigation into $17.8 million in payments for services the company did not receive.

Citizens sold its competitive local-exchange carrier (CLEC), Electric Lightwave, to Integra Telecom in mid-2006 in a deal that was valued at $247 million.

## EXECUTIVES

**Chairman and CEO:** Mary Agnes (Maggie) Wilderotter, age 52
**CFO:** Donald R. Shassian, age 51
**EVP and COO:** Daniel J. McCarthy, age 41
**EVP, Sales, Marketing, and Business Development:** Peter B. (Pete) Hayes, age 49
**EVP:** John H. (Jake) Casey III, age 50
**SVP and Chief Accounting Officer:** Robert J. Larson, age 47
**SVP, General Counsel, and Secretary:** Hilary E. Glassman, age 44
**SVP, Human Resources:** Cecilia K. McKenney, age 43
**VP, Sales and Distribution:** David M. Singer
**Investor Relations:** Michael Bromley
**Auditors:** KPMG LLP

## LOCATIONS

**HQ:** Citizens Communications Company
3 High Ridge Park, Stamford, CT 06905
**Phone:** 203-614-5600 **Fax:** 203-614-4602
**Web:** www.czn.net

## PRODUCTS/OPERATIONS

**2006 Sales**

| | % of total |
|---|---|
| Local services | 40 |
| Access services | 21 |
| Long-distance services | 8 |
| Data and Internet services | 21 |
| Directory services | 6 |
| Other | 4 |
| **Total** | **100** |

**Selected Subsidiaries**

Citizens Business Services Company
Citizens Cable Company
Citizens Directory Services Company, Inc.
Citizens Telecommunications Company
Frontier Subsidiary Telco LLC
Frontier Telephone of Rochester, Inc.
Ogden Telephone Company
Rhinelander Telecommunications, Inc.

## COMPETITORS

AT&T
Integra Telecom
McLeodUSA
Qwest
Time Warner Telecom
Verizon
Vonage
XO Holdings

## HISTORICAL FINANCIALS

Company Type: Public

**Income Statement** FYE: December 31

| | REVENUE ($ mil.) | NET INCOME ($ mil.) | NET PROFIT MARGIN | EMPLOYEES |
|---|---|---|---|---|
| **12/06** | 2,025 | 345 | 17.0% | 5,446 |
| **12/05** | 2,163 | 202 | 9.4% | 6,103 |
| **12/04** | 2,193 | 72 | 3.3% | 6,373 |
| **12/03** | 2,445 | 188 | 7.7% | 6,708 |
| **12/02** | 2,669 | (683) | — | 7,684 |
| **Annual Growth** | (6.7%) | — | — | (8.2%) |

**2006 Year-End Financials**

Debt ratio: 421.6%
Return on equity: 32.8%
Cash ($ mil.): 1,041
Current ratio: 2.99
Long-term debt ($ mil.): 4,461
No. of shares (mil.): 322
Dividends
Yield: 7.0%
Payout: 94.3%
Market value ($ mil.): 4,631

**Stock History** NYSE: CZN

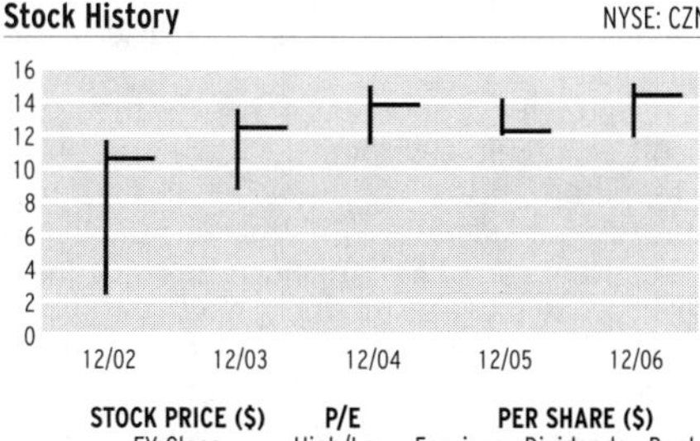


| | STOCK PRICE ($) FY Close | P/E High/Low | | PER SHARE ($) Earnings | Dividends | Book Value |
|---|---|---|---|---|---|---|
| **12/06** | 14.37 | 14 | 11 | 1.06 | 1.00 | 3.28 |
| **12/05** | 12.23 | 23 | 20 | 0.60 | 1.00 | 3.17 |
| **12/04** | 13.79 | 64 | 50 | 0.23 | 2.25 | 4.01 |
| **12/03** | 12.42 | 21 | 14 | 0.64 | — | 4.97 |
| **12/02** | 10.55 | — | — | (2.43) | 1.25 | 4.14 |
| **Annual Growth** | 8.0% | — | — | — | (5.4%) | (5.7%) |

# Cleveland-Cliffs

Cleveland-Cliffs' favorite period in history: the Iron Age; the company produces iron ore pellets, a key component of steelmaking. It owns or holds stakes in six iron ore properties, including Northshore Mining and Empire Iron, that represent more than 45% of North American iron ore pellet production capacity. Cleveland-Cliffs' mines produce more than 35 million tons of iron ore pellets annually. The company's share is about 20 million tons, and the remainder represents the holdings of other mine owners. Cleveland-Cliffs sells its iron ore pellets primarily in the US and Canada but also in Europe and China. The company owns an 80% stake in Australian iron miner Portman, which supplies the Asia/Pacific region.

As the North American steel industry struggled early in this decade, Cleveland-Cliffs began to increase its mine ownership by buying up stakes from its steel company partners. The company hopes to continue to buy out the co-owners of the mines it operates.

In addition, Cleveland-Cliffs intends to look internationally for new iron ore properties to acquire in order to supply the growing demand of the Chinese steel industry for raw materials.

In 2007 it acquired PinnOak Resources, a US metallurgical coal producer with operations in West Virginia and Alabama. The deal was for about $600 million in cash and assumed debt. While the acquired company's properties are located in the US, Cleveland Cliffs says that most of its product is slated for export sales.

## HISTORY

Samuel Mashers founded the Cleveland Iron Mining Co. in 1846, just five years after the discovery of iron ore in Michigan's Upper Peninsula. To compete in a consolidating market, the company merged with Iron Cliffs Mining in 1891 to form Cleveland-Cliffs. The company offset risks by forming joint ventures with steel companies to own and operate mines. It survived the Depression by selling all its steel and timber operations. The demands of WWII prompted Cleveland-Cliffs to invest in iron mines outside the US — in Canada, Chile, Colombia, Peru, and Venezuela (cut back after WWII to Canada and Australia).

In the 1960s the company rebuffed a takeover bid by Detroit Steel, and in the 1970s it diversified again, acquiring copper, shale oil, timber, and uranium assets. However, Cleveland-Cliffs stumbled financially and sold all its businesses not related to iron ore. The revival of the steel industry in the late 1980s and 1990s lifted Cleveland-Cliff's sales, but the financial struggles of its major customers forced losses on the company.

In 1994 the company bought Cypress Ajax Mineral's Minnesota iron mine (Northshore). In 1996 Cleveland-Cliffs closed its exhausted Australian operations. That year the company formed a joint venture with LTV and Lurgi (of Germany) to make reduced-iron briquettes in Trinidad and Tobago.

Faced with a tide of steel imports from Asia, Brazil, and Russia, the company curtailed production and deferred plans to supply steel minimills with the iron ore pellets needed to produce iron in electric furnaces — the company's planned start-up of its ferrous metallics plant in Trinidad was delayed in 2000 due to mechanical problems. During late 2000 two of Cleveland-Cliffs' mine partners — LTV and Wheeling-Pittsburgh — filed for bankruptcy protection. Cleveland-Cliffs was able to up its stake in the Empire Iron mine, previously co-owned with Wheeling-Pittsburgh, to 35%.

Later that year Canada-based Algoma Steel, co-owner with Cleveland-Cliffs of the Tilden mine, filed for bankruptcy. Also in 2001 Cleveland-Cliffs began production at its ferrous metallics plant in Trinidad; that plant was idled later in the year. In late 2001 the company, along with ALLETE subsidiary Minnesota Power, acquired the iron ore mining and processing facilities of LTV Steel Mining Co., including a rail line and dock facility on Lake Superior. In 2001 Cleveland-Cliffs increased its stake in the Tilden mine to 85%.

In late 2001 the Empire Iron mine was temporarily closed and its operations restructured. The mine reopened in 2002; Cleveland-Cliffs took a $52.7 million charge related to the closure. The following year the company increased its stake in the Empire Iron mine to 79%. In 2003 United Taconite (70% owned by Cleveland-Cliffs) was formed to hold the mining operations it purchased from bankrupt Eveleth Mines.

## EXECUTIVES

**Chairman, President, and CEO:** Joseph A. Carrabba, age 54
**SVP, CFO, and Treasurer:** Laurie Brlas, age 49
**President, North American Iron Ore:** Donald J. Gallagher, age 54
**EVP, Commercial, North American Iron Ore:** William R. Calfee, age 59
**SVP, Business Development:** James A. Trethewey, age 61
**SVP, Human Resources:** Randy L. Kummer, age 49
**VP and CTO:** Steven A. Elmquist, age 55
**VP and Controller:** Robert J. Leroux, age 56
**VP, Operations Services:** John N. (Jack) Tuomi, age 56
**VP, Public Affairs:** Dana W. Byrne, age 56
**Head Safety Initiatives, and VP; Operations, North American Iron Ore:** Duke D. Vetor, age 48
**General Counsel and Secretary:** George W. Hawk Jr., age 49
**Managing Director, Cliffs Asia-Pacific:** Richard R. Mehan, age 52
**SVP, Business Development:** William C. (Bill) Boor, age 49
**Auditors:** Deloitte & Touche LLP

## LOCATIONS

**HQ:** Cleveland-Cliffs Inc
1100 Superior Ave., Cleveland, OH 44114
**Phone:** 216-694-5700 **Fax:** 216-694-4880
**Web:** www.cleveland-cliffs.com

Cleveland-Cliffs has mining ventures in Michigan, Minnesota, and Canada (Newfoundland and Quebec).

**2006 Sales**

| | $ mil. | % of total |
|---|---|---|
| US | 1,109.2 | 57 |
| Canada | 379.7 | 20 |
| China | 367.4 | 19 |
| Japan | 74.4 | 4 |
| Other countries | 2.7 | — |
| **Total** | **1,933.4** | **100** |

## PRODUCTS/OPERATIONS

### Selected Operations

Michigan (Marquette Range)
- Empire Iron Mining Partnership (79%)
- Tilden Mine (85%)

Minnesota (Mesabi Range)
- Hibbing Taconite Company (23%)
- Northshore Mining Company
- United Taconite (70%)

Canada
- Wabush Mines (27%, Newfoundland/Quebec)

### Selected Subsidiaries

The Cleveland-Cliffs Iron Company
Cliffs Mining Company
Cliffs Minnesota Mining Company
Cliffs Natural Stone
Cliffs Oil Shale
Lake Superior & Ishpeming Railroad Company (rail transport)
Silver Bay Power Company

## COMPETITORS

BHP Billiton
Dofasco
Great Northern Iron Ore
International Briquettes
LKAB
Minerações Brasileiras Reunidas
Oglebay Norton
Rio Tinto
United States Steel
Vale do Rio Doce

## HISTORICAL FINANCIALS

Company Type: Public

**Income Statement** FYE: December 31

| | REVENUE ($ mil.) | NET INCOME ($ mil.) | NET PROFIT MARGIN | EMPLOYEES |
|---|---|---|---|---|
| **12/06** | 1,933 | 280 | 14.5% | 4,189 |
| **12/05** | 1,740 | 278 | 16.0% | 4,085 |
| **12/04** | 1,207 | 324 | 26.8% | 3,777 |
| **12/03** | 858 | (33) | — | 3,956 |
| **12/02** | 617 | (188) | — | 3,858 |
| **Annual Growth** | 33.0% | — | — | 2.1% |

**2006 Year-End Financials**

Debt ratio: —
Return on equity: 40.1%
Cash ($ mil.): 385
Current ratio: 2.09
Long-term debt ($ mil.): —
No. of shares (mil.): 41
Dividends
Yield: 1.0%
Payout: 9.0%
Market value ($ mil.): 1,981

**Stock History** NYSE: CLF

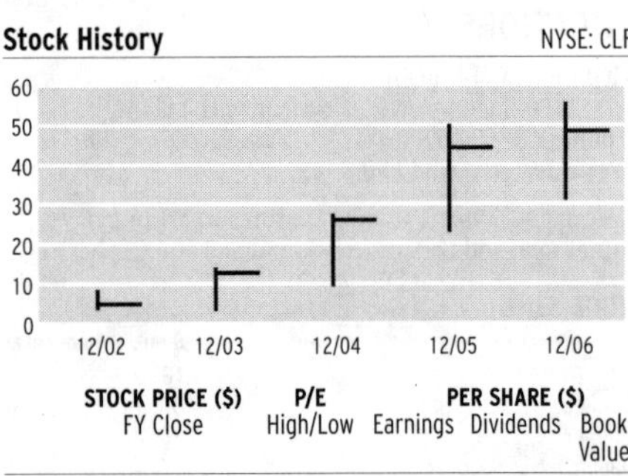


| | STOCK PRICE ($) FY Close | P/E High | P/E Low | PER SHARE ($) Earnings | Dividends | Book Value |
|---|---|---|---|---|---|---|
| **12/06** | 48.44 | 11 | 6 | 5.20 | 0.47 | 18.23 |
| **12/05** | 44.28 | 10 | 5 | 4.99 | 0.30 | 29.73 |
| **12/04** | 25.97 | 5 | 2 | 5.90 | 0.05 | 19.63 |
| **12/03** | 12.74 | — | — | (0.80) | — | 54.73 |
| **12/02** | 4.96 | — | — | (4.66) | — | 7.79 |
| **Annual Growth** | 76.8% | — | — | — | 206.6% | 23.7% |

# The Clorox Company

Bleach is the cornerstone of Clorox. It offers its namesake household cleaning products, where it is a leader worldwide, and reaches beyond bleach. Clorox makes laundry and cleaning items (Formula 409, Pine-Sol, Tilex), dressing/sauce (Hidden Valley, KC Masterpiece), cat litter (Fresh Step), car care products (Armor All, STP), the Brita water-filtration system (in North America), and charcoal briquettes (Kingsford). Its First Brands buy gave Clorox Glad-brand plastic wraps, storage bags, and containers. Chemical giant Henkel owned nearly 30% of Clorox, but Clorox bought it back in 2004 through an asset swap valued at $2.8 billion. Jerry Johnston, former chairman and CEO, retired in May 2006.

Clorox named Donald R. Knauss to suceed Johnston. A former officer in the United States Marine Corps, Knauss began his career as a brand manager for Procter & Gamble. Most recently Knauss was president and CEO of Coca-Cola North America.

Clorox sells products in more than 100 countries and makes them in more than 20 countries. Much of Clorox's foreign growth has been from Latin America and Canada. To secure its foothold there, Clorox in December 2006 agreed to buy the Latin American and Canadian bleach brands (Javex, Agua Jane, Nevex) from Colgate-Palmolive Company for $126 million plus inventory at closing. The deal also gives Clorox the license to the Ajax (bleach) brand for a short time in Colombia, the Dominican Republic, and Ecuador.

The company has been building on existing lines through acquisitions, such as its 1999 purchase of First Brands, which added 40% in total sales. Clorox also has cleaned up through the introduction of innovative products (including household items such as Clorox Disinfecting Wipes).

Henkel and Clorox negotiated a deal in late 2004 that dissolved Henkel's nearly 30% stake in Clorox through an asset swap. The $2.8 billion transaction involved Henkel's purchase of Clorox's 20% stake in Henkel Iberica, a joint venture between the two firms operating in Portugal and Spain. Henkel also bought Clorox's stake in a pesticide company.

In the meantime, Clorox partnered with iRobot to create the Scooba robotic mop, which is the wet mop version of the Roomba vacuum. It took engineers three years to get it done. Launched in early 2006, the Scooba vacuums, scrubs, and dries hard floors. It has two tanks: one with Clorox's cleaning solution and one for dirty water.

## HISTORY

Known first as the Electro-Alkaline Company, The Clorox Company was founded in 1913 by five Oakland, California, investors to make bleach using water from salt ponds around San Francisco Bay. The next year the company registered the brand name Clorox (the name combines the bleach's two main ingredients, chlorine and sodium hydroxide). At first the company sold only industrial-strength bleach, but in 1916 it formulated a household solution.

With the establishment of a Philadelphia distributor in 1921, Clorox began national expansion. The company went public in 1928 and built plants in Illinois and New Jersey in the 1930s; it opened nine more US plants in the 1940s and 1950s. In 1957 Procter & Gamble (P&G) bought Clorox. The Federal Trade Commission raised antitrust questions, and litigation ensued over the next decade. P&G was ordered to divest Clorox, and in 1969 Clorox again became an independent company.

Following its split with P&G, the firm added household consumer goods and foods, acquiring the brands Liquid-Plumr (drain opener, 1969), Formula 409 (spray cleaner, 1970), Litter Green (cat litter, 1971), and Hidden Valley (salad dressings, 1972). Clorox entered the specialty food products business by purchasing Grocery Store Products (Kitchen Bouquet, 1971) and Kingsford (charcoal briquettes, 1973).

In 1974 Henkel, a large West German maker of cleansers and detergents, purchased 15% of Clorox's stock as part of an agreement to share research. Beginning in 1977, Clorox sold off subsidiaries and brands, such as Country Kitchen Foods (1979), to focus on household goods.

During the 1980s, Clorox launched a variety of new products, including Match Light (instant-lighting charcoal, 1980), Tilex (mildew remover, 1981), and Fresh Step (cat litter, 1984). Clorox began marketing Brita water filtration systems in the US in 1988 (adding Canada in 1995). In 1990 it paid $465 million for American Cyanamid's household products group, including Pine-Sol cleaner and Combat insecticide. (It sold Combat and Soft Scrub to Henkel in 2004.)

In 1991 Clorox left the laundry detergent business (begun in 1988) after it was battered by heavyweights P&G and Unilever. Household products VP Craig Sullivan became CEO the next year (stepping down in December 2003). In 1993 Clorox dumped its frozen food and bottled water operations.

A string of acquisitions brought the company into new markets as it built on existing brands. Clorox bought Black Flag and Lestoil in 1996 and car care product manufacturer Armor All in 1997. With its 1999 purchase of First Brands — for about $2 billion in stock and debt — Clorox added four more brands of cat litter and diversified into plastic products (Glad).

In January 2001 Clorox announced a joint venture with Bombril, Brazil's leading name in steel wool, to form Detergentes Bombril; however, Clorox canceled the agreement in April 2001, claiming that various conditions of the deal had not been met.

In 2002 Clorox announced that due to the difficult economic environment in the region, it was selling its Brazil business. In 2003 it jump-started a joint venture with Procter & Gamble to take advantage of P&G's manufacturing acumen to improve its Glad products. P&G received a 10% stake in Glad. In late 2004, though, P&G boosted its share in the joint venture from 10% to 20%, which is the maximum it can invest according to the agreement.

In January 2004 Robert Matschullat, the company's nonexecutive chairman, replaced Sullivan upon his retirement. Matschullat stepped down as chairman in January 2005, passing the title to Jerry Johnston, and became a director. Matschullat reclaimed the titles of chairman and CEO on an interim basis when Johnston suffered a heart attack and retired in 2006. Former Coca-Cola executive Donald Knauss was named chairman and CEO in late 2006; Matschullat remained a director.

## EXECUTIVES

**Chairman and CEO:** Donald R. (Don) Knauss, age 56
**EVP, Functional Operations:** Frank A. Tataseo, age 52
**EVP, Strategy and Growth:** M. B. (Beth) Springer, age 42
**SVP and CFO:** Daniel J. (Dan) Heinrich, age 49, $833,250 pay
**SVP, General Counsel, and Secretary:** Laura Stein, age 44, $813,800 pay
**SVP, Human Resources and Corporate Affairs:** Jacqueline P. (Jackie) Kane, age 53
**SVP, International:** Warwick Lynton Every-Burns, age 52
**VP and General Manager, Glad Products:** Benno Dorer
**VP, Corporate Controller, and Chief Accounting Officer:** Thomas D. (Tom) Johnson, age 45
**VP and General Manager, Laundry and Home Care:** Glenn R. Savage, age 48
**VP and General Manager, Brita and Canada:** Gregory S. (Greg) Frank, age 45
**VP and General Manager, Litter, Food, and Charcoal:** George C. Roeth, age 43
**VP, CIO:** Robin A. Evitts, age 38
**VP, Research and Development:** Wayne L. Delker, age 50
**VP, Internal Audit:** Keith R. Tandowsky, age 46
**VP, Sales:** Grant J. LaMontagne
**VP, Investor Relations:** Steve Austenfeld
**VP, Marketing:** Derek A. Gordon
**Director, Finance and Accounting:** Tony Huang
**Investor Relations Analyst, Individual Investors:** Janet Hodges
**Corporate Communications and Media Relations:** Kathryn Caulfield
**Auditors:** Ernst & Young

## LOCATIONS

**HQ:** The Clorox Company
1221 Broadway, Oakland, CA 94612
**Phone:** 510-271-7000 **Fax:** 510-832-1463
**Web:** www.thecloroxcompany.com

The Clorox Company sells its products in more than 100 countries. It owns and operates 25 manufacturing plants internationally and six regional distribution centers in the US.

## PRODUCTS/OPERATIONS

### 2006 Sales

| | $ mil. | % of total |
|---|---|---|
| Household Group, North America | 2,113 | 45 |
| Specialty Group | 1,892 | 41 |
| International | 639 | 14 |
| **Total** | **4,644** | **100** |

### Selected Products

Food-Related Products
- Brita
- Glad
- Glad Press 'n Seal
- GladWare
- Hidden Valley
- K.C. Masterpiece

Household Cleaning Products
- Clorox
- Clorox 2
- Clorox Clean-Up
- Clorox Disinfecting Wipes
- Clorox FreshCare
- Clorox Oxi Magic
- Clorox ReadyMop
- Clorox Toilet Bowl Cleaner
- Formula 409
- Formula 409 Carpet Cleaner
- Handi-Wipes
- Lestoil
- Liquid-Plumr
- Pine-Sol
- S.O.S
- Stain Out
- Tilex
- ToiletWand
- Tuffy
- Ultra Clorox Bleach

International Products
- Agua Jane (bleach, Uruguay)
- Ant Rid (insecticides)
- Arela (waxes)
- Astra (disposable gloves)
- Bluebell (cleaners)
- Chux (cleaning tools)
- Clorisol (bleach)
- Clorox Gentle (color-safe bleach)
- Glad (containers)
- Glad-Lock (reclosable bags)
- Guard (shoe polish)
- Gumption (cleaners)
- Home Mat (insecticides)
- Home Keeper (insecticides)
- Javex (bleach, Canada)
- Mono (aluminum foil)
- Nevex (bleach, Venezuela)
- OSO (aluminum foil)
- Prestone (coolant)
- Selton (insecticides)
- S.O.S (cleaners)
- Super Globo (bleach)
- XLO (sponges)
- Yuhanrox (bleach)

Specialty Products
- Armor All
- BBQ Bag
- EverClean
- EverFresh
- Fresh Step
- Fresh Step Scoop
- Kingsford
- Match Light
- Rain Dance
- Scoop Away
- Son of a Gun!
- STP
- Tuff Stuff

## COMPETITORS

Alticor
CalCedar
Campbell Soup
Church & Dwight
Colgate-Palmolive
ConAgra
Del Monte Foods
Dial
Dow Chemical
JohnsonDiversey
Kraft Foods
McBride
Newman's Own
Oil-Dri
Pactiv
Procter & Gamble
Reckitt Benckiser
Reckitt Benckiser (US)
S.C. Johnson
Seventh Generation
Tree of Life
Turtle Wax
Unilever

## HISTORICAL FINANCIALS

Company Type: Public

### Income Statement

FYE: June 30

| | REVENUE ($ mil.) | NET INCOME ($ mil.) | NET PROFIT MARGIN | EMPLOYEES |
|---|---|---|---|---|
| **6/06** | 4,644 | 444 | 9.6% | 7,600 |
| **6/05** | 4,388 | 1,096 | 25.0% | 7,600 |
| **6/04** | 4,324 | 549 | 12.7% | 8,600 |
| **6/03** | 4,144 | 493 | 11.9% | 8,900 |
| **6/02** | 4,061 | 322 | 7.9% | 9,500 |
| **Annual Growth** | 3.4% | 8.4% | — | (5.4%) |

### 2006 Year-End Financials

Debt ratio: —
Return on equity: —
Cash ($ mil.): 192
Current ratio: 0.89
Long-term debt ($ mil.): 1,966
No. of shares (mil.): 151
Dividends
Yield: 1.9%
Payout: 39.3%
Market value ($ mil.): 9,225

### Stock History

NYSE: CLX

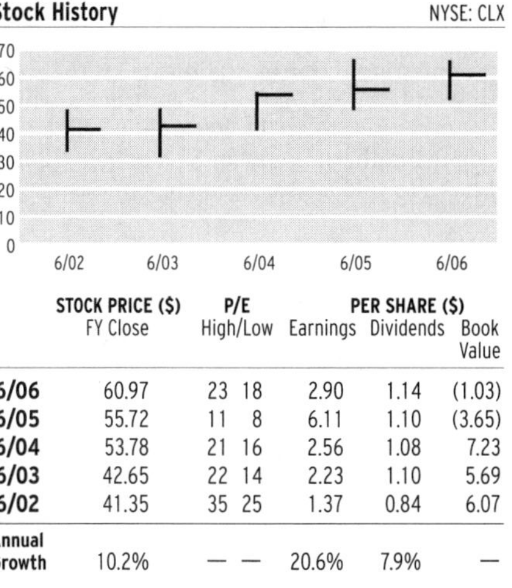


| | STOCK PRICE ($) FY Close | P/E High | P/E Low | PER SHARE ($) Earnings | Dividends | Book Value |
|---|---|---|---|---|---|---|
| **6/06** | 60.97 | 23 | 18 | 2.90 | 1.14 | (1.03) |
| **6/05** | 55.72 | 11 | 8 | 6.11 | 1.10 | (3.65) |
| **6/04** | 53.78 | 21 | 16 | 2.56 | 1.08 | 7.23 |
| **6/03** | 42.65 | 22 | 14 | 2.23 | 1.10 | 5.69 |
| **6/02** | 41.35 | 35 | 25 | 1.37 | 0.84 | 6.07 |
| **Annual Growth** | 10.2% | — | — | 20.6% | 7.9% | — |

# CMS Energy

Michigan consumers rely on CMS Energy. The energy holding company's utility, Consumers Energy, has a generating capacity of more than 6,450 MW (primarily fossil-fueled) and distributes electricity to 1.8 million customers and gas to about 1.7 million customers in Michigan. The company sells wholesale electricity, natural gas, and other commodities; its independent power projects have a gross capacity of more than 8,800 MW. CMS Energy's international interests in plants, pipelines, and utilities are mostly located in Africa, Asia, and Latin America. In 2006 CMS announced plans to sell its trouble-plagued Palisades nuclear plant (to Entergy) and its stakes in businesses in the Middle East, Africa, and India.

CMS Energy's nonregulated operations grew to account for more than half of sales in 2001 and 2002; however, as the wholesale power marketing industry has experienced a downturn, the company has refocused on its regulated energy distribution operations. The company has exited the speculative wholesale energy-trading business, which was conducted through its CMS Energy Resource Management (formerly CMS Marketing, Services and Trading) unit; it has sold its wholesale natural gas trading book to Sempra Energy, and it has sold its electricity trading book to Constellation Energy Commodities Group (formerly Constellation Power Source).

CMS Energy has faced controversy over "round trip" power trades that artificially inflated the company's sales and trading volume during 2000 and 2001. The company has reached a settlement agreement with the SEC over its energy trading activities (without admitting or denying any wrongdoing and paying no fines); however, several former CMS employees are facing penalties from the SEC.

Reining in its expansion strategy, CMS Energy is selling nonstrategic assets, including international power plants and its Latin American electric utilities. The company plans to focus its independent power production operations on the US, North African, and Middle Eastern markets.

CMS Energy has also sold its oil and gas exploration and production assets, as well as most of its domestic gas transportation assets: The company sold its CMS Panhandle companies, which together operate an 11,000-mile pipeline system, to Southern Union for $1.8 billion in 2003. It has also sold its Australian pipeline assets.

## HISTORY

In the late 1880s W. A. Foote and Samuel Jarvis formed hydroelectric company Jackson Electrical Light Works in Jackson, Michigan. After building plants in other Michigan towns, Foote formed utility holding company Consumers Power. In 1910 the firm merged with Michigan Light to create Commonwealth Power Railway and Light (CPR&L) and began building a statewide transmission system.

Foote died in 1915, and after nine years of acquisitions, successor Bernard Cobb sold the rail systems and split CPR&L into Commonwealth Power (CP) and Electric Railway Securities. In 1928 Cobb bought Southeastern Power & Light (SP&L) and merged CP with Penn-Ohio Edison to form Allied Power & Light. Commonwealth and Southern (C&S) was then created as the parent of Allied and SP&L.

In 1932 future GOP presidential nominee Wendell Willkie took the helm and became a national political figure by opposing the Public Utility Holding Company Act of 1935, which began 60 years of regulated monopolies. Consumers Power was divested from C&S after WWII.

Consumers brought a nuclear plant on line in 1962 and the next year began buying Michigan oil and gas fields. In 1967 it formed NOMECO (now CMS Oil and Gas) to guide its oil and gas efforts.

The completion of the Palisades nuke in 1971 began a 13-year run of chronic problems and lengthy shutdowns. Cost overruns and an environmental lawsuit killed the firm's third nuke (Midland) in 1984 — after $4.1 billion was spent.

A rate hike and new CEO William McCormick pointed the firm down a new path in 1985. McCormick formed a subsidiary to develop and invest in independent power projects in 1986 and created holding company CMS (short for "Consumers") Energy the next year. CMS Gas Transmission was formed in 1989.

Midland Cogeneration Venture (CMS Energy and six partners) completed converting Midland to a natural gas-fueled cogeneration plant in 1990, and CMS Energy wrote off $657 million from its losses at the former nuke. It regained profitability in 1993.

McCormick split the utilities into electric and gas divisions in 1995 and also issued stock for its gas utility and transmission businesses, Consumers Gas Group. The next year CMS Energy formed an energy marketing arm.

In 1996 and 1997 CMS Energy invested in power plants in Morocco and Australia and bought a stake in a Brazilian electric utility. The next year it began developing a gas-fired plant in Ghana and won a bid to build a plant in India.

Michigan's public service commission (PSC) issued utility restructuring orders in 1997 and 1998, but in 1999 the state Supreme Court ruled that the PSC lacked restructuring authority. Facing less-favorable proposed legislation, CMS Energy and DTE Energy moved to implement competition per the PSC's guidelines.

CMS Energy bought Panhandle Eastern Pipe Line from Duke Energy for $2.2 billion in 1999. It also grabbed a 77% stake in another Brazilian utility and began building its Powder River Basin gas pipeline. In 2000 the company partnered with Marathon Ashland Petroleum (now Marathon Petroleum) and TEPPCO to operate a pipeline transporting refined petroleum from the US Gulf Coast to Illinois.

CMS Energy agreed in 2001 to sell Consumers' high-voltage electric transmission assets to independent transmission operator Trans-Elect. It also announced plans to sell about $2.4 billion in other noncore assets.

In 2002 the company sold its Equatorial Guinea (West Africa) oil and gas assets to Marathon Oil for about $1 billion. Also that year McCormick stepped down amid controversy over "round trip" power trades that artificially inflated the company's sales and trading volume; CMS Energy later announced that it would restate its 2000 and 2001 financial results to eliminate the effects of the trades.

Later that year, the company exited the exploration and production business. It sold CMS Oil and Gas' North American and African assets to private French energy firm Perenco, and it sold the unit's Colombian properties to Spanish energy firm Compañia Española de Petróleos (Cepsa).

## EXECUTIVES

**President, CEO, and Director; CEO and Director, Consumers Energy:** David W. Joos, age 54, $1,506,615 pay
**EVP and CFO, CMS Energy, Consumers Energy, and CMS Enterprises:** Thomas J. Webb, age 54
**SVP Governmental and Public Affairs and Chief Compliance Officer:** David G. Mengebier, age 49
**SVP and General Counsel:** James E. Brunner, age 54
**SVP Human Resources and Administrative Services:** John M. Butler, age 42
**VP, Chief Accounting Officer, and Controller; VP, Chief Accounting Officer, and Controller, CMS Energy; VP and Chief Accounting Officer, CMS Enterprises:** Glenn P. Barba, age 41
**VP and Corporate Secretary; VP and Corporate Secretary, Consumers Energy and CMS Enterprises:** Catherine M. Reynolds
**VP Investor Relations and Treasurer; VP Investor Relations and Treasurer, Consumers Energy:** Laura L. Mountcastle
**President and COO, CMS Enterprises:** Thomas W. Elward, age 58
**President and COO, Consumers Energy:** John G. Russell, age 49
**Director News and Information:** Jeff Holyfield
**Director Public Information:** Dan Bishop
**VP and Controller, CMS Enterprises:** Carol A. Isles
**Auditors:** Ernst & Young LLP

## LOCATIONS

**HQ:** CMS Energy Corporation
1 Energy Plaza, Jackson, MI 49201
**Phone:** 517-788-0550 **Fax:** 517-788-1859
**Web:** www.cmsenergy.com

### Domestic Independent Power Projects

California
Connecticut
Michigan
New York
North Carolina
Oklahoma

### International Independent Power Projects

Argentina
Chile
Ghana
India
Jamaica
Morocco
Saudi Arabia
United Arab Emirates
Venezuela

## PRODUCTS/OPERATIONS

### 2006 Sales

| | $ mil. | % of total |
|---|---|---|
| Electric utility | 3,302 | 48 |
| Gas utility | 2,373 | 34 |
| Enterprises | 1,135 | 17 |
| Other | 89 | 1 |
| **Total** | **6,899** | **100** |

### Selected Subsidiaries

Consumers Energy Company (electric and gas utility)
- CMS Midland Holdings Company
- CMS Midland Inc.

CMS Enterprises Company (nonutility holding company)
- CMS Electric and Gas Company (international energy distribution)
- CMS Gas Transmission Company (gas transmission, storage, and processing)
- CMS Generation Company (independent power projects)

## COMPETITORS

AEP
AES
Allegheny Energy
Alliant Energy
Aquila
Calpine
CenterPoint Energy
Con Edison
DTE
Duke Energy
Dynegy
Edison International
FPL Group
Integrys Energy Group
ONEOK
SEMCO Energy
Sempra Energy
SUEZ-TRACTEBEL
Wisconsin Energy
Xcel Energy

## HISTORICAL FINANCIALS

Company Type: Public

### Income Statement

FYE: December 31

| | REVENUE ($ mil.) | NET INCOME ($ mil.) | NET PROFIT MARGIN | EMPLOYEES |
|---|---|---|---|---|
| **12/06** | 6,899 | (79) | — | 8,640 |
| **12/05** | 6,413 | (84) | — | 8,713 |
| **12/04** | 5,587 | 121 | 2.2% | 8,660 |
| **12/03** | 5,677 | (44) | — | 8,411 |
| **12/02** | 8,687 | (620) | — | 10,477 |
| **Annual Growth** | (5.6%) | — | — | (4.7%) |

### 2006 Year-End Financials

Debt ratio: 287.5%
Return on equity: —
Cash ($ mil.): 422
Current ratio: 1.46
Long-term debt ($ mil.): 6,422
No. of shares (mil.): 223
Dividends
Yield: —
Payout: —
Market value ($ mil.): 3,721

### Stock History

NYSE: CMS

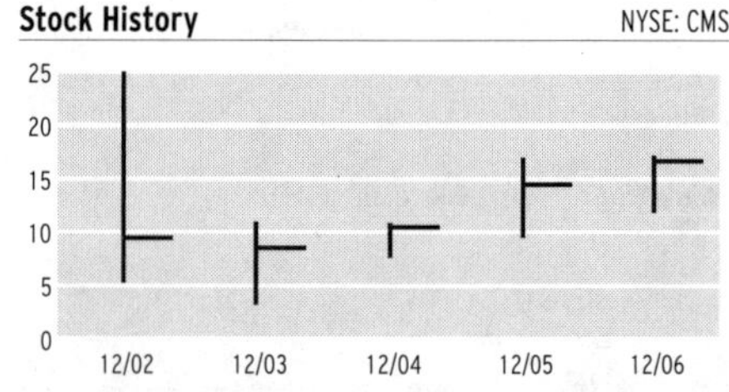

| | STOCK PRICE ($) FY Close | P/E High | P/E Low | PER SHARE ($) Earnings | Dividends | Book Value |
|---|---|---|---|---|---|---|
| **12/06** | 16.70 | — | — | (0.41) | — | 11.20 |
| **12/05** | 14.51 | — | — | (0.44) | — | 10.53 |
| **12/04** | 10.45 | 17 | 12 | 0.64 | — | 11.96 |
| **12/03** | 8.52 | — | — | (0.30) | — | 11.46 |
| **12/02** | 9.44 | — | — | (4.46) | 1.09 | 7.86 |
| **Annual Growth** | 15.3% | — | — | — | — | 9.2% |

# CNA Financial

CNA Financial is the umbrella organization for a wide range of insurance providers, including Continental Casualty and Continental Assurance. The company primarily provides commercial coverage, with such standard offerings as workers' compensation, general and professional liability, and other products for businesses and institutions. CNA also sells specialty insurance for doctors, lawyers, architects, and other professionals. Other services include risk and health care claims management, claims administration, and information services. Holding company Loews owns about 90% of CNA.

Property & casualty premiums account for more than 50% of its total revenue; its specialty lines (including CNA Surety) make up about 30%. Most of its non-core insurance products are in run-off, including a few remaining annuity and pension products, as well as accident and health insurance.

## HISTORY

When merchant Henry Bowen could not find the type of fire insurance he wanted, he began Continental Insurance. Bowen assembled a group of investors and started with about $500,000 in capital. In 1882 Continental Insurance added marine and tornado insurance. Seven years later Francis Moore became president; he was developer of the Universal Mercantile Schedule, a system of assessing fire hazards in buildings.

About the time Continental Insurance was writing the book on fire insurance, several midwestern investors were having trouble assessing risk in their own insurance field — disability. In 1897 this group founded Continental Casualty in Hammond, Indiana. In the early years its primary clients were railroads. Continental Casualty eventually merged with other companies in the field and by 1905 had branch offices in nine states and Hawaii and was writing business in 41 states and territories.

Both Continentals added new insurance lines in 1911: Continental Insurance went into personal auto, and Continental Casualty formed subsidiary Continental Assurance to sell life insurance. By 1915 Continental Insurance had four primary companies; spurred by growing prewar patriotism, they were called the America Fore Group. Both Continentals rose to the challenges presented by the World Wars and the Depression; they entered the 1950s ready for new growth.

In the 1960s the companies began to diversify. Continental Insurance added interests in Diners Club and Capital Financial Services; in 1968 it formed holding company Continental Corp. Meanwhile, Continental Assurance (which had formed its own holding company, CNA Financial) went even farther afield, adding mutual fund, consumer finance, nursing home, and residential construction companies.

By the early 1970s CNA was on the ropes because of the recession and setbacks in the housing business. In 1974 Robert and Laurence Tisch bought most of the company and cut costs ruthlessly. Continental had its own problems in the 1970s, including an Iranian joint venture that got caught up in the revolution.

Both companies suffered losses arising from Hurricane Andrew in 1992, but CNA, which did its housecleaning in the 1970s, was better able to deal with the blow than Continental, which entered the 1990s in need of restructuring.

Rising interest rates in 1994 hurt Continental, whose merger with CNA in 1995 made CNA one of the US's top 10 insurance companies. CNA consolidated the two operations, cutting about 5,000 jobs.

CNA bought Western National Warranty in 1995, followed by managed care provider CoreSource the next year. In 1997 the company spun off its surety business in a deal with Capsure Holdings and formed CNA Surety. Taking advantage of outsourcing trends, CNA created CNA UniSource (payroll and human resources services) and bought its payroll servicer, Interlogic Systems, the next year.

CNA pursued a global strategy, buying majority interests in an Argentine workers' compensation carrier and a British marine insurer, but with 1998 sales flat and earnings down the tube, the company did more slashing than accumulating. It cut 2,400 jobs and exited such lines as agriculture and entertainment insurance.

The company exited the personal insurance business to focus on the commercial market: It transferred its personal insurance lines, including its auto and homeowners coverage, to Allstate in 1999. Then, in 2000 CNA sold its life reinsurance operations to a subsidiary of Munich Re.

As part of a restructuring effort (the company reshuffled itself into three major segments: property/casualty, life, and group), CNA fired some 10% of its workforce in 2001. In 2002, CNA paid out more than $450 million in claims related to the attacks on the World Trade Center.

CNA Financial restated its earnings in 2002, after being questioned by the SEC over the accounting treatment of investment losses.

Freeing up some much needed capital, CNA sold its group benefits business to The Hartford in 2003 for some $530 million. To better focus on its remaining property & casualty lines, the company sold its individual life insurance segment to Swiss Re Life & Health in 2004.

## EXECUTIVES

**Chairman and CEO, CNA Financial and CNA Insurance:** Stephen W. (Steve) Lilienthal, age 57, $950,000 pay
**President and CEO, Property/Casualty Operations:** James R. Lewis, age 57, $800,000 pay
**EVP and CFO:** D. Craig Mense, age 55, $625,000 pay
**EVP and CIO:** John Golden
**EVP and Chief Administration Officer:** Thomas Pontarelli, age 55
**EVP, General Counsel, and Secretary:** Jonathan D. (Jon) Kantor, age 51, $950,000 pay
**Underwriting Director, Reading, Philadelphia, and Pittsburgh Branch:** Katherine Fenwick
**Corporate Communications:** Charles Boesel
**EVP, Worldwide P&C Claim:** George R. Fay
**SVP Property & Marine Operations:** James Abraham
**Auditors:** Deloitte & Touche LLP

## LOCATIONS

**HQ:** CNA Financial Corporation
333 S. Wabash, Chicago, IL 60604
**Phone:** 312-822-5000 **Fax:** 312-822-6419
**Web:** www.cna.com

CNA Financial operates primarily in the US.

## PRODUCTS/OPERATIONS

### 2006 Sales

| | $ mil. | % of total |
|---|---|---|
| Net earned premiums | 7,603 | 73 |
| Net investment income | 2,412 | 23 |
| Realized investment gains | 86 | 3 |
| Other revenues | 275 | 1 |
| **Total** | **10,376** | **100** |

### Selected Subsidiaries

Continental Casualty Company
The Continental Corporation

## COMPETITORS

21st Century
AIG
Allstate
American Financial
Chubb Corp
CIGNA
COUNTRY Insurance
GEICO
Guardian Life
The Hartford
John Hancock Financial Services
Liberty Mutual
MassMutual
MetLife
Mutual of Omaha
Nationwide
New York Life
Pacific Mutual
Prudential
State Farm
Travelers Companies
USAA
Zurich Financial Services

## HISTORICAL FINANCIALS

Company Type: Public

### Income Statement

FYE: December 31

| | ASSETS ($ mil.) | NET INCOME ($ mil.) | INCOME AS % OF ASSETS | EMPLOYEES |
|---|---|---|---|---|
| **12/06** | 60,283 | 1,108 | 1.8% | 9,800 |
| **12/05** | 58,786 | 264 | 0.4% | 10,100 |
| **12/04** | 62,411 | 446 | 0.7% | 10,600 |
| **12/03** | 68,503 | (1,433) | — | 12,100 |
| **12/02** | 61,731 | 155 | 0.3% | 15,500 |
| **Annual Growth** | (0.6%) | 63.5% | — | (10.8%) |

### 2006 Year-End Financials

Equity as % of assets: 16.2%
Return on assets: 1.9%
Return on equity: 12.3%
Long-term debt ($ mil.): 5,007
No. of shares (mil.): 271
Dividends
Yield: —
Payout: —
Market value ($ mil.): 10,931
Sales ($ mil.): 10,376

### Stock History

NYSE: CNA

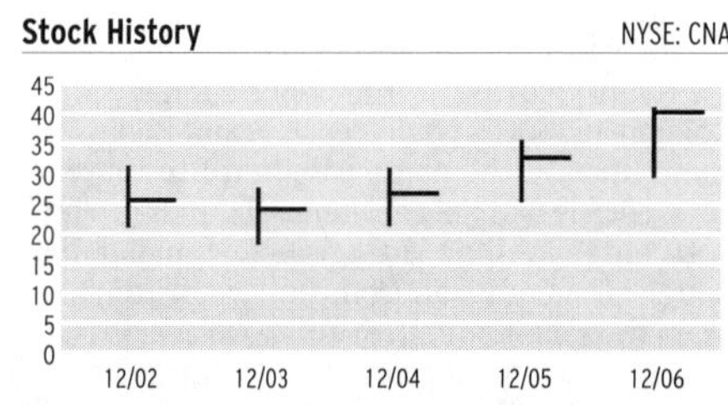


| | STOCK PRICE ($) FY Close | P/E High | P/E Low | PER SHARE ($) Earnings | PER SHARE ($) Dividends | PER SHARE ($) Book Value |
|---|---|---|---|---|---|---|
| **12/06** | 40.32 | 10 | 7 | 4.05 | — | 36.03 |
| **12/05** | 32.73 | 46 | 34 | 0.76 | — | 34.96 |
| **12/04** | 26.75 | 21 | 15 | 1.47 | — | 35.86 |
| **12/03** | 24.10 | — | — | (6.58) | — | 40.03 |
| **12/02** | 25.60 | 46 | 32 | 0.68 | — | 42.04 |
| **Annual Growth** | 12.0% | — | — | 56.2% | — | (3.8%) |

# Coca-Cola

Coke is it — "it" being the world's #1 soft-drink company. The Coca-Cola Company owns four of the top five soft-drink brands (Coca-Cola, Diet Coke, Fanta, and Sprite). Its other brands include Barq's, Minute Maid, POWERade, and Dasani water. In North America, it sells Groupe Danone's Evian. Coca-Cola sells Crush, Dr Pepper, and Schweppes outside Australia, Europe, and North America. The firm makes or licenses more than 400 drink products in more than 200 nations. Although it does no bottling itself, Coke owns 35% of Coca-Cola Enterprises (the #1 Coke bottler in the world); 32% of Mexico's bottler Coca-Cola FEMSA; and 23% of the large European bottler Coca-Cola Hellenic Bottling.

The soft-drink market being flat (no pun intended), Coca-Cola and rival PepsiCo have responded by creating a new soda categories; for example, the "midcalorie" soda. Located somewhere between their flagship brands and their diet colas, the midcalorie drinks have half the sugar, carbohydrates, and calories of the original carbonated formulas. Coke's offering is called C2 and has yet to achieve wide-scale success. Boosting its drinks in the reduced calorie category, the company introduced a so-called "calorie-burning" drink in 2006 called Enviga, a green-tea-based drink. It is marketed through a joint venture with Nestlé SA. (The joint venture, called Beverage Partners Worldwide, primarily focuses on black tea drinks.) The company is revisiting its Diet Coke flavor and plans to launch a version with vitamins.

Broadening its non-cola offerings, in 2006 the company agreed to acquire Fuze Beverage, an alternative juice and tea producer. The deal is still pending. In 2007 Coke purchased the maker of smartwater and vitaminwater, Energy Brands, (also known as Glacéau), for some $4 billion in cash. Energy Brands became a separate operating unit of Coca-Cola North America. In another move to strengthen its lineup of non-carbonated brands, the company has reportedly shown interest in buying Cadbury's Snapple.

To better represent it strategic focus and to better compete with juice and other healthier beverage makers, in 2007 Coke reorganized its North American operations into three business units: sparkling beverages, still beverages, and emerging brands.

Warren Buffett's Berkshire Hathaway owns about 9% of Coca-Cola.

## HISTORY

Atlanta pharmacist John Pemberton invented Coke in 1886. His bookkeeper, Frank Robinson, came up with the name based on two ingredients, coca leaves (later cleaned of narcotics) and kola nuts. By 1891 druggist Asa Candler had bought The Coca-Cola Company, and within four years the soda-fountain drink was available in all states; it was in Canada and Mexico by 1898.

Candler sold most US bottling rights in 1899 to Benjamin Thomas and John Whitehead of Chattanooga, Tennessee, for $1. The two designed a regional franchise bottling system that created more than 1,000 bottlers within 20 years. In 1916 Candler retired to become Atlanta's mayor; his family sold the company to Atlanta banker Ernest Woodruff for $25 million in 1919. Coca-Cola went public that year.

The firm expanded overseas and introduced the slogans "The Pause that Refreshes" (1929) and "It's the Real Thing" (1941). To keep WWII soldiers in Cokes at a nickel a pop, the government built 64 overseas bottling plants. Coca-Cola bought Minute Maid in 1960 and began launching new drinks — Fanta (1960), Sprite (1960), TAB (1963), and Diet Coke (1982).

In 1981 Roberto Goizueta became chairman. Four years later, with Coke slipping in market share, the firm changed its formula and introduced New Coke, which consumers soundly rejected (thus, Coca-Cola Classic was born). In 1986 it consolidated the US bottling operations it owned into Coca-Cola Enterprises and sold 51% of the new company to the public. Goizueta also engineered the company's purchase of Columbia Pictures in 1982. (Columbia earned Coke a $1 billion profit when it sold the studio to Sony in 1989.)

Goizueta died of lung cancer in 1997; while he was at the helm, the firm's value rose from $4 billion to $145 billion. Douglas Ivester, the architect of Coca-Cola's restructured bottling operations, succeeded him. An agreement to buy about 30 Cadbury Schweppes beverage brands — including Canada Dry, Dr Pepper, and Schweppes — outside the US and France was scaled down because of antitrust concerns. Completed in 1999, the deal also excluded Canada, much of continental Europe, and Mexico.

A battered Ivester resigned in 2000; president and COO Douglas Daft was named chairman and CEO. Coca-Cola began its largest cutbacks ever, slashing nearly 5,000 jobs, and later agreed to pay nearly $193 million to settle a race-discrimination suit filed by African-American workers.

To fortify its portfolio in the fast-growing non-carbonated drinks segment, Coca-Cola acquired Mad River Traders (teas, juices, sodas) and Odwalla (juices and smoothies) in 2001. Coca-Cola also announced that it would invest $150 million to build bottling facilities in China.

As part of the restructuring initiated by Daft in 2000, another 1,000 employees (half in Atlanta) were laid off in 2003 after the company decided to combine several business units under the Coca-Cola North America umbrella. The company laid off 2,800 employees worldwide in 2003. Later in 2003, trouble broke out for the company overseas. Claims surfaced in India that both Coke and Pepsi bottled in that country contain traces of DDT, malathion, and other pesticides that exceed government limits. Both Coke and Pepsi denied the reports in a joint press conference. Government labs cleared the colas, saying the drinks were safe, but not before both soft drink companies saw sales dip by as much as 50% in a two-week period.

Daft retired as Coca-Cola's chairman and CEO in 2004 and former Coca-Cola HBC CEO E. Neville Isdell replaced him.

In 2005 Blak, a coffee-flavored Coke (with half the calories and twice the caffeine of a regular Coke) was first tested and marketed in France and then introduced in the US. Bowing to the public's growing concern about childhood obesity, in 2006 Coke, along with Pepsi, Cadbury Schweppes, and the American Beverage Association, agreed to sell only water, unsweetened juice, and low-fat milks to public elementary and middle schools in the US.

## EXECUTIVES

**Chairman and CEO:** E. Neville Isdell, age 64, $1,500,000 pay
**President and COO:** Muhtar Kent, age 54, $773,077 pay
**EVP and CFO:** Gary P. Fayard, age 54, $616,298 pay
**EVP and President, Bottling Investments and Supply Chain:** Irial Finan, age 50
**EVP, Bottling Investments:** Mark H. Moreland, age 47
**SVP and CIO:** Jean-Michel Arès
**SVP and Chief Innovation/Research and Development Officer:** Danny L. Strickland, age 58
**SVP and President, The McDonalds Division:** Jerry S. Wilson
**SVP and Director, Corporate External Affairs; Chairperson, The Coca-Cola Foundation:** Ingrid Saunders Jones, age 61
**SVP and Director Human Resources:** Cynthia P. McCague, age 55
**SVP and Director, Worldwide Public Affairs and Communications:** Thomas G. (Tom) Mattia, age 58
**SVP and General Counsel:** Geoffrey J. (Geoff) Kelly, age 62
**SVP, North America Marketing:** John Hackett
**SVP and President, Coca-Cola North America:** J. Alexander M. (Sandy) Douglas Jr., age 45
**President, Latin America Group:** José Octavio Reyes, age 54, $543,793 pay
**Chief Marketing and Commercial Officer:** Joseph V. Tripodi, age 51
**Corporate Secretary:** Carol Crofoot Hayes
**VP and Director, Investor Relations:** Ann Taylor
**Auditors:** Ernst & Young LLP

## LOCATIONS

**HQ:** The Coca-Cola Company
1 Coca-Cola Plaza, Atlanta, GA 30313
**Phone:** 404-676-2121
**Web:** www.cocacola.com

### 2006 Sales

| | $ mil. | % of total |
|---|---|---|
| North America | 7,013 | 29 |
| Bottling investments | 5,109 | 21 |
| North Asia, Eurasia & the Middle East | 3,986 | 17 |
| European Union | 3,505 | 15 |
| Latin America | 2,484 | 10 |
| Africa | 1,103 | 5 |
| East & South Asia & the Pacific Rim | 795 | 3 |
| Corporate | 93 | — |
| **Total** | **24,088** | **100** |

## PRODUCTS/OPERATIONS

### Selected Brand Names

Carbonated Soft Drinks
- Aquarius
- Barq's
- Blak (coffee-flavored Coca-Cola)
- Canada Dry (outside Australia, Europe, North America, licensed with Cadbury Schweppes)
- Citra
- Coca-Cola (cherry, caffeine-free, lime, regular, vanilla)
- Coca-Cola classic (caffeine-free, regular)
- Coca-Cola light (outside the US)
- Coca-Cola Zero (calorie-free, North America)
- Crush (outside Australia, Europe, North America, licensed with Cadbury Schweppes)
- Diet Coke (regular, caffeine-free, lemon, lime)
- Dr Pepper (regular, diet; outside Australia, Europe, North America, licensed with Cadbury Schweppes)
- Fanta
- Fresca
- Full Throttle
- Lift
- Mello Yello
- Mr. PiBB
- Sprite (regular, diet, and light, super lemon, and ICE outside US)
- Sprite Remix (tropical-flavored)
- TAB

Other Beverages
- Bacardi (fruit mixes, licensed with Bacardi & Company Limited)
- Ciel Naturae (bottled water)
- Dannon (bottled water)
- Dasani (bottled water)
- Evian (licensed with Groupe Danone)
- Five Alive (fruit beverages)
- Fruitopia (fruit juices and teas)
- fruitwater (enhanced bottled water)
- Georgia (coffee drinks, Japan)
- Hi-C (fruit drinks)
- Minute Maid (juices and juice drinks)
- Nestea (tea-based drinks, joint venture with Nestlé S.A.)
- Odwalla (non-carbonated juices)
- POWERade (sports drink)
- Simply Orange (juice)
- smartwater (enhanced bottled water)
- Sparklettes (bottled water)
- Spring! by Dannon (bottled water)
- vitaminenergy (enhanced bottled water)
- vitaminwater (enhanced bottled water)

## COMPETITORS

American Beverage
Britvic
Cadbury Schweppes
Chiquita Brands
Clearly Canadian
Cott
Cranberries Limited
Danone
Danone Water
Energy Brands
Ferolito, Vultaggio
Florida's Natural
Fuze Beverage
Gatorade
Goya
Great Western Juice
Hansen Natural
Hawaiian Natural Water
Impulse Energy USA
IZZE
Jones Soda
Kirin Holdings Company
Kraft Foods
Mountain Valley
Naked Juice
National Beverage
National Grape Cooperative
Naumes
Nestlé
Nestlé Waters
New Attitude
Ocean Spray
Old Orchard
PepsiCo
Pernod Ricard
Procter & Gamble
Red Bull
Snapple
South Beach Beverage
Sunny Delight
Suntory Ltd.
Tree Top
Tropicana
Unilever
Virgin Group
Vitality Foodservice
Walkers Snack Foods
Welch's
Wet Planet Beverages

## HISTORICAL FINANCIALS

Company Type: Public

**Income Statement** — FYE: December 31

| | REVENUE ($ mil.) | NET INCOME ($ mil.) | NET PROFIT MARGIN | EMPLOYEES |
|---|---|---|---|---|
| **12/06** | 24,088 | 5,080 | 21.1% | 71,000 |
| **12/05** | 23,104 | 4,872 | 21.1% | 55,000 |
| **12/04** | 21,962 | 4,847 | 22.1% | 50,000 |
| **12/03** | 21,044 | 4,347 | 20.7% | 49,000 |
| **12/02** | 19,564 | 3,050 | 15.6% | 56,000 |
| **Annual Growth** | 5.3% | 13.6% | — | 6.1% |

**2006 Year-End Financials**

Debt ratio: 7.8%
Return on equity: 30.5%
Cash ($ mil.): 2,590
Current ratio: 0.95
Long-term debt ($ mil.): 1,314

No. of shares (mil.): 2,318
Dividends
Yield: 2.6%
Payout: 57.4%
Market value ($ mil.): 111,844

**Stock History** — NYSE: KO

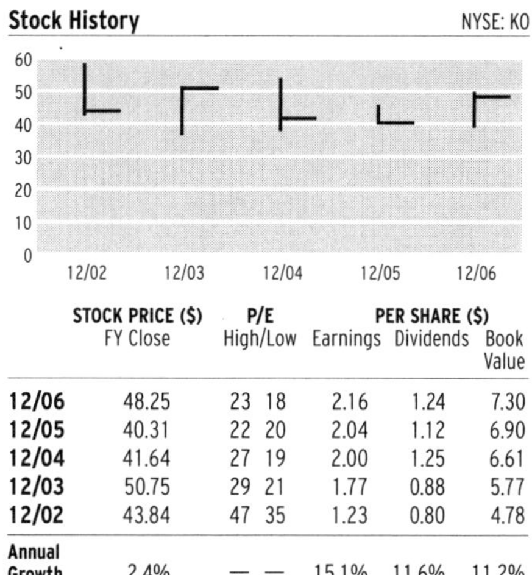


| | STOCK PRICE ($) FY Close | P/E High | P/E Low | PER SHARE ($) Earnings | Dividends | Book Value |
|---|---|---|---|---|---|---|
| **12/06** | 48.25 | 23 | 18 | 2.16 | 1.24 | 7.30 |
| **12/05** | 40.31 | 22 | 20 | 2.04 | 1.12 | 6.90 |
| **12/04** | 41.64 | 27 | 19 | 2.00 | 1.25 | 6.61 |
| **12/03** | 50.75 | 29 | 21 | 1.77 | 0.88 | 5.77 |
| **12/02** | 43.84 | 47 | 35 | 1.23 | 0.80 | 4.78 |
| **Annual Growth** | 2.4% | — | — | 15.1% | 11.6% | 11.2% |

# Coca-Cola Enterprises

The scientists and the suits at The Coca-Cola Company (TCCC) concoct the secret recipes and market the brands, but Coca-Cola Enterprises (CCE) does much of the bottling and distribution of the soft drinks. The world's #1 Coke bottler, CCE accounts for 19% of worldwide sales of Coca-Cola's beverages. CCE also bottles and distributes other beverages, including Canada Dry, Dr Pepper, Nestea, bottled waters, and juices. It sells soft drinks in 46 US states, the District of Columbia, the US Virgin Islands, Canada, and six European nations, including France and the UK. The company's territories consist of more than 412 million potential customers. The Coca-Cola Company owns approximately 35% of CCE.

An "anchor" bottler for TCCC, CCE continues to increase its share of the Coca-Cola market by acquiring other bottlers in the US, Canada, and Europe. About 54% of the company's North American product and about 43% of its European product are sold in supermarkets.

Boosting its tea offerings, Coca-Cola Enterprises struck an agreement to begin distributing new flavors of AriZona Iced Tea in 2007.

Former CCE chairman Summerfield Johnston Jr. owns about 6% of CCE.

## HISTORY

Coca-Cola Enterprises (CCE) was formed in 1986 when The Coca-Cola Company bought its two largest bottlers — JTL Corp. and BCI Holdings — and formed a single corporation. The company went public immediately, though Coca-Cola retained a significant interest in it.

CCE set about acquiring smaller bottling concerns across the US and by 1988 the company had become the #1 bottler in the world. The company centralized operations to boost its slim profit margin.

In 1991 CCE merged with the Johnston Coca-Cola Bottling Group, the #2 US Coca-Cola bottler. The acquisition cost the ailing CCE $125 million, and led a number of disaffected investors to protest. Johnston executives took control when Summerfield Johnston Jr. (whose grandfather had co-founded the first Coke bottling franchisee) assumed the post of CEO, and Henry Schimberg, a former RC Cola route salesman, became president and COO.

In 1992 the bottler was reorganized into 10 US operating regions to allow for better control of individual market dynamics. A $1.5 billion public debt offering occurred that year, and the following year the company began looking outward for growth, acquiring Nederland B.V. (the Coca-Cola bottler of the Netherlands) as well as two Tennessee bottlers. In 1994 CCE recorded its first profitable year since 1990.

The company reorganized again in 1996, forming four operating groups defined by market and geographic lines. Its acquisitions that year included bottlers in Belgium and France.

CCE bought Cadbury Schweppes' 51% stake in the Coca-Cola & Schweppes Beverages UK joint venture for $2 billion in 1997, and it also purchased Coca-Cola's shares in Coca-Cola Beverages Ltd. (Canada's leading bottler) and The Coca-Cola Bottling Company of New York.

A half-dozen deals in 1998 included the $1.1 billion purchase of Coke Southwest and other bottling acquisitions in the US and Luxembourg worth $355 million. Schimberg became CEO that year.

Also in 1998 the bottler expanded its vending-machine business, and many distributors and vending-machine owners (who use CCE as a supplier) complained that the firm was charging lower prices in its own machines than independent owners could for the same products.

Bad news came in 1999 when products bottled by CCE in Antwerp, Belgium, and Dunkirk, France, were contaminated by bad carbon dioxide and paint used on wooden pallets to prevent mold. Coca-Cola products were banned or recalled in Belgium, France, and a handful of other European countries for about two weeks, costing the company more than $100 million. Schimberg retired in 1999 and Johnston became CEO again.

In 1999 CCE acquired seven bottlers in the US for about $628 million and one in Europe. European Commission regulators raided various CCE offices in 1999 and 2000 as part of an investigation into anti-competitive marketing programs.

In 2001 Johnston stepped down as CEO, but remained chairman. Vice chairman Lowry Kline was named CEO. That same year, the company bought bottlers Hondo and Herbco Enterprises (collectively known as Herb Coca-Cola, the #3 Coke bottler in the US) for about $1.4 billion. The company also announced plans to lay off 2,000 employees as a result of stagnant sales in North America. In 2002 Kline replaced Johnston as chairman.

A banner year for acquisitions, 2002 had CCE acquiring Austin Coca-Cola Bottling Company, Brown's Beverages Ltd., Dawson Creek Beverages Ltd., Dr Pepper franchise license for parts of Arizona, and the Moark Bottling Company. The next year the company acquired Chaudfrontaine, a Belgium Water bottling and distribution company.

Having held the position for just one year, president and CEO John Alm left the company in early 2006. Chairman (and former company CEO) Lowery Kline took over temporary leadership until John Brock was appointed president and CEO later in the year. Brock is the former CEO of InBev, COO of Cadbury Schweppes, and chairman of Cadbury Schweppes Bottling Group (formerly Dr. Pepper/Seven Up Bottling). Kline continues as chairman.

The company was named (along with the Coca-Cola Company) in a suit brought by independent bottlers in 2006, seeking to bar the two companies from abandoning the tradition in which independent companies that put Coke beverages in bottles and cans also deliver the products to and stack them on the shelves of grocery stores. CCE reached a conditional settlement with Ozarks Coco-Cola and Dr. Pepper Bottling Company, wherein there will be a two-year test involving compensation to independent bottlers for the national warehouse delivery of Coke brands by CCE into the territory of said Coke bottlers (even those not involved in the litigation). The settlement also limits CCE's local warehouse delivery.

In addition, a group of shareholders filed a class-action suit against CCE, claiming that the company's practice of channel-stuffing (forcing extra product onto customers in order to boost revenue) affected CCE's financial condition. The suit is ongoing.

## EXECUTIVES

**Chairman:** Lowry F. Kline, age 66, $1,670,868 pay
**President, CEO, and Director:** John Franklin Brock, age 58, $1,790,067 pay (partial-year salary)
**EVP, Financial Services and Administration:** Vicki R. Palmer, age 53, $745,219 pay
**EVP and General Counsel:** John J. Culhane, age 61, $740,438 pay
**EVP and President, European Group:** Shaun B. Higgins, age 57, $908,558 pay
**EVP and President, North America:** Terrance M. (Terry) Marks, age 46, $884,370 pay
**SVP and CFO:** William W. (Bill) Douglas III, age 45, $747,219 pay
**SVP and CIO:** Esat Sezer, age 44
**SVP, Human Resources:** Greg A. Lee, age 57
**SVP, Public Affairs and Communications:** John H. Downs Jr., age 50
**SVP, Strategic Initiatives North America:** John R. Parker Jr., age 56
**VP, Controller, and Principal Accounting Officer:** Charles D. Lischer, age 38
**VP, Sales North America:** Mark Schortman
**Manager, Community Relations and Public Affairs:** Roy A. Potts
**Auditors:** Ernst & Young LLP

## LOCATIONS

**HQ:** Coca-Cola Enterprises Inc.
2500 Windy Ridge Pkwy., Atlanta, GA 30339
**Phone:** 770-989-3000 **Fax:** 770-989-3788
**Web:** www.cokecce.com

### 2006 Sales

| | $ mil. | % of total |
|---|---|---|
| North America | 14,221 | 72 |
| Europe | 5,583 | 28 |
| **Total** | **19,804** | **100** |

## PRODUCTS/OPERATIONS

### Selected Company Brands – North America

Barq's
Carver's Original Ginger Ale
Cherry Coke
Chippewa Water
Coca-Cola C2
Coca-Cola classic
Coca-Cola with Lime
Coca-Cola Zero
Dannon
Dasani flavored waters
Diet Barq's
Diet Cherry Coke
Diet Coke with Splenda
Diet Mello Yello'
Diet Nestea
Diet Northern Neck
Diet Rockstar
Diet Sprite Zero
Diet Vanilla Coke
Evian
Fanta
Fresca
Full Throttle
KMX
Mello Yello
Minute Maid juices & juice drinks
Minute Maid Lemonade
Minute Maid Light Lemonades
Minute Maid Light
Pibb X-tra
POWERade
Powerade Option
Red Flash
Rockstar
Seagrams Ginger Ale & Mixers
Sprite
TAB
Vanilla Coke
Vault

## COMPETITORS

Britvic
Buffalo Rock
Cadbury Schweppes
Coca-Cola Bottling
Cott
Danone
G & J Pepsi-Cola Bottlers
Georgia Crown
Honickman
Kraft Foods
Leading Brands
National Beverage
Nestlé
Ocean Spray
PepsiCo
Snapple
Southeast-Atlantic Beverage
Suntory Ltd.
Virgin Group

## HISTORICAL FINANCIALS

Company Type: Public

### Income Statement

FYE: December 31

| | REVENUE ($ mil.) | NET INCOME ($ mil.) | NET PROFIT MARGIN | EMPLOYEES |
|---|---|---|---|---|
| **12/06** | 19,804 | (1,143) | — | 74,000 |
| **12/05** | 18,706 | 514 | 2.7% | 73,000 |
| **12/04** | 18,158 | 596 | 3.3% | 74,000 |
| **12/03** | 17,330 | 676 | 3.9% | 74,000 |
| **12/02** | 16,889 | 494 | 2.9% | 74,000 |
| **Annual Growth** | 4.1% | — | — | 0.0% |

### 2006 Year-End Financials

Debt ratio: 204.0%
Return on equity: —
Cash ($ mil.): 184
Current ratio: 0.97
Long-term debt ($ mil.): 9,232
No. of shares (mil.): 480
Dividends
Yield: 1.2%
Payout: —
Market value ($ mil.): 9,795

### Stock History

NYSE: CCE

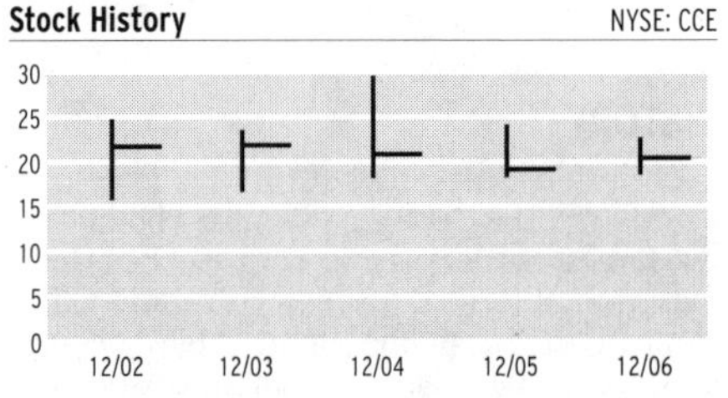


| | STOCK PRICE ($) FY Close | P/E High | P/E Low | PER SHARE ($) Earnings | Dividends | Book Value |
|---|---|---|---|---|---|---|
| **12/06** | 20.42 | — | — | (2.41) | 0.24 | 9.44 |
| **12/05** | 19.17 | 22 | 17 | 1.08 | 0.16 | 11.91 |
| **12/04** | 20.85 | 23 | 15 | 1.26 | 0.16 | 11.45 |
| **12/03** | 21.87 | 16 | 12 | 1.46 | 0.16 | 9.58 |
| **12/02** | 21.72 | 23 | 15 | 1.07 | 0.16 | 7.44 |
| **Annual Growth** | (1.5%) | — | — | — | 10.7% | 6.1% |

# Colgate-Palmolive

Colgate-Palmolive takes a bite out of grime. The company is a top maker and marketer of toothpaste and a worldwide leader in oral care products (mouthwashes, toothpaste, toothbrushes). Its Tom's of Maine unit covers the natural toothpaste niche. Colgate-Palmolive's Hill's Pet Nutrition subsidiary makes Science Diet and Prescription Diet pet foods. It also makes personal care items (deodorants, shampoos, soaps) and household cleaners (bleaches, laundry products, soaps). Colgate-Palmolive operates in some 70 countries and sells products in more than 200.

To remain competitive Colgate-Palmolive implemented a four-year restructuring plan in late 2004 that involves cutting employees and closing plants worldwide. The company's plan is to remain a top competitor by boosting its core businesses. Its three primary objectives are to increase profit, reallocate resources to promising growth areas, and leverage global market efficiencies. The initiative involves reducing its global workforce by some 12%, closing about 25 of its 78 factories, and focusing on core units. Colgate-Palmolive also looks to grow more profitable by transitioning some manufacturing operations into regional centers.

By selling its North American laundry detergent brands in 2005, Colgate-Palmolive is focusing on the high-margin pearly whites (with bite) of its portfolio — oral care and pet care. The company's purchase of natural oral care products maker Tom's of Maine in May 2006 is Colgate-Palmolive's effort to target the natural niche — a market valued at $3 billion in the US with a 15% growth rate. It bought some 84% of the firm for about $100 million. It's also purging laundry detergent brands marketed in numerous Asian and South American markets. In addition, the firm's restructuring calls for consolidation of toothpaste production in Europe, where discounted brands have lured customers away from Colgate-Palmolive's brand names.

In recent years Colgate-Palmolive brushed up its portfolio by extending its well-known brands into newer product areas. Colgate Simply White teeth whiteners, Motion battery-powered toothbrushes, and Palmolive aromatherapy dishwashing liquids are examples.

While Colgate-Palmolive leads in sales of toothpaste, consumer-goods giant P&G remains a formidable competitor. With P&G's purchase of Gillette and its greater presence in the industry, Colgate-Palmolive is likely to feel P&G flexing its marketing muscle as it negotiates positions on store shelves and contracts with retailers.

Chairman and CEO Reuben Mark handed over the title of CEO to president and COO Ian Cook in July 2007.

## HISTORY

William Colgate founded The Colgate Company in Manhattan in 1806 to produce soap, candles, and starch. Colgate died in 1857, and the company was passed to his son Samuel, who renamed it Colgate and Company. In 1873 the company introduced toothpaste in jars, and in 1896 it began selling Colgate Dental Cream in tubes. By 1906 Colgate was making 160 kinds of soap, 625 perfumes, and 2,000 other products. The company went public in 1908.

In 1898 Milwaukee's B. J. Johnson Soap Company (founded 1864) introduced Palmolive, a soap made of palm and olive oils rather than smelly animal fats. It became so popular that the firm changed its name to The Palmolive Company in 1916. Ten years later Palmolive merged with Peet Brothers, a Kansas City-based soap maker founded in 1872. Palmolive-Peet merged with Colgate in 1928, forming Colgate-Palmolive-Peet (shortened to Colgate-Palmolive in 1953). The stock market crash of 1929 prevented a planned merger of the company with Hershey and Kraft.

During the 1930s the firm purchased French and German soap makers and opened branches in Europe. Colgate-Palmolive-Peet introduced Fab detergent and Ajax cleanser in 1947, and the two brands soon became top sellers in Europe. The company expanded to Asia in the 1950s, and by 1961 foreign sales were 52% of the total.

Colgate-Palmolive introduced a host of products in the 1960s and 1970s, including Palmolive dishwashing liquid (1966), Ultra Brite toothpaste (1968), and Irish Spring soap (1972). During the same time, the company diversified by buying approximately 70 other businesses, including Kendall hospital and industrial supplies (1972), Helena Rubinstein cosmetics (1973), Ram Golf (1974), and Riviana Foods and Hill's Pet Products (1976). The strategy had mixed results, and most of these acquisitions were sold in the 1980s.

Reuben Mark became CEO of Colgate-Palmolive in 1984. The company bought 50% of Southeast Asia's leading toothpaste, Darkie, in 1985; it changed its name to Darlie in 1989 following protests of its minstrel-in-blackface trademark. Both Palmolive automatic dishwasher detergent and Colgate Tartar Control toothpaste were introduced in 1986. That year Colgate-Palmolive purchased the liquid soap lines of Minnetonka, the most popular of which is Softsoap. In 1992 the company bought Mennen, maker of Speed Stick (the leading US deodorant).

Increasing its share of the oral care market in Latin America to 79% in 1995, Colgate-Palmolive acquired Brazilian company Kolynos (from Wyeth for $1 billion) and 94% of Argentina's Odol Saic. The company also bought Ciba-Geigy's oral hygiene business in India, increasing its share of that toothpaste market. At home, however, sales and earnings in key segments were dismal, so in 1995 Colgate-Palmolive began a restructuring that included cutting more than 8% of its employees and closing or reconfiguring 24 factories in two years.

The company introduced a record 602 products in 1996 and continued to expand its operations in countries with emerging economies. In 1997 Colgate-Palmolive took the lead in the US toothpaste market for the first time in 35 years (displacing P&G).

In 1999 the company sold the rights to Baby Magic (shampoos, lotions, oils) in the US, Canada, and Puerto Rico to Playtex Products, retaining the rights in all other countries.

In 2002 Colgate-Palmolive introduced a teeth-whitening gel, Simply White, to compete with rival P&G's Crest Whitestrips. The company saw success in 2002 when its Hill's Pet Nutrition subsidiary launched new specialty foods for cats and dogs; one of its dog foods reportedly slows brain aging in canines.

## EXECUTIVES

**Chairman:** Reuben Mark, age 68, $1,871,750 pay
**President, CEO, and Director:** Ian M. Cook, age 55, $891,250 pay
**CFO:** Stephen C. Patrick, age 57, $667,500 pay
**COO, European, Greater Asia and Africa Divisions:** Michael J. Tangney, age 62, $720,667 pay
**SVP, General Counsel, and Secretary:** Andrew D. Hendry, age 59
**VP and Corporate Controller:** Dennis J. Hickey, age 58
**VP and Corporate Treasurer:** Edward J. Filusch, age 59
**VP, Global Human Resources:** Julie A. Zerbe
**VP, Investor Relations:** Delia H. (Bina) Thompson, age 57
**VP, Corporate Communications:** Jan Guifarro
**Director, Marketing:** William Kashimer
**Public Relations, Multicultural Marketing:** Allison Klimerman
**Auditors:** PricewaterhouseCoopers LLP

## LOCATIONS

**HQ:** Colgate-Palmolive Company
300 Park Ave., New York, NY 10022
**Phone:** 212-310-2000 **Fax:** 212-310-2475
**Web:** www.colgate.com

### 2006 Sales

| | $ mil. | % of total |
|---|---|---|
| Oral, personal & home care | | |
| Latin America | 3,019.5 | 25 |
| Europe/South Pacific | 2,952.3 | 24 |
| North America | 2,590.8 | 21 |
| Greater Asia/Africa | 2,006.0 | 16 |
| Pet nutrition | 1,669.1 | 14 |
| **Total** | **12,237.7** | **100** |

## PRODUCTS/OPERATIONS

### 2006 Sales

| | $ mil. | % of total |
|---|---|---|
| Oral, personal & home care | 10,568.6 | 86 |
| Pet nutrition | 1,669.1 | 14 |
| **Total** | **12,237.7** | **100** |

### 2006 Sales

| | % of total |
|---|---|
| Oral care | 38 |
| Home care | 25 |
| Personal care | 23 |
| Pet nutrition | 14 |
| **Total** | **100** |

### Personal Care Brands

Irish Spring
Mennen
Palmolive Botanicals
Softsoap
Speed Stick

### Household Surface Care Brands

Ajax
Murphy's oil soap
Palmolive

### Pet Nutrition Brands

Prescription Diet Canine b/d
Prescription Diet Feline z/d
Science Diet

## COMPETITORS

Alberto-Culver
Alticor
Avon
Chattem
Church & Dwight
Clorox
Doane Pet Care
Henkel
Johnson & Johnson
L'Oréal USA
Mars
MedPointe
Nestlé
Nu Skin
Procter & Gamble
Reckitt Benckiser
Sara Lee Household
S.C. Johnson
Unilever

## HISTORICAL FINANCIALS

Company Type: Public

### Income Statement

FYE: December 31

| | REVENUE ($ mil.) | NET INCOME ($ mil.) | NET PROFIT MARGIN | EMPLOYEES |
|---|---|---|---|---|
| **12/06** | 12,238 | 1,353 | 11.1% | 34,700 |
| **12/05** | 11,397 | 1,351 | 11.9% | 35,800 |
| **12/04** | 10,584 | 1,327 | 12.5% | 36,000 |
| **12/03** | 9,903 | 1,421 | 14.4% | 36,600 |
| **12/02** | 9,294 | 1,288 | 13.9% | 37,700 |
| **Annual Growth** | 7.1% | 1.2% | — | (2.1%) |

### 2006 Year-End Financials

Debt ratio: 229.0%
Return on equity: 118.5%
Cash ($ mil.): 490
Current ratio: 0.95
Long-term debt ($ mil.): 2,720
No. of shares (mil.): 513
Dividends
Yield: 1.9%
Payout: 50.8%
Market value ($ mil.): 33,446

### Stock History

NYSE: CL

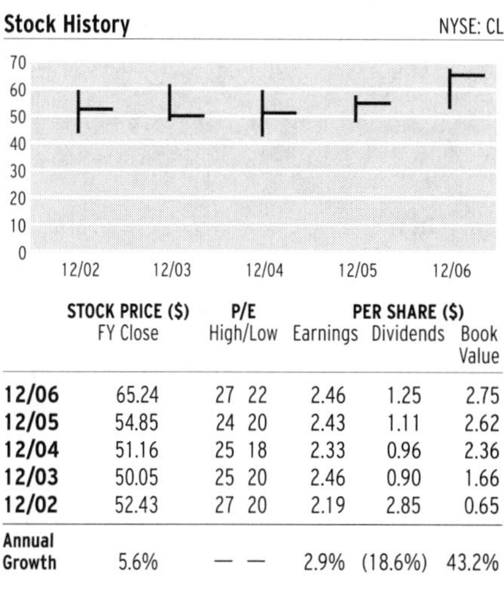


| | STOCK PRICE ($) FY Close | P/E High | P/E Low | PER SHARE ($) Earnings | PER SHARE ($) Dividends | PER SHARE ($) Book Value |
|---|---|---|---|---|---|---|
| **12/06** | 65.24 | 27 | 22 | 2.46 | 1.25 | 2.75 |
| **12/05** | 54.85 | 24 | 20 | 2.43 | 1.11 | 2.62 |
| **12/04** | 51.16 | 25 | 18 | 2.33 | 0.96 | 2.36 |
| **12/03** | 50.05 | 25 | 20 | 2.46 | 0.90 | 1.66 |
| **12/02** | 52.43 | 27 | 20 | 2.19 | 2.85 | 0.65 |
| **Annual Growth** | 5.6% | — | — | 2.9% | (18.6%) | 43.2% |

# Comcast Corporation

Commerce plus broadcasting equals Comcast. The firm's cable division has more than 23 million subscribers and is the largest in the US (well ahead of #2 Time Warner Cable). Comcast Cable brings in 95% of revenues and offers cable TV, Internet, and digital phone services. Comcast also has programming interests such as VERSUS (formerly the Outdoor Life Network), and it has majority stakes in E! Entertainment Television and Comcast SportsNet. It partially owns Philadelphia's pro sports teams, the 76ers and the Flyers. Comcast joined the Sony-led consortium that bought MGM in 2005, investing $300 million. One-third of Comcast is controlled by CEO Brian Roberts, son of founder and former chairman Ralph Roberts.

Comcast has significantly upgraded its systems, adding the capacity for two-way communications such as high-speed Internet access (11 million subscribers). The upgrades have also allowed for more varied offerings in some areas, including high-definition TV programming, on-demand programming, and digital video recorders. The company in 2005 rolled out Comcast Digital Voice, a Voice over Internet Protocol (VoIP) telephone service in 25 of its markets. Comcast has about 2.4 million voice customers, including some traditional phone subscribers, but it is transitioning all voice customers to the digital product.

In an effort to quell the growing complaints from watchdog groups and US lawmakers that cable television doesn't do enough to combat indecency, Comcast in late 2005 launched a new family-friendly tier of cable channels. The tier includes a mix of news, learning, and children's networks.

In 2007 the company agreed to purchase Patriot Media & Communications, a small New Jersey cable operator, for about $483 million. The deal would add some 81,000 video subscribers to Comcast's roster. In a bid to boost its video entertainment offerings, Comcast additionally offered to purchase movie tickets site Fandango. The new site would be rechristened Fancast.com, offering online videos for viewing and recording. Meanwhile, the company is expanding its stable of regional sports channels by purchasing two networks from Cablevision Systems. The $570 million deal included a 60% stake in FSN Bay Area and a 50% stake in FSN New England (bringing Comcast's holding to 100% in that network).

## HISTORY

In 1963 Ralph Roberts, Daniel Aaron, and Julian Brodsky bought American Cable Systems in Tupelo, Mississippi. The company soon expanded throughout the state. In 1969 the company got a new name: Comcast, combining "communications" and "broadcast." Two years later Comcast acquired franchises in western Pennsylvania, and when it went public in 1972, it moved to Philadelphia.

Comcast bought up local operations nationwide through the early 1980s and gained its first foreign cable franchise in 1983 in London (it sold its affiliate there to NTL — now Virgin Media — in 1998). It took a 26% stake in the large Group W Cable in 1986. Roberts also lent financial support that year to a fledgling home-shopping channel called QVC — for "quality, value, and convenience."

A big step into telecommunications came in 1988 when Comcast bought American Cellular Network, with Delaware and New Jersey franchises. Two years later Roberts' son Brian — who had trained as a cable installer during a summer away from college — became Comcast's president.

In 1992 Comcast bought Metromedia's Philadelphia-area cellular operations and began investing in fiber-optic and wireless phone companies. By then the company was a major QVC shareholder. With an eye toward Comcast's programming needs, Brian persuaded FOX network head Barry Diller to become QVC's chairman. But when Diller tried to use QVC to take over CBS, Comcast bought control of QVC in 1994 to quash the bid, which went against cross-ownership bans. To pay for QVC, Comcast had to sell its 20% stake in cable firm Heritage Communications in 1995. Diller left the company (he now oversees InterActiveCorp, parent of QVC's archrival HSN). Also in 1995 Comcast funded former Disney executive Richard Frank to launch the C3 (Comcast Content and Communication) programming company.

Comcast, TCI, and Cox sold Teleport, their local phone venture, to AT&T in 1998, but Comcast turned around and bought long-distance service provider GlobalCom (now Comcast Telecommunications). Comcast sold its cellular operations to SBC Communications for $1.7 billion in 1999.

The company also agreed to acquire rival MediaOne in 1999, but soon after the $54 billion deal was struck, AT&T weighed in with a $58 billion offer. Comcast dropped its bid for MediaOne when AT&T offered to sell Comcast 2 million cable subscribers. More than a million of those subscribers came from Pennsylvania cable operator Lenfest Communications, which Comcast bought in 2000 from AT&T and the Lenfest family in a $7 billion deal.

In 2001 Comcast completed a systems swap with Adelphia Communications and completed the $2.75 billion purchase of systems in six states from AT&T. Also that year Comcast offered to buy the rest of AT&T's cable operations for $44.5 billion in stock and $13.5 billion in assumed debt. AT&T's board rejected the offer, but left the door open for another bid. That December, after it had heard proposals from Time Warner and Cox, AT&T agreed to sell its cable unit to Comcast for $47 billion in stock and $25 billion in assumed debt. C. Michael Armstrong came from AT&T to Comcast, and was named chairman. About 18 months after the AT&T Broadband deal, Comcast had reduced its headcount by 10,000 people.

Also in 2001, Comcast sold its 57% stake in QVC to Liberty Media for about $7.7 billion. When Armstrong stepped down as chairman in 2004, president and CEO Brian Roberts was named successor.

Comcast had owned a 21% stake in rival Time Warner Cable (TWC), which made for strange bedfellows, but the companies managed to unwind their relationship in mid-2006. The two rivals purchased all of troubled Adelphia Communications' cable television assets. Adelphia shareholders received about $9 billion from TWC and $3.5 billion in cash from Comcast, which also contributed its TWC stake to the deal. Comcast no longer owns any part of TWC.

## EXECUTIVES

**Chairman and CEO:** Brian L. Roberts, age 47, $5,503,454 pay
**Vice Chairman:** Julian A. Brodsky, age 73
**EVP and COO; President, Comcast Cable:** Stephen B. (Steve) Burke, age 48, $2,001,000 pay
**EVP, Co-CFO, and Treasurer:** John R. Alchin, age 59, $1,183,889 pay
**EVP and Co-CFO:** Michael J. Angelakis, age 42
**EVP:** David L. Cohen, age 51, $1,201,000 pay
**SVP, Chief Accounting Officer, and Controller:** Lawrence J. Salva, age 50
**SVP, General Counsel, and Secretary:** Arthur R. Block, age 51
**SVP Content Development:** Elizabeth (Liz) Schimel
**SVP Corporate Development:** Robert S. Pick, age 53
**SVP Marketing:** Marvin O. Davis
**SVP Strategic Planning:** Mark A. Coblitz
**SVP Investor Relations:** Marlene S. Dooner
**VP and General Auditor:** Kamal Dua
**VP and Senior Deputy General Counsel:** Marc A. Rockford
**VP Administration:** Karen Dougherty Buchholz
**VP Corporate Communications:** D'Arcy Rudnay, age 50
**VP Human Resources; SVP Human Resources, Comcast Cable:** Charisse R. Lillie, age 54
**Senior Director of Public Affairs; and VP, The Comcast Foundation:** Diane Dietz
**Auditors:** Deloitte & Touche LLP

## LOCATIONS

**HQ:** Comcast Corporation
1500 Market St., Philadelphia, PA 19102
**Phone:** 215-665-1700 **Fax:** 215-981-7790
**Web:** www.comcast.com

Comcast has cable operations in 39 states.

## PRODUCTS/OPERATIONS

**2006 Sales**

| | % of total |
|---|---|
| Video | 63 |
| High-speed Internet | 21 |
| Phone | 4 |
| Advertising | 6 |
| Other | 4 |
| Franchise fees | 2 |
| **Total** | **100** |

**Selected Investments and Subsidiaries**

CN8-The Comcast Network (regional and local programming)
Comcast Cable Communications, Inc. (cable TV operations)
Comcast Spectacor, L.P. (66%, live sports, concerts, and other events)
- Philadelphia 76ers (National Basketball Association team)
- Philadelphia Flyers Hockey Club (National Hockey League team)
- Philadelphia Sports Media (78%, dba Comcast SportsNet, regional sports programming and events)
  - BravesVision
  - Comcast SportsNet Chicago
  - Comcast SportsNet Philadelphia
  - Comcast SportsNet Mid-Atlantic
  - Comcast SportsNet West (Sacramento, CA)
  - The Dallas Cowboys Channel
  - FalconsVision
  - SportsNet New York (partial stake, coverage of the New York Mets)

E! Entertainment Television, Inc. (60%, entertainment-related news and original programming)
- Style Network (fashion-related programming)

G4 Media, Inc. (83%)
- G4 — Video Game Television (video and computer game programming)

The Golf Channel (99.9%, golf-related programming)
iN DEMAND L.L.C. (54%, pay-per-view programming)
International Networks, LLC
- AZN Television (Asian American television network)

Metro-Goldwyn-Mayer (20%, film and television production)
Outdoor Life Network (outdoor activities)

## COMPETITORS

AT&T
Cablevision Systems
Charter Communications
Cox Communications
DIRECTV
EchoStar Communications
ESPN
FOX Sports
Insight Communications
Liberty Media
NBC Universal Cable
Pegasus Communications
RCN
Time Warner Cable
ValueVision Media
Viacom

## HISTORICAL FINANCIALS

Company Type: Public

**Income Statement** FYE: December 31

| | REVENUE ($ mil.) | NET INCOME ($ mil.) | NET PROFIT MARGIN | EMPLOYEES |
|---|---|---|---|---|
| **12/06** | 24,966 | 2,533 | 10.1% | 90,000 |
| **12/05** | 22,255 | 928 | 4.2% | 80,000 |
| **12/04** | 20,307 | 970 | 4.8% | 74,000 |
| **12/03** | 18,348 | 3,240 | 17.7% | 68,000 |
| **12/02** | 12,460 | (274) | — | 82,000 |
| **Annual Growth** | 19.0% | — | — | 2.4% |

**2006 Year-End Financials**

Debt ratio: 68.0%
Return on equity: 6.2%
Cash ($ mil.): 2,974
Current ratio: 0.70
Long-term debt ($ mil.): 27,992
No. of shares (mil.): 2,060
Dividends
Yield: —
Payout: —
Market value ($ mil.): 58,143

**Stock History** NASDAQ (GS): CMCSA

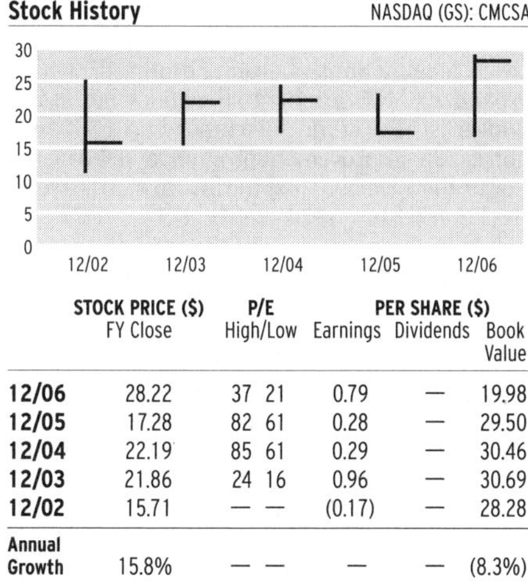


| | STOCK PRICE ($) FY Close | P/E High | P/E Low | PER SHARE ($) Earnings | Dividends | Book Value |
|---|---|---|---|---|---|---|
| **12/06** | 28.22 | 37 | 21 | 0.79 | — | 19.98 |
| **12/05** | 17.28 | 82 | 61 | 0.28 | — | 29.50 |
| **12/04** | 22.19 | 85 | 61 | 0.29 | — | 30.46 |
| **12/03** | 21.86 | 24 | 16 | 0.96 | — | 30.69 |
| **12/02** | 15.71 | — | — | (0.17) | — | 28.28 |
| **Annual Growth** | 15.8% | — | — | — | — | (8.3%) |

# Comerica Incorporated

If you have a cosigner, Comerica will be your copilot. Organized into three business lines, the bank holding company's Business Bank division focuses on business and asset-based lending to middle-market, large corporate, and government entities; it offers lines of credit and international trade finance, among other services. The Retail Bank provides small business and consumer banking services including deposits, mortgages, small-business loans, and merchant services. The Wealth and Institutional Management arm deals in private banking and asset management, trust products, insurance, and retirement services. Comerica has around 460 branches primarily in California, Arizona, Nevada, Colorado, and Washington.

The company also has offices throughout the Midwest, Northeast, and in Mexico and Canada.

Comerica has long been a leading commercial lender in the US, catering to garden-variety small and midsized firms, as well as to municipal governments and multinationals. The company remains committed to its core small- and middle-market clientele. (Around half of Comerica's assets are wrapped up in commercial real estate and operating loans.)

At the end of 2006 Comerica sold its 90% stake in asset manager Munder Capital Management to a group including private equity firms and the Munder management team for $302 million. Comerica, which kept Munder's World Asset Management unit, is Munder's biggest client.

## HISTORY

Comerica traces its history to 1849, when Michigan governor Epaphroditus Ransom tapped Elon Farnsworth to found the Detroit Savings Fund Institute. At that time Detroit was a major transit point for shipping between Lakes Huron and Erie, as well as between the US and Canada. The bank grew with the town and in 1871 became Detroit Savings Bank.

By 1899 Detroit was one of the top 10 US manufacturing centers and, thanks to a group of local tinkerers and mechanics that included Henry Ford, was on the brink of even greater growth. Detroit Savings grew also, fueled by the deposits of workers whom Ford paid up to $5 a day. Detroit Savings was not, however, the beneficiary of significant business with the auto makers; for corporate banking they turned first to eastern banks and then to large local banks in which they had an interest.

Detroit boomed during the 1920s as America went car-crazy, but after the 1929 crash Detroiters defaulted on mortgages by the thousands. By 1933 Michigan's banks were in such disarray that the governor shut them down three weeks prior to the federal bank holiday. Detroit Savings was one of only four Detroit banks to reopen. None of the major banks associated with auto companies survived.

A few months later Manufacturers National Bank, backed by a group of investors that included Edsel Ford (Henry's son), was founded. Although its start was rocky, Manufacturers National was on firm footing by 1936; around the same time, Detroit Savings Bank renamed itself the Detroit Bank to appeal to a more commercial clientele.

WWII and the postwar boom put Detroit back in gear. In the 1950s and 1960s, both banks thrived. In the 1970s statewide branching was permitted and both banks formed holding companies (DETROITBANK Corp. and Manufacturers National Corp.) and expanded throughout Michigan. As they grew, they added services; when Detroit's economy was hit by the oil shocks of the 1970s, these diversifications helped them through the lean years.

DETROITBANK opened a trust operation in Florida in 1982 to maintain its relationship with retired customers and renamed itself Comerica to be less area-specific. Manufacturers National also began operating in Florida (1983) and made acquisitions in the Chicago area (1987). Comerica went farther afield, buying banks in Texas (1988) and California (1991).

Following the national consolidation trend, in 1992 Comerica and Manufacturers National merged (retaining the Comerica name) but did not fully integrate until 1994, when the new entity began making more acquisitions. To increase sales and develop its consumer business, the company reorganized in 1996. It sold its Illinois bank and its Michigan customs brokerage business and acquired Fairlane Associates to expand its property/casualty insurance line.

As part of its strategy to have operations in all three NAFTA countries, Comerica opened a bank in Mexico in 1997 and one in Canada in 1998. That year it dropped $66 million for the naming rights to the Detroit Tigers' baseball stadium, which opened as Comerica Park in 2000. It also started a Web-based payment system for its international trade business.

To fortify its business lending operations in California, Comerica bought Imperial Bancorp in 2001. At the beginning of 2002, chairman Eugene Miller handed the CEO reins to Ralph Babb, who had been CFO. Later that year, Babb became chairman as well.

## EXECUTIVES

**Chairman, President, and CEO, Comerica Incorporated and Comerica Bank:** Ralph W. Babb Jr., age 58, $2,475,069 pay
**Vice Chairman, Business Bank, Comerica Incorporated and Comerica Bank:** Joseph J. Buttigieg III, age 61, $1,557,875 pay
**EVP and CFO:** Elizabeth S. Acton, age 55, $1,012,263 pay
**EVP and CIO:** John R. Beran, age 54
**EVP and Chief Credit Officer:** Dale E. Greene, age 60
**EVP, Corporate Human Resources:** Jacquelyn H. Wolf, age 45
**EVP and General Auditor:** David E. Duprey, age 49
**EVP, Governance, Regulatory Relations, and Legal Affairs, Chief Legal Officer, and Secretary:** Jon W. Bilstrom, age 61
**EVP, National Business Finance:** Ronald P. Marcinelli
**EVP and Director of Operations Services:** Paul R. Obermeyer
**EVP; President and CEO, Comerica Bank, Western Division:** J. Michael Fulton, age 58
**SVP, Anti-Money Laundering, Fraud Prevention, and Investigative Services:** Susan R. Joseph
**SVP, Asset Quality Review:** Edward T. Gwilt
**SVP and Chief Economist:** Dana Johnson, age 57
**Auditors:** Ernst & Young LLP

## LOCATIONS

**HQ:** Comerica Incorporated
Comerica Tower at Detroit Center,
500 Woodward Ave., MC 3391, Detroit, MI 48226
**Phone:** 313-222-4000 **Fax:** 313-965-4648
**Web:** www.comerica.com

## PRODUCTS/OPERATIONS

**2006 Sales**

| | $ mil. | % of total |
|---|---|---|
| Interest | | |
| Loans, including fees | 3,216 | 75 |
| Investments | 206 | 5 |
| Noninterest | | |
| Service charges on deposit accounts | 218 | 5 |
| Fees | 215 | 5 |
| Fiduciary income | 180 | 4 |
| Other | 255 | 6 |
| **Total** | **4,290** | **100** |

**2006 Assets**

| | $ mil. | % of total |
|---|---|---|
| Cash & due from banks | 1,434 | 2 |
| Short-term investments | 2,959 | 5 |
| Investment securities available for sale | 3,662 | 6 |
| Commercial loans | 26,265 | 45 |
| Real estate construction loans | 4,203 | 7 |
| Commercial mortgage loans | 9,659 | 17 |
| Residential mortgage loans | 1,677 | 3 |
| Consumer loans | 2,423 | 5 |
| Lease financing | 1,353 | 2 |
| International loans | 1,851 | 3 |
| Other assets | 2,515 | 5 |
| **Total** | **58,001** | **100** |

**Selected Subsidiaries**

Cass & Co.
Comerica Assurance Ltd.
Comerica Bank
Comerica Bank & Trust, National Association
Comerica do Brasil Participacoes e Servicos Ltda.
Humphrey & Co.
Pacific Bancard Association, Inc.
Professional Life Underwriters Services, Inc.
Rica & Co., Ltd.
ROC Technologies Inc.
VRB Corp.
WAM Holdings, Inc.
Wilson, Kemp & Associates, Inc.
World Asset Management, Inc.

## COMPETITORS

| | |
|---|---|
| Bank of America | National City |
| Citigroup | Northern Trust |
| Cullen/Frost Bankers | SunTrust |
| Fifth Third | SVB Financial |
| Huntington Bancshares | U.S. Bancorp |
| LaSalle Bank | Wells Fargo |

## HISTORICAL FINANCIALS

Company Type: Public

**Income Statement** FYE: December 31

| | ASSETS ($ mil.) | NET INCOME ($ mil.) | INCOME AS % OF ASSETS | EMPLOYEES |
|---|---|---|---|---|
| **12/06** | 58,001 | 893 | 1.5% | 11,270 |
| **12/05** | 53,013 | 861 | 1.6% | 11,343 |
| **12/04** | 51,766 | 757 | 1.5% | 11,514 |
| **12/03** | 52,592 | 661 | 1.3% | 11,854 |
| **12/02** | 53,301 | 601 | 1.1% | 11,808 |
| **Annual Growth** | 2.1% | 10.4% | — | (1.2%) |

**2006 Year-End Financials**

Equity as % of assets: 8.9%
Return on assets: 1.6%
Return on equity: 17.5%
Long-term debt ($ mil.): 5,949
No. of shares (mil.): 158
Dividends
Yield: 4.0%
Payout: 43.0%
Market value ($ mil.): 9,246
Sales ($ mil.): 4,290

**Stock History** NYSE: CMA

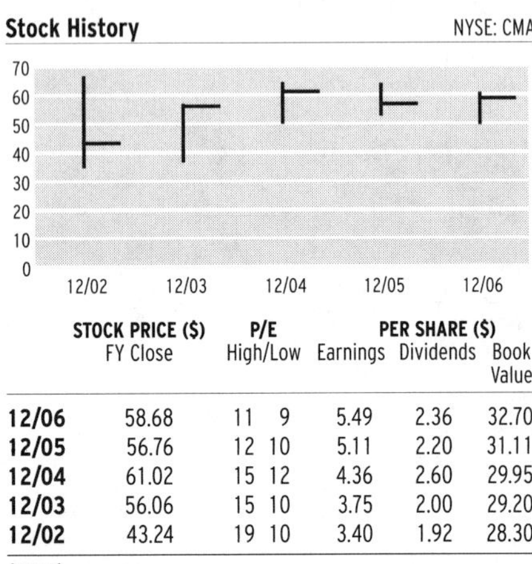

| | STOCK PRICE ($) FY Close | P/E High | P/E Low | PER SHARE ($) Earnings | Dividends | Book Value |
|---|---|---|---|---|---|---|
| **12/06** | 58.68 | 11 | 9 | 5.49 | 2.36 | 32.70 |
| **12/05** | 56.76 | 12 | 10 | 5.11 | 2.20 | 31.11 |
| **12/04** | 61.02 | 15 | 12 | 4.36 | 2.60 | 29.95 |
| **12/03** | 56.06 | 15 | 10 | 3.75 | 2.00 | 29.20 |
| **12/02** | 43.24 | 19 | 10 | 3.40 | 1.92 | 28.30 |
| **Annual Growth** | 7.9% | — | — | 12.7% | 5.3% | 3.7% |

# Commercial Metals

Commercial Metals Company (CMC) wants to steel the limelight. CMC's manufacturing segment includes domestic mills (four minimills and a copper tubing minimill) and a domestic fabrication mill (rebar and tubing minimills). The unit also runs a heat-treating plant and plants for making steel fence posts, castellated steel beams, and steel joists. Its marketing and distribution segment buys and sells primary and secondary metals, fabricated metals, and other industrial metals. CMC's recycling unit operates more than 34 secondary metals-processing plants that shred, shear, and pulverize scrap metal, which is then sold to steel mills and nonferrous ingot producers. The CMCZ facility in Poland also makes wire rod.

CMC's marketing and trading segment also operates through nearly 20 international trading offices. It brokers industrial products that include primary and secondary metals, fabricated metals, chemicals, and industrial minerals to customers in the steel, nonferrous metals, metal fabrication, chemical, refractory, and transportation industries.

Despite the gloomy outlook for the steel industry, CMC has managed to make a profit in nearly every quarter for the past 25 years. The company's vertical integration allows for a flagging segment to be compensated for by another's success in tough times. For example, when scrap prices are low, CMC's recycling centers feel the pain, but the company's minimills rake it in.

In 2006 the company acquired Tucson-based concrete products supplier Brost Forming Supply, Inc., and almost all of the assets of Yonack Iron & Metal Co. and Metallic Resources, Inc. Later that year the company bought Cherokee Supply, a provider of tools and supplies for the construction, oilfield, and industrial sectors. The acquisition has become part of CMC Construction Services division and operates under the CMC Cherokee name. Quick on the heels of the Cherokee deal came CMC's purchase of Concrete Formtek Services, a renter of concrete forming and shoring equipment. Concrete Formtek Services was renamed CMC Formtek and became part of CMC Construction Services.

In 2007 CMC bought Bouras Industries, Inc. for $146 million. The deal includes four of Bouras' operating subsidiaries: United Steel Deck (steel decking), New Columbia Joist (steel joists), ABA Trucking Corporation (delivery services for United Steel Deck and New Columbia Joist), and Nicholas J. Bouras, Inc. (sales, marketing, and engineering for the other three subsidiaries). The assets of Bouras Industries will operate as CMC Joist and Deck and will become part of CMC's Domestic Fabrication division.

## HISTORY

Russian immigrant Moses Feldman moved to Dallas in 1914 and founded scrap metal company American Iron & Metal the next year. In the 1920s Feldman suffered a heart attack, and his son Jake helped out with the business. Low metal prices hurt the company during the Depression. In 1932 Jake formed a two-man brokerage firm, Commercial Metals Company (CMC), which was combined as a partnership with his father's scrap metal operations. Moses Feldman died in 1937. CMC was incorporated in 1946 and began buying related businesses during the 1950s.

CMC was listed on the American Stock Exchange in 1960. It soon expanded geographically, buying a stake in Texas steelmaker Structural Metals (1963). In 1965 it formed Commercial Metals Europa (the Netherlands), its first overseas subsidiary, and Commonwealth Metal (New York). By 1966 CMC was one of the world's top three scrap metal companies. It bought copper tube manufacturer Howell Metals (Virginia) in 1968, the remainder of Structural Metals, and major stakes in seven affiliated businesses. Over 10 years, CMC opened trading offices around the world. Business continued to grow throughout the 1970s. The company added a small minimill in Arkansas (1971) and certain assets of General Export Iron and Metal in Texas (1976).

CMC began trading on the New York Stock Exchange in 1982. The next year the company bought Connors Steel (Alabama), its third minimill. By the end of 1984 CMC was operating 20 metal recycling plants from Texas to Florida.

The company modernized its minimills in the 1990s. CMC acquired small scrap-metal operations and Shepler's, a concrete-related products business, in 1994. Also that year CEO Stanley Rabin completed the $50 million purchase of Owen Steel (a South Carolina minimill), which expanded CMC's reach into the Mid-Atlantic and Southeast. The company wrapped up a $30 million capital improvement program at its Alabama minimill in 1995 — just in time to ride a strong steel market to record profits.

Although a correction in the steel and metals industry depressed prices in 1996, CMC achieved record sales and profits that fiscal year. However, both dipped the next year, with lower steel and scrap prices widely attributed to an influx of foreign imports. CMC strengthened its vertical integration in 1997 by acquiring Allegheny Heat Treating (heat-treatment services to steel mills) and two auto salvage plants in Florida.

During 1998 CMC moved into the Midwest, buying a metals recycling company in Missouri. It boosted global operations by purchasing a metals trading firm in Australia and entering a joint venture with Trinec, a Czech Republic steel mill, to sell steel products in Germany. The next year CMC completed construction of a rolling mill in South Carolina and renovations at an Alabama plant; both were expected to reduce production-related costs and increase efficiency to help counter slumping steel prices.

In 2000 CMC picked up three rebar fabricators — two in California (Fontana Steel and C&M Steel), and one in Florida (Suncoast Steel).

In late 2001 the company acquired Florida-based Allform, a maker of concrete-related forms and supplies. The following year Commercial Metals started manufacturing its corrosion-resistant stainless steel clad products in its new facilities in South Carolina.

Marvin Selig, founder and chairman of the company's steel group, retired in August 2002 after serving over 50 years in the steel industry.

In 2003 CMC purchased a 71% stake in Poland-based Huta Zawiercie S.A. for approximately $50 million. CMC purchased the assets of J. L. Davidson Company, a rebar fabricating operation based in California, in 2004.

## EXECUTIVES

**Chairman:** Stanley A. Rabin, age 68, $2,990,000 pay
**President, CEO, and Director:** Murray R. McClean, age 58, $1,881,250 pay
**EVP; CEO and President, Steel:** Russell B. Rinn, age 48
**EVP; President, Marketing and Distribution:** Hanns Zoellner, age 58
**EVP and Regional Manager, Rebar Fab Far East:** Jeffrey H. (Jeff) Selig, age 50
**EVP and Divisional Manager, Rebar and CRP:** Binh K. Huynh, age 53
**SVP and CFO:** William B. Larson, age 53
**SVP, General Counsel, and Secretary:** David M. Sudbury, age 61
**President, Cometals:** Eliezer Skornicki
**President, Commonwealth Metals:** Eugene L. Vastola
**President, Dallas Trading:** J. Matthew Kramer
**President, International Division, Asia and Australia:** Kevin S. Aitken
**President, Howell Metal:** James K. Forkovitch
**Treasurer:** Louis A. Federle, age 58
**Director, Public Relations:** Debbie Okle
**Director, Human Resources:** Elva Arista
**Auditors:** Deloitte & Touche LLP

## LOCATIONS

**HQ:** Commercial Metals Company
6565 N. MacArthur Blvd., Ste. 800,
Irving, TX 75039
**Phone:** 214-689-4300 **Fax:** 214-689-5886
**Web:** www.commercialmetals.com

CMC operates manufacturing and recycling facilities in Mexico, Poland, and the US; it has trading offices in Australia, China, Germany, Hong Kong, Singapore, Switzerland, the UK, and the US.

### 2006 Sales

| | $ mil. | % of total |
|---|---|---|
| US | 4,803.2 | 63 |
| Europe | 1,221.6 | 16 |
| Asia | 809.5 | 11 |
| Australia & New Zealand | 446.5 | 6 |
| Other regions | 275.1 | 4 |
| **Total** | **7,555.9** | **100** |

## PRODUCTS/OPERATIONS

### 2005 Sales

| | $ mil. | % of total |
|---|---|---|
| Marketing & distribution | 2,824.6 | 37 |
| Domestic fabrication | 1,770.3 | 24 |
| Recycling | 1,253.1 | 17 |
| Domestic mills | 1,149.7 | 15 |
| CMCZ | 553.6 | 7 |
| Corporate | 4.6 | — |
| **Total** | **7,555.9** | **100** |

## COMPETITORS

AK Steel Holding Corporation
BHP Billiton
Blue Tee
Chaparral Steel
Connell Limited Partnership
David J. Joseph
Evraz Steel Mills
Gerdau Ameristeel
Keywell
Metal Management
Metals USA
Nucor
OmniSource
Quanex Corporation
Roanoke Bar Division
Schnitzer Steel
Severstal North America
Tang Industries
Tube City
United States Steel
Worthington Industries

## HISTORICAL FINANCIALS

Company Type: Public

### Income Statement

FYE: August 31

| | REVENUE ($ mil.) | NET INCOME ($ mil.) | NET PROFIT MARGIN | EMPLOYEES |
|---|---|---|---|---|
| **8/06** | 7,556 | 356 | 4.7% | 11,734 |
| **8/05** | 6,593 | 286 | 4.3% | 11,027 |
| **8/04** | 4,768 | 132 | 2.8% | 10,604 |
| **8/03** | 2,876 | 19 | 0.7% | 7,873 |
| **8/02** | 2,447 | 41 | 1.7% | 7,728 |
| **Annual Growth** | 32.6% | 72.2% | — | 11.0% |

### 2006 Year-End Financials

Debt ratio: 26.4%
Return on equity: 33.6%
Cash ($ mil.): 181
Current ratio: 1.81
Long-term debt ($ mil.): 322

No. of shares (mil.): 118
Dividends
Yield: 0.8%
Payout: 5.9%
Market value ($ mil.): 2,545

### Stock History

NYSE: CMC

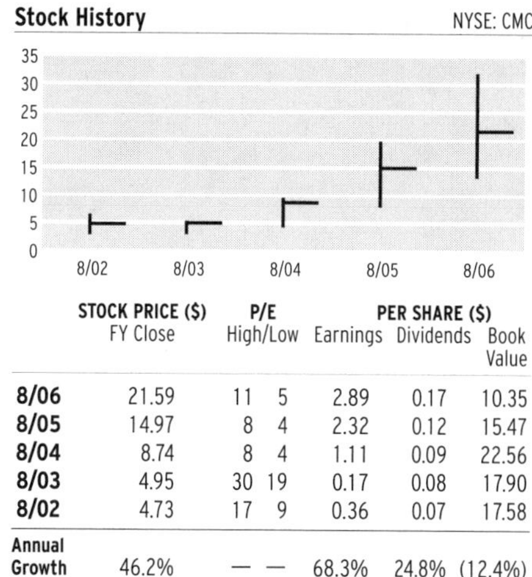


| | STOCK PRICE ($) FY Close | P/E High | P/E Low | PER SHARE ($) Earnings | Dividends | Book Value |
|---|---|---|---|---|---|---|
| **8/06** | 21.59 | 11 | 5 | 2.89 | 0.17 | 10.35 |
| **8/05** | 14.97 | 8 | 4 | 2.32 | 0.12 | 15.47 |
| **8/04** | 8.74 | 8 | 4 | 1.11 | 0.09 | 22.56 |
| **8/03** | 4.95 | 30 | 19 | 0.17 | 0.08 | 17.90 |
| **8/02** | 4.73 | 17 | 9 | 0.36 | 0.07 | 17.58 |
| **Annual Growth** | 46.2% | — | — | 68.3% | 24.8% | (12.4%) |

# Computer Sciences

Providing a wide array of consulting and outsourcing services isn't rocket science, it's computer science. Computer Sciences Corporation (CSC) is one of the world's leading providers of systems integration and other technology services, including application development, data hosting, networking, and management consulting. It is also a leading provider of business process outsourcing (BPO) services in such areas as billing and payment processing, customer relationship management (CRM), and human resources. A major government and defense contractor, federal agencies account for about a third of CSC's revenue.

CSC's board of directors has confirmed that it is exploring the potential sale of the company. CSC has also announced plans to cut 5,000 jobs.

CSC has benefited from an increased interest in outsourcing as a means to cut costs. It won several big services contracts in 2004 and 2005, including a seven-year, $1.6 billion extension on an existing outsourcing assignment with General Dynamics. It also extended its relationship with Ascension Health, inking a 10-year, $1.35 billion contract under which CSC will manage the health system's data networks and telecommunications systems. The company also managed to increase its government contracting work, winning an 11-year contract worth nearly $590 million to help the Federal Aviation Administration upgrade and modernize its air traffic control systems. It is also involved in a 15-year project to support eight Warfare Center divisions of the US Navy that could net CSC about $950 million.

The company has also made some moves to trim its own fat. In 2005 it sold some operations connected to its DynCorp Technical Services unit, including DynCorp International and DynMarine, to Varitas Capital for about $850 million.

CSC is looking to expand its presence in international markets, which now account for about 40% of the company's revenue, especially in Germany and the UK.

In late 2006 CSC acquired government solutions company Datatrac Information Services. Datatrac will operate as part of its Enforcement Security and Intelligence division and is expected to better position CSC to compete for work with the US Department of Homeland Security and other federal agencies. In 2007 the company acquired IT specialist Covansys in a deal valued at $1.3 billion.

## HISTORY

Computer Sciences Corporation (CSC) was founded in Los Angeles in 1959 by Fletcher Jones and Roy Nutt to write software for manufacturers such as Honeywell. In 1963 CSC became the first software company to go public. Three years later it signed a $5.5 million contract to support NASA's computation laboratory. Annual sales had climbed to just over $53 million by 1968.

In 1969 CSC agreed to merge with Western Union, but the deal ultimately fell through. When Jones died in a plane crash in 1972, William Hoover, a former NASA executive who had come aboard eight years earlier, became chairman and CEO. Under Hoover, CSC began transforming itself into a systems integrator. In 1986, when federal contracts still accounted for 70% of sales, the company started diversifying into the commercial sector.

In 1991 CSC signed a 10-year, $3 billion contract with defense supplier General Dynamics. In 1995 Hoover, after more than three decades with CSC, stepped down as CEO (remaining chairman until 1997); he was succeeded by president and COO Van Honeycutt. Also that year CSC bought Germany's largest independent computer services company, Ploenzke. In 1996 CSC acquired insurance services provider Continuum Company for $1.5 billion.

In 1998 CSC found itself on the other side of the bargaining table with a $9.8 billion hostile takeover bid from software giant Computer Associates (now CA). After weeks of contentious battle, CA withdrew its bid. That same year the IRS chose CSC to head the PRIME Alliance team that includes IBM, Lucent, and Unisys in a multibillion-dollar project to update the agency's computer system.

That year CSC continued its acquisition spree, buying consulting firms in Europe including Informatica Group (Italy), KMPG Peat Marwick (France), Pergamon (Germany), and SYS-AID (the Netherlands). In 1999 CSC inked an 11-year, $1 billion deal to manage the back-office functions of energy trading giant Enron's energy services unit. Also in 1999 the company acquired information technology company Nichols Research.

CSC in 2000 boosted its expertise in financial software and services with the cash acquisition of Mynd Corporation (formerly Policy Management Systems) for an estimated $570 million. Also that year CSC signed two large outsourcing contracts — a seven-year, $3 billion deal with telecom equipment maker Nortel Networks that arranged for Nortel to transfer 2,000 employees to CSC, and a $1 billion outsourcing and application development agreement with AT&T.

The company continued to make large deals in 2001, including contracts with the National Security Agency (NSA) and BAE SYSTEMS. The next year saw more of the same: CSC was contracted to operate a central data exchange for the US Environmental Protection Agency, and to collaborate on missile defense systems engineering for the US Army. CSC acquired Defense Department services contractor DynCorp for about $900 million in 2003, doubling the size of its federal services division. (The company sold off various DynCorp units two years later, recouping about $850 million.)

Also in 2003 it won a 10-year, $2.4 billion contract to provide a new network and voice, data, mobile, and Internet services to the UK's Royal Mail. However, it was beat out in 2005 by rival EDS in a bid for a $4 billion networking assignment with the British Ministry of Defence. In Asia, CSC acquired the 27% of subsidiary CSA Holdings it didn't already own.

President and COO Michael Laphen assumed the CEO's chair in 2007, inheriting the position from Honeycutt. Laphen also became chairman that year.

## EXECUTIVES

**Chairman, President, and CEO:** Michael W. (Mike) Laphen, age 56
**Corporate VP and CFO:** Michael E. Keane, age 51
**VP and Controller:** Donald G. DeBuck, age 49
**VP and Treasurer:** Thomas R. Irvin, age 57
**VP, Secretary, and General Counsel:** Hayward D. Fisk, age 64, $448,800 pay
**VP Corporate Communications and Marketing:** K. Peter Maneri
**VP Corporate Development:** Paul T. Tucker, age 58, $433,875 pay
**VP Human Resources:** Nathan (Gus) Siekierka
**VP Global Legal Compliance:** Harvey N. Bernstein, age 59
**VP Supply Chain Management:** Martin Leidemer
**Director of Communications and Marketing:** Chuck Taylor
**Director of Investor Relations:** Bill Lackey
**Auditors:** Deloitte & Touche LLP

## LOCATIONS

**HQ:** Computer Sciences Corporation
2100 E. Grand Ave., El Segundo, CA 90245
**Phone:** 310-615-0311 **Fax:** 310-322-9768
**Web:** www.csc.com

Computer Sciences Corporation has operations in more than 80 countries.

### 2007 Sales

| | $ mil. | % of total |
|---|---|---|
| US | 9,223.2 | 62 |
| Europe | | |
| UK | 1,900.3 | 13 |
| Other countries | 2,246.0 | 15 |
| Other regions | 1,487.1 | 10 |
| **Total** | **14,856.6** | **100** |

## PRODUCTS/OPERATIONS

### 2007 Sales

| | $ mil. | % of total |
|---|---|---|
| Global Commercial Sector | 9,506.3 | 64 |
| North American Public Sector | 5,350.3 | 36 |
| **Total** | **14,856.6** | **100** |

### Selected Service Areas

Application outsourcing
Business process outsourcing
Credit services (consumer credit reporting)
Customer relationship management
Data hosting
Enterprise application integration
Knowledge management
Management consulting
Risk management
Security
Supply chain management

## COMPETITORS

Accenture
ADP
Affiliated Computer Services
Atos Origin
BearingPoint
Booz Allen
Capgemini
CIBER
Convergys
Deloitte Consulting
EDS
Getronics
HP Technology Solutions Group
IBM Global Services
Infosys
Keane
LogicaCMG
Perot Systems
Titan Group
Towers Perrin
Unisys
Wipro Technologies

## HISTORICAL FINANCIALS

Company Type: Public

### Income Statement

FYE: Friday nearest March 31

| | REVENUE ($ mil.) | NET INCOME ($ mil.) | NET PROFIT MARGIN | EMPLOYEES |
|---|---|---|---|---|
| **3/07** | 14,857 | 389 | 2.6% | 79,000 |
| **3/06** | 14,616 | 634 | 4.3% | 79,000 |
| **3/05** | 14,059 | 810 | 5.8% | 79,000 |
| **3/04** | 14,768 | 519 | 3.5% | 90,000 |
| **3/03** | 11,347 | 440 | 3.9% | 90,000 |
| **Annual Growth** | 7.0% | (3.1%) | — | (3.2%) |

### 2007 Year-End Financials

| | |
|---|---|
| Debt ratio: 24.0% | No. of shares (mil.): 173 |
| Return on equity: 6.1% | Dividends |
| Cash ($ mil.): 1,050 | Yield: — |
| Current ratio: 1.28 | Payout: — |
| Long-term debt ($ mil.): 1,412 | Market value ($ mil.): 9,035 |

### Stock History

NYSE: CSC

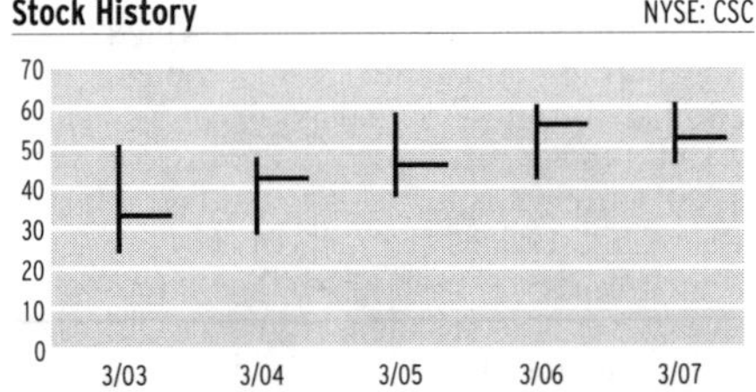


| | STOCK PRICE ($) FY Close | P/E High | P/E Low | PER SHARE ($) Earnings | Dividends | Book Value |
|---|---|---|---|---|---|---|
| **3/07** | 52.13 | 28 | 21 | 2.16 | — | 33.96 |
| **3/06** | 55.55 | 18 | 13 | 3.38 | — | 36.16 |
| **3/05** | 45.42 | 14 | 9 | 4.22 | — | 33.97 |
| **3/04** | 42.16 | 17 | 10 | 2.75 | — | 29.30 |
| **3/03** | 32.93 | 20 | 10 | 2.54 | — | 24.67 |
| **Annual Growth** | 12.2% | — | — | (4.0%) | — | 8.3% |

# ConAgra Foods

ConAgra Foods fills Americans' refrigerators, freezers, and pantries and, ultimately, their tummies. The company is a US top food producer, offering packaged and frozen foods. ConAgra's brands include Banquet, Chef Boyardee, Egg Beaters, Healthy Choice, Hunt's, Jiffy, Orville Redenbacher's, PAM, Slim Jim, and Van Camp's. It is also one of the country's largest foodservice suppliers and offers shelf-stable foods, seafood, and dairy products. The company has sold off its agricultural segments and a number of non-core brands in order to produce only branded and value-added packaged foods.

ConAgra Foods also makes shelf-stable and frozen foods under names that include Banquet, Hunt's, Marie Callender's, Peter Pan, and Wesson. The company has shifted away from its beginnings as a commodity producer and has tried to recast itself as "America's favorite food company." Brisk restructuring and shedding of nonfood-related businesses have allowed the company to better pay attention to consumer-aimed brands, including Chef Boyardee, PAM, and others.

In February 2007 salmonella was found in some of the company's Peter Pan and Great Value (a Wal-Mart product) brands of peanut butter, forcing a nation-wide recall of the peanut butter bearing the product code involved. Salmonella food poisoning was linked to some 600 people in 47 states. No deaths related to the peanut better were confirmed. The recall went back to October 2004.

ConAgra shut down the Sylvester, Georgia, plant that was involved in the outbreak and reopened it in August 2007, having spent $15 million on renovation, which included repairing the roof, installing new equipment, and creating a manufacturing process that better separated raw materials from the finished peanut butter.

AS part of its strategy to add to its brand-name offerings, in 2007 ConAgra acquired Alexia Foods, a maker of natural frozen potatoes, appetizers, and artisan breads. The price was not disclosed. Later that year the company paid a penalty of $45 million in the wake of SEC charges that alleged the company had misreported its profits for the fiscal years 1999, 2000, and 2001.

Capital Research and Management Company owns almost 8% of ConAgra; Barrow, Hanley, Mewhinney & Strauss owns 7%; and State Street Bank and Trust owns about 6%.

## HISTORY

Alva Kinney founded Nebraska Consolidated Mills in 1919 by combining the operations of four Nebraska grain mills. It did not expand outside Nebraska until it opened a mill and feed processing plant in Alabama in 1942.

Consolidated Mills developed Duncan Hines cake mix in the 1950s. But Duncan Hines failed to raise a large enough market share, and the company sold it to Procter & Gamble in 1956. Consolidated Mills used the proceeds to expand, opening a flour and feed mill in Puerto Rico the next year. In the 1960s, while competitors were moving into prepared foods, the firm expanded into animal feeds and poultry processing. By 1970 it had poultry processing plants in Alabama, Georgia, and Louisiana. In 1971 the company changed its name to ConAgra (Latin for "in partnership with the land"). During the 1970s it expanded into the fertilizer, catfish, and pet accessory businesses.

Poorly performing subsidiaries and commodity speculation caused ConAgra severe financial problems until 1974, when Mike Harper, a former Pillsbury executive, took over. Harper trimmed properties to reduce debt and had the company back on its feet by 1976. ConAgra stayed focused on the commodities side of the business, but was thus tied to volatile price cycles. In 1978 it bought United Agri Products (agricultural chemicals).

ConAgra moved into consumer food products in the 1980s. It bought Banquet (frozen food) in 1980. Other purchases included Singleton Seafood (1981), Armour Food Company (meats, dairy products, frozen food; 1983), and RJR Nabisco's frozen food business (1986). ConAgra became a major player in the red meat market with the 1987 purchases of E.A. Miller (boxed beef), Monfort (beef and lamb), and Swift Independent Packing.

Confident it had found the right path, ConAgra continued with acquisitions of consumer food makers, including Beatrice Foods (Orville Redenbacher's popcorn, Hunt's tomato products) in 1991. In 1997 the company agreed to pay $8.3 million to settle federal charges of wire fraud and watering down grain. That year ConAgra named vice chairman and president Bruce Rohde as CEO; he became chairman in 1998.

In 2000 ConAgra acquired major brand holder International Home Foods from HM Capital Partners (known as Hicks, Muse, Tate & Furst at the time) for about $2.9 billion. The company then became ConAgra Foods. During 2001 the company drew SEC attention and was forced to restate earnings for the previous three years due to accounting no-no's in its United Agri Products division.

In 2002 the USDA forced ConAgra to recall 19 million pounds of ground beef because of possible E. coli contamination, making it the second-largest food recall in US history. Later in 2002 ConAgra sold its fresh beef and pork processing business — one of the largest in the US — to Booth Creek Management and HM Capital Partners.

In 2003 ConAgra agreed to pay $1.5 million in cash and job offers to settle an EEOC lawsuit charging bias against disabled workers at the company's California-based Gilroy Foods plant. The agreement involves the largest disability settlement in the agriculture industry.

In 2005 CEO Bruce Rhode retired. His replacement was former chairman and CEO of PepsiCo Beverages and Foods North America, Gary Rodkin. ConAgra agreed to pay a $14 million shareholder settlement in 2005 regarding a lawsuit claiming fictitious sales and misreported earnings at its former subsidiary United Agri Products.

Rodkin continued the company redo, focusing on portfolio trimming, when, in early 2006, he announced plans to sell a large part of ConAgra's refrigerated-meats business. The brands involved in the sale include some of the company's best-known: Armour, Butterball, and Eckrich. (The Brown 'N Serve, Healthy Choice, Hebrew National, Pemmican, and Slim Jim brands are not included in the portfolio reduction.)

In another move to improve long-term operating performance, ConAgra announced its intention to sell off its seafood and domestic and imported cheese businesses.

## EXECUTIVES

**Chairman, President, and CEO:** Gary M. Rodkin, age 54, $2,742,308 pay (partial-year salary)
**EVP and Chief Administrative Officer:** Owen C. Johnson, age 60, $800,000 pay
**EVP and CFO:** Andre J. Hawaux, age 45
**EVP International and Chief Growth Officer:** Jacqueline K. Heslop McCook, age 49
**EVP Legal and External Affairs and Corporate Secretary:** Robert F. (Rob) Sharpe Jr., age 55, $1,084,615 pay (partial-year salary)
**EVP Research and Development and Quality:** Al Bolles, age 48
**EVP and Chief Marketing Officer:** Joan K. Chow, age 46
**SVP and Chief Litigation Counsel:** Leo A. Knowles
**SVP and Corporate Controller:** John F. Gehring, age 45
**SVP, Treasurer, and Assistant Corporate Secretary:** Scott E. Messel, age 47
**SVP Enterprise Manufacturing:** David J. (Dave) Colo
**SVP Financial Planning and Reporting:** Barry Gisser
**SVP Foodservice Sales and Business Development:** James P. (Jim) Kinnerk
**SVP Human Resources:** Peter M. (Pete) Perez, age 51
**VP Corporate Affairs; President, ConAgra Foods Foundation:** Chris Kircher
**VP Corporate Communication:** Teresa Paulsen
**VP Investor Relations:** Christopher W. (Chris) Klinefelter, age 39
**VP Marketing:** Mike McMahon
**VP, Chief Securities Counsel, and Corporate Secretary:** Colleen Batcheler
**Auditors:** KPMG LLP

## LOCATIONS

**HQ:** ConAgra Foods, Inc.
1 ConAgra Dr., Omaha, NE 68102
**Phone:** 402-595-4000 **Fax:** 402-595-4707
**Web:** www.conagra.com

## PRODUCTS/OPERATIONS

### 2007 Sales

| | $ mil. | % of total |
|---|---|---|
| Consumer foods | 6,485.3 | 54 |
| Food & ingredients | 3,481.7 | 29 |
| Trading & merchandising | 1,455.2 | 12 |
| International foods | 606.0 | 5 |
| **Total** | **12,028.2** | **100** |

### Selected Brands and Products

Dairy Foods
- Blue Bonnet
- Egg Beaters
- Fleischmann's
- Parkay
- Reddi-wip
- Banquet
- Gilardi's
- Kid Cuisine
- Marie Callender's
- Move Over Butter
- Patio
- Reddi-wip

Frozen Foods
- Alexia
- Banquet
- Gilardi's
- Kid Cuisine
- La Choy
- Marie Callender's
- Morton
- Patio
- Wolfgang Puck

Refrigerated Foods
- Brown 'N Serve
- Decker
- Healthy Choice
- Hebrew National
- Lightlife

Packaged Foods
- Act II
- Andy Capp's
- Chef Boyardee
- Chun King
- Crunch 'n Munch
- DAVID Seeds
- Fernando's
- Gebhardt
- Gulden's
- Hunt's
- J. Hungerford Smith
- Jiffy Pop
- Kid Cuisine
- Knott's Berry Farm
- La Choy
- Lamb Weston
- Libby's
- Manwich
- Orville Redenbacher's
- PAM
- Pemmican
- Penrose
- Peter Pan
- Rosarita
- Ro*Tel
- Slim Jim
- Snack Pack
- Swiss Miss
- Van Camp's
- Wesson
- Wolf Brand

## COMPETITORS

Bush Brothers
Campbell Soup
Carl Buddig
Dean Foods
Del Monte Foods
Frito-Lay
General Mills
Heinz
Hershey
Hormel
JR Simplot
Kellogg
King Arthur Flour
Kraft Foods
Kraft North America Commercial
Land O'Lakes
Link Snacks
Mars
McCain Foods
Michelina's
Nestlé
Nestlé USA
Perdue
Pilgrim's Pride
Pinnacle Foods
Sara Lee Food & Beverage
Schwan's
Smithfield Foods
Smucker
Tyson Foods
Unilever
Wholesome & Hearty Foods

## HISTORICAL FINANCIALS

Company Type: Public

### Income Statement

FYE: Last Sunday in May

| | REVENUE ($ mil.) | NET INCOME ($ mil.) | NET PROFIT MARGIN | EMPLOYEES |
|---|---|---|---|---|
| **5/07** | 12,028 | 765 | 6.4% | 24,500 |
| **5/06** | 11,579 | 534 | 4.6% | 33,000 |
| **5/05** | 14,567 | 642 | 4.4% | 38,000 |
| **5/04** | 14,522 | 811 | 5.6% | 39,000 |
| **5/03** | 19,839 | 775 | 3.9% | 63,000 |
| **Annual Growth** | (11.8%) | (0.3%) | — | (21.0%) |

### 2007 Year-End Financials

Debt ratio: 74.6%
Return on equity: 16.6%
Cash ($ mil.): 735
Current ratio: 1.87
Long-term debt ($ mil.): 3,420
No. of shares (mil.): 490
Dividends
Yield: 2.1%
Payout: 35.8%
Market value ($ mil.): 12,568

### Stock History

NYSE: CAG

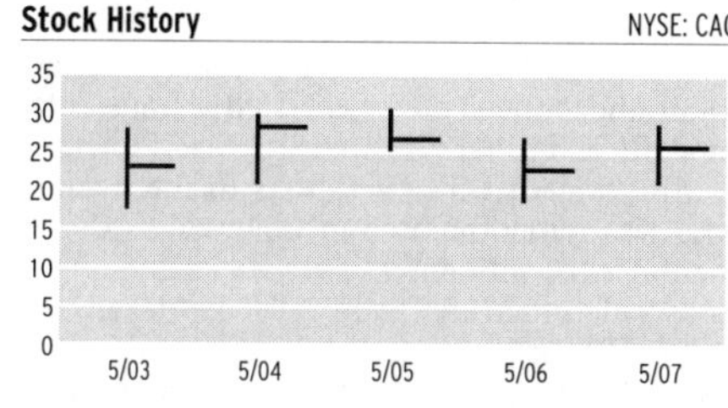


| | STOCK PRICE ($) FY Close | P/E High | P/E Low | PER SHARE ($) Earnings | PER SHARE ($) Dividends | PER SHARE ($) Book Value |
|---|---|---|---|---|---|---|
| **5/07** | 25.66 | 19 | 14 | 1.51 | 0.54 | 9.36 |
| **5/06** | 22.72 | 26 | 18 | 1.03 | 1.00 | 9.10 |
| **5/05** | 26.59 | 25 | 21 | 1.23 | 1.08 | 9.37 |
| **5/04** | 28.12 | 19 | 14 | 1.53 | 1.03 | 9.20 |
| **5/03** | 23.01 | 19 | 12 | 1.46 | 0.98 | 8.61 |
| **Annual Growth** | 2.8% | — | — | 0.8% | (13.8%) | 2.1% |

# ConocoPhillips

Formed by the merger of Conoco and Phillips Petroleum, ConocoPhillips is the #3 integrated oil and gas company in the US, behind Exxon Mobil and Chevron, and condolidated that position through the acquisition of Burlington Resources (for a reported $35 billion) in 2006. The expanded company explores for oil and gas in more than 30 countries and has estimated proved reserves of 11.5 billion barrels of oil equivalent, excluding its Syncrude (Canadian oil sands) assets. It has a refining capacity of 2.7 million barrels per day and sells petroleum at 10,600 outlets in the US under the 76, Conoco, and Phillips 66 brands. Other operations include chemicals, gas gathering, fuels technology, and power generation.

ConocoPhillips has six operating segments. Exploration and Production (which conducts business worldwide); Midstream (gathering and processing of natural gas, and fractionating and marketing natural gas liquids in the US, Canada and Trinidad, primarily through its 50% stake in DCP Midstream Partners); Refining and Marketing of crude oil and petroleum products, mainly in the US, Europe, and Asia; LUKOIL Investment (a 20% stake in Russia-based oil giant LUKOIL); Chemicals (manufacturing and marketing petrochemicals and plastics worldwide, primarily though its 50% stake in Chevron Phillips Chemical Company LLC; and Emerging Businesses (new technologies related to natural gas conversion into clean fuels, technology solutions, power generation, and emerging technologies).

In 2006 the company sold 376 of its European gas stations to LUKOIL.

In 2007 ConocoPhillips teamed up with Tyson Foods to make renewable diesel fuel from beef, pork, and poultry byproduct fats.

Under nationalization pressure from President Hugo Chavez, ConocoPhillips exited Venezuela in 2007.

## HISTORY

The roots of ConocoPhillips go back more than a century and run deep into the history of the US oil industry.

Isaac Elder Blake, an Easterner who had lost everything on a bad investment, came to Ogden, Utah, and founded Continental Oil & Transportation (CO&T) in 1875. In 1885 CO&T merged with Standard Oil's operations in the Rockies and was reincorporated in Colorado as Continental Oil. Continental tightened its grip on the Rocky Mountain area and by 1906 had taken over 98% of the western market. Its monopoly ended in 1911 when the US Supreme Court ordered Standard to divest several holdings: Continental was one of 34 independent oil companies created in 1913.

Seeing opportunity in autos, Continental built a gas station in 1914. Two years later it got into oil production when it bought United Oil, and by 1924 it had become fully integrated by merging with Mutual Oil, which owned production, refining, and distribution assets. Continental's biggest merger came in 1929 when it merged with Marland Oil of Oklahoma.

Continental diversified in the 1960s, acquiring American Agricultural Chemicals in 1963 and Consolidation Coal (Consol) in 1966. Restructuring in the 1970s into Conoco Chemical, Consol, and two petroleum divisions, the company ramped up oil exploration and entered ventures to develop uranium. In 1979 it changed its name to Conoco.

In the late 1970s, Conoco began joint ventures with chemical titan DuPont. The companies worked together well, and in 1981 Conoco was acquired by DuPont to forestall hostile takeover attempts by Mobil and Seagram. DuPont sold off $1.5 billion of Conoco's assets and absorbed Conoco Chemical. In 1998, however, DuPont spun off Conoco in what was the US's largest-ever IPO at the time (DuPont had completely divested its 70% stake by the next year).

Conoco expanded its natural gas reserves in 2001 by buying Gulf Canada Resources for $4.3 billion in cash and $2 billion in assumed debt. Also that year Conoco agreed to merge with Phillips Petroleum.

The story of Phillips Petroleum begins with Frank Phillips, a prosperous Iowa barber who married a banker's daughter in 1897 and began selling bonds. When a missionary who worked with Native Americans in Oklahoma regaled him with stories about the oil patch, Phillips migrated to Bartlesville, Oklahoma, and established Anchor Oil in 1903.

Anchor's first two wells were dry, but the next one — the Anna Anderson No. 1 — was the first of a string of 81 successful wells. Phillips and his brother L. E., doubling as bankers in Bartlesville, transformed Anchor into Phillips Petroleum in 1917.

With continued success on Native American lands in Oklahoma, Phillips moved into refining and marketing. In 1927 the company opened its first gas station in Wichita, Kansas. Frank Phillips retired after WWII and died in 1950.

During the 1980s Phillips became a target of takeover attempts. To fend off bids from corporate raiders T. Boone Pickens (1984) and Carl Icahn (1985), Phillips repurchased stock and ran its debt up to $9 billion. It then cut 8,300 jobs and sold billions of dollars' worth of assets; strong petrochemicals earnings kept it afloat.

As part of an industry trend to share costs of less-profitable operations, Phillips and Conoco flirted with the idea of merging their marketing and refining operations in 1996, but the talks failed. Discussions between Phillips and Ultramar Diamond Shamrock about merging the companies' North American oil refining and marketing operations broke down in 1999.

James Mulva took over as CEO in 1999, and Phillips decided to shift its focus to its upstream operations. The company combined its natural gas gathering and processing operations with those of Duke Energy in 2000 and received a minority stake in a new company, Duke Energy Field Services. Also that year Phillips acquired ARCO's Alaska assets for $7 billion and merged its chemicals division with that of Chevron.

In 2001, however, Phillips elected to expand its refining and marketing operations rather than spin them off, and the company bought Tosco for about $7.3 billion in stock and $2 billion in assumed debt. Big as it was, the Tosco deal was eclipsed the next year by the merger of Phillips and Conoco.

In 2003, as part of its plan to exit the retail business, the company sold its Circle K gas station chain to Alimentation Couche-Tard for $812 million.

## EXECUTIVES

**Chairman, President, and CEO:** James J. (Jim) Mulva, age 59, $8,300,274 pay
**EVP Exploration and Production, Europe, Asia, Africa, and the Middle East:** William B. (Bill) Berry, age 54, $1,845,564 pay
**EVP Finance and CFO:** John A. Carrig, age 54, $2,827,761 pay
**EVP Planning, Strategy, and Corporate Affairs:** Philip L. (Phil) Frederickson, age 50
**EVP Refining, Marketing, and Transportation:** James L. (Jim) Gallogly, age 54
**EVP; President, Exploration and Production, Americas:** Randy L. Limbacher, age 47
**SVP Services and CIO:** Eugene L. (Gene) Batchelder, age 60
**SVP Legal, General Counsel, and Acting Corporate Secretary:** Stephen F. (Steve) Gates, age 60, $1,355,055 pay
**SVP Technology:** Ryan M. Lance, age 44
**VP Human Resources:** Carin S. Knickel, age 47
**VP Health, Environment, and Safety:** Robert A. (Bob) Ridge, age 58
**VP and Controller:** Rand C. Berney, age 52
**VP and Treasurer:** J. W. Sheets
**Investor Relations:** Gary Russell
**Auditors:** Ernst & Young LLP

## LOCATIONS

**HQ:** ConocoPhillips
600 N. Dairy Ashford Rd., Houston, TX 77079
**Phone:** 281-293-1000 **Fax:** 281-293-2819
**Web:** www.conocophillips.com

ConocoPhillips has operations in more than 40 countries.

**2006 Sales**

| | $ mil. | % of total |
|---|---|---|
| US | 127,869 | 70 |
| UK | 19,510 | 11 |
| Canada | 5,554 | 3 |
| Norway | 2,480 | 1 |
| Other countries | 28,237 | 15 |
| Adjustments | 4,873 | — |
| **Total** | **188,523** | **100** |

## PRODUCTS/OPERATIONS

**2006 Sales**

| | $ mil. | % of total |
|---|---|---|
| Refining, marketing & transportation | 129,877 | 71 |
| Exploration & production | 50,166 | 27 |
| Midstream | 3,424 | 2 |
| Emerging businesses | 160 | — |
| Chemicals | 13 | — |
| Corporate & other | 10 | — |
| Adjustments | 4,873 | — |
| **Total** | **188,523** | **100** |

## COMPETITORS

Admiral Petroleum
Arabian American
Bergesen
BHP Billiton
BP
Chevron
CITGO
CVR
Eni
Exxon Mobil
Frontier Oil
George Warren
Great Lakes Carbon
Hess
Koch
Marathon Oil
Occidental Permian
Occidental Petroleum
Shell Oil Products
Sinclair Oil
Sunoco
TOTAL
Ultra Petroleum
Valero Energy

## HISTORICAL FINANCIALS

Company Type: Public

**Income Statement** FYE: December 31

| | REVENUE ($ mil.) | NET INCOME ($ mil.) | NET PROFIT MARGIN | EMPLOYEES |
|---|---|---|---|---|
| **12/06** | 188,523 | 15,550 | 8.2% | 38,400 |
| **12/05** | 183,364 | 13,529 | 7.4% | 35,600 |
| **12/04** | 136,916 | 8,129 | 5.9% | 35,800 |
| **12/03** | 105,097 | 4,735 | 4.5% | 39,000 |
| **12/02** | 57,224 | (295) | — | 57,000 |
| **Annual Growth** | 34.7% | — | — | (9.4%) |

**2006 Year-End Financials**

Debt ratio: 27.9%
Return on equity: 23.0%
Cash ($ mil.): 817
Current ratio: 0.95
Long-term debt ($ mil.): 23,091
No. of shares (mil.): 1,690
Dividends
Yield: 2.0%
Payout: 14.9%
Market value ($ mil.): 121,627

**Stock History** NYSE: COP

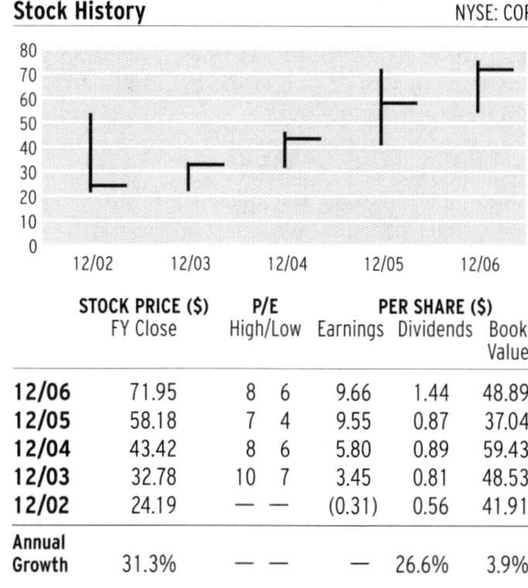


| | STOCK PRICE ($) FY Close | P/E High/Low | | PER SHARE ($) Earnings | Dividends | Book Value |
|---|---|---|---|---|---|---|
| **12/06** | 71.95 | 8 | 6 | 9.66 | 1.44 | 48.89 |
| **12/05** | 58.18 | 7 | 4 | 9.55 | 0.87 | 37.04 |
| **12/04** | 43.42 | 8 | 6 | 5.80 | 0.89 | 59.43 |
| **12/03** | 32.78 | 10 | 7 | 3.45 | 0.81 | 48.53 |
| **12/02** | 24.19 | — | — | (0.31) | 0.56 | 41.91 |
| **Annual Growth** | 31.3% | — | — | — | 26.6% | 3.9% |

# Conseco, Inc.

With a name drawn from its roots — the company began as Security National and soon acquired Consolidated National, becoming Conseco — this company has pruned and transplanted itself into a protector of working families and senior citizens. Conseco offers insurance and related products, targeted to seniors and middle-income prospects. Its three units include Bankers Life, which markets and distributes Medicare supplement, life, and long-term care insurance and annuities; Conseco Insurance Group, which offers specified disease insurance, as well as Medicare supplement and certain life insurance and annuities; and Colonial Penn, which offers life insurance to consumers through direct selling.

Over half of the company's collected premiums come from products sold by its own career agents out of 160 offices. Independent agents, insurance brokers, marketing organizations, and direct marketing account for the balance of its collected premiums.

Conseco has struggled with its growth and troubles stemming from its 1998 purchase of #1 mobile home lender Green Tree Servicing (renamed Conseco Finance and later sold). The move brought Conseco nothing but woe — clamoring creditors, unhappy stockholders, the ouster of the parent company's top officers, and what would be one of the largest Chapter 11 bankruptcy filings.

Conseco pioneered the practice of buying inefficient insurance companies at bargain-basement prices (it gobbled up about 40 firms over 15 years). But as copycats adopted the strategy, Conseco continued to buy — at premium prices — piling on the debt. In addition, the touted cross-selling synergies between the mobile home buyers and Conseco's products didn't materialize, dragging the parent company down.

The company's life insurance, supplemental health insurance, and annuities operations were not part of its Chapter 11 reorganization. However, in a continuing effort to cut costs, Conseco has sold or closed five units (including asset-based lending, vendor leasing, and bankcards). Conseco is also out of the major medical insurance business.

## HISTORY

Conseco evolved from Security National, an Indiana insurance company formed in 1979 by Stephen Hilbert. The former encyclopedia salesman and Aetna executive believed most insurance companies were bloated and the industry itself overcrowded, as well as ripe for consolidation by a smart, lean organization.

In 1982 the company began its growth-by-acquisition strategy with the purchase of Executive Income Life Insurance (renamed Security National Life Insurance). The next year it bought Consolidated National Life Insurance and renamed the expanded company Conseco.

The firm went public in 1985, using the proceeds to fund an acquisitions spree that included Lincoln American Life Insurance, Lincoln Income Life (sold 1990), Bankers National Life Insurance, Western National Life Insurance (sold 1994), and National Fidelity Life Insurance.

In 1990 the company formed Conseco Capital Partners (with General Electric and Bankers Trust) to finance acquisitions without seeming to burden the parent company with debt. This device financed the purchase of Great American Reserve and the 1991 acquisition of Beneficial Standard Life. Conseco bought Bankers Life Insurance in 1992, then sold 67% of it the next year. In 1993 it formed the Private Capital Group to invest in noninsurance companies.

In 1994 the company tried to acquire the much larger Kemper Corp., but shied away from the debt load that the $2.6 billion deal would have entailed. The aborted deal cost $36 million in bank and accounting fees and spelled the end of the company's relationship with Merrill Lynch, which had underwritten Conseco's IPO, when a Merrill Lynch analyst downgraded Conseco's stock after the fiasco.

Meanwhile, Private Capital's success led Conseco to form Conseco Global Investments. Other investments included stakes in racetrack and riverboat gambling operations in Indiana.

In 1996 and 1997 Conseco absorbed eight life, health, property/casualty, and specialty insurance companies and raised its interest in American Life Holdings to 100%.

Itching to move beyond insurance, in 1998 Conseco bought Green Tree Financial, the US's #1 mobile home financier. Charges of Green Tree's own fuzzy accounting practices helped torpedo Conseco's quest for a federal thrift charter. But the troubles had just begun. The mobile home finance industry took a dive as customers refinanced at lower rates and prepayments slammed Green Tree Financial, reducing Conseco's earnings.

Conseco tried to recoup in 1999 by launching an ad campaign portraying the company as the "Wal-Mart of financial services." It also continued the acquisition spree. But Green Tree Financial (renamed Conseco Finance that year) couldn't stanch the red ink: Buyers grew wary of the quality of the finance unit's loan securities and changes in accounting methods cost the parent company a $350 million charge against earnings for 1999.

In 2002, due to its financial woes, Gary Wendt stepped down as CEO, the NYSE suspended trading in Conseco, and the company's stock was moved to the OTC. The company also filed for Chapter 11 protection in 2002. As part of the reorganization agreement, Conseco agreed to sell Conseco Finance. The company's insurance operations were not subject to the Chapter 11 agreement. In 2003, Conseco finally unloaded its Conseco Finance unit to CFN Investment Holdings LLC, an investor group, and General Electric Co.'s consumer finance unit for $1 billion. The company emerged from bankruptcy in September 2003.

## EXECUTIVES

**Chairman:** R. Glenn Hilliard, age 64, $1,595,329 pay
**CEO and Director:** C. James Prieur, age 55, $627,534 pay
**EVP and CFO:** Edward J. Bonach
**EVP and CIO:** Russell M. (Russ) Bostick, age 50
**EVP Product Development:** Christopher J. Nickele, age 50
**EVP Corporate Communications:** Anthony B. (Tony) Zehnder, age 57
**EVP Government Relations:** William (Bill) Fritts
**EVP Human Resources:** Susan L. (Sue) Menzel, age 41
**EVP Operations:** Steven M. (Steve) Stecher, age 46
**SVP and Chief Accounting Officer:** John R. Kline, age 49, $569,319 pay
**SVP and Chief Compliance Officer:** W. Mark Johnson
**SVP Long-Term Care:** John W. Wells
**SVP and General Auditor:** Kimberly A. Roll-Wallace
**SVP Investor Relations:** Tammy Hill
**President Conseco Risk Management:** W. Michael Wells
**President Conseco Insurance Group:** Michael J. (Mike) Dubes, age 64, $400,000 pay
**President Bankers Life and Casualty:** Scott Perry, age 44, $508,333 pay
**SVP Agent Services, Conseco Insurance Group:** Michael Bottoms
**SVP Policyholder Services, Conseco Insurance Group:** Peggy Hutchison
**Secretary:** Karl W. Kindig
**Auditors:** PricewaterhouseCoopers LLP

## LOCATIONS

**HQ:** Conseco, Inc.
11825 N. Pennsylvania St., Carmel, IN 46032
**Phone:** 317-817-6100 **Fax:** 317-817-2847
**Web:** www.conseco.com

## PRODUCTS/OPERATIONS

**2006 Sales**

| | $ mil. | % of total |
|---|---|---|
| Insurance policy income | 2,989.0 | 66 |
| Net investment income | 1,506.4 | 33 |
| Net realized investment gains (losses) | (47.2) | — |
| Other revenues | 19.2 | 1 |
| **Total** | **4,467.4** | **100** |

**2006 Sales**

| | $ mil. | % of total |
|---|---|---|
| Bankers Life | 2,057.6 | 46 |
| Conseco Insurance Group | 1,709.6 | 38 |
| Colonial Penn | 151.1 | 4 |
| Other business in run-off | 508.5 | 11 |
| Corporate revenue | 40.6 | 1 |
| **Total** | **4,467.4** | **100** |

### Selected Subsidiaries

Bankers Life
Bankers Life and Casualty Company
Colonial Penn Life Insurance Company
Conseco Insurance Group
Washington National Insurance Company

## COMPETITORS

Aetna
Aflac
AIG American General
American National Insurance
AXA Financial
Fortis SA/NV
Guardian Life
John Hancock Financial Services
Lincoln Financial Group
MassMutual
MetLife
Mutual of Omaha
Nationwide Financial Network
New York Life
Northwestern Mutual
Pacific Mutual
Phoenix Companies
Protective Life
Prudential
Securian Financial

# CONSOL Energy

Consolation prizes don't interest CONSOL Energy. CONSOL is one of the US's largest coal mining companies, along with Peabody Energy and Arch Coal. The company has some 4.3 billion tons of proved reserves, mainly in northern and central Appalachia and the Illinois Basin, and produces about 70 million tons of coal annually. CONSOL primarily mines high BTU coal, which burns cleaner than lower grades. Customers include electric utilities and steel mills; Allegheny Energy is its largest customer by far. CONSOL delivers coal using its own railroad cars, export terminals, and fleet of towboats and barges. The company also engages in natural gas exploration and production; its proved reserves total 1.3 trillion cu. ft.

Aware that most planned power plants will be gas-fired, CONSOL has diversified its energy holdings by acquiring additional natural gas reserves. In 2005 CONSOL created a new subsidiary, CNX Gas, to handle the company's gas operations. It then sold a minority stake in CNX Gas to a group of institutional investors in a private transaction, and in 2006, CNX Gas filed for an IPO. CONSOL retains an 82% stake in CNX Gas. The subsidiary recovers coalbed methane gas, an increasingly popular fuel for producing electricity. Coal remains the company's core business, however.

CONSOL's Canadian coal assets (including mines and port facilities) are part of the Fording Canadian Coal Trust, which is expected to produce a fifth of the world's metallurgical coal. The trust also involves Teck Cominco and Sherritt International. CONSOL owns a 7% stake in the trust.

In 2007 the company agreed to buy AMVEST Corporation for $335 million. That company operates both coal mines and rail operations in Central Appalachia. CONSOL plans to combine AMVEST's operations with its own in the region, creating a solid base for future acquisitions.

In addition to its coal and gas businesses, CONSOL distributes mining and industrial supplies through its Fairmont Supply unit. It also operates a distribution business. In early 2006, CONSOL more than doubled its barge fleet by buying barge operators Mon River Towing and J.A.R. Barge Lines. The purchases give CONSOL a total of nearly 20 towboats and about 600 barges.

## HISTORY

When Consolidation Coal was formed in Maryland in 1864, coal was just beginning to replace wood as the world's top industrial energy source. In the 1880s Consolidation Coal, like other large coal companies, began operations in the Appalachia region of the US. During the 1920s the company built the Kentucky mining city of Van Lear. (Country music superstar Loretta Lynn's father worked as a Consolidation Coal miner nearby.) In 1945 Consolidation Coal merged with Pittsburgh Coal, and the next year the combined company took over Hanna Coal.

In 1966 Continental Oil, founded in 1875 and later renamed Conoco, bought Consolidation Coal. Two years later 78 workers were killed in a Consolidation Coal mine explosion. Also in 1968 a federal jury found the United Mine Workers (UMW) and the company guilty of conspiring to put Kentucky's South East Coal out of business. In 1971 the UMW and Consolidation Coal paid South East almost $9 million in damages, court costs, and interest. Consolidation Coal became part of DuPont when that company bought Conoco in 1981.

Ten years later the mining unit of German conglomerate RWE, Rheinbraun, bought 50% of Consolidation Coal (later increased to 74%) from DuPont. That year Consolidation Coal and Conoco formed the Pocahontas Gas Partnership to recover coalbed methane gas.

A restructuring in 1992 created CONSOL Energy as a holding company for more than 60 subsidiaries, including principal operating subsidiary Consolidation Coal. The next year the UMW initiated a strike against CONSOL, which was using more and more nonunion workers in its mines. CONSOL opened its ash disposal facility the next year and began developing ways to reuse its plant waste and byproducts.

From 1994 to 1997 the company reduced its workforce by 20% and closed six of its mining complexes. By 1997 about one-third of CONSOL's coal came from nonunion mines. In 1998 the company filed to go public and bought Rochester & Pittsburgh Coal.

CONSOL completed its IPO in 1999. The depressed coal market halved CONSOL's sales that year and the company scaled back production at some of its smaller, high-cost mines in Pennsylvania and West Virginia. During the winter of 2000 and in early 2001, coal prices improved by 36% and natural gas prices skyrocketed as cold temperatures and an energy crisis in California increased demand for energy sources. Despite the improvement in coal prices, the company continued to shut down high-cost mines.

In 2001 CONSOL acquired Conoco's half of the Pocahontas Gas joint venture. It also bought Windsor Coal, Southern Ohio Coal, and Central Ohio Coal from American Electric Power. In addition, CONSOL bought 50% of the Glennies Creek Mine, its first Australian property.

Also in 2001, CONSOL contracted with Allegheny Energy Supply (an affiliate of largest customer Allegheny Energy) to build an 88-MW electric generating plant in Virginia to be fueled by coalbed methane gas produced by CONSOL.

CONSOL in 2003 sold its Canadian operations (Cardinal River and Line Creek Mines) to Fording. The next year CONSOL sold its Glennies Creek mine interest, thus exiting Australia.

Also in 2004, RWE severed ties with CONSOL by selling its remaining 19% stake.

## EXECUTIVES

**Chairman:** John L. Whitmire, age 66
**President, CEO, and Director:** J. Brett Harvey, age 56, $956,192 pay
**COO:** Bart J. Hyita, age 48
**CFO:** William J. Lyons, age 58, $418,615 pay
**President, Coal Group:** Peter B. Lilly, age 57, $541,346 pay (prior to title change)
**EVP, Gas Operations, Land Resources, and Engineering Services:** Ronald E. Smith, age 58, $393,077 pay
**SVP, Safety:** Jack A. Holt, age 58
**SVP, Administration:** Robert P. King, age 54
**General Counsel and Secretary:** P. Jerome Richey, age 57
**VP, Engineering and Exploration:** Marshall W. Hunt
**VP, Investor and Public Relations:** Thomas F. Hoffman
**VP, Marketing Services:** James J. McCaffrey
**VP, Purchasing:** James D. Kingsley
**VP, Research and Development:** Francis P. Burke
**VP, Human Resources:** Patricia Lang, age 47
**VP, Sales:** Robert F. Pusateri
**VP, Sales:** William G. Rieland
**President and CEO, CNX Gas Corporation:** Nicholas J. Deluliss, age 38, $433,692 pay
**Auditors:** PricewaterhouseCoopers LLP

## HISTORICAL FINANCIALS

Company Type: Public

**Income Statement** — FYE: December 31

| | ASSETS ($ mil.) | NET INCOME ($ mil.) | INCOME AS % OF ASSETS | EMPLOYEES |
|---|---|---|---|---|
| **12/06** | 32,717 | 97 | 0.3% | 4,000 |
| **12/05** | 31,557 | 325 | 1.0% | 4,000 |
| **12/04** | 30,756 | 295 | 1.0% | 4,350 |
| **12/03** | 29,920 | 2,298 | 7.7% | 4,350 |
| **12/02** | 46,509 | (7,836) | — | — |
| **Annual Growth** | (8.4%) | — | — | (2.8%) |

**2006 Year-End Financials**

Equity as % of assets: 12.4%
Return on assets: 0.3%
Return on equity: 2.4%
Long-term debt ($ mil.): 1,419
No. of shares (mil.): 152
Dividends
Yield: —
Payout: —
Market value ($ mil.): 3,040
Sales ($ mil.): 4,467

**Stock History** — NYSE: CNO

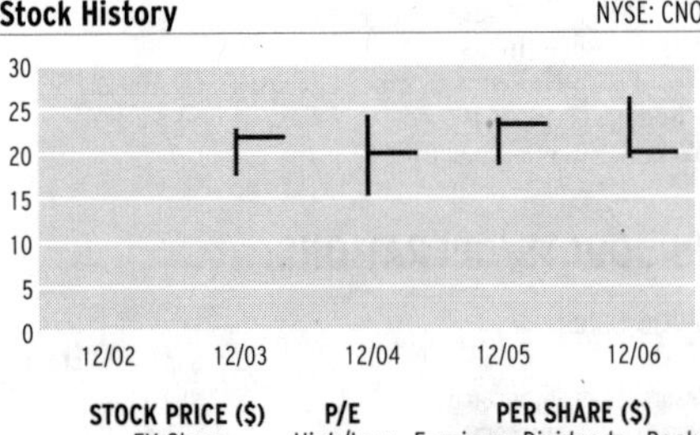


| | STOCK PRICE ($) FY Close | P/E High | P/E Low | PER SHARE ($) Earnings | Dividends | Book Value |
|---|---|---|---|---|---|---|
| **12/06** | 19.98 | 68 | 51 | 0.38 | — | 30.97 |
| **12/05** | 23.17 | 13 | 11 | 1.76 | — | 29.83 |
| **12/04** | 19.95 | 15 | 9 | 1.63 | — | 25.83 |
| **12/03** | 21.80 | 34 | 26 | 0.67 | — | 28.14 |
| **Annual Growth** | (2.9%) | — | — | — | — | 3.2% |

## LOCATIONS

**HQ:** CONSOL Energy Inc.
Consol Plaza, 1800 Washington Rd.,
Pittsburgh, PA 15241
**Phone:** 412-831-4000 **Fax:** 412-831-4103
**Web:** www.consolenergy.com

CONSOL Energy has mining operations in Appalachia, the Illinois Basin, and Utah.

### 2006 Sales

| | % of total |
|---|---|
| North America | |
| US | 90 |
| Canada | 3 |
| Europe | 6 |
| South America | 1 |
| **Total** | **100** |

## PRODUCTS/OPERATIONS

### 2006 Sales

| | $ mil. | % of total |
|---|---|---|
| Energy | | |
| Coal | 2,857.2 | 74 |
| Gas | 488.6 | 13 |
| Other | 331.7 | 9 |
| Other | 170.7 | 4 |
| Adjustments | (133.2) | — |
| **Total** | **3,715.2** | **100** |

## COMPETITORS

Alliance Resource
Arch Coal
Devon Energy
Equitable Resources
Massey Energy
Mitsui Mining
Peabody Energy
Penn Virginia
RAG
Rio Tinto
St. Mary Land & Exploration
Westmoreland Coal

## HISTORICAL FINANCIALS

Company Type: Public

### Income Statement

FYE: December 31

| | REVENUE ($ mil.) | NET INCOME ($ mil.) | NET PROFIT MARGIN | EMPLOYEES |
|---|---|---|---|---|
| **12/06** | 3,715 | 409 | 11.0% | 7,253 |
| **12/05** | 3,810 | 581 | 15.2% | 7,257 |
| **12/04** | 2,777 | 199 | 7.2% | 6,982 |
| **12/03** | 2,223 | (8) | — | 6,523 |
| **12/02** | 2,184 | 12 | 0.5% | 6,074 |
| **Annual Growth** | 14.2% | 143.1% | — | 4.5% |

### 2006 Year-End Financials

Debt ratio: 46.2%
Return on equity: 39.1%
Cash ($ mil.): 224
Current ratio: 1.24
Long-term debt ($ mil.): 493
No. of shares (mil.): 183
Dividends
Yield: 0.9%
Payout: 12.7%
Market value ($ mil.): 5,869

### Stock History

NYSE: CNX

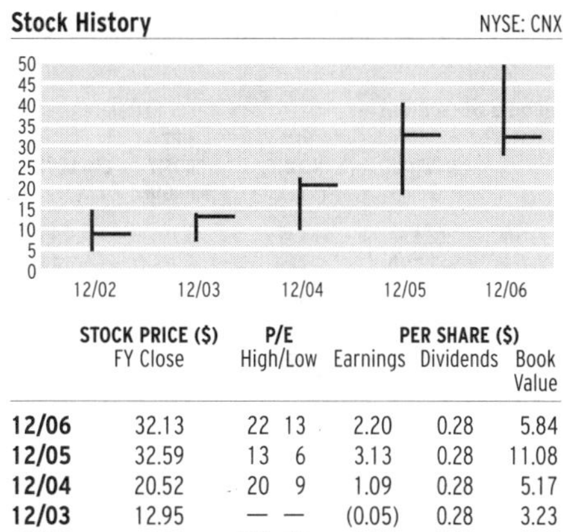


| | STOCK PRICE ($) FY Close | P/E High | P/E Low | PER SHARE ($) Earnings | Dividends | Book Value |
|---|---|---|---|---|---|---|
| **12/06** | 32.13 | 22 | 13 | 2.20 | 0.28 | 5.84 |
| **12/05** | 32.59 | 13 | 6 | 3.13 | 0.28 | 11.08 |
| **12/04** | 20.52 | 20 | 9 | 1.09 | 0.28 | 5.17 |
| **12/03** | 12.95 | — | — | (0.05) | 0.28 | 3.23 |
| **12/02** | 8.64 | 189 | 65 | 0.08 | 0.42 | 2.06 |
| **Annual Growth** | 38.9% | — | — | 129.0% | (9.6%) | 29.8% |

# Consolidated Edison

Utility holding company Consolidated Edison (Con Edison) is the night light for the city that never sleeps. Con Edison's main subsidiary, Consolidated Edison Company of New York, distributes electricity to more than 3.2 million residential and business customers in New York City; it also delivers natural gas to more than 1 million customers. Subsidiary Orange and Rockland Utilities serves almost 421,000 electric and gas customers in three states. Con Edison's nonutility operations include retail and wholesale energy marketing, independent power production, and infrastructure project development.

To prepare for deregulation, Con Edison has sold almost all of its New York power plants to focus on distribution and transmission. The company has faced some tough hurdles in the race to competition; however, Con Edison is sticking with its growth strategy. It is expanding its competitive operations and improving its regulated infrastructure assets. After evaluating strategic alternatives for its telecommunications business due to losses at the unit, in 2006 the company sold its Con Edison Communications unit (now RCN Business Solutions) to RCN Corporation for $32 million.

Competitive energy businesses include subsidiary Consolidated Edison Solutions, which markets power and gas to retail customers and provides energy procurement and management services, and Consolidated Edison Energy, which markets and trades wholesale energy. Subsidiary Consolidated Edison Development has interests in power generation facilities in North America, Latin America, and Europe.

## HISTORY

Several professionals, led by Timothy Dewey, formed The New York Gas Light Company in 1823 to illuminate part of Manhattan. In 1884 five other gas companies joined New York Gas Light to form the Consolidated Gas Company of New York.

Thomas Edison's incandescent lamp came on the scene in 1879, and The Edison Electric Illuminating Company of New York was formed in 1880 to build the world's first commercial electric power station (Pearl Street), financed by a group led by J.P. Morgan. Edison supervised the project, and in 1882 New York became the first major city with electric lighting.

Realizing electricity would replace gas, Consolidated Gas acquired electric companies, including Anthony Brady's New York Gas and Electric Light, Heat and Power Company (1900), which joined Edison's Illuminating Company in 1901 to form the New York Edison Company. More than 170 purchases followed, including that of the New York Steam Company (1930), a cheap source of steam for electric turbines.

The Public Utility Holding Company Act of 1935 ushered in the era of regulated, regional monopolies. The next year New York Edison combined its holdings to form the Consolidated Edison Company of New York (Con Ed).

Con Ed opened its first nuclear station in 1962. By then Con Ed had a reputation for inefficiency and poor service, and shareholders were angry about its slow growth and low earnings. Environmentalists joined the grousers in 1963 when Con Ed began constructing a pumped-storage plant in Cornwall near the Hudson River. Charles Luce, a former undersecretary with the Department of Interior, was recruited to rescue Con Ed in 1967. He added power plants and beefed up customer service.

In the 1970s inflation and the energy crisis drove up oil prices (Con Ed's main fuel source), and in 1974 Luce withheld dividends for the first time since 1885. He persuaded the New York State Power Authority to buy two unfinished power plants, saving Con Ed $200 million. In 1980 Luce ended the Cornwall controversy and donated the land for park use. He retired in 1982.

The utility started buying power from various suppliers and in 1984 began a two-year price freeze, a boon to rate-hike-weary New Yorkers. The New York State Public Service Commission didn't approve another rate increase until 1992.

In 1997 Con Ed, government officials, consumer groups, and other energy firms outlined the company's deregulation plan, which included the formation of the Consolidated Edison, Inc., holding company (known as Con Edison) and a power marketing unit in 1998. The next year Con Edison sold New York City generating facilities to KeySpan, Northern States Power, and Orion Power for a total of $1.65 billion.

Also in 1999 Con Edison bought Orange and Rockland Utilities for $790 million to increase its New York base and expand into New Jersey and Pennsylvania. In an effort to push into New England, the company that year agreed to buy Northeast Utilities (NU) for $3.3 billion in cash and stock and $3.9 billion in assumed debt. But the deal broke down in 2001. NU accused Con Edison of improperly trying to renegotiate terms, while Con Edison accused NU of concealing information about unfavorable power supply contracts.

Con Edison's Indian Point Unit 2 nuclear plant was shut down temporarily in 2000 after a radioactive steam leak; later that year it agreed to sell Indian Point Units 1 and 2 to Entergy for $502 million. The sale was completed in 2001. That year Con Edison also incurred an estimated $400 million in costs related to emergency response and asset damage from the September 11 terrorist attacks on New York City.

## EXECUTIVES

**Chairman and CEO; Chairman and CEO, Consolidated Edison of New York:** Kevin Burke, age 56, $1,000,000 pay
**President and COO; President and COO, Consolidated Edison of New York:** Louis L. Rana, age 58, $594,000 pay
**SVP and CFO; SVP and CFO, Consolidated Edison of New York:** Robert N. Hoglund, age 45, $535,000 pay
**VP and Treasurer; VP and Treasurer, Consolidated Edison of New York:** Joseph P. Oates, age 45
**VP, Chief Accounting Officer, and Controller; VP, Chief Accounting Officer, and Controller, Consolidated Edison of New York:** Edward J. (Ed) Rasmussen, age 58
**General Counsel; General Counsel, Consolidated Edison of New York:** Charles E. McTiernan Jr., age 62
**Secretary; Secretary and Associate General Counsel, Consolidated Edison of New York:** Saddie L. Smith
**Group President, Competitive Energy Business:** Stephen B. (Steve) Bram, age 64, $984,000 pay
**President and CEO, Orange and Rockland Utilities:** John D. McMahon, age 55, $665,000 pay
**Director Investor Relations:** Jan C. Childress
**Manager Investor Relations:** Ellen Socolow
**President and CEO, Consolidated Edison Solutions:** Jorge J. Lopez
**Manager Public Affairs:** Joseph Petta
**Auditors:** PricewaterhouseCoopers LLP

## LOCATIONS

**HQ:** Consolidated Edison, Inc.
4 Irving Place, New York, NY 10003
**Phone:** 212-460-4600 **Fax:** 212-982-7816
**Web:** www.conedison.com

Consolidated Edison subsidiary Consolidated Edison Company of New York provides electricity throughout New York City (except part of Queens) and most of Westchester County; it also provides natural gas in Manhattan, the Bronx, and parts of Queens and Westchester County, and it provides steam service in Manhattan. Subsidiary Orange and Rockland Utilities operates in southeastern New York and adjacent areas of New Jersey and Pennsylvania. Consolidated Edison also has interests in independent power projects in Maryland, Massachusetts, Michigan, New Hampshire, and New Jersey, as well as in Guatemala and the Netherlands.

## PRODUCTS/OPERATIONS

### 2006 Sales

| | $ mil. | % of total |
|---|---|---|
| Electricity | 7,634 | 63 |
| Gas | 1,849 | 15 |
| Steam | 623 | 5 |
| Other | 2,031 | 17 |
| **Total** | **12,137** | **100** |

### Selected Subsidiaries

Consolidated Edison Company of New York, Inc. (utility)
Consolidated Edison Development, Inc. (investments in power generation projects)
Consolidated Edison Energy, Inc. (wholesale energy marketing and trading)
Consolidated Edison Solutions, Inc. (retail energy marketing and services)
Orange and Rockland Utilities, Inc. (utility)

## COMPETITORS

AEP
CH Energy
CMS Energy
Delmarva Power
Duke Energy
Enbridge
Energy East
Green Mountain Energy
GridSense
KeySpan
National Fuel Gas
National Grid USA
New York Power Authority
Northeast Utilities
NSTAR
PPL
PSEG
South Jersey Industries
Syms

## HISTORICAL FINANCIALS

Company Type: Public

### Income Statement

FYE: December 31

| | REVENUE ($ mil.) | NET INCOME ($ mil.) | NET PROFIT MARGIN | EMPLOYEES |
|---|---|---|---|---|
| **12/06** | 12,137 | 737 | 6.1% | 14,795 |
| **12/05** | 11,690 | 719 | 6.2% | 14,537 |
| **12/04** | 9,758 | 537 | 5.5% | 14,096 |
| **12/03** | 9,827 | 528 | 5.4% | 14,079 |
| **12/02** | 8,482 | 659 | 7.8% | 14,293 |
| **Annual Growth** | 9.4% | 2.9% | — | 0.9% |

### 2006 Year-End Financials

Debt ratio: 105.2%
Return on equity: 9.6%
Cash ($ mil.): 234
Current ratio: 1.01
Long-term debt ($ mil.): 8,421
No. of shares (mil.): 234
Dividends
Yield: 4.8%
Payout: 78.0%
Market value ($ mil.): 11,260

### Stock History

NYSE: ED

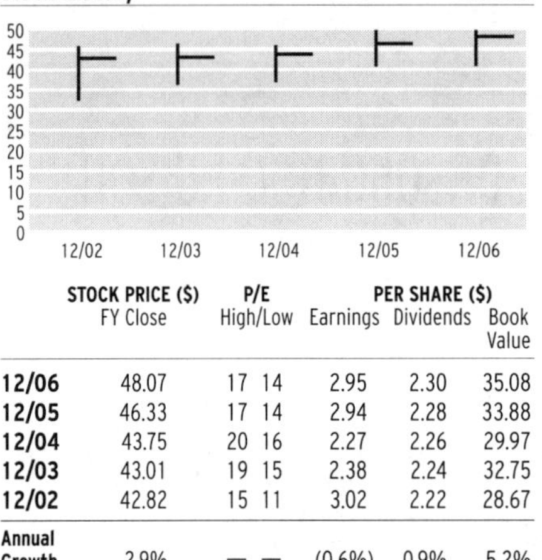


| | STOCK PRICE ($) FY Close | P/E High | P/E Low | PER SHARE ($) Earnings | Dividends | Book Value |
|---|---|---|---|---|---|---|
| **12/06** | 48.07 | 17 | 14 | 2.95 | 2.30 | 35.08 |
| **12/05** | 46.33 | 17 | 14 | 2.94 | 2.28 | 33.88 |
| **12/04** | 43.75 | 20 | 16 | 2.27 | 2.26 | 29.97 |
| **12/03** | 43.01 | 19 | 15 | 2.38 | 2.24 | 32.75 |
| **12/02** | 42.82 | 15 | 11 | 3.02 | 2.22 | 28.67 |
| **Annual Growth** | 2.9% | — | — | (0.6%) | 0.9% | 5.2% |

# Constellation Brands

Wine is at the center of this Constellation. Constellation Brands makes and distributes more than 250 brands of beer, wine, and spirits in some 150 countries. But wine is the company's shining star: its Wines division (53% of company sales) is the global leader in wine production by volume, offering brands such as Almaden, Banrock Station, Inglenook, Vendange, and Arbor Mist. It also makes premium wines including Estancia, Ravenswood, and Simi. The company imports beers such as Corona and Tsingtao, markets distilled spirits such as Fleishmann's and Barton, and produces and distributes cider, wine, and bottled water in the UK. The founding Sands family controls about 88% of Constellation's voting power.

Through its Constellation Wines U.S. subsidiary, Constellation Brands continues to make high-margin Richards Wild Irish Rose, which brought it early success. Its Constellation Europe unit is a leading producer and distributor of wine, cider, and bottled water in the UK.

Constellation joined with Brown-Forman, Lion Capital, and Blackstone in 2005 to consider making a bid for Allied Domecq. Constellation subsequently pulled out of the bidding group. Later that year, the company acquired Rex Goliath from Hahn Estates and made a number of bids to take over Canada's Vincor International.

Vincor's board rejected all offers until spring 2006, when it accepted an offer of C$1 billion dollars. As part of the integration of Vincor into the company, Constellation eliminated 230 Vincor jobs and renamed the company Vincor Canada. Also that year Constellation sold Strathmore Mineral Water to A.G. Barr for some $27 million.

Later in 2006 Constellation formed a joint venture with Grupo Modelo to import and market the Mexican brewer's beer in the US and Guam. Adding to its premium spirits portfolio, in 2007 Constellation acquired Swedish vodka label Svedka Vodka, along with its New York import operations, Spirits Marque One, for $384 million.

Another joint venture was announced in 2007. This time the deal was made with England's Punch Taverns. Constellation and Punch will become 50-50 owners of Matthew Clark, the UK's top beverage wholesaler.

Later that year, CEO Richard Sands was replaced by Robert (Rob) Sands; Richard Sands remained as chairman. (The men are brothers.)

## HISTORY

Marvin Sands, the son of wine maker Mordecai (Mack) Sands, exited the Navy in 1945 and entered distilling by purchasing an old sauerkraut factory in Canandaigua, New York. His business, Canandaigua Industries, struggled while making fruit wines in bulk for local bottlers in the East. Aiming at regional markets, the company began producing its own brands two years later. Marvin opened the Richards Wine Cellar in Petersburg, Virginia, in 1951 and put his father in charge of the unit. In 1954 Marvin developed his own brand of "fortified" wine — boosted by 190-proof brandy — and named it Richards Wild Irish Rose after his son Richard.

The company slowly expanded, buying a number of small wineries in the 1960s and 1970s. It went public in 1973, changing its name to Canandaigua Wine. A year later the company expanded to the West Coast, thus gaining access to the growing varietal market.

Canandaigua continued to grow through acquisitions and new product introductions in the early 1980s. In 1984, when wine coolers became popular, the company introduced Sun Country Coolers, doubling sales to $173 million by 1986.

The short-lived wine cooler fad made Canandaigua realize that its distribution network could handle more volume, so it began looking for additional brands. The company picked up Kosher wine maker Manischewitz and East Coast wine maker Widmer's Wine Cellars, both in 1987. The company made a major purchase in 1991 when it bought Guild Wineries & Distillers (Cook's champagne) for $60 million.

Richard Sands became CEO in 1993. Subsequent acquisitions included Barton (beer importing, branded spirits; 1993), Vintners International (Paul Masson and Taylor, 1993), Heublein's Almaden and Inglenook (1994), and 12 distilled spirits brands from United Distillers Glenmore (1995). The moves doubled Canandaigua's share of the spirits market, making it the #4 US spirits supplier. After the flurry of acquisitions, the company changed its name in 1997 to Canandaigua Brands.

In 1998 it bought Matthew Clark, a UK-based maker of cider, wine, and bottled water, for $359 million. Further stocking its cabinet, in 1999 Canandaigua bought several whiskey brands (including Black Velvet) and two Canadian production facilities from Diageo. Also in 1999, Canandaigua entered the premium wine business with the purchases of vintners Simi Winery and Franciscan Estates.

Founder Marvin Sands died in 1999. His son, Richard, who had been CEO since 1993, succeeded his father as chairman. In 2000 the firm changed its name to Constellation Brands.

In 2001 Constellation Brands acquired Turner Road Vintners, a division of Sebastiani Vineyards, including the Vendange, Talus, Heritage, Nathanson Creek, La Terre, and Farallon brands of wine, as well as two wineries in California. Also that month it acquired the Covey Run, Columbia, Ste. Chapelle, and Alice White wine brands from wine company Corus Brands for about $52 million.

Constellation Brands teamed with Australian vintner BRL Hardy in 2001 to form its Pacific Wine Partners joint venture, which targets the mid-priced wine market in the US. That year Constellation Brands also purchased Ravenswood Winery for about $148 million. In 2003 Constellation Brands acquired BRL Hardy; it then merged BRL Hardy's wine operations with those of its own wine division to form its Constellation Wines subsidiary. These moves helped move Constellation Brands' wine division to the top of the global heap. In 2004 the company completed its landmark acquisition of The Robert Mondavi Corporation, further adding to the company's dominance in the wine industry.

In 2004 the company continued to pursue several acquisitions. In addition to its $1.36 billion purchase of Robert Mondavi, Constellation Brands announced plans to buy 40% of Italy's Ruffino S.r.l. The company sold several of its brands to California-based The Legacy Estates Group in 2005, including Arrowood, Byron, Grand Archer, and IO brands.

## EXECUTIVES

**Chairman:** Richard Sands, age 56, $2,228,817 pay
**CEO and Director:** Robert S. (Rob) Sands, age 48, $1,826,944 pay
**EVP Business Development and Corporate Strategy:** F. Paul Hetterich, age 44
**EVP and CFO:** Robert (Bob) Ryder, age 44
**EVP and General Counsel:** Thomas J. Mullin, age 55
**SVP, Corporate Communications:** Philippa Dworkin
**SVP, Corporate Counsel, and Secretary:** David S. Sorce
**SVP, Channel Management, Constellation Wines US:** Abbott Wolfe
**SVP, Operations and Technology, Constellation Wines:** Angus M. Kennedy
**SVP, Sales, Pacific Wine Partners:** David Kelly
**SVP, Supply Chain:** Dave Moynihan
**SVP, West Coast Operations, Constellation Wines US:** David Hayman
**SVP and National Sales Manager, Canandaigua Wine:** Jim Kocoloski
**VP, Corporate Communications:** Michael A. (Mike) Martin
**VP, Investor Relations:** Patty Yahn-Urlaub
**CEO, Constellation Wines North America:** José Fernandez, age 51
**CEO, Constellation Beers and Spirits; President and CEO, Barton:** Alexander L. Berk, age 57, $1,078,078 pay
**Chief Administrative Officer:** W. Keith Wilson, age 56
**Director, Investor Relations:** Bob Czudak
**Auditors:** KPMG LLP

## LOCATIONS

**HQ:** Constellation Brands, Inc.
370 Woodcliff Dr., Ste. 300, Fairport, NY 14450
**Phone:** 585-218-3600 **Fax:** 585-218-3601
**Web:** www.cbrands.com

### 2007 Sales

| | $ mil. | % of total |
|---|---|---|
| North America | | |
| US | 3,012.7 | 58 |
| Canada | 326.9 | 6 |
| UK | 1,503.7 | 29 |
| Australia & New Zealand | 349.4 | 7 |
| Other regions | 23.7 | — |
| **Total** | **5,216.4** | **100** |

## PRODUCTS/OPERATIONS

### 2007 Sales

| | $ mil. | % of total |
|---|---|---|
| Branded wine | 2,755.7 | 53 |
| Wholesale & other | 1,087.7 | 21 |
| Imported beers | 1,043.6 | 20 |
| Spirits | 329.4 | 6 |
| **Total** | **5,216.4** | **100** |

### Selected Brands and Operations

Beer (imported)
Constellation Brand's, Inc.
Corona
Model Especial
Negra Modelo
Pacifico
St. Pauli Girl
Tsingtao

Spirits
Constellation Brands, Inc.
99 Schnapps
Balblair
Black Velvet
Madera
Montezuma
Mr. Boston
Svedka
Barton Brands, Ltd.
Almaden
Barton
Glenmore
Hiram Walker
J. A. Dougherty
Paul Masson

Wines
Constellation Brands, Inc.
3 Blind Moose
Almaden
Arbor Mist
Black Box
Blackstone
Brickstone
Brook Hollow
California Cellars
Canandaigua
Columbia
Cook's
Deer Valley
Estancia Estates
Excelsior
Inglenook
Madera
Manischewitz
Masson
Mendocino Creek
Monkey Bay
Paul Masson
Ravenna
Ravenswood
Saint Regis
San Marino
Talus
Trove
Vendange
Woodbridge
Yanqui

Franciscan Vineyards, Inc.
Caymus
Chantree
Columbia
Cuttings Wharf
Domaine Madeline
Estancia
Franciscan
Goldfields
Oakmont
Pickle Canyon
Simi Winescapes
Smothers Brothers
Tantalus
Veramonte
Hogue
Horse Heaven Hills
Latitudes
Olympic
Roza
Silver Falls
Sunridge
Mt.Veeder
Oakville

## COMPETITORS

Andrew Peller
Anheuser-Busch
Bacardi
Bacardi USA
Beam Global Spirits & Wine
Beam Wine Estates
Bronco Wine Co.
Brown-Forman
Carlsberg
Cruzan International
Diageo
Diageo Chateau & Estate Wines
Fortune Brands
Foster's
Foster's Americas
Future Brands
Gallo
GIV
H. P. Bulmer
Halewood
Heaven Hill Distilleries
Heineken USA
InBev
Kendall-Jackson
Labatt
LVMH
Molson Coors
National Grape Cooperative
Newton Vineyard
Pernod Ricard
Premier Pacific
SABMiller
Scheid Vineyards
Scottish & Newcastle
Sebastiani Vineyards
Skyy
Sunview Vineyards
Taittinger
Terlato Wine
Trinchero Family Estates
Vincor
Wine Group

## HISTORICAL FINANCIALS

Company Type: Public

### Income Statement

FYE: Last day in February

| | REVENUE ($ mil.) | NET INCOME ($ mil.) | NET PROFIT MARGIN | EMPLOYEES |
|---|---|---|---|---|
| **2/07** | 5,216 | 332 | 6.4% | 9,200 |
| **2/06** | 4,604 | 325 | 7.1% | 7,900 |
| **2/05** | 4,088 | 277 | 6.8% | 7,700 |
| **2/04** | 3,552 | 220 | 6.2% | 7,800 |
| **2/03** | 2,732 | 203 | 7.4% | 7,680 |
| **Annual Growth** | 17.6% | 13.0% | — | 4.6% |

### 2007 Year-End Financials

Debt ratio: 108.7%
Return on equity: 10.4%
Cash ($ mil.): 34
Current ratio: 1.90
Long-term debt ($ mil.): 3,715
No. of shares (mil.): 211
Dividends
Yield: —
Payout: —
Market value ($ mil.): 4,951

### Stock History

NYSE: STZ

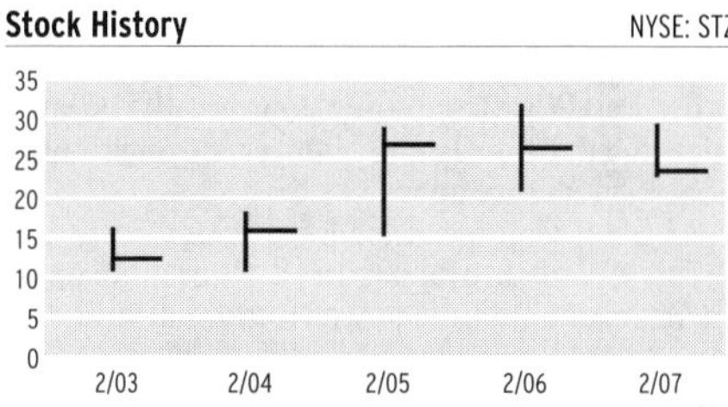

| | STOCK PRICE ($) FY Close | P/E High | P/E Low | PER SHARE ($) Earnings | PER SHARE ($) Dividends | PER SHARE ($) Book Value |
|---|---|---|---|---|---|---|
| **2/07** | 23.46 | 21 | 17 | 1.38 | — | 16.19 |
| **2/06** | 26.34 | 23 | 16 | 1.36 | — | 14.94 |
| **2/05** | 26.76 | 24 | 13 | 1.19 | — | 14.25 |
| **2/04** | 15.85 | 17 | 11 | 1.03 | — | 25.14 |
| **2/03** | 12.31 | 15 | 10 | 1.10 | — | 14.93 |
| **Annual Growth** | 17.5% | — | — | 5.8% | — | 2.0% |

# Constellation Energy Group

Constellation Energy Group's leading light is still utility Baltimore Gas and Electric (BGE), which distributes electricity and natural gas in central Maryland. The company trades and markets wholesale energy through subsidiary Constellation Energy Commodities Group, which is one of the top power marketers in North America. Constellation Energy also operates independent power plants with more than 12,300 MW of generating capacity through its Constellation Generation unit, and it competes in retail energy supply through Constellation NewEnergy. In 2007 this unit acquired Cornerstone Energy, creating one of the largest natural gas marketing companies in the US.

Other nonutility operations include a district cooling system in Baltimore, HVAC (heating, ventilation, and air-conditioning) services, appliance sales, onsite energy system installations, and energy consulting services.

Constellation Energy has been expanding its retail energy supply operations through acquisitions, including its purchase of NewEnergy, the former retail marketing unit of AES. To further expand its nonregulated operations, which have grown to account for more than half of sales, the company has purchased a New York nuclear plant for $408 million from Rochester Gas and Electric.

The company is selling off noncore assets, including its real estate investments and Latin American power projects. Constellation Energy changed Constellation Power Source's name to Constellation Energy Commodities Group in 2004 to more accurately describe the unit's activities. Constellation Energy sold Oleander power plant in Cocoa, Florida to fellow utility provider Southern Company.

In late 2005 Constellation agreed to be acquired by FPL Group Inc. However, the companies called the deal off in 2006, citing uncertainty about regulatory approvals.

In 2006 Constellation Energy agreed to sell 3,145 MW of natural gas-fired generation assets to Tenaska's Tenaska Power Fund, L.P. unit.

## HISTORY

In 1816, back when gas was made out of tar, Rembrandt Peale (an artist and son of painter Charles Willson Peale), William Lorman, and three others formed the US's first gas utility: Gas Light Company of Baltimore; Lorman was president until 1832. The firm soon ran out of money and issued stock to raise capital.

Baltimore's growth outstripped the firm's gas-main capacity, and by 1860 it had a fierce rival in the People's Gas Light Co. In 1871 the two firms divided the city up and then fought a price war with yet another rival. Finally, the three merged as the Consolidated Gas Company of Baltimore City in 1880.

The next year the Brush Electric Light Company and the United States Electric Light and Power Company were established. In 1906 their descendants merged with Consolidated Gas to form the Consolidated Gas Electric Light and Power Co.

As demand for electricity grew, the company turned from hydroelectric power to steam generators in the 1920s. Its revenues increased despite the Depression, and it later set records producing gas and electricity during WWII. Despite a postwar boom in sales, earnings fell as Consolidated spent money on new plants, shifting to natural gas, and converting downtown Baltimore from DC to AC.

In 1955 Consolidated was renamed Baltimore Gas and Electric Company (BGE). BGE announced plans in 1967 for Maryland's first nuclear power plant; Calvert Cliffs Unit 1 went on line in 1975, and Unit 2 followed two years later.

BGE began adding to the Safe Harbor Hydroelectric Project in 1981. Over the next two years it sought to form a holding company in order to diversify, but state regulators rejected the request in 1983. Undaunted, the firm formed subsidiary Constellation Holdings in 1985 and began investing in nonutility businesses and pursuing independent power projects.

Both Calvert Cliffs nukes were shut down between 1989 and 1990 for repairs, and BGE had to spend $458 million on replacement power.

The Energy Policy Act fundamentally changed the electric utility industry in 1992 by allowing wholesale power competition in monopoly territories. BGE began expanding its gas division that year, and in 1995 it ventured into Latin America and took a stake in a Bolivian power firm.

BGE formed its power marketing arm that year with Goldman Sachs as its advisor. It teamed up with Goldman Sachs again in 1998 when the duo formed joint venture Orion Power Holdings to buy electric plants in the US and Canada. In 1999 Orion bought plants from Niagara Mohawk, Con Ed, and U.S. Generating.

Meanwhile, Maryland passed deregulation legislation in 1999, and Constellation Energy Group was formed in 1999 as the holding company for BGE and its nonregulated subsidiaries. Competition began in BGE's territory in 2000, and Constellation Energy separated BGE's generation assets from its distribution assets in accordance with the state's deregulation laws.

It also announced plans to split into two companies: BGE and a merchant energy business that would retain the Constellation name. But slumping energy prices and a weakened economy caused Constellation Energy to cancel the proposed split in October 2001; it also ended its power advisory relationship with Goldman Sachs, which had planned to invest in the new merchant energy business.

Also in 2001 Constellation Energy purchased the Nine Mile Point Nuclear Station Unit 1 and 82% of Unit 2 (most of the holdings were bought from Niagara Mohawk), and sold its Guatemalan power plants to Duke Energy. In the wake of its decision not to split into two companies, Constellation Energy reorganized its management and corporate structure in 2002; it also reduced its workforce by approximately 10% and closed its BGE Home retail merchandise stores.

Constellation Energy purchased two retail supply and consulting units (Alliance Energy Services and Fellon-McCord) from Allegheny Energy in 2003; later that year it purchased two more retail energy marketing companies, Blackhawk Energy Services and Kaztex Energy Management, from Wisconsin Energy.

## EXECUTIVES

**Chairman, President, and CEO; Chairman, Baltimore Gas and Electric:** Mayo A. Shattuck III, age 52, $1,000,000 pay
**Vice Chairman; Chairman, Constellation Commodities Group:** Thomas V. (Tom) Brooks, age 43, $250,000 pay
**EVP and General Counsel:** Irving B. Yoskowitz, age 61
**EVP; President, Constellation Generation Group:** Michael J. (Mike) Wallace, age 59, $1,707,795 pay
**EVP Corporate Strategy and Retail Competitive Supply:** Thomas F. Brady, age 56
**SVP and CIO:** Beth S. Perlman, age 45
**CFO and Chief Risk Officer:** John R. Collins, age 49
**SVP and Chief Marketing Officer:** David H. Nevins
**SVP Corporate Affairs:** Paul J. Allen, age 54
**SVP Credit Risk Management:** Khalid Abedin
**SVP Human Resources:** Marc C. Ugol, age 47
**SVP Operations Services and Chief Procurement Officer:** David L. Rehn
**President, Baltimore Gas and Electric:** Kenneth W. (Ken) DeFontes Jr.
**President and CEO, BGE Home:** William H. (Bill) Munn
**President and CEO, Constellation NewEnergy:** Clement J. (Clem) Palevich
**President and CEO, Fellon-McCord & Associates and CNE, Gas Division:** Andrew R. (Drew) Fellon
**President and CEO, Constellation Energy Projects and Services Group:** Gregory S. (Greg) Jarosinski
**Co-President and Co-CEO, Constellation Commodities Group:** Felix J. Dawson, age 39, $200,000 pay
**Co-President and Co-CEO, Constellation Commodities Group:** George E. Persky, age 36, $175,000 pay
**VP, Corporate Communications:** Robert L. (Rob) Gould
**VP, Investor Relations:** Kevin W. Hadlock
**Director of Marketing:** Charles Welsh
**Auditors:** PricewaterhouseCoopers LLP

## LOCATIONS

**HQ:** Constellation Energy Group, Inc.
750 E. Pratt St., Baltimore, MD 21202
**Phone:** 410-783-2800 **Fax:** 410-783-3629
**Web:** www.constellation.com

Constellation Energy Group provides electricity and gas in Baltimore and portions of 10 counties in central Maryland. It also owns interests in power projects throughout the US.

## PRODUCTS/OPERATIONS

### 2006 Sales

| | $ mil. | % of total |
|---|---|---|
| Merchant Energy | 16,048.2 | 83 |
| Regulated electric business | 2,115.9 | 11 |
| Regulated gas business | 890.0 | 5 |
| Other nonregulated businesses | 230.8 | 1 |
| **Total** | **19,284.9** | **100** |

### Selected Subsidiaries

Merchant Energy Operations
- Constellation Energy Commodities Group (formerly Constellation Power Source, wholesale power marketing and trading)
- Constellation Generation Group, LLC (holds former BGE generation assets, plus acquired assets)
- Constellation NewEnergy (formerly AES NewEnergy, competitive retail power supply to commercial and industrial customers)

Utility and Other Unregulated Operations
- Baltimore Gas and Electric Company (BGE, gas and electric utility)
- BGE Home Products & Services, Inc. (HVAC [heating, ventilation, and air-conditioning] and plumbing, appliances, home improvements, and retail gas marketing)
- Constellation Nuclear Services, Inc. (nuclear license renewal services)
- Constellation Real Estate Group, Inc. (commercial properties)

## COMPETITORS

AEP
Allegheny Energy
AmerGen Energy
Aquila
CenterPoint Energy
Chesapeake Utilities
Dominion Resources
Duke Energy
Dynegy
Edison International
Entergy
Entergy Nuclear
Integrys Energy Services
New Jersey Resources
NiSource
Pepco Holdings
PG&E
PPL
PSEG
Sempra Energy
Southern Company
Strategic Energy
WGL Holdings
Williams Companies

## HISTORICAL FINANCIALS

Company Type: Public

### Income Statement

FYE: December 31

| | REVENUE ($ mil.) | NET INCOME ($ mil.) | NET PROFIT MARGIN | EMPLOYEES |
|---|---|---|---|---|
| **12/06** | 19,285 | 936 | 4.9% | 9,645 |
| **12/05** | 17,132 | 623 | 3.6% | 9,850 |
| **12/04** | 12,550 | 540 | 4.3% | 9,570 |
| **12/03** | 9,703 | 277 | 2.9% | 8,650 |
| **12/02** | 4,703 | 526 | 11.2% | 8,700 |
| **Annual Growth** | 42.3% | 15.5% | — | 2.6% |

### 2006 Year-End Financials

Debt ratio: 91.6%
Return on equity: 19.7%
Cash ($ mil.): 2,289
Current ratio: 1.28
Long-term debt ($ mil.): 4,222
No. of shares (mil.): 181
Dividends
Yield: 2.2%
Payout: 29.3%
Market value ($ mil.): 12,432

### Stock History

NYSE: CEG

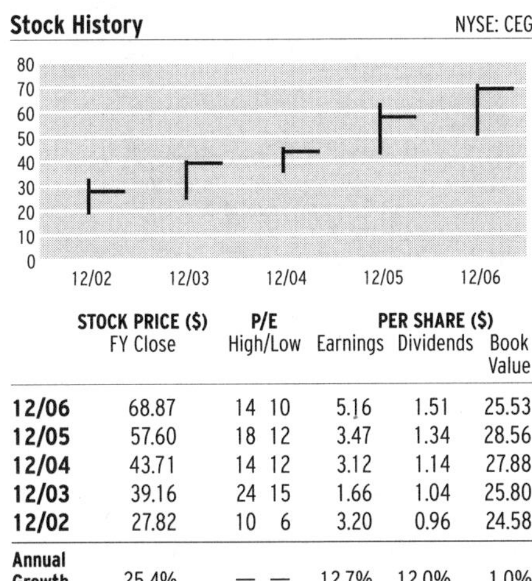


| | STOCK PRICE ($) FY Close | P/E High/Low | | PER SHARE ($) Earnings | Dividends | Book Value |
|---|---|---|---|---|---|---|
| **12/06** | 68.87 | 14 | 10 | 5.16 | 1.51 | 25.53 |
| **12/05** | 57.60 | 18 | 12 | 3.47 | 1.34 | 28.56 |
| **12/04** | 43.71 | 14 | 12 | 3.12 | 1.14 | 27.88 |
| **12/03** | 39.16 | 24 | 15 | 1.66 | 1.04 | 25.80 |
| **12/02** | 27.82 | 10 | 6 | 3.20 | 0.96 | 24.58 |
| **Annual Growth** | 25.4% | — | — | 12.7% | 12.0% | 1.0% |

# ContiGroup Companies

Knowing its place on the food chain, ContiGroup Companies (CGC) focuses on meat production. CGC operates through subsidiary Wayne Farms, a major poultry processor and Five Rivers Ranch Cattle Feeding, a 50-50 joint venture with Smithfield Foods that is one of the world's largest feedlot enterprises. Overseas it has interests in flour milling, animal feed production, aquaculture, and pork and poultry processing. CGC's investment arm, ContiInvestments, manages diverse holdings. Chairman and CEO Paul Fribourg (a descendant of founder Simon Fribourg) and his family own CGC.

CGC entered the Five Rivers joint venture with Smithfield Foods in 2005. The two companies combined their respective feedlot operations to form the new entity, which operates 10 cattle feedlots with a capacity of more than 1 million head of beef cattle in Colorado, Idaho, Kansas, Oklahoma, and Texas. CGC contributed six of the 10 feedlots, which were previously operated by its former ContiBeef subsidiary.

In 2007 Premium Standard Farms merged with Smithfield Foods. Contigroup (which owned about 39% of Premium) voted its shares in favor of the merger.

## HISTORY

Simon Fribourg founded a commodity trading business in Belgium in 1813. It operated domestically until 1848, when a drought in Belgium forced it to buy large stocks in Russian wheat.

As the Industrial Revolution swept across Europe and populations shifted to cities, people consumed more traded grain. In the midst of such rapid changes, the company prospered. After WWI, Russia, which had been Europe's primary grain supplier, ceased to be a major player in the trading game, and Western countries picked up the slack. Sensing the shift, Jules and Rene Fribourg reorganized the business as Continental Grain and opened its first US office in Chicago in 1921.

Throughout the Depression the company bought US grain elevators, often at low prices. Through its purchases, Continental Grain built a North American grain network that included major locations like Kansas City, Missouri; Nashville, Tennessee; and Toledo, Ohio.

In Europe, meanwhile, the Fribourgs were forced to endure constant political and economic upheaval, often profiting from it (they supplied food to Republican forces during the Spanish Civil War). When Nazis invaded Belgium in 1940, the Fribourgs were forced to flee, but they reorganized the business in New York City after the war.

Following the war, Continental Grain pioneered US grain trade with the Soviets. The company went on a buying spree in the 1960s and 1970s, acquiring Allied Mills (feed milling, 1965) and absorbing many agricultural and transport businesses, including Texas feedlots, a bakery, and the Quaker Oats agricultural products unit.

During the 1980s Continental Grain sold its baking units (Oroweat and Arnold) and its commodities brokerage house. Amid an agricultural bust, it formed ContiFinancial and other financial units.

Michel Fribourg stepped down as CEO in 1988 and was succeeded by Donald Staheli, the first outside CEO. The company entered a grain-handling and selling joint venture with Scoular in 1991. Three years later Staheli added the title of chairman, and Michel's son Paul became president. Continental Grain sold a stake in ContiFinancial (home equity loans and investment banking) to the public in 1996. Also in 1996 the firm formed ContiInvestments, an investment arm geared toward the parent company's areas of expertise.

That year Continental Grain and an overseas affiliate (Arab Finagrain) agreed to pay the US government $35 million, which included a $10 million fine against Arab Finagrain, to settle a fraud case involving commodity sales to Iraq.

Paul succeeded Staheli as CEO in 1997. The company bought Campbell Soup's poultry processing units that year, and in 1998 it bought a 51% stake in pork producer/processor Premium Standard Farms. Meanwhile, ContiFinancial diversified into retail home mortgage and home equity lending.

Continental Grain sold its commodities marketing business in July 1999 to #1 grain exporter Cargill. With its grain operations gone, in 1999 the company renamed itself ContiGroup Companies.

During 2000 ContiFinancial declared bankruptcy, and ContiGroup sold its Animal Nutrition Division (Wayne Foods) to feed manufacturer Ridley Inc. for $37 million. In mid-2000, Premium Standard Farms doubled its processing capacity with the purchase of Lundy Packing Company. Chairman emeritus Michel Fribourg, the founder's great-great-grandson, died in 2001. That same year ContiSea, the salmon and seafood processing joint venture between ContiGroup and Seaboard, was sold to Norway's Fjord Seafood, giving ContiGroup a significant share of Fjord.

To better focus on its food and agribusiness holdings, in early 2003 ContiGroup sold off its ContiChem LPG business.

## EXECUTIVES

**Chairman, President, and CEO:** Paul J. Fribourg, age 53
**EVP, Human Resources and Information Systems:** Teresa E. McCaslin
**EVP, Investments and Strategy and CFO; President, ContiInvestments:** Michael J. Zimmerman, age 56
**CEO, ContiBeef:** Mike Thoren
**CEO, Premium Standard Farms:** John M. Meyer, age 44
**CEO, Wayne Farms:** Elton Maddox
**SVP and Managing Director, ContiAsia:** Michael A. Hoer
**VP and General Manager, ContiLatin:** Brian Anderson

## LOCATIONS

**HQ:** ContiGroup Companies, Inc.
277 Park Ave., New York, NY 10172
**Phone:** 212-207-5100 **Fax:** 212-207-5499
**Web:** www.contigroup.com

## PRODUCTS/OPERATIONS

### Major Business Units

ContiAsia (feed milling, pork production, and poultry production; China)
ContiInvestments, LLC (investment management)
ContiLatin (feed and flour milling, poultry operations, and shrimp farming; Caribbean and Latin America)
Five Rivers Ranch Cattle Feeding LLC (joint venture with Smithfield Foods, cattle feedlot operations)
Premium Standard Farms, Inc. (39%, hog and pork production)
Wayne Farms, LLC (poultry production)

## COMPETITORS

Agri Beef
Alico
AzTx Cattle
Cactus Feeders
Cargill
CHS
ConAgra
Golden Belt Feeders
Hormel
JR Simplot
King Ranch
New Market Poultry
Pilgrim's Pride
Seaboard
Smithfield Foods
Tyson Foods

## HISTORICAL FINANCIALS

Company Type: Private

**Income Statement** FYE: March 31

| | REVENUE ($ mil.) | NET INCOME ($ mil.) | NET PROFIT MARGIN | EMPLOYEES |
|---|---|---|---|---|
| **3/05** | 1,900 | — | — | 14,500 |
| **3/04** | 2,200 | — | — | 15,500 |
| **3/03** | 2,000 | — | — | 13,500 |
| **3/02** | 3,300 | — | — | 14,500 |
| **3/01** | 4,000 | — | — | 14,500 |
| **Annual Growth** | (17.0%) | — | — | 0.0% |

**Revenue History**

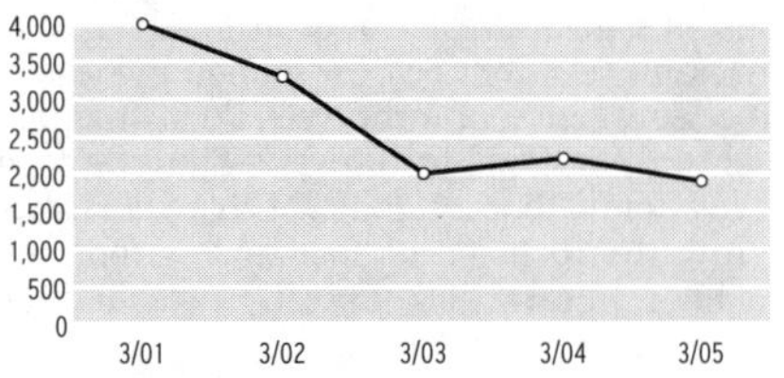


# Continental Airlines

If it's a continent, chances are it's accessible via Continental Airlines. A leading US carrier, Continental serves about 135 domestic and 125 international markets from hubs in Cleveland, Houston, and Newark, New Jersey. Subsidiary Continental Micronesia serves the western Pacific from Guam, and regional carriers operating as Continental Express and Continental Connection extend the airline's network. Overall, Continental operates a fleet of some 370 mainline jets and 270 regional jets. The carrier supplements its offerings through code-sharing with fellow members of the SkyTeam alliance, which includes carriers such as Air France, Alitalia, Delta, KLM, and Northwest Airlines, as well as with other airlines.

As has been the case with most of its peers, Continental has been forced by record fuel prices to seek significant cost reductions, primarily in the form of wage reductions and modifications to employment benefits. At the same time, the company has benefited from strong demand for international travel, where price competition on many routes is less fierce than in the US. To bolster its overseas offerings, the carrier has applied to the US government for permission to fly nonstop between Newark and Shanghai, beginning in 2009.

Continental also has been working to wring costs from its regional operations, and it has reduced its stake in former subsidiary ExpressJet to about 10%. After contract negotiations with ExpressJet for regional service fell apart, Continental said it would cut purchased capacity of ExpressJet flights, and Chautauqua Airlines, a unit of Republic Airways Holdings, has been chosen to serve as a second main regional carrier. ExpressJet will continue to lease aircraft from Continental, but the regional carrier will pay a higher rate and fly under a brand other than Continental Express.

The airline industry's troubles since the downturn in travel that followed the terrorist attacks of September 11, 2001, have led to talk of consolidation, and Continental reportedly has discussed combining with rival United Airlines and its parent, UAL Corp. A potential complication: Northwest Airlines, which used to have a majority voting stake in Continental, holds just one share, but one that allows it to block a sale of the carrier.

## HISTORY

Varney Speed Lines, the fourth airline begun by Walter Varney, was founded in 1934. It became Continental Airlines three years later when Robert Six, whose own airline had folded during the Depression, bought 40% of the carrier. Six convinced his father-in-law, chairman of drugmaker Charles Pfizer Co., to lend him $90,000 for the stake in Varney.

In 1951 Continental spent $7.6 million to update its fleet, a sum equal to its profit that year. It was a bold move for a small airline in an industry moving toward ever-larger aircraft. Two years later Continental merged with Pioneer Airlines, adding routes to 16 cities in Texas and New Mexico. It also added jets in the late 1950s to compete on cross-country routes. To maintain its small Boeing 707 fleet, Continental developed a maintenance system that enabled it to fly the planes 15 hours a day, seven days a week.

In 1962 the carrier suffered its first crash. The next year it moved its headquarters from Denver to Los Angeles. A transport service contract with the US military during the Vietnam War led to the formation of Air Micronesia in 1968.

Economic downturn, industry deregulation, and rising fuel costs left Continental with a string of losses in the late 1970s (it would lose more than $500 million between 1978 and 1983). Over the objections of Continental's unions, Frank Lorenzo's Texas Air bought the company in 1982.

Texas Air had been founded in 1947 to provide service within Texas, and by 1970 it also flew to the West Coast and Mexico. Bankrupt two years later, the company was acquired by Lorenzo, who returned it to profitability by 1976 — just in time for airline deregulation in 1978.

When Continental's union employees went on strike in 1983, Lorenzo maneuvered the airline into Chapter 11. It emerged from bankruptcy in 1986 as a low-fare carrier with the industry's lowest labor costs. That year Texas Air bought Eastern Air Lines, People Express, and Frontier Airlines.

In 1990 Lorenzo resigned as head of the company, and Texas Air changed its name to Continental Airlines Holdings. With fuel prices soaring because of the Mideast conflict, Continental again filed for bankruptcy. Gordon Bethune became CEO in 1994 and piloted Continental to a comeback with an investment by Air Partners/Air Canada and with a reduction in routes and staff.

In 1997 Bethune's honeymoon with employees ended as the pilots union negotiated for an accelerated pay-raise schedule; a five-year contract was ratified in 1998. That year Northwest Airlines paid $370 million for 13.5% of Continental, beating a takeover bid from Delta.

Northwest reduced its voting control of Continental to 5% in 2001, but maintained the right to block the sale of Continental to a third party. Also that year Continental announced plans to sell a minority stake in its ExpressJet unit, the parent of Continental Express, to the public.

Also in 2001 terrorist attacks in New York and Washington, DC, led Continental to reduce its flights and lay off more than 21% of its workforce.

The following year, ExpressJet went public, reducing Continental's stake in the regional carrier to 53%. In a unique cross-industry partnership, Continental signed a codeshare agreement with Amtrak in 2002. The agreement linked Continental's Newark International Hub to five northeastern cities.

With some 100,000 positions eliminated and $19 billion lost in the two years since September 11, 2001, Continental made more cuts to its staff, including 1,200 workers and a 20% reduction in senior management.

In the weeks after September 11, complaints against the airline for discrimination made their way to the US Transportation Department. The government and Continental reached a settlement in 2004. Also that year Continental, Northwest, and Delta received federal approval to form a marketing alliance, the largest such alliance among US carriers.

Chairman and CEO Bethune retired in January 2005 and was succeeded by Larry Kellner. The following month Continental received US Department of Transportation approval to offer service to Beijing from Newark Liberty International Airport.

## EXECUTIVES

**Chairman and CEO:** Lawrence W. (Larry) Kellner, age 47, $752,083 pay
**President and Director:** Jeffery A. (Jeff) Smisek, age 52, $600,000 pay
**EVP and CFO:** Jeffrey J. (Jeff) Misner, age 52, $375,000 pay
**EVP, Marketing:** James (Jim) Compton, age 50, $375,000 pay
**EVP, Operations:** Mark J. Moran, age 50, $375,000 pay
**SVP, Asia Pacific and Corporate Development; President and CEO, Continental Micronesia:** Mark A. Erwin, age 50
**SVP, Customer Experience:** J. David Grizzle, age 49
**SVP, Finance and Treasurer:** Gerald (Gerry) Laderman, age 47
**SVP, General Counsel, Secretary, and Corporate Compliance Officer:** Jennifer Vogel, age 43
**SVP, Government Affairs:** Rebecca G. Cox, age 50
**SVP, Human Resources and Labor Relations:** Michael P. (Mike) Bonds
**SVP, Sales:** Dave Hilfman, age 44
**SVP, Technical Operations and Purchasing:** Dante R. Marzetta II, age 61
**SVP, Worldwide Corporate Communications:** John E. (Ned) Walker, age 53
**SVP and CIO:** Ron Anderson-Lehman
**SVP, Marketing Programs and Distribution:** Mark Bergsrud
**SVP, Network Strategy:** Zane Rowe
**President and CEO, Continental Express:** James B. (Jim) Ream, age 51
**Director, Investor Relations:** DeAnne Gabel
**Auditors:** Ernst & Young LLP

## LOCATIONS

**HQ:** Continental Airlines, Inc.
1600 Smith St., Dept. HQSEO, Houston, TX 77002
**Phone:** 713-324-2950 **Fax:** 713-324-2687
**Web:** www.continental.com

**2006 Passenger Revenue**

| | $ mil. | % of total |
|---|---|---|
| Mainline | | |
| Domestic | 5,413 | 45 |
| Transatlantic | 2,085 | 17 |
| Latin America | 1,343 | 11 |
| Pacific | 888 | 8 |
| Regional | 2,274 | 19 |
| **Total** | **12,003** | **100** |

## PRODUCTS/OPERATIONS

### 2006 Sales

| | $ mil. | % of total |
|---|---|---|
| Passenger | 12,003 | 91 |
| Cargo | 457 | 4 |
| Other | 668 | 5 |
| **Total** | **13,128** | **100** |

## COMPETITORS

ACE Aviation
AirTran Holdings
Alaska Air
All Nippon Airways
AMR Corp.
British Airways
Cathay Pacific
Japan Airlines
JetBlue
Lufthansa
Qantas
SAS
Singapore Airlines
Southwest Airlines
UAL
US Airways

## HISTORICAL FINANCIALS

Company Type: Public

### Income Statement

FYE: December 31

| | REVENUE ($ mil.) | NET INCOME ($ mil.) | NET PROFIT MARGIN | EMPLOYEES |
|---|---|---|---|---|
| **12/06** | 13,128 | 343 | 2.6% | 43,770 |
| **12/05** | 11,208 | (68) | — | 42,200 |
| **12/04** | 9,899 | (409) | — | 38,255 |
| **12/03** | 8,870 | 38 | 0.4% | 37,680 |
| **12/02** | 8,402 | (441) | — | 43,900 |
| **Annual Growth** | 11.8% | — | — | (0.1%) |

### 2006 Year-End Financials

Debt ratio: 1,400.3%
Return on equity: 119.7%
Cash ($ mil.): 2,749
Current ratio: 1.04
Long-term debt ($ mil.): 4,859
No. of shares (mil.): 92
Dividends
Yield: —
Payout: —
Market value ($ mil.): 3,787

### Stock History

NYSE: CAL

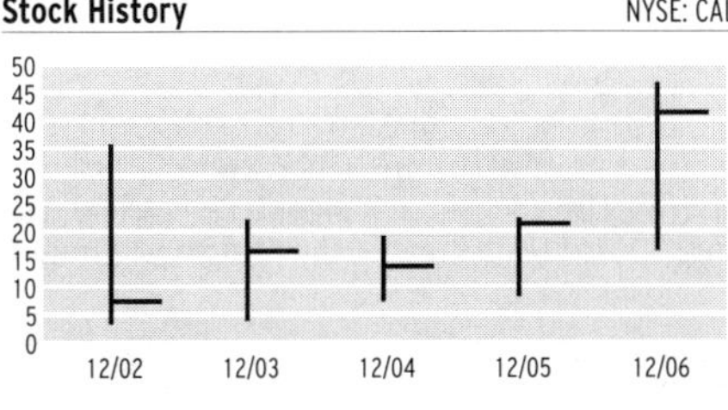

| | STOCK PRICE ($) FY Close | P/E High | P/E Low | PER SHARE ($) Earnings | PER SHARE ($) Dividends | PER SHARE ($) Book Value |
|---|---|---|---|---|---|---|
| **12/06** | 41.25 | 14 | 5 | 3.30 | — | 3.78 |
| **12/05** | 21.30 | — | — | (0.97) | — | 2.60 |
| **12/04** | 13.54 | — | — | (6.25) | — | 2.33 |
| **12/03** | 16.27 | 37 | 7 | 0.58 | — | 11.99 |
| **12/02** | 7.25 | — | — | (7.02) | — | 11.66 |
| **Annual Growth** | 54.4% | — | — | — | — | (24.6%) |

# Con-way Inc.

Con-way is a leading provider of trucking and logistics services. The company's regional less-than-truckload (LTL) carriers, which do business under the Con-way Freight brand, operate throughout North America. (LTL carriers consolidate loads from multiple shippers into a single truckload.) Con-way also offers truckload transportation services. Overall, the company operates a fleet of about 7,800 tractors and 30,500 trailers from a network of some 440 terminals. Con-way's Menlo Worldwide unit provides contract logistics, freight brokerage, and supply chain management services.

Con-way, formerly known as CNF, changed its name in 2006 in an effort to simplify its branding. In conjunction with the rebranding, Con-way moved to simplify its operations by selling its expedited transportation business and closing its freight forwarding unit. The Menlo Worldwide brand is being retained — for now. Con-way will study global trademark issues before deciding whether to rename its logistics operations.

The company hopes to grow not only via rebranding, but also by investing in its terminals and its fleet. In July 2007, Con-way agreed to acquire truckload carrier Contract Freighters, Inc., (CFI) for $750 million. Con-way plans to integrate CFI into its existing truckload division.

## HISTORY

What is now Con-way got its start in 1929, when Leland James, co-owner of a bus company in Portland, Oregon, founded Consolidated Truck Lines to serve in the Pacific Northwest. Operations extended to San Francisco and Idaho by 1934 and to North Dakota by 1936. It adopted the name Consolidated Freightways (CF) in 1939.

James formed Freightways Manufacturing that year, making CF the only trucking company to design and build its own trucks (Freightliners). In the 1940s CF extended service to Chicago, Minneapolis, and Los Angeles.

CF went public in 1951 and moved to Menlo Park, California, in 1956. It continued to buy companies (52 between 1955 and 1960) and extended its reach throughout the US and Canada. When an attempt to coordinate intermodal services with railroads and shipping lines failed in 1960, William White became president and exited intermodal operations to focus on less-than-truckload shipping.

In 1966 CF formed CF AirFreight to offer air cargo services in the US. Three years later it bought Pacific Far East Lines, a San Francisco shipping line (now a part of Con-Way).

CF sold Freightways Manufacturing to Daimler-Benz (now Daimler AG) in 1981 and started the Con-Way carriers, its regional trucking businesses, in 1983 after the US trucking industry was deregulated. In the 1980s Con-Way moved back into intermodal rail, truck, and ocean shipping.

The company bought Emery Air Freight in 1989 and combined it with CF AirFreight to form Emery Worldwide. Founded in 1946, Emery Air Freight had expanded across the US and overseas, first by using extra cargo space on scheduled airline flights, then by chartering aircraft. Later operating its own air fleet, Emery began having troubles in the 1980s, including difficulties in integrating its 1987 acquisition, Purolator Courier. A 1988 takeover attempt by former FedEx president Arthur Bass further plagued Emery; fending off the takeover resulted in losses of about $100 million in 1989. That year Emery brought CF a deal with the U.S. Postal Service (USPS) to handle its next-day express mail.

Amid the beginning of a three-year profit slump, CF formed Menlo Logistics in 1990 to provide its customers with a range of third-party logistics services. A Teamsters' strike in 1994 that halted union carriers nationwide boosted demand for Con-Way's services as customers sought nonunion carriers to move their shipments. The next year Con-Way opened 40 service centers and bought another 3,300 tractors and trailers.

In 1996 CF spun off most of its long-haul transportation businesses (including CF MotorFreight, Canadian Freightways, and Milne & Craighead) and renamed the resulting entity Consolidated Freightways. CF then changed its own name to CNF Transportation.

CNF Transportation received a five-year, $1.7 billion contract from USPS in 1997 to sort and transport two-day priority mail in the eastern US. The next year Menlo won contracts from six companies, including Intel and IBM, expected to generate more than $1 billion by 2003.

In 2000 CNF Transportation shortened its name to CNF and began renegotiating its money-losing second-day priority mail contract with USPS. (FedEx eventually got the job.) That year CNF formed Vector SCM, a supply chain management and logistics joint venture with General Motors. In 2001 CNF's Con-Way Transportation established Con-Way Air Express, an airfreight forwarder that serves the US and Puerto Rico.

Emery grounded its aircraft fleet in 2001 because of maintenance problems discovered by Federal Aviation Administration inspectors. The company hired other carriers in order to continue its airfreight services. In a settlement with the FAA, Emery agreed to pay a $1 million civil fine.

To emphasize its focus on logistics, CNF combined the operations of Emery Worldwide, Menlo Logistics, and Vector SCM into a new company, Menlo Worldwide, effective in January 2002. In 2004 CNF sold its freight forwarding unit, Menlo Worldwide Forwarding (formerly known as Emery Forwarding) and its subsidiary, Menlo Worldwide Expedite, to rival UPS for $150 million, plus the assumption of $110 million in debt. The move was an opportunity to strengthen CNF's balance sheet and exit a low-margin business.

As part of an effort to focus on its operating businesses, CNF renamed itself Con-way in 2006. In conjunction with the name change, the businesses of the former Con-Way Transportation Services were split between Con-way Freight and Con-way Transportation LLC (later renamed Con-way Truckload Services). Con-way shut down its Con-way Forwarding subsidiary, which specialized in domestic airfreight forwarding, and sold its expedited freight transportation business to Panther Expedited Services.

Also in 2006, the Vector SCM joint venture was unwound when GM exercised its option to buy out partner Menlo Worldwide for about $85 million.

## EXECUTIVES

**Chairman:** W. Keith Kennedy Jr., age 63, $1,233,669 pay
**President and CEO:** Douglas W. Stotlar, age 46, $673,569 pay
**SVP and CFO:** Kevin C. Schick, age 55, $347,705 pay
**SVP, General Counsel, and Corporate Secretary:** Jennifer W. Pileggi, age 42, $490,703 pay
**VP and CIO:** Jacquelyn (Jackie) Barretta, age 45
**VP and Chief Tax Officer:** J. Craig Boretz
**VP and Treasurer:** Mark C. Thickpenny, age 54
**VP and Corporate Controller:** Kevin S. Coel, age 48
**VP, Communications and Chief Marketing Officer:** Thomas (Tom) Nightingale
**VP, Culture and Training:** Julia P. (Pat) Jannausch, age 50
**VP, Government Relations:** C. Randal Mullett
**VP, Human Resources:** Leslie P. Lundberg
**VP, Internal Audit:** Maureen Maag, age 49
**VP, Investor Relations:** Patrick J. (Pat) Fossenier
**VP, Marketing:** Edward P. (Ned) Moritz
**VP, Procurement:** Mitchell E. (Mitch) Plaat
**VP, Strategic Planning:** Richard J. (Rich) Lunardi
**Director, Corporate Communications:** Gary N. Frantz
**Auditors:** KPMG LLP

## LOCATIONS

**HQ:** Con-way Inc.
2855 Campus Dr., Ste. 300, San Mateo, CA 94403
**Phone:** 650-378-5200 **Fax:** 650-357-9160
**Web:** www.con-way.com

**2006 Sales**

| | $ mil. | % of total |
|---|---|---|
| US | 4,072.0 | 96 |
| Canada | 67.8 | 2 |
| Other countries | 81.7 | 2 |
| **Total** | **4,221.5** | **100** |

## PRODUCTS/OPERATIONS

**2006 Sales**

| | $ mil. | % of total |
|---|---|---|
| Con-way Freight and Transportation | 2,866.2 | 68 |
| Menlo Worldwide Logistics | 1,355.3 | 32 |
| **Total** | **4,221.5** | **100** |

## COMPETITORS

APL Logistics
Arkansas Best
BAX Global
Central Freight Lines
CEVA Logistics
C.H. Robinson Worldwide
DHL
EGL Eagle Global Logistics
Estes Express
Expeditors
FedEx Freight
FedEx Trade Networks
GeoLogistics
J.B. Hunt
Old Dominion Freight
Pacer Global Logistics
Panalpina, Inc.
Ryder
Saia, Inc.
Schneider National
Transplace
UPS Freight
UPS Supply Chain Solutions
UTi Worldwide
YRC Worldwide

## HISTORICAL FINANCIALS

Company Type: Public

**Income Statement** FYE: December 31

| | REVENUE ($ mil.) | NET INCOME ($ mil.) | NET PROFIT MARGIN | EMPLOYEES |
|---|---|---|---|---|
| **12/06** | 4,222 | 266 | 6.3% | 21,800 |
| **12/05** | 4,170 | 223 | 5.3% | 21,800 |
| **12/04** | 3,712 | (116) | — | 20,100 |
| **12/03** | 5,104 | 92 | 1.8% | 26,000 |
| **12/02** | 4,762 | 102 | 2.1% | 26,200 |
| **Annual Growth** | (3.0%) | 27.2% | — | (4.5%) |

**2006 Year-End Financials**

Debt ratio: 75.3%
Return on equity: 32.2%
Cash ($ mil.): 445
Current ratio: 1.95
Long-term debt ($ mil.): 558
No. of shares (mil.): 46
Dividends
Yield: 1.1%
Payout: 10.0%
Market value ($ mil.): 2,046

**Stock History** NYSE: CNW

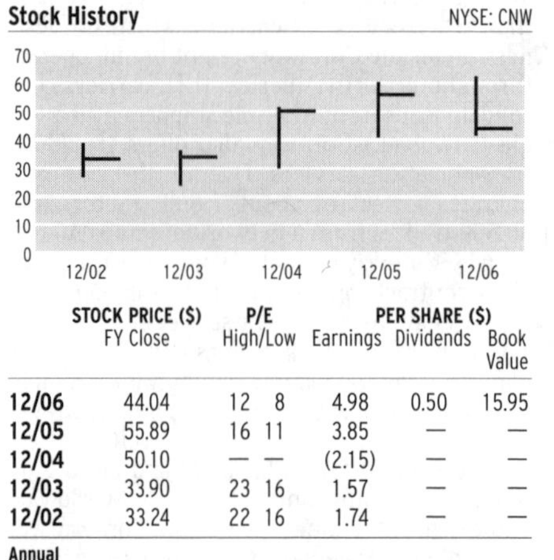


| | STOCK PRICE ($) FY Close | P/E High | P/E Low | PER SHARE ($) Earnings | Dividends | Book Value |
|---|---|---|---|---|---|---|
| **12/06** | 44.04 | 12 | 8 | 4.98 | 0.50 | 15.95 |
| **12/05** | 55.89 | 16 | 11 | 3.85 | — | — |
| **12/04** | 50.10 | — | — | (2.15) | — | — |
| **12/03** | 33.90 | 23 | 16 | 1.57 | — | — |
| **12/02** | 33.24 | 22 | 16 | 1.74 | — | — |
| **Annual Growth** | 7.3% | — | — | 30.1% | — | — |

# Cooper Industries

Cooper Industries likes to keep customers from blowing a fuse. Cooper makes electrical products, tools, hardware, and metal support products. The company's electrical products include electrical and circuit protection devices, residential and industrial lighting, and electrical power and distribution products for use by utility companies. Cooper's tool offerings include such venerable brands as Crescent wrenches and pliers, Apex impact sockets, Plumb hammers, and Weller soldering and welding supplies. Subsidiary Cooper B-Line makes metal support products that include conduits, cable trays, and fasteners.

Electrical products account for more than 80% of Cooper Industries' sales, and the company has expanded those offerings with acquisitions.

In early 2007 the company acquired WPI Interconnect Products, a manufacturer of custom connectors and cable assemblies for commercial, industrial, and military applications. WPI was added to the Crouse-Hinds division. Cooper paid about $74.5 million for WPI.

Cooper made a $29 million tender offer for Polaron, a UK-based supplier of lighting control products for the non-residential construction market, and acquired the company in early 2007.

FMR (Fidelity Instruments) owns about 10% of Cooper Industries. Barrow, Hanley, Mewhinney & Strauss holds nearly 7% of the company, as does The Vanguard Group.

## HISTORY

In 1833 Charles Cooper sold a horse for $50 and borrowed additional money to open a foundry with his brother Elias in Mount Vernon, Ohio. Known as C. & E. Cooper, the company made plows, hog troughs, maple syrup kettles, stoves, and wagon boxes.

C. & E. Cooper began making steam engines in the 1840s for mill and farm use; it later adapted its engines for wood-burning locomotives. In 1868 the company built its first Corliss steam engine, and in 1875 it introduced the first steam-powered farm tractor. By 1900 C. & E. Cooper sold its steam engines in the US and overseas. In 1909 the company debuted an internal combustion engine-compressor for natural gas pipelines.

In the 1920s the company became the #1 seller of compression engines for oil and gas pipelines. A 1929 merger with Bessemer (small engines) created Cooper-Bessemer, which made diesel engines for power boats.

Diversification began in 1959 with the purchase of Rotor Tools. Cooper adopted its current name in 1965 and moved its headquarters to Houston in 1967. It went on to buy other firms, including Lufkin Rule (measuring tapes, 1967), Crescent (wrenches, 1968), and Weller (soldering tools, 1970).

Cooper's 1979 purchase of Gardner-Denver gave it a strong footing in oil-drilling and mining equipment, and the addition of Crouse-Hinds in 1981 was key to its diversification into electrical materials. The decline in oil prices in the early 1980s caused sales to drop, but Cooper stayed profitable due to its tools and electrical products.

Cooper's electrical segment expanded with the 1985 purchase of McGraw-Edison, a maker of consumer products (Buss fuses) and heavy transmission gear for electrical utilities. Growth continued as it added RTE (electrical equipment, 1988), Cameron Iron Works (oil-drilling equipment, 1989), and Ferramentas Belzer do Brasil (hand-tool maker, 1992).

Expanding into auto parts, Cooper bought Champion Spark Plug (1989) and Moog (auto replacement parts, 1992). From 1991 to 1993, the company divested 11 businesses and bought 13. In 1994 it spun off Gardner-Denver Industrial Machinery, sold Cameron Forged Products, and added Abex Friction Products (brake materials) and Zanxx (lighting components) to its auto parts line.

Cooper spun off Cooper Cameron (petroleum equipment; now Cameron International) in 1995. The next year Cooper bought electrical fuse supplier Karp Electric, tool manufacturer Master Power, and electrical hub maker Myers Electric Products. Company veteran John Riley took over as chairman that year. Cooper added eight acquisitions in 1997, and some, such as Menvier-Swain Group (emergency lights and alarms, UK), helped to bolster its electrical segment. Despite its growth, the company trimmed its workforce by 30% that year.

Cooper completed 11 acquisitions in 1998 and 10 in 1999; among them were the tool business of Global Industrial Technologies (Quackenbush and Rotor Tool brands), Apparatebau Hundsbach (electronic sensors) and Metronix Elektronik (power tool controls), and several lighting firms. In the meantime, the company sold its automotive operations to Federal-Mogul.

In 2000 Cooper acquired B-Line Systems from Sigma-Aldrich for around $425 million. The next year tool maker Danaher offered to acquire Cooper in a deal worth about $5.5 billion. Cooper rejected the initial offer, then Danaher lost interest when Cooper's former automotive unit (sold in 1998) was named in asbestos lawsuits. (Cooper recorded a charge of about $125 million for discontinued operations in 2003 for liability exposure relating to those claims.)

In 2002 the company reincorporated in Bermuda for tax reasons and changed its name from Cooper Industries, Inc., to Cooper Industries, Ltd. As announced in 2002, the company began expensing the cost of all stock options granted after January 1, 2003.

RSA Lighting (commercial lighting fixtures) was purchased in 2004 to expand the architectural lighting product line of its Cooper Lighting division. Cooper's 2004 purchase of UK-based MEDC Limited, a privately held maker of emergency alarms and public address speakers, bolstered its Cooper Crouse-Hinds division. In 2006 Cooper acquired electrical interconnect maker G&H Technology, which also was integrated into Crouse-Hinds. Its concurrent acquisition of occupancy sensor and accessory manufacturer Novitas expanded its Cooper Wiring Devices division. Cooper also purchased fire safety and emergency communication systems maker Wheelock to bolster its Cooper Menvier operations.

## EXECUTIVES

**Chairman, President, and CEO:** Kirk S. Hachigian, age 47, $4,133,000 pay
**EVP, Cooper Connection:** Paul M. Isabella, age 51, $623,333 pay (partial-year salary)
**SVP and CFO:** Terry A. Klebe, age 51, $695,500 pay
**SVP, Business Development:** C. Thomas (Tom) O'Grady, age 55, $307,500 pay
**SVP and General Counsel:** Kevin M. McDonald
**SVP, Human Resources:** James P. Williams, age 44
**VP and Treasurer:** Alan J. Hill, age 60
**VP, Operations:** David L. Pawl, age 58
**VP, Internal Audit:** David T. Gunther, age 40
**VP, Finance:** Jeffrey B. Levos, age 46
**VP, Business Systems:** Kenneth V. Camarco, age 42
**VP, Personnel:** Brian D. Rayl, age 49
**VP, Taxes:** John B. Reed, age 55
**VP, International Operations:** Grant L. Gawronski, age 44, $306,667 pay
**VP, Environmental Affairs and Risk Management:** Robert W. Teets, age 55
**VP, Public Affairs:** Victoria B. Guennewig, age 54
**Chief Marketing Officer:** James T. Pendley, age 35
**Treasurer:** Stephen M. Kole, age 54
**Associate General Counsel and Secretary:** Terrance V. Helz, age 52
**Director, Investor Relations:** Jon Safran
**Auditors:** Ernst & Young LLP

## LOCATIONS

**HQ:** Cooper Industries, Ltd.
600 Travis, Ste. 5800, Houston, TX 77002
**Phone:** 713-209-8400 **Fax:** 713-209-8996
**Web:** www.cooperindustries.com

Cooper Industries has manufacturing and warehouse facilities in 21 countries worldwide.

### 2006 Sales

| | $ mil. | % of total |
|---|---|---|
| US | 3,781.1 | 73 |
| UK | 305.3 | 6 |
| Germany | 253.5 | 5 |
| Canada | 226.3 | 4 |
| Mexico | 172.4 | 3 |
| Other countries | 446.0 | 9 |
| **Total** | **5,184.6** | **100** |

## PRODUCTS/OPERATIONS

### 2006 Sales

| | $ mil. | % of total |
|---|---|---|
| Electrical products | 4,426.0 | 85 |
| Tools & hardware | 758.6 | 15 |
| **Total** | **5,184.6** | **100** |

### Selected Products and Brands

Electrical Products
- Architectural recessed lighting (Portfolio)
- Architectural and landscape lighting (Lumiere)
- Aviation lighting products (Crouse-Hinds)
- Current-limiting fuses (Combined Technologies)
- Distribution switchgear (Kyle)
- Electric fuses (B&S, Edison, Karp, Mercury)
- Electrical connectors (Cam-Lok)
- Electrical construction materials (CEAG, Crouse-Hinds)
- Electrical hubs (Myers)
- Electrical outlet and switch boxes (Thepitt)
- Emergency alarm systems
- Emergency lighting and fire-detection systems (CEAG, JSB, Luminox, Menvier)
- Emergency lighting and power systems (Blessing, CSA, Pretronica, Univel)
- Enclosures (B-Line)
- Exit and emergency lighting (AtLite, Sure-Lites)
- Fire-detection systems (Fulleon, Nugelec, Transmould)
- Fluorescent lighting (Metalux)
- Fasteners (B-Line)
- Fuses (Buss, Kearney)
- High-abuse, clean room, and vandal-resistant lighting fixtures (Fail-Safe)
- Indoor and outdoor HID lighting (McGraw-Edison)
- Inductors and transformers (Coiltronics)
- Lighting systems (Iris)
- Modular wiring systems (MWS)
- Plugs and receptacles (Arktite)
- Public address systems
- Recessed and track-lighting fixtures (Halo)
- Relays (Edison and Edison Pro)
- Security equipment (Menvier, Scantronic)
- Terminal strips and disconnect blocks (Magnum)
- Transformer components, cable accessories, and fuses (McGraw-Edison, RTE)
- Transient voltage protection devices (TransX)
- Wiring devices (Arrow Hart)

Tools and Hardware
- Assembly equipment, assembly stations, and transport lines (Assembly Systems, Cooper Automation, DGD/Gardner-Denver, GardoTrans)
- Chain products (Campbell)
- Cutters and tweezers (Erem)
- Farrier tools (Diamond)
- Files and saws (Nicholson)
- Hammers (Plumb)
- Industrial power tools (Airetool, Buckeye, Cleco, Dotco, Quackenbush, Rotor Tool)
- Measuring and layout products (Lufkin)
- Scissors, shears, and snips (H.K. Porter and Wiss)
- Screwdrivers and nutdrivers (Xcelite)
- Sockets, screwdriver bits, extensions, and universal joints (Apex, Geta)
- Soldering equipment (Weller)
- Torque-measuring and control equipment (Utica)
- Wrenches and pliers (Crescent)

## COMPETITORS

ABB
Acuity Brands
Atlas Copco
Black & Decker
Danaher
Dover
Eaton
Emerson Electric
Fiskars
GE
Genlyte Group
Hubbell
Illinois Tool Works
Ingersoll-Rand
Makita
Milwaukee Electric Tool
Molex
Newell Rubbermaid
Philips Electronics
Siemens AG
Simpson Manufacturing
SL Industries
Snap-on
Stanley Works
Thomas & Betts
Tinnerman Palnut
Tyco

## HISTORICAL FINANCIALS

Company Type: Public

### Income Statement

FYE: December 31

| | REVENUE ($ mil.) | NET INCOME ($ mil.) | NET PROFIT MARGIN | EMPLOYEES |
|---|---|---|---|---|
| **12/06** | 5,185 | 464 | 8.9% | 30,561 |
| **12/05** | 4,730 | 164 | 3.5% | 28,903 |
| **12/04** | 4,463 | 340 | 7.6% | 26,863 |
| **12/03** | 4,061 | 148 | 3.7% | 27,188 |
| **12/02** | 3,961 | 214 | 5.4% | 28,462 |
| **Annual Growth** | 7.0% | 21.4% | — | 1.8% |

### 2006 Year-End Financials

Debt ratio: 28.4%
Return on equity: 19.8%
Cash ($ mil.): 424
Current ratio: 1.46
Long-term debt ($ mil.): 703
No. of shares (mil.): 91
Dividends
Yield: 1.6%
Payout: 30.0%
Market value ($ mil.): 4,121

### Stock History

NYSE: CBE

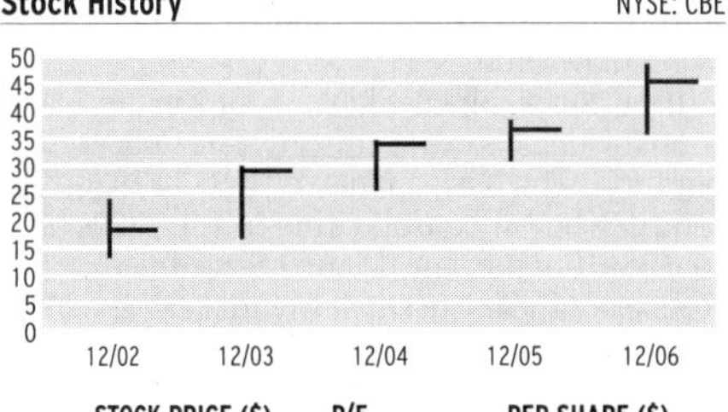


| | STOCK PRICE ($) FY Close | P/E High | P/E Low | PER SHARE ($) Earnings | Dividends | Book Value |
|---|---|---|---|---|---|---|
| **12/06** | 45.22 | 19 | 15 | 2.47 | 0.74 | 27.16 |
| **12/05** | 36.50 | 44 | 36 | 0.87 | 0.74 | 24.07 |
| **12/04** | 33.94 | 19 | 14 | 1.79 | 0.70 | 24.71 |
| **12/03** | 28.97 | 37 | 21 | 0.79 | 0.70 | 22.76 |
| **12/02** | 18.23 | 21 | 12 | 1.14 | 0.70 | 21.47 |
| **Annual Growth** | 25.5% | — | — | 21.3% | 1.4% | 6.0% |

# Cooper Tire & Rubber

Cooper Tire & Rubber is a real wheeler-dealer. As its name indicates, the company makes and distributes tires and rubber products for the transportation industry. Through its North American Tire and International Tire divisions, Cooper makes tires for passenger cars, light trucks, and medium-duty trucks. It also makes tread rubber and related equipment for the retread industry. Cooper's primary customers are independent tire dealers, wholesalers, and retailers. The company sold its Cooper-Standard Automotive subsidiary late in 2004, and has used the proceeds to fund assorted pension plans, reduce debt, and buy back a large amount of the company's stock.

In North America, Cooper has invested $32 million for new tire-making machinery with which the company expects to increase tire production by an estimated 2.5 million units. Due to increased demand, Cooper has also invested a reported $11 million to begin manufacturing racing tires in the US.

Cooper spent $107 million to purchase 11% of South Korea-based Kumho Tire in early 2005. To take advantage of the booming Chinese automotive market, Cooper announced it had purchased 51% stakes in two Chinese tire manufacturing joint ventures — Cooper Chengshan (Shandong)

Passenger Tire and Cooper Chengshan (Shandong) Tire in late 2005. The moves give Cooper a better footing in the Chinese replacement tire market. The company brought even more Chinese manufacturing capacity on line when joint venture Cooper Kenda finished construction of a new tire plant in early 2007.

In Europe, Cooper has streamlined its manufacturing operations while concentrating on two European trends — high-performance and racing tires. Also, to keep costs in check, many of the tires Cooper sells in Europe are manufactured at lower-cost facilities in Asia.

## HISTORY

John Schaefer and Claude Hart (brothers-in-law) bought M and M Manufacturing of Akron, Ohio, in 1914. M and M made tire patches, cement, and repair kits. In 1915 the two bought The Giant Tire & Rubber Company (tire rebuilding). Two years later they moved their business to Findlay, Ohio.

Ira Cooper joined Giant's board in 1917 and soon formed his own company, The Cooper Corporation, which began making tires in 1920. The industry began consolidating in the 1920s, and in 1930 Cooper and Giant merged with Falls Rubber Company (a small tire maker), and Master Tire & Rubber Company was born.

Cooper died in 1941, but the company went on to supply the war effort with tires, pontoons, life jackets, and tank decoys. After WWII the company changed its name to Cooper Tire & Rubber Company. Cooper earned sales and loyalty from retailers and private-brand customers by promising not to open its own sales outlets — a policy continued to this day. The growth of the interstate system in the postwar years meant more cars, tires, and sales. Cooper went public in 1960. In 1964 it established Cooper Industrial Products to make industrial rubber products.

The 1970s brought the radial tire into widespread use. Radials had been around since the late 1940s, but the manufacturing process hadn't been cheap or easy enough to be practical. After undertaking its own research and development, Cooper rolled out its first radial in 1974. Around the same time, it bought a Bowling Green, Ohio, plant that made extruded rubber products and reinforced hose. The plant was quickly adapted to produce rubber parts for cars.

A tire glut in the 1980s (due in part to longer-lasting tires) led to rapid downsizing in the industry. As competitors exited the tire business, Cooper was buying plants and modernizing them for about a third of the cost of building new ones. The company made its first foray outside the US with the acquisition of Rio Grande Servaas (inner tubes, Mexico). Cooper also undertook several projects in the 1980s to upgrade its research capabilities and to improve distribution. By the mid-1980s it could warehouse more than 3 million tires. By the end of the decade Cooper's stock was 68 times its 1980 level. The success came from growth in the replacement market, which was three times the size of the original equipment market.

The benefits of Cooper's capital investments became clear in the 1990s. As the decade began, the company recorded the best margins in the industry (about 33%), and investment continued. It passed the billion-dollar sales mark in 1991 and spent $110 million in capital investments in 1992.

In 1996 Cooper opened an automotive hose plant in Kentucky. The next year it bought Avon Tyres Limited (UK), its first overseas purchase.

Cooper completed its acquisition of Kentucky-based Dean Tire in 1999, expanding its sales of replacement tires for cars and light trucks to 10 countries. Cooper entered joint ventures with Italy's Pirelli in which Cooper sells and distributes Pirelli passenger car and light truck replacement tires in North America and Pirelli distributes and markets Cooper tires in South America. The company boosted its automotive sealing system business with the purchase of The Standard Products Company in a deal valued at about $750 million.

In 2000 Cooper bought Siebe Automotive, the automotive fluid-handling division of Invensys, and sold Holm Industries (acquired with Standard Products) to an affiliate of Madison Capital Partners. Cooper also sold its automotive plastic trim plant in Winnsboro, South Carolina. Cooper closed several plants and scaled back operations at other facilities during 2001. A class-action lawsuit was settled in late 2002 stemming from claims that the tire maker did not disclose adhesion problems with its steel-belted radial tires; the decision, valued at $1 billion-$3 billion, gives an estimated 40 million consumers an extended warranty. In early 2003 Cooper purchased Max Trac Tire (better known as Mickey Thompson Performance Tires & Wheels). The company introduced the Discoverer H/T Plus (truck and SUV) and the Zeon ZPT (high performance) lines of tires in early 2004.

As 2004 came to a close, Cooper Tire completed the sale of its automotive unit, Cooper Standard Automotive, to Cypress Group and Goldman Sachs Capital Partners. That year the company also sold its inner tube operations.

## EXECUTIVES

**President, CEO and Director:** Roy V. Armes, age 54
**SVP Global Human Resources:** Mark W. Krivoruchka, age 51
**VP and CFO:** Philip G. (Phil) Weaver, age 54, $400,015 pay
**VP and General Manager, China Operations:** Margaret L. Sheng
**VP, General Counsel, and Secretary:** James E. Kline, age 65, $320,985 pay
**VP, Corporate Purchasing:** Linda L. Rennels
**VP, Supply Chain Operations:** Fran Brennan
**VP; President, International Tire Division:** Harold C. (Hal) Miller, age 54, $294,297 pay
**Director, Information Technology Infrastructure:** John L. Bohnlein
**Director, Investor Relations:** Curtis Schneekloth
**Auditors:** Ernst & Young LLP

## LOCATIONS

**HQ:** Cooper Tire & Rubber Company
701 Lima Ave., Findlay, OH 45840
**Phone:** 419-423-1321 **Fax:** 419-424-4212
**Web:** www.coopertire.com

Cooper Tire & Rubber Company worldwide operations include 10 manufacturing facilities, 32 distribution centers, and 18 technical centers.

### 2006 Sales

| | $ mil. | % of total |
|---|---|---|
| North America | 2,028.9 | 76 |
| Asia | 361.9 | 13 |
| Europe | 285.4 | 11 |
| **Total** | **2,676.2** | **100** |

## PRODUCTS/OPERATIONS

### 2006 Sales

| | $ mil. | % of total |
|---|---|---|
| North American Tire | 2,096.2 | 76 |
| International Tire | 680.1 | 24 |
| Adjustments | (100.1) | — |
| **Total** | **2,676.2** | **100** |

### Selected Products

Tires (automobile, truck, motorcycle, and racing)
Tread rubber and retreading equipment

## COMPETITORS

Bandag
Bridgestone
China Enterprises
Continental AG
Continental Tire North America
Falken Tire
Goodyear
Goodyear Dunlop Tires
Hankook Tire
Kumho Tire
Manuli Rubber
Marangoni
Michelin
Sumitomo Rubber
Toyo Tire & Rubber
Yokohama Rubber

## HISTORICAL FINANCIALS

Company Type: Public

### Income Statement

FYE: December 31

| | REVENUE ($ mil.) | NET INCOME ($ mil.) | NET PROFIT MARGIN | EMPLOYEES |
|---|---|---|---|---|
| **12/06** | 2,676 | (79) | — | 13,361 |
| **12/05** | 2,155 | (9) | — | 8,762 |
| **12/04** | 2,082 | 201 | 9.7% | 8,739 |
| **12/03** | 3,514 | 74 | 2.1% | 22,899 |
| **12/02** | 3,330 | 112 | 3.4% | 23,024 |
| **Annual Growth** | (5.3%) | — | — | (12.7%) |

### 2006 Year-End Financials

Debt ratio: 80.2%
Return on equity: —
Cash ($ mil.): 222
Current ratio: 1.91
Long-term debt ($ mil.): 513
No. of shares (mil.): 61
Dividends
Yield: 2.9%
Payout: —
Market value ($ mil.): 878

### Stock History

NYSE: CTB

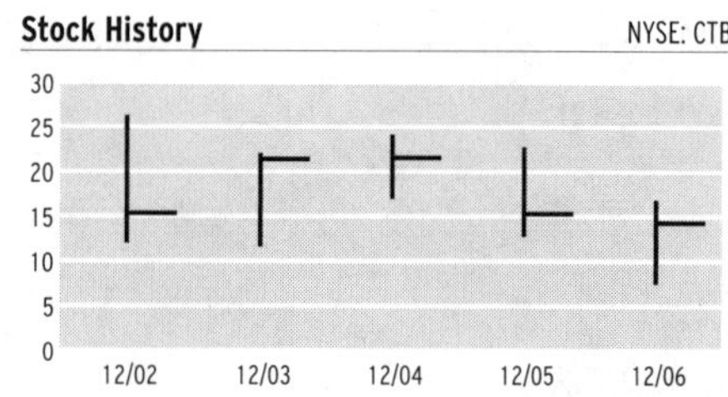


| | STOCK PRICE ($) FY Close | P/E High | P/E Low | PER SHARE ($) Earnings | Dividends | Book Value |
|---|---|---|---|---|---|---|
| **12/06** | 14.30 | — | — | (1.28) | 0.42 | 10.43 |
| **12/05** | 15.32 | — | — | (0.15) | 0.42 | 15.31 |
| **12/04** | 21.55 | 9 | 6 | 2.68 | 0.42 | 16.68 |
| **12/03** | 21.38 | 22 | 12 | 1.00 | 0.42 | 13.93 |
| **12/02** | 15.34 | 20 | 9 | 1.31 | 0.42 | 12.80 |
| **Annual Growth** | (1.7%) | — | — | — | 0.0% | (5.0%) |

# Corning Incorporated

Most of Corning's cooking is done lightly these days, and its growth is on display. The materials pioneer is the world's top maker of fiber-optic cable, which it invented more than 30 years ago. Once known mainly for its kitchenware and lab products, the company is now a leading provider of optical fiber and cable products and communications network equipment. Its display technologies unit produces glass substrates for flat-panel displays. Other major business segments include environmental technologies (ceramics for catalytic converters), and life sciences (laboratory equipment).

Corning suffered from slowing sales of telecommunications products, but a realignment of its businesses has allowed the company to regain its financial footing. Sales from its telecom segment, which accounted for 70% of revenue in 2001, now make up one-third of sales. Corning has seen significant growth from its display technologies segment. The company has stepped up manufacturing of LCD glass, which now accounts for about 40% of sales. Its LCD products are used in computer, television, cell phone, and digital camera displays.

In 2006 Corning set plans to build an LCD glass substrate finishing plant in Beijing, the first to be constructed on the Chinese mainland.

Through all of the changes in Corning's business model and strategic priorities, the company has kept Steuben Glass as a subsidiary since 1918. The fine-glass firm is named for Steuben County, New York, where Steuben maintains its design studio and glassworks.

FMR (Fidelity Investments) owns about 6% of Corning.

## HISTORY

Amory Houghton started Houghton Glass in Massachusetts in 1851 and moved it to Corning, New York, in 1868. By 1876 the company, renamed Corning Glass Works, was making several types of technical and pharmaceutical glass. In 1880 it supplied the glass for Thomas Edison's first light bulb. Other early developments included the red-yellow-green traffic light system and borosilicate glass (which can withstand sudden temperature changes) for Pyrex oven and laboratory ware.

Joint ventures have been crucial to Corning's success. Early ones included Pittsburgh Corning (with Pittsburgh Plate Glass, 1937, glass construction blocks), Owens-Corning (with Owens-Illinois, 1938, fiberglass), and Dow Corning (with Dow Chemical, 1943, silicones).

By 1945 the company's laboratories had made it the undisputed leader in the manufacture of specialty glass. Applications for its glass technology included the first mass-produced television tubes, freezer-to-oven ceramic cookware (Pyroceram, Corning Ware), and car headlights.

After World War II Corning emphasized consumer product sales and expanded globally. In the 1970s the company pioneered the development of optical fiber and auto emission technology (now two of its principal products).

Seeing maturing markets for such established products as light bulbs and television tubes, Corning began buying higher-growth laboratory services companies — MetPath in 1982, Hazleton in 1987, Enseco in 1989, and G.H. Besse-laar in 1989. Vice chairman James Houghton, who is the great-great-grandson of Corning's founder, was named chairman and CEO in 1983.

Corning established international joint ventures with Siemens, Mitsubishi, and Samsung. In 1988 the company bought Revere Ware (cookware). The next year Corning dropped Glass Works from its name.

In 1994 Corning and Siecor (joint venture with Siemens) acquired several fiber and cable businesses from Northern Telecom (now Nortel Networks), expanding the company's presence in Canada.

Joint venture Dow Corning, under assault from thousands of women seeking damages because of leaking breast implants, entered Chapter 11 bankruptcy protection in 1995. The massive losses incurred by Dow Corning due to litigation and a downturn in Corning's lab products sales prompted the company to recast itself. Corning began selling off its well-known consumer brands and putting greater emphasis on its high-tech optical and display products through acquisitions and R&D.

Company veteran Roger Ackerman was named chairman and CEO in 1996, replacing Houghton. He moved quickly to transform the company from a disjointed conglomerate to a high-tech optics manufacturer. That year the company spun off its laboratory testing division to shareholders, creating Covance and Quest Diagnostics.

After deals to sell a stake in Corning Consumer Products to AEA Investors fell through in 1997, Corning sold a majority stake in the housewares unit to Kohlberg Kravis Roberts the next year. In 1999 Corning bought UK-based BICC Group's telecom cable business.

In 2000 Corning made more than $5 billion worth of acquisitions to expand its optical fiber and hardware business. It bought Siemens' optical cable and hardware operations and the remaining 50% of the companies' Siecor joint venture. Corning acquired Oak Industries (optical components) for $1.8 billion and NetOptix (optical filters) for $2.15 billion, and purchased the 67% of microelectromechanical systems specialist IntelliSense it didn't already own.

Continuing its spending spree, the company bought part of Pirelli's fiber-optic telecom components business for about $3.6 billion; it also acquired Cisco's 10% stake in the business.

In the first half of 2001, Ackerman retired as chairman and CEO of the company. COO John Loose was named CEO, and Houghton was again appointed chairman.

Slowing demand prompted Corning to lay off about 25% of its staff, shut down plants, and discontinue its glass tubing operations that year. Houghton returned to the position of chief executive after Loose retired in 2002. That year the company made more layoffs, closed plants, and sold several non-core operations; it also bought rival Lucent's fiber-optic and cable facilities in China where demand was relatively strong.

Corning sold its photonic components business to Avanex in 2003. The next year it sold its quartz crystal frequency control products business.

Corning president Wendell Weeks succeeded Houghton as CEO in 2005. Houghton remained chairman, and retired again in 2006, becoming non-executive chairman.

In 2007 Houghton became chairman emeritus and remained on the board as a director. Weeks was elected chairman of the board.

## EXECUTIVES

**Chairman and CEO:** Wendell P. Weeks, age 47, $952,000 pay (prior to title change)
**Vice Chairman and CFO:** James B. Flaws, age 58, $759,000 pay
**President, COO and Director:** Peter F. Volanakis, age 51, $780,000 pay (prior to title change)
**EVP and Chief Administrative Officer:** Kirk P. Gregg, age 47, $535,000 pay
**EVP and CTO:** Joseph A. (Joe) Miller Jr., age 65, $563,000 pay
**EVP, Environmental Technologies:** Robert B. Brown, age 56
**SVP, Finance:** Katherine A. (Kate) Asbeck, age 50
**SVP and Treasurer:** Mark S. Rogus, age 47
**SVP, Operations Chief of Staff:** Pamela C. Schneider, age 52
**SVP Manufacturing and Performance Excellence:** Donald A. McCabe Jr.
**VP and Controller:** R. Tony Tripeny, age 47
**President and CEO, Cable Systems:** Larry Aiello Jr., age 57
**President, Display Technologies:** James P. Clappin, age 49
**Division VP and Chief Accounting Officer:** Jane D. Poulin, age 44
**National Media Communications:** Pamela W. Porter
**SVP and General Counsel:** Vincent P. Hatton
**SVP, Strategy and Corporate Development:** Lawrence D. McRae, age 48
**Auditors:** PricewaterhouseCoopers LLP

## LOCATIONS

**HQ:** Corning Incorporated
1 Riverfront Plaza, Corning, NY 14831
**Phone:** 607-974-9000 **Fax:** 800-539-3632
**Web:** www.corning.com

Corning has more than 45 manufacturing and processing facilities around the world, with operations in Australia, Belgium, Brazil, China, Denmark, the Dominican Republic, France, Germany, Hong Kong, India, Italy, Japan, Malaysia, Mexico, the Netherlands, Poland, Russia, Singapore, South Korea, Spain, Taiwan, Turkey, the UK, and the US.

### 2006 Sales

| | $ mil. | % of total |
|---|---|---|
| Asia/Pacific | | |
| Taiwan | 1,667 | 32 |
| Japan | 579 | 11 |
| China | 199 | 4 |
| South Korea | 86 | 1 |
| Other countries | 145 | 3 |
| North America | | |
| US | 1,479 | 28 |
| Canada | 117 | 2 |
| Mexico | 51 | 1 |
| Europe | | |
| Germany | 267 | 5 |
| UK | 110 | 2 |
| France | 29 | 1 |
| Italy | 28 | 1 |
| Other countries | 296 | 6 |
| Latin America | 32 | 1 |
| Other regions | 89 | 2 |
| **Total** | **5,174** | **100** |

## PRODUCTS/OPERATIONS

### 2006 Sales

| | $ mil. | % of total |
|---|---|---|
| Display technologies | 2,133 | 38 |
| Telecommunications | | |
| Optical fiber & cable | 877 | 18 |
| Hardware & equipment | 852 | 17 |
| Environmental technologies | | |
| Automotive | 451 | 11 |
| Diesel | 164 | 2 |
| Life sciences | 287 | 6 |
| Other | 410 | 8 |
| **Total** | **5,174** | **100** |

**Selected Products**

Display technologies
- Liquid crystal displays

Telecommunications
- Optical fiber and cable
- Optical networking components

Environmental technologies
- Industrial and stationary emissions products
- Mobile emissions and automotive catalytic converters products

Life sciences
- Genomics and laboratory equipment

Other
- Polarized glass
- Semiconductor materials

## COMPETITORS

3M
ADC Telecommunications
Alcatel-Lucent
Amphenol
Andrew Corporation
Asahi Glass
Avaya
BD
Belden
Carl-Zeiss-Stiftung
CommScope
DENSO
Draka Holding
Fujikura Ltd.
Furukawa Electric
General Cable
Gerresheimer Glass
Heraeus Holding
Hoya
IBIDEN
JDS Uniphase
NGK INSULATORS
Nippon Electric Glass
Nippon Sheet Glass
Nortel Networks
Pilkington
Pirelli & C.
Saint-Gobain
SCHOTT
Shin-Etsu Chemical
Sumitomo Electric
Superior Essex
SWCC SHOWA HOLDINGS
telent
Thermo Fisher Scientific
Thomas & Betts
Tyco Electronics

## HISTORICAL FINANCIALS

Company Type: Public

**Income Statement** FYE: December 31

| | REVENUE ($ mil.) | NET INCOME ($ mil.) | NET PROFIT MARGIN | EMPLOYEES |
|---|---|---|---|---|
| **12/06** | 5,174 | 1,855 | 35.9% | 24,500 |
| **12/05** | 4,579 | 585 | 12.8% | 26,000 |
| **12/04** | 3,854 | (2,165) | — | 25,000 |
| **12/03** | 3,090 | (223) | — | 20,600 |
| **12/02** | 3,164 | (1,302) | — | 23,200 |
| **Annual Growth** | 13.1% | — | — | 1.4% |

**2006 Year-End Financials**

Debt ratio: 23.4%
Return on equity: 29.1%
Cash ($ mil.): 3,167
Current ratio: 2.07
Long-term debt ($ mil.): 1,696

No. of shares (mil.): 1,565
Dividends
Yield: —
Payout: —
Market value ($ mil.): 29,281

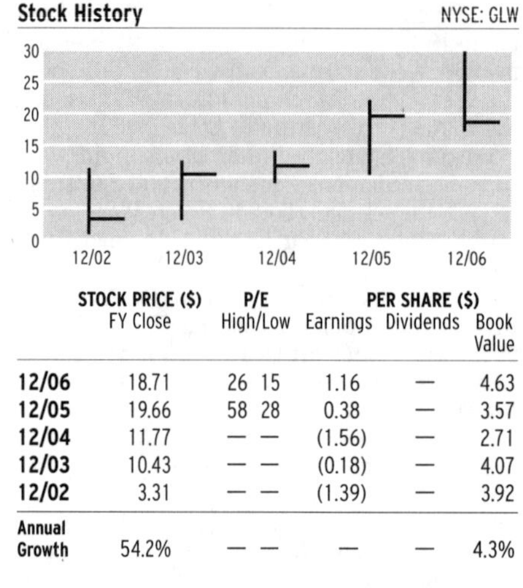

**Stock History** NYSE: GLW

| | STOCK PRICE ($) FY Close | P/E High | P/E Low | PER SHARE ($) Earnings | Dividends | Book Value |
|---|---|---|---|---|---|---|
| **12/06** | 18.71 | 26 | 15 | 1.16 | — | 4.63 |
| **12/05** | 19.66 | 58 | 28 | 0.38 | — | 3.57 |
| **12/04** | 11.77 | — | — | (1.56) | — | 2.71 |
| **12/03** | 10.43 | — | — | (0.18) | — | 4.07 |
| **12/02** | 3.31 | — | — | (1.39) | — | 3.92 |
| **Annual Growth** | 54.2% | — | — | — | — | 4.3% |

# Costco Wholesale

Wal-Mart isn't the biggest in *every* business. Costco Wholesale is the largest wholesale club operator in the US (ahead of Wal-Mart's SAM'S CLUB). The company operates nearly 490 membership warehouse stores serving more than 47 million cardholders in 37 US states and Puerto Rico, Canada, Japan, Mexico, South Korea, Taiwan, and the UK, primarily under the Costco Wholesale name.

Stores offer discount prices on, on average, 4,000 products (many in bulk packaging and a number under its private Kirkland Signature label), ranging from alcoholic beverages and appliances to fresh food, pharmaceuticals, and tires. Certain club memberships also offer products and services such as car and home insurance, mortgage and real estate services, and travel packages.

Costco's big-box stores average about 140,000 square feet and many house ancillary businesses that include food courts and hot dog stands, one-hour photo centers, optical and hearing aid centers, and pharmacies. About 250 of Costco's warehouse clubs have gas stations on the premises.

To shop at Costco customers must be members — a policy the company believes reinforces customer loyalty and provides a steady source of fee revenue. Costco's card membership renewal rate is more than 86%.

Facing competition from discounters, including Target, that don't charge a membership fee, as well as from rival SAM'S CLUB, Costco is expanding and retrofitting its warehouses to accommodate fresh food sections and other ancillary units, such as gas stations and optical departments. Costco's foray into grocery sales has been a success. Food and sundries accounted for more than half of Costco's total sales in 2006, making it the third-largest seller of groceries in the US behind Wal-Mart Supercenters and Kroger. It has struck a deal with Martha Stewart Living Omnimedia for a new line of food products exclusive to Costco, to be launched in 2008. It also plans to grow its e-commerce business, Costco.com.

In addition to its stand-alone stores, Costco has begun opening outlets in malls to grow in congested areas, such as Los Angeles. Costco also operates two Costco Home stores, which sell furniture, and has plans for a third.

In what amounts to a black eye for Costco, which enjoys its image as a benevolent employer relative to other retailers (notably Wal-Mart), a federal judge has granted class-action status to a lawsuit filed in 2004 on behalf of more than 700 female Costco employees. The suit claims the company has discriminated against women seeking promotions to store managers.

## HISTORY

From 1954 to 1974 retailer Sol Price built his Fed-Mart discount chain into a $300 million behemoth selling general merchandise to government employees. Price sold the company to Hugo Mann in 1975 and the next year, with son Robert, Rick Libenson, and Giles Bateman, opened the first Price Club warehouse, in San Diego, to sell in volume to small businesses at steep discounts.

Posting a large loss its first year prompted Price Club's decision to expand membership to include government, utility, and hospital employees, as well as credit union members. In 1978 it opened a second store, in Phoenix. With the help of his father, Sol's other son Laurence began a chain of tire-mounting stores (located adjacent to Price Club outlets on land leased from the company and using tires sold by the Price Clubs).

The company went public in 1980 with four stores in California and Arizona. Price Club moved into the eastern US with its 1984 opening of a store in Virginia and continued to expand, including a joint venture with Canadian retailer Steinberg in 1986 to operate stores in Canada; the first Canadian warehouse opened that year in Montreal.

Two years later Price Club acquired A. M. Lewis (grocery distributor, Southern California and Arizona), and the next year it opened two Price Club Furnishings, offering discounted home and office furniture.

Price Club bought out Steinberg's interest in the Canadian locations in 1990 and added stores on the East Coast and in California, Colorado, and British Columbia. However, competition in the East from ensconced rivals such as SAM'S CLUB and PACE forced the closure of two stores two years later. A 50-50 joint venture with retailer Controladora Comercial Mexicana led to the opening of two Price Clubs in Mexico City, one each in 1992 and 1993.

Price Club merged with Costco Wholesale in 1993. Founded in 1983 by Jeffrey Brotman and James Sinegal (a former EVP of Price Company), Costco Wholesale went public in 1985 and expanded into Canada.

In 1993 Price/Costco opened its first warehouse outside the Americas in a London suburb. Merger costs led to a loss the following year, and Price/Costco spun off its commercial real estate operations, as well as certain international operations as Price Enterprises (now Price Legacy). In 1995, the company launched its Kirkland Signature brand of private-label merchandise. In 1997 the company changed its corporate name to Costco Companies.

Costco began online sales and struck a deal to buy two stores in South Korea in 1998 and opened its first store in Japan in 1999. Under industry-wide pressure over the way members-only chains record fees, Costco took a $118 million charge for fiscal 1999 to change accounting practices. That year the company made yet another name change to Costco Wholesale (emphasizing its core warehouse operations).

In 2000 the company purchased private retailer Littlewoods' 20% stake in Costco UK, increasing Costco's ownership to 80%. Costco began expanding into the Midwest in 2001 as part of plans to open 40 new clubs a year, including ones in China.

During fiscal 2002 Costco opened 29 new warehouse clubs. In December 2002 the retailer opened its first home store — called Costco Home — in Kirkland, Washington, stocked with mostly high-end furniture. A second Costco Home store opened in Tempe, Arizona, in December 2004.

In October 2003, Costco increased its equity interest in Costco Wholesale UK to 100% when it purchased Carrefour Nederland's 20% stake. In 2003 the company opened 29 new warehouse clubs and closed six.

In 2004 Costco opened 20 new warehouse clubs. The year 2005 brought slower growth, with 16 new outlets added.

## EXECUTIVES

**Chairman:** Jeffrey H. (Jeff) Brotman, age 64, $450,000 pay
**President, CEO, and Director:** James D. (Jim) Sinegal, age 70, $350,000 pay
**SEVP, COO, Global Operations, Distribution and Construction, and Director:** Richard D. DiCerchio, age 63
**EVP, CFO, and Director:** Richard A. Galanti, age 50, $519,808 pay
**EVP and COO, Merchandising:** W. Craig Jelinek, age 54, $617,013 pay
**EVP and COO, Eastern and Canadian Divisions:** Joseph P. (Joe) Portera, $583,030 pay
**EVP and COO, Northern and Midwest Divisions:** Douglas W. (Doug) Schutt, age 47
**EVP and COO, Southwest Division and Mexico:** Dennis R. Zook, age 57
**EVP, Real Estate Development:** Paul G. Moulton, age 55
**SVP and Controller:** David S. Petterson
**SVP, Administration, Global Operations:** Franz E. Lazarus
**SVP, Costco Wholesale Industries and Business Development:** Richard C. Chavez
**SVP, Operations, Depots:** John D. Thelan
**SVP International Operations:** James P. (Jim) Murphy
**SVP and General Manager, Bay Area Region:** Dennis A. Hoover
**SVP and General Manager, Los Angeles Region:** Bruce A. Greenwood
**SVP, Human Resources and Risk Management:** John Matthews
**SVP, Information Systems:** Don Burdick
**SVP, Administration and Chief Legal Officer:** Joel Benoliel
**SVP, Merchandising, Fresh Foods:** Jeffrey Lyons
**Director, Financial Planning and Investor Relations:** Jeff Elliott
**VP, Legal, and General Counsel:** Richard J. Olin
**Auditors:** KPMG LLP

## LOCATIONS

**HQ:** Costco Wholesale Corporation
999 Lake Dr., Issaquah, WA 98027
**Phone:** 425-313-8100
**Web:** www.costco.com

Costco Wholesale operates stores in 37 US states and Puerto Rico. The company also operates stores in nine Canadian provinces, Japan, South Korea, Taiwan, and the UK. Costco also operates 29 outlets in Mexico via a joint venture.

### 2006 Stores

| | No. |
|---|---|
| US | 358 |
| Canada | 68 |
| UK | 18 |
| Japan | 5 |
| South Korea | 5 |
| Taiwan | 4 |
| **Total** | **458** |

## PRODUCTS/OPERATIONS

### 2006 Sales

| | % of total |
|---|---|
| Food (fresh & dry, institutionally packaged) | 30 |
| Sundries (including snacks, beverages, health/beauty aids & tobacco) | 24 |
| Hardlines (including major appliances, electronics & office & auto supplies) | 20 |
| Softlines (including apparel, books, cameras & jewelry) | 12 |
| Other (including pharmacy, optical & gas stations) | 14 |
| **Total** | **100** |

### 2006 Sales

| | $ mil. | % of total |
|---|---|---|
| Sales | 58,963.2 | 98 |
| Membership fees | 1,188.0 | 2 |
| **Total** | **60,151.2** | **100** |

### Selected Products and Services

Alcoholic beverages
Apparel
Appliances
Automotive insurance products (tires, batteries)
Automobile sales
Baby products
Books
Cameras, film, and photofinishing
Candy
Caskets
CDs
Checks and form printing
Cleaning and institutional supplies
Collectibles
Computer hardware and software
Computer training services
Copying and printing services
Credit card processing
DVDs
Electronics
Eye exams
Flooring
Floral arrangements
Fresh foods (bakery, deli, meats, produce, seafood)
Furniture
Gasoline
Gifts
Glasses and contact lenses
Groceries and institutionally packaged foods
Hardware
Health and beauty aids
Hearing aids
Home insurance
Housewares
Insurance (automobile, small-business health, home)
Jewelry
Lighting supplies
Mortgage service
Office equipment and supplies
Outdoor living products
Payroll processing
Pet supplies
Pharmaceuticals
Plumbing supplies
Real estate services
Snack foods
Soft drinks
Sporting goods
Tobacco
Tools
Toys
Travel packages and other travel services
Video games and systems

## COMPETITORS

ALDI
Army and Air Force Exchange
Aurora Wholesalers
AutoZone
Barnes & Noble
Best Buy
Big Lots
BJ's Wholesale Club
Circuit City
CompUSA
Dollar General
Family Dollar Stores
Home Depot
Kmart
Kohl's
Kroger
Lowe's
Office Depot
PETCO
PetSmart
Safeway
SAM'S CLUB
Smart & Final
Staples
Target
Toys "R" Us
Walgreen
Wal-Mart

## HISTORICAL FINANCIALS

Company Type: Public

### Income Statement

FYE: Sunday nearest August 31

| | REVENUE ($ mil.) | NET INCOME ($ mil.) | NET PROFIT MARGIN | EMPLOYEES |
|---|---|---|---|---|
| **8/06** | 60,151 | 1,103 | 1.8% | 127,000 |
| **8/05** | 52,935 | 1,063 | 2.0% | 118,000 |
| **8/04** | 48,107 | 882 | 1.8% | 113,000 |
| **8/03** | 42,546 | 721 | 1.7% | 103,000 |
| **8/02** | 38,763 | 700 | 1.8% | 92,000 |
| **Annual Growth** | 11.6% | 12.0% | — | 8.4% |

### 2006 Year-End Financials

Debt ratio: 2.4%
Return on equity: 12.2%
Cash ($ mil.): 2,833
Current ratio: 1.05
Long-term debt ($ mil.): 215
No. of shares (mil.): 462
Dividends
Yield: 1.0%
Payout: 21.3%
Market value ($ mil.): 21,889

### Stock History

NASDAQ (GS): COST

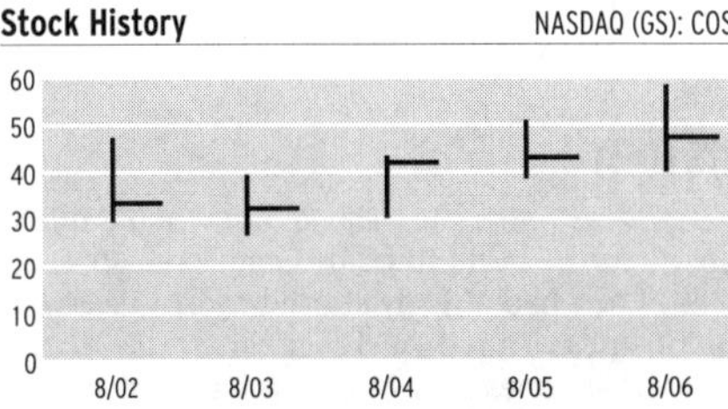


| | STOCK PRICE ($) FY Close | P/E High | P/E Low | PER SHARE ($) Earnings | Dividends | Book Value |
|---|---|---|---|---|---|---|
| **8/06** | 47.35 | 25 | 18 | 2.30 | 0.49 | 19.78 |
| **8/05** | 43.12 | 23 | 18 | 2.18 | 0.23 | 18.80 |
| **8/04** | 42.05 | 23 | 17 | 1.85 | 0.20 | 16.48 |
| **8/03** | 32.25 | 26 | 18 | 1.53 | — | 14.33 |
| **8/02** | 33.41 | 32 | 20 | 1.48 | — | 12.51 |
| **Annual Growth** | 9.1% | — | — | 11.7% | 56.5% | 12.1% |

# Countrywide Financial

Countrywide Financial gives credit where credit is due. One of the largest independent residential mortgage lending firms in the US, the company writes, sells, and services mainly prime first mortgages for single-family homes through its Countrywide Home Loans subsidiary. It also offers home equity loans, commercial mortgages, and subprime home mortgages. In addition, Countrywide Financial is a broker/dealer of mortgage-backed securities; underwrites and sells property/casualty, health, and disability insurance (mainly through Balboa Insurance Group); and runs Countrywide Bank. Countrywide Financial operates approximately 1,000 branch offices in all 50 states and Washington, DC.

Countrywide operates primarily in the US, but has a majority-owned joint venture with Barclays that services mortgages and processes mortgage loan applications in the UK. Countrywide entered into another joint venture when it bought KB Home Mortgage from KB Home in 2005. Now doing business as Countrywide KB, the unit offers mortgages to buyers of homes manufactured by KB. Countrywide also purchases loans from other lenders through a network of some 2,100 correspondents.

Countrywide gleans a larger percentage of its earnings (almost half) from mortgage banking than larger competitors like Wells Fargo and Bank of America, which are buffered by massive banking and financial services operations. To reduce this reliance on mortgages, which are subject to interest rate and market fluctuations, the company's diversification efforts have expanded to include derivatives trading and auto insurance underwriting. It bought Chicago-based futures brokerage CCM Futures in 2007.

As one of the largest mortgage lenders in the US, the company was hit hard by the subprime mortgage bust in 2006 and 2007. Bank of America invested $2 billion in Countrywide, which relieved some of the company's financial strain. The infusion of cash, however, did not prevent Countrywide from axing up to 12,000 employees (around 20% of its total workforce).

## HISTORY

Business associates David Loeb and Angelo Mozilo formed Countrywide Credit Industries in 1969. Loeb had already started mortgage banking business United Mortgage Servicing; Mozilo was his best salesman. Loeb was forced to give up his stake in United Mortgage to corporate raiders, and shortly thereafter the pair opened the first Countrywide Credit office in Anaheim, California.

The company went public in the early 1970s, but the partners raised only $800,000 in capital. Business picked up despite inflation and high interest rates. By 1974 Countrywide Credit's eight branches were doing well, but operating costs were eroding the company's bottom line.

Rather than watch Countrywide Credit slowly bleed, Loeb decided to reinvent the company. Mozilo grudgingly agreed; they closed all of the branches and fired all 95 employees except themselves and a secretary. They transformed Countrywide Credit from a sales-driven to a product-driven enterprise, dropping its commissioned sales force in favor of direct solicitation of realtors. Guaranteed low interest rates eventually drummed up enough business to reopen a California branch that was soon seeing more business than it could handle. By 1978 the company was in the black.

By the mid-1980s Countrywide Credit had more than 100 branches in about two dozen states. The company diversified, forming Countrywide Securities (1981) and Countrywide Asset Management (1985). Like other mortgage companies, it benefited from the savings and loan crisis of the late 1980s, filling a void in home loan production.

After the recession that marked the late 1980s and early 1990s, the firm's business picked up again as low interest rates prompted more refinancing. Marginally rising interest rates in 1994 resulted in a flat housing market and a shrinking volume of mortgage refinancing industrywide. In response, Countrywide Credit trimmed staff and took cost-cutting measures. By 1996 the company's profits had rebounded.

But Countrywide Credit still faced the problem of mortgage refinancing, which provides one-time fees but has little effect on loan volume. The company in 1997 responded with a nationwide ad campaign to build brand awareness and target new customer groups, including Hispanics. In an effort to diversify, the firm bought mutual funds broker and administrator Leshner Financial (renamed Countrywide Financial Services, it was sold in 1999).

Another tactic to increase loan volume was more risky. In 1998, as personal bankruptcies continued at record levels, the company moved into the subprime market through its Full Spectrum Lending subsidiary. The next year Countrywide Credit pumped up its insurance business when it bought most of the operations of Balboa Life and Casualty Group.

In preparation for a more diversified future, Countrywide Credit restructured in 2001 and changed its name to Countrywide Financial Corporation in 2002.

## EXECUTIVES

**Chairman and CEO:** Angelo R. Mozilo, age 68, $2,866,667 pay
**President and COO; Chairman and CEO, Countrywide Home Loans:** David Sambol, $1,116,667 pay
**Executive Managing Director, Banking and Insurance:** Carlos M. Garcia, age 51, $879,167 pay
**Executive Managing Director and Chief Investment Officer:** Kevin W. Bartlett, age 49
**Executive Managing Director, Capital Markets; President and CEO, Countrywide Capital Markets:** Ranjit M. (Ron) Kripalani, age 47, $566,042 pay
**Executive Managing Director and CFO:** Eric P. Sieracki, age 50, $658,333 pay
**Executive Managing Director, Residential Lending; President and COO, Countrywide Home Loans:** Andrew (Drew) Gissinger III, age 47
**Executive Managing Director, Chief Legal Officer, and Assistant Secretary:** Sandor E. Samuels, age 54
**Executive Managing Director and Chief Operations Officer:** Jack W. Schakett, age 55
**Senior Managing Director and Chief Administration Officer:** Marshall M. Gates, age 55
**Senior Managing Director and Chief Accounting Officer:** Laurie K. Milleman, age 46
**Senior Managing Director and Chief Financial Operations and Planning:** Anne D. McCallion, age 52
**Senior Managing Director and Chief Economist:** Jeffrey K. (Jeff) Speakes, age 55
**Senior Managing Director, Consumer Markets:** Joseph D. (Joe) Anderson
**Senior Managing Director, Loan Administration:** Steve Bailey
**Senior Managing Director, Marketing:** Andrew S. Bielanski
**Senior Managing Director, General Counsel, and Secretary:** Susan E. Bow
**Senior Managing Director and Chief Human Resources Officer:** Leora I. Goren
**Senior Managing Director and Treasurer:** Jennifer S. Sandefur
**Managing Director, Public Affairs:** Mary Jane M. Seebach
**Auditors:** KPMG LLP

## LOCATIONS

**HQ:** Countrywide Financial Corporation
4500 Park Granada, Calabasas, CA 91302
**Phone:** 818-225-3000 **Fax:** 818-225-4051
**Web:** www.countrywide.com

## PRODUCTS/OPERATIONS

**2006 Sales**

| | $ mil. | % of total |
|---|---|---|
| Interest income | 12,056.1 | 48 |
| Gain on sale of loans & securities | 5,681.8 | 23 |
| Net loan servicing fees & other income from retained interests | 4,960.6 | 20 |
| Net insurance premiums earned | 1,171.4 | 5 |
| Other | 1,006.9 | 4 |
| **Total** | **24,876.8** | **100** |

## COMPETITORS

ACC Capital Holdings
Bank of America
C-BASS
Citigroup
CTX Mortgage
DHI Mortgage
Fannie Mae
Freddie Mac
GMAC-RFC
HSBC Finance
JPMorgan Chase
Option One
Wachovia
Washington Mutual
Wells Fargo

## HISTORICAL FINANCIALS

Company Type: Public

**Income Statement** FYE: December 31

| | ASSETS ($ mil.) | NET INCOME ($ mil.) | INCOME AS % OF ASSETS | EMPLOYEES |
|---|---|---|---|---|
| 12/06 | 199,946 | 2,675 | 1.3% | 54,655 |
| 12/05 | 175,085 | 2,528 | 1.4% | 54,456 |
| 12/04 | 128,496 | 2,198 | 1.7% | 42,141 |
| 12/03 | 97,950 | 2,373 | 2.4% | 34,298 |
| 12/02 | 58,031 | 842 | 1.5% | 29,272 |
| Annual Growth | 36.2% | 33.5% | — | 16.9% |

**2006 Year-End Financials**

Equity as % of assets: 7.2%
Return on assets: 1.4%
Return on equity: 19.7%
Long-term debt ($ mil.): 71,488
No. of shares (mil.): 585
Dividends
Yield: 1.8%
Payout: 17.4%
Market value ($ mil.): 24,841
Sales ($ mil.): 24,877

**Stock History** NYSE: CFC

| | STOCK PRICE ($) FY Close | P/E High | P/E Low | PER SHARE ($) Earnings | Dividends | Book Value |
|---|---|---|---|---|---|---|
| 12/06 | 42.45 | 10 | 7 | 4.30 | 0.75 | 24.47 |
| 12/05 | 34.19 | 10 | 7 | 4.11 | 0.59 | 21.36 |
| 12/04 | 37.01 | 11 | 6 | 3.63 | 0.27 | 17.73 |
| 12/03 | 25.28 | 7 | 3 | 4.16 | 0.10 | 43.82 |
| 12/02 | 12.91 | 8 | 6 | 1.62 | 0.11 | 40.78 |
| Annual Growth | 34.7% | — | — | 27.6% | 61.6% | (12.0%) |

# Cox Enterprises

The Cox family has been working at this enterprise for more than 100 years. One of the largest media conglomerates in the US, family-owned Cox Enterprises publishes 17 daily newspapers (including *The Atlanta Journal-Constitution*) and about 25 non-dailies (weeklies and shoppers) and owns 15 TV stations through Cox Television. It also owns Cox Communications (which was a public company until a Cox Enterprises buyout in late 2004), one of the US's largest cable systems with more than 6.7 million subscribers. Other operations include 94% of Cox Radio, owner of about 80 radio stations in nearly 20 markets; Manheim, which sells 10 million vehicles through auctions worldwide; and a majority stake in AutoTrader.com.

While Cox Communications is the firm's biggest revenue generator (more than half of sales), Cox Enterprises has been spending a lot of money and time driving on the information superhighway. The company operates AutoTrader.com in conjunction with Manheim, a profitable Internet operation. Manheim is the world's largest used-car auctioneer, and the combination of the businesses has proved lucrative for Cox Enterprises.

Fed up with the demands of running a publicly traded cable company, Cox Enterprises in 2004 bought the 38% of Cox Communications that it didn't already own for $8.5 billion. The move gave Cox Enterprises complete control over its cable systems. The company is offering more and more broadband Internet services, VoIP (Voice over Internet Protocol) digital telephone services, and digital video recorders and related entertainment-on-demand services.

Ranked on *Forbes*' list of the richest Americans, Anne Cox Chambers, daughter of founder James Cox, controls the company. Her late sister Barbara Cox Anthony (mother of chairman and CEO James Kennedy) died in 2007.

## HISTORY

James Middleton Cox, who dropped out of school in 1886 at 16, worked as a teacher, reporter, and congressional secretary before buying the *Dayton Daily News* in 1898. In 1905 he acquired the nearby *Springfield Press-Republican* and then took up politics, serving two terms in the US Congress (1909-1913) and three terms as Ohio governor (1913-1915; 1917-1921). He even ran for president in 1920 (his running mate was future President Franklin Roosevelt) but lost to rival Ohio publisher Warren G. Harding.

Once out of politics, Cox began building his media empire. He bought the *Miami Daily News* in 1923 and founded WHIO (Dayton, Ohio's first radio station). He bought Atlanta's WSB ("Welcome South, Brother"), the South's first radio station, in 1939 and added WSB-FM and WSB-TV, the South's first FM and TV stations, in 1948. Cox founded Dayton's first FM and TV stations (WHIO-FM and WHIO-TV) the next year, and *The Atlanta Constitution* joined his collection in 1950. Cox died in 1957.

The company continued to expand its broadcasting interests in the late 1950s and early 1960s. It was one of the first major broadcasting companies to expand into cable TV when it purchased a system in Lewistown, Pennsylvania, in 1962. The Cox family's broadcast properties were placed in publicly held Cox Broadcasting in 1964. Two years later its newspapers were placed into privately held Cox Enterprises, and the cable holdings became publicly held Cox Cable Communications. The broadcasting arm diversified, buying Manheim Services (auto auctions, 1968), Kansas City Automobile Auction (1969), and TeleRep (TV ad sales, 1972).

Cox Cable had 500,000 subscribers in nine states when it rejoined Cox Broadcasting in 1977. Cox Broadcasting was renamed Cox Communications in 1982, and the Cox family took the company private again in 1985, combining it with Cox Enterprises. James Kennedy, grandson of founder James Cox, became chairman and CEO in 1987.

Expansion became the keyword for Cox in the 1990s. The company merged its Manheim unit with the auto auction business of Ford Motor Credit and GE Capital in 1991. It also formed Sprint Spectrum in 1994, a partnership with Sprint, TCI (now part of AT&T), and Comcast to bundle telephone, cable TV, and other communications services (Sprint bought out Cox in 1999). Then, in one of its biggest transactions, Cox bought Times Mirror's cable TV operations for $2.3 billion in 1995 and combined them with its own cable system into a new, publicly traded company called Cox Communications. The following year it spun off its radio holdings into a public company called Cox Radio.

To expand its online presence, the company formed Cox Interactive Media in 1996, establishing a series of city Web sites and making a host of investments in various Internet companies, including Career Path, ExciteHome, iVillage, MP3.com, and Tickets.com. Cox also applied the online strategy to its automobile auction businesses, establishing AutoTrader.com in 1998 and placing the Internet operations of Manheim Auctions (now just Manheim) into a new company, Manheim Interactive, in 2000.

In 2002 Cox dropped plans to expand its local Internet city guide business nationwide and moved its Interactive Media operations to other parts of the company. Two years later, Cox bought the 38% of Cox Communications that it didn't already own for $8.5 billion, thus ending the cable subsidiary's status as a public company.

## EXECUTIVES

**Chairman and CEO; Chairman, Cox Communications and Cox Radio:** James C. Kennedy, age 59
**Vice Chairman:** G. Dennis Berry, age 62
**President and COO:** Jimmy W. Hayes, age 54
**EVP and CFO:** Robert C. (Bob) O'Leary, age 68
**SVP Administration:** Timothy W. (Tim) Hughes, age 62
**SVP Finance:** Richard J. Jacobson, age 49
**SVP Investments and Administration:** John G. Boyette, age 60
**SVP Public Policy:** Alexander V. Netchvolodoff, age 69
**VP and CIO:** Gregory B. (Greg) Morrison, age 46
**VP and Treasurer, Cox Enterprises and Cox Communications:** Susan W. Coker, age 43
**VP and General Tax Counsel:** Preston B. Barnett, age 59
**VP Business Development:** Sanford Schwartz, age 53
**VP Corporate Communications and Public Affairs:** Roberto I. Jimenez, age 49
**VP Human Resources:** Marybeth H. Leamer, age 49
**VP Legal Affairs, General Counsel, and Corporate Secretary:** Andrew A. (Andy) Merdek
**President and CEO, AutoTrader.com:** Victor A. (Chip) Perry III, age 52
**President and CEO, Cox Radio:** Robert F. (Bob) Neil, age 48
**President and CEO, Manheim Auctions:** Dean H. Eisner, age 48
**President, Cox Communications:** Patrick J. (Pat) Esser, age 50
**President, Cox Newspapers:** Jay R. Smith, age 56
**President, Cox Television:** Andrew S. Fisher, age 58

## LOCATIONS

**HQ:** Cox Enterprises, Inc.
6205 Peachtree Dunwoody Rd., Atlanta, GA 30328
**Phone:** 678-645-0000 **Fax:** 678-645-1079
**Web:** www.coxenterprises.com

## PRODUCTS/OPERATIONS

### 2006 Sales

| | $ mil. | % of total |
|---|---|---|
| Cox Communications | 7,300 | 55 |
| Manheim | 2,800 | 21 |
| Cox Newspapers | 1,400 | 11 |
| Cox Television | 699 | 5 |
| AutoTrader.com | 519 | 4 |
| Cox Radio | 440 | 3 |
| Other | 42 | 1 |
| **Total** | **13,200** | **100** |

### Selected Operations

Cox Communications (cable television systems)
Manheim (online auto auctions)
Cox Newspapers
- Daily Newspapers
  - *The Atlanta Journal-Constitution*
  - *Austin American-Statesman* (Texas)
  - *Dayton Daily News* (Ohio)
  - *The Daily Advance* (Elizabeth City, NC)
  - *The Daily Reflector* (Greenville, NC)
  - *The Daily Sentinel* (Grand Junction, CO)
  - *The Daily Sentinel* (Nacogdoches, TX)
  - *Longview News-Journal* (Texas)
  - *The Lufkin Daily News* (Texas)
  - *The Middleton Journal* (Ohio)
  - *News Messenger* (Marshall, TX)
  - *Palm Beach Daily News* (Florida)
  - *The Palm Beach Post* (Florida)
  - *Rocky Mount Telegram* (North Carolina)
  - *Springfield News Sun* (Ohio)
  - *Waco Tribune-Herald* (Texas)
- Cox Custom Media (commercial newsletters)
- PAGAS Mailing Services
- SP Newsprint (33%)
- Valpack (direct mail advertisements)

Cox Television
- Television Stations
  - KFOX (El Paso, TX; FOX)
  - KICU (San Francisco/San Jose, CA; independent)
  - KIRO (Seattle, CBS)
  - KRXI (Reno, NV; FOX)
  - KTVU (Oakland/San Francisco, CA; FOX)
  - PCNC (cable channel, Pittsburgh, independent)
  - WAXN (Charlotte, NC; independent)
  - WFTV (Orlando, FL; ABC)
  - WHIO (Dayton, OH; CBS)
  - WJAC (Johnstown, PA; NBC)
  - WPXI (Pittsburgh, NBC)
  - WRDQ (Orlando, FL; independent)
  - WSB-TV (Atlanta, ABC)
  - WSOC (Charlotte, NC; ABC)
  - WTOV (Steubenville, OH; NBC)

Cox Auto Trader (automobile classified publications and sites)

Cox Radio
- Atlanta (WBTS-FM, WSB-AM, WSB-FM)
- Birmingham, AL (WBHJ-FM, WBHK-FM, WZZK-FM)
- Bridgeport/New Haven, CT (WEZN-FM)
- Dayton, OH (WHIO-AM, WHKO-FM)
- Greenville/Spartanburg, SC (WJMZ-FM)
- Honolulu (KRTR-FM, KXME-FM)
- Houston (KLDE-FM)
- Jacksonville (WAPE-FM, WFYV-FM, WKQL-FM)
- Long Island, NY (WBAB-FM, WBLI-FM)
- Louisville, KY (WRKA-FM, WVEZ-FM)
- Miami (WEDR-FM, WHQT-FM)
- New Haven, CT (WPLR-FM)
- Orlando, FL (WHTQ-FM, WWKA-FM)
- Richmond, VA (WKLR-FM)
- San Antonio (KCYY-FM, KISS-FM, KONO-FM)
- Stamford/Norwalk, CT (WEFX-FM, WNLK-AM)
- Tampa (WDUV-FM, WWRM-FM)
- Tulsa, OK (KRAV-FM, KRMG-AM, KRTQ-FM, KWEN-FM)

## COMPETITORS

Advance Publications
Austin Chronicle
Belo
CBS Corp
Clear Channel
Columbus Fair Auto Auction
Comcast
D-A Auto Auction
Disney
Dow Jones
E. W. Scripps
Gannett
Hearst
McClatchy Company
Media General
Morris Communications
New York Times
News Corp.
Ticketmaster
Time Warner Cable
Tribune
Washington Post

## HISTORICAL FINANCIALS

Company Type: Private

**Income Statement** FYE: December 31

| | REVENUE ($ mil.) | NET INCOME ($ mil.) | NET PROFIT MARGIN | EMPLOYEES |
|---|---|---|---|---|
| **12/06** | 13,200 | — | — | 80,000 |
| **12/05** | 12,000 | — | — | 77,000 |
| **12/04** | 11,552 | — | — | 77,000 |
| **12/03** | 10,700 | — | — | 77,000 |
| **12/02** | 9,900 | — | — | 77,000 |
| **Annual Growth** | 7.5% | — | — | 1.0% |

**Revenue History**

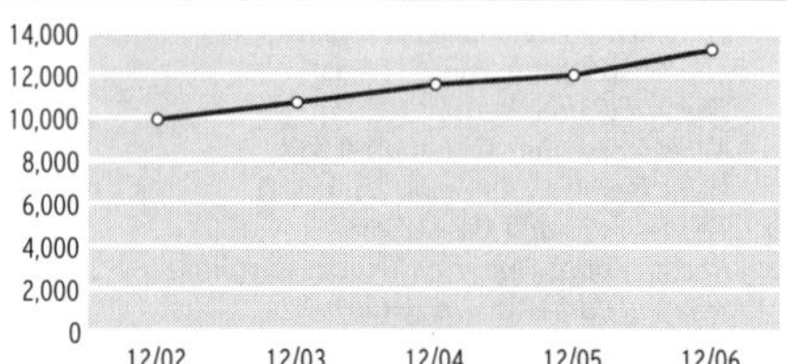


# C. R. Bard

From diagnosis to cure, C. R. Bard wants to be there. The medical devices company, which introduced the Foley urological catheter in 1934, supplies products for the continuum of care from diagnosis to cure. The company focuses on urology, vascular, and oncology products. Devices include stents, catheters, guidewires, implantable fabrics and meshes, and fluid collection systems. Bard also makes special surgical tools, including devices for laparoscopic, gynecological, and orthopedic procedures and for hernia repair. Bard primarily sells its products in the US and Europe. In 2006 the company acquired Venetec International, which sells StatLock catheter securement systems.

The Foley catheter, first sold in 1934, is the company's top-selling urology product; urology products account for 30% of the company's sales. Ever the innovator, Bard introduced the first angioplasty balloon catheter in 1980; sales of the company's vascular products now account for nearly a quarter of revenue. Popular products included the Fluency stent graft and Atlas PTA catheter. Bard sells its products in more than 100 countries through about two dozen subsidiaries and joint ventures. Sales to distributors, including Owens & Minor — the company's largest distributor — accounted for about 33% of revenues in 2006. The company continues to expand its product lines through acquisitions, research, and product development. In 2006 the company acquired Venetec International for about $170 million.

## HISTORY

When visiting Europe at the turn of the century, silk importer Charles Russell Bard discovered that gomenol, a mixture of olive oil with a eucalyptus extract, offered him relief from urinary problems caused by tuberculosis. He brought gomenol to America and began distributing it.

In 1907 C. R. Bard began selling a ureteral catheter developed by French firm J. Eynard. The company incorporated in 1923 with its present name. When Charles Bard's health declined in 1926, he sold the business to John Willits and Edson Outwin (his sales manager and accountant, respectively).

In 1934 Bard became the sole agent for Davol Rubber's new Foley catheter, which helped the company achieve $1 million in sales by 1948. During the 1950s, sales increased more than 400% when the firm introduced its first presterilized packaged product and expanded its product line to include disposable drainage tubes and an intravenous feeding device.

Bard went public in 1963. During the 1960s the firm expanded both vertically, boosting its manufacturing capabilities (it began making its own plastic tubing), and through acquisitions. It also established joint ventures with Davol to manufacture and distribute hospital and surgical supplies internationally.

The company diversified into the cardiovascular, respiratory therapy, home care products, and kidney dialysis fields in the 1970s and manufactured the first angioplasty catheter, a nonsurgical device to clear blocked arteries, in 1979.

In 1984 Bard watched its urological business go limp. In response, the company began a buying spree to gain market share in a consolidating hospital products industry. It swallowed up around a dozen companies, including Davol (maker of its best-selling Foley catheter), garnering such products as catheters and other products for angioplasty, diagnostics, and urinary incontinence. In 1988 it faced increasing competition in the coronary catheter market from such giants as Eli Lilly and Pfizer. Bard struck back with innovative products, but it was too little too late — even though the company continued to struggle for 10 more years, it finally pulled out of the cardiovascular market.

Bard agreed in 1993 to pay a then-record $61 million for mislabeling and improperly testing angioplasty catheters blamed for the deaths of two people (and later taken off the market). However, a year later Bard's sales topped $1 billion for the first time, and it purchased catheter-related companies in Canada, France, and Germany.

Purchases in 1995 and 1996 included medical device manufacturers MedChem Products and the Cardiac Assist Division of St. Jude Medical. In 1996 Bard bought a majority stake in Italy-based X-Trode and acquired IMPRA, a leading supplier of vascular grafts (its largest deal ever). That year the ongoing catheter litigation snared three former Bard executives, who received 18-month prison sentences for conspiring to hide potentially fatal flaws in the products.

In 1998 Bard reorganized along disease-state management lines. Over the next two years, it sold its cardiovascular line after deciding it was going to cost too much time and money to re-establish dominance in that field. Bard built its other fields through purchases, including ProSeed (radiation seed therapy, 1998) and Dymax (ultrasound catheter guidance systems, 1999). The next year Bard partnered with medical device distributor Owens & Minor to launch an online purchasing site.

## EXECUTIVES

**Chairman and CEO:** Timothy M. Ring, age 49, $2,083,933 pay
**President, COO, and Director:** John H. Weiland, age 51, $1,519,516 pay (prior to title change)
**SVP and CFO:** Todd C. Schermerhorn, age 46, $973,002 pay
**SVP and President, Corporate Healthcare Services:** James L. Natale, age 60
**SVP Science, Technology, and Clinical Affairs:** John A. DeFord
**Group VP:** Brian P. Kelly, age 48, $718,961 pay
**Group VP International:** Amy S. Paul, age 55, $643,327 pay
**VP and Controller:** Frank Lupisella Jr., age 45
**VP and Treasurer:** Scott T. Lowry, age 40
**VP, Government and Public Affairs:** Holly P. Glass
**VP, Human Resources:** Bronwen K. Kelly, age 53
**VP, Information Technology:** Vincent J. Gurnari Jr.
**VP, Investor Relations:** Eric J. Shick
**VP, Strategic Planning and Business Development:** Robert L. Mellen, age 50
**VP, General Counsel, and Secretary:** Stephen J. Long, age 41
**VP, Regulatory Sciences:** James M. Howard II
**VP and General Manager, Bard Europe:** P. J. Byloos
**General Manager, Bard Hellas:** G. Politis
**Auditors:** KPMG LLP

## LOCATIONS

**HQ:** C. R. Bard, Inc.
730 Central Ave., Murray Hill, NJ 07974
**Phone:** 908-277-8000 **Fax:** 908-277-8240
**Web:** www.crbard.com

C. R. Bard has facilities in Australia, Austria, Belgium, Canada, China, Denmark, Finland, France, Germany, Greece, India, Ireland, Italy, Malaysia, Mexico, the Netherlands, Norway, Portugal, Singapore, South Korea, Spain, Sweden, Switzerland, Taiwan, the UK, and the US.

**2006 Sales**

| | $ mil. | % of total |
|---|---|---|
| US | 1,388.0 | 70 |
| Europe | 364.4 | 18 |
| Japan | 101.8 | 5 |
| Other regions | 131.3 | 7 |
| **Total** | **1,985.5** | **100** |

## PRODUCTS/OPERATIONS

**2006 Sales**

| | $ mil. | % of total |
|---|---|---|
| Urology | 587.9 | 30 |
| Oncology | 481.3 | 24 |
| Vascular | 479.6 | 24 |
| Surgery | 357.4 | 18 |
| Other | 79.3 | 4 |
| **Total** | **1,985.5** | **100** |

## COMPETITORS

Arrow International
Baxter
BD
Boston Scientific
Guidant
HealthTronics
Johnson & Johnson
Medline Industries
Medtronic
St. Jude Medical
United States Surgical

## HISTORICAL FINANCIALS

Company Type: Public

**Income Statement** FYE: December 31

| | REVENUE ($ mil.) | NET INCOME ($ mil.) | NET PROFIT MARGIN | EMPLOYEES |
|---|---|---|---|---|
| **12/06** | 1,986 | 272 | 13.7% | 9,400 |
| **12/05** | 1,771 | 337 | 19.0% | 8,900 |
| **12/04** | 1,656 | 303 | 18.3% | 8,600 |
| **12/03** | 1,433 | 169 | 11.8% | 8,300 |
| **12/02** | 1,274 | 155 | 12.2% | 7,700 |
| **Annual Growth** | 11.7% | 15.1% | — | 5.1% |

**2006 Year-End Financials**

Debt ratio: 8.9%
Return on equity: 16.8%
Cash ($ mil.): 517
Current ratio: 3.83
Long-term debt ($ mil.): 151
No. of shares (mil.): 103
Dividends
Yield: 0.7%
Payout: 21.2%
Market value ($ mil.): 8,559

**Stock History** NYSE: BCR

| | STOCK PRICE ($) FY Close | P/E High | P/E Low | PER SHARE ($) Earnings | Dividends | Book Value |
|---|---|---|---|---|---|---|
| **12/06** | 82.97 | 34 | 23 | 2.55 | 0.54 | 16.46 |
| **12/05** | 65.92 | 23 | 19 | 3.12 | 0.50 | 14.77 |
| **12/04** | 63.98 | 23 | 14 | 2.82 | 0.35 | 12.99 |
| **12/03** | 40.63 | 25 | 17 | 1.60 | 0.45 | 20.20 |
| **12/02** | 29.00 | 22 | 15 | 1.47 | 0.43 | 17.06 |
| **Annual Growth** | 30.1% | — | — | 14.8% | 5.9% | (0.9%) |

# Crane Co.

Crane Co. likes to stay fluid so it can retain control of its senses while selling snack foods. The diversified company makes a variety of industrial products, including fluid handling equipment (valves and pumps), aerospace and electronic components (sensing and control systems), engineered materials (plastic composites and substrates), merchandising systems (vending machines), and controls (diagnostic, measurement, and control devices). Crane Co. serves the power generation, transportation, defense, commercial construction, food and beverage, and chemical industries, among others.

The company continues to be acquisitive. Since 2002 Crane Co. has purchased more than 20 companies. Its general strategy is to maintain a competitive advantage by building dominant positions in niche markets.

Two of the company's markets, aerospace and chemical processing, are beginning to stabilize. While pricing pressures remain tough for Crane's commercial aerospace markets, increases in defense spending have boosted the company's military and defense electronics business. Crane's fluid handling business is benefiting from cost controls including the movement of manufacturing operations to low-cost regions.

The company focused on growing its merchandising segment in 2006. Early in the year, Crane acquired CashCode, a company that makes banknote validation, storage, and recycling devices used by the gaming industry as well as vending companies, for $86 million. Crane also spent $45 million to buy Telequip, which makes coin dispensers.

Later in 2006 Crane acquired most of the assets of Automatic Products International (APi), which made and distributed vending equipment, for more than $30 million, and it paid $46 million to buy vending-machine maker Dixie-Narco from Whirlpool. APi and Dixie-Narco were both integrated into Crane's Merchandising Systems unit.

The Crane Fund, a charitable trust, owns about 13% of Crane Co.

## HISTORY

Crane was founded in 1855 by Richard Teller Crane as a small foundry in a lumberyard owned by his uncle, Martin Ryerson. Crane grew along with Chicago and its railroads. Its first big order was to supply parts to a maker of railroad cars. In 1872 the company began making passenger elevators through the Crane Elevator Company, which was sold in 1895 to a joint venture that became the Otis Elevator Company. Although it had made plumbing materials since 1886, Crane developed a broader line during the 1920s and became a household name. The company remained under the leadership of the Crane family until Thomas Mellon Evans was elected as chief executive in 1959. Evans diversified the company through acquisitions that included Huttig Sash & Door (1968) and CF&I Steel (1969). Crane also added basic materials with its purchase of Medusa (cement and aggregates) in 1979.

Evans' son, Robert, took over as Crane's chairman in 1984 and began restructuring the company. That year Crane sold its U.S. Plumbing division, and the next year it spun off CF&I Steel to its shareholders. The company then began buying manufacturing companies in the defense, aerospace, fluid controls, vending machine, fiberglass panel, and electronic components markets. Crane expanded its Ferguson Machine business with the purchase of PickOmatic Systems of Detroit (mechanical parts-handling equipment), then boosted its wood building distribution segment with the 1988 acquisitions of Pozzi-Renati Millwork Products and Palmer G. Lewis.

In 1990 Crane acquired Lear Romec (pumps for the aerospace industry) and Crown Pumps' diaphragm pump business. In the early 1990s the company continued its successful strategy of selective buying, adding Jenkins Canada (bronze and iron valves, 1992), Rondel's millwork distributions (1993), Burks Pumps (1993), and Mark Controls (valves, instruments, and controls, 1994).

Crane picked up Interpoint (DC-DC power converters) and Grenson Electronics (low-voltage power conversion components, UK) in 1996. The next year Crane bought five businesses, the largest of which was Stockham Valves & Fittings. The company's 1998 acquisitions included Environmental Products USA (water-purification systems), Consolidated Lumber Company (wholesale distributor of lumber and millwork products), Sequentia Holdings (fiberglass-reinforced plastic panels), Liberty Technologies (diagnostic equipment for the power and process industries), and the plastic-lined piping products division of Dow Chemical. Crane also sold two of its foundries in Tennessee and Alabama that year.

In 2001 Crane acquired the industrial flow business of Alfa Laval, Ventech Controls (valve repair), and Laminated Profiles (fiberglass-reinforced panels, UK). In March 2001 the investment firm led by Mario Gabelli increased its stake in Crane to nearly 8%. Crane acquired valve manufacturer Xomox (renamed Crane Process Flow) from Emerson in June and sold its Power Process Controls business (fluid and gas measurement and control) to Watts Industries (now Watts Water Technologies) in October.

Crane continued to add complementary businesses in 2002, purchasing Lasco Composites LP, a Kentucky manufacturer of fiberglass-reinforced plastic panels, from Tomkins Industries for $44 million; the US-based valve and actuator distributor Corva Corporation; and General Technology Corporation, an electronics company (printed circuit boards, customized integrated systems, cables, and wire harnesses) geared for the defense industry.

The buying spree continued in 2003 when Crane completed its announced acquisition of Signal Technology Corporation. Crane bought the pipe couplings and fittings business of Etex Group S.A. the following month.

The next year had hardly begun when Crane acquired P.L. Porter, a maker of motion control products for airline seating. A few days later Crane bought the Hattersley valve brand from Hattersley Newman Hender. Ltd., a subsidiary of Tomkins PLC. At 2004's close Crane announced it had sold the UK-based businesses and intellectual property of Victaulic (Victaulic was a subsidiary of Crane's U.K. subsidiary Crane Limited) to Euro-Victaulic B.V.B.A., a subsidiary of Victaulic Company of America, for $15.4 million.

## EXECUTIVES

**Chairman:** Robert S. Evans, age 62
**President, CEO, and Director:** Eric C. Fast, age 57, $900,000 pay
**President, Controls Group:** C. Douglas (Doug) Spitler, age 56
**President, Aerospace Group:** Gregory A. Ward, age 56, $268,799 pay
**President, Composites Group:** Thomas J. (Jeff) Craney
**President, Electronics Group:** David E. Bender, age 47
**President, Kemlite:** Daniel L. (Dan) Colbert
**Group President, Fluid Handling:** Max H. Mitchell, age 43, $283,920 pay
**Group President, Crane Merchandising Systems:** Bradly L. (Brad) Ellis, age 38
**VP, Operational Excellence:** Thomas J. Perlitz, age 38
**VP, Finance and CFO:** J. Robert Vipond, age 61, $329,600 pay
**VP, Strategic Planning and Business Development:** Curtis P. Robb, age 52
**VP, General Counsel, and Secretary:** Augustus I. duPont, age 55, $298,350 pay
**VP and Controller:** Joan Atkinson-Nano, age 51
**VP and Treasurer:** Andrew L. Krawitt, age 41
**VP, Human Resources:** Elise M. Kopczick, age 53
**VP, Taxes:** Thomas M. Noonan, age 52
**Director, Investor Relations:** Richard E. Koch
**Auditors:** Deloitte & Touche LLP

## LOCATIONS

**HQ:** Crane Co.
100 First Stamford Place, Stamford, CT 06902
**Phone:** 203-363-7300 **Fax:** 203-363-7295
**Web:** www.craneco.com

Crane Co. has manufacturing facilities in Asia, Australia, Europe, and North and South America.

### 2006 Sales

| | $ mil. | % of total |
|---|---|---|
| North America | | |
| US | 1,421.6 | 63 |
| Canada | 266.8 | 12 |
| Europe | 455.8 | 20 |
| Other regions | 112.7 | 5 |
| **Total** | **2,256.9** | **100** |

## PRODUCTS/OPERATIONS

### 2006 Sales

| | $ mil. | % of total |
|---|---|---|
| Fluid handling | 999.6 | 44 |
| Aerospace & electronics | 566.2 | 25 |
| Engineered materials | 309.3 | 14 |
| Merchandising systems | 257.8 | 11 |
| Controls | 124.0 | 6 |
| **Total** | **2,256.9** | **100** |

### Selected Business Segments and Subsidiaries

Fluid handling
- Crane Ltd. (commercial valves, UK)
- Crane Nuclear, Inc. (valve products for the nuclear power industry)
- Crane Supply (distribution)
- Crane Pumps & Systems (pumps)
- Crane Valve Group (valves, pipes, couplings, connectors, actuators)

Aerospace & electronics
- ELDEC Corporation (sensing and control systems for aircraft)
- General Technology Corporation (GTC, contract manufacturing for military and defense applications)
- Hydro-Aire, Inc. (anti-skid brake control systems)
- Interpoint Corporation (hybrid power converters)
- Lear Romec (lubrication & fuel pumps)
- P. L. Porter (motion control products for airline seating)
- Signal Technology Corporation (STC Microwave Systems, electronic radio frequency components)

Engineered materials
- Crane Composites Inc. (Kemlite, fiberglass-reinforced plastic panels)
- Polyflon (specialty components, substrates for antennas)

Merchandising systems
- Crane Merchandising Systems (Vending Solutions)
- Payment Solutions
  - CashCode Co. Inc.
  - National Rejectors, Inc. GmbH (coin changers, Germany)
  - Telquip Corporation

Controls
- Azonix Corporation (measurement and control systems)
- Barksdale Inc. (pressure switches and transducers)
- Dynalco Controls Corporation (monitoring, diagnostic, and control products)

## COMPETITORS

Automated Distribution Technologies
AZKOYEN
Chori
CIRCOR International
Colfax
Curtiss-Wright
Dover
Eaton
Emerson Electric
Flowserve
Goodrich
IMI
K&F Industries
Kohler
KSB
Kubota
Legris
Parker Hannifin
Precision Castparts
Standex
Swagelok
Tuthill
Tyco

## HISTORICAL FINANCIALS

Company Type: Public

### Income Statement

FYE: December 31

| | REVENUE ($ mil.) | NET INCOME ($ mil.) | NET PROFIT MARGIN | EMPLOYEES |
|---|---|---|---|---|
| **12/06** | 2,257 | 166 | 7.4% | 11,870 |
| **12/05** | 2,061 | 136 | 6.6% | 10,400 |
| **12/04** | 1,890 | (105) | — | 10,500 |
| **12/03** | 1,636 | 104 | 6.4% | 10,000 |
| **12/02** | 1,516 | (11) | — | 9,500 |
| **Annual Growth** | 10.5% | — | — | 5.7% |

### 2006 Year-End Financials

Debt ratio: 42.6%
Return on equity: 19.8%
Cash ($ mil.): 139
Current ratio: 1.91
Long-term debt ($ mil.): 392
No. of shares (mil.): 60
Dividends
Yield: 1.5%
Payout: 20.6%
Market value ($ mil.): 2,216

### Stock History

NYSE: CR

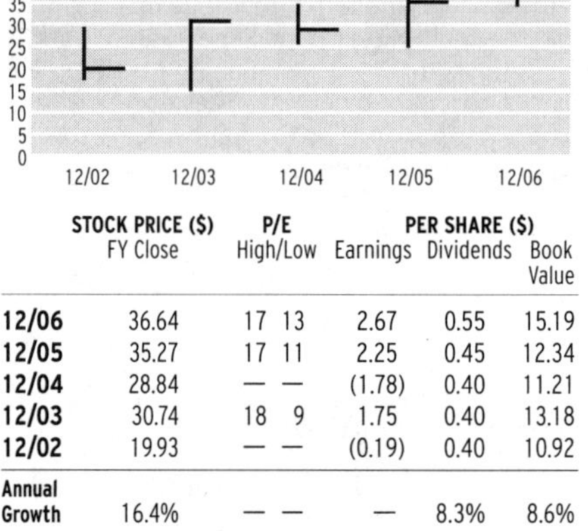


| | STOCK PRICE ($) FY Close | P/E High | P/E Low | PER SHARE ($) Earnings | Dividends | Book Value |
|---|---|---|---|---|---|---|
| **12/06** | 36.64 | 17 | 13 | 2.67 | 0.55 | 15.19 |
| **12/05** | 35.27 | 17 | 11 | 2.25 | 0.45 | 12.34 |
| **12/04** | 28.84 | — | — | (1.78) | 0.40 | 11.21 |
| **12/03** | 30.74 | 18 | 9 | 1.75 | 0.40 | 13.18 |
| **12/02** | 19.93 | — | — | (0.19) | 0.40 | 10.92 |
| **Annual Growth** | 16.4% | — | — | — | 8.3% | 8.6% |

# Crown Holdings

Crown Holdings knows how to keep a lid on it. The company is a top worldwide producer of consumer packaging; metal food and beverage cans and related packaging are the company's primary source of income. Its product portfolio also includes aerosol cans and a wide variety of metal caps, crowns, and closures, as well as specialty packaging such as decorative novelty containers and industrial paint cans. Crown Holdings also makes canmaking equipment and replacement parts. The company has divested most of its plastic closure and container operations.

In recent years Crown Holdings has focused on improving segment income, reducing debt, and reducing asbestos-related costs. For the segment income task, the company is focusing on targeting promising markets such as Latin America, Asia, and southern and central Europe. It also wants to improve selling rates, reduce costs, and develop unique new products.

The company's debt reduction plans have called for major asset sales. In line with this plan, Crown Holdings sold its plastics closures business for about $750 million in 2005. The company previously had sold several divisions and spun off its PET bottle subsidiary, Constar International. In 2006, the company sold its remaining North American and European plastics operations.

The following year Crown announced plans to build a new beverage can plant in Brazil to meet growing demand in the region.

Crown Holdings' roster of blue-chip customers includes Coca-Cola, Cadberry Schweppes, Gillette, Heinz, Nestlé, and Unilever.

## HISTORY

Formed as Crown Cork & Seal Co. (CC&S) of Baltimore in 1892, the company was consolidated into its present form in 1927 when it merged with New Process Cork and New York Patents. The next year CC&S expanded overseas and formed Crown Cork International. In 1936 CC&S acquired Acme Can and benefited from the movement at the time from home canning to processed canning. The company was the first to develop the aerosol can (1946).

By 1957 heavy debt had CC&S in trouble. Teetering on the brink of bankruptcy, the company hired John Connelly as president. Connelly immediately stopped can production (sending stockpiled inventory to customers), discontinued unprofitable product lines, and reduced costs (25% of employees were laid off in less than two years). He then directed CC&S to take advantage of new uses for aerosol cans (insecticides, hair spray, and bathroom cleaning supplies) and to expand overseas. CC&S obtained "pioneer rights" between 1955 and 1960 from foreign countries that granted it the first crack at new closure and can businesses.

The introduction of the pull-tab pop-top in 1963 hit the can business like an exploding grenade. Connelly embraced pull tabs, but he rejected getting into the production of two-piece aluminum cans (first introduced in the mid-1970s), focusing instead on existing technology for three-piece cans. He also resisted the diversification trend then popular in the can-making industry, which later led to the declining performances of competitors Continental Can and American Can.

In 1970 CC&S moved into the printing end of the industry. It gained the ability to imprint color lithography on its bottle caps and cans after buying R. Hoe.

Connelly kept CC&S debt-free through most of the 1980s, using cash flow to buy back about half of CC&S's stock. In 1989 he picked Bill Avery to succeed him. With Connelly's blessing, Avery started a buying spree that included the purchase of the plants of Continental Can. Connelly died in 1990. Acquisitions continued throughout the 1990s. CC&S's purchases included CONSTAR International, the #1 maker of polyethylene terephthalate (PET) plastic containers (1992), can maker Van Dorn (1993), and the can-manufacturing unit of Tri Valley Growers (1994). California's Northridge earthquake in 1994 ruined the company's plant in Van Nuys.

CC&S bought French packaging company CarnaudMetalbox in 1996. The purchase united CC&S's efficient operations and strong presence in North America with the French company's state-of-the-art manufacturing technology and international marketing experience. That year strikes over contract disputes halted production at eight of the company's plants. In addition, CC&S acquired Polish packaging company Fabryka Opakowan Blaszanyck.

In 1997 CC&S bought a 96% stake in Golden Aluminum from ACX Technologies, but returned the aluminum recycler in 1999 at a cost of

$10 million. Dropping sales and foreign currency fluctuations in 1998 forced the company to close seven factories and cut 7% of its workforce. CC&S closed more factories in 1999 and sold its composite can (paper cans with metal or plastic ends) business. That year the company increased its foreign presence with the purchase of two can manufacturers in Spain and Greece.

CC&S entered into a joint venture with Tempra Technology in 2000 to make and market a self-refrigerating can. The same year Avery announced his retirement; president and COO John Conway succeeded him as CEO in 2001. To reduce debt and move closer to profitability, CC&S sold three product divisions in 2001 and sold its fragrance pump unit to Rexam PLC for about $107 million in 2002. In March 2002 the company sold its Europe-based pharmaceutical packaging business. In May CC&S spun off its PET bottle subsidiary Constar in an IPO offering.

In February 2003 the company completed a refinancing plan and formed a new public holding company, Crown Holdings, Inc.; the CC&S name was retained for the company's operating subsidiary. Crown sold its Global Plastic Closures business to PAI Partners for about $750 million in 2005.

## EXECUTIVES

**Chairman, President, and CEO:** John W. Conway, age 61, $1,075,000 pay
**Vice Chairman, EVP, and CFO:** Alan W. Rutherford, age 63, $700,000 pay
**EVP, Corporate Technology and Regulatory Affairs:** Daniel A. Abramowicz
**EVP; President, European Division:** William R. Apted, age 59, $550,000 pay
**SVP, Finance:** Timothy J. Donahue, age 43
**SVP, General Counsel, and Secretary:** William T. Gallagher
**SVP, Human Resources and Secretary:** Gary L. Burgess
**VP, Corporate Affairs and Public Relations:** Michael F. Dunleavy
**VP, Corporate Risk Management:** Karen E. Berigan
**VP and Corporate Controller:** Thomas A. Kelly, age 46
**VP, Planning and Development:** Torsten Kreider
**VP and Assistant Corporate Controller:** Kevin C. Clothier
**President, North American Packaging:** Raymond L. McGowan, age 55
**President, Americas Division:** Frank J. Mechura, age 64, $550,000 pay
**President, European Division:** Chris Homfray, age 48
**Auditors:** PricewaterhouseCoopers LLP

## LOCATIONS

**HQ:** Crown Holdings, Inc.
1 Crown Way, Philadelphia, PA 19154
**Phone:** 215-698-5100 **Fax:** 215-676-7245
**Web:** www.crowncork.com

Crown Holdings operates more than 140 plants, as well as sales and service facilities, in more than 40 countries in Asia, Europe, and the US.

### 2006 Sales

| | $ mil. | % of total |
|---|---|---|
| US | 1,974 | 28 |
| UK | 778 | 11 |
| France | 629 | 9 |
| Other regions | 3,601 | 52 |
| **Total** | **6,982** | **100** |

## PRODUCTS/OPERATIONS

### 2006 Sales

| | $ mil. | % of total |
|---|---|---|
| Metal beverage cans & ends | 3,104 | 44 |
| Metal food cans & ends | 2,447 | 35 |
| Other metal packaging | 1,312 | 19 |
| Plastics packaging | 54 | 1 |
| Other products | 65 | 1 |
| **Total** | **6,982** | **100** |

### Selected Products

Metal packaging
- Aerosol cans
- Beverage cans
- Closures and caps
- Crowns
- Ends
- Food cans
- Specialty packaging (unusual containers)
- Vacuum closures

Plastics packaging

Other products
- Canmaking equipment and spares

## COMPETITORS

Alcoa
Amcor
AptarGroup
Ball Corporation
BWAY
Calmar
Metal Container
Owens-Illinois
Rexam
Silgan
Sonoco Products
Tetra Laval

## HISTORICAL FINANCIALS

Company Type: Public

### Income Statement

FYE: December 31

| | REVENUE ($ mil.) | NET INCOME ($ mil.) | NET PROFIT MARGIN | EMPLOYEES |
|---|---|---|---|---|
| **12/06** | 6,982 | 309 | 4.4% | 21,700 |
| **12/05** | 6,908 | (362) | — | 24,000 |
| **12/04** | 7,199 | 51 | 0.7% | 27,600 |
| **12/03** | 6,630 | (32) | — | 27,500 |
| **12/02** | 6,792 | (1,205) | — | 28,319 |
| **Annual Growth** | 0.7% | — | — | (6.4%) |

### 2006 Year-End Financials

Debt ratio: —
Return on equity: —
Cash ($ mil.): 407
Current ratio: 1.05
Long-term debt ($ mil.): 3,420
No. of shares (mil.): 163
Dividends
Yield: —
Payout: —
Market value ($ mil.): 3,404

### Stock History

NYSE: CCK

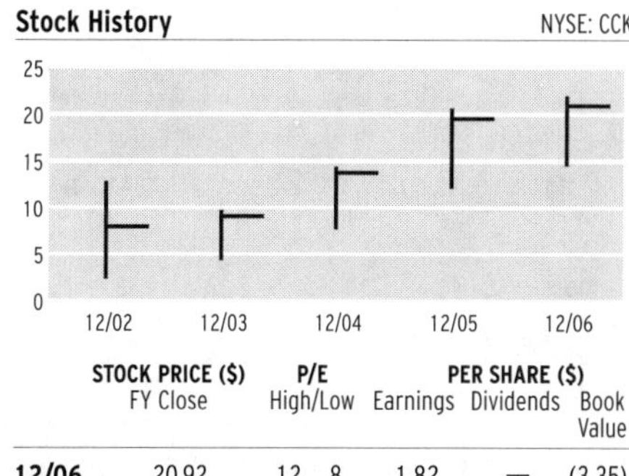


| | STOCK PRICE ($) FY Close | P/E High | P/E Low | PER SHARE ($) Earnings | PER SHARE ($) Dividends | PER SHARE ($) Book Value |
|---|---|---|---|---|---|---|
| **12/06** | 20.92 | 12 | 8 | 1.82 | — | (3.35) |
| **12/05** | 19.53 | — | — | (2.18) | — | (1.42) |
| **12/04** | 13.74 | 47 | 26 | 0.30 | — | 1.67 |
| **12/03** | 9.06 | — | — | (0.19) | — | 0.85 |
| **12/02** | 7.95 | — | — | (8.38) | — | (0.55) |
| **Annual Growth** | 27.4% | — | — | — | — | — |

# CSX Corporation

CSX banks on the railway as the right way to make money. Its main subsidiary, CSX Transportation (CSXT), operates the largest rail system (some 21,000 route miles) in the eastern US. The freight carrier links 23 states, the District of Columbia, and two Canadian provinces. Freight hauled by the company includes a wide variety of merchandise, coal, automotive products, and intermodal containers. CSX's rail segment, which accounts for more than 80% of the company's sales, also includes units that operate motor vehicle distribution centers and bulk cargo terminals. Subsidiary CSX Intermodal arranges the transportation of freight by combinations of road and rail carriers.

CSXT is concentrating on boosting the efficiency of its operations by reducing accidents and improving the rate of on-time performance. CSX Intermodal hopes to persuade more shippers to shift freight from trucks to trains, especially for cross-country journeys. Imports from the Asia/Pacific region are a key source of intermodal traffic.

The CSXT system includes tracks formerly operated by Conrail, of which CSX owns 42% and Norfolk Southern owns 58%. In 2004 the two companies reorganized Conrail so that each railroad directly owns the Conrail assets that it operates. Conrail still operates switching facilities and terminals used by both Norfolk Southern and CSX.

Besides its transportation-related assets, CSX owns The Greenbrier, a resort in West Virginia.

## HISTORY

CSX Corporation was formed in 1980, when Chessie System and Seaboard Coast Line (SCL) merged in an effort to improve the efficiency of their railroads.

Chessie's oldest railroad, the Baltimore & Ohio (B&O), was chartered in 1827 to help Baltimore compete against New York and Philadelphia for freight traffic. By the late 1800s the railroad served Chicago, Cincinnati, New York City, St. Louis, and Washington, DC. Chesapeake & Ohio (C&O) acquired it in 1962.

C&O originated in Virginia with the Louisa Railroad in 1836. It gained access to Chicago, Cincinnati, and Washington, DC, and by the mid-1900s was a major coal carrier. After B&O and C&O acquired joint control of Baltimore-based Western Maryland Railway (1967), the three railroads became subsidiaries of newly formed Chessie System (1973).

One of SCL's two predecessors, Seaboard Air Line Railroad (SAL), grew out of Virginia's Portsmouth & Roanoke Rail Road of 1832. SCL's other predecessor, Atlantic Coast Line Railroad (ACL), took shape between 1869 and 1893 as William Walters acquired several southern railroads. In 1902 ACL bought the Plant System (railroads in Georgia, Florida, and other southern states) and the Louisville & Nashville (a north-south line connecting New Orleans and Chicago), giving ACL the basic form it was to retain until 1967, when it merged with SAL to form SCL.

After CSX inherited the Chessie System and SCL, it bought Texas Gas Resources (gas pipeline, 1983), American Commercial Lines (Texas Gas' river barge subsidiary, 1984), and

Sea-Land Corporation (ocean container shipping, 1986). To improve its market value, CSX sold most of its oil and gas properties, its communications holdings (Lightnet, begun in 1983), and most of its resort properties (Rockresorts) in 1988 and 1989. American Commercial Lines acquired Valley Line in 1992.

Sea-Land struck a deal with Danish shipping company Maersk Line in 1996 to share vessels and terminals. That year CSX entered a takeover battle with rival Norfolk Southern for Conrail. Conrail decided to split its assets between the two; CSX paid $4.3 billion for 42%. (The division took place in 1999.)

CSX combined the American Commercial Lines barge business with the barge business of Vectra Group in 1998.

In 1999 CSX sold Grand Teton Lodge to Vail Resorts for $50 million. Also that year CSX divided Sea-Land into three businesses: international terminal operations (which became CSX World Terminals), domestic container shipping (CSX Lines), and global container shipping. The international shipping business was sold to Denmark's A.P. Møller (parent of Maersk Line) for $800 million.

Rail service disruptions stemming from the integration of Conrail assets were exacerbated by damage from Hurricane Floyd in 1999. The next year a federal audit found defects in CSX track. Service problems related to the Conrail takeover continued, and the company's rail unit underwent a management shake-up.

Later in 2000 CSX, looking to pay down debt, sold its CTI Logistx unit to TNT Post Group for $650 million. The next year CSX formed a new unit, Transflo, to provide intermodal services for bulk cargo.

In 2002 CSX established a CSXT office in Europe to focus on international freight and to create partnerships with European freight forwarders and ocean carriers.

CSX sold a controlling stake in its ocean container shipping unit to investment firm Carlyle Group in 2003. The former CSX Lines took the name Horizon Lines. In 2004 Carlyle sold its stake in Horizon Lines to another investment firm, Castle Harlan. The next year CSX sold its CSX World Terminals to Dubai Ports International (later DP World) for $1.14 billion.

## EXECUTIVES

**Chairman, President, and CEO; President and CEO, CSX Transportation:** Michael J. Ward, age 56, $995,833 pay
**EVP and CFO; EVP and CFO, CSX Transportation:** Oscar Munoz, age 47
**EVP and Chief Commercial Officer; EVP and Chief Commercial Officer, CSX Transportation:** Clarence W. Gooden, age 55, $495,833 pay
**SVP, Human Resources and Labor Relations; SVP, Human Resources and Labor Relations, CSX Transportation:** Robert J. Haulter, age 54
**SVP, Law and Public Affairs and Corporate Secretary; SVP, Law and Public Affairs and Corporate Secretary, CSX Transportation:** Ellen M. Fitzsimmons, age 46, $445,833 pay
**President, CSX Intermodal:** James R. (Jim) Hertwig
**President, CSX Real Property:** Stephen A. Crosby, age 52
**President, CSX Technology:** John L. West, age 47
**President, TRANSFLO:** Glen Soliah
**EVP and COO, CSX Transportation:** Tony L. Ingram, age 60, $520,833 pay
**Director, Network Control:** Dan Pinkley
**President and Managing Director, The Greenbrier Resort and Club Management Company:** Paul Ratchford
**General Counsel, Business:** Nathan Goldman
**Auditors:** Ernst & Young LLP

## LOCATIONS

**HQ:** CSX Corporation
500 Water St., 15th Fl., Jacksonville, FL 32202
**Phone:** 904-359-3200 **Fax:** 904-633-3450
**Web:** www.csx.com

## PRODUCTS/OPERATIONS

**2006 Sales**

| | $ mil. | % of total |
|---|---|---|
| Rail | 8,154 | 85 |
| Intermodal | 1,412 | 15 |
| **Total** | **9,566** | **100** |

## COMPETITORS

APL Logistics
Burlington Northern Santa Fe
Canadian National Railway
Canadian Pacific Railway
Hub Group
J.B. Hunt
Norfolk Southern
Pacer International
Schneider National
Union Pacific

## HISTORICAL FINANCIALS

Company Type: Public

**Income Statement** FYE: Last Friday in December

| | REVENUE ($ mil.) | NET INCOME ($ mil.) | NET PROFIT MARGIN | EMPLOYEES |
|---|---|---|---|---|
| **12/06** | 9,566 | 1,310 | 13.7% | 36,000 |
| **12/05** | 8,618 | 1,145 | 13.3% | 35,000 |
| **12/04** | 352 | 140 | 39.8% | 35,847 |
| **12/03** | 7,793 | 246 | 3.2% | 37,516 |
| **12/02** | 8,152 | 424 | 5.2% | 39,928 |
| **Annual Growth** | 4.1% | 32.6% | — | (2.6%) |

**2006 Year-End Financials**

Debt ratio: 60.0%
Return on equity: 15.5%
Cash ($ mil.): 900
Current ratio: 1.06
Long-term debt ($ mil.): 5,362
No. of shares (mil.): 438
Dividends
Yield: 1.0%
Payout: 11.7%
Market value ($ mil.): 15,072

**Stock History** NYSE: CSX

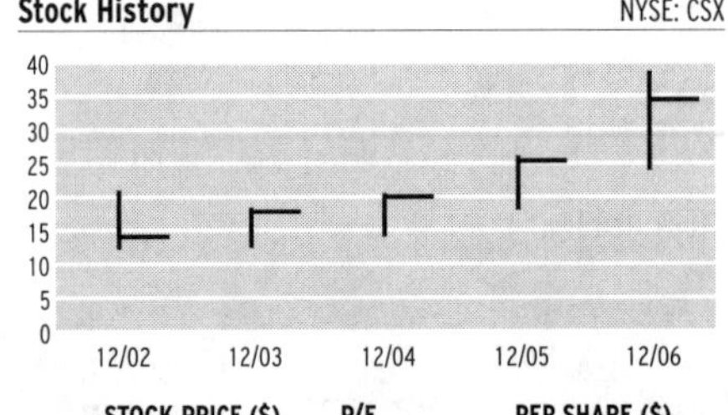


| | STOCK PRICE ($) FY Close | P/E High | P/E Low | PER SHARE ($) Earnings | Dividends | Book Value |
|---|---|---|---|---|---|---|
| **12/06** | 34.43 | 14 | 9 | 2.82 | 0.33 | 20.43 |
| **12/05** | 25.39 | 10 | 7 | 2.52 | 0.22 | 36.45 |
| **12/04** | 20.04 | 27 | 19 | 0.76 | 0.20 | 1.67 |
| **12/03** | 17.83 | 32 | 22 | 0.57 | 0.20 | 30.00 |
| **12/02** | 14.10 | 21 | 13 | 1.00 | 0.20 | 29.07 |
| **Annual Growth** | 25.0% | — | — | 29.6% | 13.3% | (8.4%) |

# Cummins, Inc.

Cummins is in it for the long haul. The company is the world's leader in the manufacture of large diesel engines. The company's engines also power school buses, medium-duty trucks, pickup trucks (primarily the Dodge Ram), and equipment for mining and construction. Cummins claims just under one-third of the North American market for heavy-duty truck engines. The company also makes power generation products such as its Onan generator sets and Stamford alternators. Other products and brands include Fleetguard (filtration), Kuss (fuel filters), and Holset (turbochargers).

The year 2006 was a banner year for Cummins. In fact it was the best year in the company's history, surpassing 2005, which up to that point had been the company's best-ever year.

Cummins has gradually been transforming itself from a company focused on North America to one whose strategy is global and aimed at seizing opportunities in emerging markets — chiefly in China and India. The new strategy aims to eliminate or lessen the cyclical booms and busts that traditionally have been the bane of the heavy-duty truck industry.

The company's strides in emerging markets have been made through the nearly 50 joint ventures Cummins has formed with overseas partners. As part of its global strategy Cummins has also opened new purchasing offices in China, India, the Czech Republic, and Brazil. Through these offices Cummins is building purchasing relationships with local manufacturers to secure high-quality, low-cost sourcing. Cummins has also opened up its newest technical center in India. To reap future rewards from its global focus, Cummins has also been tightening up its global distribution network so emerging markets can take full advantage of the Cummins brand of parts sales and service.

Cummins plans to stay on top by continuing to invest in high-growth areas, specifically in China and India — Cummins' second- and third-largest customers are located in China and India, respectively.

Barclays Global Investors owns about 12% of the company; State Street Bank and Trust Company owns 12%.

## HISTORY

Chauffeur Clessie Cummins believed that Rudolph Diesel's cumbersome and smoky engine could be improved for use in transportation. Borrowing money and work space from his employer — Columbus, Indiana, banker W. G. Irwin — Cummins founded Cummins Engine in 1919. Irwin invested more than $2.5 million and in the mid-1920s Cummins produced a mobile diesel engine. Truck manufacturers were reluctant to switch from gas to diesel, so Cummins used publicity stunts (such as racing in the Indianapolis 500) to advertise his engine.

The company was profitable by 1937, the year Irwin's grandnephew, J. Irwin Miller, took over. During WWII the Cummins engine was used in cargo trucks. From 1946 to 1956, sales jumped from $20 million to more than $100 million. The company started its first overseas plant in 1956 in Scotland, and in 1958 it bought Atlas Crankshafts. By 1967 it had 50% of the diesel engine market.

Cummins diversified in 1970 by acquiring the K2 Ski Company (fiberglass skis) and Coot Industries (all-terrain vehicles), but sold them by 1976. In the early 1980s Cummins introduced a line of midrange engines developed in a joint venture with J.I. Case (then a subsidiary of Tenneco; now a part of Fiat-controlled CNH Global). To remain competitive, Cummins cut costs by 22%, doubled productivity in its US and UK plants, and spent $1.8 billion to retool its factories.

Having twice repelled unwelcome foreign suitors in 1989, Cummins sold 27% of its stock to Ford, Tenneco, and Japanese tractor maker Kubota for $250 million in 1990. The move raised cash and protected Cummins from future takeover bids.

In 1993 Cummins established engine-making joint ventures with Tata Engineering & Locomotive, India's largest heavy-vehicle maker, and Komatsu, a leading Japanese construction equipment maker. Also in 1993 Cummins introduced a natural-gas engine for school buses and formed a joint venture to produce turbochargers in India. The company began Cummins Wartsila, a joint venture with engineering company Wartsila NSD, to develop high-speed diesel and natural gas engines in France and the UK in 1995. It also began restructuring that year, selling plants and laying off workers.

Continuing its strategy of teaming with other manufacturers, Cummins agreed in 1996 to make small and midsize diesel engines with Fiat's Iveco and New Holland (now CNH Global) subsidiaries.

In 1997 subsidiary Cadec Systems signed a license to develop and sell Montreal-based Canadian Marconi's (now BAE SYSTEMS CANADA) fleet-tracking system, which uses satellites and computers. Cummins bought diesel exhaust and air filtration company Nelson Industries for $490 million in early 1998. The company also agreed, without admission of guilt, to pay a $25 million fine and contribute $35 million to environmental programs after the EPA accused Cummins of cheating on emissions tests.

In 1999 Cummins sold its Atlas Crankshaft subsidiary to ThyssenKrupp's automotive subsidiary. Chairman and CEO James Henderson retired at the end of 1999 and was succeeded by Theodore Solso.

Early in 2001 the company announced that it had signed a long-term deal to supply PACCAR (Peterbilt and Kenworth trucks) with heavy-duty ISX, Signature, N14, ISM, and ISL engines. Cummins also formed a joint venture with Westport Innovations (Cummins Westport Inc.) for the building of low-emission, natural gas engines. Later in 2001 the company shortened its name to Cummins, Inc.

The following year Cummins and Mercury Marine formed a joint venture, Cummins MerCruiser Diesel Marine LLC, to provide diesel engines to the recreational and commercial marine markets.

In 2003 Cummins and Westport Innovations strengthened their joint venture ties by signing a technology partnership agreement that will make it easier for the two companies to develop and share alternative fuel technologies.

## EXECUTIVES

**Chairman and CEO:** Theodore M. (Tim) Solso, age 60, $1,022,500 pay
**President, COO, and Director:** F. Joseph Loughrey, age 57, $750,000 pay
**EVP and CFO:** Jean S. Blackwell, age 52, $525,000 pay
**EVP; President, Cummins Power Generation:** N. Thomas (Tom) Linebarger, age 44, $565,000 pay
**Group VP, Emerging Markets and Businesses:** Steven M. (Steve) Chapman, age 52
**VP; President, Components Group:** Rick J. Mills, age 59
**VP; President, Engine Business:** James D. (Jim) Kelly, age 54, $475,000 pay
**VP; President, Filtration Business, Components Group:** Pamela L. (Pam) Carter
**VP; President, Worldwide Distribution Business:** Rich Freeland, age 49
**VP and Corporate Controller:** Marsha L. Hunt, age 43
**VP and Controller, Engine Business:** Glyn Price
**VP and CTO:** John C. Wall, age 54
**VP and Treasurer:** Richard E. Harris, age 54
**VP, General Counsel, and Corporate Secretary:** Marya M. Rose, age 44
**VP, Human Resources:** Jill Cook
**Director, Public Relations:** Mark Land
**Auditors:** PricewaterhouseCoopers LLP

## LOCATIONS

**HQ:** Cummins, Inc.
500 Jackson St., Columbus, IN 47202
**Phone:** 812-377-5000 **Fax:** 812-377-3334
**Web:** www.cummins.com

Cummins Engine Company has major manufacturing operations in Australia, Brazil, Canada, China, France, Germany, India, Mexico, Romania, South Africa, the UK, and the US.

### 2006 Sales

| | $ mil. | % of total |
|---|---|---|
| US | 5,719 | 50 |
| Asia & Australia | 1,794 | 16 |
| Europe | 1,633 | 14 |
| Mexico & Latin America | 886 | 8 |
| Canada | 743 | 7 |
| Africa & Middle East | 587 | 5 |
| **Total** | **11,362** | **100** |

## PRODUCTS/OPERATIONS

### 2006 Sales

| | $ mil. | % of total |
|---|---|---|
| Engines | 7,511 | 55 |
| Power generation | 2,416 | 18 |
| Components | 2,281 | 17 |
| Distribution | 1,385 | 10 |
| Adjustments | (2,231) | — |
| **Total** | **11,362** | **100** |

### Selected Products

Engines
- Bus engines
- Heavy- and medium-duty truck engines
- Industrial engines for construction, mining, agricultural, rail, and marine equipment
- Light, commercial vehicle engines

Power generation
- Generator sets (Onan)

Filtration
- Fleetguard
- Nelson

## COMPETITORS

AAF-McQUAY
Caterpillar
Daimler
Detroit Diesel
Emerson Electric
Hino Motors
Invensys
Isuzu
Kohler
Mack Trucks
MAN
Navistar
Nissan Diesel
PACCAR
Regal-Beloit
Renault
Scania
ThyssenKrupp
Volvo
Weichai Power

## HISTORICAL FINANCIALS

Company Type: Public

### Income Statement

FYE: December 31

| | REVENUE ($ mil.) | NET INCOME ($ mil.) | NET PROFIT MARGIN | EMPLOYEES |
|---|---|---|---|---|
| **12/06** | 11,362 | 715 | 6.3% | 34,600 |
| **12/05** | 9,918 | 550 | 5.5% | 33,500 |
| **12/04** | 8,438 | 350 | 4.1% | 28,100 |
| **12/03** | 6,296 | 50 | 0.8% | 24,200 |
| **12/02** | 5,853 | 82 | 1.4% | 23,700 |
| **Annual Growth** | 18.0% | 71.8% | — | 9.9% |

### 2006 Year-End Financials

Debt ratio: 23.1%
Return on equity: 30.6%
Cash ($ mil.): 935
Current ratio: 1.87
Long-term debt ($ mil.): 647
No. of shares (mil.): 52
Dividends
Yield: 1.1%
Payout: 9.3%
Market value ($ mil.): 3,079

### Stock History

NYSE: CMI

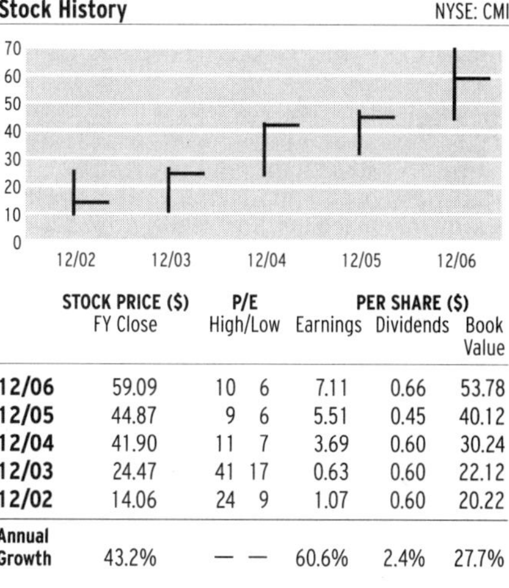

| | STOCK PRICE ($) FY Close | P/E High | P/E Low | PER SHARE ($) Earnings | Dividends | Book Value |
|---|---|---|---|---|---|---|
| **12/06** | 59.09 | 10 | 6 | 7.11 | 0.66 | 53.78 |
| **12/05** | 44.87 | 9 | 6 | 5.51 | 0.45 | 40.12 |
| **12/04** | 41.90 | 11 | 7 | 3.69 | 0.60 | 30.24 |
| **12/03** | 24.47 | 41 | 17 | 0.63 | 0.60 | 22.12 |
| **12/02** | 14.06 | 24 | 9 | 1.07 | 0.60 | 20.22 |
| **Annual Growth** | 43.2% | — | — | 60.6% | 2.4% | 27.7% |

# CVS/Caremark

CVS/Caremark (formerly CVS) interprets the scrawl of more US doctors than anyone. The CVS pharmacy chain fills more prescriptions at more drugstores than any other drugstore operator, although it trails rival Walgreen in total sales. Following its acquisitions of the Eckerd chain and stores from Albertsons, CVS operates approximately 6,200 stores in some 40 states. More recently, CVS purchased prescription benefits management (PBM) firm Caremark Rx for about $26.5 billion. Caremark was combined with CVS's PBM and specialty pharmacy subsidiary PharmaCare Management Services, which offered managed-care drug programs to insurers, employers, and other health care plan providers, to form Caremark Pharmacy Services.

The acquisition of Caremark extended CVS's buying spree beyond the retail pharmacy industry and positioned the company as a leading manager of pharmacy benefits in the US. The hard-won deal, launched in November 2006, led to a bidding war between CVS and Caremark rival Express Scripts that forced CVS to up its offer several times. Combined, CVS and Caremark create a company that's an industry leader in pharmacy and specialty pharmacy sales, PBM lives managed, mail-order pharmacy sales, and retail-based clinics (through CVS-owned MinuteClinic). Prior to the Caremark purchase, PharmaCare Management Services had been key to CVS's growth.

CVS acquired some 1,260 Eckerd drugstores in the southern US as well as Eckerd's PBM program from J. C. Penney for about $2.15 billion in 2004. The acquisition of the Eckerd stores (622 in Florida) gave CVS more stores than archrival Walgreen. CVS completed the conversion of Eckerd stores in Alabama, Arizona, Colorado, Florida, Kansas, Louisiana, Mississippi, Missouri, New Mexico, Oklahoma, and Texas to its own banner within about a year.

With its Eckerd purchase barely digested, CVS in June 2006 acquired about 700 stand-alone drugstores under the Sav-on and Osco names from Albertsons (formerly Albertson's, Inc.). CVS was part of a consortium that bought the nation's #2 supermarket chain and split it up amongst themselves. The transaction gives CVS access to Southern California and key Midwest markets. CVS plans to spend $400,000 per store on improvements to the Sav-On and Osco locations.

## HISTORY

Brothers Stanley and Sid Goldstein, who ran health and beauty products distributor Mark Steven, branched out into retail in 1963 when they opened up their first Consumer Value Store in Lowell, Massachusetts, with partner Ralph Hoagland.

The chain grew rapidly, amassing 17 stores by the end of 1964 (the year the CVS name was first used) and 40 by 1969. That year the Goldsteins sold the chain to Melville Shoe to finance further expansion.

Melville had been founded in 1892 by shoe supplier Frank Melville. Melville's son, Ward, grew the company, creating the Thom McAn shoe store chain and later buying its supplier. By 1969 Melville had opened shoe shops in Kmart stores (through its Meldisco unit), launched one apparel chain (Chess King, sold in 1993), and purchased another (Foxwood Stores, renamed Foxmoor and sold in 1985).

In 1972 CVS bought the 84-store Clinton Drug and Discount, a Rochester, New York-based chain. Two years later, when sales hit $100 million, CVS had 232 stores — only 45 of which had pharmacies. The company bought New Jersey-based Mack Drug (36 stores) in 1977. By 1981 CVS had more than 400 stores.

CVS's sales hit $1 billion in 1985 as it continued to add pharmacies to many of its older stores. In 1987 Stanley's success was recognized companywide when he was named chairman and CEO of CVS's parent company, which by then had been renamed Melville.

CVS bought the 490-store Peoples Drug Stores chain from Imasco in 1990, giving it locations in Maryland, Pennsylvania, Virginia, West Virginia, and Washington, DC. CVS created PharmaCare Management Services in 1994 to take advantage of the growing market for pharmacy services and managed-care drug programs. Pharmacist Tom Ryan was named CEO that year.

With CVS outperforming Melville's other operations, in 1995 Melville decided to concentrate on the drugstore chain. By that time Melville's holdings had grown to include discount department store chain Marshalls and furniture chain This End Up, both sold in 1995; footwear chain Footaction, spun off as part of Footstar in 1996, along with Meldisco; the Linens 'n Things chain, spun off in 1996; the Kay-Bee Toys chain, sold in 1996; and Bob's Stores (apparel and footwear), sold in 1997.

Melville was renamed CVS in late 1996. Amid major consolidation in the drugstore industry, in 1997 CVS — then with about 1,425 stores — paid $3.7 billion for Revco D.S., which had nearly 2,600 stores in 17 states, mainly in the Midwest and Southeast. The next year the company bought Arbor Drugs (200 stores in Michigan, later converted to the CVS banner) for nearly $1.5 billion. Stanley retired as chairman in 1999 and was succeeded by Ryan.

In July 2002 CVS was among the winning bidders for the remaining assets of bankrupt rival Phar-Mor. CVS acquired the majority of Phar-Mor's prescription lists.

In July 2004 CVS completed the acquisition of 1,260 Eckerd stores, Eckerd Health Services (which included Eckerd's $1 billion mail order and pharmacy benefits management businesses), and three distribution centers from J. C. Penney Company for $2.15 billion.

In June 2005 CVS agreed to pay $110 million to settle a shareholders' lawsuit filed in 2001 that alleged the company had made misleading statements to artificially raise its stock price and violated accounting practices. CVS denied the charges and said the settlement was "purely a business decision."

In June 2006 CVS completed the acquisition of some 700 stand-alone Sav-On and Osco drugstores from Albertson's. In September the company purchased the retail-based health clinic operator MinuteClinic for an undisclosed amount. The acquisition allowed CVS to provide in-store care to its customers for minor ailments.

In March 2007 CVS changed its name to CVS/Caremark Corporation following its acquisition of the pharmacy benefits manager Caremark RX, after months of bidding between CVS and Express Scripts. Ultimately, CVS paid about $26.5 billion for Caremark.

## EXECUTIVES

**Chairman:** Edwin M. (Mac) Crawford, age 58
**President, CEO, and Director:** Thomas M. (Tom) Ryan, age 54
**EVP, CFO, and Chief Administrative Officer:** David B. (Dave) Rickard, age 60, $713,750 pay
**EVP; President, Health Services:** Chris W. Bodine, age 51
**EVP; President, Retail:** Larry J. Merlo, age 51
**EVP, Strategy and Chief Legal Officer; President, CVS Realty:** Douglas A. Sgarro, age 47, $517,500 pay
**SVP, Marketing and Operations Services:** Helena B. Foulkes
**SVP, Human Resources and Corporate Communications:** V. Michael Ferdinandi, age 56
**SVP, Merchandising:** Mike Bloom
**SVP and Chief Information Officer:** Karl Taylor
**SVP and Treasurer:** Philip C. Galbo, age 51
**SVP, Supply Chain and Logistics:** Kevin Smith
**SVP and Controller:** Paula A. Price, age 45
**VP, Corporate Communications and Community Relations:** Eileen Howard-Dunn
**VP, Investor Relations:** Nancy R. Christal
**VP and Corporate Treasurer:** Carol DeNale
**Secretary:** Zenon P. Lankowsky
**Manager, Human Resources:** Caroline Garrett
**President, Caremark Pharmacy Services:** Howard A. McLure, age 50
**Auditors:** KPMG LLP

## LOCATIONS

**HQ:** CVS/Caremark Corporation
1 CVS Dr., Woonsocket, RI 02895
**Phone:** 401-765-1500 **Fax:** 401-762-9227
**Web:** www.cvs.com

CVS has stores operating under the CVS and CVS/pharmacy names in approximately 40 states and the District of Columbia, as well as four mail-order facilities and 52 specialty pharmacies operating under the PharmaCare Pharmacy name in 22 states and the District of Columbia. The company also owns six distribution centers in Alabama, California, Rhode Island, South Carolina, Tennessee, and Texas.

**2006 Stores**

| | No. |
|---|---|
| Florida | 668 |
| Texas | 476 |
| New York | 427 |
| California | 373 |
| Pennsylvania | 363 |
| Massachusetts | 329 |
| Ohio | 310 |
| North Carolina | 281 |
| Georgia | 276 |
| Indiana | 274 |
| New Jersey | 246 |
| Michigan | 234 |
| Virginia | 232 |
| Illinois | 224 |
| South Carolina | 177 |
| Maryland | 169 |
| Alabama | 145 |
| Connecticut | 131 |
| Tennessee | 125 |
| Arizona | 120 |
| Louisiana | 85 |
| Nevada | 61 |
| Kentucky | 56 |
| Rhode Island | 54 |
| District of Columbia | 51 |
| West Virginia | 48 |
| Missouri | 47 |
| Oklahoma | 33 |
| Mississippi | 29 |
| Kansas | 28 |
| New Hampshire | 27 |
| Minnesota | 25 |
| Wisconsin | 24 |
| Maine | 17 |
| Other states | 37 |
| **Total** | **6,202** |

## PRODUCTS/OPERATIONS

**2006 Sales**

| | % of total |
|---|---|
| Prescription drugs | 70 |
| Over-the-counter & personal care | 12 |
| Body/cosmetics | 3 |
| General merchandise & other | 15 |
| **Total** | **100** |

## COMPETITORS

A&P
Aetna
Ahold USA
BioScrip
CIGNA
drugstore.com
Duane Reade
Express Scripts
Humana
Kerr Drug
Kmart
Kroger
Longs Drug
Medco Health Solutions
National Medical Health Card Systems
PacifiCare
Prescription Solutions
Rite Aid
Standard Management
UnitedHealth Group
Walgreen
Wal-Mart
WellPoint

## HISTORICAL FINANCIALS

Company Type: Public

### Income Statement

FYE: December 31

| | REVENUE ($ mil.) | NET INCOME ($ mil.) | NET PROFIT MARGIN | EMPLOYEES |
|---|---|---|---|---|
| **12/06** | 43,814 | 1,369 | 3.1% | 176,000 |
| **12/05** | 37,006 | 1,225 | 3.3% | 148,000 |
| **12/04** | 30,594 | 919 | 3.0% | 145,500 |
| **12/03** | 26,588 | 847 | 3.2% | 110,000 |
| **12/02** | 24,182 | 717 | 3.0% | 105,000 |
| **Annual Growth** | 16.0% | 17.6% | — | 13.8% |

### 2006 Year-End Financials

Debt ratio: 29.6%
Return on equity: 15.4%
Cash ($ mil.): 531
Current ratio: 1.48
Long-term debt ($ mil.): 2,870
No. of shares (mil.): 826
Dividends
Yield: 0.5%
Payout: 10.0%
Market value ($ mil.): 25,524

### Stock History

NYSE: CVS

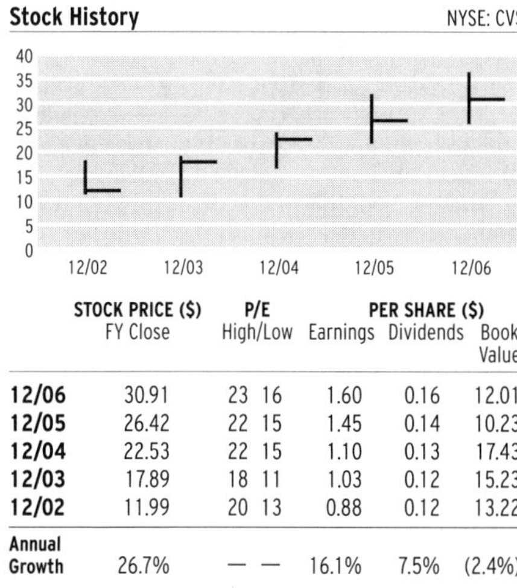


| | STOCK PRICE ($) FY Close | P/E High/Low | PER SHARE ($) Earnings | Dividends | Book Value |
|---|---|---|---|---|---|
| **12/06** | 30.91 | 23 16 | 1.60 | 0.16 | 12.01 |
| **12/05** | 26.42 | 22 15 | 1.45 | 0.14 | 10.23 |
| **12/04** | 22.53 | 22 15 | 1.10 | 0.13 | 17.43 |
| **12/03** | 17.89 | 18 11 | 1.03 | 0.12 | 15.23 |
| **12/02** | 11.99 | 20 13 | 0.88 | 0.12 | 13.22 |
| **Annual Growth** | 26.7% | — — | 16.1% | 7.5% | (2.4%) |

# Cytec Industries

Cytec Industries covers its business bases. The company produces the building-block chemicals from which it makes engineered materials (composites and adhesives for the aerospace industry), specialty chemicals (resins and coatings for metal, plastic, and wood), and additives used in treating water and in industrial processes. Cytec also sells its building-block chemicals (acrylonitrile, melamine, and sulfuric acid) to third parties. In 2006 the company sold its water treatment chemicals and acrylamide manufacturing operations to Kemira for about $240 million. The divestiture was designed to allow Cytec to pare down its operations and place its focus on core business lines.

Cytec Engineered Materials (not quite 30% of sales) includes aerospace products such as advanced composites and structural adhesives. The company's Specialty Chemicals unit makes products that are used in mining, drilling, and the manufacture of pharmaceuticals. The unit combines Cytec's Performance Chemicals and Surface Specialties segments. Cytec bought the Surface Specialties business of UCB in early 2005. Cytec paid approximately $1.8 billion in cash and stock; UCB now owns 13% of Cytec's shares.

The company had formed a joint venture with Röhm GmbH called CYRO Industries but sold the JV in 2005 for $95 million. CYRO continues to use Cytec's chemicals to make acrylic sheet and extrusion and molding compounds. Röhm is a subsidiary of Degussa.

## HISTORY

Cytec Industries was spun off of parent company American Cyanamid late in 1993. American Cyanamid had focused on agrichemical and pharmaceutical life sciences while its specialty chemicals operations languished behind its competitors. Cytec was spun off to Cyanamid stockholders, and Darryl Fry, Cyanamid's head of agriculture, became CEO of Cytec. He dumped about $300 million worth of underperforming businesses. Fry overhauled the R&D process by dragging the engineers out of their labs and having them do field work with customers. Fry also encouraged research that focused on creating products with practical applications when he realized that the last breakthrough that translated into a usable product was super glue in the 1970s. The company focused on core areas in which Cytec had expertise. Rather than go for the blockbuster product, the company aimed for an array of smaller, less-profitable but more-accessible products.

By 1996 overseas sales accounted for about 40% of revenues, up from 28% in 1993. Also in 1996 Cytec sold its aluminum sulphate operations. Cost-reduction programs and the company's improved product mix were making themselves felt; though sales were flat between 1995 and 1996, earnings were up.

David Lilley (formerly of American Home Products/Wyeth) was named COO in 1997. That year Cytec completed the sale of its acrylic-fibers business to Sterling Chemicals Holdings. Cytec also acquired Fiberite (excluding its satellite-materials business). Fiberite, a composites maker, was merged with Cytec's advanced composites and aerospace adhesives line to form Cytec Fiberite (now Cytec Engineered Materials).

In 1998 Cytec began Dyno-Cytec, a European coatings joint venture (it bought its partner's stake later in the year). It also bought composite material maker American Materials & Technologies. That year COO Lilley was named CEO; the title of chairman was added in 1999. Also in 1999 Cytec bought Inspec Mining Chemical from the UK's Laporte PLC for $25 million and BIP (amino-coating resins) for $42 million. Later that year the company sold its interest in Fortier Methanol.

The company teamed up with GE Specialty Chemicals and Albemarle in 2000 to form an online B2B joint venture to streamline the companies' purchasing. Cytec sold its stake in Criterion Catalyst to its partner CRI International, a subsidiary of Royal Dutch Shell, for $60 million. That November Cytec sold most of its paper chemicals operations, including its sizing and strength business.

In 2001 Cytec added the carbon fiber business of BP and closed up shop on joint venture AC Molding Compounds, which manufactured melamine and urea molding compounds.

With chemical companies at their lowest levels of production in about a decade, Cytec undertook some cost-cutting efforts in 2001-02, including idling an ammonia plant and reducing its staff. Problems associated with the commercial airline industry also squeezed sales.

In June 2003 the company dissolved another of its partnerships, this one with Mitsui Chemicals called Mitsui Cytec (water-treatment chemicals and melamine coating resins). Cytec kept the resins business, while Mitsui held on to the venture's water-treatment operations.

## EXECUTIVES

**Chairman, President, and CEO:** David Lilley, age 60, $828,000 pay
**CFO:** David M. Drillock, age 49
**VP, Corporate and Business Development:** William N. Avrin, age 51, $285,000 pay
**VP, General Counsel, and Secretary:** Roy Smith, age 48
**VP, Human Resources:** Joseph E. Marosits, age 54
**VP, Information Technology:** Jeffrey C. Futterman
**VP, Safety, Health, and Environment:** Karen E. Koster
**VP, Taxes:** Richard T. Ferguson
**President, Cytec Building Block Chemicals:** Jaswant S. (Jas) Gill
**President, Cytec Engineered Materials:** Steven C. (Steve) Speak, age 49, $315,000 pay
**President, Cytec Specialty Chemicals:** Shane D. Fleming, age 48, $360,000 pay
**Treasurer:** Thomas P. Wozniak, age 53
**Auditors:** KPMG LLP

## LOCATIONS

**HQ:** Cytec Industries Inc.
5 Garret Mountain Plaza, West Paterson, NJ 07424
**Phone:** 973-357-3100 **Fax:** 973-357-3065
**Web:** www.cytec.com

Cytec Industries has manufacturing facilities in Asia, Europe, North America, and South America.

### 2006 Sales

| | $ mil. | % of total |
|---|---|---|
| Europe, Middle East & Africa | 1,427.8 | 43 |
| North America | 1,246.6 | 37 |
| Asia/Pacific | 460.1 | 14 |
| Latin America | 195.0 | 6 |
| **Total** | **3,329.5** | **100** |

## PRODUCTS/OPERATIONS

### 2006 Sales and Operating Income

| | Sales $ mil. | Sales % of total | Operating Income $ mil. | Operating Income % of total |
|---|---|---|---|---|
| Cytec Surface Specialties | 1,523.4 | 46 | 95.5 | 33 |
| Cytec Performance Chemicals | 865.1 | 26 | 68.4 | 23 |
| Cytec Engineered Materials | 601.8 | 18 | 106.0 | 37 |
| Building Block Chemicals | 339.2 | 10 | 19.3 | 7 |
| **Total** | **3,329.5** | **100** | **289.2** | **100** |

### Selected Products

Cytec Surface Specialties
- Liquid coating resins (water- & solvent-borne resins, amino resins)
- Powder coating resins (conventional & ultraviolet powders)
- Radcure resins (oligomers, monomers & photo-initiators)

Performance Chemicals
- Mining chemicals (reagents, polymers)
- Phosphine and phosphine derivatives
- Polymer additives (ultraviolet light absorbers and stabilizers, antioxidants)

Cytec Engineered Materials
- Aerospace materials (structural adhesives, advanced composites)

Building-block chemicals
- Acrylamide
- Acrylonitrile
- Ammonia
- Melamine
- Sulfuric acid

## COMPETITORS

Akzo Nobel
Bayer
Ciba Specialty Chemicals
Clariant
Dow Chemical
DSM
DuPont
Georgia Gulf
H.B. Fuller
Hercules
Hexcel
Lucite
Methanex
Mitsubishi Chemical
Nalco

## HISTORICAL FINANCIALS

Company Type: Public

**Income Statement** FYE: December 31

| | REVENUE ($ mil.) | NET INCOME ($ mil.) | NET PROFIT MARGIN | EMPLOYEES |
|---|---|---|---|---|
| **12/06** | 3,330 | 195 | 5.9% | 6,700 |
| **12/05** | 2,926 | 59 | 2.0% | 7,300 |
| **12/04** | 1,721 | 126 | 7.3% | 4,500 |
| **12/03** | 1,472 | 77 | 5.3% | 4,500 |
| **12/02** | 1,346 | 79 | 5.9% | 4,250 |
| **Annual Growth** | 25.4% | 25.2% | — | 12.1% |

**2006 Year-End Financials**

Debt ratio: 57.3%
Return on equity: 13.9%
Cash ($ mil.): 24
Current ratio: 1.88
Long-term debt ($ mil.): 900
No. of shares (mil.): 48
Dividends
Yield: 0.9%
Payout: 12.5%
Market value ($ mil.): 2,691

**Stock History** NYSE: CYT

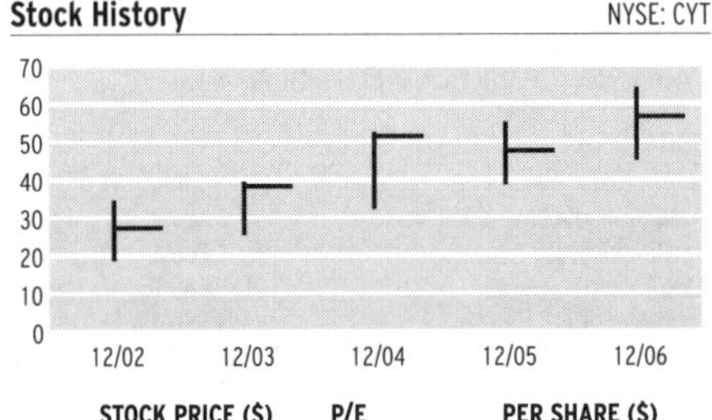


| | STOCK PRICE ($) FY Close | P/E High | P/E Low | PER SHARE ($) Earnings | Dividends | Book Value |
|---|---|---|---|---|---|---|
| **12/06** | 56.51 | 16 | 11 | 4.01 | 0.50 | 32.97 |
| **12/05** | 47.63 | 43 | 31 | 1.27 | 0.40 | 26.74 |
| **12/04** | 51.42 | 18 | 12 | 2.84 | 0.40 | 22.76 |
| **12/03** | 38.39 | 20 | 13 | 1.93 | — | 19.37 |
| **12/02** | 27.28 | 17 | 10 | 1.96 | — | 16.05 |
| **Annual Growth** | 20.0% | — | — | 19.6% | 11.8% | 19.7% |

# Danaher Corporation

If you've ever used Craftsman hand tools or bought something with a bar code on it, then odds are you've been in touch with Danaher's business. Its Professional Instrumentation group produces environmental and electronic testing technology. The Industrial Technologies unit makes motion control equipment and devices that read bar codes, and the Medical Technologies division makes dental products and medical instrumentation devices. Danaher's Tools and Components segment includes hand tools, automotive specialty tools, and accessories under brand names like Sears' Craftsman. Brothers Steven Rales (chairman) and Mitchell Rales (a director) together own approximately 20% of the company.

Danaher (from the Celtic word *dana* meaning "swift flowing") is named for a fishing stream off the Flat Head River in Montana. The term is also an appropriate description of the spotlight-averse Rales brothers. The two have proven to be fishers not only of trout but also of companies, buying underperforming companies with strong market shares and recognizable brand names.

Noted for cutting costs and improving productivity at purchased companies, Danaher plans further growth through new products, international expansion, and more acquisitions. Evidence of the company's growth strategy can be seen in its addition of medical technology as another part of its Professional Instrumentation platform.

It further expanded the medical segment through the 2005 acquisition of Leica Microsystems (surgical microscopes, diagnostic and testing equipment) and the 2006 acquisition of Sybron Dental Specialties. Later in the year it spent more than $500 million to buy Australia-based Vision Systems Limited, which makes specialized analytical gear used in medical pathology. The division was taken out of the Professional Instrumentation unit and given its status as a separate operating segment in 2007.

Danaher also has enhanced its cable installation products business, Fluke Networks, by acquiring network test and application performance management company Visual Networks in early 2006. Danaher made a move to buy British auto safety products maker First Technology for $639 million later that year, but it lost out on the bid to Honeywell.

In 2007 the company acquired ChemTreat, an industrial water treatment products maker, for $435 million. It also sold its power quality businesses, Joslyn Hi-Voltage and Power Solutions (switches and related utility products), to Thomas & Betts for $280 million.

## HISTORY

Once dubbed "raiders in short pants" by *Forbes,* Steven and Mitchell Rales began making acquisitions in their 20s. In 1981 they bought their father's 50% stake in Master Shield, a maker of vinyl building products. The brothers bought tire manufacturer Mohawk Rubber the following year. In 1983 they acquired control of publicly traded DMG, a distressed Florida real-estate firm; the next year they sold DMG's real estate holdings and folded Mohawk and Master Shield into the company, which they renamed Danaher.

Danaher then began taking over low-profile industrial firms that weren't living up to their growth potential. Backed by junk bonds from Michael Milken, it had purchased 12 more companies within two years. Among these early acquisitions were makers of tools (Jacobs, Matco Tools), controls (Partlow, Qualitrol, Veeder-Root), precision components (Allen, maker of the namesake hexagonal wrench), and plastics (A.L. Hyde). With its purchases, Danaher proceeded to cut costs and pay down debt by unloading underperforming assets.

The Rales brothers' takeover efforts weren't always successful. They lost out to Warren Buffett when they tried to buy Scott Fetzer (encyclopedias, vacuum cleaners) in 1985 and INTERCO (furniture, shoes, apparel) in 1988. They did, however, make off with $75 million for their troubles, and INTERCO was driven into dismantlement and bankruptcy in the process.

In 1989 Danaher bought Easco Hand Tools, the main maker of tools for Sears, Roebuck and Co.'s Craftsman line. (The Raleses already controlled Easco Hand Tools; a private partnership they controlled had bought the company from its parent in 1985 and taken it public in 1987.) The deal established the tool division as Danaher's largest, and two years later Sears selected Danaher as the sole manufacturer of Craftsman mechanics' hand tools.

The brothers hired Black & Decker power tools executive George Sherman as president and CEO in 1990. Between 1991 and 1995 Danaher grew through purchases such as Delta Consolidated Industries and Armstrong Brothers Tool. The firm improved its international distribution channels by adding West Instruments (UK, 1993) and Hengstler (Germany, 1994).

Danaher made its two largest purchases to date in 1998 when it bought Pacific Scientific (motion controls and safety equipment) for $460 million and Fluke (electronic tools) for $625 million.

Boosting its motion-control operations, in 2000 Danaher bought Kollmorgen for about $240 million and American Precision Industries for $185 million. In 2001 Lawrence Culp, formerly the company's COO, was named president and CEO. Later that year Danaher made a $5.5 billion offer for Cooper Industries (electric products and tools). Cooper rejected the offer and announced that it was exploring other options. Further talks with Cooper followed, but Danaher lost interest when Cooper became embroiled in asbestos lawsuits.

The following year Danaher completed the divestiture of API Heat Transfer. Also in 2002 Danaher bought motion control products maker Thomson Industries (motion control products), Gilbarco (retail automation and environmental products), and Videojet Technologies (product identification equipment).

In 2004 the company acquired Gendex, the dental imaging product manufacturer, from Dentsply International. Danaher's DH-Denmark subsidiary acquired Radiometer, a Denmark-based company that makes blood gas analyzers, later that year. Danaher also acquired a product line of telecom tool and test systems from Harris Corporation in 2004.

The summer of 2005 brought along the acquisition of German optical systems maker Leica Microsystems for about $550 million.

## EXECUTIVES

**Chairman:** Steven M. Rales, age 55
**President, CEO, and Director:** H. Lawrence (Larry) Culp Jr., age 43, $1,100,000 pay
**EVP and CFO:** Daniel L. Comas, age 43, $440,000 pay
**EVP:** Thomas P. Joyce Jr., age 46
**EVP:** Philip W. Knisely, age 52, $610,000 pay
**EVP:** James A. (Jim) Lico, age 41, $425,000 pay
**SVP, Finance and Tax:** James H. Ditkoff, age 60
**SVP, General Counsel:** Jonathan P. Graham, age 46
**VP and Group Executive; President, Videojet Technologies:** Craig B. Purse
**VP and Group Executive:** Jeffrey A. Svoboda, age 51
**VP and Chief Accounting Officer:** Robert S. Lutz, age 49
**VP, Audit:** J. David Bergman
**VP, Corporate General Manager:** Alex A. Joseph
**VP, Danaher Business System; President, Veeder-Root:** Brian E. Burnett
**VP, Strategic Development:** William H. King
**VP and Controller:** Christopher C. McMahon, age 40
**VP and Treasurer:** Frank T. McFaden
**VP and Managing Director, Europe:** Philip W. Whitehead, age 53
**VP, Corporate Development:** Daniel A. Raskas, age 40
**VP and Group Executive; President KaVo:** Alexander Granderath
**VP, Human Resources:** Henk van Duijnhoven, age 43
**VP, Investor Relations:** Andy Wilson
**Auditors:** Ernst & Young LLP

## LOCATIONS

**HQ:** Danaher Corporation
2099 Pennsylvania Ave. NW, 12th Fl.,
Washington, DC 20006
**Phone:** 202-828-0850 **Fax:** 202-828-0860
**Web:** www.danaher.com

Danaher Corporation has more than 200 manufacturing and distribution facilities in Asia, Australia, Europe, Latin America, and North America.

### 2006 Sales

| | $ mil. | % of total |
|---|---|---|
| US | 5,222.5 | 54 |
| Germany | 1,460.2 | 15 |
| UK | 369.0 | 4 |
| Other countries | 2,544.7 | 27 |
| **Total** | **9,596.4** | **100** |

## PRODUCTS/OPERATIONS

### 2006 Sales

| | $ mil. | % of total |
|---|---|---|
| Industrial Technologies | 3,119.2 | 33 |
| Professional Instrumentation | 2,906.4 | 30 |
| Medical Technologies | 2,220.0 | 23 |
| Tools & Components | 1,350.8 | 14 |
| **Total** | **9,596.4** | **100** |

### Selected Operations

Process/Environmental Controls
- Acme-Cleveland Corp.
- Dr. Bruno Lange GmbH (analytical instrumentation and reagents, Germany)
- Fisher Pierce (outdoor lighting controls)
- Fluke Corporation (electronic test tools)
- GEMS Sensors, Inc. (level, flow, and pressure sensors)
- Gendex Corporation (dental imaging)
- Hengstler GmbH (force-guided relays, Germany)
- Joslyn Manufacturing Company (pole line hardware)
- Kaltenbach & Voight GmBH (KaVo, Germany)
- Radiometer America Inc. (blood gas analyzers)
- Sybron Dental Specialties, Inc. (orthodontics)
- Videojet Technologies, Inc. (coding and labeling)
- Vision Systems, Ltd. (medical pathology)

Tools and Components
- The Allen Manufacturing Company (wrenches, hexagonal keys)
- Armstrong Tools, Inc. (industrial hand tools)
- Delta Consolidated Industries, Inc. (truck boxes and industrial gang boxes)
- Hennessy Industries Inc. (wheel-service equipment)
- Holo-Krome Company (fasteners)
- Jacobs Chuck Manufacturing Company (drill chucks and tool-holding devices)
- Jacobs Vehicle Systems Inc. (braking systems for commercial vehicles)
- Matco Tools Corporation (tools for the automotive aftermarket)

## COMPETITORS

3M Precision Optics
ABB
Baldor Electric
Black & Decker
Bosch Rexroth Corp.
Cooper Industries
Datamax
Dresser Wayne
Eaton
Emerson Electric
GE
Goodrich
Greenlee Textron
Hilti Schaan
Hitachi
Johnson Controls
Labfacility
Makita
Mettler-Toledo
Parker Hannifin
Rockwell Automation
Schneider Electric
Snap-on
SPX
Stanley Works
Tektronix
Thermo Fisher Scientific
Werner

## HISTORICAL FINANCIALS

Company Type: Public

### Income Statement

FYE: December 31

| | REVENUE ($ mil.) | NET INCOME ($ mil.) | NET PROFIT MARGIN | EMPLOYEES |
|---|---|---|---|---|
| **12/06** | 9,596 | 1,122 | 11.7% | 45,000 |
| **12/05** | 7,985 | 898 | 11.2% | 40,000 |
| **12/04** | 6,889 | 746 | 10.8% | 35,000 |
| **12/03** | 5,294 | 537 | 10.1% | 30,000 |
| **12/02** | 4,577 | 290 | 6.3% | 29,000 |
| **Annual Growth** | 20.3% | 40.2% | — | 11.6% |

### 2006 Year-End Financials

Debt ratio: 36.5%
Return on equity: 19.1%
Cash ($ mil.): 318
Current ratio: 1.38
Long-term debt ($ mil.): 2,423
No. of shares (mil.): 308
Dividends
Yield: 0.1%
Payout: 2.3%
Market value ($ mil.): 22,329

### Stock History

NYSE: DHR

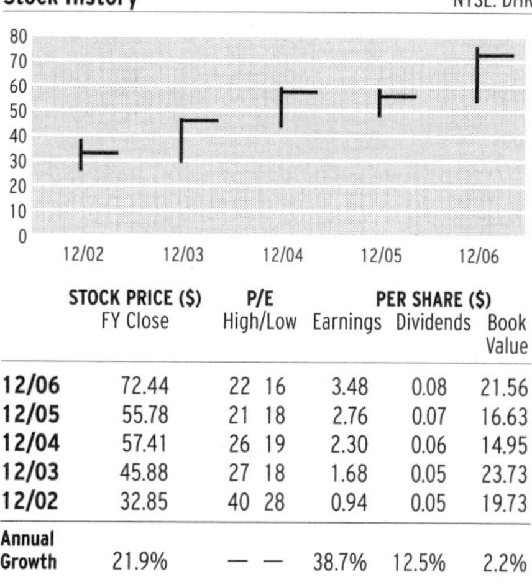


| | STOCK PRICE ($) FY Close | P/E High | P/E Low | PER SHARE ($) Earnings | Dividends | Book Value |
|---|---|---|---|---|---|---|
| **12/06** | 72.44 | 22 | 16 | 3.48 | 0.08 | 21.56 |
| **12/05** | 55.78 | 21 | 18 | 2.76 | 0.07 | 16.63 |
| **12/04** | 57.41 | 26 | 19 | 2.30 | 0.06 | 14.95 |
| **12/03** | 45.88 | 27 | 18 | 1.68 | 0.05 | 23.73 |
| **12/02** | 32.85 | 40 | 28 | 0.94 | 0.05 | 19.73 |
| **Annual Growth** | 21.9% | — | — | 38.7% | 12.5% | 2.2% |

# Darden Restaurants

This company has cornered not one but two dining markets: seafood and "Hospitaliano." Darden Restaurants is the #1 casual-dining operator (in terms of revenue) with more than 1,320 restaurants in the US and Canada. Its flagship chains include seafood segment leader Red Lobster and top Italian-themed concept Olive Garden. Both chains cater to families with mid-priced menu items, themed interiors, and primarily suburban locations. Darden also operates a small chain of tropical-themed Bahama Breeze restaurants that offer Caribbean-inspired food, along with a casual grill and wine bar concept called Seasons 52.

Both Red Lobster and Olive Garden command significant market share in the casual dining industry and continue to see increasing sales thanks in part to heavy marketing efforts centered around new or selected menu items. The chains have gained popularity for their hefty portions and occasional all-you-can-eat promotions. Darden has been focusing its expansion efforts mostly on its Olive Garden chain, opening more than 30 new locations during 2006-07 with plans to add about 40 units during 2007 and 2008.

The company shuttered its troubled Smokey Bones Barbeque & Grill concept in 2007. The chain managed to grow to almost 130 locations but struggled to find its place in the casual dining sector.

Later that year Darden agreed to acquire steakhouse operator RARE Hospitality for $1.4 billion, including debt. Darden hopes to inject some new life in RARE's 285-unit LongHorn Steakhouse in part through its ability to mount large-scale marketing campaigns. The company will also acquire the smaller, upscale Capital Grille, which will join the Bahama Breeze and Seasons 52 chains as part of a new division dubbed the Specialty Restaurant Group.

## HISTORY

Nineteen-year-old Bill Darden entered the restaurant business in the late 1930s with a 25-seat luncheonette called the Green Frog in Waycross, Georgia. The restaurant, which featured the slogan "Service with a Hop," was a hit, and his career was born. During the 1950s he owned a variety of restaurants, including several Howard Johnson's, Bonanza, and Kentucky Fried Chicken outlets.

Darden teamed with a group of investors in 1963 to buy an Orlando, Florida, restaurant, Gary's Duck Inn. The restaurant became the prototype for Darden's idea for a moderately priced, sit-down seafood chain. He decided to name the new chain Red Lobster, a takeoff on the old Green Frog.

The first Red Lobster opened in Lakeland, Florida, in 1968 with Joe Lee, who had worked in one of Darden's other restaurants, as its manager. It was such a success that within a month the restaurant had to be expanded. In 1970, when there were three Red Lobsters in operation and two under construction in Central Florida, Betty Crocker's boss, General Mills, bought the chain — keeping Darden on to run it.

Red Lobster was not General Mills' first foray into the restaurant business. The company opened Betty Crocker Tree House Restaurant in 1968 and acquired a fish-and-chips chain and a barbeque chain. But Red Lobster would be its first success. Rather than franchise the Red Lobster name, General Mills chose to develop the chain on its own. Lee was named president of Red Lobster in 1975, and Darden became chairman of General Mills Restaurants.

While General Mills continued to expand Red Lobster, it also sought another restaurant idea to complement the seafood chain. Among concepts tried and discarded were a steak house and Mexican and health-food restaurants. In 1980 the company decided on Italian. After two years of marketing questionnaires and recipe tests, General Mills opened a prototype Olive Garden in Orlando featuring moderately priced Italian food. General Mills began to add outlets in the mid-1980s, and Olive Garden became another success story of the casual-dining industry.

After testing a new Chinese restaurant concept, General Mills opened its first China Coast in Orlando in 1990. The chain grew rapidly, with more than 45 units opening in a single year. The Olive Garden drive began to cool off in 1993: Same-store sales slid as competitors added Italian items to their menus. The next year Olive Garden increased its advertising budget, introduced new menu items, and began testing new formats, including smaller cafes for malls.

General Mills decided to spin off the restaurant business as a public company in 1995 and focus on consumer foods. The restaurants were renamed Darden Restaurants in honor of Bill Darden (who had died in 1994, the same year that Joe Lee was appointed CEO). That year the company abandoned its China Coast chain.

Darden Restaurants tried again in 1997 with Bahama Breeze, opening a test restaurant in Orlando. Red Lobster's sales flagged in 1997, but the company initiated a turnaround in 1998, in part by revamping Red Lobster's menu. An ill-conceived all-you-can-eat offer at Red Lobster cost Darden in profits (and led to the ousting of chain president Edna Morris after just 18 months). The company dipped into the barbecue sauce in 1999 and opened its inaugural Smokey Bones in Orlando.

The following year Darden Restaurants began expanding its Smokey Bones concept nationally. In late 2001 Japanese noodle-shop operator Reins International agreed to buy Darden's 34 Red Lobster franchises in Japan for about $4.8 million. Dick Rivera, who had been president of the Red Lobster chain since 1997, was named company president and COO in 2002. (He resigned from the company in early 2004.)

With financial results lagging at its Bahama Breeze chain, Darden slowed growth of the concept and expanded its operating hours to include lunch business. The company also promoted former development VP Laurie Burns to lead Bahama Breeze after the unexpected resignation of Gary Heckel in 2002.

In 2004 Clarence Otis Jr. was appointed CEO, succeeding Joe Lee; the following year Otis added chairman to his title. After struggling to develop its Smokey Bones Barbeque & Grill concept, Darden shuttered the unprofitable chain in 2007.

## EXECUTIVES

**Chairman and CEO:** Clarence Otis Jr., age 51, $1,898,313 pay
**President, COO, and Director:** Andrew H. (Drew) Madsen, age 51, $1,584,856 pay
**EVP, Marketing Olive Garden:** John Caron
**EVP, Operations Olive Garden:** Valerie Insignares
**EVP, Marketing Red Lobster:** Salli Setta
**EVP, Operations Red Lobster:** Kelly Baltes
**SVP and CFO:** C. Bradford (Brad) Richmond, age 48
**SVP and CIO:** Valerie K. (Val) Collins
**SVP and Treasurer:** Bill White
**SVP, General Counsel, and Secretary:** Paula J. Shives, age 56
**SVP, Government and Community Affairs:** Robert (Bob) McAdam, age 49
**SVP, Group Human Resources:** Ronald Bojalad
**SVP, Human Resources:** Daniel M. Lyons, age 54
**SVP, Supply Chain and Development:** Barry B. Moullet, age 49
**SVP and President, Bahama Breeze:** Laurie B. Burns, age 45
**SVP and President, Olive Garden:** David T. Pickens, age 52, $830,256 pay
**SVP and President, Red Lobster:** Kim A. Lopdrup, age 49, $826,756 pay
**SVP; President, Smokey Bones:** James (J. J.) Buettgen, age 47
**VP, Investor Relations:** Matthew Stroud
**VP, Media and Communications:** Jim DeSimone
**Auditors:** KPMG LLP

## LOCATIONS

**HQ:** Darden Restaurants, Inc.
5900 Lake Ellenor Dr., Orlando, FL 32809
**Phone:** 407-245-4000 **Fax:** 407-245-5389
**Web:** www.dardenrestaurants.com

**2007 Locations**

| | No. |
|---|---|
| US | |
| Florida | 128 |
| Texas | 115 |
| California | 99 |
| Ohio | 74 |
| Pennsylvania | 63 |
| Georgia | 52 |
| Illinois | 51 |
| Michigan | 51 |
| New York | 49 |
| Virginia | 44 |
| Indiana | 38 |
| Arizona | 31 |
| New Jersey | 31 |
| North Carolina | 31 |
| Tennessee | 30 |
| Missouri | 28 |
| Colorado | 27 |
| Washington | 25 |
| Maryland | 24 |
| Minnesota | 24 |
| South Carolina | 24 |
| Alabama | 23 |
| Wisconsin | 18 |
| Oklahoma | 16 |
| Iowa | 15 |
| Kentucky | 15 |
| Utah | 14 |
| Nevada | 12 |
| Oregon | 12 |
| Arkansas | 11 |
| Kansas | 11 |
| Louisiana | 11 |
| New Mexico | 11 |
| Other states | 81 |
| Canada | 35 |
| **Total** | **1,324** |

## PRODUCTS/OPERATIONS

**2007 Locations**

| | No. |
|---|---|
| Red Lobster | 680 |
| Olive Garden | 614 |
| Bahama Breeze | 23 |
| Seasons 52 | 7 |
| **Total** | **1,324** |

## COMPETITORS

Applebee's
Bob Evans
Brinker
Carlson Restaurants
CBRL Group
Cheesecake Factory
Denny's
Hooters
Landry's
Metromedia Restaurant Group
OSI Restaurant Partners
Ruby Tuesday

## HISTORICAL FINANCIALS

Company Type: Public

**Income Statement** FYE: Last Sunday in May

| | REVENUE ($ mil.) | NET INCOME ($ mil.) | NET PROFIT MARGIN | EMPLOYEES |
|---|---|---|---|---|
| **5/07** | 5,567 | 201 | 3.6% | 157,000 |
| **5/06** | 5,721 | 338 | 5.9% | 157,300 |
| **5/05** | 5,278 | 291 | 5.5% | 150,100 |
| **5/04** | 5,003 | 227 | 4.5% | 141,300 |
| **5/03** | 4,655 | 232 | 5.0% | 140,700 |
| **Annual Growth** | 4.6% | (3.5%) | — | 2.8% |

**2007 Year-End Financials**

Debt ratio: 44.9%
Return on equity: 17.3%
Cash ($ mil.): 30
Current ratio: 0.51
Long-term debt ($ mil.): 492
No. of shares (mil.): 141
Dividends
Yield: 1.0%
Payout: 34.1%
Market value ($ mil.): 6,408

**Stock History** NYSE: DRI

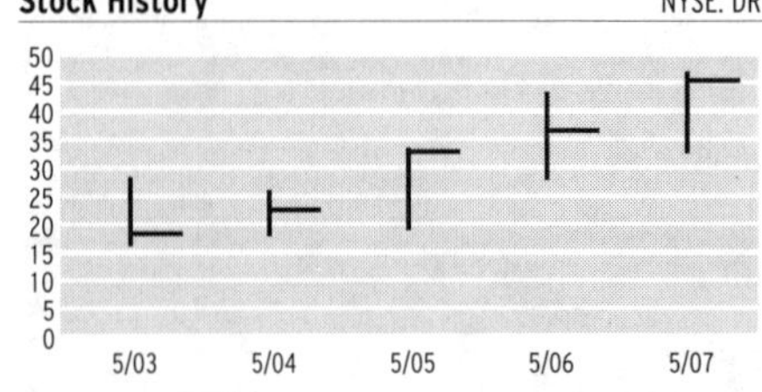


| | STOCK PRICE ($) FY Close | P/E High | P/E Low | PER SHARE ($) Earnings | Dividends | Book Value |
|---|---|---|---|---|---|---|
| **5/07** | 45.32 | 35 | 24 | 1.35 | 0.46 | 7.74 |
| **5/06** | 36.51 | 20 | 13 | 2.16 | 0.40 | 8.37 |
| **5/05** | 32.80 | 19 | 11 | 1.78 | 0.08 | 8.25 |
| **5/04** | 22.50 | 19 | 14 | 1.34 | 0.08 | 7.42 |
| **5/03** | 18.35 | 21 | 13 | 1.31 | 0.08 | 7.25 |
| **Annual Growth** | 25.4% | — | — | 0.8% | 54.9% | 1.6% |

# DaVita Inc.

DaVita — an Italian phrase which means "gives life" — provides life-sustaining dialysis treatments to patients suffering from end-stage renal disease (also known as chronic kidney failure). The company operates one of the largest chains of dialysis centers in the US. DaVita has nearly 1,300 centers in more than 40 states and Washington, DC, and provides dialysis and related services to more than 100,000 patients. The firm also offers home-based dialysis services, as well as inpatient dialysis in more than 750 hospitals, and it operates two clinical laboratories that specialize in routine testing of dialysis patients.

Along with its dialysis-based revenue (which accounts for 98% of sales), DaVita offers other services related to kidney disease, including pharmacy services and the operation of chronic kidney disease management programs for employers and health plans. Additionally, subsidiary DaVita Clinical Research conducts research trials with dialysis patients.

Nearly all of DaVita's outpatient centers are either wholly owned or majority-owned by the company. About 40 centers are owned by third parties, who pay DaVita for administrative services.

In 2005 the company acquired Gambro's Gambro Healthcare unit for about $3 billion, adding some 565 dialysis clinics to its operations. To meet FTC requirements for the deal, DaVita sold about 70 clinics to RenalAmerica, a company founded by former Gambro Healthcare executive Michael Klein. The company continues to look for acquisition opportunities to facilitate its growth.

Most of DaVita's patients receive care under Medicare and other government-sponsored programs, and a majority of the company's revenue comes from Medicare. The federal government has been looking into the way the company prescribes and files Medicare claims for certain dialysis-related drugs, including Epogen, an anti-anemia therapy made by Amgen. Proper Epogen dosing has been a subject of discussion among researchers and federal officials after a study found that too-high doses of the drug could lead to serious health problems. The FDA recommends a lower dosing regimen than DaVita (and other for-profit dialysis operators) follows, and Congress is considering changing Medicare rules to eliminate any financial incentives for providing the higher doses.

## HISTORY

Hospital chain National Medical Enterprises (NME, now Tenet) formed Medical Ambulatory Care in 1979 to run its in-hospital dialysis centers. The unit bought other centers in NME's markets. In 1994 the subsidiary's management, backed by a Donaldson, Lufkin & Jenrette (now Credit Suisse First Boston (USA)) investment fund, bought the dialysis business and renamed it Total Renal Care (TRC).

To become a leader in its consolidating field, TRC began buying other centers and soon added clinical laboratory and dialysis-related pharmacy services and home dialysis programs. It went public in 1995.

The next year the firm added 66 facilities, 32 from its acquisition of Caremark International's dialysis business. In 1997 TRC expanded abroad, buying UK-based Open Access Sonography (vein care) and partnering with UK-based Priory Hospitals Group.

In 1998 TRC bought Renal Treatment Centers, nearly doubling its size. But the acquisition costs caused a loss that year and sparked shareholder lawsuits (settled in 2000) over alleged misleading statements. The firm also became embroiled in a reimbursement dispute with Florida's Medicare program. Problems continued into 1999 as the company struggled to meld operations. The company took a charge to cover a billing shortfall, and chairman and CEO Victor Chaltiel and COO/CFO John King resigned. New management began improving billing procedures and took other cost-cutting measures.

In 2000 the company changed its name to DaVita, an Italian phrase loosely translated as "he/she gives life." It also sold its international operations to competitor Fresenius.

## EXECUTIVES

**Chairman and CEO:** Kent J. Thiry, age 51, $885,079 pay
**COO:** Joseph C. (Joe) Mello, age 48, $630,768 pay
**CFO:** Mark G. Harrison, age 50, $146,154 pay
**VP General Counsel and Corporate Secretary:** Joseph (Joe) Schohl, age 38, $682,420 pay
**VP and Controller:** James K. (Jim) Hilger, age 45
**VP Investor Relations:** LeAnne M. Zumwalt, age 49
**Chief Compliance Officer:** Christopher J. (Chris) Riopelle, age 37
**Chief Medical Officer:** Charles J. (Charlie) McAllister, age 59
**Media Relations:** Stephanie Prial
**VP Strategy:** Mary R. Kowenhoven, age 37
**Auditors:** KPMG LLP

## LOCATIONS

**HQ:** DaVita Inc.
601 Hawaii St., El Segundo, CA 90245
**Phone:** 310-536-2400 **Fax:** 310-536-2675
**Web:** www.davita.com

### 2006 Centers

| | No. |
|---|---|
| California | 153 |
| Texas | 111 |
| Florida | 107 |
| Georgia | 85 |
| Pennsylvania | 56 |
| North Carolina | 52 |
| Virginia | 50 |
| Maryland | 47 |
| Michigan | 45 |
| Illinois | 42 |
| Ohio | 35 |
| Minnesota | 32 |
| New York | 31 |
| Alabama | 30 |
| Oklahoma | 30 |
| Louisiana | 29 |
| Missouri | 29 |
| Tennessee | 28 |
| Colorado | 25 |
| South Carolina | 25 |
| New Jersey | 21 |
| Arizona | 20 |
| Indiana | 20 |
| Connecticut | 17 |
| Kansas | 16 |
| Kentucky | 16 |
| Nebraska | 13 |
| Massachusetts | 12 |
| Nevada | 12 |
| Iowa | 11 |
| Washington | 11 |
| Wisconsin | 11 |
| Other states | 40 |
| **Total** | **1,262** |

## PRODUCTS/OPERATIONS

### 2006 Sales by Payor

| | % of total |
|---|---|
| Government-based programs | |
| Medicare & Medicare-assigned HMO plans | 58 |
| Medicaid | 4 |
| Other government-based programs | 3 |
| Commercial | 35 |
| **Total** | **100** |

## COMPETITORS

Dialysis Corp.
Fresenius Medical Care
NxStage
Renal Advantage

## HISTORICAL FINANCIALS

Company Type: Public

### Income Statement

FYE: December 31

| | REVENUE ($ mil.) | NET INCOME ($ mil.) | NET PROFIT MARGIN | EMPLOYEES |
|---|---|---|---|---|
| **12/06** | 4,881 | 290 | 5.9% | 28,900 |
| **12/05** | 2,974 | 229 | 7.7% | 28,000 |
| **12/04** | 2,299 | 222 | 9.7% | 15,300 |
| **12/03** | 2,016 | 176 | 8.7% | 13,800 |
| **12/02** | 1,855 | 157 | 8.5% | 13,000 |
| **Annual Growth** | 27.4% | 16.5% | — | 22.1% |

### 2006 Year-End Financials

Debt ratio: 299.4%
Return on equity: 27.6%
Cash ($ mil.): 310
Current ratio: 1.54
Long-term debt ($ mil.): 3,730
No. of shares (mil.): 105
Dividends
Yield: —
Payout: —
Market value ($ mil.): 5,952

### Stock History

NYSE: DVA

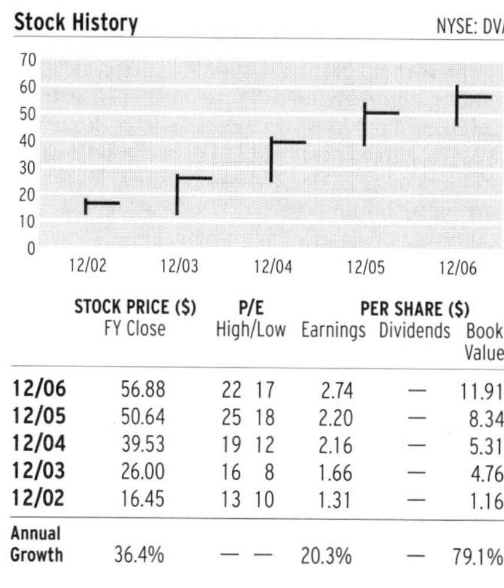


| | STOCK PRICE ($) FY Close | P/E High | P/E Low | PER SHARE ($) Earnings | Dividends | Book Value |
|---|---|---|---|---|---|---|
| **12/06** | 56.88 | 22 | 17 | 2.74 | — | 11.91 |
| **12/05** | 50.64 | 25 | 18 | 2.20 | — | 8.34 |
| **12/04** | 39.53 | 19 | 12 | 2.16 | — | 5.31 |
| **12/03** | 26.00 | 16 | 8 | 1.66 | — | 4.76 |
| **12/02** | 16.45 | 13 | 10 | 1.31 | — | 1.16 |
| **Annual Growth** | 36.4% | — | — | 20.3% | — | 79.1% |

# Dean Foods

Dean Foods has become the king of milk by taking over other dairies' thrones. The leading US producer of fluid milk and dairy products, Dean has grown and continues to grow through acquisitions. Its retail and foodservice dairy products are sold under more than 50 regional, private-label, and national brand names, including Borden, Pet, Country Fresh, and Meadow Gold. In addition, the company manufactures creamers, dips and salad dressings, and specialty dairy products (lactose-free milk, soy milk, flavored milks). Dean Foods also operates Horizon Organic and WhiteWave Foods.

To better tap the growing interest in organic dairy and dairy alternatives, Dean lapped up Horizon Organic and soy-milk maker WhiteWave and consolidated those businesses with its other nationally branded products. They were reorganized under Dean's Branded Products Group.

In 2007 WhiteWave sold the TofuTown and WhiteWave brands to Hain Celestial. Products included in the sale were baked and grilled tofu, seitan, and tempeh products. The financial terms of the purchase were not disclosed.

That year, Dean announced that it would not use milk from cloned cows in its products. Continuing its *modus operandi* of growth by purchasing regional dairies, that year Dean also agreed to acquire Friendship Dairies for about $130 million.

The company has an alliance with Land O'Lakes to market value-added dairy products under their brand, and, through licensing agreements, produces Hershey's flavored milks. In addition, Dean owns approximately 25% of Consolidated Containers (plastic beverage packaging), which supplies Dean with plastic bottles and bottle components.

The company's Dairy Group operates some 100 manufacturing sites throughout the US.

## HISTORY

Investment banker Gregg Engles formed a holding company in 1988 with other investors, including dairy industry veteran Cletes Beshears, to buy the Reddy Ice unit of Dallas-based Southland (operator of the 7-Eleven chain). The company also bought Circle K's Sparkle Ice and combined it with Reddy Ice. By 1990 it had acquired about 15 ice plants.

The company changed its name to Suiza Foods when it bought Suiza Dairy in 1993 for $99 million. The Puerto Rican dairy was formed in 1942 by Hector Nevares Sr. and named for the Spanish word for "Swiss." By 1993 it was Puerto Rico's largest dairy, controlling about 60% of the island's milk market.

Suiza Foods bought Florida's Velda Farms, manufacturer and distributor of milk and dairy products, in 1994. The company went public in 1996, the same year it bought Swiss Dairy (dairy products, California and Nevada) and Garrido y Compañía (coffee products, Puerto Rico).

The company became one of the largest players in the North American dairy industry through its acquisitions in 1997. It paid $960 million for Morningstar (Lactaid lactose-free milk, Second Nature egg substitute), which — like Suiza Foods itself — was a Dallas-based company formed in 1988 through a Southland divestiture. The company entered the Midwest with its $98 million purchase of Country Fresh and the Northeast with the Bernon family's Massachusetts-based group of dairy and packaging companies, including Garelick Farms and Franklin Plastics (packaging).

Suiza Foods strengthened its presence in the southeastern US in 1998 with its $287 million acquisition of Land-O-Sun Dairies, operator of 13 fluid-dairy and ice-cream processing facilities. Also that year Suiza Foods purchased Continental Can (plastic packaging) for about $345 million and sold Reddy Ice to Packaged Ice for $172 million.

After settling an antitrust lawsuit brought by the US Department of Justice, in 1999 Suiza Foods bought dairy processors in Colorado, Ohio, and Virginia. That year Suiza Foods combined its US packaging operations with Reid Plastics to form Consolidated Containers, retaining about 40% of the new company.

In 2001 Suiza Foods announced it had agreed to purchase rival Dean Foods for $1.5 billion and the assumption of $1 billion worth of debt. Dean Foods had begun as Dean Evaporated Milk, founded in 1925 by Sam Dean, a Chicago evaporated-milk broker. By the mid-1930s it had moved into the fresh milk industry. The company went public in 1961 and was renamed Dean Foods in 1963.

Suiza Foods completed the acquisition and took on the Dean Foods name later in 2001. The new Dean Foods bought out Dairy Farmers of America's interest in Suiza Dairy and merged it with the "old" Dean's fluid-dairy operations to create its internal division, Dean Dairy Group.

Along with the purchase of "old" Dean came a 36% ownership of soy milk maker WhiteWave, and in 2002 Dean Foods purchased the remaining 64% for approximately $189 million.

With an eye on adding organic milk, Dean purchased 13% of Horizon Organic in 2003 and acquired the remainder of the company in 2004. Dean then purchased Michael Foods' dairy products unit Kohler Mix Specialties, including three plants that produce mixes for ice cream and frozen yogurt, soy milk, and coffee creamers; it also acquired Cremora brand non-dairy creamer from Eagle Family Foods.

By 2004 sales of canned and aseptic sports drinks, meal supplement drinks, and weight-loss beverages had weakened to the point where the company predicted a loss up to $4.6 million from its largest customers and Dean decided to drop that part of its business. Expanding in the southeast, Dean purchased Milk Products of Alabama. In California the company bought Ross Swiss Dairies. Overseas, Dean acquired Tiger Foods, a dairy processing firm located in Spain.

The next year the company sold Dean's Dips and Marie's Dressings to Ventura Foods. The company spun also off its specialty foods group to its shareholders as TreeHouse Foods in 2005. TreeHouse makes private-label products such as pickles and non-dairy powdered coffee creamers and various regional brands; it also gained several former Dean Foods brands, including Mocha Mix non-dairy creamers and Second Nature egg substitute. The next year it announced the sale of its Iberian operations to Portuguese dairy Lactogal Productos Alimentares.

Dean began a concerted marketing campaign in 2006, touting its hormone-free milk sold under the Schepps brand as an alternative to organic milk, which is more expensive. It completed the sale of its operations in Iberia in early 2007.

## EXECUTIVES

**Chairman and CEO:** Gregg L. Engles, age 49, $1,200,000 pay
**Vice Chairman:** Pete Schenkel, age 71, $500,000 pay
**EVP and CFO:** Jack F. Callahan Jr., age 48, $297,620 pay
**EVP, Chief Administrative Officer, General Counsel, and Corporate Secretary:** Michelle P. Goolsby, age 49, $515,000 pay
**EVP and President, International:** Miguel M. Calado, age 51
**EVP Human Resources:** Paul Moskowitz
**SVP and COO, Dairy Group:** Harrald Kroeker, age 49
**SVP and COO, Ice Cream:** Rachel Cullen
**SVP, Corporate Development:** Ronald H. Klein, age 41
**SVP, Government and Industry Relations:** Bill Tinklepaugh
**SVP, Human Resources:** Robert Dunn
**SVP, Finance, Specialty Foods Group:** Greg Lewandowski
**SVP, Sales and Marketing, Dean Foods Group:** Curt Aust
**SVP and Chief Accounting Officer:** Ronald L. McCrummen
**President, WhiteWave Foods:** Joseph E. (Joe) Scalzo, age 48
**President, Dairy Group, and Director:** Alan J. Bernon, age 52, $620,000 pay
**Senior Director, Investor Relations:** Barry Sievert
**VP, Corporate Communications:** Marguerite Copel
**Auditors:** Deloitte & Touche LLP

## LOCATIONS

**HQ:** Dean Foods Company
2515 McKinney Ave., Ste. 1200, Dallas, TX 75201
**Phone:** 214-303-3400 **Fax:** 214-303-3499
**Web:** www.deanfoods.com

### 2006 Sales

| | % of total |
|---|---|
| US | 99 |
| Europe | 1 |
| **Total** | **100** |

## PRODUCTS/OPERATIONS

### 2006 Sales

| | $ mil. | % of total |
|---|---|---|
| Dairy group | 8,820.9 | 87 |
| WhiteWave Foods | 1,277.6 | 13 |
| **Total** | **10,098.5** | **100** |

### Selected Dairy Group Products

Cottage cheese
Half-and-half
Ice cream
Milk
Sour cream
Soymilk
Whipping cream
Yogurt

### Selected Dairy Brands

Alta Dena
Arctic Splash
Barber's
Barbe's
Berkeley Farms
Borden (licensed)
Broughton
Brown Cow
Brown's
Chug
Creamland
Country Charm
Country Delite
Country Fresh
Country Love
Dairy Fresh
Dean's
Dipzz
Fieldcrest
Foremost (licensed)
Gandy's
Garelick Farms
Hershey's (licensed)
Hygeia
Kohler
LAND O'LAKES (licensed)
LehighValley
Liberty
Louis Trauth
Mayfield
McArthur
Meadow Gold
Meadow Brook
Melody Farms
Mile High Ice Cream
Model Dairy
Mountain High
Nature's Pride
Oak Farms
Over the Moon
Pet (licensed)
Poudre Valley
Price's
Purity
Reiter
Robinson
Saudners
Schenkel's All*Star
Schepps
Sealtest (licensed)
Shenandoah's Pride
Skinny Cow
STK
Stroh's
Swiss Dairy
TG Lee
Tuscan
Verifine
Viva

## COMPETITORS

8th Continent
AMPI
Aurora Organic Dairy
B&G Foods
Blistex
California Dairies Inc.
ConAgra
Dairy Farmers of America
Dannon
Danone
Darigold, Inc.
Foremost Farms
Foster Dairy Farms
Great Lakes Cheese
Guida's
Hain Celestial
Hiland Dairy
HP Hood
Kemps
Kraft Foods
Kraft North America Commercial
Land O'Lakes
Leche Pascual
Mayfield Dairy Farms
National Dairy Holdings
Nestlé USA
Northwest Dairy
Parmalat Canada
Prairie Farms Dairy
Quality Chekd
Saputo Cheese USA Inc.
Sargento
Stonyfield Farm
Tillamook County Creamery Association

## HISTORICAL FINANCIALS

Company Type: Public

**Income Statement** FYE: December 31

| | REVENUE ($ mil.) | NET INCOME ($ mil.) | NET PROFIT MARGIN | EMPLOYEES |
|---|---|---|---|---|
| **12/06** | 10,099 | 225 | 2.2% | 26,348 |
| **12/05** | 10,506 | 328 | 3.1% | 27,030 |
| **12/04** | 10,822 | 285 | 2.6% | 28,610 |
| **12/03** | 9,185 | 356 | 3.9% | 27,466 |
| **12/02** | 8,992 | 175 | 2.0% | 27,600 |
| **Annual Growth** | 2.9% | 6.5% | — | (1.2%) |

**2006 Year-End Financials**

Debt ratio: 158.7%
Return on equity: 12.2%
Cash ($ mil.): 31
Current ratio: 1.03
Long-term debt ($ mil.): 2,872
No. of shares (mil.): 128
Dividends
Yield: —
Payout: —
Market value ($ mil.): 5,428

**Stock History** NYSE: DF

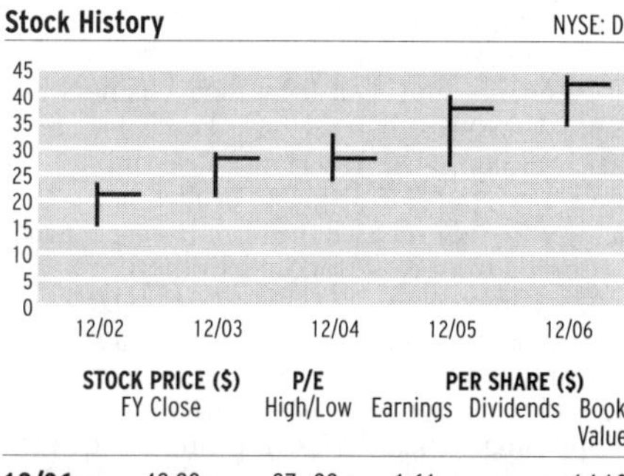


| | STOCK PRICE ($) FY Close | P/E High | P/E Low | PER SHARE ($) Earnings | Dividends | Book Value |
|---|---|---|---|---|---|---|
| **12/06** | 42.28 | 27 | 22 | 1.61 | — | 14.10 |
| **12/05** | 37.66 | 19 | 13 | 2.13 | — | 13.95 |
| **12/04** | 28.13 | 18 | 14 | 1.78 | — | 19.77 |
| **12/03** | 28.06 | 13 | 9 | 2.27 | — | 16.41 |
| **12/02** | 21.11 | 19 | 13 | 1.21 | — | 12.36 |
| **Annual Growth** | 19.0% | — | — | 7.4% | — | 3.3% |

# Deere & Company

You might say that Deere & Company enjoys its customers going to seed. The company, one of the world's two largest makers of farm equipment (CNH Global is the other), is also a leading producer of industrial, forestry, and lawn-care equipment. Its farm equipment includes tractors, tillers, harvesting machinery, and soil-preparation machinery. The construction equipment includes backhoes and excavators. Deere also makes drivetrain components, diesel engines, chain saws, and leaf- and snowblowers. To further consolidate its business operations and increase sales, Deere bought all of the outstanding shares of Nortrax (a John Deere dealer for construction, forestry, earthmoving, and material handling equipment).

Although Deere has become less dependent on the farming industry through its acquisition of forestry equipment maker Timberjack, farming is still its largest business (46% of sales). Deere has expanded its scope by acquiring Richton International Corporation, gaining its landscape irrigation equipment distributor, Century Supply (#1 in the US). However the company is weeding out non-core assets — it has sold its money-hemorrhaging Homelite consumer products division and has dissolved its farm equipment joint venture with Woods Equipment Company. Another divestiture of a non-core asset came with the early 2006 sale of John Deere Health Care to UnitedHealth Group for half a billion dollars.

Looking to address demand for small tractors in a key global market, Deere has agreed to acquire Ningbo Benye Tractor & Automobile Manufacture, which is based in southern China. Deere has been involved in the Chinese market for decades, but this deal will put the company in manufacturing low-horsepower tractors for the Chinese market. While Ningbo Benye Tractor gets most of its sales from China, it does export its 20-50 hp tractors to other countries.

Deere needs approval from Chinese authorities to conclude the transaction, which it hopes to do by the end of 2007, creating a wholly owned subsidiary called John Deere Ningbo Agricultural Machinery. Chinese regulators — loath to sell off companies that may be strategic to national interests — are not rubber-stamping acquisitions of Chinese ventures these days, however.

Deere is working with Hydrogenics Corporation (a Canadian fuel cell manufacturer) to develop its own fuel cell-powered Commercial Work Vehicles (CWVs), which could add efficiency to its current products.

The company started a wholesale landscaping division in 2001 and added to that business with the 2005 acquisition of United Green Mark. The division operates more than 250 stores throughout the US and Canada and adds United Green Mark's 41, located in the western US. The division distributes wholesale irrigation, nursery, and landscaping supplies.

## HISTORY

Vermont-born John Deere moved to Grand Detour, Illinois, in 1836 and set up a blacksmith shop. Deere and other pioneers had trouble with the rich, black soil of the Midwest sticking to iron plows designed for sandy eastern soils, so in 1837 Deere used a circular steel saw blade to create a self-scouring plow that moved so quickly, it was nicknamed the "whistling plow." He sold only three in 1838, but by 1842 he was making 25 a week.

Deere moved his enterprise to Moline in 1847. His son Charles joined the company in 1853, beginning a tradition of family management. (All five Deere presidents before 1982 were related by blood or marriage.) Charles set up an independent-dealership distribution system and added wagons, buggies, and corn planters to the product line.

Under Charles' son-in-law, William Butterworth (president, 1907-28), Deere bought agricultural equipment companies and developed harvesters and tractors with internal combustion engines. Butterworth's nephew, Charles Wiman, became president in 1928. He extended credit to farmers during the Depression and won customer loyalty. In 1931 Deere opened its first non-US plant in Canada.

William Hewitt, Wiman's son-in-law, became CEO in 1955. Deere passed International Harvester in 1958 to become the #1 US maker of farm equipment; by 1963 it led the world. Deere expanded into Argentina, France, Mexico, and Spain, and it used research and joint ventures abroad (Yanmar, small tractors, 1977; Hitachi, excavators, 1983) to diversify.

Robert Hanson became the first nonfamily CEO in 1982. He poured $2 billion into research and development during the 1980s. Despite an industry-wide sales slump resulting in losses totaling $328 million in 1986-87, Deere was the only major agricultural equipment maker to neither change ownership nor close factories during the 1980s. Instead, Deere cut its workforce 44% and improved efficiency.

During the 1990s Deere expanded its lawn-care equipment business, mainly in Europe. In 1991 it bought a majority stake in Sabo-Maschinenfabrik (commercial lawn mowers, Germany).

After spending most of the early 1990s in the doldrums because of recession and weak farm prices, Deere rebounded. Deere signed a deal to sell combines in Ukraine (1996), and it formed a joint venture in 1997 to make combines in China. Fading demand for agricultural equipment at home and jeopardized sales contracts from failing economies in Asia, Brazil, and former Soviet states caused layoffs of about 2,400 workers in 1998 and production cutbacks in 1998-99.

President and COO Robert Lane succeeded Becherer as chairman and CEO. Deere bought McGinnis Farms — the US's largest horticultural products distributor — in 2001.

That year it cut production due to soft demand. Late in 2001 Deere said it would add to its previously announced job cuts, bringing the total to about 3,000 jobs. Deere also acquired Richton International Corporation; that deal included Richton's landscape irrigation-equipment distributor Century Supply (#1 in the US) and Richton Technology Group (hardware, software, and systems support services).

Deere announced in 2004 that it, along with iRobot, would develop a battlefield vehicle for the US Army. Pilot production began in mid-2005.

In 2007 the company added to its barn-full of turf, lawn, and landscape products when it bought LESCO, Inc.

## EXECUTIVES

**Chairman, President, and CEO:** Robert W. (Bob) Lane, age 57, $3,873,609 pay
**President, Agricultural Equipment Division — Europe, Africa, South America and Global Harvesting Equipment Sourcing:** H. J. Markley, age 56, $1,262,844 pay
**President, Agricultural Division — North America, Australia, Asia and Global Tractor and Implement Sourcing:** David C. Everitt, age 54, $1,239,274 pay
**President, Worldwide Construction and Forestry Division, John Deere Power Systems:** Samuel R. (Sam) Allen, age 53, $1,213,659 pay
**President, Worldwide Commercial & Consumer Equipment Division:** Nathan J. Jones, age 50, $1,256,894 pay
**SVP and CFO:** Michael J. Mack Jr., age 50
**SVP and General Counsel:** James R. Jenkins, age 61
**EVP, Strategic Manufacturing and Engineering, Global Tractor and Implement Sourcing (Worldwide Agricultural Equipment):** Adel A. Zakaria
**SVP, John Deere Agri Services:** Daniel C. McCabe
**SVP, Engineering and Manufacturing (Worldwide Construction and Forestry):** Barry W. Schaffter R. Stamp Jr.
**SVP, Commercial Segment (Worldwide Commercial & Consumer Equipment Division):** David P. Werning
**SVP, International Financing, John Deere Credit Worldwide:** Stephen Pullin
**SVP, John Deere Power Systems:** Jean Gilles
**SVP, Agricultural Marketing, North America, Australia, and Asia (Worldwide Agricultural Operations):** Douglas C. DeVries
**SVP, Consumer Marketing & Sales (Worldwide Commercial & Consumer Equipment Division):** Robert C. Hove
**SVP, Product Marketing & Business Development (Worldwide Commercial & Consumer Equipment Division):** Vivien H. Joklik
**VP and Comptroller:** James M. Field
**VP, Corporate Communications and Brand Management:** Frances B. Emerson
**VP, Human Resources:** Mertroe B. Hornbuckle
**VP, Investor Relations:** Marie Z. Ziegler
**Corporate Secretary and Associate General Counsel:** Charles R. Stamp Jr.
**Auditors:** Deloitte & Touche LLP

## LOCATIONS

**HQ:** Deere & Company
1 John Deere Place, Moline, IL 61265
**Phone:** 309-765-8000 **Fax:** 309-765-5671
**Web:** www.deere.com

Deere & Company operates 22 factories in Canada and the US. The company also operates manufacturing plants in Argentina, Brazil, China, Finland, France, Germany, India, Mexico, the Netherlands, New Zealand, Russia, South Africa, and Spain.

### 2006 Sales

| | $ mil. | % of total |
|---|---|---|
| US & Canada | 15,506 | 70 |
| Other countries | 6,249 | 28 |
| Other sales | 393 | 2 |
| **Total** | **22,148** | **100** |

## PRODUCTS/OPERATIONS

### 2006 Sales

| | $ mil. | % of total |
|---|---|---|
| Agricultural equipment | 10,232 | 46 |
| Construction & forestry | 5,775 | 26 |
| Commercial & consumer equipment | 3,877 | 18 |
| Credit | 1,819 | 8 |
| Other | 445 | 2 |
| **Total** | **22,148** | **100** |

### Selected Products and Services

Agricultural Equipment
- Combines
- Cotton harvesting equipment
- Cutters and shredders
- Hay and forage equipment
- Material handling equipment
- Planting and seeding equipment
- Scrapers
- Sprayers
- Tillage
- Tractors

Construction and Forestry Equipment
- Articulated dump trucks
- Backhoe loaders
- Crawler dozers
- Crawler loaders
- Excavators
- Forestry harvesters
- Forklifts
- Landscape loaders
- Log skidders
- Motor graders
- Skid steers

Commercial and Consumer Equipment
- All terrain vehicles
- Golf course equipment
- Lawn and garden tractors
- Riding and walk-behind mowers
- Skid-steer loaders
- Snow equipment
- Trimmers, blowers, and saws
- Utility tractors
- Zero-turn mowers

Credit
- Leasing
- Retail and wholesale financing

Power Systems
- Diesel and natural gas engines
- Powertrain components
- Transmissions

## COMPETITORS

AGCO
Black & Decker
Buhler Industries
Caterpillar
CNH
FMC
foley
Ford
GE
Great Plains Manufacturing
Honda
Ingersoll-Rand
Kubota
Marubeni-Komatsu
Navistar
Terex
Toro
Uzel Makina Sanayi
Volvo
Woods Equipment

## HISTORICAL FINANCIALS

Company Type: Public

### Income Statement

FYE: October 31

| | REVENUE ($ mil.) | NET INCOME ($ mil.) | NET PROFIT MARGIN | EMPLOYEES |
|---|---|---|---|---|
| **10/06** | 22,148 | 1,694 | 7.6% | 46,500 |
| **10/05** | 21,931 | 1,447 | 6.6% | 47,400 |
| **10/04** | 19,986 | 1,406 | 7.0% | 46,500 |
| **10/03** | 15,535 | 643 | 4.1% | 43,200 |
| **10/02** | 13,947 | 319 | 2.3% | 43,000 |
| **Annual Growth** | 12.3% | 51.8% | — | 2.0% |

### 2006 Year-End Financials

Debt ratio: 154.6%
Return on equity: 23.6%
Cash ($ mil.): 1,688
Current ratio: 0.56
Long-term debt ($ mil.): 11,584
No. of shares (mil.): 227
Dividends
Yield: 1.8%
Payout: 21.7%
Market value ($ mil.): 19,344

### Stock History

NYSE: DE

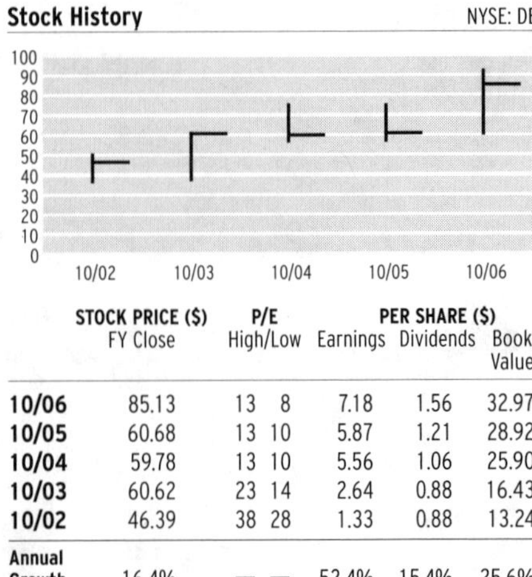

| | STOCK PRICE ($) FY Close | P/E High | P/E Low | PER SHARE ($) Earnings | Dividends | Book Value |
|---|---|---|---|---|---|---|
| **10/06** | 85.13 | 13 | 8 | 7.18 | 1.56 | 32.97 |
| **10/05** | 60.68 | 13 | 10 | 5.87 | 1.21 | 28.92 |
| **10/04** | 59.78 | 13 | 10 | 5.56 | 1.06 | 25.90 |
| **10/03** | 60.62 | 23 | 14 | 2.64 | 0.88 | 16.43 |
| **10/02** | 46.39 | 38 | 28 | 1.33 | 0.88 | 13.24 |
| **Annual Growth** | 16.4% | — | — | 52.4% | 15.4% | 25.6% |

# Del Monte Foods

How does Del Monte Foods' garden grow? Very well indeed. One of the US's largest manufacturers of branded canned fruit, vegetables, tuna, and broths, Del Monte has been harvesting acquisitions and new products. Its flagship products (canned corn, green beans, peas, peaches, pears, and pineapples) are purchased mostly from US growers. The company makes tomato-based foods such as ketchup and tomato sauce. Its retail brands include College Inn, Del Monte, Contadina, and StarKist. Del Monte makes pets grow too, with a stable of pet-food and -treat brands, including 9Lives, Gravy Train, Milk-Bone, and Meow Mix. In addition, the company makes commercial food ingredients and products for the foodservice industry.

To freshen up sales of 9Lives cat food brand, Del Monte recently reintroduced Morris the Cat to its advertising. Given Morris's finicky nature, it is unlikely he will pose any danger to Del Monte's fellow corporate spokesanimal, StarKist's Charlie the Tuna.

In order to focus on higher-margin products, in 2006 Del Monte acquired privately held cat food maker Meow Mix Holdings, Inc., for $705 million. In addition, the company sold private-label soup and baby food business Nature's Goodness to TreeHouse Foods for about $275 million. (The TreeHouse deal did not include Del Monte's College Inn broths.) Later that same year, it purchased the Milk-Bone pet product brand from Kraft for $580 million.

The company has 17 US production facilities, as well as operations in American Samoa, Mexico, and Venezuela. The Del Monte brand is licensed to other companies internationally.

Jumping on board a fast-growing trend in the bev biz, in 2007 Del Monte launched an energy drink, Bloom Energy. The drink is aimed at the female market.

Wal-Mart and SAM'S CLUB account for approximately 30% of Del Monte's sales. Atlantic Investment Management owns about 7% of Del Monte; The Bank of New York Mellon (formerly Mellon Financial Corporation) owns 5%.

## HISTORY

Fred Tillman adopted the name Del Monte (originally the name of a coffee blend made for the fancy Hotel Del Monte in Monterey, California) in 1891 for use at his newly formed Oakland Preserving Company. Brand-name labeling was becoming a significant marketing tool, and Del Monte ("of the mountain" in Spanish) became known for high value.

In 1899 Oakland Preserving merged into the California Fruit Canners Association (CFCA) with 17 other canneries (half of California's canning industry). The new company, the largest canner in the world, adopted Del Monte as its main brand name. CFCA merged with other California canneries in 1916 to form Calpak and created national demand for Del Monte products through mass advertising. The company's first ad appeared in the *Saturday Evening Post* in 1917.

Calpak expanded into the Midwest in 1925 by acquiring Rochelle Canneries (Illinois). That year it established British Sales Limited and Philippine Packing Corporation. In later years the company expanded into the Philippines. It weathered slow growth during the Depression, but WWII jump-started Calpak's operations — in 1942 about 40% of the company's products went to feed US troops — and the postwar boom kicked it into high gear.

The company bought control of Canadian Canners Limited, the world's second-largest canner, in 1956, gaining entry into the heavily protected British market. In the 1960s a venture into soft-drink products ended in failure. Calpak changed its name to Del Monte Foods in 1967.

RJR Industries bought Del Monte in 1979 as part of a diversification strategy. In 1989, after its buyout by Kohlberg Kravis Roberts, the newly named, debt-laden RJR Nabisco began selling assets, including Del Monte's Hawaiian Punch line in 1990 and its tropical fruit unit. Merrill Lynch and Del Monte executives bought Del Monte's domestic canning operations in 1990, but the transaction loaded the new company with debt.

To reduce debt, during the 1990s Del Monte sold its dried-fruit operations, its pudding division (to Kraft), and its Mexican subsidiary. Texas Pacific Group, an investment partnership known for recruiting specialists to revive companies, acquired a controlling interest in Del Monte in 1997. It installed Richard Wolford, former president of Dole Packaged Foods, as CEO. That year the company bought Contadina's canned tomato products from Nestlé (which kept the right to use the Contadina brand on refrigerated pasta and sauces).

Interested again in expanding in foreign markets, in 1998 it bought back from Nabisco the rights to the Del Monte brand in South America, and it purchased Nabisco's canned fruits and vegetables business in Venezuela. In 1999 the company completed its IPO. Later that year Del Monte purchased a vegetable processing plant from its competitor Birds Eye Foods and, like all food canners, enjoyed robust sales to Y2K-wary shoppers.

In 2000 Del Monte acquired the Sunfresh brand (citrus and tropical fruits) and a distribution center from The UniMark Group for more than $14 million. Del Monte acquired the S&W brand of canned fruits and vegetables, tomatoes, dry beans, and specialty sauces from bankrupted cooperative Tri Valley Growers for about $39 million in 2001.

Del Monte's 2002 acquisitions from Heinz shifted a mixed bag of stagnant and mature brands off Heinz's plate and more than doubled Del Monte's sales. In addition to StarKist tuna, the deal included Heinz's North American pet food business (9Lives, Kibbles 'n Bits), its US baby food business, and College Inn canned broths.

In 2004 Del Monte sold three of its pet-food brands (IVD, Medi-Cal, and Techni-Cal) to French pet-food company Royal Canin. That same year Del Monte acquired Industrias Citricolas de Montemorelos, S.A. de C.V. (ICMOSA), the Mexican subsidiary of The UniMark Group. ICMOSA is a processed tropical and citrus fruit producer and distributor.

## EXECUTIVES

**Chairman, President, and CEO:** Richard G. Wolford, age 62, $2,111,281 pay
**EVP Administration and CFO:** David L. Meyers, age 61, $828,442 pay
**EVP Operations:** Nils Lommerin, age 42, $763,954 pay
**EVP Sales:** Timothy A. (Tim) Cole, age 50, $610,451 pay
**SVP, Chief Accounting Officer, and Controller:** Richard L. French, age 50
**SVP, General Counsel, and Secretary:** James G. Potter, age 49
**SVP Consumer Products:** Apurva S. Mody, age 40
**SVP Marketing and Innovation:** Barry A. Shepard, age 41
**SVP Supply Chain Operations:** David W. (Dave) Allen, age 46
**VP Finance and Investor Relations:** Larry Bodner
**CIO:** Marc Brown
**Director, Energy and Indirect Procurement:** Glen A. Lewis
**Director, Business Systems and Decision Support:** Andrew (Andy) Wojewodka
**Director, Marketing:** Liam Farrell
**Director, National Sales, Foodservice:** Brian Crowe
**Director, Sales:** Kirk Teske
**Director, Tax:** John Ratto
**Senior Scientist, Food Product Development:** Jackie Curtis
**Press Contact:** Melissa Murphy-Brown
**Auditors:** KPMG LLP

## LOCATIONS

**HQ:** Del Monte Foods Company
One Market @ The Landmark,
San Francisco, CA 94105
**Phone:** 415-247-3000 **Fax:** 415-247-3565
**Web:** www.delmonte.com

### 2007 Sales

| | $ mil. | % of total |
|---|---|---|
| US | 3,251.6 | 95 |
| Foreign & export | 163.3 | 5 |
| **Total** | **3,414.9** | **100** |

## PRODUCTS/OPERATIONS

### 2007 Sales

| | $ mil. | % of total |
|---|---|---|
| Consumer products | 2,133.0 | 62 |
| Pet products | 1,281.9 | 38 |
| **Total** | **3,414.9** | **100** |

### Selected Brand Names

9Lives
Alley Cat
Bloom Energy
Canine Carry Outs
College Inn
Contadina
Cycle
Del Monte
Gravy Train
Jerky Treats
Kibbles 'n Bits
Meaty Bone
Meow Mix
Milk-Bone
Nature's Recipe
Pounce
Pup-Peroni
Reward
S&W
Skippy
Snausages
StarKist
Wagwells

### Selected Products

Canned soup
Canned fruit (apricots, cherries, fruit cocktail, mandarin oranges, mixed and tropical mixed fruit, peaches, pears, pineapples)
Pet food and treats
Sauces (pizza, spaghetti, sloppy joe)
Tomatoes (chunky, crushed, diced, ketchup, stewed, paste, purée, sauce)
Tuna (canned)
Vegetables (asparagus, carrots, corn, mixed and flavored vegetables, peas, potatoes, spinach, zucchini, and green, lima, and wax beans)

## COMPETITORS

Bush Brothers
Campbell Soup
Chiquita Brands
Colgate-Palmolive
ConAgra
Doane Pet Care
Dole Food
General Mills
Goya
Hanover Foods
Heinz
Kraft Foods
Mars
Maui Land & Pineapple
Morgan Foods
Nestlé Purina PetCare
Pictsweet
Procter & Gamble
Pro-Fac
Red Bull
Royal Canin
Seneca Foods
Unilever

## HISTORICAL FINANCIALS

Company Type: Public

### Income Statement

FYE: Sunday closest to April 30

| | REVENUE ($ mil.) | NET INCOME ($ mil.) | NET PROFIT MARGIN | EMPLOYEES |
|---|---|---|---|---|
| **4/07** | 3,415 | 113 | 3.3% | 18,200 |
| **4/06** | 2,999 | 170 | 5.7% | 16,700 |
| **4/05** | 3,181 | 118 | 3.7% | 17,500 |
| **4/04** | 3,130 | 165 | 5.3% | 17,200 |
| **4/03** | 2,171 | 134 | 6.1% | 17,200 |
| **Annual Growth** | 12.0% | (4.2%) | — | 1.4% |

### 2007 Year-End Financials

Debt ratio: 134.4%
Return on equity: 8.1%
Cash ($ mil.): 13
Current ratio: 2.17
Long-term debt ($ mil.): 1,952
No. of shares (mil.): 202
Dividends
Yield: 1.0%
Payout: 21.8%
Market value ($ mil.): 2,374

### Stock History

NYSE: DLM

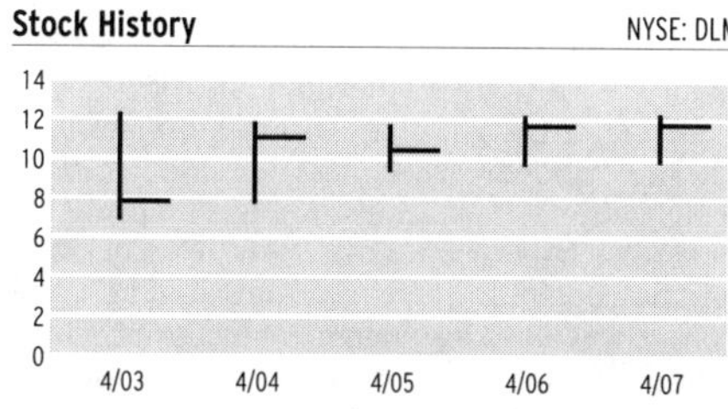


| | STOCK PRICE ($) FY Close | P/E High | P/E Low | PER SHARE ($) Earnings | PER SHARE ($) Dividends | PER SHARE ($) Book Value |
|---|---|---|---|---|---|---|
| **4/07** | 11.74 | 22 | 18 | 0.55 | 0.12 | 7.18 |
| **4/06** | 11.66 | 15 | 12 | 0.83 | 0.08 | 6.57 |
| **4/05** | 10.43 | 21 | 17 | 0.56 | — | 5.97 |
| **4/04** | 11.06 | 15 | 10 | 0.78 | — | 5.38 |
| **4/03** | 7.82 | 16 | 9 | 0.76 | — | 4.54 |
| **Annual Growth** | 10.7% | — | — | (7.8%) | 50.0% | 12.2% |

# Dell Inc.

The name Dell may be synonymous with "direct," but the computer giant has a more diverse approach to the market these days. The world's #1 direct-sale computer vendor provides a broad range of computer products for the consumer and enterprise markets. In addition to a full line of desktop and notebook PCs, Dell offers network servers, workstations, storage systems, printers, projectors, and Ethernet switches. The company also markets third-party software and peripherals. Dell's growing services unit provides systems integration, support, and training. The company announced plans to begin selling through retail stores in 2007.

Entrepreneurial wunderkind Michael Dell pioneered the direct-sales model for computers and took the company from his dorm room to the top of the PC heap by keeping it focused on a simple formula: Eliminate the middleman and sell for less. Dell's built-to-order boxes allow for lower inventories, lower costs, and higher profit margins — elements that have served it well through PC price wars and IT spending recessions. Though direct sales remain the core of Dell's business, a broader strategy has emerged since the company's founding father returned to the helm in early 2007.

Dell had ceded the CEO spot to his hand-picked successor, Kevin Rollins, in 2004. Rollins' resignation came as the company struggled with a number of difficult issues, most notably disappointing earnings and an SEC investigation into its finances. (Dell announced plans to restate four years of financial results after an audit revealed accounting irregularities.) Immediately following the shakeup, Dell announced streamlining measures including a reduction in managers and the elimination of 2006 bonuses. In mid-2007 the company announced plans to cut its workforce by 10% over the next year. It also confirmed plans to exit the flat-panel television business.

The company has made moves to increase its software portfolio. It agreed to acquire ASAP Software, a volume software acquisition and deployment specialist, for $340 million in 2007.

Dell faces intense competition from Hewlett-Packard, whose market share increased dramatically with its 2002 acquisition of Compaq. Dell generates about 80% of its sales from desktop and notebook PCs. Far from limited to PCs, the company is also a leading provider of server computers and storage devices for enterprises. Dell augmented its storage line when it reached an agreement with market leader EMC to resell that company's enterprise systems. Furthering its push beyond PCs, Dell has introduced a line of Ethernet switches. It originally partnered with Lexmark to develop a line of Dell-branded printers, and it has formed additional partnerships to quickly grow its printing line.

On the services front, Dell has mirrored its straightforward approach to hardware sales, embracing a fixed-price model for offerings such as data migration and storage systems implementation. Early in 2006 the company announced an aggressive growth plan for its Indian operations that expanded its existing call center and development units.

Michael Dell owns about 9% of the company.

## HISTORY

At age 13 Michael Dell was already a successful businessman. From his parents' home in Houston, Dell ran a mail-order stamp trading business that, within a few months, grossed more than $2,000. At 16 he sold newspaper subscriptions and at 17 bought his first BMW. When Dell enrolled at the University of Texas in 1983, he was thoroughly bitten by the entrepreneurial bug.

Dell started college as a pre-med student but found time to establish a business selling random-access memory (RAM) chips and disk drives for IBM PCs. Dell bought products at cost from IBM dealers, who were required at the time to order from IBM large monthly quotas of PCs, which frequently exceeded demand. Dell resold his stock through newspapers and computer magazines at 10%-15% below retail.

By April 1984 Dell's dorm room computer components business was grossing about $80,000 a month — enough to persuade him to drop out of college. Soon he started making and selling IBM clones under the brand name PC's Limited. Dell sold his machines directly to consumers rather than through retail outlets, as most manufacturers did. By eliminating the retail markup, Dell could sell PCs at about 40% of the price of an IBM.

The company was plagued by management changes during the mid-1980s. Renamed Dell Computer, it added international sales offices in 1987. In 1988 the company started selling to larger customers, including government agencies. That year Dell went public.

The company tripped in 1990, reporting a 64% drop in profits. Sales were growing — but so were costs, mostly because of efforts to design a PC using proprietary components and reduced instruction set computer (RISC) chips. Also, the company's warehouses were oversupplied. Within a year Dell turned itself around by cutting inventories and introducing new products.

In 1992 Xerox agreed to sell Dell machines in Latin America. Dell opened subsidiaries in Japan and Australia in 1993.

In 1996 the company started selling PCs through its Web site. The next year Dell entered the market for workstations and strengthened its consumer business by separating it from its small-business unit and launching a leasing program for consumers.

Dell began selling a $999 PC in 1999. (Dell phased out the WebPC line after just seven months due to slow sales.) That year the company made its first acquisition — storage area network equipment maker ConvergeNet — and opened a plant in Brazil.

Faced with slumping PC sales in early 2001, the company eliminated 1,700 jobs — about 4% of its workforce. Soon after, it announced it would cut as many as 4,000 additional positions. In 2003 the company shortened its name to simply Dell Inc.

Dell stepped down as CEO in mid-July 2004. Company president Kevin Rollins filled the position; Dell remained chairman of the company.

In 2006 the company announced plans to open display-only retail locations in Dallas and New York. (The Dallas store opened, but plans for the New York location were put on hold.) It also added search giant Google to its list of server customers.

Early in 2007, Rollins resigned as CEO and as a member of the board of directors, and Dell reassumed the role of CEO.

## EXECUTIVES

**Chairman and CEO:** Michael S. Dell, age 42
**Vice Chairman and CFO:** Donald J. Carty Jr., age 60
**SVP, General Counsel, and Secretary:** Lawrence P. (Larry) Tu, age 51
**SVP; President, Americas:** Paul D. Bell, age 45
**SVP and General Manager, Home and Small Business Group:** Rosendo G. (Ro) Parra, age 46
**SVP, Global Services:** Stephen F. (Steve) Schuckenbrock, age 46
**SVP, Business Product Group:** Brad Anderson, age 46
**SVP, Business Product Group:** Jeffrey W. (Jeff) Clarke, age 43
**SVP, Product Group:** Alexander (Alex) Gruzen, age 43
**SVP, Worldwide Procurement and Global Customer Experience:** Martin J. Garvin, age 53
**SVP, Worldwide Procurement and Global Customer Experience:** Glenn E. Neland, age 57
**SVP; President, Asia/Pacific and Japan:** Stephen J. Felice, age 48
**SVP, Human Resources:** Andy Esparza
**VP, Investor Relations and Global Corporate Communications:** Lynn A. Tyson
**Chief Marketing Officer:** Mark Jarvis
**VP, Finance and Chief Accounting Officer:** Thomas W. Sweet, age 47
**VP, Corporate Group Communications:** Robert Pearson
**President, Global Operations:** Michael R. Cannon, age 54
**President, Global Consumer Group:** Ronald G. (Ron) Garriques
**Auditors:** PricewaterhouseCoopers LLP

## LOCATIONS

**HQ:** Dell Inc.
1 Dell Way, Round Rock, TX 78682
**Phone:** 512-338-4400 **Fax:** 512-283-6161
**Web:** www.dell.com

### 2006 Sales

| | $ mil. | % of total |
|---|---|---|
| US | 33,028 | 59 |
| Other countries | 22,880 | 41 |
| **Total** | **55,908** | **100** |

### 2006 Sales

| | $ mil. | % of total |
|---|---|---|
| Americas | | |
| Business | 28,481 | 51 |
| US Consumer | 7,930 | 14 |
| Europe, Middle East & Africa | 12,873 | 23 |
| Asia/Pacific | 6,624 | 12 |
| **Total** | **55,908** | **100** |

## PRODUCTS/OPERATIONS

### 2006 Sales

| | % of total |
|---|---|
| Desktop PCs | 38 |
| Mobile PCs, handhelds & music players | 25 |
| Software and peripherals | 15 |
| Servers & networking | 10 |
| Enhanced services | 9 |
| Storage | 3 |
| **Total** | **100** |

### Selected Products

Computers
- Desktop (Dimension, OptiPlex, Vostro, XPS)
- Notebook (Inspiron, Latitude, Vostro, XPS)

Enterprise systems
- Network servers (PowerApp, PowerEdge)
- Storage (PowerVault)
- Workstations (Precision)

Ethernet switches (PowerConnect)
Point-of-sale systems
Printers
- Inkjet multifunction
- Laser

Projectors
Refurbished systems
Third-party peripherals and software

## COMPETITORS

3Com
Acer
Apple
Brother Industries
Canon
CDW
Cisco Systems
EMC
Enterasys
Epson
Extreme Networks
Fujitsu Siemens
Gateway
Hewlett-Packard
Hitachi
Hitachi Data Systems
IBM
Lenovo
Matsushita Electric
MPC Computers
NEC
SGI
Sony
Sun Microsystems
Toshiba
Unisys

## HISTORICAL FINANCIALS

Company Type: Public

**Income Statement** FYE: Sunday nearest January 31

| | REVENUE ($ mil.) | NET INCOME ($ mil.) | NET PROFIT MARGIN | EMPLOYEES |
|---|---|---|---|---|
| **1/06** | 55,908 | 3,572 | 6.4% | 66,100 |
| **1/05** | 49,205 | 3,043 | 6.2% | 56,000 |
| **1/04** | 41,444 | 2,645 | 6.4% | 46,000 |
| **1/03** | 35,404 | 2,122 | 6.0% | 39,100 |
| **1/02** | 31,168 | 1,246 | 4.0% | 34,600 |
| **Annual Growth** | 15.7% | 30.1% | — | 17.6% |

**2006 Year-End Financials**

| | |
|---|---|
| Debt ratio: 12.2% | No. of shares (mil.): 2,330 |
| Return on equity: 67.3% | Dividends |
| Cash ($ mil.): 9,058 | Yield: — |
| Current ratio: 1.11 | Payout: — |
| Long-term debt ($ mil.): 504 | Market value ($ mil.): 68,176 |

**Stock History** NASDAQ (GS): DELL

45 40 35 30 25 20 15 10 5 0

1/02 1/03 1/04 1/05 1/06

| | STOCK PRICE ($) FY Close | P/E High | P/E Low | PER SHARE ($) Earnings | Dividends | Book Value |
|---|---|---|---|---|---|---|
| **1/06** | 29.26 | 29 | 20 | 1.46 | — | 1.77 |
| **1/05** | 41.06 | 36 | 26 | 1.18 | — | 2.61 |
| **1/04** | 33.44 | 37 | 22 | 1.01 | — | 2.46 |
| **1/03** | 23.86 | 39 | 27 | 0.80 | — | 1.89 |
| **1/02** | 26.80 | 66 | 35 | 0.46 | — | 1.80 |
| **Annual Growth** | 2.2% | — | — | 33.5% | — | (0.4%) |

# Deloitte Touche Tohmatsu

This company is "deloitted" to make your acquaintance, particularly if you're a big business in need of accounting services. Deloitte Touche Tohmatsu (doing business as Deloitte) is one of accounting's Big Four, along with Ernst & Young, KPMG, and PricewaterhouseCoopers. Deloitte offers traditional audit and fiscal-oversight services to a multinational clientele. It also provides human resources, tax, technology, and other consulting services, as well as services to governments and international lending agencies working in emerging markets, including China and India. Units include Deloitte & Touche (the US accounting arm) and Deloitte Consulting. Consulting accounts for more than 20% of Deloitte's sales.

Deloitte spent the 1980s and 1990s pursuing a strategy of using accountants and consultants in concert to provide seamless service in auditing, accounting, strategic planning, information technology, financial management, and productivity. Deloitte Consulting became Deloitte's fastest-growing line, offering strategic and management consulting, in addition to information technology and human resources consulting services.

Increasingly, though, Deloitte and its peers came under fire for their combined accounting/consulting operations; regulators and observers wondered whether accountants could maintain objectivity when they were auditing clients for whom they also provided consulting services. Criticism mounted after Enron's collapse capsized Arthur Andersen and put the entire accounting industry under scrutiny. (Deloitte picked up new business and members in Andersen's wake.)

Deloitte in 2002 announced it would spin off its consulting business, becoming the last of the big accountants to do so; a year later it called off the split, citing a weakened market for consulting, among other woes.

Deloitte was in the headlines again in 2003, when Parmalat filed for bankruptcy in the midst of a $12 billion financial scandal, then dropped Deloitte as its auditor. Parmalat sued Deloitte in 2004, claiming its auditing procedures were inadequate and should have uncovered the fraud at Parmalat earlier. Deloitte settled the case with Parmalat for $149 million in 2007.

## HISTORY

In 1845 William Deloitte opened an accounting office in London, at first soliciting business from bankrupts. The growth of joint stock companies and the development of stock markets in the mid-19th century created a need for standardized financial reporting and fueled the rise of auditing, and Deloitte moved into the new field. The Great Western Railway appointed him as its independent auditor (the first anywhere) in 1849.

In 1890 John Griffiths, who had become a partner in 1869, opened the company's first US office in New York City. Four decades later branches had opened throughout the US. In 1952 the firm partnered with Haskins & Sells, which operated 34 US offices.

Deloitte aimed to be "the Cadillac, not the Ford" of accounting. The firm, which became Deloitte Haskins & Sells in 1978, began shedding its conservatism as competition heated up; it was the first of the major accountancy firms to use aggressive ads.

In 1984 Deloitte Haskins & Sells tried to merge with Price Waterhouse, but the deal was dropped after Price Waterhouse's UK partners objected.

In 1989 Deloitte Haskins & Sells joined the flamboyant Touche Ross (founded 1899) to become Deloitte & Touche. Touche Ross's Japanese affiliate, Ross Tohmatsu (founded 1968) rounded out the current name. The merger was engineered by Deloitte's Michael Cook and Touche's Edward Kangas, in part to unite the former firm's US and European strengths with the latter's Asian presence. Cook continued to oversee US operations, with Kangas presiding over international operations. Many affiliates, particularly in the UK, rejected the merger and defected to competing firms.

As auditors were increasingly held accountable for the financial results of their clients, legal action soared. In the 1990s Deloitte was sued because of its actions relating to Drexel Burnham Lambert junk bond king Michael Milken, the failure of several savings and loans, and clients' bankruptcies.

Nevertheless, in 1995 the SEC chose Michael Sutton, the firm's national director of auditing and accounting practice, as its chief accountant. That year Deloitte formed Deloitte & Touche Consulting to consolidate its US and UK consulting operations; its Asian consulting operations were later added to facilitate regional expansion.

In 1996 the firm formed a corporate fraud unit (with special emphasis on the Internet) and bought PHH Fantus, the leading corporate relocation consulting company. In 1997, amid a new round of industry mergers, rumors swirled that a Deloitte and Ernst & Young union had been scrapped because the firms could not agree on ownership issues. Deloitte disavowed plans to merge and launched an ad campaign directly targeted against its rivals.

The Asian economic crisis hurt overseas expansion in 1998, but provided a boost in restructuring consulting. Also that year Deloitte Consulting decided to sell its computer programming subsidiary to CGI Group, and Kangas stepped down as CEO to be succeeded by James Copeland; the following year Kangas ceded the chairman's seat to Piet Hoogendoorn.

In 2001 the SEC forced Deloitte & Touche to restate the financial results of Pre-Paid Legal Services. In an unusual move, Deloitte & Touche publicly disagreed with the SEC's findings.

The accountancy put some old trouble to bed in 2003 when it agreed to pay $23 million to settle claims it had been negligent in its auditing of failed Kentucky Life Insurance, a client in the 1980s. Later that year the UK's High Court found Deloitte negligent in audits related to the failed Barings Bank; however, the ruling was considered something of a victory for the accountancy because it essentially cleared Deloitte of the majority of charges against it and effectively limited its financial liability in the matter. Copeland retired from the global CEO's office that year and handed the reins over to Bill Parrett, who had formerly served as managing director for the US and the Americas. Parrett was succeeded in 2007 by Jim Quigley.

## EXECUTIVES

**CEO and Director:** James H. (Jim) Quigley, age 55
**CFO:** Jeffrey P. Rohr
**Deputy to the Global CEO:** Vince Cali
**Global Managing Partner, Financial Advisory Services:** Ralph G. Adams
**Global Managing Partner, Consulting:** Paul D. Robinson, age 54
**Global Managing Partner, Tax:** Alan S. Schneier
**Global Managing Director, Human Resources and Managing Director, Global Office:** James H. (Jim) Wall
**Regional Managing Partner, Japan:** Shuichiro Sekine
**Regional Managing Partner, North America; Global Managing Partner, Brand and Eminence:** Colin Taylor
**Managing Director, Finance and Administration:** S. Ashish Bali
**Executive Member, United Kingdom:** Stephen (Steve) Almond
**Executive Member, Hong Kong/China:** Manoj P. Singh
**Executive Member, United Kingdom:** Alberto E. Terol
**Executive Member, US:** Jeffrey K. (Jeff) Willemain
**Executive Member, US:** Jerry P. Leamon
**Executive Member, United Kingdom:** Vassi Naidoo
**Executive Member, United States, and Director:** Barry Salzberg, age 53
**Executive Member, US:** Ainar D. Aijala Jr.
**General Counsel:** Joseph J. Lambert

## LOCATIONS

**HQ:** Deloitte Touche Tohmatsu
1633 Broadway, New York, NY 10019
**Phone:** 212-489-1600 **Fax:** 212-489-1687
**Web:** www.deloitte.com/dtt

Deloitte Touche Tohmatsu operates through offices in about 135 countries.

### 2006 Sales

| | % of total |
|---|---|
| Americas | 52 |
| Europe/Middle East/Africa | 38 |
| Asia/Pacific/Japan | 10 |
| **Total** | **100** |

## PRODUCTS/OPERATIONS

### 2006 Sales

| | % of total |
|---|---|
| Audit | 49 |
| Consulting | 22 |
| Tax | 21 |
| Financial advisory services | 8 |
| **Total** | **100** |

### 2006 Sales By Industry

| | % of total |
|---|---|
| Financial services | 21 |
| Consumer business | 20 |
| Manufacturing | 16 |
| Telecom, media & technology | 14 |
| Energy & resources | 8 |
| Life sciences | 7 |
| Public sector | 7 |
| Aviation & transport | 2 |
| Other | 5 |
| **Total** | **100** |

### Selected Products and Services

Audit
- Auditing services
- Global offerings services
- International financial reporting conversion services

Consulting
- Enterprise applications
- Human capital
- Outsourcing
- Strategy and operations
- Technology integration

Enterprise Risk Services
- Capital markets
- Control assurance
- Corporate responsibility and sustainability
- Internal audit
- Regulatory consulting
- Security and privacy services

Financial Advisory
- Corporate finance
- Forensic services
- Reorganization services
- Transaction services
- Valuation services

Merger and Acquisition Services

Tax
- Corporate tax
- Global tax compliance
- Indirect tax
- International assignment services
- International tax
- M&A transaction services
- Research and development credits
- Tax publications
- Tax technologies
- Transfer pricing

## COMPETITORS

Accenture
BDO International
Booz Allen
Boston Consulting
Capgemini
EDS
Ernst & Young
Grant Thornton
H&R Block
KPMG
Marsh & McLennan
McKinsey & Company
PricewaterhouseCoopers
Towers Perrin
Watson Wyatt

## HISTORICAL FINANCIALS

Company Type: Partnership

### Income Statement

FYE: May 31

| | REVENUE ($ mil.) | NET INCOME ($ mil.) | NET PROFIT MARGIN | EMPLOYEES |
|---|---|---|---|---|
| **5/06** | 20,000 | — | — | 135,000 |
| **5/05** | 18,200 | — | — | 121,283 |
| **5/04** | 16,400 | — | — | 115,000 |
| **5/03** | 15,100 | — | — | 119,237 |
| **5/02** | 12,500 | — | — | 98,000 |
| **Annual Growth** | 12.5% | — | — | 8.3% |

### Revenue History



# Delphi Corporation

Delphi has taken to the road alone after being spun off from General Motors in 1999. One of the world's largest makers of auto parts, Delphi makes nearly everything mechanical and electrical/electronic that goes into cars. Its primary business divisions include Electrical/Electronic Architecture (vehicle electrical systems), Powertrain Systems (engine management, fuel, and emissions systems), Electronics and Safety (sensors, security systems, seat belts, airbags, navigation and entertainment systems), Steering (steering columns, rack and pinion gears), and Thermal Systems (climate control, radiators, heat exchangers). The bulk of Delphi's business comes from former parent GM. Delphi filed Chapter 11 in 2005.

Late in 2004 GM and Ford announced worldwide production cutbacks for 2005. In response Delphi reduced its workforce by more than 8,500. In addition to lower automotive production, high prices for commodity materials, namely steel, have contributed to Dephi's woes.

A bailout plan with help from former parent GM came too late in early fall 2005 and Delphi filed for protection under Chapter 11 bankruptcy. To survive Delphi will have to sell off or shut down much of its US manufacturing base. Delphi estimates its operations will have to become about 20% smaller by the time it emerges from bankruptcy in the first half of 2007.

To lose some of its girth Delphi will likely exit certain component sectors including chassis systems, brakes, and steering. These cuts are likely to affect Delphi's European operations as well as those in North America.

In the immediate wake of its Chapter 11 filing Delphi sought drastic concessions from UAW-represented workers. It announced it needed to cut wages from $27 an hour to as low as $9.50 an hour. The announcement triggered talk of a strike — the consequences of which would be devastating for Delphi — and GM.

To head such a possibility off at the pass, early in 2006 GM brokered a deal with the UAW and Delphi that would reduce the hourly, UAW-represented headcount at Delphi and hourly headcount at GM by offering early retirement buyouts. The program also allows UAW-represented workers to flow back to GM by September 2007. UAW-represented Delphi employees may either retire from Delphi, or flow back to GM, then retire. GM is footing the bill for the scheme.

Later in 2006, 6,300 workers represented by the IUE-CWA (International Union of Electronic, Electrical, Salaried, Machine and Furniture Workers-Communications Workers of America) union agreed to the GM-proposed early retirement buyout scheme, further reducing the chances of a Delphi strike. Possibility of a strike diminished further in mid-2007 when hourly UAW members agreed to plant closures and wage cuts. Top production wages are to drop from $27 per hour to $18.50. The plan will also close 10 US plants.

Also in 2007 Delphi struck a deal whereby an investor group led by Appaloosa Management LP will invest $2.5 billion in Delphi once it emerges from Chapter 11 in exchange for preferred and common stock. The deal would make the Appaloosa-led investor group Delphi's largest shareholder.

## HISTORY

Delphi Corporation traces its roots to the 1908 birth of General Motors, originally formed as a consortium among Buick, Oldsmobile, and Cadillac. During WWI 90% of GM's trucks were targeted for the war effort. Chevrolet joined the group in 1918, and by 1920 GM had bought more than 30 companies.

GM expanded its product line in 1936 to include radios by buying Delco Electronics (transferred to Delphi in 1997). GM spent WWII turning out defense materials, including some 1,300 airplanes and one-fourth of all US aircraft engines. In the 1950s GM introduced the V-8 engine, power steering and brakes, front-seat safety belts, and the first car air-conditioning system. GM, like other carmakers, made most of the parts for its cars.

During the mid-1960s GM diversified into home appliances, insurance, locomotives, electronics, ball bearings, and financing. Delco began to produce AM/FM car stereos. In 1961 J. T. Battenberg (Delphi's future CEO) joined the carmaker as a GM Institute student.

The 1970s oil crisis contributed to a drop in sales for GM. Additionally, new pollution-control standards forced the company to spend billions on compliance. In the early 1980s GM spent more than $60 billion on new model designs and plant updates. It bought Hughes Electronics (now The DIRECTV Group, Inc.) and placed Delco under the Hughes umbrella. GM failed to keep up with competing technological developments in the 1980s. Lagging behind, it began venturing out of its own backyard to buy cheaper car components.

Devastating losses in the early 1990s forced GM to restructure. In 1991 it began organizing its parts operations into a separate business group. The next year Battenberg took control of the parts division and began streamlining and exiting noncore operations. GM formed Automotive Components Group (ACG) Worldwide in 1994. The next year GM changed ACG's name to Delphi. As a step toward spinning Delphi off, GM began reporting the group's earnings separately in 1997. That year GM transferred its Delco operations to Delphi.

United Auto Workers (UAW) members at a Delphi plant in Flint, Michigan, joined those from GM's metal-stamping plant across town in a crippling strike in 1998 that lasted almost two months and reduced the company's income by about $726 million. In 1999 GM offered 18% of Delphi in an IPO and spun off the rest of Delphi's stock to GM shareholders.

Delphi bought Lucas Diesel Systems (the diesel engine unit of TRW) for $871 million in 2000 and renamed it Delphi Diesel Systems.

In 2001 Delphi announced that it would cut 5% of its workforce — 11,500 jobs — and close or consolidate nine plants due to slowing vehicle production in Europe and North America.

Early in 2002 Delphi shortened its name to Delphi Corporation in hopes of reflecting its efforts to expand outside the automotive industry.

Late in 2004, citing productions cuts at GM and Ford as well as increased commodity prices, Delphi announced another 8,500 job cuts for 2005 and predicted a 2005 net loss of $350 million.

In July 2005 Robert S. "Steve" Miller succeeded chairman and CEO J.T. Battenberg III, who retired after 44 years in the industry.

## EXECUTIVES

**Chairman:** Robert S. (Steve) Miller Jr., age 65
**President, CEO, COO, and Director:** Rodney O'Neal, age 53, $920,000 pay
**EVP and CFO:** Robert J. (Bob) Dellinger, age 46, $750,000 pay
**VP, Global Business Services:** Mark R. Weber, age 58
**VP and General Counsel:** David M. Sherbin, age 47
**VP and CIO:** Bette M. Walker, age 63
**VP and Treasurer:** John P. Arle, age 59
**VP; President, Automotive Holdings Group:** James A. Bertrand, age 49
**VP; President, Delphi Asia Pacific:** Choon T. Chon, age 60
**VP; President, Delphi Electronics and Safety:** Jeffrey J. Owens, age 52
**VP; President, Delphi Powertrain Systems and Delphi EMEA:** Guy C. Hachey, age 51
**VP; President, Delphi Packard Electric Systems:** James A. Spencer, age 54
**VP; President, Delphi Product and Service Solutions:** Francisco A. (Frank) Ordoñez, age 56
**VP; President, Delphi Thermal and Interior:** Ronald M. Pirtle, age 52
**VP; President, Delphi Steering:** Robert J. Remenar, age 51
**VP, Corporate Affairs, Marketing Communications, and Worldwide Facilities:** Karen L. Healy, age 52
**VP, Human Resources Management:** Kevin M. Butler, age 51
**VP, Sales and Marketing:** F. Timothy Richards, age 52
**Director, Investor Relations:** Brian Eichenlaub, age 36
**Corporate Secretary:** Marjorie Harris Loeb, age 42
**Auditors:** Ernst & Young LLP

## LOCATIONS

**HQ:** Delphi Corporation
5725 Delphi Dr., Troy, MI 48098
**Phone:** 248-813-2000 **Fax:** 248-813-2670
**Web:** www.delphi.com

### 2006 Sales

| | $ mil. | % of total |
|---|---|---|
| North America | 16,919 | 64 |
| Europe, Middle East & Africa | 6,822 | 26 |
| Asia/Pacific | 1,920 | 7 |
| South America | 731 | 3 |
| **Total** | **26,392** | **100** |

## PRODUCTS/OPERATIONS

### 2006 Sales

| | $ mil. | % of total |
|---|---|---|
| Automotive Holding Group | 5,635 | 21 |
| Electrical/Electronic Architecture | 5,365 | 20 |
| Powertrain Systems | 5,218 | 20 |
| Electronics & Safety | 4,899 | 19 |
| Steering | 2,592 | 10 |
| Thermal Systems | 2,387 | 9 |
| Other | 296 | 1 |
| **Total** | **26,392** | **100** |

### 2006 Sales

| | $ mil. | % of total |
|---|---|---|
| GM & affiliates | 11,636 | 44 |
| Other customers | 14,756 | 56 |
| **Total** | **26,392** | **100** |

### Selected Divisions and Products

Electrical/Electronic Architecture
- Complete electronic architecture and components

Powertrain Systems
- Electronics controls
- Exhaust handling
- Fuel injection systems

Electronics and Safety
- Audio, entertainment, and communications components
- Body controls
- Power electronics
- Safety systems
- Security systems

Steering
- Steering components

Thermal Systems
- Heating, ventilation, and air-conditioning systems
- Powertrain cooling and related technologies

## COMPETITORS

ArvinMeritor
Autoliv
Collins & Aikman
Continental Teves Inc.
Dana
DENSO
Eaton
Federal-Mogul
Haldex
ITT Corp.
Johnson Controls
Johnson Electric
JTEKT
Lear
LEONI
Magna International
Magneti Marelli
Molex
Motorola, Inc.
NSK
Prestolite Electric
Robert Bosch
Senior plc
Siemens VDO Automotive
Sumitomo Electric
Tenneco
ThyssenKrupp Automotive
TRW Automotive
Tyco
Valeo
Visteon
Yazaki
ZF Friedrichshafen

## HISTORICAL FINANCIALS

Company Type: Public

### Income Statement

FYE: December 31

| | REVENUE ($ mil.) | NET INCOME ($ mil.) | NET PROFIT MARGIN | EMPLOYEES |
|---|---|---|---|---|
| **12/06** | 26,392 | (5,464) | — | 171,400 |
| **12/05** | 26,947 | (2,357) | — | 184,200 |
| **12/04** | 28,622 | (4,753) | — | 185,200 |
| **12/03** | 28,096 | (56) | — | 190,000 |
| **12/02** | 27,427 | 343 | 1.3% | 192,000 |
| **Annual Growth** | (1.0%) | — | — | (2.8%) |

### 2006 Year-End Financials

Debt ratio: —
Return on equity: —
Cash ($ mil.): 1,813
Current ratio: 1.10
Long-term debt ($ mil.): 49

### Net Income History

Pink Sheets: DPHIQ

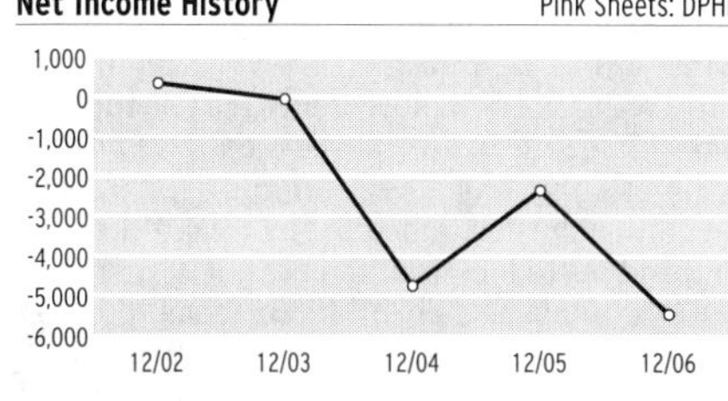


# Delta Air Lines

Just as a delta is a symbol for change in math, Delta Air Lines symbolizes the changing mathematics of the airline industry. A leading US carrier, behind AMR's American Airlines and UAL's United Airlines, Delta emerged from Chapter 11 bankruptcy protection in 2007. On its own and through its Delta Connection regional carriers (including subsidiary Comair), Delta serves about 310 destinations in more than 50 countries. It operates from hubs in Atlanta, Cincinnati, New York, and Salt Lake City. Delta extends its offerings as part of the SkyTeam code-sharing and marketing alliance, which includes carriers such as Air France, KLM, and Korean Air Lines, as well as Continental and Northwest Airlines.

After 19 months in bankruptcy, Delta exited Chapter 11 with a stronger balance sheet. In its restructuring, Delta worked not only to cut costs but also to boost its international service, and it added about 50 routes in 2005 and 2006. Demand for overseas service has increased as business activity in regions outside the US has picked up. Delta's international offerings are strongest in Europe and Latin America, which together account for more than 20% of the company's sales.

In July 2007, Delta made a move to significantly expand its international services when it applied with the US Department of Transportation for the right to operate nonstop flight services between Atlanta and both Beijing and Shanghai.

Delta CEO Gerald Grinstein said in October 2006 that he would retire after the airline's emergence from bankruptcy. His successor has not been chosen.

## HISTORY

Delta Air Lines was founded in Macon, Georgia, in 1924 as the world's first crop-dusting service, Huff-Daland Dusters, to combat boll weevil infestation of cotton fields. It moved to Monroe, Louisiana, in 1925. In 1928 field manager C. E. Woolman and two partners bought the service and renamed it Delta Air Service after the Mississippi Delta region it served.

In 1929 Delta pioneered passenger service from Dallas to Jackson, Mississippi. Flying mail without a government subsidy, Delta finally got a US Postal Service contract in 1934 to fly from Fort Worth to Charleston via Atlanta. Delta relocated to Atlanta in 1941. Woolman became president in 1945 and managed the airline until he died in 1966.

Delta added more flights, including a direct route from Chicago to New Orleans with its 1952 purchase of Chicago and Southern Airlines. The carrier offered its first transcontinental flight in 1961. In 1972 the airline bought Northeast Airlines and added service to New England and Canada; it offered service to the UK in 1978, the year that the US airline industry was deregulated.

In 1982 Delta's employees pledged $30 million to buy a Boeing 767 jet, christened *The Spirit of Delta,* as a token of appreciation. In fiscal 1983 the company succumbed to the weak US economy and posted its first loss ever; it quickly became profitable again in 1985. It bought Los Angeles-based Western Air Lines in 1986.

Delta began service to Asia in 1987, the year that longtime employee Ronald Allen became CEO. In 1990 Delta joined TWA and Northwest to form Worldspan, a computer reservation service.

Despite a slump in 1990 earnings, in 1991 Delta bought gates, planes, and Canadian routes from Eastern, as well as Pan Am's New York-Boston shuttle, European routes, and Frankfurt hub. The purchases elevated Delta from a domestic player to a top international carrier, but they also contributed to a $2 billion loss (1991-94).

Allen began a cost-reduction plan in 1994 that cut many routes and 15,000 jobs over the next three years. However, it also drove down employee morale and Delta's customer service reputation. The airline also discontinued unprofitable international routes in 1995 and introduced no-frills Delta Express in 1996. Allen was let go in 1997 and replaced by Leo Mullin, a former electric utility chief.

Spurred by the threat of emerging global alliances Oneworld and Star, Delta announced in 1999 that it would create a competing alliance with Air France and CINTRA's AeroMéxico. SkyTeam, which also included Korean Air Lines, was launched in 2000. The realignment led Delta to end code-sharing deals with Swissair Group, Sabena, and Austrian Airlines that year. At home, Delta bought regional carriers Atlantic Southeast Airlines and Comair. An 89-day pilots' strike led to flight cancellations at Comair in 2001.

In the wake of the September 11, 2001, terrorist attacks on New York and Washington, DC, and the resulting reduction in air travel, Delta cut back its flight schedule and reduced its workforce by about 15% (about 13,000 employees).

To streamline operations, the airline sold its 40% stake in reservation system Worldspan in 2003. That year CEO Leo Mullin resigned and was replaced by Gerald Grinstein, a Delta director. Delta also launched a budget carrier named Song in 2003 to compete with other low-fare carriers like Southwest and JetBlue. (Song failed to thrive on its own, however, and in 2006 the carrier's operations were folded back into those of Delta.)

Delta cut costs significantly during 2005 in an effort to avoid bankruptcy. In a last-ditch bid to raise cash, the company sold its Atlantic Southeast Airlines unit to SkyWest for $425 million in September 2005. Days later, however, the combination of high fuel prices and a string of losses from operations dating back to 2001 finally forced Delta to file for Chapter 11 protection. To keep flying Delta secured a $2 billion financing package from its creditors, chiefly GE Commercial Finance. At the end of 2005 Delta's fleet stood at about 650 aircraft — down nearly 200 planes from the year before.

A milestone in Delta's journey back to solvency was reached in May 2006 when the company's pilots voted to accept a contract with changes in pay, benefits, and work rules designed to save Delta about $280 million a year. The deal, which included the termination of the pilots' pension plan, averted a threatened strike that Delta said would have put the company out of business.

In the midst of Delta's restructuring, US Airways offered in November 2006 to pay about $8 billion — half in cash and half in stock — for the carrier. After the buyout proposal was rejected by Delta's board, US Airways upped its bid to about $10 billion in January 2007 in hopes of persuading Delta's creditors to back a deal. The creditors failed to bite, however, and US Airways withdrew its offer.

## EXECUTIVES

**Chairman:** John F. (Jack) Smith Jr., age 69
**CEO and Director:** Gerald Grinstein, age 74
**COO:** James F. (Jim) Whitehurst, age 38, $420,000 pay (prior to promotion)
**EVP and CFO:** Edward H. (Ed) Bastian, age 49
**EVP Sales and Customer Service:** Lee A. Macenczak, age 44
**EVP and Chief of Network and Revenue Management:** Glen W. Hauenstein, age 45
**EVP Operations:** Joseph C. (Joe) Kolshak, age 49, $367,917 pay (prior to promotion)
**EVP Human Resources and Labor Relations:** Michael H. (Mike) Campbell, age 57
**EVP and General Counsel:** Kenneth F. (Ken) Khoury, age 56
**SVP Airport Customer Service:** Richard W. (Rich) Cordell
**SVP Finance and Controller:** Hank Halter
**SVP Flight Operations and Chief Pilot:** Gary L. Beck
**SVP Revenue Management:** Gail Grimmett
**SVP Global Sales and Distribution:** Pam Elledge
**SVP In-Flight Service and Global Product Development:** Joanne D. Smith, age 48
**VP Consumer Marketing:** Patrice G. Miles
**VP, Deputy General Counsel, and Secretary:** Leslie P. Klemperer
**VP Human Resources:** Elizabeth H. (Beth) Johnston
**VP Public Affairs:** Doug W. Blissit
**VP Corporate Communications:** Jeff Battcher, age 45
**President, ASA Holdings and Atlantic Southeast Airlines:** W. E. (Skip) Barnette
**President, Comair Holdings and Comair:** Frederick W. P. Buttrell
**Auditors:** Ernst & Young LLP

## LOCATIONS

**HQ:** Delta Air Lines, Inc.
1030 Delta Blvd., Atlanta, GA 30320
**Phone:** 404-715-2600 **Fax:** 404-715-5042
**Web:** www.delta.com

### 2006 Sales

| | $ mil. | % of total |
|---|---|---|
| North America | 12,931 | 75 |
| Atlantic | 2,997 | 18 |
| Latin America | 1,079 | 6 |
| Pacific | 164 | 1 |
| **Total** | **17,171** | **100** |

## PRODUCTS/OPERATIONS

### 2006 Sales

| | $ mil. | % of total |
|---|---|---|
| Passenger | | |
| Mainline | 11,773 | 69 |
| Regional affiliates | 3,853 | 22 |
| Cargo | 498 | 3 |
| Other | 1,047 | 6 |
| **Total** | **17,171** | **100** |

## COMPETITORS

ACE Aviation
AirTran Holdings
Alaska Air
AMR Corp.
British Airways
Cathay Pacific
Japan Airlines
JetBlue
Lufthansa
Qantas
SAS
Singapore Airlines
Southwest Airlines
UAL
US Airways
Virgin Atlantic Airways

## HISTORICAL FINANCIALS

Company Type: Public

### Income Statement

FYE: December 31

| | REVENUE ($ mil.) | NET INCOME ($ mil.) | NET PROFIT MARGIN | EMPLOYEES |
|---|---|---|---|---|
| **12/06** | 17,171 | (6,203) | — | 51,300 |
| **12/05** | 16,191 | (3,818) | — | 55,700 |
| **12/04** | 15,002 | (5,198) | — | 69,150 |
| **12/03** | 13,303 | (773) | — | 70,600 |
| **12/02** | 13,305 | (1,272) | — | 75,100 |
| **Annual Growth** | 6.6% | — | — | (9.1%) |

### 2006 Year-End Financials

Debt ratio: —
Return on equity: —
Cash ($ mil.): 3,398
Current ratio: 0.93
Long-term debt ($ mil.): 6,509

### Net Income History

NYSE: DAL

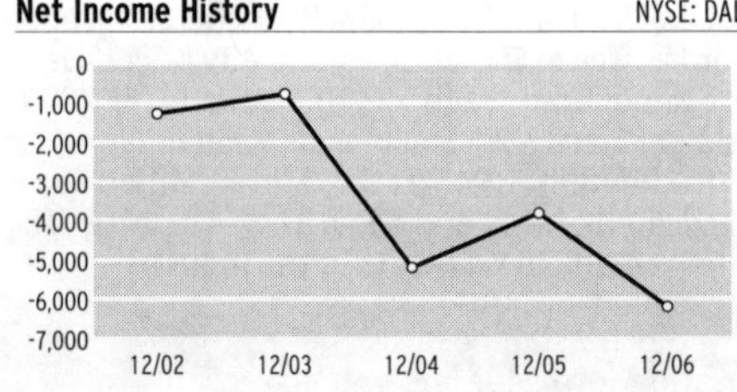

# Deluxe Corporation

When money can move at the speed of a mouse click, Deluxe wants to do more than keep its revenues in check. The company remains the largest check printer in the US, serving the nation's banks, credit unions, and financial services companies. Checks and business forms account for the majority of Deluxe's sales; it also sells checkbook covers, address labels, self-inking stamps, fraud prevention services, and customer retention programs. The company's Direct Checks division sells personal and business checks under the brands Checks Unlimited and Designer Checks.

Lee Schram, previously at NCR Corporation, replaced interim CEO Ronald Eilers in May 2006. Soon after Schram took over, Deluxe announced cost-cutting measures that will save the company some $150 million by the end of 2008. The cost-reduction initiates include consolidating its call center and check fulfillment efforts, as well as more efficient manufacturing, supply chain, and shared services.

Although it sold its greeting card, mail-order stationery, packaging, and direct-marketing operations, Deluxe offers business cards, personalized business stationery and greeting cards, and promotional specialty products online.

The company was dethroned from the top position in its industry as a result of the 2007 merger of check printers John H. Harland and Clarke American into Harland Clarke.

One step ahead of the change, Deluxe has been shifting its focus from checks to small business services, in the face of the general decline in consumers' use of checks.

Looking to grow its small business customer roster, Deluxe purchased Massachusetts-based New England Business Service (NEBS), a provider of business forms and other products to North American small businesses, in 2004. Deluxe combined the operations of NEBS with its former Business Services operations to form its Small Business Services unit. The following year Deluxe sold PremiumWear, an apparel business that was part of the NEBS purchase, to Forsyth Holdings.

## HISTORY

Deluxe Corporation began in 1915 with the determination of William Hotchkiss, a newspaper publisher turned chicken farmer, to produce one product "better, faster, and more economically than anyone else." From his office in St. Paul, Minnesota, Hotchkiss set out to provide banks with business checks within 48 hours of receiving the order. Deluxe Check Printers made just $23 that year. However, when a new Federal Reserve Bank was established in Minneapolis, the region soon became a major national banking center.

During the 1920s Hotchkiss introduced the most successful product in Deluxe's history, a pocket-sized check called the Handy. During the Depression the company cut employee hours and pay, but not jobs.

George McSweeney, a sales manager, created the Personalized Check Program in 1939 and was named president two years later. During WWII he stabilized the company by printing ration forms for banks after persuading Washington to release Deluxe's paper supply. In the 1950s Deluxe was one of the first firms to implement the government's magnetic-ink character-recognition program.

By 1960 the company was selling its printing services to 99% of US commercial banks. Deluxe went public in 1965. The company integrated computers and advanced printing technology into production during the 1970s.

In the following decade Deluxe positioned itself to profit from the increasing automation of transactions, making acquisitions such as Chex-Systems (account verification, 1984), Colwell Systems (medical business forms, 1985), A. O. Smith Data Systems (banking software, 1986), and Current (mail-order greeting cards and checks, 1987). It established a UK base in 1992 with Stockforms Ltd. (computer forms). Deluxe closed about a fourth of its check-printing plants in 1993, the first layoffs in the firm's history.

When Gus Blanchard became president and CEO of Deluxe (the first outsider to do so) the following year, he began a major reorganization. In 1996 he initiated a plan to close more than 20 check-printing plants and eliminate 1,200 jobs (completed 1999). He pursued international business, including a joint venture to provide electronic financial services to India's banking system.

Deluxe bought Fusion Marketing Group (customized database marketing services) in 1997. The next year, through a joint venture with Fair, Isaac and Company (now Fair Isaac Corporation) and Acxiom Corp., Deluxe developed FraudFinder, a computerized system to rate a merchant's risk in accepting an individual's check or debit card. Increasing its focus on financial services, the company sold off its greeting card, specialty paper, and marketing database businesses. Also in 1998 it began offering check ordering over the Internet and via voice-recognition technology.

The company bought eFunds, which provides the retail and financial sectors with electronic transaction and payment-protection technology. Deluxe also bought the remaining stake of its venture with HCL in 1999, renaming it iDLX and merging it into eFunds. eFunds went public in mid-2000 and late that same year, Deluxe spun off the unit to focus on paper payment systems.

Also in 2000 Deluxe bought Designer Checks. The next year Deluxe began offering Disney characters on checks, the first time Disney characters have been licensed to appear on personal checks. Also in 2001, Lawrence Mosner was named chairman and CEO of the company.

In 2002 Deluxe was selected as the exclusive supplier of checks and forms for Microsoft Money and Microsoft Business Solutions.

Mosner retired as chairman and CEO late in 2005. Company president Ronald Eilers succeeded Mosner as CEO on an interim basis; director Stephen Nachtsheim was named chairman. Lee Schram took over the CEO role in 2006.

## EXECUTIVES

**Chairman:** Stephen P. Nachtsheim, age 60
**CEO:** Lee J. Schram, age 45
**SVP and CFO:** Richard S. Greene, age 42
**SVP, General Counsel, and Secretary:** Anthony C. Scarfone, age 45
**SVP and Chief Sales and Marketing Officer for Financial Institutions and Small Businesses:** Luann E. Widener, age 49
**SVP, Human Resources and Corporate Communications:** Jeff Stoner, age 43
**VP, Investor Relations and Chief Accounting Officer:** Terry D. Peterson, age 42
**VP, Sales and Marketing Direct-to-Consumer:** Lynn R. Koldenhoven, age 40
**CIO:** Mike Degeneffe, age 42
**Auditors:** PricewaterhouseCoopers LLP

## LOCATIONS

**HQ:** Deluxe Corporation
3680 Victoria St. North, Shoreview, MN 55126
**Phone:** 651-483-7111 **Fax:** 651-481-4163
**Web:** www.deluxe.com

Deluxe Corporation has operations in Canada and the US.

**2006 Sales**

| | $ mil. | % of total |
|---|---|---|
| US | 1,570.8 | 96 |
| Canada | 68.9 | 4 |
| **Total** | **1,639.7** | **100** |

## PRODUCTS/OPERATIONS

**2006 Sales**

| | $ mil. | % of total |
|---|---|---|
| Checks & related services | 1,041.9 | 64 |
| Other printed products, including forms | 285.3 | 17 |
| Accessories & promotional products | 242.0 | 15 |
| Packaging supplies & other | 70.5 | 4 |
| **Total** | **1,639.7** | **100** |

**2006 Sales**

| | % of total |
|---|---|
| Small business services | 60 |
| Financial services | 27 |
| Direct checks | 13 |
| **Total** | **100** |

**Selected Products and Services**

Small Business Services (checks, forms, and related products; sold to small offices and home offices)
Financial Services
- Account conversion support
- Check merchandising
- Checks and related products
- Customized reporting
- File management
- Fraud prevention

Direct Checks (checks and related products; sold to consumers)

## COMPETITORS

American Banknote
Cenveo
Checks In The Mail
Ennis
Harland Clarke
MDC
Northstar Computer Forms
R. R. Donnelley
Standard Register

## HISTORICAL FINANCIALS

Company Type: Public

**Income Statement** — FYE: December 31

| | REVENUE ($ mil.) | NET INCOME ($ mil.) | NET PROFIT MARGIN | EMPLOYEES |
|---|---|---|---|---|
| **12/06** | 1,640 | 101 | 6.2% | 8,396 |
| **12/05** | 1,716 | 158 | 9.2% | 8,310 |
| **12/04** | 1,567 | 198 | 12.6% | 8,610 |
| **12/03** | 1,242 | 193 | 15.5% | 5,805 |
| **12/02** | 1,284 | 214 | 16.7% | 6,195 |
| **Annual Growth** | 6.3% | (17.2%) | — | 7.9% |

**2006 Year-End Financials**

Debt ratio: —
Return on equity: —
Cash ($ mil.): 25
Current ratio: 0.30
Long-term debt ($ mil.): 577
No. of shares (mil.): 52
Dividends
Yield: 5.2%
Payout: 66.3%
Market value ($ mil.): 1,298

**Stock History** NYSE: DLX

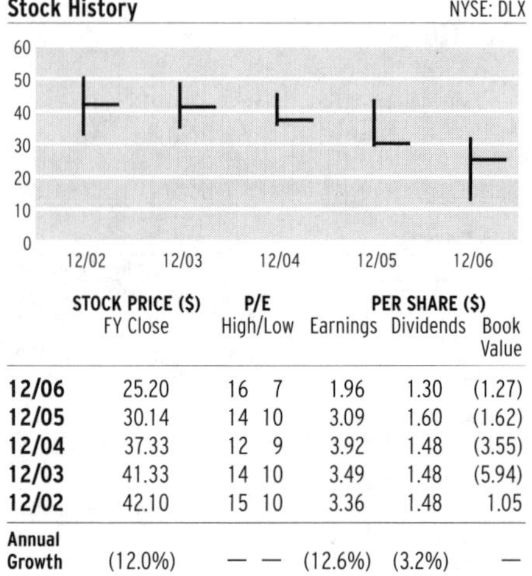


| | STOCK PRICE ($) FY Close | P/E High | P/E Low | PER SHARE ($) Earnings | Dividends | Book Value |
|---|---|---|---|---|---|---|
| **12/06** | 25.20 | 16 | 7 | 1.96 | 1.30 | (1.27) |
| **12/05** | 30.14 | 14 | 10 | 3.09 | 1.60 | (1.62) |
| **12/04** | 37.33 | 12 | 9 | 3.92 | 1.48 | (3.55) |
| **12/03** | 41.33 | 14 | 10 | 3.49 | 1.48 | (5.94) |
| **12/02** | 42.10 | 15 | 10 | 3.36 | 1.48 | 1.05 |
| **Annual Growth** | (12.0%) | — | — | (12.6%) | (3.2%) | — |

# Denny's Corporation

Feel like getting slammed for breakfast? The home of the Grand Slam Breakfast, Denny's is the leading full-service, family-style restaurant chain in the US, with about 1,550 of its signature eateries located across the country. Its family-style restaurants are typically open 24 hours a day, seven days a week, and serve breakfast, lunch, and dinner. The menu features a variety of breakfast items (which account for the majority of company sales) along with such standard fare as hamburgers, steaks, salads, and desserts. The company owns and operates about 520 of its restaurants, while the rest are franchised or operated under licensing agreements.

Denny's lives by the adage that says breakfast is the most important meal of the day: Its morning menu accounts for a majority of sales. However, the company is trying to increase its share of business coming from the lunch and dinner crowd by introducing new menu items and marketing its chain as a nighttime meal destination.

Meanwhile, the Denny's chain has been slowly contracting as the company closes underperforming units. It shuttered about 25 corporate-owned locations and lost about that number of franchised units during 2006.

In 2006 Robert Marks retired as chairman and was replaced by Debra Smithart-Ogelsby, who was formerly CFO of Chili's operator Brinker International. Marks had been elected chairman following the death of Charles Moran in 2004.

## HISTORY

Denny's traces its roots to a Lockwood, California, doughnut stand called Danny's Donuts. Opened in 1953 by serial entrepreneur Harold Butler, Danny's was an instant hit and soon began offering coffee and sandwiches along with the doughnuts. Butler changed the name of his business to Danny's Coffee Shop the next year and began expanding. By the end of the decade, Butler had 20 shops in operation. He renamed the chain Denny's in 1959. Concentrated near major highways and freeway exits, Denny's expanded rapidly to more than 80 shops in seven western states. The company went public in 1966.

Denny's pushed eastward with its expansion, reaching about 200 locations by 1968. That year the company acquired other chains such as Sandy's Restaurants and Winchell's Donut Houses. Looking to expand his business into new markets, Butler made an offer to buy Parvin-Dohrmann, the company that owned Las Vegas' landmark Caesar's Palace. The deal soured, however, after government regulators charged Butler had privately sweetened the deal to certain shareholders. Denny's stock tumbled after the scandal and Butler left the company in 1971.

Doughnut mogul Verne Winchell took over as CEO and helped rebuild Denny's fortunes. With a focused expansion plan, the company grew to more than 1,300 outlets by 1977 — about half of them were Denny's Coffee Shops and the other half were Winchell's. That year Denny's introduced its Grand Slam Breakfast. With the addition of the El Pollo Loco grilled-chicken chain in 1983, Denny's operations had expanded to more than 2,000 restaurants, including 1,200 of its signature eateries.

A group led by then president Vern Curtis took the company private for $750 million in 1985. The deal left Denny's saddled with hefty debt, however, and in 1987 the company spun off a 58% stake in its Winchell's business to the public to help raise cash. Later that year, however, Denny's was acquired by TW Services for $830 million in cash and assumed debt.

TW Services owned the hodgepodge of businesses left after Trans World Corporation had spun off its airline, TWA, in 1984. (TWA was later acquired by American Airlines parent AMR Corporation.) Its operations included the Hardee's and Quincy's Family Steakhouse chains, Canteen food and vending business, and American Medical Services. Corporate raider Coniston Partners bought TW Services for $1.7 billion in 1989 and immediately sold off the rest of Winchell's. The medical business was sold the next year. In 1992 Kohlberg Kravis Roberts bought a 47% stake in the remaining food services operations, which began doing business as Flagstar Companies the next year.

Flagstar's history got off to a rough start when patrons who claimed they were denied service because of race filed several lawsuits against its Denny's chain. Most notable was a suit filed by six African-American US Secret Service agents in Maryland. Denny's settled the suits for $54 million in 1994, one of the largest class-action settlements for a hospitality company.

In 1995 chairman and CEO Jerome Richardson stepped down from his executive position to devote more time to his new expansion football franchise, the Carolina Panthers. The company named former Burger King chief James Adamson as the new CEO. (Adamson also became chairman just four months later; in 1996 the NAACP named him Chief Executive of the Year.) That year Flagstar began unraveling other holdings left from its TW Services heritage, including stadium concessionaire Volume Services (now Centerplate). It later bought the Coco's, Jojo's, and Carrows chains from Family Restaurants in 1996.

Soft sales and continued losses, however, forced the company to file for Chapter 11 bankruptcy protection in 1997. It emerged from bankruptcy the next year with a new name, Advantica Restaurant Group. That year the company sold its nearly 600 Hardee's fast-food units to CKE Restaurants, the Hardee's franchiser, and its Quincy's chain to Buckley Acquisition. Following successful efforts to make the company more racially sensitive, Advantica ran a series of ads in 1999 to polish its public image.

In 2000 Advantica embarked on a plan to sell its Coco's and Carrows businesses and focus its resources on the Denny's chain. It refranchised nearly 150 restaurants that year, and in early 2001 Advantica sold another 28 restaurants to franchisees and added 40 new Denny's locations. Late that year James Adamson retired; director Charles Moran was named chairman and Nelson Marchioli, the former president of El Pollo Loco, was named CEO.

In 2002 Advantica sold its FRD Acquisition subsidiary (now Catalina Restaurant Group), the unit that oversaw Coco's and Carrows, for about $32.5 million. Having shed all its other operations, the company changed its name to Denny's later that year. Moran died in 2004 and was replaced by Robert Marks. The following year Denny's closed several underperforming restaurants and began beefing up its franchising efforts. Debra Smithart-Ogelsby was named chairman in 2006 when Marks retired.

## EXECUTIVES

**Chairman:** Debra Smithart-Oglesby, age 52
**President, CEO, and Director:** Nelson J. Marchioli, age 58, $734,616 pay
**EVP, Growth Initiatives and CFO:** F. Mark Wolfinger, age 52, $430,192 pay
**EVP, Chief Legal Officer, and Secretary:** Rhonda J. Parish, age 50, $391,507 pay
**SVP and Acting COO:** Samuel M. (Sam) Wilensky, age 49
**SVP, Company Operations:** Janis S. Emplit Sr., age 52, $323,031 pay
**SVP, Concept Innovation:** Mark Chmiel
**VP and Assistant General Counsel; General Counsel, Denny's Inc.:** Timothy E. Flemming
**VP, Food Safety, Quality Assurance, and Brand Standards, Denny's Inc.:** Thomas M. (Mike) Starnes
**VP, Development, Denny's Inc.:** Steven (Steve) Dunn
**VP, Information Technology and CIO, Denny's Inc.:** Susan L. Mirdamadi
**VP, Planning and Analysis, Denny's Inc.:** Enrique N. Mayor-Mora
**VP, Procurement and Distribution, Denny's Inc.:** Mark C. Smith
**VP, Product Development, Denny's Inc.:** Peter D. Gibbons, age 53
**VP, Risk Management:** Michael J. Jank
**VP and Acting Chief People Officer:** Louis Laguardia
**VP, Tax:** Ross B. Nell
**VP, Controller and Chief Accounting Officer:** Jay C. Gilmore, age 38
**VP, Investor Relations and Treasurer:** S. Alex Lewis
**Director, Public Relations:** Debbie Atkins
**Chief Diversity Officer:** Rachelle (Ray) Hood
**Auditors:** KPMG LLP

## LOCATIONS

**HQ:** Denny's Corporation
203 E. Main St., Spartanburg, SC 29319
**Phone:** 864-597-8000 **Fax:** 864-597-8780
**Web:** www.dennys.com

### 2006 Locations

| | No. |
|---|---|
| US | |
| California | 401 |
| Florida | 160 |
| Texas | 152 |
| Arizona | 72 |
| Washington | 54 |
| Illinois | 52 |
| New York | 45 |
| Pennsylvania | 37 |
| Missouri | 36 |
| Ohio | 34 |
| Indiana | 33 |
| Colorado | 26 |
| Nevada | 26 |
| Maryland | 25 |
| Oregon | 23 |
| Michigan | 22 |
| Oklahoma | 22 |
| Virginia | 22 |
| New Mexico | 20 |
| Utah | 20 |
| North Carolina | 17 |
| Wisconsin | 17 |
| Minnesota | 16 |
| Georgia | 12 |
| Kentucky | 12 |
| South Carolina | 12 |
| New Jersey | 11 |
| Arkansas | 9 |
| Connecticut | 8 |
| Kansas | 8 |
| Other states | 64 |
| Canada | 51 |
| Puerto Rico | 10 |
| Guam | 2 |
| Other countries | 14 |
| **Total** | **1,545** |

## PRODUCTS/OPERATIONS

### 2006 Sales

| | $ mil. | % of total |
|---|---|---|
| Restaurants | 904.4 | 91 |
| Franchising | 89.6 | 9 |
| **Total** | **994.0** | **100** |

### 2006 Locations

| | No. |
|---|---|
| Franchised & licensed | 1,024 |
| Company-owned | 521 |
| **Total** | **1,545** |

## COMPETITORS

Applebee's
Big Boy Restaurants
Bob Evans
Brinker
Buffets Holdings
Burger King
Carlson Restaurants
CBRL Group
CKE Restaurants
Country Kitchen
Darden
Friendly Ice Cream
Huddle House
IHOP
Jack in the Box
McDonald's
Metromedia OSI Restaurant Partners
Perkins & Marie Callender's
Ruby Tuesday
Shoney's
Steak n Shake
VICORP Restaurants
Waffle House

## HISTORICAL FINANCIALS

Company Type: Public

### Income Statement

FYE: December 31

| | REVENUE ($ mil.) | NET INCOME ($ mil.) | NET PROFIT MARGIN | EMPLOYEES |
|---|---|---|---|---|
| **12/06** | 994 | 30 | 3.0% | 27,000 |
| **12/05** | 979 | (7) | — | 27,000 |
| **12/04** | 960 | (38) | — | 27,000 |
| **12/03** | 941 | (32) | — | 27,000 |
| **12/02** | 949 | 68 | 7.2% | 28,000 |
| **Annual Growth** | 1.2% | (18.3%) | — | (0.9%) |

### 2006 Year-End Financials

Debt ratio: —
Return on equity: —
Cash ($ mil.): 26
Current ratio: 0.46
Long-term debt ($ mil.): 441
No. of shares (mil.): 93
Dividends
Yield: —
Payout: —
Market value ($ mil.): 445

### Stock History

NASDAQ (CM): DENN

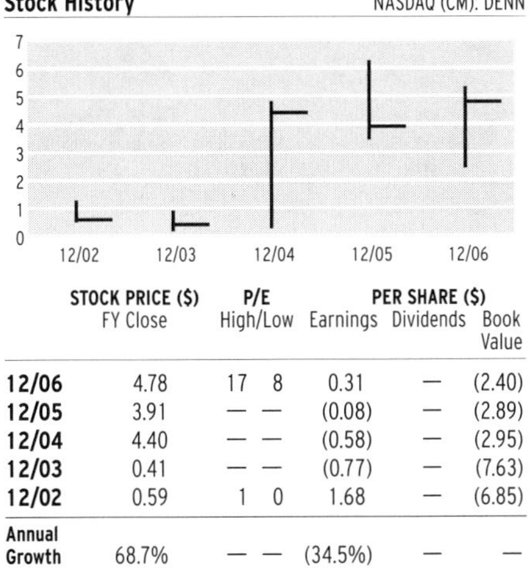


| | STOCK PRICE ($) FY Close | P/E High | P/E Low | PER SHARE ($) Earnings | PER SHARE ($) Dividends | PER SHARE ($) Book Value |
|---|---|---|---|---|---|---|
| **12/06** | 4.78 | 17 | 8 | 0.31 | — | (2.40) |
| **12/05** | 3.91 | — | — | (0.08) | — | (2.89) |
| **12/04** | 4.40 | — | — | (0.58) | — | (2.95) |
| **12/03** | 0.41 | — | — | (0.77) | — | (7.63) |
| **12/02** | 0.59 | 1 | 0 | 1.68 | — | (6.85) |
| **Annual Growth** | 68.7% | — | — | (34.5%) | — | — |

# DENTSPLY International

DENTSPLY International improves its customers' smiles. The dental equipment maker's products include dental prosthetics, crown and bridge materials, and dental implants. DENTSPLY also makes dental X-ray systems, handpieces, cutting instruments, ultrasonic scalers, and polishers, as well as other dental equipment. The company manufactures its various consumable and laboratory products under more than 100 brand names. DENTSPLY markets its goods through distributors as well as directly to dentists, dental labs, and dental schools in more than 120 countries. The company's largest customer is distributor Henry Schein, which accounts for approximately 10% of sales.

DENTSPLY grows through product innovation and acquisitions. The company's plans call for introducing approximately 30 new products each year. The company distributes more than 50% of it products through distributors and importers with a sales and technical staff of more than 2,000. It has developed a Strategic Partnership Program with 28 companies that represent more than 90% of the company's business from US distributors DENTSPLY has branched out to the Netherlands and Austria from European strongholds such as Germany, France, Italy, Switzerland, and the UK. DENTSPLY has even established itself in Russia and South Africa. The company's product in mix in various geographic regions reflects the demands of the local dental profession — highly developed markets account for greater sales related to preventive care products, cosmetic enhancements, and diagnostic and imaging equipment, while less developed markets depend on products for excavation and filling of cavities.

In mid-2006 DENTSPLY sold off its injectable anesthetic manufacturing facility in Chicago. Its supplier Pierrel S.p.A. of Italy agreed to pay $19.5 million for the facility and equipment, with $3 million settled at closing, and the balance to be paid through discounts on future products supplied by Pierrel. The company continues to have contracts with other companies to manufacture the anesthetics.

## HISTORY

DENTSPLY's roots go back to 1899 when dental business veterans Jacob Frantz, George Whiteley, Dean Osborne, and John Shepherd formed the Dentists' Supply Co. of New York. Facing a competitive market, the four bought a Pennsylvania porcelain teeth manufacturer. One of the company's first innovations was to make ceramic teeth. In 1914 Dentists' Supply introduced different-sized teeth to allow custom fitting for patients.

Between 1920 and 1950 the firm opened factories in Argentina, Australia, Brazil, Germany, Italy, Mexico, and the UK. Facing a mature denture market in the 1950s, Dentists' Supply began investing in other dental technologies. It collaborated with Dr. John Borden in the development of the Borden Airorotor, a high-speed dental drill that revolutionized dental practice. The firm changed its name to DENTSPLY in 1969.

In 1976 the company acquired its worldwide distributor, Amalgamated Dental; it purchased GE's dental X-ray division in 1983. During the 1980s and 1990s DENTSPLY opened operations in China, India, Japan, and Russia as part of its global expansion; it reorganized these operations in the late 1990s to achieve better efficiency. Moving into the information age, DENTSPLY purchased InfoSoft (dental office software). Following a protracted investigation, the Justice Department filed an antitrust suit against DENTSPLY in 1999.

In 2000 DENTSPLY decided to sell its InfoSoft LLC division. Later in the year it made plans to acquire Friadent, one of Germany's leading makers of dental implants. In 2001 the company closed that deal, and also bought AstraZeneca's dental anesthetic business.

## EXECUTIVES

**President, CEO, and Chairman:** Bret W. Wise, age 46, $477,000 pay
**SVP and CFO:** William R. Jellison, age 48, $800,000 pay
**SVP Global Human Resources:** Rachel P. McKinney, age 48
**EVP and COO:** Christopher T. (Chris) Clark, age 44, $330,000 pay
**SVP Manufacturing and Business Development:** James G. Mosch, age 48
**VP, Secretary, and General Counsel:** Brian M. Addison, age 51
**VP and Treasurer:** William E. Reardon
**VP and Corporate Controller:** Timothy S. Warady
**VP and Chief Clinical Officer:** Linda C. Niessen
**SVP:** Robert J. Size
**Auditors:** PricewaterhouseCoopers LLP

## LOCATIONS

**HQ:** DENTSPLY International Inc.
221 W. Philadelphia St., York, PA 17405
**Phone:** 717-845-7511 **Fax:** 717-849-4762
**Web:** www.dentsply.com

DENTSPLY International has manufacturing facilities in Brazil, China, France, Germany, Japan, the Netherlands, Puerto Rico, Switzerland, the UK, and the US.

| 2006 Sales | $ mil. | % of total |
|---|---|---|
| US | 687.8 | 38 |
| Europe | | |
| Germany | 399.0 | 22 |
| Switzerland | 104.2 | 6 |
| Other regions | 619.5 | 34 |
| **Total** | **1,810.5** | **100** |

## PRODUCTS/OPERATIONS

| 2006 Sales | $ mil. | % of total |
|---|---|---|
| Dental consumables | 650.0 | 36 |
| Specialty dental products | 622.2 | 34 |
| Dental laboratory products | 493.9 | 27 |
| Non-dental | 44.4 | 3 |
| **Total** | **1,810.5** | **100** |

**Selected Products**

Alloys and accessories
Anesthesia products
Bone grafting material
Burs
Cements and liners
Cosmetic dentistry
Disposables
Endodontics
Fixed prosthetics
Handpieces and accessories
Implants
Impression materials
Irrigation probes
Needles
Orthodontics
Removable prosthetics
X-ray products

## COMPETITORS

AFP Imaging
Align Technology
Astra Tech
Glidewell Laboratories
Henry Schein
National Dentex
Patterson Companies
Sirona
Sybron Dental
Young Innovations

## HISTORICAL FINANCIALS

Company Type: Public

**Income Statement** FYE: December 31

| | REVENUE ($ mil.) | NET INCOME ($ mil.) | NET PROFIT MARGIN | EMPLOYEES |
|---|---|---|---|---|
| **12/06** | 1,811 | 224 | 12.4% | 8,500 |
| **12/05** | 1,715 | 45 | 2.6% | 8,000 |
| **12/04** | 1,694 | 253 | 14.9% | 7,700 |
| **12/03** | 1,571 | 174 | 11.1% | 7,600 |
| **12/02** | 1,514 | 148 | 9.8% | 7,800 |
| **Annual Growth** | 4.6% | 10.9% | — | 2.2% |

**2006 Year-End Financials**

Debt ratio: 28.8%
Return on equity: 17.8%
Cash ($ mil.): 65
Current ratio: 2.31
Long-term debt ($ mil.): 367
No. of shares (mil.): 152
Dividends
Yield: 0.5%
Payout: 9.9%
Market value ($ mil.): 4,531

**Stock History** NASDAQ (GS): XRAY

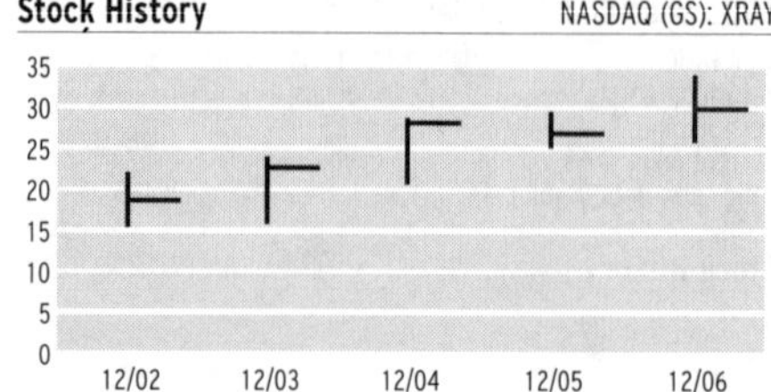


| | STOCK PRICE ($) FY Close | P/E High/Low | PER SHARE ($) Earnings | Dividends | Book Value |
|---|---|---|---|---|---|
| **12/06** | 29.85 | 24 18 | 1.41 | 0.14 | 8.39 |
| **12/05** | 26.84 | 52 45 | 0.56 | 0.13 | 15.74 |
| **12/04** | 28.10 | 18 14 | 1.54 | 0.08 | 17.92 |
| **12/03** | 22.58 | 22 15 | 1.08 | 0.10 | 14.15 |
| **12/02** | 18.60 | 24 17 | 0.93 | 0.09 | 10.66 |
| **Annual Growth** | 12.6% | — — | 11.0% | 11.7% | (5.8%) |

# Devon Energy

Independent oil and gas producer Devon Energy is buying its way into the big leagues. With acquisitions of PennzEnergy, Northstar Energy, and Santa Fe Snyder, it has become an oil and gas heavyweight. It got stouter by buying Anderson Exploration and Mitchell Energy & Development. In 2003 it acquired Ocean Energy for $3.5 billion and merged it with Devon Newco. Devon has proved reserves of 708 million barrels of oil, 8.3 trillion cu. ft. of natural gas, and 275 million barrels of natural gas liquids. It has exploration and production assets in the Gulf of Mexico, western Canada, and in other major oil patches worldwide. In 2006 Devon acquired US-based Chief Holdings LLC for $2.2 billion.

Devon is a major producer of coalbed methane gas. Acquisitions have expanded its reach from North America to the Caspian Sea, South America, Southeast Asia, and West Africa.

In 2001 the company agreed to a major deal to supply Indonesian natural gas to Singapore. It also made an unsuccessful bid for rival Barrett Resources that was trumped by a bid from Williams Companies. Undaunted, that year Devon acquired Anderson Exploration for $3.4 billion in cash and $1.2 billion in assumed debt. It also purchased Mitchell Energy & Development for $3.1 billion in cash and stock and $400 million in assumed debt.

As part of its strategy to refocus on core operations, in 2002 the company sold its Indonesian assets to PetroChina for $262 million. By mid-2002 the company had raised about $1.2 billion through the disposition of oil properties worldwide.

In 2006 the company participated with Chevron in a major oil find in the Gulf of Mexico.

In 2007 Devon Energy announced plans to divest all of its assets in West Africa. It also agreed to sell its oil and gas business in Egypt to Dana Petroleum for $375 million.

## HISTORY

Larry Nichols (a lawyer who clerked for US Supreme Court Chief Justice Earl Warren) and his father, John, founded Devon Energy in 1969. John Nichols was a partner in predecessor company Blackwood and Nichols, an oil partnership formed in 1946.

In 1981 the company bought a small stake in the Northeast Blanco Unit of New Mexico's San Juan Basin. To raise capital, Devon formed the limited partnership Devon Resource Investors and took it public in 1985. In 1988 Devon consolidated all of its units into a single, publicly traded company.

The firm increased its stake in Northeast Blanco in 1988 and again in 1989, ending up with about 25%. By 1990 Devon had drilled more than 100 wells in the area and had proved reserves of 58 billion cu. ft. of natural gas.

During the 1990s the company launched a major expansion program using a two-pronged strategy: acquiring producing properties and drilling wells in proven fields. In 1990 it bought an 88% interest in six Texas wells; two years later Devon snapped up the US properties of Hondo Oil & Gas. After its 1994 purchase of Alta Energy, which operated in New Mexico, Oklahoma, Texas, and Wyoming, Devon had proved reserves of more than 500 billion cu. ft. of gas.

Between 1992 and 1997 the company also drilled some 840 successful wells. Buoyed by new seismic techniques that raise the odds of finding oil, Devon devoted more resources to pioneering fields in regions where it already had expertise.

Continuing its buying spree, Devon bought Kerr-McGee's onshore assets in 1997. Two years later it bought Alberta, Canada-based Northstar for $775 million, creating a company with holdings divided almost evenly between oil and gas.

Also in 1999 Devon grabbed its biggest prize when it purchased PennzEnergy of Houston in a $2.3 billion stock-and-debt deal that analysts called a bargain. PennzEnergy, spun off from Pennzoil in 1998, dates back to the Texas oil boom after WWII. In addition to new US holdings, the deal gave Devon a number of international oil and gas assets in such places as Azerbaijan, Brazil, Egypt, Qatar, and Venezuela.

On a roll, Devon in 2000 bought Santa Fe Snyder for $2.35 billion in stock and $1 billion in assumed debt. The deal increased Devon's proved reserves by nearly 400 million barrels of oil equivalent.

## EXECUTIVES

**Chairman and CEO:** J. Larry Nichols, age 64, $3,300,600 pay
**President and Director:** John Richels, age 55
**SVP, Exploration and Production:** Stephen J. Hadden, age 51, $1,325,600 pay
**SVP, Marketing and Midstream:** Darryl G. Smette, age 58, $1,300,600 pay
**SVP, Administration:** Marian J. Moon, age 56
**SVP and General Counsel:** Lyndon C. Taylor, age 48
**VP, Corporate Finance and Treasurer:** Jeffrey A. (Jeff) Agosta, age 38
**VP and CIO:** Jerome Beaudoin, age 45
**VP and Controller:** R. Alan Marcum, age 39
**VP, Accounting and Chief Accounting Officer:** Danny J. Heatly, age 50
**VP, Communications and Investor Relations:** Vincent W. White, age 48

**VP, Human Resources:** Paul R. Poley, age 53
**VP, Planning and Evaluation:** Terry L. Shyer, age 38
**VP, Tax:** Gina E. Sewell, age 44
**VP and General Manager, Exploration:** William A. (Bill) Van Wie, age 60
**VP and General Manager, Marketing and Midstream Division:** Terrence L. Ruder, age 53
**Corporate Secretary and Manager, Corporate Governance:** Janice A. Dobbs, age 58
**Manager, Investor Relations:** Zack Hager
**Manager, Public Affairs:** Brian Engel
**Auditors:** KPMG LLP

## LOCATIONS

**HQ:** Devon Energy Corporation
20 N. Broadway, Oklahoma City, OK 73102
**Phone:** 405-235-3611 **Fax:** 405-552-4550
**Web:** www.devonenergy.com

Devon Energy has major operations in Central Asia, Southeast Asia, North and South America, and West Africa.

**2006 Sales**

| | $ mil. | % of total |
|---|---|---|
| US | 6,852 | 65 |
| Canada | 2,291 | 22 |
| Other countries | 1,435 | 13 |
| **Total** | **10,578** | **100** |

## PRODUCTS/OPERATIONS

**2006 Sales**

| | $ mil. | % of total |
|---|---|---|
| Gas | 4,932 | 47 |
| Oil | 3,205 | 30 |
| Marketing & midstream | 1,692 | 16 |
| Natural gas liquids | 749 | 7 |
| **Total** | **10,578** | **100** |

## COMPETITORS

Abraxas Petroleum
Apache
BHP Billiton
BP
Cabot Oil & Gas
Chesapeake Energy
Chevron
ConocoPhillips
EnCana
Exxon Mobil
Forest Oil
Hess
Imperial Oil
JKX
Marathon Oil
Occidental Petroleum
PDVSA
PETROBRAS
Royal Dutch Shell
Swift Energy
TOTAL
TXCO Resources
Williams Companies
XTO Energy

## HISTORICAL FINANCIALS

Company Type: Public

**Income Statement** FYE: December 31

| | REVENUE ($ mil.) | NET INCOME ($ mil.) | NET PROFIT MARGIN | EMPLOYEES |
|---|---|---|---|---|
| **12/06** | 10,578 | 2,846 | 26.9% | 4,600 |
| **12/05** | 10,741 | 2,930 | 27.3% | 4,075 |
| **12/04** | 9,189 | 2,186 | 23.8% | 3,900 |
| **12/03** | 7,352 | 1,747 | 23.8% | 3,924 |
| **12/02** | 4,316 | 104 | 2.4% | 3,436 |
| **Annual Growth** | 25.1% | 128.7% | — | 7.6% |

**2006 Year-End Financials**

Debt ratio: 33.7%
Return on equity: 17.6%
Cash ($ mil.): 1,313
Current ratio: 0.69
Long-term debt ($ mil.): 5,870
No. of shares (mil.): 444
Dividends
Yield: 0.7%
Payout: 7.1%
Market value ($ mil.): 29,785

**Stock History** NYSE: DVN

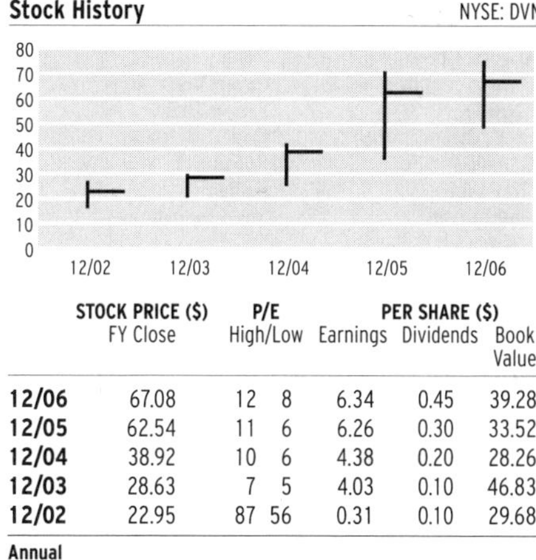

| | STOCK PRICE ($) FY Close | P/E High | P/E Low | PER SHARE ($) Earnings | Dividends | Book Value |
|---|---|---|---|---|---|---|
| **12/06** | 67.08 | 12 | 8 | 6.34 | 0.45 | 39.28 |
| **12/05** | 62.54 | 11 | 6 | 6.26 | 0.30 | 33.52 |
| **12/04** | 38.92 | 10 | 6 | 4.38 | 0.20 | 28.26 |
| **12/03** | 28.63 | 7 | 5 | 4.03 | 0.10 | 46.83 |
| **12/02** | 22.95 | 87 | 56 | 0.31 | 0.10 | 29.68 |
| **Annual Growth** | 30.8% | — | — | 112.7% | 45.6% | 7.3% |

# Diamond Offshore Drilling

This Diamond is an oiler's best friend. Diamond Offshore Drilling is a contract offshore oil and gas driller capable of descending the deep blue to depths of 7,500 feet. A leading US drilling contractor, Diamond Offshore has 30 semisubmersibles, 13 jack-up rigs (mobile drilling platforms), and one drillship. Operating in waters off six of the world's continents, Diamond Offshore contracts with major oil and gas companies, including Anadarko Petroleum and PETROBRAS. Anadarko Petroleum accounted for 10.6% of Diamond Offshore's revenues in 2006; PETROBRAS, 10.4%. Subsidiary Diamond Offshore Team Solutions provides project management and other drilling-related services. Loews Corp. owns about 51% of the company.

Although the majority of Diamond Offshore's vessels operate in the waters of the Gulf of Mexico, the company does have vessels operating in the North Sea and off the coasts of Africa, Australia, Brazil, Indonesia, New Zealand, Singapore, and Vietnam.

As oil majors increasingly pursue deepwater projects, Diamond Offshore is refitting its rigs for deepwater work and is installing advanced drilling systems. Diamond Offshore also plans to increase its fleet size by acquiring additional assets during oil and gas industry downturns. The company has purchased two additional semisubmersible drilling rigs and plans to buy more.

Diversified holding company Loews Corporation (CNA Financial Corp., insurance; Bulova Corporation, watches; Lorillard, tobacco) spun off Diamond Offshore in 1995. Diamond Offshore chairman James Tisch, son of Loews co-chairman Larry Tisch, is also president and CEO of Loews.

## HISTORY

Loews, a New York City-based holding company owned by billionaire brothers Larry and Bob Tisch, paid $48.5 million for offshore drilling rig operator Diamond M in 1989 during the depths of a major oil bust (the bust lasted from the mid-1980s through the mid-1990s). Few oil rigs were operating, and most of those were earning day rates of less than $30,000.

Diamond M was a Houston-based drilling firm that dated to the 1960s. Texas oilman and rancher Don McMahon had formed the company from several oil rigs in default when an oil bust was mirrored by a banking crisis. McMahon named the firm after his Houston area ranch, the Diamond M. (The logo used by Diamond M, and later Diamond Offshore, was styled after the ranch's brand.) At one point Diamond M was the world's largest barge drilling company, although it no longer operates drilling barges.

Kaneb Services, a Richardson, Texas-based oil pipeline and energy services company, bought Diamond M in 1978. After oil prices dropped and drilling activity slowed in the 1980s, Kaneb sold Diamond M to the Tisches, who through Loews have developed a reputation for buying companies in underperforming industries and waiting for an up cycle. Former Kaneb Services EVP Robert Rose headed Loews' new subsidiary.

With rig prices still low, Diamond M bought Odeco Drilling from Murphy Oil for $377 million in 1992. It was the first major consolidation in the offshore drilling industry; many more have followed. The Odeco acquisition gave Diamond M added deepwater capabilities and enough rigs to enter the international offshore drilling market.

In 1993 Loews' drilling interests were combined into a company named Diamond Offshore Drilling. When Loews spun Diamond Offshore off in 1995, it was operating 37 offshore rigs and 10 land rigs, all in South Texas. Also that year PETROBRAS contracted for several additional rigs off Brazil.

Diamond Offshore acquired deepwater rival Arethusa (Off-Shore) Limited in 1996 to add 11 oil rigs to its fleet. That year the company sold its land-based drilling operations in South Texas, Diamond M Onshore Inc., to DI Industries. By late 1996 day rates for deepwater rigs had rebounded to as high as $140,000. In 1997 Diamond Offshore acquired *Polyconfidence*, a semisubmersible accommodation vessel, and began converting it to an ultra-deepwater rig.

In 1998 Lawrence Dickerson, former SVP and CFO and a veteran of Diamond M, replaced Robert Rose as president; chairman James Tisch took over Rose's CEO duties. Also that year BP Amoco (now BP), citing equipment problems, canceled a Gulf of Mexico drill rig project. Undeterred, Diamond Offshore won a three-year contract in 1999 for its *Ocean Clipper* drillship (idled by the collapse of the BP Amoco deal) to provide deepwater drilling services offshore Brazil.

The next year Diamond Offshore sold one of its older jack-up drilling rigs. It also won a three-year contract from PETROBRAS for the use of one of its most modern semisubmersibles, the *Ocean Alliance*.

Lower operating day-rate contracts and underutilization of semisubmersibles led the company to post lower revenues in 2000. However, early in 2001, buoyed by higher oil prices and increased exploration activity, the company reported much stronger sales for its semisubmersible unit.

## EXECUTIVES

**Chairman and CEO:** James S. Tisch, age 54, $300,000 pay
**President, COO, and Director:** Lawrence R. Dickerson, age 54, $941,996 pay
**SVP Contracts and Marketing:** John L. Gabriel Jr., age 53, $522,941 pay
**SVP Technical Services:** John M. Vecchio, age 56
**SVP and CFO:** Gary T. Krenek, age 48
**SVP, General Counsel, and Secretary:** William C. Long, age 40
**SVP Administration:** Mark F. Baudoin, age 54
**VP Human Resources:** R. Lynn Charles
**VP Domestic Operations:** Steven A. Nelson
**SVP Worldwide Operations:** Lyndol I. Dew, age 52
**VP Tax:** Stephen G. Elwood
**VP Domestic Operations:** Morrison R. Plaisance
**VP Operations, Management Systems, and Marine Department:** Glen E. Merrifield
**VP Contracts and Marketing International:** C. Duncan Weir
**VP Contracts and Marketing, North and South America:** Robert G. Blair
**VP Engineering:** Karl S. Sellers
**VP Marketing:** Bodley P. Thornton
**Treasurer:** Lester L. Thomas
**Controller and Chief Accounting Officer:** Beth G. Gordon, age 50
**Director Investor Relations:** Lester F. (Les) Van Dyke
**Auditors:** Deloitte & Touche LLP

## LOCATIONS

**HQ:** Diamond Offshore Drilling, Inc.
15415 Katy Fwy., Houston, TX 77094
**Phone:** 281-492-5300 **Fax:** 281-492-5316
**Web:** www.diamondoffshore.com

Diamond Offshore Drilling operates drilling rigs in waters off six continents. In addition to its Houston headquarters, the company has regional offices in Louisiana, and in Africa, Australia, Brazil, Indonesia, Singapore, and Trinidad and Tobago.

### 2006 Sales

| | $ mil. | % of total |
|---|---|---|
| North America | | |
| US | 1,179.7 | 57 |
| Mexico | 96.5 | 5 |
| Australia & Southeast Asia | 323.0 | 16 |
| Europe & Africa | 250.1 | 12 |
| South America | 203.3 | 10 |
| **Total** | **2,052.6** | **100** |

## PRODUCTS/OPERATIONS

### 2006 Sales

| | $ mil. | % of total |
|---|---|---|
| Contract drilling | 1,987.1 | 97 |
| Other | 65.5 | 3 |
| **Total** | **2,052.6** | **100** |

### 2006 Sales

| | $ mil. | % of total |
|---|---|---|
| Semisubmersibles | | |
| Intermediate semisubmersibles | 785.0 | 38 |
| High-specification floaters | 766.9 | 38 |
| Jack-ups | 435.2 | 21 |
| Other | 65.5 | 3 |
| **Total** | **2,052.6** | **100** |

### Services

Contract offshore drilling
Drilling services (Diamond Offshore Team Solutions, Inc.)
- Drilling and completion operations
- Extended well tests
- Project management

## COMPETITORS

Atwood Oceanics
Dolphin Drilling
ENSCO
Fred. Olsen Energy
GlobalSantaFe
Grey Wolf
Halliburton
Helmerich & Payne
J. Ray McDermott
Nabors Industries
Noble
Ocean Rig
Parker Drilling
Pride International
Rowan
Saipem
Siem Industries
TODCO
Transocean
Weatherford International

## HISTORICAL FINANCIALS

Company Type: Public

### Income Statement

FYE: December 31

| | REVENUE ($ mil.) | NET INCOME ($ mil.) | NET PROFIT MARGIN | EMPLOYEES |
|---|---|---|---|---|
| **12/06** | 2,053 | 707 | 34.4% | 4,800 |
| **12/05** | 1,221 | 260 | 21.3% | 4,500 |
| **12/04** | 815 | (7) | — | 4,200 |
| **12/03** | 681 | (48) | — | 3,740 |
| **12/02** | 753 | 63 | 8.3% | 3,766 |
| **Annual Growth** | 28.5% | 83.4% | — | 6.3% |

### 2006 Year-End Financials

Debt ratio: 41.6%
Return on equity: 33.9%
Cash ($ mil.): 826
Current ratio: 4.44
Long-term debt ($ mil.): 964
No. of shares (mil.): 129
Dividends
Yield: 2.5%
Payout: 39.1%
Market value ($ mil.): 10,330

### Stock History

NYSE: DO

| | STOCK PRICE ($) FY Close | P/E High | P/E Low | PER SHARE ($) Earnings | Dividends | Book Value |
|---|---|---|---|---|---|---|
| **12/06** | 79.94 | 19 | 12 | 5.12 | 2.00 | 17.95 |
| **12/05** | 69.56 | 38 | 20 | 1.91 | 0.38 | 14.38 |
| **12/04** | 40.05 | — | — | (0.06) | 0.25 | 12.65 |
| **12/03** | 20.51 | — | — | (0.37) | 0.44 | 12.99 |
| **12/02** | 21.85 | 74 | 37 | 0.47 | 0.50 | 13.87 |
| **Annual Growth** | 38.3% | — | — | 81.7% | 41.4% | 6.7% |

# Diebold, Incorporated

Cash is king at Diebold. The company is one of the US's leading producers of automated teller machines (ATMs). In addition, Diebold offers automated or staffed banking facilities, such as its MicroBranch prefabricated branch offices, which can be installed in grocery stores and malls. Originally a manufacturer of safes, the company is still active in its original market, offering products ranging from vaults to security systems for financial institutions. Diebold also provides services ranging from product maintenance to installation consulting and plan design.

Diebold bolstered its maintenance and support operations when it acquired TFE Technology Holdings in 2004. That purchase was followed by the acquisition of security systems service provider Antar-Com, and in 2005 Diebold acquired another security systems integrator, TASC Security. Diebold sold its campus card systems business to CBORD Group for approximately $38 million in mid-2005. Early in 2006 the company purchased Genpass Service Solutions (GSS), a subsidiary of an ATM service and maintenance company owned by U.S. Bank. It augmented its Diebold Global Security division with the purchase of Actcom in mid-2006; Actcom provides security systems to government agencies, including the US Department of Defense.

Diebold's 2002 acquisition of Global Election Systems (now Diebold Election Systems Inc., or DESI) netted the company electronic-voting terminals. DESI made headlines in 2004 when four counties in California banned the use of its terminals after a state advisory board raised concerns about security and reliability. DESI responded to the judgment with a statement reaffirming its commitment to election systems development and support. Diebold later agreed to settle a civil action lawsuit brought by the state of California for $2.6 million; the suit accused the company of making false claims about the security and certification of its voting machines. Election systems account for less than 10% of Diebold's sales.

The company generates half of its revenues from maintenance and other services.

## HISTORY

German immigrant Charles Diebold formed safe and vault maker Diebold Bahmann in Cincinnati in 1859. The Chicago Fire of 1871 gave the company an unexpected boost: All 878 of its safes in the area (and their contents) survived the inferno. The company relocated in 1872 to North Canton, Ohio, where it was incorporated in 1876. During the next two decades, it also made jails, trapdoors for gallows, and padded cells for asylums. In the 1930s Diebold helped develop a bank-lobby tear gas system, made in part to deter the notorious John Dillinger.

Compelled to diversify after the Great Depression, Diebold made seven major acquisitions between 1936 and 1947, including bank and office equipment firms and other safe makers. WWII government arms contracts helped boost the company's sales from about $3 million per year to $40 million in 1942. Two years later former Prohibition G-man Eliot Ness (immortalized on television and in films in *The Untouchables*) joined Diebold's board, later becoming chairman and overseeing the 1946 takeover of York Safe, which had been the largest US safe maker before the war.

The 1947 acquisition of O.B. McClintock Co.'s bank equipment division moved Diebold into the drive-through teller-window business. Sales of the specialty windows and other bank equipment were stimulated by suburban growth in the 1950s. By 1957 business equipment represented about half of Diebold's sales.

Increased check use in the early 1960s led Diebold to enter check imprinting with the 1963 purchase of Consolidated Business Systems (business forms, magnetic imprinting ink for checks). Diebold went public the next year.

With security-equipment sales slowing in the early 1970s, CEO Raymond Koontz gambled on ATMs, investing heavily in R&D. In 1973 Diebold introduced its first ATM. Sales were helped by long-standing relationships with banks, and within five years Diebold had 45% of the US ATM market.

In 1990 Diebold formed InterBold, a joint venture with former rival IBM, to sell ATMs. Diebold acquired Griffin Technology, moving into the market for campus systems, in 1995. The company expanded its Asian presence in 1997 when it acquired Safetell International Security. The next year, after InterBold canceled its agreement with IBM, Diebold bought IBM's 30% interest in the venture, taking direct control over its global distribution. The InterBold purchase and heavy competition in the ATM market caused a decline in sales and earnings for 1998.

Diebold's 1999 acquisitions included Pioneer Systems, a developer of a campus ID-card system that provides links to financial institutions as well as off-campus merchants, and Procomp Amazônia Indústria Electrónica, a Brazil-based information technology company. Later that year Emerson Electric executive Walden O'Dell became CEO. Also in 1999, in a pilot program Bank United (which later became part of Washington Mutual) installed iris-based recognition technology (developed by Diebold) at three ATMs.

In 2000 the company furthered its global push by acquiring the financial self-service businesses of Amsterdam-based Getronics NV and Paris-based Bull for a combined $160 million. The following year it sold its MedSelect business, which offered systems for storing, dispensing, and tracking patient medications.

Early in 2002 Diebold acquired voting-systems maker Global Election Systems and renamed the new subsidiary Diebold Election Systems. O'Dell resigned as chairman and CEO in 2005; president Thomas Swidarski replaced him as CEO, and director John Lauer was named chairman.

## EXECUTIVES

**Chairman:** John N. Lauer, age 68
**President, CEO, and Director:** Thomas W. Swidarski, age 48, $550,000 pay
**EVP and CFO:** Kevin J. Krakora, age 51, $320,000 pay
**SVP, Customer Solutions Group:** David Bucci, age 55, $302,940 pay
**SVP, Global Security Division:** Dennis M. Moriarty, age 54, $250,000 pay
**SVP, Europe, Middle East, and Africa and Asia/Pacific Divisions:** James L. M. Chen, age 46
**SVP, Global Development and Service:** Charles E. (Chuck) Ducey, age 51
**SVP, Global Manufacturing and Supply Chain:** George S. Mayes Jr., age 48
**VP and Chief Human Resources Officer:** Sheila M. Rutt, age 38
**VP, Latin America Division; President, Diebold Procomp:** Joao Abud Jr., age 51
**VP and Managing Director, Latin America:** Miguel (Mike) Mateo
**VP, General Counsel, and Secretary:** Warren W. Dettinger, age 53
**VP and CIO:** John M. Crowther, age 50
**VP, Business Transformation:** Jim Petit
**VP, Information Technology:** Sean Forrester
**VP, Physical Security Group:** Brad Stephenson
**VP, Corporate Development:** William E. Rosenberg, age 56
**VP and Chief Communications Officer:** John D. Kristoff, age 39
**VP and Chief Tax Officer:** M. Scott Hunter, age 45
**VP and Corporate Controller:** Leslie A. Pierce
**Director Investor Relations:** Christopher Bast
**Auditors:** KPMG LLP

## LOCATIONS

**HQ:** Diebold, Incorporated
5995 Mayfair Rd., North Canton, OH 44720
**Phone:** 330-490-4000 **Fax:** 330-490-3794
**Web:** www.diebold.com

### 2006 Sales

| | $ mil. | % of total |
|---|---|---|
| Americas | 2,158.1 | 74 |
| Europe, Middle East & Africa | 458.3 | 16 |
| Asia/Pacific | 289.8 | 10 |
| **Total** | **2,906.2** | **100** |

## PRODUCTS/OPERATIONS

### 2006 Sales

| | $ mil. | % of total |
|---|---|---|
| Financial self-service | | |
| Products | 957.7 | 33 |
| Services | 941.5 | 32 |
| Security | | |
| Services | 446.9 | 16 |
| Products | 328.3 | 11 |
| Election systems/lottery | 231.8 | 8 |
| **Total** | **2,906.2** | **100** |

### Selected Products

Self-service
- Automated commercial banking systems (Merchant Banking Center)
- Automated teller machines (ATMs)
- Bill payment terminals (PayStation)
- Cash-dispensing systems (Express Delivery XT Systems)

Security
- Alarm and monitoring systems
- Bullet-resistive barriers
- Drive-up banking equipment
- Drive-up pharmacy equipment
- Modular counter equipment
- Prefabricated walls (MicroBranch Wall Systems)
- Remote bank teller kiosks (RemoteTeller System)
- Vaults, safe deposit boxes, locks, and safes

Other products
- Card-based systems
- Management software
- Voting terminals

## COMPETITORS

ACI Worldwide, Inc.
ADT Security
Advanced Voting Solutions
De La Rue
Election Systems & Software
Frisco Bay
Fujitsu
Hart InterCivic
Itautec Philco
NCR
Oki Electric
Secure Alliance Holdings
Sequoia Voting
Siemens AG
Thales e-Transactions
Tranax Technologies
Triton
Wincor Nixdorf

## HISTORICAL FINANCIALS

Company Type: Public

### Income Statement

FYE: December 31

| | REVENUE ($ mil.) | NET INCOME ($ mil.) | NET PROFIT MARGIN | EMPLOYEES |
|---|---|---|---|---|
| **12/06** | 2,906 | 87 | 3.0% | 15,451 |
| **12/05** | 2,587 | 97 | 3.7% | 14,603 |
| **12/04** | 2,381 | 184 | 7.7% | 14,376 |
| **12/03** | 2,110 | 175 | 8.3% | 13,401 |
| **12/02** | 1,940 | 99 | 5.1% | 13,072 |
| **Annual Growth** | 10.6% | (3.3%) | — | 4.3% |

### 2006 Year-End Financials

Debt ratio: 61.0%
Return on equity: 7.7%
Cash ($ mil.): 353
Current ratio: 2.67
Long-term debt ($ mil.): 665
No. of shares (mil.): 66
Dividends
Yield: 1.8%
Payout: 66.7%
Market value ($ mil.): 3,057

### Stock History

NYSE: DBD

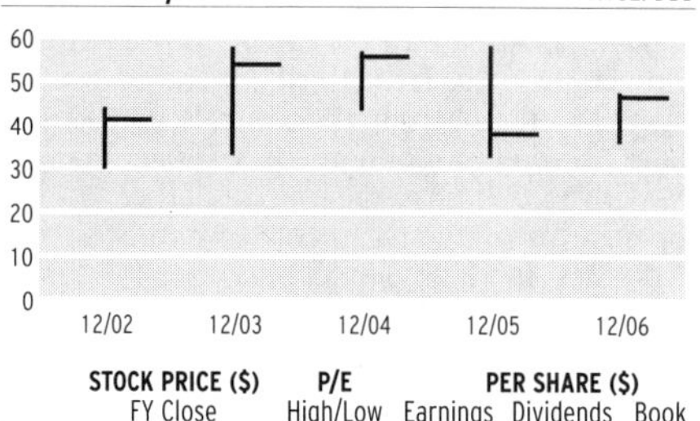


| | STOCK PRICE ($) FY Close | P/E High | P/E Low | PER SHARE ($) Earnings | PER SHARE ($) Dividends | PER SHARE ($) Book Value |
|---|---|---|---|---|---|---|
| **12/06** | 46.60 | 37 | 28 | 1.29 | 0.86 | 16.64 |
| **12/05** | 38.00 | 43 | 24 | 1.36 | 0.82 | 16.78 |
| **12/04** | 55.73 | 22 | 17 | 2.53 | 0.74 | 17.42 |
| **12/03** | 53.87 | 24 | 14 | 2.40 | 0.68 | 15.81 |
| **12/02** | 41.22 | 32 | 22 | 1.37 | 0.50 | 13.05 |
| **Annual Growth** | 3.1% | — | — | (1.5%) | 14.5% | 6.3% |

# Dillard's, Inc.

Tradition is trying to catch up with the times at Dillard's. Sandwiched between retail giant Federated Department Stores and the discount chains, such as Kohl's, Dillard's is being forced to rethink its strategy. The department store chain operates about 330 locations in nearly 30 states, covering the Sunbelt and the central US. Its stores cater to middle- and upper-middle-income women, selling name-brand and private-label merchandise with a focus on apparel and home furnishings. Women's apparel and accessories accounts for more than a third of sales. Founded in 1938 by William Dillard, today family members, through the W. D. Company, control nearly all of the company's class B voting shares.

While the company's store count has been shrinking in recent years, Dillard's plans to open nine locations this year.

Still Dillard's is closing underperforming stores — including the last of its 16 home and furniture stores — and has sold off its credit card portfolio.

One of Dillard's strategies is the dual-anchor concept: two locations in the same mall. Currently Dillard's operates about 60 dual-anchor stores. Rather than closing a store when it buys space where it already has a presence, Dillard's uses the additional store, placing women's and children's departments and home furnishings in one location and men's and juniors' departments in the other.

Dillard's prides itself on its attention to quality and its tradition as a grand old department store, but changing consumer buying habits and slumping sales are forcing the company to use new strategies, such as promoting its own private-label merchandise. In-house brands now account for about 25% of total sales in sections where private brands are sold. The company has long been averse to marking down merchandise, but competition from discount chains is forcing it to put items on sale, often at much lower prices.

Dillard's owns 241 of its 328 stores as well as six of its eight distribution centers.

## HISTORY

At age 12 William Dillard began working in his father's general store in Mineral Springs, Arkansas. After he graduated from Columbia University in 1937, the third-generation retailer spent seven months in the Sears, Roebuck manager training program in Tulsa, Oklahoma.

With $8,000 borrowed from his father, William opened his first department store in Nashville, Arkansas, in 1938. Service was one of the most important things he had to offer, he said, and he insisted on quality — he personally inspected every item and would settle for nothing but the best. William sold the store in 1948 to finance a partnership in Wooten's Department Store in Texarkana, Arkansas; he bought out Wooten and established Dillard's the next year.

Throughout the 1950s and 1960s, the company became a strong regional retailer, developing its strategy of buying well-established downtown stores in small cities; acquisitions in those years included Mayer & Schmidt (Tyler, Texas; 1956) and Joseph Pfeifer (Little Rock, Arkansas; 1963). Dillard's moved its headquarters to Little Rock after buying Pfeifer. When it went public in 1969, it had 15 stores in three states.

During the early 1960s the company began computerizing operations to streamline inventory and information management. In 1970 Dillard's added computerized cash registers, which gave management hourly sales figures.

The chain continued acquiring outlets (more than 130 over the next three decades, including stores owned by Stix, Baer & Fuller, Macy's, Joske's, and Maison Blanche). In a 1988 joint venture with Edward J. DeBartolo, Dillard's bought a 50% interest in the 12 Higbee's stores in Ohio (buying the other 50% in 1992, shortly after Higbee's bought five former Horne's stores in Ohio).

In 1991 Vendamerica (subsidiary of Vendex International and the only major nonfamily holder of the company's stock) sold its 8.9 million shares of Class A stock (25% of the class) in an underwritten public offering.

Dillard's purchase of 12 Diamond stores from Dayton Hudson in 1994 gave it a small-event ticket-sales chain in the Southwest, which it renamed Dillard's Box Office. A lawsuit filed by the FTC against Dillard's that year, claiming the company made it unreasonably difficult for its credit card holders to remove unauthorized charges from their bills, was dismissed the following year.

Dillard's continued to grow; it opened 11 new stores in 1995 and 16 more in 1996 (entering Georgia and Colorado). The next year it opened 12 new stores and acquired 20, making its way into Virginia, California, and Wyoming.

William retired in 1998 and William Dillard II took over the CEO position, while brother Alex became president. The company then paid $3.1 billion for Mercantile Stores, which operated 106 apparel and home design stores in the South and Midwest. To avoid redundancy in certain regions, Dillard's sold 26 of those stores and exchanged seven others for new Dillard's stores. The assimilation of Mercantile brought distribution problems that cut into earnings for fiscal 1999. In late 2000, with a slumping stock price and declining sales, Dillard's said it would de-emphasize its concentration on name-brand merchandise and offer deep discounts on branded items already in stock. Despite these efforts, sales and earnings continued to slide in 2001.

Founder and patriarch William Dillard (the company's guiding force) died in February 2002. Son William II became chairman of the company, which has been family-controlled for half a century. Dillard's opened four new stores and closed nine in 2002. Sales declined 3% versus the previous year.

In 2003 Dillard's shuttered 10 stores and opened five new store locations.

In November 2004 Dillard's completed the sale of Dillard National Bank, the retailer's credit card portfolio, to GE Consumer Finance for about $1.1 billion (plus debt). Dillard's had said it would use the proceeds to reduce debt, repurchase stock, and to achieve general corporate purposes.

In the spring of 2005 Dillard's shuttered the last of 16 home and furniture stores acquired when the department store chain acquired Mercantile Stores Co. in 1998. Hurricanes Katrina, Rita, and Wilma took a toll on Dillard's in 2005, interrupting business in about 60 of the company's stores at various times. At the end of 2005 three stores in Louisiana and one in Mississippi remained closed.

## EXECUTIVES

**Chairman and CEO; President, Dillard Travel:** William (Bill) Dillard II, age 62, $3,252,055 pay
**President and Director:** Alex Dillard, age 57, $3,162,055 pay
**EVP, President, Fort Worth Division, and Director:** Drue Corbusier, age 60, $1,738,234 pay
**EVP, President, Little Rock Division, and Director:** Mike Dillard, age 55, $1,778,234 pay
**SVP, CFO, and Director:** James I. Freeman, age 57, $1,778,234 pay
**VP and General Counsel:** Paul J. Schroeder Jr., age 58
**VP and CIO:** William L. (Bill) Holder Jr.
**VP, Cosmetic Merchandising:** Ann Franzke
**VP, Home Merchandising:** Richard Moore
**VP, Men's Apparel Merchandising:** Mike McNiff
**VP, Accessories and Intimate Apparel Merchandising:** William Dillard III
**VP, Product Development:** Les Chandler
**VP, Children's Apparel Merchandising:** Neil Christensen
**VP, Ladies' Apparel Merchandising:** James D. Stockman
**VP, Ladies' Apparel Merchandising:** Christine A. Ferrari
**VP, Shoes:** Joseph P. Brennan, age 61
**VP; President, Tampa Division:** Robin Sanderford, age 59
**VP; President, Phoenix Division:** Julie A. Taylor, age 54
**President, St. Louis Division:** David Terry
**Director, Investor Relations:** Julie J. Bull
**Personnel:** Molly Myers
**Auditors:** Deloitte & Touche LLP

## LOCATIONS

**HQ:** Dillard's, Inc.
1600 Cantrell Rd., Little Rock, AR 72201
**Phone:** 501-376-5200 **Fax:** 501-399-7831
**Web:** www.dillards.com

### 2007 Stores

| | No. |
|---|---|
| Texas | 59 |
| Florida | 45 |
| Ohio | 19 |
| North Carolina | 15 |
| Arizona | 14 |
| Louisiana | 14 |
| Tennessee | 14 |
| Missouri | 13 |
| Alabama | 12 |
| Georgia | 12 |
| Oklahoma | 12 |
| Colorado | 10 |
| Virginia | 10 |
| Arkansas | 9 |
| South Carolina | 8 |
| Kansas | 7 |
| Kentucky | 7 |
| New Mexico | 6 |
| Utah | 6 |
| Iowa | 5 |
| Mississippi | 5 |
| Nevada | 5 |
| Other states | 20 |
| **Total** | **327** |

## PRODUCTS/OPERATIONS

### 2007 Sales

| | % of total |
|---|---|
| Women's apparel & accessories | 36 |
| Men's apparel & accessories | 18 |
| Cosmetics | 15 |
| Shoes | 13 |
| Juniors' & children's apparel | 10 |
| Home & other | 8 |
| **Total** | **100** |

## COMPETITORS

Abercrombie & Fitch
American Eagle Outfitters
AnnTaylor
Bed Bath & Beyond
Belk
Brown Shoe
Burlington Coat Factory
Eddie Bauer Holdings
Foot Locker
Gap
J. C. Penney
J. Crew
Kohl's
Lands' End
Limited Brands
Linens 'n Things
Macy's
Men's Wearhouse
Mervyns
Neiman Marcus
Nordstrom
Saks Inc.
Sears
Stein Mart
Talbots
Target
TJX Companies
Tuesday Morning

## HISTORICAL FINANCIALS

Company Type: Public

### Income Statement

FYE: Saturday nearest January 31

| | REVENUE ($ mil.) | NET INCOME ($ mil.) | NET PROFIT MARGIN | EMPLOYEES |
|---|---|---|---|---|
| **1/07** | 7,810 | 246 | 3.1% | 51,385 |
| **1/06** | 7,708 | 122 | 1.6% | 52,056 |
| **1/05** | 7,816 | 118 | 1.5% | 53,035 |
| **1/04** | 7,864 | 9 | 0.1% | 53,598 |
| **1/03** | 8,234 | (398) | — | 55,208 |
| **Annual Growth** | (1.3%) | — | — | (1.8%) |

### 2007 Year-End Financials

Debt ratio: 45.8%
Return on equity: 10.0%
Cash ($ mil.): 194
Current ratio: 2.10
Long-term debt ($ mil.): 1,185
No. of shares (mil.): 76
Dividends
Yield: 0.5%
Payout: 5.2%
Market value ($ mil.): 2,663

**Stock History** NYSE: DDS

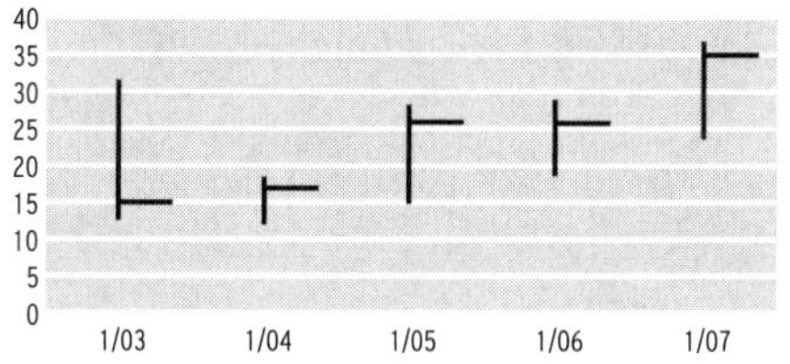

|  | STOCK PRICE ($) FY Close | P/E High | P/E Low | PER SHARE ($) Earnings | Dividends | Book Value |
|---|---|---|---|---|---|---|
| **1/07** | 34.98 | 12 | 8 | 3.05 | 0.16 | 33.98 |
| **1/06** | 25.76 | 19 | 13 | 1.49 | 0.16 | 31.09 |
| **1/05** | 25.91 | 20 | 11 | 1.41 | 0.16 | 29.35 |
| **1/04** | 16.96 | 165 | 112 | 0.11 | 0.16 | 28.15 |
| **1/03** | 15.00 | — | — | (4.67) | 0.16 | 28.04 |
| **Annual Growth** | 23.6% | — | — | — | 0.0% | 4.9% |

# The DIRECTV Group

DIRECTV takes television direct to the masses. The DIRECTV Group operates DIRECTV, the largest US direct broadcast satellite (DBS) provider, ahead of #2 EchoStar Communications' DISH Network. The DIRECTV Group provides service to more than 15 million customers in the US and about 4.1 million customers through its DIRECTV Latin America segment. To focus on the direct-to-home (DTH) satellite business, the company underwent restructuring in 2004 and 2005 and sold all other operations and investment holdings. News Corp., through its Fox Entertainment Group, owns 38% of DIRECTV but is transferring its stake to Liberty Media as part of a deal to buy News Corp. stock back from Liberty.

One of DIRECTV's distinguishing points in terms of programming (relative to cable operators and satellite rival EchoStar) is that it's the only broadcaster authorized to sell NFL Sunday Ticket, which gives subscribers access to most of the Sunday professional football games.

The company has agreements with regional local phone companies Verizon and BellSouth that allows those companies to offer DIRECTV video services in their bundle of voice and Internet communications packages. DIRECTV also has teamed up with Intel to enable remote viewing of its programming via PCs, laptops, and other electronic devices using Intel's trademarked Viiv technology. The company also has teamed up with Microsoft to allow DIRECTV's receivers to interface with PCs and Microsoft's game devices.

DIRECTV Latin America has struggled. It filed for Chapter 11 bankruptcy in early 2003, exiting in early 2004. Later in the year, the company announced plans to reorganize its Latin American operations. The reorganization is made up of various transactions between the DIRECTV Group and News Corp. in an effort to consolidate DIRECTV and Sky Latin America geographically. DIRECTV is selling its subscriber base in Mexico and acquiring operations in Brazil as well as other Latin American areas, which are to be run under the name PanAmericana.

In late 2006 News Corp. announced plans to exchange its 38% stake in DIRECTV, $550 million in cash, and three regional sports networks to Liberty Media in exchange for its 16% percent stake in News Corp.

## HISTORY

The DIRECTV Group's roots go back to 1932, when Hughes Aircraft was founded to build experimental airplanes for Howard Hughes, who set a number of world airspeed records with the company's H-1 racer. During WWII the company began building a mammoth flying boat to serve as a troop carrier, but the *Spruce Goose* wasn't completed until 1947, when Hughes piloted it for its only flight (to silence critics who claimed it couldn't fly).

After WWII the company began moving into the growing defense electronics field. In 1953 it underwent a major shake-up when about 80 of its top engineers walked out, dissatisfied with Howard Hughes, who was becoming distant and difficult. The US Air Force threatened to cancel the company's contracts because of Hughes' erratic behavior, so he transferred the company's assets to the Howard Hughes Medical Institute (with himself as its sole trustee) and hired former Bendix Aviation executive Lawrence Hyland to run the company.

Hyland rebuilt its research staff, and the institute produced the first beam of coherent laser light (1960) and placed the first communications satellite into geosynchronous orbit (1963). The Hughes-built Surveyor landed on the moon in 1966. When Hughes died in 1976, a board of trustees was created to oversee the institute.

In 1984 the Department of Defense canceled several missile contracts and the firm found it difficult to fund R&D. The next year the institute sold Hughes Aircraft to General Motors (GM) for $5.2 billion. GM teamed its Delco Electronics auto parts unit with Hughes to form GM Hughes Electronics (GMHE). GMHE acquired General Dynamics' missile business in 1992 and installed former IBM executive Michael Armstrong as CEO. He cut personnel by 25% and refocused the company on commercial electronics.

In 1995 GMHE became Hughes Electronics and launched its DIRECTV satellite service. Hughes bought a majority stake in satellite communications provider PanAmSat in 1996 (PanAmSat was acquired in 2006 by Intelsat). Armstrong left Hughes to head AT&T and was replaced by Michael Smith, whose brother John Smith was then GM's CEO. In 1998 the company boosted its stake in PanAmSat to 81% (which it offered up for sale in 2004).

To gain customers and expand its broadcast channel offerings, Hughes in 1999 bought United States Satellite Broadcasting and the satellite business of rival PRIMESTAR and folded the businesses into DIRECTV. Also that year Hughes began building its SPACEWAY broadband satellite network through its subsidiary Hughes Network Systems, which was put on the auction block in 2004. America Online (now part of Time Warner) invested $1.5 billion in Hughes.

In 2000 GM issued a tracking stock for Hughes but retained ownership of all the company's assets. That same year, GM announced that it would try to sell Hughes. Later that year Michael Smith retired abruptly, amid reports of disputes over the sale of the company. GM's Harry Pearce took over as chairman of Hughes, and Jack Shaw was named CEO.

As negotiations to sell Hughes to Rupert Murdoch's News Corp. continued in 2001, EchoStar made an unsolicited bid to buy Hughes for $30.4 billion in stock and $1.9 billion in assumed debt. After more negotiations News Corp. dropped out of the bidding and GM reached a $25.8 billion deal with EchoStar.

Despite news reports in 2002 that the Justice Department and the FCC were set to block the company's sale to EchoStar, Hughes announced that it was confident the deal would win regulatory approval by the end of the year; however, the companies terminated their merger agreement in December 2002.

Instead, GM sold its 19.8% interest in Hughes Electronics to News Corp. in 2003. News Corp. acquired another 14.2% from common stockholders, amounting to a 34% stake in Hughes Electronics, which it quickly transferred to its Fox Entertainment Group.

In 2004 Hughes Electronics changed its name to The DIRECTV Group, declaring its focus and commitment to the DIRECTV brand and DTH satellite business. The company restructured its business segments throughout 2004 and 2005 and sold all operations and investment holdings not considered core to the DTH business line including its 80% stake in satellite network operator PanAmSat, sold to a group of private equity firms (KKR, The Carlyle Group, and Providence Equity Partners) in a deal valued at $2.6 billion.

## EXECUTIVES

**Chairman:** K. Rupert Murdoch, age 76
**President, CEO, and Director:** Chase Carey, age 52, $5,034,000 pay
**EVP and CFO:** Michael W. Palkovic, age 48, $1,025,783 pay
**EVP and Chief Marketing Officer:** Paul Guyardo, age 43
**EVP and CTO:** Romulo Pontual, age 47, $1,025,783 pay
**EVP; President, New Ventures; President, DIRECTV Latin America:** Bruce B. Churchill, age 49, $1,935,434 pay
**EVP, Legal and Human Resources, General Counsel, and Secretary:** Larry D. Hunter, age 56, $1,094,225 pay
**SVP, Advertising Sales:** Bob Riordan
**SVP, Controller, Treasurer, and Chief Accounting Officer:** Patrick T. Doyle, age 51
**SVP, Sales and Distribution:** John Shelton
**SVP, Strategy and Development, DIRECTV Entertainment Group:** Derek Chang, age 38
**VP and General Auditor:** Kenneth N. Heintz
**VP, Corporate Communications:** Robert A. Marsocci
**VP, International:** Aaron McNally
**VP, Investor Relations:** Jonathan M. Rubin
**VP, Planning and Operations:** Jamie Calandruccio
**VP, Programming Acquisitions:** Daniel M. Hartman
**VP, Sports Sales and Marketing:** John O'Neill
**CIO:** Michael R. Benson, age 47
**President, DIRECTV Entertainment Group:** David Hill, age 58
**President, Sales and Services:** John Suranyi
**Auditors:** Deloitte & Touche LLP

## LOCATIONS

**HQ:** The DIRECTV Group, Inc.
2230 E. Imperial Hwy., El Segundo, CA 90245
**Phone:** 310-964-5000 **Fax:** 310-535-5225
**Web:** www.directv.com

## PRODUCTS/OPERATIONS

**2006 Sales**

|  | % of total |
|---|---|
| DIRECTV US | 93 |
| DIRECTV Latin America | 7 |
| **Total** | **100** |

## COMPETITORS

Cablevision Systems
Charter Communications
Comcast
Cox Communications
EchoStar Communications
SES AMERICOM
Time Warner Cable

## HISTORICAL FINANCIALS

Company Type: Public

### Income Statement

FYE: December 31

| | REVENUE ($ mil.) | NET INCOME ($ mil.) | NET PROFIT MARGIN | EMPLOYEES |
|---|---|---|---|---|
| **12/06** | 14,756 | 1,420 | 9.6% | 11,200 |
| **12/05** | 13,165 | 336 | 2.6% | 9,200 |
| **12/04** | 11,360 | (1,949) | — | 11,800 |
| **12/03** | 10,121 | (362) | — | 12,300 |
| **12/02** | 8,935 | (894) | — | 11,600 |
| **Annual Growth** | 13.4% | — | — | (0.9%) |

### 2006 Year-End Financials

Debt ratio: 51.5%
Return on equity: 19.4%
Cash ($ mil.): 2,669
Current ratio: 1.37
Long-term debt ($ mil.): 3,442
No. of shares (mil.): 1,226
Dividends
Yield: —
Payout: —
Market value ($ mil.): 30,589

### Stock History

NYSE: DTV

| | STOCK PRICE ($) FY Close | P/E High | P/E Low | PER SHARE ($) Earnings | Dividends | Book Value |
|---|---|---|---|---|---|---|
| **12/06** | 24.94 | 23 | 12 | 1.12 | — | 5.45 |
| **12/05** | 14.12 | 71 | 55 | 0.24 | — | 5.71 |
| **12/04** | 16.74 | — | — | (1.41) | — | 5.42 |
| **12/03** | 16.55 | — | — | (0.26) | — | 6.96 |
| **Annual Growth** | 14.6% | — | — | — | — | (98.2%) |

# Dole Food

Bananas might be Dole Food's favorite fruit because they have "a-peel," but as the world's largest producer of fresh fruits and vegetables, it grows and markets much more than the slipper-peeled fruit. The company is one of the world's leading producers of bananas and pineapples, and also markets citrus, table grapes, dried fruits, nuts, and fresh-cut flowers. Dole also offers value-added products (packaged salads, novelty canned pineapple shapes) to insulate itself from fluctuating commodity markets. It sells more than 200 products in more than 90 countries worldwide. Chairman David Murdock took the company private in 2003 and is its sole owner.

Along with being the world's largest producer of fresh fruits and vegetables, Dole is also a world-leading producer of fresh-cut flowers, offering some 500 different varieties. The company has been introducing convenience-oriented products such as bagged vegetables, ready-to-eat salads, and individual fruit servings packaged in plastic cups, as well as niche products such as organic bananas. It continues to add to its distribution channels, with a significant share of its products now available in drug and convenience stores, club stores, and mass merchandisers.

In 2006 Dole paid almost $42 million in cash to Jamaica Producers Group for the remaining 65% that it did not already own of Jamaica Producers' subsidiary, JP Fruit Distributors.

The company began test marketing the placement of vending machines in schools in 2007, offering students healthier eating options such as fresh fruit and fruit bowls. The test is being conducted in 15 schools in four US states: Arizona, Colorado, Kansas, and Texas.

## HISTORY

James Dole embarked on an unlikely career in a faraway land when he graduated from Harvard College in 1899 and sailed to Hawaii. He bought 61 acres of farmland for $4,000 in 1900 and the next year organized the Hawaiian Pineapple Company, announcing that the island's pineapples would eventually be in every US grocery store.

Others had tried and failed to sell fresh fruit to the mainland. Dole decided he would succeed by canning pineapples. He built his first cannery in 1903 and introduced a national magazine advertising campaign in 1908 designed to make consumers associate Hawaii with pineapples (then considered exotic fruits).

In 1922 Dole expanded his production by buying the island of Lanai, where he set up a pineapple plantation. He financed the purchase by selling a third interest in Hawaiian Pineapple to Waialua Agricultural Company, which was part of Castle & Cooke (C&C). Samuel Castle and Amos Cooke, missionaries to Hawaii, formed C&C in 1851 to manage their church's failing depository, which supplied outlying mission posts with staple goods. In 1858 they entered the sugar business and within 10 years served as agents for several Hawaiian sugar plantations and the ships that carried their cargoes.

C&C gained control of Hawaiian Pineapple in 1932 when it acquired an additional 21% interest in the business. The company began using the Dole name on packaging the next year. Dole became chairman of the board of the reorganized company in 1935 but pursued other business interests until he retired in 1948.

Hawaiian Pineapple was run separately until C&C bought the remainder in 1961. The company started pineapple and banana farms in the Philippines in 1963 to supply markets in East Asia. C&C began importing bananas when it purchased 55% of Standard Fruit of New Orleans in 1964. (It purchased the remainder four years later.)

Heavily in debt and limping from two hostile takeover attempts, C&C agreed in 1985 to merge with Flexi-Van, a container leasing company. The merger brought with it needed capital, Flexi-Van owner David Murdock (who became C&C's CEO), and a fleet of ships to transport produce. Murdock began trimming back, leaving C&C with its fruit and real estate operations. He then decided to end all pineapple operations on Lanai to concentrate on tourist properties. (The company took a $168 million write-off on them in 1995, when it spun off its real estate and resort operations as Castle & Cooke.)

C&C became Dole Food in 1991. The company expanded at home and internationally, adding SAMICA (dried fruits and nuts, Europe, 1992), Dromedary (dates, US, 1994), Chiquita's New Zealand produce operations (1995), and SABA Trading (60%, produce importing and distribution, Sweden, 1998; Dole acquired 100% of SABA in 2005).

In 1995 Dole sold its juice business to Seagram's Tropicana Products division, keeping its pineapple juices and licensing the Dole name to Seagram. (PepsiCo bought Tropicana in 1998.) Dole entered the fresh-flower trade in 1998 by acquiring four major growers and marketers. It is now the world's largest producer of freshly cut flowers.

A worldwide banana glut, Hurricane Mitch, and severe freezes in California hit the company hard in late 1998. The next year Dole launched cost-cutting measures, which by early 2000 had ripened into better earnings. Nonetheless, cutbacks and disposals continued throughout 2001.

In 2002 Murdock made a cash and debt takeover bid for the company worth about $2.5 billion. However, at least one minority shareholder was dissatisfied with the offer and filed a proposal calling for Murdock's resignation. The company rejected Murdock's $29.50 per share offer and negotiated with him regarding a larger price-per-share offer. In December Dole and Murdock finally signed a merger agreement. The deal, which gave stockholders $33.50 per share in cash, was approved by company stockholders in March 2003 and left Murdock in sole control of the company.

When Maui Land & Pineapple decided to sell off its Costa Rican subsidiary, Dole scooped it up in late 2003, paying $15.3 million for the pineapple-growing and marketing business. In 2004 Lawrence Kern, Dole's president and COO, left the company and chairman, CEO, and sole owner Murdock took over as president. In 2004 CFO Richard Dahl became president. Also in 2004 the company acquired frozen fruit manufacturer J.R. Wood, Inc., which it renamed Dole Packaged Frozen Foods, Inc. It also acquired fresh berry producer Coastal Berry Company (now Dole Berry Company) in 2004, making Dole a top North American strawberry producer.

## EXECUTIVES

**Chairman:** David H. Murdock, age 83
**President, CEO, and Director:** David A. DeLorenzo, age 60
**EVP, Chief of Staff, and Director:** Roberta Wieman, age 61
**EVP, Corporate Development, and Director:** Scott A. Griswold, age 53
**EVP, General Counsel, Corporate Secretary, and Director:** C. Michael Carter, age 63, $1,012,500 pay
**SVP, Manufacturing:** Danko Stambuk
**SVP, Marketing and Sales:** Brad Bartlett
**SVP, Human Resources:** Sue Hagen
**VP, Corporate Controller, and Chief Accounting Officer:** Yoon J. Hugh
**VP, Marketing, Dole Packaged Foods:** Dave Spare
**VP, Sales and Marketing, Foodservice:** Chris Lock
**VP, Worldwide Applied Research:** Thomas Farewell
**VP and CFO:** Joseph S. Tesoriero, age 53, $525,000 pay
**President, Dole Fresh Fruit:** Michael J. Cavallero, age 56
**VP and Treasurer:** Beth Potillo
**VP, Marketing and Communications:** Marty Ordman
**Auditors:** Deloitte & Touche LLP

## LOCATIONS

**HQ:** Dole Food Company, Inc.
1 Dole Dr., Westlake Village, CA 91362
**Phone:** 818-879-6600 **Fax:** 818-879-6615
**Web:** www.dole.com

### 2006 Sales

| | $ mil. | % of total |
|---|---|---|
| US | 2,752.4 | 45 |
| Euro zone countries | 1,183.1 | 19 |
| Japan | 579.1 | 9 |
| Sweden | 354.5 | 6 |
| Canada | 225.0 | 4 |
| Other regions | 1,077.4 | 17 |
| **Total** | **6,171.5** | **100** |

## PRODUCTS/OPERATIONS

### 2006 Sales

| | $ mil. | % of total |
|---|---|---|
| Fresh fruit | 3,989.5 | 65 |
| Fresh vegetables | 1,082.4 | 17 |
| Packaged foods | 938.3 | 15 |
| Fresh-cut flowers | 160.1 | 3 |
| Other | 1.2 | — |
| **Total** | **6,171.5** | **100** |

### Divisions and Selected Products

Dried fruit and nuts
- Almonds
- Dates
- Pistachios
- Prunes
- Raisins

Fresh flowers
- Alstroemeria
- Aster, Butterfly
- Aster, Matsumoto
- Campanula
- Carnations
- Chrysanthemums
- Delphiniums
- Freesia
- Gerber daisies
- Gypsophilia
- Kangaroo Paws
- Monks Hood
- Roses
- Snapdragon
- Stock
- Statice
- Sunflowers
- Tulips

Fresh fruit
- Apples
- Bananas
- Cherries
- Cranberries
- Grapefruit
- Grapes
- Kiwi
- Lemons
- Mangoes
- Melons
- Nectarines
- Oranges
- Papayas
- Pears
- Pineapples
- Raspberries
- Strawberries
- Tangelos

Fresh vegetables
- Artichokes
- Asparagus
- Broccoli
- Carrots
- Celery
- Field greens
- Green cabbage
- Iceberg lettuce
- Mushrooms
- Onions
- Plantains
- Romaine lettuce
- Snow peas
- Spinach
- Yucca root

Packaged foods
- Canned mandarin-orange segments
- Canned mixed fruits
- Canned pineapple
- Pineapple juice
- Pineapple orange banana juice
- Pineapple orange juice

Ready-to-eat foods
- Coleslaw
- Peeled mini-carrots
- Salad mixes
- Shredded lettuce

## COMPETITORS

A. Duda & Sons
Bakkavor
BBI Produce
Blue Diamond Growers
C&D Fruit and Vegetable
Calavo Growers
Chiquita Brands
Cranberries Limited
Del Monte Foods
Dixie Growers
Four Seasons Produce
Frank Capurro & Son
Fresh Del Monte Produce
Fresh Kist Produce
Frontera Produce
Fyffes
John Sanfilippo & Son
J.W. Hunt Produce
Lake Placid Groves
Mann Packing
Maui Land & Pineapple
Moonlight Packing
Nash Produce
National Grape Cooperative
Naturipe Farms
The Nunes Company
Ocean Mist Farms
Ocean Spray
O'Leary Potato
Orchard House Foods
Peace River Citrus
Performance Food
Pictsweet
Pro-Fac
Seneca Foods
Snokist Growers
Sun Growers
Sun World
Sunkist
Sunsweet Growers
Tanimura & Antle
Tropicana
UniMark Group
Worldwide Fruit

## HISTORICAL FINANCIALS

Company Type: Private

### Income Statement

FYE: Saturday nearest December 31

| | REVENUE ($ mil.) | NET INCOME ($ mil.) | NET PROFIT MARGIN | EMPLOYEES |
|---|---|---|---|---|
| **12/06** | 6,172 | 89 | 1.4% | 47,000 |
| **12/05** | 5,871 | — | — | 72,000 |
| **12/04** | 5,316 | — | — | 64,000 |
| **12/03** | 4,773 | — | — | 59,000 |
| **Annual Growth** | 8.9% | — | — | (7.3%) |

### Revenue History

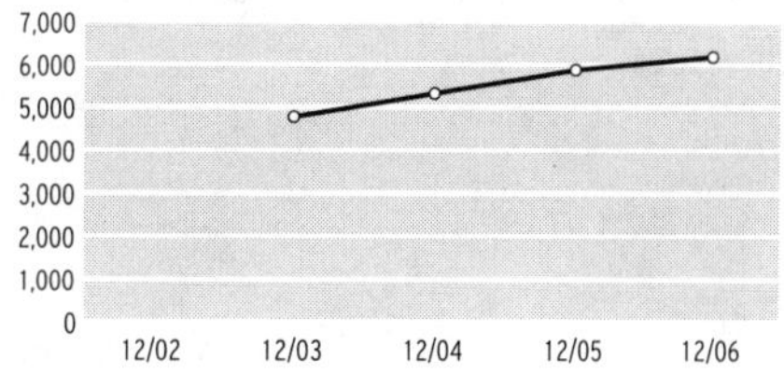


# Dominion Resources

And darkness shall have no dominion, as far as Dominion Resources is concerned. Through its Dominion Delivery unit, the company transmits and distributes electricity to 2.3 million customers and natural gas to 1.7 million customers in five states. Its Dominion Generation unit manages the company's regulated and nonregulated power plants (28,000 MW of owned or controlled capacity); subsidiary Dominion Energy trades and markets energy, oversees 7,800 miles of natural gas pipelines, and operates underground gas storage facilities (979 billion cu. ft. of capacity). In 2007 Dominion sold most of its oil and gas exploration and production assets in pieces for a total of nearly $14 billion.

Dominion has prepared for power deregulation, which is being implemented in most of its service territories, by expanding its nonregulated electric operations; however, due to poor market conditions in the power industry, it has downsized its future investment plans.

The company is divesting all of its overseas operations to focus on its businesses in the Northeast, Mid-Atlantic, and Midwest. It has sold its telecom business to private firm Elantic Networks (now a part of Cavalier Telephone); following the transaction, Dominion Telecom began operating as Elantic Networks. Dominion has also agreed to sell its district heating and cooling operations in Cleveland.

The firm has completed the acquisition of three fossil-fueled plants (2,800 MW) from USGen New England, a subsidiary of National Energy & Gas Transmission, for $656 million. Dominion had also purchased the 550-MW Kewaunee nuclear plant from WPS Resources subsidiary Wisconsin Public Service and Alliant Energy subsidiary Wisconsin Power & Light for $220 million.

At the end of 2006 Dominion Exploration & Production had proved reserves of 6.5 trillion cu. ft. of natural gas equivalent. The next year Dominion sold its offshore operations in the Gulf of Mexico to Eni for $4.75 billion; its assets in Alabama, Michigan, and Texas to Loews Corp. for $4 billion; its Mid-Continent operations to Linn Energy for $2 billion; and operations in the Rocky Mountain and Gulf Coast regions to XTO Energy for another $2.5 billion. Dominion has held onto its Appalachian operations, which control about 1 trillion cu. ft. of natural gas equivalent because they offer less risk and fit better with the company's gathering and storage systems.

## HISTORY

In 1781 the Virginia General Assembly established a group of trustees, including George Washington and James Madison, to promote navigation on the Appomattox River. The group (named the Appomattox Trustees) formed the Upper Appomattox Company in 1795 to secure its water rights. The company eventually began operating hydroelectric plants on the river, and by 1888 it had added a steam-powered plant to its portfolio.

The Virginia Railway and Power Company (VR&P), led by Frank Jay Gould, purchased the Upper Appomattox Company (which had changed its name) in 1909. The next year the firm acquired several electric and gas utilities, as well as some electric streetcar lines.

In 1925 New York engineering company Stone & Webster acquired VR&P. The company became known as Virginia Electric and Power Company (Virginia Power) and was placed under Engineers Public Service (EPS), a new holding company. Virginia Power purchased several North Carolina utilities following its acquisition.

During the 1930s the Depression (and the popularity of the automobile) led the company to exit the trolley business. The Public Utility Holding Company Act of 1935 (repealed in 2005), which ushered in an era of regulated utility monopolies, forced EPS to divest all of its operations except Virginia Power. However, the utility soon merged with the Virginia Public Service Company, thus doubling its service territory.

The company added new power plants to keep up with growing customer demand in the 1950s. Always an innovator, it also built an extra-high-voltage transmission system, the first in the world.

In the 1970s Virginia Power's first nuclear plants became operational. By 1980, however, the firm was near bankruptcy. That year William Berry, who had completed a 23-year rise through the ranks to become president, canceled two other nuclear units. He also became an early supporter of competition in the electric utility industry. In 1983 he formed Dominion Resources as a parent company for Virginia Power, and halted nearly all plant construction. Two additional subsidiaries were soon formed: Dominion Capital in 1985 and Dominion Energy in 1987.

In 1990, the year Thomas Capps took over as CEO, Dominion sold its natural gas distribution business, and in 1995 Dominion Energy began developing natural gas reserves through joint ventures and by purchasing three natural gas exploration and production companies.

In 1999 Dominion prepared for energy deregulation through reorganization. It separated its electricity generation activities from its transmission and distribution operations. In 2000 Dominion bought Consolidated Natural Gas (CNG) for $9 billion, making it one of the largest fully integrated gas and electric power companies in the US; it then sold CNG's Virginia Natural Gas to AGL Resources and the two firms' combined Latin American assets to Duke Energy.

Virginia Power moved to head off state and federal lawsuits in 2000 by agreeing to spend $1.2 billion over 12 years to reduce pollution from coal-fired plants. The company also agreed to pay $1.3 billion for Northeast Utilities' Millstone nuclear power complex that year (the deal closed in 2001). Also in 2000 Dominion changed its brand name from Dominion Resources to just Dominion and rebranded several of its subsidiaries as well.

In 2001 Dominion bought exploration and production company Louis Dreyfus Natural Gas for about $1.8 billion in cash and stock and $500 million in assumed debt; the acquisition added 1.8 trillion cu. ft. of natural gas equivalent to Dominion's proved reserves. The company also sold the assets of its financial services unit, Dominion Capital, that year.

The following year Dominion purchased a 500-MW Chicago power plant from US power producer Mirant for $182 million, and it purchased the Cove Point LNG (liquefied natural gas) import facility from The Williams Companies for $217 million.

## EXECUTIVES

**Chairman, President, and CEO:** Thomas F. Farrell II, age 52
**EVP and CFO:** Thomas N. Chewning, age 61, $1,003,200 pay
**EVP; President and CEO, Dominion E&P:** Duane C. Radtke, age 56, $926,989 pay
**EVP; President and COO, Delivery of Virginia Electric and Power Company:** Jay L. Johnson, age 60
**EVP External Affairs and Corporate Communications, DRI and CNG:** Eva S. Teig Hardy, age 62
**President and CEO, Dominion Resource Services:** Mary C. Doswell
**SVP and Treasurer; SVP and Treasurer, Virginia Electric and Power Company:** G. Scott Hetzer, age 50
**SVP Regulation:** E. Paul Hilton
**SVP Law:** James L. Sanderlin, age 65
**SVP and CIO:** Margaret E. (Lyn) McDermid
**SVP and General Counsel, DRI; VP and CNG:** James F. Stutts, age 62
**SVP Nuclear Operations and Chief Nuclear Officer, Dominion Generation:** David A. Christian, age 52
**SVP Fossil and Hydro Dominion Generation:** David Heacock
**SVP Human Resources, Dominion Resources Services:** Anne Grier
**SVP Financial Management, Dominion Generation:** Fred Wood
**CEO Dominion Energy:** Paul D. Koonce, age 46
**EVP; President and CEO, Dominion Generation:** Mark F. McGettrick, age 48
**President, Dominion Transmission:** Gary L. Sypolt, age 52
**VP and Corporate Secretary:** Patricia A. Wilkerson, age 48
**VP Budgeting, Forcasting, and Investor Relations:** Tom Wohlfarth, age 46
**Corporate Communications:** Irene Thomaidis Cimino
**Auditors:** Deloitte & Touche LLP

## LOCATIONS

**HQ:** Dominion Resources, Inc.
120 Tredegar St., Richmond, VA 23219
**Phone:** 804-819-2000 **Fax:** 804-819-2233
**Web:** www.dom.com

Dominion Resources subsidiary Dominion Delivery distributes electricity in Virginia and northeastern North Carolina and distributes natural gas in Ohio, Pennsylvania, and West Virginia. Subsidiary Dominion Generation operates power plants in Connecticut, Illinois, Indiana, Massachusetts, North Carolina, Ohio, Pennsylvania, Rhode Island, Virginia, and West Virginia. Dominion Exploration & Production operates in Canada and the US, as well as in the Gulf of Mexico.

## PRODUCTS/OPERATIONS

**2006 Sales**

| | $ mil. | % of total |
|---|---|---|
| Regulated | | |
| Electric | 5,451 | 33 |
| Gas | 1,397 | 9 |
| Nonregulated | | |
| Electric | 2,528 | 15 |
| Gas | 2,311 | 14 |
| Gas & oil production | 1,892 | 11 |
| Gas transportation & storage | 946 | 6 |
| Other | 1,957 | 12 |
| **Total** | **16,482** | **100** |

**2006 Sales**

| | $ mil. | % of total |
|---|---|---|
| Dominion Generation | 6,971 | 45 |
| Dominion Delivery | 4,226 | 27 |
| Dominion E&P | 3,026 | 19 |
| Dominion Energy | 1,369 | 9 |
| Adjustments | 890 | — |
| **Total** | **16,482** | **100** |

**Selected Subsidiaries and Business Units**

Dominion Delivery
- Consolidated Natural Gas
  - Dominion East Ohio (or The East Ohio Gas Company, gas distribution)
  - Dominion Hope (or Hope Gas, Inc., West Virginia gas distribution)
  - Dominion Peoples (or The Peoples Natural Gas Company, Pennsylvania gas distribution)
- Dominion North Carolina Power (or Virginia Electric and Power Company, electricity distribution)
- Dominion Retail, Inc. (retail energy marketing)
- Dominion Virginia Power (or Virginia Electric and Power Company, electricity distribution)

Dominion Energy (energy marketing, gas and power transmission)
- Dominion Transmission, Inc. (natural gas pipelines)

Dominion Generation Corporation (power plant management)

## COMPETITORS

AEP
Allegheny Energy
Aquila
Atlas America
CenterPoint Energy
Chevron
Columbia Gas
DPL
Duke Energy
Duquesne Light Holdings
Dynegy
Edison Mission Energy
El Paso
Entergy
E.ON U.S.
Equitable Resources
Exelon
FirstEnergy
Koch
NiSource
North Carolina Electric Membership
Northern Virginia Electric Cooperative
Pepco Energy Services
Piedmont Natural Gas
PPL
Progress Energy
PSEG Energy Holdings
RGC Resources
SCANA
UGI

## HISTORICAL FINANCIALS

Company Type: Public

**Income Statement** FYE: December 31

| | REVENUE ($ mil.) | NET INCOME ($ mil.) | NET PROFIT MARGIN | EMPLOYEES |
|---|---|---|---|---|
| **12/06** | 16,482 | 1,380 | 8.4% | 17,500 |
| **12/05** | 18,041 | 1,033 | 5.7% | 17,400 |
| **12/04** | 13,972 | 1,249 | 8.9% | 16,500 |
| **12/03** | 12,078 | 318 | 2.6% | 16,700 |
| **12/02** | 10,218 | 1,362 | 13.3% | 17,000 |
| **Annual Growth** | 12.7% | 0.3% | — | 0.7% |

**2006 Year-End Financials**

Debt ratio: 119.8%
Return on equity: 11.8%
Cash ($ mil.): 1,731
Current ratio: 0.72
Long-term debt ($ mil.): 15,472
No. of shares (mil.): 349
Dividends
Yield: 3.3%
Payout: 70.2%
Market value ($ mil.): 29,260

**Stock History** NYSE: D

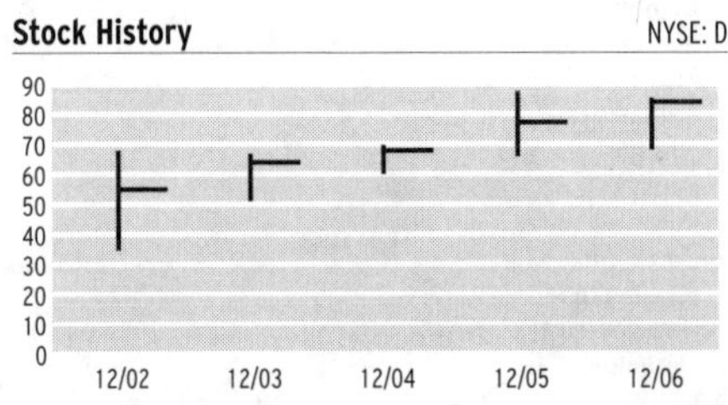

| | STOCK PRICE ($) FY Close | P/E High/Low | | PER SHARE ($) Earnings | Dividends | Book Value |
|---|---|---|---|---|---|---|
| **12/06** | 83.84 | 21 | 17 | 3.93 | 2.76 | 37.74 |
| **12/05** | 77.20 | 29 | 22 | 3.00 | 2.68 | 29.96 |
| **12/04** | 67.74 | 18 | 16 | 3.78 | 2.60 | 33.61 |
| **12/03** | 63.83 | 66 | 52 | 1.00 | 2.58 | 32.42 |
| **12/02** | 54.90 | 14 | 7 | 4.82 | 0.64 | 33.99 |
| **Annual Growth** | 11.2% | — | — | (5.0%) | 44.1% | 2.6% |

# Domino's Pizza

Domino's knows the rules of the pizza delivery game. The company is the world's #2 pizza chain (behind YUM! Brands' Pizza Hut division), with more than 8,300 locations in more than 50 countries. Domino's menu features several different styles of pizza with a wide array of topping options, as well as additional items such as bread sticks, cheese bread, and chicken wings. Its stores are principally delivery locations and generally do not have any dine-in seating. The company owns and operates about 570 locations in the US and a handful of international restaurants, while the rest are franchised. Bain Capital owns nearly 30% of the company.

While rival Pizza Hut commands the largest portion of all quick-serve pizza sales, Domino's leads the pizza delivery business with a 20% market share. Part of its success in expanding has been its focus on delivery service, meaning its restaurants tend to be smaller with less start-up and maintenance costs than other types of restaurants. Domino's continues to focus on franchising to expand its chain, with nearly 100 new units opening in the US during 2006. Its stable number of company-owned restaurants, meanwhile, account for a little more than 25% of sales.

As with any of the large fast-food chains, Domino's spends a hefty amount on advertising to maintain and increase its market share. The company's franchisees each contribute a percentage of their sales to fund both national marketing efforts and local advertising. Domino's also places a lot of emphasis on product development to steal customers away from other pizzerias. The chain introduced its Brooklyn Style Pizza in 2006.

To supply its restaurants, Domino's operates more than two dozen dough manufacturing and distribution centers, which account for more than half the company's revenue.

## HISTORY

Thomas Monaghan's early life was one of hardship. After growing up in an orphanage and numerous foster homes, Monaghan spent his young-adult life experimenting, trying everything from a Catholic seminary to a stint in the Marine Corps.

In 1960 Monaghan borrowed $500 and bought DomiNick's, a failed pizza parlor in Ypsilanti, Michigan, which he operated with the help of his brother James. In 1961 James traded his share in the restaurant to his brother for a Volkswagen Beetle, but Thomas pressed on, learning the pizza business largely by trial and error. After a brief partnership with an experienced restaurateur with whom he later had a falling out, Monaghan developed a strategy to sell only pizza and to locate stores near colleges and military bases. In 1965 the company changed its name to Domino's.

In the 1960s and 1970s, Monaghan endured setbacks that brought the company to the brink of bankruptcy. Among these were a 1968 fire that destroyed the Domino's headquarters and a 1975 lawsuit from Domino Sugar maker Amstar (now Tate & Lyle) for trademark infringement. But the company won the ensuing legal battles, and by 1978 it was operating 200 stores.

In the 1980s Domino's grew phenomenally. Between 1981 and 1983 the company doubled its number of US stores to 1,000; it went international in 1983, opening a store in Canada. The company's growth brought Monaghan a personal fortune. In 1983 he bought the Detroit Tigers baseball team and amassed one of the world's largest collections of Frank Lloyd Wright objects.

Domino's expansion continued in the mid-1980s with the help of a national advertising campaign featuring the red-suited Noid, an animated character meant to represent customers' concerns about pizza delivery ("Avoid the Noid"). With sales figures mounting, the company introduced pan pizza (its first new product) in 1989. That year Monaghan put Domino's up for sale, but his practice of linking his personal and professional finances had gotten both the founder and company into such dire fiscal straits that no one wanted to buy the chain. Monaghan installed a new management group and removed himself from day-to-day involvement.

Monaghan returned to the business in 1991 when its performance began to slide. Having experienced a religious rebirth, he sold off many of his private holdings (including his resort island and his baseball team, which went to cross-town pizza rival Michael Ilitch of Little Caesar). Monaghan also moved to reorganize management and reinvigorate the company. The next year Domino's introduced its first non-pizza menu item, bread sticks.

In 1993 a $79 million judgment was levied against the company resulting from a 1989 case in which a Domino's driver, trying to fulfill the company's 30-minute delivery guarantee, ran a red traffic light and collided with another car. The incident prompted Domino's to drop its 30-minute delivery pledge and replace it with a satisfaction guarantee.

In 1998 Monaghan announced he would retire from the business he had guided for nearly 40 years in order to to devote more time to religious pursuits. He sold 93% of his stake in the company to investment firm Bain Capital for $1 billion. (The deal left Monaghan sizable voting control in the firm, however.) David Brandon, former CEO of sales promotion company Valassis Communications, replaced Monaghan as chairman and CEO. The company also trimmed its corporate restaurant holdings by closing or selling to franchisees about 140 locations.

Further restructuring efforts in 1999 eliminated about 100 corporate positions at Domino's. The chain also introduced the first in its line of Italian Originals — specialty pizzas featuring Italian spices — and began selling pizza online through a number of franchisees.

In 2001 Domino's bought a majority stake in Dutch Pizza Beheer B.V., an operator of 52 Domino's restaurants in the Netherlands. The acquisition gave the company a base from which to manage future expansion in Europe.

Focusing in international expansion, the company added nearly 600 units between 2000 and 2003 in locations ranging from Iceland to Jamaica. The number of domestic locations grew by 275 stores during the same period.

The company went public in 2004, and soon after it used capital raised from its IPO to reduce its debt load, shrinking its $908 million debt by more than 10%. Its store growth slowed somewhat in 2004, with the addition of only about 100 domestic and about 225 international sites.

## EXECUTIVES

**Chairman and CEO:** David A. Brandon, age 54
**EVP Finance and CFO:** L. David Mounts, age 43
**EVP and CIO:** Christopher K. McGlothlin, age 42
**EVP Build the Brand and Chief Marketing Officer:** Ken C. Calwell, age 44
**EVP Communications and Investor Relations:** Lynn M. Liddle, age 50
**EVP Franchise Development:** James G. Stansik, age 51
**EVP, General Counsel, and Secretary:** Elisa D. Garcia C., age 49
**EVP International:** Michael T. Lawton, age 48
**EVP; Leader, Team USA:** J. Patrick Doyle, age 43
**EVP Franchise Operations and Supply Chain:** Michael D. Soignet, age 47
**EVP PeopleFirst:** Patricia A. (Patti) Wilmot, age 58
**VP and Corporate Controller:** Jeffrey D. Lawrence
**VP Corporate Communications:** Tim McIntyre
**VP Field Marketing:** Lori Bohlen
**Program Leader Hispanic Marketing:** Teresa Iglesias-Solomon, age 49
**Director Treasury and Tax:** Christian Dersidan
**Director Franchise Recruiting and Sales:** Mike Mettler
**Manager Public Relations:** Dana Harville
**Auditors:** PricewaterhouseCoopers LLP

## LOCATIONS

**HQ:** Domino's Pizza, Inc.
30 Frank Lloyd Wright Dr., Ann Arbor, MI 48106
**Phone:** 734-930-3030 **Fax:** 734-747-6210
**Web:** www.dominos.com

## PRODUCTS/OPERATIONS

**2006 Sales**

| | $ mil. | % of total |
|---|---|---|
| US | | |
| Distribution | 762.8 | 53 |
| Restaurants | 393.4 | 27 |
| Franchising | 157.7 | 11 |
| Other countries | 123.4 | 9 |
| **Total** | **1,437.3** | **100** |

**2006 Locations**

| | No. |
|---|---|
| US | |
| Franchised | 4,572 |
| Company-owned | 571 |
| Other countries | 3,223 |
| **Total** | **8,366** |

## COMPETITORS

Arby's
Burger King
Jack in the Box
Little Caesar's
McDonald's
Noble Roman's
Papa John's
Papa Murphys
Pizza Hut
Quiznos
Sbarro
Subway
Wendy's
YUM!

## HISTORICAL FINANCIALS

Company Type: Public

**Income Statement** FYE: Sunday nearest December 31

| | REVENUE ($ mil.) | NET INCOME ($ mil.) | NET PROFIT MARGIN | EMPLOYEES |
|---|---|---|---|---|
| **12/06** | 1,437 | 106 | 7.4% | 13,300 |
| **12/05** | 1,512 | 108 | 7.2% | 13,500 |
| **12/04** | 1,447 | 62 | 4.3% | 13,500 |
| **12/03** | 1,333 | 39 | 2.9% | — |
| **12/02** | 1,275 | 61 | 4.7% | — |
| **Annual Growth** | 3.0% | 15.1% | — | (0.7%) |

**2006 Year-End Financials**

| | |
|---|---|
| Debt ratio: — | No. of shares (mil.): 62 |
| Return on equity: — | Dividends |
| Cash ($ mil.): 38 | Yield: 1.7% |
| Current ratio: 1.07 | Payout: 29.1% |
| Long-term debt ($ mil.): 740 | Market value ($ mil.): 1,749 |

**Stock History** NYSE: DPZ

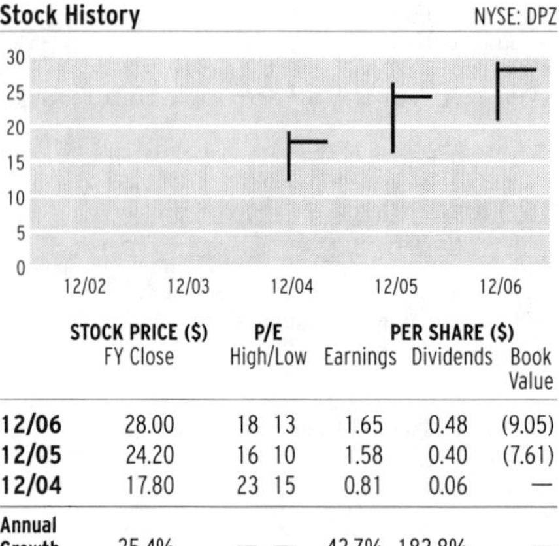


| | STOCK PRICE ($) FY Close | P/E High/Low | | PER SHARE ($) Earnings | Dividends | Book Value |
|---|---|---|---|---|---|---|
| **12/06** | 28.00 | 18 | 13 | 1.65 | 0.48 | (9.05) |
| **12/05** | 24.20 | 16 | 10 | 1.58 | 0.40 | (7.61) |
| **12/04** | 17.80 | 23 | 15 | 0.81 | 0.06 | — |
| **Annual Growth** | 25.4% | — | — | 42.7% | 182.8% | — |

# Dover Corporation

The "D" in Dover could stand for diversity. Dover manages more than 50 companies that make equipment ranging from garbage trucks to ink-jet printers. The decentralized firm's Dover Technologies makes printed circuit board assembly, ink-jet printing, and product marking equipment. Dover Industries makes transportation, food service, and waste-handling equipment. Dover Diversified turns out can-making machinery, compressors, and heat-transfer equipment. Dover Resources makes equipment for the auto, fluid-handling, and petroleum industries. Dover Electronics makes electrical and electronic components, while Dover Systems provides food refrigeration and display cases, with food and packaging equipment.

In 2006 Dover put up for sale seven businesses, including five from the Dover Technologies business. Those five are Alphasem, Hover-Davis, Universal Instruments, and Vitronics Soltec from the Circuit Assembly and Test Group and Mark Andy from the Product Identification Group. Alphasem was acquired by Kulicke & Soffa Industries, while buyout firm Francisco Partners purchased Hover-Davis, Universal Instruments, and Vitronics Soltec. Mark Andy went to a management buyout, with financial backing from Morgenthaler. The company sold Kurz-Kasch, part of Dover Electronics, to Monomoy Capital Partners, a private equity firm.

Dover has acquired Paladin Brands Holding, a manufacturer of attachments and tools for heavy and light mobile construction equipment. Paladin's products are also employed with mobile equipment used in demolition, forestry, material handling, and recycling, among other applications. Paladin Brands will operate as an independent company within Dover Resources. Dover bought the company from Norwest Equity Partners.

Overall Dover maintains a highly decentralized management culture, with a president for each division as well as for each subsidiary company. Dover Technologies and Dover Resources still are the largest segments, together accounting for nearly half of the company's sales.

Dover has maintained a long-term acquisitions and divestment strategy, participating in anywhere from about 10-20 transactions a year since 1997. The diversification means that while Dover might benefit from some changing economic tides (such as the increase in oil prices, which boosts orders for oil and gas equipment), it can be hurt concurrently by others (such as the up-and-down tech sector).

GE Asset Management owns about 6% of Dover.

## HISTORY

George Ohrstrom, a New York stockbroker, formed Dover in 1955 and took it public that year. Originally headquartered in Washington, DC, Dover consisted of four companies: C. Lee Cook (compressor seals and piston rings), Peerless (space-venting heaters), Rotary Lift (automotive lifts), and W.C. Norris (components for oil wells). In 1958 Dover made the first of many acquisitions and entered the elevator industry by buying Shepard Warner Elevator.

Dover continued to diversify throughout the 1960s. Acquisitions included OPW (gas pump nozzles) in 1961 and De-Sta-Co (industrial clamps and valves) the next year. OPW head Thomas Sutton became Dover's president in 1964 and the company moved its headquarters to New York City. Dover acquired Groen Manufacturing (food industry products) in 1967 and Ronningen-Petter (filter-strainer units) the following year.

During the 1970s Dover expanded beyond its core industries (building materials, industrial components, and equipment). In 1975 it acquired Dieterich Standard, a maker of liquid-measurement instruments. Dieterich Standard's president, Gary Roubos, became Dover's president and COO in 1977 and its CEO in 1981. The company sold Peerless in 1977 and acquired electronics assembly equipment manufacturer Universal Instruments in 1979.

Electronics became an increasingly important part of Dover's business during the 1980s. The company bought K&L Microwave, a maker of microwave filters used in satellites and cable TV equipment (1983), Dielectric Laboratories (microwave filter parts, 1985), and NURAD (microwave antennas, 1986). Between 1985 and 1990 Dover bought some 25 companies, including Weldcraft Products (welding equipment, 1985), Wolfe Frostop (salad bars, 1987), Weaver Corp. (automotive lifts, 1987), General Elevator (1988), Texas Hydraulics (1988), Security Elevator (1990), and Marathon Equipment (waste-handling equipment, 1990).

The corporation spun off its DOVatron circuit board assembly subsidiary to shareholders in 1993 after finding that DOVatron was competing with important Dover customers. That year Dover acquired The Heil Company (garbage trucks).

In 1995 it bought France-based Imaje (ink-jet printers and specialty inks) for $200 million. It was the largest purchase in the company's history at the time. In 1997 the corporation and its subsidiaries purchased 17 companies, including Vitronics Soltec (soldering equipment for circuit board assembly). The next year the company sold its Dover elevator unit — a popular brand, but a management headache — to German steel giant Thyssen (now ThyssenKrupp) for $1.1 billion.

Dover continued its acquisitive ways in 1999 and 2000, picking up 18 and 23 companies, respectively. Dover picked up Triton Systems, a maker of ATMs, in 2000. The company's prodigious acquisition rate (it completed more than 70 between 1998 and 2002) has gradually declined. Only one stand-alone company was purchased in 2002 (there were five add-ons, however) and eight were sold in 2001-02.

The Electronics segment was busy in the latter half of 2005, making a small acquisition of Colder Products (a maker of couplings for flexible tubing) and then a much larger bid for Knowles Electronics later in the year. The Knowles deal was for $750 million. It makes components for hearing aids and microphones for high-end cell phones.

Following that Dover sold Dover Diversified's Tranter, a manufacturer of heat transfer products, to the Swedish equipment maker Alfa Laval for $150 million. It marked the second disposal of a Diversified subsidiary. Early in 2005 the segment sold its Hydratight Sweeney unit to Actuant for $93 million.

## EXECUTIVES

**Chairman:** Thomas L. Reece, age 64
**President, CEO, and Director:**
Ronald L. (Ron) Hoffman, age 58, $3,300,000 pay
**VP, Finance; CFO:** Robert G. Kuhbach, age 59, $1,115,000 pay
**VP; President and CEO, Dover Technologies:**
David R. Van Loan, age 58, $1,480,000 pay
**VP; President and CEO, Dover Resources:**
David J. (Dave) Ropp, $1,450,000 pay
**VP; President and CEO, Dover Industries:**
Timothy J. (Tim) Sandker, age 58, $1,210,000 pay
**VP; President and CEO, Dover Diversified:**
William W. (Bill) Spurgeon, age 48
**VP; President and CEO, Dover Systems:**
Ralph S. Coppola
**VP; President and CEO, Dover Electronics:**
Robert A. (Bob) Livingston, age 53
**VP and Controller:** Raymond T. McKay Jr., age 53
**VP, Corporate Development:** Robert A. Tyre, age 62
**VP, General Counsel, and Secretary:** Joseph W. Schmidt, age 60
**VP, Taxation:** George Pompetzki, age 54
**Treasurer and Director of Investor Relations:**
Paul E. Goldberg, age 43
**Auditors:** PricewaterhouseCoopers LLP

## LOCATIONS

**HQ:** Dover Corporation
280 Park Ave., Fl. 34W, New York, NY 10017
**Phone:** 212-922-1640 **Fax:** 212-922-1656
**Web:** www.dovercorporation.com

Dover has more than 260 facilities in the Americas, Asia, and Europe.

**2006 Sales**

| | $ mil. | % of total |
|---|---|---|
| Americas | | |
| US | 3,716.4 | 57 |
| Other countries | 549.4 | 9 |
| Europe | 1,199.8 | 18 |
| Asia | 888.2 | 14 |
| Other regions | 157.8 | 2 |
| **Total** | **6,511.6** | **100** |

## PRODUCTS/OPERATIONS

### 2006 Sales

| | $ mil. | % of total |
|---|---|---|
| Resources | 1,841.5 | 28 |
| Technologies | 1,313.5 | 20 |
| Electronics | 880.7 | 14 |
| Industries | 876.5 | 13 |
| Systems | 834.9 | 13 |
| Diversified | 778.1 | 12 |
| Adjustments | (13.6) | — |
| **Total** | **6,511.6** | **100** |

### Selected Products

Dover Resources
- Air-operated double diaphragm pumps
- Cleaning chemical-dispensing equipment
- Factory automation and workholding devices
- Fluid transfer valves
- Gas compressors
- Gasoline nozzles and related service-station equipment
- High-pressure quartz transducers
- Liquid monitoring, valve, filtration, and control systems
- Measuring devices and connectors
- Oil and gas production equipment
- Rotary vein and progressive cavity pumps
- Winch and speed reducers

Dover Technologies
- Assembly and testing equipment
- Components for the consumer and commercial datacom and telecom communications industry (including wireless)
- Industrial marking systems
- Screen printers
- Soldering machines for the printed-circuit-board industry

Dover Electronics
- Cash-dispensing machines
- Electromechanical switches
- High-voltage ceramic capacitors
- Microwave components
- Microwave/radio-frequency filters

Dover Industries
- Auto-collision measuring and repair systems
- Automotive lifts
- Clip closures for food packaging
- Commercial refrigeration equipment
- Food service equipment
- Hydraulic cylinders
- Refuse-collecting vehicles
- Solid-waste compaction
- Touchless car-washing equipment
- Trailerized tanks
- Transporting and recycling equipment
- Welding, cutting, and laser equipment and supplies

Dover Systems
- Can-shaping and printing equipment
- Commercial refrigeration systems
- Cooking equipment and technology
- Energy distribution systems
- Refrigeration cases and systems for supermarkets
- Fire suppression systems
- Packaging equipment
- Ventilation systems

Dover Diversified
- Operator cabs for agricultural and construction machinery and electronic enclosures
- Process-industry heat exchangers
- Specialized centrifugal, oil-free screw and rotary compressors
- Specialty printing presses

## COMPETITORS

| | |
|---|---|
| Carlisle Companies | KEMET |
| Cookson Group | Mark IV |
| Cooper Industries | Oshkosh Truck |
| Crane | Sequa |
| Enodis | Snap-on |
| Gardner Denver | Thermador Groupe |
| IDEX | TurboChef |
| Ingersoll-Rand | Weatherford International |

## HISTORICAL FINANCIALS

Company Type: Public

### Income Statement

FYE: December 31

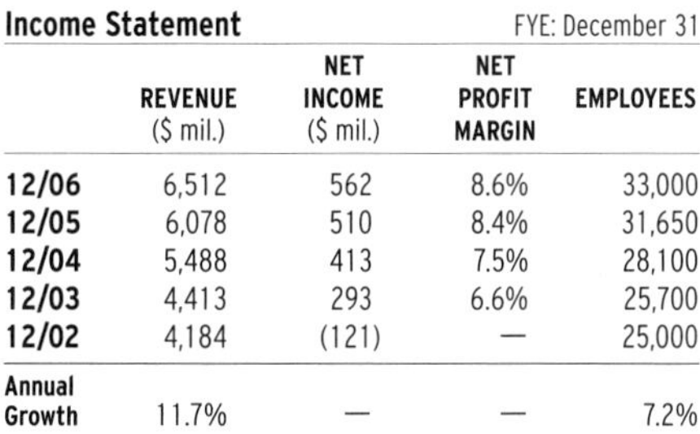

| | REVENUE ($ mil.) | NET INCOME ($ mil.) | NET PROFIT MARGIN | EMPLOYEES |
|---|---|---|---|---|
| **12/06** | 6,512 | 562 | 8.6% | 33,000 |
| **12/05** | 6,078 | 510 | 8.4% | 31,650 |
| **12/04** | 5,488 | 413 | 7.5% | 28,100 |
| **12/03** | 4,413 | 293 | 6.6% | 25,700 |
| **12/02** | 4,184 | (121) | — | 25,000 |
| **Annual Growth** | 11.7% | — | — | 7.2% |

### 2006 Year-End Financials

| | |
|---|---|
| Debt ratio: 38.8% | No. of shares (mil.): 204 |
| Return on equity: 15.7% | Dividends |
| Cash ($ mil.): 374 | Yield: 1.4% |
| Current ratio: 1.58 | Payout: 26.0% |
| Long-term debt ($ mil.): 1,480 | Market value ($ mil.): 10,016 |

### Stock History

NYSE: DOV

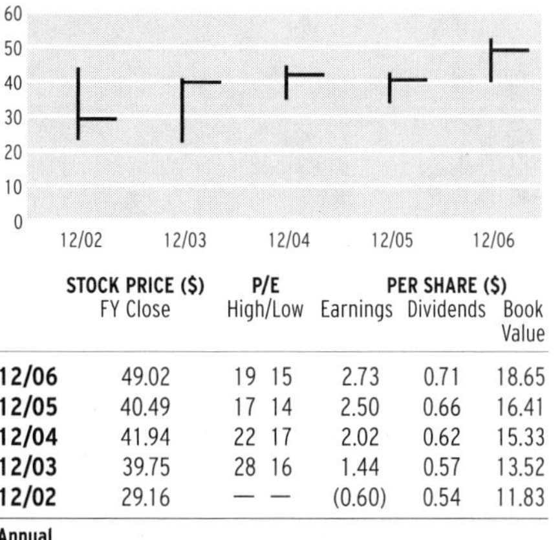


| | STOCK PRICE ($) FY Close | P/E High | P/E Low | PER SHARE ($) Earnings | Dividends | Book Value |
|---|---|---|---|---|---|---|
| **12/06** | 49.02 | 19 | 15 | 2.73 | 0.71 | 18.65 |
| **12/05** | 40.49 | 17 | 14 | 2.50 | 0.66 | 16.41 |
| **12/04** | 41.94 | 22 | 17 | 2.02 | 0.62 | 15.33 |
| **12/03** | 39.75 | 28 | 16 | 1.44 | 0.57 | 13.52 |
| **12/02** | 29.16 | — | — | (0.60) | 0.54 | 11.83 |
| **Annual Growth** | 13.9% | — | — | — | 7.1% | 12.1% |

# Dow Chemical

It's a plastic world, thanks to Dow Chemical, a leader in the production of plastics, chemicals, hydrocarbons, and agrochemicals. The largest chemical company in the US and #2 worldwide (ahead of ExxonMobil and behind BASF), Dow also is a leader in performance plastics (engineering plastics, polyurethanes, and materials for Dow Automotive). Other products include polyethylene resins for packaging (such as Styrofoam brand insulation), fibers, and films, as well as performance chemicals like acrylic acid. The company also manufactures commodity chemicals (chlor-alkalies and glycols) and agricultural chemicals. Its last unit, Hydrocarbons and Energy, makes petrochemicals. Dow makes more than 3,000 products.

Good times for performance products (both performance chemicals and performance plastics) have led the way for Dow, which will focus on growing those segments ahead of old reliables such as basic chemicals. A major move in that direction was the 2007 acquisition of Wolff Walsrode, a maker of cellulose derivatives used in construction materials and personal care products, from the Bayer Group. While the company still professes to believe in the US market for its basics, expansion in that sector will focus on Asia, and in particular China.

Dow has also been rethinking its joint ventures. In early 2005 the company agreed with DuPont to divide up their JV, DuPont Dow Elastomers. Dow took the parts of the business relating to ethylene and chlorinated elastomers and sold the remainder of the company to DuPont for $87 million. Then Dow and Cargill agreed to transfer ownership of the former Cargill Dow, and Cargill changed the name of that company to NatureWorks, after its primary product. Later in the year Dow sold its 50% interest (technically belonging to subsidiary Union Carbide) in catalysts and technology provider UOP to Honeywell for $825 million. It still, however, owns half of silicone maker Dow Corning.

In 2007 the company agreed with Chevron Phillips Chemical to combine their respective styrene businesses in the Americas into a 50-50 joint venture.

## HISTORY

Herbert Dow founded Dow Chemical in 1897 after developing a process to extract bromides and chlorides from underground brine deposits around Midland, Michigan. Its first product was chlorine bleach. Dow eventually overcame British and German monopolies on bleach, bromides, and other chemicals.

In the mid-1920s Dow rejected a takeover by DuPont. By 1930, the year of Herbert Dow's death, sales had reached $15 million. Dow started building new plants around the country in the late 1930s.

Dow research yielded new plastics in the 1940s, such as Saran Wrap, the company's initial major consumer product. In 1952 Dow built a plant in Japan (Asahi-Dow), its first subsidiary outside North America. Plastics represented 32% of sales by 1957, compared with 2% in 1940. Strong sales of plastics and silicone products propelled the company into the top ranks of US firms. Dow entered the pharmaceutical field with the 1960 purchase of Allied Labs.

Dow suffered earnings drops from 1981 to 1983 from falling chemical prices. To limit the cyclical effect of chemicals on profits, the company expanded its interests in pharmaceuticals and consumer goods. In 1989 it merged its pharmaceutical division with Marion Labs to create Marion Merrell Dow (it sold its 71% stake to Hoechst in 1995). Also in 1989 it formed DowElanco, a joint venture with Eli Lilly to produce agricultural chemicals.

Following allegations that it had put a breast implant on the market without proper testing, Dow Corning (a joint venture with glassmaker Corning Inc.), the #1 producer of silicone breast implants, stopped making the devices in 1992. In 1995 a federal judge ordered Dow to pay a Nevada woman $14 million in damages — the first breast-implant verdict against the company as a sole defendant. Facing thousands of pending cases, Dow Corning filed for bankruptcy protection. (In 1998 Dow Corning agreed to pay $3.2 billion to settle most breast-implant claims.) Dow Corning finally climbed out of bankruptcy in 2004.

Dow entered the polypropylene and polyethylene terephthalate markets with the 1996 purchase of INCA International, a subsidiary of Italy's Enichem. It also bought a stake in seed developer Mycogen.

The company sold its 80% of Destec Energy in 1997 and bought Eli Lilly's 40% stake in

DowElanco (renamed Dow AgroSciences, 1998). That year Dow bought South Africa's Sentrachem (crop-protection products), but regulators made Dow sell part of it to Akzo Nobel.

In 1998 Dow sold its DowBrands unit — maker of bathroom cleaner (Dow), plastic bags (Ziploc), and plastic wrap (Saran Wrap) — to S.C. Johnson & Son. It also paid $322 million for the rest of Mycogen, which became part of Dow AgroSciences.

The company paid $600 million in 1999 to purchase ANGUS Chemical (specialty chemicals) from TransCanada PipeLines. Dow also announced it planned to buy rival Union Carbide for $9.3 billion; it completed the acquisition early in 2001 after agreeing to divest some polyethylene assets to satisfy regulatory concerns.

In 2000 Michael Parker succeeded William Stavropoulos as president and CEO (Stavropoulos remained as chairman). Dow acquired Rohm and Haas' agricultural chemicals (fungicides, insecticides, herbicides) business for $1 billion in 2001.

A weakened economy, high raw material costs, and falling prices took a toll on Dow's sales and profits around the turn of the century. As a result of costs related to the Union Carbide takeover — such as the $830 million charge related to Union Carbide's exposure to asbestos claims — and the sputtering economy, Dow recorded its first annual loss in nearly 10 years in 2001, then reported another loss in 2002. Parker was let go and William Stavropoulos returned to his post as both chairman and CEO. Stavropoulos went to work cutting jobs and closing plants in an effort to cut at least $1 billion in costs and make the company cash-flow positive in 2003.

From 2002-2004 the company cut nearly 7,000 jobs or better than 13% of its entire workforce. By 2004 those moves, coupled with a rebounding chemicals market, had made Dow profitable again. Stavropoulos felt comfortable enough to relinquish the chief executive title and gave it to president and COO Andrew Liveris.

## EXECUTIVES

**Chairman, President, and CEO:** Andrew N. Liveris, age 52, $1,433,333 pay
**EVP, CFO, and Director:** Geoffery E. (Geoff) Merszei, age 55, $1,280,236 pay
**EVP, Basic Plastics and Chemicals Portfolio:** Michael R. (Mike) Gambrell, age 53, $648,220 pay
**SVP, Shared Services, Environment, Health, and Safety, and CIO:** David E. (Dave) Kepler II, age 54, $511,128 pay
**SVP, General Counsel, and Secretary:** Charles J. Kalil, age 55
**Corporate VP and CTO:** William F. (Bill) Banholzer, age 50
**Corporate VP and Treasurer:** Fernando Ruiz, age 51
**Corporate VP, Strategic Development and New Ventures:** Heinz Haller, age 51
**Corporate VP, Human Resources, Diversity and Inclusion, and Public Affairs:** Julie Fasone Holder, age 54
**Corporate VP, Manufacturing and Engineering:** Gary R. Veurink, age 56
**VP, Marketing:** Pam Butcher
**VP and Controller:** William H. (Bill) Weideman, age 52
**VP, Dow Core Research and Development:** Attiganal N. Sreeram
**Corporate Director, Investor Relations:** Kathleen C. Fothergill
**Director, Corporate Media Relations:** Terri F. McNeill
**Auditors:** Deloitte & Touche LLP

## LOCATIONS

**HQ:** The Dow Chemical Company
2030 Dow Center, Midland, MI 48674
**Phone:** 989-636-1463 **Fax:** 989-636-1830
**Web:** www.dow.com

Dow Chemical has more than 150 manufacturing facilities in 37 countries throughout Africa, Asia, Europe, and North and South America. It has customers in more than 175 countries.

### 2006 Sales

| | $ mil. | % of total |
|---|---|---|
| US | 18,172 | 37 |
| Europe | 17,846 | 36 |
| Other regions | 13,106 | 27 |
| **Total** | **49,124** | **100** |

## PRODUCTS/OPERATIONS

### 2006 Sales and Operating Income

| | Sales | | Operating Income | |
|---|---|---|---|---|
| | $ mil. | % of total | $ mil. | % of total |
| Performance Plastics | 13,944 | 28 | 1,629 | 27 |
| Basic Plastics | 11,833 | 24 | 2,022 | 34 |
| Performance Chemicals | 7,867 | 16 | 1,242 | 21 |
| Hydrocarbons & Energy | 6,205 | 13 | — | — |
| Basic Chemicals | 5,560 | 11 | 689 | 11 |
| Agricultural Sciences | 3,399 | 7 | 415 | 7 |
| Other | 316 | 1 | (594) | — |
| **Total** | **49,124** | **100** | **5,403** | **100** |

### Selected Products

Performance Plastics
- Dow Automotive (resins, engineering plastic materials, fluids, adhesives, sealants, acoustical systems)
- Engineering plastics (thermoplastic resins and elastomers, advanced resins, and crystalline polymers)
- Epoxy products and intermediates (acetone, acrylic monomers, epoxy resins, glycerine, and phenol)
- Fabricated products (plastic film, Styrofoam, and Weathermate house wrap)
- Polyurethanes (Great Stuff foam sealant, dispersions, carpet backings, polyurethane gloves, roof adhesives, and fiberboard products)
- Wire and cable compounds (flame-retardant compounds, wire and cable insulation compounds)

Plastics
- Polyethylene (resins, including HDPE, LDPE, and LLDPE grades, and catalysts and process technology)
- Polypropylene (resins and performance polymers)
- Polystyrene (resins and styrenic alloys)

Performance Chemicals
- Custom and fine chemicals (nitroparaffins and nitroparaffin-based specialty chemicals, printing ink distillates, contract manufacturing services)
- Emulsion polymers (synthetic latex)
- Industrial chemicals (biocides, surfactants, and deicing fluids)
- Oxide derivatives (glycol ethers and amines)
- Specialty polymers (acrylic acid/acrylic esters, epoxides, dispersants, vinyl resins, specialty monomers)
- UCAR emulsion systems (water-based emulsions)
- Water-soluble polymers (food gums and material thickeners)

Hydrocarbons and Energy
- Benzene
- Butadiene
- Butylene
- Cumene
- Ethylene
- Propylene
- Styrene

Basic Chemicals
- Caustic soda
- Chlorine
- Ethylene glycol
- Ethylene oxide
- Vinyl chloride monomer

Agricultural Products (Dow AgroSciences)
- Fumigants
- Fungicides
- Herbicides
- Insecticides

Other
- Property and casualty insurance (Liana Limited)

## COMPETITORS

Akzo Nobel
BASF AG
Bayer
Chevron Phillips Chemical
DuPont
Eastman Chemical
Eni
ExxonMobil Chemical
FMC
Formosa Plastics
Honeywell International
Imperial Chemical
Koch
Lanxess
Lucite
Lyondell Chemical
Mitsui Chemicals
Monsanto
Occidental Chemical
Olin Chlor Alkali
PPG
SABIC
Shell Chemicals
Sunoco Chemicals
Syngenta
Wellman

## HISTORICAL FINANCIALS

Company Type: Public

### Income Statement

FYE: December 31

| | REVENUE ($ mil.) | NET INCOME ($ mil.) | NET PROFIT MARGIN | EMPLOYEES |
|---|---|---|---|---|
| **12/06** | 49,124 | 3,724 | 7.6% | 42,578 |
| **12/05** | 46,307 | 4,515 | 9.8% | 42,413 |
| **12/04** | 40,161 | 2,797 | 7.0% | 43,203 |
| **12/03** | 32,632 | 1,730 | 5.3% | 46,372 |
| **12/02** | 27,609 | (338) | — | 49,959 |
| **Annual Growth** | 15.5% | — | — | (3.9%) |

### 2006 Year-End Financials

Debt ratio: 47.1%
Return on equity: 23.0%
Cash ($ mil.): 2,910
Current ratio: 1.62
Long-term debt ($ mil.): 8,036
No. of shares (mil.): 958
Dividends
Yield: 3.8%
Payout: 39.3%
Market value ($ mil.): 38,226

### Stock History

NYSE: DOW



| | STOCK PRICE ($) FY Close | P/E High | P/E Low | PER SHARE ($) Earnings | Dividends | Book Value |
|---|---|---|---|---|---|---|
| **12/06** | 39.90 | 12 | 9 | 3.82 | 1.50 | 17.81 |
| **12/05** | 43.82 | 12 | 9 | 4.62 | 1.34 | 15.84 |
| **12/04** | 49.51 | 18 | 12 | 2.93 | 1.34 | 12.88 |
| **12/03** | 41.57 | 22 | 13 | 1.87 | 1.34 | 9.89 |
| **12/02** | 29.70 | — | — | (0.37) | 1.34 | 8.36 |
| **Annual Growth** | 7.7% | — | — | — | 2.9% | 20.8% |

# Dow Jones

Dow Jones & Company has its finger on the pulse of the global economy. The company publishes *The Wall Street Journal,* the leading financial daily and one of the most widely read US newspapers with a circulation of more than 1.7 million. Dow Jones also publishes *The Wall Street Journal Europe, The Wall Street Journal Asia,* and financial magazine *Barron's*, as well as a portfolio of community newspapers through its Ottaway Newspapers subsidiary. In addition, Dow Jones offers syndicated news, financial information and stock market data. The Bancroft family (heirs of early owner Clarence Barron) controls about 65% of the voting power in the company. Dow Jones has agreed to be acquired by media giant News Corp.

The downturn in advertising that has hit the newspaper industry led some investors to begin pressuring the Bancroft family to explore other options in regard to Dow Jones, even though the company has fared better than many of its rivals thanks to its diverse syndication business, expanding Internet operations, and the continued strong performance of *The Wall Street Journal*. Initially the family spurned advances from News Corp. but finally acquiesced and agreed in 2007 to the $5.6 billion takeover.

Some members of Bancroft family did not go down without a fight, however. Fearing for the reputation of its flagship publication, they openly resisted the deal, including Leslie Hill who resigned as a board member shortly before the agreement was announced. (Another board member, Dieter von Holtzbrinck, also resigned prior to the deal being finalized.) There were also attempts to solicit bids from other companies, and while some showed interest — General Electric, Microsoft, and entrepreneur Brad Greenspan among them — no rival offer was ever made.

News Corp. chieftain Rupert Murdoch plans to use the expertise and brand identity of the *Journal* as a cornerstone for a new business news cable network that will compete with NBC Universal's CNBC. He also plans to expand the *Journal*'s bureau in Washington, DC, and to invest in international expansion to compete more with overseas rivals, such as Pearson's flagship *Financial Times*.

Murdoch is also getting an expanding portfolio of online operations that includes WSJ.com (operated through The Wall Street Journal Online), which boasts more than 810,000 subscribers, the largest paying audience of any Web site. Dow Jones owns ad-supported business news site MarketWatch and produces an online version of *Barron's*. In 2006 Dow Jones acquired the remaining 50% of online research and information service Factiva from Reuters.

News Corp. will have to deal with the challenge of Dow Jones' struggling print business, though. The company has reorganized its newspaper business several times and sold a half dozen papers from its Ottaway unit to Community Newspaper Holdings in 2006 for $280 million. Looking for other ways to cut costs, Dow Jones reduced the physical size of *The Wall Street Journal* in 2007.

## HISTORY

Charles Dow, Edward Jones, and Charles Bergstresser founded Dow Jones & Company (1882), which delivered handwritten bulletins of stock and bond trading news to New York subscribers. In 1883 Dow Jones started summarizing the trading day in the *Customers' Afternoon Letter,* which evolved into *The Wall Street Journal* (1889). Jones sold out to his partners in 1899; three years later Dow and Bergstresser sold the company to Clarence Barron. In 1921 the company introduced *Barron's National Business and Financial Weekly.*

Bernard Kilgore, who was appointed managing editor in 1941, shaped the format of *The Journal* that has endured until this day. During the 1960s the company saw the newspaper's circulation exceed 1 million. With its acquisition of the Ottaway group and investments in the *Far Eastern Economic Review* and *The Asian Wall Street Journal* during the 1970s, Dow Jones expanded into community and international publications. It launched *The Wall Street Journal Europe* in 1983 and between 1985 and 1990 acquired Telerate, a real-time financial data network that it renamed Dow Jones Markets.

Peter Kann, who joined *The Journal* as a reporter in 1964, became chairman and CEO of the company in 1991. The next year Dow Jones teamed with Hearst to launch *SmartMoney* magazine. In 1997 the company shut down its unprofitable Dow Jones Investor Network (a video news service started in 1993) and tried to revive the ailing Dow Jones Markets service by announcing a $650 million revamp.

Charges associated with Dow Jones Markets led to a sizable loss for 1997, and the company sold the unit to Bridge Information Systems for $510 million the next year. It cut staffing costs in 1998 when more than 500 employees accepted severance packages. That year Dow Jones announced it would expand the number of pages and color capacity of *The Journal,* and inked deals to distribute its newswires through Reuters, Bloomberg, and Bridge.

In 1999 Dow Jones began offering *The Wall Street Journal Sunday,* a weekly package of articles that originally appeared in more than 15 US newspapers. Dow Jones hit hard times in 2001 as the economy soured; it laid off some 200 workers as a result of declining ad revenue and increased the cover price of its flagship paper.

When the economy failed to pick up, the company eliminated another 230 jobs in 2002 (including 5% of the news staff at *The Wall Street Journal*). The company was dealt a devastating blow in 2002 when *Wall Street Journal* reporter Daniel Pearl, who had been kidnapped in Pakistan by suspected Islamic militants, was killed by his captors.

The company acquired the venture-capital news provider Alternative Investor Group, a unit of Wicks Business Information, for $85 million, in 2004. That year, the company announced that its *Far Eastern Economic Review* would move from a weekly to a monthly publication and that most of its staff would be cut. Dow Jones acquired popular financial news site MarketWatch for $519 million in 2005. The company eliminated nearly 100 jobs in the transition, mostly at MarketWatch. In late 2005 the company sold its interests in CNBC Europe and CNBC Asia to NBC Universal.

COO Richard Zannino was promoted to CEO in 2006, replacing Kann (who stayed on as chairman until 2007). Late that year Dow Jones acquired the 50% stake in Factiva owned by partner Reuters. It also sold six newspapers from its Ottaway subsidiary to Community Newspaper Holdings for $280 million.

## EXECUTIVES

**Chairman:** M. Peter McPherson, age 66
**CEO and Director:** Richard F. (Rich) Zannino, age 48
**EVP and CFO:** William B. Plummer, age 48, $131,538 pay (partial-year salary)
**EVP; President, Consumer Media Group; Publisher, The Wall Street Journal Franchise:** L. Gordon Crovitz, age 48, $588,099 pay
**EVP; President, Content Technology Solutions; Chairman, Factiva:** Clare Hart, age 46
**SVP Human Resources:** Jorge L. Figueredo, age 46
**SVP; President, Local Media Group; Chairman and CEO, Ottaway Newspapers:** John N. Wilcox, age 62
**SVP, General Counsel, and Secretary:** Joseph A. Stern, age 57, $539,423 pay
**SVP Marketing and Business Development, Consumer Electronic Publishing:** Jessica Perry
**VP and CIO:** William A. Godfrey III
**VP News Strategy; President, Dow Jones Newswires:** Paul J. Ingrassia
**VP Corporate Communications:** Amy L. Wolfcale, age 42
**VP Corporate Security:** Joseph J. Cantamessa
**VP Integrated Solutions:** Michael (Mike) Henry
**Chief Marketing Officer:** Ann Marks
**President and Editor, Barron's; Chairman and Editorial Director, SmartMoney:** Edwin A. Finn Jr.
**President, Financial Information Services:** Scott D. Schulman
**President, Licensing Services:** Jeffrey G. (Jeff) Davis
**President, Dow Jones Indexes/Ventures:** Michael A. Petronella
**President, Dow Jones Ventures:** Ann Sarnoff, age 45
**President and Publisher, Dow Jones Online:** Gordon McLeod
**Director, Investor Relations:** Mark J. Donohue
**Managing Editor, The Wall Street Journal:** Marcus Brauchli, age 45
**Auditors:** PricewaterhouseCoopers LLP

## LOCATIONS

**HQ:** Dow Jones & Company, Inc.
200 Liberty St., New York, NY 10281
**Phone:** 212-416-2000 **Fax:** 212-416-4348
**Web:** www.dj.com

### 2006 Sales

| | $ mil. | % of total |
|---|---|---|
| US | 1,618.9 | 91 |
| Other countries | 165.0 | 9 |
| **Total** | **1,783.9** | **100** |

## PRODUCTS/OPERATIONS

### 2006 Sales

| | $ mil. | % of total |
|---|---|---|
| Advertising | 957.8 | 54 |
| Information services | 397.1 | 22 |
| Circulation & other | 429.0 | 24 |
| **Total** | **1,783.9** | **100** |

### 2006 Sales

| | $ mil. | % of total |
|---|---|---|
| Consumer media | 1,123.5 | 63 |
| Enterprise media | 408.6 | 23 |
| Local media | 252.2 | 14 |
| Adjustments | (0.4) | — |
| **Total** | **1,783.9** | **100** |

**Selected Operations**

Consumer media
- *Barron's*
- Dow Jones Online
  - Barron's Online
  - BigCharts.com (stock market information)
  - Career Journal
  - College Journal
  - MarketWatch (online business news)
  - Opinion Journal
  - Real Estate Journal
  - Start Up Journal
  - WSJ.com (online edition of *The Wall Street Journal*)
- *The Wall Street Journal*
- *The Wall Street Journal Americas*
- *The Wall Street Journal Asia*
- *The Wall Street Journal Classroom Edition*
- *The Wall Street Journal Europe*
- *The Wall Street Journal Sunday*

Enterprise media
- Dow Jones Financial Information Services
- Dow Jones Indexes (stock market data)
- Dow Jones Licensing Services
- Dow Jones Newswires
- Factiva (news and business research)

Local media
- Ottaway Newspapers

Joint ventures and other interests
- Adicio (recruitment information)
- *SmartMoney* (50%, personal finance magazine)
- STOXX (33%, stock market information)
- *Vedomosti* (33%, business news, Russia)

## COMPETITORS

Advance Publications
Agence France-Presse
Associated Press
Bloomberg
Financial Times
Forbes
Gannett
Interactive Data
LexisNexis
McClatchy Company
McGraw-Hill
MSCI
New York Times
News Corp.
Reuters
Thomson Corporation
Time
Tribune
U.S. News & World Report
Washington Post

## HISTORICAL FINANCIALS

Company Type: Public

**Income Statement** FYE: December 31

| | REVENUE ($ mil.) | NET INCOME ($ mil.) | NET PROFIT MARGIN | EMPLOYEES |
|---|---|---|---|---|
| **12/06** | 1,784 | 387 | 21.7% | 7,400 |
| **12/05** | 1,770 | 60 | 3.4% | 6,900 |
| **12/04** | 1,672 | 100 | 6.0% | 6,500 |
| **12/03** | 1,549 | 171 | 11.0% | 6,975 |
| **12/02** | 1,559 | 202 | 12.9% | 6,816 |
| **Annual Growth** | 3.4% | 17.7% | — | 2.1% |

**2006 Year-End Financials**

| | |
|---|---|
| Debt ratio: 45.1% | No. of shares (mil.): 64 |
| Return on equity: 116.9% | Dividends |
| Cash ($ mil.): 13 | Yield: 2.6% |
| Current ratio: 0.38 | Payout: 21.6% |
| Long-term debt ($ mil.): 225 | Market value ($ mil.): 2,415 |

**Stock History** NYSE: DJ

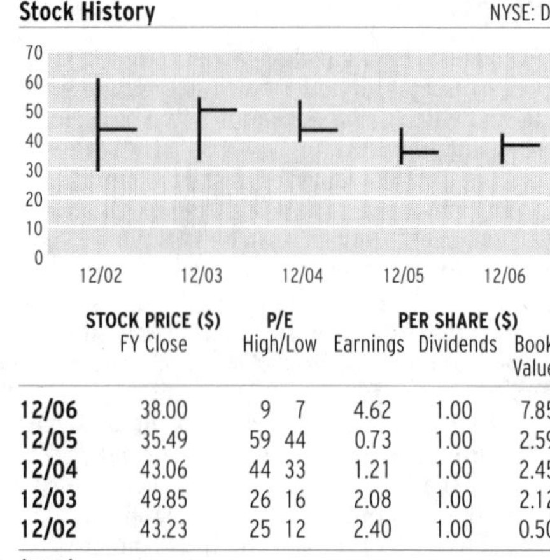


| | STOCK PRICE ($) FY Close | P/E High | P/E Low | PER SHARE ($) Earnings | Dividends | Book Value |
|---|---|---|---|---|---|---|
| **12/06** | 38.00 | 9 | 7 | 4.62 | 1.00 | 7.85 |
| **12/05** | 35.49 | 59 | 44 | 0.73 | 1.00 | 2.59 |
| **12/04** | 43.06 | 44 | 33 | 1.21 | 1.00 | 2.45 |
| **12/03** | 49.85 | 26 | 16 | 2.08 | 1.00 | 2.12 |
| **12/02** | 43.23 | 25 | 12 | 2.40 | 1.00 | 0.50 |
| **Annual Growth** | (3.2%) | — | — | 17.8% | 0.0% | 99.1% |

# D.R. Horton

When D.R. Horton heard a Who, it built the little guy a house. The top homebuilder in the US, ahead of Lennar, the company sold more than 53,000 homes in fiscal 2006. D.R. Horton mainly builds single-family homes designed for the entry-level and move-up markets. Homes range from 1,000 sq. ft. to 5,000 sq. ft., with an average selling price of about $273,000; its luxury homes can cost up to $900,000. D.R. Horton operates more than 40 divisions, building in 84 metropolitan markets in 27 states. It also provides mortgage financing and title services to homebuyers.

Despite nearly a decade of impressive results, the nationwide housing slump that hit in 2006 has affected D.R. Horton along with its fellow homebuilders. The company has suffered higher than normal cancellation rates and has had to increase sales incentives to buyers. The company has also seen a rise in the number of speculative houses; in 2005 speculative houses accounted for about 40% of D.R. Horton's inventory, whereas in 2006 it was 50%. (Speculative or "spec" houses are those that are built before being ordered by a customer.) As a result, D.R. Horton has dramatically reduced the number of speculative homes to be built.

## HISTORY

Donald R. Horton was selling homes in Fort Worth, Texas, when he hit upon a strategy for increasing sales — add options to a basic floor plan. In 1978 he borrowed $33,000 to build his first home, added a bay window for an additional charge, and sold the home for $44,000. Donald soon added floor plans and options that appealed to regional preferences.

The depressed Texas market drove the company to expand beyond the Dallas/Fort Worth area in 1987, when it entered the then-hot Phoenix market. It continued to expand into the Southeast, Mid-Atlantic, Midwest, and West in the late 1980s and early 1990s. By 1991 Horton and his family owned more than 25 companies that were combined as D.R. Horton, which went public in 1992.

D.R. Horton acquired six geographically diverse construction firms in 1994 and 1995. In 1996 the company started a mortgage services joint venture, expanded its title operations, and added three more firms.

In 1998 the company bought four builders, including Scottsdale, Arizona-based Continental Homes. Continental had been expanding beyond its Arizona and Southern California base and had entered the lucrative retirement community market. After the Continental purchase, Donald Horton stepped down as president, remaining chairman. Richard Beckwitt took over as president, and Donald Tomnitz became CEO. In 1999 the company acquired Century Title and Midwest builder Cambridge Properties.

D.R. Horton sold its St. Louis assets to McBride & Son Enterprises in 2000, after spending five years trying to break into the St. Louis homebuilding market. Tomnitz also took over the duties of president in 2000 when Beckwitt retired.

D.R. Horton gained homebuilding operations in Houston and Phoenix when it bought Emerald Builders in 2001. In February 2002 the company acquired Schuler Homes for $1.2 billion, including debt.

Sales continued to climb in fiscal 2003 and 2004. D.R. Horton experienced its 27th consecutive year of earnings and revenue growth in 2004 and broke records by being the first residential homebuilder to sell more than 45,000 homes in the US in a fiscal year; in fiscal 2005 the company closed 51,172 homes. By 2007, however it was evident that the heady days were over with a rise in cancellations and a larger value of backlog orders.

## EXECUTIVES

**Chairman:** Donald R. Horton, age 55, $13,224,804 pay
**Vice Chairman, President, and CEO:**
Donald J. (Don) Tomnitz, age 57, $13,124,804 pay
**EVP, CFO, and Director:** Bill W. Wheat, age 39
**EVP, Investor Relations and Treasurer:**
Stacey H. Dwyer, age 39
**SVP; President, West Region:** James K. (Jim) Schuler
**VP and Assistant Secretary:** Paul W. Buchschacher
**VP and Director, National Accounts:** Ric Rojas
**VP and CIO:** Robert (Bob) Koeblitz
**IT Director:** Rick Rawlings
**Operations Controller:** Steve Lovett
**Financial Reporting Controller:** Jack Simpson
**President, Financial Services:**
Randall C. (Randy) Present
**Chief Legal Officer:** Ted I. Harbour
**President, Central/Gulf Coast Region:** Rick Horton
**President, California Region:** Chris Chambers
**President, Southwest Region:** Gordon D. Jones, age 46, $2,803,691 pay (prior to title change)
**President, Southeast Region:** David Auld
**President, Midwest Region:** George W. Seagraves, age 47, $1,133,317 pay
**President, Northeast Region:** Brian Gardner
**Manager Human Resources:** Paula Hunter-Perkins
**Communication Coordinator:** Shannon B. Farrell
**Executive Assistant:** Mary Slapper
**Investor Relations:** Jessica Hansen
**Auditors:** Ernst & Young LLP

## LOCATIONS

**HQ:** D.R. Horton, Inc.
301 Commerce St., Ste. 500, Fort Worth, TX 76102
**Phone:** 817-390-8200 **Fax:** 817-390-1704
**Web:** www.drhorton.com

**2006 Homes Closed**

| | Units | % of total |
|---|---|---|
| South central | 13,444 | 25 |
| Southwest | 11,235 | 21 |
| Northeast | 8,142 | 16 |
| Southeast | 8,053 | 15 |
| California | 7,884 | 15 |
| West | 4,341 | 8 |
| **Total** | **53,099** | **100** |

## PRODUCTS/OPERATIONS

**2006 Sales**

| | $ mil. | % of total |
|---|---|---|
| Homebuilding | | |
| California | 3,643 | 24 |
| Southwest | 2,955 | 20 |
| South central | 2,311 | 15 |
| Northeast | 2,213 | 15 |
| Southeast | 2,040 | 14 |
| West | 1,598 | 11 |
| Financial services | 291 | 2 |
| **Total** | **15,051** | **100** |

**Selected Operating Units**

Cambridge Homes
Continental Homes
Dietz-Crane Homes
D.R. Horton
Emerald Builders
Emerald Homes
Keys & Schuler
Melody Homes
Milburn Homes
Schuler Homes
Stafford Homes
Torrey Homes
Trimark Communities

## COMPETITORS

Beazer Homes
Centex
Century Homebuilders
David Weekley Homes
Gehan Homes
Glennwood Custom Builders
Hovnanian Enterprises
J.F. Shea
KB Home
Lennar
Levitt Corporation
M.D.C.
Mercedes Homes
Meritage Homes
M/I Homes
NVR
Orleans Homebuilders
Pardee Homes
Pulte Homes
Ryan Building
Ryland
Standard Pacific
Toll Brothers
Weyerhaeuser Real Estate

## HISTORICAL FINANCIALS

Company Type: Public

**Income Statement** FYE: September 30

| | REVENUE ($ mil.) | NET INCOME ($ mil.) | NET PROFIT MARGIN | EMPLOYEES |
|---|---|---|---|---|
| **9/06** | 15,051 | 1,233 | 8.2% | 8,772 |
| **9/05** | 13,864 | 1,471 | 10.6% | 8,900 |
| **9/04** | 10,841 | 975 | 9.0% | 7,466 |
| **9/03** | 8,728 | 626 | 7.2% | 6,348 |
| **9/02** | 6,739 | 405 | 6.0% | 5,701 |
| **Annual Growth** | 22.2% | 32.1% | — | 11.4% |

**2006 Year-End Financials**

Debt ratio: 94.2%
Return on equity: 20.9%
Cash ($ mil.): 836
Current ratio: 5.58
Long-term debt ($ mil.): 6,079
No. of shares (mil.): 313
Dividends
Yield: 1.8%
Payout: 11.3%
Market value ($ mil.): 7,502

**Stock History** NYSE: DHI

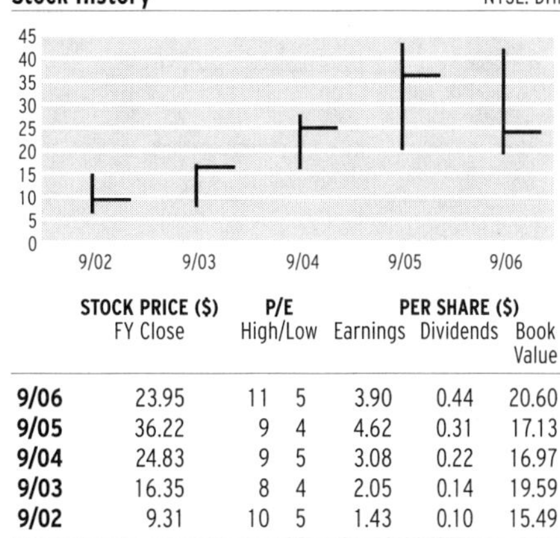


| | STOCK PRICE ($) FY Close | P/E High | P/E Low | PER SHARE ($) Earnings | Dividends | Book Value |
|---|---|---|---|---|---|---|
| **9/06** | 23.95 | 11 | 5 | 3.90 | 0.44 | 20.60 |
| **9/05** | 36.22 | 9 | 4 | 4.62 | 0.31 | 17.13 |
| **9/04** | 24.83 | 9 | 5 | 3.08 | 0.22 | 16.97 |
| **9/03** | 16.35 | 8 | 4 | 2.05 | 0.14 | 19.59 |
| **9/02** | 9.31 | 10 | 5 | 1.43 | 0.10 | 15.49 |
| **Annual Growth** | 26.6% | — | — | 28.5% | 44.8% | 7.4% |

# DRS Technologies

Methods used to track military activity are complex, but DRS Technologies makes the tasks manageable with electronic systems that process, display, and store complex military and aerospace data. Its primary offerings include surveillance and radar systems, ruggedized computers, weapons targeting systems, flight recorders, communications systems, thermal imaging systems, air combat training systems, and video recorders for defense and aerospace applications. DRS, which has acquired and integrated Integrated Defense Technologies — and has acquired Engineered Support Systems — relies on US government agencies (primarily the DoD) for 90% of sales.

DRS saw its sales and profits take off after dumping the majority of its disk drives business and expanding its core business: defense contracts. In late 2001 DRS issued an additional 3 million shares of common stock (almost 25% of all outstanding shares) to provide funds for expansion and to pay down existing debt. The company then embarked on a five-year acquisitions spree that bought nearly a dozen companies that complemented DRS's operations.

In its biggest purchase to date, DRS acquired Engineered Support Systems (military electronics and logistics) in a deal worth nearly $2 billion in January 2006; the acquisition helped increase fiscal 2007 sales over those of 2006 by more than 60%.

Following the acquisition-fest, DRS restructured to simplify and integrate its operations into four operating groups: Command, Control, Communications, Computers and Intelligence (C4I); Reconnaissance, Surveillance, and Target Acquisition (RSTA); Technical Services; and Sustainment Systems.

Exports account for less than 5% of DRS's sales.

## HISTORY

Former Loral engineers Leonard Newman and David Gross founded Diagnostic/Retrieval Systems (DRS) in 1968. (Newman died in 1998 and Gross has retired.) DRS pioneered passive sonar submarine-detection systems in 1969, and the company went public in 1981.

Contract delays and cost overruns on fixed-price contracts led to losses in the early 1990s. DRS diversified during this time, buying Technology Applications & Service (computer displays), CMC Technology (video recorders), and Ahead Technology (magnetic head products used in computer disk drives).

DRS's 1995 revenues increased from the sale of new commercial products. During 1996 and 1997 DRS continued to pursue nonmilitary acquisitions, including Mag-Head Engineering (audio recorder heads) and two commercial lines from International Tapetronics. The company's defense-related acquisitions included Pacific Technologies, a software provider to the US Navy (1996), and the Applied Systems Division of Spar Aerospace (1997). Also in 1997 the company changed its name to DRS Technologies.

In 1998 DRS bought two electro-optical firms from defense contractor Raytheon for $90 million, and the next year it expanded its offerings of ruggedized computers and peripherals for the military by acquiring NAI Technologies. The company sold its profit-draining magnetic tape head businesses in 2000. Also that year investment firm Veritas Capital made an unsuccessful attempt to acquire DRS.

DRS acquired Boeing's Systems and Electronic Systems business for about $70 million in 2001. In December of that year, the company issued an additional 3 million shares of common stock (about 25% of all outstanding shares) in order to fund expansion and to pay down existing debt. The next year DRS bought Eaton's Navy Controls (electrical power distribution and control systems for the US Navy) division for $92 million in cash. Later in 2002 the company bought Paravant, a maker of ruggedized computers.

In 2003 DRS acquired Kaman's Electromagnetics Development Center (now DRS Power Technology). Later that year DRS picked up defense electronics rival Integrated Defense Technologies for about $375 million in cash and stock and the assumption of $175 million in debt.

In 2004 DRS rejected a $42 a share buyout offer from L-3 Communications. The company stated that the deal was not in the best interests of shareholders considering DRS's growth prospects. Late in the year DRS acquired assets from Night Vision Equipment Co., Inc. and Electro Optics, Inc.

DRS sold its DRS Broadcast Technology and DRS Weather Systems units to Veritas Capital Fund II in 2005. The same year DRS added to its core business by acquiring Codem Systems, a maker of signals intelligence systems, antenna control systems, and network interface modules. DRS also acquired WalkAbout Computers, a maker of rugged computers and mobile docking stations, for an undisclosed amount.

DRS acquired Engineered Support Systems (military electronics and logistics) for about $2 billion in 2006. Engineered Support Systems is part of DRS's newest operating segment: Sustainment Systems & Services Group (S3).

## EXECUTIVES

**Chairman, President, and CEO:** Mark S. Newman, age 57, $2,174,000 pay
**EVP and COO:** Robert F. Mehmel, age 44, $892,700 pay
**EVP and CFO:** Richard A. Schneider, age 53, $789,300 pay
**EVP, General Counsel, and Secretary:** Nina Laserson Dunn, age 59, $790,660 pay
**EVP, Washington Operations:** Michael L. (Mike) Bowman, $550,000 pay
**SVP and CIO:** Louis J. Belsito
**SVP, Corporate Taxation:** Jason W. Rinsky
**SVP, Maritime Strategic Planning:** Phillip M. Balisle
**SVP, Human Resources:** Andrea J. Mandel
**SVP, Operations:** Robert Russo
**SVP, Corporate Controller:** Thomas P. Crimmins
**SVP, Contracts and Compliance:** Alan Gross
**SVP, Government Relations:** Larry K. Brewer, age 62
**SVP, Land Warfare Strategic Plans and Programs:** Jerry L. Sinn
**VP, Corporate Communications and Investor Relations:** Patricia M. Williamson
**VP, Public Affairs:** Richard Goldberg
**President, C4I Segment:** Steven T. (Steve) Schorer
**President, Tactical Systems (C4I):** Michael J. Sheehan
**President, Resonnaissance, Surveillance, and Target Acquisition Segment:** James M. Baird
**President, Sustainment Systems Segment:** Thomas G. Cornwell, age 50
**President, Technical Services Segment:** Mitchell B. (Mitch) Rambler, age 55
**Treasurer:** Donald G. Hardman
**Auditors:** KPMG LLP

## LOCATIONS

**HQ:** DRS Technologies, Inc.
5 Sylvan Way, Parsippany, NJ 07054
**Phone:** 973-898-1500 **Fax:** 973-898-4730
**Web:** www.drs.com

### 2007 Sales

| | $ mil. | % of total |
|---|---|---|
| US | 2,735.5 | 97 |
| Canada | 70.9 | 2 |
| UK | 14.7 | 1 |
| **Total** | **2,821.1** | **100** |

## PRODUCTS/OPERATIONS

### 2007 Sales

| | $ mil. | % of total |
|---|---|---|
| C4I Group | 1,139.4 | 41 |
| Technical services | 681.3 | 24 |
| RSTA | 599.6 | 21 |
| Sustainment systems | 400.8 | 14 |
| **Total** | **2,821.1** | **100** |

### 2007 Sales

| | $ mil. | % of total |
|---|---|---|
| Technical services | 681.3 | 24 |
| Reconnaissance, surveillance & target acquisition | 599.6 | 21 |
| Command, control & communications | 429.3 | 15 |
| Sustainment systems | 400.8 | 14 |
| Tactical systems | 316.6 | 11 |
| Intelligence technologies | 209.1 | 8 |
| Power systems | 184.4 | 7 |
| **Total** | **2,821.1** | **100** |

### Selected Operations

- C4I Group
  - Command, control and communications (C3)
    - Air combat training and electronic warfare and ship network systems
    - Analysis and radio frequency broadcast transmissions equipment
    - Electronics manufacturing and system integration services
    - Meteorological surveillance
    - Naval display systems
    - Radar systems
    - Secure voice and data communications
    - Ship communications systems
    - Technical support
  - Intelligence technologies
    - Signals intelligence, communications intelligence, data collection, processing, and dissemination equipment
  - Power systems
    - Naval and industrial power generation, conversion, propulsion, distribution, and control systems
  - Tactical systems
    - Battle management tactical computer systems and peripherals
- Technical services
  - Advanced technology services
  - Engineering services
  - Integration and information technology services
  - Logistics and training services
  - Power generation
  - Security and asset protection systems and services
  - Telecommunications systems
  - Vehicle armor kits
- Reconnaissance, surveillance, and target acquisition (RSTA)
  - Combat identification and laser aimer/illuminator products
  - Electronic manufacturing services
  - Electro-optical sighting
  - Image intensification night vision
  - Targeting and weapon sensor systems
- Sustainment systems
  - Heat transfer and air handling equipment
  - Integrated military electronics
  - Military support equipment
  - Power generation and distribution equipment for domestic and commercial users

## COMPETITORS

Ampex
BAE SYSTEMS
EDO
General Dynamics
Interstate Electronics
L-3 Communications
Lockheed Martin
Northrop Grumman
Raytheon
Raytheon SAS

## HISTORICAL FINANCIALS

Company Type: Public

### Income Statement

FYE: March 31

| | REVENUE ($ mil.) | NET INCOME ($ mil.) | NET PROFIT MARGIN | EMPLOYEES |
|---|---|---|---|---|
| **3/07** | 2,821 | 127 | 4.5% | 9,700 |
| **3/06** | 1,736 | 82 | 4.7% | 9,800 |
| **3/05** | 1,309 | 61 | 4.6% | 5,658 |
| **3/04** | 1,001 | 45 | 4.5% | 5,800 |
| **3/03** | 676 | 30 | 4.5% | 3,750 |
| **Annual Growth** | 42.9% | 43.2% | — | 26.8% |

### 2007 Year-End Financials

Debt ratio: 118.7%
Return on equity: 8.9%
Cash ($ mil.): 96
Current ratio: 1.46
Long-term debt ($ mil.): 1,783
No. of shares (mil.): 41
Dividends
Yield: 0.2%
Payout: 3.8%
Market value ($ mil.): 2,122

### Stock History

NYSE: DRS

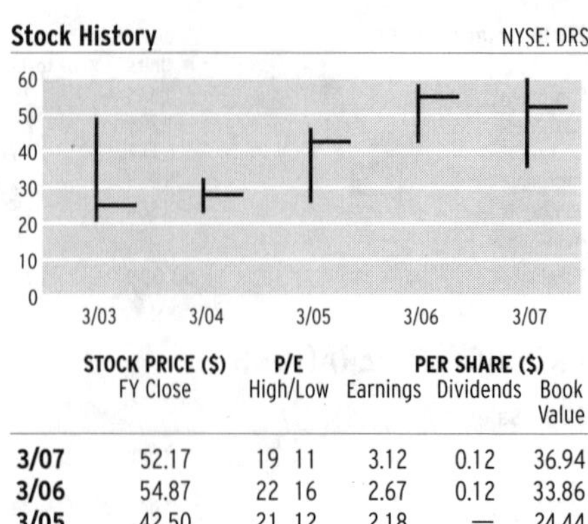


| | STOCK PRICE ($) FY Close | P/E High | P/E Low | PER SHARE ($) Earnings | Dividends | Book Value |
|---|---|---|---|---|---|---|
| **3/07** | 52.17 | 19 | 11 | 3.12 | 0.12 | 36.94 |
| **3/06** | 54.87 | 22 | 16 | 2.67 | 0.12 | 33.86 |
| **3/05** | 42.50 | 21 | 12 | 2.18 | — | 24.44 |
| **3/04** | 27.98 | 18 | 13 | 1.80 | — | 22.01 |
| **3/03** | 25.01 | 31 | 13 | 1.58 | — | 19.54 |
| **Annual Growth** | 20.2% | — | — | 18.5% | 0.0% | 17.3% |

# DST Systems

The feeling is mutual at DST Systems. A leading provider of information processing software and services for the mutual fund industry, DST's Financial Services segment processes millions of mutual fund accounts and offers software, systems, and processing services for banks, investment firms, and insurance companies. The company's Output Solutions unit manages statement and bill mailings and customer communications. DST Systems sold its billing and customer management software and services business, including the operations of DST Innovis and DST Interactive, to Amdocs in 2005.

Though DST's revenues come primarily from transaction-based service fees, the company's proprietary technology offerings are the basis for many of these fees. The company's Financial Access Network system, for instance, provides the infrastructure for a portion of its mutual fund account processing activities.

DST's Output Solutions segment, which operates primarily in the US through subsidiary DST Output, expanded its geographic reach through its purchase of DST International, a provider of customer communications and document management services in the UK.

In 2005 DST completed the sale of its Equiserve unit (shareholder services) to Australia-based financial services and technology provider Computershare. The company also acquired CSC's Health Plan Solutions (HPS) business (claims administration services).

In late 2005 DST agreed to merge its lock/line unit (administrative services for telecom carriers) with customer contact and support services provider Asurion Corporation; the deal, which closed at the beginning of 2006, left DST with a 37% stake in the combined business.

Later in 2006 the company acquired Amisys Synertech, a software developer and applications provider to the commercial health care industry. The transaction was carried out through a unit of subsidiary DST Health Solutions.

## HISTORY

After expanding into mutual funds during the early 1960s, Kansas City Southern Industries (KCSI) formed an electronic computer data processing unit to handle its mutual fund transactions, using technology designed originally for tracking railroad cars and their revenues.

In 1968 KCSI incorporated its data processing unit as DST Systems and began offering its services to the financial industry. To establish itself on the East Coast, in 1974 DST formed Boston Financial Data Services, a joint venture with State Street. Also during the 1970s DST entered the insurance market with a system for variable annuity policyholders.

In 1983 KCSI bought a majority stake in Janus Capital, a Denver-based mutual funds company. DST went public later that year; KCSI kept an 86% stake. Thomas McDonnell, president since the early 1970s, was named CEO in 1984.

By the early 1990s DST had a solid position in its markets, and it had begun to increase its service offerings and expand internationally into Canada and Europe. The company bought Vantage Computer to gain a foothold in the life and property insurance software industry, and it established joint ventures with Kemper Financial Services (now part of Zurich Financial Services) and State Street Boston, thereby pushing into portfolio accounting and stock transfer services.

In 1993 DST sold Vantage to insurance software maker Continuum, gaining a 19% stake in that company. It also bought 50% of client Argus Health Systems as well as a stake in DBS Systems (by 1997 it owned 100%). By the end of 1993 DST was the leader in mutual fund third-party services. In 1995 KCSI sold 51% of DST to the public. Information technology firm Computer Sciences Corporation (CSC) acquired Continuum in 1996, leaving DST with a minority stake in CSC.

In 1998 DST, BankBoston First Chicago Trust, and State Street formed EquiServe, the largest provider of corporate stock transfer services in the US. That year DST bought USCS International, a provider of customer management software and billing services, in an $824 million deal.

DST in 2000 took aim at fund supermarkets operated by Charles Schwab and FMR by launching a service that enabled independent commission-based financial advisers to research and trade funds over the Internet. The company also purchased a controlling stake in EquiServe from the other partners in the joint venture.

In 2001 the company acquired the remainder of EquiServe, and it sold its portfolio accounting systems business to State Street for $75 million. The following year DST bought lock/line, a provider of administrative support services for providers of insurance for telecommunications equipment and event-based debt protection programs. In 2003 Janus Capital Group sold most of its remaining stake in DST back to the company, in exchange for ownership of DST's commercial printing and graphics design unit; it sold the rest of its stake in 2004.

## EXECUTIVES

**President, CEO, and Director:** Thomas A. (Tom) McDonnell, age 61, $750,000 pay
**EVP, COO, and Director:** Thomas A. McCullough, age 64, $575,000 pay
**President and CEO, DST Output:** Steven J. (Steve) Towle, age 49
**President, DST Innovis and DST Interactive:** Peter J. (Pete) Nault
**Chairman, DST International:** J. Michael (Mike) Winn, age 60
**VP, CFO, and Treasurer:** Kenneth V. Hager, age 56, $287,500 pay
**VP, General Counsel, and Secretary:** Randall D. Young, age 50
**Group VP Mutual Funds Full Service; President, Argus Health Systems:** Jonathan J. Boehm, age 46, $270,000 pay
**Group VP Mutual Funds Remote:** Robert L. Tritt, age 51, $270,000 pay
**VP and Chief Accounting Officer:** Gregg W. Givens, age 46
**VP Automated Work Distributor:** John C. Vaughn
**VP and CIO:** Mark C. Prasifka
**President, DST Health Solutions:** A. Stephan (Steve) Sabino, age 56
**CEO, DST International:** Thomas R. (Tom) Abraham, age 55
**Auditors:** PricewaterhouseCoopers LLP

## LOCATIONS

**HQ:** DST Systems, Inc.
333 W. 11th St., Kansas City, MO 64105
**Phone:** 816-435-1000 **Fax:** 816-435-8618
**Web:** www.dstsystems.com

### 2006 Sales

| | $ mil. | % of total |
|---|---|---|
| North America | | |
| US | 2,003.6 | 90 |
| Canada | 33.1 | 1 |
| UK | 128.5 | 6 |
| Australia | 26.5 | 1 |
| Other regions | 44.1 | 2 |
| **Total** | **2,235.8** | **100** |

## PRODUCTS/OPERATIONS

### 2006 Sales

| | $ mil. | % of total |
|---|---|---|
| Output solutions | 1,155.1 | 50 |
| Financial services | 1,072.0 | 47 |
| Investments & other | 63.9 | 3 |
| Adjustments | (55.2) | — |
| **Total** | **2,235.8** | **100** |

### Selected Products and Services

Financial Services
- eLLITE (fund information access)
- Securities Transfer System (transfer agent support)
- TA2000 (mutual fund shareholder record keeping)
- TRAC-2000 (record keeping for defined contribution plans)
- Vision (Web-based mutual fund processing for independent financial advisers)

DST Output
- Call center management support
- Direct Access (instantaneous online data monitoring)
- Exact View (customer statement replica viewing)
- Info Disc (customer document replica viewing)
- Package configuration and inventory management support
- Rapid Confirm (delivery service for trade confirmations)
- Rapid NetSale (lead management for prospective online brokerage customers)

## COMPETITORS

ADP
Advent Software
Assurant
Bank of New York Mellon
Bowne
Cerner
Companion Technologies
EDS
FileNet
First Data
Fiserv
Greenway Medical Technologies
HLTH Corp.
IBM
Misys
Pegasystems
Perot Systems
PFPC
SS&C
State Street
SunGard
TIBCO Software
TriZetto

## HISTORICAL FINANCIALS

Company Type: Public

### Income Statement

FYE: December 31

| | REVENUE ($ mil.) | NET INCOME ($ mil.) | NET PROFIT MARGIN | EMPLOYEES |
|---|---|---|---|---|
| **12/06** | 2,236 | 273 | 12.2% | 10,500 |
| **12/05** | 2,515 | 425 | 16.9% | 10,500 |
| **12/04** | 2,429 | 223 | 9.2% | 11,000 |
| **12/03** | 2,416 | 321 | 13.3% | 11,400 |
| **12/02** | 2,384 | 209 | 8.8% | 11,700 |
| **Annual Growth** | (1.6%) | 6.9% | — | (2.7%) |

### 2006 Year-End Financials

Debt ratio: 86.2%
Return on equity: 51.1%
Cash ($ mil.): 186
Current ratio: 0.41
Long-term debt ($ mil.): 493
No. of shares (mil.): 95
Dividends
Yield: —
Payout: —
Market value ($ mil.): 5,969

### Stock History

NYSE: DST

| | STOCK PRICE ($) FY Close | P/E High | P/E Low | PER SHARE ($) Earnings | Dividends | Book Value |
|---|---|---|---|---|---|---|
| **12/06** | 62.63 | 17 | 14 | 3.78 | — | 6.01 |
| **12/05** | 59.91 | 12 | 8 | 5.39 | — | 6.91 |
| **12/04** | 52.12 | 20 | 16 | 2.59 | — | 9.30 |
| **12/03** | 41.76 | 15 | 9 | 2.77 | — | 8.10 |
| **12/02** | 35.55 | 30 | 14 | 1.72 | — | 11.89 |
| **Annual Growth** | 15.2% | — | — | 21.8% | — | (15.7%) |

# DTE Energy

Detroit gets a charge from its Lions, Tigers, and DTE Energy, oh my. The holding company's main subsidiary, Detroit Edison, distributes electricity to some 2.2 million customers in southeastern Michigan. The utility's power plants (mainly fossil-fueled) have a generating capacity of more than 11,100 MW. The company's Michigan Consolidated Gas (MichCon) unit distributes natural gas to 1.3 million customers. DTE Energy's nonregulated operations include energy marketing and trading; coal transportation and procurement; energy management services for commercial and industrial customers; independent and on-site power generation; and gas exploration, production, and processing.

DTE Energy is expanding its nonutility businesses. The firm has wholesale power, gas, and coal marketing operations in the Midwest, the northeastern US, and eastern Canada; it also has merchant generation facilities in Illinois, Indiana, and Michigan. Environmental pursuits by DTE Energy include waste coal and landfill gas recovery and fuel cell development.

The company expanded into natural gas distribution in 2001 by buying Detroit-based natural gas utility holding company MCN Energy; the enlarged DTE Energy is the state's biggest utility.

In 2007 the company agreed to sell its Michigan Antrim Shale gas exploration and production assets to Atlas Energy Resources for $1.2 billion.

## HISTORY

DTE Energy's predecessor threw its first switch in 1886 when George Peck and local investors incorporated the Edison Illuminating Company of Detroit. Neighboring utility Peninsular Electric Light was formed in 1891, and both companies bought smaller utilities until they merged in 1903 to form Detroit Edison. A subsidiary of holding company North American Co., Detroit Edison was incorporated in New York to secure financing for power plants.

Detroit's growth in the 1920s and 1930s led the utility to build plants and buy others in outlying areas. Detroit Edison acquired Michigan Electric Power, which had been divested from its holding company under the Public Utility Holding Company Act of 1935, and was itself divested from North American in 1940.

The post-WWII boom prompted Detroit Edison to build more plants, most of them coal-fired. In 1953 it joined a consortium of 34 companies to build Fermi 1, a nuclear plant brought on line in 1963. Still strapped for power, Detroit Edison built the coal-fired Monroe plant, which began service in 1970. In 1972 Fermi 1 had a partial core meltdown and was taken off line.

Detroit Edison began shipping low-sulfur Montana coal through its Wisconsin terminal in 1974, which reduced the cost of obtaining the fuel. The next year it began building another nuke, Fermi 2. The nuke had cost more than $4.8 billion by the time it went on line in 1988. That year the utility began its landfill gas recovery operation (now DTE Biomass Energy).

A recession pounded automakers in the early 1990s, leading to cutbacks in electricity purchases. In 1992 Congress passed the Energy Policy Act, allowing wholesale power competition. In 1993 a fire shut down Fermi 2 for almost two years. Michigan's public service commission (PSC) approved retail customer-choice pilot programs for its utilities in 1994. Detroit Edison and rival Consumers Energy (now CMS Energy) took the PSC to court.

DTE Energy became Detroit Edison's holding company in 1996. The next year it formed DTE Energy Trading (to broker power) and DTE-CoEnergy (to provide energy-management services and sell power to large customers). It also formed Plug Power with Mechanical Technology to develop fuel cells that convert natural gas to power without combustion.

In 1997 and 1998 the PSC, bolstered by state court decisions, issued orders to restructure Michigan's utilities. The transition to retail competition began in 1998. That year DTE Energy and natural gas provider Michigan Consolidated Gas (MichCon) began collaborating on some operations, including billing and meter reading. DTE and GE formed a venture to sell and install Plug Power fuel cell systems.

A higher court shot down the PSC's restructuring orders in 1999, but DTE Energy and CMS Energy decided to implement customer choice using PSC guidelines. That year the US Department of Energy selected DTE Energy to install the world's first super power-cable, which could carry three times as much electricity as conventional copper. Also in 1999, DTE Energy agreed to acquire MCN Energy, MichCon's parent.

In 2000 DTE Energy formed subsidiary International Transmission (ITC) to hold Detroit Edison's transmission assets; the next year ITC joined the Midwest Independent System Operator, which began to manage ITC's network. It also completed its $4.3 billion purchase of MCN Energy in 2001. Full deregulation of Michigan's electricity market was completed in 2002. International Transmission was sold in 2003 to affiliates of Kohlberg Kravis Roberts and Trimaran Capital Partners for $610 million.

## EXECUTIVES

**Chairman and CEO:** Anthony F. Earley Jr., age 57, $2,927,500 pay
**President and COO:** Gerard M. Anderson, age 48, $700,000 pay
**EVP and CFO:** David E. Meador, age 49, $485,000 pay
**SVP and CIO:** Lynne Ellyn, age 55
**SVP and General Counsel:** Bruce D. Peterson, age 50
**SVP, Fossil Generation:** Robert A. Richard, age 45
**SVP, Regulatory Affairs:** Daniel G. (Dan) Brudzynski, age 46
**SVP, Corporate Affairs and Communications:** Paul Hillegonds, age 57
**SVP, Energy Resources:** Knut Simonsen, age 43
**VP, Corporate and Governmental Affairs:** Frederick E. (Fred) Shell, age 55
**VP, Corporate Communications:** Michael C. Porter, age 53
**VP, Human Resources:** Larry E. Steward, age 54
**Group President; President and COO, Detroit Edison:** Robert J. Buckler, age 56, $560,000 pay
**President, DTE Gas and Oil and DTE Gas Resources:** Richard L. Redmond, age 50
**President, Midwest Energy Resources:** Fred L. Shusterich, age 52
**President, DTE Energy Trading:** Steven Mabry, age 44
**President, DTE Energy Services:** David Ruud
**President, DTE Coal Services:** Matt T. Paul, age 37
**President, DTE Biomass Energy:** Mark Cousino, age 42
**Corporate Secretary:** Sandra K. Ennis, age 50
**Auditors:** Deloitte & Touche LLP

## LOCATIONS

**HQ:** DTE Energy Company
2000 2nd Ave., Detroit, MI 48226
**Phone:** 313-235-4000 **Fax:** 313-235-8055
**Web:** www.dteenergy.com

DTE Energy provides electricity and natural gas in Michigan and has other operations throughout the US and in Canada.

## PRODUCTS/OPERATIONS

**2006 Sales**

| | $ mil. | % of total |
|---|---|---|
| Electric utility | 4,737 | 50 |
| Gas utility | 1,849 | 20 |
| Non-utility operations | | |
| Synthetic fuel | 863 | 9 |
| Energy trading | 830 | 9 |
| Coal & gas midstream | 707 | 7 |
| Power & industrial products | 409 | 4 |
| Unconventional gas production | 99 | 1 |
| Corporate & other | 5 | — |
| Adjustments | (477) | — |
| **Total** | **9,022** | **100** |

## COMPETITORS

AEP
Aquila
CMS Energy
CMS Enterprises
Dairyland Power
Distributed Energy Systems
DPL
Duke Energy
Dynegy
Exelon Energy
Integrys Energy Group
Nicor
Peabody Energy
PG&E
SEMCO Energy
Southern Company
Wisconsin Energy
Xcel Energy

## HISTORICAL FINANCIALS

Company Type: Public

**Income Statement** FYE: December 31

| | REVENUE ($ mil.) | NET INCOME ($ mil.) | NET PROFIT MARGIN | EMPLOYEES |
|---|---|---|---|---|
| **12/06** | 9,022 | 433 | 4.8% | 10,527 |
| **12/05** | 9,022 | 537 | 6.0% | 11,410 |
| **12/04** | 7,114 | 431 | 6.1% | 11,207 |
| **12/03** | 7,041 | 521 | 7.4% | 11,099 |
| **12/02** | 6,749 | 632 | 9.4% | 11,095 |
| **Annual Growth** | 7.5% | (9.0%) | — | (1.3%) |

**2006 Year-End Financials**

Debt ratio: 127.8%
Return on equity: 7.5%
Cash ($ mil.): 293
Current ratio: 0.95
Long-term debt ($ mil.): 7,474
No. of shares (mil.): 177
Dividends
Yield: 4.3%
Payout: 85.6%
Market value ($ mil.): 8,575

**Stock History** NYSE: DTE

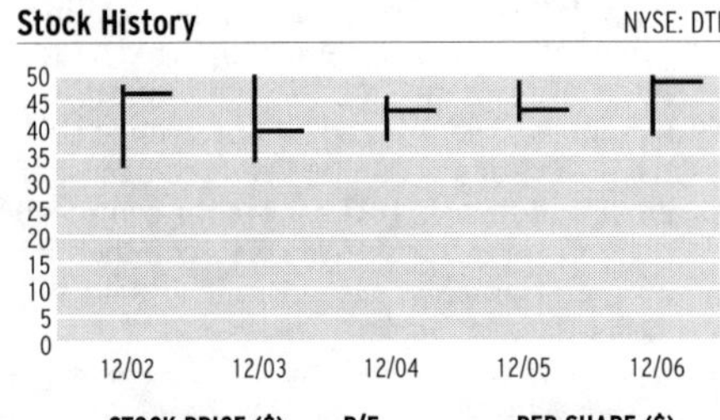


| | STOCK PRICE ($) FY Close | P/E High | P/E Low | PER SHARE ($) Earnings | Dividends | Book Value |
|---|---|---|---|---|---|---|
| **12/06** | 48.41 | 20 | 16 | 2.43 | 2.08 | 33.02 |
| **12/05** | 43.19 | 16 | 14 | 3.05 | 2.06 | 32.44 |
| **12/04** | 43.13 | 18 | 15 | 2.49 | 2.06 | 31.85 |
| **12/03** | 39.40 | 16 | 11 | 3.09 | 2.06 | 31.36 |
| **12/02** | 46.40 | 12 | 9 | 3.83 | 2.06 | 27.26 |
| **Annual Growth** | 1.1% | — | — | (10.8%) | 0.2% | 4.9% |

# Duke Energy

Duke Energy is a John Wayne-sized power business. In 2006 the company bought Cinergy in a $9 billion stock swap. Following the deal, Duke Energy has 3.9 million electric customers in the US South and Midwest. Its Commercial Power unit has 8,700 MW of unregulated generation. Duke Energy International has 4,200 MW of generation (mostly in Latin America). Crescent Resources (a joint venture with Morgan Stanley Real Estate Fund) manages land holdings and develops real estate projects. Reorganizing its operations as a pure play electric infrastucture group, in 2006 the company sold its commercial marketing and trading businesses to Fortis, and in early 2007 it spun off its natural gas businesses as Spectra Energy.

Jim Rogers, formerly Cinergy's chairman, president, and CEO, became the president and CEO of the company; the board of directors consists of 10 members from Duke Energy and five from Cinergy. In order to make the acquisition pass muster, Duke had to find a way around the Depression-era federal Public Utility Holding Company Act, legislation designed to keep ownership of public utilities in the same region as its customers.

The company has exited the European energy marketing business; it also left the proprietary (third-party) energy trading business in North America (primarily made up of Duke Energy North America or DENA, sold to LS Power Equity Partners for a reported $1.5 billion). Duke has wound down its energy-trading joint venture with Exxon Mobil. The company has also scaled back on plans to expand its power generation portfolio.

In 2006 Duke sold a 50% stake in its real estate subsidiary, Crescent Resources, to Morgan Stanley Real Estate. That year the company bought an 825-MW power plant in Rockingham County, North Carolina, from Dynegy for $195 million.

## HISTORY

Surgeon Gill Wylie founded Catawba Power Company in 1899; its first hydroelectric plant in South Carolina was on line by 1904. The next year Wylie and James "Buck" Duke (founder of the American Tobacco Company and Duke University's namesake) formed Southern Power Company with Wylie as president.

In 1910 Buck Duke became president of Southern Power and organized Mill-Power Supply to sell electric equipment and appliances. He also began investing in electricity-powered textile mills, which prospered as a result of the electric power, and continued to bring in customers. He formed the Southern Public Utility Company in 1913 to buy other Piedmont-region utilities. Wylie died in 1924, the same year the company was renamed Duke Power; Buck Duke died the next year.

Growing after WWII, the company went public in 1950 and moved to the NYSE in 1961. It also formed its real estate arm, Crescent Resources, in the 1960s. Insulating itself from the 1970s energy crises, Duke invested in coal mining and three nuclear plants, the first completed in 1974.

In 1988 Duke began to develop power projects outside its home region, and it also bought neighboring utility Nantahala Power and Light. The next year it formed a joint venture with Fluor's Fluor Daniel unit to provide engineering and construction services to power generators. Mill-Power Supply was sold in 1990.

By the 1990s Duke had moved into overseas markets, acquiring an Argentine power station in 1992. It also tried its hand at telecommunications, creating DukeNet Communications in 1994 to build fiber-optic systems, and in 1996 it joined oil giant Mobil to create a power trading and marketing business. As the US power industry traveled toward deregulation, Duke also sought natural gas operations. It targeted PanEnergy, which owned a major pipeline system in the eastern half of the US. Duke Power bought PanEnergy in 1997 to form Duke Energy Corporation.

Seeing an opportunity in 1998, Duke formed Duke Communication Services to provide antenna sites to the fast-growing wireless communications industry. It also acquired a 52% stake in Electroquil, an electric power generating company in Guayaquil, Ecuador. That year it purchased a pipeline company in Australia from PG&E; it also bought three PG&E power plants to compete in California's deregulated electric utility marketplace.

Duke sold Panhandle Eastern Pipe Line and gas-related assets in the Midwest to CMS Energy in 1999 to reduce operations in the region and made plans to build a pipeline extending from Alabama to Florida (completed in 2002).

To further enhance natural gas operations in other regions, Duke bought El Paso's East Tennessee Natural Gas pipeline unit in 2000 and a 20% stake in Canadian 88 Energy; it also purchased $1.4 billion in South American generation assets, including assets from Dominion Resources, and the gas trading operations of Mobil (now Exxon Mobil) in the Netherlands. Also in 2000, Duke and Phillips Petroleum (now ConocoPhillips) merged their gas gathering and processing and NGL operations into Duke Energy Field Services.

In 2001 Duke announced the $8 billion acquisition of Westcoast Energy; the purchase, which was completed in 2002, added more than a million natural gas customers and 6,900 miles of gas pipeline in Canada. Duke Energy Field Services purchased Chevron's 33% stake in Discovery Producer Services, which operates a Gulf of Mexico gas pipeline and nearby processing facilities.

Duke set out to sell $1.5 billion in assets in 2003 to focus on core operations. The company sold its Empire State Pipeline subsidiary to National Fuel Gas for $240 million and sold its stakes in the Alliance Pipeline, Alliance Canada Marketing, and the Aux Sable refinery to Enbridge and Fort Chicago Energy Partners for $245 million. Also that year Duke sold its stake in Foothills Pipe Lines to TransCanada for $181 million, and it sold $300 million in renewable energy facilities to privately owned Highstar Renewable Fuels.

In 2004 the company sold an Indonesian power plant to Freeport-McMoRan in a $300 million deal, and it sold its 30% interest in the Vector Pipeline to Enbridge and DTE Energy for $145 million. It also sold the assets of its merchant finance business (Duke Capital Partners), and its stake in Canadian 88 Energy (now Esprit Exploration). Following this trend in 2005, Duke Energy sold its 620-MW Grays Harbor facility (Washington) to an affiliate of Invenergy for $21 million.

## EXECUTIVES

**Chairman, President, and CEO:** James E. (Jim) Rogers, age 59
**Group Executive and Chief Nuclear Officer:** Henry B. (Brew) Barron Jr.
**Group Executive and CFO:** David L. Hauser, age 55
**Group Executive and Chief Legal Officer:** Marc E. Manly, age 52
**Group Executive and President, Commercial Businesses:** Thomas C. (Tom) O'Connor, age 51
**Group Executive and Chief Administrative Officer:** Christopher C. (Chris) Rolfe, age 56
**Group Executive and Chief Strategy, Policy, and Regulatory Officer:** B. Keith Trent, age 47
**Group Executive; President and COO, U.S. Franchised Electric and Gas:** James L. (Jim) Turner, age 45
**VP, Financial Planning and Treasurer:** Lynn J. Good, age 45
**VP and Controller:** Steven K. Young, age 46
**VP, Corporate Human Resources:** Karen R. Feld
**VP, Market and Portfolio Analysis:** Robert Irvin
**VP, Corporate Secretary and Chief Ethics and Compliance Officer:** Julia S. (Julie) Janson
**VP and Chief of Technology:** David W. Mohler
**VP and Chief Communications Officer:** Cathy S. Roche
**VP, Investor Relations:** R. Sean Trauschke, age 39
**VP, Information Technology, Duke Energy Americas:** Stan Land
**Director, Investor Relations:** John Arensdorf
**Director, External Relations:** Peter (Pete) Sheffield
**Chairman, President, and CEO, Duke Energy Field Services:** William H. (Bill) Easter III, age 57
**President and CEO, Duke Energy International:** Richard K. McGee, age 46
**President and CEO, Crescent Resources:** Arthur W. (Art) Fields
**President, DukeNet Communications:** William (Brad) Davis
**Auditors:** Deloitte & Touche LLP

## LOCATIONS

**HQ:** Duke Energy Corporation
526 S. Church St., Charlotte, NC 28202
**Phone:** 704-594-6200 **Fax:** 704-382-3814
**Web:** www.duke-energy.com

Duke Energy primarily operates in the Americas.

### 2006 Sales

| | $ mil. | % of total |
|---|---|---|
| US | 10,710 | 71 |
| Canada | 3,472 | 23 |
| Latin America | 961 | 6 |
| Other regions | 41 | — |
| **Total** | **15,184** | **100** |

## PRODUCTS/OPERATIONS

### 2006 Sales

| | $ mil. | % of total |
|---|---|---|
| US franchised electric & gas | 8,077 | 53 |
| Natural gas transmission | 4,515 | 30 |
| Commercial power | 1,396 | 9 |
| International energy | 961 | 6 |
| Crescent | 221 | 2 |
| Other | 14 | — |
| **Total** | **15,184** | **100** |

### Selected Operations

Commercial Power (unregulated power generation)
Crescent Resources (50%, real estate)
Duke Energy International (foreign asset development and marketing)
Duke Power (electric utility)

## COMPETITORS

AEP
AES
Aquila
Avista
CenterPoint Energy
Constellation Energy Group
Dynegy
El Paso
Entergy
Enterprise Products
Exelon
KeySpan
Koch
Mirant
PG&E
Piedmont Natural Gas
Progress Energy
Reliant Energy
SCANA
Southern Company
SUEZ-TRACTEBEL
TVA
TXU
Williams Companies

## HISTORICAL FINANCIALS

Company Type: Public

**Income Statement** FYE: December 31

| | REVENUE ($ mil.) | NET INCOME ($ mil.) | NET PROFIT MARGIN | EMPLOYEES |
|---|---|---|---|---|
| **12/06** | 15,184 | 1,863 | 12.3% | 25,600 |
| **12/05** | 16,746 | 1,824 | 10.9% | 20,400 |
| **12/04** | 22,503 | 1,490 | 6.6% | 21,500 |
| **12/03** | 22,154 | (1,323) | — | 23,800 |
| **12/02** | 15,663 | 1,034 | 6.6% | 22,000 |
| **Annual Growth** | (0.8%) | 15.9% | — | 3.9% |

**2006 Year-End Financials**

Debt ratio: 69.4%
Return on equity: 8.8%
Cash ($ mil.): 2,569
Current ratio: 1.05
Long-term debt ($ mil.): 18,118
No. of shares (mil.): 1,257
Dividends
Yield: 6.3%
Payout: 80.3%
Market value ($ mil.): 25,142

**Stock History** NYSE: DUK

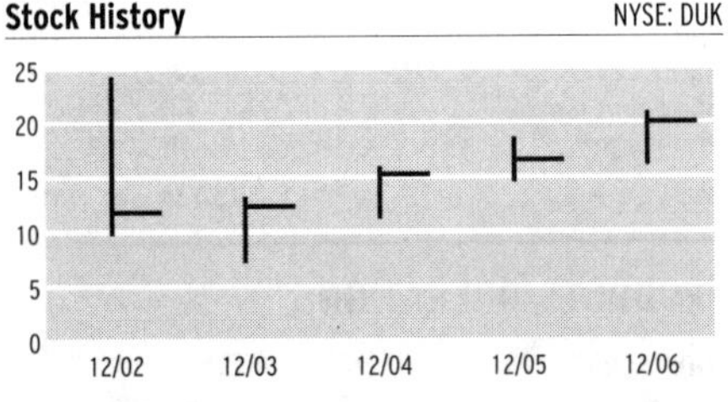


| | STOCK PRICE ($) FY Close | P/E High | P/E Low | PER SHARE ($) Earnings | Dividends | Book Value |
|---|---|---|---|---|---|---|
| **12/06** | 20.00 | 13 | 10 | 1.57 | 1.26 | 20.76 |
| **12/05** | 16.53 | 10 | 8 | 1.88 | — | 17.71 |
| **12/04** | 15.25 | 10 | 7 | 1.54 | — | 17.32 |
| **12/03** | 12.32 | — | — | (1.48) | — | 15.24 |
| **12/02** | 11.77 | 20 | 8 | 1.22 | — | — |
| **Annual Growth** | 14.2% | — | — | 6.5% | — | 10.9% |

# Dun & Bradstreet

For The Dun & Bradstreet Corporation, there's no business like "know" business. The company, known as D&B, is one of the world's leading suppliers of business information, services, and research. Its database contains statistics on more than 100 million companies in more than 200 countries, including the largest volume of business-credit information in the world. D&B sells that information and integrates it into software products and Web-based applications. D&B also offers marketing information and purchasing-support services. The company made a major commitment to provide information via the Internet in 2003 when it acquired Hoover's, the publisher of this profile.

D&B strengthened its Internet presence again in 2007 with the purchase of First Research, a Web-based provider of editorial-based industry reports aimed at sales people. (After the acquisition, First Research became a wholly owned subsidiary of Hoover's.) Hoover's and First Research are part of the E-business Solutions division, which is a key company focus because it is the fastest growing of D&B's four business segments.

The company is also making technology investments designed to expand its core businesses. D&B is improving the data capabilities of Risk Management Solutions (accounting for two-thirds of sales) and delivering more predictive indicators about credit risks to its customers. The company is also focused on making investments in and improvements to its Sales and Marketing Solutions division, which supplies lists and related data to direct mail and marketing customers.

Continuing to be a steady contributor, D&B's Supply Management Solutions segment experienced growth as a result of new customers gained from the acquisition of Open Ratings in 2006.

D&B has also instituted a financial flexibility program designed to simplify management as well as consolidate its technology infrastructure.

D&B continues to focus its international operations on a market-by-market basis, conducting business through wholly owned subsidiaries, independent correspondents, and strategic partner relationships through its D&B Worldwide Network. As a result, D&B is offering more international company records to its customers around the world.

Davis Selected Advisors owns about 15% of the company.

## HISTORY

D&B originated as Lewis Tappan's Mercantile Agency, established in 1841 in New York City. One of the first commercial credit-reporting agencies, the Mercantile supplied wholesalers and importers with reports on their customers' credit histories. The company's credit reporters included four future US presidents (Lincoln, Grant, Cleveland, and McKinley). In the 1840s it opened offices in Boston, Philadelphia, and Baltimore, and in 1857 it established operations in Montreal and London.

In 1859 Robert Dun took over the agency and renamed it R.G. Dun & Co. The first edition of the *Dun's Book* (1859) contained information on 20,268 businesses; by 1886 that number had risen to over a million. During this time Dun's was competing fiercely with the John M. Bradstreet Company, founded in 1849 by its namesake in Cincinnati. The rivalry continued until the Depression, when Dun's CEO Arthur Whiteside negotiated a merger of the two firms in 1933; the new company adopted the Dun & Bradstreet name in 1939.

In 1961 Dun & Bradstreet bought Reuben H. Donnelley Corp., a direct-mail advertiser and publisher of the Yellow Pages (first published 1886) and 10 trade magazines. In 1962 Moody's Investors Service (founded 1900) became part of Dun & Bradstreet. The company began computerizing its records in the 1960s and eventually developed the largest private business database in the world. Repackaging that information, the company began creating new products such as Dun's Financial Profiles, first published in 1979.

Dun & Bradstreet continued buying information and publishing companies during the 1970s and 1980s, including Technical Publishing (trade and professional publications, 1978), National CSS (computer services, 1979), and McCormack & Dodge (software, 1983). Later came ACNielsen (1984) and IMS International (pharmaceutical sales data, 1988).

Finding that not all information was equally profitable, Dun & Bradstreet sold its specialty industry and consumer database companies in the early 1990s. Still hoping to cash in on medical and technology information, the company formed D&B HealthCare Information and bought a majority interest in consulting firm Gartner Group. In 1993 the company consolidated its 27 worldwide data centers into four locations. The following year it settled a class-action suit involving overcharging customers for credit reports. After its second earnings decline in three years, management revamped the company in 1996, selling off ACNielsen and Cognizant (consisting of IMS Health and Nielsen Media Research). Volney Taylor was appointed chairman and CEO of Dun & Bradstreet. In 1998 it spun off R. H. Donnelley (formerly Reuben H. Donnelley).

Under pressure from unhappy shareholders, Taylor resigned in late 1999. With director Clifford Alexander Jr. acting as interim CEO, Dun & Bradstreet announced plans to spin off its Moody's unit. After completing the spinoff the following year, Allan Loren took over as chairman and CEO of Dun & Bradstreet. Loren retired from the company in mid-2005 and president Steven Alesio became chairman, president, and CEO.

The company boosted its risk management business with a $16 million acquisition of online credit management software maker LiveCapital in 2005. A similar lift was given to its Supply Management Solutions unit in 2006 after its $8.3 million purchase of Open Ratings, an Internet-based supply risk management company.

## EXECUTIVES

**Chairman and CEO:** Steven W. (Steve) Alesio, age 52, $800,000 pay
**President and COO:** Sara S. Mathew, age 51
**SVP Global Solutions and Chief Marketing Officer:** James P. (Jim) Burke, age 41, $360,000 pay
**SVP Middle Market Customer Group:** Stacy Cashman
**SVP Global Sales and Marketing Solutions:** James (Jim) Delaney
**SVP Human Resources, Winning Culture, and Team Member Communications:** Patricia A. Clifford, age 42
**SVP International Partnerships and Asia Pacific:** David J. Emery
**SVP and CFO:** Anastasios G. (Tasos) Konidaris, age 40
**SVP Small Business Marketing:** Charles E. Gottdiener, age 40
**SVP Global Reengineering:** David J. Lewinter, age 45

**SVP and Leader, Strategy and Innovation:** David Palmieri
**SVP Strategy, Business Development, and Reengineering:** Lee A. Spirer
**SVP Technology and CIO:** Byron C. Vielehr, age 43, $325,000 pay
**SVP Small Business Group Credit:** David Kieselstein
**SVP, General Counsel, and Secretary:** Jeffrey S. (Jeff) Hurwitz, age 46
**President, D&B International:** James M. (Jim) Howland, age 46
**Leader, External Communications:** Joseph Jones
**Auditors:** PricewaterhouseCoopers LLP

## LOCATIONS

**HQ:** The Dun & Bradstreet Corporation
103 JFK Pkwy., Short Hills, NJ 07078
**Phone:** 973-921-5500 **Fax:** 973-921-6056
**Web:** www.dnb.com

The Dun & Bradstreet Corporation has offices in about 30 countries and correspondents in another 140 countries.

### 2006 Sales

| | $ mil. | % of total |
|---|---|---|
| US | 1,164.2 | 76 |
| Other countries | 367.1 | 24 |
| **Total** | **1,531.3** | **100** |

## PRODUCTS/OPERATIONS

### 2006 Sales

| | $ mil. | % of total |
|---|---|---|
| Risk management solutions | 985.5 | 64 |
| Sales & marketing solutions | 412.2 | 27 |
| E-business solutions | 88.7 | 6 |
| Supply management solutions | 44.9 | 3 |
| **Total** | **1,531.3** | **100** |

## COMPETITORS

ACNielsen
Acxiom
Capgemini
Deloitte Consulting
Equifax
Experian Americas
Fair Isaac
GfK NOP
Harte-Hanks
Information Resources
infoUSA
Kreller Business Information
OneSource
S&P
Thomson Corporation

## HISTORICAL FINANCIALS

Company Type: Public

### Income Statement

FYE: December 31

| | REVENUE ($ mil.) | NET INCOME ($ mil.) | NET PROFIT MARGIN | EMPLOYEES |
|---|---|---|---|---|
| **12/06** | 1,531 | 241 | 15.7% | 4,400 |
| **12/05** | 1,444 | 221 | 15.3% | 4,350 |
| **12/04** | 1,414 | 212 | 15.0% | 4,700 |
| **12/03** | 1,386 | 175 | 12.6% | 6,100 |
| **12/02** | 1,276 | 143 | 11.2% | 6,600 |
| **Annual Growth** | 4.7% | 13.8% | — | (9.6%) |

### 2006 Year-End Financials

Debt ratio: —
Return on equity: —
Cash ($ mil.): 138
Current ratio: 0.80
Long-term debt ($ mil.): 459
No. of shares (mil.): 60
Dividends
Yield: —
Payout: —
Market value ($ mil.): 4,976

### Stock History

NYSE: DNB

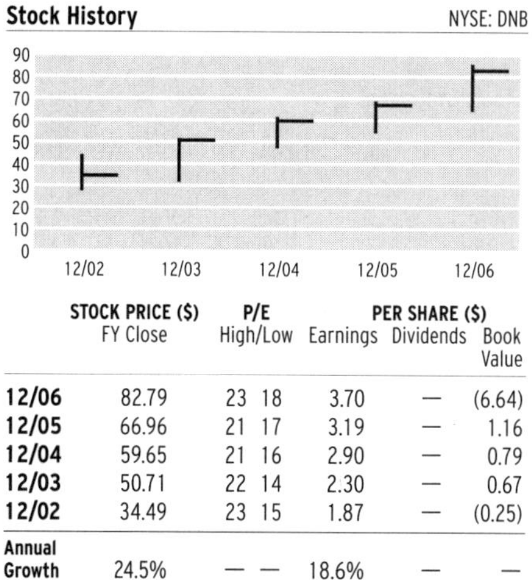

| | STOCK PRICE ($) FY Close | P/E High/Low | | PER SHARE ($) Earnings | Dividends | Book Value |
|---|---|---|---|---|---|---|
| **12/06** | 82.79 | 23 | 18 | 3.70 | — | (6.64) |
| **12/05** | 66.96 | 21 | 17 | 3.19 | — | 1.16 |
| **12/04** | 59.65 | 21 | 16 | 2.90 | — | 0.79 |
| **12/03** | 50.71 | 22 | 14 | 2.30 | — | 0.67 |
| **12/02** | 34.49 | 23 | 15 | 1.87 | — | (0.25) |
| **Annual Growth** | 24.5% | — | — | 18.6% | — | — |

# Dynegy Inc.

Power dynamo Dynegy (short for "dynamic energy") is making dynamic changes, restructuring its operations around its electricity production unit. The company's power generation portfolio consists of 11,739 MW fleet of 20 owned or leased power plants fueled by coal, fuel oil, and natural gas. Dynegy, once a top marketer of wholesale electricity, natural gas, and other commodities in North America and Europe, sold off its energy trading unit and sold its gas processing business in 2005 to Targa Resources for $2.5 billion. As part of a merger deal in 2006 Dynegy agreed to pay more than $2 billion for the power plants of private equity fund LS Power Group. Chevron owns 19% of Dynegy.

The company has sold its 50% stake in Southern California-based West Coast Power to NRG Energy; in a related deal, Dynegy acquired the 50% interest NRG owns in Rocky Road Power, a plant located near Chicago. The company is trimming costs and eliminating debt through the sale of some of its operating units to make itself a prime target for acquisition by another player in the power generation field.

The company's agreement to sell Illinois Power to Exelon was terminated in 2003; however, it completed the sale of the utility to Ameren for $500 million in cash and $1.8 billion in debt in 2004. The deal included the sale of Dynegy's 20% stake in Illinois power generator Electric Energy. Dynegy is also divesting other noncore power generation assets; it has sold stakes in plants in the US (Texas, Georgia, and Virginia), Costa Rica, and Jamaica. The company has sold its North American telecom assets to an affiliate of 360networks, and it has divested its European broadband network.

Dynegy has expanded its power generation operations in the northeastern US through the acquisition of Exelon subsidiary Sithe Energies and Sithe Independence. The acquisition included four natural gas-fired facilities and a power generation plant in New York, as well as four hydroelectric plants in Pennsylvania.

In 2007 Dynegy agreed to sell a power plant in Texas to a joint venture of PNM Resources and Cascade Investment for $470 million.

## HISTORY

Dynegy, originally Natural Gas Clearinghouse (NGC), emerged from the deregulation of the natural gas industry. In 1978 the Natural Gas Policy Act reduced interstate pipeline companies' control over the marketplace. Federal Energy Regulatory Commission (FERC) Order 380 (1984) made gas prices on the open market competitive with those of pipeline companies. NGC was founded in late 1984 to match gas buyers and sellers without taking title. Chuck Watson became president and CEO in 1985. The company grew dramatically as deregulation secured larger volumes of gas for independent marketers.

The company developed financial instruments (such as natural gas futures) to provide customers with a hedge against wide fluctuations in natural gas prices. By 1990 NGC was trading natural gas futures on NYMEX. It also branched out by buying gas gathering and processing facilities, and it formed NGC Oil Trading and Transportation to market crude oil.

FERC Order 636 (1992) required most interstate pipeline companies to offer merchant sales, transportation, and storage as separate services, on the same terms that their own affiliates received. With the low-price advantage taken away from pipeline companies, NGC began selling more to local gas utilities.

In 1994 NGC set up partnerships with Canada's NOVA (Novagas Clearinghouse, a natural gas marketer) and British Gas (Accord Energy, an energy marketer), which gave those firms sizable stakes (later reduced) in the company. It also set up an electric power marketing unit, Electric Clearinghouse.

The company changed its name to NGC and went public in 1995 after it bought Trident NGL, an integrated natural gas liquids company. The next year NGC bought Chevron's natural gas business, giving Chevron (which became ChevronTexaco in 2001 and then Chevron again in 2005) a stake in NGC.

In 1997 NGC acquired Destec Energy, a leading independent power producer. Taking the name Dynegy in 1998, the company allied with Florida Power to market wholesale electricity and gas. In 2000 Dynegy paid about $4 billion for utility holding company Illinova. The deal gave Dynegy 3,800 MW of generation capacity, which was transferred to its energy marketing unit, and utility operations in the Midwest.

In November 2001 Dynegy announced an agreement to buy energy trading giant Enron for about $9 billion in stock and $13 billion in assumed debt. Enron had seen its stock price driven down because of controversy over the way it accounted for financial transactions with partnerships controlled by company officers. Later that month, after Enron's stock price continued to plunge, Dynegy canceled the deal and announced that it would exercise its option to buy Enron's Northern Natural Gas (NNG) pipeline for $1.5 billion. Enron then filed for Chapter 11 bankruptcy protection, and the two companies filed lawsuits against each other. In early 2002 Enron let Dynegy take control of the NNG pipeline, and Dynegy agreed to pay Enron $25 million to settle the suits. Dynegy sold the NNG pipeline to MidAmerican Energy Holdings later that year for $928 million plus $950 million in assumed debt.

Also in 2002 the SEC held a formal fraud investigation into how Dynegy accounted for a multi-year natural gas transaction called Project Alpha; the company later restated its 1999-2001 earnings to eliminate a tax benefit and other accounting improprieties related to the transaction. In addition, federal authorities sought information about Dynegy's participation in round-trip energy trades with CMS Energy, which artificially drove up the companies' trading volumes. The company reduced its workforce by 15% that year.

Amid the inquiries, Watson resigned as Dynegy's chairman and CEO. Dynegy later agreed to pay a $3 million fine in relation to the Project Alpha investigation, and in 2003 Jamie Olis was the first former Dynegy executive to be convicted on fraud charges over his involvement in the project. (Olis was sentenced to 24 years in prison in 2004; also that year Dynegy joint venture West Coast Power reached a $280 million settlement — $260 million in lost payments and $20 million in fines — with the FERC over charges of manipulating the California power market during its energy crisis in 2000-01.)

In 2002 and 2003 Dynegy sold its UK gas storage assets to Centrica and Scottish and Southern for a total of $700 million.

## EXECUTIVES

**Chairman and CEO:** Bruce A. Williamson, age 47
**President and COO:** Stephen A. (Steve) Furbacher, age 58, $935,769 pay (prior to promotion)
**EVP, Strategic Planning and Corporate Business Development:** Lynn Lednicky, age 45
**EVP and CFO:** Holli C. Nichols, age 35, $454,124 pay
**EVP, General Counsel and Administration:** J. Kevin Blodgett, age 34
**SVP and Treasurer:** Chuck Cook, age 41
**SVP, Operations:** Rich Eimer
**SVP and Controller:** Carolyn J. Stone, age 33
**VP and General Auditor:** James (Jim) Horsch, age 50
**VP Tax:** Layne J. Albert, age 38
**VP, Information Technology:** Biren Kumar
**VP, Investor and Public Relations:** Norelle V. Lundy, age 32
**VP, Midwest Fleet Operations:** Keith McFarland
**VP, Fuels and Emissions:** Brian Tamplen
**VP, Commercial Power Operations:** Eric Watts
**VP, Eastern Fleet Operations:** Daniel P. Thompson
**VP, Human Resources:** Julius Cox, age 34
**VP, Strategy, Processes, and Reporting:** Mike Gray
**VP, Procurement and Business Services:** Mike Sanders
**Director, Public Relations:** David Byford
**Senior Analyst:** Hillarie Bloxom
**Auditors:** PricewaterhouseCoopers LLP

## LOCATIONS

**HQ:** Dynegy Inc.
1000 Louisiana St., Ste. 5800, Houston, TX 77002
**Phone:** 713-507-6400 **Fax:** 713-507-6808
**Web:** www.dynegy.com

## COMPETITORS

AEP
AES
Calpine
Duke Energy
Edison International
Exelon
Midwest Generation
Mirant
NRG Energy
Reliant Energy
Sempra Energy
Texas New Mexico Power

## HISTORICAL FINANCIALS

Company Type: Public

**Income Statement** FYE: December 31

| | REVENUE ($ mil.) | NET INCOME ($ mil.) | NET PROFIT MARGIN | EMPLOYEES |
|---|---|---|---|---|
| **12/06** | 2,017 | (333) | — | 1,339 |
| **12/05** | 2,313 | 90 | 3.9% | 1,371 |
| **12/04** | 6,153 | (15) | — | 2,223 |
| **12/03** | 5,787 | (667) | — | 4,103 |
| **12/02** | 5,516 | (2,737) | — | 4,626 |
| **Annual Growth** | (22.2%) | — | — | (26.7%) |

**2006 Year-End Financials**

Debt ratio: 140.7%
Return on equity: —
Cash ($ mil.): 651
Current ratio: 1.65
Long-term debt ($ mil.): 3,190
No. of shares (mil.): 403
Dividends
Yield: —
Payout: —
Market value ($ mil.): 2,919

**Stock History** NYSE: DYN

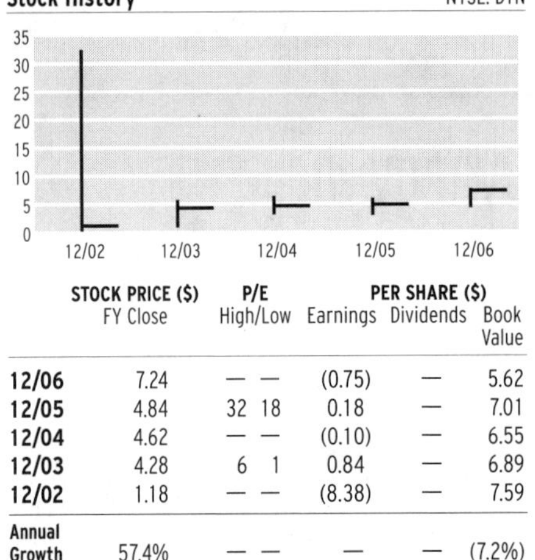


| | STOCK PRICE ($) FY Close | P/E High/Low | PER SHARE ($) Earnings | Dividends | Book Value |
|---|---|---|---|---|---|
| **12/06** | 7.24 | — — | (0.75) | — | 5.62 |
| **12/05** | 4.84 | 32 18 | 0.18 | — | 7.01 |
| **12/04** | 4.62 | — — | (0.10) | — | 6.55 |
| **12/03** | 4.28 | 6 1 | 0.84 | — | 6.89 |
| **12/02** | 1.18 | — — | (8.38) | — | 7.59 |
| **Annual Growth** | 57.4% | — — | — | — | (7.2%) |

# E. & J. Gallo Winery

E. & J. Gallo Winery brings merlot to the masses. The company is one of the world's largest wine makers and the largest in the US by cases sold, thanks in part to its inexpensive jug and box brands Carlo Rossi and Peter Vella. It also makes the fortified Thunderbird brand. The vintner cultivates more than 3,000 acres in California's Napa and Sonoma valleys. It is the leading US exporter of California wine. Among its premium wines and imports are those of Gallo Family Vineyards Sonoma Reserve and the Italian wine, Ecco Domani. For those who prefer a little kick to their wine, Gallo distills several lines of brandy. Founded in 1933, the company is still owned by the Gallo family.

In addition to using its own grapes, Gallo buys the fruit from other Sonoma County growers. Its 2002 purchase of fellow Sonoma County vintner Louis M. Martini Winery marked the first time Gallo bought another winery rather than land or wine labels. Gallo invested about $1 million in capital improvements at the winery with plans to ramp up production of cabernet under the Martini label. Along with brewing wine and spirits, the company makes its own labels and bottles at its subsidiary, Gallo Glass.

Gallo once only sold wine in the low-to-moderate price range, but now sells about 45 brands over a wide price range, from alcohol-added wines and wine coolers to upscale varietals that fetch more than $50 a bottle. It has successfully expanded premium wines such as Turning Leaf and Gossamer Bay, which don't have the Gallo name on the label. The vintner's strong affiliation with Wal-Mart has boosted wine sales in Wal-Mart markets such as Germany and the UK.

The company has tried new approaches to marketing its products, such as sponsoring pro volleyball tournaments. It also rebranded its California wines as the "Gallo Family Vineyards" and removed the Ernest & Julio tag from its packaging.

## HISTORY

Giuseppe Gallo, the father of Ernest and Julio Gallo, was born in 1882 in the wine country of northwest Italy. Around 1900 he and his brother, Michelo (they called themselves Joe and Mike), traveled to America seeking fame and fortune in San Francisco. Both brothers became wealthy growing grapes and anticipating the growth of the market during Prohibition (homemade wine was legal and popular).

Giuseppe's eldest sons, Ernest and Julio, worked with their father from the beginning, but their relationship was strained. The father was reluctant to help his sons, particularly Ernest, in business. However, the mysterious murder-suicide that ended the lives of Giuseppe and his wife in 1933 eliminated that problem: the sons inherited the business their father had been unwilling to share.

From then on Ernest ran the business end, assembling a large distribution network and building a national brand, while Julio made the wine and Joe Jr., the third, much younger, brother, worked for them. In the early 1940s Gallo opened bottling plants in Los Angeles and New Orleans, using screw-cap bottles, which then seemed more hygienic and modern than corks. Gallo lagged during WWII, when alcohol was diverted for the military. Under Julio's supervision, it upgraded its planting stock and refined its technology.

In an attempt to capitalize on the sweet wines popular in the 1950s, Gallo introduced Thunderbird, a fortified wine (its alcohol content boosted to 20%), in 1957. In the 1960s Gallo spurred its growth by heavily advertising and keeping prices low. It introduced Hearty Burgundy, a jug wine, in 1964, along with Ripple. Gallo introduced the carbonated, fruit-flavored Boone's Farm Apple Wine in 1969, creating short-term interest in "pop" wines.

The company introduced its first varietal wines in 1974. In the 1970s Gallo field workers switched unions, from the United Farm Workers to the Teamsters. Repercussions included protests and boycotts, but sales were largely unaffected. From 1976 to 1982 Gallo operated under an FTC order limiting its control over wholesalers. The order was lifted after the industry's competitive balance changed.

Through the 1970s and 1980s, Gallo expanded its production of varietals; in 1988 it began adding vintage dates to labels. But it also kept a hand in the lower levels of the market, introducing Bartles & Jaymes wine coolers.

Gallo began a legal battle in 1986 with Joe, who had been eased out of the business, over the use of the Gallo name. In 1992 Joe lost the use of his name for commercial purposes. Julio died the next year when his Jeep overturned on a family ranch.

In 1996 rival Kendall-Jackson sued Gallo for trademark infringement over Gallo's new wine brand, Turning Leaf, claiming Gallo copied its Vintner's Reserve bottle and label. A jury ruled in Gallo's favor in 1997; a federal appeals court supported that decision in 1998.

In 2000 Gallo announced plans to promote wine-cooler market leader Bartles & Jaymes with a new advertising campaign, although the category continued to wane. The next year Gallo expanded the technological end of the wine business. Gallo's research team patented a number of tools licensed to winemakers around the world; one tool, for example, can diagnose a sick vine in a matter of hours, rather than years.

The purchase of Louis M. Martini Winery in Napa Valley in 2002, furthered Gallo's expansion into premium wines. In 2004 it bought the brand name and stocks of San Jose-based wine producer, Mirassou Vineyards, one of the oldest wineries in California, and Santa Barbara company, Bindlewood Weste Winery. In 2005 Gallo added Grape Links, Inc., maker of Barefoot Cellars, to its stable of holdings.

Ernest Gallo died in 2007 at the age of 97.

## EXECUTIVES

**Co-President and CEO:** Joseph E. (Joe) Gallo, age 65
**Co-President:** James E. (Jim) Coleman, age 72
**Co-President:** Robert J. (Bob) Gallo, age 72
**EVP and General Counsel:** Jack B. Owens
**VP, Marketing:** Iain Douglas
**VP, Marketing and Chief Marketing Strategist:** Gerry Glasgow
**VP, Marketing International Americas:** Tim Roach
**VP, Supply Chain:** Ernie Chachere
**VP, Viticulture:** Nick Dokoozlian
**VP, Wine Growing:** Tom Smith
**VP and CIO:** Kent Kushar
**VP and General Manager, Europe:** Devinder Singh
**VP, Communications:** George Marsden
**VP, Public Relations:** Susan Hensley
**CTO:** Mary Wagner
**Director, Maintenanace and Engineering Gallo Glass:** Troy Wells
**Director, Marketing:** Stephanie Gallo, age 34
**Director, Marketing Western Europe:** Jane Hunter
**Director, National Trade Development:** Joseph (Joe) Farnan
**Director, Wine Education and Hospitality:** Patrick Dodd
**Director Sales, Bingham Farms:** Holly McClelland

## LOCATIONS

**HQ:** E. & J. Gallo Winery
600 Yosemite Blvd., Modesto, CA 95354
**Phone:** 209-341-3111
**Web:** www.gallo.com

## PRODUCTS/OPERATIONS

### Selected Products and Labels

Bargain generic and varietals (Carlo Rossi, Livingston Cellars, Peter Vella, Wild Vines)
Brandy (E&J, E&J Cask & Cream, E&J VSOP)
Flagship (Gallo of Sonoma — County, Estate, and Single Vineyard series)
Fortified and jug (Night Train, Ripple, Thunderbird)
French wines (Red Bicyclette, Pont d'Avignon)
Hospitality industry (Burlwood, Copperidge by E&J Gallo, Liberty Creek, William Wycliff Vineyards)
Imported varietals (Bella Sera, Ecco Domani, McWilliams Hanwood Estate, Red Bicyclette, Whitehaven)
Mid-priced varietals (Redwood Creek, Turning Leaf)
Premium (Anapamu, Bridlewood Estate, Gallo Family, Indigo Hills, MacMurray Ranch, Marcelina, Rancho Zabaco, Turning Leaf Sonoma Reserve)
Sparkling (André, Ballatore Spumante, Indigo Hills, Tott's)

## COMPETITORS

Asahi Breweries
Bacardi
Bacardi USA
Beam Global Spirits & Wine
Beam Wine Estates
Bronco Wine Co.
Brown-Forman
Concha y Toro
Constellation Brands
Diageo
Diageo Chateau & Estate Wines
Foster's
Foster's Americas
GIV
Heaven Hill Distilleries
Kendall-Jackson
Kirin Holdings Company
LVMH
Newton Vineyard
Pernod Ricard
Premier Pacific
Ravenswood Winery
R.H. Phillips
Scheid Vineyards
Sebastiani Vineyards
Sunview Vineyards
Taittinger
Terlato Wine
Trinchero Family Estates
UST
Vincor
Wine Group

## HISTORICAL FINANCIALS

Company Type: Private

**Income Statement** FYE: December 31

| | ESTIMATED REVENUE ($ mil.) | NET INCOME ($ mil.) | NET PROFIT MARGIN | EMPLOYEES |
|---|---|---|---|---|
| 12/06 | 2,700 | — | — | 4,600 |
| 12/05 | 2,700 | — | — | 4,400 |
| 12/04 | 3,000 | — | — | — |
| 12/03 | 2,000 | — | — | 4,600 |
| 12/02 | 1,800 | — | — | 4,600 |
| Annual Growth | 10.7% | — | — | 0.0% |

**Revenue History**

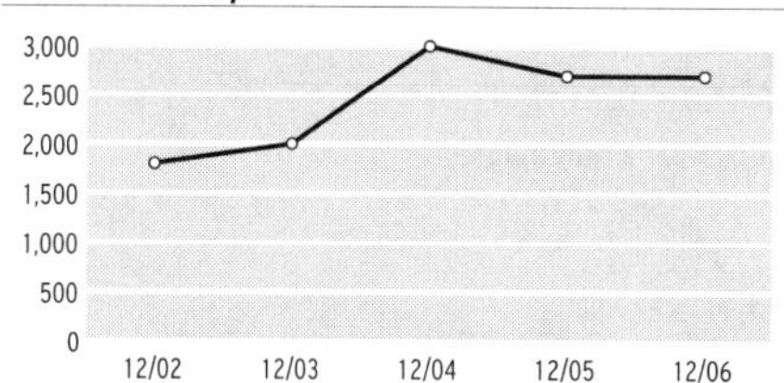


# EarthLink, Inc.

As one of the largest ISPs in the US, EarthLink is trying to bridge the gap between dial-up users and high-speed Internet access. Formerly EarthLink Network, the company has more than 5 million consumer and small-business customers. In an effort to tempt customers with faster, better services, EarthLink provides premium broadband access to more than 1.5 million of its subscribers. Web hosting services and advertising also produce revenue. The company has expanded its product offerings with the addition of wireless broadband offerings and voice over Internet protocol (VoIP) telephone service (trademarked EarthLink trueVoice), allowing customers to make and receive local and long-distance calls.

As much of the growth in Internet services is shifting to broadband access, EarthLink has forged various alliances with last-mile providers. The company, which has about 1.1 million broadband subscribers, offers cable access through agreements with companies such as Time Warner Cable and Comcast Cable, and DSL access through BellSouth, Covad, AT&T Inc. (formerly SBC Communications), and others. It uses Level 3 Communications as the carrier for its VoIP phone services.

The company has been growing through acquisitions, including PeoplePC, MindSpring, and OneMain.com, as well as e-mail appliance developer Cidco and the assets of bankrupt wireless services provider OmniSky. The company also has formed a joint venture with South Korea's leading wireless communications provider SK Telecom. The new company, formed in 2005 and dubbed HELIO, is designed to market wireless voice and data services in the US as a mobile virtual network operator (MVNO). HELIO also has teamed up with social-networking site MySpace.com and the wireless phone service will be integrated with the Web-based service.

EarthLink also acquired virtual private network (VPN) specialist New Edge Networks in 2006 in a cash-and-stock deal valued at $144 million. The purchase expands EarthLink's business in the small-to-midsized business market.

EarthLink and Sprint Nextel have ended their exclusive co-branding arrangement and Sprint has reduced its stake in EarthLink to about 12% (and is required to reduce it further). EarthLink will continue to provide Internet applications to Sprint and to use Sprint's network services, but the separation of the companies' brands was seen by some analysts as a sign that EarthLink might entertain a takeover offer from another company.

## HISTORY

After his first attempt to log onto the Internet took 80 hours in 1993, a frustrated 23-year-old Sky Dayton had an idea for a new business: an ISP focused on customer service. Dayton, who had already co-founded Los Angeles coffeehouse Cafe Mocha and graphics firm Dayton Walker Design, persuaded investors Reed Slatkin and Kevin O'Donnell to contribute $100,000. EarthLink Network was launched in Glendale, California, in 1994.

Dayton, an Ayn Rand fan who graduated from high school at 16 and never attended college, first tried to do everything — from sales to software — himself. He ultimately decided to concentrate on customer service, correctly betting that such elements as browser software and backbone networks would emerge from other providers. Offering phone help and a flat monthly rate of $19.95, EarthLink sold its first account by the end of 1994.

The next year EarthLink released TotalAccess, a package of leading Internet software that included the popular Netscape Navigator browser and QUALCOMM's Eudora, the oft-used e-mail program. Viacom's Macmillan Publishing agreed to sell TotalAccess disks in its Internet books. EarthLink was to gain similar deals with about 90 other partners.

By 1996 EarthLink had won 30,000 subscribers. The company signed a deal with PSINet giving EarthLink customers dial-up access through PSINet's more than 230 locations in the US and Canada. The next year EarthLink went public.

In 1998 EarthLink teamed with Sprint in a 10-year deal that combined the companies' Internet access services and gave Sprint 29.5% of the firm. As EarthLink passed the 1 million-subscriber mark in 1999, it agreed to offer a co-branded version of America Online's instant messaging service.

EarthLink Network agreed to merge with MindSpring in 1999 in a $1.4 billion deal (closed in 2000). The new company, EarthLink, Inc., moved to MindSpring's Atlanta headquarters. MindSpring founder Charles Brewer took over as chairman, and Dayton remained a director. Brewer left EarthLink later in 2000, however, and Dayton stepped back in as chairman.

Investments in EarthLink during 2000 included $200 million from Apple (which made EarthLink the default ISP on Macintoshes) and another $431 million from Sprint (which boosted its stake after heavy dilution from the MindSpring deal). That year, EarthLink gained 700,000 subscribers by buying OneMain.com, an ISP focused on small cities and rural communities, for $262 million.

EarthLink and Sprint stepped back from their co-branding arrangement in 2001, and Sprint sold about 40% of its stake in the company. That year EarthLink agreed to acquire Cidco, a California-based maker of personal e-mail appliances, in a $5 million deal (completed in 2002). Also in 2002 EarthLink acquired the assets of wireless Internet access provider OmniSky as well as PeoplePC, which used to sell computers with bundled Internet access and now sells value-priced narrowband Internet access (sans computer).

In 2005 Robert Kavner replaced Dayton as EarthLink's chairman of the board. Two years later the company tapped Mpower Communications chairman Rolla Huff as its new president and CEO.

## EXECUTIVES

**Chairman:** Robert M. (Bob) Kavner
**EVP and CFO:** Kevin M. Dotts, age 43, $336,154 pay
**President, New Edge Networks:** Linda W. Beck, age 43, $285,000 pay
**EVP, General Counsel, and Secretary:** Samuel R. (Sam) DeSimone Jr., age 47
**EVP; President, Municipal Networks:** Donald B. (Don) Berryman, age 48, $322,115 pay
**EVP; President, Access and Audience:** Craig I. Forman, age 45
**EVP, Public Policy:** Christopher E. Putala, age 45
**VP, Investor Relations:** Michael L. Gallentine
**President, CEO, and Director:** Rolla P. Huff, age 50
**Chief People Officer:** Stacie Hagan
**Auditors:** Ernst & Young LLP

## LOCATIONS

**HQ:** EarthLink, Inc.
1375 Peachtree St., Level A, Atlanta, GA 30309
**Phone:** 404-815-0770 **Fax:** 404-892-7616
**Web:** www.earthlink.net

EarthLink provides Internet access primarily in the US and Canada.

## PRODUCTS/OPERATIONS

### 2006 Sales

| | % of total |
|---|---|
| Narrowband access | 47 |
| Broadband access | 43 |
| Advertising & other value-added services | 7 |
| Web hosting | 3 |
| **Total** | **100** |

### Selected Subsidiaries and Affiliates

Cidco Incorporated (personal Internet communications products and services)
EarthLink/OneMain, Inc.
PeoplePC Inc.
HELIO Inc. (formerly SK-EarthLink, 50%, joint venture with SK Telecom Co., Ltd.)

## COMPETITORS

AOL
Aplus.Net
AT&T
BellSouth
Charter Communications
Comcast
Covad Communications Group
Cox Communications
Internet America
Microsoft
Qwest
ReaLLinx
Road Runner
Sprint Nextel
Time Warner Cable
United Online
Verizon
Vonage
Yahoo!

## HISTORICAL FINANCIALS

Company Type: Public

### Income Statement

FYE: December 31

| | REVENUE ($ mil.) | NET INCOME ($ mil.) | NET PROFIT MARGIN | EMPLOYEES |
|---|---|---|---|---|
| **12/06** | 1,301 | 5 | 0.4% | 2,210 |
| **12/05** | 1,290 | 143 | 11.1% | 1,732 |
| **12/04** | 1,382 | 111 | 8.0% | 2,067 |
| **12/03** | 1,402 | (62) | — | 3,335 |
| **12/02** | 1,357 | (148) | — | 5,106 |
| **Annual Growth** | (1.0%) | — | — | (18.9%) |

### 2006 Year-End Financials

Debt ratio: 56.4%
Return on equity: 1.0%
Cash ($ mil.): 373
Current ratio: 1.98
Long-term debt ($ mil.): 259
No. of shares (mil.): 123
Dividends
Yield: —
Payout: —
Market value ($ mil.): 871

### Stock History

NASDAQ (GS): ELNK

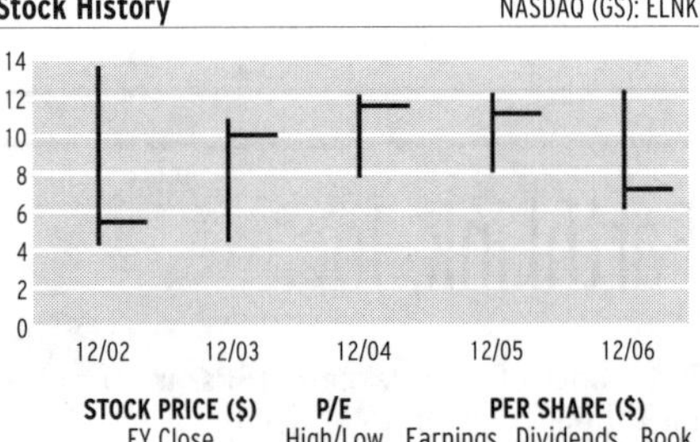


| | STOCK PRICE ($) FY Close | P/E High | P/E Low | PER SHARE ($) Earnings | PER SHARE ($) Dividends | PER SHARE ($) Book Value |
|---|---|---|---|---|---|---|
| **12/06** | 7.10 | 305 | 154 | 0.04 | — | 3.74 |
| **12/05** | 11.11 | 12 | 8 | 1.02 | — | 3.97 |
| **12/04** | 11.52 | 17 | 11 | 0.70 | — | 3.68 |
| **12/03** | 10.00 | — | — | (0.42) | — | 3.42 |
| **12/02** | 5.45 | — | — | (1.11) | — | 4.47 |
| **Annual Growth** | 6.8% | — | — | — | — | (4.4%) |

# Eastman Chemical

Eastman Chemical can recall its past through photos — it was once part of film giant Eastman Kodak. The company has developed into a major producer of chemicals, fibers, and plastics. Among Eastman's operating segments are its CASPI (coatings, adhesives, specialty polymers, and inks), Specialty Plastics (engineering polymers), and Fibers (acetate tow and textile fibers) units. Its Performance Polymers segment is the #1 maker of polyethylene terephthalate (PET), a plastic used to make packaging for soft drinks, food, and water. The last segment manufactures Performance Chemicals and Intermediates. Eastman's products go into such items as food and medical packaging, films, and toothbrushes.

Eastman Chemical has operations worldwide, with the US accounting for just more than half of sales. Eastman has expanded internationally by building plants in Asia, Europe, and Latin America. It restructured its divisional alignment in the second quarter of 2006 in an attempt to group together related product groups and technologies. In the process, Eastman disbanded its former Voridian Division. Later in the year the company sold its polyethylene business to Westlake Chemical for $255 million.

## HISTORY

Eastman Chemical went public in 1994, but the company traces its roots to the 19th century. George Eastman, after developing a method for dry-plate photography, established the Eastman Dry Plate and Film Company in 1884 in Rochester, New York (the name was changed to Eastman Kodak in 1892).

In 1886 Eastman hired scientist Henry Reichenbach to help create and manufacture new photographic chemicals. As time passed, Reichenbach and the company's other scientists came up with chemicals that were either not directly related to photography or had uses in addition to photography.

Eastman bought a wood-distillation plant in Kingsport, Tennessee, in 1920 and formed the Tennessee Eastman Corporation to make methanol and acetone for the manufacture of photographic chemicals. The company, by this time called Kodak, introduced acetate yarn and Tenite, a cellulose ester plastic, in the early 1930s. During WWII the company formed Holston Defense to make explosives for the US armed forces.

Kodak began to vertically integrate Tennessee Eastman's operations during the 1950s, acquiring A. M. Tenney Associates, Tennessee Eastman's selling agent for its acetate yarn products, in 1950. It also established Texas Eastman, opening a plant in Longview to produce ethyl alcohol and aldehydes, raw materials used in fiber and film production. At the end of 1952, Kodak created Eastman Chemical Products to sell alcohols, plastics, and fibers made by Tennessee Eastman and Texas Eastman. Also that year Tennessee Eastman developed cellulose acetate filter tow for use in cigarette filters. In the late 1950s the company introduced Kodel polyester fiber.

Kodak created Carolina Eastman Company in 1968, opening a plant in Columbia, South Carolina, to produce Kodel and other polyester products. It also created Eastman Chemicals Division to handle its chemical operations.

In the late 1970s Eastman Chemicals Division introduced polyethylene terephthalate (PET) resin used to make containers. It acquired biological and molecular instrumentation manufacturer International Biotechnologies in 1987.

Eastman Chemicals Division became Eastman Chemical Company in 1990. In 1993 it exited the polyester fiber business. When Kodak spun off Eastman Chemical in early 1994, the new company was saddled with $1.8 billion in debt.

Eastman's 1996 earnings were reduced when oversupply lowered prices for PET. Eastman opened plants in Argentina, Malaysia, and the Netherlands in 1998.

Eastman added to its international locations in 1999 by opening a plant in Singapore and an office in Bangkok. It also bought Lawter International (specialty chemicals for ink and coatings) with locations in Belgium, China, and Ireland. In 2000 the company began restructuring into two business segments (chemicals and polymers) and acquired resin and colorant maker McWhorter Technologies.

In 2001 Eastman acquired most of Hercules' resins business. In November the company announced that it has postponed plans to split into two companies (one focusing on specialty chemicals and plastics, the other concentrating on polyethylene, plastics, and acetate fibers) until mid-2002 due to the weak economy. In early 2002 the company announced that it had cancelled those plans altogether and would operate the two as separate divisions.

The following year Eastman announced it would split off part of its coatings, adhesives, specialty polymers, and inks (CASPI) segment. The division had been underperforming and had been hit particularly hard by the high costs of raw materials and a general overcapacity in the marketplace. Eastman sold a portion of CASPI to investment firm Apollo Management for $215 million. Businesses included in the sale were composites, inks and graphic arts raw materials, liquid and powder resins, and textile chemicals. (Apollo called the acquired businesses Resolution Specialty Materials, and then joined RSM with Resolution Performance Products and another of its chemical companies, Borden Chemical, to form the new Hexion Specialty Chemicals in 2005.)

## EXECUTIVES

**Chairman and CEO:** J. Brian Ferguson, age 52, $3,451,538 pay
**President; Chemicals and Fibers Business Group Head:** James P. Rogers, age 56
**EVP; Polymers Business Group Head:** Gregory O. (Greg) Nelson, age 55
**SVP and CFO:** Richard A. (Rich) Lorraine, age 61, $1,097,115 pay
**SVP and CTO:** Ronald C. Lindsay, age 49
**SVP Corporate Strategy and Marketing:** Mark J. Costa, age 40
**SVP, Chief Legal Officer, and Corporate Secretary:** Theresa K. Lee, age 54, $930,769 pay
**SVP Human Resources, Communications, and Public Affairs:** Norris P. Sneed, age 51
**VP and CIO:** Jerry Hale
**VP Corporate Development and Strategic Planning:** Prentice McKibben
**VP Finance and Chief Accounting Officer:** Curtis E. Espeland, age 42
**VP and Managing Director, Asia/Pacific, Eastman Division:** Robert Preston
**VP and General Manager, Adhesives and Coatings:** Damon Warmack
**VP and General Manager, Performance Chemicals:** Matthew Stevens
**VP and General Manager, Specialty Plastics:** Dante Rutstrom
**Director Investors Relations:** Gregory (Greg) Riddle
**Auditors:** PricewaterhouseCoopers LLP

## LOCATIONS

**HQ:** Eastman Chemical Company
200 S. Wilcox Dr., Kingsport, TN 37660
**Phone:** 423-229-2000 **Fax:** 423-229-2145
**Web:** www.eastman.com

### 2006 Sales

| | $ mil. | % of total |
|---|---|---|
| US | 4,039 | 54 |
| Other countries | 3,411 | 46 |
| **Total** | **7,450** | **100** |

## PRODUCTS/OPERATIONS

### 2006 Sales and Operating Profit

| | Sales | | Operating Profit | |
|---|---|---|---|---|
| | $ mil. | % of total | $ mil. | % of total |
| Performance Polymers | 2,642 | 36 | 54 | 8 |
| PCI | 1,659 | 22 | 132 | 19 |
| CASPI | 1,421 | 19 | 229 | 33 |
| Fibers | 910 | 12 | 226 | 33 |
| Specialty Plastics | 818 | 11 | 46 | 7 |
| Adjustments | — | — | (47) | — |
| **Total** | **7,450** | **100** | **640** | **100** |

### Selected Products

Chemicals
- Adhesives
- Agricultural chemicals
- Food and beverage ingredients
- Inks
- Performance chemicals (chemicals for agricultural products, fibers, food and beverage ingredients, photographic chemicals, pharmaceutical intermediates, polymer compounding)
- Specialty polymers and intermediates

Specialty Plastics
- Polymers
  - Container plastics
  - Specialty plastics
- Fibers
  - Estron acetate tow
  - Estron and Chromspun acetate yarns
  - Estrobond triacetin plasticizers

## COMPETITORS

Akzo Nobel
BASF AG
Bostik
Celanese
Ciba Specialty Chemicals
Clariant
Dainippon Ink
DAK Americas
Dow Chemical
DSM
DuPont
ExxonMobil Chemical
GE Plastics
Honeywell Specialty Materials
Huntsman Corp
Imperial Chemical
Lonza
Lyondell Chemical
Nan Ya Plastics
NatureWorks
Reliance Industries
Rhodia
Rohm and Haas
S.C. Johnson
Sterling Chemicals
Teijin
Wellman

## HISTORICAL FINANCIALS

Company Type: Public

### Income Statement

FYE: December 31

| | REVENUE ($ mil.) | NET INCOME ($ mil.) | NET PROFIT MARGIN | EMPLOYEES |
|---|---|---|---|---|
| **12/06** | 7,450 | 409 | 5.5% | 11,000 |
| **12/05** | 7,059 | 557 | 7.9% | 12,000 |
| **12/04** | 6,580 | 170 | 2.6% | 12,000 |
| **12/03** | 5,800 | (270) | — | 15,000 |
| **12/02** | 5,320 | 61 | 1.1% | 15,700 |
| **Annual Growth** | 8.8% | 60.9% | — | (8.5%) |

### 2006 Year-End Financials

Debt ratio: 78.3%
Return on equity: 22.5%
Cash ($ mil.): 939
Current ratio: 2.29
Long-term debt ($ mil.): 1,589
No. of shares (mil.): 84
Dividends
Yield: 3.0%
Payout: 35.8%
Market value ($ mil.): 4,954

### Stock History

NYSE: EMN

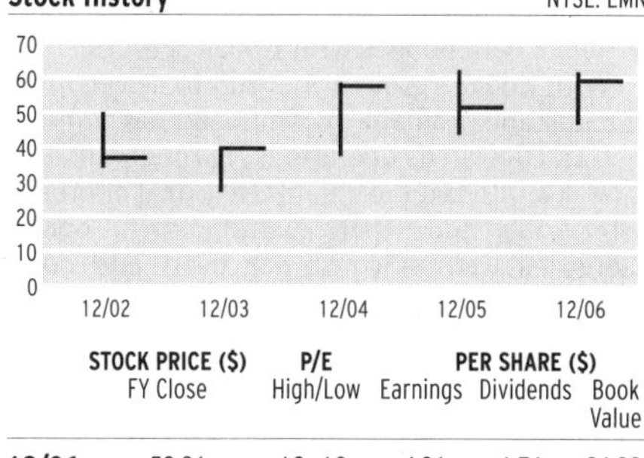


| | STOCK PRICE ($) FY Close | P/E High/Low | PER SHARE ($) Earnings | Dividends | Book Value |
|---|---|---|---|---|---|
| **12/06** | 59.31 | 12 10 | 4.91 | 1.76 | 24.29 |
| **12/05** | 51.59 | 9 6 | 6.81 | 1.76 | 19.77 |
| **12/04** | 57.73 | 27 17 | 2.18 | 2.20 | 14.95 |
| **12/03** | 39.53 | — — | (3.50) | 1.76 | 13.50 |
| **12/02** | 36.77 | 63 44 | 0.79 | 1.76 | 16.43 |
| **Annual Growth** | 12.7% | — — | 57.9% | 0.0% | 10.3% |

# Eastman Kodak

When Kodak made Brownies, folks began to say cheese. The inventor of the Brownie camera (1900), Kodak has retouched its image from a leading maker of photographic film to a provider of imaging technology products and services to the photographic and graphic communications markets. The company has restructured itself to focus less on film sales and more on digital cameras and imaging systems for consumers and professionals. Kodak's shift to become a digital technology business included purging some 30,000 employees. The firm also has long-term plans to sell ink jet printers and flat-panel displays.

As the movement toward digital technology continues to transform photography, the company is shooting for a larger share of the digital imaging market (which allows photos to be computer-altered and stored on the Internet). In addition to bundling image-manipulation software with its digital cameras, Kodak offers other computerized products, such as hot-swappable CD writers. Deals with US and European cell phone operators also allow Kodak to tap into the camera-phone market by offering online photo services and printing capabilities at Bluetooth-enabled Kodak kiosks.

Kodak slashed its stock dividend by 70%, too, to fund its effort to become the leader in digital technology. The company set aside $3 billion for acquiring and investing in digital technologies. During this time frame the firm doesn't plan to ship reloadable cameras using 35 mm film in the US, Canada, and Western Europe. However, it is investing in traditional film technology in emerging markets. For example, it purchased a 20% stake in China's leading filmmaker, Lucky Film Co. Also, the company is rolling out new designs for reloadable film cameras in China, India, Eastern Europe, and Latin America.

Having explored strategic alternatives for the Health Group since May 2006 (following consolidation in the industry's information sector), Kodak sold the group in May 2007 to an affiliate of Onex Corporation for more than $2 billion.

Its partnerships are also giving the company other avenues for revenue growth. Kodak and Motorola inked a 10-year global product, licensing, and marketing agreement in 2006 to codevelop camera phones with Kodak sensors.

With Kodak's growth and shift to newer, more popular and profitable technologies has come an ebb and flow in its operations. Throughout 2004 Kodak shuttered several international photofinishing labs and papers manufacturing operations, as well as consumer films and color photographic paper units.

## HISTORY

After developing a method for dry-plate photography, George Eastman established The Eastman Dry Plate and Film Company in 1884. In 1888 it introduced its first camera, a small, easy-to-use device that was loaded with enough film for 100 pictures. Owners mailed the camera back to the company, which returned it with the pictures and more film. The firm settled on the name Eastman Kodak in 1892, after Eastman tried many combinations of letters starting and ending with "k," which he thought was a "strong, incisive sort of letter." The user-friendly Brownie camera followed in 1900. Three years later Kodak introduced a home movie camera, projector, and film.

Ailing and convinced that his work was done, Eastman committed suicide in 1932. Kodak continued to dominate the photography industry with the introduction of color film (Kodachrome, 1935) and a handheld movie camera (1951). The company established US plants to produce the chemicals, plastics, and fibers used in its film production.

The Instamatic, introduced in 1963, became Kodak's biggest success. The camera's foolproof film cartridge eliminated the need for loading in the dark. By 1976 Kodak had sold an estimated 60 million Instamatics, 50 million more cameras than all its competitors combined. Subsequent introductions included the Kodak instant camera (1976) and the unsuccessful disc camera (1982).

In the 1980s Kodak diversified into electronic publishing, batteries, floppy disks (Verbatim, 1985, sold 1990), pharmaceuticals (Sterling Drug, sold 1994), and do-it-yourself and household products (L&F Products, sold 1994).

George Fisher, former chairman of Motorola, became Kodak's chairman and CEO in 1993. Fisher began cutting debt by selling noncore assets. Kodak spun off Eastman Chemical in 1994. Sales in 1996 included its money-losing copier sales and services business.

Kodak acquired the medical imaging business of Imation in 1998, but it also unloaded more of its noncore operations, including its 450-store Fox Photo chain.

President and COO Daniel Carp replaced Fisher as CEO in early 2000. Further hits to the economy and Kodak's revenue prompted management in 2001 to eliminate regional divisions and realign the business along product lines.

In 2003 the company announced it would cut as many as 6,000 jobs worldwide. This came after reducing as many as 2,200 jobs in the US and Western Europe earlier in the year and cutting as many as 7,000 jobs worldwide in 2002.

In 2004, on the heels of its announcement that it would stop selling film-based cameras in Western markets by year's end, Kodak said it would also stop global production of its Advantix Advanced Photo System (APS) cameras.

In mid-2005 Kodak said that it would phase out production of black-and-white photographic paper, manufactured at one of its plants in Brazil, by the end of the year. The company attributed its exit from the business to a move from chemical-based photography to digital imaging and a 25% decline in demand for black-and-white paper annually. In late 2005 Kodak announced changes related to its 2004 restructuring program that include consolidating color photographic paper manufacturing for North America, closing a Rochester operation that recycles waste to produce Estar polyester film base, and reducing capacity for the production of consumer film products at its Xiamen, China, plant.

Antonio Perez, who took over as president and CEO in mid-2005, added the title of chairman in January 2006, when Dan Carp retired. Also that year, Kodak inked a service and support agreement with now-defunct Fischer Imaging Corporation to provide post-sale support (including repair and maintenance) for Fischer's mammography products (such as SenoScan and MammoTest) installed worldwide.

## EXECUTIVES

**Chairman and CEO:** Antonio M. Perez, age 61, $1,786,693 pay (prior to promotion)
**EVP and CFO:** Frank S. Sklarsky, age 50, $99,486 pay
**SVP; President, Consumer Digital Imaging Group:** Philip J. Faraci, age 51, $648,760 pay
**SVP and CTO:** William J. (Bill) Lloyd, age 67
**SVP; President, Graphic Communications Group:** James T. Langley, age 56, $648,808 pay
**SVP; President, Film Products Group and Entertainment Imaging:** Mary Jane Hellyar, age 53
**SVP; President, Health Group:** Kevin J. Hobert, age 42
**SVP and General Manager, Film Capture, Digital and Film Imaging Systems:** Candy M. Obourn, age 56
**SVP and General Counsel:** Joyce P. Haag, age 56
**SVP and Chief Marketing Officer:** Carl E. Gustin Jr., age 55
**VP and General Manager, External Affairs, Greater Asia Region; Chairman and President, North Asia Region:** Ying Yeh
**VP; President, Kodak Graphic Solutions and Services; COO, Graphic Communications Group:** Jeff Jacobson
**SVP and Associate Director of Research and Development:** Jack C. Chang
**SVP and Director, Human Resources:** Robert L. (Bob) Berman, age 49
**VP; General Manager and VP, Prepress Consumables Graphic Communications Group:** Douglas J. Edwards, age 45
**VP and Director, Communications and Public Affairs:** Gerard K. Meuchner, age 43
**VP and Chairman, Kodak Japan Ltd.:** Yoshikazu Hori, age 67
**VP and CIO:** Kim E. VanGelder
**VP and Director, Investor Relations:** Don Flick
**VP and Director, Public Affairs:** Stephen J. Ciccone
**Corporate Secretary and Chief Governance Officer:** Laurence L. (Larry) Hickey
**Treasurer:** William G. Love
**Chief Accounting Officer and Corporate Controller:** Diane E. Wilfong, age 45
**Associate Director, Investor Relations:** Patty Yahn-Urlaub
**Manager, Sales and Marketing:** Kathryn Mazza
**Manager, Worldwide Advertising:** Sheryl Baker
**Manager, Worldwide Marketing, Kodak EASYSHARE:** Mary-Irene Marek
**Media Manager:** Kelly Kaye
**Corporate Communications:** Jim Blamphin
**Auditors:** PricewaterhouseCoopers LLP

## LOCATIONS

**HQ:** Eastman Kodak Company
343 State St., Rochester, NY 14650
**Phone:** 800-698-3324 **Fax:** 585-724-1089
**Web:** www.kodak.com

Eastman Kodak has manufacturing plants in Brazil, Bulgaria, Canada, China, France, Germany, India, Israel, Japan, Mexico, Russia, South Africa, the UK, and the US.

**2006 Sales**

| | $ mil. | % of total |
|---|---|---|
| US | 5,634 | 42 |
| Europe, Middle East & Africa | 3,995 | 30 |
| Asia/Pacific | 2,333 | 18 |
| Canada & Latin America | 1,312 | 10 |
| **Total** | **13,274** | **100** |

**2006 Sales**

| | $ mil. | % of total |
|---|---|---|
| Digital & film imaging systems | | |
| US | 3,231 | 24 |
| Other countries | 3,845 | 29 |
| Health imaging | | |
| US | 914 | 7 |
| Other countries | 1,583 | 12 |
| Graphic communications | | |
| US | 1,248 | 10 |
| Other countries | 2,384 | 18 |
| Other | | |
| US | 52 | — |
| Other countries | 17 | — |
| **Total** | **13,274** | **100** |

## PRODUCTS/OPERATIONS

**2006 Sales**

| | $ mil. | % of total |
|---|---|---|
| Digital & film imaging systems | 7,076 | 53 |
| Graphic communications | 3,632 | 27 |
| Health imaging | 2,497 | 19 |
| Other | 69 | 1 |
| **Total** | **13,274** | **100** |

## COMPETITORS

3M
Agfa
Canon
CASIO COMPUTER
FUJIFILM
Hewlett-Packard
Konica Minolta
Leica Camera
Matsushita Electric
Nature Vision
Nikon
Olympus
Pentax
Philips Electronics
PhotoWorks
Polaroid
Procter & Gamble
Ricoh
Sharp
Sony
Xerox

## HISTORICAL FINANCIALS

Company Type: Public

### Income Statement

FYE: December 31

| | REVENUE ($ mil.) | NET INCOME ($ mil.) | NET PROFIT MARGIN | EMPLOYEES |
|---|---|---|---|---|
| **12/06** | 13,274 | (601) | — | 40,900 |
| **12/05** | 14,268 | (1,362) | — | 51,100 |
| **12/04** | 13,517 | 556 | 4.1% | 54,800 |
| **12/03** | 13,317 | 265 | 2.0% | 63,900 |
| **12/02** | 12,835 | 770 | 6.0% | 70,000 |
| **Annual Growth** | 0.8% | — | — | (12.6%) |

### 2006 Year-End Financials

Debt ratio: 195.5%
Return on equity: —
Cash ($ mil.): 1,469
Current ratio: 1.12
Long-term debt ($ mil.): 2,714
No. of shares (mil.): 288
Dividends
Yield: 1.9%
Payout: —
Market value ($ mil.): 7,418

### Stock History

NYSE: EK

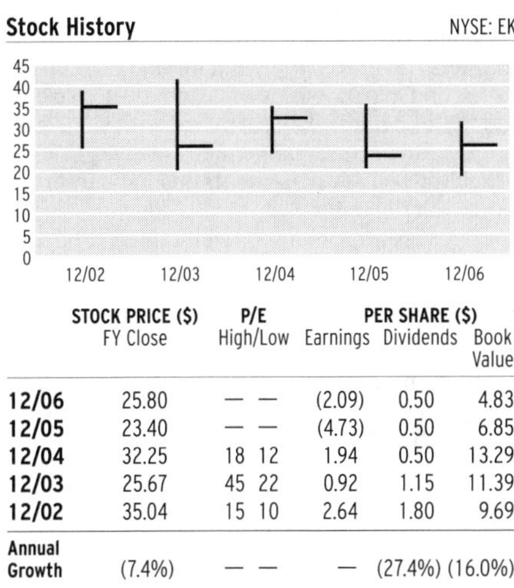


| | STOCK PRICE ($) FY Close | P/E High/Low | PER SHARE ($) Earnings | Dividends | Book Value |
|---|---|---|---|---|---|
| **12/06** | 25.80 | — — | (2.09) | 0.50 | 4.83 |
| **12/05** | 23.40 | — — | (4.73) | 0.50 | 6.85 |
| **12/04** | 32.25 | 18 12 | 1.94 | 0.50 | 13.29 |
| **12/03** | 25.67 | 45 22 | 0.92 | 1.15 | 11.39 |
| **12/02** | 35.04 | 15 10 | 2.64 | 1.80 | 9.69 |
| **Annual Growth** | (7.4%) | — — | — | (27.4%) | (16.0%) |

# Eaton Corporation

When it comes to diversification, Eaton favors an all-you-can-eat approach. The manufacturer has made dozens of acquisitions (as well as divestitures) over the past decade. Eaton's game plan calls for nurturing businesses in which it holds a strong market share. The company's product lines include electrical power distribution and control equipment, engine components, and hydraulic and fluid power products for aerospace, automotive, and other industrial uses. Eaton is also one of the world's largest manufacturers of grips for golf clubs. The company operates manufacturing facilities in dozens of countries throughout the world.

Eaton tries to beat economic downturns — and often succeeds — by constantly adjusting its product mix, keeping a close eye on costs, and making targeted acquisitions.

Innovation is another key to Eaton's growth. For example, Eaton worked with General Motors to develop a displacement on demand (DOD) system that delivers increased fuel economy by shutting down half the engine in light load situations. These systems were created for Chevy TrailBlazer EXTs and GMC Envoy XLs.

Eaton also made moves to build up its aerospace fluid and air division with two acquisitions late in 2005. First it bought that division of Cobham plc for $270 million, and then it bought a similar operation from PerkinElmer.

In 2006 Eaton continued its string of acquisitions when it purchased Synflex, a maker of thermoplastic tubing and hoses, from materials giant Saint-Gobain. Later that year Eaton bought almost all of China-based Senyuan International Holdings, which makes circuit breakers and other electrical components.

At the end of 2006 Eaton agreed to acquire the aerospace business of Argo-Tech for $695 million in cash and assumed debt, a move that will complement the fuel systems business picked up in the acquisition of Cobham Aerospace. Argo-Tech's aerospace business makes high-performance engine fuel pumps and systems, airframe fuel pumps and systems, and ground fueling systems for commercial and military aerospace markets.

Eaton bolstered its medium-voltage motor control products offerings in 2007 when it bought SMC Electrical Products. Terms of the deal were not disclosed. Later that year, the company announced plans to acquire MGE UPS SYSTEMS from Schneider Electric for $570 million. Eaton hopes to fill product gaps in its uninterruptible power supply (UPS) portfolio and access new markets through the purchase.

## HISTORY

In 1911 Joseph Eaton and Viggo Torbensen started the Torbensen Gear and Axle Company to make an internal-gear rear truck axle that Torbensen had patented in 1902. The company moved from Newark, New Jersey, to Cleveland in 1914. After Republic Motor Truck bought Torbensen (1917), Eaton formed the Eaton Axle Company (1919), repurchased Torbensen (1922), and by 1931 had bought 11 more auto parts businesses. In 1932 it became Eaton Manufacturing.

The Depression flattened auto sales, and Eaton's profits fell. WWII sparked demand that helped the company recover. Joseph Eaton died in 1949. During the 1950s and 1960s, Eaton diversified and expanded geographically. It bought Fuller Manufacturing (truck transmissions, 1958), Dole Valve (1963), and Yale & Towne Manufacturing (locks and forklifts, 1963). Eaton's international business grew, with foreign sales increasing from almost nil in 1961 to 20% of sales by 1966.

Eaton sold its lock business in 1978 and bought Cutler-Hammer (electronics), Kenway (automated storage and retrieval systems), and Samuel Moore (plastics and fluid power). Downturns in the truck and auto industries forced Eaton to close 30 plants and trim 23,000 jobs between 1979 and 1983. The company reported its first loss in 50 years in 1982 and decided to diversify into high technology and to expand operations overseas.

From 1984 to 1993 Eaton spent almost $4 billion in capital improvements and R&D. In 1986 it bought Consolidated Controls (precision instruments), Pacific-Sierra Research (computer and defense systems), and Singer Controls (valves and switches).

Eaton's acquisitions in the 1990s included Nordhauser Ventil (automotive engine valves, Germany), Control Displays (flight-deck equipment), Heinemann Electric (hydraulic-magnetic circuit breakers), and the automotive switch business of Illinois Tool Works. In 1994 Eaton tripled the size of its electrical power and controls operation with its $1.1 billion purchase of Westinghouse's electrical distribution and control business. The next year it bought Emwest Products (electrical switch gear and controls, Australia) and the IKU Group, a Dutch auto-controls firm. It purchased CAPCO Automotive Products (truck transmissions, Brazil) in 1996.

In its repositioning, the company in 1997 sold off its appliance-control business to Siebe PLC and a majority stake in its high-tech defense electronics subsidiary, AIL Systems, to management. The next year Eaton sold its heavy-axle and brake business to Dana and its suspension business to Oxford Automotive. Eaton closed and consolidated plants and laid off more than 1,000 workers in its microchip division in 1998.

The company increased its share of the hydraulics market in 1999 by spending $1.7 billion for Aeroquip-Vickers. To help pay for the purchase, Eaton sold its engineered-fasteners business to TransTechnology, its fluid power division (cooling systems for cars and trucks) to Borg-Warner (now BorgWarner), and its mobile agricultural hydraulic cylinder business to Hyco International. Eaton also unloaded Vickers' machine-tool controls business later that year.

In 20002 Eaton signed a deal with Volvo to manufacture heavy-duty transmissions for the company's South American truck market. Eaton also bought the product lines and the intellectual property of the Aerospace Division of Mechanical Products Inc. In early 2003 the company completed the acquisition of Delta plc's electrical division for a reported $215 million.

In 2004 Eaton acquired Powerware, an uninterruptible power supply and power management system manufacturer, from UK-based Invensys for $560 million. Early in 2005 the company acquired Walterscheid Rohrverbindungstechnik GmbH, the tube connecting systems business of GKN plc, for about $48 million. It also bought the Chinese hydraulic hose fitting maker Winner Group Holdings Ltd.

## EXECUTIVES

**Chairman, President, and CEO:** Alexander M. (Sandy) Cutler, age 55, $1,024,620 pay
**EVP, CFO, and Planning Officer:** Richard H. Fearon, age 51, $478,140 pay
**SVP and President, Electrical Group:** Randolph W. (Randy) Carson, age 56, $457,380 pay
**SVP and Group Executive, Fluid Power:** Craig Arnold, age 46, $451,920 pay
**SVP and President, Truck Group:** James E. Sweetnam, age 54, $429,540 pay
**SVP and President, Automotive Group:** Scott L. King
**VP and President, Electrical Components Operations:** Craig A. Black
**VP and President, Power Quality Solutions Operations:** Thomas S. Gross, age 49
**VP and President, Engine Air Management Operations:** Joseph P. Palchak
**VP and CTO:** Yannis Tsavalas, age 51
**VP and Controller:** Billie K. Rawot, age 55
**VP and CIO:** William W. Blausey Jr., age 42
**VP and General Counsel:** Mark M. McGuire, age 49
**VP and Secretary:** Earl R. Franklin, age 63
**VP and Treasurer:** Robert E. Parmenter, age 54
**VP, Communications:** Donald J. (Don) McGrath, age 54
**VP, Human Resources:** Susan J. Cook
**VP, Investor Relations:** William C. Hartman
**Auditors:** Ernst & Young LLP

## LOCATIONS

**HQ:** Eaton Corporation
Eaton Center, 1111 Superior Ave.,
Cleveland, OH 44114
**Phone:** 216-523-5000 **Fax:** 216-523-4787
**Web:** www.eaton.com

Eaton Corporation operates 202 manufacturing facilities in 32 countries across the globe.

### 2006 Sales

| | $ mil. | % of total |
|---|---|---|
| US | 8,556 | 64 |
| Europe | 2,423 | 18 |
| Latin America | 1,090 | 8 |
| Asia/Pacific | 898 | 7 |
| Canada | 337 | 3 |
| Adjustments | (934) | — |
| **Total** | **12,370** | **100** |

## PRODUCTS/OPERATIONS

### 2006 Sales

| | $ mil. | % of total |
|---|---|---|
| Electrical | 4,184 | 34 |
| Fluid power | 3,983 | 32 |
| Truck | 2,520 | 20 |
| Automotive | 1,683 | 14 |
| **Total** | **12,370** | **100** |

### Selected Brand Names

Electrical
- Cutler-Hammer
- Durant
- Heinemann
- Holec
- MEM
- Powerware

Fluid Power
- Aeroquip
- Boston
- Char-Lynn
- Eaton
- Golf Pride
- Hydro-Line
- Vickers
- Weatherhead

Truck Components
- Dana
- Eaton
- Fuller
- Roadranger
- VORAD

Automotive Components
- Aeroquip
- Eaton

## COMPETITORS

Acushnet
American Standard
ArvinMeritor
BorgWarner
Callaway Golf
Cummins
Dana
Detroit Diesel
Emerson Electric
Genus
GolfGear
Golfsmith
Honeywell International
Hubbell
INTERMET
ITT Corp.
Johnson Controls
Metaldyne
Navistar
PACCAR
Parker Hannifin
Precision Castparts
Raytheon
Robert Bosch
Rockwell Automation
Sauer-Danfoss
Schneider Electric
Siemens AG
SPX
Thomas & Betts
United Technologies
Woodhead
ZF Friedrichshafen

## HISTORICAL FINANCIALS

Company Type: Public

### Income Statement

FYE: December 31

| | REVENUE ($ mil.) | NET INCOME ($ mil.) | NET PROFIT MARGIN | EMPLOYEES |
|---|---|---|---|---|
| **12/06** | 12,370 | 950 | 7.7% | 60,000 |
| **12/05** | 11,115 | 805 | 7.2% | 59,000 |
| **12/04** | 9,817 | 648 | 6.6% | 55,000 |
| **12/03** | 8,061 | 386 | 4.8% | 51,000 |
| **12/02** | 7,209 | 281 | 3.9% | 48,000 |
| **Annual Growth** | 14.5% | 35.6% | — | 5.7% |

### 2006 Year-End Financials

Debt ratio: 43.2%
Return on equity: 24.1%
Cash ($ mil.): 785
Current ratio: 1.29
Long-term debt ($ mil.): 1,774
No. of shares (mil.): 146
Dividends
Yield: 2.0%
Payout: 23.8%
Market value ($ mil.): 10,985

### Stock History

NYSE: ETN

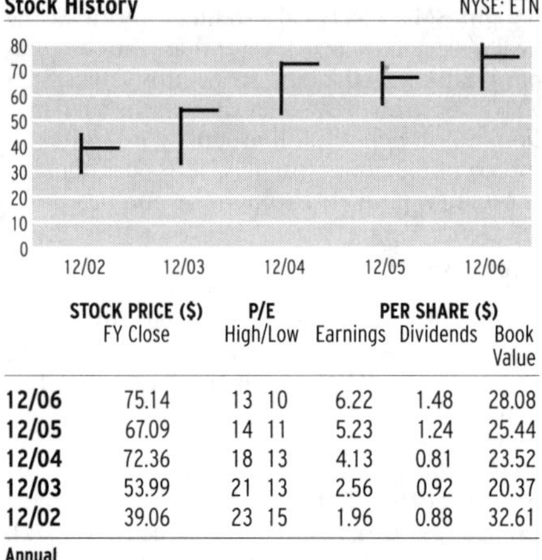


| | STOCK PRICE ($) FY Close | P/E High | P/E Low | PER SHARE ($) Earnings | PER SHARE ($) Dividends | PER SHARE ($) Book Value |
|---|---|---|---|---|---|---|
| **12/06** | 75.14 | 13 | 10 | 6.22 | 1.48 | 28.08 |
| **12/05** | 67.09 | 14 | 11 | 5.23 | 1.24 | 25.44 |
| **12/04** | 72.36 | 18 | 13 | 4.13 | 0.81 | 23.52 |
| **12/03** | 53.99 | 21 | 13 | 2.56 | 0.92 | 20.37 |
| **12/02** | 39.06 | 23 | 15 | 1.96 | 0.88 | 32.61 |
| **Annual Growth** | 17.8% | — | — | 33.5% | 13.9% | (3.7%) |

# eBay Inc.

"I got it on eBay" is barreling its way into the lexicon of the new millennium and placing a cyber-grin on the corporate face of online auctioneer extraordinaire eBay. The company is a cyber-forum for selling more than 50,000 categories of merchandise — from Beanie Babies to fine antiques — hosting about 300,000 online stores worldwide. eBay, which generates revenue through listing and selling fees and through advertising, boasts more than 220 million registered users. In early 2007, eBay acquired one of the fastest growing online ticket sellers, StubHub, for $307 million.

The StubHub deal gives eBay users the more efficient ability of sorting by individual events and by the number of seats available, as opposed to using the standard, widespread eBay interface of buying and finding tickets. StubHub had revenues of up to $400 million in 2006.

As far as an overall business strategy, fast-growing eBay is offering new services and expanding into new areas, most recently China, India, South Korea, Spain, Switzerland, and Taiwan, through site launches, acquisitions, and joint ventures. eBay also operates in Mexico and eight South American countries through its investment in MercadoLibre.com. Overall, eBay and its subsidiaries do business in almost 25 countries worldwide.

The online auction house's global payments platform, PayPal, boasts about 130 million accounts. To help secure financial transactions over the Internet, eBay acquired the payment gateway business, which enables online merchants to process and manage electronic transactions, from Internet services company VeriSign for about $374 million in late 2005.

No longer the only Internet auction site in town, eBay faces mounting competition from online powerhouses such as Amazon.com and smaller competitors like Overstock.com. In addition, the company's rising popularity created technical glitches that exposed its vulnerability to mechanical malfunctions. The manner in which eBay runs its system has also been questioned as the result of a slew of auction hoaxes (such as postings for human organs and unborn babies) and fraud.

eBay's success breaking into international markets has been largely reliant on key acquisitions and partnerships in each new market. Along these lines, eBay partnered with Google in August 2006; the arrangement involves Google providing text advertisements on eBay's international auction sites.

eBay sees huge market potential in China, the world's #2 Internet market, and India; it's spending heavily to establish its business in those countries. In late 2006, eBay shifted its China strategy when it entered a joint venture with Tom Online, a prominent online game provider. As part of the partnership, eBay will integrate its eBay Eachnet subsidiary into the venture with Tom Online owning 51% and eBay, 49%.

In late 2005 eBay acquired startup Skype Technologies S. A. of Luxembourg, for about $2.6 billion. Skype's Web-based software allows its 170 million registered users to make phone calls over the Internet.

eBay chairman and founder Pierre Omidyar owns about 14% of the company; former VP Jeffrey Skoll and CEO Meg Whitman own about 6% and 2%, respectively.

## HISTORY

Pierre Omidyar created a flea market in cyberspace when he launched online auction service Auction Web on Labor Day weekend in 1995. Making a name for itself largely through word of mouth, the company incorporated in 1996, the same year it began to charge a fee to auction items online. That year it enhanced its service with Feedback Forum (buyer and seller ratings).

The company changed the name to eBay in 1997 and began promoting itself through advertising. By the middle of that year, eBay was boasting nearly 800,000 auctions each day and Benchmark Capital came on board as a significant financial backer.

Margaret ("Meg") Whitman, a former Hasbro executive, replaced Omidyar as CEO in early 1998. eBay made a blockbuster debut as a public company later that year. The company moved closer to household name status in 1998 by launching a national ad campaign and inking alliance deals with America Online (now Time Warner) and WebTV.

A bit of the bloom came off the rose in 1999 when online service interruptions (one "brownout" in June persisted for 22 hours) revealed a chink in eBay's armor. The company called its top 10,000 users to convey its apologies and pledged to improve its Web site's performance.

In 2000 the US Department of Justice began an investigation to determine if eBay has violated antitrust laws in its dealing with competitors. In other legal news, a class-action lawsuit was filed against the company claiming that eBay is an auctioneer and therefore must authenticate the items on its site. (A trial court dismissed the case in early 2001; plaintiffs have said they'll appeal.)

Also in 2000 the company expanded into Japan through eBay Japan (computer firm NEC owned the rest) and launched Canadian and Austrian sites. eBay strengthened its European position in 2001 through the purchase of French Internet auction firm iBazar. It also launched sites in Ireland, New Zealand, and Switzerland. In 2002 eBay shuttered its eBay Japan operations after its dismal performance in that market.

In 2004 eBay took several steps toward diversifying its business. It expanded its international presence through acquisitions in China and India. The company purchased a 25% stake in online classifieds provider craigslist and announced plans to offer a music downloading service. Overall in 2004, more than 60% of eBay's new registered users were in the international business.

In February 2005 eBay acquired Internet listing site Rent.com for about $415 million. Continuing its acquisition spree eBay's international classifieds group, Kijiji (Swahili for village), in May acquired London-based Gumtree.com and Spain's LoQUo.com, a community-based listings Web site that operates sites for several Spanish cities alongside ones for France, Germany, Norway, Portugal, and the UK. In June Kijiji acquired opusforum, a local classifieds Web site based in Germany for an undisclosed sum. In August eBay acquired Shopping.com — a provider of online comparison shopping and consumer reviews with sites in France, the UK, and the US — for about $635 million. In mid-October eBay announced it had completed the acquisition of Internet-based telephone services firm Skype, for about $2.6 billion. In November eBay acquired VeriSign's payment gateway business.

## EXECUTIVES

**Chairman:** Pierre M. Omidyar, age 39
**President, CEO, and Director:** Margaret C. (Meg) Whitman, age 50, $1,216,024 pay
**SVP Finance and CFO:** Robert H. (Bob) Swan, age 46, $751,061 pay
**SVP Human Resources:** Elizabeth L. (Beth) Axelrod, age 44
**SVP, General Counsel, and Secretary:** Michael R. Jacobson, age 52, $454,066 pay
**VP Engineering and Research:** Jack Xu
**VP Global Citizenship, eBay International:** Gary Dillabough
**VP and Interim Principal Accounting Officer:** H. Baird Radford III
**CEO, Skype:** Niklas Zennström
**President, eBay International Marketplaces:** Lorrie M. Norrington, age 45
**President, eBay Marketplaces:** John J. Donahoe, age 46, $1,445,948 pay
**President, eBay Marketplaces North America:** William C. (Bill) Cobb, age 50
**President, PayPal:** Rajiv Dutta, age 45, $610,526 pay
**Head, Strategic Initiatives:** Eskander E. (Alex) Kazim, age 41
**SVP and CTO, eBay Marketplaces:** Matt Carey
**SVP and Chief Marketing Officer, eBay.com:** Gary S. Briggs, age 42
**Country Manager, Italy:** Alessandro Coppo, age 35
**General Manager, China Development Center:** Daniel Lee
**General Manager, Shopping.com:** Josh Silverman
**CTO, PayPal:** Scott Thompson
**Senior Director Brand Marketing:** Kevin McSpadden
**Media Contact:** Hani Durzy
**Investor Relations:** Tracey Ford
**Auditors:** PricewaterhouseCoopers LLP

## LOCATIONS

**HQ:** eBay Inc.
2145 Hamilton Ave., San Jose, CA 95125
**Phone:** 408-376-7400 **Fax:** 408-376-7401
**Web:** www.ebay.com

eBay operates in Australia, Austria, Belgium, Canada, China, France, Germany, Hong Kong, India, Ireland, Italy, Malaysia, the Netherlands, New Zealand, the Philippines, Singapore, South Korea, Spain, Sweden, Switzerland, Taiwan, the UK, and the US.

### 2006 Sales

| | $ mil. | % of total |
|---|---|---|
| US | 3,109.0 | 52 |
| Other countries | 2,860.7 | 48 |
| **Total** | **5,969.7** | **100** |

## PRODUCTS/OPERATIONS

### 2006 Sales

| | $ mil. | % of total |
|---|---|---|
| Marketplaces | 4,334.3 | 73 |
| Payments | 1,440.5 | 24 |
| Communications | 194.9 | 3 |
| **Total** | **5,969.7** | **100** |

### Selected Auction Categories

Antiques
Automobiles
Books, movies, and music
Coins and stamps
Collectibles
Computers
Consumer electronics
Dolls and figures
DVDs and movies
Jewelry and gemstones
Miscellaneous
Photo and electronics
Pottery and glass
Real estate
Sports memorabilia
Toys and Beanie Babies

## COMPETITORS

321 Gone
Alibaba.com
Amazon.com
Auction Concepts
Buy.com
Christie's
CityAuction
CNET Networks
Collectors Universe
Costco UK
Costco Wholesale
Costco Wholesale Canada
Curran's Select
eCom eCom
Escala Group
First Data
Gallery of History
Google
Half Price Books
HSN
J. C. Penney
K-tel
Microsoft
MSN
Northcore Technologies
Office Depot
OfficeMax
Overstock.com
The Pines
QVC
QVC UK
Rbid
SAM'S CLUB
Sears
Sotheby's
Staples
Target
Ticketmaster
Tickets.com
uBid
Visa
Walmart.com
Yahoo!

## HISTORICAL FINANCIALS

Company Type: Public

### Income Statement

FYE: December 31

| | REVENUE ($ mil.) | NET INCOME ($ mil.) | NET PROFIT MARGIN | EMPLOYEES |
|---|---|---|---|---|
| **12/06** | 5,970 | 1,126 | 18.9% | 13,200 |
| **12/05** | 4,552 | 1,082 | 23.8% | 12,600 |
| **12/04** | 3,271 | 778 | 23.8% | 8,100 |
| **12/03** | 2,165 | 442 | 20.4% | 6,200 |
| **12/02** | 1,214 | 250 | 20.6% | 4,000 |
| **Annual Growth** | 48.9% | 45.7% | — | 34.8% |

### 2006 Year-End Financials

Debt ratio: —
Return on equity: 10.7%
Cash ($ mil.): 3,218
Current ratio: 1.97
Long-term debt ($ mil.): —
No. of shares (mil.): 1,369
Dividends
Yield: —
Payout: —
Market value ($ mil.): 41,151

### Stock History

NASDAQ (GS): EBAY

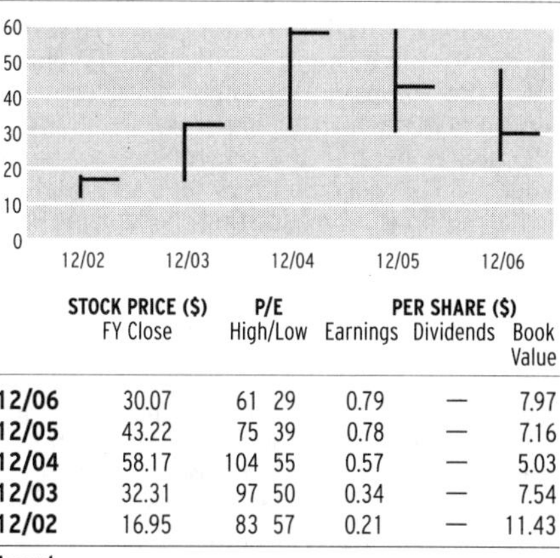


| | STOCK PRICE ($) FY Close | P/E High | P/E Low | PER SHARE ($) Earnings | PER SHARE ($) Dividends | PER SHARE ($) Book Value |
|---|---|---|---|---|---|---|
| **12/06** | 30.07 | 61 | 29 | 0.79 | — | 7.97 |
| **12/05** | 43.22 | 75 | 39 | 0.78 | — | 7.16 |
| **12/04** | 58.17 | 104 | 55 | 0.57 | — | 5.03 |
| **12/03** | 32.31 | 97 | 50 | 0.34 | — | 7.54 |
| **12/02** | 16.95 | 83 | 57 | 0.21 | — | 11.43 |
| **Annual Growth** | 15.4% | — | — | 39.3% | — | (8.6%) |

# EchoStar Communications

EchoStar Communications' DISH Network serves up fare that whets almost everyone's entertainment appetite. The company is the #2 US direct broadcast satellite (DBS) TV provider, behind DIRECTV, with the DISH Network providing programming to more than 13 million subscribers. EchoStar has formed alliances with ISPs and voice communications providers such as EarthLink, Qwest, and Sprint Nextel to offer combined services. Subsidiary EchoStar Technologies develops DBS hardware such as dishes, set-top boxes, and other digital equipment, both for the DISH Network and others. Co-founder and CEO Charlie Ergen controls the company with a 48% equity stake (and control of the vote).

EchoStar's DISH Network provides a wide range of programming (more than 2,500 digital video and audio channels) and has 14 leased and owned operational satellites in orbit and maintains sales and service locations throughout the continental US. It operates digital broadcast operations centers in Arizona and Wyoming.

The company has teamed up with Cable News Network to offer CNN Enhanced TV, an interactive news service. EchoStar's deals with various telecom providers allow the companies to offer the triple threat of TV, Internet access, and voice as bundled services, seeing how cable companies are moving in the same direction. The company has also found some success in selling digital video recorders (DVRs).

The company's engineering division — EchoStar Technologies — designs the set-top boxes used for the DISH Network's satellite reception (outsourcing the manufacturing activities). The unit also serves other satellite TV operators, supplying similar receiver systems and providing design and construction supervision of uplink centers in Canada and Europe.

EchoStar's Satellite Services unit leases satellite capacity for audio, data, and video services. The company is developing interactive TV services through a partnership with OpenTV. To thwart increased competition from regional cable companies, DISH Network has been working to provide customers with local TV channels. The company now offers local channel service to markets in all 50 states.

EchoStar became the second-largest shareholder of TU Media, South Korea's sole satellite digital multimedia broadcasting operator, in 2007. The $40 million investment was made through EchoStar subsidiary EchoStar Asia Holdings.

## HISTORY

Charlie Ergen, a former financial analyst for Frito-Lay, founded a Denver company called Echosphere, a retailer of large-dish, C-band satellite TV equipment, with his wife, Cantey, and James DeFranco (currently an EVP) in 1980. Echosphere evolved into a national manufacturer and distributor, which in 1987 began its move toward the new direct broadcast satellite (DBS) delivery system. It filed for a DBS license and set up subsidiary EchoStar Communications Corporation to build, launch, and operate DBS satellites. In 1992 the FCC granted the company an orbital slot.

By 1994 Echosphere was the US's largest distributor of conventional home satellite equipment, but the future clearly rested with DBS and EchoStar. A 1995 reorganization renamed the firm EchoStar Communications; the Echosphere distributor business became a subsidiary. EchoStar also created the DISH (Digital Sky Highway) Network brand, aiming for an easier-to-remember name than its rivals' "DSS" and "USSB."

The company launched the EchoStar I satellite in 1995, followed a year later by EchoStar II. Commencing DISH Network service in 1996, EchoStar competed against other DBS providers, including DIRECTV, to win 350,000 subscribers by year's end.

In 1997 Rupert Murdoch scrubbed a deal that called for News Corp. to buy half of EchoStar for $1 billion; Ergen sued for $5 billion in damages. EchoStar also went public in 1997 and reached the 1-million-customer mark.

The next year EchoStar tangled again with Murdoch, winning FCC approval to access programming from FX Networks (owned by News Corp. and the former TCI, now AT&T's cable unit), despite FX Networks' claims that it was locked up in exclusive programming agreements with cable companies. That issue and the 1997 lawsuit were put to rest in 1999 when News Corp. and MCI WorldCom (now WorldCom) traded DBS assets, including an orbital slot, for a combined 15% stake in EchoStar.

That year EchoStar and DIRECTV joined forces to successfully lobby for federal legislation allowing local TV signals to be delivered by satellites nationwide. The company entered the Internet business, providing WebTV Internet access via satellite to customers through an agreement with US software giant Microsoft. EchoStar also bought Media4 (now EchoStar Data Networks), which specializes in providing Internet and data transmission over satellite networks.

In 2000, the company reached an agreement to distribute two-way broadband Internet access using technology developed by the Israel-based Gilat Satellite Networks and Microsoft in a joint venture called StarBand Communications. In addition, EchoStar paid $50 million for a 13% stake in startup WildBlue Communications, which has planned to launch two geostationary satellites used to offer the two-way data services. EchoStar later backed out of those alliances.

When Hughes Electronics, at that time the parent of DIRECTV, was put up for sale in 2001, EchoStar expressed interest. After months of negotiations, EchoStar appeared to have given up but instead made an unsolicited offer. Hughes' parent, General Motors, agreed to sell the company to EchoStar after News Corp. dropped out of the bidding. Regulators rejected the deal in 2002, and the companies abandoned their merger plans (To help in the effort to purchase DIRECTV, Vivendi Universal had acquired a 10% stake in EchoStar in a $1.5 billion deal that included a distribution alliance, but it sold the stake back to EchoStar after the merger failed).

As part of its attempt to compete with regional cable companies that have the capability to provide regional TV channels, DISH Network began offering local channels to towns in California, Idaho, Maryland, Montana, North Carolina, South Carolina, Virginia, and Wisconsin in 2003. The next year EchoStar announced it had made local channels available in markets in all 50 states.

## EXECUTIVES

**Chairman and CEO:** Charles W. (Charlie) Ergen, age 54, $550,000 pay
**Vice Chairman and President:** Carl E. Vogel, age 49, $383,079 pay
**EVP and CFO:** Bernard L. (Bernie) Han, age 42, $88,077 pay (partial-year salary)
**EVP, Sales and Distribution and Director:** James DeFranco, age 54
**EVP, Strategic Initiatives:** O. Nolan Daines, age 47, $266,539 pay
**EVP, Installation and Service:** David J. Rayner, age 49, $300,000 pay
**EVP, Commercial and Business Services:** Michael Kelly, age 45
**EVP, General Counsel, Secretary, and Director:** David K. Moskowitz, age 48, $350,772 pay
**EVP, Human Resources:** Stephen Wood, age 48
**EVP, Corporate Development:** Thomas A. Cullen, age 47
**EVP, Operations:** Carol J. Kline, age 42
**VP and Corporate Controller:** Paul W. Orban
**VP, Programming:** Susan Arnold
**President, EchoStar International Corporation:** Steven B. Schaver, age 52
**President, EchoStar Technologies Corporation:** Mark W. Jackson, age 46
**Media Relations:** Kevin Hubbard
**Investor Relations:** Jason Kiser
**Auditors:** KPMG LLP

## LOCATIONS

**HQ:** EchoStar Communications Corporation
9601 S. Meridian Blvd., Englewood, CO 80112
**Phone:** 303-723-1000 **Fax:** 303-723-1999
**Web:** www.dishnetwork.com

### 2006 Sales

| | % of total |
|---|---|
| US | 99 |
| Other countries | 1 |
| **Total** | **100** |

## PRODUCTS/OPERATIONS

### 2006 Sales

| | % of total |
|---|---|
| Subscriber-related revenue | 95 |
| Equipment sales | 4 |
| Other | 1 |
| **Total** | **100** |

### 2006 Sales

| | % of total |
|---|---|
| DISH Network | 97 |
| EchoStar Technologies | 2 |
| Other | 1 |
| **Total** | **100** |

### Selected Subsidiaries and Affiliations

EchoStar DBS Corporation
- Dish Network Service L.L.C.
- Echosphere L.L.C.
- EchoStar Satellite L.L.C.
- EchoStar Technologies Corporation

EchoStar Orbital Corporation
EchoStar Orbital Corporation II
NagraStar LLC (50%, smart-card encryption security access devices)

## COMPETITORS

Cablevision Systems
Charter Communications
Comcast
Cox Communications
DIRECTV
Pegasus Communications
Rainbow Media
RCN
ReplayTV
Time Warner Cable
TiVo

## HISTORICAL FINANCIALS

Company Type: Public

### Income Statement

FYE: December 31

| | REVENUE ($ mil.) | NET INCOME ($ mil.) | NET PROFIT MARGIN | EMPLOYEES |
|---|---|---|---|---|
| **12/06** | 9,819 | 608 | 6.2% | 21,000 |
| **12/05** | 8,426 | 1,515 | 18.0% | 21,000 |
| **12/04** | 7,151 | 215 | 3.0% | 20,000 |
| **12/03** | 5,739 | 225 | 3.9% | 15,000 |
| **12/02** | 4,821 | (882) | — | 15,000 |
| **Annual Growth** | 19.5% | — | — | 8.8% |

### 2006 Year-End Financials

| | |
|---|---|
| Debt ratio: — | No. of shares (mil.): 207 |
| Return on equity: — | Dividends |
| Cash ($ mil.): 3,033 | Yield: — |
| Current ratio: 1.28 | Payout: — |
| Long-term debt ($ mil.): 5,929 | Market value ($ mil.): 7,890 |

**Stock History** NASDAQ (GS): DISH

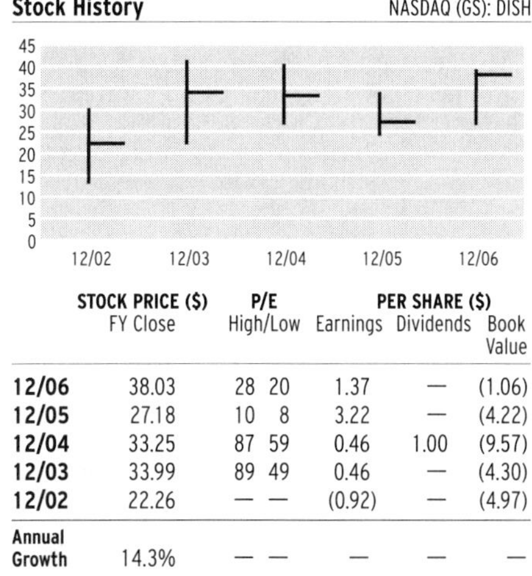


| | STOCK PRICE ($) FY Close | P/E High/Low | | PER SHARE ($) Earnings | Dividends | Book Value |
|---|---|---|---|---|---|---|
| **12/06** | 38.03 | 28 | 20 | 1.37 | — | (1.06) |
| **12/05** | 27.18 | 10 | 8 | 3.22 | — | (4.22) |
| **12/04** | 33.25 | 87 | 59 | 0.46 | 1.00 | (9.57) |
| **12/03** | 33.99 | 89 | 49 | 0.46 | — | (4.30) |
| **12/02** | 22.26 | — | — | (0.92) | — | (4.97) |
| **Annual Growth** | 14.3% | — | — | — | — | — |

# Ecolab Inc.

Ecolab cleans up by cleaning up. The company offers cleaning, sanitation, pest-elimination, and maintenance products and services to hospitality, institutional, and industrial customers. Its institutional division serves hotels and restaurants, food service and health care facilities, schools, and commercial and institutional laundries. Other divisions focus on products for textile care, water care, fast food, and pest control. Ecolab makes most of its products, although the company sells some products made by other manufacturers. Henkel owns 29% of the company.

The company has grown through several acquisitions over the years, which have granted Ecolab access to geographic areas as well as business sectors it previously did not have. Ecolab has plans to keep up with its acquisitive ways, and acquired biocides maker Alcide, which manufactures sanitation products that protect and clean livestock and food, in 2004.

And early the next year the company acquired a small water care company based in Kansas, Midland Research Laboratories. The new subsidiary provides services to the hospitality and health care industries. In 2006 Ecolab made acquisitions in both the UK (contamination control products for pharmaceutical makers and a commercial laundry company) and the US (sanitation products for the food industry).

The following year saw Ecolab agree to another acquisition in the health care field, buying Microtek Medical Holdings, which makes infection control products for health care facilities. The deal was for about $275 million.

## HISTORY

Salesman Merritt Osborn founded Economics Laboratory in 1924 as a specialty chemical maker; its first product was a rug cleaner for hotels. It added industrial and institutional cleaners and consumer detergents in the 1950s. The company went public in 1957. By 1973 it had been organized into five divisions: industrial (cleaners and specialty chemical formulas), institutional (dishwasher products, sanitation formulas), consumer (dishwasher detergent and laundry aids, coffee filters, floor cleaners), food-processing (detergents), and international (run by future CEO Fred Lanners Jr.).

At the time household dishwasher detergent was Economics Laboratory's top seller, second to Procter & Gamble in the US and #1 overseas. The company began offering services and products as packages in the early 1970s, including on-premise laundry services for hotels and hospitals and sanitation and cleaning services for the food industry.

E. B. Osborn, son of the founder, retired in 1978, and Lanners became the company's first CEO outside the Osborn family. Sales of dishwashing detergent had fallen, while the institutional cleaning business had become its primary segment, quadrupling in sales between 1970 and 1980. International sales were growing rapidly. In 1979 the company bought Apollo Technologies (chemicals and pollution-control equipment) to improve its share of the industrial market.

A depressed industrial sector caused Apollo's sales to drop in early 1980. The man expected to save Apollo, Richard Ashley, succeeded Lanners in 1982 but died in a car crash that year. Pierson "Sandy" Grieve became CEO in 1983 and shut down Apollo. Meanwhile, debt was up, the institutional market had shrunk, and the company was slipping in the dishwashing-detergent market. Grieve sold the firm's coffee-filters unit and several plants, laid off employees, and began new packaging processes. The company changed its name to Ecolab in 1986, and in 1987 it sold its dishwashing-detergent unit and bought lawn-service provider ChemLawn. (ChemLawn was sold in 1992.)

As 1990 neared, Grieve introduced what's now known as "Circle the Customer — Circle the Globe," the aim being to become a worldwide leader in core businesses and broaden product offerings. The company concentrated on building its presence in Africa, the Asia/Pacific region, Latin America, and the Middle East. In 1991 Ecolab also began a highly successful joint venture, Henkel-Ecolab, with German consumer-products company Henkel to better exploit European markets.

Ecolab acquired Kay Chemical (cleaning and sanitation products for the fast-food industry, 1994), Monarch (cleaning and sanitation products for food processing, 1996), Huntington Laboratories (janitorial products, 1996), and Australia-based Gibson (cleaning and sanitation products, 1997). In 1995 Grieve stepped down, and president Allan Schuman became CEO. Adding a few more degrees to its circle of services, in 1998 Ecolab bought GCS Service (commercial kitchen equipment repair).

The company further secured footholds in Asia and South America in 2000 by acquiring industrial and institutional cleaning firms Dong Woo Deterpan (South Korea), Spartan de Chile, and Spartan de Argentina. At home, it bought kitchen-equipment companies ARR/CRS and Southwest Sanitary Distributing. Late in 2000 Ecolab sold its Johnson dish machines unit to Endonis and announced a restructuring that was soon followed by the departure of several top executives, including president and COO Bruno Deschamps.

In 2001 Ecolab purchased the 50% of Henkel-Ecolab that it didn't own from Henkel for about $435 million; the move greatly expanded the company's international business.

In mid-2004 Schuman stepped down as CEO (retaining the chairman's role); president Doug Baker took over and became a director in addition to his role as president and CEO. Two years later Allan Schuman retired as chairman, ending his 49-year tenure with Ecolab. The company named Baker to replace Schuman.

## EXECUTIVES

**Chairman, President, and CEO:**
Douglas M. (Doug) Baker Jr., age 48, $800,000 pay
**EVP and CFO:** Steven L. Fritze, age 52, $420,000 pay
**EVP, Asia/Pacific and Latin America:** Phillip J. Mason, age 56
**EVP, Institutional Sector North America:**
James A. Miller, age 50, $350,000 pay
**EVP, Specialty Sector:** Thomas W. Handley, age 52
**EVP, Global Services Sector:** C. William Snedeker, age 61, $437,000 pay
**SVP, Human Resources:** Diana D. Lewis, age 60
**SVP, Research, Development, and Engineering; CTO:**
Susan K. Nestegard, age 46
**SVP, General Counsel, and Secretary:** Lawrence T. Bell, age 59, $342,000 pay
**SVP, Global Supply Chain:** Robert K. Gifford, age 49
**SVP, Global Business Development:** Michael A. Hickey, age 45
**VP and CIO:** Robert P. Tabb, age 55
**VP and Controller:** Daniel J. Schmechel, age 47
**Auditors:** PricewaterhouseCoopers LLP

## LOCATIONS

**HQ:** Ecolab Inc.
370 Wabasha St. North, St. Paul, MN 55102
**Phone:** 651-293-2233 **Fax:** 651-293-2092
**Web:** www.ecolab.com

Ecolab has manufacturing facilities worldwide.

**2006 Sales**

| | $ mil. | % of total |
|---|---|---|
| US | 2,635 | 54 |
| Other countries | 2,261 | 46 |
| **Total** | **4,896** | **100** |

## PRODUCTS/OPERATIONS

**2006 Sales and Operating Income**

| | Sales $ mil. | Sales % of total | Operating Income $ mil. | Operating Income % of total |
|---|---|---|---|---|
| International | 2,261 | 47 | 234 | 39 |
| US Cleaning & Sanitizing | 2,152 | 44 | 329 | 55 |
| US Other Services | 411 | 9 | 39 | 6 |
| Effect of foreign currency translations | 72 | 1 | — | — |
| **Total** | **4,896** | **100** | **602** | **100** |

## COMPETITORS

ABM Industries
Acuity Specialty Products
Chemed
CPAC
Healthcare Services
ISS A/S
JohnsonDiversey
Reckitt Benckiser (US)
Rentokil Initial
Rollins
ServiceMaster
Tranzonic
UNICCO Service
Unilever
Unisource

## HISTORICAL FINANCIALS

Company Type: Public

**Income Statement** FYE: December 31

| | REVENUE ($ mil.) | NET INCOME ($ mil.) | NET PROFIT MARGIN | EMPLOYEES |
|---|---|---|---|---|
| **12/06** | 4,896 | 369 | 7.5% | 23,130 |
| **12/05** | 4,535 | 320 | 7.0% | 22,400 |
| **12/04** | 4,185 | 311 | 7.4% | 21,300 |
| **12/03** | 3,762 | 277 | 7.4% | 20,800 |
| **12/02** | 3,404 | 210 | 6.2% | 20,400 |
| **Annual Growth** | 9.5% | 15.1% | — | 3.2% |

**2006 Year-End Financials**

| | |
|---|---|
| Debt ratio: 33.2% | No. of shares (mil.): 251 |
| Return on equity: 22.1% | Dividends |
| Cash ($ mil.): 484 | Yield: 0.9% |
| Current ratio: 1.23 | Payout: 28.7% |
| Long-term debt ($ mil.): 557 | Market value ($ mil.): 11,360 |

**Stock History** NYSE: ECL

| | STOCK PRICE ($) FY Close | P/E High | P/E Low | PER SHARE ($) Earnings | Dividends | Book Value |
|---|---|---|---|---|---|---|
| **12/06** | 45.20 | 32 | 24 | 1.43 | 0.41 | 6.69 |
| **12/05** | 36.27 | 30 | 25 | 1.23 | 0.36 | 6.49 |
| **12/04** | 35.13 | 30 | 22 | 1.19 | 0.41 | 6.07 |
| **12/03** | 27.37 | 26 | 22 | 1.06 | 0.30 | 5.03 |
| **12/02** | 24.75 | 32 | 23 | 0.80 | 0.28 | 8.46 |
| **Annual Growth** | 16.2% | — | — | 15.6% | 10.0% | (5.7%) |

# Edison International

Although Edison International has been around the world, the company's largest subsidiary is still Southern California Edison (SCE), which distributes electricity to a population of more than 13 million people in central, coastal, and southern California. Edison has created a cosmopolitan image through Edison Mission Energy (EME), but it has pulled back on most of its international operations. After having sold off plants in Asia and Europe, it now markets energy in only North America and Turkey. The company also provides consulting, management, and maintenance services for energy projects.

The deregulation of California's energy market took a heavy toll on SCE. Prices on the wholesale power market began to soar in 2000, and SCE was unable to pass along the increase to customers because of a rate freeze. After the rate freeze was lifted in 2001, the utility reached a settlement with state regulators that allowed it to keep high rates in place until its debts were paid off. Rates were lowered again in 2003.

## HISTORY

In 1896 a group including Elmer Peck and George Baker organized West Side Lighting to provide electricity in Los Angeles. The following year the company merged with Los Angeles Edison Electric, which owned rights to the Edison name and patents in the region; Baker became president. Edison Electric installed the Southwest's first DC-power underground conduits.

John Barnes Miller took over the top spot in 1901. During his 31-year reign the firm bought many neighboring utilities and built several power plants. In 1909 it took the name Southern California Edison (SCE).

SCE doubled its assets by buying Southern California electric interests from rival Pacific Light & Power in 1917. However, in 1912 the City of Los Angeles had decided to develop its own power distribution system, and by 1922 SCE's authority in the city had ended. A 1925 earthquake and the 1928 collapse of the St. Francis Dam severely damaged SCE's facilities.

SCE built 11 fossil-fueled power stations (1948-1973) and moved into nuclear power in 1963, when it broke ground on the San Onofre plant with San Diego Gas & Electric (brought online in 1968). It finished consolidating its service territory with the 1964 purchase of California Electric Power. In the late 1970s SCE began to build solar, geothermal, and wind power facilities.

Edison Mission Energy (EME) was founded in 1986 to develop, buy, and operate power plants around the world. The next year investment arm Edison Capital was formed, as well as a holding company for the entire group, SCEcorp. EME began to build its portfolio in 1992 when it snagged a 51% stake in an Australian plant (now 100%-owned) and bought hydroelectric facilities in Spain. In 1995 it bought UK hydroelectric company First Hydro; it also began building plants in Italy, Turkey, and Indonesia.

The 1994 Northridge earthquake that cut power to a million SCE customers was nothing compared to the industry's seismic shifts. In 1996 SCEcorp became the more worldly Edison International. California's electricity market opened to competition in 1998, and the utility began divesting SCE's generation assets; it sold 12 gas-fired plants. Overseas EME picked up 25% of a power plant being built in Thailand and a 50% stake in a cogeneration facility in Puerto Rico.

SCE got regulatory approval to offer telecom services in its utility territory in 1999. That year EME snapped up several plants in the Midwest from Unicom for $5 billion. Overseas it purchased two UK coal-fired plants from PowerGen (which it sold to American Electric Power in 2001 for $960 million). The next year EME CEO Edward Muller (who had held the post since 1994) abruptly resigned, and Edison bought Citizens Power from the Peabody Group.

In 2000 SCE got caught in a price squeeze brought on in part by deregulation. Prices on the wholesale power market soared, but the utility was unable to pass along the increase to customers because of a rate freeze. The company gained some prospect of relief in 2001 when California's governor signed legislation to allow a state agency to buy power from wholesalers under long-term contracts. In addition, the California Public Utilities Commission (CPUC) approved a substantial increase in retail electricity rates, and the Federal Energy Regulatory Commission approved a plan to limit wholesale energy prices during periods of severe shortage in 11 western states.

To reduce debt, Edison International agreed to sell its transmission grid to the state for $2.8 billion. While the California legislature debated the agreement, however, the CPUC announced a settlement in which SCE would be allowed to keep its current high rates in place until its debts are paid off. The settlement, which was approved in 2002, eliminated the need for the sale of the company's transmission grid.

Also in 2001, the company sold most of its Edison Enterprises businesses, including home security services unit Edison Select, which was sold to ADT Security Services.

## EXECUTIVES

**Chairman, President, and CEO; Chairman, Southern California Edison; Chairman, Edison Capital:** John E. Bryson, age 63, $3,260,000 pay

**EVP, CFO, and Treasurer:** Thomas R. (Tom) McDaniel, age 55, $1,287,500 pay

**EVP and General Counsel:** J.A. (Lon) Bouknight Jr., age 61

**SVP and CIO; Edison International and Southern California Edison:** Mahvash Yazdi, age 55, $684,400 pay

**SVP Public Affairs; SVP Public Affairs, Southern California Edison:** Polly L. Gault

**VP and General Auditor; VP and General Auditor, Southern California Edison:** Diane L. Featherstone, age 48

**VP Corporate Communications; VP Corporate Communications, Southern California Edison:** Barbara J. Parsky

**VP Human Resources and Labor Relations, Edison International and Southern California Edison:** Frederick J. Grigsby Jr., age 56

**VP Tax; VP Tax, Southern California Edison:** Anthony L. Smith

**Chairman, President, and CEO, Edison Mission Energy; CEO, Edison Capital:** Theodore F. (Ted) Craver Jr., age 55, $1,368,000 pay

**CEO, Southern California Edison:** Alan J. Fohrer, age 46, $1,363,000 pay

**President, Southern California Edison:** John R. Fielder, age 61, $763,340 pay

**VP and Chief Ethics and Compliance Officer:** Kenneth S. Stewart

**VP and Controller; VP and Controller, Southern California Edison:** Linda G. Sullivan

**VP Investor Relations:** Scott S. Cunningham

**Auditors:** PricewaterhouseCoopers LLP

## LOCATIONS

**HQ:** Edison International
2244 Walnut Grove Ave., Rosemead, CA 91770
**Phone:** 626-302-2222 **Fax:** 626-302-2517
**Web:** www.edison.com

Southern California Edison operates primarily in central, coastal, and southern California.

**2006 Sales**

| | $ mil. | % of total |
|---|---|---|
| US | 12,563 | 99 |
| Other countries | 59 | 1 |
| **Total** | **12,622** | **100** |

## PRODUCTS/OPERATIONS

**2006 Sales**

| | $ mil. | % of total |
|---|---|---|
| Electric utility | 10,312 | 82 |
| Nonutility power generation | 2,228 | 18 |
| Financial services & other | 82 | — |
| **Total** | **12,622** | **100** |

### Selected Subsidiaries

Edison Capital (capital and financial services for energy and infrastructure projects)
Edison Mission Energy (power generation, energy trading and marketing)
Edison Mission Marketing & Trading
Midwest Generation
Southern California Edison Company (SCE, electric utility)

## COMPETITORS

AES
Aquila
Avista
Calpine
CMS Energy
Constellation Energy Group
Dynegy
Electricité de France
Endesa S.A.
Enel
Entergy
FPL Group
IBERDROLA
Los Angeles Water and Power
MidAmerican Energy
Mirant
NRG Energy
PacifiCorp
PG&E
Portland General Electric
Reliant Energy
Sacramento Municipal
Sempra Energy
Sierra Pacific Resources

## HISTORICAL FINANCIALS

Company Type: Public

### Income Statement

FYE: December 31

| | REVENUE ($ mil.) | NET INCOME ($ mil.) | NET PROFIT MARGIN | EMPLOYEES |
|---|---|---|---|---|
| 12/06 | 12,622 | 1,181 | 9.4% | 16,139 |
| 12/05 | 11,852 | 1,137 | 9.6% | 15,838 |
| 12/04 | 10,199 | 916 | 9.0% | 15,293 |
| 12/03 | 12,135 | 821 | 6.8% | 15,407 |
| 12/02 | 11,488 | 1,192 | 10.4% | 15,038 |
| Annual Growth | 2.4% | (0.2%) | — | 1.8% |

### 2006 Year-End Financials

Debt ratio: 121.2%
Return on equity: 16.5%
Cash ($ mil.): 2,864
Current ratio: 1.27
Long-term debt ($ mil.): 9,347
No. of shares (mil.): 326
Dividends
Yield: 2.4%
Payout: 30.8%
Market value ($ mil.): 14,818

### Stock History

NYSE: EIX

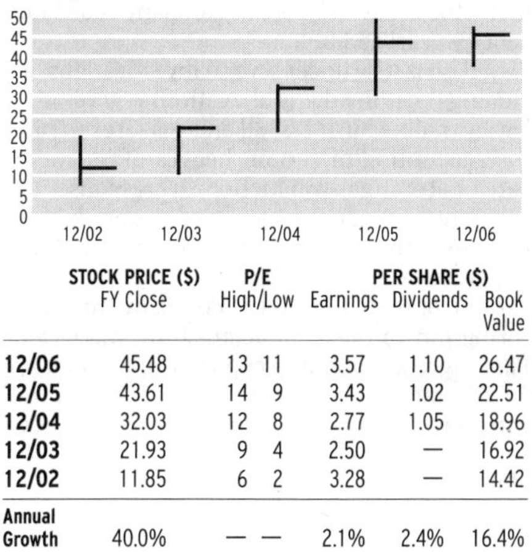


| | STOCK PRICE ($) FY Close | P/E High | P/E Low | PER SHARE ($) Earnings | Dividends | Book Value |
|---|---|---|---|---|---|---|
| 12/06 | 45.48 | 13 | 11 | 3.57 | 1.10 | 26.47 |
| 12/05 | 43.61 | 14 | 9 | 3.43 | 1.02 | 22.51 |
| 12/04 | 32.03 | 12 | 8 | 2.77 | 1.05 | 18.96 |
| 12/03 | 21.93 | 9 | 4 | 2.50 | — | 16.92 |
| 12/02 | 11.85 | 6 | 2 | 3.28 | — | 14.42 |
| Annual Growth | 40.0% | — | — | 2.1% | 2.4% | 16.4% |

# E. I. duPont de Nemours

E. I. du Pont de Nemours (DuPont) is focusing on chemicals and profits. The #3 US chemical maker (behind Dow and ExxonMobil Chemicals) has undergone a restructuring that consolidated eight business units into five. These segments produce coatings (automotive finishes and coatings), crop protection chemicals and genetically modified seeds, electronic materials (LCDs, sensors, and fluorochemicals), polymers and resins for packaging and other uses, and safety and security materials. The company has slimmed down, exiting the pharmaceutical business and spinning off its fibers operations (as INVISTA, owner of the Lycra and Stainmaster brands), and is focusing more and more on biotechnology and safety and protection.

The company gets about 40% of sales from the US; internationally it operates throughout Europe and Asia as well as in Canada and Mexico. Though it no longer makes pharmaceutical products, having sold those operations to Bristol-Myers Squibb in 2001, DuPont still receives nearly a billion dollars of income from two anti-hypertension drugs, Cozaar and Hyzaar, that are licensed to Merck.

In the spring of 2004 the company sold INVISTA to Koch, withdrawing DuPont completely from the fibers business. It still is, however, very much in the chemicals business. In fact, a month after the INVISTA deal closed, DuPont announced that it was initiating a joint venture with British ingredients maker Tate & Lyle to create a renewable alternative to some petrochemicals. Called DuPont Tate & Lyle BioProducts, the JV's first manufacturing facility was up and running by the end of 2006. The intent is to use renewable resources, like corn, as the base material for building block chemicals like propanediol 1,3 that currently are built from petrochemicals.

In 2007 the company agreed to sell part of its fluorochemical products business to Huntsman. The unit sold provides fluoro-products for nonwovens to the textiles industry. They are used to repel water, alcohol, and oil-based fluids in medical, filtration, and automotive applications.

## HISTORY

Eleuthère Irénée du Pont de Nemours fled to America in 1800 after the French Revolution. Two years later he founded a gunpowder plant in Delaware. Within a decade the DuPont plant was the largest of its kind in the US. After Irénée's death in 1834, his sons Alfred and Henry took over. DuPont added dynamite and nitroglycerine in 1880, guncotton in 1892, and smokeless powder in 1894.

In 1902 three du Pont cousins bought DuPont. By 1906 the company controlled most of the US explosives market, but a 1912 antitrust decision forced it to sell part of the powder business. WWI profits were used to diversify into paints, plastics, and dyes.

DuPont acquired an interest in General Motors in 1917; the stake increased to 37% by 1922 (the company surrendered its stake in 1962 due to antitrust regulations). In the 1920s the firm bought and improved French cellophane technology and began producing rayon. DuPont's inventions include neoprene synthetic rubber (1931), Lucite (1937), nylon (1938), Teflon (1938), and Dacron. The last du Pont to head the company resigned as chairman in 1972. DuPont got into the energy business by acquiring Conoco for $7.6 billion in 1981.

In 1991 DuPont and Merck created DuPont Merck Pharmaceutical to focus on non-US markets. After record earnings in 1994, DuPont spent $8.8 billion the next year to buy back shares of the corporation from Seagram. In 1997 DuPont purchased Protein Technologies International (soy proteins) from Ralston Purina and Imperial Chemical's polyester-resins and intermediates operations (1997) and polyester-film business (1998).

DuPont president Chad Holliday became CEO in early 1998. That year DuPont purchased a 20% stake in Pioneer Hi-Bred International (corn seed) for $1.7 billion and Merck's 50% stake in DuPont Merck Pharmaceutical (now DuPont Pharmaceuticals) for $2.6 billion. DuPont's public offering of Conoco in 1998 raised $4.4 billion, the largest US IPO at the time. In 1999 DuPont bought the Herberts paints and coatings unit from Hoechst. It also bought the remaining 80% of Pioneer Hi-Bred for $7.7 billion and biotechnology research firm CombiChem. Making a clean break with its oil business, DuPont sold its remaining 70% stake in Conoco.

In late 2001 Bristol-Myers Squibb bought DuPont's pharmaceutical operations (HIV, heart disease, nerve disorder, and cancer drugs) for $7.8 billion in cash. In early 2002 DuPont initiated a restructuring that included the eventual spin-off of its fibers businesses (now called INVISTA) and the reorganization of its remaining business units into five segments: Electronics & Communication Technologies, Performance Materials, Coatings & Color Technologies, Safety & Protection, and Agriculture & Nutrition.

Later that year DuPont acquired TOTAL's surface protection and fluoroadditives business to become the largest integrated fluorotelomer protectants maker in both Europe and North America. DuPont also acquired semiconductor chemicals maker ChemFirst and packaging company Liqui-Box in 2002.

Excluding the former pharmaceutical operations, DuPont wasn't profitable for the first few years of the new century. Much of its losses were due to employee severance costs and the write-down of assets. In 2003 the company took a large hit from the separation of INVISTA, among other costs. And so despite a 12% increase in sales, the company saw no real profit.

DuPont announced in late 2003 an initiative that it hoped would deliver $900 million in growth by the end of 2005. In addition to workforce cuts and product consolidation, DuPont also began to shift its focus to emerging markets, by which it meant Asia. The company announced a substantial shift in management in January 2004 to follow up on the initiative, which included appointing a head of global sales for the first time and rearranging its leadership in Asia. The workforce cuts were announced in April; 3,500 jobs were cut in 2004, mostly in the US and Western Europe.

Preparing to separate INVISTA, DuPont reabsorbed DuPont Canada (which had been a separate, public company) into the fold. In early 2004 the company completed the sale of INVISTA; with that, DuPont was completely out of the fibers business.

## EXECUTIVES

**Chairman and CEO:** Charles O. (Chad) Holliday Jr., age 59, $1,293,000 pay
**EVP and COO:** Richard R. Goodmanson, age 59, $811,000 pay
**EVP and CFO:** Jeffrey L. Keefer, age 54, $451,014 pay
**EVP and Chief Innovation Officer; Group VP, DuPont Electronic & Communication Technologies and DuPont Bio-Based Materials:** Thomas M. (Tom) Connelly Jr., age 54, $566,640 pay
**EVP, DuPont Safety & Protection and Coatings; DuPont Coatings & Color Technologies; Marketing & Sales; Safety and Sustainability; Pharmaceuticals; and Risk Management:** Ellen J. Kullman, age 51, $537,640 pay
**SVP and Chief Science and Technology Officer:** Uma Chowdhry, age 55
**SVP, DuPont Operations & Engineering:** Mathieu Vrijsen
**SVP, Chief Administrative Officer, and General Counsel:** Stacey J. Mobley, age 61
**SVP, DuPont Human Resources:** James C. Borel, age 51
**President, U.S. Region; VP, Diversity and Work/Life and Human Resources Development for Operations:** Willie C. Martin
**President and CEO, DuPont Performance Elastomers:** John R. (Jack) Lewis, age 61
**Group VP, DuPont Performance Materials:** Diane H. Gulyas, age 47
**Group VP, DuPont Agriculture and Nutrition:** J. Erik Fyrwald, age 48
**Group VP, DuPont Coatings and Color Technologies:** Terry Caloghiris, age 55
**Group VP, Dupont Safety and Protection:** Mark P. Vergnano, age 48
**VP, DuPont Investor Relations:** Carl J. Lukach, age 50
**Chief Marketing and Sales Officer:** David G. Bills, age 45
**Auditors:** PricewaterhouseCoopers LLP

## LOCATIONS

**HQ:** E. I. du Pont de Nemours and Company
1007 Market St., Wilmington, DE 19898
**Phone:** 302-774-1000 **Fax:** 302-999-4399
**Web:** www.dupont.com

E. I. du Pont de Nemours has about 200 manufacturing and processing facilities. It has operations in about 80 countries throughout the Americas, Europe, and Asia.

### 2006 Sales

| | % of total |
|---|---|
| US | 41 |
| Europe | 29 |
| Asia/Pacific | 17 |
| Canada & Latin America | 13 |
| **Total** | **100** |

## PRODUCTS/OPERATIONS

### 2006 Sales

| | $ mil. | % of total |
|---|---|---|
| Performance Materials | 6,892 | 23 |
| Agriculture & Nutrition | 6,329 | 21 |
| Coatings & Color Technologies | 6,309 | 21 |
| Safety & Protection | 5,584 | 18 |
| Electronic & Communication Technologies | 3,814 | 12 |
| Other | 1,618 | 5 |
| Adjustments | (1,564) | — |
| **Total** | **28,982** | **100** |

### Selected Operations

Performance Materials
- DuPont Dow Elastomers
- DuPont Engineering Polymers
- DuPont Packaging & Industrial Polymers (includes Polyester Resins, formerly part of Polyester)
- DuPont Teijin Films

Agriculture & Nutrition
- DuPont Crop Protection
- DuPont Nutrition & Health
- DuPont Protein Technologies
- DuPont Qualicon
- Pioneer HiBred International

Coatings & Color Technologies
- DuPont Performance Coatings
- DuPont Titanium Technologies

Safety & Protection
- DuPont Advanced Fiber Systems
- DuPont Chemical Solutions Enterprise
- DuPont Nonwovens
- DuPont Safety Resources
- DuPont Surfaces

Electronic & Communication Technologies
- DuPont Displays Technologies
- DuPont Electronic Technologies
- DuPont Fluoroproducts
- DuPont Imaging Technologies

## COMPETITORS

3M
Akzo Nobel
Asahi Kasei
Ashland
BASF AG
Bayer
Cargill
Chevron Phillips Chemical
Clorox
ConAgra
Dainippon Ink
Degussa
Dow Chemical
Eastman Chemical
FMC
Formosa Plastics
Henkel
Hercules
Honeywell International
Imperial Chemical
Lyondell Chemical
Occidental Chemical
PPG
Reliance Industries
Rohm and Haas
Sherwin-Williams
Shin-Etsu Chemical
Syngenta
W. R. Grace
Wellman

## HISTORICAL FINANCIALS

Company Type: Public

### Income Statement

FYE: December 31

| | REVENUE ($ mil.) | NET INCOME ($ mil.) | NET PROFIT MARGIN | EMPLOYEES |
|---|---|---|---|---|
| **12/06** | 28,982 | 3,148 | 10.9% | 59,000 |
| **12/05** | 28,491 | 2,053 | 7.2% | 60,000 |
| **12/04** | 27,995 | 1,780 | 6.4% | 60,000 |
| **12/03** | 27,730 | 973 | 3.5% | 81,000 |
| **12/02** | 24,522 | (1,103) | — | 79,000 |
| **Annual Growth** | 4.3% | — | — | (7.0%) |

### 2006 Year-End Financials

Debt ratio: 65.5%
Return on equity: 35.3%
Cash ($ mil.): 1,893
Current ratio: 1.62
Long-term debt ($ mil.): 6,013
No. of shares (mil.): 922
Dividends
Yield: 3.0%
Payout: 43.8%
Market value ($ mil.): 44,914

### Stock History

NYSE: DD

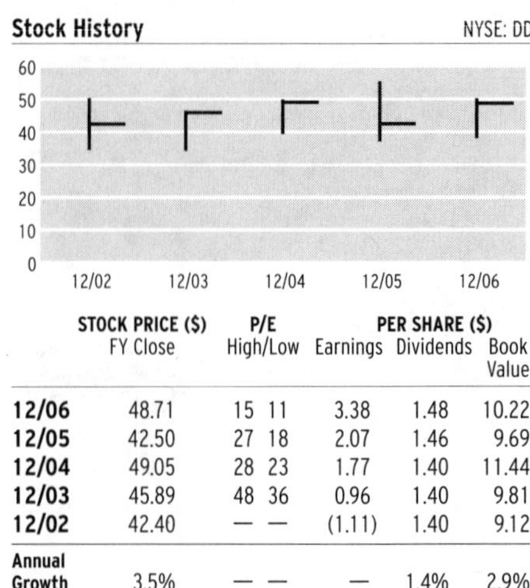

| | STOCK PRICE ($) FY Close | P/E High | P/E Low | PER SHARE ($) Earnings | Dividends | Book Value |
|---|---|---|---|---|---|---|
| **12/06** | 48.71 | 15 | 11 | 3.38 | 1.48 | 10.22 |
| **12/05** | 42.50 | 27 | 18 | 2.07 | 1.46 | 9.69 |
| **12/04** | 49.05 | 28 | 23 | 1.77 | 1.40 | 11.44 |
| **12/03** | 45.89 | 48 | 36 | 0.96 | 1.40 | 9.81 |
| **12/02** | 42.40 | — | — | (1.11) | 1.40 | 9.12 |
| **Annual Growth** | 3.5% | — | — | — | 1.4% | 2.9% |

# El Paso Corporation

Out in the West Texas town of El Paso this company fell in love with the natural gas industry. Founded in 1928 in its namesake Texas city, El Paso Corp. is primarily engaged in gas transportation and storage, oil and gas exploration and production, and gas gathering and processing. Operator of the largest gas transportation system in the US, El Paso has interests in 55,000 miles of interstate pipeline. Subsidiary El Paso Exploration and Production has estimated proved reserves of 2.4 trillion cu. ft. of natural gas equivalent in Brazil, Egypt, and the US. The company also has interests in global energy projects, including power plants, and it markets wholesale energy commodities.

After expanding into various nonregulated sectors, the company is going back to its roots — natural gas — and is selling its Asian and Central American power plants.

Additionally, in 2007 it sold ANR Pipeline, its Michigan storage assets, and its 50% interest in Great Lakes Gas Transmission, which comprised approximately 12,600 miles of pipeline. The year before, El Paso sold some of its Central American power assets to Globeleq Ltd. for $88 million.

Selling assets, combined with issuing common stock, has helped the company reduce its debt by nearly $3 billion.

El Paso is now under several investigations, including those involving allegations regarding its legacy trading business, oil and gas reserves, and the accounting of certain hedges of its anticipated natural gas production. In response, the company has reduced its oil and gas production workforce and restructured its reserve accounting processes.

None of that stopped the company from venturing out to make an acquisition. In 2007 El Paso agreed to buy Peoples Production for $875 million from Integrys Energy. The acquired company controls 300 billion cu. ft. of natural gas proved reserves and will fit within El Paso Exploration & Production.

## HISTORY

In 1928 Paul Kayser, a Houston attorney, started the El Paso Natural Gas Company and got the rights to sell natural gas to that West Texas town a year later. Despite the 1929 stock market crash, the company built a 200-mile pipeline, first connecting El Paso, Texas, with natural gas wells in Jal, New Mexico. In 1931 it laid pipe again to reach the copper mines of Arizona and Mexico, and three years later expanded to Phoenix and Tucson.

After World War II the company began a 700-mile pipeline to bring natural gas from Texas' Permian Basin to California. As the Golden State's population exploded, sales soared. El Paso also ventured into new business areas, first chemicals and later textiles, mining, land development, and insurance.

In 1974 the Supreme Court ruled that El Paso had to divest its pipeline holdings north of New Mexico and Arizona. Federal regulators had granted the company the right to buy the holdings two decades earlier but later rescinded. Other operations, such as fiber manufacturing, were posting losses, so the company jettisoned some non-gas businesses. El Paso received a boost in 1978 when the Natural Gas Policy Act allowed it more freedom to purchase its own reserves, but later weak demand, coupled with oversupply brought on by the 1970s spike in energy prices, cut into its business by 1982.

Conglomerate Burlington Northern acquired El Paso Natural Gas in 1983. Many of El Paso's operations were spun off when federal regulations required pipeline companies to break apart their sales and transportation businesses and open up interstate pipelines to third parties. El Paso became mainly a gas transportation company.

The company became independent again when Burlington spun it off in 1992. It entered the big leagues in 1996 by buying Tenneco Energy for $4 billion. With some 16,000 miles of pipeline, Tenneco more than doubled El Paso's transportation capacity and gave it the only coast-to-coast natural gas pipeline in the US. El Paso Natural Gas began using the name El Paso Energy and moved from its namesake town to Houston, Tenneco's headquarters.

Refocusing on Gulf Coast assets, El Paso sold its Anadarko pipeline gas gathering system in Oklahoma and Texas in 1998.

In 1999 El Paso bought Sonat, a natural gas transportation and marketing firm that also had an exploration and production unit, in a $6 billion deal. To gain regulators' approval of the Sonat deal, El Paso sold three pipeline systems in 2000, including East Tennessee Natural Gas (to Duke Energy for $386 million) and Sea Robin Pipeline (to CMS Energy for $72 million).

El Paso bought PG&E's natural gas and natural gas liquids businesses for about $900 million in 2000. Also that year the company agreed to buy diversified energy company Coastal in a $24 billion deal. The company changed its name from El Paso Energy to El Paso that year.

Following the collapse of #1 energy trader Enron in 2001, El Paso, along with many other wholesale energy companies, fell under financial scrutiny from investors and regulators. As a result, the company scaled back operations at its El Paso Marketing unit (formerly named El Paso Merchant Energy).

To raise cash to help offset its heavy debt load, the company began selling noncore assets in 2002, including the $782 million sale of midstream oil and gas assets in the Southwest to 27%-owned El Paso Energy Partners (now GulfTerra Energy Partners). The company sold a total of nearly $4 billion in assets in 2002.

In 2003 El Paso was engaged in an unsuccessful proxy contest with dissident shareholders who attempted to replace the company's board of directors. The company reached a $1.7 billion settlement agreement with the California government and the FERC over charges of withholding natural gas supplies from the troubled California market in 2000 and 2001, although it admitted no wrongdoing. In addition, the SEC launched an investigation into El Paso's accounting methods for power plant contracts that it restructured in 2002. El Paso sold more than $3 billion in assets that year to further pay down debt, including $500 million in mid-continent gas reserves to Chesapeake Energy; it also sold a 900-MW power plant in New Jersey to The Goldman Sachs Group for $450 million.

The following year, the company sold its Coastal Eagle Point refinery to Sunoco and its Aruba refinery to Valero Energy. El Paso also sold its Canadian exploration and production assets to BG Group. Reversing its trend of selling properties, El Paso acquired the Denver-based Medicine Bow Energy Corporation in late 2005 for a reported $814 million.

## EXECUTIVES

**Chairman:** Ronald L. Kuehn Jr., age 71
**President, CEO, and Director:** Douglas L. (Doug) Foshee, age 47, $2,350,004 pay
**EVP and CFO:** David M. (Mark) Leland, age 45, $973,800 pay
**EVP; President, Pipeline Group and Southern Natural Gas Company:** James C. (Jim) Yardley, age 57, $955,216 pay
**EVP and General Counsel:** Robert W. Baker, age 50, $834,692 pay
**SVP and Chief Accounting Officer:** John R. (J. R.) Sult
**SVP, Human Resources and Administration:** Susan B. (Sue) Ortenstone, age 50
**SVP, Pipeline Operations:** Daniel B. Martin, age 52
**VP, Gulf of Mexico Operations, El Paso Production:** Albert W. Erxleben, age 59
**VP and Corporate Secretary:** Marguerite Woung-Chapman
**VP, Investor and Public Relations:** Bruce L. Connery
**President, Eastern Pipeline Group:** Stephen C. Beasley, age 55
**President, Western Pipeline Group:** James J. Cleary, age 52
**President, El Paso Exploration & Production Company:** Brent J. Smolik, age 45, $727,008 pay
**CFO, Exploration and Production Division:** Dane E. Whitehead
**Director, Shareholder Relations:** Alan Bishop
**Manager, Investor Relations:** Bill Baerg
**Manager, Media Relations:** Richard Wheatley
**Auditors:** Ernst & Young LLP

## LOCATIONS

**HQ:** El Paso Corporation
El Paso Bldg., 1001 Louisiana St.,
Houston, TX 77002
**Phone:** 713-420-2600 **Fax:** 713-420-4417
**Web:** www.elpaso.com

## PRODUCTS/OPERATIONS

**2006 Sales**

| | $ mil. | % of total |
|---|---|---|
| Pipelines | 2,402 | 55 |
| Exploration & production | 1,854 | 43 |
| Field services | 77 | 2 |
| Power | 6 | — |
| Adjustments | (58) | — |
| **Total** | **4,281** | **100** |

## COMPETITORS

AEP
AES
Apache
Aquila
BP
CenterPoint Energy
DCP Midstream Partners
Dominion Resources
Duncan Energy
Dynegy
Enbridge
Enron
Enterprise Products
EOG
Equitable Resources
Exxon Mobil
Kinder Morgan
Mirant
NiSource
ONEOK Partners
Peabody Energy
Royal Dutch Shell
SandRidge Energy
Sempra Energy
Southern Union
SUEZ-TRACTEBEL
TransCanada
TransMontaigne
Williams Companies

## HISTORICAL FINANCIALS

Company Type: Public

**Income Statement** FYE: December 31

| | REVENUE ($ mil.) | NET INCOME ($ mil.) | NET PROFIT MARGIN | EMPLOYEES |
|---|---|---|---|---|
| **12/06** | 4,281 | 475 | 11.1% | 5,050 |
| **12/05** | 4,017 | (606) | — | 5,700 |
| **12/04** | 6,543 | (947) | — | 6,400 |
| **12/03** | 6,711 | (1,928) | — | 7,574 |
| **12/02** | 12,194 | (1,467) | — | 11,855 |
| **Annual Growth** | (23.0%) | — | — | (19.2%) |

**2006 Year-End Financials**

Debt ratio: 392.4%
Return on equity: 15.6%
Cash ($ mil.): 665
Current ratio: 1.17
Long-term debt ($ mil.): 13,483
No. of shares (mil.): 697
Dividends
Yield: 1.0%
Payout: 25.0%
Market value ($ mil.): 10,652

**Stock History** NYSE: EP

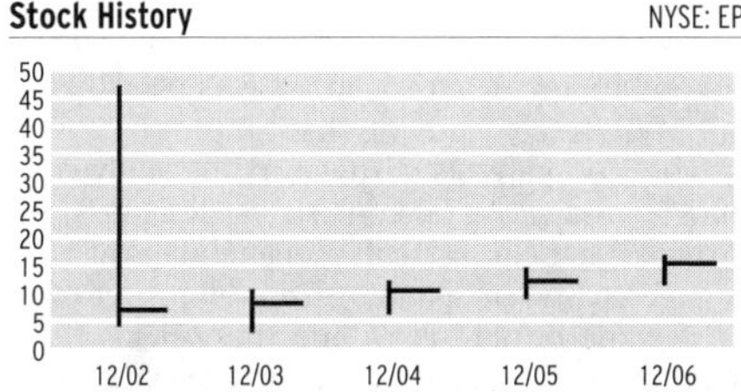


| | STOCK PRICE ($) FY Close | P/E High/Low | PER SHARE ($) Earnings | Dividends | Book Value |
|---|---|---|---|---|---|
| **12/06** | 15.28 | 26 18 | 0.64 | 0.16 | 6.00 |
| **12/05** | 12.16 | — — | (0.98) | 0.16 | 5.14 |
| **12/04** | 10.40 | — — | (1.48) | 0.16 | 5.34 |
| **12/03** | 8.19 | — — | (3.23) | 0.16 | 7.08 |
| **12/02** | 6.96 | — — | (2.62) | 0.87 | 13.98 |
| **Annual Growth** | 21.7% | — — | — | (34.5%) | (19.0%) |

# Electronic Arts

Electronic Arts (EA) has a knack for the craft of creating video games. EA is a leading video game publisher, with popular titles such as *NFL Head Coach, Madden NFL 2006, The Sims, Need for Speed: Most Wanted,* and *Medal of Honor*. It develops games under such brand names as EA GAMES, EA SPORTS, and EA SPORTS BIG. It also distributes titles for third-party labels and publishes games based on Hollywood franchises, including *The Lord of the Rings*, *The Godfather*, Harry Potter, and Batman. EA develops its games for PCs and console systems such as Sony's PlayStation 2, Nintendo's GameCube, and Microsoft's Xbox.

In a move to enter the cell phone game market, EA has teamed up with mobile phone maker QUALCOMM's gaming division, Brew, to develop titles aimed at gamers on the go. An agreement with Amp'd Mobile will offer over 15 EA titles to its customers over Verizon Wireless' network, including *Madden NFL 06*, *The Sims 2*, and puzzle games from Pogo.com.

The company is also expanding its presence in mobile markets overseas; TOM Online subsidiary Indiagames will distribute EA's games to a number of mobile phone carriers in the Indian market. In its most aggressive move to snatch up a portion of the mobile gaming market, the company acquired mobile gaming leader JAMDAT Mobile in early 2006 and created a new division, EA Mobile.

Previously offering titles for online gaming through Sony's PlayStation2 system, EA ended a long standoff and announced that it will also offer some of its titles for online network play via Xbox Live, Microsoft's subscription-based gaming service.

When EA suffered a challenge to its popular Madden NFL franchise from Take-Two and SEGA (which had joined up to create a set of low-priced, ESPN-branded sports titles), it fired back by procuring a five-year exclusive license to use NFL players and teams in its games as well as acquiring the exclusive rights to the ESPN trademark in 2006. Take-Two retaliated to these challenges with a two-year exclusive license to use MLB teams in its games, essentially putting an end to any new versions of EA's blockbuster hit MVP Baseball during that time.

The company is also courting Hollywood movie production talent (writers, designers, animators) to help create its games and has already signed up Steven Spielberg to develop three original game franchises. Along these lines, Electronic Arts is expanding its LA-based studios by consolidating development operations from Bel Air, Las Vegas, and Irvine. Its new facilities will rival movie studios as the company adds more than 1,000 designers, engineers, and animators by 2010. Development is centered in Los Angeles, Vancouver, and Redwood City, California.

It's been said that EA is an attractive property to big media companies, since games are increasingly seen as an important distribution channel for content. Rumors abounded that Viacom was interested, until that company's chairman and CEO, Sumner Redstone, quelled them in 2004, saying the company was too expensive.

## HISTORY

After four years with Apple, video game pioneer Trip Hawkins left in 1982, raised $5 million, and founded Electronic Arts to explore the entertainment potential of PCs. The company went public in 1989. Sales exploded the next year when Electronic Arts began designing games for SEGA's Genesis video game system. Hawkins stepped down as CEO in 1991 and was replaced by president Larry Probst. (Hawkins remained chairman until 1994; he left to devote time to a new games company, 3DO, which later went bankrupt.) The company bought game developer ORIGIN Systems in 1992 and began marketing its games in Japan with partner JVC. By 1995 more than 40% of Electronic Arts' sales were from outside the US. That year Sony introduced its PlayStation game system in the US.

In 1997 the company bought US publisher Maxis (*SimCity*) for about $215 million. That year ORIGIN introduced *Ultima Online,* an online fantasy game in which players interact with each other. In 1998 Electronic Arts bought Westwood Studios for $122 million. The next year it established EA.com, an Internet division to develop games for online players. It also agreed to pay America Online (now part of Time Warner) about $80 million to operate AOL's game channel.

In 2000 the company bought DreamWorks Interactive, a joint venture between Microsoft and DreamWorks. It also launched EA.com's Web site and released six titles for Sony's PlayStation 2. It later agreed to develop titles for Microsoft's new Xbox game system. In 2001 Electronic Arts bought online gaming site pogo.com and launched *Majestic* (an interactive, subscription-based game played online) only to terminate the game in 2002 because of its failure to catch on with fans.

Electronic Arts was banking on the success of the Internet incarnation of its popular Sims franchise, *The Sims Online*, which charges players a monthly subscription fee. The game was launched in late 2002; the response — including negative reviews and sluggish sales — was a letdown. In 2003 Electronic Arts consolidated its money-losing online unit (EA.com) into its core operations. However, the company continues to experiment with online gaming; it makes some of its titles available for online play via the PlayStation 2 and Xbox systems.

John Riccitiello stepped down as president and COO in April 2004 to start his own private equity business. Also in 2004 Electronic Arts moved the operations of ORIGIN Systems from Austin, Texas, to Redwood City, California, as part of a larger move towards consolidation of development in California and Vancouver.

## EXECUTIVES

**Chairman:** Lawrence F. (Larry) Probst III, age 55
**CEO and Director:** John S. Riccitiello, age 47
**EVP, CFO, and Chief Administration Officer:** Warren C. Jenson, age 48, $575,073 pay
**EVP and COO, EA Worldwide Studios:** David P. Gardner, age 40
**EVP, Business and Legal Affairs:** Joel Linzner, age 53
**EVP and General Manager, International Publishing:** Gerhard Florin, age 46, $506,318 pay
**SVP and Managing Director, Asia Publishing:** Jon Niermann, age 41
**SVP, General Counsel, and Corporate Secretary:** Stephen G. Bené, age 41
**SVP, Human Resources:** Gabrielle Toledano, age 39
**SVP and General Manager, EA Mobile:** Michael Marchetti, age 35
**SVP and General Manager EA Mobile, EA Casual Entertainment:** Barry Cottle
**VP, Public Relations:** Jeff Brown
**Director, Investor Relations:** Karen Sansot
**Corporate Communications Manager:** Trudy Muller
**President, The Sims:** Nancy L. Smith, age 52, $496,800 pay
**President, EA Games:** Frank D. Gibeau, age 37
**President, Online, Asia:** Hubert Larenaudie
**President, EA Casual Entertainment:** Kathy Vrabeck, age 44
**President, EA SPORTS:** Peter Moore
**Auditors:** KPMG LLP

## LOCATIONS

**HQ:** Electronic Arts Inc.
209 Redwood Shores Pkwy.,
Redwood City, CA 94065
**Phone:** 650-628-1500 **Fax:** 650-628-1422
**Web:** www.ea.com

Electronic Arts has offices throughout Asia, Europe, and North America.

## PRODUCTS/OPERATIONS

**2007 Sales**

| | $ mil. | % of total |
|---|---|---|
| Consoles | | |
| PlayStation 2 & 3 | 980 | 32 |
| Xbox & Xbox 360 | 637 | 20 |
| Wii | 65 | 2 |
| Nintendo GameCube | 60 | 2 |
| Mobility | | |
| PSP | 258 | 8 |
| Cellular handsets | 140 | 6 |
| Nintendo DS | 104 | 3 |
| Game Boy Advance | 38 | 1 |
| PC | 498 | 16 |
| Co-publishing & distribution | 175 | 6 |
| Internet services, licensing & other | | |
| Subscription services | 79 | 2 |
| Licensing, advertising & other | 57 | 2 |
| **Total** | **3,091** | **100** |

**Selected Titles**

*Def Jam Vendetta*
*EA SPORTS Fight Night 2004*
*EA SPORTS Rugby 2004*
*FIFA Soccer 2004*
*Harry Potter: Quidditch World Cup*
*The Lord of the Rings: The Return of the King*
*Madden NFL 2004*
*Medal of Honor Rising Sun*
*MVP Baseball 2004*
*NASCAR Thunder 2004*
*NBA Live 2004*
*NBA Street Vol. 2*
*NCAA Football 2004*
*NCAA March Madness 2004*
*Need for Speed Underground*
*NFL Street*
*NHL 2004*
*The Sims Bustin' Out*
*SSX 3*
*SSX Tricky*
*Tiger Woods PGA TOUR 2004*

## COMPETITORS

Activision
Capcom
Eidos
Infogrames
Konami
LucasArts
Midway Games
Namco
Nintendo
SEGA
Sony Online Entertainment
Take-Two
THQ
Ubisoft
Valve Corporation
Vivendi Games

## HISTORICAL FINANCIALS

Company Type: Public

**Income Statement** FYE: March 31

| | REVENUE ($ mil.) | NET INCOME ($ mil.) | NET PROFIT MARGIN | EMPLOYEES |
|---|---|---|---|---|
| **3/07** | 3,091 | 76 | 2.5% | 7,900 |
| **3/06** | 2,951 | 236 | 8.0% | 7,200 |
| **3/05** | 3,129 | 504 | 16.1% | 6,100 |
| **3/04** | 2,957 | 577 | 19.5% | 4,800 |
| **3/03** | 2,482 | 317 | 12.8% | 4,000 |
| **Annual Growth** | 5.6% | (30.0%) | — | 18.5% |

**2007 Year-End Financials**

Debt ratio: —
Return on equity: 2.0%
Cash ($ mil.): 2,976
Current ratio: 3.51
Long-term debt ($ mil.): —
No. of shares (mil.): 311
Dividends
Yield: —
Payout: —
Market value ($ mil.): 15,662

**Stock History** NASDAQ (GS): ERTS

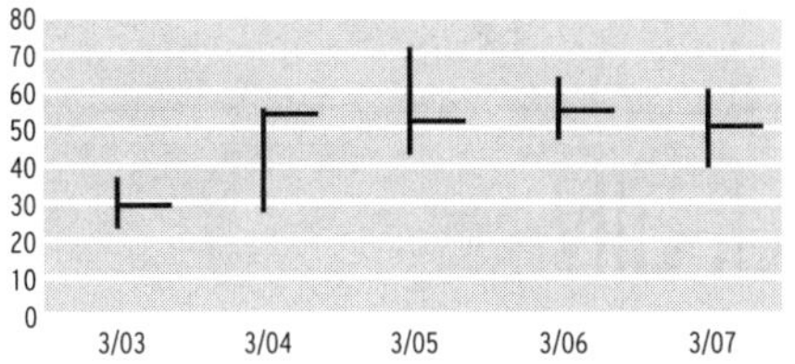

| | STOCK PRICE ($) FY Close | P/E High | P/E Low | PER SHARE ($) Earnings | PER SHARE ($) Dividends | PER SHARE ($) Book Value |
|---|---|---|---|---|---|---|
| **3/07** | 50.36 | 249 | 167 | 0.24 | — | 12.96 |
| **3/06** | 54.72 | 84 | 63 | 0.75 | — | 11.17 |
| **3/05** | 51.78 | 45 | 27 | 1.59 | — | 11.27 |
| **3/04** | 53.74 | 29 | 15 | 1.87 | — | 8.89 |
| **3/03** | 29.32 | 33 | 22 | 1.09 | — | 12.38 |
| **Annual Growth** | 14.5% | — | — | (31.5%) | — | 1.2% |

# Electronic Data Systems

They started it! Electronic Data Systems (EDS) pioneered the computer outsourcing business, and now it is the largest independent systems management and services firm in the US (rival IBM is #1 worldwide). EDS delivers such services as systems integration, network and systems operations, data center management, application development, and outsourcing. It serves customers in a number of different industries, including health care, manufacturing, and transportation; EDS is also one of the largest federal government contractors. The company was spun off in 1996 from General Motors, which still accounts for almost 10% of revenues.

The company in late 2006 sold its European global field services business to A&O Systems and Services and agreed to receive services from A&O. It also plans to outsource thousands of jobs to India and additional countries in 2007.

In 2005 EDS struck a major deal with accounting and financial management giant Towers Perrin to launch ExcellerateHRO, a joint venture to offer human resources outsourcing and benefits administration management services. EDS owns 85% of the new business. Meanwhile, the company has been shedding business units not central to its technology consulting and outsourcing mission. EDS sold its UGS PLM Solutions subsidiary (now UGS Corp.) in 2004 to three private investment firms for $2.05 billion in cash. Early in 2006, the company sold its A.T. Kearney consulting unit to a management group. That same year EDS won a five-year, $3.8 billion systems services contract from GM and a three-year, $3 billion extension to its ongoing contract to provide technical services to the US Navy and Marine Corps.

In a twist, the company in 2006 acquired a 52% stake in Bangalore, India-based applications and BPO services firm MphasiS BFL and later took full ownership of the company. The deals were seen as confirmation that EDS has further plans to expand its overseas outsourcing business. MphasiS continues to operate independently. In 2007 it closed on its purchase of Indian software testing firm RelQ Software for about $40 million and agreed to acquire 75% of IT firm Itellium Systems & Services from Karstadt Quelle.

The company was originally founded by Texas billionaire Ross Perot (now chairman emeritus of rival Perot Systems).

## HISTORY

After five years with IBM, disgruntled salesman Ross Perot founded Electronic Data Systems (EDS) in 1962. IBM executives had dismissed Perot's idea of providing electronic data processing management that would relieve clients' data management worries.

Perot took five months to find his first customer, Collins Radio of Cedar Rapids, Iowa. In 1963 EDS pioneered the long-term, fixed-price contract with snack food maker Frito-Lay, writing a five-year contract instead of the 60- to 90-day contracts usually offered by service companies. EDS then got into Medicare and Medicaid claims processing (mid-1960s), data processing for insurance providers (1963), and data management for banks (1968) — moves that would make it the #1 provider of data management services in these markets.

EDS went public in 1968. It established regional data centers and central data processing stations in the early 1970s to pioneer the notion of distributed processing. In 1975 EDS signed one of its first offshore contracts, with Iran. But by 1978 Iran was behind in its payments, and EDS halted operations there. When two EDS employees were later arrested amid the disorder of the Islamic revolution, Perot assembled a rescue team that spirited them out of the country.

On EDS's 22nd anniversary, in 1984, General Motors (GM) bought the company for $2.5 billion. GM promised EDS its independence as well as contract work managing its lumbering data processing system. While EDS prospered, Perot and GM chairman Roger Smith had different managerial styles, resulting in an uneasy alliance and, ultimately, divorce. GM bought Perot's EDS shares in 1986 for more than $700 million. Perot formed competitor Perot Systems in 1988.

In 1993 the company launched its management consulting service. Two years later EDS acquired management consulting firm A.T. Kearney and securities industry consultant FCI.

The company won independence from GM in mid-1996 in a spin-off that involved paying $500 million to GM and agreeing to extend the automaker more favorable computer services contracts. In 1998 CEO Lester Alberthal resigned and was replaced by Cable and Wireless executive Richard Brown, who became chairman and CEO in 1999. Brown cut thousands of jobs (including a third of the sales force), and reversed a trend at EDS of spending more money on philanthropy than advertising, launching a $100 million global ad campaign to present a reinvented, more nimble EDS.

In 1999 the company exchanged assets and services from its networking business for communications management services and employees from MCI WorldCom (now Verizon Business) in a $17 billion alliance. As one part of that deal, EDS paid $1.65 billion to buy MCI Systemhouse, a move that thrust EDS into the electronic commerce arena. In 2000 EDS scored a record contract with the US Navy, the Navy-Marine Corps Intranet (NMCI) program. NMCI has since soared to a value of nearly $9 billion but has been an unprofitable millstone for the company.

In 2001 EDS signed a 10-year, $2.2 billion service contract with Sabre. As part of the deal EDS acquired Sabre's airline infrastructure outsourcing business and its information technology assets for $670 million. EDS continued to expand its territory that year, purchasing Structural Dynamics Research Corporation for $950 million in cash and reacquiring the publicly traded shares of Unigraphics Solutions it spun off in 1998.

However, in 2002 EDS faced a string of bad news: the bankruptcies of two large clients, WorldCom and US Airways; a drop in new contracts; an unsuccessful hedging strategy; and a credit rating downgrade. As a result, the company cut jobs and sold off noncore assets. In 2003 former CBS Corporation chairman Michael Jordan replaced Brown as CEO.

US Airways went into Chapter 11 for a second time in September 2004, and EDS was one of its largest creditors, along with General Electric. Early in 2006, EDS sold A.T. Kearney to a management group.

In 2007 Ronald Rittenmeyer, the company's president and COO, was tapped to replace outgoing CEO Jordan, who remained as chairman.

## EXECUTIVES

**Chairman:** Michael H. (Mike) Jordan, age 70, $1,572,000 pay
**Vice Chairman:** Jeffrey M. (Jeff) Heller, age 67, $172,350 pay
**President and CEO:** Ronald A. (Ron) Rittenmeyer, age 60, $1,080,833 pay
**EVP and CFO:** Ronald P. (Ron) Vargo, age 52, $654,083 pay
**EVP and General Counsel:** Storrow M. Gordon, age 54
**EVP and General Manager, EDS Europe, Middle East, and Africa; Managing Director, Electronic Data Systems Limited:** William G. (Bill) Thomas, age 47
**SEVP, Chief Administrative Officer, and Global Leader, Energy Industry Group:** Tina M. Sivinski, age 50
**SEVP, Applications Services:** Charles S. (Charlie) Feld, age 65, $1,265,419 pay
**VP and Global Leader, Financial Products:** Paul W. Currie, age 49
**VP and Treasurer:** Anthony (Tony) Glasby
**VP and Global Leader, Healthcare Industry Group:** Sean Kenny
**VP and CFO, EDS Europe, Middle East, and Africa:** Thomas A. (Tom) Haubenstricker, age 43, $505,000 pay
**VP and Global Leader, Communications Industry Group:** Sue Chevins

**VP Global Government Affairs:** William R. (Bill) Sweeney Jr.
**VP and Global Leader, Consumer and Retail Industries:** Michael (Mike) Klaus
**VP, Chief Risk Officer, and Chief Security Officer:** David Morrow
**VP and Global Leader, Government Services Industry Group:** Suparno Banerjee
**VP and Global Leader, Manufacturing Industry Group:** Jeffrey D. (Jeff) Kelly, age 50
**VP and Global Leader, Financial Services Industry Group:** Steve Ingram
**VP and Global Leader, Transportation Industry Group:** Jim Dullum
**VP Investor Relations:** David (Dave) Kost
**CTO:** Stan Alexander
**Director of Public Relations:** Robert Brand
**Auditors:** KPMG LLP

## LOCATIONS

**HQ:** Electronic Data Systems Corporation
5400 Legacy Dr., Plano, TX 75024
**Phone:** 972-604-6000 **Fax:** 972-605-6033
**Web:** www.eds.com

Electronic Data Systems has operations in about 60 countries.

### 2006 Sales

| | % of total |
|---|---|
| US | 52 |
| UK | 20 |
| Other countries | 28 |
| **Total** | **100** |

## PRODUCTS/OPERATIONS

### 2006 Sales

| | % of total |
|---|---|
| Infrastructure services | 56 |
| Applications services | 28 |
| Business process outsourcing services | 14 |
| Other | 2 |
| **Total** | **100** |

### Selected Services

Infrastructure services
- Business continuity management
- Converged network services
- Data hosting
- E-mail archive
- Enterprise risk management
- Extended connected office
- Managed storage services
- Mobile information protection
- Network management
- Security and privacy consulting
- Workplace management
- Workplace messaging and collaboration
- Workplace migration services
- Workplace support services

Applications services
- Applications development
- Applications modernization
- Applications outsourcing
- Applications rationalization
- Business exchange services
- Business intelligence
- Contact center transformation
- Enterprise application implementation
- Enterprise application integration
- Enterprise application management
- Enterprise content management integration
- Financial services assessment
- Mobile applications
- Passenger rail solutions
- Portals and dashboards
- Web services

Business process outsourcing
- Benefits administration
- Commercial card services
- Consumer card services
- Consumer loan services
- Contact center outsourcing
- Content management
- Converged billing services
- Customer intelligence
- Customer relationship management
- Demand management and distribution
- Finance and accounting
- Health care payer administrative
- Human resources outsourcing
- Interactive billing services
- Life and annuity services
- Merchant acquirer services
- Mortgage loan services
- Payroll services
- Relocation and assignment services
- Revenue cycle management
- Reverse mortgage services
- Supply chain management
- Surveyor application processing
- Warranty services

## COMPETITORS

Accenture
ADP
Affiliated Computer Services
Bain & Company
BearingPoint
Booz Allen
Boston Consulting
CACI International
Capgemini
CGI Group
CIBER
Computer Sciences Corp.
Convergys
Deloitte Consulting
First Data
Fiserv
Fujitsu Services
Getronics
Hewitt Associates
HP Technology Solutions Group
IBM Global Services
Infosys
Keane
Lockheed Martin Information & Technology
LogicaCMG
McKinsey & Company
Perot Systems
SunGard
Tata Consultancy
Titan Group
T-Systems International
Unisys
Wipro Technologies

## HISTORICAL FINANCIALS

Company Type: Public

### Income Statement

FYE: December 31

| | REVENUE ($ mil.) | NET INCOME ($ mil.) | NET PROFIT MARGIN | EMPLOYEES |
|---|---|---|---|---|
| **12/06** | 21,268 | 470 | 2.2% | 131,000 |
| **12/05** | 19,757 | 150 | 0.8% | 117,000 |
| **12/04** | 20,669 | 158 | 0.8% | 117,000 |
| **12/03** | 21,476 | (1,698) | — | 132,000 |
| **12/02** | 21,502 | 1,116 | 5.2% | 137,000 |
| **Annual Growth** | (0.3%) | (19.4%) | — | (1.1%) |

### 2006 Year-End Financials

Debt ratio: 37.6%
Return on equity: 6.1%
Cash ($ mil.): 3,017
Current ratio: 1.58
Long-term debt ($ mil.): 2,965
No. of shares (mil.): 514
Dividends
Yield: 0.7%
Payout: 22.5%
Market value ($ mil.): 14,169

### Stock History

NYSE: EDS

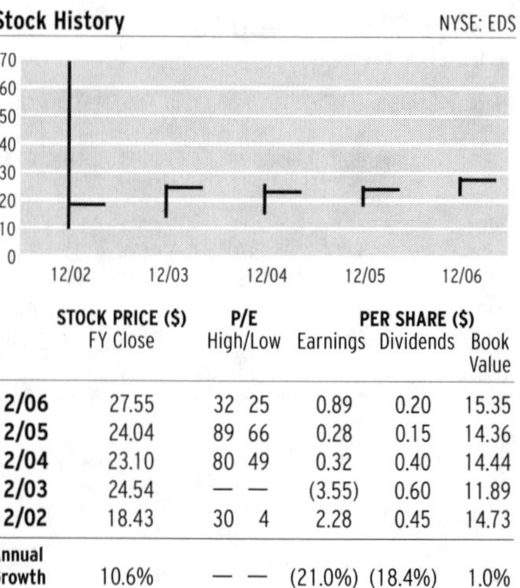

| | STOCK PRICE ($) FY Close | P/E High | P/E Low | PER SHARE ($) Earnings | Dividends | Book Value |
|---|---|---|---|---|---|---|
| **12/06** | 27.55 | 32 | 25 | 0.89 | 0.20 | 15.35 |
| **12/05** | 24.04 | 89 | 66 | 0.28 | 0.15 | 14.36 |
| **12/04** | 23.10 | 80 | 49 | 0.32 | 0.40 | 14.44 |
| **12/03** | 24.54 | — | — | (3.55) | 0.60 | 11.89 |
| **12/02** | 18.43 | 30 | 4 | 2.28 | 0.45 | 14.73 |
| **Annual Growth** | 10.6% | — | — | (21.0%) | (18.4%) | 1.0% |

# Eli Lilly

Eli Lilly hopes everything will come up roses for you, healthwise. Although best known for its widely popular antidepressants Prozac and Serafem, the company develops medicines for a wide variety of ailments. Its top drugs include schizophrenia therapy Zyprexa, pancreatic cancer treatment Gemzar, antidepressant Cymbalta, osteoporosis medication Evista, Humalog insulin, and erectile dysfunction treatment Cialis (developed with ICOS). In addition to neurological, oncological, and diabetes drugs, the company also makes antibiotics, growth hormones, antiulcer agents, and cardiovascular therapies, as well as animal health products.

Eli Lilly knows the value of patents: After the company lost its lucrative patent protection for Prozac in August 2001, it saw sales drop dramatically. Lilly's fortunes were reversed in regards to its bestseller Zyprexa (nearly 30% of sales) — federal courts ruled that the drug's patents remain valid until 2011. As a result, Eli Lilly has started making its own "knockoff" drugs so that other companies will be less able to come up with generic versions of Lilly's drugs.

The power of Zyprexa was diminished in early 2007 when Eli Lilly agreed to settle with more than 18,000 patients complaining of health-threatening side-effects of the drug, including diabetes, dangerous levels of weight gain, and dangerous increases in cholesterol. Settlement figures reached $500 million, while additional suits are still pending.

The drugmaker's pipeline has become increasingly important to make up for sales lost to generics. The company has some 40 candidates in development, including treatments for sepsis, cancer, and diabetes. Released in 2006 was generalized anxiety disorder drug Cymbalta, and slated for release was Evista, a treatment already on the market for osteoporosis which Eli Lilly wants to apply as a preventative breast cancer treatment for postmenopausal women. Evista, however, was found to raise the occurrence of blood clots and strokes in patients at risk for those events.

Early in 2007, the company acquired development partner ICOS for $2.1 billion; the deal gave Lilly full ownership of Viagra-competitor Cialis. Lilly is systematically laying off all ICOS employees. Also in 2007, Lilly made a move to reinforce its veterinarian pharmaceuticals division, Elanco Animal Health, by bolstering it with the planned acquisition of Ivy Animal Health.

The Lilly Endowment, a charitable foundation, owns 12% of the company.

## HISTORY

Colonel Eli Lilly, pharmacist and Union officer in the Civil War, started Eli Lilly and Company in 1876 with $1,300. His process of gelatin-coating pills led to sales of nearly $82,000 in 1881. Later, the company made gelatin capsules, which it still sells. Lilly died in 1898, and his son and two grandsons ran the business until 1953.

Eli Lilly began extracting insulin from the pancreases of hogs and cattle in 1923; 6,000 cattle glands or 24,000 hog glands made one ounce of the substance. Other products created in the 1920s and 1930s included antiseptic Merthiolate, sedative Seconal, and treatments for pernicious anemia and heart disease. In 1947 the company began selling diethylstilbestrol (DES), a drug to prevent miscarriages. Eli Lilly researchers isolated the antibiotic erythromycin from a species of mold found in the Philippines in 1952. Lilly was also the major supplier of Salk polio vaccine.

The company enjoyed a 70% share of the DES market by 1971, when researchers noticed that a rare form of cervical cancer afflicted many of the daughters of women who had taken the drug. The FDA restricted the drug's use and Lilly found itself on the receiving (and frequently losing) end of a number of trailblazing product-liability suits that stretched into the 1990s.

The firm diversified in the 1970s, buying Elizabeth Arden (cosmetics, 1971; sold 1987) and IVAC (medical instruments, 1977). It launched such products as analgesic Darvon and antibiotic Ceclor.

Lilly's 1982 launch of Humulin, a synthetic insulin developed by Genentech, made it the first company to market a genetically engineered product. In 1986 the company introduced Prozac; that year it also bought biotech firm Hybritech for $300 million (sold in 1995 for less than $10 million). In 1988 Lilly introduced anti-ulcerative Axid. It founded pesticides and herbicides maker DowElanco with Dow Chemical in 1989.

Eli Lilly in 1995 bought medical communications network developer Integrated Medical Systems. The next year it launched antipsychotic Zyprexa, Humalog, and Gemzar, and Prozac was approved to treat bulimia nervosa.

In 1997 the firm sold its DowElanco stake to Dow. In 1998 the Lilly Endowment passed the Ford Foundation as the US's largest charity, largely due to Prozac (it has since been passed by the Bill & Melinda Gates Foundation).

In 1999 a US federal judge found the firm illegally promoted osteoporosis drug Evista as a breast cancer preventative similar to AstraZeneca's Nolvadex. Lilly halted tests on its variation of heart drug Moxonidine after 53 patients died. Also that year Zyprexa was approved to treat bipolar disorder.

In 2000 the firm began marketing Prozac under the Sarafem name for severe premenstrual syndrome. A federal appeals court knocked more than two years off Prozac's patent, reducing the expected 2003 expiration date to 2001.

While the firm fretted over Prozac and its patents, it continued work to find its next blockbuster. In 2000 Lilly and partner ICOS announced favorable results from a study of erectile dysfunction treatment Cialis, which was approved in Europe in 2002 and the US in 2004. (Several years later, Lilly acquired ICOS and, with it, full ownership of the Cialis franchise, which competes with Pfizer's market-leading erectile disfunction drug Viagra.) In 2001 Lilly bought a minority stake in Isis Pharmaceuticals, a developer of antisense drugs, and licensed from it an antisense lung cancer drug. In 2002 the company settled with eight states in an infringement-of-privacy case involving the company's accidental disclosure of e-mail addresses for more than 600 Prozac patients.

In late 2004 the druggernaut was one of several pharmas hit by bad news about drug side effects. Lilly announced its attention-deficit disorder drug Strattera had been linked to rare liver problems. The company agreed to add warning labels about the potential side effects to the drug's packaging and advertisements.

After a lengthy lawsuit regarding its patents for its top seller, Zyprexa, a federal judge ruled in Lilly's favor against generic manufacturers IVAX, Dr. Reddy's Laboratories, and Teva Pharmaceutical Industries.

## EXECUTIVES

**Chairman and CEO:** Sidney Taurel, age 58, $3,832,020 pay
**President, COO, and Director:** John C. Lechleiter, age 53, $2,005,917 pay
**EVP, Science and Technology; President, Lilly Research Laboratories:** Steven M. Paul, age 56, $1,682,468 pay
**SVP and General Counsel:** Robert A. Armitage, age 58, $1,171,771 pay
**SVP, Human Resources:** Anthony (Tony) Murphy, age 56
**SVP, Corporate Strategy and Policy:** Gino Santini, age 50
**SVP and CFO:** Derica Rice
**SVP, Corporate Affairs and Communications:** Alex M. Azar II, age 41
**Group VP and Chief Marketing Officer:** Richard D. Pilnik
**VP, Business-to-Business Division:** Jack Bailey
**VP, Medical and Chief Medical Officer:** Alan Breier
**VP, Global Regulatory Affairs:** Timothy R. Franson
**VP, Information Technology and CIO:** Michael C. (Mike) Heim
**VP, Six Sigma:** Elizabeth H. Klimes
**VP, Compliance and Enterprise Risk Management and Chief Compliance Officer:** Anne Nobles, age 50
**VP, Global Marketing and Sales:** Steven R. Plump
**VP, Process and Product Development:** Thomas Verhoeven
**VP, Human Resources and Global Compensation:** Sharon L. Sullivan
**VP, Discovery Biology Research and Clinical Investigation:** William W. Chin
**VP and Treasurer:** Thomas W. Grein, age 55
**Chief Accounting Officer:** Arnold C. Hanish
**Secretary:** James B. Lootens
**Auditors:** Ernst & Young LLP

## LOCATIONS

**HQ:** Eli Lilly and Company
Lilly Corporate Center, 893 S. Delaware, Indianapolis, IN 46285
**Phone:** 317-276-2000
**Web:** www.lilly.com

Eli Lilly has facilities in Brazil, Canada, France, Germany, Ireland, Italy, Mexico, Puerto Rico, Spain, the UK, and the US.

**2006 Sales**

| | $ mil. | % of total |
|---|---|---|
| US | 8,599.2 | 55 |
| Europe | 3,894.3 | 25 |
| Other regions | 3,197.5 | 20 |
| **Total** | **15,691.0** | **100** |

## PRODUCTS/OPERATIONS

**2006 Sales**

| | $ mil. | % of total |
|---|---|---|
| Zyprexa | 4,363.6 | 28 |
| Gemzar | 1,408.1 | 9 |
| Cymbalta | 1,316.4 | 8 |
| Humalog | 1,299.5 | 8 |
| Evista | 1,045.3 | 7 |
| Humulin | 925.3 | 6 |
| Animal health products | 875.5 | 5 |
| Alimta | 611.8 | 4 |
| Forteo | 594.3 | 4 |
| Strattera | 579.0 | 4 |
| Actos | 448.5 | 3 |
| Humatrope | 415.6 | 3 |
| Fluoxetine | 315.1 | 2 |
| ReoPro | 280.4 | 2 |
| Anti-infectives | 274.6 | 2 |
| Byetta | 219.0 | 1 |
| Cialis | 215.8 | 1 |
| Xigris | 192.2 | 1 |
| Other pharmaceuticals | 311.0 | 2 |
| **Total** | **15,691.0** | **100** |

**Selected Products**

Neuroscience
- Cymbalta (depression, with Quintiles Transnational and Boehringer Ingelheim)
- Darvon (line of analgesic products)
- Permax (Parkinson's disease)
- Prozac (depression)
- Sarafem (premenstrual dysphoric disorder)
- Strattera (attention-deficit hyperactivity disorder)
- Symbyax (bipolar disorder-related depression)
- Zyprexa (schizophrenia)

Endocrinology
- Actos (type 2 diabetes, with Takeda Pharmaceutical)
- Evista (osteoporosis in post-menopausal women)
- Forteo (osteoporosis)
- Humalog (insulin)
- Humatrope (human growth hormone)
- Humulin (insulin)

Oncology
- Alimta (mesothelioma)
- Gemzar (breast, lung, and pancreatic cancer)

Animal Health
- Apralan (enteric infections in calves and swine)
- Coban (anticoccidial agents for use in poultry)
- Maxiban (anticoccidial agents for use in poultry)
- Micotil (bovine respiratory disease)
- Monteban (anticoccidial agents for use in poultry)
- Optaflexx (leanness and performance enhancer for cattle)
- Paylean (leanness and performance enhancer for swine)
- Pulmotil (respiratory disease in swine)
- Rumensin (production efficiency)
- Surmax/Maxus (performance enhancer for swine and poultry)
- Tylan (animal respiratory disease)

Cardiovascular
- Cynt (hypertension)
- Dobutrex (cardiac decompensation)
- ReoPro (angioplasty adjunct, with Centocor)
- Xigris (sepsis)

Anti-infectives
- Ceclor (antibiotic)
- Keftab (antibiotic)
- Lorabid (antibiotic)
- Vancocin HCl (staphylococcal infections)

Other
- Axid (anti-ulcer agent)
- Cialis (erectile dysfunction, sold by Lilly ICOS)

## COMPETITORS

Abbott Labs
Amgen
AstraZeneca
Baxter
Bayer
Boehringer Ingelheim
Bristol-Myers Squibb
Genentech
GlaxoSmithKline
Johnson & Johnson
Merck
Novartis
Novo Nordisk
Pfizer
Roche
Schering-Plough
Wyeth

## HISTORICAL FINANCIALS

Company Type: Public

**Income Statement** FYE: December 31

| | REVENUE ($ mil.) | NET INCOME ($ mil.) | NET PROFIT MARGIN | EMPLOYEES |
|---|---|---|---|---|
| **12/06** | 15,691 | 2,663 | 17.0% | 41,500 |
| **12/05** | 14,645 | 1,980 | 13.5% | 42,600 |
| **12/04** | 13,858 | 1,810 | 13.1% | 44,500 |
| **12/03** | 12,583 | 2,561 | 20.4% | 46,100 |
| **12/02** | 11,078 | 2,708 | 24.4% | 43,700 |
| **Annual Growth** | 9.1% | (0.4%) | — | (1.3%) |

**2006 Year-End Financials**

Debt ratio: 31.8%
Return on equity: 24.5%
Cash ($ mil.): 3,891
Current ratio: 1.91
Long-term debt ($ mil.): 3,494
No. of shares (mil.): 1,132
Dividends
Yield: 3.1%
Payout: 65.3%
Market value ($ mil.): 58,960

**Stock History** NYSE: LLY

90 80 70 60 50 40 30 20 10 0
12/02 12/03 12/04 12/05 12/06

| | STOCK PRICE ($) FY Close | P/E High | P/E Low | PER SHARE ($) Earnings | Dividends | Book Value |
|---|---|---|---|---|---|---|
| **12/06** | 52.10 | 24 | 20 | 2.45 | 1.60 | 9.70 |
| **12/05** | 56.59 | 34 | 27 | 1.81 | 1.52 | 9.55 |
| **12/04** | 56.75 | 46 | 30 | 1.66 | 1.42 | 9.65 |
| **12/03** | 70.33 | 31 | 22 | 2.37 | 1.34 | 8.69 |
| **12/02** | 63.50 | 32 | 18 | 2.50 | 1.24 | 7.37 |
| **Annual Growth** | (4.8%) | — | — | (0.5%) | 6.6% | 7.1% |

# EMC Corporation

EMC has braced itself for an all-out raid. Long a leading provider of RAID (redundant array of independent disks) storage systems, the company has its hands full trying to stay a step ahead in a crowded market. Banks, manufacturers, Internet service providers, retailers, and government agencies use EMC's systems to store and retrieve massive amounts of data. The company also sells a line of network attached storage (NAS) file servers, and a wide array of software designed to manage, protect, and share data. EMC sells its products directly and through distributors and manufacturers. Its biggest resale partner, PC leader Dell, sells co-branded EMC systems.

EMC built its storage empire with refrigerator-sized systems used to store data for huge mainframe computers. While the company's high-end Symmetrix and mid-size CLARiiON storage arrays are still EMC's bread and butter, its hardware portfolio has expanded into complementary NAS devices (Celerra). The company's Centera content-addressed storage systems are designed to manage huge archives of fixed data.

Since taking over as CEO in 2001, Joe Tucci has led an effort to expand EMC's software offerings, largely through acquisitions. Its software offerings now encompass a wide range of information lifecycle management applications for storing, managing, protecting, and sharing data. Key purchases include LEGATO Software and Documentum (2003); VMware and Dantz Development (2004); System Management ARTS, Rainfinity, and Captiva Software (2005); and Internet security specialist RSA Security and data protection software developer Avamar Technologies (2006). In 2007 EMC sold off 10% of VMware with an IPO.

In addition to software developers, EMC purchased IT services firms Internosis and Interlink Group in 2006.

EMC has kept its head above the competitive waters by leading the development of new storage technologies. It has been at the forefront of the movement away from direct-attached storage configurations, with products optimized for use in storage area networks (SANs). Acquisitions have provided footholds in emerging storage technologies, and it has placed particular emphasis on growing its software products. The company has also pursued an open-system strategy that encourages greater interoperability with competitors' products.

Essentially a pure-play storage company, EMC must compete against larger companies such as HP, IBM, and Sun Microsystems that can offer storage systems as part of a package that includes servers and other hardware.

## HISTORY

Former Intel executive Dick Egan and his college roommate, Roger Marino, founded EMC in 1979. (Their initials gave the company its name.) Egan, a feisty entrepreneur whose first job was shining shoes, served as a Marine in Korea and later worked at MIT on the computer system for NASA's Apollo program. Egan also helped found Cambridge Memory Systems (later Cambex).

EMC was started with no business plan, only the idea that Egan and Marino would be better off working for themselves. At first, they sold office furniture, which in short order led to contacts at technology companies and recognition of the niche market for add-on memory boards for minicomputers.

EMC grew steadily throughout the early 1980s and went public in 1986. Two years later Michael Ruettgers, a former COO of high-tech publishing and research company Technical Financial Services, joined the company as EVP of operations. Ruettgers spent his first year and a half at EMC dealing with a crisis that almost ruined the company: Defective disk drives in some of its products were losing customers' files. Ruettgers stepped up quality control and guided EMC through the crisis period. In 1989 he became the company's president and COO.

In the late 1980s EMC expanded into data storage, developing a system that employed small hard disks rather than larger, more expensive disks and tapes used in IBM mainframes. EMC then separated itself from competitors by providing systems with a large cache — a temporary storage area used for quicker data retrieval.

In 1990 EMC pioneered redundant array of independent disks (RAID) storage and eliminated nearly a dozen major product lines, focusing on storage for large IBM computers in a bid to beat Big Blue by undercutting prices. The company introduced its original Symmetrix system, based on the new integrated cached disk array technology that held data from a variety of computer types. Marino left the company in 1990.

Ruettgers became CEO in 1992. The next year the company acquired Epoch Systems, a provider of data management software, and in 1994 it bought storage products company Array Technology and Magna Computer, a leader in tape storage technology for IBM computers. EMC also introduced its first storage product for open systems, the Centriplex series, and its sales passed the $1 billion mark.

EMC increased its presence in this fast-growing data switching and computer connection market with the 1995 acquisition of McDATA. In 1999 the company moved into the market for midrange storage when it acquired data storage and server specialist Data General.

EMC took McDATA public in 2000; the following year it distributed its majority stake in that company to EMC shareholders. In early 2001 the company's corporate ladder shifted. Joe Tucci, who had joined EMC in 2000 as president, added CEO to his title. Ruettgers became chairman and Egan was named chairman emeritus. (Tucci suceeded Ruettgers as chairman at the end of 2005.)

EMC began a major push to expand its software offerings in 2003. The company acquired LEGATO Software for $1.3 billion, and Documentum for approximately $1.5 billion. The following year it purchased server software maker VMware for approximately $625 million, and backup and recovery software developer Dantz Development for about $50 million. EMC acquired System Management ARTS (SMARTS) for approximately $260 million early in 2005. It also acquired Rainfinity (storage virtualization software), the assets of Maranti Networks (storage network switches), and input management software maker Captiva Software. EMC purchased IT services firm Internosis in 2006, as well as data replication software developer Kashya, IT services provider Interlink Group, and application discovery and mapping software maker nLayers. Also in 2006 EMC acquired RSA Security for about $2.1 billion, and Network Intelligence for approximately $175 million.

## EXECUTIVES

**Chairman, President, and CEO:** Joseph M. (Joe) Tucci, age 59

**Vice Chairman and Head of Customer Operations, Worldwide Sales, and Distribution:** William J. (Bill) Teuber Jr., age 54

**EVP and CFO:** David I. Goulden, age 47

**EVP; President, Customer Operations and Content Management Software:** David G. (Dave) DeWalt, age 43

**EVP; President, RSA:** Arthur W. (Art) Coviello Jr., age 52

**EVP; President, VMware:** Diane B. Greene, age 51

**EVP, Global Services and Resource Management Software Group:** Howard D. Elias, age 48

**EVP, Global Marketing and Customer Quality:** Frank M. Hauck, age 46

**EVP and Chief Development Officer:** Mark S. Lewis, age 43

**EVP, Storage Product Operations:** David A. Donatelli, age 40
**EVP and General Counsel:** Paul T. Dacier, age 48
**EVP, Global Sales Programs:** Bill Scannell
**EVP, Human Resources:** John T. (Jack) Mollen
**SVP, EMEA:** Rainer Erlat
**SVP and CTO:** Jeffrey M. (Jeff) Nick
**SVP, Emerging Markets and International Development:** Sanjay Mirchandani
**SVP and Treasurer:** Irina Simmons
**SVP; President, APJ:** Steve Leonard
**SVP; Co-General Manager, Content Management and Archive Business:** Michael (Mike) DeCesare, age 41
**SVP; Co-General Manager, Content Management and Archives Business:** Balaji Yelamanchili
**Auditors:** PricewaterhouseCoopers LLP

## LOCATIONS

**HQ:** EMC Corporation
176 South St., Hopkinton, MA 01748
**Phone:** 508-435-1000 **Fax:** 508-497-6912
**Web:** www.emc.com

### 2006 Sales

| | $ mil. | % of total |
|---|---|---|
| US | 6,319.7 | 57 |
| Europe, Middle East & Africa | 3,232.6 | 29 |
| Asia/Pacific | 1,126.2 | 10 |
| Latin America & Canada | 476.6 | 4 |
| **Total** | **11,155.1** | **100** |

## PRODUCTS/OPERATIONS

### 2006 Sales

| | $ mil. | % of total |
|---|---|---|
| Information storage | 9,608.6 | 86 |
| VMware Virtual Infrastructure | 709.0 | 6 |
| Content management & archiving | 685.8 | 6 |
| RSA Information Security | 151.7 | 2 |
| **Total** | **11,155.1** | **100** |

### 2006 Sales

| | $ mil. | % of total |
|---|---|---|
| Systems | 5,140.6 | 46 |
| Services | 3,077.1 | 28 |
| Software | 2,937.4 | 26 |
| **Total** | **11,155.1** | **100** |

### Selected Products and Services

Information Storage Products
- Storage systems
  - Content-addressed storage (Centera)
  - Data storage arrays (CLARiiON, Symmetrix)
  - Fibre Channel switches and directors (Connectrix)
  - Network file and media servers (Celerra)
- EMC platform-based software (networked storage system management)

Services
- Customer education
- Customer service
- Technology solutions

Multi-platform Software
- Backup and archive
- Content management
- Resource management

VMware

## COMPETITORS

CA
Dell
Fujitsu
Hewlett-Packard
Hitachi Data Systems
IBM
Microsoft
NetApp
SGI
Sun Microsystems
Symantec

## HISTORICAL FINANCIALS

Company Type: Public

### Income Statement

FYE: December 31

| | REVENUE ($ mil.) | NET INCOME ($ mil.) | NET PROFIT MARGIN | EMPLOYEES |
|---|---|---|---|---|
| 12/06 | 11,155 | 1,224 | 11.0% | 31,100 |
| 12/05 | 9,664 | 1,133 | 11.7% | 26,500 |
| 12/04 | 8,230 | 871 | 10.6% | 22,700 |
| 12/03 | 6,237 | 496 | 8.0% | 20,000 |
| 12/02 | 5,438 | (119) | — | 17,400 |
| Annual Growth | 19.7% | — | — | 15.6% |

### 2006 Year-End Financials

Debt ratio: 33.4%
Return on equity: 10.9%
Cash ($ mil.): 3,350
Current ratio: 1.68
Long-term debt ($ mil.): 3,450
No. of shares (mil.): 2,122
Dividends
Yield: —
Payout: —
Market value ($ mil.): 28,015

### Stock History

NYSE: EMC

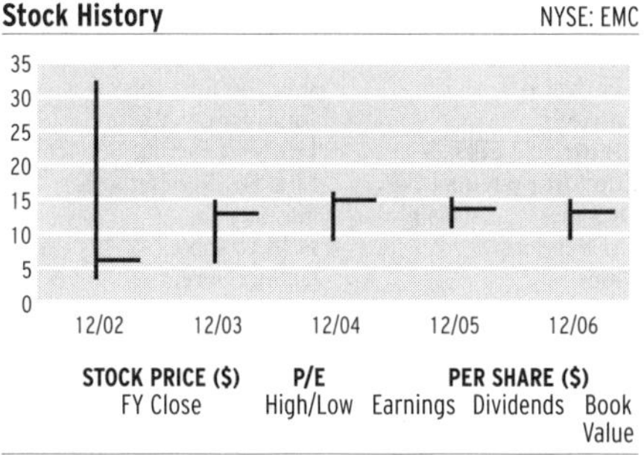


| | STOCK PRICE ($) FY Close | P/E High | P/E Low | PER SHARE ($) Earnings | PER SHARE ($) Dividends | PER SHARE ($) Book Value |
|---|---|---|---|---|---|---|
| 12/06 | 13.20 | 27 | 17 | 0.54 | — | 4.87 |
| 12/05 | 13.62 | 32 | 24 | 0.47 | — | 5.06 |
| 12/04 | 14.87 | 44 | 26 | 0.36 | — | 4.92 |
| 12/03 | 12.92 | 67 | 27 | 0.22 | — | 4.51 |
| 12/02 | 6.14 | — | — | (0.05) | — | 3.31 |
| Annual Growth | 21.1% | — | — | — | — | 10.1% |

# EMCOR Group

The core of EMCOR Group is electrical and mechanical construction. One of the world's largest specialty construction firms, EMCOR designs, installs, operates, and maintains complex mechanical and electrical systems. These include systems for power generation and distribution, lighting, voice and data communications, plumbing, and heating, ventilation, and air-conditioning (HVAC). It also provides facilities services, including management and maintenance support. Through about 70 subsidiaries and joint ventures, the company serves various commercial, industrial, institutional, and utility customers. EMCOR operates primarily in the US (more than three-fourths of sales), Canada, and the UK.

EMCOR's mechanical and electrical construction services account for the lion's share of its business. In 2005 US mechanical and electrical construction services accounted for around 60% of sales; UK and Canadian mechanical and electrical services, more than 10%. Of the US sales 65% were related to new construction (versus renovation or retrofit) projects.

One of the largest union employers in the US, about 70% of EMCOR's 27,000 employees belong to a union.

## HISTORY

EMCOR's forerunner, Jamaica Water Supply Co., was incorporated in 1887 to supply water to some residents of Queens and Nassau Counties in New York. In 1902 it bought Jamaica Township Water Co., and by 1906 it was generating revenue — reaching $1.6 million by 1932. Over the next 35 years, the company kept pace with the population of its service area.

In 1966 the enterprise was acquired by Jamaica Water and Utilities, which then bought Sea Cliff Water Co. In 1969 and 1970 it acquired Welsbach (electrical contractors) and A to Z Equipment (construction trailer suppliers); it briefly changed its name in 1974 to Welsbach Corp. before becoming Jamaica Water Properties in 1976.

Diversification proved unprofitable, however, and in 1977, Martin Dwyer and his son Andrew took over the management of the struggling firm. Despite posting million-dollar losses in 1979, it was profitable by 1980.

The Dwyers acquired companies in the electrical and mechanical contracting, security, telecommunications, computer, energy and environmental businesses. In 1985 Andrew Dwyer became president, and the firm changed its name the next year to JWP.

Between 1986 and 1990 JWP acquired more than a dozen companies, including Extel (1986), Gibson Electric (1987), Dynalectric (1988), Drake & Scull (1989), NEECO and Compumat (1990), and Comstock Canada (1990).

In 1991 JWP capped its strategy of buying up US computer systems resellers by acquiring Businessland. It then bought French microelectronics distributor SIVEA. Later that year JWP bought a 34% stake in Resource Recycling Technologies (a solid-waste recycler).

JWP's shopping spree extended the firm's reach, but the company began to struggle when several sectors turned sour. A price war in the information services business and a weak construction market led to a loss of more than $600 million in 1992. That year president David Sokol resigned after questioning JWP's accounting practices. He turned over to the SEC a report that claimed inflated profits.

Cutting itself to about half its former size, the company sold JWP Information Services in 1993. (JWP Information Services later became ENTEX Information Services, which was acquired by Siemens in 2000.) However, JWP continued to struggle, and in early 1994 it filed for bankruptcy. Emerging from Chapter 11 protection in December 1994, the reorganized company took the name EMCOR. That year Frank MacInnis, former CEO of electrical contractor Comstock Group, stepped in to lead EMCOR.

In 1995 the SEC, using Sokol's information, charged several former JWP executives with accounting fraud, claiming they had overstated profits to boost the value of their company stock and their bonuses. EMCOR later reached a nonmonetary settlement with the SEC. The company sold Jamaica Water Supply and Sea Cliff in 1996; it also achieved profitability that year.

Focusing on external growth, EMCOR acquired a number of firms in 1998 and 1999, including Marelich Mechanical Co. and Mesa Energy Systems, BALCO, Inc., and the Poole & Kent group of mechanical contracting companies based in Baltimore and Miami. To meet increased demands for facilities services, in 2000 EMCOR consolidated the operations of three of its mechanical contractors (BALCO, J.C. Higgins, and Tucker Mechanical) into one company, EMCOR Services, which operates in New England.

That year, about six years after emerging from bankruptcy, EMCOR began trading on the New York Stock Exchange. In 2002 EMCOR bought 19 subsidiaries from its financially troubled rival, Comfort Systems USA, including its largest unit, Shambaugh & Son. Later that year it expanded its facilities services operations with the acquisition of Consolidated Engineering Services (CES), an Archstone-Smith subsidiary that operated in 20 states.

EMCOR broadened its facilities services operations by acquiring the US facility management services unit of Siemens Building Technologies in 2003; in 2005 it added Fluidics, Inc., a mechanical services company based in Philadelphia.

## EXECUTIVES

**Chairman and CEO:** Frank T. MacInnis, age 60, $870,000 pay
**President and COO:** Anthony J. (Tony) Guzzi, age 42, $600,000 pay
**EVP and CFO:** Mark A. Pompa, age 42, $366,250 pay (prior to promotion)
**EVP, General Counsel, and Secretary:** Sheldon I. (Shelly) Cammaker, age 67, $445,000 pay
**SVP Shared Services:** R. Kevin Matz, age 48, $1,085,016 pay
**VP and CIO:** Joseph A. (Joe) Puglisi
**VP Marketing and Communications:** Mava K. Heffler
**VP Consolidated Engineering Services, Department of Government:** Michael W. (Mike) Shelton
**VP and Controller:** William Feher
**President and CEO, EMCOR Construction Services:** Michael (Mike) Parry, age 58
**President and CEO, EMCOR Facilities Services:** William A. (Bill) Rodgers Jr.
**EVP, EMCOR Construction Services:** John Warga, age 62
**Treasurer:** Joseph A. Serino
**Auditors:** Ernst & Young LLP

## LOCATIONS

**HQ:** EMCOR Group, Inc.
301 Merritt Seven Corporate Park, 6th Fl., Norwalk, CT 06851
**Phone:** 203-849-7800 **Fax:** 203-849-7900
**Web:** www.emcorgroup.com

## PRODUCTS/OPERATIONS

### 2006 Sales

| | $ mil. | % of total |
|---|---|---|
| US | | |
| Mechanical construction & facilities services | 1,820.9 | 36 |
| Electrical construction & facilities services | 1,280.2 | 25 |
| Facilities services | 960.7 | 19 |
| UK | | |
| Construction & facilities services | 671.4 | 13 |
| Canada | | |
| Construction & facilities services | 287.8 | 7 |
| **Total** | **5,021.0** | **100** |

### Selected Operations

Mechanical and Electrical Construction
- Building plant and lighting systems
- Data communications systems
- Electrical power distribution systems
- Energy recovery
- Heating, ventilation, and air-conditioning (HVAC) systems
- Lighting systems
- Low-voltage systems (alarm, security, communications)
- Piping and plumbing systems
- Refrigeration systems
- Voice communications systems

Facilities Services
- Facilities management
- Installation and support for building systems
- Mobile maintenance and service
- Program development and management for energy systems
- Remote monitoring
- Site-based operations and maintenance
- Small modification and retrofit projects
- Technical consulting and diagnostic services

### Major Subsidiaries

Dyn Specialty Contracting, Inc.
EMCOR Construction Services, Inc.
EMCOR-CSI Holding Co.
EMCOR Facilities Services, Inc.
EMCOR Group (UK) plc
EMCOR International, Inc.
EMCOR Mechanical/Electrical Services (East), Inc.
MES Holdings Corporation
Monumental Investment Corporation

## COMPETITORS

ABM Industries
APi Group
Carrier
CB Richard Ellis
Comfort Systems USA
Dycom
FACServices
Fluor
Hoffman Corporation
Honeywell International
InfrastruX
Integrated Electrical Services
Jacobs
Johnson Controls
Jones Lang LaSalle
Limbach Facility Services
Linc Facility Services
MasTec
MYR Group
Quanta Services
Schneider Electric
Siemens AG
Trammell Crow Company
Trane
UNICCO Service

## HISTORICAL FINANCIALS

Company Type: Public

### Income Statement

FYE: December 31

| | REVENUE ($ mil.) | NET INCOME ($ mil.) | NET PROFIT MARGIN | EMPLOYEES |
|---|---|---|---|---|
| **12/06** | 5,021 | 87 | 1.7% | 27,000 |
| **12/05** | 4,715 | 60 | 1.3% | 26,000 |
| **12/04** | 4,748 | 33 | 0.7% | 26,000 |
| **12/03** | 4,535 | 21 | 0.5% | 26,000 |
| **12/02** | 3,968 | 63 | 1.6% | 26,000 |
| **Annual Growth** | 6.1% | 8.3% | — | 0.9% |

### 2006 Year-End Financials

Debt ratio: 24.0%
Return on equity: 13.1%
Cash ($ mil.): 274
Current ratio: 1.38
Long-term debt ($ mil.): 170
No. of shares (mil.): 32
Dividends
Yield: —
Payout: —
Market value ($ mil.): 905

### Stock History

NYSE: EME

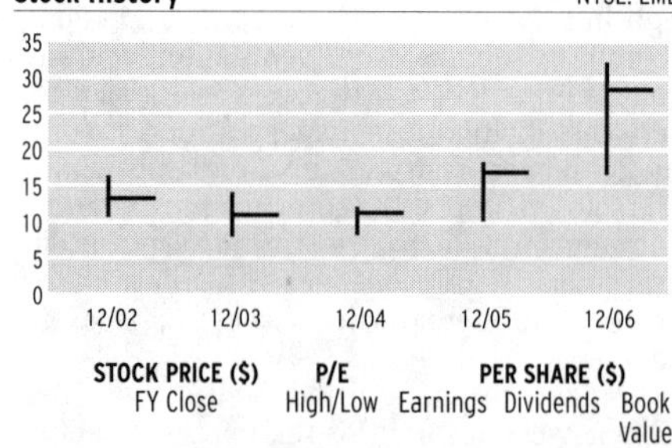


| | STOCK PRICE ($) FY Close | P/E High | P/E Low | PER SHARE ($) Earnings | Dividends | Book Value |
|---|---|---|---|---|---|---|
| **12/06** | 28.42 | 24 | 13 | 1.33 | — | 22.32 |
| **12/05** | 16.88 | 19 | 11 | 0.94 | — | 19.79 |
| **12/04** | 11.30 | 22 | 16 | 0.53 | — | 36.91 |
| **12/03** | 10.98 | 42 | 25 | 0.33 | — | 34.68 |
| **12/02** | 13.25 | 16 | 11 | 1.02 | — | 32.82 |
| **Annual Growth** | 21.0% | — | — | 6.9% | — | (9.2%) |

# Emerson Electric

Ralph Waldo Emerson wrote, "Work and acquire, and thou hast chained the wheel of Chance." Emerson Electric would agree. The company, generally known as just Emerson, makes a host of electrical, electromechanical, and electronic products, many of which are used to control gases, liquids, and electricity. Emerson has pursued an active, aggressive acquisition strategy (with select divestitures along the way) in building up its global business with dozens of subsidiaries. The company has gathered its 60-plus business units and divisions under eight Emerson Brands. As old Ralph Waldo once said, "Make yourself necessary to somebody," and Emerson Electric follows that adage.

The company has acquired Stratos International for $83.5 million, net of acquired cash. The purchase expands the product portfolios of the Emerson Network Power and Emerson Connectivity Solutions units. Stratos makes radio-frequency and microwave components, as well as optical subsystems, components, and interconnect products for a variety of applications.

Emerson serves a wide variety of industries, including commercial refrigeration, computers, food and beverages, health care, heating and air conditioning, home appliances, industrial manufacturing, mining, oil and gas, paper and pulp, petrochemical, pharmaceuticals, municipal utilities, retail, and telecommunications. The US accounts for more than half of sales.

## HISTORY

Emerson Electric was founded in 1890 in St. Louis by brothers Alexander and Charles Meston, inventors who developed uses for the alternating-current electric motor, which was new at the time. The company was named after former Missouri judge and US marshal John Emerson, who financed the enterprise and became its first president. Emerson's best-known product was an electric fan introduced in 1892. Between 1910 and 1920 the company helped develop the first forced-air circulating systems.

The Depression and labor problems in the 1930s brought Emerson close to bankruptcy, but new products, including a hermetic motor for refrigerators, revived it. The company's electric motors were adapted for additional uses during WWII, including powering the gun turrets in B-24 bombers.

Emerson suffered in postwar years, having grown dependent on military business. Wallace Persons took over as president in 1954 and reorganized the company's commercial product line, seeking to bring in customers from outside the consumer appliance market.

In the early 1960s Persons bought a number of smaller companies to produce thermostats and gas controls, welding and cutting tools, and power transmission products. Emerson's sales increased from $56 million in 1954 to $800 million in 1973. Persons retired in 1974, and Chuck Knight became CEO. Knight took the company into high-tech fields and expanded its hardware segment with six acquisitions between 1976 and 1986.

In 1989 Emerson expanded its electrical offerings by acquiring a 45% stake in Hong Kong-based Astec (power supplies). The company spun off its defense systems, electronics, and other businesses in 1990 as ESCO Electronics.

Emerson bought Fisher Controls International in 1992 and formed S-B Power Tool with Robert Bosch. It also acquired Buehler International (destructive testing equipment). From 1993 through 1995 Emerson expanded globally by targeting the Asia/Pacific market, setting up operations in China and Eastern Europe, and forming joint ventures in China and India.

Emerson and Caterpillar invested in plants in Northern Ireland in 1996 through their power-generating equipment joint venture, F. G. Wilson. Bosch bought out Emerson's interest in S-B Power Tool (now Robert Bosch Tool) in 1996.

In 1998 Emerson bought CBS Corporation's Westinghouse Process Control division. It also acquired PC&E to enhance its monitoring, diagnostic, and testing capabilities.

Emerson sold its F. G. Wilson stake to partner Caterpillar in 1999 in exchange for that company's Kato Engineering electric generator subsidiary. Purchases that year included Daniel Industries (measurement and flow-control equipment) and the rest of Astec.

Early in 2000 Emerson acquired the telecom products division of Jordan Industries for about $980 million and later bought European telecommunications power provider Ericsson Energy Systems from Ericsson for $725 million. Later that year the company dropped "Electric" from its everyday name to reflect its diverse product line. Also in 2000 Emerson executive David Farr replaced long-time CEO Chuck Knight.

Emerson sold its Chromalox division (electric heating and control products) to JPMorgan Partners in late 2001 for a reported $165 million.

In 2004 Farr assumed the additional title of chairman when Knight retired (Knight was named chairman emeritus).

Emerson acquired Metran Industrial, a provider of flow products and services in Russia and Eastern Europe, in 2004. Emerson also acquired the US-based outside plant and power systems businesses of Marconi (now telent) for $375 million, which it combined with its Emerson Network Power business. The acquisition strengthened Emerson's presence in DC power products and services, particularly with the regional Bell operating companies, as well as wireless and cable firms, in the North American market.

Emerson acquired process measurement and control equipment maker Solartron Mobrey from the Roxboro Group in 2005. The company renamed the unit Mobrey Measurement and integrated it into the Emerson Process Management group. The following year Emerson purchased Knurr, a German manufacturer of racks and enclosures for data centers, for approximately $97 million; Knurr became part of Emerson's Network Power segment, which also includes Liebert. In a move that further expanded its Network Power group, Emerson also acquired power conversion equipment maker Artesyn Technologies. Emerson sold the wireline test systems business of Emerson Network Power to Tollgrade Communications early in 2006. It then acquired Bristol Babcock, a unit of British diversified manufacturer FKI, for about $120 million; the purchase added measurement and control products for the energy and utilities markets to Emerson's Process Management segment. Also in 2006, Emerson sold its Buehler materials testing business.

## EXECUTIVES

**Chairman, President, and CEO:** David N. Farr, age 52, $3,300,000 pay
**Chairman Emeritus:** Charles F. (Chuck) Knight, age 71
**COO:** Edward L. Monser, age 56
**EVP, Secretary, and General Counsel:** Walter W. Withers, age 66, $1,100,000 pay
**SEVP, CFO, and Director:** Walter J. Galvin, age 60, $1,520,000 pay
**SEVP and Director:** Charles A. Peters, age 51, $1,100,000 pay
**SVP, Secretary, and General Counsel:** Frank L. Steeves, age 53
**SVP and CTO:** Randall D. Ledford, age 56
**SVP and Controller:** B. N. Eckhardt
**SVP, Acquisitions and Development:** Frank J. Dellaquila
**SVP, Administration:** Robert M. Cox Jr.
**SVP, Development:** James D. Switzer
**SVP, Human Resources:** Philip A. Hutchison
**SVP, Planning and Development:** Craig W. Ashmore
**VP and Chief Accounting Officer:** Richard J. Schlueter, age 52
**VP and CIO:** Stephen C. (Steve) Hassell
**VP and Chief Marketing Officer:** Katherine Button Bell
**VP and Treasurer:** D. J. Rabe
**President, Emerson Canada:** L.C. Barrett
**President, Emerson Greater China:** Peter K. Yam
**President, Emerson India:** Pradipta Sen
**President, Emerson Latin America:** L. A. Rodriguez
**President and CEO, Stratos International:** Phillip A. (Andy) Harris, age 60
**Corporate Media Relations:** Mark Polzin
**Assistant Treasurer and Director, Investor Relations:** C. L. Tucker
**Auditors:** KPMG LLP

## LOCATIONS

**HQ:** Emerson Electric Co.
PO Box 4100, 8000 W. Florissant Ave.,
St. Louis, MO 63136
**Phone:** 314-553-2000 **Fax:** 314-553-3527
**Web:** www.gotoemerson.com

Emerson Electric has 275 manufacturing locations around the world, of which about 170 are outside the US, primarily in Europe and also in Asia, Canada, and Latin America.

### 2006 Sales

| | $ mil. | % of total |
|---|---|---|
| US | 10,588 | 53 |
| Europe | 4,334 | 22 |
| Asia | 2,920 | 14 |
| Latin America | 857 | 4 |
| Other regions | 1,434 | 7 |
| **Total** | **20,133** | **100** |

## PRODUCTS/OPERATIONS

### 2006 Sales

| | $ mil. | % of total |
|---|---|---|
| Process management | 4,875 | 23 |
| Network power | 4,350 | 21 |
| Appliance & tools | 4,313 | 21 |
| Industrial automation | 3,767 | 18 |
| Climate technologies | 3,424 | 17 |
| Adjustments | (596) | — |
| **Total** | **20,133** | **100** |

### Selected Products and Services

Process Management
- Measurement and analytical
- Software, services, and systems
- Valves and regulators

Network Power
- AC power systems
- Connectivity
- DC power systems
- Inbound power
- OEM power
- Precision air
- Service

Appliance and Tools
- Appliance controls
- Hand/power tools and wet/dry vacuums
- Motors
- Plumbing products and disposers

Industrial Automation
- Alternators
- Fluid control
- Industrial equipment
- Mechanical power transmission
- Motors and drives
- Power distribution

Climate Technologies
- Compressors
- Flow controls
- Terminal assemblies
- Thermal controls
- Thermostats and valve controls

Storage Solutions
- Bins
- Cabinets
- Display and storage shelving
- Inventory storage racks
- Stock-picking and kitting carts

## COMPETITORS

ABB
American Power Conversion
AMETEK
Black & Decker
Cooper Industries
Cummins
Dana
Dresser
Eaton
Endress + Hauser
GE
Hitachi
Honeywell ACS
Illinois Tool Works
Ingersoll-Rand
Interpump
Invensys
Johnson Controls
Kinetek
Lennox
Mark IV
McDermott
MGE UPS
NEC
Power-One
Raytheon
Rockwell Automation
Rolls-Royce
Siemens AG
Sino-American Electronics
Snap-on
SPX
Stanley Works
Tecumseh Products
Toshiba
Trippe Manufacturing
United Technologies

## HISTORICAL FINANCIALS

Company Type: Public

### Income Statement

FYE: September 30

| | REVENUE ($ mil.) | NET INCOME ($ mil.) | NET PROFIT MARGIN | EMPLOYEES |
|---|---|---|---|---|
| **9/06** | 20,133 | 1,845 | 9.2% | 127,800 |
| **9/05** | 17,305 | 1,422 | 8.2% | 114,200 |
| **9/04** | 15,615 | 1,257 | 8.0% | 107,800 |
| **9/03** | 13,958 | 1,089 | 7.8% | 106,700 |
| **9/02** | 13,824 | 122 | 0.9% | 111,500 |
| **Annual Growth** | 9.9% | 97.2% | — | 3.5% |

## 2006 Year-End Financials

Debt ratio: 38.4%
Return on equity: 23.7%
Cash ($ mil.): 810
Current ratio: 1.36
Long-term debt ($ mil.): 3,128
No. of shares (mil.): 402
Dividends
Yield: 2.1%
Payout: 39.7%
Market value ($ mil.): 16,870

## Stock History — NYSE: EMR

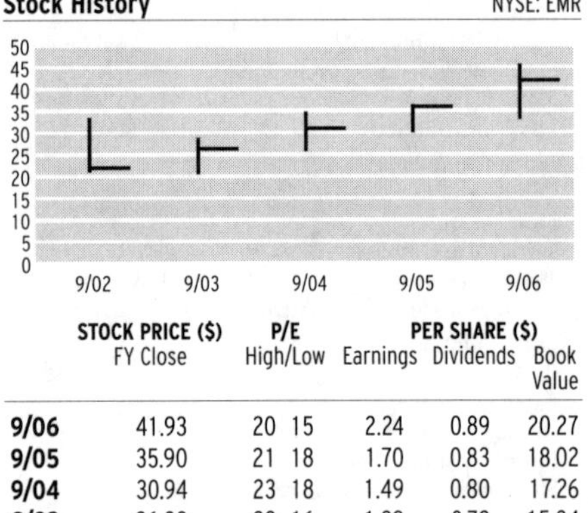

| | STOCK PRICE ($) FY Close | P/E High | P/E Low | PER SHARE ($) Earnings | Dividends | Book Value |
|---|---|---|---|---|---|---|
| 9/06 | 41.93 | 20 | 15 | 2.24 | 0.89 | 20.27 |
| 9/05 | 35.90 | 21 | 18 | 1.70 | 0.83 | 18.02 |
| 9/04 | 30.94 | 23 | 18 | 1.49 | 0.80 | 17.26 |
| 9/03 | 26.33 | 22 | 16 | 1.29 | 0.79 | 15.34 |
| 9/02 | 21.97 | 228 | 147 | 0.14 | 0.77 | 13.65 |
| Annual Growth | 17.5% | — | — | 100.0% | 3.7% | 10.4% |

# ENSCO International

ENSCO International is well-ensconced as a leading offshore drilling contractor. The company owns a fleet of 46 offshore rigs, including 44 jack-ups, one barge rig, one platform rig, and one semisubmersible (capable of drilling in up to 8,500 ft. of water). ENSCO conducts most of its domestic drilling business in the Gulf of Mexico, but also operates in the North Sea; offshore West Africa, Indonesia, and Trinidad; and in the Asia/Pacific region. In order to focus on its core business, ENSCO has sold its Marine unit, which provided support services to oil and gas firms in the Gulf with a fleet of 27 vessels, to Tidewater. The company took delivery of its 44th jack-up rig in 2007.

ENSCO pursues growth by expanding its drilling fleet through both acquisitions and construction of additional rigs. It also continues to evaluate its current fleet to determine if its rigs are optimized for handling the greater production metrics it desires.

## HISTORY

A former executive of oil field equipment manufacturer Dresser Industries (now part of Halliburton), John Blocker formed contract drilling firm Blocker Energy in 1975 with only six rigs. The young company had more business than its six rigs could handle because of increased drilling activity after the Arab oil embargo of the early 1970s. Blocker borrowed money to build another 30 rigs over the next four years.

Blocker Energy was soon steeped in debt, and the company went public in 1980 to raise capital. However, Blocker Energy continued to fall on hard times during the oil bust of the 1980s, and in 1986 Texas investor Richard Rainwater bought a controlling stake in the firm. The next year Rainwater renamed the firm Energy Service Company and brought in the former president of Sedco-Forex (Schlumberger's drilling unit), Carl Thorne, as CEO.

Thorne began focusing the firm on building a fleet of offshore drilling rigs. In 1989 Energy Services, known as ENSCO, began buying up the debt of another driller, Penrod Holding. By 1993 ENSCO had acquired Penrod, which added several rigs to its fleet. ENSCO also shed its noncore assets, including a marine supply business (1993), its land rigs (1994), and its technical services operation (1995).

Meanwhile, the firm had new rigs constructed, including eight barge rigs (1993-94), and added three harsh environment jack-ups to its North Sea fleet (1994-95). In 1995 the firm was renamed ENSCO International, and the next year it bought Dual Drilling, which added 20 more rigs to ENSCO's portfolio.

In 1998 ENSCO ordered the construction of three barge rigs, and the firm's first semisubmersible (capable of deepwater drilling to 8,000 feet of water depth). Also that year the company sold four barge rigs to Venezuela's state-owned oil company PDVSA, but ENSCO's new barge rigs began operating in 1999 off the coast of Venezuela, under contract to a Chevron affiliate.

The company completed the construction of a harsh environment jackup rig, earmarked for service in the North Sea, in 2000. The next year ENSCO's newly completed semisubmersible rig, *ENSCO 7500*, began a three-year contract with Burlington Resources in the Gulf of Mexico.

In 2002 ENSCO moved two of its jackups from the Gulf of Mexico to the Asia/Pacific region to capitalize on the better rig rates there. Later that year ENSCO added two offshore rigs, five oilfield support vessels, and five jackup rigs to its fleet by acquiring Chiles Offshore.

ENSCO teamed with Keppel FELS in 2004 to construct an additional high-performance drilling rig, which was completed in 2005. Also in 2005, the company sold its Venezuela barge rig fleet, which consisted of six rigs operating in Lake Maracaibo, to a unit of A.P. Møller — Mærsk for about $60 million.

## EXECUTIVES

**Chairman, President, and CEO:** Daniel W. Rabun, age 52
**EVP and COO:** William S. Chadwick Jr., age 58
**SVP and CFO:** James W. (Jay) Swent III, age 55, $566,586 pay
**SVP Business Development and Marketing, and Safety, Health, and Environment:** Jon C. Cole, age 52, $430,000 pay
**SVP, Business Development and SHE:** Philip J. Saile, age 53, $581,666 pay
**VP, Corporate Finance, Investor Relations, and Treasurer:** Richard A. LeBlanc, age 55
**President, ENSCO Offshore International Company:** Paul Mars, age 47, $451,805 pay
**VP, Finance:** H. E. Malone Jr., age 62
**VP, General Counsel, and Secretary:** Cary A. Moomjian Jr., age 58
**VP, Human Resources and Security:** Charles A. Mills, age 56
**Controller:** David A. Armour, age 48
**Treasurer:** Ramon Yi, age 52
**Auditors:** KPMG LLP

## LOCATIONS

**HQ:** ENSCO International Incorporated
500 N. Akard St., Ste. 4300, Dallas, TX 75201
**Phone:** 214-397-3000 **Fax:** 214-397-3370
**Web:** www.enscous.com

ENSCO International operates offshore drilling rigs in the Asia/Pacific region, the Gulf of Mexico, and the North Sea.

## 2006 Sales

| | $ mil. | % of total |
|---|---|---|
| US | 709.9 | 39 |
| UK | 325.9 | 18 |
| Qatar | 79.5 | 4 |
| Other countries | 698.2 | 39 |
| **Total** | **1,813.5** | **100** |

## PRODUCTS/OPERATIONS

### 2006 Sales

| | $ mil. | % of total |
|---|---|---|
| Jackup rigs | 1,731.6 | 96 |
| Semisubmersible rig | 60.9 | 3 |
| Barge rig | 21.0 | 1 |
| **Total** | **1,813.5** | **100** |

## COMPETITORS

Atwood Oceanics
Diamond Offshore
GlobalSantaFe
Helmerich & Payne
Nabors Industries
Noble
Parker Drilling
Pride International
Rowan
Saipem
Schlumberger
Tidewater
Transocean

## HISTORICAL FINANCIALS

Company Type: Public

### Income Statement — FYE: December 31

| | REVENUE ($ mil.) | NET INCOME ($ mil.) | NET PROFIT MARGIN | EMPLOYEES |
|---|---|---|---|---|
| 12/06 | 1,814 | 770 | 42.4% | 3,900 |
| 12/05 | 1,047 | 294 | 28.1% | 3,700 |
| 12/04 | 768 | 103 | 13.4% | 3,600 |
| 12/03 | 791 | 108 | 13.7% | 3,600 |
| 12/02 | 698 | 59 | 8.5% | 4,300 |
| Annual Growth | 27.0% | 89.8% | — | (2.4%) |

### 2006 Year-End Financials

Debt ratio: 9.6%
Return on equity: 26.8%
Cash ($ mil.): 570
Current ratio: 2.56
Long-term debt ($ mil.): 309
No. of shares (mil.): 152
Dividends
Yield: 0.2%
Payout: 2.0%
Market value ($ mil.): 7,599

### Stock History — NYSE: ESV

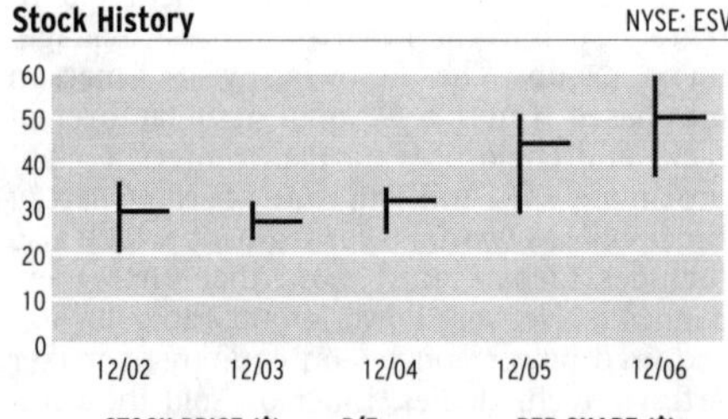

| | STOCK PRICE ($) FY Close | P/E High | P/E Low | PER SHARE ($) Earnings | Dividends | Book Value |
|---|---|---|---|---|---|---|
| 12/06 | 50.06 | 12 | 7 | 5.04 | 0.10 | 21.19 |
| 12/05 | 44.35 | 26 | 15 | 1.93 | 0.10 | 16.51 |
| 12/04 | 31.74 | 50 | 37 | 0.68 | 0.10 | 14.44 |
| 12/03 | 27.17 | 43 | 33 | 0.72 | 0.10 | 13.83 |
| 12/02 | 29.45 | 85 | 50 | 0.42 | 0.08 | 13.20 |
| Annual Growth | 14.2% | — | — | 86.1% | 5.7% | 12.6% |

# Entergy Corporation

If Entergy had an Entergizer bunny for a mascot, it would stay fully charged. The integrated utility holding company's subsidiaries distribute electricity to 2.6 million customers in four southern states (Arkansas, Louisiana, Mississippi, and Texas) and provide natural gas to 157,000 customers in Louisiana. Entergy has interests in regulated and nonregulated power plants in North America that have a combined generating capacity of about 30,000 MW. The company markets wholesale energy commodities; however, it has divested its primary marketing and trading operations. As a result of Hurricane Katrina, more than 1 million of Entergy's customers in Mississippi and Louisiana lost power.

Entergy is one of the largest nuclear power generators in the US. The company is increasing its generating capacity (to support its utilities and its marketing and trading operations) through domestic nuclear plant acquisitions. Entergy had also been focused on new plant construction; however, poor conditions in the wholesale power market have prompted the company to delay or cancel most of its developments. Entergy has sold its Latin American and European power plant interests.

Entergy and Koch Industries exited their Entergy-Koch's joint venture in 2004 through the sale of the unit's marketing operations to Merrill Lynch for an undisclosed amount and the sale of its gas transportation and storage assets to TGT Pipeline, a subsidiary of Loews, for approximately $1.1 billion.

In 2006 the company agreed to buy Consumers Energy's 798 MW Palisades Nuclear Plant in Michigan for $380 million.

## HISTORY

Arkansas Power & Light (AP&L, founded in 1913) consolidated operations with three other Arkansas utilities in 1926. Also that year, New Orleans Public Service Inc. (NOPSI, founded in 1922) merged with two other Big Easy electric companies. Louisiana Power & Light (LP&L) and Mississippi Power & Light (MP&L) were both formed in 1927, also through consolidation of regional utilities.

AP&L, LP&L, MP&L, NOPSI, and other utilities were combined into a Maine holding company, Electric Power and Light, which was dissolved in 1949. A new holding company, Middle South Utilities, emerged that year to take over the four utilities' assets.

In 1971 the company bought Arkansas-Missouri Power. In 1974 it brought its first nuclear plant on line and formed Middle South Energy (now System Energy Resources) to develop two more nuclear facilities, Grand Gulf 1 and 2. Unfortunately, Grand Gulf 1 was completed behind schedule and about 400% over budget. When Middle South tried to pass on the costs to customers, controversy ensued. Construction of Grand Gulf 2 was halted, and the CFO, Edwin Lupberger, took charge in 1985. Two years later, nuke-related losses took the company to the brink of bankruptcy.

The company moved to settle the disputes by absorbing a $900 million loss on Grand Gulf 2 in 1989. To distance itself from the controversy, Middle South changed its name to Entergy. In 1991 NOPSI settled with the City of New Orleans over Grand Gulf 1 costs.

That year Entergy, anticipating deregulation, branched out into nonregulated industries and looked abroad for growth opportunities. In 1993 a consortium including Entergy acquired a 51% interest in Edesur, a Buenos Aires electric utility. In 1995 Entergy agreed to buy a 20% stake in a power plant under construction in India, but the state government soon halted the project, accusing the participating US companies of exploiting India.

Entergy completed its acquisition of CitiPower, an Australian electric distributor, in 1996, and the next year it bought the UK's London Electricity.

But diversification had drained funds. Lupberger resigned in 1998, and a new management team began selling noncore businesses, such as CitiPower and London Electricity. It contracted out construction on two UK power plants, to be owned by Entergy, and moved into Eastern Europe through a joint venture with Bulgaria's National Electricity Company. NYMEX began trading electricity futures in 1998, using Entergy and Cinergy as contract-delivery points.

In 1999 Wayne Leonard, Cinergy's former CFO, stepped in as Entergy's CEO. The company bought the Pilgrim nuclear reactor in Massachusetts, its first plant outside its utility territory, from BEC Energy (now NSTAR); it also contracted to operate the Nine Mile Point nuclear plants in New York. Entergy sold its security monitoring business and its interest in a telecom joint venture to partner Adelphia Business Solutions.

Entergy continued its push into the Northeast by buying two nuclear plants — Indian Point 3 and James Fitzpatrick — from the New York Power Authority for $967 million in 2000, and it announced that it would purchase Indian Point 1 and 2 from Consolidated Edison (completed in 2001). In 2001 the company agreed to buy the Vermont Yankee nuclear plant from a group of New England utilities; the deal was completed in 2002 for $180 million.

Entergy agreed to merge with FPL Group in 2000, but the deal was called off the next year. The company also moved to expand through joint ventures. In 2000 Entergy and The Shaw Group, a piping systems fabricator, formed Entergy-Shaw, which designs and builds power plants. Entergy announced an agreement with Framatome to create a nuclear operations company, and in 2001 Entergy and Koch Industries formed an energy marketing and trading joint venture.

In 2002 Entergy sold its power plant interests in Argentina, Chile, and Peru to Southern Cone Power for $136 million. It also sold interests in projects in Spain and the UK.

## EXECUTIVES

**Chairman and CEO:** J. Wayne Leonard, age 55, $8,597,625 pay
**EVP and CFO:** Leo P. Denault, $1,597,825 pay
**EVP, Secretary, and General Counsel, Entergy, Entergy Arkansas, Entergy Gulf States, Entergy Louisiana, Entergy Mississippi, and Entergy New Orleans:** Robert D. Sloan
**EVP External Affairs:** Curtis L. (Curt) Hébert Jr., age 43
**EVP Operations:** Mark T. Savoff, $1,594,755 pay
**SVP Fossil Operations:** Michael D. Bakewell
**SVP Human Resources and Administration:** Terry Seamons
**VP Investor Relations:** Michele Lopiccolo
**President and COO:** Richard J. (Rick) Smith, age 55, $536,650 pay (prior to title change)
**President and CEO; Entergy Arkansas:** Hugh T. McDonald, age 47, $298,870 pay
**President and CEO, Entergy Gulf States — Texas:** Joseph F. (Joe) Domino, $365,576 pay
**President and CEO, Entergy Louisiana and Entergy Gulf States — Louisiana:** E. Renae Conley
**President and CEO, Entergy Mississippi:** Carolyn C. Shanks, age 44, $365,539 pay
**Group President, Utility Operations:** Gary J. Taylor, $515,967 pay (prior to title change)
**Chief Nuclear Officer; President and CEO, Entergy Operations:** Michael R. (Mike) Kansler
**President, Entergy Nuclear South:** John R. McGaha
**President and CEO, Entergy New Orleans:** Roderick K. (Rod) West
**VP and CFO, Entergy Arkansas, Gulf States, Louisiana, Mississippi, and New Orleans:** Jay A. Lewis, $193,122 pay
**Director Investor Relations:** Paul LaRosa
**Auditors:** Deloitte & Touche LLP

## LOCATIONS

**HQ:** Entergy Corporation
639 Loyola Ave., New Orleans, LA 70113
**Phone:** 504-576-4000 **Fax:** 504-576-4428
**Web:** www.entergy.com

Entergy Corporation primarily provides energy in Arkansas, Louisiana, Mississippi, and Texas.

## PRODUCTS/OPERATIONS

### 2006 Sales

| | $ mil. | % of total |
|---|---|---|
| Domestic electric | 9,063.2 | 83 |
| Competitive businesses | 1,784.8 | 16 |
| Natural gas | 84.2 | 1 |
| **Total** | **10,932.2** | **100** |

### 2006 Fuel Supply

| | % of total |
|---|---|
| Purchased power | 41 |
| Nuclear | 33 |
| Natural gas | 15 |
| Coal | 11 |
| **Total** | **100** |

### Selected Subsidiaries

Domestic Utilities
- Entergy Arkansas, Inc. (electric utility)
- Entergy Gulf States, Inc. (electric and gas utility)
- Entergy Louisiana, Inc. (electric utility)
- Entergy Mississippi, Inc. (electric utility)
- Entergy New Orleans, Inc. (electric and gas utility)
- Entergy Operations, Inc. (plant management and maintenance for Entergy utilities)
- Entergy Services, Inc. (management services for Entergy utilities)
- System Energy Resources, Inc. (plant management and supply to Entergy utilities)
- System Fuels, Inc. (fuel storage and delivery to Entergy utilities)

Competitive and Other Businesses
- Entergy Commodity Services
  - Entergy Asset Management, Inc. (power plant development)
  - Entergy-Koch L.P. (gas transportation and storage)
- Entergy Nuclear, Inc. (nuclear plant operation)
- Entergy-Shaw, LLC (power plant construction joint venture)

## COMPETITORS

AEP
AES
AmerGen Energy
Aquila
Atmos Energy
Avista
Brazos Electric Power
CenterPoint Energy
Cleco
Constellation Energy Group
Dominion Resources
Duke Energy
Edison International
El Paso Electric
Exelon
FPL Group
MidAmerican Energy
Mirant
OGE Energy
Peabody Energy
PG&E
Progress Energy
Reliant Energy
Sempra Energy
Southern Company
TVA
TXU
Williams Companies
Xcel Energy

## HISTORICAL FINANCIALS

Company Type: Public

### Income Statement

FYE: December 31

| | REVENUE ($ mil.) | NET INCOME ($ mil.) | NET PROFIT MARGIN | EMPLOYEES |
|---|---|---|---|---|
| 12/06 | 10,932 | 1,133 | 10.4% | 13,800 |
| 12/05 | 10,106 | 924 | 9.1% | 14,100 |
| 12/04 | 10,124 | 933 | 9.2% | 14,425 |
| 12/03 | 9,195 | 951 | 10.3% | 14,800 |
| 12/02 | 8,305 | 623 | 7.5% | 15,601 |
| Annual Growth | 7.1% | 16.1% | — | (3.0%) |

### 2006 Year-End Financials

| | |
|---|---|
| Debt ratio: 109.6% | No. of shares (mil.): 203 |
| Return on equity: 14.2% | Dividends |
| Cash ($ mil.): 1,016 | Yield: 2.3% |
| Current ratio: 1.35 | Payout: 40.3% |
| Long-term debt ($ mil.): 8,986 | Market value ($ mil.): 18,710 |

### Stock History

NYSE: ETR

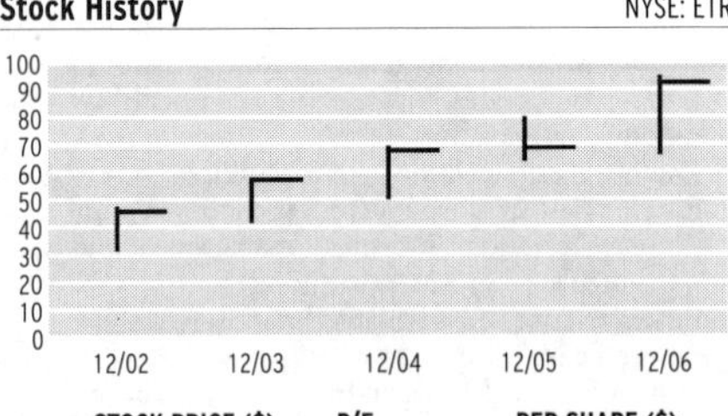


| | STOCK PRICE ($) FY Close | P/E High/Low | | PER SHARE ($) Earnings | Dividends | Book Value |
|---|---|---|---|---|---|---|
| 12/06 | 92.32 | 18 | 12 | 5.36 | 2.16 | 40.45 |
| 12/05 | 68.65 | 19 | 15 | 4.19 | 2.16 | 39.46 |
| 12/04 | 67.59 | 17 | 13 | 3.93 | 1.89 | 39.95 |
| 12/03 | 57.13 | 14 | 11 | 4.01 | 1.60 | 39.58 |
| 12/02 | 45.59 | 18 | 12 | 2.64 | 1.34 | 35.24 |
| Annual Growth | 19.3% | — | — | 19.4% | 12.7% | 3.5% |

# EOG Resources

EOG Resources hogs a resource — natural gas. The independent oil and gas company is engaged in exploring for natural gas and crude oil and developing, producing, and marketing those resources. EOG, an independent offspring of the once powerful Enron, has total estimated reserves of 6.8 trillion cu. ft. equivalent, including 6.1 trillion cu. ft. of natural gas reserves and 118 million barrels of crude oil, condensate, and natural gas liquid (NGL) reserves. The company operates in major production basins in Canada, offshore Trinidad, the US, and the UK sector of the North Sea. EOG is boosting its North American exploration activities and expanding its reserves.

In 2003 the company enhanced its drilling inventory in Canada with the acquisition of gas properties in southeastern Alberta from Husky Energy for $320 million (US). The purchase has complemented EOG's assets in southern Alberta. In Trinidad, the company has been supplying gas to an ammonia plant and plans to supply to another ammonia plant and to a methanol plant. EOG has also stepped up its drilling and exploration efforts to find additional reserves offshore Trinidad.

The group's strategy is to focus on growth through internal generation and strategic acquisitions in North America, Trinidad, and the North Sea.

## HISTORY

In 1987 Enron formed Enron Oil & Gas from its existing InterNorth and Houston Natural Gas operations to concentrate on exploration for oil and natural gas and their production. Enron maintained full ownership until 1989, when it spun off 16% of Enron Oil & Gas to the public, raising about $200 million. Later offerings reduced its holdings to just over 50%.

Enron Oil & Gas in 1992 was awarded a 95% working interest in three fields off Trinidad that previously had been held by government-owned companies. Two years later the company assumed the operations of three drilling blocks off Bombay (including the Tapti field), as well as a 30% interest in them. Natural gas prices fell in the winter of 1994, causing Enron Oil & Gas to focus its 1995 drilling on crude oil exploitation and the enhancement of its natural gas reserves. Natural gas prices rebounded in 1996. That year Enron Oil & Gas was awarded a 90% interest in an offshore area of Venezuela. In 1997 the company inked a 30-year production contract with China. The company made a major discovery of natural gas in offshore Trinidad in 1998. That year Mark Papa succeeded Forrest Hoglund as CEO (Papa became chairman in 1999).

In 1999 Enron traded most of its remaining stake in Enron Oil & Gas to the company in exchange for Enron Oil & Gas' operations and assets in India and China. Consequently, the company changed its name from Enron Oil & Gas to EOG Resources.

The next year EOG won contracts to develop properties in Canada's Northwest Territories. It also moved into the Appalachian Basin in 2000, through the acquisition of Somerset Oil & Gas. Buoyed by a strong performance that year, the company increased its capital spending on North American exploration by more than 30%, and in 2001 it bought Energy Search, a small natural gas exploration and production company that operated in the Appalachian Basin.

## EXECUTIVES

**Chairman and CEO:** Mark G. Papa, age 60, $1,940,000 pay
**EVP Exploration and Development:** Loren M. Leiker, age 52, $1,026,055 pay
**EVP Operations:** Gary L. Thomas, age 56, $1,026,055 pay
**SVP and General Counsel:** Barry Hunsaker Jr., age 55, $616,923 pay
**SVP Law:** Lewis P. Chandler Jr.
**SVP and General Manager, Fort Worth:** William R. Thomas
**SVP and General Counsel:** Frederick J. (Rick) Plaeger
**SVP and General Manager, Corpus Christi:** Robert K. Garrison
**SVP and General Manager, Denver:** Kurt D. Doerr
**SVP and General Manager, Tyler:** Steven B. Coleman
**VP and CFO:** Timothy K. Driggers, age 44
**VP Acquisitions and Engineering:** William E. Albrecht
**VP Investor Relations:** Maire A. Baldwin
**VP and CIO:** Sandeep Bhakhri
**VP and General Manager, International Division; President, EOG Resources International:** Gerald R. Colley
**VP Business Development:** Phil C. DeLozier
**VP Human Resources, Administration, and Corporate Secretary:** Patricia L. Edwards
**VP Audit:** Kevin S. Hanzel
**VP Marketing and Regulatory Affairs:** Andrew N. Hoyle
**VP and Treasurer:** Helen Lim
**Auditors:** Deloitte & Touche LLP

## LOCATIONS

**HQ:** EOG Resources, Inc.
1111 Bagby, Sky Lobby 2, Houston, TX 77002
**Phone:** 713-651-7000 **Fax:** 713-651-6995
**Web:** www.eogresources.com

### 2006 Sales

| | $ mil. | % of total |
|---|---|---|
| US | 2,878.1 | 74 |
| Canada | 593.7 | 15 |
| Trinidad | 345.7 | 9 |
| UK | 86.9 | 2 |
| **Total** | **3,904.4** | **100** |

## PRODUCTS/OPERATIONS

### 2006 Sales

| | $ mil. | % of total |
|---|---|---|
| Natural gas | 2,803.2 | 72 |
| Crude oil, condensate & NGLs | 761.6 | 19 |
| Gains on commodity derivative contracts | 334.3 | 9 |
| Other | 5.3 | — |
| **Total** | **3,904.4** | **100** |

## COMPETITORS

Adams Resources
Anadarko Petroleum
Apache
BP
Cabot Oil & Gas
Chevron
El Paso
Exxon Mobil
Murphy Oil
Occidental Petroleum
Pioneer Natural Resources
Royal Dutch Shell
Talisman Energy

## HISTORICAL FINANCIALS

Company Type: Public

**Income Statement** FYE: December 31

| | REVENUE ($ mil.) | NET INCOME ($ mil.) | NET PROFIT MARGIN | EMPLOYEES |
|---|---|---|---|---|
| **12/06** | 3,904 | 1,300 | 33.3% | 1,570 |
| **12/05** | 3,620 | 1,260 | 34.8% | 1,400 |
| **12/04** | 2,271 | 625 | 27.5% | 1,250 |
| **12/03** | 1,825 | 430 | 23.6% | 1,100 |
| **12/02** | 1,144 | 87 | 7.6% | 1,000 |
| **Annual Growth** | 35.9% | 96.5% | — | 11.9% |

**2006 Year-End Financials**

Debt ratio: 13.2%
Return on equity: 26.6%
Cash ($ mil.): 218
Current ratio: 1.08
Long-term debt ($ mil.): 733
No. of shares (mil.): 244
Dividends
Yield: 0.4%
Payout: 4.2%
Market value ($ mil.): 15,221

**Stock History** NYSE: EOG

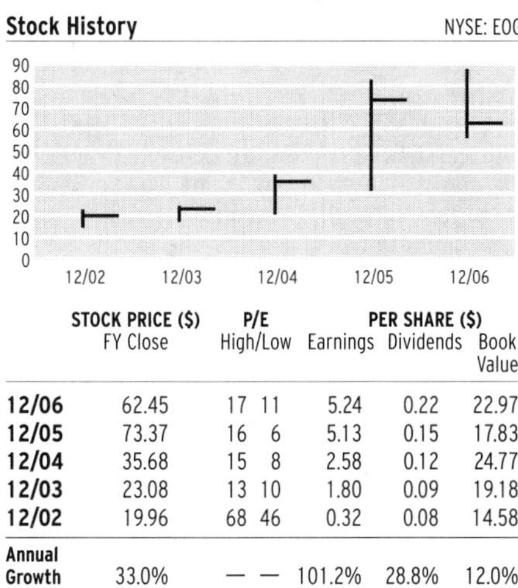

| | STOCK PRICE ($) FY Close | P/E High | P/E Low | PER SHARE ($) Earnings | Dividends | Book Value |
|---|---|---|---|---|---|---|
| **12/06** | 62.45 | 17 | 11 | 5.24 | 0.22 | 22.97 |
| **12/05** | 73.37 | 16 | 6 | 5.13 | 0.15 | 17.83 |
| **12/04** | 35.68 | 15 | 8 | 2.58 | 0.12 | 24.77 |
| **12/03** | 23.08 | 13 | 10 | 1.80 | 0.09 | 19.18 |
| **12/02** | 19.96 | 68 | 46 | 0.32 | 0.08 | 14.58 |
| **Annual Growth** | 33.0% | — | — | 101.2% | 28.8% | 12.0% |

# Equifax Inc.

Equifax knows you. Yes, you. One of the US's largest credit reporting agencies (alongside Experian and TransUnion), the company has information on more than 400 million worldwide credit holders (about three-quarters of which are consumers). In addition to credit reports, Equifax provides credit card marketing and fraud detection services and offers database marketing, credit risk consulting, and such products as credit scoring software through a host of subsidiaries. Founded in 1899, Equifax does business in more than a dozen countries. Its customers include retailers, insurance firms, health care providers, utilities, government agencies, banks, and other financial institutions.

With the maturity of its markets (particularly the US), the company has increasingly looked to expand its services and its reach through acquisitions, including human resources and payroll outsourcing firm TALX, direct-marketing firm Naviant (renamed Equifax eMarketing Solutions), and marketing-technology firm BeNOW.

Equifax is also targeting such emerging markets as Latin America, where the infrastructure for consumer credit reporting is nascent, but fast-growing economies have created a need for Equifax's services.

## HISTORY

Brothers Cator and Guy Woolford started Retail Credit Co. in Atlanta in 1899. They compiled credit records of local residents into their Merchants Guide, which they sold to retailers for $25 a year. The brothers extended their services to the insurance industry in 1901, investigating applicants' backgrounds. The company grew steadily and by 1920 had offices across the US and Canada. After several decades, Retail Credit branched into other information sectors, partly through acquisitions of regional credit reporters.

The company came under scrutiny in 1973 when the FTC filed an antimonopoly suit (dropped in 1982) against its consumer credit division and a complaint against its investigative practices (Retail Credit used field investigators to probe people's backgrounds). In 1976 the company became Equifax, short for "equitability in the gathering and presentation of facts."

In the 1980s and 1990s, Equifax continued to buy small businesses in the US and Europe. As the Information Age matured, businesses clamored for its services. By the end of the 1980s, Equifax had passed TRW (now part of Experian) as the largest provider of consumer information.

Receptive to consumer concerns in the late 1980s, the company ended list sales to US direct marketers and scrapped Marketplace, a 1991 joint venture with Lotus Development to compile a database of the shopping habits of 100 million Americans. During the 1990s Equifax acquired regional credit and collection firms in Florida, Georgia, and Texas. The company restructured in 1992, merging its US and Canadian operations, closing field offices, and expanding its international operations.

In 1992 and 1993 it settled cases with several states over intrusive and inaccurate credit and job reference reports. The California State Lottery ended its scratch ticket terminal contract with an Equifax unit, claiming the subsidiary ran substandard operations. The contract was reinstated in 1995 after Equifax threatened to sue, but the lottery business left a bad impression on Equifax. In 1996 it subcontracted most of its contract obligations to GTECH.

Also in 1996 Equifax exited the health care information business; the next year it spun off its insurance services business as Choicepoint. As part of this effort it reassigned CDB Infotek (acquired 1996) to ChoicePoint. After CDB was alleged to have improperly sold voter registration and social security number lists, shareholders wondered whether Equifax's management had been unaware of the supposed activities, or if it had bought CDB knowing that it could be assuming legal responsibility for them. Equifax spokespeople gave contradictory explanations. At least partially in response to these woes, Equifax helped launch a self-policing initiative for the industry.

Equifax turned to building its Latin American business, buying the remaining 50% of South American credit company DICOM in 1997. It also bought 80% of Brazil's largest credit information firm, Segurança ao Crédito e Informações (1998), Chilean card processing firm Procard (2000), and one of Uruguay's largest credit information providers, Clearing de Informes (2001).

In 1999 the company entered the UK credit card market with a card-processing contract with IKANO Financial Services. The next year it expanded its direct marketing prowess with its acquisition of R.L. Polk's consumer information database. Also in 2000 the company agreed to pay $500,000 to the FTC for blocking or not responding promptly enough to consumers' phone calls.

In 2001 the company spun off credit-card processing and check-management unit Centegy (since acquired by Fidelity National Information Services) to shareholders, sold its city directory business (acquired in the R.L. Polk acquisition) to infoUSA, and underwent a restructuring that included cutting some 700 jobs, primarily outside the US.

In 2005 Equifax acquired APPRO Systems, a provider of automated credit risk management and financial technologies, for approximately $92 million. That year, Richard F. Smith (former COO of GE Insurance Solutions) succeeded Thomas F. Chapman as CEO of the company. Smith also took on the role of chairman when Chapman retired from the firm.

## EXECUTIVES

**Chairman and CEO:** Richard F. (Rick) Smith, age 47, $4,325,444 pay
**SVP, Corporate Development:** Joseph M. (Trey) Loughran
**SVP, Investor Relations:** Jeffrey L. (Jeff) Dodge, age 55
**SVP and Controller:** Nuala M. King, age 53
**VP and CFO:** Lee Adrean, age 55
**VP and General Counsel:** Kent E. Mast, age 63, $750,708 pay
**VP and Chief Marketing Officer:** Paul J. Springman, age 61, $691,057 pay
**VP and Chief Administrative Officer:** Coretha M. Rushing, age 50
**VP, Communications:** David Rubinger
**CTO:** Robert J. Webb, age 38
**Global Operations Officer:** Owen V. Flynn, age 56
**President, U.S. Consumer Information Solutions:** J. Dann Adams, age 49
**President, North American Personal Solutions:** Steven P. (Steve) Ely, age 51
**Group Executive, Enabling Technologies:** Steven L. (Steve) Uffman, age 55
**President, International:** Rodolfo O. Ploder, age 46
**President, North America Commercial Solutions:** Michael S. Shannon, age 51
**Office of the Corporate Secretary, Shareholder Services:** Kathryn J. Harris
**President, TALX Corporation:** William W. (Bill) Canfield, age 68
**President, Equifax Enabling Technologies:** Rajib Roy, age 41
**Auditors:** Ernst & Young LLP

## LOCATIONS

**HQ:** Equifax Inc.
1550 Peachtree St. NW, Atlanta, GA 30309
**Phone:** 404-885-8000 **Fax:** 404-885-8988
**Web:** www.equifax.com

Equifax has operations in Argentina, Brazil, Canada, Chile, Costa Rica, El Salvador, Honduras, Ireland, Peru, Portugal, Spain, the UK, the US, and Uruguay.

**2006 Sales**

| | % of total |
|---|---|
| US | 72 |
| UK | 9 |
| Canada | 8 |
| Brazil | 5 |
| Other countries | 6 |
| **Total** | **100** |

## PRODUCTS/OPERATIONS

**2006 Sales By Segment**

| | % of total |
|---|---|
| North America | |
| Information Services | 54 |
| Marketing Services | 18 |
| Personal Solutions | 8 |
| Latin America | 10 |
| Europe | 10 |
| **Total** | **100** |

### Selected Subsidiaries and Affiliates

Acrofax Inc. (Canada)
Austin Consolidated Holdings, Inc.
Clearing de Informes S.A. (Uruguay)
Compliance Data Center LLC
Computer Ventures, Inc.
Credit Bureau Services, Inc.
The Infocheck Group Ltd. (UK)
Light Signatures, Inc.
New Management Services LLC
Propago S.A. (Chile)
Soluciones Veraz Asnef Equifax, S.L. (Spain)
Verdad Informatica de Costa Rica, S.A.

## COMPETITORS

Acxiom
D&B
Experian
Fair Isaac
First Data
Harte-Hanks
infoUSA
Marmon Group
Moody's
NOVA
Total System Services
TransUnion

## HISTORICAL FINANCIALS

Company Type: Public

**Income Statement** FYE: December 31

| | REVENUE ($ mil.) | NET INCOME ($ mil.) | NET PROFIT MARGIN | EMPLOYEES |
|---|---|---|---|---|
| **12/06** | 1,546 | 275 | 17.8% | 4,960 |
| **12/05** | 1,443 | 247 | 17.1% | 4,600 |
| **12/04** | 1,273 | 235 | 18.4% | 4,400 |
| **12/03** | 1,225 | 165 | 13.5% | 4,600 |
| **12/02** | 1,109 | 178 | 16.0% | 5,000 |
| **Annual Growth** | 8.7% | 11.4% | — | (0.2%) |

**2006 Year-End Financials**

Debt ratio: 20.7%
Return on equity: 33.1%
Cash ($ mil.): 68
Current ratio: 0.59
Long-term debt ($ mil.): 174
No. of shares (mil.): 125
Dividends
Yield: 0.4%
Payout: 7.5%
Market value ($ mil.): 5,063

**Stock History** NYSE: EFX

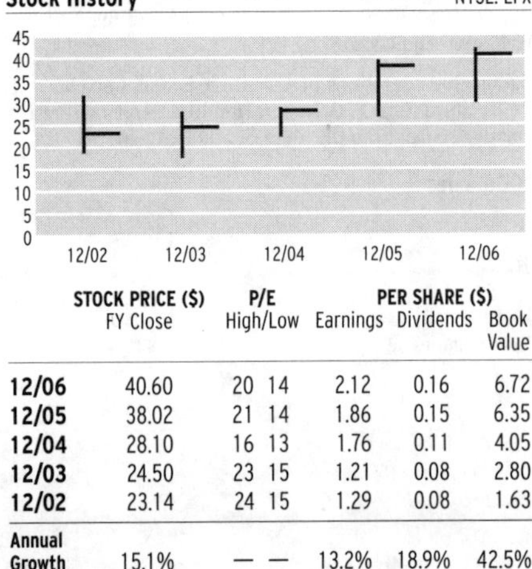


| | STOCK PRICE ($) FY Close | P/E High/Low | PER SHARE ($) Earnings | Dividends | Book Value |
|---|---|---|---|---|---|
| **12/06** | 40.60 | 20 14 | 2.12 | 0.16 | 6.72 |
| **12/05** | 38.02 | 21 14 | 1.86 | 0.15 | 6.35 |
| **12/04** | 28.10 | 16 13 | 1.76 | 0.11 | 4.05 |
| **12/03** | 24.50 | 23 15 | 1.21 | 0.08 | 2.80 |
| **12/02** | 23.14 | 24 15 | 1.29 | 0.08 | 1.63 |
| **Annual Growth** | 15.1% | — — | 13.2% | 18.9% | 42.5% |

# Equity Group Investments

Equity Group Investments is the apex of financier Sam Zell's pyramid of business holdings. The Chicago-based private investment group controls a multi-billion dollar mix of private and public, domestic and foreign businesses, including real estate investment trusts (REITs), and much, much more. Zell's REIT portfolio makes him one of the US's largest owners of apartments (Equity Residential), and of property leased by manufactured homeowners (Equity LifeStyle Properties, formerly Manufactured Home Communities). Zell is buying Tribune Company, but plans to unload that firm's holdings in the Chicago Cubs. Zell co-founded Equity Group Investments in 1968 and has a controlling interest in it.

In one of the biggest private equity deals ever, Blackstone Group bought Equity Office Properties Trust — one of the largest landlords in the US — for some $39 billion, including the assumption of $16 billion in debt. Zell's Equity Residential continues to build its portfolio through acquisitions. Equity Lifestyle Properties has also grown rapidly through acquisitions. Zell has made his niche — and a lot of money — by purchasing distressed properties and turning them into profitable investments (for which he earned the nickname "Grave Dancer"). Affiliate Equity International Properties invests in commercial and residential real estate outside the US. It established Mexico Retail Partners, a joint venture with the Black Creek Group, to develop big-box retail south of the border. Equity International Properties also pursues real estate deals throughout the rest of Latin America, and other far-flung markets, targeting both the commercial and residential sectors.

Equity Group Investments, which often buys during downturns, has rescued many companies floundering in bankruptcy. Acquisitions are frequently made through the Zell/Chilmark Fund.

## HISTORY

Sam Zell's first business endeavor was photographing his eighth-grade prom. In 1953 he graduated to reselling 50-cent *Playboy* magazines to schoolmates at a 200% markup.

While at the University of Michigan in the 1960s, Zell teamed with fraternity brother Robert Lurie to manage off-campus student housing. In graduate school, they invested in residential properties and formed Equity Financial and Management Co. after graduation. Their collection of distressed properties grew in the 1970s as Zell made the deals and Lurie made them work. Zell's hands-off management style had its drawbacks, however. In 1976 Zell and three others (including his brother-in-law) were indicted on federal tax-related charges after selling a Reno, Nevada, hotel and apartment complex. The charges were later dropped against Zell and another defendant (only the brother-in-law was convicted).

In the 1980s tax-law changes led the team to begin buying troubled companies. They started in 1983 with Great American Management and Investment, a foundering real estate manager they turned into an investment vehicle. Other targets included Itel (1984, now Anixter International) and oil and gas company Nucorp (1988, now part of insurer CNA Surety). The true attraction in many of these acquisitions, however, lay in tax-loss carryforwards that could be applied against future earnings.

Lurie died in 1990, after which Zell began to consolidate his power and ease out old friends. (Lurie's estate still owns shares of many Zell enterprises.) That year Zell and David Schulte formed the Zell/Chilmark Fund, which soon owned or controlled such companies as Schwinn (sold 1997), Sealy (sold 1997), and Revco (sold 1997). Among the fund's failures was West Coast retailer Broadway Stores, which Zell bought out of bankruptcy in 1992; when California's slumping economy prevented a rapid turnaround, Zell sold it (once again near bankruptcy) in 1995.

Starting in 1987, Zell formed four real estate funds with Merrill Lynch; six years later, both Equity Residential and Equity Lifestyle Properties (formerly Manufactured Home Communities) went public. As REITs became popular with investors, more trusts began vying for distressed assets — Zell's traditional lifeblood. In 1997 Zell melded four of his commercial real estate funds into another REIT, Equity Office Properties Trust, and took it public.

In 1998, as investors and financiers looked for fresh opportunities, Zell launched Equity International Properties, a fund targeting acquisitions in Latin America and elsewhere. That year a civil racketeering suit brought against Zell by former executive Richard Perlman shed light on "handshake" loans to top executives and other informal business deals. In 1999 Zell sold Jacor Communications to radio industry consolidator Clear Channel Communications. Equity Group Investments remained diversified, however. That year Equity Office Properties teamed with venture capital firm Kleiner Perkins Caufield & Byers to form Broadband Office to offer Internet and phone services to Zell's tenants and those of other property owners. Not surprisingly, Broadband Office bit the dust in the dot-com blowout.

Equity Office Properties Trust continued its buying into the 21st century, claiming New York-based Cornerstone Properties (2000) and California's Spieker Properties (2001).

Another holding, American Classic Voyages, filed for bankruptcy in 2001, victim both to a softening Hawaiian cruise market and to the general travel slow-down in the wake of the 2001 terrorist attacks. The company's assets were later sold.

## EXECUTIVES

**Chairman:** Samuel (Sam) Zell, age 65
**President:** Donald J. (Don) Liebentritt, age 57
**CFO:** Philip G. Tinkler, age 40
**Managing Director:** William C. (Bill) Pate, age 42

## LOCATIONS

**HQ:** Equity Group Investments, L.L.C.
2 N. Riverside Plaza, Ste. 600, Chicago, IL 60606
**Phone:** 312-454-0100 **Fax:** 312-454-0335
**Web:** www.equityinternational.com/home.html

## PRODUCTS/OPERATIONS

### Selected Affiliates

Anixter International, Inc. (communications network equipment)
Capital Trust, Inc. (commercial real estate finance)
Equity International Properties (overseas buyout fund)
Equity LifeStyle Properties (manufactured home community REIT)
Equity Office Properties Trust (office property REIT)
Equity Residential Properties Trust (apartment REIT)
Rewards Network, Inc. (loyalty marketing program)
Zell/Chilmark Fund L.P. (investment vulture fund)

## COMPETITORS

Apollo Advisors
Blackstone Group
The Carlyle Group
CD&R
Goldman Sachs
JMB Realty
KKR
MSD Capital
Thomas H. Lee Partners
Trump
Vulcan

# Ernst & Young International

Accounting may actually be the *second*-oldest profession, and Ernst & Young is one of the oldest practitioners. Ernst & Young is also one of the world's largest accounting firms (third in revenue of the Big Four behind PricewaterhouseCoopers and Deloitte Touche Tohmatsu) with some 700 offices in 140 countries, offering auditing and accounting services. The firm also provides legal services and services relating to emerging growth companies, human resources issues, and corporate transactions (mergers and acquisitions, IPOs, and the like). Ernst & Young has one of the world's largest tax practices, serving multinational clients that have to comply with multiple local tax laws.

After spending decades building their consultancies, the big accountancies have all moved toward shedding them, because of internal and regulatory pressures, as well as the perceived conflict of interest in providing auditing and consulting services to the same clients. Ernst & Young was the first to split off its consultancy, selling it in 2000 to what is now Cap Gemini Ernst & Young.

Ernst & Young, which gained an impressive amount of weight in former rival Andersen's diaspora, has also boosted its legal services, assembling some 2,000 lawyers in dozens of countries.

But the firm has faced Andersen-style trouble of its own as client suits against auditors have become more common in the wake of corporate scandals at Enron and other troubled companies. Both Avis Budget Group, Inc. (formerly Cendant) and HealthSouth have sued Ernst & Young in connection with alleged accounting missteps. As a result, the accounting firms are seeking help from Washington to protect themselves from the threat of litigation and ending up like Andersen.

## HISTORY

In 1494 Luca Pacioli's *Summa di Arithmetica* became the first published text on double-entry bookkeeping, but it was almost 400 years before accounting became a profession.

In 1849 Frederick Whinney joined the UK firm of Harding & Pullein. His ledgers were so clear that he was advised to take up accounting, which was a growth field as stock companies proliferated. Whinney became a name partner in 1859 and his sons followed him into the business. The firm became Whinney, Smith & Whinney (WS&W) in 1894.

After WWII, WS&W formed an alliance with Ernst & Ernst (founded in Cleveland in 1903 by brothers Alwin and Theodore Ernst), with each firm operating on the other's behalf across the Atlantic. Whinney merged with Brown, Fleming & Murray in 1965 to become Whinney Murray. In 1979 Whinney Murray, Turquands Barton Mayhew (also a UK firm), and Ernst & Ernst merged to form Ernst & Whinney.

But Ernst & Whinney wasn't done merging. Ten years later, when it was the fourth-largest accounting firm, it merged with #5 Arthur Young, which had been founded by Scotsman Arthur Young in 1895 in Kansas City. Long known as "old reliable," Arthur Young fell on hard times in the 1980s because its audit relationships with failed S&Ls led to expensive litigation (settled in 1992 for $400 million).

Thus the new firm of Ernst & Young faced a rocky start. In 1990 it fended off rumors of collapse. The next year it slashed payroll, even thinning its partner roster. Exhausted by the S&L wars, in 1994 the firm replaced its pugnacious general counsel, Carl Riggio, with the more cost-conscious Kathryn Oberly.

In the mid-1990s Ernst & Young concentrated on consulting, particularly in software applications, and grew through acquisitions. In 1996 the firm bought Houston-based Wright Killen & Co., a petroleum and petrochemicals consulting firm, to form Ernst & Young Wright Killen. It also entered new alliances that year, including ones with Washington-based ISD/Shaw, which provided banking industry consulting, and India's Tata Consulting.

In 1997 Ernst & Young was sued for a record $4 billion for its alleged failure to effectively handle the 1993 restructuring of the defunct Merry-Go-Round Enterprises retail chain (it settled for $185 million in 1999). On the heels of a merger deal between Coopers & Lybrand and Price Waterhouse, Ernst & Young agreed in 1997 to merge with KPMG International. But Ernst & Young called off the negotiations in 1998, citing the uncertain regulatory process they faced.

The firm reached a settlement in 1999 in lawsuits regarding accounting errors at Informix and Avis Budget Group and sold its UK and southern African trust and fiduciary businesses to Royal Bank of Canada (now RBC Financial Group).

In 2000 Ernst & Young became the first of the (then) Big Five firms to sell its consultancy, dealing it to France's Cap Gemini Group for about $11 billion. The following year the UK accountancy watchdog group announced it would investigate Ernst & Young for its handling of the accounts of UK-based The Equitable Life Assurance Society. The insurer was forced to close to new business in 2000 because of massive financial difficulties.

Ernst & Young made headlines and gave competitors plenty to talk about in 2002 when closely held financial records were made public during a divorce case involving executive Rick Bobrow (who in 2003 abruptly retired as global CEO after just a year on the job).

Also in 2002 the firm allied with former New York City mayor Rudy Giuliani to launch a business consultancy bearing the Giuliani name. Ernst & Young later helped the venture to build its investment banking capabilities by selling its corporate finance unit (as well as its stake in Giuliani Partners) to that firm in 2004.

In 2005 Ernst & Young's UK arm emerged victorious from a torrid legal battle with insurer Equitable Life, which in 2003 had sued the accountancy for professional negligence related to work performed when Ernst & Young was its auditor. Another highlight for that year was the fee bonanza fueled by changes in international accounting standards required by the Sarbanes-Oxley Act in the US.

## EXECUTIVES

**Chairman and CEO, Ernst & Young International and Ernst & Young L.L.P.:** James S. (Jim) Turley, age 51
**Global Vice Chair, Strategy, Communications, and Regulatory Affairs:** Beth A. Brooke
**Global COO:** John Ferraro
**Global Managing Partner, Quality and Risk Management:** Sue Frieden
**Global CFO and Global Managing Partner, Operations and Finance:** Jeffrey H. (Jeff) Dworken
**Global Managing Partner, People:** Pierre Hurstel
**Global Vice Chair, Assurance and Advisory Business Services:** Christian Mouillon
**Global Vice Chair, Tax:** Sam Fouad
**Global Vice Chair, Transaction Advisory Services:** Dave Read
**Global Vice Chair, Technology, Communications, and Entertainment:** Stephen E. (Steve) Almassy
**Global Vice Chair, Strategic Growth Markets:** Gregory Ericksen
**Global Vice Chair, Global Financial Services:** Robert W. (Bob) Stein
**Global Director, Automotive:** Michael S. (Mike) Hanley
**Global Director, Business Risk Services:** Thomas (Tom) Bussa
**Global Director, Insurance Industry Services:** Peter R. (Pete) Porrino
**Global Managing Partner, Client Service and Accounts:** Herman Hulst
**CEO, Ernst & Young AG:** Peter Athanas

## LOCATIONS

**HQ:** Ernst & Young International
5 Times Sq., New York, NY 10036
**Phone:** 212-773-3000 **Fax:** 212-773-6350
**Web:** www.eyi.com

Ernst & Young International has approximately 700 offices in 140 countries.

## PRODUCTS/OPERATIONS

### Selected Services

Assurance and Advisory
- Actuarial services
- Audits
- Accounting advisory
- Business risk services
- Internal audit
- Real estate advisory services
- Technology and security risk services

Emerging Growth Companies
- Corporate finance services
- Mergers and acquisitions advisory
- Operational consulting
- Strategic advisory
- Transactions advisory

Human Capital
- Compensation and benefits consulting
- Cost optimization and risk management
- Transaction support services

Law
- Corporate and M&A
- Employment
- Finance
- Information technology services
- Intellectual property
- International trade and anti-trust
- Litigation and arbitration
- Real estate

Tax
- Global tax operations
- Indirect tax
- International tax

Transactions
- Capital management
- Corporate development advisory
- Financial and business modeling
- M&A advisory
- Post-deal advisory
- Strategic finance
- Transaction management
- Valuation

## COMPETITORS

Baker Tilly International
BDO International
Deloitte
Grant Thornton International
Horwath International
IBM
KPMG
Moore Stephens International
PKF International
PricewaterhouseCoopers

## HISTORICAL FINANCIALS

Company Type: Partnership

**Income Statement** FYE: June 30

| | REVENUE ($ mil.) | NET INCOME ($ mil.) | NET PROFIT MARGIN | EMPLOYEES |
|---|---|---|---|---|
| **6/06** | 18,400 | — | — | 114,000 |
| **6/05** | 16,902 | — | — | 106,650 |
| **6/04** | 14,547 | — | — | 100,601 |
| **6/03** | 13,136 | — | — | 103,000 |
| **6/02** | 10,124 | — | — | 87,206 |
| **Annual Growth** | 16.1% | — | — | 6.9% |

**Revenue History**

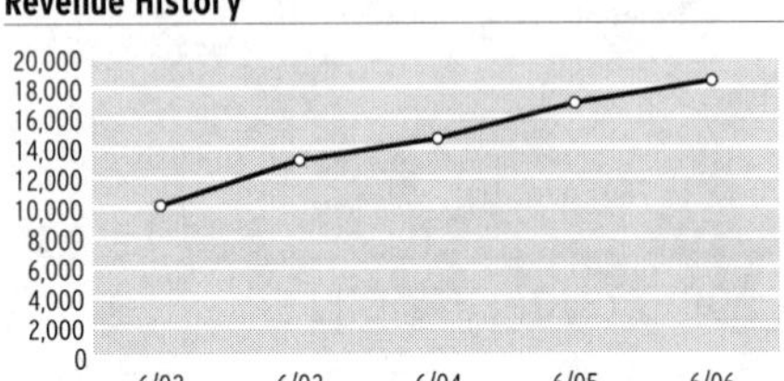


# Estée Lauder

The firm's Estée and Bobbi are counted among some of the closest friends to women worldwide. Estée Lauder sells cosmetics, fragrances, and skin care products, with brands including upscale Estée Lauder and Clinique and professional-style Bobbi Brown *essentials*. Its high-end lines are sold in department stores, company stores, and by specialty retailers. The company has expanded its chain of freestanding retail stores (primarily for its M.A.C, Origins, and Aveda brands). Estée Lauder also sells products online. The founding Lauder family controls about 88% of its voting shares.

With its products available in more than 130 countries, Estée Lauder is a world leader in upscale personal care products. It captures nearly half of all US prestige cosmetics sales. The company has expanded its customer base to include younger shoppers by acquiring the M.A.C cosmetics line.

Estée Lauder and the Lauder family have been working to revive the company's flagship brand as competition heats up in the industry. While Coty, Elizabeth Arden, and L'Oréal are enlisting the help of celebrities to elevate and give credibility to their brands, Estée Lauder has sewn up its brand rejuvenation with a boost from the fashion world. In early 2005 the company partnered with former Gucci Group creative director and fashion talent Tom Ford to develop a Tom Ford-inspired Estée Lauder line. Products designed by Ford debuted in November 2005 for the holiday season.

The company is targeting teens with a new line of skin care by Clinique that launched in spring 2007. The aim is to draw potential new customers to the brand at a younger age.

In addition to widening its customer base, Estée Lauder has expanded its distribution channels to include mass merchandisers and salons. The company has been gradually shifting business from department stores to its own stores and other outlets.

An agreement, inked in late 2006 with Coach, gave Estée Lauder's BeautyBank the rights to develop fragrances and related items to be sold in Coach's US retail outlets.

In addition to its partnerships with retailers, Estée Lauder has been penning licensing agreements to boost its brand and reach. In May 2004 Estée Lauder and Sean John, the private company formed by Sean "Diddy" Combs, signed an agreement to create and market a line of fragrances under the Sean John name. The first fragrance, called Unforgivable, is a $300 couture version. Estée Lauder signed on mogul Donald Trump in late 2004.

While the company is busy signing fragrance deals, Estée Lauder is also jockeying for position in the doctor-based skin care arena. In 2006 the firm opened the Clinique Skin Wellness Center through a partnership with Weill Cornell Medical College.

It's also extending its reach internationally. In mid-2006 Estée Lauder established a presence in Turkey and operates a unit in Istanbul named ELCA Kozmetik Ltd. Sti. A year later, in mid-2007, Estée Lauder inked a deal to purchase privately held Ojon Corporation, based in Canada. Ojon sells high-end hair care products through fast-growing QVC, specialty retailers (such as Sephora, Ulta, and Nordstrom), as well as hundreds of upscale salons.

## HISTORY

Estée Lauder (then Josephine Esther Mentzer) started her beauty career by selling skin care products formulated by her Hungarian uncle, John Schotz, during the 1930s. Eventually she packaged and peddled her variations of his formulas, which included face cream and a cleansing oil.

With the help of her husband, Joseph Lauder, she set up her first office in Queens, New York, in 1944, and added lipstick, eye shadow, and face powder to the line. Joseph oversaw production, and Estée sold her wares to beauty salons and department stores, using samples and gifts to win customers. Throughout the 1950s Estée traveled cross-country, at first to sell her line to high-profile department stores such as Neiman Marcus, I. Magnin, and Saks, and later to train saleswomen in these stores.

Estée Lauder created her first fragrance, Youth Dew perfume and bath oil, in 1953. In the late 1950s US cosmetics firms introduced European skin care lines with scientific names and supposedly advanced skin repair properties. Estée Lauder's contribution was Re-Nutriv cream, which sold for $115 a pound in 1960. The cream's advertising campaign established the sophisticated "Lauder look" — an image that Estée herself cultivated.

In 1964 Estée Lauder introduced Aramis, a fragrance for men, and in 1968, with the help of a *Vogue* editor, it launched Clinique, a hypoallergenic skin care line. In 1972 Estée's son Leonard became president; Estée remained CEO.

Estée Lauder created the Prescriptives skin care and makeup line for young professional women in 1979. Leonard was named CEO in 1983. By 1988 the company had captured a third of the US market in prestige cosmetics.

Estée Lauder unveiled its Origins botanical cosmetics line in 1990. The company launched the All Skins cosmetics line in 1991 and in 1994 bought a controlling stake in hip Make-Up Art Cosmetics (M.A.C).

Leonard became chairman in 1995. The company's IPO that year was structured to allow Estée and her son Ronald (previously an unsuccessful candidate for mayor of New York) to avoid a potential $95 million tax bill (inspiring a 1997 revision of the federal tax law). Filling out a busy year, Estée Lauder acquired the Bobbi Brown *essentials* line of cosmetics, bought botanical beauty products concern Aveda for $300 million (broadening its distribution into hair salons), and entered the mass market with its purchase of Sassaby (*jane* cosmetics, which was sold in early 2004). In 1998 Estée Lauder bought the rest of M.A.C.

In 1999 Estée Lauder bought Jo Malone Limited, a London-based seller of some 200 skin care and fragrance products. Company president Fred Langhammer succeeded Leonard Lauder as CEO in 2000; Leonard remained chairman. Also in 2000 Estée Lauder bought a majority interest in Bumble and bumble, a hair salon and products company.

Estée Lauder bought Paris-based Laboratories Darphin in 2003, adding the high-end Darphin skin care line to its portfolio. In July 2003 Estée Lauder acquired the Rodan & Fields skin care line, launched by two dermatologists in 2002, bringing with it the Proactiv skin care line.

Langhammer retired and assumed the role of chairman of global affairs in July 2004, when William Lauder was promoted to CEO. Also that year company founder Estée Lauder died of a heart attack at the age of 97.

## EXECUTIVES

**Chairman:** Leonard A. Lauder, age 74, $2,809,000 pay
**President, CEO, and Director:** William P. Lauder, age 46, $3,021,100 pay
**COO:** Daniel J. (Dan) Brestle, age 61, $2,695,000 pay
**Group President, Estée Lauder, M.A.C, Sean John, Prescriptives, and Tom Ford Beauty:** John Demsey, age 50
**Group President, Aramis and Designer Fragrances:** Patrick Bousquet-Chavanne, age 48, $2,048,900 pay
**Group President, Aveda, Bumble and bumble, Clinique, Origins, and Online Operations:** Philip Shearer, age 53, $2,003,000 pay
**Group President, International:** Cedric Prouvé, age 46
**EVP and CFO:** Richard W. Kunes, age 53
**EVP, Global Operations:** Malcolm Bond, age 56
**EVP, Global Research and Development:** Harvey Gedeon, age 63
**EVP, General Counsel, and Secretary:** Sara E. Moss, age 60
**EVP, Global Communications:** Sally Susman, age 45
**SVP, Global Packaging:** Roger Caracappa, age 57
**SVP, Global Communications:** Marianne Diorio
**SVP, Global Creative Directions and Director:** Aerin Lauder, age 36
**SVP, Global Creative Director, Aramis and Designer Fragrance Division:** Marc Benhamou
**SVP, Global Product Innovation:** Anne Carullo
**SVP, Global Human Resources:** Amy DiGeso, age 54
**VP, Investor Relations:** Dennis D'Andrea
**Chief Marketing Officer:** Joseph Gubernick
**Auditors:** KPMG LLP

## LOCATIONS

**HQ:** The Estée Lauder Companies Inc.
767 Fifth Ave., New York, NY 10153
**Phone:** 212-572-4200 **Fax:** 212-572-3941
**Web:** www.elcompanies.com

Estée Lauder sells its products in more than 130 countries and operates plants and research facilities in Belgium, Canada, Japan, South Africa, Switzerland, the UK, and the US.

### 2007 Sales

| | $ mil. | % of total |
|---|---|---|
| Americas | 3,560.9 | 51 |
| Europe, Middle East, Africa | 2,493.4 | 35 |
| Asia/Pacific | 983.2 | 14 |
| **Total** | **7,037.5** | **100** |

## PRODUCTS/OPERATIONS

### 2007 Sales

| | $ mil. | % of total |
|---|---|---|
| Makeup | 2,712.7 | 38 |
| Skin care | 2,601.0 | 37 |
| Fragrance | 1,308.6 | 19 |
| Hair care | 377.1 | 5 |
| Other | 38.1 | 1 |
| **Total** | **7,037.5** | **100** |

### Selected Brands

Aramis
Aveda
Beyond Paradise
Bobbi Brown
Bumble and bumble
Clinique
Darphin
DKNY for Women
Donna Karan (licensed)
Estée Lauder
Jo Malone
Kate Spade (licensed)
La Mer
M.A.C
Michael Kors Fragrances
Origins
Pleasures
Prescriptives
Proactiv
Rodan & Fields
Tommy Hilfiger (licensed)

## COMPETITORS

Alberto-Culver
Alticor
Avon
Baxter of California
BeautiControl
Beiersdorf
BeneFit Cosmetics
Body Shop
Bristol-Myers Squibb
Canderm Pharma
Chanel
Clarins
Coty Inc.
Dana Classic Fragrances
E Com Ventures
Elizabeth Arden Inc
Gap
Helen of Troy
Hydron
Inter Parfums
Joh. A. Benckiser
Kanebo
Kiehl's
Limited Brands
L'Oréal
LVMH
Mary Kay
Neiman Marcus
Nu Skin
OrthoNeutrogena
Procter & Gamble
Revlon
Sephora
Shiseido
Unilever NV

## HISTORICAL FINANCIALS

Company Type: Public

### Income Statement — FYE: June 30

| | REVENUE ($ mil.) | NET INCOME ($ mil.) | NET PROFIT MARGIN | EMPLOYEES |
|---|---|---|---|---|
| **6/07** | 7,038 | 449 | 6.4% | 28,500 |
| **6/06** | 6,464 | 244 | 3.8% | 26,200 |
| **6/05** | 6,336 | 406 | 6.4% | 23,700 |
| **6/04** | 5,790 | 342 | 5.9% | 22,200 |
| **6/03** | 5,118 | 320 | 6.2% | 21,500 |
| **Annual Growth** | 8.3% | 8.9% | — | 7.3% |

### 2007 Year-End Financials

Debt ratio: 85.7%
Return on equity: 31.8%
Cash ($ mil.): 254
Current ratio: 1.49
Long-term debt ($ mil.): 1,028
No. of shares (mil.): 113
Dividends
Yield: 1.1%
Payout: 23.1%
Market value ($ mil.): 5,121

### Stock History — NYSE: EL

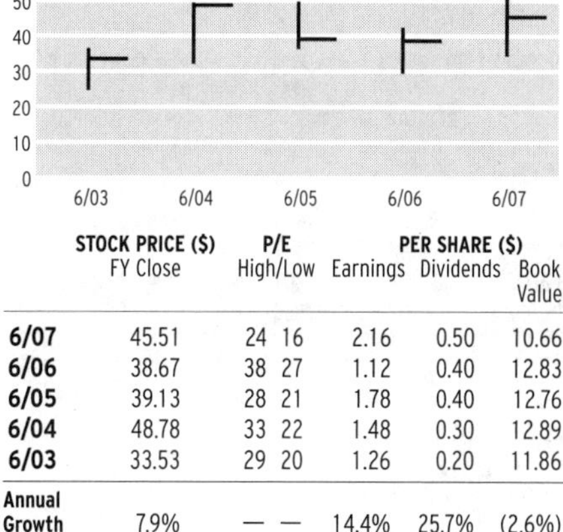


| | STOCK PRICE ($) FY Close | P/E High | P/E Low | PER SHARE ($) Earnings | Dividends | Book Value |
|---|---|---|---|---|---|---|
| **6/07** | 45.51 | 24 | 16 | 2.16 | 0.50 | 10.66 |
| **6/06** | 38.67 | 38 | 27 | 1.12 | 0.40 | 12.83 |
| **6/05** | 39.13 | 28 | 21 | 1.78 | 0.40 | 12.76 |
| **6/04** | 48.78 | 33 | 22 | 1.48 | 0.30 | 12.89 |
| **6/03** | 33.53 | 29 | 20 | 1.26 | 0.20 | 11.86 |
| **Annual Growth** | 7.9% | — | — | 14.4% | 25.7% | (2.6%) |

# E*TRADE Financial

E*TRADE wants you to use its services for E*VERYTHING financial. A top online brokerage, the company has more than 4 million account holders who can trade stock over the Internet (the majority of transactions) and by phone. The company also offers online and retail banking, mutual funds, market making, and stock plan administration services. It also performs trade-clearing services.

Active primarily in North America, E*TRADE Financial is trying to tap international markets through 16 retail brokerage Web sites in more than a dozen countries throughout Europe, Australia, and the Pacific Rim.

International growth target markets include China, India, and the United Arab Emirates. At home, the company is targeting affluent individuals with premium trading and money management services, including a flat commission rate and reduced fees for active traders. In order to keep pace with TD Ameritrade (the result of the merger of rivals Ameritrade and TD Waterhouse), the company has been expanding its client base and product menu through acquisitions. In 2005 it bought US-based online brokerage Harris*direct* from Bank of Montreal, as well as the J.P. Morgan Invest unit BrownCo, which served experienced online traders. The acquisitions have been integrated and their clients converted to the E*TRADE platform. To build its wealth management business, E*TRADE in 2005 and 2006 purchased several money managers, including Boston-area investment advisory firm Kobren Insight Management. Subsidiary E*TRADE Bank offers deposits, loans, credit cards, insurance, and other services online, and customers can transfer funds between their banking and brokerage accounts in real-time. Its banking clients are concentrated in metropolitan areas, and the company has some two dozen retail financial centers in major cites throughout the US.

Although it had built one of the largest ATM networks in the US, E*TRADE decided that business didn't jibe with its core brokerage and banking activities. In 2004 the company sold its ATM operations to Cardtronics, but retained some branding rights. The following year E*TRADE sold its consumer finance operations to what is now GE Money and exited the institutional trading business.

## HISTORY

In 1982 physicist William Porter created Trade Plus, an electronic brokerage service for stockbrokers; clients included Charles Schwab & Co. and Fidelity Brokerage Services. A decade later subsidiary E*TRADE Securities became CompuServe's first online securities trader.

In 1996 E*TRADE moved from the institutional side to retail when it launched its Web site. Christos Cotsakos (a Vietnam and FedEx veteran) became CEO and took the firm public. But there were problems: E*TRADE covered $1.7 million in customer losses and added backup systems after computer failure stymied user access. In 1997 it formed alliances with America Online and BANK ONE and ended the year with 225,000 accounts.

The firm began to position itself globally in 1997 and 1998, opening sites for Australian, Canadian, German, Israeli, and Japanese customers. It offered its first IPO (Sportline USA) in

1997. Volume grew as Internet trading increased, but technical glitches dogged E*TRADE. In 1999 day trading became fashionable and the company began running ads promoting prudent trading to counter criticism that online trading fosters a get-rich-quick mentality.

The company also continued to add services. In 1999 it teamed with Garage.com to offer affluent clients venture capital investments in young companies and launched online investment bank E*OFFERING with former Robertson Stephens & Co. chairman Sanford Robertson. (E*TRADE sold its stake in the bank to Wit Soundview — which later became SoundView Technology Group — the next year.) It also bought TIR Holdings, which executes and settles multi-currency securities transactions.

Retail banking was a major focus in 2000. The company bought Telebanc Financial (now E*TRADE Financial), owner of Telebank, an online bank with more than 100,000 depositors, and started E*TRADE Bank, which offers retail banking products on the E*TRADE Web site. To provide clients with "real-world" access to their money, it bought Card Capture Services, an operator of more than 9,000 ATMs across the US.

Continuing to expand its global reach, E*TRADE bought the part of its E*TRADE UK joint venture it didn't already own; acquired Canadian firm VERSUS Technologies, a provider of electronic trading services; and teamed with UBS Warburg to allow non-US investors to buy US securities without needing to trade in dollars. Later its E*Trade International Capital announced plans to offer IPOs to European investors.

In 2001 E*TRADE entered consumer lending when it bought online mortgage originator LoansDirect (now E*TRADE Mortgage). Also that year the company bought online brokerage Web Street, and moved to the NYSE. In late 2002 E*TRADE Bank purchased Ganis Credit Corp. (a US-based unit of Germany's Deutsche Bank) to boost its consumer finance business.

E*TRADE purchased the online trading operations of Tradescape in mid-2002. The deal, which cost E*TRADE $280 million, was hashed out the previous April — just days after rival Ameritrade announced its acquisition of online brokerage Datek.

Cotsakos resigned in early 2003, days after the company issued a gloomy forecast (he also had been criticized for his 2001 pay of $80 million, although he subsequently gave up about $20 million). He was replaced by company president Mitch Caplan, who has been viewed as instrumental in the company's effort to integrate brokerage and banking operations.

## EXECUTIVES

**Chairman:** George A. Hayter, age 68
**CEO and Director:** Mitchell H. (Mitch) Caplan, age 48, $4,300,000 pay
**President, COO, and Director:** R. Jarrett Lilien, age 43, $3,900,000 pay (prior to title change)
**CFO:** Robert J. (Rob) Simmons, age 43, $2,006,000 pay
**SVP, Corporate Communications:** Pam Erickson
**SVP, Investor Relations:** Adam Townsend
**Chief Administrative and Banking Officer; President, E*TRADE Bank:** Arlen W. Gelbard, age 49, $2,006,000 pay
**Chief Technology and Operations Officer; President, E*TRADE Technologies:** Joshua S. (Josh) Levine, age 52
**Chief Government Affairs Officer:** Betsy Barclay
**Chief Communications Officer:** Connie M. Dotson
**Chief Marketing Officer:** Nicholas A. (Nick) Utton
**General Counsel and Corporate Secretary:** Russell S. (Russ) Elmer, age 41
**Chairman, E*TRADE Futures:** John F. (Jack) Sandner, age 65
**Division President, E*TRADE Capital Markets:** Dennis Webb, age 41, $2,453,845 pay
**Senior Director, Interactive and Alliance Marketing:** Alison Mittelstadt
**Managing Director, International Development:** James R. (Jim) Bidwell
**Auditors:** Deloitte & Touche LLP

## LOCATIONS

**HQ:** E*TRADE Financial Corporation
135 E. 57th St., New York, NY 10022
**Phone:** 646-521-4300 **Fax:** 212-826-2803
**Web:** www.etrade.com

### 2006 Sales

| | $ mil. | % of total |
|---|---|---|
| North America | | |
| US | 2152.2 | 89 |
| Canada | 66.8 | 3 |
| Europe | 147.8 | 6 |
| Asia | 53.5 | 2 |
| **Total** | **2,420.3** | **100** |

## PRODUCTS/OPERATIONS

### 2006 Sales

| | $ mil. | % of total |
|---|---|---|
| Net operating interest income after provision for loan losses | 1,355.1 | 56 |
| Commissions | 625.3 | 26 |
| Service charges & fees | 137.4 | 6 |
| Principal transactions | 110.2 | 4 |
| Gain on sales of loans & securities | 56.0 | 2 |
| Other | 136.3 | 6 |
| **Total** | **2,420.3** | **100** |

### 2006 Sales By Segment

| | $ mil. | % of total |
|---|---|---|
| Retail business | 1,654.1 | 68 |
| Institutional business | 777.4 | 32 |
| Eliminations | (11.2) | — |
| **Total** | **2,420.3** | **100** |

## COMPETITORS

A.G. Edwards
Charles Schwab
FMR
Merrill Lynch
Morgan Stanley
NetBank
Scottrade
ShareBuilder
Siebert Financial
TD Ameritrade
UBS Financial Services

## HISTORICAL FINANCIALS

Company Type: Public

### Income Statement

FYE: December 31

| | REVENUE ($ mil.) | NET INCOME ($ mil.) | NET PROFIT MARGIN | EMPLOYEES |
|---|---|---|---|---|
| **12/06** | 2,420 | 629 | 26.0% | 4,100 |
| **12/05** | 2,537 | 430 | 17.0% | 3,400 |
| **12/04** | 2,083 | 381 | 18.3% | 3,300 |
| **12/03** | 2,008 | 203 | 10.1% | 3,500 |
| **12/02** | 1,902 | (186) | — | 3,500 |
| **Annual Growth** | 6.2% | — | — | 4.0% |

### 2006 Year-End Financials

Debt ratio: 170.8%
Return on equity: 16.6%
Cash ($ mil.): 1,672
Current ratio: —
Long-term debt ($ mil.): 7,166
No. of shares (mil.): 426
Dividends
Yield: —
Payout: —
Market value ($ mil.): 9,558

### Stock History

NASDAQ (GS): ETFC

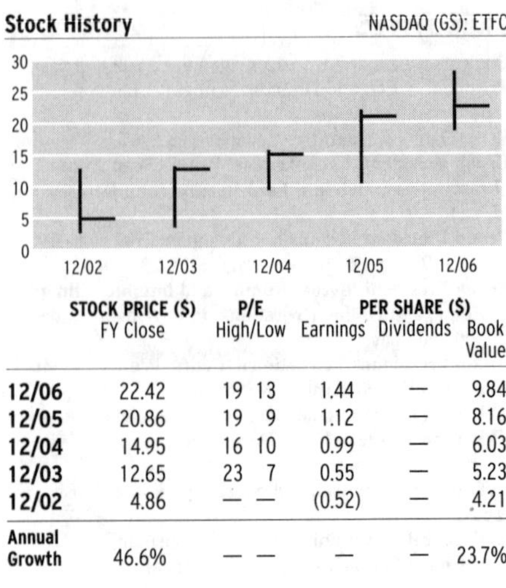


| | STOCK PRICE ($) FY Close | P/E High | P/E Low | PER SHARE ($) Earnings | PER SHARE ($) Dividends | PER SHARE ($) Book Value |
|---|---|---|---|---|---|---|
| **12/06** | 22.42 | 19 | 13 | 1.44 | — | 9.84 |
| **12/05** | 20.86 | 19 | 9 | 1.12 | — | 8.16 |
| **12/04** | 14.95 | 16 | 10 | 0.99 | — | 6.03 |
| **12/03** | 12.65 | 23 | 7 | 0.55 | — | 5.23 |
| **12/02** | 4.86 | — | — | (0.52) | — | 4.21 |
| **Annual Growth** | 46.6% | — | — | — | — | 23.7% |

# E. W. Scripps

There sure is a lot of TV watching going on at this newspaper company. The E. W. Scripps Company is a venerable newspaper publisher with a portfolio of about 20 daily papers including *The Commercial Appeal* (Memphis, Tennessee) and the *Denver Rocky Mountain News*. However, the lion's share of the company's revenue comes from its Scripps Networks unit which operates a collection of cable TV channels including Home & Garden Television (HGTV) and the Food Network (70%-owned). In addition, Scripps owns 10 TV stations around the country; its United Media subsidiary syndicates more than 150 comic strips, including *Peanuts* and *Dilbert*. Trusts benefiting the Scripps family own almost 90% of the company.

In addition to making up the bulk of its business, Scripps' television operations have also been helping support the company while its newspaper businesses struggle. Its popular lifestyle channels, by targeting such niche interests as food and home improvement, have gained a solid foothold in the fragmented world of cable television. Its channels also operate popular Web sites offering advice and information, further strengthening their popularity among fans.

Not all of Scripps' TV ventures have been so popular, however. In 2006 the company shuttered the money-losing Shop At Home network, selling most of its assets to Jewelry Television for $17 million. Scripps later sold its five Shop At Home affiliate television stations to Multicultural Television Broadcasting for $170 million.

The company has made additional moves to branch out into interactive media, acquiring comparison shopping site Shopzilla in 2005 and UK-based shopping site uSwitch the following year. Both have delivered strong revenue gains as online advertising continues to grow; Internet businesses now account for about 10% of Scripps' revenue.

The company was also one of a group of newspaper publishers to strike a deal with Yahoo's HotJobs in 2006, allowing them to sell listings on the online classified company's site. The newspapers can sell combined print and online ads, or just the online ads. The deal also allows the company to sell access to HotJobs' resume database.

In 2007 former chairman and family scion Charles Scripps died.

## HISTORY

Edward Willis "E. W." Scripps launched a newspaper empire in 1878 with his creation of *The Penny Press* in Cleveland. While adding to his string of inexpensive newspapers, Scripps demonstrated his fondness for economy by shunning "extras" such as toilet paper and pencils for his employees.

In 1907 Scripps gave the Associated Press a new rival, combining three wire services to form United Press. E. W. Scripps' health began deteriorating in the 1920s, and Roy Howard was named chairman. Howard's contribution to the burgeoning media enterprise soon was acknowledged when the company's name was changed to the Scripps Howard League. E. W. Scripps died in 1926, leaving a newspaper chain second in size only to Hearst.

In the 1930s Scripps made a foray into radio, buying WCPO (Cincinnati) and KNOX (Knoxville, Tennessee). Roy Howard placed his son Jack in charge of Scripps' radio holdings; under Jack's leadership, Scripps branched into TV. Its first TV station, Cleveland's WEWS, began broadcasting in 1947. Scripps also made Charlie Brown a household name when it launched the *Peanuts* comic strip in 1950. By the time Charles Scripps (E. W. Scripps' grandson) became chairman and Jack Howard was appointed president in 1953, the company had amassed 19 newspapers and a handful of radio and TV stations.

United Press merged with Hearst's International News Service in 1958 to become United Press International (UPI). In 1963 Scripps took its broadcasting holdings public as Scripps Howard Broadcasting Company (Scripps retained controlling interest). Scripps Howard Broadcasting expanded its TV station portfolio in the 1970s and 1980s, buying KJRH (Tulsa, Oklahoma; 1971), KSHB (Kansas City; 1977), KNXV (Phoenix; 1985), WFTS (Tampa; 1986), and WXYZ (Detroit; 1986).

With UPI facing mounting losses, Scripps sold the news service in 1982. Under leadership of chief executive Lawrence Leser, Scripps began streamlining, jettisoning extraneous investments and refocusing on its core business lines. In 1988 after decades of family ownership, the company went public as The E. W. Scripps Company (the Scripps family retained a controlling interest).

In 1994 Scripps Howard Broadcasting merged back into E. W. Scripps Company. That year Scripps branched into cable TV when its Home & Garden Television network went on the air. Former newspaper editor William Burleigh became CEO in 1996. Scripps' 1997 purchase of the newspaper and broadcast operations of Harte-Hanks marked the largest acquisition in its history. Scripps promptly traded Harte-Hanks' broadcasting operations for a controlling interest in the Food Network.

Scripps sold television production unit Scripps Howard Productions in 1998. The company sold its Dallas Community Newspaper Group in 1999 and launched the Do It Yourself cable network and affiliated Web site later that year. In 2000 Scripps' financially struggling *Rocky Mountain News* entered into a joint operating agreement with rival *The Denver Post* (owned by MediaNews). The Justice Department approved the agreement in 2001. Scripps launched cable channel Fine Living, aimed at affluent households, in 2002. That year the company shuttered its Scripps Ventures fund, which invested in Internet and online commerce businesses.

In late 2002 the company bought a 70% stake in home shopping network company Summit America Television (owner of the Shop At Home cable network) for $49 million. It bought the remaining 30% of the company in 2004.

Scripps made a foray into online shopping when it acquired comparison shopping site Shopzilla in 2005. The following year Scripps bought UK-based shopping site uSwitch.

The Shop At Home network came to an end in 2006 when Scripps shut down the network after several years of nothing but losses at the channel.

## EXECUTIVES

**Chairman:** William R. Burleigh, age 71
**President, CEO, and Director:** Kenneth W. (Ken) Lowe, age 56, $1,050,000 pay
**EVP and COO:** Richard A. (Rich) Boehne, age 50, $1,273,312 pay
**EVP Finance and Administration and CFO:** Joseph G. (Joe) NeCastro, age 50, $550,000 pay
**SVP and General Counsel:** Anatolio B. Cruz III, age 48
**SVP; President, Scripps Networks:** John F. Lansing, age 49, $575,000 pay
**SVP Human Resources:** Jennifer L. Weber, age 40
**SVP Interactive Media:** Tim A. Peterman, age 39
**SVP Newspapers:** Mark G. Contreras, age 45, $473,250 pay
**SVP Technology Operations:** Mark S. Hale, age 48
**SVP Television Station Group:** William B. (Bill) Peterson, age 63
**VP and Controller:** Lori A. Hickok, age 43
**VP and Treasurer:** E. John Wolfzorn, age 61
**VP, Corporate Secretary, and Director Legal Affairs:** Mary Denise Kuprionis, age 51
**VP Communications and Investor Relations:** Timothy E. (Tim) Stautberg, age 44
**VP Human Resources Operations:** Lisa Knutson, age 40
**Auditors:** Deloitte & Touche LLP

## LOCATIONS

**HQ:** The E. W. Scripps Company
312 Walnut St., Cincinnati, OH 45202
**Phone:** 513-977-3000 **Fax:** 513-977-3721
**Web:** www.scripps.com

## PRODUCTS/OPERATIONS

### 2006 Sales

| | $ mil. | % of total |
|---|---|---|
| Scripps networks | 1,052.4 | 42 |
| Newspapers | 718.5 | 29 |
| Broadcast television | 363.5 | 14 |
| Interactive media | 271.1 | 11 |
| Licensing | 94.6 | 4 |
| Other | (2.0) | — |
| **Total** | **2,498.1** | **100** |

### Selected Operations

Scripps networks
- DIY Network
- Fine Living (90%)
- Food Network (70%)
- FOX Sports Net South (12%)
- Great American Country
- HGTV (Home and Garden Television)

Newspapers
- *Abilene Reporter-News* (Texas)
- *Albuquerque Tribune* (jointly operated, New Mexico)
- *Anderson Independent-Mail* (South Carolina)
- *Cincinnati Post* (jointly operated)
- *Corpus Christi Caller-Times* (Texas)
- *Denver Rocky Mountain News* (jointly operated)
- *Evansville Courier & Press* (Indiana)
- *Ft. Pierce Tribune* (Florida)
- *Henderson Gleaner* (Kentucky)
- *Kitsap Sun* (Washington)
- *Knoxville News Sentinel* (Tennessee)
- *Memphis Commercial Appeal* (Tennessee)
- *Naples Daily News* (Florida)
- *Redding Record-Searchlight* (California)
- *San Angelo Standard-Times* (Texas)
- *Stuart News* (Florida)
- *Ventura County Star* (California)
- *Vero Beach Press Journal* (Florida)
- *Wichita Falls Times Record News* (Texas)

Television stations
- KJRH (NBC; Tulsa, OK)
- KMCI (Ind; Lawrence, KS)
- KNXV (ABC, Phoenix)
- KSHB (ABC, Kansas City)
- WCPO (ABC, Cincinnati)
- WEWS (ABC, Cleveland)
- WFTS (ABC, Tampa)
- WMAR (ABC, Baltimore)
- WPTV (NBC; West Palm Beach, FL)
- WXYZ (ABC, Detroit)

Interactive media
- Shopzilla (comparison shopping site)
- uSwitch (comparison shopping service, UK)

## COMPETITORS

A&E Networks
Advance Publications
CBS
Community Newspaper Holdings
Discovery Communications
Dow Jones
FOX Broadcasting
Gannett
Hearst-Argyle Television
ION Media Networks
McClatchy Company
MediaNews
Meredith
MTV Networks
NBC Universal Cable
New York Times
Raycom
Sinclair Broadcast Group
Tribune
Turner Broadcasting
Washington Post

## HISTORICAL FINANCIALS

Company Type: Public

### Income Statement

FYE: December 31

| | REVENUE ($ mil.) | NET INCOME ($ mil.) | NET PROFIT MARGIN | EMPLOYEES |
|---|---|---|---|---|
| **12/06** | 2,498 | 353 | 14.1% | 9,000 |
| **12/05** | 2,514 | 249 | 9.9% | 9,600 |
| **12/04** | 2,168 | 304 | 14.0% | 8,900 |
| **12/03** | 1,875 | 271 | 14.4% | 7,800 |
| **12/02** | 1,619 | 188 | 11.6% | 7,700 |
| **Annual Growth** | 11.5% | 17.0% | — | 4.0% |

### 2006 Year-End Financials

Debt ratio: 29.7%
Return on equity: 14.5%
Cash ($ mil.): 33
Current ratio: 2.19
Long-term debt ($ mil.): 766
No. of shares (mil.): 127
Dividends
Yield: 0.9%
Payout: 22.0%
Market value ($ mil.): 6,341

**Stock History** NYSE: SSP

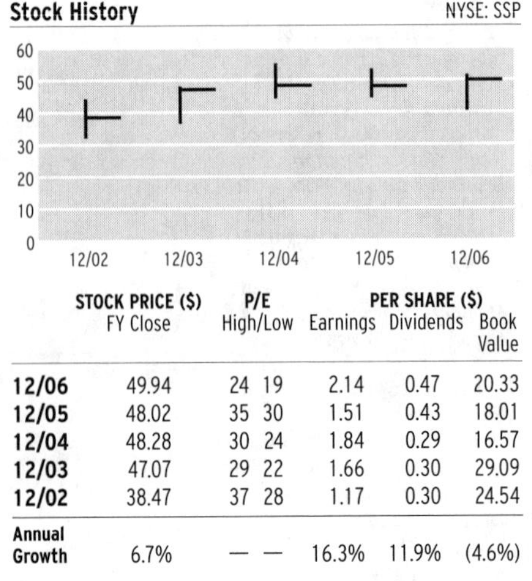


| | STOCK PRICE ($) FY Close | P/E High/Low | | PER SHARE ($) Earnings | Dividends | Book Value |
|---|---|---|---|---|---|---|
| **12/06** | 49.94 | 24 | 19 | 2.14 | 0.47 | 20.33 |
| **12/05** | 48.02 | 35 | 30 | 1.51 | 0.43 | 18.01 |
| **12/04** | 48.28 | 30 | 24 | 1.84 | 0.29 | 16.57 |
| **12/03** | 47.07 | 29 | 22 | 1.66 | 0.30 | 29.09 |
| **12/02** | 38.47 | 37 | 28 | 1.17 | 0.30 | 24.54 |
| **Annual Growth** | 6.7% | — | — | 16.3% | 11.9% | (4.6%) |

# Exelon Corporation

The City of Brotherly Love meets the Windy City in utility holding company Exelon. The company distributes electricity to 5.4 million customers in northern Illinois (including Chicago) and in southeastern Pennsylvania (including Philadelphia) through subsidiaries Commonwealth Edison (ComEd) and PECO Energy. PECO also distributes natural gas to 480,000 customers.

Subsidiary Exelon Generation holds the firm's power plants, which produce 25,543 MW of capacity. Exelon Power Team is a top wholesale energy marketer, and Exelon Energy markets retail power and offers other energy-related services.

Exelon was formed in 2000 when Philadelphia-based PECO Energy bought Chicago-based Unicom. Both PECO and Unicom were leading nuclear plant operators, and about 60% of Exelon's generating capacity comes from nuclear plants. The company is expanding its Exelon Generation unit through new plant construction and acquisitions. Exelon has also been looking to expand its regulated utility operations through the acquisition of a smaller utility company. In 2006 Exelon dropped its bid to buy New Jersey utility Public Service Enterprise Group (PSEG).

To focus on core utility operations, the company has sold its infrastructure construction business, InfraSource, and its facility and infrastructure management business, Exelon Solutions. Exelon has completed the sale of its interest in telecommunications joint venture PECO TelCove, which provides voice and data services, to its partner TelCove, and it has sold its district heating and cooling division (Thermal Chicago) to Macquarie Bank. The company plans to sell additional noncore assets.

## HISTORY

Thomas Dolan and local investors formed the Brush Electric Light Company of Philadelphia in 1881 to provide street and commercial lighting. Competitors sprang up, and in 1885 Brush merged with the United States Electric Lighting Company of Pennsylvania to form a secret "electric trust," or holding company. Dolan became president in 1886 and bought four other utilities.

In 1895 Martin Maloney formed Pennsylvania Heat Light and Power to consolidate the city's electric companies. By the next year it had acquired, among other businesses, Columbia Electric Light, Philadelphia Edison, and the electric trust. In 1899 a new firm, National Electric, challenged Maloney by acquiring neighboring rival Southern Electric Light. Before retiring, Maloney negotiated the merger of the two firms, forming Philadelphia Electric in 1902.

Demand rose rapidly into the 1920s, fueled in part by the company's promotion of electric appliances. In 1928, the year after it completed the Conowingo Hydroelectric Station, Philadelphia Electric was absorbed by the much larger United Gas Improvement. United Gas avoided large layoffs during the Depression, but passage of the Public Utility Holding Company Act (PUHCA) in 1935 sounded its death knell. (PUHCA was repealed in 2005.) In 1943 the SEC forced United Gas to divest Philadelphia Electric.

Philadelphia Electric built several plants in the 1950s and 1960s in response to a postwar electricity boom. A small experimental nuclear reactor was completed at Peach Bottom, Pennsylvania, in 1967, and in 1974 the company placed two nuclear units in service at the plant. The Salem (New Jersey) nuke (Unit 1) followed in 1977. The company relied on these plants during the OPEC oil crisis. Another one, Limerick Unit 1, began operations in 1986, and Unit 2 went on line in 1990, but the Peach Bottom plant was shut down from 1989 to 1991 because of management problems (later resolved).

The company began reorganizing in 1993 and the next year changed its name to PECO Energy Company. It also sold Maryland retail subsidiary Conowingo Power, retaining the hydroelectric plant. In 1995 rival PP&L rejected PECO's acquisition bid, citing PECO's nuclear liabilities.

A year later PECO teamed with AT&T Wireless to offer PCS in Philadelphia (service was launched in 1997). EnergyOne, a national venture formed in 1997 by PECO, UtiliCorp United (now Aquila), and AT&T, offered consumers a package of power, phone, and Internet services on one bill. However, the slow deregulation process caused the venture to fail.

PECO also joined with British Energy in 1997 to form AmerGen, hoping to buy nukes at rock-bottom prices from utilities eager to unload them. AmerGen purchased three nuclear facilities in 1999 and 2000: Unit 1 of the Three Mile Island (Pennsylvania) facility; the Clinton, Illinois, facility; and the Oyster Creek (New Jersey) facility.

In 1999 PECO announced plans to acquire Chicago's Unicom, the parent company of Commonwealth Edison (ComEd). After the deal was completed in 2000, the combined company took the name Exelon and established its headquarters in Chicago.

Pennsylvania's utility markets were fully deregulated in 2000. To expand its power generation business, Exelon that year bought 49.9% of Sithe Energies for $682 million. In 2001 Exelon agreed to buy two gas-fired power plants (2,300 MW) in Texas from TXU for $443 million; the deal was completed in 2002.

Also in 2002, Exelon purchased Sithe Energies' stakes in six New England power plants with 2,000 MW of capacity (plus 2,400 MW under construction) for $543 million plus the assumption of $1.15 billion in debt. The company also sold its Philadelphia PCS venture interest to former partner AT&T Wireless Services (now part of AT&T Mobility). Sithe Energies was sold to Dynegy in 2005 for $135 million.

## EXECUTIVES

**Chairman, President, and CEO:** John W. Rowe, age 61
**EVP Finance and Markets and CFO; EVP Finance and Markets and CFO, PECO; EVP Finance and Markets and CFO, Generation:** John F. Young, age 50, $546,767 pay
**EVP and Chief Human Resources Officer:** S. Gary Snodgrass, age 55
**EVP, Chief Administrative Officer, and Chief Legal Officer:** Randall E. Mehrberg, age 50, $556,767 pay
**EVP Government and Environmental Affairs and Public Policy:** Elizabeth Ann (Betsy) Moler, age 58
**EVP and Chief of Staff; President, ComEd:** Frank M. Clark Jr., age 61, $440,000 pay
**EVP; President, Exelon Energy Delivery; President, Exelon Generation:** John L. (Jack) Skolds, age 56, $630,959 pay
**EVP; President, Exelon Power Team:** Ian P. McLean, age 57
**SVP, Exelon Generation; President, Exelon Power:** Mark A. Schiavoni, age 51
**SVP; President and Chief Nuclear Officer, Exelon Nuclear:** Christopher M. (Chris) Crane, age 48
**SVP and Corporate Controller:** Matthew F. Hilzinger, age 43
**SVP and CIO:** Dan Hill
**SVP and Treasurer:** Michael Metzner
**VP Investor Relations:** Chaka Patterson, age 38
**President, ComEd:** J. Barry Mitchell, age 59
**President, PECO Energy:** Denis P. O'Brien, age 46
**Manager External Communications:** Jennifer Medley
**Auditors:** PricewaterhouseCoopers LLP

## LOCATIONS

**HQ:** Exelon Corporation
10 S. Dearborn St., 37th Fl., Chicago, IL 60680
**Phone:** 312-394-7398 **Fax:** 312-394-7945
**Web:** www.exeloncorp.com

Exelon distributes electricity in Illinois and Pennsylvania.

## PRODUCTS/OPERATIONS

### 2006 Sales

| | $ mil. | % of total |
|---|---|---|
| Generation | 9,143 | 43 |
| ComEd | 6,101 | 29 |
| PECO | 5,168 | 24 |
| Other | 807 | 4 |
| Adjustments | (5,564) | — |
| **Total** | **15,655** | **100** |

### Major Operating Units, Subsidiaries, and Affiliates

Exelon Energy Delivery
- Commonweath Edison Company (ComEd, electric utility)
- PECO Energy Company (PECO, electric and gas utility)

Exelon Generation Company, LLC
- AmerGen Energy Company, LLC (independent power producer)
- Exelon Energy (nonregulated retail power sales)
- Exelon Nuclear (nuclear power generation)

## COMPETITORS

AES
Allegheny Energy
Alliant Energy
Ameren
American Transmission
Aquila
CenterPoint Energy
Delmarva Power
Dominion Resources
Duke Energy
Duquesne Light Holdings
Dynegy
Entergy
FirstEnergy
FPL Group
Green Mountain Energy
Indeck Energy
Integrys Energy Group
Nicor
PG&E
PPL
PSEG
Reliant Energy
UGI

## HISTORICAL FINANCIALS

Company Type: Public

**Income Statement** FYE: December 31

| | REVENUE ($ mil.) | NET INCOME ($ mil.) | NET PROFIT MARGIN | EMPLOYEES |
|---|---|---|---|---|
| **12/06** | 15,655 | 1,592 | 10.2% | 17,200 |
| **12/05** | 15,357 | 923 | 6.0% | 17,200 |
| **12/04** | 14,515 | 1,864 | 12.8% | 17,300 |
| **12/03** | 15,812 | 905 | 5.7% | 20,000 |
| **12/02** | 14,955 | 1,440 | 9.6% | 25,200 |
| **Annual Growth** | 1.2% | 2.5% | — | (9.1%) |

**2006 Year-End Financials**

Debt ratio: 120.2%
Return on equity: 16.7%
Cash ($ mil.): 1,700
Current ratio: 0.86
Long-term debt ($ mil.): 11,989
No. of shares (mil.): 670
Dividends
Yield: 2.6%
Payout: 68.1%
Market value ($ mil.): 41,466

**Stock History** NYSE: EXC

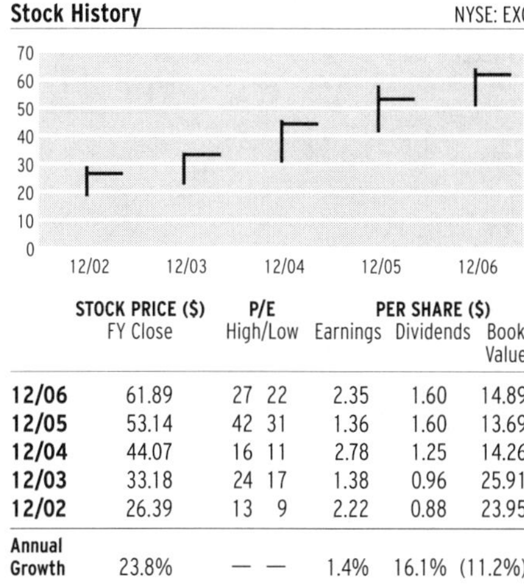


| | STOCK PRICE ($) FY Close | P/E High/Low | PER SHARE ($) Earnings | Dividends | Book Value |
|---|---|---|---|---|---|
| **12/06** | 61.89 | 27 22 | 2.35 | 1.60 | 14.89 |
| **12/05** | 53.14 | 42 31 | 1.36 | 1.60 | 13.69 |
| **12/04** | 44.07 | 16 11 | 2.78 | 1.25 | 14.26 |
| **12/03** | 33.18 | 24 17 | 1.38 | 0.96 | 25.91 |
| **12/02** | 26.39 | 13 9 | 2.22 | 0.88 | 23.95 |
| **Annual Growth** | 23.8% | — — | 1.4% | 16.1% | (11.2%) |

# Exide Technologies

Exide Technologies hopes you'll get a charge out of its products. The company makes lead-acid automotive and industrial batteries for customers that include retailers such as Wal-Mart and NAPA, and transportation giants such as Ford and Toyota. The company also makes batteries for boats, farm equipment, golf carts, locomotives, and wheelchairs, as well as backup power supply batteries for telecommunications, computer, and power plant systems. Brand names include Classic, Marathon, NASCAR Extreme, Sunlyte, and Super Crank. Exide emerged from Chapter 11 bankruptcy in 2004 a leaner organization. The company is challenged by rising prices for lead and other raw materials.

While in bankruptcy, Exide consolidated manufacturing and distribution facilities, reduced its workforce, and improved its supply chain processes.

Operations outside of the US account for more than half of sales.

The Securities and Exchange Commission opened a preliminary inquiry into statements made by Exide in 2005. The SEC's Enforcement Division is looking at what the company had to say about its ability to comply with fiscal 2005 loan covenants and about the "going concern" notice provided by its auditor for the 2005 10-K filing.

Sterling Capital Management owns about 14% of Exide Technologies, while Wells Fargo holds more than 10% of the company. Tontine Capital Management and Donald Smith & Co. each have equity stakes of nearly 10%. Stanfield Capital Partners owns nearly 8%. David J. Greene and Co. holds around 7%. Arklow Capital has an equity stake of more than 6%.

## HISTORY

Exide got its start in 1888 when Thomas Edison founded The Electric Storage Battery Company (ESB) in Gloucester, New Jersey, to develop a backup battery for steam engines and dynamos. By 1890 ESB had installed the first practical battery backup in a Philadelphia utility, and that year it also provided batteries for the US's first streetcars. Sales picked up as the versatility of the battery was recognized, and in 1898 ESB batteries powered the US Navy's first submarine. The company was soon the world's top battery maker.

The Exide brand name (short for "excellent oxide") debuted in 1900, and the firsts kept coming: the first automobile ignition battery (1903), the batteries used in the first transcontinental telephone services (1915), and the batteries used for the first air-conditioned train (1931). WWII saw the beginning of ESB's vertical integration, with the purchases of a maker of battery chargers and testers (1938) and a maker of battery containers (1946). ESB also developed battery-powered torpedoes used in WWII.

In 1951 Exide batteries assured the continuous operation of many Bell Systems relay stations for the first coast-to-coast wireless telephone network. In 1957 it entered the dry-cell battery business by acquiring the Ray-O-Vac Company. NASA used Exide batteries throughout the Apollo missions of the 1960s and 1970s, including the 1969 moon landing.

Inco Limited of Toronto purchased ESB in 1974. Management reorganized ESB in 1978 as a holding company, ESB Ray-O-Vac. The Exide brand stagnated, losing market share. In 1980 ESB Ray-O-Vac became INCO Electro Energy, with Exide as a subsidiary.

Investors led by the Spectrum Group and First Chicago Investment rescued Exide's North American operations in 1983. In 1985 the company hired ITT executive Arthur Hawkins as CEO and began a turnaround. Exide bought General Battery in 1987 to become #1 in the US auto battery market. The company acquired Speedclip Manufacturing (battery cables, terminals, and accessories; 1989) and Shadwood Industries (automotive battery chargers; fully acquired 1991) and went public in 1993.

Exide expanded into Europe in the mid-1990s, buying firms in France, Spain, and the UK, including two of the continent's largest battery makers. In 1997 it completed its European expansion by buying three battery-making units from Germany's CEAG AG.

Despite market dominance, Exide lost about 75% of its share value from 1996 to 1998. Some shareholders sued management, alleging misrepresentation, and the Florida attorney general and the SEC launched probes into whether the company sold used batteries as new. (In 1999 Exide settled with Florida, without admitting wrongdoing and it also settled with shareholders.) Amid these problems, Hawkins resigned as chairman and CEO and former Chrysler exec Robert Lutz replaced him.

In 2000 it acquired Pacific Dunlop's (now Ansell Limited) global battery business, GNB Technologies. Exide also sold its remanufactured starter and alternator business (Sure Start).

In 2001 Exide agreed to a plea deal with federal prosecutors whereby the company would pay out $27.5 million in fines over five years. The company admitted to making defective batteries, covering up the defects, and bribing a Sears, Roebuck buyer. That year the company changed its name from Exide Corporation to Exide Technologies.

Early in 2002 Exide filed Chapter 11 bankruptcy as a result of its acquisitions bender and poor conditions in the automotive sector. Later in the year Exide inked a deal to become the exclusive battery supplier to Volvo Truck Australia, giving the battery maker a 74% market share for heavy truck batteries in Australia.

Arthur Hawkins, the former CEO of Exide, was convicted in 2002 of fraudulently selling defective batteries to Sears Automotive Marketing Services, a subsidiary of Sears, Roebuck. He was sentenced to 10 years in federal prison; the sentence was upheld in 2005. Three other Exide executives were convicted of various federal charges.

When Exide emerged from Chapter 11 bankruptcy in 2004, the company had cut its debt by a reported 70%. That year the company combined its Motive Power and Network Power operations into one segment, Industrial Energy.

While Exide exited Chapter 11, it still experienced corporate pain — the company continued to lose money, and it shut down its lead-acid battery manufacturing plant in Shreveport, Louisiana, in mid-2006. The plant served Ford Motor and other after-market customers. The Shreveport factory had been operating since 1968. Production was shifted to other Exide facilities.

## EXECUTIVES

**Chairman:** John P. Reilly, age 63
**President, CEO, and Director:** Gordon A. Ulsh, age 61, $1,475,000 pay
**EVP and CFO:** Francis M. (Fran) Corby Jr., age 63
**EVP Human Resources and Communications:** George S. Jones Jr., age 54
**EVP and General Counsel:** Barbara A. Hatcher, age 51
**SVP and Controller:** Phillip A. Damaska, age 52, $64,169 pay (partial-year salary)
**VP US Aftermarket Sales and Branch System:** Jeff Barna
**VP Global Procurement:** Douglas Gillespie
**President Industrial Energy Europe:** Joel M. Campbell, age 60
**President Industrial Energy Americas:** Mitchell S. Bregman, age 53, $288,000 pay
**President Transportation Americas:** Edward J. (E.J.) O'Leary, age 51, $367,292 pay
**President Transportation Europe:** Rodolphe Reverchon, age 48
**Managing Director Asia Pacific:** Allan Moore
**Auditors:** PricewaterhouseCoopers LLP

## LOCATIONS

**HQ:** Exide Technologies
13000 Deerfield Pkwy., Bldg. 200,
Alpharetta, GA 30004
**Phone:** 678-566-9000 **Fax:** 678-566-9188
**Web:** www.exide.com

Exide Technologies has distribution and manufacturing facilities in Australia, Belgium, Canada, France, Germany, Italy, the Netherlands, New Zealand, Poland, Portugal, Spain, the UK, and the US.

## 2007 Sales

| | $ mil. | % of total |
|---|---|---|
| US | 1,296.8 | 44 |
| Germany | 376.1 | 13 |
| Spain | 244.1 | 8 |
| France | 224.2 | 8 |
| Italy | 197.5 | 7 |
| UK | 120.6 | 4 |
| Other countries | 480.5 | 16 |
| **Total** | **2,939.8** | **100** |

## PRODUCTS/OPERATIONS

### 2007 Sales

| | $ mil. | % of total |
|---|---|---|
| Transportation | 1,762.6 | 60 |
| Industrial Energy | 1,177.2 | 40 |
| **Total** | **2,939.8** | **100** |

### Selected Products

Automotive batteries (for agricultural equipment, buses, commercial trucks, construction equipment, and emergency and passenger vehicles)
Industrial batteries
Motive power batteries (for forklifts, golf carts, and wheelchairs)
Network power batteries (for telecommunication, industrial, and military applications)
Standby/backup batteries (for hospitals, security systems, traffic control, and elevators)

## COMPETITORS

BAE SYSTEMS
C&D Technologies
Douglas Battery
Eagle-Picher
East Penn
EnerSys
GS Yuasa
Hitachi
Imsa
Interstate Batteries
iQ Power
Johnson Controls Power Solutions
Matsushita Electric
SAFT
Valence Technology

## HISTORICAL FINANCIALS

Company Type: Public

### Income Statement

FYE: March 31

| | REVENUE ($ mil.) | NET INCOME ($ mil.) | NET PROFIT MARGIN | EMPLOYEES |
|---|---|---|---|---|
| **3/07** | 2,940 | (106) | — | 13,862 |
| **3/06** | 2,820 | (173) | — | 13,982 |
| **3/05** | 2,476 | (467) | — | 14,268 |
| **3/04** | 2,501 | (114) | — | — |
| **3/03** | 2,361 | (141) | — | — |
| **Annual Growth** | 5.6% | — | — | (1.4%) |

### 2007 Year-End Financials

Debt ratio: 201.7%
Return on equity: —
Cash ($ mil.): 76
Current ratio: 1.71
Long-term debt ($ mil.): 667
No. of shares (mil.): 61
Dividends
Yield: —
Payout: —
Market value ($ mil.): 528

### Stock History

NASDAQ (GM): XIDE

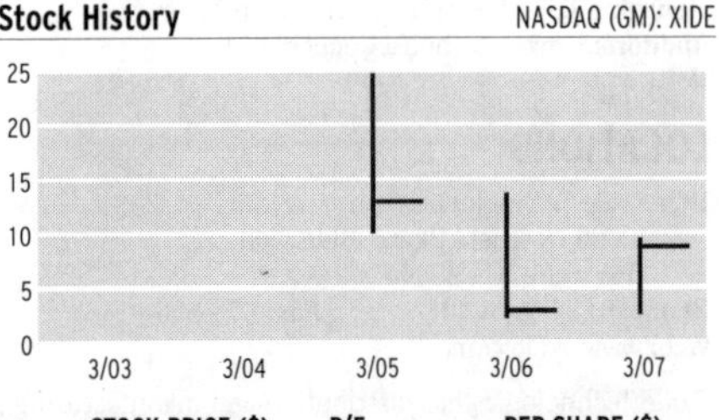


| | STOCK PRICE ($) FY Close | P/E High/Low | PER SHARE ($) Earnings | Dividends | Book Value |
|---|---|---|---|---|---|
| **3/07** | 8.70 | — — | (2.39) | — | 5.45 |
| **3/06** | 2.86 | — — | (6.91) | — | 9.16 |
| **3/05** | 12.90 | — — | (18.68) | — | 17.43 |
| **Annual Growth** | (17.9%) | — — | — | — | (44.1%) |

# Expeditors International

Need your goods moved expeditiously? Freight forwarder Expeditors International of Washington can help. As a freight forwarder, the company purchases air and ocean cargo space on a volume basis and resells that space to its customers at lower rates than they could obtain directly from the carriers. The company also acts as a customs broker for air and ocean freight shipped by its customers and offers supply chain management services. Expeditors operates from some 320 facilities, including those of agents, in more than 50 countries worldwide. More than half of the company's sales come from the Asia/Pacific region.

In its rapid development, Expeditors has favored internal growth over expansion by acquisition. The company continues to open new offices and to invest in its information technology infrastructure.

In the investment community, Expeditors and CEO Peter Rose have developed a reputation for straight shooting, thanks to the company's periodic filings with the SEC of answers to questions from analysts. One answer reads, in part: "We are freight forwarders not a seventh grade science project. We have read this question several times but for the life of us we cannot imagine what possible good would come from trying to calculate this number."

## HISTORY

After leaving the freight forwarding company that became Circle International (later acquired by EGL), Peter Rose used $55,000 in seed money to start his own company, Expeditors International of Washington, in 1979. Two years later Rose met with several fellow shipping veterans to implement their idea of combining freight forwarding and customs clearing services.

Expeditors soon had people beating a path to its door. It grew quickly to become a leading importer of goods made in Asia. Expeditors added export services in 1982 and went public in 1984. The next year it added ocean freight services to its offerings, and in 1986 it entered the European market. As the 1980s ended, the company had offices in 42 countries. Expeditors expanded into the Middle East in 1991 and, despite the economic doldrums of the early 1990s, opened 14 offices in 1992.

Expeditors also diversified with services such as long-term customs brokerage contracts and distribution. In 1997 it added truck and rail border brokerage services for the US, Mexico, and Canada. Expeditors continued to expand rapidly: In 1997 it added 22 offices and in 1999 opened still more, including five in Turkey and others in Greece, Lebanon, and the UK.

In 2000 Expeditors and other freight forwarders urged the US Department of Transportation to allow more dedicated air freighter service for the US-China market.

## EXECUTIVES

**Chairman and CEO:** Peter J. Rose, age 63, $110,000 pay
**President and COO:** Glenn M. Alger, age 50, $100,000 pay
**EVP, CFO, Treasurer, and Director:** R. Jordan Gates, age 51, $100,000 pay
**EVP, Global Customs:** Rosanne Esposito, age 55
**EVP, Global Sales:** Timothy C. Barber, age 47
**SVP, General Counsel, and Secretary:** Jeffrey J. King, age 51
**SVP and CIO:** Jeffrey S. Musser, age 41
**SVP and Corporate Controller:** Charles J. Lynch, age 46
**SVP, Air Cargo:** Roger A. Idiart, age 53
**SVP, Ocean Cargo:** William J. Coogan, age 49
**SVP, Ocean Services:** Daniel R. Wall, age 38
**SVP, South Asia:** Andrew Goh
**VP, General Counsel, and Secretary:** Amy J. Tangeman, age 38
**VP, Americas, Sales and Marketing:** Carol Kijac
**VP, Training and Personnel Development:** Samuel R. Bokor
**President, Asia and Director:** James L. K. Wang, age 59, $105,879 pay
**President, Europe, Africa, Near/Middle East, and Indian Subcontinent:** Rommel C. Saber, age 49
**President, The Americas:** Robert L. Villanueva, age 54, $100,000 pay
**COO, Asia:** Sandy K. Y. Liu, age 59
**Auditors:** KPMG LLP

## LOCATIONS

**HQ:** Expeditors International of Washington, Inc.
1015 3rd Ave., 12th Fl., Seattle, WA 98104
**Phone:** 206-674-3400 **Fax:** 206-674-3459
**Web:** www.expeditors.com

### 2006 Sales

| | $ mil. | % of total |
|---|---|---|
| Asia | 2,616.1 | 57 |
| North America | | |
| US | 932.2 | 20 |
| Other countries | 120.4 | 3 |
| Europe | 619.0 | 13 |
| Middle East | 215.9 | 5 |
| Latin America | 67.5 | 1 |
| Australia & New Zealand | 54.9 | 1 |
| **Total** | **4,626.0** | **100** |

## PRODUCTS/OPERATIONS

### 2006 Sales

| | $ mil. | % of total |
|---|---|---|
| Airfreight | 2,229.5 | 48 |
| Ocean freight & ocean services | 1,553.1 | 34 |
| Customs brokerage & other services | 843.4 | 18 |
| **Total** | **4,626.0** | **100** |

## COMPETITORS

APL Logistics
C.H. Robinson Worldwide
DHL
EGL Eagle Global Logistics
FedEx Trade Networks
GeoLogistics
Kintetsu World Express
Kuehne + Nagel
Mitsui-Soko
Nippon Express
Panalpina
Schenker
Sinotrans
UPS Supply Chain Solutions
UTi Worldwide

## HISTORICAL FINANCIALS

Company Type: Public

**Income Statement** FYE: December 31

| | REVENUE ($ mil.) | NET INCOME ($ mil.) | NET PROFIT MARGIN | EMPLOYEES |
|---|---|---|---|---|
| **12/06** | 4,626 | 235 | 5.1% | 11,600 |
| **12/05** | 3,902 | 219 | 5.6% | 10,600 |
| **12/04** | 3,318 | 156 | 4.7% | 9,400 |
| **12/03** | 2,625 | 122 | 4.6% | 8,600 |
| **12/02** | 2,297 | 113 | 4.9% | 8,000 |
| **Annual Growth** | 19.1% | 20.2% | — | 9.7% |

**2006 Year-End Financials**

Debt ratio: —
Return on equity: 23.7%
Cash ($ mil.): 512
Current ratio: 1.89
Long-term debt ($ mil.): —
No. of shares (mil.): 213
Dividends
Yield: 0.5%
Payout: 20.8%
Market value ($ mil.): 8,630

**Stock History** NASDAQ (GS): EXPD

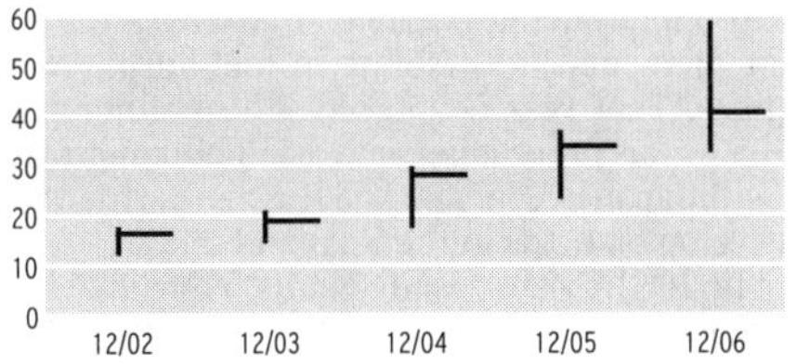

| | STOCK PRICE ($) FY Close | P/E High | P/E Low | PER SHARE ($) Earnings | PER SHARE ($) Dividends | PER SHARE ($) Book Value |
|---|---|---|---|---|---|---|
| **12/06** | 40.50 | 55 | 31 | 1.06 | 0.22 | 5.02 |
| **12/05** | 33.76 | 37 | 24 | 0.98 | 0.15 | 8.57 |
| **12/04** | 27.94 | 41 | 25 | 0.70 | 0.11 | 7.57 |
| **12/03** | 18.83 | 36 | 26 | 0.56 | 0.08 | 6.14 |
| **12/02** | 16.33 | 33 | 24 | 0.51 | 0.06 | 5.03 |
| **Annual Growth** | 25.5% | — | — | 20.1% | 38.4% | (0.0%) |

# Express Scripts

Express Scripts knows its customers like their drugs fast. One of the largest pharmacy benefits management (PBM) companies in North America, Express Scripts has about 50 million members in the US and Canada. Members have access to a network of about 57,000 retail pharmacies and several home delivery pharmacies. Express Scripts processes more than 400 million prescriptions per year, designs formularies, and offers such services as disease management programs and consumer drug data analysis. Its pharma business solutions segment offers specialty drug packaging, drug sample distribution, and other services. Clients include HMOs and other health insurers, self-insured businesses, and union benefits plans.

Express Scripts launched a hostile takeover bid for its larger rival Caremark Rx (now Caremark Pharmacy Services) in late 2006, topping a previous offer made by drug store chain CVS. However, Caremark's board and its shareholders rejected the bid the following year.

The company is especially keen to develop its specialty pharmacy division, CuraScript, which provides distribution of injectable, infusible, and other high-cost specialty drugs to patients' homes, doctors' offices, and other health care providers. It grew the unit significantly in 2005 with the acquisition of rival Priority Healthcare.

The company owns a third of RxHub, which provides software enabling doctors to write electronic prescriptions and submit them electronically to pharmacies. The technology also allows pharmacies to communicate electronically with PBMs and health plans. Rivals AdvancePCS (now part of Caremark) and Medco Health Solutions also have stakes in the IT firm.

## HISTORY

In 1986 St. Louis-based drugstore chain Medicare-Glaser and HMO Sanus joined forces to create Express Scripts, which would manage the HMO's prescription program. Express Scripts began managing third-party programs in 1988 and later developed other operations: Mail-order prescription, infusion therapy, and vision services. New York Life bought Sanus and picked up the rest of Express Scripts in 1989 when Medicare-Glaser went into bankruptcy.

In 1992 Express Scripts went public. The next year the company formed subsidiary Practice Patterns Science to begin profiling providers and tracking treatment outcomes.

In the late 1990s, the company continued to expand, adding customers in Canada (1996) and building operations — with varying success. A 1996 expansion of its eyecare management services was abandoned in 1998. Although Express Scripts has traditionally grown through big-ticket contracts, such as its 1997 pact with RightCHOICE Managed Care, it has also bought books of business. In 1998 it bought Columbia/HCA's (now HCA) ValueRx unit. The next year Express Scripts bought SmithKline Beecham's Diversified Pharmaceutical Services (DPS); however, it lost DPS's largest customer when United Healthcare began moving its more than 8 million enrollees to Merck-Medco in 2000.

The company suffered another setback in 2000 when it wrote down its 20% interest in online pharmacy PlanetRx. It had bought into the company in 1999, when dot-coms were soaring, transferring its own Internet pharmacy operations (YourPharmacy.com) into the fledgling company. In 2001 Express Scripts joined rivals AdvancePCS and Merck-Medco (now Medco Health Solutions) to form RxHub to create technology to allow physicians to file prescriptions electronically.

In 2001 the firm began a bit of an acquisition spree. In 2001, it bought Phoenix Marketing Group, one of the biggest prescription drug sample fulfillment companies in the US. National Prescription Administrators, a top private pharmacy benefits management company in the US, joined the family in 2002. In 2004 Express Scripts expanded its specialty pharmacy capabilities with CuraScript, a leading specialty pharmacy.

## EXECUTIVES

**Chairman, President, and CEO:** George Paz, age 51
**COO:** David A. Lowenberg, age 57, $1,106,350 pay
**SVP and CFO:** Edward J. Stiften, age 52, $790,065 pay
**SVP and CIO:** Patrick (Pat) McNamee, age 47, $676,515 pay
**SVP, Secretary, and General Counsel:** Thomas M. Boudreau, age 55, $881,330 pay
**SVP, Client and Patient Services:** Douglas (Doug) Porter, age 48
**SVP, Research and Product Management:** Brenda Motheral, age 36
**SVP, Strategy and Business Development:** Agnes Rey-Giraud, age 42
**SVP, Specialty Services:** Domenic A. Meffe, age 42
**SVP, Sales and Account Management:** Edward (Ed) Ignaczak, age 41
**SVP, Supply Chain Management:** C. K. Casteel, age 56
**VP, Communications:** Elaine Branding
**VP, Controller, and Chief Accouting Officer:** Kelley Elliott, age 33
**VP, Corporate and Marketing Communications:** Larry Zarin
**VP, Human Resources:** Karen Matteuzzi
**VP, Human Resources:** Glenda Knebel
**VP, Investor Relations:** David Myers
**Director, Communications Content and Development:** Guy Jacobs
**Auditors:** PricewaterhouseCoopers LLP

## LOCATIONS

**HQ:** Express Scripts, Inc.
1 Express Way, St. Louis, MO 63121
**Phone:** 314-996-0900
**Web:** www.express-scripts.com

Express Scripts has facilities in Arizona, California, Colorado, Florida, Georgia, Kentucky, Massachusetts, Michigan, Minnesota, Missouri, New Jersey, New Mexico, New York, Nevada, Ohio, Pennsylvania, Texas, and Canada.

## PRODUCTS/OPERATIONS

**2006 Sales**

| | $ mil. | % of total |
|---|---|---|
| Product | | |
| Network | 8,797.4 | 50 |
| Home delivery | 8,451.8 | 47 |
| Other | 115.2 | 1 |
| Service | 295.6 | 2 |
| **Total** | **17,660** | **100** |

**Selected Subsidiaries**

Acuity Health Solutions, Inc.
Byfield Drug, Inc.
Central Fill, Inc.
CFI New Jersey, Inc.
Chesapeake Infusion, Inc.
Comprehensive Renal Care, Inc.
CuraScript PBM Services, Inc.
CuraScript Pharmacy, Inc.
Custom Medical Products, Inc.
Diversified NY IPA, Inc.
Diversified Pharmaceutical Services, Inc.
Diversified Pharmaceutical Services (Puerto Rico), Inc.
ESI Canada, Inc.
ESI Claims, Inc.
ESI Home Delivery Service, Inc.
Express Scripts Canada Co.
Express Scripts Insurance Company
Express Scripts Sales Development Co.
Express Scripts Senior Care, Inc.
Express Scripts Specialty Distribution Services, Inc.
Express Scripts Utilization Management Co.
iBIOLogic, Inc.
Intecare Pharmacies, Ltd.
Integrity Healthcare Services, Inc.
Intecare Pharmacies, Ltd. (Canada)
IVTx, Inc.
Lynnfield Drug, Inc.
Matrix Oncology, LLC
National Prescription Administrators, Inc.
Priority Healthcare Corporation
Priority Healthcare Distribution, Inc.
Specialty Infusion Pharmacy, Inc.
Value Health, Inc.
ValueRx of Michigan, Inc.
YourPharmacy.com, Inc.

## COMPETITORS

Aetna
BioScrip
Caremark Pharmacy Services
CIGNA
HealthExtras
Medco Health Solutions
National Medical Health Card Systems
Omnicare
PharMerica
Prescription Solutions
UnitedHealth Group
WellPoint

## HISTORICAL FINANCIALS

Company Type: Public

**Income Statement** FYE: December 31

| | REVENUE ($ mil.) | NET INCOME ($ mil.) | NET PROFIT MARGIN | EMPLOYEES |
|---|---|---|---|---|
| **12/06** | 17,660 | 474 | 2.7% | 11,300 |
| **12/05** | 16,266 | 400 | 2.5% | 11,100 |
| **12/04** | 15,115 | 278 | 1.8% | 10,828 |
| **12/03** | 13,295 | 250 | 1.9% | 8,575 |
| **12/02** | 12,261 | 203 | 1.7% | 7,561 |
| **Annual Growth** | 9.6% | 23.7% | — | 10.6% |

**2006 Year-End Financials**

Debt ratio: 112.9%
Return on equity: 36.6%
Cash ($ mil.): 131
Current ratio: 0.73
Long-term debt ($ mil.): 1,270
No. of shares (mil.): 136
Dividends
Yield: —
Payout: —
Market value ($ mil.): 4,856

**Stock History** NASDAQ (GS): ESRX

| | STOCK PRICE ($) FY Close | P/E High | P/E Low | PER SHARE ($) Earnings | Dividends | Book Value |
|---|---|---|---|---|---|---|
| **12/06** | 35.80 | 28 | 18 | 1.67 | — | 8.29 |
| **12/05** | 41.90 | 34 | 14 | 1.34 | — | 10.01 |
| **12/04** | 19.11 | 23 | 16 | 0.90 | — | 16.20 |
| **12/03** | 16.61 | 24 | 15 | 0.79 | — | 15.39 |
| **12/02** | 12.01 | 26 | 15 | 0.64 | — | 12.56 |
| **Annual Growth** | 31.4% | — | — | 27.1% | — | (9.9%) |

# Exxon Mobil

It's not necessarily the oil standard, but Exxon Mobil is the world's largest integrated oil company (ahead of BP and Royal Dutch Shell). Exxon Mobil engages in oil and gas exploration, production, supply, transportation, and marketing worldwide. It has proved reserves of 13.6 billion barrels of oil equivalent. Exxon Mobil's 40 refineries in 20 countries have a capacity of producing 6.4 million barrels per day. The company supplies refined products to more than 35,000 service stations in 100 countries. It also provides fuel to 700 airports and more than 200 ports. Exxon Mobil is also a major petrochemical producer. The company posted consecutive US records for annual corporate earnings for 2005 and 2006.

Shortages caused by Hurricane Katrina prompted Exxon Mobil to receive a 6 million barrel of crude oil loan, primarily from the US Strategic Petroleum Reserve, and increase gasoline production at its Baton Rouge facility.

Through ExxonMobil Chemical, the company develops and sells petrochemicals (including ethylene, olefin, polyolefin, and paraxylene). Another unit mines coal and other minerals. Exxon Mobil also has stakes in electric power plants in China.

With significant oil and gas holdings in Europe, the US, and eastern Canada, the company is looking for new opportunities in West Africa, both onshore and off; in the former Soviet Union; and in South America. It is also investing heavily in deepwater exploration (i.e., in water depths greater than 1,350 feet). Exxon Mobil is divesting coal and other mining assets in order to focus on its core oil and gas businesses.

Under nationalization pressure from President Hugo Chavez, Exxon Mobil exited Venezuela in 2007.

## HISTORY

Exxon's 1999 acquisition of Mobil reunited two descendants of John D. Rockefeller's Standard Oil Company. Rockefeller, a commodity trader, started his first oil refinery in 1863 in Cleveland. Realizing that the price of oil at the well would shrink with each new strike, Rockefeller chose to monopolize oil refining and transportation. In 1870 he formed Standard Oil, and in 1882 he created the Standard Oil Trust, which allowed him to set up new, ostensibly independent, companies, including the Standard Oil Company of New Jersey (Jersey Standard); Rochester, New York-based Vacuum Oil; and Standard Oil of New York (nicknamed Socony).

Initially capitalized at $70 million, the Standard Oil Trust controlled 90% of the petroleum industry. In 1911, after two decades of political and legal wrangling, the Supreme Court broke up the trust into 34 companies, the largest of which was Jersey Standard.

Walter Teagle, who became president of Jersey Standard in 1917, secretly bought half of Humble Oil of Texas (1919) and expanded operations into South America. In 1928 Jersey Standard joined in the Red Line Agreement, which reserved most Middle East oil for a few companies. Teagle resigned in 1942 after the company was criticized for a prewar research pact with German chemical giant I.G. Farben.

The 1948 purchase of a 40% stake in Arabian American Oil Company, combined with a 7% share of Iranian production bought in 1954, made Jersey Standard the world's #1 oil company at that time.

Meanwhile, Vacuum Oil and Socony reunited in 1931 as Socony-Vacuum, and the company adopted the Flying Red Horse (Pegasus — representing speed and power) as a trademark. The fast-growing, diversifying company changed its name to Socony Mobil Oil in 1955 and became Mobil in 1976.

Other US companies, still using the Standard Oil name, objected to Jersey Standard's marketing in their territories as Esso (derived from the initials for Standard Oil). To end the confusion, in 1972 Jersey Standard became Exxon, a name change that cost $100 million.

Nationalization of oil assets by producing countries reduced Exxon's access to oil during the 1970s. Though it increased exploration that decade and the next, Exxon's reserves shrank.

Oil tanker *Exxon Valdez* spilled some 11 million gallons of oil into Alaska's Prince William Sound in 1989. Exxon spent billions on the cleanup, and in 1994 a federal jury in Alaska ordered the company to pay $5.3 billion in punitive damages to fishermen and others affected by the spill. (Exxon appealed, and in 2001 the jury award was overturned.)

With the oil industry consolidating, Exxon merged its worldwide oil and fuel additives business with that of Royal Dutch/Shell in 1996. The next year, under FTC pressure, Exxon agreed to run ads refuting claims that its premium gas enabled car engines to run more efficiently. Another PR disaster followed in 1998 when CEO Lee Raymond upset environmentalists by publicly questioning the global warming theory.

Still, Exxon was unstoppable. It acquired Mobil for $81 billion in 1999; the new company had Raymond at the helm and Mobil's Lucio Noto as vice chairman. (Noto retired in 2001.) To get the deal done, Exxon Mobil had to divest $4 billion in assets. It agreed to end its European gasoline and lubricants joint venture with BP and to sell more than 2,400 gas stations in the US.

In 2000 Exxon Mobil sold 1,740 East Coast gas stations to Tosco for $860 million. It sold a California refinery and 340 gas stations to Valero Energy for about $1 billion.

More than a decade after the *Exxon Valdez* wreaked environmental havoc off the shores of Alaska, Exxon Mobil attempted to atone in 2001 by joining the California Fuel Cell Partnership, a group studying possible alternatives to, and supplements for, gasoline in fuel-burning engines. That year Exxon Mobil also announced that it was proceeding with a $12 billion project (with Japanese, Indian, and Russian partners) to develop oil fields in the Russian Far East.

In 2002 Exxon Mobil sold its 50% stake in a Colombian coal mine as part of its strategy to divest coal assets in order to focus on its core businesses. That year the company sold its Chilean copper mining subsidiary (Disputada de Las Condes) to mineral giant Anglo American for $1.3 billion. Exxon Mobil sold its 3.7% stake in China Petroleum & Chemical Corp. (Sinopec) in early 2005. Later that year the company was ordered to pay $1.3 billion to about 10,000 gas station owners for overcharges dating back to 1983; the average amount for each station owner was about $130,000.

## EXECUTIVES

**Chairman and CEO:** Rex W. Tillerson, age 55, $2,416,667 pay (prior to promotion)
**SVP and Director:** J. Stephen (Steve) Simon, age 62
**SVP and Treasurer:** Donald D. (Don) Humphreys, age 59
**VP Human Resources:** Lucille J. Cavanaugh
**VP; President, ExxonMobil Chemical:** Michael J. (Mike) Dolan, age 52
**VP; President, ExxonMobil Exploration:** A. T. Cejka, age 54
**VP Public Affairs:** K. P. Cohen
**VP; President, ExxonMobil Fuels Marketing:** Hal R. Cramer, age 55
**VP; President, ExxonMobil Lubricants & Petroleum Specialties:** Gerry L. Kohlenberger, age 53
**VP; President, ExxonMobil Production:** Morris E. Foster, age 62
**VP; President, ExxonMobil Refining & Supply:** Stephen D. (Steve) Pryor, age 56
**VP and Controller:** Patrick T. (Pat) Mulva, age 54
**VP and General Counsel:** Charles W. Matthews Jr., age 61
**VP and General Tax Counsel:** Paul E. Sullivan, age 62
**VP Investor Relations and Secretary:** Henry H. Hubble, age 53
**VP Safety, Health, and Environment:** S. K. Stuewer
**Chairman, President, and CEO, Imperial Oil:** Timothy J. (Tim) Hearn, age 62
**President, ExxonMobil Development:** Mark W. Albers, age 49
**President, ExxonMobil Global Services:** T. R. Walters
**President, ExxonMobil Research and Engineering:** R. V. Pisarczyk
**President, ExxonMobil Upstream Research and ExxonMobil Upstream Technical Computing:** Steve M. Cassiani
**President, ExxonMobil Gas & Power Marketing Company:** Andrew P. (Andy) Swiger, age 50
**Auditors:** PricewaterhouseCoopers LLP

## LOCATIONS

**HQ:** Exxon Mobil Corporation
5959 Las Colinas Blvd., Irving, TX 75039
**Phone:** 972-444-1000 **Fax:** 972-444-1350
**Web:** www.exxon.mobil.com

Exxon Mobil operates in about 200 countries. Its oil and gas assets are in countries across the globe, including Angola, Argentina, Australia, Azerbaijan, Cameroon, Canada, Chad, Equatorial Guinea, France, Germany, Indonesia, Italy, Japan, Kazakhstan, Malaysia, the Netherlands, Nigeria, Norway, Papua New Guinea, Qatar, Russia, Thailand, the UK, the US (including the Gulf of Mexico), and Yemen.

### 2006 Sales

| | $ mil. | % of total |
|---|---|---|
| US | 112,787 | 31 |
| Japan | 27,368 | 8 |
| Canada | 25,281 | 7 |
| UK | 24,646 | 7 |
| Germany | 19,458 | 5 |
| Belgium | 16,271 | 4 |
| Italy | 15,332 | 4 |
| France | 13,537 | 4 |
| Other countries | 110,787 | 30 |
| Adjustments | 12,168 | — |
| **Total** | **377,635** | **100** |

## PRODUCTS/OPERATIONS

### 2006 Sales

| | $ mil. | % of total |
|---|---|---|
| Downstream | 298,457 | 82 |
| Chemicals | 34,098 | 9 |
| Upstream | 32,875 | 9 |
| Other | 37 | — |
| Adjustments | 12,168 | — |
| **Total** | **377,635** | **100** |

### Selected Subsidiaries and Affiliates

Aera Energy, LLC (48%)
Al-Jubail Petrochemical Company (50%)
Esso Deutschland GmbH
Esso Petroleum Company, Limited (UK)
ExxonMobil Chemical Company
ExxonMobil Pipeline Company
TonenGeneral Sekiyu K.K. (50%, Japan)

## COMPETITORS

7-Eleven
Ashland
BHP Billiton
BP
Chevron
ConocoPhillips
Costco Wholesale
Dow Chemical
DuPont
Eastman Chemical
Eni
Hess
Huntsman
Imperial Chemical
Koch
Lyondell Chemical
Marathon Oil
Norsk Hydro
Occidental Petroleum
PDVSA
PEMEX
PETROBRAS
Racetrac Petroleum
Repsol YPF
Royal Dutch Shell
Saudi Aramco
Sunoco
TOTAL
Valero Energy

## HISTORICAL FINANCIALS

Company Type: Public

### Income Statement

FYE: December 31

| | REVENUE ($ mil.) | NET INCOME ($ mil.) | NET PROFIT MARGIN | EMPLOYEES |
|---|---|---|---|---|
| **12/06** | 377,635 | 39,500 | 10.5% | 82,100 |
| **12/05** | 370,680 | 36,130 | 9.7% | 83,700 |
| **12/04** | 298,035 | 25,330 | 8.5% | 85,900 |
| **12/03** | 246,738 | 21,510 | 8.7% | 88,300 |
| **12/02** | 204,506 | 11,460 | 5.6% | 92,500 |
| **Annual Growth** | 16.6% | 36.3% | — | (2.9%) |

### 2006 Year-End Financials

Debt ratio: 5.8%
Return on equity: 35.1%
Cash ($ mil.): 32,848
Current ratio: 1.55
Long-term debt ($ mil.): 6,645
No. of shares (mil.): 5,729
Dividends
Yield: 2.1%
Payout: 24.2%
Market value ($ mil.): 439,013

### Stock History

NYSE: XOM

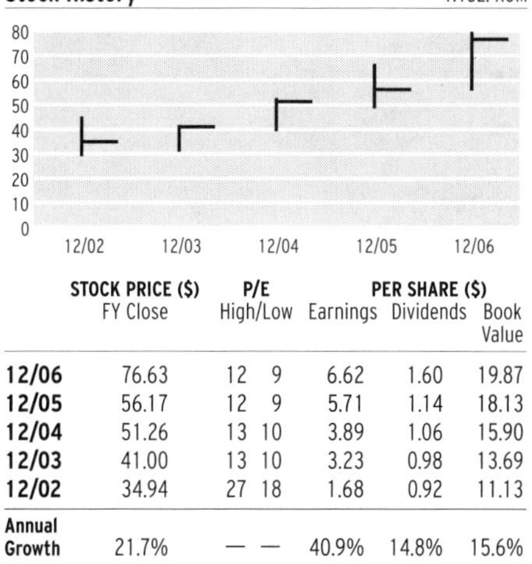


| | STOCK PRICE ($) FY Close | P/E High | P/E Low | PER SHARE ($) Earnings | Dividends | Book Value |
|---|---|---|---|---|---|---|
| **12/06** | 76.63 | 12 | 9 | 6.62 | 1.60 | 19.87 |
| **12/05** | 56.17 | 12 | 9 | 5.71 | 1.14 | 18.13 |
| **12/04** | 51.26 | 13 | 10 | 3.89 | 1.06 | 15.90 |
| **12/03** | 41.00 | 13 | 10 | 3.23 | 0.98 | 13.69 |
| **12/02** | 34.94 | 27 | 18 | 1.68 | 0.92 | 11.13 |
| **Annual Growth** | 21.7% | — | — | 40.9% | 14.8% | 15.6% |

# Family Dollar Stores

Penny-pinching moms are important to Family Dollar Stores. The nation's #2 dollar store (behind Dollar General) targets women shopping for a family that earns around $25,000 a year. Fast-growing Family Dollar operates about 6,300 stores in 44 states and the District of Columbia. Consumables (food, health and beauty aids, and household products) account for more than half of sales; the stores also sell apparel, shoes, and linens. Family Dollar emphasizes neighborhood stores near its low- and middle-income customers in rural and urban areas. Most merchandise (national brands, Family Dollar private labels, and unbranded items) is less than $10. Family Dollar was founded in 1959 by the father of CEO Howard Levine.

Levine and his family own about 7% of the discount chain.

In the face of increased competition from mass discounters such as Wal-Mart, the company has shifted to an everyday-low-pricing strategy (as opposed to short-lived promotional advertising), while increasing the number of brand-name goods it carries. While Family Dollar has been expanding rapidly, adding freestanding stores and strip mall stores without accumulating long-term debt, the pace of new store openings has slowed in recent years. After opening some 275 stores (net of closings) in fiscal 2006, Family Dollar Stores plans to open another 250 this year. Also, the discount chain has been increasing its retail presence in urban areas, with 50% of the new stores added in 2006 in urban markets.

The retailer is expanding its food offering to include milk and other perishables. To that end, Family Dollar has installed refrigerated coolers in about 3,800 stores. In addition to selling more groceries, the dollar chain will also begin accepting food stamps to attract more low-income customers to its stores.

Eventually, Family Dollar would like to expand westward into California, Idaho, Montana, Oregon, and Washington. International expansion may also be on the horizon, management says.

## HISTORY

Leon Levine came from a retailing family. His father, who founded The Hub, a general store-style department store in Rockingham, North Carolina, in 1908, died when Levine was 13. Leon and his older brother Al helped their mother run the store. (Al went on to found the Pic 'n Pay self-service shoe stores in 1957.) In 1959, when he was 25, Levine (with his cousin Bernie) opened his own store in Charlotte, with nothing priced over a dollar, targeting low- and middle-income families. The concept of low prices and small neighborhood stores was immediately popular, and Levine began adding stores. By 1970, when he took Family Dollar Stores public, it had 100 stores in five states. That year Levine brought his cousin Lewis into the business.

Family Dollar's profits plummeted in the mid-1970s as the chain's low-income customers, hit by recession, cut back on spending — even though all merchandise was priced at $3 or less. Such pricing made for tight margins, so the company dropped the policy. Family Dollar also improved inventory controls to make operations more efficient and began moving into other states. Sales picked up, topping $100 million in 1977, and the next year the firm bought the 40-store Top Dollar chain from Sav-A-Stop.

As the 1980s began, Family Dollar had nearly 400 stores in eight southern states; rapidly expanding, it was adding more than 100 stores a year. But in an effort to boost margins, the company had lost its pricing edge to a new threat — Wal-Mart's truckload prices and quick domination of the southern discount retailing market.

After Family Dollar sales were flat in 1986 and dropped 10% in 1987, Levine finally took action. He found his prices were sometimes as much as 10% higher than Wal-Mart's and his stores were often insufficiently stocked with advertised products. He lowered prices, declaring that Family Dollar would not be undersold, and again instituted new inventory controls. But the action had not come quickly enough, argued president and COO Lewis, who left the company in 1987. (He was also upset over a huge salary disparity: Leon — noted for being a hard bargainer with suppliers — was making $1.8 million a year, compared to Lewis' $260,000.) Leon's son Howard, who joined the firm in 1981, also left; he returned to the fold in 1996 and became CEO in 1998.

Family Dollar picked up momentum in the 1990s. It implemented a major renovation of stores and phased out low-margin items such as motor oil and tools in favor of such high-margin items as toys and electronics. The company also accelerated its growth plans, opening stores in a number of new markets and setting up a second distribution center, in Arkansas, in 1994 to support its westward expansion. Also that year Family Dollar began offering everyday low prices and scaled back its sales promotions.

The pace of expansion was steady during the late 1990s, as the company opened hundreds of new stores and more distribution centers and closed underperforming locations. Family Dollar added 165 stores in fiscal 1996, 186 in fiscal

1997, 250 in fiscal 1998, and 366 in fiscal 1999 (its largest single-year increase in stores). It continued adding stores in 2000 and 2001 (although the rate of growth began slowing) and it began emphasizing food, household products, and gift and seasonal items rather than clothing.

Family Dollar increased its presence in urban areas by locating 40% of the 475 stores added in 2002 in cities. Historically about 25% of its stores have been placed in urban markets.

Founder Leon Levine retired in January 2003, 43 years after starting the company. His son Howard (CEO) succeeded him as chairman. In 2003 Family Dollar Stores opened its seventh distribution center and 475 new stores, including its first outlets in Wyoming and North Dakota. In 2004 the chain opened an additional 500 outlets, increasing its store count by about 10%.

President and COO David Alexander resigned in August 2005. (James Kelly replaced him in 2006.) In 2005 the company installed refrigerated coolers in about 1,000 of its stores.

In April 2006 an Alabama jury found Family Dollar guilty of violating the Federal Labor Standards Act by misclassifying hourly employees as salaried managers to avoid paying overtime. As a result the company was fined $16.6 million. Also that year Family Dollar opened a new Northeast regional distribution center in Rome, New York.

## EXECUTIVES

**Chairman and CEO:** Howard R. Levine, age 47, $728,409 pay
**President and COO:** R. James (Jim) Kelly, age 59
**EVP and Chief Merchandising Officer:** Robert A. George, age 44
**EVP, Supply Chain:** Charles S. Gibson Jr., age 45, $277,640 pay
**SVP and CFO:** Kenneth T. (Ken) Smith, age 45
**SVP, Strategy and Business Development:** Dorlisa K. Flur, age 41
**SVP and CIO:** Joshua R. (Josh) Jewett, age 37
**SVP, Finance:** C. Martin Sowers, age 48
**SVP, General Counsel, and Secretary:** Janet G. Kelley, age 53, $262,390 pay (prior to promotion)
**SVP, Human Resources:** Kathi S. Child
**SVP, Hardlines and Marketing:** John J. Scanlon, age 56
**SVP, New Stores:** Thomas M. (Tom) Nash
**SVP, Planning, Allocation, and Replenishment:** Bryan P. Causey
**SVP, Softlines:** Mike Kvitko
**SVP, Store Operations:** Barry W. Sullivan, age 42
**VP, Investor Relations and Communications:** Kiley F. Rawlins
**VP and General Merchandise Manager, Hardlines:** Richard P. (Rick) Siliakus
**VP, Information Technology:** Michael Laurenti
**VP, Information Technology Operations:** Elizabeth M. Austin
**VP, Marketing:** Samuel J. Bernstein
**Manager, Human Resources Information Systems:** Michael Lariosa
**Auditors:** PricewaterhouseCoopers LLP

## LOCATIONS

**HQ:** Family Dollar Stores, Inc.
10401 Monroe Rd., Matthews, NC 28105
**Phone:** 704-847-6961 **Fax:** 704-847-0189
**Web:** www.familydollar.com

Family Dollar Stores operates more than 6,200 stores in 44 states and the District of Columbia, with distribution facilities in Arkansas, Florida, Iowa, Kentucky, New York, North Carolina, Oklahoma, Texas, and Virginia.

**2006 Stores**

| | No. |
|---|---|
| Texas | 780 |
| Ohio | 389 |
| Florida | 330 |
| North Carolina | 327 |
| Michigan | 324 |
| Georgia | 296 |
| New York | 271 |
| Pennsylvania | 241 |
| Illinois | 222 |
| Louisiana | 218 |
| Virginia | 205 |
| Tennessee | 198 |
| Kentucky | 185 |
| South Carolina | 183 |
| Indiana | 177 |
| Alabama | 144 |
| Wisconsin | 139 |
| Arizona | 125 |
| Oklahoma | 123 |
| West Virginia | 113 |
| Mississippi | 108 |
| Colorado | 99 |
| Arkansas | 98 |
| Missouri | 94 |
| Massachusetts | 92 |
| Maryland | 90 |
| New Mexico | 87 |
| New Jersey | 73 |
| Minnesota | 62 |
| Utah | 58 |
| Connecticut | 51 |
| Maine | 43 |
| Iowa | 35 |
| Kansas | 33 |
| Idaho | 28 |
| Nebraska | 26 |
| Nevada | 22 |
| Delaware | 21 |
| Other states | 98 |
| **Total** | **6,208** |

## PRODUCTS/OPERATIONS

**2006 Sales**

| | % of total |
|---|---|
| Consumables | 58 |
| Home products | 15 |
| Apparel & accessories | 14 |
| Seasonal & electronics | 13 |
| **Total** | **100** |

**2006 Sales**

| | % of total |
|---|---|
| Nationally advertised brands | 37 |
| Family Dollar brands | 4 |
| Other brands or unlabeled | 59 |
| **Total** | **100** |

**Selected Products**

Hardlines
- Automotive supplies
- Candy, snacks, and other foods
- Electronics
- Gifts
- Hardware
- Health and beauty aids
- Household chemical products
- Household paper products
- Housewares
- Seasonal goods
- Stationery and school supplies
- Toys

Soft goods
- Apparel (men's, women's, children's, and infants')
- Domestics (blankets, sheets, and towels)
- Shoes

## COMPETITORS

7-Eleven
Big Lots
Bill's Dollar Stores
BJ's Wholesale Club
Costco Wholesale
CVS/Caremark
Dollar General
Dollar Tree
Duckwall-ALCO
Fred's
J. C. Penney
Kmart
Meijer
Pamida
The Pantry
Retail Ventures
Rite Aid
Sears
ShopKo Stores
Simply Amazing
Target
Toys "R" Us
Variety Wholesalers
Walgreen
Wal-Mart

## HISTORICAL FINANCIALS

Company Type: Public

**Income Statement** FYE: August 31

| | REVENUE ($ mil.) | NET INCOME ($ mil.) | NET PROFIT MARGIN | EMPLOYEES |
|---|---|---|---|---|
| **8/06** | 6,395 | 195 | 3.1% | 44,000 |
| **8/05** | 5,825 | 218 | 3.7% | 42,000 |
| **8/04** | 5,282 | 258 | 4.9% | 39,000 |
| **8/03** | 4,750 | 248 | 5.2% | 37,000 |
| **8/02** | 4,163 | 217 | 5.2% | 39,400 |
| **Annual Growth** | 11.3% | (2.6%) | — | 2.8% |

**2006 Year-End Financials**

Debt ratio: 20.7%
Return on equity: 14.8%
Cash ($ mil.): 216
Current ratio: 1.44
Long-term debt ($ mil.): 250
No. of shares (mil.): 150
Dividends
Yield: 1.7%
Payout: 31.7%
Market value ($ mil.): 3,542

**Stock History** NYSE: FDO

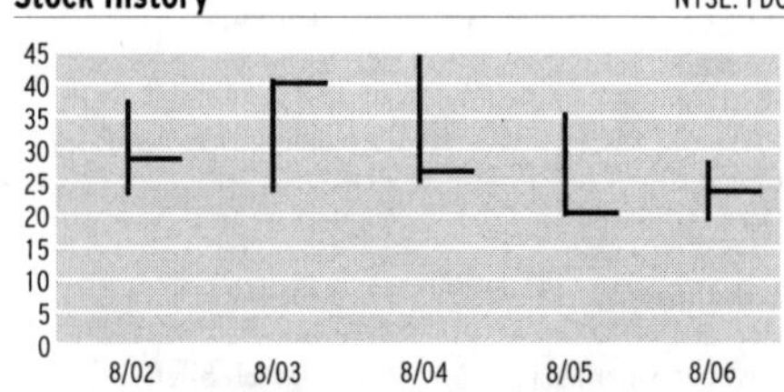


| | STOCK PRICE ($) FY Close | P/E High | P/E Low | PER SHARE ($) Earnings | Dividends | Book Value |
|---|---|---|---|---|---|---|
| **8/06** | 23.58 | 22 | 15 | 1.26 | 0.40 | 8.04 |
| **8/05** | 20.24 | 27 | 15 | 1.30 | 0.36 | 8.64 |
| **8/04** | 26.63 | 29 | 17 | 1.50 | 0.32 | 7.99 |
| **8/03** | 40.12 | 28 | 17 | 1.43 | 0.28 | 7.61 |
| **8/02** | 28.55 | 30 | 19 | 1.25 | 0.19 | 6.66 |
| **Annual Growth** | (4.7%) | — | — | 0.2% | 20.5% | 4.8% |

# Fannie Mae

The Federal National Mortgage Association, or Fannie Mae, has helped 50 million low- to middle-income families realize the American Dream. A public company operating under federal charter, it is the US's #1 source for mortgage funding, financing more than one in five home loans. The firm, like brother Freddie Mac, provides liquidity in the mortgage market by buying mortgages from lenders and packaging them for resale, transferring risk from lenders and allowing them to offer mortgages to those who may not otherwise qualify. Fannie Mae borrows from the government at low rates and is exempt from certain taxes, but the company's accounting policies have come under scrutiny from US regulators.

Criticism has become Fannie Mae's companion of late. Bureaucrats and mortgage-market competitors have called for an end to Fannie Mae's federal charter status because it gives the company an advantage over its competitors in attracting investors and building market share.

In 2006 federal regulators hit Fannie Mae with a whopping $400 million fine. Investigators claimed that the company's former executives willfully overstated earnings by more than $10 billion — and then tried to impede an investigation into the discrepancies — in order to reap performance bonuses. CEO Daniel Mudd and chairman Stephen Ashley were brought to task by the Senate Banking Committee that June in regard to accounting misdeeds.

In response, Fannie Mae agreed to major changes in its accounting, internal controls, and management practices. It additionally agreed to appoint an independent chief risk officer as well as an organizational review overseen by a compliance committee. Meanwhile, the lender suspended its home construction loan program — worth about $10 billion — while it got its financial house in order.

Good news finally arrived in August 2006 for the lender. The Justice Department announced it would not pursue criminal charges, effectively ending its two-year investigation. Fannie Mae still faced the threat of shareholder litigation while its former executives remained under investigation — the Office of Federal Housing Enterprise Oversight hinted it would file suit against former CEO Franklin Raines and former CFO Timothy Howard.

## HISTORY

In 1938 President Franklin Roosevelt created Fannie Mae as part of the government-owned Reconstruction Finance Corporation; its mandate was to buy FHA (Federal Housing Administration) loans. Fannie Mae began buying VA (Veterans Administration) mortgages in 1948. It was rechartered as a public-private, mixed-ownership corporation in 1954.

The Housing Act of 1968 divided the corporation into the Government National Mortgage Association (Ginnie Mae, which retained explicit government backing) and Fannie Mae, which went public (with only an implicit US guarantee). Fannie Mae retained its treasury backstop authority, whereby the secretary of the treasury can purchase up to $2.24 billion of the company's obligations.

The company introduced uniform conventional loan mortgage documents in 1970, began to buy conventional mortgages in 1972, and started buying condo and planned unit development mortgages in 1974. By 1976 it was buying more conventional loans than FHA and VA loans.

As interest rates rose in the 1970s, Fannie Mae's profits declined, and by 1981 it was losing more than $1 million a day. Then it began offering mortgage-backed securities (MBSs) — popular as an investment product because of their implicit guarantee from the government. By 1982 the company funded 14% of US home mortgages.

Fannie Mae began borrowing money overseas and buying conventional multifamily and co-op housing loans in 1984. The next year it tightened credit rules and began issuing securities aimed at foreign investors, such as yen-denominated securities. Fannie Mae issued its first real estate mortgage investment conduit (REMIC) securities (shares in mortgage pools of specific maturities and risk classes) and introduced a program to allow small lenders to pool loans with other lenders to create MBSs in 1987.

After CEO David Maxwell's 1991 retirement with a reported $29 million pension package, Fannie Mae's powerful Washington lobby squelched calls to limit executive salaries. Other attempts to make the company more competitive with private concerns were more successful. In 1992 Fannie Mae's capital requirements were raised; a new mandate also required the organization to lend greater support to inner-city buyers.

In 1997 Fannie Mae officially adopted its longtime nickname. The next year Fannie Mae named White House budget chief Franklin Raines to succeed CEO James Johnson.

In 1999 the Department of Housing and Urban Development began investigating charges that the company's automated underwriting systems were racially biased. The next year the agency released a study that found it to be negligent in promoting homeownership in low-income neighborhoods. In response, Fannie Mae eased credit requirements in an effort to boost minority homeownership (1999) and announced plans to loan some $2 trillion to minority and low-income homebuyers (2000). This move, however, invoked criticism that the company was exposing itself to increased risk from buyers more likely to default.

Following the lead of rival Freddie Mac, in 2000 Fannie Mae offered securities for sale over the Internet. In 2002 it tightened standards for mortgage refinance cash-out loans it would buy as mortgage defaults rose (even as home sales and mortgage refinancings were helping prop up the sagging US economy).

In response to those who thought it was in bed with the federal government, Fannie Mae kicked off the covers and put one foot on the floor. In 2003 it fulfilled a voluntary commitment to register its common stock with the SEC and came permanently under that organization's disclosure and oversight requirements.

But the move did not stop controversy from swirling around the lender. Chairman and CEO Franklin Raines, CFO Timothy Howard, and auditor KPMG were ousted in December 2004 after the SEC determined Fannie Mae had violated accounting rules. The inquiry was prompted by accusations Fannie Mae had manipulated earnings; earnings from 2001 through 2003 were restated and those from 2004 and 2005 were each released more than a year late.

## EXECUTIVES

**Chairman:** Stephen B. Ashley, age 67
**President and CEO:** Daniel H. (Dan) Mudd, age 48, $3,499,996 pay
**EVP and CFO:** Stephen M. (Steve) Swad, age 45
**EVP and COO:** Michael J. (Mike) Williams, age 49, $3,547,394 pay
**EVP and Chief Business Officer:** Robert J. (Rob) Levin, age 51, $4,597,192 pay
**EVP and Chief Risk Officer:** Enrico Dallavecchia, age 45
**EVP and CIO:** Rahul N. Merchant, age 50
**EVP Enterprise Operations:** Linda K. Knight, age 57
**EVP, General Counsel, and Secretary:** Beth A. Wilkinson, age 44
**EVP Capital Markets:** Peter S. Niculescu, age 47
**EVP Single-Family Mortgage Business:** Thomas A. (Tom) Lund, age 48, $2,203,236 pay
**SVP and Chief Compliance Officer:** William B. (Bill) Senhauser, age 44
**SVP and Controller:** David C. Hisey, age 44
**SVP Accounting:** Gregory H. Kozich
**SVP, Business Analytics and Decisions:** Mark Winer
**SVP Communications:** Charles V. (Chuck) Greener
**SVP, Credit Risk Oversight:** Michael Shaw
**SVP, Finance:** Paul A. Noring
**SVP Government and Industry Relations:** Duane S. Duncan
**SVP Housing and Community Development Credit Risk:** David Worley
**SVP Operational Risk Oversight:** Angela H. Isaac
**SVP Strategy:** Carolyn Groobey
**SVP Investor Relations:** Mary Lou Christy
**Managing Director Communications:** Brian Faith
**Auditors:** Deloitte & Touche LLP

## LOCATIONS

**HQ:** Federal National Mortgage Association
3900 Wisconsin Ave. NW, Washington, DC 20016
**Phone:** 202-752-7000
**Web:** www.fanniemae.com

## HISTORICAL FINANCIALS

Company Type: Public

### Income Statement

FYE: December 31

| | REVENUE ($ mil.) | NET INCOME ($ mil.) | NET PROFIT MARGIN | EMPLOYEES |
|---|---|---|---|---|
| 12/05 | 50,149 | 6,347 | 12.7% | 5,600 |
| 12/04 | 51,826 | 4,967 | 9.6% | 5,400 |
| 12/03 | 53,768 | 7,905 | 14.7% | 5,055 |
| 12/02 | 52,901 | 4,619 | 8.7% | 4,800 |
| Annual Growth | (1.8%) | 11.2% | — | 5.3% |

### 2005 Year-End Financials

Debt ratio: 1,994.7%
Return on equity: 21.2%
Cash ($ mil.): 12,475
Current ratio: —
Long-term debt ($ mil.): 602,269
No. of shares (mil.): 971
Dividends
Yield: 2.1%
Payout: 17.3%
Market value ($ mil.): 47,372

### Stock History

NYSE: FNM

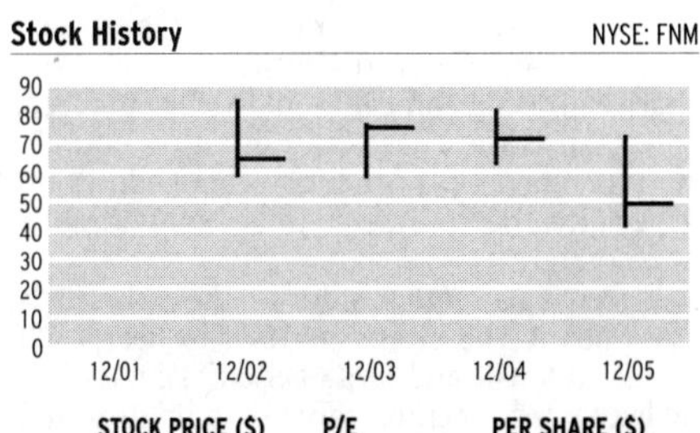


| | STOCK PRICE ($) FY Close | P/E High | P/E Low | PER SHARE ($) Earnings | PER SHARE ($) Dividends | PER SHARE ($) Book Value |
|---|---|---|---|---|---|---|
| 12/05 | 48.81 | 12 | 7 | 6.01 | 1.04 | 40.50 |
| 12/04 | 71.21 | 16 | 13 | 4.94 | 2.08 | 40.14 |
| 12/03 | 75.06 | 10 | 7 | 7.91 | 1.68 | 23.06 |
| 12/02 | 64.33 | 19 | 13 | 4.53 | 1.32 | 16.47 |
| Annual Growth | (8.8%) | — | — | 9.9% | (7.6%) | 35.0% |

# Fastenal Company

Some might say it has a screw loose, but things are actually pretty snug at Fastenal. The company operates about 2,000 stores in all 50 US states, Canada, China, Mexico, the Netherlands, Puerto Rico, and Singapore. Its stores stock about 690,000 items in 10 product categories, including threaded fasteners such as screws, nuts, and bolts. Other sales come from fluid-transfer parts for hydraulic and pneumatic power; janitorial, electrical, and welding supplies; material handling items; metal-cutting tool blades; and power tools. Its customers are typically construction, manufacturing, and other industrial professionals. Fastenal Company was founded by its chairman Bob Kierlin in 1967 and went public in 1987.

The company has been one of the fastest-growing companies in the US — adding about 200 stores annually over the past several years — primarily by selling threaded fasteners, which account for nearly half of sales. Products manufactured by other companies account for about 95% of Fastenal's sales; the remainder comes from items custom-made or modified by Fastenal. Fastenal stores are moving away from their traditional focus on wholesaling. The company's Customer Service Project calls for more business with retail customers.

Fast-growing Fastenal believes it has plenty of room to continue to grow. The company estimates the North American market can support at least 3,500 of its stores. The company locates stores in small, medium, and large markets.

Fastenal is expanding internationally, most recently into China. Currently about 7% of the company's revenue is generated outside the US.

Founder and chairman Bob Kierlin, a former Minnesota state senator, owns nearly 7% of Fastenal; director Stephen Slaggie owns about 4%.

## HISTORY

Peace Corps veteran Robert Kierlin led four friends and Winona Cotter High School classmates in founding Fastenal in 1967 as a distributor of threaded fasteners. (Kierlin's inspiration was customers' inquiries at his father's auto parts store.) The company and its lone store lost money its first two years, but it was able to open another store by 1970. Fastenal then changed its retail focus from regular consumers to contractors and professionals.

The company expanded, locating stores on the outskirts of small and medium-sized cities where real estate and operating costs are lower. By 1987 it had 58 stores. Fastenal went public that year, using some 40% of the IPO proceeds to establish the Hiawatha Education Foundation to support private high school education, especially the founders' financially troubled alma mater.

Fastenal grew quickly during the early 1990s, from about 100 stores in 1990 to nearly 400 stores in small and large US cities in 1995. It added tool-sharpening services to its stores the next year. The firm also added new product lines as it expanded, including FastTool tools and safety supplies (1993), SharpCut blades and PowerFlow fluid-transfer components (1996), and FastArc welding supplies (1997). In 1997 Fastenal opened its first store in Puerto Rico.

In 1998 the company printed its first catalog and formed a subsidiary to sell its products in Mexico. Fastenal started selling online in 1999. In 2000 the company opened about 90 stores, and the next year opened more than 125, including one in Singapore. In 2002 the company made a move into the retail market through its purchase of the retail fastener and related hardware business of two Textron subsidiaries. The company sold that business, however, to Hillman Companies later that year.

In 2004 Fastenal opened 219 stores (including its first in the Netherlands) compared to 151 new outlets in 2003. In 2005 the company opened its first store in China and added, overall, about 220 stores. 2006 saw the opening of 225 additional stores.

## EXECUTIVES

**Chairman:** Robert A. (Bob) Kierlin, age 67
**President, CEO, and Director:** Willard D. (Will) Oberton, age 48, $350,000 pay
**EVP and COO:** Nicholas J. Lundquist, age 49, $300,000 pay
**EVP and CFO:** Daniel L. (Dan) Florness, age 43, $235,000 pay
**VP, Product Development, Supply Chain, Global Procurement, and Trading:** Steven L. Appelwick, age 47, $175,000 pay
**VP, Information Systems:** Tim Albrecht
**Director, Employee Development and Director:** Reyne K. Wisecup, age 44
**Auditors:** KPMG LLP

## LOCATIONS

**HQ:** Fastenal Company
2001 Theurer Blvd., Winona, MN 55987
**Phone:** 507-454-5374 **Fax:** 507-453-8049
**Web:** www.fastenal.com

Fastenal operates a dozen distribution centers throughout North America in California, Georgia, Indiana, Kansas, Minnesota, North Carolina, Ohio, Pennsylvania, Texas, Utah, and Washington, and in Toronto, Canada.

**2006 Sales**

| | % of total |
|---|---|
| US | 93 |
| International | 7 |
| **Total** | **100** |

**2006 Stores**

| | No. |
|---|---|
| US | 1,829 |
| Canada | 137 |
| Mexico | 22 |
| Puerto Rico | 8 |
| Netherlands | 2 |
| China | 1 |
| Singapore | 1 |
| **Total** | **2,000** |

## PRODUCTS/OPERATIONS

**Selected Brands, Products, and Services**

CleanChoice
- Janitorial and paper products

EquipRite
- Material handling and storage products

FastArc
- Welding supplies

Fastenal
- Threaded fasteners (bolts, nuts, screws, and washers)
- Concrete anchors
- Struts

FastTool
- Power tools and accessories

PowerPhase
- Electrical supplies

SharpCut
- Cutting tools

## COMPETITORS

Ace Hardware
Anixter Pentacon
Applied Industrial Technologies
HD Supply
Home Depot
Lawson Products
Lowe's
Menard
MSC Industrial Direct
Noland
Park-Ohio Holdings
Penn Engineering
Production Tool Supply
Snap-on
True Value
WinWholesale
W.W. Grainger

## HISTORICAL FINANCIALS

Company Type: Public

**Income Statement** FYE: December 31

| | REVENUE ($ mil.) | NET INCOME ($ mil.) | NET PROFIT MARGIN | EMPLOYEES |
|---|---|---|---|---|
| **12/06** | 1,809 | 199 | 11.0% | 10,415 |
| **12/05** | 1,523 | 167 | 10.9% | 9,306 |
| **12/04** | 1,239 | 131 | 10.6% | 7,946 |
| **12/03** | 995 | 84 | 8.5% | 6,851 |
| **12/02** | 905 | 76 | 8.3% | 7,108 |
| **Annual Growth** | 18.9% | 27.4% | — | 10.0% |

**2006 Year-End Financials**

Debt ratio: —
Return on equity: 23.3%
Cash ($ mil.): 30
Current ratio: 7.39
Long-term debt ($ mil.): —
No. of shares (mil.): 151
Dividends
Yield: 1.1%
Payout: 30.3%
Market value ($ mil.): 5,425

**Stock History** NASDAQ (GS): FAST

| | STOCK PRICE ($) FY Close | P/E High | P/E Low | PER SHARE ($) Earnings | Dividends | Book Value |
|---|---|---|---|---|---|---|
| **12/06** | 35.88 | 37 | 25 | 1.32 | 0.40 | 6.10 |
| **12/05** | 39.13 | 38 | 23 | 1.10 | 0.31 | 5.19 |
| **12/04** | 30.78 | 37 | 26 | 0.86 | 0.20 | 9.02 |
| **12/03** | 24.88 | 46 | 25 | 0.56 | 0.10 | 7.60 |
| **12/02** | 18.69 | 43 | 27 | 0.50 | 0.03 | 6.59 |
| **Annual Growth** | 17.7% | — | — | 27.5% | 91.1% | (1.9%) |

# FedEx Corporation

Holding company FedEx hopes its package of subsidiaries will keep delivering significant market share. Its FedEx Express unit is the world's #1 express transportation provider, delivering some 3.3 million packages daily to more than 220 countries and territories. It maintains a fleet of about 670 aircraft and more than 43,000 motor vehicles. Complementing the express delivery business, FedEx Ground provides ground delivery of small packages in North America, and less-than-truckload (LTL) carrier FedEx Freight hauls larger shipments. FedEx Kinko's locations, in addition to providing document services, serve as retail hubs for other FedEx businesses.

FedEx continues to invest in its signature express delivery business, which accounts for about two-thirds of sales. The unit is working to expand outside the US, particularly in China and India. In 2007 FedEx Express spent about $430 million to buy out its joint venture partner in China, DTW Group, and acquire DTW Group's domestic delivery network. It also acquired PAFEX, which had provided express delivery service in India under contract with FedEx since 2002. In 2006 FedEx bought UK-based express transportation company ANC Holdings for about $240 million, gaining a fleet of 2,200 vehicles and a network of 80 offices.

In the US, FedEx has been building out the networks of both FedEx Ground and FedEx Freight, which have been the company's fastest-growing units. To boost FedEx Freight's long-haul capabilities, FedEx in 2006 paid about $790 million for LTL carrier Watkins Motor Lines and the assets of Watkins' Canadian unit, Watkins Canada Express. The latest additions to the FedEx stable in North America have been renamed FedEx National LTL and FedEx Freight Canada, respectively.

FedEx also is opening additional FedEx Kinko's retail locations. In 2006 FedEx Kinko's established a major printing facility near the FedEx Express hub in Memphis, allowing for efficient distribution of big commercial print jobs.

Founder and CEO Fred Smith owns about 6% of FedEx.

## HISTORY

From his undergraduate classes at Yale and his experience as a charter airplane pilot, Fred Smith got the idea that increased automation of business processes would create the need for a reliable overnight delivery service, and he presented his case in a term paper in 1965. After serving in the Marine Corps in Vietnam, Smith began raising money to develop the overnight delivery idea. He founded Federal Express in 1971 with $4 million inherited from his father and $80 million from investors. Overnight and second-day delivery to two dozen US cities began in 1973.

Several factors contributed to FedEx's early success: Airlines turned their focus from parcels to passengers; United Parcel Service (UPS) union workers went on strike in 1974; and competitor REA Express went bankrupt. FedEx went public in 1978.

Spotting e-mail's threat to express delivery in the early 1980s, FedEx invested heavily in satellite-based system ZapMail. However, the humble fax machine blindsided FedEx, and it lost over $300 million in 1986 on the short-lived service. The 1987 launch of PowerShip, which processed shipments electronically, was more successful.

FedEx expanded internationally in the late 1980s, buying Italy's SAMIMA and three Japanese freight carriers in 1988 and Tiger International (Flying Tigers line) in 1989. That year it doubled overseas sales to become the #1 air cargo company.

In 1991 FedEx introduced EXPRESSfreighter, an international air-express cargo service, but suffered a setback when its loss-making European delivery service was scrapped the next year. However, FedEx was back on its feet in 1995 when it created Latin American and Caribbean divisions and became the first US express carrier with direct flights to China.

FedEx jumped back into the Web in 1996 and introduced Internet-based shipping management system interNetShip. It also began selling BusinessLink, a software package that helps businesses use the Internet to sell goods, which are delivered by FedEx.

The 1997 UPS strike put an extra 850,000 packages a day into FedEx's hands. Turning the screws on UPS, FedEx bought ground carrier Caliber System in 1998 and reorganized into holding company FDX. FedEx pilots (unionized in 1993) threatened their own strike during the 1998 holiday season, prompting FedEx to outsource more of its flight operations. Nevertheless, the pilots ratified a five-year contract in 1999.

Focusing on the supply chain, in 1999 FedEx restructured Caliber's logistics unit and formed a business-to-business logistics alliance with KPMG. The company also bought freight forwarder GeoLogistics Air Services (renamed Caribbean Transportation Services). Internationally, FedEx opened its first European hub in Paris and launched a joint venture in China.

In 2000 FDX changed its name to FedEx. As part of a major rebranding effort, RPS became FedEx Ground, and Roberts Express became FedEx Custom Critical. Also that year the company formed FedEx Trade Networks to offer customs brokerage and trade consulting services.

In a landmark deal with the United States Postal Service, FedEx Express began transporting mail shipments (but not making deliveries) in 2001, and FedEx drop boxes were placed in post offices. (In 2004 FedEx won a contract to deliver international express shipments for the Postal Service.) Also that year FedEx phased out its FedEx Logistics subsidiary, shifting its operations into other subsidiaries.

FedEx acquired less-than-truckload (LTL) carrier American Freightways in 2001, and FedEx Freight was created to operate American Freightways and Viking Freight, which the company had acquired in the Caliber deal. (By 2002, both carriers were using the FedEx Freight brand name.)

FedEx, which already operated service counters in more than 130 Kinko's locations, gained more than 1,000 additional outlets in 2004 by buying the document services company. The $2.4 billion cash deal followed UPS's 2001 acquisition of Mail Boxes Etc. and its retail locations, most of which have been rebranded as The UPS Store. In turn, FedEx adopted a new brand for Kinko's stores: FedEx Kinko's Office and Print Center.

FedEx expanded its ground delivery business in 2004 by acquiring Parcel Direct, a unit of Quad/Graphics, for about $120 million. Parcel Direct was rebranded as FedEx SmartPost.

## EXECUTIVES

**Chairman, President, and CEO:** Frederick W. (Fred) Smith, age 62, $3,999,530 pay
**EVP and CFO:** Alan B. Graf Jr., age 53, $1,772,597 pay
**EVP FedEx Information Services and CIO:** Robert B. (Rob) Carter, age 48
**EVP, General Counsel, and Secretary:** Christine P. Richards, age 52
**EVP Market Development and Corporate Communications; President and CEO, FedEx Services:** T. Michael Glenn, age 51, $1,651,513 pay
**Corporate VP Human Resources:** William J. Cahill III
**Corporate VP and Principal Accounting Officer:** John L. Merino
**VP Investor Relations:** James Clippard Jr.
**VP US Marketing:** Karen Rogers
**President and CEO, FedEx Custom Critical:** John G. (Jack) Pickard
**President and CEO, FedEx Express:** David J. Bronczek, age 53, $2,074,480 pay
**President and CEO, FedEx Freight:** Douglas G. Duncan, age 56
**President and CEO, FedEx Global Supply Chain Services; SVP FedEx Solutions:** Tom Schmitt
**President and CEO, FedEx Ground:** David F. (Dave) Rebholz, age 54
**President and CEO, FedEx Kinko's Office and Print Services:** Kenneth A. (Ken) May, age 46
**President and CEO, FedEx Trade Networks:** G. Edmond (Ed) Clark
**Director Advertising:** Steve Pacheco
**Auditors:** Ernst & Young LLP

## LOCATIONS

**HQ:** FedEx Corporation
942 S. Shady Grove Rd., Memphis, TN 38120
**Phone:** 901-818-7500 **Fax:** 901-395-2000
**Web:** www.fedex.com

### 2007 Sales

| | $ mil. | % of total |
|---|---|---|
| US | 26,132 | 74 |
| Other countries | 9,082 | 26 |
| **Total** | **35,214** | **100** |

## PRODUCTS/OPERATIONS

### 2007 Sales

| | $ mil. | % of total |
|---|---|---|
| FedEx Express | 22,681 | 64 |
| FedEx Ground | 6,043 | 17 |
| FedEx Freight | 4,586 | 13 |
| FedEx Kinko's | 2,040 | 6 |
| Adjustments | (136) | — |
| **Total** | **35,214** | **100** |

### Primary Business Units

FedEx Express segment
- Federal Express Corporation (FedEx Express, express package delivery)
- FedEx Trade Networks, Inc. (customs brokerage and freight forwarding)

FedEx Ground segment
- FedEx Ground Package System, Inc. (ground-based small-package delivery)
- FedEx SmartPost (small-parcel consolidator)

FedEx Freight segment
- FedEx Freight Corporation
  - FedEx Freight East, Inc. (less-than-truckload freight)
  - FedEx Freight West, Inc. (less-than-truckload freight)
  - FedEx National LTL (less-than-truckload freight)
- FedEx Custom Critical, Inc. (time-specific carrier)
- Caribbean Transportation Services, Inc. (regional airfreight forwarding)

FedEx Kinko's segment
- FedEx Kinko's Office and Print Services, Inc. (document services)

## COMPETITORS

Allegra
AlphaGraphics
Arkansas Best
BAX Global
Canada Post
Con-way Inc.
DHL
IKON
Japan Post
Mail Boxes Etc.
Nippon Express
Office Depot
Pitney Bowes
Ryder
TNT
UPS
US Postal Service
Xerox
YRC Worldwide

## HISTORICAL FINANCIALS

Company Type: Public

**Income Statement** FYE: May 31

| | REVENUE ($ mil.) | NET INCOME ($ mil.) | NET PROFIT MARGIN | EMPLOYEES |
|---|---|---|---|---|
| **5/07** | 35,214 | 2,016 | 5.7% | 143,000 |
| **5/06** | 32,294 | 1,806 | 5.6% | 260,000 |
| **5/05** | 29,363 | 1,449 | 4.9% | 250,000 |
| **5/04** | 24,710 | 838 | 3.4% | 195,838 |
| **5/03** | 22,487 | 830 | 3.7% | 190,918 |
| **Annual Growth** | 11.9% | 24.8% | — | (7.0%) |

**2007 Year-End Financials**

Debt ratio: 15.9%
Return on equity: 16.7%
Cash ($ mil.): 1,569
Current ratio: 1.22
Long-term debt ($ mil.): 2,007
No. of shares (mil.): 308
Dividends
Yield: 0.3%
Payout: 5.6%
Market value ($ mil.): 34,379

**Stock History** NYSE: FDX

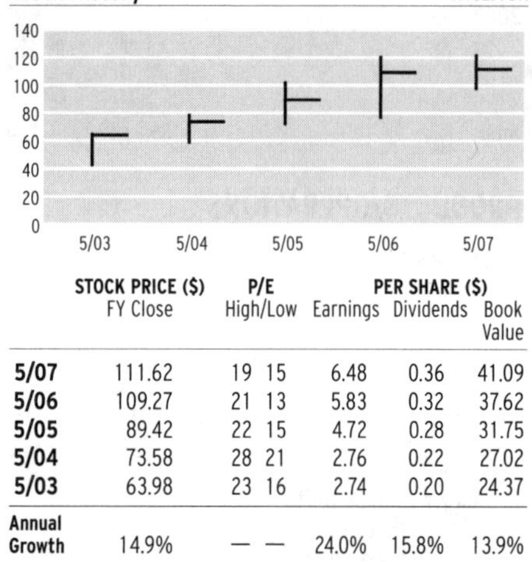


| | STOCK PRICE ($) FY Close | P/E High/Low | | PER SHARE ($) Earnings | Dividends | Book Value |
|---|---|---|---|---|---|---|
| **5/07** | 111.62 | 19 | 15 | 6.48 | 0.36 | 41.09 |
| **5/06** | 109.27 | 21 | 13 | 5.83 | 0.32 | 37.62 |
| **5/05** | 89.42 | 22 | 15 | 4.72 | 0.28 | 31.75 |
| **5/04** | 73.58 | 28 | 21 | 2.76 | 0.22 | 27.02 |
| **5/03** | 63.98 | 23 | 16 | 2.74 | 0.20 | 24.37 |
| **Annual Growth** | 14.9% | — | — | 24.0% | 15.8% | 13.9% |

# Ferrellgas Partners

Ferrellgas Partners' flame is burning brightly as the second-largest US retail marketer of propane, behind AmeriGas. The company sells 809 million gallons of propane a year to more than 1 million industrial, commercial, and agricultural customers in 50 states, primarily in the Midwest and the Southeast. It operates about 830 retail outlets, and its delivery fleet includes 2,750 trucks and trailers. Ferrellgas also trades propane and natural gas, markets wholesale propane, provides liquid natural gas storage, and markets chemical feedstock. About 32% of the company's stock is held in trust for employees.

Ferrellgas Partners has ferreted out a way to become a leader in the US retail propane business: Buy up the competition. The company has acquired 155 businesses since 1986, including Crow's LP Gas located in Granger, Iowa, and Hilltop Supply located in Guatay, California. The company has also acquired ProAm, the propane operations of DQE, and Louisiana-based Aeropres Propane. Ferrellgas plans to focus on acquisition activities in strategic geographical areas in an effort to expand its current operations. It has acquired Suburban Propane's retail propane operations located in Kansas, Missouri, Oklahoma, and Texas. Ferrellgas has also expanded its propane operations by acquiring Blue Rhino Corp.

In 2005 the company sold some non-strategic storage and terminal assets to Enterprise Products Partners for about $144 million.

In 2006 Ferrellgas acquired propane companies in Washington and Massachusetts.

## HISTORY

A. C. Ferrell began the company in 1939 as a single retail propane outlet in Atchison, Kansas. It was incorporated in 1954. When Ferrell retired in 1965, his son, current chairman and CEO James Ferrell, took over the business. Ferrellgas grew by acquiring small propane dealers in rural areas of Iowa, Kansas, Minnesota, Missouri, South Dakota, and Texas.

In 1984 Ferrellgas bought propane operations with annual retail sales volume of 33 million gallons, then followed that up in 1986 with another major buy that added 395 million gallons per year. Ferrellgas acquired more than 100 smaller independent propane retailers in the next 12 years, including Vision Energy Resources (1994) and Skelgas Propane (1996).

The company formed a limited partnership in 1994, Ferrellgas Partners, to acquire and manage the operations of Ferrellgas, Inc. Ferrellgas Partners went public that year. The company created trading and marketing subsidiary Ferrell Resources in 1996. In 1998 Ferrellgas implemented an employee stock ownership plan that placed a majority of the company's stock in a trust for its employees.

Ferrellgas acquired #5 retail propane distributor ThermoGas from energy and communications giant Williams Companies for $432.5 million in 1999, making it one of the largest propane retailers in the US. (Rival AmeriGas kept pace in 2001, however, with a major acquisition of its own.)

In 2000 the company ventured into a new direction by launching Bluebuzz.com, an ISP that serves rural communities where few services offer local dial-up phone numbers, thus forcing users to pay long-distance charges to connect to the Internet. In 2001, Ferrellgas sold this ISP to Wisconsin-based network service provider Network Innovations.

In November 2002 the company expanded it operations geographically by acquiring Northstar Propane of Reno, Nevada, and the Des Moines, Iowa branch of Cenex Propane Partners. Later that year, Ferrellgas acquired ProAm from DQE.

In 2003 Ferrellgas acquired Bud's Propane Service and Louisiana-based Aeropres Propane, representing its 63rd and 64th acquisitions since 1994. In 2004 Ferrellgas acquired an additional 11 customer service centers from Suburban Propane. Later that year the company acquired a 71% stake in Blue Rhino.

## EXECUTIVES

**Chairman and CEO:** James E. Ferrell, age 66, $1,085,000 pay
**President and COO:** Stephen L. (Steve) Wambold, age 38, $571,000 pay
**SVP and CFO:** Kevin T. Kelly, age 41, $459,000 pay
**SVP and CIO:** Patrick J. Walsh, age 52
**Special Advisor to CEO and Director:** Billy D. Prim, age 50
**Director, Propane Acquisitions:** Daryl McClendon
**Investor Relations:** Ryan VanWinkle
**Media Relations:** Scott Brockelmeyer
**Auditors:** Deloitte & Touche LLP

## LOCATIONS

**HQ:** Ferrellgas Partners, L.P.
7500 College Blvd., Ste. 1000,
Overland Park, KS 66210
**Phone:** 913-661-1500
**Web:** www.ferrellgas.com

Ferrellgas Partners sells products to customers in 50 US states, as well as in Canada, Puerto Rico, and the US Virgin Islands. Its activities are concentrated in the midwestern, northeastern, and southern regions of the US. Ferrellgas' underground storage tanks are in Arizona, Kansas, and Utah, and the trading and wholesale marketing operations are in Houston.

## PRODUCTS/OPERATIONS

**2006 Sales**

| | $ mil. | % of total |
|---|---|---|
| Propane & other gas liquids | 1,698.0 | 90 |
| Other | 197.5 | 10 |
| **Total** | **1,895.5** | **100** |

## COMPETITORS

AmeriGas Partners
Energy Transfer
Energy West
MDU Resources
RGC Resources
Star Gas Partners
Suburban Propane
Transammonia

## HISTORICAL FINANCIALS

Company Type: Public

**Income Statement** FYE: July 31

| | REVENUE ($ mil.) | NET INCOME ($ mil.) | NET PROFIT MARGIN | EMPLOYEES |
|---|---|---|---|---|
| **7/06** | 1,896 | 25 | 1.3% | 3,669 |
| **7/05** | 1,754 | 89 | 5.1% | 3,704 |
| **7/04** | 1,379 | 29 | 2.1% | 4,348 |
| **7/03** | 1,222 | 57 | 4.6% | 5,220 |
| **7/02** | 1,035 | 60 | 5.8% | 5,073 |
| **Annual Growth** | 16.3% | (19.7%) | — | (7.8%) |

**2006 Year-End Financials**

Debt ratio: 370.1%
Return on equity: 8.3%
Cash ($ mil.): 17
Current ratio: 1.10
Long-term debt ($ mil.): 984
No. of shares (mil.): 61
Dividends
Yield: 8.9%
Payout: 487.8%
Market value ($ mil.): 1,369

**Stock History** NYSE: FGP

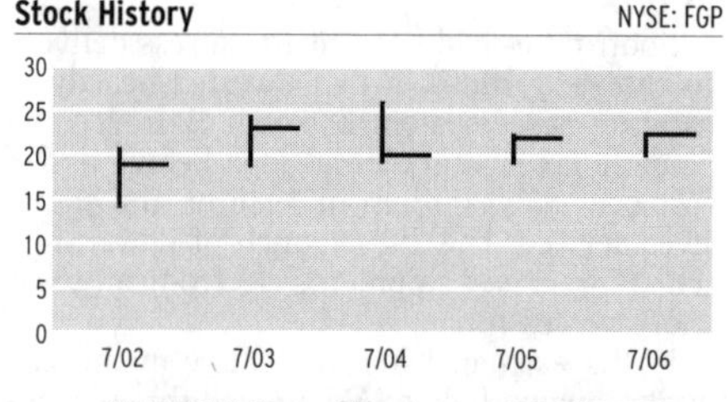


| | STOCK PRICE ($) FY Close | P/E High/Low | | PER SHARE ($) Earnings | Dividends | Book Value |
|---|---|---|---|---|---|---|
| **7/06** | 22.49 | 55 | 49 | 0.41 | 2.00 | 4.36 |
| **7/05** | 22.00 | 15 | 13 | 1.50 | 2.00 | 5.55 |
| **7/04** | 20.04 | 53 | 39 | 0.49 | 2.00 | 4.14 |
| **7/03** | 23.03 | 19 | 15 | 1.25 | 2.00 | 0.08 |
| **7/02** | 18.90 | 15 | 11 | 1.34 | 2.00 | 0.59 |
| **Annual Growth** | 4.4% | — | — | (25.6%) | 0.0% | 65.2% |

# Fifth Third Bancorp

Fifth Third Bancorp wants to be first in the hearts and minds of its customers. The holding company operates more than 1,150 Fifth Third Bank branches in the Midwest and Florida. Fifth Third operates through five segments: branch banking, commercial banking, processing solutions, consumer lending, and investment advisors. It provides consumer and business banking (including deposit accounts, loans, and credit cards); investment advisory services (mutual funds, private banking, and securities brokerage); and ATM and merchant transaction processing. The company also runs the Jeanie ATM network and offers foreign exchange trading and life insurance, among other products. Fifth Third is buying First Charter.

The deal will give the company nearly 60 branches in North Carolina, as well as locations in the Atlanta metropolitan area. Also in 2007 Fifth Third arranged to expand in Florida with the purchase of R-G Crown Bank from R&G Financial. The move will add some 30 branches in Florida and give Fifth Third additional branches in Georgia.

Fifth Third is emphasizing customer service by beefing up its consultative call expertise as well as its customer resolution process. This is a move away from the high-pressure, transaction-oriented sales process of past years, and it may have something to do with the company's recent underperformance.

The company operates on an affiliate model, dividing its business operations into separate geographic regions. Each affiliate has considerable autonomy, on the grounds that local executives can make better business decisions applicable to their regions.

Fifth Third traces its unusual name to the 1908 merger of Cincinnati's Fifth National Bank and Third National Bank. Another financial services firm from the company's hometown, insurer Cincinnati Financial Corporation, owns approximately 13% of Fifth Third.

## HISTORY

In 1863 a group of Cincinnati businessmen opened the Third National Bank inside a Masonic temple to serve the Ohio River trade. Acquiring the Bank of the Ohio Valley (founded 1858) in 1871, the firm progressed until the panic of 1907. Third National survived and in 1908 consolidated with Fifth National, forming the Fifth Third National Bank of Cincinnati. The newly organized bank acquired two local banks in 1910.

A second bank consolidation, in 1919, resulted in Fifth Third's affiliation with Union Savings Bank and Trust Company, permitting the bank to establish branches, theretofore forbidden by regulators. The company acquired the assets and offices of five more banks and thrifts that year, operating them as branches.

In 1927 the bank merged its operations with the Union Trust Company, forming the Fifth Third Union Trust. With its combined strength, it weathered the Great Depression and acquired three more banks between 1930 and 1933. However, the Depression also brought massive banking regulations to the industry, limiting Fifth Third's acquisitions.

In the postwar years and during the 1950s and 1960s, the bank expanded its consumer banking services, offering traveler's checks. Under CEO Bill Rowe, son of former CEO John Rowe, the firm emphasized the convenience of its locations and increased hours of operations.

In the 1970s Fifth Third shifted its lending program's emphasis from commercial loans to consumer credit and launched its ATM and telephone banking services. Aware that the bank was technologically unprepared for the onslaught of electronic information, Fifth Third expanded its data processing and information services resources, forming the basis for its Midwest Payment Systems division.

The company formed Fifth Third Bancorp, a holding company, and began to branch within Ohio (branching had previously been limited to the home county) in 1975. Ten years later, more deregulation allowed the bank to move into contiguous states. Focused on consumer banking, and with cautious underwriting policies, Fifth Third weathered the real estate bust and leveraged-buyout problems of the 1980s and acquired new outlets cheaply by buying several small banks, as well as branches from larger banks. It acquired the American National Bank in Kentucky and moved further afield with its purchase of the Sovereign Savings Bank in Palm Harbor, Florida, in 1991.

The company continued to expand, buying several banks and thrifts in Ohio in 1997 and 1998. In 1999 Fifth Third moved into Indiana in a big way with its purchase of CNB Bancshares, then solidified its position in the state with the acquisition of Peoples Bank of Indianapolis. Fifth Third also moved into new business areas, buying mortgage banker W. Lyman Case, broker-dealer The Ohio Company (1998), and Cincinnati-based commercial mortgage banker Vanguard Financial (1999). The company began to offer online foreign exchange via its FX Internet Trading Web in 2000.

In 2001 Fifth Third bought money manager Maxus Investments and added some 300 bank branches with its purchase of Capital Holdings (Ohio and Michigan) and Old Kent Financial (Michigan, Indiana, and Illinois), its largest-ever acquisition.

Fifth Third exited the property/casualty insurance brokerage business in 2002, selling its operations to Hub International.

Also that year, Fifth Third arranged to enter Tennessee via its planned purchase of Franklin Financial. But the deal was stalled as industry regulators investigated Fifth Third's risk management procedures and internal controls. A moratorium on acquisitions was placed on the bank during the investigation. It was lifted in 2004 and the purchase of Franklin was completed not long afterwards. That opened the door for Fifth Third's acquisition of First National Bankshares of Florida in 2005.

## EXECUTIVES

**Chairman, Fifth Third Bancorp and Fifth Third Bank:** George A. Schaefer Jr., age 61, $990,018 pay (prior to title change)
**President, CEO, and Director; President and CEO, Fifth Third Bank:** Kevin T. Kabat, age 50, $601,693 pay (prior to promotion)
**EVP and COO:** Greg D. Carmichael, age 45, $968,227 pay
**EVP and CFO:** Christopher G. (Chris) Marshall, age 47, $707,686 pay
**EVP and Controller:** Daniel T. Poston, age 48
**EVP, Secretary, and General Counsel:** Paul L. Reynolds, age 45
**EVP; President, Fifth Third Processing Solutions:** Charles D. Drucker, age 43, $493,747 pay
**EVP and Chief Risk Officer:** Mary E. Tuuk, age 35
**EVP, Employee Development:** Lauris Woolford
**SVP, Corporate Healthcare Lending:** Kevin P. Lavender, age 45
**SVP and Director of Community Affairs:** Ed Owens III
**SVP, Indirect Lending:** David A. Jackson
**SVP, Retail Administration:** Richard (Rick) Lucas
**SVP and Treasurer:** Mahesh Sankaran, age 45
**SVP and City Executive, Fifth Third Bank:** L. Thomas Bulla
**SVP and Auditor:** Robert Shaffer
**Head of Retail Banking:** Karen L. Dee, age 45
**Head of Strategic Initiatives:** John M. Presley, age 46
**Chief Marketing Officer:** Larry S. Magnesen, age 49
**Director of Investor Relations and Corporate Analysis:** Jeff Richardson, age 42
**CIO:** Raymond C. Dury, age 46
**Auditors:** Deloitte & Touche LLP

## LOCATIONS

**HQ:** Fifth Third Bancorp
38 Fountain Sq. Plaza, Fifth Third Center, Cincinnati, OH 45263
**Phone:** 513-579-5300 **Fax:** 513-534-0629
**Web:** www.53.com

Fifth Third Bancorp has bank branches in Florida, Illinois, Indiana, Kentucky, Michigan, Missouri, Ohio, Pennsylvania, Tennessee, and West Virginia.

## PRODUCTS/OPERATIONS

### 2006 Sales

| | $ mil. | % of total |
|---|---|---|
| Interest | | |
| Loans & leases | 5,000 | 59 |
| Securities | 934 | 11 |
| Other | 21 | — |
| Noninterest | | |
| Electronic payment processing revenue | 857 | 10 |
| Service charges on deposits | 517 | 6 |
| Investment advisory revenue | 367 | 5 |
| Mortgage banking net revenue | 155 | 2 |
| Other | 621 | 7 |
| **Total** | **8,472** | **100** |

### 2006 Assets

| | $ mil. | % of total |
|---|---|---|
| Cash & due from banks | 2,737 | 3 |
| Securities held for sale | 11,053 | 11 |
| Other securities | 1,352 | 1 |
| Loans | | |
| Consumer | 23,311 | 23 |
| Commercial | 20,725 | 21 |
| Commercial mortgages | 10,405 | 10 |
| Other loans & leases | 19,912 | 20 |
| Other | 11,174 | 11 |
| **Total** | **100,669** | **100** |

**Selected Subsidiaries**

Fifth Third Financial Corporation
- Fifth Third Bank
  - Fifth Third Asset Management, Inc.
  - The Fifth Third Company
  - Fifth Third Holdings, LLC
  - Fifth Third Insurance Agency, Inc.
  - Fifth Third International Company
    - Fifth Third Trade Services Limited (Hong Kong)
  - The Fifth Third Leasing Company
    - The Fifth Third Auto Leasing Trust
    - Fifth Third Foreign Lease Management, LLC
  - Fifth Third Mortgage Company
    - Fifth Third Real Estate Investment Trust, Inc.
  - Fifth Third Mortgage Reinsurance Company
  - Fifth Third Real Estate Capital Markets Company
  - Fifth Third Securities, Inc.
- Fifth Third Bank (Michigan)
  - Community Financial Services, Inc.
  - Fifth Third Auto Funding, LLC
  - Fifth Third Funding, LLC
  - GNB Management, LLC
    - FNB Investment Company, Inc.
    - GNB Realty, LLC
  - Home Equity of America, Inc.
  - Old Kent Investment Corporation
  - Old Kent Mortgage Services, Inc.
- Fifth Third Bank, National Association
- Fifth Third Community Development Corporation
  - Fifth Third New Markets Development Co., LLC
- Fifth Third Investment Company
- Fifth Third Reinsurance Company, LTD (Turks and Caicos Islands)
- Fountain Square Life Reinsurance Company, Ltd. (Turks and Caicos Islands)
- Old Kent Financial Life Insurance Company

## COMPETITORS

BA Merchant Services
Comerica
EDS
First Data
FirstMerit
Harris Bankcorp
Huntington Bancshares
KeyCorp
LaSalle Bank
Marshall & Ilsley
National City
Northern Trust
PNC Financial
U.S. Bancorp
Wells Fargo

## HISTORICAL FINANCIALS

Company Type: Public

**Income Statement** FYE: December 31

| | ASSETS ($ mil.) | NET INCOME ($ mil.) | INCOME AS % OF ASSETS | EMPLOYEES |
|---|---|---|---|---|
| **12/06** | 100,669 | 1,188 | 1.2% | 21,362 |
| **12/05** | 105,225 | 1,549 | 1.5% | 22,901 |
| **12/04** | 94,456 | 1,525 | 1.6% | 21,027 |
| **12/03** | 91,143 | 1,755 | 1.9% | 20,211 |
| **12/02** | 80,894 | 1,635 | 2.0% | 19,119 |
| **Annual Growth** | 5.6% | (7.7%) | — | 2.8% |

**2006 Year-End Financials**

Equity as % of assets: 9.9%
Return on assets: 1.2%
Return on equity: 12.2%
Long-term debt ($ mil.): 12,558
No. of shares (mil.): 556
Dividends
Yield: 3.9%
Payout: 74.2%
Market value ($ mil.): 22,767
Sales ($ mil.): 8,472

**Stock History** NASDAQ (GS): FITB

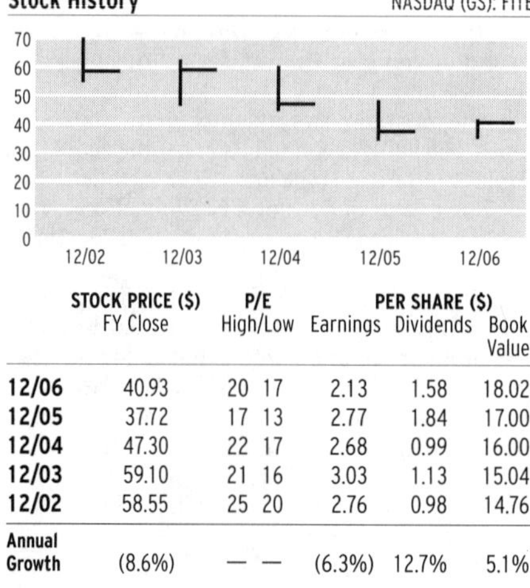


| | STOCK PRICE ($) FY Close | P/E High | P/E Low | PER SHARE ($) Earnings | Dividends | Book Value |
|---|---|---|---|---|---|---|
| **12/06** | 40.93 | 20 | 17 | 2.13 | 1.58 | 18.02 |
| **12/05** | 37.72 | 17 | 13 | 2.77 | 1.84 | 17.00 |
| **12/04** | 47.30 | 22 | 17 | 2.68 | 0.99 | 16.00 |
| **12/03** | 59.10 | 21 | 16 | 3.03 | 1.13 | 15.04 |
| **12/02** | 58.55 | 25 | 20 | 2.76 | 0.98 | 14.76 |
| **Annual Growth** | (8.6%) | — | — | (6.3%) | 12.7% | 5.1% |

# First American

The First American Corporation believes that when you're buying real estate, more information is better. In addition to its flagship title insurance subsidiary (First American Title), the company offers real estate-related financial and information services. First American provides real estate tax-valuation services, flood-zone certification, appraisal services, and credit-reporting services for property buyers and mortgage lenders. Along with good old title insurance, First American also provides property/casualty insurance, equity loans, and home warranties. The company is making use of its extensive databases to offer employee screening and credit reporting for landlords and automotive lenders.

Although First American makes the majority of its money in the US (the company underwrites almost 25% of all title insurance policies in the US), it provides title insurance in countries and territories around the world and has put extra sales efforts in Australia, Canada, Hong Kong, South Korea, and the UK. However, its information services businesses are still limited to the US.

Acquisitions have been key to First American's expansion across the real estate services and information technology services industries. Through the acquisitions of such firms as Data Tree, owner of an extensive database of imaged property records; Data Trace Information Services, a joint venture with LandAmerica; and First American Real Estate Solutions, a joint venture with Experian (a unit of GUS), First American Financial is closer to reaching its goal: eliminating costly local searches by providing a central source for property titles.

Title insurance policies represent an average of 75% of the company's annual earnings.

Chairman emeritus D. P. and chairman and CEO Parker Kennedy are descendants of the founder of the company, C. E. Parker. Fidelity Management Trust holds about 10% of the company's shares as trustee of First American's employee 401(k) plan.

## HISTORY

In 1889, when Los Angeles was on its way to becoming a real city, the more countrified residents to the south (including the Irvine Company's founding family) formed Orange County, a peaceful realm of citrus groves where land transactions were assisted by title companies Orange County Abstract and Santa Ana Abstract. In 1894 the firms merged under the leadership of local businessman C. E. Parker. For three decades, the resulting Orange County Title limited its business to title searches.

In 1924, as real estate transactions became more complex (in part because of mineral-rights issues related to Southern California's oil boom), Orange County Title began offering title insurance and escrow services. The company remained under Parker family management until 1930, when H. A. Gardner took over and guided it through the Depression. In 1943 the company returned to Parker family control.

In 1957 the company began a major expansion beyond Orange County. The new First American Title Insurance and Trust name acknowledged the firm's expansion into trust and custody operations. Donald Kennedy (C. E. Parker's grandson) took over in 1963 and took the company public the next year.

In 1968 First American Financial was formed as a holding company for subsidiaries First American Title Insurance and First American Trust. This structure facilitated growth as the firm began opening new offices and buying all or parts of other title companies, including Title Guaranty Co. of Wyoming, Security Title & Trust (San Antonio), and Ticore, Inc. (Portland, Oregon), all purchased in 1968.

The 1970s were a quiet time for the company, but it began growing again in the 1980s as savings and loan deregulation jump-started the commercial real estate market in Southern California. First American diversified into home warranty and real estate tax services. In 1988, on the brink of the California meltdown, the company bought an industrial loan corporation to make commercial real estate loans.

Reduced property sales during California's early 1990s real estate crash and recession rocked company results. Fluctuating interest rates didn't help the tremulous bottom lines. In 1994 Donald Kennedy became chairman; his son Parker became president.

As part of its expansion effort, First American bought CREDCO (mortgage credit reporting) and Flood Data Services (flood zone certification) in 1995. A year later it acquired Ward Associates, a property inspection and preservation service provider. In 1997 the company merged its real estate information subsidiaries with those of the Experian Information Solutions, a leading supplier of real estate data; it also bought Strategic Mortgage Services (mortgage information and document preparation), whose software formed the core of software operations for First American's title division.

Earnings jumped in 1998's hot real estate market. That year and the next, First American's acquisitions brought into the company's fold resident-screening services and providers of mortgage loan and loan default management software. In 1999 American Financial and Wells Fargo teamed to provide title insurance and appraisal services nationwide.

In 2000 the company bought National Information Group, a provider of tax service, flood certification, and insurance tracking for the mortgage industry. That year the company partnered with Transamerica to create the US's largest property database. The company remained acquisitive in 2002, buying two providers of tax searches and real estate valuation service company SourceOne Services.

Following a Colorado Division of Insurance investigation into the company's First American Title Insurance subsidiary's alleged practice of offering kickbacks in exchange for business, First American reached a settlement in 2005 to pay $24 million back to US consumers affected by its practices, which the company has discontinued.

First American restructured itself a bit during 2005. The company combined its credit information and screening operations into its risk mitigation and business solutions segment. It also moved its credit information group over to risk mitigation and business services firm First Advantage. As part of the deal, First American bumped its stake in First Advantage up to 80%. That year the company also acquired San Francisco-based LoanPerformance, a leading provider of mortgage analytics.

## EXECUTIVES

**Chairman Emeritus:** Donald P. (D.P.) Kennedy, age 88
**Chairman and CEO; Chairman, First American Title Insurance Company:** Parker S. Kennedy, age 59, $3,114,600 pay
**Vice Chairman and CFO:** Frank V. McMahon, age 47
**President:** Craig I. DeRoy, age 54, $2,978,950 pay
**COO:** Dennis J. Gilmore, age 48, $2,603,800 pay
**EVP; SEVP and COO, First American Title Insurance Company; EVP, First American Real Estate Information Services, Inc.:** Curt A. Caspersen, age 51
**EVP; Vice Chairman, First American Title Insurance Company:** Gary L. Kermott, age 53
**EVP, Technology; SEVP, First American Title Insurance Company:** John M. Hollenbeck, age 45
**EVP and CIO:** Roger S. Hull
**SVP and General Counsel:** Kenneth D. (Ken) DeGiorgio, age 36
**SVP, Director of Corporate Compliance, Special Counsel, and Assistant Secretary:** Kathleen M. (Katy) Collins
**SVP and Chief Accounting Officer:** Max O. Valdes, age 52
**SVP Corporate Communication:** Jo Etta Bandy
**SVP Operations, First American International Services Group:** Russ Watts
**SVP National Litigation Counsel:** Timothy P. Sullivan
**SVP and Director, Market Development:** Landon V. Taylor
**VP and Chief Marketing Officer:** Sandra Bell
**President, First Advantage Corporation:** Anand K. Nallathambi, age 46
**President, Mortgage Information Segment:** Barry M. Sando, age 47
**President, First American Title Insurance:** Curt G. Johnson
**President, First American Property Information and Services Group:** George S. Livermore
**President, Data Trace; President, DataTree, LLC:** Michael T. Henney
**Chief Actuary:** David L. Ruhm
**Director, Investor Relations:** Mark E. Seaton
**Corporate Communications:** Carrie Gaska
**Auditors:** PricewaterhouseCoopers LLP

## LOCATIONS

**HQ:** The First American Corporation
1 First American Way, Santa Ana, CA 92707
**Phone:** 714-800-3000 **Fax:** 714-800-3135
**Web:** www.firstam.com

The First American Corporation operates in Australia, the Bahamas, Canada, Guam, Ireland, Mexico, Puerto Rico, South Korea, the UK, and the US.

## PRODUCTS/OPERATIONS

### 2006 Sales

| | $ mil. | % of total |
|---|---|---|
| Financial services | | |
| Title insurance & services | 6,245.1 | 74 |
| Specialty insurance | 328.4 | 4 |
| Information technology | | |
| First Advantage | 827.7 | 9 |
| Property information | 622.8 | 7 |
| Mortgage information | 531.6 | 6 |
| Corporate | 10.1 | — |
| Eliminations | (66.6) | — |
| **Total** | **8,499.1** | **100** |

### Selected Subsidiaries

Mortgage information
- First American Centralized Services, Inc.
- First American Default Information Services LLC
- First American Flood Data Services
- First American Nationwide Documents
- First American Real Estate Information Services, Inc.

Property information
- Data Trace
- Data Tree LLC
- eAppraiseIT, LLC
- First American Real Estate Solutions, LP
- First American Residential Value View

Risk mitigation and business solutions
- First Advantage Corporation

Specialty insurance
- First American Home Buyers Protection Corporation
- First American Property & Casualty Insurance Company
- First American Specialty Insurance Company

Title insurance and services
- First American Residential Group, Inc.
- First American SMS
- First American Title Insurance Company
- First American Transportation Title Insurance Company
- Metropolitan Title Company
- Pacific Northwest Title Holding Company
- The Talon Group
- United General Title Insurance Company

## COMPETITORS

AHS
Capital Title
Fidelity National Financial
Investors Title
LandAmerica Financial Group
North American Title
Old Republic
PMI Group
Stewart Information Services
Ticor Title Co.
Transnation Title Insurance

## HISTORICAL FINANCIALS

Company Type: Public

### Income Statement

FYE: December 31

| | ASSETS ($ mil.) | NET INCOME ($ mil.) | INCOME AS % OF ASSETS | EMPLOYEES |
|---|---|---|---|---|
| **12/06** | 8,224 | 288 | 3.5% | 39,670 |
| **12/05** | 7,599 | 485 | 6.4% | 35,444 |
| **12/04** | 6,208 | 349 | 5.6% | 30,994 |
| **12/03** | 4,892 | 451 | 9.2% | 29,802 |
| **12/02** | 3,398 | 234 | 6.9% | 24,886 |
| **Annual Growth** | 24.7% | 5.3% | — | 12.4% |

### 2006 Year-End Financials

Equity as % of assets: 38.9%
Return on assets: 3.6%
Return on equity: 9.3%
Long-term debt ($ mil.): 848
No. of shares (mil.): 96
Dividends
Yield: 1.8%
Payout: 24.7%
Market value ($ mil.): 3,925
Sales ($ mil.): 8,499

### Stock History

NYSE: FAF

| | STOCK PRICE ($) FY Close | P/E High | P/E Low | PER SHARE ($) Earnings | Dividends | Book Value |
|---|---|---|---|---|---|---|
| **12/06** | 40.68 | 16 | 12 | 2.92 | 0.72 | 33.19 |
| **12/05** | 45.30 | 10 | 6 | 4.97 | 0.72 | 31.36 |
| **12/04** | 35.14 | 9 | 6 | 3.83 | 0.60 | 27.36 |
| **12/03** | 29.77 | 6 | 4 | 5.22 | 0.50 | 23.84 |
| **12/02** | 22.20 | 8 | 6 | 2.92 | 0.34 | 18.53 |
| **Annual Growth** | 16.3% | — | — | 0.0% | 20.6% | 15.7% |

# FirstEnergy Corp.

FirstEnergy's first goal is to deliver power, but its second goal is to survive deregulation. Its utilities provide electricity to 4.5 million customers in Ohio, Pennsylvania, and New Jersey, three states that are ushering in power industry competition. The company's domestic power plants have a total generating capacity of more than 13,940 MW; most generated by coal-fired plants. Subsidiary FirstEnergy Solutions trades energy commodities in deregulated markets throughout the US. FirstEnergy's other nonregulated operations include electrical and mechanical contracting and energy planning and procurement.

In response to deregulation of the US utility market, the company has not only branched out into new non-utility activities, but it has also expanded its regulated utility operations into new territories. FirstEnergy's strategy led to its 2001 acquisition of GPU, which made it one of the largest electric utility holding companies in the US and nearly doubled its customer count.

To focus on its domestic operations, FirstEnergy has sold the international energy assets gained through its acquisition of GPU. It has divested its Australian utility (GasNet) and its UK utility (Midlands Electricity), and it has exited its Argentine utility business (Emdersa) and sold its stakes in Latin American, European, and Asian power plants. The company has also sold some of its facilities services businesses, and its 50% stake in Great Lakes Energy Partners, which explores for and produces oil and gas in the Appalachian Basin, for $200 million.

The US-Canada Power System Outage Task Force, which investigated the massive August 14, 2003, blackout that affected eight states and one Canadian province, has released its interim and final reports. The task force's interim report found that FirstEnergy violated four voluntary standards set by the North American Electric Reliability Council, and stated that the blackout was largely caused by FirstEnergy's failure to set up proper communication and monitoring procedures for its transmission assets. The report also cited the company's failure to trim trees that caused several major transmission lines in its service territory to short-circuit on August 14.

The task force's final report did not lay any additional blame on the utility, but stated that the blackout could have been prevented if utilities had followed voluntary reliability standards. FirstEnergy paid a total of $90 million to settle federal lawsuits over its involvement in the blackout, as well as other securities and derivative issues, without admitting any wrongdoing. FirstEnergy faced a formal SEC investigation into financial restatements (in 2003) and an extended nuclear power plant outage (2002-2004); the investigation was not related to the blackout and was an extension of an informal SEC inquiry.

To settle with the US Environmental Protection Agency, FirstEnergy agreed to pay an estimated $1.1 billion in fines and for anti-pollution devices to be installed at its coal-burning plants in Ohio and Pennsylvania.

## HISTORY

FirstEnergy (as Ohio Edison) came to light in 1893 as the Akron Electric Light and Power Company. After several mergers, the business went bankrupt and was sold in 1899 to Akron Traction and Electric Company, which became Northern Ohio Power and Light (NOP&L).

In 1930 Commonwealth and Southern (C&S) bought NOP&L and merged it with four other Ohio utility holding companies to form Ohio Edison. The new firm increased sales during the Depression by selling electric appliances.

The Public Utility Holding Company Act of 1935 (passed to rein in the uncontrolled utilities) caught up with C&S in 1949, forcing it to divest Ohio Edison. Rival Ohio Public Service was also divested from its holding company, and in 1950 Ohio Edison bought it.

In 1967, after two decades of expansion, Ohio Edison and three other Ohio and Pennsylvania utilities formed the Central Area Power Coordination Group (CAPCO) to share new power plant costs, including the construction of the Beaver Valley nuclear plant (1970-76). Although the CAPCO partners agreed in 1980 to cancel four planned nukes, in 1985 Ohio Edison took part in building the Perry Unit 1 and Beaver Valley Unit 2 nuclear plants.

The federal Energy Policy Act of 1992 allowed wholesale power competition, and to satisfy new federal requirements, Ohio Edison formed a six-state transmission alliance in 1996 with fellow utilities Centerior Energy, Allegheny Power System, and Dominion Resources' Virginia Power to coordinate their grids.

Ohio Edison paid about $1.5 billion in 1997 for Centerior Energy, formed in 1986 as a holding company for Toledo Edison and Cleveland Electric. Ohio Edison and Centerior, both burdened by high-cost generating plants, merged to cut costs, and the expanded energy concern was renamed FirstEnergy Corp.

Looking toward deregulation, FirstEnergy began buying mechanical construction, contracting, and energy management companies in 1997. FirstEnergy then ventured into natural gas operations by purchasing MARBEL Energy.

Power marketers Federal Energy Sales and the Power Co. of America couldn't deliver the juice to FirstEnergy during the summer of 1998's hottest days. FirstEnergy later sued Federal Energy for $25 million in damages. The next year it bought electricity outage insurance.

Pennsylvania began large-scale electric power competition in 1999, when the Ohio legislature passed deregulation legislation. To comply with state laws, FirstEnergy agreed to trade power plants, including Beaver Valley, with DQE (now Duquesne Light Holdings). That year brought trouble when the EPA named FirstEnergy and six other utilities in a suit that charged the utility with noncompliance of the Clean Air Act.

In 2000 FirstEnergy agreed to acquire New Jersey-based electric utility GPU in an $11.9 billion deal; it became one of the largest US utilities in 2001 when it completed the acquisition, which added three utilities (Jersey Central Power & Light, Metropolitan Edison, and Pennsylvania Electric) that serve 2.1 million electricity customers.

Following the acquisition, FirstEnergy agreed to sell an 80% stake in GPU's UK utility, Midlands Electricity, to UtiliCorp (later Aquila) in a $2 billion deal, which was completed in 2002.

FirstEnergy sold its remaining 20% stake in Midlands Electricity to Powergen in early 2004.

Also in late 2003 former FirstEnergy chairman and CEO Peter Burg began treatment for leukemia, and president and COO Anthony Alexander was named acting CEO. Burg died in January 2004, and Alexander became president and CEO.

## EXECUTIVES

**Chairman:** George M. Smart, age 61
**President, CEO, and Director; President and COO, First Energy Service; President, The Illuminating Company, Met-Ed, Ohio Edison, Toledo Edison, Penelec, and Penn Power:** Anthony J. Alexander, age 55, $1,216,923 pay
**EVP and COO, FirstEnergy and FirstEnergy Service:** Richard R. (Dick) Grigg, age 58, $749,154 pay
**SVP and CFO, FirstEnergy, FirstEnergy Service, FirstEnergy Solutions, and FirstEnergy Nuclear Operating; SVP, The Illuminating Company, JCP&L, Met-Ed, Ohio Edison, Toledo Edison, Penelec, and Penn Power:** Richard H. (Rich) Marsh, age 56, $461,865 pay
**SVP and General Counsel, FirstEnergy, FirstEnergy Service, FirstEnergy Solutions, and FirstEnergy Nuclear Operating; SVP, The Illuminating Company, JCP&L, Metropolitan Edison, Ohio Edison, Penelec, Penn Power, and Toledo Edison:** Leila L. Vespoli, age 47, $457,769 pay
**SVP Strategic Planning and Operations, FirstEnergy and FirstEnergy Service:** Mark T. Clark, age 56
**SVP Energy Delivery and Customer Service; President, FirstEnergy Solutions:** Charles E. Jones, age 51
**SVP:** Carole B. Snyder, age 61
**SVP External Affairs:** Thomas M. Welsh, age 57
**SVP Governmental Affairs:** David C. Luff, age 59
**SVP Human Resources:** Lynn M. Cavalier, age 55
**SVP Operations:** Gary R. Leidich, age 56
**VP and Chief Information Officer:** Bennett L. Gaines
**VP, Controller, and Chief Accounting Officer; VP and Controller, FirstEnergy Service, FirstEnergy Solutions, FirstEnergy Nuclear Operating, The Illuminating Company, JCP&L, Met-Ed, Ohio Edison, Penelec, Penn Power, and Toledo Edison:** Harvey L. Wagner, age 54
**VP Federal Energy Regulatory Commission (FERC) Policy and Chief FERC Compliance Officer, FirstEnergy Service:** Stanley F. Szwed
**Director, Investor Relations:** Kurt E. Turosky
**Public Relations:** Keith Hancock
**Auditors:** PricewaterhouseCoopers LLP

## LOCATIONS

**HQ:** FirstEnergy Corp.
76 S. Main St., Akron, OH 44308
**Phone:** 800-633-4766 **Fax:** 330-384-3866
**Web:** www.firstenergycorp.com

FirstEnergy serves electricity customers in New Jersey, Ohio, and Pennsylvania.

## PRODUCTS/OPERATIONS

**2006 Sales**

| | $ mil. | % of total |
|---|---|---|
| Power supply management services | 7,029 | 61 |
| Regulated services | 4,441 | 39 |
| Other | 31 | — |
| **Total** | **11,501** | **100** |

**Electric Utility Subsidiaries**

American Transmission Systems, Inc.
The Cleveland Electric Illuminating Company (The Illuminating Company)
Jersey Central Power & Light Company (JCP&L)
Metropolitan Edison Company (Met-Ed)
Ohio Edison Company
Pennsylvania Electric Company (Penelec)
Pennsylvania Power Company (Penn Power)
The Toledo Edison Company

**Selected Unregulated Subsidiaries**

FirstEnergy Nuclear Operating Co. (nuclear generation facilities)
FirstEnergy Properties, Inc.
FirstEnergy Securities Transfer Company
FirstEnergy Service Company
FirstEnergy Solutions Corp. (retail and wholesale energy marketing and management services)
FirstEnergy Ventures Corp.
GPU Diversified Holdings, LLC
GPU Nuclear, Inc. (nuclear plant management and decommissioning)

## COMPETITORS

AEP
Allegheny Energy
Aquila
Delmarva Power
Dominion Resources
DPL
Duke Energy
Duquesne Light
Duquesne Light Holdings
Dynegy
EnergySolve
Exelon
Exelon Energy
Integrys Energy Group
NewPower Holdings
Peabody Energy
PG&E
PPL
PSEG
PSEG Energy Holdings
Southern Company
Vectren

## HISTORICAL FINANCIALS

Company Type: Public

**Income Statement** FYE: December 31

| | REVENUE ($ mil.) | NET INCOME ($ mil.) | NET PROFIT MARGIN | EMPLOYEES |
|---|---|---|---|---|
| **12/06** | 11,501 | 1,254 | 10.9% | 13,739 |
| **12/05** | 11,989 | 861 | 7.2% | 14,586 |
| **12/04** | 12,453 | 878 | 7.1% | 15,245 |
| **12/03** | 12,307 | 423 | 3.4% | 15,905 |
| **12/02** | 12,231 | 553 | 4.5% | 17,560 |
| **Annual Growth** | (1.5%) | 22.7% | — | (6.0%) |

**2006 Year-End Financials**

Debt ratio: 94.5%
Return on equity: 13.8%
Cash ($ mil.): 90
Current ratio: 0.40
Long-term debt ($ mil.): 8,535
No. of shares (mil.): 319
Dividends
Yield: 3.0%
Payout: 47.2%
Market value ($ mil.): 19,248

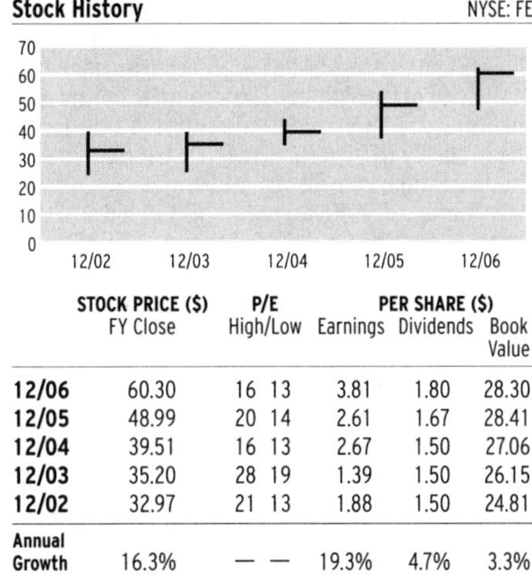


| | STOCK PRICE ($) FY Close | P/E High | P/E Low | PER SHARE ($) Earnings | PER SHARE ($) Dividends | PER SHARE ($) Book Value |
|---|---|---|---|---|---|---|
| **12/06** | 60.30 | 16 | 13 | 3.81 | 1.80 | 28.30 |
| **12/05** | 48.99 | 20 | 14 | 2.61 | 1.67 | 28.41 |
| **12/04** | 39.51 | 16 | 13 | 2.67 | 1.50 | 27.06 |
| **12/03** | 35.20 | 28 | 19 | 1.39 | 1.50 | 26.15 |
| **12/02** | 32.97 | 21 | 13 | 1.88 | 1.50 | 24.81 |
| **Annual Growth** | 16.3% | — | — | 19.3% | 4.7% | 3.3% |

# Fiserv, Inc.

It's 10:30, America. Do you know where your money is? Fiserv does. A leading processor of financial data, Fiserv provides check processing, software development, business support, insurance claims processing, health plan management services, transaction processing, and other data processing and related services to the financial industry, including banks, thrifts, credit unions, insurance firms, self-funded employers, and leasing companies. Acquisitive Fiserv has bundled its myriad business units into three segments centered around client industries: Financial Institution Services, Insurance Services, and Investment Support Services. Fiserv has offices in the US and about 15 other countries.

Approximately 150 acquisitions since Fiserv's founding in 1984 have broadened the company's menu and brought in new customers. Its acquisition targets are typically well-run, profitable operations with strong management willing to stay on. Through its purchases, the company has expanded into new areas (including employee benefit plan administration, pharmacy benefits management, and care management) and continues to develop new software. Fiserv signed up for a big purchase in 2007, agreeing to pay more than $4 billion for electronic bill payment and presentation company CheckFree.

Fiserv, which grew by serving community banks, now targets consolidation-engorged megabanks and international firms. Fiserv is also capitalizing on the banking industry's increasing reliance on transaction-oriented, fee-based services, which typically demand a large data-processing capability.

## HISTORY

When First Bank System of Minneapolis bought Milwaukee-based Midland Bank in 1984, the head of Midland's data processing operation, George Dalton, bought the unit and then merged that operation with Sunshine State Systems, a newly independent Florida processing company headed by Leslie Muma. Christened Fiserv, the company went public in 1986. It grew by providing outsourcing services to small banks and thrifts.

In the 1990s, Fiserv began targeting larger clients. But industry consolidation sometimes hurt the company, as when the 12-year term of a 1995 contract with Chase Manhattan was reduced to three after Chase and Chemical Bank merged in 1996.

As banks moved into new areas, Fiserv went along. In the late 1990s it acquired BHC Financial and Hanifen, Imhoff Holdings (securities transaction processing). Other purchases that broadened its service list included Automated Financial Technology (credit union software) and Network Data Processing (administrative software for insurance companies). The push into software continued with 1999 purchases in the field of workers' compensation systems.

Also in 1999 Fiserv bolstered its client list by buying QuestPoint's check servicing business. It moved into retirement plan administration with the purchase of a unit from what is now AIG Retirement Services. In 2000 a deal announced a year earlier to provide back-office services for American Express' online Membership Banking unit fell apart, but Fiserv recovered its momentum with enhanced mortgage servicing offerings and an agreement to provide technology services to cahoot, the online banking unit of the UK's Abbey National.

Fiserv continued its acquisitive activities the next year, buying Benefit Planners (a leading employee benefit program administrator with operations in Europe, the Middle East, South America, and the US), Facilities and Services Corporation (a California-based insurance software maker), NCSI (information and services targeting the flood insurance industry), and the bank processing operations of NCR Corporation. The company that year also sold its Human Resources Information Services unit to buyout firm Gores Technology Group.

Fiserv boosted its ATM and EFT (electronic funds transfer) business with the 2002 purchase of Electronic Data Systems' Consumer Network Services unit.

The company sold its securities clearing operations to a unit of FMR in 2005.

## EXECUTIVES

**Chairman:** Donald F. (Don) Dillon, age 66
**President, CEO, and Director:** Jeffery W. (Jeff) Yabuki, age 47, $280,000 pay
**SEVP and COO:** Norman J. (Norm) Balthasar, age 60, $1,366,120 pay
**EVP and Operating Group CFO:** Douglas J. (Doug) Craft, age 53
**EVP and CFO:** Thomas J. Hirsch, age 43
**EVP, Chief Administrative Officer, General Counsel, and Secretary:** Charles W. Sprague, age 57, $631,450 pay
**EVP, Human Resources:** Bridie A. Fanning, age 38
**EVP, Consultant Services, Item Processing Group:** Thomas R. Taylor, age 59
**Group President, Credit Union and Industry Products:** Thomas A. (Tom) Neill, age 57, $634,665 pay
**Group President, Investment Support Services:** Robert H. (Bob) Beriault, age 55
**Group President, Fiserv Health:** James W. Cox, age 43
**Group President, Item Processing:** Mark J. Damico, age 38
**Group President, Bank Servicing and ePayments:** Patrick C. (Pat) Foy, age 52
**Group President, Lending Systems and Services:** James C. Puzniak, age 60
**Group President, Marketing and Sales:** Dean C. Schmelzer, age 56
**Group President, Insurance Solutions:** Terry R. Wade, age 46
**Corporate SVP and Director of Audit:** Daniel F. Murphy, age 57
**Corporate SVP, Product and Technologies:** Thomas E. Wachtl
**Corporate SVP, Tax:** Nancy H. Wedelstaedt, age 41
**SVP, Business Development:** Mark Sievewright
**SVP and Corporate Controller:** Joseph (Joe) Gibson
**Chief Medical Officer:** Elaine H. Mischler, age 63
**Auditors:** Deloitte & Touche LLP

## LOCATIONS

**HQ:** Fiserv, Inc.
255 Fiserv Dr., Brookfield, WI 53045
**Phone:** 262-879-5000 **Fax:** 262-879-5013
**Web:** www.fiserv.com

## PRODUCTS/OPERATIONS

**2006 Sales**

| | % of total |
|---|---|
| Processing & services | 67 |
| Product | 33 |
| **Total** | **100** |

**2006 Sales By Segment**

| | % of total |
|---|---|
| Financial Institution Services | 63 |
| Insurance Services | 34 |
| Investment Support Services | 3 |
| **Total** | **100** |

## COMPETITORS

Accenture
Aetna
BA Merchant Services
BISYS
Blue Cross
CGI Group
Charles Schwab
ChoicePoint
CIGNA
Computer Sciences Corp.
DST
EDS
Fidelity National Information Services
First Data
FMR
IBM
ISO
Jack Henry
Metavante
NCR
Open Solutions
Perot Systems
SAP
State Street
SunGard
Total System Services
UnitedHealth Group
Vertafore

## HISTORICAL FINANCIALS

Company Type: Public

**Income Statement** FYE: December 31

| | REVENUE ($ mil.) | NET INCOME ($ mil.) | NET PROFIT MARGIN | EMPLOYEES |
|---|---|---|---|---|
| **12/06** | 4,544 | 450 | 9.9% | 23,000 |
| **12/05** | 4,060 | 516 | 12.7% | 22,000 |
| **12/04** | 3,730 | 378 | 10.1% | 22,000 |
| **12/03** | 3,034 | 315 | 10.4% | 21,700 |
| **12/02** | 2,569 | 266 | 10.4% | 19,400 |
| **Annual Growth** | 15.3% | 14.0% | — | 4.3% |

**2006 Year-End Financials**

Debt ratio: 30.8%
Return on equity: 18.4%
Cash ($ mil.): 185
Current ratio: 1.28
Long-term debt ($ mil.): 747
No. of shares (mil.): 171
Dividends
Yield: —
Payout: —
Market value ($ mil.): 8,969

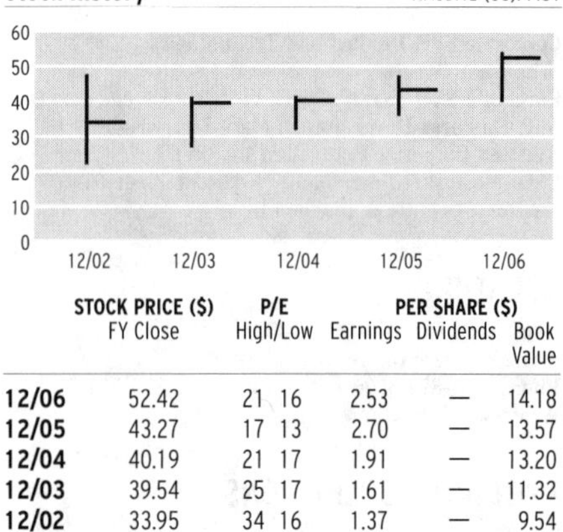


| | STOCK PRICE ($) FY Close | P/E High/Low | | PER SHARE ($) Earnings | Dividends | Book Value |
|---|---|---|---|---|---|---|
| **12/06** | 52.42 | 21 | 16 | 2.53 | — | 14.18 |
| **12/05** | 43.27 | 17 | 13 | 2.70 | — | 13.57 |
| **12/04** | 40.19 | 21 | 17 | 1.91 | — | 13.20 |
| **12/03** | 39.54 | 25 | 17 | 1.61 | — | 11.32 |
| **12/02** | 33.95 | 34 | 16 | 1.37 | — | 9.54 |
| **Annual Growth** | 11.5% | — | — | 16.6% | — | 10.4% |

# Fleetwood Enterprises

Fleetwood Enterprises gets revved up over recreational vehicles (RVs). The company is also a leading maker of manufactured housing. Fleetwood's RVs come in three types: motor homes (brands such as American Eagle, American Heritage, Southwind, and Tioga), travel trailers (Mallard, Pioneer, and Wilderness), and folding trailers. Fleetwood's manufactured homes feature vaulted ceilings, walk-in closets, and porches. Fleetwood operates manufacturing facilities in 14 US states and in Canada; sales are made through both company-owned outlets and independent distributors.

In order to focus its efforts on manufacturing operations, Fleetwood sold its manufactured housing retail operations as well as its HomeOne Credit Corp. financial services subsidiary to Clayton Homes in 2006.

The company is consolidating manufacturing operations and closing some plants to bring its travel trailer production capacity into line with its share of the travel trailer market. Fleetwood has had market share problems with its line of travel trailers due to increased competition, lack of competitiveness on features and pricing, and the growing demand for products in segments of the market in which Fleetwood did not participate. In 2006 the company began to update its product portfolio and lowered prices. The company further refined its lineup of travel trailers for the 2008 model year.

As gas prices climb, Fleetwood has also lost Class-C motor home market share as it did not participate in the low-end and fuel-efficient segments of the market. The company is responding by introducing two lower-priced models, and plans to launch a fuel-efficient model in 2008.

## HISTORY

In 1950 John Crean started Coach Specialties Company, a California business that made venetian blinds for use by motor-home manufacturers. Headquartered in Riverside, this company was the forerunner of Fleetwood Enterprises, Crean's 1957 entry into the manufactured-housing industry. The company entered the RV market in 1964 by buying a small plant that produced the Terry travel trailer. The firm went public in 1965.

Between 1968 and 1973 sales grew nearly 55% annually. In 1969 the company bought motorhome maker Pace Arrow to expand its offerings in the fast-growing RV market. An industry-wide recession caused by the 1973 oil shock and subsequent credit crunch dropped Fleetwood's stock from a 1972 high of $49.50 to $3.50 in 1974. Intensive cost-cutting helped position the company for an eventual upturn, and in 1976 it bought Avion Coach (luxury-class travel trailers and motor homes).

In 1980 Fleetwood closed nine factories in response to a recession, high interest rates, and high gas prices. COO Glenn Kummer became president in 1982. Strong RV sales helped pull the company out of a mild recession in the mid-1980s.

Fleetwood opened a credit office in Southern California in 1987 to finance customers' RV purchases; this enabled the company to avoid riskier loans made to mobile-home buyers. Fleetwood added to its existing supply operations (fiberglass and lumber) by buying a maker of cabinet doors in 1988 and a maker of aluminum windows in 1989.

Also in 1989 the company became the first to surpass the $1 billion sales mark in RVs by increasing market share during an industry slump while continuing to avoid long-term debt. Fleetwood also added two new models to its RV line: the lower-priced Flair and the curved-wall Cambria. Another 1989 acquisition included Coleman's folding-trailer business — the largest in the industry, with a 30% market share.

Fleetwood received an order from Saudi Arabia for 2,000 manufactured homes in 1990. Recession and the Persian Gulf War inhibited demand for RVs and manufactured housing, but sales began to rebound by mid-1991. Fleetwood and Ford Motor Credit formed a joint venture that year to offer financing to manufactured-housing dealers.

The company bought 80% of Niesmann & Bischoff (luxury motor homes, Germany) in 1992. The next year Fleetwood finished a plant in Tennessee, followed by a plant near Waco, Texas, in 1994. The travel trailer unit introduced a lightweight line in 1994 for customers with limited towing capacity. Fleetwood began producing manufactured homes in Wichita Falls, Texas, in 1995, and the company broke ground for a housing manufacturing center in Winchester, Kentucky.

Streamlining its operations in 1996, Fleetwood sold its finance subsidiary, Fleetwood Credit, and its money-losing German RV subsidiary. In 1997 Fleetwood became the first US homebuilder to construct a million houses.

Kummer succeeded Crean as chairman and CEO in 1998; Crean became chairman emeritus (he left to start another business in 1999). Also that year the company bought more than half a dozen retailers, including HomeUSA (65 outlets), Better Homes (Kansas), Central Homes (Oregon), and Jasper Homes, Classic City Homes, and America's Best Homes (all in Georgia). Acquisitions continued in 1999 with the purchases of Viking Homes (New Mexico), JR's Mobile Homes (Illinois), and D&D Homes (California).

Because of slowing sales, Fleetwood closed five factories and laid off more than 800 employees in 2000. A 2001 restructuring included several management departures.

In 2002 Kummer retired and Thomas Pitcher became interim chairman in February, before he was elected chairman in September. PACCAR VP Edward Caudill was named president and CEO. The company had 21 idle manufacturing facilities at the end of fiscal 2002. That year the company's manufactured housing group suffered along with the industry in general due to restrictive financing (particularly in Texas) and competition from new home sales. Fleetwood announced in 2004 that it would begin using Caterpillar engines in all its diesel RVs by the end of 2005.

In March 2005 Caudill stepped down and was replaced by former Fleetwood SVP Elden Smith.

## EXECUTIVES

**Chairman:** Thomas B. Pitcher, age 67
**President, CEO, and Director:** Elden L. Smith, age 66, $1,803,637 pay
**EVP and CFO:** Boyd R. Plowman, age 62, $828,739 pay
**EVP, RV Group:** Christopher J. Braun, age 46, $459,514 pay
**SVP and CIO:** Todd L. Inlander, age 41
**SVP, General Counsel, and Secretary:** Leonard J. McGill, age 47, $533,385 pay
**SVP and Chief Accounting Officer:** Andrew M. (Andy) Griffiths, age 40
**SVP Human Resources and Administration:** Michael B. Shearin
**VP, Treasurer, and Assistant Secretary:** Lyle N. Larkin, age 61
**VP, Controller-Operations:** James F. Smith, age 58
**Director, Investor Relations:** Kathy A. Munson
**Director, Marketing Services, Housing:** JoAnna Foist
**Marketing Manager, Recreational Vehicles:** Amy Coleman
**President, Fleetwood Housing Group:** Charles E. (Charley) Lott, age 58
**President, Fleetwood Recreational Vehicle Group:** Paul Eskritt
**President, Fleetwood Supply Group:** Larry L. Mace, age 63
**Auditors:** Ernst & Young LLP

## LOCATIONS

**HQ:** Fleetwood Enterprises, Inc.
3125 Myers St., Riverside, CA 92503
**Phone:** 951-351-3500 **Fax:** 951-351-3312
**Web:** www.fleetwood.com

## PRODUCTS/OPERATIONS

### 2007 Sales

| | $ mil. | % of total |
|---|---|---|
| Recreational vehicles | | |
| Motor homes | 961.9 | 48 |
| Travel trailers | 391.3 | 20 |
| Folding trailers | 88.6 | 4 |
| Manufactured housing | | |
| Housing group | 518.3 | 26 |
| Supply group | 47.9 | 2 |
| **Total** | **2,008.0** | **100** |

### Selected Products and Brands

Recreational vehicles
- Folding trailers
- Motor homes (American Eagle, American Heritage, American Tradition, Bounder, Discovery, Expedition, Flair, Jamboree, Pace Arrow, Southwind, Storm, Tioga)
- Travel trailers (Gear Box, Mallard, Nitrous, Pegasus, Pioneer, Prowler, Terry, Wilderness)

Manufactured housing

## COMPETITORS

American Homestar
Cavalier Homes
Cavco
Champion Enterprises
Clayton Homes
Coachmen
Dynamic Homes
Featherlite
Forest River
General Housing
Horton Industries
Keystone RV
Liberty Homes
Monaco Coach
Motor Coach Industries
National RV
Newmar Corporation
Nobility Homes
Palm Harbor Homes
Patriot Homes
Rexhall
Skyline
Southern Energy Homes
Sunshine Homes
Supreme Industries
Thor Industries
Tiffin Motorhomes
TRIGANO
Wells Cargo
Winalta
Winnebago

## HISTORICAL FINANCIALS

Company Type: Public

**Income Statement** FYE: Last Sunday in April

| | REVENUE ($ mil.) | NET INCOME ($ mil.) | NET PROFIT MARGIN | EMPLOYEES |
|---|---|---|---|---|
| **4/07** | 2,008 | (90) | — | 9,300 |
| **4/06** | 2,432 | (28) | — | 11,500 |
| **4/05** | 2,375 | (162) | — | 12,700 |
| **4/04** | 2,608 | (22) | — | 13,800 |
| **4/03** | 2,318 | (71) | — | 13,000 |
| **Annual Growth** | (3.5%) | — | — | (8.0%) |

**2007 Year-End Financials**

| | |
|---|---|
| Debt ratio: 329.9% | No. of shares (mil.): 64 |
| Return on equity: — | Dividends |
| Cash ($ mil.): 76 | Yield: — |
| Current ratio: 1.54 | Payout: — |
| Long-term debt ($ mil.): 278 | Market value ($ mil.): 553 |

**Stock History** NYSE: FLE

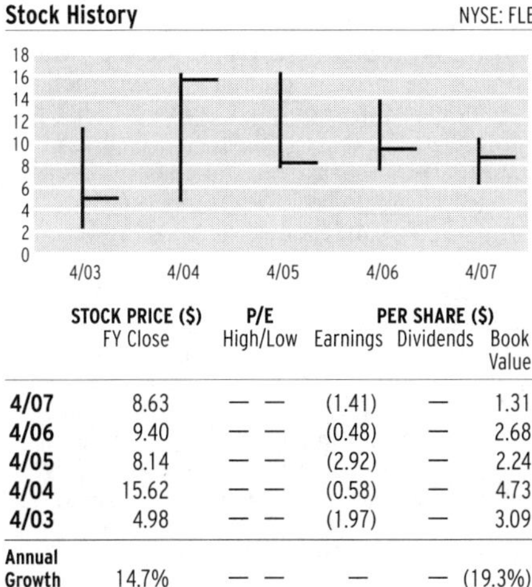


| | STOCK PRICE ($) FY Close | P/E High/Low | PER SHARE ($) Earnings | Dividends | Book Value |
|---|---|---|---|---|---|
| **4/07** | 8.63 | — — | (1.41) | — | 1.31 |
| **4/06** | 9.40 | — — | (0.48) | — | 2.68 |
| **4/05** | 8.14 | — — | (2.92) | — | 2.24 |
| **4/04** | 15.62 | — — | (0.58) | — | 4.73 |
| **4/03** | 4.98 | — — | (1.97) | — | 3.09 |
| **Annual Growth** | 14.7% | — — | — | — | (19.3%) |

# Flowers Foods

Look for Flowers Foods in your breadbox, not your garden — the company is one of the largest wholesale bakeries in the US. Its Flowers Bakeries unit produces, markets, and distributes fresh breads, buns, rolls, and bakery goodies to retail and foodservice customers throughout the southern US. The company's brand names include ButterKrust, Cobblestone Mill, and Nature's Own. The company's Flowers Specialty division makes snack cakes and frozen bread products for retail, vending, and co-pack customers nationwide. Flowers Bakeries also rolls out hamburger buns for foodservice chains such as Burger King, Hardee's, Outback Steakhouse, Wendy's, and Whataburger.

Flowers Bakeries also makes private-label breads for food retailers. Wal-Mart is the company's largest customer, representing about 19% of sales.

The company has a long-term strategy of organic and strategic growth that includes developing new products, expanding its distribution system, and acquiring other bakeries. It has completed over 100 acquisitions in the past 40 years. In 2005 Flowers Foods acquired bankrupt snack maker Royal Cake and renamed it Flowers Bakery of Winston-Salem, LLC. The following year the company acquired Derst Baking, a private company that distributes fresh bread products under the Captain John Derst's Old Fashioned Bread and Sunbeam brands in the southeastern US.

Although Flower Foods' New Orleans bakery sustained some damage from Hurricane Katrina in August 2005, it was back in business by that December.

The company introduced a line of specialty breads aimed at the health sector in 2006. Available under the Nature's Own label, the breads are whole grain and contain no artificial ingredients.

## HISTORY

Georgia native William Flowers and his brother Joseph opened the Flowers Ice Cream Co. in the winter resort town of Thomasville, Georgia, in 1914 to serve wealthy visitors from the North. Seeing that there was no bakery in the town (the nearest bakery was more than 200 miles away), the brothers opened Flowers Baking Co. in 1919. During the 1920s William took charge of the bakery, while Joseph continued to run the ice-cream operation. In 1928 Flowers moved into the production of sweet rolls and cakes. As its reputation for high-quality baked goods spread, the firm established a regional network of customers. William died in 1934, and his 20-year-old son, Bill, took over.

Amidst the difficult Depression years, Bill led the company in its first acquisition, a bakery in Florida. Flowers operated its bakeries around the clock during WWII to supply military bases in the Southeast. Bill's brother Langdon joined the firm after the war and helped take the company on a major expansion drive in the 1950s and 1960s.

Flowers acquired additional southeastern bakers in the mid-1960s and bought the Atlanta Baking Co. in 1967. The next year the company changed its name to Flowers Industries and went public.

In 1976 the company diversified, entering the frozen-food business by acquiring Stilwell Foods (frozen fruits, battered vegetables) in Oklahoma and its subsidiary, Rio Grande Foods, in Texas. The firm also expanded its fresh bread line, including the Nature's Own brand of variety breads (1978).

During the 1970s and 1980s, the company expanded beyond its southeastern regional base by acquiring bakeries in the Southwest and Midwest. Company veteran Amos McMullian became CEO in 1981 and chairman in 1985, when both Bill and Langdon retired. (Langdon died in 2007 at the age of 85.) In 1989 Flowers bought out Winn-Dixie's bakery operations.

The company launched a $377 million, six-year capital investment program in 1991 to upgrade and automate its bakeries. Flowers began a major expansion strategy with the 1996 acquisition of Mrs. Smith's, the US's top frozen-pie brand, from J.M. Smucker. Later that year Flowers and joint venture partners Artal Luxembourg and Benmore acquired cookie maker Keebler Foods (which it sold to Kellogg in 2001). In 1997 the company acquired Allied Bakery Products, a baker of frozen bread and rolls for food service customers in the Northeast US. When Keebler went public in 1998, Flowers increased its controlling stake to 55%.

Further acquisitions included Home Baking Company (food service buns, 1999) and Kroger's bakery operations in Memphis (2000). Weakened by equipment glitches in newly upgraded Mrs. Smith's facilities, earnings suffered at the end of 1999. Flowers snubbed an acquisition inquiry by Sara Lee in early 2000, but as other mega-food company acquisitions dominoed around it, Flowers agreed to sell Keebler to Kellogg in 2000.

Upon completion of the Keebler/Kellogg deal in 2001, Flowers Industries recreated itself, spinning off its Flowers Bakeries and Mrs. Smith's Bakeries businesses under the Flowers Foods name; it kept the same FLO stock ticker.

To better control costs, the company cut jobs at Mrs. Smiths in mid-2002, and initiated a restructuring of its operating units. Later that same year, the company acquired family-owned Ideal Baking of Arkansas and the snack-cake maker Bishop Baking Company.

In 2003 Flowers sold the frozen dessert segment of Mrs. Smith's to The Schwan Food Company for $240 million. Flowers retained the frozen bread and roll dough portion of Mrs. Smith's. That same year it also introduced a line of snack cakes under the names Tesoritos and Pan Dulce de Mi Casa, which are aimed at the Latino and Hispanic markets.

In 2004 the company acquired the Houston operations of the Sara Lee Bakery Group. The terms of the deal were not disclosed. However, the company in early 2005 did disclose the settlement of a million-dollar class-action lawsuit brought against the company for producing non-kosher food items on a kosher pie shell line at its production facility in Pembroke, North Carolina. To settle, the company apologized for failing to notify the Orthodox Union for occasions when the error occurred and agreed to donate more than $2 million in cash and bread products to charitable groups.

## EXECUTIVES

**Chairman, President, and CEO:** George E. Deese, age 61
**SVP and CFO:** Jimmy M. Woodward, age 46
**SVP, Corporate Relations:** Marta Jones Turner, age 52
**SVP, Secretary, and General Counsel:**
Stephen R. (Steve) Avera, age 50
**SVP, Supply Chain:** Michael A. (Mike) Beaty, age 56

**VP and Corporate Controller:** R. Steve Kinsey
**VP, Communications:** Mary Krier
**VP, Diversity and Recruitment:** Leny J. Garcia-Hill
**VP, Marketing, Flowers Bakeries Group:** Janice Anderson
**VP, Sales:** Randy Brock
**VP, Sales:** Bobby Priest
**VP and Treasurer:** Kirk L. Tolbert
**VP Environmental and Regulatory Affairs:** Jerry F. Hancock II
**President and COO, Flowers Bakeries Group:** Gene D. Lord, age 59
**President and COO, Flowers Foods Specialty Group:** Allen L. Shiver, age 51
**Auditors:** PricewaterhouseCoopers LLP

## LOCATIONS

**HQ:** Flowers Foods, Inc.
1919 Flowers Cir., Thomasville, GA 31757
**Phone:** 229-226-9110 **Fax:** 229-225-3806
**Web:** www.flowersfoods.com

## PRODUCTS/OPERATIONS

### 2006 Sales

| | $ mil. | % of total |
|---|---|---|
| Flowers Bakeries | 1,535.7 | 78 |
| Flowers Specialty | 440.8 | 22 |
| Eliminations | (87.8) | — |
| **Total** | **1,888.7** | **100** |

### Selected Brands

Flowers Bakeries Brands
- BlueBird
- ButterKrust
- Cobblestone Mill
- Dandee
- Evangeline Maid
- Flowers
- Ideal
- Mary Jane
- Mi Casa
- Nature's Own
- Whitewheat

Flowers Bakeries Regional Franchised Brands
- Bunny
- Holsum
- Roman Meal
- Sunbeam

Flowers Specialty Brands
- European Bakers
- Mrs. Freshley's
- Snack Away

## COMPETITORS

Alpha Baking
Bimbo
Bimbo Bakeries
Campbell Soup
Columbia Bakeries
Frito-Lay
General Mills
George Weston
Heinemann's Bakeries
Interstate Bakeries
Kellogg Snacks
King's Hawaiian
Kraft Foods
Kraft North America Commercial
Lance Snacks
McKee Foods
Otis Spunkmeyer
RAB Holdings
Ralcorp
Rich Products
Sara Lee Food & Beverage
Tasty Baking
United States Bakery

## HISTORICAL FINANCIALS

Company Type: Public

### Income Statement

FYE: Saturday nearest December 31

| | REVENUE ($ mil.) | NET INCOME ($ mil.) | NET PROFIT MARGIN | EMPLOYEES |
|---|---|---|---|---|
| **12/06** | 1,889 | 81 | 4.3% | 7,800 |
| **12/05** | 1,716 | 61 | 3.6% | 7,500 |
| **12/04** | 1,551 | 51 | 3.3% | 7,000 |
| **12/03** | 1,453 | 15 | 1.0% | 6,900 |
| **12/02** | 1,652 | (17) | — | 8,100 |
| **Annual Growth** | 3.4% | — | — | (0.9%) |

### 2006 Year-End Financials

Debt ratio: 14.1%
Return on equity: 15.1%
Cash ($ mil.): 14
Current ratio: 1.31
Long-term debt ($ mil.): 79
No. of shares (mil.): 60
Dividends
Yield: 1.8%
Payout: 36.8%
Market value ($ mil.): 1,088

### Stock History

NYSE: FLO

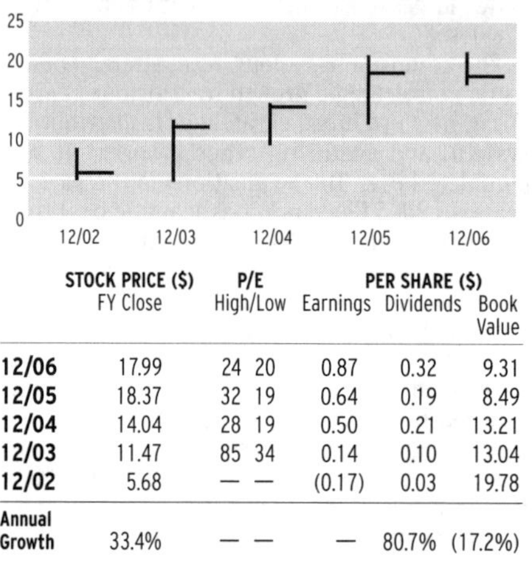


| | STOCK PRICE ($) FY Close | P/E High | P/E Low | PER SHARE ($) Earnings | Dividends | Book Value |
|---|---|---|---|---|---|---|
| **12/06** | 17.99 | 24 | 20 | 0.87 | 0.32 | 9.31 |
| **12/05** | 18.37 | 32 | 19 | 0.64 | 0.19 | 8.49 |
| **12/04** | 14.04 | 28 | 19 | 0.50 | 0.21 | 13.21 |
| **12/03** | 11.47 | 85 | 34 | 0.14 | 0.10 | 13.04 |
| **12/02** | 5.68 | — | — | (0.17) | 0.03 | 19.78 |
| **Annual Growth** | 33.4% | — | — | — | 80.7% | (17.2%) |

# Fluor Corporation

There's construction, and then there's *construction*, and Fluor ranks among the leading international design, engineering, and contracting firms. The company oversees construction projects for a large range of industrial sectors worldwide, focusing on its core strengths: engineering, procurement, construction, and maintenance. Its projects include designing and building manufacturing facilities, refineries, pharmaceutical facilities, health care buildings, power plants, and telecommunications and transportation infrastructure. Fluor also provides operations and maintenance services for its projects, as well as administrative and support services to the US government.

Fluor's oil and gas segment provides design, engineering, and construction and project management services to markets including upstream oil and gas producers, refiners, petrochemical manufacturers, and producers of specialty and fine chemicals.

The company's industrial and infrastructure segment provides design, engineering, procurement, and construction services for pharmaceutical and biotechnology facilities, commercial and institutional buildings, and mining, telecommunications, and transportation projects.

Fluor has jumped into the growing outsourcing market with its global services segment, which provides operations and maintenance support, temporary staffing, and asset management. The segment provides services to nearly 200 facilities and project sites worldwide. Fluor also provides construction equipment, tools, and fleet outsourcing for construction projects and plant sites worldwide through its American Equipment Company (AMECO) subsidiary. Fluor has exited from the nonconstruction-related temporary staffing services (accounting, information technology, and finance) of its TRS Staffing Solutions (TRS) unit.

Fluor's government services segment offers project management primarily to the US Departments of Energy and Defense. It provides environmental restoration, engineering and construction, and operations and maintenance services for two former nuclear weapons complexes that are now DOE cleanup sites: the Fernald Environmental Management Project near Cincinnati and the Hanford Environmental Management Project in Richland, Washington. Other projects of the group range from construction services for US ground-based missile defense facilities in Alaska to the upgrading of Afghanistan airports with radar and runway lighting for the US Air Force. In Iraq the company is one of the prime US contractors and has helped upgrade military facilities and electrical infrastructure. It has partnered with UK-based AMEC (FluorAMEC) to reconstruct public works and water infrastructure in Iraq.

Although Fluor is continuing to dispose of noncore operations, it has expanded through niche acquisitions in key markets, including operations and maintenance for US industrial plants and outsourced services to the federal government.

Fluor moved its headquarters from California to Dallas in 2006. The move resulted in the elimination of about 100 jobs.

## HISTORY

Fluor's history began in 1890 when three Fluor brothers, immigrants from Switzerland, opened a Wisconsin lumber mill under the name Rudolph Fluor & Brothers. In 1912 John Simon Fluor formed a construction firm in Santa Ana, California. Fluor's company soon began a relationship with Southern California Gas, which led it to specialize in oil and gas construction. The company, incorporated as Fluor Construction in 1924, later began making engine mufflers. In 1930 it expanded outside of California with a contract to build Texas pipelines.

After WWII, Middle East oil reserves were aggressively developed by Western companies. Fluor cashed in on the stampede, winning major contracts in Saudi Arabia. During the early 1960s it continued to emphasize oil and gas work, establishing a contract drilling unit, and in the 1970s it began work on giant energy projects.

In 1977 Fluor made its biggest purchase: Daniel International, a South Carolina engineering and construction firm with more than $1 billion in annual revenues. The contracting firm, founded by Charles Daniel in 1934, initially did construction work for the textile industry, then later worked for the chemical, pharmaceutical, metal, and power industries.

Flush with cash, Fluor bought St. Joe Minerals in 1981. A drop in oil prices in the 1980s killed demand for the big projects that were its bread and butter. As metal prices fell, St. Joe didn't help the bottom line either. John Robert Fluor, the last of the founding family to head the firm, died in 1984.

When David Tappan stepped in as CEO, he faced a $573 million loss the first year. The white-haired son of missionaries to China, Tappan — known as the Ice Man — dumped subsidiaries and halved the payroll. In 1986 he merged Daniel into Fluor's engineering unit, forming Fluor Daniel.

Leslie McCraw succeeded Tappan as CEO in 1991. McCraw saw Fluor as overly conservative, and three years later he began setting up offices around the world while decentralizing Fluor's structure and adding new business such as temporary staffing and equipment leasing. Fluor also shed some of its commodity companies, including its lead business in 1994. In 1996 Fluor's environmental services unit merged with Groundwater Technology and was spun off as a public company, Fluor Daniel GTI.

Ill with cancer, McCraw stepped down in 1998, and Philip Carroll, who had overhauled Shell Oil, took over as CEO. Fluor in 1999 cut 5,000 jobs, further streamlined operations, and focused on growth industries such as biotechnology and telecommunications. The next year the company split its construction and coal mining operations into two separate publicly traded companies, one to concentrate on engineering and construction and one on coal mining. Former Fluor subsidiary A. T. Massey Coal was spun off as Massey Energy.

Carroll, his restructuring job complete, announced in December 2001 that he would retire the following February. Alan Boeckmann, who had been president and COO, succeeded Carroll in 2002.

The next year Fluor acquired Del-Jen, a provider of outsourced services to US military bases and to the US Department of Labor. It also picked up five specialty operations and maintenance business groups from Philip Services. And in 2003 the company decided to dissolve its Duke/Fluor Daniel joint venture.

## EXECUTIVES

**Chairman and CEO, Fluor Corporation and Fluor Federal Services:** Alan L. Boeckmann, age 58, $1,088,009 pay
**EVP and CIO:** Ray F. Barnard, age 48
**SVP and CFO:** D. Michael (Mike) Steuert, age 58, $677,278 pay
**SVP, Business Development and Strategy, Infrastructure:** Robert (Bob) Prieto
**SVP, Corporate Strategy & Emerging Markets:** Ian Thomas
**SVP, Industrial Relations, Security, and Health, Safety, and Environment:** Garry W. Flowers
**SVP Government Relations:** David (Dave) Marventano
**SVP Human Resources and Administration:** H. Steven (Steve) Gilbert, age 59, $420,198 pay
**Chief Legal Officer and Secretary, Fluor Corporation and Fluor Federal Services:** Lawrence N. (Larry) Fisher, age 63, $561,432 pay
**VP Corporate Communications:** Lee C. Tashjian
**VP Corporate Finance and Investor Relations:** Kenneth H. (Ken) Lockwood
**VP Global Public Affairs:** J. Robert (Bob) Fluor II
**Group President, Government: Group President, Corporate Strategy & Emerging Markets:** John L. Hopkins, age 52
**Senior Group President, Industrial and Infrastructure, Government and Global Services:** Stephen B. Dobbs, age 50
**Senior Group President, Energy and Chemicals and Power:** Jeffery L. (Jeff) Faulk, age 56, $462,938 pay (prior to promotion)
**Group President, Global Services:** Kirk D. Grimes, age 49
**Group President, Power:** David E. Constable
**Group President, Industrial and Infrastructure:** Dwayne A. Wilson, age 48
**Group President, Energy and Chemicals:** David T. Seaton, age 45
**Auditors:** Ernst & Young LLP

## LOCATIONS

**HQ:** Fluor Corporation
6700 Las Colinas Blvd., Irving, TX 75039
**Phone:** 469-398-7000 **Fax:** 469-398-7255
**Web:** www.fluor.com

### 2006 Sales

| | $ mil. | % of total |
|---|---|---|
| US | 6,339 | 45 |
| Canada | 1,090 | 8 |
| Asia/Pacific (including Australia) | 1,346 | 9 |
| Europe | 1,717 | 12 |
| Central & South America | 1,805 | 13 |
| Middle East & Africa | 1,782 | 13 |
| **Total** | **14,079** | **100** |

## PRODUCTS/OPERATIONS

### 2006 Sales

| | $ mil. | % of total |
|---|---|---|
| Oil & gas | 5,368 | 38 |
| Industrial & infrastructure | 3,171 | 23 |
| Government | 2,860 | 20 |
| Global services | 2,138 | 15 |
| Power | 542 | 4 |
| **Total** | **14,079** | **100** |

### Selected Services

Construction management
Design
Engineering, procurement, and construction (EPC)
Operations and maintenance
Program management
Project development and finance
Project management
Staffing

### Selected Industries Served

Biotechnology
Chemicals and petrochemicals
Commercial and institutional
Equipment
Gas processing
Government
Manufacturing
Mining
Oil and gas production
Petroleum refining
Pharmaceuticals
Power generation
Telecommunications
Transportation

### Selected Subsidiaries

American Construction Equipment Company, Inc.
Fluor Constructors International, Inc.
Fluor Enterprises, Inc.
  Daniel International Corporation
  Del-Jen, Inc.
  ICA-Fluor Daniel, S. de R.L. de C.V. (49%, Mexico)
Fluor Holding Company LLC
TRS Staffing Solutions, Inc.

## COMPETITORS

ABB
ARCADIS
Balfour Construction
BE&K
Bechtel
Bilfinger Berger
Black & Veatch
Bouygues
CH2M HILL
Dragados
Earth Tech
Foster Wheeler
Halliburton
Hitachi
Jacobs Engineering
KBR
Marelich Mechanical
McDermott
Michael Baker
Parsons
POSCO
Raytheon
Shaw Group
Technip
Tetra Tech
Tyco
University Mechanical & Engineering
URS
Vecellio & Grogan
Washington Group
WFI Government Services
WorleyParsons Corp.

## HISTORICAL FINANCIALS

Company Type: Public

### Income Statement

FYE: December 31

| | REVENUE ($ mil.) | NET INCOME ($ mil.) | NET PROFIT MARGIN | EMPLOYEES |
|---|---|---|---|---|
| **12/06** | 14,079 | 264 | 1.9% | 37,560 |
| **12/05** | 13,161 | 227 | 1.7% | 34,836 |
| **12/04** | 9,380 | 187 | 2.0% | 35,000 |
| **12/03** | 8,806 | 157 | 1.8% | 29,011 |
| **12/02** | 9,959 | 164 | 1.6% | 44,809 |
| **Annual Growth** | 9.0% | 12.7% | — | (4.3%) |

### 2006 Year-End Financials

Debt ratio: 10.8%
Return on equity: 15.7%
Cash ($ mil.): 976
Current ratio: 1.38
Long-term debt ($ mil.): 187
No. of shares (mil.): 88
Dividends
  Yield: 1.0%
  Payout: 27.1%
Market value ($ mil.): 7,189

### Stock History

NYSE: FLR

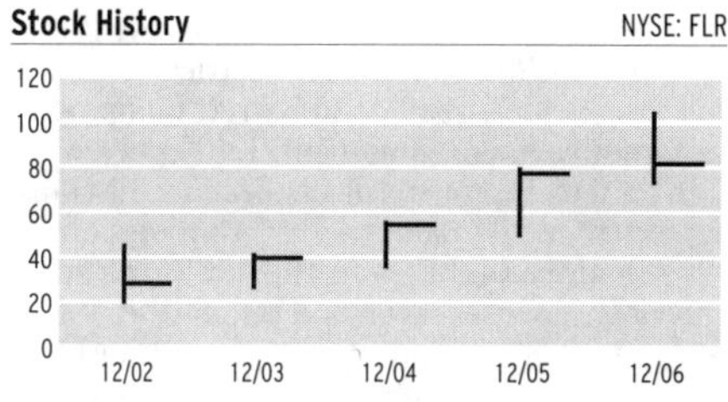


| | STOCK PRICE ($) FY Close | P/E High | P/E Low | PER SHARE ($) Earnings | Dividends | Book Value |
|---|---|---|---|---|---|---|
| **12/06** | 81.65 | 35 | 25 | 2.95 | 0.80 | 19.66 |
| **12/05** | 77.26 | 30 | 19 | 2.62 | 0.64 | 18.72 |
| **12/04** | 54.51 | 25 | 16 | 2.25 | 0.64 | 15.61 |
| **12/03** | 39.64 | 21 | 14 | 1.95 | 0.64 | 13.17 |
| **12/02** | 28.00 | 22 | 10 | 2.05 | 0.64 | 11.02 |
| **Annual Growth** | 30.7% | — | — | 9.5% | 5.7% | 15.6% |

# FMC Corporation

E may = mc2, but FMC = chemicals. Once in areas as diverse as oil field equipment and food machinery, FMC Corporation now focuses on industrial, specialty, and agricultural chemicals. The company's industrial chemicals include soda ash (it's one of the largest producers), hydrogen peroxide, and phosphorus chemicals. The rest of its sales come from agricultural products (insecticides and herbicides) and specialty chemicals (food and pharmaceutical additives). FMC and partner Solutia sold Astaris (now called ICL Performance Products LP), its phosphorus compounds joint venture, to Israel Chemicals Limited in late 2005.

FMC's equation lately has improved after a few years' effort to increase its efficiency, profitability, and credit rating. The company cut costs across the board and re-focused on strong growth areas.

The specialty chemicals sectors of food and pharmaceutical additives are the areas of choice where FMC sees a real opportunity to improve its fortunes. Product development has been concentrated on specialty chemicals product areas like energy storage (lithium products for batteries) and agricultural products like home and garden pesticides.

## HISTORY

After retiring to California, inventor John Bean developed a pump to deliver a continuous spray of insecticide in 1884. This invention led to the Bean Spray Pump Company in 1904. In 1928 Bean Spray Pump went public and bought Anderson-Barngrover (food-growing and -processing equipment). The company became Food Machinery Corporation the next year. It bought Peerless Pump (agricultural and industrial pumps) in 1933.

During WWII the company began making military equipment. It entered the agricultural chemical field when it bought Niagara Sprayer & Chemical (1943). After the war it added Westvaco Chemical (1948) and changed its name to Food Machinery & Chemical.

The Bean family ran the company until 1956, when John Bean's grandson, John Crummey, retired as chairman. The company extended its product line, buying Oil Center Tool (wellhead equipment, 1957), Sunland Industries (fertilizer and insecticides, 1959), and Barrett Equipment (automotive brake equipment, 1961).

In light of its growing diversification, the company changed its name to FMC Corporation in 1961. Major purchases in the 1960s included American Viscose (rayon and cellophane, 1963) and Link-Belt (equipment for power transmission and for bulk-material handling, 1967).

To be centrally located, FMC moved its headquarters from San Jose to Chicago in 1972. Through the 1970s and early 1980s, the company sold several slow-growing businesses, including its pump and fiber divisions (1976), semiconductor division (1979), industrial packaging division (1980), Niagara Seed Operation (1980), and Power Transmission Group (1981).

It moved into other markets just as quickly. These included a Nevada gold mine (through a 1979 joint venture with Freeport Minerals), Bradley armored personnel carriers (through an early-1980s contract with the US Army), and lithium (by acquiring Lithium Corp. of America, 1985). In a 1986 antitakeover move, FMC gave employees a larger stake in the company.

FMC bought Ciba-Geigy's flame-retardant and water-treatment businesses in 1992 and combined its defense operations with Harsco as United Defense. FMC's 1994 acquisitions included Abex's Jetway Systems Division (aircraft support systems) and Caterpillar's Automated Vehicle Systems group. FMC formed a joint venture with Nippon Sheet Glass and Sumitomo Corporation in 1995 to mine for soda ash.

FMC made a deal with DuPont in 1996 to commercialize new herbicides. The company debuted its composite (nonmetallic) prototype armored vehicle in 1997. In the long shadow of reduced defense budgets, FMC and Harsco sold their stagnant defense operation for $850 million to The Carlyle Group investment firm.

The sale of its defense division didn't protect FMC from a $310 million damage award in a whistleblower suit against the company in 1998. A federal jury found that FMC had misled the Army about the safety of the Bradley armored infantry vehicle. The court later lowered the penalty to about $90 million.

In 1999 the company agreed to combine its phosphorus operations with Solutia to form a joint venture called Astaris. That year FMC sold its process-additives unit to Great Lakes Chemical (now called Chemtura).

FMC bought Northfield Freezing Systems (food processing) in 2000. The following year the company split into separate chemical and machinery companies by spinning off its machinery business as FMC Technologies; FMC Corporation then moved its headquarters from Chicago to Philadelphia. In early 2002 FMC sold its sodium cyanide business to Cyanco Company, a joint venture between Degussa Corporation and Winnemucca Chemicals (a subsidiary of Nevada Chemicals).

In 2005 FMC and Solutia sold Astaris (now called ICL Performance Products) to Israel Chemicals Limited for $255 million.

## EXECUTIVES

**Chairman, President, and CEO:** William G. (Bill) Walter, age 61, $891,667 pay
**SVP and CFO:** William K. Foster, age 58, $497,551 pay
**VP and Corporate Controller:** Graham R. Wood, age 53
**VP and General Manager, Agricultural Products:** Milton Steele, age 58, $406,442 pay
**VP and General Manager, Industrial Chemicals:** D. Michael Wilson, age 44, $364,457 pay
**VP and General Manager, Specialty Chemicals:** Theodore H. (Ted) Butz, age 48, $364,457 pay
**VP and Treasurer:** Thomas C. Deas Jr., age 56
**VP General Counsel and Secretary:** Andrea E. Utecht, age 58
**CIO:** Michael F. Giesler
**VP Government and Public Affairs:** Gerald R. Prout, age 52
**VP Human Resources and Communications:** Kenneth R. Garrett
**Director, Investor Relations:** Brennen Arndt
**Auditors:** KPMG LLP

## LOCATIONS

**HQ:** FMC Corporation
1735 Market St., Philadelphia, PA 19103
**Phone:** 215-299-6000 **Fax:** 215-299-5998
**Web:** www.fmc.com

FMC operates more than 30 manufacturing facilities and mines in 18 countries.

### 2006 Sales

| | $ mil. | % of total |
|---|---|---|
| North America | | |
| US | 908.2 | 39 |
| Other countries | 51.9 | 2 |
| Europe/Middle East/Africa | 652.8 | 28 |
| Latin America | | |
| Brazil | 280.8 | 12 |
| Other countries | 176.5 | 7 |
| Asia/Pacific | 276.8 | 12 |
| **Total** | **2,347.0** | **100** |

## PRODUCTS/OPERATIONS

### 2006 Sales and Operating Income

| | Sales | | Operating Income | |
|---|---|---|---|---|
| | $ mil. | % of total | $ mil. | % of total |
| Industrial Chemicals | 990.9 | 42 | 96.7 | 27 |
| Agricultural Products | 767.0 | 33 | 151.0 | 41 |
| Specialty Chemicals | 592.8 | 25 | 118.8 | 32 |
| Adjustments | (3.7) | — | (.1) | — |
| **Total** | **2,347.0** | **100** | **366.4** | **100** |

### Selected Products

Industrial chemicals
- Hydrogen peroxide
- Phosphorus chemicals
- Soda ash
- Sodium bicarbonate
- Sodium sesquicarbonate

Agricultural products
- Herbicides
- Pesticides

Specialty chemicals
- Cellulose (alginate, carrageenan, and microcrystalline)
- Lithium

## COMPETITORS

Agrium
Arkema
Asahi Glass
Asahi Kasei
BASF AG
Bayer CropScience
Cargill
CP Kelco
Degussa
Dow Chemical
DuPont
Hercules
Imperial Chemical
PPG
Rohm and Haas
Solvay
SQM
Sumitomo Chemical
Syngenta
Terra Industries

## HISTORICAL FINANCIALS

Company Type: Public

### Income Statement

FYE: December 31

| | REVENUE ($ mil.) | NET INCOME ($ mil.) | NET PROFIT MARGIN | EMPLOYEES |
|---|---|---|---|---|
| **12/06** | 2,347 | 132 | 5.6% | 5,000 |
| **12/05** | 2,150 | 117 | 5.4% | 5,000 |
| **12/04** | 2,051 | 160 | 7.8% | 5,100 |
| **12/03** | 1,921 | 27 | 1.4% | 5,300 |
| **12/02** | 1,853 | 66 | 3.6% | 5,500 |
| **Annual Growth** | 6.1% | 19.0% | — | (2.4%) |

### 2006 Year-End Financials

Debt ratio: 51.3%
Return on equity: 13.3%
Cash ($ mil.): 166
Current ratio: 1.52
Long-term debt ($ mil.): 524
No. of shares (mil.): 38
Dividends
Yield: 0.9%
Payout: 21.6%
Market value ($ mil.): 2,933

**Stock History** NYSE: FMC

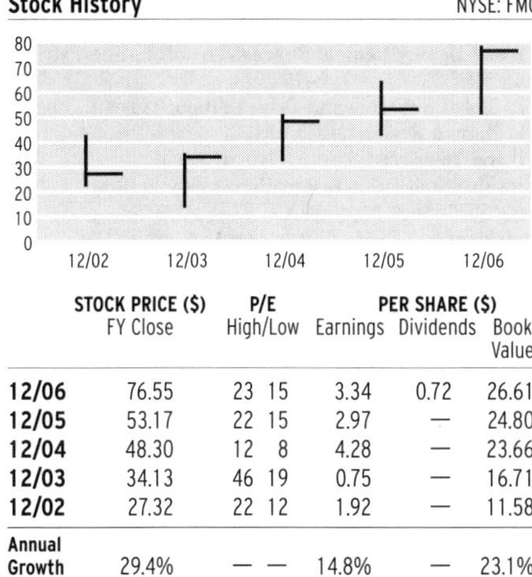


| | STOCK PRICE ($) FY Close | P/E High | P/E Low | PER SHARE ($) Earnings | Dividends | Book Value |
|---|---|---|---|---|---|---|
| **12/06** | 76.55 | 23 | 15 | 3.34 | 0.72 | 26.61 |
| **12/05** | 53.17 | 22 | 15 | 2.97 | — | 24.80 |
| **12/04** | 48.30 | 12 | 8 | 4.28 | — | 23.66 |
| **12/03** | 34.13 | 46 | 19 | 0.75 | — | 16.71 |
| **12/02** | 27.32 | 22 | 12 | 1.92 | — | 11.58 |
| **Annual Growth** | 29.4% | — | — | 14.8% | — | 23.1% |

# FMR Corp.

FMR is *semper fidelis* (ever faithful) to its core business. The financial services conglomerate, better known as Fidelity Investments, is one of the world's largest mutual fund firms. Serving more than 22 million individual and institutional clients, Fidelity manages more than 300 funds and has more than $1.2 trillion of assets under management. It also operates a leading online discount brokerage and has investor centers in about 100 cities throughout the US and Canada, as well in Europe and Asia. The founding Johnson family controls most of FMR; Abigail Johnson, CEO Ned's daughter and perhaps his successor (not to mention one of the richest women in America), is the company's largest single shareholder.

Fidelity's nonfund offerings include life insurance, trust services, securities clearing, and retirement services. It is one of the largest administrators of 401(k) plans, and the firm continues to grow this segment, which includes other services related to benefits outsourcing. The company had been reluctant to give direct investment advice to 401(k) plan participants, but under pressure from customers struck an agreement with Financial Engines Inc., who now provides those services to Fidelity's clients.

FMR has major holdings in telecommunications (COLT Telecom Group) and transportation (BostonCoach). Like many institutional investors, Fidelity uses its clout to sway the boards of companies in which it has significant holdings. In 2007 the company's Fidelity Equity Partners arm launched a $500 million buyout fund that targets middle-market firms involved in media, software, health care, and service industries in North America and Europe.

FMR acquired about a 15% stake in venerable British investment bank Lazard in 2005.

The following year the company announced that it would pay $42 million into its mutual funds after an internal investigation showed that some of its traders had guided business to brokers who had given the traders gifts.

## HISTORY

Boston money management firm Anderson & Cromwell formed Fidelity Fund in 1930. Edward Johnson became president of the fund in 1943, when it had $3 million invested in Treasury bills. Johnson diversified into stocks, and by 1945 the fund had grown to $10 million. In 1946 he established Fidelity Management and Research to act as its investment adviser.

In the early 1950s Johnson hired Gerry Tsai, a young immigrant from Shanghai, to analyze stocks. He put Tsai in charge of Fidelity Capital Fund in 1957. Tsai's brash, go-go investment strategy in such speculative stocks as Xerox and Polaroid paid off; by the time he left to form his own fund in 1965, he was managing more than $1 billion.

The Magellan Fund started in 1962. The company entered the corporate pension plans market (FMR Investment Management) in 1964, and retirement plans for self-employed individuals (Fidelity Keogh Plan) in 1967. It began serving investors outside the US (Fidelity International) in 1968.

Holding company FMR was formed in 1972, the same year Johnson gave control of Fidelity to his son Ned, who vertically integrated FMR by selling directly to customers rather than through brokers. In 1973 he formed Fidelity Daily Income Trust, the first money market fund to offer check writing.

Peter Lynch was hired as manager of the Magellan Fund in 1977. During his 13-year tenure, Magellan grew from $20 million to $12 billion in assets and outperformed all other mutual funds. Fidelity started Fidelity Brokerage Services in 1978, becoming the first mutual fund company to offer discount brokerage.

In 1980 the company launched a nationwide branch network and in 1986 entered the credit card business. The Wall Street crash of 1987 forced its Magellan Fund to liquidate almost $1 billion in stock in a single day. That year FMR moved into insurance by offering variable life, single premium, and deferred annuity policies. In 1989 the company introduced the low-expense Spartan Fund, targeted toward large, less-active investors.

Magellan's performance faded in the early 1990s, dropping from #1 performer to #3. Most of Fidelity's best performers were from its 36 select funds, which focus on narrow industry segments. FMR founded London-based COLT Telecom in 1993. In 1994 Johnson gave his daughter and heir apparent, Abigail, a 25% stake in FMR.

Jeffrey Vinik resigned as manager of Magellan in 1996, one of more than a dozen fund managers to leave the firm that year and the next. Robert Stansky took the helm of the $56 billion fund, which FMR decided to close to new investors in 1997. Fidelity had a first that year when it went with an outside fund manager, hiring Bankers Trust (now part of Deutsche Bank) to manage its index funds.

FMR did some housecleaning in the late 1990s. It sold its Wentworth art galleries (1997) and *Worth* magazine (1998). Despite continued management turnover, it entered Japan and expanded its presence in Canada.

In 1999 the firm teamed with Internet portal Lycos (now part of Terra Networks) to develop its online brokerage. FMR opened savings and loan Fidelity Personal Trust Co. in 2000.

## EXECUTIVES

**Chairman and CEO:** Edward C. (Ned) Johnson III
**President:** Rodger A. Lawson, age 60
**EVP and CFO:** Clare S. Richer
**EVP, Fidelity Employer Services Company:** Laura B. Cronin
**EVP and Director, Corporate Affairs:** Thomas E. Eidson
**EVP and General Counsel:** Lena G. Goldberg
**EVP, Fidelity Government Relations:** David C. Weinstein
**EVP, Fidelity Human Resources:** D. Ellen Wilson
**EVP, Fidelity Risk Oversight:** Kenneth A. Rathgeber
**President, Fidelity Employer Services Company:** Abigail P. (Abby) Johnson, age 45
**President, Fidelity Registered Investment Advisor Group:** John W. Callahan
**President, Fidelity Human Resources Services Company:** Jim MacDonald
**President, Fidelity Real Estate:** Sarah K. Abrams
**President, Registered Investment Advisor Group:** William C. (Bill) Carey
**President, Investment Services, Fidelity Management & Research:** Dwight D. Churchill
**Venture Partner, Fidelity Ventures:** Donald A. (Don) Haile
**President, Devonshire Investors:** Timothy T. Hilton, age 54
**President, Fidelity Strategic Initiatives:** Robert A. Lawrence
**President, Fidelity Investments Institutional Services Company:** Joseph P. LoRusso
**President, National Financial:** Norman R. Malo
**Managing Partner, Fidelity Ventures:** Robert C. (Rob) Ketterson
**President, Fidelity Personal Investments:** Steven P. (Steve) Akin
**Manager, Fidelity Contrafund:** William Danoff
**Manager, Fidelity Magellan Fund:** Harry W. Lange, age 53
**Interim Chief Administrative Officer:** John Remondi
**Auditors:** PricewaterhouseCoopers LLP

## LOCATIONS

**HQ:** FMR Corp.
82 Devonshire St., Boston, MA 02109
**Phone:** 617-563-7000 **Fax:** 617-476-6150
**Web:** www.fidelity.com

## PRODUCTS/OPERATIONS

### Selected Subsidiaries and Divisions

Fidelity Employer Services Company
Fidelity Institutional Retirement Services Company
Fidelity Investments Canada, Limited
Fidelity Investments Institutional Services Company, Inc.
Fidelity Management and Research Company
Fidelity Management Trust Company
Fidelity Personal Investments
Fidelity Registered Investment Advisor Group
Fidelity Ventures
National Financial
National Financial Markets Group

## COMPETITORS

AllianceBernstein Holding
American Century
AXA Financial
Barclays
BlackRock
Charles Schwab
Citigroup
Dow Jones
E*TRADE Financial
Goldman Sachs
John Hancock
Lehman Brothers
Marsh & McLennan
MassMutual
MetLife
Morgan Stanley
Northwestern Mutual
Prudential
Putnam
Raymond James Financial
T. Rowe Price
TD Ameritrade
TIAA-CREF
UBS Financial Services
The Vanguard Group

# Foot Locker

Foot Locker leads the pack in the race to capture the biggest share of the athletic footwear market. The company is a leading retailer of athletic shoes and apparel. Foot Locker has about 4,000 specialty stores in 20 countries in North America and Europe, as well as Australia and New Zealand, led by Foot Locker (the #1 athletic footwear retailer in the US). Foot Locker also operates Lady Foot Locker and Kids Foot Locker; Champs Sports, an athletic wear retail chain; Eastbay, a catalog retailer of athletic equipment and apparel; and the Footlocker.com Web site. The company also has about 360 Footaction stores in the US and Puerto Rico, which sell footwear and apparel to young urbanites.

About a quarter of the company's revenue is earned outside the US.

Foot Locker is expanding in Europe, where it expects to open as many as 30 new stores in 2008, while continuing to reduce its US store count. After shuttering stores in 2006, the company again plans to close about 250 underperforming stores in 2007 (about twice the number it originally planned to close this year) in a bid to enhance profitability.

Foot Locker has hired Lehman Brothers to advise it on strategic alternatives, including inquiries from private-equity firms looking to buy the company.

In 2007 the company announced a new partnership with NIKE to launch a new store focused purely on basketball called "House of Hoops by Foot Locker." The stores will sell only NIKE products and about 50 are planned over the next three years.

In early 2007 Foot Locker made an unsolicited $1.2 billion bid for rival Genesco that was rejected by Genesco's board.

The company's direct-to-consumer business is enjoying healthy growth in online sales but is experiencing a steep decline in sales from catalogs.

Financial services giant FMR Corp. owns nearly 8% of Foot Locker's shares.

## HISTORY

With the idea of selling merchandise priced at no more than five cents, Frank Woolworth opened the Great Five Cent Store in Utica, New York, in 1879; it failed. That year he moved to Lancaster, Pennsylvania, and created the first five-and-dime. Woolworth moved his headquarters to New York City (1886) and spent the rest of the century acquiring other dime-store chains. He later expanded to Canada (1897), England (1909), France (1922), and Germany (1927).

The 120-store chain, with $10 million in sales, incorporated as F.W. Woolworth & Company in 1905, with Woolworth as president. In 1912 the company merged with five rival chains and went public with 596 stores, making $52 million in sales the first year. The next year, paying $13.5 million in cash, Woolworth finished construction of the Woolworth Building, then the world's tallest building (792 feet). When he died in 1919, the chain had 1,081 stores, with sales of $119 million.

Woolworth became more competitive after WWII by advertising, establishing revolving credit and self-service, moving stores to suburbs, and expanding merchandise selections. In 1962 it opened Woolco, a US and Canadian discount chain.

From the 1960s through the 1980s, the company grew by acquiring and expanding in the US and abroad. It picked up Kinney (shoes, 1963), Richman Brothers (men's clothing, 1969), Holtzman's Little Folk Shop (children's clothing, 1983), Champs Sports (sporting goods, 1987), and Mathers (shoes, Australia, 1988).

The company introduced Foot Locker, the athletic shoe chain, in 1974, later developing Lady Foot Locker (1982) and Kids Foot Locker (1987). In 1993 Woolworth launched an ambitious restructuring plan, focusing on specialty stores (mostly apparel and shoes). It also closed 400 US stores and sold 122 Canadian Woolco stores to Wal-Mart that year. Former Macy's president Roger Farah became CEO in 1994. Farah eliminated 16 divisions and dozens of executives.

A year later the firm sold its Kids Mart/Little Folks children's wear chain. In 1996 Woolworth began a major remodeling program that included removing its venerable lunch counters. (Another alleged renovation at the Woolworth chain — the firing of older workers, who were replaced by teenagers — led to an Equal Employment Opportunity Commission lawsuit against the company in 1999.) The changes failed, and the next year the company closed its US Woolworth stores and bought athletic-products catalog company Eastbay.

In 1998 Woolworth changed its name to Venator Group and sold the Woolworth Building, a national landmark (headquarters remained in the building). The company then shed itself of more than 1,400 stores, including Kinney shoes and Footquarters (both closed).

Internet site eVenator was launched in 1999 to sell Eastbay, Champs, and Foot Locker merchandise. Venator came out the champ in a proxy fight against investment group Greenway Partners in July 1999. Shortly thereafter, Farah was replaced as CEO (he remained chairman) by president Dale Hilpert.

In 2000 Venator slashed 7% of its workforce in the US and Canada (a small part of the planned 30% cut) and closed 465 stores. COO Matt Serra became president, and Hilpert became chairman when Farah resigned later that year.

In March 2001 Hilpert resigned, replaced by Carter Bacot as chairman, and Serra added CEO to his title. Venator later sold its Canadian Northern Group unit to investment firm York Management Services and closed its Northern Reflections stores in the US. Venator changed its name to Foot Locker in November. It also sold gift retailer San Francisco Music Box Co. and its hospitality division's fast-food franchises before the end of the year.

In November 2003 the company announced that in February 2004 chairman Bacot would become lead director, and president and CEO Serra would add chairman to his title.

In 2004 Foot Locker, capitalizing on the Chapter 11 filing of Footstar, Inc., purchased from the company 350 of its Footaction stores. The company also acquired 11 stores in Ireland from Champion Sports Group later in the same year.

## EXECUTIVES

**Chairman, President, and CEO:** Matthew D. (Matt) Serra, age 62, $1,500,000 pay
**SVP and CFO:** Robert W. McHugh, age 48, $500,000 pay
**SVP, General Counsel, and Secretary:** Gary M. Bahler, age 55, $517,400 pay
**SVP, Human Resources:** Laurie J. Petrucci, age 48, $436,538 pay
**SVP, CIO, and Investor Relations:** Peter D. Brown, age 52
**SVP, Strategic Planning:** Lauren B. Peters, age 45
**VP and Chief Accounting Officer:** Giovanna Cipriano, age 37
**VP and Deputy General Counsel:** Dennis E. Sheehan, age 50
**VP, Global Sourcing and Team Edition:** James T. Bulzis
**VP, Human Resources:** Patricia A. Peck
**VP and Treasurer:** John A. Maurer, age 47
**President and CEO, International:** Ronald (Ron) Halls, age 53, $530,909 pay (partial-year salary)
**President and CEO, Foot Locker U.S.:** Keith Daly
**President and CEO, Lady Foot Locker:** Marla Anderson
**President and CEO, Foot Locker Europe:** Dick Johnson
**Auditors:** KPMG LLP

## LOCATIONS

**HQ:** Foot Locker, Inc.
112 W. 34th St., New York, NY 10120
**Phone:** 212-720-3700 **Fax:** 212-720-4397
**Web:** www.footlocker-inc.com

Foot Locker operates more than 3,900 stores throughout North America and in 20 other countries in Europe, as well as in Australia and New Zealand.

**2007 Sales**

| | $ mil. | % of total |
|---|---|---|
| US | 4,356 | 76 |
| Other countries | 1,394 | 24 |
| **Total** | **5,750** | **100** |

## PRODUCTS/OPERATIONS

**2007 Stores**

| | No. |
|---|---|
| Foot Locker | 2,101 |
| Champs Sports | 576 |
| Lady Foot Locker | 557 |
| Footaction | 373 |
| Kids Foot Locker | 335 |
| **Total** | **3,942** |

**2007 Sales**

| | $ mil. | % of total |
|---|---|---|
| Athletic stores | 5,370 | 93 |
| Direct-to-consumer | 380 | 7 |
| **Total** | **5,750** | **100** |

## COMPETITORS

Academy Sports
Brown Shoe
Dick's Sporting Goods
Dillard's
DSW
Finish Line
Forzani Group
Gap
Genesco
Hibbett Sports
J. C. Penney
Kmart
L.L. Bean
Macy's
Modell's
NIKE
Sears
Shoe Carnival
Sports Authority
Target
TJX Companies
Wal-Mart

## HISTORICAL FINANCIALS

Company Type: Public

**Income Statement** FYE: Saturday nearest January 31

| | REVENUE ($ mil.) | NET INCOME ($ mil.) | NET PROFIT MARGIN | EMPLOYEES |
|---|---|---|---|---|
| **1/07** | 5,750 | 251 | 4.4% | 45,406 |
| **1/06** | 5,653 | 264 | 4.7% | 44,276 |
| **1/05** | 5,355 | 293 | 5.5% | 44,109 |
| **1/04** | 4,779 | 207 | 4.3% | 40,298 |
| **1/03** | 4,509 | 153 | 3.4% | 40,151 |
| **Annual Growth** | 6.3% | 13.2% | — | 3.1% |

**2007 Year-End Financials**

Debt ratio: 10.1%
Return on equity: 11.6%
Cash ($ mil.): 485
Current ratio: 3.94
Long-term debt ($ mil.): 232
No. of shares (mil.): 156
Dividends
Yield: 1.7%
Payout: 25.0%
Market value ($ mil.): 3,528

**Stock History** NYSE: FL

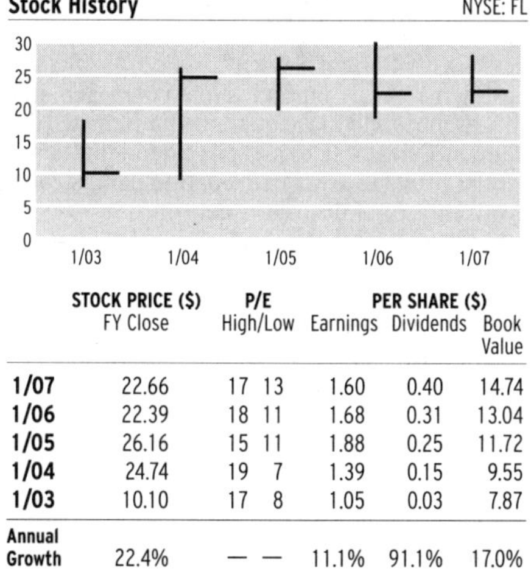


| | STOCK PRICE ($) FY Close | P/E High/Low | | PER SHARE ($) Earnings | Dividends | Book Value |
|---|---|---|---|---|---|---|
| **1/07** | 22.66 | 17 | 13 | 1.60 | 0.40 | 14.74 |
| **1/06** | 22.39 | 18 | 11 | 1.68 | 0.31 | 13.04 |
| **1/05** | 26.16 | 15 | 11 | 1.88 | 0.25 | 11.72 |
| **1/04** | 24.74 | 19 | 7 | 1.39 | 0.15 | 9.55 |
| **1/03** | 10.10 | 17 | 8 | 1.05 | 0.03 | 7.87 |
| **Annual Growth** | 22.4% | — | — | 11.1% | 91.1% | 17.0% |

# Ford Motor

Ford Motor began a manufacturing revolution with its mass production assembly lines in the early 1900s. Now the company is firmly entrenched in the status quo as one of the world's largest makers of cars and trucks. It makes vehicles with such brands as Ford, Lincoln, and Mercury. Among its biggest successes are the redesigned Ford Mustang and F-Series pickup. Ford owns a controlling (33%) stake in Mazda and also controls the Land Rover, Jaguar, and Volvo nameplates through Premier Automotive Group. Finance subsidiary Ford Motor Credit is the US's #1 auto finance company. Ford has sold Hertz, the world's #1 car-rental firm. The Ford family owns about 40% of the company's voting stock.

Severe pricing pressures, rising health care and raw materials costs, skyrocketing fuel prices and a consumer shift away from large SUVs, and brutal competition (chiefly from Japanese rivals) led to a staggering company-wide loss of $12.7 billion in 2006.

Late in 2006 Ford made a drastic move to ensure mid-term liquidity as it sought $22 to $23 billion in secured and unsecured financing. The bulk of the financing, about $19 billion, will be in the form of secured loans and Ford is putting up many of its domestic assets — such as plants and offices, as well as entire subsidiaries (including Ford Motor Credit and Volvo) — as collateral. About $3 billion in financing will be in unsecured notes. The move is seen as a last ditch effort to save the company; if the move fails the company risks its independence, and the Ford family risks losing control.

Ford's first priority is to reduce costs in North America. Manufacturing capacity will be trimmed by 1.2 million units or 26%. To do this, Ford will idle 16 plants and reduce its workforce by cutting as many as 45,000 jobs between 2006 and 2012. Ford is also cutting its executive ranks by about a third and is trimming its number of global suppliers from 2,500 to about 800 over the next few years.

To increase consumer appeal, Ford is de-emphasizing large SUVs while working to develop more small cars and crossover vehicles (half car, half SUV). Entry into the hybrid market has been a somewhat surprising product bright spot for Ford. Its hybrids currently include the Escape Hybrid and the Mercury Mariner. The success of these vehicles in North America has prompted the company to fast-track the development of more hybrids.

In 2007 Ford sold Aston Martin to a group including British race-shop owner David Richards, Aston Martin racing backer John Sinders, and two Kuwaiti investment firms — Investment Dar and Adeem Investment Co., although Ford retained a small stake in Aston Martin. Ford is also looking at options for selling Jaguar and Land Rover.

Amid all the swirling rumors and speculation regarding Ford's future plans, former Boeing executive Alan Mulally was named president and CEO. Bill Ford remains executive chairman. Not long after the naming of Mulally as CEO, the UAW announced its members and Ford had reached an agreement whereby Ford would extend buyout packages to 75,000 UAW workers — or virtually all of Ford's UAW-represented labor force (by late 2006 about 38,000 Ford workers had accepted the buyout offer).

## HISTORY

Henry Ford started the Ford Motor Company in 1903 in Dearborn, Michigan. In 1908 Ford introduced the Model T, produced on a moving assembly line that revolutionized both carmaking and manufacturing. By 1920 some 60% of all vehicles on the road were Fords.

After Ford omitted its usual dividend in 1916, stockholders sued. Ford responded by buying back all of its outstanding shares in 1919 and didn't allow outside ownership again until 1956.

Ford bought Lincoln in 1922 and discontinued the Model T in 1927. Its replacement, the Model A, came in 1932. With Henry Ford's health failing, his son Edsel became president that year. Despite the debut of the Mercury (1938), market share slipped behind GM and Chrysler. After Edsel's death in 1943, his son, Henry II, took over and decentralized Ford, following the GM model. In 1950 the carmaker recaptured second place. Ford rolled out the infamous Edsel in 1958 and launched the Mustang in 1964.

Hurt by the oil crisis of the 1970s, Ford cut its workforce and closed plants during the 1980s. It also diversified into agricultural equipment by purchasing New Holland (1986) and Versatile (1987). Ford added luxury sports cars in 1987 by buying 75% of Aston Martin (it bought the rest in 1994). The 1988 introduction of the Taurus and Sable spurred Ford to its largest share of the US car market (21.7%) in 10 years. In 1989 it bought Jaguar (luxury cars).

Ford acquired Hertz in 1994 and two years later bought #3 rental agency Budget Rent a Car (sold 1997). Also in 1996 it increased its stake in Mazda to one-third. Ford began building a minibus line in China in 1997, beating GM in the race to produce vehicles for the Chinese market. Henry Ford's great-grandson, William Clay Ford Jr., became chairman in 1998. Company veteran Jacques Nasser became president and CEO in early 1999.

Ford bought Volvo's carmaking operations for $6.45 billion in 1999, and it bought BMW's Land Rover SUV operations for about $2.7 billion in 2000. In 2001 Ford recalled some 300,000 cars, including 1995-96 Ford Contour and Mercury Mystique sedans, which posed possible fire danger linked to engine overheating problems.

Citing a study showing that the tires failed three times more frequently than the industry average, in May 2001 Ford announced that it would take a $2.1 billion charge to cover the replacement of up to 13 million Firestone Wilderness AT tires already on its vehicles. The news led Firestone to announce that it would no longer do business with Ford, thus ending a 95-year relationship.

In late 2001 Nasser resigned and was replaced as CEO by chairman William Clay Ford Jr. A week or so into 2002, Ford announced far-reaching cost-cutting measures, including 35,000 worldwide job cuts (22,000 in North America) and the closure of three North American assembly plants. Early in 2004 Ford signed a deal with the Chinese government to secure rights to land in Nanjing, where the company plans to build a second Ford plant in China.

In March 2005 Ford took full control of its operations in India with the purchase of a nearly 16% stake from its Indian partner, Mahindra & Mahindra Ltd. (Ford Motor set up its Indian subsidiary in Madras in 1995 as a 50-50 joint venture with Mahindra. But Ford later raised its stake.)

In order to focus on its struggling automotive operations, in 2005 Ford sold its Hertz car rental business to a private equity group made up of Clayton Dubilier & Rice, The Carlyle Group, and Merrill Lynch Global Private Equity.

## EXECUTIVES

**Chairman:** William Clay (Bill) Ford Jr., age 49
**President, CEO, and Director:** Alan R. Mulally, age 61, $2,516,667 pay
**EVP and CFO:** Donat R. (Don) Leclair, age 55, $1,000,933 pay
**EVP; President, The Americas:** Mark Fields, age 46, $1,250,933 pay
**EVP, Ford of Europe and Premier Automotive Group; Chairman, Ford Europe, Jagaur, and Land Rover:** Lewis W.K. Booth, age 58, $850,933 pay
**SVP; President, Ford Customer Service Division:** Darryl B. Hazel, age 58
**SVP, Sustainability, Environment, and Safety Engineering:** Susan M. (Sue) Cischke
**SVP and Controller:** Peter J. Daniel, age 60
**SVP, Global Purchasing:** Thomas K. (Tony) Brown
**Group VP; Chairman and CEO, Ford Motor Credit Company:** Michael E. (Mike) Bannister, age 57
**Group VP; President and CEO, Ford of Europe:** John Fleming, age 56
**Group VP and Chief Creative Officer:** J. C. Mays, age 52
**Group VP, Global Product Development and CTO:** Richard Parry-Jones, age 55
**Group VP, Global Product Development:** Derrick M. Kuzak, age 55
**Group VP, Corporate Human Resources and Labor Affairs:** Joe W. Laymon, age 54
**Group VP, North America, Marketing, Sales and Service:** Francisco N. (Cisco) Codina
**Group VP, Asia Pacific and Africa Operations:** John G. Parker, age 59
**VP and CIO:** Nick Smither, age 48
**VP and Chief Communications Officer:** Charles B. (Charlie) Holleran
**VP and Treasurer:** Ann Marie Petach
**VP; CEO, Jaguar and Land Rover:** Geoff Polites
**VP; CEO, Volvo Car:** Fredrik Arp
**VP, Human Resources:** Felicia J. Fields, age 39
**Secretary:** Peter J. Sherry Jr.
**Auditors:** PricewaterhouseCoopers LLP

## LOCATIONS

**HQ:** Ford Motor Company
1 American Rd., Dearborn, MI 48126
**Phone:** 313-322-3000 **Fax:** 313-845-6073
**Web:** www.ford.com

### 2006 Sales

| | $ mil. | % of total |
|---|---|---|
| North America | | |
| US | 81,155 | 51 |
| Canada | 8,075 | 5 |
| Mexico | 3,461 | 2 |
| Europe | | |
| UK | 15,850 | 10 |
| Germany | 7,006 | 4 |
| Sweden | 4,290 | 3 |
| Other countries | 22,934 | 14 |
| Other regions | 17,352 | 11 |
| **Total** | **160,123** | **100** |

## PRODUCTS/OPERATIONS

### 2006 Sales

| | $ mil. | % of total |
|---|---|---|
| Automotive | | |
| Ford North America | 69,425 | 43 |
| Ford Europe | 30,394 | 19 |
| Premier Automotive Group | 30,028 | 19 |
| Ford Asia Pacific, Africa & Mazda | 7,763 | 5 |
| Ford South America | 5,697 | 4 |
| Finacial Services | | |
| Ford Credit | 16,553 | 10 |
| Other | 263 | — |
| **Total** | **160,123** | **100** |

### 2006 Sales by Vehicle Type

| | % of total |
|---|---|
| Cars | |
| Medium | 12 |
| Small | 12 |
| Large | 8 |
| Premium | 6 |
| Trucks | |
| Full-size pickup | 28 |
| SUV | 22 |
| Bus/van | 8 |
| Compact pickup | 3 |
| Medium/heavy | 1 |
| **Total** | **100** |

### Selected Operations

Ford Automotive
Ford Motor Credit

### Selected Auto Brands

Ford
Jaguar
Land Rover
Lincoln
Mazda (33%)
Mercury
Volvo

## COMPETITORS

AM General
AutoNation
Bank of America
BMW
Chrysler
Citigroup
Daimler
DENSO
Fiat
General Motors
GKN
Honda
Isuzu
JPMorgan Chase
Navistar
Nissan
Peugeot Motors of America, Inc.
Renault
Saab Automobile
Saturn
Suzuki Motor
Toyota
Volkswagen

## HISTORICAL FINANCIALS

Company Type: Public

### Income Statement FYE: December 31

| | REVENUE ($ mil.) | NET INCOME ($ mil.) | NET PROFIT MARGIN | EMPLOYEES |
|---|---|---|---|---|
| **12/06** | 160,123 | (12,613) | — | 283,000 |
| **12/05** | 176,896 | 1,440 | 0.8% | 300,000 |
| **12/04** | 171,652 | 3,487 | 2.0% | 324,864 |
| **12/03** | 165,066 | 495 | 0.3% | 327,531 |
| **12/02** | 163,420 | (980) | — | 350,321 |
| **Annual Growth** | (0.5%) | — | — | (5.2%) |

### 2006 Year-End Financials

Debt ratio: —
Return on equity: —
Cash ($ mil.): 28,894
Current ratio: 0.94
Long-term debt ($ mil.): 172,049
No. of shares (mil.): 1,837
Dividends
Yield: 3.3%
Payout: —
Market value ($ mil.): 13,796

### Stock History NYSE: F

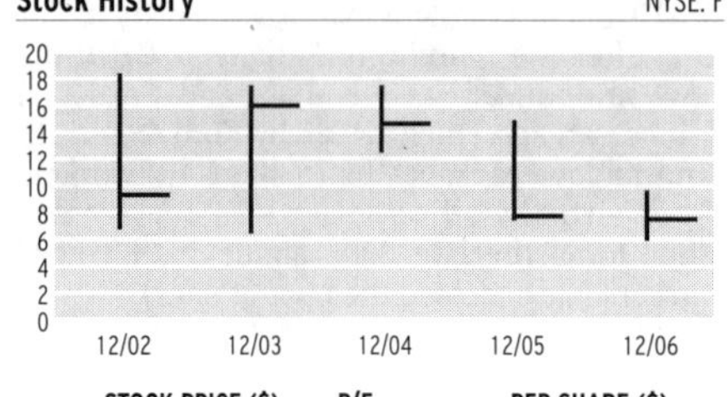


| | STOCK PRICE ($) FY Close | P/E High/Low | | PER SHARE ($) Earnings | Dividends | Book Value |
|---|---|---|---|---|---|---|
| **12/06** | 7.51 | — | — | (6.72) | 0.25 | (1.89) |
| **12/05** | 7.72 | 19 | 10 | 0.77 | 0.40 | 7.32 |
| **12/04** | 14.64 | 10 | 7 | 1.73 | 0.40 | 8.73 |
| **12/03** | 16.00 | 64 | 24 | 0.27 | 0.40 | 6.34 |
| **12/02** | 9.30 | — | — | (0.55) | 0.40 | 3.04 |
| **Annual Growth** | (5.2%) | — | — | — | (11.1%) | — |

# Forest Laboratories

Forest Laboratories doesn't just blend in with the trees. The company develops and manufactures name-brand as well as generic prescription and over-the-counter pharmaceutical products. The company's central nervous system pharmaceutical line includes antidepressants Celexa and Lexapro, as well as Namenda, which treats Alzheimer's disease. Other products include treatments for irritable bowel syndrome, hypertension, and pain. Forest Laboratories, which has subsidiaries in the UK and Ireland, markets directly to doctors, drugstore chains, managed care organizations, and distributors through its own sales force.

Despite competing with such household names as Prozac, Zoloft, and Paxil, Forest Laboratories has found a niche in the antidepressant market. With Celexa's recent conversion to generic status, however, the company has become more dependent on Lexapro's, which accounted for close to 70% of the company's sales. In 2006, a federal judge reinforced the patent on Lexapro (and therefore shot down a proposed generic version from Teva Pharmaceutical Industries subsidiary Ivax Diagnostics), which expires in 2012.

The firm has also recently released three new drugs, hypertension treatment Benicar (marketed with Daiichi Sankyo), Campral (alcohol abstinence), and Combunox (pain management) that it hopes will make up for the anticipated decline in Celexa's sales. Its pipeline includes potential drugs to treat neuropathic pain, stroke, gastrointestinal disorders, central nervous system disorders, asthma, and schizophrenia.

In 2006 the FDA issued a non-approvable letter for faropenem medoxomil, an antibiotic for sinusitis, bronchitis, and pneumonia that Forest Laboratories was seeking to market with Replidyne. The companies plan to conduct additional trials requested by the FDA and seek approval at a later date.

Forest began to lose its grip on the thyroid treatment market in the beginning of 2007 when the FDA approved a generic version of its Levothroid, produced by competitor Mylan Laboratories. To bolster its biopharmaceutical research capabilities, the company at around the same time purchased Cerexa, Inc. for a sum of nearly a half-billion dollars. Cerexa brought with it a series of injectable antibiotics designed to combat MRSA and PSRP, two common but increasingly communicable and deadly bacteria.

About 85% of the company's sales revenues come from large pharmaceutical distributors McKesson (35%), Cardinal Health (33%), and AmerisourceBergen (28%).

Subsidiary Inwood Laboratories markets the company's generic products.

## HISTORY

Forest Laboratories began as a drug research and development firm in 1956. The company diversified into the food business, but when company attorney Howard Solomon took charge in 1977, he sold the food holdings and moved from drug development to drug commercialization. It acquired drugs from other companies and improved them through its proprietary Synchron continuous-release drug-delivery technology.

In 1984 Forest bought scandal-ridden drug company O'Neal, Jones, & Feldman to grow its sales force. The next year it bought headache formula ESGIC (later pulled because it qualified as a new drug needing FDA approval). In 1986 it acquired Aerobid from Schering-Plough.

The company continued to grow through acquisitions, buying UAD Laboratories and its analgesic Lorcet in 1989, Pharmasciences' labor-induction agent Cervidil, and other drugs. Although the firm had mostly successes, one of its failures was Micturin, an incontinence treatment whose dangerous side effects led the company to discontinue it in 1991.

In 1998 the FDA approved antidepressant citalopram (Celexa). Celexa was to be marketed by Warner-Lambert, but when that firm was acquired by Pfizer (which makes rival antidepressant Prozac), Forest Labs bought its way out of the deal and grew its own sales force. Celexa proved worthy of such effort, becoming Forest Labs' biggest seller. The following year the company entered into an alliance with 3M's pharmaceutical unit to make asthma treatment Aerospan. In 2000 the company expanded its research facilities and licensed drugs to treat hypertension, dementia, and irritable bowel syndrome.

In 2002 the company launched hypertension drug Benicar through an alliance with Sankyo and failed to win FDA approval for alcohol dependence treatment acamprosate (licensed from Merck KGaA).

## EXECUTIVES

**Chairman and CEO:** Howard Solomon, age 79, $1,592,500 pay
**President and COO:** Lawrence S. Olanoff, age 56
**EVP, Global Marketing and CEO, Forest Laboratories Europe:** Raymond Stafford
**SVP, Finance and CFO:** Francis I. Perier Jr., age 47, $670,000 pay
**SVP, Marketing:** Elaine Hochberg, age 50, $715,000 pay
**SVP, Scientific Affairs; President, Forest Research Institute:** Ivan Gergel, age 47, $706,830 pay
**VP, Human Resources:** Bernard J. McGovern
**VP, Information Systems:** Kevin Walsh
**VP, Investor Relations:** Charles E. Triano
**VP, Licensing and Corporate Development:** Mary E. Prehn
**VP, Operations and Facilities:** Richard S. Overton
**VP and Controller:** Rita Weinberger
**VP and General Counsel:** Herschel S. Weinstein
**Secretary and Director:** William J. Candee III, age 80
**EVP, Trade Sales and Development, Forest Pharmaceuticals:** Michael F. Baker
**EVP and Chief Medical Officer, Forest Research Institute:** Jeffrey Jonas
**Auditors:** BDO Seidman, LLP

## LOCATIONS

**HQ:** Forest Laboratories, Inc.
909 3rd Ave., New York, NY 10022
**Phone:** 212-421-7850 **Fax:** 212-750-9152
**Web:** www.frx.com

Forest Laboratories has facilities in Missouri, New Jersey, New York, and Ohio, as well as in Ireland and the UK.

### 2007 Sales

| | % of total |
|---|---|
| US | 98 |
| UK & Ireland | 2 |
| **Total** | **100** |

## PRODUCTS/OPERATIONS

### 2007 Sales

| | $ mil. | % of total |
|---|---|---|
| Products | | |
| Central nervous system | 2,794.7 | 81 |
| Cardiovascular | 50.2 | 1 |
| Other | 338.4 | 10 |
| Other income | 258.5 | 8 |
| **Total** | **3,441.8** | **100** |

### Selected Products

Benicar (antihypertensive)
Campral (alcohol dependence)
Celexa (antidepressant)
Combunox (pain)
Lexapro (antidepressant)
Namenda (Alzheimer's disease)
Neramexane (central nervous system disorders)
Tiazac (antihypertensive)

## COMPETITORS

AstraZeneca
Bristol-Myers Squibb
Eli Lilly
GlaxoSmithKline
Hi-Tech Pharmacal
Johnson & Johnson
Merck
Novartis
Pfizer
Sandoz International GmbH
Schering-Plough
Teva Pharmaceuticals
Warner Chilcott, Inc.
Watson Pharmaceuticals

## HISTORICAL FINANCIALS

Company Type: Public

### Income Statement

FYE: March 31

| | REVENUE ($ mil.) | NET INCOME ($ mil.) | NET PROFIT MARGIN | EMPLOYEES |
|---|---|---|---|---|
| **3/07** | 3,442 | 454 | 13.2% | 5,126 |
| **3/06** | 2,962 | 709 | 23.9% | 5,050 |
| **3/05** | 3,160 | 839 | 26.5% | 5,136 |
| **3/04** | 2,680 | 736 | 27.5% | 4,967 |
| **3/03** | 2,246 | 622 | 27.7% | 4,240 |
| **Annual Growth** | 11.3% | (7.6%) | — | 4.9% |

### 2007 Year-End Financials

Debt ratio: —
Return on equity: 15.9%
Cash ($ mil.): 1,353
Current ratio: 3.86
Long-term debt ($ mil.): —
No. of shares (mil.): 320
Dividends
Yield: —
Payout: —
Market value ($ mil.): 16,438

### Stock History

NYSE: FRX

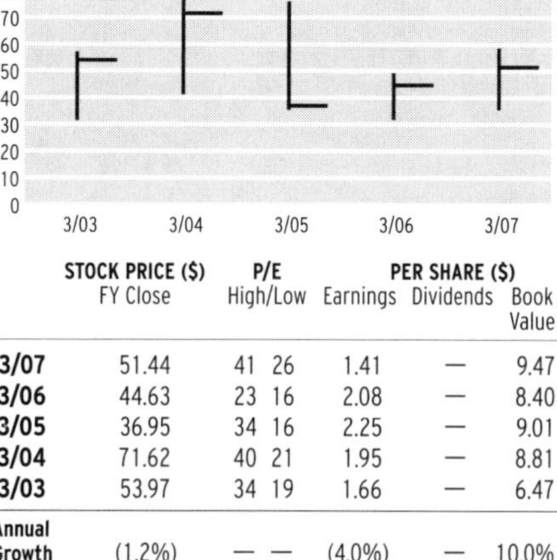


| | STOCK PRICE ($) FY Close | P/E High | P/E Low | PER SHARE ($) Earnings | Dividends | Book Value |
|---|---|---|---|---|---|---|
| **3/07** | 51.44 | 41 | 26 | 1.41 | — | 9.47 |
| **3/06** | 44.63 | 23 | 16 | 2.08 | — | 8.40 |
| **3/05** | 36.95 | 34 | 16 | 2.25 | — | 9.01 |
| **3/04** | 71.62 | 40 | 21 | 1.95 | — | 8.81 |
| **3/03** | 53.97 | 34 | 19 | 1.66 | — | 6.47 |
| **Annual Growth** | (1.2%) | — | — | (4.0%) | — | 10.0% |

# Fortune Brands

Execs at Fortune Brands have good reason to meet over a game of golf and a glass of bourbon. The holding company is a leading US producer and distributor of distilled spirits (Jim Beam, DeKuyper, Knob Creek, Maker's Mark) and golf equipment (Titleist, Cobra, FootJoy, Pinnacle). However, Fortune's largest segment is home products and hardware, where its holdings include Moen faucets, MasterBrand cabinets, Master Lock padlocks, and Therma-Tru doors. The firm, which spun off office products company ACCO World Corporation (Day-Timers, Swingline, Kensington) in 2005, added former Allied Domecq brands Sauza, Courvoisier, Canadian Club, and Clos du Bois to its stable of potent potables later that year.

Fortune Brands teamed up with Pernod Ricard in the deal, which also added several local European brands, including Teacher's, Harvey's, and Cockburn's in the UK; DYC and Fundador in Spain; and Kuemmerling in Germany to Fortune's portfolio. The company also gained Larios gin (Spain) from Pernod in the transaction.

In less intoxicating businesses, Fortune bolstered its Home and Hardware division in 2006 when it bought vinyl-framed window replacements maker Simonton Building Products.

Fortune Brands spun off its Office segment to focus on its Home and Hardware, Spirits & Wine, and Golf segments. The company had previously tried to sell ACCO World but abandoned the idea when it didn't receive an acceptable offer. Instead, Fortune spun off the company and merged it with General Binding Corporation. The resulting firm, ACCO Brands Corporation, trades publicly on the New York Stock Exchange.

## HISTORY

Fortune Brands began in 1864 as W. Duke and Sons, a small tobacco company started by North Carolina farmer Washington Duke. James Buchanan Duke joined his father's business at age 14, and by age 25 was its president. James advertised to expanding markets, bought rival tobacco firms, and by 1904 controlled the industry. That year he merged all the competitive groups as American Tobacco Company. In a 1911 antitrust suit, the US Supreme Court dissolved American Tobacco into its original constituents, ordering them to operate independently.

James left American Tobacco the next year. He established a $100 million trust fund composed mainly of holdings in his power company, Duke Power and Light (now Duke Energy Corporation), for Trinity College. The school became Duke University in 1924.

George Washington Hill became president of American Tobacco in 1925. For the next 19 years until his death, George proved himself a consummate adman, pushing Lucky Strike, Pall Mall, and Tareyton cigarettes to top sales.

Smokers began switching to filter-tipped cigarettes in the 1950s because of health concerns. American Tobacco, however, ignored the trend and continued to rely on its popular filterless brands until the mid-1960s. In 1962 the firm sold J. Wix and Sons (Kensitas cigarettes) to UK tobacco firm Gallaher Group for a stake in Gallaher.

The company remained solely in the tobacco business until 1966, when it purchased Sunshine Biscuits (sold 1988) and Jim Beam Distillery. Reflecting its increasing diversity, the firm became American Brands in 1969. The next year it added Swingline (office supplies) and Master Lock. Meanwhile, American Brands increased its stake in Gallaher, controlling 100% by 1975. In 1976 the company bought Acushnet (Titleist and Bulls Eye); it added FootJoy in 1986.

Threatened with a takeover by E-II Holdings (a conglomerate of brands split from Beatrice), American Brands bought E-II in 1988. It kept five of E-II's companies — Day-Timers (time management products), Aristokraft (cabinets), Waterloo (tool boxes), Twentieth Century (plumbing supplies), and Vogel Peterson (office partitions; sold 1995) — and sold the rest (Culligan, Samsonite) to Riklis Family Corporation. Acquisitions in 1990 included Moen (faucets) and Whyte & Mackay (distillers). The company bought seven liquor brands in 1991 from Seagram.

American Brands sold its American Tobacco subsidiary, including the Pall Mall and Lucky Strike brands, to onetime subsidiary B.A.T Industries in 1994. The firm acquired publicly held Cobra Golf in 1996.

The following year American Brands changed its name to Fortune Brands and completed the spinoff of its Gallaher tobacco subsidiary. In 1998 Fortune bought kitchen and bathroom cabinetmaker Schrock from Electrolux, doubling its sales in that category. Also that year it bought Geyser Peak Winery and Apollo Presentation Products (overhead projectors).

Seeking to trim costs, in 1999 Fortune relocated its headquarters to Lincolnshire, Illinois. Norman Wesley was named chairman and CEO in July. In August 1999 Fortune formed Maxxium Worldwide, a non-US wine/spirits sales and distribution joint venture, with Rémy Cointreau and Highland Distillers. Also in 1999 the company bought Boone International (presentation products) and NHB Group, a manufacturer of ready-to-assemble kitchen and bath cabinetry.

In 2001 Fortune and Swedish company Vin & Sprit formed Future Brands, a joint venture to distribute Absolut vodka in the US. That year Fortune's Jim Beam Brands Worldwide unit unloaded its UK-based Scotch business for $290 million as part of its strategy to focus on fast-growing, premium brands. Fortune Brands bought The Omega Group, a manufacturer of kitchen and bath cabinetry, for $538 million in 2002.

About 20,000 barrels of Fortune's Jim Beam bourbon went up in smoke during a warehouse fire in the summer of 2003. The Bardstown, Kentucky, facility was believed to be the victim of a lighting strike from a passing thunderstorm. In November 2003 the company expanded its home and hardware division by acquiring privately held doormaker Therma-Tru Corp. for approximately $925 million.

In July of 2005 Fortune spent about $5 billion (subsequent adjustments added $350 million more) to acquire more than 20 wine and liquor brands formerly owned by Allied Domecq. First, Pernod Ricard acquired Allied Domecq with Fortune's monetary help; Pernod Ricard then began transferring a group of previously agreed-upon assets — including Sauza tequila, Canadian Club whiskey, Courvoisier Cognac, Laphroaig single-malt Scotch, and Clos du Bois wines — to Fortune.

## EXECUTIVES

**Chairman and CEO:** Norman H. (Norm) Wesley, age 57, $1,166,000 pay
**President and COO:** Bruce A. Carbonari, age 51
**SVP and CFO:** Craig P. Omtvedt, age 57, $575,000 pay
**SVP Finance and Treasurer:** Mark Hausberg, age 57, $335,000 pay
**SVP Strategy and Corporate Development:** Christopher J. Klein, age 43, $425,000 pay
**SVP, General Counsel, and Secretary:** Mark A. Roche, age 52, $478,000 pay
**VP and Associate General Counsel:** Lauren S. Tashma
**VP and Chief Internal Auditor:** Gary L. Tobison
**VP Business Development:** Allan J. Snape
**VP Corporate Communications:** C. Clarkson Hine
**VP Investor Relations:** Anthony J. Diaz
**VP Strategy:** Daniel J. Waters
**Corporate Director, Human Resources:** Rosalyn D. Wesley
**Auditors:** PricewaterhouseCoopers LLP

## LOCATIONS

**HQ:** Fortune Brands, Inc.
520 Lake Cook Rd., Deerfield, IL 60015
**Phone:** 847-484-4400 **Fax:** 847-478-0073
**Web:** www.fortunebrands.com

### 2006 Sales

| | $ mil. | % of total |
|---|---|---|
| US | 6,898.2 | 79 |
| Canada | 446.7 | 5 |
| UK | 266.8 | 3 |
| Australia | 233.4 | 3 |
| Spain | 181.2 | 2 |
| Other countries | 742.7 | 8 |
| **Total** | **8,769.0** | **100** |

## PRODUCTS/OPERATIONS

### 2006 Sales

| | $ mil. | % of total |
|---|---|---|
| Home & Hardware | 4,694.2 | 54 |
| Spirits & Wine | 2,761.4 | 31 |
| Golf | 1,313.4 | 15 |
| **Total** | **8,769.0** | **100** |

### Selected Brands

Home & Hardware
- Aristokraft (cabinets)
- Master Lock (padlocks)
- MasterBrand (cabinets)
- Moen (faucets)
- Omega (cabinets)
- Schrock (cabinets)
- Waterloo (toolboxes)

Spirits & Wine
- After Shock (cordial)
- Ardmore (scotch)
- Atlas Peak (wines)
- Calvert (gin)
- Canadian Club (whiskey)
- Chinaco (tequila)
- Clos du Bois (wines)
- Cockburn's (port)
- Courvoisier (cognac)
- The Dalmore (scotch)
- DeKuyper (cordials)
- DYC (whiskey)
- El Tosoro (tequila)
- Fundador (brandy)
- Geyser Peak (wine)
- Gilbey's (gin and vodka)
- Harveys (sherry)
- Jim Beam (bourbon)
- Kamchatka (vodka)
- Kessler (whiskey)
- Knob Creek (bourbon)
- Kuemmerling (cordials)
- Laphroaig (Scotch)
- Larios (gin)
- Leroux (cordials)
- Lord Calvert (whiskey
- Maker's Mark (bourbon)
- Old Crow (bourbon)
- Old Grand-Dad (bourbon)
- Old Overholt (bourbon)
- Ronrico (rum)
- Sauza (tequila)
- Teacher's (whiskey)
- VOX (vodka)
- William Hill Estate (wines)
- Windsor (whiskey)
- Wolfschmidt (vodka)

Golf
- Cobra (clubs)
- FootJoy (shoes and gloves)
- Pinnacle (balls)
- Scotty Cameron (putters)
- Titleist (balls, clubs, bags, and accessories)

## COMPETITORS

American Standard
American Woodmark
Armstrong World Industries
Bacardi USA
Black & Decker
Brown-Forman
Brunswick
Callaway Golf
Carbite Golf
Constellation Brands
Diageo
Eastern Company
Franklin Covey
Grohe
Huffy
K2
Kohler
KraftMaid Cabinetry
Masco
Newell Rubbermaid
Reebok
Skyy
Snap-on
Stanley Works
Waxman

## HISTORICAL FINANCIALS

Company Type: Public

### Income Statement

FYE: December 31

| | REVENUE ($ mil.) | NET INCOME ($ mil.) | NET PROFIT MARGIN | EMPLOYEES |
|---|---|---|---|---|
| **12/06** | 8,769 | 830 | 9.5% | 36,251 |
| **12/05** | 7,061 | 621 | 8.8% | 30,298 |
| **12/04** | 6,145 | 784 | 12.8% | 31,851 |
| **12/03** | 6,215 | 579 | 9.3% | 30,988 |
| **12/02** | 5,678 | 526 | 9.3% | 28,592 |
| **Annual Growth** | 11.5% | 12.1% | — | 6.1% |

### 2006 Year-End Financials

Debt ratio: 106.6%
Return on equity: 19.9%
Cash ($ mil.): 183
Current ratio: 1.56
Long-term debt ($ mil.): 5,035
No. of shares (mil.): 235
Dividends
Yield: 1.8%
Payout: 27.7%
Market value ($ mil.): 20,058

### Stock History

NYSE: FO

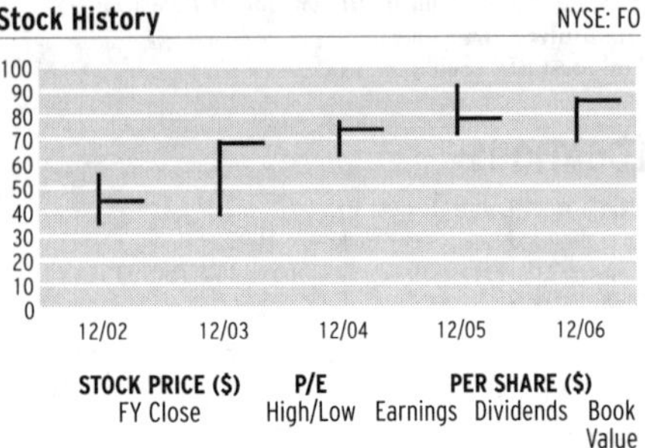


| | STOCK PRICE ($) FY Close | P/E High | P/E Low | PER SHARE ($) Earnings | Dividends | Book Value |
|---|---|---|---|---|---|---|
| **12/06** | 85.39 | 16 | 13 | 5.42 | 1.50 | 20.13 |
| **12/05** | 78.02 | 22 | 17 | 4.13 | 1.38 | 24.92 |
| **12/04** | 73.53 | 15 | 12 | 5.23 | 1.26 | 21.70 |
| **12/03** | 68.11 | 18 | 10 | 3.86 | 1.14 | 18.59 |
| **12/02** | 44.31 | 16 | 10 | 3.41 | 1.02 | 10.07 |
| **Annual Growth** | 17.8% | — | — | 12.3% | 10.1% | 18.9% |

# Foster Wheeler

International engineering, construction, and energy specialist Foster Wheeler builds business process and power generating facilities. The company operates through two business groups. The Engineering & Construction group designs and builds facilities for the oil and gas, chemical, pharmaceutical, and other industrial markets. Foster Wheeler's Global Power Group makes steam-generating units and related equipment for power and industrial plants, including fluidized-bed and conventional boilers. In addition, the group builds, owns, and leases cogeneration and independent power projects. Europe accounts for two-thirds of sales.

This global engineering and construction giant is run from offices in New Jersey, but is domiciled in Bermuda.

As reflected in its revenues, the company has an international bent. Recent contracts have ranged from soil remediation in Italy to petrochemical plant design and construction in farflung Tatarstan.

## HISTORY

In 1884 Pell and Ernest Foster started Water Works Supply (which became Power Specialty Company in 1900); Ernest hoped to market a European technology that used superheated steam for power. Cousins Frederick and Clifton Wheeler founded Wheeler Condenser & Engineering in New York in 1891 to build condensers and pumps for the marine and power industries.

Power Specialty acquired Wheeler Condenser & Engineering in 1927 and became Foster Wheeler Corporation. That year the company launched a UK subsidiary and in 1928 established a Canadian branch. Foster Wheeler went public in 1929 and bought D. Connelly Boiler in 1931.

US military contracts helped the firm weather the Depression, and the experience won it record business during WWII. After the war Foster Wheeler expanded internationally with subsidiaries in France (1949), Italy (1957), Spain (1965), and Australia (1967).

During the 1960s shortages in many of Foster Wheeler's core industries (energy, fertilizer, and petrochemicals) boosted sales and prompted diversification. In 1967 the company acquired Glitsch International, which made auto and chemical products and electronics.

The company formed Foster Wheeler Energy and Foster Wheeler International in 1973 and acquired Ullrich Copper, a fabricator of industrial copper products. In 1979 it ducked a takeover attempt by McDonnell Douglas.

In the 1980s Foster Wheeler moved into China and Thailand. In 1987 it set up its headquarters in New Jersey and formed Foster Wheeler Constructors to handle Western Hemisphere projects. In the late 1980s it avoided another takeover attempt by New York investor Asher Edelman.

Foster Wheeler opened a Chile subsidiary in 1991 and two years later organized its business into three groups. In 1994 the company acquired Enserch Environmental and formed Foster Wheeler Environmental. It also bought Optimized Process Designs, a construction firm serving the oil industry. That year longtime company executive Richard Swift became CEO.

Continuing its buying spree, Foster Wheeler acquired boilermaker Pyropower in 1995 from Finland's Ahlstrom. In 1996 it won a contract to build a polyethylene plant in the Philippines.

In 1997 the international builder struggled with the Asian collapse and sold Glitsch to Koch Engineering. It also took a blow on an Illinois waste-to-energy plant (Robbins Resource Recovery) when that state withdrew an interest-free loan and rescinded tax rebates for using that type of energy. The plant cost Foster Wheeler $235 million in charges over the next two years.

Although global sales grew in 1998 (with new contracts in Turkey, Mexico, and China), the oil slump and the Robbins plant were blamed for a $31.5 million loss. That year the company agreed to build a steam generating plant in Ohio and began building Vietnam's first oil refinery.

In 1999 Foster Wheeler formed a recovery plan: It received Chapter 11 bankruptcy protection for the Robbins plant, which it agreed to operate for two years or until sold to a third party, and it filed suit against the State of Illinois. It also cut 1,600 jobs, slashed its quarterly dividend, and closed some facilities. The next year it reorganized its operations, combining the Power Systems Group with the Energy Equipment Group. It also settled a discrimination suit involving about 100 African-American and female employees at the Robbins plant.

In 2001 the company reorganized in Bermuda as Foster Wheeler Ltd. That year Swift retired and was replaced by Raymond Milchovich, a former chairman and CEO of Kaiser Aluminum. To trim down the company, Milchovich launched an aggressive cost-reduction plan in 2002. A decline in the energy sector led subsidiary Foster Wheeler Energy to decide to close its Dansville, New York, manufacturing plant by early 2003. In 2002 the company also consolidated the engineering and construction operations of its New Jersey-based pharmaceutical center under its Reading, UK, office.

The next year Foster Wheeler completed the sale of its environmental management services unit to Tetra Tech for $80 million. In 2004 UK subsidiary Foster Wheeler Energy Limited won a program management contract to provide support for design and construction activities within Iraq's oil sector.

## EXECUTIVES

**Chairman and CEO; Acting CEO, Global Power Group:** Raymond J. (Ray) Milchovich, age 57, $2,847,382 pay (prior to title change)
**EVP and CFO:** Franco Baseotto
**EVP, General Counsel, and Secretary:** Peter J. Ganz, age 45, $1,039,630 pay
**VP Corporate Development and Treasurer:** Thierry Desmaris, age 48
**VP and Treasurer:** Peter D. Rose, age 60
**VP Investor Relations:** W. Scott Lamb, age 52
**VP and Controller:** Lisa Wood
**EVP, Global Sales and Marketing, Global Power Group:** David J. Parham
**Managing Director, Foster Wheeler Iberia:** Jesus Cadenas
**Managing Director, Global Sales and Marketing, Global Engineering and Construction Group:** Giuseppe Bonadies
**Chairman and CEO, Foster Wheeler Energy Limited:** Stephen J. (Steve) Davies, age 54
**President and COO:** Umberto della Sala, age 58, $1,140,254 pay (prior to promotion)
**President and CEO, Foster Wheeler USA Corporation:** W. Troy Roder
**CEO, Foster Wheeler Asia Pacific (APAC):** Franco Anselmi
**President and CEO, Foster Wheeler France:** André Robini
**President and CEO, Foster Wheeler North America; CEO, Power Group Asia:** Gary T. Nedelka
**President and CEO, Foster Wheeler Power Group Europe:** James E. Stone
**Chief Accounting Officer:** Edward (Ed) Carr
**Corporate Communications:** Maureen Bingert
**Auditors:** PricewaterhouseCoopers LLP

## LOCATIONS

**HQ:** Foster Wheeler Ltd.
Perryville Corporate Park, Clinton, NJ 08809
**Phone:** 908-730-4000 **Fax:** 908-730-5315
**Web:** www.fwc.com

### 2006 Sales

| | $ mil. | % of total |
|---|---|---|
| Europe | 2,286.2 | 65 |
| North America | 943.3 | 27 |
| Asia | 253.5 | 7 |
| South America | 12.1 | 1 |
| **Total** | **3,495.1** | **100** |

## PRODUCTS/OPERATIONS

### 2006 Sales

| | $ mil. | % of total |
|---|---|---|
| Engineering & Construction | 2,219.1 | 63 |
| Global Power | 1,276.0 | 37 |
| **Total** | **3,495.1** | **100** |

### Selected Operations

Engineering and Construction Group
- Environmental technologies
- Fired heaters
- Licensed technologies to the petrochemical markets
- Process (oil refining) technologies

Global Power Group
- Fluidized-bed, pulverized-coal, and package boilers
- Gasification of biomass
- Heat recovery steam generators
- Specialty products
  - Coal pulverizers
  - Condensers
  - Feedwater heaters
  - Selective catalytic reduction

## COMPETITORS

ABB
Aker Kværner
ALSTOM
AMEC
Babcock & Wilcox
Barr & Barr
Bechtel
Bilfinger Berger
Black & Veatch
Bouygues
Campenon Bernard
Chiyoda Corp.
Covanta
Doosan Heavy Industries
Dresser-Rand
Duke Energy
Fluor
GE
Halliburton
Hitachi
HOCHTIEF
ITOCHU
Jacobs Engineering
JGC
KBR
McDermott
Mitsubishi Heavy Industries
Parsons
Parsons Brinckerhoff
Saipem
Skanska
Technip
Tetra Tech
University Mechanical & Engineering
Washington Group
WorleyParsons Corp.
Zimmermann Group

## HISTORICAL FINANCIALS

Company Type: Public

### Income Statement

FYE: Last Friday in December

| | REVENUE ($ mil.) | NET INCOME ($ mil.) | NET PROFIT MARGIN | EMPLOYEES |
|---|---|---|---|---|
| **12/06** | 3,495 | 262 | 7.5% | 11,992 |
| **12/05** | 2,200 | (110) | — | 8,953 |
| **12/04** | 2,661 | (285) | — | 6,723 |
| **12/03** | 3,801 | (157) | — | 6,661 |
| **12/02** | 3,575 | (525) | — | 8,945 |
| **Annual Growth** | (0.6%) | — | — | 7.6% |

### 2006 Year-End Financials

Debt ratio: 289.3%
Return on equity: —
Cash ($ mil.): 611
Current ratio: 1.11
Long-term debt ($ mil.): 181
No. of shares (mil.): 69
Dividends
Yield: —
Payout: —
Market value ($ mil.): 3,810

### Stock History

NASDAQ (GS): FWLT

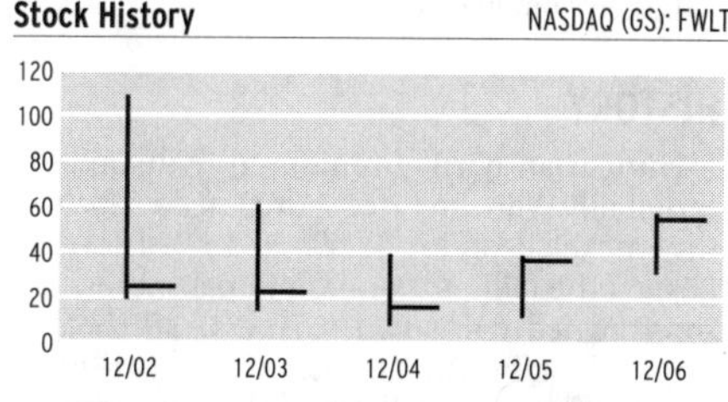


| | STOCK PRICE ($) FY Close | P/E High | P/E Low | PER SHARE ($) Earnings | Dividends | Book Value |
|---|---|---|---|---|---|---|
| **12/06** | 55.14 | 17 | 9 | 3.43 | — | 0.91 |
| **12/05** | 36.78 | — | — | (2.36) | — | (5.94) |
| **12/04** | 15.87 | — | — | (57.84) | — | (12.96) |
| **12/03** | 22.40 | — | — | (76.60) | — | (21.40) |
| **12/02** | 24.60 | — | — | (256.40) | — | (19.15) |
| **Annual Growth** | 22.4% | — | — | — | — | — |

# Fox Entertainment Group

This Fox has cunning ways to keep TV and movie fans entertained. Fox Entertainment Group oversees a broad collection of entertainment assets owned by media giant News Corp., including Fox Filmed Entertainment, the FOX television network, and about 35 broadcasting stations. It also owns a portfolio of cable channels, such as FX and the regional sports stations of Fox Sports Net. In addition, Fox Entertainment owns international satellite broadcaster STAR Group, a 38% stake in British Sky Broadcasting, and a 38% stake in US satellite provider DIRECTV.

Fox Entertainment's film and TV operations account for the largest share of News Corp.'s revenue (about 45%) and both continue to be strong performers in the media world. Fox Filmed Entertainment is also a successful producer of television shows, including *24* and *The Simpsons* (both of which air on FOX), and *My Name Is Earl* (NBC).

On the small screen, the FOX network nabbed the #2 ratings spot behind CBS for the 2006-07 season thanks to *American Idol, House*, and *24*. It also claims the top position in the all-important 18-49 age group — the demographic most coveted by advertisers.

FOX is also banking on continued interest in sports, renewing its relationship with Major League Baseball in 2006 with a seven-year, $1.8 billion rights deal for regular season games, one League Championship Series and the World Series. The network is also a major broadcast partner of the National Football League, along with CBS, Walt Disney's ESPN, NBC, and its own DIRECTV.

News Corp. rocked the broadcast television boat once again when it launched a new, limited-distribution television network in 2006 called MyNetworkTV. (Its launch of the FOX network in 1986 was a gutsy move at the time, engaging in a business dominated by ABC, CBS, and NBC.) News Corp. signed affiliation agreements with more than 95 stations (reaching 63% of the US) left without programming following UPN and The WB's merger into a new network called The CW. MyNetworkTV airs in primetime Monday through Saturday and broadcasts about 12 hours of content a week, most of it serialized dramas similar to Spanish-language telenovelas.

## HISTORY

Hungarian-born immigrant William Fox (originally Wilhelm Fried) purchased a New York City nickelodeon for $1,600 in 1904. He transformed the failing operation into a success and soon owned (with two partners) 25 theaters across the city. The partners opened a film exchange, The Greater New York Rental Company, and in 1913 began making movies through the Box Office Attraction Company.

Fox became the first to combine film production, leasing, and exhibition when he founded the Fox Film Corporation in 1915. Soon after, he moved the studio to California. One of the first to recognize the value of individual actors, Fox is credited with developing the "star system."

Throughout the 1920s, Fox Film continued to grow. The company began experiencing trouble in 1927, and by 1930 William Fox was forced out.

In 1935 the company was merged with Twentieth Century Pictures, a studio started two years earlier by Darryl Zanuck, former head of production at Warner Brothers. Under Zanuck's leadership, the studio flourished in the 1930s and 1940s, producing such films as *The Grapes of Wrath* and *All About Eve.* By the early 1950s, however, TV was dulling some of Hollywood's shine. Zanuck left the studio in 1956, only to return in 1962 to help it recover from the disastrously overbudget *Cleopatra.*

The 1960s brought both good (*The Sound of Music*) and bad (*Tora! Tora! Tora!*). By 1971 infighting between Darryl Zanuck and his son Richard, who had been president of the studio, resulted in the resignation of both men. The studio prospered during the 1970s, culminating in 1977 with the release of *Star Wars,* the biggest box office hit in history at that time.

Oilman Marvin Davis bought Twentieth Century Fox for $722 million in 1981. In 1985 the studio changed hands again when it was purchased by Rupert Murdoch. The next year Murdoch bought six TV stations from Metromedia and launched the FOX Broadcasting Company.

Murdoch became CEO in 1995. In 1996 and 1997, respectively, Murdoch created the Fox News Channel and purchased Pat Robertson's International Family Entertainment. The company also joined Liberty Media in 1996 to create a rival to Disney's ESPN sports network.

Fox Entertainment Group went public in November 1998, raising $2.8 billion — one of the largest offerings in American history. That year Murdoch bought the Los Angeles Dodgers and acquired 40% of the Staples Center sports arena, thereby acquiring options to buy minority interests in the Los Angeles Kings and Los Angeles Lakers. (Fox sold its interest in the Staples Center to Anschutz Entertainment Group in 2004.)

In 1999 News Corp. bought the 50% of the Fox/Liberty Networks business that it didn't already own from Liberty Media and transferred ownership to Fox (the operation was renamed FOX Sports Net). The deal gave Liberty Media an 8% stake in News Corp. Doug Herzog, Fox's fifth entertainment president in eight years, left in 2000 after only 14 months as programming chief. Gail Berman took over the position in mid-2000. (Berman quit in 2005 and became president of Paramount Pictures.)

In 2001 Fox and partner Saban sold the Fox Family Channel, which they jointly owned, to Walt Disney for about $5.2 billion. In 2003 News Corp. bought 34% of DIRECTV owner Hughes Electronics from General Motors. It transferred the stake in Hughes (renamed The DIRECTV Group) to Fox Entertainment after the acquisition closed. The following year the company sold the Los Angeles Dodgers to real estate developer Frank McCourt for $430 million.

In the early part of 2005, News Corp. purchased the rest of Fox Entertainment that it didn't already own for about $6.2 billion. At that time Murdoch passed Fox's top post to president Peter Chernin. The company acquired the Turner South regional cable network the following year from Turner Broadcasting for $375 million and relaunched the channel as SportSouth.

## EXECUTIVES

**President and COO:** Peter F. Chernin, age 55
**SEVP and CFO:** David F. DeVoe, age 60
**Chairman and CEO, FOX News Network; and Chairman, Fox Television Stations:** Roger Ailes, age 66
**CEO, Fox Television Stations Group:** Jack Abernethy, age 48
**President, Engineering:** Andrew G. (Andy) Setos
**President, Fox Baseball Holdings:** Frank McCourt
**President, Fox Searchlight Pictures:** Peter Rice
**President, FOX National Cable Sports Networks:** Robert (Bob) Thompson, age 43
**President, FOX Television Network and Fox Broadcasting:** Ed Wilson
**Vice Chairman, Twentieth Century Fox Film Group:** Hutch Parker
**President, Twentieth Television:** Rick Jacobson
**President, FOX Regional Cable Sports Networks:** Randy Freer
**President, Digital Media:** Dan Fawcett, age 43
**President, Twentieth Century Fox Animation:** Vanessa Morrison
**Auditors:** Ernst & Young LLP

## LOCATIONS

**HQ:** Fox Entertainment Group, Inc.
10201 W. Pico Blvd., Los Angeles, CA 90035
**Phone:** 310-369-1000
**Web:** www.fox.com

## PRODUCTS/OPERATIONS

### Selected Operations

Filmed entertainment
- Feature film production and distribution
  - Fox Filmed Entertainment
    - Fox 2000
    - Fox Searchlight Pictures
    - Twentieth Century Fox
    - Twentieth Century Fox Animation
  - Twentieth Century Fox Home Entertainment
- Television production and distribution
  - Fox Television Studios
  - Twentieth Century Fox Television
  - Twentieth Television

Television
- FOX Broadcasting
- Fox Television Stations
  - KCOP (MyNetworkTV, Los Angeles)
  - KDFI (FOX, Dallas)
  - KDFW (FOX, Dallas)
  - KDVR (FOX, Denver)
  - KMSP (FOX, Minneapolis)
  - KRIV (FOX, Houston)
  - KSAZ (FOX, Phoenix)
  - KSTU (FOX, Salt Lake City)
  - KTBC (FOX; Austin, TX)
  - KTTV (FOX, Los Angeles)
  - KTVI (FOX, St. Louis)
  - KUTP (MyNetworkTV, Phoenix)
  - WAGA (FOX, Atlanta)
  - WBRC (FOX; Birmingham, AL)
  - WDAF (FOX, Kansas City)
  - WDCA (MyNetworkTV; Washington, DC)
  - WFLD (FOX, Chicago)
  - WFTC (MyNetworkTV, Minneapolis)
  - WFXT (FOX, Boston)
  - WGHP (FOX; Greensboro, NC)
  - WHBQ (FOX, Memphis)
  - WITI (FOX, Milwaukee)
  - WJBK (FOX, Detroit)
  - WJW (FOX, Cleveland)
  - WNYW (FOX, New York City)
  - WOFL (FOX; Orlando, FL)
  - WOGX (FOX; Gainesville, FL)
  - WPWR (MyNetworkTV, Chicago)
  - WTTG (FOX; Washington, DC)
  - WTVT (FOX, Tampa)
  - WTXF (FOX, Philadelphia)
  - WUTB (MyNetworkTV, Baltimore)
  - WWOR (MyNetworkTV, New York City)
- MyNetworkTV
- STAR Group (international televison broadcasting, Asia)

Cable network programming
Fox College Sports
Fox International Channels
Fox Movie Channel
Fox News Channel
Fox Reality
Fox Sports International
Fox Pan American Sports (38%)
Fox Sports en Español
Fox Sports Latin America
Fox Soccer Channel
Fox Sports Middle East
Fox Sports Net
FUEL TV
FX
SPEED
Direct broadcast satellite
British Sky Broadcasting (38%, UK)
DIRECTV (38%)
SKY Italia
Other operations and investments
Colorado Rockies (14%, baseball team)
LAPTV (23%, Latin American pay television)
National Geographic Channel (67%)
NGC Network Latin America (67%, National Geographic Channel)
NGC Network International (75%, National Geographic Channel International)
Premium Movie Partnership (20%, pay televison, Australia)
Sky Network Television (44%, direct broadcast satellite service, New Zealand)
Telecine (13%, pay televison, Brazil)

## COMPETITORS

A&E Networks
Carsey-Werner
CBS Corp
Disney
DreamWorks
Hearst-Argyle Television
Liberty Media
Lucasfilm
MGM
NBC Universal
Rainbow Media
Sony Pictures Entertainment
Time Warner
Viacom

# FPL Group

For a Florida company without any oranges, FPL Group produces a lot of juice. It has operations across the US, including independent power production and telecommunications businesses, but most of its revenues are produced by its utility subsidiary, Florida Power & Light (FPL). FPL distributes electricity to more than 4.4 million customers and has more than 20,980 MW of generating capacity from interests in nuclear and fossil-fueled power plants. Subsidiary FPL Group Capital owns nonutility businesses, including FPL Energy, an independent power producer and wholesale energy marketer. In 2006 the company agreed to buy the Point Beach Nuclear Plant in Two Rivers from Wisconsin Energy for $998 million.

Green power producer FPL Energy gets about 30% of its 11,000-MW generating capacity from wind, solar, hydroelectric, and waste-to-energy facilities; the rest comes from traditional nuclear and thermal plants. The unit owns plants in more than 20 states, and it is expanding its generation portfolio. FPL Energy had agreed to purchase British Energy's 50% stake in nuclear power generation firm AmerGen Energy; however, Exelon, which owns the other half of AmerGen, exercised its right of first refusal and purchased the remainder of AmerGen.

Subsidiary FPL FiberNet leases wholesale fiber-optic capacity to telephone, cable, and Internet providers; the unit operates a 2,500-mile network. FPL Group has canceled plans to expand its telecom operations.

Late in 2005 FPL agreed to buy rival power concern Constellation Energy Group Inc. in an $11 billion stock deal. However, the companies called the deal off in 2006, citing uncertainty about regulatory approvals.

## HISTORY

During Florida's land boom of the early 1920s, new homes and businesses were going up fast. But electric utilities were sparse, and no transmission lines linked systems.

In 1925 American Power & Light Company (AP&L), which operated utilities throughout the Americas, set up Florida Power & Light (FPL) to consolidate the state's electric assets. AP&L built transmission lines linking 58 communities — from Miami to Stuart on the Atlantic and from Arcadia to Punta Gorda on the Gulf.

FPL accumulated many holdings, including a limestone quarry, streetcars, phone companies, and water utilities, and purchases in 1926 and 1927 nearly doubled its electric properties. In 1927 the company used an electric pump to demonstrate how swamplands could be drained and cultivated.

During the 1940s and 1950s FPL sold its nonelectric properties. The Public Utility Holding Company Act of 1935 forced AP&L to spin off FPL in 1950. The company was listed on the NYSE that year.

FPL grew with Florida's booming population. In 1972 its first nuclear plant (Turkey Point, south of Miami) went on line. In the 1980s it began to diversify with the purchase of real estate firm W. Flagler Investment in 1981, and FPL Group was created in 1984 as a holding company. It subsequently acquired Telesat Cablevision (1985), Colonial Penn Group (1985, insurance), and Turner Foods (1988, citrus groves). FPL Group formed ESI Energy in 1985 to develop nonutility energy projects.

Diversification efforts didn't pan out, and in 1990 the firm wrote off about $750 million. That year, sticking to electricity, the utility snagged its first out-of-state power plant, in Georgia, acquiring a 76% stake (over five years). FPL Group sold its ailing Colonial Penn unit in 1991; two years later it sold its real estate holdings and some of its cable TV businesses.

The utility gave environmentalists cause to complain in 1995. First, the St. Lucie nuclear plant was fined by the NRC for a series of problems. FPL also wanted to burn orimulsion, a cheap, tarlike fuel. (Barred by the governor, the utility gave up the plan in 1998.)

In 1997 FPL Group created FPL Energy, an independent power producer (IPP), out of its ESI Energy and international operations; FPL Energy teamed up with Belgium-based Tractebel the next year to buy two gas-fired plants in Boston and Newark, New Jersey.

FPL Energy built wind-power facilities in Iowa in 1998 and in Wisconsin and Texas in 1999; it also bought 35 generating plants in Maine in 1999. That year FPL Group sold its Turner Foods citrus unit and the rest of its cable TV holdings. By 2000, FPL Energy owned interests in plants in 12 states.

Out of its fiber-optic operations, FPL Group in 2000 created subsidiary FPL FiberNet to market wholesale capacity. That year talks of Spanish utility giant Iberdrola purchasing FPL Group ended when Iberdrola's shareholders objected; in 2001 plans to merge with New Orleans-based Entergy fell through after a series of disagreements. The deal would have created one of the US's largest power companies.

In 2002 FPL Group purchased an 88% interest in the Seabrook Nuclear Generating Station in New Hampshire for $837 million from a consortium of US utilities, including Northeast Utilities and BayCorp Holdings. In 2005 FPL Group acquired Gexa Corp., a Houston-based electric utility.

## EXECUTIVES

**Chairman and CEO; Chairman and CEO, Florida Power & Light and FPL Energy:** Lewis (Lew) Hay III, age 51
**President and COO:** James L. (Jim) Robo, age 44
**SVP Business Management:** T. J. Tuscai
**VP and Chief Development Officer:** Michael L. Leighton
**VP Finance and CFO; SVP Finance and CFO, Florida Power & Light:** Moray P. Dewhurst, age 51
**VP Marketing and Corporate Communications:** Mary Lou Kromer
**VP Tax:** James P. Higgins
**VP and General Counsel:** Edward F. Tancer, age 45
**VP and Corporate Secretary:** Alissa E. Ballot
**VP Governmental Affairs Federal:** Michael M. Wilson
**VP Regulatory Affairs:** William G. Walker
**President, Florida Power & Light:** Armando J. Olivera, age 56
**President, FPL Energy:** Mitchell (Mitch) Davidson, age 60
**President, Commodities Marketing and Retail Markets:** Mark Maisto
**Chief Accounting Officer and Controller; VP, Accounting, Chief Accounting Officer, and Controller, Florida Power & Light:** K. Michael Davis, age 60
**SVP Development, FPL Energy:** Michael O'Sullivan
**SVP Nuclear Division, Florida Power & Light:** John A. Stall, age 52
**SVP Power Generation, Florida Power & Light:** Antonio Rodriguez, age 64
**VP and General Counsel, FPL Energy, LLC:** Scott D. Cousins
**VP Enviromental Services, Florida Power & Light:** Randall R. LaBauve
**Director, Investor Relations:** Jim von Riesemann
**Auditors:** Deloitte & Touche LLP

## LOCATIONS

**HQ:** FPL Group, Inc.
700 Universe Blvd., Juno Beach, FL 33408
**Phone:** 561-694-4000 **Fax:** 561-694-4620
**Web:** www.fplgroup.com

FPL Group provides electric utility services in southern and eastern Florida through Florida Power & Light (FPL), which owns generating facilities in Florida and Georgia. It also has operating US power plants in Alabama, California, Iowa, Kansas, Maine, Massachusetts, Minnesota, New Hampshire, New Jersey, New Mexico, New York, North Dakota, Oklahoma, Oregon, Pennsylvania, Rhode Island, South Carolina, South Dakota, Texas, Virginia, Washington, West Virginia, Wisconsin, and Wyoming, through FPL Energy. FPL FiberNet markets fiber-optic network capacity in Florida.

## PRODUCTS/OPERATIONS

### 2006 Sales

| | $ mil. | % of total |
|---|---|---|
| Florida Power & Light | 11,988 | 76 |
| FPL Energy | 3,558 | 23 |
| Corporate & other | 164 | 1 |
| **Total** | **15,710** | **100** |

**Selected Subsidiaries and Divisions**

Florida Power & Light Company
  Energy Marketing and Trading
FPL Group Capital Inc.
  FPL Energy, LLC
    FPL Energy Power Marketing, Inc.
  FPL FiberNet, LLC

## COMPETITORS

AES
Bangor Hydro-Electric
BellSouth
Calpine
Chesapeake Utilities
CMS Energy
Delmarva Power
Duke Energy
Edison International
Entergy
Exelon
Florida East Coast Industries
Florida Public Utilities
JEA
MidAmerican Energy
Mirant
Narragansett
Oglethorpe Power
Progress Energy
PSEG
SCANA
Seminole Electric
Sempra Energy
Southern Company
TECO Energy

## HISTORICAL FINANCIALS

Company Type: Public

**Income Statement** FYE: December 31

| | REVENUE ($ mil.) | NET INCOME ($ mil.) | NET PROFIT MARGIN | EMPLOYEES |
|---|---|---|---|---|
| **12/06** | 15,710 | 1,281 | 8.2% | 10,400 |
| **12/05** | 11,846 | 885 | 7.5% | 10,200 |
| **12/04** | 10,522 | 887 | 8.4% | 11,921 |
| **12/03** | 9,630 | 890 | 9.2% | 11,500 |
| **12/02** | 8,311 | 473 | 5.7% | 9,612 |
| **Annual Growth** | 17.3% | 28.3% | — | 2.0% |

**2006 Year-End Financials**

Debt ratio: 96.6%
Return on equity: 13.9%
Cash ($ mil.): 1,917
Current ratio: 0.77
Long-term debt ($ mil.): 9,591

No. of shares (mil.): 405
Dividends
  Yield: 2.8%
  Payout: 46.4%
Market value ($ mil.): 22,040

**Stock History** NYSE: FPL

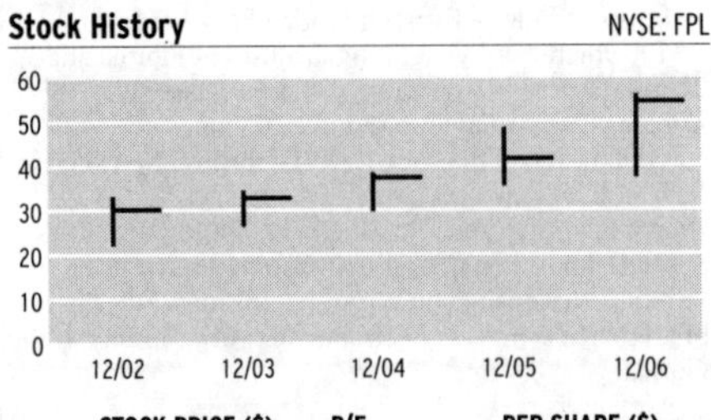


| | STOCK PRICE ($) FY Close | P/E High | P/E Low | PER SHARE ($) Earnings | Dividends | Book Value |
|---|---|---|---|---|---|---|
| **12/06** | 54.42 | 17 | 12 | 3.23 | 1.50 | 24.52 |
| **12/05** | 41.56 | 21 | 16 | 2.29 | 1.07 | 21.52 |
| **12/04** | 37.38 | 15 | 12 | 2.45 | 1.30 | 40.48 |
| **12/03** | 32.71 | 14 | 11 | 2.50 | 1.20 | 37.89 |
| **12/02** | 30.07 | 24 | 16 | 1.37 | 1.16 | 36.20 |
| **Annual Growth** | 16.0% | — | — | 23.9% | 6.6% | (9.3%) |

# Franklin Resources

Franklin Resources believes a penny saved is a penny lost — if it's not invested. The firm manages a family of more than 100 funds that invest in international and domestic stocks; taxable and tax-exempt money market instruments; and corporate, municipal, and US government bonds. The investment products are sold under the Franklin, Templeton, Mutual Series, Bissett, Darby, and Fiduciary Trust banners. Franklin Resources also offers separately managed accounts. Descendants of founder Rupert Johnson Sr. and their families own about a third of Franklin Resources.

The company, which manages more than $500 billion in assets and more than 17 million shareholder accounts, continues to expand its product portfolio and strengthen its geographic reach; it operates mainly in North America and Europe, but is adding assets under management in Asia. In addition to its core business, Franklin Resources also provides shareholder services and manages investments for pension plans, trusts, and other institutions. Its banking subsidiaries offer clients such services as lending and deposit accounts. Retail banking, private banking, consumer lending, auto-loan securitization, and trust services are offered through subsidiaries Franklin Templeton Bank & Trust, Franklin Capital, and Fiduciary Trust Company International. The company also has an offshore trust subsidiary in the Cayman Islands.

## HISTORY

Rupert Johnson Sr. founded Franklin Distributors (capitalizing on Benjamin Franklin's reputation for thrift) in New York in 1947; it launched its first fund, Franklin Custodian, in 1948. Custodian grew into five funds, including conservatively managed equity and bond funds. In 1968 Johnson's son Charles (who had joined the firm in 1957) became president and CEO. The company went public in 1971 as Franklin Resources.

In 1973 Franklin bought San Mateo-based investment firm Winfield & Co. and relocated to the Golden State. The buy provided additional products, including the Franklin Gold Fund (made possible by the end of the prohibition in the US against private interests owning commodity gold). With interest rate spikes in the late 1970s and early 1980s, money drained from savings accounts was poured into more lucrative money market mutual funds.

The Franklin Money Fund, launched in 1975, fueled the firm's tremendous asset growth in the 1980s. In 1981 the Franklin Tax-Free Income Fund (introduced in 1977) began investing solely in California municipal bonds. The fund's success led Franklin to introduce 43 tax-free income funds in later years.

In 1985 Franklin bought Pacific Union Bank and Trust (now Franklin Bank), allowing it to offer consumers such services as credit cards and to compete with financial services supermarkets, such as Merrill Lynch. It also bought real estate firm Property Resources (now Franklin Properties).

The 1987 stock crash and the California real estate slump forced Franklin to focus on its funds businesses. In 1992 it bought Bahamas-based Templeton, Galbraith & Hansberger, the manager of Templeton Funds, a major international funds business. The Templeton deal added an aggressive investment management unit to complement the conservatively managed Franklin funds.

In 1940 Sir John Templeton gained control of investment company Templeton, Dobbrow and Vance (TDV). TDV launched Templeton Growth Fund in 1954. In 1969 Templeton sold his interest in TDV but continued to manage the Templeton Growth Fund. John Galbraith became president of Securities Fund Investors (SFI), the distribution company for Templeton Growth Fund, in 1974. In 1977 Galbraith bought SFI from Templeton and began building the Templeton funds broker-dealer network in the US. The Templeton World Fund was formed in 1978. Templeton Investment Counsel was launched to provide investment advice in 1979. In 1986 these companies were combined to form Templeton, Galbraith & Hansberger Ltd.

In 1996 Franklin bought Heine Securities, previous investment adviser to Mutual Series Fund Inc. Max Heine, a leading investor, had established Mutual Shares Corp. in 1949. Heine Securities was formed in 1975. Following the purchase, Franklin set up subsidiary Franklin Mutual Advisers as the investment adviser for the Mutual Series Fund.

In 1997 the weak Asian economy hurt Templeton's international funds, prompting liquidation of a Japanese stocks-based fund. Franklin cut jobs and shuffled management in 1999; the restructuring acknowledged the clash between the firm's value-investing style and investors' bull-market optimism.

In 2000 the firm gained a foothold in Canada with its purchase of Bissett & Associates Investment Management. Franklin's purchase of Fiduciary Trust the following year gave the firm greater access to institutional investors and affluent individuals.

Franklin Resources boosted its alternative investment offerings with the 2003 acquisition of Darby Overseas, which focuses on private equity, mezzanine, and fixed-income investment products, and specializes in Asian and Latin American fixed-income securities.

Chairman Charles Johnson retired from the CEO's office in 2004, turning the reins over to a new generation; his son Gregory was named CEO. Also that year Franklin Resources agreed to pay $50 million to settle market-timing allegations and reached a $20 million settlement with the SEC and an $18 million settlement with the state of California over commissions paid to brokers for mutual fund sales.

## EXECUTIVES

**Chairman:** Charles B. (Charlie) Johnson, age 73
**Vice Chairman:** Harmon E. Burns, age 62
**Vice Chairman:** Rupert H. Johnson Jr., age 66
**President and CEO:** Gregory E. (Greg) Johnson, age 45, $3,430,132 pay
**EVP, Portfolio Operations:** John M. Lusk, age 48
**EVP, Technology and Operations:** Jennifer J. (Jenny) Bolt, age 42
**SVP and Assistant Secretary:** Leslie M. Kratter, age 61
**SVP and Chief Administrative Officer:** Norman R. Frisbie Jr., age 39
**SVP and General Counsel:** Craig S. Tyle, age 46
**VP, Enterprise Risk Management; Interim CFO, and Treasurer:** Kenneth A. Lewis, age 45
**VP, Corporate Communications:** Holly E. Gibson Brady, age 40
**VP, Deputy General Counsel, and Secretary:** Barbara J. Green, age 59

**VP, Human Resources — US:** Penelope S. Alexander, age 46
**VP, Human Resources — International:** Donna S. Ikeda, age 50
**VP and Director, Registered Investment Advisor:** Lincoln Baca
**President, Fiduciary Trust Company International:** Henry P. Johnson
**President and CEO, Franklin Templeton Sealand Fund Management:** Michael X. Lin
**Director, Public Relations:** Lisa Gallegos
**Auditors:** PricewaterhouseCoopers LLP

## LOCATIONS

**HQ:** Franklin Resources, Inc.
1 Franklin Pkwy., Bldg. 970, 1st Fl.
San Mateo, CA 94403
**Phone:** 650-312-2000 **Fax:** 650-312-5606
**Web:** www.franklintempleton.com

### 2006 Sales

| | $ mil. | % of total |
|---|---|---|
| North America | | |
| US | 3,262.4 | 65 |
| Bahamas | 815.2 | 16 |
| Canada | 324.8 | 6 |
| Europe | 187.2 | 4 |
| Other regions | 461.1 | 9 |
| **Total** | **5,050.7** | **100** |

### 2006 Assets Under Management

| | % of total |
|---|---|
| North America | |
| US | 71 |
| Canada | 7 |
| Europe | 11 |
| Asia/Pacific & other regions | 11 |
| **Total** | **100** |

## PRODUCTS/OPERATIONS

### 2006 Sales

| | $ mil. | % of total |
|---|---|---|
| Investment management fees | 2,963.9 | 59 |
| Underwriting & distribution fees | 1,756.0 | 35 |
| Shareholder servicing fees | 259.3 | 5 |
| Other | 71.5 | 1 |
| **Total** | **5,050.7** | **100** |

### 2006 Sales by Segment

| | $ mil | % of total |
|---|---|---|
| Investment management & related services | 4,997.6 | 99 |
| Banking/finance | 53.1 | 1 |
| **Total** | **5,050.7** | **100** |

## COMPETITORS

AllianceBernstein
American Century
AXA Financial
BlackRock
Capital Group
Citigroup
FMR
INVESCO
John Hancock Financial Services
JPMorgan Chase
Morgan Stanley
Nationwide Financial
New York Life
Old Mutual (US)
PIMCO
Pioneer Investment Management
Principal Financial
Putnam
T. Rowe Price
Torchmark
USAA
The Vanguard Group

## HISTORICAL FINANCIALS

Company Type: Public

### Income Statement

FYE: September 30

| | ASSETS ($ mil.) | NET INCOME ($ mil.) | INCOME AS % OF ASSETS | EMPLOYEES |
|---|---|---|---|---|
| **9/06** | 9,500 | 1,268 | 13.3% | 8,000 |
| **9/05** | 8,894 | 1,058 | 11.9% | 7,200 |
| **9/04** | 8,228 | 707 | 8.6% | 6,700 |
| **9/03** | 6,971 | 503 | 7.2% | 6,500 |
| **9/02** | 6,423 | 433 | 6.7% | 6,700 |
| **Annual Growth** | 10.3% | 30.8% | — | 4.5% |

### 2006 Year-End Financials

Equity as % of assets: 70.4%
Return on assets: 13.8%
Return on equity: 20.5%
Long-term debt ($ mil.): 860
No. of shares (mil.): 253
Dividends
Yield: 0.3%
Payout: 7.4%
Market value ($ mil.): 26,781
Sales ($ mil.): 5,051

### Stock History

NYSE: BEN

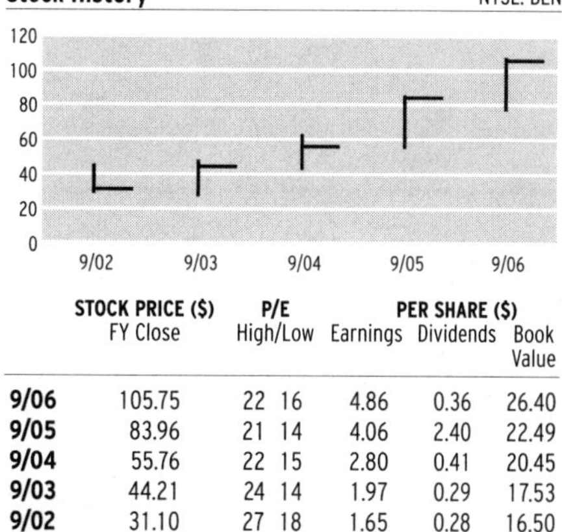


| | STOCK PRICE ($) FY Close | P/E High | P/E Low | PER SHARE ($) Earnings | Dividends | Book Value |
|---|---|---|---|---|---|---|
| **9/06** | 105.75 | 22 | 16 | 4.86 | 0.36 | 26.40 |
| **9/05** | 83.96 | 21 | 14 | 4.06 | 2.40 | 22.49 |
| **9/04** | 55.76 | 22 | 15 | 2.80 | 0.41 | 20.45 |
| **9/03** | 44.21 | 24 | 14 | 1.97 | 0.29 | 17.53 |
| **9/02** | 31.10 | 27 | 18 | 1.65 | 0.28 | 16.50 |
| **Annual Growth** | 35.8% | — | — | 31.0% | 6.5% | 12.5% |

# Freddie Mac

Uncle Sam's nephew is somewhat of a real estate tycoon. Officially known as the Federal Home Loan Mortgage Corporation, Freddie Mac is a shareholder-owned, government-sponsored enterprise that, along with sister Fannie Mae, creates liquidity in the residential mortgage market by guaranteeing, purchasing, securitizing, and investing in such loans. The company, which is prohibited from originating loans, buys conventional residential mortgages from mortgage bankers, transferring risk from them and allowing them to provide mortgages to those who otherwise wouldn't qualify. It also provides assistance for affordable rental housing. Freddie Mac indirectly finances one out of every six homes in the US.

Although not part of the US government, Freddie Mac enjoys an implicit guarantee of government support should the company fall on hard times. Because of the perceived backing, investors are willing to lend to Freddie Mac at below-market rates. Consequently, private-sector competitors (and, increasingly, government critics) are growing more vocal with their complaints. Lenders accuse Freddie Mac and Fannie Mae of using their special status to fund expansion into activities outside the scope of their congressional charter.

In 2006 Freddie Mac paid a record $3.8 million fine to settle allegations by the Federal Election Commission that the company made illegal campaign contributions to members of the US House Financial Services Committee. It also agreed to pay $4.65 million to settle a lawsuit related to its employee 401(k) plan. The suit stated Freddie Mac failed to give complete and accurate information to program participants.

The Department of Justice dropped criminal charges against Freddie Mac in 2006 after the lender revealed in 2003 it had misstated earnings by about $5 billion for 2000 to 2002. The news came on the heels of the Justice Department's earlier decision to rescind criminal charges against Fannie Mae.

Freddie Mac stopped buying subprime mortgages in 2007.

## HISTORY

Ah, the 1960s — free love, great tunes, and a war nobody wanted to pay for with taxes. By the 1970s, inflation was rising and real income was starting to fall. To divert a construction industry recession, Congress created a new entity to buy home mortgages and boost the flow of money into the housing market.

Fannie Mae had been buying mortgages since 1938, but focused on Federal Housing Administration (FHA) and Veterans Administration loans. In 1970 Congress created Freddie Mac and enlarged Fannie Mae's field of action to include conventional mortgages. Still, rising interest rates in the 1970s were brutal to the US real estate market.

In the early 1980s dealers devised a way to securitize the company's loans — seen as somewhat frumpy investments — by packaging them into more alluring, bond-like investments, made even sexier by the implicit government guarantee. When three major government securities dealers collapsed in 1985, ownership of some Freddie Mac securities was in doubt, and the Federal Reserve Bank of New York quickly automated registration of government securities.

In 1984 Freddie Mac issued shares to members of the Federal Home Loan Bank (the overseer of US savings and loans). By 1989 the shares had been converted to common stock and were traded on the NYSE. Freddie Mac's board expanded from three political appointees to 18 members.

Nationwide real estate defaults (rampant in the wake of the late 1980s crash) kindled concern about Freddie Mac's reserve levels and whether it might need to tap its US Treasury line of credit. In response, Congress in 1992 created the Office of Federal Housing Enterprise Oversight to regulate Freddie Mac and Fannie Mae. Initial examinations sounded no alarms. A 1996 Congressional Budget Office report questioned whether the government should continue its implicit guarantees of the pair's debt securities.

In 1997 Freddie Mac officially adopted its longtime nickname. The next year, it launched a system to cut loan approval time from weeks to minutes (it agreed to develop a similar version for the FHA). The streamlining was crucial to pacts in which mortgage lenders (including one of the US's largest, Wells Fargo) promised to sell Freddie Mac their loan originations. In 1999 Freddie Mac hired former House Speaker Newt Gingrich as a consultant.

Freddie Mac made a major Internet push in 2000 with its first online taxable bond offering. A wired venture involving Freddie Mac, Microsoft, and such big lenders as Chase Manhattan (now part of JPMorgan Chase & Co.), Bank of America, and Wells Fargo drew fire from small banks that said it would push them out of the online lending business.

In 2001 Freddie Mac bought Tuttle Decision Systems, a loan-pricing software system provider. Critics responded that Freddie Mac overstepped its government charter with such a move.

In a move initiated by its auditor, Freddie Mac re-audited its earnings from 2000 to 2003, uncovering accounting irregularities and employee misconduct. Further investigations, executive oustings, restructuring, and numerous lawsuits followed. In late 2003 Freddie Mac announced the findings of its re-audit. The company admitted to understating earnings by $4.4 billion between 2000 and 2002 and overstating profits by $989 million in 2001, all in an attempt to smooth out results and show steady profit growth.

## EXECUTIVES

**Chairman and CEO:** Richard F. (Dick) Syron, age 60
**President, COO, and Director:** Eugene M. (Gene) McQuade, age 58
**CFO:** Anthony S. (Buddy) Piszel, age 52
**EVP Community Relations; Chairman, Freddie Mac Foundation:** Ralph F. Boyd Jr., age 50, $875,000 pay (prior to title change)
**EVP and General Counsel:** Robert Bostrom
**EVP Human Resources:** Paul G. George, age 56
**EVP Investments and Capital Markets:** Patricia L. Cook, age 52
**EVP Operations and Technology:** Joseph A. (Joe) Smialowski, age 58
**SVP Enterprise Operational Risk:** Gareth Davies
**SVP and CIO:** James D. Hughes
**SVP Technology:** James P. (Jim) Witkins, age 54
**SVP and CTO:** Milton E. Moore
**SVP Strategy and Administration and Chief Administrative Officer:** Margaret A. Colon, age 47
**SVP and Chief Compliance Officer:** Jerry Weiss, age 47
**SVP and Chief of Staff:** Hollis S. McLoughlin, age 54
**SVP and Chief Enterprise Risk Officer, Enterprise Risk Oversight:** David A. Andrukonis, age 47
**SVP and Treasurer, Funding and Investor Relations:** Timothy S. (Tim) Bitsberger
**SVP and General Auditor:** Stanley J. D. (Stan) Martin, age 58
**SVP and General Auditor:** Kirk Die
**SVP Risk Management and Capital Strategy:** Nazir G. Dossani, $884,583 pay
**VP Community Relations; President and CEO, Freddie Mac Foundation:** Maxine B. Baker
**VP Corporate and Marketing Communications:** David R. Palombi
**Auditors:** PricewaterhouseCoopers LLP

## LOCATIONS

**HQ:** Federal Home Loan Mortgage Corporation
8200 Jones Branch Dr., McLean, VA 22102
**Phone:** 703-903-2000
**Web:** www.freddiemac.com

## PRODUCTS/OPERATIONS

### 2006 Sales

| | $ mil. | % of total |
|---|---|---|
| Mortgage-related securities in retained portfolio | 34,673 | 80 |
| Cash & investments | 4,262 | 10 |
| Mortgage loans | 4,152 | 10 |
| **Total** | **43,087** | **100** |

## HISTORICAL FINANCIALS

Company Type: Public

**Income Statement** — FYE: December 31

| | REVENUE ($ mil.) | NET INCOME ($ mil.) | NET PROFIT MARGIN | EMPLOYEES |
|---|---|---|---|---|
| **12/06** | 43,087 | 2,211 | 5.1% | 5,535 |
| **12/05** | 36,327 | — | — | — |
| **12/04** | 35,603 | — | — | — |
| **12/03** | 37,098 | — | — | — |
| **Annual Growth** | 5.1% | — | — | — |

**Revenue History** — NYSE: FRE

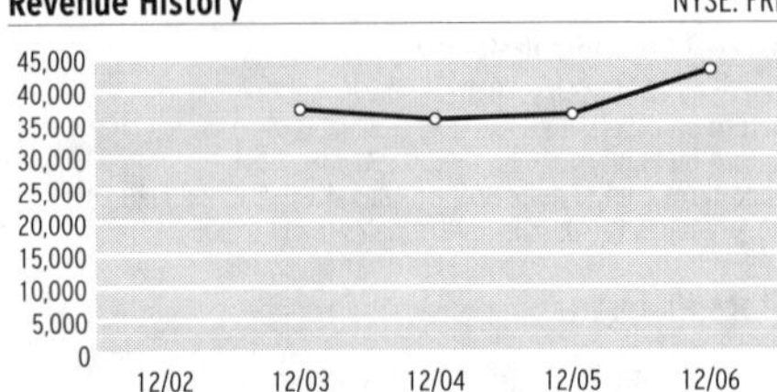


# Freeport-McMoRan Copper & Gold

Freeport-McMoRan Copper & Gold (FCX) really digs its profits. Its 91%-owned subsidiary, PT Freeport Indonesia (PT-FI), operates the vast open-pit Grasberg gold, copper, and silver mine in Indonesia. (The Indonesian government owns the other 9%.) Through its stake in PT-FI, FCX controls proved and probable reserves of about 35 billion pounds of copper and about 35 million ounces of gold. Copper, in the form of concentrates and in refined products such as cathodes and anodes, accounts for most of FCX's sales. In 2007 the company acquired Phelps Dodge for $26 billion, creating the world's #2 copper company behind Codelco. That deal brought Phelps Dodge's global copper, gold, and molybdenum business into the fold.

FCX also engages in smelting and refining. It owns a 25% stake in PT Smelting, which operates a copper smelter and refinery in Indonesia. Other FCX units include PT Irja Eastern Minerals, which explores for minerals in Indonesia, and Atlantic Copper, which operates a copper smelter in Spain.

Political and environmental controversy in Indonesia has dogged FCX since its major protector, former president Suharto, was forced to resign in 1998 after more than 30 years in power. Terrorism in Indonesia, where FCX is one of the largest employers, makes the company vulnerable to work stoppages. British mining giant Rio Tinto is jointly involved with FCX in developing mineral properties in Indonesia's politically and environmentally sensitive Papua region.

The Phelps Dodge deal came in the wake of that company's failed attempt at a three-way merger with the former Inco and Falconbridge and in the middle of a vast wave of consolidation within the greater metals and mining industry. Freeport is well placed following the deal to thrive as a global competitor in the rank just below such metals and mining giants like BHP Billiton, Rio Tinto, and ArcelorMittal. Freeport's chairman and CEO — James Moffett and Richard Adkerson, respectively — were placed in charge of the merged company, while Phelps Dodge chairman and CEO Steven Whisler retired.

## HISTORY

The Freeport Sulfur Company was formed in Texas in 1912 by Francis Pemberton, banker Eric Swenson, and several investors to develop a sulfur field. The next year Freeport Texas was formed as a holding company for Freeport Sulfur and other enterprises.

During the 1930s the company diversified. In 1936 Freeport pioneered a process to remove hydrocarbons from sulfur. The company joined Consolidated Coal in 1955 to establish the National Potash Company. In 1956 Freeport formed an oil and gas subsidiary, Freeport Oil.

Internationally, Freeport formed an Australian minerals subsidiary in 1964 and a copper-mining subsidiary in Indonesia in 1967. The company changed its name to Freeport Minerals in 1971 and merged with Utah-based McMoRan Oil & Gas (formerly McMoRan Explorations) in 1982.

McMoRan Explorations had been formed in 1969 by William McWilliams, Jim Bob Moffett, and Byron Rankin. In 1973 McMoRan formed an exploration and drilling alliance with Dow Chemical and signed a deal with Indonesia to mine in the remote Irian Jaya region. McMoRan went public in 1978.

Moffett became chairman and CEO of Freeport-McMoRan in 1984. The company formed Freeport-McMoRan Copper in 1987 to manage its Indonesian operations. The unit assumed the Freeport-McMoRan Copper & Gold name in 1991. Two years later Freeport-McMoRan acquired Rio Tinto Minera, a copper-smelting business with operations in Spain.

To support expansion in Indonesia, Freeport-McMoRan spun off its copper and gold division in 1994. In 1995 Freeport-McMoRan Copper & Gold (FCX) formed an alliance with the UK's RTZ Corporation to develop its Indonesian mineral reserves. Local riots that year closed the Grasberg Mine, and FCX's political risk insurance was canceled. Despite these setbacks, higher metal prices and growing sales in 1995 helped the company double its operating income.

An Indonesian tribal leader filed a $6 billion lawsuit in 1996 charging FCX with environmental, human rights, and social and cultural violations. The company called the suit baseless but offered to set aside 1% of its annual revenues, or about $15 million, to help local tribes. Tribal leaders rejected the offer, and in 1997 a judge dismissed the lawsuit.

In 1997 FCX pulled out of Bre-X Minerals' Busang gold mine project, which independent tests later proved to be a fraud of historic proportions. Amid widespread rioting, Indonesia's embattled president Suharto was forced out of office in 1998. The new government investigated charges of cronyism involving FCX.

FCX received permission from the Indonesian government in 1999 to expand the Grasberg Mine and increase ore output up to 300,000 metric tons per day. However, the next year an overflow accident killed four workers in Grasberg and, as a result of the accident, the Indonesian government ordered FCX to reduce its production at the mine by up to 30%. Normal production at the mine resumed in early 2001.

FM Services (administrative, legal, and financial services) was added as a subsidiary in 2002. In 2003 FCX bought an 86% stake in PT Puncakjaya Power, a supplier of power to PT-FI.

## EXECUTIVES

**Chairman and President Commissioner, PT Freeport Indonesia:** James R. (Jim Bob) Moffett, age 68, $21,906,000 pay
**Vice Chairman:** B. M. Rankin Jr., age 77
**President, CEO and Director; EVP, PT Freeport Indonesia:** Richard C. Adkerson, age 60
**COO of the merged company:** Timothy R. Snider, age 56
**CFO of the merged company:** Ramiro G. Peru, age 51
**SVP, CFO, and Treasurer; Commissioner, PT Freeport Indonesia; and Director, Atlantic Copper:** Kathleen L. Quirk, age 43
**SVP and COO; Named COO, Indonesian Operations:** Mark J. Johnson, age 46
**SVP, Marketing; President, Atlantic Copper S.A.:** Javier Targhetta
**SVP, International Relations and Federal Government Affairs:** W. Russell King
**VP, Assistant to the Chairman:** Lynne M. Cooney
**VP and General Counsel:** Dean T. Falgoust
**VP, Communications:** William L. Collier III
**VP, Exploration:** George D. MacDonald
**President Director, PT Freeport Indonesia and PT Irja Eastern Minerals:** Adrianto Machribie, age 64, $2,559,000 pay
**President Director and General Manager, PT Freeport Indonesia:** Armando Mahler
**Deputy President Director and EVP, PT Freeport Indonesia:** Rusdian Lubis
**Deputy President Director and EVP, PT Freeport Indonesia:** August Kafiar
**EVP, Exploration, PT Freeport Indonesia:** David R. Potter
**EVP, Security, PT Freeport Indonesia:** Frank D. Reuneker
**Auditors:** Ernst & Young LLP

## LOCATIONS

**HQ:** Freeport-McMoRan Copper & Gold Inc.
One North Central Ave., Phoenix, AZ 85004
**Phone:** 602-366-8100
**Web:** www.fcx.com

### 2006 Sales

| | $ mil. | % of total |
|---|---|---|
| Spain | 1,380.1 | 24 |
| Japan | 1,242.2 | 22 |
| Indonesia | 1,202.2 | 21 |
| India | 387.5 | 7 |
| South Korea | 376.6 | 7 |
| Belgium | 214.7 | 3 |
| Switzerland | 176.8 | 3 |
| Other countries | 810.4 | 13 |
| **Total** | **5,790.5** | **100** |

## PRODUCTS/OPERATIONS

### 2006 Sales and Operating Income

| | Sales | | Operating Income | |
|---|---|---|---|---|
| | $ mil. | % of total | $ mil. | % of total |
| Mining & Exploration | 4,394.8 | 72 | 2,709.7 | 94 |
| Smelting & Refining | 2,241.8 | 28 | 74.5 | 3 |
| Adjustments | (846.1) | — | 84.6 | 3 |
| **Total** | **5,790.5** | **100** | **2,868.8** | **100** |

### 2006 Sales

| | $ mil. | % of total |
|---|---|---|
| Copper in concentrates | 2,720.5 | 46 |
| Refined copper products | 1,865.0 | 32 |
| Gold in concentrates | 784.2 | 13 |
| Gold & silver in slimes | 349.3 | 6 |
| Silver in concentrates | 25.8 | — |
| Sulphur & other | 171.7 | 3 |
| Royalties | (126.0) | — |
| **Total** | **5,790.5** | **100** |

### Selected Subsidiaries and Affiliates

Atlantic Copper Holding, SA (smelting and refining, Spain)
FM Service Company (administrative and financial services)
PT Freeport Indonesia Co. (90%, mining)
PT Smelting (Gresik) Co. (25%, smelting, Indonesia)
PT Irja Eastern Minerals Corp. (mining, Indonesia)
PT Puncakjaya Power (86%, supplies power to PT Freeport Indonesia)

## COMPETITORS

Barrick Gold
BHP Billiton
Centromin
Codelco
CVRD Inco
Encore Wire
International Wire
Newmont Mining
Rio Tinto
Southern Copper

## HISTORICAL FINANCIALS

Company Type: Public

### Income Statement

FYE: December 31

| | REVENUE ($ mil.) | NET INCOME ($ mil.) | NET PROFIT MARGIN | EMPLOYEES |
|---|---|---|---|---|
| 12/06 | 5,791 | 1,457 | 25.2% | 7,000 |
| 12/05 | 4,179 | 995 | 23.8% | 26,938 |
| 12/04 | 2,372 | 202 | 8.5% | 14,988 |
| 12/03 | 2,212 | 182 | 8.2% | 14,803 |
| 12/02 | 1,911 | 165 | 8.6% | 10,107 |
| Annual Growth | 31.9% | 72.5% | — | (8.8%) |

### 2006 Year-End Financials

Debt ratio: 49.1%
Return on equity: 139.5%
Cash ($ mil.): 907
Current ratio: 2.21
Long-term debt ($ mil.): 661
No. of shares (mil.): 381
Dividends
Yield: 8.5%
Payout: 71.6%
Market value ($ mil.): 21,226

### Stock History

NYSE: FCX

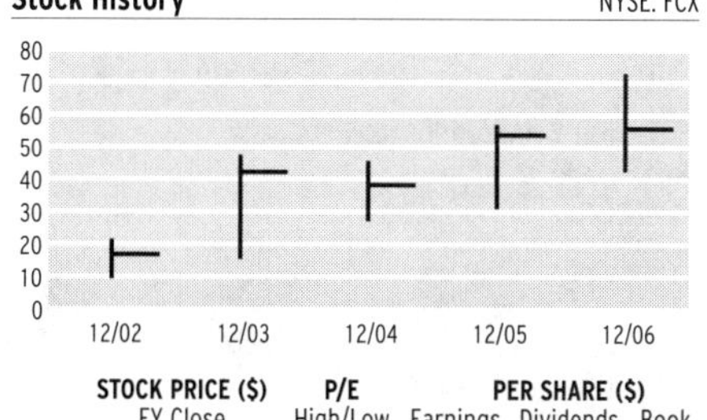


| | STOCK PRICE ($) FY Close | P/E High | P/E Low | PER SHARE ($) Earnings | Dividends | Book Value |
|---|---|---|---|---|---|---|
| 12/06 | 55.73 | 11 | 7 | 6.63 | 4.75 | 6.42 |
| 12/05 | 53.80 | 12 | 7 | 4.67 | 2.50 | 9.87 |
| 12/04 | 38.23 | 53 | 33 | 0.85 | 1.10 | 6.50 |
| 12/03 | 42.13 | 48 | 17 | 0.97 | 0.27 | 4.23 |
| 12/02 | 16.78 | 24 | 11 | 0.87 | — | 1.84 |
| Annual Growth | 35.0% | — | — | 66.1% | 160.1% | 36.6% |

# Freescale Semiconductor

Freescale Semiconductor just wants to be free. Freescale, formerly Motorola's Semiconductor Products Sector, is one of the oldest and most diverse makers of microchips in the world. It produces many different kinds of chips for use in automobiles, computers, industrial equipment, wireless communications and networking equipment, and other applications. The company's global client roster includes such blue-chip companies as Alcatel-Lucent, Cisco Systems, Fujitsu, Hewlett-Packard, QUALCOMM, Robert Bosch, and Siemens; former parent Motorola remains a substantial customer. Two years after going public, Freescale went private in a 2006 buyout valued at $17.6 billion.

Perhaps looking to be freed from the headaches of being a publicly held company, Freescale was acquired by an investment group consisting of The Blackstone Group, The Carlyle Group, Permira Advisers, and Texas Pacific Group, in the largest private-equity transaction in the technology sector since the $11.3 billion acquisition of SunGard Data Systems in 2005. Apax Partners, Bain Capital, Kohlberg Kravis Roberts (KKR), and Silver Lake Partners were said to have submitted a competing consortium bid.

The Blackstone-led group reportedly offered $16 billion for Freescale after months of negotiations and lining up financing for the deal. The rival bidders are said to have stepped in at the last moment, offering a higher price, but lacking full financing. The Blackstone "club" of investors apparently then upped its offer by 10%. Freescale, however, reserved the right to entertain alternative offers for 50 days.

KKR and Silver Lake have together successfully bid to buy two other semiconductor manufacturers, Avago Technologies (the chip business of Agilent Technologies) and NXP (the semiconductor division of Philips). Bain Capital bought the controls and sensors business of Texas Instruments, spinning it off as Sensata Technologies. The KKR "club" is said to have withdrawn from talks with Freescale after the deal with the Blackstone consortium was disclosed.

Freescale is focusing on the automotive, networking, and wireless communications markets for growth.

To revamp operations for more efficiency as a freestanding company, Freescale has reduced its headcount significantly, discontinued product lines, and consolidated manufacturing operations.

## HISTORY

Freescale is the successor to the Semiconductor Products Sector (SPS) of electronics giant Motorola, which began as a supplier of radio products in 1928. Motorola began offering semiconductors in 1953, just six years after the invention of the transistor. As of the late 1950s, Motorola used nine-tenths of the semiconductors it produced in its own wide variety of electronic gear. Already a leader in automotive radios, during the 1950s and 1960s Motorola introduced many designs for semiconductor-based automotive electronics, a market in which it is still one of the foremost players.

Early in the 1960s, Motorola pioneered the epitaxial method of semiconductor wafer production, in which silicon crystals are grown layer by layer onto wafers; epitaxy became an industry-standard process that still endures. By the late 1960s, Motorola sold $200 million per year of its chips, and vied with fellow industry titan Texas Instruments as the top chip maker in the world.

Motorola entered the microprocessor (MPU) market in 1974 with its 8-bit 6800 model, which was used in computers, video games, and automotive systems. (Intel had introduced the first MPU in 1971.) While Intel and Advanced Micro Devices ultimately captured most of the market for computer processors, Motorola went on to become a top maker of embedded processors for many kinds of electronic equipment, especially portable devices such as wireless phones (in which Motorola has always been a world leader) and PDAs.

In 1979 the company introduced a 16-bit MPU, successors of which were used in the 1980s in early models of Apple's Macintosh computer. Motorola introduced its first 32-bit MPU in 1984. In 1991 Motorola began collaborating with IBM on the PowerPC family of processors, which have powered Macintoshes ever since. Four years later Motorola debuted its DragonBall line of processors designed for portable consumer electronics applications.

In 1999 Motorola SPS acquired Metrowerks, a supplier of software development tools for embedded electronics.

SPS lost nearly $4 billion in 2001 and 2002 amid the worst downturn in chip industry history. During this period, it announced that it would move to an "asset light" strategy, under which it would operate fewer chip fabrication plants and outsource more of its production.

Late in 2003 Motorola announced plans to spin off SPS as a separate company; it subsequently dubbed the unit Freescale. Initially Motorola named veteran SPS executive Scott Anderson to lead Freescale, but several months later it appointed long-time IBM veteran Michel Mayer as CEO. (Anderson remained president and COO until 2005.)

Freescale debuted on the New York Stock Exchange in mid-2004. Motorola owned most of it until late in 2004, when it distributed its stake to Motorola shareholders.

The company sold a chip fabrication plant (fab) in China to Shanghai-based SMIC in 2004. It sold its timing products group to Integrated Device Technology the following year.

Freescale's wireless operations got a boost early in 2005 when the company acquired the assets of PrairieComm, a developer of software and chipsets for cellular phones. That same year it also acquired the assets of content processing semiconductor developer Seaway Networks.

Also in 2005 Freescale absorbed the free-standing Metrowerks subsidiary and its CodeWarrior line into the company, redubbing Metrowerks as the Developer Technology Organization, or DevTech.

Freescale agreed to a $17.6 billion buyout by a consortium of private equity firms in September 2006, which was approved by shareholders two months later, and the transaction was completed in late 2006.

## EXECUTIVES

**Chairman and CEO:** Michel Mayer, age 47
**SVP and CFO:** Alan Campbell, age 49
**SVP, General Counsel, and Secretary:** John D. Torres, age 49
**SVP and General Manager, Asia:** Joe Yiu
**SVP and General Manager, EMEA:** Denis Griot
**SVP and General Manager, Japan:** Tsuneo Takahashi
**SVP, Global Sales and Marketing:** David Perkins, age 45
**SVP and General Manager, Transportation and Standard Products:** Paul E. Grimme, age 47
**SVP, Business Operations:** Janelle S. (Jan) Monney, age 50
**SVP, Human Resources:** Kurt Twining, age 53
**SVP, Manufacturing:** Alex Pepe, age 45
**SVP, Americas Sales and Marketing:** William R. (Bill) Bradford, age 43
**SVP, Strategy and Business Development:** Sumit Sadana, age 39
**SVP and General Manager, Wireless and Mobile Systems:** Sandeep Chennakeshu
**SVP and General Manager, Networking and Computing Systems:** Lynelle McKay
**VP and CIO:** Sam Coursen
**VP, Corporate Communications and Marketing Services:** Timothy J. (Tim) Doke
**VP and Treasurer:** Gregory J. Heinlein
**Investor Relations:** Mitch Haws
**Auditors:** KPMG LLP

## LOCATIONS

**HQ:** Freescale Semiconductor, Inc.
6501 William Cannon Dr. West, Austin, TX 78735
**Phone:** 512-895-2000 **Fax:** 512-895-2652
**Web:** www.freescale.com

Freescale Semiconductor has facilities in Denmark, France, Germany, Hong Kong, India, Ireland, Israel, Japan, Malaysia, Romania, Russia, the UK, and the US.

## PRODUCTS/OPERATIONS

**2006 Sales**

| | $ mil. | % of total |
|---|---|---|
| Transportation & standard products | 2,710 | 43 |
| Wireless & mobile solutions | 2,137 | 34 |
| Networking & computing systems | 1,433 | 22 |
| Other | 83 | 1 |
| **Total** | **6,363** | **100** |

**Selected Semiconductor Products**

8-, 16-, and 32-bit microcontrollers (MCUs)
Analog
- Power management integrated circuits (ICs)
- Power switching ICs
- Network transceivers

Application-specific Standard Products (ASSPs)
- Digital video encoders
- Display drivers

Clock drivers
Digital signal processors
Embedded processors
Memory
- Content-addressable memory
- Magnetoresistive random-access memory (MRAM)

Networking processors
Radio-frequency
- Amplifier ICs and modules
- Transistors

Sensors
Wireless receivers and transmitters

## COMPETITORS

AMD
Analog Devices
Atmel
Avago Technologies
Broadcom
Conexant Systems
Cypress Semiconductor
IBM Microelectronics
Infineon Technologies
Intel
Linear Technology
LSI Corp.
Marvell Technology
Maxim Integrated Products
Microchip Technology
National Semiconductor
NVIDIA
NXP
ON Semiconductor
QUALCOMM CDMA
RF Micro Devices
Sensata
STMicroelectronics
Texas Instruments
VIA Technologies
Vishay Intertechnology
ZiLOG

## HISTORICAL FINANCIALS

Company Type: Private

**Income Statement** FYE: December 31

| | REVENUE ($ mil.) | NET INCOME ($ mil.) | NET PROFIT MARGIN | EMPLOYEES |
|---|---|---|---|---|
| **12/06** | 6,363 | — | — | 24,000 |
| **12/05** | 5,843 | — | — | 22,700 |
| **12/04** | 5,715 | — | — | 22,200 |
| **12/03** | 4,864 | — | — | 22,300 |
| **12/02** | 5,001 | — | — | — |
| **Annual Growth** | 6.2% | — | — | 2.5% |

**Revenue History**

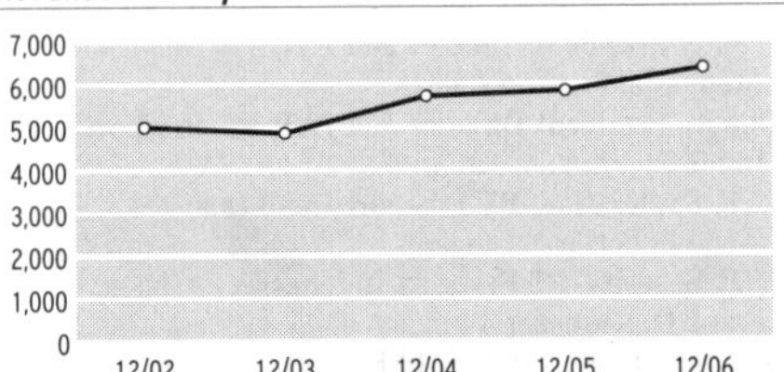


# Furniture Brands International

Furniture Brands International runs a furniture-making empire. The company ranks as one of the top US makers of residential furniture. Furniture Brands' subsidiaries offer a lineup of nationally recognized brands. Broyhill makes medium-priced bedroom, dining room, and other furnishings. Lane (offering 18th-century reproductions and cedar chests) and Thomasville (wood and upholstered furniture) target the premium-priced furniture market. Furniture Brands distributes its products through a network of furniture centers, independent dealers, national and local chains, and department stores.

In early 2007 an affiliate of Sun Capital Partners acquired a 5% stake in Furniture Brands.

The company sells its products through four operating units: Broyhill Furniture Industries, Lane Furniture Industries, Thomasville Furniture Industries, and HDM Furniture Industries. Once acquired in 2001, Henredon, Drexel Heritage, and Maitland-Smith were folded into the firm's HDM Furniture Industries subsidiary.

In response to financial troubles at major furniture retailers, Furniture Brands is expanding its network of free-standing independently owned stores such as Thomasville Home Furnishings, which exclusively sell Thomasville products. To strengthen brand awareness and more keenly focus distribution and sales, Furniture Brands also is boosting its share of Drexel Heritage Home Inspiration Stores, Lane Home Furnishings Stores, and Broyhill Home Collections Stores.

Due in part to the residential furniture industry trend of shifting to offshore sourcing (primarily to Asia), Thomasville has reorganized its domestic manufacturing operations. The company has closed or announced the closing of more than 35 domestic manufacturing facilities since 2001. In 2007 the company announced the pending shutdown of three plants in North Carolina and the elimination of about 330 executive, administrative, and factory jobs there. The closings, set for July and August, impact two upholstery plants (Hickory and Troutman, North Carolina) and a case goods plant in Thomasville.

The company announced that CEO Mickey Holliman would step down in 2008. His replacement, gum and candy supplier executive Ralph Scozzafava, has already been hired and will act as vice chairman and CEO designate, until then.

## HISTORY

Although already a diversified firm, INTERCO's purchase of Ethan Allen in 1980 took the company in a direction that would eventually become its only business. INTERCO (now Furniture Brands International) traces its roots to the pairing of two shoe manufacturers and made a name for itself by running men's shoemaker and retailer Florsheim, which it acquired in 1953. It added other operations, including department stores and apparel, beginning in the 1960s. The Ethan Allen purchase gave INTERCO 24 furniture factories and 300 retail outlets.

Later in 1980, the company purchased Broyhill Furniture Industries, which was founded by J. E. Broyhill as Lenoir Chair Company in 1926. The Broyhill line first became popular during the 1930s. The Broyhill family built the company into the largest privately owned maker of furniture, with 20 manufacturing facilities when INTERCO bought it.

In 1986, after acquiring furniture maker Highland House (Hickory), INTERCO made its largest acquisition in the home furnishings and furniture market when it gained control of the Lane Company for approximately $500 million. Founded in 1912 by Ed Lane to make cedar chests, Virginia-based Lane had grown into a full-line maker of furniture with 16 plants in operation. The acquisition of Lane lifted furniture and furnishings to 33% of INTERCO's total sales in 1987.

Meanwhile, INTERCO hadn't neglected its shoe business, adding Converse in 1986. Richard Loynd, the Converse CEO, served as INTERCO's CEO from 1989 to 1996. In 1988, under a takeover threat by the Rales brothers of Washington, DC, the company retained the investment banking firm of Wasserstein Perella, which advised payment of a $76 special dividend, for which INTERCO borrowed $1.8 billion via junk bonds. To repay the debt, the firm began selling off assets, including its apparel businesses and Ethan Allen. However, the sales yielded low prices and some businesses failed to attract buyers.

After fighting off the hostile takeover, INTERCO filed bankruptcy in 1991 — one of the largest bankruptcy cases in US history. It also filed a malpractice suit against Wasserstein Perella when it emerged from Chapter 11; the suit was settled the following year, and Apollo Investment Fund acquired a large stake in the firm.

INTERCO sold the last of its 80-year-old shoemaking sole with the spinoff of its Florsheim and Converse units in 1994. The company acquired Thomasville Furniture from Armstrong World Industries for $331 million in 1993, a purchase that made it the leading shaker in residential furniture. Founded in 1904, the Finch brothers ran Thomasville until Armstrong acquired it in 1968.

W. G. "Mickey" Holliman became CEO in 1996, and INTERCO's board decided to change the company's name to Furniture Brands International. In 1997 Apollo Investment Fund, its largest shareholder, sold its 38% stake. The next year Furniture Brands and retailer Haverty Furniture signed a deal (terminated in 2003) whereby Havertys would allocate up to half its retail space for Furniture Brands' items.

In 2000 the company started selling kitchen and bathroom cabinets under the Thomasville brand in Home Depot. In 2001 Furniture Brands bought Drexel Heritage, Henredon, and Maitland-Smith units from LifeStyle Furnishings for $275 million. Overall economic pressures, as well as the residential furniture industry's shift to offshore sourcing (in countries with lower labor costs), led Thomasville to shut down 21 domestic manufacturing facilities in 2003.

Overall, Furniture Brands-owned companies have closed or have announced the closing of 31 domestic manufacturing facilities between 2001 and the end of 2005. In August 2006 Broyhill and Thomasville both closed domestic manufacturing plants in North Carolina.

## EXECUTIVES

**Chairman and CEO:** Wilbert G. (Mickey) Holliman, age 69
**Vice Chairman:** Ralph P. Scozzafava, age 48
**President, COO, and Director; Interim President and CEO, Lane Furniture Industries; Interim CEO, Broyhill Furniture Industries:** John T. (Tom) Foy, age 59, $961,252 pay
**SVP and General Counsel:** Lynn Chipperfield, age 55
**SVP Human Resources:** Mary E. Sweetman, age 42
**President and CEO, Drexel Heritage HDM Furniture Industries:** C. Jeffrey (Jeff) Young, age 56
**President and COO, Drexel Heritage:** Lenwood Rich
**President, Henredon Furniture Industries:** Thomas G. (Tom) Tilley Jr., age 58, $560,387 pay
**President and CEO, Thomasville Furniture Industries:** Nancy W. Webster, age 53
**President, Maitland-Smith Furniture Industries:** Larry Milan
**EVP and CFO, HDM Furniture Industries:** Bryan Milleson
**SVP, IT, HDM Furniture Industries:** Triche Leander
**SVP, Upholstery Manufacturing, HDM Furniture Industries:** Thad Monroe
**SVP, Wood Manufacturing, HDM Furniture Industries:** Tom Mangum
**Director of Employee Benefits and Risk Management:** Richard Lockard
**Manager of Corporate Communications:** Marty Richmond
**General Counsel:** Jerry Lybarger
**President, Broyhill Furniture Industries:** Jeffrey L. (Jeff) Cook
**Controller, Principal Financial Officer, and Chief Accounting Officer:** Richard R. (Rick) Isaak, age 39
**Auditors:** KPMG LLP

## LOCATIONS

**HQ:** Furniture Brands International, Inc.
101 S. Hanley Rd., St. Louis, MO 63105
**Phone:** 314-863-1100 **Fax:** 314-863-5306
**Web:** www.furniturebrands.com

Furniture Brands International's products, which are sold worldwide, are manufactured in plants in Mississippi, North Carolina, and Virginia in the US, as well as in Indonesia and the Philippines.

## PRODUCTS/OPERATIONS

### Subsidiaries

Broyhill Furniture
Drexel Heritage
Henredon Furniture
Lane Furniture
MaitlandSmith Furniture
Thomasville Furniture

### Selected Products

Case Goods Furniture
- Bedroom
- Dining room
- Living room

Occasional Furniture
- Accent items
- Freestanding home entertainment centers
- Home office items
- Wood tables

Stationary Upholstery Products
- Chairs
- Love seats
- Sectionals
- Sofas

Other
- Motion furniture
- Recliners
- Sleep sofas

## COMPETITORS

Ashley Furniture
Bassett Furniture
Berkline/BenchCraft
Bombay Company
Brown Jordan International
Bush Industries
Chromcraft Revington
Decorize
DMI Furniture
Dorel Industries
Ethan Allen
Flexsteel
Home Meridian
Hooker Furniture
Kimball International
Klaussner Furniture
La-Z-Boy
Masco
Meadowcraft
O'Sullivan Industries Inc.
Rowe Furniture
Sauder Woodworking
Stanley Furniture

## HISTORICAL FINANCIALS

Company Type: Public

### Income Statement

FYE: December 31

| | REVENUE ($ mil.) | NET INCOME ($ mil.) | NET PROFIT MARGIN | EMPLOYEES |
|---|---|---|---|---|
| **12/06** | 2,418 | 55 | 2.3% | 13,800 |
| **12/05** | 2,387 | 61 | 2.6% | 15,150 |
| **12/04** | 2,447 | 92 | 3.7% | 17,800 |
| **12/03** | 2,368 | 95 | 4.0% | 20,250 |
| **12/02** | 2,398 | 119 | 5.0% | 23,600 |
| **Annual Growth** | 0.2% | (17.5%) | — | (12.6%) |

### 2006 Year-End Financials

Debt ratio: 33.0%
Return on equity: 6.1%
Cash ($ mil.): 27
Current ratio: 4.99
Long-term debt ($ mil.): 301
No. of shares (mil.): 48
Dividends
Yield: 3.9%
Payout: 56.6%
Market value ($ mil.): 784

**Stock History** NYSE: FBN

| | STOCK PRICE ($) FY Close | P/E High | P/E Low | PER SHARE ($) Earnings | Dividends | Book Value |
|---|---|---|---|---|---|---|
| **12/06** | 16.23 | 22 | 14 | 1.13 | 0.64 | 18.84 |
| **12/05** | 22.33 | 22 | 14 | 1.18 | 0.60 | 18.20 |
| **12/04** | 25.05 | 21 | 13 | 1.66 | 0.52 | 17.99 |
| **12/03** | 29.33 | 18 | 10 | 1.68 | 0.13 | 17.28 |
| **12/02** | 23.85 | 20 | 9 | 2.11 | — | 15.63 |
| **Annual Growth** | (9.2%) | — | — | (14.5%) | 70.1% | 4.8% |

# GameStop Corp.

GameStop holds the top score in the video game retailing industry. The company is the largest retailer of new and used games, hardware, entertainment software, and accessories through nearly 4,800 outlets in the US and nearly a dozen other countries. A majority of sales come from new and used video games; stores carry an average of 1,000 new titles and 3,500 used ones. The company also has e-commerce Web sites (GameStop.com, ebgames.com) and publishes *Game Informer*, a video game magazine that reaches more than 2.7 million subscribers. The company's 2005 purchase of rival Electronics Boutique doubled GameStop's size.

Prior to buying Electronics Boutique, GameStop had planned to expand by adding about 400 stores a year. The company vastly improved on those plans with the purchase of its rival. GameStop's sales have skyrocketed as a result (the firm now earns about $5 billion a year).

GameStop is poised to take advantage of an increased demand for video games thanks to the launch of next generation game consoles such as Nintendo's Wii, Microsoft's Xbox 360 and Sony's PlayStation 3.

## HISTORY

NeoStar Retail Group resulted from the 1994 combination of software retailers Babbage's and Software Etc. Babbage's had been founded by James McCurry and Gary Kusin in 1983. Named for 19th-century mathematician Charles Babbage (considered the father of the computer), it went public in 1988.

Software Etc. began as a division of B. Dalton Bookseller in 1984. Bookstore chain Barnes & Noble and Dutch retailer Vendex acquired B. Dalton two years later. Software Etc. went public in 1992.

Both companies focused on mall retailing: Babbage's on game software, and Software Etc. on a broader variety of PC software. Both saw growth spurred by the rising popularity of Nintendo and Sega game systems and by falling PC prices. The two merged in 1994 in an effort to stave off growing competition from big retail chains such as Best Buy and Wal-Mart. NeoStar opened 122 stores in 1995.

Amid flat sales the following year, several senior executives left. Also in 1996 NeoStar lost its contract to operate software departments at 136 Barnes & Noble sites, and it soon filed for Chapter 11. Late that year a group led by Barnes & Noble's head honcho Leonard Riggio purchased about 460 of NeoStar's 650 stores for $58.5 million and renamed the company Babbage's, Etc. Former Software Etc. chief Dick Fontaine was named CEO.

By 1997 the company began concentrating on popular games and software, and in 1999 it formed its e-commerce site GameStop.com. In late 1999 Barnes & Noble paid Riggio's group $210 million for Babbage's Etc. In June 2000 the company fortified its position and became the #1 US video game retailer with the purchase of rival game retailer Funco (about 400 stores) for $161.5 million. The company changed its name to GameStop in August 2001 and filed to go public, which it accomplished in February 2002. Though public, it was still under the majority control of Barnes & Noble until 2004 when GameStop bought back its shares.

GameStop bought rival Electronics Boutique in 2005, virtually doubling its size from 2,000 to about 4,500 stores. Steven R. Morgan, a former executive with Electronics Boutique, became president of GameStop later that year.

## EXECUTIVES

**Chairman and CEO:** R. Richard (Dick) Fontaine, age 65, $1,011,593 pay
**Vice Chairman and COO:** Daniel A. (Dan) DeMatteo, age 59, $810,385 pay
**President:** Steven R. Morgan, age 55, $467,308 pay
**EVP, CFO, and Assistant Secretary:** David W. Carlson, age 44, $358,846 pay
**EVP Distribution:** Ronald Freeman, age 59, $278,754 pay
**EVP Merchandising and Marketing:** Tony Bartel, age 43
**SVP and Chief Accounting Officer:** Robert A. Lloyd, age 45
**SVP, Marketing and Merchandising:** John C. (Jack) Beuttell, age 56
**VP, Human Resources:** David Shuart
**Secretary and Director:** Michael N. Rosen, age 66
**VP Marketing:** Tom DeNapoli
**Auditors:** BDO Seidman, LLP

## LOCATIONS

**HQ:** GameStop Corp.
625 Westport Pkwy., Grapevine, TX 76051
**Phone:** 817-424-2000 **Fax:** 817-424-2002
**Web:** www.gamestop.com

GameStop has about 4,500 locations in Australia, Canada, Denmark, Finland, Germany, Italy, Ireland, New Zealand, Norway, Puerto Rico, Spain, Sweden, Switzerland, the UK, and the US.

**2007 Sales**

| | $ mil. | % of total |
|---|---|---|
| US | 4,269.5 | 80 |
| Europe | 441.6 | 8 |
| Canada | 319.7 | 6 |
| Australia | 288.1 | 6 |
| **Total** | **5,318.9** | **100** |

## PRODUCTS/OPERATIONS

**2007 Sales**

| | $ mil. | % of total |
|---|---|---|
| New video game software | 2,012.5 | 38 |
| Used video game products | 1,316.0 | 25 |
| New video game hardware | 1,073.7 | 20 |
| Other | 916.7 | 17 |
| **Total** | **5,318.9** | **100** |

**Selected Merchandise**

Accessories
- PC entertainment accessories (video cards, joysticks, mice)
- Video game accessories (controllers, memory cards, add-ons)
- Other (strategy guides, magazines, action figures, trading cards)

PC entertainment software and other software
Used video games
Video game hardware
Video game software

## COMPETITORS

Amazon.com
Best Buy
Blockbuster
Borders
Buy.com
Circuit City
CompUSA
Fry's Electronics
GAME Group
Hollywood Entertainment
KB Toys
Kmart
Movie Gallery
RadioShack
Target
Toys "R" Us
Wal-Mart
Zones

## HISTORICAL FINANCIALS

Company Type: Public

**Income Statement** FYE: Saturday nearest January 31

| | REVENUE ($ mil.) | NET INCOME ($ mil.) | NET PROFIT MARGIN | EMPLOYEES |
|---|---|---|---|---|
| **1/07** | 5,319 | 158 | 3.0% | 32,000 |
| **1/06** | 3,092 | 101 | 3.3% | 42,000 |
| **1/05** | 1,843 | 61 | 3.3% | 22,800 |
| **1/04** | 1,579 | 64 | 4.0% | 18,100 |
| **1/03** | 1,353 | 52 | 3.9% | 13,500 |
| **Annual Growth** | 40.8% | 31.8% | — | 24.1% |

**2007 Year-End Financials**

Debt ratio: 61.3%
Return on equity: 12.7%
Cash ($ mil.): 652
Current ratio: 1.32
Long-term debt ($ mil.): 844
No. of shares (mil.): 152
Dividends
Yield: —
Payout: —
Market value ($ mil.): 4,105

**Stock History** NYSE: GME

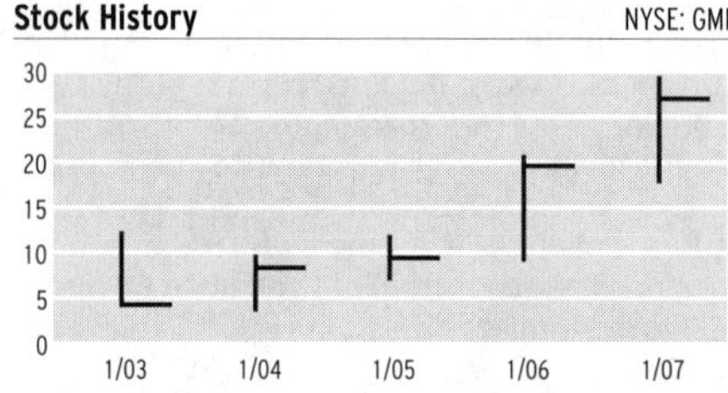


| | STOCK PRICE ($) FY Close | P/E High | P/E Low | PER SHARE ($) Earnings | Dividends | Book Value |
|---|---|---|---|---|---|---|
| **1/07** | 26.95 | 29 | 18 | 1.00 | — | 9.03 |
| **1/06** | 19.57 | 26 | 12 | 0.81 | — | 25.99 |
| **1/05** | 9.40 | 22 | 14 | 0.52 | — | 25.95 |
| **1/04** | 8.30 | 18 | 7 | 0.53 | — | 28.71 |
| **1/03** | 4.25 | 28 | 10 | 0.44 | — | 26.07 |
| **Annual Growth** | 58.7% | — | — | 22.8% | — | (23.3%) |

# Gannett Co.

Gannett satisfies news junkies with a stash of daily US papers. The company is the nation's largest newspaper publisher with about 90 daily papers boasting a total circulation of 7.2 million. Its flagship *USA TODAY*, with a circulation of 2.3 million, is the nation's largest newspaper. Some other big papers in Gannett's holdings include *The Arizona Republic* and the *Detroit Free Press*. The company also owns about 1,000 non-daily publications, as well as about 300 papers in the UK (through subsidiary Newsquest). In addition, Gannett owns 23 television stations in 20 markets, publishes periodicals and inserts (including *USA WEEKEND*), and operates Web sites for many of its papers.

While many companies in the newspaper industry struggle against declining advertising revenue, Gannett has been able to buck that trend in part through acquisitions and also through its sheer size. The company has been able to withstand regional economic downturns since it has papers in almost every part of the country, and it is able to sell space across all its local publications to national advertisers through a centralized sales force.

The company has also been keen to make acquisitions to expand and diversify its operations. It bought the *Detroit Free Press* in 2005 from Knight Ridder (later acquired by rival McClatchy), and it acquired about 60 community newspapers from Hometown Communications Network. The following year it bought TV stations in Atlanta and Denver.

Gannett has also been focused on non-traditional media as well as print and TV, taking stakes in such enterprises as CareerBuilder (43%), ShopLocal (43%), and new aggregation site Topix (32%). It is also working to build a digital news distribution business to deliver information from newspapers, television, and Web sources to mobile devices and Internet users.

## HISTORY

In 1906 Frank Gannett started a newspaper empire when he and his associates purchased a stake in New York's *Elmira Gazette*. In 1923 Gannett bought out his associates' interests and formed the Gannett Company. The company's history of technical innovation dates to the 1920s, when Frank Gannett invested in the development of the Teletypesetter; some of his newspapers were printing in color by 1938. The company continued to buy small and medium-sized dailies in the Northeast, and by Gannett's death in 1957, it had accumulated 30 newspapers.

In the 1960s Gannett expanded nationally through acquisitions. It was not until 1966, however, that it started its own paper, *TODAY* (now *FLORIDA TODAY*), in Cocoa Beach, Florida. Gannett went public in 1967.

The company's greatest period of growth came during the 1970s and 1980s under the direction of Allen Neuharth (CEO from 1973 to 1986). Gannett captured national attention in 1979 when it merged with Phoenix-based Combined Communications Corporation (CCC), whose holdings included TV and radio stations, an outdoor advertising business, and pollster Louis Harris & Associates.

In 1982 Gannett started *USA TODAY*, a national newspaper whose splashy format and mini-stories made it an industry novelty. Critics branded it "McPaper," but circulation passed a million copies a day by the end of 1983. (It wasn't profitable until 1993, however.)

In 1990 declines in newspaper advertising, primarily among US retailers, broke the company's string of 89 consecutive quarters of positive earnings. USA TODAY-On-Demand, a fax news service, began in 1992. Gannett bought Multimedia Inc., a newspaper, TV, cable, and program syndication company, for about $2.3 billion in 1995.

Web site *USA TODAY Online* debuted in 1995. The next year Gannett teamed up with newspaper publisher Knight Ridder and privately held media firm Landmark Communications to form Internet service provider InfiNet. In 1996 Gannett sold Louis Harris & Associates and its outdoor advertising operations and traded six radio stations to Jacor Communications for one Tampa TV station.

Gannett exited the radio industry in 1998 by selling its last five stations. That year the company expanded its TV holdings through purchases of three stations in Maine and South Carolina. Gannett's integrity took a blow in 1998 when a reporter for one of its newspapers (*The Cincinnati Enquirer*) illegally obtained information for a report accusing Chiquita Brands International of unscrupulous business practices. Gannett retracted the story and settled with Chiquita to the tune of about $14 million.

The company broke new ground in 1999 when Karen Jurgensen was named editor of *USA TODAY* (she was the first woman to head a national newspaper). Also that year Gannett acquired Newsquest, one of the largest regional newspaper publishers in the UK. In early 2000 Gannett sold its cable operations to Cox Communications for $2.7 billion. The company also formed TV and Web venture USA Today Live to produce news stories for its TV stations. Later that year chairman John Curley passed the title of CEO to president Douglas McCorkindale (McCorkindale would become chair the next year).

Also in 2000 Gannett made a slew of acquisitions, including a purchase of the UK's News Communications & Media, *Arizona Republic* publisher Central Newspapers, and 21 newspapers from Canada's Thomson Corp. The company moved its headquarters in 2001 from Arlington to McLean, Virginia. Amid an industry-wide advertising recession, Gannett saw its profits decline in 2001, and *USA TODAY* cut more than 5% of its staff (about 100 employees). In early 2002 Gannett sold nearly $2 billion in debt in unsecured global notes in order to use the funds to repay short-term loans. Later that year the company bought a stake in the online job site, CareerBuilder.

In 2004 Gannett also purchased more than 30 newspapers and specialty publications from Brown County Publishing in Wisconsin. Jurgensen stepped down as editor of *USA Today* in the fallout of a scandal involving reporter Jack Kelley. Broadcasting chief Craig Dubow took over as president and CEO in 2005. In late 2005 Gannett acquired a TV station in Denver (KTVD-TV).

In 2006 McCorkindale retired and Dubow added chairman to his title. Later that year, the company acquired WATL-TV in Atlanta from the Tribune Company for $180 million.

## EXECUTIVES

**Chairman, President, and CEO:** Craig A. Dubow, age 52, $2,950,000 pay
**EVP and CFO:** Gracia C. Martore, age 55, $1,256,250 pay (prior to promotion)
**SVP and General Counsel:** Kurt Wimmer, age 47
**SVP Human Resources:** Roxanne V. Horning, age 57
**SVP Labor Relations:** Wendell J. Van Lare, age 62
**VP and Controller:** George R. Gavagan, age 60
**VP, Chief Governance Officer, Associate General Counsel, and Secretary:** Todd A. Mayman
**VP Compensation and Benefits:** Robert B. Oliver
**VP Corporate Communications:** Tara J. Connell
**VP Leadership Development and Diversity:** José A. Berrios
**VP Planning and Development:** Daniel S. Ehrman Jr., age 60
**VP and Associate General Counsel:** Barbara W. Wall
**VP and Treasurer:** Michael A. Hart
**President and Publisher, USA TODAY:** Craig A. Moon, age 57, $931,000 pay
**President, Newspaper Division:** Susan Clark-Johnson, age 60, $1,195,000 pay
**President, Gannett Broadcasting:** David Lougee
**President, Gannett Digital:** John A. (Jack) Williams, age 56
**Auditors:** Ernst & Young LLP

## LOCATIONS

**HQ:** Gannett Co., Inc.
7950 Jones Branch Dr., McLean, VA 22107
**Phone:** 703-854-6000 **Fax:** 703-854-2046
**Web:** www.gannett.com

## PRODUCTS/OPERATIONS

### 2006 Sales

| | $ mil. | % of total |
|---|---|---|
| Newspapers | | |
| Advertising | 5,370.5 | 67 |
| Circulation | 1,306.6 | 16 |
| Broadcasting | 854.8 | 11 |
| Other | 501.5 | 6 |
| **Total** | **8,033.4** | **100** |

### Selected Operations

Newspapers
- *Asbury Park Press* (New Jersey)
- *Detroit Free Press*
- *Rochester Democrat and Chronicle* (New York)
- *The Arizona Republic* (Phoenix)
- *The Cincinnati Enquirer*
- *The Courier-Journal* (Louisville, KY)
- *The Des Moines Register* (Iowa)
- *The Honolulu Advertiser*
- *The Indianapolis Star*
- *The Journal News* (Westchester County, NY)
- *The News Journal* (Wilmington, DE)
- *The Tennessean* (Nashville)
- *USA TODAY* (McLean, VA)

Broadcasting
- KNAZ-TV (NBC; Flagstaff, AZ)
- KARE-TV (NBC, Minneapolis)
- KPNX-TV (NBC, Phoenix)
- KSDK-TV (NBC, St. Louis)
- KTHV-TV (CBS; Little Rock, AR)
- KTVD-TV (MyNetworkTV, Denver)
- KUSA-TV (NBC, Denver)
- KXTV-TV (ABC; Sacramento, CA)
- WATL-TV (MyNetworkTV, Atlanta)
- WBIR-TV (NBC; Knoxville, TN)
- WCSH-TV (NBC; Portland, ME)
- WFMY-TV (CBS; Geensboro, NC)
- WGRZ-TV (NBC; Buffalo, NY)
- WJXX-TV (ABC, Jacksonville)
- WKYC-TV (NBC, Cleveland)
- WLBZ-TV (NBC; Bangor, ME)
- WLTX-TV (CBS; Columbia, SC)
- WMAZ-TV (CBS; Macon, GA)
- WTLV-TV (NBC, Jacksonville)
- WTSP-TV (CBS, Tampa)
- WUSA-TV (CBS; Washington, DC)
- WXIA-TV (NBC, Atlanta)
- WZZM-TV (ABC; Grand Rapids, MI)

Other holdings and investments
- Army Times Publishing Company (newspapers)
- California Newspaper Publishing (19%, community newspapers)
- CareerBuilder (42%, online job recruitment)
- Classified Ventures (24%, online content publishing)
- Clipper Magazine (direct mail advertising)
- Gannett Healthcare Group (periodical publishing)
- Gannett Offset (commercial printing)
- Newsquest plc (newspaper publishing, UK)
- Planet Discover (Internet search and advertising)
- PointRoll (digital media marketing services)
- Ponderay Newsprint (14%)
- ShopLocal.com (42%, online shopping portal)
- Texas-New Mexico Newspaper Partnership (41%, community newspapers)
- Topix.net (32%, news monitoring service)
- USA WEEKEND (weekly newspaper insert)

## COMPETITORS

Advance Publications
Associated Press
Belo
Cox Enterprises
Dow Jones
E. W. Scripps
Journal Communications
Landmark Communications
Lee Enterprises
McClatchy Company
Media General
MediaNews
New York Times
News Corp.
Reuters
Sun-Times
Tribune
Washington Post

## HISTORICAL FINANCIALS

Company Type: Public

**Income Statement** FYE: Last Sunday in December

| | REVENUE ($ mil.) | NET INCOME ($ mil.) | NET PROFIT MARGIN | EMPLOYEES |
|---|---|---|---|---|
| **12/06** | 8,033 | 1,161 | 14.4% | 49,675 |
| **12/05** | 7,599 | 1,245 | 16.4% | 52,600 |
| **12/04** | 7,381 | 1,317 | 17.8% | 52,500 |
| **12/03** | 6,711 | 1,211 | 18.0% | 53,000 |
| **12/02** | 6,422 | 1,160 | 18.1% | 51,000 |
| **Annual Growth** | 5.8% | 0.0% | — | (0.7%) |

**2006 Year-End Financials**

Debt ratio: 62.2%
Return on equity: 14.6%
Cash ($ mil.): 94
Current ratio: 1.37
Long-term debt ($ mil.): 5,210
No. of shares (mil.): 235
Dividends
Yield: 2.0%
Payout: 24.5%
Market value ($ mil.): 14,193

**Stock History** NYSE: GCI

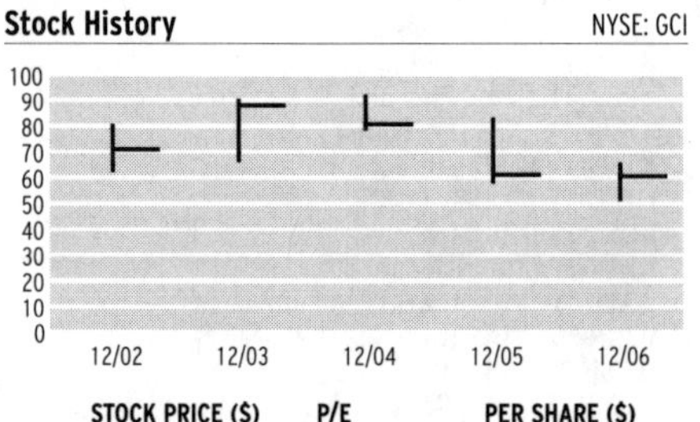

| | STOCK PRICE ($) FY Close | P/E High | P/E Low | PER SHARE ($) Earnings | Dividends | Book Value |
|---|---|---|---|---|---|---|
| **12/06** | 60.46 | 13 | 11 | 4.90 | 1.20 | 35.71 |
| **12/05** | 61.09 | 16 | 12 | 5.05 | 1.12 | 31.80 |
| **12/04** | 80.69 | 19 | 16 | 4.92 | 1.04 | 32.10 |
| **12/03** | 87.90 | 20 | 15 | 4.46 | 0.98 | 30.92 |
| **12/02** | 70.85 | 19 | 15 | 4.31 | 0.94 | 25.80 |
| **Annual Growth** | (3.9%) | — | — | 3.3% | 6.3% | 8.5% |

# The Gap Inc.

From Flauntywood to Slouchville, no slots are left exposed by ubiquitous clothing retailer Gap. The company has built its brand on basic, casual styles for men, women, and children (T-shirts, jeans, and khakis), but over the years has expanded through the urban chic chain Banana Republic and fast-growing budgeteer Old Navy. Gap runs 3,100-plus stores worldwide. Other chains include GapBody, GapKids, and babyGap; each chain also has its own online incarnation. All Gap clothing is private-label merchandise made specifically for the company. From the design board to store displays, Gap controls all aspects of its trademark casual look. The founding Fisher family owns about a third of Gap Inc.

After more than two years of slumping sales, failed turnaround attempts, and fashion missteps the US's largest specialty apparel retailer is weighing its options, including a possible sale of the company or the spin-off of one or more of its brands: struggling Old Navy or Banana Republic. The Gap has hired investment bank Goldman Sachs to advise it. The need for a new direction was further solidified in early 2007 when Paul Pressler, CEO since 2002, left the company. In July Gap named a former drugstore and supermarket executive, Glenn Murphy, chairman and CEO of the company. Murphy, a Canadian, succeeds Robert Fisher — son of The Gap's founder — as chairman. (Fisher had also served as interim chief executive after Pressler's departure.)

In another blow to the company, Gap shut down Forth & Towne — its newest store concept launched in August 2005 — in June 2007. The Forth & Towne stores catered to women over 35.

Pressler's long-expected exit came after the retail icon had become an industry poster child for a titan that has lost its way. Sales at the chain have suffered due to uninspired fashion since 2004. After a failed foray into clothing lines aimed at the Britney Spears and bubblegum set that alienated the company's core clientele, The Gap got back to the basics: khaki pants, denim, T-shirts, polos, and other casual fashions. In a bid to regain its merchandising edge, the company has made revamping its Gap-brand women's apparel collection a top priority. As a result, Gap has replaced its chief designer for Gap brand clothing and added petite and tall sizes.

Outside the US, Gap stores reach foreign customers mainly in Canada, France, Japan, and the UK. However, sales in Germany were such an overall flop that all 10 units were sold to H&M. Gap Inc. plans to deploy Old Navy stores overseas in coming years. Banana Republic opened its first store in Tokyo in 2005. Filling in gaps in the Asian market, the company has entered into a franchise agreement (its first) with the Singaporean retailer F J Benjamin to open Gap and Banana Republic stores in Singapore and Malaysia. Some 30 stores are slated to open in those markets by 2010. Subsequent franchise agreements with companies in Dubai (Al Tayer Group), Saudi Arabia (Fawaz Alhokair Group), and Turkey (Fiba Holding) will lead to the opening of Gap and Banana Republic stores in the Middle East and Turkey. Gap is also exploring the vast Chinese market.

## HISTORY

Donald Fisher and his wife, Doris, opened a small store in 1969 near what is now San Francisco State University. The couple named their store The Gap (after "the generation gap") and concentrated on selling Levi's jeans. The couple opened a second store in San Jose, California, eight months later, and by the end of 1970 there were six Gap stores. The Gap went public six years later.

In the beginning the Fishers catered almost exclusively to teenagers, but in the 1970s they expanded into activewear that would appeal to a larger spectrum of customers. Nevertheless, by the early 1980s The Gap — which had grown to about 500 stores — was still dependent upon its largely teenage customer base. However, it was less dependent on Levi's (about 35% of sales), thanks to its growing stable of private labels.

In a 1983 effort to revamp the company's image, Donald hired Mickey Drexler, a former president of AnnTaylor with a spotless apparel industry track record, as The Gap's new president. Drexler immediately overhauled the motley clothing lines to concentrate on sturdy, brightly colored cotton clothing. He also consolidated the stores' many private clothing labels into the Gap brand. As a final touch, Drexler replaced circular clothing racks with white shelving so clothes could be neatly stacked and displayed.

Also in 1983 The Gap bought Banana Republic, a unique chain of jungle-themed stores that sold safari clothing. The company expanded the chain, which enjoyed tremendous success in the mid-1980s but slumped after the novelty of the stores wore off late in the decade. In response, Drexler introduced a broader range of clothes (including higher-priced leather items) and dumped the safari lines in 1988. By 1990 Banana Republic was again profitable.

The first GapKids opened in 1985 after Drexler couldn't find clothing that he liked for his son. In 1990 it introduced babyGap in 25 GapKids stores, featuring miniature versions of its GapKids line. The Gap announced in 1991 it would no longer sell Levi's (which had fallen to less than 2% of total sales) and would sell nothing but private-label items.

In 1994 it launched Old Navy Clothing Co., named after a bar Drexler saw in Paris. Robert Fisher (the founders' son) became the new president of the Gap division (including babyGap and GapKids) in 1997 and was charged with reversing the segment's sales decline. The company refocused its Gap chain on basics (jeans, T-shirts, and khakis).

In late 1999, amid sluggish Gap division sales, Robert resigned and Drexler took over his duties. After a 10% reduction in its workforce, the company returned to a more conservative fashion approach. In 2002 Drexler retired and was replaced by Paul Pressler, a veteran of The Walt Disney Company.

In January 2007 CEO Paul Pressler left the company and the board after four years in the top job. Pressler was succeeded as CEO on an interim basis by Robert Fisher, previously the non-executive chairman of the retailer. In June the company shutdown its Forth & Towne retail format after less than two years in business. In July Gap named a new chairman and CEO, Glenn Murphy. Murphy joined the company from Canadian drugstore chain Shoppers Drug Mart where he retired as chairman and chief executive in March.

## EXECUTIVES

**Chairman and CEO:** Glenn K. Murphy, age 45
**Director:** Robert J. (Bob) Fisher, age 52
**EVP, Chief Compliance Officer, General Counsel, and Secretary:** Lauri M. Shanahan, age 44
**EVP and CFO:** Byron H. Pollitt Jr., age 55, $710,096 pay
**EVP and CIO:** Michael B. Tasooji, age 46
**EVP, Corporate Strategy and Business Development:** Art Peck, age 51
**EVP Human Resources:** Eva Sage-Gavin, age 48, $522,211 pay
**SVP, Design and Product Development, Women's Division:** Austyn Zung
**SVP, Merchandising, Gap Adult:** Karyn Hillman, age 39
**SVP, Sourcing and Vendor Development:** Stan Raggio, age 50
**SVP, International Strategic Alliances:** Ron Young
**SVP, Treasury and Investor Relations:** Sabrina Simmons, age 38
**President, Gap North America:** Marka Hansen, age 52
**President, Europe, Gap Inc. International:** Stephen (Steve) Sunnucks
**President, Gap Inc. Direct:** Toby Lenk
**President, Gap Inc. Outlet:** John T. (Tom) Wyatt, age 51
**President, GapKids, babyGap, and Gap Maternity:** Pamela B. Wallack, age 46
**President, Old Navy:** Dawn Robertson, age 51
**Interim President and EVP, Merchandising and Marketing, Banana Republic:** Jack Calhoun, age 38
**Chief Foundation Officer, Gap Foundation:** Roberta H. (Bobbi) Silten, age 44
**Director of Investor Relations:** Evan Price
**Director of Public Relations and Promotions, Gap:** Rebecca Weill
**Auditors:** Deloitte & Touche LLP

## LOCATIONS

**HQ:** The Gap Inc.
2 Folsom St., San Francisco, CA 94105
**Phone:** 650-952-4400 **Fax:** 415-427-2553
**Web:** www.gap.com

Gap sells casual apparel, shoes, and personal care items through more than 3,100 Gap, Banana Republic, and Old Navy stores in Canada, France, Ireland, Japan, the UK, and the US.

### 2007 Stores

| | No. |
|---|---|
| North America | 2,858 |
| Europe | 168 |
| Asia | 105 |
| **Total** | **3,131** |

## PRODUCTS/OPERATIONS

### 2007 Stores

| | No. |
|---|---|
| Gap North America | 1,293 |
| Old Navy North America | 1,012 |
| Banana Republic North America | 521 |
| Gap Europe | 168 |
| Gap Asia | 105 |
| Forth & Towne | 19 |
| Banana Republic Japan | 13 |
| **Total** | **3,131** |

### 2007 Sales

| | $ mil. | % of total |
|---|---|---|
| Old Navy | 6,829 | 43 |
| Gap | 6,507 | 41 |
| Banana Republic | 2,548 | 16 |
| International | 59.0 | — |
| **Total** | **15,943** | **100** |

### Stores

babyGap (clothing for infants and toddlers)
Banana Republic (upscale clothing and accessories)
Gap (casual and active clothing and body care products)
GapBody (intimate apparel)
GapKids (clothing for children)
Old Navy (lower-priced family clothing)

## COMPETITORS

Abercrombie & Fitch
Aéropostale
American Eagle Outfitters
Benetton
Calvin Klein
Dillard's
Eddie Bauer
Express
Fast Retailing
Foot Locker
Fruit of the Loom
Guess
Gymboree
H&M
Inditex
J. C. Penney
J. Crew
J. Jill Group
Juicy Couture
Lands' End
Levi Strauss
Limited Brands
L.L. Bean
Macy's
Nautica Enterprises
NIKE
Nordstrom
OshKosh B'Gosh
Phillips-Van Heusen
Polo Ralph Lauren
Reebok
Retail Brand Alliance
Saks Inc.
Sears
Target
TJX Companies
Tommy Hilfiger
Toys "R" Us
VF
Wal-Mart
Zappos.com

## HISTORICAL FINANCIALS

Company Type: Public

**Income Statement** FYE: Saturday closest to January 31

| | REVENUE ($ mil.) | NET INCOME ($ mil.) | NET PROFIT MARGIN | EMPLOYEES |
|---|---|---|---|---|
| **1/07** | 15,943 | 778 | 4.9% | 154,000 |
| **1/06** | 16,023 | 1,113 | 6.9% | 153,000 |
| **1/05** | 16,267 | 1,150 | 7.1% | 152,000 |
| **1/04** | 15,854 | 1,030 | 6.5% | 153,000 |
| **1/03** | 14,455 | 478 | 3.3% | 169,000 |
| **Annual Growth** | 2.5% | 13.0% | — | (2.3%) |

**2007 Year-End Financials**

Debt ratio: 3.6%
Return on equity: 14.7%
Cash ($ mil.): 2,644
Current ratio: 2.21
Long-term debt ($ mil.): 188
No. of shares (mil.): 814
Dividends
Yield: 1.6%
Payout: 34.4%
Market value ($ mil.): 15,846

**Stock History** NYSE: GPS

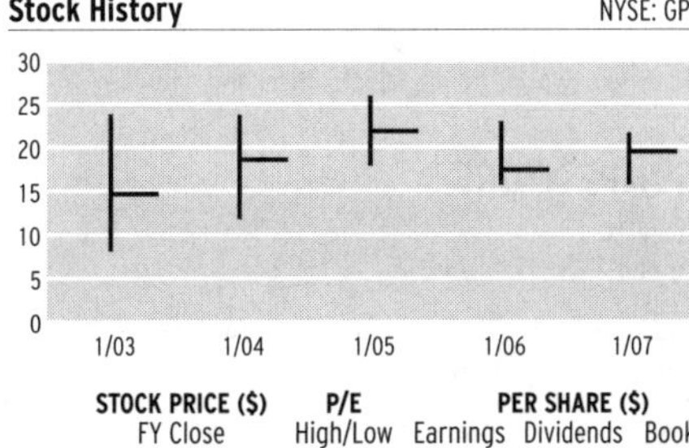


| | STOCK PRICE ($) FY Close | P/E High | P/E Low | PER SHARE ($) Earnings | Dividends | Book Value |
|---|---|---|---|---|---|---|
| **1/07** | 19.47 | 23 | 17 | 0.93 | 0.32 | 6.36 |
| **1/06** | 17.38 | 18 | 13 | 1.24 | 0.20 | 6.33 |
| **1/05** | 21.81 | 21 | 15 | 1.21 | 0.09 | 5.74 |
| **1/04** | 18.58 | 22 | 11 | 1.09 | 0.09 | 5.33 |
| **1/03** | 14.63 | 44 | 15 | 0.54 | 0.09 | 4.12 |
| **Annual Growth** | 7.4% | — | — | 14.6% | 37.3% | 11.4% |

# Gateway, Inc.

Gateway has found a new way. The company makes desktop and portable PCs and network servers for customers in the consumer, corporate, education, and government markets. It also offers third-party consumer electronics and peripherals including printers, storage drives, and networking equipment. Its services include training, support, and financing. Gateway acquired rival eMachines in 2004. Following the acquisition Gateway overhauled its management team and closed its stores. It now sells directly by phone and through its Web site, and through PC retailers. eMachines PCs serve as Gateway's value brand. Founder Ted Waitt owns more than a quarter of the company. Gateway agreed to be acquired by Taiwan-based Acer for $710 million in 2007.

In 2004 Gateway acquired competitor eMachines in a cash and stock deal valued at approximately $235 million. The merger expanded Gateway's distribution channels, providing access to large electronics retailers such as Best Buy and Circuit City where eMachines was entrenched. eMachines CEO Wayne Inouye took over as CEO of Gateway when the deal closed. (He resigned early in 2006.) A number of other former eMachines executives joined the Gateway management team following the acquisition. Consequently, Gateway moved its headquarters to Orange County where eMachines is based. In 2006 eMachines founder and Gateway shareholder Lap Shun Hui offered to acquire Gateway's retail operations for $450 million. (Gateway sells its eMachines-branded PCs exclusively through the retail channel.) Gateway rejected the offer.

Gateway has returned its focus to PCs and reestablished its retail presence, now utilizing electronics chains instead of its own stores. It has largely shifted manufacturing to contractors, but the company also serves corporate customers with a US-based custom assembly and configuration plant that it opened in 2006. Gateway has also re-entered international markets, selling through distributors and retailers in Canada, China, France, Japan, Mexico, and the UK.

Early in 2006 Gateway agreed to pay rival HP $47 million to settle a patent dispute involving personal computer technologies.

## HISTORY

Apparently college and billion-dollar PC businesses don't mix. Like his main competitor, Michael Dell, Ted Waitt dropped out of college to get into the computer business. Waitt had gone to Des Moines, Iowa, to see his roommates' band one weekend. He met a friend who was working for a computer retailer, liked the sound of the job, and left school to go to work. After nine months, he quit to start his own company.

Using his grandmother's certificate of deposit as collateral, Waitt borrowed $10,000 and in 1985 set up shop in the South Dakota barn of his father, a fourth-generation cattleman. There, with his brother Norm and friend Mike Hammond, he founded the TIPC Network, which sold add-on parts by phone for Texas Instruments' PCs.

However, Ted's goal was to sell PCs himself, and in 1987 the three men jumped into the fray. Ted and Hammond put together a fully configured computer system at a price that was near what other companies were charging for a barebones system. Sales took off. The next year they changed the enterprise's name to Gateway 2000 to express the belief that their computers were the gateway to the 21st century.

The company's customers were savvy buyers willing to dig through catalogs to find the best price for the exact system they wanted, and much of Gateway's success was rooted in Ted's ability to predict which standard features would sell.

Gateway distinguished itself from competitors with eye-catching ads. Some featured cows and another depicted Ted dressed as Robin Hood. He wanted to convince potential customers that Gateway would be around in the future to service the computers it sold.

In 1990 Gateway moved to North Sioux City, South Dakota. Two years later it introduced a line of notebook computers and created a division to handle component add-ons. Gateway went public in 1993, and opened a manufacturing facility in Ireland. In 1994 it added retail showrooms in Europe.

In 1995 Gateway expanded into Australia when it purchased 80% of the country's largest computer maker. Gateway introduced a cross between a PC and a big-screen TV (called a PCTV) in 1996 and opened two US retail showrooms.

The next year Ted, balking at the thought of his staff becoming subordinate to Compaq's management, rejected a $7 billion takeover bid from the PC giant.

Gateway dropped the "2000" from its name in 1998 to avoid appearing behind the times as the millennium approached, and moved its headquarters to San Diego.

In 1999 America Online (now Time Warner) made an $800 million investment in Gateway that stipulated a deal for the online services giant to run Gateway.net. As 1999 ended, so did Waitt's reign as CEO — but not as chairman. He turned over the duties to company president and AT&T veteran Jeff Weitzen.

At the beginning of 2001 Gateway reduced its workforce by 10% and moved its headquarters to Poway, California, when an industrywide sales slowdown led to heavy losses. Gateway also overhauled its management team, a move that included the departure of Weitzen. Waitt returned to the helm as CEO of a greatly reduced staff. Gateway then began closing many of its Gateway Country stores in North America. The company's next restructuring push included plans to cut its workforce by as much as a quarter worldwide, the closing of manufacturing plants throughout the Pacific Rim, and a withdrawal from European markets. Despite its increased focus on domestic operations, Gateway also announced it would reduce its US call centers and close its Salt Lake City manufacturing plant.

In 2004 Gateway acquired competitor eMachines in a cash and stock deal valued at approximately $235 million. eMachines CEO Wayne Inouye took over as CEO of Gateway when the deal closed, but Waitt retained his chairman title. Following the eMachines acquisition, Gateway closed all of the remaining locations, cutting about 2,500 jobs. It announced another 1,500 job cuts soon after the store closings.

Waitt stepped down as chairman in 2005. Early in 2006 Inouye resigned and chairman Richard Snyder was named interim CEO. Later that year Edward Coleman, a veteran of Arrow Electronics, was named CEO; Snyder retained his chairmanship.

## EXECUTIVES

**Chairman:** Richard D. (Rick) Snyder, age 48
**CEO and Director:** J. Edward (Ed) Coleman, age 55, $377,000 pay (partial-year salary)
**SVP and CFO:** John P. Goldsberry, age 52, $529,000 pay
**SVP Human Resources and Customer Support Services:** Lazane Smith, age 52
**SVP Marketing:** Bart R. Brown, age 41
**SVP Retail:** Robert V. (Bob) Davidson, age 52, $421,227 pay
**SVP, Chief Legal and Administrative Officer, and Secretary:** Michael R. (Mike) Tyler, age 47
**SVP Professional and Consumer Direct:** James R. Burdick, age 47
**SVP Product Planning-Retail:** Charles H. (Chuck) May, age 54
**VP Products:** Gary Elsasser, age 38
**VP and Corporate Controller:** Neal West, age 47
**VP and Treasurer; VP Finance, Professional and Direct Segments:** Craig Calle, age 46
**VP Quality Assurance:** Kyle J. Price, age 46
**VP Supply Chain:** Jack Baikie, age 50
**Investor Relations:** Marlys Johnson
**Media Relations:** David Hallisey
**Auditors:** Deloitte & Touche LLP

## LOCATIONS

**HQ:** Gateway, Inc.
7565 Irvine Center Dr., Irvine, CA 92618
**Phone:** 949-471-7000 **Fax:** 949-471-7041
**Web:** www.gateway.com

## PRODUCTS/OPERATIONS

### 2006 Sales

| | $ mil. | % of total |
|---|---|---|
| Retail & International | 2,739.9 | 69 |
| Professional | 895.8 | 22 |
| Direct | 345.1 | 9 |
| **Total** | **3,980.8** | **100** |

### 2006 Sales

| | $ mil. | % of total |
|---|---|---|
| Computers | | |
| Desktop | 1,868.3 | 47 |
| Notebook | 1,437.0 | 36 |
| Servers & other | 32.1 | 1 |
| Other | 643.4 | 16 |
| **Total** | **3,980.8** | **100** |

### Selected Products

Personal Computers
- Desktop
- Notebook

Servers
Third-party peripherals, electronics, and software

## COMPETITORS

Acer
Apple
Dell
Fujitsu
Hewlett-Packard
IBM
Lenovo
Matsushita Electric
MPC Computers
NEC
Samsung Group
Sharp Electronics
Sony
Sun Microsystems
Toshiba

## HISTORICAL FINANCIALS

Company Type: Public

### Income Statement

FYE: December 31

| | REVENUE ($ mil.) | NET INCOME ($ mil.) | NET PROFIT MARGIN | EMPLOYEES |
|---|---|---|---|---|
| **12/06** | 3,981 | 10 | 0.2% | 1,700 |
| **12/05** | 3,854 | 6 | 0.2% | 1,800 |
| **12/04** | 3,650 | (568) | — | 1,900 |
| **12/03** | 3,402 | (515) | — | 7,407 |
| **12/02** | 4,171 | (298) | — | 11,500 |
| **Annual Growth** | (1.2%) | — | — | (38.0%) |

### 2006 Year-End Financials

Debt ratio: 111.5%
Return on equity: 3.7%
Cash ($ mil.): 416
Current ratio: 1.23
Long-term debt ($ mil.): 300
No. of shares (mil.): 372
Dividends
Yield: —
Payout: —
Market value ($ mil.): 747

### Stock History

NYSE: GTW

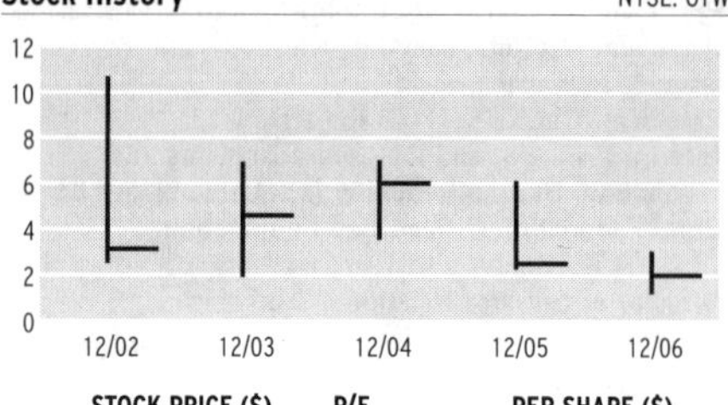


| | STOCK PRICE ($) FY Close | P/E High | P/E Low | PER SHARE ($) Earnings | Dividends | Book Value |
|---|---|---|---|---|---|---|
| **12/06** | 2.01 | 99 | 43 | 0.03 | — | 0.72 |
| **12/05** | 2.51 | 302 | 117 | 0.02 | — | 0.68 |
| **12/04** | 6.01 | — | — | (1.45) | — | 0.66 |
| **12/03** | 4.60 | — | — | (1.62) | — | 2.23 |
| **12/02** | 3.14 | — | — | (0.95) | — | 3.85 |
| **Annual Growth** | (10.6%) | — | — | — | — | (34.1%) |

# GATX Corporation

GATX never tried to unite Georgia and Texas, but the holding company does bring together some diverse businesses. After reorganizing in late 2003, and selling nearly all its aircraft holdings in 2006, the company now operates three divisions: rail (tank and freight car and locomotive leasing), specialty (leases, affiliate investments, and loans), and American Steamship Company (a shipping company with a fleet of self-unloading ships operating on the Great Lakes for nearly 100 years). GATX sold its information technology leasing business to CIT Group in 2004. The company chose to exit the aircraft leasing business in late 2006. Insurance giant State Farm owns about 12% of GATX.

The company also offers rail leasing and financial services to the marine, shipping, and industrial equipment industries.

GATX's aircraft leasing business was not performing as well as the company would like, so GATX made some adjustments. Realizing it could not compete head-to-head with deep-pocketed competitors that order up large numbers of new aircraft, GATX focused its strategy on the services associated with managing aircraft for its customers. As part of the strategy GATX sold nearly half a billion dollars worth of older aircraft.

Then in late 2006 the company essentially exited the aircraft leasing segment completely when it sold the majority of its aircraft assets as well as the aircraft leasing joint ventures that GATX manages to an investment consortium which includes Macquarie Bank and affiliated funds of Och Ziff Capital Management Group.

The following year, in order to streamline its operations, GATX decided to merge the activities of GATX Financial Corp. into its parent, GATX Corporation. As a result, GATX Financial ceased operations as an ongoing concern.

## HISTORY

Max Epstein, a worker in the Chicago Stockyards, founded the Atlantic Seaboard Dispatch in 1898. He used the $1,000 commission he received for arranging the sale of 20 old railway freight cars as a down payment to purchase 28 cars for himself. In 1902 he incorporated his German-American Car Co., the first to lease specialty railcars on a long-term basis.

By 1907 Epstein had 433 railcars and had begun to specialize in building customized freight cars. In 1916 the firm offered stock under the name General American Tank Car (GATC); its railcars carried the initials GATX (the "X" meant that a car belonged to a private line). In 1925 GATC began a bulk-liquid storage business.

Epstein purchased 13 firms between 1926 and 1931. The Depression was good to GATC: Epstein declared that conditions allowed him to make better deals, and the petroleum and food products hauled in GATC cars were always in demand, despite economic pressures. By the 1940s the company was the US's largest freight-car lessor. It also owned the US's largest public liquid-storage terminal facility and began operating cargo ships on the Great Lakes.

The company was the US's fourth-largest maker of freight cars by 1952. In 1954 GATC acquired Fuller Co., a builder of cement plants, which produced steady profits until its sale in 1986.

In 1968 GATC formed GATX Leasing, an airplane lessor. That year, as the demand for railcars plummeted, the firm reduced manufacturing and began refocusing. In 1973 GATC acquired American Steamship, which helped expand its role in Great Lakes shipping. The company changed its name to GATX Corporation in 1975.

GATX exited manufacturing and became more service-oriented in the 1980s by expanding its railcar and aircraft fleets and bulk-liquid storage operations. It narrowly escaped several takeover attempts. GATX Terminals expanded rapidly toward the end of the 1980s.

GATX purchased Associated Unit Companies in 1989 (later the Unit Companies and then GATX Logistics) and Sealand Oil Services Ltd. (Scotland) in 1993. It continued to expand overseas by forming a joint venture with EnviroLease in 1994 to provide equipment for moving wastes and recyclables. In 1995 the company leased the 1,200-tank-car fleet of Mexico's state-owned railroad.

CEO James Glasser, head of GATX since 1978, turned over the reins to Ronald Zech in 1996. The next year mailing-machine maker Pitney Bowes sold part of its lease portfolio to GATX and put other equipment in a joint venture with the company.

Also in 1997, as part of a three-year strategy to sell underperforming units, the company began to sell some of its terminals. By 1999 it had sold six UK terminals. In 2000 GATX changed the name of its main operating unit, General American Transportation Corp., to GATX Rail. It also sold its GATX Logistics subsidiary to two investment groups.

To trim down its operations even further, the firm sold its GATX Terminals subsidiary in 2001 and reorganized its leasing businesses.

Also in 2001, GATX expanded its European rail operations into Poland with the acquisition of Dyrekcja Eksploatacji Cystern (DEC). Late in 2002 the company acquired the remaining interests of European railcar lessors KVG Kesselwagen Vermietgesellschaft (Germany) and KVG Kesselwagen Vermietgesellschaft (Austria).

## EXECUTIVES

**Chairman, President, and CEO:** Brian A. Kenney, age 47, $625,000 pay
**SVP Human Resources:** Gail L. Duddy, age 54, $292,300 pay
**EVP and COO:** James F. (Jim) Earl, age 50, $371,212 pay
**VP and CFO:** Robert C. Lyons, age 43, $291,667 pay
**VP Corporate Strategy:** Clifford J. Porzenheim, age 38
**VP and CIO:** S. Yvonne Scott, age 48
**VP and Treasurer:** William J. Hasek, age 50
**VP and General Counsel:** Deborah A. Golden, age 52, $303,542 pay
**VP, Controller, and Chief Accounting Officer:** William M. Muckian, age 47
**President and CEO, American Steamship Company:** Jerome K. Welsch Jr.
**President, GATX Rail Europe:** Johannes Mansbart
**President, GATX Technology Services:** Thomas K. (Tom) McGreal
**Managing Director, GATX Specialty Finance:** Charles (Charly) Freeman
**Managing Director, Industrial Equipment Finance, Specialty Finance:** Jeffrey D. Walsh
**Chief Commercial Officer, Rail:** Thomas (Tom) Ellman
**Director, Investor Relations:** Rhonda S. Johnson
**Auditors:** Ernst & Young LLP

## LOCATIONS

**HQ:** GATX Corporation
500 W. Monroe St., Chicago, IL 60661
**Phone:** 312-621-6200 **Fax:** 312-621-6648
**Web:** www.gatx.com

## PRODUCTS/OPERATIONS

### 2006 Sales

| | $ mil. | % of total |
|---|---|---|
| Rail | 883.0 | 72 |
| American Steamship Company | 209.8 | 17 |
| Specialty | 135.7 | 11 |
| Other | 0.6 | — |
| **Total** | **1,229.1** | **100** |

### Selected Operations

American Steamship Company (commodity transportation on the Great Lakes)
GATX Rail (railcar leasing)
GATX Specialty (investing and brokering of financial services)

## COMPETITORS

ACF
CIT Transportation Finance
Electro Rent
Eurofima
Forsythe Technology
GE Equipment Services
General Motors
Greenbrier
IAF Group
Interpool
Oglebay Norton
Stolt-Nielsen
Transtar
Trinity Industries
TTX
XTRA

## HISTORICAL FINANCIALS

Company Type: Public

### Income Statement

FYE: December 31

| | REVENUE ($ mil.) | NET INCOME ($ mil.) | NET PROFIT MARGIN | EMPLOYEES |
|---|---|---|---|---|
| **12/06** | 1,229 | 112 | 9.1% | 2,340 |
| **12/05** | 1,135 | (14) | — | 1,870 |
| **12/04** | 1,231 | 170 | 13.8% | 2,680 |
| **12/03** | 1,315 | 77 | 5.9% | 2,250 |
| **12/02** | 1,341 | 0 | 0.0% | 2,800 |
| **Annual Growth** | (2.1%) | 339.3% | — | (4.4%) |

### 2006 Year-End Financials

Debt ratio: 190.4%
Return on equity: 10.2%
Cash ($ mil.): 244
Current ratio: 4.86
Long-term debt ($ mil.): 2,215
No. of shares (mil.): 52
Dividends
Yield: 1.9%
Payout: 42.0%
Market value ($ mil.): 2,253

### Stock History

NYSE: GMT

| | STOCK PRICE ($) FY Close | P/E High | P/E Low | PER SHARE ($) Earnings | Dividends | Book Value |
|---|---|---|---|---|---|---|
| **12/06** | 43.33 | 24 | 18 | 2.00 | 0.84 | 22.37 |
| **12/05** | 36.08 | — | — | (0.29) | 0.80 | 20.20 |
| **12/04** | 29.56 | 10 | 7 | 3.04 | 1.00 | 21.82 |
| **12/03** | 27.98 | 19 | 9 | 1.56 | 1.28 | 18.05 |
| **12/02** | 22.82 | — | — | — | 1.28 | 16.34 |
| **Annual Growth** | 17.4% | — | — | 8.6% | (10.0%) | 8.2% |

# Gemstar-TV Guide

Gemstar-TV Guide International is a friend to couch potatoes everywhere. The company operates the TV Guide Channel, which provides program listings to millions of cable subscribers. Its TV Guide On Screen technology allows users to review onscreen TV listings and use them to program their TVs or digital video recorders (DVRs). Its TV Guide Interactive licenses technologies and services related to TV interactive program guides (IPGs). Gemstar's tight grip on the listings market extends to TV Guide, publisher of *TV Guide* magazine. The company has expanded its Web presence with TV Guide Online, which offers TV listings, features, and e-commerce services. News Corp. owns 41% of Gemstar, which has put itself up for sale.

The company's invention of VCR Plus+ (which lets users record TV programs using a simple numeric code) made it one of the earliest leaders in interactive programming technologies. But the rise of DVD players, TiVo, and other DVRs have made the VCR virtually obsolete, so the company is relying more than ever on its TV Guide Interactive and TV Guide On Screen IPGs.

Along these lines, the company is developing a cross-platform suite of products and services to offer a more personalized experience for consumers, including targeted programming recommendations, customizable user interfaces, and the ability to receive content and information about favorite shows and stars. The suite will provide services such as DVR recording, customizable grid listings, and text message prompts to manage a user's viewing experience.

Gemstar-TV Guide is also focused on creating new content. Its TV Guide Channel produces content for distribution across multiple outlets, including TV Guide SPOT (a behind-the-scenes entertainment program), TV Guide Broadband (Internet content for tvguide.com and major video portals such as AOL Video and Google Video), and TV Guide Mobile (content for mobile devices through deals with Verizon, Sprint, and AT&T).

The company has been tied up in court for the past several years due to accounting scandals. Former Gemstar-TV Guide CEO Henry Yuen was found guilty of committing fraud that led the company to overstate revenue by more than $225 million between 2000 and 2002. (Former co-president and CFO Elsie Leung was also involved in the scandal. She later settled with the SEC.) In 2006 a federal judge ordered Yuen to pay some $22 million for his involvement in the scandal. The ruling is one of the largest civil penalties the SEC has ever obtained against an individual in an accounting-fraud case.

## HISTORY

Frustrated by a failed attempt to record a Red Sox game, Henry Yuen founded Gemstar Development in 1989 with Daniel Kwoh to simplify VCR programming. Yuen and Kwoh, fellow researchers at TRW, invented a system to translate data about when and where a show aired into a single number. The company introduced the VCR Plus+ system in 1990, selling converter boxes at about $60 and persuading daily newspapers to list coding numbers.

In 1993 the company embarked on a long series of legal battles to protect its patents, exchanging lawsuits with rivals. Its ferocious defense of its technology earned the company the epithet "patent terrorist."

In 1994 Gemstar debuted its VCR Plus+ with CallSet (enabling VCR Plus+ technology via the telephone) and VCR Plus+ Control Tower (a universal remote with built-in VCR Plus+ with CallSet). The company went public in 1995, and changed its name to Gemstar International Group. Through acquisitions of VideoGuide (1996) and StarSight (1997), Gemstar branched into electronic program guides (EPGs). In 1997 THOMSON Multimedia agreed to use the company's EPG technology (called Gemstar Guide Technology) as the industry standard in North and South America.

In 2000 Gemstar strengthened its grip on the couch potato market when it purchased TV Guide in a stock deal valued at around $14 billion. In acquiring TV Guide, Gemstar gobbled up one of its longtime foes — two years earlier, United Video Satellite Group had purchased TV Guide and adopted the TV Guide name. The deal gave News Corp. and Liberty Media each a 21.5% stake in the new company. (News Corp. later bought Liberty Media's stake.)

2002 was not a good year for Gemstar. Early in the year the company acknowledged that revenue had been inflated, and the stock price collapsed. The SEC launched a probe, and federal prosecutors began a criminal investigation. News Corp. waged a successful campaign to oust most of Gemstar's top management including then-CEO Yuen, and co-president and CFO Elsie Leung. Yuen was replaced as CEO by former News Corp. executive Jeff Shell.

Yuen initially refused to testify for the SEC about possible Gemstar accounting irregularities, and the government filed civil lawsuits against Yuen and Leung. The SEC later amended the indictment to include three other former company officers, most of which have since settled. (Both Yuen and Leung initially remained on the board of directors, but the company eventually fired them both.)

In 2004 Shell left the company and was replaced by Fox Entertainment executive Rich Battista, becoming Gemstar's third CEO in as many years.

Also that year the company formed a joint venture with US cable TV provider Comcast called Guideworks to develop on-screen cable TV program guides using Gemstar technology. Comcast paid Gemstar $250 million to license its program-guide technology and gain rights to the TV Guide name. Gemstar owns 49% of the venture, and Comcast owns 51%.

Gemstar-TV agreed to pay about $68 million in 2004 to settle lawsuits by shareholders who alleged they were misled by the company's accounting and financial practices. Also that year in another lawsuit the company agreed to pay a $10 million penalty fee to settle SEC allegations of revenue fraud, but did not admit or deny the claims. (By early 2006, Leung had settled her case and agreed to pay a $1.3 million fine.)

Also that year Gemstar drastically revamped its TV Guide magazine. The company relaunched the publication as a large-format lifestyle and entertainment magazine, focusing less on TV listings and more on entertainment news and features. The redesign forced the company to reduce its circulation from 9 million to less than 5 million. Circulation continued to decline to 3.5 million at the end of 2006.

## EXECUTIVES

**Chairman:** Anthea Disney, age 62
**CEO and Director:** Richard (Rich) Battista, age 42, $1,540,678 pay
**COO; President, Interactive Program Guides:** Michael (Mike) McKee, age 52, $1,116,782 pay
**EVP and CFO:** Bedi A. Singh, age 47, $696,757 pay
**EVP and Chief Content Officer; Editor-in-Chief, TV Guide:** Ian Birch
**EVP and Chief Marketing Officer:** Alan Cohen
**EVP, Secretary, and General Counsel:** Stephen H. Kay, age 46, $1,010,028 pay
**EVP; General Manager, Product Development:** Steve Shannon, age 42
**EVP Distribution:** Tonia O'Connor, age 37
**SVP and Chief Accounting Officer:** Peter C. Halt
**SVP Corporate Communications:** Eileen Murphy
**SVP Affiliate Sales and Marketing:** John High
**SVP Business Development and Strategic Planning:** Sanjay Reddy, age 40
**SVP Human Resources:** Dustin K. Finer
**SVP Technical and Operations:** Jean Francois Grasset
**SVP Technology:** Michael Starkenburg
**SVP; General Manager, Digital Media:** Richard (Rich) Cusick, age 36
**SVP; General Manager, ODS Technologys (TVG Network):** David Nathanson, age 29
**VP Communications and Public Affairs:** Bo Park
**President, TV Guide Channel:** Ryan O'Hara, age 38
**President, North American Interactive Programming Guide:** Thomas (Tom) Carson
**President, TV Guide Publishing Group:** J. Scott Crystal, age 50, $1,080,938 pay
**President, Gemstar Multimedia (Japan):** Akitaka Nishimura
**Director Investor Relations:** Robert L. Carl
**Auditors:** Ernst & Young LLP

## LOCATIONS

**HQ:** Gemstar-TV Guide International, Inc.
6922 Hollywood Blvd., 12th Fl.,
Los Angeles, CA 90028
**Phone:** 323-817-4600 **Fax:** 212-852-7301
**Web:** www.gemstartvguide.com

## PRODUCTS/OPERATIONS

### 2006 Sales

| | $ mil. | % of total |
|---|---|---|
| Cable & satellite | 302.2 | 53 |
| Publishing | 162.1 | 28 |
| Consumer electronics licensing | 107.0 | 19 |
| **Total** | **571.3** | **100** |

### Selected Products and Operations

Cable and Satellite
- TV Guide Channel
- TV Guide Interactive
- TV Guide Mobile Entertainment
- TV Guide SPOT
- TVG Network

Consumer Electronics Licensing
- TV Guide On Screen
- VCR Plus+

Publishing
- *TV Guide* magazine
- TV Guide Data Solutions
- TV Guide Online

## COMPETITORS

Cablevision Systems
Charter Communications
Cox Communications
Magna Entertainment
Motorola, Inc
Personalized Media
ReplayTV
Scientific-Atlanta
Time Warner
TiVo
TVData
Zap2it.com

## HISTORICAL FINANCIALS

Company Type: Public

### Income Statement

FYE: December 31

| | REVENUE ($ mil.) | NET INCOME ($ mil.) | NET PROFIT MARGIN | EMPLOYEES |
|---|---|---|---|---|
| **12/06** | 571 | 73 | 12.7% | 1,691 |
| **12/05** | 604 | 55 | 9.1% | 1,780 |
| **12/04** | 732 | (95) | — | 2,011 |
| **12/03** | 879 | (577) | — | 2,166 |
| **12/02** | 1,001 | (6,423) | — | 2,209 |
| **Annual Growth** | (13.1%) | — | — | (6.5%) |

### 2006 Year-End Financials

Debt ratio: 2.7%
Return on equity: 17.5%
Cash ($ mil.): 545
Current ratio: 2.64
Long-term debt ($ mil.): 12
No. of shares (mil.): 428
Dividends
Yield: —
Payout: —
Market value ($ mil.): 1,716

**Stock History** NASDAQ (GS): GMST

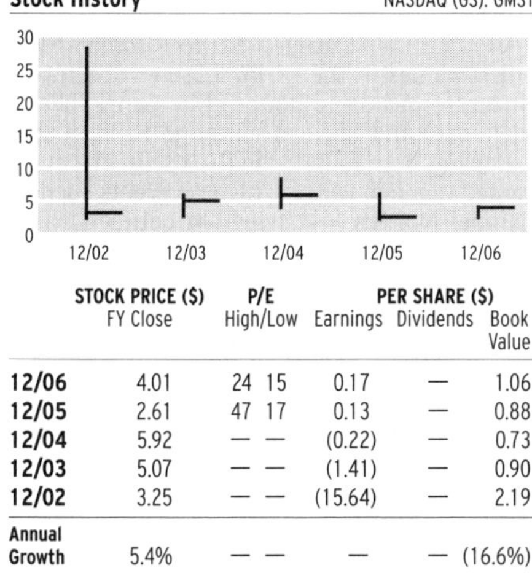


| | STOCK PRICE ($) FY Close | P/E High/Low | | PER SHARE ($) Earnings | Dividends | Book Value |
|---|---|---|---|---|---|---|
| **12/06** | 4.01 | 24 | 15 | 0.17 | — | 1.06 |
| **12/05** | 2.61 | 47 | 17 | 0.13 | — | 0.88 |
| **12/04** | 5.92 | — | — | (0.22) | — | 0.73 |
| **12/03** | 5.07 | — | — | (1.41) | — | 0.90 |
| **12/02** | 3.25 | — | — | (15.64) | — | 2.19 |
| **Annual Growth** | 5.4% | — | — | — | — | (16.6%) |

# Genentech, Inc.

"The few, the proud, the profitable" could be Genentech's motto. One of the world's most successful biotechs (in an industry full of money-losers), the firm has three billion-dollar blockbusters: Rituxan, which fights non-Hodgkin's lymphoma; Avastin, a treatment for colorectal and non-small cell lung cancers; and Herceptin for breast cancer. Lung cancer drug Tarceva rounds out the company's oncology portfolio. Genentech's other marketed drugs include cardiovascular therapies Activase and TNKase, human growth hormone Nutropin, cystic fibrosis drug Pulmozyme, and asthma drug Xolair, developed with Novartis and Tanox. Top customers are AmerisourceBergen, Cardinal Health, and McKesson. Roche owns 56% of the firm.

Though not not normally an acquisitive company, Genentech in 2007 bought its Xolair partner Tanox in a deal worth nearly a billion dollars. The acquisition makes Xolair more profitable for Genentech, since it won't have to pay royalties to Tanox; Genentech also will receive the royalty and profit-sharing payments Tanox has been getting from Novartis.

Instead of acquisitions, Genentech mostly relies on its own internal efforts (sometimes with research partners) to develop and commercialize new drugs. Its efforts met with success in mid-2006 when it won FDA approval for Lucentis, a treatment for the wet form of age-related macular degeneration (AMD). New drugs in clinical trials include treatments for rheumatoid arthritis, lupus, growth hormone deficiency, and cancers.

While its long-term success depends on its ability to develop novel compounds, Genentech is also seeking shorter-term success in its commercialization efforts for recently approved drugs Avastin (approved in 2004) and Lucentis, which is already rapidly gaining market share. Additionally, the company is working to expand the number of approved uses of its currently approved drugs; it is developing Avastin as a breast cancer treatment and Rituxan for immunological disorders. The latter drug was approved as a treatment for rheumatoid arthritis in 2006.

Sales to drug distributor AmerisourceBergen account for half of Genentech's US product sales, while Cardinal Health and McKesson contribute 18% and 17%, respectively.

Through its 33% stake in Roche, Novartis is an indirect shareholder in Genentech.

## HISTORY

Venture capitalist Robert Swanson and molecular biologist Herbert Boyer founded Genentech in 1976 to commercialize Boyer's patented gene-splicing techniques that could mass-produce genetically engineered substances. The company went public in 1980.

Genentech's market debut (the first FDA-approved biotech product) was a bioengineered form of human insulin in 1982. Eli Lilly bought the license and sold it as Humulin. Genentech sold marketing rights for royalties and focused on research; the company next developed the human immune system protein alpha interferon and licensed it to Hoffmann-La Roche, which sold the cancer treatment as Roferon-A. The first product to bear the Genentech name was human growth hormone Protropin, approved by the FDA in 1985.

Genentech released Activase in 1987. Its $180 million in sales was the best first year of any new drug at the time. Roche bought 60% of Genentech for $2.1 billion in 1990, including nearly $500 million to maintain the long-term research pipeline. In 1993 Genentech and Merck developed a compound to prevent activation of the RAS oncogene, a trigger for cancerous cells in the pancreas, colon, and lungs. Merck began human tests of anti-RAS drugs in 1998.

Genentech began shipping human growth hormone Nutropin in early 1994. The next year CEO Kirk Rabb was ousted after trying to secure a $2 million personal loan from Roche. Rabb was replaced by scientist Arthur Levinson (seen as a sign of Roche's R&D commitment). That year the companies signed a pact that gave Roche Genentech's Canadian and European operations, with a provision allowing Roche to buy the rest of the company by mid-1999.

After spending $100 million in 10 years on AIDS-related research, Genentech in 1996 formed a new company to develop its sidetracked HIV vaccine. That year the FDA approved Activase as the first effective treatment for acute stroke. In 1997 lymphoma treatment Rituxan (developed with IDEC Pharmaceuticals) became the first monoclonal antibody of its kind approved for cancer. The FDA approved breast cancer drug Herceptin in 1998.

That year saw the demise of Neuleze, once thought to hold promise to treat diabetes-related nerve damage; the company took comfort in the accolades pouring in for Herceptin and the skyrocketing sales of Rituxan. Meanwhile, charges that Genentech marketed human growth hormone for non-approved uses led to a federal court fine of $50 million.

In 1999 co-founder Swanson died of cancer. Also that year Roche bought the shares of Genentech that it didn't own, then spun off 16% of the company and 26% more in 2000. Genentech issued a warning to physicians in 2000 after Herceptin was linked to several deaths; together with the FDA, it set about relabeling the drug. That year the FDA approved TNKase to treat heart attacks, and Genentech formed two collaborative agreements with ImmunoGen to develop cancer treatments.

The firm won a patent dispute with GlaxoSmithKline in 2001 over how Genentech makes Herceptin and Rituxan. The next year, though, it lost a royalty dispute with the City of Hope research organization and was hit with $500 million damages from the suit. (Genetech appealed, but the verdict was upheld in 2004.) The firm declared victory in another battle to keep its revenues for itself: Chiron had sued Genentech over a patent for Herceptin and sought 30% of the drug's sales, but a California jury ruled in Genentech's favor.

## EXECUTIVES

**Chairman, President, and CEO:** Arthur D. (Art) Levinson, age 57, $2,975,833 pay
**President, Product Development:** Susan D. Desmond-Hellmann, age 49, $1,386,875 pay
**EVP and CFO:** David A. Ebersman, age 36
**EVP, General Counsel, Secretary, and Chief Compliance Officer:** Stephen G. Juelsgaard, age 57, $937,667 pay
**EVP, Commercial Operations:** Ian T. Clark, age 45
**EVP, Product Operations:** Patrick Y. (Pat) Yang, age 58
**EVP, Research:** Richard H. Scheller, age 52, $980,021 pay
**SVP, Development and Chief Medical Officer:** Hal Barron, age 40
**SVP, Regulatory, Quality, and Compliance:** Robert L. Garnick, age 56
**SVP, Sales and Marketing, BioOncology:** John Orwin, age 42
**SVP and General Counsel:** Sean A. Johnston, age 44
**SVP, Biochemical Manufacturing:** Markus Gemuend, age 48
**SVP, Global Supply Chain:** Timothy L. (Tim) Moore, age 45
**VP, Business Development:** Joseph S. McCracken, age 49
**VP, Regulatory Affairs, Clinical and Commercial:** Todd W. Rich, age 49
**VP, Human Resources:** Denise Smith-Hams
**Chief Accounting Officer and Controller:** Robert E. Andreatta, age 45
**Treasurer:** Thomas T. Thomas II, age 45
**Director, Corporate Relations:** Mary Strutts
**Investor Relations:** Kathee Litrell
**Auditors:** Ernst & Young LLP

## LOCATIONS

**HQ:** Genentech, Inc.
1 DNA Way, South San Francisco, CA 94080
**Phone:** 650-225-1000 **Fax:** 650-225-6000
**Web:** www.gene.com

**2006 Sales**

| | $ mil. | % of total |
|---|---|---|
| US | 7,838 | 84 |
| Europe | | |
| Switzerland | 561 | 6 |
| Germany | 133 | 1 |
| France | 100 | 1 |
| UK | 61 | 1 |
| Italy | 57 | 1 |
| Spain | 49 | 1 |
| Other countries | 121 | 1 |
| Japan | 119 | 1 |
| Canada | 64 | 1 |
| Other countries | 181 | 2 |
| **Total** | **9,284** | **100** |

## PRODUCTS/OPERATIONS

### 2006 Sales

| | $ mil. | % of total |
|---|---|---|
| Products | | |
| Rituxan | 2,071 | 22 |
| Avastin | 1,746 | 19 |
| Herceptin | 1,234 | 13 |
| Xolair | 425 | 5 |
| Tarceva | 402 | 4 |
| Lucentis | 380 | 4 |
| Nutropin products | 378 | 4 |
| Thrombolytics | 243 | 3 |
| Pulmozyme | 199 | 2 |
| Raptiva | 91 | 1 |
| Sales to collaborators | 471 | 5 |
| Royalties | 1,354 | 15 |
| Contracts | 290 | 3 |
| **Total** | **9,284** | **100** |

### Selected Products

Approved
- Activase (heart attack, ischemic stroke)
- Avastin (colon and rectal cancer)
- Herceptin (breast cancer)
- Lucentis (age-related macular degeneration)
- Nutropin (human growth hormone)
- Nutropin AQ (liquid form of Nutropin)
- Pulmozyme (cystic fibrosis)
- Raptiva (psoriasis)
- Rituxan (non-Hodgkin's lymphoma and rheumatoid arthritis, with Biogen Idec)
- Tarceva (non-small cell lung cancer and pancreatic cancer, with OSI Pharmaceuticals)
- TNKase (heart attack)
- Xolair (asthma, with Novartis Pharma)

In Development
- Anti-CD40 (non-Hodgkin's lymphoma, with Seattle Genetics)
- Avastin/Tarceva combination therapy (non-small cell lung cancer, with Roche and OSI Pharmaceuticals)
- HAE1 (allergic asthma)
- Omnitarg (breast, ovarian, and non-small cell lung cancers, with Roche)

## COMPETITORS

Abbott Labs
Amgen
Astellas
AstraZeneca
Bayer Corp.
Bayer HealthCare
Biogen Idec
Bristol-Myers Squibb
Cell Therapeutics
Centocor
Chiron
Critical Therapeutics
Eli Lilly
Genmab
Genzyme
GlaxoSmithKline
ImClone
Johnson & Johnson
Merck Serono
Millennium Pharmaceuticals
Novartis
Novo Nordisk
Onyx Pharmaceuticals
OSI Pharmaceuticals
PDL
Pfizer
Roche
Sandoz
Sanofi-Aventis
Savient
Telik
Teva Pharmaceuticals
Wyeth Pharmaceuticals

## HISTORICAL FINANCIALS

Company Type: Public

### Income Statement

FYE: December 31

| | REVENUE ($ mil.) | NET INCOME ($ mil.) | NET PROFIT MARGIN | EMPLOYEES |
|---|---|---|---|---|
| **12/06** | 9,284 | 2,113 | 22.8% | 10,533 |
| **12/05** | 6,633 | 1,279 | 19.3% | 9,500 |
| **12/04** | 4,621 | 785 | 17.0% | 7,646 |
| **12/03** | 3,300 | 563 | 17.0% | 6,226 |
| **12/02** | 2,719 | 64 | 2.3% | 5,252 |
| **Annual Growth** | 35.9% | 139.9% | — | 19.0% |

### 2006 Year-End Financials

Debt ratio: 23.3%
Return on equity: 24.9%
Cash ($ mil.): 2,493
Current ratio: 2.64
Long-term debt ($ mil.): 2,204
No. of shares (mil.): 1,053
Dividends
Yield: —
Payout: —
Market value ($ mil.): 85,430

### Stock History

NYSE: DNA

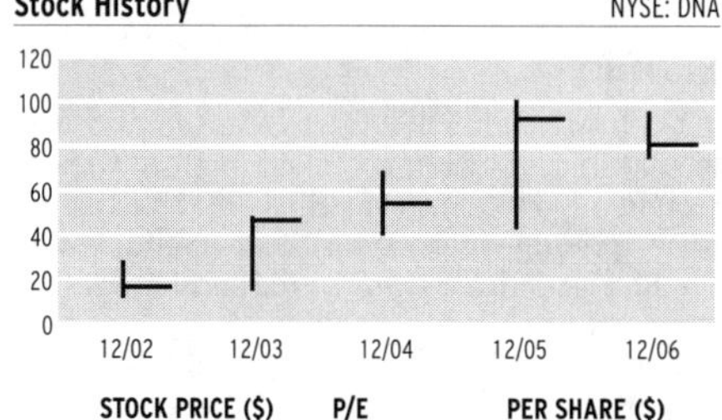


| | STOCK PRICE ($) FY Close | P/E High | P/E Low | PER SHARE ($) Earnings | Dividends | Book Value |
|---|---|---|---|---|---|---|
| **12/06** | 81.13 | 48 | 38 | 1.97 | — | 9.00 |
| **12/05** | 92.50 | 85 | 37 | 1.18 | — | 7.09 |
| **12/04** | 54.44 | 93 | 56 | 0.73 | — | 6.48 |
| **12/03** | 46.78 | 90 | 30 | 0.53 | — | 12.43 |
| **12/02** | 16.58 | 460 | 209 | 0.06 | — | 10.41 |
| **Annual Growth** | 48.7% | — | — | 139.4% | — | (3.6%) |

# General Cable

General Cable helps all sorts of companies get wired for business. The company makes aluminum, copper, and fiber-optic wire and cable, including electric utility (cables used for low-, medium- and high-voltage power distribution and power transmission), electrical infrastructure (for industrial and commercial power and control applications), and telecommunications products (low-voltage signal wire for voice, data, video, and control applications). Brand names include Carol, BICC, and Helix/HiTemp. General Cable also produces power cables, automotive wire, mining cables, and custom-designed cables for medical equipment and other products.

A rise in materials costs (especially aluminum and copper) in 2005 and 2006 led General Cable to reorganize some of its manufacturing facilities and to consolidate product lines. The company has also divested non-core and underperforming operations.

Late in 2005 General Cable expanded its European operations when it bought Silec, which had been the wire and cable business of SAFRAN. The following year the company acquired French power cable maker E.C.N. Cable Group.

The company expanded into China in 2007 with the acquisition of Jiangyin Huaming Specialty Cable, which makes automotive and industrial cables. Later that year it purchased German submarine cable system maker Norddeutsche Seekabelwerke (NSW) from Corning — NSW was part of Corning's Cable Systems unit. General Cable plans to continue growth through strategic acquisitions.

## HISTORY

General Cable originated from some of the oldest names in the wiring business: Standard Underground Cable (founded by George Westinghouse) and Phillips Wire and Safety Cable Company, both founded in the 1800s. The companies supplied wire for historic events such as Samuel Morse's first telegram between Baltimore and Washington, DC, in 1844, the lighting the Statute of Liberty in 1886, and the first Chicago World's Fair in 1892.

The company's best-known brand of nonmetallic sheathed cable, Romex, was invented at the company's Rome, New York, facility in 1922. Five years later, Phillips Wire and Standard Underground Cable joined to form General Cable Corporation. In 1935 the company's cables were used for power lines connecting the Hoover Dam to Los Angeles.

In the early 1980s the company was purchased by Penn Central Corporation (now known as American Premier Underwriters, part of American Financial Group). Later that decade Penn Central added the Carol brand when it purchased the Carol Cable Company (1989) and bought other wiring companies. The construction industry declined in the early 1990s, leaving wire inventories overstocked. In 1992 Penn Central spun off General Cable to shareholders, but the Lindner family (which owned Penn Central) continued to control most of the stock. The company also made news in 1992 when it moved its corporate headquarters from Cincinnati to northern Kentucky, representing a win in the battle for companies being waged between the bordering states. That year General Cable also sold its equipment-making subsidiary, Marathon LeTourneau, because it was not directly tied to the wire and cable business.

In 1994 Wassall, a British holding company, bought General Cable, which had lost more than $130 million in the previous two years. (Wassall sold its interest in 1997.) Soon afterward the company hired a new CEO, Stephen Rabinowitz, who had been president of General Electric's electrical distribution and control unit and president of the braking-systems business of Allied-Signal (now Honeywell International). He began integrating the company's many units, which previously had been run separately. He also consolidated the company's distribution sites and closed five manufacturing plants.

General Cable went public in 1997. That year it formed a joint venture with glass company Spectran Corporation (since acquired by Lucent) to create fiber-optic cable under the name General Photonics. In 1999 General Cable bought the energy cable businesses of BICC Plc for $440 million, which made General Cable one of the largest makers of wire and cable in the world. (It briefly operated under the BICCGeneral name.)

When its energy cable businesses in Europe, Africa, and Asia failed to perform up to expectations, General Cable agreed to sell some of those businesses (in the UK, Italy, Africa, and Asia) to Italy-based Pirelli for $216 million in 2000. Fearing Pirelli's dominant position, the European Commission opened an in-depth investigation of the takeover, but the deal was approved and completed later that year.

In 2001 General Cable sold its Pyrotenax unit to Raychem HTS Canada, Inc. (a division of Tyco International) for $60 million. The company also freed up $175 million in that same year by selling its building wire interests and exiting the cordset (indoor and outdoor extension cords) business. In early 2002 General Cable acquired the New Zealand-based data cable manufacturer Brand-Rex from Novar plc. Later that same year General cable sold its building wire operations to Southwire Company.

The company acquired certain specialty electronics and datacom assets from Draka Comteq in 2005. It also purchased Cuernavaca, Mexico-based Beru S.A. de C.V., which is an automotive aftermarket assembly and distribution enterprise.

## EXECUTIVES

**Nonexecutive Chairman:** John E. Welsh III, age 56
**President, CEO, and Director:** Gregory B. Kenny, age 54, $699,231 pay
**SVP, CFO, Treasurer, and Controller:** Brian J. Robinson, age 38
**EVP, General Counsel, and Secretary:** Robert J. Siverd, age 58, $346,252 pay
**SVP and General Manager, Telecommunications Business and Corporate Development:** James W. (Jim) Barney
**SVP and CIO:** Elizabeth W. Taliaferro
**SVP and General Manager, Utility and Industrial Cables:** J. Michael Andrews
**SVP, Human Resources:** Peter J. Olmsted
**SVP, North American Operations:** Larry E. Fast
**SVP, Sales and Business Development:** Roderick Macdonald
**SVP and General Manager, Specialty Wire Harnesses:** Roger A. Roundhouse
**SVP and General Manager, Data Communications Cables and Carol Brand Products:** Gregory J. Lampert
**SVP, International Sales:** Josep M. Martinez
**SVP; President and CEO, General Cable Europe:** Domingo Goenaga
**VP, Corporate Communications:** Lisa B. Lawson
**VP and Chief Learning Officer:** Tedd C. Simmons
**VP, Tax:** Jeffrey J. Whelan
**VP, Technology, North America:** James Freestone
**VP, Utility Sales:** Patrick Gorman
**VP, Finance and Investor Relations:** Michael P. Dickerson
**President and CEO, General Cable Oceania:** Campbell Whyte
**Auditors:** Deloitte & Touche LLP

## LOCATIONS

**HQ:** General Cable Corporation
4 Tesseneer Dr., Highland Heights, KY 41076
**Phone:** 859-572-8000 **Fax:** 859-572-8458
**Web:** www.generalcable.com

General Cable operates more than 25 facilities in Angola, Australia, Brazil, Canada, China, France, Mexico, New Zealand, Portugal, Spain, and the US.

**2006 Sales**

| | $ mil. | % of total |
|---|---|---|
| North America | 2,058.6 | 56 |
| Other regions | 1,606.5 | 44 |
| **Total** | **3,665.1** | **100** |

## PRODUCTS/OPERATIONS

**2006 Sales**

| | $ mil. | % of total |
|---|---|---|
| Electric utility | | |
| North American | 779.2 | 21 |
| Other regions | 617.2 | 17 |
| Electrical infrastructure | | |
| North American | 313.4 | 9 |
| Other regions | 876.8 | 24 |
| Telecommunications | 349.1 | 10 |
| Networking | 315.8 | 8 |
| Portable power & control | 297.8 | 8 |
| Transportation & industrial harnesses | 115.8 | 3 |
| **Total** | **3,665.1** | **100** |

**Selected Products**

Electric utility
- Power transmission & distribution cables

Electrical infrastructure
- Industrial instrumentation cables
- Maintenance cords & cables
- Power & control cables

Telecommunications
- Outside plant wires & cables (aerial, buried & duct)

Networking
- Fiber-optic cables
- Information technology cables
- Network cables

Portable power & control
- Electronic cables (signal, control, sound & security)

Transportation & industrial harnesses
- Automotive wires & cables
- Wire harnesses & assemblies (application specific)

## COMPETITORS

Alcatel-Lucent
Andrew Corporation
Balfour Beatty
Belden
Carlisle Companies
Coleman Cable
CommScope
Corning
Encore Wire
Furukawa Electric
Genesis Cable
Hubbell
Huber + Suhner, Inc.
Kalas Manufacturing
LEONI
Nexans
Owl Wire & Cable
Quabbin Wire
Southwire
Sumitomo Electric
Superior Essex
Tyco
Volex

## HISTORICAL FINANCIALS

Company Type: Public

**Income Statement** FYE: December 31

| | REVENUE ($ mil.) | NET INCOME ($ mil.) | NET PROFIT MARGIN | EMPLOYEES |
|---|---|---|---|---|
| **12/06** | 3,665 | 135 | 3.7% | 7,700 |
| **12/05** | 2,381 | 39 | 1.6% | 7,300 |
| **12/04** | 1,971 | 38 | 1.9% | 6,300 |
| **12/03** | 1,538 | (5) | — | 6,000 |
| **12/02** | 1,454 | (24) | — | 5,900 |
| **Annual Growth** | 26.0% | — | — | 6.9% |

**2006 Year-End Financials**

Debt ratio: 159.6%
Return on equity: 37.8%
Cash ($ mil.): 311
Current ratio: 1.74
Long-term debt ($ mil.): 685
No. of shares (mil.): 52
Dividends
Yield: —
Payout: —
Market value ($ mil.): 2,273

**Stock History** NYSE: BGC

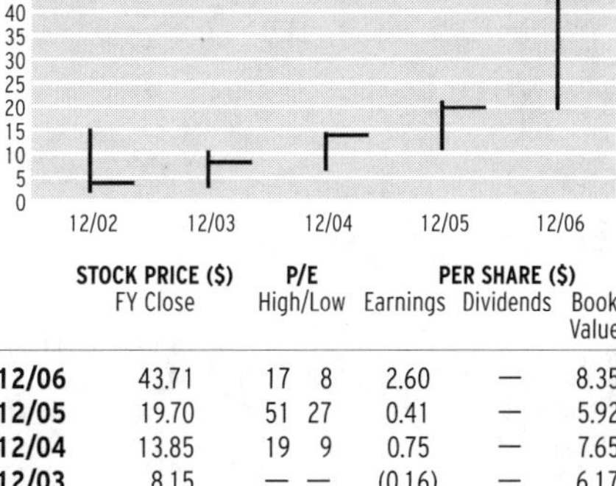


| | STOCK PRICE ($) FY Close | P/E High | P/E Low | PER SHARE ($) Earnings | Dividends | Book Value |
|---|---|---|---|---|---|---|
| **12/06** | 43.71 | 17 | 8 | 2.60 | — | 8.35 |
| **12/05** | 19.70 | 51 | 27 | 0.41 | — | 5.92 |
| **12/04** | 13.85 | 19 | 9 | 0.75 | — | 7.65 |
| **12/03** | 8.15 | — | — | (0.16) | — | 6.17 |
| **12/02** | 3.80 | — | — | (0.73) | 0.15 | 1.84 |
| **Annual Growth** | 84.2% | — | — | — | — | 46.0% |

# General Dynamics

Defense contractor General Dynamics brings it on by land, air, and sea. It operates in four areas: Information Systems & Technology (command and control systems), Marine Systems (warships and nuclear submarines), Combat Systems (tanks, amphibious assault vehicles, and munitions), and Aerospace (business jets). General Dynamics' Electric Boat subsidiary builds nuclear submarines (Seawolf, Ohio, Los Angeles classes); Bath Iron Works builds DDG 51 destroyers and LPD 17 landing craft; Land Systems builds the Abrams M1A1 and M1A2 main battle tanks and Fox reconnaissance vehicles; and Gulfstream Aerospace makes business jets. The US government accounts for more than two-thirds of sales.

General Dynamics has been focusing on its satellite communications and defense-related electronics operations and IT operations — as evidenced by its acquisitions of Veridian, Tri-Point Global Communications (ground-based satellite communications systems), and Spectrum Astro (satellite and ground-base integration). General Dynamics has also acquired IT specialist Anteon International. Anteon's operations are being rolled into those of General Dynamics Network Systems as a new division called General Dynamics Information Technology.

The company hasn't been ignoring its roots, though; it has broadened its "traditional" military operations by expanding into munitions for tanks and other weapons systems and by adding to its armored vehicle offerings through acquisitions. Early in 2006 General Dynamics agreed to acquire SNC Technologies, a Canadian ammunition maker, from SNC-Lavalin Group for about $275 million (the deal was completed early in 2007); it also sold Material Service Corporation, its aggregates subsidiary, to Hanson PLC for $300 million in 2006.

The war in Iraq and the push to improve military intelligence systems has been of particular benefit to General Dynamic's Information Systems & Technology unit. Veridian's four business groups have been integrated into General Dynamics' Information Systems & Technology division.

The chaos in Iraq has also led to increased orders for the Combat Systems unit. On the downside, expected Pentagon spending cuts are likely to hurt the company's Marine Systems unit in the future.

General Dynamics is the US Navy's #2 shipbuilder behind Northrop Grumman. The company's 2001 bid for rival shipmaker Newport News was thwarted by the Department of Justice, which sued to block General Dynamics' bid on antitrust grounds. General Dynamics then withdrew its bid and Northrop Grumman acquired Newport News.

## HISTORY

In 1899 John Holland founded Electric Boat Company, a New Jersey ship and submarine builder. The company built ships, PT boats, and submarines during WWII, but faced with waning postwar orders, CEO John Jay Hopkins diversified with the 1947 purchase of aircraft builder Canadair. Hopkins formed General Dynamics in 1952, merging Electric Boat and Canadair and buying Consolidated Vultee Aircraft (Convair), a major producer of military and civilian aircraft, in 1954.

Electric Boat launched the first nuclear submarine, the *Nautilus,* in the mid-1950s. In 1955, at the urging of Howard Hughes, Convair began designing its first commercial jetliners. Weakened by the planes' production costs, General Dynamics merged with building-materials supplier Material Service Corporation (1959). Nuclear subs became a mainstay for the company, and it abandoned jetliners in 1961 after losses on the planes reached the staggering sum of $425 million.

During the 1960s General Dynamics developed the controversial F-111 fighter. Despite numerous problems, the aircraft proved financially and militarily successful (F-111s participated in the 1986 US bombing raid on Libya).

In the following years the company won contracts for the US Navy's 688-class attack submarine (1971), liquefied natural gas tankers for Burmah Oil Company (1972), the Trident ballistic-missile submarine (1974), and the F-16 lightweight fighter aircraft (1975). The company sold Canadair in 1976 and bought Chrysler Defense, which had a contract to build the US Army's new M1 tank, in 1982.

The company bought Cessna Aircraft in 1986. The next year it won a contract to design and build the upper stage of the Titan IV space-launch rocket. Facing defense cuts, General Dynamics sold off pieces of the company: In 1992 it sold Cessna Aircraft to Textron and sold its missile operations to Hughes Aircraft; its electronics business was sold to The Carlyle Group in 1993. The company sold its space-systems business to Martin Marietta in 1994.

The next year General Dynamics began a buying spree with the purchase of shipbuilder Bath Iron Works. In 1996 it added Teledyne's combat vehicle unit, followed in 1997 by Lockheed Martin's Defense Systems and Armament Systems units and defense electronics units from Ceridian and Lucent. Also that year Nicholas Chabraja, director of Ceridian and former general counsel for General Dynamics, became CEO.

In 1999 General Dynamics bought business-jet maker Gulfstream Aerospace. In 2001 General Dynamics completed the $520 million acquisition of munitions maker Primex Technologies — now General Dynamics Ordnance and Tactical Systems (GD-OTS). The company also paid $330 million (plus contingency payments) to acquire Galaxy Aerospace, thus adding midsize aircraft to its Gulfstream lineup. Additionally, General Dynamics acquired Empresa Nacional Santa Bárbara de Industrias Militares (ENSB) of Spain.

In 2003 General Dynamics acquired General Motors' armored vehicle operations (for about $1.1 billion) and Austria's Steyr Spezialfahrzeug, maker of the Pandur line of wheeled armored vehicles. General Dynamics also acquired government security and intelligence specialist Veridian for about $1.5 billion in 2003.

In 2005 General Dynamics sold its aeronautics services business, which provides aeronautic testing, engineering, and support services, to Wyle Laboratories. Later that year it boosted its rugged computer operations by acquiring Itronix Corporation. Late in 2005 subsidiary Electric Boat said it would cut 2,400 jobs.

The following year General Dynamics acquired the large-caliber artillery and mortar projectile operations of Chamberlain Manufacturing for an undisclosed sum. Chamberlain is a subsidiary of Duchossois Industries.

## EXECUTIVES

**Chairman and CEO:** Nicholas D. (Nick) Chabraja, age 64, $4,500,000 pay
**EVP and Group Executive, Combat Systems:** Charles M. Hall, age 55
**EVP and Group Executive, Information Systems:** Gerard J. DeMuro, age 51, $1,262,500 pay
**EVP and Group Executive, Marine Systems:** Michael W. Toner, age 63
**SVP and CFO:** L. Hugh Redd, age 49, $778,333 pay
**SVP, General Counsel, and Secretary:** David A. Savner, age 63, $1,162,500 pay
**SVP, Planning and Development:** Phebe N. Novakovic, age 49
**SVP, Human Resources and Administration:** Walter M. Oliver, age 61
**SVP; President, Land Systems:** David K. Heebner
**VP and Controller:** John W. Schwartz, age 50
**VP and Treasurer:** David H. Fogg
**VP, Communications:** Kendell M. Pease, age 60
**VP, Government Relations:** Cordis (Cork) Colburn, age 61
**VP; President, Advanced Information Systems:** Lewis A. Von Thaer, age 46
**VP; President, European Land Combat Systems:** John C. Ulrich
**VP; President, European Land Combat System:** H. Michael Malzacher
**VP; President, Armament and Technical Products:** Michael J. Mulligan, age 43
**VP; President, Aviation Services:** Larry R. Flynn
**VP; President, Electric Boat Corporation:** John P. Casey, age 55
**VP; President, Network Systems:** Michael E. Chandler, age 62
**President, Bath Iron Works:** John F. (Dugan) Shipway
**President, National Steel and Shipbuilding Company:** Frederick J. (Fred) Harris, age 61
**President, General Dynamics C4 Systems:** Christopher Marzilli, age 47
**Auditors:** KPMG LLP

## LOCATIONS

**HQ:** General Dynamics Corporation
2941 Fairview Park Dr., Ste. 100,
Falls Church, VA 22042
**Phone:** 703-876-3000 **Fax:** 703-876-3125
**Web:** www.gendyn.com

General Dynamics has operations in more than 20 US states, as well as in Austria, Canada, Germany, Mexico, Spain, Switzerland, and the UK.

### 2006 Sales

| | $ mil. | % of total |
|---|---|---|
| North America | | |
| US | 20,241 | 84 |
| Canada | 429 | 2 |
| Other countries | 96 | — |
| Europe | | |
| UK | 1,000 | 4 |
| Spain | 700 | 3 |
| Other countries | 573 | 2 |
| Asia/Pacific | 639 | 3 |
| Africa/Middle East | 242 | 1 |
| South America | 143 | 1 |
| **Total** | **24,063** | **100** |

## PRODUCTS/OPERATIONS

### 2006 Sales

| | $ mil. | % of total |
|---|---|---|
| Information systems & technology | 9,024 | 37 |
| Combat systems | 5,983 | 25 |
| Marine systems | 4,940 | 21 |
| Aerospace | 4,116 | 17 |
| **Total** | **24,063** | **100** |

### 2006 Sales

| | $ mil. | % of total |
|---|---|---|
| US government | 16,415 | 67 |
| US commercial | 3,833 | 17 |
| International | 3,815 | 16 |
| **Total** | **24,063** | **100** |

### Selected Operations

Information systems and technology
- Actionable intelligence, surveillance, and reconnaissance
- Homeland security
- Information assurance
- Integrated space systems
- Maritime combat systems

Combat systems
- Armament Systems
  - Advanced materials (composites)
  - Detection systems (biological and chemical detection systems)
  - Gun and munition systems
  - Hydra 70 2.75" air-to-ground rocket
- Land systems
  - Advanced Amphibious Assault Vehicle (AAAV)
  - M1A1 and M1A2 Abrams Main Battle Tank
  - Pandur 6x6 and 8x8 wheeled armored vehicles
  - Stryker Mobile Gun System
- Ordnance and tactical systems
  - Electronic products
  - Munitions
  - Propellants
  - Satellite propulsion systems

Marine systems
- American Overseas Marine (ship-management services)
- Bath Iron Works Corp.
  - Arleigh Burke class DDG 51 destroyer
  - Class DD 21 land attack destroyer
  - Class LPD 17 amphibious assault transport
- Electric Boat Corp.
  - New Attack submarine (Virginia class)
  - Seawolf attack submarine
- General Dynamics Defense Systems, Inc.
- National Steel and Shipbuilding Company

Aerospace
- Gulfstream Aerospace
  - Large-cabin business jet (Gulfstream IV-SP; up to 4,220 nautical miles distance)
  - Long-range, large-cabin business jet (Gulfstream V; up to 6,500 nautical miles distance)

## COMPETITORS

Airbus
BAE SYSTEMS
Boeing
Bombardier
Dassault Aviation
Dewey Electronics
EDS
Harris Corp.
Harsco
Herley Industries
Interstate Electronics
ITT Corp.
L-3 Communications
Lockheed Martin
Northrop Grumman
Park Air Systems
Peugeot
Raytheon
Renco
Rockwell Collins
Sperry Marine
Textron
Westwood

## HISTORICAL FINANCIALS

Company Type: Public

### Income Statement

FYE: December 31

| | REVENUE ($ mil.) | NET INCOME ($ mil.) | NET PROFIT MARGIN | EMPLOYEES |
|---|---|---|---|---|
| **12/06** | 24,063 | 1,856 | 7.7% | 81,000 |
| **12/05** | 21,244 | 1,461 | 6.9% | 72,200 |
| **12/04** | 19,178 | 1,227 | 6.4% | 70,200 |
| **12/03** | 16,617 | 1,004 | 6.0% | 67,600 |
| **12/02** | 13,829 | 917 | 6.6% | 54,000 |
| **Annual Growth** | 14.9% | 19.3% | — | 10.7% |

### 2006 Year-End Financials

Debt ratio: 28.2%
Return on equity: 20.7%
Cash ($ mil.): 1,604
Current ratio: 1.26
Long-term debt ($ mil.): 2,774
No. of shares (mil.): 406
Dividends
Yield: 1.2%
Payout: 19.5%
Market value ($ mil.): 30,171

**Stock History** NYSE: GD

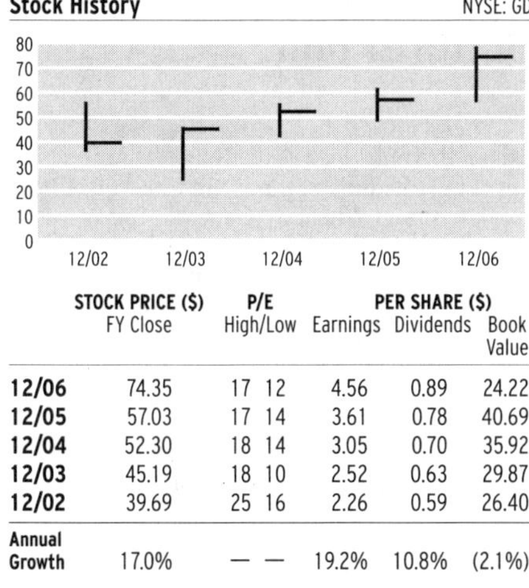


| | STOCK PRICE ($) FY Close | P/E High/Low | | PER SHARE ($) Earnings | Dividends | Book Value |
|---|---|---|---|---|---|---|
| **12/06** | 74.35 | 17 | 12 | 4.56 | 0.89 | 24.22 |
| **12/05** | 57.03 | 17 | 14 | 3.61 | 0.78 | 40.69 |
| **12/04** | 52.30 | 18 | 14 | 3.05 | 0.70 | 35.92 |
| **12/03** | 45.19 | 18 | 10 | 2.52 | 0.63 | 29.87 |
| **12/02** | 39.69 | 25 | 16 | 2.26 | 0.59 | 26.40 |
| **Annual Growth** | 17.0% | — | — | 19.2% | 10.8% | (2.1%) |

# General Electric

From turbines to TV, from household appliances to power plants, General Electric (GE) is plugged in to most of the businesses that have shaped the modern world. The company produces — take a deep breath — aircraft engines, locomotives and other transportation equipment, kitchen and laundry appliances, lighting, electric distribution and control equipment, generators and turbines, and medical imaging equipment. GE is also one of the largest financial services companies in the US, offering commercial finance, consumer finance, and equipment financing. Other operations include the NBC television network. The company is selling its GE Plastics unit to SABIC for more than $11 billion.

GE is organized into six industry-focused lines: GE Money, GE Commercial Finance, GE Healthcare, GE Infrastructure, GE Industrial, and NBC Universal (80% owned).

CEO Jeff Immelt is emerging from the considerable shadow of his predecessor, Jack Welch, by not being shy about making sweeping changes. He has diverged somewhat from Welch's slavish obsession with the bottom line and encourages managers to innovate and take more risks. As a result, GE has been growing in such areas as biotech, renewable energy, nanotechnology, and digital technology. Immelt has, however, taken a page from his former boss' playbook by pursuing growth outside the US, particularly in emerging markets like India, China, Eastern Europe, Africa, and the Middle East.

Immelt has set about reshaping GE, spinning off its life and mortgage insurance businesses into a new entity, Genworth Financial, which went public in 2004; it completely divested its remaining stake in Genworth in 2006. Also that year, GE sold off most of its remaining insurance businesses, including GE Insurance Solutions and Employers Reinsurance, in a sale to Swiss Re. The company kept its US life reinsurance business.

Meanwhile, GE has also been building some of its traditional businesses through acquisitions. In early 2007 the company's aviation division acquired aircraft systems manufacturer Smiths Aerospace from Smiths Group. GE Energy bought oil and gas production equipment supplier Vetco Gray and US retail natural gas distribution network of Kinder Morgan, while GE Industrial acquired Microwave Data Systems.

Later that year GE announced that it will buy PHH Corporation; GE will retain the company's fleet management unit, PHH Arval, but will sell PHH Mortgage to Blackstone Group.

## HISTORY

General Electric (GE) was established in 1892 in New York, the result of a merger between Thomson-Houston and Edison General Electric. Charles Coffin was GE's first president, and Thomas Edison, who left the company in 1894, was one of the directors.

GE's financial strength (backed by the Morgan banking house) and its research focus contributed to its initial success. Early products included such Edison legacies as light bulbs, elevators, motors, toasters, and other appliances under the GE and Hotpoint labels. In the 1920s GE joined AT&T and Westinghouse in a radio broadcasting venture, Radio Corporation of America (RCA), but GE sold off its RCA holdings in 1930 because of an antitrust ruling.

By 1980 GE had reached $25 billion in revenues from plastics, consumer electronics, nuclear reactors, and jet engines. But it had become rigid and bureaucratic. Jack Welch became president in 1981 and shook up the company. He decentralized operations and adopted a strategy of pursuing only high-achieving ventures and dumping those that didn't perform. GE shed air-conditioning (1982), housewares (1984), and semiconductors (1988), and with the proceeds acquired Employers Reinsurance (1984); RCA, including NBC (1986, but sold RCA in 1987); CGR medical equipment (1987); and investment banker Kidder, Peabody (1990).

In the early 1990s GE grew its lighting business. It bought mutual fund wholesaler GNA in 1993, and GE Investment Management (now GE Financial Network) began selling mutual funds to the public.

GE sold scandal-plagued Kidder, Peabody to Paine Webber in 1994. General Electric Capital Services (GECS) expanded its lines, buying Amex Life Insurance (Aon's Union Fidelity unit) and Life Insurance Co. of Virginia in 1995 and First Colony the next year. The company formed an NBC and Microsoft venture, the MSNBC cable news channel in 1996.

GE acquired Lockheed Martin's medical imaging unit in 1997. In 1998 GECS became the first foreign company to enter Japan's life insurance market when it bought assets from Toho Mutual Life Insurance and set up GE Edison Life.

In 1999 GECS bought the 53% of Montgomery Ward it didn't already own, along with the retailer's direct-marketing arm, as Montgomery Ward emerged from bankruptcy. (Ward declared bankruptcy again in 2000.) In 2000 it reorganized GE Information Systems to form an e-commerce unit, Global eXchange Services (GXS). (GE sold 90% of GXS to buyout firm Francisco Partners in 2002.)

Later in 2000 the company announced its biggest acquisition of the Welch era. Moving in at the last minute, GE trumped a rival bid from United Technologies and agreed to pay $45 billion in stock for manufacturing giant Honeywell International and to assume $3.4 billion in Honeywell debt.

Welch, by then viewed as one of the best corporate leaders in the US, had agreed to postpone his retirement from April 2001 until the end of that year in order to oversee the completion of the Honeywell acquisition. But European regulators, concerned about the potential strength of the combined GE-Honeywell aircraft-related businesses, blocked the Honeywell deal that summer. Welch then stepped down, and Jeff Immelt, formerly president and CEO of GE Medical Systems, succeeded him in September 2001.

Also in 2001 GE Capital expanded by buying commercial lender Heller Financial for $5.3 billion. The next year former business segment GE Industrial Systems acquired electronic security company Interlogix for $777 million.

In a move intended to provide a clearer picture for investors, Immelt in 2002 divided the former GE Capital into four units — GE Commercial Finance, GE Consumer Finance, GE Equipment Management, and GE Insurance.

In 2003 GE acquired UK-based Amersham, a medical diagnostics and life sciences company, as well as First National Bank, Allbank, and the retail sales finance business of Conseco.

## EXECUTIVES

**Chairman and CEO:** Jeffrey R. (Jeff) Immelt, age 51, $8,300,000 pay
**Director:** Sir William M. (Bill) Castell, age 59
**Vice Chairman:** Robert C. (Bob) Wright, age 64, $9,400,000 pay
**Vice Chairman; President and CEO, Commercial Finance; Chairman, Capital Services:** Michael A. (Mike) Neal, age 53, $4,700,000 pay
**Vice Chairman; President and CEO, Infrastructure:** John G. Rice, age 50, $3,950,000 pay
**Vice Chairman; President and CEO, Industrial:** Lloyd G. Trotter, age 61
**Vice Chairman, SVP, and CFO:** Keith S. Sherin, age 48, $3,775,000 pay
**SVP Human Resources:** John F. Lynch, age 54
**SVP Corporate Business Development:** Pamela Daley, age 54
**SVP and CIO:** Gary M. Reiner, age 52
**SVP and Director of Global Research:** Mark M. Little, age 53
**SVP and General Counsel:** Brackett B. Denniston III, age 59
**SVP; President and CEO, GE Money:** David R. (Dave) Nissen, age 55
**SVP; President and CEO, Energy:** John Krenicki Jr., age 45
**SVP; President and CEO, GE Real Estate:** Ronald R. (Ron) Pressman, age 49
**VP and Chief Intellectual Property Counsel:** Q. Todd Dickinson
**VP and Chief Marketing Officer:** Daniel S. (Dan) Henson, age 44
**VP and Comptroller:** Philip D. Ameen, age 58
**VP Corporate Investor Communications:** Daniel C. Janki, age 37
**VP and Treasurer:** Kathryn A. (Kathy) Cassidy, age 52
**President and CEO, Consumer and Industrial:** James P. (Jim) Campbell
**President and CEO, Healthcare:** Joseph M. (Joe) Hogan, age 50
**President and CEO, GE Enterprise Solutions:** Charlene T. Begley, age 40
**President and CEO, NBC Universal:** Jeffrey A. (Jeff) Zucker, age 41
**Executive Director, Communications and Public Affairs:** Gary Sheffer
**Auditors:** KPMG LLP

## LOCATIONS

**HQ:** General Electric Company
3135 Easton Tpke., Fairfield, CT 06828
**Phone:** 203-373-2211 **Fax:** 203-373-3131
**Web:** www.ge.com

## PRODUCTS/OPERATIONS

### 2006 Sales

| | $ mil. | % of total |
|---|---|---|
| Infrastructure | 47,429 | 29 |
| Industrial | 33,494 | 20 |
| Commercial finance | 23,792 | 15 |
| GE Money | 21,759 | 13 |
| Healthcare | 16,562 | 10 |
| NBC Universal | 16,188 | 10 |
| Corporate items & eliminations | 4,167 | 3 |
| **Total** | **163,391** | **100** |

### 2006 Sales

| | $ mil. | % of total |
|---|---|---|
| Sales of goods | 64,297 | 39 |
| GE Capital Services | 60,154 | 37 |
| Sales of services | 36,403 | 22 |
| Other | 2,537 | 2 |
| **Total** | **163,391** | **100** |

### Selected Subsidiaries

Amersham plc (UK)
Bently Nevada, LLC
Caribe GE International of Puerto Rico, Inc.
Cardinal Cogen, Inc.
Datex-Ohmeda, Inc.
GE Canada Company
GE Drives and Controls, Inc.
GE Druck Holdings Limited (UK)
GE Energy Europe, B.V. (the Netherlands)
GE Energy Parts, Inc.
GE Energy Products France SNC
GE Energy Services, Inc.
GE Energy Services-Dallas, LP
GE Engine Services Distribution, LLC
GE Engine Services, Inc.
GE Fanuc Automation Corporation
GE Healthcare AS (Norway)
GE Healthcare Bio-Sciences AB (Sweden)
GE Healthcare Finland Oy
GE Healthcare Ltd. (UK)
GE Hungary Co., Ltd.
GE Infrastructure, Inc.
GE Ionics, Inc.
GE Lighting/Plastics Austria GmbH & Co KG
GE Medical Systems Global Technology Company, LLC
GE Medical Systems Information Technologies, Inc.
GE Medical Systems, Inc.
GE Medical Systems, Ultrasound & Primary Care Diagnostics LLC
GE Military Systems
GE Osmonics, Inc.
GE Packaged Power L.P.
GE Security, Inc.
GE Transportation Parts, LLC
GE Transportation Systems Global Signaling, LLC
GE Wind Energy, LLC
General Electric Capital Services, Inc.
General Electric Capital Corporation
General Electric International, Inc.
Granite Services, Inc.
NBC Universal
Nuclear Fuel Holding Co., Inc.
Nuovo Pignone Holdings S.p.A. (99%, Italy)
OEC Medical Systems, Inc.
PII Limited (UK)
Reuter-Stokes, Inc.
Unison Industries LLC
Viceroy, Inc.

## COMPETITORS

Agilent Technologies
AIG
ALSTOM
Bank of America
Capital One
Caterpillar
CBS Corp
CIGNA
CIT Group
Citigroup
Cooper Industries
Disney
Electrolux
General Motors
General Re
Hitachi
ITT Corp.
Jacuzzi Brands
Johnson Controls
JPMorgan Chase
Matsushita Electric
News Corp.
Philips Electronics
Polaroid
Raytheon
Rockwell Automation
Rohm and Haas
Rolls-Royce
Siemens AG
Sony
Textron
ThyssenKrupp
Toshiba
United Technologies
Viacom
Washington Group
Wells Fargo
Whirlpool

## HISTORICAL FINANCIALS

Company Type: Public

### Income Statement

FYE: December 31

| | ASSETS ($ mil.) | NET INCOME ($ mil.) | INCOME AS % OF ASSETS | EMPLOYEES |
|---|---|---|---|---|
| **12/06** | 697,239 | 20,829 | 3.0% | 319,000 |
| **12/05** | 673,321 | 16,711 | 2.5% | 316,000 |
| **12/04** | 750,507 | 16,819 | 2.2% | 307,000 |
| **12/03** | 647,483 | 15,002 | 2.3% | 305,000 |
| **12/02** | 575,244 | 14,118 | 2.5% | 315,000 |
| **Annual Growth** | 4.9% | 10.2% | — | 0.3% |

### 2006 Year-End Financials

Equity as % of assets: 16.1%
Return on assets: 3.0%
Return on equity: 18.8%
Long-term debt ($ mil.): 260,804
No. of shares (mil.): 10,277
Dividends
Yield: 2.8%
Payout: 51.2%
Market value ($ mil.): 382,421
Sales ($ mil.): 163,391

### Stock History

NYSE: GE

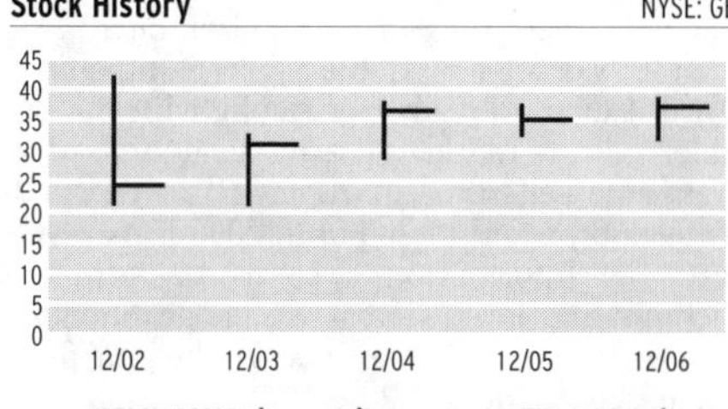

| | STOCK PRICE ($) FY Close | P/E High/Low | PER SHARE ($) Earnings | Dividends | Book Value |
|---|---|---|---|---|---|
| **12/06** | 37.21 | 19 16 | 2.01 | 1.03 | 10.93 |
| **12/05** | 35.05 | 24 21 | 1.57 | 0.91 | 10.43 |
| **12/04** | 36.50 | 24 18 | 1.60 | 0.82 | 10.47 |
| **12/03** | 30.98 | 22 14 | 1.49 | 0.77 | 7.87 |
| **12/02** | 24.35 | 30 15 | 1.41 | 0.73 | 6.39 |
| **Annual Growth** | 11.2% | — — | 9.3% | 9.0% | 14.4% |

# General Mills

General Mills gets its Kix as the US's #2 cereal maker (behind *uber*-rival Kellogg). Among its Big G Cereals unit's brands are Cheerios, Chex, Total, Kix, and Wheaties. General Mills is also a brand leader in flour (Gold Medal), baking mixes (Betty Crocker, Bisquick), dinner mixes (Hamburger Helper), fruit snacks (Fruit Roll-Ups), and grain snacks (Chex Mix, Pop Secret). It is also a leader in branded yogurt (Colombo, Go-Gurt, and Yoplait). Through joint ventures, the company's products are available worldwide. Its 2001 acquisition of Pillsbury (refrigerated dough products, frozen vegetables) from Diageo doubled the company's size, making General Mills one of the world's largest food companies.

While most of its brands are best found in supermarkets, the company has entered the natural foods niche by acquiring its Small Planet subsidiary which makes natural foods brands Muir Glen (canned tomato products) and Cascadian Farms (frozen fruits and vegetables).

Acknowledging that the low-carb trend of the early 2000s had peaked, General Mills began concentrating on more healthy and convenient offerings. The company now makes all of its Big G cereals using whole grains. (Big G brands include Cinnamon Toast Crunch, Golden Grahams, Honey Nut Cheerios, Lucky Charms, and Trix.). In 2007 it partnered with Curves International to introduce a weight-management brand (Curves) of cereal and granola bars.

After more than 10 years of being ignored, the Jolly Green Giant came out of retirement in 2005 as part of a multi-million dollar marketing campaign by General Mills to up its veggie sales. The next year, General Mills declined to renew its licensing agreement with Archer Daniels Midland regarding the sale and marketing of Pillsbury Bakery Flour to the industrial and foodservice sectors. General Mills integrated the brand, which consists of mixes and frozen bakery products, into its bakery ingredients segment.

In order to develop healthier products, in 2006 the company entered a supply agreement for DAH (an omega-3 fatty acid said to play a role in mental and cardiovascular health) with Martek Biosciences, maker of DAH (which is already widely used in infant formula).

General Mills pulled its reduced-sugar children's cereal from the market in 2007 due to poor sales. Sweetened with Splenda, the cereals never took off with consumers, perhaps due to resistance to the sugar replacement. (Kellogg and Kraft use sugar in their reduced-sugar cereal offerings.)

General Mills products are manufactured in 18 countries and available in 130 countries throughout the world.

## HISTORY

Cadwallader Washburn built his first flour mill in 1866 in Minneapolis, which eventually became the Washburn Crosby Company. After winning a gold medal for flour at an 1880 exposition, the company changed the name of its best flour to Gold Medal Flour.

In 1921 advertising manager Sam Gale created fictional spokeswoman Betty Crocker so that correspondence to housewives could go out with her signature. The firm introduced Wheaties cereal in 1924. James Bell, named president in 1925, consolidated the company with other US mills in

1928 to form General Mills, the world's largest miller. The companies operated independently of one another, with corporate headquarters coordinating advertising and merchandising.

General Mills began introducing convenience foods such as Bisquick (1931) and Cheerios (1941). During WWII it produced war goods such as ordnance equipment and developed chemical and electronics divisions.

When Edwin Rawlings became CEO in 1961, he closed half of the flour mills and divested such unprofitable lines as electronics. This cost $200 million in annual sales but freed resources for such acquisitions as Kenner Products (toys, 1967) and Parker Brothers (board games, 1968), which made General Mills the world's largest toy company.

Through the next 20 years the company made many acquisitions, including Gorton's (frozen seafood, 1968), Monet (jewelry, 1968), Eddie Bauer (outerwear, 1971), and The Talbots (women's clothing, 1973). It bought Red Lobster in 1970 and acquired the US rights to Yoplait yogurt in 1977. When the toy and fashion divisions' profits fell in 1984, they were spun off as Kenner Parker Toys and Crystal Brands (1985). Reemphasizing food in 1989, the firm sold many businesses, including Eddie Bauer and Talbots.

To expand into Europe, General Mills struck two important joint ventures: Cereal Partners Worldwide (with Nestlé in 1989) and Snack Ventures Europe (with PepsiCo in 1992).

As part of a cereal price war, in 1994 the company cut coupon promotion costs by $175 million and lowered prices on many cereals. But some retailers did not pass on the price cuts to consumers due to shortages that developed after the FDA found an unauthorized pesticide in some cereals. General Mills destroyed 55 million boxes of cereal at a cost of $140 million. Stephen Sanger became CEO in 1995. That year the company sold Gorton's to Unilever and spun off its restaurant businesses as Darden Restaurants.

In the late 1990s, focused on a food-only future, the company picked up several smaller businesses, including Ralcorp Holdings' Chex cereal and snack lines and Gardetto's Bakery snack mixes. Entering the natural foods market in 2000, General Mills launched Sunrise organic cereal and bought organic foods producer Small Planet Foods.

Big changes came in 2001 when General Mills became the #1 cereal maker in the US, overtaking Kellogg for the first time since 1906. The company then completed its $10.5 billion purchase of Pillsbury from Diageo in October 2001. A month later General Mills sold competing product lines to International Multifoods.

In 2004 Diageo sold part of its approximate 20% stake in General Mills. General Mills, in turn, sold an $835 million stake to an affiliate of Lehman Brothers Holding and used $750 million to buy back the Diageo shares and $85 million to pay down debt.

Also in 2004 the company sold its US Häagen-Dazs ice cream shop franchise business to Dreyer's Grand Ice Cream. In 2005 it sold its stake in Snack Ventures Europe joint venture to PepsiCo for $750 million.

In 2005 Diageo sold two-thirds of its 20% stake in General Mills. In 2006 Cereal Partners Worldwide (joint venture with Nestlé) acquired the Australian breakfast cereal operations of Uncle Tobys from Burns Philp.

## EXECUTIVES

**Chairman and CEO:** Stephen W. Sanger, age 61, $3,359,810 pay
**President, COO, and Director:** Kendall J. (Ken) Powell, age 52, $1,273,731 pay
**EVP and COO, U.S. Retail:** Ian R. Friendly, age 46
**EVP and COO, International:** Christopher D. O'Leary, age 47
**EVP and CFO:** Donal L. (Don) Mulligan, age 46
**EVP, Worldwide Health, Brand and New Business Development:** Y. Marc Belton, age 45
**EVP, Worldwide Operations and Technology:** Randy G. Darcy, age 55, $1,006,875 pay
**EVP, Worldwide Sales and Channel Development:** Jeffrey J. (Jeff) Rotsch, age 55, $966,135 pay
**SVP; President, Europe, Latin America, and Africa:** Giuseppe A. D'Angelo
**SVP, Human Resources and Corporate Services:** Michael A. (Mike) Peel, age 56
**SVP, General Counsel, Chief Governance and Compliance Officer, and Secretary:** Siri S. Marshall, age 58
**SVP; President, Bakeries and Foodservice:** John T. Machuzick
**SVP; President, Big G Cereals:** Peter J. Capell
**SVP; President, Greater China:** Gary Chu
**SVP; President, International:** Lucio Rizzi
**SVP, Strategic Technology Development:** Rory A. M. Delaney, age 61
**SVP; President and CEO, Cereal Partners Worldwide:** Christianne L. (Christi) Strauss
**SVP; President, Yoplait-Colombo:** Robert P. (Bob) Waldron
**SVP; President, Pillsbury USA:** Juliana L. Chugg, age 39
**VP, Corporate Communications:** Thomas (Tom) Forsythe
**Auditors:** KPMG LLP

## LOCATIONS

**HQ:** General Mills, Inc.
1 General Mills Blvd., Minneapolis, MN 55426
**Phone:** 763-764-7600 **Fax:** 763-764-7384
**Web:** www.generalmills.com

### 2007 Sales

| | $ mil. | % of total |
|---|---|---|
| US | 10,258 | 82 |
| Other countries | 2,184 | 18 |
| **Total** | **12,442** | **100** |

## PRODUCTS/OPERATIONS

### 2007 Sales

| | $ mil. | % of total |
|---|---|---|
| US retail | 8,491 | 68 |
| International | 2,124 | 17 |
| Bakeries & foodservice | 1,827 | 15 |
| **Total** | **12,442** | **100** |

### Selected Brands

Dessert and baking mixes
- Betty Crocker
- Bisquick
- Creamy Deluxe
- Gold Medal
- SuperMoist
- Warm Delights

Dry dinners and shelf stable and frozen vegetable products
- Bac*O's
- Betty Crocker Complete Meals
- Chicken Helper
- Diablitos
- Green Giant
- Hamburger Helper
- Old El Paso
- Potato Buds
- Simply Steam
- Suddenly Salad
- Tuna Helper

Frozen pizza and pizza snacks
- Jeno's
- Pillsbury Pizza Minis
- Pizza Rolls
- Totino's

Grain, fruit, and savory snacks
- Bugles
- Chex Mix
- Fiber One
- Fruit Roll-Ups
- Gardetto's
- Gushers
- Nature Valley

Ice cream and frozen desserts
- Häagen-Dazs

Microwave popcorn
- PopSecret

Organic products
- Cascadian Farm
- Muir Glen

Ready-to-eat cereals
- Basic 4
- Cheerios
- Chex
- Cinnamon Toast Crunch
- Clusters
- Cocoa Puffs
- Cookie Crisp
- Fiber One
- Golden Grahams
- Kix
- Lucky Charms
- Nature Valley
- Oatmeal Crisp
- Reese's Puffs
- Total
- Trix
- Uncle Tobys
- Wheaties

Ready-to-serve soup
- Progresso

Refrigerated and frozen dough products
- Forno de Minas
- Frescarini
- Golden Layers
- Grands!
- Jus-Rol
- La Salteña
- Latina
- Pillsbury
- Saxby's
- Toaster Strudel
- Wanchai Ferry

Refrigerated yogurt
- Colombo
- Go-GURT
- Yoplait Kids
- Yoplait

## COMPETITORS

Bay State Milling
Campbell Soup
Chelsea Milling
ConAgra
Danone
Del Monte Foods
Frito-Lay
Gilster-Mary Lee
Heinz
Heinz Canada
Heinz Foodservice
Heinz North America Consumer Products
H.J. Heinz Limited
Kellogg
King Arthur Flour
Kraft Foods
Malt-O-Meal
Mars
McKee Foods
Pinnacle Foods
Procter & Gamble
Pro-Fac
Ralcorp
Stonyfield Farm

## HISTORICAL FINANCIALS

Company Type: Public

### Income Statement

FYE: Last Sunday in May

| | REVENUE ($ mil.) | NET INCOME ($ mil.) | NET PROFIT MARGIN | EMPLOYEES |
|---|---|---|---|---|
| **5/07** | 12,442 | 1,144 | 9.2% | 28,500 |
| **5/06** | 11,640 | 1,090 | 9.4% | 28,100 |
| **5/05** | 11,244 | 1,240 | 11.0% | 27,800 |
| **5/04** | 11,070 | 1,055 | 9.5% | 27,580 |
| **5/03** | 10,506 | 917 | 8.7% | 27,300 |
| **Annual Growth** | 4.3% | 5.7% | — | 1.1% |

### 2007 Year-End Financials

Debt ratio: 60.5%
Return on equity: 20.6%
Cash ($ mil.): 417
Current ratio: 0.52
Long-term debt ($ mil.): 3,218

No. of shares (mil.): 340
Dividends
Yield: 2.4%
Payout: 45.3%
Market value ($ mil.): 20,451

### Stock History

NYSE: GIS

70
60
50
40
30
20
10
0
5/03 5/04 5/05 5/06 5/07

| | STOCK PRICE ($) FY Close | P/E High/Low | | PER SHARE ($) Earnings | Dividends | Book Value |
|---|---|---|---|---|---|---|
| **5/07** | 60.15 | 19 | 15 | 3.18 | 1.44 | 15.64 |
| **5/06** | 51.79 | 18 | 15 | 2.90 | 1.34 | 16.21 |
| **5/05** | 49.68 | 17 | 14 | 3.08 | 1.24 | 15.38 |
| **5/04** | 46.05 | 18 | 16 | 2.75 | 1.10 | 13.85 |
| **5/03** | 46.56 | 20 | 15 | 2.43 | 1.10 | 11.28 |
| **Annual Growth** | 6.6% | — | — | 7.0% | 7.0% | 8.5% |

# General Motors

So far General Motors (GM) has steered around competitors to remain the world's #1 maker of cars and trucks, with brands such as Buick, Cadillac, Chevrolet, GMC, Pontiac, Saab, and Saturn. GM also produces cars through its Holden, Opel, and Vauxhall units. GM also has stakes in Suzuki Motor, and GM Daewoo Auto & Technology. Subsidiary GMAC provides financing. GM has been selling off non-core assets including stakes in Fiat and Fuji Heavy Industries (Subaru), as well as its locomotive manufacturing business. GM is in the midst of restructuring its sprawling North American operations.

The Chapter 11 filing of former GM parts subsidiary Delphi Corp. cast a shadow of potential bankruptcy on GM after the automaker reported a staggering 2005 loss of $10.6 billion. GM has said it needs to reach 100% plant capacity by 2008, saying it will have to reduce its workforce by as many as 30,000 and close 12 plants.

Health care costs have been an albatross hanging over GM's head for years. To address its health care woes GM has hammered out a tentative deal with the United Auto Workers (UAW) union that would reduce GM's payout for retiree health care by about $15 billion while cutting employee health care costs by about $3 billion. In another UAW-GM scheme, GM offered to finance the early retirement of thousands of unionized GM and Delphi workers. By mid-2006 GM had reached its target of more than 20,000 blue-collar workers accepting the buyouts. Ultimately, about 35,000 hourly employees, or about one-third of GM's hourly workforce, accepted the buyouts. In addition to hourly job cuts, GM has also announced it would cut 7% of its white collar positions, or about 2,500 jobs.

To help pay the bills while it restructures GM has sold some assets. GM's finance arm, GMAC, sold a 78% equity stake in its commercial mortgage business to a private equity consortium including Kohlberg Kravis Roberts & Co., Five Mile Capital Partners, and Goldman Sachs Partners. The deal raised nearly $9 billion for GMAC. GM has also sold a 51% stake in GMAC to a consortium of investors led by Cerberus Capital Management for $14 billion.

GM has also unloaded its entire stake in Fuji Heavy Industries and reduced its stake in Suzuki from 20% to 3%. The company has also sold its 8% stake in Isuzu to Mitsubishi Corp., ITOCHU Corp., and Mizuho Corporate Bank for $300 million. Mitsubishi Corp. and ITOCHU Corp. sold the stake in Isuzu to Toyota Motor in late 2006. In 2007 GM also sold its Allison Transmission commercial and military business to The Carlyle Group and Onex Corp. for about $5.6 billion.

Outside of North America GM's fortunes don't look as bleak. GM's unit sales keep climbing in China and in 2006 the company increased its market share for the fifth consecutive year and is the leading foreign car maker in China.

To maintain its leadership position, GM plans to double its production capacity, introduce new models, and has set up a financing venture with Chinese partner Shanghai Automotive Industry Corporation.

## HISTORY

In the early years of the auto industry, hundreds of carmakers each produced a few models. William Durant, who bought a failing Buick Motors in 1904, reasoned that manufacturers could benefit from banding together and formed the General Motors Company in Flint, Michigan, in 1908.

Durant bought 17 companies (including Oldsmobile, Cadillac, and Pontiac) by 1910, the year a bankers' syndicate forced him to step down. In 1915 he regained control when he formed a company with racecar driver Louis Chevrolet. They soon formed GM Acceptance Corporation (GMAC, financing) and bought businesses including Frigidaire (sold in 1979) and Hyatt Roller Bearing.

With Hyatt came Alfred Sloan (president, 1923-37), who built GM into a corporate colossus via a decentralized management system. Unlike Ford — which offered cars in any color you liked as long as it was black — GM offered a range of models and colors; by 1927 it was the industry leader. It bought Vauxhall Motors (UK, 1925), merged with Adam Opel (Germany, 1931), added defense products for WWII, and diversified into home appliances and locomotives.

In the post-war boom years GM expanded with the nation; the good times rolled until Japanese automakers became established in the 1970s. GM spent much of the decade trying to emulate the Japanese while making its cars meet federal pollution-control mandates. CEO Roger Smith laid off thousands of workers.

GM bought Electronic Data Systems (1984), Hughes Aircraft (1986), and 50% of Saab Automobile (1989). GM launched the Saturn car in 1990; that year Robert Stempel became CEO. In 1992 Jack Smith replaced Stempel as CEO.

GM spun off Electronic Data Systems the next year in 1996. In 1997 it sold the defense electronics business of Hughes Electronics to Raytheon.

UAW walkouts at two Michigan GM parts plants in 1998 forced the shutdown of virtually all of the company's North American production lines. In 1999 GM spun off Delphi and boosted its stake in small-truck partner Isuzu to 49%. The next year GM acquired the 50% of Saab Automobile that it didn't already own (from Investor AB).

President Rick Wagoner replaced Smith as CEO in June 2000. In 2001 GM paid about $600 million to double its stake in Suzuki to 20%. The following year GM took a 42% stake in South Korea's bankrupt Daewoo Motor. GM later increased its stake to 50%.

2004 marked the last model year for GM's Oldsmobile brand. The world's last Oldsmobile rolled off the assembly line in June 2004 — almost 100 years after GM first bought the brand. That year GM announced it would trim 12,000 jobs in Europe (one-fifth of its European workforce).

Early in 2006 GM also sold the bulk of its stake in Suzuki Motor back to the Japanese carmaker for about $2 billion. The deal cut GM's stake in Suzuki from 20% to 3%. Later in 2006 billionaire GM investor Kirk Kerkorian (owned about a 10% stake) suggested GM might improve its fortunes by hooking up a three-way alliance with Nissan Motor and Renault, both of which are helmed by automotive turnaround guru Carlos Ghosn. Kerkorian's advise quickly prompted board meetings at all three companies to consider the idea. After a 90-day examination of an alliance's potential, Renault and GM walked away from the table in the midst of the 2006 Paris Auto Show without a deal.

As 2006 wound to a close Kerkorian slowly reduced his stake; first to about 7%, then to 5%, and finally he sold the entire stake, officially ending his influence on the company.

## EXECUTIVES

**Chairman and CEO:** G. Richard (Rick) Wagoner Jr., age 54, $2,200,000 pay
**Vice Chairman, Global Product Development:** Robert A. (Bob) Lutz, age 74, $1,550,000 pay
**Vice Chairman and CFO:** Frederick A. (Fritz) Henderson, age 47
**Group VP; Chairman, General Motors Acceptance Corporation:** Eric A. Feldstein, age 46
**Group VP; President, GM Asia Pacific:** David N. (Nick) Reilly, age 56
**Group VP; President, GM Latin America, Africa, and Middle East:** V. Maureen Kempston-Darkes, age 58
**Group VP, Global Manufacturing and Labor:** Gary L. Cowger, age 58, $850,000 pay
**Group VP, Global Product Planning:** John F. Smith Jr.
**Group VP and CIO:** Ralph J. Szygenda, age 58
**Special Advisor to the CEO and CFO:** Stephen Girsky
**Group VP, Global Engineering:** James E. Queen, age 58

**VP, Global Human Resources:** Kathleen S. (Katy) Barclay, age 51
**VP, Global Sales, Service, and Marketing Operations:** John G. Middlebrook
**VP, Global Public Policy and Government Relations:** Kenneth W. (Ken) Cole
**VP, GM North America, Engineering:** Edward Koerner
**VP, GM North America, Vehicle Sales, Service, and Marketing:** Mark LaNeve
**VP, Research and Development and Strategic Planning:** Lawrence D. (Larry) Burns, age 55
**VP, GM North America Manufacturing and Labor Relations:** Timothy E. Lee, age 56
**Secretary:** Nancy E. Polis, age 53
**Treasurer:** Walter G. Borst, age 45
**Controller and Chief Accounting Officer:** Nicholas S. (Nick) Cyprus, age 53
**President and Managing Director, GM de Mexico:** Kevin W. Williams, age 44
**Auditors:** Deloitte & Touche LLP

## LOCATIONS

**HQ:** General Motors Corporation
300 Renaissance Center, Detroit, MI 48265
**Phone:** 313-556-5000 **Fax:** 313-556-5108
**Web:** www.gm.com

General Motors has about 300 locations in the US (excluding financing and insurance operations), about 25 in Canada, and a number of others in more than 50 additional countries, including major manufacturing or assembly operations in Argentina, Australia, Belgium, Brazil, China, Germany, India, Mexico, Poland, South Africa, South Korea, Spain, Sweden, Thailand, and the UK.

### 2006 Sales

| | $ mil. | % of total |
|---|---|---|
| North America | | |
| US | 129,041 | 62 |
| Canada & Mexico | 19,979 | 10 |
| Europe | | |
| UK | 7,975 | 4 |
| Germany | 7,687 | 4 |
| Spain | 2,866 | 1 |
| France | 2,411 | 1 |
| Other countries | 13,407 | 7 |
| Asia Pacific | | |
| Korea | 7,550 | 4 |
| Australia | 301 | — |
| Other countries | 3,353 | 2 |
| Latin America | | |
| Brazil | 4,961 | 2 |
| Other countries | 4,768 | 2 |
| Other regions | 3,050 | 1 |
| **Total** | **207,349** | **100** |

## PRODUCTS/OPERATIONS

### 2006 Sales

| | $ mil. | % of total |
|---|---|---|
| Manufactured products | | |
| GM North America | 109,779 | 53 |
| GM Europe | 33,193 | 16 |
| GM Asia Pacific | 15,499 | 8 |
| GM Latin America, Africa, & Middle East | 14,618 | 7 |
| Financing | | |
| GMAC | 33,629 | 16 |
| Other | 793 | — |
| Adjustments | (162) | — |
| **Total** | **207,349** | **100** |

### Selected Brands

Buick
Cadillac
Chevrolet
GMC
Holden
Hummer
Isuzu
Opel
Pontiac
Saab
Saturn
Subaru
Vauxhall

### Selected Operations

Adam Opel GmbH (Germany)
General Motors Acceptance Corp. (49%)
GM Automotive
GM Daewoo Auto & Technology Company
Isuzu Motors Limited (8%, Japan)
Saab Automobile AB (Sweden)
Saturn Corporation

## COMPETITORS

BMW
Chrysler
Daimler
Fiat
Ford
Fuji Heavy Industries
Honda
Hyundai
Kia Motors
Land Rover
Mazda
Nissan
Peugeot
Renault
Suzuki Motor
Toyota
Volkswagen

## HISTORICAL FINANCIALS

Company Type: Public

### Income Statement

FYE: December 31

| | REVENUE ($ mil.) | NET INCOME ($ mil.) | NET PROFIT MARGIN | EMPLOYEES |
|---|---|---|---|---|
| **12/06** | 207,349 | (1,978) | — | 280,000 |
| **12/05** | 192,604 | (10,567) | — | 335,000 |
| **12/04** | 193,517 | 2,804 | 1.4% | 324,000 |
| **12/03** | 185,524 | 3,822 | 2.1% | 326,000 |
| **12/02** | 186,763 | 1,736 | 0.9% | 350,000 |
| **Annual Growth** | 2.6% | — | — | (5.4%) |

### 2006 Year-End Financials

Debt ratio: —
Return on equity: —
Cash ($ mil.): 24,261
Current ratio: 0.93
Long-term debt ($ mil.): 42,505
No. of shares (mil.): 566
Dividends
Yield: 3.3%
Payout: —
Market value ($ mil.): 17,377

### Stock History

NYSE: GM

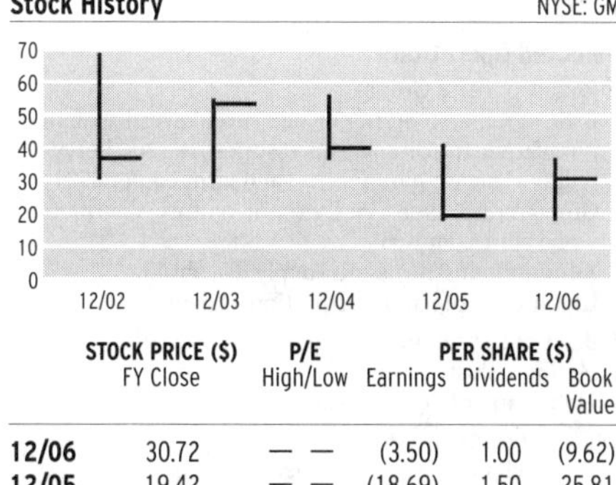


| | STOCK PRICE ($) FY Close | P/E High | P/E Low | PER SHARE ($) Earnings | Dividends | Book Value |
|---|---|---|---|---|---|---|
| **12/06** | 30.72 | — | — | (3.50) | 1.00 | (9.62) |
| **12/05** | 19.42 | — | — | (18.69) | 1.50 | 25.81 |
| **12/04** | 40.06 | 11 | 7 | 4.94 | 2.00 | 48.41 |
| **12/03** | 53.40 | 8 | 4 | 7.14 | 2.00 | 44.96 |
| **12/02** | 36.86 | 20 | 9 | 3.35 | 1.50 | 12.16 |
| **Annual Growth** | (4.5%) | — | — | — | (9.6%) | — |

# Genuine Parts

What do spark plugs, hydraulic hoses, note pads, and magnet wire have in common? They're all Genuine Parts. The diversified company is the largest member and majority owner of the National Automotive Parts Association (NAPA), a voluntary trade association that distributes auto parts nationwide. Genuine Parts Company (GPC) operates about 1,100 NAPA Auto Parts stores in more than 40 US states. North of the border, NAPA Canada runs about 225 auto parts and TRACTION stores. GPC's Auto Todo subsidiary operates distribution centers and auto and tire stores in Mexico. Other subsidiaries include Balkamp, Motion Industries, S.P. Richards Company, and UAP Inc.

GPC's Rayloc division rebuilds automotive parts. In addition to the automotive market, GPC distributes industrial replacement parts, including bearings, belts, and hoses for transmissions and hydraulic equipment. With about a dozen distribution centers, the division serves about 465 branches in the US and Canada.

Overall, the company's auto parts group accounts for half of GPC's total sales.

GPC also distributes office products through S.P. Richards, one of the oldest office supply wholesalers in the country. The office products group supplies schools, offices, and other institutions in North America with computer and imaging supplies, office furniture and machines, general office and school supplies, and more. The division has seven proprietary brands including: Sparco, NATURE SAVER, and Compucessory. Another subsidiary, EIS, manufactures and distributes electronic and electrical products such as copper foil, magnet wire, and thermal management materials to more than 20,000 electrical and electronic manufacturers in North America.

## HISTORY

Genuine Parts Company (GPC) got its start in Atlanta in 1928 when Carlyle Fraser bought a small auto parts store. That year GPC had the only loss in its history. Three years earlier a group that included Fraser had founded the National Automotive Parts Association (NAPA), an organization of automotive manufacturers, remanufacturers, distributors, and retailers.

The Depression was a boon for GPC because fewer new-car sales meant more sales of replacement parts. During the 1930s GPC's sales rose from less than $350,000 to more than $3 million. One tool it developed to spur sales during the Depression was its monthly magazine, *Parts Pups*, which featured pretty girls and corny jokes (discontinued in the 1990s). GPC acquired auto parts rebuilder Rayloc in 1931 and established parts distributor Balkamp in 1936.

WWII boosted sales at GPC because carmakers were producing for the war effort, but scarce resources limited auto parts companies to producing functional parts. GPC went public in 1948.

The postwar boom in car sales boosted GPC's sales in the 1950s and 1960s. It expanded during this period with new distribution centers across the country. GPC bought Colyear Motor Sales (NAPA's West Coast distributor) in 1965 and introduced a line of filters and batteries in 1966 that were the first parts to carry the NAPA name.

GPC moved into Canada in 1972 when it bought Corbetts, a Calgary-based parts distributor. That acquisition included Oliver Industrial Supply. During the mid-1970s GPC began to broaden its distribution businesses, adding S. P. Richards (office products, 1975) and Motion Industries (industrial replacement parts, 1976). In the late 1970s GPC acquired Bearing Specialty and Michigan Bearing as part of Motion Industries.

In 1982 the company introduced its now familiar blue-and-yellow NAPA logo. Canadian parts distributor UAP (formerly United Auto Parts) and GPC formed a joint venture, UAP/NAPA, in 1988, with GPC acquiring a 20% stake in UAP.

During the 1990s GPC diversified its product lines and its geographic reach. Its 1993 acquisition of Berry Bearing made the company a leading distributor of industrial parts. The next year GPC formed a joint venture with Grupo Auto Todo of Mexico.

NAPA formed an agreement in 1995 with Penske Corporation to be the exclusive supplier of auto parts to nearly 900 Penske Auto Centers. GPC purchased Horizon USA Data Supplies that year, adding computer supplies to S. P. Richards' product mix.

A string of acquisitions in the late 1990s increased GPC's industrial distribution business (including Midcap Bearing, Power Drives & Bearings, and Amarillo Bearing).

GPC paid $200 million in 1998 for EIS, a leading wholesale distributor of materials and supplies to the electrical and electronics industries. Late in 1998, after a 10-year joint venture, it bought the remaining 80% of UAP it didn't already own. GPC continued to expand its auto parts distribution network in 1999, acquiring Johnson Industries, an independent distributor of auto supplies for large fleets and car dealers. GPC also acquired Oklahoma City-based Brittain Brothers, a NAPA distributor that serves about 190 auto supply stores in Arkansas, Missouri, Oklahoma, and Texas.

In 2000 the company bought a 15% interest in Mitchell Repair Information (MRIC), a subsidiary of Snap-on Incorporated that provides diagnostic and repair information services. The next year Johnson Industries acquired Coach and Motors, a distribution center in Detroit.

In 2003 GPC acquired NAPA Hawaii, which serves more than 30 independently owned NAPA stores and four company-owned ones in Hawaii and Samoa. Also that year GPC sold its interest in the partnership that distributes industrial parts in Mexico, Refacciones Industriales de Mexico.

President Thomas Gallagher became the company's fourth CEO in more than 75 years when he was named to the position in August 2004. Former CEO Larry Prince remained as chairman until early in 2005 when Gallagher was elected chairman; Prince remains on the board. Also during 2005 the company acquired a 25% interest in Altrom Canada Corp.

GPC subsidiary Motion Industries in mid-2006 acquired Lewis Supply Co., a provider of casters, cutting tools, machinery accessories and other general mill supplies. In October the company merged HorizonUSA Data Supplies, previously a wholly owned subsidiary of S. P. Richards, into S.P. Richards.

## EXECUTIVES

**Chairman, President, and CEO:** Thomas C. (Tom) Gallagher, age 59, $2,108,661 pay
**Vice Chairman, EVP, Finance, and CFO:** Jerry W. Nix, age 61, $969,868 pay
**SVP, Human Resources:** R. Bruce Clayton, age 60, $476,138 pay
**SVP and Treasurer:** Frank M. Howard
**VP, Planning and Acquisitions:** Treg S. Brown
**VP, Compensation and Benefits:** Phillip C. Johnson
**VP, Investor Relations:** Sidney G. Jones
**VP and Corporate Counsel:** Scott C. Smith
**VP, Finance and Corporate Secretary:** Carol B. Yancey
**Director; Chairman, UAP:** Jean Douville, age 63
**President, Rayloc:** J. Richard Borman
**President, Automotive Parts Group; Vice Chairman and CEO, UAP:** Larry R. Samuelson, age 60, $758,445 pay
**EVP, Operations, U.S. Automotive Parts Group:** Glenn M. Chambers
**SVP and CIO, US Automotive Parts Group:** R. Craig Bierman
**SVP, Global Product Management, U.S. Automotive Parts Group:** D. Gary Silva
**SVP Technology and Process Improvement:** Charles A. Chesnutt, age 48
**Auditors:** Ernst & Young LLP

## LOCATIONS

**HQ:** Genuine Parts Company
2999 Circle 75 Pkwy., Atlanta, GA 30339
**Phone:** 770-953-1700 **Fax:** 770-956-2211
**Web:** www.genpt.com

### 2006 Sales

| | $ mil. | % of total |
|---|---|---|
| US | 9,314.9 | 89 |
| Canada | 1,071.1 | 10 |
| Mexico | 94.6 | 1 |
| Adjustments | (22.7) | — |
| **Total** | **10,457.9** | **100** |

## PRODUCTS/OPERATIONS

### 2006 Sales

| | $ mil. | % of total |
|---|---|---|
| Automotive | 5,185.1 | 50 |
| Industrial | 3,107.6 | 30 |
| Office products | 1,779.8 | 17 |
| Electrical/electronic materials | 408.1 | 3 |
| Adjustments | (22.7) | — |
| **Total** | **10,457.9** | **100** |

### Selected Operations

Automotive Parts Group
- Balkamp, Inc. (majority-owned subsidiary; distributes replacement parts and accessories for cars, heavy-duty vehicles, motorcycles, and farm equipment)
- Grupo Auto Todo SA de CV (joint venture, distribution and stores, Mexico)
- Johnson Industries (auto supply distribution)
- UAP Inc. (auto parts distribution, Canada)

Industrial Parts Group
- Motion Industries, Inc.
- Motion Industries (Canada), Inc.

Office Products Group
- S. P. Richards Company (office products)

Electrical/Electronic Materials Group
- EIS, Inc. (products for electrical and electronic equipment, including adhesives, copper foil, and thermal management materials)

## COMPETITORS

Advance Auto Parts
Applied Industrial Technologies
Arrow Electronics
AutoZone
Avnet
CARQUEST
Corporate Express
D&H Distributing
Ford
General Motors
General Parts
Graybar Electric
Hahn Automotive
Hillman Companies
Ingersoll-Rand
Office Depot
OfficeMax
O'Reilly Automotive
Staples
United Stationers

## HISTORICAL FINANCIALS

Company Type: Public

### Income Statement

FYE: December 31

| | REVENUE ($ mil.) | NET INCOME ($ mil.) | NET PROFIT MARGIN | EMPLOYEES |
|---|---|---|---|---|
| **12/06** | 10,458 | 475 | 4.5% | 32,000 |
| **12/05** | 9,783 | 437 | 4.5% | 31,700 |
| **12/04** | 9,097 | 396 | 4.3% | 31,200 |
| **12/03** | 8,449 | 334 | 4.0% | 30,800 |
| **12/02** | 8,259 | (28) | — | 30,700 |
| **Annual Growth** | 6.1% | — | — | 1.0% |

### 2006 Year-End Financials

Debt ratio: 20.1%
Return on equity: 18.1%
Cash ($ mil.): 136
Current ratio: 3.20
Long-term debt ($ mil.): 512
No. of shares (mil.): 171
Dividends
Yield: 2.8%
Payout: 48.9%
Market value ($ mil.): 8,088

### Stock History

NYSE: GPC

| | STOCK PRICE ($) FY Close | P/E High | P/E Low | PER SHARE ($) Earnings | Dividends | Book Value |
|---|---|---|---|---|---|---|
| **12/06** | 47.43 | 18 | 14 | 2.76 | 1.35 | 14.95 |
| **12/05** | 43.92 | 19 | 16 | 2.50 | 1.25 | 15.57 |
| **12/04** | 44.06 | 20 | 14 | 2.25 | 1.20 | 14.54 |
| **12/03** | 33.20 | 18 | 14 | 1.91 | 1.18 | 13.29 |
| **12/02** | 30.80 | — | — | (0.16) | 1.16 | 12.21 |
| **Annual Growth** | 11.4% | — | — | — | 3.9% | 5.2% |

# Genzyme Corporation

Genzyme makes big money off small-time diseases. The company's product portfolio focuses on rare genetic disorders as well as organ transplant, cancer, and kidney disease. One of its main products, Cerezyme, is a leading (and pricey) treatment for Gaucher's disease, a rare enzyme-deficiency condition. Founded in 1981, Genzyme also is involved in drug development and genetic testing and other services. In addition, the company develops gene-based cancer diagnosis and treatment products and it makes orthopedic medical and surgical products. Genzyme provides products and services for patients in some 90 countries.

Cerezyme is one of the most expensive drugs in the world; it accounted for 35% of Genzyme's sales in 2006. Genzyme is intent on diversifying its product line in case this radical treatment turns out not to be effective in the long-term.

The company started marketing Myozyme, a treatment for Pompe disease (a genetic disorder caused by a deficiency in the enzymes needed to break down glycogen), following its 2006 FDA approval. Its pipeline also includes therapies for the treatment of hereditary angiodema, kidney disease, osteoarthritis, and leukemia.

Genzyme has been honing in on its cancer treatments and testing over the last couple of years. In 2006 Genzyme brought to market a new non-small cell lung cancer test for the KRAS gene (and mutations thereof), which will help doctors determine why certain patients don't respond to traditional lung cancer therapies. That same year, Genzyme acquired AnorMED, which is close to developing a treatment for cancer patients undergoing stem cell transplants. A year later, it agreed to acquire Bioenvision, mostly for the worldwide rights to Bioenvision's acute lymphoblastic leukemia treatment for pediatric patients, Clofarabine (sold in the US and Canada under the brand name Clolar). The two companies worked collaboratively to develop the drug; Clolar has orphan drug status in the US and EU.

## HISTORY

From little oaks, mighty biotech companies may grow. In 1981 Tufts professor Henry Blair (now a board member) teamed up with Sherman Snyder and Oak Venture Partners to buy biotech businesses. (The first purchase was an English company that made diagnostic enzymes and had an agreement with the National Institutes of Health to make an enzyme for Gaucher's disease patients.) Armed both with a good therapeutic candidate and a salable product to help fund its development, Genzyme became profitable in 1984 and went public in 1986.

Genzyme diversified through purchases, adding fine chemicals (for use in clinical chemistry testing; exited 1997), diagnostics (such as cholesterol testing), and biotherapeutics. In 1989 the firm bought prenatal testing company Integrated Genetics, which had molecular biology capabilities, and took it public in 1991. Genzyme's development efforts paid off that year when Ceredase was approved to treat Gaucher's disease. The product's protected orphan drug status quickly made it a cash cow. The company later made purchases in such areas as tissue repair (1995), surgical specialties (1996), and cancer treatments (1997).

In 1998 it began selling newly approved Renagel kidney disease treatment (developed with GelTex Pharmaceuticals, which it bought in 2000), as well as Biogen's AVONEX multiple sclerosis drug in Japan. In 1999 the company increased its niche focus by buying Peptimmune, which developed drugs for rare genetic disorders.

In 2000 Genzyme bought Biomatrix and combined it with Genzyme Tissue Repair and Genzyme Surgical Products to form Genzyme Biosurgery. The next year it bought a private Brazilian pharmaceutical company to regain Renagel distribution rights in that key market. In August 2001 its Fabry disease drug Fabrazyme won European approval, marking the firm's entrance into a niche market; Genzyme then geared up to win FDA approval and claim a large share of this limited market.

Looking to capitalize on some R&D, the firm in 2002 created subsidiary Peptimmune to create new therapies for autoimmune and allergy disorders. That year the company settled a 1991 suit with Genentech disputing royalty rights to Genentech's TNKase; Genzyme's buy of Integrated Genetics gave it patents the company alleged were key to TNKase. The FDA helped the company in 2003 expand its product portfolio: The agency approved Fabrazyme and Aldurazyme, another niche drug co-developed with BioMarin. That year it bought antibody drugmaker SangStat Medical.

As part of plans to simplify its structure, Genzyme consolidated its tracking stocks under its primary GENZ ticker in 2003. Instead of three units that included Genzyme General, the company established five business units: Renal, Therapeutics, Biosurgery, Transplant, and Diagnostic Products and Services.

With the 2004 purchase of ILEX Oncology, valued at $1 billion, Genzyme aims to augment its oncology pipeline with two late-stage products and a first-class clinical organization. The next year it bought Verigen, which had developed a cartilage repair cell therapy available in Europe and Australia.

## EXECUTIVES

**Chairman, President, and CEO:** Henri A. Termeer, age 61, $3,124,500 pay
**EVP, Finance, CFO, and Chief Accounting Officer:** Michael S. Wyzga, age 52, $895,000 pay
**EVP, Legal, Corporate Development, and Drug Discovery and Development, Chief Legal Officer, and Secretary:** Peter Wirth, age 56, $1,095,000 pay
**EVP, Cardiovascular and Oncology:** Earl M. (Duke) Collier Jr., age 59, $930,000 pay
**EVP, Therapeutics, Transplant, and Renal:** Georges Gemayel, age 47, $885,000 pay
**EVP; President, International Group:** Sandford D. (Sandy) Smith, age 60
**SVP and General Manager, Genzyme Oncology:** Mark J. Enyedy
**SVP and General Manager, Endocrine Business:** Michael W. Heslop
**SVP and General Manager, Pharmaceuticals:** Daniel O. (Dan) Hayden
**SVP and General Manager, Transplant:** Joseph M. Lobacki
**SVP, Cardiovascular:** James A. (Jim) Geraghty, age 51
**SVP, Cell and Protein Research and Development:** John M. McPherson
**SVP, Corporate Affairs:** Elliott D. Hillback Jr.
**SVP, Clinical, Medical, and Regulatory Affairs and Chief Medical Officer:** Richard A. Moscicki, age 56
**SVP, Corporate Development:** Richard H. Douglas, age 54
**SVP, Corporate Operations and Pharmaceuticals:** Mark R. Bamforth
**SVP, General Counsel, and Chief Patent Counsel:** Thomas J. DesRosier
**SVP and Chief Human Resources Officer:** Zoltan A. Csimma, age 66
**SVP, Regulatory Affairs and Corporate Quality Systems:** Alison Lawton
**SVP, Research and Chief Scientific Officer:** Alan E. Smith, age 62
**VP and Treasurer:** Evan M. Lebson
**VP, Investor Relations:** Sally J. Curley
**Senior Director, Corporate Communications:** Bo Piela
**Auditors:** PricewaterhouseCoopers LLP

## LOCATIONS

**HQ:** Genzyme Corporation
500 Kendall St., Cambridge, MA 02142
**Phone:** 617-252-7500 **Fax:** 617-252-7600
**Web:** www.genzyme.com

Genzyme has operations in Argentina, Australia, Belgium, Brazil, Canada, Colombia, Denmark, France, Germany, Greece, Hong Kong, Ireland, Israel, Italy, Japan, Jordan, Luxemborg, Mexico, the Netherlands, South Korea, Spain, Sweden, Switzerland, Taiwan, the UK, and the US.

## PRODUCTS/OPERATIONS

### Subsidiaries

BioMarin/Genzyme LLC (50%)
Genzyme GmbH (Germany)
Genzyme Limited (UK)
Genzyme Luxembourg S.à.r.l.
Genzyme Europe B.V. (The Netherlands)
Genzyme Ireland Limited
Genzyme Pharmaceuticals (Switzerland)
Genzyme Securities Corporation
GLBC LLC
SangStat Medical Corp.

## COMPETITORS

Abbott Labs
ACON Laboratories
Actelion
Amgen
Amicus Therapeutics
Anika Therapeutics
Baxter
BD
Beckman Coulter
Bristol-Myers Squibb
Chiron
Ferring Pharmaceuticals
Fidia
Fresenius
GlaxoSmithKline
Hoffmann-La Roche
Innovata
Inverness Medical
Johnson & Johnson
LabCorp
Merck
Nabi
Novartis
Ortho Biotech
Pfizer
Quest Diagnostics
Quidel
Roche
Shire
Smith & Nephew
Teva Pharmaceuticals
Toyobo
UCB

## HISTORICAL FINANCIALS

Company Type: Public

### Income Statement

FYE: December 31

| | REVENUE ($ mil.) | NET INCOME ($ mil.) | NET PROFIT MARGIN | EMPLOYEES |
|---|---|---|---|---|
| 12/06 | 3,187 | (17) | — | 9,000 |
| 12/05 | 2,735 | 442 | 16.1% | 8,200 |
| 12/04 | 2,201 | 87 | 3.9% | 7,100 |
| 12/03 | 1,714 | (68) | — | 5,625 |
| 12/02 | 1,330 | (13) | — | 5,600 |
| Annual Growth | 24.4% | — | — | 12.6% |

### 2006 Year-End Financials

Debt ratio: 14.3%
Return on equity: —
Cash ($ mil.): 612
Current ratio: 3.05
Long-term debt ($ mil.): 810
No. of shares (mil.): 263
Dividends
Yield: —
Payout: —
Market value ($ mil.): 16,197

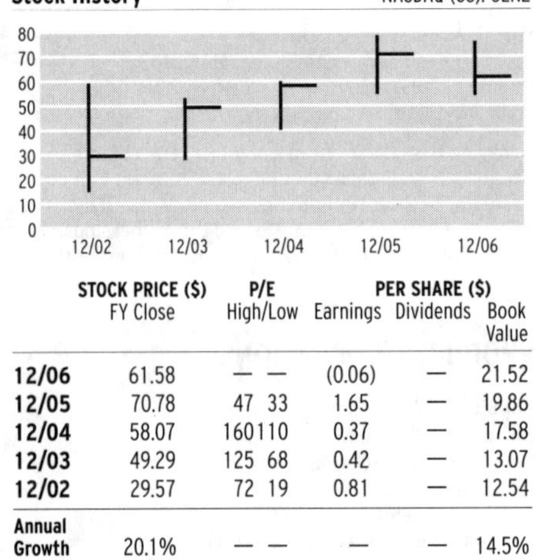


| | STOCK PRICE ($) FY Close | P/E High/Low | PER SHARE ($) Earnings | Dividends | Book Value |
|---|---|---|---|---|---|
| **12/06** | 61.58 | — — | (0.06) | — | 21.52 |
| **12/05** | 70.78 | 47 33 | 1.65 | — | 19.86 |
| **12/04** | 58.07 | 160 110 | 0.37 | — | 17.58 |
| **12/03** | 49.29 | 125 68 | 0.42 | — | 13.07 |
| **12/02** | 29.57 | 72 19 | 0.81 | — | 12.54 |
| **Annual Growth** | 20.1% | — — | — | — | 14.5% |

# Gilead Sciences

Gilead Sciences has biotech balms for infectious diseases, including hepatitis, HIV, and AIDS-related infections. Viread is an HIV therapy used with other antiretrovirals; the drug is approved in both the US and Europe. The company's newest anti-HIV drug, Truvada, is a combination of Viread and another HIV drug Emtriva. Other products on the market including AmBisome, used to treat systemic fungal infections, such as those that accompany AIDS; Vistide, to treat AIDS-related eye infections; and hepatitis B antiviral Hepsera. The company has marketing alliances with Pfizer and GlaxoSmithKline. In 2006 it acquired Myogen.

Gilead paid about $2.5 billion for Myogen, which was developing drug candidate ambrisentan for the treatment of pulmonary arterial hypertension. In 2007 the purchase began to pay off when Gilead received FDA approval for the drug, which it will sell under the trade name Letairis. The Myogen acquisition, as well as Gilead's buyout of Corus Pharma the same year, expanded the company's development pipeline to include drugs for cardiovascular and respiratory diseases. Corus' lead drug candidate is an inhaled antibiotic that aims to fight cystic fibrosis-related infections.

Also in 2006, Gilead Sciences bought Raylo Chemicals, a Canada-based subsidiary of Degussa AG. Raylo is a manufacturer of active pharmaceutical ingredients and other chemicals used in drug development.

Gilead uses its own commercial sales force to sell many of its products, but it also relies on marketing and development collaborations with other drug companies to sell its wares and beef up its product pipeline. Astellas Pharma, for instance, promotes AmBisome in the US, and GlaxoSmithKline markets Hepsera in Asia, Africa, and Latin America.

Additionally, the firm receives royalties on influenza treatment Tamiflu, which it developed with Hoffmann-La Roche. Gilead transferred worldwide marketing rights for the drug to its partner, but sparred with the firm in 2005, claiming it had not put forth enough effort to make the antiviral a blockbuster. The two companies reached a new agreement late that year, with Hoffmann-La Roche agreeing to a one-time $62.5 million payment and increased royalties.

Through a joint venture with Bristol-Myers Squibb (BMS), Gilead developed an antiretroviral therapy combining BMS' Sustiva with Gilead's Truvada. The two companies market the FDA-approved combo drug (known as Atripla) in the US; in a separate joint venture that also includes Merck, Gilead is seeking regulatory approval for Atripla in the European Union.

Gilead partnered with Royalty Pharma to acquire the rights to emtricitabine, an AIDS drug developed at Emory University and approved by the FDA. Gilead's holds a 65% share.

Gilead has other marketing and development agreements with Achillion Pharmaceuticals (for hepatitis C therapies), Japan Tobacco (to develop HIV drugs in Japan), Pfizer (to market Vistide internationally), and OSI Pharmaceuticals (to market age-related macular degeneration drug Macugen).

## HISTORY

Dr. Michael Riordan started Gilead Sciences in 1987, backed by venture capital firm Menlo Ventures. The name was derived from the Biblical phrase, "Is there no balm in Gilead?" In 1990 Glaxo Wellcome (now GlaxoSmithKline) agreed to fund Gilead's research into code-blocking treatments for cancer. Gilead went public in 1992.

In 1994 Gilead formed an alliance with American Home Products' Storz Instruments (now part of Bausch & Lomb) to develop and market a topical treatment for an ophthalmic virus. Two years later Gilead joined forces with Hoffmann-La Roche to develop a cure for influenza.

Vistide was approved in the US in 1996 and in Europe in 1997. But more-effective HIV therapies brought declining demand for Vistide.

The company bounced back with Tamiflu, which was approved in 1999. Sales were brisk during that flu season. Also that year Gilead expanded its pipeline and geographic reach with the $550 million, all-stock acquisition of NeXstar Pharmaceuticals, which focused on antifungals, antibiotics, and cancer treatments.

In 2000 Gilead sought approval for Tamiflu in Japan and Europe (it withdrew the European application after regulators there asked for more information) and also sought approval for pediatric uses for the drug, which it was granted. The following year it resubmitted Tamiflu for approval in Europe.

Chairman Donald Rumsfeld resigned in 2001 to become US secretary of defense and was replaced by retired Sears, Roebuck executive James Denny. Perhaps the Defense connection has helped: Vistide become one of the many drugs researchers began studying as a possible alternative to vaccines should a smallpox bio-attack occur in the US.

Also in 2001 Gilead sold its oncology pipeline to OSI Pharmaceuticals to focus on infection-control products and its hepatitis B lead drug candidate. The sale was a smart move — the FDA approved Hepsera less than a year later.

To help alleviate the AIDS epidemic, in 2003 the company announced plans to sell Viread at cost to all African nations and some 15 other impoverished countries striken by the disease. That year Gilead won FDA approval for another weapon to battle AIDS: antiretroviral Emtriva, which is taken once a day like sister product Viread.

To acquire new ammo in its battle against HIV, the firm bought Triangle Pharmaceuticals in 2003.

## EXECUTIVES

**Chairman:** James M. Denny, age 74
**President, CEO, and Director:** John C. Martin, age 55, $2,078,583 pay
**COO and CFO:** John F. Milligan, age 46
**EVP, Commercial Operations:** Kevin Young, age 51, $964,313 pay
**EVP, Research and Development and Chief Scientific Officer:** Norbert W. Bischofberger, age 51
**SVP and General Counsel:** Gregg H. Alton, age 41
**SVP, Clinical Research:** John J. Toole, age 53
**SVP, Manufacturing and Operations:** Anthony D. Caracciolo, age 51
**SVP, Pharmaceutical Development and Manufacturing:** Taiyin Yang, age 53
**SVP, Research:** William A. Lee, age 51
**SVP and Head of Respiratory Therapeutics:** A. Bruce Montgomery
**SVP, Commercial Operations, North America:** James R. Meyers
**SVP International Commercial Operations:** Paul Carter
**VP, Human Resources:** Kristen M. Metza
**Senior Director, Investor Relations:** Susan Hubbard
**Media Relations:** Erin Edgley
**Auditors:** Ernst & Young LLP

## LOCATIONS

**HQ:** Gilead Sciences, Inc.
333 Lakeside Dr., Foster City, CA 94404
**Phone:** 650-574-3000 **Fax:** 650-578-9264
**Web:** www.gilead.com

Gilead Sciences has facilities in California and North Carolina, as well as in Australia, Canada, and Europe.

**2006 Sales**

| | $ mil. | % of total |
|---|---|---|
| Europe | | |
| Switzerland | 382.4 | 13 |
| France | 228.8 | 7 |
| Spain | 169.8 | 6 |
| UK | 157.4 | 5 |
| Italy | 149.4 | 5 |
| Germany | 126.4 | 4 |
| Other countries | 172.9 | 6 |
| US | 1,467.3 | 48 |
| Other countries | 171.7 | 6 |
| **Total** | **3,026.1** | **100** |

## PRODUCTS/OPERATIONS

**2006 Sales**

| | $ mil. | % of total |
|---|---|---|
| Products | | |
| Truvada | 1,194.3 | 40 |
| Viread | 689.4 | 23 |
| Hepsera | 230.5 | 8 |
| AmBisome | 223.0 | 7 |
| Atripla | 205.7 | 7 |
| Emtriva | 36.4 | 1 |
| Other | 8.9 | — |
| Royalties | 416.5 | 14 |
| Contract revenue | 21.4 | — |
| **Total** | **3,026.1** | **100** |

### Selected Products

Approved
- AmBisome (antifungal)
- Emtriva (HIV)
- Hepsera (hepatitis B)
- Tamiflu (influenza, with Hoffmann-La Roche)
- Truvada (fixed-dose combination of Viread and Emtriva for HIV)
- Viread (HIV)
- Vistide (AIDS-related cytomegalovirus retinitis)

In Development
- Aztreonam lysine (cystic fibrosis)
- Tenofovir disoproxil fumarate (chronic hepatitis B)

## COMPETITORS

Abbott Labs
Actelion
AstraZeneca
Bausch & Lomb
BioCryst Pharmaceuticals
Boehringer Ingelheim
Bristol-Myers Squibb
CIBA Vision
Encysive Pharmaceuticals
Enzon
Genentech
GlaxoSmithKline
Idenix Pharmaceuticals
InterMune
Merck
Novartis
Pfizer
Roche
Schering-Plough
Shire
Three Rivers Pharmaceuticals
Valeant
Zeneus Pharma

## HISTORICAL FINANCIALS

Company Type: Public

### Income Statement

FYE: December 31

| | REVENUE ($ mil.) | NET INCOME ($ mil.) | NET PROFIT MARGIN | EMPLOYEES |
|---|---|---|---|---|
| **12/06** | 3,026 | (1,190) | — | 2,515 |
| **12/05** | 2,028 | 814 | 40.1% | 1,900 |
| **12/04** | 1,325 | 449 | 33.9% | 1,654 |
| **12/03** | 868 | (72) | — | 1,425 |
| **12/02** | 467 | 72 | 15.4% | 1,250 |
| **Annual Growth** | 59.6% | — | — | 19.1% |

### 2006 Year-End Financials

| | |
|---|---|
| Debt ratio: 71.6% | No. of shares (mil.): 461 |
| Return on equity: — | Dividends |
| Cash ($ mil.): 937 | Yield: — |
| Current ratio: 3.18 | Payout: — |
| Long-term debt ($ mil.): 1,300 | Market value ($ mil.): 14,970 |

### Stock History

NASDAQ (GS): GILD

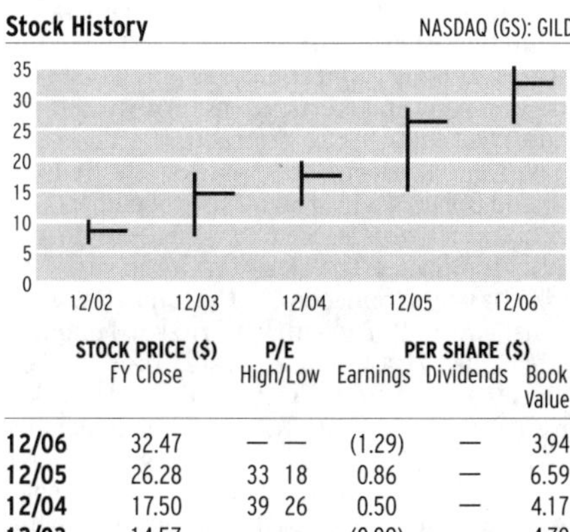


| | STOCK PRICE ($) FY Close | P/E High/Low | | PER SHARE ($) Earnings | Dividends | Book Value |
|---|---|---|---|---|---|---|
| **12/06** | 32.47 | — | — | (1.29) | — | 3.94 |
| **12/05** | 26.28 | 33 | 18 | 0.86 | — | 6.59 |
| **12/04** | 17.50 | 39 | 26 | 0.50 | — | 4.17 |
| **12/03** | 14.57 | — | — | (0.09) | — | 4.70 |
| **12/02** | 8.50 | 114 | 75 | 0.09 | — | 2.89 |
| **Annual Growth** | 39.8% | — | — | — | — | 8.0% |

# Global Crossing

Born to bridge the Atlantic, Global Crossing has emerged from the murky depths of the sea of bankruptcy to surf the bandwidth wave. The global Internet protocol (IP)-based telecommunications carrier operates an integrated global system of major IP-based networks. Its network systems connect the Americas and Europe, and link to Asia through Asia Netcom, which purchased assets of former subsidiary Asia Global Crossing. This massive fiber stream supports a range of services, including Internet access and other data offerings to businesses, along with voice and managed network services for multinational corporations, government, service providers, and telecom carriers.

Global Crossing built its network of facilities-based and leased capacity into a global force, hoping to ride a surge of Internet-driven demand for data transport. But the market for bandwidth capacity has been slow to develop. However times are changing and demand is growing for those long-held network assets.

Global Crossing has refocused its attentions on large-volume users of its IP network and on Voice over Internet Protocol (VoIP). In 2006 the company expanded its VoIP service for enterprise customers across Europe. It also acquired UK-based Fibernet Group in a deal valued at about $95 million, enhancing its UK operations with Fibernet's client list of financial, insurance, and retail companies. Later that year it bought Argentina-based IMPSAT Fiber Networks.

With the focus on multinationals and other high-capacity clients, the company has sold its small business group to Matrix Telecom in a 2005 deal valued at $40.5 million. It also sold its trader voice business, which specializes in services for the financial markets industry, in 2005 to WestCom Corporation, in a cash deal valued at $25 million. In 2004 Global Crossing sold its Global Marine Systems subsidiary and its 49% stake in the SB Submarine Systems Company joint venture, to Bridgehouse Marine.

Singapore-based investment company Temasek Holdings owns nearly 70% of Global Crossing after acquiring Singapore Technologies, parent company to ST Telemedia, in a 2004 corporate restructuring; the family of Mexican entrepreneur Carlos Slim Helú owns about 10%.

## HISTORY

In glamorous Beverly Hills in 1997, Pacific Capital founder Gary Winnick (who was also a former colleague of ex-junk-bond king Michael Milken) teamed with retired ARCO CEO Lodwrick Cook to form Global Crossing. Their goal was to lay a fiber-optic cable, Atlantic Crossing (AC-1), from the US to Europe. Undersea cables had traditionally been laid by consortia of big telecommunications companies, generally monopolies. AT&T (which wanted to exit the undersea cable laying business and needed fast revenues) agreed to construct AC-1 if Winnick could find $750 million.

Winnick put up $15 million and sold demo videos to lure investors. He also trumpeted his plan to undercut competitors' prices ($20 million per 155 Mbps circuit) by charging only $8 million. Global Crossing soon recouped about half of the $750 million debt.

Telecom veteran Jack Scanlon was tapped as CEO in 1998, and the company mapped out plans for the Pacific Crossing (PC-1) and Mid-Atlantic Crossing (MAC). When AC-1 was finished, Global Crossing went public.

In 1999 Robert Annunziata left AT&T to become CEO of Global Crossing, and he brought visions of transforming the company from wholesale carrier to full-fledged telecom operator. Just 17 days after he arrived, he began acquisition talks with Frontier, which the company agreed to buy in a stock swap.

Global Crossing sweetened the Frontier offer after its share price fell; it wrapped up the deal for $10 billion. Frontier's key assets were its substantial US fiber network and its fast-growing Web hosting unit, GlobalCenter. Global Crossing also bought Cable & Wireless' undersea-cable operations that year, and in 2000 the company bought IPC Communications and its IXnet subsidiary for about $3.8 billion, gaining a suite of Internet-based services for financial institutions.

Cable TV veteran Leo Hindery, who had become CEO of GlobalCenter in 1999, replaced Annunziata in 2000. Hindery stepped down later that year, however, and vice chairman Thomas Casey became the company's fourth CEO since 1998.

Demand for services grew far more slowly than the industry had hoped, and Global Crossing was forced to retrench. To cut costs, the company in 2001 began cutting jobs and looking for noncore assets to sell. It sold GlobalCenter to Exodus Communications in early 2001 for stock that was originally worth $6.5 billion, but whose value later collapsed as Exodus slid toward bankruptcy. Global Crossing sold its local-exchange carrier business (also gained in the Frontier deal) to Citizens Communications for about $3.5 billion in cash.

The next year Global Crossing sought reorganization under Chapter 11 bankruptcy protection. Winnick, who owned 10% of Global Crossing before the bankruptcy filing, was known as a hands-on leader who worked through five CEOs in his company's brief history — three in 2000 alone. However, by the end of 2002 Winnick himself had tendered his resignation in the wake of an investigation into his stock sales, before news had surfaced that the company faced a $1 billion revenue shortfall.

Global Crossing emerged from bankruptcy in 2003 after a lengthy and highly-publicized reorganization. Domiciled in Bermuda, Global Crossing moved its operating headquarters from posh surroundings in Beverly Hills, California, to New Jersey. That year Global Crossing completed construction of its core worldwide network and announced plans to cut 2,000 jobs as part of a cost-control effort. Asia Global Crossing CEO John Legere replaced Casey as head of the parent company.

The company reached a bankruptcy court approval to sell a 61.5% majority stake to the telecom unit of Hutchison Whampoa and Singapore Technologies' Telemedia unit. After Hutchison pulled out of the deal, ST Telemedia said it would make good on the $250 million offer on its own, and a nod of approval from the US president seemed to seal the deal.

In 2004, Temasek Holdings, which handles investment business for the Singapore government, acquired Singapore Technologies, including its subsidiary ST Telemedia, in a corporate restructuring, thereby taking control of Global Crossing.

## EXECUTIVES

**Chairman:** Lodewijk Christiaan van Wachem, age 74
**Vice Chairman:** Peter L. H. Seah, age 60
**CEO and Director:** John J. Legere, age 47, $2,525,600 pay
**EVP and CFO:** Jean F. H. P. Mandeville, age 46, $893,603 pay
**EVP and Chief Marketing Officer:** Anthony D. Christie, age 45
**EVP, Business Infrastructure, and CIO:** Daniel J. (Dan) Wagner, age 41
**EVP, Worldwide Carrier Services:** Edward T. (Ted) Higase, age 39
**EVP, Global Operations:** Daniel J. (Dan) Enright, age 46, $803,600 pay
**EVP, Strategy and Corporate Development:** David R. (Dave) Carey, age 52, $861,000 pay
**EVP and General Counsel, and Director, Global Crossing UK:** John B. McShane, age 44
**SVP, Business Development:** Jeffrey Curtachio
**SVP, Corporate Communications:** Gerald (Jerry) Santos, age 62
**SVP, Global Wholesale Voice and Access Management:** John R. Mulhearn Jr., age 55
**SVP, Global Enterprise and Collaboration Services:** Michael Toplisek, age 36
**VP, Investor Relations:** Laurinda Pang
**VP, Media & Analyst Relations:** Rebecca (Becky) Yeamans
**VP, Secretary, and Deputy General Counsel:** Mitchell C. Sussis
**Chief Accounting Officer:** Robert A. Klug, age 38
**Auditors:** Ernst & Young LLP

## LOCATIONS

**HQ:** Global Crossing Limited
200 Park Ave., Ste. 300, Florham Park, NJ 07932
**Phone:** 973-937-0100 **Fax:** 973-360-0148
**Web:** www.globalcrossing.com

### 2006 Sales

| | % of total |
|---|---|
| US | 65 |
| UK | 29 |
| Other countries | 6 |
| **Total** | **100** |

## PRODUCTS/OPERATIONS

### 2006 Sales

| | % of total |
|---|---|
| Enterprise, carrier data & indirect channels | 67 |
| Carrier voice | 33 |
| **Total** | **100** |

### Selected Services

Data
- Asynchronous Transfer Mode (ATM)
- Colocation
- Dedicated Internet access
- Frame relay
- Internet dial-up
- Internet Protocol Virtual Private Network (IP VPN) service
- IP transit
- Managed services
  - Equipment procurement, provisioning, and installation
  - Network monitoring and management
  - Pre-sales engineering and customer premises equipment ("CPE") design
- Metro access
- Private lines
- Wavelength services

Voice
- Calling cards
- Commercial managed voice services (UK only)
- Dedicated outbound and inbound domestic and international long-distance traffic
- Switched outbound and inbound domestic and international long-distance traffic
- Toll-free enhanced routing services

Conferencing
- Event call (operator assisted conference calls)
- Ready-Access (audio on-demand, reservation-free audio conferencing service)
- Videoconferencing

## COMPETITORS

AT&T
BT
Cable & Wireless
COLT Telecom
Deutsche Telekom AG
France Telecom
Genesys
IDT
Intercall
Level 3 Communications
Orange Business
Premiere Global Services
Qwest
Sprint Nextel
Telecom Italia
Telefónica
Telmex
Telstra
Verizon
XO Holdings

## HISTORICAL FINANCIALS

Company Type: Public

### Income Statement

FYE: December 31

| | REVENUE ($ mil.) | NET INCOME ($ mil.) | NET PROFIT MARGIN | EMPLOYEES |
|---|---|---|---|---|
| **12/06** | 1,871 | (324) | — | 3,700 |
| **12/05** | 1,968 | (354) | — | 3,400 |
| **12/04** | 2,487 | (336) | — | 3,600 |
| **12/03** | 2,932 | 24,728 | 843.4% | 5,000 |
| **12/02** | 3,116 | 654 | 21.0% | 5,644 |
| **Annual Growth** | (12.0%) | — | — | (10.0%) |

### 2006 Year-End Financials

Debt ratio: —
Return on equity: —
Cash ($ mil.): 469
Current ratio: 0.89
Long-term debt ($ mil.): 1,042
No. of shares (mil.): 37
Dividends
Yield: —
Payout: —
Market value ($ mil.): 899

### Stock History

NASDAQ (GM): GLBC

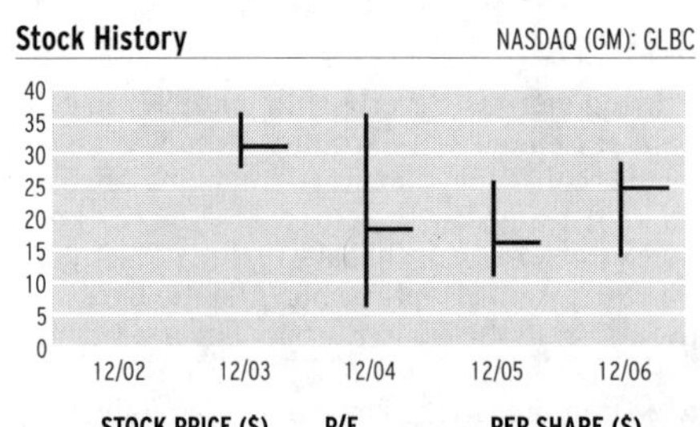

| | STOCK PRICE ($) FY Close | P/E High | P/E Low | PER SHARE ($) Earnings | Dividends | Book Value |
|---|---|---|---|---|---|---|
| **12/06** | 24.55 | — | — | (10.50) | — | (5.33) |
| **12/05** | 16.03 | — | — | (15.94) | — | (7.66) |
| **12/04** | 18.14 | — | — | (15.45) | — | 2.27 |
| **12/03** | 31.00 | 1 | 1 | 25.47 | — | 17.86 |
| **Annual Growth** | (7.5%) | — | — | — | — | — |

# Global Hyatt

Travelers interested in luxury lodgings can check in for the Hyatt touch. Global Hyatt is one of the world's top operators of full-service luxury hotels and resorts with more than 700 locations in some 40 countries. Its core Hyatt Regency brand offers hospitality services targeted primarily to business travelers and upscale vacationers. The firm also operates properties under the names Grand Hyatt, Park Hyatt, Hyatt Place, Hyatt Summerfield Suites, Hyatt Resorts, and Andaz. Its resort destinations offer golf, spas, and other upmarket rest and relaxation activities. Although Global Hyatt was formed in 2004, the Hyatt chain traces its roots back to 1957. It is owned by the wealthy Pritzker family of Chicago.

As part of an ongoing effort to restructure H Group Holding, the holding company that oversees the family's various business enterprises, Global Hyatt was formed to consolidate the Pritzker's hospitality interests. The reorganization brought together the operations of Hyatt Hotels Corporation (domestic hotels), Hyatt International (international hotels), Hyatt Equities (hotel ownership), and Hyatt Vacation Ownership (timeshares) under one umbrella.

Global Hyatt has been busy expanding beyond the luxury segment. Its operations in this arena include U.S. Franchise Systems, which franchises the smaller Hawthorn Suites and Microtel Inns & Suites chains. In 2005 Hyatt expanded its reach into the limited-service hotel business when it acquired the AmeriSuites chain previously owned by Prime Hospitality. The hotelier announced a $175 million initiative to rebrand the more than 140 locations under the Hyatt Place banner, a new brand designed to attract younger travelers with wireless Internet access, flat screen televisions, and contemporary interiors.

Other developments have followed: in 2006 the company acquired the Summerfield Suites chain from The Blackstone Group, which it rebranded as Hyatt Summerfield Suites. In 2007, Hyatt launched Andaz, a new luxury hotel brand.

## HISTORY

Nicholas Pritzker left Kiev for Chicago in 1881, where his family's ascent to the ranks of America's wealthiest families began. His son A. N. left the family law practice in the 1930s and began investing in a variety of businesses. He turned a 1942 investment (Cory Corporation) worth $25,000 into $23 million by 1967. A. N.'s son Jay followed in his father's wheeling-and-dealing footsteps. In 1953, with the help of his father's banking connections, Jay purchased Colson Company and recruited his brother Bob, an industrial engineer, to restructure a company that made tricycles and US Navy rockets. By 1990 Jay and Bob had added 60 industrial companies, with annual sales exceeding $3 billion, to the entity they called The Marmon Group.

The family's connection to Hyatt hotels was established in 1957 when Jay Pritzker bought a hotel called Hyatt House, located near the Los Angeles airport, from Hyatt von Dehn. Jay added five locations by 1961 and hired his gregarious youngest brother, Donald, to manage the hotel company. Hyatt went public in 1967, but the move that opened new vistas for the hotel chain was the purchase that year of an 800-room hotel in Atlanta that both Hilton and Marriott had turned down. John Portman's design, incorporating a 21-story atrium, a large fountain, and a revolving rooftop restaurant, became a Hyatt trademark.

The Pritzkers formed Hyatt International in 1969 to operate hotels overseas, and the company grew rapidly in the US and abroad during the 1970s. Donald Pritzker died in 1972, and Jay assumed control of Hyatt. The family decided to take the company private in 1979. Much of Hyatt's growth in the 1970s came from contracts to manage Hyatt hotels built by other investors. When Hyatt's earnings on those contracts shrank in the 1980s, the company launched its own hotel and resort developments under Nick Pritzker, a cousin to Jay and Bob. In 1988, with US and Japanese partners, it built the Hyatt Regency Waikoloa on Hawaii's Big Island for $360 million — a record at the time for a hotel.

The Pritzkers took a side-venture into air travel in 1983 when they bought bedraggled Braniff Airlines through Hyatt subsidiaries as it emerged from bankruptcy. After a failed 1987 attempt to merge the airline with Pan Am, the Pritzkers sold Braniff in 1988.

Hyatt opened Classic Residence by Hyatt, a group of upscale retirement communities, in 1989. The company joined Circus Circus (now part of MGM MIRAGE) in 1994 to launch the Grand Victoria, the nation's largest cruising gaming vessel. The next year, as part of a new strategy to manage both freestanding golf courses and those near Hyatt hotels, the company opened its first freestanding course: an 18-hole, par 71 championship course in Aruba.

President Thomas Pritzker, Jay's son, took over as Hyatt chairman and CEO following his father's death in early 1999. In 2000 Hyatt announced plans to join rival Marriott International in launching an independent company to provide an online procurement network serving the hospitality industry. The following year the company announced plans to build a 47-story skyscraper in downtown Chicago. Construction for the new building, named the Hyatt Center, began at the end of 2002.

In 2004 the Pritzker family consolidated its hospitality holdings to form Global Hyatt Corporation. The following year the company bought the AmeriSuites limited-service hotel chain from Prime Hospitality.

Mark Hoplamazian, president of The Pritzker Organization, a merchant-banking firm serving the family's business activities, took over as president and CEO in 2006; Thomas Prtizker remained chairman.

## EXECUTIVES

**Chairman, Global Hyatt and Hyatt International:** Thomas J. (Tom) Pritzker, age 56
**Vice Chairman; Chairman and CEO, Hyatt Development and Hyatt Equities:** Nicholas J. (Nick) Pritzker
**President and CEO:** Mark S. Hoplamazian, age 43
**EVP Acquisitions and Development:** Steve Goldman
**SVP and General Counsel:** Susan T. Smith, age 53
**SVP Acquisitions and Development:** James R. (Jim) Abrahamson, age 49
**President and CEO, U.S. Franchise Systems:** Michael A. (Mike) Leven, age 69
**President, Hyatt Hotels:** Edward W. Rabin Jr., age 60
**President, Hyatt International:** Bernd Chorengel
**EVP and COO, Hyatt Hotels:** Chuck Floyd
**SVP Field Operations, Hyatt Hotels:** Pete Sears
**SVP Marketing, Hyatt Hotels:** Thomas F. (Tom) O'Toole, age 48
**VP Corporate Communications:** Katie Meyer
**VP Electronic Distribution, Hyatt Hotels:** Joan Lowell
**VP Finance:** Kirk A. Rose
**VP Human Resources, Hyatt Hotels:** Doug Patrick
**VP Marketing, Hyatt Hotels:** Amy Weyman
**Director Corporate Public Relations:** Lori Armon

## LOCATIONS

**HQ:** Global Hyatt Corporation
71 S. Wacker Dr., Chicago, IL 60606
**Phone:** 312-750-1234 **Fax:** 312-750-8550
**Web:** www.hyatt.com

Global Hyatt Corporation operates more than 200 hotels and resorts in nearly 40 countries.

## PRODUCTS/OPERATIONS

### Selected Operations

Hyatt Regency (core hotel format)
Hyatt Summerfield Suites (extended stay)
Hyatt Vacation Ownership (timeshares)
U.S. Franchise Systems (mid-priced hotels)
- Hawthorn Suites
- Microtel Inns and Suites

## COMPETITORS

Accor
Carlson Hotels
Club Med
Four Seasons Hotels
Hilton
InterContinental Hotels
Ladbrokes
LXR Luxury Resorts
Marriott
Millennium & Copthorne Hotels
Starwood Hotels & Resorts
Wyndham

## HISTORICAL FINANCIALS

Company Type: Private

**Income Statement** FYE: January 31

| | REVENUE ($ mil.) | NET INCOME ($ mil.) | NET PROFIT MARGIN | EMPLOYEES |
|---|---|---|---|---|
| 1/05 | 6,438 | — | — | 88,647 |
| 1/04 | 5,812 | — | — | — |
| 1/03 | 3,600 | — | — | 40,000 |
| 1/02 | 3,400 | — | — | 37,000 |
| 1/01 | 3,500 | — | — | 36,632 |
| Annual Growth | 16.5% | — | — | 24.7% |

**Revenue History**

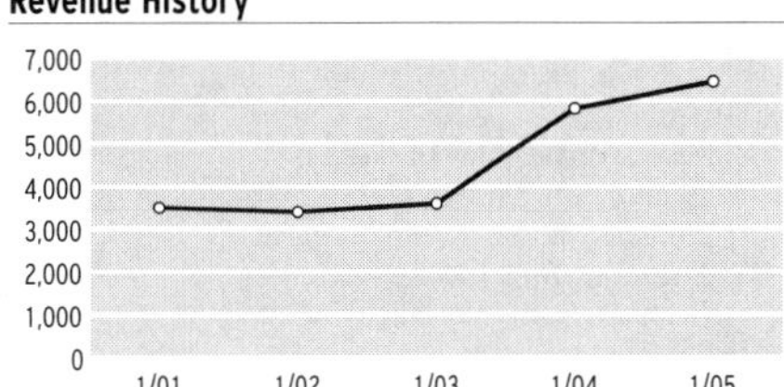


# Goldman Sachs

Goldman Sachs has traditionally possessed the Midas touch in the investment banking world. A global leader in mergers and acquisitions advice and securities underwriting, Goldman offers a gamut of investment banking and asset management services to corporate and government clients, as well as institutional and individual investors. It owns Goldman Sachs Execution & Clearing (formerly Spear, Leeds & Kellogg Specialists), one of the largest market makers on the NYSE, and is also a leading market maker for fixed income products, currencies, and commodities. Among its other business units are private equity firm GS Capital Partners and Queens Moat Houses, a UK-based hotel chain.

Former president and COO Lloyd Blankfein was named chairman and CEO in 2006 when Henry "Hank" Paulson was named as the US treasury secretary.

Goldman's business falls into three segments: Investment Banking; Trading and Principal Investments; and Asset Management and Securities Services.

The firm's distinct business culture and unparalleled prestige attracts the Street's top talent. Teamwork is paramount at Goldman, along with an attitude that the firm is the best at what it does. As Goldman's perennial rank among the top companies in its industry attests, the world's most venerable and profitable companies entrust Goldman with their corporate financial and advisory needs. Goldman has some government and high-net-worth individual clients, but unlike rivals that are rushing to diversify operations and income sources, Goldman has focused almost exclusively on institutional clients.

Whether Goldman remains untarnished amid charges of conflicts-of-interest and investigations into so-called IPO "spinning" (giving special IPO allocations to key clients in exchange for investment banking business) remains to be seen. The firm was fined $50 million as part of a far-reaching settlement involving conflict-of-interest allegations that encompassed virtually all of Wall Street's top firms. Goldman also was ordered to pay $60 million to provide independent research and education to investors. When the regulatory scrutiny turned to the mutual fund industry, Goldman again was one of several investment and brokerage firms investigated for possible trading abuses.

Partnering Canada's Borealis Infrastructure Management and the Singapore-based GIC Special Investments, Goldman has acquired Associated British Ports for a reported $4.6 billion.

Goldman is constructing a $1.8 billion headquarters building in New York City's lower Manhattan. The new tower is expected to be complete by 2010.

## HISTORY

German immigrant-cum-Philadelphia retailer Marcus Goldman moved to New York in 1869 and began buying customers' promissory notes from jewelers to resell to banks. Goldman's son-in-law came aboard in 1882, and the firm became Goldman, Sachs & Co. in 1885.

Two years later Goldman Sachs began offering US-UK foreign exchange and currency services. To serve such clients as Sears, Roebuck, it expanded to Chicago and St. Louis. In 1896 it joined the NYSE.

While the firm increased its European contracts, Goldman's son Henry made it a major source of financing for US industry. In 1906 it co-managed its first public offering, United Cigar Manufacturers (later General Cigar). By 1920 it had underwritten IPOs for Sears, B.F. Goodrich, and Merck.

Sidney Weinberg made partner in 1927 and stayed until his death in 1969. In the 1930s Goldman Sachs entered securities dealing and sales. After WWII it became a leader in investment banking, co-managing Ford's 1956 IPO. In the 1970s it pioneered buying blocks of stock for resale.

Under Weinberg's son John, Goldman Sachs became a leader in mergers and acquisitions. The 1981 purchase of J. Aron gave the firm a significant commodities presence and helped it grow in South America.

Seeking capital after 1987's market crash, Goldman Sachs raised more than $500 million from Sumitomo for a 12% nonvoting interest in the firm (since reduced to 3%). The Kamehameha Schools/Bishop Estate of Hawaii, an educational trust, also invested.

The 1994 bond crash and a decline in new debt issues led Goldman Sachs to cut staffing for the first time since the 1980s. But problems went deeper. Partners began leaving and taking their equity. Cost cuts, a stronger bond market, and the long bull market helped the firm rebound; firm members sought protection through limited liability partnership status. The firm also extended the period during which partners can cash out (slowing the cash drain) and limited the number of people entitled to a share of profits. Overseas growth in 1996 and 1997 focused on the UK and Asia.

After three decades of resistance, the partners in 1998 voted to sell the public a minority stake in the firm, but market volatility led to postponement. Goldman Sachs also suffered from involvement with Long-Term Capital Management, ultimately contributing $300 million to its bailout.

In 1999 Jon Corzine, then co-chairman and co-CEO, announced that he would leave the group after seeing it through its IPO, and Goldman Sachs finally went public that year in an offering valued at close to $4 billion. In 2000 Corzine was elected to a US Senate seat. The New Jersey Democrat spent more than $64 million on his campaign (a record), nearly $61 million of it from his own personal wealth (also a record). Corzine went on to win New Jersey's gubernatorial race in 2005.

In early 2004, Goldman president and COO John Thain left the firm to assume the helm of the New York Stock Exchange. Lloyd Blankfein was named his successor. Blankfein was named chairman and CEO in 2006 after his predecessor, Henry "Hank" Paulson, left for the US Department of the Treasury.

## EXECUTIVES

**Chairman and CEO:** Lloyd C. Blankfein, age 52, $19,720,500 pay (prior to title change)
**Co-Head, Global Investment Banking:** John S. Weinberg
**President, Co-COO and Director:** Gary D. Cohn, age 45
**President, Co-COO and Director:** Jon Winkelried, age 48
**EVP and Chief Administrative Officer:** Edward C. Forst, age 45
**EVP and Global Head of Compliance:** Alan M. Cohen, age 55
**EVP and CFO:** David A. Viniar, age 50
**EVP, General Counsel, Secretary, and Co-Head of the Legal Department:** Gregory K. Palm, age 57
**EVP, General Counsel, and Co-Head of the Legal Department:** Esta Eiger Stecher, age 48
**EVP, Human Capital Management:** Kevin W. Kennedy, age 57
**Chairman, Global Investment Banking:** Christopher A. Cole
**Chairman, Goldman Sachs International:** Peter D. Sutherland, age 61
**Co-CEO, Goldman Sachs International:** Richard J. Gnodde
**CEO, Goldman Sachs International:** Michael S. Sherwood, age 41
**Head, Global Financing:** David M. Solomon
**Co-Head, Investment Management:** Peter S. Kraus
**Co-Head, Investment Management:** Eric S. Schwartz
**Co-Head, Investment Banking, Russia:** Magomed Galaev
**Head, Merchant Banking:** Richard A. Friedman
**Chief US Investment Strategist:** Abby Joseph Cohen
**Principal Accounting Officer:** Sarah E. Smith
**Auditors:** PricewaterhouseCoopers LLP

## LOCATIONS

**HQ:** The Goldman Sachs Group, Inc.
85 Broad St., New York, NY 10004
**Phone:** 212-902-1000 **Fax:** 212-902-3000
**Web:** www.goldmansachs.com

The Goldman Sachs Group has operations in Argentina, Australia, Brazil, Canada, China, France, Germany, Hong Kong, Ireland, Italy, Japan, Mexico, New Zealand, Russia, Singapore, South Africa, South Korea, Spain, Sweden, Switzerland, Taiwan, the UK, and the US.

### 2006 Sales

| | % of total |
|---|---|
| Americas | 54 |
| Europe, Middle East, & Africa | 25 |
| Asia | 21 |
| **Total** | **100** |

## PRODUCTS/OPERATIONS

### 2006 Sales

| | $ mil. | % of total |
|---|---|---|
| Interest income | 35,186 | 51 |
| Trading & principal investments | 24,027 | 35 |
| Investment banking | 5,613 | 8 |
| Asset management & securities services | 4,527 | 6 |
| **Total** | **69,353** | **100** |

### Selected Subsidiaries

Goldman, Sachs & Co.
  Goldman Sachs (Asia) Finance Holdings L.L.C.
Goldman Sachs Credit Partners L.P. (Bermuda)
Goldman Sachs Financial Markets, L.P.
Goldman Sachs (Japan) Ltd. (British Virgin Islands)
Goldman Sachs (UK) L.L.C.
  Goldman Sachs Group Holdings (UK)
    Goldman Sachs Holdings (UK)
      Goldman Sachs International Bank (UK)
GS Financial Services L.P.
  Goldman Sachs Capital Markets, L.P.
    William Street Equity LLC
      William Street Funding Corporation
  GS Global Funding, Inc.
      Goldman Sachs Mortgage Company
J. Aron Holdings, L.P.
  J. Aron & Company
SLK LLC
  Goldman Sachs Execution & Clearing, L.P.

## COMPETITORS

Bear Stearns
Charles Schwab
CIBC World Markets
Citigroup Global Markets
Credit Suisse (USA)
FMR
JPMorgan Chase
Lehman Brothers
Merrill Lynch
MF Global
Morgan Stanley
UBS Financial Services

## HISTORICAL FINANCIALS

Company Type: Public

### Income Statement

FYE: Last Friday in November

| | REVENUE ($ mil.) | NET INCOME ($ mil.) | NET PROFIT MARGIN | EMPLOYEES |
|---|---|---|---|---|
| **11/06** | 69,353 | 9,537 | 13.8% | 26,467 |
| **11/05** | 43,391 | 5,626 | 13.0% | 31,005 |
| **11/04** | 29,839 | 4,553 | 15.3% | 21,928 |
| **11/03** | 23,623 | 3,005 | 12.7% | 19,476 |
| **11/02** | 22,854 | 2,114 | 9.3% | 19,739 |
| **Annual Growth** | 32.0% | 45.7% | — | 7.6% |

### 2006 Year-End Financials

Debt ratio: 598.0%
Return on equity: 32.4%
Cash ($ mil.): 169,409
Current ratio: —
Long-term debt ($ mil.): 195,474
No. of shares (mil.): 413
Dividends
  Yield: 0.6%
  Payout: 6.6%
Market value ($ mil.): 83,193

### Stock History

NYSE: GS

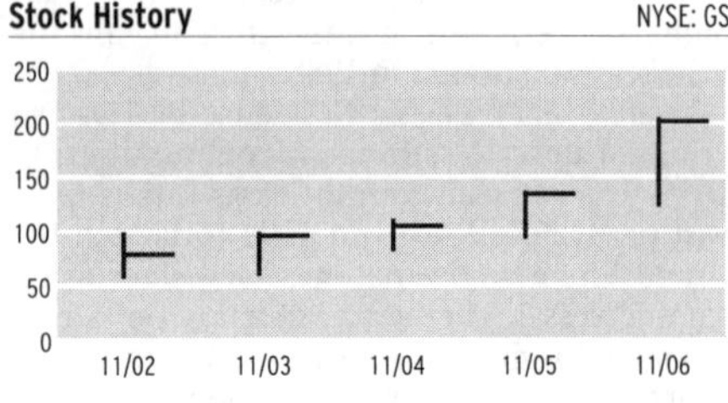


| | STOCK PRICE ($) FY Close | P/E High | P/E Low | PER SHARE ($) Earnings | Dividends | Book Value |
|---|---|---|---|---|---|---|
| **11/06** | 201.60 | 10 | 6 | 19.69 | 1.30 | 86.72 |
| **11/05** | 134.12 | 12 | 8 | 11.21 | 1.00 | 64.05 |
| **11/04** | 104.84 | 12 | 9 | 8.92 | 1.00 | 52.14 |
| **11/03** | 96.08 | 17 | 10 | 5.87 | 0.74 | 45.73 |
| **11/02** | 78.87 | 24 | 15 | 4.03 | 0.48 | 40.18 |
| **Annual Growth** | 26.4% | — | — | 48.7% | 28.3% | 21.2% |

# Goodrich Corporation

Goodrich Corporation is a tireless leader in aerospace systems. The company, formerly tire maker BFGoodrich, is now focused on its three aerospace divisions. Goodrich's largest unit, Engine Systems, makes aerostructures (nacelles, pylons, and thrust reversers), engine and fuel controls, fuel systems, pumps, and turbine components. Next largest, Airframe Systems makes aircraft wheels, brakes, landing gear, and flight control and actuation systems; it also provides aircraft maintenance, repair, and overhaul services. Finally, Electronic Systems makes interior products, de-icing and specialty systems, monitoring systems, lighting products, avionics systems, telemetry systems, sensors, and reconnaissance systems.

2006 marked Goodrich's third consecutive year of solid sales and earnings growth as the defense sector continues to perform well, and the commercial aerospace sector continues to recover.

The US government accounts for about 18% of sales; Airbus, 16%; and Boeing, 12%.

## HISTORY

Orphan, doctor, Civil War veteran, and entrepreneur Benjamin Franklin Goodrich bought stock in the Hudson River Rubber Co. in 1869 and moved the firm to Akron, Ohio, in 1870. Its rubber products included fire hoses, bottle stoppers, rubber rings for canning jars, and billiard cushions. After the depression of the mid-1870s, the company reorganized as B.F. Goodrich & Co (BFG).

BFG's new uses for rubber galvanized the industry, but it was the advent of rubber tires that secured the company's future. In 1896 bicycle maker Alexander Winton asked BFG to make tires for his "horseless carriage." (A British company named Silvertown had invented the pneumatic tire, and BFG acquired the patent.) As the automobile's popularity grew, BFG continued to improve its tires. It added fabric cords and carbon black to make tires tougher and give them black coloring.

BFG introduced the first rubber sponge in 1902 and began making aircraft tires in 1909 (standard on WWI airplanes). In the 1920s the company added sliding fasteners made by Universal Fastener to its rubber galoshes and began calling the boots "zippers." In 1926 BFG scientists formulated polyvinyl chloride (PVC). The following year the company supplied tires for Charles Lindbergh's *Spirit of St. Louis,* and in the 1930s BFG introduced the first commercial aircraft de-icer.

BFG was at the forefront of the effort to manufacture synthetic rubber, especially after Japan cut the US's supply of natural rubber during WWII. The company's chemicals division was organized in 1943. During the war BFG introduced continuous rubber tracks for tanks, as well as the technology used in pilots' "Mae West" life vests.

The company began selling tubeless tires in 1947, and by the mid-1950s new cars came equipped with the safer tires. In 1956 it formed its aerospace division. A few years later the company provided the space suit worn by Alan Shepard, the first American in space. BFG also made P-F Flyers, sneakers popular with children in the 1960s.

John Ong became chairman in 1979 and reduced the company's dependence on tires. In 1986 BFG and Uniroyal formed the Uniroyal Goodrich Tire Co. When Michelin bought the unit in 1990, BFG was out of the tire business.

BFG sold Geon, its vinyl division, in 1993, and Ong poured the proceeds back into chemical and aerospace businesses. Acquisitions since 1990 include Hercules Aircraft and Electronics Group (1990), Eastern Airlines Avionics (test equipment, 1991), GE Specialty Heating and Avionics Power (heated and electrical components, 1994), and Rohr (commercial airline engine nacelles, 1997). David Burner, an executive at BFG since 1983, replaced Ong as chairman in 1997.

BFG acquired Freedom Chemical (specialty chemicals) in 1998 and Coltec Industries (aerospace components and engineered industrial products) the next year. BFG then moved its headquarters from Richfield, Ohio, to Coltec's home — Charlotte, North Carolina.

BFG and Boeing agreed in 2000 to cooperate in airplane maintenance and landing-gear overhauling. BFG bought Boeing's airplane ejection-seat maker, IBP Aerospace Group. Late in the year the company bought Raytheon's optical systems business and Autoliv's OEA aerospace operations (propellant-actuated devices).

Early in 2001 BFGoodrich sold its performance materials operations (industrial plastics and additives) to an investor group for $1.4 billion. In June 2001 the company changed its name to Goodrich Corporation. The same year Goodrich bolstered its aerospace lighting operations with the acquisition of Hella Aerospace GmbH (from privately held Hella KG Hueck & Co.) and announced that it was spinning off its engineered industrial products business as EnPro Industries (completed in 2002). In October Goodrich announced that it was closing 16 plants and cutting its workforce by about 10% because of the slowdown in the aircraft manufacturing business.

Late in 2002 Goodrich paid $1.5 billion in cash for TRW's Aeronautical Systems unit (flight controls, cargo systems, engine control systems, power/utility systems, missile actuation). The company divested its Avionics Systems (integrated flight controls and displays) operations in 2003.

In 2004 Goodrich won a large deal to supply Boeing with thrust reversers, engine coverings, wheels, brake systems, lighting, and cargo handling systems for its upcoming 787 airplane, which could bring Goodrich up to $4 billion in revenue over the life of the contract. Early the next year Airbus selected Goodrich to supply engine coverings and thrust reversers for its upcoming A350 (which will compete directly with Boeing's 787) in a deal that could be worth $6 billion.

In 2005 Goodrich sold its Test Systems business to Aeroflex Incorporated for $35 million and acquired imaging products specialist Sensors Unlimited for $61 million.

The following year Goodrich agreed to sell its Turbomachinery Products division to Admiralty Partners, Inc. for $83 million. The deal was called off two months later, however.

## EXECUTIVES

**Chairman, President, and CEO:** Marshall O. Larsen, age 59, $970,000 pay
**EVP, Operational Excellence and Technology:** John J. Grisik, age 60, $480,000 pay
**EVP, Administration and General Counsel:** Terrence G. Linnert, age 60, $475,000 pay
**SVP and CFO:** Scott E. Kuechle, age 47, $370,000 pay
**SVP, Human Resources:** Jennifer Pollino, age 42
**SVP, Strategy and Business Development:** Stephen R. (Steve) Huggins, age 62
**VP and Segment President, Actuation and Landing Systems:** John J. (Jack) Carmola, age 51, $460,000 pay
**VP and Segment President, Nacelles and Interior Systems:** Cynthia M. (Cindy) Egnotovich, age 49, $390,000 pay (prior to title change)
**VP and General Manager, Lighting Systems:** Steve Chalmers
**VP, Associate General Counsel, and Secretary:** Sally L. Geib
**VP, Business Development and Tax:** Joseph F. Andolino
**VP, Corporate Communications:** Lisa Bottle
**VP, Investor Relations:** Paul S. Gifford
**VP and Controller:** Scott A. Cottrill, age 41
**VP and Treasurer:** Houghton Lewis
**Auditors:** Ernst & Young LLP

## LOCATIONS

**HQ:** Goodrich Corporation
Four Coliseum Centre, 2730 W. Tyvola Rd., Charlotte, NC 28217
**Phone:** 704-423-7000 **Fax:** 704-423-5540
**Web:** www.goodrich.com

Goodrich Corporation has operations in about 10 states in the US, and in Canada, France, Germany, Singapore, and the UK.

## PRODUCTS/OPERATIONS

### 2006 Sales

| | $ mil. | % of total |
|---|---|---|
| Engine Systems | 2,455.3 | 42 |
| Airframe Systems | 1,950.6 | 33 |
| Electronic Systems | 1,472.4 | 25 |
| **Total** | **5,878.3** | **100** |

### Selected Businesses

Airframe Systems
- Actuation systems
- Aviation technical services
- Brakes
- Engineered polymer products
- Landing gear
- Wheels

Electronic Systems
- Aircraft interior products
- De-icing systems
- Fuel and utility systems
- Lighting systems
- Optical and space systems
- Power systems
- Propulsion systems
- Sensor systems

Engine Systems
- Aerostructures (nacelles, pylons, thrust reversers)
- Cargo systems
- Engine controls
- Fuel controls
- Gas turbine fuel technologies
- Gas turbine components (discs, blisks, shafts, airfoils)

## COMPETITORS

AAR
AeroMechanical Services
Argo-Tech
BAE SYSTEMS
BAE Systems Inc.
Banner Aerospace
BE Aerospace
Boeing
Breeze-Eastern
Crane
Crane Aerospace & Electronics
Danaher
Ducommun
EADS
Esterline
GE
General Dynamics
Gulfstream Aerospace
Héroux-Devtek
Honeywell International
Hydro-Aire
ITT Corp.
Kaman Aerospace
L-3 Vertex
Lockheed Martin
Lufthansa Technik
Marshall Aerospace
Martin-Baker Aircraft
Meggitt
Meggitt USA
Midcoast Aviation
Moog
MRAS
Northrop Grumman
Parker Hannifin
Pemco Aviation
Raytheon
SAFRAN
Samsung Group
Singapore Technologies
Smiths Group
Spirit AeroSystems
Telair
Teleflex
TIMCO Aviation
United Technologies
Volvo Aero Services
Vought Aircraft
Woodward
Zodiac

## HISTORICAL FINANCIALS

Company Type: Public

### Income Statement

FYE: December 31

| | REVENUE ($ mil.) | NET INCOME ($ mil.) | NET PROFIT MARGIN | EMPLOYEES |
|---|---|---|---|---|
| **12/06** | 5,878 | 482 | 8.2% | 23,400 |
| **12/05** | 5,397 | 264 | 4.9% | 22,600 |
| **12/04** | 4,725 | 172 | 3.6% | 21,300 |
| **12/03** | 4,383 | 100 | 2.3% | 20,600 |
| **12/02** | 3,910 | 118 | 3.0% | 22,900 |
| **Annual Growth** | 10.7% | 42.2% | — | 0.5% |

## 2006 Year-End Financials

| | |
|---|---|
| Debt ratio: 87.1% | No. of shares (mil.): 125 |
| Return on equity: 28.0% | Dividends |
| Cash ($ mil.): 201 | Yield: 1.8% |
| Current ratio: 1.84 | Payout: 21.0% |
| Long-term debt ($ mil.): 1,722 | Market value ($ mil.): 5,692 |

## Stock History

NYSE: GR

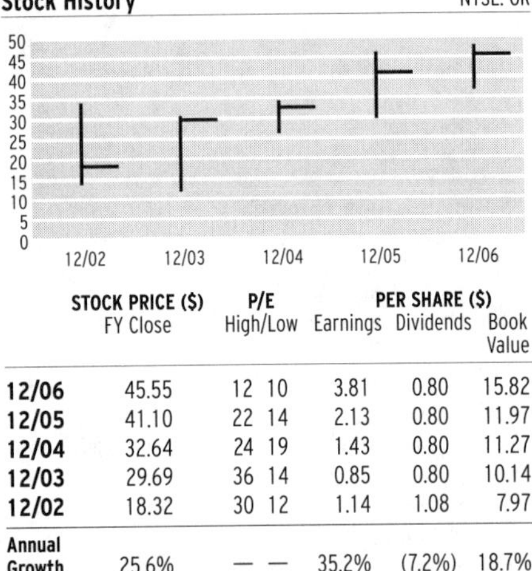


| | STOCK PRICE ($) FY Close | P/E High | P/E Low | PER SHARE ($) Earnings | Dividends | Book Value |
|---|---|---|---|---|---|---|
| **12/06** | 45.55 | 12 | 10 | 3.81 | 0.80 | 15.82 |
| **12/05** | 41.10 | 22 | 14 | 2.13 | 0.80 | 11.97 |
| **12/04** | 32.64 | 24 | 19 | 1.43 | 0.80 | 11.27 |
| **12/03** | 29.69 | 36 | 14 | 0.85 | 0.80 | 10.14 |
| **12/02** | 18.32 | 30 | 12 | 1.14 | 1.08 | 7.97 |
| **Annual Growth** | 25.6% | — | — | 35.2% | (7.2%) | 18.7% |

# Goodyear Tire & Rubber

Despite a worldwide alliance with Sumitomo Rubber Industries designed to dominate the tire industry, The Goodyear Tire & Rubber Company is the #3 tire maker in the world, behind Bridgestone and Michelin. The company operates about 60 plants worldwide, and has nearly 1,800 retail tire and auto centers. Goodyear sells tires for the replacement market as well as to the world's automakers. In addition to its own brand of tires, Goodyear makes Dunlop tires for sale in North America and Europe through its alliance with Japan's Sumitomo. The company has sold its Engineered Products division to The Carlyle Group.

Goodyear has called off plans to sell its Chemical Products division. Instead the company has integrated its chemical operations with those of its North American Tire division to take greater advantage of operational synergies.

The company has, however, gone forward with plans to jettison its Engineered Products division. Goodyear secured the services of J.P. Morgan Securities and Goldman Sachs to help it explore opportunities for the sale of Engineered Products in 2005.

Shortly after the Engineered Products decision was announced, Goodyear said it would close an undisclosed number of plants as part of a sweeping restucturing of its North American operations. The plan aims to save $1 billion by mid-2008. In 2006 Goodyear made another move that aimed to lower costs. The company announced it would cut 1,500 jobs in the UK and Poland as it shuttered unprofitable operations in those countries.

Later in 2006 Goodyear sold its global tire fabric operations to South Korea's Hyosung Corporation for about $80 million.

In early 2007 Goodyear said it would invest more than $100 million over four years in expanding production of high-value tires at T C Debica, Poland's largest tire manufacturer. The company holds a 60% stake in Debica and has previously invested almost $200 million in the Polish tire maker since acquiring an interest in Debica in 1995.

Later in 2007 the company struck a deal for The Carlyle Group to buy its Engineered Products division for about $1.5 billion. The division makes rubber automotive hoses and belts, conveyor belts, and tank tracks for military and off-road vehicles.

## HISTORY

In 1898 Frank and Charles Seiberling founded a tire and rubber company in Akron, Ohio, and named it after Charles Goodyear (inventor of the vulcanization process, 1839). The debut of the Quick Detachable tire and the Universal Rim (1903) made Goodyear the world's largest tire maker by 1916.

Goodyear began manufacturing in Canada in 1910, and over the next two decades it expanded into Argentina, Australia, and the Dutch East Indies. The company established its own rubber plantations in Sumatra (now part of Indonesia) in 1916.

Financial woes led to reorganization in 1921, and investment bankers forced the Seiberlings out. Succeeding caretaker management, Paul Litchfield began three decades as CEO in 1926, a time in which Goodyear had emerged to become the world's largest rubber company.

Goodyear blimps served as floating billboards nationwide by the 1930s. During that decade Goodyear opened company stores, acquired tire maker Kelly-Springfield (1935), and began producing tires made from synthetic rubber (1937). After WWII Goodyear was an innovative leader in technologies such as polyester tire cord (1962) and the bias-belted tire (1967).

By 1980 Goodyear had introduced radial tire brands such as the all-weather Tiempo, the Eagle, and the Arriva, as it led the US market.

Thwarting British financier Sir James Goldsmith's takeover attempt in 1986, CEO Robert Mercer raised $1.7 billion by selling the company's non-tire businesses (Motor Wheel, Goodyear Aerospace) and by borrowing heavily.

Recession, overcapacity, and price-cutting in 1990 led to hard times for tire makers. After suffering through 1990, its first money-losing year since the Depression, Goodyear lured Stanley Gault out of retirement. He ceased marketing tires exclusively through Goodyear's dealer network by selling tires through Wal-Mart, Kmart, and Sears. Gault also cut costs through layoffs, plant closures, and spending reductions and returned Goodyear to profitability in 1991.

The company increased its presence in the US retail market in 1995 when it began selling tires through 860 Penske Auto Centers and 300 Montgomery Ward auto centers. President Samir Gibara succeeded chairman Gault as CEO in 1996. That year Goodyear bought Poland's leading tire maker, T C Debica, and a 60% stake in South African tire maker Contred (acquiring the rest in 1998).

In 1997 Goodyear formed an alliance with Kobe, Japan-based Sumitomo Rubber Industries, under which the companies agreed to make and market tires for one another in Asia and North America. The company acquired Sumitomo Rubber Industries' North American and European Dunlop tire businesses in 1999. The acquisition returned Goodyear to its #1 position in the tire-making industry.

Despite record sales in 2000, the company's profits hit some hard road, prompting Goodyear to lay off 10% of its workforce and implement other cost-cutting efforts.

Early in 2001 the company announced that it would close its Mexican tire plant. The same year the company agreed to replace Firestone Wilderness AT tires with Goodyear tires for Ford owners as part of Ford's big Firestone tire recall. In 2002 the tire maker became embroiled in an age discrimination lawsuit claiming unfair job evaluations for the company's older employees. Blaming a slow US economy, Goodyear announced plans to cut 450 jobs at its Union City, Tennessee, manufacturing plant. Later in the year as the company was embroiled in a lengthy debate with the United Steelworkers union it was announced that the Huntsville, Alabama, tire manufacturing plant would be closed. Goodyear also announced that it would cut 500 nonunion salaried employees in North America.

Qantas Airways announced in 2004 that it has chosen Goodyear to provide tires for its Jetstar Airways unit. Also that year Goodyear announced more job cuts in its engineered products and chemicals sectors.

In 2005 Goodyear sold its stake in Goodyear Sumatra Plantations (rubber plantations in Indonesia) to Bridgestone Corporation. Later that year the company sold its Wingtack adhesive resin business to Sartomer Company Inc. (a subsidiary of France's TOTAL S.A.).

## EXECUTIVES

**Chairman, President, and CEO:** Robert (Bob) Keegan, age 59, $3,377,333 pay
**President, North American Tire:** Richard J. (Rich) Kramer, age 43, $1,174,433 pay (prior to title change)
**EVP, Quality Systems and CTO:** Joseph M. (Joe) Gingo, age 60, $733,000 pay
**EVP and CFO:** W. Mark Schmitz, age 56
**SVP, Finance and Strategy:** Darren R. Wells, age 41
**SVP, General Counsel, and Secretary:** C. Thomas Harvie, age 62, $865,167 pay
**SVP, Human Resources:** Kathleen T. Geier, age 49
**SVP, Global Sourcing:** Christopher W. (Chris) Clark, age 54
**VP and Controller:** Thomas A. Connell, age 57
**VP, Business Development:** Laura K. Thompson, age 37
**VP, Commercial Sales, North American Tire:** Steve McCellan
**VP, Consumer Sales, North American Tire:** Jack Winterton
**VP Finance, North American Tire:** Marc O. Voorhees, age 50
**VP, Global Engineering and Manufacturing Technology:** Robert A. (Bob) Novotny
**VP, Information Technology and CIO:** Stephanie K. Wernet
**VP and General Manager, Original Equipment Tires, North American Tire:** Johann Finkelmeier, age 53
**VP, Purchasing and Chief Procurement Officer:** Gary A. Miller, age 59
**VP, Public Relations and Communications, North American Tire:** Edward W. (Ed) Markey
**VP and Treasurer:** Damon J. Audia, age 36
**Auditors:** PricewaterhouseCoopers LLP

## LOCATIONS

**HQ:** The Goodyear Tire & Rubber Company
1144 E. Market St., Akron, OH 44316
**Phone:** 330-796-2121 **Fax:** 330-796-2222
**Web:** www.goodyear.com

**2006 Sales**

| | $ mil. | % of total |
|---|---|---|
| US | 8,664 | 43 |
| Germany | 2,170 | 11 |
| Other countries | 9,424 | 46 |
| **Total** | **20,258** | **100** |

## PRODUCTS/OPERATIONS

**2006 Sales**

| | $ mil. | % of total |
|---|---|---|
| Tire Business | | |
| North American Tire | 9,089 | 45 |
| European Tire | 4,990 | 25 |
| Latin American Tire | 1,604 | 8 |
| Eastern Europe, Middle East, & Africa Tire | 1,562 | 8 |
| Asia Pacific Tire | 1,503 | 7 |
| Engineered Products | 1,510 | 7 |
| **Total** | **20,258** | **100** |

**Selected Products**

Chemical products (coating resins, latex polymers, and rubber chemicals)
Tires
- Automotive
- Aviation
- Buses
- Earthmoving, farm, and industrial equipment
- Motorcycles
- Trucks

## COMPETITORS

AirBoss of America
Bandag
BFS Retail & Commercial
Bridgestone
Bridgestone Americas
Continental AG
Cooper Tire & Rubber
Hankook Tire
Kumho Tire
Marangoni
Michelin
Michelin North America
Midas
Pep Boys
Pirelli & C.
Sime Darby
SmarTire Systems
TBC
Titan International
Toyo Tire & Rubber
Yokohama Rubber
Zeon

## HISTORICAL FINANCIALS

Company Type: Public

**Income Statement** FYE: December 31

| | REVENUE ($ mil.) | NET INCOME ($ mil.) | NET PROFIT MARGIN | EMPLOYEES |
|---|---|---|---|---|
| **12/06** | 20,258 | (330) | — | 77,000 |
| **12/05** | 19,723 | 228 | 1.2% | 80,000 |
| **12/04** | 18,370 | 115 | 0.6% | 84,000 |
| **12/03** | 15,119 | (802) | — | 86,000 |
| **12/02** | 13,850 | (1,106) | — | 92,742 |
| **Annual Growth** | 10.0% | — | — | (4.5%) |

**2006 Year-End Financials**

Debt ratio: —
Return on equity: —
Cash ($ mil.): 4,113
Current ratio: 2.18
Long-term debt ($ mil.): 6,563
No. of shares (mil.): 178
Dividends
Yield: —
Payout: —
Market value ($ mil.): 3,741

**Stock History** NYSE: GT

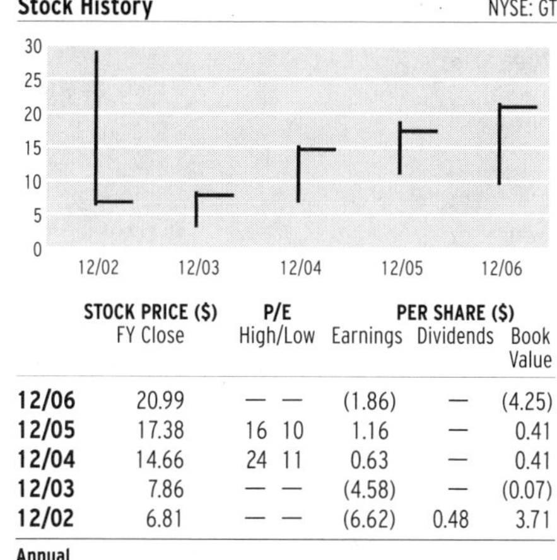


| | STOCK PRICE ($) FY Close | P/E High/Low | PER SHARE ($) Earnings | Dividends | Book Value |
|---|---|---|---|---|---|
| **12/06** | 20.99 | — — | (1.86) | — | (4.25) |
| **12/05** | 17.38 | 16 10 | 1.16 | — | 0.41 |
| **12/04** | 14.66 | 24 11 | 0.63 | — | 0.41 |
| **12/03** | 7.86 | — — | (4.58) | — | (0.07) |
| **12/02** | 6.81 | — — | (6.62) | 0.48 | 3.71 |
| **Annual Growth** | 32.5% | — — | — | — | — |

# Google Inc.

If you've never Googled, you probably aren't finding what you want online. Google operates the leading Internet search engine, offering targeted search results from more than 8 billion Web pages. The site, which ranks results based on a proprietary algorithm, offers search results in more than 35 languages and attracts an audience of more than 380 million people worldwide. The company generates revenue through ads that are targeted by keywords. Google also sells ads across a network of more than 200,000 affiliated Web sites. Founders Sergey Brin and Larry Page each have nearly 30% voting control of the company.

While Google's core business includes search engine services and advertising, the company also provides Web portal services such as Webmail, blogging, photo sharing, and instant messaging. Other tools Google offers to help its users make the most of their digital life include comparison shopping services (Froogle), an online image library (Google Images), general news stories (Google News), financial news (Google Finance), interactive maps (Google Maps), and Internet discussion groups (Google Groups).

The heart of Google's business, however, is its advertising system, comprised of its AdWords and AdSense products. Customers of Google AdWords consist of advertisers who seek to drive qualified traffic from Google to their sites and generate leads. Advertisers bid on keywords and have their ads appear as links on the right-hand column of Google's search results page under the sponsored links heading. Google powers the search capabilities of other publishers' Web sites and search engines through its AdSense for Search product.

With Google's AdSense for Content, Google automatically delivers ads to a publisher's Web site that are precisely targeted to its content, and the publisher shares in the revenue generated when readers click on the ads. Customers of Google AdSense include publishers of third-party Web sites that comprise the Google AdSense Network. The AdSense Network includes many small Web sites but has also attracted several big players in online publishing and e-commerce, including AOL, IAC Search & Media (Ask.com), and NYTimes.com.

The company opened up its well-stuffed wallet with the purchase of YouTube for more than $1.6 billion in 2006 in order to complement its online video offering (Google Video). In addition, Google has announced plans to acquire digital ad firm DoubleClick for $3.1 billion, solidifying Google's dominance in the online ad industry, and e-mail security company Postini for $625 million in cash, furthuring Google's push into business software.

Google has announced a Chinese-language brand name and is expanding a Beijing research center to develop new products to take on Baidu.com, the Chinese market leader.

Google takes its name from "googol," the mathematical term for the value represented by a one followed by 100 zeros. (In keeping with that theme, the company's headquarters is referred to as "the Googleplex," a play on googolplex — a one followed by a googol zeros.)

Chairman and CEO Eric Schmidt has about 10% voting control through his 5% equity stake.

## HISTORY

Google is the product of two computer science grad students, Sergey Brin and Larry Page, who met in 1995 at Stanford University where they studied methods of searching and organizing large datasets. They discovered a formula to rank the order of random search results by relevancy, and in 1997 they adopted the name Google to their findings.

In 1998 the two presented their discovery at the World Wide Web Conference, and by 1999 they had raised almost $30 million in funding from private investors, venture capital firms, and Stanford University. Later that year the Google site was launched.

Brin and Page hired tech industry veteran Eric Schmidt (former CTO at Sun Microsystems and former CEO of Novell) in 2001 as Google's CEO. Brin, previously the company's chairman, adopted the role of president of technology, and Page, previously CEO of Google, became president of product. Also in 2001 Google launched AdWords, its search-based advertising service. The following year the company launched another advertising service, the context-based AdSense.

In 2003 Google purchased Applied Semantics, a software company that makes applications for online advertising and managing domain names and other information. Also that year the company hired 100 additional software engineers to work in its New York office. Google next purchased Kaltix Corp., a Palo Alto, California-based startup that focuses on developing personalized and context-sensitive search technologies.

And in 2004, the once highly secretive company went public in one of the most anticipated IPOs ever, raising $1.6 billion.

With rivals (and former technology licensees) Yahoo! and MSN launching their own search engines and targeted advertising systems, Google is locked in a race to develop new search tools to attract users and to expand its advertising networks. In 2005 it agreed to invest $1 billion for a 5% stake in AOL, gaining ad distribution throughout the content portal's network of sites. Under the deal, AOL continues to use Google's search technology and the two companies work together to make their instant messaging software compatible with one another. AOL also gets about $300 million in promotional advertising for its online properties through Google's AdSense Network.

In addition to these deals, in 2006 the company made high-profile agreements with News Corp.'s Fox Interactive Media (FIM) and Viacom's MTV Networks. FIM selected Google as the $900 million high bidder for providing search on MySpace.com and other Fox properties in a multiyear search agreement, and Google will distribute MTV video (shows such as *Laguna Beach* and *Sponge Bob Square Pants*) to a variety of sites. Google separately announced agreements with Warner Music Group and Sony BMG to make music videos and other content available for free through its video service and on partner sites.

The company acquired Adscape Media (a technology company focused on placing advertising within videogames) in 2007.

## EXECUTIVES

**Chairman and CEO:** Eric E. Schmidt, age 51, $1,724 pay
**Director; President, Products:** Larry E. Page, age 34, $1,724 pay
**Director; President, Technology:** Sergey Brin, age 33, $1,724 pay
**SVP and CFO:** George Reyes, age 52, $421,052 pay
**SVP Business Operations:** Shona L. Brown, age 40, $421,339 pay
**SVP Corporate Development, Chief Legal Officer, and Secretary:** David C. Drummond, age 43, $421,052 pay
**SVP Engineering and Research:** Robert A. (Alan) Eustace, age 50
**SVP Global Sales and Business Development:** Omid Kordestani, age 43
**SVP Operations and Google Fellow:** Urs Hölzle
**SVP Product Management:** Jonathan J. Rosenberg, age 45, $457,116 pay
**VP and Chief Internet Evangelist:** Vinton G. (Vint) Cerf, age 63
**VP and General Counsel:** Kent Walker
**VP Advertising Sales:** Tim Armstrong
**VP Systems Infrastructure Engineering:** W. M. (Bill) Coughran Jr.
**VP Engineering:** Jeff Huber
**VP Engineering:** Udi Manber
**VP Engineering, Product, and Public Affairs; President, Google China:** Kai-Fu Lee
**VP Global Communications and Public Affairs:** Elliot Schrage, age 46
**Director Human Resources:** Stacy Sullivan
**Director Marketing:** Doug Edwards
**Investor Relations:** Maria Shim
**Auditors:** Ernst & Young LLP

## LOCATIONS

**HQ:** Google Inc.
1600 Amphitheatre Pkwy., Mountain View, CA 94043
**Phone:** 650-253-0000 **Fax:** 650-253-0001
**Web:** www.google.com

Google has offices in Atlanta; Boston; Chicago; Dallas; Denver; Detroit; Irving, Mountain View, and Santa Monica, California; Kirkland and Seattle, Washington; New York City; Phoenix; and Pittsburgh. It also has international operations in Australia, Brazil, Canada, Denmark, France, Germany, India, Italy, Japan, Mexico, the Netherlands, Spain, South Korea, Sweden, Switzerland, Turkey, and the UK.

**2006 Sales**

| | % of total |
|---|---|
| US | 57 |
| UK | 15 |
| Other countries | 28 |
| **Total** | **100** |

## PRODUCTS/OPERATIONS

**2006 Sales**

| | $ mil. | % of total |
|---|---|---|
| Advertising | | |
| Google sites | 6,333 | 60 |
| Google networks | 4,160 | 39 |
| Licensing & other | 112 | 1 |
| **Total** | **10,605** | **100** |

**Selected Operations and Products**

Advertising programs
- AdSense (network ad program for online publishers)
- AdWords (text-based ad placement for advertisers)

Internet search and content
- Google Alerts (news and search e-mail alerts)
- Google Answers (fee-based expert help)
- Google Catalogs (searchable mail-order catalogs)
- Google Earth (3-D satellite imagery)
- Google Groups (message boards)
- Google Image Search
- Google Labs (online services research and development)
- Google Local (localized search)
- Google Mobile (wireless device content)
- Google News
- Google Scholar (academic materials search)
- Google Video
- Google Web Directory
- Google Web Search
- Froogle (comparison shopping)
- YouTube

Tools and applications
- Blogger (Web logging tools)
- Gmail (Web-based e-mail)
- Google Analytics (Web traffic measurement)
- Google Desktop Search
- Google Language Tools (translation tools)
- Google Talk (instant messaging)
- Google Toolbar (browser plug-in application)
- Picasa (digital photo organization and sharing)

## COMPETITORS

24/7 Real Media
aQuantive
Citysearch
CNET Networks
craigslist
Daum Communications
DoubleClick
IAC Search & Media
InfoSpace
LookSmart
MIVA
MSN
NetEase.com
Shopping.com
Shopzilla
SINA
Sohu.com
ValueClick
Yahoo!

## HISTORICAL FINANCIALS

Company Type: Public

**Income Statement** FYE: December 31

| | REVENUE ($ mil.) | NET INCOME ($ mil.) | NET PROFIT MARGIN | EMPLOYEES |
|---|---|---|---|---|
| **12/06** | 10,605 | 3,077 | 29.0% | 10,674 |
| **12/05** | 6,139 | 1,465 | 23.9% | 5,680 |
| **12/04** | 3,189 | 399 | 12.5% | 3,021 |
| **12/03** | 1,466 | 106 | 7.2% | — |
| **12/02** | 440 | 100 | 22.7% | — |
| **Annual Growth** | 121.6% | 135.7% | — | 88.0% |

**2006 Year-End Financials**

Debt ratio: —
Return on equity: 23.3%
Cash ($ mil.): 11,244
Current ratio: 10.00
Long-term debt ($ mil.): —
No. of shares (mil.): 228
Dividends
Yield: —
Payout: —
Market value ($ mil.): 104,837

**Stock History** NASDAQ (GS): GOOG

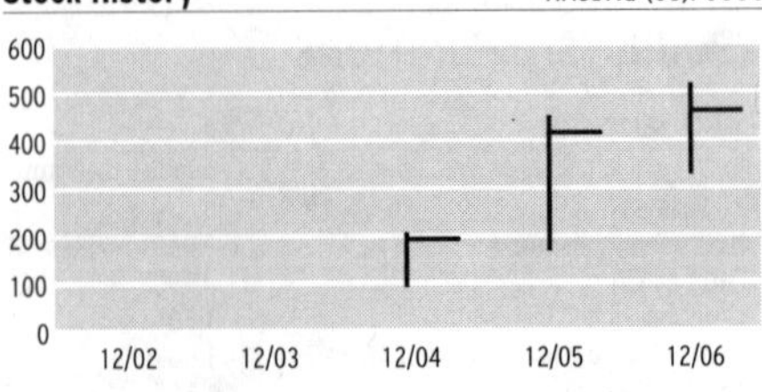


| | STOCK PRICE ($) FY Close | P/E High | P/E Low | PER SHARE ($) Earnings | Dividends | Book Value |
|---|---|---|---|---|---|---|
| **12/06** | 460.48 | 52 | 33 | 9.94 | — | 74.84 |
| **12/05** | 414.86 | 89 | 34 | 5.02 | — | 32.14 |
| **12/04** | 192.79 | 138 | 66 | 1.46 | — | 30.66 |
| **Annual Growth** | 54.5% | — | — | 160.9% | — | 56.2% |

# Green Bay Packers

On the frozen tundra of Lambeau Field, the Green Bay Packers battle for pride in the National Football League. The team, founded in 1919 by Earl "Curly" Lambeau, has been home to such football icons as Bart Starr, Ray Nitschke, and legendary coach Vince Lombardi. The Packers boast a record 12 championship titles, including three Super Bowl victories (its last in Super Bowl XXXI after the 1996 season). The team is also the only community-owned franchise in American professional sports, being a not-for-profit corporation with about 112,000 shareholders. The shares do not increase in value nor pay dividends, and can only be sold back to the team. No individual is allowed to own more than 200,000 shares.

Win or lose, Green Bay remains a very popular team: Regular season games have been sold out since 1960 and the waiting list for season tickets boasts about 74,000 names. (Get on the list now and you'll only have to wait 35 years to get your seats.) Nationally, the team regularly places near the top of popularity polls, and it is one of the top NFL teams in terms of merchandise sales.

The current success and popularity of the Packers is due in part to three-time MVP quarterback Brett Favre, who holds the league record for consecutive starts by a QB as well as several NFL passing records. However, retirement stories continue to dominate the headlines surrounding the ironman player as he enters his 16th season with the team.

Green Bay has also faced several changes in its front office in recent years. In 2007 the team scuttled a succession plan that would have seen president John Jones replacing longtime CEO Bob Harlan. Concerns about Jones' management abilities were initially reported as the reason for the sea change, though an official statement later cited health concerns arising from Jones' 2006 emergency open heart surgery.

Meanwhile, the franchise has settled into a new head coaching regime under Mike McCarthy. The former San Francisco 49ers assistant was hired as the team's 14th head coach in 2006, replacing Mike Sherman after a dismal 2005 campaign. (Sherman had lost his position as general manager the previous year when Ted Thompson was hired from the Seattle Seahawks.)

## HISTORY

In 1919 Earl "Curly" Lambeau helped organize a professional football team in Green Bay, Wisconsin, with the help of George Calhoun, the sports editor of the *Green Bay Press-Gazette.* At 20 years old, Lambeau was elected team captain and convinced the Indian Packing Company to back the team, giving the squad its original name, the Indians. The local paper, however, nicknamed the team the Packers and the name stuck. Playing on an open field at Hagemeister Park, the team collected fees by passing the hat among the fans. In 1921 the franchise was admitted into the American Professional Football Association (later called the National Football League), which had been organized the year before.

The Packers went bankrupt after a poor showing its first season in the league and Lambeau and Calhoun bought the team for $250. With debts continuing to mount, *Press-Gazette* general manager Andrew Turnbull helped reorganize the team as the not-for-profit Green Bay Football Corporation and sold stock at $5 a share. Despite winning three straight championships from 1929-31, the team again teetered on the brink of bankruptcy, forcing another stock sale in 1935. With fortunes on and off the field dwindling, Lambeau retired in 1950 after leading the team to six NFL championships (prior to the creation of the Super Bowl which pitted the NFL against rival American Football League). A third stock sale was called for that year, raising $118,000. City Stadium (renamed Lambeau Field in 1965) was opened in 1957. In 1959 the team hired New York Giants assistant Vince Lombardi as head coach.

Under Lombardi, the Packers dominated football in the 1960s, winning five NFL titles. With players such as Bart Starr and Ray Nitschke, the team defeated the Kansas City Chiefs in the first Super Bowl after the 1966 season. Lombardi resigned after winning Super Bowl II and five NFL championships. He died in 1970 and football commissioner Pete Rozelle named the Super Bowl championship trophy the Vince Lombardi trophy. But the team again fell into mediocrity. Former MVP Starr was called upon to coach in 1974 but couldn't turn the tide before he was released in 1983.

Bob Harlan, who had joined the Packers as assistant general manager in 1971, became president and CEO in 1989. He hired Ron Wolf as general manager in 1991, who in turn hired Mike Holmgren as head coach early the next year. With a roster including Brett Favre, Reggie White, and Robert Brooks, the Packers posted six straight playoff appearances and won its third Super Bowl (and 12th NFL title) in 1997. A fourth stock sale (preceded by a 1,000:1 stock split) netted the team more than $24 million.

After Holmgren resigned in 1999 (he left to coach the Seattle Seahawks), former Philadelphia Eagles coach Ray Rhodes tried to lead the team but lasted only one dismal season. In 2000 Mike Sherman, a former Holmgren assistant, was named the team's 13th head coach.

Prompted by falling revenue, the team announced plans to renovate Lambeau Field, and voters in Brown County later approved a sales tax increase to help finance the $295 million project. (The work was completed in 2003.) The next year Wolf retired and coach Sherman added general manager to his title. The team also signed quarterback Favre to a 10-year, $100 million contract extension.

While Sherman managed to lead the team to the playoffs in four of his first five seasons, the Packers were a disappointing 2-4 in postseason play. The team hired Ted Thompson from Seattle in 2005 to take over the general manager duties. That season turned out to be one of the worst in recent team history, however, and Sherman was replaced as head coach by San Francisco 49ers assistant coach Mike McCarthy in 2006.

## EXECUTIVES

**Chairman and CEO:** Robert E. (Bob) Harlan, age 70
**EVP, General Manager, and Director of Football Operations:** Ted Thompson, age 54
**VP and Director:** John J. Fabry
**VP Player Finance and General Counsel:** Andrew Brandt, age 47
**VP Finance:** Vicki Vannieuwenhoven, age 40
**VP Administration:** Jason Wied, age 35
**Head Coach:** Michael (Mike) McCarthy, age 42
**Director of Accounting:** Duke Copp
**Secretary, Executive Committee and Director:** Peter M. Platten III, age 67
**Director of Administrative Affairs:** Mark Schiefelbein
**Director of College Scouting:** John Dorsey, age 46
**Director of Marketing and Corporate Sales:** Craig Benzel
**Director of Pro Personnel:** Reggie McKenzie, age 44
**Director of Public Relations:** Jeff Blumb
**Director of Research and Development:** Mike Eayrs, age 56
**Team Historian:** Lee Remmel, age 83
**Marketing Manager:** Michelle Palubicki
**Pro Personnel Coordinator:** Autumn Thomas-Beenenga
**College Scouting Coordinator:** Danny Mock
**Head Trainer:** Pepper Burruss
**Team Physician:** Patrick McKenzie
**Treasurer and Director:** Larry L. Weyers, age 61
**Equipment Manager:** Gordon (Red) Batty
**Member, Executive Committee and Director:** Carl W. Kuehne
**Member, Executive Committee and Director:** John F. Bergstrom, age 60
**Member, Executive Committee and Director:** Edward N. Martin
**Auditors:** Wipfli Ullrich Bertelson LLP

## LOCATIONS

**HQ:** The Green Bay Packers, Inc.
1265 Lombardi Ave., Green Bay, WI 54304
**Phone:** 920-569-7500 **Fax:** 920-569-7301
**Web:** www.packers.com

The Green Bay Packers play at 72,928-seat capacity Lambeau Field in Green Bay, Wisconsin.

## PRODUCTS/OPERATIONS

### Championship Titles

Super Bowl Championships
- Super Bowl XXXI (1997)
- Super Bowl II (1968)
- Super Bowl I (1967)

NFC Championships (1996-97)
NFC North Division (2002-04)
NFC Central Division (1972, 1995-97)
NFL Championships (1929-31, 1936, 1939, 1944, 1961-62, 1965-67)
NFL Western Conference (1936, 1938-39, 1944, 1960-62, 1965-67)

## COMPETITORS

Chicago Bears
Detroit Lions
Minnesota Vikings

## HISTORICAL FINANCIALS

Company Type: Not-for-profit

**Income Statement** FYE: March 31

| | REVENUE ($ mil.) | NET INCOME ($ mil.) | NET PROFIT MARGIN | EMPLOYEES |
|---|---|---|---|---|
| **3/07** | 218 | — | — | 200 |
| **3/06** | 208 | — | — | 150 |
| **3/05** | 200 | — | — | 150 |
| **3/04** | 179 | — | — | 150 |
| **3/03** | 153 | — | — | 150 |
| **Annual Growth** | 9.2% | — | — | 7.5% |

**Revenue History**

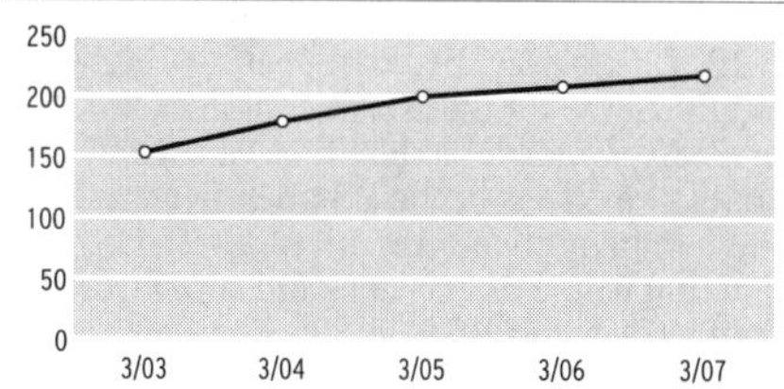


# Greif, Inc.

Good Greif! Greif (rhymes with "life") produces containers and containerboard, mainly for bulk shippers in the chemical, food, petroleum, and pharmaceutical industries. The firm's industrial shipping products include shipping drums, drum closure systems, and pallets, while its containerboard segment makes containerboard, corrugated sheets and containers, and multiwall packaging. Greif's multiwall bag products are used to ship a wide range of industrial and consumer products, such as chemicals, flour, pet foods, seed, and sugar. Greif also manages timber properties in the US and Canada. Michael Dempsey, the son of former company chairman Jack Dempsey (not the boxer), owns about 54% of Greif.

The purchase of Van Leer Industrial's packaging operations from Finnish firm Huhtamäki (in 2001) nearly doubled the size of Greif's business and satisfied the company's longtime desire for expansion into Europe. The acquisition vastly increased Greif's presence in Europe, Africa, Asia, Australia, and Latin America. Greif operates from about 200 locations in 40 countries.

In 2006 Greif expanded further when it acquired Delta Petroleum Company, which blends and packages lubricants and other chemical mixtures. Later that year, Greif spent $270 million to buy the European and Asian steel drum manufacturing business of Blagden Packaging Group.

## HISTORY

Charles Greif cofounded Vanderwyst and Greif, a Cleveland-based maker of casks, kegs, and barrels, in 1877. The next year his brothers William, Louis, and Thomas joined the company, which was renamed Greif Bros. to reflect the sibling involvement. The thriving company bought timberland as a source for raw materials and in 1926 went public as Greif Bros. Cooperage. In 1946 Jack Dempsey became chairman (his wife and mother-in-law owned minority stakes) and acquired a controlling interest. Dempsey moved Greif beyond barrels and kegs into fiber containers and steel drums. The company relocated to Delaware, Ohio, in 1951.

Greif entered the multiwall bag and corrugated packaging businesses in the 1960s and cut "Cooperage" from its name in 1969. In the early 1970s, it began making plastic containers. Greif teamed with Robert Macauley to form Virginia Fibre in 1974 and bought the supplier outright in 1992. In 1994, after 48 years at the helm, Dempsey was succeeded by COO Michael Gasser.

Greif bought three corrugated container firms and a pair of steel drum makers during 1997. Low paper prices and excess capacity dropped containerboard prices to a 19-year low in 1997. Dempsey died that year. In 1998 Greif bought Sonoco's industrial container business for $225 million in a deal that gave Greif control of two-thirds of the US fiber drum market. The company then announced a restructuring plan that would close plants and lay off workers. Greif joined with RDJ Holdings in a corrugated sheet joint venture, CorrChoice. In 1999 Greif bought Sonoco's intermediate bulk containers business and box maker Great Lakes Corrugated.

Late in 2000 Greif agreed to buy Finland-based Huhtamäki's industrial packaging operations. The deal, worth about $555 million, closed in 2001.

In 2003 the company changed its name to Greif Inc. The company felt that Greif Bros. had a regional sounding name unworthy of a global industrial giant.

## EXECUTIVES

**Chairman, President, and CEO:** Michael J. Gasser, age 55, $1,427,523 pay
**EVP and CFO:** Donald S. (Don) Huml, age 60, $760,555 pay
**SVP; President, Industrial Packaging and Services, Americas, Asia, Africa and Australia:** David B. Fischer, age 44, $574,874 pay
**SVP, General Counsel, and Secretary; President, Soterra LLC:** Gary R. Martz, age 48
**SVP, Global Sourcing and Supply Chain:** Ronald L. Brown, age 59, $613,391 pay
**SVP, Global Human Resources:** Michael L. Roane, age 52
**VP, CIO, and Controller:** Kenneth B. (Ken) Andre III, age 41
**SVP, Paper, Packaging & Services and Transformation Worldwide:** Michael C. (Mike) Patton, age 45, $579,234 pay
**VP and Treasurer:** John K. Dieker, age 43
**VP, Taxes:** Robert A. Young, age 52
**SVP, Industrial Packaging and Services, Europe:** Ivan Signorelli, age 54
**Director, Communications:** Debra (Deb) Strohmaier
**Assistant Secretary:** Sharon R. Maxwell, age 57
**SVP, People Services and Talent Development:** Karen L. Lane
**Auditors:** Ernst & Young LLP

## LOCATIONS

**HQ:** Greif, Inc.
425 Winter Rd., Delaware, OH 43015
**Phone:** 740-549-6000 **Fax:** 740-549-6100
**Web:** www.greif.com

### 2006 Sales

| | $ mil. | % of total |
|---|---|---|
| North America | 1,546.4 | 59 |
| Europe | 711.6 | 27 |
| Other regions | 370.5 | 14 |
| **Total** | **2,628.5** | **100** |

## PRODUCTS/OPERATIONS

### 2006 Sales

| | $ mil. | % of total |
|---|---|---|
| Industrial Packaging & Services | 1,945.3 | 74 |
| Paper, Packaging & Services | 668.1 | 25 |
| Timber | 15.1 | 1 |
| **Total** | **2,628.5** | **100** |

### Selected Products

Industrial shipping containers
  Drums (fiber, plastic, and steel)
  Industrial shipping containers
  Intermediate bulk containers

Containerboard
  Containerboard
  Corrugated containers
  Multiwall packaging
  Specialty and protective packaging products
  Transit protection products

## COMPETITORS

Cascades SA
Georgia-Pacific
Longview Fibre
Pactiv
SCA Packaging
Smurfit-Stone
Temple-Inland
Weyerhaeuser

## HISTORICAL FINANCIALS

Company Type: Public

### Income Statement

FYE: October 31

| | REVENUE ($ mil.) | NET INCOME ($ mil.) | NET PROFIT MARGIN | EMPLOYEES |
|---|---|---|---|---|
| **10/06** | 2,629 | 142 | 5.4% | 9,025 |
| **10/05** | 2,424 | 105 | 4.3% | 9,100 |
| **10/04** | 2,209 | 48 | 2.2% | 9,400 |
| **10/03** | 1,916 | 10 | 0.5% | 9,800 |
| **10/02** | 1,653 | 31 | 1.9% | 9,800 |
| **Annual Growth** | 12.3% | 46.3% | — | (2.0%) |

### 2006 Year-End Financials

Debt ratio: 57.0%
Return on equity: 18.0%
Cash ($ mil.): 187
Current ratio: 1.61
Long-term debt ($ mil.): 481
No. of shares (mil.): 12
Dividends
  Yield: 1.3%
  Payout: 24.8%
Market value ($ mil.): 1,090

### Stock History

NYSE: GEF

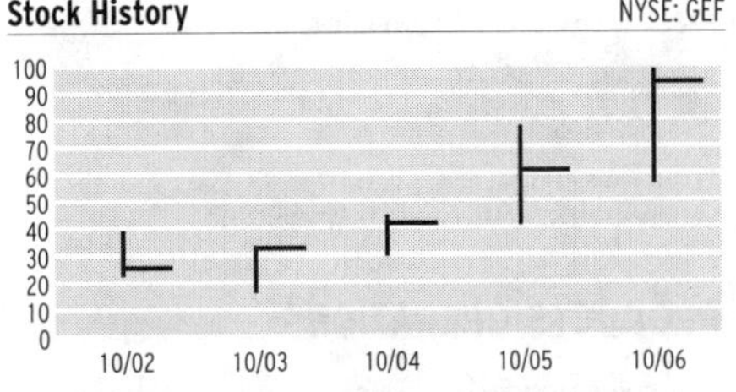


| | STOCK PRICE ($) FY Close | P/E High | P/E Low | PER SHARE ($) Earnings | Dividends | Book Value |
|---|---|---|---|---|---|---|
| **10/06** | 93.71 | 20 | 12 | 4.83 | 1.20 | 72.55 |
| **10/05** | 61.00 | 22 | 12 | 3.56 | 0.80 | 63.38 |
| **10/04** | 41.55 | 26 | 18 | 1.66 | 0.60 | 57.06 |
| **10/03** | 32.53 | 96 | 49 | 0.34 | 0.56 | 54.03 |
| **10/02** | 25.39 | 35 | 21 | 1.10 | 0.56 | 53.88 |
| **Annual Growth** | 38.6% | — | — | 44.8% | 21.0% | 7.7% |

# Halliburton Company

Ah, that feels better. Oilfield services giant Halliburton is feeling a lot lighter now that it has divested its KBR engineering and military contracts division. The company made the move so it can concentrate on its own dream — to be the largest oilfield services company in the world. Halliburton's Energy Services Group provides production optimization, drilling evaluation, fluid services, and oilfield drilling software and consulting. It combines tried and true well drilling and optimization techniques with high-tech analysis and modeling software and services. Halliburton works in established oilfields from the North Sea to the Middle East as well as in newer sites in Southeast Asia and Africa.

Halliburton took KBR public in 2006 by offering a 20% stake in an IPO and later divested the rest, cutting all ties with the company in 2007. It reorganized its management in anticipation of the deal by promoting former KBR CEO Andrew Lane to COO of Halliburton and putting him in charge of all Halliburton subsidiaries. Former CEO of Halliburton's Energy Services Group John Gibson left the company.

Halliburton hoped that spinning off KBR would protect it from the division's declining sales — KBR saw sales fall due to lower government services contracts in the Middle East, the end of fixed-price projects, and the resolution of disputed Iraqi contracts.

In 2006 Halliburton was awarded a multimillion dollar contract by Saudi Aramco as part of the Khurais oilfield development project, the largest in the region since the 1950s.

The company made headlines in 2007 when it announced that it would open a corporate headquarters office in the United Arab Emirates, and that its CEO David Lesar would move to Dubai. The move will allow Halliburton to foster better relations with Middle East oil companies as well as to grow its business in the region.

## HISTORY

Erle Halliburton began his oil career in 1916 at Perkins Oil Well Cementing. He moved to oil boomtown Burkburnett, Texas, to start his Better Method Oil Well Cementing Company in 1919. Halliburton used cement to hold a steel pipe in a well, which kept oil out of the water table, strengthened well walls, and reduced the risk of explosions. Though the contribution would later be praised, his technique was considered useless at the time.

In 1920 Halliburton moved to Oklahoma. Incorporating Halliburton Oil Well Cementing Company in 1924, he patented its products and services, forcing oil companies to employ his firm if they wanted to cement wells.

Erle died in 1957, and his company grew through acquisitions between the 1950s and the 1970s. In 1962 it bought Houston construction giant Brown & Root, an expert in offshore platforms. After the 1973 Arab oil embargo Halliburton benefited from the surge in global oil exploration, and later, as drilling costs surged, it became a leader in well stimulation.

When the oil industry slumped in 1982, the firm halved its workforce. Three years later a suffering Brown & Root coughed up $750 million to settle charges of mismanagement at the South Texas Nuclear Project.

In the 1990s Halliburton expanded abroad, entering Russia in 1991 and China in 1993. The next year Brown & Root was named contractor for a pipeline stretching from Qatar to Pakistan. Halliburton drilled the world's deepest horizontal well (18,860 ft.) in Germany in 1995.

Also in 1995 Dick Cheney, a former US defense secretary, became CEO. Brown & Root began providing engineering and logistics services to US Army peacekeeping troops in the Balkans in 1995 and won a major contract to develop an offshore Canadian oil field the next year.

The company nearly doubled in size in 1998 with its $7.7 billion acquisition of oil field equipment manufacturer Dresser Industries. The purchase, coupled with falling oil prices in 1998 and 1999, prompted Halliburton to ax more than 9,000 workers.

Cheney resigned as chairman and CEO that year after he was chosen as George W. Bush's vice presidential running mate. President and COO David Lesar was named to succeed him.

In 2001 a group consisting of investment firms First Reserve and Odyssey Investment Partners and Dresser managers paid $1.55 billion for Dresser Equipment Group. That year a number of multimillion dollar verdicts against Halliburton in asbestos cases sparked rumors that the company was going to file for bankruptcy (flatly denied by Halliburton) and caused the firm's stock price to tumble.

In 2002, in part to protect the company's assets from the unresolved asbestos claims issue, Lesar announced plans to restructure Halliburton into two independent subsidiaries, separating the Energy Services Group from Halliburton's KBR engineering and construction operations.

Halliburton settled more than 300,000 asbestos-related lawsuits by paying about $4 billion in cash and in stock. As a result, Halliburton placed its subsidiaries, Dresser Industries and Kellogg Brown & Root, under Chapter 11 bankruptcy protection. Later that year, in an effort to boost its newly formed Energy Services unit, Halliburton purchased Pruett Industries, a fiber optic sensor technology company.

In 2003 Halliburton announced plans to divest its noncore assets in an effort to return its focus to its main operating divisions. In 2004 the company's KBR subsidiary was awarded nearly $1.4 billion worth of contracts to aid in the repair and restoration of Iraq's oil fields during the US-led invasion of Iraq. The US Army Corps of Engineers later withdrew the contracts after allegations that they were awarded to the subsidiary due to Halliburton's relationship to Cheney. KBR also came under fire when the Pentagon claimed the company overcharged US taxpayers $61 million to supply fuel to Iraq. After an investigation by the US Army Corp of Engineers, Halliburton was cleared of any wrongdoing. The investigation was picked up by the Pentagon's criminal investigative unit and the US State Department. Following an internal audit, Halliburton repaid $6 million after discovering an overcharge from one of its subcontractor companies.

The company agreed to pay more than $4 billion in cash and stock to settle more than 300,000 asbestos and silica-related personal injury lawsuits filed against its DII Industries and KBR subsidiaries. Halliburton has reorganized its DII and KBR subsidiaries and finalized its asbestos settlements. DII and KBR emerged from Chapter 11 bankruptcy protection in January 2005.

## EXECUTIVES

**Chairman, President, and CEO:** David J. (Dave) Lesar, age 53, $1,300,000 pay
**EVP and COO:** Andrew R. (Andy) Lane, age 47, $650,000 pay
**EVP and CFO:** C. Christopher (Cris) Gaut, age 50, $575,000 pay
**EVP and General Counsel:** Albert O. (Bert) Cornelison Jr., age 57, $525,000 pay
**SVP and Chief Accounting Officer:** Mark A. McCollum, age 48, $395,000 pay
**SVP and Treasurer:** Craig W. Nunez, age 45
**SVP Business Development and Marketing:** Peter Bernard
**SVP Strategy:** James B. (Jim) Renfroe Jr.
**SVP Product Optimization:** David King
**SVP Eastern Hemisphere Operations:** Ahmed Lofty
**SVP and CTO:** Vik Rao
**SVP Western Hemisphere Operations:** Jim Brown
**VP Government Affairs:** Donald A. Deline
**VP and Corporate Secretary:** Sherry D. Williams
**VP Investor Relations:** Evelyn M. Angelle
**VP Human Resources and Administration:** Lawrence J. Pope, age 38
**VP Tax:** David R. Smith, age 60
**VP Strategic Procurement and Logistics for Supply Chain Management:** Mark McDaniel
**Director of Communications:** Cathy G. Mann
**Senior Representative, Public Relations, Trade Media:** Zelma Branch
**Manager, Public Relations:** Melissa Norcross
**Auditors:** KPMG LLP

## LOCATIONS

**HQ:** Halliburton Company
5 Houston Center, 1401 McKinney, Ste. 2400
Houston, TX 77010
**Phone:** 713-759-2600 **Fax:** 713-759-2635
**Web:** www.halliburton.com

### 2006 Sales

| | $ mil. | % of total |
|---|---|---|
| US | 7,216 | 32 |
| Iraq | 4,331 | 19 |
| UK | 1,594 | 7 |
| Kuwait | 330 | 2 |
| Other countries | 9,105 | 40 |
| **Total** | **22,576** | **100** |

## PRODUCTS/OPERATIONS

### 2006 Sales

| | $ mil. | % of total |
|---|---|---|
| KBR | | |
| Government & infrastructure | 7,248 | 32 |
| Energy & chemicals | 2,373 | 11 |
| Energy Services | | |
| Production optimization | 5,360 | 24 |
| Fluid systems | 3,598 | 16 |
| Drilling & formation evaluation | 3,221 | 14 |
| Digital & consulting solutions | 776 | 3 |
| **Total** | **22,576** | **100** |

### Selected Subsidiaries

BITC (US) LLC
Breswater Marine Contracting B.V.
Devonport Management Limited
DII Industries, LLC
Halliburton Canada Holdings, Inc.
Halliburton de Mexico, S. de R.L. de C.V.
KBR, Inc.
Landmark Graphics Corporation
Oilfield Telecommunications, LLC.

## COMPETITORS

ABB
Baker Hughes
Bechtel
BJ Services
Black & Veatch
Bouygues
Cameron
CGGVeritas
Diamond Offshore
ENSCO
Fluor
FMC
Foster Wheeler
GlobalSantaFe
IAP Worldwide Services
IHI Corp.
McDermott
Nabors Industries
National Oilwell Varco
Noble
Nuovo Pignone Industrie Meccaniche
Parsons
Peter Kiewit Sons'
Petroleum Geo-Services
Pride International
Raytheon
Saipem
Schlumberger
Smith International
Technip
Transocean
Weatherford International
WFI Government Services
Wilson

## HISTORICAL FINANCIALS

Company Type: Public

### Income Statement

FYE: December 31

| | REVENUE ($ mil.) | NET INCOME ($ mil.) | NET PROFIT MARGIN | EMPLOYEES |
|---|---|---|---|---|
| **12/06** | 22,576 | 2,348 | 10.4% | 104,000 |
| **12/05** | 20,994 | 2,358 | 11.2% | 106,000 |
| **12/04** | 20,466 | (979) | — | 97,000 |
| **12/03** | 16,271 | (820) | — | 101,000 |
| **12/02** | 12,498 | (998) | — | 83,000 |
| **Annual Growth** | 15.9% | — | — | 5.8% |

### 2006 Year-End Financials

Debt ratio: 37.8%
Return on equity: 34.2%
Cash ($ mil.): 4,379
Current ratio: 2.37
Long-term debt ($ mil.): 2,786
No. of shares (mil.): 998
Dividends
Yield: 1.0%
Payout: 13.5%
Market value ($ mil.): 30,988

### Stock History

NYSE: HAL

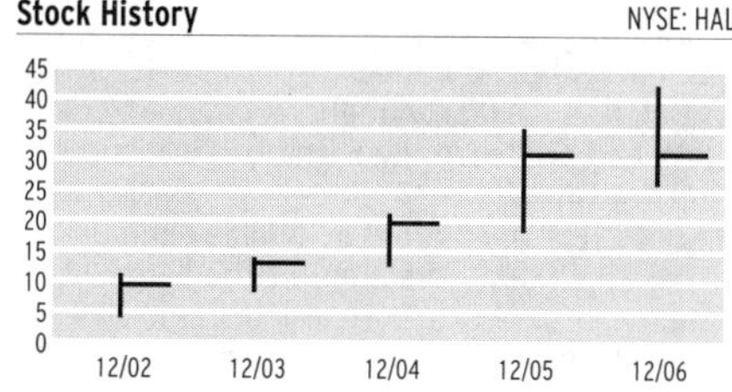


| | STOCK PRICE ($) FY Close | P/E High | P/E Low | PER SHARE ($) Earnings | PER SHARE ($) Dividends | PER SHARE ($) Book Value |
|---|---|---|---|---|---|---|
| **12/06** | 31.05 | 19 | 12 | 2.23 | 0.30 | 7.39 |
| **12/05** | 30.98 | 15 | 8 | 2.27 | 0.25 | 12.40 |
| **12/04** | 19.62 | — | — | (1.11) | 0.25 | 8.90 |
| **12/03** | 13.00 | — | — | (0.94) | 0.25 | 5.80 |
| **12/02** | 9.35 | — | — | (1.15) | 0.25 | 8.16 |
| **Annual Growth** | 35.0% | — | — | — | 4.7% | (2.4%) |

# Hallmark Cards

As the #1 producer of warm fuzzies, Hallmark Cards is the Goliath of greeting cards. The company's cards are sold under brand names such as Hallmark, Shoebox, and Ambassador and can be found in more than 43,000 US retail stores (about 4,000 of these stores bear the Hallmark Gold Crown name; the majority of these stores are independently owned). Hallmark also owns crayon manufacturer Crayola (formerly known as Binney & Smith). It offers electronic greeting cards and flowers through its Web site. It also owns a controlling stake of Crown Media. Members of the founding Hall family own two-thirds of Hallmark.

Not resting on well-engraved laurels, Hallmark has announced its intention to triple its revenue by 2010. While it plans to continue expanding its greeting card empire, the company is also intent on stretching its reach in markets such as personal development and family entertainment. The company is working on the image of its Gold Crown stores, changing store designs and layouts to reflect a homier image and differentiate the stores from other retail shops.

In 2005 the company's Crown Media unit sold its overseas operations as well as foreign rights to its program library. Hallmark also sold its portrait studio operation, The Picture People. The following year the company decided not to put itself up for sale following a strategic review.

In 2006 the company launched a women's lifestyle periodical called *Hallmark Magazine* and picked up the assets of Paramount Cards, a Rhode Island-based card manufacturer.

Hallmark had success with a pilot program of musical cards in mid-2006, seeing sales increase nearly 10%. In response to the positive news, the company introduced sound to more cards for the Christmas card rush. The cards are more expansive than regular non-musical cards, and the sound lasts about two years.

## HISTORY

Eighteen-year-old Joyce Hall started selling picture postcards from two shoe boxes in his room at the Kansas City, Missouri, YMCA in 1910. His brother Rollie joined him the next year, and the two added greeting cards to their line in 1912. The brothers opened Hall Brothers, a store that sold postcards, gifts, books, and stationery, but it was destroyed in a 1915 fire. The Halls got a loan, bought an engraving company, and produced their first original cards in time for Christmas.

In 1921 a third brother, William, joined the firm, which started stamping the backs of its cards with the phrase "A Hallmark Card." By 1922 Hall Brothers had salespeople in all 48 states. The firm began selling internationally in 1931.

Hall Brothers patented the "Eye-Vision" display case for greeting cards in 1936 and sold it to retailers across the country. The company aired its first radio ad in 1938. The next year it introduced a friendship card, displaying a cart filled with purple pansies. The card became the company's best-seller. During WWII Joyce Hall persuaded the government not to curtail paper supplies, arguing that his greeting cards were essential to the nation's morale.

The company opened its first retail store in 1950. The following year marked the first production of *Hallmark Hall of Fame,* TV's longest-running dramatic series and winner of more Emmy awards than any other program. Hall Brothers changed its name to Hallmark Cards in 1954 and introduced its Ambassador line of cards five years later.

Hallmark introduced paper party products and started putting *Peanuts* characters on cards in 1960. Donald Hall, Joyce Hall's son, was appointed CEO in 1966. Two years later Hallmark opened Crown Center, which surrounded company headquarters in Kansas City. Disaster struck in 1981 when two walkways collapsed at Crown Center's Hyatt Regency hotel, killing 114 and injuring 225.

Joyce Hall died in 1982, and Donald Hall became both chairman and CEO. Hallmark acquired Crayola Crayon maker Binney & Smith in 1984. It introduced Shoebox Greetings, a line of nontraditional cards, in 1986. Irvine Hockaday replaced Donald Hall as CEO the same year (Hall continued as chairman).

The company joined with Information Storage Devices in 1993 to market recordable greeting cards. It unveiled its Web site, Hallmark.com, in 1996 and began offering electronic greeting cards. Hallmark's 1998 acquisition of UK-based Creative Publications boosted the company into the top spot in the British greeting card market. The following year the company acquired portrait studio chain The Picture People (sold in 2005) and Christian greeting card maker DaySpring Cards. Hallmark also introduced Warm Wishes, a line of 99-cent cards. The company also unveiled the Hallmark Home Collection, a line of home furnishings.

The company began testing overnight flower delivery in the US just in time for Valentine's Day 2000. Hockaday retired as president and CEO at the end of 2001; vice chairman Donald Hall Jr. took the additional title of CEO in early 2002.

Hallmark decided to move some of its IT operations in 2004 to Affiliated Computer Services in a seven-year deal worth $230 million; the Dallas-based company opened a center near the Hallmark headquarters to handle the work. Binney & Smith announced it would change its name to Crayola effective 2007.

## EXECUTIVES

**Chairman:** Donald J. Hall
**Vice Chairman, President, and CEO:** Donald J. (Don) Hall Jr., age 51
**EVP and General Counsel:** Brian E. Gardner, age 54
**EVP Corporate Strategy:** Anil Jagtiani, age 43
**SVP Creative:** Paul Barker
**SVP Human Resources:** Tom Wright
**SVP Greetings:** Steve Hawn
**SVP Public Affairs and Communication:** Steve Doyal
**SVP Customer Development:** Steve Paoletti
**VP Business Research and One-to-One Consumer Marketing:** Jay Dittmann
**Group VP Operations:** Margaret Keating
**VP Trade Development:** Vince G. Burke
**President and CEO, Crayola:** Mark J. Schwab
**President, Personal Expression Group:** David E. Hall, age 44
**President, Retail:** James E. (Jim) Boike
**Public Relations Director, Public Affairs and Communications:** Julie O'Dell

## LOCATIONS

**HQ:** Hallmark Cards, Inc.
2501 McGee St., Kansas City, MO 64108
**Phone:** 816-274-5111 **Fax:** 816-274-5061
**Web:** www.hallmark.com

Hallmark Cards has operations in Australia, Belgium, Canada, Denmark, Japan, the Netherlands, New Zealand, Puerto Rico, the UK, and the US.

## PRODUCTS/OPERATIONS

### Selected Product Lines

Fresh Ink (greeting cards)
Hallmark.com (electronic greeting cards, gifts, flowers)
Hallmark Flowers (flower delivery)
Keepsake (holiday ornaments and other collectibles)
Mahogany (products celebrating African-American heritage)
Nature's Sketchbook (cards and gifts)
Shoebox (greeting cards)
Sinceramente (Spanish-language greeting cards)
Tree of Life (products celebrating Jewish heritage)

### Selected Subsidiaries

Crayola (crayons and markers)
Crown Center Redevelopment (retail complex)
Crown Media Holdings (controlling stake, pay television channels)
DaySpring Cards (Christian greeting cards)
Gold Crown (retail stores)
Hallmark Insights (business and consumer gift certificates)
Halls Merchandising (department store)
Image Arts (discount greeting card distribution)
InterArt (specialized cards)
Irresistible Ink (handwriting and marketing service)
Litho-Krome (lithography)
William Arthur (invitations, stationery)

## COMPETITORS

1-800-FLOWERS.COM
American Greetings
Amscan
Andrews McMeel Universal
Blyth
Build-A-Bear
Celebrate Express
CPI Corp.
CSS Industries
Disney
Dixon Ticonderoga
Enesco
Faber-Castell
iParty
Lifetouch
NobleWorks
Olan Mills
Party City
PCA International
SPS Studios
Syratech
Taylor Corporation
Thomas Nelson
Time Warner

## HISTORICAL FINANCIALS

Company Type: Private

**Income Statement** FYE: December 31

| | REVENUE ($ mil.) | NET INCOME ($ mil.) | NET PROFIT MARGIN | EMPLOYEES |
|---|---|---|---|---|
| 12/06 | 4,100 | — | — | 16,000 |
| 12/05 | 4,200 | — | — | 18,000 |
| 12/04 | 4,400 | — | — | 18,000 |
| 12/03 | 4,300 | — | — | 18,000 |
| 12/02 | 4,000 | — | — | 18,645 |
| Annual Growth | 0.6% | — | — | (3.8%) |

**Revenue History**

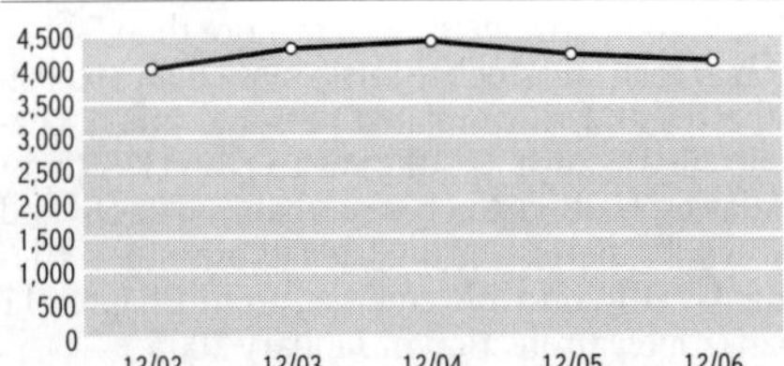

# H&R Block

Only two things are certain in this life, and H&R Block has a stranglehold on one. The company, which boasts nearly 23 million tax customers, is the leading tax return preparer in the US with 12,000-plus national retail offices; it also prepares tax returns in Canada, Australia, and the UK through some 1,400 offices. A third of its network is franchised. H&R Block also operates nearly 1,500 shared locations in Wal-Mart, Sears, and other stores. Average fee per client is $165. In addition to its ubiquitous tax-preparation services, the company provides a number of other products and services; these include tax-preparation software and residential mortgage loans.

Throughout its history H&R Block has sought to reduce its dependence on its tax services, which provide the bulk of its sales. The company has bought — and sold — many operations that it has hoped would balance its revenue stream. For example, it acquired wholesale lending business Option One Mortgage in the mid-90s, only to sell it in 2007. It will continue to offer mortgages through H&R Block Bank, which it opened in 2006, but has otherwise pulled out of the mortgage business.

The move away from tax preparation and advice has been a point of contention with some shareholders, namely Connecticut-based hedge fund Breeden Partners. Headed up by former SEC chairman Richard Breeden, Breeden Partners claims that more than $4 billion in potential profits have been lost due to poor decisions made by H&R Block. Breeden Partners is demanding seats on the H&R Block board of directors, a move opposed by H&R Block.

The company continues to offer other financial products and services through its various subsidiaries. Its H&R Block Financial Advisors unit offers brokerage and other investment services to individuals.

It is committed to growing its business services operations. Its RSM McGladrey Business Services subsidiary provides accounting, consulting, tax planning, and other services to midsized companies. H&R Block acquired the Tax and Business Services division of American Express for about $190 million in 2006 and combined it with RSM McGladrey to increase its offerings in this market. The company broadened its presence yet again when it acquired TaxWorks in 2007.

H&R Block's refund anticipation loan (RAL) program continues to be the target of numerous lawsuits that claim disclosures in the RAL applications are inadequate and that interest rates are excessive. The company has settled dozens of lawsuits, with more cases still pending.

H&R Block has also come under fire from New York Attorney General Eliot Spitzer who has sued the firm for $250 million, accusing it of "fraudulent marketing" and alleging that the majority of its customers who purchased its Express IRA product paid more in fees than they earned in interest on the accounts.

## HISTORY

Brothers Henry and Richard Bloch opened the United Business Co. in Kansas City, Missouri, in 1946 to provide accounting services. As tax preparation monopolized their time, a client suggested they specialize in taxes. The Blochs bought two ads, which brought a stampede of customers.

In 1955 the company became H&R Block (the Blochs didn't want customers to read the name as "blotch"). Basing charges on the number and complexity of tax forms resulted in a low-fee, high-volume business. The first tax season was a success, and the next year the brothers successfully tested their formula in New York City. But neither brother wanted to move to New York, so they worked out a franchise-like agreement with local CPAs. It was the first step toward becoming a nationwide chain.

As the chain grew, H&R Block began training preparers at H&R Block Income Tax Schools. By 1969, when Richard retired, the company had more than 3,000 offices in the US and Canada.

Henry began appearing in company ads in the 1970s; his reassuring manner inspired confidence and aided expansion. Fearing saturation of the tax preparer market, he pushed the company into new areas. H&R Block bought Personnel Pool of America in 1978 (taken public in 1994 as part of Interim Services) and two years later bought 80% of law office chain Hyatt Legal Services (sold in 1987).

In 1980 the firm bought CompuServe, which evolved from a computer time-share firm to a major online service by the 1990s. (H&R Block spun off CompuServe in 1996 and had sold all of its stake in the company by 1998.)

In 1992 Henry was succeeded as president by his son, Thomas, who built on the nontax side of the business to try for more even revenue distribution. Thomas stepped down in 1994. That year H&R Block bought Fleet Financial Group's Option One Mortgage, boosting its financial services. Frank Salizzoni became CEO in 1996.

In 1999 the firm formed RSM McGladrey by purchasing the non-consulting assets of the #7 US accounting firm, McGladrey & Pullen.

The McGladrey & Pullen deal didn't please everyone. In May 1999 — even before the McGladrey deal had been reached — a group of franchisees sued H&R Block to ensure that they receive their fair share of royalties from any sales generated in their territories by both the accounting group and H&R Block's tax software.

In 2000 H&R Block's online operations suffered some technology glitches, while its bottom line was blitzed by its string of purchases expanding the firm's financial services offerings. That year co-founder Henry Bloch became honorary chairman, ceding the chairman slot to Salizzoni. In 2001 H&R Block and Time Warner inked a cross-marketing agreement that gave the firms access to each other's customer base. Mark Ernst became CEO in 2001 and was named chairman in 2002, when Salizzoni retired.

In 2003 H&R Block settled a Texas RAL case for $43.5 million. Accounting errors caused H&R Block to overstate net income for the 2004 and 2003 fiscal years by $91.1 million.

Company co-founder Richard Bloch, who retired from the business in 1969, died in 2004. His brother (and company co-founder) Henry Bloch continues to serve as H&R Block's honorary chairman.

The company in 2004 was charged by the NASD with defrauding investors by selling them Enron bonds in the weeks leading up to that company's collapse.

In 2006 the tax preparer announced that it had gotten its own taxes wrong in recent years. As a result, H&R Block restated results for fiscal years 2004 and 2005 and parts of 2006 because of mistakes in calculating its income tax rate.

## EXECUTIVES

**Co-Founder and Honorary Chairman:** Henry W. Bloch, age 85
**Chairman, President, and CEO:** Mark A. Ernst, age 49, $854,167 pay
**EVP and CFO:** William L. (Bill) Trubeck, age 61, $757,920 pay
**EVP and General Counsel:** Carol F. Graebner, age 51
**SVP and CIO:** Richard (Rich) Agar
**SVP and Chief Marketing Officer:** Brad C. Iversen, age 57
**SVP and Corporate Controller:** Jeffrey E. (Jeff) Nachbor, age 42
**SVP Corporate Tax:** Peter F. Simpson
**SVP Human Resources:** Tammy S. Serati, age 48
**SVP and General Manager, Digital Tax Solutions:** Thomas A. (Tom) Allanson, age 45
**VP and Secretary:** Bret G. Wilson, age 48
**VP and Treasurer:** Becky S. Shulman, age 42
**VP Communications:** Linda M. McDougall, age 54
**VP Corporate Tax:** Timothy R. Mertz, age 56
**VP Government Relations:** Robert A. Weinberger, age 63
**VP Investor Relations:** Pam Kearney
**VP Tax, Mortgage, and Business Development:** Scott Ragan
**President and CEO, Option One Mortgage:** Robert E. (Bob) Dubrish, age 55, $579,692 pay
**President, Consumer Financial Services:** Steven L. (Steve) Nadon, age 50
**President, H&R Block Financial Advisors:** Joan K. Cohen
**President, Retail Tax Services:** Timothy C. (Tim) Gokey, age 45
**President, RSM McGladrey Business Services:** Steven (Steve) Tait, age 47, $757,920 pay
**President, RSM McGladrey Employer Services:** Robert M. Digby
**Group President, Commercial Tax Markets:** Marc West, age 48
**Director, Communications:** Nick Iammartino

## LOCATIONS

**HQ:** H&R Block, Inc.
1 H&R Block Way, Kansas City, MO 64105
**Phone:** 816-854-3000 **Fax:** 816-854-8500
**Web:** www.hrblock.com

H&R Block operates in Australia, Canada, the UK, and the US.

### 2007 Offices

| | No. |
|---|---|
| US | 12,784 |
| Canada | 1,070 |
| Australia | 360 |
| **Total** | **14,214** |

## PRODUCTS/OPERATIONS

### 2007 Sales

| | $ mil. | % of total |
|---|---|---|
| Services | 3,356.4 | 83 |
| Products & other | 529.9 | 13 |
| Interest | 135.0 | 4 |
| **Total** | **4,021.3** | **100** |

### Selected Subsidiaries and Affiliates

AcuLink Mortgage Solutions, LLC
AcuLink of Alabama, LLC
BFC Transactions, Inc.
Birchtree Financial Services, Inc.
Birchtree Insurance Agency, Inc.
Block Financial Corporation
Companion Insurance, Ltd.
Companion Mortgage Corporation
Credit Union Jobs, LLC
Equico Europe Limited
Equico, Inc.
Financial Marketing Services, Inc.
Financial Stop, Inc.

FM Business Services, Inc. (d/b/a Freed Maxick ABL Services)
Franchise Partner, Inc.
HRB Financial Corporation
O'Rourke Career Connections, LLC (50%)
OLDE Discount of Canada
Option One Mortgage Corporation
PDI Global, Inc.
Pension Resources, Inc.
RSM McGladrey, Inc.
TaxNet Inc.
The Tax Man, Inc.
West Estate Investors, LLC

## COMPETITORS

BDO International
CBIZ
Deloitte
Ernst & Young
Gilman + Ciocia
Grant Thornton International
Intuit
Jackson Hewitt
KPMG
Liberty Tax Service
Microsoft Business Solutions
PricewaterhouseCoopers
Universal Tax

## HISTORICAL FINANCIALS

Company Type: Public

**Income Statement** FYE: April 30

| | REVENUE ($ mil.) | NET INCOME ($ mil.) | NET PROFIT MARGIN | EMPLOYEES |
|---|---|---|---|---|
| **4/07** | 4,021 | (434) | — | 136,600 |
| **4/06** | 4,873 | 490 | 10.1% | 134,500 |
| **4/05** | 4,420 | 624 | 14.1% | 133,800 |
| **4/04** | 4,206 | 698 | 16.6% | 111,300 |
| **4/03** | 3,780 | 580 | 15.3% | 118,300 |
| **Annual Growth** | 1.6% | — | — | 3.7% |

**2007 Year-End Financials**

Debt ratio: 36.7%
Return on equity: —
Cash ($ mil.): 1,254
Current ratio: 0.67
Long-term debt ($ mil.): 520
No. of shares (mil.): 436
Dividends
Yield: 2.3%
Payout: —
Market value ($ mil.): 9,853

**Stock History** NYSE: HRB

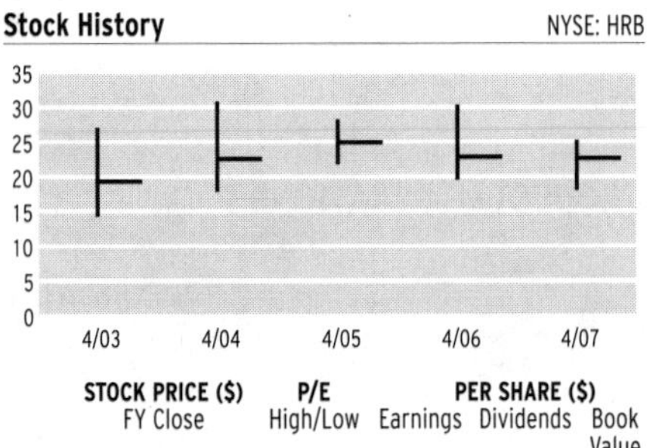

| | STOCK PRICE ($) FY Close | P/E High | P/E Low | PER SHARE ($) Earnings | Dividends | Book Value |
|---|---|---|---|---|---|---|
| **4/07** | 22.61 | — | — | (1.33) | 0.53 | 3.25 |
| **4/06** | 22.83 | 20 | 13 | 1.47 | 0.49 | 6.54 |
| **4/05** | 24.91 | 15 | 12 | 1.85 | 0.43 | 5.88 |
| **4/04** | 22.56 | 16 | 9 | 1.93 | 0.49 | 10.96 |
| **4/03** | 19.31 | 17 | 9 | 1.58 | 0.35 | 9.26 |
| **Annual Growth** | 4.0% | — | — | — | 10.9% | (23.1%) |

# Hanover Insurance Group

The Hanover Insurance Group, formerly known as Allmerica Financial Corporation, is an all-around property/casualty insurance holding company. Through its Hanover Insurance Company, it provides personal and commercial automobile, homeowners, workers' compensation, and commercial multiple-peril insurance coverage. In Michigan, it operates as Citizens Insurance Company. It sells its products through a network of independent agents in the midwestern, northeastern, and southeastern US, but Michigan and Massachusetts account for more than 50% of the company's business.

To better focus on its property/casualty lines, in late 2005 the company sold off its life insurance and annuity subsidiary First Allmerica Financial Life Insurance Company (FAFLIC) to Goldman Sachs.

Hanover Insurance kept two smaller businesses: its AMGRO commercial property finance company and Opus Investment Management which provides institutional investment management services.

Wriggling into a niche is one method of expanding, which explains the company's 2007 acquisition of Professionals Direct, a provider of professional liability insurance for small and mid-sized law firms.

## HISTORY

In 1842 a group of Worcester, Massachusetts, businessmen tried to form a mutual life insurance company. After a failed first attempt, they succeeded with the help of lobbyist Benjamin Balch. In 1844 the State Mutual Life Assurance Co. of Worcester set up business in the back room of Secretary Clarendon Harris' bookstore. The first president was John Davis, a US senator. The company issued its first policy in 1845.

In the early years State Mutual reduced risk by issuing policies only for residents of such "civilized" areas as New England, New Jersey, New York, Pennsylvania, and Ohio. It also restricted movement, requiring policyholders to get permission for travel outside those areas. By the 1850s the company had begun issuing policies in the Midwest (with a 25% premium surcharge), the South (for 30% extra), and California (for a pricey extra $25 per $1,000), with a maximum coverage of $5,000.

The Civil War was a problem for many insurers, who had to decide what to do about Southern policyholders and payment on war-related claims. State Mutual chose to pay out its Northern policyholders' benefits, despite the extra cost. In 1896 the firm began offering installment payout plans for policyholders afraid that their beneficiaries would fritter away the whole payment.

The first 30 years of the 20th century were, for the company, a time of growth that was stopped short by the Depression. But despite a great increase in the number of policy loans and surrenders for cash value, State Mutual's financial footing remained solid.

After WWII the company entered group insurance and began offering individual sickness and accident coverage. In 1957 it was renamed State Mutual Life Assurance Co. of America. The firm added property/casualty insurance in the late 1950s through alliances with such firms as Worcester Mutual Fire Insurance. During the 1960s State Mutual continued to develop property/casualty, buying interests in Hanover Insurance and Citizens Corp.

The firm followed the industry-wide shift into financial services in the 1970s, adding mutual funds, a real estate investment trust, and an investment management firm. This trend accelerated in the 1980s, and State Mutual began offering financial planning services, as well as administrative and other services for the insurance and mutual fund industries (the mutual fund administration operations were sold in 1995). Managing this growth was another story: Its buys left it bloated and disorganized. Technical systems were in disarray by the early 1990s, and the agency force had grown to more than 1,400. In response, the company began a five-year effort to upgrade systems, cut fat, and reduce sales positions.

In view of its shifting focus, State Mutual became Allmerica Financial in 1992. Three years later it demutualized. In 1997 it bought the 40% of Allmerica Property & Casualty that it didn't already own. The next year heavy spring storms hammered Allmerica's bottom line, and the company incurred $15 million in catastrophe losses. Also in 1998 it bought the portion of Citizens it didn't already own.

In 1999 Allmerica announced plans to sell its group life and health insurance operations to concentrate on its core businesses; Great-West Assurance bought them the next year. Its 1999 purchase of Advantage Insurance Network, a group of affiliated life insurance agencies, grew its distribution channels. In 2000 the firm reduced its workforce by 5% (some 6,000 employees) in an efficiency move. In 2001 Allmerica sold its 401(k) business to Minnesota Life.

Raising some much needed capital, the company sold a large chunk of its life insurance and annuities operations in 2002, which led to an improved bottom line the following year.

Deep in the red, the company in 2003 sold its fixed universal life insurance operations to John Hancock. The declining stock market forced the company to stop selling new variable annuities and life insurance products. The company rebounded somewhat, thanks in part to the discontinuation of unprofitable lines of business.

The company changed its name from Allmerica Financial Corporation to The Hanover Insurance Group in late 2005.

## EXECUTIVES

**Chairman:** Michael P. Angelini, age 64
**President, CEO, and Director:** Frederick H. (Fred) Eppinger, age 48, $1,184,000 pay
**EVP and CFO:** John J. Leahy
**EVP; President, Property & Casualty Companies:** Marita Zuraitis, age 46, $765,000 pay
**SVP, General Counsel, and Assistant Secretary:** J. Kendall Huber, age 52, $531,000 pay
**VP and COO:** Richard W. Lavey
**VP and CIO:** Gregory D. Tranter, age 50
**VP and Corporate Controller:** Warren W. Barnes
**VP and Chief Human Resources Officer:** Bonnie K. Haase, age 43
**VP and Chief Investment Officer:** Ann Tripp
**VP and Chief Marketing Officer:** John W. Chandler
**VP and Secretary:** Charles F. Cronin
**VP, Investor Relations:** Sujata Mutalik
**President, Commercial Lines:** David J. Firstenberg
**President, Personal Lines:** James S. (Jim) Hyatt
**Media Relations:** Michael Buckley
**Chief Actuary:** Kristen Albright
**Auditors:** PricewaterhouseCoopers LLP

## LOCATIONS

**HQ:** The Hanover Insurance Group, Inc.
440 Lincoln St., Worcester, MA 01653
**Phone:** 508-855-1000 **Fax:** 508-853-6332
**Web:** www.hanover.com

The Hanover Insurance Group operates throughout the US, primarily in the Northeast, Midwest, and Southeast.

## PRODUCTS/OPERATIONS

**2006 Sales**

| | $ mil. | % of total |
|---|---|---|
| Premiums | 2,254.6 | 85 |
| Net investment income | 318.9 | 12 |
| Fees & other income | 74.9 | 3 |
| Net realized investment losses | (4.3) | — |
| **Total** | **2,644.1** | **100** |

**Selected Subsidiaries**

Allmerica Funding Corp.
First Allmerica Financial Life Insurance Company
First Sterling Limited (Bermuda)
Opus Investment Management, Inc.
Allmerica Financial Insurance Brokers
The Hanover Insurance Company
Citizens Insurance Company of America
Hanover Texas Insurance Management Company, Inc.
AMGRO Receivables Corporation
VeraVest Investments, Inc.

## COMPETITORS

AIG
Allstate
American Automobile Association (AAA)
American Financial
Auto-Owners Insurance
Chubb Corp
GEICO
Liberty Mutual
Nationwide
Progressive Corporation
State Farm
Travelers Companies
USAA

## HISTORICAL FINANCIALS

Company Type: Public

**Income Statement** FYE: December 31

| | ASSETS ($ mil.) | NET INCOME ($ mil.) | INCOME AS % OF ASSETS | EMPLOYEES |
|---|---|---|---|---|
| **12/06** | 9,857 | 170 | 1.7% | 4,000 |
| **12/05** | 10,634 | (325) | — | 4,100 |
| **12/04** | 23,719 | 125 | 0.5% | 4,300 |
| **12/03** | 25,113 | 87 | 0.3% | 4,700 |
| **12/02** | 26,579 | (306) | — | 5,300 |
| **Annual Growth** | (22.0%) | — | — | (6.8%) |

**2006 Year-End Financials**

Equity as % of assets: 20.3%
Return on assets: 1.7%
Return on equity: 8.6%
Long-term debt ($ mil.): 509
No. of shares (mil.): 51
Dividends
Yield: 0.6%
Payout: 9.2%
Market value ($ mil.): 2,494
Sales ($ mil.): 2,644

**Stock History** NYSE: THG

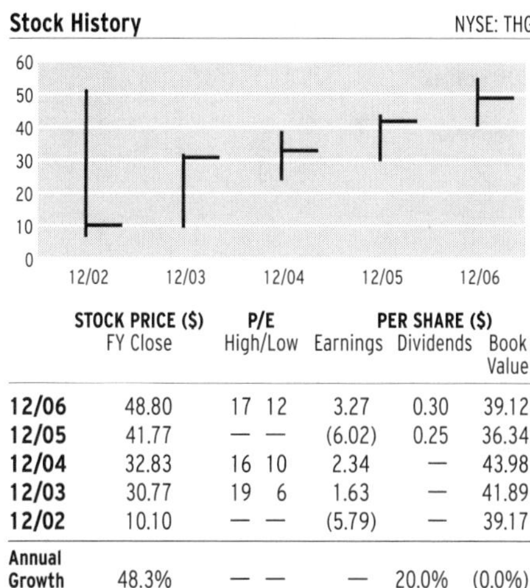


| | STOCK PRICE ($) FY Close | P/E High/Low | | PER SHARE ($) Earnings | Dividends | Book Value |
|---|---|---|---|---|---|---|
| **12/06** | 48.80 | 17 | 12 | 3.27 | 0.30 | 39.12 |
| **12/05** | 41.77 | — | — | (6.02) | 0.25 | 36.34 |
| **12/04** | 32.83 | 16 | 10 | 2.34 | — | 43.98 |
| **12/03** | 30.77 | 19 | 6 | 1.63 | — | 41.89 |
| **12/02** | 10.10 | — | — | (5.79) | — | 39.17 |
| **Annual Growth** | 48.3% | — | — | — | 20.0% | (0.0%) |

# Harley-Davidson

"Put your ass on some class," reads one (not necessarily official) Harley-Davidson T-shirt. Harley-Davidson is the only major US maker of motorcycles and the nation's #1 seller of heavyweight motorcycles. The company offers 35 models of touring and custom Harleys through a worldwide network of more than 1,500 dealers. Harley models include the Electra Glide, the Sportster, and the Fat Boy. The company also makes motorcycles under the Buell nameplate. Besides its bikes, Harley-Davidson sells attitude — goods licensed with the company name include a line of clothing and accessories (MotorClothes). Harley-Davidson Financial Services offers financing to dealers and consumers in the US and Canada.

If Harley-Davidson has a problem, it's with supply, not demand. Devoted customers sometimes wait a while for a new bike, depending on the model. To address the lag time, the company has steadily increased its annual production.

Harley has steadily grown sales and profits every year since 1995. However, the company's largest markets are mature (North America, Europe, and Japan) and therefore will not likely generate the sales volume necessary to take the company to the next level.

The company's major first step toward solving this issue came in April 2006 when it opened its first Chinese Harley dealership in Beijing. Near term the move is more about protecting the Harley brand in China against counterfeiting and just getting a footprint in the country. But if Harley sales eventually emulate the extremely brisk sales of American, European, and Japanese luxury automobile brands, Harley could be on the cusp of a major growth spurt. To take full advantage of such a situation, however, Harley would need to find a local manufacturing partner in order to keep retail prices down.

Later in 2006 Harley announced it would enter into a partnership with Lehman Trikes USA (a subsidiary of Lehman Trikes Inc. of Canada) to make Harley-branded trikes — or three-wheeled cycles. Harley did not specify when the trikes would go into production, but did say they would be distributed through its regular dealer network.

## HISTORY

In 1903 William Harley and the Davidson brothers (Walter, William, and Arthur) of Milwaukee sold their first Harley-Davidson motorcycles, which essentially were motor-assisted bicycles that required pedaling uphill. Demand was high, and most sold before leaving the factory. Six years later the company debuted its trademark two-cylinder, V-twin engine. By 1913 it had 150 competitors.

WWI created a demand for US motorcycles overseas that made foreign sales important. During the 1920s Harley-Davidson was a leader in innovative engineering, introducing models with a front brake and the "teardrop" gas tank that became part of the Harley look.

The Depression took a heavy toll on the motorcycle industry. As one of only two remaining companies, Harley-Davidson survived through exports and sales to the police and military. To improve sales, the company added styling features such as art deco decals and three-tone paint. The 1936 EL model, with its "knucklehead" engine (named for the shape of its valve covers), was a forerunner of today's models.

During WWII Harley-Davidson prospered from military orders. It introduced new models after the war to cater to a growing recreational market of consumers with money to spend: the K-model (1952), Sportster "superbike" (1957), and Duo-Glide (1958). Ever since competitor Indian Motorcycle Company gave up the ghost in the 1950s, Harley-Davidson has been the US's only major motorcycle manufacturer. (Indian Motorcycle was revived in 1998, however.)

The company began making golf carts (since discontinued) in the early 1960s. It went public in 1965, and American Machine and Foundry (AMF) bought the company in 1969. But by the late 1970s, sales and quality were slipping. Certain that Harley-Davidson would lose to Japanese bikes flooding the market, AMF put the company up for sale. There was no buyer until 1981, when Vaughn Beals and other AMF executives purchased it. Minutes away from bankruptcy in 1985, then-CFO Richard Teerlink convinced lenders to accept a restructuring plan.

Facing falling demand and increasing imports, Harley-Davidson made one of the greatest comebacks in US automotive history (helped in part by a punitive tariff targeting Japanese imports). Using Japanese management principles, it updated manufacturing methods, improved quality, and expanded the model line. Harley-Davidson again went public in 1986, and by the next year it had control of 25% of the US heavyweight-motorcycle market, up from 16% in 1985.

In 1993 the company acquired a 49% stake in Eagle Credit (financing, insurance, and credit cards for dealers and customers; it bought the rest in 1995) and a 49% share of Wisconsin-based Buell Motorcycle, gaining a niche in the performance-motorcycle market. (It bought most of Buell's remaining stock in 1998.) The recreational vehicle business, Holiday Rambler, was sold to Monaco Coach Corp. in 1996.

Jeffrey Bleustein, who had headed Harley-Davidson's manufacturing unit, was named the company's chairman and CEO in 1997. Two years later the company began production at its new assembly plant in Brazil, with an eye on increasing sales in Latin America. Harley-Davidson bested Honda in the US in 1999 for the first time in 30 years.

In 2000 Harley-Davidson's production increased by more than 15% over 1999, reaching just over 200,000 bikes. Despite the slowing economy in 2001, demand for Hogs continued to grow. To meet demand, Harley-Davidson again increased production by about 15% — making more than 240,000 bikes in 2001. Also in 2001 Harley introduced the V-Rod. The V-Rod draws design inspiration from Harley's legendary drag racing heritage.

Harley-Davidson marked its 100th year in operation in 2002. To celebrate, all 2003 model Harleys were designated 100th anniversary models. Harley-Davidson introduced two new lines of Buell motorcycles in 2003, the Firebolt and the Lightning.

In 2006 Harley acquired its Australian supplier of wheels and hubs, Castalloy.

## EXECUTIVES

**Chairman:** Jeffrey L. Bleustein, age 67
**President, CEO, and Director; CEO, Motor Company:** James L. Ziemer, age 57, $824,551 pay
**VP and CFO:** Thomas E. (Tom) Bergmann, age 40, $370,110 pay
**VP, Chief Credit Officer, and Chief Administrative Officer, Harley-Davidson Financial Services:** Kathryn H. Marczak
**VP, Treasurer and Acting CFO:** James M. Brostowitz, age 54, $290,645 pay
**VP, General Counsel, Secretary, and Chief Compliance Officer; VP, General Counsel, and Secretary, Motor Company:** Gail A. Lione, age 57, $353,715 pay
**VP, Strategic Planning and New Business Development, Motor Company:** John A. Hevey, age 49
**Chairman and CTO, Buell Motorcycle:** Erik F. Buell
**President and COO, Motor Company:** James A. (Jim) McCaslin, age 58
**VP Operations and CFO, Harley-Davidson Financial Services:** Lawrence G. Hund
**VP and Director, Harley Owners Group, Motor Company:** Michael D. Keefe
**VP, Customer Relationships and Motorcycle Product Planning, Motor Company:** Jerry G. Wilke
**VP, Advanced Operations, Motor Company:** Leroy Coleman
**VP and Controller, Motor Company:** John A. Olin
**VP and Director, Styling, Motor Company:** Louis N. Netz
**VP, North American Sales, Motor Company:** William B. Dannehl, age 48
**VP, Communication, Motor Company:** Kathleen A. Lawler
**VP, Enthusiast Services, Motor Company:** Lara L. Lee
**VP, Engineering, Motor Company:** W. Kenneth Sutton Jr., age 58
**VP, Human Resources, Motor Company:** Harold A. Scott, age 59
**Auditors:** Ernst & Young LLP

## LOCATIONS

**HQ:** Harley-Davidson, Inc.
3700 W. Juneau Ave., Milwaukee, WI 53208
**Phone:** 414-342-4680 **Fax:** 414-343-8230
**Web:** www.harley-davidson.com

Harley-Davidson operates manufacturing facilities in Missouri, Pennsylvania, and Wisconsin, as well as Brazil.

### 2006 Sales

| | $ mil. | % of total |
|---|---|---|
| US | 4,975.6 | 81 |
| Europe | 632.1 | 10 |
| Japan | 207.9 | 3 |
| Canada | 206.3 | 3 |
| Other regions | 163.7 | 3 |
| **Total** | **6,185.6** | **100** |

## PRODUCTS/OPERATIONS

### 2006 Sales

| | % of total |
|---|---|
| Motorcycles | |
| Harley-Davidson | 78 |
| Buell | 2 |
| Parts & accessories | 15 |
| General merchandise | 5 |
| **Total** | **100** |

### 2006 Unit Shipments

| | Units |
|---|---|
| Harley-Davidson | |
| Custom motorcycles | 161,195 |
| Touring motorcycles | 123,444 |
| Sportster motorcycles | 64,557 |
| Buell motorcycles | 12,460 |
| **Total** | **361,656** |

### Selected Motorcycles

Harley-Davidson
- Dyna
  - Low Rider
  - Super Glide Custom
  - Super Glide
  - Wide Glide
- Softail
  - Deuce
  - Fat Boy
  - Heritage Softail Classic
  - Night Train
  - Softail Standard
  - Springer Softail
- Sportster
  - 883 — XL 883
  - 1200 Custom — XL 1200C
  - 1200 Roadster — XL 1200R
- Touring
  - Electra Glide Classic
  - Electra Glide Standard
  - Road Glide
  - Road King
  - Road King Classic
  - Road King Custom
  - Street Glide
  - Ultra Classic Electra Glide
- VRSC
  - Night Rod
  - Street Rod
  - V-Rod

Buell
- Blast
- Firebolt
  - XB9R
  - XB12R
- Lightning
  - XB12S
  - XB12Ss
  - XB12STT
- Ulysses
  - XB12X

### Selected Operations

Buell Motorcycle Company
Harley Davidson Financial Services, Inc.
Harley-Davidson Motor Company

## COMPETITORS

BMW
Ducati
Ek Chor China Motorcycle
Honda
Kawasaki Heavy Industries
Norton Motorsports
Polaris Industries
Suzuki Motor
Triumph Motorcycles
Yamaha Motor

## HISTORICAL FINANCIALS

Company Type: Public

### Income Statement

FYE: December 31

| | REVENUE ($ mil.) | NET INCOME ($ mil.) | NET PROFIT MARGIN | EMPLOYEES |
|---|---|---|---|---|
| **12/06** | 6,186 | 1,043 | 16.9% | 9,000 |
| **12/05** | 5,674 | 960 | 16.9% | 9,700 |
| **12/04** | 5,321 | 890 | 16.7% | 9,580 |
| **12/03** | 4,904 | 761 | 15.5% | 8,800 |
| **12/02** | 4,303 | 580 | 13.5% | 8,500 |
| **Annual Growth** | 9.5% | 15.8% | — | 1.4% |

### 2006 Year-End Financials

Debt ratio: 31.6%
Return on equity: 35.7%
Cash ($ mil.): 897
Current ratio: 2.23
Long-term debt ($ mil.): 870
No. of shares (mil.): 258
Dividends
Yield: 1.1%
Payout: 20.6%
Market value ($ mil.): 18,185

### Stock History

NYSE: HOG

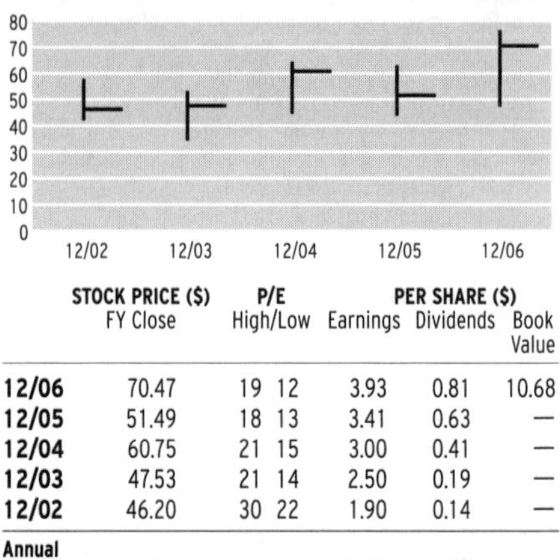


| | STOCK PRICE ($) FY Close | P/E High | P/E Low | PER SHARE ($) Earnings | Dividends | Book Value |
|---|---|---|---|---|---|---|
| **12/06** | 70.47 | 19 | 12 | 3.93 | 0.81 | 10.68 |
| **12/05** | 51.49 | 18 | 13 | 3.41 | 0.63 | — |
| **12/04** | 60.75 | 21 | 15 | 3.00 | 0.41 | — |
| **12/03** | 47.53 | 21 | 14 | 2.50 | 0.19 | — |
| **12/02** | 46.20 | 30 | 22 | 1.90 | 0.14 | — |
| **Annual Growth** | 11.1% | — | — | 19.9% | 55.1% | — |

# Harris Corporation

Hail Harris for a high-flying, high-tech hookup. The company, which develops communications products for government and commercial customers worldwide, makes microwave, satellite, and other wireless network transmission equipment; air traffic control systems; mobile radio systems; and digital network broadcasting and management systems. The company's largest customer is the US government. Harris' commercial clients include radio and TV broadcasters, utilities providers, construction companies, and oil producers. Clear Channel Communications, Sony, and Lockheed Martin are customers.

Harris has strengthened its line of communications products with acquisitions and has adapted technologies created for its government customers to other markets. The company has drawn on its expertise in broadcast, high-frequency, and radio-frequency transmission to build up its wireless broadband communications systems portfolio in an effort to expand its presence in commercial markets. Harris still makes about 60% of sales to the US government.

The company's acquisition of broadcast video systems provider Leitch Technology gave Harris a stake in the transition to high-definition digital services. In 2007 Harris' Microwave Communication Division is merging with Stratex Networks to form a new company, in which it will hold a 56% stake. It further acquired Multimax — a provider of IT and communication services — for $400 million. Multimax primarily serves government customers.

To concentrate on the communications equipment market, Harris has sold its semiconductor and office equipment businesses and acquired complementary commercial wireless equipment and software businesses.

## HISTORY

Harris was founded in Niles, Ohio, in 1895 by brothers Alfred and Charles Harris, both jewelers and inventors. Among their inventions was a printing press that became Harris Automatic Press Company's flagship product.

Harris remained a small, family-run company until 1944, when engineer George Dively was hired as general manager. Under Dively the company began manufacturing bindery, typesetting, and paper-converting equipment while remaining a leading supplier of printing presses. Harris merged with Intertype, a manufacturer of typesetting equipment, in 1957 and became known as Harris-Intertype Corporation.

During the 1960s and 1970s Harris-Intertype grew through acquisitions. In 1967 it bought electronics and data processing equipment maker Radiation, a company heavily dependent on government contracts, and relocated to Radiation's headquarters in Melbourne, Florida. The company also bought RF Communications (two-way radios, 1969), General Electric's broadcast equipment line (1972), and UCC-Communications Systems (data processing equipment, 1972).

The company changed its name to Harris Corporation in 1974. In 1980 Harris bought Farinon, a manufacturer of microwave radio systems, and Lanier Business Products, the leading maker of dictating equipment. In 1983 it sold its printing equipment business.

Harris formed a joint venture with 3M, called Harris/3M Document Products, in 1986 to market copiers and fax machines, and in 1989 it acquired the entire operation, which became Lanier Worldwide. Other 1980s acquisitions included Scientific Calculations, a CAD software developer (1986), and GE's Solid State group (1988).

Harris won a contract with the FAA in 1992 to modernize voice communications between airports and airplanes. Later that year Harris acquired Westronic, a supplier of automated control systems for electric utilities. In 1994 Harris began installing the world's largest private digital telephone network, along Russia's gas pipeline, and it spun off its computer products division as Harris Computer Systems.

In 1996 Harris became the first company to demonstrate a digital TV transmitter. That year it acquired NovAtel, a maker of cellular and wireless local-loop systems for rural areas, and it bought a stake in the Chile-based phone company Compañia de Teléfonos. In 1997 it purchased digital broadcasting specialist Innovation Telecommunications Image and Sound.

The company in 1998 purchased German chemical manufacturer Bayer's Agfa-Gevaert photocopier business, which doubled Lanier's share of the European office equipment market. Hurt by a tough semiconductor market that year, Harris laid off about 8% of its workforce.

Shifting toward a strictly communications-related operation in 1999, Harris sold its semiconductor operation (which now does business as Intersil) in a deal valued at about $600 million and spun off Lanier to shareholders. It also sold its photomask manufacturing unit to Align-Rite.

In 2000 Harris expanded its broadcasting and wireless transmission product lines with the acquisitions of Louth Automation and Wavtrace. That year the company began outsourcing the assembly of its commercial printed circuit boards and folded its telephone switching and alarm management product lines.

The company broadened its communications product portfolio in 2001 with the acquisitions of Exigent, a provider of satellite tracking and control software, and Hirschmann, a maker of digital broadcasting radio transmitters and cable systems. That year Harris sold its minority stakes in two industrial electronics joint ventures to majority owner General Electric.

The company also sold its telecom testing product lines, which accounted for about $30 million in revenue, to Danaher Corporation in mid-2004. Later that year the company bought Encoda, a developer of software and services to customers in the broadcast media industry, for $340 million.

## EXECUTIVES

**Chairman, President, and CEO:** Howard L. Lance, age 51, $2,762,020 pay
**EVP and COO:** Robert K. Henry, age 57
**VP and CFO:** Gary L. McArthur, age 44, $543,231 pay
**VP, Tax and Treasurer:** Charles J. (Chuck) Greene, age 51
**VP, Corporate Communications:** Jim Burke
**VP, Corporate Development:** Ricardo A. (Rick) Navarro, age 55
**VP, Corporate Technology and Development and Chief Growth Officer:** R. Kent Buchanan, age 55
**VP, Human Resources and Corporate Relations:** Jeffrey S. (Jeff) Shuman, $676,923 pay
**VP, Information Services, and CIO:** William H. Miller Jr.
**VP, Investor Relations and Corporate Communications:** Pamela (Pam) Padgett
**VP and General Counsel:** Eugene S. (Gene) Cavallucci, age 65
**VP; Counsel; and Director, Business Conduct:** John D. Gronda, age 48
**VP, Associate General Counsel, and Corporate Secretary:** Scott T. Mikuen, age 43
**VP Human Resources:** David Cunningham
**Principal Accounting Officer:** Lewis A. Schwartz, age 42
**President, Broadcast Communications Division:** Timothy E. (Tim) Thorsteinson
**President, Microwave Communications Division:** Guy M. Campbell, age 55, $607,500 pay
**President, RF Communications Division:** Dana A. Mehnert, age 44
**President, Department of Defense Programs:** Sheldon J. Fox, age 47
**Auditors:** Ernst & Young LLP

## LOCATIONS

**HQ:** Harris Corporation
1025 W. NASA Blvd., Melbourne, FL 32919
**Phone:** 321-727-9100 **Fax:** 321-674-4740
**Web:** www.harris.com

## PRODUCTS/OPERATIONS

### Selected Products and Services

Government
- Advanced avionics systems
- Aircraft, shipboard, spacecraft, and missile communications
- Airborne and spaceborne systems for processing, displaying, and communicating information
- Civil and military air traffic control systems
- Command, control, communication, and intelligence systems, products, and services
- Electronic warfare simulation
- Global Positioning System-based control systems
- Information assurance and security systems, products, and services
- Information technology systems and support
- Signal and image processing
- Terrestrial and satellite communication antennas, terminals, and networks
- Weather support systems

Commercial
- Broadband wireless access systems
- Digital and analog AM and FM radio studio and transmission systems and products
- High-frequency (HF), very-high-frequency (VHF), and ultrahigh-frequency (UHF) radio communication equipment
- Integrated communications management solutions
- Law enforcement communication systems
- Microwave communications products and systems
- Network automation solutions
- Secure communications systems
- Telephone line test systems and subscriber-loop test systems equipment
- Transmitters and studio equipment for digital and analog television

## COMPETITORS

ADC Telecommunications
Alcatel-Lucent
Cisco Systems
Ericsson
Fujitsu
General Dynamics
GigaBeam
Hitachi
L-3 Communications
Motorola, Inc.
NEC Corporation
Nera
Nokia
Nortel Networks
Northrop Grumman
Raytheon
Rockwell Collins
Rohde & Schwarz
Siemens AG
telent
Tellabs
Terabeam Inc

## HISTORICAL FINANCIALS

Company Type: Public

### Income Statement

FYE: Friday nearest June 30

| | REVENUE ($ mil.) | NET INCOME ($ mil.) | NET PROFIT MARGIN | EMPLOYEES |
|---|---|---|---|---|
| **6/07** | 4,243 | 480 | 11.3% | 16,000 |
| **6/06** | 3,475 | 238 | 6.8% | 13,900 |
| **6/05** | 3,001 | 202 | 6.7% | 12,600 |
| **6/04** | 2,519 | 133 | 5.3% | 10,900 |
| **6/03** | 2,093 | 60 | 2.8% | 10,200 |
| **Annual Growth** | 19.3% | 68.6% | — | 11.9% |

### 2007 Year-End Financials

Debt ratio: 21.5%
Return on equity: 26.9%
Cash ($ mil.): 429
Current ratio: 1.12
Long-term debt ($ mil.): 409
No. of shares (mil.): 130
Dividends
Yield: 0.8%
Payout: 12.8%
Market value ($ mil.): 7,068

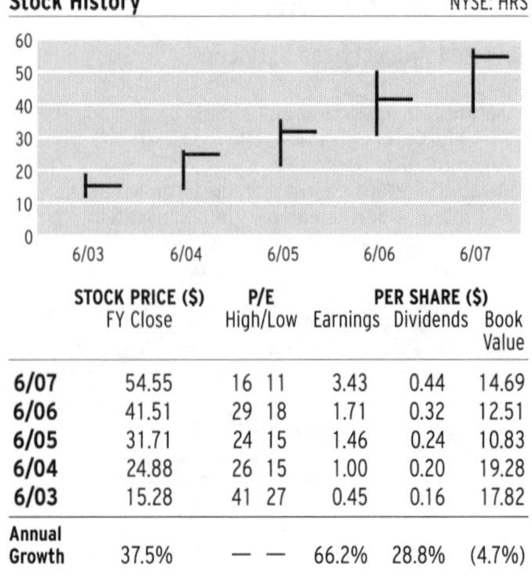


| | STOCK PRICE ($) FY Close | P/E High/Low | | PER SHARE ($) Earnings | Dividends | Book Value |
|---|---|---|---|---|---|---|
| **6/07** | 54.55 | 16 | 11 | 3.43 | 0.44 | 14.69 |
| **6/06** | 41.51 | 29 | 18 | 1.71 | 0.32 | 12.51 |
| **6/05** | 31.71 | 24 | 15 | 1.46 | 0.24 | 10.83 |
| **6/04** | 24.88 | 26 | 15 | 1.00 | 0.20 | 19.28 |
| **6/03** | 15.28 | 41 | 27 | 0.45 | 0.16 | 17.82 |
| **Annual Growth** | 37.5% | — | — | 66.2% | 28.8% | (4.7%) |

# Hartford Financial Services Group

This buck makes bucks by offering a variety of personal and commercial life and property/casualty insurance products, including homeowners, auto, and workers' compensation. Through its Hartford Life subsidiary, the company offers individual and group life insurance, annuities, employee benefits administration, asset management, and mutual funds (managed both in-house and by Wellington Management). Its property/casualty operations include both personal and business coverage, including specialty commercial coverage for large companies. The Hartford, in business since 1810, sells its products through about 11,000 independent agencies and more than 100,000 registered broker-dealers.

As the lucrative baby-boomer generation ages, Hartford Life is targeting the retirement savings market and seeking marketing alliances, such as its agreement to provide auto and homeowners polices to members of AARP (the American Association of Retired Persons).

Focusing on the US market, the company has exited virtually all of its international property and casualty operations. The company has boosted its position in other areas, buying a large chunk of property/casualty insurer Kemper's group captives business, and paying some $500 million for CNA's group benefits business.

Like other insurers, The Hartford boosted its asbestos reserves, setting aside some $2.6 billion for liability claims, and exiting the property & casualty reinsurance business (it sold a large chunk of its HartRe unit to Endurance Specialty). Reinsurance has grown increasingly less profitable due to asbestos claims and weather and terrorism-related disasters.

## HISTORY

In 1810 a group of Hartford, Connecticut, businessmen led by Walter Mitchell and Henry Terry founded the Hartford Fire Insurance Co. Frequent fires in America's wooden cities and executive ignorance of risk assessment and premium-setting often left the firm on the edge of insolvency. (In 1835 stockholders staged a coup and threw management out.) Still, each urban conflagration — including the Great Chicago Fire of 1871 — gave the Hartford an opportunity to seek out and pay all its policyholders, thus teaching the company to underwrite under fire, as it were, and to use such disasters to refine its rates.

The company's stag logo was initially a little deer, as shown on a policy sold to Abraham Lincoln in 1861. A few years later, however, Hartford began using the majestic creature (from a Landseer painting) now familiar to customers. By the 1880s Hartford operated nationwide, as well as in Canada and Hawaii.

The company survived both world wars and the Depression but emerged in the 1950s in need of organization. It set up new regional offices and added life insurance, buying Columbian National Life (founded 1902), which became Hartford Life Insurance Co.

In 1969 Hartford was bought by ITT (formerly International Telephone and Telegraph), whose CEO, Harold Geneen, was an avid conglomerateur. Consumer advocate Ralph Nader strongly opposed the acquisition — he fought the merger in court for years and felt vindicated when ITT spun off Hartford in 1995. Others opposed it, too, because ITT had engineered the merger based on an IRS ruling (later revoked) that Hartford stockholders wouldn't have to pay capital gains taxes on the purchase price of their stock.

Insurance operations consolidated under the Hartford Life Insurance banner in 1978. Through the 1980s, Hartford Life remained one of ITT's strongest operations. A conservative investment policy kept Hartford safe from the junk bond and real estate manias of the 1980s.

Hartford reorganized its property/casualty operations along three lines in 1986, and in 1992 it organized its reinsurance business into one unit. The company faced some liability in relation to Dow Corning's breast-implant litigation, but underwriting standards after 1985 reduced long-term risk. In 1994 the company began selling insurance products to AARP members under an exclusive agreement. In 1996 the company finished its spinoff from ITT, which was acquired by Starwood Hotels & Resorts two years later.

To grow its reinsurance operation, Hartford acquired the reinsurance business of Orion Capital (now Royal & SunAlliance USA) in 1996. It posted a loss of $99 million, due in large part to asbestos and pollution liabilities. Late that year the firm changed its name to The Hartford Financial Services Group.

To shore up reserves and fund growth, in 1997 the company spun off 19% of Hartford Life. The next year The Hartford expanded into nonstandard auto insurance, buying Omni Insurance Group, and sold its London & Edinburgh Insurance Group to Norwich Union (now part of Aviva, formerly CGNU). In 1999 Hartford acquired the reinsurance business of Vesta Fire Insurance, a subsidiary of Vesta Insurance Group.

In 2000 Hartford bought back the part of Hartford Life it had spun off. Hartford also bought the financial products and excess and surplus specialty insurance lines of Reliance Group Holdings. Assurances Générales de France bought the company's Dutch subsidiary, Zwolsche Algemeene. In 2001 the company bought Fortis Financial, a US subsidiary of Belgian insurer Fortis, and sold Hartford Seguros, its Spanish subsidiary, to Liberty Mutual.

## EXECUTIVES

**Chairman and CEO; Chairman, Hartford Life:** Ramani Ayer, age 59
**President, COO, and Director:** Thomas M. Marra, age 48
**EVP; President and COO, Hartford Property Casualty:** David K. Zwiener, age 52, $2,964,417 pay
**EVP and CFO:** David M. Johnson, age 46, $2,048,417 pay
**EVP and Chief Investment Officer; President, Hartford Investment Management Co.:** David M. Znamierowski, age 46
**EVP Human Resources:** Eileen G. Whelley, age 53
**EVP and General Counsel:** Alan J. Kreczko, age 56
**VP, Marketing, Personal Insurance Division:** George P. Thacker
**Co-COO, U.S. Wealth Management, International Wealth Management, and Group Benefits:** Lizabeth H. (Liz) Zlatkus, age 48
**VP Brand and Advertising:** Michael Johnson
**VP Media Relations:** Joshua A. King
**Co-COO, U.S. Wealth Management, International Wealth Management, and Group Benefits:** John C. Walters, age 45
**Director National Accounts:** Tom Tooley
**President and COO, Property Casualty Operations:** Neal S. Wolin, age 45
**President, Heritage Holdings, Inc.:** Andrew J. Pinkes
**SVP U.S. Wealth Management Group, Canadian Retail Business:** Rob Arena
**SVP U.S. Wealth Management Group, Hartford's Institutional Solutions Group:** Ken McCullum
**EVP Sales and Distribution, Hartford Property and Casualty Insurance Operations:** Dan Brown
**SVP Controller and Chief Accounting Officer:** Beth A. Bombara, age 39
**Investor Relations:** Kim Johnson
**Auditors:** Deloitte & Touche LLP

## LOCATIONS

**HQ:** The Hartford Financial Services Group, Inc.
One Hartford Plaza, 690 Asylum Ave.,
Hartford, CT 06115
**Phone:** 860-547-5000 **Fax:** 860-547-2680
**Web:** www.thehartford.com

Hartford Financial Services operates primarily in North America, but also has operations in Brazil, Ireland, Japan, and the UK.

### 2006 Sales

| | $ mil. | % of total |
|---|---|---|
| North America | 23,840 | 90 |
| Other regions | 2,660 | 10 |
| **Total** | **26,500** | **100** |

## PRODUCTS/OPERATIONS

### 2006 Sales

| | $ mil. | % of total |
|---|---|---|
| Earned premiums | 15,023 | 56 |
| Net investment income | | |
| Equity securities held for trading | 1,824 | 7 |
| Securities available for sale & other | 4,691 | 18 |
| Fee income | 4,739 | 18 |
| Net realized capital gains | (251) | — |
| Other revenue | 474 | 1 |
| **Total** | **26,500** | **100** |

## 2006 Sales

| | $ mil. | % of total |
|---|---|---|
| Life | | |
| Premiums | | |
| Group Benefits | 4,150 | 16 |
| Retail | 2,611 | 10 |
| Institutional | 731 | 3 |
| Individual Life | 830 | 3 |
| International | 700 | 2 |
| Retirement plans | 211 | 1 |
| Other | 83 | — |
| Net investment income | 5,008 | 19 |
| Net realized capital losses | (260) | — |
| Property/casualty | | |
| Ongoing operations | | |
| Business insurance | 5,118 | 19 |
| Personal lines | 3,760 | 14 |
| Specialty commercial | 1,550 | 6 |
| Net investment income | 1,486 | 5 |
| Servicing revenue | 473 | 2 |
| Net realized capital gains | 9 | — |
| Other operations | 5 | — |
| Other revenue | 35 | — |
| **Total** | **26,500** | **100** |

## COMPETITORS

AEGON USA
AIG
Allstate
Berkshire Hathaway
CNA Financial
ING
Liberty Mutual
MetLife
Nationwide Financial
New York Life
Northwestern Mutual
Prudential
State Farm Financial Services
TIAA-CREF
Travelers Companies
Zurich Financial Services

## HISTORICAL FINANCIALS

Company Type: Public

### Income Statement

FYE: December 31

| | ASSETS ($ mil.) | NET INCOME ($ mil.) | INCOME AS % OF ASSETS | EMPLOYEES |
|---|---|---|---|---|
| **12/06** | 326,710 | 2,745 | 0.8% | 31,000 |
| **12/05** | 285,557 | 2,274 | 0.8% | 30,000 |
| **12/04** | 259,735 | 2,115 | 0.8% | 30,000 |
| **12/03** | 225,853 | (91) | — | 30,000 |
| **12/02** | 182,043 | 1,000 | 0.5% | 29,000 |
| **Annual Growth** | 15.7% | 28.7% | — | 1.7% |

### 2006 Year-End Financials

Equity as % of assets: 5.8%
Return on assets: 0.9%
Return on equity: 16.1%
Long-term debt ($ mil.): 3,762
No. of shares (mil.): 323
Dividends
Yield: 1.8%
Payout: 19.6%
Market value ($ mil.): 30,169
Sales ($ mil.): 26,500

### Stock History

NYSE: HIG

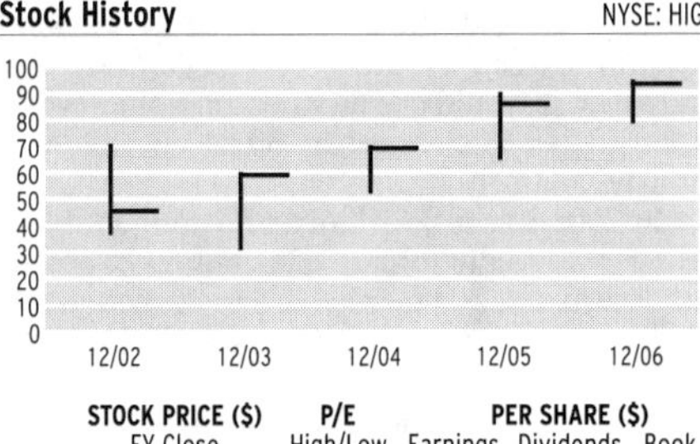


| | STOCK PRICE ($) FY Close | P/E High | P/E Low | PER SHARE ($) Earnings | Dividends | Book Value |
|---|---|---|---|---|---|---|
| **12/06** | 93.31 | 11 | 9 | 8.69 | 1.70 | 58.38 |
| **12/05** | 85.89 | 12 | 9 | 7.44 | 1.17 | 50.72 |
| **12/04** | 69.31 | 10 | 7 | 7.12 | 1.13 | 48.39 |
| **12/03** | 59.03 | — | — | (0.33) | 1.09 | 41.07 |
| **12/02** | 45.43 | 18 | 9 | 3.97 | 1.05 | 42.05 |
| **Annual Growth** | 19.7% | — | — | 21.6% | 12.8% | 8.5% |

# Hartmarx Corporation

Hartmarx fills its pockets by outfitting well-heeled customers with its tailored clothing and sportswear. It's a top maker of men's suits and sports coats under the Hart Schaffner & Marx and Hickey-Freeman labels, as well as Austin Reed- and Barrie Pace-branded women's suits and separates. Best known for its tailored items, the firm also makes and markets Bobby Jones golfwear and Sansabelt slacks. It manufactures clothing under license from Tommy Hilfiger, Kenneth Cole, and other designers. Hartmarx sells its suits and sport coats primarily to upscale retailers; the balance is distributed to department and specialty stores, pro shops, resorts, and catalogs in the US and more than a dozen other countries.

Hartmarx consolidated all of its men's tailored clothing divisions, except Hickey-Freeman, into a single unit. The company is diversifying its non-tailored division, as it did with the 2005 acquisition of Simply Blue and Seymour J. Blue, makers of women's denim apparel.

After flirting with marketing its tailored suits and premium casualwear through mainstream department stores and other similar retail formats, Hartmarx has abandoned that strategy due to extremely low margins. It now plans to market premium clothing solely through the upscale retail market. The company's purchase of Monarchy, in August 2007, represents its step toward achieving higher margins for one of its largest product lines. Monarchy's apparel — upscale men's and women's clothing — is sold through Nordstrom and Bloomingdale's.

Saudi Arabian investor Abdullah Taha Bakhsh owns about 15% of Hartmarx.

## HISTORY

Harry Hart, 21, and his brother Max, 18, of Chicago, opened a men's clothing store, Harry Hart and Brother, in 1872. In 1887, after Marcus Marx and Joseph Schaffner had joined the company, the enterprise was renamed Hart Schaffner & Marx.

The young clothiers contracted with independent tailors to produce suits for their new store. Recognizing the potential of the wholesale garment industry, they began selling to other merchants and in 1897 launched a national ad campaign in leading publications.

A walkout by female workers in 1910 protesting low wages and poor working conditions in one of the company's 48 tailoring shops sparked a citywide garment workers' strike. Schaffner and Harry successfully negotiated a settlement (not honored by other major Chicago companies) in January 1911.

Hart Schaffner & Marx in 1935 began a pattern of purchases over the next three decades that included Wallach Brothers (New York clothing chain), Hastings (a California clothier, 1952), Hanny's (Arizona, 1962), Hickey-Freeman (stores in Chicago, New York, and Detroit; 1964), and Field Brothers (New York, 1968). A 1970 antitrust decree forced it to sell 30 of its 238 men's clothing stores and refrain for 10 years from further purchases without court approval. The company made several approved purchases during the period. In 1981 Hart Schaffner & Marx bought the Country Miss chain and expanded into women's clothing. A year later it bought Kuppenheimer, a leading maker of lower-priced suits.

The company changed its name to Hartmarx in 1983, creating a holding company to oversee the variety of businesses it had acquired. A costly 1986 reorganization of administrative functions and the retail stores resulted in the loss of 800 jobs; earnings fell 42%. After a brief recovery in 1987 and 1988, earnings declined by more than half to $17 million in 1989, largely because of a dramatic increase in wool prices. Further restructuring, in 1990, Hartmarx reorganized its women's lines into a new unit under the name Barrie Pace and began experimenting with placing Kuppenheimer outlets in Sears stores. It entered the golf wear industry the next year with the introduction of its Bobby Jones line; golf wear grew to $50 million in sales in just five years.

Despite the financial birdie hit by golf wear, CEO Harvey Weinberg was ousted in 1992 due to continued losses (blamed largely on retail operations). President Elbert Hand became chairman and CEO and immediately upped the restructuring pace, expanding Hartmarx's core men's apparel business and further divesting retail operations. The company completely exited retailing in 1995, even as some of its retail customers (Barneys, Today's Man) filed for bankruptcy protection. It also closed 10 domestic factories and began moving production to countries such as Costa Rica and Mexico.

Hartmarx in 1996 bought Plaid Clothing Group, a bankrupt supplier of men's tailored clothing. In 1998 the company acquired the tropical sportswear wholesale business of Pusser's, as well as Canadian men's apparel maker and Hartmarx licensee Coppley, Noyes and Randall. Hartmarx bought Canada's Royal Shirt in 1999.

Emphasizing the importance of sportswear in a dress-down world, the company brought its various sportswear lines under one roof in early 2000. Late in the year Hartmarx formed a partnership with UK designer Ted Baker to offer the designer's apparel and home furnishings in North and South America. Hartmarx acquired men's sportswear manufacturer Consolidated Apparel Group in August 2001. The Lincoln Company, a group of investors (including suit manufacturer The Tom James Company), made an offer to buy Hartmarx, but the deal fell through.

In July 2004 Hartmarx acquired Exclusively Misook, a marketer of women's designer knitwear.

In August 2006 the company acquired Sweater.com, Inc., which designs and sells women's knitwear, tops, and related apparel to specialty stores and via its Sweater.com Web site. The purchase price was about $12 million.

## EXECUTIVES

**Chairman, President, and CEO:** Homi B. Patel, age 57, $880,990 pay
**EVP, CFO, and Treasurer:** Glenn R. Morgan, age 59, $300,326 pay
**SVP, General Counsel, and Secretary:** Taras R. Proczko, age 52, $246,505 pay
**VP, Controller, and Chief Accounting Officer:** Andrew A. Zahr, age 63, $145,140 pay
**VP Sourcing Operations, HMX Tailored:** Greg Mergel
**VP and Managing Director, International Licensing:** Raymond C. Giuriceo, age 63, $148,574 pay
**Group President, Hickey-Freeman:** Paulette Garafolo
**Group President, HMX Sportswear:** Eric G. Prengel
**Group President, Womenswear:** Susan G. Falk
**Group President:** Steve Weiner
**CEO, International Women's Apparel:** Tom Hall
**Director Compensation and Benefits:** Michael Pickelny
**Director of Human Resources:** Susan Klawitter
**Auditors:** PricewaterhouseCoopers LLP

## LOCATIONS

**HQ:** Hartmarx Corporation
101 N. Wacker Dr., Chicago, IL 60606
**Phone:** 312-372-6300 **Fax:** 312-444-2710
**Web:** www.hartmarx.com

**2006 Sales**

| | % of total |
|---|---|
| US | 96 |
| Canada | 4 |
| **Total** | **100** |

## PRODUCTS/OPERATIONS

**2006 Sales**

| | $ mil. | % of total |
|---|---|---|
| Apparel | 597.9 | 99 |
| Licensing & other | 2.6 | 1 |
| **Total** | **600.5** | **100** |

## COMPETITORS

Armani
Ashworth
Brooks Brothers
Calvin Klein
Capital Mercury Apparel
Cutter & Buck
Donna Karan
Ellen Tracy
Gap
Haggar
Hugo Boss
J. Crew
Jones Apparel
Jos. A. Bank
Lands' End
Levi Strauss
Men's Wearhouse
Nautica Enterprises
Oxford Industries
Perry Ellis International
Phillips-Van Heusen
Polo Ralph Lauren
S&K Famous Brands

## HISTORICAL FINANCIALS

Company Type: Public

**Income Statement** FYE: November 30

| | REVENUE ($ mil.) | NET INCOME ($ mil.) | NET PROFIT MARGIN | EMPLOYEES |
|---|---|---|---|---|
| **11/06** | 601 | 7 | 1.2% | 4,000 |
| **11/05** | 600 | 24 | 3.9% | 4,100 |
| **11/04** | 589 | 16 | 2.7% | 4,000 |
| **11/03** | 564 | 9 | 1.5% | 4,100 |
| **11/02** | 573 | 1 | 0.2% | 4,200 |
| **Annual Growth** | 1.2% | 68.8% | — | (1.2%) |

**2006 Year-End Financials**

Debt ratio: 33.9%
Return on equity: 2.9%
Cash ($ mil.): 2
Current ratio: 3.08
Long-term debt ($ mil.): 88
No. of shares (mil.): 37
Dividends
Yield: —
Payout: —
Market value ($ mil.): 241

**Stock History** NYSE: HMX

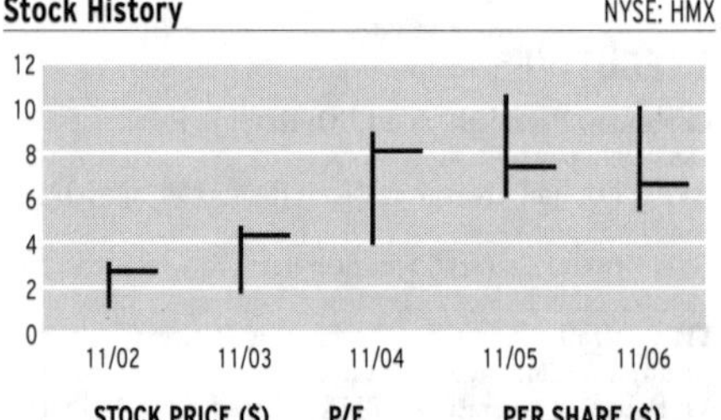


| | STOCK PRICE ($) FY Close | P/E High | P/E Low | PER SHARE ($) Earnings | Dividends | Book Value |
|---|---|---|---|---|---|---|
| **11/06** | 6.58 | 50 | 27 | 0.20 | — | 7.13 |
| **11/05** | 7.34 | 17 | 10 | 0.63 | — | 6.62 |
| **11/04** | 8.07 | 20 | 9 | 0.44 | — | 6.13 |
| **11/03** | 4.30 | 18 | 7 | 0.25 | — | 5.49 |
| **11/02** | 2.72 | 151 | 59 | 0.02 | — | 5.21 |
| **Annual Growth** | 24.7% | — | — | 77.8% | — | 8.2% |

# Hasbro, Inc.

It's all fun and games at Hasbro, the #2 toy maker in the US (after Mattel) and the producer of such childhood favorites as G.I. Joe, Play-Doh, Tonka toys, Nerf balls, and Weebles. Besides toys, Hasbro makes board games under its Milton Bradley (*Scrabble, Candy Land*) and Parker Brothers (*Monopoly, Trivial Pursuit*) brands, as well as trading cards such as *Pokémon, Harry Potter*, and *Magic: The Gathering* (through its Wizards of the Coast unit). Hasbro also makes *Star Wars* action figures and is the licensee of action figures and games for the prequels, as well as toys related to Disney and other movie and television characters. Hasbro is making a live-action, full-length film based on the G.I. Joe brand.

Hasbro has tapped into cross-marketing for movies and other forms of media, paying at least $600 million for the right to make most of the toys for the *Star Wars* prequels (not to mention giving producer George Lucas warrants to buy about 8% of the company). In 2007 Hasbro struck a deal with Electronic Arts to create electronic versions of some of its popular toys and games including Scrabble and Monopoly.

The toy maker has access to some 5,000 Marvel characters (such as Spider-Man, Fantastic Four, X-Men, Captain America, and Ghost Rider) thanks to a five-year agreement it inked with Marvel Entertainment in 2006 to sell Marvel-branded toys and games.

Hasbro also inked licensing deals for Dreamworks' *Shrek 2* and Disney and Pixar's *The Incredibles*. Also, in 2006 Hasbro partnered with G4 to produce an hour-long animation show called *Action Blast!* in association with Tango Pix. The production spotlights new and old Hasbro characters, such as Transformers, G.I. Joe, Beastwars, and B-Daman. G4 and Hasbro are also in talks to produce a late night show and are discussing deals related to other content formats, such as broadband, VOD, and wireless platforms. However, the company is narrowing its focus on licensing, and in the face of losses caused by the fading *Pokémon* craze, Hasbro is focusing on favorites such as G.I. Joe, Tonka, and Nerf.

Tapping into the company's research and development capabilities, Hasbro launched a Tooth Tunes toothbrush that includes a song stored in a microchip, which began selling for $10 apiece at CVS stores in late 2005.

And while Hasbro is getting busy in the oral care arena, it's also brushing up on film debuts. The Transformers toy line is getting its own live-action film. Slated for a summer 2007 release, the movie is being produced by Dreamworks and Paramount (in association with Hasbro) with Steven Spielberg serving as executive producer.

In 2006 nearly 50% of Hasbro's sales came from its top three customers — Wal-Mart (24%), Toys "R" Us (11%), and Target (13%).

Chairman Alan Hassenfeld, the third generation of Hassenfelds to control the company, owns nearly 10% of Hasbro.

## HISTORY

Henry and Helal Hassenfeld formed Hassenfeld Brothers in Pawtucket, Rhode Island, in 1923 to distribute fabric remnants. By 1926 the company was manufacturing fabric-covered pencil boxes and shortly thereafter, pencils.

Hassenfeld Brothers branched into the toy industry during the 1940s by introducing toy nurse and doctor kits. The company's toy division was the first to use TV to promote a toy product (Mr. Potato Head in 1952).

Expansion continued in the mid-1960s with the introduction of the G.I. Joe doll, which quickly became its primary toy line. Hassenfeld Brothers went public in 1968 and changed its name to Hasbro Industries. It bought Romper Room (TV productions) the next year.

In the 1970s the toy and pencil divisions, led by different family members, disagreed over the company's finances, future direction, and leadership. The dispute caused the company to split in 1980. The toy division continued to operate under the Hasbro name; the pencil division (Empire Pencil Corporation in Shelbyville, Tennessee, led by Harold Hassenfeld) became a separate corporation.

Hasbro expanded rapidly in the 1980s under new CEO Stephen Hassenfeld. He reduced the number of products by one-third to concentrate on developing a line of toys aimed at specific markets. During that decade the firm released a number of successful toys, including a smaller version of G.I. Joe (1982) and Transformers (small vehicles that transform into robots, 1984). Hasbro acquired Milton Bradley, a major producer of board games (*Chutes and Ladders, Candy Land*), puzzles, and preschool toys (Playskool) in 1984.

The company acquired Cabbage Patch Kids, *Scrabble, Parcheesi,* and other product lines in 1989. Stephen died that year. His brother Alan, who had spearheaded Hasbro's international sales growth in the late 1980s, became CEO.

Hasbro bought Tonka (including the Kenner and Parker Brothers brands) in 1991 and established operations in Greece, Mexico, and Hungary. Hasbro blocked a $5.2 billion hostile takeover attempt by Mattel in 1996 and in 1997 began cutting about 2,500 jobs (20% of Hasbro's employees) that year.

Expanding in the high-tech toys niche, in 1998 Hasbro made several acquisitions, including Tiger Electronics (Giga Pets), the rights to some 75 Atari home console game titles (*Missile Command, Centipede*), MicroProse (3-D video games for PCs), and Galoob Toys, a fellow *Star Wars* prequel licensee and maker of Micro Machines and Pound Puppies. Tiger Electronics had the hit of the 1998 holiday season: a chattering interactive doll called Furby.

In 1999 Hasbro bought game maker and retailer Wizards of the Coast (maker of *Pokémon* trading cards). In late 1999 the company announced it would can another 19% of its workforce (2,200 jobs). Another 750 job cuts followed in late 2000.

In 2002 Hasbro was fined $7.7 million in the UK for allegedly forcing distributors to fix toy and game prices; however, due to the company's full cooperation during the investigation, the fine was waived in 2003. Later that year Hasbro announced it would close its manufacturing plant in Valencia, Spain, and shift operations to China and Ireland, affecting about 500 employees. In December 2004 Hasbro laid off about 125 employees across several departments.

The release in May 2005 of *Star Wars Episode III: Revenge of the Sith* and subsequent DVD release gave Hasbro's line of licensed Star Wars products a huge boost. Star Wars products contributed 16% of the year's revenues.

## EXECUTIVES

**Chairman:** Alan G. Hassenfeld, age 58
**President, CEO, and Director:** Alfred J. Verrecchia, age 64, $1,000,000 pay
**COO:** Brian Goldner, age 43, $794,616 pay
**EVP Finance and Global Operations and CFO:** David D. R. Hargreaves, age 54, $494,231 pay (prior to promotion)
**SVP and Controller:** Deborah Thomas Slater
**SVP and Treasurer:** Martin R. Trueb
**SVP, General Counsel, and Secretary:** Barry Nagler, age 50, $475,000 pay
**SVP Human Resources:** Bob Carniaux
**SVP Marketing:** Ira Hernowitz
**VP Community Relations:** Karen Davis
**President, North American Sales:** Frank P. Bifulco Jr.
**President, Hasbro Europe:** Simon Gardner, age 46, $521,289 pay
**President, Hasbro Properties:** Jane Ritson Parsons
**President, Wizards of the Coast:** Loren Greenwood
**SVP, Americas, Hasbro Properties Group:** Bryony Bouyer
**SVP Marketing, Hasbro Games:** Mark Blecher
**SVP Marketing and Product Development, Hasbro Games:** Phil Jackson
**VP Corporate Media:** Deborah Boyd
**Corporate Communications:** Audrey DeSimone
**Investor Relations:** Karen A. Warren
**Auditors:** KPMG LLP

## LOCATIONS

**HQ:** Hasbro, Inc.
1027 Newport Ave., Pawtucket, RI 02862
**Phone:** 401-431-8697 **Fax:** 401-431-8535
**Web:** www.hasbro.com

Hasbro has operations in the US and more than 20 other countries, and manufacturing facilities in Massachusetts and Ireland.

### 2006 Sales

| | $ mil. | % of total |
|---|---|---|
| US | 1,898.9 | 60 |
| Other countries | 1,252.6 | 40 |
| **Total** | **3,151.5** | **100** |

## PRODUCTS/OPERATIONS

### 2006 Sales

| | $ mil. | % of total |
|---|---|---|
| Games & puzzles | 1,294.1 | 41 |
| Boys' toys | 575.8 | 18 |
| Girls' toys | 540.3 | 17 |
| Preschool toys | 406.7 | 13 |
| Tweens' toys | 266.9 | 9 |
| Other | 67.7 | 2 |
| **Total** | **3,151.5** | **100** |

### Selected Brands and Products

Electronics
- Tiger Electronics
  - Furby
  - Giga Pets
  - Hitclips (micro music systems)
  - Kidclips Disney Tunes
  - Luv Cubs
  - Thintronix (ultra-thin speakerphone, FM radio)
  - VideoNow (personal video player)

Games and Puzzles
- Avalon Hill
  - Acquire
  - Axis & Allies
  - Cosmic Encounter
  - Diplomacy
  - History of the World
  - Risk 2210 A.D.
  - Stratego Legends
- Jigsaw Puzzles
- Milton Bradley
  - Battleship
  - Candy Land
  - Chutes and Ladders
  - Connect Four
  - The Game of Life
  - Hungry Hungry Hippos
  - Jenga
  - Mousetrap
  - Operation
  - Scattergories
  - Scrabble
- Tiger Games
  - Trouble
  - Twister
  - Yahtzee
- Parker Brothers
  - Boggle
  - Clue
  - Monopoly
  - Ouija
  - Risk
  - Sorry!
  - Trivial Pursuit
- Wizards of the Coast
  - Dungeons and Dragons
  - *Harry Potter* trading cards
  - Magic: The Gathering
  - Magic: The Gathering Online
  - NeoPets
  - *Pokémon*
- Wrebbit
  - PERFALOCK
  - PUZZ-3D

Boys' Toys
- BTR (Built To Rule action building sets)
- G.I. Joe action figures
- Hard Metal System spinning tops
- *Star Wars* action figures
- Tonka (toy trucks)
- *Transformers* (small vehicles that transform into robots)

Preschool Toys
- *Bob the Builder* toys
- Busy Ball Popper
- Gloworm
- Mr. Potato Head
- Playskool
- Sit 'N Spin
- Weebles

Creative Play
- Easy-Bake Oven
- Lite-Brite
- Play-Doh
- Spirograph
- Tinkertoys

Girls' Toys
- Makeup Mindy (dolls)
- My Little Pony
- Raggedy Ann and Raggedy Andy dolls
- Secret Central (dolls)
- TwinkleTwirls Dance Studio

Other
- Nerf (soft play toys)
- Super Soaker water products

## COMPETITORS

Atari
Build-A-Bear
Corgi International
Electronic Arts
The First Years
Graco Children's Products
Gund
JAKKS Pacific
LeapFrog
LEGO
Marvel Entertainment
Mattel
MGA Entertainment
Nakajima USA
Namco Bandai
Ohio Art
Playmates
Playmobil
Poof-Slinky
Radio Flyer
RC2
Sanrio
SMOBY
Spin Master
TakaraTomy
Toy Quest
Ty
VTech Holdings
WHAM-O

## HISTORICAL FINANCIALS

Company Type: Public

### Income Statement

FYE: Last Sunday in December

| | REVENUE ($ mil.) | NET INCOME ($ mil.) | NET PROFIT MARGIN | EMPLOYEES |
|---|---|---|---|---|
| **12/06** | 3,152 | 230 | 7.3% | 5,800 |
| **12/05** | 3,088 | 212 | 6.9% | 5,900 |
| **12/04** | 2,998 | 196 | 6.5% | 6,000 |
| **12/03** | 3,139 | 158 | 5.0% | 6,900 |
| **12/02** | 2,816 | (171) | — | 7,200 |
| **Annual Growth** | 2.9% | — | — | (5.3%) |

### 2006 Year-End Financials

Debt ratio: 32.2%
Return on equity: 14.1%
Cash ($ mil.): 715
Current ratio: 1.90
Long-term debt ($ mil.): 495
No. of shares (mil.): 161
Dividends
Yield: 1.7%
Payout: 34.9%
Market value ($ mil.): 4,377

### Stock History

NYSE: HAS

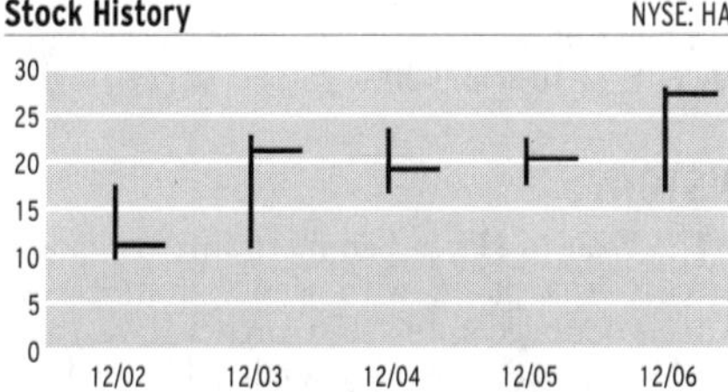


| | STOCK PRICE ($) FY Close | P/E High | P/E Low | PER SHARE ($) Earnings | Dividends | Book Value |
|---|---|---|---|---|---|---|
| **12/06** | 27.25 | 21 | 13 | 1.29 | 0.45 | 9.57 |
| **12/05** | 20.36 | 21 | 16 | 1.09 | 0.33 | 9.69 |
| **12/04** | 19.19 | 24 | 18 | 0.96 | 0.21 | 9.25 |
| **12/03** | 21.22 | 26 | 13 | 0.88 | 0.12 | 8.01 |
| **12/02** | 11.12 | — | — | (0.98) | 0.09 | 6.88 |
| **Annual Growth** | 25.1% | — | — | — | 49.5% | 8.6% |

# Hayes Lemmerz International

Steel Wheels is more than a Stones album — it's a living for Hayes Lemmerz. The company rolls along as the world's #1 maker of steel and aluminum wheels for automobiles. The company has restructured its operations into three segments: automotive wheels, components, and other products. Its wheel segment makes steel and aluminum wheels for cars and light trucks. The company's Automotive Components Group makes automotive parts such as brake and structural components. Other products include wheels, rims, and brakes for commercial vehicles. GM, Ford, Daimler, and Chrysler together account for half of sales.

After emerging from Chapter 11 in June 2003, Hayes Lemmerz is back on a roll. The company still holds a leading position in the steel and aluminum wheel market for passenger cars as well as commercial vehicles. The company plans to remain competitive by maintaining its global reach — it serves every major carmaker in North America, Europe, and Asia.

Part of its strategy is to serve these global markets from low-cost regions. The company serves the Japanese market with its plant in Thailand; European customers are served by Hayes Lemmerz' plants in the Czech Republic, Poland, and Turkey. As part of a cost-control effort, the company moved to close an aluminum wheel plant in Huntington, Indiana, in 2006.

In 2007 the company announced additional measures to increase efficiency. Hayes Lemmerz said it would exit the suspensions business by selling its two suspension plants (Bristol, Indiana and Montague, Michigan) to Diversified Machine. The company is also combining its Automotive Components Group headquarters and technical center with its Northville, Michigan World Headquarters in order to eliminate its facility in Ferndale, Michigan.

In addition to restructuring, the company is trimming costs by reducing base pay for US employees by 7%. Sharing in the sacrifice, Hayes Lemmerz officers and directors are also taking pay cuts of 10% and 20%, respectively.

## HISTORY

The road to Hayes Lemmerz International's success was paved with wood. Both Hayes Wheels (founded in 1908 by Clarence Hayes) and the K.H. Wheel Company (founded in 1909 by John Kelsey and John Herbert) got their starts making wooden-spoked wheels, which became standard on Henry Ford's Model T cars. During WWI sales of artillery wheels put K.H. Wheel solidly in the black.

Meanwhile, Hayes Wheels grew quickly. By 1920 the company had claimed 60% of the US auto wheel business, but wheel production was shifting from wood to wire. The threat to makers of wooden wheels was a motivating factor for the merger of Hayes Wheels with K.H. Wheel in 1927.

The new company, Kelsey-Hayes Wheel Corporation, survived the Depression, in part, by acquiring a General Motors (GM) subsidiary, Jaxon Steel Products Company. Still, Kelsey-Hayes Wheel lost $1.1 million in 1932. By the end of the 1930s, it had added brakes and brake drums to its product line to help it stay afloat.

During WWII Kelsey-Hayes Wheel built machine guns, tank parts, and aircraft wheels. Anticipating the change to a postwar economy, it bought leading agricultural wheel maker French & Hecht.

The postwar boom was slow to start. In 1946 unemployment rose and wages fell when GIs returned home. A wildcat strike by 4,500 United Auto Workers members closed down Kelsey-Hayes Wheel for 46 days. In 1947 the company acquired brake-parts maker Lather Company. It began supplying Chrysler and Buick with power brakes and started cost-cutting operations.

In the early 1950s the company began developing antilock brakes and wheels and brakes for buses and other large vehicles. It changed its name to the Kelsey-Hayes Corporation. Kelsey-Hayes pioneered the development of disc brakes during the 1960s. After the oil crunch of the early 1970s, the company was challenged to develop parts for smaller cars. With its credit overextended and its stock falling, the company was taken over by truck-trailer maker Fruehauf Corporation in 1973. Kelsey-Hayes soon accounted for 60% of its parent's sales. In 1978 the Federal Trade Commission ruled that the acquisition violated antitrust laws and ordered Fruehauf to divest some of its subsidiary's assets.

In 1986 Kelsey-Hayes merged with wheel and brake maker Motor Wheel Corporation, whose parent company, MWC, was controlled by Joseph Littlejohn & Levy. The leveraged recapitalization left the investment firm in control of 43% of the combined company, which retained the Hayes Wheels name. The company was acquired by brake and diesel-engine maker Varity Corporation in 1989. It was spun off in 1992 as Varity restructured to reduce debt.

Consistent with the industry trend toward consolidation, Hayes bought Motor Wheel Corporation in 1996 and, after acquiring Lemmerz in 1997, was renamed Hayes Lemmerz. The acquisitions, combined with a 17-day GM strike, caused the company to lose money in fiscal 1997.

In 1998 the company took control of its Brazilian and South African joint ventures and bought Mexican truck-wheel maker Min-Cer. The next year Hayes Lemmerz paid about $600 million for the automotive division of CMI International, which enabled the company to offer complete corner suspension modules to automakers. The company also moved its headquarters to Northville, Michigan.

Late in the year Hayes Lemmerz announced that it planned to cut about 1,200 jobs due to slower auto sales. In 2001 the company received a long-term commitment from DaimlerChrysler Corporation to supply two aluminum wheels for its 2002 Jeep Liberty sport utility vehicle. Later in 2001 the company realigned its North American wheel businesses into a single operating division — North American Wheels Business Unit. Days later Hayes Lemmerz announced it would trim 11% of its North American salaried workforce. Within weeks of announcing the job cuts, Hayes Lemmerz' US operations filed for Chapter 11 bankruptcy protection.

Early in 2002 Hayes Lemmerz sold its System Service business to German-based Schedl Automotive System Service Beteiligungsgesellschaft GmbH & Co. Verwaltungs-KG.

Hayes Lemmerz closed its Howell, Michigan, plant in 2004 and moved production to other locations in the US to trim costs. The Howell plant employed 180 people.

## EXECUTIVES

**Chairman, President, and CEO:** Curtis J. Clawson, age 47, $1,310,762 pay
**EVP and CFO:** James A. (Jim) Yost, age 57, $534,055 pay
**VP, General Counsel, and Secretary:** Patrick C. Cauley, age 46
**VP Business Development:** John A. Salvette, age 50
**VP, Human Resources and Administration:** Larry Karenko, age 54
**VP, President, Commercial Highway and Aftermarket Services; President, North American Wheel Group:** Edward Kopkowski, age 41
**VP; President, North American Wheels:** James L. Stegemiller, age 52, $608,855 pay
**VP Global Material and Logistics; President, Automotive Components Group:** Daniel M. Sandberg, age 44, $489,454 pay (prior to promotion)
**COO; President, Hayes Global Wheel Group:** Fred Bentley, age 42, $416,313 pay (prior to promotion)
**Managing Director, South American Operations, International Wheel Group:** Don Septer
**Director of Taxes:** Christine M. Sweda
**Corporate Controller:** Mark A. Brebberman
**Auditors:** KPMG LLP

## LOCATIONS

**HQ:** Hayes Lemmerz International, Inc.
15300 Centennial Dr., Northville, MI 48168
**Phone:** 734-737-5000 **Fax:** 734-737-2003
**Web:** www.hayes-lemmerz.com

Hayes Lemmerz International operates facilities in Belgium, Brazil, the Czech Republic, Germany, India, Italy, Japan, Mexico, South Africa, Spain, Thailand, Turkey, and the US.

### 2007 Sales

| | $ mil. | % of total |
|---|---|---|
| US | 562.1 | 27 |
| Germany | 268.7 | 13 |
| Other regions | 1,225.4 | 60 |
| **Total** | **2,056.2** | **100** |

## PRODUCTS/OPERATIONS

### 2007 Sales

| | $ mil. | % of total |
|---|---|---|
| Automotive wheels | 1,671.6 | 81 |
| Components | 384.6 | 19 |
| **Total** | **2,056.2** | **100** |

### Selected Products

Automotive wheels
- Aluminum wheels
- Steel wheels

Components
- Automotive brake components
- Crossmembers
- Ductile iron exhaust manifolds
- Engine covers
- Intake manifolds
- Water pump housings

Other
- Commercial highway vehicle wheels, rims, and brake products

## COMPETITORS

Accuride
Alcoa
American Axle & Manufacturing
ArvinMeritor
CRAGAR
Ford
GKN
Metaldyne
Michelin
NGK INSULATORS
Superior Industries
Titan International
Topy
Ube
Volkswagen
Yokohama Rubber

## HISTORICAL FINANCIALS

Company Type: Public

**Income Statement** FYE: January 31

| | REVENUE ($ mil.) | NET INCOME ($ mil.) | NET PROFIT MARGIN | EMPLOYEES |
|---|---|---|---|---|
| **1/07** | 2,056 | (167) | — | 8,500 |
| **1/06** | 2,277 | (458) | — | 10,500 |
| **1/05** | 2,245 | (62) | — | 11,000 |
| **1/04** | 2,056 | 997 | 48.5% | 11,000 |
| **1/03** | 2,002 | (635) | — | — |
| **Annual Growth** | 0.7% | — | — | (8.2%) |

**2007 Year-End Financials**

Debt ratio: 647.7%
Return on equity: —
Cash ($ mil.): 38
Current ratio: 1.32
Long-term debt ($ mil.): 659
No. of shares (mil.): 38
Dividends
Yield: —
Payout: —
Market value ($ mil.): 176

**Stock History** NASDAQ (GM): HAYZ

| | STOCK PRICE ($) FY Close | P/E High/Low | PER SHARE ($) Earnings | Dividends | Book Value |
|---|---|---|---|---|---|
| **1/07** | 4.57 | — — | (4.36) | — | 2.65 |
| **1/06** | 3.73 | — — | (12.07) | — | 4.82 |
| **1/05** | 8.02 | — — | (1.66) | — | 18.52 |
| **1/04** | 18.35 | — — | (1.55) | — | 19.86 |
| **Annual Growth** | (37.1%) | — — | — | — | — |

# HCA Inc.

The top for-profit hospital operator in the US, HCA operates about 170 acute care, psychiatric, and rehabilitation hospitals (with more than 40,000 beds) in the US and abroad. It also runs about 100 ambulatory surgery centers, as well as diagnostic imaging, cancer treatment, and outpatient rehab centers that form health care networks in some communities. The company operates in about 20 states, with about three-quarters of its hospitals located in the southern US. (About 70 are in Florida and Texas.) The hospital giant's HCA International operates eight hospitals in Switzerland and the UK. In 2006 a group of investors took the company private in a $30 billion leveraged buyout.

The private investor group included HCA co-founder Thomas Frist, Jr., as well as Bain Capital, Kohlberg Kravis Roberts, the private equity arm of Merrill Lynch, and other members of HCA management.

Most of HCA's hospitals are in high-growth urban and suburban markets. The company divested ten rural hospitals over the course of 2005 and 2006 in order to focus on its key markets. Four Virginia and West Virginia facilities went to LifePoint Hospitals in 2006; it had sold five non-urban hospitals in Louisiana, Oklahoma, Tennessee, and Washington to Capella Healthcare the previous year.

The company plans to grow in its selected markets by acquiring hospitals and by luring patients to its existing facilities with high-quality care and a broad range of services. It is particularly interested in expanding its outpatient offerings, as well as specialty services in high-margin fields such as orthopedics and cardiology.

HCA also tries to take advantage of its national scale (and its position as the leading health care provider in many communities) to negotiate advantageous purchasing contracts, as well as favorable deals with managed care companies. Its attempts to demand rate increases in some renegotiated contracts with UnitedHealth in 2006, however, led to a bitter dispute that was finally resolved late that year, but not before UnitedHealth filed suit against HCA for alleged anti-competitive practices.

Like most hospital operators, HCA has had to deal with the rising rate of uninsured patients it treats, a phenomenon that leads to increasing amounts of bad debt when patients can't pay their bills. To combat the problem (and in response to criticism over how the hospital industry bills the uninsured), HCA instituted a discount plan for such patients in 2005.

## HISTORY

In 1987 Dallas lawyer Rick Scott and Fort Worth, Texas, financier Richard Rainwater founded Columbia Hospital Corp. to buy two hospitals in El Paso, Texas. The partners eventually sold 40% of the hospitals to local doctors, hoping that ownership would motivate physicians to increase productivity and efficiency.

The company entered the Miami market the next year and by 1990 had four hospitals. After merging with Smith Laboratories that year, Columbia went public and then acquired Sutter Laboratories (orthopedic products). By the end of 1990 it had 11 hospitals.

Columbia moved into Florida in a bigger way in 1992 with the purchase of several hospitals and facilities. The next year it acquired Galen Health Care, which operated 73 hospitals and had been spun off from health plan operator Humana earlier in the year. The merger thrust the hospital chain into about 15 new markets.

Columbia bought Hospital Corporation of America (HCA) in 1994. Thomas Frist, his son Thomas Frist Jr., and Jack Massey (former owner of Kentucky Fried Chicken, now part of TRICON) founded HCA in Nashville, Tennessee, in 1968. By 1973 the company had grown to 50 hospitals.

Meanwhile, the medical industry was changing as insurers, Medicare, and Medicaid began scrutinizing payment procedures, while the growth of HMOs (which aimed to restrict hospital admissions) cut hospital occupancy rates. HCA began paring operations in the late 1980s, selling more than 100 hospitals. In 1989 the younger Frist led a $5.1 billion leveraged buyout of the company. He sold more assets and in 1992 took HCA public again, but losses and a tumbling stock price made it a takeover target.

Later in 1994 the newly christened Columbia/HCA acquired the US's largest operator of outpatient surgery centers, Dallas-based Medical Care America. A year later it bought 117-hospital HealthTrust, a 1987 offshoot of HCA. Columbia/HCA was unstoppable in 1996, with some 150 acquisitions.

In 1997 the government began investigating the company's business practices. After executive indictments, the company fired Scott and several other top officers. Frist Jr. became chairman and CEO, pledging to shrink the company and tone down its aggressive approach. Columbia/HCA sold its home care business, more than 100 of its less-desirable hospitals, and almost all the operations of Value Health, a pharmacy benefits and behavioral health care management firm it had recently bought.

In 1998 Columbia/HCA sued former financial executive Samuel Greco and several vendors, accusing them of defrauding the company of several million dollars. In 2000 the firm settled with the federal government for about $800 million overcharges of fraudulent Medicare billing. It also bought out partner Sun Life and Provincial Holdings' (now AXA UK) interest in several London hospitals and bought three hospitals there from St. Martins Healthcare. That year it became HCA — The Healthcare Company. In 2001 the company changed its name again — this time to simply HCA Inc.

HCA seems to be shaking off its shaky past. In 2002 the bottom line was more kind to the company, allowing it to reinvest millions into modernizing facilities and equipment at its hospitals and surgery centers. In 2003 the company closed the books on the numerous government investigations launched in 1997 into its business practices. Over the five years ended in 2003, HCA paid out some $2 billion in settlements for Medicare fraud and other claims.

The devastating hurricane season of 2005 took a toll on HCA's operations, concentrated as they are in the southern US. When Hurricane Katrina hit, the devastation caused HCA to evacuate its Tulane University Hospital and Clinic (it re-opened in early 2006). Hurricane Rita spurred HCA to evacuate three Houston-area hospitals (Mainland Medical Center in Texas City, East Houston Regional Medical Center in Houston, and Clear Lake Regional Medical Center in Webster) and partially evacuate two others.

## EXECUTIVES

**Chairman and CEO:** Jack O. Bovender Jr., age 62, $1,404,959 pay
**President, COO, and Director:** Richard M. Bracken, age 54, $817,667 pay
**EVP and CFO:** R. Milton Johnson, age 50, $578,373 pay
**SVP:** Victor L. Campbell, age 60
**SVP and CIO; President, HCA Information Technology & Services:** Noel Brown Williams, age 52
**SVP and General Counsel:** Robert A. (Bob) Waterman, age 53, $569,988 pay
**SVP Development:** V. Carl George, age 63
**SVP and Chief Ethics and Compliance Officer:** Alan R. Yuspeh, age 57
**SVP Finance and Treasurer:** David G. Anderson, age 59
**SVP Government Programs:** Patricia T. Lindler, age 60
**SVP Human Resources:** John M. Steele, age 51
**SVP Internal Audit Services:** Joseph N. Steakley, age 53
**SVP Operations Finance:** Rosalyn S. Elton, age 46
**SVP Quality and Chief Medical Officer:** Jonathan B. (Jon) Perlin, age 46
**SVP Supply Chain Operations:** James A. Fitzgerald Jr., age 52
**VP and Corporate Secretary:** John M. Franck II
**VP Investor Relations:** Mark Kimbrough
**President, Outpatient Services Group:** A. Bruce Moore Jr., age 47
**President, Financial Services Group:** Beverly B. Wallace, age 56
**President, Eastern Group:** Charles J. (Chuck) Hall, age 54
**President, Western Group:** Samuel N. (Sam) Hazen, age 47, $569,981 pay
**Auditors:** Ernst & Young LLP

## LOCATIONS

**HQ:** HCA Inc.
1 Park Plaza, Nashville, TN 37203
**Phone:** 615-344-9551 **Fax:** 615-344-2266
**Web:** www.hcahealthcare.com

**2006 Locations**

| | No. |
|---|---|
| US | |
| Florida | 38 |
| Texas | 35 |
| Tennessee | 13 |
| Georgia | 12 |
| Louisiana | 11 |
| Virginia | 10 |
| Colorado | 7 |
| Missouri | 7 |
| Utah | 6 |
| California | 5 |
| Kansas | 4 |
| Nevada | 3 |
| South Carolina | 3 |
| Idaho | 2 |
| Kentucky | 2 |
| New Hampshire | 2 |
| Oklahoma | 2 |
| Alaska | 1 |
| Indiana | 1 |
| Mississippi | 1 |
| Other countries | |
| England | 6 |
| Switzerland | 2 |
| **Total** | **173** |

## PRODUCTS/OPERATIONS

**2006 Sales**

| | % of total |
|---|---|
| Managed care & other insurers | 53 |
| Medicare | 26 |
| Uninsured | 8 |
| Medicaid | 5 |
| Managed Medicare | 5 |
| Managed Medicaid | 3 |
| **Total** | **100** |

**2006 Sales**

| | $ mil. | % of total |
|---|---|---|
| Western group | 10,495 | 41 |
| Eastern group | 8,609 | 34 |
| Central group | 5,514 | 22 |
| Corporate & other | 859 | 3 |
| **Total** | **25,477** | **100** |

## COMPETITORS

Ascension Health
Banner Health
Catholic Health Initiatives
Catholic Healthcare West
CHRISTUS Health
Health Management Associates
HealthSouth
Kaiser Permanente
SSM Health Care
Tenet Healthcare
Trinity Health (Novi)
Universal Health Services

## HISTORICAL FINANCIALS

Company Type: Private

**Income Statement** FYE: December 31

| | REVENUE ($ mil.) | NET INCOME ($ mil.) | NET PROFIT MARGIN | EMPLOYEES |
|---|---|---|---|---|
| **12/06** | 25,477 | 1,036 | 4.1% | 186,000 |
| **12/05** | 24,455 | 1,424 | 5.8% | 191,100 |
| **12/04** | 23,502 | 1,246 | 5.3% | 191,400 |
| **12/03** | 21,808 | 1,332 | 6.1% | 188,000 |
| **12/02** | 19,729 | 833 | 4.2% | 178,000 |
| **Annual Growth** | 6.6% | 5.6% | — | 1.1% |

**Net Income History**

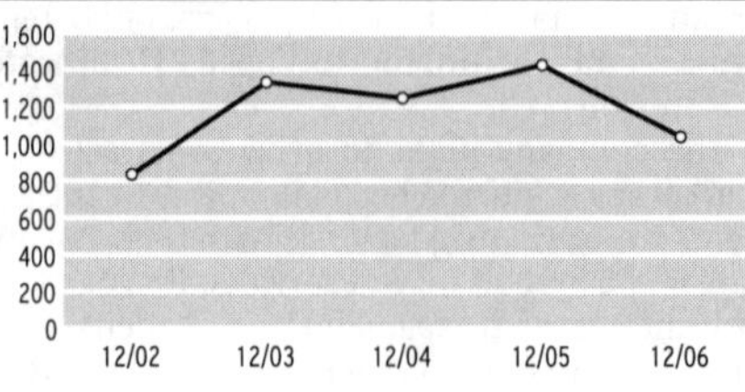


# Health Management Associates

William Schoen, chairman of Health Management Associates (HMA) once described his company as the "Wal-Mart of the hospital business" because, like Sam Walton's empire, HMA thrives in small-town America. The company operates a network of about 60 acute care and psychiatric hospitals in 15 mainly southern states (although its territory extends as far north as Washington). Combined, the facilities have about 8,500 beds. HMA also specializes in acquiring and upgrading rural hospitals and equipment in order to attract business from patients who would previously have been forced to travel to receive medical treatment.

Each year HMA buys a number of hospitals, most of which are financially struggling, but which are the main source of primary care in their areas. HMA works to quickly turn around the acquisitions. The company implements its own management information system, introduces strict cost controls, upgrades facilities and equipment, and begins volume purchasing under company-wide agreements. HMA also recruits new doctors, often specialists, allowing it to offer services previously unavailable in its market.

In 2006 HMA's acquisitions included Gulf Coast Medical Center in Mississippi (sold by Tenet Healthcare), Cleveland Clinic — Naples Hospital in Florida, and Barrow Community Hospital in Georgia. The same year it sold off two psychiatric hospitals in Florida to Psychiatric Solutions. In 2007 it sold two Virginia hospitals to Wellmont Health System.

## HISTORY

From its founding in 1977 by Joseph Greene until 1985, Health Management Associates (HMA) owned only a handful of hospitals, mostly in urban areas. In 1983 CEO Greene brought aboard William Schoen, an ex-Marine who ran a beer company in New York before founding a bank in Florida. Schoen became president and COO that year, took a co-CEO position in 1985, and assumed full leadership in 1986 when Greene retired.

Schoen sold the urban hospitals and refocused on small-town hospitals in underserved, mainly southern communities with growing populations. To finance acquisitions and hospital overhauls, HMA went public in 1986. Two years later Schoen took it private, but it went public again in 1991. In the early 1990s it had a growth spurt, adding 10 hospitals.

HMA continued buying, adding two facilities in 1996, another two in 1997, and five in 1998 (three in Mississippi and two in Florida). The acquisitions continued in 1999 as Medicare cutbacks and costly Y2K computer fixes forced many small hospitals to seek buyers; the company bought facilities in Florida, Mississippi (two), and Pennsylvania. In 2000 HMA continued to be acquisitive, buying three medical centers (in Florida, North Carolina, and Pennsylvania), although it shut down its treatment center for at-risk youth in Kansas due to security concerns. In 2001 HMA bought some hospitals from the financially troubled Clarent Hospital.

In 2003, HMA acquired five hospitals from Tenet and expanded into the US northwest by purchasing two hospitals in Washington. The next year, the company bought Chester County Hospital in South Carolina. In 2005 HMA acquired five hospitals in Florida, Mississippi, and Virginia.

## EXECUTIVES

**Chairman:** William J. Schoen, age 71, $300,000 pay
**Vice Chairman:** Joseph V. Vumbacco, age 60
**President and CEO:** Burke W. Whitman, age 50
**EVP and COO:** Kelly E. Curry
**EVP Hospital Operations:** Peter M. Lawson, age 44, $480,000 pay
**EVP Hospital Operations:** Jon P. Vollmer, age 48, $480,000 pay
**SVP MIS:** James L. Jordan
**SVP Administration and Operations:** Stanley D. McLemore
**SVP and CFO:** Robert E. Farnham, age 51, $450,000 pay
**SVP, General Counsel, and Corporate Secretary:** Timothy R. Parry
**SVP Human Resources:** Frederick L. Drow
**VP Administration and Operations:** David A. Beardsley
**VP Financial Relations:** John C. Merriwether
**VP Operations Finance and Division CFO:** Douglas E. (Doug) Browning
**Corporate Treasurer:** Joseph C. Meek
**Director Marketing:** Susan Sartain
**Auditors:** Ernst & Young LLP

## LOCATIONS

**HQ:** Health Management Associates, Inc.
5811 Pelican Bay Blvd., Ste. 500, Naples, FL 34108
**Phone:** 239-598-3131 **Fax:** 239-598-2705
**Web:** www.hma-corp.com

**Selected Hospitals**

Alabama
- Riverview Regional Medical Center (Gadsden)
- Stringfellow Memorial Hospital (Anniston)

Arkansas
- Crawford Memorial Hospital (Van Buren)
- Southwest Regional Medical Center (Pulaski County)

Florida
- Brooksville Regional Hospital
- Fishermen's Hospital (Marathon)
- Heart of Florida Regional Medical Center (Haines City)
- Highlands Regional Medical Center (Sebring)
- Lehigh Regional Medical Center (Lehigh Acres)
- Lower Keys Medical Center (Key West)
- Charlotte Regional Medical Center Hospital (Punta Gorda)
- Pasco Regional Medical Center (Dade City)
- Santa Rosa Medical Center (Milton)
- Sebastian River Medical Center (Sebastian)
- Seven Rivers Regional Medical Center (Crystal River)
- Spring Hill Regional Hospital

Georgia
- East Georgia Regional Medical Center (Statesboro)
- Walton Regional Medical Center (Monroe)

Kentucky
- Paul B. Hall Regional Medical Center (Paintsville)

Mississippi
- Biloxi Regional Medical Center
- Central Mississippi Medical Center (Jackson)
- Natchez Community Hospital
- Northwest Mississippi Regional Medical Center (Clarksdale)
- Rankin Medical Center (Brandon)
- Riley Hospital (Meridian)
- River Oaks East (Jackson)
- River Oaks Hospital (Jackson)

North Carolina
- Davis Regional Medical Center (Statesville)
- Franklin Regional Medical Center (Louisburg)
- Lake Norman Regional Medical Center (Mooresville)
- Sandhills Regional Medical Center (Hamlet)

Oklahoma
- Medical Center of Southeastern Oklahoma (Durant)
- Midwest Regional Medical Center

Pennsylvania
- Carlisle Regional Medical Center (Carlisle)
- Heart of Lancaster Regional Medical Center

South Carolina
- Carolina Pines Regional Medical Center
- Upstate Carolina Medical Center (Gaffney)

West Virginia
- Williamson Memorial Hospital

## PRODUCTS/OPERATIONS

### 2006 Payments

| | % of total |
|---|---|
| Commercial insurance | 47 |
| Medicare | 35 |
| Medicaid | 9 |
| Self pay & other | 9 |
| **Total** | **100** |

## COMPETITORS

Ascension Health
Catholic Health East
Catholic Health Initiatives
Community Health Systems
Greenville Hospital System
HCA
LifePoint
Methodist Healthcare
SSM Health Care
Tenet Healthcare

## HISTORICAL FINANCIALS

Company Type: Public

### Income Statement

FYE: December 31

| | REVENUE ($ mil.) | NET INCOME ($ mil.) | NET PROFIT MARGIN | EMPLOYEES |
|---|---|---|---|---|
| **12/06*** | 4,057 | 183 | 4.5% | 34,500 |
| **9/05** | 3,589 | 353 | 9.8% | 31,000 |
| **9/04** | 3,206 | 325 | 10.1% | 28,000 |
| **9/03** | 2,561 | 283 | 11.1% | 24,000 |
| **9/02** | 2,263 | 246 | 10.9% | 23,000 |
| **Annual Growth** | 15.7% | (7.2%) | — | 10.7% |

*Fiscal year change

### 2006 Year-End Financials

Debt ratio: 53.9%
Return on equity: 7.8%
Cash ($ mil.): 87
Current ratio: 2.14
Long-term debt ($ mil.): 1,297
No. of shares (mil.): 241
Dividends
Yield: 1.1%
Payout: 32.0%
Market value ($ mil.): 5,081

### Stock History

NYSE: HMA

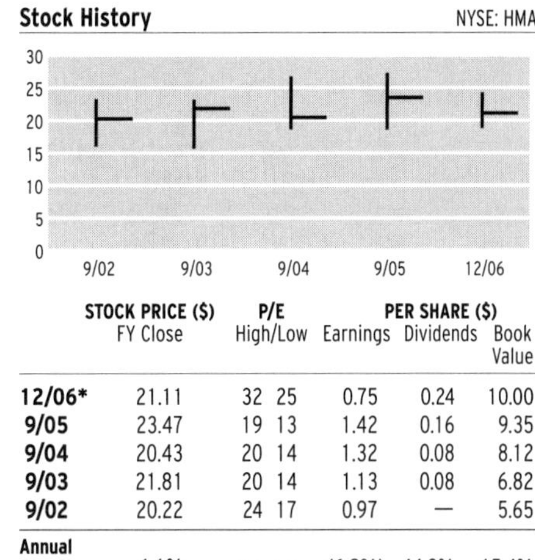


| | STOCK PRICE ($) FY Close | P/E High/Low | | PER SHARE ($) Earnings | Dividends | Book Value |
|---|---|---|---|---|---|---|
| **12/06*** | 21.11 | 32 | 25 | 0.75 | 0.24 | 10.00 |
| **9/05** | 23.47 | 19 | 13 | 1.42 | 0.16 | 9.35 |
| **9/04** | 20.43 | 20 | 14 | 1.32 | 0.08 | 8.12 |
| **9/03** | 21.81 | 20 | 14 | 1.13 | 0.08 | 6.82 |
| **9/02** | 20.22 | 24 | 17 | 0.97 | — | 5.65 |
| **Annual Growth** | 1.1% | — | — | (6.2%) | 44.2% | 15.4% |

*Fiscal year change

# Health Net

Health Net is not another Web site trying to give you health advice, it's a web of health services. The company provides managed health care and other medical coverage to more than 6 million members in 27 states and Washington, DC. The company's Health Plan Services unit offers HMO, PPO, Medicare, and Medicaid plans. The Government Contracts/Specialty Services unit provides health care coverage for almost 3 million military and other government personnel and their dependents through TRICARE contracts. This segment also offers behavioral health, vision, and dental care plans, as well as pharmacy benefits management and workers' compensation administrative services.

California comprises Health Net's largest market, accounting for more than 60% of the company's medical membership. HN California, Health Net's California HMO is part of the State Children's Health Insurance Program (known as Healthy Families) and insures over 90,000 children.

In an effort to further expand its business in the Golden State, the company acquired the health plan assets of Universal Care in 2006, adding another 20,000 Medi-Cal and Healthy Families members to its ranks (as well as some 5,000 Medicare Advantage and 75,000 commercial members).

Also that year, the company exited the Pennsylvania market and it has plans to divest non-core businesses.

Legg Mason owns about 18% of the company.

## HISTORY

Foundation Health started as the not-for-profit Foundation Community Health Plan in the 1960s. In 1984 it was bought by AmeriCare Health, which had HMOs in six states. The acquisition was a coup: Foundation Health soon accounted for the bulk of AmeriCare's sales.

AmeriCare went public in 1985. The next year it lost the rights to its name to another firm. Redubbed Foundation Health, it expanded into new states and unrelated businesses: commercial real estate, silk flowers, and furniture.

In late 1986 senior management led a $140 million LBO that left Foundation Health hobbled with debt when the industry started to slide. A 1988 Department of Defense (DOD) CHAMPUS contract brightened prospects, but the five-year, $3 billion contract to provide health care to 860,000 military retirees and dependents in California and Hawaii provided little short-term relief against the effects of high debt and rapid growth: The company lost money again.

The CEO slot had been vacant a year when Dan Crowley, a trained accountant with a good turnaround record, came aboard in 1989. He cut staff, slashed budgets, sold unrelated and non-performing units, and kicked off a huge sales effort. To satisfy bankers and the DOD, which was threatening to rescind its contract, Crowley refinanced Foundation's debt. In a little over a year, Foundation Health recorded its best results ever. In 1990 the company went public.

Back on solid ground, the company expanded its services and markets, buying such firms as Western Universal Life Insurance (renamed Foundation Health Benefit Life Insurance, 1991), Occupational Health Services (employee assistance and substance abuse programs, 1992), and California Compensation Insurance (workers' compensation insurance, 1993).

Foundation Health lost the DOD Hawaii/California contract (almost half its revenues) in 1993, but managed to cope until it regained the business — by then worth $2.5 billion — two years later. Also that year Foundation Health won DOD's five-year, $1.8 billion managed-care contract for Oklahoma and parts of Arkansas, Louisiana, and Texas.

Meanwhile, the company had formed Integrated Pharmaceutical Services and bought CareFlorida Health Systems, Intergroup Healthcare, and Thomas-Davis Medical Centers in 1994.

In 1995 the company dropped an offer to buy Health Systems International. The next year it added behavioral health and employee assistance programs with the purchase of Managed Health Network.

Renewed discussions with Health Systems International resulted in the companies merging to become Foundation Health Systems in 1997. Crowley — whose aggressive style garnered profits but was denounced as brutal by some critics — resigned after the merger.

In 1998 the company pushed into the Northeast, buying Connecticut-based HMO Physicians Health Services. It then sold its workers' compensation insurance operations. Chairman Malik Hasan (founder of Health Systems' nucleus, QualMed) resigned that year, partly because president Jay Gellert planned to focus on Arizona and California health plans, CHAMPUS, and behavioral health and pharmacy benefit management.

The financial aftershocks of the companies' merger continued, and FHS pruned its operations in 1999 and 2000, exiting such states as Colorado, New Mexico, and Texas, trimming its Medicare operations, and selling certain non-core administrative business lines. In 2000 the California Medical Association sued the company under RICO statutes, claiming it coerced doctors and interfered in doctor-patient relationships. Later that year, the company changed its name to Health Net in its effort to build a national brand name.

In 2002, the company continued to divest certain non-core businesses by selling its EOS Claims Services subsidiary.

## EXECUTIVES

**Chairman:** Roger F. Greaves, age 68
**President, CEO, and Director:** Jay M. Gellert, age 53, $1,715,000 pay
**Acting CFO; President, Government and Specialty Services Division:** James P. (Jim) Woys, age 48
**SVP, Organization Effectiveness:** Karin D. Mayhew, age 55
**SVP, Corporate Communications:** David W. Olson, age 55
**SVP and Chief Medical Officer:** Jonathan Scheff, age 53
**SVP and Controller, Corporate Finance:** Bret A, Morris
**SVP; President, Health Net Pharmaceutical Services:** John Sivori
**SVP, General Counsel, and Secretary:** Linda V. Tiano, age 49
**Chief Actuarial Officer:** Joyce Li
**Chief Senior Products Officer:** Mark S. El-Tawil, age 41
**President, MHN:** Steven (Steve) Sell, age 40
**President, Health Net Federal Services:** Steve D. Tough
**President, Regional Health Plans and Health Net of California:** Stephen (Steve) Lynch, age 55
**President, Health Net of the Northeast:** Steven H. (Steve) Nelson, age 47
**VP, Chief Compliance Officer, Deputy General Counsel, and Corporate Ethics Officer:** Philip G. (Phil) Davis, age 55
**Auditors:** Deloitte & Touche LLP

## LOCATIONS

**HQ:** Health Net, Inc.
21650 Oxnard St., Woodland Hills, CA 91367
**Phone:** 818-676-6000 **Fax:** 818-676-8591
**Web:** www.healthnet.com

Health Net operates both commercial and government-sponsored health plans in Alaska, Arizona, Arkansas, California, Connecticut, Hawaii, Idaho, Louisiana, New Jersey, New York, Oklahoma, Oregon, Pennsylvania, Texas, and Washington.

## PRODUCTS/OPERATIONS

### 2006 Sales

| | % of total |
|---|---|
| Health plan | 81 |
| Government contracts | 19 |
| **Total** | **100** |

### Selected Subsidiaries

East Los Angeles Doctors Hospital, Inc.
FH Surgery Centers, Inc.
FH Surgery Limited, Inc.
Foundation Health Facilities, Inc.
Health Net Federal Services, Inc.
Health Net of Arizona, Inc
Health Net of California, Inc.
Health Net of the Northeast, Inc.
Health Net of Oregon, Inc.
Health Net One Payment Services, Inc.
Health Net Pharmaceutical Services
Health Net Services, Inc.
HSI Advantage Eastern Holdings, Inc.
Intercare, Inc.
Managed Health Network, Inc.
Memorial Hospital of Gardena, Inc.
National Pharmacy Services, Inc.
QualMed, Inc.
QualMed Plans for Health of Pennsylvania, Inc.
Questium, Inc.

## COMPETITORS

Aetna
Blue Cross Blue Shield of Arizona
Blue Shield Of California
CIGNA
ConnectiCare
Health Insurance of New York
Horizon Healthcare
Humana
Kaiser Foundation Health
Kaiser Permanente
LifeWise Health Plan
Oxford Health
PacifiCare
Pacificare of California
Providence Health System
Regence BlueCross BlueShield
UnitedHealth Group
WellPoint

## HISTORICAL FINANCIALS

Company Type: Public

### Income Statement

FYE: December 31

| | REVENUE ($ mil.) | NET INCOME ($ mil.) | NET PROFIT MARGIN | EMPLOYEES |
|---|---|---|---|---|
| **12/06** | 12,908 | 329 | 2.6% | 10,068 |
| **12/05** | 11,941 | 230 | 1.9% | 9,286 |
| **12/04** | 11,646 | 43 | 0.4% | 8,569 |
| **12/03** | 11,065 | 234 | 2.1% | 9,053 |
| **12/02** | 10,195 | 226 | 2.2% | 9,400 |
| **Annual Growth** | 6.1% | 9.9% | — | 1.7% |

### 2006 Year-End Financials

Debt ratio: 16.9%
Return on equity: 19.6%
Cash ($ mil.): 2,121
Current ratio: 1.53
Long-term debt ($ mil.): 300
No. of shares (mil.): 112
Dividends
Yield: —
Payout: —
Market value ($ mil.): 5,444

### Stock History

NYSE: HNT

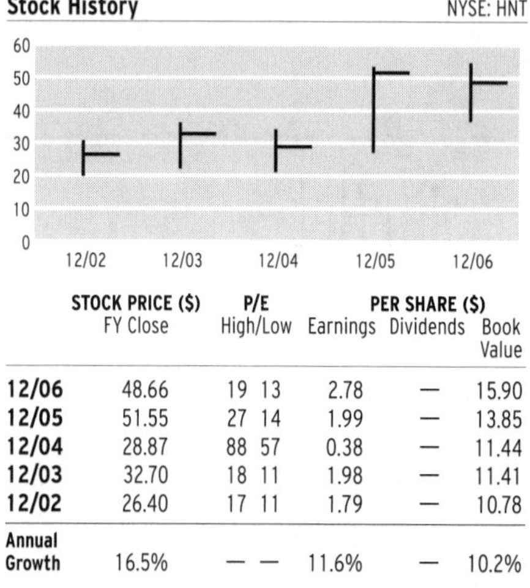


| | STOCK PRICE ($) FY Close | P/E High | P/E Low | PER SHARE ($) Earnings | Dividends | Book Value |
|---|---|---|---|---|---|---|
| **12/06** | 48.66 | 19 | 13 | 2.78 | — | 15.90 |
| **12/05** | 51.55 | 27 | 14 | 1.99 | — | 13.85 |
| **12/04** | 28.87 | 88 | 57 | 0.38 | — | 11.44 |
| **12/03** | 32.70 | 18 | 11 | 1.98 | — | 11.41 |
| **12/02** | 26.40 | 17 | 11 | 1.79 | — | 10.78 |
| **Annual Growth** | 16.5% | — | — | 11.6% | — | 10.2% |

# HealthSouth

Embattled HealthSouth is looking for a way to rehabilitate its own fortunes. A leading provider of rehabilitative health care, the firm has facilities throughout the US and in Puerto Rico. A 2003 SEC investigation of accounting fraud at HealthSouth led to the firing of chairman and CEO Richard Scrushy and the company's stock delisting by the NYSE (it has since been relisted). Hoping for a full recovery in the wake of the scandals, it is engaged in an intensive restructuring plan that includes the sale of its surgery, outpatient, and diagnostic imaging assets, in order to pay down debt and focus on growing its inpatient rehab business.

HealthSouth ended up paying out a total of about $3 billion to avoid criminal prosecution for the accounting fraud. Under terms of the agreement, the company accepted responsibility for crimes committed by its executives and is enacting more strict internal controls; it remains on probation until 2009. The scandal, through payout, debt, and company devaluation, pushed HealthSouth to the brink of bankruptcy and led to a massive shakeup of its board of directors and senior executive team.

The company took the first step in its divestiture plan in 2007, selling its outpatient rehabilitation division — which comprises more than 550 facilities in about 35 states — to privately owned Select Medical. Also that year it sold its outpatient surgery unit, consisting of more than 135 surgery centers and three surgical hospitals, to private investment firm TPG. Later, HealthSouth offloaded its diagnostics unit to private equity firm The Gores Group.

With all the sales completed, HealthSouth is focused on providing post-acute care services, including inpatient rehabilitative care. Its inpatient rehab unit operates about 90 wholly or jointly owned inpatient facilities in 27 states, with the largest concentrations in Alabama, Florida, Pennsylvania, Tennessee, and Texas. The unit also includes about 10 long-term care hospitals and a number of outpatient centers located adjacent to or inside of its inpatient facilities. The inpatient operations provide nursing and therapy to patients who have experienced significant disabilities as a result of stroke, spinal cord injury, neuromuscular disease, and other conditions.

Government-funded health programs are the largest source of revenues for HealthSouth; about 70% of inpatient revenues are paid by Medicare.

## HISTORY

A one-time service station worker (when he was a 17-year-old married man with a baby on the way), Richard Scrushy got into the health care industry by working in respiratory therapy; he earned a degree in the subject in 1974. Recruited for a job with a Texas health care management firm, Scrushy saw the convergence of several trends: Lowered reimbursements for medical care; a new emphasis on rehabilitation as a way to reduce the need for surgery and get employees back to work faster; and a dearth of brand names in health care. Scrushy decided to establish a national health care brand of rehabilitation hospitals, and in 1984 he and four of his co-workers founded Amcare and built its first outpatient center in Birmingham, Alabama.

From the beginning Scrushy wanted to make his rehabilitation centers less like hospitals and more like upscale health clubs. He also sought workers' compensation and rehabilitation contracts from self-insured companies and managed care operations. The strategies worked. The company had revenues of $5 million in 1985, the year it became HealthSouth. Other strategies included specializing in specific ailments, such as back problems and sports injuries, and using the same floor plan and furnishings for all HealthSouth locations to save money. The company went public in 1986.

By 1988 HealthSouth had nearly 40 facilities in 15 states and kept shopping for more. A merger with its biggest rival, Continental Medical Systems, fell through in 1992, but HealthSouth became the #1 provider of rehabilitative services the next year with its acquisition of most of the rehabilitation services of National Medical Enterprises (now Tenet Healthcare). (Scrushy and other officers formed MedPartners, a physician management company, in 1993.) Additional acquisitions included the inpatient rehabilitation hospitals of ReLife (1994) and NovaCare (now NAHC) and Caremark's rehabilitation services (1995). HealthSouth became the #1 operator of outpatient surgery centers with its acquisition of Surgical Care Affiliates in 1995. The $1.1 billion stock swap was the company's largest acquisition ever.

In 1997 HealthSouth acquired Horizon/CMS Healthcare, the US's largest provider of specialty health care. After completing the Horizon/CMS deal, HealthSouth sold Horizon's 139 long-term-care facilities, 12 specialty hospitals, and 35 institutional pharmacies to Integrated Health Services; it kept about 30 inpatient and 275 outpatient rehabilitation facilities.

In the late 1990s HealthSouth built its outpatient operations through acquisitions, buying nearly three dozen outpatient centers from what is now HCA.

In 2003 the SEC initiated an investigation of HealthSouth's accounting practices which led to the firing of chairman and CEO Richard Scrushy, removal of the company's auditor, and delisting of the company's stock by the NYSE. The company settled with the SEC for the charges brought specifically against the company itself and not any of its officers in 2005 to the tune of $100 million.

Scrushy was brought to trial in 2005 on 86 criminal counts (later reduced to 36 counts) related to the $2.7 billion, seven-year run of accounting fraud at the firm. Scrushy did not take the stand in his defense during the trial; his lawyers maintained that the fraud was carried out against his knowledge by subordinates. After the jury deliberated for nearly a month, Scrushy was found not guilty on all 36 charges, including charges of falsifying financial reports under the Sarbanes-Oxley Act. Meanwhile, Aaron Beam, the co-founder of the company and its first CFO, was convicted and remanded to three months in prison in August 2005; Bill Owens, another HealthSouth CFO who secretly recorded Scrushy for federal agents, was sentenced to five years in prison in December 2005. Some 15 other former HealthSouth executives have pleaded guilty to fraud charges since 2003.

Scrushy finally resigned from the board of directors in December 2005; after being dismissed from his executive position at the company, he had refused to give up his seat on the board. In the months thereafter, the company replaced the entire board of directors and its senior-level executive roster.

## EXECUTIVES

**Chairman:** Jon F. Hanson, age 69
**President, CEO, and Director:** Jay Grinney, age 55, $1,398,100 pay
**EVP and COO:** Michael D. (Mike) Snow, age 51, $996,178 pay
**EVP and CFO:** John L. Workman, age 54, $854,941 pay
**EVP and Chief Administrative Officer:** James C. (Jim) Foxworthy, age 54
**EVP and Chief Compliance Officer:** John Markus, age 54, $559,832 pay
**EVP, General Counsel, and Corporate Secretary:** John P. Whittington
**SVP, Human Resources:** Cheryl Levy
**President, Inpatient Division:** Mark J. Tarr, age 44
**President, Diagnostic Division:** R. Gregory (Greg) Brophy
**Auditors:** PricewaterhouseCoopers

## LOCATIONS

**HQ:** HealthSouth Corporation
1 HealthSouth Pkwy., Birmingham, AL 35243
**Phone:** 205-967-7116 **Fax:** 205-969-3543
**Web:** www.healthsouth.com

HealthSouth operates inpatient rehabilitation facilities in 27 states.

## PRODUCTS/OPERATIONS

**2006 Sales**

| | $ mil. | % of total |
|---|---|---|
| Inpatient | 1,725 | 57 |
| Surgery centers | 737 | 24 |
| Outpatient | 327 | 11 |
| Diagnostic | 187 | 6 |
| Corporate & other | 48 | 2 |
| Adjustments | (24) | — |
| **Total** | **3,000** | **100** |

**2006 Revenue Sources**

| | % of total |
|---|---|
| Medicare | 47 |
| Managed care & other discount plans | 35 |
| Workers' compensation | 7 |
| Other third-party payers | 5 |
| Medicaid | 2 |
| Patients | 1 |
| Other income | 3 |
| **Total** | **100** |

## COMPETITORS

Ascension Health
Burke Rehabilitation Hospital
HCA
Kindred Healthcare
Manor Care
RehabCare
Select Medical
Tenet Healthcare

## HISTORICAL FINANCIALS

Company Type: Public

**Income Statement** FYE: December 31

| | REVENUE ($ mil.) | NET INCOME ($ mil.) | NET PROFIT MARGIN | EMPLOYEES |
|---|---|---|---|---|
| **12/06** | 3,000 | (625) | — | 33,000 |
| **12/05** | 3,208 | (446) | — | 37,000 |
| **12/04** | 3,754 | (175) | — | 40,000 |
| **12/03** | 3,958 | (435) | — | 40,000 |
| **12/02** | 3,960 | (467) | — | 51,000 |
| **Annual Growth** | (6.7%) | — | — | (10.3%) |

**2006 Year-End Financials**

Debt ratio: —
Return on equity: —
Cash ($ mil.): 178
Current ratio: 0.70
Long-term debt ($ mil.): 3,365
No. of shares (mil.): 79
Dividends
Yield: —
Payout: —
Market value ($ mil.): 1,782

**Stock History** NYSE: HLS

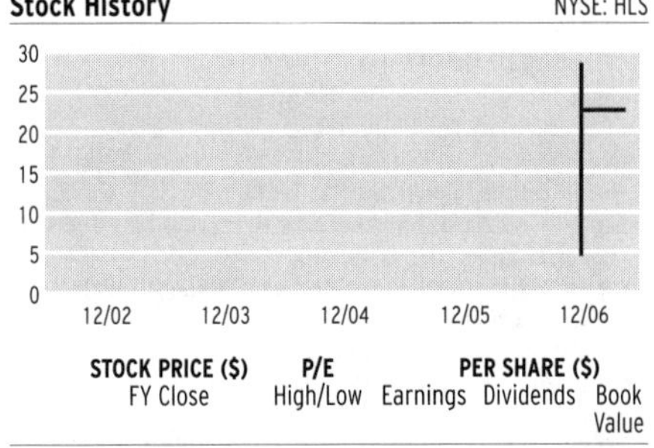


| | STOCK PRICE ($) FY Close | P/E High/Low | PER SHARE ($) Earnings | Dividends | Book Value |
|---|---|---|---|---|---|
| **12/06** | 22.65 | — — | (8.14) | — | (27.76) |

# The Hearst Corporation

Like founder William Randolph Hearst's castle, The Hearst Corporation is sprawling. The company owns 12 daily newspapers (such as the *San Francisco Chronicle* and the *Houston Chronicle*) and eight weekly newspapers; nearly 20 US consumer magazines (such as *Cosmopolitan*, *Seventeen*, and *Esquire*) with nearly 200 international editions; TV and radio stations (through majority-owned Hearst Argyle Television); and a cartoon and features syndication service (King Features). Hearst is also active in cable networks through stakes in A&E, Lifetime, and ESPN. In 2006 it sold its 25% stake in women's Web network iVillage. The Hearst Corporation is owned by the Hearst family, but managed by a board of trustees.

*Cosmopolitan* is published in 34 languages and sold in more than 100 countries, making it the largest magazine franchise in the world.

Through its Interactive Media unit, the company makes strategic investments in online properties such as drugstore.com, Gather, and Hire.com. In 2007 it ponied up about $100 million to acquire UGO Networks, which operates a Web site targeting young men in the 18-34 demographic with a mix of movie reviews, sports stories, video game previews, and racy pictorals. In 2007 Hearst announced plans to acquire Kaboodle, a social shopping community where consumers recommend and share products.

Although the company no longer owns Hearst Castle (deeded to the State of California in 1951), it has extensive real estate holdings. Projects include the Hearst Ranch in San Simeon, California and the Hearst Tower in New York.

Upon his death, William Randolph Hearst left 99% of the company's common stock to two charitable trusts controlled by a 13-member board that includes five family and eight nonfamily members. The will includes a clause that allows the trustees to disinherit any heir who contests the will.

## HISTORY

William Randolph Hearst, son of a California mining magnate, started as a reporter — having been expelled from Harvard in 1884 for playing jokes on professors. In 1887 he became editor of the *San Francisco Examiner,* which his father had obtained as payment for a gambling debt. In 1895 he bought the *New York Morning Journal* and competed against Joseph Pulitzer's *New York World*. The "yellow journalism" resulting from that rivalry characterized American-style reporting at the turn of the century.

Hearst branched into magazines (1903), film (1913), and radio (1928). Also during this time it created the Hearst International News Service (it was sold to E.W. Scripps' United Press in 1958 to form United Press International). By 1935 Hearst was at its peak, with newspapers in 19 cities, the largest syndicate (King Features), international news and photo services, 13 magazines, eight radio stations, and two motion picture companies. Two years later Hearst relinquished control of the company to avoid bankruptcy, selling movie companies, radio stations, magazines, and, later, most of his San Simeon estate. (Hearst's rise and fall inspired the 1941 film *Citizen Kane.*)

In 1948 Hearst became the owner of one of the US's first TV stations, WBAL-TV in Baltimore. When Hearst died in 1951, company veteran

Richard Berlin became CEO. Berlin sold off failing newspapers, moved into television, and acquired more magazines.

Frank Bennack, CEO since 1979, expanded the company, acquiring newspapers, publishing firms (notably William Morrow, 1981), TV stations, magazines (*Redbook,* 1982; *Esquire,* 1986), and 20% of cable sports network ESPN (1991). Hearst branched into video via a joint venture with Capital Cities/ABC (1981) and helped launch the Lifetime and Arts & Entertainment cable channels (1984).

In 1991 Hearst launched a New England news network with Continental Cablevision. The following year Hearst brought on board former Federal Communications Commission chairman Alfred Sikes, who quickly moved the company onto the Internet. In 1996 Randolph A. Hearst passed the title of chairman to nephew George Hearst (the last surviving son of the founder, Randolph died in 2000). Broadcaster Argyle Television merged with Hearst's TV holdings in 1997 to form publicly traded Hearst-Argyle Television.

In 1999 Hearst combined its HomeArts Web site with Women.com to create one of the largest online networks for women. In addition, it joined with Walt Disney's Miramax Films to publish entertainment magazine *Talk* (shut down in 2001) and Oprah Winfrey's Harpo Entertainment to publish *O, The Oprah Magazine* (launched in 2000). The company sold its book publishing operations to News Corp.'s HarperCollins unit in 1999. It also agreed to buy the *San Francisco Chronicle* from rival Chronicle Publishing. That deal was called into question over concerns that the *San Francisco Examiner* would not survive and the city would be left with one major paper. To resolve the issue, the next year Hearst sold the *Examiner* to ExIn (a group of investors affiliated with the Ted Fang family and other owners of the *San Francisco Independent*). Also in 2000 Hearst bought the UK magazines of Gruner + Jahr, the newspaper and magazine unit of German media juggernaut Bertelsmann.

The following year Hearst gained a 30% stake in iVillage following that company's purchase of rival Women.com Networks. In mid-2002 Victor Ganzi took over as CEO and president following Bennack's retirement from these positions.

Using the selling power of its popular *Cosmopolitan* magazine, the company capitalized with a TV channel in Spain based on the magazine. It then added another one in Latin America. Hearst hasn't been so lucky when trying to take the trend in the other direction. The firm launched *Lifetime* magazine in 2003 with women's cable channel Lifetime. However, the magazine fared poorly and ceased publication in late 2004. This came on the heels of the high-profile failure of *Talk* magazine, a joint venture with movie studio Miramax. Led by Tina Brown, the famous former editor of *The New Yorker*, the magazine only lasted two years before the partners shut it down, citing the downturn in the economy and poor circulation.

Hearst further expanded its potent stable of magazines in 2003 by purchasing *Seventeen* magazine from PRIMEDIA. In addition to the magazine, the deal (valued at $182 million) included the purchase of *Teen* magazine and school marketing business Cover Concepts. Hearst also became a major player in yellow page publishing with its 2004 purchase of White Directory Publishers, one of the largest telephone directory companies in the US.

## EXECUTIVES

**Chairman:** George R. Hearst Jr., age 79
**Vice Chairman:** Frank A. Bennack Jr., age 74
**President and CEO; Chairman, Hearst-Argyle Television:** Victor F. Ganzi, age 60
**SVP and CFO:** Ronald J. Doerfler
**SVP and Chief Legal and Development Officer:** James M. Asher
**SVP; President, Hearst Newspapers:** George B. Irish
**VP; President and CEO, Hearst Magazines International; EVP, Hearst Magazines:** George J. Green
**VP; EVP, Hearst Entertainment and Syndication; President, Hearst Entertainment:** Bruce Paisner
**Chairman and Editorial Director, SmartMoney:** Edwin A. Finn Jr.
**President and CEO, Hearst-Argyle Television:** David J. Barrett, age 59
**President, Hearst Business Media:** Richard P. Malloch
**President, Hearst Interactive Media:** Kenneth A. Bronfin, age 47
**President, Hearst Magazines:** Cathleen P. (Cathie) Black, age 62
**EVP, Hearst Newspapers:** Steven R. Swartz
**SVP and Director Digital Media, Hearst Newspapers:** Lincoln Millstein
**SVP, Advertising, Hearst Newspapers:** Mark Adkins
**SVP, Finance, Hearst Newspapers:** John (Jack) Condon
**VP, Hearst Interactive Media:** Michael Dunn
**Executive Director, Corporate Communications; VP, Communications, Hearst Magazines:** Paul Luthringer

## LOCATIONS

**HQ:** The Hearst Corporation
959 8th Ave., New York, NY 10019
**Phone:** 212-649-2000 **Fax:** 212-649-2108
**Web:** www.hearstcorp.com

Hearst newspapers are located throughout the US. Hearst Magazines are distributed in more than 100 countries.

## PRODUCTS/OPERATIONS

### Selected Operations

Broadcasting
- Hearst-Argyle Television (majority owned)

Business Publications
- *Black Book*
- *Diversion*
- *Electronic Products*
- *First DataBank*
- *MOTOR Magazine*

Entertainment and Syndication
- A&E Television Networks (joint venture with ABC and NBC)
  - A&E
  - The Biography Channel
  - The History Channel
  - History Channel International
- Cosmopolitan Television (Latin America)
- Cosmopolitan Television Iberia (Spain)
- ESPN (20%)
- King Features Syndicate
- Hearst Entertainment (content library and production operations)
- Lifetime Entertainment Services (50%, with Walt Disney Company)
  - Lifetime Movie Network
  - Lifetime Online
  - Lifetime Television
- New England Cable News (with Comcast)
- Reed Brennan Media Associates (custom electronic and pagination services for newspapers)

Interactive Media
- Circles (online loyalty marketing programs)
- drugstore.com (online pharmacy site)
- Gather (social networking)
- Hire.com (job site)

Magazines
- *CosmoGIRL!*
- *Cosmopolitan*
- *Country Living*
- *Esquire*
- *Good Housekeeping*
- *Harper's BAZAAR*
- *House Beautiful*
- *Marie Claire*
- *O, The Oprah Magazine* (with Harpo)
- *Popular Mechanics*
- *Quick & Simple*
- *Redbook*
- *Seventeen*
- *SmartMoney* (with Dow Jones)
- *Teen*
- *Weekend*

Major Newspapers
- *Albany Times Union* (New York)
- *Houston Chronicle*
- *Huron Daily Tribune* (Michigan)
- *Laredo Morning Times* (Texas)
- *Midland Daily News* (Michigan)
- *San Antonio Express-News*
- *San Francisco Chronicle*
- *Seattle Post-Intelligencer*

Other Operations
- Real estate
- White Directory Publishers (telephone directories)

## COMPETITORS

| | |
|---|---|
| Advance Publications | McClatchy Company |
| Andrews McMeel Universal | McGraw-Hill |
| Belo | MediaNews |
| Bertelsmann | Meredith |
| Bloomberg | New York Times |
| Cox Enterprises | News Corp. |
| Dennis Publishing | PRIMEDIA |
| Disney | Reader's Digest |
| E. W. Scripps | Reed Elsevier Group |
| Emap | Rodale |
| Freedom Communications | Seattle Times |
| Gannett | Time Warner |
| infoUSA | Tribune |
| IPC Group | Viacom |
| Lagardère Active Media | Washington Post |
| Liberty Media | Yellow Book USA |

## HISTORICAL FINANCIALS

Company Type: Private

### Income Statement

FYE: December 31

| | ESTIMATED REVENUE ($ mil.) | NET INCOME ($ mil.) | NET PROFIT MARGIN | EMPLOYEES |
|---|---|---|---|---|
| **12/05** | 4,550 | — | — | 17,016 |
| **12/04** | 4,000 | — | — | 16,667 |
| **12/03** | 4,100 | — | — | 20,000 |
| **12/02** | 3,565 | — | — | 17,320 |
| **12/01** | 3,300 | — | — | 17,170 |
| **Annual Growth** | 8.4% | — | — | (0.2%) |

### Revenue History

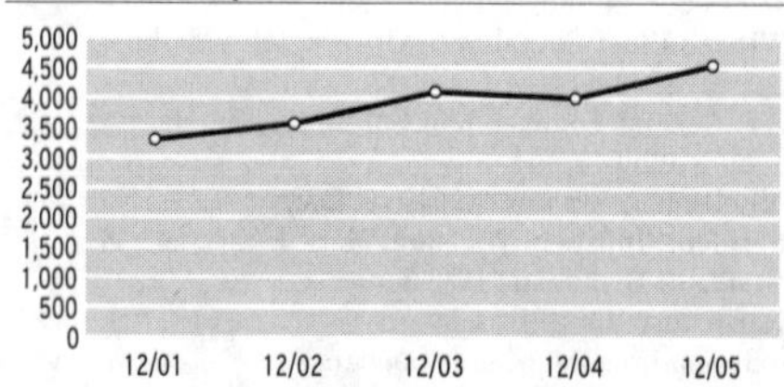

# Henry Schein

Henry Schein helps dentists get your sparkly whites to shine. The company is a leading distributor of dental supplies and equipment; it claims to serve over 80% of dental offices in North America. Henry Schein provides such dental items as impression materials, X-ray equipment, anesthetics, and dental practice management software. In addition to dental products, the company provides supplies and equipment to medical offices, including diagnostic kits, surgical tools, and generic and brand-name pharmaceuticals. The company also serves veterinary offices with supplies and equipment.

Not content with its nearly half a million customers worldwide and a strong presence in North America, the company aggressively pursues acquisitions to further build its business. The company's purchases have expanded its array of products and its geographic reach.

The company offers pharmaceutical products in addition to equipment to its medical customers. It also expanded its veterinary distribution business in 2006 with the acquisition of NLS Animal Health, which provides some 12,000 products (including pharmaceuticals, instruments, supplies, and equipment) to over 8,000 companion animal and equine clinics in 26 states.

The same year its acquisitions included Island Dental, Darby Medical Supply, and Darby Dental Laboratory Supply from the Darby Group. Schein also divested its hospital supply business.

## HISTORY

For more than 50 years, Henry Schein distributed drugs made by Schein Pharmaceuticals. In 1992 management spun off the drug business and, led by former accountant Stanley Bergman, began acquiring other dental supply companies at a terrific rate: 34 between 1994 and 1996 alone.

The company went public in 1995 and bought more than a dozen businesses. These purchases, which included product marketer Vertex Corporation's distribution unit, moved Henry Schein into the medical and veterinary supply fields. The purchase of Schein Dental Equipment (founded by Marvin Schein) boosted per-customer sales by adding big-ticket merchandise to the product mix.

Acquisitions continued hot and heavy as the company boosted operations abroad. The purchases hit the bottom line; Schein avoided bloat by restructuring operations, closing facilities, and developing new systems. The company consolidated 13 distribution centers into five in 1997. The following year the firm expanded into Canada, and bought a controlling stake in UK direct marketer Porter Nash.

To boost profits, the company announced in 2000 that it would cut 5% of its workforce. It also shut down some facilities and sold its software development business as part of its overall restructuring plan. In 2001 the firm resumed its acquisitions when it bought the dental supply business of Zila, maker of over-the-counter and prescription drugs.

## EXECUTIVES

**Chairman, President, and CEO:** Stanley M. Bergman, age 57, $1,000,000 pay
**President, COO, and Director:** James P. Breslawski, age 53, $564,676 pay
**EVP, CFO, and Director:** Steven Paladino, age 50, $423,940 pay
**EVP, Chief Administrative Officer, and Director:** Gerald A. Benjamin, age 54, $328,282 pay
**EVP Corporate Business Development Group and Director:** Mark E. Mlotek, age 51, $446,671 pay
**President, International Group:** Michael Zack, age 54
**VP Global Human Resources:** Carole M. DeMayo, age 50
**VP and Chief Compliance Officer:** Leonard A. David, age 58
**VP Corporate Communications:** Susan Vassallo
**VP Investor Relations:** Neal Goldner
**President, Medical Group:** Michael Racioppi, age 52
**CTO:** Jim Harding
**Senior Advisor:** Stanley Komaroff, age 71
**Auditors:** BDO Seidman, LLP

## LOCATIONS

**HQ:** Henry Schein, Inc.
135 Duryea Rd., Melville, NY 11747
**Phone:** 631-843-5500 **Fax:** 631-843-5658
**Web:** www.henryschein.com

Henry Schein has distribution facilities in Canada, Germany, the UK, and the US. The company operates in nearly 20 countries and has offices in Australia, Austria, Belgium, Canada, the Czech Republic, France, Germany, Luxembourg, Ireland, Italy, the Netherlands, New Zealand, Portugal, Spain, the UK, and the US.

### 2006 Sales

| | $ mil. | % of total |
|---|---|---|
| US | 3,536.6 | 69 |
| Germany | 642.6 | 12 |
| Other countries | 973.9 | 19 |
| **Total** | **5,153.1** | **100** |

## PRODUCTS/OPERATIONS

### 2006 Sales

| | $ mil. | % of total |
|---|---|---|
| Health care distribution | | |
| Dental | 2,136.8 | 41 |
| Medical | 1,516.2 | 30 |
| International | 1,401.9 | 27 |
| Technology | 98.2 | 2 |
| **Total** | **5,153.1** | **100** |

### Selected Products

Dental products
- Acrylics
- Alloys
- Anesthetics
- Articulators
- Bridges
- Composites
- Crowns
- Gypsum
- Impression materials
- Preventatives
- Surgical equipment
- X-ray equipment

Medical products
- Diagnostic kits
- Office equipment
- Pharmaceuticals (generic and brand-name)
- Surgical tools
- Vitamins

Technology
- Dental practice management software

Veterinary products
- Dental equipment
- Pharmaceuticals
- Surgical tools

## COMPETITORS

Benco Dental
Burns Veterinary Supply
Cardinal Health
Cardinal Medical Products
Darby Dental
DENTSPLY
IDEXX Labs
McKesson
Moore Medical
MWI Veterinary Supply
Omega Pharma
Owens & Minor
Patterson Companies
PSS World Medical
Sybron Dental

## HISTORICAL FINANCIALS

Company Type: Public

### Income Statement

FYE: Last Saturday in December

| | REVENUE ($ mil.) | NET INCOME ($ mil.) | NET PROFIT MARGIN | EMPLOYEES |
|---|---|---|---|---|
| **12/06** | 5,153 | 164 | 3.2% | 11,000 |
| **12/05** | 4,636 | 151 | 3.3% | 11,000 |
| **12/04** | 4,060 | 128 | 3.2% | 9,600 |
| **12/03** | 3,354 | 138 | 4.1% | 7,900 |
| **12/02** | 2,825 | 118 | 4.2% | 6,900 |
| **Annual Growth** | 16.2% | 8.5% | — | 12.4% |

### 2006 Year-End Financials

Debt ratio: 31.0%
Return on equity: 12.1%
Cash ($ mil.): 297
Current ratio: 2.03
Long-term debt ($ mil.): 456
No. of shares (mil.): 88
Dividends
Yield: —
Payout: —
Market value ($ mil.): 4,335

### Stock History

NASDAQ (GS): HSIC

| | STOCK PRICE ($) FY Close | P/E High | P/E Low | PER SHARE ($) Earnings | Dividends | Book Value |
|---|---|---|---|---|---|---|
| **12/06** | 48.98 | 30 | 24 | 1.82 | — | 16.62 |
| **12/05** | 43.64 | 27 | 19 | 1.70 | — | 14.12 |
| **12/04** | 33.82 | 28 | 20 | 1.43 | — | 12.77 |
| **12/03** | 33.83 | 23 | 11 | 1.53 | — | 22.95 |
| **12/02** | 22.41 | 22 | 13 | 1.32 | — | 19.58 |
| **Annual Growth** | 21.6% | — | — | 8.4% | — | (4.0%) |

# Hercules Incorporated

Hercules labors to strengthen products such as paper, paint, and textiles. The company's paper technologies division supplies water-treatment and functional performance chemicals and services to the pulp and paper industry. Its Aqualon subsidiary makes thickeners for water-based products such as latex paints, printing inks, and oral hygiene products. The company's Pinova unit — which makes wood and gum rosin resins for adhesives, food and beverages, and construction materials — was moved within Aqualon in 2006. Hercules owns a minority stake in FiberVisions, a business that makes staple fibers used in disposable diapers and automotive textiles.

The company is focused on improving competitive advantages, increasing cash flows and profitability, and reducing financial leverages and legacy liabilities (including asbestos-related claims). Hercules has been streamlining some operations, shutting down its pulp and paper facility in Indonesia and its Pendlebury plant in the UK. The company also sold Pinova's terpenes specialties business, which served the flavors and fragrance industry.

To enhance its existing operations, Aqualon acquired, in 2006, the guar gum (a thickener) manufacturing business of Benchmark Polymer. The division also acquired the remaining 40% of a venture with two Chinese companies — called Shanghai Hercules Chemicals Company — to manufacture methylcellulose thickeners.

Hercules sold a 51% stake in FiberVisions to Snow, Phipps & Guggenheim, an affiliate of private equity firm SPG Partners, for $109 million in 2006.

## HISTORY

In 1912 a federal court decision forced DuPont (which controlled two-thirds of the US's explosives production) to spin off half its business into two companies: Hercules Powder and Atlas Powder.

Hercules began operating explosives plants across the US in 1913. During WWI it became the largest US producer of TNT. After the war Hercules diversified into nonexplosive products, which included nitrocellulose for the manufacture of plastics, lacquers, and films.

By the late 1920s Hercules' core business had changed from powders to chemicals. Its resin products were marketed to dozens of industries, including the paper industry, the largest user.

In the early 1950s Hercules developed a new process for making phenol, a substance in plastics, paints, and pharmaceuticals. Its explosives unit made important contributions in rocketry by developing propellants for Nike rockets and by making motors for Minuteman and Polaris missiles. By the late 1950s Hercules was making chemical propellants, petrochemical plastics, synthetic fibers, agricultural and paper chemicals, and food additives.

During the 1960s and early 1970s, the company, renamed Hercules Incorporated (1966), increased plastic resin and fabricated plastic production. Hercules also developed foreign markets, doubling export sales between 1962 and 1972. Following the 1970s energy crisis, Hercules reduced its dependence on petrochemicals and expanded its specialty chemical and defense-related rocket propulsion businesses. In 1989 Hercules took full ownership of the Aqualon Group, which had been a 50-50 joint venture with Germany's Henkel.

Hercules sold its aerospace business (26% of 1994 sales) in 1995 to Alliant Techsystems for $440 million. The deal left Hercules with 30% ownership of Alliant.

In 1997 Hercules and Mallinckrodt sold their Tastemaker joint venture. Also in 1997 Hercules began selling its stake in Alliant.

The company's acquisitions in 1998 included Houghton International's Citrus Colloids pectin business and, for $2.4 billion and the assumption of $700 million in debt, BetzDearborn, a maker of chemicals for paper production and wastewater treatment. In 1999 president and COO Vincent Corbo replaced R. Keith Elliott as CEO.

In 2000 Hercules combined its food gums business with Pharmacia's (Monsanto) Kelco biogums unit to form CP Kelco, a joint venture with Lehman Brothers Holdings. The company received about $600 million through the sale. Also in 2000 Elliott retired and Corbo became chairman; later the same year Corbo resigned and former CEO Gossage was named interim chairman and CEO. Not long afterwards Hercules let it be known that it was looking for a buyer.

Hercules sold its hydrocarbon resins business — and most of its other resin assets — to Eastman Chemical early in 2001. The same year CP Kelco sued Pharmacia for more than $400 million, plus punitive damages, alledging fraud in the joint venture deal. In May former Union Carbide head William Joyce replaced Gossage as CEO.

To reduce its approximately $2.8 billion in debt (due in part to its purchase of BetzDearborn), Hercules revisited that 1998 decision and sold the water treatment portion of BetzDearborn to GE Specialty Materials (now part of GE Industrial) for about $1.8 billion (except the paper process chemicals business operations). The sale was often criticized because the company bought BetzDearborn for $3.1 billion.

International Specialty Products (ISP), which had a 10% stake in Hercules, led a proxy fight for control of the company throughout the first half of 2003. It withdrew its efforts at the July annual meeting when it became clear its four board nominees would not all win spots as directors. ISP had been highly critical of Hercules' board and management, specifically the sale of the company's BetzDearborn subsidiary and Hercules' poison pill that would go in effect in the event of a takeover attempt.

In October 2003 Joyce resigned from the company to take over the chairman and CEO roles at water treatment chemicals manufacturer Nalco (formerly Ondeo Nalco). Joyce had been Heyman's chief target of criticism but came out of the proxy fight looking strong. The company started its search for a replacement immediately but split the chairman and CEO positions between John Wulff and Craig Rogerson, respectively, in the interim. In December the board gave the permanent jobs to Wulff and Rogerson.

Also in 2003, Aqualon reduced production costs and increased its production volumes through the acquisition of Chinese manufacturing firm Jiangmen Quantum Hi-Tech Biochemical Engineering.

## EXECUTIVES

**Chairman:** John K. Wulff, age 58
**President, CEO, and Director:** Craig A. Rogerson, age 50, $712,508 pay
**VP and CFO:** Allen A. Spizzo, age 49, $345,838 pay
**VP and Controller:** Fred G. Aanonsen, age 59
**VP; President, Aqualon:** John E. Panichella, age 47, $313,807 pay
**VP; President, Paper Technologies and Ventures Group:** Paul C. Raymond III, age 42, $312,500 pay
**VP and Treasurer:** Stuart C. Shears, age 56
**VP, Human Resources:** Edward V. (Ed) Carrington, age 64, $271,678 pay
**VP, Safety, Health, Environment, Regulatory Affairs, and Manufacturing Excellence:** Thomas H. Strang, age 54
**VP, Taxes:** Vincenzo M. Romano, age 53
**Chief Legal Officer:** Richard G. Dahlen, age 67
**Corporate Secretary and General Counsel:** Israel J. Floyd, age 60
**Director, Hercules Paper Technologies, Americas:** Chet Cross
**Director, Investor Relations and Corporate Analysis:** Stuart L. (Stu) Fornoff
**Director, Public Affairs:** John S. Riley
**Global Business Development, Ventures:** Lori Palmer
**Corporate Communications:** Susan R. Cavanaugh
**Auditors:** BDO Seidman, LLP

## LOCATIONS

**HQ:** Hercules Incorporated
Hercules Plaza, 1313 N. Market St.,
Wilmington, DE 19894
**Phone:** 302-594-5000 **Fax:** 302-594-5400
**Web:** www.herc.com

Hercules operates 30 manufacturing plants throughout Asia, Europe, North America, and South America. The company's products are sold in more than 135 countries worldwide.

### 2006 Sales

| | $ mil. | % of total |
|---|---|---|
| Americas | | |
| US | 897.2 | 44 |
| Other countries | 214.7 | 11 |
| Europe | 696.0 | 34 |
| Asia/Pacific | 227.4 | 11 |
| **Total** | **2,035.3** | **100** |

## PRODUCTS/OPERATIONS

### 2006 Sales

| | $ mil. | % of total |
|---|---|---|
| Paper Technologies & Ventures | 1,075.3 | 53 |
| Aqualon Group | 890.8 | 44 |
| FiberVisions | 69.2 | 3 |
| **Total** | **2,035.3** | **100** |

### Business Units

Paper Technologies & Ventures
- Pulp and paper (functional, process, and water management chemicals)

Aqualon
- Pinova (wood and gum rosin resins)
- Thickeners for water-based products (from personal care products to food additives to paints and coatings)

FiberVisions (49%; biocomponent fibers, polypropylene monocomponent fibers)

## COMPETITORS

3M
Akzo Nobel
BASF AG
Ciba Specialty Chemicals
Cytec
Dow Chemical
DuPont
Eastman Chemical
FMC
International Specialty Products
Lanxess
Nalco
Rohm and Haas
Siemens Water Technologies
W. R. Grace

## HISTORICAL FINANCIALS

Company Type: Public

### Income Statement

FYE: December 31

| | REVENUE ($ mil.) | NET INCOME ($ mil.) | NET PROFIT MARGIN | EMPLOYEES |
|---|---|---|---|---|
| **12/06** | 2,035 | 239 | 11.7% | 4,430 |
| **12/05** | 2,069 | (41) | — | 4,650 |
| **12/04** | 1,997 | 27 | 1.4% | 4,950 |
| **12/03** | 1,846 | 45 | 2.4% | 5,116 |
| **12/02** | 1,705 | (616) | — | 5,095 |
| **Annual Growth** | 4.5% | — | — | (3.4%) |

**2006 Year-End Financials**

Debt ratio: 395.1%
Return on equity: 218.8%
Cash ($ mil.): 172
Current ratio: 1.56
Long-term debt ($ mil.): 960
No. of shares (mil.): 116
Dividends
Yield: —
Payout: —
Market value ($ mil.): 2,241

**Stock History** NYSE: HPC

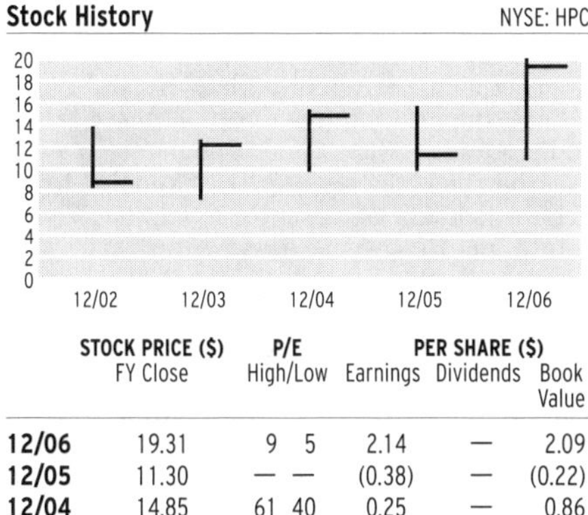


| | STOCK PRICE ($) FY Close | P/E High | P/E Low | PER SHARE ($) Earnings | Dividends | Book Value |
|---|---|---|---|---|---|---|
| **12/06** | 19.31 | 9 | 5 | 2.14 | — | 2.09 |
| **12/05** | 11.30 | — | — | (0.38) | — | (0.22) |
| **12/04** | 14.85 | 61 | 40 | 0.25 | — | 0.86 |
| **12/03** | 12.20 | 30 | 18 | 0.42 | — | 0.07 |
| **12/02** | 8.80 | — | — | (5.65) | — | (1.12) |
| **Annual Growth** | 21.7% | — | — | — | — | — |

# Herman Miller

Desk jockeys can ride Herman Miller's products all the way up the corporate ladder and home again. A top US manufacturer of office furniture, the firm is known for developing designs for corporate, government, home office and leisure, and health care environments. Herman Miller's products include ergonomic devices, filing and storage systems, freestanding furniture, lighting, seating, textiles, and wooden casegoods. It manufactures its products in the UK and the US and sells worldwide through its sales staff and dealer network, as well as through independent dealers and the Internet. Ariel Capital Management owns about 13% of capital stock.

Previously focused on landing big contracts with major corporations, Herman Miller has developed new designs to grab medium-sized companies and small startups. However, amid a slowing economy during the past few years the company has cut costs through layoffs and by consolidating some brands and operations.

Most of Herman Miller's worldwide sales come from independent dealers (69%). The company's furniture is known for its contemporary designs and upscale prices; collectors still seek pieces designed and manufactured in the 1940s and 1950s.

## HISTORY

In 1923 Herman Miller lent his son-in-law, D. J. De Pree, enough money to buy Star Furniture, started in 1905 in Zeeland, Michigan. (De Pree renamed the furniture maker after Miller.) Designer Gilbert Rohde led Herman Miller's transformation from traditional to more modern styles in the 1930s.

Rohde designed the company's first office component line, the Executive Office Group (introduced in 1942). Rohde died two years later, and in 1946 George Nelson was named Herman Miller's design director. Nelson brought in a number of notable designers, including Charles Eames and Isamu Noguchi.

Throughout its history, the company has maintained a reputation for being open to suggestions and comments from its workers. This policy dates back to De Pree's learning that one of his millwrights who had died had also been a poet; De Pree began to value his employees for their innate talents rather than just for the work they did for him.

Herman Miller grew, largely unimpeded by national competitors, except for neighboring Steelcase. In 1950 the company adopted the Scanlon plan, an employee participation plan that included bonuses based on helpful participation, such as cost-cutting suggestions.

De Pree retired in 1962 and was succeeded by his son, Hugh. Two years later Herman Miller introduced the Action Office, a collection of panels, work surfaces, and storage units that could be moved about to create custom-designed work spaces within an open-plan office; this line has been the company mainstay ever since.

The firm, which went public in 1970, introduced its Ergon ergonomic chair in 1976. Hugh retired in 1980 and was succeeded by his brother Max, who capped executive salaries at 20 times the average wage of factory-line workers. Max became chairman in 1988 and resigned from day-to-day management duties to pursue teaching opportunities.

Max's successor, 33-year company veteran Richard Ruch, began restructuring to sharpen Herman Miller's focus. Then the commercial real estate market collapsed and, with it, the need for new office furnishings. Earnings tumbled in 1991 and 1992. Ruch retired in 1992 to become vice chairman and was succeeded by first-ever company outsider Kermit Campbell.

In 1994 Herman Miller acquired German furniture company Geneal. Earnings plummeted in 1995 and chairman Campbell was forced out. Despite his commitment to its traditionally employee-friendly corporate culture, CEO Michael Volkema led Herman Miller in a shake-up, cutting 180 jobs and closing underperforming plants. The company introduced its cubicle systems office furniture unit, Miller SQA ("simple, quick, and affordable"), in 1995.

Herman Miller and leading carpet tile maker Interface formed a joint venture in 1997 to provide integrated office furniture and carpeting systems for commercial clients. The next year the company became the first major office furniture maker to target customers over the Internet. Herman Miller acquired wood furniture maker Geiger Brickel in 1999. The company launched a low-cost line of office furniture, dubbed RED, aimed at fledgling Internet-oriented firms in late 2000, shortly before the bubble burst for Web startups.

A slowdown in the US economy prompted cut after cut in 2001; by March 2002 the company had eliminated some 3,900 positions (or 37% of its workforce). The company also phased out its SQA and RED lines that year amidst slowing sales; in 2003, it consolidated two of its manufacturing sites (Holland, Michigan and Canton, Georgia) into existing facilities. President and COO Brian Walker succeeded Volkema as CEO in July 2004. Volkema remains as chairman.

## EXECUTIVES

**Chairman:** Michael A. Volkema, age 51, $397,569 pay
**President, CEO, and Director:** Brian C. Walker, age 44, $1,453,446 pay
**CFO:** Curt Pullen
**EVP; President, Herman Miller Healthcare:** Elizabeth A. (Beth) Nickels, age 45, $529,603 pay
**EVP and Chief Administrative Officer:** Andrew J. (Andy) Lock, age 52, $601,490 pay
**EVP, Creative Office:** Gary S. Miller, age 56, $571,164 pay
**EVP, North American Emerging Markets:** Charles J. Vranian, age 56
**EVP, North American Office Learning Environments:** Kristen L. (Kris) Manos, age 47
**EVP, Operations:** Kenneth L. Goodson Jr., age 54
**EVP, Research, Design, and Development:** Donald D. Goeman, age 49
**VP, Investor Relations and Treasurer:** Joseph M. Nowicki, age 44
**President, Geiger:** David S. Guy
**President, Herman Miller International:** John P. Portlock, age 60, $589,740 pay
**Director, External Communications:** Mark Sherman
**Auditors:** Ernst & Young LLP

## LOCATIONS

**HQ:** Herman Miller, Inc.
855 E. Main Ave., Zeeland, MI 49464
**Phone:** 616-654-3000 **Fax:** 616-654-5234
**Web:** www.hermanmiller.com

Herman Miller designs and manufactures furniture in the UK and the US. It has distribution subsidiaries in Canada, France, Germany, Italy, Japan, Mexico, the Netherlands, and the UK. Independent dealers sell the company's products in Asia, the Middle East, and South America.

**2007 Sales**

| | $ mil. | % of total |
|---|---|---|
| US | 1,510.0 | 79 |
| Other countries | 408.9 | 21 |
| **Total** | **1,918.9** | **100** |

## PRODUCTS/OPERATIONS

**2007 Sales**

| | $ mil. | % of total |
|---|---|---|
| Systems | 565.2 | 30 |
| Seating | 481.7 | 25 |
| International | 408.9 | 21 |
| Freestanding & storage | 288.0 | 15 |
| Other | 175.1 | 9 |
| **Total** | **1,918.9** | **100** |

**Selected Products and Brands**

Accessories (Accents, Aalto, Eames)
Freestanding furniture (Passage, Aalto, Abak, Burdick, Eames, Arrio, Kiva)
Health care systems (Ethospace)
Modular systems (Action Office, Ethospace, Q System, Resolve)
Screens (Eames)
Seating (Aeron, Ambi, Equa, Ergon, Mirra, Reaction)
Storage and filing (Meridian, Eames)
Textiles (Ituri, Meinecke)
Wooden casegoods (Geiger)

## COMPETITORS

Anderson Hickey
CFGroup
Global Furniture
Haworth
HighPoint Furniture
HNI
Inscape corp
Jami
Kewaunee Scientific
KI
Kimball International
Knoll
MITY
Neutral Posture
Open Plan Systems
Reconditioned Systems
Shelby Williams
Steelcase
TAB Products
Teknion
Virco Mfg.
Vitra

## HISTORICAL FINANCIALS

Company Type: Public

**Income Statement** FYE: Saturday nearest May 31

| | REVENUE ($ mil.) | NET INCOME ($ mil.) | NET PROFIT MARGIN | EMPLOYEES |
|---|---|---|---|---|
| **5/07** | 1,919 | 129 | 6.7% | 6,574 |
| **5/06** | 1,737 | 99 | 5.7% | 6,242 |
| **5/05** | 1,516 | 68 | 4.5% | 6,234 |
| **5/04** | 1,338 | 42 | 3.2% | 6,286 |
| **5/03** | 1,337 | 23 | 1.7% | 6,315 |
| **Annual Growth** | 9.5% | 53.4% | — | 1.0% |

**2007 Year-End Financials**

Debt ratio: 111.5%
Return on equity: 87.9%
Cash ($ mil.): 92
Current ratio: 1.35
Long-term debt ($ mil.): 173

No. of shares (mil.): 63
Dividends
Yield: 0.9%
Payout: 16.7%
Market value ($ mil.): 2,298

**Stock History** NASDAQ (GS): MLHR

45 40 35 30 25 20 15 10 5 0

5/03 5/04 5/05 5/06 5/07

| | STOCK PRICE ($) FY Close | P/E High/Low | PER SHARE ($) Earnings | Dividends | Book Value |
|---|---|---|---|---|---|
| **5/07** | 36.53 | 21 13 | 1.98 | 0.33 | 2.47 |
| **5/06** | 30.34 | 23 18 | 1.45 | 0.31 | 2.10 |
| **5/05** | 29.80 | 33 23 | 0.96 | 0.22 | 2.45 |
| **5/04** | 24.08 | 51 32 | 0.58 | 0.18 | 2.71 |
| **5/03** | 19.34 | 77 47 | 0.31 | 0.14 | 2.62 |
| **Annual Growth** | 17.2% | — — | 59.0% | 23.9% | (1.5%) |

# The Hershey Company

The Hershey Company (formerly Hershey Foods) will cover you in Kisses and bring you Almond Joy. The company makes such well-known chocolate and candy brands as Hershey's Kisses, Reese's peanut butter cups, Swizzles licorice, Mounds, York Peppermint Patty, and Kit Kat (licensed from Nestlé). Hershey also makes grocery goods such as baking chocolate, ice-cream toppings, chocolate syrup, cocoa mix, cookies, snack nuts, hard candies, lollipops, and peanut butter. Its products are sold throughout North America and exported overseas. The Hershey Trust — which benefits the Milton Hershey School for disadvantaged children — controls approximately 79% of Hershey's voting power.

Chocolate may be the name of the game but the company is also a growing presence in the hard- and non-chocolate candy markets, offering such brands as Good & Plenty and Jolly Rancher. The company is expanding its products with new versions of old favorites, such as Jolly Rancher lollipops and bite-sized bits of its popular chocolate bars.

It introduced sugar-free chocolate and expanded the snack-food and Hispanic markets, as well as producing packaged cookies whose flavors are based on the flavors of its Almond Joy, Reese's, and York products.

Hershey has been attempting to join the quickly expanding premium chocolate market. It has introduced its own SpecialDark, Extra Dark, and Cacao Reserve brands. It has also acquired such top-of-the-line chocolate manufacturers as Artisan Confections Company (Scharffen Berger brand) and Joseph Schmidt (Dagoba brand).

The company formed a joint venture with South Korean confectioner, Lotte, in 2007 to manufacture and sell Hershey's products in China. Later in the year, Hershey announced a total revamp of its supply-chain operations. The three-year project involves closing some plants and cutting about 1,500 jobs.

Continuing to expand its geographical reach, in 2007 Hershey agreed to acquire a 51% interest in the food and beverage operations of the Indian conglomerate Godrej Industries for $54 million for the purpose of distributing Hershey's products in India.

## HISTORY

The Hershey Company is the legacy of Milton Hershey, of Pennsylvania Dutch origin. Apprenticed in 1872 at age 15 to a candy maker, Hershey started Lancaster Caramel Company at age 30. In 1893, at the Chicago Exposition, he saw a new chocolate-making machine, and in 1900 he sold the caramel operations for $1 million to start a chocolate factory.

The factory was completed in 1905 in Derry Church, Pennsylvania, and renamed Hershey Foods the next year. Chocolate Kisses, individually hand wrapped in silver foil, were introduced in 1907. Two years later the candy man founded the Milton Hershey School, an orphanage; the company was donated to a trust in 1918 and for years existed solely to fund the school. Although Hershey went public in 1927, the school still controls the majority of shareholder votes.

The candy company pioneered mass-production techniques for chocolates and developed much of the machinery for making and packaging its own products. At one time Hershey supplied its own sugar cane from Cuba and enlarged the world's almond supply six fold through nut farm ownership. The Hershey bar became so universally familiar that it was used overseas during WWII as currency. Milton refused to advertise, believing that quality would speak for itself. Even after his death in 1945, the company continued his policy. Then, in 1970, facing a sluggish candy market and a diet-conscious public, the company lost share to Mars and management relented.

During the 1960s and 1970s, Hershey diversified in order to stabilize the effects of changing commodity prices. The company got into the pasta business with its 1966 purchase of San Giorgio Macaroni, and it bought the Friendly Ice Cream chain in 1979 (sold 1988). The company expanded candy operations by bringing out large-sized bars (1980) and buying Cadbury's US candy business (Peter Paul, Cadbury, Caramello; 1988).

Kenneth Wolfe was named chairman and CEO in 1994. In 1999 the company sold its pasta business to New World Pasta for $450 million and a 6% interest in that company. Also that year the Hershey Trust, wanting to diversify its holdings, sold $100 million of its stock to Hershey.

In 2001 Nabisco veteran Rick Lenny replaced Wolfe as CEO. The company cut about 400 salaried positions and closed three plants and a distribution facility.

In 2002 Wolfe retired as chairman and Lenny was selected to replace him. Also that year Hershey settled a bitter six-week factory-worker strike, the longest in company history. It subsequently sold its non-chocolate Heide brands (Heide, Jujyfruits, Wunderbeans, Amazin' Fruit) to Farley's & Sathers Candy Company.

Also in 2002 the Hershey Trust said that to diversify its holdings, it wanted to sell its 77% interest in Hershey. However, the sale was temporarily blocked while the state of Pennsylvania reviewed the impact it would have on the community. Despite the injunction against the sale, the trust continued to look for a buyer and was considering a $12.5 billion offer from chewing gum giant Wm. Wrigley Jr. and a $10.5 billion joint offer from Nestlé and Cadbury Schweppes.

Amid the community outcry and legal wrangling, the sale was finally called off later in 2002, after 10 of the trust's 17 members changed their minds. Due to the uproar surrounding the proposed sale, the trust board promised to restructure itself. Among the outgoing board members was William Lepley, president and chief executive of the Milton Hershey School.

In order to expand its sales in the Hispanic market, in 2004 Hershey announced a new line of Latin-inspired candies including those with chili-based flavors and *dulce de leche* fillings. The company also signed an endorsement deal with Latin singer Thalia. And in 2004 Hershey's Mexican subsidiary bought one of Mexico's top confectionery companies, Grupo Lorena.

The company changed its name to The Hershey Company in 2005, dropping the "Foods" from its name to reflect the company's move away from coffee, pasta, and restaurant businesses and the concentration on confectionery.

In 2006 the company purchased organic chocolate confectioner, Dagoba.

The company established the Hershey Center for Health and Nutrition in 2006 in order to research and develop new products that help provide consumers with heart health, weight management, and mental and physical energy.

## EXECUTIVES

**Chairman, President, and CEO:**
Richard H. (Rick) Lenny, age 55, $1,100,000 pay
**SVP, Global Operations:** Gregg A. Tanner, age 50
**EVP and COO:** David J. (Dave) West, age 44, $485,000 pay
**SVP and CFO:** Humberto P. (Bert) Alfonso, age 50
**SVP and Global Chief Growth Officer:**
Thomas K. (Tom) Hernquist, age 49, $420,000 pay
**SVP and Chief Marketing Officer, U.S.:** Michele B. Buck
**SVP and Chief People Officer:** Marcella K. Arline, age 54, $375,000 pay
**SVP; President, International Commercial Group:**
John P. (J.P.) Bilbrey, age 50, $370,000 pay
**SVP; President, North American Commercial Group:**
Christopher J. Baldwin, age 44
**SVP, General Counsel, and Secretary:**
Burton H. (Burt) Snyder, age 59
**VP, Business Development:** Bryon L. Klemens
**VP, Global Confectionery and New Platforms:**
Andreas J. (Drew) Panayiotou
**VP, Global Convenience Stores and Specialty Retail:**
David G. Onorato
**VP, Global Sourcing and Operations Strategy:**
Robert J. Woelfling

**VP, Global Strategy and Integrated Business Intelligence:** Robert P. Goodpaster
**VP, The Hershey Experience:** Michelle J. Gloeckler
**VP and Chief Accounting Officer:** David W. Tacka, age 53
**VP and Global Chief Customer Officer:** E. Daniel Vucovich Jr.
**VP and CIO:** George F. Davis, age 58
**Treasurer:** Rosa C. Stroh
**Director, Investor Relations:** Mark K. Pogharian
**Auditors:** KPMG LLP

## LOCATIONS

**HQ:** The Hershey Company
100 Crystal A Dr., Hershey, PA 17033
**Phone:** 717-534-4200
**Web:** www.thehersheycompany.com

### 2006 Sales

| | % of total |
|---|---|
| US | 89 |
| Other countries | 11 |
| **Total** | **100** |

## PRODUCTS/OPERATIONS

### Selected Subsidiaries

Artisan Confections Company
Dagoba Organic Chocolates, LLC
Grupo Lorena, SA de CV (Mexico)
Hershey Canada, Inc.
Hershey Chocolate & Confectionery Corporation
Hershey Chocolate of Virginia, Inc.
Hershey México, SA de CV
Joseph Schmidt Confactions, Inc.
Mauna Loa Macadamia Nut Holdings, Inc.
Scharffen Berger Chocolate Maker, Inc.

## COMPETITORS

Barry Callebaut
Brach's
Cadbury Schweppes
Cadbury Trebor Bassett
Campbell Soup
Chase General
Chocolates à la Carte
Chupa Chups
Cloetta Fazer
ConAgra
Dynamic Confections
Endangered Species Chocolate
Ferrero
Ghirardelli
Godiva Chocolatier
Guittard
Harry London Candies
Interstate Bakeries
Jelly Belly Candy
Kellogg
Kellogg Snacks
Kellogg USA
Kraft Foods
Kraft North America Commercial
Laura Secord
Lindt & Sprüngli
Mars
Nestlé
Otis Spunkmeyer
Perfetti Van Melle
Purdy's Chocolates
Rocky Mountain Chocolate
Russell Stover
See's Candies
Smucker
Spangler Candy
The Sweet Shop USA
Tasty Baking
Tootsie Roll
Unilever
Warrell Corporation
World's Finest Chocolate
Wrigley

## HISTORICAL FINANCIALS

Company Type: Public

### Income Statement

FYE: December 31

| | REVENUE ($ mil.) | NET INCOME ($ mil.) | NET PROFIT MARGIN | EMPLOYEES |
|---|---|---|---|---|
| **12/06** | 4,944 | 559 | 11.3% | 15,000 |
| **12/05** | 4,836 | 493 | 10.2% | 13,750 |
| **12/04** | 4,429 | 591 | 13.3% | 16,000 |
| **12/03** | 4,173 | 458 | 11.0% | 14,800 |
| **12/02** | 4,120 | 404 | 9.8% | 15,400 |
| **Annual Growth** | 4.7% | 8.5% | — | (0.7%) |

### 2006 Year-End Financials

Debt ratio: 182.6%
Return on equity: 65.6%
Cash ($ mil.): 97
Current ratio: 0.98
Long-term debt ($ mil.): 1,248
No. of shares (mil.): 169
Dividends
Yield: 2.1%
Payout: 44.0%
Market value ($ mil.): 8,438

### Stock History

NYSE: HSY

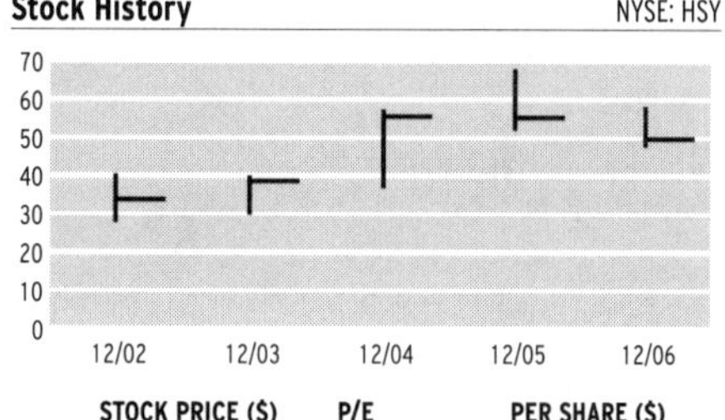


| | STOCK PRICE ($) FY Close | P/E High | P/E Low | PER SHARE ($) Earnings | Dividends | Book Value |
|---|---|---|---|---|---|---|
| **12/06** | 49.80 | 25 | 21 | 2.34 | 1.03 | 4.03 |
| **12/05** | 55.25 | 34 | 26 | 1.99 | 0.93 | 5.68 |
| **12/04** | 55.54 | 25 | 16 | 2.30 | 0.64 | 5.86 |
| **12/03** | 38.49 | 23 | 18 | 1.73 | 0.53 | 12.91 |
| **12/02** | 33.72 | 27 | 19 | 1.47 | 0.63 | 13.22 |
| **Annual Growth** | 10.2% | — | — | 12.3% | 13.1% | (25.7%) |

# Hertz Global Holdings

If you've ever said, "Don't worry about it, it's just a rental," guess who hurts: Hertz Global Holdings, one of the world's leading car rental companies. On its own and through agents and licensees, Hertz operates about 7,600 rental locations in about 145 countries. The company's fleet includes some 478,000 cars from Ford, General Motors, and other manufacturers. Car rental accounts for about 80% of the company's sales. Hertz also rents a variety of heavy equipment through some 360 locations in North America and Europe. Investment firms Clayton Dubilier & Rice, The Carlyle Group, and Merrill Lynch Global Private Equity each own about 19% of Hertz.

The investment firms bought Hertz from Ford in 2005 and took the car rental company public in 2006.

Airport locations account for about 80% of Hertz's car rental revenue in the US, but the company is boosting its presence in the off-airport rental market. It operates about 1,400 facilities to serve customers who want to rent cars for reasons unrelated to air travel, such as to use while their own vehicles are being repaired. Expanding in the off-airport market makes the company less dependent on trends in the travel industry. Hertz's car rental revenue is split evenly between business and leisure rentals.

Subsidiary Hertz Equipment Rental Corporation (HERC) is a major renter of construction and industrial equipment, primarily in the US and Canada but also in France and Spain. HERC's inventory includes earthmoving equipment, material-handling equipment, and aerial and electrical equipment. Unlike the airport car rental industry, where several national brands dominate, the US equipment-rental market is fragmented, and Hertz sees opportunities for HERC to gain market share. HERC also has been expanding its inventory of smaller equipment, such as air compressors and generators, in order to serve more of its customers' needs.

At the same time, Hertz is moving to cut costs, mainly in its US car rental operations. In separate announcements in January and February 2007, the company said it would eliminate about 1,550 jobs, or about 5% of the workforce, a move expected to save some $140 million annually. Hoping to add an additional $24 million in savings to that number, Hertz announced another 480 job cuts in June 2007.

Hertz is attempting to expand geographically through acquisitions and joint ventures. To that end, it recently acquired the UK-based car-rental firm Autotravel. The acquisition increases the number of Hertz's U.K. locations by more than 25%.

## HISTORY

In 1918, 22-year-old John Jacobs opened a Chicago car rental business with 12 Model T Fords that he had repaired. By 1923, when Yellow Cab entrepreneur John Hertz bought Jacobs' business, it had revenues of about $1 million. Jacobs continued as top executive of the company, renamed Hertz Drive-Ur-Self System. Three years later General Motors acquired the company when it bought Yellow Truck from John Hertz. Hertz introduced the first car rental charge card in 1926, opened its first airport location at Chicago's Midway Airport in 1932, and initiated the first one-way (rent-it-here/leave-it-there) plan in 1933. The company expanded into Canada in 1938 and Europe in 1950.

Omnibus bought Hertz from GM in 1953, sold its bus interests, and focused on vehicle leasing and renting. The next year Omnibus changed its name to The Hertz Corporation and was listed on the NYSE. Also in 1954 the company purchased Metropolitan Distributors, a New York-based truck leasing firm. In 1961 Hertz began operations in South America.

The company formed its Hertz Equipment Rental subsidiary in 1965. RCA bought Hertz two years later but allowed the company to maintain its board of directors and management. In 1972 it introduced the first frequent traveler's club, the #1 Club, which allowed the rental location to prepare a rental agreement before the customer arrived at the counter. Three years later Hertz began defining the company's image through TV commercials featuring football star/celebrity O. J. Simpson running through airports. (Hertz canceled Simpson's contract in 1994 after his arrest on murder charges — the TV ads had stopped in 1992.) Frank Olson became CEO in 1977 after serving in the same position at United Airlines.

United Airlines bought Hertz from RCA in 1985, then sold it in 1987 for $1.3 billion to Park

Ridge, which had been formed by Hertz management and Ford Motor specifically for the purchase. (Hertz was Ford's largest customer.) In 1988 Ford, which held 80% of Park Ridge, sold 20% to Volvo North America for $100 million. (Ford later reduced its stake to 49% when it sold shares to Volvo.) Also that year Hertz sold its stock in the Hertz Penske truck leasing joint venture for $85.5 million and issued Penske a license to use its name.

Ford bought all the shares of Hertz it didn't already own in 1994. Ford sold 17% of Hertz to the public in 1997. Olson retired as CEO in 1999, and president Craig Koch was named his successor.

Lackluster performance of Hertz stock in 2001 prompted Ford to pay about $735 million to buy back shares held by the public — once again making the car rental company a wholly owned Ford subsidiary. Also that year Hertz opened about 200 new suburban rental locations. In April 2001 Hertz eliminated commissions for negotiated corporate and government accounts in the US and Canada.

The decline in air travel that followed the terrorist attacks of September 11, 2001, hampered Hertz's business in 2001 and 2002.

As part of an effort to strengthen its balance sheet and focus on its core automotive manufacturing operations, Ford sold Hertz to a group of investment firms — Clayton Dubilier & Rice, The Carlyle Group, and Merrill Lynch Global Private Equity — in December 2005 for $5.6 billion and nearly $10 billion in assumed debt.

Ford had filed for an IPO of the car rental company in June 2005, but that offering was withdrawn in favor of a new proposed IPO in July 2006. Proceeds of the offering, which was completed in November 2006, were to be used to reduce debt — including a $1 billion loan taken out by the company in June 2006 — and to pay an additional dividend to the investment firms.

Koch stepped down as CEO in 2006. He was named chairman, and Tenneco's Mark Frissora was hired to be CEO of Hertz. Frissora became chairman upon Koch's retirement in 2007.

## EXECUTIVES

**Chairman and CEO:** Mark P. Frissora, age 52
**EVP and CFO:** Paul J. Siracusa, age 62, $545,673 pay
**EVP; President, HERC:** Gerald A. Plescia, age 51, $425,481 pay
**EVP; President, Hertz Europe:** Michel Taride, age 50, $529,345 pay
**EVP; President, Vehicle Rental and Leasing, The Americas and Pacific:** Joseph R. Nothwang, age 60, $565,385 pay
**EVP, Marketing and Sales:** Brian J. Kennedy, age 65
**SVP, General Counsel, and Secretary:** Harold E. Rolfe, age 49
**SVP, Quality Assurance and Administration:** Charles L. Shafer, age 62
**SVP and Chief Human Resources Officer:** LeighAnne Baker
**SVP and CIO:** Joseph F. (Joe) Eckroth Jr., age 47
**VP and Treasurer:** Elyse Douglas, age 51
**VP, Global Tax:** Anthony Fiore
**Senior Director, Marketing and Advertising:** Lisa Diliberto
**Director, Sales and Marketing, Hertz Canada:** Geno Diraddo
**Manager, Public Relations:** Paula Rivera
**Auditors:** PricewaterhouseCoopers LLP

## LOCATIONS

**HQ:** Hertz Global Holdings, Inc.
225 Brae Blvd., Park Ridge, NJ 07656
**Phone:** 201-307-2000 **Fax:** 201-307-2644
**Web:** www.hertz.com

### 2006 Sales

| | $ mil. | % of total |
|---|---|---|
| US | 5,631 | 70 |
| Other countries | 2,427 | 30 |
| **Total** | **8,058** | **100** |

## PRODUCTS/OPERATIONS

### 2006 Sales

| | $ mil. | % of total |
|---|---|---|
| Car rental | 6,273 | 78 |
| Equipment rental | 1,672 | 21 |
| Corporate & other | 113 | 1 |
| **Total** | **8,058** | **100** |

## COMPETITORS

Avis Budget
Avis Europe
Dollar Thrifty Automotive
Enterprise Rent-A-Car
Neff
NES Rentals
RSC Holdings Inc.
Sixt
United Rentals
Vanguard Car Rental

## HISTORICAL FINANCIALS

Company Type: Public

### Income Statement

FYE: December 31

| | REVENUE ($ mil.) | NET INCOME ($ mil.) | NET PROFIT MARGIN | EMPLOYEES |
|---|---|---|---|---|
| **12/06** | 8,058 | 116 | 1.4% | 31,500 |
| **12/05** | 7,469 | 350 | 4.7% | 32,200 |
| **12/04** | 6,676 | 366 | 5.5% | 31,400 |
| **12/03** | 5,208 | 159 | 3.0% | 29,300 |
| **12/02** | 4,968 | (150) | — | 28,900 |
| **Annual Growth** | 12.9% | — | — | 2.2% |

### 2006 Year-End Financials

Debt ratio: 484.4%
Return on equity: 4.8%
Cash ($ mil.): 1,227
Current ratio: 1.95
Long-term debt ($ mil.): 12,276
No. of shares (mil.): 321
Dividends
Yield: —
Payout: —
Market value ($ mil.): 5,576

### Stock History

NYSE: HTZ

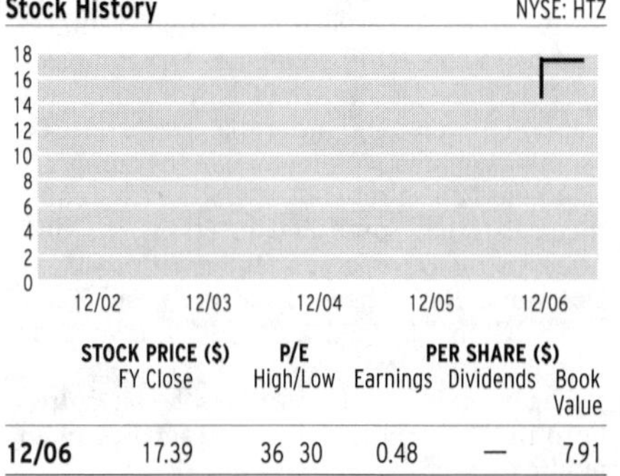


| | STOCK PRICE ($) FY Close | P/E High | P/E Low | PER SHARE ($) Earnings | Dividends | Book Value |
|---|---|---|---|---|---|---|
| **12/06** | 17.39 | 36 | 30 | 0.48 | — | 7.91 |

# Hess Corporation

Hess Corporation (formerly Amerada Hess) has what it takes. The integrated oil and gas company conducts exploration and production in Denmark, Gabon, Norway, the UK, and the US; it also operates in Indonesia, Thailand, and other countries. Hess' proved reserves total 832 million barrels of oil, and 2.5 billion cu. ft. of natural gas, and it has gained assets in West Africa, Latin America, and Southeast Asia by buying exploration and production company Triton Energy. It operates a 50%-owned refinery (HOVENSA) in the US Virgin Islands and a smaller one in New Jersey, and it markets gasoline through 1,350 HESS gas stations, chiefly in the eastern US. CEO John Hess owns about 14% of the company.

Hess' North Sea and Russian properties account for 43% of its proved oil and gas reserves. The company is looking to exploit attractive properties in Algeria, Azerbaijan, Latin America, and Southeast Asia (particularly in Malaysia and Thailand).

On the downstream side, Hess' refinery in the US Virgin Islands is operated as a joint venture with Venezuela's state oil company Petróleos de Venezuela S.A (PDVSA).

In 2006 the company re-entered its former oil and gas production operations in the Waha concessions in Libya.

## HISTORY

In 1919 British oil entrepreneur Lord Cowdray formed Amerada Corporation to explore for oil in North America. Cowdray soon hired geophysicist Everette DeGolyer, a pioneer in oil geology research. DeGolyer's systematic methods helped Amerada not only find oil deposits faster but also pick up fields missed by competitors. DeGolyer became president of Amerada in 1929 but left in 1932 to work independently.

After WWII Amerada began exploring overseas and during the 1950s entered pipelining and refining. It continued its overseas exploration through Oasis, a consortium formed in 1964 with Marathon, Shell, and Continental to explore in Libya.

Leon Hess began to buy stock in Amerada in 1966. The son of immigrants, he had entered the oil business during the Depression, selling "resid" — thick refining leftovers that refineries discarded — from a 1929 Dodge truck in New Jersey. He bought the resid cheap and sold it as heating fuel to hotels. Hess also speculated, buying oil at low prices in the summer and selling it for a profit in the winter. He later bought more trucks, a transportation network, refineries, and gas stations and went into oil exploration. Expansion pushed up debt, so in 1962 Leon's company went public as Hess Oil and Chemical after merging with Cletrac Corporation.

Hess acquired Amerada in 1969, after an ownership battle with Phillips Petroleum. During the 1970s Arab oil embargo, Amerada Hess began drilling on Alaska's North Slope. Oilman T. Boone Pickens bought up a chunk of Amerada Hess stock during the 1980s, spurring takeover rumors. They proved premature.

Amerada Hess completed a pipeline in 1993 to carry natural gas from the North Sea to the UK. In 1995 Leon Hess stepped down as CEO (he died in 1999), and his son John took the position. Amerada Hess sold its 81% interest in the Northstar oil field in Alaska to BP, and the next year Petro-Canada bought the company's Canadian operations. In 1996 the company acquired a 25% stake (sold in 2002) in UK-based Premier Oil.

The company teamed with Dixons Stores Group in 1997 to market gas in the UK. It also purchased 66 Pick Wick convenience store/service stations.

In 1998 Amerada Hess signed production-sharing contracts with a Malaysian oil firm as part of its strategy to move into Southeast Asia and began to sell natural gas to retail customers in the UK.

To offset losses brought on by depressed oil prices, Amerada Hess sold assets worth more than $300 million in 1999, including its southeastern pipeline network, gas stations in Georgia and South Carolina, and Gulf Coast terminals. It also moved into Latin America, acquiring stakes in fields in offshore Brazil.

In 2000 Amerada Hess acquired Statoil Energy Services, which markets natural gas and electricity to industrial and commercial customers in the northeastern US. It also announced its intention to buy LASMO, a UK-based exploration and production company, before Italy's Eni topped the Amerada Hess offer.

Undeterred, in 2001 the company bought Dallas-based exploration and production company Triton Energy for $2.7 billion in cash and $500 million in assumed debt. Amerada Hess also acquired the Gulf of Mexico assets of LLOG Exploration Company for $750 million. That year, however, stiff competition prompted Amerada Hess to put its UK gas and electricity supply business on the auction block. The unit was sold to TXU in 2002.

In 2003 Amerada Hess sold 26 oil and gas fields in the Gulf of Mexico to Anadarko Petroleum. Amerada Hess was granted permission by the Equatorial Guinea government in 2004 to develop 29 new wells in that country. That year Amerada Hess acquired a 65% stake in Trabant Holdings International, a Russia-based production and exploration company.

## EXECUTIVES

**Chairman and CEO:** John B. Hess, age 52, $2,497,978 pay
**EVP and Director; President, Worldwide Exploration and Production:** John J. O'Connor, age 60, $1,912,969 pay
**EVP and Director; President, Marketing and Refining:** F. Borden Walker, age 53, $1,055,446 pay
**EVP, General Counsel, and Director:** J. Barclay Collins II, age 62, $1,001,847 pay
**SVP, Global Exploration and New Ventures:** Bill Drennen
**SVP, Human Resources:** Brian J. Bohling, age 46
**SVP, Exploration and Production, Worldwide Technology:** E. Clyde Crouch, age 58
**SVP, Energy Marketing:** John A. Gartman, age 59
**SVP, Refining and Marketing Supply and Financial Controls:** Lawrence H. Ornstein, age 55
**SVP, Global New Business Development:** Howard Paver, age 56
**SVP and CFO:** John P. Rielly, age 44, $765,960 pay
**SVP, Europe, North Africa, and Asia Production:** George F. Sandison, age 50
**SVP, Finance and Corporate Development:** John J. Scelfo, age 49
**VP, Secretary, and Deputy General Counsel:** G. C. Barry
**VP and Treasurer:** Robert J. Vogel, age 47
**VP, Tax:** J. J. Lynett
**VP, Investor Relations:** Jay R. Wilson
**VP and Chief Information Officer:** P. R. Walton
**VP, Retail Marketing:** R. J. Lawlor
**VP, Corporate Communications:** James R. Allen
**Auditors:** Ernst & Young LLP

## LOCATIONS

**HQ:** Hess Corporation
1185 Avenue of the Americas, New York, NY 10036
**Phone:** 212-997-8500 **Fax:** 212-536-8593
**Web:** www.hess.com

Hess conducts exploration and production activities in Algeria, Azerbaijan, Denmark, Equatorial Guinea, Gabon, Indonesia, Libya, Malaysia, Russia, Thailand, the UK, and the US. It operates refineries in New Jersey and on St. Croix in the US Virgin Islands.

### 2006 Sales

| | $ mil. | % of total |
|---|---|---|
| US | 22,599 | 81 |
| Europe | 3,108 | 11 |
| Africa | 1,677 | 6 |
| Asia & other regions | 683 | 2 |
| Adjustments | 653 | — |
| **Total** | **28,720** | **100** |

## PRODUCTS/OPERATIONS

### 2006 Sales

| | $ mil. | % of total |
|---|---|---|
| Refining & marketing | 21,480 | 77 |
| Exploration & production | 6,585 | 23 |
| Adjustments | 655 | — |
| **Total** | **28,720** | **100** |

## COMPETITORS

BP
CAMAC Holdings
Chevron
CMA CGM
ConocoPhillips
Continental Energy
Desire Petroleum
Devon Energy
Eni
Eni Lasmo
ERHC
Exxon Mobil
Getty Petroleum
Gulf Oil
Koch
Marathon Oil
Marathon Petroleum
Norsk Hydro
Occidental Petroleum
PDVSA
PEMEX
PETROBRAS
Royal Dutch Shell
Serica Energy
Sinclair Oil
Sunoco
TOTAL
United Refining

## HISTORICAL FINANCIALS

Company Type: Public

### Income Statement

FYE: December 31

| | REVENUE ($ mil.) | NET INCOME ($ mil.) | NET PROFIT MARGIN | EMPLOYEES |
|---|---|---|---|---|
| **12/06** | 28,720 | 1,916 | 6.7% | 13,700 |
| **12/05** | 23,255 | 1,242 | 5.3% | 11,610 |
| **12/04** | 17,126 | 977 | 5.7% | 11,119 |
| **12/03** | 14,480 | 643 | 4.4% | 11,481 |
| **12/02** | 12,093 | (218) | — | 11,662 |
| **Annual Growth** | 24.1% | — | — | 4.1% |

### 2006 Year-End Financials

Debt ratio: 46.2%
Return on equity: 26.6%
Cash ($ mil.): 383
Current ratio: 0.87
Long-term debt ($ mil.): 3,745
No. of shares (mil.): 315
Dividends
Yield: 0.8%
Payout: 6.6%
Market value ($ mil.): 15,615

### Stock History

NYSE: HES

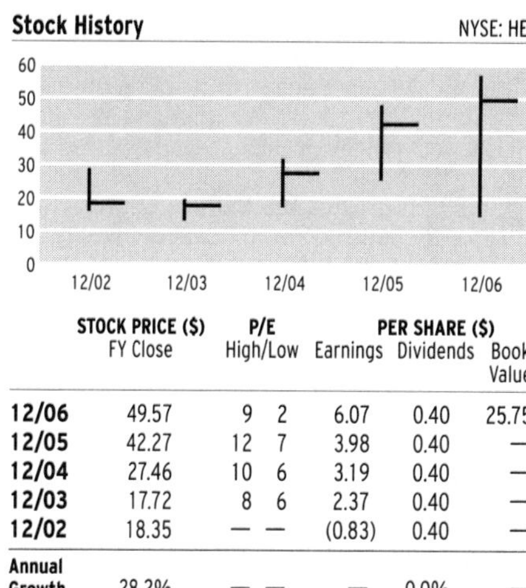


| | STOCK PRICE ($) FY Close | P/E High | P/E Low | PER SHARE ($) Earnings | Dividends | Book Value |
|---|---|---|---|---|---|---|
| **12/06** | 49.57 | 9 | 2 | 6.07 | 0.40 | 25.75 |
| **12/05** | 42.27 | 12 | 7 | 3.98 | 0.40 | — |
| **12/04** | 27.46 | 10 | 6 | 3.19 | 0.40 | — |
| **12/03** | 17.72 | 8 | 6 | 2.37 | 0.40 | — |
| **12/02** | 18.35 | — | — | (0.83) | 0.40 | — |
| **Annual Growth** | 28.2% | — | — | — | 0.0% | — |

# Hewitt Associates

If any of a company's resources are human, chances are it'll need the assistance of Hewitt Associates. As one of the primary leaders in its industry, the company provides a variety of HR related services including payroll, organizational change management, talent and reward consulting, and the largest portion of the company's business — benefits outsourcing. Hewitt Associates administers medical, 401(k), and pension plans on an outsourced basis for mainly larger companies with complex benefit programs. The company also provides consulting for the design, implementation, and operation of many of the same human resources programs. Hewitt Associates was founded by Ted Hewitt in 1940.

Hewitt's outsourcing services account for about 70% of its total revenue. The company has expanded its operations internationally through a number of acquisitions over the years. In 2006, international revenue represented 22% of the company's overall sales — a percentage that has steadily been growing over the past few years. While the company does look to acquisitions for potential growth, it largely depends on its strong client retention rate, which on any given year, typically exceeds 95%.

## HISTORY

Edwin "Ted" Hewitt founded Hewitt Associates in 1940 to offer personal estate property and financial services. In the 1950s it became one of the first to measure defined-plan investment performance and offer personalized benefit statements. Hewitt also worked for the government, designing forms for the Welfare and Pension Plans Disclosure Act and serving on the Federal Interagency Task Force from 1964 to 1968.

Hewitt Associates developed the first flexible benefit plans and the Benefit Index (for measuring the competitive value between benefit plans) in the 1970s. It also established its investment consultancy, Hewitt Investment Group, in 1974. The company developed computerized employee benefit program systems and benefits software packages in the 1980s for integrated compensation management, defined contribution administration, pension management, and retirement plan simulation. Hewitt Technologies, its information technology division, became part of the firm in 1988.

In 1992 it created the Defined Contribution Alliance to bundle communication, investment management, record keeping, and trustee services for 401(k) plans. The company's new benefits management center opened near Orlando, Florida, in 1997. The following year Hewitt Associates teamed with online investment adviser Financial Engines to offer its clients Internet-based investment advice. In 2000 the company arranged with investment consulting firm James P. Marshall to establish a new Hewitt venture in Canada. Later that year, the company announced a merger with UK consulting firm Bacon & Woodrow.

After nearly 60 years as a privately held company, the company registered to trade on the New York Stock Exchange in 2002. Hewitt Associates bought HR management software and payroll services provider Cyborg Worldwide in 2003. In 2004 Hewitt Associates acquired Exult, a human resources and consulting firm.

## EXECUTIVES

**Chairman and CEO:** Russell P. (Russ) Fradin, age 52, $68,654 pay (partial-year salary)
**CFO:** John J. Park, age 46, $592,695 pay (partial-year salary)
**SVP Corporate Development and Strategy:** Matthew C. (Matt) Levin, age 33
**SVP Global Business Services:** Kristi A. Savacool, age 47
**SVP Strategy and Chief Legal Officer:** John M. Ryan, age 59, $488,413 pay
**SVP Human Resources:** Stephen Dale (Steve) King, age 55
**Chief Diversity Officer:** Andrés Tapia
**Chief of Staff and Global Corporate Relations Leader:** Esther K. Laspisa
**President, HR Consulting:** Perry O. Brandorff, age 48, $741,425 pay
**Acting President, HR Outsourcing and Director:** Julie S. Gordon, age 49, $488,823 pay
**HR Consulting, Sales and Client Management Leader:** Michael R. Lee, age 45, $660,000 pay
**Global Chief, Consulting Operations:** Monica M. Burmeister, age 53
**General Counsel:** C. Lawrence Connolly III
**Public Relations:** Joe Micucci
**Media Contact:** Kelly Zitlow
**Auditors:** Ernst & Young LLP

## LOCATIONS

**HQ:** Hewitt Associates, Inc.
100 Half Day Rd., Lincolnshire, IL 60069
**Phone:** 847-295-5000 **Fax:** 847-295-7634
**Web:** www.hewittassociates.com

Hewitt Associates maintains more than 85 offices in about 30 countries.

### 2006 Sales

| | $ mil. | % of total |
|---|---|---|
| US | 2,238.9 | 78 |
| UK | 344.6 | 12 |
| Other countries | 273.7 | 10 |
| **Total** | **2,857.2** | **100** |

## PRODUCTS/OPERATIONS

### 2006 Sales

| | $ mil. | % of total |
|---|---|---|
| Outsourcing | 1,983.2 | 69 |
| Consulting | 842.6 | 29 |
| Reimbursements | 68.5 | 2 |
| Adjustments | (37.1) | — |
| **Total** | **2,857.2** | **100** |

### Selected Services

Health Care
HR, Payroll, and Benefits Outsourcing
Retirement and Financial Management
Talent and Organizational Change

## COMPETITORS

Accenture
Administaff
ADP
Affiliated Computer Services
BearingPoint
Ceridian
Convergys
EDS
Envestnet
GatesMcDonald
Marsh & McLennan
Right Management
Schloss & Company
T. Rowe Price
Towers Perrin
United Benefit Consulting
The Vanguard Group
Watson Wyatt

## HISTORICAL FINANCIALS

Company Type: Public

### Income Statement

FYE: September 30

| | REVENUE ($ mil.) | NET INCOME ($ mil.) | NET PROFIT MARGIN | EMPLOYEES |
|---|---|---|---|---|
| **9/06** | 2,857 | (116) | — | 24,000 |
| **9/05** | 2,898 | 135 | 4.6% | 22,000 |
| **9/04** | 2,262 | 123 | 5.4% | 17,000 |
| **9/03** | 2,031 | 94 | 4.6% | 15,000 |
| **9/02** | 1,750 | 190 | 10.9% | 14,600 |
| **Annual Growth** | 13.0% | — | — | 13.2% |

### 2006 Year-End Financials

Debt ratio: 20.3%
Return on equity: —
Cash ($ mil.): 449
Current ratio: 1.53
Long-term debt ($ mil.): 255
No. of shares (mil.): 111
Dividends
Yield: —
Payout: —
Market value ($ mil.): 2,689

### Stock History

NYSE: HEW

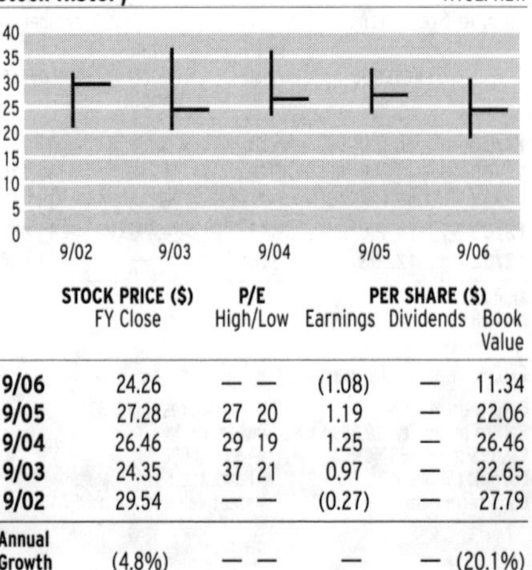


| | STOCK PRICE ($) FY Close | P/E High | P/E Low | PER SHARE ($) Earnings | Dividends | Book Value |
|---|---|---|---|---|---|---|
| **9/06** | 24.26 | — | — | (1.08) | — | 11.34 |
| **9/05** | 27.28 | 27 | 20 | 1.19 | — | 22.06 |
| **9/04** | 26.46 | 29 | 19 | 1.25 | — | 26.46 |
| **9/03** | 24.35 | 37 | 21 | 0.97 | — | 22.65 |
| **9/02** | 29.54 | — | — | (0.27) | — | 27.79 |
| **Annual Growth** | (4.8%) | — | — | — | — | (20.1%) |

# Hewlett-Packard

While Hewlett-Packard may be known for product innovation, the company's corporate development is a tale of reinvention. HP provides enterprise and consumer customers a full range of high-tech equipment, including personal computers, servers, storage devices, printers, and networking equipment. Its software portfolio includes operating systems, print management tools, and OpenView, a suite that encompasses application, business, network infrastructure, and product lifecycle management. HP also boasts an IT service organization that is among the world's largest.

Years after its acquisition of Compaq Computer — a deal valued at approximately $19 billion — HP continues to integrate its operations. Debate over to the wisdom of the merger and speculation about the possibility of spinning off certain divisions of HP also continues, but CEO Mark Hurd has so far opted to keep HP intact. Since taking over in 2005, Hurd has been charged with streamlining operations, and soon after his appointment he split the printer and personal systems units that his predecessor, Carly Fiorina, had combined only months earlier. Other restructuring measures include a workforce reduction of roughly 10%.

HP's Technology Solutions Group (TSG) encompasses its enterprise storage and servers, services, and software segments. HP's services unit provides technical support, consulting and systems integration, and managed services such as technology outsourcing. In 2006 HP acquired IT management software provider Mercury Interactive for approximately $4.5 billion in cash. The following year HP agreed to purchase Opsware, a developer of data center automation software, for approximately $1.6 billion.

HP's Personal Systems Group (PSG) markets desktop and notebook PCs to consumer, businesses, government agencies, and schools. PSG, which jockeys with Dell for PC supremacy, sells both HP and Compaq-branded products.

HP's Imaging and Printing Group (IPG) provides inkjet, laser, and large-format printers. Its comprehensive line also includes copiers, digital presses, scanners, multifunction devices, software, and supplies. IPG also oversees HP's digital photography products and services, including cameras, digital photo printers, and online services.

## HISTORY

Encouraged by professor Frederick Terman (considered the founder of Silicon Valley), in 1938 Stanford engineers Bill Hewlett and David Packard started Hewlett-Packard (HP) in a garage in Palo Alto, California, with $538. Hewlett was the idea man, while Packard served as manager; the two were so low-key that the company's first official meeting ended with no decision on exactly what to manufacture. Finding good people took priority over finding something to sell. The first product ended up being an audio oscillator. Walt Disney Studios, one of HP's first customers, bought eight to use in the making of *Fantasia*.

Demand for HP's electronic testing equipment during WWII spurred sales growth from $34,000 in 1940 to nearly $1 million just three years later. HP went public in 1957. The company expanded beyond the US during 1959, establishing a marketing organization in Switzerland and a manufacturing plant in West Germany. HP entered the medical field in 1961 by acquiring Sanborn, and the analytical instrumentation business in 1965 with the purchase of F&M Scientific. Chairman Packard in 1969 began serving two years as deputy defense secretary.

In 1972 the company pioneered personal computing with the world's first handheld scientific calculator. Under the leadership of John Young, the founders' chosen successor (named CEO in 1978), HP introduced its first PCs, the first desktop mainframe, and the LaserJet printer. Its initial PCs were known for their rugged build, tailored for factory operations. They were also more expensive than rival versions and, consequently, didn't enjoy strong sales.

By 1986 a five-year, $250 million R&D project — the company's largest to date — had produced a family of HP computers based on the reduced instruction set computing (RISC) architecture. Hewlett retired in 1987 (he died in 2001); sons of both Hewlett and Packard were named that year to the company's board of directors. HP became a leader in workstations with the 1989 purchase of market pioneer Apollo Computer, despite technology delays with the merger that resulted in the loss of nearly $750 million in new business.

Lewis Platt, an EVP since 1987, was named president and CEO that year. Packard retired in 1993 (he died in 1996).

In 1999 HP formed Agilent Technologies for its test and measurement and other noncomputer operations, and spun off 15% of the company to the public. (HP distributed to its shareholders its remaining 85% in mid-2000.) Also in 1999 Platt retired and HP — one of the first major US corporations to be headed by a woman — appointed Lucent executive Carly Fiorina president and CEO. She was named chairman the following year.

In 2001 HP agreed to pay $400 million to Pitney Bowes to settle a 1995 patent-infringement case related to printer technology. HP said in mid-2002 that it was cutting about 6,000 jobs.

Next came the announcement of a blockbuster deal: HP agreed to buy rival Compaq in a stock transaction initially valued at about $25 billion. At the time of closing, the deal was valued at approximately $19 billion.

Fiorina soon had to address the clash of disparate corporate cultures and subsequent morale problems without Michael Capellas; the former Compaq CEO, who initially served as president under Fiorina and helped champion the deal, left HP in late 2002 to become CEO of troubled telecom giant WorldCom.

Fiorina's differences with HP's board over strategic direction finally came to a head early in 2005, and she stepped down as chairman and CEO. HP's CFO, Robert Wayman, was named interim CEO, and director Patricia Dunn took over as non-executive chairman. Mark Hurd, formerly CEO of NCR, was named to lead HP in March 2005.

HP's leadership experienced another shakeup the following year, this time prompted by negative attention related to tactics used in an investigation of boardroom leaks. The company's board came under fire after it was revealed that third-party investigators employed by the company impersonated board members and journalists to obtain their phone records (a practice known as "pretexting"). Dunn was asked to resign from the board in September 2006, and Hurd replaced her as chairman. HP settled a related dispute with the California Attorney General later that year, agreeing to pay $14.5 million. ($13.5 million of the settlement was earmarked to create a Privacy and Piracy Fund to assist state prosecutors.)

## EXECUTIVES

**Chairman, President, and CEO:** Mark V. Hurd, age 49, $10,024,000 pay
**EVP and CFO:** Catherine A. (Cathie) Lesjak, age 47
**EVP and CIO:** Randall D. (Randy) Mott, age 49
**EVP and Chief Marketing Officer:** Catherine T. (Cathy) Lyons, age 50
**EVP, CTO, and Chief Strategy Officer:** Shane V. Robison, age 53, $3,358,125 pay
**EVP, Human Resources:** Marcela Perez de Alonso, age 52
**EVP, HP Imaging and Printing Group:** Vyomesh (V.J.) Joshi, age 53, $3,163,093 pay
**EVP, Personal Systems Group:** R. Todd Bradley, age 48
**EVP, Technology Solutions Group:** Ann M. Livermore, age 48, $3,556,000 pay
**EVP and Chief Administrative Officer:** Jon E. Flaxman, age 49
**EVP and General Counsel:** Michael J. Holston, age 44
**SVP and Chief Sales Officer, Technology Solutions Group:** Andreas W. (Andy) Mattes, age 46
**SVP, Controller, and Principal Accounting Officer:** Jim Murrin, age 46
**SVP and General Manager, Enterprise Storage and Software:** Robert L. (Bob) Schultz Jr., age 49
**SVP, Enterprise Storage and Servers:** Scott J. Stallard, age 53
**SVP, Solutions Partners Organization:** Jim McDonnell
**SVP and Treasurer:** John McMullen, age 48
**SVP, Operations, Infrastructure, Architecture, and Security IT:** Pete Karolczak
**SVP, Data Management and Product Engineering Support:** Charlie McMurtry
**SVP, Research; Director HP Labs:** Prith Banerjee, age 46
**SVP, Corporate Affairs:** Diana Bell
**SVP, HP Financial Services IT; Chairman, HP Financial Services:** Matt Minetola
**President and CEO, HP Financial Services:** Irv Rothman
**VP, Assistant Secretary, and Acting General Counsel:** Charles N. Charnas, age 47
**VP, Investor Relations:** Brian Humphries, age 33
**Auditors:** Ernst & Young LLP

## LOCATIONS

**HQ:** Hewlett-Packard Company
3000 Hanover St., Palo Alto, CA 94304
**Phone:** 650-857-1501 **Fax:** 650-857-5518
**Web:** www.hp.com

### 2006 Sales

| | $ mil. | % of total |
|---|---|---|
| US | 32,244 | 35 |
| Other countries | 59,414 | 65 |
| **Total** | **91,658** | **100** |

## PRODUCTS/OPERATIONS

### 2006 Sales

| | $ mil. | % of total |
|---|---|---|
| Products | 73,557 | 80 |
| Services | 17,773 | 19 |
| Financing | 328 | 1 |
| **Total** | **91,658** | **100** |

### 2006 Sales

| | $ mil. | % of total |
|---|---|---|
| Technology Solutions Group | | |
| Enterprise storage & servers | 17,308 | 19 |
| HP Services | 15,617 | 17 |
| Software | 1,301 | 1 |
| Personal Systems Group | 29,166 | 31 |
| Imaging & Printing | 26,786 | 29 |
| HP Financial Services | 2,078 | 2 |
| Investments | 566 | 1 |
| Adjustments | (1,164) | — |
| **Total** | **91,658** | **100** |

### Selected Products and Services

Enterprise Systems
- Management software (OpenView)
- Networking equipment
- Servers (Linux, Unix, Windows)
  - Blade
  - Carrier-grade
  - Rack-optimized
  - Server appliances
  - Super-scalable
  - Tower
- Storage
  - Disks and disk arrays
  - Network-attached storage (NAS) devices
  - Optical disk drives
  - Storage area network (SAN) systems
  - Tape drives and libraries

Services
- Consulting
- Design and installation
- Education
- Financing
- Outsourcing
- Printing
- Support and maintenance
- Web hosting

Personal Systems
- Calculators
- Desktop PCs
- Digital audio devices
- Handheld computers
- Notebook computers
- Workstations

Imaging and Printing
- Commercial printing
  - Digital presses
  - Printers
- Digital imaging
  - Cameras
  - Projectors
  - Scanners
- Personal printing
  - All-in-ones (copier, fax, printer, scanner)
  - Ink jet printers
  - Laser printers
- Shared printing
  - Networked inkjet, laser, and multifunction printers
  - Office all-in-ones
  - Services
- Supplies

## COMPETITORS

3Com
Acer
Apple
Canon
Canon USA
Cisco Systems
Computer Sciences Corp.
Dell
Eastman Kodak
EDS
EMC
Epson
Fuji Xerox
Fujitsu
Fujitsu Siemens
Gateway
Heidelberg
Hitachi
IBM
Konica Minolta
Lenovo
Lexmark
Matsushita Electric
Microsoft
NEC
Océ
Palm
Ricoh
SGI
Sharp
Siemens AG
Sony
Sun Microsystems
Toshiba
Unisys
Xerox

## HISTORICAL FINANCIALS

Company Type: Public

**Income Statement** FYE: October 31

| | REVENUE ($ mil.) | NET INCOME ($ mil.) | NET PROFIT MARGIN | EMPLOYEES |
|---|---|---|---|---|
| **10/06** | 91,658 | 6,198 | 6.8% | 156,000 |
| **10/05** | 86,696 | 2,398 | 2.8% | 150,000 |
| **10/04** | 79,905 | 3,497 | 4.4% | 151,000 |
| **10/03** | 73,061 | 2,539 | 3.5% | 142,000 |
| **10/02** | 56,588 | (903) | — | 141,000 |
| **Annual Growth** | 12.8% | — | — | 2.6% |

**2006 Year-End Financials**

Debt ratio: 6.5%
Return on equity: 16.5%
Cash ($ mil.): 16,422
Current ratio: 1.35
Long-term debt ($ mil.): 2,490
No. of shares (mil.): 2,732
Dividends
Yield: 0.8%
Payout: 14.7%
Market value ($ mil.): 105,839

**Stock History** NYSE: HPQ

| | STOCK PRICE ($) FY Close | P/E High/Low | PER SHARE ($) Earnings | Dividends | Book Value |
|---|---|---|---|---|---|
| **10/06** | 38.74 | 18 13 | 2.18 | 0.32 | 13.96 |
| **10/05** | 28.04 | 36 23 | 0.82 | 0.32 | 13.10 |
| **10/04** | 18.66 | 23 14 | 1.15 | 0.32 | 12.90 |
| **10/03** | 22.31 | 29 17 | 0.83 | 0.32 | 12.40 |
| **10/02** | 15.80 | — — | (0.36) | 0.24 | 11.91 |
| **Annual Growth** | 25.1% | — — | — | 7.5% | 4.0% |

# Highmark Inc.

Highmark has staked its claim as the largest health insurer in the Keystone state. A licensee of the Blue Cross and Blue Shield Association, the firm covers some 4 million people in central and western Pennsylvania, as well as the Lehigh Valley. It operates elsewhere in the state through partnerships with other insurers and provides administrative and network access services nationally. In Pennsylvania and neighboring West Virginia, Highmark sells Medicare Advantage and prescription drug plans to seniors. Other subsidiaries (not operating under the BCBS license) provide dental insurance, vision care, and other products and services nationwide. The firm agreed to merge with Independence Blue Cross in 2007.

The merged company will cover some 7 million Pennsylvanians, more than half the state's population. The companies hope that resulting economies of scale will allow it to expand its operations (particularly in the areas of third-party administration, pharmacy benefits management, and national accounts), as well as increase its support of Pennsylvania's state programs for the uninsured.

Not everyone is as sanguine about the deal, however. Some Pennsylvania regulators and politicians, as well as other players in the health care industry, have voiced concerns that the mega-company will stifle competition in the state and lead to higher premiums and lower payments to hospitals and doctors.

Prior to the merger deal, Highmark has co-marketed Blue-branded coverage in southeastern Pennsylvania with Independence Blue Cross. It operates similarly in the northeastern part of the state through a partnership with Blue Cross of Northeastern Pennsylvania.

Outside of its core Pennsylvania service areas, the company manages the benefits of self-insured employers and provides third-party administrative and claims processing services to other BCBS plans.

It also provides an impressive array of specialty services through its non-Blue subsidiaries. Its Eye Care Centers of America unit, acquired in 2006, operates a nationwide network of some 400 retail vision care chains. HM Insurance Group offers health risk solutions, such as stop loss insurance and a limited benefit medical plan, to employers; HM Insurance has sold its life and disability insurance operations to Fort Dearborn Life Insurance. Yet another subsidiary United Concordia Companies provides dental coverage to about 7 million members across the US.

Highmark sold its Medmark specialty pharmacy unit to Walgreens in 2006. The same year, the company acquired third-party administrator Employee Benefit Data Services.

## HISTORY

Highmark was created from the merger of Blue Cross of Western Pennsylvania (founded in 1937) and Pennsylvania Blue Shield, created in 1964 when the Medical Service Association of Pennsylvania (MSAP) adopted the Blue Shield name.

The Pennsylvania Medical Society, in conjunction with the state of Pennsylvania, had formed MSAP to provide medical insurance to the poor and indigent. MSAP borrowed $25,000 from the Pennsylvania Medical Society to help set up its operations, and Chauncey Palmer (who had originally proposed the organization) was named president. Individuals paid 35 cents per month, and families paid $1.75 each month to join MSAP, which initially covered mainly obstetrical and surgical procedures.

In 1945 Arthur Daugherty replaced Palmer as president (he served until his death in 1968) and helped MSAP recruit major new accounts, including the United Mine Workers and the Congress of Industrial Organizations. MSAP in 1946 became a chapter of the national Blue Shield association, which was started that year by the medical societies of several states to provide prepaid health insurance plans.

In 1951 MSAP signed up the 150,000 employees of United States Steel, bringing its total enrollment to more than 1.6 million. Growth did not lead to prosperity, though, as the organization had trouble keeping up with payments to its doctors. This shortfall in funds led MSAP to raise its premiums in 1961, at which point the state reminded the association of its social mission and suggested it concentrate on controlling costs instead of raising rates.

MSAP changed its name to Pennsylvania Blue Shield in 1964. Two years later the association began managing the state's Medicare plan and started the 65-Special plan to supplement Medicare coverage. In the 1970s Pennsylvania Blue Shield again could not keep up with the cost of paying its doctors, which led to more rate increases and closer scrutiny of its expenses. Competition increased in the 1980s as HMOs cropped up around the state. Pennsylvania Blue Shield fought back by creating its own HMO plans — some of which it owned jointly with Blue Cross of Western Pennsylvania — in the 1980s.

After years of slowly collecting noninsurance businesses, Blue Cross of Western Pennsylvania changed its name to Veritus in 1991 to reflect the growing importance of its for-profit operations.

In 1996 Pennsylvania Blue Shield overcame physicians' protests and state regulators' concerns to merge with Veritus. The company adopted the name Highmark to represent its standards for high quality; it took a loss as it failed to meet cost-cutting goals and suffered early-retirement costs related to the merger consolidation. To gain support for the merger, Highmark sold for-profit subsidiary Keystone Health Plan East to Independence Blue Cross in 1997.

In 1999 Highmark teamed with Mountain State Blue Cross Blue Shield to become West Virginia's primary licensee. Rate hikes and investment returns helped propel the company into the black as the decade closed.

In 2001 Highmark announced that it had uncovered almost $5 million in health care insurance fraud against the company over the course of the previous year.

As a result of some belt-tightening in 2004, the company shut down its Alliance Ventures (administrative and information services) and Lifestyle Advantage subsidiaries.

## EXECUTIVES

**Chairman:** J. Robert Baum
**President, CEO, and Director:** Kenneth R. Melani, age 53
**EVP, CFO, and Treasurer:** Nanette P. (Nan) DeTurk
**EVP, Human Resources and Administrative Services:** S. Tyrone Alexander
**EVP, Subsidiary Services:** Robert C. Gray, age 59
**EVP, Health Services:** James Klingensmith
**SVP, Information Services and CIO:** Tom Tabor, age 55
**SVP and Chief Audit Executive:** Elizabeth A. Farbacher
**SVP and Corporate Compliance Officer:** Michael A. Romano
**SVP, Corporate Secretary, and General Counsel:** Gary R. Truitt
**SVP, Corporate Affairs:** Aaron A. Walton
**SVP and Chief Medical Officer:** Donald R. Fischer
**President and CEO, United Concordia:** Thomas A. Dzuryachko
**Assistant Secretary:** Carrie J. Pecht
**Assistant Treasurer:** Joseph F. Reichard
**Auditors:** PricewaterhouseCoopers LLP

## LOCATIONS

**HQ:** Highmark Inc.
120 5th Ave., Pittsburgh, PA 15222
**Phone:** 412-544-7000 **Fax:** 412-544-8368
**Web:** www.highmark.com

## PRODUCTS/OPERATIONS

**Selected Subsidiaries**

Davis Vision, Inc. (vision insurance and ophthalmic laboratories)
Employee Benefit Data Services Co. (benefit administration)
Eye Care Centers of America, Inc. (retail vision care centers)
Highmark Blue Cross Blue Shield (health care plans, western Pennsylvania)
Highmark Blue Shield (health care plans, central Pennsylvania and the Lehigh Valley)
Highmark Foundation (community health charitable organization)

Highmark Medicare Services, Inc. (Medicare claims administration and financial management)
Highmark Senior Resources, Inc. (Medicare Part D prescription drug plans, Pennsylvania and West Virginia)
HM Insurance Group (stop loss insurance, HMO reinsurance, and other health risk solutions)
Keystone Health Plan West, Inc. (HMO, western Pennsylvania)
United Concordia Companies, Inc. (dental insurance)
Viva International Group (eyewear manufacturing)

## COMPETITORS

Aetna
American United Mutual
AmeriChoice of Pennsylvania
Blue Cross of Northeastern Pennsylvania
Capital BlueCross
CIGNA
DeCare
Delta Dental Plans
Dental Benefit Providers
DentaQuest
Emerging Vision
Genworth Financial
HealthAmerica
Humana
Independence Blue Cross
Independence Holding
LensCrafters
National Vision
Pearle Vision
UnitedHealth Group
UPMC
U.S. Healthcare, Inc.
U.S. Vision
Wal-Mart

## HISTORICAL FINANCIALS

Company Type: Not-for-profit

**Income Statement** FYE: December 31

| | REVENUE ($ mil.) | NET INCOME ($ mil.) | NET PROFIT MARGIN | EMPLOYEES |
|---|---|---|---|---|
| **12/06** | 11,084 | 398 | 3.6% | 18,500 |
| **12/05** | 9,847 | 342 | 3.5% | 12,000 |
| **12/04** | 9,118 | 311 | 3.4% | 11,000 |
| **12/03** | 8,140 | 76 | 0.9% | 11,000 |
| **12/02** | 7,482 | (83) | — | 11,000 |
| **Annual Growth** | 10.3% | — | — | 13.9% |

**Net Income History**

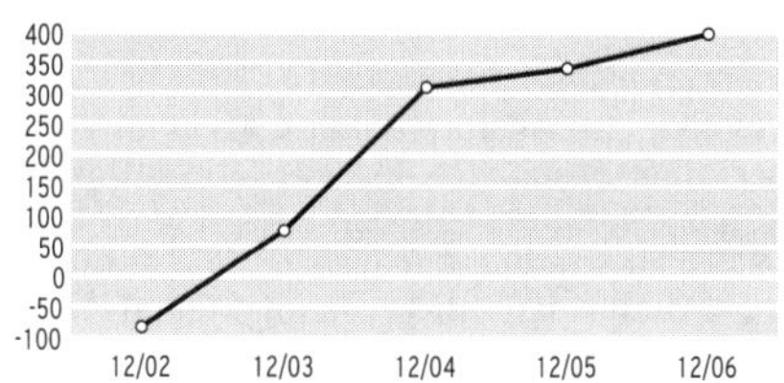


# Hillenbrand Industries

Whether it's funerals or equipment for health care facilities, Hillenbrand Industries buries the competition. The holding company operates two major subsidiaries. Its Hill-Rom unit makes, sells, and rents hospital beds and other patient-room furniture and equipment, along with stretchers, surgical table accessories, and non-invasive care equipment for pulmonary and circulatory conditions and wounds. Its customers are acute and long-term care facilities around the world. Hillenbrand's Batesville Casket is the leading casket maker in the US. Coffins aren't Batesville's only products: The unit also sells urns and other cremation products, along with merchandise display fixtures for funeral homes.

In 2007 Hillenbrand announced plans to split its two operating units into separate publicly traded companies, in order to increase value for shareholders and tighten industry focus for each unit. By early 2008 the company will spin off Hill-Rom into a new public company; Batesville Casket will continue as the sole operating unit of Hillenbrand Industries.

Hillenbrand had been considering strategic alternatives for the company since 2006. It had also announced several other strategic initiatives that year, including improving its sales force effectiveness and focusing on product solutions that reduce the side effects of long hospital stays, such as bed sores and infections; it has an ongoing collaboration with Ascension Health to address these issues. Additionally, Hillenbrand is trying to kick-start its rental business by cutting costs, improving efficiency, and investing in its out-of-date truck fleet. The company also sees room for growth in the post-acute care market (long-term care facilities and home care) and in some international markets. It expanded into Australia with the 2006 acquisition of Medicraft, a maker of hospital beds.

Both of the company's subsidiaries have recognized how they can gain from the growing girth of the US population: Hill-Rom has introduced beds and other equipment made for overweight patients, and Batesville launched Dimensions by Batesville, a line of caskets made for larger bodies.

Rolf Classon was the first leader of the company outside the Hillenbrand family when he took on the role of chairman in February 2006. At the same time, Peter Soderberg was appointed CEO.

## HISTORY

In 1906 John A. Hillenbrand, a banker, newspaperman, and general store owner in Batesville, Indiana, bought the ailing Batesville Casket Company (founded 1884) to save it from bankruptcy. Under Hillenbrand, and later his four sons (John W., who succeeded his father as president of the company; William; George; and Daniel), the casket company flourished.

In 1929 William Hillenbrand established the Hill-Rom Company in Batesville to make hospital furniture. Hill-Rom made its furniture out of wood instead of tubular steel and quickly became a leader in innovative hospital furnishings.

During the following decades George Hillenbrand created several patented products for both Batesville Casket and Hill-Rom. By the 1940s, for example, the company had developed corrosion-, air-, and water-resistant metal caskets. George constantly sought ways to improve manufacturing techniques and product quality, giving the company a competitive edge in sales and productivity.

Daniel, the youngest son, became president of Batesville Casket in 1964 and consolidated Batesville Casket and Hill-Rom into Hillenbrand Industries five years later. Hoping to make the company more competitive nationally (and eventually globally), Daniel took Hillenbrand public in 1971.

The company acquired Dominion Metalware Industries (1972) and luggage maker American Tourister (1978; sold to Astrum International, maker of Samsonite luggage, in 1993). In 1984 it bought Medeco Security Locks (sold 1998) and a year later purchased Support Systems International (SSI), provider of specialty rental mattresses for critically ill and immobile patients. (In 1994 SSI was integrated into Hill-Rom.)

Hillenbrand founded the Forethought Group in 1985 to provide special life insurance to cover prearranged funerals. In 1991 it entered the European market by acquiring Le Couviour, a French maker of hospital beds. The company also bought Block Medical, a maker of home infusion-therapy products, that year. August Hillenbrand, nephew of Daniel, became CEO in 1989.

In 1992 Batesville Casket set out to consolidate its market, buying casket producer Cormier & Gaudet (Canada). It then bought Bridge Casket (New Jersey), Lincoln Casket (Hamtramck, Michigan); and Industrias Arga (Mexico City), all in 1993. That year Hillenbrand also purchased L & C Arnold, one of the biggest and oldest hospital furniture makers in Germany.

With the casket market flat in the mid-1990s, Hillenbrand grew its business by going after market share in cremation products.

As the 20th century drew to a close, Medicare reimbursement cutbacks bit into Hill-Rom's sales. The company cut jobs in both 2000 and 2001. Those years also brought the retirement of both August and Daniel Hillenbrand. Frederick Rockwood became president and CEO in 2000; Ray Hillenbrand (nephew of Daniel) was named chairman in 2001.

Hillenbrand sold its piped medical gas unit (to Beacon Medical Products in late 2003) and the Air-Shields infant care products business of Hill-Rom, since those operations were not key to Hill-Rom's success. It acquired Advanced Respiratory, a maker of airway management equipment, in 2003 and MEDIQ, a company that provides medical equipment outsourcing, asset management, and rentals to the health care industry, in 2004.

To focus on Hill-Rom and Batesville, Hillenbrand sold its Forethought Financial Services subsidiary in July 2004. As its name suggests, Forethought offered funeral prepayment products and services.

Hillenbrand simplified Hill-Rom's structure in 2005, bringing more of its support operations under the parent company and realigning its commercial divisions into two geographically focused units.

Rockwood retired in 2005; Peter Soderberg replaced him the following year.

## EXECUTIVES

**Chairman, Hillenbrand Industries and Hill-Rom:** Rolf A. Classon, age 61
**Vice Chairman:** Joanne C. Smith, age 46
**President, CEO, and Director, Hillenbrand Industries; President and CEO, Hill-Rom:** Peter H. Soderberg, age 60, $1,104,165 pay
**SVP; President and CEO, Batesville Casket:** Kenneth A. Camp, age 61, $723,540 pay
**SVP and CFO:** Gregory N. Miller, age 43, $522,504 pay
**VP, Corporate Tax:** Larry V. Baker, age 51
**VP, Business Development and Strategy:** Michael J. Grippo, age 37
**VP, Corporate Information Technology:** Todd P. Brabender
**VP, General Counsel, and Secretary:** Patrick D. de Maynadier, age 46, $490,393 pay
**VP, Human Resources:** John Dickey, age 52
**VP; SVP, Post Acute Care (North America) and Information Technology of Hill-Rom Company, Inc:** Kimberly K. Dennis, age 39, $384,551 pay
**VP, International Business and Technology Development:** Abel Ang
**VP, Investor Relations, Corporate Communications, and Global Brand Development:** Blair A. (Andy) Rieth
**VP, Controller, and Chief Accounting Officer:** Richard G. Keller, age 45
**VP and Treasurer:** Mark R. Lanning, age 52
**VP, Internal Audit:** Gary L. Larson, age 45
**Auditors:** PricewaterhouseCoopers LLP

## LOCATIONS

**HQ:** Hillenbrand Industries, Inc.
700 State Rte. 46 East, Batesville, IN 47006
**Phone:** 812-934-7000 **Fax:** 812-931-3533
**Web:** www.hillenbrand.com

**2006 Sales**

| | $ mil. | % of total |
|---|---|---|
| US | 1,710.2 | 87 |
| Other countries | 252.7 | 13 |
| **Total** | **1,962.9** | **100** |

## PRODUCTS/OPERATIONS

**2006 Sales**

| | $ mil. | % of total |
|---|---|---|
| Hill-Rom | | |
| North America | 954.1 | 49 |
| International | 217.2 | 11 |
| Home care & surgical | 117.0 | 6 |
| Batesville Casket | 674.6 | 34 |
| **Total** | **1,962.9** | **100** |

**Selected Subsidiaries**

Batesville Services, Inc.
Batesville Casket Company, Inc.
Batesville Casket de Mexico, S.A. de C.V.
Batesville International Corporation
Batesville Logistics, Inc.
Batesville Manufacturing, Inc.
Green Tree Manufacturing, Inc.
Modern Wood Products, Inc.
Hill-Rom, Inc.
Advanced Respiratory, Inc.
Hill-Rom Company, Inc.
Hill-Rom International B.V. (The Netherlands)
Hill-Rom Ltd. (UK)
Hillrom S.A. (Switzerland)
Hill-Rom Austria GmbH
Hill-Rom International, Inc.
Hill-Rom Asia Limited (Hong Kong)
Hill-Rom Australia Pty, Ltd
Hill-Rom Manufacturing, Inc.
Hill-Rom SARL (France)
NaviCare Systems, Inc.
MEDIQ, Incorporated
The Acorn Development Group, Inc.

## COMPETITORS

Aurora Casket
BGI (California)
Freedom Medical
Gaymar
Getinge USA
Huntleigh Healthcare
Invacare
Kinetic Concepts
Matthews International
Medline Industries
Rauland-Borg
Stryker
Sunrise Medical
Universal Hospital
Wilbert
York Group

## HISTORICAL FINANCIALS

Company Type: Public

**Income Statement** FYE: September 30

| | REVENUE ($ mil.) | NET INCOME ($ mil.) | NET PROFIT MARGIN | EMPLOYEES |
|---|---|---|---|---|
| **9/06** | 1,963 | 221 | 11.3% | 9,300 |
| **9/05** | 1,938 | (94) | — | 9,800 |
| **9/04** | 1,829 | 143 | 7.8% | 10,400 |
| **9/03** | 2,042 | 138 | 6.8% | 9,900 |
| **9/02** | 1,757 | (10) | — | 10,300 |
| **Annual Growth** | 2.8% | — | — | (2.5%) |

**2006 Year-End Financials**

Debt ratio: 30.7%
Return on equity: 21.1%
Cash ($ mil.): 82
Current ratio: 2.35
Long-term debt ($ mil.): 347
No. of shares (mil.): 61
Dividends
Yield: 2.0%
Payout: 31.5%
Market value ($ mil.): 3,499

**Stock History** NYSE: HB

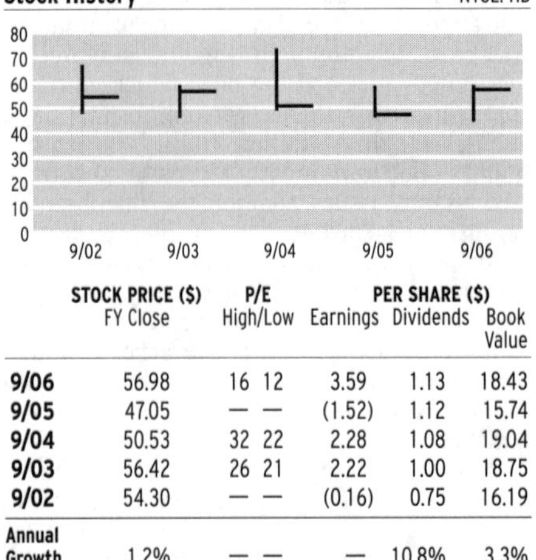


| | STOCK PRICE ($) FY Close | P/E High/Low | PER SHARE ($) Earnings | Dividends | Book Value |
|---|---|---|---|---|---|
| **9/06** | 56.98 | 16 12 | 3.59 | 1.13 | 18.43 |
| **9/05** | 47.05 | — — | (1.52) | 1.12 | 15.74 |
| **9/04** | 50.53 | 32 22 | 2.28 | 1.08 | 19.04 |
| **9/03** | 56.42 | 26 21 | 2.22 | 1.00 | 18.75 |
| **9/02** | 54.30 | — — | (0.16) | 0.75 | 16.19 |
| **Annual Growth** | 1.2% | — — | — | 10.8% | 3.3% |

# Hilton Hotels

If you need a bed for the night, Hilton Hotels has a few hundred thousand of them. One of the largest hoteliers in the world, the company's lodging empire includes about 2,800 hotels and resorts in more than 80 countries operating under such names as Doubletree, Embassy Suites, and Hampton, as well as its flagship Hilton brand. Many of its hotels serve the mid-market segment, though its Hilton and Conrad hotels offer full-service, upscale lodging. In addition, its Homewood Suites chain offers extended-stay services. Hilton owns or has stakes in about 110 properties and either franchises, leases, or manages the rest. Private equity firm The Blackstone Group plans to buy Hilton for about $20 billion plus debt.

The Blackstone deal represents the biggest private equity buyout in the hotel industry. As a result of the acquisition, the equity firm will assume about $6 billion in debt, bringing the total purchase price to some $26 billion. Blackstone already owns hotel assets such as LaQuinta Inns and Suites and LXR Luxury Resorts & Hotels.

Hilton's largest chain is its Hampton Inn and Hampton Inn & Suites, with more than 1,300 locations offering moderately priced rooms with limited amenities. Hilton does not own the majority of its hotels, but it makes half of its profit from those that it does own, like the Waldorf-Astoria, the New York Hilton, and the Hilton Hawaiian Village. Nearly all its Hampton hotels are operated by franchisees or by the company under management contracts with third-party owners. At the other end of the scale, its Hilton and Conrad chains offer luxury services and distinctive locations. Its Hilton Grand Vacations subsidiary operates more than 30 time-share vacation resorts located mostly in Florida.

In 2006 the company acquired Hilton International, the lodging operations of UK-based Hilton Group (now Ladbrokes). The $5.7 billion deal re-unified the Hilton Hotel brand throughout the world and added about 400 new locations to Hilton's portfolio. The purchase solidified the company's plans for significant international expansion. The company additionally brought into the Hilton fold about 80 LivingWell Health Clubs and more than 140 hotels operating under the Scandic brand. Following the acquisition, Hilton in 2007 sold its Scandic Hotels business to private equity firm EQT for $1.1 billion.

After leading the company for more than a decade, CEO Stephen Bollenbach has announced his resignation from Hilton. He plans to step down at the end of 2007 to become CEO at troubled home builder KB Home, though he'll remain co-chairman of the hotel business through 2010.

The company has introduced a new brand of luxury hotels, the Waldorf-Astoria Collection. The elite brand debuted with New York's Waldorf-Astoria, along with three luxury resorts newly managed by Hilton: the Grand Wailea Resort Hotel & Spa in Hawaii; the Arizona Biltmore Resort & Spa in Phoenix, and La Quinta Resort & Club in La Quinta, California.

The family of co-chairman William Barron Hilton, son of founder Conrad Hilton, owns about 5% of the company.

## HISTORY

Conrad Hilton got his start in hotel management by renting out rooms in his family's New Mexico home. He served as a state legislator and started a bank before leaving for Texas in 1919, hoping to make his fortune in banking. Hilton was unable to shoulder the cost of purchasing a bank, however, but recognized a high demand for hotel rooms and made a quick change in strategy, buying his first hotel in Cisco, Texas. Over the next decade he bought seven more Texas hotels.

Hilton lost several properties during the Depression, but began rebuilding his empire soon thereafter through the purchase of hotels in California (1938), New Mexico (1939), and Mexico (1942). He even married starlet Zsa Zsa Gabor in 1942 (they later divorced, of course). Hilton Hotels Corporation was formed in 1946 and went public. The company bought New York's Waldorf-Astoria in 1949 (a hotel Hilton called "the greatest of them all") and opened its first European hotel in Madrid in 1953. Hilton paid $111 million for the 10-hotel Statler chain the following year.

Hilton took his company out of the overseas hotel business in 1964 by spinning off Hilton International and began franchising the following year to capitalize on the well-known Hilton name. Barron Hilton, Conrad's son, was appointed president in 1966 (he became chairman upon Conrad Hilton's death in 1979). Hilton bought two Las Vegas hotels (the Las Vegas Hilton and the Flamingo Hilton) in 1970 and launched its gaming division. The company returned to the international hotel business with Conrad International Hotels in 1982 and opened its first suite-only Hilton Suites hotel in 1989.

Hilton expanded its gaming operations in the 1990s, buying Bally's Casino Resort in Reno in 1992 and launching its first riverboat casino, the Hilton Queen of New Orleans, in 1994. Two years later it acquired all of Bally Entertainment, making it the largest gaming company in the world. Also that year, Stephen Bollenbach, the former Walt Disney CFO who negotiated the $19 billion acquisition of Capital Cities/ABC, was named CEO — becoming the first non-family member to run the company.

Hilton formed an alliance with Ladbroke Group in 1997 (later Hilton Group, owner of Hilton International and the rights to the Hilton name outside the US) to promote the Hilton brand worldwide. Hilton also put in a bid that year to acquire ITT, owner of Sheraton hotels and Caesars World, but was thwarted when ITT accepted a higher offer from Starwood Hotels & Resorts. With a downturn in the gambling industry translating into sluggish results in Hilton's gaming segment, the company spun off its gaming interests as Park Place Entertainment (later Caesars Entertainment, now owned by Harrah's) later that year.

In 1999 Hilton made a massive acquisition with the $3.7 billion purchase of Promus Hotel Corp.

Following an extended downturn in the hospitality business brought on by recession and post-9/11 fears about terrorism, Hilton began to invest in refurbishments for many of its properties and added about 150 locations in 2004.

Two years later the company re-unified the Hilton Hotels brand internationally by acquiring Hilton International from Hilton Group (now Ladbrokes) for about $5.7 billion.

## EXECUTIVES

**Co-Chairman:** William Barron Hilton, age 80
**Co-Chairman and CEO:** Stephen F. Bollenbach, age 64, $1,137,830 pay
**President, COO, and Director:** Matthew J. Hart, age 54, $850,000 pay
**EVP and CFO:** Robert M. La Forgia, age 48, $1,150,000 pay
**EVP; CEO, Hilton International:** Ian R. Carter, age 45, $2,906,543 pay
**EVP; CEO, Americas and Global Brands:** Thomas L. (Tom) Keltner, age 60
**EVP Global Distribution Services and CIO:** James T. (Tim) Harvey, age 48
**EVP, General Counsel, and Corporate Secretary:** Madeleine A. Kleiner, age 55, $1,025,000 pay
**EVP Human Resources, Diversity, and Administration:** Molly McKenzie-Swarts
**SVP and Controller:** David A. Thomson
**SVP and Deputy General Counsel:** Tim S. Glassett
**SVP and Treasurer:** Mariel A. Joliet
**SVP Architecture and Construction:** Patrick Terwilliger
**SVP Corporate Affairs:** Marc A. Grossman
**SVP Customer, Quality, and Performance Support:** Jim Hartigan
**SVP Development and Finance:** Ted Middleton
**SVP Distribution and Brand Integration:** Bala Subramanian
**SVP Franchise Development:** William B. (Bill) Fortier
**SVP Hilton Brand Management:** Jeffrey (Jeff) Diskin
**SVP Sales and Development:** Bob Dirks
**SVP Sales:** Steven (Steve) Armitage
**SVP Tax:** W. Steven Standefer
**VP Corporate Communications:** Kathy Shepard
**VP Investor Relations:** Atish Shah
**Auditors:** Ernst & Young LLP

## LOCATIONS

**HQ:** Hilton Hotels Corporation
9336 Civic Center Dr., Beverly Hills, CA 90210
**Phone:** 310-278-4321 **Fax:** 310-205-7678
**Web:** www.hiltonworldwide.com

## PRODUCTS/OPERATIONS

### 2006 Sales

| | $ mil. | % of total |
|---|---|---|
| Management & franchise revenue | 2,527 | 31 |
| Owned hotels | 2,521 | 31 |
| Leased hotels | 2,347 | 29 |
| Time-share & other | 767 | 9 |
| **Total** | **8,162** | **100** |

### 2006 Locations

| | No. |
|---|---|
| Franchised & managed | 2,585 |
| Owned, joint venture & leased | 316 |
| Time-share | 34 |
| **Total** | **2,935** |

### 2006 Locations

| | No. |
|---|---|
| Hampton | 1,392 |
| Hilton | 498 |
| Hilton Garden Inn | 302 |
| Homewood Suites by Hilton | 192 |
| Embassy Suites | 185 |
| Doubletree | 173 |
| Scandic | 129 |
| Time-share | 34 |
| Other | 30 |
| **Total** | **2,935** |

## COMPETITORS

Accor North America
Best Western
Carlson Hotels
Choice Hotels
Hyatt
InterContinental Hotels
LXR Luxury Resorts
Marriott
Starwood Hotels & Resorts
Wyndham

## HISTORICAL FINANCIALS

Company Type: Public

### Income Statement

FYE: December 31

| | REVENUE ($ mil.) | NET INCOME ($ mil.) | NET PROFIT MARGIN | EMPLOYEES |
|---|---|---|---|---|
| **12/06** | 8,162 | 572 | 7.0% | 105,000 |
| **12/05** | 4,437 | 460 | 10.4% | 61,000 |
| **12/04** | 4,146 | 238 | 5.7% | 70,000 |
| **12/03** | 3,819 | 164 | 4.3% | 70,000 |
| **12/02** | 3,847 | 198 | 5.1% | 74,000 |
| **Annual Growth** | 20.7% | 30.4% | — | 9.1% |

### 2006 Year-End Financials

Debt ratio: 186.4%
Return on equity: 17.5%
Cash ($ mil.): 431
Current ratio: 0.77
Long-term debt ($ mil.): 6,946
No. of shares (mil.): 387
Dividends
Yield: 0.5%
Payout: 11.5%
Market value ($ mil.): 13,506

### Stock History

NYSE: HLT

| | STOCK PRICE ($) FY Close | P/E High | P/E Low | PER SHARE ($) Earnings | PER SHARE ($) Dividends | PER SHARE ($) Book Value |
|---|---|---|---|---|---|---|
| **12/06** | 34.90 | 26 | 16 | 1.39 | 0.16 | 9.63 |
| **12/05** | 24.11 | 23 | 17 | 1.13 | 0.12 | 7.36 |
| **12/04** | 22.74 | 38 | 25 | 0.60 | 0.08 | 6.60 |
| **12/03** | 17.13 | 41 | 24 | 0.43 | 0.08 | 5.88 |
| **12/02** | 12.71 | 32 | 18 | 0.53 | 0.08 | 5.46 |
| **Annual Growth** | 28.7% | — | — | 27.3% | 18.9% | 15.2% |

# H. J. Heinz

Forget those original 57 varieties: H. J. Heinz now has thousands of products. One of the world's largest food producers, Heinz produces ketchup, condiments, sauces, frozen foods, beans, pasta meals, infant food, and other processed food products. Its flagship product is ketchup, of course, and the company dominates the US ketchup market. The company's customers include food retailers, the foodservice industry, and the US military. Its leading brands include the aforementioned ketchup, Lea & Perrins sauces, Ore-Ida frozen potatoes, Boston Market, T.G.I. Friday's, and Weight Watchers foods.

Ketchup, condiments, and sauces account for some 40% of its sales and Heinz (which supplies McDonald's with ketchup) is banging on the bottom of the bottle, trying to get more sales out of ketchup, as well as its other core brands. Heinz's products are in mature markets in the US.

Heinz said that in order to focus on its core business (ketchup and sauces, meals and snacks, and infant nutrition), in 2006 it sold its 16% interest in The Hain Celestial Group and its New Zealand poultry operations, Tegel Foods, to Pacific Equity Partners for $165 million.

In a continuing effort to concentrate on its core business, that year Heinz also agreed to sell the ethnic foods sector of Lea & Perrins maker, HP Foods (which it acquired the year before and which supplies products to the Chinese, Indian, and Thai restaurant sectors under the brand names Cathay, Dynasty, Green Dragon, Lotus, and Rajah), to Associated British Foods for an undisclosed sum.

Later in 2006, Heinz sold its European seafood business to Lehman Brothers Merchant Banking for $506 million. The brands involved in the seafood sale include the canned tuna brands Mareblu (in Italy), John West (in the UK, Ireland, and the Netherlands), and Petit Navire (in France) canned tunas. Continuing to shed noncore operations, Heinz sold its UK chilled prepared foods business (including the Linda McCartney brand of frozen vegetarian entrees) to Hain Celestial. Terms of the transaction were not disclosed.

Heinz announced changes in 2006 to its corporate governance policy as a result of its proxy battle with dissident shareholders led by billionaire and former corporate raider Nelson Peltz and investment-management firm Trian Fund Management (of which Peltz is a principal). The changes, which Heinz disclosed after discussions with CalPERS and other large Heinz shareholders, included adding two independent board members and the adoption of a majority voting process with regard to the election of directors.

After many Heinz and Trian press-release statements back and forth and much press surrounding the bitter struggle between Peltz and Heinz leadership, it was announced that Heinz's board elected to add two of Trian's five nominees to its board: Nelson Peltz and Michael Weinstein.

Capital Research and Management Company owns 11% of the company and Peltz's Trian Fund owns almost 6%.

## HISTORY

In 1852 8-year-old Henry J. Heinz started selling produce from the family garden to neighbors in Sharpsburg, Pennsylvania. The young entrepreneur formed a partnership with his friend

L. C. Noble in 1869, bottling horseradish sauce in clear glass, but the business went bankrupt in 1875. The following year, with the help of his brother John and his cousin Frederick, Heinz created F. & J. Heinz; the enterprise developed ketchup (1876) and sweet pickles (1880). He gained financial control of the firm in 1888 and changed the name to the H. J. Heinz Company.

Heinz developed a reputation as an advertising and marketing genius. He introduced pickle pins, a popular promotion at the 1893 Chicago World's Fair; coined the catchy "57 Varieties" slogan in 1897 (despite already having 60 products); and in 1900 raised New York City's first large electric advertising sign (a 40-ft. pickle). By 1905 Heinz was manufacturing food products in the UK.

After Heinz's death in 1919 the business, under the direction of his son and later his grandson, continued to rely on its traditional product lines for the next four decades, although some new ones were introduced, such as baby food in 1931. The company went public in 1946.

Heinz changed its strategy in 1958 when it made its first acquisition, a Dutch food processor. Major purchases that followed included Star-Kist (tuna and pet food, 1963) and Ore-Ida (potatoes, 1965). In 1966 Burt Gookin became CEO, the first non-family member to hold that position.

The company bought Weight Watchers in 1978. The next year former rugby star Anthony O'Reilly became the company's fifth CEO. He intensified the focus on international expansion and presided over a string of acquisitions throughout the 1980s. O'Reilly became chairman in 1987.

Acquisitions in the 1990s included Wattie's Limited (New Zealand, 1992); Borden's food service business (1994); and pet food divisions from Quaker Oats (1995). However, faced with weak sales growth in its stable markets, in 1997 Heinz began shedding domestic units as it made global acquisitions. It sold its Ore-Ida food service operations (to McCain Foods, 1997) and its bakery products division (to Pillsbury, 1998).

William Johnson, who had turned around stagnant brands such as 9-Lives, succeeded O'Reilly as CEO in 1998. In 1999 Heinz announced a restructuring intended to eliminate jobs and close or sell about 20 factories over several years. Heinz sold the diet business of Weight Watchers, and, seeking greater access to the US natural foods market, purchased nearly 20% of The Hain Celestial Group

In 2000 O'Reilly retired and Johnson was named chairman. In an effort to focus on its core food products (sauces, ketchup, frozen foods), Heinz spun off a number of its North American businesses to Del Monte Foods in 2002. The all-stock transaction included the company's pet food (Kibbles 'n Bits) and snacks, tuna (StarKist), private-label soup, and infant feeding (Nature's Goodness) businesses.

Heinz acquired a majority stake in Russian condiment and margarine maker Petrosoyuz and the HP Foods Group from Groupe Danone in 2005. The HP group (for which Heinz paid $820 million in cash) included Lea & Perrins, HP, and Amoy Asian sauces.

## EXECUTIVES

**Chairman, President, and CEO:** William R. Johnson, age 58, $3,440,000 pay
**EVP and CFO:** Arthur B. (Art) Winkleblack, age 50, $1,065,183 pay
**EVP and President and CEO, Heinz Europe:** C. Scott O'Hara, age 46
**EVP and Chairman, Global Foodservice:** Jeffrey P. (Jeff) Berger, age 57
**EVP; President and CEO, Heinz North America:** David C. Moran, age 49
**SVP, Chief Administrative Officer, and Corporate and Government Affairs:** D. Edward I. (Ted) Smyth, age 57
**SVP, Finance and Corporate Controller:** Edward J. McMenamin, age 50
**SVP, Heinz Asia:** Christopher (Chris) Warmoth, age 48
**SVP, Heinz Australia, New Zealand, and Rest of World:** Michael D. Milone, age 51, $845,072 pay
**SVP and General Counsel:** Theodore N. Bobby, age 56
**SVP, Business Development:** Mitchell A. Ring, age 55
**VP, Investor Relations:** Margaret R. Nollen
**Chief People Officer:** Steve Clark
**Corporate Secretary:** Rene Biedzinski
**Manager, Communications:** Mike Yeomans
**Auditors:** PricewaterhouseCoopers LLP

## LOCATIONS

**HQ:** H. J. Heinz Company
600 Grant St., Pittsburgh, PA 15219
**Phone:** 412-456-5700 **Fax:** 412-456-6128
**Web:** www.heinz.com

### 2007 Sales

| | $ mil. | % of total |
|---|---|---|
| Europe | 3,076.8 | 34 |
| North American consumer products | 2,739.5 | 31 |
| US foodservice | 1,556.3 | 17 |
| Asia/Pacific | 1,202.0 | 13 |
| Other | 427.0 | 5 |
| **Total** | **9,001.6** | **100** |

## PRODUCTS/OPERATIONS

### 2007 Sales

| | $ mil. | % of total |
|---|---|---|
| Meals & snacks | 4,026.1 | 45 |
| Ketchup & sauces | 3,682.1 | 41 |
| Infant foods | 929.1 | 10 |
| Other | 364.3 | 4 |
| **Total** | **9,001.6** | **100** |

### Selected Brand Names

Amoy (Asian sauces)
Bagel Bites (frozen pizza and pizza snacks)
Boston Market (frozen meals)
Chef Francisco (frozen soups)
Classico (pasta sauce)
Delimex (frozen foods, Mexico)
Heinz (ketchup, organic ketchup, pickles, relishes, sauces)
HP (sauces)
Jack Daniel's Grilling Sauce (licensed, barbecue marinades)
Lea & Perrins (Worchestershire sauce)
Ore-Ida (frozen potatoes and potato products)
Orlando (tomato products, Europe)
Plasmon (baby food, Europe)
Smart Ones (diet frozen entrees)
Wattie's (grocery products and frozen foods, Australasia)
Weight Watchers (diet foods)
Wyler's (bouillon and soups)

## COMPETITORS

Associated British Foods
B&G Foods
Barilla
Campbell Soup
ConAgra
Del Monte Foods
Hain Celestial
Jenny Craig
John Sanfilippo & Son
Kraft Foods
La Doria
McIlhenny
Michelina's
Milnot
Nestlé
NutriSystem
Ralcorp
Slim-Fast
Smucker

## HISTORICAL FINANCIALS

Company Type: Public

### Income Statement

FYE: Wednesday nearest April 30

| | REVENUE ($ mil.) | NET INCOME ($ mil.) | NET PROFIT MARGIN | EMPLOYEES |
|---|---|---|---|---|
| **4/07** | 9,002 | 786 | 8.7% | 33,000 |
| **4/06** | 8,643 | 646 | 7.5% | 36,000 |
| **4/05** | 8,912 | 753 | 8.4% | 41,000 |
| **4/04** | 8,415 | 804 | 9.6% | 37,500 |
| **4/03** | 8,237 | 566 | 6.9% | 38,900 |
| **Annual Growth** | 2.2% | 8.5% | — | (4.0%) |

### 2007 Year-End Financials

Debt ratio: 239.7%
Return on equity: 40.4%
Cash ($ mil.): 653
Current ratio: 1.21
Long-term debt ($ mil.): 4,414
No. of shares (mil.): 322
Dividends
Yield: 3.0%
Payout: 59.3%
Market value ($ mil.): 14,998

### Stock History

NYSE: HNZ

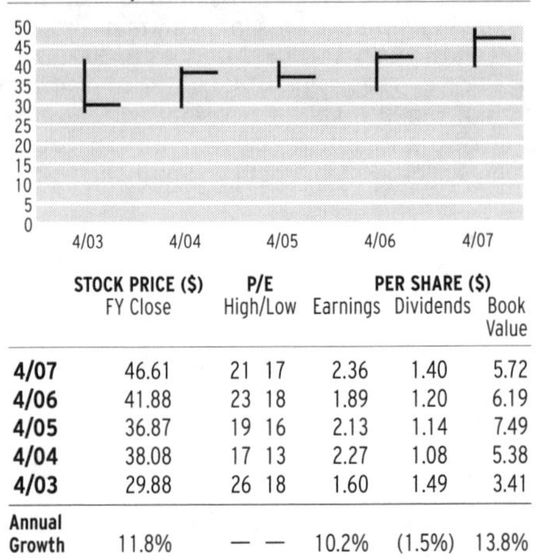


| | STOCK PRICE ($) FY Close | P/E High | P/E Low | PER SHARE ($) Earnings | PER SHARE ($) Dividends | PER SHARE ($) Book Value |
|---|---|---|---|---|---|---|
| **4/07** | 46.61 | 21 | 17 | 2.36 | 1.40 | 5.72 |
| **4/06** | 41.88 | 23 | 18 | 1.89 | 1.20 | 6.19 |
| **4/05** | 36.87 | 19 | 16 | 2.13 | 1.14 | 7.49 |
| **4/04** | 38.08 | 17 | 13 | 2.27 | 1.08 | 5.38 |
| **4/03** | 29.88 | 26 | 18 | 1.60 | 1.49 | 3.41 |
| **Annual Growth** | 11.8% | — | — | 10.2% | (1.5%) | 13.8% |

# HNI Corporation

Tired of your office furniture? HNI Corporation can supply you with replacements, along with a fireplace to burn the old set. HNI is a leading US manufacturer of office furniture. About three-quarters of the firm's sales come from its office furniture. It sells primarily to furniture dealers, wholesalers, and retail superstores (OfficeMax, Corporate Express, Office Depot, and Staples).True to its name, the company's Hearth & Home subsidiary makes fireplaces. HNI also has a division devoted to international marketing and distribution. The company sells its products primarily in Canada and the US.

Through its Hearth & Home Technologies subsidiary, HNI is one of the largest US makers of wood- and gas-burning fireplaces for the home, selling brands such as Heatilator, Heat-N-Glo, and Quadra-Fire. It also makes stoves under the Aladdin brand. Fireplaces and stoves are sold though dealers, distributors, and company-owned retail stores.

HNI has grown through acquisitions. Early in 2006 the company acquired Lamex, a Chinese office furniture manufacturer. Other smaller purchases in 2006 included an office furniture services company, a office furniture dealer, and a manufacturer of fireplace facings.

## HISTORY

Friends Maxwell Stanley, Clement Hanson, and Wood Miller founded The Home-O-Nize Co. (a name that suggested "modernize" and "economize") in 1944, planning to make home freezers and steel kitchen cabinets. These two products were never made, however, because of a steel shortage.

The first Home-O-Nize product was an aluminum hood used in the installation of natural gas systems. More important than the aluminum hood was the aluminum scrap left behind, which the company made into beverage coasters. These coasters, which could be imprinted with a company's name, were sold to businesses to give out as gifts. Home-O-Nize also transformed the aluminum scraps into boxes for file cards and, due to favorable response, decided to plunge into the office products business.

This move began in earnest in 1951, in an effort dramatically labeled "Operation Independence Home-O-Nize." The program was successful, and in 1952 the company started an unbroken string of profitable years. Helping this streak were such products as Unifile, a file cabinet that featured a single key that would lock all drawers simultaneously (1953). Home-O-Nize added cabinets, coat racks, and desks to its product line during this time and began marking all its products with the "H-O-N" label. Miller retired in 1958.

Home-O-Nize grew during the 1960s under the control of Stanley Howe, a Home-O-Nize employee since 1948. Howe had been appointed president in 1964 and made the company a national manufacturer by purchasing a plant in Georgia in 1967. The firm changed its name to HON INDUSTRIES the next year. Hanson left the company in 1969.

HON INDUSTRIES continued its expansion by purchasing California-based Holga Metal Products in 1971. Acquiring facilities in Pennsylvania and the opening of a plant in Virginia the next year gave HON INDUSTRIES a considerable presence on both US coasts. Howe replaced founder Maxwell Stanley as CEO in 1979.

In 1981 HON INDUSTRIES moved into the fireplace market by acquiring Heatilator, a leading brand of prefabricated fireplaces. By 1987, four decades after shipping its first product, HON INDUSTRIES had become a *FORTUNE* 500 company that many regarded as the most efficient in the making of office furniture. (It could produce a desk a minute and a chair every 20 seconds.) HON INDUSTRIES acquired Gunlocke, a maker of wooden office furniture, in 1989.

The rise of the office products superstore at the start of the 1990s did not go unnoticed by the company, which quickly positioned itself as a supplier to these businesses. Yet no action could spare HON INDUSTRIES from the office supply bust that occurred soon afterward, as oversupply and a lagging national economy dragged the industry downward.

Jack Michaels became the new CEO in 1991 as the company's sales dropped for the first time in decades. It adapted by investing in new products, and by 1992 sales were climbing again. In 1996 HON INDUSTRIES acquired rival fireplace maker Heat-N-Glo, which it merged with Heatilator to form Hearth Technologies. The next year it acquired three furniture makers, including Allsteel, and further bolstered Hearth by buying stove maker Aladdin Steel Products in 1998. HON INDUSTRIES closed three plants in 1999 to cut costs.

The company acquired hearth products distributors American Fireplace Company and the Allied Group in 2000, and wood case goods manufacturer Paoli (2004).

HON INDUSTRIES has been recognized repeatedly for its excellence; it was twice named as one of the "400 Best Big Companies in America" by *Forbes* magazine (2000, 2001) and was honored as the most admired company in the furniture industry by *FORTUNE* magazine (2003).

In 2004 the company changed its name to HNI in an attempt to reduce confusion between itself (HON INDUSTRIES Inc.) and its largest subsidiary (The HON Company). Its 2004 purchases included Paoli (wood case goods and seating, from Klaussner Furniture), Edward George (fireplace and stone products), and Omni Remanufacturing (panel systems).

## EXECUTIVES

**Chairman, President, and CEO:**
Stanley A. (Stan) Askren, age 46, $714,788 pay
**EVP; President, Hearth & Home Technologies:**
Bradley D. (Brad) Determan, age 45
**EVP; President, The HON Company:** Eric K. Jungbluth, age 46, $296,849 pay
**VP and CFO:** Jerald K. (Jerry) Dittmer, age 49, $300,908 pay
**VP and CIO:** Douglas L. Jones, age 48
**VP, Business Analysis and General Auditor:**
Robert D. Hayes, age 63
**VP, Continuous Improvement:** Thomas E. Hammer
**VP and Controller:** Robert J. Driessnack, age 48
**VP, Financial Reporting:** Tamara S. Feldman, age 46
**VP, General Counsel, and Secretary:** Jeffrey D. Lorenger, age 41
**VP, Investor Relations and Treasurer:**
Melinda C. Ellsworth, age 48
**VP, Manufacturing, Seating and Woodcase Goods:**
Timothy R. Summers, age 41
**VP, Member and Community Relations:** Donald T. Mead
**President, Maxon Furniture:** Jean M. Reynolds, age 48
**President, Omni Workspace Company:**
Timothy J. Anderson
**President, Paoli:** Thomas A. (Tom) Tolone
**President, Gunlocke:** Donald C. Wharton
**EVP; President, Allsteel:** Eugene Sung
**Auditors:** PricewaterhouseCoopers LLP

## LOCATIONS

**HQ:** HNI Corporation
408 E. 2nd St., Muscatine, IA 52761
**Phone:** 563-272-7400 **Fax:** 563-272-7655
**Web:** www.hnicorp.com

## PRODUCTS/OPERATIONS

### 2006 Sales

| | $ mil. | % of total |
|---|---|---|
| Office furniture | 2,077.0 | 78 |
| Hearth products | 602.8 | 22 |
| **Total** | **2,679.8** | **100** |

### Selected Products

Office Furniture
- Desks and related products (tables, bookcases, credenzas)
- Office systems (modular and moveable workspaces)
- Seating (task, executive, conference/training, and side chairs)
- Storage (filing cabinets, pedestals)

Hearth Products
- Accessories
- Fireplaces and stoves (wood, electric, gas, and pellet)
- Fireplace inserts
- Gas logs

### Selected Subsidiaries

Allsteel Inc. (office furniture)
Maxon Furniture Inc. (panel systems products and specialized services)
The Gunlocke Company (high-quality wood office furniture)
Hearth & Home Technologies Inc. (fireplaces and other hearth products)
The HON Company (value-priced office furniture)
HON International Inc. (worldwide distribution of all office furniture brands)
Omni Workspace Company (manufacturing services)
Paoli Inc. (wood case goods, modular desks, conference products, seating)

## COMPETITORS

CFM Corporation
Chromcraft Revington
Global Group
Haworth
Herman Miller
KI
Kimball International
Knoll
Lennox
Steelcase
Teknion

## HISTORICAL FINANCIALS

Company Type: Public

### Income Statement

FYE: Saturday nearest December 31

| | REVENUE ($ mil.) | NET INCOME ($ mil.) | NET PROFIT MARGIN | EMPLOYEES |
|---|---|---|---|---|
| 12/06 | 2,680 | 123 | 4.6% | 14,200 |
| 12/05 | 2,451 | 137 | 5.6% | 11,304 |
| 12/04 | 2,093 | 114 | 5.4% | 10,600 |
| 12/03 | 1,756 | 98 | 5.6% | 8,900 |
| 12/02 | 1,693 | 91 | 5.4% | 8,800 |
| Annual Growth | 12.2% | 7.8% | — | 12.7% |

### 2006 Year-End Financials

Debt ratio: 57.7%
Return on equity: 22.6%
Cash ($ mil.): 37
Current ratio: 1.41
Long-term debt ($ mil.): 286
No. of shares (mil.): 48
Dividends
Yield: 1.6%
Payout: 29.4%
Market value ($ mil.): 2,128

### Stock History

NYSE: HNI

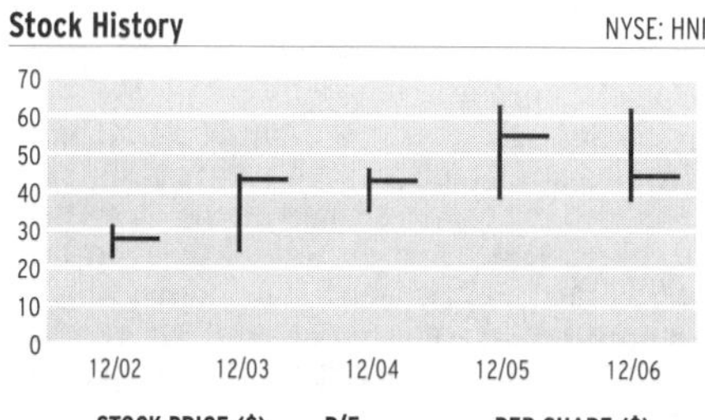


| | STOCK PRICE ($) FY Close | P/E High | P/E Low | PER SHARE ($) Earnings | Dividends | Book Value |
|---|---|---|---|---|---|---|
| 12/06 | 44.41 | 25 | 16 | 2.45 | 0.72 | 10.35 |
| 12/05 | 54.93 | 25 | 16 | 2.50 | 0.62 | 11.46 |
| 12/04 | 43.05 | 23 | 18 | 1.97 | 0.42 | 12.10 |
| 12/03 | 43.33 | 26 | 15 | 1.68 | — | 12.19 |
| 12/02 | 27.49 | 20 | 15 | 1.55 | — | 11.08 |
| Annual Growth | 12.7% | — | — | 12.1% | 30.9% | (1.7%) |

# Holly Corporation

Like a good, productive buddy, Holly Corporation refines crude oil to produce gasoline, diesel fuel, and jet fuel, which it sells in the southwestern US, northern Mexico, and Montana. Subsidiary Navajo Refining (New Mexico) has a refining capacity of 83,000 barrels a day. Holly's Woods Cross refinery (Utah) has a crude oil capacity of 25,200 barrels per day. In 2004 the company spun off its Navajo refinery-related refined petroleum pipeline and other distribution assets as Holly Energy Partners, L.P.; it retains a 45% interest in the company. In 2006 Holly sold its Montana Refining unit to a subsidiary of Connacher Oil and Gas, for about $55 million.

Holly Corporation buys crude from independents or on the spot market. In a move to expand its production capacity, in 2003 Holly acquired ConocoPhillips' Woods Cross refinery and related assets for $25 million. Holly agreed to be acquired by Frontier Oil for about $450 million that year, but the companies terminated the agreement, and litigation between the parties resulted.

In 2005 the Delaware Chancery Court ruled that Frontier Oil had not proved that Holly had repudiated the merger agreement, and awarded Frontier Oil only $1 in damages. Also that year, Holly acquired the remaining 51% of NK Asphalt Producers that it did not already own. The company sold its intermediate feedstock pipelines connecting two refining facilities in Lovington and Artesia, New Mexico to Holly Energy Partners for $81.5 million.

## HISTORY

Holly was founded in 1947 as General Appliance Corp. to process other companies' crude oil; the current name was adopted in 1952. Holly grew with the number of gas-guzzling cars in the 1950s and 1960s, and in the 1970s it developed its Navajo refinery in New Mexico. (Current CEO Lamar Norsworthy, whose family has had large stakes in the company since 1960, became a top executive in 1971 at age 24.) In 1981 Holly began producing higher-grade gasoline and started an asphalt company at Navajo.

In 1984 Holly became a partner in Montana Refining and later bought the entire business. It upgraded the Navajo refinery in the early 1990s to meet the demand for unleaded gasoline. In 1995 Amoco, Mapco, and Holly formed a joint venture, the 265-mile Rio Grande Pipeline (completed in 1997), to transport natural gas liquids to Mexico.

Also in 1997, FINA and Holly allied to expand and use Holly's pipelines in the southwestern US. A proposed merger with another southwestern refiner, Giant Industries, died in 1998 because of federal antitrust concerns and a billion-dollar lawsuit filed against Holly by Longhorn Partners Pipeline. Court papers revealed in 2000 that Holly had paid $4 million to fight Longhorn's request for a permit to transport gasoline in its Houston-to-El Paso pipeline. The permit, if approved, would compete with Holly's own interests in western Texas.

Later in 2000 the company cut its workforce by about 10%, mostly at Navajo Refining. The next year Navajo Refining secured a $122 million contract to provide JP-8 jet fuel to the Defense Department.

## EXECUTIVES

**Chairman:** Lamar Norsworthy, age 60, $1,953,509 pay (prior to title change)
**CEO and Chairman:** Matthew P. (Matt) Clifton, age 55, $1,617,958 pay (prior to promotion)
**EVP Refining and Marketing:** David L. Lamp, age 49, $724,334 pay (prior to promotion)
**SVP and General Counsel:** W. John Glancy, age 65, $509,894 pay
**VP and CFO:** Stephen J. McDonnell, age 55, $425,718 pay
**VP and Chief Accounting Officer:** P. Dean Ridenour, age 65
**SVP Holly Logistic Services, L.L.C.:** David G. Blair, age 48
**VP Environmental Affairs Holly Corporation and Holly Refining & Marketing Company:** Philip L. Youngblood
**VP Risk Management Holly Corporation:** Scott C. Surplus
**VP Asphalt Operations Holly Refining & Marketing Company:** Mark A. Plake, age 46
**VP Investor Relations Holly Corporation and Holly Logistic Services, L.L.C.:** M. Neale Hickerson, age 54
**VP Engineering and Process Development Holly Refining & Marketing Company:** Randall R. Howes
**VP International Crude Oil and Refined Products Holly Refining & Marketing Company:** Mike Mirbagheri
**VP Lease Crude Oil Holly Refining & Marketing Company:** R. Scott Louderback
**VP Marketing and Product Supply Holly Refining & Marketing Company:** Gregory A. White
**VP Human Resources Holly Refining & Marketing Company, Holly Logistic Services, L.L.C., and Holly Corporation:** Nancy F. Hartmann
**Auditors:** Ernst & Young LLP

## LOCATIONS

**HQ:** Holly Corporation
100 Crescent Ct., Ste. 1600, Dallas, TX 75201
**Phone:** 214-871-3555 **Fax:** 214-871-3560
**Web:** www.hollycorp.com

Holly sells its products in the southwestern US, and in northern Mexico.

## PRODUCTS/OPERATIONS

**2006 Sales**

| | $ mil. | % of total |
|---|---|---|
| Refining | 4,022.0 | 100 |
| Corporate & other | 1.7 | — |
| Adjustments | (0.5) | — |
| **Total** | **4,023.2** | **100** |

**Selected Subsidiaries**

Black Eagle, Inc.
Holly Logistics
 Holly Energy Partners, L.P. (45%)
Holly Petroleum, Inc.
Navajo Corp.
Navajo Holdings, Inc.
Navajo Pipeline Co.
 Navajo Southern, Inc.
Navajo Refining Co.
 Lorefco, Inc.
  Lea Refining Co.
 Navajo Northern, Inc.
 Navajo Western Asphalt Co.
Woods Cross Refining Co., L.L.C.

## COMPETITORS

BP
Crown Central
Exxon Mobil
George Warren
Marathon Petroleum
Sunoco
Tesoro
Valero Energy
Western Refining, Inc.
Williams Companies

## HISTORICAL FINANCIALS

Company Type: Public

**Income Statement** FYE: December 31

| | REVENUE ($ mil.) | NET INCOME ($ mil.) | NET PROFIT MARGIN | EMPLOYEES |
|---|---|---|---|---|
| 12/06 | 4,023 | 267 | 6.6% | 859 |
| 12/05 | 3,213 | 168 | 5.2% | 881 |
| 12/04 | 2,246 | 84 | 3.7% | 845 |
| 12/03* | 1,403 | 46 | 3.3% | 735 |
| 7/02 | 889 | 32 | 3.6% | 560 |
| Annual Growth | 45.9% | 69.9% | — | 11.3% |

*Fiscal year change

**2006 Year-End Financials**

Debt ratio: —
Return on equity: 63.2%
Cash ($ mil.): 250
Current ratio: 1.44
Long-term debt ($ mil.): —
No. of shares (mil.): 55
Dividends
 Yield: 0.6%
 Payout: 6.3%
Market value ($ mil.): 2,843

**Stock History** NYSE: HOC

| | STOCK PRICE ($) FY Close | P/E High | P/E Low | PER SHARE ($) Earnings | Dividends | Book Value |
|---|---|---|---|---|---|---|
| 12/06 | 51.40 | 12 | 6 | 4.58 | 0.29 | 8.43 |
| 12/05 | 29.43 | 12 | 5 | 2.65 | 0.19 | 12.85 |
| 12/04 | 13.94 | 11 | 5 | 1.30 | 0.14 | 10.86 |
| 12/03* | 6.88 | 10 | 7 | 0.72 | 0.11 | — |
| 7/02 | 4.21 | 11 | 7 | 0.50 | 0.10 | — |
| Annual Growth | 86.9% | — | — | 74.0% | 30.5% | (11.9%) |

*Fiscal year change

# Home Depot

Lots of folks embark on household projects from The Home Depot. As the world's largest home improvement chain and second-largest retailer in the US after Wal-Mart, the firm operates more than 2,150 stores in all 50 US states, the District of Columbia, Canada, Mexico, and Puerto Rico. It targets the do-it-yourself and professional markets with a broad product assortment (up to 45,000 items, including lumber, floor and wall coverings, plumbing, gardening supplies, tools, paint, and even appliances). Its construction supply business, HD Supply, caters to professional builders. Home Depot has reshuffled its top management in response to angry shareholders and has lined up investors to buy its HD Supply.

Home Depot began 2007 by taking a good look in the mirror. In January Home Depot parted ways with six-year chairman and chief executive Robert Nardelli as the board yielded to pressure from investors upset over the direction of the company. During his tenure Nardelli led a near-doubling in sales and a more than 140% increase in earnings per share. Despite this, Home Depot's stock had declined while competitor

Lowe's saw triple-digit growth during the same period. What seemed to be the nail in Nardelli's coffin and what had continued to cause speculation was his autocratic management style and hefty compensation package (strategically based on options rather than shareholder returns and estimated at $245 million over five years). Nardelli left Home Depot that month with a $210 million severance package. Nardelli was replaced by vice chairman and EVP Frank Blake.

The company avoided a proxy fight threatened by one of its large shareholders by granting San Diego-based Relational Investors a seat on its board and agreeing that four directors involved in the hiring of Nardelli will leave the board in 2008.

To diversify, the home improvement retailer has been aggressively growing its services business, which includes roofing, and flooring and kitchen fixtures installation, and HD Supply. By 2010 the company had expected that up to 6% of its revenue will come from services. It had anticipated 20% of sales would be generated by its HD Supply business, before deciding to re-evaluate the supply unit's place in the company.

Three suitors — Bain Capital, The Carlyle Group, and Clayton, Dubilier & Rice — lined up to buy the retailer's HD Supply unit in mid-2007. Disbanding its efforts to follow through with Nardelli's services expansion, Home Depot agreed to unload its supply business to the three private equity firms in a deal valued at some $10 billion to focus on its core retail operations.

The US's #2 retailer is expanding and looking to grow its operations overseas, including China. Lured by the growth potential of the vast Chinese market, the US home improvement giant plans to purchase a majority stake in Taiwan-based HomeWay for about $100 million. HomeWay operates about a dozen DIY warehouse stores in northern China.

## HISTORY

Bernard Marcus and Arthur Blank founded The Home Depot in 1978 after they were fired (under disputed circumstances) from Handy Dan Home Improvement Centers. They joined Handy Dan co-worker Ronald Brill to launch a "new and improved" home center for the do-it-yourselfer (DIY). In 1979 they opened three stores in the fast-growing Atlanta area and expanded to four stores in 1980.

Home Depot went public, opened four stores in South Florida, and posted sales of $50 million in 1981. The chain entered Louisiana and Arizona next. By 1983 sales were more than $250 million.

In 1984 Home Depot's stock was listed on the NYSE and the company acquired nine Bowater Home Centers in the South. Through subsequent stock and debenture offerings, Home Depot continued to grow, entering California (Handy Dan's home turf) with six new stores in 1985.

Back on track in 1986, sales exceeded $1 billion in the firm's 60 stores. Home Depot began the current policy of "low day-in, day-out pricing" the following year, achieving Marcus' dream of eliminating sales events. The company entered the competitive northeastern market with stores in Long Island, New York, in 1988 and opened its first EXPO Design Center in San Diego.

Home Depot's sales continued to rise during the 1990-92 recession and the retailer kept opening stores. It entered Canada in 1994 when it acquired a 75% interest in Aikenhead's, a DIY chain that it converted to the Home Depot name (it bought the remaining 25% in 1998).

A series of gender-bias lawsuits plagued the company in 1994 as female workers claimed they were not treated on an equal basis with male employees. Home Depot reached a $65 million out-of-court settlement in 1997, but not before the company was ordered to pay another female employee $1.7 million in a case in California.

In 1997 Blank succeeded Marcus as the company's CEO; Marcus remained chairman. Home Depot bought National Blind & Wallpaper Factory (a mail-order firm) and Maintenance Warehouse (a direct-mail marketer) that year.

Home Depot named General Electric executive Robert Nardelli as its president and CEO in 2000. Marcus and Blank were named co-chairmen. The next year Marcus was named chairman after Blank stepped down. Later that year Marcus retired, and Nardelli became chairman. The company agreed to settle discrimination claims on the part of some Colorado employees for $5.5 million in 2004.

In 2005 the company shuttered 15 EXPO Design Center stores, which cater to affluent homeowners, and converted five others to The Home Depot format. In all, in 2005 Home Depot spent about $2.5 billion to acquire 21 companies.

In January 2006 Home Depot acquired carpet and upholstery cleaning franchisor Chem-Dry, which it will add to its At-Home Services division. (Chem-Dry has nearly 4,000 franchises worldwide, including 2,500 in the US. In March the company completed its largest acquisition to date: the construction, repair, and maintenance products distributor Hughes Supply Inc., for $3.2 billion. That purchase was followed in May by the acquisition of Cox Lumber Co., a Tampa, Florida-based provider of trusses, doors, and lumber-related products.

In early 2007 Nardelli left the company and vice chairman and EVP Frank Blake took the top spot. Home Depot decided to close its handful of flooring-only stores that year. It also closed a call center in Texas, affecting 550 employees.

## EXECUTIVES

**Chairman and CEO:** Francis S. (Frank) Blake, age 57
**EVP and COO; CEO, HD Supply:** Joseph J. (Joe) DeAngelo, age 46
**EVP, Corporate Services and CFO:** Carol B. Tomé, age 50
**EVP and CIO:** Robert P. (Bob) DeRodes, age 56, $940,192 pay
**EVP, General Counsel, and Corporate Secretary:** Jack A. Van Woerkom, age 53
**EVP, Merchandising:** Craig Menear, age 49
**EVP, Human Resources:** Timothy M. (Tim) Crow, age 51
**SVP, Corporate Communications and External Affairs:** Brad Shaw
**SVP and Chief Marketing Officer:** Roger W. Adams, age 50
**SVP, Merchandising Lumber and Building Materials:** Eric Peterson
**SVP, Supply Chain:** Mark Holifield, age 49
**SVP, Store Merchandising:** Kim McKesson
**VP and Controller:** Kelly H. Barrett, age 37
**VP, Litigation and Risk Management:** James C. (Jim) Snyder Jr., age 43
**VP, Merchandising, Garden-Live Goods/Landscaping:** Scott Manning
**VP, Investor Relations:** Dianne S. Dayhoff
**Senior Director, Merchandising Operations:** Mark Healy
**Senior Public Relations Manager:** Jerry Shields
**Marketing Manager:** Kenneth Rye
**Auditors:** KPMG LLP

## LOCATIONS

**HQ:** The Home Depot, Inc.
2455 Paces Ferry Rd. NW, Atlanta, GA 30339
**Phone:** 770-433-8211 **Fax:** 770-384-2356
**Web:** www.homedepot.com

### 2007 Locations

| | No. |
|---|---|
| US | |
| California | 214 |
| Texas | 172 |
| Florida | 140 |
| New York | 97 |
| Georgia | 81 |
| Illinois | 70 |
| Michigan | 70 |
| Ohio | 70 |
| Pennsylvania | 66 |
| New Jersey | 64 |
| Mexico | 61 |
| Arizona | 52 |
| Virginia | 45 |
| Colorado | 44 |
| Massachusetts | 42 |
| Washington | 42 |
| North Carolina | 41 |
| Maryland | 40 |
| Tennessee | 34 |
| Missouri | 33 |
| Minnesota | 31 |
| Wisconsin | 30 |
| Alabama | 26 |
| Connecticut | 26 |
| Indiana | 26 |
| Louisiana | 25 |
| South Carolina | 25 |
| Oregon | 22 |
| New Hampshire | 19 |
| Utah | 19 |
| Nevada | 17 |
| Kansas | 16 |
| Oklahoma | 16 |
| Kentucky | 15 |
| Arkansas | 14 |
| Mississippi | 14 |
| New Mexico | 13 |
| Other states | 113 |
| Canada | 155 |
| **Total** | **2,100** |

## PRODUCTS/OPERATIONS

### 2007 Sales

| | $ mil. | % of total |
|---|---|---|
| Retail | 79,027.0 | 87 |
| HD Supply | 12,070.0 | 13 |
| Adjustments | (260.0) | — |
| **Total** | **90,837.0** | **100** |

### 2007 Sales by Product

| | % of total |
|---|---|
| Plumbing, electrical & kitchen | 31 |
| Hardware & seasonal | 27 |
| Building materials, lumber & millwork | 24 |
| Paint, flooring & wall covering | 18 |
| **Total** | **100** |

### Selected Private Labels and Proprietary Brands

BEHR Premium Plus (paint)
Hampton Bay (lighting)
Mill's Pride (cabinets)
Traffic Master (carpet)
Vigoro (fertilizer)

### Selected Subsidiaries

HD Supply (wholesale supplier of plumbing, HVAC, appliances, and related professional products; building supplies, tools, and services for multihousing, lodging, and commercial properties)
Home Depot Landscape Supply (retailer of garden and nursery products)

## COMPETITORS

84 Lumber
Abbey Carpet
Ace Hardware
Amazon.com
Best Buy
Building Materials Holding
CCA Global
Costco Wholesale
Do it Best
F.W. Webb
Guardian Building Products Distribution
Kelly-Moore
Kmart
Lowe's
Menard
Northern Tool
Pacific Coast Building Products
Reno-Depot
Sears
Sherwin-Williams
Stock Building Supply
Sutherland Lumber
Target
Tractor Supply
True Value
Wal-Mart
W.E. Aubuchon
Wolseley

## HISTORICAL FINANCIALS

Company Type: Public

### Income Statement

FYE: Sunday nearest January 31

| | REVENUE ($ mil.) | NET INCOME ($ mil.) | NET PROFIT MARGIN | EMPLOYEES |
|---|---|---|---|---|
| 1/07 | 90,837 | 5,761 | 6.3% | 364,000 |
| 1/06 | 81,511 | 5,838 | 7.2% | 345,000 |
| 1/05 | 73,094 | 5,001 | 6.8% | 325,000 |
| 1/04 | 64,816 | 4,304 | 6.6% | 299,000 |
| 1/03 | 58,247 | 3,664 | 6.3% | 280,000 |
| Annual Growth | 11.7% | 12.0% | — | 6.8% |

### 2007 Year-End Financials

Debt ratio: 46.5%
Return on equity: 22.2%
Cash ($ mil.): 614
Current ratio: 1.39
Long-term debt ($ mil.): 11,643
No. of shares (mil.): 1,970
Dividends
Yield: 1.7%
Payout: 24.4%
Market value ($ mil.): 78,682

### Stock History

NYSE: HD

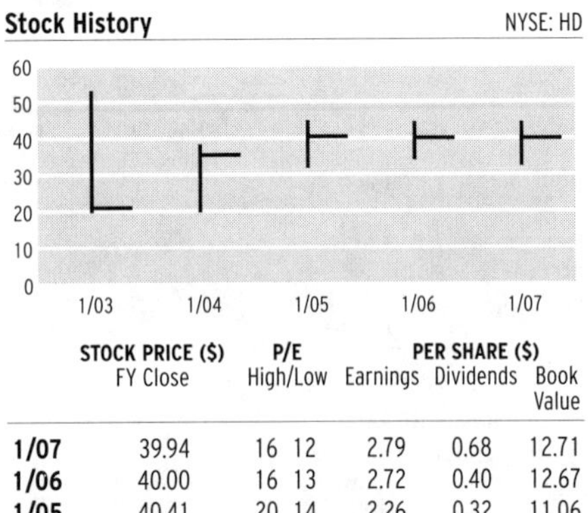


| | STOCK PRICE ($) FY Close | P/E High/Low | PER SHARE ($) Earnings | Dividends | Book Value |
|---|---|---|---|---|---|
| 1/07 | 39.94 | 16 12 | 2.79 | 0.68 | 12.71 |
| 1/06 | 40.00 | 16 13 | 2.72 | 0.40 | 12.67 |
| 1/05 | 40.41 | 20 14 | 2.26 | 0.32 | 11.06 |
| 1/04 | 35.47 | 20 11 | 1.88 | 0.26 | 9.44 |
| 1/03 | 20.90 | 34 13 | 1.56 | 0.21 | 8.38 |
| Annual Growth | 17.6% | — — | 15.6% | 34.1% | 11.0% |

# Honeywell International

Jet engines and thermostats seem worlds apart, but they're Honeywell International's bread and butter. The company's largest business segment, Honeywell Aerospace, makes products such as turbofan and turboprop engines and flight safety and landing systems. Close behind is Honeywell's Automation and Control segment, which includes home and industrial heating, ventilation, and manufacturing process products. Honeywell, through its Specialty Materials segment, also makes performance materials used in semiconductors, polymers for electronics and fibers, and specialty friction materials. Lastly, the company turns out consumer car care products (Prestone, FRAM) through its Transportation Systems segment.

Honeywell agreed to be acquired by General Electric in 2001, but EU regulators vetoed the deal on antitrust concerns. In the aftermath, former AlliedSignal CEO Lawrence Bossidy (a GE alum) replaced Michael Bonsignore at Honeywell's helm. Bossidy was replaced the next year by David Cote (another GE alum).

Facing the economic slowdown — and the fallout from the aborted GE deal — Honeywell closed about 50 plants and reduced its workforce. Speculation about possible mergers or the sale of operations surfaced in the wake of the scuttled GE deal, but CEO Cote insisted that he wants to run a diverse, independent company.

Honeywell acquired UK-based Novar plc for $1.7 billion early in 2005. Also that year Honeywell sold its nylon carpet fibers unit to Shaw Industries, a unit of Berkshire Hathaway.

In mid-2007 Honeywell acquired Dimensions International, a provider of logistics support to the US military and other defense agencies. The deal was valued at about $230 million. Dimensions became part of the Honeywell Technology Solutions subsidiary.

Later in 2007 Honeywell completed the purchase of the Netherlands-based Enraf Holding B.V. for about $260 million. Enraf, a maker of measurement and controls solutions used in the exploration, production, and transportation of energy products, became part of Honeywell's Process Solutions division.

## HISTORY

During WWI Germany controlled much of the world's chemical industry, causing dye and drug shortages. In response, *Washington Post* publisher Eugene Meyer and scientist William Nichols organized the Allied Chemical & Dye Corporation in 1920.

Allied opened a synthetic ammonia plant in 1928 near Hopewell, Virginia, and became the world's leading producer of ammonia. After WWII Allied began making nylon, refrigerants, and other products. The company became Allied Chemical Corporation in 1958.

Seeking a supplier of raw materials for its chemical products, in 1962 Allied bought Union Texas Natural Gas. In the early 1970s CEO John Connor sold many of the firm's unprofitable businesses and invested in oil and gas exploration. By 1979, when Edward Hennessy became CEO, Union Texas produced 80% of Allied's income.

Hennessy led the company into the electronics and technical markets. Under a new name, Allied Corporation (1981), it bought the Bendix Corporation, an aerospace and automotive company, in 1983. In 1985 Allied merged with Signal Companies (founded by Sam Mosher in 1922) to form AlliedSignal. The company spun off more than 40 unprofitable chemical and engineering businesses over the next two years.

Larry Bossidy, hired from General Electric in 1991 as the new CEO, began to cut waste and buy growth businesses. In 1998 alone the company made 13 acquisitions. Late in 1999 the company acquired Honeywell in a deal valued at $15 billion and changed its name to Honeywell International. Honeywell, after trying to make a go of it in the computer and telecommunications industries, had refocused on its bread and butter — thermostats, security systems, and other automation equipment. The chairman and CEO of the original Honeywell, Michael Bonsignore, took the same titles in the combined company.

In 2000 Honeywell picked up building-security and fire systems company Pittway for $2 billion. The same year Honeywell agreed to sell its fluid-connectors business (to Eaton Corporation). Then, amid lower than expected earnings, the company announced plans to cut an additional 6,000 jobs on top of the 11,000 cuts already planned.

Late in the year Honeywell was reportedly close to inking a deal to be acquired by United Technologies, but the talks ended when industrial behemoth GE made a better offer. Honeywell then agreed to be acquired by GE in a stock deal worth about $45 billion.

In 2001 Honeywell's shareholders approved the deal with GE; the US Justice Department also approved the deal (if Honeywell sold its helicopter engine business and authorized other companies to perform maintenance and repair services on some of its aircraft engines). European Union regulators saw things differently and the deal apparently collapsed in June when GE — which had offered to sell assets that generate about $2.2 billion a year — balked at demands that it sell virtually all of Honeywell's avionics operations. Honeywell then offered itself at a reduced price, but GE declined. The EU formally rejected the acquisition in July, and Honeywell ousted CEO Bonsignore, replacing him with Bossidy.

In September the company said that it would take cost-cutting measures with charges of almost $1 billion and increased the total of previously announced layoffs, cutting about 16,000 jobs (about 13% of its workforce) by year's end. In December Honeywell agreed to pay Northrop Grumman $440 million to settle an antitrust and patent infringement lawsuit filed against it by Litton (now a part of Northrop) in 1990.

In 2002 David Cote the former chairman, president, and CEO of TRW, was named president and CEO of Honeywell, replacing Bossidy (Cote also replaced Bossidy as chairman in July 2002).

Late in 2005 Honeywell sold its US nylon fibers business to Shaw Industries and its Clarke American Checks (check printing) business to M&F Worldwide for $800 million. It also bought Dow Chemical's 50% stake in UOP, their energy refining joint venture, for $825 million.

Honeywell sold Novar's Indalex Aluminum Solutions operations to Sun Capital Partners for $425 million early in 2006. Not long after, Honeywell completed the acquisition of First Technology PLC, a maker of gas sensing, automotive, and safety equipment, for $718 million.

## EXECUTIVES

**Chairman and CEO:** David M. Cote, age 54, $1,610,192 pay
**SVP and CFO:** David J. (Dave) Anderson, age 56, $753,365 pay
**SVP and General Counsel:** Peter M. Kreindler, age 62
**SVP, Technology and Operations:** Larry E. Kittelberger, age 60, $594,692 pay
**SVP, Government Relations:** Timothy J. (Tim) Keating
**SVP, Human Resources and Communications:** Thomas W. (Tom) Weidenkopf, age 48
**VP, Secretary, and Deputy Corporate Counsel:** Thomas F. Larkins
**VP, Six Sigma and Operations:** William L. (Bill) Ramsey
**VP, Strategy and Business Development:** Rhonda G. Germany
**VP and Treasurer:** John J. Tus
**VP, Investor Relations:** Nick Noviello
**President and CEO, Aerospace:** Robert J. (Rob) Gillette, age 47, $585,769 pay
**President and CEO, Automation and Control Solutions:** Roger Fradin, age 54, $645,077 pay
**President and CEO, Specialty Materials:** Nance K. Dicciani, age 58
**President and CEO, Transportation Systems:** Adriane M. Brown, age 48
**President, Engines, Systems, and Services, Aerospace:** Russell D. (Russ) Turner
**President, Environmental Combustion and Control, Automation and Control Solutions:** Andreas Kramvis
**President, Honeywell Life Safety, Automation and Control Solutions:** Mark Levy
**President, Honeywell Building Solutions, Automation and Control Solutions:** Joesph (Joe) Puishys
**President, Honeywell Process Solutions, Automation and Control Solutions:** Jack Bolick
**President, Honeywell Security, Automation and Control Solutions:** Ben Cornett
**Auditors:** PricewaterhouseCoopers LLP

## LOCATIONS

**HQ:** Honeywell International Inc.
101 Columbia Rd., Morristown, NJ 07962
**Phone:** 973-455-2000 **Fax:** 973-455-4807
**Web:** www.honeywell.com

Honeywell International maintains approximately 1,300 manufacturing, sales, and research locations, mainly in Asia, Europe, and North and South America; its principal manufacturing plants are in France, Germany, Italy, the UK, and the US.

### 2006 Sales

| | $ mil. | % of total |
|---|---|---|
| US | 19,821 | 63 |
| Europe | 7,781 | 25 |
| Other regions | 3,765 | 12 |
| **Total** | **31,367** | **100** |

## PRODUCTS/OPERATIONS

### 2006 Sales

| | $ mil. | % of total |
|---|---|---|
| Aerospace | 11,124 | 36 |
| Automation & Control Solutions | 11,020 | 35 |
| Specialty Materials | 4,631 | 15 |
| Transportation Systems | 4,592 | 14 |
| **Total** | **31,367** | **100** |

## COMPETITORS

Akzo Nobel
American Standard
ArvinMeritor
BAE Systems Inc.
Barber-Coleman
BASF AG
Bayer
Beaulieu
BorgWarner
Carrier
Dana
Delphi
Dow Chemical
DuPont
Eastman Chemical
Eaton
Emerson Electric
Endress + Hauser
Federal-Mogul
GE
GE Aircraft Engines UK
GE Fanuc Automation
Goodrich
Hamilton Sundstrand
Hercules
Hexcel
ITT Corp.
Johnson Controls
Lockheed Martin
Northrop Grumman
Parker Hannifin
Pratt & Whitney
Raytheon
Robert Bosch
Rockwell Automation
Rolls-Royce
Sextant Avionique
Siemens AG
Tenneco
Tyco
United Technologies

## HISTORICAL FINANCIALS

Company Type: Public

### Income Statement

FYE: December 31

| | REVENUE ($ mil.) | NET INCOME ($ mil.) | NET PROFIT MARGIN | EMPLOYEES |
|---|---|---|---|---|
| **12/06** | 31,367 | 2,083 | 6.6% | 118,000 |
| **12/05** | 27,653 | 1,655 | 6.0% | 116,000 |
| **12/04** | 25,601 | 1,281 | 5.0% | 109,000 |
| **12/03** | 23,103 | 1,324 | 5.7% | 108,000 |
| **12/02** | 22,274 | (220) | — | 108,000 |
| **Annual Growth** | 8.9% | — | — | 2.2% |

### 2006 Year-End Financials

Debt ratio: 40.2%
Return on equity: 19.9%
Cash ($ mil.): 1,224
Current ratio: 1.21
Long-term debt ($ mil.): 3,909
No. of shares (mil.): 801
Dividends
Yield: 2.0%
Payout: 36.1%
Market value ($ mil.): 36,219

### Stock History

NYSE: HON

| | STOCK PRICE ($) FY Close | P/E High | P/E Low | PER SHARE ($) Earnings | Dividends | Book Value |
|---|---|---|---|---|---|---|
| **12/06** | 45.24 | 18 | 14 | 2.52 | 0.91 | 12.14 |
| **12/05** | 37.25 | 20 | 17 | 1.94 | 0.82 | 13.57 |
| **12/04** | 35.41 | 26 | 21 | 1.49 | 0.75 | 13.24 |
| **12/03** | 33.43 | 22 | 13 | 1.54 | 0.75 | 12.44 |
| **12/02** | 24.00 | — | — | (0.27) | 0.75 | 10.44 |
| **Annual Growth** | 17.2% | — | — | — | 5.0% | 3.8% |

# Hormel Foods

Now that Hormel Foods has stocked its pantry with ethnic convenience foods, can we look forward to SPAM enchiladas or SPAM curry? Along with its famous canned "spiced ham," SPAM, Hormel is a top US turkey processor and a major pork processor, making Jennie-O turkey products, Cure 81 hams, and Always Tender fresh pork, as well as canned Stagg chili and Dinty Moore beef stews. Hormel has branched into convenience, ethnic, and frozen foods such as Chi-Chi's Mexican, Patak's Indian, and House of Tsang Asian products. As more people eat out, sales of Hormel's foodservice products have increased as well. The Hormel Foundation, a charitable trust formed during WWII, owns about 46% of the company's stock.

Hormel is expanding globally, forming joint ventures in Australia, Canada, China (the world's biggest market for pork), Japan, and the Philippines. It added another to its list of countries in which it has joint ventures in 2006, when it formed a JV with San Miguel to raise and market hogs and animal feed in Vietnam. The JV is 49%-owned by Hormel.

Back home, the company has formed Precept Foods, a 51% joint venture with Cargill to market case-ready fresh beef and pork under the Always Tender brand.

Hormel's growing HealthLabs division creates texture-modified foods for hospital and nursing home patients who have difficulty swallowing.

Adding to its grocery product offerings, in 2006 the company acquired canned, ready-to-eat chicken producer Valley Fresh Foods for $78 million. It also bought pepperoni and pasta maker Provena Foods and sausage and sliced meat maker, Saag's Products.

## HISTORY

George Hormel opened his Austin, Minnesota, slaughterhouse in an abandoned creamery in 1891. By 1900 Hormel had modernized his facilities to compete with larger meat processors. In 1903 the enterprise introduced its first brand name (Dairy Brand) and a year later began opening distribution centers nationwide. The scandal that ensued after the discovery in 1921 that an assistant controller had embezzled over $1 million almost broke the company, causing Hormel to initiate tighter controls. By 1924 it was processing more than a million hogs annually. Hormel introduced canned ham two years later.

Jay Hormel, George's son, became president in 1929; under his guidance Hormel introduced Dinty Moore beef stew (1936) and SPAM (1937). A Hormel executive won a contest, and $100, by submitting the name, a contraction of "spiced ham." During WWII the US government bought over half of Hormel's output; it supplied SPAM to GIs and Allied forces.

In 1959 Hormel introduced its Little Sizzlers pork sausage and sold its billionth can of SPAM. New products rolled out in the 1960s included Hormel's Cure 81 ham (1963). By the mid-1970s the firm had more than 750 products.

The company survived a violent, nationally publicized strike triggered by a pay cut in 1985. In the end only 500 of the original 1,500 strikers returned to accept lower pay scales.

Sensing the consumer shift toward poultry, Hormel purchased Jennie-O Foods in 1986. Later acquisitions included the House of Tsang and Oriental Deli (1992), Dubuque (processed pork, 1993) and Herb-Ox (bouillon and dry soup mix, 1993). After more than a century as Geo. A. Hormel & Co., the company began calling itself Hormel Foods in 1993 to reflect its expansion into non-pork foods. Former General Foods executive Joel Johnson was named president and CEO that year (and chairman two years later).

Hormel proved it could take a joke with the 1994 debut of its tongue-in-cheek SPAM catalog, featuring dozens of SPAM-related products. But when a 1996 Muppets movie featured a porcine character named Spa'am, Hormel sued Jim Henson Productions; a federal court gave Spa'am the go-ahead.

Also in 1996 Hormel teamed up with Mexican food processor Grupo Herdez to sell Herdez sauces and other Mexican food products in the US. It then formed a joint venture with Indian food producer Patak Spices (UK) to market its products in the US. Late that year Hormel paid $64 million for a 21% interest in Spanish food maker Campofrio Alimentacion.

Earnings fell in 1996, due in part to soaring hog prices. The company was hit hard again in 1998 when production contracts with hog growers meant it wound up paying premium rates, despite a market glut. In 1998 the Smithsonian Institution accepted two cans of SPAM (one from 1937, the other an updated 1997 version) for its History of Technology collection.

SPAM sales soared in 1999 as nervous consumers stockpiled provisions for the millennium. To build its growing HealthLabs division, Hormel acquired Cliffdale Farms (2000) and Diamond Crystal Brands nutritional products (a division of Imperial Sugar) in 2001 — boosting its share of the market for easy-to-swallow foods sold to hospitals and nursing homes.

In early 2001 Hormel acquired family-owned The Turkey Store for approximately $334 million and folded it into its Jennie-O division.

Hormel produced its 6 billionth can of SPAM in 2002 and traded $115 million in stock to acquire the rest of Imperial Sugar's Diamond Crystal Brands unit, which packages single-serve packets of sugar, sweeteners, seasonings, and plastic cutlery for the foodservice industry.

To further diversify, in 2003 Hormel acquired food manufacturer Century Foods International (whey-based protein powders, beverages, and nutrition bars) and added it to its burgeoning specialty foods group. In 2004 Hormel sold off its stake in Campofrio to Smithfield Foods.

Its last act of business in 2004 was to purchase Southern California's Clougherty Packing for about $186 million. The pork processor's facilities help extend Hormel's capacity for further-processed foods in the southwestern US.

In 2005 the company purchased Mexican food manufacturer Arriba Foods for $47 million in cash. Later that year it purchased Lloyd's Barbecue Company from General Mills for an undisclosed sum.

Responding to the growing trend of the US population to dine out, Hormel expanded its foodservice segment (which it refers to as its specialty foods business) with the 2005 purchase of foodservice food manufacturer and distributor Mark-Lynn Foods. Mark-Lynn's products include salt and pepper packets, ketchup, mustard, sauces and salad dressings, creamers, and sugar packets, as well as jellies, desserts, and drink mixes.

Johnson retired in 2006; company veteran Jeffrey Ettinger was tapped to be the new chairman and CEO.

## EXECUTIVES

**Chairman, President, and CEO:** Jeffrey M. Ettinger, age 48, $1,575,300 pay (prior to title change)
**SVP and CFO:** Jody H. Feragen, age 50
**SVP, External Affairs, General Counsel, and Corporate Secretary:** James W. Cavanaugh, age 58
**SVP, Supply Chain:** William F. Snyder, age 49
**Group VP; President and CEO, Jennie-O Turkey Store:** Michael D. (Mike) Tolbert, age 50
**Group VP; President, Consumer Products Sales:** Larry L. Vorpahl, age 43
**Group VP; President, Hormel Foods International:** Richard A. Bross, age 55
**Director; President, Protein Business:** Gary J. Ray, age 60, $1,378,162 pay
**VP, Asia-Pacific:** David L. Longacre
**VP, Corporate Communications:** Julie H. Craven, age 51
**VP, Engineering:** Larry J. Pfeil, age 57
**VP, Foodservice Marketing:** Dennis B. Goettsch, age 53
**VP, Human Resources:** David P. Juhlke, age 47
**VP, Legislative Affairs and Marketing Services:** Joe C. Swedberg, age 51
**VP, Marketing, Consumer Products/Refrigerated Foods:** James Splinter, age 44
**VP, Marketing Grocery Products:** D. Scott Aakre, age 42
**VP, Quality Management:** Bryan D. Farnsworth, age 49
**VP, Research and Development:** Phillip L. (Phil) Minerich, age 52
**VP, Finance and Treasurer:** Roland G. Gentzler, age 52
**VP and Controller:** James N. Sheehan, age 50
**Director, Investor Relations:** Fred D. Halvin
**Auditors:** Ernst & Young LLP

## LOCATIONS

**HQ:** Hormel Foods Corporation
1 Hormel Place, Austin, MN 55912
**Phone:** 507-437-5611 **Fax:** 507-437-5129
**Web:** www.hormel.com

### 2006 Sales

| | $ mil. | % of total |
|---|---|---|
| US | 5,528 | 96 |
| Other countries | 218 | 4 |
| **Total** | **5,746** | **100** |

## PRODUCTS/OPERATIONS

### 2006 Sales

| | $ mil. | % of total |
|---|---|---|
| Refrigerated foods | 2,958 | 51 |
| Jenny-O Turkey Store | 1,105 | 19 |
| Grocery products | 847 | 15 |
| Specialty foods | 625 | 11 |
| Other | 211 | 4 |
| **Total** | **5,746** | **100** |

### Selected Brands

Deli
- DI LUSS Deli Products
- HORMEL Deli Beef
- HORMEL Deli Dry Sausage
- HORMEL Deli Ham
- HORMEL Deli Turkey
- HORMEL Party Trays

Ethnic
- BUFALO Authentic Mexican Products
- CARAPELLI Olive Oils
- CHI-CHI'S Mexican Products
- DOÑA MARÍA Authentic Mexican Products
- EL TORITO Mexican Products
- HERDEZ Authentic Mexican Products
- HOUSE OF TSANG Asian Sauces and Oils
- MANNY'S Tortilla Products
- MARRAKESH EXPRESS Mediterranean Products
- PATAK'S Indian Products
- PELOPONNESE Mediterranean Products

Pantry
- DINTY MOORE Products
- HERB-OX Bouillon
- HORMEL Bacon Toppings
- HORMEL Chili
- HORMEL Chunk Meats
- HORMEL Dried Beef
- HORMEL Hash
- HORMEL KID'S KITCHEN Microwave Meals
- HORMEL Microwave Meals and Soups
- HORMEL Microwave Trays
- NOT-SO-SLOPPY-JOE Sloppy Joe Sauce
- SPAM Family of Products
- STAGG Chili
- VALLEY FRESH Premium Canned Poultry Products

Refrigerated
- HORMEL ALWAYS TENDER Flavored Pork and Beef
- HORMEL Bacon
- HORMEL CURE 81 Ham
- HORMEL Fully Cooked Entrees
- HORMEL NATURAL CHOICE Deli Lunch Meats
- HORMEL OLD SMOKEHOUSE Summer Sausage
- HORMEL Pepperoni
- HORMEL WRANGLERS Smoked Franks
- JENNIE-O TURKEY STORE Turkey Products
- LITTLE SIZZLERS Pork Sausage
- LLOYD'S BBQ Products

## COMPETITORS

Boar's Head
Bob Evans
Bridgford Foods
Butterball
Campbell Soup
Cargill
ConAgra
Dial
Foster Farms
JBS Swift
Kraft Foods
Perdue
Pilgrim's Pride
Pinnacle Foods
Sanderson Farms
Sara Lee Food & Beverage
Seaboard
Smithfield Foods
Tyson Foods

## HISTORICAL FINANCIALS

Company Type: Public

### Income Statement

FYE: Last Saturday in October

| | REVENUE ($ mil.) | NET INCOME ($ mil.) | NET PROFIT MARGIN | EMPLOYEES |
|---|---|---|---|---|
| **10/06** | 5,746 | 286 | 5.0% | 18,100 |
| **10/05** | 5,414 | 254 | 4.7% | 17,600 |
| **10/04** | 4,780 | 232 | 4.8% | 15,600 |
| **10/03** | 4,200 | 186 | 4.4% | 16,000 |
| **10/02** | 3,910 | 189 | 4.8% | 15,500 |
| **Annual Growth** | 10.1% | 10.9% | — | 4.0% |

### 2006 Year-End Financials

Debt ratio: 19.4%
Return on equity: 16.9%
Cash ($ mil.): 172
Current ratio: 1.95
Long-term debt ($ mil.): 350
No. of shares (mil.): 137
Dividends
Yield: 1.6%
Payout: 27.3%
Market value ($ mil.): 4,951

### Stock History

NYSE: HRL

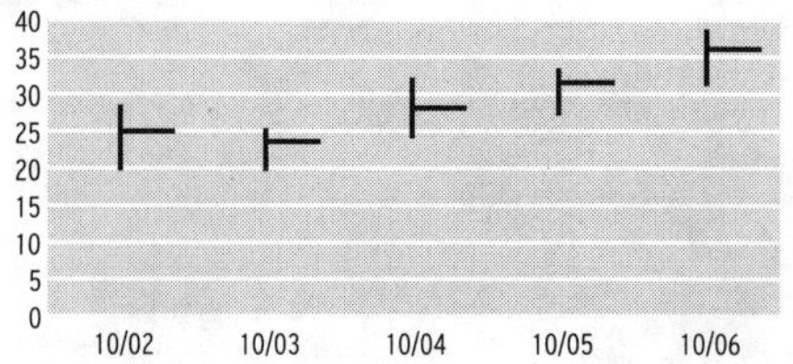

| | STOCK PRICE ($) FY Close | P/E High | P/E Low | PER SHARE ($) Earnings | PER SHARE ($) Dividends | PER SHARE ($) Book Value |
|---|---|---|---|---|---|---|
| **10/06** | 36.05 | 19 | 15 | 2.05 | 0.56 | 13.13 |
| **10/05** | 31.53 | 18 | 15 | 1.82 | 0.52 | 11.42 |
| **10/04** | 28.11 | 19 | 15 | 1.65 | 0.45 | 10.15 |
| **10/03** | 23.58 | 19 | 15 | 1.33 | 0.42 | 9.04 |
| **10/02** | 24.95 | 21 | 15 | 1.35 | 0.39 | 8.06 |
| **Annual Growth** | 9.6% | — | — | 11.0% | 9.5% | 13.0% |

# Hovnanian Enterprises

Gimme shelter. Hovnanian Enterprises designs, builds, and markets single-family detached homes, condominiums, and townhomes for first-time, move-up, and luxury buyers as well as for empty-nesters and active adults. Hovnanian builds about 20,000 homes a year, with base prices ranging from $42,000 to $2.1 million and averaging about $329,000. It operates mainly along the eastern seaboard, California, and Texas and develops homes under names including Oster, Four Seasons, K. Hovnanian, Metro Homes, CraftBuilt, First Homes, and Town & Country Homes. Its K. Hovnanian Mortgage unit offers mortgage financing and title services. Members of the Hovnanian family control more than 90% of the company.

Like its peers, Hovnanian was caught in the almost epic real estate downturn of 2005-2006 when interest rates started to rise. Unsold inventory and falling sales were the norm across the sector, and Hovnanian was not alone in offering steep incentives to reluctant buyers to prevent cancellations.

## HISTORY

After fleeing revolution in his home of Iraq in the 1950s, Kevork Hovnanian came to America and began building homes in New Jersey in 1959 with his three brothers (including brother Vahak, later to become founder of Internet service provider SPEEDUS.COM). His firm incorporated as K. Hovnanian Enterprises in 1967, and Kevork's son Ara came on board in 1979. (Ara became president in 1988 and CEO in 1997.) The company's 1983 IPO helped Hovnanian take advantage of New Jersey's strong housing market, which peaked in 1986. However, the boom had declined dramatically by 1990, and Hovnanian landed in the red.

Responding to the setback, Hovnanian expanded geographically in the 1990s. It moved into the Washington, DC, area in 1992 and into Southern California in 1994. But the new markets did not add much to the bottom line, thanks to a slowdown in North Carolina and a recession in California.

Hovnanian crews traveled to Armenia in 1988 to help rebuild the country after devastating earthquakes wreaked havoc. The trip convinced Kevork, an Armenian who grew up in Iraq, to expand Hovnanian operations into the emerging economies of Eastern Europe. Because of its relatively more advanced real estate and mortgage laws, Poland was chosen, and Hovnanian began constructing townhouses there in 1996.

Sales and earnings slipped in 1997, in part because Hovnanian wrote down several Florida properties. The company began to divest itself of commercial holdings to focus on housing; by 1998 Hovnanian had exited the investment properties business.

With cash to plow into homebuilding, Hovnanian strengthened its Washington, DC, operations in 1998 by acquiring Virginia's P.C. Homes. The next year the builder purchased New Jersey luxury homebuilder Matzel & Mumford and entered Texas with the purchase of Dallas-based Goodman Family of Builders. In 2001 Hovnanian bought Washington Homes, which operated primarily in North Carolina and the Washington, DC, metropolitan area.

In early 2002 Hovnanian acquired the homebuilding assets of The Forecast Group, increasing Hovnanian's presence in California and adding nearly $500 million in annual revenue. The company was listed that year as one of the 100 fastest-growing companies in the US by *FORTUNE* magazine. Also that year Hovnanian expanded its presence in Texas, entering the Houston homebuilding market with its purchase of Parkside Homes. The company saw its fifth consecutive year of record sales and earnings.

Hovnanian initiated plans in 2003 to stop selling homes in Poland and to liquidate its homebuilding operations in the mid-south (US) region. On the expansion side, the company acquired Brighton Homes to strengthen its position in the Houston area. (Hovnanian's two Houston-area acquisitions operate as separate divisions.) It also acquired Great Western Homes, expanding its market into the Phoenix area and the Southwest, and Tampa, Florida-based Windward Homes, expanding its southeastern US market into Florida. Hovnanian's earnings per share increased by 83% in 2003.

CEO of the company for seven years, Ara Hovnanian was named "Executive of the Year" in 2004 by *BUILDER* magazine. That year Hovnanian established a presence in the Midwest by entering the Minneapolis/St. Paul, Minnesota, market. It also expanded its metro DC presence by acquiring the homebuilding assets of McLean, Virginia-based Rocky Gorge Homes for an undisclosed amount. In 2004 the company's earnings and revenue increased by 36% and 30%, respectively, for its fiscal year.

In 2005 Hovnanian entered the Chicago market by acquiring homebuilder Town and Country Homes. It also entered the Orlando market and expanded its operations in Florida and Minnesota by acquiring Cambridge Homes. Hovnanian also acquired Oster Homes (Ohio) and First Home Builders (Florida) in 2005.

## EXECUTIVES

**Chairman:** Kevork S. Hovnanian, age 83, $2,838,427 pay
**President, CEO, and Director:** Ara K. Hovnanian, age 49, $6,937,809 pay
**SVP Finance and Treasurer:** Kevin C. Hake, age 47, $625,344 pay
**SVP Human Resources:** Robyn T. Mingle, age 41
**SVP and Corporate Controller:** Paul W. Buchanan, age 56, $408,780 pay
**SVP and General Counsel:** Peter S. Reinhart, age 56
**EVP, CFO, and Director:** J. Larry Sorsby, age 51, $665,257 pay
**SVP Corporate Operations:** Mark S. Hodges
**VP and CIO:** John F. Ulen
**Assistant VP and Assistant Treasurer:** Nancy A. Marrazzo
**Director, Investor Relations:** Jeffrey T. (Jeff) O'Keefe
**Auditors:** Ernst & Young LLP

## LOCATIONS

**HQ:** Hovnanian Enterprises, Inc.
110 W. Front St., Red Bank, NJ 07701
**Phone:** 732-747-7800 **Fax:** 732-747-6835
**Web:** www.khov.com

Hovnanian Enterprises operates in the following regions: Northeast (New Jersey, New York, Pennsylvania), Mid-Atlantic (Delaware, Maryland, Virginia, West Virginia, Washington, DC), Midwest (Illinois, Kentucky, Michigan, Minnesota, Ohio), Southeast (Florida, Georgia, North Carolina, South Carolina), Southwest (Arizona, Texas), and West (California).

### 2006 Home Sales

| | $ mil. | % of total |
|---|---|---|
| West | 1,586.9 | 27 |
| Southeast | 1,243.5 | 21 |
| Northeast | 992.7 | 17 |
| Mid-Atlantic | 980.7 | 17 |
| Southwest | 925.9 | 16 |
| Midwest | 173.7 | 2 |
| **Total** | **5,903.4** | **100** |

### 2006 Homes Delivered

| | No. | % of total |
|---|---|---|
| Southeast | 5,074 | 25 |
| Southwest | 4,252 | 21 |
| West | 3,587 | 18 |
| Northeast | 2,188 | 11 |
| Mid-Atlantic | 1,984 | 10 |
| Midwest | 855 | 4 |
| Joint ventures | 2,261 | 11 |
| **Total** | **20,201** | **100** |

## PRODUCTS/OPERATIONS

### 2006 Sales

| | $ mil. | % of total |
|---|---|---|
| Homebuilding | | |
| Sale of homes | 5,903.4 | 96 |
| Land sales & other | 155.3 | 3 |
| Financial services | 89.6 | 1 |
| **Total** | **6,148.3** | **100** |

### Selected Trade Names

Brighton Homes
Cambridge Homes
First Home Builders
Forecast Homes
Great Western Homes
K. Hovnanian Homes
K. Hovnanian Homes Build On Your Lot
K. Hovnanian's Four Seasons (active-adult communities)
Matzel and Mumford
Oster Homes
Parkside Homes
Town & Country Homes
Westminster Homes
Windward Homes

## COMPETITORS

Beazer Homes
Centex
D.R. Horton
KB Home
Lennar
M/I Homes
NVR
Orleans Homebuilders
Pulte Homes
Rottlund
Ryland
Toll Brothers
Weyerhaeuser Real Estate

## HISTORICAL FINANCIALS

Company Type: Public

### Income Statement

FYE: October 31

| | REVENUE ($ mil.) | NET INCOME ($ mil.) | NET PROFIT MARGIN | EMPLOYEES |
|---|---|---|---|---|
| **10/06** | 6,148 | 150 | 2.4% | 6,239 |
| **10/05** | 5,348 | 472 | 8.8% | 6,084 |
| **10/04** | 4,160 | 349 | 8.4% | 3,837 |
| **10/03** | 3,202 | 257 | 8.0% | 3,249 |
| **10/02** | 2,551 | 138 | 5.4% | 2,370 |
| **Annual Growth** | 24.6% | 2.1% | — | 27.4% |

### 2006 Year-End Financials

Debt ratio: 131.2%
Return on equity: 8.3%
Cash ($ mil.): 56
Current ratio: 5.40
Long-term debt ($ mil.): 2,370
No. of shares (mil.): 47
Dividends
Yield: —
Payout: —
Market value ($ mil.): 1,455

**Stock History** NYSE: HOV

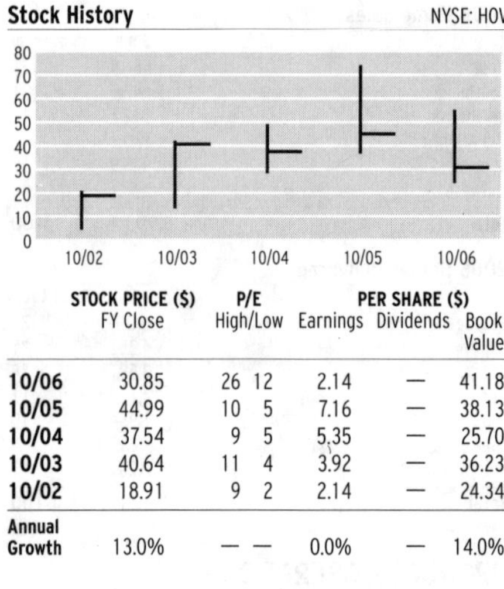


| | STOCK PRICE ($) FY Close | P/E High/Low | | PER SHARE ($) Earnings | Dividends | Book Value |
|---|---|---|---|---|---|---|
| **10/06** | 30.85 | 26 | 12 | 2.14 | — | 41.18 |
| **10/05** | 44.99 | 10 | 5 | 7.16 | — | 38.13 |
| **10/04** | 37.54 | 9 | 5 | 5.35 | — | 25.70 |
| **10/03** | 40.64 | 11 | 4 | 3.92 | — | 36.23 |
| **10/02** | 18.91 | 9 | 2 | 2.14 | — | 24.34 |
| **Annual Growth** | 13.0% | — | — | 0.0% | — | 14.0% |

# Humana Inc.

Humana is counting on Medicare to make it a national player in the health insurance game. The company provides Medicare Advantage health plans and prescription drug coverage to more than 4 million members in all 50 states and Puerto Rico. It also administers managed care plans for other government programs, including Medicaid plans in Florida and Puerto Rico and TRICARE (a program for military personnel) in 10 southern states. Additionally, Humana offers health plans and some specialty products (group life and disability insurance, for example) to commercial employers and individuals, primarily in 18 southern and midwestern states. All told, it covers more than 13 million members in the US.

The company has been aggressive in signing up Medicare recipients for prescription drug coverage under the Medicare Part D provisions that took effect in 2006. It has also been expanding the geographic reach of its Medicare Advantage plans; it grew its Medicare Advantage membership by 80% in 2006 and now offers its private-fee-for-service version of the plans in every state in the US. (It offers HMO and PPO versions in select markets.)

In 2007 the company, along with UnitedHealth and several other health plans, agreed to temporarily stop marketing its Medicare Advantage private-fee-for-service plans. The voluntary suspension came amid complaints that some agents were using shady practices to enroll seniors in the plans.

The company has partnered with Wal-Mart to reach even more seniors eligible for the Medicare Part D prescription drug benefit by offering a co-branded prescription drug card with the discount retailer.

Two-thirds of Humana's sales come from government program premiums, and more than half come from Medicare-related premiums alone. The company's growing reliance on its government business has brought it significant growth, but also leaves it vulnerable to cuts in reimbursement rates. And as pressures to balance the government's budget grow, Congress has noted the cost-cutting potential in rate reductions for Medicare Advantage programs, which are more costly than traditional government-run Medicare.

The commercial unit offers health coverage to employer groups on a fully-insured basis or with an "administrative services only" model to self-funded groups. Its products include HMO, PPO, and fee-for-service plans, as well as consumer-directed products such as health savings accounts. The company's SmartSuite and SmartExpress lines let employers offer a menu of coverage options to their employees. Additionally, the firm offers a major medical plan for individuals under the HumanaOne brand.

In 2007 Humana agreed to acquire Atlanta-based CompBenefits, a provider of dental and vision benefits to nearly 5 million members. The acquisition gives Humana a full-service vision offering and expands its dental benefits operations.

## HISTORY

In 1961 Louisville, Kentucky, lawyers David Jones and Wendell Cherry bought a nursing home as a real estate investment. Within six years their company, Extendicare, was the largest nursing home chain in the US (with only eight homes).

Faced with a glutted nursing home market, the partners noticed that hospitals received more money per patient per day than nursing homes, so they took their company public in 1968 to finance hospital purchases (one per month from 1968 to 1971). The company then sold its 40 nursing homes. Sales rose 13 times over in the next five years, and in 1973 the firm changed its name to Humana.

By 1975 Humana had built 27 hospitals in the South and Southwest. It targeted young, privately insured patients and kept its charity caseload and bad-debt expenses low. Three years later #3 for-profit hospital operator Humana moved up a notch when it bought #2 American Medicorp.

In 1983 the government began reimbursing Medicare payments based on fixed rates. Counting on its high hospital occupancy, in 1984 the company launched Humana Health Care Plans, rewarding doctors and patients who used Humana hospitals. However, hospital occupancy dropped, and the company closed several clinics. When its net income fell 75% in 1986, the firm responded by lowering premiums to attract employers.

In 1991 co-founder Cherry died. With hospital profits down, in 1993 Jones spun off Humana's 76 hospitals as Galen Healthcare, which formed the nucleus of what is now HCA — The Healthcare Company. Humana used the cash to expand its HMO membership, buying Group Health Association (an HMO serving metropolitan Washington, DC) and CareNetwork (a Milwaukee HMO). The next year Humana added 1.3 million members when it bought EMPHESYS.

In the mid-1990s cutthroat premiums failed to cover rising health care costs as members' hospital use soared out of control, particularly in the company's new Washington, DC, market. Profits dropped 94%, and Humana's already tense relationship with doctors and members worsened. President and COO Wayne Smith and CFO Roger Drury resigned as part of a management shake-up, and newly appointed president Gregory Wolf offered to drop the company's gag clause after the Florida Physicians Association threatened to sue.

A reorganized Humana rebounded in 1997. The company pulled out of 13 unprofitable markets, including Alabama (though it did not drop TRICARE, its military health coverage program, in that state) and Washington, DC. Refocusing on core markets in the Midwest and Southeast, Wolf replaced Jones as CEO in 1997.

Humana did everything *but* party in 1999. The company faced RICO charges for allegedly overcharging members for co-insurance; it agreed to repay $15 million in Medicare overpayments to the government; and it became the first health insurance firm to be slapped with a class-action suit over its physician incentives and other coverage policies.

In 2001 Humana sold its underperforming Florida Medicaid HMO to Well Care HMO, and agreed to pay more than $14 million to the government for submitting false Medicare payment information. Also in 2001 Humana bought a unit of Anthem (now WellPoint) that provides health benefits to the military.

Expanding its holdings in the southeast, Humana acquired Louisiana's Ochsner Health Plan in 2004.

## EXECUTIVES

**Chairman:** David A. Jones Jr., age 49
**President, CEO, and Director:** Michael B. (Mike) McCallister, age 54, $2,201,479 pay
**COO:** James E. (Jim) Murray, age 52
**SVP, CFO, and Treasurer:** James H. (Jim) Bloem, age 56, $941,722 pay
**SVP and Chief Service and Information Officer:** Bruce J. Goodman, age 65, $941,316 pay
**SVP and Chief Marketing Officer:** Steven O. (Steve) Moya, age 56
**SVP and Chief Human Resources Officer:** Bonita C. (Bonnie) Hathcock, age 57
**SVP and General Counsel:** Arthur P. (Art) Hipwell, age 57
**SVP, Government Programs:** R. Eugene (Gene) Shields, age 58
**SVP, Corporate Communications:** Thomas J. (Tom) Noland Jr.
**SVP, Strategy and Corporate Development; Head Partner, Humana Ventures:** Thomas J. (Tom) Liston, age 44
**SVP, Government Relations:** Heidi S. Margulis, age 52
**SVP, National Contracting; President, ChoiceCare Network:** Bruce Perkins
**SVP, Senior Products:** Douglas R. (Doug) Carlisle
**VP and Controller:** Steven E. McCulley, age 44
**VP, General Counsel, and Secretary:** Walter E. Neely
**VP, Investor Relations:** Regina C. Nethery
**VP Senior Products:** Stefen F. (Steve) Brueckner
**VP, Product Innovation:** Beth Bierbower
**VP and Chief Learning Officer:** Ray Vigil
**Chief Actuary:** Michael W. (Mike) Fedyna
**Auditors:** PricewaterhouseCoopers LLP

## LOCATIONS

**HQ:** Humana Inc.
500 W. Main St., Louisville, KY 40202
**Phone:** 502-580-1000 **Fax:** 502-580-3677
**Web:** www.humana.com

## PRODUCTS/OPERATIONS

### 2006 Sales

| | $ mil. | % of total |
|---|---|---|
| Government | | |
| Premiums | | |
| Medicare Advantage | 8,499.1 | 40 |
| Medicare prescription drug plan | 3,050.3 | 14 |
| TRICARE | 2,543.9 | 12 |
| Medicaid | 520.5 | 3 |
| Administrative services fees | 49.4 | — |
| Investment & other income | 117.9 | 1 |
| Commercial | | |
| Premiums | | |
| PPO | 3,684.4 | 17 |
| HMO | 2,019.9 | 9 |
| Specialty | 411.0 | 2 |
| Administrative services fees | 291.8 | 1 |
| Investment & other income | 228.3 | 1 |
| **Total** | **21,416.5** | **100** |

### 2006 Medical Membership

| | Members (thou.) | % of total |
|---|---|---|
| Government | | |
| Medicare | 4,539.2 | 40 |
| TRICARE | 1,716.4 | 15 |
| TRICARE ASO | 1,163.6 | 10 |
| Medicaid | 569.1 | 5 |
| Commercial | | |
| Fully insured | 1,754.2 | 16 |
| ASO | 1,529.6 | 14 |
| **Total** | **11,272.1** | **100** |

### Selected Products and Services

Government
- Medicaid managed care plans
- Medicare Advantage plans
- Medicare prescription drug plans
- TRICARE (military personnel)

Commercial
- Administrative services only
- Health care spending accounts
- HMO plans
- Humana Classic (traditional indemnity plan)
- HumanaOne (individual insurance)
- POS (point-of-service) plans
- PPO plans
- Specialty products
  - Dental insurance
  - Life insurance
  - Short-term disability insurance

## COMPETITORS

Aetna
Blue Cross
Caremark Pharmacy Services
CIGNA
HCSC
Health Net
Kaiser Foundation Health Plan
Medco Health Solutions
New York Life
Oxford Health
PacifiCare
Prudential
Sierra Health
UnitedHealth Group
WellCare
WellPoint

## HISTORICAL FINANCIALS

Company Type: Public

### Income Statement

FYE: December 31

| | REVENUE ($ mil.) | NET INCOME ($ mil.) | NET PROFIT MARGIN | EMPLOYEES |
|---|---|---|---|---|
| **12/06** | 21,417 | 487 | 2.3% | 22,300 |
| **12/05** | 14,418 | 309 | 2.1% | 18,700 |
| **12/04** | 13,104 | 280 | 2.1% | 13,700 |
| **12/03** | 12,226 | 229 | 1.9% | 13,700 |
| **12/02** | 11,261 | 143 | 1.3% | 13,500 |
| **Annual Growth** | 17.4% | 35.9% | — | 13.4% |

### 2006 Year-End Financials

Debt ratio: 41.6%
Return on equity: 17.6%
Cash ($ mil.): 5,561
Current ratio: 1.41
Long-term debt ($ mil.): 1,269
No. of shares (mil.): 167
Dividends
Yield: —
Payout: —
Market value ($ mil.): 9,217

### Stock History

NYSE: HUM

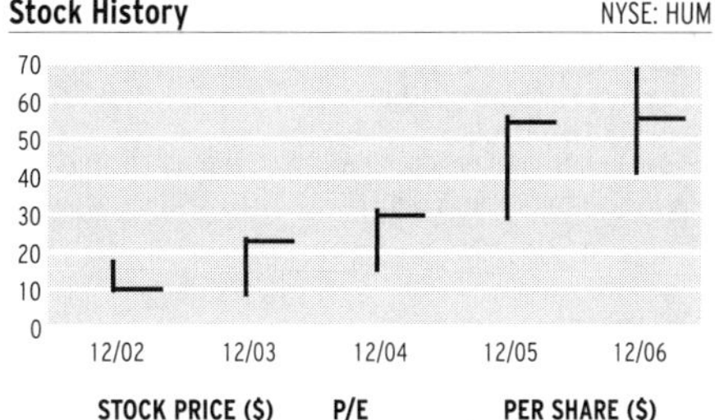


| | STOCK PRICE ($) FY Close | P/E High | P/E Low | PER SHARE ($) Earnings | Dividends | Book Value |
|---|---|---|---|---|---|---|
| **12/06** | 55.31 | 24 | 14 | 2.90 | — | 18.33 |
| **12/05** | 54.33 | 30 | 15 | 1.87 | — | 15.16 |
| **12/04** | 29.69 | 18 | 9 | 1.72 | — | 13.04 |
| **12/03** | 22.85 | 17 | 6 | 1.41 | — | 11.34 |
| **12/02** | 10.00 | 21 | 12 | 0.85 | — | 9.86 |
| **Annual Growth** | 53.4% | — | — | 35.9% | — | 16.8% |

# Huntington Bancshares

Huntington Bancshares is the holding company for The Huntington National Bank, which operates some 700 offices mainly in Ohio and Michigan, but also in Indiana, Kentucky, Pennsylvania, and West Virginia. Huntington Bancshares operates in two other segments besides regional banking: Dealer Sales and Private Financial and Capital Markets. Its Dealer Sales unit finances auto sales and leases through some 3,500 car dealerships throughout the Midwest and other states. Private Financial and Capital Markets provides investment banking and wealth management services to wealthy customers.

Huntington Bancshares acquired Unizan Financial in 2006, two years and one month after initially announcing it.

The next year the company added Pennsylvania to its regional presence with the acquisition of Sky Financial, which has around 300 branches in Ohio and in Indiana, as well as the Keystone State.

## HISTORY

Pelatiah Webster (P. W.) Huntington, descendant of both a Revolutionary War leader and a Declaration of Independence signer, went to work at sea in 1850 at age 14. He returned to go into banking and in 1866 founded what would become Huntington National Bank of Columbus. As the business grew, he conscripted four of his five sons. The bank took a national charter in 1905 and became The Huntington National Bank of Columbus. It survived the hard times of 1907 and 1912 through the Huntington philosophy of sitting on piles of cash. P. W. died in 1918 and his son Francis became president. Francis expanded the company into trust services. Unlike many bankers in the 1920s, he refused to make speculative loans based on the stock market. Francis died in 1928 and was succeeded by brother Theodore. By 1930 Huntington's trust assets accounted for more than half of the total. The family's conservative philosophy helped the bank sail through the 1933 bank holiday, although when it reopened the amount of cash it could pay out was restricted to 10% of deposits.

P. W.'s son Gwynne chaired the bank during its post-WWII expansion. His death in 1958 ended the Huntington family reign. The bank began opening branches and adding new services, such as mortgage and consumer loans. In 1966, in order to expand statewide, the bank formed a holding company, Huntington Bancshares. In the 1960s and 1970s, the corporation added new operations, including mortgage and leasing companies and an international division to help clients with foreign exchange.

In 1979 the company consolidated its 15 affiliates into The Huntington National Bank. Three years later the company bit off more than it could chew with the acquisitions of Reeves Banking and Trust Company of Dover and Union Commerce Corporation of Cleveland. The latter purchase loaded the company with debt. Nevertheless, it continued to expand, particularly after 1985 when banking regulations allowed interstate branch banking, and soon had operations in Florida, Indiana, Kentucky, Michigan, and West Virginia.

Huntington Bancshares was largely insulated from the real estate problems of the late 1980s and early 1990s thanks to its continuing conservative lending policies. But the company was at risk from the nationwide consolidation of the banking industry, which made it a potential takeover target. It increased its service offerings and bolstered its place in the market through acquisitions. In 1996 Huntington Bancshares bought life insurance agency Tice & Associates and began cross-selling bank and insurance products. Important banking acquisitions in 1997 included First Michigan Bank and several Florida companies.

Also in 1997 the company took advantage of deregulation to consolidate its interstate operations (except The Huntington State Bank) into a single operating company. In 1998 Huntington Bancshares continued to build its Huntington insurance services unit with the acquisition of Pollock & Pollock. In 1999 the bank launched a mortgage program aimed at wealthy clients and sold its credit card receivables portfolio to Chase Manhattan (now J.P. Morgan Chase & Co.). In 2000 the company bought Michigan's Empire Banc Corporation and added commercial property/casualty coverage to its product menu with the purchase of J. Rolfe Davis Insurance Agency.

Former BANK ONE executive Thomas Hoaglin was named president and CEO in 2001. Later that year he became chairman when Frank Wobst retired after leading the company for 20 years.

In 2002 the company consolidated some branches in the Midwest to cut costs and exited the retail banking market in Florida, selling some 140 retail branches there to SunTrust.

## EXECUTIVES

**Chairman and CEO, Huntington Bancshares and The Huntington National Bank:** Thomas E. Hoaglin, age 57, $1,114,035 pay
**President, COO, and Director:** Marty E. Adams, age 54
**SEVP and Regional Banking Group President, The Huntington National Bank:** Mary W. Navarro, age 51, $457,339 pay (prior to title change)
**SEVP and Group Manager, Dealer Sales, The Huntington National Bank:** Nicholas G. (Nick) Stanutz, age 52
**EVP, Finance Administration and CFO:** Donald R. Kimble, age 47, $531,502 pay (prior to title change)
**EVP and Chief Credit Officer:** Richard (Dick) Witherow
**EVP and Chief Risk Officer:** James W. (Jim) Nelson, age 47, $561,104 pay
**EVP and Human Resources Director:** Melinda S. Ackerman, age 58
**EVP, Customer Experience, The Huntington National Bank:** Jane Ashley
**EVP, Operations and Technology Services:** Wilton W. Dolloff
**EVP and Chief Auditor:** Eric N. Sutphin
**SVP, Special Assets and Senior Lender:** Michael (Mike) Cross
**Controller:** Thomas P. Reed, age 48
**General Counsel and Secretary; EVP, General Counsel, Secretary, and Cashier, The Huntington National Bank:** Richard A. Cheap, age 55, $489,533 pay
**Auditors:** Deloitte & Touche LLP

## LOCATIONS

**HQ:** Huntington Bancshares Incorporated
Huntington Center, 41 S. High St.,
Columbus, OH 43287
**Phone:** 614-480-8300 **Fax:** 614-480-5284
**Web:** www.huntington.com

### 2006 Branches

| | No. |
|---|---|
| Ohio | 202 |
| Michigan | 112 |
| West Virginia | 26 |
| Indiana | 25 |
| Kentucky | 12 |
| Florida | 4 |
| Cayman Islands | 1 |
| Hong Kong | 1 |
| **Total** | **383** |

## PRODUCTS/OPERATIONS

### 2006 Sales

| | $ mil. | % of total |
|---|---|---|
| Interest | | |
| Loans & direct financing leases | 1,777.6 | 66 |
| Securities | 255.2 | 9 |
| Other | 37.7 | 1 |
| Noninterest | | |
| Service charges on deposit accounts | 185.7 | 7 |
| Trust services | 90.0 | 3 |
| Brokerage & insurance | 58.8 | 2 |
| Other service charges & fees | 51.3 | 2 |
| Bank-owned life insurance income | 43.8 | 2 |
| Mortgage banking | 41.5 | 2 |
| Other | 163.2 | 6 |
| **Total** | **2,704.8** | **100** |

### 2006 Assets

| | $ mil. | % of total |
|---|---|---|
| Cash & equivalents | 1,080.2 | 3 |
| Investment & other securities | 4,839.5 | 14 |
| Loans held for sale | 270.4 | 1 |
| Loans & leases | | |
| Commercial & industrial | 7,849.9 | 22 |
| Commercial real estate | 4,504.5 | 13 |
| Automobile loans | 2,125.8 | 6 |
| Automobile leases | 1,769.4 | 5 |
| Home equity | 4,926.9 | 14 |
| Residential mortgage | 4,548.9 | 13 |
| Other consumer | 427.9 | 1 |
| Other assets | 2,985.6 | 8 |
| **Total** | **35,329.0** | **100** |

### Selected Subsidiaries

Bosgraaf Capital Company, LLC
CB&T Capital Investment Company
First Sunset Development, Inc.
Haberer Registered Investment Advisor, Inc.
Hatco, LLC
HBI Payments Holdings, Inc.
Heritage Service Corporation
The Huntington National Bank
Inner City Partnerships, LLC
LeaseNet Group, LLC
Lodestone Realty Management, Inc.
Mezzanine Opportunities LLC
WS Realty, Inc.

## COMPETITORS

Bank of America
Citigroup
Comerica
Fifth Third
KeyCorp
National City
PNC Financial
Regions Financial
U.S. Bancorp

## HISTORICAL FINANCIALS

Company Type: Public

### Income Statement — FYE: December 31

| | ASSETS ($ mil.) | NET INCOME ($ mil.) | INCOME AS % OF ASSETS | EMPLOYEES |
|---|---|---|---|---|
| **12/06** | 35,329 | 461 | 1.3% | 8,081 |
| **12/05** | 32,765 | 412 | 1.3% | 7,602 |
| **12/04** | 32,566 | 399 | 1.2% | 7,812 |
| **12/03** | 30,484 | 372 | 1.2% | 7,983 |
| **12/02** | 27,432 | 324 | 1.2% | 8,177 |
| **Annual Growth** | 6.5% | 9.3% | — | (0.3%) |

### 2006 Year-End Financials

Equity as % of assets: 8.5%
Return on assets: 1.4%
Return on equity: 16.6%
Long-term debt ($ mil.): 3,556
No. of shares (mil.): 235
Dividends
Yield: 4.2%
Payout: 52.1%
Market value ($ mil.): 5,593
Sales ($ mil.): 2,705

### Stock History — NASDAQ (GS): HBAN

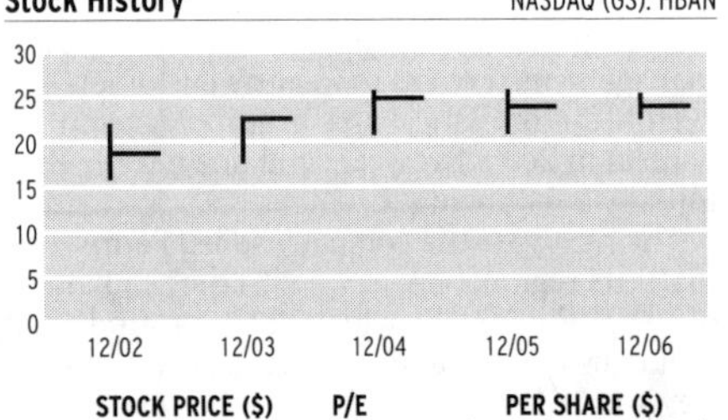


| | STOCK PRICE ($) FY Close | P/E High | P/E Low | PER SHARE ($) Earnings | Dividends | Book Value |
|---|---|---|---|---|---|---|
| **12/06** | 23.75 | 13 | 12 | 1.92 | 1.00 | 12.80 |
| **12/05** | 23.75 | 14 | 12 | 1.77 | 0.43 | 11.45 |
| **12/04** | 24.74 | 15 | 12 | 1.71 | 0.55 | 10.96 |
| **12/03** | 22.50 | 14 | 11 | 1.61 | 0.67 | 9.93 |
| **12/02** | 18.71 | 16 | 12 | 1.33 | 0.64 | 9.40 |
| **Annual Growth** | 6.1% | — | — | 9.6% | 11.8% | 8.0% |

# IAC/InterActiveCorp

IAC/InterActiveCorp (IAC) satisfies shop-aholics who fantasize about taking in a show, meeting the right partner, and financing a home. The Internet conglomerate owns some 65 interactive brands including HSN (formerly Home Shopping Network), which pipes on-air sales reps into some 89 million US homes; US ticket retailer Ticketmaster; and Match.com and LendingTree, the online dating and loan Web sites, respectively. Surrounded by billion-dollar media conglomerates, IAC (then USA Interactive) once coveted a spot with the big shot entertainment companies, but it has since sold out to selling and now is pushing into the market for online content. IAC is controlled by its CEO Barry Diller.

A string of acquisitions has positioned IAC as a big player in e-commerce. Some of the company's more recent purchases include a majority stake in Connected Ventures, LLC, the parent company of racy college entertainment site CollegeHumor.com; Cornerstone Brands, a portfolio of print catalogs and online retailing sites; and Ask.com (formerly Ask Jeeves), the nation's fourth-largest search engine company. IAC also operates the Citysearch Web-based city guides.

In mid-2005 IAC spun off its online travel subsidiary Expedia, which included travel-related businesses, such as Hotels.com and travel-advice site TripAdvisor.com, among others.

The company has also let go of its Home Shopping Europe TV channel, selling it to German firm KarstadtQuelle for some $270 million.

TV mogul Diller is the alchemist at IAC and controls the majority (about 59%) of the company's voting power. Under his reign, the company completed the Vivendi deal, which combined the USA Networks entertainment businesses (Studios USA, Focus, USA Network, and SCI-FI Channel) with Universal Pictures to create a new company called Vivendi UNIVERSAL Entertainment (since renamed Vivendi). In mid-2005 IAC sold its 5.4% stake in VUE to NBC Universal for $3.4 billion in cash and stock, putting an end to a long and contentious relationship between IAC and VUE.

Liberty Interactive Group owns a 26% stake in IAC.

## HISTORY

TV networks aren't built in a day; but if anyone could do it, it's probably Barry Diller. Since dropping out of UCLA in 1958 to work in the mailroom at the William Morris talent agency (he was promoted to agent in 1961), Diller has been all over Tinseltown. He got into television in 1968 as the VP of programming for ABC, where he developed the concepts of the mini-series and the made-for-TV movie. Diller's next step took him into movies as chairman of Paramount Pictures in 1974. His 10-year Paramount stint produced films including *Raiders of the Lost Ark*. But Diller's biggest claim to fame is his tenure at FOX. Beginning in 1984, Diller led the brash television network from joke to jewel. After a scrape with FOX boss Rupert Murdoch in 1992, he moved on to home shopping as head of QVC in 1993.

Diller built a company of his own in 1995 after leaving QVC. With financial backing from TCI (later bought by AT&T Broadband), Diller took over the Home Shopping Network (now HSN) and its separately traded distribution unit, Silver King Communications. Silver King merged with Savoy Pictures and Home Shopping Network in 1996, calling the new company HSN. In 1997 HSN bought Microsoft co-founder Paul Allen's 47% interest in Ticketmaster. Diller followed that up with the $4 billion purchase of USA Networks in 1998.

USA Networks dates back to 1977, when Kay Koplovitz founded the all-sports Madison Square Garden Network cable channel. In 1980, after shifting its focus from sports to syndicated TV shows and feature films, she sold the channel (now USA Network) to Time, MCA, and Paramount. After years of reruns, USA began developing original programming in 1988. By that time Paramount (later bought by Viacom) and MCA (later bought by Seagram and renamed Universal Studios) had become equal owners in USA. After a bitter courtroom struggle in which Universal accused Viacom of running its MTV and Nickelodeon networks in competition with USA, Universal bought out Viacom's interest in 1997.

Diller bought USA Networks (USA Network and the SCI-FI Channel) and Vivendi UNIVERSAL Entertainment's TV production and US distribution business as well. The deal gave Seagram a 45% stake in HSN, which changed its name to USA Networks. USA Networks bought the remainder of Ticketmaster in 1998, then purchased online entertainment guide publisher Citysearch, merging it with Ticketmaster Online into a new company called Ticketmaster Online-Citysearch. USA Networks then spun off the new company to the public, retaining a 60% interest (later reduced to about 50%).

In 1999 Diller bought parts of PolyGram Filmed Entertainment and independent film companies Gramercy and October from Seagram, renaming them Focus. French utility and media firm Vivendi (now Vivendi UNIVERSAL) bought Seagram in 2000, gaining Seagram's 43% stake in USA Networks.

In 2001 Ticketmaster Online bought its former parent Ticketmaster Corporation. USA Networks retained 68% of the combined company. USA Networks also agreed to sell its TV stations to Univision for $1.1 billion.

At the end of 2001, Diller decided to shift USA Interactive's focus entirely to retailing. He agreed to sell USA Networks' entertainment assets to Vivendi UNIVERSAL for $10.3 billion. The deal was completed in May 2002 and the company changed its name to USA Interactive with Diller retaining his voting control of the firm.

In 2003 USA Interactive bought the remaining 33% stake in Ticketmaster that it didn't already own. In November 2003 IAC acquired discount travel Web site hotwire.com. In 2004, in a move to round out its travel-related entities, IAC acquired TripAdvisor; over the course of the year, IAC also purchased a total of 52% of Beijing-based travel site eLong. Also that year the company changed its name to IAC/InterActiveCorp.

In March 2005 IAC launched gifts.com, a gift-shopping Web site. In April the company completed the acquisition of Cornerstone Brands, a portfolio of leading print catalogs and online retailing sites for $720 million. On August 9, IAC completed the spin-off to IAC shareholders of its travel businesses, which included its Expedia subsidiary, as well as Hotels.com, Hotwire, and TripAdvisor.

In 2006 IAC purchased a 51% stake in Connected Ventures, LLC, the parent company of CollegeHumor.com.

## EXECUTIVES

**Chairman and CEO:** Barry Diller, age 65, $2,250,000 pay
**Vice Chairman:** Victor A. Kaufman, age 63, $2,250,000 pay
**President and COO:** Douglas R. (Doug) Lebda, age 37, $2,050,000 pay
**EVP and CFO:** Thomas J. (Tom) McInerney, age 38, $2,150,000 pay
**EVP, General Counsel, and Secretary:** Gregory R. (Greg) Blatt, age 35, $1,550,000 pay
**SVP, Strategy and Mergers & Acquisitions:** Shana Fisher, age 33
**SVP and Chief Communications Officer:** Jonathan L. Sanchez
**SVP and Controller:** Michael H. Schwerdtman
**VP, Corporate Communications:** Deborah Roth
**VP, Partner Marketing:** Andrew Zucker
**VP, Investor Relations:** Roger Clark
**Chairman, Ticketmaster:** Terry R. Barnes
**President, Citysearch:** Jay Herratti
**President, Programming:** Michael Jackson, age 43
**CEO, Pronto:** Daniel C. (Dan) Marriott, age 35
**CEO, Ask.com:** James (Jim) Lanzone
**CEO, Entertainment Publications:** MaryAnn D. Rivers, age 39
**CEO, Precision Response Corp. (PRC):** John G. Hall
**CEO, Citysearch:** Briggs Ferguson
**CEO, IAC Advertising Solutions:** Paul Gardi, age 38
**CEO, Match.com:** Jim Safka
**CEO, IAC Local Services and Media Services:** Anne M. Busquet, age 53
**CEO, Retailing:** Mindy F. Grossman, age 49
**Chief Administrative Officer:** Jason Stewart
**Auditors:** Ernst & Young LLP

## LOCATIONS

**HQ:** IAC/InterActiveCorp
152 W. 57th St., New York, NY 10019
**Phone:** 212-314-7300
**Web:** www.iac.com

## PRODUCTS/OPERATIONS

### 2006 Sales

| | $ mil. | % of total |
|---|---|---|
| Retailing | 3,291.6 | 52 |
| Services | 1,634.7 | 26 |
| Membership & subscriptions | 805.5 | 13 |
| Media & advertising | 544.2 | 9 |
| Emerging businesses | 7.5 | — |
| Adjustment | (5.9) | — |
| **Total** | **6,277.6** | **100** |

### Selected Operations

Electronic Retailing
- America's Store
- Cornerstone Brands
- HSN U.S.
- HSN.com
- Shoebuy.com

Financial Services and Real Estate
- Lending Tree
- RealEstate.com

Local Services
- Ask.com
- Citysearch
- Evite
- ServiceMagic

Personals
- Chemistry.com
- Match.com
- uDate

Ticketing
- Ticketmaster

## COMPETITORS

Access TV
Amazon.com
AOL
Countrywide Financial
Cox Enterprises
craigslist
ditech.com
eBay
eHarmony.com
E-LOAN
Friendster
Google
MSN
QVC
Shopping.com
Tickets.com
Tickle
ValueVision Media
Yahoo!

## HISTORICAL FINANCIALS

Company Type: Public

### Income Statement

FYE: December 31

| | REVENUE ($ mil.) | NET INCOME ($ mil.) | NET PROFIT MARGIN | EMPLOYEES |
|---|---|---|---|---|
| **12/06** | 6,278 | 193 | 3.1% | 20,000 |
| **12/05** | 5,754 | 876 | 15.2% | 28,000 |
| **12/04** | 4,188 | 165 | 3.9% | 26,000 |
| **12/03** | 6,328 | 167 | 2.6% | 25,700 |
| **12/02** | 4,621 | 1,953 | 42.3% | 23,200 |
| **Annual Growth** | 8.0% | (44.0%) | — | (3.6%) |

### 2006 Year-End Financials

Debt ratio: 9.8%
Return on equity: 2.1%
Cash ($ mil.): 2,354
Current ratio: 1.69
Long-term debt ($ mil.): 857
No. of shares (mil.): 267
Dividends
Yield: —
Payout: —
Market value ($ mil.): 9,930

### Stock History

NASDAQ (GS): IACI

| | STOCK PRICE ($) FY Close | P/E High | P/E Low | PER SHARE ($) Earnings | Dividends | Book Value |
|---|---|---|---|---|---|---|
| **12/06** | 37.16 | 64 | 39 | 0.60 | — | 32.81 |
| **12/05** | 28.31 | 12 | 10 | 2.46 | — | 31.59 |
| **12/04** | 30.35 | 94 | 51 | 0.41 | — | 46.14 |
| **12/03** | 37.28 | 205 | 99 | 0.23 | — | 22.80 |
| **12/02** | 25.18 | 8 | 4 | 4.54 | — | 20.56 |
| **Annual Growth** | 10.2% | — | — | (39.7%) | — | 12.4% |

# IDT Corporation

IDT keeps a corporate finger in several pies. The company makes most of its money through IDT Telecom, which provides retail and wholesale phone services. In 2006 the company acquired the remaining shares of Net2Phone. The formerly publicly traded company has become a privately held subsidiary of IDT. Net2Phone, which is a leading provider of global hosted VoIP services for service providers, is a success story in IDT's telecom industry investment strategy. Net2Phone is being integrated into IDT's Telecom division. Founder and chairman Howard Jonas controls IDT with 40% ownership.

Also in 2006 the company sold its IDT Entertainment unit, now known as Starz Media, to Liberty Media. In the deal, IDT received all of Liberty Media's shareholdings in IDT, including a 5% stake in IDT Telecom, plus $186 million in cash and some assumed debt. The company has cashed in on a unit that it has built through multiple acquisitions over the past several years. IDT Entertainment has been the company's second-largest unit. It included animation and live-action production studios and operates a home entertainment distribution business.

Earlier in 2006, IDT had increased its equity stake in Net2Phone from around 40% to nearly 83% through a tender offer before buying the rest. In fact, IDT could stand for Invest in Distressed Telecom companies. It has pieced together remnants of struggling competitive carriers Teligent, ICG Communications, and long-distance firm STAR Telecommunications. It once offered to buy parts of WorldCom (MCI).

But IDT's investments have provided mixed results. It hoped to repeat the success of Net2Phone with the spinoff of IDT Spectrum (the reorganized IDT Solutions division made up of assets acquired from the bankrupt Winstar), but it discontinued IDT Spectrum in 2006. The company has also written off or sold its stakes in money-losing firms Teligent and ICG.

The company's IDT Telecom unit provides retail domestic and international long-distance access in the US as well as wholesale voice and data services. It has been a leader in the fast-growing calling card industry and has acquired the Global One prepaid phone card business from France Telecom and Belgacom's prepaid phone card business, Expercom.

IDT entered the teleservices business by acquiring two call center firms, Provo, Utah-based Marketing Ally, and Contact America, based in La Jolla, California.

IDT pioneered international callback technology, sometimes known as call re-origination, which allows international phone callers to bypass overseas carriers (and their high rates) by rerouting calls through less expensive US exchanges. These days, to connect callers around the globe, IDT operates a network that includes switches in Europe and the US. The company leases additional capacity from other carriers, including 14 undersea fiber-optic cables that connect to the facilities of IDT's partners in Asia, Europe, and Latin America.

## HISTORY

Howard Jonas started a trade publishing business in 1978; when he ran up an $8,000 phone bill establishing a sales office in Israel, the 33-year-old entrepreneur bought $300 worth of components and rigged up a callback device. That feat of ingenuity led Jonas to start International Discount Telecommunications (IDT) in 1990. The next year the company began selling its international call reorigination services, which took advantage of cheaper US rates. By 1993 it had more than 1,000 customers in some 60 countries and had begun reselling long-distance services to its US customers.

In 1994 IDT added Internet access to its service portfolio. Jonas renamed the company IDT Corporation in 1995. That year IDT took advantage of the volume of callers that used its callback services and began reselling to other long-distance carriers. The company went public the next year and also acquired the Genie online service. Continuing to experiment with telephony services, IDT formed Net2Phone in 1997 to provide long-distance phone service over the Internet.

IDT dropped its rates in 1998, offering long-distance rates of 5 cents per minute in some markets. It introduced Net2Fax, which routes faxes over the Internet, and Click2Talk, which connects Web-surfing customers directly to live customer service representatives. Also in 1998 it acquired InterExchange, a debit card company that complemented IDT's calling card services.

The next year IDT spun off Net2Phone then sold a stake in the former subsidiary to AT&T. It formed a joint venture with Spain's Terra Networks (spun off from Telefónica) to provide Internet products and services to the US Hispanic population. Also in 1999 Chattle, IDT's wholly owned subsidiary, joined with Westmintech to provide high-speed voice and data services, cable TV, and Internet access worldwide.

In 2000 IDT reorganized into two divisions: IDT Telecom, with its international retail and wholesale telecom services, and IDT Ventures and Investments, to pursue other opportunities, including branded wireless services using the Sprint PCS network. That year Liberty Media bought a stake in IDT. In addition, the company raised $1.1 billion by selling most of its remaining stake in Net2Phone to AT&T.

When its joint venture with Terra Networks crumbled in 2001, IDT launched a lawsuit. That year the company bought the debit card business of PT-1 Communications (part of STAR Telecommunications) and invested $1.2 million in STAR. Still flush with cash, IDT traded some of its own stock to Liberty Media for stakes in struggling competitive local-exchange carriers ICG and Teligent. It regained control of its Net2Phone spinoff that year when it took the lead in a consortium with AT&T and Liberty Media that holds a 49% stake in Net2Phone and controls about 64% of the voting power (AT&T later sold its stake to the other two).

In 2003 IDT was outbid in a plan to offer $255 million to acquire fiber-optic network operator Global Crossing. It also entered discussions over acquiring ITXC after dropping a hostile stock offer valued at about $60 million. ITXC, however, rejected the buyout offer (ITXC has since been acquired by Teleglobe).

The company in 2006 sold operating subsidiaries Winstar Communications, Winstar Government Solutions, and Winstar Wireless, entities that provide telecom services under US government contracts, to Detroit-based GVC Networks.

## EXECUTIVES

**Chairman:** Howard S. Jonas, age 49
**Vice Chairman and CEO:** James A. (Jim) Courter, age 64, $1,549,247 pay
**President:** Ira A. Greenstein, age 46, $1,069,375 pay
**CFO and Treasurer:** Stephen R. Brown, age 49
**EVP and COO; Chairman, IDT Telecom, Inc.:** Morris Lichtenstein, age 41, $3,916,765 pay (prior to promotion)
**EVP, Business Development:** Morris Berger, age 47
**EVP, Business Development; CEO and Treasurer, IDT Telecom, Inc.:** Yona Katz, age 35, $1,446,250 pay
**EVP, Strategic Planning, and Director:** Moshe Kaganoff, age 34
**EVP, Technology; COO, IDT Telecom:** Kathleen B. Timko, age 45
**EVP, General Counsel, and Secretary:** Joyce J. Mason, age 46
**EVP and Director:** Marc E. Knoller, age 44
**Chairman, IDT Telecom:** Mikhail Leibov
**CEO, IDT Spectrum, Inc.:** John C. Petrillo, age 57
**President, Engineering and Operations, IDT Spectrum, Inc.:** Peter B. Atwal, age 49
**Chief Accounting Officer and Controller:** Mitch Silberman, age 38
**Chief Tax Officer:** Douglas (Doug) Mauro, age 63
**Chief Legal Officer:** Eli D. Tendler, age 37
**Auditors:** Ernst & Young LLP

## LOCATIONS

**HQ:** IDT Corporation
520 Broad St., Newark, NJ 07102
**Phone:** 973-438-1000 **Fax:** 973-482-3971
**Web:** www.idt.net

## PRODUCTS/OPERATIONS

### 2006 Sales

| | $ mil. | % of total |
|---|---|---|
| IDT Telecom | | |
| Retail | 1,434.0 | 64 |
| Wholesale | 526.5 | 24 |
| IDT Capital | 168.1 | 8 |
| Voice over IP (Net2Phone) | 94.2 | 4 |
| IDT Solutions | 3.6 | — |
| **Total** | **2,226.4** | **100** |

### Selected Subsidiaries and Affiliates

IDT Capital, Inc. (formerly IDT Media, Inc., 94%, media-related holdings)
  IDT Carmel, Inc. (management of aged receivables)
  IDT Energy, Inc. (resale of natural gas and electricity)
  IDT Global Services, Inc. (call center operations)
  IDT Local Media
    CTM Brochure Display, Inc.
    WMET 1160 AM (talk radio station)
IDT Solutions
  IDT Spectrum, Inc. (commercial fixed wireless spectrum licenses holding company)
  Winstar Holdings, LLC (private line services)
IDT Telecom, Inc. (retail and wholesale telecommunications services holdings)
  IDT America, Corp. (IDT America Unlimited, consumer phone services)
  Tuyo Mobile, LLC (TúYo Mobile, virtual mobile network operatos (MVNO))
  Union Telecard Alliance, LLC (51%, prepaid calling card distribution)
    Ethnic Grocery Brands (90%, ethnic food products, primarily the Vitarroz brand)
Net2Phone, Inc. (voice over Internet Protocol (VoIP) services)

## COMPETITORS

Arbinet
AT&T
Con Edison
France Telecom
Goya
KeySpan
National Fuel Gas
National Grid
Orange & Rockland Utilities
Qwest
Rapid Link
Rochester Gas and Electric
Sprint Nextel
Telefónica
TracFone
Verizon

## HISTORICAL FINANCIALS

Company Type: Public

### Income Statement

FYE: July 31

| | REVENUE ($ mil.) | NET INCOME ($ mil.) | NET PROFIT MARGIN | EMPLOYEES |
|---|---|---|---|---|
| **7/06** | 2,226 | (179) | — | 3,000 |
| **7/05** | 2,469 | (44) | — | 5,951 |
| **7/04** | 2,217 | (96) | — | 4,434 |
| **7/03** | 1,835 | (18) | — | 3,805 |
| **7/02** | 1,584 | (303) | — | 2,533 |
| **Annual Growth** | 8.9% | — | — | 4.3% |

**2006 Year-End Financials**

Debt ratio: 15.2%
Return on equity: —
Cash ($ mil.): 515
Current ratio: 1.83
Long-term debt ($ mil.): 122

No. of shares (mil.): 71
Dividends
Yield: —
Payout: —
Market value ($ mil.): 955

**Stock History** NYSE: IDT

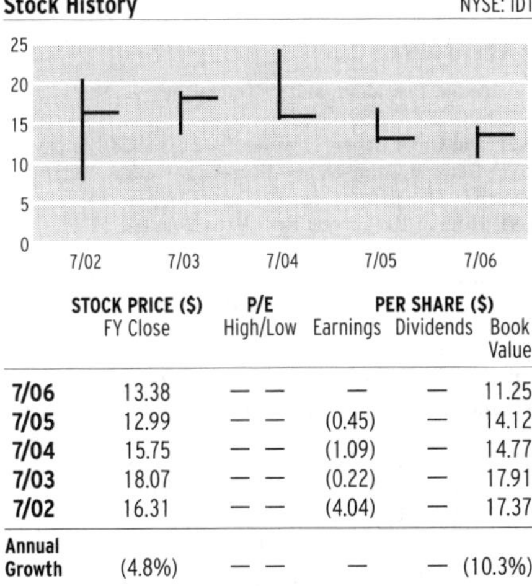

| | STOCK PRICE ($) FY Close | P/E High/Low | PER SHARE ($) Earnings | Dividends | Book Value |
|---|---|---|---|---|---|
| **7/06** | 13.38 | — — | — | — | 11.25 |
| **7/05** | 12.99 | — — | (0.45) | — | 14.12 |
| **7/04** | 15.75 | — — | (1.09) | — | 14.77 |
| **7/03** | 18.07 | — — | (0.22) | — | 17.91 |
| **7/02** | 16.31 | — — | (4.04) | — | 17.37 |
| **Annual Growth** | (4.8%) | — — | — | — | (10.3%) |

# IGA, Inc.

IGA grocers are independent, but not that independent. The world's largest voluntary supermarket network, IGA has more than 4,000 stores, including members in 48 US states and more than 40 other countries, including China. Collectively, its members are among North America's leaders in terms of supermarket sales. IGA (for either International or Independent Grocers Alliance, the company says) is owned by about 50 worldwide distribution companies, including SUPERVALU. Members can sell IGA Brand private-label products (some 2,300 items) and take advantage of joint operations and services, such as advertising and volume buying. Some stores in the IGA alliance, which primarily caters to smaller towns, also sell gas.

The first US grocer in China and Singapore, the company hopes to have 500 IGA-affiliated stores in China by the end of 2006 and double that number by year end 2007. IGA is also present in Europe with operations in Poland and Spain. Its international operations, including Canada, account for nearly 70% of its total sales.

In 2006 the company reorganized by splitting itself into three companies: IGA USA, IGA International, and the IGA Coca-Cola Institute. All three operate under IGA Inc. As a result of the reorganization, Thomas Haggai became chairman and CEO of IGA International and Mark Batenic — formerly of Clemens Markets — joined the company as chairman, president, and CEO of IGA USA. (Previously, IGA realigned its corporate structure in 2001.)

By separating IGA's 1,152 domestic stores from its 2,890 stores overseas the company hopes to improve communications among IGA's US retailers.

One of Batenic's first moves was to establish a presence for IGA in San Francisco with the acquisition of eight supermarkets there from Ralphs Grocery. The stores are slated to reopen as IGA supermarkets by March 2007.

IGA claims that it doesn't try to fight large chains such as Wal-Mart and Publix, instead preferring to keep the focus on its own niche of hometown and family-owned grocery stores.

## HISTORY

IGA was founded in Chicago in 1926 by a group led by accountant Frank Grimes. During the 1920s chains began to dominate the grocery store industry. Grimes, an accountant for many grocery wholesalers, saw an opportunity to develop a network of independent grocers that could compete with the burgeoning chains. Grimes and five associates — Gene Flack, Louis Groebe, W. K. Hunter, H. V. Swenson, and William Thompson — created IGA.

Their idea was to "level the playing field" for independent grocers and chain stores by taking advantage of volume buying and mass marketing. IGA originally acted as a purchasing agent for its wholesalers but eventually passed that duty to the wholesalers. The group's first members were Poughkeepsie, New York-based grocery distributor W. T. Reynolds Company and the 69 grocery stores it serviced.

IGA focused on adding distributors and retailers, and it soon added wholesaler Fleming-Wilson (now Fleming Companies) and Winston & Newell (now SUPERVALU). In 1930 it hired Babe Ruth as a spokesman; other celebrity endorsers during the period included Jackie Cooper, Jack Dempsey, and Popeye. IGA also sponsored a radio program called the IGA Home Town Hour.

In 1945 the company introduced the Foodliner format, a design for stores larger than 4,000 sq. ft. The next year IGA introduced the 30-ft.-by-100-ft. Precision Store — designed so customers had to pass all the other merchandise in the store to get to the dairy and bread sections.

Grimes retired as president in 1951. He was succeeded by his son, Don, who continued to expand the company. Don was succeeded in 1968 by Richard Jones, head of IGA member J. M. Jones Co.

Thomas Haggai was named chairman of the company in 1976. A Baptist minister, radio commentator, and former CIA employee, Haggai had come to the attention of Grimes in 1960 when he praised Christian Scientists in one of his radio broadcasts. Grimes, a Christian Scientist, asked Haggai to speak at an IGA convention and eventually asked him to join the IGA board. Haggai, who became CEO in 1986, tightened the restrictions for IGA members, weeding out many of the smaller, low-volume mom-and-pop stores making up much of the group's network.

Haggai also began a push for international expansion. In 1988 the organization signed a deal with Japanese food company C. Itoh (now ITOCHU) to open a distribution outlet in Tokyo.

The 1990s saw expansion into Australia, Papua New Guinea, the Caribbean, China, Singapore, South Africa, and Brazil. IGA also expanded outside the continental US when it entered Hawaii. In 1993 IGA began an international television advertising campaign, a first for the supermarket industry. The next year the company launched its first line of private-label products for an ethnic food market, introducing several Mexican food products. In 1998 the group developed a new format for its stores that included on-site gas pumps.

SUPERVALU signed 54 independent grocery stores (primarily in Mississippi and Arkansas, and Trinidad in the Caribbean) to the IGA banner in August 1999.

With more than 60% of sales coming from international operations, IGA realigned its corporate structure in 2001, setting up IGA North America, IGA Southern Hemisphere/Europe/Caribbean, and IGA Asia, each with its own president.

IGA suffered the loss of Fleming (one of the grocery chain's principal wholesale distributors) and 300 stores in 2003. On the plus side, four Julian's Supermarkets on the Caribbean island of St. Lucia converted to IGA, giving IGA a presence in 45 countries worldwide.

## EXECUTIVES

**Chairman and CEO:** Thomas S. Haggai
**National Accounts Manager:** Jim Collins
**EVP, IGA International, and President, IGA Institute:** Paulo Goelzer
**Chairman, President, and CEO, IGA USA:** Mark K. Batenic
**VP, Administration, Events, and Communication:** Barbara G. Wiest
**VP, Information Technology:** Nick Liakopulos
**VP, U.S. Chief Growth Officer:** Doug Fritsch
**Senior Director, Branding and Business Development:** James J. (Jim) Walz
**Director, Packaging:** Tim Considine
**Area Director:** Bill Overman
**Area Director:** Ricky St. John
**Area Director:** Jim Griffin
**Area Director:** Shane Maue
**Manager, Events Marketing:** Zorona Chapman
**Controller:** John Collins
**Editor, Grocergram Magazine:** Flontina Miller
**Editor-at-Large, Grocergram Magazine and Director, Red Oval Partner Relations:** Pat Sylvester
**Public Relations Contact:** Ashley M. Page

## LOCATIONS

**HQ:** IGA, Inc.
8725 W. Higgins Rd., Chicago, IL 60631
**Phone:** 773-693-4520 **Fax:** 773-693-4532
**Web:** www.igainc.com

IGA has operations in 48 US states and about 45 countries, including Anguilla, Antigua, Aruba, Australia, Barbados, Barbuda, Botswana, Brazil, Cambodia, Canada, Cayman Islands, China, the Czech Republic, Dominica, Dominican Republic, Grenada, Indonesia, Jamaica, Japan, Kenya, Lesotho, Malaysia, Malawi, Mauritius, Mozambique, Namibia, Papua New Guinea, the Philippines, Poland, St. Kitts, Singapore, South Africa, South Korea, Spain, Swaziland, Thailand, Trinidad, Tobago, Turks & Caicos, Vietnam, Zambia, and Zimbabwe. IGA is supported by 52 distribution companies and more than 55 major manufacturers.

## PRODUCTS/OPERATIONS

**Selected Joint Operations and Services**

Advertising
Community service programs
Equipment purchase
IGA Brand (private-label products)
IGA Grocergram (in-house magazine)
Internet services
Marketing
Merchandising
Red Oval Family (manufacturer/IGA collaboration on sales, marketing, and other activities)
Volume buying

## COMPETITORS

A&P
Albertsons
Associated Wholesale Grocers
BJ's Wholesale Club
C&S Wholesale
Carrefour
Casino Guichard
Coles Group
Daiei
Dairy Farm International
Delhaize
George Weston
Hannaford Bros.
H-E-B
Ito-Yokado
Kroger
Meijer
Penn Traffic
Publix
Roundy's Supermarkets
Royal Ahold
Safeway
Spartan Stores
Wakefern Food
Wal-Mart
Winn-Dixie

## HISTORICAL FINANCIALS

Company Type: Holding company

**Income Statement** FYE: December 31

| | ESTIMATED REVENUE ($ mil.) | NET INCOME ($ mil.) | NET PROFIT MARGIN | EMPLOYEES |
|---|---|---|---|---|
| 12/07 | 21,000 | — | — | — |

# IKON Office Solutions

This company works to ensure that when it comes to buying business equipment, its customers say, "I can and I will." IKON Office Solutions sells and leases Canon, Hewlett-Packard, Ricoh, and other brands of copiers, printers, fax machines, and additional office equipment. It also provides an assortment of related office supplies, such as ink and toner cartridges, labels, paper, document management software, and mailroom supplies. In addition, the company offers such services as document management outsourcing, electronic file conversions, facilities management, and training.

IKON serves primarily large and small businesses and government entities throughout North America and Western Europe. To grow, IKON is focusing on the mid-market and growing its national accounts program, which includes *FORTUNE* 500 and other large companies.

IKON has been focused on streamlining its business and increasing operating efficiencies. During 2005 it sold its business document printing unit as well as operations serving Mexico and France. It has also expanded the number of products and services that it offers, placing an emphasis on high-end products with greater margins. The company continues to push into high-end printers, forging alliances with leading hardware makers such as Hewlett-Packard. IKON has rapidly shifted away from analog products; digital devices account for almost all of its product sales. More than 80% of sales are generated in the US.

## HISTORY

Tinkham Veale, a mechanical engineer from Cleveland, married the daughter of A. C. Ernst of the Ernst & Ernst accounting firm in 1941. Ernst helped Veale buy a stake in an engineered goods manufacturer, which prospered during WWII. Veale retired at age 37 to breed and race horses. He invested his earnings, became a millionaire by 1951, and joined the board of Alco Oil and Chemical (formerly Rainbow Production Company). In 1960 Veale and his associates formed a holding company, V & V Associates, and bought a large minority share in Alco.

Alco (renamed Alco Chemical in 1962) acquired four fertilizer companies and in 1965 (renamed Alco Standard) merged with V & V, which had bought stakes in several machinery producers. Veale then implemented the partnership strategy that would serve the company for 25 years: He bought small, privately owned businesses, usually with cash and Alco Standard stock, and let the owners continue to run them. By 1968 Alco Standard had bought 52 companies in this way and had branched into electrical, metallurgical, and distribution businesses.

Alco Standard expanded into coal mining in the 1970s. The company also bought several paper distributors and formed a national paper distributor called Unisource. The division's profitability prompted Alco Standard to enter other distribution businesses, including pharmaceuticals, steel products, auto parts, food service equipment, and liquor. By 1981 distribution provided 75% of sales.

Veale had also acquired several manufacturers (plastics, machinery, rubber, and chemicals), but they had not grown as rapidly as the distribution units. In 1984 he merged the manufacturers into Alco Industries and sold the new company to its managers; he kept a minority stake. Ray Mundt (who succeeded Veale as chairman) switched Alco Standard's focus in 1986 to office products and paper distribution, cutting seven divisions, including health services and ice cream.

John Stuart succeeded Mundt as CEO in 1993 (and as chairman in 1995) and oversaw a restructuring. Although a 1992 joint venture with Europe-based IMM Office Systems (IMMOS) didn't work out, the dissolution agreement gave Alco two IMMOS subsidiaries: Denmark's Eskofot and France-based STR.

Alco's largest purchase in 1995 was UK-based copier distribution and service company Southern Business Group PLC — renamed A:Copy (UK) PLC. Alco bought 97 businesses in fiscal 1996. The following year it spun off Unisource, which had by then acquired 100 local sales and service operations. After the spinoff Alco Standard changed its name to IKON Office Solutions. It continued a searing rate of acquisitions, including a total of 123 companies for fiscal 1997 and 1998.

Trouble integrating all of its purchases into a united company pushed IKON off its axis, and profits dropped for fiscal 1997. In 1998 EVP James Forese replaced Stuart as president and CEO. Forese, an IBM veteran of 36 years, cut IKON's workforce by 1,500 positions to reduce expenses that year. Charges from this and other restructuring moves caused a loss for 1998. The next year the company's sales force shrank by about 20% thanks to layoffs and attrition. About 1,500 more job cuts — 5% of the workforce — were announced in 2000.

In early 2001 IKON said it would sell and support e-business software from leading vendors through its Sysinct e-business consulting unit (sold in 2004). The next year Forese announced that he would step down as CEO in September 2002 and as chairman in February of the following year; IKON tapped Matthew Espe, former head of GE Lighting, as its new president and CEO. The company in 2004 sold its IOS Capital leasing subsidiary to GE Commercial Finance that year. The following year it shuttered certain subsidiaries in Mexico and France, and sold its coffee vending business, Kafevend Group PLC, in the UK.

## EXECUTIVES

**Chairman, President, and CEO:** Matthew J. (Matt) Espe, age 48, $1,683,450 pay
**SVP and CFO:** Robert F. Woods, age 51, $958,125 pay
**SVP, General Counsel, and Secretary:** Mark A. Hershey, age 37
**SVP Human Resources:** Beth B. Sexton, age 51
**SVP North American Sales and Services:** Brian D. Edwards, age 43, $717,950 pay
**SVP Operations:** Jeffrey W. Hickling, age 51, $636,100 pay
**VP and CIO:** Tracey Rothenberger
**VP and Controller:** Theodore E. (Ted) Strand, age 62
**VP and Treasurer:** Richard (Dick) Obetz
**VP Enterprise Solutions and Strategy:** Dan Murphy
**VP IKON Europe:** David D. Mills, age 48, $678,110 pay
**VP and General Manager, Western Region:** Mark Bottini
**President, IKON UK:** Phil Keoghan
**Director of Marketing Communications:** Wendy Pinckney
**Auditors:** PricewaterhouseCoopers LLP

## LOCATIONS

**HQ:** IKON Office Solutions, Inc.
70 Valley Stream Pkwy., Malvern, PA 19355
**Phone:** 610-296-8000 **Fax:** 610-408-7025
**Web:** www.ikon.com

IKON Office Solutions has operations in Canada, the US, and Western Europe.

**2006 Sales**

| | $ mil. | % of total |
|---|---|---|
| US | 3,516.7 | 83 |
| UK | 350.4 | 8 |
| Canada | 207.7 | 5 |
| Other countries | 153.5 | 4 |
| **Total** | **4,228.3** | **100** |

## PRODUCTS/OPERATIONS

**2006 Sales**

| | $ mil. | % of total |
|---|---|---|
| Equipment | 1,790.2 | 42 |
| Customer service & supplies | 1,445.6 | 34 |
| Managed & professional services | 741.0 | 18 |
| Rental & fees | 151.2 | 4 |
| Other | 100.3 | 2 |
| **Total** | **4,228.3** | **100** |

**Selected Operations**

Services
- Digital conversion
- Facilities management
- Financing
- Legal document services

Products
- Copiers (color, monochrome)
- Fax machines
- Printers (color, large-format, monochrome)
- Raster image processors
- Workflow management systems

## COMPETITORS

Canon
Corporate Express
Danka
Distribution Management
Epson
Global Imaging Systems
Hewlett-Packard
Ingram Micro
Kinko's
Konica Minolta
Lexmark
Océ
Office Depot
Pitney Bowes
Ricoh
Sharp
Tech Data
Xerox

## HISTORICAL FINANCIALS

Company Type: Public

**Income Statement** FYE: September 30

| | REVENUE ($ mil.) | NET INCOME ($ mil.) | NET PROFIT MARGIN | EMPLOYEES |
|---|---|---|---|---|
| **9/06** | 4,228 | 106 | 2.5% | 25,000 |
| **9/05** | 4,377 | 61 | 1.4% | 26,000 |
| **9/04** | 4,614 | 84 | 1.8% | 29,400 |
| **9/03** | 4,711 | 116 | 2.5% | 30,250 |
| **9/02** | 4,828 | 150 | 3.1% | 33,200 |
| **Annual Growth** | (3.3%) | (8.3%) | — | (6.8%) |

**2006 Year-End Financials**

Debt ratio: 39.0%
Return on equity: 6.5%
Cash ($ mil.): 414
Current ratio: 1.82
Long-term debt ($ mil.): 658
No. of shares (mil.): 129
Dividends
Yield: 1.2%
Payout: 19.8%
Market value ($ mil.): 1,733

**Stock History** NYSE: IKN

| | STOCK PRICE ($) FY Close | P/E High | P/E Low | PER SHARE ($) Earnings | Dividends | Book Value |
|---|---|---|---|---|---|---|
| **9/06** | 13.44 | 18 | 12 | 0.81 | 0.16 | 13.08 |
| **9/05** | 9.98 | 28 | 20 | 0.43 | 0.16 | 11.57 |
| **9/04** | 12.02 | 24 | 13 | 0.55 | 0.16 | 11.87 |
| **9/03** | 7.31 | 13 | 9 | 0.75 | 0.16 | 11.17 |
| **9/02** | 7.88 | 14 | 7 | 0.99 | 0.16 | 10.66 |
| **Annual Growth** | 14.3% | — | — | (4.9%) | 0.0% | 5.2% |

# Illinois Tool Works

Don't let the name fool you — Illinois Tool Works (ITW) hammers out a lot more than just tools, and it operates well beyond the Land of Lincoln, all around the globe. With some 750 separate companies in about 50 nations, ITW makes a range of products used in the automotive, construction, electronics, food and beverage, paper products, and pharmaceuticals industries. The company's engineered products segment offers fasteners, nail guns, industrial adhesives, and automotive transmission components. The specialty systems unit's products include paint application equipment and welding machines.

Although ITW focuses on buying small, often niche, companies and then making them more efficient, it has sold its consumer products holdings (appliances and cookware, exercise equipment, and ceramic tile). The always acquisitive company set a corporate record for itself in 2006, buying more than 50 companies at a cost of around $1.7 billion.

With its arsenal of diversified operating units, ITW's performance is often viewed as a yardstick with which to measure the health of the overall economy. The prognosis is encouraging. Slowing demand across the industries that ITW serves had caused the company to trim jobs at some of its businesses in the early 21st century. The company also sold its fitness equipment business and other consumer products holdings, many of which it had gained through the acquisition of Premark International, to cut operating costs and to relieve debt. Freed from businesses subject to fickle consumer buying, ITW has sought to acquire industrial and technology ventures that are more complementary to its corporate portfolio. After the company reduced its workforce by about 14% over three years, employment at the corporation is on the rise again.

Among the company's subsidiaries and brands are: Hobart (commercial kitchen appliances), Binks (spray guns), Simco (industrial static control products), Chemtronics (electronics chemicals), Vulcan-Hart (ovens), Southland (automotive engine sealants), Foilmark (hot-stamped packaging foil), and Hi-Cone (recyclable six-pack rings).

The Northern Trust Company owns about 13% of Illinois Tool Works. Capital Research and Management holds 7% of the company. UBS has an equity stake of around 6%.

## HISTORY

In the early years of the 20th century, Byron Smith, founder of Chicago's Northern Trust Company, recognized that rapid industrialization was outgrowing the capacity of small shops to supply machine tools. Smith encouraged two of his four sons to launch Illinois Tool Works (ITW) in 1912. Harold C. Smith became president of ITW in 1915 and expanded its product line into automotive parts.

ITW developed the Shakeproof fastener, the first twisted-tooth lock washer, in 1923. When Harold C. died in 1936, the torch passed to his son Harold B., who decentralized the company and exhorted salesmen to learn customers' businesses so they could develop solutions even before the customers recognized the problems. Smith plowed profits back into research as WWII spurred demand.

In the 1950s the company began exploring plastics and combination metal and plastic fasteners, as well as electrical controls and instruments, to become a leader in miniaturization. Its major breakthrough came in the early 1960s with the development of flexible plastic collars to hold six-packs of beverage cans. This item, under a new division called Hi-Cone, was ITW's most-profitable offering.

Silas Cathcart became CEO in 1970. Smith's son, another Harold B., was president and COO until 1981 (he remains on the board of directors and is chairman of the board's executive committee). By the early 1980s ITW had become bureaucratic and susceptible to foreign competition. It was forced to lower prices to hold on to customers. Wary after the 1982 recession, ITW hired John Nichols as CEO.

Nichols broadened the company's product line, introduced more-effective production methods, and doubled ITW's size by buying 27 companies, the largest being Signode Industries, bought for $524 million (1986). Nichols broke Signode into smaller units to speed development of 20 new products.

ITW purchased Ransburg Corporation (electrostatic finishing systems, 1989) and the DeVilbiss division of Eagle Industries (1990) and merged the two to form its Finishing Systems and Products division. In 1992 the company introduced the Ring Leader Recycling Program to recycle its plastic six-pack rings.

Through a stock swap, ITW acquired ownership of the Miller Group (arc welding equipment and related systems) in 1993. In 1995 ITW named president James Farrell as CEO. He replaced Nichols as chairman in 1996. ITW acquired Hobart Brothers (welding products) and Medalists Industries (industrial fasteners) in 1996 and made 28 acquisitions and joint ventures in 1997.

In 1999 ITW paid $3.5 billion, Premark International. Early in 2001 the company added to its welding operations by buying four welding component businesses from Dover Corporation. In early 2002 the company's board of directors gave its stamp of approval for the divestiture of ITW's consumer products segment. That decision led to the sale of its Precor fitness equipment business to Finland's Amer Sports in October for about $180 million.

Farrell retired as CEO, though he remained chairman, in 2005; he was replaced by president David Speer. Farrell retired as chairman in 2006 and was succeeded by Speer in that post. EVP Thomas Hansen was elevated to vice chairman, as well.

In 2005 ITW purchased the Wynn Oil segment of industrial products maker Parker Hannifin. Wynn Oil makes chemical car care products and maintenance technology for the auto industry.

In early 2006 ITW bought Alpine Engineered Products, a maker of connectors, design software, and related machinery from Stonebridge Partners. Also that year ITW acquired CFC International for about $90 million in cash. CFC makes multilayer coatings for a variety of markets, including furniture. The company then acquired Click Commerce, a developer of supply chain management software, for about $292 million in cash. In late 2006 ITW also purchased Speedline Technologies, a manufacturer of printed circuit board assembly and semiconductor packaging equipment.

## EXECUTIVES

**Chairman, President, and CEO:** David B. Speer, age 55, $815,385 pay
**Vice Chairman:** Thomas J. Hansen, age 58, $402,244 pay
**EVP, Global Finishing and Software:** Jane L. Warner, age 60
**EVP, Worldwide Welding, Electronic Component Fabrication, and Aircraft Ground Support Equipment Group:** E. Scott Santi, age 45
**EVP, Automotive Engineered Components Businesses:** Robert E. Brunner, age 49
**EVP, Polymers and Fluids Businesses:** David C. Parry, age 53
**EVP, Automotive Fastener Business:** Roland M. Martel, age 52
**SVP and CFO:** Ronald D. Kropp, age 41, $217,727 pay
**SVP, Leasing and Investments:** Allan C. Sutherland, age 43
**SVP, General Counsel, and Secretary:** James H. Wooten Jr., age 58
**SVP, Human Resources:** Sharon M. Brady, age 55
**VP, Investor Relations:** John L. Brooklier, age 55
**VP, Research and Development:** Lee A. Sheridan
**VP, Patents and Technology:** Mark W. Croll
**Auditors:** Deloitte & Touche LLP

## LOCATIONS

**HQ:** Illinois Tool Works Inc.
3600 W. Lake Ave., Glenview, IL 60026
**Phone:** 847-724-7500 **Fax:** 847-657-4261
**Web:** www.itw.com

Illinois Tool Works has principal plants in Australia, Belgium, Brazil, Canada, China, the Czech Republic, Denmark, France, Germany, Ireland, Italy, the Netherlands, Spain, Switzerland, the UK, and the US. It has operations in nearly 50 countries.

### 2006 Sales

| | $ mil. | % of total |
|---|---|---|
| North America | | |
| US | 7,009.6 | 50 |
| Other countries | 944.8 | 7 |
| Europe | 4,039.9 | 29 |
| Asia/Pacific | | |
| Asia | 1,085.9 | 8 |
| Australia & New Zealand | 604.1 | 4 |
| Other regions | 370.7 | 2 |
| **Total** | **14,055.0** | **100** |

## PRODUCTS/OPERATIONS

### 2006 Sales

| | $ mil. | % of total |
|---|---|---|
| Specialty Systems | | |
| North America | 4,627.6 | 32 |
| International | 2,947.6 | 20 |
| Engineered Products | | |
| North America | 4,118.5 | 28 |
| International | 2,914.7 | 20 |
| Adjustments | (553.4) | — |
| **Total** | **14,055.0** | **100** |

### Selected Products

Specialty Systems
- Arc welding equipment
- Food-preparation equipment
- Industrial adhesive-application equipment
- Paint application equipment
- Recyclable ring packaging
- Steel and plastic strapping systems

Engineered Products
- Adhesives
- Fasteners and assemblies
- Fastening tools
- Laminates

## COMPETITORS

3M
BASF AG
Black & Decker
Cooper Industries
DuPont
Emerson Electric
Enodis
Entegris
ESAB
GE
Graco Inc.
Ingersoll-Rand
Koch Enterprises
Lincoln Electric
Marmon Group
NCH
Nordson
Park-Ohio Holdings
Penn Engineering
Snap-on
Stanley Works
Textron
Thermadyne
TriMas Corporation
Tyco
W. R. Grace

## HISTORICAL FINANCIALS

Company Type: Public

### Income Statement

FYE: December 31

| | REVENUE ($ mil.) | NET INCOME ($ mil.) | NET PROFIT MARGIN | EMPLOYEES |
|---|---|---|---|---|
| **12/06** | 14,055 | 1,718 | 12.2% | 55,000 |
| **12/05** | 12,922 | 1,495 | 11.6% | 50,000 |
| **12/04** | 11,731 | 1,339 | 11.4% | 49,000 |
| **12/03** | 10,036 | 1,024 | 10.2% | 47,500 |
| **12/02** | 9,468 | 713 | 7.5% | 48,700 |
| **Annual Growth** | 10.4% | 24.6% | — | 3.1% |

### 2006 Year-End Financials

Debt ratio: 11.1%
Return on equity: 20.7%
Cash ($ mil.): 590
Current ratio: 1.97
Long-term debt ($ mil.): 1,000
No. of shares (mil.): 559
Dividends
Yield: 1.6%
Payout: 24.9%
Market value ($ mil.): 25,812

### Stock History

NYSE: ITW

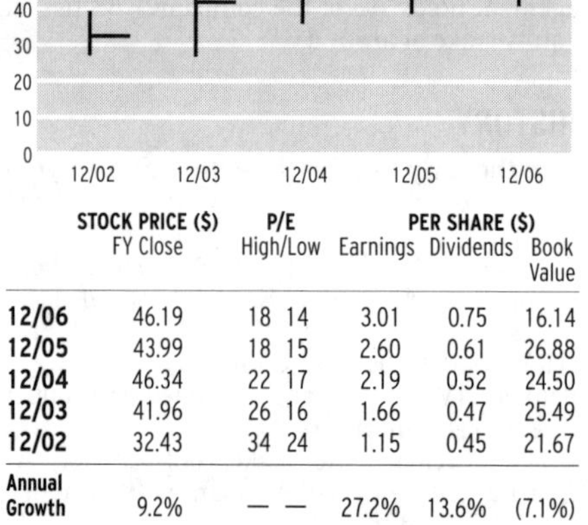


| | STOCK PRICE ($) FY Close | P/E High/Low | PER SHARE ($) Earnings | Dividends | Book Value |
|---|---|---|---|---|---|
| **12/06** | 46.19 | 18 14 | 3.01 | 0.75 | 16.14 |
| **12/05** | 43.99 | 18 15 | 2.60 | 0.61 | 26.88 |
| **12/04** | 46.34 | 22 17 | 2.19 | 0.52 | 24.50 |
| **12/03** | 41.96 | 26 16 | 1.66 | 0.47 | 25.49 |
| **12/02** | 32.43 | 34 24 | 1.15 | 0.45 | 21.67 |
| **Annual Growth** | 9.2% | — — | 27.2% | 13.6% | (7.1%) |

# IMS Health

IMS Health has the dope on drugs. The company is a leading provider of sales management and market research services to clients in the pharmaceutical and health care industries. It tracks not only the sale of prescription drugs and over-the-counter products but also the productivity of individual sales representatives that work for its client companies. It offers market forecasts and surveys physicians and hospitals about drugs they are prescribing to patients. In addition, IMS Health offers consulting and other professional services. The company serves clients worldwide and operates through about 100 offices in more than 75 countries.

Being a dominant player in its market, IMS Health sees acquisitions or joint ventures as a major part of its growth strategy. A former acquisition, PharMetrics, researches patient data in order to provide new market opportunities for its clients.

IMS Health's most lucrative business segment remains its Sales Force Effectiveness operations, which track sales of not only prescription drugs but also over-the-counter products. Clients can access the data via the Internet or CD-ROM, or they can get hardcopy reports. IMS Health also provides decision support software (Sales Insight) to make the data more useful for its clients.

IMS Health is comprised of two additional operating segments: Portfolio Optimization and Launch, Brand Management and Other. The former unit specializes in identifying and developing pharmaceutical product portfolios, while the latter segment offers clients consulting and brand planning tools and services during each step of the pharmaceutical brands marketing process.

## HISTORY

IMS Health (IMS is short for International Marketing Services) was founded in 1954 by Ludwig Wilhelm Frohlich, who headed the New York-based prescription drug advertising agency L.W. Frohlich (founded in the 1930s) and was considered one of the fathers of the drug marketing business. As the post-WWII prescription drug industry grew, drug manufacturers turned to market research to monitor promotions and sales. Frohlich created IMS in 1954 to extend the drug marketing business internationally.

IMS expanded into market research in 1957 under research chief David DuBow, who completed the first syndicated study of the pharmaceutical market. By 1966 IMS had operations throughout Europe. IMS expanded through purchases of research firms RA Gosselin & Co., Lea Associates, and Medical Data Service, and went public in 1972.

Dun & Bradstreet (D&B) bought IMS in 1988, one of several data and publishing companies it added during the 1970s and 1980s. But D&B reversed its growth strategy soon after, and in 1996 it split into three corporations: Cognizant (IMS's parent), ACNielsen, and Dun & Bradstreet Corporation.

IMS continued expanding internationally in 1997. The following year *Advertising Age* identified IMS as the #1 research company in terms of US revenue. The same year Cognizant announced it would split into two entities: Nielsen Media Research and IMS Health. Cognizant chairman and CEO Robert Weissman became IMS' chairman and CEO. IMS continued to grow, buying Walsh International, a developer of sales force automation for pharmaceutical companies; ChinaMetrik, a pharmaceutical tracker focusing on the Chinese market; and the non-US assets of Pharmaceutical Marketing Services. Also in 1998 IMS formed a joint venture with Institut fur Marktanalysen to enhance health care information services in Switzerland.

In 1999 IMS launched I2 (I-squared), an Internet portal for pharmaceutical companies. Victoria Fash became CEO that year (Weissman remained as chairman). IMS also spun off its interest in IT research and consulting firm Gartner Group. The following year IMS agreed to be acquired by The TriZetto Group, an Internet portal developer for the health care industry, for about $8 billion. However, the companies soon called off the deal, and IMS instead sold its Erisco Managed Care Technologies unit to TriZetto in a stock swap deal valued at $255 million that gave IMS a 33% stake in TriZetto. IMS also spun off its Strategic Technologies and Clark-O'Neill divisions as SYNAVANT (later acquired by Dendrite International). In late 2000 former IBM executive David Thomas took over as CEO. The following year IMS sold its DataEdge unit, a provider of clinical trial databases, to clinical trial services firm Fast Track Systems.

IMS also became involved in a bitter dispute with European competition authorities in 2000.

The European Union ordered IMS to license its system that tracks drug sales in Germany to competitors, claiming the dominance of IMS in that market prevented anyone from entering or staying in the business. IMS Health won its appeal in 2001 and a European Commission ended its probe into IMS in 2002 after finding that IMS no longer engaged in activities adverse to competition.

In early 2003 IMS Health sold its stake in Cognizant Technology Solutions, leaving the company with pharmaceutical sales management and market research services as its primary businesses. David Carlucci, who joined the company as president in 2002, was named CEO when Thomas stepped down from the chief executive position in 2005.

A proposed deal for the company to be acquired by marketing research firm VNU was scrapped in 2005 after several large VNU shareholders expressed opposition. Also that year IMS Health acquired PharMetrics, a provider of health care market data.

## EXECUTIVES

**Chairman, President, and CEO:** David R. (Dave) Carlucci, age 52, $801,250 pay
**EVP and COO:** Gilles V. J. Pajot, age 57
**SVP and CFO:** Leslye G. Katz, age 52
**SVP Corporate Strategy:** Murray L. Aitken, age 46
**SVP, General Counsel, and Corporate Secretary:** Robert H. Steinfeld, age 52, $373,400 pay
**SVP Customer Delivery and Development:** Kevin S. McKay, age 53
**SVP Global Marketing and External Affairs:** Bruce F. Boggs, age 54, $346,325 pay
**SVP Business Line Management:** Kevin Knightly, age 45
**VP and General Manager, Asia Pacific:** Stephen Phua
**VP and Treasurer:** Jeffrey J. Ford, age 41
**VP Corporate Development:** John R. (Jack) Walsh, age 52
**VP Communications and Public Affairs:** Bill Hughes
**VP Investor Relations:** Darcie Peck
**VP and Controller:** Harshan Bhangdia
**VP Global Human Resources:** Marie B. Sonde, age 42
**Manager, Public Relations:** Lance Longwell
**President, IMS Americas:** William J. Nelligan, age 46
**President and Representative Director, IMS Japan:** Tatsuyuki Saeki
**Auditors:** PricewaterhouseCoopers LLP

## LOCATIONS

**HQ:** IMS Health Incorporated
901 Main Ave., Ste. 612, Norwalk, CT 06851
**Phone:** 203-845-5200 **Fax:** 203-845-5304
**Web:** www.imshealth.com

IMS Health has about 100 offices in more than 75 countries.

### 2006 Sales

| | $ mil. | % of total |
|---|---|---|
| Americas | 880.7 | 45 |
| Europe | 812.9 | 42 |
| Asia/Pacific | 265.0 | 13 |
| **Total** | **1,958.6** | **100** |

## PRODUCTS/OPERATIONS

### 2006 Sales

| | $ mil. | % of total |
|---|---|---|
| Sales Force Effectiveness | 927.2 | 48 |
| Portfolio Optimization | 555.6 | 28 |
| Launch, Brand & Other | 475.8 | 24 |
| **Total** | **1,958.6** | **100** |

### 2006 Sales

| | $ mil. | % of total |
|---|---|---|
| Information & analytics revenue | 1,599.1 | 82 |
| Consulting & services revenue | 359.5 | 18 |
| **Total** | **1,958.6** | **100** |

### Selected Products and Services

Market research
- Hospital audits (product sales to hospitals)
- Medical audits (physician surveys)
- MIDAS (data analysis tools)
- Pharmaceutical audits (product sales to pharmacies)
- Prescription audits (product sales by pharmacies)
- Promotional audits (promotional campaign effectiveness)

Sales management
- Consumer health (market share and pricing of over-the-counter drugs and personal care products)
- Prescription tracking reporting
- Sales territory reporting

Other services
- Consulting
- Market trend reports

## COMPETITORS

Advisory Board
Cegedim
GfK
GfK NOP
GfK V2
Information Resources
Ipsos
The Nielsen Company
Taylor Nelson
Verispan

## HISTORICAL FINANCIALS

Company Type: Public

### Income Statement

FYE: December 31

| | REVENUE ($ mil.) | NET INCOME ($ mil.) | NET PROFIT MARGIN | EMPLOYEES |
|---|---|---|---|---|
| **12/06** | 1,959 | 316 | 16.1% | 7,400 |
| **12/05** | 1,755 | 284 | 16.2% | 6,900 |
| **12/04** | 1,569 | 285 | 18.2% | 6,400 |
| **12/03** | 1,382 | 639 | 46.2% | 6,000 |
| **12/02** | 1,428 | 266 | 18.6% | 5,900 |
| **Annual Growth** | 8.2% | 4.3% | — | 5.8% |

### 2006 Year-End Financials

Debt ratio: 2,876.5%
Return on equity: 140.5%
Cash ($ mil.): 157
Current ratio: 1.28
Long-term debt ($ mil.): 975
No. of shares (mil.): 201
Dividends
Yield: 0.4%
Payout: 7.8%
Market value ($ mil.): 5,515

### Stock History

NYSE: RX

| | STOCK PRICE ($) FY Close | P/E High | P/E Low | PER SHARE ($) Earnings | Dividends | Book Value |
|---|---|---|---|---|---|---|
| **12/06** | 27.48 | 20 | 16 | 1.53 | 0.12 | 0.17 |
| **12/05** | 24.92 | 23 | 18 | 1.22 | 0.08 | 1.82 |
| **12/04** | 23.21 | 22 | 17 | 1.20 | 0.08 | 1.12 |
| **12/03** | 24.86 | 10 | 5 | 2.58 | 0.08 | 0.80 |
| **12/02** | 16.00 | 24 | 14 | 0.93 | 0.08 | 0.79 |
| **Annual Growth** | 14.5% | — | — | 13.3% | 10.7% | (32.0%) |

# Ingersoll-Rand

Known for its tools and machinery — which carved the faces on Mount Rushmore — Ingersoll-Rand also would like to be known for its other business segments. With about 100 plants worldwide, the company makes refrigeration equipment (Thermo King, Hussmann) used mostly in trucks and supermarkets, locks and security systems (Schlage, Kryptonite), construction equipment (Bobcat skid steers, light towers, portable compressors), industrial equipment (generators, turbines, and the like), and heavy equipment and golf carts (Compact Vehicle Technologies). Ingersoll-Rand has sold its Torrington and Dresser-Rand subsidiaries, which included the manufacture of precision bearings and fluid-control devices, respectively.

The company is emphasizing less-cyclical product lines such as security systems, industrial components, and refrigeration equipment, while selling off its more-cyclical businesses. That explains the Torrington and Dresser-Rand divestments, the latter of which came in late 2004 to private equity group First Reserve Corporation for about $1.2 billion.

Early in 2007 IR sold its road construction equipment division to AB Volvo for $1.3 billion in cash. Later that year the company said it was exploring options for Bobcat and its other construction equipment businesses, citing the fact that these operations no longer complement its core business. IR found a buyer later in 2007 in a teaming of two sister companies of the Doosan Group — Doosan Infracore and Doosan Engine. The two companies will pay $4.9 billion for the businesses which include Bobcat, utility equipment, and attachments.

The company has customers in more than 100 countries around the world. Sales to these customers bring in about 40% of revenues.

## HISTORY

Simon Ingersoll invented the steam-driven rock drill in New York City in 1871. In 1874 he sold the patent to Jose Francisco de Navarro, who financed the organization of the Ingersoll Rock Drill Company. Three years later it merged with Sergeant Drill, a company created by Henry Clark Sergeant, Navarro's former foreman.

Meanwhile, the Rand brothers were also establishing a drill company. The companies merged in 1905 to become Ingersoll-Rand.

Ingersoll-Rand initially produced air compressors and a basic line of rock drills. In 1912 the company added centrifugal compressors and turbo blowers. Later, portable air tools were added. After WWII Ingersoll-Rand, which had mostly served US mining operations, expanded internationally. From the 1960s on, the company diversified into specialized machinery and products. Acquisitions in the 1970s and 1980s made Ingersoll-Rand the largest bearing manufacturer in the US.

The company also developed small air compressors and water-jet systems capable of cutting steel and concrete. In 1986 Ingersoll-Rand formed a joint venture with Dresser Industries called Dresser-Rand to produce gas turbines, compressors, and similar equipment. Ingersoll-Rand and Dresser Industries combined pump operations to form another joint venture, Ingersoll-Dresser Pump, in 1992.

In 1993 16-year Ingersoll-Rand veteran James Perrella became CEO. That year the company bought the German needle- and cylindrical-bearing business of FAG Kugelfischer Georg Schafer; it also sold its underground coal-mining machinery business (to Long-Airdox), as well as its domestic jet-engine bearing operation. ECOAIR, a unit of MAN GHH, was among several 1994 acquisitions.

Ingersoll-Rand acquired Clark Equipment for $1.5 billion in 1995 in a deal that included the businesses of Bobcat (skid-steer loaders), Clark-Hurth Components (axles and transmissions, sold 1997), Club Car (golf cars), and Blaw-Knox Construction Equipment (asphalt-paving equipment). In 1996 Ingersoll-Rand bought Metaldyne's (formerly Mascotech) Steelcraft Division (steel doors). In 1997 Ingersoll-Rand bought Newman Tonks Group (UK) and technology from the Master Lock unit of Fortune Brands, which boosted its architectural hardware line and extended its distribution in Europe and Asia. That year Ingersoll-Rand bought Thermo King from Westinghouse (now CBS) for $2.6 billion.

In 1999 Ingersoll-Rand bought Harrow Industries (access controls, architectural hardware, decorative bath fixtures). The company's industrial production equipment was enhanced when it struck a deal with Cadence Design Systems, a world-leading supplier of electronic design and automation software. James Perrella stepped down as CEO that year; Herbert Henkel, formerly of Textron, succeeded him.

In 2000 Ingersoll-Rand bought Halliburton's stake in its joint ventures with Dresser-Rand and Ingersoll-Dresser Pump. Ingersoll-Rand then sold Ingersoll-Dresser Pump to Flowserve for about $775 million and bought Neal Manufacturing, which makes compact road-paving equipment. It also acquired Hussmann International (refrigeration equipment) for about $1.8 billion. That same year, Ingersoll-Rand sold the reciprocating gas compressor packaging and rental business of its Dresser-Rand unit to Hanover Compressor Company for $190 million.

The company closed 20 plants and laid off more than 3,900 employees the next year. But acquisitions continued. Ingersoll-Rand's 2001 purchases included refrigeration company National Refrigeration Services and lock maker Kryptonite Corporation (originator of the U-shaped bicycle lock), as well as companies in the Czech Republic, France, the Netherlands, and Turkey.

Ingersoll-Rand reincorporated in Bermuda in late 2001; the move could save the company nearly $40 million in US taxes every year.

The company sold its Torrington Co. unit (bearings and motion-control components) to The Timken Co. for $840 million in 2003. It then sold its drilling business to Atlas Copco for $225 million. A bigger divestment came in late 2004 with the sale of Dresser-Rand to private equity group First Reserve Corporation for about $1.2 billion.

## EXECUTIVES

**Chairman, President, and CEO:** Herbert L. (Herb) Henkel, age 59, $1,200,000 pay
**SVP and CFO:** Timothy R. (Tim) McLevish, age 51, $537,500 pay
**SVP; President, Industrial Technologies:** James R. (Jim) Bolch, age 49
**SVP, General Counsel, and Director:** Patricia Nachtigal, age 60, $468,333 pay
**SVP; President, Construction Technologies:** Christopher P. (Chris) Vasiloff, age 55, $460,000 pay
**SVP; President, Security Technologies:** Michael W. (Mike) Lamach, age 43, $488,333 pay
**SVP; President, Compact Vehicle Technologies:** Richard F. (Dick) Pedtke, age 58
**SVP and President, Climate Control Technologies:** Steven R. (Steve) Shawley, age 54
**SVP, Enterprise Services:** William B. (Bill) Gauld, age 53
**SVP, Human Resources and Communications:** Marcia J. Avedon, age 45
**VP and CIO:** Barry Libenson
**VP and Controller:** Richard (Rich) Randall, age 56
**VP and Director, Audit Services:** Timothy E. (Tim) Scofield
**VP, Investor Relations and Treasurer:** Barbara L. Brasier
**VP, Corporate Governance and Secretary:** Barbara A. Santoro
**VP, Tax:** Larry Kurland
**Director, Investor Relations:** Joseph P. Fimbianti
**Auditors:** PricewaterhouseCoopers LLP

## LOCATIONS

**HQ:** Ingersoll-Rand Company Limited
155 Chestnut Ridge Rd., Montvale, NJ 07645
**Phone:** 201-573-0123 **Fax:** 201-573-3172
**Web:** www.irco.com

Ingersoll-Rand's operations include 16 plants in Asia, one in Canada, 31 in Europe, eight in Latin America, and 39 in the US.

### 2006 Sales

| | $ mil. | % of total |
|---|---|---|
| US | 6,438.7 | 56 |
| Other countries | 4,970.6 | 44 |
| **Total** | **11,409.3** | **100** |

## PRODUCTS/OPERATIONS

### 2006 Sales

| | $ mil. | % of total |
|---|---|---|
| Climate Control Technologies | 3,171.0 | 28 |
| Compact Vehicle Technologies | 2,641.2 | 23 |
| Security Technologies | 2,285.0 | 20 |
| Industrial Technologies | 1,949.8 | 17 |
| Construction Technologies | 1,362.3 | 12 |
| **Total** | **11,409.3** | **100** |

### Segments and Selected Products

Climate Control Technologies
- Case refrigeration equipment (Hussmann)
- Transport temperature control equipment (Thermo King)

Compact Vehicle Technologies
- Industrial products (Club Car golf cars and utility vehicles, tools, and related industrial production equipment)
- Skid-steer loaders (Bobcat)

Security Technologies
- Architectural locks (Schlage)
- Biometric access control, time and attendance, and personal identification products (Recognition Systems)
- Door-control hardware
- Electronic-access control technologies (power-operated doors and architectural columns)
- Exit devices (Von Durpin)
- Portable and recreational locks (Kryptonite)
- Steel doors (Steelcraft)

Industrial Technologies
- Air solutions (compressed air systems)
- Gas compressors and turbines
- Portable power products
- Steam turbines

Construction Technologies
- Compact hydraulic excavators
- Compactors (Ingersoll)
- Pavers (Blaw-Knox and ABG)

## COMPETITORS

Astec Industries
Baker Hughes
Bamford Excavators
Black & Decker
Caterpillar
Cooper Industries
Crown Equipment
Deere
Dover
Eaton
Emerson Electric
E-Z-GO
Gardner Denver
Gehl
ITT Corp.
JLG Industries
Johnson Controls
Joy Global
Liebherr International
NESCO
Robert Bosch
SPX
Stanley Works
Terex
Toyota Material Handling
Tyco
Wacker Construction Equipment
W.W. Grainger

## HISTORICAL FINANCIALS

Company Type: Public

### Income Statement

FYE: December 31

| | REVENUE ($ mil.) | NET INCOME ($ mil.) | NET PROFIT MARGIN | EMPLOYEES |
|---|---|---|---|---|
| **12/06** | 11,409 | 1,033 | 9.0% | 43,000 |
| **12/05** | 10,547 | 1,054 | 10.0% | 40,000 |
| **12/04** | 9,394 | 1,219 | 13.0% | 36,000 |
| **12/03** | 9,876 | 645 | 6.5% | 42,000 |
| **12/02** | 8,951 | (174) | — | 45,000 |
| **Annual Growth** | 6.3% | — | — | (1.1%) |

### 2006 Year-End Financials

Debt ratio: 16.7%
Return on equity: 18.5%
Cash ($ mil.): 363
Current ratio: 1.13
Long-term debt ($ mil.): 905
No. of shares (mil.): 307
Dividends
Yield: 1.7%
Payout: 21.3%
Market value ($ mil.): 12,004

### Stock History

NYSE: IR

| | STOCK PRICE ($) FY Close | P/E High | P/E Low | PER SHARE ($) Earnings | PER SHARE ($) Dividends | PER SHARE ($) Book Value |
|---|---|---|---|---|---|---|
| **12/06** | 39.13 | 15 | 11 | 3.20 | 0.68 | 17.62 |
| **12/05** | 40.37 | 14 | 11 | 3.09 | 0.44 | 15.97 |
| **12/04** | 40.15 | 12 | 8 | 3.47 | 0.44 | 33.13 |
| **12/03** | 33.94 | 18 | 9 | 1.87 | 0.36 | 25.76 |
| **12/02** | 21.53 | — | — | (0.51) | 0.25 | 20.55 |
| **Annual Growth** | 16.1% | — | — | — | 28.4% | (3.8%) |

# Ingram Micro

There's nothing micro about Ingram. Ingram Micro is the world's largest wholesale distributor of computer products. It provides thousands of products — desktop and notebook PCs, servers, storage devices, CD-ROM drives, monitors, printers, and software — to 159,000 reseller customers around the globe. The company also provides a wide range of services for its resellers and suppliers, including contract manufacturing and warehousing, customer care, financing, logistics, and enterprise network support services. Customers include resellers such as CompUSA, Wal-Mart.com, Staples, and Office Depot.

Ingram Micro has reduced its inventory, consolidated distribution facilities, outsourced certain service and support functions, and trimmed its workforce to streamline its operations, but it continues to make acquisitions to expand its presence in certain markets. In 2005 the company acquired select assets of consumer electronics distributor AVAD. The following year it expanded its reach in Northern Europe when it purchased the assets of SymTech Nordic. It also formed a new North American services division focused on professional IT services, warranty contract management, and managed services. Ingram agreed to purchase consumer electronics distributor DBL Distributing for $96 million in 2007.

The Ingram family, led by Ingram Industries chairman Martha Ingram (one of America's wealthiest active businesswomen), controls about 20% of Ingram Micro.

## HISTORY

There is no love lost between the former Micro D and Ingram Industries. Micro D was founded in Fountain Valley, California, in 1979 by husband-and-wife entrepreneurs Geza Csige and Lorraine Mecca. As the company grew, Mecca sought to merge the computer distributor with a partner that could take over daily operations. She relinquished control of Micro D to Linwood "Chip" Lacy in 1986 and sold her 51% share of the company to minority shareholder Ingram Distribution Group.

Sales bottomed out for Micro D that year. Lacy tightened Micro D's belt and took huge charges for outdated inventory it sold at a discount and overdue payments from customers that had gone bankrupt.

At the same time, Ingram Industries was busy merging recently acquired Ingram Software Distribution Services of Buffalo, New York, with Compton, California-based Softeam. The merger made the company one of the nation's largest wholesale distributors of computer software. Lacy saw Ingram's purchase of Micro D shares as a conflict of interest, but he was too busy returning Micro D to profitability: centralizing its marketing and distribution functions, cutting costs, and expanding its market to include more small retailers, which provided higher margins. Micro D went from the fourth-largest distributor of microcomputer products to #1 in just one year.

The surging PC market in the late 1980s fueled Micro D's growth. By 1988 the firm had expanded outside the US for the first time, acquiring Canadian company Frantek Computer Products.

Ingram Industries offered to acquire the 41% of outstanding Micro D stock it did not own in 1988, but Lacy resisted, preferring to let Ingram wait. Though Ingram owned a majority of Micro D stock, it only controlled three of seven seats on the board. Ingram was forced to play Lacy's game and finally acquired the company at a higher cost in 1989. The new company, which controlled 20% of the computer distribution market, was called Ingram Micro D. The merger was anything but smooth, and several Micro D executives jumped ship.

As the PC took hold in the US in the 1990s, Ingram Micro D became the dominant industry player, but relations between Lacy and the Ingram family never improved. The company shortened its name to Ingram Micro in 1991, and two years later, as it was hitting stride, Lacy announced plans to leave. To keep him, Ingram Industries CEO Bronson Ingram (much to his distaste) promised to let Lacy take the company public.

Bronson Ingram died in 1995 and the next year his widow, Martha, forced Lacy's resignation. Lacy was replaced by Jerre Stead, formerly CEO of software maker LEGENT (bought by Computer Associates), who devised a compensation package for himself consisting solely of stock options (no salary) and listed "Head Coach" on his business card. Ingram went public a few months after Stead took over.

In 1998 Ingram Micro forged a distribution alliance with Japanese computer giant SOFTBANK and bought a majority stake in German computer products distributor Macrotron. It also expanded into build-to-order PC manufacturing. Amid softer PC sales industrywide, Ingram Micro in 1999 terminated nearly 600 employees as part of a worldwide realignment and signed a deal (worth an estimated $10 billion) with CompUSA to be its primary PC manufacturer and distributor.

Later in 1999 Stead — with Ingram Micro's sales slipping and its stock slumping — made plans to step down as CEO. The search ended in 2000 when the company named GTE veteran Kent Foster to the post.

Ingram Micro expanded its portfolio of services for enterprises and began offering more extensive network and product support services. The next year the company outsourced certain IT infrastructure operations, along with the related personnel, to Affiliated Computer Services (ACS) in late 2002. Ingram Micro continued to expand international operations in 2002, acquiring the 49% of a Singapore exporter it did not previously own, and purchasing operations in Belgium and the Netherlands. In a move to expand its presence in the Asia/Pacific region, Ingram acquired Australian distributor Tech Pacific in 2004.

Company president Greg Spierkel replaced Foster as CEO in 2005.

## EXECUTIVES

**Chairman:** Dale R. Laurance, age 61
**CEO and Director:** Gregory M.E. (Greg) Spierkel, age 50
**President and COO:** Alain Monie, age 54
**EVP; President, North America:** Keith Bradley, age 43
**EVP and CFO:** William D. Humes, age 42
**EVP; President, Ingram Micro Europe:** Henri T. (Hans) Koppen, age 64, $863,383 pay
**EVP; President, Ingram Micro Asia/Pacific:** Alain Monié, age 56
**SVP and CFO, Ingram Micro Europe:** Karen Griffiths
**SVP and CIO:** Karen E. Salem, age 45
**SVP; President, Ingram Micro Latin America:** Alain Maquet, age 56
**SVP, General Counsel, and Secretary:** Larry C. Boyd, age 54
**SVP, Human Resources Worldwide:** Matthew A. (Matt) Sauer, age 59
**SVP, Legal Services:** Mark K. Slater
**SVP, Sales:** Brian Wiser
**SVP, Vendor Management:** Paul Bay
**VP and Treasurer:** James F. Ricketts, age 60
**VP, Strategy and Communications:** Ria Marie Carlson, age 45
**Director, Public Relations:** Jennifer Baier
**Auditors:** PricewaterhouseCoopers LLP

## LOCATIONS

**HQ:** Ingram Micro Inc.
1600 E. St. Andrew Place, Santa Ana, CA 92705
**Phone:** 714-566-1000 **Fax:** 714-566-7900
**Web:** www.ingrammicro.com

### 2006 Sales

| | $ mil. | % of total |
|---|---|---|
| North America | 13,585.0 | 43 |
| Europe | 10,754.0 | 34 |
| Asia/Pacific | 5,537.5 | 18 |
| Latin America | 1,481.0 | 5 |
| **Total** | **31,357.5** | **100** |

## PRODUCTS/OPERATIONS

### Selected Products

CD-ROM, CD-RW, and DVD drives
Computer supplies and accessories
Consumer electronics
Desktop and notebook PCs, servers, and workstations
Mass storage devices
Modems
Monitors
Networking hubs, routers, and switches
Network interface cards
PDAs
Printers
Scanners
Software (business and entertainment)
Wireless devices

### Selected Services

Supply chain
Contract manufacturing
Credit and collection management
Customer care
End-to-end order fulfillment
Logistics and transportation management
Marketing services
Product procurement
Warehouse services

## COMPETITORS

Agilysys
Arrow Electronics
ASI Corp.
Avnet
Bell Microproducts
Black Box
Communications Supply
CompuCom
Computacenter
Computech Systems
D&H Distributing
Digiland
Flextronics
GTSI
MA Laboratories
Menlo Worldwide
Merisel
MicroAge
New Age Electronics
Otto
ScanSource
SED International
Softmart
Software House
Solectron
Supercom
SYNNEX
Tech Data
United Stationers
UPS Supply Chain Solutions
Westcon

## HISTORICAL FINANCIALS

Company Type: Public

**Income Statement** — FYE: Saturday nearest December 31

| | REVENUE ($ mil.) | NET INCOME ($ mil.) | NET PROFIT MARGIN | EMPLOYEES |
|---|---|---|---|---|
| **12/06** | 31,358 | 266 | 0.8% | 13,700 |
| **12/05** | 28,808 | 217 | 0.8% | 13,000 |
| **12/04** | 25,462 | 220 | 0.9% | 13,600 |
| **12/03** | 22,613 | 149 | 0.7% | 11,300 |
| **12/02** | 22,459 | (275) | — | 12,700 |
| **Annual Growth** | 8.7% | — | — | 1.9% |

**2006 Year-End Financials**

Debt ratio: 9.3%
Return on equity: 9.9%
Cash ($ mil.): 333
Current ratio: 1.51
Long-term debt ($ mil.): 271
No. of shares (mil.): 169
Dividends
Yield: —
Payout: —
Market value ($ mil.): 3,458

**Stock History** — NYSE: IM

| | STOCK PRICE ($) FY Close | P/E High | P/E Low | PER SHARE ($) Earnings | Dividends | Book Value |
|---|---|---|---|---|---|---|
| **12/06** | 20.41 | 14 | 11 | 1.56 | — | 17.24 |
| **12/05** | 19.93 | 16 | 11 | 1.32 | — | 15.02 |
| **12/04** | 20.80 | 15 | 8 | 1.38 | — | 14.12 |
| **12/03** | 15.88 | 16 | 9 | 0.98 | — | 12.32 |
| **12/02** | 12.20 | — | — | (1.81) | — | 10.85 |
| **Annual Growth** | 13.7% | — | — | — | — | 12.3% |

# Insight Enterprises

With this company around the end of your technology woes could be in sight. Insight Enterprises is one of the leading distributors of computer hardware and software in North America, carrying about 300,000 products from major manufacturers such as Hewlett-Packard, IBM, and Microsoft. The company uses direct telesales and field sales agents to reach customers in business, government, and education markets. Insight also offers products for sale through catalogs and its Web site. In addition to North America, the company sells some 65,000 products in the UK. It bought software and mobile solutions firm Software Spectrum.

The deal, which closed in 2006, was valued at some $287 million in cash. The acquisition from Level 3 Communications gives Insight a foothold in the software and wireless niche of the industry. It also allows Insight Enterprises to redirect its revenue streams — from mostly hardware sales to 60% hardware, 39% software, and 1% services.

The company sold the PC Wholesale division (acquired in 2002) of its subsidiary Insight Direct USA Inc. to Synnex Corp. in 2007 for about $10 million, plus approximately $20 million for net assets acquired (subject to adjustments).

To stay ahead of the competition and to expand its revenue streams, the company has been focused on expanding its technology services business, which now accounts for about 5% of revenue. Insight Enterprises in 2006 sold its business process outsourcing (BPO) division, Direct Alliance, to TeleTech Holdings for $46 million so Insight can focus on its other operations.

The company is forging ahead with its plans under the leadership of former IBM executive Richard Fennessy, who was appointed in 2004 to replace co-founder Tom Crown as CEO. Crown, now chairman of the company, started Insight with his brother, Eric (now chairman emeritus).

As part of its marketing strategy, Insight sponsors the Insight Bowl, a college football bowl game.

## HISTORY

Eric Crown worked for a small computer retail chain in the mid-1980s before leaving to market PCs. In 1986 he and his brother, Tim, pooled $2,000 from credit cards and $1,300 in savings and, anticipating a drop in hard drive prices, placed an ad for low-cost hard drives in a computer magazine. The ad pulled in $20,000 worth of sales and, since costs did indeed drop, the profit was enough to start a new company, Hard Drives International. In 1988 they changed the name to Insight Enterprises; by 1991 the Crowns also sold Insight-branded PCs, software, and peripherals (discontinued in 1995). The company passed the $100 million revenue mark in 1992.

Insight shifted its marketing focus to catalogs in 1993 and had a circulation of more than 7 million by 1995. The company went public that year and entered an alliance with Computer City (acquired by CompUSA in 1998) to handle its mail-order fulfillment. It also launched its Web site. The next year subsidiary Insight Direct began to offer on-site service warranties, and in 1997 retailing subsidiary Direct Alliance was chosen to provide product fulfillment for Internet software firm Geo Publishing. That year the company began sponsoring the Copper Bowl, a college football game played in Arizona, which was renamed the Insight.com Bowl (and later the Insight Bowl).

Looking beyond the US, in 1998 Insight established operations in Canada and acquired direct marketers Choice Peripherals (UK) and Computerprofis Computersysteme (Germany). At home it added direct marketer Treasure Chest Computers. Sales passed the billion dollar mark that year.

The company formed an alliance with Daisytek International in 1999 that expanded its product line by more than 10,000. Soon thereafter, Insight walked away from a merger with UK-based computer wholesaler Action Computer Supplies when Action's profits slumped.

Insight withdrew its planned IPO and spinoff of Direct Alliance in 2001 due to poor market conditions. Also that month Eric became chairman and Tim became CEO (they had previously shared the title of co-CEO). Insight ended up buying Action Computer Supplies in 2001. It also shut down its German operations and acquired computer direct marketers in both the UK and Canada in late 2001.

In April 2002 Insight acquired Comark, a leading private reseller of computers, peripherals, and computer supplies in the US, and began integrating its operations into Insight North America's existing operational structure.

Tim stepped down as president and CEO and became chairman in late 2004, while Eric assumed the title of chairman emeritus. The company appointed IBM veteran Richard Fennessy to the position of president and CEO. That same year Insight spun off its UK-based Internet service provider PlusNet.

Two years later Insight sold its outsourcing subsidiary, Direct Alliance, to TeleTech for about $46 million.

## EXECUTIVES

**Chairman:** Timothy A. (Tim) Crown, age 42
**President, CEO, and Director:** Richard A. Fennessy, age 41, $1,845,000 pay
**EVP, CFO, Secretary, Treasurer, and Director:** Stanley Laybourne, age 57, $998,250 pay
**EVP and Chief People Officer:** Gary M. Glandon, age 47
**Chief Accounting Officer:** Karen K. McGinnis
**SVP Corporate Sales:** John Thomas
**VP and General Manager, Insight Canada:** Carmela Orlando, age 40, $386,370 pay
**Chief Marketing Officer:** Catherine W. (Cathy) Eckstein, age 48
**CIO:** David B. Rice, age 53
**President, Insight Direct North America and APAC:** Mark T. McGrath, $407,199 pay (partial-year salary)
**President, Insight EMEA:** Stuart A. Fenton, age 37
**Investor Relations:** Nancy M. Stephens
**Auditors:** KPMG LLP

## LOCATIONS

**HQ:** Insight Enterprises, Inc.
1305 W. Auto Dr., Tempe, AZ 85284
**Phone:** 480-902-1001 **Fax:** 480-902-1157
**Web:** www.insight.com

**2006 Sales**

| | $ mil. | % of total |
|---|---|---|
| North America | 3,076.8 | 80 |
| Europe, Middle East & Africa | 710.3 | 19 |
| Asia/Pacific | 30.0 | 1 |
| **Total** | **3,817.1** | **100** |

## PRODUCTS/OPERATIONS

**Selected Products**

Computer memory and processors
Desktop computers
Displays
Laptop computers
Networking equipment
Servers
Software
Storage devices

**Selected Services**

Business process outsourcing
- Collections
- Credit card processing
- Customer support
- Direct marketing
- Fulfillment
- Inbound and outbound call handling
- Supply chain management

Information technology
- Consulting
- Help desk support
- Maintenance
- Network administration
- Project management
- Systems integration

## COMPETITORS

Amazon.com
Best Buy
Buy.com
CDW
CompuCom
CompUSA
Convergys
Dell
Digital River
DSG International
Fry's Electronics
Gateway
Hewlett-Packard
IBM
Micro Electronics
ModusLink
Office Depot
OfficeMax
PC Connection
PC Mall
PC Warehouse
PFSweb
RadioShack
Staples
Systemax
Zones

## HISTORICAL FINANCIALS

Company Type: Public

**Income Statement** FYE: December 31

| | REVENUE ($ mil.) | NET INCOME ($ mil.) | NET PROFIT MARGIN | EMPLOYEES |
|---|---|---|---|---|
| **12/06** | 3,817 | 77 | 2.0% | 4,568 |
| **12/05** | 3,261 | 55 | 1.7% | 3,967 |
| **12/04** | 3,083 | 81 | 2.6% | 3,914 |
| **12/03** | 2,914 | 38 | 1.3% | 4,018 |
| **12/02** | 2,891 | (43) | — | 4,424 |
| **Annual Growth** | 7.2% | — | — | 0.8% |

**2006 Year-End Financials**

Debt ratio: 32.5%
Return on equity: 12.2%
Cash ($ mil.): 55
Current ratio: 1.50
Long-term debt ($ mil.): 224
No. of shares (mil.): 49
Dividends
Yield: —
Payout: —
Market value ($ mil.): 922

**Stock History** NASDAQ (GS): NSIT

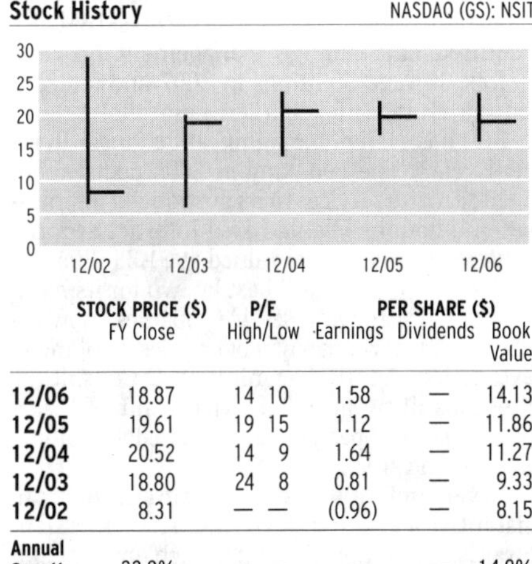


| | STOCK PRICE ($) FY Close | P/E High | P/E Low | PER SHARE ($) Earnings | Dividends | Book Value |
|---|---|---|---|---|---|---|
| **12/06** | 18.87 | 14 | 10 | 1.58 | — | 14.13 |
| **12/05** | 19.61 | 19 | 15 | 1.12 | — | 11.86 |
| **12/04** | 20.52 | 14 | 9 | 1.64 | — | 11.27 |
| **12/03** | 18.80 | 24 | 8 | 0.81 | — | 9.33 |
| **12/02** | 8.31 | — | — | (0.96) | — | 8.15 |
| **Annual Growth** | 22.8% | — | — | — | — | 14.8% |

# Intel Corporation

Intel — still #1 in semiconductors, and no longer complacent about holding the top spot. The company holds the lion's share in the market for microprocessors that go into desktop and notebook computers, and also into computer servers. Archrival AMD has eaten into Intel's market share in recent years, but the big guy has fought back with faster processors and advanced manufacturing technology. Intel also makes flash memories and embedded semiconductors for the industrial equipment and networking gear markets.

While remaining the world's largest semiconductor manufacturer, Intel has been humbled by a series of events, including increased competition in its core chip business, temporary shortages of chipsets, and unsuccessful forays into niche markets. The company has responded with aggressive cost cutting, corporate reorganizations and brand initiatives, and the rollout of new devices meant to re-establish not only its market lead, but also its manufacturing and technical pre-eminence.

In the wake of operational gaffes early in the 21st century, former CEO Craig Barrett launched companywide initiatives to refocus Intel on flawless execution. Among other changes, the company reorganized its communications chips units and R&D operations; terminated the online services (such as server farms and Web hosting); and shuttered or sold some of its many acquisitions from the years of the tech boom. Barrett won a sterling reputation as Intel's manufacturing chief before succeeding legendary CEO Andy Grove. Barrett handed over the CEO reins to president Paul Otellini in 2005. (Barrett succeeded Grove as chairman at that time.) Otellini is just the fifth CEO in the company's 39-year history, and the first non-engineer.

Intel's processor market share stands around 75%, but the company's long-running battle with AMD has heated up as that company's successful Athlon processor has taken market share away from Intel's Pentium models. Intel struck back with rounds of price cuts and an unusually aggressive schedule for introducing faster Pentium models. AMD filed an antitrust suit against Intel in 2005, alleging that its rival has used improper subsidies and coercion to secure sales. In 2007 the European Commission brought formal anticompetitive charges against Intel on behalf of AMD.

In late 2006 the company doubled down on dual-core processors by launching the Xeon 5300 processor for computer servers — packaging four computing engines in one microprocessor.

Intel decided in early 2007 to build a 300mm wafer fabrication plant in Dalian, a city in northeast China. The $2.5 billion project, dubbed Fab 68, will be the company's first wafer fab in Asia. The facility is scheduled to begin production of chipsets in the first half of 2010. Intel also is building a $1 billion assembly and test facility in Vietnam.

## HISTORY

In 1968 three engineers from Fairchild Semiconductor created Intel in Mountain View, California, to develop technology for silicon-based chips. ("Intel" is a contraction of "integrated electronics.") The trio consisted of Robert Noyce (who co-invented the integrated circuit, or IC, in 1958), Gordon Moore, and Andy Grove.

Intel initially provided computer memory chips such as DRAMs (1970) and EPROMs (1971). These chips' success funded the microprocessor designs that revolutionized the electronics industry. In 1971 Intel introduced the 4004 microprocessor, introduced as "a microprogrammable computer on a chip."

In 1979 Moore became Intel's chairman and Grove its president. (Grove became CEO in 1987.) When Intel's 8088 chip was chosen for IBM's PC in 1981, Intel secured its place as the microcomputer standard-setter.

Cutthroat pricing by Japanese competitors forced Intel out of the DRAM market in 1985; in a breathtaking strategy shift that has become the subject of countless business school case studies, the company refocused on microprocessors. It licensed its 286 chip technology to Advanced Micro Devices (AMD) and others in an effort to create an industry standard. Reacting to AMD's escalating market share (which stood at more than half by 1990), Intel fiercely protected the technology of its 386 (1985) and 486 (1989) chips; AMD sued for breach of contract.

Grove handed the CEO reins to president Craig Barrett in 1998; Grove replaced Moore as chairman, while Moore became chairman emeritus. (Thanks to a mandatory retirement age he helped set, Moore retired from Intel's board in 2001.) Also in 1998 Intel unveiled its low-end Celeron chip. Late in 1999 the company began shipping prototypes of its Itanium 64-bit processor; Itanium's general release was delayed repeatedly, ultimately into mid-2001.

A string of problems beset Intel in 2000. The company recalled hundreds of thousands of its motherboards that were distributed with a defective chip, and later cancelled development of a low-cost microprocessor for budget PCs.

In 2004 it announced plans to spend $2 billion to add a cutting-edge production plant in Ireland. The following year Intel unveiled plans for its second plant in Israel; the $3.5 billion project is expected to be operational in 2008. In 2005 Grove retired from the board, Barrett retired as CEO and succeeded Grove as chairman, and Otellini succeeded Barrett as CEO.

Intel announced late in 2005 that it would join with Micron Technology to form a new company devoted to NAND flash memory. Each contributed roughly $1.3 billion to create IM Flash Technologies, which will manufacture memory exclusively for Micron and Intel.

In 2006, in the face of stiff competition and lower demand for personal computers, the company taid it would reduce its headcount by 10,500 jobs, through attrition and workforce reductions, particularly in management, marketing, and IT functions.

In 2006 Intel sold its communications and application processor line. Later in 2006 Intel sold its optical-networking components business to Cortina Systems for around $115 million in cash and stock. It received a minority equity stake in Cortina as part of the transaction. Intel acquired the business as part of its 1999 acquisition of Level One Communications.

## EXECUTIVES

**Chairman and Director Emeritus:** Gordon E. Moore, age 78
**Chairman:** Craig R. Barrett, age 67, $436,000 pay
**President, CEO, and Director:** Paul S. Otellini, age 56, $700,000 pay
**EVP, CFO, and Chief Enterprise Services Officer:** Andy D. Bryant, age 56, $355,000 pay
**EVP and General Manager, Sales and Marketing Group, and Chief Sales and Marketing Officer:** Sean M. Maloney, age 51, $290,000 pay
**SVP; General Manager, Digital Enterprise Group:** Patrick P. (Pat) Gelsinger, age 45
**SVP and General Counsel:** D. Bruce Sewell, age 48
**SVP; General Manager, Mobility Group:** David (Dadi) Perlmutter, age 54
**SVP; General Manager, Ultra Mobility Group:** Anand Chandrasekher, age 44
**SVP; General Manager, Digital Home Group:** Eric B. Kim, age 52
**SVP; General Manager, Technology and Manufacturing Group:** Robert J. (Bob) Baker, age 51, $265,000 pay
**SVP; Director, Human Resources:** Patricia Murray, age 53
**SVP; Co-General Manager, Technology and Manufacturing Group:** William M. (Bill) Holt, age 54
**SVP; President, Intel Capital:** Arvind Sodhani, age 52
**VP; Director, Corporate Affairs Group:** William A. Swope, age 59
**VP; Director, Corporate Finance:** Leslie S. Culbertson, age 56
**Auditors:** Ernst & Young LLP

## LOCATIONS

**HQ:** Intel Corporation
2200 Mission College Blvd., Santa Clara, CA 95054
**Phone:** 408-765-8080 **Fax:** 408-765-3804
**Web:** www.intel.com

Intel has manufacturing plants in China, Costa Rica, Ireland, Israel, Malaysia, the Philippines, and the US, and sales offices in more than 40 countries worldwide.

### 2006 Sales

| | $ mil. | % of total |
|---|---|---|
| Asia/Pacific | | |
| Taiwan | 7,200 | 20 |
| China | 4,969 | 14 |
| Japan | 3,806 | 11 |
| Other countries | 5,308 | 15 |
| Americas | | |
| US | 5,486 | 15 |
| Other countries | 2,026 | 6 |
| Europe | 6,587 | 19 |
| **Total** | **35,382** | **100** |

## PRODUCTS/OPERATIONS

### 2006 Sales

| | $ mil. | % of total |
|---|---|---|
| Digital Enterprise Group | | |
| Microprocessors | 14,606 | 41 |
| Chipsets, motherboards & other | 5,270 | 15 |
| Mobility Group | | |
| Microprocessors | 9,212 | 26 |
| Chipsets & other | 3,097 | 9 |
| Flash Memory Group | 2,163 | 6 |
| Other | 1,034 | 3 |
| **Total** | **35,382** | **100** |

### Selected Products

Chipsets (consumer electronics, desktop, embedded, laptop, modem, server, workstation)
Communication infrastructure components
- Network processors
- Networked storage products

Flash memory (embedded, wireless)
Microprocessors (control plane, desktop, embedded, laptop, network, server, wireless, workstation)
- Celeron
- Core Duo
- Core Quad
- Itanium
- Pentium
- Xeon

Motherboards
Wired and wireless connectivity components

## COMPETITORS

AMD
Analog Devices
Applied Micro Circuits
Atmel
Broadcom
Cisco Systems
Conexant Systems
Creative Technology
Freescale Semiconductor
Hynix
IBM Microelectronics
Infineon Technologies
Intersil
LSI Corp.
Marvell Technology
Maxim Integrated Products
Microchip Technology
Micron Technology
Mitsubishi Electric
National Semiconductor
NEC Electronics
NVIDIA
NXP
Opnext
PMC-Sierra
QUALCOMM
Samsung Electronics
Silicon Integrated Systems
Spansion
STMicroelectronics
Sun Microsystems
Texas Instruments
Toshiba
Transmeta
VIA Technologies

## HISTORICAL FINANCIALS

Company Type: Public

### Income Statement

FYE: Last Saturday in December

| | REVENUE ($ mil.) | NET INCOME ($ mil.) | NET PROFIT MARGIN | EMPLOYEES |
|---|---|---|---|---|
| **12/06** | 35,382 | 5,044 | 14.3% | 94,100 |
| **12/05** | 38,826 | 8,664 | 22.3% | 99,900 |
| **12/04** | 34,209 | 7,516 | 22.0% | 85,000 |
| **12/03** | 30,141 | 5,641 | 18.7% | 79,700 |
| **12/02** | 26,764 | 3,117 | 11.6% | 78,700 |
| **Annual Growth** | 7.2% | 12.8% | — | 4.6% |

### 2006 Year-End Financials

Debt ratio: 5.0%
Return on equity: 13.8%
Cash ($ mil.): 10,002
Current ratio: 2.15
Long-term debt ($ mil.): 1,848
No. of shares (mil.): 5,766
Dividends
Yield: 2.0%
Payout: 46.5%
Market value ($ mil.): 116,762

### Stock History

NASDAQ (GS): INTC

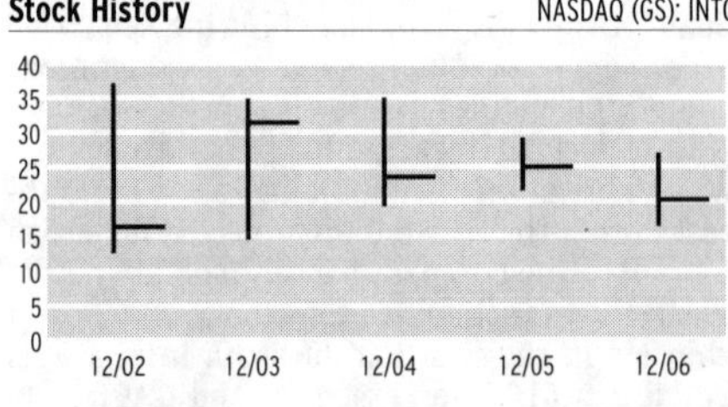


| | STOCK PRICE ($) FY Close | P/E High | P/E Low | PER SHARE ($) Earnings | Dividends | Book Value |
|---|---|---|---|---|---|---|
| **12/06** | 20.25 | 31 | 19 | 0.86 | 0.40 | 6.37 |
| **12/05** | 24.96 | 21 | 16 | 1.40 | 0.24 | 6.11 |
| **12/04** | 23.54 | 30 | 17 | 1.16 | 0.12 | 6.17 |
| **12/03** | 31.36 | 41 | 18 | 0.85 | 0.08 | 5.83 |
| **12/02** | 16.40 | 80 | 28 | 0.46 | 0.08 | 5.39 |
| **Annual Growth** | 5.4% | — | — | 16.9% | 49.5% | 4.3% |

# International Business Machines

Big Blue? Try Huge Blue. International Business Machines (IBM) is the world's top provider of computer products and services. Among the leaders in almost every market in which it competes, the company makes mainframes and servers, storage systems, and peripherals. Its service arm is the largest in the world and accounts for more than half of its revenue. IBM is also one of the largest providers of both software (ranking #2, behind Microsoft) and semiconductors. The company continues to use acquisitions to augment its software and service businesses, while streamlining its hardware operations with divestitures and organizational reengineering.

Acquisitions play an especially important role in IBM's software strategy. A pioneer in server operating system software, IBM made an early move into messaging and network management software with its acquisitions of Lotus Development (1995) and Tivoli (1996). Its software operations now focused primarily on e-commerce infrastructure, IBM has continued its push beyond OS software, purchasing the database operations of Informix (2001) and application integration products from CrossWorlds Software (2002). In 2003 it acquired development tool maker Rational Software for $2.1 billion in cash, and it acquired supply chain software developer Trigo Technologies early in 2004. Soon after came the purchase of software partner Candle, and in 2005 it acquired Ascential Software for about $1.1 billion in cash. The next year the company bought FileNet, a maker of content management software, in a deal valued at $1.6 billion.

In 2007 IBM acquired Vallent Corporation, a software firm that develops network performance monitoring and service management applications for wireless carriers. Vallent was integrated into its Software Group as part of its Tivoli Software business unit. Hoping to improve its data mobility technology offerings, IBM also acquired data storage management provider Softek Storage Solutions in 2007 and folded it into its storage and data services unit.

IBM has seen other significant changes in recent years. The company in 2006 added managed security services to its portfolio of offerings when it bought Atlanta-based Internet Security Systems in a cash deal valued at $1.3 billion.

Though perhaps still best known for its hardware, IBM's growing services business now accounts for more than half of its sales. Looking to extend its lead, IBM acquired PwC Consulting, the consulting and IT services unit of PricewaterhouseCoopers, for an estimated $3.5 billion in cash and stock.

Never content to rest on its laurels, IBM consistently leads the tech industry in patent awards. It is at the forefront of such diverse fields as nanotechnology and quantum computing.

## HISTORY

In 1914 National Cash Register's star salesman, Thomas Watson, left to rescue the flagging Computing-Tabulating-Recording (C-T-R) Company, the pioneer in US punch card processing that had been incorporated in 1911. Watson aggressively marketed C-T-R's tabulators, supplying them to the US government during WWI and tripling company revenues to almost $15 million by 1920. The company became International Business Machines (IBM) in 1924 and soon dominated the global market for tabulators, time clocks, and electric typewriters. It was the US's largest office machine maker by 1940.

IBM perfected electromechanical calculation (the Harvard Mark I, 1944) but initially dismissed the potential of computers. When Remington Rand's UNIVAC computer (1951) began replacing IBM machines, IBM quickly responded.

The company unveiled its first computer in 1952. With its superior research and development and marketing, IBM built a market share near 80% in the 1960s and 1970s. Its innovations included the STRETCH systems, which eliminated vacuum tubes (1960), and the first compatible family of computers, the System/360 (1964). IBM also developed floppy disks (1971) and the first laser printer for computers (1975). The introduction of the IBM PC in 1981 ignited the personal computer industry, sparking a barrage of PC clones. Through it all IBM was the subject of a 12-year government antitrust investigation that ended in 1982.

The shift to smaller, open systems, along with greater competition in all of IBM's segments, caused wrenching change. Instead of responding to the market need for cheap PCs and practical business applications, IBM stubbornly stuck with mainframes, and rivals began capitalizing on Big Blue's technology. After posting profits of $6.6 billion in 1984, the company began a slow slide. It sold many noncomputer businesses, including its copier division to Kodak in 1988 and its Lexmark typewriter business in 1991. Closing the book on its heritage, IBM shuttered the last of its punch card plants that year.

In 1993 CEO John Akers was replaced by Louis Gerstner, the first outsider to run IBM. He began to turn the ailing, artifact-status company around by slashing costs and nonstrategic divisions, cutting the workforce, shaking up entrenched management, and pushing services. His $1 billion R&D budget cut caused an exodus of IBM scientists and created an operation geared more toward quick turnaround than lengthy research (However, the company still leads the business world in patents each year). In 1994 Big Blue reported its first profit in four years. It also began making computer chips that year.

Beefing up its software offerings, IBM bought spreadsheet pioneer Lotus in 1995 and network management specialist Tivoli the next year. In 1997 an IBM supercomputer, Deep Blue, made headlines when it bested chess champion Garry Kasparov. Expanding its Web focus to include small businesses, IBM in 1999 bought Internet communications server maker Sequent.

Hoping to turn around its ailing PC business, IBM in 1999 axed manufacturing staff and halted sales of its PCs through US retailers.

Looking to bolster its data management division, IBM in 2001 purchased the database software unit of Informix for $1 billion. In early 2002, IBM announced it would outsource a significant amount of the manufacturing of its NetVista PC line to Sanmina-SCI; as part of the deal, Sanmina-SCI agreed to purchase IBM's desktop manufacturing operations in the US and Europe. IBM then completed its acquisition of longtime partner CrossWorlds Software.

Later in 2002 COO Samuel Palmisano succeeded Gerstner as CEO (The succession plan called for Palmisano to take over the additional role as chairman the following year).

## EXECUTIVES

**Chairman, President, and CEO:** Samuel J. Palmisano, age 55, $1,750,000 pay
**EVP Innovation and Technology:** Nicholas M. (Nick) Donofrio, age 61, $971,667 pay
**SVP and CFO:** Mark Loughridge, age 53, $859,167 pay
**SVP; Group Executive, Sales and Distribution:** Douglas T. (Doug) Elix, age 58, $968,751 pay
**SVP; Group Executive, Software:** Steven A. (Steve) Mills, age 55, $641,250 pay
**SVP; Group Executive, Systems and Technology:** William M. (Bill) Zeitler, age 59
**SVP Legal and Regulatory Affairs and General Counsel:** Robert C. Weber, age 56
**SVP Research:** John E. Kelly III, age 53
**SVP Communications:** Jon C. Iwata, age 44
**SVP Enterprise On Demand Transformation:** Linda S. Sanford, age 54
**SVP Human Resources:** J. Randall (Randy) MacDonald, age 58
**SVP Integrated Operations:** Robert W. (Bob) Moffat Jr., age 51
**SVP Marketing and Strategy:** J. Bruce Harreld, age 56
**VP ISC Global Procurement and Chief Procurement Officer:** John Paterson
**VP and Treasurer:** Jesse J. Greene Jr., age 61
**VP, Assistant General Counsel, and Secretary:** Daniel E. O'Donnell, age 59
**VP and Controller:** Timothy S. Shaughnessy, age 49
**VP Corporate Affairs and Chief Privacy Officer:** Harriet Pearson
**VP Deep Computing:** Dave Turek
**VP Sales, IBM Software:** Michael J. (Mike) Borman
**VP Worldwide Engineering:** Robert (Bob) Cancilla
**Auditors:** PricewaterhouseCoopers LLP

## LOCATIONS

**HQ:** International Business Machines Corporation
1 New Orchard Rd., Armonk, NY 10504
**Phone:** 914-499-1900 **Fax:** 914-765-7382
**Web:** www.ibm.com

International Business Machines operates in more than 150 countries.

## PRODUCTS/OPERATIONS

### 2006 Sales by Service

| | % of total |
|---|---|
| Global services | 53 |
| Hardware | 25 |
| Software | 20 |
| Global financing | 2 |
| **Total** | **100** |

### 2006 Sales by Sector

| | % of total |
|---|---|
| Financial services | 28 |
| Public | 15 |
| Industrial | 13 |
| Distribution | 10 |
| Communications | 9 |
| Small & medium-sized business | 19 |
| OEM | 4 |
| Other | 2 |
| **Total** | **100** |

### Selected Products

Microelectronics
- Application-specific integrated circuits (ASICs)
- Foundry services
- Memory chips
- Microprocessors and embedded processors
- Packaging and interconnect products and services

Printing systems

Servers

Software
- Application development
- Database and data management
- E-commerce
- Graphics and multimedia
- Groupware
- Networking and communication
- Operating systems
- Product life cycle management
- Security
- Speech recognition
- System management
- Transaction system
- Web application servers

Storage
- Hard drive systems
- Optical libraries
- Storage networking
- Tape drives, systems, and libraries

### Selected Services

Business services
- E-business
- Strategic consulting

Financing

IT services
- Infrastructure
- Outsourcing
- Systems management
- Web hosting

Training

## COMPETITORS

Accenture
Alcatel-Lucent
BEA Systems
BearingPoint
CA
Canon
Capgemini
Computer Sciences Corp.
Dell
Deloitte Consulting
EDS
EMC
Epson
Ericsson
Fujitsu
Hewlett-Packard
Hitachi
Hitachi Data Systems
Intel
Lexmark
Matsushita Electric
McKinsey & Company
Microsoft
Motorola, Inc.
NEC
Novell
NTT DATA
Oracle
Ricoh
SAP
SGI
Siemens AG
Sony
Sun Microsystems
Texas Instruments
Toshiba
TSMC
Unisys
Xerox

## HISTORICAL FINANCIALS

Company Type: Public

**Income Statement** FYE: December 31

| | REVENUE ($ mil.) | NET INCOME ($ mil.) | NET PROFIT MARGIN | EMPLOYEES |
|---|---|---|---|---|
| **12/06** | 91,424 | 9,492 | 10.4% | 355,766 |
| **12/05** | 91,134 | 7,934 | 8.7% | 366,345 |
| **12/04** | 96,293 | 8,430 | 8.8% | 369,277 |
| **12/03** | 89,131 | 7,583 | 8.5% | 355,157 |
| **12/02** | 81,186 | 3,579 | 4.4% | 355,421 |
| **Annual Growth** | 3.0% | 27.6% | — | 0.0% |

**2006 Year-End Financials**

Debt ratio: 48.3%
Return on equity: 30.8%
Cash ($ mil.): 10,656
Current ratio: 1.11
Long-term debt ($ mil.): 13,780
No. of shares (mil.): 1,506
Dividends
Yield: 1.1%
Payout: 18.0%
Market value ($ mil.): 146,355

**Stock History** NYSE: IBM

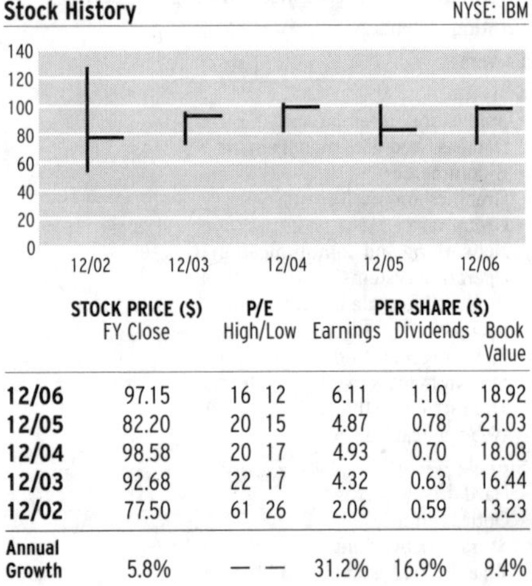


| | STOCK PRICE ($) FY Close | P/E High | P/E Low | PER SHARE ($) Earnings | Dividends | Book Value |
|---|---|---|---|---|---|---|
| **12/06** | 97.15 | 16 | 12 | 6.11 | 1.10 | 18.92 |
| **12/05** | 82.20 | 20 | 15 | 4.87 | 0.78 | 21.03 |
| **12/04** | 98.58 | 20 | 17 | 4.93 | 0.70 | 18.08 |
| **12/03** | 92.68 | 22 | 17 | 4.32 | 0.63 | 16.44 |
| **12/02** | 77.50 | 61 | 26 | 2.06 | 0.59 | 13.23 |
| **Annual Growth** | 5.8% | — | — | 31.2% | 16.9% | 9.4% |

# International Flavors & Fragrances

*Iff* you've got a taste for the sweet and the salty, then International Flavors & Fragrances (IFF) is your kind of company. It's one of the world's leading creators and manufacturers of artificial aromas and flavors, producing fragrances used in the manufacture of perfumes, cosmetics, soaps, and other personal care and household products. The company has 12% of the world market, placing it right behind Givaudan as the #2 flavor and fragrance maker. IFF sells its flavors principally to producers of prepared foods, dairy foods, beverages, confections, and pharmaceuticals. The company sells its fragrances and flavors in solid and liquid forms in amounts that range from a few pounds to several tons.

The company has manufacturing, sales, and distribution facilities in more than 30 countries. Sales outside North America account for nearly 70% of revenues. The compounds used in IFF's products are made both synthetically and from natural ingredients such as flowers and fruits.

The company operates about 30 fragrance and flavor laboratories in more than 20 countries. While IFF's flavor products represent 60% of the total production volume, fragrances contribute more than half of the company's sales.

IFF continues to introduce new products and to invest heavily in product development; R&D spending amounts to about 10% of sales. The company opened new creative centers for fragrances in Paris and Mumbai in 2005. IFF has expanded its fragrance plant in Singapore to support its growth in the Asia/Pacific region.

## HISTORY

International Flavors & Fragrances (IFF) began in 1929 when Dutch immigrant and perfumer A. L. van Ameringen (who originally came to the US to work for the agent of the Dutch firm Polak & Schwarz, later leaving to form his own business) and William Haebler formed a fragrance company, van Ameringen-Haebler, in New York City.

The company produced the fragrance for Youth Dew, Estée Lauder's first big cosmetics hit, in 1953. One biographer of Estée Lauder linked her romantically with van Ameringen after her 1939 divorce (she later remarried Joseph Lauder). The business association with van Ameringen's company endured, and by the late 1980s it had produced an estimated 90% of Estée Lauder's fragrances.

In 1958 the company changed its name to International Flavors & Fragrances after it bought Polak & Schwarz. The US market for fragrances grew as consumers bought items such as air fresheners and manufacturers began adding fragrances to household cleaning items.

Henry Walter, who became CEO when van Ameringen retired in 1963, expanded IFF's presence overseas. Walter boasted, "Most of the great soap fragrances have been ours." So have many famous French perfumes, but most perfume companies wanted to cultivate product mystique, preventing IFF from taking credit for its scents.

Most of IFF's products were made for manufacturers of consumer goods. But under Walter's direction in the 1970s, IFF's R&D team experimented to find scents for museum exhibits and participated in Masters & Johnson research on the connection between sex and smell. Said Walter, "Our business is sex and hunger."

During the early 1980s IFF conducted fragrance research for relieving stress, lowering blood pressure, and alleviating depression. In 1982 IFF researchers developed a way to bind odors to plastic, a process used by makers of garbage bags and toys.

Walter retired in 1985 and Eugene Grisanti became CEO. After a three-year slump in new creations, IFF developed fragrances for several prestigious perfumes (Eternity and Halston) in 1988. IFF enhanced its position in dairy flavors with its 1991 purchase of Wisconsin-based Auro Tech. In 1993 IFF's Living Flower process successfully synthesized the fragrance of growing flowers for perfumes.

IFF inaugurated its flavor and fragrance facility in China (Guangzhou) and formed a joint venture with China's Hangzhou Xin'anjiang Perfumery Factory. The company reasserted its leadership in the US fragrance market in 1996 with the launch of two IFF-developed fragrances: Elizabeth Taylor's Black Pearls and Escada's Jardin de Soleil.

Sales and profits dipped in 1997, prompting IFF to consolidate production. Asia's economic crisis and turmoil in Russia continued to hurt profits in 1998, and in 1999 IFF was hit by the devaluation of Brazil's currency, weak demand for aroma chemicals, and the US dollar's strength against the euro.

In 2000 Unilever executive Richard Goldstein was appointed chairman and CEO. Boosting its natural ingredients operations, IFF bought Laboratoire Monique Remy (France). The same year IFF acquired rival fragrance and flavor maker Bush Boake Allen in a deal worth about $1 billion. The acquisition led to a company-wide reorganization, including the closing of some manufacturing, distribution, and sales facilities worldwide.

In 2001 the company sold its US and Brazilian formulated fruit and vegetable preparation businesses and its aroma chemicals business in the UK. Continuting its product development strategy, IFF launched a high-intensity cooling technology (CoolTek) for use in the food, beverage, and pharmaceutical industries that does not use the traditional mint-based technology in 2003. The following year it opened a new culinary and baking center to support customers' product development programs.

IFF sold its fruit preparations operations in Switzerland and Germany in August 2004 to Israel's Frutarom. The deal was for $36.5 million. Later that year, it sold the remainder of its fruit preparations business (located in France) to Frutarom. It also closed its Canadian manufacturing facility and its plant in Dijon, France.

Chairman and CEO Goldstein retired in 2006. Former Sears chairman and CEO Arthur Martinez, an IFF director, took over on an interim basis until International Paper's Robert Amen was named chairman and CEO.

## EXECUTIVES

**Chairman and CEO:** Robert M. (Rob) Amen, age 56
**Group President, Flavors:** Hernan Vaisman, age 47
**Group President, Fragrances:** Nicolas Mirzayantz, age 43
**EVP, Global Operations:** D. Wayne Howard, age 49, $474,150 pay
**SVP and Chief Transition Officer:** James H. (Jim) Dunsdon, age 59
**SVP and CFO:** Douglas J. Wetmore, age 49, $459,000 pay
**SVP, Aroma Chemicals:** Robert J. M. (Rob) Edelman, age 44
**SVP, Human Resources:** Steven J. Heaslip, age 48
**SVP, Research and Development:** Clint D. Brooks, age 54
**SVP and Regional Manager, Europe:** Robert Burns, age 48
**SVP, General Counsel, and Secretary:** Dennis M. Meany, age 58
**VP and CIO:** John Kirven
**VP and Treasurer:** Charles D. Weller
**VP and Chief Marketing Officer:** Joseph (Joe) Faranda, age 52

## LOCATIONS

**HQ:** International Flavors & Fragrances Inc.
521 W. 57th St., New York, NY 10019
**Phone:** 212-765-5500 **Fax:** 212-708-7132
**Web:** www.iff.com

International Flavors & Fragrances has 30 manufacturing facilities in 22 countries, with major facilities in Argentina, Australia, Brazil, China, India, Indonesia, Ireland, Japan, Mexico, the Netherlands, Singapore, Spain, the UK, and the US. The company has sales and distribution facilities in 30 countries.

**2006 Sales**

| | $ mil. | % of total |
|---|---|---|
| Europe | 780.4 | 37 |
| North America | 648.6 | 31 |
| Asia/Pacific | 341.4 | 16 |
| Latin America | 265.9 | 13 |
| India | 59.1 | 3 |
| **Total** | **2,095.4** | **100** |

## PRODUCTS/OPERATIONS

**2006 Sales**

| | $ mil. | % of total |
|---|---|---|
| Fragrances | 1,200 | 57 |
| Flavors | 895 | 43 |
| **Total** | **2,095** | **100** |

**Selected Applications for IFF's Products**

Fragrance Chemical Uses
- Aftershave lotions
- Air fresheners
- All-purpose cleaners
- Colognes
- Cosmetic creams
- Deodorants
- Detergents
- Hair care products
- Lipsticks
- Lotions
- Perfumes
- Powders
- Soaps

Flavor Chemical Uses
- Alcoholic beverages
- Baked goods
- Candies
- Dairy products
- Desserts
- Diet foods
- Drink powders
- Pharmaceuticals
- Prepared foods
- Snacks
- Soft drinks

## COMPETITORS

Ajinomoto
BASF AG
Bayer
Danisco A/S
Firmenich
Frutarom
Givaudan
Henkel
Human Pheromone Sciences
International Specialty Products
Kerry Group
M & F Worldwide
McCormick
Newly Weds Foods
PCAS
Robertet
Sensient
Symrise
Takasago International
Wrigley

## HISTORICAL FINANCIALS

Company Type: Public

**Income Statement** FYE: December 31

| | REVENUE ($ mil.) | NET INCOME ($ mil.) | NET PROFIT MARGIN | EMPLOYEES |
|---|---|---|---|---|
| **12/06** | 2,095 | 227 | 10.8% | 5,087 |
| **12/05** | 1,993 | 193 | 9.7% | 5,160 |
| **12/04** | 2,034 | 196 | 9.6% | 5,212 |
| **12/03** | 1,902 | 173 | 9.1% | 5,454 |
| **12/02** | 1,809 | 176 | 9.7% | 5,728 |
| **Annual Growth** | 3.7% | 6.5% | — | (2.9%) |

**2006 Year-End Financials**

Debt ratio: 87.4%
Return on equity: 24.9%
Cash ($ mil.): 115
Current ratio: 2.42
Long-term debt ($ mil.): 791
No. of shares (mil.): 89
Dividends
Yield: 1.6%
Payout: 30.6%
Market value ($ mil.): 4,396

**Stock History** NYSE: IFF

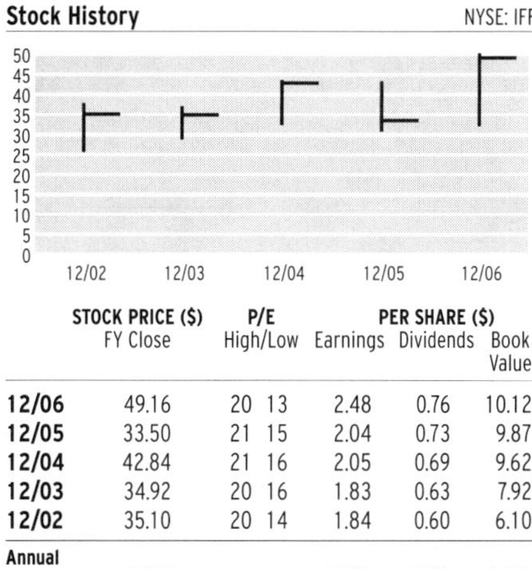


| | STOCK PRICE ($) FY Close | P/E High/Low | PER SHARE ($) Earnings | Dividends | Book Value |
|---|---|---|---|---|---|
| **12/06** | 49.16 | 20 13 | 2.48 | 0.76 | 10.12 |
| **12/05** | 33.50 | 21 15 | 2.04 | 0.73 | 9.87 |
| **12/04** | 42.84 | 21 16 | 2.05 | 0.69 | 9.62 |
| **12/03** | 34.92 | 20 16 | 1.83 | 0.63 | 7.92 |
| **12/02** | 35.10 | 20 14 | 1.84 | 0.60 | 6.10 |
| **Annual Growth** | 8.8% | — — | 7.7% | 6.1% | 13.5% |

# International Game Technology

International Game Technology (IGT) wants to hit the jackpot in the slot machine business. The company is the #1 designer and manufacturer of slot machines (it controls about two-thirds of the North American market). It also produces video gaming, player tracking, and accounting systems. Other IGT products include reel-type slot machines (the S2000 series), video gaming machines (Game King), video gaming terminals for government-sponsored lotteries, and progressive jackpot slot-machine networks (MegaJackpots) that link slot machines from several casinos to increase jackpot payoffs. IGT is also active in the Internet gambling industry.

In 2004, IGT expanded into Canada with its purchase of Hi-Tech Gaming, a leading Canadian provider of gaming equipment and services. The acquisition results in the creation of IGT-Canada, with offices in Toronto, Montreal, Winnipeg, and Moncton.

IGT's other focus is an expansion into the online gaming market. In 2005 it bought WagerWorks, a company which provides Internet-based online games, and related technology and content. IGT wants to distribute its gaming brands through new mediums like interactive television and mobile devices, and the $90 million purchase of WagerWorks helps IGT break into that arena without having to launch a new business itself.

In 2007 IGT agreed to invest in Digideal Corporation, a privately held gaming technology company whose main product is an electronic table game platform.

## HISTORY

International Game Technology (IGT) was formed in 1980 by William "Si" Redd, a veteran of the slot machine industry. Lady Luck was good to Redd for five years before turning fickle. Rather than fold, Redd dealt himself a king (hiring Charles Mathewson, a retired top executive from investment firm Jefferies & Co.). Mathewson flushed top management, cinched IGT's belt, and dealt new managers a fresh hand (stock options rather than cash). IGT developed its Telnaes patent-based slot machine — a reel-type slot with higher payouts and higher odds — featuring flashy themes, fewer breakdowns, and improved reporting systems. Slots went from a nickel-and-dime game to a major source of casino revenue, and the Telnaes patent is used in almost every modern reel-type machine.

Legalized gambling on riverboats, Indian reservations, cruise ships, and in foreign markets has increased IGT's take (sales to foreign countries account for almost a quarter of revenue).

In 1997 IGT debuted Mega$ports, which accepts unique wagers on sports (such as which quarterback will throw the most yards in a game). That year IGT's vast new headquarters became fully operational (five plants and seven warehouses were moved under one roof). In 1998 IGT beefed up its Australian operations with the $114 million acquisition of Olympic Amusements, a Melbourne-based supplier of gaming equipment and services. IGT also bought the UK-based Barcrest gaming machine business from Bass (now split into Mitchells & Butlers and InterContinental Hotel Group) for $70 million.

In 1999 the company acquired Sodak Gaming, a supplier of gaming machines to Native American casinos and other clients. In 2001 IGT bought rivals Silicon Gaming (for about $45 million) and Anchor Gaming. The latter buy was part of the company's strategy of expanding into the lottery business. The following year it created a new division, IGT Lottery, to house its lottery operations, including the former Anchor companies AWI, United Tote, and VLC, and its own Oregon lottery route operations and SAMS lottery system.

In 2003 IGT purchased gaming software development company Acres Gaming for $130 million. Also that year, the company sold its online lottery operations to Scientific Games for $143 million. In late 2004 IGT created its IGT-Canada unit with the acquisition of Canadian gaming equipment provider Hi-Tech Gaming. It also expanded into online gaming that same year through the purchase of WagerWorks.

## EXECUTIVES

**Chairman, President, and CEO:** Thomas J. Matthews, age 41
**COO:** Steven W. (Steve) Morro, age 49
**Interim CFO, Chief Accounting Officer, and Treasurer:** Daniel R. Siciliano, age 38
**EVP, General Counsel, and Secretary:** David D. (Dave) Johnson, age 54, $1,214,430 pay
**EVP Engineering:** Jon Wade
**EVP Operations:** Anthony Ciorciari, age 59
**EVP Corporate Strategy:** Richard (Rich) Pennington, age 44
**EVP Product Strategy and Director:** Robert A. (Bob) Bittman, age 52, $999,566 pay
**SVP Finance:** Eric Vetter
**SVP Product Development:** Jean Venneman
**SVP Sales:** Ron Rivera
**VP and General Manager, IGT Gaming Systems:** Rick Rowe
**VP and Firmware Engineer:** Ali Saffari
**VP Human Resources:** Tami Corbin
**VP Investor Relations:** Patrick W. (Pat) Cavanaugh, age 43
**Auditors:** Deloitte & Touche LLP

## LOCATIONS

**HQ:** International Game Technology
9295 Prototype Dr., Reno, NV 89521
**Phone:** 775-448-7777 **Fax:** 775-448-0719
**Web:** www.igt.com

International Game Technology has offices in Australia, Canada, Europe, Japan, Latin America, New Zealand, Russia, South Africa, the UK, and the US.

### 2006 Sales

| | $ mil. | % of total |
|---|---|---|
| North America | 1,978.2 | 79 |
| Other regions | 533.5 | 21 |
| **Total** | **2,511.7** | **100** |

## PRODUCTS/OPERATIONS

### 2006 Sales

| | $ mil. | % of total |
|---|---|---|
| Product sales | 1,260.3 | 50 |
| Gaming operations | 1,251.4 | 50 |
| **Total** | **2,511.7** | **100** |

### Selected Products

IGT Systems (casino control, information tracking, and casino management systems)
MegaJackpots (slot-machine network linking machines from several casinos)
- *American Bandstand*
- *Austin Powers in Goldmember*
- Elvis
- *Jeopardy!*
- Megabucks
- Marilyn Monroe
- Megabucks
- Quartermania
- UNO
- *Wheel of Fortune*
- *Young Frankenstein*

Spinning-reel slot machines
- S2000 Series

Video gaming products
- Game King

Video gaming terminals for government-sponsored gaming

## COMPETITORS

Aristocrat Leisure
Aruze Gaming
Atronic Americas
Bally Technologies
Escor
Konami
Lottomatica
Multimedia Games
Progressive Gaming
Scientific Games
Shuffle Master
WMS Industries

## HISTORICAL FINANCIALS

Company Type: Public

**Income Statement** FYE: September 30

| | REVENUE ($ mil.) | NET INCOME ($ mil.) | NET PROFIT MARGIN | EMPLOYEES |
|---|---|---|---|---|
| **9/06** | 2,512 | 474 | 18.9% | 5,200 |
| **9/05** | 2,379 | 437 | 18.3% | 5,000 |
| **9/04** | 2,485 | 489 | 19.7% | 4,900 |
| **9/03** | 2,128 | 391 | 18.4% | 5,300 |
| **9/02** | 1,848 | 271 | 14.7% | 6,200 |
| **Annual Growth** | 8.0% | 15.0% | — | (4.3%) |

**2006 Year-End Financials**

Debt ratio: 9.8%
Return on equity: 24.0%
Cash ($ mil.): 636
Current ratio: 1.10
Long-term debt ($ mil.): 200
No. of shares (mil.): 334
Dividends
Yield: 1.2%
Payout: 37.3%
Market value ($ mil.): 13,869

**Stock History** NYSE: IGT

| | STOCK PRICE ($) FY Close | P/E High/Low | | PER SHARE ($) Earnings | Dividends | Book Value |
|---|---|---|---|---|---|---|
| **9/06** | 41.50 | 32 | 19 | 1.34 | 0.50 | 6.11 |
| **9/05** | 27.00 | 31 | 20 | 1.20 | 0.48 | 5.63 |
| **9/04** | 35.95 | 35 | 21 | 1.34 | 0.30 | 5.71 |
| **9/03** | 28.15 | 26 | 14 | 1.11 | 0.17 | 4.88 |
| **9/02** | 17.40 | 23 | 13 | 0.79 | — | 16.51 |
| **Annual Growth** | 24.3% | — | — | 14.1% | 43.3% | (22.0%) |

# International Paper

International Paper is the world's largest forest products company. It produces uncoated paper, industrial and consumer packaging, and pulp. Together, paper and packaging account for nearly two-thirds of the company's sales. International Paper also distributes printing, packaging, and graphic-art supplies in North America through subsidiary xpedx and in Europe through multiple subsidiaries. Slimming down, the company has sold its specialty chemicals operations, the majority of its lumber and wood products business, and most of the 6.3 million acres of US forestland it once owned. It retains 500,000 acres of US land and owns or has harvesting rights to nearly 900,000 acres of forestland in Brazil and Russia.

To focus on its core paper and packaging businesses, International Paper has been shedding non-core operations. Divestitures between 2000 and 2005 include its retail and flexible packaging operations, subsidiary Bush Boake Allen, and door and building products maker Masonite. It sold about $11 billion in assets in 2006 alone.

A zealous consolidator, International Paper's notable purchases have included Union Camp, Shorewood Packaging, and papermaker Champion International.

In mid-2006 International Paper moved its headquarters to Memphis, Tennessee.

Early in 2006 International Paper sold 218,000 acres of forest to The Nature Conservancy and the Conservation Fund for about $300 million. Soon thereafter it announced agreements to sell 4.2 million acres of forestland to an investor group led by Resource Management Service and another 900,000 acres of forestland to an investor group led by TimberStar; it completed both deals before the end of 2006. Together, the two deals brought International Paper more than $6 billion.

In mid-2006 International Paper sold its business in coated and supercalendared papers to Verso Paper, an affiliate of investment firm Apollo Management, for about $1.4 billion. It later sold its coated papers business in Brazil to Stora Enso for $420 million, a deal including 50,000 hectares (around 124,000 acres) of forestland in Brazil's Parana state. Later in 2006, International Paper announced that it would swap more than $1 billion worth of factories and forestland in Brazil with Votorantim Celulose e Papel. (It completed the swap early in 2007.)

Near the end of 2006, International Paper announced three more big divestitures, all of which were completed by April 2007. In the first deal the company sold its beverage packaging operations to Carter Holt Harvey for approximately $500 million. In the second deal, the paper giant sold its Arizona Chemical subsidiary to Rhone Capital for about $485 million. Lastly, IP sold five wood products plants to rival Georgia-Pacific for $237 million.

IP formed a joint venture with Ilim Holding in 2007. The company has agreed to buy 50% of Ilim Holding for about $650 million. The JV, Ilim Group, will operate pulp and paper mills in the European and Siberian regions of Russia.

## HISTORY

In 1898 18 northeastern pulp and paper firms consolidated to lower costs. The resulting International Paper had 20 mills in Maine, Massachusetts, New Hampshire, New York, and Vermont. The mills relied on forests in New England and Canada for wood pulp. When Canada enacted legislation to stop the export of pulpwood in 1919, International Paper formed Canadian International Paper.

In the 1920s International Paper built a hydroelectric plant on the Hudson River. Between 1928 and 1941 the company called itself International Paper & Power. It entered the market for kraft paper (paper sacks) in 1925 with the purchase of Bastrop Pulp & Paper (Louisiana).

During the 1940s and 1950s, the company bought Agar Manufacturing (shipping containers, 1940), Single Service Containers (Pure-Pak milk containers, 1946), and Lord Baltimore Press (folding cartons, 1958). It diversified in the 1960s and 1970s, buying Davol (hospital products, 1968; sold to C. R. Bard, 1980), American Central (land development, 1968; sold to developers, 1974), and General Crude Oil (gas and oil, 1975; sold to Mobil Oil, 1979).

In the 1980s International Paper modernized its plants to focus on less-cyclical products. After selling Canadian International Paper in 1981, the company bought Hammermill Paper (office paper, 1986), Arvey (paper manufacturing and distribution, 1987), and Masonite (composite wood products, 1988). International Paper entered the European paper market in 1989 by buying Aussedat Rey (France), Ilford Group (UK), and Zanders (West Germany). In 1990 it bought Dixon Paper (distributor of paper and graphic arts supplies), Nevamar (laminates), and the UK's Cookson Group (printing plates).

International Paper expanded in the early 1990s with acquisitions such as Scaldia Papier (the Netherlands, 1991) and Western Paper (1992) and through investments in Carter Holt Harvey (New Zealand) and Scitex (Israel), a leading maker of electronic prepress systems. In 1994 International Paper formed a Chinese packaging joint venture and bought two Mexican paper-distributing companies. The next year it bought Seaman-Patrick Paper and Carpenter Paper (paper distribution), and DSM (inks and adhesives resins).

After recording a loss in 1997, International Paper began downsizing: It sold $1 billion in marginal assets and cut its workforce by 10%.

International Paper paid $7.9 billion in 1999 for rival Union Camp, annd it acquired Shorewood Packaging for $850 million in 2000. That year it made an unsolicited $6.2 billion bid for Champion International — which had previously agreed to be acquired by UPM-Kymmene — igniting a bidding war. UPM withdrew its offer, however, and International Paper acquired Champion for about $9.6 billion. Also in 2000, the company sold its 68% stake in Bush Boake Allen for about $640 million.

International Paper closed its mill in Natchez, Mississippi, and exited the Chemical Cellulose pulp business in 2003. (The Natchez plant is the world's second-largest producer of acetate pulps.) Layoffs affected about 600 workers, or 6% of International Paper's workforce.

At the close of 2004 International Paper sold more than 1 million acres of its Maine and New Hampshire forestlands to private forest investment management company GMO Renewable Resources, LLC. It also completed the sale of its Weldwood of Canada, Ltd. subsidiary to West Fraser Timber Co. Ltd. of Vancouver, Canada, for about $950 million (C$1.26 billion).

In 2005 the company sold its 50.5% stake in Carter Holt Harvey for $1.14 billion.

## EXECUTIVES

**Chairman and CEO:** John V. Faraci Jr., age 57, $1,173,750 pay
**EVP and CFO:** Marianne Miller Parrs, age 62, $588,700 pay
**EVP, Manufacturing and Technology:** Newland A. Lesko, age 61, $563,296 pay
**SVP and CIO:** John N. Balboni, age 58
**SVP; President, Shorewood Packaging:** Michael J. (Mike) Balduino, age 56
**SVP, Corporate Development:** C. Cato Ealy, age 50
**SVP, General Counsel, and Secretary:** Maura Abeln Smith, age 51, $552,150 pay
**SVP, Human Resources:** Jerome N. (Jerry) Carter, age 58
**SVP, Internal Audit:** Andrew R. (Andy) Lessin, age 64
**SVP, Packaging Solutions:** Carol L. Roberts, age 47
**SVP, Printing and Communication Papers:** H. Wayne Brafford, age 55
**SVP, Strategic Initiatives:** Paul Herbert, age 57, $485,688 pay
**SVP; President, IP Asia:** Thomas E. (Tom) Gestrich, age 60
**SVP; President, International Paper, Brazil:** Maximo Pacheco, age 54
**SVP; President, xpedx:** Thomas G. (Tom) Kadien, age 50
**SVP; President, European Operations:** Mary A. Laschinger, age 46
**VP, Finance, and Controller:** Robert J. Grillet, age 51
**VP, Investor Relations:** Brian N. McDonald
**Media Relations Manager:** Amy J. Sawyer
**Auditors:** Deloitte & Touche LLP

## LOCATIONS

**HQ:** International Paper Company
6400 Poplar Ave., Memphis, TN 38197
**Phone:** 901-419-7000 **Fax:** 901-214-9682
**Web:** www.ipaper.com

### 2006 Sales

| | $ mil. | % of total |
|---|---|---|
| Americas | | |
| US | 17,811 | 81 |
| Other countries | 846 | 4 |
| Europe | 3,030 | 14 |
| Pacific Rim | 308 | 1 |
| **Total** | **21,995** | **100** |

## PRODUCTS/OPERATIONS

### 2006 Sales

| | $ mil. | % of total |
|---|---|---|
| Printing Papers | 6,930 | 30 |
| Distribution | 6,785 | 30 |
| Industrial packaging | 4,925 | 22 |
| Consumer packaging | 2,455 | 11 |
| Forest products | 765 | 3 |
| Specialty businesses & other | 935 | 4 |
| Adjustments | (800) | — |
| **Total** | **21,995** | **100** |

### Selected Operations and Products

Printing papers
- Commercial printing papers
- Office and consumer papers

Distribution
- Business products for copiers and computers
- Food service disposables
- Graphic arts equipment and supplies
- Industrial packaging and supplies
- Printing papers

Industrial Packaging
- Containerboard

Consumer Packaging
- Bleached board
- Food service packaging

## COMPETITORS

Alcoa
Amcor
Cascades Inc.
Domtar
ENCE
Environmental Mill & Supply
Georgia-Pacific
Louisiana-Pacific
McFarland Cascade
MeadWestvaco
Myllykoski Paper
NewPage
Nippon Paper
OfficeMax
Potlatch
Pratt Industries USA
Smurfit-Stone Container
Temple-Inland
UPM-Kymmene
Weyerhaeuser

## HISTORICAL FINANCIALS

Company Type: Public

### Income Statement — FYE: December 31

| | REVENUE ($ mil.) | NET INCOME ($ mil.) | NET PROFIT MARGIN | EMPLOYEES |
|---|---|---|---|---|
| **12/06** | 21,995 | 1,050 | 4.8% | 60,600 |
| **12/05** | 24,097 | 1,100 | 4.6% | 68,700 |
| **12/04** | 25,548 | (35) | — | 80,000 |
| **12/03** | 25,179 | 302 | 1.2% | 83,000 |
| **12/02** | 24,976 | (880) | — | 91,000 |
| **Annual Growth** | (3.1%) | — | — | (9.7%) |

### 2006 Year-End Financials

Debt ratio: 82.0%
Return on equity: 12.9%
Cash ($ mil.): 1,624
Current ratio: 1.86
Long-term debt ($ mil.): 6,531
No. of shares (mil.): 454
Dividends
Yield: 2.9%
Payout: 45.9%
Market value ($ mil.): 15,464

### Stock History — NYSE: IP

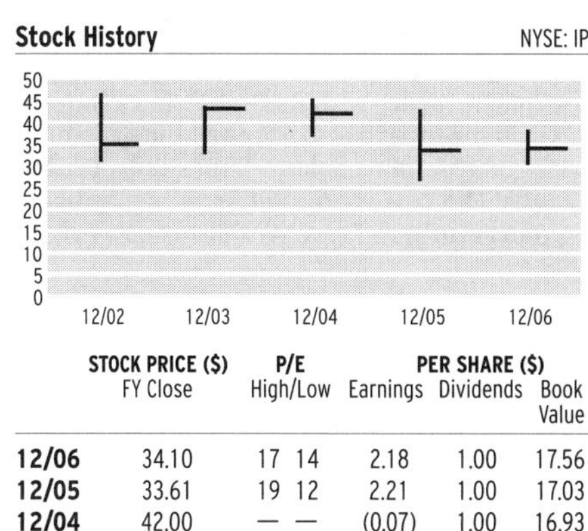


| | STOCK PRICE ($) FY Close | P/E High | P/E Low | PER SHARE ($) Earnings | Dividends | Book Value |
|---|---|---|---|---|---|---|
| **12/06** | 34.10 | 17 | 14 | 2.18 | 1.00 | 17.56 |
| **12/05** | 33.61 | 19 | 12 | 2.21 | 1.00 | 17.03 |
| **12/04** | 42.00 | — | — | (0.07) | 1.00 | 16.93 |
| **12/03** | 43.11 | 69 | 53 | 0.63 | 1.00 | 17.11 |
| **12/02** | 34.97 | — | — | (1.83) | 1.00 | 15.39 |
| **Annual Growth** | (0.6%) | — | — | — | 0.0% | 3.3% |

# Interpublic Group

Subsidiaries of this company come between brands and the general public. The Interpublic Group of Companies is the world's third-largest advertising and marketing services conglomerate (behind Omnicom Group and WPP Group), operating through offices in more than 100 countries. Its flagship creative agencies include McCann Worldgroup, DraftFCB, and Lowe & Partners, while such firms as Campbell-Ewald; Deutsch; and Hill, Holliday are leaders in the US advertising business. Interpublic also offers direct marketing, media services, and public relations through such agencies as Initiative Media and Weber Shandwick. Its largest clients include General Motors, Johnson & Johnson, Microsoft, and Unilever.

Once the largest of the global ad holding companies, Interpublic has been in a downward spiral as a result of both internal and external strife. The company's rapid expansion through acquisitions in the late 1990s left it bloated and unable to integrate its disparate agencies. Accounting discrepancies brought to light in 2002 damaged its reputation both on Wall Street and Madison Avenue, while a revolving door in the executive ranks has hobbled its efforts to right the ship.

In 2005 new chief executive Michael Roth was tasked with straightening out Interpublic's financial controls and improving its balance sheet. Later that year, the company revealed extensive bookkeeping problems, primarily in its overseas operations, leading to a financial restatement going back to 2000.

Looking to optimize its infrastructure, Interpublic integrated direct marketer Draft, Inc. with advertising agency Foote, Cone & Belding (forming DraftFCB) in mid-2006.

Interpublic has also been keeping its eye on one of the world's fastest growing economies, India. In mid-2007, it bought all the shares of

FCB Ulka, a top five ad agency in India that operates from six offices. Interpublic will integrate the Indian agency with its DraftFCB operations. At the same time, it also acquired the remaining 51% stake it didn't hold in Lintas India Private Limited at a cost of $50 million in cash and integrated it into its Lowe Worldwide network.

## HISTORY

Standard Oil advertising executive Harrison McCann opened the H. K. McCann Company in 1911 and signed Standard Oil of New Jersey (later Exxon) as his first client. McCann's ad business boomed as the automobile became an integral part of American life. His firm merged with Alfred Erickson's agency (created 1902) in 1930, forming the McCann-Erickson Company. At the end of the decade, the firm hired Marion Harper, a top Yale graduate, as a mailroom clerk. Harper became president in 1948.

Harper began acquiring other ad agencies and by 1961 controlled more than 20 companies. That year he unveiled a plan to create a holding company that would let the ad firms operate separately, allowing them to work on accounts for competing products, but give them the parent firm's financial and informational resources. He named the company Interpublic Inc. after a German research company owned by the former H. K. McCann Co. The conglomerate continued expanding and was renamed The Interpublic Group of Companies in 1964. Harper's management capabilities weren't up to the task, however, and the company soon faced bankruptcy. In 1967 the board replaced him with Robert Healy, who saved Interpublic and returned it to profitability. The company went public in 1971.

The 1970s were fruitful years for Interpublic; its ad teams created memorable campaigns for Coke ("It's the Real Thing" and "Have a Coke and a Smile") and Miller Beer ("Miller Time" and Miller Lite ads). After Philip Geier became chairman in 1980, the company gained a stake in Lowe Howard-Spink (1983; it later became The Lowe Group) and bought Lintas International (1987). Interpublic bought the rest of The Lowe Group in 1990.

In 1994 Interpublic bought Western International Media (now Initiative Media Worldwide), and Ammirati & Puris (merged with Lintas to form Ammirati Puris Lintas). As industry consolidation picked up in 1996, Interpublic kept pace with acquisitions of PR company Weber Group and DraftWorldwide. Interpublic bought a majority stake in artist management and film production company Addis-Wechsler & Associates (now Industry Entertainment) in 1997 and later formed sports marketing and management group Octagon.

Interpublic acquired US agencies Carmichael Lynch and Hill, Holliday, Connors, Cosmopulos in 1998. It also boosted its PR presence with its purchase of International Public Relations (UK), the parent company of public relations networks Shandwick and Golin/Harris. Interpublic strengthened its position in the online world in 1999 when it purchased 20% of Internet services company Icon Medialab International of Stockholm. That year the company merged agencies Ammirati and Lowe & Partners Worldwide to form Lowe Lintas & Partners Worldwide (in 2002 they changed the name to just Lowe & Partners Worldwide).

Interpublic bought market research firm NFO Worldwide for $580 million in 2000 and merged Weber Public Relations with Shandwick International to form Weber Shandwick Worldwide, one of the world's largest PR firms. Later that year the company bought ad agency Deutsch for about $250 million. John Dooner took the position of chairman and CEO at the end of the year after Geier resigned. His first move proved a big one: Interpublic acquired True North Communications for $2.1 billion in stock in 2001.

The honeymoon was short lived; facing a recession, the mounting debt from its buying spree, and with the revelation of accounting discrepancies at McCann-Erickson WorldGroup (renamed McCann Worldgroup in 2004), Dooner stepped aside as chairman and CEO in 2003. Interpublic chose vice chairman David Bell (former CEO of True North) as Dooner's replacement. After almost two years of work to improve Interpublic's balance sheet, Bell was replaced by former MONY Group chief Michael Roth.

## EXECUTIVES

**Chairman Emeritus:** David A. Bell, age 63
**Chairman and CEO:** Michael I. Roth, age 61
**EVP and CFO:** Frank Mergenthaler, age 46
**EVP and Chief Growth Officer:** Marjorie Altschuler
**EVP and Chief Human Resources Officer:** Timothy A. Sompolski, age 54
**EVP Strategy and Network Operations; CEO, Lowe Worldwide:** Stephen J. (Steve) Gatfield, age 49
**EVP Strategy and Corporate Relations:** Philippe Krakowsky, age 44
**SVP and Managing Director:** Terry D. Peigh
**SVP and Treasurer:** Ellen T. Johnson
**President, Futures Marketing Group:** Bant Breen, age 35
**SVP, Controller, and Chief Accounting Officer:** Christopher Carroll, age 40
**SVP, General Counsel, and Secretary:** Nicholas J. (Nick) Camera, age 60
**SVP Finance and Development:** Jonathan B. (Jon) Burleigh
**SVP Leadership and Organizational Development:** Frank Guglielmo
**SVP Business Development and Strategic Information Resources:** David I. Weiss
**SVP Investor Relations:** Jerome J. (Jerry) Leshne
**SVP and CIO:** Joseph W. (Joe) Farrelly, age 62
**SVP Corporate Services:** Richard J. Haray
**Chairman, Deutsch:** Donny J. Deutsch, age 49
**Chairman, Lowe Worldwide:** Tony Wright, age 43
**Chairman and CEO, Campbell-Ewald:** Anthony J. (Tony) Hopp
**Chairman and CEO, DraftFCB:** Howard Draft, age 54
**Chairman and CEO, The Martin Agency:** John B. Adams Jr.
**Chairman and CEO, McCann-Erickson Worldgroup:** John J. Dooner Jr., age 59
**Chairman and CEO, ID Media:** Lynn Fantom
**CEO, North America:** Richard Beaven
**Auditors:** PricewaterhouseCoopers LLP

## LOCATIONS

**HQ:** The Interpublic Group of Companies, Inc.
1114 Avenue of the Americas, New York, NY 10036
**Phone:** 212-704-1200 **Fax:** 212-704-1201
**Web:** www.interpublic.com

The Interpublic Group of Companies has offices in more than 100 countries.

### 2006 Sales

| | $ mil. | % of total |
|---|---|---|
| US | 3,441.2 | 56 |
| Europe | | |
| UK | 565.6 | 9 |
| Other countries | 1,043.0 | 17 |
| Asia Pacific | 512.0 | 8 |
| Latin America | 303.4 | 5 |
| Other regions | 325.6 | 5 |
| **Total** | **6,190.8** | **100** |

## PRODUCTS/OPERATIONS

### 2006 Sales

| | $ mil. | % of total |
|---|---|---|
| Advertising & marketing services | 5,230.6 | 84 |
| Public relations & corporate communications | 960.2 | 16 |
| **Total** | **6,190.8** | **100** |

### Selected Operations

Advertising and marketing services
- Advertising agencies
  - Austin-Kelly
  - Avrett Free & Ginsberg
  - Campbell-Ewald
  - Campbell Mithun
  - Carmichael Lynch
  - Dailey & Associates
  - Deutsch
  - Foote, Cone & Belding Worldwide
  - Gotham
  - Hill, Holiday
  - Jay Advertising
  - Lowe & Partners (UK)
  - The Martin Agency
  - McCann Erickson Worldwide
  - Mullen
  - Tierney Communications
  - TM Advertising
- Marketing agencies
  - DraftFCB
  - The Hacker Group
  - MRM Partners
  - Momentum
  - Zipatoni
- Media services
  - Initiative Media
  - MAGNA Global
  - Universal McCann

Public relations and corporate communications
- DeVries Public Relations
- MWW Group
- Weber Shandwick

## COMPETITORS

Aegis Group
Dentsu
Hakuhodo
Havas
Omnicom
Publicis
WPP Group

## HISTORICAL FINANCIALS

Company Type: Public

### Income Statement

FYE: December 31

| | REVENUE ($ mil.) | NET INCOME ($ mil.) | NET PROFIT MARGIN | EMPLOYEES |
|---|---|---|---|---|
| **12/06** | 6,191 | (32) | — | 42,000 |
| **12/05** | 6,274 | (263) | — | 43,000 |
| **12/04** | 6,387 | (538) | — | 43,700 |
| **12/03** | 5,863 | (452) | — | 43,400 |
| **12/02** | 6,204 | 100 | 1.6% | 50,800 |
| **Annual Growth** | (0.1%) | — | — | (4.6%) |

### 2006 Year-End Financials

Debt ratio: 158.8%
Return on equity: —
Cash ($ mil.): 2,001
Current ratio: 1.08
Long-term debt ($ mil.): 2,249
No. of shares (mil.): 469
Dividends
Yield: —
Payout: —
Market value ($ mil.): 5,736

**Stock History** NYSE: IPG

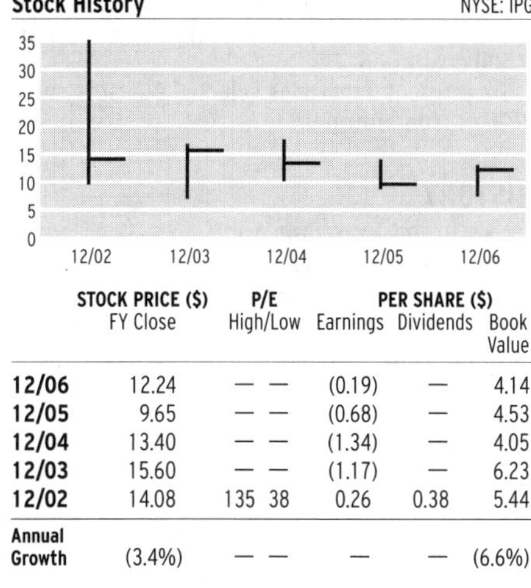

| | STOCK PRICE ($) FY Close | P/E High/Low | | PER SHARE ($) Earnings | Dividends | Book Value |
|---|---|---|---|---|---|---|
| **12/06** | 12.24 | — | — | (0.19) | — | 4.14 |
| **12/05** | 9.65 | — | — | (0.68) | — | 4.53 |
| **12/04** | 13.40 | — | — | (1.34) | — | 4.05 |
| **12/03** | 15.60 | — | — | (1.17) | — | 6.23 |
| **12/02** | 14.08 | 135 | 38 | 0.26 | 0.38 | 5.44 |
| **Annual Growth** | (3.4%) | — | — | — | — | (6.6%) |

# Intuit Inc.

Intuit knows that good accounting takes more than a pocket calculator. The company is a leading provider of personal finance (Quicken), small business accounting (QuickBooks), and consumer tax preparation (TurboTax) software for consumers, accountants, and small businesses. Other software offerings include industry-specific accounting and management applications for construction, real estate, retail, and wholesale distribution organizations. Intuit also provides payroll services, financial supplies, and software for professional tax preparation.

The company operates through five major business segments: QuickBooks, Payroll and Payments, Consumer Tax, Professional Tax, and Other Businesses.

The company's growth strategy is centered on catering to what the company defines as "self-directed" customers that are comfortable using software and performing assorted financial tasks themselves, as well as aggressively targeting "self-directed with assistance" clients (who are comfortable performing the tasks themselves but need more assistance and assurance).

Due to the nature of Intuit's tax preparation products, the company's financial results are very seasonal. Its net revenue is usually highest in the company's second quarter ending January 31 and third quarter ending April 30, with losses typically reported in its first quarter ending October 31 and fourth quarter ending July 31.

Intuit has used a string of acquisitions to expand its product lines and services beyond the consumer finance and accounting markets, adding offerings for small and midsized businesses and industry-specific accounting and management applications. The company has added new products and services through its purchases of CBS Employer Services, Management Reports (property management software), Eclipse (enterprise management software for wholesale distributors), and Innovative Merchant Solutions (small business debit and credit processing services). In 2007 the company acquired online banking software provider Digital Insight for about $1.35 billion.

The company has also sold and exited certain other business lines — including its 2005 sale of Intuit Information Technology Solutions and its 2006 sale of its Master Builder software line — in order to focus on its core products and services. In 2007 the company agreed to sell its Eclipse management software unit, which serves the wholesale distribution market, to Activant for $100 million.

Founder Scott Cook owns 8% of the company.

## HISTORY

After earning his Harvard MBA, Scott Cook spent three years in marketing at Procter & Gamble and four years with consultancy Bain & Company before founding Intuit in 1983. Research showed that consumers wanted an easy-to-use personal finance software package. Quicken was introduced in 1984.

Intuit was near collapse in 1986 when it received its first big order from software retailer Egghead.com. Intuit released QuickBooks in 1992 and went public in 1993. The next year Intuit acquired a number of firms, including tax preparation software developer ChipSoft, which brought TurboTax onboard. Cook stepped down as CEO in 1994, as former Apple executive William Campbell took the helm.

In 1995 Microsoft's $2 billion bid to buy Intuit was halted by a Justice Department antitrust lawsuit. Also in 1995 Intuit launched an online banking service and forged its first ties with the Web by bundling a browser and free Internet access with Quicken.

Intuit sold its online banking and bill presentation business to CheckFree in 1997. The next year Campbell became chairman, passing the CEO torch to ChipSoft-ex and Intuit EVP William Harris. Also in 1998 the company bought Lacerte Software, a provider of software and services to tax professionals.

In 1999 Intuit bought Computing Resources, which had been providing the company's online payroll services, for about $200 million. The company also purchased Rock Financial, an online consumer mortgage company, for about $370 million and renamed it Quicken Loans. Harris resigned and Campbell took over as interim CEO, remaining chairman.

Stephen Bennett, a former GE Financial Services executive, replaced Campbell as CEO in 2000. Later that year Intuit sold its Quicken-Insurance business to InsWeb, an online insurance service. Intuit also bought small business services provider EmployeeMatters for $39 million in stock from FrontLine Capital Group.

Moving to boost its small business offerings, in 2001 the company expanded its QuickBooks software to include industry-specific versions designed for retailers and accountants, and it acquired OMware, a provider of business management software for the construction industry.

In 2002 the company completed a string of acquisitions, purchasing American Fundware (public-sector accounting software), Management Reports (property management software), Eclipse (business management software), CBS Payroll (outsourced payroll services), and Blue Ocean Software (information technology asset management software).

In late 2002 the company sold its Quicken Loans mortgage operation, followed by the sale of its wholly owned Japanese subsidiary Intuit KK in 2003.

Intuit continued to pare down its product line over the next few years in order to focus on its core products, selling its Intuit Public Sector Solutions and Intuit Information Technology Solutions businesses in 2005, as well as its Master Builder operations in 2006.

## EXECUTIVES

**Chairman:** William V. (Bill) Campbell, age 66
**Chairman, Executive Committee and Director:** Scott D. Cook, age 54, $899,039 pay
**President, CEO, and Director:** Stephen M. (Steve) Bennett, age 53, $4,270,000 pay
**SVP, CFO, and General Manager, Consumer Tax and TurboTax:** Kiran Patel, age 59
**SVP and CIO:** Jim Fitzpatrick
**SVP, Product Development, Small Business Division:** Richard W. (Bill) Ihrie, age 56
**SVP and General Manager, Small Business Division:** Brad D. Smith, age 42, $1,150,000 pay
**SVP, Human Resources:** Sherry Whiteley
**SVP, Product Management:** Daniel J. (Dan) Levin, age 41
**SVP, Strategy and Corporate Development:** Alexander M. (Alex) Lintner, age 44
**SVP, General Counsel, and Corporate Secretary:** Laura A. Fennell, age 45
**SVP and Chief Marketing and Product Management Officer:** Peter J. Karpas, age 38
**SVP and CTO:** Per-Kristian (Kris) Halvorsen, age 55
**SVP and Financial Institutions Division President:** Jeff Stiefler
**VP and Corporate Controller:** Jeffrey P. Hank, age 46
**VP and Treasurer:** Peter Campagna
**VP, Business Operations:** Ginny Lee
**VP, Communications:** Harry Pforzheimer
**VP, Corporate Development:** Greg Paulsen
**VP, Corporate Business Applications:** John P. Courtney
**VP, Investor Relations:** Jessica Kourakos
**Marketing Director:** Rob Lips
**Auditors:** Ernst & Young LLP

## LOCATIONS

**HQ:** Intuit Inc.
2700 Coast Ave., Mountain View, CA 94043
**Phone:** 650-944-6000 **Fax:** 650-944-3699
**Web:** www.intuit.com

Intuit has offices in Canada, France, Germany, the UK, and the US.

## PRODUCTS/OPERATIONS

**2006 Sales**

| | $ mil. | % of total |
|---|---|---|
| Consumer Tax products & services | 710.5 | 30 |
| QuickBooks products & services | 534.6 | 23 |
| Payroll & Payments products & services | 462.0 | 20 |
| Professional Tax products & services | 272.9 | 12 |
| Other businesses | 362.3 | 15 |
| **Total** | **2,342.3** | **100** |

**2006 Sales**

| | $ mil. | % of total |
|---|---|---|
| Products | 1,351.6 | 58 |
| Services | 910.5 | 39 |
| Other | 80.2 | 3 |
| **Total** | **2,342.3** | **100** |

### Selected Software and Services

Small Business
- Check forms, tax forms, and other supplies
- QuickBooks (accounting software)
  - QuickBooks Basic
  - QuickBooks Credit Check Services (for access to credit reports)
  - QuickBooks Enterprise Solutions Business Management Software (for businesses with up to 250 employees)
  - QuickBooks Merchant Account Service (for enabling credit card payments)
  - QuickBooks Online Billing (for enabling electronic billing and customer payments)
  - QuickBooks Point of Sale (for retail businesses)
  - QuickBooks Premier (for small businesses)
  - QuickBooks Premier: Accountant Edition (for professional accountants)
  - QuickBooks Pro (for up to five simultaneous users)

Consumer Tax
- TurboTax (desktop tax preparation software for individuals and small businesses)
- TurboTax for the Web (Internet-based tax preparation and filing service)
- TurboTax Premier (tax preparation software for investors and rental property owners)

Professional Accounting Solutions
- EasyACCT Professional Accounting Series (software for helping accountants prepare financial statements and tax forms)
- IntuitAdvisor (subscription-based information and tools for accounting business growth)
- Lacerte (professional tax preparation software)
- Lacerte Tax Planner (tax planning service software for accountants)
- ProSeries (professional tax preparation software)

Employer Services
- Payroll processing
  - Intuit Payroll Services — Complete Payroll (full service payroll processing, tax payment, and check delivery service)
  - QuickBooks Assisted Payroll Service (online payroll processing service)
  - QuickBooks Do-It-Yourself Payroll (subscription-based payroll tax tables)

Small Business Verticals
- Intuit Construction Business Solutions (business management software for the construction industry)
- Intuit Eclipse Distribution Management Solutions (business management software for the wholesale durable goods industry)
- Intuit MRI Real Estate Solutions (business management software for commercial and residential property managers)

Personal Finance
- Quicken (desktop personal finance software)
- Quicken Brokerage (online and phone-based securities brokerage service powered by Siebert)
- Quicken Financial Planner (retirement planning)
- Quicken Lite
- Quicken Premier (Quicken with added investment and tax planning tools)
- Quicken.com (online personal finance information and tools)

Global Business
- Canada and UK
  - Localized versions of Quicken, QuickBooks, and tax preparation software
  - Localized personal finance Web sites
- Other locations
  - Localized versions of Quicken and QuickBooks for Australia, Europe, Hong Kong, New Zealand, and Singapore

## COMPETITORS

2nd Story Software
ADP
CA
CCH Incorporated
Deluxe
H&R Block
Jackson Hewitt
Microsoft
MYOB
Paychex
Sage Group
SAP
Thomson

## HISTORICAL FINANCIALS

Company Type: Public

### Income Statement

FYE: July 31

| | REVENUE ($ mil.) | NET INCOME ($ mil.) | NET PROFIT MARGIN | EMPLOYEES |
|---|---|---|---|---|
| 7/06 | 2,342 | 417 | 17.8% | 7,500 |
| 7/05 | 2,038 | 382 | 18.7% | 7,000 |
| 7/04 | 1,868 | 317 | 17.0% | 6,700 |
| 7/03 | 1,651 | 343 | 20.8% | 6,700 |
| 7/02 | 1,358 | 140 | 10.3% | 6,500 |
| Annual Growth | 14.6% | 31.3% | — | 3.6% |

### 2006 Year-End Financials

Debt ratio: 0.9%
Return on equity: 24.3%
Cash ($ mil.): 1,197
Current ratio: 1.79
Long-term debt ($ mil.): 15
No. of shares (mil.): 344
Dividends
Yield: —
Payout: —
Market value ($ mil.): 10,625

### Stock History

NASDAQ (GS): INTU

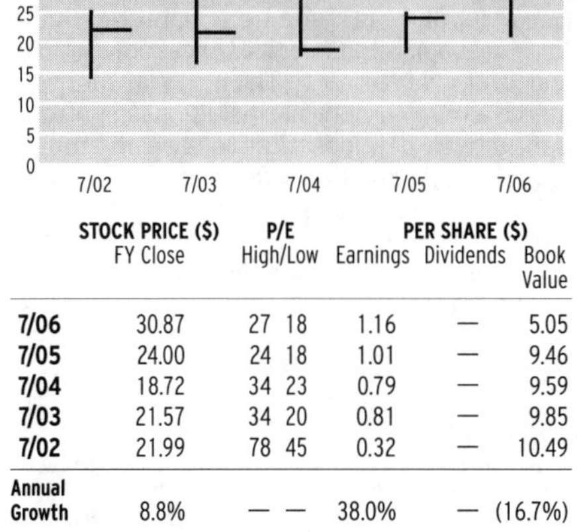


| | STOCK PRICE ($) FY Close | P/E High | P/E Low | PER SHARE ($) Earnings | Dividends | Book Value |
|---|---|---|---|---|---|---|
| 7/06 | 30.87 | 27 | 18 | 1.16 | — | 5.05 |
| 7/05 | 24.00 | 24 | 18 | 1.01 | — | 9.46 |
| 7/04 | 18.72 | 34 | 23 | 0.79 | — | 9.59 |
| 7/03 | 21.57 | 34 | 20 | 0.81 | — | 9.85 |
| 7/02 | 21.99 | 78 | 45 | 0.32 | — | 10.49 |
| Annual Growth | 8.8% | — | — | 38.0% | — | (16.7%) |

# Iron Mountain

You think you have a mountain of paperwork to deal with? Iron Mountain is one of the largest records storage and information management companies in the world. The company stores paper documents, computer disks and tapes, microfilm and microfiche, audio and videotapes, film, X-rays, and blueprints for more than 90,000 corporate customers. It provides such services as records filing, secure shredding, digital conversion, database management, packing, transportation, and disaster recovery. Its COMAC unit stores, builds, and mails information packets for companies. Iron Mountain traces its paper trail back to when it was established — in 1951.

The company sees acquisitions and joint ventures as a key business strategy when it comes to expansion. In 2005, the company added to its data protection services when it bought backup and recovery solutions provider LiveVault for $36 million. In 2006, it cast its eye on the Pacific Rim when it bought Australia-based DigiGuard, an offsite data storage provider. It also expanded its Asia/Pacific presence later that year when it entered a joint venture with Transnational Company Pte. Ltd, a provider of information storage services headquartered in Singapore. In mid-2007, Iron Mountain focused on the US once more when it announced it was acquiring ArchivesOne, a smaller rival serving more than 8,500 customers.

Investment firm Davis Selected Advisors owns 20% of Iron Mountain.

## HISTORY

Leo W. Pierce founded L.W. Pierce in 1957. Based in Philadelphia, the company sold filing systems and other storage equipment. In 1969 Pierce made the move into document storage, keeping other companies' records in his basement. Off-site document storage caught on during the 1980s, when a depressed economy forced managers to find creative ways to reduce costs.

The company doubled its size in 1990 by paying $36 million to buy Leahy Business Archives. The first corporate records storage firm, Leahy was founded in the 1950s in New York City. Pierce Leahy went public in 1997.

Pierce Leahy's sales increased in the mid-1990s, aided by acquisitions. The company was intent on consolidating the records management market, grabbing up as many smaller firms as it could. Pierce Leahy bought two more data storage companies, Archive (Canada) and Amodio (Connecticut), in 1998. The company made several acquisitions in 1999, including Datavault, a UK records management company, and ImageMax, a digital imaging company.

In early 2000 Pierce Leahy was acquired by its primary competitor, Iron Mountain, for $1.2 billion. Pierce Leahy was the surviving entity of the reverse merger, taking the Iron Mountain name. Richard Reese, chairman of the former Iron Mountain, became chairman and CEO of the new company. The company acquired Canadian record management company FACS Records Centre in late 2000.

In 2004 Iron Mountain created a new business unit — Iron Mountain Intellectual Property Management — by combining its DSI Technology Escrow and Arcemus subsidiaries. The new unit extended the Iron Mountain brand name to services such as online trademark protection, management of domain name records, and technology escrow. Iron Mountain also purchased Mentmore's interest in joint venture Iron Mountain Europe in 2004, making the company a wholly owned subsidiary. That year Iron Mountain acquired Connected Corp., a maker of data storage and recovery software. The next year the company bought Pickfords Records Management, the Australian and New Zealand operations of SIRVA, for $87 million.

## EXECUTIVES

**Chairman and CEO:** C. Richard Reese, age 61, $920,221 pay
**President and COO:** Robert T. (Bob) Brennan, age 46, $497,596 pay
**CFO:** Brian P. McKeon, age 45
**EVP Corporate Development:** John F. Kenny Jr., age 49, $406,020 pay (prior to title change)
**EVP and CIO:** Kevin B. Roden
**EVP Asia-Pacific Development:** Robert G. (Bob) Miller, age 47
**EVP Human Resources:** Linda Rossetti
**EVP Marketing:** Kenneth A. (Ken) Rubin
**VP Information Technology:** Dave Weldon
**VP Investor Relations:** Stephen Golden

**President, Americas:** John J. Connors, age 51, $331,731 pay (prior to promotion)
**President, Iron Mountain Digital:** John Clancy
**President, Iron Mountain Europe:** Marc A. Duale, age 55, $486,462 pay
**President, Iron Mountain South America and Comac Fulfillment Divisions:** Ross Engelman
**Group President, North American Operations:** Harold E. Ebbighausen, age 52
**Public Relations Manager:** Laura Sudnik
**Auditors:** Deloitte & Touche LLP

## LOCATIONS

**HQ:** Iron Mountain Incorporated
745 Atlantic Ave., Boston, MA 02111
**Phone:** 617-535-4766 **Fax:** 617-350-7881
**Web:** www.ironmountain.com

Iron Mountain has more than 900 records management facilities in Australia, Europe, and the Americas.

**2006 Sales**

| | $ mil. | % of total |
|---|---|---|
| US | 1,647.3 | 70 |
| UK | 312.3 | 13 |
| Canada | 154.8 | 7 |
| Other countries | 235.9 | 10 |
| **Total** | **2,350.3** | **100** |

## PRODUCTS/OPERATIONS

**2006 Sales**

| | $ mil. | % of total |
|---|---|---|
| Storage | 1,327.2 | 56 |
| Service & storage materials | 1,023.1 | 44 |
| **Total** | **2,350.3** | **100** |

**Selected Services**
Archiving
Consulting
Conversion
Database management
Disaster recovery
Electronic vaulting
Fulfillment
Packing
Shredding
Transportation

## COMPETITORS

Administaff
AmeriVault
Anacomp
ArchivesOne
DataBank IMX
IPSA
Lason
Per-Se Technologies
Recall
SOURCECORP
TAB Products
Xerox

## HISTORICAL FINANCIALS

Company Type: Public

**Income Statement** FYE: December 31

| | REVENUE ($ mil.) | NET INCOME ($ mil.) | NET PROFIT MARGIN | EMPLOYEES |
|---|---|---|---|---|
| **12/06** | 2,350 | 129 | 5.5% | 18,600 |
| **12/05** | 2,078 | 111 | 5.3% | 5,800 |
| **12/04** | 1,818 | 94 | 5.2% | 14,500 |
| **12/03** | 1,501 | 85 | 5.6% | 13,000 |
| **12/02** | 1,319 | 58 | 4.4% | 11,800 |
| **Annual Growth** | 15.5% | 21.9% | — | 12.0% |

**2006 Year-End Financials**

Debt ratio: 167.8%
Return on equity: 8.8%
Cash ($ mil.): 45
Current ratio: 1.06
Long-term debt ($ mil.): 2,606
No. of shares (mil.): 199
Dividends
Yield: —
Payout: —
Market value ($ mil.): 5,487

**Stock History** NYSE: IRM

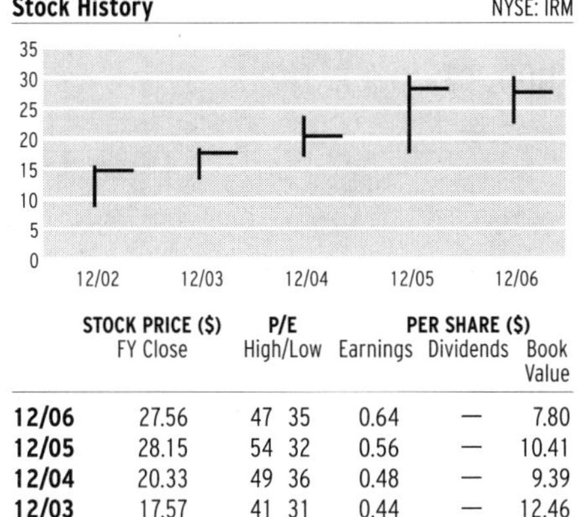


| | STOCK PRICE ($) FY Close | P/E High/Low | | PER SHARE ($) Earnings | Dividends | Book Value |
|---|---|---|---|---|---|---|
| **12/06** | 27.56 | 47 | 35 | 0.64 | — | 7.80 |
| **12/05** | 28.15 | 54 | 32 | 0.56 | — | 10.41 |
| **12/04** | 20.33 | 49 | 36 | 0.48 | — | 9.39 |
| **12/03** | 17.57 | 41 | 31 | 0.44 | — | 12.46 |
| **12/02** | 14.67 | 50 | 30 | 0.30 | — | 11.21 |
| **Annual Growth** | 17.1% | — | — | 20.9% | — | (8.7%) |

# ITT Corporation

ITT Corporation (formerly ITT Industries) doesn't get defensive when you associate its name with fluid motion. The company has three primary segments: defense electronics (combat radios, night-vision devices, airborne electronic-warfare systems), fluid technology (pumps, mixers, heat exchangers, and valves for water and wastewater systems), and motion and flow control (connectors, boat pumps, shock absorbers, friction pads for communication and transportation applications). ITT, which traces its corporate roots more than 80 years to the old ITT phone empire, also provides repair and maintenance services for the products it manufactures.

The company has enjoyed strong organic sales growth in its defense products and water/wastewater businesses while making selective acquisitions. The defense electronics segment has grown to account for nearly half of the company's sales.

The acquisition of WEDECO through 2004 and 2005 share purchases gave ITT the world's largest manufacturer of ultraviolet disinfection and ozone oxidation systems, a tool that is increasingly seen as a better alternative than chlorine treatment. The company further added to its water treatment business with the 2005 acquisition of Ellis K. Phelps & Company, which for years has been the #1 distributor of ITT's Flygt brand for the wastewater pumping and treatment industry, and the 2006 purchase of F.B. Leopold, a provider of pre-treatment filtration technologies.

Early in 2006 ITT exited the automotive tubing (steel and plastic tubing for fuel and brake lines) business by selling those operations to Cooper-Standard Automotive for $205 million.

In mid-2006 the company changed its name to ITT Corporation to coincide with an international branding initiative that includes a new corporate slogan — "Engineered for Life."

The company was fined $100 million in 2007 for illegally providing classified night-vision equipment to foreign countries, including China. ITT pled guilty to felony charges under the Arms Export Control Act after an extensive investigation by the Departments of Defense and Justice.

In mid-2007 ITT said it would purchase International Motion Control (IMC) of Buffalo, New York for about $395 million. The addition of IMC will complement the product mix and global footprint of ITT's motion and flow control business. Buying IMC gives ITT 11 new plants — five of them overseas (three in the Asia/Pacific region, and two in Europe).

## HISTORY

Colonel Sosthenes Behn founded International Telephone and Telegraph (ITT) in 1920 to build a global telephone company. After three small acquisitions, Behn bought International Western Electric (renamed International Standard Electric, or ISE) from AT&T in 1925, making ITT an international maker of phone equipment. In the late 1920s ITT bought Mackay, a US company that made telegraph, cable, radio, and other equipment.

In the 1930s sales outside the US made up two-thirds of revenues. To increase US opportunities during WWII, Behn arranged for a Mackay subsidiary, Federal AT&T Telegraph (later Federal Electric), to become part of ITT. Behn took charge of Federal and created Federal Telephone & Radio Laboratories. Meanwhile, ISE scientists who fled war-torn Europe gravitated to ITT's research and development operations and laid the foundation for its high-tech electronics business.

ITT became a diverse and unwieldy collection of companies by the 1950s. In mid-decade ISE, its biggest unit, developed advanced telephone-switching equipment.

During the 1960s and 1970s, ITT added auto-part makers such as Teves (brakes, West Germany), Ulma (trim, Italy), and Altissimo (lights and accessories, Italy). ITT's electronics acquisitions included Cannon Electric (electrical connectors) and National Computer Products (satellite communications). It also bought Bell & Gossett (the US's #1 maker of commercial and industrial pumps). When ITT bought Sheraton's hotel chain in 1968, it also got auto-parts supplier Thompson Industries. By 1977 its Engineered Products division consisted of nearly 80 automotive and electrical companies. In 1979 ITT began selling all or part of 250 companies, including the last of its telecom operations.

In the 1980s ITT became a major supplier of antilock brakes and, with the 1988 purchase of the Allis-Chalmers pump business, a global force in fluid technology. Its Defense & Electronics unit earned contracts to make equipment used in the Gulf War. In 1994 ITT Automotive purchases solidified its position as the world's top maker of electric motors and wiper systems.

ITT split into three independent companies in 1995: ITT Corporation (hospitality, entertainment, and information services; now part of Starwood Hotels & Resorts), ITT Hartford (insurance; now Hartford Financial Services), and ITT Industries (auto parts, defense and electric systems, and fluid-control products).

In 1997 ITT Industries acquired Goulds Pumps, establishing it as the world's largest pump maker. After the $815 million takeover, ITT reorganized into four segments: Connectors & Switches, Defense Products & Services, Pumps & Complementary Products, and Specialty Products. The company sold its automotive electrical systems unit to Valeo for $1.7 billion and its brake and chassis unit to Germany's Continental for about $1.9 billion.

Beefing up its specialty and defense units, ITT in 1999 bought Hydro Air Industries (spa and swimming pool accessories) and K&M Electronics. In 2000 ITT bought C&K Components, a privately owned switch maker, for about $117 million. ITT acquired the assets of Waterlink's Pure Water Division in 2002. Later that year it bought submersible pump manufacturer Svedala Robot from Finland-based Metso Corporation and PCI Membrane (pumps, mixers, aeration equipment, and wastewater process systems) from UK-based Thames Water.

In 2004 ITT acquired the Remote Sensing Systems business of Eastman Kodak Company for $725 million. It also acquired water treatment businesses Shanghai Hengtong and Cleghorn Waring, as well as GPS receivers maker Allen Osborne Associates.

In mid-2006 the company changed its name from ITT Industries to ITT Corporation. Later that year the company said it was selling its switches business to private equity firm Littlejohn & Co. LLC.

## EXECUTIVES

**Chairman, President, and CEO:** Steven R. Loranger, age 55, $983,846 pay
**CFO:** Denise L. Ramos, age 50
**SVP and General Counsel:** Vincent A. Maffeo, age 56, $437,092 pay
**SVP and Director, Corporate Relations:** Thomas R. Martin, age 53
**SVP and Director, Global Workforce Strategy:** Usha Wright
**SVP and Director, Human Resources:** Scott A. Crum, age 50
**SVP, Treasurer, and Director, Taxes:** Donald E. Foley, age 55
**SVP; President, Defense:** Steven F. (Steve) Gaffney, age 47, $422,578 pay
**SVP, CTO, and Director of Engineering:** Brenda L. Reichelderfer, age 48
**SVP; President, Motion & Flow Control:** Nicholas P. (Nick) Hill, age 52
**VP, Associate General Counsel:** Lawrence J. Swire
**VP, Finance:** Robert J. (Bob) Pagano Jr., age 44
**VP, Strategy:** Robert M. Powers
**VP and Director, Strategy and Corporate Development:** Aris C. Chicles
**VP; Director, Corporate Relations:** Angela A. Buonocore
**VP, Secretary, and Associate General Counsel:** Kathleen S. Stolar
**President, Space Systems Division:** James (Jim) Manchisi
**President, ITT China:** William E. Taylor, age 54
**President, Fluid Technology and Director:** Gretchen McClain, age 44
**President, Residential and Commercial Water, Fluid Technology:** John P. Williamson, age 46
**Chief Accounting Officer:** Janice M. Klettner, age 46
**Director, Investor Relations:** Peter J. Milligan
**Director, Public Relations:** Thomas E. (Tom) Glover
**Auditors:** Deloitte & Touche LLP

## LOCATIONS

**HQ:** ITT Corporation
4 W. Red Oak Ln., White Plains, NY 10604
**Phone:** 914-641-2000 **Fax:** 914-696-2950
**Web:** www.itt.com

ITT Corporation has operations throughout the world.

### 2006 Sales

| | $ mil. | % of total |
|---|---|---|
| US | 5,041.2 | 64 |
| Western Europe | 1,683.9 | 22 |
| Asia/Pacific | 411.2 | 5 |
| Other regions | 671.6 | 9 |
| **Total** | **7,807.9** | **100** |

## PRODUCTS/OPERATIONS

### 2006 Sales

| | $ mil. | % of total |
|---|---|---|
| Defense Electronics & Services | 3,659.3 | 47 |
| Fluid Technology | 3,070.1 | 39 |
| Motion & Flow Control | 1,092.9 | 14 |
| Adjustments | (14.4) | — |
| **Total** | **7,807.9** | **100** |

### Selected Products

Defense Electronics
- Electronic warfare systems
- Imaging and navigation systems
- Night-vision devices
- Tactical communications equipment

Fluid Technology
- Controls
- Heat exchangers
- Mixers
- Pumps
- Treatment systems
- Valves

Motion and Flow Control
- Aerospace controls
- Cable assemblies
- Connectors
- Friction pads
- Interconnects
- Precision valves
- Pumps for boat and spa baths
- Shock absorbers

## COMPETITORS

Alliant Techsystems
BAE SYSTEMS
Dana
Delphi
DENSO
Dresser
Eaton
Ebara
Flowserve
GE
GenCorp
General Dynamics
Harris Corp.
Honeywell International
Interpump
KSB
L-3 Communications
Lockheed Martin
Marmon Group
Molex
Northrop Grumman
Oilgear
Parker Hannifin
Raytheon
Robert Bosch
Siemens AG
SPX
Swagelok
Texas Instruments
Tyco

## HISTORICAL FINANCIALS

Company Type: Public

### Income Statement

FYE: December 31

| | REVENUE ($ mil.) | NET INCOME ($ mil.) | NET PROFIT MARGIN | EMPLOYEES |
|---|---|---|---|---|
| **12/06** | 7,808 | 581 | 7.4% | 37,500 |
| **12/05** | 7,427 | 360 | 4.8% | 40,900 |
| **12/04** | 6,764 | 432 | 6.4% | 44,000 |
| **12/03** | 5,627 | 404 | 7.2% | 39,000 |
| **12/02** | 4,985 | 380 | 7.6% | 38,000 |
| **Annual Growth** | 11.9% | 11.2% | — | (0.3%) |

### 2006 Year-End Financials

Debt ratio: 17.5%
Return on equity: 20.8%
Cash ($ mil.): 937
Current ratio: 1.21
Long-term debt ($ mil.): 500
No. of shares (mil.): 183
Dividends
Yield: 0.8%
Payout: 14.2%
Market value ($ mil.): 10,399

### Stock History

NYSE: ITT

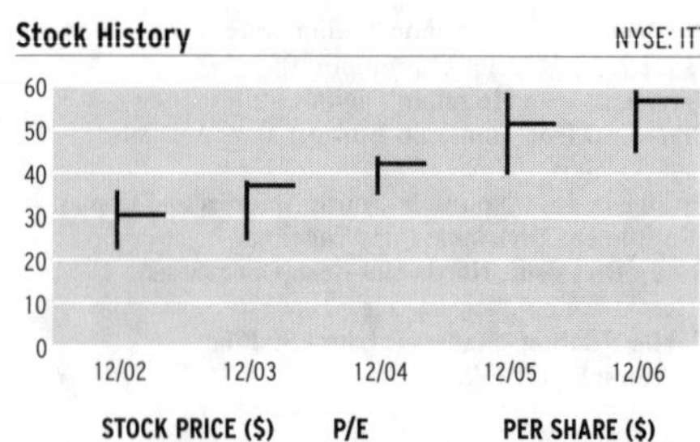


| | STOCK PRICE ($) FY Close | P/E High | P/E Low | PER SHARE ($) Earnings | Dividends | Book Value |
|---|---|---|---|---|---|---|
| **12/06** | 56.82 | 19 | 15 | 3.10 | 0.44 | 15.65 |
| **12/05** | 51.41 | 30 | 21 | 1.91 | 0.36 | 14.75 |
| **12/04** | 42.22 | 19 | 16 | 2.29 | 0.34 | 25.39 |
| **12/03** | 37.10 | 18 | 12 | 2.14 | 0.32 | 20.02 |
| **12/02** | 30.34 | 17 | 11 | 2.03 | 0.30 | 12.39 |
| **Annual Growth** | 17.0% | — | — | 11.2% | 10.0% | 6.0% |

# Jabil Circuit

Jabil Circuit takes more than a jab at contract electronics manufacturing. The company is one of the leading providers of electronics manufacturing services (EMS) in the world. Parts made by Jabil on a contract basis are used in communications products, computers and computer peripherals, and automobiles. Services range from product design and component procurement to order fulfillment and supply chain management. The company has been rapidly expanding into Asian and Eastern European markets in recent years, through acquisitions and new plants. Top customers include Cisco Systems, Hewlett-Packard, Nokia (21% of sales), and Philips (12%).

Bringing a more specialized approach to its customer base, Jabil is reorganizing into two divisions, Consumer Electronics and EMS. Consumer Electronics will make cell phones and other mobile electronic products, TVs, set-top boxes, and computer peripherals. The EMS division essentially will manufacture everything else, from electronic components to printed circuit boards, serving both traditional and emerging markets.

To compete in a rapidly consolidating industry, Jabil provides global parallel production and uses a "workcell" approach, in which semi-autonomous business units are dedicated to individual customers. The company continues to add services and to expand globally through acquisitions, including deals to acquire manufacturing operations from Lucent Technologies (now Alcatel-Lucent), NEC, and Philips.

The company has acquired Taiwan Green Point Enterprises, a contract manufacturer with plants in China, Malaysia, and Taiwan. Jabil made a tender offer of NT$109 ($3.32) a share in cash for all shares of Green Point, valuing the deal at nearly $900 million. Green Point specializes in plastic parts for cell phones and other portable electronics products. Jabil plans to operate Green Point as an autonomous subsidiary, hiring about 30,000 employees and keeping the company's management in place.

Further expanding into Asian markets, Jabil opened a facility in Vietnam in mid-2007.

Jabil initiated an internal review of its historical practices in granting stock options during 2006, a process that caused the company to delay filing its 2006 10-K annual report for six months. The review found no egregious examples of backdating or other shady transactions, but the company did pinpoint inadequate documentation of $6 million in revenue during the third quarter of fiscal 2001. Jabil continues to cooperate with the SEC and the US Department of Justice in probing stock option practices of the past.

Chairman William Morean and his family own about 15% of Jabil Circuit. Capital Group International holds nearly 11% of the company. William Blair & Company has an equity stake of around 5%.

## HISTORY

Jabil Circuit was named for founders James Golden and Bill Morean. The duo, who originally ran an excavation business, started Jabil in suburban Detroit in 1966 to provide assembly and reworking services to electronics manufacturers. Jabil incorporated in 1969 and began making circuit boards for Control Data Corporation (later renamed Control Data Systems) that year.

William D. Morean, the founder's son who had worked summers at Jabil while in high school, joined the company in 1977. The next year the younger Morean took over Jabil's day-to-day operations. The company entered the automotive electronics business in 1976 through a $12 million contract with General Motors.

During the 1980s Jabil began building computer components, adding such customers as Dell, NEC, Sun Microsystems, and Toshiba. Jabil moved its headquarters to St. Petersburg, Florida, in 1983. William Morean became Jabil's chairman and CEO in 1988.

Production design accounted for most of Jabil's sales for the first time in 1992. The next year the company went public and also opened a factory in Scotland. A major laptop computer manufacturing contract from Epson soured when, in 1995, cracks appeared in the casings of the laptops and Epson balked at paying its tab.

Disk drive maker Quantum, then Jabil's biggest client, canceled production orders worth about $60 million in 1996. Jabil quickly filled production gaps by shifting its focus to the booming communications market. By 1997 it had successfully diversified beyond low-margin PC manufacturing, becoming one of the top US circuit board manufacturers while adding higher-margin products, such as networking hardware.

In 1999 the company expanded into China when it acquired electronics manufacturing services provider GET Manufacturing. The next year William Morean stepped down as CEO (he remains chairman); he was succeeded by president Timothy Main.

In 2001 Jabil announced it would cut about 3,000 jobs, or about 10% of its staff. In 2002 Jabil acquired most of the assets of Lucent Technologies of Shanghai, a joint venture among Lucent (now Alcatel-Lucent) and three Chinese partners, for $75 million; the deal included an agreement to supply Lucent with optical switching and other communications components for three years. Also that year the company bought Philips Contract Manufacturing Services, an arm of the Dutch electronics giant, for around $210 million. Philips signed a four-year product supply agreement with Jabil, valued at €4 billion.

Two Jabil plants in Florida and Massachusetts were certified in 2003 under the international AS 9100 standard for aerospace manufacturing.

In late 2004 Jabil began expanding its manufacturing capacity in Asia by breaking ground on new plants in India and China.

In 2005 the company paid about $195 million to acquire the contract manufacturing business of Varian, Inc., the instrument vendor.

Together with Carl Zeiss, Jabil created a joint venture in early 2006 to manufacture optical modules for computer displays and other applications. Jabil took the majority interest in the JV.

In 2006 Jabil exercised a purchase option to acquire Celetronix International, an India-based electronics manufacturer. The company paid about $150 million in cash for Celetronix, which has operations in India, the UK, and the US. Late in the year Jabil started building a new facility in Uzhgorod, Ukraine. The plant was its second in the former Soviet republic and joined other Eastern European facilities in Hungary and Poland.

In 2007 the company sold Celetronix International's switching power supply business to Red Rocket Inc.

## EXECUTIVES

**Chairman:** William D. Morean, age 51
**Vice Chairman:** Thomas A. Sansone, age 57
**President, CEO, and Director:** Timothy L. Main, age 49, $895,385 pay
**COO:** Mark T. Mondello, age 42, $498,077 pay
**CFO:** Forbes I. J. Alexander, age 46
**SVP, Jabil Technology Services:** Scott D. Brown, age 44
**SVP; President, Americas:** William E. (Bill) Peters, age 43
**Senior Advisor, Europe:** Michel Charriau, age 64, $769,820 pay
**SVP, Global Business Units:** Joseph A. (Joe) McGee, age 44
**SVP; President, Asia:** William D. (Bill) Muir Jr., age 38
**SVP, Global Supply Chain:** Courtney J. Ryan, age 37
**SVP, Tools, Systems, and Training:** Wesley B. (Butch) Edwards, age 54
**VP, Jabil Automotive Group:** Brian Althaver, age 50
**VP, Business and Technology Development:** Jeffrey J. Lumetta, age 43
**VP, Communications and Investor Relations:** Beth A. Walters, age 46
**VP, Corporate Development:** Donald J. Myers
**VP, Engineering Services:** Ralph T. Leimann
**VP, Human Resources:** Thomas T. (Tom) O'Connor
**VP, Sales and Marketing, Americas:** David S. Emerson, age 49
**President, Global Services:** Hartmut Liebel
**Regional President, Europe:** John P. Lovato, age 46
**General Counsel and Secretary:** Robert L. Paver, age 50
**Controller:** Meheryar (Mike) Dastoor, age 39
**Treasurer:** Sergio A. Cadavid
**Auditors:** KPMG LLP

## LOCATIONS

**HQ:** Jabil Circuit, Inc.
10560 Dr. Martin Luther King Jr. St. North, St. Petersburg, FL 33716
**Phone:** 727-577-9749 **Fax:** 727-579-8529
**Web:** www.jabil.com

Jabil Circuit has manufacturing and repair operations in Austria, Belgium, Brazil, China, France, Hungary, India, Ireland, Italy, Japan, Malaysia, Mexico, the Netherlands, Poland, Singapore, Taiwan, Ukraine, the UK, the US, and Vietnam.

### 2006 Sales

| | $ mil. | % of total |
|---|---|---|
| Americas | 3,942.0 | 38 |
| Europe | 3,046.3 | 30 |
| Asia | 2,851.7 | 28 |
| Other regions | 425.5 | 4 |
| **Total** | **10,265.5** | **100** |

## PRODUCTS/OPERATIONS

### 2006 Sales

| | % of total |
|---|---|
| Consumer | 36 |
| Instrumentation & medical | 17 |
| Networking | 13 |
| Computing & storage | 12 |
| Peripherals | 7 |
| Telecommunications | 6 |
| Automotive | 5 |
| Other | 4 |
| **Total** | **100** |

### Services

Component selection, sourcing, and procurement
Design and prototyping
Engineering
Printed circuit board assembly
Repair and warranty services
Systems assembly
Test development

## COMPETITORS

Benchmark Electronics
BenQ
Celestica
CTS
Elcoteq
Flextronics
Hon Hai
Inventec
Merix
Nam Tai
Plexus
Sanmina-SCI
SMTC
Solectron
Suntron
SYNNEX
Sypris Solutions
Viasystems
Wistron

## HISTORICAL FINANCIALS

Company Type: Public

### Income Statement

FYE: August 31

| | REVENUE ($ mil.) | NET INCOME ($ mil.) | NET PROFIT MARGIN | EMPLOYEES |
|---|---|---|---|---|
| **8/06** | 10,266 | 165 | 1.6% | 74,000 |
| **8/05** | 7,524 | 232 | 3.1% | 40,000 |
| **8/04** | 6,253 | 167 | 2.7% | 34,000 |
| **8/03** | 4,730 | 43 | 0.9% | 26,000 |
| **8/02** | 3,546 | 35 | 1.0% | 20,000 |
| **Annual Growth** | 30.4% | 47.6% | — | 38.7% |

### 2006 Year-End Financials

Debt ratio: 14.4%
Return on equity: 7.4%
Cash ($ mil.): 774
Current ratio: 1.36
Long-term debt ($ mil.): 330
No. of shares (mil.): 203
Dividends
Yield: 0.5%
Payout: 18.2%
Market value ($ mil.): 5,445

### Stock History

NYSE: JBL

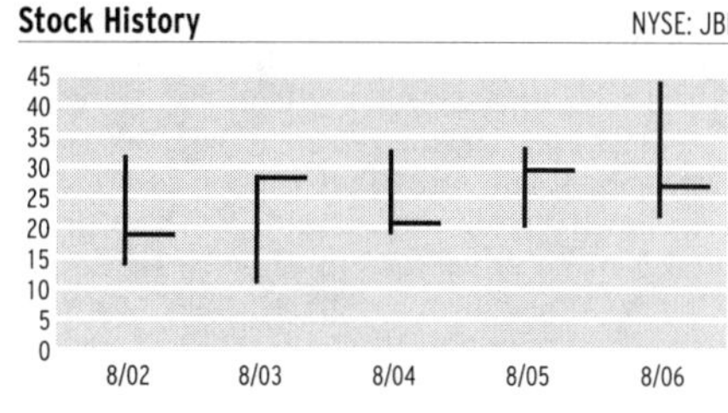


| | STOCK PRICE ($) FY Close | P/E High | P/E Low | PER SHARE ($) Earnings | Dividends | Book Value |
|---|---|---|---|---|---|---|
| **8/06** | 26.83 | 57 | 29 | 0.77 | 0.14 | 11.31 |
| **8/05** | 29.44 | 29 | 18 | 1.12 | — | 10.44 |
| **8/04** | 20.63 | 40 | 24 | 0.81 | — | 9.04 |
| **8/03** | 28.15 | 134 | 53 | 0.21 | — | 7.97 |
| **8/02** | 18.71 | 185 | 82 | 0.17 | — | 7.61 |
| **Annual Growth** | 9.4% | — | — | 45.9% | — | 10.4% |

# Jack in the Box

Led by a pugnacious "CEO" with a Ping-Pong ball for a head, Jack in the Box is among the leading quick-service restaurant businesses in the US. The company operates and franchises more than 2,000 of its flagship hamburger outlets in California, Texas, and about 15 other states. Jack in the Box offers such standard fast-food fare as burgers, fries, and soft drinks, as well as salads, tacos, and breakfast items. About 1,500 locations are company-owned, while the rest are franchised. In addition to its mainstay burger business, the company runs a chain of more than 300 Qdoba Mexican Grill fast-casual eateries through its subsidiary, Qdoba Restaurant Corporation.

Jack in the Box continues to lean on quirky marketing efforts and an almost constant stream of new menu items to help it compete with such larger rivals as McDonald's and Burger King. Its advertising campaign featuring the company's off-kilter, fictional CEO, Jack, strikes a balance somewhere between the family friendly image of the Golden Arches and the marketing efforts of BK, which skews more towards the young male demographic. Meanwhile, Jack in the Box is working to upgrade many of its outlets with modern interior designs, complete with flat-screen televisions and ceramic tile floors.

The company's expansion has been mostly in its core markets, with more than 35 new locations opening during 2005-06. It hopes to add about 45 new Jack in the Box restaurants in 2007, including some locations in new territories.

As for the company's Qdoba chain, Jack in the Box plans to open about 90 new locations in 2007, mostly through franchising. The concept, acquired in 2003, is the #2 quick-casual Mexican chain behind Chipotle Mexican Grill (spun off from McDonald's in 2006).

## HISTORY

Robert Peterson founded his first restaurant, Topsy's Drive-In, in 1941 in San Diego. He soon renamed it Oscar's (his middle name) and began to expand the restaurant. By 1950 he had four Oscar's drive-in restaurants. That year he changed the name again to Jack in the Box and in 1951 opened one of the country's first drive-through restaurants, which featured a speaker mounted in the chain's signature clown's head.

The drive-through concept took off, and by the late 1960s the company, renamed Foodmaker, operated about 300 Jack in the Box restaurants. In 1968 Peterson sold Foodmaker to Ralston Purina (now Nestlé Purina PetCare). To differentiate itself from competitors, Foodmaker added new food items, including the first breakfast sandwich (1969). The company continued to expand during the 1970s, and by 1979 it had more than 1,000 restaurants. That year it decided to concentrate on the western and southwestern US, selling 232 restaurants in the East and Midwest.

To attract more adult customers, in 1980 Foodmaker began remodeling its stores and adding menu items geared toward adult tastes. The company ran a series of TV ads showing its trademark clown logo being blown up. The ads were meant to show that Jack in the Box was not just for children anymore, but they drew protests from parents worried about the violence in the advertisements.

In 1985 Foodmaker's management acquired the company in a $450 million LBO. The company went public in 1987, but management took it private again the next year. Led by then-CEO Jack Goodall, Foodmaker expanded its number of franchises. (Unlike most of its competitors, the company had previously owned almost all of its restaurants.) By 1987 about 30% of the company's 900 stores were owned by franchisees.

The next year Foodmaker paid about $230 million for the Chi-Chi's chain of 200 Mexican restaurants. It made its first move outside the US in 1991, opening restaurants in Mexico and Hong Kong. The company went public again the following year.

In 1993 four people died, and more than 700 became ill, after eating *E. coli*-tainted hamburgers from Jack in the Box restaurants in several states, the largest such contamination in US history. Customers, shareholders, and franchisees sued Foodmaker, which in turn sued meat supplier and supermarket chain Vons and Vons' suppliers. Foodmaker's stock and profits plummeted, and the company subsequently enacted a stringent food safety program, which became a model for the fast-food industry and won kudos from the FDA.

Foodmaker sold its Chi-Chi's chain to Family Restaurants (later renamed Prandium, which dissolved in 2004) in 1994 for about $200 million and briefly held a stake in that company. In 1996 Goodall retired as CEO, and Robert Nugent succeeded him. The next year Foodmaker announced a major expansion to add 200 Jack in the Box restaurants, primarily in the western US. Foodmaker put the *E. coli* episode farther behind it in 1998 when it accepted a $58.5 million settlement from Vons and others. In 1999 the company began building units in selected southeastern markets. Also that year Foodmaker dropped its generic moniker and renamed the firm Jack in the Box. The following year it got a nice break from Uncle Sam in the form of a nearly $23 million tax benefit related to the 1995 selling of its stake in Family Restaurants Inc. The company also opened 120 new stores, many in the southeastern US.

In 2001 Goodall stepped down from the board and was replaced by Nugent as chairman. With same-store sales down amidst a sagging economy and fewer tourist dollars, the company scaled down its expansion plans. In 2002 it built 100 new locations (down from 126 the previous year), including about 30 in the Southeast.

Following the lead of its competitors, Jack in the Box acquired fast-casual restaurant operator Qdoba Restaurant Corporation in 2003 for about $45 million.

In 2004 the company announced it would restate earnings dating back to 2002 as a result of adjustments in its accounting practices. In addition, Nugent announced his 2005 retirement. He was replaced by company president Linda A. Lang.

## EXECUTIVES

**Chairman and CEO:** Linda A. Lang, age 48, $1,750,000 pay
**President and COO:** Paul L. Schultz, age 52, $1,139,750 pay
**EVP and CFO:** Jerry P. Rebel, age 49, $803,000 pay
**EVP, General Counsel, and Secretary:** Lawrence E. Schauf, age 61, $777,416 pay
**SVP Human Resources and Strategic Planning:** Carlo E. Cetti, age 62
**SVP Quality and Logistics:** David M. Theno, age 56, $679,100 pay
**VP and Chief Marketing Officer:** Terri F. Graham, age 41
**VP and CIO:** Stephanie E. Cline, age 61
**VP and Controller:** Paul D. Melancon, age 50
**VP and Treasurer:** Harold L. (Hal) Sachs, age 61
**VP Financial Planning and Analysis:** Pamela S. Boyd, age 51
**VP Financial Strategy:** John F. Hoffner, age 59
**VP Franchise Services:** Karen G. Gentry
**VP Restaurant Development:** Charles E. Watson
**VP Systems Development:** Debra Jensen
**Corporate VP Human Resources:** Mark Blankenship, age 44
**President and CEO, Qdoba Restaurant Corporation:** Gary J. Beisler, age 50
**Director, Corporate Communications:** Brian Luscomb
**Senior Manager, Marketing:** Teka O'Rourke
**Auditors:** KPMG LLP

## LOCATIONS

**HQ:** Jack in the Box Inc.
9330 Balboa Ave., San Diego, CA 92123
**Phone:** 858-571-2121 **Fax:** 858-571-2101
**Web:** www.jackinthebox.com

## PRODUCTS/OPERATIONS

**2006 Sales**

| | $ mil. | % of total |
|---|---|---|
| Jack in the Box | 2,691 | 97 |
| Qdoba Mexican Grill | 75 | 3 |
| **Total** | **2,766** | **100** |

**2006 Sales**

| | $ mil. | % of total |
|---|---|---|
| Restaurants | 2,101 | 76 |
| Distribution & other sales | 513 | 18 |
| Franchise rents & royalties | 101 | 4 |
| Other | 51 | 2 |
| **Total** | **2,766** | **100** |

**2006 Locations**

| | No. |
|---|---|
| Jack in the Box | 2,079 |
| Qdoba Mexican Grill | 318 |
| **Total** | **2,397** |

**2006 Locations**

| | No. |
|---|---|
| Company-owned | 1,545 |
| Franchised | 852 |
| **Total** | **2,397** |

## COMPETITORS

AFC Enterprises
American Dairy Queen
Arby's
Burger King
Cajun Operating Company
Checkers Drive-In
Chick-fil-A
Chipotle
CKE Restaurants
Del Taco
Fresh Enterprises
In-N-Out Burgers
McDonald's
Quiznos
Schlotzsky's
Sonic
Subway
Wendy's
Whataburger
YUM!

## HISTORICAL FINANCIALS

Company Type: Public

**Income Statement** FYE: Sunday nearest September 30

| | REVENUE ($ mil.) | NET INCOME ($ mil.) | NET PROFIT MARGIN | EMPLOYEES |
|---|---|---|---|---|
| **9/06** | 2,766 | 108 | 3.9% | 44,300 |
| **9/05** | 2,507 | 92 | 3.6% | 44,600 |
| **9/04** | 2,322 | 75 | 3.2% | 45,000 |
| **9/03** | 2,058 | 74 | 3.6% | 45,730 |
| **9/02** | 1,966 | 83 | 4.2% | 44,100 |
| **Annual Growth** | 8.9% | 6.8% | — | 0.1% |

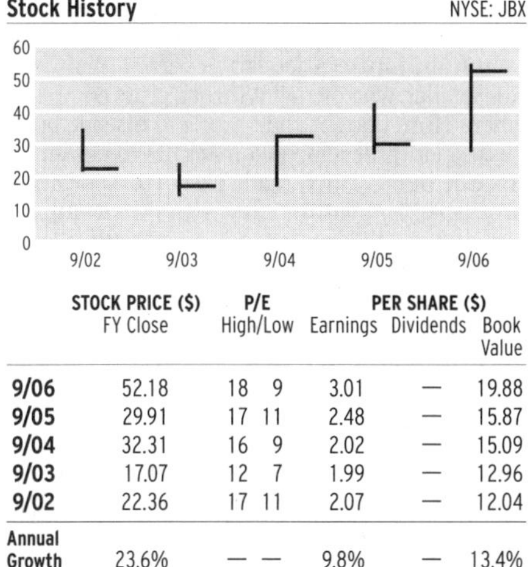

**2006 Year-End Financials**

Debt ratio: 35.8%
Return on equity: 16.9%
Cash ($ mil.): 234
Current ratio: 1.19
Long-term debt ($ mil.): 254
No. of shares (mil.): 36
Dividends
Yield: —
Payout: —
Market value ($ mil.): 1,866

**Stock History** NYSE: JBX



| | STOCK PRICE ($) FY Close | P/E High/Low | | PER SHARE ($) Earnings | Dividends | Book Value |
|---|---|---|---|---|---|---|
| **9/06** | 52.18 | 18 | 9 | 3.01 | — | 19.88 |
| **9/05** | 29.91 | 17 | 11 | 2.48 | — | 15.87 |
| **9/04** | 32.31 | 16 | 9 | 2.02 | — | 15.09 |
| **9/03** | 17.07 | 12 | 7 | 1.99 | — | 12.96 |
| **9/02** | 22.36 | 17 | 11 | 2.07 | — | 12.04 |
| **Annual Growth** | 23.6% | — | — | 9.8% | — | 13.4% |

# Jacobs Engineering Group

Jacobs Engineering Group keeps climbing a ladder of success by expanding its services and markets. The company has evolved from a one-person engineering firm into a global provider of diverse professional technical services. Engineering and construction projects for the chemical, petroleum, and pharmaceutical and biotech industries generate much of its revenues. US government contracts, chiefly for aerospace and defense, also add significantly to Jacobs' bottom line. Projects include buildings, process plants, manufacturing facilities, and paper and pulp plants. Jacobs also works on roads, highways, railways, ports, and other infrastructure projects, and it provides operations and maintenance services.

Its specialty consulting includes pricing studies, project feasibility reports, and automation and control system analysis. The oil, gas, and refining industries account for nearly 40% of sales. More than 15% of the group's annual revenues come from government contracts for environmental, aerospace and defense, and building programs. US government agencies involved in defense and aerospace programs have been pivotal to Jacobs' growth. The Air Force's Arnold Engineering Development Center (AEDC) has been a key client for 50 years, almost as long as the engineering firm itself has existed. Jacobs is a managing partner in a joint venture performing work for AEDC, including support in developing such next-generation defense-based airships as the F-35 Joint Strike Fighter (now called the F-35 Lightning II). Jacobs helped design and build modifications of the test cells used in performance testing of the F-35 aircraft.

Another long-term client for Jacobs is NASA, for which the company has a 40-year history of contract work. Some of its current activities for NASA include design and construction support for the Propulsion Research Laboratory, which studies new propulsion concepts for future space travel.

The group also participates in the environmental restoration of former weapons production and defense sites. Its strategy to speed up environmental cleanup at the Department of Energy's Oak Ridge site has earned it contracts to help accelerate cleanup at other major DOE facilities. Jacobs has also been providing services for the Air Force Center for Environmental Excellence (AFCEE) to help the agency with its environmental cleanup goals since 1991.

Recent acquisitions for Jacobs include Scottish engineering firm Babtie Group. Babtie (now Jacobs U.K.), with 50 offices worldwide, has performed road-building projects in China, the Czech Republic, and India and has expanded Jacobs' presence in Southeast Asia and China. In 2006 the company was awarded a contract to enhance London's famed Underground in advance of the 2012 Olympic Games.

## HISTORY

Joseph Jacobs graduated from the Polytechnic Institute of Brooklyn in 1942 with a doctorate in engineering. He went to work for Merck, designing processes for pharmaceutical production. Later he moved to Chemurgic Corp. near San Francisco, where he worked until 1947, when he founded Jacobs Engineering as a consulting firm. Jacobs also sold industrial equipment, avoiding any apparent conflict of interest by simply telling his consulting clients.

When equipment sales outstripped consulting work by 1954, Jacobs hired four salesmen and engineer Stan Krugman, who became his right-hand man. Two years later the company got its first big chemical design job for Kaiser Aluminum. Jacobs incorporated his sole proprietorship in 1957.

In 1960 the firm won its first construction contract to design and build a potash flotation plant, and Jacobs Engineering became an integrated design and construction firm. In 1967 it opened its first regional office but kept management decentralized to replicate the small size and hard-hitting qualities of its home office. Three years later Jacobs Engineering went public.

The firm merged with Houston-based Pace Companies, which specialized in petrochemical engineering design, in 1974. Also that year the firm became Jacobs Engineering Group and began building its first major overseas chemical plant in Ireland.

By 1977 sales had reached $250 million. A decade of lobbying paid off that year when the firm won a contract for the Arab Potash complex in Jordan. Jacobs began to withdraw from his firm's operations in the early 1980s, but the 1982-83 recession and poor management decisions pounded earnings. Jacobs returned from retirement in 1985, fired 14 VPs, cut staff in half, and pushed the firm to pursue smaller process-plant jobs and specialty construction.

After abandoning a 1986 attempt to take the company private, Jacobs began making acquisitions to improve the firm's construction expertise. In 1992 he relinquished his role as CEO to president Noel Watson. The next year the company expanded its international holdings by acquiring the UK's H&G Process Contracting and H&G Contractors.

Continuing its acquisition drive, the company bought a 49% interest in European engineering specialist Serete Group in 1996; it bought the rest the next year. Also in 1997 it gained control of Indian engineering affiliate Humphreys & Glasgow (now Jacobs H&G), increasing its 40% stake to 70%. In 1999 the company paid $198 million for St. Louis construction and design firm Sverdrup, which had completed projects in some 65 countries.

After being accused of overcharging the US government, Jacobs Engineering settled a whistleblower lawsuit (for $35 million) in 2000 while continuing to deny the allegations. However, the next year Jacobs continued to receive federal contracts, including contracts for boosting security at the US Capitol complex and providing logistics to the US Special Operations Command. Jacobs completed its acquisition of the UK-based GIBB unit of engineering consulting firm LawGibb Group in 2001, as well as the purchase of McDermott Engineers and Constructors (Canada).

Jacobs went on a shopping spree in 2003, acquiring a controlling stake in Finland's largest engineering firm, Neste Engineering, and picking up Glasgow-based engineering firm Babtie Group.

In 2004 the group's founder and chairman died at the age of 88. He was succeeded as chairman by Watson, who retained the CEO post until 2005.

## EXECUTIVES

**Chairman:** Noel G. Watson, age 70, $2,031,830 pay
**President, CEO, and Director:** Craig L. Martin, age 57, $1,824,660 pay
**EVP Operations:** Thomas R. (Tom) Hammond, age 55, $1,260,110 pay
**EVP Operations:** George A. Kunberger Jr., age 54, $920,200 pay
**EVP Finance and Administration and Treasurer:** John W. Prosser Jr., age 61, $1,018,080 pay
**Group VP Asia:** Arlan C. Emmert, age 61
**Group VP Federal Operations:** Michael J. Higgins, age 62
**Group VP Federal Operations:** James W. (Jim) Thiesing, age 62
**Group VP Middle East:** Walter C. Barber, age 65
**Group VP International Operations:** Andrew F. (Andy) Kremer, age 49
**Group VP United Kingdom and Ireland:** Philip J. (Phil) Stassi, age 51
**SVP and Controller:** Nazim G. Thawerbhoy, age 59
**SVP Acquisitions and Strategy:** John McLachlan, age 60
**SVP, General Counsel, and Secretary:** William C. Markley III, age 61
**SVP Global Sales:** Robert M. (Bob) Clement, age 58
**SVP Global Human Resources:** Patricia H. Summers, age 49
**SVP Information Technology:** Mark S. Williams, age 48
**President, Jacobs Technology:** Rogers F. Starr, age 63
**Auditors:** Ernst & Young LLP

## LOCATIONS

**HQ:** Jacobs Engineering Group Inc.
1111 S. Arroyo Pkwy., Pasadena, CA 91105
**Phone:** 626-578-3500 **Fax:** 626-578-6827
**Web:** www.jacobs.com

Jacobs Engineering Group operates worldwide from more than 60 offices.

**2006 Sales**

| | $ mil. | % of total |
|---|---|---|
| US | 4,827.3 | 65 |
| Europe | 1,694.7 | 23 |
| Canada | 745.1 | 10 |
| Asia | 117.8 | 2 |
| Other regions | 36.4 | — |
| **Total** | **7,421.3** | **100** |

## PRODUCTS/OPERATIONS

**2006 Sales**

| | $ mil. | % of total |
|---|---|---|
| Oil, gas & refining | 2,802.6 | 38 |
| National government programs | 1,259.4 | 17 |
| Chemicals & polymers | 1,124.2 | 15 |
| Pharmaceuticals & biotechnology | 679.0 | 9 |
| Infrastructure | 547.0 | 8 |
| Buildings | 395.2 | 5 |
| Technology & manufacturing | 137.8 | 2 |
| Pulp & paper | 102.4 | 1 |
| Other | 373.7 | 5 |
| **Total** | **7,421.3** | **100** |

**2006 Sales**

| | $ mil. | % of total |
|---|---|---|
| Construction | 3,239.6 | 44 |
| Project services | 2,894.3 | 39 |
| Operations & maintenance | 805.0 | 11 |
| Process, scientific & systems consulting | 482.4 | 6 |
| **Total** | **7,421.3** | **100** |

## COMPETITORS

AECOM
Aker Kværner
AMEC
BE&K
Bechtel
CH2M HILL
Computer Sciences Corp.
Earth Tech
Fluor
Foster Wheeler
HDR
HNTB Companies
HOK
Honeywell International
KBR
Lockheed Martin
Louis Berger
Parsons
Parsons Brinckerhoff
Peter Kiewit Sons'
Raytheon
SAIC
Shaw Group
Technip
Tetra Tech
Turner Construction
URS
Washington Group
Weston
Zimmermann Group

## HISTORICAL FINANCIALS

Company Type: Public

**Income Statement** FYE: September 30

| | REVENUE ($ mil.) | NET INCOME ($ mil.) | NET PROFIT MARGIN | EMPLOYEES |
|---|---|---|---|---|
| **9/06** | 7,421 | 197 | 2.7% | 31,700 |
| **9/05** | 5,635 | 151 | 2.7% | 38,600 |
| **9/04** | 4,594 | 129 | 2.8% | 35,400 |
| **9/03** | 4,616 | 128 | 2.8% | 33,700 |
| **9/02** | 4,556 | 110 | 2.4% | 34,900 |
| **Annual Growth** | 13.0% | 15.7% | — | (2.4%) |

**2006 Year-End Financials**

Debt ratio: 5.5%
Return on equity: 15.4%
Cash ($ mil.): 434
Current ratio: 1.75
Long-term debt ($ mil.): 78
No. of shares (mil.): 59
Dividends
Yield: —
Payout: —
Market value ($ mil.): 2,204

**Stock History** NYSE: JEC

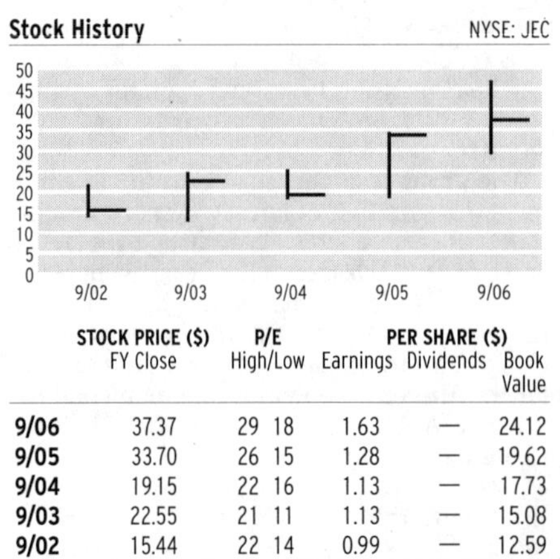


| | STOCK PRICE ($) FY Close | P/E High/Low | | PER SHARE ($) Earnings | Dividends | Book Value |
|---|---|---|---|---|---|---|
| **9/06** | 37.37 | 29 | 18 | 1.63 | — | 24.12 |
| **9/05** | 33.70 | 26 | 15 | 1.28 | — | 19.62 |
| **9/04** | 19.15 | 22 | 16 | 1.13 | — | 17.73 |
| **9/03** | 22.55 | 21 | 11 | 1.13 | — | 15.08 |
| **9/02** | 15.44 | 22 | 14 | 0.99 | — | 12.59 |
| **Annual Growth** | 24.7% | — | — | 13.3% | — | 17.6% |

# J.B. Hunt Transport

As one of the largest truckload carriers in the US, J. B. Hunt Transport Services is a leader of the pack. The company's trucking unit, which has a fleet of about 4,300 tractors, provides dry van freight transportation service in the US, Canada, and Mexico. J. B. Hunt's intermodal unit, which maintains some 1,600 tractors and 27,600 containers, moves customers' freight by combinations of train and truck. The company's dedicated contract services unit supplies customers with drivers and equipment; it operates some 5,200 company-controlled tractors.

Freight transported by J. B. Hunt includes automotive parts, building materials, chemicals, food and beverages, forest and paper products, and general merchandise.

J. B. Hunt hopes to grow by concentrating on its truckload, intermodal, and dedicated contract services units as separate, but overlapping, businesses and by selling more value-added services to its customers. The company has seen strong growth in its intermodal unit, which has partnerships with several major North American railroads. In addition, J. B. Hunt is the largest shareholder in Transplace, a company formed from the logistics units of several truckload carriers.

J. B. Hunt's top customer is its Arkansas neighbor, Wal-Mart, which accounts for about 15% of sales.

The family of founder J. B. Hunt, who retired as senior chairman in 2004 and died in 2006, owns 24% of the company. His widow, Johnelle Hunt, and son, Bryan Hunt, are board members. Company chairman Wayne Garrison holds a 5% stake.

## HISTORY

Johnnie Bryan (J. B.) Hunt's life was a classic tale of rolling from rags to riches — with a little help from a Rockefeller.

Hunt grew up in a family of sharecroppers during the Depression, and he left school at age 12 to work for his uncle's Arkansas sawmill. In the late 1950s, after driving trucks for more than nine years, Hunt noticed that the rice mills along his eastern Arkansas route were burning rice hulls. Believing the hulls could be used as poultry litter, Hunt got a contract to haul away the hulls and began selling them to chicken farmers.

In 1961 he began the J. B. Hunt Company with help from future Arkansas governor Winthrop Rockefeller, who owned Winrock grass company, where Hunt bought sod for one of his side businesses. Hunt developed a machine to compress the rice hulls, which made their transportation profitable, and within a few years the company was the world's largest producer of rice hulls for poultry litter.

Still looking for new opportunities, Hunt bought some used trucks and refrigerated trailers in 1969, though the company continued to focus on its original business. In the 1970s it found that the ground rice hulls made a good base for livestock vitamins and medications. Buyers of the ground hulls included Pfizer and Eli Lilly. J. B. Hunt, with Pfizer's backing, soon began selling a vitamin premix to feed companies.

In the 1980s J. B. Hunt's trucking division grew dramatically and became lucrative as the trucking industry was being deregulated. In 1981-82 the Hunt trucking business had higher margins than most trucking firms. In 1983, when J. B. Hunt Transport Services went public, Hunt sold the rice hull business to concentrate on trucking.

By 1986 J. B. Hunt was the US's third-largest irregular-route trucking company. The time was ripe to expand, and it began trucking in Canada (1988) and Mexico (1989). It also formed an alliance in 1989 with Santa Fe Pacific Railroad (now Burlington Northern Santa Fe) to provide intermodal services between the West Coast and the Midwest.

The company began adding computers to its trucks in 1992 to improve data exchange and communication on the road. J. B. Hunt also formed a joint venture with Latin America's largest transportation company, Transportación Marítima Mexicana. Founder Hunt retired in 1995 and became senior chairman.

J. B. Hunt tried hauling automobiles in 1996 but abandoned the idea when it found that cars were easily dented on intermodal trailers. More in line with the trucking company's long-term goals was an effort to stabilize its roster of drivers. It raised wages by one-third in 1997 to counteract driver shortages and high turnover. That year J. B. Hunt sold its underperforming flatbed-trucking unit (renamed Charger Inc.).

In 1998 the company reaped the benefits from its efforts to retain drivers with greater profits. The next year it began testing a satellite system from ORBCOMM Global to track empty trailers.

The company combined its J.B. Logistics (JBL) unit with the logistics businesses of five other truckers in 2000 to form Transplace.com (later known as Transplace). Also that year J. B. Hunt inked a $100 million deal with Wal-Mart to increase its full-truckload services to the retailer by 50%.

In 2002 J. B. Hunt bought a 10% stake in Transplace from Werner Enterprises, increasing its stake in the logistics company to 37%.

Founder Hunt stepped down from the company's board in 2004. He died in 2006.

## EXECUTIVES

**Chairman:** Wayne Garrison, age 54, $500,000 pay
**President, CEO, and Director:** Kirk Thompson, age 53, $605,769 pay
**EVP, Operations and COO:** Craig Harper, age 49, $311,365 pay
**EVP, Finance and Administration and CFO:** Jerry W. Walton, age 60, $358,269 pay
**EVP and CIO:** Kay J. Palmer, age 43
**EVP, Equipment and Properties:** Bob D. Ralston, age 60
**EVP, Marketing and Chief Marketing Officer; President, Intermodal:** Paul R. Bergant, age 59, $317,884 pay
**EVP, Enterprise Solutions; President, Dedicated Contract Services:** John N. Roberts III, age 42
**SVP, Finance, Controller, and Chief Accounting Officer:** Donald G. Cope, age 56
**SVP, Marketing:** Terrence D. Matthews, age 48
**SVP, Tax and Risk Management:** David G. Mee, age 46
**VP and Treasurer:** David N. Chelette, age 43
**Corporate Secretary and Director:** Johnelle D. Hunt, age 75
**Auditors:** Ernst & Young LLP

## LOCATIONS

**HQ:** J.B. Hunt Transport Services, Inc.
615 J.B. Hunt Corporate Dr., Lowell, AR 72745
**Phone:** 479-820-0000 **Fax:** 479-820-3418
**Web:** www.jbhunt.com

## PRODUCTS/OPERATIONS

**2006 Sales**

| | $ mil. | % of total |
|---|---|---|
| Intermodal | 1,430 | 43 |
| Trucking | 1,008 | 30 |
| Dedicated contract services | 915 | 27 |
| Adjustments | (25) | — |
| **Total** | **3,328** | **100** |

## COMPETITORS

APL Logistics
Best Drivers
Burlington Northern Santa Fe
Canadian National Railway
Con-way Inc.
CSX
EGL Eagle
Hub Group
Kansas City Southern
Landstar System
Norfolk Southern
Pacer International
Ryder
Schneider National
Swift Transportation
Union Pacific
U.S. Xpress
Werner Enterprises
YRC Worldwide

## HISTORICAL FINANCIALS

Company Type: Public

**Income Statement** FYE: December 31

| | REVENUE ($ mil.) | NET INCOME ($ mil.) | NET PROFIT MARGIN | EMPLOYEES |
|---|---|---|---|---|
| **12/06** | 3,328 | 220 | 6.6% | 5,916 |
| **12/05** | 3,128 | 207 | 6.6% | 16,367 |
| **12/04** | 2,786 | 146 | 5.3% | 15,850 |
| **12/03** | 2,434 | 96 | 3.9% | 15,700 |
| **12/02** | 2,248 | 52 | 2.3% | 16,265 |
| **Annual Growth** | 10.3% | 43.5% | — | (22.3%) |

**2006 Year-End Financials**

Debt ratio: 24.0%
Return on equity: 27.9%
Cash ($ mil.): 7
Current ratio: 0.98
Long-term debt ($ mil.): 182
No. of shares (mil.): 145
Dividends
Yield: 1.9%
Payout: 27.8%
Market value ($ mil.): 3,002

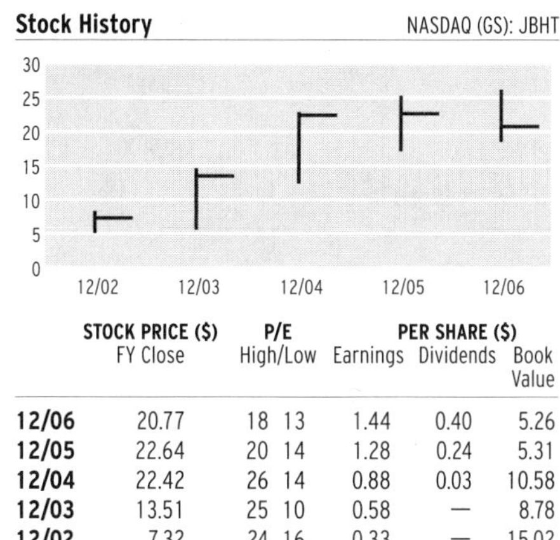


| | STOCK PRICE ($) FY Close | P/E High | P/E Low | PER SHARE ($) Earnings | Dividends | Book Value |
|---|---|---|---|---|---|---|
| **12/06** | 20.77 | 18 | 13 | 1.44 | 0.40 | 5.26 |
| **12/05** | 22.64 | 20 | 14 | 1.28 | 0.24 | 5.31 |
| **12/04** | 22.42 | 26 | 14 | 0.88 | 0.03 | 10.58 |
| **12/03** | 13.51 | 25 | 10 | 0.58 | — | 8.78 |
| **12/02** | 7.32 | 24 | 16 | 0.33 | — | 15.02 |
| **Annual Growth** | 29.8% | — | — | 44.5% | 265.1% | (23.1%) |

# J. C. Penney

An old name in retailing, J. C. Penney has been busy reinventing itself to bring style to Middle America's department store shoppers. The company's chain of about 1,035 JCPenney department stores in the US and Puerto Rico has found itself squeezed between upscale competitors and major discounters (Target, Wal-Mart). Following the sale of its ailing Eckerd drugstore chain (formerly 45% of Penney's sales) to The Jean Coutu Group and CVS for $4.5 billion in 2004, the retailer has focused on fashion. The firm runs one of the top catalog operations in the US. J. C. Penney Corporation is a wholly owned subsidiary of holding company J. C. Penney Company (created in 2002), which is the publicly traded entity.

Penney has used the proceeds from the Eckerd sale and the sale of its stake in the Renner department store chain in Brazil to pay down debt and invest in its stores and merchandising efforts. Penney's latest move is the launch in early 2007 of a private-label line of intimate apparel called Ambrielle.

Like its rival Federated Department Stores, which aims to make Macy's the department store brand of choice for Middle America, Penney is also trying to recapture the middle ground between discount chains and more upscale department stores. Instead of expanding through acquisitions — as Federated did with its purchase of May Department Stores — Penney has earmarked about $3 billion to build enough new stores (mainly off-mall locations) to reach 1,200 total stores by 2011.

In a bid to attract younger shoppers, Penney has teamped up with beauty purveyor Sephora USA, to open Sephora ministores inside its department stores. The first of five Sephora ministores opened in the fall of 2006 at a new Penney's department store in Fort Worth, Texas.

CEO Myron Ullman, an experienced retail veteran and former chief executive of Macy's, has focused on fashion to boost Penney's fortunes. To that end, he has expanded Penney's private-label brand offerings and signed exclusive deals with well-known designers, including Liz Claiborne and Nicole Miller. Penney's newest partnership is with Polo Ralph Lauren's Global Brand Concepts for a new lifestyle brand called American Living. Recent private label launches include Liz & Co. for women and Concepts by Claiborne for men; as well as Nicole by Nicole Miller, a dressy casual line of apparel; and W, an expansion of the Worthington career brand for men.

## HISTORY

In 1902 James Cash Penney and two former employers opened the Golden Rule, a dry goods store, in Kemmerer, Wyoming. Penney bought out his partners in 1907 and opened stores that sold soft goods in small towns. Basing his customer service policy on his Baptist heritage, he held employees (called "associates") to a high moral code.

The firm incorporated in Utah in 1913 as the J. C. Penney Company, with headquarters in Salt Lake City, but it moved to New York City the next year to improve buying and financial operations. It expanded to nearly 1,400 stores in the 1920s and went public in 1929. The company grew during the Depression with its reputation for high quality and low prices.

J. C. Penney rode the postwar boom, and by 1951 sales had surpassed $1 billion. It introduced credit plans in 1958 and entered catalog retailing in 1962 with its purchase of General Merchandise Co. The next year the stores added hard goods, which allowed them to compete with Sears and Montgomery Ward.

The company formed J. C. Penney Insurance in the mid-1960s and bought Thrift Drug in 1969. The chain continued to grow, and in 1973, two years after Penney's death, there were 2,053 stores. Also in the 1970s J. C. Penney began its ill-fated foray overseas by buying chains in Belgium and Italy in hopes of duplicating its US formula — giant department stores.

It bought Delaware-based First National Bank in 1983 (renamed J. C. Penney National Bank in 1984) to issue MasterCard and Visa cards. Stores refocused on soft goods during the 1980s and stopped selling automotive services, appliances, paint, hardware, and fabrics in 1983. It discontinued sporting goods, consumer electronics, and photographic equipment in 1987.

The next year J. C. Penney Telemarketing was formed to take catalog phone orders and provide telemarketing services for other companies. Also in 1988 the company moved its headquarters to Plano, Texas. J. C. Penney tried to move upmarket in the 1980s, enlisting fashion designer Halston. The line failed, however, so the company developed its own brands.

James Oesterreicher was named CEO in 1995, and J. C. Penney opened its first Mexican department store in Monterrey that year. Facing a slow-growing department store business back home, it then bought 272 drugstores from Fay's Inc. and 200 more from Rite Aid. In 1997 it acquired Eckerd (nearly 1,750 stores) for $3.3 billion, converting its other drugstores to the Eckerd name. It also sold its $740 million credit card portfolio of J. C. Penney National Bank to Associates First Capital and dealt its bank branches to First National Bank of Wyoming in 1997.

The retailer struggled in 1998, closing 75 underperforming department stores that year. In 2000 the company closed about 50 department stores and 300 Eckerd drugstores. That year Oesterreicher retired and was replaced by Allen Questrom; the company hired Questrom because of the work he did turning around Federated Department Stores and Barneys New York.

In 2001 the company shuttered about 50 more department stores and drugstores. Also that year Dutch insurer AEGON acquired J. C. Penney's Direct Marketing Services (DMS) unit, including its life insurance subsidiaries, for $1.3 billion. The company changed its name to J. C. Penney Corporation in January 2002 and formed a holding company under its former name.

Despite a major initiative to remodel hundreds of Eckerd stores and centralize the drugstore chain's distribution and merchandising systems, sales gains continued to lag behind rivals Walgreen, CVS, and Rite Aid. Also J. C. Penney's discount store rivals (Target, Wal-Mart, and wholesale club Costco) all began building their drugstore businesses. Ultimately the department store operator sold its Eckerd drugstores operations to The Jean Coutu Group and CVS for $4.5 billion in cash in August 2004.

In December 2004 Questrom stepped down and was succeeded by Myron E. "Mike" Ullman III.

In July 2005 J. C. Penney's Brazilian subsidiary, J. C. Penney Brazil, sold its controlling stake in the 60-store Brazilian department store chain through an IPO.

## EXECUTIVES

**Chairman and CEO:** Myron E. (Mike) Ullman III, age 60
**President and Chief Merchandising Officer:** Kenneth C. (Ken) Hicks, age 53
**EVP and CFO:** Robert B. Cavanaugh, age 55
**EVP, Chief Human Resources and Administration Officer:** Michael T. Theilmann, age 42
**EVP and CIO:** Thomas M. Nealon, age 46
**EVP and Chief Marketing Officer:** Michael J. (Mike) Boylson, age 48
**EVP, Planning and Allocation:** Clarence Kelley
**EVP and President, JCPenney Direct:** John W. Irvin, age 52
**EVP and Director, Product Development and Sourcing:** Peter M. McGrath
**EVP and General Merchandise Manager, Fine Jewelry:** Beryl B. Raff, age 56
**EVP and General Merchandise Manager, Home and Custom Decorating:** Jeffrey J. Allison
**EVP and General Merchandise Manager, Men's and Children's Division:** Lana Cain, age 51
**EVP and General Merchandise Manager, Women's Apparel:** Elizabeth H. (Liz) Sweney
**EVP, General Counsel, and Secretary:** Joanne L. Bober, age 54
**SVP, Chief Technology Officer:** Andrew T. Cowan
**SVP, Director of Communications and Public Affairs:** Wynfred C. Watkins
**VP and Director, Investor Relations:** Robert (Bob) Johnson
**Auditors:** KPMG LLP

## LOCATIONS

**HQ:** J. C. Penney Corporation, Inc.
6501 Legacy Dr., Plano, TX 75024
**Phone:** 972-431-1000 **Fax:** 972-431-1362
**Web:** www.jcpenney.net

J. C. Penney Corporation operates more than 1,030 JCPenney department stores in 49 US states and Puerto Rico. It has five catalog distribution centers.

## PRODUCTS/OPERATIONS

### 2007 Sales

| | % of total |
|---|---|
| Women's apparel | 22 |
| Home | 21 |
| Men's apparel & accessories | 20 |
| Children's apparel | 11 |
| Women's accessories | 10 |
| Family footwear | 6 |
| Fine jewelry | 5 |
| Services & other | 5 |
| **Total** | **100** |

### 2007 Sales

| | $ mil. | % of total |
|---|---|---|
| Retail | 16,948 | 85 |
| Direct | 2,955 | 15 |
| **Total** | **19,903** | **100** |

### Major Product Lines

Accessories
Family apparel
Home furnishings
Jewelry
Shoes

### Selected Private and Exclusive Labels

a.n.a. (casual women's apparel)
Arizona Jean Co.
Crazy Horse by Liz Claiborne (exclusive third-party brand)
Delicates
Hunt Club
Jacqueline Ferrar
JCPenney Home Collection (bedding, furniture, window coverings)
nicole by Nicole Miller
St. John's Bay
Stafford
The Chris Madden for JCPenney Home
USA Olympic
Worthington

## COMPETITORS

Bed Bath & Beyond
Belk
Brown Shoe
Costco Wholesale
Dillard's
Dress Barn
Eddie Bauer Holdings
Foot Locker
Gap
J. Crew
J. Jill Group
Kmart
Kohl's
Lands' End
Limited Brands
Macy's
Nine West
Nordstrom
Otto
Ross Stores
Saks Inc.
Sears
Signet
Stage Stores
Target
TJX Companies
Wal-Mart
Wickes Furniture

## HISTORICAL FINANCIALS

Company Type: Subsidiary

### Income Statement

FYE: Saturday closest to January 31

| | REVENUE ($ mil.) | NET INCOME ($ mil.) | NET PROFIT MARGIN | EMPLOYEES |
|---|---|---|---|---|
| **1/07** | 19,903 | 1,153 | 5.8% | 155,000 |
| **1/06** | 18,781 | 1,088 | 5.8% | 151,000 |
| **1/05** | 18,424 | 524 | 2.8% | 151,000 |
| **1/04** | 17,786 | (928) | — | 147,000 |
| **1/03** | 32,347 | 405 | 1.3% | 228,000 |
| **Annual Growth** | (11.4%) | 29.9% | — | (9.2%) |

### Net Income History

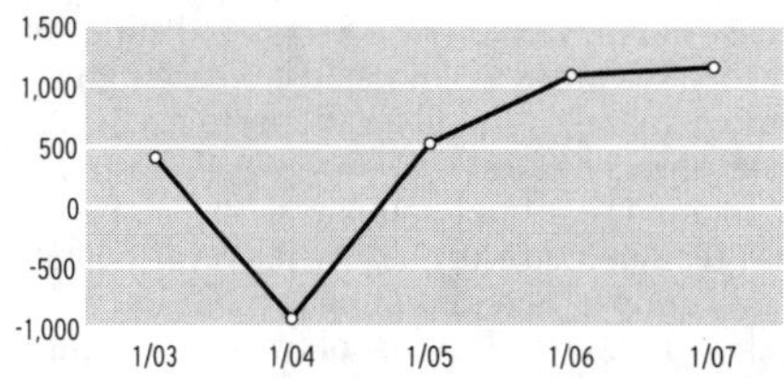


# Jefferies Group

Because smaller companies need hostile takeover advice, too. Jefferies Group raises capital, does research, and provides advisory services for small and mid-sized companies through its Jefferies & Company subsidiary. The firm also underwrites stock and bond offerings, primarily high-yield debt issues (i.e., junk bonds) and brokers trades of large blocks of securities for institutional investors; its Jefferies Execution Services subsidiary trades some 25 billion shares per year. The company also has been building its asset management business, and now oversees more than $3 billion on behalf of its clients. Jefferies Group is active in the US, Canada, Europe, and Asia.

The company's Jefferies Quarterdeck unit specializes in mergers and acquisitions (M&A) advice for the aerospace, defense, and clean technology industries, while Jefferies Broadview provides M&A expertise mainly to the tech, transportation, and oil services sectors.

Jefferies' 2005 purchase of M&A advisor Randall & Dewey (now Jefferies Randall & Dewey) added some muscle to its energy industry practice. Meanwhile, the company enhanced its capital-raising capabilities by acquiring Helix Associates, a UK-based private equity fund placement firm, that same year.

In 2007 Jefferies acquired the financial services investment banking business of Putnam Lovell from National Bank of Canada.

Jefferies & Company was fined $5.5 million by the NASD and $4.2 million by the SEC in 2006 for giving nearly $2 million worth of improper gifts to equity traders at Fidelity.

## HISTORY

Former cowboy and stock exchange clerk Boyd Jefferies founded Jefferies & Company in 1962. The firm referred customers to brokers in exchange for cuts of their commissions. In 1969 mutual fund giant Investors Diversified Services (IDS) acquired the upstart. Because IDS was not a broker, Jefferies was kicked off the NYSE and increased its off-exchange activities.

Boyd Jefferies bought back his company in 1973 and took it public in 1983. Because the SEC had less control over off-exchange trades, Jefferies was a popular stop for greenmailers amassing stock for hostile takeovers. By 1986 the firm was in Japan, Switzerland, and the UK.

After 1987's "Black Monday" stock crash it was revealed that Jefferies had illegally "parked" stocks for Ivan Boesky. Boyd Jefferies pleaded guilty to SEC rules violations, resigned, and sold his interest in the company. New CEO Frank Baxter launched subsidiary Investment Technology Group (ITG). When Michael Milken's Drexel Burnham Lambert failed in 1990, Baxter hired scores of former Drexelites.

During the 1990s, ITG grew along with demand for off-exchange trading. In 1999 Jefferies merged ITG into a separate company, spinning off its other operations as the new Jefferies Group. Jefferies formed an alliance with Crédit Lyonnais' US brokerage subsidiary and bought a stake in online bond trading system LIMITrader.com, which had substantially ceased operations by 2001.

At the end of 2000 Baxter retired as CEO but stayed on as chairman until 2002. He was succeeded in both capacities by Jefferies Group veteran Richard Handler. Also in 2000, Jefferies bought The Europe Company to boost its international operations.

The company's Helfant Group subsidiary (which was renamed Jefferies Execution Services in 2004) was created from the 2002 merger of Lawrence Helfant and W&D Securities.

## EXECUTIVES

**Chairman and CEO, Jefferies Group and Jefferies & Company:** Richard B. Handler, age 45, $1,000,000 pay
**Chairman of the Executive Committee:** Brian P. Friedman, age 51, $500,000 pay
**EVP and CFO:** Joseph A. (Joe) Schenk, age 48, $1,000,000 pay
**EVP, General Counsel, and Secretary:** Lloyd H. Feller, age 64, $900,000 pay
**EVP and Co-Head of Investment Banking:** Chris M. Kanoff, age 49
**EVP and Head of Convertible Division:** Jonathan R. Cunningham, age 43
**EVP and Head of Equities:** Scott W. Jones, age 49
**SVP and Global Head of Compliance:** Robert J. (Bob) Albano
**SVP and Deputy General Counsel:** Cathleen Shine
**VP and Senior Research Analyst, Healthcare:** Brian M. Wright
**Controller; EVP and CFO, Jefferies & Company:** Maxine Syrjamaki, age 62, $161,500 pay
**Vice Chairman, Jefferies & Company:** Roy L. Furman
**Vice Chairman, Jefferies & Company:** Robert H. (Bob) Lessin, age 49
**Vice Chairman and Co-Head of Investment Banking, Jefferies & Company:** Andrew R. Whittaker, age 44
**CEO, Jefferies International:** Clifford A. (Cliff) Siegel, age 48
**Co-President, Jefferies Financial Products:** Adam De Chiara
**Co-President, Jefferies Asset Management:** Bradford L. (Brad) Klein
**Director, Marketing Communications:** Thomas E. (Tom) Tarrant
**Auditors:** KPMG LLP

## LOCATIONS

**HQ:** Jefferies Group, Inc.
520 Madison Ave., 12th Fl., New York, NY 10022
**Phone:** 212-284-2300 **Fax:** 212-284-2111
**Web:** www.jefco.com

### US Offices

Atlanta
Boston
Chicago
Dallas
Denver
Foster City, CA
Houston
Jersey City, NJ
Los Angeles
Nashville, TN
New Orleans
New York (2)
Richmond, VA
San Francisco
Short Hills, NJ
Stamford, CT
Washington, DC

### International Offices

Calgary
Dubai
London (2)
Melbourne
Paris
Shanghai
Sydney
Tokyo
Zurich

## PRODUCTS/OPERATIONS

### 2006 Sales

| | $ mil. | % of total |
|---|---|---|
| Investment banking | 540.6 | 27 |
| Interest | 528.9 | 27 |
| Principal transactions | 468.0 | 24 |
| Commissions | 280.7 | 14 |
| Asset management fees & investment income from managed funds | 109.5 | 6 |
| Other | 35.5 | 2 |
| **Total** | **1,963.2** | **100** |

## COMPETITORS

Baird
Banc of America Securities
Bear Stearns
Deutsche Bank Alex. Brown
Friedman, Billings, Ramsey Group
Houlihan Lokey
JPMorgan Chase
Lazard
Lincoln International
Piper Jaffray
RBC Dain Rauscher
Thomas Weisel Partners
UBS Financial Services
Unterberg, Towbin
Wedbush Morgan
WR Hambrecht

## HISTORICAL FINANCIALS

Company Type: Public

### Income Statement

FYE: December 31

| | REVENUE ($ mil.) | NET INCOME ($ mil.) | NET PROFIT MARGIN | EMPLOYEES |
|---|---|---|---|---|
| **12/06** | 1,963 | 206 | 10.5% | 2,254 |
| **12/05** | 1,498 | 157 | 10.5% | 2,045 |
| **12/04** | 1,199 | 131 | 11.0% | 1,783 |
| **12/03** | 927 | 84 | 9.1% | 1,626 |
| **12/02** | 755 | 63 | 8.3% | 1,357 |
| **Annual Growth** | 27.0% | 34.7% | — | 13.5% |

### 2006 Year-End Financials

Debt ratio: 510.0%
Return on equity: 14.4%
Cash ($ mil.): 1,265
Current ratio: —
Long-term debt ($ mil.): 8,063
No. of shares (mil.): 120
Dividends
Yield: 1.7%
Payout: 31.7%
Market value ($ mil.): 3,206

### Stock History

NYSE: JEF

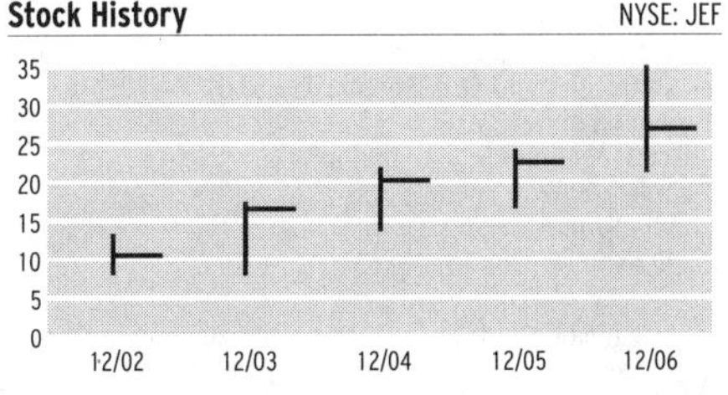


| | STOCK PRICE ($) FY Close | P/E High | P/E Low | PER SHARE ($) Earnings | PER SHARE ($) Dividends | PER SHARE ($) Book Value |
|---|---|---|---|---|---|---|
| **12/06** | 26.82 | 25 | 15 | 1.42 | 0.45 | 13.23 |
| **12/05** | 22.49 | 21 | 14 | 1.16 | 0.19 | 22.14 |
| **12/04** | 20.14 | 21 | 13 | 1.03 | 0.18 | 18.14 |
| **12/03** | 16.51 | 24 | 11 | 0.71 | 0.10 | 13.15 |
| **12/02** | 10.49 | 23 | 15 | 0.57 | 0.05 | 23.32 |
| **Annual Growth** | 26.5% | — | — | 25.6% | 73.2% | (13.2%) |

# J. M. Smucker

The J. M. Smucker Company is known for the sweet, sticky stuff, but hopes shortening and biscuits will fatten its bottom line. The #1 US producer of jams, jellies, and preserves also makes dessert toppings, juices, and specialty fruit spreads under names such as Laura Scudder's and Dickinson's. To diversify, the company has added market leaders Jif peanut butter and Crisco oils and shortening. Smucker owns other brands as well. Parent of International Multifoods, the company's roster also includes baking-goods brands Hungry Jack, Martha White, and Pillsbury, along with Pet evaporated milk.

To quench any thirst with that PB&J, Smucker Quality Beverages stocks natural juices under the After the Fall, Santa Cruz Organic, and R.W. Knudsen brands. As sales of jam and jelly slowed, Smucker started selling the stuff to other food companies to put in processed foods. The company's own new product introductions include a crustless frozen peanut butter and jelly sandwich, which sells briskly to consumers, schools, and other foodservice providers. However, it was Smucker's acquisition of the Jif and Crisco brands that nearly doubled the company's sales.

Turning to consumers for increased sales, the company sold its Canadian grain-based foodservice operations and industrial businesses in 2006 to Cargill and CHS Inc. The operations were integrated into leading US flour miller Horizon Milling (which is jointly owned by Cargill and CHS). The company acquired the White Lily brand of flours, baking mixes and frozen biscuits from C.H. Guenther in 2006.

In 2007 Smucker reformulated its popular Crisco brand of vegetable shortening to contain no trans fats. The revamped-formula shortening included traditional and butter-flavored varieties of Crisco. (Its Crisco oils and sprays needed no redo, having never contained trans fats.)

Further adding to its baking offerings and accompanying its Pet milk products, Smucker acquired sweetened condensed and evaporated milk producer Eagle Family Foods Holdings in 2007. Smucker paid $133 million in cash and assumed $115 million in debt for Eagle.

Given Smucker's size and therefore, bargaining power with food retailers (including Wal-Mart) and Eagle's domination of the North American canned milk sector (it is the largest producer of evaporated and sweetened condensed milk in the US and Canada), the pairing of the two companies was a sensible move for both.

## HISTORY

Jerome Smucker began operating a steam-powered cider mill in 1897 for farmers in Orrville, Ohio, but he found that his biggest business was selling apple butter from a secret Smucker family recipe. By the 1920s The J. M. Smucker Company had begun producing a full line of preserves and jellies, and in 1935 it acquired its first fruit processing operations.

Under Jerome's grandson, Paul Smucker, the company gained widespread national distribution by the mid-1960s. Tim Smucker succeeded his father, Paul, as president in 1981, then as chairman in 1987, when his brother Richard became president.

The company's recent growth has come from the development of its industrial fruit fillings business and acquisitions of domestic natural juice and peanut butter companies, including Knudsen & Sons (1984), After the Fall (1994), and Laura Scudder's (from National Grape Co-op, 1994). It has gradually expanded internationally through acquisitions. In 1993 it acquired the jam, preserves, and pie-filling unit of Canada's Culinar. In a 1998 deal Smucker purchased Australia's Allowrie jam and Lackersteens marmalade lines.

Smucker sold its flagging Mrs. Smith's frozen pie business to Flowers in 1997, less than two years after buying the unit from Kellogg. It bought Kraft's domestic fruit spread unit in 1997 and in early 1999 purchased the northwestern Adams peanut butter business from Pro-Fac Cooperative. Smucker kept the Adams name but shifted packaging to its Pennsylvania peanut butter plant.

Spreading into retail, the company opened its first store in 1999 in hometown Orrville and then launched online and catalog sales. Also that year Smucker bought a fruit filling plant in Brazil from Groupe Danone, a major customer. During 2000 the company's Henry Jones Foods subsidiary (Australia) purchased Taylor Foods (sauces, marinades).

Smucker acquired International Flavors & Fragrances' formulated fruit and vegetable preparation businesses in 2001. Moving beyond its stronghold on natural peanut butter brands, Smucker purchased the Jif peanut butter and Crisco cooking oil and shortening brands from Procter & Gamble in 2002. The $670 million purchase price for Jif and Crisco included shifting 53% of Smucker stock into the hands of P&G shareholders.

A decision to concentrate on North America led to the $37 million sale of Australian subsidiary Henry Jones Foods in 2004. Also that year, Smucker sold its operations in Brazil to Cargill and closed down two fruit processing plants in California and Oregon. Its purchase of International Multifoods that year added an array of US brands to the Smucker family, including Pillsbury flour, baking mixes, and ready-to-spread frostings; Hungry Jack pancake mixes, syrup, and potato side dishes; Martha White baking mixes and ingredients; and Pet evaporated milk brands. Canadian brands included Robin Hood flour and baking mixes, Bick's pickles and condiments, and Golden Temple flour and rice.

In 2005 Smucker sold the US foodservice and bakery business, and the Canadian operations of Gourmet Baker (all part of its International Multifoods acquisition) to Value Creation Partners.

## EXECUTIVES

**Chairman and Co-CEO:** Timothy P. Smucker, age 63, $1,293,600 pay
**President, Co-CEO, and Director:** Richard K. Smucker, age 58, $1,293,600 pay
**SVP Consumer Market and Director:** Vincent C. Byrd, age 52, $522,554 pay
**VP, CFO, and Treasurer:** Mark R. Belgya, age 44
**VP International:** Mark T. Smucker, age 37
**VP Corporate Development:** Barry C. Dunaway, age 44
**VP Customer Development:** John F. Mayer, age 51
**VP Human Resources:** Robert E. Ellis, age 60
**VP Information Services:** Mark J. Thome
**VP Marketing Services:** Christopher R. Resweber, age 45
**VP Sales, Grocery Market:** Donald D. Hurrle Sr., age 58
**VP, General Counsel, and Secretary:** M. Ann Harlan
**VP Information Services and CIO:** Andrew G. Platt, age 51
**VP and General Manager, Consumer Oils and Baking:** Steven T. Oakland, age 46, $402,838 pay
**VP and General Manager, Smucker Quality Beverages:** Julia L. Sabin, age 47
**Auditors:** Ernst & Young LLP

## LOCATIONS

**HQ:** The J. M. Smucker Company
1 Strawberry Ln., Orrville, OH 44667
**Phone:** 330-682-3000 **Fax:** 330-684-3370
**Web:** www.smucker.com

### 2007 Sales

| | $ mil. | % of total |
|---|---|---|
| US | 1,819.7 | 85 |
| Canada | 282.1 | 13 |
| Other countries | 46.2 | 2 |
| **Total** | **2,148.0** | **100** |

## PRODUCTS/OPERATIONS

### 2007 Sales

| | % of total |
|---|---|
| Peanut butter | 21 |
| Shortening & oils | 15 |
| Fruit spreads | 14 |
| Baking mixes & frostings | 11 |
| Flour & baking ingredients | 11 |
| Juices & beverages | 5 |
| Portion control | 5 |
| Toppings & syrups | 5 |
| Uncrustables brand frozen sandwiches | 4 |
| Pickles & condiments | 3 |
| Other | 6 |
| **Total** | **100** |

### Selected Products

Baking mixes
Condiments
Dessert toppings
Eggnog
Evaporated milk
Frozen sandwiches
Fruit and vegetable juices
Fruit spreads
Gift packages
Instant coffee
Jams
Jellies
Juice beverages
Oils
Peanut butter
Pie fillings
Potato side dishes
Preserves
Ready-to-spread frostings
Shortening
Sweetened, condensed milk
Syrups

### Selected Brands

Adams (peanut butter)
After The Fall (juice beverages)
Bick's (pickles and condiments, Canada)
Borden (eggnog)
Crisco (cooking oils, shortening)
Dickinson's (fruit spreads)
Double Fruit (Canada)
Eagle (canned milk products, dessert kits)
Golden Temple (flour and rice)
Goober (peanut butter and jelly combination)
Good Morning (Canada)
Hungry Jack (pancake mix, syrup, and potato side dishes)
Jif (peanut butter)
Kava (instant coffee)
Laura Scudder's (peanut butter)
Lost Acres (fruit spreads)
Martha White (baking mixes and ingredients)
Magic Shell (dessert topping)
Magnolia (sweetened condensed milk)
None Such (pie fillings)
Pet (canned milk products)
Pillsbury (flour, frostings, and refrigerated doughs)
Rocket Juice (juice beverages)
Robin Hood (flour and baking mixes, Canada)
R.W. Knudsen (juice beverages)
Santa Cruz Natural (juice beverages)
Shirriff (fruit spreads, Canada)
Simply Fruit (fruit spreads)
Smucker's (dessert topping, jam, jelly, preserves, peanut butter)
Smucker's Snackers (peanut butter, jelly, and cracker snacks)
Smucker's Uncrustables (frozen peanut butter and jelly sandwiches)

## COMPETITORS

B&G Foods
Birds Eye
Chiquita Brands
Coca-Cola North America
ConAgra
Cranberries Limited
Darigold, Inc.
Dean Foods
E.D. Smith
General Mills
Glanbia Foods
Goya
Hansen Natural
Hershey
Kraft Foods
Milnot
National Grape Cooperative
Nestlé
Nestle Canada
Nestlé USA
Ocean Spray
PepsiCo
Pinnacle Foods
Procter & Gamble
Ralcorp
Spectrum Organic Products
Tropicana
Unilever
Welch's

## HISTORICAL FINANCIALS

Company Type: Public

### Income Statement

FYE: April 30

| | REVENUE ($ mil.) | NET INCOME ($ mil.) | NET PROFIT MARGIN | EMPLOYEES |
|---|---|---|---|---|
| **4/07** | 2,148 | 157 | 7.3% | 3,025 |
| **4/06** | 2,155 | 143 | 6.7% | 3,500 |
| **4/05** | 2,044 | 129 | 6.3% | 3,700 |
| **4/04** | 1,417 | 111 | 7.9% | 2,950 |
| **4/03** | 1,312 | 96 | 7.3% | 2,775 |
| **Annual Growth** | 13.1% | 13.0% | — | 2.2% |

### 2007 Year-End Financials

Debt ratio: 21.9%
Return on equity: 8.9%
Cash ($ mil.): 200
Current ratio: 2.70
Long-term debt ($ mil.): 393
No. of shares (mil.): 57
Dividends
Yield: 2.0%
Payout: 40.6%
Market value ($ mil.): 3,169

### Stock History

NYSE: SJM

| | STOCK PRICE ($) FY Close | P/E High | P/E Low | PER SHARE ($) Earnings | PER SHARE ($) Dividends | PER SHARE ($) Book Value |
|---|---|---|---|---|---|---|
| **4/07** | 55.82 | 21 | 14 | 2.76 | 1.12 | 31.62 |
| **4/06** | 39.26 | 21 | 15 | 2.45 | 0.81 | 30.34 |
| **4/05** | 49.62 | 24 | 18 | 2.24 | 1.00 | 28.88 |
| **4/04** | 52.30 | 24 | 16 | 2.21 | 0.92 | 24.13 |
| **4/03** | 36.28 | 21 | 14 | 2.02 | 0.76 | 22.59 |
| **Annual Growth** | 11.4% | — | — | 8.1% | 10.2% | 8.8% |

# Jo-Ann Stores

Jo-Ann Stores has sewn up the leadership of the fabric store market. The company is the #1 fabric retailer in the US, well ahead of Hancock Fabrics. Jo-Ann Stores sells fabrics and sewing supplies, craft materials, decorating and floral items, and seasonal goods. Most of the company's roughly 630 stores, located mainly in strip shopping centers, operate under the Jo-Ann Fabrics and Crafts name. The company also operates nearly 175 Jo-Ann superstores. Jo-Ann Stores has been closing shops in response to weak sales. Recognizing that sewing these days is more often a hobby than a necessity, the company is luring creative customers with arts and crafts and home-decorating items.

Jo-Ann Stores is pinning its hopes for future growth on its 35,000-sq.-ft. Jo-Ann superstores — more than twice the size of the company's 14,900 sq. ft. traditional stores. Last year the company added about 20 superstores vs. five traditional stores. (The company decreased the size of its superstore format from 45,000 sq. ft. to 35,000 sq. ft. in 2003.)

Sales have been a major disappointment at Jo-Ann Stores lately. As a result, the firm has been closing stores (so has competitor Hancock Fabrics) and has scaled down its expansion plans to focus instead on improving margins. Consequently, the retailer's store count has been shrinking. In 2007 Jo-Ann Stores plans to open only five superstores and one traditional location, while shuttering about 20 shops.

The company has also shaken up its top management in an effort to turn its business around. Alan Rosskamm, formerly chairman and CEO of the company, owns about 9% of the shares of Jo-Ann Stores.

## HISTORY

Jo-Ann Stores' predecessor began in 1943 when the German immigrant Rohrbach family started Cleveland Fabric with the help of fellow immigrants, the Reichs. Alma, daughter of the Rohrbachs, worked at the store and was joined by Betty Reich in 1947.

Betty's and Alma's respective husbands, Martin Rosskamm and Freddy Zimmerman, also joined the company. At the urging of Martin (who eventually became chairman), Cleveland Fabric opened more stores, mainly in malls. As it moved beyond Cleveland, it adopted a new store name — Jo-Ann — devised from the names of Alma and Freddy's daughter Joan and Betty and Martin's daughter Jackie Ann. It changed its name to Fabri-Centers of America in 1968 and went public the following year.

The very postwar boom that brought Alma and Betty into the workforce worked against the company in the 1970s, as women tucked away their sewing baskets in favor of jobs outside their homes. As department stores responded to the trend and stopped offering sewing supplies, specialty fabric stores found a niche. But they soon faced competition from fabric superstores and heavily discounted ready-made clothing.

Martin and Betty's son Alan took over as president and CEO in 1985 and began to modernize the company and the stores. Trained in real estate law, he began focusing on opening larger stores in strip shopping centers, which offered cheaper leases than malls. The company had about 625 stores by mid-1989.

As its industry consolidated, Fabri-Centers held on, despite missteps such as its 1984 launch of the Cargo Express housewares chain (the money-losing venture, with about 40 stores at its peak, ended in 1994). The firm became the nation's #1 fabrics and crafts chain in 1994 when it bought 300-plus Cloth World stores. At the close of that deal, Fabri-Centers had nearly 1,000 stores, with locations in every state except Hawaii.

In 1995 Fabri-Centers opened a store on its home turf in Hudson, Ohio, that offered not only a range of fabric and craft items, but also home decorating merchandise, furniture, craft classes, and day care. At three times the size of its other stores, the Jo-Ann etc superstore helped the company pull in non-sewers looking for art supplies, picture frames, and decorating ideas. Jo-Ann etc became the focus of the company's growth.

Fabri-Centers paid $3.8 million in 1997 to settle SEC charges that it had overstated its profits during a 1992 debt offering. In 1998 it paid nearly $100 million for ailing Los Angeles-based fabric and craft company House of Fabrics, adding about 260 locations and strengthening its West Coast presence. Fabri-Centers then renamed itself Jo-Ann Stores and began placing all of its stores under the Jo-Ann name.

Jo-Ann continued relocating traditional stores and opening new shops while snipping underperforming locations. In 1999 the company signed a pact with Martha Stewart Living Omnimedia to sell fancy decorating fabrics under the Martha Stewart Home name. (As of 2003 the company no longer offers Martha Stewart's fabrics.)

Jo-Ann invested in and partnered with Idea Forest, an Internet-based arts and crafts retailer, in 2000 to run Jo-Ann's e-commerce site. In 2001 the company reported a $13.2 million loss (only the second in its history), in part because of inventory and distribution problems. As a result, Jo-Ann closed more than 90 underperforming stores and reduced the number of items carried in the shops.

In 2003 Jo-Ann Stores bought three stores in the Dallas-Fort Worth area from bankrupt MJDesigns. Those stores had a combined revenue of $16 million during the last fiscal year they operated under the former name.

In September 2005 CFO Brian P. Carney left the firm to join supermarket operator BI-LO.

In January 2006 Jo-Ann Stores eliminated 75 administrative jobs. In April construction of the company's new 700,000 sq. ft. distribution center in Opelika, Alabama, was completed. It's designed to support growth in the South, specifically in Florida, Georgia, and Texas. Jo-Ann Stores operates two other distribution centers in California and Ohio. In July, Alan Rosskamm stepped down as chairman, president, and CEO (although he remains a director of the company) when Darrell Webb, formerly with Fred Meyer, was appointed to the positions. James Kerr became CFO in August. Previously Kerr was the retailer's VP, controller, and chief accounting officer.

## EXECUTIVES

**Chairman, President, and CEO:** Darrell D. Webb, age 49, $807,692 pay
**EVP and CFO:** James C. Kerr, age 44, $378,272 pay (partial-year salary)
**EVP Human Resources:** Rosalind Thompson, age 55, $402,871 pay
**EVP Merchandising and Marketing:** Travis Smith, age 34, $446,635 pay
**SVP, General Counsel, and Secretary:** David B. Goldston
**SVP Marketing:** Kevin Brown
**SVP Store Operations:** James Eisen
**SVP Supply Chain Management and Logistics:** Anthony (Tony) Dissinger
**VP Finance and Treasurer:** Donald R. (Don) Tomoff
**VP Advertising:** Michele Watkins
**VP and General Merchandise Manager, Craft:** Rebecca (Becky) Jones
**VP and General Merchandise Manager, Sewing:** Michelle Christensen
**VP and General Merchandise Manager, Decor:** Charles S. Domingue
**VP and CIO:** Kevin Stack
**VP Human Resources Services:** Thomas Williams
**VP Controller:** Christopher Beem
**VP Marketing:** Riddianne Kline
**VP Operations:** Richard Chapman
**VP and Treasurer:** Scott Roubic
**Public Relations:** Tom Biltz
**Auditors:** Ernst & Young LLP

## LOCATIONS

**HQ:** Jo-Ann Stores, Inc.
5555 Darrow Rd., Hudson, OH 44236
**Phone:** 330-656-2600 **Fax:** 330-463-6675
**Web:** www.joann.com

Jo-Ann Stores has about 800 locations in 47 states, including about 175 superstores.

**2007 Stores**

| | No. |
|---|---|
| California | 91 |
| Ohio | 57 |
| Florida | 52 |
| Michigan | 48 |
| Pennsylvania | 45 |
| Texas | 41 |
| New York | 40 |
| Illinois | 38 |
| Washington | 31 |
| Indiana | 26 |
| Oregon | 24 |
| Massachusetts | 23 |
| Virginia | 22 |
| Minnesota | 20 |
| Maryland | 19 |
| Wisconsin | 18 |
| Arizona | 17 |
| Colorado | 14 |
| Connecticut | 13 |
| New Jersey | 13 |
| Missouri | 12 |
| Georgia | 11 |
| Iowa | 11 |
| Utah | 10 |
| Idaho | 9 |
| Kansas | 8 |
| New Hampshire | 8 |
| Montana | 7 |
| North Carolina | 7 |
| Alaska | 6 |
| Nevada | 6 |
| New Mexico | 6 |
| Louisiana | 5 |
| Maine | 5 |
| Nebraska | 5 |
| West Virginia | 5 |
| Other states | 28 |
| **Total** | **801** |

## PRODUCTS/OPERATIONS

### 2007 Sales

| | % of total |
|---|---|
| Hardlines & seasonal | 50 |
| Softlines | 50 |
| **Total** | **100** |

### Softlines

Fabrics
- Apparel fabrics used in the construction of garments (cottons, linens, wools, fleece, and outerwear)
- Craft fabrics (for quilting, craft, and holiday projects)
- Home-decorating fabrics (for window treatments, furniture, and bed coverings)
- Printed fabrics (juvenile designs, seasonal designs, National Football League logo prints, and proprietary print designs)
- Special-occasion fabrics (satins, metallics, and other fabrics for evening wear and bridal gowns)

Patterns
Sewing machines
Sewing notions
- Buttons
- Cutting implements
- Elastics
- Pins
- Ribbons

Tapes
Threads
Trims
Zippers

### Hardlines

Accessories for arranging flowers and making wreaths
Craft materials (for making stencils, dolls, jewelry, wood projects, wall décor, rubber stamps, memory books, and plaster)
Custom floral arrangements
Decorations
Fine art materials
- Brushes
- Canvas
- Easels
- Paints (pastels, water colors, oils, and acrylics)

Floral products line
Framed art
Full-service framing
Gifts
Hobby items
Holiday supplies
Home accessories
- Baskets
- Candles
- Potpourri

Needlecraft items
Needles
Paint-by-number kits
Paper
Photo albums
Picture-framing materials (custom frames, mat boards, glass, and backing materials)
Plastic model kits and supplies
Ready-made frames
Seasonal products
Silk, dried, and artificial flowers
Wooden model kits and supplies
Yarns and threads (for knitting, needlepoint, embroidery, cross-stitching, crocheting, and other stitchery)

## COMPETITORS

A.C. Moore
Burnes
Garden Ridge
Hancock Fabrics
Hobby Lobby
Home Interiors & Gifts
Kirkland's
Kmart
Martha Stewart Living
Michaels Stores
Pier 1 Imports
Target
Wal-Mart

## HISTORICAL FINANCIALS

Company Type: Public

### Income Statement

FYE: Saturday nearest January 31

| | REVENUE ($ mil.) | NET INCOME ($ mil.) | NET PROFIT MARGIN | EMPLOYEES |
|---|---|---|---|---|
| **1/07** | 1,851 | (2) | — | 22,280 |
| **1/06** | 1,883 | (23) | — | 24,060 |
| **1/05** | 1,812 | 46 | 2.5% | 22,250 |
| **1/04** | 1,734 | 41 | 2.4% | 21,750 |
| **1/03** | 1,682 | 45 | 2.7% | 21,200 |
| **Annual Growth** | 2.4% | — | — | 1.2% |

### 2007 Year-End Financials

Debt ratio: 30.6%
Return on equity: —
Cash ($ mil.): 18
Current ratio: 2.40
Long-term debt ($ mil.): 125

No. of shares (mil.): 24
Dividends
Yield: —
Payout: —
Market value ($ mil.): 611

### Stock History

NYSE: JAS

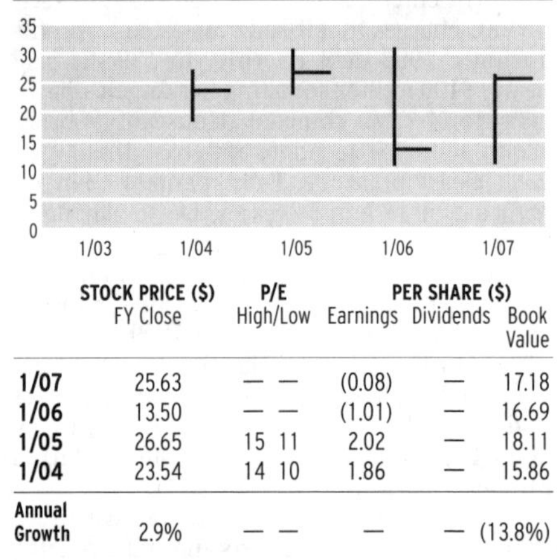


| | STOCK PRICE ($) FY Close | P/E High/Low | | PER SHARE ($) Earnings | Dividends | Book Value |
|---|---|---|---|---|---|---|
| **1/07** | 25.63 | — | — | (0.08) | — | 17.18 |
| **1/06** | 13.50 | — | — | (1.01) | — | 16.69 |
| **1/05** | 26.65 | 15 | 11 | 2.02 | — | 18.11 |
| **1/04** | 23.54 | 14 | 10 | 1.86 | — | 15.86 |
| **Annual Growth** | 2.9% | — | — | — | — | (13.8%) |

# Johnson & Johnson

It's nearly impossible to get well without Johnson & Johnson (J&J). The diversified health care giant operates in three segments through more than 250 operating companies. Its pharmaceuticals unit makes drugs — including best-selling schizophrenia medication Risperdal — for an array of ailments, such as neurological conditions, blood disorders, autoimmune diseases, and chronic pain. J&J's medical devices and diagnostics division offers surgical equipment, monitoring devices, orthopedic products, and disposable contact lenses, among other things. Its consumer products segment makes over-the-counter drugs and products for skin and hair care, baby care, oral care, first aid, and women's health.

Within its pharmaceuticals division, sales for blockbuster drug Risperdal are up, accounting for 8% of J&J's total sales and close to 20% of its pharmaceutical sales. Other drugs experiencing strong growth are Crohn's disease treatment Remicade (which the FDA approved for treatment of psoriasis in 2006); epilepsy drug Topamax; and attention deficit disorder drug CONCERTA. Looming generic competition may hurt CONCERTA's sales, however, as it has the contraceptives business of subsidiary Ortho-McNeil.

In 2006 J&J purchased the consumer health care unit of Pfizer, adding about 40 brands to J&J's offerings. The company plans to combine its own consumer brands (including Tylenol pain reliever, Neutrogena skin products, and Johnson's baby shampoo) with Pfizer's lineup (Listerine, Sudafed, Rolaids antacid, Benadryl allergy medicine, Rogaine baldness treatment, Zantac antacid, Bengay analgesic, and Lubriderm skin lotion). In order to clear some FTC hurdles, the companies agreed to sell US marketing rights for Zantac to Boehringer Ingelheim Pharmaceuticals for a little more than $500 million. J&J has also sold five brands (Act mouthwash, Unisom sleep aid, Cortizone anti-itch treatment, Kaopectate anti-diarrhea medication, and Balmex for diaper rash) to Chattem.

In 2006 J&J aggressively pushed to add cardiac defibrillator maker Guidant to its medical device portfolio, but was thwarted at every turn by counter-bids from niche rival Boston Scientific. Boston Scientific emerged victorious from that battle, paying some $27 billion for Guidant.

The company had better luck on the acquisition market in 2007, acquiring drug-coated stent maker Conor Medsystems. The acquired company will become part of J&J's Cordis cardiac device business.

## HISTORY

Brothers James and Edward Mead Johnson founded their medical products company in 1885 in New Brunswick, New Jersey. In 1886 Robert joined his brothers to make the antiseptic surgical dressings he developed. The company bought gauze maker Chicopee Manufacturing in 1916. In 1921 it introduced two of its classic products, the Band-Aid and Johnson's Baby Cream.

Robert Jr. became chairman in 1932 and served until 1963. A WWII Army general, he believed in decentralization; managers were given substantial freedom, a principle still used today. Product lines in the 1940s included Ortho (birth control products) and Ethicon (sutures). In 1959 Johnson & Johnson bought McNeil Labs, which launched Tylenol (acetaminophen) as an OTC drug the next year. Foreign acquisitions included Switzerland's Cilag-Chemie (1959) and Belgium's Janssen (1961). The company focused on consumer products in the 1970s, gaining half the feminine protection market and making Tylenol the top-selling painkiller.

J&J bought Iolab, a developer of intraocular lenses used in cataract surgery, in 1980. Trouble struck in 1982 when someone laced Tylenol capsules with cyanide, killing eight people. The company's response is now a damage-control classic: It immediately recalled 31 million bottles and totally redesigned its packaging to prevent future tampering. The move cost $240 million but saved the Tylenol brand. The next year prescription painkiller Zomax was linked to five deaths and was pulled.

New products in the 1980s included ACUVUE disposable contact lenses and Retin-A. The company bought LifeScan (blood-monitoring products for diabetics) in 1986. In 1989 it began a joint venture with Merck to sell Mylanta and other drugs bought from ICI Americas.

The firm continued its acquisition and diversification strategy in the 1990s. After introducing the first daily-wear, disposable contact lenses in 1993, it bought skin-care product maker Neutrogena (1994) to enhance its consumer lines. To diversify its medical products and better compete for hospital business, it bought Mitek Surgical Products (1995) and heart disease product maker Cordis (1996). The FDA cleared J&J's Renova wrinkle and fade cream in 1996. The company also began selling at-home HIV test Confide but pulled it the next year after low sales and other problems.

In 1997 J&J bought the OTC rights to Motrin from Pharmacia (now Pfizer). In 1998 the FDA approved artificial sweetener sucralose and its Indigo LaserOptic system to treat prostate enlargement. That year it bought DePuy and launched Benecol, a margarine said to cut "bad" cholesterol by up to 15%.

In response to numerous negative events in 1998 — several drugs in late development fell through, rights to an anemia drug were lost, and the company's share of the coronary stent market fell — the firm cut jobs and consolidated plants worldwide to control inventory and improve service. In 1999 it purchased S.C. Johnson & Son's skin care business, including the Aveeno line. That year the Ethicon Endo-Surgery unit settled three patent-infringement suits with Tyco International's U.S. Surgical. J&J also pulled its Hismanal antihistamine and bought biotechnology firm Centocor.

In 2000, after more than 80 deaths were linked to its use, J&J pulled heartburn drug Propulsid from the US market. That year the company started a health care services information-technology joint venture with Merrill Lynch.

In 2001 J&J bought minimally invasive heart-surgery equipment maker Heartport. Other buys included drug and drug-delivery system maker ALZA; and the diabetes-care businesses of Inverness Medical Technology, which it merged with its LifeScan division.

The company made headlines in 2002 with its INDEPENDENCE iBOT, a robotic wheelchair capable of climbing staircases and traversing rough terrain, made by subsidiary Independence Technology. That same year, J&J acquired OraPharma, a maker of oral antibiotics and other periodontal therapies.

## EXECUTIVES

**Chairman and CEO:** William C. (Bill) Weldon, age 58, $1,670,000 pay
**Vice Chairman; Worldwide Chairman, Medicines and Nutritionals:** Christine A. (Chris) Poon, age 54, $975,000 pay
**CFO:** Dominic J. Caruso, age 49
**VP, General Counsel, and Chief Compliance Officer:** Russell C. Deyo, age 57
**VP, Corporate Affairs:** Brian D. Perkins, age 53
**VP, Corporate Development:** David P. Holveck
**VP, Investor Relations:** Louise Mehrotra
**VP, Government Affairs and Policy:** Thomas M. Gorrie
**VP, Human Resources:** Kaye I. Foster-Cheek, age 47
**VP, Public Affairs and Corporate Communications:** Raymond Jordan
**VP, Science and Technology:** Theodore J. Torphy
**VP, Technical Resources and Corporate Compliance Officer:** Brenda S. Davis
**VP, Worldwide Operations:** Donnie Young
**VP, Worldwide Advertising, Marketing, and Communications:** Joseph McCarthy
**Worldwide Chairman, Consumer and Personal Care Group:** Colleen A. Goggins, age 52
**Worldwide Chairman, Medical Devices and Diagnostics:** Nicholas J. Valeriani, age 50
**Worldwide Chairman, Pharmaceuticals Group:** Joseph C. Scodari, age 53
**Consumer Company Group Chairman; President, Personal Products Company:** Michael E. Sneed
**Chief Science and Technology Officer, Device and Diagnostic Unit:** Harlan Weisman
**President and Head Mom, BabyCenter:** Mari J. Baker
**Secretary and Associate General Counsel:** Michael H. Ullmann
**Treasurer:** John A. Papa
**Principal Scientist:** Jennifer Jensen
**Company Group Chairman, Pharmaceutical Research and Development:** Paul Stoffels
**Group President, Research and Development:** Jay P. Siegel
**Auditors:** PricewaterhouseCoopers LLP

## LOCATIONS

**HQ:** Johnson & Johnson
1 Johnson & Johnson Plaza,
New Brunswick, NJ 08933
**Phone:** 732-524-0400 **Fax:** 732-214-0332
**Web:** www.jnj.com

### 2006 Sales

| | $ mil. | % of total |
|---|---|---|
| US | 29,775 | 56 |
| Europe | 12,786 | 24 |
| Asia/Pacific & Africa | 7,221 | 14 |
| Canada & Latin America | 3,542 | 6 |
| **Total** | **53,324** | **100** |

## PRODUCTS/OPERATIONS

### 2006 Sales

| | $ mil. | % of total |
|---|---|---|
| Pharmaceuticals | 23,267 | 44 |
| Medical devices & diagnostics | 20,283 | 38 |
| Consumer products | 9,774 | 18 |
| **Total** | **53,324** | **100** |

### Selected Products

Pharmaceuticals
- Concerta (ADHD)
- Consta (schizophrenia)
- Duragesic (pain management; Durogesic outside the US)
- Floxin (anti-infective)
- Levaquin (anti-infective)
- Natrecor (congestive heart failure)
- Ortho Evra (patch contraceptive)
- Ortho Tri-cyclen (oral contraceptive)
- Procrit (anemia, Eprex outside the US)
- Remicade (rheumatoid arthritis and Crohn's disease)
- Risperdal (antipsychotic)
- Topamax (epilepsy)

Medical devices and diagnostics
- Diagnostic cardiology products
- Diagnostic equipment and supplies
- Disposable contact lenses
- Infection prevention products
- Interventional cardiology products
- Joint replacements
- Mechanical wound closure products
- Surgical equipment and devices
- Sutures
- Wound management products

Consumer products
- Aveeno skin care products
- Band-Aid bandages
- Benecol food products
- Carefree feminine hygiene products
- Clean & Clear skin care products
- Imodium A-D antidiarrheal
- Johnson's baby care products
- Lactaid nutritional products
- Listerine mouthwash
- Monistat vaginal yeast infection treatment
- Motrin IB analgesic
- Mylanta gastrointestinal aid
- Neutrogena skin and hair care products
- Pepcid AC gastrointestinal aid
- Reach toothbrushes
- RoC skin care products
- Splenda non-caloric sugar substitute
- Stayfree feminine hygiene products
- Sudafed cold, flu, and allergy medications
- Tylenol acetaminophen
- Viactiv calcium supplements

## COMPETITORS

3M
Abbott Labs
Affymetrix
Alberto-Culver
Amgen
Bausch & Lomb
Baxter
Bayer
BD
Beckman Coulter
Bristol-Myers Squibb
Colgate-Palmolive
Dade Behring
Dial
Eli Lilly
Genentech
GlaxoSmithKline
Kimberly-Clark
L'Oréal USA
Medtronic
Merck
Nestlé
Novartis
Perrigo
Pfizer
Procter & Gamble
Roche
Sanofi-Aventis
St. Jude Medical
Unilever
United States Surgical
Wyeth

## HISTORICAL FINANCIALS

Company Type: Public

### Income Statement

FYE: Sunday nearest December 31

| | REVENUE ($ mil.) | NET INCOME ($ mil.) | NET PROFIT MARGIN | EMPLOYEES |
|---|---|---|---|---|
| **12/06** | 53,324 | 11,053 | 20.7% | 122,200 |
| **12/05** | 50,514 | 10,411 | 20.6% | 115,600 |
| **12/04** | 47,348 | 8,509 | 18.0% | 109,900 |
| **12/03** | 41,862 | 7,197 | 17.2% | 110,600 |
| **12/02** | 36,298 | 6,597 | 18.2% | 108,300 |
| **Annual Growth** | 10.1% | 13.8% | — | 3.1% |

### 2006 Year-End Financials

Debt ratio: 5.1%
Return on equity: 28.6%
Cash ($ mil.): 4,084
Current ratio: 1.20
Long-term debt ($ mil.): 2,014
No. of shares (mil.): 2,893
Dividends
Yield: 2.2%
Payout: 39.1%
Market value ($ mil.): 191,011

### Stock History

NYSE: JNJ

| | STOCK PRICE ($) FY Close | P/E High | P/E Low | PER SHARE ($) Earnings | Dividends | Book Value |
|---|---|---|---|---|---|---|
| **12/06** | 66.02 | 19 | 15 | 3.73 | 1.46 | 13.59 |
| **12/05** | 60.10 | 20 | 17 | 3.46 | 0.94 | 12.73 |
| **12/04** | 63.42 | 23 | 17 | 2.84 | 1.10 | 10.71 |
| **12/03** | 50.62 | 25 | 20 | 2.40 | 0.93 | 9.05 |
| **12/02** | 53.11 | 31 | 19 | 2.16 | 0.80 | 7.65 |
| **Annual Growth** | 5.6% | — | — | 14.6% | 16.2% | 15.5% |

# Johnson Controls

Johnson Controls wants to put you in the driver's seat. The company makes car seats, interior systems, and batteries, as well as environmental control systems for commercial buildings and HVAC systems through York International. Interior components include consoles and instrument panels. Major OEM customers include GM (11% of sales), Daimler and Chrysler (11%), and Ford (10%). The battery unit makes car batteries for retailers such as Wal-Mart, Advance Auto, AutoZone, Pep Boys, and Sears. The building efficiency division makes, installs, and services control systems that monitor temperatures and detect fires in non-residential buildings. The unit also offers on-site facility management for buildings.

Like most automotive suppliers, Johnson Controls is beefing up its presence in China to be near its customers' greatest geographic growth. Johnson Controls opened its first Chinese factory in 1997, and has since added 11 more to command the largest share of the Chinese seating market. The company has announced it would expand capacity at its Shanghai seat plant to meet increased demand. The company also plans to expand its component offerings beyond seating in China by entering the interior electronics, overhead systems, and cockpits markets. Johnson Controls' purchase of Delphi Corporation's global auto battery operations has also increased its footprint in Asia, particularly in China. The deal, valued at about $202 million, is tied to a long-term, global contract to supply GM with batteries.

Johnson Controls' battery business grew in 2004 when it bought out partner Imsa. The company now has full control of the most popular battery brands in Mexico and South America. Johnson Controls is working on low-weight lithium ion batteries for use in the next generation of gas-electric hybrid vehicles. The company is also developing the under-hood electronics for the necessary communication between a hybrid vehicle's batteries and engine.

The company's controls division will be complemented by Johnson Controls' late 2005 acquisition of York International, the US's third-largest supplier of heating, ventilation, air-conditioning, and refrigeration equipment. The deal was valued at $3.2 billion. The controls division will also benefit from Johnson Controls' 2005 purchase of corporate real estate services firm United Systems Integrators Corporation (USI) for $80 million. The move allows Johnson Controls to offer customers a single source for facilities management and real estate services.

In mid-2006 Johnson Controls announced it would take an estimated after-tax charge of between $130 and $140 million in the third quarter for restructuring. The revamping is aimed at reducing costs at its automotive interiors and facilities management businesses. The plan includes the cutting of 5,000 jobs and the closure of 16 plants over one year.

## HISTORY

Professor Warren Johnson developed the electric telethermoscope in 1880 so that janitors at Whitewater, Wisconsin's State Normal School could regulate room temperatures without disturbing classrooms. His device, the thermostat, used mercury to move a heat element that opened and shut a circuit. Milwaukee hotelier William Plankinton believed in the invention and invested $150,000 to start production.

The two men formed Johnson Electric Service Company in 1885. They sold the marketing, installation, and service rights to concentrate on manufacturing. Johnson also invented other devices such as tower clocks, and he experimented with the telegraph before becoming intrigued with the automobile and beginning production of steam-powered cars. He won the US Postal Service's first automotive contract, but never gained support within his own company. Johnson continued to look elsewhere for financing until his death in 1911.

The renamed Johnson Services regained full rights to its thermostats in 1912 and sold its other businesses. During the Depression it produced economy systems, which regulated building temperatures. Johnson Services became a public company in 1940. During WWII it aided the war effort, building weather-data gatherers and test radar sets.

In the 1960s Johnson Services began to develop centralized control systems for temperature, fire alarm, lighting, and security regulation. The company was renamed Johnson Controls in 1974; it acquired automotive battery maker Globe-Union in 1978.

Johnson Controls bought auto seat makers Hoover Universal and Ferro Manufacturing in 1985. It expanded its controls business through the purchases of ITT's European controls group (1982) and Pan Am World Services (1989).

The company sold its car-door components business in 1990 and bought battery maker Varta's Canadian plant. The next year Johnson Controls purchased several car-seat component makers in Europe.

In 1996 Johnson Controls bought most of Roth Frères (auto components) and Prince Automotive (interior systems), becoming a major interior-systems integrator.

The company bought Becker Group (automotive interior parts), Creative Control Designs (HVAC and lighting-control systems), and Italy-based Commerfin SpA (door systems) in 1998.

The company announced in 1999 that it would develop integrated electronics for car interiors through a *keiretsu*-like partnership with Gentex Corporation (mirrors), Jabil Circuit (semiconductors and transistors), and Microchip Technology (microcontrollers). The next year Johnson Controls agreed to buy Nissan's 38% stake in seat maker Ikeda Bussan. Late in 2000 the company bought a 15% stake in Donnelly Corporation (automotive components).

In 2002 Johnson Controls acquired the automotive electronics business of Sagem SA (France) and the automotive battery operations of Varta AG (Germany). In 2004 the company bought out its joint venture partner Grupo IMSA, S.A. de C.V.'s share in the two companies' Mexican battery making operations.

Early the following year Johnson Controls sold its engine electronics division (engine management systems and components) to France's Valeo for $437 million. It also sold its Johnson Controls World Services subsidiary to IAP Worldwide Services for $260 million.

In 2006 the company bought Environmental Technologies Inc., a supplier of HVAC equipment.

## EXECUTIVES

**Chairman, President, and CEO:** John M. Barth, age 60, $4,302,500 pay
**Vice Chairman and EVP:** Stephen A. Roell, age 57, $2,506,000 pay
**President and COO:** Keith E. Wandell, age 56, $1,654,500 pay
**EVP; President, Controls Group:** John P. Kennedy, age 63
**EVP; President, Johnson Controls International:** Giovanni (John) Fiori, age 63
**Group VP and General Manager, North America:** Jeff Williams
**VP; Group VP and General Manager, Battery Business:** Gregg M. Sherrill, age 53
**VP and CFO:** R. Bruce McDonald, age 46, $1,584,500 pay
**VP and CIO:** Subhash (Sam) Valanju, age 63
**VP; President, Building Efficiency:** C. David (Dave) Myers, age 43, $1,438,252 pay
**VP and President, Interior Experience:** Beda-Helmut Bolzenius, age 50
**VP; President, Power Solutions:** Alex A. Molinaroli, age 47
**VP and Corporate Controller:** Jeffrey G. Augustin, age 44
**VP and Treasurer:** Frank A. Voltolina, age 46
**VP, Diversity and Public Affairs:** Charles A. Harvey, age 54
**VP, Secretary, and General Counsel:** Jerome D. Okarma, age 54
**VP, Human Resources:** Susan F. Davis, age 53
**VP, Strategy, Investor Relations, and Corporate Communication:** Denise M. Zutz, age 55
**VP and General Manager, Hybrid Systems; CEO, Johnson Controls-Saft Advanced Power Solutions:** Mary Ann Wright
**VP and Corporate Controller:** Susan M. Kreh, age 45
**Auditors:** PricewaterhouseCoopers LLP

## LOCATIONS

**HQ:** Johnson Controls, Inc.
5757 N. Green Bay Ave., Milwaukee, WI 53209
**Phone:** 414-524-1200 **Fax:** 414-524-2077
**Web:** www.johnsoncontrols.com

### 2006 Sales

| | $ mil. | % of total |
|---|---|---|
| US | 12,822 | 40 |
| Europe | | |
| Germany | 3,390 | 10 |
| Other countries | 9,208 | 29 |
| Other regions | 6,815 | 21 |
| **Total** | **32,235** | **100** |

## PRODUCTS/OPERATIONS

### 2006 Sales

| | $ mil. | % of total |
|---|---|---|
| Automotive experience | 18,274 | 57 |
| Building efficiency | 10,245 | 32 |
| Power solutions | 3,716 | 11 |
| **Total** | **32,235** | **100** |

### Selected Products

Automotive experience
- Cockpits
- Door systems
- Floor consoles
- Instrument panels
- Overhead systems
- Seating systems

Building efficiency
- Actuators
- Air handlers
- Building automation systems
- Chillers
- Control panels, consoles, and instrumentation
- Dampers
- Digital electronic controllers
- Electronic sensor controls
- HVAC systems
- Pneumatic controls
- Refrigeration controls
- Valves

Power solutions
- Batteries
- Plastic battery containers

### Selected Subsidiaries

Hoover Universal, Inc. (automotive seating and plastic machinery)
Johnson Controls Battery Group (automotive batteries)
York International Corporations (HVAC systems and service)

## COMPETITORS

Alcatel-Lucent
Ansell
Carrier
Collins & Aikman
Comfort Systems USA
Delphi
DENSO
Eagle-Picher
East Penn
Eaton
Exide
Faurecia
Fedders Addison
General Motors
Goodman Global
GS Yuasa
Hitachi
Honeywell International
Invensys
Johnson Electric
Landis & Gyr
Lear
Lennox
Magna International
Paloma
Rieter Automotive
Robert Bosch
Siemens AG
SPX
Textron
Trane
Valeo
Varta
Visteon
Yazaki North America

## HISTORICAL FINANCIALS

Company Type: Public

### Income Statement

FYE: September 30

| | REVENUE ($ mil.) | NET INCOME ($ mil.) | NET PROFIT MARGIN | EMPLOYEES |
|---|---|---|---|---|
| **9/06** | 32,235 | 1,028 | 3.2% | 136,000 |
| **9/05** | 27,479 | 909 | 3.3% | 114,000 |
| **9/04** | 26,553 | 818 | 3.1% | 123,000 |
| **9/03** | 22,646 | 683 | 3.0% | 118,000 |
| **9/02** | 20,103 | 601 | 3.0% | 111,000 |
| **Annual Growth** | 12.5% | 14.4% | — | 5.2% |

### 2006 Year-End Financials

Debt ratio: 56.6%
Return on equity: 15.3%
Cash ($ mil.): 293
Current ratio: 1.14
Long-term debt ($ mil.): 4,166
No. of shares (mil.): 196
Dividends
- Yield: 1.6%
- Payout: 21.4%

Market value ($ mil.): 14,045

### Stock History

NYSE: JCI

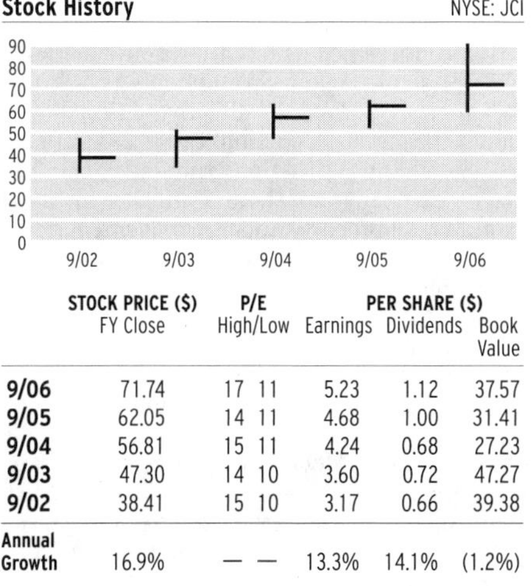


| | STOCK PRICE ($) FY Close | P/E High | P/E Low | PER SHARE ($) Earnings | Dividends | Book Value |
|---|---|---|---|---|---|---|
| **9/06** | 71.74 | 17 | 11 | 5.23 | 1.12 | 37.57 |
| **9/05** | 62.05 | 14 | 11 | 4.68 | 1.00 | 31.41 |
| **9/04** | 56.81 | 15 | 11 | 4.24 | 0.68 | 27.23 |
| **9/03** | 47.30 | 14 | 10 | 3.60 | 0.72 | 47.27 |
| **9/02** | 38.41 | 15 | 10 | 3.17 | 0.66 | 39.38 |
| **Annual Growth** | 16.9% | — | — | 13.3% | 14.1% | (1.2%) |

# Jones Apparel Group

While some are busy keeping up with the Joneses, Jones Apparel Group is too busy buying up firms to take notice. It provides a wide range of women's and men's clothing and shoes. Brands include Jones New York and Evan-Picone. Subsidiary Nine West Group designs shoes under names Easy Spirit, Enzo Angiolini, Bandolino, and Gloria Vanderbilt. Gloria Vanderbilt and l.e.i. design twill and denim casualwear, swimwear, and accessories, among other items. Retailer Barneys New York was a surprise acquisition that helped Jones capture the luxury niche, although it's now selling it. Jones currently owns and operates more than 1,100 stores.

Turnover at the top began at Jones in mid-2007. Veteran executive Peter Boneparth, who joined Jones when it acquired McNaughton in 1997, stepped down in July 2007. Wesley Card, the company's president and CEO and an executive with nearly three decades of retail experience, was appointed as the firm's CEO. Soon after Card took the top seat, he announced plans for an executive management reorganization within its women's sportswear unit.

Jones Apparel has taken down the "for sale" sign after failing to find a private- equity buyer for the company to meet its asking price. In March 2006 the firm said that it was exploring the sale of the entire business, as opposed to divesting parts of the company. Private equity firms — including Cerberus Capital Management, Bain Capital, and Texas Pacific Group — had expressed interest but ultimately passed on the opportunity to acquire the midtier apparel maker.

It's now speculated that Jones in 2007 is resigned to splitting up the entire company and has been looking for interest in Nine West.

Jones has been restructuring various parts of its businesses to reduce excess capacity and decrease its dependency on licensed wholesale products. To that end, the company sold its luxury department store chain Barneys in late 2007. (Jones plans to use some of the proceeds from the $945 million Barneys sale to buy back its slumping stock.) Previously in 2006 the firm sold its Polo Jeans Company apparel business to Polo Ralph Lauren. Its Maxwell Shoe Company unit, purchased in 2004 through a leveraged buyout, was dissolved into the Jones footwear segment.

The company's retail operations include more than 400 specialty footwear and apparel stores (Bandolino, Easy Spirit, Nine West), and about 700 outlet stores (Jones New York, Nine West, Kasper).

Jones's products are manufactured — mainly by third parties — in Asia (89%), Latin America, and the US. Footwear is primarily made in China, but also in Brazil.

Jones got a stronger foothold in the Hispanic clothing market in early 2005. The company partnered with Hispanic publisher Latina Media Ventures to design a Latina Life line of apparel, footwear, and handbags that is being sold by Sears Holdings in some 425 Sears stores. The publisher's *Latina* magazine will serve as fashion director.

## HISTORY

When diversifying chemical firm W. R. Grace & Co. began a brief foray into the fashion world in 1970, it hired Sidney Kimmel to run the show. Kimmel had worked in a knitting mill in the 1950s and served as president of women's sportswear maker Villager in the 1960s. He and his companion, designer Rena Rowan, created Grace's fashionable but moderately priced Jones New York line.

Kimmel and Grace accountant Gerard Rubin bought Grace's fashion division in 1975, incorporating it as Jones Apparel Group. Jones expanded quickly by bringing out new labels and licensing others, such as Christian Dior. Talks to sell the company to underwear maker Warnaco fell through in 1981.

Tapping into two trends of the early 1980s, Jones Apparel offered the sweatsuit fashions of Norma Kamali and in 1984 acquired the license for the Gloria Vanderbilt line from Murjani. Swan-adorned Gloria Vanderbilt jeans had been must-haves early in the decade, but the deal turned into an ugly duckling as costs beyond Jones Apparel's control pushed the company into the red. (Meanwhile, Kimmel produced the films *9 1/2 Weeks* and *Clan of the Cave Bear* and led a group that briefly controlled the Famous Amos Cookie Co.)

Creditors forced Jones Apparel to unload most of its brands — all but Jones New York, Saville, and Christian Dior — and cut jobs, and by 1988 it was profitable again. Kimmel bought Rubin's interest in the company in 1989 and took it public in 1991, retaining about half of the stock.

In the early 1990s, as recession-minded shoppers looked for bargains and the American workplace became more casual, Jones again took off. The company expanded with new lines, such as Rena Rowan (inexpensive suits) and Jones & Co. (career casuals). Jones Apparel moved into women's accessories with the 1993 purchase of the Evan-Picone brand name.

Two years later the company struck its first licensing agreement with Polo Ralph Lauren, for the Lauren by Ralph Lauren line of women's sportswear. Propelled by the new line, Jones reached $1 billion in sales in 1996. The company ended its long-held licensing agreement with Christian Dior the next year.

Jones Apparel licensed Ralph by Ralph Lauren, a lower-priced juniors' line, in 1998. That year it purchased Sun Apparel, picking up the rights to Todd Oldham and Polo jeans, and in 1999 it bought the remaining clothing, footwear, cosmetics, and apparel rights to the youth-oriented Oldham name.

The firm then made its biggest acquisition by far when it paid $1.4 billion for shoe designer and retailer Nine West Group (Easy Spirit, Enzo Angiolini, Bandolino, Amalfi). With the Nine West purchase, Jones Apparel inherited an FTC investigation into the footwear designer's pricing policies. The company closed several Nine West facilities in 1999, cutting about 1,900 jobs, followed by the sale of its retail operations in Canada (1999), Asia (2000), and the UK (2001).

Continuing its acquisition spree, the company agreed to purchase Gloria Vanderbilt Apparel in March 2002 for about $140 million. In May president Peter Boneparth was named CEO, after Kimmel stepped down (he remains as chairman). Jones Apparel bought RSV Sport, maker of l.e.i. jeanswear for girls, in 2002 and with it came a foray into swimwear, watches, belts, sunglasses, outerwear, and children's apparel that went beyond licensing.

In 2003 Jones announced plans to close some of its manufacturing facilities, cut jobs, and convert most of its Angiolini shoe stores into more successful Bandolino stores. In 2004 Jones acquired Barneys New York for nearly $400 million.

The company has held the exclusive license to produce Lauren-branded apparel in Canada, Mexico, and the US for the Polo Ralph Lauren Corp. The deal, however, spurred litigation over control of the brand. In 2006 Jones and Polo Ralph Lauren agreed to a settlement. Polo Ralph Lauren paid Jones some $355 million for the Jones Sun Apparel subsidiary that operates the brand and for a controlling ownership of the brand in the US.

In September 2007 Jones Apparel sold Barneys New York to an affiliate of the Dubai-based private equity firm Istithmar for about $945 million, booking a nice return on its original $400 million investment. The sale followed a bidding war between Istithmar and Japan's Fast Retailing Co.

## EXECUTIVES

**Chairman:** Sidney Kimmel, age 79, $1,200,000 pay
**President, CEO, and Director:** Wesley R. (Wes) Card, age 59
**CFO:** John T. McClain, age 46
**EVP and CTO:** Paul Lanham
**EVP Production, Better Sportwear Divisions:** Douglas (Doug) Means, age 41
**COO:** Cynthia (Cindy) DiPietrantonio
**EVP, Distribution Operations:** Mike Kauffman
**EVP Corporate Quality and Production:** Ronald Harrison, age 59
**EVP, General Counsel, and Secretary:** Ira M. Dansky, age 61, $1,025,000 pay
**EVP, Human Resources:** Aida Tejero-DeColli
**EVP Marketing:** Stacy Lastrina
**EVP Management Information Services:** Norman (Norm) Veit
**SVP Corporate Taxation and Risk Management and Treasurer:** Joseph Donnalley
**Group President, l.e.i. and Energie:** Barry Bates
**President and CEO, Canadian Division:** Mary Ann Curran
**President and CEO, Costume Jewelry Division:** Robert Andreoli
**Group CEO, Jones Moderate Sportswear:** Howard Zwilling
**CEO, Women's Better Sportswear:** Susan Metzger, age 53
**CEO, Retail Footwear and Apparel:** Heather Pech
**CEO, Wholesale Footwear and Accessories:** Andrew (Andy) Cohen
**CEO, Victoria + Co and Handbags and Small Leather Goods Division:** Jackie Corso
**Group President, Nine West Accessories and Victoria + Co.:** Lisa Geardino
**President, Licensing:** Mary Belle
**President, Company-Owned Retail Footwear and Apparel:** Jay Friedman
**Auditors:** BDO Seidman, LLP

## LOCATIONS

**HQ:** Jones Apparel Group, Inc.
250 Rittenhouse Cir., Bristol, PA 19007
**Phone:** 215-785-4000 **Fax:** 215-785-1795
**Web:** www.jny.com

**2006 Sales**

| | $ mil. | % of total |
|---|---|---|
| US | 4,456.8 | 94 |
| International | 286.0 | 6 |
| **Total** | **4,742.8** | **100** |

## PRODUCTS/OPERATIONS

**2006 Sales**

| | $ mil. | % of total |
|---|---|---|
| Wholesale better apparel | 1,127.4 | 24 |
| Retail | 1,477.9 | 31 |
| Wholesale moderate apparel | 1,142.0 | 24 |
| Wholesale footwear & accessories | 941.1 | 20 |
| Licensing & other | 54.4 | 1 |
| **Total** | **4,742.8** | **100** |

**2006 Stores**

| | No. |
|---|---|
| Outlet | 701 |
| Specialty retail | 411 |
| Luxury (Barneys) | 20 |
| **Total** | **1,132** |

**Selected Brand Affiliates**

9 & Co.
Albert Nipon
Anne Klein
Bandolino
Capezio (licensed)
Easy Spirit
Enzo Angiolini
Evan-Picone
Givenchy (jewelry) (licensed)
Gloria Vanderbilt
J.G. Hook (licensed)
Kasper
Mootsies Tootsies
JNY Sport
Joan & David
Jones New York
Jones Wear
Judith Jack
Kasper
Napier
Nine West
Sam & Libby
Westies

## COMPETITORS

AnnTaylor
Bally
bebe stores
Berkshire Hathaway
Bernard Chaus
Bill Blass
Brown Shoe
Caché
Calvin Klein
Chico's FAS
Coach
Coldwater Creek
Collective Brands
Donna Karan
Ellen Tracy
Etienne Aigner Group
Gucci
Hampshire Group
Iconix Brand Group
IT Holding
J. Jill Group
Kenneth Cole
Levi Strauss
Liz Claiborne
Nordstrom
Phillips-Van Heusen
Polo Ralph Lauren
Salvatore Ferragamo
Skechers U.S.A.
St. John Knits
Steven Madden
Talbots
VF

## HISTORICAL FINANCIALS

Company Type: Public

**Income Statement** FYE: December 31

| | REVENUE ($ mil.) | NET INCOME ($ mil.) | NET PROFIT MARGIN | EMPLOYEES |
|---|---|---|---|---|
| **12/06** | 4,743 | (144) | — | 16,485 |
| **12/05** | 5,074 | 274 | 5.4% | 18,430 |
| **12/04** | 4,650 | 302 | 6.5% | 22,500 |
| **12/03** | 4,375 | 329 | 7.5% | 21,845 |
| **12/02** | 4,341 | 319 | 7.3% | 20,785 |
| **Annual Growth** | 2.2% | — | — | (5.6%) |

**2006 Year-End Financials**

Debt ratio: 35.7%
Return on equity: —
Cash ($ mil.): 72
Current ratio: 2.08
Long-term debt ($ mil.): 789
No. of shares (mil.): 108
Dividends
Yield: 1.5%
Payout: —
Market value ($ mil.): 3,627

**Stock History** NYSE: JNY

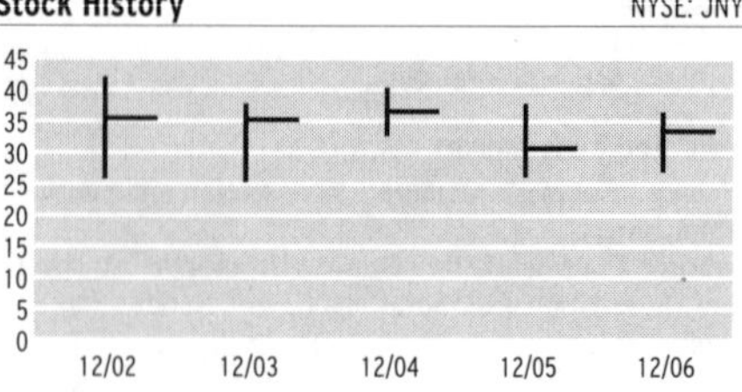

| | STOCK PRICE ($) FY Close | P/E High | P/E Low | PER SHARE ($) Earnings | Dividends | Book Value |
|---|---|---|---|---|---|---|
| **12/06** | 33.43 | — | — | (1.30) | 0.50 | 20.39 |
| **12/05** | 30.72 | 16 | 12 | 2.30 | 0.44 | 23.01 |
| **12/04** | 36.57 | 17 | 14 | 2.39 | 0.36 | 21.72 |
| **12/03** | 35.23 | 15 | 10 | 2.48 | 0.16 | 20.11 |
| **12/02** | 35.44 | 18 | 11 | 2.36 | — | 17.94 |
| **Annual Growth** | (1.4%) | — | — | — | 46.2% | 3.2% |

# Jones Lang LaSalle

Borders are nothing to Jones Lang LaSalle; the giant real estate services company helps its customers buy, sell, and manage property in 50 countries. It offers property management, leasing, project management, and tenant representation. Jones Lang LaSalle's financial services include investment banking, corporate finance, and real estate finance. The firm also offers real estate investment management services to pension funds, insurance companies, and money managers; it has $30 billion in assets under management. With the acquisition of real estate and investment firm Spaulding & Slye, Jones Lang LaSalle increased its expertise in leasing, project management, investment sales, and consulting and development.

Jones Lang LaSalle and Trammell Crow Meghraj have merged their operations in India and created Jones Lang LaSalle Meghraj (JLLM). The new company will have operations in 10 cities on the subcontinent and some 44 million sq. ft. under management.

It also increased its footprint in the lucrative New England region, Spaulding & Sly's home territory, and retained the Spaulding brand under the names Spaulding & Slye Investments and Spaulding & Slye Construction.

The company has about 1 million sq. ft. of commercial property under management.

Ariel Capital Management owns about 9% of the company, down from more than 20% in 2006.

## HISTORY

Jones Lang Wootton had roots in London's Paternoster Row auction houses in 1783. LaSalle Partners, originally known as IDC Real Estate, was founded in El Paso, Texas in 1968. The two companies could not have started out in a more disparate fashion; yet their combined force is now one of the largest real estate services firms in the world.

Richard Winstanley opened an auction house in 1783, and his son James joined him in that business in 1806. In 1840, the Joneses entered the picture — the Winstanleys created a partnership with one James Jones. The business moved to King Street (in the Guildhall section of London) in 1860 and remained in that location for some 100 years in various incarnations — James' son Frederick took over the business, renaming it Frederick Jones and Co. When James retired in 1872, the firm was again renamed, to Jones Lang and Co., and was controlled by C. A. Lang. Jones Lang merged with Wootton and Son in 1939, becoming Jones Lang Wootton and Sons.

Jones Lang Wootton was active in redrawing the property lines in London after the Blitz. In 1945, the firm began contacting small landowners and by combining small parcels of land, secured development, leasing, and/or purchase contracts. When the rebuilding of London began in 1954, Jones Lang Wootton was in a secure place to be right at the forefront of that new development. The firm began engaging in speculative development in the West End and in the City of London.

1958 saw the expansion of Jones Lang Wootton into Australia; the firm had offices throughout the Asia Pacific region by 1968. Further expansion took place closer to home in Scotland (1962) and Ireland (1965), and the first continental European office in Brussels (also 1965). The firm moved into the Manhattan market in 1975.

On the other side of the story, IDC Real Estate (the name change to LaSalle Partners came in 1977) was a group of partnerships, initially focused on investment banking, investment management, and land. The firm began offering development management services in 1975; it moved into property management, leasing, and tenant representation in 1978 and facility management operations in 1980.

It built market share by buying other firms, including Kleinwort Benson Realty Advisors Corp. (1994) and UK-based investment adviser CIN Property Management (1996).

The firm leveraged its experience and long-term client base to pursue an acquisition strategy, taking advantage of trends shaping commercial real estate — globalization, consolidation, and merchant banking. LaSalle went public in 1997, amalgamating the Galbreath Company (a property and development management firm with which it merged that year) with its other partnerships and becoming a corporation.

In 1998 it acquired the project management business of Satulah Group and two retail management business units from Lend Lease, and took real estate investment trust LaSalle Hotel Properties public. In 1999 the firm strengthened its world position by merging with Jones Lang Wootton; the company was renamed Jones Lang LaSalle.

The merger with Jones Lang Wootton combined Wootton's strength in Asia and Europe with LaSalle Partners' large presence in North America to create a worldwide real estate services firm.

## EXECUTIVES

**Chairman:** Sheila A. Penrose, age 61, $100,000 pay
**President, CEO, and Director:** Colin Dyer, age 54, $2,550,000 pay
**COO, CFO, and Director:** Lauralee E. Martin, age 56, $1,545,000 pay
**EVP and Chief Human Resources Officer:** Nazneen Razi, age 54
**EVP, General Counsel, and Secretary:** Mark J. Ohringer, age 48
**EVP and Treasurer:** Brian P. Hake
**SVP and Global Controller:** Stanley Stec, age 48
**International Director and CIO:** David A. Johnson, age 44
**Chairman, Asia Pacific:** Christopher M. G. (Chris) Brown, age 56
**Chairman, Corporate Solutions:** John Phillips
**CEO, Asia Pacific; Chairman, Jones Lang Lasalle Hotels:** Peter A. Barge, age 56, $1,365,000 pay
**CEO, Americas:** Peter C. Roberts, age 46
**CEO, Capital Markets:** Earl E. Webb, age 46
**CEO, International Capital Group:** Tony Horrell
**CEO, Europe:** Alastair Hughes, age 41
**Chairman, LaSalle Investment Management:** Lynn C. Thurber, age 59
**CEO, LaSalle Investment Management:** Jeff A. Jacobson, age 45
**Chief Marketing and Communications Officer:** Margaret A. (Molly) Kelly, age 48
**Auditors:** KPMG LLP

## LOCATIONS

**HQ:** Jones Lang LaSalle Incorporated
200 E. Randolph Dr., Chicago, IL 60601
**Phone:** 312-782-5800 **Fax:** 312-782-4339
**Web:** www.joneslanglasalle.com

### 2006 Sales

| | $ mil. | % of total |
|---|---|---|
| Europe, Middle East & Africa | 679.3 | 33 |
| Americas | 625.4 | 31 |
| Asia/Pacific | 337.1 | 17 |
| Investment management | 384.3 | 19 |
| Adjustments | (12.5) | — |
| **Total** | **2,013.6** | **100** |

## PRODUCTS/OPERATIONS

### Selected Services

Agency leasing
Buying and selling properties
Capital markets
Corporate finance
Facilities management
Hotel advisory
Outsourcing
Project and development
Property management
Real estate investment banking and merchant banking
Space acquisition and disposition (tenant representation)
Strategic consulting
Valuations

## COMPETITORS

CB Richard Ellis
Colliers International
Cushman & Wakefield
Grubb & Ellis
Hines
Inland Group
Lend Lease
Realogy
Shorenstein
Staubach
Studley
Trammell Crow Company

## HISTORICAL FINANCIALS

Company Type: Public

### Income Statement

FYE: December 31

| | REVENUE ($ mil.) | NET INCOME ($ mil.) | NET PROFIT MARGIN | EMPLOYEES |
|---|---|---|---|---|
| **12/06** | 2,014 | 176 | 8.8% | 25,500 |
| **12/05** | 1,391 | 104 | 7.5% | 22,000 |
| **12/04** | 1,167 | 64 | 5.5% | 19,300 |
| **12/03** | 950 | 36 | 3.8% | 17,300 |
| **12/02** | 840 | 27 | 3.2% | 16,900 |
| **Annual Growth** | 24.4% | 59.7% | — | 10.8% |

### 2006 Year-End Financials

Debt ratio: 4.3%
Return on equity: 27.4%
Cash ($ mil.): 51
Current ratio: 0.97
Long-term debt ($ mil.): 32
No. of shares (mil.): 37
Dividends
Yield: 0.7%
Payout: 11.5%
Market value ($ mil.): 3,373

### Stock History

NYSE: JLL

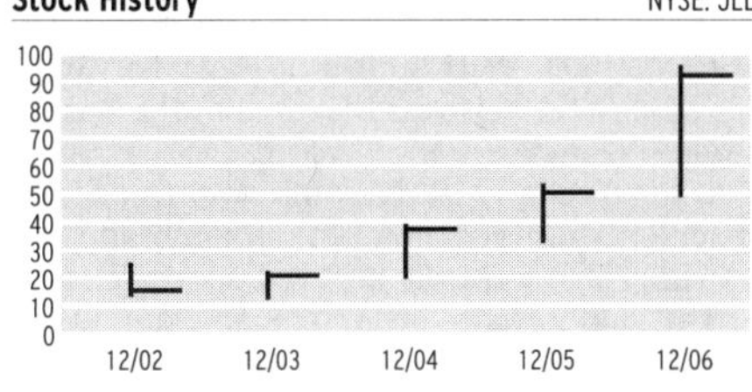


| | STOCK PRICE ($) FY Close | P/E High | P/E Low | PER SHARE ($) Earnings | Dividends | Book Value |
|---|---|---|---|---|---|---|
| **12/06** | 92.17 | 18 | 9 | 5.24 | 0.60 | 20.51 |
| **12/05** | 50.35 | 17 | 11 | 3.12 | 0.25 | 15.23 |
| **12/04** | 37.41 | 20 | 10 | 1.96 | — | 15.28 |
| **12/03** | 20.73 | 19 | 12 | 1.12 | — | 13.57 |
| **12/02** | 15.38 | 29 | 17 | 0.85 | — | 11.88 |
| **Annual Growth** | 56.5% | — | — | 57.6% | 140.0% | 14.6% |

# Joy Global

Joy Global is pretty peppy for a company that builds equipment that is destined to spend the majority of its life down in a hole. The company makes heavy equipment for the mining industry through two subsidiaries. Its Joy Mining Machinery subsidiary makes underground coal-mining equipment that includes armored face conveyors, roof supports, longwall shearers, and shuttle cars. Subsidiary P&H Mining Equipment makes draglines, blasthole drills, and other equipment used by surface miners; it also provides parts and services to mines through its P&H MinePro Services distribution group. Joy Global operates manufacturing and service facilities worldwide.

Joy Global suffered as its Asian customers retrenched following the implosion of that region's economy. The company incurred heavy debt while diversifying into the replacement parts business, slipped into bankruptcy, and sold its Beloit unit (replacement parts for papermaking machinery). In 2001 the company emerged from bankruptcy sporting the Joy Global moniker. Although Joy Global operates globally, the US accounts for about half of its total sales.

With its fortunes on the mend, in 2006 the company purchased the Stamler line of mining machinery from Oldenburg Group. The Stamler product line includes feeder-breakers, battery haulers, continuous haulage systems, and underground crushers and sizers. The deal adds breadth to Joy Global's existing line of mining machinery offerings.

Boston-based FMR Corp. owns about 10% of the company.

## HISTORY

In the mid-1880s German immigrant Henry Harnischfeger and partner Alonzo Pawling started Pawling and Harnischfeger (P&H), a small machine and pattern shop, in Milwaukee. The company shipped its first overhead electric crane in 1888. After a fire destroyed its main shop in 1903, P&H built a new plant in West Milwaukee the next year that became the world's leading manufacturer of overhead cranes. After Pawling died in 1914, the company became Harnischfeger Corporation. In remembrance of Pawling, Harnischfeger kept its P&H trademark.

The highly cyclical heavy-equipment industry encountered a big upswing with WWI. After the war, Harnischfeger began selling excavating and mining equipment to help weather downturns in the industry. Harnischfeger died in 1930, and his son Walter became president. The Depression was hard for the company, as it lost money every year from 1931 to 1939. Harnischfeger diversified into welding equipment, diesel engines, and prefabricated houses during the 1930s and 1940s.

WWII and the postwar period boosted the company, and Harnischfeger was listed on the AMEX in 1956. Walter became chairman in 1959, and his son, Henry, became president. Harnischfeger streamlined operations in the 1960s, keeping its construction and mining division and its industrial and electrical division.

Harnischfeger was listed on the NYSE in 1971. After the 1973 oil embargo, its machinery sales increased with the opening of coal reserves and the construction of oil pipelines and mass transit systems. By the end of the 1970s, however, recession and high-interest rates took their toll on the company.

On the verge of bankruptcy in the early 1980s, Harnischfeger revived itself by trimming down, diversifying, and making key acquisitions. It formed Harnischfeger Engineering in 1984 (sold in the early 1990s), and in 1986 the company bought Beloit (papermaking equipment) and formed Harnischfeger Industries as a holding company.

Harnischfeger began moving away from systems handling in the early 1990s. It bought underground mining equipment maker Joy Technologies (now Joy Mining Machinery) in 1994 and Longwall International (through the acquisition of Dobson Park Industries) in 1995. The next year Harnischfeger bought Ingersoll-Rand's pulp machinery division. In 1997 the company's $631 million bid for Giddings & Lewis (machine tools) was thwarted when Giddings & Lewis agreed to be acquired by Thyssen (now ThyssenKrupp AG).

After the Asian economic crisis and other factors weakened demand for its papermaking and mining equipment, Harnischfeger announced in 1998 it would be laying off about 20% of its workforce — about 3,100 jobs. Harnischfeger also sold an 80% stake in P&H Material Handling to Chartwell Investments for $340 million that year.

In 1999 Harnischfeger rearranged the terms of $500 million in loans and obtained an additional $250 million term loan. CEO Jeffery Grade, also chairman since 1993, stepped down. Grade had spearheaded the company's aggressive growth strategy, which had been stymied by slips in demand for the company's machinery due to weak prices for metal and paper. President John Nils Hanson succeeded Grade as CEO. Unable to keep up with its debt, the company filed for Chapter 11 bankruptcy protection.

Creditors accepted a $160 million offer from Metso Corporation in 2000 to buy Beloit's assets, including its roll cover division, paper machine aftermarket assets, and related paper machine technology. Harnischfeger emerged from bankruptcy and changed its name to Joy Global Inc. in 2001.

Orders for new equipment were soft in 2002, although limited sales were offset by paced revenue growth through the company's operations in China. In 2003 Joy Global completed the purchase of the remaining 25% interest in P&H-Australia (surface mining equipment) that it didn't already own.

P&H sold its subsidiary The Horsburgh & Scott Co., a manufacturer of industrial gears and mechanical gear drives, in November 2005. The following year Joy Global agreed to purchase the Stamler business of Oldenburg Group, Inc. for $118 million. Stamler's products, used in underground and surface coal mining, include feeder breakers, battery haulers, and continuous haulage systems.

## EXECUTIVES

**Chairman:** John N. Hanson, age 65, $2,282,400 pay
**President and CEO:** Michael W. Sutherlin, age 60, $1,072,077 pay
**CFO and Treasurer:** James H. Woodward Jr., age 54
**EVP, Human Resources:** Dennis R. Winkleman, $543,167 pay
**EVP; President and COO, P&H Mining Equipment:** Mark E. Readinger, $761,000 pay
**VP, Controller, and Chief Accounting Officer:** Michael S. (Mike) Olsen
**Investor Relations:** Sandra L. McKenzie
**Secretary:** Oren B. Azar
**General Counsel:** Sean D. Major, age 42
**Auditors:** Ernst & Young LLP

## LOCATIONS

**HQ:** Joy Global Inc.
100 E. Wisconsin Ave., Ste. 2780,
Milwaukee, WI 53202
**Phone:** 414-319-8500 **Fax:** 414-319-8520
**Web:** www.joyglobal.com

Joy Global's Joy Mining Machinery subsidiary has manufacturing and service facilities in Australia, Poland, South Africa, the UK, and the US, as well as sales offices and service facilities in China, India, and Russia. Subsidiary P&H Mining Equipment has facilities in Australia, Brazil, Canada, Chile, China, South Africa, and the US, as well as sales offices in India, Mexico, Peru, Russia, the UK, and Venezuela.

### 2006 Sales

| | $ mil. | % of total |
|---|---|---|
| US | 1,498.3 | 51 |
| Europe | 524.3 | 18 |
| Australia | 419.8 | 14 |
| Other regions | 488.2 | 17 |
| Adjustments | (528.9) | — |
| **Total** | **2,401.7** | **100** |

## PRODUCTS/OPERATIONS

### 2006 Sales

| | $ mil. | % of total |
|---|---|---|
| Underground mining equipment | 1,424.8 | 59 |
| Surface mining equipment | 976.9 | 41 |
| **Total** | **2,401.7** | **100** |

### Selected Products

Underground mining machinery
- Armored face conveyors
- Continuous chain haulage systems
- Continuous miners
- Flexible conveyor trains
- Longwall shearers
- Roof bolters
- Roof supports
- Shuttle cars

Surface mining equipment
- Electric mining shovels
- Rotary blasthole drills
- Walking draglines

## COMPETITORS

Bucyrus
Caterpillar
Hitachi
Ingersoll-Rand
Komatsu
Marmon Group
Metso
Rowan
Tampella Corporation
Terex

## HISTORICAL FINANCIALS

Company Type: Public

### Income Statement

FYE: Saturday nearest October 31

| | REVENUE ($ mil.) | NET INCOME ($ mil.) | NET PROFIT MARGIN | EMPLOYEES |
|---|---|---|---|---|
| **10/06** | 2,402 | 416 | 17.3% | 8,900 |
| **10/05** | 1,928 | 148 | 7.7% | 7,900 |
| **10/04** | 1,432 | 55 | 3.9% | 7,700 |
| **10/03** | 1,216 | 19 | 1.5% | 7,200 |
| **10/02** | 1,151 | (28) | — | 6,800 |
| **Annual Growth** | 20.2% | — | — | 7.0% |

### 2006 Year-End Financials

Debt ratio: 10.7%
Return on equity: 52.5%
Cash ($ mil.): 101
Current ratio: 2.05
Long-term debt ($ mil.): 98
No. of shares (mil.): 118
Dividends
Yield: 1.3%
Payout: 15.7%
Market value ($ mil.): 4,805

### Stock History

NASDAQ (GS): JOYG

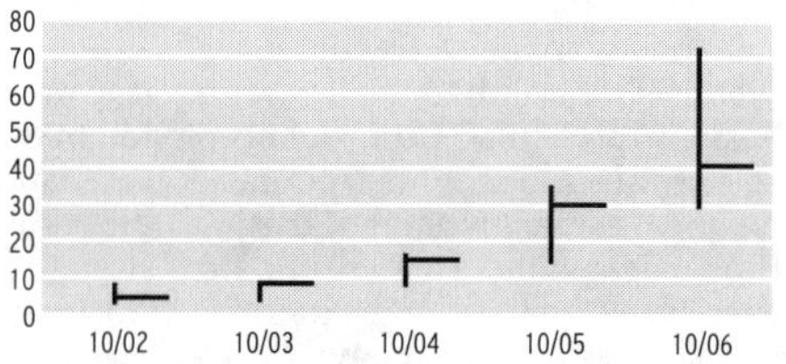

| | STOCK PRICE ($) FY Close | P/E High | P/E Low | PER SHARE ($) Earnings | PER SHARE ($) Dividends | PER SHARE ($) Book Value |
|---|---|---|---|---|---|---|
| **10/06** | 40.88 | 21 | 9 | 3.38 | 0.53 | 7.82 |
| **10/05** | 30.15 | 29 | 12 | 1.20 | 0.15 | 5.48 |
| **10/04** | 15.02 | 35 | 18 | 0.46 | 0.12 | 8.49 |
| **10/03** | 8.56 | 52 | 25 | 0.16 | — | 7.53 |
| **10/02** | 4.71 | — | — | (0.25) | — | 7.56 |
| **Annual Growth** | 71.6% | — | — | — | 110.2% | 0.8% |

# JPMorgan Chase

JPMorgan Chase was born with a silver spoon in its mouth but hasn't let that stop it. The #3 financial services firm in the US (behind Citigroup and Bank of America) expanded nationwide with the acquisition of BANK ONE and now has some 3,000 branches and growing. The bank is keen on its retail operations and is also among the nation's top mortgage lenders, automobile loan writers, and credit card issuers. Formed in 2001 by the blockbuster merger of retail banking behemoth Chase Manhattan and venerable investment bank J.P. Morgan, JPMorgan Chase boasts formidable investment banking and asset management operations as well. Wunderkind BANK ONE chief Jamie Dimon took the reins of JPMorgan Chase at the end of 2005.

The company's subsidiaries include the prestigious JPMorgan Private Bank and institutional investment manager JPMorgan Asset Management (with $1.1 trillion in assets under management). JPMorgan Chase also owns 43% of mutual fund company American Century and has a stake in Chase Paymentech Solutions, a transaction processing joint venture with First Data.

In keeping with its focus on retail operations, in 2006 JPMorgan Chase swapped its corporate trust business for Bank of New York's 338-branch network in the New York metropolitan area. Banks like branches because they can upsell customers face to face. Both units were valued at about $2 billion, with JPMorgan Chase paying Bank of New York up to $150 million more to make up the difference.

That year the company cut ties with private equity investment arm JPMorgan Partners, which divided into two companies, CCMP Capital and Panorama Capital. JPMorgan Chase retained the former private equity operations of BANK ONE, One Equity Partners.

In keeping with the lesson learned regarding its $2 billion fine to settle claims in the WorldCom debacle, in 2006 the bank was quick to settle its part of another class-action lawsuit, this time brought by investors claiming they were cheated in the dot-com IPO boom. JPMorgan Chase paid $425 million to settle that case. It paid a much smaller settlement of $3.8 million for its part in the demise of the ill-fated telecom Global Crossing.

The company got good news regarding its alleged involvement with the Enron collapse when the class action suit against it was dismissed.

## HISTORY

JPMorgan Chase & Co.'s roots are in The Manhattan Company, created in 1799 to bring water to New York City. A provision buried in its incorporation documents let the company provide banking services; investor and future US Vice President Aaron Burr brought the company (eventually the Bank of Manhattan) into competition with The Bank of New York, founded by Burr's political rival Alexander Hamilton. JPMorgan Chase still owns the pistols from the notorious 1804 duel in which Burr mortally wounded Hamilton.

In 1877 John Thompson formed Chase National, naming it for Salmon Chase, Abraham Lincoln's secretary of the treasury and the architect of the national bank system. Chase National merged with John D. Rockefeller's Equitable Trust in 1930, becoming the world's largest bank and beginning a long relationship with the Rockefellers. Chase National continued growing after WWII, and in 1955 it merged with the Bank of Manhattan. Christened Chase Manhattan, the bank remained the US's largest into the 1960s.

When soaring 1970s oil prices made energy loans attractive, Chase invested in Penn Square, an obscure oil-patch bank in Oklahoma and the first notable bank failure of the 1980s. (The legal aftereffects of Penn Square's 1982 failure dragged on until 1993.) Losses following the 1987 foreign loan crisis hit the company hard, as did the real estate crash. In 1995 the bank went looking for a partner. After talks with Bank of America, it settled on Chemical Bank.

Chemical Bank opened in 1824 and was one of the US's largest banks by 1900. As with Chase, Chemical Bank began as an unrelated business (New York Chemical Manufacturing) in 1823, largely in order to open a bank (it dropped its chemical operations in 1844). Chemical would merge with Manufacturers Hanover in 1991.

After its 1996 merger with Chase, Chemical Bank was the surviving entity but assumed Chase's more prestigious name. In 1997 Chase acquired the credit business of The Bank of New York and the corporate trustee business of Mellon Financial, but underwent another round of belt-tightening the next year when it took a $320 million charge and cut 4,500 jobs. The bank also suffered losses related to its involvement with the ill-starred Long-Term Capital Management hedge fund.

In 1999 Chase focused on lending, buying two mortgage originators and forming a marketing alliance with subprime auto lender AmeriCredit. Chase also bought Mellon Financial's residential mortgage unit and Huntington Bancshares' credit card portfolio.

In 2001 it closed its $30 billion buy of J.P. Morgan and renamed itself JPMorgan Chase & Co. Chairman Sandy Warner (who ran J.P. Morgan) retired at year-end and was replaced by former Chase Manhattan leader CEO William Harrison.

JPMorgan Chase had more than $1 billion in exposure to Enron, but in 2003 recovered some $600 million after a court battle with the failed energy trader's insurers, which claimed the losses stemmed from loans by JPMorgan Chase disguised as oil and gas transactions. Nonetheless, JPMorgan Chase ended up paying some $135 million to settle actions relating to the questionable loans.

In 2005 JPMorgan Chase and its investment banking arm, JPMorgan Securities, avoided a trial by paying some $2 billion to settle claims from investors who lost money on bonds that the firm underwrote in 2000 and 2001 for scandal-ridden WorldCom (now MCI), which eventually declared bankruptcy.

The following year the company acquired student lender Collegiate Funding Services, which JPMorgan Chase combined with its existing Chase Education Finance division. The company also got the go-ahead from the FTC and bought Kohl's $1.6 billion credit card portfolio.

Enron continued to haunt the company: later that year it forked over $2.2 billion to settle part of an investor class-action suit over fraud charges related to the Enron debacle and paid another $350 million to the infamous energy trading firm, which asserted that JPMorgan Chase and about 10 other banks aided and abetted the company's collapse.

William Harrison retired as chairman at the end of 2006; he was succeeded by president and CEO (and the CEO of BANK ONE when it was acquired) Jamie Dimon.

## EXECUTIVES

**Chairman, President, and CEO:** James (Jamie) Dimon, age 50, $9,400,000 pay (prior to promotion)
**CFO:** Michael J. Cavanaugh, age 38
**Chief Administrative Officer:** Frank J. Bisignano, age 46
**Chief Investment Officer:** Ina R. Drew, age 49
**EVP, Global Government Relations and Public Policy:** Enrico A. (Rick) Lazio, age 47
**EVP and CEO, Treasury and Securities Services:** Heidi G. Miller, age 54
**EVP, Worldwide Securities Services:** Michael K. (Mike) Clark
**EVP and General Counsel:** Stephen M. (Steve) Cutler, age 45
**CEO, Consumer Banking:** Scott Powell
**Head of Office of Corporate Social Responsibility and Chairman, Midwest Region:** William M. (Bill) Daley, age 58
**Chairman, JPMorgan Asset Management:** Paul Bateman
**Chairman, Europe, Middle East, and Africa:** Walter A. Gubert
**Co-CEO, Investment Bank:** Steven D. Black, age 54, $9,865,000 pay
**Co-CEO, Investment Bank:** William T. (Bill) Winters, age 45, $10,005,291 pay
**CEO, J.P. Morgan Private Bank:** Mary E. Erdoes, age 39
**CEO, Retail Financial Services:** Charles W. (Charlie) Scharf, age 40, $6,350,000 pay
**CEO, JPMorgan Asset Management:** James E. (Jes) Staley, age 49
**Global Head Credit, Investment Bank:** Donald H. (Don) McCree III, age 41
**Managing Director and Head, Investment Bank:** Carlos M. Hernandez, age 45
**Head, Strategy and Business Development:** Jay Mandelbaum, age 43
**Managing Director, One Equity Partners:** Richard M. (Dick) Cashin Jr., age 53
**Secretary:** Anthony J. Horan
**Treasurer:** Mark I. Kleinman
**Senior Advisor and Director:** Robert I. (Bob) Lipp
**Director Human Resources:** John F. Bradley, age 45
**Head, Corporate Communications:** Joseph Evangelisti
**Auditors:** PricewaterhouseCoopers LLP

## LOCATIONS

**HQ:** JPMorgan Chase & Co.
270 Park Ave., New York, NY 10017
**Phone:** 212-270-6000 **Fax:** 212-270-1648
**Web:** www.jpmorganchase.com

**2006 Sales**

| | % of total |
|---|---|
| Americas | 51 |
| Europe, Middle East & Africa | 40 |
| Asia/Pacific | 9 |
| **Total** | **100** |

## PRODUCTS/OPERATIONS

**2006 Sales**

| | $ mil. | % of total |
|---|---|---|
| Interest income | | |
| Loans | 33,121 | 33 |
| Trading assets | 10,942 | 11 |
| Federal funds sold & securities purchased | 5,578 | 6 |
| Securities | 4,147 | 4 |
| Securities borrowed | 3,402 | 3 |
| Deposits with banks | 1,265 | 1 |
| Interest in purchased receivables | 652 | 1 |
| Noninterest income | | |
| Asset management, administration & commissions | 11,725 | 12 |
| Principle transactions | 10,346 | 10 |
| Credit cards | 6,913 | 7 |
| Investment banking fees | 5,520 | 6 |
| Lending & deposit-related fees | 3,468 | 3 |
| Mortgage fees & related income | 591 | 1 |
| Other | 2,175 | 2 |
| **Total** | **99,845** | **100** |

**2006 Assets**

| | $ mil. | % of total |
|---|---|---|
| Cash & equivalents | 40,412 | 3 |
| Securities borrowed | 73,688 | 6 |
| Trading assets | 365,738 | 27 |
| Federal funds sold & securities purchased under resale agreements | 140,524 | 10 |
| Securities | 91,975 | 7 |
| Net loans | 475,848 | 35 |
| Other | 163,335 | 12 |
| **Total** | **1,351,520** | **100** |

## COMPETITORS

ABN AMRO
American Express
Bank of America
Bear Stearns
Capital One
CIBC
Citigroup
Citigroup Global Markets
Credit Suisse (USA)
Deutsche Bank
Goldman Sachs
HSBC Finance
HSBC Holdings
HSBC USA
ING DIRECT
Lehman Brothers
Merrill Lynch
MF Global
Morgan Stanley
RBC Financial Group
UBS

## HISTORICAL FINANCIALS

Company Type: Public

**Income Statement** FYE: December 31

| | ASSETS ($ mil.) | NET INCOME ($ mil.) | INCOME AS % OF ASSETS | EMPLOYEES |
|---|---|---|---|---|
| **12/06** | 1,351,520 | 14,444 | 1.1% | 174,360 |
| **12/05** | 1,198,942 | 8,483 | 0.7% | 168,847 |
| **12/04** | 1,157,248 | 4,466 | 0.4% | 160,968 |
| **12/03** | 770,912 | 6,719 | 0.9% | 110,453 |
| **12/02** | 758,800 | 1,663 | 0.2% | 94,335 |
| **Annual Growth** | 15.5% | 71.7% | — | 16.6% |

**2006 Year-End Financials**

Equity as % of assets: 8.6%
Return on assets: 1.1%
Return on equity: 13.0%
Long-term debt ($ mil.): 182,532
No. of shares (mil.): 3,462
Dividends
Yield: 2.8%
Payout: 33.7%
Market value ($ mil.): 167,199
Sales ($ mil.): 99,845

**Stock History** NYSE: JPM

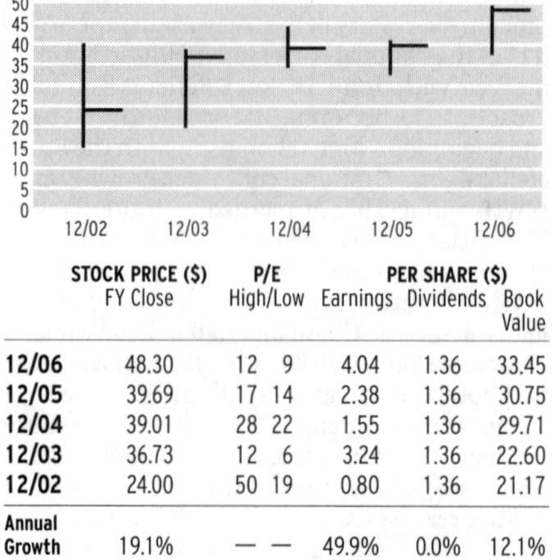


| | STOCK PRICE ($) FY Close | P/E High/Low | | PER SHARE ($) Earnings | Dividends | Book Value |
|---|---|---|---|---|---|---|
| **12/06** | 48.30 | 12 | 9 | 4.04 | 1.36 | 33.45 |
| **12/05** | 39.69 | 17 | 14 | 2.38 | 1.36 | 30.75 |
| **12/04** | 39.01 | 28 | 22 | 1.55 | 1.36 | 29.71 |
| **12/03** | 36.73 | 12 | 6 | 3.24 | 1.36 | 22.60 |
| **12/02** | 24.00 | 50 | 19 | 0.80 | 1.36 | 21.17 |
| **Annual Growth** | 19.1% | — | — | 49.9% | 0.0% | 12.1% |

# Kaiser Foundation Health Plan

Kaiser Foundation Health Plan aims to be the emperor of the HMO universe. With more than 8.5 million members in nine states and the District of Columbia, it is one of the largest not-for-profit managed health care companies in the US. Kaiser has an integrated care model, offering both hospital and physician care through a network of hospitals and physician practices operating under the Kaiser Permanente name. Members of Kaiser health plans have access to hospitals and some 400 other health care facilities operated by Kaiser Foundation Hospitals and Permanente Medical Groups, associations consisting of about 12,000 doctors.

California is the company's largest market, accounting for more than 75% of its members.

A string of losses due to skyrocketing costs and stiff competition from commercial providers of managed care have prompted Kaiser to raise rates and divest underperforming units.

Kaiser's strategy for growth and profitability consists of strengthening its integrated care model via increased use of technology, and construction of new health care facilities.

## HISTORY

Henry Kaiser — shipbuilder, war profiteer, builder of the Hoover and Grand Coulee dams, and founder of Kaiser Aluminum — was a bootstrap capitalist who did well by doing good. A high school dropout from upstate New York, Kaiser moved to Spokane, Washington, in 1906 and went into road construction. During the Depression, he headed the consortium that built the great WPA dams.

It was in building the Grand Coulee Dam that, in 1938, Kaiser teamed with Dr. Sidney Garfield, who earlier had devised a prepayment health plan for workers on California public works projects. As Kaiser moved into steelmaking and shipbuilding during WWII (turning out some 1,400 bare-bones Liberty ships — one per day at peak production), Kaiser decided healthy workers produce more than sick ones, and he called on Garfield to set up on-site clinics funded by the US government as part of operating expenses. Garfield was released from military service by President Roosevelt for the purpose.

After the war, the clinics became war surplus. Kaiser and his wife bought them — at a 99% discount — through the new Kaiser Hospital Foundation. His vision was to provide the public with low-cost, prepaid medical care. He created the health plan — the self-supporting entity that would administer the system — and the group medical organization, Permanente (named after Kaiser's first cement plant site). He then endowed the health plan with $200,000. This health plan, the classic HMO model, was criticized by the medical establishment as socialized medicine performed by "employee" doctors.

But the plan flourished, becoming California's #1 medical system. In 1958 Kaiser retired to Hawaii and started his health plan there. However, physician resistance limited national growth; HMOs were even illegal in some states well into the 1970s.

As health care costs rose, Congress legalized HMOs in all states. Kaiser expanded in the 1980s; as it moved outside its traditional geographic areas, the company contracted for space in hospitals rather than build them. Growth slowed as competition increased.

Some health care costs in California fell in the early 1990s as more medical procedures were performed on an outpatient basis. Specialists flooded the state, and as price competition among doctors and hospitals heated up, many HMOs landed advantageous contracts. Kaiser, with its own highly paid doctors, was unable to realize the same savings and was no longer the best deal in town. Its membership stalled.

To boost membership and control expenses, Kaiser instituted a controversial program in 1996 in which nurses earned bonuses for cost-cutting. Critics said the program could lead to a decrease in care quality; Kaiser later became the focus of investigations into wrongful death suits linked to cost-cutting in California (where it has since beefed up staffing and programs) and Texas (where it has agreed to pay $1 million in fines).

In 1997 Kaiser and Washington-based Group Health Cooperative of Puget Sound formed Kaiser/Group Health to handle administrative services in the Northwest. Kaiser also tried to boost membership by lowering premiums, but the strategy proved *too* effective: Costs linked to an unwieldy 20% enrollment surge brought a loss in 1997 — Kaiser's first annual loss ever.

A second year in the red in 1998 prompted Kaiser to sell its Texas operations to Sierra Health Services. It also entered the Florida market via an alliance with Miami-based AvMed Health Plan. In 1999 Kaiser announced plans to sell its unprofitable North Carolina operations (it closed the deal the following year).

In 2000 Kaiser announced plans to charge premiums for its Medicare HMO, Medicare Advantage, to offset the shortfall in federal reimbursements. Kaiser also responded to rising costs by selling its unprofitable operations in North Carolina (2000) and Kansas (2001). In 2001 the company's hospital division bought the technology and assets of defunct Internet grocer Webvan in an effort to increase its distribution activity. Also that year the son of a deceased anthrax victim sued a Kaiser facility for failing to recognize and treat his father's symptoms.

## EXECUTIVES

**Chairman and CEO:** George C. Halvorson
**SVP, Research and Policy Development:** Robert M. Crane
**SVP, Strategic Planning and CFO:** Kathy Lancaster
**SVP, Human Resources:** Laurence G. O'Neil
**SVP, Product and Market Management:** Arthur M. Southam
**SVP, Health Plan and Hospital Operations:** Bernard J. Tyson, age 47
**SVP, Brand Strategy, Communications and Public Relations:** Diane Gage Lofgren
**SVP and CIO:** Philip (Phil) Fasano, age 48
**VP and Treasurer:** Tom Meier
**VP, Clinical Information System (CIS) Project:** Bruce Turkstra
**President, Southern California Region:** Benjamin K. Chu, age 54
**President, Kaiser Foundation Health Plan of The Mid-Atlantic States:** Marilyn J. Kawamura
**President, Kaiser Foundation Health Plan of Ohio:** Patricia D. Kennedy-Scott
**President, Kaiser Foundation Health Plan of GA:** Carolyn Kenny
**Executive Director, The Permanente Federation:** Francis J. Crosson
**President, Kaiser Foundation Health Plan of Colorado:** Donna Lynne
**Auditors:** KPMG LLP

## LOCATIONS

**HQ:** Kaiser Foundation Health Plan, Inc.
1 Kaiser Plaza, Oakland, CA 94612
**Phone:** 510-271-5800 **Fax:** 510-271-6493
**Web:** www.kaiserpermanente.org

Kaiser Foundation Health Plan operates in California, Colorado, Georgia, Hawaii, Maryland, Ohio, Oregon, Virginia, Washington, and the District of Columbia.

## COMPETITORS

Aetna
Blue Cross
Blue Cross of California
Blue Shield Of California
CIGNA
Health Net
Humana
Molina Healthcare
Oxford Health
PacifiCare
Premera Blue Cross
Regence BlueShield
Regence Group
Sharp Health Plan
Sierra Health
UnitedHealth Group
UnitedHealthcare of Colorado
WellPoint

## HISTORICAL FINANCIALS

Company Type: Subsidiary

**Income Statement** FYE: December 31

| | REVENUE ($ mil.) | NET INCOME ($ mil.) | NET PROFIT MARGIN | EMPLOYEES |
|---|---|---|---|---|
| **12/06** | 34,400 | — | — | 156,000 |
| **12/05** | 31,100 | — | — | — |
| **12/04** | 28,000 | — | — | — |
| **12/03** | 25,300 | — | — | 54,300 |
| **12/02** | 22,500 | — | — | 47,300 |
| **Annual Growth** | 11.2% | — | — | 34.8% |

**Revenue History**

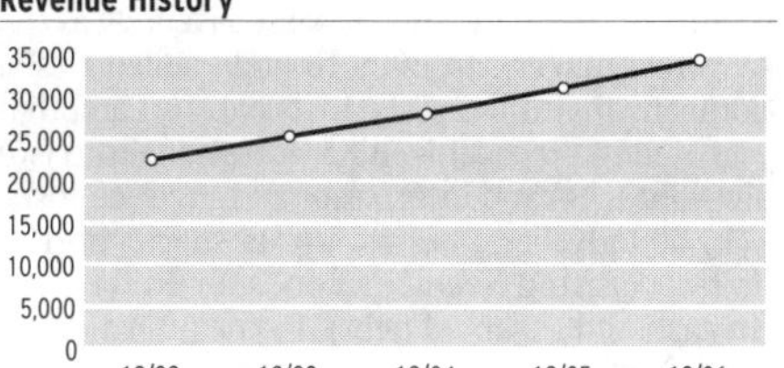


# KB Home

KB Home continues to hammer out the details in the homebuilding industry. The acquisitive company (formerly Kaufman and Broad Home) has grown to become one of the largest homebuilders in the US. KB Home builds mainly for first-time and trade-up buyers in Arizona, California, the Carolinas, Colorado, Florida, Georgia, Illinois, Nevada, New Mexico, and Texas. Its homes range in size from about 1,400 sq. ft. to over 5,000 sq. ft. The company offers financing, mortgage assistance, and home insurance through Countrywide Mortgage Ventures, a joint venture with Countrywide Financial.

Although the housing market outside of the US remains strong, KB Home in 2007 sold its 49% stake in Kaufman & Broad to PAI Partners for about $800 million. Kaufman & Broad builds single-family homes, condos, and commercial projects in France.

KB Home is known for its many innovations in design and financing. Moving away from speculative building of look-alike homes, the company assembles KB Home Studios that display standard features and options — and the prices of each of those items — allowing prospective homebuyers to customize their homes. It was the first in the industry to offer a "lease-to-own" option for new homebuyers and the first to create a mortgage company for its customers.

KB Home ended 2006 with a backlog of 17,384 units, down more than 30% over 2005's 25,722 units. Inside the US, KB Home has been particularly active in the Southeast. Outside the US, the company has been expanding its operations in France, where KB Home is now a leading homebuilder; operations there now account for about 15% of the company's sales.

The company announced in 2005 that it was selling essentially all of its KB Home Mortgage subsidiary to Countrywide Home Loans. Simultaneously, KB Home and Countrywide Home Loans announced that they were forming a 50-50 joint venture to provide residential lending services to KB Home customers. In 2006 KB Home and Martha Stewart Living Omnimedia opened its first two Martha Stewart-designed communities. KB has also formed KB Urban, California housing developments found in mixed-use dwellings.

Former chairman and CEO Bruce Karatz retired in late 2006 amidst rumors of irregularities in the handling of stock options.

## HISTORY

Kaufman and Broad Building Co. was founded in Detroit in 1957 by Eli Broad and Donald Kaufman. Broad, an accountant, parlayed an initial $25,000 investment into sales of $250,000 on the first weekend of business. By the end of its first year, Kaufman and Broad was posting revenues of $1.7 million.

The company expanded rapidly and went public in 1961. A year later it was the first homebuilder to be listed on the NYSE. Kaufman and Broad moved into California in 1963. Through acquisitions, it rapidly became a top US homebuilder, expanding into New York, San Francisco, and Chicago. In 1965 it formed a mortgage subsidiary to arrange loans for its customers.

In the early 1970s the firm entered Europe and Canada. Sales passed the $100 million mark in 1971 and the company diversified, buying Sun Life Insurance. Housing operations were renamed Kaufman and Broad Development Group (KBDG).

In 1980 the flamboyant Bruce Karatz, who had joined the firm in 1972, was appointed president. Karatz steered the company through the recession of the early 1980s, focusing on California, France, and Canada. KBDG acquired Bati-Service, a major French developer of affordable homes, in 1985.

The company was renamed Kaufman and Broad Home Corporation in 1986. In 1989 it reorganized into two separate billion-dollar companies: Broad Inc. (now SunAmerica), an insurance firm with Eli Broad as its chairman and CEO, and Kaufman and Broad Home, with Karatz as CEO (and later chairman), which was spun off to shareholders in 1989.

When the California real estate market crashed in 1990, earnings plummeted. Karatz diversified by buying up strong regional builders. Kaufman and Broad entered Arizona, Colorado, and Nevada in 1993 and Utah in 1994. Profits dropped in 1995-96 because of weakness in the California and Paris markets and the company's winding down of Canadian operations. But expansion continued, including the acquisition of Rayco, a Texas builder, in 1996.

Borrowing from the methods of Rayco, Kaufman and Broad began surveying homebuyers for suggestions to incorporate into new designs. In 1998 the company began to build its New Home Showrooms. The corporation continued its expansion drive that year when it paid about $165 million for Dover/Ideal, PrideMark, and Estes, privately held builders based in Houston, Denver, and Tucson, respectively. In 1999 Kaufman and Broad bought Lewis Homes, a major California builder and the #1 builder in Las Vegas, for about $545 million.

The company raised $117 million in 2000 by taking half of its French subsidiary public, but retained a controlling interest. In 2001 the company changed its name again, shortening it to KB Home. Later that year it expanded into the northern Florida market by buying Jacksonville-based Trademark Home Builders.

KB Home expanded in other markets, which included Tucson (by acquiring assets of New World Homes, gaining more than 1,600 lots in 12 new home communities there) and the Rio Grande Valley of Texas (by opening a division in the fast-growing McAllen region, about four miles from the Mexican border).

KB Home continued to build its empire in 2003 by acquiring Atlanta-based Colony Homes, one of the Southeast's largest privately owned homebuilders, with principal operations in Atlanta, Raleigh, and Charlotte, which are among the largest markets in the Southeast for new-home permits. The company also moved into the Midwest with the $33 million purchase of privately held homebuilder Zale Homes (Chicago).

In 2004 KB Home expanded its operations in the Southeast by acquiring South Carolina-based Palmetto Traditional Homes. It also acquired Indianapolis builder Dura Builders and two French-owned builders, Groupe Avantis and Foncier Investissement.

When charges of fraud surrounding company stock options were leveled against Karatz in 2006, the chairman and president retired from KB Home; former COO Jeff Mezger was then named president and CEO.

## EXECUTIVES

**Chairman:** Stephen F. Bollenbach, age 64
**President, CEO, and Director:** Jeffrey T. (Jeff) Mezger, age 51, $3,068,750 pay
**EVP and CFO:** Domenico (Dom) Cecere, age 57, $1,298,333 pay (prior to promotion)
**SVP and Chief Accounting Officer:** William R. (Bill) Hollinger, age 48, $1,062,633 pay
**SVP and Treasurer:** Kelly Masuda, age 39, $912,604 pay
**SVP, Asset Management Group:** Albert Z. Praw
**SVP, Corporate Communications:** Caroline Shaw
**SVP, Sales and Marketing:** Wendy Marlett
**SVP, Studios:** Lisa M. Kalmbach
**SVP, Tax:** Cory F. Cohen
**SVP, Human Resources:** John Staines, age 45
**VP and CIO:** Brian Bruce
**Regional General Manager, Georgia and North Carolina (Atlanta, Charlotte and Raleigh Divisions):** Steven M. (Steve) Davis, age 48
**Regional General Manager, Southern California (Los Angeles/Ventura, Riverside, San Bernardino, Orange County and San Diego):** Jay L. Moss, $1,519,167 pay
**Regional General Manager, Tampa, Jacksonville, Orlando, Treasure Coast, and Fort Myers (FL):** John E. (Buddy) Goodwin, age 55
**Regional General Manager, Texas (Austin, Dallas, Fort Worth, Houston, Rio Grande Valley, and San Antonio):** Larry Oglesby
**Regional General Manager, Phoenix, Las Vegas, and Tucson:** Jim Widner, $1,496,667 pay
**Regional General Manager, Las Vegas, Phoenix, and Tucson Divisions:** Leah S. W. Bryant, age 59
**Chairman and CEO, Kaufman and Broad S.A.:** Guy Nafilyan, age 59
**Managing Director (President and COO), Kaufman & Broad S.A.:** Joël Monribot
**President, KB Home Mortgage Company:** Richard D. (Rick) Powers
**Auditors:** Ernst & Young LLP

## LOCATIONS

**HQ:** KB Home
10990 Wilshire Blvd., 7th Fl.,
Los Angeles, CA 90024
**Phone:** 310-231-4000 **Fax:** 310-231-4222
**Web:** www.kbhome.com

## PRODUCTS/OPERATIONS

**2006 Sales**

| | $ mil. | % of total |
|---|---|---|
| Construction | | |
| US | | |
| West Coast | 3,531.3 | 32 |
| Southwest | 2,183.9 | 20 |
| Southeast | 2,091.4 | 19 |
| Central | 1,553.3 | 14 |
| France | 1,623.7 | 15 |
| Financial services | 20.2 | — |
| **Total** | **11,003.8** | **100** |

## COMPETITORS

Beazer Homes
Capital Pacific
Centex
Centex Homes
Champion Enterprises
Clayton Homes
David Weekley Homes
D.R. Horton
Drees
Highland Homes
Hovnanian Enterprises
Kimball Hill inc
Lennar
Levitt Corporation
Maisons France Confort
M.D.C.
Mercedes Homes
Meritage Homes
NVR
Pulte Homes
Ryland
Shapell Industries
Standard Pacific
Toll Brothers
Weyerhaeuser Real Estate
William Lyon Homes

## HISTORICAL FINANCIALS

Company Type: Public

**Income Statement** FYE: November 30

| | REVENUE ($ mil.) | NET INCOME ($ mil.) | NET PROFIT MARGIN | EMPLOYEES |
|---|---|---|---|---|
| **11/06** | 11,004 | 482 | 4.4% | 5,100 |
| **11/05** | 9,442 | 842 | 8.9% | 6,700 |
| **11/04** | 7,053 | 481 | 6.8% | 6,000 |
| **11/03** | 5,851 | 371 | 6.3% | 5,100 |
| **11/02** | 5,031 | 314 | 6.2% | 4,500 |
| **Annual Growth** | 21.6% | 11.3% | — | 3.2% |

**2006 Year-End Financials**

Debt ratio: 106.9%
Return on equity: 16.7%
Cash ($ mil.): 655
Current ratio: 2.80
Long-term debt ($ mil.): 3,126
No. of shares (mil.): 89
Dividends
Yield: 1.9%
Payout: 17.2%
Market value ($ mil.): 4,620

**Stock History** NYSE: KBH

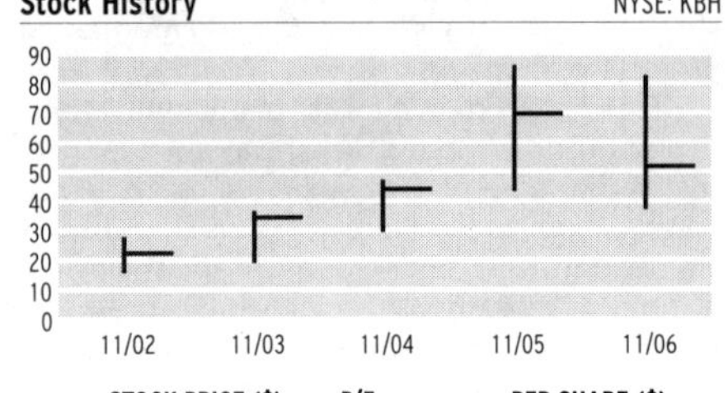


| | STOCK PRICE ($) FY Close | P/E High | P/E Low | PER SHARE ($) Earnings | Dividends | Book Value |
|---|---|---|---|---|---|---|
| **11/06** | 51.69 | 14 | 7 | 5.82 | 1.00 | 32.70 |
| **11/05** | 69.77 | 9 | 5 | 9.53 | 0.75 | 30.05 |
| **11/04** | 43.94 | 8 | 5 | 5.70 | 0.50 | 37.28 |
| **11/03** | 34.44 | 8 | 5 | 4.40 | 0.15 | 29.46 |
| **11/02** | 22.34 | 8 | 5 | 3.58 | 0.15 | 23.85 |
| **Annual Growth** | 23.3% | — | — | 12.9% | 60.7% | 8.2% |

# Kellogg Company

Kellogg does more business before 8 a.m. than most companies do all day. It is the #1 US breakfast cereal maker (a mere corn flake ahead of General Mills). Among its well-known brands are Frosted Flakes and Rice Krispies. As on-the-go consumers grow impatient with the traditional cereal-milk combo, Kellogg increasingly relies on snacks and convenience foods such as Eggo waffles, Nutri-Grain cereal bars, and Pop-Tarts to buff up its bottom line. Furthering its non-cereal offerings, the company bought cookie and cracker giant Keebler Foods (Fudge Shoppe, Cheez-It), which became its Kellogg Snacks Division. The W. K. Kellogg Foundation, one of the world's largest private charities, owns about 27% of the company.

Kellogg briefly snapped under the pressure of ongoing cereal wars (for a while General Mills led the market), and the company still crackles under fierce store-brand competition. Kellogg continued its pursuit of new markets by acquiring Worthington Foods, owner of the Morningstar Farms meat alternative brand.

The company began using oils derived from genetically modified soybeans in some of its products in 2006, in order to lower their fat content — a real toss-up move considering consumer concern about obesity and heart disease and the fear of scientists altering genes.

The company's largest customer, Wal-Mart and its subsidiaries, account for about 18% of Kellogg's sales. The Gund family, which sold its coffee business (later Sanka) to Kellogg in 1927, owns about 9% of the company.

## HISTORY

Will Keith (W. K.) Kellogg first made wheat flakes in 1894 while working for his brother, Dr. John Kellogg, at Battle Creek, Michigan's famed homeopathic sanitarium. While doing an experiment with grains (for patients' diets), the two men were interrupted; by the time they returned to the dough, it had absorbed water. They rolled it anyway, toasted the result, and accidentally created the first flaked cereal. John sold the flakes via mail order (1899) in a partnership that W. K. managed. In 1906 W. K. started his own firm to produce corn flakes.

As head of the Battle Creek Toasted Corn Flake Company, W. K. competed against 42 cereal companies in Battle Creek (one run by former patient C. W. Post) and roared to the head of the pack with his innovative marketing ideas. A 1906 *Ladies' Home Journal* ad helped increase demand from 33 cases a day earlier that year to 2,900 a day by year-end. W. K. soon introduced Bran Flakes (1915), All-Bran (1916), and Rice Krispies (1928). International expansion began in Canada (1914) and followed in Australia (1924) and England (1938). Diversifying a little, the company introduced the Pop-Tart in 1964 and acquired Eggo waffles in the 1970s. By the early 1980s Kellogg's US market share dipped, due to strong competition from General Mills and other rivals. The company pitched new cereals to adults and aggressively pursued the fast-growing European market.

Kellogg spent the mid-1990s reengineering itself, creating the USA Convenience Foods Division and selling such non-core assets as its carton container and Argentine snack-food makers (1993). It teamed with ConAgra in 1994 to create a cereal line sold under the latter's popular Healthy Choice label.

In 1997-98 the company expanded operations in Australia, the UK, Asia, and Latin America, and it slashed about 25% of its salaried North American workforce and hiked prices on about two-thirds of its cereals. Several top officers left in 1998-99, and Cuban-born president and COO Carlos Gutierrez became CEO.

The company sold the disappointing Lender's division to Aurora Foods in 1999 for just $275 million. (Aurora later merged with Pinnacle Foods to become Pinnacle Foods Group.) Kellogg took another crack at non-breakfast foods when it bought Worthington Foods (Morningstar Farms meat alternatives, Harvest Burgers) for $307 million.

By the beginning of 2000, cereal competitor General Mills had closed the gap with Kellogg in US market share (in 2001 it passed Kellogg as the #1 cereal maker). In 2000 Kellogg added Kasha Company (natural cereals) to its pantry. Later that year Kellogg reorganized its operations into two divisions (USA and International) to reduce costs.

In 2001 Kellogg bulked up its snacks portfolio by acquiring Keebler's Foods for $4.5 billion (in cash and assumed debt). In the aftermath of the acquisition, the company trimmed jobs at Keebler and its own headquarters.

To boost enthusiasm among kids for breakfast, in 2002 Kellogg launched new cereals featuring Disney characters Buzz Light-year, Mickey Mouse, and Winnie the Pooh — the first such alliance for The Walt Disney Company. That move, combined with better marketing and General Mills being distracted by its purchase of Pillsbury, helped Kellogg grab back the top spot in the US.

As part of Kellogg's digestion of Keebler's, it consolidated some manufacturing operations and reconfigured parts of Keebler's distribution system in 2002. To better focus on its branded products, the company sold off Keebler's private-label Bake-Line division to Atlantic Baking Group for $65 million in cash.

In 2004 Kellogg sold the Athens Re-packaging business of Keebler to Total Logistics. Later that year, Kellogg reached an agreement with then New York Attorney General Eliot Spitzer to stop using promotional toys identified as a possible environmental risk in its cereal products. In addition the company agreed to phase out the sale or distribution of promotional products containing mercury by the end of 2004, recycle mercury batteries returned by consumers, and educate consumers as to the need to dispose of mercury properly.

Continuing its integration of Keebler Foods, in 2004 the company did some juggling: The US snack division was relocated from Elmhurst, Illinois, to Kellogg's main headquarters in Battle Creek, Michigan. The Food Away From Home (FAFH) business unit and the Information Technology Center remained in Elmhurst.

In 2005 Gutierrez resigned from Kellogg to become secretary of the Department of Commerce in the George W. Bush administration. He was succeeded at the cereal behemoth by advertising executive and Kellogg board member James Jenness. In 2006 David Mackay was appointed Kellogg's CEO, replacing Jenness who remained as chairman.

## EXECUTIVES

**Chairman:** James M. (Jim) Jenness, age 61, $1,103,720 pay
**President, CEO, and Director:** A. D. David Mackay, age 52, $898,743 pay
**EVP and CFO; President, Kellogg North America:** John A. Bryant, age 41, $561,948 pay
**EVP; President, Kellogg International:** Jeffrey W. Montie, age 46, $594,361 pay
**SVP; President, Asia/Pacific; EVP, Kellogg International:** Jeffrey M. (Jeff) Boromisa, age 52, $467,599 pay
**SVP and CIO:** Ruth E. Bruch, age 54
**SVP Corporate Development, General Counsel, and Secretary:** Gary H. Pilnick, age 42
**SVP, Global Nutrition and Corporate Affairs:** Celeste A. Clark, age 53
**SVP; EVP Kellogg International and President, Kellogg Latin America:** Juan Pablo Villalobos
**SVP; President, U.S. Morning Foods and Frozen Foods:** Paul Norman
**SVP; President, US Snacks; President, Kellogg Canada:** Bradford J. (Brad) Davidson, age 46
**SVP, Global Human Resources:** Kathleen Wilson-Thompson, age 49
**SVP, Global Supply Chain:** Donna J. Banks, age 50
**SVP, Marketing:** Mark Baynes
**SVP, US Marketing Services:** Kevin Smith
**VP and Corporate Controller:** Alan R. Andrews, age 51
**VP; EVP, Kellogg International; President, Kellogg Europe:** Timothy P. Mobsby, age 52
**VP, Corporate Social Responsibility:** Tim Knowlton
**VP, Nutrition and Corporate Affairs:** Christine (Chris) Lowry
**Senior Director, Advertising and Media Services:** Andrew (Andy) Jung
**Senior Director, Marketing Communications:** Jenny Taylor-Enochson
**Director, Investor Relations:** Simon Burton
**Auditors:** PricewaterhouseCoopers LLP

## LOCATIONS

**HQ:** Kellogg Company
1 Kellogg Sq., Battle Creek, MI 49016
**Phone:** 269-961-2000 **Fax:** 269-961-2871
**Web:** www.kelloggcompany.com

### 2006 Sales

| | $ mil. | % of total |
|---|---|---|
| North America | 7,348.8 | 67 |
| Europe | 2,143.8 | 20 |
| Latin America | 890.8 | 8 |
| Asia Pacific | 523.3 | 5 |
| **Total** | **10,906.7** | **100** |

## PRODUCTS/OPERATIONS

### 2006 Sales

| | $ mil. | % of total |
|---|---|---|
| Cereal | 5,677.3 | 52 |
| Snacks | 3,318.4 | 30 |
| Frozen, specialty & convenience foods | 1,911.0 | 18 |
| **Total** | **10,906.7** | **100** |

### Selected Brands and Products

Kellogg-brand cereals
- All-Bran
- Apple Jacks
- BeBig
- Bran Buds
- Chex
- Cocoa Rice Krispies
- Complete
- Corn Pops
- Country Store
- Cracklin' Oat Bran
- Crispix
- Crusli
- Froot Loops
- Frosted Mini-Wheats
- Honey Loops
- Just Right
- Kashi
- Kellogg's Corn Flakes
- Kellogg's Frosted Bran
- Kellogg's Frosted Flakes
- Kellogg's Iron Man Food
- Kellogg's Raisin Bran
- Kellogg's Two Scoops Raisin Bran
- Mueslix
- Nutri-Grain
- Optima
- Product 19
- Rice Bubbles
- Rice Krispies
- Smacks
- Special K
- Sucrilhos
- Sultana Bran
- Supercharged
- Vector
- Zucaritas

Keebler-brand products
- Chips Deluxe cookies
- Club crackers
- Fudge Shoppe cookies
- Keebler ice-cream cones
- Munch'ems crackers
- Ready Crust piecrusts
- Sandies cookies
- Town House crackers
- Vienna Fingers cookies
- Wheatables crackers
- Zesta crackers

Sunshine-brand products
- Cheez-It crackers
- Krispy crackers
- Sunshine

Other brands and products
- Austin (snacks)
- Carr's (licensed and distributed in the US)
- Eggo (frozen waffles)
- E. L. Fudge
- Famous Amos
- Girl Scout cookies
- Kellogg's Corn Flake Crumbs (breading)
- Kellogg's Nutri-Grain (cereal bars, frozen waffles)
- Loma Linda (meat alternatives)
- Morningstar Farms (meat alternatives)
- Murray Sugar Free cookies
- Natural Touch (meat alternatives)
- Pop-Tarts (toaster pastries)
- Pop-Tarts Pastry Swirls (toaster Danish pastries)
- Rice Krispies Treats (marshmallow snacks)
- Worthington (meat alternatives)

## COMPETITORS

Boca Foods
ConAgra
Frito-Lay
General Mills
Gilster-Mary Lee
Grist Mill Company
Hain Celestial
Interstate Bakeries
Kraft Foods
Lance Snacks
Malt-O-Meal
McKee Foods
Nestlé
Parmalat Canada
Patty King
Pinnacle Foods
PowerBar
Ralcorp
Weetabix
Wessanen
Weston Foods
Wholesome & Hearty Foods

## HISTORICAL FINANCIALS

Company Type: Public

### Income Statement

FYE: December 31

| | REVENUE ($ mil.) | NET INCOME ($ mil.) | NET PROFIT MARGIN | EMPLOYEES |
|---|---|---|---|---|
| **12/06** | 10,907 | 1,004 | 9.2% | 26,000 |
| **12/05** | 10,177 | 980 | 9.6% | 25,600 |
| **12/04** | 9,614 | 891 | 9.3% | 25,171 |
| **12/03** | 8,812 | 787 | 8.9% | 25,250 |
| **12/02** | 8,304 | 721 | 8.7% | 25,700 |
| **Annual Growth** | 7.1% | 8.6% | — | 0.3% |

### 2006 Year-End Financials

Debt ratio: 147.6%
Return on equity: 46.1%
Cash ($ mil.): 411
Current ratio: 0.60
Long-term debt ($ mil.): 3,053
No. of shares (mil.): 398
Dividends
Yield: 1.7%
Payout: 34.3%
Market value ($ mil.): 19,909

**Stock History** NYSE: K

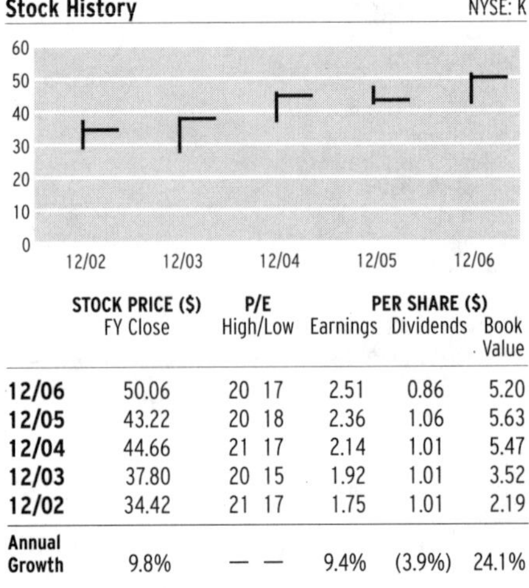


| | STOCK PRICE ($) FY Close | P/E High/Low | | PER SHARE ($) Earnings | Dividends | Book Value |
|---|---|---|---|---|---|---|
| **12/06** | 50.06 | 20 | 17 | 2.51 | 0.86 | 5.20 |
| **12/05** | 43.22 | 20 | 18 | 2.36 | 1.06 | 5.63 |
| **12/04** | 44.66 | 21 | 17 | 2.14 | 1.01 | 5.47 |
| **12/03** | 37.80 | 20 | 15 | 1.92 | 1.01 | 3.52 |
| **12/02** | 34.42 | 21 | 17 | 1.75 | 1.01 | 2.19 |
| **Annual Growth** | 9.8% | — | — | 9.4% | (3.9%) | 24.1% |

# Kelly Services

These days a lot of "Kelly Girls" are men. Once a business that supplied only female clerical help, Kelly Services has expanded to include light industrial, technical, and professional employees of both genders, including information technology specialists, engineers, and accountants. It also places lawyers (Kelly Law Registry), scientists (Kelly Scientific Resources), substitute teachers (Kelly Educational Staffing), nurses and other medical staff (Kelly Healthcare Resources), and teleservices personnel (KellyConnect). Kelly Services provides some 750,000 employees through some 2,500 offices in more than 30 countries. Chairman Terence Adderley controls more than 90% of the company.

Kelly Services continues to grow by opening new offices in target markets across the US and abroad. The company provides additional personnel in areas such as automotive (Kelly Automotive Services Group), electronics (Kelly Electronic Assembly Services), merchandising (Kelly Marketing Services), and security clearance (Kelly FedSecure).

In order to augment its portfolio of career transition services and business effectiveness consulting, Kelly Services bought New York-based The Ayers Group for $10 million in mid-2006. It also expanded its reach to the Czech Republic and Poland with the buyout of executive search firm Talents Technology in 2007. Its presence in Japan was also augmented when it acquired all the shares of a former joint venture — Tempstaff Kelly, headquartered in Tokyo — the same year. Looking to China, Hong Kong, and Singapore, Kelly Services subsequently acquired executive search and HR outsourcing services firm P-Serv, which projects an estimated 2007 revenue of $12 million.

At the same time, the company is shedding noncore operations. At the end of 2006, Kelly Services sold its staff leasing operations to Oasis Outsourcing Holdings for $6.5 million, and early in 2007 the company sold its Home Care Services unit to Res-Care for $12.5 million.

Citing medical reasons, Terence Adderley stepped down as chairman and CEO in February 2006. President and COO Carl Camden took over as CEO, and by May 2006, Adderley had recovered and was named chairman again.

## HISTORY

William Russell Kelly, a college dropout and former car salesman, went to Detroit after WWII to seek his fortune. An owner of modern business equipment, he set up Russell Kelly Office Service in 1946 to provide copying, typing, and inventory services for other businesses; first-year sales from 12 customers totaled $848.

Although companies began to acquire their own machines, Kelly knew that they still needed people to work at their offices. He reincorporated his rapidly expanding business as Personnel Service in 1952 and opened the company's first branch office in Louisville, Kentucky, in 1955; by the end of that year, he had 35 offices throughout the US. In 1957 the company was renamed Kelly Girl Service to reflect its all-female workforce.

In the 1960s Kelly ventured beyond office services and began placing convention hostesses, blue-collar workers, data processors, door-to-door marketers, and drafters, among others. Kelly Girl went public in 1962, boasting 148 branches at the time. In 1966 the company adopted its present name, Kelly Services. It opened its first non-US office in Toronto in 1968, and one in Paris followed in 1972.

A tough US economy in the 1970s saw a surge in corporate interest in temporary employees. Employers saw the benefits of hiring "Kelly Girls" to meet seasonal needs and special projects. In 1976 Kelly Services acquired a modest health care services company and used it to form Kelly Home Care. In the 1980s this division abandoned the Medicaid and Medicare markets and shifted to private-sector care. Renamed Kelly Assisted Living Services in 1984 (and later known as Kelly Home Care Services), the unit offered aides to perform household duties and nurses to conduct home visits for the elderly and disabled. Also in the 1980s Kelly Services began hiring retired people as part of its ENCORE Program.

The company developed specialty services in the US in the 1990s. It acquired ComTrain (testing and training software products) and Your Staff (an employee-leasing firm providing companies with entire human resources departments, including benefits and payroll services) in 1994. The following year it bought the Wallace Law Registry (later renamed Kelly Law Registry), which provides lawyers, paralegals, and clerks. Kelly also established Kelly Scientific Resources to place science professionals. In 1996 that subsidiary acquired Oak Ridge Research Institute, which provided scientists to the defense and energy industries.

Kelly continued its international expansion as well. Since 1988 more than a dozen acquisitions expanded the company in Asia, Australia, Europe, and elsewhere. In response to new legislation allowing companies to hire temporary workers, Kelly opened five offices in Italy and acquired a personnel placement firm in Russia in 1997.

William Kelly died at the age of 92 in 1998, and the company named president and CEO Terence Adderley, his adopted son, to replace him as chairman (Adderley relinquished the title of president in late 2001). The next year the company made four additions to its staffing services: Kelly Healthcare Resources, Kelly Financial Resources, Kelly Educational Staffing (substitute teachers), and KellyConnect (teleservices).

In 2000 the company made three acquisitions: Extra ETT in Spain (automotive staffing), ProStaff Group in the US (general staffing), and Business Trends Group in Singapore (general staffing). Kelly Services continued with its acquisition strategy the following year, purchasing the engineering services business of Compuware, among others. In 2002 the company opened new offices in the US, Europe, and Canada. In 2003 Kelly Services launched Kelly FedSecure, which provides professionals with security clearances to companies and government contractors.

Carl Camden took over as CEO in 2006 after Adderley had medical problems.

## EXECUTIVES

**Chairman:** Terence E. (Terry) Adderley, age 73, $950,000 pay
**President, CEO, and Director:** Carl T. Camden, age 52, $868,750 pay
**EVP and CFO:** William K. (Bill) Gerber, age 53, $570,000 pay
**EVP and Chief Administrative Officer:** Michael L. Durik, age 58, $650,000 pay
**SVP and Regional General Manager, Western Europe:** Bernard Tommasini
**SVP and General Manager, Strategic Customer Relations:** Joan M. Brancheau
**SVP, Corporate Controller, and Chief Accounting Officer:** Michael E. Debs, age 50
**SVP, General Counsel, and Corporate Secretary:** Daniel T. Lis, age 60, $373,333 pay
**SVP, Administration:** James H. Bradley
**SVP, Global Sales:** Carol J. Johnson
**SVP, Human Resources:** Nina M. Ramsey
**SVP, Information Technology:** Allison M. Everett
**SVP, International:** Rolf E. Kleiner
**SVP, Marketing:** Michael S. Morrow
**SVP, Professional, Technical, and Staffing Alternatives:** Michael S. Webster
**SVP, Asia/Pacific:** Dhirendra Shantilal
**Director, Investor Relations:** James M. Polehna
**Manager, Public Relations:** Renee Walker
**Auditors:** PricewaterhouseCoopers LLP

## LOCATIONS

**HQ:** Kelly Services, Inc.
999 W. Big Beaver Rd., Troy, MI 48084
**Phone:** 248-362-4444 **Fax:** 248-244-4360
**Web:** www.kellyservices.com

## PRODUCTS/OPERATIONS

### 2006 Sales

| | $ mil. | % of total |
|---|---|---|
| US commercial staffing | 2,524.5 | 45 |
| International | 1,943.5 | 35 |
| PTSA | 1,137.8 | 20 |
| **Total** | **5,605.8** | **100** |

### Selected Services

Kelly Automotive Services Group
Kelly Educational Staffing (substitute teachers)
Kelly Electronic Assembly Services
Kelly Engineering Resources (engineers)
Kelly FedSecure
Kelly Financial Resources (accounting, analysts)
Kelly Healthcare Resources (nurses, medical technicians)
Kelly Home Care Services (in-home caregivers)
Kelly Information Technology Resources
Kelly Law Registry
Kelly Light Industrial
Kelly Management Services
Kelly Marketing Services
Kelly Office Services (clerical staffing)
Kelly Scientific Resources (science staffing)

## COMPETITORS

Adecco
Administaff
Allegis Group
ATC Healthcare
CDI
Gevity HR
Labor Ready
Manpower
MPS
On Assignment
Randstad
Robert Half
Spherion
TAC Worldwide
Vedior
Volt Information

## HISTORICAL FINANCIALS

Company Type: Public

**Income Statement** FYE: Sunday nearest December 31

| | REVENUE ($ mil.) | NET INCOME ($ mil.) | NET PROFIT MARGIN | EMPLOYEES |
|---|---|---|---|---|
| **12/06** | 5,606 | 64 | 1.1% | 750,000 |
| **12/05** | 5,290 | 39 | 0.7% | 708,600 |
| **12/04** | 4,984 | 21 | 0.4% | 708,400 |
| **12/03** | 4,325 | 5 | 0.1% | 707,900 |
| **12/02** | 4,324 | 19 | 0.4% | 708,200 |
| **Annual Growth** | 6.7% | 35.9% | — | 1.4% |

**2006 Year-End Financials**

Debt ratio: —
Return on equity: 8.9%
Cash ($ mil.): 118
Current ratio: 1.82
Long-term debt ($ mil.): —
No. of shares (mil.): 33
Dividends
Yield: 1.6%
Payout: 25.7%
Market value ($ mil.): 953

**Stock History** NASDAQ (GS): KELYA

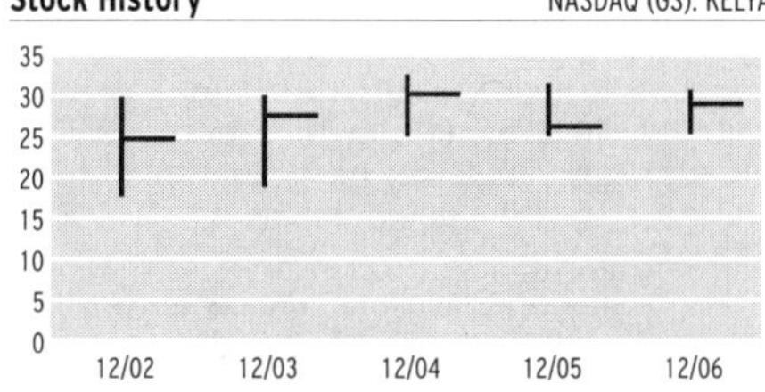


| | STOCK PRICE ($) FY Close | P/E High/Low | PER SHARE ($) Earnings | Dividends | Book Value |
|---|---|---|---|---|---|
| **12/06** | 28.94 | 17 15 | 1.75 | 0.45 | 23.03 |
| **12/05** | 26.22 | 29 23 | 1.09 | 0.20 | 20.77 |
| **12/04** | 30.18 | 54 42 | 0.60 | 0.30 | 20.37 |
| **12/03** | 27.52 | 212136 | 0.14 | 0.40 | 19.61 |
| **12/02** | 24.72 | 57 34 | 0.52 | 0.30 | 19.31 |
| **Annual Growth** | 4.0% | — — | 35.4% | 10.7% | 4.5% |

# Kennametal Inc.

Kennametal welcomes cutting-edge remarks. The company offers a host of metal-cutting tools, mining and highway construction equipment, and engineering services across its two divisions: the Metalworking Solutions and Services Group and the Advanced Materials Solutions Group. Kennametal's products include cutting, milling, and drilling tools used in metalworking; drums, bits, and accessories used in mining; and bits, grader blades, and snowplow blades used in construction. Kennametal and its subsidiaries sell products worldwide under the Cleveland, Conforma Clad, Drill-Fix, Fix-Perfect, Greenfield, Kendex, Kenloc, Kennametal, and Kyon brand names.

The company has acquired the metal-cutting tool business of Federal Signal for about $67 million. The business comprises Manchester Tool Company, ClappDiCO Corporation, and On Time Machine, Inc. (OTM). The company sees the purchase as a "bolt-on" acquisition that will be easily integrated into its Metalworking Solutions and Services Group.

Kennametal's bottom line had been hurt by weak demand in the oil and gas industries, the agricultural market, and the overall depressed market. In response the company cut costs by reducing its salaried workforce and consolidated eight North American warehouses to a single, central location near Cleveland. The company believes these moves will help bolster future profits.

Franklin Resources and Transamerica Investment Management each own more than 6% of Kennametal. Barclays Global Investors holds nearly 6% of the company.

## HISTORY

In 1832 Irish immigrant and coppersmith Robert McKenna came to Pittsburgh and opened a copper works. His three sons took over the business after he died in 1852. In 1900 Robert's grandson, A. G. McKenna, developed a revolutionary cutting tool made of steel and tungsten (and, later, of vanadium). The family set up Vanadium Alloys Steel Co. in 1910.

In 1938 Philip McKenna, A. G.'s son, formed a new business called Kennametal, based on a tungsten-titanium carbide alloy for cutting tools. The family incorporated the company in 1943. WWII and the Korean War brought strong US military demand for the company's products. Kennametal expanded overseas during the 1960s and 1970s and went public in 1977. Quentin McKenna was named CEO in 1979. During the 1980s, Kennametal bought Bristol Erickson (UK), as well as companies in Belgium, Canada, France, and the Netherlands.

The company was accused of illegally selling equipment to an Iraqi-controlled firm in the UK in 1991, in violation of a trade embargo imposed by the first Bush Administration in 1990. While the US Department of Justice ultimately concluded that no export laws had been broken by Kennametal, the company settled the case in 1997 by paying a fine of $13,457, without admitting any wrongdoing.

The firm bought J & L Industrial Supply, a Detroit-based catalog supplier of metalwork tools, in 1991, and continued to grow by buying a majority stake in German toolmaker Hertel (1993) and by forming a marketing alliance with industrial supplies distributor W.W. Grainger (1994). During fiscal 1995, Kennametal invested in Asia, Mexico, and Poland. The next year William Newlin became the first outsider to become chairman. He succeeded Quentin McKenna, a nephew of Philip McKenna, who had been chairman for 13 years.

Kennametal added JLK Direct Distribution to its supply operations in 1997 and then spun off the unit, retaining about 80% ownership. It also bought rival toolmaker Greenfield Industries. Weak product demand caused by slumps in the oil and paper industries and Asian economic woes contributed to Kennametal's job cuts (about 5% of its workforce) and its plans for plant closures in 1998 and 1999.

In mid-1999 Markos Tambakeras succeeded Robert McGeehan as president and CEO. McGeehan had served 10 years as president of Kennametal, and was the first person outside the McKenna family to hold that post.

Kennametal had been considering selling its stake in JLK, but shelved the idea in 2000 amid market turbulence, opting instead to buy the company back. In 2001 Kennametal announced that it would cut between 6% and 8% of its salaried workforce.

In mid-2002 Kennametal purchased Widia Group, a metalworking toolmaker with operations in Europe and India. Newlin stepped down as chairman, remaining on the board as lead director, and was succeeded by Tambakeras as chairman. In 2003 the company named its global technology center in Latrobe the Quentin C. McKenna Technology Center, after its former chief executive, who died that year at the age of 76.

In early 2005 Kennametal added Pennsylvania-based Extrude Hone, which provides engineered component process technologies to a variety of industries, in a deal valued at $137 million. The next year Kennametal again added to that same electro chemical machining (ECM) technologies unit with the purchase of European supplier VMB/Diva-Tec.

In 2006 the company made a move to narrow its focus, selling its distribution subsidiary, J & L Industrial Supply, to MSC Industrial Direct for about $350 million. With the closing of the J & L sale, Kennametal exited completely the distribution business.

EVP/COO Carlos Cardoso was promoted to president and CEO at the outset of 2006, after one year as chief of manufacturing operations. Markos Tambakeras remained as executive chairman following the management transition.

In mid-2006 the company acquired Sintec Group of Germany, a manufacturer of ceramic engineered components for the aerospace, medical, and metalizing markets. Kennametal next purchased the Camco Group, a Canadian supplier of specialized saw tips for forestry and woodworking, adding the business to its Engineered Products Group. It also increased its equity ownership in its Italian and Spanish affiliates.

Tambakeras served one year as executive chairman before leaving the board at the end of 2006. Larry Yost, the former chairman and CEO of ArvinMeritor and a Kennametal director since 1987, was elected to succeed Tambakeras as chairman.

## EXECUTIVES

**Chairman:** Larry D. Yost, age 68
**President, CEO, and Director:** Carlos M. Cardoso, age 48, $1,381,117 pay
**VP and CFO:** Frank P. Simpkins, age 43
**VP and CTO:** William Y. (Bill) Hsu, age 58
**VP and CIO:** Raj Datt
**VP and Chief Administrative Officer:** Stanley B. Duzy Jr., age 59, $548,816 pay
**VP and Chief Human Resources Officer:** Kevin R. Walling
**VP, Corporate Strategy and MSSG Global Marketing:** R. Daniel Bagley, age 45
**VP, Global Sales Metalworking Solutions and Services Group:** John Q. Stang, age 51
**VP, Secretary, and General Counsel:** David W. Greenfield, age 56, $546,040 pay
**VP, Mergers and Acquisitions:** James E. Morrison, age 55
**VP, Value Business System and Lean Enterprise:** Philip H. Weihl, age 50

**VP; President, Advanced Components Group:** James R. Breisinger, age 56, $658,875 pay
**VP and Treasurer:** Lawrence J. Lanza, age 57
**VP, Finance and Corporate Controller; CFO, Europe:** Wayne D. Moser, age 53
**VP; President, Advanced Materials Solutions Group:** Gary W. Weismann, age 51
**Director, Manufacturing, Europe:** Brendan Drummond
**Director, Sales and Service, Europe:** Gerald Goubau
**Director, Marketing, Europe:** Doug Phillips
**Auditors:** PricewaterhouseCoopers LLP

## LOCATIONS

**HQ:** Kennametal Inc.
1600 Technology Way, Latrobe, PA 15650
**Phone:** 724-539-5000 **Fax:** 724-539-6657
**Web:** www.kennametal.com

Kennametal has manufacturing facilities in Brazil, Canada, China, France, Germany, India, Israel, Italy, Mexico, the Netherlands, Spain, the UK, and the US, and joint venture operations in China, Poland, and Russia.

### 2007 Sales

| | $ mil. | % of total |
|---|---|---|
| North America | | |
| US | 1,134.7 | 48 |
| Canada | 83.0 | 3 |
| Europe | | |
| Germany | 441.7 | 18 |
| UK | 76.5 | 3 |
| Asia | 252.8 | 11 |
| Other regions | 396.8 | 17 |
| **Total** | **2,385.5** | **100** |

## PRODUCTS/OPERATIONS

### 2007 Sales

| | $ mil. | % of total |
|---|---|---|
| Metalworking Solutions & Services | 1,577.2 | 66 |
| Advanced Materials Solutions | 808.3 | 34 |
| **Total** | **2,385.5** | **100** |

### Selected Products

Metalworking Tools
- Boring tools
- Combination tools
- Metal-cutting inserts
- Milling kits
- Tool management software

Mining, Construction, and Other Equipment
- Agricultural implements
- Auger tooling and drilling products
- Face and roof augers
- Motor grader blades
- Pining-rod systems
- Scraper and grader blades
- Snowplow blades
- Soil stabilization tooling
- Two-prong bits

Industrial Supply
- Bandsaws
- Boring bars
- Calipers
- Dies
- Drills and drill bits
- Lathes
- Milling cutters
- Reamers
- Safety wear and equipment
- Taps

### Selected Brand Names

Block Style K
Chicago Latrobe
Cleveland
Conforma Clad
Drill-Fix
Ecogrind
Erickson
Fix-Perfect
Greenfield
Heinlein
Hertel
Kendex
Kenloc
KennaMAX
Kennametal
Kennametal Hertel
KM
KM Micro
Kyon
RTW
Top Notch
Widia
Widma

## COMPETITORS

Actuant
Allegheny Technologies
Atlas Copco
Flow
Giddings & Lewis
GILDEMEISTER
Hardinge
Jore
L. S. Starrett
Sandvik
Seco Tools
Walter

## HISTORICAL FINANCIALS

Company Type: Public

### Income Statement

FYE: June 30

| | REVENUE ($ mil.) | NET INCOME ($ mil.) | NET PROFIT MARGIN | EMPLOYEES |
|---|---|---|---|---|
| **6/07** | 2,386 | 174 | 7.3% | 13,947 |
| **6/06** | 2,330 | 256 | 11.0% | 13,300 |
| **6/05** | 2,304 | 119 | 5.2% | 14,000 |
| **6/04** | 1,971 | 74 | 3.7% | 13,700 |
| **6/03** | 1,759 | 18 | 1.0% | 13,970 |
| **Annual Growth** | 7.9% | 76.1% | — | (0.0%) |

### 2007 Year-End Financials

Debt ratio: 24.3%
Return on equity: 12.5%
Cash ($ mil.): 50
Current ratio: 2.09
Long-term debt ($ mil.): 361
No. of shares (mil.): 39
Dividends
Yield: 1.0%
Payout: 18.5%
Market value ($ mil.): 3,198

### Stock History

NYSE: KMT

| | STOCK PRICE ($) FY Close | P/E High | P/E Low | PER SHARE ($) Earnings | Dividends | Book Value |
|---|---|---|---|---|---|---|
| **6/07** | 82.03 | 19 | 11 | 4.44 | 0.82 | 38.08 |
| **6/06** | 62.25 | 10 | 7 | 6.48 | 0.76 | 33.55 |
| **6/05** | 45.85 | 17 | 13 | 3.13 | 0.68 | 25.52 |
| **6/04** | 45.80 | 23 | 16 | 2.02 | 0.51 | 24.22 |
| **6/03** | 33.84 | 72 | 53 | 0.51 | 0.68 | 20.34 |
| **Annual Growth** | 24.8% | — | — | 71.8% | 4.8% | 17.0% |

# KeyCorp

Financial services giant KeyCorp has the clout of mean Henry Potter of Bedford Falls, but wants to be the sweet George Bailey of bankers. With a focus on relationship banking and retail operations, flagship subsidiary KeyBank operates some 950 branches (KeyCenters) in 16 states. KeyBank's operations are divided into two groups — Community Banking and National Banking. Community Banking offers local banking services including deposits, loans, and financial planning; National Banking provides real estate capital, equipment financing, and capital markets services to large investors. Nonbank subsidiaries offer insurance, brokerage, investment banking, and credit card processing for small businesses.

KeyCorp has been paring away its nonbanking subsidiaries to focus on its consumer and corporate businesses. As part of this focus on local banking, it sold its mortgage unit, Champion Mortgage, which specializes in high-risk customers, to HSBC Holdings and its financial services unit McDonald Investments to UBS Financial Services in 2007.

The company agreed to buy U.S.B. Holding Co. Inc., for some $550 million in 2007. The deal nearly doubles KeyCorp's footprint in the Hudson River Valley region.

## HISTORY

KeyCorp predecessor Commercial Bank of Albany was chartered in 1825. In 1865 it joined the new national banking system and became National Commercial Bank of Albany. After WWI National Commercial consolidated with Union National Bank & Trust as National Commercial Bank and Trust, which then merged with First Trust and Deposit in 1971.

In 1973 Victor Riley became president and CEO. Under Riley, National Commercial grew during the 1970s and 1980s through acquisitions. Riley sought to make the company a regional powerhouse but was thwarted when several New England states passed legislation barring New York banks from buying banks in the region.

As a result, the company, renamed Key Bank in 1979, turned west, targeting small towns with less competition. Thus situated, it prospered, despite entering Alaska just in time for the 1986 oil price collapse. Its folksy image and small-town success earned it a reputation as the "Wal-Mart of banking."

Meanwhile, in Cleveland, Society for Savings followed a different path. Founded as a mutual savings bank in 1849, the institution succeeded from the start. It survived the Civil War and postwar economic turmoil and built Cleveland's first skyscraper in 1890. It continued to grow even during the Depression and became the largest savings bank outside the Northeast in 1949.

In 1955 the bank formed a holding company, Society National. Society grew through the acquisitions of smaller banks in Ohio until 1979, when Ohio allowed branch banking in contiguous counties. Thereafter, Society National opened branches as well. In the mid-1980s and the early 1990s, the renamed Society Corporation began consolidating its operations and continued growing.

A 1994 merger of National Commercial with Society more than doubled assets for the surviving KeyCorp; systems and software compatibility simplified the companies' consolidation. KeyCorp sold its mortgage-servicing unit to NationsBank (now Bank of America) in 1995 and over the next year bought investment management, finance, and investment banking companies.

In 1997 KeyCorp began trimming its branch network, divesting 200 offices, including its 28-branch KeyBank Wyoming subsidiary. It expanded its consumer lending business that year by buying Champion Mortgage. In cooperation with USF&G (now part of The St. Paul Travelers Companies) and three HMOs, KeyCorp began offering health insurance to the underserved small-business market.

In 1998 the company bought Leasetec, which leases computer storage systems globally through its StorageTek subsidiary; it also bought McDonald & Company Investments (now McDonald Investments; sold in 2007), with an eye toward reaching its goal of earning half of its revenues from fees. Also in 1998, KeyCorp began offering business lines of credit to customers of Costco Wholesale, the nation's largest wholesale club.

As part of a restructuring effort, KeyCorp sold 28 Long Island, New York, branches to Dime Bancorp in 1999. The next year the company sold its credit card portfolio to Associates First Capital (now part of Citigroup) and bought National Realty Funding, a securitizer of commercial mortgages. In 2001 it acquired Denver-based investment bank The Wallach Company.

The company expanded further in the Denver area with its 2002 purchase of Union Bankshares. Two years later KeyCorp bought Seattle-area bank EverTrust Financial Group.

## EXECUTIVES

**Chairman, President, and CEO:** Henry L. Meyer III, age 57, $4,450,000 pay
**Vice Chair; President, Key National Banking; President, McDonald Investments:** Thomas W. Bunn, age 53, $2,819,230 pay
**Vice Chairman and Chief Administrative Officer:** Thomas C. (Tom) Stevens, age 57, $1,619,230 pay
**Vice Chair:** Beth E. Mooney, age 51
**SEVP and CFO:** Jeffrey B. Weeden, age 50, $1,519,230 pay
**EVP and Chief Risk Officer:** Charles S. (Chuck) Hyle, age 55, $900,000 pay
**EVP Client Services Group:** Michael P. (Mike) Barnum
**EVP, Corporate Development and Strategic Planning:** Andrew R. (Andy) Tyson
**EVP, General Counsel, and Secretary:** Paul N. Harris, age 48
**EVP Public Affairs and Chief Communications Officer:** Michael J. Monroe
**EVP; President, Retail Banking:** Timothy J. (Tim) King
**EVP; Chairman, KeyBank National Association; CEO, McDonald Financial Group:** Robert B. (Yank) Heisler Jr., age 58
**EVP; Chief Fiduciary Officer and Manager, Wealth Management and Trust Services, McDonald Financial Group:** Carol L. Klimas
**EVP and CIO:** Stephen E. Yates, age 58
**EVP and Chief Human Resources Officer:** Thomas E. (Tom) Helfrich, age 54
**EVP and National Sales Manager, KeyBank Real Estate Capital:** John E. Case
**EVP Investor Relations:** Vernon L. (Vern) Patterson
**EVP and Director, Client Experience:** Michael L. (Mike) Evans
**EVP and Director, Call Center Sales and Service:** Dean Kontul
**EVP and Treasurer:** Joseph M. Vayda
**Chief Accounting Officer:** Robert L. Morris, age 54
**Chief Bank Secrecy Act Officer; EVP, Risk Management Group:** Linda A. Grandstaf
**Chief Marketing Officer:** Karen R. Haefling
**Auditors:** Ernst & Young LLP

## LOCATIONS

**HQ:** KeyCorp
127 Public Sq., Cleveland, OH 44114
**Phone:** 216-689-6300 **Fax:** 216-689-0519
**Web:** www.key.com

## PRODUCTS/OPERATIONS

### 2006 Sales

| | $ mil. | % of total |
|---|---|---|
| Interest | | |
| Loans | 4,561 | 61 |
| Other | 819 | 11 |
| Noninterest | | |
| Trust & investment services | 553 | 7 |
| Service charges on deposits | 304 | 4 |
| Investment banking & capital markets | 230 | 3 |
| Operating lease income | 229 | 3 |
| Other | 811 | 11 |
| **Total** | **7,507** | **100** |

### 2006 Assets

| | $ mil. | % of total |
|---|---|---|
| Cash & equivalents | 2,264 | 2 |
| Securities available for sale | 7,827 | 9 |
| Short-term investments | 1,407 | 2 |
| Other investments | 1,352 | 1 |
| Net loans | 64,882 | 70 |
| Corporate-owned life insurance | 2,782 | 3 |
| Other | 11,823 | 13 |
| **Total** | **92,337** | **100** |

## COMPETITORS

Associated Banc-Corp
Bank of America
Bank of New York Mellon
Citigroup
Citizens Financial Group
Comerica
Fifth Third
Flagstar Bancorp
HSBC USA
Huntington Bancshares
JPMorgan Chase
LaSalle Bank
M&T Bank
Marshall & Ilsley
National City
Northern Trust
Sovereign Bancorp
U.S. Bancorp
Washington Mutual
Wells Fargo

## HISTORICAL FINANCIALS

Company Type: Public

### Income Statement

FYE: December 31

| | ASSETS ($ mil.) | NET INCOME ($ mil.) | INCOME AS % OF ASSETS | EMPLOYEES |
|---|---|---|---|---|
| **12/06** | 92,337 | 1,055 | 1.1% | 20,006 |
| **12/05** | 93,126 | 1,129 | 1.2% | 19,485 |
| **12/04** | 90,739 | 954 | 1.1% | 19,576 |
| **12/03** | 84,487 | 903 | 1.1% | 20,034 |
| **12/02** | 85,202 | 976 | 1.1% | 20,437 |
| **Annual Growth** | 2.0% | 2.0% | — | (0.5%) |

### 2006 Year-End Financials

Equity as % of assets: 8.3%
Return on assets: 1.1%
Return on equity: 13.8%
Long-term debt ($ mil.): 16,647
No. of shares (mil.): 399
Dividends
Yield: 4.5%
Payout: 67.3%
Market value ($ mil.): 15,180
Sales ($ mil.): 7,507

### Stock History

NYSE: KEY

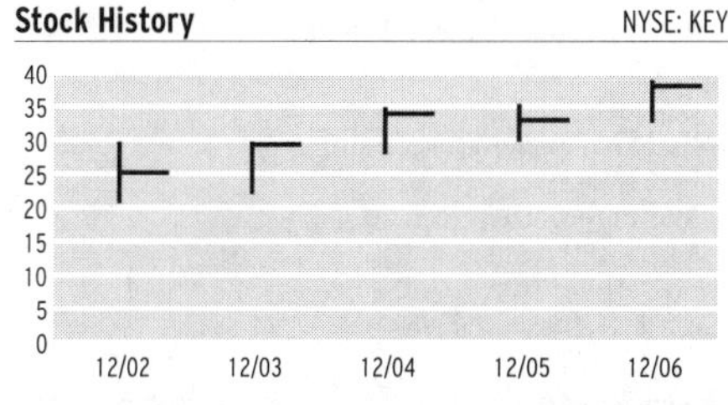

| | STOCK PRICE ($) FY Close | P/E High | P/E Low | PER SHARE ($) Earnings | Dividends | Book Value |
|---|---|---|---|---|---|---|
| **12/06** | 38.03 | 15 | 13 | 2.57 | 1.73 | 19.30 |
| **12/05** | 32.93 | 13 | 11 | 2.73 | 1.30 | — |
| **12/04** | 33.90 | 15 | 12 | 2.30 | 1.24 | — |
| **12/03** | 29.32 | 14 | 11 | 2.12 | 1.22 | — |
| **12/02** | 25.14 | 13 | 9 | 2.27 | 1.20 | — |
| **Annual Growth** | 10.9% | — | — | 3.2% | 9.6% | — |

# Kimberly-Clark

Nobody knows noses and diapering babies better than Kimberly-Clark, the world's top maker of personal paper products. Under brand names such as Cottonelle, Kleenex, and Scott, it makes facial and bathroom tissues, paper towels, and other household items. Its personal care products include Huggies, Kotex, and Depend. The firm also makes WypAll and Kimwipes commercial wipes. It spun off its paper (Neenah Paper, Technical Paper), pulp, and timber operations to create Neenah Paper. The firm kicked off a multiyear reorganization in 2005 and bought Germany's Microcuff GmbH.

Using its momentum from reorganization efforts, Kimberly-Clark has continued to restructure its operations. The company combined its North Atlantic Personal Care and Family Care businesses in 2005 to form a North Atlantic Consumer Products unit, which serves North America and Europe. Later that year Kimberly-Clark announced that it would purge about 10% of its workforce (some 6,000 employees) worldwide, close or sell more than 20 plants (representing about 17% of its manufacturing facilities), and streamline its operations — all by the close of 2008 — as it progresses deeper into its Global Business Plan.

Best known for its consumer products, Kimberly-Clark has seen wealth in the health and medical sectors. The company has been expanding into medical products and is now a leading US maker of disposable medical goods. Kimberly-Clark also has been adding products for the health care market through acquisitions. The firm makes sterilization wrap, face masks, surgical drapes and gowns, and closed-suction respiratory products. Its purchase of Safeskin (for approximately $750 million) made it a leading manufacturer of examination gloves. Its 2005 $16 million acquisition of Microcuff extended Kimberly-Clark's reach into medical devices and catheter technology.

The company also makes specialty and technical papers. Products, such as its Huggies Little Swimmers disposable swimpants and Depend and Poise incontinence care products, have helped fuel the company's sales growth. In its ongoing battle with rival Pampers for dominance of the diaper market, in mid-2006 Huggies introduced two new diapers (Huggies Supreme Gentle Care and Huggies Supreme Natural Fit) to replace its Huggies Supreme line.

## HISTORY

John Kimberly, Charles Clark, Havilah Babcock, and Frank Shattuck founded Kimberly, Clark & Company in Neenah, Wisconsin, in 1872 to manufacture newsprint from rags. The company incorporated as Kimberly & Clark Company in 1880 and built a pulp and paper plant on the Fox River in 1889.

In 1914 the company developed cellu-cotton, a cotton substitute used by the US Army as surgical cotton during WWI. Army nurses used cellu-cotton pads as disposable sanitary napkins, and six years later the company introduced Kotex, the first disposable feminine hygiene product. Kleenex, the first throwaway handkerchief, followed in 1924. Kimberly & Clark joined with The New York Times Company in 1926 to build a newsprint mill (Spruce Falls Power and

Paper) in Ontario, Canada. Two years later the company went public as Kimberly-Clark.

The firm expanded internationally during the 1950s, opening plants in Mexico, Germany, and the UK. It began operations in 17 more foreign locations in the 1960s.

CEO Guy Minard, who retired in 1971, sold the four mills that handled Kimberly-Clark's unprofitable coated-paper business and entered the paper towel and disposable diaper markets. Minard's successor, Darwin Smith, introduced Kimbies diapers in 1968, but they leaked and were withdrawn from the market. An improved version came out in 1976, followed by Huggies, a premium-priced diaper with elastic leg bands, two years later.

The company formed Midwest Express Airlines from its corporate flight department in 1984 (a business it exited in 1996). Smith moved Kimberly-Clark's headquarters from Neenah to Irving, Texas, the following year.

In 1991 Kimberly-Clark and The New York Times Company sold Spruce Falls Power and Paper. Smith retired as chairman in 1992 and was succeeded by Wayne Sanders, who was largely responsible for designing Huggies Pull-Ups (introduced in 1989). Kimberly-Clark entered a joint venture to make personal care products in Argentina in 1994 and also bought the feminine hygiene units of VP-Schickedanz (Germany) and Handan Comfort and Beauty Group (China).

Kimberly-Clark bought Scott Paper in 1995 for $9.4 billion. The move boosted its market share in bathroom tissue from 5% to 31% and its share in paper towels from 6% to 18%, but led to some headaches as the company absorbed Scott's operations.

In 1997 Kimberly-Clark sold its 50% stake in Canada's Scott Paper to forest products company Kruger and bought diaper operations in Spain and Portugal and disposable surgical face masks maker Tecnol Medical Products. A tissue price war in Europe bruised the company's bottom line that year and the company began massive job cuts. (By the end of 1999, nearly 4,000 jobs, mostly in the tissue-based businesses, had been axed.)

In part to focus on its health care business, which it entered in 1997, the company in 1999 sold some of its timber interests and its timber fleet to Cooper/T. Smith Corp. Augmenting its presence in Germany, Switzerland, and Austria, in 1999 the company paid $365 million for the tissue business of Swiss-based Attisholz Holding. Adding to its lineup of medical products, the company bought Ballard Medical Products in 1999 for $744 million and examination glove maker Safeskin in 2000 for about $800 million.

Also in 2000 the company bought virtually all of Taiwan's S-K Corporation; the move made Kimberly-Clark one of the largest manufacturers of consumer packaged goods in Taiwan and set the stage for expanded distribution in the Asia/Pacific region. The company later purchased Taiwan Scott Paper Corporation for about $40 million and merged the two companies, forming Kimberly-Clark Taiwan. In 2001 Kimberly-Clark bought Italian diaper maker Linostar, and announced it was closing four Latin American manufacturing plants.

In 2002 Kimberly-Clark purchased paper-packaging rival Amcor's stake in their Kimberly-Clark Australia joint venture. Adding to its global consumer tissue business, in 2003 Kimberly-Clark acquired the Polish tissue-maker Klucze.

## EXECUTIVES

**Chairman, President, and CEO:** Thomas J. (Tom) Falk, age 48, $1,175,000 pay
**SVP and CFO:** Mark A. Buthman, age 46, $507,517 pay
**SVP and Chief Marketing Officer:** Anthony J. Palmer
**SVP and Chief Strategy Officer:** Robert W. (Bob) Black, age 47
**SVP, Human Resources:** Lizanne C. (Liz) Gottung, age 50
**Group President:** Juan Ernesto de Bedout, age 62
**Group President, Developing and Emerging Markets:** Robert E. Abernathy, age 52, $521,285 pay
**Group President, North Atlantic Consumer Products:** Steven R. Kalmanson, $618,000 pay
**VP and Controller:** Randy J. Vest
**VP and Secretary:** Timothy C. Everett, age 40
**VP and Treasurer:** Jolene L. Varney
**VP, Corporate Communications:** Tina S. Barry
**VP, Corporate Diversity and Inclusion:** Edwin Garcia
**VP, Global Healthcare Sales and Marketing, Kimberly-Clark Health Care:** John Amat
**VP, Finance and Administration, Europe:** Simon Newton
**VP, Investor Relations:** Michael D. (Mike) Masseth
**President, North American Baby Care:** Bruce Paynter
**President, Global K-C Professional:** Jan B. Spencer, age 51
**President, Global Health Care:** Joanne B. Bauer
**President, North Atlantic Customer Development:** Don Quigley
**Director, Corporate Communications:** David J. (Dave) Dickson
**Auditors:** Deloitte & Touche LLP

## LOCATIONS

**HQ:** Kimberly-Clark Corporation
351 Phelps Dr., Irving, TX 75038
**Phone:** 972-281-1200 **Fax:** 972-281-1490
**Web:** www.kimberly-clark.com

### 2006 Sales

| | $ mil. | % of total |
|---|---|---|
| US | 9,405.6 | 54 |
| Europe | 3,153.4 | 18 |
| Canada | 538.0 | 3 |
| Asia, Latin America & other regions | 4,480.9 | 25 |
| Adjustment | (831.0) | — |
| **Total** | **16,746.9** | **100** |

## PRODUCTS/OPERATIONS

### 2006 Sales

| | $ mil. | % of total |
|---|---|---|
| Personal care products | 6,740.9 | 40 |
| Consumer tissue | 5,982.0 | 36 |
| K-C professional & other | 2,718.7 | 16 |
| Health care | 1,331.8 | 8 |
| Corporate & other | 32.3 | — |
| Adjustment | (58.8) | — |
| **Total** | **16,746.9** | **100** |

### Selected Products and Brands

Medical
- Closed-suction respiratory products
- Examination gloves (Safeskin)
- Face masks
- Infection-control products
- Scrub suits and apparel
- Sterile wrap (Kimguard)
- Surgical drapes and gowns

Personal Care
- Baby wipes (Huggies)
- Disposable diapers (Huggies, Pull-Ups)
- Feminine hygiene products (Kotex, New Freedom, Lightdays)
- Incontinence products (Depend, Poise)
- Swimpants (Little Swimmers)

Tissue-Based
- Bathroom tissue (Cottonelle, Scott)
- Commercial wipes (Kimwipes, WypAll)
- Facial tissue (Kleenex)
- Paper napkins (Scott)
- Paper towels (Kleenex, Scott, Viva)

## COMPETITORS

3M
BD
Bristol-Myers Squibb
Cardinal Medical Products
CCA Industries
DSG International Ltd
Georgia-Pacific
Johnson & Johnson
Medline Industries
Nice-Pak Products
Playtex
Potlatch
Procter & Gamble
SSI Surgical Services

## HISTORICAL FINANCIALS

Company Type: Public

### Income Statement

FYE: December 31

| | REVENUE ($ mil.) | NET INCOME ($ mil.) | NET PROFIT MARGIN | EMPLOYEES |
|---|---|---|---|---|
| **12/06** | 16,747 | 1,500 | 9.0% | 55,000 |
| **12/05** | 15,903 | 1,568 | 9.9% | 57,000 |
| **12/04** | 15,083 | 1,800 | 11.9% | 60,000 |
| **12/03** | 14,348 | 1,694 | 11.8% | 62,000 |
| **12/02** | 13,566 | 1,675 | 12.3% | 63,900 |
| **Annual Growth** | 5.4% | (2.7%) | — | (3.7%) |

### 2006 Year-End Financials

Debt ratio: 37.3%
Return on equity: 25.7%
Cash ($ mil.): 625
Current ratio: 1.05
Long-term debt ($ mil.): 2,276
No. of shares (mil.): 456
Dividends
Yield: 2.9%
Payout: 60.3%
Market value ($ mil.): 30,958

### Stock History

NYSE: KMB

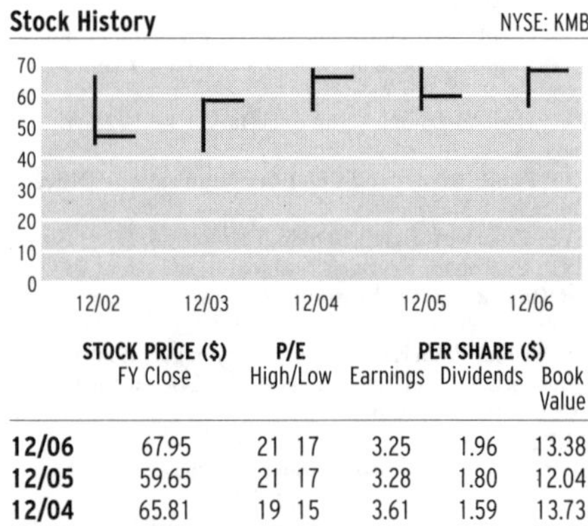


| | STOCK PRICE ($) FY Close | P/E High | P/E Low | PER SHARE ($) Earnings | Dividends | Book Value |
|---|---|---|---|---|---|---|
| **12/06** | 67.95 | 21 | 17 | 3.25 | 1.96 | 13.38 |
| **12/05** | 59.65 | 21 | 17 | 3.28 | 1.80 | 12.04 |
| **12/04** | 65.81 | 19 | 15 | 3.61 | 1.59 | 13.73 |
| **12/03** | 58.33 | 18 | 13 | 3.33 | 1.34 | 13.49 |
| **12/02** | 46.86 | 20 | 14 | 3.22 | 1.18 | 11.06 |
| **Annual Growth** | 9.7% | — | — | 0.2% | 13.5% | 4.9% |

# Kindred Healthcare

Kindred Healthcare is one of the largest long-term health care providers in the US. Kindred operates some 240 nursing homes (more than 30,000 beds) in 28 states and about 80 long-term acute care hospitals (about 6,400 beds) in 24 states. The company also operates a contract rehabilitation therapy business, which serves its own and other long-term care facilities, through its People*first* Rehabilitation division. In 2007 Kindred spun off its Kindred Pharmacy Services unit, which distributes drugs to long-term care facilities, and combined it with the spun-off institutional pharmacy business of Amerisource-Bergen; the new company is called PharMerica.

The deal created the #2 institutional pharmacy nationwide (behind Omnicare). Kindred

Pharmacy Services contributed more than 40 institutional pharmacies in 26 states to the combined company.

The company's Health Services division, which accounts for about 40% of sales, operates nursing home facilities and provides specialized treatment for certain diseases such as Alzheimer's. It also provides rehabilitative care, often through contracts with Kindred's own rehabilitation division. (About 75% of the rehab unit's sales come from such contracts.)

The Hospital division includes both freestanding hospitals and "hospitals-within-hospitals," which are co-located with short-term acute care facilities and sometimes receive patients as they are discharged from the host facility. All of Kindred's hospitals care for patients with complex medical conditions: those who are recovering from major surgery, are experiencing multiple organ failure, or have brain or spinal cord injuries, for instance.

Providing high quality care, recruiting qualified medical personnel, and improving operating efficiencies are key to Kindred's strategy across all its divisions. The company also wants to capitalize on marketing opportunities within "cluster markets" where it has multiple facilities.

Additionally, Kindred tries to manage its portfolio of facilities to rid itself of underperforming assets and acquire or build new ones. It announced in 2006 plans to divest 11 unprofitable nursing homes; it sold off nine of them that year. Also in 2006 Kindred acquired the long-term care operations of Commonwealth Communities Holdings, gaining six long-term acute care hospitals and 11 nursing homes in Massachusetts. It has a handful of new hospital facilities under development.

Director Michael Embler is an officer of Franklin Mutual Advisers (FMA), an investment advisory firm that owns about 25% of Kindred; FMA owns warrants that, if exercised, would boost ownership to 36%.

Medicare and Medicaid reimbursements make up nearly 70% of Kindred's revenue.

## HISTORY

After a stint as Kentucky's commerce secretary in the 1980s, Bruce Lunsford was approached by respiratory therapist Michael Barr with the idea of establishing long-term hospitals for ventilator-dependent patients. Barr contended these hospitals would be cheaper to run than full-service facilities, which require additional equipment. Lunsford (who became chairman, president, and CEO) and Barr (who was COO) founded Vencare in 1983 with backing from Gene Smith (a wealthy political associate of Lunsford). They bought a money-losing, 62-bed Indiana hospital and soon turned the operation around.

Vencare expanded into Florida and Texas and, by the end of the 1980s, operated more than 420 beds in seven facilities. Revenues jumped from less than $1 million in 1985 to $54 million by 1989, the year it changed its name to Vencor.

During the early 1990s, Vencor added facilities in Arizona, California, Colorado, Georgia, and Missouri. Vencor ran 29 facilities by the end of 1993, the same year it launched its Vencare respiratory care program.

Vencor acquisitions in 1995 included hospital respiratory and cardiopulmonary departments in seven states. Later that year it bought the much-larger Hillhaven, the US's #2 nursing home operator at that time. (In 1990 Hillhaven had been spun off from what is now Tenet Healthcare.) When Vencor bought it, Hillhaven owned 310 nursing homes, 60 pharmacies, and 23 retirement communities. The buy furthered Lunsford's vision of creating a network of long-term-care facilities and services. Vencor also debuted VenTouch, an electronic-pad-based record keeping system for its facilities, in 1995.

In 1996 Vencor spun off its assisted and independent living properties as Atria Communities; as part of the Hillhaven assimilation, it also consolidated its MediSave pharmacy unit into its hospital operations and sold 34 nursing homes to Lennox Healthcare.

Vencor's 1997 buys included TheraTx (216 rehabilitation centers, 28 nursing centers, 16 occupational health clinics), and Transitional Hospitals (long-term acute care hospitals). That year Vencor formed an alliance with insurer CNA to develop an insurance product for long-term care.

In 1998 the company split into Ventas (real estate) and Vencor (operations). It also sold most of its remaining interest in an assisted living company (now called Atria Senior Quarters) it had spun off in 1996. To attract wealthier residents, it also launched a program in 1998 to turn away — and turn out — Medicaid patients. Vencor soon abandoned the plan amid heated attacks from advocacy groups. (Welcoming back the evictees didn't stop Florida regulators from fining Vencor.) Several other states and the federal government also began probing Vencor's practices; in 1999 the affair prompted Congressional action designed to protect Medicaid patients. Lunsford and Barr were ousted in the turmoil. The government also demanded that Vencor return $90 million in overpayments over 60 months ($2 million a month) or risk losing Medicare payments.

The company filed for Chapter 11 bankruptcy later in 1999. Despite bankruptcy protection, the Justice Department in 2000 filed claims for more than $1 billion from Vencor for Medicare fraud since 1992. In 2001, Vencor settled the majority of these claims. The company emerged from bankruptcy in April 2001 and changed its name to Kindred Healthcare. In 2003 the company sold all of its Texas and Florida nursing center operations. Kindred Healthcare began operating its contract rehabilitation business as a separate division in 2004.

## EXECUTIVES

**Chairman:** Edward L. Kuntz, age 62
**President, CEO, and Director:** Paul J. Diaz, age 45, $847,906 pay
**EVP and CFO:** Richard A. (Rich) Lechleiter, age 49, $398,513 pay
**EVP, CIO, and Chief Administrative Officer:** Richard E. Chapman, age 58, $369,893 pay
**EVP and President, Health Services Division:** Lane M. Bowen, age 56, $927,409 pay
**EVP and President, Hospital Division:** Frank J. Battafarano, age 56, $418,226 pay
**SVP and General Counsel:** M. Suzanne Riedman, age 55
**SVP, Compliance and Government Programs:** William M. Altman, age 47
**SVP, Corporate Development and Financial Planning:** Gregory C. (Greg) Miller, age 36
**SVP, Corporate Legal Affairs and Corporate Secretary:** Joseph L. Landenwich, age 42
**VP, Corporate Communications:** Susan E. Moss
**VP, Finance and Corporate Controller:** John J. Lucchese
**VP, Pharmacy Operations, Pharmacy Services Division:** Bob Weir
**President, Peoplefirst Rehabilitation:** Benjamin A. Breier, age 35
**Auditors:** PricewaterhouseCoopers LLP

## LOCATIONS

**HQ:** Kindred Healthcare, Inc.
680 S. 4th St., Louisville, KY 40202
**Phone:** 502-596-7300 **Fax:** 502-596-4170
**Web:** www.kindredhealthcare.com

### 2006 Nursing Home Locations

| | No. |
|---|---|
| Massachusetts | 42 |
| Indiana | 26 |
| North Carolina | 23 |
| California | 18 |
| Kentucky | 14 |
| Ohio | 14 |
| Wisconsin | 12 |
| Maine | 10 |
| Idaho | 9 |
| Tennessee | 9 |
| Washington | 9 |
| Arizona | 6 |
| Connecticut | 6 |
| Utah | 6 |
| Georgia | 5 |
| Alabama | 4 |
| Colorado | 4 |
| Virginia | 4 |
| Wyoming | 4 |
| New Hampshire | 3 |
| Other states | 14 |
| **Total** | **242** |

### 2006 Hospital Locations

| | No. |
|---|---|
| Texas | 12 |
| California | 11 |
| Florida | 8 |
| Massachusetts | 8 |
| Illinois | 5 |
| Pennsylvania | 5 |
| Arizona | 3 |
| Missouri | 3 |
| Nevada | 3 |
| New Jersey | 3 |
| Ohio | 3 |
| Indiana | 2 |
| Kentucky | 2 |
| Oklahoma | 2 |
| Tennessee | 2 |
| Other states | 9 |
| **Total** | **81** |

## PRODUCTS/OPERATIONS

### 2006 Sales

| | $ mil. | % of total |
|---|---|---|
| Health services division | 1,957.2 | 42 |
| Hospital division | 1,726.8 | 37 |
| Pharmacy division | 652.6 | 14 |
| Rehabilitation division | 300.1 | 7 |
| Adjustments | (370.0) | — |
| **Total** | **4,266.7** | **100** |

### 2006 Sales by Payor

| | $ mil. | % of total |
|---|---|---|
| Medicare | 1,973.3 | 42 |
| Private & other | 1,524.4 | 33 |
| Medicaid | 1,139.0 | 25 |
| Adjustments | (370.0) | — |
| **Total** | **4,266.7** | **100** |

## COMPETITORS

Ascension Health
Catholic Healthcare Partners
Extendicare
Genesis HealthCare
Golden Horizons
HCA
HealthSouth
Life Care Centers
Manor Care
Mariner Health Care
National HealthCare
RehabCare
Select Medical
Sun Healthcare
Tenet Healthcare

## HISTORICAL FINANCIALS

Company Type: Public

**Income Statement** FYE: December 31

| | REVENUE ($ mil.) | NET INCOME ($ mil.) | NET PROFIT MARGIN | EMPLOYEES |
|---|---|---|---|---|
| **12/06** | 4,267 | 79 | 1.8% | 55,000 |
| **12/05** | 3,924 | 145 | 3.7% | 51,600 |
| **12/04** | 3,531 | 71 | 2.0% | 50,700 |
| **12/03** | 3,284 | (75) | — | 50,900 |
| **12/02** | 3,358 | 35 | 1.0% | 53,400 |
| **Annual Growth** | 6.2% | 22.6% | — | 0.7% |

**2006 Year-End Financials**

Debt ratio: 13.1%
Return on equity: 8.4%
Cash ($ mil.): 254
Current ratio: 1.65
Long-term debt ($ mil.): 130
No. of shares (mil.): 40
Dividends
Yield: —
Payout: —
Market value ($ mil.): 799

**Stock History** NYSE: KND

35 30 25 20 15 10 5 0
12/02 12/03 12/04 12/05 12/06

| | STOCK PRICE ($) FY Close | P/E High | P/E Low | PER SHARE ($) Earnings | Dividends | Book Value |
|---|---|---|---|---|---|---|
| **12/06** | 19.98 | 13 | 8 | 1.92 | — | 24.90 |
| **12/05** | 20.38 | 10 | 6 | 3.20 | — | 23.32 |
| **12/04** | 23.70 | 15 | 11 | 1.67 | — | 19.35 |
| **12/03** | 20.57 | — | — | (2.15) | — | 32.89 |
| **12/02** | 7.18 | 21 | 4 | 0.96 | — | 35.79 |
| **Annual Growth** | 29.2% | — | — | 18.9% | — | (8.7%) |

# King Ranch

Meanwhile, back at the ranch . . . the sprawling King Ranch, to be exact. Founded in 1853, King Ranch's operations extend beyond its original 825,000 cattle-raising acres. The ranch is still home to cattle and horses, of course. However, King Ranch oversees considerable farming interests in Texas and Florida (cotton, sorghum, sod, citrus, vegetables, and cane sugar). It also has varied retail operations (hardware, designer saddles and other leather goods, publishing and printing). In addition, King Ranch also beefs up revenues with tourist dollars from birdwatchers, hunters, and sightseers who visit its Texas ranch lands. The descendants of founder Richard King own King Ranch.

Considered the birthplace of the American ranching industry, King Ranch introduced the highly fertile breed of beef cattle: the King Ranch Santa Cruz, which is one-fourth Gelbvieh, one-fourth Red Angus, and one-half Santa Gertrudis. Raising animals isn't the only thing King Ranch cottons to — this sprawl of four noncontiguous ranches is also one of the US's largest cotton producers. In addition to its cattle, King Ranch has about 300 quarter horses. Its quarter horse and thoroughbred programs can be traced back to Richard King and his son-in-law, Robert Kleberg Sr.

The company owns the Kingsville Publishing Company, which offers printing services and publishes several local newspapers, including the *Kingsville Record* and *Bishop News*. It also owns the Robstown Hardware Company.

The company's operations are managed from its Houston corporate headquarters.

## HISTORY

King Ranch was founded in 1853 by former steamboat captain Richard King and his wife Henrietta, the daughter of a Brownsville, Texas, missionary. On the advice of his friend Robert E. Lee, King used his steamboating profits and occasional strong-arm tactics to buy land — miles of flat, brush-filled, coastal plain and desert south of Corpus Christi, Texas, valued at pennies an acre.

The next year King relocated the residents of an entire drought-ravaged village to the ranch and employed them as ranch hands, known ever after as *kineños* ("King's men"). The Kings built their homestead in 1858 at a site recommended by Lee.

King Ranch endured attacks from Union guerrillas during the Civil War and Mexican bandits after the war. Times were tough, but King was up to the challenge, always traveling armed and with outriders.

In 1867 the ranch used its famed Running W brand for the first time. After King's death in 1885, Robert Kleberg, who married King's daughter Alice, managed the 1.2 million-acre ranch for his mother-in-law. Henrietta died in 1925 and left three-fourths of the ranch to Alice. Before Robert's death in 1932, control of the ranch passed to sons Richard and Bob. In 1933 Bob negotiated an exclusive oil and gas lease with Houston-based Humble Oil, which later became part of Exxon.

While Richard served in Congress, Bob ran the ranch. He developed the Santa Gertrudis, the first breed of cattle ever created in the US, by crossing British shorthorn cattle with Indian Brahmas. The new breed was better suited to the hot, dry South Texas climate.

Bob made King Ranch a leading breeder of quarter horses, which worked cattle, and Thoroughbreds, which he raced. He bought Kentucky Derby winner Bold Venture in 1936 and a Kentucky breeding farm in 1946; that year a King Ranch horse, Assault, won racing's Triple Crown.

When Bob died in 1974, the family asked James Clement, husband of one of the founders' great-granddaughters, to become CEO and bypassed Robert Shelton, a King relative and orphan whom Bob had raised as his own son. Shelton severed ties with the ranch in 1977 over a lawsuit he filed against Exxon, and partially won, alleging underpayment of royalties.

Under Clement, King Ranch became a multinational corporation. In 1980 it formed King Ranch Oil and Gas (also called King Ranch Energy) to explore for and produce oil and gas in five states and the Gulf of Mexico. In 1988 Clement retired, and Kimberly-Clark executive Darwin Smith became the first CEO not related to the founders. Smith left after one year, and the reins passed to petroleum geologist Roger Jarvis and then to Jack Hunt in 1995.

With the help of scientists, in the early 1990s the company developed a leaner, more fertile Santa Gertrudis called the Santa Cruz.

In 1998 Stephen "Tio" Kleberg, the only King descendant still actively working the ranch, was pushed from the saddle of daily operations to a seat on the board. King Ranch sold its Kentucky horse farm in 1998 and teamed up with Collier Enterprises that year to purchase citrus grower Turner Foods from utility holding company FPL Group. In 2000 King Ranch sold King Ranch Energy to St. Mary Land and Exploration Co. for $60 million.

Like a good western movie, some things ride into the sunset at King Ranch. The company sold its 670-acre Kentucky Thoroughbred breeding and racing farm, most of its foreign ranches, and its primary oil and gas subsidiary.

## EXECUTIVES

**Chairman:** James H. Clement Jr.
**President and CEO:** Jack Hunt, age 61
**CFO:** Bill Gardiner
**VP Audit:** Richard Nilles
**VP Livestock and Ranch Operations:** Paul Genho
**Secretary and General Counsel:** Frank Perrone
**Director Human Resources:** Martha McGee
**Director Security and Wildlife:** Butch Thompson
**VP Farming Operations:** Robert J. Underbrink

## LOCATIONS

**HQ:** King Ranch, Inc.
3 River Way, Ste. 1600, Houston, TX 77056
**Phone:** 832-681-5700 **Fax:** 832-681-5759
**Web:** www.king-ranch.com

King Ranch operates ranching and farming interests in South Texas, as well as in Florida.

**Selected Operations**

Florida
- 3,100 acres (St. Augustine sod)
- 12,000 acres (sugar cane)
- 40,000 acres (orange and grapefruit groves)

Texas
- 60,000 acres (cotton and grain)
- 825,000 acres (cattle)

## PRODUCTS/OPERATIONS

**Selected Operations**

Caesar Kleberg Wildlife Research Institute
Consolidated Citrus L.P.
Kingsville Publishing
Robstown Hardware Company
King Ranch — Florida
King Ranch — Texas
King Ranch Institute of Ranch Management
King Ranch Museum
King Ranch Nature Tour Program
King Ranch Saddle Shop

## COMPETITORS

A. Duda & Sons
Ace Hardware
Alico
AzTx Cattle
Bartlett and Company
Cactus Feeders
Chiquita Brands
Coleman Natural Foods
ContiGroup
Dakota
Dole Food
Home Depot
Laura's Lean Beef
Lowe's
Lykes Bros.
M A Patout
Maverick Ranch
Niman Ranch
Organic Valley
Pederson's
SMBSC
Southern States
Sugar Cane Growers
Sugar Cane Growers Cooperative of Florida
Sun Growers
Sun-Maid
Tejon Ranch

## HISTORICAL FINANCIALS

Company Type: Private

**Income Statement** FYE: December 31

| | ESTIMATED REVENUE ($ mil.) | NET INCOME ($ mil.) | NET PROFIT MARGIN | EMPLOYEES |
|---|---|---|---|---|
| 12/06 | 34 | — | — | 683 |

# KKR & Co.

Have the barbarians at the gate become civilized? KKR (formerly Kohlberg Kravis Roberts), the master of the leveraged buyout, has shed its old name and is going public in a $1.25 billion IPO. The company long ago updated its hostile takeover image for a kinder, gentler, buy-and-build strategy. The firm assembles funds from institutional and wealthy investors and profits from management fees and its direct interests. An active investor, it often supervises or installs new management and revamps strategy and corporate structure, selling underperforming units or adding new ones. KKR has some $53 billion in assets under management.

After the IPO, an as-yet-to-be-determined stake in the company will be owned by current and former KKR insiders through a holding company.

KKR intends to use the proceeds from the IPO to fund new business, capitalize on its research, reduce its reliance on third-party capital, and expand through the acquisition of other equity firms.

The company is no stranger to the public equity process. In 2005 it took its real estate investment trust (REIT) unit, KKR Financial, public. The next year it raised some $5 billion by listing its KKR Private Equity Investors fund on the Euronext stock market, a strategy that is gaining popularity among private equity firms.

The IPO is not the only big deal around for KKR. Along with TPG, the company is leading an investor group that is buying Dallas-based utility TXU in one of the largest private equity buyouts ever. The $45 billion dollar price tag, which includes the assumption of TXU's debt, dwarfs the approximately $30 billion that KKR paid in its legendary 1988 takeover of RJR Nabisco, which remained the largest-ever deal for more than a decade.

In another huge buyout, KKR is teaming up with Bain Capital and Merrill Lynch Global Private Equity to buy hospital operator HCA for about $33 billion. Acting alone, the company announced it will purchase credit card payment processor First Data for some $29 billion.

## HISTORY

In 1976 Jerome Kohlberg left investment bank Bear Stearns to form his own leveraged buyout firm; with him he brought protégé Henry Kravis and Kravis' cousin George Roberts. They formed Kohlberg Kravis Roberts & Co. (KKR).

Kohlberg believed LBOs, by giving management ownership stakes in their companies, would yield better results. KKR orchestrated friendly buyouts funded by investor groups and debt. The firm's first buyout was machine-toolmaker Houdaille Industries in 1979.

KKR lost money on its 1981 investment in the American Forest Products division of Bendix. But by 1984 the firm had raised its fourth fund and made its first $1 billion buyout: Wometco Enterprises.

The next year KKR turned mean with a hostile takeover of Beatrice. The deal depended on junk bond financing devised by Drexel Burnham Lambert's Michael Milken and on the sale of pieces of the company. KKR funded the buyouts of Safeway Stores and Owens-Illinois (1986), Jim Walter Homes (1987), and Stop & Shop (1988, sold in 1996).

Unhappy with the firm's hostile image, Kohlberg left in 1987 to form Kohlberg & Co. His suit against KKR over the alleged undervaluing of companies in relation to his departure settlement was resolved for an undisclosed amount.

The Beatrice LBO triggered a rash of similar transactions as the financial industry sought fat fees. The frenzy culminated in 1988 with the $31 billion RJR Nabisco buyout, which brought KKR $75 million in fees.

In 1991 KKR joined with FleetBoston to buy Bank of New England. The next year it picked up 47% of what was then Advantica Restaurant Group (now just plain Denny's). It sold that holding in 1997. In 1994 KKR freed itself from the RJR morass by swapping its investment in RJR for troubled food company Borden.

In the latter half of the decade, KKR reaped mixed results on its investments, including what is now Spalding Holdings (sporting goods and Evenflo baby products), supermarket chain Bruno's, and KinderCare Learning Centers. The $600 million that KKR had invested in magazine group K-III (now PRIMEDIA) between 1990 and 1994 didn't do anything to revive interest in the stock, and Bruno's filed for bankruptcy in 1998. Disgruntled investors complained about low returns, and in 1996 KKR booted activist mega-fund CalPERS from its investor ranks.

In 1998 KKR's niche buying continued when it joined with HM Capital (then known as Hicks, Muse, Tate & Furst) to buy Regal Cinemas, which it combined with Act III to form the biggest theater chain in the US. The chain's expansion left it on the brink of bankruptcy, and investor Philip Anschutz bought a chunk of its debt and possible control of the company in 2001.

The next year KKR departed from course and unveiled online mortgage lender Nexstar Financial, its first company built from the ground up.

Focused on Europe, in 2000 the firm claimed the telecommunications business of Robert Bosch (now Tenovis, and sold to Avaya in 2004), UK private equity fund Wassall PLC, and Siemens' banking systems unit. The next year it bought the specialty chemicals and pigments operations of Laporte plc to create Rockwood Specialties.

Also in 2000, KKR joined with Internet VC firm Accel Partners to form Accel KKR to invest in companies that combine traditional business and Internet assets. It lost its place as the top fund-raiser to Thomas H. Lee, which closed a record-setting $6.1 billion fund in early 2001. Kohlberg acquired major divisions from Laporte for about $1.2 billion in that same year.

After a failed attempt to take Borden Chemical public in 2004, KKR sold the firm to private equity group Apollo Management. KKR acquired Masonite International, a profitable Canadian building products company in 2005 for about $2.7 billion. Meanwhile, in Europe, it acquired German recycler Duales System Deutschland GmbH. KKR also teamed with Permira Advisers Limited to acquire SBS Broadcasting.

A slew of high-dollar, high-profile deals characterized 2005. KKR, Bain Capital, and Vornado Realty Trust acquired Toys "R" Us, the #2 US toy retailer. KKR also joined with a group of seven private investment companies (led by Silver Lake Partners) to acquire SunGard Data Systems for $11.3 billion. KKR again teamed with Silver Lake Partners to buy Agilent Technologies' chip business (now operating as Avago Technologies). KKR bought medical device maker Accellent and Canadian building products company Masonite International, as well.

## EXECUTIVES

**Co-Chairman and Co-CEO:** Henry R. Kravis, age 63
**Co-Chairman and Co-CEO:** George R. Roberts, age 63
**CFO:** William J. Janetschek, age 45
**Auditors:** Deloitte & Touche LLP

## LOCATIONS

**HQ:** KKR & Co. L.P.
9 W. 57th St., Ste. 4200, New York, NY 10019
**Phone:** 212-750-8300 **Fax:** 212-750-0003
**Web:** www.kkr.com

## PRODUCTS/OPERATIONS

**Selected Investments**

Accellent Inc.
Accuride Corporation
Alea Group Holdings (Bermuda) Ltd.
Alliance Imaging, Inc.
Auto-Teile-Unger Holding AG
Avago Technologies
The Boyds Collection, Ltd.
Bristol West Holdings, Inc.
Broadnet Mediascape Communications AG
Capmark Financial
Demag Holding
- Argillon
- Demag Cranes and Components
- Gottwald Port Technology
- Mannesman Plastics Machines

Duales System Deutschland GmbH
FL Selenia
Flextronics Software Systems
HCA
Jazz Pharmaceuticals, Inc.
KSL Holdings
Legrand Holding SA
Masonite International Inc.
MedCath Corporation
MTU Aero Engines GmbH
NuVox Communications (formerly NewSouth Holdings, Inc.)
NXP
PRIMEDIA Inc.
ProSiebenSat1. Media AG
Rockwood Holdings, Inc.
Royal Vendex KBB
SBS Broadcasting S.a.r.l.
Sealy Corporation
SunGard Data Systems Inc.
Toys "R" Us, Inc.
Visant Corporation
- ARCADE Marketing
- Jostens

Zohne Technologies, Inc.
Zumtobel AG

## COMPETITORS

AEA Holdings
American Financial
Apollo Advisors
Bear Stearns
Berkshire Hathaway
Blackstone Group
The Carlyle Group
CD&R
Citigroup Global Markets
CVC Capital Partners
Equity Group Investments
Forstmann Little
Goldman Sachs
Haas Wheat
Heico Companies
Hellman & Friedman
HM Capital Partners
Interlaken Investment
Investcorp
Jordan Company
Lehman Brothers
Leonard Green
MacAndrews & Forbes
Merrill Lynch
Silver Lake Partners
Thomas H. Lee Partners
TPG
Veronis Suhler Stevenson
Vestar Capital Partners
Wingate Partners

## HISTORICAL FINANCIALS

Company Type: Private

**Income Statement** FYE: December 31

| | REVENUE ($ mil.) | NET INCOME ($ mil.) | NET PROFIT MARGIN | EMPLOYEES |
|---|---|---|---|---|
| **12/06** | 4,411 | 1,113 | 25.2% | 399 |
| **12/05** | 3,974 | 942 | 23.7% | — |
| **12/04** | 3,278 | 773 | 23.6% | — |
| **Annual Growth** | 16.0% | 19.9% | — | — |

**2006 Year-End Financials**

Debt ratio: 4.7%
Return on equity: 7.0%
Cash ($ mil.): —
Current ratio: —
Long-term debt ($ mil.): 949

**Net Income History**

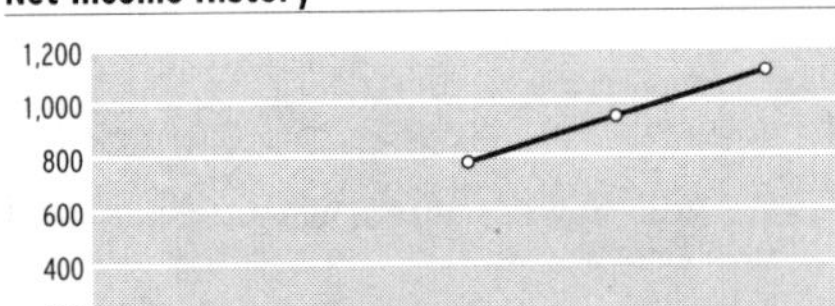


# KLA-Tencor

KLA-Tencor is hard-core when it comes to hunting down flaws in chips. The company — one of the world's largest makers of semiconductor equipment — offers yield management systems that monitor and analyze wafers at various stages of chip production, inspecting reticles (which make circuit patterns) and measuring crucial microscopic layers. The systems' feedback allows flaws to be corrected before they can ruin the costly wafers. KLA-Tencor has long dominated the market for equipment that inspects semiconductor photomasks and reticles. The company gets more than three-quarters of its sales from outside the US, and uses selective acquisitions as well as intensive R&D to keep up with advances in chip fabrication.

The company's software includes products for factorywide yield management and for test floor automation and control. KLA-Tencor's systems are used by most of the world's major semiconductor makers, as well as by silicon wafer and data storage product manufacturers.

KLA-Tencor is the undisputed leader in its niche; it tries to position itself as a one-stop shop for its customers' yield management needs, particularly by complementing its technology offerings with consulting services.

Broadening its portfolio of semiconductor metrology tools, KLA-Tencor has acquired competitor Therma-Wave for around $75 million in cash. The transaction was expected to close in the first quarter of 2007. German regulators, however, extended their review of the proposed merger before finally granting their approval in May 2007. The transaction closed soon after that regulatory hurdle was cleared.

Entities affiliated with The Capital Group Companies own about 36% of KLA-Tencor. FMR (Fidelity Investments) holds around 7% of the company.

## HISTORY

In the semiconductor industry's early years, chip defects rendered about half of some product runs unusable. Silicon Valley entrepreneurs Kenneth Levy — who helped develop image processing equipment pioneer Computervision (later merged into Parametric Technology) — and Robert Anderson founded KLA Instruments in 1975. ("KLA" originally stood for Kenneth Levy Associates.) Their goal was to develop inspection equipment to improve semiconductor factory yields. In 1978 KLA introduced a first-of-its-kind inspection system that employed advanced optical and image processing technology to test the templates used to etch circuit designs onto silicon wafers. It cut inspection time from eight hours to about 15 minutes.

KLA went public in 1980; within two years it had introduced wafer inspection and wafer metrology systems. As chip yields jumped, so did KLA's sales, shooting past $60 million by mid-decade. When increased competition left US demand faltering, Levy began targeting markets in Europe and Asia. By 1987, 40% of KLA's sales came from those two regions.

Levy named former Hewlett-Packard executive Kenneth Schroeder president in 1991 (Schroeder would later become CEO) to take more day-to-day control of the company. (Anderson by then had given up his executive duties; he retired in 1994.) Also in 1994 KLA bought Metrologix, a maker of advanced electron beam measurement equipment. In 1995 KLA launched an electron beam-based system that doubled wafer production yields.

Seeking an edge in an increasingly splintered market, the company merged with Tencor Instruments (and changed its name to KLA-Tencor) in 1997. The $1.3 billion deal created a company with the broadest line of wafer inspection equipment, film measurement systems, and yield management software in the industry.

Czechoslovakian Karel Urbanek had started Tencor in 1976 to make semiconductor measurement and test instruments. Tencor's first product was the Alpha-Step, a film layer profiler, but the company became known for a system that detected and analyzed wafer defects measuring as small as 1/100,000th the width of a human hair. Tencor went public in 1993.

Following the merger, Levy gave up his CEO duties (he remained chairman) to top Tencor executive Jon Tompkins. The two switched titles in 1998 to better reflect their strengths.

Tompkins retired as chairman in 1999 but remained on the board. Levy resumed the chairmanship, and Schroeder became CEO. That year KLA-Tencor bought Taiwan-based ACME Systems (engineering analysis software). In 2000 KLA-Tencor bought FINLE Technologies, another maker of yield management software.

Aiming to expand outside the bounds of the semiconductor equipment industry, KLA-Tencor purchased Candela Instruments, which made inspection gear used in the production of data storage equipment, in 2004.

KLA-Tencor in early 2005 made a bid to purchase August Technology, a supplier of semiconductor inspection and metrology systems. Rival Rudolph Technologies, however, closed the deal with August in mid-2005. Perhaps as a consolation prize, KLA-Tencor in 2006 acquired competitor ADE Corporation in a transaction valued at approximately $474 million.

Kenneth Schroeder retired as CEO at the end of 2005 and became a special advisor to the company. His successor, COO Richard Wallace, had joined KLA in 1988.

Following a special board committee's review of historical practices in granting stock options, co-founder Ken Levy retired from the board in late 2006 and was named chairman emeritus. Edward Barnholt, a director since 1995 and the former CEO of Agilent Technologies, was named non-executive chairman to succeed Levy. The company repriced all outstanding retroactively priced stock options held by Levy and other executives following the probe, which resulted in KLA-Tencor restating financial results from mid-1997 to mid-2002 and taking a non-cash charge of $370 million.

KLA-Tencor also "terminated all aspects of its employment relationship" with former CEO Kenneth Schroeder after the conclusion of the options probe and canceled all options held by Schroeder. Stuart Nichols, the company's general counsel for six years, resigned his post. Other top executives were exonerated of wrongdoing by the board committee.

KLA-Tencor put an end to the stock-options mess in mid-2007, reaching a settlement with the SEC but didn't pay any fine, penalty, or monetary damages to settle the case.

Kenneth Schroeder didn't get off as easy, however; the SEC charged him with fraud, accusing the former CEO of backdating more than $200 million worth of stock options.

## EXECUTIVES

**Chairman:** Edward W. (Ned) Barnholt, age 63
**CEO and Director:** Richard P. (Rick) Wallace, age 46, $1,741,123 pay
**President and COO:** John H. Kispert, age 43, $1,408,357 pay
**SVP and CFO:** Jeffrey L. Hall, age 39, $611,939 pay
**Group VP, Parametric Solutions Group; President, KLA-Tencor (Israel):** Avi Cohen, age 53, $765,607 pay
**EVP and CTO:** Benjamin B.M. Tsai, age 48
**EVP and Interim General Counsel:** Lawrence A. Gross, age 54
**Senior Director, Corporate Communications:** Kyra Whitten
**Manager, Investor Relations:** Chris Brocoum
**SVP and Chief Administrative Officer:** Jorge L. Titinger, age 45
**SVP, General Counsel, and Secretary:** Brian M. Martin, age 45
**Auditors:** PricewaterhouseCoopers LLP

## LOCATIONS

**HQ:** KLA-Tencor Corporation
160 Rio Robles, San Jose, CA 95134
**Phone:** 408-875-3000 **Fax:** 408-875-4144
**Web:** www.kla-tencor.com

KLA-Tencor has manufacturing facilities in Israel and the US. It also has offices in China, France, Germany, India, Italy, Japan, Malaysia, Singapore, South Korea, Taiwan, the UK, and the US.

### 2007 Sales

| | $ mil. | % of total |
|---|---|---|
| Asia/Pacific | | |
| Japan | 600.9 | 22 |
| Taiwan | 559.1 | 20 |
| South Korea | 288.7 | 11 |
| Other countries | 362.9 | 13 |
| US | 647.8 | 24 |
| Europe & Israel | 271.8 | 10 |
| **Total** | **2,731.2** | **100** |

## PRODUCTS/OPERATIONS

### 2007 Sales

| | % of total |
|---|---|
| Defect inspection | 61 |
| Metrology | 19 |
| Services | 15 |
| Software & other | 5 |
| **Total** | **100** |

### Selected Products

Metrology systems
- Critical dimension scanning electron microscopes (SEMs)
- Film and film stress measurement
- Optical overlay measurement
- Surface profiling

Reticle (circuit pattern mask) inspection systems

Wafer inspection systems
- Automated defect classification
- Defect analysis software
- In-line monitoring
- Optical and SEM defect review
- Process tool performance monitoring

Yield management software
- Factorywide yield management software
- Test floor automation/control software

## COMPETITORS

Applied Materials
Carl Zeiss
Cascade Microtech
Cognex
Dainippon Screen
Electroglas
FEI
Hitachi High-Technologies
ICOS Vision Systems
Keithley Instruments
Nanometrics
Nova Measuring
Orbotech
PDF Solutions
Rudolph Technologies
Veeco Instruments
Zygo

## HISTORICAL FINANCIALS

Company Type: Public

### Income Statement

FYE: June 30

| | REVENUE ($ mil.) | NET INCOME ($ mil.) | NET PROFIT MARGIN | EMPLOYEES |
|---|---|---|---|---|
| **6/07** | 2,731 | 528 | 19.3% | 6,000 |
| **6/06** | 2,071 | 381 | 18.4% | 5,900 |
| **6/05** | 2,085 | 467 | 22.4% | 5,500 |
| **6/04** | 1,497 | 244 | 16.3% | 5,200 |
| **6/03** | 1,323 | 137 | 10.4% | 4,900 |
| **Annual Growth** | 19.9% | 40.1% | — | 5.2% |

### 2007 Year-End Financials

| | |
|---|---|
| Debt ratio: — | No. of shares (mil.): 191 |
| Return on equity: 14.8% | Dividends |
| Cash ($ mil.): 1,711 | Yield: 0.9% |
| Current ratio: 3.03 | Payout: 18.4% |
| Long-term debt ($ mil.): — | Market value ($ mil.): 10,515 |

### Stock History

NASDAQ (GS): KLAC

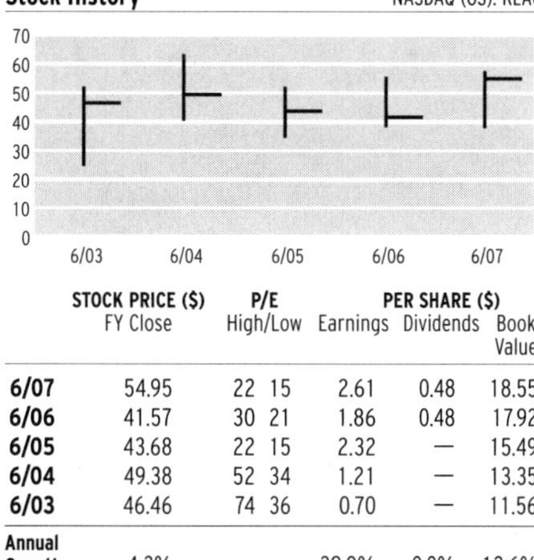


| | STOCK PRICE ($) FY Close | P/E High | P/E Low | PER SHARE ($) Earnings | Dividends | Book Value |
|---|---|---|---|---|---|---|
| **6/07** | 54.95 | 22 | 15 | 2.61 | 0.48 | 18.55 |
| **6/06** | 41.57 | 30 | 21 | 1.86 | 0.48 | 17.92 |
| **6/05** | 43.68 | 22 | 15 | 2.32 | — | 15.49 |
| **6/04** | 49.38 | 52 | 34 | 1.21 | — | 13.35 |
| **6/03** | 46.46 | 74 | 36 | 0.70 | — | 11.56 |
| **Annual Growth** | 4.3% | — | — | 39.0% | 0.0% | 12.6% |

# Kmart Corporation

Attention Kmart shoppers: Kmart is the #3 discount retailer in the US, behind Wal-Mart and Target. It sells name-brand and private-label goods (including its Martha Stewart label), mostly to low- and mid-income families. It runs nearly 1,400 off-mall stores (including 55 Supercenters) in 49 US states, Puerto Rico, Guam, and the US Virgin Islands. About 1,100 Kmart stores contain in-store pharmacies. The company also operates the kmart.com Web site. Dismal sales and the erosion of supplier confidence led Kmart to file for Chapter 11 bankruptcy in 2002. (It emerged from Chapter 11 in 2003.) Kmart then bought and merged with Sears, Roebuck in 2005 to form both chains' parent company, Sears Holdings.

In a bid to move its Sears chain out of the mall environment, Sears Holdings wasted no time converting about 400 of Kmart's stand-alone stores to Sears outlets. Most recently, about a dozen Kmart stores have been converted to Sears Grand outlets. Sears is also taking advantage of cross-selling opportunities by offering proprietary Sears brands, including Craftsman, Diehard, and Kenmore products, in Kmart stores. The sale of Kenmore brand appliances should help Kmart differentiate itself from its larger rivals Wal-Mart and Target, which stock a more limited range of appliances. To date, about 180 Kmart stores have been remodeled to offer Sears brand appliances.

Kmart continues to offer the Martha Stewart Everyday line, as well as Joe Boxer and Jaclyn Smith brand clothing. The retailer also has a deal with Mexican superstar Thalia to carry her line of women's clothing and accessories in some 335 Kmart stores. Martha Stewart Living Omnimedia recently launched its first collection of ready-to-assemble furniture — called Everyday Rooms — in Kmart stores.

Parent company, Sears Holdings, is the third-largest retailer in the US with about $55 billion in annual sales. Following the megamerger, the combined company operated about 3,770 full-line and specialty stores in the US and Canada (Sears Canada). Edward Lampert, who was the largest shareholder in both Kmart and Sears, became chairman of Sears Holdings and owns about 42% of that company through ESL Investments.

## HISTORY

Sebastian Kresge and John McCrorey opened five-and-dime stores in Memphis and Detroit in 1897. When the partners split two years later, Kresge got Detroit and McCrorey took Memphis. By the time Kresge incorporated as S. S. Kresge Company in 1912, it had become the second-largest dime store chain in the US, with 85 stores. Kresge expanded rapidly in the next several decades, forming S. S. Kresge, Ltd., in 1929 to operate stores in Canada. In the late 1920s and 1930s, the company opened stores in suburban shopping centers. By the 1950s Kresge was one of the largest general merchandise retailers in the US.

A marketing study prompted management to enter discount retailing in 1958, and three unprofitable locations were transformed into Jupiter Discount stores in 1961. The company judged this a success and opened the first Kmart discount store in Detroit in 1962; by 1966 the company had more than 160 Kmart stores. Kresge formed a joint venture with G. J. Coles & Coy (later Coles Myer) to operate Kmart stores in Australia (1968; sold in 1994). The company expanded the Kmart format swiftly in the 1970s, opening more than 270 stores in 1976 alone. With about 95% of its sales coming from Kmart stores, the company changed its name to Kmart in 1977.

Kmart diversified during the 1980s and early 1990s, adding various retailers, including Walden Book Company, then the #1 US bookstore chain, and Builders Square (formerly Home Centers of America) in 1984; PayLess Drug Stores Northwest in 1985; PACE Membership Warehouse in 1989; The Sports Authority in 1990; a 90% stake in OfficeMax by 1991; and the Borders bookstore chain in 1992.

Meanwhile, in 1987 the company sold most of its remaining Kresge and Jupiter locations in the US to McCrory's, the chain started by Kresge's former partner.

In 1994 and 1995, amid falling earnings, the company began shedding operations, spinning off or selling OfficeMax, The Sports Authority, PACE, its US automotive service centers (to Penske, which still runs them), and Borders. In 1995 CEO Joseph Antonini — architect of the diversification strategy — was replaced by Floyd Hall. More than 200 US stores were closed.

The company then sold Kmart Mexico, a joint venture with El Puerto de Liverpool, and an 87.5% stake in Kmart Canada in 1997 (it sold the rest in 1998). The company also sold woebegone 162-store Builders Square to Leonard Green & Partners (owners of the Hechinger chain) for a mere $10 million, but retained a $761 million liability for the stores' lease obligations. (Hechinger filed for bankruptcy in 1999, and Kmart assumed the obligations of 115 stores.)

In May 2000 Hall was replaced by former CVS president and COO Charles Conaway. In July 2001 Kmart said it would close 72 stores (in about 30 states) in locations that did not fit with expansion plans.

In a management shakeup that followed downgrades in Kmart's credit rating in 2002, director James Adamson replaced Conaway as chairman. Soon after, key vendors suspended shipments to the troubled discounter saying Kmart failed to make regular weekly payments. Kmart filed for Chapter 11 bankruptcy protection that month. Soon after, Adamson was also named CEO. After filing for bankruptcy Kmart closed 283 stores, resulting in 22,000 job losses. Nearly a year after filing for bankruptcy, Kmart's shares were delisted in December after 84 years on the New York Stock Exchange.

In January 2003 Adamson was succeeded as CEO by COO Julian Day. Later in the month Kmart won final approval from the bankruptcy court to close another 316 stores and proceed with a $2 billion exit financing package. In May 2003, 15 months after filing Chapter 11, Kmart emerged from bankruptcy protection with the help of its largest shareholder, ESL Investments.

Aylwin Lewis, a 13-year veteran of YUM! Brands, succeeded Day as CEO of Kmart Holding Corp. in October 2004. In August 2005 two former Kmart executives (Conaway and ex-CFO John McDonald) were accused by the Securities and Exchange Commission of misleading investors about the company's finances prior to its 2002 bankruptcy filing.

The company settled a class-action lawsuit regarding disabled-shopper access for $13 million in 2006.

## EXECUTIVES

**CEO, Kmart Retail:** Aylwin B. Lewis, age 52
**EVP, Interim CFO, Chief Administrative Officer, and Director; Chairman, Sears Canada:** William C. Crowley, age 49
**SVP, Kmart Retail:** Donald J. Germano
**SVP, Kmart Apparel:** Irving (Irv) Neger, age 53
**SVP and Chief Marketing Officer:** Bill Stewart
**SVP and Chief Legal Officer:** William R. Harker, age 34
**Merchandising Officer; SVP, Sears Holdings Corporation:** Peter J. Whitsett, age 41
**Divisional VP, Geo-Demographic Merchandising:** Tom Downs
**District Manager, New York City and Long Island:** Mike Lorbino
**Auditors:** Deloitte & Touche LLP

## LOCATIONS

**HQ:** Kmart Corporation
3333 Beverly Rd., Hoffman Estates, IL 60179
**Phone:** 847-286-2500 **Fax:** 847-286-5500
**Web:** www.kmartcorp.com

Kmart operates nearly 1,400 retail stores in 49 US states, Puerto Rico, the US Virgin Islands, and Guam.

## PRODUCTS/OPERATIONS

### 2007 Stores

| | No. |
|---|---|
| Kmart discount stores | 1,333 |
| Kmart Supercenters | 55 |
| **Total** | **1,388** |

### Selected Private Labels

Craftsman (tools)
DieHard (car batteries)
Jaclyn Smith (ladies' apparel)
Joe Boxer (men's and women's apparel)
Kenmore (appliances)
Martha Stewart Everyday (home fashions, kitchenware)
Route 66 (casual wear and shoes)

### Retail Divisions

Kmart discount store (general merchandise/small grocery section)
Kmart Supercenter (general merchandise/supermarkets)

## COMPETITORS

Bed Bath & Beyond
Best Buy
Big Lots
BJ's Wholesale Club
Circuit City
Costco Wholesale
CVS/Caremark
Dollar General
Family Dollar Stores
J. C. Penney
Kohl's
Kroger
Linens 'n Things
Office Depot
PETCO
Retail Ventures
Rite Aid
Ross Stores
ShopKo Stores
Staples
Target
TJX Companies
Toys "R" Us
Walgreen
Wal-Mart

## HISTORICAL FINANCIALS

Company Type: Subsidiary

### Income Statement

FYE: Last Wednesday in January

| | REVENUE ($ mil.) | NET INCOME ($ mil.) | NET PROFIT MARGIN | EMPLOYEES |
|---|---|---|---|---|
| **1/07** | 18,647 | — | — | — |
| **1/06** | 19,094 | — | — | — |
| **1/05** | 19,701 | — | — | 133,000 |
| **1/04** | 23,253 | — | — | 158,000 |
| **1/03** | 30,762 | — | — | 212,000 |
| **Annual Growth** | (11.8%) | — | — | (20.8%) |

### Revenue History

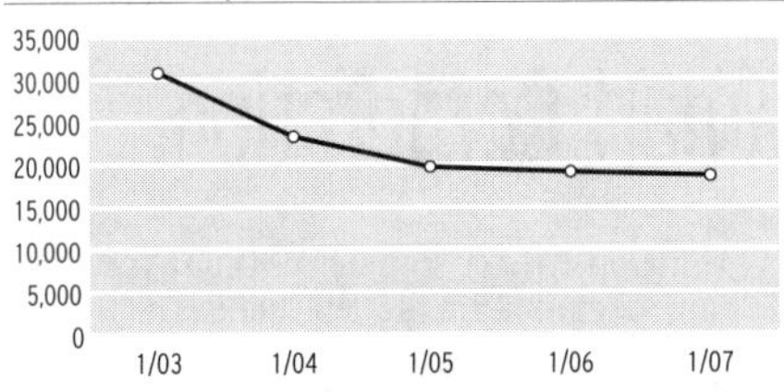


# Koch Industries

Now that is has completed the purchase of forest products giant Georgia-Pacific (for a reported $21 billion), Koch Industries has become a real paper tiger. Koch (pronounced "coke") is one of the largest private companies in the US. Koch Industries' operations include refining and chemicals, process equipment, and technologies; fibers and polymers; commodity and financial trading; and forest and consumer products. Its Flint Hills Resources subsidiary owns three refineries that process 800,000 barrels of crude oil daily. Koch operates crude gathering systems and pipelines across North America as well as cattle ranches in Kansas, Montana, and Texas. Brothers Charles and David Koch control the company.

Koch's numerous subsidiary companies leverage capabilities such as its proprietary Market Based Management system; innovation; and a high level of operational, trading, transaction, and public sector skills to create long-term value for customers.

## HISTORY

Fred Koch grew up poor in Texas and worked his way through MIT. In 1928 Koch developed a process to refine more gasoline from crude oil, but when he tried to market his invention, the major oil companies sued him for patent infringement. Koch eventually won the lawsuits (after 15 years in court), but the controversy made it tough to attract many US customers. In 1929 Koch took his process to the Soviet Union, but he grew disenchanted with Stalinism and returned home to become a founding member of the anticommunist John Birch Society.

Koch launched Wood River Oil & Refining in Illinois (1940) and bought the Rock Island refinery in Oklahoma (1947). He folded the remaining purchasing and gathering network into Rock Island Oil & Refining (though he later sold the refineries).

After Koch's death in 1967, his 32-year-old son Charles took the helm and renamed the company Koch Industries. He began a series of acquisitions, adding petrochemical and oil trading service operations.

During the 1980s Koch was thrust into various arenas, legal and political. Charles' brother David, also a Koch Industries executive, ran for US vice president on the Libertarian ticket in 1980. That year the other two Koch brothers, Frederick and William (David's fraternal twin), launched a takeover attempt, but Charles retained control, and William was fired from his job as VP.

In a 1983 settlement Charles and David bought out the dissident family members for just over $1 billion. William and Frederick continued to challenge their brothers in court, claiming they had been shortchanged in the deal (the two estranged brothers eventually lost their case in 1998, and their appeals were rejected in 2000).

Despite this legal wrangling, Koch Industries continued to expand, purchasing a Corpus Christi, Texas, refinery in 1981. It expanded its pipeline system, buying Bigheart Pipe Line in Oklahoma (1986) and two systems from Santa Fe Southern Pacific (1988).

In 1991 Koch purchased the Corpus Christi marine terminal, pipelines, and gathering systems of Scurlock Permian (a unit of Ashland Oil). In 1992 the company bought United Gas Pipe Line (renamed Koch Gateway Pipeline) and its pipeline system extending from Texas to Florida.

To strengthen its engineering services presence worldwide, Koch acquired Glitsch International (a maker of separation equipment) from engineering giant Foster Wheeler in 1997. It also acquired USX-Delhi Group, a natural gas processor and transporter.

In 1998 Koch bought Purina Mills, the largest US producer of animal feed, and formed the KoSa joint venture with Mexico's Saba family to buy Hoechst's Trevira polyester unit. (Koch acquired the Saba family's stake in KoSa in 2001.) Lethargic energy and livestock prices in 1998 and 1999, however, led Koch to lay off several hundred employees, sell its feedlots, and divest portions of its natural gas gathering and pipeline systems. Purina Mills filed for bankruptcy protection in 1999 (later, it emerged from bankruptcy and held an IPO in 2000, and was acquired by #2 US dairy co-op Land O'Lakes in 2001).

William Koch sued Koch Industries in 1990, claiming the company had underreported the amount of oil purchased on US government and Native Americans lands. A jury found for William, but he, Charles, and David agreed to settle the case in 2001 — and sat down to dinner together for the first time in 20 years.

In other legal matters, in 2000 Koch agreed to pay a $30 million civil fine and contribute $5 million toward environmental projects to settle complaints over oil spills from its pipelines in the

1990s. The company agreed to pay $20 million in 2001 to settle a separate environmental case concerning a Texas refinery.

The company acquired INVISTA in 2004 for $4.2 billion and merged it with its KoSa unit. In 2005 SemGroup acquired all of Koch Materials Company's US and Mexico asphalt operations and ONEOK, Inc. acquired the natural gas liquids businesses owned by several Koch companies.

In 2005, a Koch subsidiary completed the $21 billion acquisition of Georgia-Pacific.

## EXECUTIVES

**Chairman and CEO:** Charles G. Koch, age 71
**President, COO, and Director:** David L. (Dave) Robertson
**CFO and Director:** Steve Feilmeier
**EVP and Director; Chairman and CEO, INVISTA; President, Koch Mineral Services, LLC:** Jeff Gentry
**EVP and Director:** David H. Koch, age 67
**EVP and Director:** Rich Fink
**SVP, Corporate Strategy:** John C. Pittenger
**SVP and General Counsel:** Mark Holden
**VP, Operations:** Jim Mahoney
**VP, Human Resources; Director, Georgia-Pacific:** Dale Gibbens
**VP, Business Development:** Ron Vaupel
**Chairman and CEO, Georgia-Pacific:** Joseph W. (Joe) Moeller, age 63
**President and COO, Koch Chemical Technology Group, LLC:** John M. Van Gelder
**President, Koch Financial Corporation:** Randall A. (Randy) Bushman
**President, Koch Supply & Trading:** Steve Mawer
**President, Koch Pipeline Company:** Bob O'Hair
**Controller:** Richard Dinkel
**Treasurer:** David May
**Communication Coordinator and Public Affairs:** Patti Parker

## LOCATIONS

**HQ:** Koch Industries, Inc.
4111 E. 37th St. North, Wichita, KS 67220
**Phone:** 316-828-5500 **Fax:** 316-828-5739
**Web:** www.kochind.com

Koch Industries has operations in Argentina, Australia, Belgium, Brazil, Canada, China, the Czech Republic, France, Germany, India, Italy, Japan, Luxembourg, the Netherlands, Poland, South Africa, Spain, Switzerland, the UK, the US, and Venezuela.

## PRODUCTS/OPERATIONS

### Selected Operations

Flint Hills Resources (formerly Koch Petroleum, crude oil, petrochemicals, and refined products)
Georgia-Pacific Corporation
Koch Chemical Technology Group (specialty equipment and services for refining and chemical industry)
- Iris Power Engineering, Inc.
- The John Zink Company
- Koch-Glitsch, Inc.
- Koch Heat Transfer Group (formerly Brown Fintube Company)
- Koch Membrane Systems Inc.
- Koch-Partners
- Koch Modular Process Systems, LLC
- Quest Tru-Tec Services (formerly Tru-Tec Services)

Koch Financial Corp.
Koch Genesis Company (investment in noncore businesses)
Koch Mineral Services (bulk ocean transportation and terminalling and trading)
- Koch Fertilizer Storage & Terminal Co.
- Koch Nitrogen Co.

Koch Pipeline Co. LP
Koch Specialty Chemicals (high-octane missile fuel)
Koch Supply & Trading, LLC
Matador Cattle Co.

## COMPETITORS

ADM
AEP
Aquila
Ashland
Avista
Bowater
BP
Cargill
CenterPoint Energy
Chevron
ConocoPhillips
ContiGroup
Duke Energy
Dynegy
Enron
Exxon Mobil
Gypsum Products
Hesperia Holding
Imperial Oil
International Paper
Kimberly-Clark
King Ranch
Lyondell Chemical
Marathon Oil
Motiva Enterprises
Occidental Petroleum
OfficeMax
Peabody Energy
PEMEX
PG&E
Royal Dutch Shell
Shell Oil Products
Smurfit-Stone Container
Southern Company
SUEZ-TRACTEBEL
Sunoco
Weyerhaeuser
Williams Companies

## HISTORICAL FINANCIALS

Company Type: Private

### Income Statement

FYE: December 31

| | ESTIMATED REVENUE ($ mil.) | NET INCOME ($ mil.) | NET PROFIT MARGIN | EMPLOYEES |
|---|---|---|---|---|
| **12/06** | 90,000 | — | — | 80,000 |
| **12/05** | 80,000 | — | — | 80,000 |
| **12/04** | 40,000 | — | — | 30,000 |
| **12/03** | 40,000 | — | — | 30,000 |
| **12/02** | 40,000 | — | — | 17,000 |
| **Annual Growth** | 22.5% | — | — | 47.3% |

### Revenue History

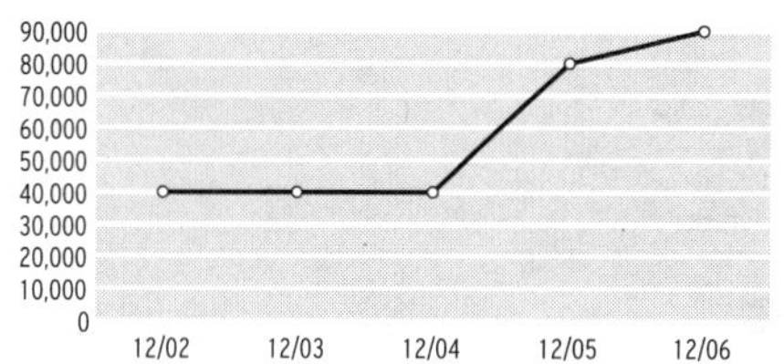


# Kohl's Corporation

Kohl's wants to be easy on shoppers and tough on competition. The company operates about 825 discount department stores in 45 states. Nearly a third of its stores are in the Midwest, where Kohl's continues to grow while rapidly expanding into other markets. Moderately priced name-brand and private-label apparel, shoes, accessories, and housewares are sold through centrally located cash registers, designed to expedite checkout and keep staff costs down. Kohl's competes with discount and mid-level department stores. Merchandising relationships allow Kohl's to carry top brands (NIKE, Levi's, OshKosh B'Gosh) not typically available to discounters; it sells them cheaper than department stores by controlling costs.

Kohl's stores are generally located in strip malls where rents are cheaper and competition is scarce; customers get easier access to the stores.

After several years of expanding on its native Midwestern turf and in the mid-Atlantic region, Kohl's is aggressively moving west and south. It entered the Florida market in 2005 and opened its first stores in Pacific Northwest in 2006. The fast-growing retailer also introduced a more appealing, modern store format in the fall of 2006 designed to broaden its appeal beyond its current customer base. In 2007 the company plans to open between 110 and 115 new stores, including its first in Idaho and Wyoming. By 2010, Kohl's plans to expand to more than 1,200 locations.

Private-label offerings are key to Kohl's growth strategy. The discount retailer has signed a licensing agreement with Lagardère Active Media Licensing, a division of the company that publishes *ELLE* magazine, to develop an ELLE-branded line of women's clothing. Set to launch this spring in some 300 Kohl's stores, the line will be rolled out to all Kohl's stores in 2008. Also, Kohl's recently signed a licensing agreement with sportswear maker Quicksilver to gain exclusive rights to the Tony Hawk (of skateboarding fame) brand of boys and young men's fashions. Other private-label lines include the Genuine Sonoma and Croft & Barrow brands. In 2004 Kohl's launched a new private label, Apt. 9, which was designed to compete with the likes of Banana Republic, Liz Claiborne, and Perry Ellis.

In a bid to emulate its "cheap chic" rivals Target and J. C. Penney, Kohl's has been busy adding big-name designers to its floors. In August 2006 the company inked a deal with Vera Wang. As part of the agreement, Wang provides the design inspiration and Kohl's sources the apparel production. The collection comprises women's apparel, intimate apparel, handbags, leather accessories, footwear, jewelry, linens, and towels.

## HISTORY

Max Kohl (father of Sen. Herbert Kohl of Wisconsin) opened his first grocery store in Milwaukee in the late 1920s. Over the years he and his three sons developed it into a chain and in 1938 Kohl's incorporated.

Kohl opened a department store (half apparel, half hard goods) in 1962 next door to a Kohl's grocery. In the mid-1960s he hired William Kellogg, a twentysomething buyer in the basement discount department at Milwaukee's Boston Store, for his expertise in budget retailing. Kellogg came from a retailing family (his father was VP of merchandising at Boston Store; the younger Kellogg had joined that firm out of high school). Kohl and Kellogg began developing the pattern for the store, carving out a niche between upscale department stores and discounters (offering department store quality at discount store prices).

The Kohl family entered real estate development in 1970, building the largest shopping center in the Milwaukee area. By 1972 the family's 65 food stores and five department stores were generating about $90 million in yearly sales. That year the Kohls sold 80% of the two operations to British American Tobacco's Brown & Williamson Industries division (later called BATUS), the first in a string of department store acquisitions that would eventually include Marshall Field's and Saks Fifth Avenue.

BATUS bought the rest of Kohl's in 1978. Herb and Allen Kohl left the business to concentrate on real estate and politics, and Kellogg was named president and CEO. The next year BATUS separated the food and department store operations and eventually sold the food store chain to A&P in 1983.

Kohl's discount image did not fit in with BATUS's other retail operations, so it decided to sell the department store chain. In 1986 Kellogg and two other executives, with the backing of mall developers Herbert and Melvin Simon, led an LBO to acquire the chain's 40 stores and a distribution center; annual sales were about $288 million.

Two years later Kohl's acquired 26 Main Street department stores from Federated Department Stores, moving the company into new cities such as Chicago and Detroit. When Kohl's went public in 1992, it had 81 stores in six states, and sales topped $1 billion.

In 1996 Kohl's began its mid-Atlantic expansion by opening stores in North Carolina. Early in 1997 the firm acquired a former Bradlees store to enter New Jersey and opened stores in Washington, DC; Philadelphia; New York; and Delaware. Kohl's continued its expansion in 1998, entering Tennessee and building its mid-Atlantic presence. In early 1999 Kohl's named Larry Montgomery as CEO. The company also bought 30 stores from bankrupt Caldor (mostly in the New York City area) and reopened them as Kohl's in 2000.

Montgomery was named chairman of Kohl's in February 2003, succeeding William Kellogg, who retired after 34 years with the company. Kohl's, which had become one of the fastest-growing and most successful US department store chains in the last decade, hit some serious bumps in 2003, including excess inventory (built up based on previous years of strong sales).

Kohl's opened its eighth distribution center in Macon, Georgia in the spring of 2005.

On October 5, 2006 the company opened 65 stores (with three more slated to open in November), making fall 2006 a record season for store openings.

In 2006 Kohl's sold its private-label credit card business to JPMorgan Chase for about $1.6 billion. (Kohl's continues to handle all customer and marketing services for JPMorgan Chase as they relate to credit card customers.)

## EXECUTIVES

**Chairman and CEO:** R. Lawrence (Larry) Montgomery, age 58, $1,087,067 pay
**President and Director:** Kevin B. Mansell, age 54, $946,283 pay
**SEVP:** Thomas A. (Tom) Kingsbury, age 54, $375,000 pay
**EVP and CFO:** Wesley S. (Wes) McDonald, age 43, $615,833 pay
**EVP and General Merchandise Manager, Home and Footwear:** Chris Capuano, age 45
**EVP and General Merchandise Manager, Men's and Children's:** Donald A. Brennan, age 44
**EVP and General Merchandise Manager, Women's Apparel and Accessories:** Jack H. Boyle, age 36
**EVP, Administration:** John J. Lesko, age 52
**EVP, General Counsel, and Secretary:** Richard D. (Rick) Schepp, age 44
**EVP, Human Resources:** Telvin Jeffries, age 36
**EVP, Marketing:** Gary Vasques, age 57
**EVP, Planning and Allocation:** Jon K. Nordeen, age 49
**EVP, Product Development:** Peggy Eskenasi, age 49, $895,833 pay
**SVP, Marketing:** Julie Gardner
**VP Public Relations:** Vicki Shamion
**Auditors:** Ernst & Young LLP

## LOCATIONS

**HQ:** Kohl's Corporation
N56 W17000 Ridgewood Dr., Menomonee Falls, WI 53051
**Phone:** 262-703-7000 **Fax:** 262-703-6143
**Web:** www.kohls.com

Kohl's has distribution centers in Blue Springs, Missouri; Corsicana, Texas; Findlay, Ohio; Macon, Georgia; Mamakating, New York; Menomonee Falls, Wisconsin; Patterson and San Bernardino, California; and Winchester, Virginia.

### 2007 Stores

| | No. |
|---|---|
| California | 79 |
| Texas | 61 |
| Illinois | 55 |
| Ohio | 51 |
| Michigan | 42 |
| New York | 39 |
| Pennsylvania | 39 |
| Wisconsin | 36 |
| New Jersey | 33 |
| Indiana | 30 |
| Georgia | 24 |
| Minnesota | 24 |
| Virginia | 22 |
| North Carolina | 21 |
| Colorado | 20 |
| Massachusetts | 20 |
| Missouri | 19 |
| Arizona | 18 |
| Connecticut | 17 |
| Maryland | 15 |
| Tennessee | 15 |
| Florida | 14 |
| Iowa | 11 |
| Kentucky | 11 |
| Arkansas | 8 |
| Kansas | 8 |
| Oklahoma | 8 |
| New Hampshire | 7 |
| South Carolina | 7 |
| Utah | 7 |
| Alabama | 6 |
| Nebraska | 6 |
| Nevada | 6 |
| Maine | 5 |
| Oregon | 5 |
| Washington | 5 |
| West Virginia | 5 |
| Other states | 18 |
| **Total** | **817** |

## PRODUCTS/OPERATIONS

### 2007 Sales

| | % of total |
|---|---|
| Women's | 33 |
| Men's | 19 |
| Home | 18 |
| Children's | 13 |
| Accessories | 9 |
| Footwear | 8 |
| **Total** | **100** |

## COMPETITORS

Belk
BJ's Wholesale Club
Dillard's
Dunlap
J. C. Penney
Kmart
Linens 'n Things
Macy's
Men's Wearhouse
Mervyns
Old Navy
Retail Ventures
Ross Stores
Saks Inc.
Sears
ShopKo Stores
Syms
Target
TJX Companies
Wal-Mart

## HISTORICAL FINANCIALS

Company Type: Public

### Income Statement

FYE: Saturday closest to January 31

| | REVENUE ($ mil.) | NET INCOME ($ mil.) | NET PROFIT MARGIN | EMPLOYEES |
|---|---|---|---|---|
| **1/07** | 15,544 | 1,109 | 7.1% | 114,000 |
| **1/06** | 13,402 | 842 | 6.3% | 107,000 |
| **1/05** | 11,701 | 730 | 6.2% | 95,000 |
| **1/04** | 10,282 | 591 | 5.7% | 85,000 |
| **1/03** | 9,120 | 643 | 7.1% | 75,000 |
| **Annual Growth** | 14.3% | 14.6% | — | 11.0% |

### 2007 Year-End Financials

Debt ratio: 18.6%
Return on equity: 19.2%
Cash ($ mil.): 620
Current ratio: 1.77
Long-term debt ($ mil.): 1,040
No. of shares (mil.): 321
Dividends
Yield: —
Payout: —
Market value ($ mil.): 23,480

### Stock History

NYSE: KSS

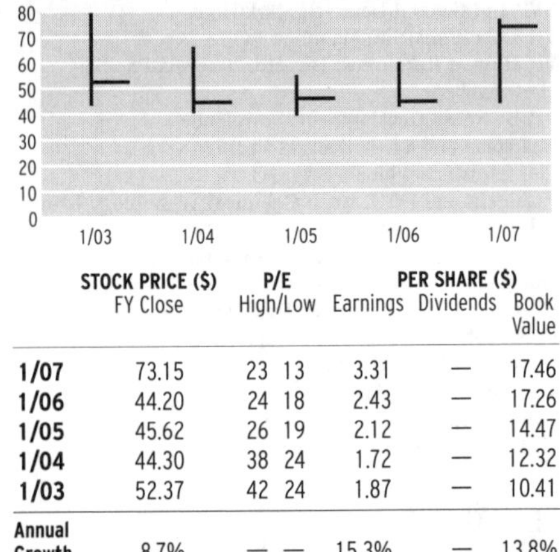


| | STOCK PRICE ($) FY Close | P/E High | P/E Low | PER SHARE ($) Earnings | Dividends | Book Value |
|---|---|---|---|---|---|---|
| **1/07** | 73.15 | 23 | 13 | 3.31 | — | 17.46 |
| **1/06** | 44.20 | 24 | 18 | 2.43 | — | 17.26 |
| **1/05** | 45.62 | 26 | 19 | 2.12 | — | 14.47 |
| **1/04** | 44.30 | 38 | 24 | 1.72 | — | 12.32 |
| **1/03** | 52.37 | 42 | 24 | 1.87 | — | 10.41 |
| **Annual Growth** | 8.7% | — | — | 15.3% | — | 13.8% |

# KPMG International

Businesses all over the world count on KPMG for accounting. KPMG is the smallest, yet one of the most geographically dispersed of accounting's Big Four, which also includes Deloitte Touche Tohmatsu, Ernst & Young, and PricewaterhouseCoopers. KPMG, a cooperative that operates as an umbrella organization for its member firms, has organized its structure into three operating regions: the Americas; Asia/Pacific; and Europe, Middle East, Africa. Member firms' offerings include audit, tax, and advisory services; KPMG focuses on clients in such industries as financial services, consumer products, and government. KPMG has discontinued its KLegal International network.

KPMG's UK and German operations in 2006 announced they would merge to form KPMG Europe, which will continue to operate under the KPMG International umbrella. The move is seen as the first step in a plan to unite KPMG's European units into a single firm.

## HISTORY

Peat Marwick was founded in 1911, when William Peat, a London accountant, met James Marwick during an Atlantic crossing. University of Glasgow alumni Marwick and Roger Mitchell had formed Marwick, Mitchell & Company in New York in 1897. Peat and Marwick agreed to ally their firms temporarily, and in 1925 they merged as Peat, Marwick, Mitchell, & Copartners.

In 1947 William Black became senior partner, a position he held until 1965. He guided the firm's 1950 merger with Barrow, Wade, Guthrie, one of the US's oldest firms, and built its consulting practice. Peat Marwick restructured its international practice as PMM&Co. (International) in 1972 (renamed Peat Marwick International in 1978).

The next year several European accounting firms led by Klynveld Kraayenhoff (the Netherlands) and Deutsche Treuhand (Germany) began forming an international accounting federation. Needing an American member, the European firms encouraged the merger of two American firms founded around the turn of the century, Main Lafrentz and Hurdman Cranstoun. Main Hurdman & Cranstoun joined the Europeans to form Klynveld Main Goerdeler (KMG), named after two of the member firms and the chairman of Deutsche Treuhand, Reinhard Goerdeler. Other members were Thorne Riddel (Canada), C. Jespersen (Denmark), Thomson McLintok (UK), and Fides Revision (Switzerland).

Peat Marwick merged with KMG in 1987 to form Klynveld Peat Marwick Goerdeler (KPMG). KPMG lost 10% of its business as competing client companies departed. Professional staff departures followed in 1990 when, as part of a consolidation, the firm trimmed its partnership rolls.

In the 1990s the then-Big Six accounting firms all faced lawsuits arising from an evolving standard holding auditors responsible for the substance, rather than merely the form, of clients' accounts. KPMG was hit by suits stemming from its audits of defunct S&Ls and litigation relating to the bankruptcy of Orange County, California (settled for $75 million in 1998). Nevertheless KPMG kept growing; it expanded its consulting division with the acquisition of banking consultancy Barefoot, Marrinan & Associates in 1996.

In 1997, after Price Waterhouse and Coopers & Lybrand announced their merger, KPMG and Ernst & Young announced one of their own. But they called it quits the next year, fearing that regulatory approval of the deal would be too onerous.

The creation of PricewaterhouseCoopers (PwC) and increasing competition in the consulting sides of all of the Big Five brought a realignment of loyalties in their national practices. KPMG Consulting's Belgian group moved to PwC and its French group to Computer Sciences Corporation. Andersen nearly wooed away KPMG's Canadian consulting group, but the plan was foiled by the ever-sullen Andersen Consulting group (now Accenture) and by KPMG's promises of more money. Against this background, KPMG sold 20% of its consulting operations to Cisco Systems for $1 billion. In addition to the cash infusion, the deal allowed KPMG to provide installation and system management to Cisco's customers.

Even while KPMG worked on the IPO of its consulting group (which took place in 2001), it continued to rail against the SEC as it called for relationships between consulting and auditing organizations to be severed. In 2002 KPMG sold its British and Dutch consultancy units to France's Atos Origin.

In 2003 the SEC charged US member firm KPMG L.L.P. and four partners with fraud in relation to alleged profit inflation at former client Xerox in the late 1990s. (In April 2005 the accounting firm paid almost $22.5 million, including a $10 million civil penalty, to settle the charges.) KPMG exited various businesses around the globe during fiscal 2004, including full-scope legal services and certain advisory services, to focus on higher-demand services.

## EXECUTIVES

**Chairman:** Sir Michael D. V. (Mike) Rake, age 59
**CEO:** Michael P. (Mike) Wareing
**Chairman, Asia Pacific; Senior Partner, China and Hong Kong, SAR:** John B. Harrison
**Chairman and CEO, KPMG L.L.P.:** Timothy P. (Tim) Flynn, age 48
**Chairman, Europe, Middle East and Africa:** Ben van der Veer
**Chairman, Australia:** Douglas K. (Doug) Jukes
**Chairman and CEO, Canada:** William A. (Bill) MacKinnon
**Senior Partner, KPMG UK:** John Griffith-Jones
**Senior Partner, Brazil:** David Bunce
**Senior Partner, Singapore:** Danny Teoh
**Senior Partner, Mexico:** Guillermo García Naranjo
**Senior Partner, Italy:** L. Renato Guerini
**Senior Partner, Denmark:** Finn L. Meyer
**Senior Partner and CEO, Japan:** Masanori Sato
**Senior Partner, Sweden:** Thomas Thiel
**Senior Partner, Germany:** Rolf Nonnenmacher
**CEO, KPMG UK:** Colin Cook
**CEO, Switzerland:** Hubert Achermann
**CEO, South Africa:** Tom W. Grieve
**President, France:** Jean-Luc Decornoy
**Managing Partner, Ireland:** Denis O'Connor
**Managing Partner, Global Markets:** Alistair Johnston

## LOCATIONS

**HQ:** KPMG International
Burgemeester Rijnderslaan 10-20,
1185 MC Amstelveen, The Netherlands
**Phone:** +31-20-656-7890 **Fax:** +31-20-656-7700
**US HQ:** 3 Chestnut Ridge Road, Montvale, NJ 07645
**US Phone:** 201-307-7000 **US Fax:** 212-758-9819
**Web:** www.kpmg.com

KPMG International has offices in nearly 150 countries.

**2006 Sales**

| | $ mil. | % of total |
|---|---|---|
| Europe, Middle East & Africa | 8,820 | 52 |
| Americas | 5,960 | 35 |
| Asia/Pacific | 2,100 | 13 |
| **Total** | **16,880** | **100** |

## PRODUCTS/OPERATIONS

**2006 Sales**

| | $ mil. | % of total |
|---|---|---|
| Audit | 8,270 | 49 |
| Advisory | 5,280 | 31 |
| Tax | 3,330 | 20 |
| **Total** | **16,880** | **100** |

**2006 Sales**

| | $ mil. | % of total |
|---|---|---|
| Financial Services | 4,130 | 24 |
| Industrial Markets | 3,910 | 23 |
| Information, Communication & Entertainment | 3,450 | 21 |
| Infrastructure, Government & Healthcare | 3,350 | 20 |
| Consumer Markets | 2,040 | 12 |
| **Total** | **16,880** | **100** |

**Selected Services**

Audit services
- Financial statement audit
- Internal audit services

Tax services
- Corporate and business tax
- Global tax
- Indirect tax
- Personal tax

Advisory services
- Audit support services
- Financial risk management
- Information risk management
- Process improvement
- Regulatory and compliance

## COMPETITORS

Aon
Bain & Company
Baker Tilly
BDO International
Booz Allen
Deloitte
Ernst & Young
Grant Thornton
H&R Block
Hewitt Associates
Marsh & McLennan
McKinsey & Company
PricewaterhouseCoopers
Towers Perrin
Watson Wyatt

## HISTORICAL FINANCIALS

Company Type: Partnership

**Income Statement** FYE: September 30

| | REVENUE ($ mil.) | NET INCOME ($ mil.) | NET PROFIT MARGIN | EMPLOYEES |
|---|---|---|---|---|
| **9/06** | 16,880 | — | — | 113,000 |
| **9/05** | 15,690 | — | — | 103,621 |
| **9/04** | 13,440 | — | — | 93,983 |
| **9/03** | 12,160 | — | — | 93,470 |
| **9/02** | 10,720 | — | — | 98,000 |
| **Annual Growth** | 12.0% | — | — | 3.6% |

**Revenue History**

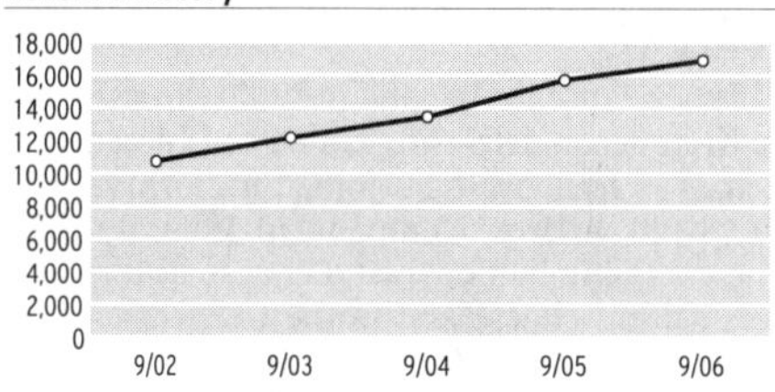


# Kraft Foods

Mac & cheese if you please. Kraft Foods, the #1 food company in the US and #2 in the world (behind Nestlé), finally extricated itself from the haze of second-hand tobacco smoke litigation when it was spun off from Altria in 2007. Kraft's North America business includes the world's most popular cheese brand (Kraft) and the planet's largest cookie and cracker business (Nabisco). Reaching more than 155 countries worldwide, the company's international business offers most of Kraft's US brands, plus national favorites. Seven of Kraft's brands (Jacobs, Kraft, Milka, Nabisco, Oscar Mayer, Philadelphia, and Post) have revenues of $1 billion; more than 50 hit the $100-million mark.

Having edged toward splitting from its former parent company for years, the separation relieves the food maker of many headaches. The spinoff freed Kraft from any tobacco-related liability that Altria may be found guilty of post-spinoff. It also eliminated a significant layer of management, which makes it easier for Kraft to improve its recent sluggish sales. Kraft's plan for boosting its fortune includes streamlining operations and introducing new products.

In order to improve its European operations, in 2007 Kraft announced it was moving its European headquarters to Zurich. Currently the company has two headquarters in Europe, one in London and one in Vienna, Austria. To begin in the summer of 2007, the move is expected to be completed sometime in 2008.

Focusing on sharpening its brand portfolio, Kraft sold off its hot cereals business in 2007. The $200-million-dollar sale to B&G Foods included the old favorites, Cream of Wheat and Cream of Rice.

Also in 2007 Kraft announced that rather than use traditional media (television, magazines, radio), it would launch 70 new products via the online world, at a virtual supermarket on the Web site, secondlife.com.

On the expansion front, Kraft bought the Spanish and Portuguese operations of United Biscuits; the deal returned to Kraft the rights to Nabisco trademarks such as Oreo, Ritz, and Chips Ahoy! in Europe, the Middle East, and Africa. In 2007 it announced plans to purchase the cookie business of Groupe Danone for some $7.2 billion. The purchase would give the company brands such as Petit Ecolier and Crème Roulee.

Billionaire Warren Buffet (of Berkshire-Hathaway fame) acquired a small percentage (less than 5%) of Kraft in 2007, joining the also famously rich and famous-on-Wall Street corporate raiders, Nelson Peltz (3%) and Carl Ichan (percentage unknown), in ownership of the Velveeta vendor.

## HISTORY

The Kraft tale began in 1903 when James L. Kraft began delivering cheese to Chicago grocers. His four brothers joined in, forming the J.L. Kraft & Bros. Company, in 1909. By 1914 the company had opened a cheese factory and was selling cheese across the US. Kraft developed its first blended, pasteurized cheese the following year.

Kraft went public in 1924; four years later it merged with Philadelphia cream-cheese maker, Phoenix, and also created Velveeta cheese spread. In 1930 Kraft was bought by National Dairy, but its operations were kept separate. New and notable products included Miracle Whip salad dressing (1933), macaroni and cheese dinners (1937), and Parkay margarine (1940). In the decades that followed, Kraft expanded into foreign markets.

National Dairy became Kraftco in 1969 and Kraft in 1976, hoping to benefit from its internationally known trademark. To diversify, Kraft merged with Dart Industries in 1980; Dart's subsidiaries (including Duracell batteries) and Kraft kept separate operations. With non-food sales sagging, Dart & Kraft split up in 1986. Kraft kept its original lines; the rest became Premark International. Tobacco giant Philip Morris Companies bought Kraft in 1988 for $12.9 billion. The next year Philip Morris joined Kraft with another unit, General Foods.

General Foods began when Charles Post, who marketed a wheat/bran health beverage, established the Postum Cereal Co. in 1896; he expanded the firm with such cereals as Grape-Nuts and Post Toasties. The company went public in 1922. Postum bought the makers of Jell-O (1925), Log Cabin syrup (1927), and Maxwell House coffee (1928), and in 1929 it acquired control of General Foods (owned by frozen vegetable pioneer Clarence Birdseye) and changed its own name to General Foods.

Its later purchases included Perkins Products (Kool-Aid, 1953) and Kohner Brothers (toys, 1970). Most of its non-food lines proved unsuccessful and were sold throughout the years. General Foods bought Oscar Mayer, the US's #1 hot dog maker, in 1981. Philip Morris bought General Foods for $5.6 billion in 1985.

The 1989 combination of Kraft and General Foods (the units still ran independently) created the largest US food maker, Kraft General Foods.

To streamline management, Philip Morris integrated Kraft and General Foods in 1995. Newly named Kraft Foods sold off lower-margin businesses, including its bakery unit and its North American table spreads business.

In 2000 parent Philip Morris (which renamed itself the Altria Group in 2003) outbid Danone and Cadbury Schweppes and agreed to buy Nabisco Holdings. It completed the deal that December for $18.9 billion and began integrating those operations into Kraft Foods and Kraft Foods International. Then Philip Morris created a holding company for the newly combined food operations under the Kraft Foods Inc. name in 2001. The original Kraft Foods was renamed Kraft Foods North America.

Kraft Foods International CEO Roger Deromedi was appointed co-CEO of the new holding company, along with Betsy Holden. Kraft Foods Inc. was spun off by Altria in 2001 in what was the US's second-largest IPO ever at the time (behind AT&T Wireless, now AT&T Mobility). Kraft cut 7,500 jobs in 2002 as a result of the integration of Nabisco operations.

Deromedi shared the CEO slot with Holden until 2003, at which time he was named sole CEO. As part of Deromedi's plan to refashion Kraft's product line-up, in 2005 the company sold its Altoids breath mints, LifeSavers and CremeSavers candies brands to Wm. Wrigley Jr. Company for about $1.4 billion. Despite his best efforts to improve the bottom line, Deromedi was shown the door in 2006. He was replaced by Frito-Lay's CEO Irene Rosenfeld.

The long partnership with Altria finally came to an end in 2007 when the tobacco giant shed Kraft in a spinoff.

## EXECUTIVES

**Chairman and CEO:** Irene B. Rosenfeld, age 53
**President, Commercial Operations European Union:** Pascal Houssin, age 54
**EVP and CFO:** James P. (Jim) Dollive, age 55
**EVP, Global Human Resources:** Karen J. May, age 49
**EVP, General Counsel and Corporate and Legal Affairs:** Marc S. Firestone, age 47
**EVP, Global Business Services and Strategy:** David Brearton, age 46
**EVP, Global Supply Chain:** Franz-Josef H. Vogelsang, age 56, $1,091,262 pay
**EVP, Global Technology and Quality:** Jean E. Spence, age 49
**EVP; President, International Commercial:** Sanjay Khosla, age 55
**EVP; President, North America Commercial:** Richard G. (Rick) Searer, age 53
**SVP and Controller:** Pamela King, age 45
**SVP and President, Kraft Canada:** Dino Bianco, age 45
**SVP, Global Health and Wellness and New Category Development:** Lance Friedmann
**SVP, Sales, International Commercial:** Franco Suardi, age 53
**SVP, Customer Development Organization, Kraft North America:** Brian J. Driscoll, age 48
**SVP and President, North America Foodservice:** Thomas H. (Tom) Sampson, age 48
**SVP and General Manager, Kraft Pizza Co.:** Michael Pellegrino
**SVP, Global Integrated Marketing and Communications:** Carole Irgang
**Group VP and President, US Cheese and Dairy:** Kevin Ponticelli, age 49
**Group VP; President Beverage Sector:** Mary Beth West, age 44
**Group VP and President, US Snacks and Cereals:** John F. Baxter, age 46
**Auditors:** PricewaterhouseCoopers LLP

## LOCATIONS

**HQ:** Kraft Foods Inc.
3 Lakes Dr., Northfield, IL 60093
**Phone:** 847-646-2000 **Fax:** 847-646-6005
**Web:** www.kraft.com

Kraft Foods has 159 manufacturing facilities (54 in the US; 105 in other countries).

**2006 Sales**

| | $ mil. | % of total |
|---|---|---|
| US | 20,931 | 61 |
| Europe | 7,817 | 23 |
| Other countries | 5,608 | 16 |
| **Total** | **34,356** | **100** |

## PRODUCTS/OPERATIONS

**2006 Sales**

| | $ mil. | % of total |
|---|---|---|
| Snacks | 10,028 | 29 |
| Beverages | 7,325 | 21 |
| Cheese & dairy | 6,414 | 19 |
| Convenient meals | 5,508 | 16 |
| Grocery | 5,081 | 15 |
| **Total** | **34,356** | **100** |

**Selected Brands**

A.1.
Bull's-Eye
Capri Sun (licensed)
Cheese Nips
Cheez Whiz
Chips Ahoy!
Cool Whip
Country Time
Cracker Barrel
Crystal Light
DiGiorno
Grey Poupon
Honey Maid
Jell-O
Kool-Aid
Kraft Macaroni & Cheese
Lunchables
Louis Rich
Maxwell House
Minute Rice
Miracle Whip
Newtons
Nilla
Nutter Butter
Oreo
Oscar Mayer
Philadelphia
Planters
Post
Ritz
Premium
Sanka
Shake' N Bake
SnackWell's
South Beach Diet (licensed)
Stove Top
Tang
Tazo (licensed)
Teddy Grahams
Toblerone
Tombstone
Triscuit
Velveeta
Veryfine
Wheat Thins
Yuban

## COMPETITORS

ADM
Bongrain
Cadbury Schweppes
Campbell Soup
Cargill
Cheesemakers, Inc.
Cold Stone Creamery
ConAgra
Dairy Crest
Dairy Farmers of America
Danone
Dean Foods
Del Monte Foods
Diageo
Eden Foods
Farmland Dairies
Frito-Lay
Fromageries Bel
Galaxy Nutritional Foods
General Mills
George Weston
Goya
Great Lakes Cheese
Hain Celestial
Heinz
Hershey
Hormel
HP Hood
Interstate Bakeries
JBS Swift
Kellogg
Kellogg Snacks
Kerry Group
Lactalis
Lance Snacks
Land O'Lakes
Lindt & Sprüngli
Maple Leaf Foods
Marathon Cheese
Mars
McCain Foods
Michael Foods, Inc.
Nestlé
Nestlé USA
Northern Foods
Old Home Foods
Parmalat Canada
Procter & Gamble
Ralcorp
Rich Products
Saputo
Saputo Cheese USA Inc.
Sara Lee
Sara Lee Food & Beverage
Sargento
Schreiber Foods
Schwan's
Seneca Foods
Smithfield Foods
Smucker
Stonyfield Farm
Tofutti Brands
Tyson Foods
Unilever
Uniq
United Biscuits
WhiteWave

## HISTORICAL FINANCIALS

Company Type: Public

### Income Statement

FYE: December 31

| | REVENUE ($ mil.) | NET INCOME ($ mil.) | NET PROFIT MARGIN | EMPLOYEES |
|---|---|---|---|---|
| **12/06** | 34,356 | 3,060 | 8.9% | 90,000 |
| **12/05** | 34,113 | 2,632 | 7.7% | 94,000 |
| **12/04** | 32,168 | 2,665 | 8.3% | 98,000 |
| **12/03** | 31,010 | 3,476 | 11.2% | 106,000 |
| **12/02** | 29,723 | 3,394 | 11.4% | 109,000 |
| **Annual Growth** | 3.7% | (2.6%) | — | (4.7%) |

### 2006 Year-End Financials

Debt ratio: 24.8%
Return on equity: 10.5%
Cash ($ mil.): 239
Current ratio: 0.79
Long-term debt ($ mil.): 7,081
No. of shares (mil.): 456
Dividends
Yield: 2.7%
Payout: 51.9%
Market value ($ mil.): 16,278

### Stock History

NYSE: KFT

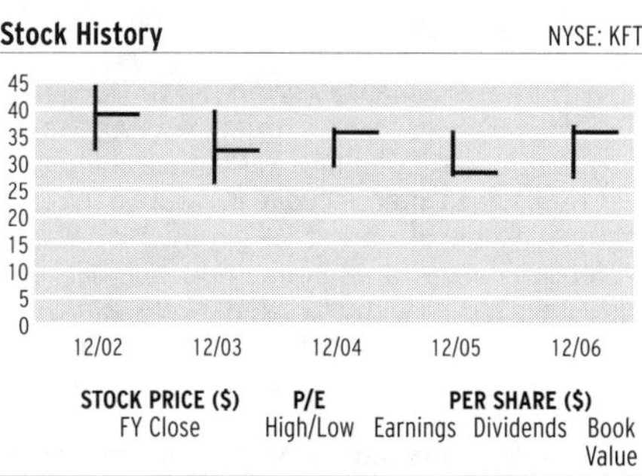

| | STOCK PRICE ($) FY Close | P/E High | P/E Low | PER SHARE ($) Earnings | Dividends | Book Value |
|---|---|---|---|---|---|---|
| **12/06** | 35.70 | 20 | 15 | 1.85 | 0.96 | 62.62 |
| **12/05** | 28.17 | 23 | 18 | 1.55 | 0.87 | 60.41 |
| **12/04** | 35.61 | 23 | 19 | 1.55 | 0.77 | 56.93 |
| **12/03** | 32.22 | 20 | 13 | 2.01 | 0.66 | 52.64 |
| **12/02** | 38.93 | 22 | 17 | 1.96 | 0.56 | 46.91 |
| **Annual Growth** | (2.1%) | — | — | (1.4%) | 14.4% | 7.5% |

# The Kroger Co.

Kroger is the nation's #1 pure grocery chain, but it still must watch out for falling prices; Wal-Mart has overtaken Kroger as the largest seller of groceries in the US. While Kroger has diversified through acquisitions, adding jewelry and general merchandise to its mix, food stores still account for about 85% of sales. The company operates about 3,650 stores, including nearly 2,470 supermarkets and multi-department stores, under two dozen banners, in about 30 states. It also runs some 780 convenience stores under names such as Quik Stop and Kwik Shop. Kroger's Fred Meyer Stores subsidiary operates more than 120 supercenters, which offer groceries, general merchandise, and jewelry, in the western US.

In response to intense competition from non-traditional grocery sellers, such as Wal-Mart Supercenters and Costco Wholesale (the #1 and #3 sellers of groceries in the US, respectively), Kroger has been cutting prices while improving service and product selection to hang on to customers, with some success. Wal-Mart operates supercenters in more than half of Kroger's markets.

Kroger owns about 42 food processing plants that supply its supermarkets with a growing stable of some 10,000 private-label products (accounting for about 25% of its grocery sales), including Naturally Preferred, Kroger's own brand of natural and organic products. Digging deeper into the organics market, Kroger has launched a second line of some 60 organic items (including pasta, tea, waffles, peanut butter, snacks, and milk) called "Organics for Everyone". The new line, which targets mainstream consumers, is priced lower than Kroger's Naturally Preferred brand.

Kroger is also a major pharmacy operator, with pharmacies in about 75% of its food stores. Prescription sales account for close to 10% of Kroger's sales volume. About 630 of the company's supermarkets sell gas.

Acquisitive Kroger agreed in April 2007 to acquire 18 Scott's Food & Pharmacy stores in Indiana from rival SUPERVALU for an undisclosed amount.

Kroger's 1999 acquisition of Fred Meyer not only added three supermarket chains (Ralphs, Smith's Food & Drug Centers, and QFC), it gave the company several new retailing formats: multi-department stores (Fred Meyer), price-impact warehouse outlets (Food 4 Less and Foods Co.), and jewelry stores (under the Barclay, Fred Meyer, and Littman names). The purchase gave Kroger a significant presence in the western US.

Its namesake chain has outlets in more than 40 major markets and a sizable share of the market in large cities such as Dallas/Fort Worth and Atlanta. The grocer's newest store concept, Kroger Marketplace, opened in Columbus, Ohio, in late 2004. The Marketplace stores are twice the size of its standard grocery outlets and stock plenty of non-grocery items.

## HISTORY

Bernard Kroger was 22 when he started the Great Western Tea Company in 1883 in Cincinnati. Kroger lowered prices by cutting out middlemen, sometimes by making products such as bread. Growing to 40 stores in Cincinnati and northern Kentucky, the company became Kroger Grocery and Baking Company in 1902. It expanded into St. Louis in 1912 and grew rapidly during the 1910s and 1920s by purchasing smaller, cash-strapped companies. Kroger sold his holdings in the company for $28 million in 1928, the year before the stock market crash, and retired.

The company acquired Piggly Wiggly stores in the late 1920s and bought most of Piggly Wiggly's corporate stock, which it held until the early 1940s. The chain reached its largest number of stores — a whopping 5,575 — in 1929. (The Depression later trimmed that total.) A year later Kroger manager Michael Cullen suggested opening self-service, low-price supermarkets, but company executives demurred. Cullen left Kroger and began King Kullen, the first supermarket. If he was ahead of his time at Kroger, it wasn't by much; within five years, the company had 50 supermarkets.

During the 1950s Kroger acquired companies with stores in Texas, Georgia, and Washington, DC. It added New Jersey-based Sav-on drugstores in 1960 and it opened its first SupeRx drugstore in 1961. The company began opening larger supermarkets in 1971; between 1970 and 1980 Kroger's store count grew just 5%, but its selling space nearly doubled.

In 1983 the grocer bought Kansas-based Dillons Food Stores (supermarkets and convenience stores) and Kwik Shop convenience stores. Kroger sold most of its interests in the Hook and SupeRx drug chains (which became Hook-SupeRx) in 1987 and focused on its food-and-drugstores. (It sold its remaining stake to Revco in 1994.) The next year it faced two separate takeover bids from the Herbert Haft family and from Kohlberg Kravis Roberts. The company warded off the raiders by borrowing $4.1 billion to pay a special dividend to shareholders and to buy shares for an employee stock plan.

To reduce debt, Kroger sold most of its equity in Price Saver Membership Wholesale Clubs and its Fry's California stores. Joseph Pichler became CEO in 1990.

Kroger sold its Time Saver Stores unit in 1995. In 1999 Kroger acquired Fred Meyer, operator of about 800 stores mainly in the West, in a $13 billion deal. Late in 1999 it announced it was buying nearly 75 stores (mostly in Texas) from Winn-Dixie Stores; the deal was called off in 2000 shortly after the FTC withheld its approval. In late 2001 Kroger said it would cut 1,500 jobs. With mega-discounter Wal-Mart breathing down its neck, Kroger cut prices in December 2001.

In June 2003, Joseph Pichler stepped down as CEO (but remained chairman) and was succeeded by David B. Dillon. A four-and-a-half month long strike by grocery workers at Kroger's Ralphs chain in Southern California ended in March 2004. The dispute pitted workers' demands for continued generous health care benefits against management's call to control costs in the face of increasing non-union competition.

Pichler retired as chairman in June 2004 and was succeeded by Dillon. Also that year Kroger opened its newest store concept, Kroger Marketplace, in Columbus, Ohio.

In August 2006, Kroger sold 11 Cala Foods and Bell Markets in the San Francisco Bay area to DeLano Retail Partners, headed by Hartley DeLano the former president of the Cala chain, for an undisclosed sum.

In July 2007 Kroger bought 20 Farmer Jack stores in the Detroit area from A&P.

## EXECUTIVES

**Chairman and CEO:** David B. Dillon, age 56, $1,155,991 pay
**Vice Chairman:** W. Rodney McMullen, age 46, $809,969 pay
**President, COO, and Director:** Don W. (Donnie) McGeorge, age 52, $809,969 pay
**EVP, Merchandising:** Donald E. Becker, age 57, $575,413 pay
**EVP, Secretary, and General Counsel:** Paul W. Heldman, age 55
**SVP and CFO:** J. Michael Schlotman, age 49, $499,099 pay
**SVP and CIO:** Christopher T. (Chris) Hjelm, age 45
**SVP; President, Kroger Manufacturing:** William T. Boehm, age 59
**SVP, Retail Operations:** Paul J. Scutt, age 58
**Group VP, Human Resources:** Della Wall, age 55
**Group VP, Perishables Merchandising and Procurement:** Joseph A. Grieshaber Jr., age 49
**Group VP, Corporate Affairs:** Lynn Marmer, age 54
**VP and Controller:** M. Elizabeth Van Oflen, age 49
**VP, Drug, Pharmacy and General Merchandising:** Lisa E. Holsclaw, age 46
**VP and Treasurer:** Scott M. Henderson, age 51
**VP, Convenience Store Division:** Van Tarver
**VP, Pharmacy Merchandising and Procurement:** Lincoln Lutz
**Manager, Investor Relations:** Carin Fike
**Auditors:** PricewaterhouseCoopers LLP

## LOCATIONS

**HQ:** The Kroger Co.
1014 Vine St., Cincinnati, OH 45202
**Phone:** 513-762-4000 **Fax:** 513-762-1160
**Web:** www.kroger.com

The Kroger Co. operates supermarkets in 31 states and convenience stores in 16 states.

## PRODUCTS/OPERATIONS

### 2007 Sales

| | $ mil. | % of total |
|---|---|---|
| Food stores | 57,712 | 87 |
| Food store fuel sales | 4,455 | 7 |
| Other stores & manufacturing | 3,944 | 6 |
| **Total** | **66,111** | **100** |

### 2007 Stores

| | No. |
|---|---|
| Supermarkets & multi-department stores | 2,468 |
| Convenience stores | 779 |
| Jewelry | 412 |
| **Total** | **3,659** |

### 2007 Supermarkets

| | No. |
|---|---|
| Combo stores | 2,171 |
| Price-impact & warehouse stores | 145 |
| Multi-department stores | 122 |
| Marketplace stores | 30 |
| **Total** | **2,468** |

### Selected Kroger Stores

Multidepartment Stores
- Fred Meyer
- Fry's Marketplace

Supermarkets
- City Market Food & Pharmacy
- Dillon Food Stores
- Fry's Food & Drug Stores
- Gerbes Supermarkets
- Hilander Food Stores
- Jay C Food Stores
- King Soopers
- Kroger
- Pay Less Super Markets
- Quality Food Centers (QFC)
- Ralphs
- Smith's Food & Drug Centers

Warehouse Stores
- Food 4 Less
- FoodsCo

Convenience Stores
- Kwik Shop
- Loaf 'N Jug
- Quik Stop Markets
- Tom Thumb Food Stores
- Turkey Hill Minit Markets

Jewelry Stores
- Barclay Jewelers
- Fred Meyer Jewelers
- Littman Jewelers

### Selected Private-Label Brands

Bath & Body Therapies (body and bath)
Banner brands (Kroger, Ralphs, King Soopers)
Everyday Living (kitchen gadgets)
FMV (For Maximum Value)
HD Design (upscale kitchen gadgets)
Moto Tech (automotive)
Naturally Preferred (premium quality natural and organic brand)
Office Works (office and school supplies)
Private Selection (premium quality brand)
Splash Spa (body and bath)
Splash Sport (body and bath)

## COMPETITORS

| | |
|---|---|
| 7-Eleven | Meijer |
| 99 Cents Only | Publix |
| A&P | Raley's |
| Ahold USA | Randall's |
| Albertsons | Rite Aid |
| Bruno's Supermarkets | Safeway |
| Costco Wholesale | Save Mart |
| CVS/Caremark | Stater Bros. |
| Delhaize America | Sterling Jewelers |
| Dollar General | SUPERVALU |
| Family Dollar Stores | Target |
| Giant Eagle | Walgreen |
| H-E-B | Wal-Mart |
| Hy-Vee | Wegmans |
| IGA | Whole Foods |
| Kmart | Winn-Dixie |
| Marsh Supermarkets | Zale |

## HISTORICAL FINANCIALS

Company Type: Public

### Income Statement

FYE: Saturday nearest January 31

| | REVENUE ($ mil.) | NET INCOME ($ mil.) | NET PROFIT MARGIN | EMPLOYEES |
|---|---|---|---|---|
| **1/07** | 66,111 | 1,115 | 1.7% | 310,000 |
| **1/06** | 60,553 | 958 | 1.6% | 290,000 |
| **1/05** | 56,434 | (100) | — | 289,000 |
| **1/04** | 53,791 | 312 | 0.6% | 290,000 |
| **1/03** | 51,760 | 1,205 | 2.3% | 290,000 |
| **Annual Growth** | 6.3% | (1.9%) | — | 1.7% |

### 2007 Year-End Financials

Debt ratio: 125.0%
Return on equity: 23.9%
Cash ($ mil.): 803
Current ratio: 0.89
Long-term debt ($ mil.): 6,154
No. of shares (mil.): 705
Dividends
Yield: 0.8%
Payout: 12.3%
Market value ($ mil.): 18,224

### Stock History

NYSE: KR

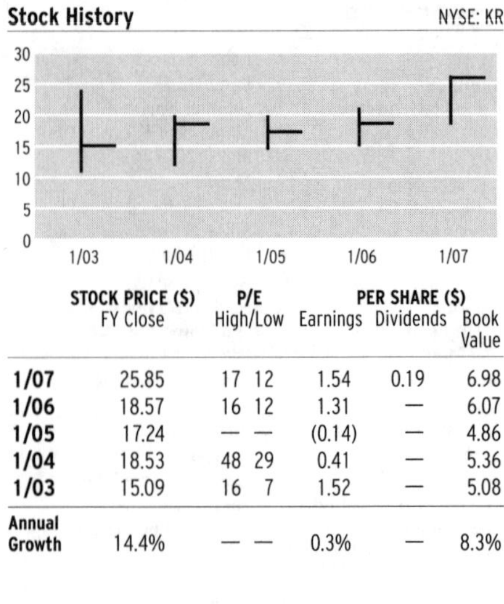

| | STOCK PRICE ($) FY Close | P/E High | P/E Low | PER SHARE ($) Earnings | Dividends | Book Value |
|---|---|---|---|---|---|---|
| **1/07** | 25.85 | 17 | 12 | 1.54 | 0.19 | 6.98 |
| **1/06** | 18.57 | 16 | 12 | 1.31 | — | 6.07 |
| **1/05** | 17.24 | — | — | (0.14) | — | 4.86 |
| **1/04** | 18.53 | 48 | 29 | 0.41 | — | 5.36 |
| **1/03** | 15.09 | 16 | 7 | 1.52 | — | 5.08 |
| **Annual Growth** | 14.4% | — | — | 0.3% | — | 8.3% |

# L-3 Communications

L-3's good defense is its best commercial offense. L-3 Communications Holdings makes secure and specialized systems for satellite, avionics, and marine communications. The US government (primarily the military) accounts for about 80% of the company's business, but L-3 is using acquisitions to expand its commercial offerings. Commercial products include flight recorders (black boxes), display systems, and wireless telecom gear. L-3 has added to its aircraft repair, overhaul, and technical services with the purchase of Spar Aerospace and what are now L-3 Communications Integrated Systems, L-3 Communications Vertex Aerospace, and L-3 Communications Cincinnati Electronics.

CEO Frank Lanza died suddenly in June 2006. Prior to his passing he had championed the idea of continuing to add to L-3's product lines by acquiring niche technology companies and by adapting L-3's defense technologies to commercial markets, primarily transportation and communications, which account for a quarter of sales. L-3 has developed such products as data recorders for passenger aircraft and explosives detectors used by the Federal Aviation Administration in airports.

Within days of Lonza's death L-3 CFO Michael T. Strianese was named interim CEO. Board member Robert B. Millard was named chairman.

Frank Lanza announced in early 2005 that L-3 planned to spend around $900 million on acquisitions in the upcoming year. In July of that year, however, L-3 Communications went *way* over its intended acquisition budget and acquired defense IT specialist The Titan Corporation in a deal worth about $2.6 billion.

In 2006 L-3 created a new Homeland Security division as an organization of its security-related businesses.

Citigroup, through Smith Barney Fund Management LLC, owns almost 12% of L-3.

## HISTORY

In the early 1970s, Frank Lanza caught defense giant Lockheed's eye by building Loral Corporation into an aerospace industry contender through acquisitions of smaller defense technology firms. Lockheed (now Lockheed Martin) eventually bought Loral in 1996 and made Lanza the head of defense electronics. Looking for more action, Lanza formed L-3 Communications Holdings in 1997 by convincing Lockheed Martin's CEO to spin off a group of 10 communications technology units and put him at the helm. The operations were units from General Electric and Loral acquired by Lockheed Martin in 1993 and 1996, respectively.

In charge were two of the L's in the L-3 name: 20-year Loral executives Lanza (chairman and CEO, by then old enough to retire) and Robert LaPenta (president and CFO). The third L stands for major backer Lehman Brothers. The company embarked on an acquisition binge (just as Loral had originally done) in 1997. L-3 targeted strapped independent companies and the potential noncore operations of large corporate mergers.

Much as he had at Loral, Lanza remained a hands-off executive, a surprising approach in a red tape-wrapped industry. As a result, L-3's divisions developed an entrepreneurial freedom. In 1998, the year L-3 went public, it purchased the Ocean Systems unit of AlliedSignal (now Honeywell International; sonar products), ILEX Systems (information technology and support for the US government), SPD Technologies (electronics and power products), and the satellite transmission systems unit of California Microwave. The next year L-3 bought Microdyne (telemetry receivers) and AYDIN (electronic products for military, government, and aerospace).

In 2000 L-3 sold its network security software division to Symantec. Its 10 acquisitions that year included Honeywell's Traffic Alert and Collision Avoidance System (TCAS) avionics safety technology, 53% of wireless network infrastructure equipment maker LogiMetrics, and Raytheon's training devices and services division.

In 2002 L-3 made its largest acquisition to date, buying Raytheon's Aircraft Integration Systems unit for $1.13 billion in cash. Also in 2002 L-3 acquired Canadian aircraft repair and overhaul firm Spar Aerospace, the Detection Systems (X-ray screening) business of PerkinElmer, and Westwood Corporation (shipboard power systems). Late in the year L-3 acquired some Northrop Grumman operations (electron devices and displays-navigation systems) as well as Wescam Inc (image capture/transmission).

L-3 acquired Vertex Aerospace, a company that provides technical services for government agencies, for about $650 million in 2003 and renamed it L-3 Communications Vertex Aerospace. L-3's acquisition of optical/homeland defense businesses continued late in 2004 with a $43 million deal for Raytheon's commercial infrared unit.

The acquisition roll continued in 2005 as L-3 acquired the Marine Controls division (shipboard control systems) of CAE, the Propulsion Systems business unit (transmissions, engines, suspensions, and turret drives) of General Dynamics, and most of Boeing's Electron Dynamic Devices, Inc. business, including the space and military traveling wave tubes, traveling wave tube amplifiers, passive microwave devices, and electric propulsion operations. L-3 also acquired Mobile-Vision Inc., a maker of video surveillance systems used in police cars.

Early in 2006 L-3 completed its $150 million acquisition of SAM Electronics, a German naval electronics company. Later that year the company acquired Germany's Magnet-Motor GmbH, a maker of high-tech electric and energy systems for propulsion of commercial and combat vehicles, and marine vessels. Later that year L-3 acquired radio and satellite communications systems maker TRL Electronics PLC of the UK for about $176 million.

L-3 then kept the 2006 acquisitions spree going with the agreement to purchase Crestview Aerospace Corporation (airframe assemblies and military aircraft modifications) for $135 million. Crestview became part of L-3's Aircraft Modernization and Maintenance division when the transaction closed in late 2006.

In June 2006 Lanza died suddenly. Shortly after Lonza's death, L-3 completed its acquisition of Nautronix Defence Group, a provider of mine warfare and anti-submarine systems. L-3 purchased Nautronix Defence Group from Nautronics Holdings PLC for $65 million in cash. Later in 2006 L-3 purchased Nova Engineering, a maker of communication systems for network-centric warfare and technology applications.

The following year L-3 acquired Global Communications Solutions, a maker of portable satellite communications equipment.

## EXECUTIVES

**Chairman:** Robert B. Millard, age 56
**President, CEO, and Director:** Michael T. Strianese, age 51, $2,425,192 pay
**SVP; President, Products Group:** Charles J. Schafer, age 59
**SVP, General Cousel and Corporate Secretary:** Kathleen E. Karelis, age 46
**SVP and General Counsel Mergers and Acquisitions:** Christopher C. Cambria
**SVP; President, Sensors and Simulation Group:** James W. Dunn, age 63, $1,004,000 pay
**SVP; President, L-3 Integrated Systems Group:** Robert W. (Bob) Drewes, age 64, $1,275,000 pay
**SVP; President, L-3 Services Group:** Carl E. Vuono, age 72, $951,052 pay
**SVP, Washington DC Operations:** Jimmie V. Adams, age 70
**SVP, Corporate Strategy and Development:** Curtis Brunson, age 59
**SVP:** Robert W. RisCassi, age 71
**VP and Chief Technology Officer:** A. Michael Andrews II
**VP and Chief Information Officer:** Vincent T. Taylor
**VP and CFO:** Ralph G. D'Ambrosio, age 39
**VP and Treasurer:** Stephen M. Souza, age 54
**VP; President, Microwave Group:** John S. Mega
**VP, Administration:** Sheila M. Sheridan
**VP, Business Development:** Jill J. Wittels
**VP, Business Review:** Michael R. (Mike) Orlowski
**VP, Corporate Communications:** Cynthia Swain
**VP, Human Resources:** Kenneth W. Manne
**Auditors:** PricewaterhouseCoopers LLP

## LOCATIONS

**HQ:** L-3 Communications Holdings, Inc.
600 3rd Ave., New York, NY 10016
**Phone:** 212-697-1111 **Fax:** 212-867-5249
**Web:** www.l-3com.com

L-3 Communications Holdings has operations in 531 locations; its major operations are located in Canada and the US.

### 2006 Sales

| | $ mil. | % of total |
|---|---|---|
| US | 10,682.8 | 86 |
| Canada | 350.7 | 3 |
| Germany | 257.6 | 2 |
| South Korea | 193.5 | 2 |
| UK | 177.8 | 1 |
| New Zealand | 111.1 | 1 |
| Australia | 86.9 | — |
| Other countries | 616.5 | 5 |
| **Total** | **12,476.9** | **100** |

## PRODUCTS/OPERATIONS

### 2006 Sales

| | $ mil. | % of total |
|---|---|---|
| Specialized products | 4,289.7 | 34 |
| Government services | 3,834.4 | 31 |
| Aircraft modernization & maintenance | 2,327.5 | 19 |
| Command, Control & Communications (C3), Intelligence, Surveillance & Reconnaissance | 2,025.3 | 16 |
| **Total** | **12,476.9** | **100** |

### Selected Operations

Specialized Products
- Acoustic undersea warfare products
- Forward looking infrared sensors, laser range finders, illuminators, and designators
- Fusing products
- Naval power distribution, conditioning, switching, and protection equipment
- Ruggedized displays
- Telemetry, instrumentation, space, and navigation products
- Training simulators
- Video surveillance and display systems

Government Services
- Acquisition management and staff augmentation
- Battlefield and weapon simulation
- Communication software support
- Information management and IT systems support and software design, development, and systems integration
- Information technology systems
- Linguistic interpretation, translation, and analysis services
- Network and enterprise administration and management
- Surveillance systems and products, installation, logistics, and support
- System support and concept operations
- Systems acquisition and advisory support and comprehensive operational support services
- Systems engineering, operations analysis, research and technical analysis
- Weapons training

Aircraft Modernization & Maintenance
- Aircraft maintenance and modification services
- Airborne traffic and collision avoidance systems
- Ruggedization of displays, computers, and electronics
- Voice recorders, flight data recorders, and maritime hardened voyage recorders

Command, Control & Communications & Intelligence, Surveillance, and Reconnaissance
- Airborne, space, and surface data link terminals, ground stations, and transportable tactical SATCOM systems
- Fleet management of special mission aircraft
- Ground-based satellite communications terminals and payloads
- Prime mission systems integration, sensor development, and operations and support
- Satellite command and control sustainment and support
- Satellite communication and tracking systems
- Secure communication terminals and equipment, and secure network encryption products
- Shipboard communications

## COMPETITORS

AeroMechanical Services
BAE SYSTEMS
BAE Systems Inc.
Boeing Space and Intelligence Systems
C4 Systems
DIRECTV
DRS Technologies
Ericsson
GE
General Dynamics
General Dynamics UK
Harris Corp.
Herley Industries
Honeywell International
JPS Communications
LMCSS
Lockheed Martin
Lockheed Martin Transportation & Security
Meggitt USA
Motorola, Inc.
Northrop Grumman
Northrop Grumman Electronic Systems
Northrop Grumman IT
Northrop Grumman Mission Systems
Raytheon
Raytheon IIS
Raytheon NCS
Rockwell Collins
Sierra Nevada Corp.
Sperry Marine
telent
ThalesRaytheonSystems

# Land O'Lakes

Land O'Lakes butters up its customers, and shows you what life is like if everyone cooperates. Owned by and serving more than 7,000 dairy farmer members and 1,300 community cooperatives, Land O'Lakes is the one of the largest dairy co-ops in the US (along with Dairy Farmers of America and California Dairies). It provides its members with wholesale fertilizer and crop protection products, seed, and animal feed. Its oldest and best known product, LAND O' LAKES butter, is the top butter brand in the US. Land O'Lakes also produces packaged milk, margarine, sour cream, and cheese. The co-op's animal-feed division, Land O'Lakes Purina Feed, is a leading animal and pet food maker.

Land O'Lakes also owns egg producer MoArk. (MoArk sold its liquid egg products operations to Golden Oval Eggs in 2006.) In addition, the company's subsidiary, Land O'Lakes Finance, provides financing services for beef, dairy, pork, and poultry producers.

In 2007 the company sold its international cheese and protein operations (known as CPI) to Saputo Cheese USA for about $216 million. The sale included the Golden Valley Dairy Products cheese manufacturing and cut-and-wrap operations. The deal also included a long-term milks agreement, such that Land O'Lakes is the sole milk supplier for CPI.

Also in 2007 Land O'Lakes and CHS realigned the businesses of their 50-50 joint venture Agriliance in 2007, with CHS acquiring its crop-nutrients wholesale-products business and Land O'Lakes acquiring the crop-protection products business. The two companies are looking for a buyer for the one remaining Agriliance operation, retail agronomy.

Outside of the US, Land O'Lakes has taken aim at the largest emerging market: China, where the company is working to establish the Land O'Lakes brand of cheese and cultured dairy products in supermarkets.

## HISTORY

In the old days, grocers sold butter from communal tubs and it often went bad. Widespread distribution of dairy products had to await the invention of fast, reliable transportation. By 1921 the necessary transportation was available. That year about 320 dairy farmers in Minnesota formed the Minnesota Cooperative Creameries Association and launched a membership drive with $1,375, mostly borrowed from the US Farm Bureau.

The co-op arranged joint shipments for members; imposed strict hygiene and quality standards; and aggressively marketed its sweet cream butter nationwide, packaged for the first time in the familiar box of four quarter-pound sticks. A month after the co-op's New York sales office opened, it was ordering 80 shipments a week.

Minnesota Cooperative Creameries, as part of its promotional campaigns, ran a contest in 1924 to name that butter. Two contestants offered the winning name — Land O'Lakes. The distinctive Indian Maiden logo first appeared about the same time, and in 1926 the co-op changed its name to Land O'Lakes Creameries. By 1929, when it began supplying feed, its market share approached 50%.

During WWII civilian consumption dropped, but the co-op increased production of dried milk to provide food for soldiers and newly liberated concentration camp victims.

In the 1950s and 1960s, Land O'Lakes added ice cream and yogurt producers to its membership and fought margarine makers, yet butter's market share continued to melt. The co-op diversified in 1970 through acquisitions, adding feeds and agricultural chemicals. Two years later Land O'Lakes threw in the towel and came out with its own margarine. Despite the decreasing use of butter nationally, the co-op's market share grew.

Land O'Lakes formed a marketing joint venture, Cenex/Land O'Lakes Agronomy, with fellow co-op Cenex in 1987. As health consciousness bloomed in the 1980s, Land O'Lakes launched reduced-fat dairy products. It also purchased a California cheese plant, doubling its capacity. Land O'Lakes began ramping up its international projects at the same time: It built a feed mill in Taiwan, introduced feed products in Mexico, and established feed and cheese operations in Poland.

In 1997 the co-op bought low-fat cheese maker Alpine Lace Brands. Land O'Lakes took on the eastern US when it merged with the 3,600-member Atlantic Dairy Cooperative (1997), and it bulked up on the West Coast when California-based Dairyman's Cooperative Creamery Association joined its fold (1998).

During 2000 the co-op sold five plants to Dean Foods with an agreement to continue supplying the plants with raw milk. Also in 2000 Land O'Lakes combined its feed business with those of Farmland Industries to create Land O'Lakes Farmland Feed, LLC, with a 69% ownership. That same year, Land O'Lakes and CHS joined their agronomy operations to create a 50-50 joint venture, Agriliance LLC.

In late 2001 the company spent $359 million to acquire Purina Mills (pet and livestock feeds). Purina Mills was folded into Land O'Lakes Farmland Feed and, as part of the purchase, Land O'Lakes increased its ownership of the feed business to 92%. In 2004 it purchased the remaining 8%.

To take advantage of its nationally recognized brand, Land O'Lakes formed an alliance with Dean Foods in 2002 to develop and market value-added dairy products.

Exiting the meat business, Land O'Lakes sold its swine operations in 2005 to private pork producer, Maschhoff West LLC, for an undisclosed sum. That same year, it sold its interest in fertilizer manufacturer, CF Industries. Long-time president and CEO Jack Gherty retired that year; he was replaced by Chris Policinski. In 2006 the company acquired 100% ownership of MoArk.

## EXECUTIVES

**Chairman:** Peter (Pete) Kappelman, age 44
**First Vice Chairman:** Ronnie Mohr, age 58
**President and CEO:** Chris Policinski, age 48, $750,000 pay
**EVP; COO, Dairy Foods Industrial:** Alan Pierson, age 56
**EVP; COO, Dairy Foods Value-Added:** Steve Dunphy, age 49
**EVP; COO, Feed:** Fernando Palacios, age 47, $445,303 pay
**EVP; COO, Seed:** David L. (Dave) Seehusen, age 60, $265,700 pay
**SVP and CFO:** Daniel E. Knutson, age 50, $451,690 pay

## HISTORICAL FINANCIALS

Company Type: Public

### Income Statement

FYE: December 31

| | REVENUE ($ mil.) | NET INCOME ($ mil.) | NET PROFIT MARGIN | EMPLOYEES |
|---|---|---|---|---|
| **12/06** | 12,477 | 526 | 4.2% | 63,700 |
| **12/05** | 9,445 | 509 | 5.4% | 59,500 |
| **12/04** | 6,897 | 382 | 5.5% | 44,200 |
| **12/03** | 5,062 | 278 | 5.5% | 38,700 |
| **12/02** | 4,011 | 178 | 4.4% | 27,000 |
| **Annual Growth** | 32.8% | 31.1% | — | 23.9% |

### 2006 Year-End Financials

Debt ratio: 86.1%
Return on equity: 10.7%
Cash ($ mil.): 348
Current ratio: 1.65
Long-term debt ($ mil.): 4,566
No. of shares (mil.): 125
Dividends
Yield: 0.9%
Payout: 17.8%
Market value ($ mil.): 10,242

### Stock History

NYSE: LLL

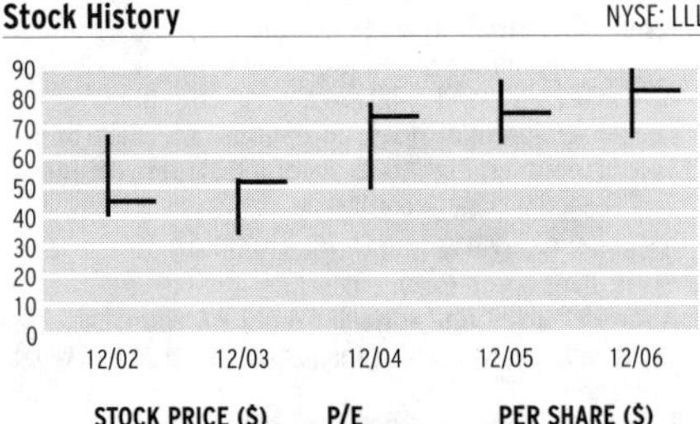


| | STOCK PRICE ($) FY Close | P/E High/Low | PER SHARE ($) Earnings | Dividends | Book Value |
|---|---|---|---|---|---|
| **12/06** | 81.78 | 21 16 | 4.22 | 0.75 | 42.37 |
| **12/05** | 74.35 | 20 15 | 4.20 | 0.50 | 37.31 |
| **12/04** | 73.24 | 23 15 | 3.33 | 0.40 | 32.85 |
| **12/03** | 51.36 | 19 13 | 2.71 | — | 26.52 |
| **12/02** | 44.91 | 35 21 | 1.93 | — | 23.28 |
| **Annual Growth** | 16.2% | — — | 21.6% | 36.9% | 16.1% |

**VP and General Counsel:** Peter Janzen, age 47, $352,008 pay
**VP, Corporate Strategy and Business Development:** Barry Wolfish, age 50
**VP, Foodservice Sales:** Mark Blabac
**VP, Human Resources:** Karen Grabow, age 57
**VP, Public Affairs:** James D. (Jim) Fife, age 57
**Secretary and Director:** Douglas (Doug) Reimer, age 56
**Director, Corporate Communications:** Lydia Botham
**Auditors:** KPMG LLP

## LOCATIONS

**HQ:** Land O'Lakes, Inc.
4001 Lexington Ave. North, Arden Hills, MN 55112
**Phone:** 651-481-2222 **Fax:** 651-481-2000
**Web:** www.landolakesinc.com

## PRODUCTS/OPERATIONS

### 2006 Sales

| | % of total |
|---|---|
| Dairy foods | 46 |
| Feed | 38 |
| Seed | 11 |
| Layers | 5 |
| **Total** | **100** |

### Selected Brands
Alpine Lace (low-fat cheese)
CROPLAN GENETICS (crop seed)
LAND O' LAKES (consumer dairy products)
Land O'Lakes (animal feed)
New Yorker (cheese)

### Dairy Products
Butter
Cheese
Flavored butter
Light butter
Margarine
Milk
Sour cream

### Selected Joint Ventures
Advanced Food Products (35%, with Bongrain, S.A.)
Agriliance LLC (50%, with CHS, Inc.)

## COMPETITORS

ADM
AMPI
Blue Seal Feeds
Breeder's Choice
California Dairies Inc.
Cal-Maine Foods
Cargill
Dairy Farmers of America
Darigold, Inc.
Dean Foods
Doane Pet Care
Fonterra
Foremost Farms
Frontier Agriculture
Hartz Mountain
Hill's Pet Nutrition
HP Hood
Iams
Keller's Creamery
Kent Feeds
Kraft Foods
Meow Mix Company
Michael Foods Egg Products
Michael Foods, Inc.
Monsanto
MSC
National Dairy Holdings
Nestlé
Nestlé Purina PetCare
Nestlé USA
Northwest Dairy
Parmalat
Pioneer Hi-Bred
Prairie Farms Dairy
Rose Acre Farms
Royal Canin
Saputo
Sargento
Schreiber Foods
Syngenta Seeds
Unilever

## HISTORICAL FINANCIALS

Company Type: Cooperative

### Income Statement
FYE: December 31

| | REVENUE ($ mil.) | NET INCOME ($ mil.) | NET PROFIT MARGIN | EMPLOYEES |
|---|---|---|---|---|
| 12/06 | 7,275 | 89 | 1.2% | 8,500 |
| 12/05 | 7,557 | 129 | 1.7% | 7,500 |
| 12/04 | 7,677 | 21 | 0.3% | 8,000 |
| 12/03 | 6,321 | 84 | 1.3% | 8,000 |
| 12/02 | 5,847 | 99 | 1.7% | 8,000 |
| Annual Growth | 5.6% | (2.7%) | — | 1.5% |

### Net Income History

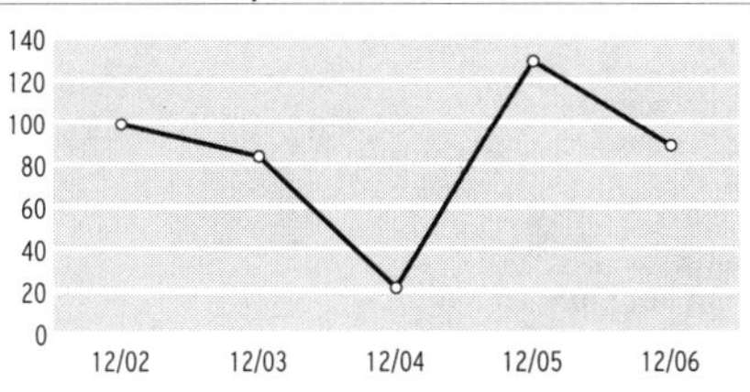


# La-Z-Boy

The kickback that La-Z-Boy gives its customers is perfectly legal. The top US maker of upholstered furniture, La-Z-Boy sells its ubiquitous recliners (#1 in the world), plus chairs, sofas, tables, and modular seating units. A new recliner sports a drink cooler, phone, and massage and heat system. La-Z-Boy sells through more than 70 company-owned stores, almost 250 independent La-Z-Boy Furniture Galleries, and about 300 in-store galleries at furniture dealers, department stores, and other outlets. La-Z-Boy also makes wood furniture (desks, cabinets, and bedroom items) and licenses its name for use on furniture for the health care industry. Its brands include La-Z-Boy, Bauhaus USA, Hammary, Lea, and Kincaid. La-Z-Boy also owns LADD Furniture, which makes furniture under such names as American Drew.

In recent years, La-Z-Boy has made strategic moves to stay competitive and maintain a profitable portfolio. In early 2007 the furniture maker announced a restructuring that eliminated some 500 positions. As part of the reorganization, the company will close several upholstery manufacturing facilities and a rough mill lumber operation, as well as consolidate three upholstery operations into one.

As it re-evaluated its products portfolio, La-Z-Boy sold off its Sam Moore Furniture unit to Hooker Furniture in May 2007.

## HISTORY

Carpenter Edward Knabusch repaired and built furniture in his family's garage in Monroe, Michigan, in the early 1920s. When people began clamoring for Knabusch's repair expertise, he quit his job, hired his cousin, Edwin Shoemaker, and in 1927 formed Floral City Furniture.

The duo specialized in new designs, including a telephone stand with seat that they dubbed "the Gossiper." Their first recliner, a wooden porch chair that shaped itself to body contours, was developed in 1928. Positive response prompted family and friends to raise money (Shoemaker's dad mortgaged the farm) for a manufacturing plant. At a customer's urging, the pair upholstered the chair, and Knabusch drummed up even more interest with a contest to name the new piece. Entries included Slack-Back, Sit-N-Snooze, and the moniker that would help define an industry, La-Z-Boy.

In the midst of the Depression, the company thrived, turning the bottom factory floor into a showroom and offering entertainment and circus tents stuffed with merchandise to attract out-of-state visitors. The cousins amassed a petting zoo of farm animals collected, instead of money, from cash-strapped customers.

To separate manufacturing and a burgeoning retail operation, La-Z-Boy Chair was incorporated in 1941. Production stopped during WWII while Knabusch and Shoemaker made tank seats and crash pads.

Its one-of-a-kind product styles helped to distinguish the company through the 1950s and 1960s. Its reputation grew, thanks to products such as a love seat fashioned in the form of a car seat, replete with lights, horns, fins, and tires (1959), and a chair that both rocked and reclined (1961). La-Z-Boy also began what would become a long-lived marketing campaign by using such celebrity spokesmen as football player Joe Namath and talk-show host Johnny Carson.

Sales reached nearly $53 million in 1971, and La-Z-Boy went public the next year. It diversified through the late 1970s into sleeper sofas (1977) and other products. Knabusch's adopted son Charles became chairman in 1985 and vowed to increase female clientele. La-Z-Boy also began making business furniture and began a continuing buying binge, including table maker Hammary Furniture (1986) and dining room and bedroom furniture specialist Kincaid Furniture (1988). Knabusch died in 1988, and the company's largest investor, Prescott Investors, made a failed takeover bid in 1989. That year La-Z-Boy opened its first superstore gallery.

Thinking globally, the company targeted the Asian market by redesigning its recliners for smaller physiques in 1993. It changed its name to La-Z-Boy in 1996. Charles Knabusch, Edward's son and company CEO, died in 1997; COO Gerald Kiser was made president. (He was later named CEO in July 2001.) The next year co-founder Shoemaker, who still held the EVP of engineering and VC titles, died in his recliner at the age of 90. Acquisitions continued, including Centurion Furniture (UK) and upscale Sam Moore Furniture Industries (1998), mid-priced furniture maker Bauhaus USA (1999), and LADD Furniture (2000).

In mid-2001 the company restructured into two main groups (upholstery and casegoods), combined LADD divisions into those groups, and began phasing out the LADD name. Restructuring plans, implemented in 2001, mandated the closure of three manufacturing facilities and the elimination of nearly 600 jobs. In December 2001 La-Z-Boy entered a joint venture with the Steinhoff Group (a leading household goods manufacturer in Europe, Australia, and South Africa); the resulting company, La-Z-Boy Europe, makes and sells furniture throughout Europe.

In August 2002 La-Z-Boy's subsidiary, England Inc., acquired the Englander Sleep Products name and trademarks from Schottenstein Stores of Ohio. (It sold the Englander bedding brand to Englander Sleep Products, a group of licensees, in late 2005.) Also in the summer of 2002 La-Z-Boy further restructured its casegoods operations by shuttering a Virginia plant and eliminating several hundred jobs. In 2003 another three casegoods manufacturing facilities were shut down, resulting in the elimination of an additional 400 positions. In 2004 production facilities in Pennsylvania, North Carolina, and Mississippi were shut down, putting about 650 La-Z-Boy employees out of work.

The company exited the office furniture manufacturing industry in mid-2005 so it could focus on the home furnishings business. Also that year it sold its La-Z-Boy Contract Unit, which manufactures furnishings used in commercial and health care settings, to the owners of Best Home Furnishings.

Also in 2005 the company acquired 13 stores (four in the New Generation format and the balance in the older format), all located in the Chicago area. The purchase gave La-Z-Boy a broader share of one of its top markets.

In July 2006 the company sold American of Martinsville, a maker of furniture for the hospitality industry, to private equity firm Hancock Park Associates for an undisclosed sum. American of Martinsville accounted for about 5% of the La-Z-Boy's sales in 2006.

## EXECUTIVES

**Chairman:** James W. Johnston, age 67
**Chairman Emeritus:** Patrick H. Norton, age 84
**President, CEO, and Director:** Kurt L. Darrow, age 51, $917,259 pay
**SVP, CFO, and Chief Accounting Officer:** Louis M. (Mike) Riccio Jr., age 44
**SVP, Corporate Operations:** Otis S. Sawyer
**SVP; President, Casegoods Product and Kincaid Furniture Company:** Steven M. (Steve) Kincaid, age 57, $419,621 pay
**SVP; President, Non-Branded Upholstery Product and England, Inc.; Interim President, Bauhaus USA:** Rodney D. (Rod) England, age 54, $470,718 pay
**SVP, Operations, Residential:** David A. (Dave) Layman
**SVP Sales and Marketing, La-Z-Boy Residential:** Steve Matlock
**SVP, Retail Operations, Kincaid:** Todd Hady
**VP, Brand Marketing:** Jennifer (Jen) Sievertsen
**VP, Corporate Human Resources:** Steven P. (Steve) Rindskopf, age 45
**VP, Process Improvement:** Roger L. Miller
**VP, Merchandising and Sales:** Gregory D. (Greg) White
**VP, Residential Global Merchandising, Tables, Lamps, and Accessories:** Bob Ireland
**VP, Store Development and Marketing:** Mark Wagner
**VP, Upholstery Merchandising:** Paula Hoyas
**VP and Chief Marketing Officer:** Doug Collier, age 40
**VP, Sales, American Drew/Lea:** Jeffrey W. Bowler
**VP and Treasurer:** Michael Skrzypczak, age 51
**Secretary and General Counsel:** James P. Klarr
**Director of Investor Relations and Corporate Communications:** Kathy Liebmann
**Auditors:** PricewaterhouseCoopers LLP

## LOCATIONS

**HQ:** La-Z-Boy Incorporated
1284 N. Telegraph Rd., Monroe, MI 48162
**Phone:** 734-242-1444 **Fax:** 734-457-2005
**Web:** www.lazboy.com

### 2007 Sales

| | % of total |
|---|---|
| US | 90 |
| Canada & other countries | 10 |
| **Total** | **100** |

## PRODUCTS/OPERATIONS

### 2007 Sales

| | $ mil. | % of total |
|---|---|---|
| Upholstery group | 1,194.2 | 74 |
| Casegoods group | 262.7 | 16 |
| Retail group | 220.3 | 13 |
| Other | (59.9) | (3) |
| **Total** | **1,617.3** | **100** |

### Selected Products

Bedroom furniture
Chairs
Dining room furniture
Entertainment units
Leather furniture
Love seats
Modular seating groups
Recliners
Reclining sofas
Sleep sofas
Sofas
Tables
Wall systems
Youth furniture

### Divisions and Brands

Upholstery Group
- Bauhaus USA (upholstered furniture, convertible sofas)
- Centurion (recliners, and leather-upholstered furniture, motion seating in Europe)
- England (mid-priced upholstered and motion furniture for living, family rooms)
- HickoryMark (fabric and leather upholstered furniture)
- La-Z-Boy (residential and health care furniture)

Casegoods Group
- Alexvale (upholstered furniture)
- American Drew (wood furniture for bedroom, dining room, occasional use)
- Hammary (tables, entertainment units, wall units, and upholstered furniture for living, family rooms)
- Kincaid (wood furniture)
- Lea (bedroom furniture)

## COMPETITORS

Art Van Furniture
Ashley Furniture
Bassett Furniture
Berkline/BenchCraft
Brown Jordan International
Chromcraft Revington
DFS Furniture
Ethan Allen
Flexsteel
Furniture Brands International
Herman Miller
HNI
Home Meridian
Hooker Furniture
IKEA
KI
Kimball International
Klaussner Furniture
Natuzzi
Rooms To Go
Rowe Furniture
Shelby Williams
Stanley Furniture
Steelcase
W. S. Badcock
Wickes Furniture

## HISTORICAL FINANCIALS

Company Type: Public

### Income Statement

FYE: last Saturday in April

| | REVENUE ($ mil.) | NET INCOME ($ mil.) | NET PROFIT MARGIN | EMPLOYEES |
|---|---|---|---|---|
| **4/07** | 1,617 | 4 | 0.3% | 11,729 |
| **4/06** | 1,917 | (3) | — | 13,404 |
| **4/05** | 2,048 | 37 | 1.8% | 14,822 |
| **4/04** | 1,999 | (6) | — | 16,034 |
| **4/03** | 2,112 | 36 | 1.7% | 16,800 |
| **Annual Growth** | (6.5%) | (42.0%) | — | (8.6%) |

### 2007 Year-End Financials

Debt ratio: 23.0%
Return on equity: 0.8%
Cash ($ mil.): 52
Current ratio: 2.37
Long-term debt ($ mil.): 112
No. of shares (mil.): 51
Dividends
Yield: 4.0%
Payout: 600.0%
Market value ($ mil.): 617

### Stock History

NYSE: LZB

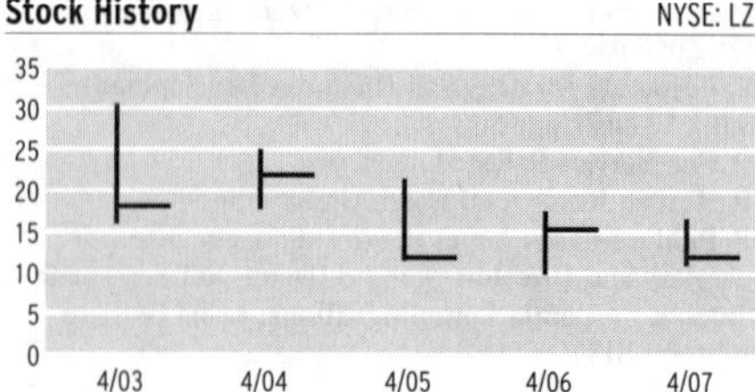


| | STOCK PRICE ($) FY Close | P/E High | P/E Low | PER SHARE ($) Earnings | Dividends | Book Value |
|---|---|---|---|---|---|---|
| **4/07** | 12.01 | 205 | 141 | 0.08 | 0.48 | 9.45 |
| **4/06** | 15.32 | — | — | (0.06) | 0.44 | 9.86 |
| **4/05** | 11.84 | 30 | 17 | 0.71 | 0.44 | 10.10 |
| **4/04** | 21.85 | — | — | (0.11) | 0.40 | 10.04 |
| **4/03** | 18.07 | 48 | 26 | 0.63 | 0.40 | 11.08 |
| **Annual Growth** | (9.7%) | — | — | (40.3%) | 4.7% | (3.9%) |

# Lear Corporation

Lear Corporation doesn't take a back seat to anyone when it comes to manufacturing automotive seats. A major supplier of automotive interiors, the company is a leader in the global market for car seat systems. It also makes interior components including floor and acoustic systems, door panels, headliners, and instrument panels, offering one-stop shopping for major automakers. Lear, which has more than 260 facilities in 33 countries, sells to automakers such as Ford and General Motors, BMW, DaimlerChrysler, Fiat, Toyota, and Volkswagen. The US is Lear's largest market.

Like many companies in the sector, Lear is feeling the pinch as the woes of its North American customers — primarily Ford and GM — trickle down. As gas prices soar, consumers are reevaluating their love affairs with SUVs and Lear has been hurt by Detroit's cutback on the manufacture of high-margin gas-guzzling utility vehicles. The company is also caught in the balancing act of paying high materials costs while complying with automakers' demands for low prices.

To minimize the damage Lear has announced factory closures, as well as the transfer of some manufacturing to lower-cost regions such as Eastern Europe. Plant closures in North America and Western Europe will cut about 7,700 jobs.

Some relief is coming from Asia (specifically China) which quickly has become a focal point for industry growth across the spectrum of global carmakers and suppliers. Asia is Lear's fastest growing geographic segment. The company has formed several joint ventures in Japan, South Korea, and China, and plans to grow its Asian market share by further leveraging joint venture operations and increasing content per vehicle.

Lear is also focused on the trend of increasing an automobile's electronic equipment content, as the company's research indicates that by 2010 electronic components will account for up to 35% of a car's total value. To take advantage of the trend, Lear is developing innovative safety, communications, and information/entertainment electronics products.

Lear was dealt a heavy blow in early 2006 when Chrysler said it would replace Lear as its seat and interiors supplier on the next-generation Dodge Ram pickup which is scheduled for production in 2008.

Lear has sold $200 million in common stock to activist investor Carl Icahn, whose funds already held 5% of the company. The sale gave Icahn's interests a 16% stake in Lear. Early in 2007 Icahn offered to buy the entire company in a deal valued at $2.8 billion. Amid skepticism among shareholders, Icahn raised his bid to $37.25 per share, or $2.9 billion. However, shareholders voted to reject the offer.

## HISTORY

Lear dates back to 1917, when American Metal Products began supplying seats to Detroit's fledgling car industry. The seat maker incorporated in 1928 and grew during the 1950s and 1960s by buying other auto parts makers.

Siegler Heating, an industrial conglomerate with interests in the aerospace, auto parts, and manufacturing industries, was founded in 1950 as a maker of climate-control equipment. Entrepreneur John Brooks and a group of associates bought the company (renamed Siegler Corporation) in 1954 and led it through a series of acquisitions, including that of aerospace firm Lear in 1962. The company then became Lear Siegler.

Lear Siegler acquired American Metal in 1966. Beset by project delays, the company's aerospace unit sputtered in the 1970s, but the seat business did well. By 1985 metal seat frames had become Lear Siegler's major auto parts revenue producer. Spurred by growing competition with Japanese carmakers, the company built a plant near a GM factory in Michigan to allow swift delivery of its car seats.

In 1986 Forstmann Little bought the financially troubled Lear Siegler and began selling off the parts. Two years later the investment firm offered Lear Seating to its management (including Ken Way, who had been with the company since 1966). Way took the company private in a $500 million LBO, with the help of Kidder, Peabody. Kidder sold its stake in Lear Seating to Lehman Brothers in 1991.

Lear Seating bought a slice of Ford's North American automotive and trim operation and manufacturing factory in Ciudad Juárez, Mexico, in 1993. As a result of the purchase, the company entered a long-term supply agreement with Ford.

In another strategic buy of a customer's seat business, Lear Seating acquired Fiat's seat operations in 1994. This purchase encompassed Sepi Poland, Sepi S.p.A. (Italy), and a 35% stake in a Turkish joint venture, giving Lear Seating a presence in those countries. The purchase also made the company Europe's largest seat maker and gave it access to Fiat's 5% of the global automotive market. That year Lear Seating went public.

In 1995 Lear Seating bought Automotive Industries and inked a contract to provide seats for Brazil's top-selling car, the Volkswagen Gol. To reflect the broader scope of its business, the company dropped "Seating" from its name and became Lear Corporation in 1996. That year the company acquired Pennsylvania-based Masland for $475 million and formed a joint venture with China's Jiangling Motors to make seats and interior trim for Ford and Isuzu vehicles.

In 1998 Lear bought the automotive seating unit of GM's then-subsidiary Delphi Automotive Systems (now Delphi Corporation), giving it a bigger chunk of GM's business; it also bought parts companies in the UK and Italy. To cut costs, Lear announced that it would shut down 18 plants and cut 2,800 jobs (4% of its workforce) in the US, Europe, and South America. Acquisitions continued, however.

The company paid $2.3 billion for United Technologies' auto unit (but sold the electric motors unit to Johnson Electric Holdings for $310 million) to complete its instrument-panel offerings in 1999. Lear also bought Hyundai Motor's seat business to boost Pacific Rim sales. The following year Lear sold its sealants and foam rubber business to GSC Industries' AcoustiSeal.

Early in 2002 Lear announced it would cut 6,500 more jobs and close 21 manufacturing facilities. In light of the tightening automotive market, Lear plans to shutter older plants and move work to more cost efficient locations.

In 2004 Lear acquired German automotive electronics maker Grote & Hartmann GmbH & Co. for $220 million.

## EXECUTIVES

**Chairman, President, and CEO:** Robert E. Rossiter, age 61, $1,232,000 pay
**Vice Chairman and CFO:** James H. (Jim) Vandenberghe, age 57, $999,000 pay
**EVP, General Counsel, and Chief Administrative Officer:** Daniel A. (Dan) Ninivaggi, age 42, $742,767 pay (prior to title change)
**SVP; President, Electric and Electronics Systems Product Group:** Miguel Herrera-Lasso
**SVP; President, Global Asian Customer Group:** Louis R. Salvatore, age 47
**SVP; President, Global Seating Systems Product Group:** P. Joseph Zimmer, age 47
**SVP, Operational Finance, and Chief Accounting Officer:** Matthew J. (Matt) Simoncini, age 46
**SVP; President, European Operations:** James Brackenbury, age 48
**SVP; President, North American Seating Systems Group:** Raymond E. Scott, age 41, $476,518 pay
**SVP, Human Resources:** Roger A. Jackson, age 60
**VP and Corporate Controller:** James L. Murawski, age 55
**VP and Treasurer:** Shari Burgess, age 48
**VP, China:** Russ Hall
**VP, Investor Relations and Corporate Communications:** Mel Stephens
**VP Finance and Adminsitration and Corporate Secretary:** Wendy L. Foss
**Chief Diversity Officer:** Marina Williams
**Director, Corporate Communications:** Andrea Puchaslsky
**Auditors:** Ernst & Young LLP

## LOCATIONS

**HQ:** Lear Corporation
21557 Telegraph Rd., Southfield, MI 48034
**Phone:** 248-447-1500 **Fax:** 248-447-1772
**Web:** www.lear.com

Lear operates 265 facilities in 33 countries worldwide.

### 2006 Sales

| | $ mil. | % of total |
|---|---|---|
| North America | | |
| US | 6,624.3 | 37 |
| Canada | 1,375.3 | 8 |
| Germany | 2,034.3 | 11 |
| Mexico | 1,789.5 | 10 |
| Other countries | 6,015.5 | 34 |
| **Total** | **17,838.9** | **100** |

## PRODUCTS/OPERATIONS

### 2006 Sales

| | $ mil. | % of total |
|---|---|---|
| Seating | 11,624.8 | 65 |
| Interior | 3,217.2 | 18 |
| Electronic & Electrical | 2,996.9 | 17 |
| **Total** | **17,838.9** | **100** |

### 2006 Sales by Customer

| | % of total |
|---|---|
| General Motors | 32 |
| Ford | 23 |
| DaimlerChrysler | 10 |
| Others | 35 |
| **Total** | **100** |

### Selected Products

Seating
- Automotive seats and head restraints

Interior
- Door panels and trim
- Flooring and acoustic systems
- Instrument panels and cockpit systems
- Overhead systems

Electronic & Electrical
- Electrical distribution systems
- Interior control and entertainment systems
- Wireless systems

## COMPETITORS

Alps Automotive
Cherry
Collins & Aikman
Delphi
DENSO
Eaton
Faurecia
Flexsteel
Jason
Johnson Controls
Lacks Enterprises
LEONI
Magna International
Methode Electronics
OMRON
Rieter Holding
Robert Bosch
Siemens VDO Automotive
Sumitomo
Textron
Tokai Rika
Toyota Boshoku
TRW Automotive
Valeo
Visteon
Yazaki

## HISTORICAL FINANCIALS

Company Type: Public

### Income Statement

FYE: December 31

| | REVENUE ($ mil.) | NET INCOME ($ mil.) | NET PROFIT MARGIN | EMPLOYEES |
|---|---|---|---|---|
| **12/06** | 17,839 | (708) | — | 104,000 |
| **12/05** | 17,089 | (1,382) | — | 115,000 |
| **12/04** | 16,960 | 422 | 2.5% | 110,000 |
| **12/03** | 15,747 | 381 | 2.4% | 111,000 |
| **12/02** | 14,425 | 13 | 0.1% | 115,000 |
| **Annual Growth** | 5.5% | — | — | (2.5%) |

### 2006 Year-End Financials

Debt ratio: 404.4%
Return on equity: —
Cash ($ mil.): 503
Current ratio: 1.00
Long-term debt ($ mil.): 2,435
No. of shares (mil.): 76
Dividends
Yield: 0.8%
Payout: —
Market value ($ mil.): 2,252

### Stock History

NYSE: LEA

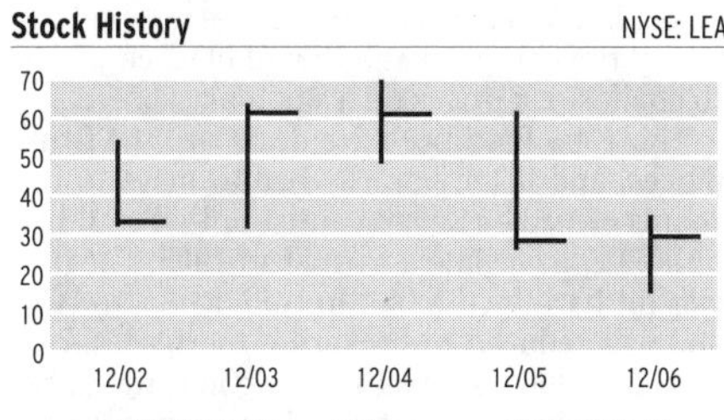


| | STOCK PRICE ($) FY Close | P/E High | P/E Low | PER SHARE ($) Earnings | Dividends | Book Value |
|---|---|---|---|---|---|---|
| **12/06** | 29.53 | — | — | (10.31) | 0.25 | 7.89 |
| **12/05** | 28.46 | — | — | (20.57) | 1.00 | 16.54 |
| **12/04** | 61.01 | 12 | 8 | 5.77 | 0.80 | 40.50 |
| **12/03** | 61.33 | 11 | 6 | 5.55 | 0.20 | 33.12 |
| **12/02** | 33.28 | 283 | 172 | 0.19 | — | 25.29 |
| **Annual Growth** | (2.9%) | — | — | — | 7.7% | (25.2%) |

# Legg Mason

Legg Mason's feats include wealth management and mutual fund management. The financial services firm has several subsidiaries that offer asset management, trust services, and annuities to retail and institutional investors. The company manages more than 150 mutual funds under the Legg Mason, Legg Mason Partners, Western Asset, and The Royce Funds banners. Other offerings include closed-end funds and separate accounts. Legg Mason distributes its products through its own offices, retirement plans, insurance companies, and other channels. The company operates primarily in the US and the UK, but has locations in about 15 other countries.

In a deal worth some $3.7 billion, Legg Mason swapped its brokerage and capital markets operations for most of the mutual fund and asset management business of Citigroup in 2005. The company also bought 80% of The Permal Group, a large funds-of-hedge-funds administrator.

Legg Mason announced the latter agreement the same day it unveiled the unusual Citigroup transaction. These two significant deals allowed Legg Mason to focus solely on asset management and made it one of the largest such companies in the US with about $1 trillion of assets under management. Prior to the transactions, Legg Mason had less than $400 billion in assets under management. The acquisitions also significantly increased the company's assets under management overseas.

In 2006 Legg Mason changed the name of the former Citigroup Asset Management US Equity Group to ClearBridge Advisors. The Smith Barney funds, also acquired in the Citi deal, were renamed Legg Mason Partners Funds. Later that year, Legg Mason restructured into three segments: US Asset Management, International Asset Management, and Global Managed Investments.

Legg Mason offers wealth management services to affluent clients through several subsidiaries, including Cincinnati's Bartlett & Co., Florida-based Private Capital Management, and Legg Mason Investment Counsel & Trust.

Institutional investor AXA Financial owns nearly 10% of Legg Mason.

## HISTORY

In 1899 George Mackubin and G. Clem Goodrich joined together to form brokerage firm Mackubin & Goodrich. The next year John Legg joined the company as a "board boy," employed to chalk stock prices on a small blackboard.

The 1904 Baltimore fire destroyed the firm's offices, and it temporarily had to move to two rooms owned by Legg's dentist until it could rebuild. Legg became a partner in 1905. The firm was hit hard by the halt in trading due to WWI and was reduced to brokering mortgages for a local homebuilder. In 1925 the company started what may have been the first real estate investment trust, National Union Mortgage Company. The company established a new department in 1930 devoted exclusively to women investors and hired A. Catherine Overbeck to run it.

The 1929 stock market crash and Depression devastated the firm, and in 1930 the partners liquidated their own portfolios to inject cash into the company. After Goodrich died in 1932, the firm was renamed Mackubin, Legg & Co. It lost its other founder in 1942 when Mackubin argued with Legg and left to join a competitor. The firm became John C. Legg & Co.

The company flourished in the postwar boom. In 1962 Raymond "Chip" Mason founded his own brokerage in Virginia and eight years later merged it with Legg to form Legg Mason & Co. In 1973 the firm acquired New York broker-dealer Wood Walker & Co. and became Legg Mason Wood Walker.

The company introduced a money market mutual fund in 1979 and its first equity fund in 1982. Between those two events, it established Legg Mason, Inc. as a holding company for its growing list of subsidiaries; it went public in 1983. During the 1980s and 1990s, the firm added to its straight brokerage business by buying a string of asset management companies.

Targeting wealthy individuals, in 1999 the company obtained a national thrift charter, allowing it to take on trust business outside Maryland. Expanding outside the US at century's end, it bought UK investment firm Johnson Fry Holdings and Canadian pension fund manager Perigee; both acquisitions were ultimately rebranded under the Legg Mason name. Also that year, the company merged Howard, Weil, Labouisse, Friedrichs into Legg Mason Wood Walker.

Legg Mason bought New York-based investment manager Barrett Associates in 2000 and purchased Private Capital Management and Royce & Associates the following year.

In 2004, Legg Mason was one of several companies that settled NASD and SEC charges of failing to pay mutual fund customers discounts to which they were entitled.

## EXECUTIVES

**Chairman, President, and CEO:** Raymond A. (Chip) Mason, age 70
**CEO, Western Asset Management:** James W. (Jim) Hirschmann III, age 46
**SEVP; President, U.S. Asset Management:** Peter L. Bain, age 48, $2,839,000 pay
**SEVP; President, Global Managed Investments:** Mark R. Fetting, age 52, $3,519,000 pay
**SVP, Treasurer, and CFO:** Charles J. Daley Jr., age 45
**SVP Business Development:** F. Barry Bilson, age 54
**SVP Business Strategy:** Elisabeth N. Spector, age 59
**SVP and General Counsel:** Thomas P. Lemke
**SVP and Head of International Marketing and Distribution; CEO, Legg Mason Investments:** Deepak Chowdhury, age 48, $1,585,000 pay
**Secretary:** Robert F. Price
**Chairman and Chief Investment Officer, Legg Mason Capital Management:** William H. (Bill) Miller III
**CEO, Legg Mason Capital Management:** Kyle Prechtl Legg
**CEO, Legg Mason Investment Counsel:** Harry O'Mealia
**CEO, ClearBridge Advisors:** Brian Posner
**Chairman, Asset Management Committee, Western Asset Management:** D. Daniel Fleet
**Manager, Salomon Brothers Investors Value Fund:** Mark McAllister
**Co-Portfolio Manager, Salomon Brothers Capital Fund:** Brian Angerame
**Managing Director and Head, US Distribution:** Donald E. (Don) Froude
**Corporate Communications:** Mary Athridge
**Auditors:** PricewaterhouseCoopers LLP

## LOCATIONS

**HQ:** Legg Mason, Inc.
100 Light St., Baltimore, MD 21202
**Phone:** 410-539-0000 **Fax:** 410-454-4923
**Web:** www.leggmason.com

Legg Mason and its subsidiaries have offices in Australia, Brazil, Canada, Chile, Dubai, France, Germany, Hong Kong, Japan, Luxembourg, Poland, Singapore, Spain, Taiwan, the UK, and the US.

**2007 Sales**

| | $ mil. | % of total |
|---|---|---|
| US | 3,272.9 | 75 |
| UK | 829.4 | 19 |
| Other | 241.4 | 6 |
| **Total** | **4,343.7** | **100** |

## PRODUCTS/OPERATIONS

**2007 Sales**

| | $ mil. | % of total |
|---|---|---|
| Investment advisory fees | | |
| Funds | 2,023.1 | 47 |
| Separate accounts | 1,445.8 | 33 |
| Performance fees | 142.3 | 3 |
| Distribution & service fees | 716.4 | 17 |
| Other | 16.1 | — |
| **Total** | **4,343.7** | **100** |

## COMPETITORS

A.G. Edwards
AllianceBernstein
AllianceBernstein Holding
Bear Stearns
BlackRock
Charles Schwab
Citigroup
Credit Suisse (USA)
Deutsche Bank
E*TRADE Financial
Edward Jones
Federated Investors
FMR
Goldman Sachs
Janus Capital
JPMorgan Chase
Lehman Brothers
Morgan Keegan
Morgan Stanley
Phoenix Companies
Piper Jaffray
Principal Financial
Raymond James Financial
T. Rowe Price
TD Ameritrade
UBS Financial Services
The Vanguard Group
Wells Fargo

## HISTORICAL FINANCIALS

Company Type: Public

**Income Statement** FYE: March 31

| | ASSETS ($ mil.) | NET INCOME ($ mil.) | INCOME AS % OF ASSETS | EMPLOYEES |
|---|---|---|---|---|
| **3/07** | 9,605 | 647 | 6.7% | 4,030 |
| **3/06** | 9,303 | 1,144 | 12.3% | 3,800 |
| **3/05** | 8,220 | 408 | 5.0% | 5,580 |
| **3/04** | 7,263 | 298 | 4.1% | 5,250 |
| **3/03** | 6,068 | 191 | 3.1% | 5,290 |
| **Annual Growth** | 12.2% | 35.7% | — | (6.6%) |

**2007 Year-End Financials**

Equity as % of assets: 68.1%
Return on assets: 6.8%
Return on equity: 10.4%
Long-term debt ($ mil.): 1,108
No. of shares (mil.): 130
Dividends
Yield: 0.9%
Payout: 18.1%
Market value ($ mil.): 12,220
Sales ($ mil.): 4,344

**Stock History** NYSE: LM

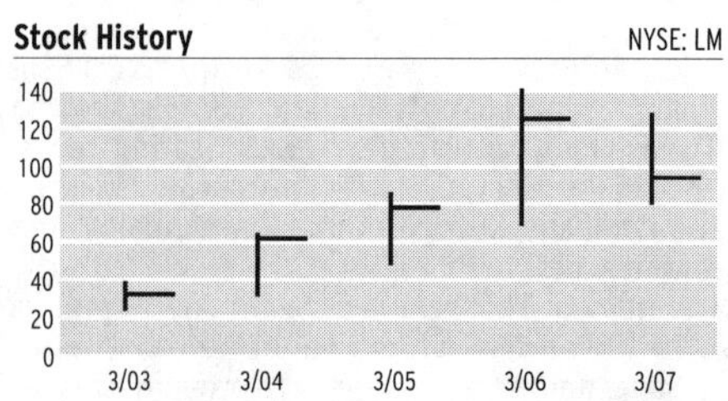


| | STOCK PRICE ($) FY Close | P/E High | P/E Low | PER SHARE ($) Earnings | Dividends | Book Value |
|---|---|---|---|---|---|---|
| **3/07** | 94.21 | 28 | 18 | 4.48 | 0.81 | 50.43 |
| **3/06** | 125.33 | 16 | 8 | 8.80 | 0.69 | 45.10 |
| **3/05** | 78.14 | 24 | 14 | 3.53 | 0.55 | 21.49 |
| **3/04** | 61.85 | 24 | 12 | 2.71 | 0.37 | 23.44 |
| **3/03** | 32.49 | 21 | 13 | 1.85 | 0.29 | 19.25 |
| **Annual Growth** | 30.5% | — | — | 24.7% | 29.3% | 27.2% |

# Leggett & Platt

That spring in your step after a good night's sleep may be there courtesy of Leggett & Platt — the pioneer of coiled bedsprings. Primarily using aluminum and steel, it makes finished furniture (headboards), commercial furnishings (store displays, shelving), and die-cast products (components for gas barbecue grills and outdoor lighting fixtures). Leggett & Platt also produces industrial materials (wire, steel tubing) and specialized items (quilting machinery, commercial truck equipment). Customers include furniture retailers and manufacturers of automobiles, construction-related products, furniture and bedding, and garden and yard equipment.

Leggett & Platt has boosted its profitability and grown through acquisitions, strengthening its presence in the residential and commercial furnishings and specialized product markets. Leggett & Platt has bought more than 100 companies since 1996.

The firm hadn't kicked its acquisition habit. After numerous acquisitions in 2005, it continued in 2006 with the purchase of a rubber carpet underlay company. It also acquired two geo components makers, boosting its geographic presence and offerings in soil stabilization, drainage, erosion and flood control products. The company also divested several smaller companies in 2006 including an industrial sewing machine manufacturer and a steel coil slitter business.

As part of its recent strategy to only operate in areas where the company can be a market leader, Leggett & Platt in early 2007 exited the foam business. The company sold its Prime Foam unit to Comfort Co., a Catterton Partners firm. The foam business manufactured cushions for upholstered furniture and bedding. Leggett still makes foam for carpet underlay.

## HISTORY

Carthage, Missouri resident J. P. Leggett, an inventor with several patents, took his coiled bedspring to his businessman/manufacturer brother-in-law, C. B. Platt, in 1883. The two formed a partnership and began selling bedsprings (patented in 1885) to retailers who incorporated them into their mattresses (previous mattresses were made of cotton, horsehair, or feathers). They had two plants when they incorporated as Leggett & Platt Spring Bed & Manufacturing Co. in 1901.

Leggett was president until 1921, when Platt took over. Leggett's son got the nod in 1929, and though he headed the company for only three years, he initiated the production of both innerspring mattress springs (the original coiled spring had been the company's sole product) and coiled springs for upholstered furniture.

By this time Leggett & Platt was selling to manufacturers rather than retailers, and sales and profits took off along with the innerspring market, though the conservative company didn't open another plant until 1942. Another plant opening in 1947 was the last expansion until 1960. That year CEO Harry Cornell (grandson of J. P. Leggett), who joined the company in 1950, took the reins. By then Leggett & Platt had three plants and $7 million in annual sales.

Cornell envisioned the company as a national low-cost supplier of furnishings components. He acquired a woodworking plant in 1960, giving the firm the ability to make wooden bed frames. Acquisitions steadily increased the company's range of products and its geographic scope, and by the early 1970s (the company went public in 1967) Leggett & Platt had 17 plants and annual sales of about $50 million. The increasing size of the company, along with vertical integration (it began making its own wire in 1970), gave it economies of scale and cost advantages in the fragmented industry.

In 1970 bedding components accounted for about 70% of sales; just four years later — as Leggett & Platt focused on finished furniture and furniture components — they accounted for only 43%. Leggett & Platt also made investments in new plants, equipment, and products. By 1980 the company had about 60 plants and sales of more than $250 million. Leggett & Platt introduced its continuous coil innerspring — which contributed to the company's good performance in an otherwise slumping industry — around the middle of the decade.

The recession at the beginning of the 1990s hurt the company's sales, but Leggett & Platt bounced back with the economy and had over $1 billion in sales in 1992. The next year the company added to its 135 plants with the acquisitions of Hanes Holding Company and VWR Textiles & Supplies (bedding and furniture fabrics).

About 75% of the company's 1995 sales increase resulted from acquisitions; the following year Leggett & Platt acquired 14 more companies, including Pace Holdings (aluminum die-cast components). Cornell's 47-year-old strategy continued in 1997 and into 1998 as the company acquired over 39 businesses (28 furnishings-related) with aggregate annual sales of about $560 million.

President Felix Wright added CEO to his duties in 1999 and Cornell remained chairman. Throughout 1999 Leggett & Platt bought 29 companies with a combined revenue of about $480 million. In 2000 the company kept up its buying habit, purchasing 21 companies. By 2001, however, Leggett & Platt began to reverse that trend, closing or selling off facilities it deemed unprofitable.

In 2005, as sales improved, Leggett & Platt bought (the assets of) Ikex; (the membership interests of) Jarex Distribution; a Jia Jiang, China, furniture mechanism facility; Toronto-based Westex International; and Mississippi's Everwood Products. Also, it purchased a Shanghai, China, fixtures facility.

Leggett & Platt's acquisition of America's Body Company (ABC) in late 2005 gave the company a leg up in the commercial truck equipment segment of the industry and spurred the firm to restructure its operations. ABC designs, makes, and markets bodies for vans, flatbed trucks, utility work vehicles, and dump trucks, as well as interiors for vans and equipment for snow and ice control. Leggett & Platt folded ABC into its existing van interiors operations to form the Commercial Vehicle Products Group, which is estimated to generate some $250 million in revenue. The group's rolled up into the company's Specialized Products business segment.

Cornell became chairman emeritus in May 2006, when Wright resigned as CEO and took the title of chairman. President David Haffner became CEO as part of the succession.

## EXECUTIVES

**Chairman Emeritus:** Harry M. Cornell Jr., age 77
**Chairman:** Felix E. Wright, age 71
**President, CEO, and Director:** David S. (Dave) Haffner, age 54
**EVP, COO, and Director:** Karl G. Glassman, age 48
**EVP, Sales and Marketing, Consumer Products Business Unit:** Stephen Sczubelek
**SVP and CFO:** Matthew C. (Matt) Flanigan, age 45
**SVP; President, Residential Furnishings:** Paul R. Hauser, age 55
**SVP; President, Aluminum Products:** Daniel R. (Dan) Hebert, age 63
**SVP; President, Fixture and Display Group:** Robert G. (Bob) Griffin, age 53
**SVP; President, Industrial Materials:** Joseph D. Downes Jr., age 62, $323,817 pay
**SVP; President, Specialized Products:** Jack D. Crusa, age 52
**SVP; President, Commercial Fixturing and Components:** Dennis S. Park, age 52
**SVP, Business Development:** Dick Ralston
**SVP, General Counsel, and Secretary:** Ernest C. Jett, age 61
**SVP, Human Resources:** John A. Hale
**VP, Corporate Controller, and Chief Accounting Officer:** William S. Weil, age 48
**VP and Treasurer:** Sheri L. Mossbeck
**VP, Investor Relations and Assistant Treasurer:** David M. (Dave) DeSonier
**Group President, Commercial Vehicle Products:** Elliott J. Lyons, age 40
**Group EVP, Sales and Marketing, Bedding:** Mark Quinn
**Auditors:** PricewaterhouseCoopers LLP

## LOCATIONS

**HQ:** Leggett & Platt, Incorporated
No. 1 Leggett Rd., Carthage, MO 64836
**Phone:** 417-358-8131 **Fax:** 417-358-5840
**Web:** www.leggett.com

### 2006 Sales

| | $ mil. | % of total |
|---|---|---|
| North America | | |
| US | 4,360.7 | 79 |
| Canada | 419.9 | 8 |
| Mexico | 161.0 | 3 |
| Europe | 353.7 | 6 |
| China | 157.3 | 3 |
| Other regions | 52.8 | 1 |
| **Total** | **5,505.4** | **100** |

## PRODUCTS/OPERATIONS

### 2006 Sales

| | $ mil. | % of total |
|---|---|---|
| Residential furnishings | 2,745.8 | 50 |
| Commercial fixturing & components | 1,018.8 | 18 |
| Specialized products | 708.7 | 13 |
| Aluminum products | 543.3 | 10 |
| Industrial materials | 488.8 | 9 |
| **Total** | **5,505.4** | **100** |

### Selected Products

Residential Furnishings
- Finished products
  - Adjustable electric beds
  - Bed frames
  - Bunk beds
  - Carpet underlay
  - Daybeds
  - Fashion beds
  - Headboards
  - Non-slip products
- Foam, textile, fiber, and other cushioning materials (bedding, furniture, industrial applications)
- Innerspring and box spring units
- Springs and seating suspensions (chairs, sofas)
- Steel mechanisms and hardware (reclining chairs, sleeper sofas)

Commercial Furnishings
- Component products
  - Chair controls, bases, columns, backrests, and casters
- Finished products
  - Point-of-purchase displays
  - Storage products
  - Store counters, carts, fixtures, and shelving

Aluminum Products
- Aluminum die-cast components (including items for gas barbecue grills, outdoor lighting fixtures, computers, power tools, and engines)

Industrial Materials
- Drawn steel wire
- Steel tubing

Specialized Products
- Quilting machinery
- Seating suspension, lumbar support, and control cable systems (automobile industry)

### Selected Trademarks

ADJUSTAMAGIC (adjustable electric beds)
DYNA-Lock, LOK-Fast, and SEMI-FLEX (box spring components and foundations)
Gribetz and Porter (quilting and sewing manufacturing machines)
Hanes (fiber materials)
Masterack, Amco, and RHC Spacemaster (fixtures and displays)
Mira-Coil, Lura-Flex, and Superlastic (mattress innersprings)
No-Sag (sinuous wire)
Nova-Bond and Rollout (insulators for mattresses)
Schukra, Pullmaflex, and Flex-O-Lators (automotive products)
Spuhl (mattress innerspring manufacturing machines)
SUPER SAGLESS (motion and sofa sleeper mechanisms)
Tack & Jump and Patternlink (quilting machines)
Wallhugger (recliner chairs)

## COMPETITORS

Advance Auto Parts
Alcoa
AutoZone
Burlington WorldWide
Diam International
Flexsteel
Foamex
Genuine Parts
Holophane
Kaiser Aluminum
Keystone Consolidated
Knape & Vogt
Louisville Bedding
Lozier
Wal-Mart

## HISTORICAL FINANCIALS

Company Type: Public

**Income Statement** FYE: December 31

| | REVENUE ($ mil.) | NET INCOME ($ mil.) | NET PROFIT MARGIN | EMPLOYEES |
|---|---|---|---|---|
| **12/06** | 5,505 | 300 | 5.5% | 32,828 |
| **12/05** | 5,299 | 251 | 4.7% | 33,000 |
| **12/04** | 5,086 | 285 | 5.6% | 33,000 |
| **12/03** | 4,388 | 206 | 4.7% | 33,000 |
| **12/02** | 4,272 | 233 | 5.5% | 31,000 |
| **Annual Growth** | 6.5% | 6.5% | — | 1.4% |

**2006 Year-End Financials**

Debt ratio: 45.1%
Return on equity: 13.1%
Cash ($ mil.): 132
Current ratio: 2.74
Long-term debt ($ mil.): 1,060
No. of shares (mil.): 178
Dividends
Yield: 2.8%
Payout: 41.6%
Market value ($ mil.): 4,254

**Stock History** NYSE: LEG

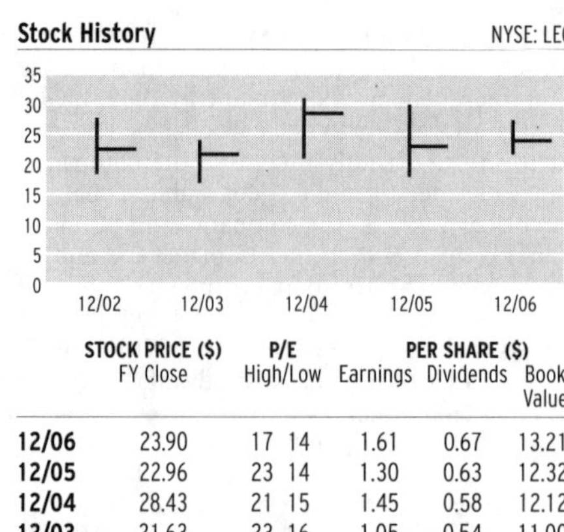


| | STOCK PRICE ($) FY Close | P/E High | P/E Low | PER SHARE ($) Earnings | Dividends | Book Value |
|---|---|---|---|---|---|---|
| **12/06** | 23.90 | 17 | 14 | 1.61 | 0.67 | 13.21 |
| **12/05** | 22.96 | 23 | 14 | 1.30 | 0.63 | 12.32 |
| **12/04** | 28.43 | 21 | 15 | 1.45 | 0.58 | 12.12 |
| **12/03** | 21.63 | 23 | 16 | 1.05 | 0.54 | 11.00 |
| **12/02** | 22.44 | 23 | 16 | 1.17 | 0.50 | 10.16 |
| **Annual Growth** | 1.6% | — | — | 8.3% | 7.6% | 6.8% |

# Lehman Brothers Holdings

Lehman Brothers is a lean, mean, investment banking machine. One of the top bulge-bracket firms, the company is perennially among the industry leaders in mergers and acquisition advice, debt and equity underwriting, and global finance. Capital markets activities (by far its largest segment) entail institutional brokerage, market making, equity and debt research, securities lending, and mortgage banking. Its investment management business, which oversees approximately $225 billion for clients, includes private banking, trust services, private equity, and money manager Neuberger Berman.

Lehman Brothers has more than 120 offices in the Americas, Europe, and Asia. Traditionally a participant in the business world's largest mergers and acquisitions, the company is taking advantage of increased deal-making activity, particularly in Europe and Asia. It has also remained relatively unscathed by many of the controversies (conflicts of interest, Enron) that have plagued competitors in recent years. In fiscal year 2006, Lehman Brothers reported record earnings for the third year in a row, as well as record levels of net income.

The company also runs Lehman Brothers Bancorp, which serves as the holding company for mortgage banking subsidiaries Aurora Loan Services and BNC Mortgage in addition to providing traditional banking services.

In 2006 Lehman inaugurated a new private equity real estate fund that will invest up to 50% of its £4 billion stake in Asia. The company bought a 20% stake in massive hedge fund D.E. Shaw & Co. and agreed to purchase LightPoint Capital Management, a Chicago-based leveraged specialist in 2007.

## HISTORY

Henry Lehman came to the US in 1844. After a year in New York, he moved to Montgomery, Alabama to open a dry goods store. Younger brothers Emanuel and Mayer had joined him by 1850. The brothers often accepted raw cotton instead of cash for merchandise and developed a thriving cotton business on the side. Soon cotton trading dominated the firm, and in 1858 the company opened a New York office.

Despite the effects of the Civil War, in 1862 the Lehman brothers joined fellow cotton merchant John Durr to form Lehman, Durr & Co. The company helped finance Alabama's postwar reconstruction and, in 1870, helped form the New York Cotton Exchange.

The firm continued to grow and diversify, underwriting its first IPO in 1899 for International Steam Pump Co. Seven years later Lehman joined with Goldman Sachs to take Sears, Roebuck public. In the 1920s and during the Depression, Lehman continued its investment operations, pioneering private placements during the long eclipse of the stock market in the 1930s. The company remained under family management until the death of Robert Lehman (Emanuel's grandson) in 1969.

In 1977 Lehman merged with Kuhn Loeb & Co., which had helped finance the railroad industry. Kuhn Loeb had significant business overseas dating from the turn of the century, when it helped the Japanese government finance the Russo-Japanese War.

But the late 1970s were a precarious time in the financial world, and the firms did not meld well. By 1984 Lehman Brothers Kuhn Loeb was torn by infighting among its partners and managers and was ripe for a sellout to the right suitor. Along came Sandy Weill, who had sold his Shearson brokerage to American Express and become that company's president. He was attempting to assemble a financial supermarket and needed an investment banking firm.

Lehman Brothers Kuhn Loeb had trouble adjusting to Shearson and mass defections ensued. Shearson's go-getting ethos improved results, but they remained spotty, and the firm splurged on employee perks. The 1987 stock market crash hit Shearson hard, yet Travel Related Services (the core business of American Express) remained profitable.

In 1992 American Express began to divest its financial services by business lines. Lehman kept investment banking but lost brokerage. American Express spun off Lehman in 1994, but Lehman's independence came at a price. It had to struggle to increase sales and cut costs as management shake-ups rippled through. The firm overhauled leadership, cut extravagant personnel costs, and introduced its Restricted Stock Unit employee ownership program.

In 2002, the firm bolstered its Asian operations by purchasing a minority stake (in convertible bonds) in South Korea's Woori Financial Holding Co. — one of the country's largest financial services firms — along with a portfolio of Woori's non-performing loans. Also in 2002, Lehman created a $1.6 billion real estate fund. And the idea of driving a Ferrari apparently wasn't enough: the company acquired a 6.5% stake in the automaker from Italian merchant banker Mediobanca in September 2002.

The company's World Trade Center offices were destroyed by the 2001 terrorist attacks, displacing 6,400 employees. After operating temporarily from a hotel, the company bought Morgan Stanley's newly completed office building in Manhattan. While the relocation costs initially had a negative impact on financials, the company's 2002 earnings were bolstered by gains related to insurance settlements.

Lehman Brothers acquired Neuberger Berman, private equity fund manager The Crossroads Group (now Lehman Crossroads), and fixed-income asset management firm Lincoln Capital in 2003.

## EXECUTIVES

**Chairman and CEO:** Richard S. (Dick) Fuld Jr., age 60, $7,000,000 pay
**EVP and Chief Legal Officer; Vice Chairman, Lehman Brothers Inc.:** Thomas A. Russo, age 63, $5,000,000 pay
**President and COO, Lehman Brothers Holdings and Lehman Brothers Inc.:** Joseph M. (Joe) Gregory, age 54, $5,950,000 pay
**Global Head of Strategic Partnerships, Principal Investing and Risk:** David (Dave) Goldfarb, age 48, $3,000,000 pay
**EVP and CFO, Lehman Brothers Holdings and Lehman Brothers Inc.:** Christopher M. (Chris) O'Meara, age 45, $2,500,000 pay
**EVP and Co-Chief Administrative Officer:** Scott J. Freidheim, age 41, $2,500,000 pay (prior to title change)
**Chairman, European Luxury Goods Investment Banking:** Roberto Vedovotto, age 42
**Chairman and CEO, Lehman Brothers Bank:** William E. (Bill) Lighten
**Global Head, Fixed Income:** Roger B. Nagioff, age 41
**Global Head of Investment Management:** George H. Walker
**Global Head of Equities:** Herbert H. (Bart) McDade III, age 46
**Global Head of Investment Banking:** Hugh E. (Skip) McGee III, age 46
**Global Head of Private Investment Management:** Alan P. Marantz
**Global Head of Equity and Fixed Income Research:** Ravi Mattu
**Global Head of Foreign Exchange Research:** Jim McCormick
**Global Head of Strategy and Corporate Communications, Advertising, and Brand and Marketing Strategy, New York:** Scott Friedman
**Head of Global Finance:** Larry Wieseneck
**Managing Director and Global Head of Merchant Banking:** Charles Ayres
**Managing Director and Head of Private Equity:** Michael J. Odrich, age 43
**Managing Director and Head of Private Fund Investments:** Anthony D. Tutrone
**Corporate Secretary:** Jeffrey A. Welikson
**Investor Relations:** Shaun K. Butler
**Auditors:** Ernst & Young LLP

## LOCATIONS

**HQ:** Lehman Brothers Holdings Inc.
745 7th Ave., New York, NY 10019
**Phone:** 212-526-7000 **Fax:** 212-526-8766
**Web:** www.lehman.com

## PRODUCTS/OPERATIONS

**2006 Sales**

| | $ mil. | % of total |
|---|---|---|
| Capital Markets | 41,074 | 88 |
| Investment banking | 3,160 | 7 |
| Investment management | 2,475 | 5 |
| **Total** | **46,709** | **100** |

**2006 Sales**

| | $ mil. | % of total |
|---|---|---|
| Interest & dividends | 30,284 | 65 |
| Principal transactions | 9,802 | 21 |
| Investment banking | 3,160 | 7 |
| Commissions | 2,050 | 4 |
| Asset management & other | 1,413 | 3 |
| **Total** | **46,709** | **100** |

## COMPETITORS

AXA Financial
Bank of America
Bear Stearns
Citigroup
Citigroup Global Markets
Cowen Group
Credit Suisse (USA)
Deutsche Bank
Goldman Sachs
ING
JPMorgan Chase
Merrill Lynch
Morgan Stanley
UBS
UBS Financial Services

## HISTORICAL FINANCIALS

Company Type: Public

**Income Statement** FYE: November 30

| | REVENUE ($ mil.) | NET INCOME ($ mil.) | NET PROFIT MARGIN | EMPLOYEES |
|---|---|---|---|---|
| **11/06** | 46,709 | 4,007 | 8.6% | 25,900 |
| **11/05** | 32,420 | 3,260 | 10.1% | 22,900 |
| **11/04** | 21,250 | 2,369 | 11.1% | 19,600 |
| **11/03** | 17,287 | 1,699 | 9.8% | 16,200 |
| **11/02** | 16,781 | 975 | 5.8% | 12,343 |
| **Annual Growth** | 29.2% | 42.4% | — | 20.4% |

**2006 Year-End Financials**

Debt ratio: 686.3%
Return on equity: 23.7%
Cash ($ mil.): 12,078
Current ratio: —
Long-term debt ($ mil.): 124,188
No. of shares (mil.): 533
Dividends
Yield: 0.7%
Payout: 7.0%
Market value ($ mil.): 39,293

**Stock History** NYSE: LEH

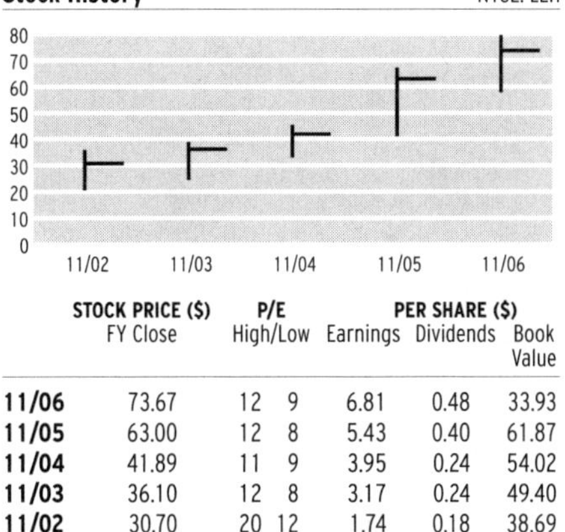


| | STOCK PRICE ($) FY Close | P/E High | P/E Low | PER SHARE ($) Earnings | PER SHARE ($) Dividends | PER SHARE ($) Book Value |
|---|---|---|---|---|---|---|
| **11/06** | 73.67 | 12 | 9 | 6.81 | 0.48 | 33.93 |
| **11/05** | 63.00 | 12 | 8 | 5.43 | 0.40 | 61.87 |
| **11/04** | 41.89 | 11 | 9 | 3.95 | 0.24 | 54.02 |
| **11/03** | 36.10 | 12 | 8 | 3.17 | 0.24 | 49.40 |
| **11/02** | 30.70 | 20 | 12 | 1.74 | 0.18 | 38.69 |
| **Annual Growth** | 24.5% | — | — | 40.7% | 27.8% | (3.2%) |

# Lennar Corporation

Lennar is one of the largest homebuilding, land-owning, loan-making leviathans in the US. The company joins D.R. Horton, Pulte Homes, and Centex in the top tier of US homebuilders. Lennar builds about 49,000 homes annually for first-time buyers, move-up, and active adults in nearly 20 states. Home prices average $315,000. Lennar also provides financial services (residential mortgage, title, and closing services). Lennar markets its homes through its Everything's Included program, in which houses come complete with most top-of-the-line features. CEO Stuart Miller controls some 49% of the company.

The company ran into trouble in 2006 along with the rest of the housing industry when rising interest rates and overbuilding took their toll. At the beginning of 2007 Lennar and partner LNR Properties sold a 62% stake in their LandSource joint venture (which owns Newhall Land and Farming Company) for $900 million in cash and property to MW Housing Partners, a group that includes the California Public Employees' Retirement System.

## HISTORY

Lennar is the creation of Leonard Miller and Arnold Rosen, and the name of the company is a combination of their given names. Rosen, a Miami homebuilder, formed F&R Builders in 1954. A year later Miller graduated from Harvard with no firm career plans. Having worked summers in Florida, Miller decided it would be a good place to make his fortune, and the 23-year-old began selling real estate there.

With $10,000 earned from commissions, Miller bought 42 lots and in 1956 entered a joint venture with Rosen to build homes on the lots. They worked well together, and Miller soon joined F&R. The operation grew, emphasizing marketing and concentrating on low- and medium-priced single-family homes for first-time buyers and retirees.

After expanding into commercial real estate in the late 1960s, the duo folded F&R into a new company — Lennar Corporation — in 1971 and went public. During the 1970s and 1980s, the company hawked Jacuzzi tubs and designer homes (such as the Calvin and the Liz) and promised customers "$10,000 worth of extras" free at Midnight Madness shopping mall sales. Lennar also began expanding, acquiring land and builders in the Phoenix area in 1973. Rosen retired in 1977.

Spurred by a recession, Lennar began offering mortgage services nationwide in 1981, keeping the potentially lucrative servicing for itself and selling its mortgages to Fannie Mae, Ginnie Mae, and Freddie Mac, among others. In 1984 it dissolved its construction operations and began subbing out its work (a practice that it continues today). Lennar was relatively unscathed by the recession of the late 1980s, in part because Miller had foreseen a slump and had cut corporate debt and overhead. When other builders were overextending themselves by buying land in good times, Miller had used profit to pay down debt so he would have the resources to buy land cheap when bad times arrived.

During the 1990s Lennar targeted other Sun Belt markets and began buying portfolios of distressed property in partnership with heavy hitters like Morgan Stanley. Although Miller had looked at Texas as a development site since 1987, it was not until 1991 that Lennar entered the state, beginning in Dallas.

The company bought up the secured debt of Bramalea Homes in Southern California in 1995 and entered Northern California with its acquisition of Renaissance Homes. Lennar's acquisition of Village Homes and Exxon's Friendswood Development in 1996 made it Houston's top home builder, and Lennar surpassed $1 billion in sales.

In 1997 Stuart Miller became president and CEO (Leonard, his father, remained chairman). That year Lennar also spun off its commercial real estate operations as LNR Property, a separately traded public company, and acquired Pacific Greystone, a Los Angeles builder.

The following year the company strengthened its position in the western US, acquiring three California homebuilders: Winncrest Homes

(Sacramento), ColRich Communities (San Diego), and Polygon Communities (Southern California and Sacramento). Lennar also purchased North American Title, an escrow and title services company operating in Arizona, California, and Colorado.

In 2000 Lennar bought fellow builder U.S. Home for about $1.1 billion in a deal that expanded its operations into 13 states. The company acquired the North and South Carolina operations of The Fortress Group in late 2001, giving Lennar the Don Galloway Homes and Sunstar Homes brands. Through its FG Acquisition Corporation subsidiary, Lennar acquired 93% of The Fortress Group in 2002; it also added Maryland-based Patriot Homes and assets of California homebuilders Pacific Century Homes and Cambridge Homes to bring its homebuilding operations to 16 states.

In July 2002 Leonard Miller died of liver cancer. Stuart Miller continues to lead the company as its president and CEO. The company acquired nine homebuilders that year, which expanded its operations into markets in Chicago (Concord Homes and Summit Homes), Baltimore, the Carolinas, and California's Central Valley; some of the acquisitions strengthened Lennar's position in its existing markets.

Lennar continued to acquire in 2003, adding Seppala Homes and Coleman Homes (with a backlog of about 300 homes and 3,000 owned or controlled homesites), expanding its positions, respectively, in South Carolina and the Central Valley of California.

In mid-2003 an entity jointly owned by Lennar and LNR Property Corporation (real estate investment, finance, and management) agreed to acquire The Newhall Land and Farming Company (master-planned communities) for about $1 billion. The deal closed in January 2004, enabling LNR to buy existing income-producing commercial assets from the venture, and Lennar to option certain current homesites. Also in 2004 Lennar's Texas operations grew with its cash purchase of San Antonio-based Connell-Barron Homes and the company expanded into Jacksonville, Florida, by acquiring Classic American Homes, Inc., for an undisclosed cash price.

Lennar has continued to acquire regional builders, mortgage operations, and title and closing businesses. During 2005 Lennar entered the Boston, New York City, and Reno markets; it also expanded its Jacksonville operations by acquiring Admiral Homes. The condo and apartment buildings in New York and Boston were valued at more than $2 billion.

## EXECUTIVES

**President, CEO, and Director:** Stuart A. Miller, age 49, $5,713,200 pay
**EVP:** Richard Beckwitt, age 47, $4,881,600 pay
**VP and COO:** Jonathan M. (Jon) Jaffe, age 47, $2,685,300 pay
**VP and CFO:** Bruce E. Gross, age 48, $1,868,800 pay
**VP and Controller:** Diane J. Bessette, age 46, $743,800 pay
**VP and Treasurer:** Waynewright Malcolm
**VP Investor Relations:** Marshall H. Ames, age 63
**VP; Chairman, Lennar Financial Services, LLC:** Allan J. Pekor
**VP; President and CEO, Lennar Financial Services, LLC:** David B. McCain, age 45
**VP, Community Development; President, Strategic Technologies, Inc.:** Craig M. Johnson, age 51, $1,122,000 pay
**CIO:** John R. Nygard III
**Chief Human Resources Officer:** Anthony S. Marino
**Director, Communications:** Kay L. Howard
**Director, Tax:** Ronald L. George
**Secretary and General Counsel:** Mark Sustana, age 45
**President, Lennar Communications Ventures:** David J. Kaiserman
**President, Universal American Mortgage Company:** James T. Timmons
**President, Eagle Home Mortgage, Inc.:** Gary E. Carlson
**EVP and CFO, Lennar Financial Services, LLC:** Nancy A. Kaminsky
**EVP, Lennar Financial Services, LLC, and President, North American Title Group, Inc.:** Linda Reed
**Auditors:** Deloitte & Touche LLP

## LOCATIONS

**HQ:** Lennar Corporation
700 NW 107th Ave., Ste. 400, Miami, FL 33172
**Phone:** 305-559-4000 **Fax:** 305-229-6453
**Web:** www.lennar.com

Lennar has operations in Arizona, California, Colorado, Delaware, Florida, Illinois, Maryland, Minnesota, Nevada, New Jersey, New York, North Carolina, Pennsylvania, South Carolina, Texas, Virginia, and Wisconsin.

### 2006 Homes Delivered

| | Units (No.) | % of total |
|---|---|---|
| Central (AZ, CO & TX) | 17,069 | 34 |
| East (FL, MD, NJ & VA) | 14,859 | 30 |
| West (CA & NV) | 13,333 | 27 |
| Other (IL, MN, NY, NC & SC) | 4,307 | 9 |
| **Total** | **49,568** | **100** |

### Selected Markets

Arizona
- Phoenix-Mesa
- Tucson

California
- Bakersfield
- Desert Resort Country
- Fresno
- Los Angeles-Long Beach
- Oakland
- Orange County
- Palm Springs
- Riverside-San Bernardino
- Sacramento
- San Diego

Colorado
- Colorado Springs
- Denver
- Northern Colorado

Delaware
- Bridgeville
- Millsboro
- Ocean View
- Rehoboth

Florida
- Clermont
- Fort Lauderdale
- Fort Myers
- Jacksonville
- Lakeland
- Miami
- Naples
- Orlando
- Palm Beach
- Sarasota
- Space Coast
- Tampa
- Winterhaven

Nevada
- Las Vegas
- Reno

New Jersey
- Atlantic
- Camden
- Cape May
- Cumberland
- Gloucester
- Hudson County
- Middlesex
- Monmouth
- Morris County
- Ocean County

New York
- Duchess County
- Orange County

North and South Carolina
- Charlotte, NC
- Raleigh-Durham, NC
- Charleston, SC
- Greenville, SC
- Myrtle Beach, SC

Texas
- Austin-San Marcos
- Dallas
- Fort Worth-Arlington
- Houston
- San Antonio

Other
- Baltimore
- Chicago
- Minneapolis-St. Paul, MN
- River Falls, WI
- Washington, DC
- Williamsburg, VA
- York County, PA

## PRODUCTS/OPERATIONS

### 2006 Sales

| | $ mil. | % of total |
|---|---|---|
| Homebuilding | 15,623.1 | 96 |
| Financial services | 643.6 | 4 |
| **Total** | **16,266.7** | **100** |

## COMPETITORS

Beazer Homes
Centex
D.R. Horton
Hovnanian Enterprises
KB Home
Levitt Corporation
M.D.C.
NVR
Pulte Homes
Ryland
Standard Pacific
Toll Brothers
Weyerhaeuser Real Estate

## HISTORICAL FINANCIALS

Company Type: Public

### Income Statement

FYE: November 30

| | REVENUE ($ mil.) | NET INCOME ($ mil.) | NET PROFIT MARGIN | EMPLOYEES |
|---|---|---|---|---|
| **11/06** | 16,267 | 594 | 3.7% | 12,605 |
| **11/05** | 13,867 | 1,355 | 9.8% | 13,687 |
| **11/04** | 10,505 | 946 | 9.0% | 11,796 |
| **11/03** | 8,908 | 751 | 8.4% | 10,572 |
| **11/02** | 7,320 | 545 | 7.4% | 9,419 |
| **Annual Growth** | 22.1% | 2.2% | — | 7.6% |

### 2006 Year-End Financials

Debt ratio: 66.0%
Return on equity: 10.8%
Cash ($ mil.): 803
Current ratio: 8.62
Long-term debt ($ mil.): 3,763
No. of shares (mil.): 127
Dividends
Yield: 1.2%
Payout: 17.3%
Market value ($ mil.): 6,664

### Stock History

NYSE: LEN

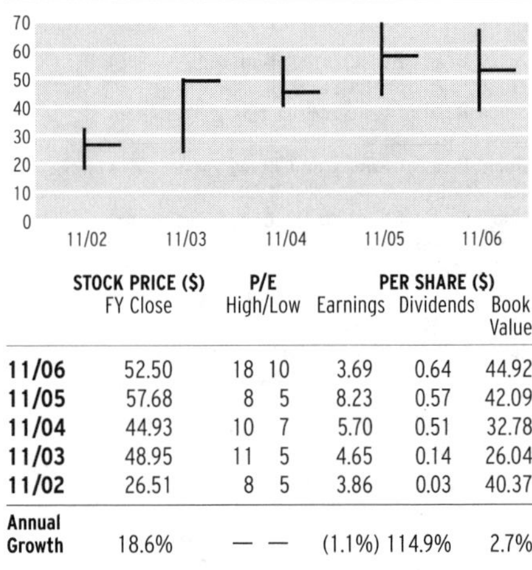


| | STOCK PRICE ($) FY Close | P/E High | P/E Low | PER SHARE ($) Earnings | Dividends | Book Value |
|---|---|---|---|---|---|---|
| **11/06** | 52.50 | 18 | 10 | 3.69 | 0.64 | 44.92 |
| **11/05** | 57.68 | 8 | 5 | 8.23 | 0.57 | 42.09 |
| **11/04** | 44.93 | 10 | 7 | 5.70 | 0.51 | 32.78 |
| **11/03** | 48.95 | 11 | 5 | 4.65 | 0.14 | 26.04 |
| **11/02** | 26.51 | 8 | 5 | 3.86 | 0.03 | 40.37 |
| **Annual Growth** | 18.6% | — | — | (1.1%) | 114.9% | 2.7% |

# Lennox International

Lennox International (LII) makes products so cool they're hot — and vice versa. The company makes air-conditioning, heating, and fireplace systems for residential and commercial uses, as well as commercial refrigeration equipment. Its brands include Lennox, Armstrong Air, and Ducane. Subsidiary Lennox Industries distributes the company's products in the US and Canada through independent dealers; additionally, Lennox's Service Experts unit runs about 120 company-owned service centers. Lennox also has interests and facilities in Asia, Australia, Europe, and South America.

Named after inventor Dave Lennox, the company in 1904 was sold to newspaper publisher D.W. Norris. Norris's descendants own around 8% of Lennox.

When it comes to air-conditioning, Lennox knows that its fortunes lie in the US Sunbelt and is focusing on expanding sales in the region. The company is also improving the efficiency of its manufacturing operations in Europe and reorganizing its Service Center locations for better results. It is actively looking for joint venture partners and other alliances, although how much of that has come to fruition remains to be seen; it has not announced any joint ventures in the last few years.

## HISTORY

Inventors Ernest Bryant and Ezra Smith developed and patented a riveted-steel sheet metal coal furnace in Marshalltown, Iowa, in the 1890s. The cast iron furnaces in use at the time tended to warp with usage; their sheet metal furnace did not. The inventors hired machine shop operator Dave Lennox to build the manufacturing equipment necessary to produce the new furnace. They were underfunded, however, and Lennox took over the patents in lieu of payment and redesigned the furnace. Lennox didn't warm to the furnace business and sold out to D. W. Norris, the local newspaper publisher, and three other people for $40,000 in 1904.

Norris, the company's first president, incorporated the business as Lennox Furnace Company and sold about 600 units the first year. Norris soon established the company's method of selling and delivering directly to authorized dealers.

Lennox built a manufacturing plant in New York in 1925 and acquired Armstrong Furnace, a steel coal furnace plant in Ohio, in 1927. That year John Norris, D. W.'s son, joined the company after graduating from MIT. The younger Norris pushed for new innovations such as oil burners, gas furnaces, and blowers. He set up a research department in the 1930s and soon developed a line of gas- and oil-burning furnaces. The company opened another Ohio plant in 1940 and bought a machine shop there in 1942 to make bomb and aircraft parts for WWII. John Norris became president after the death of his father in 1949.

The company established Lennox Industries (Canada) Ltd. in 1952. Norris began developing an air conditioner the same year, after shopping the idea around to his dealers. Soon the company was turning out residential, commercial, and industrial air conditioners and compressors. In 1955 the company's name was changed to Lennox Industries Inc. to reflect its broader product range. The international division was created in 1962. Soon manufacturing facilities were established outside London and other offices were opened in the Netherlands and West Germany.

Lennox acquired Heatcraft, a maker of heating and cooling components, in 1973. Headquarters were moved to Dallas in 1978; in 1980 John Norris Jr. was named CEO. Lennox International Inc. (LII) was formed as the parent company for Heatcraft and Lennox Industries in 1986. The company reacquired Armstrong Air Conditioning (which it had owned in the 1920s and sold in the mid-1950s) in 1988.

LII underwent restructuring in 1989 and 1991, leading to the consolidation of production to four locations and the grouping of the sales, management, product ordering, and marketing teams at its headquarters in Dallas. In 1995 the company formed Lennox Global and rededicated itself to international expansion through joint ventures with foreign companies. LII formed HCF-Lennox, a joint venture with France's Brancher group, in 1996. The company agreed in 1998 to pay $6.2 million to settle an age bias lawsuit filed by 11 former employees. LII went public in 1999 and began buying HVAC dealers.

In 2000 the company more than doubled its number of owned retail outlets with the $300 million acquisition of Service Experts, a HVAC installation and sales business with 120 locations. However, the acquisition disappointed, and some of the locations were later closed.

COO Robert Schjerven succeeded John W. Norris Jr. as CEO in early 2001; Norris remained as chairman. Every operating segment but its commercial segment saw significant sales declines in 2001. The company restructured its service experts operations and some of its manufacturing and distribution operations that year. LII closed plants in Canada and Australia and closed retail centers to cut costs.

In 2002 LII continued restructuring its noncore heat transfer engineering business and made moves to focus on its core operations. That year it formed a joint venture with Outokumpu Oyj (Finland), selling 55% of its former heat transfer business segment in the US and Europe to Outokumpu. (In 2005 Outokumpu exercised its option to buy the remainder of the venture, however.) LII also sold its 50% interest in its underperforming commercial HVAC joint venture in Argentina. Sales overall continued to decline, although slight increases were made in the residential heating and cooling segment and in the refrigeration segment.

## EXECUTIVES

**Chairman:** Richard L. (Rich) Thompson, age 67
**CEO and Director:** Todd M. Bluedorn, age 44
**EVP and CFO:** Susan K. Carter, age 48, $436,814 pay
**EVP and Chief Supply Chain, Logistics, and Technology Officer:** Linda A. Goodspeed, age 45, $365,827 pay
**EVP, Chief Legal Officer, and Secretary:** William F. (Bill) Stoll Jr., age 58
**EVP; President and COO, Service Experts:** Scott J. Boxer, age 56, $462,127 pay
**EVP; President and COO, LII Commercial Heating & Cooling:** Harry J. Bizios, age 56
**EVP; President and COO, LII Residential Heating & Cooling:** Douglas L. (Doug) Young, age 44
**EVP; President and COO, Worldwide Refrigeration:** David W. Moon, age 45
**VP, Controller, and Chief Accounting Officer:** Roy A. Rumbough Jr., age 51
**VP Communications and Public Relations:** Karen O'Shea
**VP and Treasurer:** Gary Larson
**VP Investor Relations:** Karen Fugate
**Chief Human Resources Officer:** Daniel M. Sessa
**Auditors:** KPMG LLP

## LOCATIONS

**HQ:** Lennox International Inc.
2140 Lake Park Blvd., Richardson, TX 75080
**Phone:** 972-497-5000 **Fax:** 972-497-5299
**Web:** www.lennoxinternational.com

### 2006 Sales

| | % of total |
|---|---|
| Americas | 87 |
| Europe | 8 |
| Asia/Pacific | 5 |
| **Total** | **100** |

## PRODUCTS/OPERATIONS

### 2006 Sales

| | % of total |
|---|---|
| Residential | 49 |
| Commercial | 19 |
| Service experts | 18 |
| Refrigeration | 14 |
| **Total** | **100** |

### Selected Products and Brand Names

Heating and cooling
- Residential products
  - Air conditioners
  - Fireplace inserts and accessories
  - Free-standing stoves
  - Furnaces
  - Heat pumps
  - Indoor air quality equipment
  - Packaged heating and cooling systems
  - Prefabricated fireplaces
- Brand names
  - Advanced Distributor Products (ADP)
  - Aire-Flo
  - Armstrong Air
  - Concord
  - Ducane
  - Lennox
  - Magic-Pak
  - Security Chimneys
  - Superior
  - Whitfield
- Commercial products
  - Unitary air conditioning and applied systems
- Brand names
  - Allied Commercial
  - Lennox

Service experts
- Installation
- Maintenance
- Repair

Refrigeration
- Products
  - Air-cooled condensers
  - Air handlers
  - Chillers
  - Condensing units
  - Fluid coolers
  - Unit coolers
- Brand names
  - Bohn
  - Chandler Refrigeration
  - Climate Control
  - Friga-Bohn
  - Frigus-Bohn
  - Heatcraft Worldwide Refrigeration
  - HK Refrigeration
  - Kirby
  - Larkin
  - Lovelocks

## COMPETITORS

AAON
American Standard
CFM Corporation
Comfort Systems USA
Daikin
Electrolux
Emerson Electric
Fireplace Manufacturers
Goodman Global
Goodman Manufacturing
HNI
Hong Leong Asia
Hussmann International
Ingersoll-Rand
Johnson Controls
Linde
Mestek
NorthWestern
ServiceMaster
Tecumseh Products
Thermador Groupe
United Electric Company
United Technologies
Watsco
Whirlpool
Yazaki Energy Systems

## HISTORICAL FINANCIALS

Company Type: Public

**Income Statement** FYE: December 31

| | REVENUE ($ mil.) | NET INCOME ($ mil.) | NET PROFIT MARGIN | EMPLOYEES |
|---|---|---|---|---|
| **12/06** | 3,671 | 166 | 4.5% | 16,000 |
| **12/05** | 3,366 | 151 | 4.5% | 16,000 |
| **12/04** | 2,983 | (134) | — | 15,000 |
| **12/03** | 3,085 | 84 | 2.7% | 18,000 |
| **12/02** | 3,026 | (190) | — | 18,000 |
| **Annual Growth** | 5.0% | — | — | (2.9%) |

**2006 Year-End Financials**

Debt ratio: 12.0%
Return on equity: 20.8%
Cash ($ mil.): 144
Current ratio: 1.56
Long-term debt ($ mil.): 97

No. of shares (mil.): 67
Dividends
Yield: 1.5%
Payout: 20.4%
Market value ($ mil.): 2,056

**Stock History** NYSE: LII

35
30
25
20
15
10
5
0
12/02 12/03 12/04 12/05 12/06

| | STOCK PRICE ($) FY Close | P/E High/Low | | PER SHARE ($) Earnings | Dividends | Book Value |
|---|---|---|---|---|---|---|
| **12/06** | 30.61 | 15 | 9 | 2.26 | 0.46 | 11.98 |
| **12/05** | 28.20 | 15 | 9 | 2.11 | 0.41 | 11.18 |
| **12/04** | 20.35 | — | — | (2.24) | 0.38 | 7.47 |
| **12/03** | 16.70 | 13 | 8 | 1.40 | 0.38 | 9.55 |
| **12/02** | 12.55 | — | — | (3.23) | 0.38 | 7.54 |
| **Annual Growth** | 25.0% | — | — | — | 4.9% | 12.3% |

# Level 3 Communications

Level 3 Communications is several steps ahead of the cutting edge. The global communications and information services company operates one of the world's first and largest Internet protocol (IP)-based fiber-optic networks. Built for the Internet age, Level 3 is a leading provider of wholesale dial-up service and it provides broadband Internet connectivity for millions of high-speed Internet users, specializing in service for data-intensive customers such as ISPs and telecom carriers. Level 3 also offers fiber-optic and satellite video delivery services through subsidiary Vyvx. It continued its buying spree with its early 2007 purchase of Austin, Texas-based Broadwing Corporation.

Level 3 is pursuing growth through acquisition. Its Broadwing purchase expands its enterprise market. Half of Broadwing's revenues are from business clients. Level 3 paid approximately $744 million in cash and issued more than 100 million shares of common stock. Level 3 also completed its purchase of SAVVIS Inc.'s content delivery network services business (including customer contracts, intellectual property, and network elements) for approximately $132 million.

To expand its metro services business unit, Level 3 has acquired metro transport services provider Looking Glass Networks in a cash-stock-and-debt deal valued at $165 million.

Other recent expansion efforts include TelCove ($1.2 billion), ICG Communications ($163 million), Progress Telecom ($137 million), and the nationwide long-haul transport business of 360networks (including the contract to provide optical wavelength services to T-Systems North America). Vyvx was acquired in 2005 when Level 3 bought WilTel Communications Group from Leucadia National. The deal, valued at about $680 million, extended Level 3's long-haul telecom network services to an additional 50 markets and about 23,000 route-miles of network.

The buying spree has prompted Level 3 to cut costs. It announced it would eliminate 1,000 jobs in early 2007, on top of 900 jobs cut the year before. A year earlier it sold its Software Spectrum subsidiary, and released its computer outsourcing services unit (i)Structure in 2005.

## HISTORY

Thoroughly modern Level 3 Communications was the brainchild of an Omaha, Nebraska, construction company that traces its roots to 1884 — the multinational Peter Kiewit Sons'. With cash to invest in the 1980s, Kiewit acquired Metropolitan Fiber Systems, which built fiber-optic networks for phone companies. In 1986, Kiewit executive James Crowe convinced CEO Walter Scott that Kiewit should build some phone circuits of its own, and by 1987 Kiewit had created MFS Communications, headed by Crowe, to build networks in business districts. Kiewit slated $500 million for the project in 1989.

By 1995 MFS had gone public and was the biggest of the competitive local-exchange carriers (CLECs). That year Crowe and Scott heard Bill Gates speak on the power of the Internet to destroy traditional phone traffic. MFS launched "Project Silver" to decide how to respond. The answer: buy UUNET. In 1996 MFS acquired the giant ISP and Internet backbone operator, and in the process made itself an acquisition target. WorldCom bought MFS for $14 billion by year's end. Within a month Crowe left WorldCom (with several MFS execs in tow) to head Kiewit Diversified Group, which had holdings in telecommunications, technology, and energy.

In 1998 Kiewit split into the Peter Kiewit Sons' construction group, headed by Ken Stinson, and a diversified company called Level 3 Communications, headed by Crowe. Level 3 kept stakes in telecom companies RCN and C-TEC (now Commonwealth Telephone Enterprises). The Level 3 name came from the seven-layer Open Systems Interconnect (OSI) network model: the company saw its field of play in the bottom three levels — the physical plant, data link, and network layers.

Kiewit provided Crowe with a $2.5 billion grubstake; Level 3 went public and sold its oil interests and Michigan cable TV operation. It retained its coal-mining and toll-road interests to help fund the buildout of a new fiber-optic network to be based on Internet protocol (IP) technology instead of the old circuit-switching system.

Level 3 secured rights-of-way from Burlington Northern and Union Pacific. The company found a new angel in Craig McCaw, whose INTERNEXT agreed to plunge $700 million into the Level 3 network in return for capacity. By year's end the company had begun local networks in 25 US cities and had completed gateway sites in 17.

In 1999 Level 3 moved from Omaha to Broomfield, Colorado. Level 3 hired Tyco International to develop an Atlantic undersea cable and agreed to participate in the building of the Japan-US Cable Network across the Pacific.

Fellow fiber baron Global Crossing agreed to buy a 50% interest in the transatlantic cable in 2000. By mid-year Level 3 had installed fiber across more than a third of its planned US intercity network. In early 2001 the company announced the completion of its network construction and said it would expand its European network to eight additional markets despite cutting about 6% of its workforce.

For Level 3, as for many of its rivals, demand for bandwidth capacity and services failed to reach expected levels and the company in 2001 scaled back its revenue estimates and cut almost 25% of its workforce.

However, Level 3 received a shot in the arm in 2002 when an investment group that included Warren Buffett's Berkshire Hathaway invested $500 million in the company (it sold the stake in 2004). Level 3 acquired most of the assets of network services provider Genuity in a deal valued at $242 million.

Also in 2002 Level 3 acquired Massachusetts-based software distributor CorpSoft and Software Spectrum, a business software distributor based in Texas. The companies were combined and Level 3 soon derived much of its revenues from software distribution, which provided relief from the telecom sector's hard times.

In 2003 Level 3 agreed to provide Internet access through its satellite platform to the 500,000 Internet access customers of Hughes Electronics' DIRECTV unit.

To reduce costs, the company reduced its workforce in early 2005 and exited the hosted IP Centrex business that it called (3)Tone, which provided the resale of VoIP service.

## EXECUTIVES

**Chairman:** J. Walter (Walter) Scott Jr., age 75
**CEO and Director:** James Q. (Jim) Crowe, age 56, $4,125,000 pay
**President and COO:** Kevin J. O'Hara, age 45, $1,870,000 pay
**EVP and CTO:** John F. (Jack) Waters Jr., age 41
**EVP, Chief Legal Officer, and Secretary:** Thomas C. Stortz, age 54, $1,320,000 pay
**EVP, Global Operations:** Edward F. McLaughlin, age 53
**EVP, Sales and Marketing:** J. Neil Hobbs, age 46
**EVP, Softswitch Services:** Sureel A. Choksi, age 33
**SVP and Treasurer:** Robin Grey
**SVP and Controller:** Eric J. Mortensen, age 47
**SVP and General Manager, Government Markets:** Jerry Hogge
**Group VP, Corporate Marketing:** Josh Howell
**Group VP, Corporate Strategy:** Donald H. (Don) Gips, age 45
**Group VP, Global Systems Development and CIO:** Kevin T. Hart, age 39
**Group VP, Corporate Marketing:** Joseph M. Howell III, age 59
**Group VP, Emerging Opportunities:** Ronald J. Vidal, age 43
**Group VP, Human Resources:** Christopher P. Yost, age 42
**Group VP and CFO:** Sunit S. Patel, age 44
**VP, Corporate Communications:** Chris Hardman
**President and CEO, Europe Operations:** Brady Rafuse, age 42
**CEO, Broadwing:** Stephen E. Courter
**Director, Investor Relations:** Sandra Curlander
**Manager, Public Relations:** Jennifer Daumler
**Auditors:** KPMG LLP

## LOCATIONS

**HQ:** Level 3 Communications, Inc.
1025 Eldorado Blvd., Broomfield, CO 80021
**Phone:** 720-888-1000 **Fax:** 720-888-5085
**Web:** www.level3.com

### 2006 Sales

| | % of total |
|---|---|
| North America | 94 |
| Europe | 6 |
| **Total** | **100** |

## PRODUCTS/OPERATIONS

### 2006 Sales

| | % of total |
|---|---|
| Transport and infrastructure | 31 |
| Wholesale IP and data | 9 |
| Voice | 16 |
| Vyvx | 4 |
| Managed modem | 9 |
| Reciprocal compensation | 3 |
| Managed IP | 2 |
| SBC contract services | 26 |
| **Total** | **100** |

### Selected Services

Backhaul services
Colocation
Dark fiber
Dedicated access
Dedicated wavelengths (virtual fibers in a wavelength division multiplexed system)
Internet protocol (IP) and data services
Managed modem (outsourced local points of presence for ISPs)
Managed security
Private lines (dedicated circuits, from T1 to OC48 speeds)
Softswitch services
Transoceanic services
Transport and infrastructure services
Virtual private networks (VPNs)

## COMPETITORS

360networks
ASAP Software
AT&T
CDW
COLT Telecom
CompuCom
Deutsche Telekom AG
France Telecom
Global Crossing
Hewlett-Packard
Insight Enterprises
Qwest
Redbus Interhouse
SAVVIS
Softchoice
Sprint Nextel
Switch and Data Facilities
TeleCity
TeliaSonera
Verizon

## HISTORICAL FINANCIALS

Company Type: Public

### Income Statement

FYE: December 31

| | REVENUE ($ mil.) | NET INCOME ($ mil.) | NET PROFIT MARGIN | EMPLOYEES |
|---|---|---|---|---|
| **12/06** | 3,378 | (744) | — | 7,400 |
| **12/05** | 3,613 | (638) | — | 4,800 |
| **12/04** | 3,712 | (458) | — | 4,500 |
| **12/03** | 4,026 | (711) | — | 4,650 |
| **12/02** | 3,148 | (858) | — | 6,275 |
| **Annual Growth** | 1.8% | — | — | 4.2% |

### 2006 Year-End Financials

Debt ratio: 1,967.1%
Return on equity: —
Cash ($ mil.): 1,962
Current ratio: 2.57
Long-term debt ($ mil.): 7,357
No. of shares (mil.): 1,178
Dividends
Yield: —
Payout: —
Market value ($ mil.): 6,599

### Stock History

NASDAQ (GS): LVLT

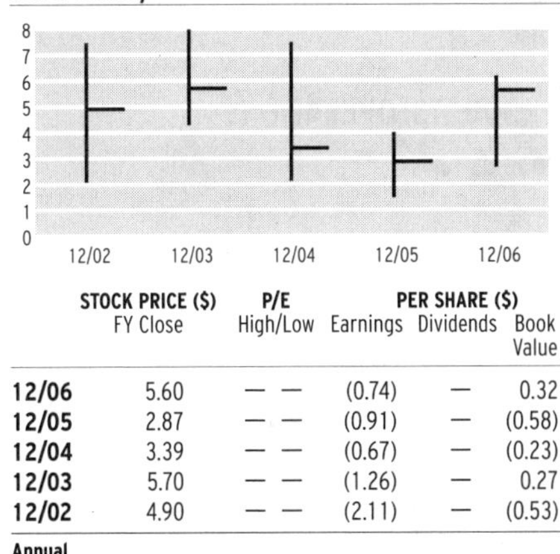


| | STOCK PRICE ($) FY Close | P/E High/Low | PER SHARE ($) Earnings | Dividends | Book Value |
|---|---|---|---|---|---|
| **12/06** | 5.60 | — — | (0.74) | — | 0.32 |
| **12/05** | 2.87 | — — | (0.91) | — | (0.58) |
| **12/04** | 3.39 | — — | (0.67) | — | (0.23) |
| **12/03** | 5.70 | — — | (1.26) | — | 0.27 |
| **12/02** | 4.90 | — — | (2.11) | — | (0.53) |
| **Annual Growth** | 3.4% | — — | — | — | — |

# Levi Strauss

Levi Strauss & Co. (LS&CO.) strives to provide the world's casual workday wardrobe, inside and out. LS&CO., the #1 maker of brand-name clothing globally, sells jeans and sportswear under the Levi's, Dockers, and Levi Strauss Signature names in more than 110 countries. It also markets men's and women's underwear and loungewear. Levi's jeans — department store staples — were once the uniform of American youth, but LS&CO. has been working to reconnect with the niche in recent years. In response, it transformed its product offerings to include wrinkle-free and stain-resistant fabrics used in the making of some of its Levi's and Dockers slacks. The Haas family (relatives of founder Levi Strauss) owns LS&CO.

Levi Strauss overhauled its marketing strategy by expanding its products portfolio. Rather than relying on its basic one or two styles and brands, Levi's hoped to regain some of the market share lost to VF Corporation (maker of Lee and Wrangler) and others over the past decade.

Levi's Superlow jeans and Levi Strauss Signature jeans were created for the mass market, although their distribution in the US was short-lived. Dockers Flat Front Mobile pants (with secret pockets for cell phones, PDAs, and other gadgets) and Dockers Go Khaki pants (with Stain Defender, a Teflon treatment preventing stains) target the 25 to 39 age group. Undaunted by a slate of disappointing and stale brands, Levi Strauss revamped a number of its basic products, including Levi's 501, 550, and 515. And in 2006 it debuted denim and other items made from organic materials.

Through licensing deals the company has extended its reach into other niche markets. Through a licensing agreement with Dehli, India-based M&B Footwear, LS&CO. launched men's and women's casual shoes and sneakers in 2005. LS&CO. under license by Signature Apparel Group added Levi-brand underwear and loungewear to its portfolio.

Due to noteworthy dips in net sales over the years, Levi Strauss has also taken measures to recoup some of its losses by closing more than 35 of its factories worldwide and, instead, using independent contract manufacturers.

Transitions with the company's operations weren't relegated to the firm's manufacturing facilities. Pinpointing 2006 as the best time to step down as the company's chief executive, Philip Marineau announced in July his plans to retire at the end of the year. John Anderson, president of LS&CO.'s Asia Pacific Division and head of the firm's global supply chain unit, was named to replace Marineau as president and CEO. Executive ranks on the US level are seeing some tailoring, as well. To jump-start business in wholesale and retail operations, the company separated the two units in December 2006 and appointed two leaders to run them.

J.C. Penney Company represents 9% of overall sales; retailer Target carries Levi's Signature line.

## HISTORY

Levi Strauss arrived in New York City from Bavaria in 1847. In 1853 he moved to San Francisco to sell dry goods to the gold rushers. Shortly after, a prospector told Strauss of miners' problems in finding sturdy pants. Strauss made a pair out of canvas for the prospector; word of the rugged pants spread quickly.

Strauss continued his dry-goods business in the 1860s. During this time he switched the pants' fabric to a durable French cloth called serge de Nimes, soon known as denim. He colored the fabric with indigo dye and adopted the idea from Nevada tailor Jacob Davis of reinforcing the pants with copper rivets. In 1873 Strauss and Davis produced their first pair of waist-high overalls (later known as jeans). The pants soon became *de rigueur* for lumberjacks, cowboys, railroad workers, oil drillers, and farmers.

Strauss continued to build his pants and wholesaling business until he died in 1902. Levi Strauss & Co. (LS&CO.) passed to four nephews who carried on their uncle's jeans business while maintaining the company's philanthropic reputation.

After WWII Walter Haas and Peter Haas (a fourth-generation Strauss family member) assumed leadership of LS&CO. In 1948 they ended the company's wholesaling business to concentrate on Levi's clothing. In the 1950s Levi's jeans ceased to be merely functional garments for workers: They became the uniform of American youth. In the 1960s LS&CO. added women's attire and expanded overseas.

The company went public in 1971. That year it added a women's career line and bought Koret sportswear (sold in 1984). By the mid-1980s profits declined. Peace Corps-veteran-turned-McKinsey-consultant Robert Haas (Walter's son) grabbed the reins of LS&CO. in 1984 and took the company private the next year. He also instilled a touchy-feely corporate culture often at odds with the bottom line.

In 1986 LS&CO. introduced Dockers casual pants. The company's sales began rising in 1991 as consumers forsook designer duds of the 1980s for more practical clothes. LS&CO. says seven out of every ten American men own a pair of Dockers. However, LS&CO. missed out on the birth of another trend: the split between the fashion sense of US adolescents and their Levi's-loving, baby boomer parents.

In 1996 the company introduced Slates dress slacks. That year LS&CO. bought back nearly one-third of its stock from family and employees for $4.3 billion. Grappling with slipping sales and debt from the buyout, in 1997 LS&CO. closed 11 of its 37 North American plants, laying off 6,400 workers and 1,000 salaried employees; it granted generous severance packages even to those earning minimum wage.

In 1998, citing improved labor conditions in China, LS&CO. announced it would step up its use of Chinese subcontractors. Further restructuring added a third of its European plants to the closures list that year. LS&CO.'s sales fell 13% in fiscal 1998. The next year LS&CO. closed 11 of 22 remaining North American plants. It also unleashed several new jeans brands that eschewed the company's one-style-fits-all approach of old.

In 1999 Haas handed his CEO title to Pepsi executive Philip Marineau.

In April 2002 LS&CO. announced it would close six of its last eight US plants and cut 20% of its worldwide staff (3,300 workers). In September 2003 it cut another 5% of its worldwide staff (650 workers). Also in September the company opened its first girls-only store, located in Paris. In December LS&CO. replaced CFO Bill Chiasson with an outside turnaround specialist.

## EXECUTIVES

**Chairman:** Robert D. (Bob) Haas, age 64
**President, CEO, and Director:** R. John Anderson, age 55, $1,493,951 pay (prior to promotion)
**SVP and CFO:** Hans Ploos van Amstel, age 41, $1,033,885 pay
**SVP and CIO:** David G. Bergen, age 50
**SVP and General Counsel:** Hilary K. Krane, age 43
**SVP, Strategy and Worldwide Marketing and Global Marketing Officer:** Lawrence W. (Larry) Ruff, age 50
**SVP, Dockers Men's Merchandising, Design, and Licensing:** Jim Tibbs
**SVP; President, Asia/Pacific:** Alan Hed, age 47
**SVP; President, Levi Strauss Europe:** Armin Broger, age 45
**SVP, Global Sourcing:** David Love, age 44
**VP, Finance, Levi Strauss North America:** Mary Boland, age 49
**VP, Sales:** Donna Paulo
**VP, Worldwide and US Communications:** Dan Chew
**President and Commercial General Manager, Dockers Brand, US:** John D. Goodman, age 42, $1,258,055 pay
**President and General Manager, Levi Strauss Signature Brand, US:** Scott A. LaPorta, age 43
**President, North America; President and Commercial General Manager, Levi's Brand, US:** Robert L. Hanson, age 43, $1,285,569 pay
**President, Retail:** Mark Breitbard, age 38
**President, Wholesale:** Loreen Zakern, age 53
**Auditors:** KPMG LLP

## LOCATIONS

**HQ:** Levi Strauss & Co.
1155 Battery St., San Francisco, CA 94111
**Phone:** 415-501-6000 **Fax:** 415-501-7112
**Web:** www.levistrauss.com

### 2006 Sales

| | $ mil. | % of total |
|---|---|---|
| US | 2,326.9 | 55 |
| Other countries | 1,866.0 | 45 |
| Adjustments | (86.3) | — |
| **Total** | **4,106.6** | **100** |

### 2006 Sales

| | $ mil. | % of total |
|---|---|---|
| North America | | |
| US | 2,326.9 | 55 |
| Canada & Mexico | 206.6 | 5 |
| Europe | 898.0 | 21 |
| Asia/Pacific | 761.4 | 18 |
| Adjustments | (86.3) | — |
| **Total** | **4,106.6** | **100** |

## PRODUCTS/OPERATIONS

### 2006 US Sales

| | % of total |
|---|---|
| US Levi's brand | 55 |
| US Dockers brand | 31 |
| US Levi Strauss Signature brand | 14 |
| **Total** | **100** |

### Selected Brand Names

501
505
Dockers
Dockers K-1
Dockers Premium
Dockers Recode
Dress Mobile
Flat Front Mobile
Go Khaki
Levi's
Levi's Engineered
Levi's Red
Levi's Silvertab
Levi's Type 1
ProStyle
Pure Blue
Red Tab
Superlow

## COMPETITORS

Abercrombie & Fitch
adidas
American Eagle Outfitters
Benetton
Blue Holdings
Calvin Klein
Diesel
Eddie Bauer
Fruit of the Loom
FUBU
Gap
Guess
Haggar
Hugo Boss
Innovo
J. C. Penney
J. Crew
Jockey International
Jones Apparel
Kmart
Kohl's
Lands' End
Limited Brands
Liz Claiborne
Macy's
Nautica Enterprises
NIKE
OshKosh B'Gosh
Oxford Industries
Perry Ellis International
Phillips-Van Heusen
Playtex
Polo Ralph Lauren
Sean John
Sears
Target
Tommy Hilfiger
True Religion Apparel
Under Armour
VF
Victoria's Secret Stores
Wacoal
Wal-Mart
Warnaco Group

## HISTORICAL FINANCIALS

Company Type: Private

### Income Statement

FYE: November 26

| | REVENUE ($ mil.) | NET INCOME ($ mil.) | NET PROFIT MARGIN | EMPLOYEES |
|---|---|---|---|---|
| **11/06** | 4,107 | 239 | 5.8% | 10,680 |
| **11/05** | 4,125 | 156 | 3.8% | 9,635 |
| **11/04** | 4,073 | 30 | 0.7% | 8,850 |
| **11/03** | 4,091 | (349) | — | 12,300 |
| **11/02** | 4,137 | 25 | 0.6% | 12,400 |
| **Annual Growth** | (0.2%) | 75.8% | — | (3.7%) |

### Net Income History

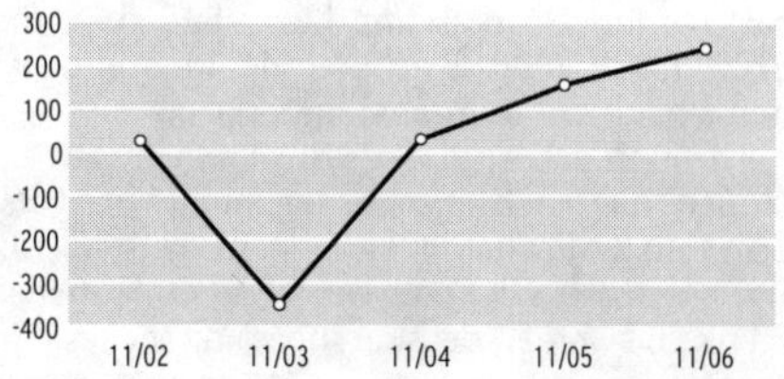


# Lexmark International

Lexmark attacks printing with a host of jets and lasers. Lexmark International is a leading maker of computer printers and related products. Its printer line includes laser printers (designed primarily for corporate networks and desktops) and ink jet printers (for home and business use). Unlike many of its competitors, Lexmark develops and manufactures its own devices, thereby speeding product cycles. The company sells its products in more than 150 countries through distributors including Ingram Micro and Tech Data, and through retailers in the US (CompUSA and Best Buy), France (Carrefour), and the UK (DSG International); it also supplies products to other equipment manufacturers.

Lexmark points to its singular focus on printing products as an advantage it holds in a sector that features diverse players such as market leader Hewlett-Packard. The company continues to grow its printer supplies business, which accounts for about 60% of sales. Lexmark also maintains partnerships with key manufacturers such as IBM and Lenovo. An agreement with Dell has Lexmark manufacturing printers that the PC leader sells under its own brand.

## HISTORY

During the late 1980s, as a horde of Davids took aim at Goliath IBM, the computer giant began downsizing to become more competitive. IBM cut its workforce by 100,000 between 1986 and 1992 and began to sell off its peripherals businesses. One of these was Lexmark ("Lex" as in "lexicon" and "mark" as in "marks on paper").

In early 1991 IBM sold Lexmark to a group led by investment firm Clayton, Dubilier & Rice for $1.5 billion. Martin Dubilier, who helped found the firm in 1978, had learned the leveraged buyout (LBO) ropes as a turnaround expert for Jerome Kohlberg, founder of investment firm Kohlberg Kravis Roberts, during the 1970s. Clayton, Dubilier's LBO of Lexmark was financed primarily with bank loans, leaving the new company over $1 billion in debt. Marvin Mann, a 32-year IBM veteran, was appointed Lexmark's chairman.

Mann took a cue from his former bosses and did some downsizing of his own at Lexmark, cutting the number of employees from 5,000 to 3,000. Mann also put more of the responsibility for running the company in the hands of his line managers, allowing them to come up with their own goals and business plans rather than take strategy from above.

Although many employees were given their walking papers, Mann put up a "Help Wanted" sign in his sales department. As an IBM subsidiary, Lexmark had relied on Big Blue's general sales force and Mann now needed to create one from scratch. By the end of 1991, staff had risen to 4,000.

As another sign of Lexmark's break from IBM, where it had sometimes gotten lost in the shuffle, Mann reorganized the company into four operating groups and made each group's financial information available to everyone in the company.

Lexmark began to flex its muscles as an independent in 1992, when it introduced the first products (IBM PC-compatible keyboards) bearing its own name rather than the IBM logo. That year Lexmark's first color printer debuted. Lexmark's operating profits doubled in 1992, its second year of operation. Using the additional cash flow, the company reduced its debt ahead of schedule, to about $750 million. In 1993 it made its first acquisition when it bought Australian printer maker Gestetner Lasers; the purchase increased Lexmark's presence in the Pacific Rim.

Lexmark began removing the IBM logo from its printers in 1994 and kicked off retail distribution of its own brand of ink jet printers and low-end laser printers. In 1995 the company went public and introduced its first color laser printer. In 1996 Lexmark doubled the number of its manufacturing facilities, opening ink jet plants in the US, Mexico, and the UK to help keep up with rising demand and put its products closer to burgeoning markets.

In continuing efforts to swipe market share from Hewlett-Packard, Lexmark in 1997 revamped its line of office and home printers. Clayton, Dubilier & Rice sold its remaining 23% stake in Lexmark in 1998. COO Paul Curlander, who had developed IBM's first laser printer, replaced Mann as CEO that year and as chairman the next.

Lexmark in 2000 opened an ink jet plant in the Philippines and a second such plant in Mexico. Later that year the company announced it would move some manufacturing operations to Mexico and China and cut about 900 jobs. In 2001 the company announced further jobs cuts — about 1,600 — and the closure of one of its plants in Mexico.

## EXECUTIVES

**Chairman and CEO:** Paul J. Curlander, age 54, $1,000,000 pay
**EVP and CFO:** John W. Gamble Jr., age 44, $450,000 pay
**EVP; President, Consumer Printer Division:** Paul A. Rooke, age 49, $530,000 pay
**VP and General Manager, EMEA:** Najib Bahous, age 51, $440,000 pay
**VP and Controller:** Gary D. Stromquist, age 51
**VP and Treasurer:** Richard A. (Rick) Pelini, age 48
**VP, Secretary, and General Counsel:** Vincent J. (Vinny) Cole, age 50, $390,000 pay
**VP Corporate Communications:** Tim Fitzpatrick
**VP Asia/Pacific and Latin America:** David L. Goodnight, age 54
**VP Human Resources:** Jeri I. Stromquist, age 51
**VP Tax:** Daniel P. (Dan) Bork, age 55
**VP; President, Printing Solutions and Services Division:** Marty Canning, age 44
**Auditors:** PricewaterhouseCoopers LLP

## LOCATIONS

**HQ:** Lexmark International, Inc.
One Lexmark Centre Dr., 740 W. New Circle Rd., Lexington, KY 40550
**Phone:** 859-232-2000 **Fax:** 859-232-2403
**Web:** www.lexmark.com

### 2006 Sales

| | $ mil. | % of total |
|---|---|---|
| US | 2,245.3 | 44 |
| Europe | 1,843.1 | 36 |
| Other regions | 1,019.7 | 20 |
| **Total** | **5,108.1** | **100** |

## PRODUCTS/OPERATIONS

### 2006 Sales

| | $ mil. | % of total |
|---|---|---|
| Business | 2,869.1 | 56 |
| Consumer | 2,239.0 | 44 |
| **Total** | **5,108.1** | **100** |

### 2006 Sales

| | $ mil. | % of total |
|---|---|---|
| Supplies | 3,211.6 | 63 |
| Printers | 1,663.0 | 33 |
| Other | 233.5 | 4 |
| **Total** | **5,108.1** | **100** |

### Selected Products

Networking Hardware
- Adapters
- Print servers

Printers
- Dot matrix
- Ink jet
- Laser
- Multifunction
- Refurbished
- Wide-format

Software
- Drivers
- Network management

Supplies
- Labels
- Paper
- Print cartridges

Typewriters

## COMPETITORS

Brother Industries
Canon
Eastman Kodak
Epson
Hewlett-Packard
IBM
Konica Minolta
Kyocera Mita
NEC
Oki Data
Ricoh
Samsung Electronics
Sharp
Xerox

## HISTORICAL FINANCIALS

Company Type: Public

### Income Statement

FYE: December 31

| | REVENUE ($ mil.) | NET INCOME ($ mil.) | NET PROFIT MARGIN | EMPLOYEES |
|---|---|---|---|---|
| **12/06** | 5,108 | 338 | 6.6% | 14,900 |
| **12/05** | 5,222 | 356 | 6.8% | 13,600 |
| **12/04** | 5,314 | 569 | 10.7% | 13,400 |
| **12/03** | 4,755 | 439 | 9.2% | 11,800 |
| **12/02** | 4,356 | 367 | 8.4% | 12,100 |
| **Annual Growth** | 4.1% | (2.0%) | — | 5.3% |

### 2006 Year-End Financials

Debt ratio: 14.5%
Return on equity: 27.5%
Cash ($ mil.): 562
Current ratio: 1.38
Long-term debt ($ mil.): 150
No. of shares (mil.): 97
Dividends
Yield: —
Payout: —
Market value ($ mil.): 7,100

### Stock History

NYSE: LXK

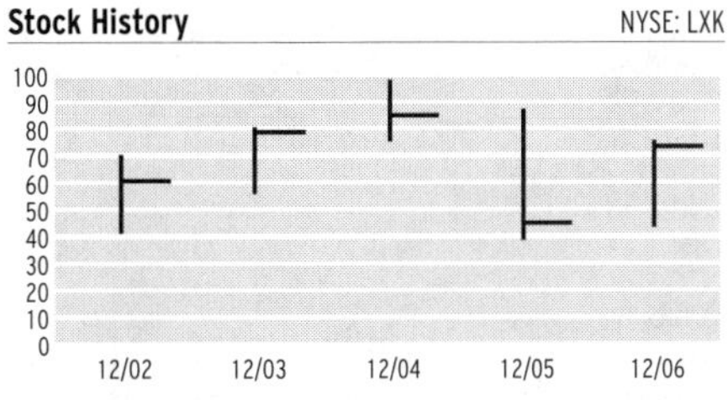


| | STOCK PRICE ($) FY Close | P/E High | P/E Low | PER SHARE ($) Earnings | Dividends | Book Value |
|---|---|---|---|---|---|---|
| **12/06** | 73.20 | 23 | 13 | 3.27 | — | 10.67 |
| **12/05** | 44.83 | 30 | 14 | 2.91 | — | 12.77 |
| **12/04** | 85.00 | 23 | 18 | 4.28 | — | 16.32 |
| **12/03** | 78.64 | 24 | 17 | 3.34 | — | 12.78 |
| **12/02** | 60.50 | 25 | 15 | 2.79 | — | 8.57 |
| **Annual Growth** | 4.9% | — | — | 4.0% | — | 5.6% |

# Liberty Media

Liberty Media Holding Corp. (LMHC, formerly Liberty Media) takes the freedom to arrange its varied businesses as it pleases. The holding company comprises publicly traded Liberty Interactive Group and Liberty Capital Group. The arrangement effectively splits the fast-growing video and online commerce operations from the company's less robust cable TV and entertainment businesses. Liberty Interactive's largest holding is home shopping network QVC, as well as flower and food e-tailer Provide Commerce and online costume shop Buyseasons. Movie channel Starz Entertainment, FUN Technologies, and TruePosition fall under Liberty Capital's umbrella. LMHC is chaired by John Malone.

The formation in May 2006 of LMHC, Liberty Interactive, and Liberty Capital is the latest reconfiguration of the company's disparate holdings. Over the past few years, Liberty Media has attempted to simplify its structure through a variety of spinoffs and asset sales. Previously the company spun off its stake in Discovery Communications, as well as Ascent Media Group, to form a new company (Discovery Holding Company). It completed the deal in mid-2005 and no longer has any stake in Discovery Holding. In late 2006 LMHC agreed to sell On Command to rival LodgeNet for approximately $380 million. The deal will give LMHC a 10% stake in LodgeNet upon completion.

The company also formed Liberty Broadband Interactive Television, to focus on developing and investing in the interactive television sector. The unit manages interactive television company OpenTV, in which LMHC owns a controlling stake.

Liberty Capital's various equity positions include a 50% stake in GSN (the Game Show Network), WildBlue Communications, and a 16% stake in News Corporation (valued at $11 billion). LMHC agreed in December 2006 to swap its News Corp. stake for a more than 38% stake (and controlling interest) in The DirecTV Group, as well as three regional sports networks and $550 million in cash. The deal restores Rupert Murdoch's control of News Corp.

Other Liberty Interactive holdings include about 21% of online travel firm Expedia and 25% of Barry Diller's Internet conglomerate IAC/InterActiveCorp. In May 2007 LMHC acquired the Atlanta Braves baseball team from Time Warner. The baseball club will be attributed to Liberty Capital Group.

## HISTORY

The man who would be king of cable programming got his start on the hardware end of the business. In 1970 John Malone became president of General Instrument's Jerrold Communications subsidiary, which supplied equipment to the then-new cable TV industry. One of Jerrold's customers was Bob Magness, a former Texas rancher who in the 1950s started the company that eventually became Denver-based cable operator Tele-Communications, Inc. (TCI). In the early 1970s, TCI struggled, in need of leadership. In 1973 the 32-year-old Malone was named CEO of TCI.

Malone restructured TCI's debt in 1977, paving the way for expansion into bigger cable markets after deregulation in 1984. He also acquired programming, buying stakes in Black Entertainment

Television (33%, 1979, sold to Viacom in 2001), the Discovery Channel (14%, 1986), and American Movie Classics (50%, 1986). In 1987 TCI helped save debt-plagued Turner Broadcasting and came away with 12% of Turner Broadcasting's stock.

Due in part to antitrust pressure from government regulators, in 1991 TCI spun off much of its programming assets, along with interests in 14 cable systems, as Liberty Media. Malone became chairman and principal shareholder. In its first year the company launched Court TV in a joint venture, and introduced film channel Encore. The next year it bought an interest in the Home Shopping Network (which became USA Networks in 1998, and later changed names to USA Interactive in 2002, InterActiveCorp in 2003, and finally IAC/InterActiveCorp in 2004).

In 1994 TCI reacquired Liberty Media; it issued a tracking stock the next year to reflect the value of Liberty's program assets. Also in 1995 Liberty Media and News Corp. joined forces to create FOX/Liberty Networks, a national sports network designed to compete with Disney's ESPN.

Control of TCI's stake in Turner Broadcasting was passed to Liberty Media after Turner was acquired by Time Warner in 1996, giving Liberty Media a 9% holding in entertainment giant Time Warner. (AOL acquired Time Warner in 2001 to form AOL Time Warner, but the company resumed the Time Warner name in 2003.) Magness died in 1996, and Malone became TCI's chairman. In 1998 Liberty Media and BET's former chairman Robert Johnson bought out BET in a $380 million deal.

AT&T bought TCI for $55 billion in 1999 to form AT&T Broadband. As part of the deal, AT&T folded TCI Ventures into Liberty Media, including stakes in Sprint PCS (now Sprint FON), United Video Satellite Group (now Gemstar-TV Guide), General Instrument (Motorola bought General Instrument in 2000), and TCI International, and issued a new tracking stock for Liberty Media. The company later traded its interest in FOX/Liberty Networks (now called FOX Sports Net) for an 8% interest (later increased to 19%) in News Corp. and agreed to buy Associated Group and a stake in wireless communications company Teligent (the deal closed in early 2000).

In 2001 AT&T spun off Liberty Media as part of a plan to restructure the phone giant into four separate companies. The firm came solely under Malone's control.

The company restructured its deal with European cable operator UnitedGlobalCom in late 2001, upping its stake to 72% and retaining its Latin American assets. Liberty Media completed its purchase of the remaining UnitedGlobalCom stake that it did not own in 2004. Later that year, the company spun off all of its international assets (including UnitedGlobalCom) into a new firm called Liberty Media International.

In August 2005 CEO Robert Bennett announced that he would retire. Former TCI head Malone took over the CEO position briefly until the company named former Oracle executive Gregory Maffei near the end of 2005.

Liberty Media bought Provide Commerce, an e-tailer of flowers and perishable food items, early in 2006. The purchase furthered Liberty Media's push into online and television shopping. In May the company changed its name to Liberty Media Holding Corp. and reorganized to form two tracking stocks: Liberty Interactive Group and Liberty Capital Group. Also in May, the company sold its 50% stake in Court TV to Time Warner for $735 million.

## EXECUTIVES

**Chairman:** John C. Malone, age 66, $627,600 pay
**President, CEO, and Director:** Gregory B. (Greg) Maffei, age 46, $1,625,000 pay
**SVP:** Mark D. Carleton
**SVP:** Michael P. Zeisser, age 41
**SVP and Controller:** Christopher W. (Chris) Shean, age 42, $700,000 pay
**EVP, General Counsel, and Secretary:** Charles Y. Tanabe, age 55
**SVP Tax Strategy, Planning, and Compliance:** Albert E. Rosenthaler, age 47, $681,000 pay
**SVP and Treasurer:** David J. A. Flowers, age 52, $668,000 pay
**VP Business Development:** John A. Orr
**VP Investor and Media Relations:** Michael Erickson
**Auditors:** KPMG LLP

## LOCATIONS

**HQ:** Liberty Media Corporation
12300 Liberty Blvd., Englewood, CO 80112
**Phone:** 720-875-5400 **Fax:** 720-875-5401
**Web:** www.libertymedia.com

## PRODUCTS/OPERATIONS

### 2006 Sales

| | $ mil. | % of total |
|---|---|---|
| QVC | 7,074 | 82 |
| Starz Entertainment | 1,033 | 12 |
| Corporate & other | 506 | 6 |
| **Total** | **8,613** | **100** |

### Selected Subsidiaries and Investments

Corporate Assets
- News Corporation (16%, media and entertainment)

Capital Group
- FUN Technologies, Inc. (53%, online and interactive casual games and sports content)
- Starz, LLC
- Starz Entertainment, LLC
- Starz Media, LLC
- TruePosition, Inc. (89%, wireless technology services)
- WildBlue Communications, Inc. (32%, broadband satellite network)

Interactive Group
- BuySeasons, Inc. (100%, online costume and party supply retail)
- Provide Commerce, Inc. (100%, e-commerce)
- QVC (98%, home shopping network)

## COMPETITORS

1-800-FLOWERS.COM
American Express
Comcast
Cox Communications
Disney
Disney Studios
DreamWorks
Fox Entertainment
FTD
Hearst
HSN
KaBloom
NBC
NDS Group
Orbitz Worldwide
Oxygen Media
Pixar
priceline.com
Rainbow Media
Teleflora
Time Warner
Travelocity
Turner Broadcasting
Twentieth Century Fox
ValueVision Media
Viacom

## HISTORICAL FINANCIALS

Company Type: Holding company

### Income Statement

FYE: December 31

| | REVENUE ($ mil.) | NET INCOME ($ mil.) | NET PROFIT MARGIN | EMPLOYEES |
|---|---|---|---|---|
| **12/06** | 8,613 | 840 | 9.8% | 14,765 |
| **12/05** | 7,960 | — | — | — |
| **12/04** | 7,051 | — | — | — |
| **12/03** | 3,230 | — | — | — |
| **Annual Growth** | 38.7% | — | — | — |

### Revenue History

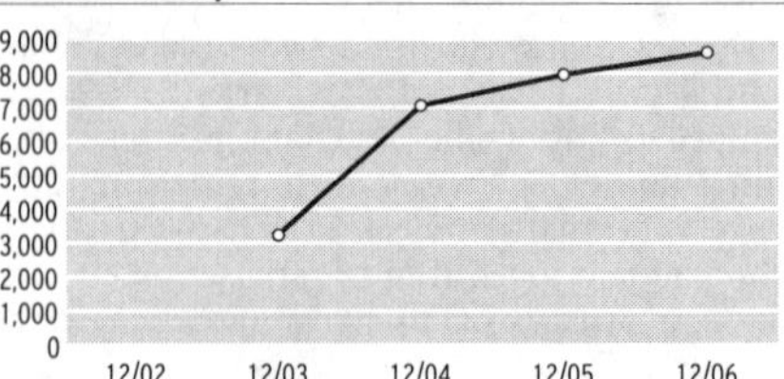


# Liberty Mutual

Boston boasts of baked beans, the Red Sox, and the Liberty Mutual Group. Liberty Mutual Holding is the parent company for the Liberty Mutual Group and its three principal mutual insurance companies, Liberty Mutual Insurance, Liberty Mutual Fire Insurance, and Employers Insurance Company of Wausau. Liberty Mutual is one of the top property/casualty insurers in the US and among the top 10 providers of automobile insurance. The company also offers homeowners' insurance and commercial lines for small to large companies. Liberty Mutual Group is a diversified global insurer with operations in nearly 900 offices throughout the world.

The Personal Market group offers personal lines property/casualty insurance including private auto and homeowners' insurance. Much of its new business comes from relationships with affinity groups such as credit unions, employers, and professional and alumni associations.

The Commercial Markets division provides commercial property/casualty products. The division includes the National Market unit, which serves large businesses, and the Business Market unit, serving mid-sized businesses. The Commercial Markets division also includes Liberty Mutual Property (commercial property coverage) and Group Market (group disability products and administration).

The Agency Markets division is focused on small and mid-sized employers and individuals. It operates through smaller regional businesses as well as Wausau Insurance, Summit Holding Southeast, and Liberty Mutual Surety. Commercial customers account for more than 80% of Agency Markets' business, with workers compensation premiums accounting for more than 40% of its total premiums.

Liberty's International unit has grown in importance as part of a planned long-term expansion outside of the US. The International division includes local companies that offer personal and commercial insurance to local markets in more than 20 countries and Liberty International Underwriters, which provides specialty commercial lines worldwide.

Liberty Mutual has announced that it intends to acquire property/casualty insurer Ohio Casualty. When the $2.6 billion deal closes, Ohio Casualty will become part of Liberty Mutual's Agency Markets division.

## HISTORY

The need for financial aid to workers injured on the job was recognized in Europe in the late 19th century but did not make its way to the US until a workers' compensation law for federal employees was passed in 1908. Massachusetts was one of the first states to enact similar legislation. Liberty Mutual was founded in Boston in 1912 to fill this newly recognized niche.

Liberty Mutual followed the fire insurance practice of taking an active part in loss prevention. It evaluated clients' premises and procedures and recommended ways to prevent accidents. The company rejected the budding industry practice of limiting medical fees, instead studying the most effective ways to reduce the long-term cost of a claim by getting the injured party back to work.

In 1942 the company acquired the United Mutual Fire Insurance Company (founded 1908, renamed Liberty Mutual Fire Insurance Company in 1949). The next year it founded a rehabilitation center in Boston to treat injured workers and to test treatments.

In the 1960s and 1970s, Liberty Mutual expanded its line to include life insurance (1963), group pensions (1970), and IRAs (1975).

Seeking to increase its national presence, the company formed Liberty Northwest Insurance Corporation in 1983. It continued expanding its offerings, with new subsidiaries in commercial, personal, and excess lines and, in 1986, by moving into financial services by buying Stein Roe & Farnham (founded 1958).

The expansion/diversification strategy seemed to work. Earnings between 1984 and 1986 more than tripled. Then the downturn: Recession was followed by a string of natural disasters, and Liberty Mutual's income fell sharply between 1986 and 1988. In 1992 and 1993 the firm lost suits to Coors and Outboard Marine for failing to back those companies in environmental litigation cases.

In 1995 Liberty Mutual gained a foothold in the UK when it received permission to invest in a Lloyd's of London syndicate management company. In 1997 Liberty Mutual acquired bankrupt workers' comp provider Golden Eagle Insurance of California; the next year the firm bought Florida's Summit Holding Southeast. Mutual funds were also on the shopping list: Purchases included Société Générale's US mutual funds unit, led by international money dean Jean-Marie Eveillard.

In 1999 the company bought Guardian Royal Exchange's US operations. In a new international initiative that year, Liberty Mutual bought 70% of Singapore-based insurer Citystate Holdings (to be renamed Liberty Citystate) as its foothold in Asia.

After failing to find a buyer, asset management subsidiary Liberty Financial in 2001 began liquidating assets. Canadian insurer Sun Life acquired Keyport Life Insurance and mutual fund distributor Independent Financial Marketing Group. Liberty Financial's investment management segment (including subsidiaries Crabbe Huston, Stein Roe & Farnham, and Liberty Wanger Asset Management) was snapped up by FleetBoston (now part of the Bank of America empire). Liberty Mutual then bought the nearly 30% of Liberty Financial it did not already own and merged the remains into its subsidiary operations.

The company's diversification efforts included Liberty International, which expanded operations in such countries as Canada, Japan, Mexico, Singapore, and the UK. The company also grew its international presence in areas such as China and southern Europe.

Slumping property/casualty lines and the events of September 11 hit Liberty Mutual in 2001 (the company paid out some $500 million in claims). In 2001 and 2002 the company reorganized into a mutual holding company structure with its three principal operating companies (Liberty Mutual Insurance, Liberty Mutual Fire Insurance, and Employers Insurance Company of Wausau) each becoming separate stock insurance companies with Liberty Mutual Holding Company as the parent.

Strengthening its personal lines business, Liberty Mutual in 2003 bought Prudential's domestic property/casualty operations. The deal included some 1,400 Prudential agents which were added to the company's distribution mix.

## EXECUTIVES

**Chairman, President, and CEO:** Edmund F. (Ted) Kelly, age 61
**Special Consultant to the CEO:** Roger L. Jean
**EVP, Liberty International:** Thomas C. Ramey
**EVP and Chief Investment Officer:** A. Alexander Fontanes
**EVP; President and COO, Wausau Insurance:** Mark Fiebrink
**SVP and CFO:** Dennis J. Langwell
**SVP and General Counsel:** Christopher C. Mansfield
**SVP, Human Resources and Administration:** Helen E. R. Sayles
**VP and Comptroller:** John D. Doyle
**VP and Secretary:** Dexter R. Legg
**VP and Treasurer:** Laurance H. S. Yahia
**VP and Manager, External Relations:** John Cusolito
**VP and Director, Investor Relations:** Matthew T. Coyle
**President and CEO, Montgomery Insurance:** Michael Plavnicky
**Auditors:** Ernst & Young LLP

## LOCATIONS

**HQ:** Liberty Mutual Holding Company Inc.
175 Berkeley St., Boston, MA 02116
**Phone:** 617-357-9500 **Fax:** 617-350-7648
**Web:** www.libertymutual.com

Liberty Mutual Insurance has nearly 900 offices in the US, as well as in Argentina, Brazil, Chile, China, Colombia, Hong Kong, Poland, Portugal, Singapore, Spain, Thailand, Turkey, and Venezuela.

## PRODUCTS/OPERATIONS

### 2006 Sales

| | $ mil. | % of total |
|---|---|---|
| Personal market | 6,695 | 28 |
| Agency markets | 6,246 | 27 |
| Liberty International | 4,900 | 21 |
| Commercial markets | 4,771 | 20 |
| Other revenues | 908 | 4 |
| **Total** | **23,520** | **100** |

### 2006 Sales

| | $ mil. | % of total |
|---|---|---|
| Premiums earned | 19,867 | 84 |
| Net investment income | 2,548 | 11 |
| Net realized investment gains | 343 | 2 |
| Fees & other revenues | 762 | 3 |
| **Total** | **23,520** | **100** |

### Selected Subsidiaries and Affiliates

Liberty International
- Liberty ART SA (Argentina)
- Liberty Direct (Poland)
- Liberty Insurance PTE. LTD. (Singapore)
- Liberty International Underwriters
- Liberty Paulista de Seguros (Brazil)
- Liberty Seguros SA (Colombia)
- Seguros Caracas de Liberty Mutual C.A. (Venezuela)
- Seker Sigorta A.S. (Turkey)

Liberty Mutual Group Inc.
- America First Insurance
- Colorado Casualty
- Employers Insurance Company of Wausau
- Golden Eagle Insurance Co.
- Hawkeye-Security Insurance
- Indiana Insurance Company
- Merchants and Businessmen's Insurance Company
- Montgomery Mutual Insurance Company
- Peerless Insurance
- Summit Holding Southeast
- Wausau Insurance Companies

## COMPETITORS

21st Century
ACE Limited
AEGON USA
AIG
Allianz
Allstate
CIGNA
Citigroup
CNA Financial
GEICO
The Hartford
ING
Lincoln Financial Group
MassMutual
MetLife
Northwestern Mutual
Progressive Corporation
State Farm
Travelers Companies
Washington National
Zurich Financial Services

## HISTORICAL FINANCIALS

Company Type: Mutual company

### Income Statement

FYE: December 31

| | ASSETS ($ mil.) | NET INCOME ($ mil.) | INCOME AS % OF ASSETS | EMPLOYEES |
|---|---|---|---|---|
| **12/06** | 85,498 | 1,626 | 1.9% | 39,000 |
| **12/05** | 78,824 | 1,027 | 1.3% | 39,000 |
| **12/04** | 72,359 | 1,245 | 1.7% | 38,000 |
| **12/03** | 64,422 | 851 | 1.3% | 38,000 |
| **12/02** | 55,877 | 508 | 0.9% | 35,000 |
| **Annual Growth** | 11.2% | 33.8% | — | 2.7% |

### 2006 Year-End Financials

Equity as % of assets: —
Return on assets: 2.0%
Return on equity: —
Long-term debt ($ mil.): —
Sales ($ mil.): 23,520

### Net Income History

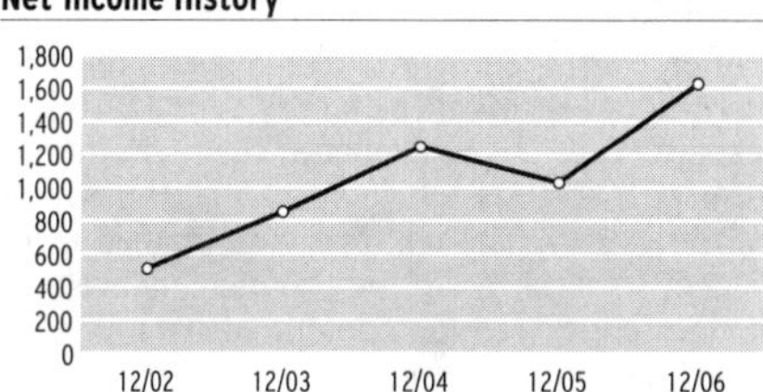

# Limited Brands

Limited Brands is as much of a shopping-mall mainstay as food courts and teenagers. The company operates some 3,750 stores throughout North America. Originally focused on apparel, Limited Brands has evolved into a personal care, beauty, and lingerie company (more than 70% of sales). It recently boosted its lingerie share with the purchase of Canada's La Senza. Its shrinking apparel business includes The Limited and Henri Bendel chains. Its Intimate Brands business segment is known for its Victoria's Secret, Bath & Body Works, and White Barn Candle units. It also owns apparel maker MAST Industries. Limited Brands is controlled by founder and chairman Leslie Wexner, whose family owns about 13% of the firm.

Vice chairman and COO Len Schlesinger resigned in July 2007 after eight years with the firm. Wexner and administrative executive Martyn Redgrave took over Schlesinger's responsibilities.

To better focus on its intimate apparel and personal care brands, the firm has sold controlling interests in its Express and Limited apparel chains to affiliates of Golden Gate Capital and Sun Capital Partners, respectively.

To better fit its shrinking size, Limited Brands has announced that it will reduce its corporate staff in Columbus and New York by 10% (about 530 jobs).

Wexner announced in mid-2006 that he wants to see Victoria's Secret blossom into a $10 billion brand. Despite the lofty goal (Victoria's Secret generated a little more than $5.1 billion in sales last year), the company began to integrate its operations and pool top management. Limited Brands grouped Victoria's Secret Stores, Victoria's Secret Beauty, Victoria's Secret Direct, PINK, Intimissimi, and Sexy Sport under one entity (Victoria's Secret Megabrand and Intimate Apparel) led by president and CEO Sharen Jester Turney (from Victoria's Secret Direct).

In early 2007 Limited Brands completed its acquisition of lingerie maker and retailer La Senza, based in Montreal, for about $600 million. With more than 300 stores that it owns and operates and roughly 300 others that operate by licensees in 34 countries, La Senza is key to Wexner's goal to enhance its lingerie holdings internationally.

To speed product development in its beauty business, Limited Brands has formed Beauty Avenue, a personal care sourcing company. The in-house division is charged with creating personal care and beauty brands for Bath & Body Works and Victoria's Secret Beauty, as well as PINK and a new Henri Bendel concept.

## HISTORY

After a disagreement with his father in 1963 over the operation of the family store (Leslie's), Leslie Wexner, then 26, opened the first Limited store in Columbus, Ohio, with $5,000 borrowed from his aunt. The company was named from Wexner's desire to do one product line well — moderately priced fashionable attire for teenagers and young women.

When The Limited went public in 1969, it had only five stores, but the rapid development of large, covered malls spurred growth to 100 stores by 1976. Two years later The Limited acquired MAST Industries, an international apparel purchasing and importing company. The company opened Express in 1980 to serve the teen market.

The Limited grew with acquisitions, including the 1982 purchases of Lane Bryant (large sizes) and Victoria's Secret (lingerie). That year it formed the Brylane fashion catalog division and acquired Roaman's, a bricks-and-mortar and catalog merchandiser.

Wexner bought The Lerner Stores (budget women's apparel) and Henri Bendel (high fashion) in 1985, sportswear retailer Abercrombie & Fitch (A&F) in 1988, and London-based perfumer Penhaligon's in 1990 (sold in 1997). The Limited introduced several in-store shops, including Cacique (French lingerie) in 1988 and Limited Too (girls' fashions), which were later expanded into stand-alone stores. It also launched Structure (men's sportswear) in 1989 and Bath & Body Works shops in 1990. All of these stores were in malls, often strategically clustered together.

The Limited in 1993 closed many The Limited and Lerner stores and sold 60% of its Brylane catalog unit to Freeman Spogli (taking it public in 1997). It opened four Bath & Body Works stores in the UK (its first non-US stores) to compete with British rival The Body Shop.

In 1994 The Limited bought Galyan's Trading Company, a chain of sporting goods superstores. The company began spinning off its businesses while keeping controlling stakes; it spun off Intimate Brands (Victoria's Secret, Cacique, and Bath & Body Works) in 1995 and A&F in 1996.

In 1997 the company closed more than 100 of its women's apparel stores; the next year it closed nearly 300 more companywide (excluding the Intimate Brands chains) and the majority of its Henri Bendel stores.

The Limited in 1998 launched White Barn Candle Co. (candle and home fragrance stores). The following year the company spun off Limited Too, its most successful chain, as Too, Inc., and reduced its interest in Galyan's to 40%. (Galyan's management and buyout firm Freeman Spogli own 60% of the sporting goods chain.)

To boost profits, in 2001 The Limited folded the Structure brand into the Express unit and spun off its Galyan's and Alliance Data Systems subsidiaries, retaining 22% and 20%, respectively. The Limited sold its Lane Bryant unit to Charming Shoppes for $335 million that year.

In March 2002 The Limited bought back the remaining shares of Intimate Brands it did not already own and, over the course of the year, phased it into a business segment. In May 2002 the company changed its name to Limited Brands. Later that year Limited Brands sold off its remaining stake in Lerner New York and in late 2003 sold its Structure label to Sears, Roebuck and Co.

In May 2004 Limited Brands acquired New York-based Slatkin & Co., a prestige home fragrance company that distributes scented candles, potpourris, and room sprays under the names Slatkin & Co., Oscar Home, Elton John, C.Z. Guest, and Kabbalah. That year the company laid off 25% of its headquarters workforce — including managers and support personnel — in the face of slipping earnings.

In 2007 Limited Brands sold a 75% interest in its Express chain to affiliates of Golden Gate Capital for about $425 million. Limited Brands retained a 25% stake in the 625-store chain. In a similar transaction completed in August, Limited Brands sold a 75% stake in its 251-store Limited Stores business to Sun Capital Partners, taking a loss on the sale.

## EXECUTIVES

**Chairman and CEO:** Leslie H. Wexner, age 69, $1,823,269 pay
**CFO:** Stuart Burgdoerfer
**EVP and Chief Administrative Officer:** Martyn R. Redgrave, age 54, $975,962 pay
**EVP, Corporate Development:** V. Ann Hailey, age 55, $934,615 pay (partial-year salary)
**EVP Human Resources:** Jane L. Ramsey, age 49
**EVP, Retail Real Estate:** Jamie Bersani
**EVP Retail Operations:** Mark A. Giresi, age 49
**SVP and General Counsel:** Douglas L. Williams
**SVP, Law, Policy and Governance and Secretary:** Samuel P. Fried
**SVP, Investor, Media and Community Relations:** Thomas (Tom) Katzenmeyer
**SVP, Lingerie Projects:** Jeanette Cantone
**SVP and Counsel Company Affairs:** Bruce A. Soll, age 49
**VP Investor Relations:** Amie Preston
**VP, Marketing and Media:** Pattie Glod
**VP, Treasury, and Mergers and Acquisitions:** Timothy J. Faber
**President and CEO, Victoria's Secret Group:** Sharen Jester Turney, age 50, $1,086,731 pay
**President and CEO, Henri Bendel; President, Limited Brands Accessories:** Edward (Ed) Bucciarelli, age 47
**CEO, Bath & Body Works:** Diane L. Neal, age 50
**President, White Barn Candle Co.:** Christiane Michaels
**President and Chief Marketing Officer, Brand and Creative Services:** Edward G. Razek
**President, Home Design:** Harry Slatkin
**President, Logistics Services, The Limited:** Nicholas J. LaHowchic, age 59
**President and General Merchandise Manager, Limited Stores:** Avra Myers
**Communications Specialist:** Jennifer Ortiz
**Auditors:** Ernst & Young LLP

## LOCATIONS

**HQ:** Limited Brands, Inc.
3 Limited Pkwy., Columbus, OH 43230
**Phone:** 614-415-7000 **Fax:** 614-415-7440
**Web:** www.limitedbrands.com

## PRODUCTS/OPERATIONS

### 2007 Stores

| | No. |
|---|---|
| Bath & Body Works | 1,546 |
| Victoria's Secret | |
| Victoria's Secret Stores | 1,003 |
| La Senza | 323 |
| Apparel business | |
| Express dual gender | 394 |
| Express women's | 195 |
| Express men's | 69 |
| Limited stores | 260 |
| Diva London | 6 |
| Henri Bendel | 2 |
| **Total** | **3,798** |

### 2007 Sales

| | $ mil. | % of total |
|---|---|---|
| Victoria's Secret | | |
| Victoria's Secret Stores | 3,700 | 35 |
| Victoria's Secret Direct | 1,416 | 13 |
| La Senza | 23 | — |
| Bath & Body Works | 2,556 | 24 |
| Apparel | | |
| Express | 1,749 | 16 |
| Limited | 493 | 5 |
| Other | 734 | 7 |
| **Total** | **10,671** | **100** |

## COMPETITORS

Abercrombie & Fitch
American Eagle Outfitters
AnnTaylor
Avon
Benetton
Body Shop
Burlington Coat Factory
Charming Shoppes
The Children's Place
CVS/Caremark
Dillard's
Dress Barn
Eddie Bauer Holdings
Estée Lauder
Frederick's of Hollywood
Fruit of the Loom
Gap
Guess
H&M
Hanesbrands
J. C. Penney
J. Crew
Jockey International
Kiehl's
Lands' End
Levi Strauss
Liz Claiborne
L.L. Bean
Macy's
Mary Kay
Mervyns
Nautica Enterprises
Nordstrom
Pacific Sunwear
Polo Ralph Lauren
Retail Brand Alliance
Revlon
Saks Inc.
Sears
Sephora
Shiseido Cosmetics
Talbots
Target
TJX Companies
Tommy Hilfiger
VF
Warnaco Group
Wet Seal

## HISTORICAL FINANCIALS

Company Type: Public

**Income Statement** FYE: Saturday nearest January 31

| | REVENUE ($ mil.) | NET INCOME ($ mil.) | NET PROFIT MARGIN | EMPLOYEES |
|---|---|---|---|---|
| **1/07** | 10,671 | 676 | 6.3% | 125,500 |
| **1/06** | 9,699 | 683 | 7.0% | 110,000 |
| **1/05** | 9,408 | 705 | 7.5% | 115,300 |
| **1/04** | 8,934 | 717 | 8.0% | 111,100 |
| **1/03** | 8,445 | 502 | 5.9% | 98,900 |
| **Annual Growth** | 6.0% | 7.7% | — | 6.1% |

**2007 Year-End Financials**

Debt ratio: 56.3%
Return on equity: 24.9%
Cash ($ mil.): 500
Current ratio: 1.62
Long-term debt ($ mil.): 1,665
No. of shares (mil.): 398
Dividends
Yield: 2.1%
Payout: 35.7%
Market value ($ mil.): 11,367

**Stock History** NYSE: LTD

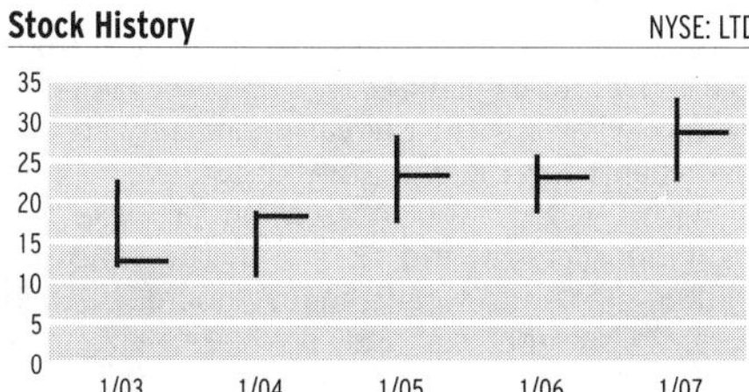


| | STOCK PRICE ($) FY Close | P/E High | P/E Low | PER SHARE ($) Earnings | Dividends | Book Value |
|---|---|---|---|---|---|---|
| **1/07** | 28.56 | 19 | 14 | 1.68 | 0.60 | 7.42 |
| **1/06** | 23.02 | 15 | 11 | 1.66 | 0.60 | 6.26 |
| **1/05** | 23.23 | 19 | 12 | 1.47 | 1.71 | 5.74 |
| **1/04** | 18.20 | 14 | 8 | 1.36 | 0.40 | 10.17 |
| **1/03** | 12.59 | 23 | 13 | 0.96 | 0.30 | 9.29 |
| **Annual Growth** | 22.7% | — | — | 15.0% | 18.9% | (5.5%) |

# Lincoln Electric Holdings

With this thing, I thee weld. The Lincoln Electric Company is a leading manufacturer of arc-welding and cutting products, as well as welding supplies that include arc-welding power sources, automated wire-feeding systems, and consumable electrodes for arc welding. Lincoln Electric also makes coated manual electrodes, solid electrodes produced in coil form, and cored electrodes produced in solid form. Lincoln Electric's welding products unit accounts for the majority of its revenues. The company operates more than 30 manufacturing facilities in the US and 18 other countries.

Lincoln Electric has focused on expanding internationally through acquisitions — especially equipment makers in Europe and Asia. Although its bid to acquire rival Charter plc in 2000 didn't work out, it has gone on to purchase several companies in recent years.

Royce & Associates owns more than 12% of Lincoln Electric. Former director David C. Lincoln holds about 5% of the company.

## HISTORY

John Lincoln founded The Lincoln Electric Company in 1895 to make and repair electric motors. By the time his younger brother James joined the company as a salesman in 1907, John had expanded into rechargeable batteries and had also begun researching arc welding. John dedicated himself to research and left James to handle management.

In the workplace, James formed an advisory board made up of elected employee representatives from each department. Its twice-monthly meetings became a cornerstone of the company's Incentive Management System, which Lincoln based on six tenets: people as assets, Christian ethics, principles, simplicity, competition, and customer satisfaction. As part of the system, piecework pay and group life insurance (unusual at the time) were begun in 1915. Meanwhile, John perfected the electric arc welding machine that soon became the company's chief product, and in 1917 he formed The Lincoln Electric Welding School.

In 1934 workers offered to work longer hours during the Depression in exchange for a share of the company's profits; that year bonuses averaged 30% of pay. By the 1940s Lincoln was the world's #1 maker of arc-welding equipment, with subsidiaries in Australia, Canada, and the UK and licensees in Argentina, Brazil, Canada, and Mexico. Lincoln added a pension plan and an internal promotion program during WWII as ship manufacturing fueled demand for its products.

William Irrgang, a German engineer with 26 years at the company, succeeded James Lincoln as president in 1954 (James became chairman). Under Irrgang and Lincoln the company practiced conservative policies: It prohibited capital spending projects with paybacks greater than one year. Irrgang became chairman in 1965 and was named CEO (a new title) in 1972, the same year George Willis, a Harvard MBA and devotee of the Incentive Management System, became president. Willis was constrained by Irrgang's conservatism and the economic woes of the early 1980s. Sales dropped and though Lincoln's policy of not laying off workers was strained, workers shifted jobs into maintenance or sales work.

Irrgang died in 1986, leaving Willis in control. Willis quickly expanded product lines and geographic coverage. Soon the company's offerings included robotic and gas-based welding products. When he retired the next year, Willis left a legacy of expansion and debt. Though sales had doubled and the company's international presence had grown to 15 countries, debt had risen from about $18 million in 1988 to $222 million in 1993. Lincoln also had trouble exporting its incentive system to other countries. The company returned to profitability in 1994, cutting jobs and closing factories in Europe and Latin America and adding jobs in the US.

Anthony Massaro became CEO in 1996. He looked overseas for opportunities, including deals in China, Indonesia, and Italy. In 1997 Lincoln consolidated production at its European plants and agreed to settle some of the lawsuits alleging that a type of its welding wire contributed to building damage in California's 1994 Northridge earthquake.

In 1998 the company acquired Indalco, a Canada-based maker of aluminum welding wire, and Germany-based Uhrhan & Schwill, which made pipe-welding systems. It also obtained a 50% stake in Turkish welding company AS Kaynak and opened a distribution center near Johannesburg, South Africa. In 1999 Lincoln sold its electric motors business to Regal-Beloit.

In 2000 Lincoln bought a 35% stake in Kuang Tai Metal Industrial, a Taiwan-based company that made mild and stainless-steel welding wires. That year Lincoln acquired Italian welding consumables maker C.I.F.E. It then went after UK-based welding-equipment maker Charter plc, but was unable to complete the transaction after the US Federal Trade Commission ruled it would require Lincoln to divest certain operations if it acquired Charter. In 2001 the company opened a new research facility in Cleveland; the next year it acquired 85% of Polish welding equipment maker Bester S.A.

In 2004 John Stropki replaced Anthony Massaro as president and CEO of Lincoln Electric. Stropki also became chairman when Massaro retired near the end of 2004.

In 2005 Lincoln Electric purchased brazing and soldering alloys manufacturer J.W. Harris Co. for about $71 million in cash and $15 million of assumed debt.

In 2006 the company purchased Metrode Products, a UK-based firm that makes specialty consumables for the process and power generation industries. Metrode rang up annual sales of about $24 million with its alloyed welding consumables.

## EXECUTIVES

**Chairman, President, and CEO:** John M. Stropki Jr., age 56, $750,000 pay
**SVP, CFO, and Treasurer:** Vincent K. Petrella, age 46, $325,000 pay
**SVP, Global Engineering:** George D. Blankenship, age 44, $403,470 pay
**SVP, Sales, Marketing, Middle East, and Africa:** Richard J. Seif
**SVP, Secretary, and General Counsel:** Frederick G. Stueber, age 53, $325,000 pay

**VP and Corporate Controller:** Gabriel Bruno
**VP, Corporate Tax:** Michele R. Kuhrt
**VP, Global Operations Development:** Vinod K. Kapoor
**VP and Group President, Brazing, Cutting, and Retail Subsidiaries:** David J. Nangle
**VP, Human Resources:** Gretchen Farrell, age 44
**VP, Machine Division:** Ronald A. Nelson
**VP; President and CEO, Lincoln Electric Canada:** Joseph G. Doria
**VP; President, Lincoln Electric Latin America:** Ralph C. Fernandez, age 60, $265,000 pay
**VP and President, Lincoln Electric Asia Pacific:** Thomas A. (Tom) Flohn, age 46
**VP; President, Lincoln Electric Europe:** David M. LeBlanc, age 42, $235,000 pay
**VP, Strategic Planning and Acquisitions:** Robert K. Gudbranson, age 43
**Auditors:** Ernst & Young LLP

## LOCATIONS

**HQ:** Lincoln Electric Holdings, Inc.
22801 St. Clair Ave., Cleveland, OH 44117
**Phone:** 216-481-8100 **Fax:** 216-486-1751
**Web:** www.lincolnelectric.com

Lincoln Electric Holdings has manufacturing facilities in Australia, Brazil, Canada, China, Colombia, France, Germany, Indonesia, Ireland, Italy, Mexico, the Netherlands, Poland, Spain, Taiwan, Turkey, the UK, the US, and Venezuela.

### 2006 Sales

| | $ mil. | % of total |
|---|---|---|
| North America | 1,305.5 | 66 |
| Europe | 372.3 | 19 |
| Other regions | 294.1 | 15 |
| **Total** | **1,971.9** | **100** |

## PRODUCTS/OPERATIONS

### Selected Products

Arc-welding power sources
Consumable electrodes and fluxes
Fume-extraction equipment
Oxy-fuel welding and cutting regulators and torches
Robotic welding packages
Wire-feeding systems

## COMPETITORS

Airgas
Charter
Emerson Electric
ESAB
FANUC
Flow
Franklin Electric
Illinois Tool Works
Indel
Iwatani International
Kobe Steel
KUKA
Pentair
Schumacher
Shinsho
Thermadyne
Uniweld Products

## HISTORICAL FINANCIALS

Company Type: Public

### Income Statement

FYE: December 31

| | REVENUE ($ mil.) | NET INCOME ($ mil.) | NET PROFIT MARGIN | EMPLOYEES |
|---|---|---|---|---|
| **12/06** | 1,972 | 175 | 8.9% | 8,430 |
| **12/05** | 1,601 | 122 | 7.6% | 7,485 |
| **12/04** | 1,334 | 81 | 6.0% | 6,835 |
| **12/03** | 1,041 | 55 | 5.2% | 5,992 |
| **12/02** | 994 | 29 | 2.9% | 6,097 |
| **Annual Growth** | 18.7% | 56.3% | — | 8.4% |

### 2006 Year-End Financials

Debt ratio: 13.4%
Return on equity: 23.3%
Cash ($ mil.): 120
Current ratio: 2.45
Long-term debt ($ mil.): 114
No. of shares (mil.): 43
Dividends
Yield: 1.3%
Payout: 19.4%
Market value ($ mil.): 2,586

### Stock History

NASDAQ (GS): LECO

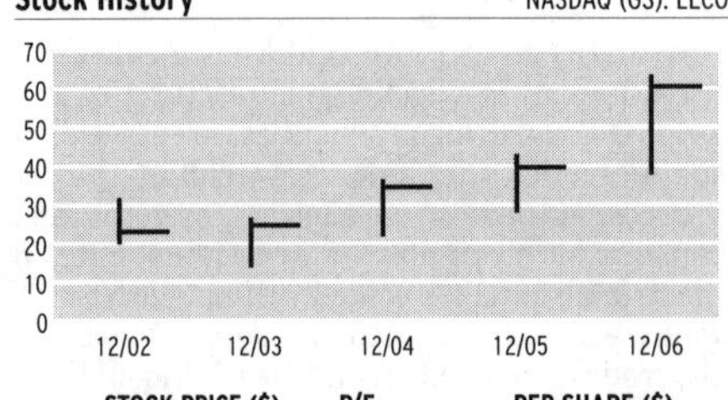


| | STOCK PRICE ($) FY Close | P/E High | P/E Low | PER SHARE ($) Earnings | Dividends | Book Value |
|---|---|---|---|---|---|---|
| **12/06** | 60.42 | 15 | 9 | 4.07 | 0.79 | 19.93 |
| **12/05** | 39.66 | 15 | 10 | 2.90 | 0.73 | 15.46 |
| **12/04** | 34.54 | 19 | 11 | 1.94 | 0.69 | 13.86 |
| **12/03** | 24.74 | 20 | 11 | 1.31 | 0.64 | 11.78 |
| **12/02** | 23.15 | 46 | 30 | 0.68 | 0.61 | 10.20 |
| **Annual Growth** | 27.1% | — | — | 56.4% | 6.7% | 18.2% |

# Lincoln National

Who better to trust with your nest egg than the company that took its name from Honest Abe? Lincoln National, which operates as Lincoln Financial Group, offers retirement planning and life insurance with a focus on annuities and a variety of life insurance products, through such subsidiaries as Lincoln National Life Insurance, First Penn-Pacific Life Insurance Company, and Lincoln Life & Annuity Company of New York. The company is also active in the investment management business, offering individual and institutional clients such financial services as pension plans, trusts, and mutual funds through Delaware Investments and other subsidiaries.

Lincoln National sells through its own system of financial advisors, as well as through a variety of third parties (brokerages, independent financial advisors, financial institutions). It also provides financial services in the UK through subsidiary Lincoln National (UK).

Its subsidiary Lincoln Financial Media owns and operates television and radio stations while its Lincoln Financial Sports provides syndication and marketing of televised regional college sporting events.

Lincoln National has stepped up its advertising efforts (including paying to put the name Lincoln Financial Field on the Philadelphia Eagles' stadium), hoping to improve brand recognition.

Lincoln National completed a merger/acquisition of Jefferson-Pilot in early 2006. The $7.5 billion deal combined the Lincoln Financial Group with the Jefferson Pilot Financial group (the operating brand for Jefferson-Pilot Corporation) and created a new company, operating as Lincoln Financial Group. Led by management from both former organizations, the new group has expanded insurance and financial products offerings and national retail and wholesale distribution platforms.

## HISTORY

Wilbur Wynant, a sort of Johnny Appleseed of shady fraternal benefits societies, arrived in Fort Wayne, Indiana, in 1902. He persuaded several respected businessmen and professionals to help him found the Fraternal Assurance Society of America, an assessable mutual organization in which surviving members contributed to the death benefits of deceased members. Wynant absconded within a couple of years, and the local organizers restructured the society's remains as a stock company in 1905. To clean up the organization's reputation, they obtained permission from Abraham Lincoln's son Robert to use his father's name and image.

In 1905, when the company wrote its first policy, it had three agents, including its leading executive, Arthur Hall. By 1911 the company had 106 agents. Careful risk assessment was an early hallmark of the company and allowed it to accept business that other companies rejected based on more superficial analysis.

From a very early period, the company grew through acquisitions. WWI increased claims, but not as much as the global flu epidemic that followed the war. Internal growth continued in the 1920s.

Death and disability claims increased abnormally during the Depression, and the company's underwriting became more stringent. Lincoln National used the financial turmoil of the period to buy other troubled insurers. Reinsurance became the firm's primary line until after WWII.

The company continued buying other firms in the 1950s and 1960s, and in 1968 it formed holding company Lincoln National. Soon it began diversifying, buying Chicago Title and Trust (1969; sold 1985) as well as more life and reinsurance companies. Lincoln National also went into the health benefits business, setting up its own HMO and investing in EMPHESYS (which it took public in 1994, divesting the remainder of its stock in 1995).

The collapse of the real estate market in many areas nicked results in the late 1980s, and in 1990 the company accepted an infusion of cash from Dai-Ichi Mutual Life Insurance. Property/casualty results were hurt in the early 1990s by an unprecedented string of natural disasters.

With the growth of retirement savings from baby boomers hitting their 50s, the company shifted gears into wealth management. In 1995 Lincoln National expanded its investment management capacities by purchasing Delaware Management Holdings and Laurentian Financial Group. The next year it bought the group tax-qualified annuity business of disability insurer UNUM (now UNUMProvident) and in 1997 bought Voyageur Fund Managers, a tax-free-bond fund business. The company also took a 49% stake in a Mexican insurance company owned by Grupo Financiero Santander Serfin (sold in 2000). It sold its 83% interest in property/casualty firm American States Financial in 1996.

Lincoln National bought CIGNA's annuity and individual life insurance business and Aetna's US individual life insurance operations in 1998. It reorganized that year to help it absorb these businesses, causing earnings to take a substantial hit.

In 1999, after nearly a century in the heartland, the company moved to Philadelphia. Lincoln National sold its individual disability income business and cut its "excess of loss" and group carrier medical reinsurance.

As sluggish sales and fines related to a pension scandal weakened its bottom line, it put its UK operations up for sale in 2000. The sale was abandoned after the potential acquirer ceased negotiations. However, Lincoln National stopped writing new business for new customers in the UK.

The company sold its reinsurance business to Swiss Re in 2001 to re-focus on wealth and asset accumulation products and services.

In 2002, the company acquired employee benefits record-keeping firm The Administrative Management Group.

## EXECUTIVES

**Chairman:** J. Patrick Barrett, age 70
**President, CEO, and Director:** Dennis R. Glass, age 56
**SVP and CFO:** Frederick J. (Fred) Crawford, age 43, $400,000 pay
**SVP and General Counsel:** Dennis L. Schoff, age 47
**SVP and Chief Human Resources Officer:** Elizabeth L. (Beth) Reeves, age 53
**VP and Treasurer:** Duane L. Bernt
**President and CEO, Lincoln Financial Advisors:** Robert W. (Bob) Dineen, age 57
**President, Lincoln Employer Markets:** Westley V. (Wes) Thompson, age 52, $500,000 pay
**President and Managing Director, Lincoln National (UK):** Michael Tallett-Williams, age 53
**President, Individual Markets:** Mark E. Konen, age 47
**President, Lincoln National Investment Company, Inc. and Delaware Management Holdings, Inc:** Patrick P. Coyne, age 43, $395,000 pay
**SVP Distribution for Retirement, Executive Benefits and Group Protection, Lincoln Employer Markets:** Don Roberson
**SVP, Sales and Marketing, Lincoln Employer Markets:** Len Cavallaro
**SVP, Strategic Investment Relationships and Initiatives, Delaware Investments:** David P. O'Connor
**SVP, Shared Services and CIO:** Charles C. (Chuck) Cornelio, age 47
**Secretary:** C. Suzanne Womack
**Chief Risk Officer and Treasurer:** Randy Freitag
**Auditors:** Ernst & Young LLP

## LOCATIONS

**HQ:** Lincoln National Corporation
1500 Market St., Ste. 3900, Philadelphia, PA 19102
**Phone:** 215-448-1400 **Fax:** 215-448-3962
**Web:** www.lfg.com

Lincoln National has operations throughout the US and in the UK.

## PRODUCTS/OPERATIONS

### 2006 Sales

| | $ mil. | % of total |
|---|---|---|
| Individual markets | | |
| Life insurance | 3,256 | 36 |
| Annuities | 2,161 | 24 |
| Employer markets | | |
| Retirement products | 1,360 | 15 |
| Group protection | 1,032 | 12 |
| Investment management | 564 | 6 |
| Lincoln UK | 308 | 3 |
| Lincoln Financial Media | 188 | 2 |
| Other operations | 196 | 2 |
| Net realized investment losses | (3) | — |
| Reinsurance amortization | 1 | — |
| **Total** | **9,063** | **100** |

### 2006 Sales

| | $ mil. | % of total |
|---|---|---|
| Net investment income | 3,981 | 44 |
| Insurance fees | 2,604 | 29 |
| Insurance premiums | 1,406 | 15 |
| Investment advisory fees | 328 | 4 |
| Net communications revenue | 187 | 2 |
| Amortization of deferred gain | 76 | 1 |
| Other revenues & fees | 484 | 5 |
| Realized loss on investments | (3) | — |
| **Total** | **9,063** | **100** |

### Selected Subsidiaries and Affiliates

The Lincoln National Life Insurance Company
Finetre Corporation (formerly AnnuityNet, Inc.)
Corporate Benefit Systems, Inc.
First Penn-Pacific Life Insurance Company
Lincoln National (UK) PLC
Lincoln Assurance Limited
Barnwood Property Group Limited
IMPCO Properties G.B. Ltd.
Lincoln Financial Group PLC
Lincoln Milldon Limited
Lincoln General Insurance Co. Ltd.
Lincoln Insurance Services Limited
Chapel Ash Financial Services Ltd.

## COMPETITORS

AEGON
AIG
AIG American General
Aon
AXA Financial
FMR
Guardian Life
The Hartford
Hartford Life
John Hancock
Manulife Financial
MassMutual
MetLife
Nationwide
Nationwide
New York Life
Northwestern Mutual
Pacific Mutual
Principal Financial
Prudential
Prudential plc
Safeco
TIAA-CREF
Torchmark

## HISTORICAL FINANCIALS

Company Type: Public

**Income Statement** FYE: December 31

| | ASSETS ($ mil.) | NET INCOME ($ mil.) | INCOME AS % OF ASSETS | EMPLOYEES |
|---|---|---|---|---|
| **12/06** | 178,494 | 1,316 | 0.7% | 10,744 |
| **12/05** | 124,788 | 831 | 0.7% | 5,259 |
| **12/04** | 116,219 | 707 | 0.6% | 5,441 |
| **12/03** | 106,745 | 512 | 0.5% | 5,644 |
| **12/02** | 93,133 | 92 | 0.1% | 5,830 |
| **Annual Growth** | 17.7% | 94.7% | — | 16.5% |

**2006 Year-End Financials**

Equity as % of assets: 6.8%
Return on assets: 0.9%
Return on equity: 14.2%
Long-term debt ($ mil.): 3,687
No. of shares (mil.): 276
Dividends
Yield: 2.3%
Payout: 29.6%
Market value ($ mil.): 18,310
Sales ($ mil.): 9,063

**Stock History** NYSE: LNC

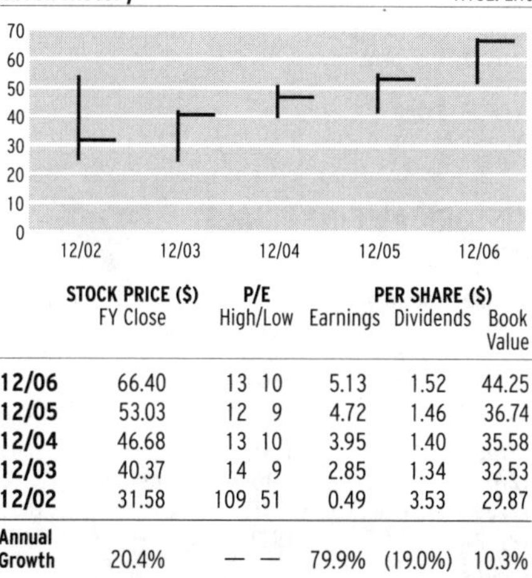


| | STOCK PRICE ($) FY Close | P/E High | P/E Low | PER SHARE ($) Earnings | Dividends | Book Value |
|---|---|---|---|---|---|---|
| **12/06** | 66.40 | 13 | 10 | 5.13 | 1.52 | 44.25 |
| **12/05** | 53.03 | 12 | 9 | 4.72 | 1.46 | 36.74 |
| **12/04** | 46.68 | 13 | 10 | 3.95 | 1.40 | 35.58 |
| **12/03** | 40.37 | 14 | 9 | 2.85 | 1.34 | 32.53 |
| **12/02** | 31.58 | 109 | 51 | 0.49 | 3.53 | 29.87 |
| **Annual Growth** | 20.4% | — | — | 79.9% | (19.0%) | 10.3% |

# Live Nation

Live Nation (formerly CCE Spinco, and Clear Channel Entertainment before that) holds center stage as the world's largest producer and promoter of live entertainment. Once a subsidiary of radio giant Clear Channel Communications, the company owns or operates some 160 venues in North America and Europe. It produces concerts, touring Broadway shows, and sports events. Annually, about 60 million people attend the company's some 26,000 events. Clear Channel Communications spun off Live Nation into an independent entity in late 2005. Live Nation purchased House of Blues owner HOB Entertainment in 2006.

The company operates through three business segments: events; venues and sponsorship; and digital distribution. Through its event segment, in 2006 Live Nation promoted or produced over 10,000 live music events, including tours for the Rolling Stones, Madonna, and Barbra Streisand. It also presented and/or produced over 5,000 theatrical performances, such as *Phantom of the Opera* in Las Vegas, and tours of *Cats, Starlight Express,* and *Chicago* in the UK. Live Nation owns a 50% interest in a joint venture with Cirque du Soleil to develop, produce, and promote a new type of live entertainment musical and visual event. Live Nation's venues and sponsorship operations include the management and operation of its owned and/or operated venues, and the sale of various types of sponsorships and advertising.

In 2006 the company acquired rival HOB Entertainment for $354 million. Live Nation used the acquisition to expand its presence in the midsize venue business and fill in geographic gaps in its existing amphitheater network. As part of the deal, Live Nation gained high profile House of Blues-branded music venues such as San Francisco's Fillmore Auditorium, Jones Beach in New York, and London's Apollo Theatre and Wembley Arena.

The company's digital distribution business involves the management of third-party ticketing relationships, in-house ticketing operations, and online and wireless distribution activities, including the development of Live Nation's Web site.

## HISTORY

Robert Sillerman began his career teaching advertisers how to reach young consumers. He started investing in radio and TV stations and founded SFX Broadcasting (named for a scrambling of his initials) in 1992. In early 1997 the firm entered the live entertainment field with the formation of SFX Concerts and the purchase of concert promoter Delsener/Slater.

When SFX Broadcasting agreed to be bought in 1997 by Capstar Broadcasting, 87% controlled by investment firm Hicks, Muse, Tate & Furst (now HM Capital), SFX Entertainment was formed to house the live entertainment operations (it was spun off in 1998). In 1998 the company continued its rapid acquisition rate with the purchases of sports marketing and management team FAME, New England concert promoter Don Law, and national concert producer PACE Entertainment.

In 1999 the company bought concert promoter The Cellar Door Companies (which almost doubled SFX's size), sports marketing firm Integrated Sports International, sporting event management company The Marquee Group, sports talent agency Hendricks Management, 50% of urban-music producer A.H. Enterprises, and troubled theatrical producer Livent. SFX also made its first foray abroad through its purchase of Apollo Leisure, a UK-based live entertainment firm. The company rolled all of its sports talent and marketing businesses into a new division, SFX Sports Group, that year.

In 2000 SFX jumped on the other side of the acquisition train when it was bought by radio station owner Clear Channel Communications for about $4 billion. Sillerman stepped down as chairman and CEO and was replaced by Clear Channel EVP Brian Becker. Later that year SFX acquired Philadelphia-based concert promoter and venue operator Electric Factory Concerts; Core Audience Entertainment, Canada's second-largest concert promoter and events marketer; and the Cotter Group, a North Carolina-based motorsports marketing agency.

In 2001 SFX acquired a majority interest in the International Hot Rod Association. It also bought professional golf talent agency Signature Sports Group. Later that year the company changed its name to Clear Channel Entertainment. It also continued expansion into Europe with the acquisition of Trident Agency and Milano Concerti music promotion businesses in Italy.

While operating as Clear Channel Entertainment, Live Nation spent nearly $2 billion on acquisitions (Pace Entertainment, Livent), almost single-handedly consolidating the live entertainment industry.

Before being spun off in December 2005, the company changed its name to CCE Spinco, then Live Nation. Also that year Randall Mays became chairman and Michael Rapino replaced Becker as CEO. As part of the Clear Channel spinoff, the company relocated from Houston to headquarters in tony Beverly Hills. It trimmed the fat by shutting down operating divisions such as museum exhibitions and music publishing (and laying off about 400 employees in the process), in order to focus on its core businesses of live music concerts, venue management, and Web site brand development. In 2006 Live Nation acquired HOB Entertainment.

## EXECUTIVES

**Chairman:** Randall T. Mays, age 41
**Vice Chairman:** Mark P. Mays, age 43
**President, CEO, and Director:** Michael (Mike) Rapino, age 41, $636,083 pay
**CFO:** Alan Ridgeway, age 40, $1,440,000 pay
**EVP and General Counsel:** Michael G. Rowles, age 41, $425,799 pay (partial-year salary)
**EVP Direct Marketing and Research:** Jeff Schroeder
**EVP; Executive Producer, Interactive Products:** Scott Fedewa
**SVP Corporate Finance:** Lee Ann Gliha
**SVP Interactive Technology:** Dave Kochbeck
**VP Communications:** John Vlautin
**Chief Accounting Officer:** Kathy Willard, age 40
**Chairman, International Music:** Thomas O. Johansson, age 58
**CEO, North American Music:** Bruce Eskowitz, age 48, $755,250 pay
**Chairman, Global Theatre; CEO, European Theatre:** David I. Lane
**CEO, North American Theater:** Steven K. (Steve) Winton, age 45
**Chairman, Global Theatrical:** David Ian
**President and Chief Creative Officer, Merchandising; CEO and Creative Director, TRUNK:** Brad Beckerman
**Chairman, Global Music:** Arthur Fogel, age 53
**President, Local Alliances:** Maureen Ford
**President Marketing, Artist Marketing Products:** Faisel Durrani, age 41
**Auditors:** Ernst & Young LLP

## LOCATIONS

**HQ:** Live Nation, Inc.
9348 Civic Center Dr., Beverly Hills, CA 90210
**Phone:** 310-867-7000 **Fax:** 310-867-7001
**Web:** www.livenation.com

## PRODUCTS/OPERATIONS

### 2006 Sales

| | $ mil. | % of total |
|---|---|---|
| Events | 2,923.4 | 79 |
| Venues & sponsorship | 635.8 | 17 |
| Digital distribution | 99.0 | 3 |
| Other | 33.4 | 1 |
| **Total** | **3,691.6** | **100** |

### Selected Concerts

Aerosmith
Jimmy Buffett
Cher
Dave Matthews Band
Josh Groban
Toby Keith
Linkin Park
Madonna
Bette Midler
The Rolling Stones
Barbra Streisand
Sting

### Selected Theatrical Productions

*Cats*
*Chicago*
*Fosse*
*Grease*
*Phantom of the Opera*
*The Producers*
*Starlight Express*

## COMPETITORS

Anschutz Entertainment
Dodger Stage Holding Theatricals
Feld Entertainment
Gaylord Entertainment
IMG
Independent Promoters
Indy Racing League
Interpublic Group
Jujamcyn Theaters
NASCAR
Nederlander Producing Company
Octagon
On Stage Entertainment
Shubert Organization
SMG Management
TBA Global
Westwood One
William Morris

## HISTORICAL FINANCIALS

Company Type: Public

### Income Statement

FYE: December 31

| | REVENUE ($ mil.) | NET INCOME ($ mil.) | NET PROFIT MARGIN | EMPLOYEES |
|---|---|---|---|---|
| **12/06** | 3,692 | (31) | — | 4,400 |
| **12/05** | 2,937 | (131) | — | 3,000 |
| **12/04** | 2,802 | 16 | 0.6% | 3,200 |
| **12/03** | 2,704 | 57 | 2.1% | 3,600 |
| **12/02** | 2,470 | (3,929) | — | — |
| **Annual Growth** | 10.6% | — | — | 6.9% |

### 2006 Year-End Financials

Debt ratio: 95.1%
Return on equity: —
Cash ($ mil.): 338
Current ratio: 0.95
Long-term debt ($ mil.): 607
No. of shares (mil.): 67
Dividends
Yield: —
Payout: —
Market value ($ mil.): 1,505

### Stock History

NYSE: LYV

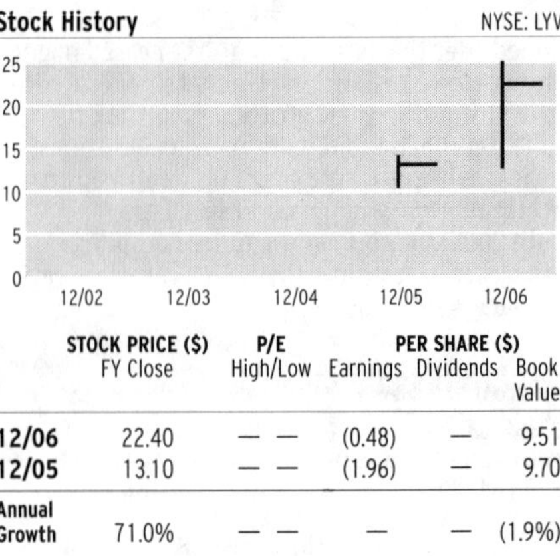


| | STOCK PRICE ($) FY Close | P/E High/Low | PER SHARE ($) Earnings | Dividends | Book Value |
|---|---|---|---|---|---|
| **12/06** | 22.40 | — — | (0.48) | — | 9.51 |
| **12/05** | 13.10 | — — | (1.96) | — | 9.70 |
| **Annual Growth** | 71.0% | — — | — | — | (1.9%) |

# Liz Claiborne

Liz Claiborne is dressed for success as a leading US seller of clothes and accessories for women. It markets its products as designer items but prices them for a broader market. Its brands — including Ellen Tracy, Laundry, Liz & Co., Concepts by Claiborne, kate spade, and Dana Buchman — are sold worldwide in department stores, in some 400 specialty stores, in more than 330 outlets, and among numerous brand Web sites. Liz Claiborne also makes men's clothing and licenses its name for shoes, sunglasses, swimwear, formalwear, home furnishings, and stationery. Liz Claiborne has bought kate spade and activewear maker Skylark Sport Marketing (dba prAna). It's cutting jobs and restructuring its operations.

Liz Claiborne's reorganization involves purging some 8% of its global workforce, or 700 positions, as well as shuttering or repurposing about 20 retail locations. Most staff reductions are expected in senior-level positions. The company says that the move is necessary to make it more nimble, to increase operating efficiencies, and to provide "for more growth opportunities."

Liz Claiborne is pulling the plug on retail formats that don't have the potential to support a minimum of 100 stores. Other casualties include the July 2007 shuttering of the last four Mexx retail stores in the US. (In 2006 Liz Claiborne closed seven US Mexx stores.) The company also closed its three Laundry retail stores in New York and California to focus on Laundry's wholesale business.

As part of the restructuring, Liz Claiborne is separating its power brands — brands the company defines as having the most potential — from its other brand names. Its power brands include direct-to-consumer names Juicy Couture and Lucky Brands and these are the operations that will receive the most attention and funding.

Liz Claiborne is boosting its direct-to-consumer business, as a result of the changes. It's also putting out to pasture some brand names, such as Crazy Horse, and developing new lines for its partnerships with certain department stores. In late 2006 Liz Claiborne announced that it would discontinue production of the Crazy Horse line, having manufactured the line for JCPenney since 1998.

The firm has a history of increasing its product offerings by licensing or acquiring new brands. In December 2006 the apparel giant acquired handbag and accessories maker kate spade from Neiman Marcus for some $124 million. The purchase is designed to build Liz Claiborne's handbag business, which is one of the hottest segments of the accessories unit. Since 1999 Claiborne has purchased about a dozen firms including Mexx, Juicy Couture, and Enyce.

Liz Claiborne got into men's formalwear in mid-2006 with its licensing deal with After Hours Formalwear.

Drug industry veteran William McComb, formerly with Johnson & Johnson, succeeded retiring CEO Paul Charron in November 2006.

## HISTORY

In 1975 Liz Claiborne, a dress designer in Jonathan Logan's Youth Guild division, had a vision of stylish, sporty, affordable clothes for working women. Unable to sell the concept to her employer, Claiborne quit and, with husband Arthur Ortenberg and partners Jerome Chazen and Leonard Boxer, founded Liz Claiborne in 1976 with $250,000.

Born just as women were beginning to flood the workforce, Liz Claiborne became an immediate success by rescuing them from drab business suits. Making money its first year, Liz Claiborne remained the fastest-growing, most profitable US apparel maker in the 1980s. In 1981 it went public and by 1986 had made the *FORTUNE* 500, with sales topping $800 million.

The company expanded into men's clothing (Claiborne, 1985), cosmetics (Liz Claiborne, a 1986 joint venture with Avon; in 1988 it acquired full rights to the line), women's plus sizes (Elisabeth, 1989), and knit sportswear (Liz & Co., 1989). Higher-priced sportswear by in-house designer Dana Buchman was introduced in 1987. Liz Claiborne moved into retailing the following year, opening First Issue boutiques.

Claiborne and Ortenberg began withdrawing from the business side in 1989 and left the board the next year. About this time the retail business began to slow down as a recession loomed. In addition, baby boomers' clothing tastes began to shift toward comfort and versatility.

Liz Claiborne acquired the Crazy Horse, Russ Togs, Villager, and Red Horse brand names in 1992 and took over 16 outlet stores from bankrupt Russ Togs. The new fashion realities and a lack of differentiation between its lines caught up with the company in 1993, when earnings plunged. In response, Liz Claiborne brought in VF veteran Paul Charron as COO. Named CEO in 1995, Charron closed the First Issue stores and moved production from US union plants to foreign factories.

In 1997 Liz Claiborne signed its first agreement to produce apparel under another company's brand name: jeans and activewear under Donna Karan International's DKNY label. In response to sagging sales, the company took a $27 million charge that year to close 30 retail stores, and cut 400 jobs in 1998.

Charron set out to give Liz Claiborne a broader appeal. In 1999 the company bought trendy Laundry (women's sportswear and dresses) and teen-targeted Lucky Brand Dungarees.

Liz Claiborne bought Mexx Canada and Ellen Tracy in 2002. The next year the company bought Travis Jeans (now named Juicy Couture).

In 2004 the company made a foray into the high-end luggage arena with a licensing agreement with luggage maker Bandanco Enterprises for the design and production of luggage under the Liz Claiborne and Claiborne names.

In 2005 and 2006 the firm extended its reach across North America. It acquired California-inspired men's and women's apparel maker C & C California. It also inked a deal with Bardwil Industries, which designs and makes table linens and kitchen textiles for the Liz Claiborne Home Collection. Also in 2005 Liz Claiborne was brand-focused. It rolled out six mid-level brands at retailers such as Sears, JCPenney, and Kohl's.

In 2006 a deal with Nourison brought Liz Claiborne area and accent rugs that coordinate with the company's home and furniture collections. That year Liz Claiborne picked up Vancouver, Canada-based Westcoast Contempo Fashions Limited and Mac and Jac Holdings Limited. The deal was inked at a purchase price of $23.6 million with additional payments based on earnings for fiscal years 2006, 2008, 2009, and 2010.

Company namesake Liz Claiborne died at the age of 78 in mid-2007.

## EXECUTIVES

**Chairman:** Kay Koplovitz, age 61
**CEO and Director:** William L. McComb, age 44, $577,500 pay
**COO:** Michael (Mike) Scarpa, age 51
**CFO:** Andrew C. Warren, age 40
**EVP Direct Brands:** Jill Granoff, age 45
**EVP Partnered Brands:** Dave McTague, age 45
**SVP:** Robert J. (Bob) Zane, age 65
**SVP, Corporate Affairs and General Counsel:** Roberta Schuhalter Karp
**SVP, Human Resources:** Lawrence D. (Larry) McClure, age 58, $464,583 pay
**SVP Business Development and Legal/Corporate Affairs:** Roberta Karp
**Corporate VP, Global Manufacturing and Sourcing:** Gary Ross
**VP, Corporate Communications:** Jane Randel
**VP, Corporate Controller, and Chief Accounting Officer:** Elaine H. Goodell
**VP, Corporate Merchandising and Design:** Anne Cashill
**VP, Finance and Investor Relations and Treasurer:** Robert J. Vill
**VP, Investor Relations:** Dana Stambaugh
**VP and Group Manufacturing Director, Liz Claiborne Apparel and Special Markets:** Mary Ellen Prentis
**VP Marketing:** Lilach Asofsky
**VP, General Counsel, and Secretary:** Nicholas Rubino
**Group President, International Alliances and Licensing:** Karen Murray
**Group President, Non-Apparel:** Susan Davidson
**President, Licensing:** Barbara J. Friedman
**President, Liz Claiborne Accessories:** Dina Battipaglia
**President and Chief Merchandising Officer, Liz Claiborne Apparel:** Michele Parsons
**Chief Creative Officer:** Tim Gunn
**Auditors:** Deloitte & Touche LLP

## LOCATIONS

**HQ:** Liz Claiborne, Inc.
1441 Broadway, New York, NY 10018
**Phone:** 212-354-4900 **Fax:** 212-626-3416
**Web:** www.lizclaiborne.com

Liz Claiborne sells its clothing and accessories in more than 30,000 retail locations worldwide.

**2006 Sales**

| | % of total |
|---|---|
| US | 72 |
| Other countries | 28 |
| **Total** | **100** |

## PRODUCTS/OPERATIONS

**2006 US Retail Specialty Stores**

| | No. |
|---|---|
| Lucky Brand Dungarees | 131 |
| Sigrid Olsen | 55 |
| Elisabeth | 23 |
| Kate Spade | 19 |
| Juicy Couture | 18 |
| Dana Buchman | 4 |
| Mexx | 4 |
| Laundry by Shelli Segal | 2 |
| Kensie / Mac & Jac | 1 |
| Jack Spade | 1 |
| **Total** | **258** |

**2006 Foreign Retail Specialty Stores**

| | No. |
|---|---|
| Mexx | 96 |
| Mexx Canada | 32 |
| Monet Europe | 5 |
| Sigrid Canada | 4 |
| Lucky Brand Europe | 2 |
| Lucky Brand Canada | 2 |
| **Total** | **141** |

**2006 US Outlet Stores**

| | No. |
|---|---|
| Liz Claiborne | 134 |
| Ellen Tracy | 18 |
| DKNY Jeans | 14 |
| Liz Claiborne Woman | 11 |
| Juicy Couture | 9 |
| Lucky Brand Dungarees | 7 |
| Dana Buchman | 6 |
| Kate Spade | 4 |
| Claiborne | 3 |
| **Total** | **206** |

### Selected Labels

Claiborne (men's business casual and sportswear)
Classic Accessories (Monet, Sigrid Olsen, and Ellen Tracy)
Contemporary Accessories (Juicy Couture)
Dana Buchman (bridge career wear)
Dana Buchman Luxe (upscale, specialty store products)
DKNY Active (sportswear under license for Donna Karan International)
DKNY Jeans (denim wear under license for Donna Karan International)
Emma James (casual separates)
First Issue (sportswear sold at Sears)
kate spade (handbags, accessories, stationery)
Laundry By Shelli Segal (sportswear and dresses)
Liz & Co. (informal knitwear)
Liz Claiborne (misses' career wear)
Liz Claiborne Accessories
Liz Claiborne Woman
Lizsport (sportswear)
Lizwear (denim sportswear)
Marvella (jewelry)
Modern Brands Accessories (Lucky Brand, Kenneth Cole, and Enyce)
prAna (activewear for men and women)
Russ (casual separates, sold at Wal-Mart)
Special Markets Accessories (Villager, Axcess, Crazy Horse, Monet 2, and Trifari)
Tapemeasure (contemporary, value-conscious)

### Other Products

Accessories (handbags, leather goods, scarves, jewelry)
Cosmetics (fragrances and body care products)
Dresses (licensed to Kellwood's Halmode division)
Eyewear (licensed; sunglasses and frames)
Home furnishings (licensed)
Shoes (licensed)
Slippers (licensed to R.G. Barry Corporation)

## COMPETITORS

AnnTaylor
bebe stores
Benetton
Bernard Chaus
Calvin Klein
Chico's FAS
Donna Karan
Esprit Holdings
French Connection
Gap
H&M
Hartmarx
Inditex
J. Crew
J. Jill Group
Jones Apparel
Lands' End
Limited Brands
Nautica Enterprises
NEXT
Polo Ralph Lauren
St. John Knits
Talbots
Tommy Hilfiger
Urban Outfitters
Warnaco Group
Zara

## HISTORICAL FINANCIALS

Company Type: Public

**Income Statement** — FYE: Saturday nearest December 31

| | REVENUE ($ mil.) | NET INCOME ($ mil.) | NET PROFIT MARGIN | EMPLOYEES |
|---|---|---|---|---|
| **12/06** | 4,994 | 255 | 5.1% | 17,000 |
| **12/05** | 4,848 | 317 | 6.5% | 15,400 |
| **12/04** | 4,633 | 314 | 6.8% | 14,500 |
| **12/03** | 4,241 | 280 | 6.6% | 13,000 |
| **12/02** | 3,718 | 231 | 6.2% | 12,000 |
| **Annual Growth** | 7.7% | 2.4% | — | 9.1% |

**2006 Year-End Financials**

| | |
|---|---|
| Debt ratio: 26.8% | No. of shares (mil.): 103 |
| Return on equity: 12.3% | Dividends |
| Cash ($ mil.): 195 | Yield: 0.5% |
| Current ratio: 2.18 | Payout: 8.9% |
| Long-term debt ($ mil.): 570 | Market value ($ mil.): 4,483 |

**Stock History** — NYSE: LIZ

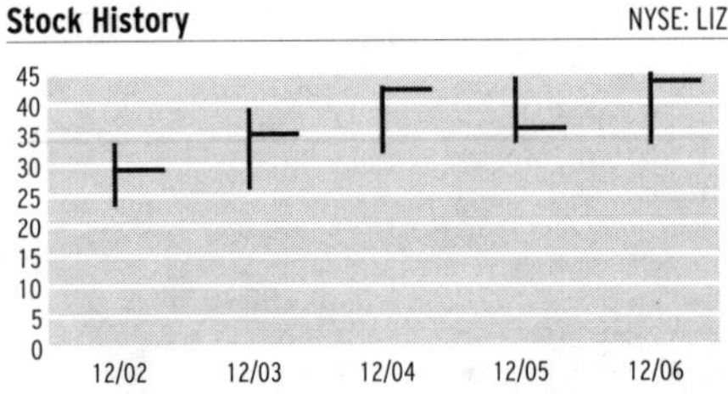


| | STOCK PRICE ($) FY Close | P/E High/Low | PER SHARE ($) Earnings | Dividends | Book Value |
|---|---|---|---|---|---|
| **12/06** | 43.46 | 18 14 | 2.46 | 0.22 | 20.65 |
| **12/05** | 35.82 | 15 11 | 2.94 | 0.22 | 19.08 |
| **12/04** | 42.21 | 15 11 | 2.85 | 0.22 | 16.66 |
| **12/03** | 34.97 | 15 10 | 2.55 | 0.17 | 14.40 |
| **12/02** | 29.15 | 15 11 | 2.16 | 0.22 | 12.02 |
| **Annual Growth** | 10.5% | — — | 3.3% | 0.0% | 14.5% |

# Lockheed Martin

Lockheed Martin moves product in times of crisis — the company is the world's #1 defense contractor (ahead of Boeing and Northrop Grumman). Its business segments: Aeronautics, which includes the F-16 and F-22 fighters, and the upcoming F-35 Joint Strike Fighter (now officially named the Lightning II); Electronic Systems, encompassing everything from missiles and submarine warfare systems to homeland security systems, radar, and postal automation systems; Space Systems, which includes satellites, strategic missiles, and airborne defense systems; Integrated Systems & Solutions, which makes command, control, and communication systems and reconnaissance/surveillance systems; and Information & Technology Services.

Lockheed is firmly on the defense/government side of the aerospace industry; in fact, the US government accounts for about 85% of sales. This reliance on the US government is a double-edged sword: Lockheed has largely avoided turbulence in the commercial aerospace sector, but the company is vulnerable to military spending cuts. Aeronautics and Electronic Systems account for nearly 60% of Lockheed's sales.

Lockheed Martin has reorganized, consolidating its divisions to better reflect its core activities as part of a plan to cut $3 billion in costs.

The recent conflicts in Afghanistan and Iraq, along with increased spending on homeland security, have buoyed the company thus far, but looming military program cuts may affect some of Lockheed's largest programs. Lockheed is the prime contractor for the US military's two most recent jet fighters, the $200 billion F-35 Lightning II (formerly called the Joint Strike Fighter) program and the F-22 Raptor, but one or both of the projects may be scaled back due to budget constraints. Despite its uncertain future, the Raptor was approved for full-scale production in April 2005 and was rated "Mission Capable" early in 2006. The inaugural flight of the F-35 Lightning II took place in late 2006.

Late in the summer of 2006, Lockheed got a bonanza of business when NASA awarded the company with the coveted Orion manned lunar spaceship contract. Lockheed beat out competing bids by Northrop Grumman and Boeing. Orion is planned to be NASA's next generation of manned spacecraft and is slated to eventually replace the space shuttle. Orion is also anticipated to take astronauts to the moon, and possibly to Mars.

## HISTORY

Brothers Allan and Malcolm Loughead (pronounced "Lockheed") joined Fred Keeler in 1926 to form Lockheed Aircraft. John Northrop (who later founded Northrop Corporation) designed Lockheed's first airplane, the Vega (flown by Amelia Earhart).

Robert Gross, Carl Squier, and Lloyd Stearman bought Lockheed in 1932. The company produced such aviation classics as the P-38 Lightning fighter, the U-2 spy plane, and the SR-71 Blackbird spy plane. It also produced submarine-launched ballistic missiles (Polaris, 1958), military transports (C-5 Galaxy, 1968), and the L-1011 TriStar airliner (1971).

Lockheed suffered from the cancellation of its Cheyenne attack helicopter, the C-5A cost-overrun scandal, and financial problems with the L-1011. Government loans saved the firm from bankruptcy in 1971.

In the late 1970s Lockheed was at the center of a corporate bribery scandal that overturned governments in Japan and Italy and led to tougher US anti-bribery laws. During the 1970s and 1980s, Lockheed developed the Hubble Space Telescope and the F-117A stealth fighter. Shrinking orders forced Lockheed to close its main aircraft plant in 1990. Lockheed merged with Martin Marietta in 1995 to form Lockheed Martin.

Glenn Martin started Martin Marietta in 1917. Martin Marietta made the first US-built bombers, as well as military and commercial flying boats. During the 1950s Martin Marietta made missiles, electronics, and nuclear systems. In 1961 it merged with American-Marietta Company (construction materials and chemical products).

Strapped with debt after defeating a hostile takeover by Bendix in 1982, Martin Marietta sold many of its businesses. It bought General Electric's aerospace business (1992) and became part of Lockheed in 1995.

In 1996 Lockheed Martin sold its Defense Systems and Armament Systems units to General Dynamics and bought most of Loral Corporation (advanced electronics). A prospective deal to buy Northrop Grumman for $11.6 billion ended in 1998 when the US government raised antitrust issues. In 1999 it acquired a 49% stake in COMSAT, a satellite network company that is the centerpiece of Lockheed Martin's communications business.

A series of launch failures in 1999 destroyed about $4 billion in rockets and payloads and led to an inquiry that blamed poor management oversight and quality-control problems.

In 2000 the Pentagon bailed out Lockheed Martin by agreeing to buy 24 C-130J transports. The company also won a $3.97 billion contract from the Pentagon to develop the Theater High-Altitude Area Defense (THAAD) anti-missile defense system. Lockheed sold some defense electronics units, including its Sanders unit (aerial electronic warfare and countermeasure systems), to UK-based BAE SYSTEMS for around $1.67 billion; in a separate deal it also sold its Lockheed Martin Control Systems unit to BAE. That year Lockheed Martin purchased the 51% of COMSAT it didn't already own.

In 2001 Lockheed Martin (along with TRW) was awarded a $2.7 billion contract for the US military's next-generation communications satellite system. In 2002 the company was awarded a $12.7 billion US defense contract (spread out over 23 years) to provide support work for single-seat F-16s flown by 16 different countries. Lockheed Martin acquired the government technology-services business of Affiliated Computer Services (ACS) for about $650 million in August 2003.

In 2005 the US Navy selected Lockheed (prime contractor) and AgustaWestland to build a new fleet of 23 Presidential Marine One helicopters in a deal worth about $6.1 billion. Lockheed also acquired the SYTEX Group (now SYTEX Lockheed), a provider of IT services and technical support services to the US government, for $462 million.

In 2006 Lockheed Martin acquired ISX Corporation, a privately held provider of military decision systems and other government IT systems. Later that year the company bought Pacific Architects and Engineers Incorporated (PAE), a provider of services that support military readiness, peacekeeping missions, and disaster relief.

## EXECUTIVES

**Chairman, President, and CEO:** Robert J. Stevens, age 55, $5,165,145 pay
**EVP and CFO:** Bruce L. Tanner, age 48
**EVP and General Manager, F-35 Joint Strike Fighter Program Integration:** Charles T. (Tom) Burbage
**EVP, Aeronautics:** Ralph D. Heath, age 58, $1,457,685 pay
**EVP, Electronic Systems:** Christopher E. Kubasik, age 45, $1,868,131 pay (prior to title change)
**EVP, Information Systems and Global Services (IS&GS):** Linda R. Gooden, age 53
**EVP, Space Systems:** Joanne M. Maguire
**SVP, Finance:** Mary Margaret (Meg) VanDeWeghe, age 47
**SVP and General Counsel:** James B. Comey, age 46
**SVP, Strategic Development:** Arthur E. (Art) Johnson, age 60
**SVP, Human Resources:** Kenneth J. Disken
**VP and CIO; President, Enterprise Information Systems:** Joseph R. Cleveland
**VP and President, Lockheed Martin Systems Integration, Owego:** Frank C. Meyer
**VP and President, Maritime Systems & Sensors (MS2):** Fred P. Moosally
**VP and Treasurer:** Anthony G. Van Schaick, age 60
**VP, Advanced Platforms, Maritime Systems & Sensors:** Dave Broadbent
**VP, Atlas Program, Lockheed Martin Space Systems Company:** James V. Sponnick
**VP, Corporate Secretary, and Associate General Counsel:** Lillian M. Trippett
**VP, Ethics and Business Conduct:** Maryanne R. Lavan
**VP, Investor Relations:** James R. Ryan
**VP, Media Relations and Chief Spokesperson:** Thomas J. Jurkowsky
**President, Continental Europe:** Scott A. Harris
**President, Maritime Systems & Sensors Undersea Systems:** John O'Neill
**President, Lockheed Martin Transportation & Security Solutions:** Judy F. Marks
**Auditors:** Ernst & Young LLP

## LOCATIONS

**HQ:** Lockheed Martin Corporation
6801 Rockledge Dr., Bethesda, MD 20817
**Phone:** 301-897-6000 **Fax:** 301-897-6704
**Web:** www.lockheedmartin.com

Lockheed Martin operates 500 facilities worldwide. Aeronautics maintains major operations in California, Georgia, and Texas; Electronics Systems has major operations in Alabama, Arkansas, Florida, Maryland, Minnesota, New Jersey, New York, Ohio, Pennsylvania, Texas, and Virginia as well as the UK; Space Systems maintains major operations in California, Colorado, Florida, Louisiana, and Pennsylvania; Integrated Systems & Solutions has major operations in Arizona, California, Colorado, the District of Columbia, Maryland, Pennsylvania, and Virginia; and Information & Technology Services maintains major operations in California, the District of Columbia, New Jersey, New Mexico, New York, South Carolina, and Texas.

### 2006 Sales

| | $ mil. | % of total |
|---|---|---|
| US | 34,469 | 87 |
| Other countries | 5,151 | 13 |
| **Total** | **39,620** | **100** |

## PRODUCTS/OPERATIONS

### 2006 Sales by Customer

| | $ mil. | % of total |
|---|---|---|
| US government | 33,281 | 84 |
| Foreign governments | 5,151 | 13 |
| Commercial | 1,188 | 3 |
| **Total** | **39,620** | **100** |

### 2006 Sales by Business Segment

| | $ mil. | % of total |
|---|---|---|
| Aeronautics | 11,401 | 29 |
| Electronic Systems | 11,304 | 28 |
| Space Systems | 7,923 | 20 |
| Information Technology & Global Services | 4,605 | 12 |
| Integrated Systems & Solutions | 4,387 | 11 |
| **Total** | **39,620** | **100** |

### Selected Products and Services

Aeronautics
- C-5 (strategic airlift aircraft)
- C-130J (tactical airlift aircraft)
- F-2 (Japanese combat aircraft)
- F-16 (multi-role fighter)
- F-22 (air-superiority fighter)
- F-35 Joint Strike Fighter (next-generation multi-role fighter)
- Special mission and reconaissance aircraft (S-3 Viking, U-2, P-3 Orion)
- T-50 (Korean advanced trainer)

Electronic Systems
- Advanced aviation management
- Air and theater missile defense systems
- Anti-submarine and undersea warfare systems
- Avionics and ground combat vehicle integration
- Homeland security systems
- Missiles and fire control systems
- Platform integration systems
- Postal automation systems
- Radars
- Security and information technology solutions
- Simulation and training systems
- Surface ship and submarine combat systems
- Surveillance and reconnaissance systems

Space Systems
- Airborne defense systems
- Defensive missiles
- Missile launch vehicles
- Satellites (for commercial and government use)
- Satellite launch services
- Strategic missiles

Information Technology & Global Services
- Aircraft and engine maintenance and modification services
- Application development
- Engineering, science, and information services for NASA
- Engineering, science, and technology services
- Enterprise solutions
- Government technology services
- Information technology integration and management
- Launch, mission, and analysis services for military, classified, and commercial satellites
- Nuclear operations and materials management (Oak Ridge, Tennessee, and other locations)
- Operation, maintenance, training, and logistics support for military, homeland security, and civilian systems

Integrated Systems & Solutions (IS&S)
- Command, control, and communication systems
- Computer system design and service
- Intelligence
- Reconnaissance
- Surveillance

## COMPETITORS

Alcatel-Lucent
Alliant Techsystems
Arianespace
BAE SYSTEMS
Boeing
Daimler
DIRECTV
EADS
EADS North America
Finmeccanica
GE
General Dynamics
Herley Industries
Honeywell International
Interstate Electronics
MBDA
Northrop Grumman
Orbital Sciences
Park Air Systems
Raytheon
Saab AB
Sextant Avionique
Siemens AG
Textron
ThalesRaytheonSystems
URS

## HISTORICAL FINANCIALS

Company Type: Public

### Income Statement

FYE: December 31

| | REVENUE ($ mil.) | NET INCOME ($ mil.) | NET PROFIT MARGIN | EMPLOYEES |
|---|---|---|---|---|
| **12/06** | 39,620 | 2,529 | 6.4% | 140,000 |
| **12/05** | 37,213 | 1,825 | 4.9% | 135,000 |
| **12/04** | 35,526 | 1,266 | 3.6% | 130,000 |
| **12/03** | 31,824 | 1,053 | 3.3% | 130,000 |
| **12/02** | 26,578 | 500 | 1.9% | 125,000 |
| **Annual Growth** | 10.5% | 50.0% | — | 2.9% |

### 2006 Year-End Financials

Debt ratio: 64.0%
Return on equity: 34.3%
Cash ($ mil.): 2,293
Current ratio: 1.06
Long-term debt ($ mil.): 4,405
No. of shares (mil.): 421
Dividends
Yield: 1.4%
Payout: 21.6%
Market value ($ mil.): 38,761

### Stock History

NYSE: LMT

| | STOCK PRICE ($) FY Close | P/E High | P/E Low | PER SHARE ($) Earnings | Dividends | Book Value |
|---|---|---|---|---|---|---|
| **12/06** | 92.07 | 16 | 11 | 5.80 | 1.25 | 16.35 |
| **12/05** | 63.63 | 16 | 13 | 4.10 | 1.05 | 18.01 |
| **12/04** | 55.55 | 22 | 15 | 2.83 | 0.91 | 15.96 |
| **12/03** | 51.40 | 25 | 17 | 2.34 | 0.58 | 15.11 |
| **12/02** | 57.75 | 64 | 41 | 1.11 | 0.44 | 12.87 |
| **Annual Growth** | 12.4% | — | — | 51.2% | 29.8% | 6.2% |

# Loews Corporation

This diversified holding company not only drills deep, tells time, rolls its own, and makes the bed — it'll insure others that do, too. Loews' main interest is insurance through publicly traded subsidiary CNA Financial. Its Carolina Group tracking subsidiary covers tobacco company Lorillard which includes the Kent, Newport, and True US cigarette brands. Other holdings include hotels in the US and Canada (through subsidiary Loews Hotels), watchmaker Bulova, contract oil-drilling subsidiary Diamond Offshore Drilling (which operates about 50 oil rigs), and natural gas transmission pipeline systems operator Boardwalk Pipelines.

Despite Loews' eclectic collection of businesses, its flagship unit CNA Financial still accounts for nearly two-thirds of the corporation's revenues. CNA's affiliates, which include The Continental Insurance Company and Continental Assurance Company, offer property & casualty insurance, as well as life and group insurance. Tobacco distributor Lorillard makes up an additional 21% of Loews' revenues.

The old Loews magic has faded over the past few years, as a steady stream of tobacco-related litigations and downturns in the insurance and oil industries have pummeled its holdings.

## HISTORY

In 1946 Larry Tisch, who earned a business degree from New York University at age 18, dropped out of Harvard Law to run his parents' New Jersey resort. Younger brother Bob joined him in creating a new entity, Tisch Hotels. The company bought two Atlantic City hotels in 1952, quickly making them profitable. Later Tisch purchased such illustrious hotels as the Mark Hopkins, The Drake, the Belmont Plaza, and the Regency.

Moving beyond hotels, the brothers bought money-losing companies with poor management. Discarding the management along with underperforming divisions, they tightened operational control and eliminated such frills as fancy offices, company planes, and even memos.

In 1960 Tisch Hotels gained control of MGM's ailing Loew's Theaters to take advantage of their desirable city locations. The company then began demolishing more than 50 stately movie palaces and selling the land to developers. In 1968 the company bought Lorillard, the oldest US tobacco company; it shed Lorillard's unprofitable pet food and candy operations and reversed its slipping tobacco market share.

Taking the Loews name in 1971, the company bought CNA Financial in 1974. The Tisch method turned losses of more than $200 million to profits of more than $100 million the very next year. It bought Bulova Watch in 1979, and guided by Larry's son Andrew, it gradually returned to profitability.

In the early 1980s Loews entered the energy business by investing in oil supertankers. The company sold its last movie theaters in 1985. Then in 1987 Loews helped CBS fend off a takeover attempt by Ted Turner and ended up with about 25% of the company. Larry became president of the broadcaster.

In 1989 Loews acquired Diamond M Offshore, a Texas drilling company, and with the acquisition of Odeco Drilling in 1992, the company amassed the world's largest fleet of offshore rigs. The next year Loews grouped its drilling interests as Diamond Offshore Drilling.

In 1994 CNA expanded its insurance empire, buying The Continental Corp. The next year Loews sold its interest in CBS, and the following year Diamond Offshore Drilling merged with Arethusa (Off-Shore) Limited.

As deft as the Tisch brothers had been in accumulating their riches, Larry's bearish investment strategy (short-selling stocks) cost Loews in the late 1990s (more than $900 million alone during 1997's bull market). Larry and Bob retired as co-CEOs at the end of 1998; Larry's son James, already president and COO, became CEO.

That year Lorillard signed on to the 46-state tobacco lawsuit settlement; the first payment cost the company $325 million (payments continue until 2025). Facing a softened insurance market, CNA sold unprofitable lines to focus on commercial insurance; in 1999 it transferred its auto and homeowners lines to Allstate (it continues writing and renewing these policies) and put its life and life reinsurance units up for sale in 2000. Also that year Lorillard was hit with $16 billion of a record-breaking $144 billion punitive damage award in a smokers' class-action suit in Florida. CNA Financial paid out over $450 million in 2001-02 for claims related to the attacks on the World Trade Center.

In 2004 the company continued to expand its natural resource offerings when its subsidiary Boardwalk Pipelines (formerly known as TGT Pipeline) acquired Gulf South Pipeline, which operates natural gas pipeline and gathering systems in Texas, Louisiana, Mississippi, Alabama, and Florida, including several major supply hubs. Loews had acquired gas pipeline operator Texas Gas Transmission in 2003. Texas Gas operates natural gas pipeline systems reaching from the Louisiana Gulf Coast and East Texas north through Louisiana, Arkansas, Mississippi, Tennessee, Kentucky, Indiana, and into Ohio and Illinois.

Larry Tisch died at the age of 80 in 2003. Chairman Bob Tisch died of cancer in late 2005. Tisch also was co-owner of the New York Giants of the National Football League.

## EXECUTIVES

**Co-Chairman, Office of the President, and Chairman, Executive Committee:** Andrew H. Tisch, age 57, $975,000 pay
**Co-Chairman and Office of the President; Chairman and CEO, Loews Hotels:** Jonathan M. Tisch, age 53, $975,000 pay
**President, CEO, Office of the President, and Director:** James S. Tisch, age 54, $1,275,000 pay
**SVP and CFO:** Peter W. Keegan, age 62, $1,240,000 pay
**SVP, General Counsel, Secretary:** Gary W. Garson, age 60
**SVP:** Arthur L. Rebell, age 66, $1,475,000 pay
**SVP:** David B. Edelson, age 47
**SVP; President and CEO, Bulova:** Herbert C. Hofmann, age 64
**VP, Human Resources:** Alan Momeyer
**VP, Internal Audit:** Richard E. Piluso
**VP, Public Affairs:** Candace Leeds
**VP, Real Estate:** Jason Boxer
**Controller:** Mark S. Schwartz, age 48
**Investor Relations:** Darren Daugherty
**Auditors:** Deloitte & Touche LLP

## LOCATIONS

**HQ:** Loews Corporation
667 Madison Ave., New York, NY 10021
**Phone:** 212-521-2000 **Fax:** 212-521-2525
**Web:** www.loews.com

Loews operates primarily in North America.

## PRODUCTS/OPERATIONS

### 2006 Sales

| | $ mil. | % of total |
|---|---|---|
| Insurance premiums | 7,603.1 | 42 |
| Manufactured products | 3,961.8 | 22 |
| Net investment income | 2,911.1 | 16 |
| Investment gains | 91.5 | 1 |
| Gain on issuance of stock | 9 | — |
| Other | 3,334.5 | 19 |
| **Total** | **17,911** | **100** |

### 2006 Sales

| | $ mil. | % of total |
|---|---|---|
| CNA Financial | 10,381.7 | 58 |
| Lorillard | 3,858.6 | 22 |
| Diamond Offshore | 2,102.0 | 12 |
| Boardwalk Pipeline | 618.4 | 3 |
| Loews Hotels | 371.3 | 2 |
| Corporate & other | 579.0 | 3 |
| **Total** | **17,911** | **100** |

### Selected Subsidiaries

CNA Financial Corporation (89%)
The Continental Corporation
Continental Casualty Company
Diamond Offshore Drilling, Inc. (51%)

## COMPETITORS

AIG
Allstate
Altria
American Financial
Berkshire Hathaway
Chubb Corp
CIGNA
Citigroup
Citizen Watch
Fossil
Four Seasons Hotels
The Hartford
Hilton
Hyatt
Marriott
Movado Group
Prudential
Reynolds American
Ritz-Carlton
Safeco
Starwood Hotels & Resorts
Swatch
Timex
Travelers Companies
Vector
Wyndham

## HISTORICAL FINANCIALS

Company Type: Public

### Income Statement

FYE: December 31

| | ASSETS ($ mil.) | NET INCOME ($ mil.) | INCOME AS % OF ASSETS | EMPLOYEES |
|---|---|---|---|---|
| **12/06** | 76,881 | 2,491 | 3.2% | 21,600 |
| **12/05** | 70,676 | 1,212 | 1.7% | 21,600 |
| **12/04** | 73,635 | 1,235 | 1.7% | 22,000 |
| **12/03** | 77,881 | (611) | — | 22,700 |
| **12/02** | 70,520 | 912 | 1.3% | 25,800 |
| **Annual Growth** | 2.2% | 28.6% | — | (4.3%) |

### 2006 Year-End Financials

Equity as % of assets: 21.5%
Return on assets: 3.4%
Return on equity: 16.8%
Long-term debt ($ mil.): 10,216
No. of shares (mil.): 544
Dividends
Yield: 0.6%
Payout: 6.4%
Market value ($ mil.): 22,568
Sales ($ mil.): 17,911

### Stock History

NYSE: LTR

45 40 35 30 25 20 15 10 5 0

12/02 12/03 12/04 12/05 12/06

| | STOCK PRICE ($) FY Close | P/E High | P/E Low | PER SHARE ($) Earnings | Dividends | Book Value |
|---|---|---|---|---|---|---|
| **12/06** | 41.47 | 11 | 8 | 3.75 | 0.24 | 30.32 |
| **12/05** | 31.62 | 19 | 13 | 1.72 | 0.20 | 70.45 |
| **12/04** | 23.43 | 13 | 9 | 1.89 | 0.20 | 65.50 |
| **12/03** | 16.48 | — | — | (1.30) | 0.20 | 59.61 |
| **12/02** | 14.82 | 15 | 9 | 1.37 | 0.20 | 60.59 |
| **Annual Growth** | 29.3% | — | — | 28.6% | 4.7% | (15.9%) |

# Longs Drug Stores

Longs Drug Stores wants to be known for being short on hassle and long on service. A leading drugstore chain with about 500 stores in the western US and Hawaii, Longs prides itself on customer service. Known for giving store managers autonomy to select merchandise, its stores add local flavor by carrying specialty items popular in the neighborhoods they serve. With larger stores than its rivals — such as CVS and Walgreen — the company surpasses the industry average when it comes to selling higher-margin, front-store items such as cosmetics, food, greeting cards, and over-the-counter medications. Longs Drug's RxAmerica subsidiary provides pharmacy benefit management services.

The company's announcement in early 2007 that it will shutter 31 stores this year, including all of its locations in Washington, Oregon, and Colorado, is a geographic retreat for the drugstore operator. Amid shrinking profits, Longs Drug says it plans to focus on its markets with a higher concentration of stores. To that end, five Longs stores in Oregon and Washington were transferred to Rite Aid in a store swap between the two drugstore operators in mid-2007. Longs exchanged those stores, and another in California, in return for six Rite Aid stores in the Reno, Nevada, area.

On the plus side, Longs Drug recently agreed to acquire four pharmacies in Hawaii and California from PharMerica, a subsidiary of AmerisourceBergen Corp. Previous purchases include two dozen pharmacies in Southern California from Redlands, California-based Network Pharmaceuticals. Longs, which already operates some 65 drug stores in the Los Angeles area, will run the stores under the Network banner. The Network pharmacies are located in or near medical offices or hospitals.

Front-of-store items account for nearly 50% of sales; pharmaceuticals and pharmacy services account for the rest. Longs drugstores also offer in-store photo processing and mail centers.

RxAmerica manages pharmacy benefit plans covering more than 5 million people in all 50 US states, Puerto Rico, and the US Virgin Islands. The company also owns American Diversified Pharmacies, a mail order pharmacy operation.

The founding Long family owns more than 5% of the company; employees own about 13%.

## HISTORY

Joseph Long (son-in-law of Marion Skaggs, who developed the Safeway chain) and his brother Thomas opened their first store, Longs Self-Service Drug Store, in Oakland, California, in 1938; their second store opened a year later in nearby Alameda. The Oakland store (still operating today) was the first to introduce the idea of self-service to drugstores. The brothers believed that the manager of each store should make the decisions regarding its operation, and each store manager was given freedom in setting prices, selecting inventory, and promoting sales. The stores offered the lowest prices in their neighborhoods.

By 1950 the company had six stores in the Oakland area and one in Fresno. It opened 10 more stores during the 1950s in California and Hawaii. Longs Drug Stores went public in 1961. In 1975 Joseph became chairman and his son, Robert, president. The company continued to add stores; it expanded into other western states in the late 1970s and had 132 outlets by 1980.

Seven years later Longs acquired one Osco Drug store in Denver and 11 in California from American Stores, increasing its market share in California to 20%. At the same time, it sold all 15 Longs locations in Arizona to Osco. In 1989 a pharmacy distribution center was opened in Southern California. To speed up prescription dispensing, some high-volume stores were upgraded to "superpharmacy" status. Joseph died the next year and was succeeded as chairman by Robert. In 1993 co-founder Thomas died at age 82.

Longs acquired 21-store Bill's Drugs for $12 million in 1993, the same year government agencies investigated Longs for inaccurate Medicaid billings in Hawaii and Nevada. The company admitted inaccuracies and a settlement was reached with Nevada for $750,000 and with Hawaii for $2.4 million. Longs was one of several retailers named in a 1994 lawsuit over a distribution scheme in which a former employee confirmed nonexistent transactions. (A $14 million settlement of the lawsuit in 1996 ate into earnings.)

In 1995 Longs bought six drugstores in Hawaii and established Integrated Health Concepts, a pharmacy benefits management service, as a wholly owned subsidiary. The company introduced a computer-aided prescription-filling system in 1996. In 1997 Integrated Health Concepts merged with American Stores' RxAmerica in a joint venture. (Albertson's acquired American Stores in 1999.)

Longs settled a lawsuit filed by druggists alleging the company cheated them out of overtime pay ($3.1 million was divided by 1,000 employees) in 1998. (Management-level employees filed a similar lawsuit in 1999.) Longs lengthened its presence in the west in 1998 when it bought Drug Emporium franchisee Western Drug Distributors, which operated 18 stores in Washington and two in Oregon.

In 1999 the company bought 31 stores in California from rival Rite Aid for about $150 million. In 2000 CEO Robert Long, son of co-founder Joseph, stepped down as CEO; president Stephen Roath replaced him. In 2001 Longs jointly launched an online pharmacy and also exercised its purchase option, acquiring Albertson's stake in their RxAmerica joint venture.

In February 2002 Roath retired and board member Harold Somerset was named president and CEO. Somerset became vice chairman of the company in October when former Kroger executive Warren Bryant was named president and CEO.

In April 2003 Longs Drug acquired American Diversified Pharmacies, a mail order pharmacy service, for an undisclosed sum. In August CEO Bryant was elected chairman of the company, succeeding Robert Long, who became chairman emeritus. To revive its flagging financial performance, Longs cut about 170 jobs, primarily in its California headquarters, in 2003 and offered store managers a voluntary separation program.

In June 2006 Longs Drug acquired 24 pharmacies in Southern California from Redlands, California-based Network Pharmaceuticals for about $10 million. Also in 2006, the company built a new 800,000-sq.-ft. front-end distribution center in Patterson, California.

## EXECUTIVES

**Chairman, President, and CEO:** Warren F. Bryant, age 61, $843,750 pay
**EVP and COO, Longs Drug Stores California:** Karen L. Stout, age 48
**EVP and CFO:** Steven F. (Steve) McCann, age 54, $428,269 pay
**EVP, Business Development and Managed Care, Longs Drug Stores California:** Bruce E. Schwallie, age 52, $426,500 pay
**SVP and CIO, Longs Drug Stores California:** Michael M. Laddon, age 53
**SVP, General Counsel, and Secretary:** William J. (Bill) Rainey, age 60, $412,385 pay
**SVP and Chief Merchandising Officer, Longs Drug Stores California:** Todd J. Vasos, age 45, $353,500 pay
**SVP, Human Resources, Longs Drug Stores California:** Linda M. Watt, age 50
**SVP, Finance, Controller, and Treasurer:** Roger L. Chelemedos, age 44
**Group VP, Store Operations:** Martin A. Bennett
**Group VP, RxAmerica:** John Gardynik
**Group VP, Store Operations:** W. Allan Torres
**Group VP, Marketing:** Lawrence J. Gatta Jr.
**Group VP, Store Operations:** Marlon D. Bradford
**Group VP, Financial Planning and Analysis:** Daniel R. Thorson
**VP, Real Estate:** Brian T. McAndrews
**VP, Information Technology:** Edward R. Puskas
**VP, Administration and Special Projects:** Grover L. White
**VP, Pharmacy Operations:** Frank V. Scorpiniti
**VP, Professional Services:** Michael L. Cantrell
**VP, Investor Relations and Corporate Communications:** Phyllis J. Proffer
**Auditors:** Deloitte & Touche LLP

## LOCATIONS

**HQ:** Longs Drug Stores Corporation
141 N. Civic Dr., Walnut Creek, CA 94596
**Phone:** 925-937-1170 **Fax:** 925-210-6886
**Web:** www.longs.com

Longs Drug Stores operates more than 500 stores in California, Colorado, Hawaii, Nevada, Oregon, and Washington.

### 2007 Stores

| | No. |
|---|---|
| California | 437 |
| Hawaii | 32 |
| Nevada | 17 |
| Washington | 12 |
| Colorado | 9 |
| Oregon | 2 |
| **Total** | **509** |

## PRODUCTS/OPERATIONS

### 2007 Sales

| | $ mil. | % of total |
|---|---|---|
| Pharmacy | 2,408.8 | 47 |
| Front-end | 2,367.8 | 47 |
| Pharmacy benefit services | 320.4 | 6 |
| **Total** | **5,097.0** | **100** |

### Selected Divisions

Cosmetics
Food and beverage
Greeting cards
Groceries
Health and beauty products
Mail centers
Over-the-counter medications
Pharmacy
Photo and photo processing
Specialty items (watches, jewelry, sporting goods)

## COMPETITORS

7-Eleven
Albertsons
Costco Wholesale
CVS/Caremark
Kmart
Kroger
Medicap
Medicine Shoppe
Raley's
Rite Aid
Safeway
Save Mart
Stater Bros.
Target
Walgreen
Wal-Mart

## HISTORICAL FINANCIALS

Company Type: Public

**Income Statement** FYE: Last Thursday in January

| | REVENUE ($ mil.) | NET INCOME ($ mil.) | NET PROFIT MARGIN | EMPLOYEES |
|---|---|---|---|---|
| **1/07** | 5,097 | 75 | 1.5% | 21,900 |
| **1/06** | 4,670 | 74 | 1.6% | 22,000 |
| **1/05** | 4,608 | 37 | 0.8% | 22,000 |
| **1/04** | 4,527 | 30 | 0.7% | 22,900 |
| **1/03** | 4,426 | 7 | 0.2% | 22,200 |
| **Annual Growth** | 3.6% | 82.6% | — | (0.3%) |

**2007 Year-End Financials**

Debt ratio: 15.7%
Return on equity: 9.4%
Cash ($ mil.): 28
Current ratio: 1.36
Long-term debt ($ mil.): 128
No. of shares (mil.): 37
Dividends
Yield: 1.3%
Payout: 28.7%
Market value ($ mil.): 1,604

**Stock History** NYSE: LDG

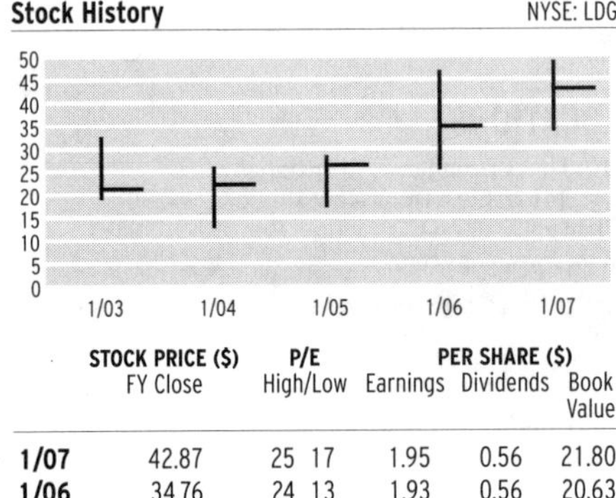


| | STOCK PRICE ($) FY Close | P/E High | P/E Low | PER SHARE ($) Earnings | Dividends | Book Value |
|---|---|---|---|---|---|---|
| **1/07** | 42.87 | 25 | 17 | 1.95 | 0.56 | 21.80 |
| **1/06** | 34.76 | 24 | 13 | 1.93 | 0.56 | 20.63 |
| **1/05** | 26.26 | 29 | 18 | 0.97 | 0.56 | 19.43 |
| **1/04** | 22.08 | 32 | 17 | 0.79 | 0.56 | 19.02 |
| **1/03** | 21.17 | 179 | 107 | 0.18 | 0.56 | 18.61 |
| **Annual Growth** | 19.3% | — | — | 81.4% | 0.0% | 4.0% |

# Louisiana-Pacific

Orient yourself to the fact that Louisiana-Pacific (LP) is one of the world's largest producers of oriented strand board (OSB) siding and other OSB-based products. LP also produces hardboard siding products, engineered/composite wood products (I-joists, laminated veneer lumber), plastic building products (vinyl siding, composite decking products, and mouldings), trim products, radiant barrier sheathing, and concrete form products. LP sells to wholesale distributors, building material dealers, retail "do-it-yourself" home centers, manufactured housing producers, and industrial manufacturers.

After hemorrhaging cash in the early years of the new millennium, LP adopted a plan to radically restructure its operations to focus on its core structural products business. After losing $62 million in 2002, the restructured company made $272 million in 2003, $421 million in 2004, and $476 million in 2005. The next year started off hot, but a weakening housing market affected LP drastically: It ended 2006 making only $124 million.

LP's restructuring plan included the sale of several businesses, including its plywood, industrial panel, lumber, fee timber and timberlands, distribution, and wholesale operations. The drastic cuts reduced the company's workforce by nearly 50%. OSB products accounted for more than 50% of sales in 2006 and 2005. The company has forged a number of joint-venture and partnership deals to build new OSB and other facilities in the US and Canada. The company has continued to experience setbacks — in 2006 it closed a Quebec OSB mill and adjacent sawmill, citing high transportation, fuel, and materials costs.

## HISTORY

Louisiana-Pacific (LP) was spun off in 1972 from Georgia-Pacific after the Federal Trade Commission contended that Georgia-Pacific had created a monopoly in the softwood plywood industry. Harry Merlo, the company's first CEO, became chairman in 1974.

In 1978 the company acquired Fibreboard Corporation, a maker of asbestos and other products used in furniture and cabinets. (Despite spinning off Fibreboard in 1988, LP has been a co-defendant in hundreds of asbestos-related lawsuits.) Also in 1978 the US government acquired some of LP's timberlands as part of the expansion of the Redwood National Park in California.

Facing a shortage of Douglas fir and southern pine trees, LP experimented with making wood products from fast-growing, less-expensive trees, including aspen and cottonwood. Oriented strand board (OSB) — pieces of logs mixed with resin and pressed into sheets — was developed in the late 1970s and was touted as a cheaper, stronger alternative to plywood.

LP profited from a housing boom and a strong pulp market in the 1980s. It began marketing OSB as an exterior siding alternative in 1985. Between 1990 and 1994, however, thousands of property owners in Florida complained that its OSB siding deteriorated in the humid climate. Three class-action suits were filed. The attorney general of Minnesota sued the company over defective siding in 1991. LP settled that case in 1992, and by the end of that year LP had paid $22 million to settle OSB claims throughout the US. But consumers, armed with the siding's 25-year warranty, continued to complain about rotting and cracking boards. The company paid out another $15 million in 1993 and 1994. After a 1995 grand jury indicted LP for environmental violations and product misrepresentation, Merlo and other top executives were dismissed. International Paper EVP Mark Suwyn was named chairman and CEO in 1996 and immediately became the subject of a non-compete lawsuit filed by his former employer. (In 1997 a federal judge ruled in Suwyn's favor.)

In 1996 the company agreed to pay at least $275 million to 800,000 homeowners who had used its wood siding. LP also started growing its complementary building-products business by purchasing companies such as wood-coating and chemical producer Associated Chemists (sold in 1999) and cellulose insulation maker GreenStone Industries. Meanwhile, a weak OSB market prompted LP to close several of its OSB plants. LP chopped operations and some 25% of its workforce in 1997 to focus on its core building products.

LP sold its Northern California lumber operations in 1998 and closed down its fiber-cement roofing operations. In 1999 LP acquired ABT Building Products (paneling and siding), as well as Canadian companies Le Groupe Forex (OSB) for $510 million and Evans Forest Products (laminated veneer and plywood). The following year the company added Hoff Companies' composite decking assets and the Sawyer Lumber Company (low-cost lumber for residential construction). In 2001 the company sold a controlling interest in its Samoa, California, pulp mill to LaPointe Partners.

LP continued to trim operations in 2002 by selling its controlling interest in an OSB plant in Ireland; the company recorded a $2 million gain on the sale and reduced its debt by $6.5 million. LP bought out its joint venture in Chile for $3 million that year. Also in 2002, due to low paper demand and falling profits, LP announced a radical restructuring plan in which the company would cut 45% of its workforce (or 4,400 jobs) and close unprofitable businesses to focus on its core structural products business.

The company in 2003 sold more than 600,000 acres of timberland in a series of deals. Also that year LP sold six lumber facilities, an industrial panel facility, and a veneer facility, in part because of an industrywide oversupply of lumber and historically low prices for lumber.

In 2004 LP sold a hardboard plant in Michigan, a decorative panel facility in Ohio, and a Washington sawmill. The following year, the selling continued, with several operations siphoned off.

## EXECUTIVES

**Chairman:** E. Gary Cook, age 62
**CEO and Director:** Richard W. (Rick) Frost, age 55, $1,352,320 pay
**EVP Administration and CFO:** Curtis M. Stevens, age 54, $755,520 pay
**EVP Oriented Strand Board (OSB):** Jeffrey N. (Jeff) Wagner, $373,019 pay (prior to promotion)
**EVP Specialty Products, Sales and Marketing:** Richard S. (Rick) Olszewski
**VP, CIO, and Director, Technology:** F. Jeff Duncan Jr., age 49
**VP Corporate Engineering and Technology:** David (Dave) Crowe
**VP and General Manager, Engineered Wood Products:** Brian Luoma
**VP Human Resources:** Ann P. Harris
**VP Marketing:** John Neilson
**VP, Procurement, Logistics, and Supply Management:** Neil Sherman
**VP and General Manager Siding:** Brad Southern
**VP Oriented Strand Board (OSB) Manufacturing:** Jamey Barnes, age 56
**VP Sales:** Mike Sims
**VP and General Counsel:** Mark Fuchs
**Director, Human Resources:** William Strom
**Media Relations:** Mary Cohn
**Investor Relations:** Becky Barckley
**Corporate Controller:** Jeffrey Poloway, age 50
**Auditors:** Deloitte & Touche LLP

## LOCATIONS

**HQ:** Louisiana-Pacific Corporation
414 Union St., Ste. 2000, Nashville, TN 37219
**Phone:** 615-986-5600 **Fax:** 615-986-5666
**Web:** www.lpcorp.com

Louisiana-Pacific operates about 30 manufacturing facilities in the US and Canada and one in Chile.

**2006 Sales**

| | $ mil. | % of total |
|---|---|---|
| US | 1,857 | 72 |
| Canada & other countries | 717 | 28 |
| Intersegment US sales | (339) | — |
| **Total** | **2,235** | **100** |

## PRODUCTS/OPERATIONS

**2006 Sales**

| | $ mil. | % of total |
|---|---|---|
| OSB | 1,212.2 | 54 |
| Siding | 493.4 | 22 |
| Engineered wood products | 392.0 | 18 |
| Other | 139.0 | 6 |
| Adjustments | (1.5) | — |
| **Total** | **2,235.1** | **100** |

## COMPETITORS

Amos-Hill Associates
Boise Cascade
Georgia-Pacific Corporation
Hesperia Holding
International Paper
Norbord
Potlatch
Pratt Industries USA
Smurfit-Stone Container
South Coast Lumber Co.
Temple-Inland
USG
Weyerhaeuser

## HISTORICAL FINANCIALS

Company Type: Public

**Income Statement** FYE: December 31

| | REVENUE ($ mil.) | NET INCOME ($ mil.) | NET PROFIT MARGIN | EMPLOYEES |
|---|---|---|---|---|
| **12/06** | 2,235 | 124 | 5.5% | 5,600 |
| **12/05** | 2,599 | 456 | 17.5% | 5,600 |
| **12/04** | 2,849 | 421 | 14.8% | 6,500 |
| **12/03** | 2,300 | 273 | 11.8% | 7,100 |
| **12/02** | 1,943 | (62) | — | 7,900 |
| **Annual Growth** | 3.6% | — | — | (8.2%) |

**2006 Year-End Financials**

Debt ratio: 31.2%
Return on equity: 6.0%
Cash ($ mil.): 1,063
Current ratio: 5.68
Long-term debt ($ mil.): 645
No. of shares (mil.): 104
Dividends
Yield: 2.8%
Payout: 51.3%
Market value ($ mil.): 2,244

**Stock History** NYSE: LPX

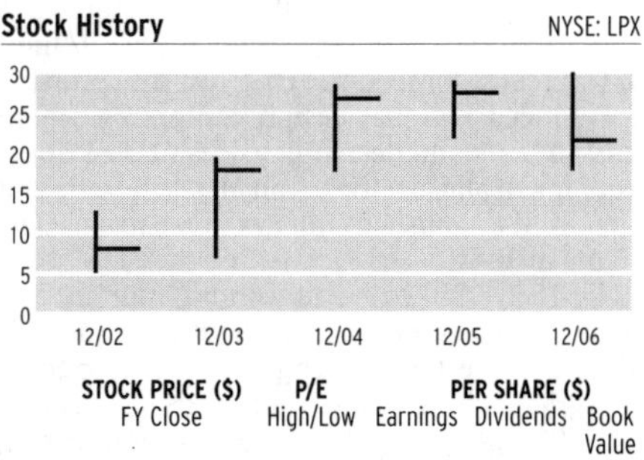


| | STOCK PRICE ($) FY Close | P/E High/Low | | PER SHARE ($) Earnings | Dividends | Book Value |
|---|---|---|---|---|---|---|
| **12/06** | 21.53 | 25 | 15 | 1.17 | 0.60 | 19.84 |
| **12/05** | 27.47 | 7 | 5 | 4.15 | 0.35 | 19.31 |
| **12/04** | 26.74 | 7 | 5 | 3.84 | 0.30 | 16.05 |
| **12/03** | 17.88 | 8 | 3 | 2.56 | — | 12.31 |
| **12/02** | 8.06 | — | — | (0.59) | — | 9.62 |
| **Annual Growth** | 27.8% | — | — | — | 41.4% | 19.8% |

# Lowe's Companies

No longer a low-profile company, Lowe's Companies has evolved from a regional hardware store operator into a nationwide chain of home improvement superstores. The #2 US home improvement chain (after The Home Depot), Lowe's has more than 1,380 superstores in 49 states and has announced plans to expand into Canada in 2007. The company's stores sell about 40,000 products for do-it-yourselfers and professionals for home improvement and repair projects, such as gardening products, home fashion items, lumber, millwork, plumbing and electrical supplies, and tools, as well as appliances and furniture. Lowe's is the second-largest US home appliance retailer after Sears.

In the past, Lowe's concentrated on small and medium-sized markets, but that trend is changing. Lowe's is expanding in large metro areas (with populations of 500,000 or more). But the company is not forgetting its traditional customer base either. About 20% of the new stores Lowe's plans to open will be smaller stores in rural markets.

Despite the recent slowdown in the US housing market, Lowe's continues to expand to gain market share. The company plans to open more than 150 stores in 2007, after adding about 155 locations in 2006. To supply all those new stores the home improvement chain is expanding its distribution network. It opened a distribution center in Rockford, Illinois, in mid-2007 and is building another in Lebanon, Oregon, with additional centers planned for 2008. It is also building a new flatbed distribution center in St. Joseph, Missouri, bringing the number of regional flatbed centers Lowe's operates throughout the US to 14. Lowe's is also trying to attract more female customers, who, the company claims, call the shots on about 80% of home improvement decisions.

North of the border Lowe's plans to open six to 10 stores in the Toronto market in 2007. The company's long term plan for Canada calls for as many as 100 Lowe's stores there. Longer-term, the US home improvement chain plans to open five stores in Monterrey, Mexico in 2009. (Rival Home Depot is Mexico's #1 do-it-yourself operator with more than 55 stores there.)

While rival Home Depot diversified to focus on professional customers and expanded internationally, Lowe's remained focused on the domestic market. The company's stores make effective use of lighting and signage and cater to women and baby boomers with an attractive store design. In addition, the company has been increasing exclusive product arrangements with suppliers. Like its rival Home Depot, Lowe's is putting more emphasis on services, offering installation service in more than 40 categories, such as flooring and cabinet installation.

## HISTORY

Lowe's Companies was founded in 1921 as Mr. L. S. Lowe's North Wilkesboro Hardware in North Wilkesboro, North Carolina. A family operation by 1945, Mr. Lowe's store (which also sold groceries, snuff, and harnesses) was run by his son Jim and his son-in-law H. Carl Buchan. Buchan bought Lowe's share of the company in 1956 and incorporated as Lowe's North Wilkesboro Hardware; he wanted Lowe's as part of the company name because he liked the slogan "Lowe's Low Prices." The chain expanded from North Carolina into Tennessee, Virginia, and West Virginia. By 1960 Buchan had 15 stores and sales of $31 million — up $4 million from a decade before.

Buchan planned to create a profit-sharing plan for Lowe's employees, but in 1960 he died of a heart attack at age 44. In 1961 Lowe's management and the executors of Buchan's estate established the Lowe's Employees Profit Sharing and Trust, which bought Buchan's 89% of the company (later renamed Lowe's Companies). That year they financed the transaction through a public offering, which diluted the employees' stock. Lowe's was listed on the NYSE in 1979.

Robert Strickland, who had joined the company in 1957, became chairman in 1978. Revenues increased from $170 million in 1971 to more than $900 million, with a net income of $25 million, in 1979. Traditionally, the majority of Lowe's business was in sales to professional homebuilders, but in 1980 housing starts fell, and company profits dropped. Concurrently, The Home Depot introduced its low-price warehouse concept. Instead of building warehouse stores of its own, Strickland changed the stores' layouts and by 1982 had redesigned half of the 229 stores to be more oriented toward do-it-yourself (DIY) consumers. The new designs featured softer lighting and displays of entire room layouts to appeal to women, who made up over half of all DIY customers. In 1982 Lowe's made more than half of its sales to consumers for the first time in its history.

Although Lowe's had more than 300 stores by 1988, its outlets were only about 20,000 sq. ft. (one-fifth the size of Home Depot's warehouse stores). By 1989 Lowe's, which had continued to target contractors as well as DIYers, was overtaken by Home Depot as the US's #1 home retail chain.

Since 1989 the company has focused on building larger stores, taking a charge of $71 million in 1991 to phase out smaller stores and build warehouse outlets. In 1993 Lowe's opened 57 large stores (half were replacements for existing stores), almost doubling its total floor space.

In 1997 president and CEO Leonard Herring retired and was replaced by former COO Robert Tillman, who also took the post of chairman when Strickland stepped down in 1998.

Also in 1998 the company entered a joint venture to sell an exclusive line of Kobalt-brand professional mechanics' tools produced by Snap-on and, to better serve commercial customers, began allowing them to special order items not stocked in stores. In addition, Lowe's announced it would spend $1.5 billion over the next several years on a 100-store push into the western US. Lowe's westward expansion was fueled when it purchased Washington-based, 38-store Eagle Hardware & Garden in 1999 in a stock swap deal worth $1.3 billion. The company gradually converted the Eagle stores into Lowe's.

In 2001 the company earmarked $2.4 billion of its $2.7 billion capital budget for store expansions and new distribution centers.

Robert Niblock was promoted from CFO to president in March 2003. Lowe's sold its some 30 outlets operating as The Contractor Yard to The Strober Organization in 2004. Also that year it opened its first predominantly urban-oriented store, suited to the needs of city dwellers and building superintendents, in Brooklyn.

Chairman and CEO Robert Tillman retired in January 2005. He was succeeded by president Robert Niblock.

## EXECUTIVES

**Chairman and CEO:** Robert A. Niblock, age 44, $950,000 pay
**President and COO:** Larry D. Stone, age 54, $770,039 pay
**EVP and CFO:** Robert F. (Bob) Hull Jr., age 41, $480,000 pay
**EVP, Business Development:** Gregory M. (Greg) Bridgeford, age 51, $480,000 pay
**EVP, Store Operations:** Michael K. (Mike) Brown, age 41
**SVP and CIO:** Steven M. Stone, age 44
**SVP and General Merchandising Manager, Building Products:** J. David Steed, age 52
**SVP and General Merchandising Manager, Kitchen and Bath:** John L. Kasberger, age 59
**SVP and General Merchandising Manager, Home Décor:** Theresa A. Anderson, age 47
**SVP and General Merchandising Manager, Hardlines:** Clinton T. (Clint) Davis
**SVP and General Merchandising Manager, Outdoor Living:** Patricia M. (Patti) Price
**SVP and Chief Accounting Officer:** Matthew V. Hollifield, age 39
**SVP, General Counsel, and Secretary:** Gaither M. Keener Jr.
**SVP, Corporate Affairs:** N. Brian Peace
**SVP, Distribution:** Stephen J. Szilagyi
**SVP, Merchandising and Store Support:** Marshall A. Croom, age 44
**SVP, Product Development and Global Sourcing; President, LG Sourcing:** Michael K. Menser, age 51
**SVP, General Counsel, and Secretary:** Ross W. McCanless, age 48
**SVP, Human Resources:** Maureen K. Ausura, age 50
**SVP, Marketing and Advertising:** Robert J. Gfeller Jr., age 43
**SVP, Real Estate, Engineering and Construction:** David E. Shelton, age 58
**SVP, Specialty Sales:** K. Scott Plemmons
**Investor Relations Specialist:** Vicki C. Heitman
**Auditors:** Deloitte & Touche LLP

## LOCATIONS

**HQ:** Lowe's Companies, Inc.
1000 Lowe's Blvd., Mooresville, NC 28117
**Phone:** 704-758-1000 **Fax:** 336-658-4766
**Web:** www.lowes.com

## PRODUCTS/OPERATIONS

**2007 Sales**

| | $ mil. | % of total |
|---|---|---|
| Appliances | 4,193 | 9 |
| Lumber | 3,690 | 8 |
| Flooring | 3,214 | 7 |
| Millwork | 3,137 | 7 |
| Paint | 3,073 | 7 |
| Building materials | 3,002 | 6 |
| Fashion plumbing | 2,893 | 6 |
| Lighting | 2,573 | 5 |
| Tools | 2,563 | 5 |
| Lawn & landscape | 2,356 | 5 |
| Hardware | 2,296 | 5 |
| Seasonal living | 2,154 | 5 |
| Cabinets & countertops | 1,903 | 4 |
| Outdoor power equipment | 1,805 | 4 |
| Rough plumbing | 1,664 | 4 |
| Rough electrical | 1,479 | 3 |
| Nursery | 1,454 | 3 |
| Home environment | 1,145 | 2 |
| Walls/windows | 1,101 | 2 |
| Home organization | 1,001 | 2 |
| Other | 231 | 1 |
| **Total** | **46,927** | **100** |

## COMPETITORS

84 Lumber
Abbey Carpet
Ace Hardware
Best Buy
CCA Global
Do it Best
E.N. Beard Hardwood
F.W. Webb
Guardian Building Products
Home Depot
McCoy
Menard
Northern Tool
Sears
Sherwin-Williams
Sutherland Lumber
True Value
Wal-Mart
Wolseley

## HISTORICAL FINANCIALS

Company Type: Public

**Income Statement** FYE: Friday nearest January 31

| | REVENUE ($ mil.) | NET INCOME ($ mil.) | NET PROFIT MARGIN | EMPLOYEES |
|---|---|---|---|---|
| **1/07** | 46,927 | 3,105 | 6.6% | 210,000 |
| **1/06** | 43,243 | 2,765 | 6.4% | 185,000 |
| **1/05** | 36,464 | 2,176 | 6.0% | 162,000 |
| **1/04** | 30,838 | 1,877 | 6.1% | 147,000 |
| **1/03** | 26,491 | 1,471 | 5.6% | 153,000 |
| **Annual Growth** | 15.4% | 20.5% | — | 8.2% |

**2007 Year-End Financials**

Debt ratio: 27.5%
Return on equity: 20.7%
Cash ($ mil.): 796
Current ratio: 1.27
Long-term debt ($ mil.): 4,325
No. of shares (mil.): 1,525
Dividends
Yield: 0.4%
Payout: 6.5%
Market value ($ mil.): 52,079

**Stock History** NYSE: LOW

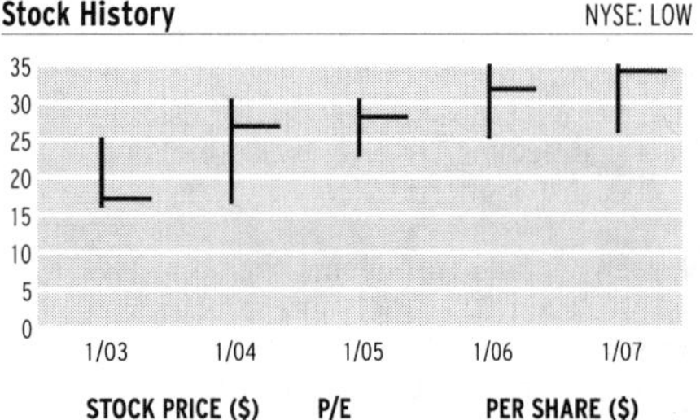


| | STOCK PRICE ($) FY Close | P/E High | P/E Low | PER SHARE ($) Earnings | Dividends | Book Value |
|---|---|---|---|---|---|---|
| **1/07** | 34.15 | 18 | 13 | 1.99 | 0.13 | 10.31 |
| **1/06** | 31.76 | 20 | 15 | 1.73 | 0.11 | 9.12 |
| **1/05** | 28.09 | 22 | 17 | 1.36 | 0.08 | 14.91 |
| **1/04** | 26.77 | 26 | 14 | 1.17 | 0.05 | 13.10 |
| **1/03** | 17.09 | 27 | 18 | 0.93 | 0.04 | 10.62 |
| **Annual Growth** | 18.9% | — | — | 20.9% | 34.3% | (0.7%) |

# LSI Corporation

LSI Corp. (formerly LSI Logic) offers lots more than logic chips. The fabless semiconductor developer provides standard integrated circuits (ICs) and custom-designed application-specific ICs (ASICs), focusing on broadband and wireless communications, consumer electronics, and data networking markets. LSI was a pioneer of system-on-a-chip (SoC) devices, which combine elements of an electronic system — especially a microprocessor, memory, and logic — onto a single chip. LSI's top customers include Hewlett-Packard, IBM (19% of sales), and Seagate (12%). LSI also provides hardware and software for storage area networks. The company has acquired rival Agere Systems for stock valued at nearly $4 billion.

While Agere and LSI were key competitors to each other in chips for hard-disk drives (both have Seagate as a leading customer), they expect to find complementary strengths in the areas of consumer electronics and networking technology.

The acquisition agreement called for LSI to issue approximately 379 million shares of its common stock for all of Agere's shares. Following the merger, previous shareholders of LSI own about 52% of the combined company. LSI retained its headquarters in California, and CEO Abhi Talwalkar will serve as CEO of the merged company. LSI will name six of the nine directors on the board.

LSI's SoC leadership is based on its CoreWare library of industry-standard building blocks (including analog and digital cores, transceivers, and digital signal processor cores). CoreWare's standardization is designed to save customers time and money by allowing them to mix and match components to develop new ICs.

The company was extending this approach with its RapidChip product line, behind which it put lots of engineering and marketing muscle. LSI touted RapidChip, which allows customers to combine chip building blocks with customized logic features, as offering time and cost savings in comparison to other custom-chip alternatives, such as ASICs and field-programmable gate arrays (FPGAs). In early 2006, however, LSI decided to cease development of the RapidChip product line, choosing to focus corporate R&D resources on consumer electronics and data storage products.

Softness in business during the first half of 2007 led LSI to eliminate approximately 900 jobs, a 10% reduction for the combined Agere-LSI workforce. As part of a general corporate restructuring, LSI has sold its consumer products business to Magnum Semiconductor, a venture-funded chip company.

BlackRock owns nearly 12% of LSI. Morgan Stanley holds about 7% of the company. Paulsen & Co. has an equity stake of around 6%.

## HISTORY

Wilfred (Wilf) Corrigan, an engineer and former CEO of Fairchild Camera & Instrument (the original parent company of Fairchild Semiconductor), founded LSI Logic in 1981. (Its name is the acronym for large-scale integration, describing a chip that has up to 100,000 transistors.) LSI Logic went public in 1983 with a $152 million IPO, a record for its time. That year the company introduced regional design centers — where customers could design chips using LSI Logic equipment and facilities — in Massachusetts and the UK. It established affiliates in Japan and Germany in 1984.

By 1985 LSI Logic had won big military and aerospace customers and, with sales of $140 million, was the US's leading application-specific integrated circuit (ASIC) maker. By the end of the 1980s, however, LSI Logic was foundering after heavy investment in factories (it had geared up for a boom that failed to materialize). In 1992 the company began developing its CoreWare mix-and-match standardization technology.

A trimmer, smarter LSI Logic emerged in 1993 — the year it introduced the 0.5-micron CMOS (complementary metal oxide semiconductor) ASIC chip. Also that year LSI Logic penned 10-year technology sharing agreements with electronic design automation leaders Synopsys and Cadence Design Systems. LSI Logic passed the $1 billion sales mark in 1995.

LSI Logic paid $804 million to acquire Symbios, a US electronics subsidiary of cash-strapped Hyundai, in 1998. It also entered a DVD development joint venture with SANYO.

In 1999 LSI Logic won a lucrative contract to make chips for Sony's PlayStation consoles, and teamed up with Hitachi to develop embedded hybrid chips. The next year the company purchased C-Cube Microsystems (chips for digital set-top boxes and DVDs) in a deal valued at about $850 million. Also in 2001 LSI Logic bought a business unit of American Megatrends that makes hardware and software for redundant array of independent disks (RAID) systems used in networking and storage applications.

Early in 2002 the company shed two product lines and cut 1,400 positions in an effort to return to profitability. As part of its restructuring, LSI divested itself of fabrication plants in Colorado and Japan.

The company acquired the assets of CrossLayer Networks, a maker of Gigabit Ethernet switch products, and acquired communications chip maker Velio Communications, both in 2004.

Intel veteran Abhi Talwalkar succeeded Wilf Corrigan as CEO in 2005. Corrigan remained chairman of the board. In 2006, however, LSI Logic's founder retired from the board of directors, officially ending his 25-year association with the company. Including stock options, Corrigan owns about 3% of LSI Logic.

James Keyes, the former CEO of Johnson Controls and an LSI Logic director since 1983, succeeded Corrigan as non-executive chairman.

In 2006 LSI sold its Oregon fab to ON Semiconductor for about $105 million in cash. Among other agreements between the companies, LSI will pay ON Semi around $100 million a year for two years for ON to make chips for LSI.

In 2006 LSI said it would sell its ZSP digital signal processor business. It had acquired ZSP seven years earlier, in 1999. ZSP's assets were acquired by VeriSilicon Holdings, an ASIC design house based in China, for $13 million in cash and stock. Most of the ZSP workforce was hired by VeriSilicon.

In late 2006 LSI acquired StoreAge Networking Technologies, a developer of network storage management and data protection software, for around $50 million in cash. The company hired all of StoreAge's employees.

In early 2007 LSI Logic completed its $4 billion acquisition of rival Agere Systems and changed its name to LSI Corporation. Also that year Gregorio Reyes became non-executive chairman.

## EXECUTIVES

**Chairman:** Gregorio Reyes, age 66
**President, CEO, and Director:** Abhijit Y. (Abhi) Talwalkar, age 42, $800,000 pay
**EVP and CFO:** Bryon Look, age 53, $400,000 pay
**EVP, Consumer Products:** Umesh Padval, age 49, $368,174 pay
**EVP, Worldwide Operations:** Donald J. Esses, age 55
**EVP, Custom Solutions Group:** D. Jeffrey (Jeff) Richardson, age 42, $400,000 pay
**EVP, Storage Sales and Marketing:** Flavio Santoni, age 48, $347,074 pay
**EVP, Sales:** Jeffery L. Hoogenboom, age 41
**EVP and CTO:** Claudine Simson, age 53
**SVP Corporate Planning and Marketing:** Philip G. Brace, age 36
**SVP, Engenio Storage Group:** Philip W. (Phil) Bullinger, age 42
**VP, Human Resources:** Jon R. Gibson, age 60
**Auditors:** PricewaterhouseCoopers LLP

## LOCATIONS

**HQ:** LSI Corporation
1621 Barber Ln., Milpitas, CA 95035
**Phone:** 408-433-8000 **Fax:** 408-954-3220
**Web:** www.lsi.com

LSI has operations in Australia, Austria, Canada, China, France, Germany, Hong Kong, India, Ireland, Israel, Italy, Japan, Russia, Singapore, South Korea, Spain, Sweden, Taiwan, Thailand, the United Arab Emirates, the UK, and the US.

### 2006 Sales

| | $ mil. | % of total |
|---|---|---|
| North America | 956.7 | 48 |
| Asia/Pacific | 797.2 | 40 |
| Europe, Middle East & Africa | 228.3 | 12 |
| **Total** | **1,982.2** | **100** |

## PRODUCTS/OPERATIONS

### 2006 Sales

| | $ mil. | % of total |
|---|---|---|
| Semiconductors | 1,223.2 | 62 |
| Storage systems | 759.0 | 38 |
| **Total** | **1,982.2** | **100** |

### Selected Semiconductor Products and Markets

Broadband and wireless networking (analog and digital chip cores, ASICs, and baseband processors)
- Wide-area network (WAN) equipment
- Wireless local-area network (LAN) equipment
- Wireless phones

Broadband entertainment (analog and digital chip cores, ASICs, and software)
- Digital set-top boxes
- DVD players
- Home video games
- Satellite and terrestrial television broadcasting

Networking infrastructure
- Analog equipment (Ethernet physical-layer devices)
- Digital equipment (ARM- and MIPS-based microprocessors, Ethernet controllers, and high-speed content-addressable memory)

Storage components (ASICs, software, and standard input/output components)
- Fibre Channel (host adapters and adapter boards, physical-layer components, protocol controllers, SAN switches, and transceivers)
- Hard disk drives and tape peripherals (controllers)

## COMPETITORS

Adaptec
Altera
AMD
AMI Semiconductor
Atmel
Avago Technologies
Broadcom
Cirrus Logic
Conexant Systems
Dot Hill
EMC
Epson
ESS Technology
Freescale Semiconductor
Genesis Microchip
Hitachi Data Systems
IBM Microelectronics
Intel
Marvell Technology
MediaTek
NEC Electronics
NetApp
NXP
Philips Electronics
Pixelworks
PMC-Sierra
QLogic
Samsung Electronics
STMicroelectronics
Sunplus
Texas Instruments
Toshiba
Trident Microsystems
Xilinx
Xiotech
Xyratex
Zoran

## HISTORICAL FINANCIALS

Company Type: Public

### Income Statement

FYE: December 31

| | REVENUE ($ mil.) | NET INCOME ($ mil.) | NET PROFIT MARGIN | EMPLOYEES |
|---|---|---|---|---|
| **12/06** | 1,982 | 170 | 8.6% | 4,010 |
| **12/05** | 1,919 | (6) | — | 4,322 |
| **12/04** | 1,700 | (464) | — | 4,414 |
| **12/03** | 1,693 | (309) | — | 4,722 |
| **12/02** | 1,817 | (292) | — | 5,281 |
| **Annual Growth** | 2.2% | — | — | (6.7%) |

### 2006 Year-End Financials

Debt ratio: 18.5%
Return on equity: 9.6%
Cash ($ mil.): 1,009
Current ratio: 3.11
Long-term debt ($ mil.): 350
No. of shares (mil.): 404
Dividends
Yield: —
Payout: —
Market value ($ mil.): 3,633

### Stock History

NYSE: LSI

| | STOCK PRICE ($) FY Close | P/E High | P/E Low | PER SHARE ($) Earnings | Dividends | Book Value |
|---|---|---|---|---|---|---|
| **12/06** | 9.00 | 28 | 18 | 0.42 | — | 4.70 |
| **12/05** | 8.00 | — | — | (0.01) | — | 4.13 |
| **12/04** | 5.48 | — | — | (1.21) | — | 4.17 |
| **12/03** | 8.87 | — | — | (0.82) | — | 5.35 |
| **12/02** | 5.77 | — | — | (0.79) | — | 6.13 |
| **Annual Growth** | 11.8% | — | — | — | — | (6.5%) |

# The Lubrizol Corporation

Lubrizol is a smooth operator — the company is the world's #1 maker of additives for lubricants and fuels. Its Lubrizol Additives segment includes engine oil additives that fight sludge buildup, viscosity breakdown, and component wear; fuel additives designed to control deposits and improve combustion; and additives for paints, inks, greases, metalworking, and other industrial markets. Lubrizol's Advanced Materials segment sends its products to the personal care and rubber and plastics markets. The company bought Noveon in mid-2004; Noveon's former businesses make up the bulk of the Advanced Materials segment. (That segment bore the Noveon name until late 2006 when Lubrizol quit using that trademark.)

The company markets nearly 3,000 products in more than 100 countries. Lubrizol operates research facilities and testing labs in Canada, Germany, Japan, the UK, and the US. More than half of its sales are outside the US.

In the summer of 2005 the company announced its intention to divest its noncore operations, which totaled $500 million in annual sales. The first move came later that year with the sale of Lubrizol Performance Systems to the Dutch medical and industrial technology company Delft Instruments. Later in the year it sold a much smaller piece of Noveon when it divested its Telene resins business line to TIMTEC, a joint venture of ZEON and Teijin Chemicals.

The following year brought the sale of Noveon's consumer specialties line of chemical products to Sun Capital Partners. The unit provided chemicals and performance materials to the food and beverage, personal care, and textiles industries and had annual sales of about $400 million. Sun Capital formed a new company called Emerald Performance Materials to operate the business. Lubrizol then sold the active pharmaceutical ingredients and intermediate compounds business of Noveon (with facilities in Germany and India) to a German private equity firm called Auctus Management. The move is the last in the planned divestiture of its non-core businesses. It then ceased to use the Noveon name for its specialty chemicals business.

## HISTORY

The company that eventually became Lubrizol was founded in 1928 by the Smith (Kelvin, Kevin, and Vincent) and Nason (Alex and Frank) brothers, along with their friend, Thomas James. Chemistry was in the Smiths' blood; all three had worked at Dow Chemical, a company their chemist father helped start. Known originally as The Graphite Oil Products Company, Lubrizol's first product, Lubri-graph, was a suspended graphite and oil product designed to keep car springs quiet. Following the success of their anti-squeak product, the principals turned their attention to the gunk that built up from the mineral oil used in car engines. Cars of the era overheated often and pistons frequently became stuck from excessive heat or sludge build-up. Graphite Oil chemists discovered that the addition of chlorine to lubricants solved the overheating problem. The new product (and later the company) was named Lubrizol.

Alex Nason went to Detroit in 1935 and convinced General Motors to add Lubrizol to its list of recommended products. Following that success Lubrizol was used extensively during WWII by the military, which established performance standards. During the war the company stopped producing lubricants and concentrated solely on additives, including rust inhibitors, detergents, and chemicals to slow oil breakdown.

After WWII performance standards for cars were set, and Lubrizol cleaned up, having patented many ingredients and processes used to manufacture lubricants. By the 1950s the privately held corporation was the #1 petroleum additive company in the world. It was during this time that the company made its first acquisition, R.O. Hull Company, a rustproofing chemicals manufacturer (it has since been sold). Lubrizol went public in 1960.

The company benefited as environmental regulations grew, since unleaded gas and catalytic converters required new additives. Lubrizol also benefited from the oil crisis in the early 1970s because the more fuel-efficient cars that resulted required new transmission fluids, fuel additives, and gear lubricants. Even the recession helped the slippery company, as industrial companies relied more on quality lubricants and additives to protect costly machinery.

Lubrizol purchased lithium battery maker Althus Corporation in 1979 and moved into biotechnology soon afterward. In 1985 the firm bought Agrigenetics Corporation and focused its biotechnology efforts on genetically altered plants. Biotechnology seemed to offer vast patent potential, whereas additives had become so effective that growth opportunities there seemed limited in comparison. However, after seven costly years, Lubrizol sold a controlling interest in Agrigenetics, which had become the sixth-largest seed company in the US, to Mycogen (acquired by Dow Chemical in 1998).

Lubrizol continued divesting noncore interests, and by 1996 it was back to being an additives company. Despite the turmoil in Asia, the company formed two joint ventures in China in 1997. Shrinking profits caused the company to cut production by approximately 20% and its workforce by 11% between 1999 and 2000.

In 2000 Lubrizol bought RPM's Alox metalworking additive business. The next year it acquired ROSS Chem, a privately held maker of antifoam and defoaming agents used by the coatings, inks, textile, food, and metalworking industries. The company's 2002 acquisitions have included Kabo International (defoaming products), Chemron (specialty surfactants), and Lambent Technologies (silicone defoamers).

Lubrizol bought the additives business of Avecia in a deal that closed in January 2004. The former Avecia unit makes pigment and color dispersants for inks and coatings under the brand names Solsperse, Solplus, and Solthix. Later that year it bought up the formerly private company Noveon, which had announced its intention to go public. Noveon makes polymers and additives used in food and pharmaceuticals. The total price Lubrizol paid for the company was $1.84 billion (about $900 million cash and the assumption of another $900 million in debt). The deal triggered a restructuring that resulted in Lubrizol's two main operating segments: its former activities called Lubricant Additives and Noveon's operations making up the Specialty Chemicals segment.

## EXECUTIVES

**Chairman, President, and CEO:** James L. Hambrick, age 52, $840,044 pay
**SVP; President, Lubricant Additives:** Stephen F. (Steve) Kirk, age 57, $355,935 pay
**SVP; President, Lubrizol Advanced Materials:** Donald W. Bogus, age 59, $355,565 pay
**SVP, CFO, and Treasurer:** Charles P. Cooley, age 51, $404,626 pay
**VP, Operations, Lubricant Additives:** Larry Norwood, age 54
**VP, Information Systems and Business Processes:** Patrick H. Saunier, age 51
**VP and General Counsel:** Joseph W. Bauer, age 53, $305,774 pay
**VP and General Counsel, Specialty Chemicals:** Gregory R. Lewis, age 46
**VP, Human Resources and Chief Ethics Officer:** Mark W. Meister, age 52
**Corporate Controller:** W. Scott Emerick, age 42
**Corporate Secretary:** Leslie M. Reynolds, age 46
**Chief Tax Officer:** Jeffrey A. Vavruska, age 46
**VP, Finance, Lubricant Additives:** Gregory P. Lieb, age 52
**SVP and COO, Specialty Chemicals:** Julian M. Steinberg
**VP and General Manager, Performance Coatings:** Eric Schnur
**VP, Corporate Planning, Development, and Communications:** Gregory D. Taylor, age 48
**Director, Investor Relations and Corporate Communications:** Mark Sutherland
**Auditors:** Deloitte & Touche LLP

## LOCATIONS

**HQ:** The Lubrizol Corporation
29400 Lakeland Blvd., Wickliffe, OH 44092
**Phone:** 440-943-4200 **Fax:** 440-943-5337
**Web:** www.lubrizol.com

### 2006 Sales

| | $ mil. | % of total |
|---|---|---|
| North America | | |
| US | 1,637.0 | 41 |
| Other countries | 187.2 | 5 |
| Europe | 1,144.7 | 28 |
| Asia/Pacific & Middle East | 823.5 | 20 |
| Latin America | 248.4 | 6 |
| **Total** | **4,040.8** | **100** |

## PRODUCTS/OPERATIONS

### 2006 Sales and Operating Income

| | Sales | | Operating Income | |
|---|---|---|---|---|
| | $ mil. | % of total | $ mil. | % of total |
| Lubrizol Additives | 2,600.5 | 64 | 306.1 | 65 |
| Lubrizol Advanced Materials | 1,440.3 | 36 | 167.6 | 35 |
| **Total** | **4,040.8** | **100** | **473.7** | **100** |

### Selected Products and Services

Lubrizol Additives
- Compression lubricants
- Corrosion control products
- Fuel additives
  - E-diesel products (non-petroleum based)
- Lubricant additives
  - Engine oils
  - Driveline lubricants
  - Industrial lubricants
  - Viscosity modifiers
- Metalworking additives
- Refinery and oilfield products
- Specialty surfactants
- Terminals
- Toll manufacturing
- Warehousing

Lubrizol Advanced Materials
- Engineered Polymers
  - Chlorinated polyvinyl chloride (TempRite)
  - Foam control additives
  - Reactive liquid polymers (Hycar)
  - Specialty monomers
  - Thermoplastic polyurethane (Estane)
- Performance Coatings
  - Acrylic-based coatings for textiles
  - Dye thickeners and binders
  - Emulsions for specialty paper
  - Glyoxal and glyoxal resins
  - Ink additives
    - Dispersants
    - Ink vehicles
    - Waxes
    - Paints and coatings
    - Polymers for inks and packaging
- Consumer Specialties
  - Food and Beverage
    - Benzoates (sodium and potassium)
    - Flavor and fragrance enhancers
    - Intermediates (phenol, benzaldehyde, benzyl alcohol, and benzoic acid)
    - Natural colors and pigments
  - Personal care and pharmaceuticals
    - Acrylic thickener (Carbopol)
    - Advanced intermediates
    - Amino acid-based actives
    - Cassia gum
    - Colorants
    - Polymeric emulsifier (Pemulen)
    - Polymers for cosmetics and skin care products (Avalure)
    - Resins for hair styling (Fixate)
    - Specialty silicones

## COMPETITORS

Afton Chemical
Avecia
BASF AG
Bayer MaterialScience
Chevron Oronite
Cognis
CP Kelco
Dow Chemical
DSM
FUCHS
Infineum
Reichhold
Rhodia
Rohm and Haas
Symrise

## HISTORICAL FINANCIALS

Company Type: Public

**Income Statement** FYE: December 31

| | REVENUE ($ mil.) | NET INCOME ($ mil.) | NET PROFIT MARGIN | EMPLOYEES |
|---|---|---|---|---|
| **12/06** | 4,041 | 106 | 2.6% | 6,700 |
| **12/05** | 4,043 | 189 | 4.7% | 7,500 |
| **12/04** | 3,160 | 94 | 3.0% | 7,800 |
| **12/03** | 2,052 | 91 | 4.4% | 5,032 |
| **12/02** | 1,984 | 119 | 6.0% | 5,231 |
| **Annual Growth** | 19.5% | (2.8%) | — | 6.4% |

**2006 Year-End Financials**

Debt ratio: 90.1%
Return on equity: 6.4%
Cash ($ mil.): 576
Current ratio: 2.91
Long-term debt ($ mil.): 1,538
No. of shares (mil.): 69
Dividends
Yield: 2.6%
Payout: 85.5%
Market value ($ mil.): 3,460

**Stock History** NYSE: LZ

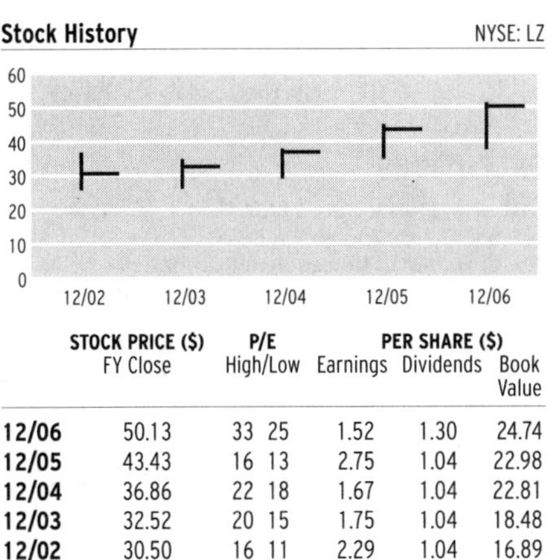


| | STOCK PRICE ($) FY Close | P/E High/Low | PER SHARE ($) Earnings | Dividends | Book Value |
|---|---|---|---|---|---|
| **12/06** | 50.13 | 33 25 | 1.52 | 1.30 | 24.74 |
| **12/05** | 43.43 | 16 13 | 2.75 | 1.04 | 22.98 |
| **12/04** | 36.86 | 22 18 | 1.67 | 1.04 | 22.81 |
| **12/03** | 32.52 | 20 15 | 1.75 | 1.04 | 18.48 |
| **12/02** | 30.50 | 16 11 | 2.29 | 1.04 | 16.89 |
| **Annual Growth** | 13.2% | — — | (9.7%) | 5.7% | 10.0% |

# MacAndrews & Forbes

Through MacAndrews & Forbes Holdings, financier Ron Perelman is focused on cosmetics and cash. The holding company has investments in an array of public and private companies, most notably Revlon (the #3 cosmetics company in the US) and M&F Worldwide (licorice flavors). Perelman is intent on reversing the fortunes of Revlon, which he has controlled since 1985. He made a hefty sum when Consolidated Cigar Holdings (the #1 US cigar maker) was sold to French tobacco maker Seita. Perelman acquired a majority stake in AM General, maker of Humvee and HUMMER vehicles through MacAndrews AMG Holdings. It bought The Rank Group's Deluxe Film operation for some $750 million.

With an 83% stake in Panavision (the #1 provider of cameras for shooting movies and TV shows) through its investment firm PX Holding, MacAndrews & Forbes' purchase of Deluxe Film (which has operations in Hollywood, Rome, and London) in 2006 pairs well in the company's portfolio alongside cosmetics. MacAndrews & Forbes' other holdings include the drug-development company TransTech Pharma (in which it is the largest shareholder) and privately held Allied Security, one of the biggest providers of security guards and systems.

Perelman's holdings have dwindled in value since 1999. Most of the investor's business strategy involves improving his cash position and paying down debt — hence his IPO of Revlon (1996), the sale of The Coleman Company to American Household (formerly Sunbeam Corp., 1998), and the sale of two of Revlon's noncore units. Perelman has committed a $215 million debt-and-equity funding package to rescue Revlon, which is struggling with debt and dwindling market share.

Perelman's sale of The Coleman Company — in the late 1990s — is helping the investor improve his cash flow today. In his suit against Morgan Stanley, Perelman alleged that the investment bank withheld its knowledge of Sunbeam's accounting fraud when Perelman sold The Coleman Company to Sunbeam in 1998 for about $1.5 billion. Perelman's investment (he held 14.1 million shares of Sunbeam stock as part of the sale) later tanked as news broke of the accounting irregularities. Despite an attempt to settle the dispute with Morgan Stanley in 2003 for $20 million, Perelman took the bank to court and was awarded more than $1.5 billion in damages by a Florida jury in mid-2005.

Around the time of his public breakup with wife #4, actress Ellen Barkin, Perelman's MacAndrews & Forbes sold WeddingChannel.com to The Knot in late 2006.

## HISTORY

Ron Perelman grew up working in his father's Philadelphia-based conglomerate, Belmont Industries, but he left at the age of 35 to seek his fortune in New York. In 1978 he bought 40% of jewelry store operator Cohen-Hatfield Industries. The next year Cohen-Hatfield bought a minority stake in MacAndrews & Forbes (licorice flavoring). Cohen-Hatfield acquired MacAndrews & Forbes in 1980.

In 1984 Perelman reshuffled his assets to create MacAndrews & Forbes Holdings, which acquired control of Pantry Pride, a Florida-based supermarket chain, in 1985. Pantry Pride then bought Revlon for $1.8 billion with the help of (convicted felon) Michael Milken. After Perelman acquired Revlon, he added several other cosmetics vendors, including Max Factor and Yves Saint Laurent's fragrance and cosmetic lines.

In 1988 MacAndrews & Forbes agreed to invest $315 million in five failing Texas savings and loans (S&Ls), which Perelman combined and named First Gibraltar (sold to BankAmerica, now Bank of America, in 1993). The next year MacAndrews & Forbes bought The Coleman Company, a maker of outdoor equipment.

With a growing reputation for buying struggling companies, revamping them, and then selling them at a higher price, Perelman bought Marvel Entertainment Group (Marvel Comics) in 1989 and took it public in 1991. That year he sold Revlon's Max Factor and Betrix units to Procter & Gamble for more than $1 billion.

MacAndrews & Forbes acquired 37.5% of TV infomercial producer Guthy-Renker and SCI Television's seven stations and merged them to create New World Television. That company was combined with TV syndicator Genesis Entertainment and TV production house New World Entertainment to create New World Communications Group, which Perelman took public in 1994. That year MacAndrews & Forbes and partner Gerald J. Ford bought Ford Motor's First Nationwide, the US's fifth-largest S&L at that time.

Subsidiaries Mafco Worldwide and Consolidated Cigar Holdings merged with Abex (aircraft parts) to create Mafco Consolidated Group in 1995. Following diminishing comic sales, Perelman placed Marvel in bankruptcy in 1996 and subsequently lost control of the company.

In 1997 First Nationwide bought California thrift Cal Fed Bancorp for $1.2 billion. In addition, Perelman sold New World to Rupert Murdoch's News Corp.

In 1998 Perelman orchestrated a $1.8 billion deal in which First Nationwide merged with Golden State Bancorp to form the US's third-largest thrift. Sunbeam Corp. (now American Household) bought Perelman's stake in Coleman that year, making Perelman a major American Household shareholder. Also in 1998 MacAndrews & Forbes bought a 72% stake in Panavision (movie camera maker, later increased to 91%), invested in WeddingChannel.com (sold in 2006), and sold its 64% stake in Consolidated Cigar to French tobacco giant Seita (netting Perelman a smoking $350 million profit).

Still burdened by debt, Revlon sold its professional products business in 2000.

Perelman's stock in American Household was rendered worthless when the company initiated bankruptcy proceedings in February 2001. (It would emerge from bankruptcy, however, in December 2002.) He also was sued by angry shareholders after the board of M&F Worldwide, the licorice company he controls, bought Perelman's stock in Panavision at more than five times its market value. In order to settle the litigation surrounding the purchase, in 2002 M&F agreed to return Perelman's 83% stake in Panavision to Mafco. Golden State Bancorp also left the MacAndrews fold in 2002 when it was acquired by Citigroup.

MacAndrews & Forbes Holdings acquired Allied Security, the largest independent provider of contract security services and products in the US, from Gryphon Investors in February 2003 for an undisclosed sum.

## EXECUTIVES

**Chairman and CEO:** Ronald O. (Ron) Perelman, age 64
**Co-Chairman; President and CEO, Panavision:** Robert L. (Bob) Beitcher
**Co-Vice Chairman and Chief Administrative Officer:** Howard Gittis, age 73
**EVP and General Counsel:** Barry F. Schwartz, age 58
**SVP, Corporate Affairs:** Christine Taylor
**VP and Controller:** Norman J. Ginstling
**President, MacAndrews & Forbes Acquisition Holdings:** Samuel L. (Sam) Katz

## LOCATIONS

**HQ:** MacAndrews & Forbes Holdings Inc.
35 E. 62nd St., New York, NY 10021
**Phone:** 212-572-8600 **Fax:** 212-572-8400
**Web:** www.macandrewsandforbes.com

MacAndrews & Forbes Holdings' consumer products operations are principally in the US.

## PRODUCTS/OPERATIONS

**Selected Holdings**

AM General (70%, multipurpose and military vehicles)
Allied Security (leading provider of security guards and systems)
American Household (about 37%, small appliances and Coleman camping gear)
Deluxe Film (film production)
M&F Worldwide Corp. (32%, licorice extract)
Revlon Inc. (83%, cosmetics and personal care products)
TransTech Pharma (drug development company)

## COMPETITORS

Alberto-Culver
Alticor
Avon
BAE Systems
Body Shop
Boeing
Chattem
Colgate-Palmolive
Dial
Estée Lauder
General Dynamics
Guardsmark
iRobot
Johnson & Johnson
Kellwood
Lockheed Martin
L'Oréal USA
LVMH
Mary Kay
Procter & Gamble
Ulta
Unilever
Wackenhut

## HISTORICAL FINANCIALS

Company Type: Private

**Income Statement** FYE: December 31*

| | ESTIMATED REVENUE ($ mil.) | NET INCOME ($ mil.) | NET PROFIT MARGIN | EMPLOYEES |
|---|---|---|---|---|
| 6/07 | 2,148 | — | — | 44,000 |

*Fiscal year change

# Macy's, Inc.

The nation's #1 department store chain has adopted the name of its most famous brand and cash cow: Macy's. Macy's, Inc. (formerly Federated Department Stores) operates more than 825 stores nationwide and rings up some $27 billion in annual sales. The name change comes on the heels of its acquisition of rival May Department Stores in 2005. The retail giant operates seven regional divisions: Macy's East, Macy's Florida, Macy's Midwest, Macy's North, Macy's Northwest, Macy's South, and Macy's West, and the upscale Bloomingdale's chain. The department stores sell men's, women's, and children's apparel and accessories, cosmetics, and home furnishings, among other things.

CEO Terry Lundgren is on a mission to reinvent the American department store by making it more relevant to younger consumers, who tend to shop elsewhere. In fact, the plan for Macy's is to promote it as "America's department store."

In a deal with Martha Stewart Living Omnimedia, the domestic diva's design team has agreed to develop a new line of Martha Stewart Collection merchandise for the home that includes bed and bath textiles, housewares, casual dinnerware, flatware and glassware, cookware, and more, slated to debut in all Macy's stores in the fall of 2007.

But the road to success has been bumpy. Amid slow sales in early 2007, the company decided to take its advertising to a wider audience via TV advertisements to aggressively promote sales at its Macy's stores, instead of relying on direct mail avenues. Also, disgruntled Chicagoans, upset over renaming of the 62-store Marshall Field's chain to Macy's, have been boycotting its stores.

With its future clearly staked on its Macy's stores, the company has cleaned house of some 65 overlapping stores and divested extraneous businesses, including its bridal division. In early 2007, the David's Bridal chain of 270 stores was sold to buyout firm Leonard Green & Partners for about $750 million. (The deal also included 10 Priscilla of Boston locations.) Soon after unloading David's Bridal, Federated sold the 500-plus store After Hours Formalwear business to The Men's Wearhouse for about $100 million.

AXA Financial owns 11% of the company.

## HISTORY

In 1929 Fred Lazarus, who controlled Columbus, Ohio's giant F&R Lazarus department store and the John Shillito Company (the oldest department store west of the Alleghenies; 1830), met with three other great retailers on a yacht in Long Island Sound: Walter Rothschild of Brooklyn-based Abraham & Straus; Louis Kirstein of Boston-based Filene's; and Samuel Bloomingdale, head of Manhattan's Bloomingdale's. Lazarus, Rothschild, and Kirstein agreed to merge their stores into a loose federation. Bloomingdale joined the next year.

Though Federated set up headquarters in Cincinnati in 1945, it continued to be run by powerful merchants in each city where it operated. Under Lazarus' leadership, it was among the first to see the coming growth of the Sunbelt, acquiring Foley's (Houston, 1945), Burdines (Miami, 1956), Sanger's (Dallas, 1958), Bullock's and I. Magnin (California, 1964), and Rich's (Atlanta, 1976).

Federated's growth stalled after Lazarus' son Ralph stepped down in 1981. The company faced stiffer competition from rival department store operators and chains, including May Department Stores, Nordstrom, and Dillard's. By 1989 Federated was no longer a leader, although it was still financially strong.

Years before, when Federated was leader of the department store industry, Allied Stores was #2. Allied was made up mostly of stores that were in small towns or were #2 in their market, with a few leaders (Maas Brothers, The Bon Marché, Jordan Marsh). It had a mediocre track record until Thomas Macioce took the helm in 1971. He closed unprofitable stores, downsized others, and went on an acquisition spree (Brooks Brothers, Ann Taylor).

Campeau Corporation bought Allied and Federated in 1988. Saddled with more than $8 billion in debt from the purchase, both companies declared bankruptcy in 1990. Allen Questrom became Federated's CEO, and in 1992 the companies emerged from bankruptcy as Federated Department Stores.

The next year, after being rebuffed in a bid to merge with Macy's, Federated purchased 50% of Macy's unsecured debt, setting the stage for Federated's 1994 acquisition of the respected department store.

Rowland Macy opened a store under his name in Manhattan in 1858. After Macy's death, the Strauses, a New York china merchant family, bought the department store in 1896 and expanded it across the US. In 1986 chairman Edward Finkelstein led a $3.5 billion buyout of Macy's and took it private. Its debt load increased into the early 1990s, and Macy's entered bankruptcy proceedings in 1992.

In 1995 Federated bought the 82-store Broadway Stores. Questrom quit (under longstanding tensions with Federated) in 1997, succeeded by president James Zimmerman. In 1998 the firm paid $10.6 million to settle complaints that it illegally collected debts from bankrupt credit card holders.

In February 2003 COO Terry J. Lundgren succeeded Zimmerman as CEO of the company. Zimmerman remained chairman of Federated and five vice chairs were appointed in a major reorganization of Federated's top management. Zimmerman resigned in January 2004, and Lundgren took on the chairman title.

On August 30, 2005, Federated completed its $11 billion acquisition of rival May Department Stores. In 2006 Federated completed the first of two transactions in its sale of the May Company's credit card receivables to Citigroup, for about $753 million. The second transaction was completed in mid-July for $1 billion.

In October Federated completed the sale of its 48-store Lord & Taylor department store chain to NRDC Equity Partners LLC for nearly $1.1 billion. Lord & Taylor operates stores in a dozen states and the District of Columbia.

Adopting the name of its most famous brand, Federated changed its corporate name to Macy's, Inc. in June 2007. Along with its name, the department store operator changed its ticker symbol to "M" on the New York Stock Exchange.

## EXECUTIVES

**Chairman, President, and CEO:** Terry J. Lundgren, age 55, $1,383,333 pay
**Vice Chair, Legal, Human Resources, Internal Audit and External Affairs:** Thomas G. Cody, age 65, $1,017,500 pay
**Vice Chair, Support Operations; Chairman, Federated Logistics, Federated Systems Group, and Financial, Administrative, and Credit Services:** Thomas L. (Tom) Cole, age 56, $908,333 pay
**Vice Chair, Merchandising, Private Brand and Product Development; Chairman and CEO, Macy's Merchandising Group (MMG):** Janet E. Grove, age 56, $908,333 pay
**Vice Chair, Department Store Divisions:** Susan D. Kronick, age 55, $1,067,500 pay
**EVP and CFO:** Karen M. Hoguet, age 50, $766,667 pay
**EVP, Ready-to-Wear and Children's:** Marcia Haimbach
**SVP, General Counsel, and Secretary:** Dennis J. Broderick, age 58
**SVP, Human Resources:** David W. Clark, age 51
**VP, Area Research:** Cynthia Ray Walker
**VP and Controller:** Joel A. Belsky, age 53
**VP, Corporate Communications and External Affairs:** James A. (Jim) Sluzewski, age 48
**VP, Diversity and Deputy General Counsel:** William L. (Bill) Hawthorne III, age 48
**VP, Employee Relations:** John Michael (Michael) Zorn, age 48
**VP, Internal Audit:** Felicia Williams, age 38
**VP, Investor Relations:** Susan Robinson
**VP, Tax:** Bradley R. Mays
**Chairman and CEO, Bloomingdale's:** Michael (Mike) Gould
**Chairman and CEO, macys.com, President, Macy's Corporate Marketing, and Chief Marketing Officer:** Peter R. Sachse, age 49
**Chairman and CEO, Macy's Home Store:** Timothy M. (Tim) Adams, age 51
**Auditors:** KPMG LLP

## LOCATIONS

**HQ:** Macy's, Inc.
7 W. 7th St., Cincinnati, OH 45202
**Phone:** 513-579-7000 **Fax:** 513-579-7555
**Web:** www.federated-fds.com

Federated Department Stores operates more than 850 department stores in 45 states, the District of Columbia, Guam, and Puerto Rico.

## PRODUCTS/OPERATIONS

### 2007 Sales

| | % of total |
|---|---|
| Women's accessories, intimate apparel, shoes & cosmetics | 35 |
| Women's apparel | 28 |
| Men's & children's | 22 |
| Home & miscellaneous | 15 |
| **Total** | **100** |

### 2007 Stores

| | No. |
|---|---|
| Macy's East | 190 |
| Macy's West | 190 |
| Macy's South | 133 |
| Macy's Midwest | 114 |
| Macy's Northwest | 68 |
| Macy's North | 63 |
| Macy's Florida | 60 |
| Bloomingdale's | 38 |
| **Total** | **856** |

### Private Labels

Alfani (women's and men's apparel)
American Rag Cie. (casual sportswear for juniors and young men)
Charter Club (women's and men's apparel, home furnishings)
First Impressions (infant and layette apparel)
Greendog (children's apparel)
Hotel Collection (sheets, towels, tabletop, and barware)
I.N.C (casual and career fashions for men and women)
ML/Material London (men's sportswear, suits, shoes)
Style & Co. (sportswear & casual apparel)
Tasso Elba (menswear)
The Cellar (housewares and related home merchandise)
Tools of the Trade (cookware, bakeware, cutlery, and kitchen gadgets)

## COMPETITORS

AnnTaylor
Bed Bath & Beyond
Belk
Brown Shoe
Dillard's
Eddie Bauer Holdings
Foot Locker
Gap
J. C. Penney
J. Crew
Jos. A. Bank
Kohl's
Lands' End
Limited Brands
Linens 'n Things
Men's Wearhouse
Neiman Marcus
Nine West
Nordstrom
Old Navy
Polo Ralph Lauren
Saks Inc.
Sears
Stage Stores
Talbots
Target
TJX Companies
Wal-Mart
Zale

## HISTORICAL FINANCIALS

Company Type: Public

**Income Statement** FYE: Saturday nearest January 31

| | REVENUE ($ mil.) | NET INCOME ($ mil.) | NET PROFIT MARGIN | EMPLOYEES |
|---|---|---|---|---|
| **1/07** | 26,970 | 995 | 3.7% | 188,000 |
| **1/06** | 22,390 | 1,406 | 6.3% | 232,000 |
| **1/05** | 15,630 | 689 | 4.4% | 112,000 |
| **1/04** | 15,264 | 693 | 4.5% | 111,000 |
| **1/03** | 15,435 | 818 | 5.3% | 113,000 |
| **Annual Growth** | 15.0% | 5.0% | — | 13.6% |

### 2007 Year-End Financials

Debt ratio: 64.0%
Return on equity: 7.7%
Cash ($ mil.): 1,211
Current ratio: 1.17
Long-term debt ($ mil.): 7,847
No. of shares (mil.): —
Dividends
Yield: —
Payout: —
Market value ($ mil.): —

### Stock History NYSE: M

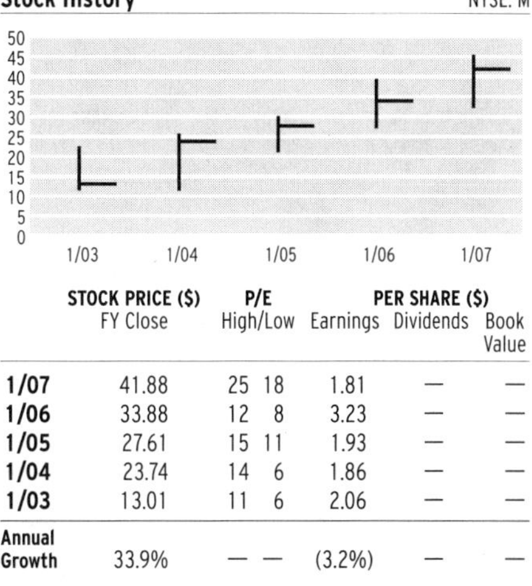


| | STOCK PRICE ($) FY Close | P/E High | P/E Low | PER SHARE ($) Earnings | Dividends | Book Value |
|---|---|---|---|---|---|---|
| **1/07** | 41.88 | 25 | 18 | 1.81 | — | — |
| **1/06** | 33.88 | 12 | 8 | 3.23 | — | — |
| **1/05** | 27.61 | 15 | 11 | 1.93 | — | — |
| **1/04** | 23.74 | 14 | 6 | 1.86 | — | — |
| **1/03** | 13.01 | 11 | 6 | 2.06 | — | — |
| **Annual Growth** | 33.9% | — | — | (3.2%) | — | — |

# Magellan Health Services

Magellan Health Services has a new charter. Once a power in the psychiatric hospital field, the company has repositioned itself as one of the largest managed behavioral health care companies in the nation. The company manages mental health, employee assistance, and work/life programs through its nationwide provider network that consists of about 70,000 behavioral health professionals. Magellan also provides specialty pharmaceutical management and radiology benefits management, with all programs serving more than 100 million members. Magellan emerged from Chapter 11 bankruptcy in January 2004.

Magellan sold its human services unit, which offered at-home care for sufferers of chronic disorders. The company plans to expand by developing new products, as well as growing through acquisitions. In 2006 Magellan bought National Imaging Associates (NIA), a provider of radiology benefits management services. ICORE Healthcare's specialty pharmaceutical management was also added to the fold in 2006. Both companies now operate as subsidiaries of Magellan. Magellan has targeted radiology benefits management and specialty pharmaceutical management for future growth opportunities.

## HISTORY

William Fickling, once a star basketball player at Auburn University, started his career in his father's real estate office in Georgia. In 1969 Fickling founded Charter Medical as a holding company for the family's six nursing homes and one hospital. The company went public in 1971 as an owner/manager of general acute care hospitals. By the mid-1980s it had focused on psychiatric facilities and was adding addiction treatment centers to its portfolio. Charter had 63 psychiatric and 13 acute care hospitals by 1987, when Fickling engineered a $1.4 billion LBO, largely funded by the company's employee stock ownership plan (ESOP), which ended up owning 68% of the company, with Fickling owning the rest.

By 1989 Charter was in trouble. Not only was it dogged by Medicare and Medicaid fraud probes, but Fickling was accused of cheating the ESOP, which had purchased another 13% of the company from him at allegedly inflated prices. (A month after that sale, Fickling announced accounting errors that cut operating income by $26 million and the ESOP's stake plummeted.) In 1992 the Medicare fraud charges were settled for $1.9 million; a suit related to the ESOP stock sale was settled for $82 million.

But Charter's problems ran deeper — the industry itself was in flux. New treatments and managed care restrictions reduced the average stay for psychiatric patients from 26 days to 20 by 1991. Stories of abuses in the psychiatric industry surfaced, and payers were demanding fewer hospitalizations and more outpatient care. Undaunted, but deeply in debt, Charter continued to build inpatient facilities, bringing losses.

The company went into Chapter 11 in 1991, emerging in 1992 with a plan to focus on behavioral health care; it also went public again. The next year Fickling left Charter and was eventually replaced by E. Mac Crawford. As part of its plan, Charter sold its general hospitals and bought 40 psychiatric hospitals from National Medical Enterprises (now Tenet Healthcare) in 1994; it also began offering outpatient and home care services. That year Charter relocated to Atlanta.

As part of its reorganization, Charter in 1995 bought Magellan Health Services and took that name. It also bought 51% of Green Spring Health Services, a managed care company specializing in mental health and substance abuse. (It bought the rest in 1998.)

Reorganization costs and corporate cutbacks on mental health benefits brought losses until 1996, when it posted its only profit of the decade amid the increasing privatization of government psychiatric care. Seeing fast growth in managed care, Magellan sold its psychiatric hospitals to Crescent Operating in 1997, using the money to buy two more managed behavioral care companies. Magellan and Crescent created joint venture Charter Behavioral Health Systems (CBHS) to run the psychiatric facilities under the Charter name.

In 1998 Crawford was succeeded by Henry Harbin, a founder of Green Spring. In 1999 Magellan sold its European operations, and relocated to Columbia, Maryland. With CBHS flailing, Magellan gave Crescent all but 10% of the hospital firm, which filed for bankruptcy in 2000. While making plans to sell its specialty managed health care segment, Magellan also agreed to sell human services segment National Mentor in a management buyout. The National Mentor sale closed in 2001, when Magellan also began its exit from its stake in CBHS. The company is now engaged in the managed behavioral health care business only.

In 2003, weak earnings and high debt prompted Magellan to file for Chapter 11 bankruptcy.

In January 2004, Magellan emerged from Chapter 11 bankruptcy.

## EXECUTIVES

**Chairman and CEO:** Steven J. (Steve) Shulman, age 53, $3,492,949 pay
**President, COO, and Director:** René Lerer, age 49, $1,645,769 pay
**EVP and CFO:** Mark S. Demilio, age 49, $1,174,295 pay
**SVP, Aetna Division:** Dennis P. Moody, age 44
**SVP and Controller:** Jeffrey N. West
**SVP, Employer Solutions:** Michael Alexander
**SVP, Health Plan Solutions East:** Suzanne Kunis
**SVP, Investor Relations:** Melissa L. Rose
**SVP, Sales, Health and Insurance Markets:** Jay Youell
**VP, Public Relations and Communications:** Erin S. Somers
**Chief Branding and Communications Officer:** Christopher W. (Chris) Cooney
**Chief Human Resources Officer:** Caskie Lewis-Clapper
**CIO:** Jeff D. Emerson, age 57, $570,000 pay
**Chief Sales and Marketing Officer:** Michael Majerik
**Chief Medical Officer:** Alex Rodriguez
**Chairman, National Imaging Associates:** John J. Donahue
**CEO, National Imaging Associates:** Eric Reimer
**COO, Public Sector Solutions:** Russell C. Petrella
**General Counsel:** Daniel N. Gregoire
**Media Relations Specialist:** Kristin L. Brunnworth
**Auditors:** Ernst & Young LLP

## LOCATIONS

**HQ:** Magellan Health Services, Inc.
55 Nod Rd., Avon, CT 06001
**Phone:** 860-507-1900 **Fax:** 860-507-1990
**Web:** www.magellanhealth.com

Magellan Health Services operates nationwide.

## PRODUCTS/OPERATIONS

**2006 Sales**

| | $ mil. | % of total |
|---|---|---|
| Public sector solutions | 808.7 | 48 |
| Health plan solutions | 656.0 | 39 |
| Employer solutions | 128.8 | 8 |
| Specialty pharmaceutical management | 55.2 | 3 |
| Radiology benefits management | 41.6 | 2 |
| **Total** | **1,690.3** | **100** |

## COMPETITORS

APS Healthcare
Comprehensive Care
Horizon Health
Mental Health Network
Premier Behavioral Solutions
US Oncology
ValueOptions

## HISTORICAL FINANCIALS

Company Type: Public

**Income Statement** FYE: December 31

| | REVENUE ($ mil.) | NET INCOME ($ mil.) | NET PROFIT MARGIN | EMPLOYEES |
|---|---|---|---|---|
| **12/06** | 1,690 | 86 | 5.1% | 3,900 |
| **12/05** | 1,808 | 131 | 7.2% | 3,900 |
| **12/04** | 1,795 | 88 | 4.9% | 4,300 |
| **12/03*** | 1,511 | 452 | 29.9% | 4,700 |
| **9/02** | 1,753 | (729) | — | 4,620 |
| **Annual Growth** | (0.9%) | — | — | (4.1%) |

*Fiscal year change

**2006 Year-End Financials**

Debt ratio: 1.8%
Return on equity: 12.4%
Cash ($ mil.): 357
Current ratio: 1.67
Long-term debt ($ mil.): 14
No. of shares (mil.): 38
Dividends
Yield: —
Payout: —
Market value ($ mil.): 1,633

**Stock History** NASDAQ (GS): MGLN

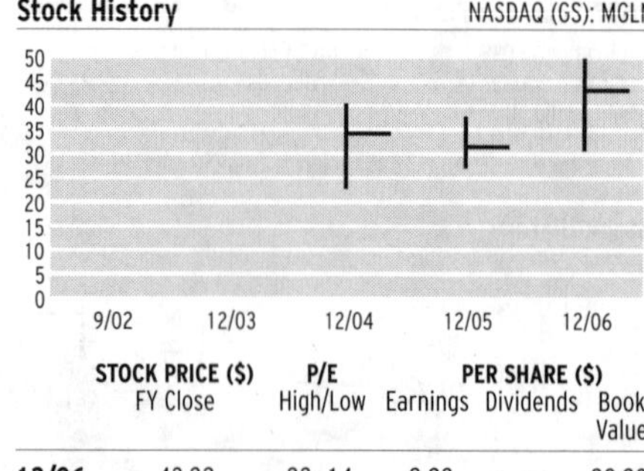


| | STOCK PRICE ($) FY Close | P/E High | P/E Low | PER SHARE ($) Earnings | Dividends | Book Value |
|---|---|---|---|---|---|---|
| **12/06** | 43.22 | 22 | 14 | 2.23 | — | 20.20 |
| **12/05** | 31.45 | 11 | 8 | 3.46 | — | 17.30 |
| **12/04** | 34.16 | 16 | 10 | 2.43 | — | 18.49 |
| **Annual Growth** | 12.5% | — | — | (4.2%) | — | 4.5% |

# The Manitowoc Company

Ice, cranes, and ship repairs — no, it's not a sequel to the movie *Titanic;* it's the business of The Manitowoc Company. The company makes ice-making, beverage-dispensing, and refrigerating products, as well as cranes and other material-handling equipment. Its ice-making and beverage-dispensing machines serve the restaurant, hospitality, and convenience store markets. Manitowoc sells its boom cranes, tower cranes, telescopic cranes, and related equipment to companies in the construction and mining industries. The company, which began at the turn of the 20th century as a shipbuilder, also has a marine segment with shipyards that build, service, and repair commercial and military vessels.

Manitowoc tends to be acquisitive — particularly in the foodservice and crane sectors.

In 2006 Manitowoc attempted to make a $1.8 billion bid for the UK commercial foodservice concern Enodis; the offer was rebuffed. Enodis then warmed to the idea after Manitowoc said informally that any future bid would be higher. Enodis granted Manitowoc due diligence access to its books, but after a period of looking more closely at each others' operations, the two companies walked away from discussions.

The following year the company picked up the Carrydeck line of mobile industrial cranes from privately held Marine Travelift. The move enhances Manitowoc's position in industrial cranes with the addition of six models. Later in 2007 the company bolstered its international presence with the purchase of India's Shirke Construction Equipments Pvt. Ltd., a maker of tower cranes.

## HISTORY

Manitowoc began in 1902 when naval architect Charles West and shipbuilder Elias Gunnell bought a shipyard. The company grew during WWI, but the government canceled its contracts at war's end. After feuding with Gunnell, West bought Manitowoc (he would run it until his death in 1957) and diversified into industrial equipment. Crane manufacturing helped Manitowoc survive the Depression. During WWII Manitowoc built submarines and landing craft. After the war the company branched out into freezers and dry-cleaning machines.

A recession and oil-patch bust in the 1980s caused Manitowoc's sales to plummet. By the decade's end, aging product lines had stalled earnings growth. CEO Fred Butler ended the company's shipbuilding operations and focused it on repairing vessels instead. It also modernized its cranes and broadened its product line through acquisitions in 1990. From 1994 to 1998 the company grew six-fold, largely through acquisitions.

In 1998 Manitowoc improved earnings by buying boom truck and forklift maker Powerscreen USC and by expanding into Europe with a 50% stake in Italy-based ice-machine maker F.A.G. That year Butler retired and Terry Growcock, president of subsidiary Manitowoc Ice, became CEO.

Manitowoc bought Purchasing Support Group, a beverage equipment distributor with broad US regional reach, in 1999. The next year Manitowoc boosted its cranes and related equipment business by acquiring Pioneer Holdings (hydraulic boom trucks). It also acquired Harford Duracool, a maker of walk-in refrigerators and freezers in the eastern US, and Marinette Marine, a Great Lakes shipyard (which added a significant shipbuilding business to its marine repair operations).

In 2001 the company bought Legris Industries' Potain tower crane unit. Manitowoc then added mobile cranes to its crane business in 2002 by acquiring Grove Worldwide for about $270 million. In 2002 Terry Growcock, the company's CEO, was also named as chairman, a post that had been vacant for 10 years.

In early 2003 Manitowoc sold its Manitowoc Boom Trucks unit to Quantum Heavy Equipment, LLC. The company sold this unit in order to satisfy an order set by the Justice Department to complete the acquisition of Grove Worldwide.

In 2004 the company sold its Delta Manlift subsidiary to JLG Industries, exiting the aerial platform business. The following year it sold its Diversified Refrigeration, Inc. (DRI) subsidiary to a subsidiary of GE.

## EXECUTIVES

**Chairman:** Terry D. Growcock, age 61
**President, CEO, and Director:** Glen E. Tellock, age 46
**SVP, CFO, and Treasurer:** Carl J. Laurino, age 45, $275,000 pay
**SVP, Human Resources and Administration:** Thomas G. Musial, age 55, $315,000 pay
**SVP, Secretary, and General Counsel:** Maurice D. Jones, age 47
**SVP; President, Manitowoc Marine:** Robert P. (Bob) Herre, age 54
**SVP; President, Foodservice Group:** Mike Kachmer, age 48
**VP, Corporate Development:** Mary Ellen Bowers, age 50
**VP, Finance and Controller:** Dean J. Nolden, age 38
**VP, Global Procurement:** Robert E. Ward
**Director, Investor Relations and Corporate Communications:** Steven C. Khail
**Auditors:** PricewaterhouseCoopers LLP

## LOCATIONS

**HQ:** The Manitowoc Company, Inc.
2400 S. 44th St., Manitowoc, WI 54221
**Phone:** 920-684-4410 **Fax:** 920-652-9778
**Web:** www.manitowoc.com

The Manitowoc Company has operations in the US in Arkansas, California, Indiana, Maryland, Nevada, Ohio, Pennsylvania, Tennessee, and Wisconsin, and international operations in China, France, Germany, Italy, Mexico, Portugal, and the UK.

### 2006 Sales

| | $ mil. | % of total |
|---|---|---|
| North America | | |
| US | 1,535.1 | 52 |
| Other countries | 80.5 | 2 |
| Europe | 817.0 | 30 |
| Asia | 170.4 | 5 |
| Middle East | 167.8 | 5 |
| Central & South America | 54.0 | 2 |
| Australia | 52.9 | 2 |
| Africa | 50.6 | 2 |
| South Pacific & Caribbean | 5.0 | — |
| **Total** | **2,933.3** | **100** |

## PRODUCTS/OPERATIONS

### 2006 Sales

| | $ mil. | % of total |
|---|---|---|
| Cranes & related products | 2,235.4 | 76 |
| Foodservice equipment | 415.4 | 14 |
| Marine | 282.5 | 10 |
| **Total** | **2,933.3** | **100** |

### Selected Products and Services

Cranes and Related Products
- Aftermarket replacement parts
- Crane rebuilding and remanufacturing services
- Hydraulically powered telescopic boom trucks
- Lattice-boom crawler cranes
- Mobile telescopic cranes
- Mountable telescopic cranes
- Slewing and self-erecting cranes
- Tower cranes
- Truck-mounted lattice-boom cranes

Food Service Equipment
- Cast aluminum cold plates
- Commercial ice-cube machines
- Compressor racks
- Food-prep tables
- Ice-storage bins
- Ice and beverage dispensers
- Ice-cube machines
- Long-draw beer dispensing systems
- Post mix beverage-dispensing valves
- Reach-in refrigerators and freezers
- Refrigerated undercounters
- Walk-in refrigerators and freezers

Marine Operations
- Ballasting systems
- Cargo handling
- Conversion services
- Drydocking
- Inspections and surveys
- New construction services
- Repowering
- Retrofitting
- Ship repair services

## COMPETITORS

Aga Foodservice
Altec Industries
American Panel
BAE Systems Ship Repair
Baltija Shipbuilding
Bollinger Shipyards
Delfield
Enodis Corp.
Furukawa
Hitachi
Ingersoll-Rand Climate Control
JLG Industries
Kobelco Construction Machinery America
Lancer
Liebherr International
Reddy Ice
Scotsman Group
Sumitomo Heavy Industries
Terex
UpRight
VT Shipbuilding

## HISTORICAL FINANCIALS

Company Type: Public

### Income Statement

FYE: December 31

| | REVENUE ($ mil.) | NET INCOME ($ mil.) | NET PROFIT MARGIN | EMPLOYEES |
|---|---|---|---|---|
| **12/06** | 2,933 | 166 | 5.7% | 9,500 |
| **12/05** | 2,254 | 66 | 2.9% | 8,000 |
| **12/04** | 1,964 | 39 | 2.0% | 7,600 |
| **12/03** | 1,571 | 4 | 0.2% | 7,700 |
| **12/02** | 1,407 | (21) | — | 7,800 |
| **Annual Growth** | 20.2% | — | — | 5.1% |

### 2006 Year-End Financials

Debt ratio: 34.1%
Return on equity: 25.2%
Cash ($ mil.): 191
Current ratio: 1.22
Long-term debt ($ mil.): 264
No. of shares (mil.): 62
Dividends
Yield: 0.2%
Payout: 3.8%
Market value ($ mil.): 3,692

### Stock History

NYSE: MTW

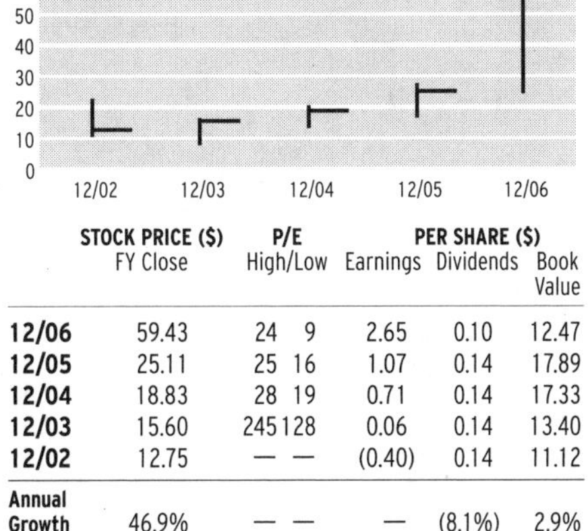


| | STOCK PRICE ($) FY Close | P/E High | P/E Low | PER SHARE ($) Earnings | PER SHARE ($) Dividends | PER SHARE ($) Book Value |
|---|---|---|---|---|---|---|
| **12/06** | 59.43 | 24 | 9 | 2.65 | 0.10 | 12.47 |
| **12/05** | 25.11 | 25 | 16 | 1.07 | 0.14 | 17.89 |
| **12/04** | 18.83 | 28 | 19 | 0.71 | 0.14 | 17.33 |
| **12/03** | 15.60 | 245 | 128 | 0.06 | 0.14 | 13.40 |
| **12/02** | 12.75 | — | — | (0.40) | 0.14 | 11.12 |
| **Annual Growth** | 46.9% | — | — | — | (8.1%) | 2.9% |

# Manor Care

Manor Care is a lord of the manor in the nursing home kingdom. Operating as HCR Manor Care, the company runs about 275 nursing homes in 30 states under the Heartland and ManorCare names, along with another 65 assisted-living and outpatient facilities (some operating under the Arden Courts and Springhouse names). Some of its centers house specialty units that provide post-acute medical care, rehabilitation therapy, and services for Alzheimer's patients. Manor Care also offers hospice and home health services through offices in 25 states. It has sold its medical transcription business, which converted medical dictation into electronic patient records.

More than 60% of Manor Care's long-term care facilities are in Florida, Illinois, Michigan, Ohio, and Pennsylvania.

In addition to its long-term care, hospice, and home health operations, Manor Care provides rehabilitation therapy at its own outpatient clinics, as well as third-party sites, such as schools, workplaces, and hospitals. Its outpatient business operates in the Midwest and Mid-Atlantic states, as well as Texas and Florida.

Manor Care gets two-thirds of its long-term care revenue from Medicare and Medicaid. In response to falling reimbursement rates, the company has shifted its focus to seeking out patients that require more complex care (over a shorter period of time) that is reimbursed at higher levels. This shift in patient mix has resulted in the growth of its post-acute business, which cares for patients recovering from chronic illness, serious injury, or surgery.

The company also intends to grow through selective acquisitions and construction of new facilities. It opened one new nursing facility in 2005 and built two more the following year. It has grown its home health and hospice segment during the same time period through a number of small acquisitions.

Manor Care has announced that it has agreed to be acquired and taken private by private equity firm The Carlyle Group.

Janus Capital holds about 11% of the company. T. Rowe Price owns 7% of Manor Care. Iridian Asset Management and Wellington Management each own about 6%.

## HISTORY

The new Manor Care has its roots in an Ohio lumber company bought by the Wolfe family in the mid-1940s. Over the next two decades the business diversified into mortgages and real estate development. By 1975 the company (by then renamed Wolfe Industries) had begun acquiring nursing homes. In 1981 Wolfe spun off its non-nursing home interests and created Health Care and Retirement Corporation of America (HCR) from what remained. HCR went public that year and continued making acquisitions.

Looking to diversify, glass and plastics maker Owens-Illinois bought HCR in 1984 and later added other health care operations, including long-term skilled nursing care, rehabilitation, and specialty care services. Owens-Illinois was taken private in a Kohlberg Kravis Roberts leveraged buyout in 1987; in 1991 HCR and related health care operations were sold to a group led by Paul Ormond, who had headed Owens-Illinois' health care business since 1986. Ormond took HCR public again that year.

HCR's acquisition strategy expanded to include partnerships and other ventures, as well as the opening of specialty units and the construction and development of new facilities. Under Ormond, HCR concentrated on attracting Medicare and private-pay patients, who were more profitable than Medicaid (i.e., public aid) patients.

As part of the effort to diversify beyond nursing homes, HCR in the 1990s added vision care (forming Vision Management Services to provide financing and management for eye-related medical practices, 1991), short-term rehabilitation, home health care (Heartland Home Health Services, 1991; enlarged through the acquisition of Allan Home Health Care and Hospice, 1995), and pharmacy services (through a joint venture to supply nursing homes, 1994).

In 1997 the company acquired MileStone Healthcare, a top provider of program management services for subacute care and acute rehabilitation programs. But it was still not enough. The company's 1998 purchase of larger rival Manor Care more than doubled its size, although related costs hammered earnings.

The next year the company took the more widely recognized Manor Care name. It partnered with Alterra Healthcare (formerly Alternative Living Services) to build and operate Alzheimer's and assisted-living residences and to provide management services for about 30 assisted-living and Alzheimer's care residences located outside Manor Care's core operating areas.

Also in 1999, Manor Care was hit with a suit by Genesis Health Ventures, claiming that it had bought Vitalink, a nursing home pharmacy services company, from Manor Care with the understanding that service contracts with Manor Care homes would remain in effect for several years (the new Manor Care terminated the contracts soon after the merger). The company also faced regulatory and legal actions in several states over infractions of patient care rules.

In 2000, Manor Care nixed separate buyout bids led by chairman Stewart Bainum Jr. and another management group. It also bought the percentage of In Home Health (a home health care provider) that it didn't already own, and absorbed the firm into its own operations. Also in 2000, the company opened 10 new Alzheimer's assisted living centers. In 2001, the company was less acquisitive.

## EXECUTIVES

**Chairman, President, and CEO:** Paul A. Ormond, age 57, $2,761,531 pay
**EVP, COO, and Director:** Stephen L. Guillard, age 56
**VP and CFO:** Steven M. (Steve) Cavanaugh, age 36
**VP and General Manager of Central Division:** Nancy A. Edwards, age 55
**VP, Procurement:** R. Michael Ferguson
**VP and General Manager Mid-Atlantic Division:** Jeffrey A. Grillo, age 47
**VP and General Manager Midwest Division, and Director of Marketing:** Larry C. Lester, age 63
**VP and Controller:** Spencer C. Moler, age 58
**VP and General Manager West Division:** F. Joseph Schmitt, age 57
**VP and General Manager Southeast Division:** Lynn M. Hood, age 44
**VP and General Manager Assisted Living Division:** Michael J. Reed, age 54
**VP and General Counsel:** Richard A. Parr II, age 49
**Auditors:** Ernst & Young LLP

## LOCATIONS

**HQ:** Manor Care, Inc.
333 N. Summit St., Toledo, OH 43604
**Phone:** 419-252-5500 **Fax:** 419-252-5554
**Web:** www.hcr-manorcare.com

## PRODUCTS/OPERATIONS

### 2006 Sales

| | $ mil. | % of total |
|---|---|---|
| Long-term care | 3,009.0 | 83 |
| Hospice & home health | 479.3 | 13 |
| Other | 124.9 | 4 |
| **Total** | **3,613.2** | **100** |

### Selected Subsidiaries and Affiliates

HCR Home Health Care and Hospice, Inc.
Health Care and Retirement Corporation of America
Heartland Rehabilitation Services, Inc.
ManorCare Health Services, Inc.
MileStone Healthcare, Inc.

## COMPETITORS

Advocat
American HomePatient
Assisted Living Concepts
Balanced Care
Emeritus
Extendicare
Gentiva
Golden Horizons
Kindred Healthcare
Life Care Centers
Mariner Health Care
Sun Healthcare
Sunrise Senior Living
Tender Loving Care

## HISTORICAL FINANCIALS

Company Type: Public

### Income Statement

FYE: December 31

| | REVENUE ($ mil.) | NET INCOME ($ mil.) | NET PROFIT MARGIN | EMPLOYEES |
|---|---|---|---|---|
| **12/06** | 3,613 | 167 | 4.6% | 59,500 |
| **12/05** | 3,417 | 161 | 4.7% | 58,000 |
| **12/04** | 3,209 | 168 | 5.2% | 59,400 |
| **12/03** | 3,029 | 119 | 3.9% | 61,000 |
| **12/02** | 2,905 | 131 | 4.5% | 61,000 |
| **Annual Growth** | 5.6% | 6.4% | — | (0.6%) |

### 2006 Year-End Financials

Debt ratio: 166.6%
Return on equity: 24.8%
Cash ($ mil.): 18
Current ratio: 1.18
Long-term debt ($ mil.): 955
No. of shares (mil.): 73
Dividends
Yield: 1.4%
Payout: 29.9%
Market value ($ mil.): 3,411

### Stock History

NYSE: HCR

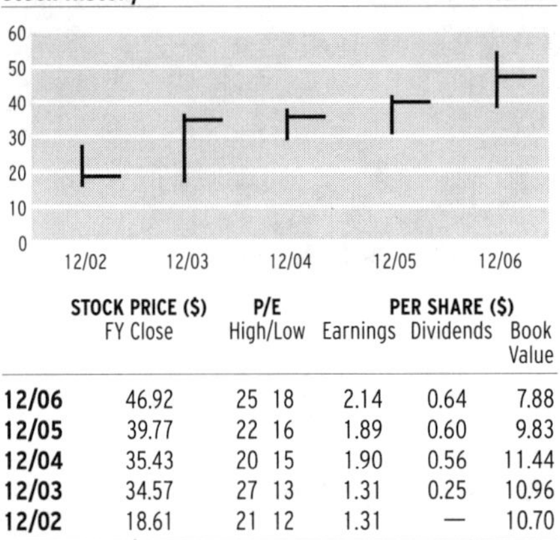


| | STOCK PRICE ($) FY Close | P/E High/Low | | PER SHARE ($) Earnings | Dividends | Book Value |
|---|---|---|---|---|---|---|
| **12/06** | 46.92 | 25 | 18 | 2.14 | 0.64 | 7.88 |
| **12/05** | 39.77 | 22 | 16 | 1.89 | 0.60 | 9.83 |
| **12/04** | 35.43 | 20 | 15 | 1.90 | 0.56 | 11.44 |
| **12/03** | 34.57 | 27 | 13 | 1.31 | 0.25 | 10.96 |
| **12/02** | 18.61 | 21 | 12 | 1.31 | — | 10.70 |
| **Annual Growth** | 26.0% | — | — | 13.1% | 36.8% | (7.3%) |

# Manpower Inc.

Millions of workers have helped power this firm to the upper echelon of the staffing industry. Manpower is the world's second-largest provider of temporary employees (behind Adecco), placing about 2 million people in office, industrial, and professional positions. It has some 4,400 owned or franchised offices in more than 70 countries (mainly France, the UK, and the US). The company also provides employee testing, training, and other contract services. Its Global Learning Centers give employees access to training materials over the Internet. Subsidiary Right Management offers career transition and organizational consulting services.

Manpower, which generates about 70% of its sales overseas, supplies temporary employees to businesses on an as-needed basis. The company generates most of its sales from office and light-industrial placements, but its professional placement division is the fastest-growing area.

The staffing giant offers its products and services across five primary brands: Manpower, Manpower Professional, Elan, Jefferson Wells, and Right Management.

The Jefferson Wells segment provides consulting and staffing services for the finance services industry, while its Manpower UK branch operates through a network of about 120 offices. Another segment, Brook Street Bureau, targets the UK as well, operating across some 140 branch offices.

## HISTORY

Milwaukee lawyers Elmer Winter and Aaron Scheinfeld founded Manpower in 1948. It originally concentrated on supplying temporary help to industry during the first few years of the postwar boom. In the next few years, the company expanded, and in 1956 it began franchising. During the 1960s Manpower opened franchises in Europe, Asia, and South America. Unlike many of its competitors, however, it continued to emphasize blue-collar placements.

Manpower embarked on a series of acquisitions in the 1970s and began to shift its emphasis from industrial to clerical placements. It was Mitchell Fromstein, Manpower's advertising account executive in the 1960s, who orchestrated the company's growth into a powerhouse. Fromstein joined the board in 1971 and became president and CEO in 1976.

Mid-decade, with Scheinfeld deceased and Winter eager to sell, Parker Pen came along. Parker, also based in Wisconsin, was trying to re-energize its fading fortunes after the arrival of the disposable pen. Parker bought Manpower in 1976, sold the pen business 10 years later, and became Manpower Inc. Fromstein continued as president and CEO, with a 20% interest in the company.

In the late 1970s Manpower entered the computer age, instituting a computer training program for its temporary employees. The company grew as the character of employment in the US changed from career-long employment with one company to a series of shorter-term jobs with many employers. In addition to providing short-term workers, Manpower began offering hiring and training services for permanent employees, thus saving companies in-house recruitment and training costs.

Blue Arrow, a temporary-employment agency based in the UK, acquired the firm in 1987. The combined companies operated as Manpower, and almost immediately tensions arose between Fromstein and his new boss, Antony Berry, who accused Fromstein of obstructing efforts to unite the two companies. Fromstein was fired in 1988.

Manpower's worldwide franchisees revolted against Berry, and the UK began an investigation of how the acquisition of Manpower was financed — a $1.5 billion stock sale by UK bank NatWest (now Royal Bank of Scotland Group). Berry was ousted in 1989, and Fromstein regained control. A push by US interests changed the US composition of the company's ownership during that year from just 9% in January to over 60% by the end of the year. This gave Fromstein the support he needed to move Manpower back to Wisconsin in 1991.

Fromstein then worked to disentangle the two companies by selling off all Blue Arrow holdings not related to employment. During the mid-1990s the company opened hundreds of new offices in the US and abroad. It spent more than $15 million in 1995 to upgrade its computerized worker-to-job matching system. An alliance with Drake Beam Morin the following year gave the company access to more than 200,000 new clients.

Manpower began two pilot programs in 1997 — one to place inner-city welfare recipients in the workforce, and one offering free technology-related training to company applicants via the

Internet. In 1998 the company acquired Australia's Kirby Contract Labour, which added 15 branches to the 55 already operating in Australia and New Zealand. The following year Fromstein retired after leading Manpower for 23 years. Jeffrey Joerres took over as CEO (and added chairman to his title in 2001).

Later in 1999, Manpower changed the name of its Manpower Technical division to Manpower Professional to better indicate the variety of disciplines it supported and compete in an increasingly tight market for professional workers. In 2001 the company bought financial services provider Jefferson Wells International. Manpower started a program that provides internships for high school students in 2002. In 2003 the company launched its Business Resource Center, which offers online human resources information for small and midsized businesses. Manpower acquired Right Management in 2004.

## EXECUTIVES

**Chairman, President, and CEO:** Jeffrey A. (Jeff) Joerres, age 47, $1,000,000 pay
**EVP; President, Europe, Middle East, and Africa:** Barbara J. Beck, age 46, $420,000 pay
**EVP, CFO, and Secretary:** Michael J. (Mike) Van Handel, age 47, $500,000 pay
**EVP; CEO, Right Management Consultants and Jefferson Wells International:** Owen J. Sullivan, age 49, $500,000 pay
**EVP; President, US and Canadian Operations:** Jonas Prising, age 42, $350,000 pay
**EVP; President Asia and Pacific:** Darryl E. Green, age 46
**EVP; President, France:** Françoise Gri
**SVP Corporate Affairs:** David Arkless
**SVP and Global CIO:** Rick Davidson
**SVP Global Human Resources:** Mara E. Swan, age 45
**SVP Workforce Strategy:** Tammy Johns
**SVP Global Marketing and Branding:** Varina Nissen
**President and COO, Jefferson Wells:** Michael E. (Mike) Touhey
**Auditors:** Deloitte & Touche LLP

## LOCATIONS

**HQ:** Manpower Inc.
5301 N. Ironwood Rd., Milwaukee, WI 53217
**Phone:** 414-961-1000 **Fax:** 414-906-7985
**Web:** www.manpower.com

## PRODUCTS/OPERATIONS

### 2006 Sales

| | $ mil. | % of total |
|---|---|---|
| France | 6,019.1 | 35 |
| Other Europe, Middle East & Africa | 6,363.3 | 36 |
| US | 2,114.9 | 12 |
| Right Management | 387.3 | 2 |
| Jefferson Wells | 373.0 | 2 |
| Other operations | 2,304.9 | 13 |
| **Total** | **17,562.5** | **100** |

### Selected Services

Staffing
Industrial trades
Manpower Professional
- Engineering
- Finance
- Information technology
- Telecommunications

Office and clerical

### Other Services

Brook Street (office and light industrial staffing in the UK)
Elan Group (IT staffing in UK)
Global Learning Center (online employee testing and training)
Jefferson Wells (financial services)
Right Management Consultants (career consulting)

## COMPETITORS

Adecco
CDI
Kelly Services
Labor Ready
MPS
Randstad
Robert Half
Spherion
Vedior
Volt Information

## HISTORICAL FINANCIALS

Company Type: Public

### Income Statement

FYE: December 31

| | REVENUE ($ mil.) | NET INCOME ($ mil.) | NET PROFIT MARGIN | EMPLOYEES |
|---|---|---|---|---|
| **12/06** | 17,563 | 398 | 2.3% | 4,030,000 |
| **12/05** | 16,080 | 260 | 1.6% | 4,027,000 |
| **12/04** | 14,930 | 246 | 1.6% | 2,027,100 |
| **12/03** | 12,185 | 138 | 1.1% | 2,351,600 |
| **12/02** | 10,611 | 113 | 1.1% | 1,621,400 |
| **Annual Growth** | 13.4% | 36.9% | — | 25.6% |

### 2006 Year-End Financials

Debt ratio: 32.0%
Return on equity: 17.2%
Cash ($ mil.): 688
Current ratio: 1.62
Long-term debt ($ mil.): 791
No. of shares (mil.): 85
Dividends
Yield: 0.8%
Payout: 13.0%
Market value ($ mil.): 6,374

### Stock History

NYSE: MAN

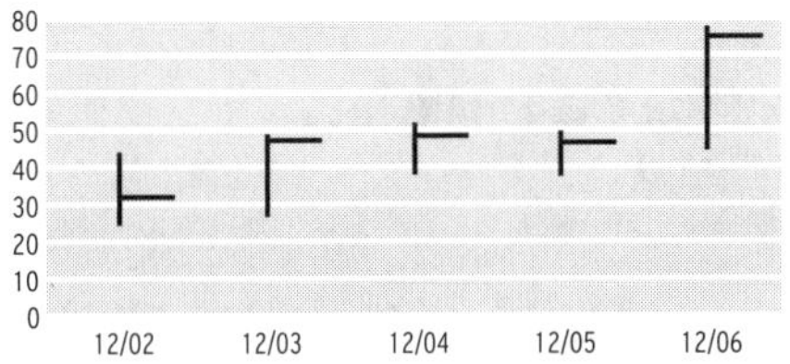

| | STOCK PRICE ($) FY Close | P/E High | P/E Low | PER SHARE ($) Earnings | Dividends | Book Value |
|---|---|---|---|---|---|---|
| **12/06** | 74.93 | 17 | 10 | 4.54 | 0.59 | 29.08 |
| **12/05** | 46.50 | 17 | 13 | 2.87 | 0.47 | 24.57 |
| **12/04** | 48.30 | 20 | 15 | 2.59 | 0.30 | 24.08 |
| **12/03** | 47.08 | 28 | 16 | 1.74 | 0.20 | 16.66 |
| **12/02** | 31.90 | 30 | 17 | 1.46 | 0.20 | 12.97 |
| **Annual Growth** | 23.8% | — | — | 32.8% | 31.1% | 22.4% |

# Marathon Oil

In the long-running competition for profits in the oil and gas industry, Marathon Oil (formerly USX Corporation) is keeping up a steady pace. Through its Marathon Oil Company subsidiary, the company explores for and produces oil and gas primarily in Angola, Equatorial Guinea, Gabon, Ireland, Libya, Norway, the UK, and the US. It has net proved reserves of 1.3 billion barrels of oil equivalent. Marathon Oil's Marathon Petroleum (formerly Marathon Ashland Petroleum, or MAP) operates seven refineries with an aggregate capacity of 974,000 barrels of crude oil a day. Marathon Petroleum supplies about 4,200 Marathon-branded US retail gas outlets. Marathon Oil also services 1,636 Speedway SuperAmerica gas stations.

In 2005 Ashland sold its 38% stake in Marathon Ashland to Marathon Oil for about $3.7 billion.

In addition to acquiring MAP, Marathon Oil also obtained Ashland's maleic anhydride business, a share of its Valvoline Instant Oil Change business in Michigan and Ohio, and other assets.

In 2006 the company sold its oil and gas assets in the Khanty-Mansiysk autonomous region of western Siberia to LUKOIL for $787 million. That year Marathon Oil announced plans to spend $3.2 billion to expand the crude oil refining capacity of its refinery in Garyville, Louisiana.

In 2007 the company agreed to acquire Canada's Western Oil Sands for about $5.6 billion.

## HISTORY

Marathon Oil was founded in 1887 in Lima, Ohio, as The Ohio Oil Company by 14 independent oil producers to compete with Standard Oil. Within two years Ohio Oil was the largest producer in the state. This success did not go unnoticed by Standard Oil, which proceeded to buy Ohio Oil in 1889. In 1905 the company moved to Findlay, Ohio, where it remained until it relocated to Houston in 1990.

When the US Supreme Court broke up Standard Oil in 1911, Ohio Oil became independent once again and expanded its exploration activities to Kansas, Louisiana, Texas, and Wyoming.

In a 1924 attempt to drill three wells west of the Pecos River in Texas, Ohio Oil mistakenly drilled three dry holes to the east. The company was on the verge of abandoning the project until a geologist reported the error. Ohio Oil drilled in the right area and the wells flowed. That year the company bought Lincoln Oil Refining — its first venture outside crude oil production.

Ohio Oil continued its expansion into refining and marketing operations in 1927. Following WWII the company began international exploration. Through Conorada Petroleum (later Oasis), a partnership with Continental Oil (later Conoco and then ConocoPhillips) and Amerada Hess, the company explored in Africa and South and Central America. Conorada's biggest overseas deal came in 1955, when it acquired concessions on more than 60 million acres in Libya.

In 1962 the company acquired Plymouth Oil and changed its name to Marathon Oil Company; it had been using the Marathon name in its marketing activities since the late 1930s. Marathon added a 200,000-barrel-a-day refinery in Louisiana to its operations in 1976 when it acquired ECOL Ltd.

After a battle with Mobil, U.S. Steel acquired Marathon in 1982 for $6.5 billion. U.S. Steel changed its name to USX in 1986 and acquired Texas Oil & Gas. That year the US government introduced economic sanctions against Libya, putting Marathon's Libyan holdings in suspension.

USX consolidated Texas Oil and Marathon in 1990. After a protracted struggle with corporate raider Carl Icahn, USX split Marathon and U.S. Steel into two separate stock classes in 1991. A third offering, USX-Delhi Group (the pipeline operator division), followed the next year. (Koch Industries bought USX-Delhi in 1997.)

A consortium led by USX-Marathon signed an agreement with the Russian government in 1994 to develop oil and gas fields off Sakhalin Island (although USX-Marathon sold its stake in the project in 2000). In 1996 Marathon formed a venture, ElectroGen International, with East Coast utility DQE to develop power generation projects in the Asia/Pacific region.

In 1998 Marathon and Ashland merged their refining and retail operations, creating Marathon Ashland Petroleum (MAP), with Marathon owning 62%. That year Marathon, in a deal that boosted its reserves by 18%, acquired Calgary-based Tarragon Oil and Gas.

As part of a restructuring drive, in 1999 MAP sold its crude oil gathering business, Scurlock Permian, to Plains All American Pipeline. With oil prices rebounding, Marathon ramped up its oil exploration in 2000, buying more deepwater leases in the Gulf of Mexico and acquiring an interest in an oil and gas play offshore the Republic of Congo.

The company bought Pennaco Energy, a Colorado-based producer of coalbed methane gas, for about $500 million in 2001, and it agreed to buy CMS Energy's Equatorial Guinea (West Africa) oil and gas assets in a $993 million deal that was completed in 2002. At the end of 2001, USX spun off U.S. Steel and changed the name of the remaining company to Marathon Oil Corporation. In 2002 Marathon acquired Globex Energy, a privately held exploration and production company with assets in West Africa, for $155 million.

## EXECUTIVES

**Chairman:** Thomas J. Usher, age 64
**President, CEO, and Director:** Clarence P. Cazalot Jr., age 56, $1,175,000 pay
**EVP; President, Marathon Petroleum:** Gary R. Heminger, age 53, $1,391,976 pay
**EVP and CFO:** Janet F. Clark, age 52, $513,000 pay
**SVP Business Development:** David E. (Dave) Roberts Jr., age 46
**SVP Corporate Affairs:** Jerry Howard, age 58
**SVP Worldwide Exploration:** Philip G. Behrman, age 55, $384,000 pay
**SVP Worldwide Production:** Steven B. Hinchman, age 47, $422,000 pay
**VP, General Counsel, and Secretary:** William F. Schwind Jr., age 62
**VP Accounting and Controller:** Michael K. Stewart
**VP Corporate Responsibility:** Daniel J. Sullenbarger, age 51
**VP Finance and Treasurer:** Paul C. Reinbolt, age 51
**VP Human Resources:** Eileen M. Campbell, age 45
**VP Investor Relations and Public Affairs:** Kenneth L. Matheny, age 59
**VP Major Projects:** Alard (Al) Kaplan, age 56
**VP Tax:** James F. Meara, age 50
**CIO:** Thomas K. Sneed
**Auditors:** PricewaterhouseCoopers LLP

## LOCATIONS

**HQ:** Marathon Oil Corporation
5555 San Felipe Rd., Houston, TX 77056
**Phone:** 713-629-6600 **Fax:** 713-296-2952
**Web:** www.marathon.com

Marathon Oil conducts exploration and development activities in Angola, Canada, the Republic of Congo, Equatorial Guinea, Gabon, Ireland, the Netherlands, Norway, Russia, the UK, and the US.

**2006 Sales**

| | % of total |
|---|---|
| US | 92 |
| Other countries | 8 |
| **Total** | **100** |

## PRODUCTS/OPERATIONS

**2006 Sales**

| | % of total |
|---|---|
| Refining, marketing & transportation | 86 |
| Exploration & production | 14 |
| **Total** | **100** |

**Selected Subsidiaries**

Marathon Petroleum Company LLC
Speedway SuperAmerica LLC
Marathon Canada Limited
Marathon International Oil Company
Marathon International Petroleum Ireland Limited
Marathon Oil Company
Marathon Oil U.K., Ltd
Marathon Petroleum Gabon LDC (Cayman Islands)
Marathon Petroleum Investment, Ltd.

## COMPETITORS

7-Eleven
BP
Chevron
ConocoPhillips
Crested
Ergon
Exxon Mobil
Hess
J.M. Huber
Koch
Lyondell Chemical
Norsk Hydro
Occidental Petroleum
PDVSA
PEMEX
Royal Dutch Shell
Sibir Energy
Sinclair Oil
Sunoco
TransCanada

## HISTORICAL FINANCIALS

Company Type: Public

**Income Statement** FYE: December 31

| | REVENUE ($ mil.) | NET INCOME ($ mil.) | NET PROFIT MARGIN | EMPLOYEES |
|---|---|---|---|---|
| **12/06** | 65,449 | 5,234 | 8.0% | 28,195 |
| **12/05** | 63,673 | 3,032 | 4.8% | 27,756 |
| **12/04** | 49,907 | 1,261 | 2.5% | 25,804 |
| **12/03** | 41,234 | 1,321 | 3.2% | 27,007 |
| **12/02** | 31,720 | 516 | 1.6% | 28,166 |
| **Annual Growth** | 19.9% | 78.5% | — | 0.0% |

**2006 Year-End Financials**

Debt ratio: 21.0%
Return on equity: 39.8%
Cash ($ mil.): 2,585
Current ratio: 1.25
Long-term debt ($ mil.): 3,061
No. of shares (mil.): 348
Dividends
Yield: 1.7%
Payout: 10.5%
Market value ($ mil.): 16,084

**Stock History** NYSE: MRO

| | STOCK PRICE ($) FY Close | P/E High | P/E Low | PER SHARE ($) Earnings | Dividends | Book Value |
|---|---|---|---|---|---|---|
| **12/06** | 46.25 | 7 | 4 | 7.25 | 0.76 | 42.00 |
| **12/05** | 30.49 | 9 | 4 | 4.22 | 0.47 | 31.92 |
| **12/04** | 18.81 | 11 | 8 | 1.87 | 0.51 | 23.40 |
| **12/03** | 16.55 | 8 | 5 | 2.13 | 0.48 | 19.57 |
| **12/02** | 10.65 | 18 | 11 | 0.83 | 0.34 | 16.40 |
| **Annual Growth** | 44.4% | — | — | 71.9% | 22.3% | 26.5% |

# Markel Corporation

Have you ever thought about who insures the manicurist or an antique motorcycle? Markel Corporation takes on the risks its competition won't touch, from amusement parks to thoroughbred horses and summer camps. Coverage is also available for one-time events, such as golf tournaments and auto races. Markel's subsidiaries include Essex Insurance Company (excess and surplus lines), Shand Professional/Products Liability (excess and surplus, professional and products liability), Markel Insurance (specialty program insurance), and Markel Southwest Underwriters (excess and surplus, brokered). Markel International provides specialty insurance internationally, primarily in the UK.

Higher premium volume (primarily in its excess and surplus segment) and improved results by its previously struggling international business have helped to increase Markel's underwriting profits. However, in 2005 the company was faced with some $245 million in losses due to hurricanes Katrina, Rita, and Wilma. President Anthony Markel and vice chairman Steven Markel control about 8% of the company.

## HISTORY

In the 1920s Sam Markel formed a mutual insurance company for "jitneys" (passenger cars refurbished as public transportation buses). In 1930 he founded Markel Service to expand nationally. To keep up with industry growth, the company revamped itself as a managing general agent and independent claims service organization in the late 1950s. In 1978 Markel began covering taverns, restaurants, and vacant buildings. It created excess and surplus lines underwriter Essex Insurance in 1980.

Markel went public in 1986. The next year it invested in Shand Morahan and Evanston Insurance (specialty coverage, including architects, engineers, and lawyers professional liability; officers and directors insurance; errors and omissions; and medical malpractice). It bought summer camp insurer Rhulen Agency in 1989.

In the 1990s Markel began buying insurers with their own offbeat niches. In 1990 it bought the rest of Shand Morahan and Evanston Insurance. In 1995 it bought Lincoln Insurance (excess and surplus lines) from media giant Thomson. The next year the company bought Investors Insurance Holding (excess and surplus lines). Markel, which already owned nearly 10% of Gryphon Holdings (commercial property/casualty), bought the rest in 1999.

Expanding internationally, Markel bought Bermuda-based Terra Nova Holdings, a reinsurer and a Lloyd's managing agency, in 2000. The company experienced heavy losses in 2001, not only related to the events of September 11 but also to its slumping international business (the company took a $100 million charge).

## EXECUTIVES

**Chairman and CEO:** Alan I. Kirshner, age 71, $600,000 pay
**Vice Chairman:** Steven A. Markel, age 58, $575,000 pay
**President, COO, and Director:** Anthony F. (Tony) Markel, age 65, $575,000 pay
**EVP and Chief Investment Officer:** Thomas Gayner, age 45, $462,019 pay
**EVP:** Paul W. Springman, age 55, $462,019 pay

**SVP and CFO:** Richard R. Whitt III, age 43, $353,462 pay
**SVP, Operations:** John Latham
**VP, Sales and Marketing, Shand Morahan & Co., Inc:** Letha Heaton
**VP, eCommerce:** Robert DuFour
**VP, Human Resources:** Pam Perrott
**VP, Investor Relations:** Bruce Kay
**VP, Marketing:** Brenda Phillips
**VP, Marketing, Markel American Insurance:** Audrey Hanken
**VP, Marketing, Essex Insurance:** Andrea D. Nash
**VP, Marketing, Markel Southwest Underwriters:** Scott Delatorre
**President and COO, Markel International:** Gerald (Gerry) Albanese
**Director, Marketing and Public Relations, Markel International:** Tamara Cutting
**Director, Business Development:** Jeff Lamb
**Secretary:** Gregory B. Nevers
**Auditors:** KPMG LLP

## LOCATIONS

**HQ:** Markel Corporation
4521 Highwoods Pkwy., Glen Allen, VA 23060
**Phone:** 804-747-0136 **Fax:** 804-965-1600
**Web:** www.markelcorp.com

Markel operates primarily in North America and the UK.

## PRODUCTS/OPERATIONS

### 2006 Sales

| | $ mil. | % of total |
|---|---|---|
| Earned premiums | 2184.4 | 87 |
| Net investment income | 271.0 | 11 |
| Net realized investment gains | 63.6 | 2 |
| **Total** | **2,519.0** | **100** |

### Selected Subsidiaries

Essex Insurance Company
Gryphon Holding Inc.
  Associated International Insurance Company
  Deerfield Insurance Company
Markel American Insurance Company
Markel Insurance Company
Shand/Evanston Group, Inc.
  Evanston Insurance Company
Terra Nova (Bermuda) Holdings Ltd.
  Markel International Limited (UK)
    Markel International Insurance Company Limited
Markel Capital Limited (UK)

## COMPETITORS

AIG
American Financial
Assurant
Chubb Corp
CNA Financial
Fireman's Fund Insurance
HCC Insurance
Medical Liability Mutual
Nationwide
Penn-America
Philadelphia Consolidated
Travelers Companies
XL Capital

## HISTORICAL FINANCIALS

Company Type: Public

### Income Statement

FYE: December 31

| | ASSETS ($ mil.) | NET INCOME ($ mil.) | INCOME AS % OF ASSETS | EMPLOYEES |
|---|---|---|---|---|
| **12/06** | 10,088 | 393 | 3.9% | 1,897 |
| **12/05** | 9,814 | 148 | 1.5% | 1,866 |
| **12/04** | 9,398 | 165 | 1.8% | 1,834 |
| **12/03** | 8,532 | 124 | 1.4% | 1,759 |
| **12/02** | 7,409 | 75 | 1.0% | 1,621 |
| **Annual Growth** | 8.0% | 51.1% | — | 4.0% |

### 2006 Year-End Financials

Equity as % of assets: 22.8%
Return on assets: 3.9%
Return on equity: 19.6%
Long-term debt ($ mil.): 858
No. of shares (mil.): 10
Dividends
  Yield: —
  Payout: —
Market value ($ mil.): 4,798
Sales ($ mil.): 2,519

### Stock History

NYSE: MKL

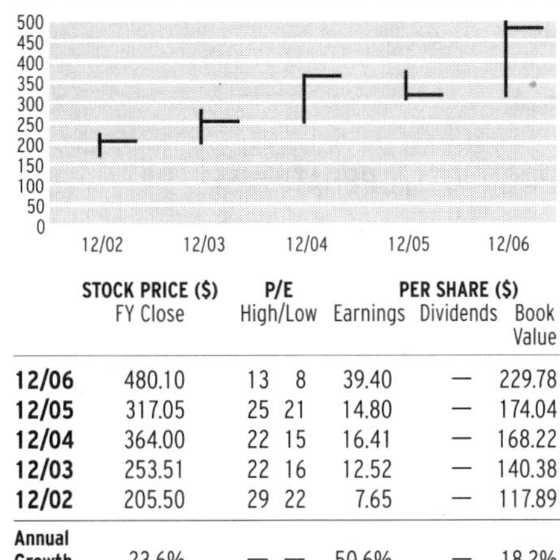


| | STOCK PRICE ($) FY Close | P/E High | P/E Low | PER SHARE ($) Earnings | PER SHARE ($) Dividends | PER SHARE ($) Book Value |
|---|---|---|---|---|---|---|
| **12/06** | 480.10 | 13 | 8 | 39.40 | — | 229.78 |
| **12/05** | 317.05 | 25 | 21 | 14.80 | — | 174.04 |
| **12/04** | 364.00 | 22 | 15 | 16.41 | — | 168.22 |
| **12/03** | 253.51 | 22 | 16 | 12.52 | — | 140.38 |
| **12/02** | 205.50 | 29 | 22 | 7.65 | — | 117.89 |
| **Annual Growth** | 23.6% | — | — | 50.6% | — | 18.2% |

# Marriott International

Marriott International signs in at the top of the lodging industry. The company is one of the world's leading hoteliers with more than 2,800 operated or franchised properties in more than 65 countries. Marriott's hotels include such full-service brands as Renaissance Hotels and its flagship Marriott Hotels & Resorts, as well as select-service and extended-stay brands Courtyard and Fairfield Inn. It also owns the Ritz-Carlton luxury hotel chain and several resort and time-share properties operated by Marriott Vacation Club International. The Marriott family, including CEO J. W. Marriott Jr., owns about 15% of the company.

Marriott operates more than 1,000 of its hotels and gets most of its revenue through lease agreements and management fees collected from property owners. It has more than 1,700 franchised hotels that pay the company fees and royalties as well as a percentage of their food and beverage revenue. While the bulk of its hotels are located in the US, Marriott gets about 10% of its revenue from international operations. In addition to its hotel business, Marriott provides more than 2,000 rental units for corporate housing and it manages 45 golf courses.

Marriott has rebounded as a result of stronger demand for hotel rooms worldwide after struggling through a recession in travel. The company has benefited from a weak US dollar that continues to drive international travelers to the US. In 2006 the company added 13 managed properties (4,126 rooms), and 77 franchised properties (11,286 rooms) to its holdings.

Marriott is keen to increase its share of the extended-stay and select-service market, which typically has higher margins since those hotels offer fewer amenities. The company has also seen healthy increases in its vacation and time-share businesses. Trying to eliminate guest complaints about cigarette odor, the company announced in 2006 that it would ban smoking in every room and public area at all of its hotels. In 2007 it announced plans to develop a boutique chain (small, upscale, stylish hotels in prime locations) designed by Ian Schrager, the hotelier behind hip properties such as Manhattan's Morgans Hotel.

## HISTORY

The company began in 1927 as a Washington, DC, root beer stand operated by John and Alice Marriott. Later they added hot food and named their business the Hot Shoppe. In 1929 the couple incorporated and began work on building a regional chain.

Hot Shoppes opened its first hotel, the Twin Bridges Marriott Motor Hotel, in Arlington, Virginia, in 1957. When the Marriotts' son Bill became president in 1964 (CEO in 1972, chairman in 1985), he focused on expanding the hotel business. The company changed its name to Marriott Corp. in 1967. With the rise in airline travel, Marriott built several airport hotels during the 1970s. By 1977 sales had topped $1 billion.

Marriott became the #1 operator of airport food, beverage, and merchandise facilities in the US with its 1982 acquisition of Host International, and it introduced moderately priced Courtyard hotels in 1983. Acquisitions in the 1980s included a time-share business, food service companies, and competitor Howard Johnson. (Marriott later sold the hotels but kept the restaurants and turnpike units.)

The company entered three new market segments in 1987: Marriott Suites (full-service suites), Residence Inn (moderately priced suites), and Fairfield Inn (economy hotels). It also began developing "life-care" communities, which provide apartments, meals, and limited nursing care to the elderly, in 1988.

Marriott split its operations into two companies in 1993: Host Marriott to own hotels, and Marriott International primarily to manage them. However, Marriott International still owned some of the properties, and in 1995 it bought 49% of the Ritz-Carlton luxury hotel group.

In 1996 Marriott purchased the Forum Group (assisted living communities and health care services) and merged it into Marriott Senior Living Services.

Marriott introduced its Marriott Executive Residences in 1997. Also that year the firm expanded overseas operations with its purchase of the 150-unit Hong Kong-based Renaissance Hotel Group, a deal that included branding rights to the Ramada chain.

In 1998, after the division of its lodging and food distribution services, the new Marriott International then began trading as a separate company. Also in 1998 Marriott acquired the rest of Ritz-Carlton and established SpringHill Suites by Marriott.

Marriott entered the corporate housing business in 1999 through its acquisition of ExecuStay Corporation (renamed ExecuStay by Marriott), which provides fully furnished and accessorized apartments for stays of 30 days or more. The following year the company set up a $3.7 billion investment fund with Ripplewood Holdings (Marriott owns about 20%) that would buy Japanese hotels to operate under Marriott management. It also agreed to pay $400 million to settle a lawsuit brought by stockholders who contended the company defrauded them. Marriott also announced plans in 2000 to join rival Hyatt in launching a joint venture to provide an electronic procurement network serving the hospitality industry. The following year it joined Italy's Bulgari, the world's #3 jeweler, in a $140 million venture of luxury hotels sporting the Bulgari name.

Marriott refocused its operations on the lodging market in 2003 when it exited both the senior living and distribution services businesses. It sold Marriott Distribution Services (food and beverage distribution) to Services Group of America, and sold Marriott Senior Living Services to Sunrise Assisted Living (the management business) and CNL Retirement Properties (nine communities). The following year Marriott sold the international branding rights to the Ramada and Days Inn chains to Cendant (now Avis Budget Group) for about $200 million.

In 2005 Marriott acquired about 30 properties from CTF Holdings (an affiliate of Hong Kong-based New World Development) for nearly $1.5 billion. It sold 14 properties immediately to Sunstone Hotel Investors and Walton Street Capital. The deal put an end to an ongoing legal battle between Marriott and CTF Holdings, which alleged that the hotelier had pocketed kickbacks and fees from outside vendors.

It invested about $200 million in 2005 to upgrade its hotel beds with higher thread-count sheets and triple-sheeted tops, and it renovated and upgraded many of its Courtyard and Residence Inn locations during 2006.

## EXECUTIVES

**Chairman and CEO:** J. W. (Bill) Marriott Jr., age 74
**Vice Chairman:** John W. Marriott III, age 45
**President, COO, and Director:** William J. Shaw, age 61
**President, North American Lodging Operations and Global Brand Management:** Robert J. (Bob) McCarthy, age 53
**EVP and CFO; President, Continental European Lodging:** Arne M. Sorenson, age 48
**EVP and CIO:** Carl Wilson
**EVP and General Counsel:** Edward A. (Ed) Ryan, age 53
**EVP Brand Management:** Michael E. Jannini
**EVP Taxes:** M. Lester Pulse Jr.
**EVP Development Planning and Feasibility:** Scott E. Melby
**EVP Enterprise Accounting Services:** Pamela G. Murray
**EVP Finance:** Kevin M. Kimball
**EVP Finance and Global Treasurer:** Carolyn B. Handlon
**EVP Global Communications and Public Affairs:** Kathleen Matthews
**EVP Global Human Resources:** David A. Rodriguez, age 48
**EVP Mergers, Acquisitions, and Development Planning:** Richard S. Hoffman
**EVP Sales and Marketing:** Amy C. McPherson
**SVP Investor Relations:** Laura E. Paugh
**VP, Corporate Secretary, and Assistant General Counsel:** Terri L. Turner
**VP International Public Relations:** June Farrell
**President, Marriott Vacation Club International:** Stephen P. (Steve) Weisz, age 55
**President and COO, Ritz-Carlton Hotel Company:** Simon F. Cooper, age 61
**President, Marriott Leisure:** Robert A. (Bob) Miller
**Auditors:** Ernst & Young LLP

## LOCATIONS

**HQ:** Marriott International, Inc.
10400 Fernwood Rd., Bethesda, MD 20817
**Phone:** 301-380-3000 **Fax:** 301-380-3969
**Web:** www.marriott.com

Marriott International has operations in more than 65 countries.

### 2006 Locations

| | No. |
|---|---|
| Americas | |
| US | 2,471 |
| Other countries | 54 |
| Europe | |
| UK and Ireland | 77 |
| Other countries | 109 |
| Asia | 79 |
| Middle East & Africa | 34 |
| Australia | 8 |
| **Total** | **2,832** |

## PRODUCTS/OPERATIONS

### 2006 Sales

| | $ mil. | % of total |
|---|---|---|
| Lodging | | |
| North American full-service | 5,196 | 43 |
| North American limited-service | 2,060 | 17 |
| Timeshare | 1,840 | 15 |
| Luxury | 1,423 | 12 |
| International | 1,411 | 12 |
| Other | 230 | 1 |
| **Total** | **12,160** | **100** |

### 2006 Locations

| | No. |
|---|---|
| North American limited-service | 1,968 |
| North American full-service | 415 |
| International | 330 |
| Luxury | 62 |
| Timeshare | 57 |
| **Total** | **2,832** |

### 2006 Locations

| | No. |
|---|---|
| Franchised | 1,784 |
| Company-owned | 1,048 |
| **Total** | **2,832** |

### Selected Operations and Brands

International lodging
- Courtyard by Marriott
- Fairfield Inn by Marriott
- JW Marriott Hotels & Resorts
- Marriott Executive Apartments
- Marriott Hotels & Resorts
- Ramada International
- Renaissance Hotels & Resorts
- Residence Inn by Marriott

Luxury hotels
- Bulgari Hotels & Resorts
- The Ritz-Carlton

North American full-service hotels
- JW Marriott Hotels & Resorts
- Marriott Conference Centers
- Marriott Hotels & Resorts
- Renaissance ClubSport
- Renaissance Hotels & Resorts

North American limited-service hotels
- Courtyard by Marriott
- Fairfield Inn by Marriott
- Marriott ExecuStay
- Residence Inn by Marriott
- SpringHill Suites by Marriott
- TownePlace Suites by Marriott

Timeshare resorts
- Horizons by Marriott Vacation Club International
- Grand Residences by Marriott
- Marriott Vacation Club International
- The Ritz-Carlton Club

## COMPETITORS

Accor
Best Western
Carlson Hotels
Choice Hotels
Club Med
Fairmont Raffles
Four Seasons Hotels
Hilton
Hilton International
HVM
Hyatt
InterContinental Hotels
Loews Hotels
LXR Luxury Resorts
Starwood Hotels & Resorts

## HISTORICAL FINANCIALS

Company Type: Public

### Income Statement

FYE: Friday nearest December 31

| | REVENUE ($ mil.) | NET INCOME ($ mil.) | NET PROFIT MARGIN | EMPLOYEES |
|---|---|---|---|---|
| **12/06** | 12,160 | 608 | 5.0% | 150,600 |
| **12/05** | 11,550 | 669 | 5.8% | 143,000 |
| **12/04** | 10,099 | 596 | 5.9% | 133,000 |
| **12/03** | 9,014 | 502 | 5.6% | 128,000 |
| **12/02** | 8,441 | 277 | 3.3% | 144,000 |
| **Annual Growth** | 9.6% | 21.7% | — | 1.1% |

### 2006 Year-End Financials

Debt ratio: 69.4%
Return on equity: 20.7%
Cash ($ mil.): 193
Current ratio: 1.31
Long-term debt ($ mil.): 1,818
No. of shares (mil.): 390
Dividends
Yield: 0.5%
Payout: 17.0%
Market value ($ mil.): 18,587

### Stock History

NYSE: MAR

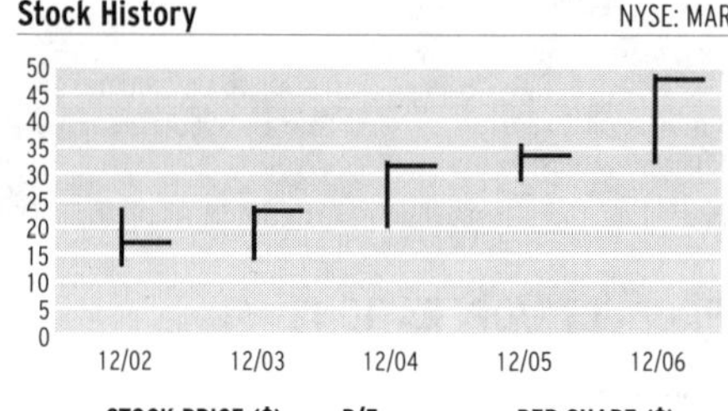


| | STOCK PRICE ($) FY Close | P/E High | P/E Low | PER SHARE ($) Earnings | Dividends | Book Value |
|---|---|---|---|---|---|---|
| **12/06** | 47.72 | 34 | 23 | 1.41 | 0.24 | 6.72 |
| **12/05** | 33.49 | 24 | 20 | 1.45 | 0.20 | 15.61 |
| **12/04** | 31.49 | 26 | 16 | 1.24 | 0.17 | 18.08 |
| **12/03** | 23.08 | 23 | 14 | 1.02 | 0.15 | 16.68 |
| **12/02** | 17.14 | 42 | 24 | 0.55 | 0.14 | 15.15 |
| **Annual Growth** | 29.2% | — | — | 26.5% | 14.4% | (18.4%) |

# Mars, Incorporated

Mars knows chocolate sales are nothing to snicker at. The company makes such worldwide favorites as M&M's, Snickers, and the Mars bar. Its other confections include 3 Musketeers, Dove, Milky Way, Skittles, Twix, and Starburst sweets; Combos and Kudos snacks; Uncle Ben's rice; and pet food under the names Pedigree, Sheba, and Whiskas. Mars also provides office beverage services and makes drink vending equipment. The Mars family (including siblings and retired company CEO Forrest Mars Jr., chairman John Franklyn Mars, and VP Jacqueline Badger Mars) owns the highly secretive firm, making the family one of the richest in the US.

Mars makes non-chocolate confections including breath mints such as AquaDrops, and snack foods like Combos and Kudos. It also makes ice-cream versions of several of its candy bars. It swallows a large bite of the pet-food market with its Royal Canin, Pedigree, and Whiskas brands. In conjunction with Unilever, Mars' Pedigree dog food offers dairy-based Pedigree Ice Cream Sandwich Treats for Dogs. Mars' other brands include Uncle Ben's, Seeds of Change, and Flavia Beverage Systems.

The company sold off its payment-processing subsidiary, MEI Conlux (which has headquarters in Pennsylvania and Japan) in 2006 to investment firms Bain Capital and Advantage Partners for more than $500 million.

Adding to its fast-growing pet-products sector, in 2006 Mars purchased dog-treat manufacturer S&M Nu Tec, maker of Greenies, a bone-shaped treat with a toothbrush on one end that is a hot item in the pet-product market. The purchase price was not disclosed.

Still barking up the pet-product tree, Mars acquired private-label dry pet food manufacturer Doane Pet Care Company that year as well. Doane's products are sold in the US and Europe.

The company discontinued brands in 2006, including Pop'ables and Cookies &, for an estimated $300 million savings, which it invested in advertising. The company introduced new Dove varieties and a dark chocolate version of M&Ms that year as well.

Mars stays virtually debt free and uses its profits for international expansion. It has operations in 65 countries and sells its products in more than 100.

## HISTORY

Frank Mars invented the Milky Way candy bar in 1923 after his previous three efforts at the candy business left him bankrupt. After his estranged son, Forrest, graduated from Yale, Mars hired him to work at his candy operation. When Forrest demanded one-third control of the company and Frank refused, Forrest moved to England with the foreign rights to Milky Way and started his own company (Food Manufacturers) in the 1930s. He made a sweeter version of Milky Way for the UK, calling it a Mars bar. Forrest also ventured into pet food with the 1934 purchase of Chappel Brothers (renamed Pedigree). At one point he controlled 55% of the British pet food market.

During WWII Forrest returned to the US and introduced Uncle Ben's rice (the world's first brand-name raw commodity) and M&M's (a joint venture between Forrest and Bruce Murrie, son of Hershey's then-president). The idea for M&M's was borrowed from British Smarties, for which Forrest obtained rights (from Rowntree Mackintosh) by relinquishing similar rights to the Snickers bar in some foreign markets. The ad slogan "Melts in your mouth, not in your hand" (and the candy's success in non-air-conditioned stores and war zones) made the company an industry leader. Mars introduced M&M's Peanut in 1954. It was one of the first candy companies to sponsor a television show — *Howdy Doody* in the 1950s.

Forrest merged his firm with his deceased father's company in 1964, after buying his dying half-sister's controlling interest. (He renamed the business Mars at her request.) The merger was the end of an alliance with Hershey, who had supplied Frank with chocolate since his Milky Way inception.

In 1968 Mars bought Kal Kan. In 1973 Forrest, then 69 years old, delegated his company responsibilities to sons Forrest Jr. and John. Five years later the brothers, looking for snacks to offset dwindling candy resulting from a more diet-conscious America, bought the Twix chocolate-covered cookie brand. During the late 1980s they bought ice-cream bar maker Dove Bar International and Ethel-M Chocolates, producer of liqueur-flavored chocolates, a business their father had begun in his retirement.

Hershey surpassed Mars as the US's largest candy maker in 1988 when it acquired Cadbury Schweppes' US division (Mounds and Almond Joy). In response to the success of Hershey's Symphony Bar, Mars introduced its dark-chocolate Dove bar in 1991.

While Hershey chose to stick close to home, Mars ventured abroad. The company entered the huge confectionery market of India in 1989 by building a $10 million factory there. In 1996 the company opened a confectionery processing plant in Brazil. Back home, in 1997 the company launched new ad campaigns, including M&M's spots featuring a trio of animated M&M candies.

Forrest Sr. died in 1999, spurring rumors that Mars would go public or be sold. Instead, the company dismantled most of its sales force, opting to use less costly food brokers. Also in 1999 Forrest Jr. retired, leaving brother John Franklyn as president and CEO. Still far behind its rival, Mars received a modest boost in US market share when Hershey experienced computer troubles.

In 2000 the company established a subsidiary, Effem India, to market Mars' products in India. In 2003 Mars acquired French pet food producer Royal Canin. The company also acquired Japanese vending machine parts manufacturer Nippon Conlux in 2003.

Moving into the drink sector, in 2004 Mars licensed its Milky Way, Starburst, and 3 Musketeers brands to Bravo!, which uses the brand names to market vitamin-enhanced milk drinks using the brand names. That year the company appointed two co-presidents, Peter Cheney and Paul Michaels, leaving John Franklyn Mars as chairman. Cheney retired in 2005.

Responding to public concerns about healthy eating, Mars started phasing out its "king size" candy bars in 2005. Mars also jumped on the "chocolate as health food" bandwagon that year, introducing CocoaVia, a line of confections containing flavanols, which are said to have antioxidant qualities, and plant sterols, which the company claims is good for hearts and arteries. Unlike Mars' other products, the CocoaVia line is shelved in retailers' health-food sections.

## EXECUTIVES

**Chairman:** John Franklyn Mars, age 70
**President:** Paul S. Michaels
**VP:** Jacqueline Badger Mars
**VP, Chocolate:** Mark Mattia
**VP and General Manager, My M&M's:** Jim Cass
**VP, Treasurer, and CFO:** R. E. Barnes
**President, Gourmet Chocolate and Retail:** John Haugh
**President, Mars Nutrition for Health and Well-Being:** James (Jamie) Mattikow
**President, Masterfoods Australia-New Zealand:** Andy Weston-Webb
**President, Masterfoods Europe:** Pierre Laubies
**President, Masterfoods North America:** Bob Gamgort
**VP, Sales Snack Channels Masterfoods USA:** Larry Lupo
**VP, Marketing, Masterfoods USA:** Michele Kessler
**VP, Marketing Masterfoods USA Pet Care:** Chris Jones
**VP, Sales Strategy Masterfoods USA:** Timothy LeBel
**Chief Science Officer:** Harold Schmitz
**Director, Cocoa Sustainability:** Roger Dehnel
**Director, Masterfoods USA:** Doug Milne
**Director, Marketing, Flavia Beverage Systems:** Frank LaRusso
**Director, Corporate Health and Nutrition Affairs, Masterfoods Europe:** Matthias Berninger, age 36

## LOCATIONS

**HQ:** Mars, Incorporated
6885 Elm St., McLean, VA 22101
**Phone:** 703-821-4900 **Fax:** 703-448-9678
**Web:** www.mars.com

## PRODUCTS/OPERATIONS

### Selected Brands

Beverages
- Flavia

Ice Cream Bars
- 3 Musketeers
- DoveBars
- Milky Way
- Snickers

Main Meals
- Dolmio
- Ebly
- Uncle Ben's

Petcare
- Buckeye
- Catscan
- Cesar
- Doane
- Frolic
- Pedigree
- Royal Canin
- Sheba
- Spillers
- Waltham
- Whiskas
- Winergy

Snackfoods
- 3 Musketeers
- Bounty
- Celebrations
- CocoaVia
- Combos
- Dove
- Ethel-M
- Kudo
- M&M'S
- Marathon
- Milky Way
- Skittles
- Snickers
- Starburst
- Twix

Other Products
- Flavia office beverage systems
- Klix beverage vending equipment

## COMPETITORS

American Licorice
Annabelle Candy
Anthony-Thomas Candy
Asher's Chocolates
Avani International Group
Barry Callebaut
Betsy Ann Candies
Brach's
Breeder's Choice
Butterfields Candy
Cadbury Adams USA
Cadbury Schweppes
Cadbury Trebor Bassett
Campbell Soup
Caribou Coffee
Chase General
Chocolates à la Carte
Chupa Chups
Cloetta Fazer
Colgate-Palmolive
ConAgra
Concord Confections
CSM
Dynamic Confections
Elmer Candy
Endangered Species Chocolate
Enstrom
Eurochoc Americas
Ezaki Glico
Farley's & Sathers
Ferrara Pan Candy
Ferrero
General Mills
Ghirardelli
Gilster-Mary Lee
Godiva Chocolatier
Goetze's Candy
Green & Black's
Green Mountain Coffee
Grupo Corvi
Guittard
HARIBO
Haribo of America
Harry London Candies
Heinz
Hershey
Hill's Pet Nutrition
Iams
Jelly Belly Candy
Just Born
Kraft Foods
Laura Secord
Lindt & Sprüngli
Madelaine Chocolate
Meiji Seika
Meow Mix Company
Millstone
NECCO
Nestlé
Nestlé Purina PetCare
Nestlé USA
Perfetti Van Melle
Perfetti Van Melle USA
PETCO (Holding)
PEZ Candy
Purdy's Chocolates
Riviana Foods
Rocky Mountain Chocolate
Royal Cup Coffee
Russell Stover
S&D Coffee
See's Candies
Sherwood Brands
Smucker
Spangler Candy
Starbucks
Strauss
The Sweet Shop USA
SweetWorks
Tootsie Roll
Unilever
Warrell Corporation
World's Finest Chocolate
Wrigley
Zachary Confections

## HISTORICAL FINANCIALS

Company Type: Private

**Income Statement** FYE: December 31

| | REVENUE ($ mil.) | NET INCOME ($ mil.) | NET PROFIT MARGIN | EMPLOYEES |
|---|---|---|---|---|
| 12/07 | 21,000 | — | — | 40,000 |

# Marsh & McLennan

Marsh & McLennan Companies is the ultimate middleman. The company is the world's largest insurance broker by total revenue (rival Aon is #2). Through core insurance subsidiary Marsh, the company provides a broad array of insurance and risk management services; its reinsurance business is handled by subsidiary Guy Carpenter. Kroll is Marsh & McLennan's risk consulting and technology services arm. It also owns Mercer Consulting Group, which provides human resources and management consulting services to customers worldwide. Marsh & McLennan in 2007 sold its money management operation, Putnam Investments, to Power Financial Corporation subsidiary Great-West Lifeco.

Citing such recent high profile natural disasters as tsunamis and hurricanes as well as international terrorism, Marsh & McLennan plans to expand its role as a risk consultant; its paring of other operations is part of a greater plan to focus on this business sector. In addition, the company re-organized its management consultancy operations, melding three firms under the tutelage of one new brand. Mercer Oliver Wyman, Mercer Management Consulting, and Mercer Delta Organizing in 2007 merged into one unit, called Oliver Wyman.

As part of an effort to relieve possible conflicts of interest following an investigation into allegations of pricing and disclosure improprieties, the company sold off its wholesale brokerage units. To this end, MMC divested its US-based wholesale insurance brokerage Crump Group in late 2005. It also sold its private equity subsidiary, MMC Capital (now Stone Point Capital), to the unit's management team.

Meanwhile, the company's Marsh insurance subsidiary (more than one third of sales) is restyling itself as a strategic risk adviser while maintaining its primary mission as a broker. In 2007 CEO Cherasky replaced about a third of the subsidiary's office managers nationwide; as a result, Marsh lost a substantial number of customers, a price Cherasky says will be worth paying in the long-term.

## HISTORY

Marsh & McLennan Companies dates back to the Dan H. Bomar Company, founded in 1871 after the Great Chicago Fire. In 1885 a plucky Harvard dropout named Henry Marsh joined the company, then known as R.A. Waller and Company. When Robert Waller died in 1889, Marsh and fellow employee Herbert Ulmann bought a controlling stake and renamed the company Marsh Ulmann & Co. Marsh pioneered insurance brokering and in 1901 set up U.S. Steel's self-insurance program.

In 1904 different directors at Burlington Northern Railroad promised their account to Marsh Ulmann, as well as Manley-McLennan of Duluth (railroad insurance), and D.W. Burrows (a small Chicago-based railroad insurance firm). Rather than fight over it, the firms joined forces to form the world's largest insurance brokerage. When Burrows retired in 1906, the firm became Marsh & McLennan.

In the early 20th century, Marsh won AT&T's business and McLennan landed the account of Armour Meat Packing.

In 1923 Marsh & McLennan became a closely held corporation. Marsh sold out to McLennan in 1935. The company weathered the Depression without major layoffs by cutting pay and branching into life insurance and employee-benefits consulting after passage of the Social Security Act (1935).

The firm grew through acquisitions in the 1950s, went public in 1962, and in 1969 formed a holding company that became Marsh & McLennan Companies. In the 1970s it diversified, buying Putnam Management (investment management). It set up subsidiary William M. Mercer's employee-benefits consulting business in 1975, and in 1980 it acquired a foothold in the UK with C.T. Bowring Reinsurance. In 1982 Marsh & McLennan formed Seabury & Smith to manage its insurance group programs.

As the insurance business slowed in the 1980s, the financial and consulting fields grew. In 1992 the firm formed Mercer Consulting Group as an umbrella for its various consulting companies. With J.P. Morgan (now J.P. Morgan Chase & Co.), the company (through Marsh & McLennan Risk Capital) formed Mid Ocean Reinsurance and Underwriters Capital (Merrett) Ltd. in 1993 and the Trident Fund in 1994.

In 1997 the company expanded its insurance brokering and money management by buying Johnson & Higgins. In 1998 a group of Johnson & Higgins' retired directors filed suit over alleged manipulation of the partnership's rules, which they charged prevented them from participating in the vote to join Marsh & McLennan. The same year the company bought Sedgwick Group, a UK-based insurance services firm.

The next year the firm named Jeffrey Greenberg, the son of AIG chairman Hank Greenberg, to replace chairman and CEO A. J. C. Smith. In 2000 Marsh & McLennan launched MMC Enterprise Risk, an enterprise risk management unit.

With offices in the World Trade Center, the company lost some 300 employees in the September 11 terrorist attacks. Following the attacks on the World Trade Center, Marsh & McLennan launched a new subsidiary (AXIS Specialty) to deal with the capacity shortage in the insurance industry.

Two major Marsh & McLennan units came under legal fire in probes of the mutual fund and insurance brokerage industries, respectively. In 2003 Putnam agreed to settle securities fraud charges with the SEC and reimburse investors; many of Putnam's top officers were replaced and its compliance procedures were restructured.

The following year, Marsh found itself at the center of a price-fixing investigation that involved several insurance companies, including AIG and ACE Limited. At least nine employees of March and AIG pled guilty to criminal charges. Jeffery Greenberg, the son of outspoken AIG CEO Maurice Greenberg who had served as Marsh & McLennan's chairman and CEO, resigned in 2004 as a result of the price-fixing allegations.

Strengthening its risk management operations, Marsh & McLennan acquired risk consulting company Kroll for about $2 billion in 2004.

Michael Cherkasky was named as Greenberg's successor. Before entering the insurance industry, Cherkasky had headed the investigations unit of the New York County District Attorney's Office; at one point, he was supervisor to future New York attorney general Elliot Spitzer; Spitzer launched the investigation into Marsh's alleged involvement in price-fixing and bid-rigging that ended in a settlement agreement reached in early 2005. Following the $850 million settlement agreement, the company slashed its dividend and cut jobs.

## EXECUTIVES

**Chairman:** Stephen R. Hardis, age 71
**Vice Chairman; Chairman, MMC International:** Mathis Cabiallavetta, age 62
**Vice Chairman:** David A. Nadler, age 58
**President, CEO, and Director:** Michael G. Cherkasky, age 56, $973,965 pay
**CFO:** Matthew B. Bartley, age 49
**SVP and Chief Marketing Officer:** James D. Speros
**SVP, General Counsel, and Corporate Secretary:** Peter J. Beshar, age 44
**SVP and Chief Administrative Officer:** Michael A. (Mike) Petrullo, age 37
**SVP and Chief Strategic Development Officer:** Michael A. Beber, age 46
**SVP and Chief Compliance Officer:** E. Scott Gilbert, age 50
**VP and Controller:** Robert J. Rapport
**Chairman and CEO, Marsh Inc.:** Brian M. Storms, age 51, $3,100,000 pay (prior to title change)
**Chairman and CEO, Mercer Human Resource Consulting:** M. Michele Burns, age 49
**Chairman and CEO, Guy Carpenter & Company, Inc.:** Salvatore D. (Sal) Zaffino, age 60
**President and CEO, Kroll Inc.:** Simon Freakley, age 44, $3,378,050 pay
**Director, Corporate Development:** Steven Spiegel, age 59
**Director, Utilities Consulting Practice, Mercer Management Consulting:** Andrew W. Patterson
**Deputy General Counsel and Corporate Secretary:** Lucy Fato, age 39
**Managing Director and COO, Mercer Management Consulting:** John P. Drzik
**Director, Corporate Communications, Mercer Management Consulting:** Chris Schmidt
**CFO, Marsh Inc.:** Mark C. McGivney
**CEO, US Business, Marsh Inc.:** Mark Feuer, age 38
**Auditors:** Deloitte & Touche LLP

## LOCATIONS

**HQ:** Marsh & McLennan Companies, Inc.
1166 Avenue of the Americas, New York, NY 10036
**Phone:** 212-345-5000
**Web:** www.marshmac.com

**2006 Sales**

| | $ mil. | % of total |
|---|---|---|
| US | 6,772 | 56 |
| Europe | | |
| UK | 2,029 | 17 |
| Other countries | 1,547 | 13 |
| Other regions | 1,704 | 14 |
| Adjustments | (131) | — |
| **Total** | **11,921** | **100** |

## PRODUCTS/OPERATIONS

**2006 Sales**

| | $ mil. | % of total |
|---|---|---|
| Risk & insurance services | | |
| Insurance services | 4,390 | 37 |
| Reinsurance services | 880 | 7 |
| Risk capital holdings | 193 | 1 |
| Consulting | | |
| Human resource consulting | 3,021 | 25 |
| Specialty consulting | 1,204 | 10 |
| Investment management | 1,385 | 12 |
| Risk consulting & technology | 979 | 8 |
| Adjustments | (131) | — |
| **Total** | **11,921** | **100** |

### Selected Subsidiaries

Kroll Inc.
Marsh & McLennan Securities Corporation
Marsh, Inc.
- Guy Carpenter & Co., Inc.
- Marsh & McLennan Capital, Inc.
- Seabury & Smith, Inc.
- Sedgwick Group PLC

MMC Enterprise Risk, Inc.
MMC International
Mercer Consulting Group, Inc.
- Mercer Human Resource Consulting, Inc.
- Oliver Wyman
- National Economic Research Associates (NERA)
- William M. Mercer Companies LLC

## COMPETITORS

Accenture
AIG
Allianz
Aon
Arthur Gallagher
AXA
Benfield Group
Booz Allen
GE
General Re
Hilb Rogal & Hobbs
ING
Jardine Lloyd
Lloyd's
McKinsey & Company
Morgan Stanley
T. Rowe Price
Towers Perrin
UBS Financial Services
Watson Wyatt
Wells Fargo Insurance
Willis Group
Zurich Financial Services

## HISTORICAL FINANCIALS

Company Type: Public

### Income Statement

FYE: December 31

| | REVENUE ($ mil.) | NET INCOME ($ mil.) | NET PROFIT MARGIN | EMPLOYEES |
|---|---|---|---|---|
| **12/06** | 11,921 | 990 | 8.3% | 55,200 |
| **12/05** | 11,652 | 404 | 3.5% | 55,000 |
| **12/04** | 12,159 | 176 | 1.4% | 61,800 |
| **12/03** | 11,588 | 1,540 | 13.3% | 60,500 |
| **12/02** | 10,440 | 1,365 | 13.1% | 59,500 |
| **Annual Growth** | 3.4% | (7.7%) | — | (1.9%) |

### 2006 Year-End Financials

Debt ratio: 66.3%
Return on equity: 17.7%
Cash ($ mil.): 2,089
Current ratio: 1.05
Long-term debt ($ mil.): 3,860
No. of shares (mil.): 552
Dividends
- Yield: 2.2%
- Payout: 38.6%

Market value ($ mil.): 16,922

### Stock History

NYSE: MMC

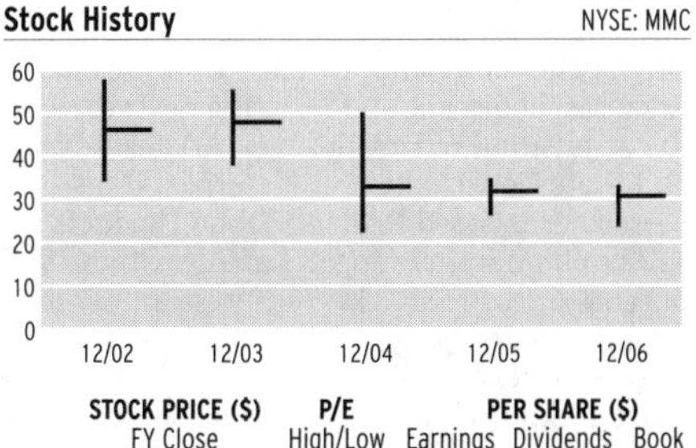

| | STOCK PRICE ($) FY Close | P/E High | P/E Low | PER SHARE ($) Earnings | Dividends | Book Value |
|---|---|---|---|---|---|---|
| **12/06** | 30.66 | 19 | 14 | 1.76 | 0.68 | 10.54 |
| **12/05** | 31.76 | 46 | 36 | 0.74 | 0.68 | 9.82 |
| **12/04** | 32.90 | 151 | 69 | 0.33 | 0.99 | 9.60 |
| **12/03** | 47.89 | 20 | 14 | 2.81 | 1.49 | 10.35 |
| **12/02** | 46.21 | 23 | 14 | 2.45 | 1.09 | 9.32 |
| **Annual Growth** | (9.7%) | — | — | (7.9%) | (11.1%) | 3.1% |

# Martha Stewart Living

If anyone could turn a stay in jail into a good thing, it's legendary lifestyle maven Martha Stewart. Following the completion of her sentence on federal criminal charges, Stewart has not shied away from the limelight. Rather, she and her company, Martha Stewart Living Omnimedia (MSLO), have embraced the spotlight. The company has its fingers in many money-making pies: publishing (magazines and books), TV (programs), radio (satellite radio network channel), and merchandising. Stewart was accused of insider trading relating to the sale of her ImClone stock, and was later convicted for lying to investigators and obstruction of justice. Stewart controls about 55% of MSLO's stock and about 92% of voting stock.

The scandal around her sale of ImClone stock, allegedly based on an insider trading tip, rocked Stewart's seemingly perfect world, and her persona (which had been her most successful recipe to date) briefly suffered a hit. Stewart served less than six months in jail; she saw her company struggle: its stock price dropped, her TV show was put on hold, and for a time executives carefully tried to de-emphasize the "Martha-ness" of its products. But following the end of her jail and home confinement sentence in 2005, Stewart and her company then made a flurry of deals, and she has spent even more time in the public eye.

Her recipe: Mix equal parts Julia Child, Miss America, and P. T. Barnum; stir in liberal amounts of ambition and chutzpah; and serve with a flourish to a public hungry for a more gracious existence. Ever the model of organization, Stewart arranged MSLO's activities into four tidy divisions: publishing, broadcasting, merchandising, and Internet.

Magazines such as *Martha Stewart Living* and *Martha Stewart Weddings*, and a series of more than 30 books (*Entertaining*, *Martha Stewart's Christmas*) illustrate MSLO's reach into publishing (55% of sales).

MSLO's syndicated daytime show *The Martha Stewart Show* has garnered solid ratings. Stewart's classic shows (*Martha Stewart Living*, cable series *From Martha's Kitchen* and *From Martha's Home*) still air on cable networks. A TV series based on MSLO's *Everyday Food* magazine airs on PBS. Broadcasting operations also include the satellite radio channel *Martha Stewart Living Radio*, found on SIRIUS Satellite Radio.

Retail partnerships with companies such as Kmart (The Martha Stewart Everyday Home collection) and Sherwin-Williams (Martha Stewart Everyday Colors) fall into MSLO's merchandising division. MSLO has resolved a complaint filed against it by Kmart concerning possible excessive royalty payments, and the two firms have extended their licensing agreement to 2009. MSLO has additional merchandising agreements with companies such as Bernhardt Furniture Company, Macy's, Lowe's, Kodak, and KB Home.

## HISTORY

A former model and stockbroker, Martha Stewart's entry into the commerce of gracious living can be traced back to 1972 when she launched a Westport, Connecticut, catering business. Culling her experiences as a caterer, Stewart published her first book, *Entertaining,* in 1982.

The resounding success of *Entertaining* (the book has gone into 30 printings) propelled Stewart into the public spotlight. Kmart appointed Stewart as its lifestyle consultant in 1987, and in 1991 her notoriety led media giant Time Inc. to begin publishing the *Martha Stewart Living* magazine. Though beautiful to look at, the publication was expensive to produce; it did not achieve profitability until 1996.

Stewart rode the coattails of her magazine's success into a variety of other ventures. Her syndicated TV show, *Martha Stewart Living,* premiered in 1993. Stewart's first prime-time TV Christmas special (featuring Hillary Rodham Clinton and Miss Piggy) aired in 1995. Expanding further into merchandising, Stewart introduced Martha by Mail, a direct-mail catalog business, in 1995.

Frustrated with what she saw as Time's inability to keep pace with the growth of her burgeoning empire and desirous of a hefty equity stake in her collection of companies, Stewart wrested her operation (then called Martha Stewart Enterprises) away from Time in 1997. Stewart's friend Sharon Patrick (and later a MSLO CEO) negotiated a buyout valuing the company at about $53 million.

Christening her new undertaking Martha Stewart Living Omnimedia (MSLO), Stewart wasted no time in expanding the company. MSLO entered into an alliance with Kmart to market the Martha Stewart Everyday line of merchandise. When MSLO went public in 1999, Stewart greeted harried Wall Street traders with a breakfast of brioches stuffed with scrambled eggs.

Stewart resigned as CEO and chairman in 2003 after being indicted on insider trading charges related to a bio-tech stock. She remained on the board and was given the new title of chief creative officer. Stewart was replaced by COO Sharon Patrick as CEO, and managing partner of ValueAct Capital Partners Jeffrey Ubben as chairman.

Stewart was found guilty on all charges in 2004 after a federal jury deliberated for three days following a five-week trial. Shortly after her conviction, Stewart stepped down as chief creative officer and director.

In September 2004, Stewart, who had been free pending appeal, asked to begin serving her jail sentence immediately in order to "put this nightmare behind me" and "reclaim my good life" and "return to my good works" as soon as possible. Following her request, she began serving her sentence in October 2004 at a prison in West Virginia.

Patrick stepped down from her position in 2004 and was replaced by director Susan Lyne, a former ABC television executive. Ubben served as chairman until July 2004 when board member Thomas Siekman was named as his replacement. Charles Koppelman took over as chairman in 2005.

Stewart completed the prison sentence in March 2005, a time that her company referred to as her "homecoming." She then served another five months of house arrest.

In 2006 Stewart struck a deal with the Securities and Exchange Commission to settle her insider-trading case in which she will pay $5 million and will not be able to serve as a director of a public company for five years. Also limited for five years in her service as an officer or employee of a public company, Stewart assumed the title of founder at the company.

MSLO announced a new deal in 2006 to create a line of craft products called "Martha Stewart Crafts," to be sold in craft stores and online.

## EXECUTIVES

**Chairman:** Charles A. Koppelman, age 67
**President, CEO, and Director:** Susan Lyne, age 56, $900,000 pay
**CFO:** Howard Hochhauser, age 36, $311,500 pay
**Chief Creative Officer:** Gael Towey, age 55
**Founder:** Martha Stewart, Age 66, $900,000 pay
**EVP and Editor-in-Chief:** Margaret Roach, age 49
**EVP Print Production:** Dora Braschi Cardinale, age 47
**SVP and Chief Marketing Officer:** Amy Stanton
**SVP; Publisher, Martha Stewart Living:** Sally Preston
**SVP; Executive Producer, Martha Stewart Living Television:** Linda Corradina
**SVP Corporate Communications and Media Relations:** Diana Pearson
**SVP Consumer Marketing Director:** Richard P. Fontaine
**SVP and Editorial Business Manager:** Rita Christiansen
**SVP; Founding Publisher, Martha Stewart Weddings:** Marcia E. Miller
**VP and Controller:** Alison Jacques
**VP Human Resources:** Laura A. Schmidt
**VP Information Technology:** Jeff Frasure
**VP Marketing and Broadcasting:** Jill Boulet-Gercourt
**VP Programming and Broadcasting:** Richard Claflin
**Assistant VP Corporate Communications:** Elizabeth J. Estroff
**President, Merchandising:** Robin Marino, age 52, $495,000 pay
**President, Broadcasting:** Sheraton Kalouria, age 41, $475,000 pay
**Secretary and General Counsel:** John R. Cuti, age 41
**Auditors:** Ernst & Young LLP

## LOCATIONS

**HQ:** Martha Stewart Living Omnimedia Inc.
11 W. 42nd St., New York, NY 10036
**Phone:** 212-827-8000 **Fax:** 212-827-8204
**Web:** www.marthastewart.com

## PRODUCTS/OPERATIONS

### 2006 Sales

| | $ mil. | % of total |
|---|---|---|
| Publishing | 156.5 | 55 |
| Merchandising | 69.5 | 24 |
| Broadcasting | 46.5 | 16 |
| Internet | 15.8 | 5 |
| **Total** | **288.3** | **100** |

### Selected Operations

Broadcasting
- *Everyday Food*
- *Martha Stewart Living* (licensed syndicated series)
- Martha Stewart Living Radio (on Sirius Satellite Radio)
- *The Martha Stewart Show*

Internet
- Marthastewart.com
- marthastewartflowers.com

Merchandising
- KB Home / Martha Stewart Homes
- Martha Stewart Collection at Macy's
- Martha Stewart Colors at Lowe's
- Martha Stewart Everyday at Kmart & Sears Canada
- Martha Stewart Furniture with Bernhardt

Publishing
- *Blueprint: Design Your Life* (magazine)
- *Body + Soul* (healthy living magazine)
- *Everyday Food* (magazine)
- *Martha Stewart's Homekeeping Handbook: The Essential Guide to Caring for Everything in Your Home* (book)
- *Martha Stewart Living* (magazine)
- *Martha Stewart Weddings* (magazine)

## COMPETITORS

Advance Publications
Bertelsmann
Disney
Dwell
Euromarket Designs
Hanover Direct
Harpo
Harry & David Holdings
Hearst Magazines
Hobby Lobby
iVillage
Lagardère Active Media
Lifetime
Meredith
Michaels Stores
News Corp.
Oxygen Media
Pampered Chef
PRIMEDIA
Reader's Digest
Smith & Hawken
Time Warner

## HISTORICAL FINANCIALS

Company Type: Public

### Income Statement — FYE: December 31

| | REVENUE ($ mil.) | NET INCOME ($ mil.) | NET PROFIT MARGIN | EMPLOYEES |
|---|---|---|---|---|
| **12/06** | 288 | (17) | — | 755 |
| **12/05** | 210 | (76) | — | 656 |
| **12/04** | 187 | (60) | — | 480 |
| **12/03** | 246 | (3) | — | 544 |
| **12/02** | 295 | 7 | 2.5% | 580 |
| **Annual Growth** | (0.6%) | — | — | 6.8% |

### 2006 Year-End Financials

Debt ratio: —
Return on equity: —
Cash ($ mil.): 64
Current ratio: 1.97
Long-term debt ($ mil.): —
No. of shares (mil.): 26
Dividends
Yield: 2.3%
Payout: —
Market value ($ mil.): 570

### Stock History — NYSE: MSO

| | STOCK PRICE ($) FY Close | P/E High | P/E Low | PER SHARE ($) Earnings | Dividends | Book Value |
|---|---|---|---|---|---|---|
| **12/06** | 21.90 | — | — | (0.33) | 0.50 | 5.03 |
| **12/05** | 17.43 | — | — | (1.49) | — | 6.47 |
| **12/04** | 29.02 | — | — | (1.20) | — | 8.69 |
| **12/03** | 9.85 | — | — | (0.06) | — | 11.95 |
| **12/02** | 9.87 | 140 | 35 | 0.15 | — | 12.27 |
| **Annual Growth** | 22.0% | — | — | — | — | (20.0%) |

# Martin Marietta Materials

Martin Marietta Materials (MMM) is a rock star. The company is the #2 US producer (behind Vulcan Materials) of aggregates for highway, infrastructure, commercial, and residential construction. MMM's Martin Marietta Aggregates division (more than 90% of sales) produces about 200 million tons of granite, limestone, sand, and gravel annually. The division also has ready-mixed concrete, asphalt, and road-paving operations. MMM has a Magnesia Specialties unit that produces dolomitic lime and magnesia-based products, including chemicals for industrial, environmental, and agricultural uses. The company also makes fiber-reinforced composite materials.

MMM's aggregate markets include 31 states, as well as Canada, the Bahamas, and the Caribbean. The firm gets more than half of its sales from customers in five key states: Georgia, Iowa, North Carolina, South Carolina, and Texas. Since the mid-1990s MMM has expanded geographically via acquisitions, focusing on businesses near rail facilities or navigable waterways. The company believes its lower transportation costs give it a competitive advantage locally, while allowing it to ship aggregates to more-distant customers economically. In 2005 MMM formed a venture (Hunt Martin Materials) with Hunt Midwest Enterprises to jointly operate 15 quarries in the Kansas City area. The company has also continued to close underperforming aggregates facilities, even as it beefs up operations in other areas. In 2006 it opened new or expanded facilities in Georgia, Kentucky, and Oklahoma, and plans to continue its capital spending program with a focus on the Southeast.

## HISTORY

Aerospace giant Martin Marietta Corporation kept its aggregates business out of the fray during the industry's acquisition binge of the 1980s, during which quarry prices became inflated. When recession hit at the beginning of the 1990s, the company was able to pick up quarries at fire-sale prices before spinning off the group as Martin Marietta Materials (MMM) in 1993. An initial public offering of 19% was completed in 1994.

The next year the company acquired Dravo Corporation's aggregates business for about $121 million, a move that added production and distribution operations in nine states and the Bahamas, as well as new distribution methods (by barge) and nonconstruction markets. Lockheed Martin Corporation (formed by the merger of Martin Marietta and Lockheed in 1995) owned 81% of the company until 1996, when it spun off its stake to shareholders.

In 1997 MMM shelled out $242 million for American Aggregates Corporation to add distribution and production facilities in Indiana and Ohio. The company extended its reach to Arkansas, Louisiana, and Texas the next year with the acquisition of Hot Springs, Arkansas-based Mid-State Construction & Materials. It also acquired Texas-based Redland Stone Products for $272 million from France's Lafarge. Other 1998 purchases included a 14% interest in Meridian Aggregates Company.

Rival Vulcan Materials sued MMM in 1999; Vulcan claimed it had rights to some of the leased reserves MMM had acquired in its purchase of Redland Stone Products. (The suit was dropped in 2000.) Also in 1999 MMM bought another Texas aggregates company, Marock.

In 2000 MMM completed four deals that added three asphalt plants and an aggregate company in Texas, as well as limestone operations in Ohio and West Virginia. The next year MMM bought Brauntex Materials, a limestone facility in Texas, and the part of Meridian Aggregates Company it didn't already own. Also in 2001 MMM sold its Magnesia Specialties refractories business to Minerals Technologies.

From 2002 to 2005, while continuing to pursue strategic acquisitions, the company divested several noncore and underperforming operations, as well as two nonstrategic magnesia business lines. In 2002 MMM began selling noncore aggregates businesses; it also made acquisitions in key markets, including quarries in Texas and North Carolina and an asphalt plant in Texas. It sold facilities in Illinois, Iowa, Ohio, Oklahoma, Tennessee, and Virginia.

The company sold additional noncore aggregate assets in 2003 and 2004. In 2005 it divested underperforming asphalt operations in Arkansas and Texas and closed aggregates plants in North Carolina and Ohio.

## EXECUTIVES

**Chairman and CEO; Chairman, Magnesia Specialties Business; President, Aggregates Business:** Stephen P. (Steve) Zelnak Jr., age 62, $1,508,333 pay
**President and COO:** C. Howard (Ward) Nye, age 44
**EVP; CEO, Magnesia Specialties:** Daniel G. (Dan) Shephard, age 48
**EVP; EVP, Aggregates Division:** Philip J. (Phil) Sipling, age 59, $691,621 pay
**EVP; President, Martin Marietta Materials West:** Bruce A. Vaio, age 46
**SVP, CFO, and Treasurer:** Anne H. Lloyd, age 45
**SVP, General Counsel, and Corporate Secretary:** Roselyn R. Bar, age 48, $464,508 pay
**SVP:** J. Michael (Mike) Pertsch
**SVP Human Resources:** Jonathan T. (Jon) Stewart, age 58
**VP Operations:** George S. Seaman
**VP, Controller, and Chief Accounting Officer:** Dana F. Guzzo
**Auditors:** Ernst & Young LLP

## LOCATIONS

**HQ:** Martin Marietta Materials, Inc.
2710 Wycliff Rd., Raleigh, NC 27607
**Phone:** 919-781-4550 **Fax:** 919-783-4695
**Web:** www.martinmarietta.com

Martin Marietta Materials operates about 310 quarries, plants, and distribution yards in 31 US states and in Canada and the Bahamas.

## PRODUCTS/OPERATIONS

### 2006 Sales By Business Segment

| | $ mil. | % of total |
|---|---|---|
| Aggregates | | |
| West Group | 769 | 35 |
| Southeast Group | 639 | 29 |
| Mideast Group | 632 | 29 |
| Specialty products | 166 | 7 |
| **Total** | **2,206** | **100** |

### 2006 Sales By Product Line

| | $ mil. | % of total |
|---|---|---|
| Aggregates | 1,931 | 88 |
| Specialty products | 166 | 7 |
| Asphalt | 49 | 2 |
| Ready-mixed concrete | 35 | 2 |
| Road paving & other | 25 | 1 |
| **Total** | **2,206** | **100** |

### Selected Operations

Aggregates Division
- Aggregates (granite, gravel, limestone, and sand)
- Asphalt
- Ready-mixed concrete
- Road paving

Specialty Products Division
- Magnesia Specialties (dolomitic lime, magnesia-based chemicals)
- Structural Composite Products (fiber-reinforced polymer composites)

### Selected Subsidiaries and Affiliates

Alamo Gulf Coast Railroad Company
Alamo North Texas Railroad Company
American Aggregates Corporation
American Stone Company (50%)
Bahama Rock Limited
Fredonia Valley Railroad, Inc.
Granite Canyon Quarry (51%)
Harding Street Corporation
Hunt Martin Materials, LLC (50%)
J.W. Jones Materials, LLC
Martin Bauerly Materials, LLC (67%)
Material Producers, Inc.
Meridian Aggregates Company
Meridian Granite Company
Mid South-Weaver Joint Venture (50%
Mid-State Construction & Materials, Inc.
MTD Pipeline LLC (50%)
Powderly Transportation, Inc.
R&S Sand & Gravel, LLC
Rocky Ridge, Inc.
Sha-Neva, LLC
Theodore Holding, LLC (61%)
Valley Stone LLC (50%)
Wycliff Holding, LLC

## COMPETITORS

Aggregate Industries
Ashland
BPB
Carmeuse North America
CEMEX
Chemical Lime
Cookson Group
CRH
CSR Limited
Eagle Materials
Florida Rock
Giant Cement
Hanson Building Products
Holcim
Lafarge North America
MDU Resources
Minerals Technologies
Oglebay Norton
Ready Mix USA
Rinker Materials
Rogers
Trinity Industries
TXI
Vulcan Materials

## HISTORICAL FINANCIALS

Company Type: Public

### Income Statement

FYE: December 31

| | REVENUE ($ mil.) | NET INCOME ($ mil.) | NET PROFIT MARGIN | EMPLOYEES |
|---|---|---|---|---|
| **12/06** | 2,206 | 245 | 11.1% | 5,500 |
| **12/05** | 2,004 | 193 | 9.6% | 5,754 |
| **12/04** | 1,760 | 129 | 7.3% | 5,778 |
| **12/03** | 1,711 | 94 | 5.5% | 5,900 |
| **12/02** | 1,692 | 86 | 5.1% | 6,400 |
| **Annual Growth** | 6.9% | 29.9% | — | (3.7%) |

### 2006 Year-End Financials

Debt ratio: 46.2%
Return on equity: 20.2%
Cash ($ mil.): 32
Current ratio: 1.88
Long-term debt ($ mil.): 579
No. of shares (mil.): 45
Dividends
Yield: 1.0%
Payout: 19.1%
Market value ($ mil.): 4,660

### Stock History

NYSE: MLM

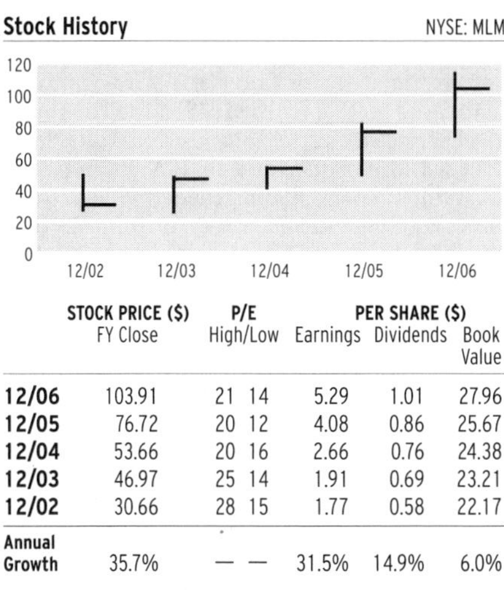

| | STOCK PRICE ($) FY Close | P/E High | P/E Low | PER SHARE ($) Earnings | Dividends | Book Value |
|---|---|---|---|---|---|---|
| **12/06** | 103.91 | 21 | 14 | 5.29 | 1.01 | 27.96 |
| **12/05** | 76.72 | 20 | 12 | 4.08 | 0.86 | 25.67 |
| **12/04** | 53.66 | 20 | 16 | 2.66 | 0.76 | 24.38 |
| **12/03** | 46.97 | 25 | 14 | 1.91 | 0.69 | 23.21 |
| **12/02** | 30.66 | 28 | 15 | 1.77 | 0.58 | 22.17 |
| **Annual Growth** | 35.7% | — | — | 31.5% | 14.9% | 6.0% |

# Masco Corporation

Masco's ideal customer is a lazy home-improvement junkie with a thing for cabinets — and a hand-washing fetish. The company's cabinet and faucet businesses account for more than half its sales: cabinet brands include KraftMaid, Merillat, and Mill's Pride in the US (and Moore Group and Tvilum-Scanbirk in Europe); faucet brands include Delta and Peerless in the US (and Bristan and Hansgrohe in Europe). Masco also makes bath and shower accessories, BEHR paints and stains, windows, patio doors, staple guns, locksets, and HVAC products. If you're more comfortable on the couch, Masco also provides installation and other services. The Home Depot accounts for about 20% of sales.

Masco adds to its broad line of products through acquisitions. It has capitalized on the popularity of home-center retail chains such as The Home Depot and Lowe's by offering a single source for a wide range of home-improvement products. It has added to its core offerings by purchasing companies that make hand tools and stains, varnishes, and paints, including BEHR Process. The company's services segment, its fastest-growing segment, was expanded significantly with the purchase of insulation installer BSI Holdings.

After reorganizing its European business operations, Masco sold off several of its operating units, including Gebhardt Consolidated (HVAC) and GMU Group (cabinets). The company also disposed of North American businesses that were not core to its long-term growth strategy, which included Computerized Security Systems (CSS) and Zenith Products (bathroom storage).

## HISTORY

Masco founder Alex Manoogian moved to the US at age 19 in 1920. He wound up in Detroit, and with partners Harry Adjemian and Charles Saunders, he started Masco (the first letters of their last names plus "co" for "company") Screw Products Company eight days before the crash of 1929. Manoogian's partners left within the year.

Largely reliant on Detroit's auto industry, Masco grew slowly during the Depression, making custom parts for Chrysler, Ford, and others. With sales of $200,000 by 1937, it went public on the Detroit Stock Exchange. During WWII Masco focused on defense, and in 1942 sales passed $1 million. A new plant opened in 1948 in Dearborn, Michigan, as Masco resumed peacetime business, mainly in the auto industry.

In 1954 Masco began selling Manoogian's one-handle kitchen faucet (Delta). Sales of faucets passed $1 million by 1958, and Masco opened a new faucet factory in Indiana.

Under Manoogian's son Richard — whose dinner was often delayed while his father used the stove to test the heat tolerance of new faucet parts — Masco Corporation (so renamed in 1961) diversified. From 1964 to 1980 it bought more than 50 companies, concentrating on tool and metal casting, energy exploration, and air compressors. In 1984 the firm split. Masco Corporation pursued the course set by its successful faucet sales, expanding its interests in home improvement and furnishings. The industrial products business was spun off as Masco Industries, a separate public corporation (later Metaldyne) in which Masco maintained a sizable stake.

Masco Corporation became the #1 US furniture maker in the late 1980s by buying Lexington Furniture (1987) and Universal Furniture (1989), both of North Carolina. In 1990 Masco acquired KraftMaid cabinets.

Two years later the company sold its interests in Mechanical Technology, Payless Cashways, and Emco Limited of Canada (Masco bought back 40% of Emco in 1997).

Masco sought to establish itself in Europe, and in 1994 it bought a German cabinetmaker and a UK producer of handheld showers. In 1996 founder Manoogian died, but the company flowed on. It added a UK cabinetmaker, a German shower manufacturer, and a German insulation firm. The same year Masco sold its troubled furniture unit to a group of investors and executives (who renamed the unit LifeStyle Furnishings International) for about $1 billion and further reduced its stake in Metaldyne to less than 20% (and later sold it all).

To increase its geographic reach, Masco bought Tvilum-Scanbirk (ready-to-assemble furniture, Denmark), Masterchem Industries (specialty paint products), and Glass Idromassaggio (bathroom equipment, Italy), in 2000.

During 2002 Masco acquired home improvement products and service companies that included Bristan Ltd. (kitchen and bath faucets and shower and bath accessories), Brasstech, Inc. (faucets, plumbing specialties, and bath accessories; California), Cambrian Windows Ltd. (vinyl window frames), Duraflex Ltd. (extruded vinyl frame components), Premier Manufacturing Ltd. (vinyl window and door frames), SCE Unlimited (siding, shutters, gutters; Illinois), IDI Group (fireplaces, garage doors, shower enclosures; Atlanta), Service Partners LLC (insulation and other building products, Virginia), several small installation and other service companies, and Diversified Cabinet Distributors (cabinets and countertops, Atlanta).

Masco's president and COO since 1996, Raymond Kennedy, died of an apparent heart attack in early 2003. Chairman and CEO Richard Manoogian assumed Kennedy's responsibilities until company group president Alan Barry assumed the role of president and COO in 2003. Also that year, Masco increased its ownership interest in Hansgrohe AG (kitchen and bath faucets, hand-held and fixed showerheads, luxury shower systems, and steam showers; Germany) to 64% from 27%. The company established Color Solutions Centers in more than 1,500 Home Depot stores throughout the US. Masco sold its Baldwin Hardware and Weiser Lock businesses (builders' hardware and locksets) to Black & Decker and The Marvel Group (specialty products including office workstations and machine stands) to key members of Marvel's management team (led by president John Dellamore) for $289 million in total. Acquisitions in 2003 included PowerShot Tool Company, Inc. (fastening products, New Jersey) and several small installation service companies for a combined $63 million.

In 2004 Masco sold its Jung Pumpen (pumps), The Alvic Group (kitchen cabinets), Alma Kuchen (kitchen cabinets), E. Missel (acoustic insulation), and SKS Group (shutters and ventilation systems) businesses for $199 million. Masco continued its business review in 2005, selling two operating companies that made and distributed cabinets, vanities, medicine cabinets, shower rods, and bath accessories.

## EXECUTIVES

**Chairman:** Richard A. Manoogian, age 70, $2,925,000 pay
**CEO and Director:** Timothy (Tim) Wadhams, age 59, $718,942 pay
**President and COO:** Alan H. Barry, age 63, $1,001,827 pay
**Group President, Architectural Coatings and Windows Group:** Clay H. Kiefaber, age 50
**Group President, Europe:** Lau Frandsen
**Group President:** Ronald W. (Ron) Ayers
**Group President:** Charles A. Dowd Jr.
**EVP; Group President, Installation Services and Other Services:** Donald J. DeMarie Jr., age 44
**EVP, Europe:** Thomas Voss
**SVP and General Counsel:** John R. Leekley, age 62, $747,500 pay
**VP and Associate General Counsel:** Barry J. Silverman
**VP and Secretary:** Eugene A. Gargaro Jr., age 62
**VP and Senior Financial Advisor:** Richard G. Mosteller
**VP and CIO:** Timothy J. Monteith, age 52
**VP Corporate Development, CFO, and Treasurer:** John G. Sznewajs, age 39
**VP Corporate Affairs:** Sharon Rothwell
**VP Corporate Taxes:** Jerry W. Mollien
**VP International:** David W. Van Hise
**VP Investor Relations:** Maria C. Duey, age 42
**VP Sales and Marketing:** Karen R. Mendelsohn
**VP and Secretary:** Eugene A. Gorgaro Jr.
**Auditors:** PricewaterhouseCoopers LLP

## LOCATIONS

**HQ:** Masco Corporation
21001 Van Born Rd., Taylor, MI 48180
**Phone:** 313-274-7400 **Fax:** 313-792-6135
**Web:** www.masco.com

### 2006 Sales

| | $ mil. | % of total |
|---|---|---|
| North America | 10,537 | 82 |
| Other regions | 2,241 | 18 |
| **Total** | **12,778** | **100** |

## PRODUCTS/OPERATIONS

### 2006 Sales

| | $ mil. | % of total |
|---|---|---|
| Cabinets & Related Products | 3,286 | 26 |
| Plumbing Products | 3,296 | 26 |
| Installation & Other Services | 3,158 | 24 |
| Decorative Architectural Products | 1,777 | 14 |
| Other Specialty Products | 1,261 | 10 |
| **Total** | **12,778** | **100** |

### Selected Brand Names

Kitchen and Bath Products
- Alsons (hand showers and shower heads)
- American Shower & Bath (bath and shower units and accessories)
- Aqua Glass (bath and shower units)
- BrassCraft (components)
- Delta (faucets)
- Home Plumber (components)
- Huppe (luxury bath and shower units)
- KraftMaid (cabinets)
- Liberty Hardware (cabinet hardware)
- Melard (components)
- Merillat (cabinets)
- Mill's Pride (cabinets)
- Mixet (valves and accessories)
- Peerless (faucets)
- Plumb Shop (components)
- Quality Cabinets
- Scanbirk (ready-to-assemble cabinetry, shelving, and storage products)
- Systema (cabinetry and related products)
- Trayco (bath and shower units and accessories)
- Tvilum (ready-to-assemble cabinetry, shelving, and storage products)
- Zenith Products (bath and shower accessories)

Specialty Products
- BEHR (paints and varnishes)
- Brilliance (brass finish)
- The Lifetime Finish (brass finish)
- Saflok (hardware)
- Winfield (hardware)

## COMPETITORS

American Standard
American Woodmark
Armstrong World Industries
Benjamin Moore
Black & Decker
Columbia Pipe
Elkay Manufacturing
Fortune Brands
Furniture Brands International
Gerber Plumbing Fixtures
Grohe
Helen of Troy
Home Solutions of America
ICI Paints in North America
Ingersoll Rand Security Technologies
Jacuzzi Brands
Jones-Blair
Kohler
Marmon Group
Master Lock
MasterBrand Cabinets
Moen
Nordyne
NTK Holdings
Omega Cabinets
PPG
Price Pfister
Republic National Cabinet
Richelieu Hardware
RSI Holding Corporation
Sherwin-Williams
Simpson Manufacturing
Simpson Strong-Tie
Spear & Jackson
Stanley Works
US Home Systems
Valspar
Water Pik Technologies
Waxman

## HISTORICAL FINANCIALS

Company Type: Public

**Income Statement** FYE: December 31

| | REVENUE ($ mil.) | NET INCOME ($ mil.) | NET PROFIT MARGIN | EMPLOYEES |
|---|---|---|---|---|
| **12/06** | 12,778 | 488 | 3.8% | 57,000 |
| **12/05** | 12,642 | 940 | 7.4% | 62,000 |
| **12/04** | 12,074 | 893 | 7.4% | 62,000 |
| **12/03** | 10,936 | 806 | 7.4% | 61,000 |
| **12/02** | 9,419 | 590 | 6.3% | 61,000 |
| **Annual Growth** | 7.9% | (4.6%) | — | (1.7%) |

**2006 Year-End Financials**

Debt ratio: 79.0%
Return on equity: 10.5%
Cash ($ mil.): 1,958
Current ratio: 1.51
Long-term debt ($ mil.): 3,533
No. of shares (mil.): 384
Dividends
Yield: 2.9%
Payout: 70.5%
Market value ($ mil.): 11,467

**Stock History** NYSE: MAS

| | STOCK PRICE ($) FY Close | P/E High | P/E Low | PER SHARE ($) Earnings | Dividends | Book Value |
|---|---|---|---|---|---|---|
| **12/06** | 29.87 | 28 | 21 | 1.22 | 0.86 | 11.65 |
| **12/05** | 30.19 | 18 | 12 | 2.19 | 0.78 | 11.57 |
| **12/04** | 36.53 | 19 | 13 | 1.96 | 0.66 | 12.14 |
| **12/03** | 27.41 | 17 | 10 | 1.64 | 0.58 | 11.90 |
| **12/02** | 21.05 | 26 | 15 | 1.15 | 0.55 | 10.83 |
| **Annual Growth** | 9.1% | — | — | 1.5% | 11.8% | 1.8% |

# Massachusetts Mutual Life Insurance

Massachusetts Mutual Life Insurance (known as MassMutual) is the flagship firm of the MassMutual Financial Group, a global organization of companies that provide financial services including life insurance, annuities, money management, and retirement planning. Founded in 1851, MassMutual's clients include individuals and businesses. The company also offers disability income insurance, long-term care insurance, structured settlement annuities, and trust services (through The MassMutual Trust Company). Other subsidiaries include OppenheimerFunds (mutual funds), David L. Babson & Co. (investor services), and Cornerstone Real Estate (real estate equities).

Like so many other insurance firms, MassMutual is determined to transform into a financial services firm. However, you won't catch the firm issuing stock to get the job done; its management and policyholders have reaffirmed their intention to keep MassMutual a mutual company despite the efforts of some policyholders.

MassMutual has acquired the operations of Baring Asset Management from ING Groep.

MassMutual International is exporting the company's operations worldwide, having established subsidiaries in Asia, Europe, and South America. It focuses on new product development (the majority of sales come from products or channels developed within the last couple of years) and broadened distribution.

## HISTORY

Insurance agent George Rice formed Massachusetts Mutual in 1851 as a stock company based in Springfield. The firm converted to a mutual in 1867. For its first 50 years MassMutual sold only individual life insurance, but after 1900 it branched out, offering first annuities (1917) and then disability coverage (1918).

The early 20th century was rough on MassMutual, which was forced to raise premiums on new policies during WWI, then faced the high costs of the 1918 flu epidemic. The firm endured the Great Depression despite policy terminations, expanding its product line to include income insurance. In 1946 MassMutual wrote its first group policy, for Jack Daniel's maker Brown-Forman Distillers. By 1950 the company had diversified into medical insurance.

MassMutual began investing in stocks in the 1950s, switching from fixed-return bonds and mortgages for higher returns. It also decentralized and in 1961 began automating operations. By 1970 the firm had installed a computer network linking it to its independent agents. During this period, whole life insurance remained the core product.

With interest rates increasing during the late 1970s, many insurers diversified by offering high-yield products like guaranteed investment contracts funded by high-risk investments. MassMutual resisted as long as it could, but as interest rates soared to 20%, the company experienced a rash of policy loans, which led to a cash crunch. In 1981, with its policy growth rate trailing the industry norm, MassMutual developed new products, including some that offered higher dividends in return for adjustable interest on policy loans.

In the 1980s MassMutual reduced its stock investment (to about 5% of total investments by 1987), allowing it to emerge virtually unscathed from the 1987 stock market crash.

The firm changed course in 1990 and entered financial services. It bought a controlling interest in mutual fund manager Oppenheimer Management. MassMutual announced in 1993 that, with legislation limiting rates, it would stop writing new individual and small-group policies in New York.

The next year the company targeted the neglected family-owned business niche; in 1995 it sponsored the American Alliance of Family-Owned Businesses and rolled out new whole life products aimed at this segment. That year it bought David L. Babson & Company, a Massachusetts-based investment management firm, and opened life insurance companies in Chile and Argentina.

In 1996 MassMutual merged with Connecticut Mutual. It also acquired Antares Leveraged Capital Corp. (commercial finance) and Charter Oak Capital Management (investment advisory services). The next year MassMutual sold its Life & Health Benefits Management subsidiary.

Still in the mood to merge, the company entered discussions with Northwestern Mutual in 1998, but culture clashes terminated the talks. Also that year the company helped push through legislation that would allow insurers to issue stock through mutual holding companies, a move which MassMutual itself contemplated in 1999.

MassMutual expanded outside the US at the turn of the century. In 1999 it issued securities in Europe, opened offices in such locales as Bermuda and Luxembourg, and bought the Argentina operations of Jefferson-Pilot. A year later it expanded into Asia when it bought Hong Kong-based CRC Protective Life Insurance (now MassMutual Asia). In 2001 the company entered the Taiwanese market, buying a stake in Mercuries Life Insurance (now MassMutual Mercuries Life Insurance) and acquiring Japanese insurer Aetna Heiwa Life (a subsidiary of US health insurer Aetna).

Also in 2001 MassMutual policyholders defeated a proposal by some to convert the company to stockholder ownership.

The company's board of directors terminated former CEO Robert O'Connell in 2005, citing a laundry list of reasons that included using company assets improperly and the use of retaliatory behavior against employees. Stuart Reese was named his replacement.

## EXECUTIVES

**Chairman, President, and CEO:** Stuart H. Reese
**EVP and CFO:** Michael T. Rollings, age 42
**EVP and Chief Administrative Officer; President and CEO, MassMutual International:** Elaine A. Sarsynski, age 51
**EVP, Chief Investment Officer, and Co-COO; Office of the CEO:** Roger W. Crandall, age 42
**COO, Retirement Services Division:** Marie M. Augsberger
**EVP and CIO:** James E. Miller
**EVP; Chairman, President, and CEO, OppenheimerFunds, Inc.:** John V. Murphy
**EVP, Retirement, Financial, Disability and Long-Term Care Products:** Toby J. Slodden
**EVP and General Counsel:** Mark D. Roellig, age 51
**EVP U.S. Insurance Group and Co-COO:** William Glavin, age 47
**SVP and COO, U.S. Insurance Group:** Michael R. Fanning, age 43
**SVP and CFO, U.S. Insurance Group:** Gregory (Greg) Deavens
**SVP, Corporate Financial Operations:** Richard D. Bourgeois
**SVP; Managing Director and CEO, MassMutual Asia:** Elroy Chan
**SVP, Retirement Services:** Beverly A. Holmes
**SVP, Life Marketing:** Steven S. Holstein
**SVP and Actuary, Corporate Actuarial:** Isadore Jermyn
**SVP, Secretary, and Deputy General Counsel:** Stephen L. Kuhn
**SVP, Annuity Strategic Business/Trust Company:** David W. O'Leary
**SVP, Mergers & Acquisitions:** Larry N. Port
**SVP, Corporate Human Resources:** Nancy M. Roberts
**SVP and Chief Actuary:** John R. Skar
**SVP and General Auditor:** Donald B. Robitaille
**Public Relations Contact:** Marty McDonough

## LOCATIONS

**HQ:** Massachusetts Mutual Life Insurance Company
1295 State St., Springfield, MA 01111
**Phone:** 413-744-1000 **Fax:** 413-744-6005
**Web:** www.massmutual.com

## PRODUCTS/OPERATIONS

**2006 Sales**

| | $ mil. | % of total |
|---|---|---|
| Premium income | 13,043 | 72 |
| Net investment income | 4,473 | 25 |
| Fees & other income | 504 | 3 |
| **Total** | **18,020** | **100** |

**Selected Subsidiaries and Affiliates**

Babson Capital Management LLC
Baring Asset Management Limited (UK)
C.M. Life Insurance Company
Cornerstone Real Estate Advisers LLC (real estate equities)
Fuh Hwa Securities Investment Trust Co., Ltd. (Taiwan)
MassMutual Asia Ltd. (Hong Kong)
MassMutual Europe S.A. (Luxembourg)
MassMutual International, Inc.
MassMutual Life Insurance Co. (Japan)
MassMutual Mercuries Life Insurance Co., Ltd. (Taiwan)
MML Bay State Life Insurance Company
MML Investors Services, Inc.
OppenheimerFunds, Inc. (mutual funds)
The MassMutual Trust Company, FSB
Tremont Capital Management, Inc.

## COMPETITORS

AIG
AIG American General
Allianz
Allstate
American Financial
AXA Financial
Charles Schwab
CIGNA
Citigroup
CNA Financial
Conseco
FMR
Genworth Financial
Guardian Life
The Hartford
John Hancock Financial Services
Liberty Mutual
Merrill Lynch
MetLife
Nationwide
New York Life
Northwestern Mutual
Principal Financial
Prudential
State Farm
TIAA-CREF
Torchmark
Travelers Companies
UBS Financial Services

## HISTORICAL FINANCIALS

Company Type: Mutual company

**Income Statement** FYE: December 31

| | ASSETS ($ mil.) | NET INCOME ($ mil.) | INCOME AS % OF ASSETS | EMPLOYEES |
|---|---|---|---|---|
| **12/06** | 122,155 | 810 | 0.7% | — |
| **12/05** | 113,552 | 753 | 0.7% | 10,000 |
| **12/04** | 108,216 | 335 | 0.3% | 10,000 |
| **12/03** | 96,779 | 461 | 0.5% | 10,000 |
| **12/02** | 84,102 | 1,408 | 1.7% | 9,000 |
| **Annual Growth** | 9.8% | (12.9%) | — | 3.6% |

**2006 Year-End Financials**

Equity as % of assets: —
Return on assets: 0.7%
Return on equity: —
Long-term debt ($ mil.): —
Sales ($ mil.): 18,020

**Net Income History**

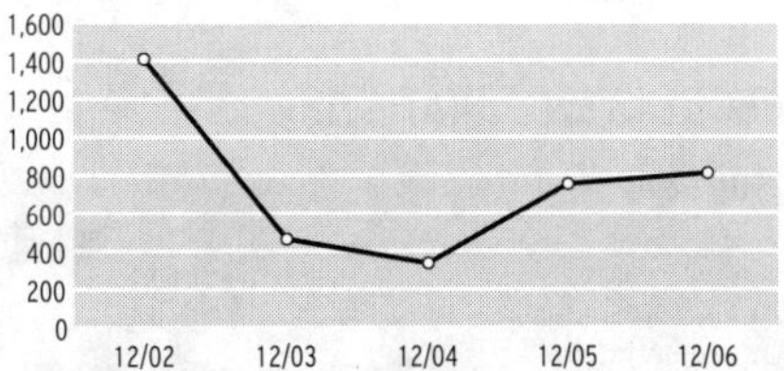


# MasterCard

Surpassing Visa in market share — now *that* would be priceless. Serving nearly 25,000 member financial institutions worldwide, MasterCard is the #2 payment system in the US. The company does not issue credit or its namesake cards; rather, it markets the MasterCard (credit and debit cards) and Maestro (debit cards) brands, provides the transaction authorization network, establishes guidelines for use, and collects fees from members. The company provides services in more than 210 countries and territories; its cards are accepted at more than 23 million locations around the globe. MasterCard also operates the Cirrus ATM network.

After some 40 years as a private entity, MasterCard went public in 2006 in one of the largest IPOs in recent history. Some of the IPO proceeds will go to fight antitrust lawsuits from such rivals as American Express and Discover, as well as other payment processors. The company's legal woes deepened in 2006 when the European Union (EU) charged MasterCard with fixing the prices that retailers must pay for accepting the company's cards. Post-IPO, the approximately 1,400 financial institutions that wholly owned MasterCard before the offering retained a stake of more than 40%. Two of the top three US banks (Citigroup and JPMorgan Chase) are among MasterCard's largest shareholders. There are more than 630 million MasterCard-branded cards in circulation worldwide and the company processes more than 16 billion transactions worth some $2 trillion. Long considered more down-market than Visa, MasterCard has worked to lure affluent users by offering such products as the World MasterCard, which has no spending limit and offers other elite services. The company offers its computer chip-enabled cards in several markets, including Europe, Latin America/Caribbean, and Asia/Pacific. US consumers have been slower to adopt this technology, but not for MasterCard's lack of trying. One "smart" product, however, that's showing signs of success stateside is the company's MasterCard PayPass, which allows customers to quickly tap or swipe their payment cards at specially equipped terminals.

The company's MasterCard Advisors unit conducts payment industry research and offers consulting services. MasterCard also has programs that assist businesses in expense reporting and accounts-payable management.

## HISTORY

A group of bankers formed The Interbank Card Association (ICA) in 1966 to establish authorization, clearing, and settlement procedures for bank credit card transactions. This was particularly important to banks left out of the rapidly growing BankAmericard (later Visa) network sponsored by Bank of America.

By 1969, ICA was issuing the Master Charge card throughout the US and had formed alliances in Europe and Japan. In the mid-1970s ICA modernized its system, replacing telephone transaction authorization with a computerized magnetic strip system. ICA had members in Africa, Australia, and Europe by 1979. That year the organization changed its name (and the card's) to MasterCard.

In 1980 Russell Hogg became president when John Reynolds resigned after disagreeing with the board over company performance and direction. Hogg made major organizational changes and consolidated data processing in St. Louis. MasterCard began offering debit cards in 1980 and traveler's checks in 1981.

MasterCard issued the first credit cards in China in 1987. The next year it bought Cirrus, then the world's largest ATM network. It also secured a pact with Belgium-based card company Eurocard (which later became Europay) to supervise MasterCard's European operations and help build the brand.

Hogg resigned in 1988 after disagreements with the board, and was succeeded by Alex Hart. In 1991 the Maestro debit card was unveiled.

The 1990s were marked by trouble in Europe: The pact with Europay hadn't resulted in the boom MasterCard had hoped for, customer service was below par, and competition was keen. Alex Hart retired in 1994 and was succeeded by Eugene Lockhart, who tackled the European woes. Lockhart considered ending the relationship but eventually worked things out with Europay. By the end of the decade, Europay was locked in a vicious battle to undercut Visa's market share through lower fees.

MasterCard in 1995 invested in UK-based Mondex International, maker of electronic, set-value, refillable smart cards. But US consumer resistance to cash cards and competition in the more advanced European market delayed growth in this area.

In October 1996 a group of merchants, including Wal-Mart and Sears, filed class-action lawsuits against both MasterCard and Visa, challenging the "honor all cards" rule. Because usage fees are higher, merchants balked at accepting consumers' MasterCard- or Visa-branded off-line, or signature-based debit cards, and claimed the card issuers violated antitrust laws by tying acceptance of debit to that of credit. In a dramatic twist, minutes before the trial was set to begin in 2003, MasterCard announced a settlement (the card issuer was required to pay $125 million in 2003 and $100 million annually from 2004 through 2012). Just months later, armed with the lawsuit's settlement which also freed merchants to pick which credit and debit card services they use, Wal-Mart (along with a handful of others) stopped accepting signature debit cards issued by MasterCard.

Lockhart resigned in 1997 and was succeeded by former head of overseas operations Robert Selander. Yet another management upheaval began in 1999 as the company moved to streamline its organizational structure and shift away from geographical divisions. It also said member banks could boost visibility by putting their logos on card fronts and moving MasterCard's logo to the back.

In 2002 MasterCard merged with Europay, with which it already had close ties. As part of the transaction, holding company MasterCard Incorporated was formed; MasterCard International become the company's main subsidiary and MasterCard Europe (formerly Europay) became its European subsidiary.

## EXECUTIVES

**Chairman:** Richard Haythornthwaite, age 50
**President, CEO, and Director:**
Robert W. (Bob) Selander, age 56, $900,000 pay
**COO:** Alan J. Heuer, age 65, $1,750,000 pay
**CFO:** Chris A. McWilton, age 48, $495,833 pay

**EVP and Chief Marketing Officer Global Marketing:** Lawrence (Larry) Flanagan
**EVP Advanced Payment Solutions:** Arthur D. (Art) Kranzley
**EVP Central Resources and Chief Administrative Officer:** Michael W. Michl, age 61, $447,917 pay
**SVP Worldwide:** Stephen Orfei
**VP, Global Communications and Corporate Public Relations:** Sharon Gamsin
**VP, Global Marketing Communications:** Chris Monteiro
**President Global Technology and Operations:** W. Roy Dunbar, age 46, $2,595,000 pay
**President Americas:** Walter M. (Walt) Macnee
**President Asia Pacific, Middle East, and Africa:** André Sekulic
**President Canada:** Kevin J. Stanton
**President Europe:** Javier Perez
**President Advisors:** Keith Stock
**General Counsel and Corporate Secretary:** Noah J. Hanft, age 54, $445,733 pay
**Corporate Controller and Principal Accounting Officer:** Tara Maguire, age 37
**General Manager Northern Europe, UK, and Ireland:** John Bushby
**General Manager Southern Europe:** Gaetano Carboni
**General Manager Central Europe:** Norbert Gebhard
**Chief Product Officer Global Product:** Wendy J. Murdock
**Auditors:** PricewaterhouseCoopers LLP

## LOCATIONS

**HQ:** MasterCard Incorporated
2000 Purchase St., Purchase, NY 10577
**Phone:** 914-249-2000 **Fax:** 914-249-4206
**Web:** www.mastercard.com

### 2006 Sales

| | % of total |
|---|---|
| US | 52 |
| Other countries | 48 |
| **Total** | **100** |

## PRODUCTS/OPERATIONS

### 2006 Sales

| | $ mil. | % of total |
|---|---|---|
| Net operations fees | 2,430 | 73 |
| Net assessments | 896 | 27 |
| **Total** | **3,326** | **100** |

### Selected Subsidiaries and Affiliates

Bright Skies LLC
Cirrus System, LLC
Clear Skies LLC
EMVCo, LLC
euro travellers cheque International S.A. (Belgium)
Eurocard Limited (UK)
European Payment Systems Services sprl (Belgium)
GVP Holding Incorporated
JNS Corporation Yugen Kaisha (Japan)
Maestro International Incorporated
MAOSCO Limited (UK)
Mastermanager LLC
MC Indonesia, Inc.
Mondex International Limited (UK)
MXI Management Limited (UK)
Purchase Street Research, LLC
SET Secure Electronic Transaction LLC
The Tower Group, Inc.
Towergroup Europe Limited (UK)

## COMPETITORS

American Express
Discover
Fifth Third
First Data
JCBI
NYCE Payments Network
PULSE EFT
Total System Services
Visa
Wells Fargo

## HISTORICAL FINANCIALS

Company Type: Public

### Income Statement

FYE: December 31

| | REVENUE ($ mil.) | NET INCOME ($ mil.) | NET PROFIT MARGIN | EMPLOYEES |
|---|---|---|---|---|
| **12/06** | 3,326 | 50 | 1.5% | 4,600 |
| **12/05** | 2,938 | 267 | 9.1% | 4,300 |
| **12/04** | 2,593 | 238 | 9.2% | 4,000 |
| **12/03** | 2,231 | (386) | — | 4,000 |
| **12/02** | 1,892 | 116 | 6.2% | 4,000 |
| **Annual Growth** | 15.2% | (19.0%) | — | 3.6% |

### 2006 Year-End Financials

Debt ratio: 9.7%
Return on equity: 2.8%
Cash ($ mil.): 2,594
Current ratio: 1.97
Long-term debt ($ mil.): 230
No. of shares (mil.): 80
Dividends
Yield: 0.1%
Payout: 24.3%
Market value ($ mil.): 7,843

### Stock History

NYSE: MA

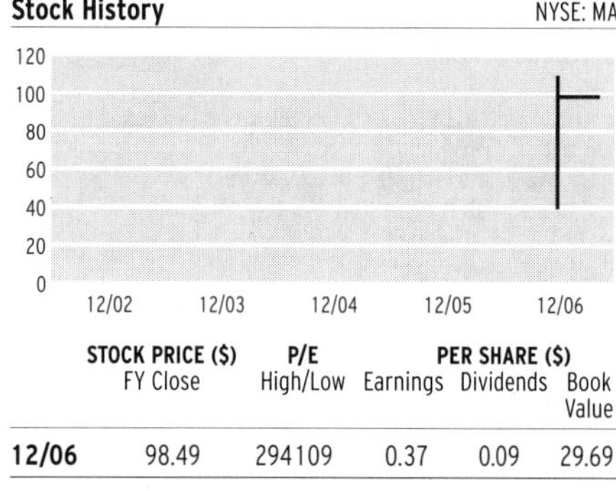


| | STOCK PRICE ($) FY Close | P/E High/Low | PER SHARE ($) Earnings | Dividends | Book Value |
|---|---|---|---|---|---|
| **12/06** | 98.49 | 294109 | 0.37 | 0.09 | 29.69 |

# Mattel, Inc.

Barbie is the platinum blonde in power at Mattel, the #1 toy maker in the world. Its products include Barbie dolls, Fisher-Price toys, Hot Wheels and Matchbox cars, American Girl dolls and books, and various *Sesame Street*, *Barney*, Ferrari, and other licensed items. Mattel also produces action figures and toys based on Walt Disney movies and the Harry Potter children's books. To satisfy techie kids, Mattel has accessorized Barbie with interactive games, software, and now a line of Barbie MP3 players. The company has even licensed the Barbie name for eyewear. Mattel is trying to reduce its reliance on its biggest customers — Wal-Mart, Toys "R" Us, and Target — through its own catalog and Internet sales.

Mattel is capitalizing on its core brands, particularly with licensing deals. For example, REM Eyewear developed a line of Barbie eyewear for little girls. Other licensing deals include a plethora of purple playthings featuring TV's Barney character for its littlest customers; toys based on Warner Bros. characters, including Looney Tunes, Batman, and Superman; and Innovo Group adult apparel and accessories under the Hot Wheels brand. In 2006 Mattel selected Activision in a multiyear deal to be the exclusive worldwide distributor for Barbie-branded video games. A new line of Barbie MP3 players, called Barbie Girls, went on sale in 2007.

Looking to further its presence in the electronic toys business, Mattel acquired Hong Kong-based Radica Games for $230 million.

Mattel had to recall 1 million Chinese-made Fisher-Price toys in August 2007, after learning that they may contain hazardous levels of lead paint. The recall was the latest in a number of recalls in the toy industry involving Chinese-made products. The recalled products include some of Mattel's most popular characters, such as Dora the Explorer, Elmo, and Big Bird.

Compounding the problem, the company announced additional recalls later in August also due to lead paint and magnet problems. The newest recall included nearly 440,000 die cast toys from the *Cars* movie. Mattel also recalled more than 18 million toys due to potentially hazardous small magnets. These toys include certain Polly Pocket and Barbie dolls and Batman action figures.

A class action suit related to the recalls has been filed against Mattel. Attorney Jeffrey Kilino is seeking payment for medical testing for children who have been exposed to the recalled toys containing elevated levels of lead paint.

Three customers (Wal-Mart, Toys "R" Us, and Target) account for almost 45% of Mattel's sales.

## HISTORY

A small California toy manufacturer began operating out of a converted garage in 1945, producing dollhouse furniture. Harold Matson and Elliot Handler named their new company Mattel, using letters from their last and first names. Matson soon sold his share to Handler and his wife, Ruth, who incorporated the business in 1948.

By 1952 the company's toy line had expanded to include burp guns and musical toys, and sales exceeded $5 million. Sponsorship of Walt Disney's *Mickey Mouse Club* (debuted 1955), a first in toy advertising, was a shrewd marketing step for Mattel, providing direct, year-round access to millions of young potential customers.

In 1959 Mattel introduced the Barbie doll, named after the Handlers' daughter, Barbara, and later introduced Ken, named after their son. Barbie, with her fashionable wardrobe and extensive line of accessories, was an instant hit and eventually became the most successful brand-name toy ever sold.

Mattel went public in 1960, and within two years sales had jumped from $25 million to $75 million. It launched the popular Hot Wheels miniature cars line in 1968.

The Handlers were ousted from management in 1974 after an investigation by the SEC found irregularities in reports of the company's profits. The new management moved into non-toy businesses, adding Western Publishing (Golden Books) and the Ringling Brothers-Barnum & Bailey Combined Shows circus in 1979.

By the 1980s Mattel was a high-volume business with heavy overhead expenses and high development costs. By 1984, in an effort to recapitalize, the company had sold all its non-toy assets. Sales were more than $1 billion in 1987, but Mattel lost $93 million. Toying with bankruptcy, newly appointed chairman John Amerman cut Mattel's manufacturing capacity by 40% and fired 22% of its corporate staff.

The early 1990s saw several acquisitions — Fisher-Price (toys for preschoolers), and Kransco (battery-powered ride-on vehicles). But Mattel backed down from a 1996 hostile bid for rival Hasbro when it realized the purchase would be too costly.

Amerman relinquished his roles as chairman and CEO in 1997 and was replaced by COO Jill Barad, who had enlivened the Barbie brand. Also in 1997 the company bought #3 US toy maker Tyco Toys (Tickle Me Elmo and Matchbox cars). In 1998 Mattel bought mail-order firm Pleasant Company (now known as American Girl), maker of American Girl-brand books, dolls, and clothing, and the UK's Bluebird Toys.

Barad started restructuring Mattel in 1999, closing plants and laying off 3,000 workers.

The company entered unfamiliar territory in 1999, paying $3.6 billion for leading educational software maker The Learning Company (*Carmen Sandiego, Reader Rabbit*) in a deal that would be Barad's downfall. The Learning Company unexpectedly lost money, leading to the resignations of the unit's top brass. Additional losses followed, and Barad left in 2000. Mattel soon put its software business (mostly consisting of The Learning Company) up for sale, and it named Kraft Foods veteran Bob Eckert chairman and CEO.

Later in 2000 Mattel finally found a buyer for its beleaguered Learning Company software business — an affiliate of privately owned Gores Technology Group. Mattel also cut 350 jobs.

Co-founder Ruth Handler, credited with the creation of the Barbie doll, died in April 2002.

Mattel and two former employees agreed in December 2002 to pay $477,000 in fines for making political donations in other people's names, the third-largest fine imposed by the Federal Election Commission. Also that year the company closed its Kentucky manufacturing and distribution facilities and in early 2003 consolidated two of its manufacturing facilities in Mexico.

## EXECUTIVES

**Chairman and CEO:** Robert A. Eckert, age 52, $1,250,000 pay
**CFO:** Kevin M. Farr, age 49, $721,154 pay
**EVP; President, American Girl:** Ellen L. Brothers
**EVP, International:** Bryan G. Stockton, age 53, $675,000 pay
**EVP, Worldwide Operations:** Thomas A. Debrowski, age 56, $706,154 pay
**SVP, General Counsel, and Secretary:** Robert (Bob) Normile, age 47
**SVP and Corporate Controller:** H. Scott Topham, age 46
**SVP, Operations Finance and Strategy:** Douglas E. Kerner, age 47
**SVP, External Affairs and CIO:** Dianne Douglas
**SVP, Human Resources:** Alan Kaye, age 53
**SVP, Worldwide Quality Assurance:** Jim Walter
**SVP, External Affairs and Treasurer:** Michael A. (Mike) Salop, age 42
**SVP and General Manager, Fisher-Price:** David Allmark
**SVP, Mattel Brands:** Jerry Bossick
**SVP, Inventor Relations, Licensing and New Business, Fisher-Price Brands:** Stan Clutton
**SVP, Mattel Brands Consumer Products:** Richard Dickson
**VP, Corporate Communications:** Lisa Marie Bongiovanni
**President, Mattel Brands:** Neil B. Friedman, age 59, $1,000,000 pay
**Director, Investor Relations:** Joleen Jackson
**Auditors:** PricewaterhouseCoopers LLP

## LOCATIONS

**HQ:** Mattel, Inc.
333 Continental Blvd., El Segundo, CA 90245
**Phone:** 310-252-2000 **Fax:** 310-252-2179
**Web:** www.mattel.com

Mattel's main factories are located in China, Indonesia, Malaysia, Mexico, and Thailand. It utilizes independent manufacturing contractors in Asia, Australia, Europe, Latin America, and the US. Its toys are sold around the world.

### 2006 Sales

| | $ mil. | % of total |
|---|---|---|
| United States | 3,419.1 | 56 |
| International | | |
| Europe | 1,544.6 | 25 |
| Latin America | 739.9 | 12 |
| Asia/Pacific | 239.6 | 4 |
| Other | 214.9 | 3 |
| Sales adjustments | (507.9) | — |
| **Total** | **5,650.2** | **100** |

## PRODUCTS/OPERATIONS

### 2006 Sales

| | $ mil. | % of total |
|---|---|---|
| Domestic | | |
| Mattel Girls & Boys Brands US | 1,507.5 | 25 |
| Fisher-Price Brands US | 1,471.6 | 24 |
| American Girl Brands | 440.0 | 7 |
| International | 2,739.0 | 44 |
| Adjustments | (507.9) | — |
| **Total** | **5,650.2** | **100** |

### Selected Brands

Girls
- American Girl (books, dolls, clothing, accessories, and activity products)
- Barbie (fashion dolls and accessories)
- Cabbage Patch Kids (large dolls)
- Diva Starz (interactive dolls)
- ello (creative kits)
- Flavas (hip-hop fashion dolls)
- Polly Pocket! (dolls)
- What's Her Face (designable dolls)

Infant and Preschool
- *Barney* (licensed)
- *Blue's Clues* (licensed)
- Disney (licensed preschool and plush)
- *Dora the Explorer* (licensed)
- ESPN GameStation (ESPN and Fisher-Price)
- Fisher-Price
- Kasey the Kinderbot
- Little People
- Magna Doodle
- PowerTouch Learning System
- Power Wheels
- See 'N Say
- *Sesame Street* (licensed)
- *Veggie Tales*
- View Master
- Winnie the Pooh (licensed)

Boys — Entertainment
- Batman (licensed)
- Disney (licensed)
- Harry Potter (licensed)
- *He-Man and Masters of the Universe* (licensed)
- Hot Wheels
- Matchbox
- Max Steel
- Nickelodeon (licensed)
- Pictionary
- Tyco Electric Racing
- Tyco Radio Control
- *Yu-Gi-Oh!* (licensed)

## COMPETITORS

Electronic Arts
Hasbro
JAKKS Pacific
LeapFrog
LEGO
Marvel Entertainment
MGA Entertainment
Motorsports Authentics
Namco Bandai
Ohio Art
Playmobil
Radica Games
Radio Flyer
RC2
Sanrio
TakaraTomy
Toy Quest
Ty
VTech Holdings

## HISTORICAL FINANCIALS

Company Type: Public

### Income Statement

FYE: December 31

| | REVENUE ($ mil.) | NET INCOME ($ mil.) | NET PROFIT MARGIN | EMPLOYEES |
|---|---|---|---|---|
| **12/06** | 5,650 | 593 | 10.5% | 32,000 |
| **12/05** | 5,179 | 417 | 8.1% | 26,000 |
| **12/04** | 5,103 | 573 | 11.2% | 25,000 |
| **12/03** | 4,960 | 538 | 10.8% | 25,000 |
| **12/02** | 4,885 | 230 | 4.7% | 25,000 |
| **Annual Growth** | 3.7% | 26.7% | — | 6.4% |

### 2006 Year-End Financials

Debt ratio: 26.1%
Return on equity: 26.1%
Cash ($ mil.): 1,206
Current ratio: 1.80
Long-term debt ($ mil.): 636
No. of shares (mil.): 384
Dividends
Yield: 2.9%
Payout: 42.5%
Market value ($ mil.): 8,708

### Stock History

NYSE: MAT

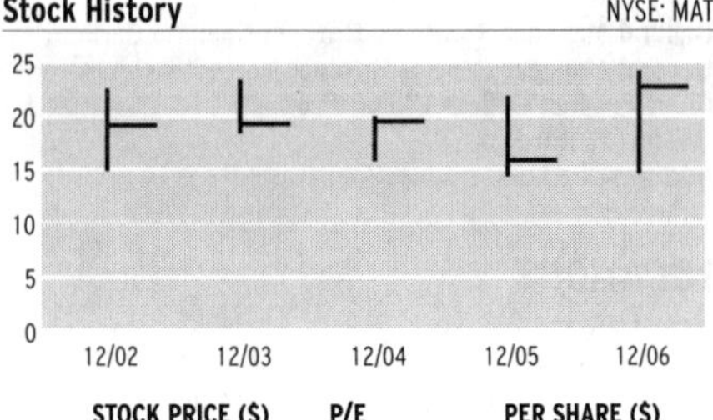


| | STOCK PRICE ($) FY Close | P/E High | P/E Low | PER SHARE ($) Earnings | Dividends | Book Value |
|---|---|---|---|---|---|---|
| **12/06** | 22.66 | 16 | 10 | 1.53 | 0.65 | 6.33 |
| **12/05** | 15.82 | 21 | 14 | 1.01 | 0.50 | 5.41 |
| **12/04** | 19.49 | 15 | 12 | 1.35 | — | 5.74 |
| **12/03** | 19.27 | 19 | 15 | 1.22 | 0.40 | 5.17 |
| **12/02** | 19.15 | 43 | 29 | 0.52 | 0.05 | 4.60 |
| **Annual Growth** | 4.3% | — | — | 31.0% | 89.9% | 8.3% |

# MBIA Inc.

For MBIA, it's largely about the bonds. Through subsidiaries MBIA Insurance and Capital Markets Assurance, MBIA is a leading provider of insurance for municipal bonds, asset- and mortgage-based securities, and stable corporate bonds (such as utility bonds). Its insurance can be bought either at the time of issue or on the secondary market. MBIA also manages assets (including cash raised by bond issues) for public-sector clients, guarantees bank deposits for government entities, and insures insurance companies' guaranteed investment contracts. Other lines of business include tax compliance services and buying and servicing municipal real estate tax liens.

MBIA has expanded internationally for long-term growth although it still writes more than 70% of its business in the US. California and New York represent nearly 20% of the company's portfolio. The company's MBIA Assurance S.A. writes insurance in Europe and MBIA UK does business in the United Kingdom.

Investment advisor Wellington Management owns 12% of the company.

## HISTORY

In 1974 such insurers as Aetna, CIGNA, Fireman's Fund (now part of Allianz), and Continental (now part of CNA) formed consortium Municipal Bond Insurance Association. The insurance was intended to reduce investor risk and to boost ratings and cut costs for bond issuers. Holding company MBIA was incorporated and went public in 1986. Three years later it absorbed rival Bond Investors Group.

As bond insurance gained wide acceptance, MBIA moved into coverage of investment-grade corporate bonds, and asset- and mortgage-backed bonds. It also began offering institutional brokerage services and money market funds to municipal customers. But with acceptance came competition, forcing MBIA to take on riskier bond issues. It joined forces with Ambac Indemnity in 1995 to offer bond insurance abroad; the decision pricked MBIA three years later when a Thai company defaulted.

Since 1996 MBIA has invested in real estate tax lien and tax compliance companies, including asset-backed bond insurer CapMAC Holdings in 1998, despite that company's exposure in Asia. In 1998 MBIA formed an alliance with Japan's Mitsui Marine & Fire and bought 1838 Investment Advisors, which oversees assets of $6 billion.

In 1999 the company inked a deal to be the exclusive insurer of municipal bonds on Trading Edge's BondLink trading service. That year MBIA sold its bond administration and consulting firm MBIA MuniFinancial, saying it no longer fit with its strategy.

In 2000 MBIA's venture with Trading Edge opened for online business. That year the company exited its alliance with Mitsui Marine & Fire (now Mitsui Sumitomo Insurance).

Due to its decision to discontinue equity advisory services operations, MBIA sold subsidiary 1838 Investment Advisors to that company's management in 2004; MBIA then focused its advisory services on fixed-income asset management.

## EXECUTIVES

**Chairman, President, and CEO:** Gary C. Dunton, age 51
**Vice Chairman and CFO:** C. Edward (Chuck) Chaplin, age 47, $250,000 pay
**VP and CTO:** Andrea E. Randolph, age 54
**VP and Chief Administrative Officer:** Kevin D. Silva, age 53
**VP and Chief Investment Officer; President, MBIA Asset Management:** Clifford D. Corso, age 45, $950,000 pay
**VP and Head of Insured Portfolio Management and Government Relations:** Mitchell I. Sonkin, age 54
**VP, Global Public Finance:** Thomas G. (Tom) McLoughlin, age 46
**VP, International:** Christopher E. (Chris) Weeks, age 46
**VP, Secretary, and General Counsel:** Ram D. Wertheim, age 52, $1,075,000 pay
**Head of Consumer Asset Finance, Global Structured Finance Division:** Joseph L. Sevely
**Managing Director, Corporate Strategy:** William C. (Bill) Fallon
**Managing Director and Treasurer, MBIA Inc. and MBIA Insurance:** Richard R. Thevenet
**Auditors:** PricewaterhouseCoopers LLP

## LOCATIONS

**HQ:** MBIA Inc.
113 King St., Armonk, NY 10504
**Phone:** 914-273-4545 **Fax:** 914-765-3163
**Web:** www.mbia.com

MBIA has operations in Australia, France, Italy, Japan, Spain, the UK, and the US.

## PRODUCTS/OPERATIONS

### 2006 Sales

| | % of total |
|---|---|
| Insurance | 54 |
| Investment management services | 45 |
| Corporate | 1 |
| **Total** | **100** |

### Selected Subsidiaries

CAH Asset Holdings, Inc.
Capital Markets Assurance Corporation
CapMAC Asia Ltd.
CapMAC Financial Services, Inc.
CapMAC Holdings Inc.
CapMAC Investment Management, Inc.
Colorado Investor Services Corporation
Euro Asset Acquisition Limited
KOP Management LLC
MBIA Insurance Corporation
MBIA U.K. (Holdings) Limited
MBIA UK Insurance Limited
Meridian Funding Company, LLC
Municipal Issuers Service Corporation
Municipal Tax Collection Bureau, Inc.
Polaris Funding Company, LLC
Triple-A One Funding Corporation

## COMPETITORS

Ambac
Assured Guaranty
FGIC
Financial Security Assurance
Radian Asset Assurance
St. Paul Travelers Bond

## HISTORICAL FINANCIALS

Company Type: Public

### Income Statement

FYE: December 31

| | ASSETS ($ mil.) | NET INCOME ($ mil.) | INCOME AS % OF ASSETS | EMPLOYEES |
|---|---|---|---|---|
| **12/06** | 39,763 | 819 | 2.1% | 492 |
| **12/05** | 34,561 | 711 | 2.1% | 626 |
| **12/04** | 33,036 | 843 | 2.6% | 623 |
| **12/03** | 30,268 | 814 | 2.7% | 701 |
| **12/02** | 18,852 | 579 | 3.1% | 694 |
| **Annual Growth** | 20.5% | 9.1% | — | (8.2%) |

### 2006 Year-End Financials

Equity as % of assets: 18.1%
Return on assets: 2.2%
Return on equity: 11.9%
Long-term debt ($ mil.): 14,765
No. of shares (mil.): 135
Dividends
Yield: 1.7%
Payout: 20.7%
Market value ($ mil.): 9,851
Sales ($ mil.): 2,689

### Stock History

NYSE: MBI

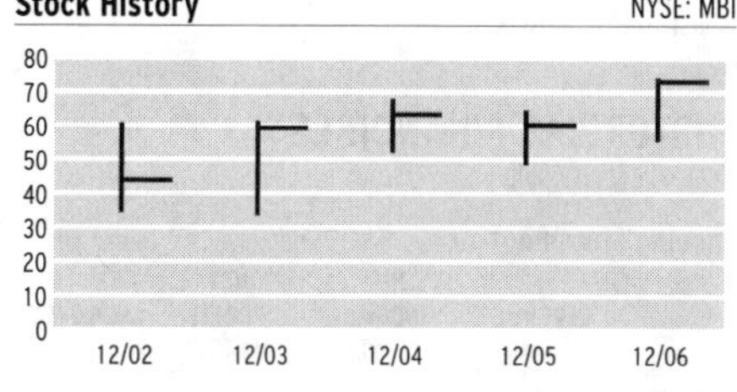


| | STOCK PRICE ($) FY Close | P/E High | P/E Low | PER SHARE ($) Earnings | Dividends | Book Value |
|---|---|---|---|---|---|---|
| **12/06** | 73.06 | 12 | 9 | 5.99 | 1.24 | 53.43 |
| **12/05** | 60.16 | 12 | 9 | 5.18 | 1.12 | 49.54 |
| **12/04** | 63.28 | 12 | 9 | 5.82 | 0.96 | 47.05 |
| **12/03** | 59.23 | 11 | 6 | 5.61 | 0.80 | 43.50 |
| **12/02** | 43.86 | 15 | 9 | 3.92 | 0.68 | 37.94 |
| **Annual Growth** | 13.6% | — | — | 11.2% | 16.2% | 8.9% |

# The McClatchy Company

This company has gotten its clutches on quite a few newspapers. The McClatchy Company is the #3 newspaper publisher in the US (behind *USA TODAY* publisher Gannett and Tribune Company), with more than 30 daily papers with a combined circulation of nearly 3 million. Its portfolio includes the *Sacramento Bee, The Miami Herald,* and the *Star-Telegram* (Fort Worth, Texas), as well as about 50 non-daily newspapers in several states. McClatchy has online publishing and multimedia holdings through McClatchy Interactive, which publishes regional portal sites and provides technology and content to the firm's newspaper Web sites. The McClatchy family holds more than 90% of the firm's voting power.

McClatchy briefly leapt into the second spot among US newspaper companies in 2006 after it acquired rival Knight-Ridder for $4.5 billion in cash and the assumption of $2 billion in debt. Following the mega deal, McClatchy has been busy evaluating its new papers, retaining those located in strategic and growing markets and selling others.

In 2007 the company sold subsidiary The Star Tribune Company to private equity firm Avista Capital Partners for $530 million. The unit publishes the *Star Tribune* in Minneapolis, which with a weekday circulation of about 377,000, had accounted for about a third of McClatchy's sales.

It also shed the *Philadelphia Inquirer* and the *Philadelphia Daily News*, selling the papers for $562 million to Philadelphia Media Holdings, a group of Philadelphia investors led by Brian P. Tierney, an advertising and public relations executive, and Bruce Toll, co-founder of luxury home builder Toll Brothers. In a move to reduce debt following the Knight-Ridder transaction, McClatchy had to sell 12 other papers, including the *San Jose Mercury News*, the *Contra Costa Times*, the *Monterey County Herald*, and the *St. Paul Pioneer Press*, which were bought by MediaNews for $1 billion.

Later that year the company joined a Yahoo consortium, which requires member newspapers to use Yahoo search on their Web sites. In addition, Yahoo and the newspapers sell ads on each other's Web sites and revenue is shared among the partners. Content from the newspapers are featured on Yahoo's individual channels, such as news and technology. Other members of the consortium include Calkins Media, Media General, Morris Communications, and Paddock Publications.

## HISTORY

In the 1840s James McClatchy was a reporter for Horace Greeley's *New York Tribune*. When Greeley exhorted young men to go west, McClatchy went. He worked for several newspapers in Sacramento before co-founding *The Bee* (named to liken reporters to industrious insects) in 1857. The paper gained a reputation as a crusader and was known for its antislavery stance. During the 1920s the company expanded with sister *Bees* in Fresno and Modesto, California.

The McClatchy family bought out the other owners, and the company grew under its watch. Granddaughter Eleanor McClatchy ran the company from 1936 until 1978. It went public in 1988.

McClatchy bought three South Carolina dailies from The News and Observer Publishing Co. in 1990. Five years later, it bought the Raleigh-based publisher — giving it a toehold in North Carolina's fast-growing Research Triangle area — as well as Nando.net (renamed Nando Media in 1998), its Internet publishing company. In 1996 and 1997 the company sold five of its community newspapers. Also in 1996 Gary Pruitt, who joined the company in 1984, was named CEO.

In 1997 McClatchy became the surprise winner in the bidding for Cowles Media Company (*Star Tribune*), for which it paid $1.4 billion. In 1998 the company sold Cowles' magazine and book publishing divisions. The company also changed its name from McClatchy Newspapers to The McClatchy Company.

The company made several Web-related investments in 2000; it took equity stakes in StreamSearch.com (a now defunct online audio and video search engine) and BrightStreet.com (online loyalty programs). McClatchy continued to focus on the Internet in 2001 even as it cut costs to combat a slump in ad spending.

In 2003 the company sold its Newspaper Network unit in two parts to news service Associated Press and ad services company Vertis (now called Vertis Communications). The McClatchy Company acquired six California newspapers, including the *Merced Sun-Star*, for $41 million in early 2004. The following year Nando changed its name once again when it became McClatchy Interactive.

Former chairman and patriarch of the family James McClatchy, great-grandson of the company's founder, died in 2006 at the age of 85. McClatchy became the second-largest newspaper publisher in the US that year after it purchased rival Knight-Ridder for $4.5 billion in cash and the assumption of $2 billion in debt. Following the deal, the company sold several of the newly acquired newspapers, as well as the *Star Tribune*.

## EXECUTIVES

**Chairman, President, and CEO:** Gary B. Pruitt, age 49, $2,050,000 pay
**VP Finance and CFO:** Patrick J. Talamantes, age 42, $689,000 pay
**VP Interactive Media:** Christian A. Hendricks
**VP, General Counsel, and Corporate Secretary:** Karole Morgan-Prager, age 44, $602,000 pay
**VP Human Resources:** Heather L. Fagundes, age 38
**VP News:** Howard C. Weaver, age 56
**VP Operations:** Lynn Dickerson, age 49
**VP Operations:** Robert J. (Bob) Weil, age 56, $632,000 pay
**VP Operations:** Frank R. J. Whittaker, age 57, $632,000 pay
**Publisher:** James B. McClatchy, age 84
**President and Publisher, The Bradenton Herald (Florida):** William H. (Will) Fleet, age 48
**President and Publisher, Miami Herald Media:** David Landsberg
**President and Publisher, The Star Tribune:** J. Keith Moyer
**Publisher, Idaho Statesman:** Mi-Ai Parrish, age 35
**Publisher, Tri-City Herald:** Rufus M. Friday, age 43
**President and Publisher, Anchorage Daily News:** Mike Sexton
**President and Publisher, The Fresno Bee:** Ray Steele
**Publisher, The Tribune:** Joseph (Chip) Visci
**President and Publisher, The Modesto Bee:** Margaret Randazzo
**President and Publisher, The Sacramento Bee:** Janis Heaphy
**Director Communications:** Peter Tira
**Treasurer:** Elaine Lintecum
**Auditors:** Deloitte & Touche LLP

## LOCATIONS

**HQ:** The McClatchy Company
2100 Q St., Sacramento, CA 95816
**Phone:** 916-321-1846 **Fax:** 916-321-1964
**Web:** www.mcclatchy.com

## PRODUCTS/OPERATIONS

**2006 Sales**

| | $ mil. | % of total |
|---|---|---|
| Advertising | 1,432.9 | 85 |
| Circulation | 195.0 | 12 |
| Other | 47.3 | 3 |
| **Total** | **1,675.2** | **100** |

**Selected Daily Newspapers**

*Anchorage Daily News* (Alaska)
*The Beaufort Gazette* (South Carolina)
*Belleville News-Democrat* (Illinois)
*The Bellingham Herald* (Washington)
*The Bradenton Herald* (Florida)
*Centre Daily Times* (State College, PA)
*Charlotte Observer* (North Carolina)
*El Nuevo Herald* (Miami)
*The Fresno Bee* (California)
*The Herald* (Rock Hill, SC)
*Idaho Statesman* (Boise)
*The Island Packet* (Bluffton, SC)
*The Kansas City Star*
*Ledger-Enquirer* (Columbus, GA)
*Lexington Herald-Leader* (Kentucky)
*Merced Sun-Star* (California)
*The Miami Herald*
*The Modesto Bee* (California)
*The News & Observer* (Raleigh, NC)
*The News Tribune* (Tacoma, WA)
*The Olathe News* (Kansas)
*The Olympian* (Olympia, WA)
*The Sacramento Bee* (California)
*Star-Telegram* (Fort Worth, TX)
*The State* (Columbia, SC)
*Sun Herald* (Biloxi, MS)
*The Sun News* (Myrtle Beach, SC)
*The Telegraph* (Macon, GA)
*Tri-City Herald* (Kennewick, WA)
*The Tribune* (San Luis Obispo, CA)
*The Wichita Eagle* (Kansas)

## COMPETITORS

Advance Publications
Belo
Cox Newspapers
Dispatch Printing
Dow Jones
Gannett
Landmark Communications
Media General
New York Times
Tribune
Washington Post

## HISTORICAL FINANCIALS

Company Type: Public

**Income Statement** FYE: Sunday nearest December 31

| | REVENUE ($ mil.) | NET INCOME ($ mil.) | NET PROFIT MARGIN | EMPLOYEES |
|---|---|---|---|---|
| **12/06** | 1,675 | (156) | — | 16,791 |
| **12/05** | 1,186 | 161 | 13.5% | 8,948 |
| **12/04** | 1,163 | 156 | 13.4% | 9,171 |
| **12/03** | 1,099 | 150 | 13.7% | 9,093 |
| **12/02** | 1,082 | 131 | 12.1% | 9,332 |
| **Annual Growth** | 11.6% | — | — | 15.8% |

**2006 Year-End Financials**

Debt ratio: 100.9%
Return on equity: —
Cash ($ mil.): 20
Current ratio: 1.42
Long-term debt ($ mil.): 3,132
No. of shares (mil.): 56
Dividends
Yield: 1.7%
Payout: —
Market value ($ mil.): 2,416

**Stock History** NYSE: MNI

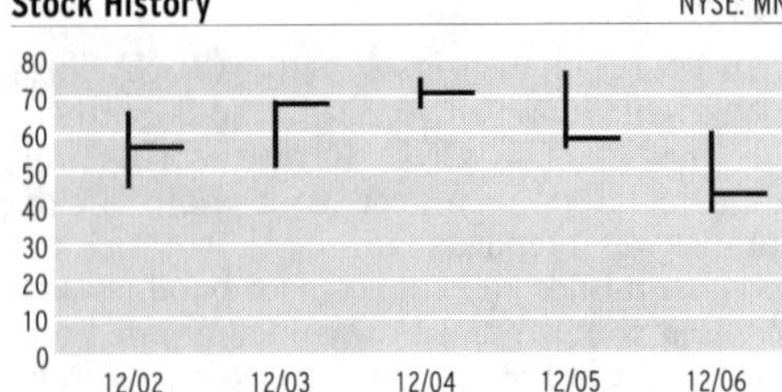

| | STOCK PRICE ($) FY Close | P/E High/Low | PER SHARE ($) Earnings | Dividends | Book Value |
|---|---|---|---|---|---|
| **12/06** | 43.30 | — — | (2.41) | 0.72 | 55.63 |
| **12/05** | 58.39 | 22 16 | 3.42 | 0.67 | 76.27 |
| **12/04** | 70.90 | 22 20 | 3.33 | 0.50 | 70.45 |
| **12/03** | 67.99 | 21 16 | 3.23 | 0.44 | 61.12 |
| **12/02** | 56.40 | 23 16 | 2.84 | 0.40 | 54.30 |
| **Annual Growth** | (6.4%) | — — | — | 15.8% | 0.6% |

# McCormick & Company

More than just the flavor of the month, McCormick & Company is the world's #1 spice maker. It makes a tasty assortment of spices, seasonings, flavorings, sauces, and extracts. McCormick distributes its own products, which are sold to consumers under brands including Club House, Ducros, McCormick, and Schwartz, as well as under private labels. It handles the Paul Newman brand of foods under license. The company's customers include retailers, the foodservice industry, and industrial food processors worldwide. An employee profit-sharing plan owns about 50% of McCormick.

The company's earnings were erratic in the 1990s, partly because of a price war with then-rival Burns, Philp, but also due to the decline of home cooking in the US. McCormick countered with increased advertising and a growing emphasis on industrial sales to flavor the foods eaten outside the home. McCormick also has been expanding internationally through its Decors spice business and operations in China.

About 39% of McCormick's sales came from its international operations in 2005. The year was not the company's best, however, as a drop in vanilla prices and the effects of Hurricane Katrina both cut into sales. In 2006 McCormick acquired Epicurean International for $97 million in cash, adding the Thai Kitchen and Simply Asia brands to its stable.

The company's foodservice customers include Darden Restaurants, Doctor's Associates, Wendy's, McDonald's, and YUM! Brands. McCormick is known for scenting its annual reports with one of its more pleasing products, such as vanilla or Chinese five-spice.

Chairman and CEO Robert Lawless owns about 9% of McCormick.

## HISTORY

McCormick & Company was founded in 1889 by 25-year-old Willoughby McCormick, who crafted fruit syrups, root beer, and nerve and bone liniment in his Baltimore home. He employed three assistants to hawk his wares door-to-door. His company soon expanded its product line to include food coloring, cream of tartar, and blood purifier. By 1894 McCormick was exporting, and two years later it acquired the F.G. Emmett Spice Company of Philadelphia, firmly committing itself to the spice industry. By the turn of the century, McCormick was trading around the world.

Willoughby's nephew, Charles McCormick, joined the company as a part-time shipping clerk in 1912. When Willoughby died in 1932, Charles succeeded him as CEO. He increased employee wages, shortened the workweek, and established the Multiple Management system (still an integral part of the company's management structure), which solicited employee input. By 1933 McCormick was on a growth track that continued unabated through the 1930s. In 1938 Charles wrote a book expounding his participative management philosophy.

The company opened its first international office in 1940 and achieved coast-to-coast distribution seven years later with the acquisition of A. Schilling & Co., producers of spices and extracts. In 1959 McCormick purchased Gorman Eckert & Co., Canada's largest spice business and the precursor to Club House Foods. It acquired Gilroy Foods in 1961 and rival Baker Extract in 1962. From 1962 until its sale in 1988 McCormick ran a real estate subsidiary, Maryland Properties (renamed McCormick Properties, 1979).

Charles died in 1970. Though the years following his death were characterized by acquisitions and joint venture agreements in the US and abroad, profits slumped until his son, Charles "Buzz" McCormick, took over as CEO in 1987.

In 1989 Australia's Burns, Philp began challenging McCormick by buying up spice companies in the US and Europe, including the Spice Islands and Durkee French brands. Buzz — succeeded twice as CEO in the mid-1990s, only to return when one successor died and the other left for health reasons — responded with a bruising battle for shelf space that led to Burns, Philp's near-collapse in 1997. The company also sold garlic and onion processing subsidiary Gilroy Foods, Minipack Systems (UK), and several smaller, noncore operations. In 1997 Buzz yielded the CEO's post — for good — to Robert Lawless.

Economic woes in Venezuela caused McCormick to cease manufacturing operations there in 1998. In 1999 Lawless succeeded Buzz as chairman. In June 1999 the company announced it would cut costs by eliminating 300 jobs (mostly overseas) and closing a British plant.

McCormick's sweet victory over Burns, Philp was soured by an FTC investigation into its alleged practice of offering some grocery chains low prices in exchange for up to 90% of their shelf space for spices. The investigation brought scrutiny on a common supermarket practice known as slotting fees. McCormick settled with the FTC in 2000, agreeing not to illegally discriminate against retailers in its pricing. Also that year the company bought France-based Ducros (spices, herbs, dessert aid products) from Béghin-Say for about $380 million.

In 2003 McCormick's UK subsidiary acquired condiment maker Uniqsauces, adding the Beswicks and Hammonds, as well as the licensed Newman's Own brands to its European product line. That year the company also acquired New Orleans-style cuisine product maker Zatarain's. Saying that the packaging business was not a strategic part of the company, McCormick also sold its packaging business (Setco and Tubed Products) to Kerr Group in 2003.

Acquisitions continued in 2004 with McCormick's purchase of C.M. van Sillevoldt B.V. and its Silvo brand of spices, herbs, and seasonings, which is sold in the Netherlands and Belgium. In 2006 the company consolidated its North American operations with the closure of its manufacturing facility in California.

McCormick acquired Dessert Products International (DPI) in 2006. DPI markets the Vahine brand dessert toppings in Europe. That year it also bought Epicurean International (which makes Thai Kitchen and Simply Asia brand products) for $97 million in cash.

## EXECUTIVES

**Chairman and CEO:** Robert J. Lawless, age 59
**President and COO:** Alan D. Wilson, age 48
**EVP, Strategic Planning, CFO, and Director:** Francis A. Contino, age 61, $623,625 pay
**SVP, General Counsel, and Secretary:** Robert W. Skelton, age 58
**VP, Corporate Operations:** Michael J. Navarre
**VP, Finance and Treasurer:** Paul C. Beard, age 51
**VP, Financial Shared Services:** Sharon H. Mirabelle
**VP, Finance, Europe:** Gordon M. Stetz Jr., age 41
**VP, Quality Assurance:** Roger T. Lawrence
**VP, Research and Development:** Hamed Faridi
**VP, Strategic Sourcing:** Stephen J. Donohue
**VP, Supply Chain, and CIO:** Jeryl (Jerry) Wolfe
**VP and Controller:** Kenneth A. Kelly Jr., age 51
**VP, Corporate Communications and Community Relations:** John G. McCormick
**President, Europe, Middle East and Africa:** Lawrence Kurzius, age 48
**President, North American Consumer Foods:** Mark T. Timbie, age 52
**President, McCormick Canada:** Keith Gibbons
**President, U.S. Industrial Group:** Charles T. Langmead, age 48
**Managing Director, McCormick Foods Australia Consumer:** Graham Robertson
**Manager, Investor Relations:** Dorothy Powe
**Manager, Marketing:** Abe Sendros
**Auditors:** Ernst & Young LLP

## LOCATIONS

**HQ:** McCormick & Company, Incorporated
18 Loveton Cir., Sparks, MD 21152
**Phone:** 410-771-7301 **Fax:** 410-771-7462
**Web:** www.mccormick.com

McCormick & Company brands can be found in nearly 100 countries. The company has operations in Australia, Canada, China, France, the Netherlands, Mexico, the UK, and the US.

### 2006 Sales

| | $ mil. | % of total |
|---|---|---|
| US | 1,678.7 | 62 |
| Europe | 643.6 | 24 |
| Other countries | 394.1 | 14 |
| **Total** | **2,716.4** | **100** |

## PRODUCTS/OPERATIONS

### 2006 Sales

| | $ mil. | % of total |
|---|---|---|
| Consumer | 1,556.4 | 57 |
| Industrial | 1,160.0 | 43 |
| **Total** | **2,716.4** | **100** |

### Selected Brands

Aeroplane
Baker's Imitation Vanilla
Club House
Ducros
Golden Dipt
Grill Mates
McCormick
Mojave
Old Bay
Produce Partners
Schwartz
Silvo
Zatarain's

### Selected Products

Coating systems
- Batters
- Breaders
- Glazes
- Marinades
- Rubs

Compound flavors
- Beverage flavors
- Confectionery flavors
- Dairy flavors

Condiments
- Flavored oils
- Jams and jellies
- Ketchup
- Mustards
- Salad dressings
- Sandwich sauces
- Seafood cocktail sauces

Ingredients
- Extracts
- Essential oils and oleoresins
- Fruit and vegetable powders
- Spices and herbs
- Tomato powder

Processed flavors
- Meat flavors
- Savory flavors

Seasonings
- Sauces and gravies
- Salty snack seasonings
- Seasoning blends
- Side dish seasonings
- Simply Asia
- Thai Kitchen

## COMPETITORS

ACH Food Companies
Adams Extract & Spice
Alberto-Culver
ALK-Abelló
Associated British Foods
B&G Foods
Bolner's Fiesta Products
D. D. Williamson
Danisco A/S
Flayco Products
Givaudan
Goya
The Great Spice Company
Heinz
International Flavors
Kerry Group
La Flor
M & F Worldwide
Magic Seasoning Blends
Newly Weds Foods
Nielsen-Massey
Penzeys
RFI Ingredients
Sensient
Sterling Extract
Tone's
Unilever

## HISTORICAL FINANCIALS

Company Type: Public

**Income Statement** FYE: November 30

| | REVENUE ($ mil.) | NET INCOME ($ mil.) | NET PROFIT MARGIN | EMPLOYEES |
|---|---|---|---|---|
| **11/06** | 2,716 | 202 | 7.4% | 7,500 |
| **11/05** | 2,592 | 215 | 8.3% | 8,000 |
| **11/04** | 2,526 | 215 | 8.5% | 8,000 |
| **11/03** | 2,270 | 211 | 9.3% | 8,000 |
| **11/02** | 2,320 | 180 | 7.8% | 9,000 |
| **Annual Growth** | 4.0% | 3.0% | — | (4.5%) |

**2006 Year-End Financials**

Debt ratio: 61.0%
Return on equity: 23.3%
Cash ($ mil.): 49
Current ratio: 1.15
Long-term debt ($ mil.): 570

No. of shares (mil.): 117
Dividends
Yield: 1.9%
Payout: 48.0%
Market value ($ mil.): 4,524

**Stock History** NYSE: MKC

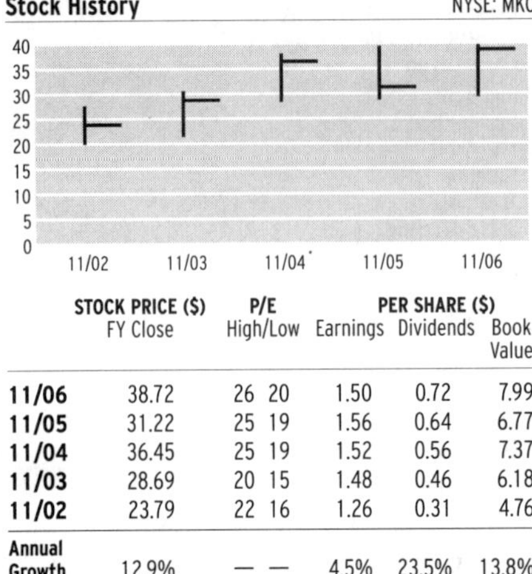


| | STOCK PRICE ($) FY Close | P/E High/Low | | PER SHARE ($) Earnings | Dividends | Book Value |
|---|---|---|---|---|---|---|
| **11/06** | 38.72 | 26 | 20 | 1.50 | 0.72 | 7.99 |
| **11/05** | 31.22 | 25 | 19 | 1.56 | 0.64 | 6.77 |
| **11/04** | 36.45 | 25 | 19 | 1.52 | 0.56 | 7.37 |
| **11/03** | 28.69 | 20 | 15 | 1.48 | 0.46 | 6.18 |
| **11/02** | 23.79 | 22 | 16 | 1.26 | 0.31 | 4.76 |
| **Annual Growth** | 12.9% | — | — | 4.5% | 23.5% | 13.8% |

# McDermott International

Getting into deep water? Getting fired up? All in a day's work for McDermott International, a global engineering and construction firm active in offshore oil and gas construction, power generation systems, and government contracting. The offshore business segment includes subsidiary J. Ray McDermott, which builds deepwater and subsea oil and gas facilities. McDermott International's power segment is led by Babcock & Wilcox and builds fossil-fuel, nuclear, and other generation systems. Subsidiary BWX Technologies is the driving force in the company's government segment, which provides nuclear components and services to US government agencies (accounting for about 15% of the parent company's business).

The company formed the Babcock & Wilcox Companies unit in 2007, rolling into it the operations of subsidiaries BWX Technologies and Babcock & Wilcox, which filed for Chapter 11 protection because of asbestos liabilities in 2000 and emerged in 2006 after negotiating a revised settlement. McDermott International continued to manage Babcock & Wilcox during its bankruptcy, but the subsidiary was deconsolidated from the parent company's financial statements during that period.

## HISTORY

When R. Thomas McDermott won a contract to supply drilling rigs to a Texas wildcatter in 1923, he started J. Ray McDermott & Co., named after his father. Following the oil industry's expansion into Louisiana, J. Ray McDermott made New Orleans its headquarters in the 1930s. When the company incorporated in 1946, it supplied services for oil and natural gas production.

After WWII McDermott became a pioneer in the construction of offshore drilling platforms. Spurred by increased demand for oil in the 1960s and by price inflation in the 1970s, the company's offshore business boomed. McDermott supplied the US Navy and the salvage and subsea markets.

In 1978 McDermott diversified. That year it bought Babcock & Wilcox (B&W), which had been founded as a boilermaker in 1867, then later focused on nuclear energy and built the reactor for the first nuclear-powered merchant ship. It made major contributions to the US Navy's nuclear program during the 1950s.

J. Ray McDermott became McDermott Inc. in 1980, and in 1983, McDermott International, Inc. Unprepared for industry changes of the 1980s, McDermott had to shrink its workforce 57% by selling its insulation, controls, trading, and seamless-tube operations.

In a sweeping reorganization, McDermott consolidated its marine construction operations into a subsidiary, J. Ray McDermott, which in 1995 merged with Offshore Pipeline; McDermott owned a majority stake in the resulting company. A consortium including McDermott won a $275 million power plant contract with Huaneng International Power Development, the largest independent power producer in China, in 1996.

In 1997 Roger Tetrault became chairman and CEO as McDermott swallowed about $123 million in charges, including $72 million in asbestos claims. It also sold its interests in Sakhalin Energy Investment and Unifab International. Under government pressure, the company dissolved its joint ventures with Heerema Offshore in 1997 (an employee of the JV was later fined after pleading guilty to criminal charges) and ETPM in 1998 (amid allegations of anti-competitive activity in the marine construction business).

As oil prices (and McDermott's profits) slumped during fiscal 1999, the company sought ways to cut costs. In 1999 the company paid $513 million for the remainder of oil platform installer J. Ray McDermott and consolidated its management. Also that year, plans to build a 650-kilometer underwater natural gas pipeline from gas fields in the southeast China Sea to Singapore came under scrutiny by the Indonesian government. A committee recommended the contract be voided because of McDermott's connections to Mohammed Hasan, an 18% owner of McDermott Indonesia and close friend of Indonesia's former president Suharto. The project was later approved by the country's minister of mines and energy.

Babcock & Wilcox, weighed down by 20 years of asbestos liability claims (and having paid $1.6 billion), filed for Chapter 11 bankruptcy protection early in 2000. With the company's marine construction division suffering losses, Bruce Wilkinson replaced Roger Tetrault as chairman and CEO the same year. In 2002 a judge ruled that McDermott didn't have to return the $622 million that Babcock & Wilcox transferred to it in 1998. (The ruling suggested that McDermott might be able to limit the claims to its subsidiary.) Later that year, McDermott discontinued its Hudson Products subsidiary.

Babcock & Wilcox emerged from bankruptcy in 2006.

## EXECUTIVES

**Chairman and CEO:** Bruce W. Wilkinson, age 62, $866,687 pay
**EVP and CFO:** Francis S. (Frank) Kalman, age 59, $539,846 pay
**EVP and Chief Administrative and Legal Officer:** John T. Nesser III, age 58
**EVP, Human Resources, Health, Safety and Environmental:** Louis J. (Lou) Sannino, age 58
**SVP and CFO:** Michael S. Taff, age 45
**VP and Chief Risk Officer:** Tim Woodard
**VP Litigation, Claims, and Compliance:** Claire Hunter
**VP and Controller, Babcock & Wilcox:** Marvin D. Sehn
**VP and Treasurer:** James C. (Jim) Lewis, age 51
**VP, General Counsel, and Corporate Secretary:** Liane K. Hinrichs, age 49
**VP and Corporate Compliance Officer:** Thomas A. Henzler, age 50
**VP, Corporate Development and Strategic Planning:** James R. Easter, age 50
**VP, Internal Audit; VP and Controller, J. Ray McDermott:** Louis W. Burkart, age 55
**VP, Investor Relations and Communications:** John E. (Jay) Roueche III
**President and COO, The Babcock & Wilcox Company:** David L. (Dave) Keller, age 53
**President and CEO, The Babcock & Wilcox Companies:** John A. Fees, age 49
**President and COO, J. Ray McDermott:** Robert A. (Bob) Deason, age 61, $495,751 pay
**President and General Manager, BWXT Services:** Rhonnie L. Smith
**President, Babcock & Wilcox Canada:** Richard E. Reimels
**President, Diamond Power International, Babcock & Wilcox:** Eileen M. Competti
**Auditors:** Deloitte & Touche LLP

## LOCATIONS

**HQ:** McDermott International, Inc.
777 N. Eldridge Pkwy., Houston, TX 77079
**Phone:** 281-870-5000 **Fax:** 281-870-5095
**Web:** www.mcdermott.com

McDermott International maintains major operations in Azerbaijan, Canada, China, Denmark, Indonesia, Mexico, the United Arab Emirates, and the US. The company operates worldwide.

**2006 Sales**

| | % of total |
|---|---|
| US | 53 |
| Azerbaijan | 10 |
| Qatar | 6 |
| Saudi Arabia | 6 |
| Canada | 6 |
| Indonesia | 4 |
| Thailand | 3 |
| Vietnam | 2 |
| Malaysia | 2 |
| Sweden | 1 |
| Denmark | 1 |
| China | 1 |
| Mexico | 1 |
| Other countries | 4 |
| **Total** | **100** |

## PRODUCTS/OPERATIONS

**2006 Sales**

| | % of total |
|---|---|
| Power Generation Systems | 46 |
| Offshore Oil & Gas Construction | 39 |
| Government Operations | 15 |
| **Total** | **100** |

**Selected Products and Services**

Power Generation Systems
- Aftermarket goods and services
- Boiler Auxiliary Equipment
- Nuclear equipment operations
- Original equipment manufacturers (OEMs) operations

Offshore Oil and Gas Construction
- Fabrication
- Offshore operations
- Procurement
- Project services and engineering

Government Operations
- Contract research
- Government facilities management and operation
- Nuclear component program
- Nuclear environmental services

## COMPETITORS

ABB
Acergy
Aker Kværner
ALSTOM
Bechtel National
CH2M HILL
Daewoo Engineering
Doosan Babcock
Emerson Electric
Fluor
Foster Wheeler
GE Aviation
Global Industries
Gulf Island Fabrication
Halliburton
Hitachi
Horizon Offshore
Hyundai Heavy Industries
Kiewit Offshore
Lockheed Martin
Mitsubishi Heavy Industries
National Oilwell Varco
NFS
Nippon Steel
Oceaneering International
Raytheon
Saipem
Technip
Tidewater
Vetco Gray
Washington Group

## HISTORICAL FINANCIALS

Company Type: Public

**Income Statement** FYE: December 31

| | REVENUE ($ mil.) | NET INCOME ($ mil.) | NET PROFIT MARGIN | EMPLOYEES |
|---|---|---|---|---|
| **12/06** | 4,120 | 342 | 8.3% | 27,800 |
| **12/05** | 1,856 | 198 | 10.7% | 14,200 |
| **12/04** | 1,923 | 62 | 3.2% | 12,500 |
| **12/03** | 2,335 | (95) | — | 16,000 |
| **12/02** | 1,749 | (776) | — | 18,200 |
| **Annual Growth** | 23.9% | — | — | 11.2% |

**2006 Year-End Financials**

Debt ratio: 3.9%
Return on equity: 224.4%
Cash ($ mil.): 880
Current ratio: 0.86
Long-term debt ($ mil.): 15

No. of shares (mil.): 111
Dividends
Yield: —
Payout: —
Market value ($ mil.): 5,637

**Stock History** NYSE: MDR

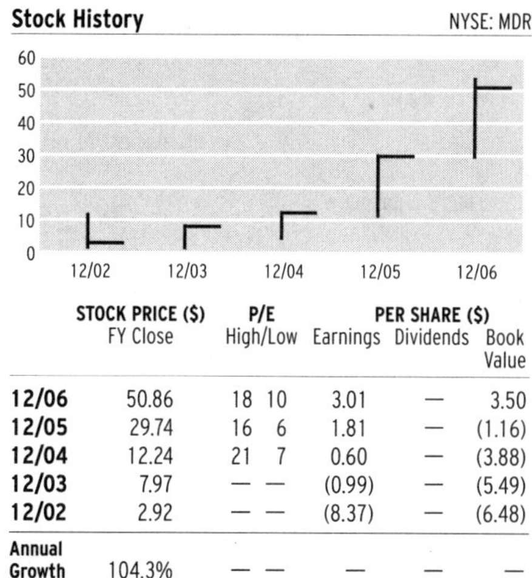


| | STOCK PRICE ($) FY Close | P/E High/Low | | PER SHARE ($) Earnings | Dividends | Book Value |
|---|---|---|---|---|---|---|
| **12/06** | 50.86 | 18 | 10 | 3.01 | — | 3.50 |
| **12/05** | 29.74 | 16 | 6 | 1.81 | — | (1.16) |
| **12/04** | 12.24 | 21 | 7 | 0.60 | — | (3.88) |
| **12/03** | 7.97 | — | — | (0.99) | — | (5.49) |
| **12/02** | 2.92 | — | — | (8.37) | — | (6.48) |
| **Annual Growth** | 104.3% | — | — | — | — | — |

# McDonald's

"Billions served," indeed. McDonald's is the world's #1 fast-food company by sales, with more than 31,000 flagship restaurants serving burgers and fries in almost 120 countries. The popular chain is well-known for its Big Macs, Quarter Pounders, and Chicken McNuggets. Most of its outlets are free-standing units, but McDonald's also has many quick-service kiosk units located in airports and retail areas. Each unit gets its food and packaging from approved suppliers and uses standardized procedures to ensure that a Big Mac purchased in Pittsburgh tastes the same as one bought in Beijing. About 75% of its restaurants are run by franchisees. McDonald's also owns the Boston Market fast-casual dining chain.

Despite its size and leading position in the fast food industry, McDonald's has only recently recovered from a long slump in sales. It managed to reverse its course by focusing on food quality and improving sales at existing locations rather than rapid expansion. Its strategy of being better rather than bigger has been the cornerstone of CEO Jim Skinner's administration since taking the reigns at McDonald's in 2004.

In addition to upgrading the facilities at its eateries, the Golden Arches has also been reducing the number of company-owned restaurants in its system. It is currently working to transfer about 2,300 locations to licensee ownership and hopes to complete the process by 2008. The company's growth plans are also focused on international markets, especially in China where McDonald's is trying to build a significant stronghold in time for the 2008 Olympics.

Many challenges stand in the way of the fast-food leader, however, not the least of which is an ongoing public relations battle to fight negative perceptions of its brand. McDonald's has come under fire in recent years for the low nutritional quality of its food, notably through such films and books as *Super Size Me* and *Fast Food Nation*. It has tried introducing healthier menu items and shifting its marketing toward children to show a more active Ronald McDonald.

The company has also reaped some benefits from earlier investments in alternative chains. It spun off Chipotle Mexican Grill in 2006 through an IPO and a later time disposed of its remaining stake in the quick-casual leader, adding about $670 million to McDonald's coffers. The following year it agreed to sell Boston Market to private equity firm Sun Capital Partners.

## HISTORY

The first McDonald's opened in 1948 in San Bernardino, California. In 1954 owners Dick and Mac McDonald signed a franchise agreement with 52-year-old Ray Kroc (a malt machine salesman), and a year later Kroc opened his first restaurant in Des Plaines, Illinois. By 1957 Kroc was operating 14 McDonald's restaurants in Illinois, Indiana, and California. In 1961 Kroc bought out the McDonald brothers for $2.7 million.

In 1962 the now-ubiquitous Golden Arches appeared for the first time, and the company sold its billionth burger. Ronald McDonald made his debut the following year, and the company introduced its first new menu item — the Filet-O-Fish. Two years later McDonald's went public and ran its first TV ads. The company opened its first stores outside the US (in Canada) in 1967, and the next year it added the Big Mac to the menu and opened its 1,000th restaurant.

During the 1970s McDonald's grew at the rate of about 500 restaurants per year, and the first Ronald McDonald House (a temporary residence for families of hospitalized children) opened in 1974. The drive-through window appeared in 1975.

McDonald's introduced Chicken McNuggets in 1983. Kroc, who had become senior chairman in the 1970s, died the next year. Growing competition slowed the company's US sales growth to about 5% per year at the end of the 1980s. In response, McDonald's added specially priced "value menu" items.

In 1990 the company made history and headlines when it opened the first McDonald's in Moscow. Two years later the Golden Arches expanded into China. In 1997 US division CEO Edward Rensi retired and was replaced by division chairman Jack Greenberg.

The next year Greenberg launched the Made For You food preparation system, designed to reduce waste and produce a better tasting burger. He was named CEO later that year. McDonald's also made its first investment in another restaurant concept in 1998 when it bought a stake in Chipotle Mexican Grill, a Denver-based chain of Mexican food restaurants. That same year saw the death of co-founder Dick McDonald, who died at age 89.

In 1999 McDonald's added a third brand to its family when it acquired the Ohio-based Donatos Pizzeria chain. The company's biggest deal, though, came in 2000 when it bought the Boston Market chain from struggling Boston Chicken.

But the company suffered from ill-thought product changes, less-than-successful marketing plans, and the growing public preference for lighter fast-food options, such as sub sandwiches and salads. Following three quarters of declining profits, in 2001 McDonald's announced a major restructuring of its US operations. It cut about 700 corporate jobs, hired five new managers, and consolidated its service regions.

Business failed to improve, however, and in 2002 it laid off approximately 600 corporate employees and closed about 175 underperforming units. At the end of 2002, after the company posted its first quarterly loss in history, vice chairman and president Jim Cantalupo, a veteran of McDonald's international operation, replaced Jack Greenberg as chairman and CEO.

McDonald's business began to improve during 2003 with the introduction of healthier menu fare. Late that year the company sold Donatos Pizzeria back to its founder Jim Grote and closed all Boston Market locations outside the US in order to focus more attention on its core chains.

Cantalupo died in April 2004. Director Andrew McKenna was named chairman and president. Charlie Bell became CEO. Diagnosed with cancer and undergoing surgery in May 2004, Bell curtailed his workload but returned to his job full-time later that month. However, he later stepped down in November in order to devote all his time to fighting cancer. (Bell died in January 2005.) Vice chairman Jim Skinner assumed the mantle of CEO, becoming the company's third chief executive in seven months.

The Venezuelan government ordered all 80 of the country's McDonald's restaurants closed for three days in 2005 as punishment for not following the country's tax laws.

## EXECUTIVES

**Chairman:** Andrew J. McKenna, age 77
**Vice Chairman and CEO:** James A. (Jim) Skinner, age 62, $1,177,692 pay
**President and COO:** Ralph Alvarez, age 51, $703,077 pay
**Corporate SEVP and CFO:** Matthew H. (Matt) Paull, age 55, $683,333 pay
**Corporate EVP, General Counsel, and Secretary:** Gloria Santona, age 56
**Corporate EVP and Worldwide Chief Restaurant Officer:** Jeffrey P. (Jeff) Stratton, age 51
**Corporate EVP and Global Chief Marketing Officer:** Mary Dillon, age 45
**Corporate EVP and Chief Human Resources Officer:** Richard R. (Rich) Floersch, age 49
**Corporate SVP Social Responsibility; President and CEO, Ronald McDonald House Charities:** Kenneth L. (Ken) Barun
**SVP Global Consumer and Business Insights:** Eric Leininger
**SVP Global Marketing:** Dean Barrett
**VP Corporate Communications:** Walt Riker
**President and CEO, Boston Market:** Michael D. (Mike) Andres
**President, McDonald's Asia/Pacific, Middle East, and Africa:** Timothy J. (Tim) Fenton, age 49, $462,500 pay
**President, McDonald's Europe:** Denis Hennequin, age 48, $534,427 pay
**President, McDonald's Latin America:** Jose Armario, age 47
**President, McDonald's USA:** Donald (Don) Thompson, age 44
**VP Training, McDonald's USA; Dean, Hamburger University:** Diana Thomas
**Chief Information Officer:** Dave Weick
**Chief Marketing Officer:** Bill Lamar Jr.
**Chief Creative Officer:** Marlena Peleo-Lazar
**Executive Chef:** Dan Coudreaut
**Auditors:** Ernst & Young LLP

## LOCATIONS

**HQ:** McDonald's Corporation
McDonald's Plaza, Oak Brook, IL 60523
**Phone:** 630-623-3000 **Fax:** 630-623-5004
**Web:** www.mcdonalds.com

**2006 Sales**

| | $ mil. | % of total |
|---|---|---|
| Europe | 7,638 | 35 |
| US | 7,464 | 35 |
| Asia/Pacific, the Middle East & Africa | 3,053 | 14 |
| Latin America | 1,659 | 8 |
| Canada | 1,081 | 5 |
| Other regions & corporate | 691 | 3 |
| **Total** | **21,586** | **100** |

**2006 Locations**

| | No. |
|---|---|
| US | 13,774 |
| Asia/Pacific, the Middle East & Africa | 7,822 |
| Europe | 6,403 |
| Latin America | 1,656 |
| Canada | 1,391 |
| Other regions & corporate | 621 |
| **Total** | **31,667** |

## PRODUCTS/OPERATIONS

**2006 Sales**

| | $ mil. | % of total |
|---|---|---|
| Restaurants | 16,083 | 75 |
| Franchising | 5,503 | 25 |
| **Total** | **21,586** | **100** |

**2006 Locations**

| | No. |
|---|---|
| McDonald's | |
| Franchised & affiliated | 22,880 |
| Company-owned | 8,166 |
| Boston Market | 621 |
| **Total** | **31,667** |

## COMPETITORS

AFC Enterprises
Arby's
Burger King
Cajun Operating Company
Chick-fil-A
CKE Restaurants
Dairy Queen
Jack in the Box
Quiznos
Subway
Wendy's
YUM!

## HISTORICAL FINANCIALS

Company Type: Public

**Income Statement** FYE: December 31

| | REVENUE ($ mil.) | NET INCOME ($ mil.) | NET PROFIT MARGIN | EMPLOYEES |
|---|---|---|---|---|
| **12/06** | 21,586 | 3,544 | 16.4% | 465,000 |
| **12/05** | 20,460 | 2,602 | 12.7% | 447,000 |
| **12/04** | 19,065 | 2,279 | 12.0% | 438,000 |
| **12/03** | 17,141 | 1,471 | 8.6% | 418,000 |
| **12/02** | 15,406 | 894 | 5.8% | 413,000 |
| **Annual Growth** | 8.8% | 41.1% | — | 3.0% |

**2006 Year-End Financials**

Debt ratio: 54.4%
Return on equity: 23.2%
Cash ($ mil.): 2,136
Current ratio: 1.21
Long-term debt ($ mil.): 8,417
No. of shares (mil.): 1,204
Dividends
Yield: 2.3%
Payout: 35.3%
Market value ($ mil.): 53,360

**Stock History** NYSE: MCD

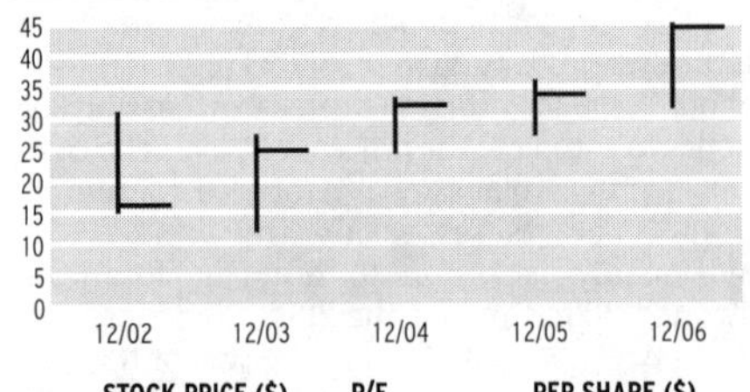

| | STOCK PRICE ($) FY Close | P/E High | P/E Low | PER SHARE ($) Earnings | Dividends | Book Value |
|---|---|---|---|---|---|---|
| **12/06** | 44.33 | 16 | 11 | 2.83 | 1.00 | 12.84 |
| **12/05** | 33.72 | 17 | 13 | 2.04 | 0.67 | 11.99 |
| **12/04** | 32.06 | 18 | 14 | 1.79 | — | 11.18 |
| **12/03** | 24.83 | 23 | 11 | 1.15 | 0.40 | 9.50 |
| **12/02** | 16.08 | 44 | 22 | 0.70 | 0.23 | 8.11 |
| **Annual Growth** | 28.9% | — | — | 41.8% | 44.4% | 12.2% |

# McGraw-Hill

As a successful publishing operation, McGraw-Hill is a textbook case. The company is one of the world's largest producers of textbooks, tests, and related materials, serving the elementary, secondary, and higher education markets. McGraw-Hill is also a leading supplier of financial and business information services, providing indexes and ratings for both domestic and overseas markets through Standard & Poor's. In addition, it publishes *BusinessWeek* magazine. The company also publishes a number of industry trade journals (*Aviation Week, Engineering News-Record*), creates professional training and development materials, and operates nine TV stations (four ABC affiliates and five Azteca America affiliates).

McGraw Hill's operations consist of three business segments: McGraw-Hill Education, Financial Services, and Information & Media.

McGraw-Hill Education's School Education Group (SEG), which serves the elementary and high school markets, is investing heavily in math, reading, social studies, and science programs in 2007. The group is influenced by The federal "No Child Left Behind" act, which is expanding from reading and math to science in the 2007-2008 school year.

The Financial Services unit operates under the Standard & Poor's brand and provides global credit ratings, indices, risk evaluation, and investment research and data to investors, corporations, governments, financial institutions, and investment managers.

In addition to its television stations, trade publications, and magazines, the Information & Media holdings include J.D. Power and Associates, a company that offers automobile ratings. In this area McGraw Hill is placing greater emphasis on digital asset management and Web-based content. Along these lines the company bought a stake in social networking site Gather Inc. in 2006.

The company took some cost-cutting measures in 2006 when it announced 500 layoffs, mainly from its educational testing and BusinessWeek divisions.

Chairman, president, and CEO Harold "Terry" McGraw III is the great grandson of the company's founder.

## HISTORY

James H. McGraw bought his first industry journal, *American Journal of Railway Appliances*, in 1888 and incorporated The McGraw Publishing Company in 1899. Journal editor John Hill started The Hill Publishing Company (*American Machinist, Locomotive Engineer*) in 1902. The two men merged their book publishing operations into the McGraw-Hill Book Company in 1909. The rest of the companies merged as the McGraw-Hill Publishing Company in 1917 following Hill's death the previous year. In 1929, two months before the stock market crash, McGraw-Hill launched *BusinessWeek,* which bucked popular opinion in its first issue with concerns about the economy's health. The company also went public that year. James McGraw retired as chairman in 1935; he was succeeded by his son, Jay.

During the 1930s and 1940s, McGraw-Hill produced trade journals for aviation, health care, and atomic energy. In 1947, its trade division published *Betty Crocker's Picture Cook Book,* which sold 2.3 million copies its first two years. The company's textbook operations began printing for the elementary and secondary school markets to capitalize on booming enrollment in the 1950s and 1960s. In 1966 it bought Standard & Poor's financial services and bought four TV stations from Time in 1972. Harold McGraw, grandson of founder James, became president in 1974 and successfully fended off a takeover attempt by American Express in 1979.

Harold retired as CEO in 1983 (he remained chairman until 1988) and was replaced by Joseph Dionne. During the 1980s the company expanded its electronic information services and sold its trade books division in 1989. That year McGraw-Hill began Primis Custom Publishing, a partnership with Kodak and printer R. R. Donnelley to produce customized college textbooks, and it started textbook and educational software joint venture Macmillan/McGraw-Hill School Publishing. (McGraw-Hill bought Macmillan's share in 1993 after Macmillan's parent, Maxwell Communications, went bankrupt.)

Its financial services unit expanded with the purchases of J.J. Kenny (municipal securities information) in 1990 and 25% of Liberty Brokerage in 1993, which gave McGraw-Hill access to US Treasury securities pricing information. In 1995 it rechristened itself The McGraw-Hill Companies and launched its corporate Internet site the next year.

When Dionne retired in 1998, the company named Harold McGraw III (the founder's great-grandson) CEO. In 1999 McGraw-Hill bought medical publisher Appleton & Lange from Pearson for $46 million and sold some trade magazines (*Modern Plastics*) and related trade show businesses to Veronis Suhler (now named Veronis Suhler Stevenson). The next year it sold Tower Group International (customs consulting) to FedEx for $140 million.

After a belt-tightening period in the early 2000s that included a restructuring as well as layoffs of nearly 1,000 employees, the company rebounded by refocusing on its core markets — education and financial — and reducing its stakes in e-commerce and emerging technology firms. Amid a topsy-turvy stock market and well-publicized corporate scandals, the company saw strong growth in its credit rating and investment services as investors do their homework before putting their money down.

The federal "No Child Left Behind" act, passed in 2001, was a boost for the company as the law opened up additional federal funds for education and created additional testing and assessment opportunities.

In early 2002 the company closed its Lifetime Learning unit as part of a restructuring, letting go 100 employees. The company sold some of its Lifetime Learning assets to The Thomson Corporation. That year McGraw-Hill's Education division bought UK academic book publisher, Open University Press.

As it regrouped around core products, the company divested certain units. In 2003 the company sold its financial data provider, S&P ComStock, to Interactive Data Corp. for $155 million. McGraw-Hill said the divestiture allowed Standard & Poor's to direct its resources to its investment services group.

McGraw-Hill sold its Healthcare Information Group in 2005 to the Vendome Group. Also that year the company acquired J.D. Power and Associates, a provider of automobile ratings.

## EXECUTIVES

**Chairman, President, and CEO:** Harold W. (Terry) McGraw III, age 58
**EVP and CFO:** Robert J. (Bob) Bahash, age 62
**EVP and CIO:** Bruce D. Marcus, age 58
**EVP and General Counsel:** Kenneth M. (Ken) Vittor, age 57
**EVP Global Strategy:** Peter C. Davis, age 52
**EVP Human Resources:** David L. Murphy, age 61, $1,340,000 pay
**SVP Corporate Affairs and Executive Assistant to the Chairman, President, and CEO:** David B. Stafford, age 44
**SVP Investor Relations:** Donald S. Rubin
**VP Corporate Communications:** Steven H. Weiss
**VP and Publisher, Wright Group:** Stephen Mico
**VP and Group Editorial Director, Literacy, Wright Group:** Marianne Hiland
**President, Information and Media:** Glenn S. Goldberg, age 48
**President, McGraw-Hill Education:** Henry Hirschberg
**President, Business Week:** Keith Fox, age 42
**President, Platts:** Victoria Chu Pao
**President, School Education:** Buzz Ellis
**President, Standard & Poor's:** Kathleen A. Corbet, age 47
**President, McGraw-Hill Learning Group:** Daniel Caton
**Auditors:** Ernst & Young LLP

## LOCATIONS

**HQ:** The McGraw-Hill Companies, Inc.
1221 Avenue of the Americas, New York, NY 10020
**Phone:** 212-512-2000 **Fax:** 212-512-3840
**Web:** www.mcgraw-hill.com

McGraw-Hill has more than 350 offices in more than 35 countries.

## PRODUCTS/OPERATIONS

### 2006 Sales

| | $ mil. | % of total |
|---|---|---|
| Financial services | 2,746.4 | 44 |
| Education | 2,524.2 | 40 |
| Information & media services | 984.5 | 16 |
| **Total** | **6,255.1** | **100** |

### Selected McGraw-Hill Education Holdings

Higher Education
- McGraw-Hill Dushkin
- McGraw-Hill/Irwin
- McGraw-Hill/Primis Custom Publishing
- McGraw-Hill Science, Engineering & Mathematics
- McGraw-Hill Social Sciences and World Languages

School Education Group
- Glencoe/McGraw-Hill
- Macmillan/McGraw-Hill
- McGraw-Hill Digital Learning
- McGraw-Hill Professional Development
- SRA/McGraw-Hill
- Wright Group/McGraw-Hill

### Selected Financial Services Holdings

Credit Market Services
Investment Services
Standard & Poor's

### Selected Information and Media Services Holdings

Aviation Week Group
- AviationNow.com
- Conferences & Exhibitions
- Custom Media
- Education
- Magazines
- Newsletters
- References & Directories
- Television & Video

Broadcasting Group
- KERO-TV (Bakersfield, CA)
- KGTV (San Diego)
- KMGH-TV (Denver)
- WRTV (Indianapolis)

Business Week Group
- BusinessWeek/Golf Digest Partnership
- BusinessWeek/USA Today Partnership
- BusinessWeek Events
- BusinessWeek Investor Workshops
- *BusinessWeek* Magazine
- BusinessWeek Online
- BusinessWeek TV

J.D. Power and Associates (marketing information provider)

McGraw-Hill Construction Group
- *Architectural Record*
- Construction.com
- *Design-Build*
- *Engineering News-Record*
- F.W. Dodge
- Sweet's Group

Platts
- Coal
- Electric Power
- Energy Information Technology
- Energy Policy
- Engineering
- Metals
- Natural Gas
- Nuclear
- Oil
- Petrochemicals
- Utility Data Institute

## COMPETITORS

Advance Publications
Advanstar
Bloomberg
Crain Communications
D&B
Disney Publishing
Dow Jones
Educational Development
Educational Testing Service
FactSet
Fitch
Forbes
Hanley Wood
Houghton Mifflin
IHS
Informa
John Wiley
Media General
Moody's
Morningstar
The Nielsen Company
Pearson
Penton Media
PRIMEDIA
RD School & Educational Services
Reed Elsevier Group
Reuters
Riverdeep
Scholastic
Thomas Publishing
Thomson Corporation
Time
U.S. News & World Report
Value Line
Washington Post
Wolters Kluwer
W.W. Norton

## HISTORICAL FINANCIALS

Company Type: Public

### Income Statement

FYE: December 31

| | REVENUE ($ mil.) | NET INCOME ($ mil.) | NET PROFIT MARGIN | EMPLOYEES |
|---|---|---|---|---|
| **12/06** | 6,255 | 882 | 14.1% | 20,214 |
| **12/05** | 6,004 | 844 | 14.1% | 19,600 |
| **12/04** | 5,251 | 756 | 14.4% | 17,000 |
| **12/03** | 4,999 | 688 | 13.8% | 16,068 |
| **12/02** | 4,788 | 577 | 12.0% | 16,505 |
| **Annual Growth** | 6.9% | 11.2% | — | 5.2% |

**2006 Year-End Financials**

Debt ratio: 0.0%
Return on equity: 30.5%
Cash ($ mil.): 354
Current ratio: 0.91
Long-term debt ($ mil.): 0

No. of shares (mil.): 354
Dividends
Yield: 1.1%
Payout: 30.4%
Market value ($ mil.): 24,076

**Stock History** NYSE: MHP

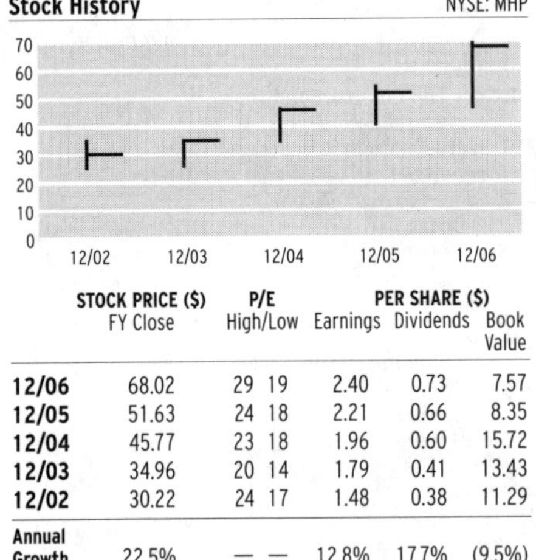


| | STOCK PRICE ($) FY Close | P/E High | P/E Low | PER SHARE ($) Earnings | Dividends | Book Value |
|---|---|---|---|---|---|---|
| **12/06** | 68.02 | 29 | 19 | 2.40 | 0.73 | 7.57 |
| **12/05** | 51.63 | 24 | 18 | 2.21 | 0.66 | 8.35 |
| **12/04** | 45.77 | 23 | 18 | 1.96 | 0.60 | 15.72 |
| **12/03** | 34.96 | 20 | 14 | 1.79 | 0.41 | 13.43 |
| **12/02** | 30.22 | 24 | 17 | 1.48 | 0.38 | 11.29 |
| **Annual Growth** | 22.5% | — | — | 12.8% | 17.7% | (9.5%) |

# McKesson Corporation

McKesson moves medicine. The largest pharmaceuticals distributor in the US, McKesson delivers prescription and generic drugs, as well as health and beauty care products, to retail and institutional pharmacies throughout the US and Canada. The company is also a major North American medical supplies wholesaler, providing medical and surgical equipment to alternate health care sites, such as doctors' offices, surgery centers, and long-term care facilities. In addition to distribution services, McKesson offers software and technical services to health care providers and insurers that help them manage supply chain, clinical, administrative, and financial operations.

McKesson's distribution businesses bring in most of the company's money. Along with getting drugs and other health care items to retailers and health care institutions, the company also offers disease management programs for insurers and employers, as well as specialty pharmacy distribution for patients who need high-cost, injectable drugs on a regular basis. Additionally, the company supplies automated pharmacy dispensing systems through its minority stake in North Carolina-based Parata Systems and first aid kits and workplace safety training through subsidiary Zee Medical. Pharmacy benefits manager Caremark (which accounts for about 10% of sales) and Wal-Mart are among the company's key clients.

Though retail chains and institutional pharmacies still account for a larger percentage of revenue, the company has been expanding its service offering aimed at independent pharmacies, acquiring D&K Healthcare Resources — a regional distributor with a strong independent pharmacy customer base — in 2005. Additionally, its Health Mart franchising program, revamped in 2006, gives independents the clout of a national brand and purchasing organization. The Health Mart program has grown by leaps and bounds — from 350 to 1,300 stores in less than a year.

McKesson is also responding to the growth in the generic drug industry with its OneStop purchasing program, which gives its pharmacy customers discounts on generics and helps them keep up with new generic product launches.

Strategic acquisitions have been important to the growth of each of the company's units. In addition to D&K, McKesson added Sterling Medical Services (a distributor of disposable medical supplies) in 2006 and Per-Se Technologies (which provides technology and outsourcing solutions to doctors and other health care providers) in 2007. In 2005 it bought Israeli technology company Medcon, which provides cardiac imaging and information management solutions.

McKesson has trimmed some operations, too. It sold the hospital-oriented part of its medical equipment distribution business to Owens & Minor in 2006 and is instead focusing on serving doctor's offices, clinics, and other nonhospital customers.

## HISTORY

John McKesson opened a Manhattan drugstore in 1833, and Daniel Robbins joined him as a partner in 1840. McKesson-Robbins soon expanded into chemical and drug production, and the enterprise grew steadily. In 1926, after differences arose between the McKesson and Robbins heirs, the company was sold to Donald Coster.

Coster was actually convicted felon Philip Musica, who purchased McKesson-Robbins with fraudulently obtained bank loans. For more than a decade his real identity remained secret from all but one blackmailer. By 1930 McKesson-Robbins had wholesale drug operations in 33 states. The company appeared to be growing, but a treasurer discovered a Musica-orchestrated accounting scam and a cash shortfall of $3 million. Faced with exposure, Musica killed himself in 1939; company bankruptcy followed. McKesson-Robbins emerged from bankruptcy in 1941.

In a hostile takeover in 1967, San Francisco-based Foremost Dairies bought McKesson-Robbins to form Foremost-McKesson. Over the next 20 years, the company bought liquor, chemical, and software wholesalers, as well as several bottled-water companies. It sold Foremost Dairies in 1983 to focus on distribution, changed its name to McKesson the next year, and continued to build its drug wholesaling business through acquisitions. By 1985 it was the US's largest distributor of drugs and medical equipment, wine and liquor, bottled water, and car waxes and polishes.

In 1986 McKesson narrowed its focus to the health industry by selling its liquor and chemical distributors. It acquired Canadian drug distributor Medis by halves in 1990 and 1991, and a 23% stake in Mexican drug distributor Nadro in 1993.

McKesson sold PCS, the US's #1 prescription claims processor (acquired in 1970), to Eli Lilly in 1994. In 1996 the firm bought bankrupt distributor FoxMeyer Drug and sold its stake in Armor All (auto and home products) to Clorox.

In 1997 the company purchased General Medical, the US's largest distributor of medical surgical supplies, for about $775 million. The company began to focus on health care, selling its Millbrook Distribution Services unit (health and beauty products, general merchandise, and specialty foods).

Under new CEO Mark Pulido, it agreed to buy drug wholesaler AmeriSource Health (now AmerisourceBergen), but withdrew the offer in 1998, facing FTC opposition. Instead, McKesson moved into information systems, paying $14 billion for health care information top dog HBO & Company, forming McKesson HBOC. HBO, a high-flyer in the high-growth health information systems segment, balanced its rather dowdy drug and medical distribution operations.

But just months after the deal closed, accounting inconsistencies at HBO prompted McKesson to restate fourth-quarter results for fiscal 1999 twice, triggering shareholder lawsuits and a housecleaning of top brass. Five ex-HBO executives, including McKesson HBOC chairman Charlie McCall (who was later indicted for securities fraud), were canned for using improper accounting methods. McKesson's veteran CEO Pulido and CFO Richard Hawkins were forced to resign for not seeing the problems coming.

The company changed its name to McKesson Corporation in 2001.

To catch former #1 pharmaceutical distributor Cardinal Health, McKesson built up its core areas in 2003 and 2004, while trimming away some of the dead weight (Abaton.com, Amysis Managed Care Systems, and ProDental Corp.). The company bought PMO, a specialty mail order prescription business. It also acquired Canadian firm A.L.I. Technologies, which provides systems for managing medical images.

## EXECUTIVES

**Chairman, President, and CEO:** John H. Hammergren, age 46, $5,309,615 pay
**EVP and Group President; President, McKesson Supply Solutions:** Paul C. Julian, age 51, $2,329,231 pay
**EVP and CFO:** Jeffrey C. Campbell, age 46, $1,623,923 pay
**EVP and CIO:** Randall N. (Randy) Spratt, age 55
**EVP General Counsel, and Secretary:** Laureen E. Seeger, age 45
**EVP Corporate Strategy and Business Development:** Marc E. Owen, age 47
**EVP Human Resources:** Paul E. Kirincic, age 56
**EVP; President, McKesson Provider Technologies:** Pamela J. Pure, age 47, $1,592,192 pay
**VP and Controller:** Nigel A. Rees
**VP, Corporate Communications:** Katherine (Kate) Rohrbach
**VP Investor Relations:** Larry Kurtz
**VP and Treasurer:** Nicholas A. Loiacono
**President, McKesson Canada:** Claudio F. Bussandri
**President, McKesson Health Solutions:** Emad Rizk
**President, McKesson Medication Management:** Eleonore Saenger
**President, McKesson Medical-Surgical:** Brian S. Tyler, age 39
**President, McKesson Specialty Pharmaceutical, McKesson Pharmacy Systems and Automated Prescription Systems:** Patrick Blake
**President, U.S. Pharmaceutical Distribution, Pharmaceutical Solutions Division:** John Figueroa
**Chief Nursing Officer:** Billie Waldo
**General Manager, McKesson New Zealand:** Lesley Clarke
**Director Public Relations:** James Larkin
**Auditors:** Deloitte & Touche LLP

## LOCATIONS

**HQ:** McKesson Corporation
1 Post St., San Francisco, CA 94104
**Phone:** 415-983-8300 **Fax:** 415-983-7160
**Web:** www.mckesson.com

McKesson distributes pharmaceuticals and medical supplies primarily in the US and Canada. Its Provider Technologies segment has operations in Europe, Israel, and North America.

## 2007 Sales

| | $ mil. | % of total |
|---|---|---|
| US | 86,026 | 93 |
| Other countries | 6,951 | 7 |
| **Total** | **92,977** | **100** |

## PRODUCTS/OPERATIONS

### 2007 Sales

| | $ mil. | % of total |
|---|---|---|
| Pharmaceutical Solutions | 88,708 | 95 |
| Medical-Surgical Solutions | 2,364 | 3 |
| Provider Technologies | 1,905 | 2 |
| **Total** | **92,977** | **100** |

### Selected Products and Services

Pharmaceutical/Medical-Surgical Solutions
- Disease management programs
- Drug distribution
- Fulfill-Rx (ordering and inventory management for hospitals)
- Health Mart (independent retail pharmacy franchising program)
- Inventory management
- Medical equipment and supplies distribution
- OneStop (generic drug purchasing program)
- Pharmacy robotics
- Specialty pharmaceutical distribution
- RxPak (bulk repackaging)
- ZEE Medical (first-aid supplies distribution and training )

Provider Technologies
- Billing and accounting software
- Clinical management software
- Document imaging software
- Outsourcing services
- Patient accounting and processing software
- Supply chain management software
- Technical consulting and services

## COMPETITORS

Accredo Health
AmerisourceBergen
athenahealth
Bellco Health
Cardinal Health
CuraScript
GE Healthcare
HLTH Corp.
Kinray
Medline Industries
Owens & Minor
PolyMedica
PSS World Medical
Quality King
Siemens Medical
Surgical Express

## HISTORICAL FINANCIALS

Company Type: Public

### Income Statement

FYE: March 31

| | REVENUE ($ mil.) | NET INCOME ($ mil.) | NET PROFIT MARGIN | EMPLOYEES |
|---|---|---|---|---|
| **3/07** | 92,977 | 913 | 1.0% | 31,800 |
| **3/06** | 88,050 | 751 | 0.9% | 26,400 |
| **3/05** | 80,515 | (157) | — | 25,200 |
| **3/04** | 69,506 | 647 | 0.9% | 24,600 |
| **3/03** | 57,121 | 555 | 1.0% | 24,500 |
| **Annual Growth** | 13.0% | 13.2% | — | 6.7% |

### 2007 Year-End Financials

Debt ratio: 28.7%
Return on equity: 15.0%
Cash ($ mil.): 2,938
Current ratio: 1.18
Long-term debt ($ mil.): 1,803
No. of shares (mil.): 295
Dividends
Yield: 0.4%
Payout: 8.0%
Market value ($ mil.): 17,269

### Stock History

NYSE: MCK

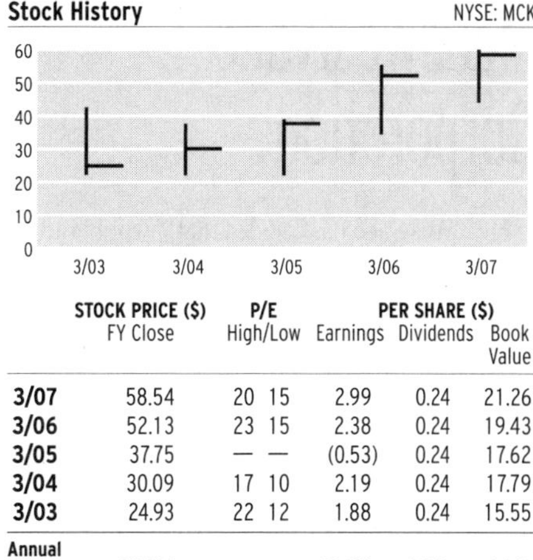

| | STOCK PRICE ($) FY Close | P/E High | P/E Low | PER SHARE ($) Earnings | Dividends | Book Value |
|---|---|---|---|---|---|---|
| **3/07** | 58.54 | 20 | 15 | 2.99 | 0.24 | 21.26 |
| **3/06** | 52.13 | 23 | 15 | 2.38 | 0.24 | 19.43 |
| **3/05** | 37.75 | — | — | (0.53) | 0.24 | 17.62 |
| **3/04** | 30.09 | 17 | 10 | 2.19 | 0.24 | 17.79 |
| **3/03** | 24.93 | 22 | 12 | 1.88 | 0.24 | 15.55 |
| **Annual Growth** | 23.8% | — | — | 12.3% | 0.0% | 8.1% |

# McKinsey & Company

One of the world's top management consulting firms, McKinsey & Company has more than 85 offices in some 45 countries around the globe. The company advises corporate enterprises, government agencies, and foundations on a variety of issues. It groups its practices into six main areas: business technology, corporate finance, marketing and sales, operations, organization, and strategy. McKinsey serves clients in numerous industry sectors, from automotive to high tech to nonprofit to telecommunications. Founded by James McKinsey in 1926, the company is owned by its partners.

McKinsey takes advantage of its global reach to gain business from multinational companies that want help in harmonizing their diverse operations. In addition, strategic consulting continues to be an important revenue source for the firm, as it has been since McKinsey's inception.

In addition to being one of the oldest consulting firms, McKinsey is considered one of the most prestigious (along with Boston Consulting Group and Bain) as measured in surveys of aspiring consultants. Contributing to McKinsey's allure as an employer is the firm's network of 15,000-plus alumni, many of whom have been tapped for C-level jobs in the course of their careers. Alumni running companies, in turn, represent a potential source of business for the firm.

## HISTORY

McKinsey & Company was founded in Chicago in 1926 by University of Chicago accounting professor James McKinsey. The company evolved from an auditing practice of McKinsey and his partners, Marvin Bower and A.T. Kearney, who began analyzing business and industry and offering advice. McKinsey died in 1937; two years later, Bower, who headed the New York office, and Kearney, in Chicago, split the firm. Kearney renamed the Chicago office A.T. Kearney & Co. (later acquired by Electronic Data Systems), and Bower kept the McKinsey name and built up a practice structured like a law firm.

Bower focused on the big picture instead of on specific operating problems, helping boost billings to $2 million by 1950. He hired staff straight out of prestigious business schools, reinforcing the firm's theoretical bent. Bower implemented a competitive up-or-out policy requiring employees who are not continually promoted to leave the firm.

The firm's prestige continued to grow during the booming 1950s along with demand for consulting services. Before becoming president in 1953, Dwight Eisenhower asked McKinsey to find out exactly what the government did. By 1959 Bower had opened an office in London, followed by others in Amsterdam; Dusseldorf, Germany; Melbourne; Paris; and Zurich.

In 1964 the company founded management journal *The McKinsey Quarterly*. When Bower retired in 1967, sales were $20 million, and McKinsey was the #1 management consulting firm. During the 1970s it faced competition from firms with newer approaches and lost market share. In response, then-managing director Ronald Daniel started specialty practices and expanded foreign operations.

The consulting boom of the 1980s was spurred by mergers and buyouts. By 1988 the firm had 1,800 consultants, sales were $620 million, and 50% of billings came from overseas.

The recession of the early 1990s hit white-collar workers, including consultants. McKinsey, scrambling to upgrade its technical side, bought Information Consulting Group (ICG), its first acquisition. But the corporate cultures did not meld, and most ICG people left by 1993.

In 1994 the company elected its first managing director of non-European descent, Indian-born Rajat Gupta. Two years later the traditionally hush-hush firm found itself at the center of that most public 1990s arena, the sexual discrimination lawsuit. A female ex-consultant in Texas sued, claiming McKinsey had sabotaged her career (the case was dismissed).

In 1998 McKinsey partnered with Northwestern University and the University of Pennsylvania to establish a business school in India. The following year graduating seniors surveyed in Europe, the UK, and the US named the company as their ideal employer.

Also in 1999 the company created McKinsey to help "accelerate" Internet startups. The next year it increased salaries and offered incentives to better compete with Internet firms for employees. In 2001 the company expanded its branding business with the acquisition of Envision, a Chicago-based brand consultant.

Like its rivals in the consulting industry, McKinsey took a hit from the dot-com bust and the economic downturn of 2001 and 2002, as many companies were slower to sign up for costly long-term strategy consulting engagements and mergers and acquisitions work dried up.

In 2003 Ian Davis was elected as managing director of the firm, succeeding Rajat Gupta, who had served as McKinsey's top executive for nine years. (Managing directors serve for three years and are limited to three terms.) Davis had previously served as the head of the firm's UK office.

## EXECUTIVES

**Managing Director:** Ian Davis, age 56
**Senior Partner Worldwide:** Rajat Gupta, age 58
**Chairman, Americas:** Michael Patsalos-Fox
**Chairman, Asia:** Dominic Barton
**Director, Frankfurt Offices and Co-Leader European Chemical Practice:** Florian Budde
**Director, McKinsey Global Institute:** Diana Farrell

**Media Contact, Asia (Singapore):** Patricia Welch
**Media Contact, North and South America (New York):** Mitch Kent
**Media Contact, Europe, Middle East, and Africa (Düsseldorf):** Rolf Antrecht
**Media Contact, McKinsey Global Institutue (US):** Rebeca Robboy
**Media Contact, Europe, Middle East, and Africa (London):** Andrea Minton Beddoes
**Director, Greater China Office:** Andrew Grant
**Director, New York Office:** Vikram Malhotra
**German Office Manager:** Frank Mattern

## LOCATIONS

**HQ:** McKinsey & Company
55 E. 52nd St., 21st Fl., New York, NY 10022
**Phone:** 212-446-7000 **Fax:** 212-446-8575
**Web:** www.mckinsey.com

## PRODUCTS/OPERATIONS

### Selected Industry Practices

Automotive and assembly
Banking and securities
Chemicals
Consumer packaged goods
Electric power and natural gas
Health care
Information technology
Insurance
Media and entertainment
Metals and mining
Nonprofit organizations
Petroleum
Pharmaceuticals and medical products
Private equity
Pulp and paper
Retail
Telecommunications
Travel and logistics

## COMPETITORS

Accenture
A.T. Kearney
Bain & Company
BearingPoint
Booz Allen
Boston Consulting
Capgemini
Computer Sciences Corp.
Deloitte Consulting
EDS
ESource
IBM
PA Consulting
Perot Systems
PRTM
Roland Berger

## HISTORICAL FINANCIALS

Company Type: Private

**Income Statement** FYE: December 31

| | ESTIMATED REVENUE ($ mil.) | NET INCOME ($ mil.) | NET PROFIT MARGIN | EMPLOYEES |
|---|---|---|---|---|
| **12/05** | 3,800 | — | — | 12,900 |
| **12/04** | 3,150 | — | — | 12,100 |
| **12/03** | 3,000 | — | — | 11,500 |
| **12/02** | 3,000 | — | — | 12,000 |
| **12/01** | 3,400 | — | — | 13,000 |
| **Annual Growth** | 2.8% | — | — | (0.2%) |

**Revenue History**

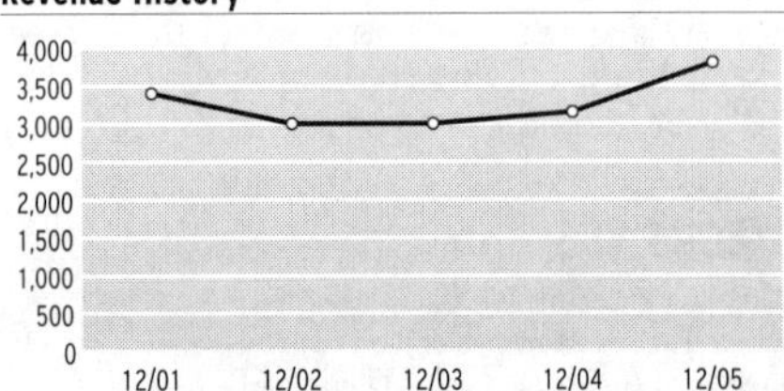


# MeadWestvaco Corporation

MeadWestvaco has decided that it would rather box than shuffle paper: It sold its Papers business — which made labels, book/catalog/magazine papers, and business forms — to investment firm Cerberus Capital Management in 2005 for $2.3 billion. The company's packaging operations (folding cartons, corrugated boxes, printed plastics) account for nearly three-fourths of sales. The company also makes school supplies (Mead, Five Star, Trapper Keeper), consumer office products (AT-A-GLANCE, Cambridge), and specialty chemicals (activated carbons, asphalt emulsifiers, tall oil).

MeadWestvaco owns about 1.25 million acres of timber (primarily in the US), but it has announced plans to sell 300,000 acres that it holds in the southeastern US. The company reached a deal to sell 228,000 acres, plus another 95,000 acres worth of harvesting rights, to Wells Timberland REIT for $400 million in mid-2007.

MeadWestvaco had been selling assets, cutting jobs, and consolidating operations and restructuring even before it sold its entire Papers segment. Papers accounted for a little under 30% of MeadWestvaco's sales prior to the deal, but the segment had been a consistent money loser. Cerberus set up the divested business as an independent company, NewPage Holding Corporation.

Focusing on its packaging business going forward, MeadWestvaco is particularly interested in fast-growing markets in Latin America, Asia, and Eastern Europe.

In 2006 MeadWestvaco realigned its packaging operations into two groups (Packaging Resources and Consumer Solutions); established a packaging research facility in Raleigh, North Carolina; and moved its headquarters to Richmond, Virginia. Under the new structure, Packaging Resources specializes in paperboard products while Consumer Solutions tackles all manner of consumer packaging products.

The company also spent about $714 million that year to acquire Saint-Gobain Calmar (now MeadWestvaco Calmar), which makes plastic dispensing and spraying goods used for packaging, from Compagnie de Saint-Gobain.

## HISTORY

Late in August 2001 Mead agreed to merge with Westvaco to form MeadWestvaco. Together, the two companies had combined annual sales of about $7 billion and a market capitalization of some $6 billion; their combined debt tallied to $4.4 billion. The combined company — 50.2%-owned by former Mead shareholders — had an equally-split board. Westvaco executives occupied the new CEO, CFO, and transition officer positions, while the new corporate headquarters were Westvaco's Connecticut offices. The two companies merged as MeadWestvaco Corporation in January 2002.

To quickly expand its production capability in Europe, MeadWestvaco also bought Kartoncraft Limited, near Dublin, Ireland, a leading pharmaceutical packaging producer. In July 2002 the company reported that it had eliminated 2,100 jobs of the 2,500 it expected to cut by the end of the year. As part of its plan to divest 950,000 non-strategic acres, the company sold 95,500 acres of forest land in West Virginia for $50 million; the purchase was made through The Forestland Group LLC for Heartwood Forestland Fund IV Limited Partnership in December 2002.

In 2003 the company bought AMCAL, a maker of stationery products including journals, notepads, decorative calendars, and holiday cards.

Sticking with its consolidation and realignment strategy, in mid-2004 MeadWestvaco eliminated some 600 jobs by closing both its Garland, Texas and St. Joseph, Missouri facilities. Also in 2004, MeadWestvaco acquired Brazilian-based Tilibra S.A. Produtos de Papelaria, a maker of office products.

MeadWestvaco sold its papers business to Cerberus Capital Management in January 2005. The deal included mills in Kentucky, Maine, Maryland, Michigan, and Ohio and about 900,000 acres of forest land in Illinois, Kentucky, Michigan, Missouri, Ohio, and Tennessee.

## EXECUTIVES

**Chairman and CEO:** John A. Luke Jr., age 58, $985,000 pay
**President:** James A. Buzzard, age 52, $654,000 pay
**SVP and CFO:** E. Mark Rajkowski, age 48, $550,008 pay
**SVP Enterprise Human Resources:** Linda V. Schreiner, age 47
**SVP, Secretary, and General Counsel:** Wendell L. Willkie II, age 55, $441,000 pay
**SVP Technology and Forestry:** Mark T. Watkins, age 53, $433,850 pay
**SVP Global Market Strategy and Emerging Markets:** Bruce V. Thomas, age 50
**SVP; President, Community Development and Land Management Group:** Kenneth T. Seeger
**VP Communications:** Donna O. Cox, age 43
**VP and CIO:** James M. McGrane, age 57
**VP Corporate Affairs:** Ned W. Massee, age 56
**VP Marketing, Consumer and Office Products:** John Draper
**President, Consumer & Office Products Group:** Neil A. McLachlan, age 50
**President, Global Business Services:** Mark V. Gulling, age 53
**President and CEO, Paxonix:** Donald F. Armagnac, age 57
**President, Packaging Resources Group:** Robert A. (Bob) Feeser, age 44
**President, Consumer Solutions Group:** William J. (Bill) Biedenharn, age 52
**President, Forestry Division:** Marvin E. (Gene) Hundley, age 52
**President and General Manager, Specialty Papers Division:** Michael J. Huth
**President, Specialty Chemicals Division:** Robert Beckler
**Treasurer:** Robert E. Birkenholz, age 46
**Controller:** John E. Banu, age 60
**Media Relations:** Alison von Puschendorf
**Auditors:** PricewaterhouseCoopers LLP

## LOCATIONS

**HQ:** MeadWestvaco Corporation
11013 W. Broad St., Glen Allen, VA 23060
**Phone:** 804-327-5200 **Fax:** 404-897-6383
**Web:** www.meadwestvaco.com

MeadWestvaco has production facilities in Austria, Brazil, Canada, China, the Czech Republic, France, Germany, Japan, Mexico, the Netherlands, Poland, Russia, Spain, the UK, and the US. It owns 1.1 million acres of forestland in the US and 135,000 acres in Brazil; it also manages another 102,000 acres in the US.

**2006 Sales**

| | % of total |
|---|---|
| US | 72 |
| Other countries | 28 |
| **Total** | **100** |

## PRODUCTS/OPERATIONS

### 2006 Sales

| | $ mil. | % of total |
|---|---|---|
| Packaging | | |
| Packaging resources | 2,564 | 39 |
| Consumer solutions | 2,169 | 33 |
| Consumer & office products | 1,143 | 18 |
| Specialty chemicals | 468 | 7 |
| Corporate & other | 186 | 3 |
| **Total** | **6,530** | **100** |

### Selected Products

Packaging
- Packaging resources
  - Bleached paperboard
  - Consumer products packaging (media, beverage and dairy, cosmetics, tobacco, pharmaceuticals, health care)
  - Kraft paperboard
  - Linerboard
- Consumer solutions
  - Multi-pack cartons (beverages and tobacco)
  - Plastic dispensing and spraying systems
  - Printed plastic packaging

Consumer and office products
- School and office products (AT-A-GLANCE, AMCAL, Cambridge, COLUMBIAN, Day Runner, Five Star, Mead, Trapper Keeper)

Specialty chemicals
- Activated carbon
- Emulsifiers
- Printing ink resins

## COMPETITORS

3M
ACCO Brands
Alcoa
Amcor
Anglo American
Ball Corporation
Bemis
Boise Cascade
Cascades Inc.
Chesapeake Corporation
Disc Graphics
Georgia-Pacific Corporation
Graphic Packaging
Iggesund Paperboard
International Paper
Pratt Industries USA
Smurfit-Stone Container
Sonoco Products
Temple-Inland
UPM-Kymmene
Weyerhaeuser

## HISTORICAL FINANCIALS

Company Type: Public

### Income Statement

FYE: December 31

| | REVENUE ($ mil.) | NET INCOME ($ mil.) | NET PROFIT MARGIN | EMPLOYEES |
|---|---|---|---|---|
| **12/06** | 6,530 | 93 | 1.4% | 24,000 |
| **12/05** | 6,170 | 28 | 0.5% | 22,200 |
| **12/04** | 8,227 | (349) | — | 29,400 |
| **12/03** | 7,553 | 18 | 0.2% | 29,400 |
| **12/02** | 7,242 | (389) | — | 30,700 |
| **Annual Growth** | (2.6%) | — | — | (6.0%) |

### 2006 Year-End Financials

Debt ratio: 88.0%
Return on equity: 2.7%
Cash ($ mil.): 156
Current ratio: 1.38
Long-term debt ($ mil.): 3,110
No. of shares (mil.): 182
Dividends
Yield: 3.1%
Payout: 176.9%
Market value ($ mil.): 5,474

### Stock History

NYSE: MWV

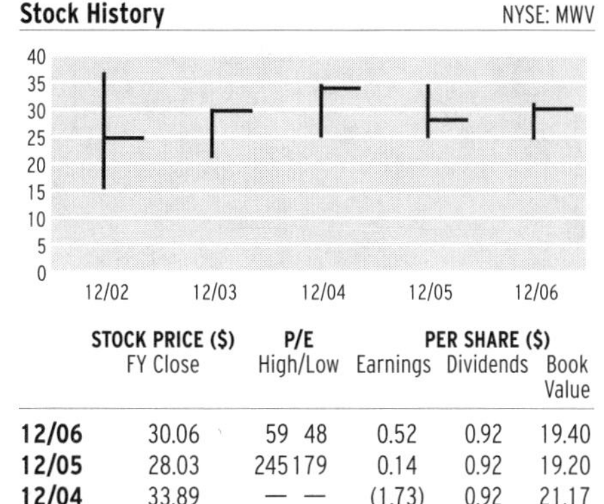

| | STOCK PRICE ($) FY Close | P/E High/Low | | PER SHARE ($) Earnings | Dividends | Book Value |
|---|---|---|---|---|---|---|
| **12/06** | 30.06 | 59 | 48 | 0.52 | 0.92 | 19.40 |
| **12/05** | 28.03 | 245 | 179 | 0.14 | 0.92 | 19.20 |
| **12/04** | 33.89 | — | — | (1.73) | 0.92 | 21.17 |
| **12/03** | 29.75 | 331 | 237 | 0.09 | 0.92 | 23.46 |
| **12/02** | 24.71 | — | — | (2.02) | 0.92 | 24.15 |
| **Annual Growth** | 5.0% | — | — | — | 0.0% | (5.3%) |

# Medco Health Solutions

Medco Health Solutions is the top pharmacy benefits management company and the top specialty pharmacy in the US, dispensing some 550 million prescriptions yearly. (It snagged the top spot after the acquisition of specialty pharmacy Accredo Health in 2005.) The company assists health plans in managing drug costs by designing drug formularies, negotiating discounts with pharmaceutical companies, and processing claims. Patients may fill their prescriptions through a network of close to 60,000 pharmacies, a mail-order program, or the company's Internet pharmacy. Medco Health Solutions manages drug benefits for clients that include unions, corporations, HMOs, insurance companies, and federal employees.

Customer cost containment forms the cornerstone of the company's business strategy. Medco Health Solutions is able to control costs through the use of technology to process prescription claims, automation to fill and distribute prescriptions, and volume purchasing of pharmaceuticals. It also encourages the use of its mail order pharmacies and of generic equivalents (in place of more expensive brand name drugs).

Another key component of the company's strategy is the growth of its specialty pharmacy unit, which provides pharmacy and disease management services for chronic and serious conditions that require complicated or expensive drug regimens (usually biotechnology drugs). The company bought Accredo Health, a top specialty pharmacy, in 2005. The two companies had formed an alliance in 2004 to deliver biopharmaceuticals to Medco's clients.

Medco has been trying to take advantage of the Medicare prescription drug benefit (Medicare Part D), implemented in 2006, by tailoring some services to clients offering Medicare Part D programs or other drug coverage to their Medicare-eligible members. It has also contracted with the Centers for Medicare & Medicaid Services to offer a Medicare Part D drug plan of its own.

In 2007 the company won back a contract with the Blue Cross and Blue Shield Association to administer the mail-order and specialty pharmaceuticals portions of that organization's Federal Employee Program, an insurance plan for government workers. Medco had lost the Blue Cross contract in 2004 to Caremark. Under the new deal, which takes effect in 2008, Medco will handle the mail order and specialty pharmacy benefit for some four million federal employees and their families.

## HISTORY

MedcoHealth Solutions (aka Medco Containment Services) was started in 1983 by former Wall Street investment banker Martin Wygod. Wygod believed that a mail order pharmacy could improve efficiency, increase sales volume, and reduce prescription costs. Medco Containment Services became a publicly traded company in 1984. The firm acquired retail pharmacy management company, PAID Prescriptions, in 1985. As a result, the company became the first pharmacy in the nation to provide its customers with both retail and mail order pharmacy services.

Wygod's vision proved to be right on target as the company exceeded $1 billion in sales in 1990 and had more than 25 million members by 1991. In 1993 the company was acquired by Merck & Co. and changed its name to Medco Health.

For Medco Health, 1996 proved to be a breakthrough year. The firm received a contract to provide pharmacy benefit management services to a purchasing group consisting of *FORTUNE* 500 companies. As a result, Medco Health managed more than 200 million prescriptions.

In the late 1990s the company used the Internet to improve its efficiency and cut costs. The firm opened its Internet pharmacy and formed partnerships with Healtheon (now part of WebMD Health), CVS, and Reader's Digest.

In 2000 the company acquired ProVantage Health Services, a health care information and benefits management company. The acquisition increased the company's customer base by 5 million members. The next year Medco Health became the first Internet pharmacy to exceed $1 billion in prescription sales.

Accounting issues with parent Merck delayed the planned 2002 spin-off of Medco. The next year, however, the deal was completed; Merck retained no ownership stake in Medco.

## EXECUTIVES

**Chairman and CEO:** David B. Snow Jr., age 51, $1,183,224 pay
**President and COO:** Kenneth O. Klepper, age 52, $673,158 pay
**SVP and Chief Pharmacist:** Roger W. Anderson
**SVP Products and Business Development:** John P. Driscoll, age 46, $386,881 pay
**SVP Medical Affairs and Chief Medical Officer:** Robert S. Epstein, age 50
**SVP eCommerce and Chief Web Officer:** Tom Feitel
**SVP General Counsel, and Secretary:** David S. Machlowitz, age 52
**SVP Pharmaceutical Contracting:** Arthur H. Nardin, age 46
**SVP Human Resources:** Karin Princivalle, age 49
**SVP Finance and CFO:** JoAnn A. Reed, age 50, $486,619 pay
**SVP and Chief Marketing Officer:** Jack A. Smith, age 58
**SVP, Controller, and Chief Accounting Officer:** Richard J. Rubino, age 48
**SVP Channel and Generic Strategy:** Laizer Kornwasser
**VP Public Affairs:** Jeffrey (Jeff) Simek
**Chairman, Accredo Health Group and Director:** David D. Stevens, age 54

**President Employer Accounts Customer Group:** Bryan D. Birch, age 40, $420,887 pay
**President, Customer Respect Group:** Terry Golesworthy
**President and CEO Accredo Health Group:** Timothy C. Wentworth, age 45
**Group President Health Plans:** Brian T. Griffin, age 47, $500,000 pay
**Group President Key Accounts:** Glenn C. Taylor, age 54, $769,766 pay
**Manager, Investor Relations:** Judith Pirro
**Auditors:** PricewaterhouseCoopers LLP

## LOCATIONS

**HQ:** Medco Health Solutions, Inc.
100 Parsons Pond Dr., Franklin Lakes, NJ 07417
**Phone:** 201-269-3400 **Fax:** 201-269-1109
**Web:** www.medco.com

Medco Health Solutions has facilities in Florida, Nevada, New Jersey, Ohio, Pennsylvania, Texas, and Washington.

## PRODUCTS/OPERATIONS

### 2006 Sales

| | $ mil. | % of total |
|---|---|---|
| Products | | |
| Retail | 25,880.1 | 61 |
| Mail order | 16,142.5 | 38 |
| Services | | |
| Client & other | 344.1 | 1 |
| Manufacturer | 177.0 | — |
| **Total** | **42,543.7** | **100** |

### Selected Subsidiaries

Accredo Health, Incorporated
BioPartners In Care, Inc.
Hemophilia Resources of America, Inc.
Medco Health, L.L.C
medcohealth.com, L.L.C.
Systemed, L.L.C.

## COMPETITORS

Aetna
BioScrip
Caremark Pharmacy Services
CIGNA
CVS/Caremark
drugstore.com
Express Scripts
HealthExtras
Humana
National Medical Health Card Systems
Omnicare
Option Care
Prescription Solutions
UnitedHealth Group
ValueOptions
Walgreen
Wal-Mart

## HISTORICAL FINANCIALS

Company Type: Public

### Income Statement

FYE: December 31

| | REVENUE ($ mil.) | NET INCOME ($ mil.) | NET PROFIT MARGIN | EMPLOYEES |
|---|---|---|---|---|
| **12/06** | 42,544 | 630 | 1.5% | 15,700 |
| **12/05** | 37,871 | 602 | 1.6% | 15,300 |
| **12/04** | 35,352 | 482 | 1.4% | 13,500 |
| **12/03** | 34,265 | 426 | 1.2% | 13,650 |
| **Annual Growth** | 7.5% | 14.0% | — | 4.8% |

### 2006 Year-End Financials

Debt ratio: 11.5%
Return on equity: 8.3%
Cash ($ mil.): 887
Current ratio: 1.21
Long-term debt ($ mil.): 866
No. of shares (mil.): 288
Dividends
Yield: —
Payout: —
Market value ($ mil.): 15,415

### Stock History

NYSE: MHS

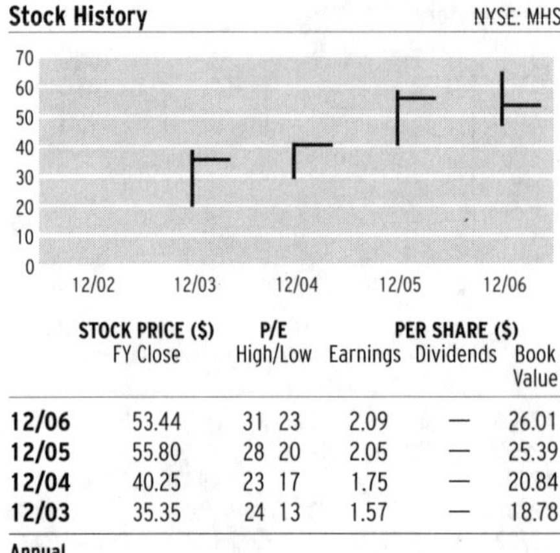


| | STOCK PRICE ($) FY Close | P/E High | P/E Low | PER SHARE ($) Earnings | Dividends | Book Value |
|---|---|---|---|---|---|---|
| **12/06** | 53.44 | 31 | 23 | 2.09 | — | 26.01 |
| **12/05** | 55.80 | 28 | 20 | 2.05 | — | 25.39 |
| **12/04** | 40.25 | 23 | 17 | 1.75 | — | 20.84 |
| **12/03** | 35.35 | 24 | 13 | 1.57 | — | 18.78 |
| **Annual Growth** | 14.8% | — | — | 10.0% | — | 11.5% |

# Medtronic, Inc.

Sometimes the best medicine is a short, sharp shock; that's why Medtronic's products reside in its customers' hearts and minds (among other places). A leading maker of implantable biomedical devices, the company makes defibrillators and pacemakers that help the heart beat normally. Subsidiary Medtronic Sofamor Danek makes spinal implant devices, and its neurological division makes neurostimulation devices and products that treat urinary incontinence. Products made by Medtronic CardioVascular include catheters, stents, valves, and surgical ablation technologies used to treat vascular and heart disease. Medtronic also makes devices for diabetes; ear, nose, and throat (ENT) conditions; and emergency medicine.

Medtronic got its start treating heart diseases (it was a leader in the development of pacemakers in the 1950s), and a majority of its revenue still comes from sales of products used to treat heart or vascular conditions. However, it has expanded its product lines over the years, through both in-house development and acquisitions, to include devices that treat a wide range of chronic diseases. The acquisition of MiniMed (now Medtronic MiniMed) brought it into the diabetes care business, for instance, and other acquisitions (Sofamor Danek and Xomed Surgical Products) led the company into the areas of orthopedics and ENT.

It added to its ENT offerings in 2007 by acquiring some assets (including worldwide distribution rights) of Vision-Sciences' EndoSheath product line, which features sterile disposable sheaths used with fiber optic endoscopes. Later that year the company agreed to acquire Kyphon, a maker of orthopedic medical devices used to treat compression fractures of the spine.

The company's Neurological division accounts for about 10% of total sales and makes electrical stimulation devices and drug delivery systems that help control chronic pain, tremors, and urinary incontinence. Medtronic began exploring the use of electrical stimulation to treat obesity with the 2005 acquisition of Transneuronix, which is developing a pacemaker-like device that sends electronic pulses to the stomach.

In 2006 Medtronic announced plans to spin off its Physio-Control business, which makes external defibrillators, into a separate, publicly traded entity. The spin-off plans were delayed after the company had to halt shipments from the division's Redmond, Washington, manufacturing facility and deal with some related quality control issues.

It also created its Medtronic CardioVascular division in 2007 by combining its former Cardiac Surgery and Vascular business units. The division has developed a drug-eluting stent it hopes will compete with market-dominating products made by Johnson & Johnson and Boston Scientific. The stent (branded Endeavor) has already received approval in Europe.

At right around the same time, Medtronic acquired the MRI safety portfolio of Biophan. The technologies include those that make pacemakers and other medical devices safe for MRIs (standard pacemakers fail to operate during an MRI procedure). Once the sale is complete, the portfolio will transfer to Medtronic CardioVascular.

## HISTORY

In 1949 electrical engineer Earl Bakken and brother-in-law Palmer Hermundslie founded Medtronic in Minneapolis as a medical equipment repair outfit. After branching into custom-made products, Bakken made history in 1957 by crafting the world's first external, battery-powered cardiac pacemaker. In 1960 Medtronic began making and selling the first implantable pacemakers; the company quickly claimed about 80% of the market.

In the late 1960s and early 1970s Medtronic acquired other medical devices companies. Calamity struck in 1976 when the firm had to recall more than 35,000 Xytron pacemakers (some of which were already in patients) because body moisture was seeping into the battery chamber. Market share plunged to about 35%.

Medtronic recruited former Pillsbury COO Winston Wallin as chairman and CEO in 1985. The next year Medtronic released its Activitrax pacemaker, which snagged about 20% of the market. Under Wallin (who retired in 1996), the firm opened facilities in Europe and Asia and resumed acquisitions, adding companies in Italy, the Netherlands, and the US.

In the early 1990s Medtronic sought to expand its position in the vascular market. Its 1990 purchase of Bio-Medicus made the company the world's top maker of centrifugal blood pumps; it also entered the lucrative cardiac defibrillator market (1992) and increased other lines with the purchase of a maker of blood recycling devices and a company that produced disposable tubing and detection kits for breast and prostate cancer.

With an eye on the hot stent market, Medtronic in 1996 acquired InStent and AneuRx, makers of devices used to keep diseased arteries open. The company failed to become a leader in the market because its new units did not perform.

Using its expertise in implant devices, the company developed (and in 1997 received FDA approval for) devices aimed at the growing tremor control and incontinence markets.

In the late 1990s Medtronic undertook a flurry of acquisitions, both to solidify its leadership in the cardiovascular market and to broaden its operations. These purchases included external defibrillator maker Physio-Control International, as well as a maker of power instruments for neurological, bone, and plastic surgery procedures in 1998. The next year Medtronic bought #1 spinal implant product maker Sofamor Danek to boost its neurosurgical business. The company took one more stab at the stent market, buying market-leader Arterial Vascular Engineering. Its share of the market fell after it was acquired, however, so Medtronic closed five facilities. Later that year the company bought Xomed Surgical Products (renamed Medtronic Xomed), a maker of products for ear, nose, and throat specialists.

In 2000 the company announced a partnership with health care companies — including Johnson & Johnson and GE Medical Systems — to provide online product ordering. Medtronic also partnered with WebMD (now WebMD Health) to provide health care information on the Internet.

The following year the firm bought medical device makers MiniMed and Medical Research Group and combined them to form Medtronic MiniMed. The company also made news when Vice President Dick Cheney bought one of its pacemaker-defibrillators. In 2002 Medtronic bought VidaMed to grow its urology offerings.

## EXECUTIVES

**Chairman and CEO:** Arthur D. (Art) Collins Jr., age 59, $3,002,125 pay
**President, COO, and Director:** William A. (Bill) Hawkins III, age 53
**EVP and President, Cardiac Rhythm Management:** Stephen H. Mahle, age 60, $1,106,191 pay
**SVP and CIO:** H. James Dallas, age 47
**SVP CFO and Treasurer:** Gary L. Ellis, age 50
**SVP and President, Asia/Pacific:** Jean-Luc Butel, age 50
**SVP General Counsel, and Secretary:** Terrance L. Carlson, age 53
**SVP and President, Europe, Canada, Latin America and Emerging Markets:** Michael F. DeMane, age 51, $961,901 pay
**SVP and President, Neurological, Gastrointestinal and Urology, and Obesity Management:** Richard Kuntz, age 50
**SVP and President, Medtronic Europe, Emerging Markets and Canada:** Oern R. Stuge, age 53
**SVP and President, CardioVascular:** Scott R. Ward, age 47
**SVP International Affairs:** Barry W. Wilson, age 63
**SVP and President Diabetes:** Christopher J. O'Connell, age 41
**SVP Human Resources:** Carol McCormick, age 53
**Senior Director Diabetes Public & Media Relations:** Jeff Newton
**Senior Director Corporate Public Relations:** Marybeth Thorsgaard
**Senior Director CardioVascular Public Relations & State Government Affairs:** Rob Clark
**Auditors:** PricewaterhouseCoopers LLP

## LOCATIONS

**HQ:** Medtronic, Inc.
710 Medtronic Pkwy., Minneapolis, MN 55432
**Phone:** 763-514-4000 **Fax:** 763-514-4879
**Web:** www.medtronic.com

Medtronic markets its products in more than 120 countries.

### 2007 Sales

| | $ mil. | % of total |
|---|---|---|
| US | 7,900 | 64 |
| Europe | 2,811 | 23 |
| Asia/Pacific | 1,195 | 10 |
| Other regions | 393 | 3 |
| **Total** | **12,299** | **100** |

## PRODUCTS/OPERATIONS

### 2007 Sales

| | $ mil. | % of total |
|---|---|---|
| Cardiac rhythm disease management (CRDM) | 4,876 | 40 |
| Spinal & navigation | 2,544 | 21 |
| Vascular | 1,205 | 10 |
| Neurological | 1,183 | 9 |
| Diabetes | 863 | 7 |
| Cardiac surgery | 704 | 6 |
| ENT | 539 | 4 |
| Physio-Control (Medtronic Emergency Response Systems) | 385 | 3 |
| **Total** | **12,299** | **100** |

### Selected Products

CRDM
- Cardiac resynchronization therapy devices
- Implantable defibrillators
- Pacemakers, pacing systems, leads and monitors
- Patient management tools

Spinal and navigation
- Computer-assisted surgery guidance systems
- Bone grafts
- Retractors
- Spinal plates

Vascular
- Ablation systems
- Cannulae
- Coronary stents
- Drug-eluting stents
- Embolic protection systems
- Endovascular stent grafts
- Heart stabilizers
- Heart valves
- Peripheral stents

Neurological
- Implantable neurostimulation devices

Diabetes
- Glucose monitoring systems
- Insulin pumps

Cardiac Surgery

Ear, nose, and throat (ENT)
- Ear ventilation tubes
- Middle ear prostheses
- Nerve integrity monitors
- Sinus micro-endoscopy systems

Physio-Control (Medtronic Emergency Response Systems)
- Non-invasive emergency defibrillators

## COMPETITORS

Abbott Labs
American Medical
Arrow International
ATS Medical
Boston Scientific
C. R. Bard
Cardiac Science
Cook Incorporated
Cyberonics
Datascope
DexCom
Edwards Lifesciences
Gyrus
Integra LifeSciences
Johnson & Johnson
Kyphon
Philips Electronics
ReAble Therapeutics
Roche
Smiths Group
Sorin
St. Jude Medical
Stryker
Synthes
Urologix
Welch Allyn
W.L. Gore
Zimmer
ZOLL Medical

## HISTORICAL FINANCIALS

Company Type: Public

### Income Statement

FYE: Last Friday in April

| | REVENUE ($ mil.) | NET INCOME ($ mil.) | NET PROFIT MARGIN | EMPLOYEES |
|---|---|---|---|---|
| **4/07** | 12,299 | 2,802 | 22.8% | 38,000 |
| **4/06** | 11,292 | 2,547 | 22.6% | 36,000 |
| **4/05** | 10,055 | 1,804 | 17.9% | 33,000 |
| **4/04** | 9,087 | 1,959 | 21.6% | 31,000 |
| **4/03** | 7,665 | 1,600 | 20.9% | 30,000 |
| **Annual Growth** | 12.5% | 15.0% | — | 6.1% |

### 2007 Year-End Financials

Debt ratio: 50.8%
Return on equity: 27.5%
Cash ($ mil.): 3,078
Current ratio: 3.09
Long-term debt ($ mil.): 5,578
No. of shares (mil.): 1,143
Dividends
Yield: 0.6%
Payout: 13.7%
Market value ($ mil.): 61,287

### Stock History

NYSE: MDT

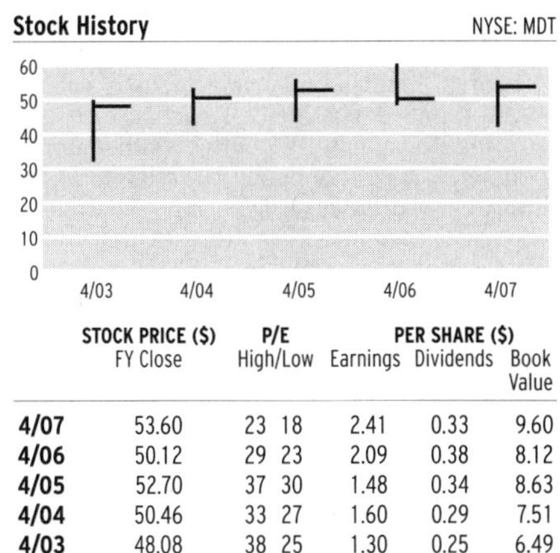


| | STOCK PRICE ($) FY Close | P/E High | P/E Low | PER SHARE ($) Earnings | PER SHARE ($) Dividends | PER SHARE ($) Book Value |
|---|---|---|---|---|---|---|
| **4/07** | 53.60 | 23 | 18 | 2.41 | 0.33 | 9.60 |
| **4/06** | 50.12 | 29 | 23 | 2.09 | 0.38 | 8.12 |
| **4/05** | 52.70 | 37 | 30 | 1.48 | 0.34 | 8.63 |
| **4/04** | 50.46 | 33 | 27 | 1.60 | 0.29 | 7.51 |
| **4/03** | 48.08 | 38 | 25 | 1.30 | 0.25 | 6.49 |
| **Annual Growth** | 2.8% | — | — | 16.7% | 7.2% | 10.3% |

# Men's Wearhouse

With a business strategy tailored for growth, The Men's Wearhouse has made alterations even a haberdasher would be hard-pressed to follow. One of the largest discount retailers of men's business and formal attire, the firm operates more than 1,200 stores throughout North America. Its primary operations are Men's Wearhouse, which has about 545 stores (mostly in strip malls), Moores Clothing, and some 500 newly acquired After Hours Formalwear stores that sell and rent tuxes. Men's Wearhouse sells tailored suits priced 20% to 30% less than competitors, as well as shoes, formal wear, and casual clothes. Its K&G subsidiary caters to thriftier shoppers and sells women's career apparel in about half of its stores.

In April 2007, Men's Wearhouse paid about $100 million to buy the 507-store men's formalwear business, which includes Mr. Tux stores in New England, from Federated Department Stores (now Macy's, Inc.). The tux rental business attracts men younger than Men's Wearhouse's typical customers.

Nearly a quarter of Men's Wearhouse stores are located in California and Texas.

Tailored clothing accounts for more than half of sales, although the firm is selling more casual apparel, shoes, and accessories. The Men's Wearhouse stresses attentive, low-pressure customer service to attract the man with little knowledge of buying suits.

The company plans to open about 20 new Men's Wearhouse stores and 15 K&G stores this year. Also in 2007, the retailer plans to open five retail dry cleaning and laundry facilities in the Houston area, where it already has 30 such outlets in operation.

Moores Clothing for Men is a chain of about 115 stores in 10 Canadian provinces. Almost half of the stores have been expanded to offer tuxedo rentals.

The company also has a corporate apparel and uniform program that serves about 10 contract customers.

Chairman and CEO George Zimmer owns 8% of The Men's Wearhouse.

## HISTORY

George Zimmer, an apparel industry veteran at 23, founded The Men's Wearhouse in fast-growing Houston in 1973 with his father, Robert Zimmer, and college buddy Harry Levy. By the time George debuted on TV in 1986 with his now popular "I guarantee it" motto, the company had 25 stores. It went public in 1992 and continued to grow at a slower but more sustainable pace than its competitors, some of which went bankrupt as a result of overexpansion.

In 1997, through its newly formed Value Price Clothing division, The Men's Wearhouse bought C & R Clothiers, adding 17 stores and a new, lower-priced segment to its operations. The division added four Suit Warehouse stores in the Detroit area the next year.

An on-again-off-again deal to grow into Canada was back on (for good) in early 1999 when The Men's Wearhouse paid $127 million for the Montreal-based Moores Retail Group. The company later began offering tuxedo rentals at some of its Men's Wearhouse stores. Also in that year The Men's Wearhouse bought K&G Men's Center, operator of 34 superstores in 16 states. In 2000 it combined its other discount operations with K&G, renaming most of the stores K&G Men's Center. After 2001's economic downturn hit the company hard, CEO Zimmer announced a return to focusing on the suits, rather than casualwear, and not carrying anything priced more than $500.

In 2002 the company acquired the Wilke-Rodriguez brand and became its sole distributor. Plans to launch a 100-store chain catering to Latino men under the Eddie Rodriguez name were abandoned in 2005.

On the lookout for complementary products and services, the company entered the dry-cleaning business in December 2003 when it bought Nesbit's Cleaners and Craig's Cleaners of Houston.

In April 2007 Men's Wearhouse acquired After Hours Formalwear from Federated Department Stores for about $100 million.

## EXECUTIVES

**Chairman and CEO:** George Zimmer, age 58, $428,077 pay
**Vice Chairman:** David H. Edwab, age 52, $560,000 pay
**President:** Charles Bresler, age 58, $428,077 pay
**EVP, CFO, and Principal Financial Officer:** Neill P. Davis, age 50, $375,534 pay
**EVP and COO:** Douglas S. Ewert, age 43, $424,616 pay
**President, Moores Retail Group:** Pasquale De Marco, age 46, $324,271 pay
**President, K&G Men's Company:** Chris Zender, age 43
**SVP and Chief Compliance Officer:** Gary G. Ckodre, age 57
**EVP, Manufacturing:** William C. (Will) Silveira, age 49
**SVP, Employee Relations:** Carole Souvenir, age 41
**SVP, Merchandising:** James E. Zimmer, age 55
**SVP and Principal Accounting Officer:** Diana M. Wilson, age 59
**SVP Marketing:** Jayme Maxwell
**VP Human Resources, Houston:** Claudia Pruitt
**Secretary:** Michael W. Conlon
**Auditors:** Deloitte & Touche LLP

## LOCATIONS

**HQ:** The Men's Wearhouse, Inc.
5803 Glenmont Dr., Houston, TX 77081
**Phone:** 713-592-7200 **Fax:** 713-664-1957
**Web:** www.menswearhouse.com

### 2007 US Stores

| | Men's Wearhouse | K&G |
|---|---|---|
| California | 85 | — |
| Texas | 47 | 11 |
| Florida | 39 | 3 |
| New York | 28 | 4 |
| Illinois | 22 | 7 |
| Pennsylvania | 22 | 4 |
| Michigan | 22 | 7 |
| Ohio | 19 | 4 |
| Georgia | 17 | 6 |
| Virginia | 17 | 2 |
| Massachusetts | 15 | 5 |
| Colorado | 14 | 2 |
| Washington | 14 | 2 |
| Maryland | 14 | 7 |
| New Jersey | 13 | 8 |
| North Carolina | 13 | 3 |
| Arizona | 12 | — |
| Missouri | 11 | 1 |
| Tennessee | 10 | 2 |
| Minnesota | 9 | 2 |
| Wisconsin | 9 | 1 |
| Oregon | 9 | — |
| Connecticut | 8 | 2 |
| Indiana | 8 | 1 |
| Louisiana | 7 | 3 |
| Utah | 7 | — |
| Alabama | 5 | 1 |
| Nevada | 5 | — |
| Oklahoma | 5 | 2 |
| New Mexico | 4 | — |
| Kansas | 4 | 1 |
| Kentucky | 4 | 1 |
| South Carolina | 4 | 1 |
| Other states | 21 | — |
| **Total** | **543** | **93** |

## PRODUCTS/OPERATIONS

### Merchandise

Accessories
Dress shirts
Formal wear
Outerwear
Shoes
Slacks
Sport coats
Sport shirts
Suits

### Store Names

After Hours Formalwear
K&G Men's Company
Men's Wearhouse
Moores
Mr. Tux

## COMPETITORS

Brooks Brothers
Burlington Coat Factory
Dillard's
Eddie Bauer Holdings
Harold's Stores
Hudson's Bay
J. Crew
Jos. A. Bank
Kohl's
Macy's
Neiman Marcus
Nordstrom
Ross Stores
S&K Famous Brands
Saks Inc.
Sears
Syms

## HISTORICAL FINANCIALS

Company Type: Public

### Income Statement

FYE: Saturday nearest January 31

| | REVENUE ($ mil.) | NET INCOME ($ mil.) | NET PROFIT MARGIN | EMPLOYEES |
|---|---|---|---|---|
| **1/07** | 1,882 | 149 | 7.9% | 14,900 |
| **1/06** | 1,725 | 104 | 6.0% | 13,800 |
| **1/05** | 1,547 | 71 | 4.6% | 13,200 |
| **1/04** | 1,393 | 50 | 3.6% | 12,300 |
| **1/03** | 1,295 | 42 | 3.3% | 11,500 |
| **Annual Growth** | 9.8% | 36.8% | — | 6.7% |

### 2007 Year-End Financials

Debt ratio: 9.7%
Return on equity: 21.5%
Cash ($ mil.): 180
Current ratio: 3.01
Long-term debt ($ mil.): 73
No. of shares (mil.): 54
Dividends
Yield: 0.5%
Payout: 7.4%
Market value ($ mil.): 2,363

### Stock History

NYSE: MW

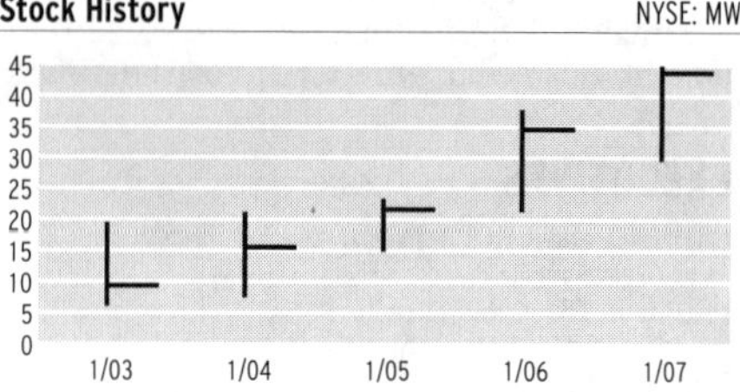


| | STOCK PRICE ($) FY Close | P/E High | P/E Low | PER SHARE ($) Earnings | Dividends | Book Value |
|---|---|---|---|---|---|---|
| **1/07** | 43.82 | 16 | 11 | 2.71 | 0.20 | 13.98 |
| **1/06** | 34.64 | 20 | 12 | 1.88 | — | 11.82 |
| **1/05** | 21.63 | 18 | 12 | 1.29 | — | 15.70 |
| **1/04** | 15.53 | 25 | 9 | 0.85 | — | 13.68 |
| **1/03** | 9.34 | 28 | 9 | 0.69 | — | 13.38 |
| **Annual Growth** | 47.2% | — | — | 40.8% | — | 1.1% |

# Merck

Merck helps those who are hooked on hamburgers. Drugs treating ailments associated with American eating habits — high cholesterol, hypertension, and heart failure — are among Merck's biggest sellers. Its drugs include hypertension fighters Cozaar and Hyzaar and cholesterol combatants Vytorin, Zetia, and Zocor. Merck makes drugs in a broad range of other therapeutic areas as well: Propecia treats male pattern baldness, Singulair treats asthma, and Fosamax fights osteoporosis. In addition to pharmaceuticals, the company makes childhood and adult vaccines for such diseases as measles, mumps, hepatitis, and shingles. In 2006 Merck was awarded FDA approval for its cervical cancer vaccine Gardasil.

Merck is still feeling the effects of its 2004 withdrawal of blockbuster pain drug Vioxx from the market, after the drug (one of a category of pain medications called Cox-2 inhibitors) was linked to increased risk of stroke and heart attack. Merck is facing some 27,000 personal injury lawsuits over Vioxx and is fighting each case individually, rather than working for a collective settlement. It has received mixed results in the cases that have come to trial.

But despite its Vioxx hangover, the company has enjoyed some recent successes, receiving FDA approvals for five new drugs in 2006. In addition to Gardasil (the world's first anti-cancer vaccine), Merck got the regulatory green light to market diabetes drug Januvia, shingles vaccine Zostavax, pediatric vaccine Rotateq, and cancer drug Zolinza. The following year it won approval for Janumet, a diabetes medication that combines Januvia with generic anti-diabetes drug metformin.

Merck has several drugs awaiting approval, including an injectable form of Emend (which treats chemotherapy-related nausea and vomiting). Other drugs in late stages of development include treatments for HIV and high cholesterol.

Merck uses licensing and collaboration agreements with other drug firms and biotechs to fill its R&D pipeline. It has external alliances with the likes of Neuromed Pharmaceuticals, ARIAD Pharmaceuticals, NiCox, FoxHollow, and Ambrilia BioPharma. A co-development agreement with Schering-Plough yielded anti-cholesterol drug Vytorin.

In addition, the company acquires firms it believes will beef up its internal development efforts. In 2006, it acquired GlycoFi, which specializes in optimizing biologic drug molecules, and Abmaxis, which develops monoclonal antibodies. Later that year, Merck bought California-based biotech Sirna Therapeutics. Sirna is developing drugs using cutting-edge RNA interference (RNAi) technology, which has shown promise in finding treatments for cancer and other diseases.

The company hopes all this effort to find new drugs will ensure success over the long term, as more of its currently marketed drugs lose patent protection. Zocor, once its best-seller, began facing generic competition in 2006, leading to a precipitous drop in the drug's sales. Merck will lose patent protection on its popular osteoporosis drug Fosamax in 2008.

Merck plans to eliminate about 7,000 jobs and closing five production plants by the end of 2008.

## HISTORY

Merck was started in 1887 when German chemist Theodore Weicker came to the US to set up a branch of E. Merck AG of Germany. George Merck (grandson of the German company's founder) came in 1889 and formed a partnership with Weicker. At first the firm imported and sold drugs and chemicals from Germany, but in 1903 it opened a plant in Rahway, New Jersey, to make alkaloids. Weicker sold out to Merck the next year and bought a controlling interest in competitor Squibb. During WWI, Merck gave the US government the 80% of company stock owned by family in Germany (George kept his shares). After the war, the stock was sold to the public.

The company acquired Powers-Weightman-Rosengarten of Philadelphia (a producer of antimalarial quinine) in 1927. Merck opened a research lab in 1933; Merck scientists there developed the first steroid, cortisone, in 1944. Five Merck scientists received Nobel Prizes in the 1940s and 1950s. In 1953 Merck bought drugmaker Sharp & Dohme of Philadelphia, which brought with it a strong sales force.

The 1958 introduction of Diuril (antihypertensive) and several other drugs in the early 1960s was followed by a 10-year dry spell. John Horan, who took over in 1976, accelerated R&D to create new products. By the late 1970s Merck had produced Clinoril (antiarthritic), Flexeril (muscle relaxant), and Timoptic (for glaucoma).

Biochemist Roy Vagelos, who became CEO in 1985, continued the commitment to R&D. Merck introduced 10 major new drugs in the 1980s, including Mevacor (high cholesterol) and Vasotec (high blood pressure).

In 1990 the company bought the nonprescription drug segment of ICI Americas; products from the purchase are marketed through a joint venture with Johnson & Johnson.

Merck bought pharmacy benefits manager Medco Containment Services in 1993. The firm brought eight new drugs to market in 1995 and 1996, including Cozaar (for reducing hypertension) and Pepcid AC (antacid).

In 1997 Merck and Rhône-Poulenc (now part of Sanofi-Aventis) merged their animal health units to form Merial; Merck sold its insecticide and fungicide business to Novartis that year.

In 1999 Merck-Medco partnered with Internet health network Healtheon (now part of WebMD Health), CVS, and Reader's Digest (the following year) to sell drugs and provide drug information online. Also that year the FDA approved Merck's preservative-free hepatitis B vaccine, Recombivax HB.

In 2000 Merck's Fosamax, already in use for female osteoporosis, became the first FDA-approved male osteoporosis treatment. The firm lost patent protection for its hypertension drug Vasotec, high-cholesterol drug Mevacor, and ulcer drug Pepcid in 2001. The next year it reportedly scaled back its marketing perks to doctors in order to avoid any appearance of impropriety. The FDA also explored a possible link between Vioxx, the company's painkiller, and cases of meningitis. Merck spun off its highly successful Medco Health Solutions drug distribution subsidiary in 2003.

Merck announced restructuring plans in 2005 to reduce its workforce by more than 10% and close a handful of manufacturing facilities. The announcement was the first major move by CEO Richard Clark, a long-time Merck executive who had replaced Raymond Gilmartin as president and CEO earlier that year.

## EXECUTIVES

**Chairman, President, and CEO:** Richard T. (Dick) Clark, age 61
**EVP and President, Global Human Health:** Kenneth C. Frazier, age 52
**EVP and CFO:** Peter N. Kellogg, age 49
**EVP, Strategy Initiatives:** David W. Anstice, age 58, $686,758 pay
**EVP, Oncology:** Stephen H. Friend
**SVP and General Counsel:** Bruce N. Kuhlik, age 50
**SVP, Global Process and Services, and CIO:** J. Chris Scalet, age 48
**SVP, Human Resources:** Mirian M. Graddick-Weir, age 52
**VP, Public Affairs:** Steven Kelmar, age 53
**VP and Treasurer:** Mark E. McDonough, age 42
**VP, Secretary, and Assistant General Counsel:** Celia A. Colbert, age 50
**VP, Finance, Global Human Health:** Richard C. Henriques Jr., age 51
**VP and Controller:** John Canan, age 50
**VP, Basic Research; Site Head, Merck Research Laboratories Boston:** Lex van der Ploeg
**VP, Clinical Research:** Jeffrey Chodakewitz
**President, US Human Health:** Adam Schechter, age 42
**President, Merck Manufacturing Division:** Willie A. Deese, age 51
**President, Merck Research Laboratories:** Peter S. Kim, age 48, $821,334 pay
**President, Merck Vaccines:** Margaret G. (Margie) McGlynn, age 47
**President, Europe, Middle East, Africa, and Canada:** Stefan Oschmann
**Investor Relations:** Graeme Bell
**Auditors:** PricewaterhouseCoopers LLP

## LOCATIONS

**HQ:** Merck & Co., Inc.
1 Merck Dr., Whitehouse Station, NJ 08889
**Phone:** 908-423-1000 **Fax:** 908-735-1253
**Web:** www.merck.com

### 2006 Sales

| | $ mil. | % of total |
|---|---|---|
| US | 13,776.8 | 61 |
| Europe, Middle East & Africa | 4,977.1 | 22 |
| Japan | 1,479.0 | 6 |
| Other regions | 2,403.1 | 11 |
| **Total** | **22,636.0** | **100** |

## PRODUCTS/OPERATIONS

### 2006 Sales

| | $ mil. | % of total |
|---|---|---|
| Singulair | 3,579.0 | 16 |
| Cozaar/Hyzaar | 3,163.1 | 14 |
| Fosamax | 3,134.4 | 14 |
| Zocor | 2,802.7 | 12 |
| Vaccines/biologicals | 1,859.4 | 8 |
| Primaxin | 704.8 | 3 |
| Cosopt/Trusopt | 697.1 | 3 |
| Proscar | 618.5 | 3 |
| Vasotec/Vaseretic | 547.2 | 2 |
| Cancidas | 529.8 | 2 |
| Maxalt | 406.4 | 2 |
| Propecia | 351.8 | 2 |
| Other | 4,241.8 | 19 |
| **Total** | **22,636.0** | **100** |

### Selected Products

Cardiology
- Cozaar (hypertension)
- Hyzaar (hypertension)
- Vasotec (hypertension/heart failure)
- Vytorin (elevated cholesterol)
- Zetia (elevated cholesterol)
- Zocor (elevated cholesterol)

Endocrinology
- Fosamax (osteoporosis)
- Propecia (male pattern hair loss)
- Proscar (benign prostate enlargement)

Gastrointestinal
- Pepcid (ulcers, marketed with Johnson & Johnson)

Infection
- Cancidas (antifungal)
- Crixivan (HIV)
- Invanz (antibacterial)
- Primaxin (antibiotic)
- Stocrin (HIV)

Neurological
- Maxalt (migraine)

Ophthalmic
- Cosopt (glaucoma)
- Trusopt (glaucoma)

Respiratory
- Singulair (asthma and allergic rhinitis)

Vaccines
- Comvax (hepatitis B)
- Gardasil (cervical cancer caused by HPV virus)
- M-M-R II (measles, mumps, and rubella)
- Pneumovax (pneumococcal disease)
- ProQuad (measles, mumps, rubella, varicella)
- Recombivax HB (hepatitis B)
- RotaTeq (rotavirus gastroenteritis)
- Vaqta (hepatitis A)
- Varivax (chicken pox)
- Zostavax (shingles)

## COMPETITORS

Abbott Labs
Allergan
Amgen
AstraZeneca
Barr Pharmaceuticals
Bausch & Lomb
Baxter
Bayer
Boehringer Ingelheim
Bristol-Myers Squibb
Eli Lilly
Forest Labs
Genzyme
Gilead Sciences
GlaxoSmithKline
Johnson & Johnson
Mylan Labs
Novartis
Pfizer
Roche
Sandoz International GmbH
Sanofi-Aventis
Schering-Plough
Teva Pharmaceuticals
Watson Pharmaceuticals
Wyeth

## HISTORICAL FINANCIALS

Company Type: Public

### Income Statement

FYE: December 31

| | REVENUE ($ mil.) | NET INCOME ($ mil.) | NET PROFIT MARGIN | EMPLOYEES |
|---|---|---|---|---|
| **12/06** | 22,636 | 4,434 | 19.6% | 60,000 |
| **12/05** | 22,012 | 4,631 | 21.0% | 61,500 |
| **12/04** | 22,939 | 5,813 | 25.3% | 63,000 |
| **12/03** | 22,486 | 6,831 | 30.4% | 30,828 |
| **12/02** | 51,790 | 7,150 | 13.8% | 62,000 |
| **Annual Growth** | (18.7%) | (11.3%) | — | (0.8%) |

### 2006 Year-End Financials

Debt ratio: 31.6%
Return on equity: 25.0%
Cash ($ mil.): 8,713
Current ratio: 1.20
Long-term debt ($ mil.): 5,551
No. of shares (mil.): 2,168
Dividends
Yield: 3.5%
Payout: 74.9%
Market value ($ mil.): 94,515

### Stock History

NYSE: MRK

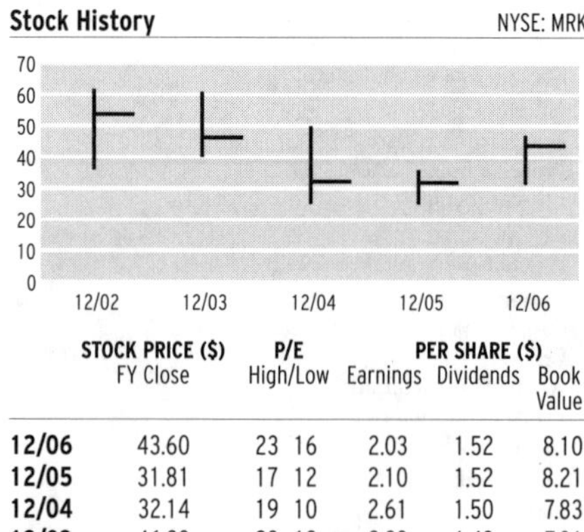


| | STOCK PRICE ($) FY Close | P/E High | P/E Low | PER SHARE ($) Earnings | Dividends | Book Value |
|---|---|---|---|---|---|---|
| **12/06** | 43.60 | 23 | 16 | 2.03 | 1.52 | 8.10 |
| **12/05** | 31.81 | 17 | 12 | 2.10 | 1.52 | 8.21 |
| **12/04** | 32.14 | 19 | 10 | 2.61 | 1.50 | 7.83 |
| **12/03** | 46.20 | 20 | 13 | 3.03 | 1.42 | 7.01 |
| **12/02** | 53.66 | 19 | 12 | 3.14 | 1.35 | 8.11 |
| **Annual Growth** | (5.1%) | — | — | (10.3%) | 3.0% | (0.0%) |

# Merrill Lynch

Merrill Lynch is the matador of investment firms. The company (famous for its bull logo) offers financial services for private, institutional, and government clients, including mutual fund, insurance, annuity, trust, and clearing services, besides traditional investment banking and brokerage. Merrill Lynch operates in two segments: the Global Markets and Investment Banking Group, and Global Wealth Management. The latter combines Merrill's Global Private Client group and Global Investment Management units. The company also owns 45% of asset manager BlackRock, Inc., which absorbed Merrill Lynch's Investment Managers division, uniting Merrill's equity and mutual fund offerings and BlackRock's fixed-income prowess.

The resulting company has approximately $1 trillion in assets under management.

The company has refrained from resting on its laurels. In 2006 it unveiled expansion plans that included buying a mortgage lender. Those plans came to fruition when it acquired National City's First Franklin Financial Corp. mortgage unit for $1.3 billion in 2007.

It also made the move back into energy trading, acquiring Petrie Parkman & Co., an energy industry investment bank. It kept up this acquisitive streak with the announcement that it was buying First Republic Bank for $1.8 billion in cash and stock. San Francisco-based First Republic serves wealthy clients.

Like many of its peers, the bank was caught up in the Enron and Global Crossing debacles and forced to pay some $50 million in fines. The firm also agreed to forgive some $74 million in claims it had against Enron.

## HISTORY

Wall Street bond salesman Charles Merrill opened an underwriting firm in 1914 and made his friend Edmund Lynch partner. In the 1920s the firm pursued investors by offering personal service. Merrill became known as the man who brought Wall Street to Main Street.

In 1930 the firm sold its retail business to Wall Street's largest brokerage, E. A. Pierce, and survived the Depression as an investment banker. Merrill Lynch reacquired the retail business in a 1940 merger with Pierce; the next year it merged with Fenner and Beane.

Merrill Lynch was the first New York Stock Exchange member to incorporate (1959) and go public (1971). In the 1960s it diversified into government securities, real estate financing, and asset management.

In the 1970s Donald Regan (later treasury secretary and President Ronald Reagan's chief of staff) led the firm's buildup in investment banking, insurance, and foreign operations. The firm simultaneously pursued the consumer market. Its underwriting business boomed in the 1980s, and it became the global leader in offerings. It advised on Kohlberg Kravis Roberts' LBO of RJR Nabisco.

After the 1987 crash Merrill Lynch reorganized, cutting less-profitable segments. In 1993 it began to pump up its mergers and acquisitions department by raiding other firms for key personnel.

In the late 1990s the firm expanded in Europe and Asia. Despite its brokerage dominance, Merrill Lynch was slow to log onto the Internet. In 1997, the firm launched Merrill Lynch OnLine with limited trading capabilities, but later bolstered its Internet presence with the 1999 purchase of D.E. Shaw's online brokerage unit. Maintaining that investors need skilled human guidance, the company was pressured by rising competition to beef up its online services and Web site alacrity. The company exited commodities trading in 2000 and jumped into banking services after Congress removed Depression-era restrictions on financial companies.

In 2001, in response to industry-wide criticism, Merrill Lynch barred its analysts (as well as their immediate family members) from owning stock in companies they cover. The company also began taking a variety of cost-cutting measures in order to cope with the slowing economy. Like most of its peers, Merrill's investment banking arm suffered from a frigid dealmaker climate. The terrorist attacks of September 11 and economic woes incapacitated M&A and other trading activity.

In the wake of the downturn, the firm concluded that the explosive growth of 1999 and 2000 was an aberration and adjusted its strategy accordingly, cutting costs to increase margins in a more perilous environment. Merrill streamlined operations in late 2001 and early 2002, paring jobs to 1997 levels (57,000) from a high of 72,600 in 2000. By the end of 2002, the company had reduced staff home and abroad by about 30%, or more than 21,000 jobs.

The Bull was forced to yield to the bears yet again when it decided to cut the number of Nasdaq stocks it trades from 10,000 to 2,400 of the most widely held, actively traded shares. The firm said it would stop trading shares listed on the Pink Sheets and the Bulletin Board, along with some smaller Nasdaq issues.

Merrill Lynch was an unwitting player in the ImClone insider trader scandal. Domestic doyenne Martha Stewart sold off her ImClone stake through a Merrill Lynch broker a day before the stock tanked in 2001. Merrill Lynch subsequently fired Stewart's broker and his assistant.

In early 2002 Merrill Lynch struck a $100 million settlement in New York over questionable investment research, which was followed by another $100 million fine later in the year to pay for programs for independent research and investor education. In response, the firm reorganized its research and investment banking operations and implemented new policies and procedures.

Former Merrill head David Komansky stepped down as CEO in December 2002 and as chairman in April 2003. Stan O'Neal, who had been president, was named Komansky's successor.

Merrill Lynch bought brokerage firm The Advest Group from AXA Financial in late 2005. That year it acquired the retirement business of AMVESCAP (now INVESCO) and the pension business of Philips, and bought institutional brokerage Wave Securities from Archipelago Holdings early the following year.

## EXECUTIVES

**Chairman and CEO:** E. Stanley (Stan) O'Neal, age 55
**Vice Chairman, Co-President, and Chief Administrative Officer:** Ahmass L. Fakahany, age 48
**Vice Chairman:** Richard (Dick) McCormack
**Vice Chairman, Global Equity Financing and Services:** Gary Yetman
**Vice Chairman, Public Markets; Counselor to the Chairman:** Paul W. Critchlow, age 56
**Vice Chairman and Special Advisor to the Chairman:** William J. McDonough, age 73
**Vice Chairman and President, Global Private Client Group:** Robert J. (Bob) McCann, age 47, $7,200,000 pay (prior to promotion)

**Vice Chairman, Executive Client Coverage Group:** Samuel R. (Sam) Chapin
**Vice Chairman, Executive Client Coverage Group:** Brian P. Hull
**Vice Chairman, Executive Client Coverage Group:** Jerome P. (Jerry) Kenney
**Vice Chairman, Executive Client Coverage Group:** Harry McMahon
**Vice Chairman, Executive Client Coverage Group:** James B. Quigley
**Vice Chairman, Executive Client Coverage Group:** Gregg Seibert
**Vice Chairman, Executive Client Coverage Group:** Hugh Sullivan
**Vice Chairman and General Counsel:** Rosemary T. Berkery, age 53
**EVP and Co-President; Co-President, Global Markets and Investment Banking:** Gregory J. (Greg) Fleming, age 42
**EVP; Co-President, Global Markets and Investment Banking:** Dow Kim, age 42, $11,200,000 pay
**SVP and CFO:** Jeffrey N. (Jeff) Edwards, age 45
**COO Global Markets and Investment Banking:** Laurence A. Tosi
**SVP; President and Chief Investment Officer, Merrill Lynch Investment Managers:** Robert C. (Bob) Doll, age 52
**SVP, Communications and Public Affairs:** Jason H. Wright, age 46
**SVP, Head of Americas Region, Global Private Client:** H. McIntyre (Mac) Gardner
**SVP; President, Merrill Lynch Global Research:** Candace Browning
**SVP, Tax Policy and Product Development:** D. Kevin Dolan
**First VP, Corporate Marketing:** Eileen Lynch
**Chairman, Europe, Middle East, and Africa:** Robert (Bob) Wigley
**President, Merrill Lynch Capital:** Robert E. Radway
**Co-Head of Global Bank Group:** Scott A. Kisting, age 59
**Co-Head of Global Bank Group:** John Qua
**Head of Investor Relations:** Tina Madon
**Finance Director and Principal Accounting Officer:** Christopher Hayward, age 41
**Auditors:** Deloitte & Touche LLP

## LOCATIONS

**HQ:** Merrill Lynch & Co., Inc.
4 World Financial Center, 250 Vesey St.,
New York, NY 10080
**Phone:** 212-449-1000 **Fax:** 212-449-9418
**Web:** www.merrilllynch.com

Merrill Lynch has operations in Europe, the Middle East and Africa (EMEA), the Pacific Rim, Canada, Latin America, and the US.

### 2006 Sales

| | % of total |
|---|---|
| US | 65 |
| Europe, Middle East & Africa | 20 |
| Pacific Rim | 11 |
| Latin America | 3 |
| Canada | 1 |
| **Total** | **100** |

## PRODUCTS/OPERATIONS

### 2006 Sales

| | $ mil. | % of total |
|---|---|---|
| Interest & dividends | 40,588 | 57 |
| Principal transactions | 7,034 | 10 |
| Managed accounts & fee-based revenues | 6,539 | 9 |
| Commissions | 5,952 | 8 |
| Investment banking | 4,680 | 7 |
| Gain on merger | 1,969 | 3 |
| Other | 3,829 | 6 |
| **Total** | **70,591** | **100** |

## COMPETITORS

A.G. Edwards
AIG
AXA Financial
Bear Stearns
Brown Brothers Harriman
Charles Schwab
Citigroup Global Markets
Credit Suisse (USA)
Deutsche Bank
E*TRADE Financial
Edward Jones
FMR
Goldman Sachs
INVESCO
JPMorgan Chase
Lehman Brothers
MF Global
Morgan Stanley
Nomura Securities
Old Mutual (US)
Prudential
Raymond James Financial
TD Ameritrade
UBS Financial Services
USAA

## HISTORICAL FINANCIALS

Company Type: Public

### Income Statement

FYE: Last Friday in December

| | REVENUE ($ mil.) | NET INCOME ($ mil.) | NET PROFIT MARGIN | EMPLOYEES |
|---|---|---|---|---|
| **12/06** | 70,591 | 7,499 | 10.6% | 56,200 |
| **12/05** | 47,783 | 5,116 | 10.7% | 54,600 |
| **12/04** | 32,467 | 4,436 | 13.7% | 50,600 |
| **12/03** | 27,745 | 3,988 | 14.4% | 48,100 |
| **12/02** | 28,253 | 2,513 | 8.9% | 50,900 |
| **Annual Growth** | 25.7% | 31.4% | — | 2.5% |

### 2006 Year-End Financials

Debt ratio: 982.1%
Return on equity: 21.8%
Cash ($ mil.): 223,926
Current ratio: —
Long-term debt ($ mil.): 352,496
No. of shares (mil.): 865
Dividends
Yield: 1.1%
Payout: 13.2%
Market value ($ mil.): 80,502

### Stock History

NYSE: MER

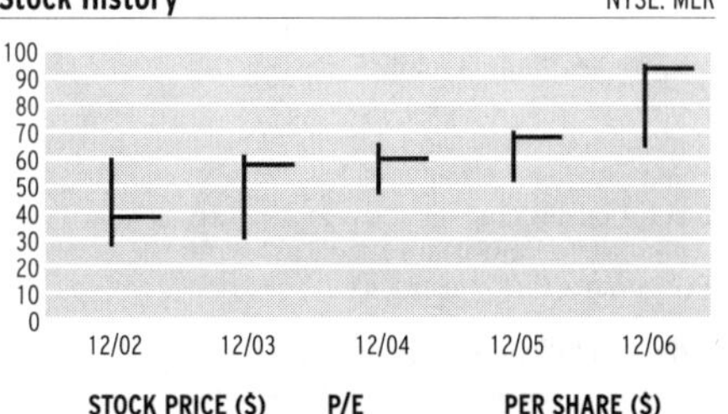


| | STOCK PRICE ($) FY Close | P/E High | P/E Low | PER SHARE ($) Earnings | Dividends | Book Value |
|---|---|---|---|---|---|---|
| **12/06** | 93.10 | 12 | 9 | 7.59 | 1.00 | 45.15 |
| **12/05** | 67.73 | 13 | 10 | 5.16 | 0.76 | 38.88 |
| **12/04** | 59.77 | 15 | 11 | 4.38 | 0.48 | 33.90 |
| **12/03** | 57.60 | 15 | 8 | 4.05 | 0.64 | 29.23 |
| **12/02** | 38.30 | 23 | 11 | 2.63 | 0.48 | 26.49 |
| **Annual Growth** | 24.9% | — | — | 30.3% | 20.1% | 14.3% |

# MetLife, Inc.

The name says "city," but the company is coast-to-coast and then some. MetLife is one of the US's largest insurers. The company's flagship insurance subsidiary is Metropolitan Life Insurance Company. MetLife's Institutional segment offers group benefits products (life and disability insurance, retirement products, prepaid legal plans); its Individual segment offers consumers many of the same types of products; and its International segment offers the same to groups and individuals in the Asia/Pacific region, Europe, and Latin America. The company's reinsurance business operates as Reinsurance Group of America, but serves customers around the world.

MetLife also provides personal auto and homeowners coverage through its Metropolitan Property and Casualty Insurance (MPC) subsidiary. By acquiring a small regional bank in 2004, the company established MetLife Bank, which provides FDIC insured individual banking services online.

MetLife is focusing on emerging markets, increasing its already strong presence in the Asia/Pacific region and in Latin America. It acquired Hidalgo, Mexico's largest life insurer, in 2002, and its 2005 acquisition of Citigroup's international insurance operations deepened its penetration in Europe and the Asia/Pacific region.

While MetLife is primarily known as an insurance company, it also holds a global real estate portfolio valued around $40 billion. However, it is steadily selling off some of its largest properties, including Chicago's Sears Tower (2004), its own landmark headquarters in New York (2005), and the Peter Cooper and Stuyvesant Town housing complexes which it helped build with government funding in 1947. Tishman Speyer Properties and BlackRock paid $5.4 billion for the property in late 2006.

## HISTORY

New York merchant Simeon Draper tried to form National Union Life and Limb Insurance to cover Union soldiers in the Civil War, but investors were scared away by heavy casualties. After several reorganizations and name changes, the enterprise emerged in 1868 as Metropolitan Life Insurance (MetLife), a stock company.

Sustained at first by business from mutual assistance societies for German immigrants, MetLife went into industrial insurance with workers' burial policies. The firm was known for its aggressive sales methods. Agents combed working-class neighborhoods, collecting small premiums. If a worker missed one payment, the company could cancel the policy and keep all premiums paid, a practice outlawed in 1900.

MetLife became a mutual company (owned by its policyholders) in 1915 and began offering group insurance two years later.

After a period of conservative management under the Eckers family from 1929 to 1963, MetLife began to change, dropping industrial insurance in 1964. It started offering auto and homeowners insurance in 1974.

To diversify, the company bought State Street Research & Management (1983), Century 21 Real Estate (1985, sold 1995), London-based Albany Life Assurance (1985), and Allstate's group life and health business (1988). In 1987 it took over the annuities segment of the failed Baldwin United Co., and expanded into Spain and Taiwan in 1988. During the early 1990s, MetLife reemphasized insurance, adding such new products as long-term-care insurance.

In 1993 MetLife was charged with improper sales practices in 13 states. Legal fees, fines, and refunds in these cases exceeded $100 million; bad publicity had a chilling effect on sales. MetLife in turn instituted new training and sales practices. (In 1998 it agreed to pay an additional $25 million civil penalty to settle the federal investigation.)

In 1996 MetLife bought New England Mutual Life Insurance, expanding its customer base to include wealthier middle-class customers (it also sought to obliterate its 1995 loss by retroactively restating results on combined sales).

MetLife's problems continued with a suit over its sales of insurance to Americans in Europe and an investigation in Florida related to churning.

In 1997 MetLife acquired Los Angeles-based Security First Group (annuity contracts for public employees). In 1998 it sold its UK insurance operations and its Canadian business, then cut 10% (about 1,900) of its administrative employees.

In 1999 MetLife followed the industry trend of buying and selling single product lines rather than whole companies. Also in 1999, the company agreed to pay $1.7 billion to settle policyholder lawsuits related to churning allegations.

MetLife saw numerous changes in 2000. Most notably, it went public, bought fellow insurer GenAmerica, and purchased Grand Bank, a one-office nationally chartered bank in New Jersey, which was renamed MetLife Bank. Plans to use Grand Bank as a ticket into the financial services arena met with opposition from community and consumer groups concerned about how MetLife's ownership would comply with the Community Reinvestment Act. The Federal Reserve Board approved the acquisition in 2001.

To trim expenses, MetLife cut employees and consolidated some offices and in 2001 it exited the large-market 401(k) business and sold asset manager Conning to Swiss Re.

Solidifying its position as a major group benefits provider, MetLife bought John Hancock's group life insurance operations in 2003.

MetLife in 2005 exited the asset management business when it sold State Street Research, to BlackRock. That same year it acquired The Travelers Life and Annuity Company, a unit of Citigroup, in a cash and equity deal valued at $11.8 billion. The deal, which included Citigroup's international insurance businesses, made MetLife North America's largest individual life insurer. In 2006 it changed the acquired business' name to MetLife Life and Annuity Company of Connecticut.

## EXECUTIVES

**Chairman, President, and CEO:**
C. Robert (Rob) Henrikson, age 60
**SEVP and Chief Administrative Officer:**
Catherine A. Rein, age 64
**EVP and CFO:** William J. (Bill) Wheeler, age 45, $1,770,833 pay
**EVP and CIO:** Steven L. Sheinheit
**EVP and General Counsel:** James L. Lipscomb, age 60
**EVP and Chief Investment Officer:**
Steven A. Kandarian, age 55
**SVP:** Stanley J. Talbi
**SVP, Finance Operations and Chief Accounting Officer:** Joseph J. Prochaska Jr.
**SVP and CIO, Corporate Systems:** Georgette A. Piligian, age 41
**SVP and Secretary:** Gwenn L. Carr
**VP, Marketing, MetLife Bank:** William J. Raczko
**VP, Public Relations:** John Calagna
**VP, International Communications:** Peter Stack
**President, International:** William J. Toppeta, age 58, $2,291,667 pay
**President, Individual Business:** Lisa M. Weber, age 44, $2,291,667 pay
**President, Institutional Business:** William J. Mullaney, age 47
**President, MetLife Bank:** Donnalee A. DeMaio
**Auditors:** Deloitte & Touche LLP

## LOCATIONS

**HQ:** MetLife, Inc.
200 Park Ave., New York, NY 10166
**Phone:** 212-578-2211 **Fax:** 212-578-3320
**Web:** www.metlife.com

MetLife and its affiliates operate primarily in the US but also in Argentina, Australia, Belgium, Brazil, Chile, China, Hong Kong, India, Ireland, Japan, Mexico, Poland, South Korea, Taiwan, the UK, and Uruguay.

## PRODUCTS/OPERATIONS

### 2006 Sales

| | $ mil. | % of total |
|---|---|---|
| Premiums | | |
| Institutional | 11,867 | 24 |
| Individual | 4,516 | 9 |
| Auto & home | 2,924 | 6 |
| International | 2,722 | 5 |
| Reinsurance | 4,348 | 9 |
| Corporate & other | 35 | 34 |
| Net investment income | 17,192 | |
| Universal life & investment-type product policy fees | 4,780 | 10 |
| Net investment gains (losses) | (1,350) | — |
| Other | 1,362 | 3 |
| **Total** | **48,396** | **100** |

### Business Segments

Auto & Home (auto, home, boat, RV, mobile home, and personal liability insurance)
Banking (online consumer savings products)
Individual (annuities; life, disability, and long-term care insurance; mutual funds)
International (annuities; life, accident, and health insurance; savings and retirement products; property and casualty insurance)
Institutional (group insurance; retirement and savings products; administrative services)
Reinsurance (life reinsurance)

### Selected Subsidiaries and Affiliates

GenAmerica Financial LLC (distribution)
Hyatt Legal Plans, Inc. (prepaid legal plans)
MetLife Bank, N.A. (consumer banking)
MetLife Investors Group, Inc. (distribution)
Metropolitan Property and Casualty Insurance Company
New England Life Insurance Company
Reinsurance Group of America, Incorporated
Texas Life Insurance Company
Tower Square Securities (affiliated broker)
Walnut Street Securities, Inc. (mutual funds, securities)

## COMPETITORS

AEGON USA
Aetna
Aflac
AIG
AIG American General
Allianz
Allstate
Aon
AXA
AXA Financial
CIGNA
CNA Financial
COUNTRY Insurance
GEICO
Guardian Life
The Hartford
ING
John Hancock Financial Services
Liberty Mutual
Lincoln Financial Group
MassMutual
Mutual of Omaha
Nationwide
New York Life
Northwestern Mutual
Pacific Mutual
Principal Financial
Prudential
State Farm
TIAA-CREF
USAA
Zurich Financial Services

## HISTORICAL FINANCIALS

Company Type: Public

### Income Statement

FYE: December 31

| | ASSETS ($ mil.) | NET INCOME ($ mil.) | INCOME AS % OF ASSETS | EMPLOYEES |
|---|---|---|---|---|
| **12/06** | 527,715 | 6,293 | 1.2% | 47,000 |
| **12/05** | 481,645 | 4,714 | 1.0% | 65,500 |
| **12/04** | 356,808 | 2,758 | 0.8% | 54,000 |
| **12/03** | 326,841 | 2,217 | 0.7% | 49,000 |
| **12/02** | 277,385 | 1,605 | 0.6% | 48,500 |
| **Annual Growth** | 17.4% | 40.7% | — | (0.8%) |

### 2006 Year-End Financials

Equity as % of assets: 6.4%
Return on assets: 1.2%
Return on equity: 20.0%
Long-term debt ($ mil.): 13,759
No. of shares (mil.): 752
Dividends
Yield: 1.0%
Payout: 7.4%
Market value ($ mil.): 44,375
Sales ($ mil.): 48,396

### Stock History

NYSE: MET

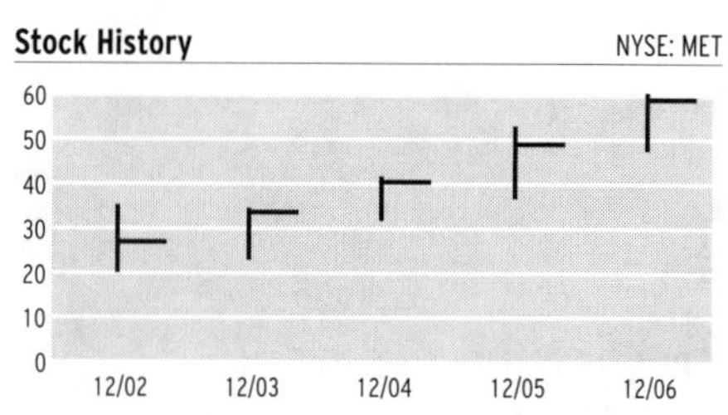


| | STOCK PRICE ($) FY Close | P/E High | P/E Low | PER SHARE ($) Earnings | Dividends | Book Value |
|---|---|---|---|---|---|---|
| **12/06** | 59.01 | 8 | 6 | 7.99 | 0.59 | 44.95 |
| **12/05** | 49.00 | 9 | 6 | 6.16 | 0.52 | 38.42 |
| **12/04** | 40.51 | 11 | 9 | 3.65 | 0.46 | 31.16 |
| **12/03** | 33.67 | 12 | 8 | 2.94 | 0.23 | 27.93 |
| **12/02** | 27.04 | 16 | 9 | 2.20 | 0.21 | 24.83 |
| **Annual Growth** | 21.5% | — | — | 38.0% | 29.5% | 16.0% |

# MGM MIRAGE

It's not your imagination — MGM MIRAGE is one of the world's largest gaming firms. The company's 26 partially or wholly owned properties include Las Vegas' MGM Grand, Luxor, Bellagio, The Mirage, New York-New York, and the Monte Carlo. MGM MIRAGE also owns casinos in about five other Nevada cities, as well as in Michigan and Mississippi. In addition, the company operates the Borgata casino in Atlantic City through a joint venture with Boyd Gaming. In 2005 MGM MIRAGE acquired rival Mandalay Resort Group for $7.9 billion, shooting the firm to the top of the gaming world. However, Harrah's surpassed MGM MIRAGE after its merger with Caesars. Founder Kirk Kerkorian owns about 56% of MGM MIRAGE.

MGM MIRAGE has embarked on its most ambitious development plan to date with the announcement that it will build a $7 billion mega-resort in Las Vegas on a 66-acre site between the company's Bellagio and Monte Carlo casinos. The site, dubbed Project CityCenter, will feature a 4,000-room casino resort, two 400-room boutique hotels, 470,000 sq. ft. of retail space, restaurants and entertainment venues, and a 1,650-unit condominium complex. MGM MIRAGE expects to open the first phase of the project in 2009.

The company's lavish Beau Rivage casino in Biloxi, Mississppi, includes a barge-bound gambling floor with a waterside compound of restaurants, bars, a hotel, and convention center. While Beau Rivage weathered Hurricane Katrina better than its competitors' casinos, the hotel remained closed for a full year as a result of the disaster.

MGM MIRAGE also owns 50% of a company that is building a hotel and casino resort in Macao, China. Plans are set for the property, named MGM Grand Macau, to open in late 2007.

Kerkorian's Tracinda Corp. had entered into talks with MGM Mirage in 2007 to purchase the Bellagio and CityCenter properties. However, it later scrapped those plans, reportedly in part because Tracinda disagrees with the valuation of separate development deal between MGM Mirage and Kerzner International.

MGM MIRAGE was formed when MGM Grand acquired Mirage Resorts in 2000. The acquisition of Mandalay Resort Group in 2005 gave MGM MIRAGE a portfolio of properties that pull in about $7 billion in revenues a year. In 2006 MGM Mirage and Boyd Gaming debuted a $200 million expansion of its Borgata casino.

## HISTORY

Billionaire Kirk Kerkorian purchased a stake in famed movie studio Metro-Goldwyn-Mayer (MGM; formed in 1924) for just over $80 million in 1970. Around the same time, he began acquiring property in Las Vegas and started construction on the city's largest hotel.

Financial difficulties led Kerkorian to sell his new hotel as well as many of MGM's assets in the early 1970s. But he kept the MGM name and used it for MGM Grand hotels in Las Vegas and Reno, Nevada. In 1986 Kerkorian sold MGM Grand Hotels to Bally, but he retained the rights to the MGM Grand name and logo. That year Kerkorian founded MGM Grand, Inc. and took the company public in 1987. He set about snapping up Las Vegas property in the late 1980s and early 1990s.

In 1993 Kerkorian and company unveiled Las Vegas' MGM Grand, a $1.1 billion complex featuring a 33-acre theme park and, at the time, the largest casino on the planet (171,500 sq. ft.). It was a success ($742 million in revenues its first year) and spawned plans for expansion.

The 1990s proved a challenge for MGM Grand, however, as attendance figures at the theme park dropped off and the company struggled to maintain profitability. In 1996 MGM Grand began planning for an Atlantic City casino and signed on as developer and manager for gaming company Tsogo Sun, which was opening casinos in South Africa. The following year, through its joint venture with Primadonna Resorts, it opened the 2,035-room hotel and casino New York-New York. In 1998 MGM Grand narrowly won its bid to become one of three groups to build casinos in Detroit. (The MGM Grand Detroit opened the following year and pulled in $4.8 million in its first three days.)

In 1999 the company bought Primadonna Resorts, which gave MGM Grand complete ownership of New York-New York and three casino properties in Primm, Nevada. (In 2007 it sold the Primm properties.) The company appointed co-CEOs John Redmond and Daniel Wade to their posts in late 1999. (Redmond and Wade moved to other positions in the company when Terrence Lanni became CEO in 2001.)

In a landmark deal, MGM Grand bought rival Mirage Resorts for $6.4 billion (including $2 billion in debt) in 2000 and became one of the top gaming companies in the world. (Mirage Resorts' newer casinos had posted less-than-exciting financial results, and the company had become an attractive acquisition target.)

The purchase of Mirage Resorts allowed MGM Grand to add a string of opulent casinos to its collection. Among the casinos the deal brought to the MGM Grand fold were Las Vegas strip properties Bellagio, a luxurious European-style casino, and The Mirage, a tropical-themed casino. The Mirage Resorts acquisition also put Las Vegas' Treasure Island, the Golden Nugget, and Monte Carlo (50%-owned with Mandalay Resort Group) under the MGM Grand umbrella. Mirage Resorts' Beau Rivage in Biloxi, Mississippi, and the Golden Nugget in Laughlin, Nevada, also became MGM Grand properties.

Steven Wynn, who had propelled Mirage Resorts from a single casino (the Golden Nugget) to its spot as one of the world's leading gaming companies, opted not to join the merged firm. Later in 2000 MGM Grand changed its name to MGM MIRAGE. MGM MIRAGE laid off over 6,700 employees after declining guest numbers in the wake of the September 11th terrorist attacks. In 2002 the company withdrew its $615 million bid for Chicago's Emerald Casino after the Illinois legislature passed a bill to increase gaming taxes by as much as 50%. Also that year the company ended its operations in South Africa where it managed four casinos.

In 2003 MGM MIRAGE closed its online casino, citing an absence of sound regulatory policies regarding Internet gambling. The following year the company sold its Golden Nugget properties in Las Vegas and Laughlin to a private investment firm for $215 million.

The following year MGM MIRAGE purchased rival Mandalay Resort Group for about $7.9 billion, briefly creating the world's largest gaming company. (It was surpassed later in 2005 when Harrah's bought Caesars.)

## EXECUTIVES

**Chairman and CEO:** J. Terrence (Terry) Lanni, age 63, $2,000,000 pay
**President, CFO, Treasurer, and Director:** James J. (Jim) Murren, age 45, $1,500,000 pay
**EVP, General Counsel, Secretary, and Director:** Gary N. Jacobs, age 61, $700,000 pay
**EVP and Chief Administrative Officer:** Aldo Manzini
**SVP and CIO:** Tom Peck
**SVP, Assistant General Counsel, and Assistant Secretary:** Bryan L. Wright, age 43
**SVP and Senior Counsel:** Phyllis A. James, age 54
**SVP Accounting:** Robert C. Selwood, age 51
**SVP Corporate Diversity and Community Affairs:** Punam Mathur, age 46
**SVP Finance:** Daniel J. D'Arrigo, age 38
**SVP Global Security:** Bruce Gebhardt, age 58
**SVP Public Affairs:** Alan Feldman, age 48
**SVP Taxes:** Shawn T. Sani, age 41
**SVP Human Resources:** Cynthia Kiser Murphy, age 49
**VP Corporate Diversity, Communications, and Community Affairs:** Debra Nelson
**Director; President and CEO, MGM Grand Resorts:** John T. Redmond, age 48, $1,500,000 pay
**President and COO, New York-New York Hotel & Casino:** Lorenzo Creighton
**President, Beau Rivage Resort and Casino:** George P. Corchis Jr.
**Director; President and CEO, Mirage Resorts; President, Project CityCenter:** Robert H. Baldwin, age 56, $1,500,000 pay
**National Diversity Sales Manager:** Dzidra Junior
**Auditors:** Deloitte & Touche LLP

## LOCATIONS

**HQ:** MGM MIRAGE
3600 Las Vegas Blvd. South, Las Vegas, NV 89109
**Phone:** 702-693-7111 **Fax:** 702-693-8626
**Web:** www.mgmmirage.com

MGM Mirage owns or operates casinos in Illinois, Michigan, Mississippi, Nevada, and New Jersey.

## PRODUCTS/OPERATIONS

### 2006 Sales

| | $ mil. | % of total |
|---|---|---|
| Casino | 3,130.4 | 40 |
| Rooms | 1,991.5 | 26 |
| Food & beverage | 1,483.9 | 19 |
| Entertainment | 459.5 | 6 |
| Retail | 278.7 | 3 |
| Other | 452.7 | 6 |
| Promotional allowances | (620.7) | — |
| **Total** | **7,176.0** | **100** |

### Selected Properties

Bellagio (Las Vegas)
Beau Rivage (Biloxi, MS)
Boardwalk Hotel & Casino (Las Vegas)
Borgata (50%; Atlantic City, NJ)
Circus Circus (Las Vegas)
Circus Circus Reno (Nevada)
The Colorado Belle Hotel and Casino (Laughlin, NV)
The Edgewater Hotel and Casino (Laughlin, NV)
Excalibur (Las Vegas)
Gold Strike (Tunica County, MS)
Gold Strike Hotel and Gambling Hall (Jean, NV)
Luxor (Las Vegas)
Mandalay Bay Resort & Casino (Las Vegas)
MGM Grand (Las Vegas)
MGM Grand Detroit
The Mirage (Las Vegas)
Monte Carlo (Las Vegas)
Nevada Landing Hotel and Casino (Jean)
New York-New York (Las Vegas)
Railroad Pass Hotel & Casino (Henderson, NV)
Silver Legacy (50%; Reno, NV)
Slots-A-Fun (Las Vegas)
Treasure Island (Las Vegas)

## COMPETITORS

Aztar
Boyd Gaming
Harrah's Entertainment
Las Vegas Sands
Pinnacle Entertainment
Riviera Holdings
Star City
Station Casinos
Stratosphere
Trump Resorts

## HISTORICAL FINANCIALS

Company Type: Public

**Income Statement** FYE: December 31

| | REVENUE ($ mil.) | NET INCOME ($ mil.) | NET PROFIT MARGIN | EMPLOYEES |
|---|---|---|---|---|
| **12/06** | 7,176 | 648 | 9.0% | 70,000 |
| **12/05** | 6,482 | 443 | 6.8% | 66,500 |
| **12/04** | 4,238 | 412 | 9.7% | 40,000 |
| **12/03** | 3,909 | 244 | 6.2% | 43,000 |
| **12/02** | 4,031 | 292 | 7.3% | 43,000 |
| **Annual Growth** | 15.5% | 22.0% | — | 13.0% |

**2006 Year-End Financials**

Debt ratio: 337.6%
Return on equity: 18.3%
Cash ($ mil.): 453
Current ratio: 0.92
Long-term debt ($ mil.): 12,995
No. of shares (mil.): 284
Dividends
Yield: —
Payout: —
Market value ($ mil.): 16,282

**Stock History** NYSE: MGM

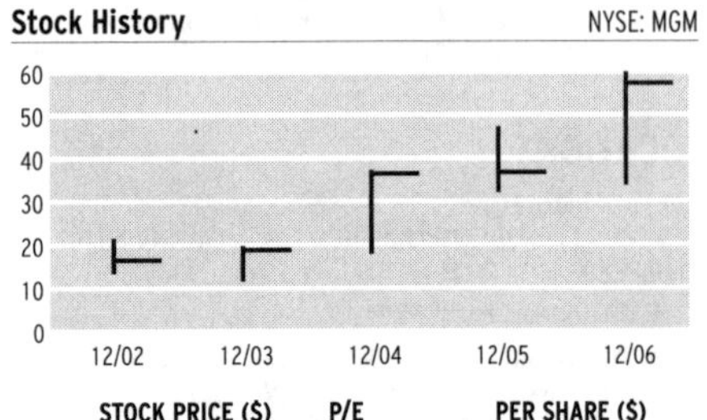


| | STOCK PRICE ($) FY Close | P/E High | P/E Low | PER SHARE ($) Earnings | Dividends | Book Value |
|---|---|---|---|---|---|---|
| **12/06** | 57.35 | 27 | 15 | 2.22 | — | 13.56 |
| **12/05** | 36.67 | 31 | 22 | 1.50 | — | 11.35 |
| **12/04** | 36.37 | 26 | 13 | 1.42 | 4.00 | 19.75 |
| **12/03** | 18.81 | 24 | 15 | 0.81 | — | 17.71 |
| **12/02** | 16.49 | 23 | 15 | 0.92 | — | 17.24 |
| **Annual Growth** | 36.6% | — | — | 24.6% | — | (5.8%) |

# Micron Technology

Don't let Micron Technology's name mislead you: The circuits on its chips are well under one micron across, but the company is one of the biggest semiconductor makers in the world. Micron is among the four largest memory chip makers in the semiconductor industry. It makes dynamic random-access memories (DRAMs), flash memory chips, and memory modules, as well as image sensor chips. The company sold its MicronPC business (now called MPC Computers), but continues to offer PC memory upgrades to consumers though its Crucial Technology subsidiary. Micron has acquired flash memory maker Lexar Media for about $850 million.

The Lexar acquisition will bolster Micron's position in NAND flash memory, which is the type of memory found in many MP3 players (such as the iPod Nano and the iPod Shuffle), digital still cameras, and other portable electronics. The closing of the transaction came as Gartner, a market research firm, was predicting NAND flash shortages for the fourth quarter of 2006, based on demand for iPods and other popular gadgets.

Micron CEO Steve Appleton, who has been known to fly stunt jets for fun, has steered Micron through the wild cycles of the memory chip market with an intense focus on cost control.

Micron has joined with Intel to form a new company devoted to NAND flash memory. Each contributed roughly $1.2 billion to create IM Flash Technologies, which will manufacture memory exclusively for Micron and Intel. Apple Computer has already agreed to prepay $250 million to each company. Apple uses flash memory in some of its iPod digital music players. The partners behind IM Flash Technologies announced in late 2006 that they plan to build a fourth wafer fabrication facility (or fab) in Singapore to make NAND flash memory chips. IM Flash has existing fabs in Idaho and Virginia, with a third facility in Utah coming online.

Micron will further its push into NAND with the purchase of Lexar, gaining USB flash drives and memory cards and readers from the acquisition.

Photronics has formed a joint venture with Micron Technology called MP Mask Technology Center. The memory chip manufacturer will own slightly more than half of MP Mask. The JV will operate Micron's mask shop in Boise, Idaho. The two companies plan to build a "NanoFab" in Boise to conduct R&D on advanced technology in photomasks.

Brandes Investment Partners owns nearly 10% of Micron Technology. PrimeCap Management holds more than 7% of the company. CAM North America has an equity stake of about 6%. Capital Research and Management owns around 5% of Micron.

## HISTORY

Micron Technology was founded in 1978 by twins Joe and Ward Parkinson and colleague Doug Pitman in the basement of a dentist's office. They started it as a semiconductor design firm but dreamed of manufacturing their own chips. In 1980 they persuaded several local businessmen, including J. R. Simplot and Allen Noble, to provide financial backing. They built their own production facility and sold their first dynamic random-access memory (DRAM) products in 1982.

Micron went public in 1984. The following year Japanese chip makers began dumping chips on the US market to capture market share, causing huge losses for US DRAM makers. Micron filed an antidumping petition with the International Trade Commission, and in 1986 the US and Japan agreed to a semiconductor trade pact to curb dumping.

By 1988 a shortage of memory chips had developed, and Micron cashed in. The company began to diversify into SRAM (static random-access memory) chips and other add-in memory products for PCs. (The company wound down its SRAM product line in 2003 in the face of a dire industry slump.)

In the 1990s Micron expanded into PC manufacturing, in part to soften the impact of the volatile cycles of the memory chip industry. It bought PC manufacturer ZEOS in 1995, merging it with two other Micron units to form Micron Electronics (now Interland), which it took public that year.

Also in 1995 Micron CEO and co-founder Joe Parkinson left the company after a clash with Simplot. Steve Appleton, who had started as a production operator in 1983, became the new CEO. In early 1996 an internal power struggle triggered by longtime director Noble resulted in Appleton's ouster. But within a few days, as several executives loyal to Appleton threatened to revolt, Simplot wooed the CEO back. Noble resigned.

In 2001 the company acquired full ownership of Japan-based DRAM maker KMT Semiconductor when it bought out joint venture partner Kobe Steel for about $350 million. (KMT was subsequently renamed Micron Japan, Ltd.)

Also that year the company acquired Photobit, a small developer of complementary metal oxide semiconductor (CMOS) image sensors, an image-capturing chip that would become widely used in camera phones and digital still cameras, among other uses. The acquisition launched Micron into a new semiconductor business line that would help the company withstand the volatile cycles of the memory chip business.

At the end of 2001 Micron struck a surprise deal with Toshiba to acquire the Japanese giant's Dominion Semiconductor unit in Virginia. (The deal was closed in 2002; Micron paid about $300 million in cash and stock for Dominion.)

The company used a strong balance sheet to grow capacity during the steep industry swoon of the early 21st century, but also stumbled a bit with slow product introductions. Micron surprised the industry in 2002 by announcing an agreement to buy the DRAM operations of Toshiba. The Toshiba purchase, which cost Micron about $300 million in cash and stock, saddled Micron with too much production capacity in the midst of an especially soft DRAM market. Micron rose on improved industry conditions after the chip industry slump ended in 2003, and returned to black ink by 2004.

In 2004 Intel made a $450 million investment in Micron, giving the chip giant rights to a 5% ownership stake in the company.

In early 2006 Micron merged its mobile memory and systems memory business units into one memory products group, responsible for NAND flash memory, DRAM, and specialty memory devices. The company also paid nearly $5 million to acquire a wafer fabrication facility in Nampa, Idaho, from ZiLOG. Micron will use the fab to make image sensor chips for camera phones, digital still cameras, and machine vision equipment, among other applications.

## EXECUTIVES

**Chairman and CEO:** Steven R. (Steve) Appleton, age 47, $1,914,500 pay
**President and COO:** D. Mark Durcan, age 45, $750,183 pay
**VP Finance and CFO:** Wilbur G. (Bill) Stover Jr., age 53, $751,405 pay
**VP, Legal Affairs, General Counsel, and Corporate Secretary:** Roderic W. Lewis, age 51, $630,941 pay
**VP, Systems Memory Group:** Robert M. Donnelly, age 67
**VP, DRAM Development:** John Schreck, age 47
**VP, Investor Relations:** Kipp A. Bedard, age 47
**VP, Human Resources:** JoAnne S. Arnold
**VP, Imaging Group:** Robert J. (Bob) Gove, age 52, $819,346 pay
**VP, Information Systems:** James E. (Ed) Mahoney
**VP, Market Development:** Dean A. Klein
**VP, Memory:** Brian Shirley
**VP, Memory Marketing:** Jan du Preez, age 49

**VP, NAND Development:** Frankie F. Roohparvar, age 44
**VP, Operations:** Jay L. Hawkins, age 46
**VP, Worldwide Wafer Fabrication:** Brian J. Shields
**VP, Worldwide Sales:** Michael W. Sadler, age 48
**Treasurer:** Norman L. Schlachter
**Director, Media Relations:** Daniel Francisco
**Director, Federal Government Affairs:** Melika D. Carroll, age 33
**Auditors:** PricewaterhouseCoopers LLP

## LOCATIONS

**HQ:** Micron Technology, Inc.
8000 S. Federal Way, Boise, ID 83707
**Phone:** 208-368-4000 **Fax:** 208-368-2536
**Web:** www.micron.com

Micron Technology has manufacturing facilities in Italy, Japan, Puerto Rico, Singapore, the UK, and the US. It has sales and marketing offices in more than a dozen countries worldwide.

### 2006 Sales

| | $ mil. | % of total |
|---|---|---|
| US | 1,721 | 33 |
| Asia/Pacific | | |
| China | 1,049 | 20 |
| Japan | 494 | 9 |
| Other countries | 1,068 | 20 |
| Europe | 719 | 14 |
| Other regions | 221 | 4 |
| **Total** | **5,272** | **100** |

## PRODUCTS/OPERATIONS

### 2006 Sales

| | $ mil. | % of total |
|---|---|---|
| Memory | 4,523 | 86 |
| Imaging | 749 | 14 |
| **Total** | **5,272** | **100** |

### Semiconductor Products

Dynamic random-access memories (DRAMs)
Direct Rambus DRAMs (RDRAMs)
Synchronous DRAMs (SDRAMs)
Double data rate synchronous DRAMs (DDR SDRAMs)
Flash memory devices
Image sensors
Memory modules

### Selected Operations

Crucial Technology (memory module upgrade supplier)
IM Flash Technologies, LLC (joint venture with Intel; NAND flash memory devices)
Lexar Media, Inc. (memory cards, USB flash drives)
MP Mask Technology Center, LLC (joint venture with Photronics; photomask production)
TECH Semiconductor Singapore Pte. Ltd. (joint venture with Canon and others; wafer fabrication)

## COMPETITORS

Atmel
Cypress Semiconductor
Elpida
Hynix
Intel
Kingston Technology
MagnaChip
Matsushita Electric
Mosel Vitelic
Nanya
OmniVision Technologies
PNY Technologies
Qimonda
Rambus
Samsung Electronics
SanDisk
Sharp
SMART Modular
Sony
Spansion
STMicroelectronics
Toshiba
Viking InterWorks

## HISTORICAL FINANCIALS

Company Type: Public

### Income Statement

FYE: Thursday nearest August 31

| | REVENUE ($ mil.) | NET INCOME ($ mil.) | NET PROFIT MARGIN | EMPLOYEES |
|---|---|---|---|---|
| **8/06** | 5,272 | 408 | 7.7% | 23,500 |
| **8/05** | 4,880 | 188 | 3.9% | 18,800 |
| **8/04** | 4,404 | 157 | 3.6% | 17,900 |
| **8/03** | 3,091 | (1,273) | — | 16,600 |
| **8/02** | 2,589 | (907) | — | 18,700 |
| **Annual Growth** | 19.5% | — | — | 5.9% |

### 2006 Year-End Financials

Debt ratio: 5.0%
Return on equity: 5.8%
Cash ($ mil.): 3,079
Current ratio: 3.07
Long-term debt ($ mil.): 405
No. of shares (mil.): 749
Dividends
Yield: —
Payout: —
Market value ($ mil.): 12,950

### Stock History

NYSE: MU

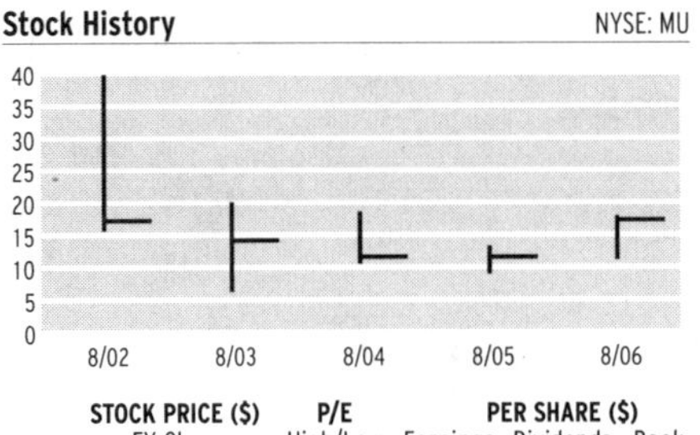


| | STOCK PRICE ($) FY Close | P/E High | P/E Low | PER SHARE ($) Earnings | PER SHARE ($) Dividends | PER SHARE ($) Book Value |
|---|---|---|---|---|---|---|
| **8/06** | 17.28 | 31 | 20 | 0.57 | — | 10.83 |
| **8/05** | 11.62 | 45 | 32 | 0.29 | — | 9.49 |
| **8/04** | 11.65 | 76 | 45 | 0.24 | — | 9.18 |
| **8/03** | 14.19 | — | — | (2.11) | — | 8.15 |
| **8/02** | 17.25 | — | — | (1.51) | — | 10.46 |
| **Annual Growth** | 0.0% | — | — | — | — | 0.9% |

# Microsoft Corporation

Microsoft's ambitions are anything but small. The world's #1 software company provides a variety of products and services, including its Windows operating systems and Office software suite. The company has expanded into markets such as video game consoles, interactive television, and Internet access. With its core markets maturing, Microsoft is targeting services for growth, looking to transform its software applications into Web-based services for enterprises and consumers. Microsoft has reached settlements to end a slew of antitrust investigations and lawsuits, including agreeing to uniformly license its operating systems and allowing manufacturers to include competing software with Windows.

While desktop applications and platforms remain the cornerstone of its operations, Microsoft has inexorably expanded its product lines, which include video game consoles, enterprise software, computer peripherals, software development tools, and Internet access services. In 2006 the company launched its Zune brand of digital entertainment products and services. The first Zune product, a digital media player, competes directly against Apple's iPod.

In mid-2007 Microsoft announced it would take a $1 billion charge to cover extended warranties and repairs to its Xbox 360 game consoles. Earlier in the year the company was ordered to pay Alcatel-Lucent about $1.5 billion as part of a patent dispute between the two companies over digital music technology.

Microsoft has also reached major settlement agreements with Netscape (paying the company about $750 million); Sun Microsystems ($1.6 billion in addition to royalty payments on certain technologies); Novell ($536 million to settle a suit tied to Novell's NetWare software); Gateway ($150 million); IBM ($775 million and extending $75 million in credit towards Microsoft software deployment); and RealNetworks ($761 million in cash and promotions).

Microsoft has used selective acquisitions (including the purchases of Navision and Great Plains Software) to expand its enterprise software offerings, which include applications for customer relationship management and accounting. And in an attempt to keep pace with Google and other competitors in a consolidating online advertising market, in May 2007 the company announced plans to acquire aQuantive for about $6 billion.

Chairman Bill Gates owns about 10% of Microsoft; CEO Steve Ballmer owns nearly 4%. Gates stepped down from his role as chief software architect in June 2006 to concentrate on his charitable work through the Bill & Melinda Gates Foundation.

## HISTORY

Bill Gates founded Microsoft (originally known as Micro-soft) in 1975 after dropping out of Harvard at age 19 and teaming with high school friend Paul Allen to sell a version of the programming language BASIC. While Gates was at Harvard, the pair wrote the language for Altair, the first commercial microcomputer. The company was born in an Albuquerque, New Mexico, hotel room and grew by modifying BASIC for other computers.

Gates moved Microsoft to his native Seattle in 1979 and began developing software that let others write programs. The modern PC era dawned in 1980 when IBM chose Microsoft to write the operating system for its new machines. Although hesitant at first, Gates bought QDOS, short for "quick and dirty operating system," for $50,000 from a Seattle programmer, renaming it the Microsoft Disk Operating System (MS-DOS).

Allen fell ill with Hodgkin's disease and left Microsoft in 1983. In the mid-1980s Microsoft introduced Windows, a graphics-based version of MS-DOS that borrowed from rival Apple's Macintosh system. The company went public in 1986, and Gates became the industry's first billionaire a year later. Microsoft introduced Windows NT in 1993 to compete with the UNIX operating system, popular on mainframes and large networks.

The early 1990s brought monopoly charges from inside and outside the industry. In 1995 antitrust concerns scotched a $1.5 billion acquisition of personal finance software maker Intuit.

When the Internet began transforming business practices, holdout Gates at last embraced the medium; the Microsoft Network (MSN) debuted in 1995. That year Microsoft licensed the Java Web programming language from Sun and introduced its Internet Explorer Web browser.

In 1998 the US Justice Department, backed by 18 states, filed antitrust charges against the software giant, claiming it stifled Internet browser competition and limited consumer choice.

In 1999 Microsoft agreed to invest $5 billion for a minority stake in AT&T as part of that company's move to acquire cable operator MediaOne. In addition, Microsoft bought Windows-based technical drawing software specialist Visio for $1.3 billion.

Gates named president Steve Ballmer CEO in 2000. Gates, who had held the CEO spot since the company's founding, remained chairman and added the title of chief software architect.

A federal judge's ruling later that year that Microsoft used its monopoly powers to violate antitrust laws left the prospect of two (smaller) Microsofts, a decision the company aggressively appealed. (The initial ruling to split Microsoft into two companies was later struck down, leading to a settlement between the company and the US Justice Department.)

In 2001 Microsoft completed the acquisition of longtime partner Great Plains Software, a specialist in applications for midsized and small businesses, in a $1.1 billion deal. A federal appeals court struck down the initial ruling to break up Microsoft, leading to a tentative settlement (pending approval by the 18 US states involved in the trial) between the company and the US Justice Department. The settlement would leave Microsoft intact, but impose restrictions on the company's licensing policies for its operating systems.

Netscape Communications filed suit in 2002 against Microsoft, seeking unspecified damages and injunctions against the company's alleged antitrust actions. The company also acquired enterprise software provider Navision for about $1.5 billion.

Microsoft settled the suit with Netscape in 2003, agreeing to pay AOL $750 million as part of a larger settlement that includes AOL licensing Microsoft's Internet Explorer browser and its digital media technology.

In part due to increasing demands from shareholders to explore alternatives for its ever-growing cash hoard, in 2003 the company declared its first ever dividend for common stock. Microsoft also eliminated stock options, instead moving to a system of distributing shares of its stock directly to employees.

## EXECUTIVES

**Chairman:** William H. (Bill) Gates III, age 51, $966,667 pay
**CEO and Director:** Steven A. (Steve) Ballmer, age 51, $966,667 pay
**COO:** B. Kevin Turner, age 41, $839,205 pay
**SVP; President, Microsoft International:** Jean-Philipe Courtois, age 47
**SVP and CTO, Business Platform:** David Vaskevitch, age 54
**SVP and General Counsel, Corporate Secretary, Legal and Corporate Affairs:** Bradford L. (Brad) Smith, age 47
**SVP; Chairman Emeritus, Microsoft Europe, Middle East, and Africa:** Bernard P. Vergnes, age 55
**SVP and Chief Advertising Strategist:** Yusuf Mehdi
**SVP, Central Marketing Group:** Michelle (Mich) Mathews, age 39
**SVP, Finance and Administration and CFO:** Christopher P. (Chris) Liddell, age 48
**SVP, Market Expansion Group, Platforms & Services Division:** Will Poole
**VP, Human Resources:** Lisa Brummel, age 46
**VP and CIO:** Stuart L. Scott
**Chairman and VP, Microsoft EMEA:** Umberto Paolucci
**President, Microsoft Business Division, and Group VP:** Jeffrey S. (Jeff) Raikes, age 49, $1,095,000 pay
**President, Microsoft Entertainment and Devices and Chief Xbox Officer:** Robert J. (Robbie) Bach, age 44
**Co-President, Microsoft Platform Products and Services, and Group VP:** Kevin R. Johnson, age 46, $1,095,000 pay
**Chairman, Microsoft Business Solutions Group:** Douglas J. (Doug) Burgum, age 51
**CTO and Chief Software Architect:** Ray Ozzie
**Chief Research and Strategy Officer:** Craig J. Mundie, age 58
**Auditors:** Deloitte & Touche LLP

## LOCATIONS

**HQ:** Microsoft Corporation
1 Microsoft Way, Redmond, WA 98052
**Phone:** 425-882-8080 **Fax:** 425-936-7329
**Web:** www.microsoft.com

Microsoft has offices in more than 80 countries.

### 2007 Sales

| | $ mil. | % of total |
|---|---|---|
| US | 31,346 | 61 |
| Other countries | 19,776 | 39 |
| **Total** | **51,122** | **100** |

## PRODUCTS/OPERATIONS

### 2007 Sales

| | $ mil. | % of total |
|---|---|---|
| Microsoft Business | 16,397 | 32 |
| Client | 14,973 | 29 |
| Server & Tools | 11,175 | 22 |
| Entertainment & Devices | 6,083 | 12 |
| Online Services | 2,474 | 5 |
| **Total** | **51,122** | **100** |

### Selected Products

Desktop Applications
- Access (relational database management)
- Excel (integrated spreadsheet)
- FrontPage (Web site publishing)
- MS Office (business productivity software suite)
- Outlook (messaging and collaboration)
- PowerPoint (presentation graphics)
- Project (project scheduling and resource allocation)
- Word (word processing)

Enterprise Software
- BackOffice (server software suite)
- Content Management Server (content management)
- Exchange Server (messaging server)
- Proxy Server (Internet gateway)
- Site Server (Web site management)
- SQL Server (database and data analysis management)
- Systems Management Server (centralized management)
- Visio (visualization and diagramming suite)

Consumer Software, Services, and Devices
- Flight Simulator (flight simulation software)
- Xbox (video game console)

Other
- Avanade (20%, information technology services)
- Microsoft Network (MSN, interactive online service)
- MSNBC Cable (18%, 24-hour cable news channel)
- MSNBC Interactive News (50%, Internet news site)
- Exchange Server (messaging server)
- Proxy Server (Internet gateway)
- Site Server (Web site management)
- SQL Server (database and data analysis management)
- Systems Management Server (centralized management)
- Visio (visualization and diagramming suite)

## COMPETITORS

ACCESS
Adobe
AOL
Apple
BASF Corporation
CA
EarthLink
EMC
Google
Hewlett-Packard
IBM
Logitech
Nintendo
Nokia
Novell
Oracle
Red Hat
SAP
Sony
Sun Microsystems
Symbian
Time Warner
Yahoo!

## HISTORICAL FINANCIALS

Company Type: Public

### Income Statement

FYE: June 30

| | REVENUE ($ mil.) | NET INCOME ($ mil.) | NET PROFIT MARGIN | EMPLOYEES |
|---|---|---|---|---|
| **6/07** | 51,122 | 14,065 | 27.5% | 79,000 |
| **6/06** | 44,282 | 12,599 | 28.5% | 71,000 |
| **6/05** | 39,788 | 12,254 | 30.8% | 61,000 |
| **6/04** | 36,835 | 8,168 | 22.2% | 57,000 |
| **6/03** | 32,187 | 9,993 | 31.0% | 55,000 |
| **Annual Growth** | 12.3% | 8.9% | — | 9.5% |

### 2007 Year-End Financials

Debt ratio: —
Return on equity: 39.5%
Cash ($ mil.): 23,411
Current ratio: 1.69
Long-term debt ($ mil.): —
No. of shares (mil.): 9,380
Dividends
Yield: 1.7%
Payout: 34.5%
Market value ($ mil.): 276,429

### Stock History

NASDAQ (GS): MSFT

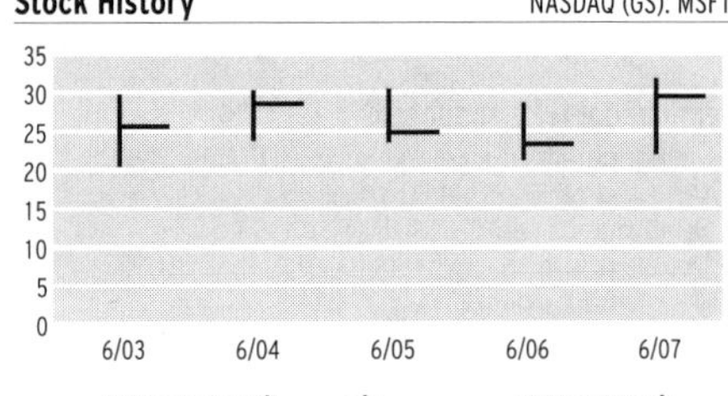


| | STOCK PRICE ($) FY Close | P/E High | P/E Low | PER SHARE ($) Earnings | Dividends | Book Value |
|---|---|---|---|---|---|---|
| **6/07** | 29.47 | 22 | 16 | 1.42 | 0.49 | 3.32 |
| **6/06** | 23.30 | 24 | 18 | 1.20 | 0.34 | 3.99 |
| **6/05** | 24.84 | 27 | 21 | 1.12 | 3.16 | 4.49 |
| **6/04** | 28.56 | 40 | 32 | 0.75 | 0.16 | 6.89 |
| **6/03** | 25.64 | 45 | 31 | 0.66 | 0.08 | 5.69 |
| **Annual Growth** | 3.5% | — | — | 21.1% | 57.3% | (12.6%) |

# Mohawk Industries

Mohawk Industries doesn't mind being trampled under foot. The company is the second-largest maker of commercial and residential carpets and rugs in the US (after Shaw Industries) and one of the largest carpet makers in the world. It produces woven and tufted broadloom carpets and rugs under such names as Mohawk, Aladdin, Durkan, Karastan, and Bigelow. Mohawk's Dal-Tile International division is one of the US's largest makers of ceramic tile and stone flooring. Laminate, wood, and vinyl flooring round out Mohawk's operations. The company sells its wares to more than 39,000 customers, including carpet retailers, home centers, mass merchandisers, department stores, and dealers.

In 2007 Mohawk bought the wood flooring plants of Columbia Forest Products. The deal included three plants in the US and one in Malaysia. The two companies are no strangers; Columbia was the manufacturer of the wood flooring Mohawk distributes.

Investment firm Ruane, Cunniff & Goldfarb, Inc. controls nearly 20% of the company. Chairman, president, and CEO Jeffrey Lorberbaum owns about 18%.

## HISTORY

Mohawk Carpet was an ailing unit of Mohasco until 1988, when division president David Kolb led an LBO to separate Mohawk from its parent and became CEO of the new company. Mohawk traces its origins to the Shuttleworth family who founded the company in Amsterdam, New York, in 1878, setting up their business with 14 second-hand looms imported from England. The company was incorporated as Shuttleworth Brothers in 1902. It introduced the popular Karnak carpet design in 1908.

The firm acquired carpet maker McLeary, Wallin and Crouse and began to consolidate the fragmented carpet industry in the Northeast. The company renamed itself Mohawk Carpet Mills and was the only maker of a complete line of domestic carpets, under the Wilton, Axminster, Velvet, and Chenille styles. Over the next three decades the company pioneered a number of carpet industry firsts: the first texture design (Shuttlepoint), the first sculptured weave (Raleigh), and the first knitted carpet (Woven Interlock).

Mohawk Carpet Mills, like the rest of the industry, moved into synthetics such as nylon and acrylics during the late 1940s and early 1950s. The company merged with Alexander Smith in 1956 to form Mohasco Industries, the largest carpet maker in the world at the time.

By 1980 the company was facing a fiercely competitive market. Mohasco had failed to keep up with changing fashions and was no longer the leading carpet maker. Allied Fibers veteran David Kolb was brought in to turn Mohasco's unprofitable Mohawk division around. He moved the company's headquarters to the carpet-making center of the US, Georgia. Kolb began modernizing equipment and refocused the company on its high-margin carpet products and emphasized direct sales to retailers.

Kolb took Mohawk public in 1992 and began acquiring other carpet makers, including Horizon Industries (carpet mills, 1992), American Rug Craftsmen (household rugs and mats, 1993), and Fieldcrest Cannon's Karastan and Bigelow divisions (carpets and rugs, 1993).

In 1994 Mohawk bought Aladdin Mills, then the fourth-largest carpet maker in the US. Jeffrey Lorberbaum, son of Aladdin founder Alan Lorberbaum, became Mohawk's president and COO.

The company's spending spree continued, acquiring Galaxy Carpet Mills in 1995. In 1996 Mohawk added capacity at all its plants: The acquisition of Fiber One boosted Mohawk's annual polypropylene extrusion capacity by 40 million pounds and in 1997 Mohawk added approximately 100 million pounds of annual polypropylene extrusion capacity by acquiring certain assets of Diamond Rug. In 1998 Mohawk purchased American Weavers and floorcoverings maker World Carpets.

In 1999 the company paid $232 million for Image Industries, a unit of Maxim Group that makes residential polyester carpet from recycled plastic bottles, and $98 million for commercial carpet supplier Durkan Patterned Carpets. Mohawk entered the market for hardwood floors by introducing a product line in 2000. Also that year the company purchased the Wovens Division of Crown Crafts (woven throws, bedspreads, and coverlets). Lorberbaum succeeded Kolb as CEO in 2001.

Early in 2002 Mohawk acquired ceramic tile maker Dal-Tile International for $1.5 billion. Dal-Tile added nearly $1 billion in sales (or nearly a quarter of Mohawk's total revenues) and gave the company an automatic stronghold in the hard flooring business. Mohawk followed that up by acquiring bankrupt Burlington Industries' carpet division, Lees Carpet, for about $350 million in 2003. In 2005 Mohawk acquired Unilin Holding NV, a European manufacturer of laminate flooring. The purchase price for Unilin, which has about $1 billion in annual sales, was $2.6 billion.

## EXECUTIVES

**Chairman, President, and CEO:** Jeffrey S. Lorberbaum, age 52, $825,000 pay
**COO and Director:** W. Christopher (Chris) Wellborn, age 51, $934,032 pay
**VP, Finance and CFO:** Frank H. Boykin, age 51, $460,000 pay
**VP, Operations:** Joe W. Yarbrough Jr.
**President, Carpet Group:** Herbert Monte Thornton, age 66, $588,800 pay
**President, Dal-Tile:** Harold G. Turk, age 60
**President, Mohawk Home:** William B. Kilbride
**VP, Corporate Controller and Chief Accounting Officer:** Thomas J. Kanuk, age 54
**President, Unilin and Director:** Frans G. De Cock, age 64, $564,375 pay
**Secretary:** Barbara M. Goetz
**Auditors:** KPMG LLP

## LOCATIONS

**HQ:** Mohawk Industries, Inc.
160 S. Industrial Blvd., Calhoun, GA 30701
**Phone:** 706-629-7721 **Fax:** 706-624-3825
**Web:** www.mohawkind.com

Mohawk Industries has factories in Georgia and Oklahoma in the US, as well as in Belgium and Mexico.

### 2006 Sales

| | $ mil. | % of total |
|---|---|---|
| North America | 6,974.5 | 88 |
| Other regions | 931.3 | 12 |
| **Total** | **7,905.8** | **100** |

## PRODUCTS/OPERATIONS

### 2006 Sales

| | $ mil. | % of total |
|---|---|---|
| Mohawk | 4,742.0 | 60 |
| Dal-Tile | 1,941.8 | 24 |
| Unilin | 1,236.9 | 16 |
| Adjustments | (14.9) | — |
| **Total** | **7,905.8** | **100** |

### Selected Operations

Mohawk
- Bath rugs
- Blankets
- Carpet
- Ceramic tile
- Decorative throws and pillows
- Doormats
- Hardwood flooring
- Laminate flooring
- Resilient flooring
- Rugs
- Woven and tufted rugs
- Woven bedspreads

Dal-Tile
- Ceramic tile
- Glazed floor tile
- Glazed wall tile
- Glazed and unglazed ceramic mosaic tile
- Porcelain tile
- Quarry tile
- Stone products

Unilin
- Insulated roofing
- Laminate flooring
- Wood paneling

### Selected Brand Names

Mohawk
- Aladdin
- Bigelow Commercial
- Durkan
- Helios
- Horizon
- Karastan
- Lees
- Merit
- Mohawk
- Mohawk Home
- Ralph Lauren

Dal-Tile
- American Olean
- Dal-Tile

Unilin
- Mohawk
- Quick-Step

## COMPETITORS

Armstrong World Industries
Beaulieu
Couristan
Dixie Group
Formica
Guilford Mills
Interface
Mannington Mills
Perstorp
Shaw Industries
Tarkett Inc.
Wilsonart International

## HISTORICAL FINANCIALS

Company Type: Public

### Income Statement

FYE: December 31

| | REVENUE ($ mil.) | NET INCOME ($ mil.) | NET PROFIT MARGIN | EMPLOYEES |
|---|---|---|---|---|
| **12/06** | 7,906 | 456 | 5.8% | 37,100 |
| **12/05** | 6,620 | 358 | 5.4% | 37,700 |
| **12/04** | 5,880 | 369 | 6.3% | 34,300 |
| **12/03** | 5,005 | 310 | 6.2% | 33,300 |
| **12/02** | 4,522 | 285 | 6.3% | 31,780 |
| **Annual Growth** | 15.0% | 12.5% | — | 3.9% |

### 2006 Year-End Financials

Debt ratio: 59.4%
Return on equity: 13.5%
Cash ($ mil.): 63
Current ratio: 1.49
Long-term debt ($ mil.): 2,208
No. of shares (mil.): 68
Dividends
Yield: —
Payout: —
Market value ($ mil.): 5,073

**Stock History** NYSE: MHK

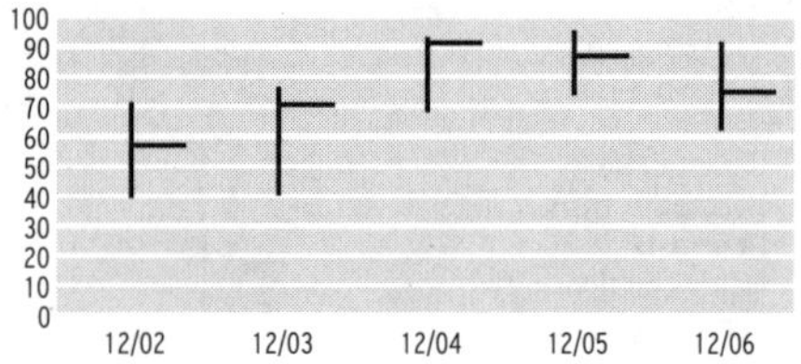

| | STOCK PRICE ($) FY Close | P/E High | P/E Low | PER SHARE ($) Earnings | Dividends | Book Value |
|---|---|---|---|---|---|---|
| **12/06** | 74.86 | 14 | 9 | 6.70 | — | 54.83 |
| **12/05** | 86.98 | 18 | 14 | 5.30 | — | 44.85 |
| **12/04** | 91.25 | 17 | 13 | 5.46 | — | 39.94 |
| **12/03** | 70.54 | 16 | 9 | 4.62 | — | 34.54 |
| **12/02** | 56.95 | 16 | 9 | 4.39 | — | 29.88 |
| **Annual Growth** | 7.1% | — | — | 11.1% | — | 16.4% |

# Molex Incorporated

Molex makes mountains out of connections. The company is the world's #2 maker (behind Tyco Electronics) of plugs and other electrical connectors. It makes more than 100,000 kinds of electronic, electrical, and fiber-optic connectors and switches. Its miniature plugs, jacks, and other complex connectors are used in a wide variety of products including computers, consumer electronics, home appliances, automobiles, telecommunications equipment, and industrial machinery. Molex's customers are primarily manufacturers and include Cisco, Dell, Ford, General Motors, Hewlett-Packard, IBM, Matsushita, Motorola, and Nokia. Asian customers, primarily in China and Japan, account for about half of sales.

In 2006 Molex acquired Woodhead Industries for about $256 million plus debt and outstanding stock options. Woodhead is a manufacturer of network and electrical infrastructure products.

Like many other electronics manufacturers, Molex has seen sales slump in the first half of 2007, due to some larger customers continuing to burn off inventory and to lower-than-expected demand in the mobile phone, consumer electronics, and data networking equipment markets. Molex is responding with a corporate reorganization and a variety of cost-cutting measures, including layoffs and plant closures.

The Krehbiel family, including co-chairmen Fred and John Jr., grandsons of Molex's founder, owns a controlling interest in the company.

FMR (Fidelity Investments) owns nearly 7% of Molex. Cooke & Bieler holds nearly 6%.

## HISTORY

In 1938 Frederick Krehbiel, the son of Swiss Mennonites, on a lark began mixing waste substances coal tar and asbestos. The result was a thick, black plastic material that he called Molex, combining a reference to its "mol"-ded state with the modern-sounding "ex." That year he founded Molex Products Company in Brookfield, Illinois. Soon the substance was being used to make everything from flower pots and salt shakers to moisture-resistant bushings.

Frederick's son, John Sr. (known simply as Senior), joined the company in the 1940s and, recognizing the material's electrical insulating properties, expanded its uses to include coatings for US Army land mines (masking them from enemy detectors) and sheathing for electrical components. Senior also shifted the company's focus to connectors that linked electronic components. Because it was still unproven by the start of WWII, Molex was one of the few plastic substances not restricted to use by the war effort; manufacturers flocked to it as a substitute. (The original Molex product later became obsolete due to newer materials, such as nylon.)

By the 1950s and 1960s, Molex, under Senior's leadership, had targeted its connector sales toward manufacturers of televisions, ranges, washer-dryers, and other consumer electronics and appliances.

When Senior asked his son Frederick to use his foreign experience (he had attended school in England) to the company's advantage, Molex in the late 1960s began an international expansion. Frederick thought it wise to build plants overseas to lower costs and be closer to customers; in 1970 the company opened its first non-US factory, in Japan. Molex went public in 1972 and relocated its headquarters to Lisle, Illinois. Senior's older son, John Krehbiel Jr., was named president in 1975.

By the 1980s Molex was the world's 10th-largest maker of electronic connectors. Long cautious in dealings, the company in the late 1980s went on a spending spree. Molex bought stakes in a variety of small companies to position itself in such lucrative locations as China. In 1989 the company bought an 85% interest in Ulti Mate and gained a stronger connector presence in the military market. Fred Krehbiel was named CEO in 1988.

Chairman John Sr. died in 1993. Molex, which more than doubled its global manufacturing capacity in the 1990s, opened new factories in China and Puerto Rico in 1997. In 1999 the company acquired Cardell Corporation, a privately held maker of automotive connectors; it also bought Silent Systems (heat sinks) and Indian connector maker Mafatlal Micron. That year Fred and John Jr. became co-chairmen and co-CEOs.

In 2000 Molex reported record sales thanks to a wide variety of new products and strong growth in its telecommunications and automotive offerings. During that year the company bought Axsys Technologies' Beau Interconnects division for about $30 million. Fred and John Jr. handed over the CEO reins to Joseph King in 2001 (Fred and John Jr. remained co-chairmen).

Facing dismal conditions across its target markets in 2001-02, Molex instituted a variety of cost-cutting measures including reductions in executive pay, shortened work-weeks, and a small number of plant closures and layoffs. Molex closed facilities in Puerto Rico, Slovakia, the UK, and the US.

In 2004 Molex acquired France-based Connecteurs Cinch SA, adding manufacturing facilities in France, Portugal, India, and China. That year Molex also acquired privately held INCEP Technologies, a maker of power delivery interconnect, high-density packaging, and thermal management products for the semiconductor industry.

An accounting irregularity in inventory calculations — and the resulting request by company auditors for a management representation letter from a different CFO — led Molex to name an acting CFO in late 2004, make adjustments to 2004 financial results, and delay filing its quarterly SEC report. The auditors also asked that both the CEO and CFO no longer serve as officers of the company and requested additional disclosures; Molex initially refused, and auditor Deloitte & Touche resigned. Late in 2004, however, Molex announced King's resignation and Fred Krehbiel's assumption of the CEO post. (Krehbiel served as CEO until mid-2005, when Martin Slark was named to the position.) Ernst & Young was appointed as auditor.

In mid-2006 Molex acquired Woodhead Industries, one of the biggest acquisitions the company has ever attempted.

## EXECUTIVES

**Co-Chairman:** Frederick A. (Fred) Krehbiel, age 66, $450,000 pay
**Co-Chairman:** John H. Krehbiel Jr., age 69, $793,935 pay
**Vice Chairman and CEO:** Martin P. Slark, age 52, $1,367,775 pay
**President and COO:** Liam McCarthy, age 51, $957,443 pay
**EVP:** James E. Fleischhacker, age 63
**EVP; President, Americas:** Ronald L. Schubel, age 63
**VP; President, Far East North:** Goro Tokuyama, age 72, $550,753 pay
**VP, CFO, and Treasurer:** David D. Johnson, age 51
**SVP, Investor Relations:** Neil Lefort
**VP; President, Americas and VP, Sales, Americas:** Dave B. Root, age 53
**VP; Regional President, Europe:** Graham C. Brock, age 53
**VP and CIO:** Gary Matula
**President, Connector Products, Americas and Director:** Frederick L. (Fred) Krehbiel, age 41
**Controller:** K. Travis George, age 37
**Secretary and General Counsel:** Louis A. Hecht, age 62
**Auditors:** Ernst & Young LLP

## LOCATIONS

**HQ:** Molex Incorporated
2222 Wellington Ct., Lisle, IL 60532
**Phone:** 630-969-4550 **Fax:** 630-968-8356
**Web:** www.molex.com

Molex operates manufacturing facilities in Australia, Brazil, China, France, Germany, India, Ireland, Italy, Japan, Malaysia, Mexico, Poland, Singapore, Slovakia, South Korea, Taiwan, Thailand, and the US.

**2007 Sales**

| | $ mil. | % of total |
|---|---|---|
| Asia/Pacific | | |
| South | 1,128.0 | 34 |
| North | 510.3 | 16 |
| Americas | 783.5 | 24 |
| Europe | 556.1 | 17 |
| Other regions | 288.0 | 9 |
| **Total** | **3,265.9** | **100** |

## PRODUCTS/OPERATIONS

**2007 Sales**

| | % of total |
|---|---|
| Telecommunications | 26 |
| Data products | 21 |
| Consumer | 18 |
| Automotive | 18 |
| Industrial | 15 |
| Other | 2 |
| **Total** | **100** |

## COMPETITORS

3M
Amphenol
Cooper Industries
Hon Hai
Innovex
ITT Corp.
Kyocera
Methode Electronics
Northrop Grumman
Oki Electric
Parlex
Thomas & Betts
Tyco Electronics
Viasystems

## HISTORICAL FINANCIALS

Company Type: Public

**Income Statement** FYE: June 30

| | REVENUE ($ mil.) | NET INCOME ($ mil.) | NET PROFIT MARGIN | EMPLOYEES |
|---|---|---|---|---|
| **6/07** | 3,266 | 241 | 7.4% | 33,200 |
| **6/06** | 2,861 | 236 | 8.3% | 32,400 |
| **6/05** | 2,549 | 154 | 6.1% | 27,525 |
| **6/04** | 2,247 | 176 | 7.8% | 21,225 |
| **6/03** | 1,843 | 85 | 4.6% | 17,275 |
| **Annual Growth** | 15.4% | 29.8% | — | 17.7% |

**2007 Year-End Financials**

Debt ratio: 5.1%
Return on equity: 10.0%
Cash ($ mil.): 461
Current ratio: 3.00
Long-term debt ($ mil.): 128
No. of shares (mil.): 99
Dividends
Yield: 1.0%
Payout: 23.1%
Market value ($ mil.): 2,984

**Stock History** NASDAQ (GS): MOLX

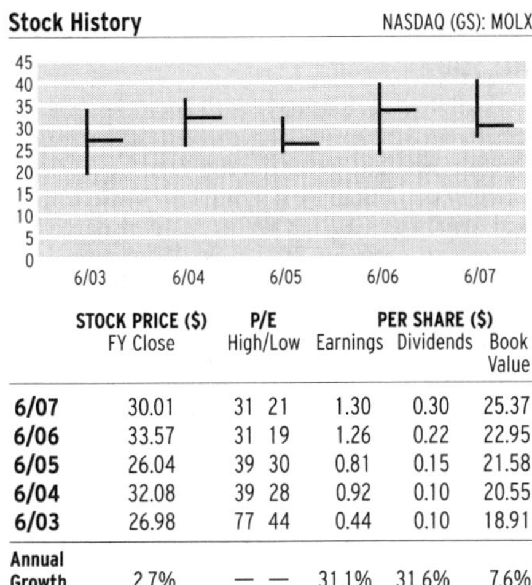


| | STOCK PRICE ($) FY Close | P/E High | P/E Low | PER SHARE ($) Earnings | Dividends | Book Value |
|---|---|---|---|---|---|---|
| **6/07** | 30.01 | 31 | 21 | 1.30 | 0.30 | 25.37 |
| **6/06** | 33.57 | 31 | 19 | 1.26 | 0.22 | 22.95 |
| **6/05** | 26.04 | 39 | 30 | 0.81 | 0.15 | 21.58 |
| **6/04** | 32.08 | 39 | 28 | 0.92 | 0.10 | 20.55 |
| **6/03** | 26.98 | 77 | 44 | 0.44 | 0.10 | 18.91 |
| **Annual Growth** | 2.7% | — | — | 31.1% | 31.6% | 7.6% |

# Molson Coors Brewing

Molson Coors Brewing Company plays with the big boys: The Company is among the largest brewers by volume in the world, producing 42 million barrels of beer in 2006. Its most popular brand is Coors Light, nicknamed "The Silver Bullet." The company markets about a dozen beers in the US, including George Killian's Irish Red Lager, and Keystone. Molson Coors also makes Zima and Coors Non-Alcoholic (Coors NA). In 2005 Coors merged with Canadian brewer Molson, adding such brands as Black Ice and Rickard's Red Ale to the company's refreshment roster. The Coors family owns about 26% of the company.

Most of Molson Coors' beers are brewed in Colorado; its Golden, Colorado, plant is the world's largest single-site brewery. The company also has brewing operations at six sites in Canada. The company is adding brewing operations to its packaging facility in Virginia.

Once known as a single-product, regional beer maker, the brewer has not been afraid to try new varieties, although it discontinued several that fell short (Blue Moon Abbey Ale, Keystone Dry, and Killian's Irish Honey). It also has a low-carb beer, Aspen Edge, and a caffeinated beer, Molson Kick, which is available only in Canada and sold in an aluminum bottle.

With the 2005 merger of Coors and Molson, the company added control of three more well-known brands: Coors Light, Carling, and Molson Canadian.

It began selling Coors Fine Light Beer in Russia during 2005, its first foray into that country. However, due to poor sales, it pulled out of the country in 2006. The company sold a 68% stake in its Brazilian brewing operation to FEMSA Cerveza for $68 million in 2006.

Company vice-chairman and director Pete Coors made headlines in 2006 when he was charged with driving under the influence. He admitted to having a beer shortly before leaving a friend's wedding and apologized publicly for not using alcohol responsibly.

## HISTORY

Adolph Coors landed in Baltimore in 1868, a 21-year-old stowaway fleeing Germany's military draft. He worked his way west to Denver, where he bought a bottling company in 1872 and became partners with Jacob Schueler, a local merchant, in 1873. The partners built a brewery in Golden, Colorado, a small town in the nearby Rocky Mountain foothills. Coors became sole owner of the Adolph Coors Company in 1880.

For most of its history, Coors confined its sales to western states. The cost of nationwide distribution was prohibitive because the company used a single brewery, natural brewing methods, and no preservatives; Coors beer was made, transported, and stored under refrigeration, with a shelf life of only one month.

The brewer survived Prohibition by making near beer and malted milk and by entering cement and porcelain chemical ware production. The Coors family built a vertically integrated company that did everything from growing brewing ingredients to pumping the oil that powered its breweries. By 1929, when Adolph died, son Adolph Jr. was running the company. After repeal of the 18th Amendment, beer sales grew steadily in the company's 11-state market.

By the 1960s Coors beer had achieved cult status. Another result of the company's national reputation was that the Coors family had become notoriously private. In 1960 Adolph III was kidnapped and murdered, sending the clan into an even deeper state of secrecy.

Adolph Jr. died in 1970; his son Bill was named chairman and started the country's first aluminum-recycling program. Coors beer was the top seller in 10 of its 11 state markets by 1975, when the company went public. However, sales began to decline as Miller Brewing and Anheuser-Busch introduced new light and super premium beers. Coors responded by introducing its own light and super premium brands and expanding its market area to 16 states.

In the late 1970s and 1980s, the company began rapid expansion while enduring boycotts and strikes due to alleged discriminatory labor practices. The brewer eventually developed progressive employment policies.

It spun off its packaging and ceramics firm ACX Technologies in 1992. Also that year it introduced Zima, a clear, malt-based brew. Leo Kiely became the first president of the company's brewing operations from outside the Coors family in 1993. The company also cut its workforce by nearly 700 positions; the severance program cost $70 million and resulted in its first loss in more than 10 years.

Specialty Blue Moon products were piloted at its Sandlot microbrewery in 1995. The company formed a partnership with Molson Breweries and Foster's in 1997 to manage the distribution of its brands in Canada. (Foster's later sold its stake to Molson.)

In 2000 Peter Coors (Adolph's great-grandson) was named president and CEO of Adolph Coors Company and chairman of Coors Brewing Company. In 2001 the brewer formed a joint venture with Molson to distribute Molson's beers in the US. In 2002 Belgium's Interbred (now known as InBev) sold the Carling division of its Bass Brewers holding to Coors for nearly $1.8 billion. The purchase led to the creation of Coors Brewers Limited, which makes the Carling, Worthington's, and Jaffrey's beer brands, as well as Grolsch (under license).

The company announced in 2003 that it would cut the workforce at its Memphis brewery by 20%. In 2004 chairman Peter Coors failed to capture a seat in the US Senate. Coors was replaced by Eric Molson as chairman upon the company's merger with Molson. Kiely remained as CEO. Following the merger, 11 top executives left the company, including CFO David Barnes.

Molson signed a contract with the NFL in 2005, making its subsidiary Coors Brewing Company the "Official Beer Sponsor" of the league through the 2010 football season.

## EXECUTIVES

**Chairman:** Eric H. Molson, age 69
**CEO and Director:** W. Leo Kiely III, age 60, $945,000 pay
**VP and Global CFO:** Timothy V. (Tim) Wolf, age 53, $539,000 pay
**VP and Treasurer:** Michael J. (Mike) Gannon, age 40
**VP and Global Controller:** Martin L. (Marty) Miller, age 44
**VP Global Investor Relations:** David (Dave) Dunnewald
**Global Chief Legal Officer and Corporate Secretary:** Samuel D. Walker, age 48
**Global Chief People Officer:** Ralph P. Hargrow, age 55
**Chief Global Strategy and Commercial Officer:** David (Dave) Perkins, age 54
**Global Chief Public Affairs Officer:** Dan A. Lewiss
**Global Chief Synergies Officer:** Cathy Noonan, age 50
**Global Chief Technical Officer:** Gregory L. Wade, age 58
**Chief Marketing Officer:** Andrew J. (Andy) England
**President and CEO, Coors Brewing Company:** Frits D. van Paasschen, age 46, $637,500 pay
**President and CEO, Coors Europe and Asia:** Peter Swinburn, age 54, $613,018 pay
**President and CEO, Molson Canada:** Kevin T. Boyce, age 51, $592,901 pay
**VP Marketing, Coors Brewing Company:** Jim Sabia
**Chief Brewing Officer, Molson Canada:** Daniel Pelland
**Chief Commercial Officer, Molson Canada:** Mark Hunter
**Director Hispanic Marketing:** Paul Mendieta
**Brewmaster, Coors Brewing Co.:** Keith Villa
**Auditors:** PricewaterhouseCoopers LLP

## LOCATIONS

**HQ:** Molson Coors Brewing Company
1225 17th St., Denver, CO 80202
**Phone:** 303-279-6565 **Fax:** 303-277-5415
**Web:** www.molsoncoors.com

### 2006 Sales

| | % of total |
|---|---|
| US | 45 |
| Canada | 31 |
| Europe | 24 |
| **Total** | **100** |

## PRODUCTS/OPERATIONS

### 2006 Sales

| | % of total |
|---|---|
| Coors Light | 45 |
| Carling | 19 |
| Molson Canadian | 8 |
| Other | 28 |
| **Total** | **100** |

### Selected Brands

Canada
- Amstel Light (licensed)
- Asahi Select (licensed)
- Carling
- Coors Light
- Corona (licensed)
- Creemore Springs
- Foster's (licensed)
- Foster's Special Bitter (licensed)
- Heineken (licensed)
- Miller Genuine Draft (licensed)
- Miller Lite (licensed)
- Milwaukee's Best (licensed)
- Molson Canadian
- Molson Dry
- Molson Export
- Murphy's (licensed)
- Pilsner
- Rickard's Red Ale

UK
- C2
- Caffrey's
- Carling
- Coors Fine Light Beer
- Grolsch
- Reef
- Screamers
- Stones
- Worthington's

US
- Belgian White Ale
- Blue Moon
- Coors
- Coors Light
- Coors Non-Alcoholic
- George Killian's
- Irish Red Lager
- Keystone
- Keystone Ice
- Keystone Light
- Molson
- Zima

## COMPETITORS

Anchor Brewing
Anheuser-Busch
Boston Beer
Brick Brewing
Carlsberg
Constellation Brands
Diageo
FEMSA
Foster's
Gambrinus
Grupo Modelo
Heineken
Heineken USA
InBev
InBev USA
Kirin Brewery of America
Labatt
Mendocino Brewing
Miller Brewing
Pabst
SABMiller
Scottish & Newcastle
Yuengling & Son

## HISTORICAL FINANCIALS

Company Type: Public

### Income Statement

FYE: Last Sunday in December

| | REVENUE ($ mil.) | NET INCOME ($ mil.) | NET PROFIT MARGIN | EMPLOYEES |
|---|---|---|---|---|
| **12/06** | 5,845 | 361 | 6.2% | 9,550 |
| **12/05** | 5,507 | 135 | 2.4% | 10,200 |
| **12/04** | 4,306 | 197 | 4.6% | 8,400 |
| **12/03** | 4,000 | 175 | 4.4% | 8,500 |
| **12/02** | 3,776 | 162 | 4.3% | 8,700 |
| **Annual Growth** | 11.5% | 22.3% | — | 2.4% |

### 2006 Year-End Financials

Debt ratio: 41.2%
Return on equity: 6.5%
Cash ($ mil.): 182
Current ratio: 0.81
Long-term debt ($ mil.): 2,399
No. of shares (mil.): 67
Dividends
Yield: 1.4%
Payout: 30.7%
Market value ($ mil.): 5,929

### Stock History

NYSE: TAP

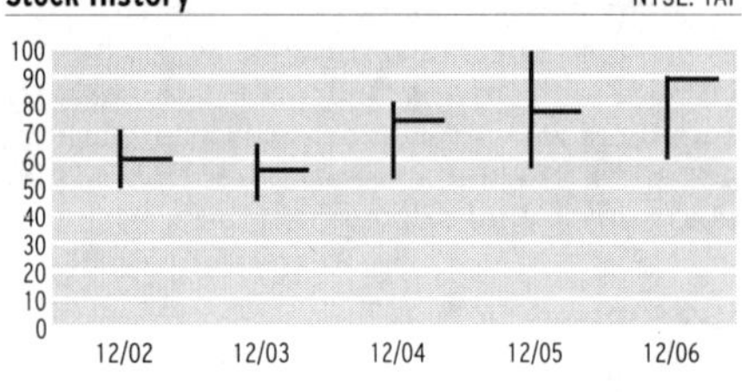


| | STOCK PRICE ($) FY Close | P/E High | P/E Low | PER SHARE ($) Earnings | Dividends | Book Value |
|---|---|---|---|---|---|---|
| **12/06** | 89.01 | 21 | 15 | 4.17 | 1.28 | 87.34 |
| **12/05** | 77.33 | 58 | 34 | 1.69 | 1.28 | 86.23 |
| **12/04** | 74.07 | 15 | 10 | 5.19 | 0.82 | 28.94 |
| **12/03** | 56.11 | 14 | 10 | 4.77 | 0.82 | 36.05 |
| **12/02** | 60.04 | 16 | 11 | 4.42 | 0.82 | 27.99 |
| **Annual Growth** | 10.3% | — | — | (1.4%) | 11.8% | 32.9% |

# Monsanto Company

Corn the size of a Trident missile? Not quite, but Monsanto *is* all about bioengineered crops. Monsanto helps farmers grow more crops by applying biotechnology and genomics to seeds and herbicides. It produces genetically altered seeds that tolerate Roundup — its flagship chemical product — and resist bugs. Monsanto estimates that more than 70% of the world's herbicide-resistant crops bear its stamp. The company also produces Asgrow and DEKALB seeds. Roundup is the world's #1 herbicide. In this decade Monsanto has been re-making itself as a seed and biotech company, as opposed to one focused on agrochemicals, a transition that was sped up with the acquisition of Delta and Pine Land.

Monsanto used to get about 40% of its sales from Roundup and other glyphosate products, but its US patent on glyphosate expired in 2000, and the company has seen its share of the market shrink. Roundup and its brethren now account for less than a third of sales.

Monsanto announced in the spring of 2005 that it had acquired fruit and vegetable seed maker Seminis for about $1.4 billion in cash and assumed debt. Seminis is among the world's largest fruit and vegetable seed producers, with about 3,500 varieties of seed sold in more than 150 countries. It continues as a wholly owned subsidiary of Monsanto with its own management remaining in place. The deal furthered the company's recent emphasis on growing its seeds business and changing its focus from agricultural chemicals.

Many analysts saw the move for Seminis as an indication Monsanto was trying to broaden its seed portfolio, to give the company something to balance out its biotech business. Perhaps, but Monsanto isn't content with the size of its GM seed business either. Later in 2005 the company purchased the cotton business of Emergent Genetics for $300 million. That business gives Monsanto a foothold in the cotton seed business similar to its existing corn and soybean product lines. Emergent ranked among the top three cotton seed companies with 12% of the market.

The acquisition of Delta and Pine Land only furthered the seed build-up; the company is the #1 cotton seed producer in the US. The deal, which was for $1.5 billion, required Monsanto to sell its Stoneville cottonseed business to Bayer CropScience for about $300 million.

In early 2007 the company announced a $1.5 billion joint R&D initiative with BASF to develop genetically modified crops with an emphasis on meeting the demand for biofuels. The two companies foresee the venture's first products being delivered in the first half of the next decade.

## HISTORY

Realizing he had only a German source for saccharin and foreseeing growing US demand for the product, in 1901 drug firm buyer John Queeny spent $5,000 to found Monsanto Chemical Works (using his wife's maiden name) to make saccharin in St. Louis. Monsanto soon added caffeine, vanillin, antiseptic phenol, and aspirin; it went public in 1927.

Queeny's son Edgar became president in 1928. He branched out into rubber additives and plastics through acquisitions. In 1943 Monsanto began making styrene monomer used to produce the US Army's first synthetic rubber tires.

Monsanto and American Viscose joined forces to form synthetic-fiber firm Chemstrand in 1949 (Monsanto bought it in 1961). Chemstrand also developed Acrilan fibers (1952) and the synthetic surface AstroTurf (first used commercially in Houston's Astrodome, 1966). In 1954 Monsanto and Bayer formed a joint venture to develop urethane foams (sold to Bayer, 1967). Monsanto debuted the herbicides Lasso (1969) and Roundup (1973) and stopped making saccharin in 1972.

Monsanto bought drugmaker G. D. Searle (founded 1868) in 1985, inheriting lawsuits relating to its Copper-7 contraceptive IUD. It also got the rights to artificial sweetener aspartame (NutraSweet). In 1994 Monsanto launched its first biotech product (to increase milk yields).

Searle's Robert Shapiro became CEO in 1995 and set out to create genetically altered foods. That year Monsanto bought Merck's specialty chemicals unit, Syntex (birth-control pills), and 50% of biotech firm Calgene (it bought the rest in 1997).

In 1996 Monsanto bought a stake in DEKALB Genetics (it bought the rest in 1998) and introduced a Roundup-tolerant soybean. It bought Holden's Foundation Seeds (corn seed) in 1997 and spun off chemicals unit Solutia. Purchases in 1998 included the seed business of Cargill and the wheat-breeding business of Unilever (UK). It also said it would buy #1 cottonseed producer

Delta and Pine Land, but that deal was delayed by regulators and dropped altogether in 1999.

In 1999 Monsanto launched Celebrex, an arthritis drug that set new prescription records. Meanwhile, concerns about genetically modified foods prompted bans in the UK and Brazil (and later in other countries). Negative public reaction led Monsanto to stop developing seeds with a terminator gene that rendered them sterile.

Late in 1999 activists stepped up protests over bioengineered crops, and lawyers filed a class-action suit alleging inadequate testing and unfair price influence.

Monsanto merged with Pharmacia & Upjohn in 2000, and the new entity, Pharmacia Corporation (with Monsanto now a wholly owned subsidiary), set about restructuring, selling Monsanto's NutraSweet, Equal, and Canderel sweeteners (in part to a group led by Michael Dell), as well as its biogums (food texturing and processing) business. The "new" Monsanto is focused solely on using advanced technology to grow better crops — the pharmaceutical and other operations of the old Monsanto have been assumed by Pharmacia. Consumer apprehension over so-called "Frankenfoods" and the like prompted Pharmacia to spin off about 15% of Monsanto to the public in 2000; the company spun off the remainder as a dividend to shareholders in 2002.

After two disappointing years of results, in December 2002 CEO Hendrik Verfaillie resigned and chairman Frank AtLee assumed the position. In late May 2003 COO Hugh Grant was named president and CEO, with AtLee returning to chair the board of directors. Less than a month later, Grant initiated a reorganization of Monsanto, placing focus on growing the company's seed business and redefining its goals and strategies for public acceptance of biotechnology. The company elected Grant chairman at its annual meeting in October of that year, with AtLee staying on the board as a director.

## EXECUTIVES

**Chairman, President, and CEO:** Hugh Grant, age 48, $3,045,500 pay
**EVP and CFO:** Terrell K. (Terry) Crews, age 51, $1,105,269 pay
**EVP and CTO:** Robert T. (Robb) Fraley, age 53, $1,173,673 pay
**EVP, Commercial Acceptance:** Gerald A. Steiner, age 46
**EVP, International Commercial:** Brett D. Begemann, age 45
**EVP, Manufacturing:** Mark J. Leidy, age 50
**EVP, North America Commercial:** Carl M. Casale, age 45, $1,090,192 pay
**SVP, Corporate Strategy:** Cheryl P. Morley, age 52
**SVP, Human Resources:** Steven C. Mizell, age 46
**SVP, Secretary, and General Counsel:** David F. Snively, age 52
**VP and Chief of Staff:** Janet M. Holloway, age 52
**VP and Controller:** Richard B. Clark, age 54
**VP and Treasurer:** Robert A. Paley, age 58
**VP, Investor Relations:** Scarlett Lee Foster, age 49
**President, American Seeds:** Dennis M. Plummer
**President, Seminis:** Kerry Preete
**President and Managing Director, Monsanto Brazil:** Richard A. (Rick) Greubel Jr., age 43
**Special Assistant and Counsel to the CEO:** Charles W. Burson, age 61
**Auditors:** Deloitte & Touche LLP

## LOCATIONS

**HQ:** Monsanto Company
800 N. Lindbergh Blvd., St. Louis, MO 63167
**Phone:** 314-694-1000 **Fax:** 314-694-8394
**Web:** www.monsanto.com

Monsanto Company has operations in more than 50 countries, including major chemical manufacturing facilities in Argentina, Belgium, Brazil, and the US.

**2006 Sales**

| | $ mil. | % of total |
|---|---|---|
| US | 4,201 | 57 |
| Latin America | 1,281 | 17 |
| Europe/Africa | 1,061 | 15 |
| Asia/Pacific | 528 | 7 |
| Canada | 273 | 4 |
| **Total** | **7,344** | **100** |

## PRODUCTS/OPERATIONS

**2006 Sales**

| | $ mil. | % of total |
|---|---|---|
| Seeds & Genomics | | |
| Corn seed and traits | 1,793 | 24 |
| Soybean seed & traits | 960 | 13 |
| Vegetable & fruit seed | 569 | 8 |
| Other | 706 | 10 |
| Agricultural Productivity | | |
| Roundup & other herbicides | 2,262 | 31 |
| Other | 1,054 | 14 |
| **Total** | **7,344** | **100** |

### Selected Products

Seeds (modified to be drought, insect, and herbicide resistant; Roundup Ready)
Herbicides (designed to be used in conjunction with its seeds; Roundup)

### Selected Brand/Trade Names

Agroceres (seeds)
Apyros (sulfosulfuron herbicide)
Asgrow (seeds)
Bollgard (trait in cotton)
Degree (acetanilide-based herbicide)
DEKALB (seeds)
Guardian (acetanilide-based herbicide)
Harness (acetanilide-based herbicide)
Hartz (seeds)
Holden's (seeds)
Lasso (acetanilide-based herbicide)
Leader (sulfosulfuron herbicide)
Machete (butachlor herbicide)
Manage (halosulfuron herbicide)
Maverick (sulfosulfuron herbicide)
Monitor (sulfosulfuron herbicide)
Monsoy (seeds)
Outrider (sulfosulfuron herbicide)
PBI (seeds)
Permit (halosulfuron herbicide)
Posilac (bovine somatotropin)
Roundup
Roundup DryPosilac
Roundup Ready (trait in soybeans, canola, cotton, and corn)
Roundup Ultra
Sempra (halosulfuron herbicide)
Sundance (sulfosulfuron herbicide)
YieldGard (Corn Borer trait in corn)

## COMPETITORS

BASF AG
Bayer CropScience
Dow AgroSciences
DuPont Agriculture & Nutrition
FMC
Nippon Soda
Scotts Miracle-Gro
Syngenta

## HISTORICAL FINANCIALS

Company Type: Public

**Income Statement** FYE: August 31

| | REVENUE ($ mil.) | NET INCOME ($ mil.) | NET PROFIT MARGIN | EMPLOYEES |
|---|---|---|---|---|
| **8/06** | 7,344 | 689 | 9.4% | 17,500 |
| **8/05** | 6,294 | 255 | 4.1% | 16,500 |
| **8/04** | 5,457 | 267 | 4.9% | 12,600 |
| **8/03*** | 3,373 | (23) | — | 13,200 |
| **12/02** | 4,673 | (1,693) | — | 13,700 |
| **Annual Growth** | 12.0% | — | — | 6.3% |

*Fiscal year change

**2006 Year-End Financials**

Debt ratio: 25.1%
Return on equity: 11.4%
Cash ($ mil.): 1,482
Current ratio: 2.40
Long-term debt ($ mil.): 1,639
No. of shares (mil.): 543
Dividends
Yield: 0.8%
Payout: 30.4%
Market value ($ mil.): 25,768

**Stock History** NYSE: MON

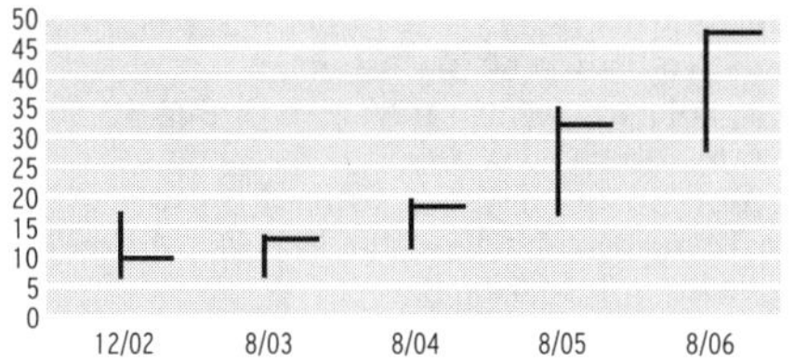

| | STOCK PRICE ($) FY Close | P/E High | P/E Low | PER SHARE ($) Earnings | Dividends | Book Value |
|---|---|---|---|---|---|---|
| **8/06** | 47.44 | 38 | 22 | 1.25 | 0.38 | 12.01 |
| **8/05** | 31.92 | 74 | 36 | 0.47 | 0.33 | 20.93 |
| **8/04** | 18.30 | 39 | 23 | 0.50 | 0.27 | 19.89 |
| **8/03*** | 12.85 | — | — | (0.05) | 0.25 | 19.63 |
| **12/02** | 9.63 | — | — | (3.22) | 0.24 | 19.82 |
| **Annual Growth** | 49.0% | — | — | — | 12.2% | (11.8%) |

*Fiscal year change

# Morgan Stanley

One of the world's top investment banks, Morgan Stanley serves up a whole smorgasbord of financial services. The company operates through several primary business segments, comprising institutional securities (capital raising, corporate lending, financial advisory services for corporate and institutional investors); global wealth management group (brokerage and investment advisory services, and financial planning for individual investors and small-to-medium businesses); and asset management (asset management services in alternative investments, equity, fixed income). It also has in-house private equity operations.

Morgan Stanley had been one of the largest credit card operators through Discover Financial Services. However, it spun off those operations in 2007, despite the credit card division posting some of its best results in recent years. Discover was the last remnant of the company's merger with the venerable Dean Witter at the end of the previous century.

In 2006 the firm agreed to pay a $15 million fine to settle charges that it did not produce documents and was uncooperative during investigations performed by the Securities and Exchange Commission (SEC). Also that year it sold its aircraft leasing business to UK-based Terra Firma Capital Partners for some $2.5 billion.

Morgan Stanley signed a definitive agreement that year to acquire TransMontaigne, a Denver-based oil and gas transportation company, and Heidmar Group, a Connecticut-based marine transportation and logistics firm (it sold Heidmar's lightering business in 2007). Later in 2006 the company acquired Saxon Capital, a Virginia-based residential mortgage lender, for a reported $706 million.

Taking part in one of the largest hotel chain sales in recent history, Morgan Stanley Real Estate Fund has agreed to purchase eight luxury resorts from CNL Hotels & Resorts for a reported $4.2 billion (Ashford Properties is set to acquire the remaining 51 properties from CNL).

It is also buying the San Francisco property portfolio of Equity Office Properties after the latter's acquisition by Blackstone.

It sold UK wealth manager Quilter to Citigroup at the end of 2006.

Morgan Stanley has teamed up with Apax Partners Worldwide to buy insurance brokerage Hub International.

## HISTORY

The San Francisco brokerage founded by Dean Witter in 1924 remained regional for 40 years, serving wealthy customers.

In 1977 the firm merged with Reynolds Securities, another regional retail brokerage started by Richard Reynolds Jr., the son of the founder of Reynolds Metals (now part of Alcoa) and grandnephew of the founder of R.J. Reynolds Tobacco. The new company, Dean Witter Reynolds, became the #2 US brokerage after Merrill Lynch and one of the top 10 US underwriters.

Dean Witter needed capital in the early 1980s and sold itself to Sears, which hoped to turn it into a financial Allstate. Sears put in a retail-oriented management team and tried to shoehorn Dean Witter into in-store brokerages. Sears' indifference to the investment side hobbled operations.

The Discover card, introduced by Sears and Dean Witter in 1986, was a hit, but by the late 1980s it was obvious Sears would never be a financial giant. The retailer spun off Allstate Insurance and the newly renamed Dean Witter, Discover in 1993. In 1997, prior to merging with Morgan Stanley, the firm bought Internet broker Lombard Brokerage.

In 1934 the Glass-Steagall Act required the J. P. Morgan bank (now part of JPMorgan Chase & Co.) to sell its securities-related activities. The next year Henry Morgan, Harold Stanley, and others established Morgan Stanley as an investment bank. Capitalizing on old ties to major corporations, the firm handled $1 billion in issues its first year. By 1941, when it joined the NYSE, it had managed 25% of all bond issues underwritten since Glass-Steagall took effect.

In the 1950s Morgan Stanley was known for handling large issues alone. Clients included General Motors, U.S. Steel, General Electric, and DuPont.

The firm avoided the merger wave of the 1960s, but in the early 1970s it formed Wall Street's first mergers and acquisitions (M&A) department. In 1974 Morgan Stanley handled its first hostile takeover, International Nickel's (now Inco) buy of ESB, the world's #1 battery maker.

Morgan Stanley went public in 1986. It escaped the carnage of the 1987 crash, but a lawsuit arising from investor dissatisfaction with its M&A and LBO activities during that period lasted well into the 1990s. By 1994 it was talking to possible merger mates, including Dean Witter, and finally merged with Dean Witter, Discover in 1998, creating Morgan Stanley Dean Witter & Co. The firm dropped the public use of "Dean Witter" in 2001 for promotional purposes and then dropped it completely in June 2002.

Hoping to capitalize on deregulations and privatizations in Europe, as well as the rise of the individual investor, Morgan Stanley acquired UK-based private bank Quilter & Co. in 2001.

Amazingly, all but six of the firm's 3,700 World Trade Center employees survived the September 11, 2001, terrorist attack on the towers.

When regulatory scrutiny fell on the mutual fund industry, Morgan Stanley was charged with failing to adequately disclose the incentives its brokers and managers received for selling certain funds. In November 2003 the firm agreed to pay a $50 million fine and adopt a "plain English" approach to informing investors about its product fees and broker compensation.

In mid-2004 the firm agreed to pay $54 million to settle a sex discrimination lawsuit filed on behalf of more than 300 female employees who claimed they were denied promotions and salary raises.

Unhappy with the firm's performance, eight former Morgan Stanley executives (dubbed the Group of Eight) publicly called for the ouster of chairman and CEO Philip Purcell in 2005; Purcell was replaced by John Mack. That same year a jury ordered Morgan Stanley to pay more than $1.5 billion to Ronald Perelman, now the chairman of cosmetics giant Revlon. (Morgan Stanley in 2003 rejected an offer from Perelman to settle the dispute for $20 million.) Perelman contended that Morgan Stanley withheld knowledge of massive accounting fraud at appliance maker Sunbeam when he sold his camping gear firm, Coleman, to that company for some $1.5 billion in cash and stock in 1998; a Florida appeals court overturned the verdict in 2007.

## EXECUTIVES

**Chairman and CEO:** John J. Mack, age 62, $800,000 pay
**Vice Chairman:** David W. Heleniak, age 60
**Co-President:** Zoe Cruz, age 52, $10,825,000 pay
**Co-President:** Robert (Bob) Scully, age 57, $7,162,500 pay
**EVP and CFO:** David H. Sidwell, age 53
**EVP, Chief Administrative Officer, and Secretary:** Thomas R. (Tom) Nides, age 45
**SVP Finance and Controller:** Alexander C. Frank
**VP and Counsel:** Ronald T. Carman
**VP and Global Head of Corporate Services and Security:** Jessica Gorman Taylor
**VP and Global Head of Human Resources:** Karen C. Jamesley
**Chief Compliance Officer:** Stuart Breslow
**Chief Legal Officer:** Gary G. Lynch, age 56
**Chief Risk Officer:** Thomas V. Daula, age 54
**Global Controller and Principal Accounting Officer:** Paul C. Wirth, age 47
**Head of Global Operations and Technology:** Eileen K. Murray, age 48
**Global Head of Global Mergers and Acquisitions:** Paul J. Taubman
**Head of Investment Banking:** Walid Chammah, age 51
**Co-Head of Institutional Sales and Trading and Head of Worldwide Fixed Income:** Neal A. Shear, age 51, $12,445,000 pay
**Co-Head of Institutional Sales and Trading:** Jerker M. Johansson, age 51
**Chairman, Morgan Stanley International:** Jonathan Chenevix-Trench, age 45
**Managing Director and Vice Chairman, Institutional Securities:** Christopher R. (Chris) Carter, age 57
**Chairman and CEO, Discover Financial Services:** David W. Nelms, age 44
**Co-Chairman, Global Mergers and Acquisitions:** Steve Munger
**Co-Chairman, Global Mergers and Acquisitions:** Simon Robey, age 45
**Auditors:** Deloitte & Touche LLP

## LOCATIONS

**HQ:** Morgan Stanley
1585 Broadway, New York, NY 10036
**Phone:** 212-761-4000 **Fax:** 212-762-8131
**Web:** www.morganstanley.com

Morgan Stanley has more than 600 offices in about 30 countries.

## PRODUCTS/OPERATIONS

**2006 Sales**

| | $ mil. | % of total |
|---|---|---|
| Interest & dividends | 45,216 | 59 |
| Principal transactions | | |
| Trading | 11,738 | 15 |
| Investments | 1,669 | 2 |
| Asset management, distribution & administration fees | 5,288 | 7 |
| Investment banking | 4,755 | 6 |
| Commissions | 3,810 | 5 |
| Servicing & securitization income | 2,338 | 3 |
| Merchant, cardmember & other fees | 1,167 | 2 |
| Other | 570 | 1 |
| **Total** | **76,551** | **100** |

## COMPETITORS

A.G. Edwards
Bear Stearns
Brown Brothers Harriman
Charles Schwab
CIBC
Citigroup
Citigroup Global Markets
Deutsche Bank
FMR
Franklin Resources
Goldman Sachs
JPMorgan Chase
Lehman Brothers
Marsh & McLennan
Merrill Lynch
MF Global
Nomura Securities
Oppenheimer Holdings
Raymond James Financial
State Street
T. Rowe Price
TD Bank
UBS
Wachovia Capital Markets

## HISTORICAL FINANCIALS

Company Type: Public

**Income Statement** FYE: November 30

| | REVENUE ($ mil.) | NET INCOME ($ mil.) | NET PROFIT MARGIN | EMPLOYEES |
|---|---|---|---|---|
| 11/06 | 76,551 | 7,472 | 9.8% | 55,310 |
| 11/05 | 52,081 | 4,939 | 9.5% | 53,218 |
| 11/04 | 39,549 | 4,486 | 11.3% | 53,284 |
| 11/03 | 34,933 | 3,787 | 10.8% | 51,196 |
| 11/02 | 32,450 | 2,988 | 9.2% | 55,726 |
| Annual Growth | 23.9% | 25.8% | — | (0.2%) |

**2006 Year-End Financials**

Debt ratio: 1,183.1%
Return on equity: 23.6%
Cash ($ mil.): 225,037
Current ratio: —
Long-term debt ($ mil.): 405,379
No. of shares (mil.): 1,049
Dividends
Yield: 1.7%
Payout: 15.3%
Market value ($ mil.): 67,559

**Stock History** NYSE: MS

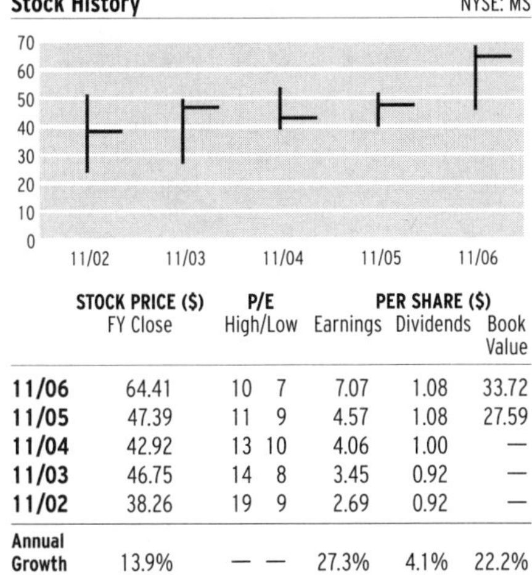


| | STOCK PRICE ($) FY Close | P/E High/Low | | PER SHARE ($) Earnings | Dividends | Book Value |
|---|---|---|---|---|---|---|
| **11/06** | 64.41 | 10 | 7 | 7.07 | 1.08 | 33.72 |
| **11/05** | 47.39 | 11 | 9 | 4.57 | 1.08 | 27.59 |
| **11/04** | 42.92 | 13 | 10 | 4.06 | 1.00 | — |
| **11/03** | 46.75 | 14 | 8 | 3.45 | 0.92 | — |
| **11/02** | 38.26 | 19 | 9 | 2.69 | 0.92 | — |
| **Annual Growth** | 13.9% | — | — | 27.3% | 4.1% | 22.2% |

# Motorola, Inc.

Motorola is continuing its drive down the information superhighway, but with a slimmer load and a new driver at the wheel. The company's reorganization has continued after the highly publicized spin-off of its semiconductor unit. Its remaining operations have been focused on three business segments: Enterprise mobility solutions; mobile devices; and home and networks mobility. Motorola is the #2 manufacturer of wireless handsets after global leader Nokia. The company also is a leading supplier of such wireless infrastructure equipment as cellular transmission base stations, amplifiers, and servers.

The company generates nearly 70% of sales through the manufacture and sales of wireless handsets and related products. Its largest customers include wireless carriers Sprint Nextel, AT&T Mobility (formerly Cingular), China Mobile, América Móvil, and T-Mobile. A leading supplier of cell phones to the burgeoning markets of China and Mexico, the company does about two-thirds of its business outside the US. Its largest international markets are Brazil, China, Germany, Mexico, and the UK.

Motorola originated the clamshell handset and has set its hopes on its new innovative RAZR and PEBL models to keep its place among the market leaders. It also has released SLVR, a new candy bar-type phone.

Motorola is leading in the drive to create mobile communications that cross multiple technologies such as cellular, passive optical networks (PONs), and wireless broadband. The company also is an industry leader in popular push-to-talk over cellular (PoC) technology.

In an effort to expand its product lines, Motorola purchased Netopia, a maker of broadband routers and software based on DSL technology, in 2007 for $208 million. Also the same year, Motorola bought Symbol Technologies, a manufacturer of bar-code scanner and other devices, for about $3.9 billion; the Symbol purchase formed the core of Motorola's enterprise mobility business, and aiming to boost its home video and network technology business, Motorola paid $140 million to purchase Terayon Communication Systems in 2007.

Motorola's restructuring has included selling some IT services units, shifting some production to contractors, and using extensive layoffs to reduce costs. The company also sold its automotive products unit, which manufactured telematics products used for vehicle safety and navigation, to German auto supplier Continental, in a 2006 deal valued at about $1 billion. The auto unit also made sensors used in power doors and windows, brake systems, and steering. The unit employed 5,000 people and contributed more than $1.6 billion in annual sales. It additionally announced it would axe up to 7,500 jobs by the end of 2008 to help realize cost savings.

Activist investor Carl Icahn began buying up Motorola shares in 2007 in a failed attempt to obtain a seat on the company's board of directors. Icahn had indicated his intent to help increase Motorola's debt and return cash to investors in an effort to counter weakened sales and profits.

## HISTORY

Born entrepreneur Paul Galvin started his first business as a popcorn vendor when he was 13. In 1928, at age 33, he founded Galvin Manufacturing in Chicago to make battery eliminators, so early radios could run on household current instead of batteries. The following year Galvin began making car radio receivers and trying to develop a mobile radio for the police. In 1940 the company developed the first handheld two-way radio for the US Army.

In 1947 Galvin renamed the company Motorola, after its car radios. In the late 1950s Motorola started making integrated circuits and microprocessors, stepping outside its auto industry mainstay. Galvin died in 1959, and his son Robert became CEO. The company's purchase that year of a hospital communications systems maker led it to produce some of the first pagers.

Motorola began to change focus in the 1970s. The company invested in the data communications hardware market by acquiring Codex (1977) and Universal Data Systems (1978). In 1977 Motorola began developing its first cellular phone system. By 1985 sales of the company's cellular systems had taken off. In 1987 Motorola made its last car radio.

In 1990 Motorola organized the 66-satellite Iridium communication system (which went on line in 1998). The company began developing the PowerPC chip with Apple and IBM in 1991. In 1996 China adopted Motorola's technology as its national paging standard.

The founder's grandson, Christopher Galvin, took over as CEO in 1997 on the heels of a major drop in profits — the result of increasing competition in the cellular phone market and a downturn in semiconductor sales. Chris, who had sold police radios for the company as a university student, began a full-scale restructuring that included the sale of noncore assets and the layoffs of 15,000 employees.

The next year Motorola recorded a $2 billion restructuring charge that contributed to a loss. The vestiges of the PowerPC alliance evaporated that year when Motorola and IBM announced plans to work separately on the technology.

In 2000 Motorola acquired General Instrument in a deal valued at $17 billion. That spring Iridium went out of business, leaving Motorola to oversee the de-orbiting and destruction of its satellites. Also that year Motorola agreed to outsource about 15% of its manufacturing to Flextronics. As part of the $30 billion deal (the largest outsourcing contract to date), Motorola took a small stake in Flextronics.

In early 2001 Motorola, led by Chris Galvin, cut more than 30,000 jobs amid slow sales of semiconductors and mobile phones. Motorola also cut back on its manufacturing outsourcing and sold its stake in Flextronics back to that company; it also sold its North American IT operations.

Faced with continuing weak sales, the company continued to make layoffs through 2002.

Motorola acquired the shares of network equipment manufacturer Next Level Communications that it did not already own in 2003. After disagreeing with the board of directors about Motorola's future in late 2003, Chris Galvin retired as chairman and CEO and Ed Zander, the former head of Sun Microsystems, took over in 2004 becoming the first person from outside the Galvin family to lead the company.

Also in 2004 Motorola handed off its stake in StarCore when it spun off its semiconductor operations as Freescale Semiconductor, a publicly traded company.

## EXECUTIVES

**Chairman and CEO:** Edward J. (Ed) Zander, age 60, $4,500,000 pay
**President, COO, and Director:** Gregory Q. (Greg) Brown, age 46, $1,418,981 pay
**EVP; President, Connected Home Solutions:** Daniel M. (Dan) Moloney, age 47
**EVP and CTO:** Padmasree Warrior, age 45
**EVP and Chief Marketing Officer:** Kenneth C. (Casey) Keller Jr., age 45
**EVP and Chief Strategy Officer:** Richard N. (Rich) Nottenburg, age 52
**EVP, General Counsel, and Secretary:** A. Peter Lawson, age 60
**EVP, Human Resources:** Ruth A. Fattori, age 54
**SVP; Chairman and General Manager, Motorola Israel:** Elisha Yanay
**EVP and CIO:** Patricia B. (Patty) Morrison, age 47
**SVP Finance and Treasurer:** Steven J. (Steve) Strobel, age 49
**SVP Global Governance:** Patrick J. (Pat) Canavan
**SVP and Director, Investor Relations:** Edward (Ed) Gams
**VP; Chairman and President, Motorola Electronics Taiwan; General Manager, Motorola University, Asia Pacific:** Tom Sun
**VP; President and Representative Director, Motorola Korea:** Jae Ha Park
**VP; President, Motorola Japan:** Takashi Kitagawa
**VP; President, Motorola Latin America North:** Omar E. Villarreal
**VP and Director, Corporate Development and Strategic Transactions:** Donald F. (Don) McLellan
**VP and Director, Middle East and Africa Region:** Hassan Alex Tavakoli
**VP, Equity Investments:** Warren Holtsberg
**VP, Marketing:** George Neill
**Auditors:** KPMG LLP

## LOCATIONS

**HQ:** Motorola, Inc.
1303 E. Algonquin Rd., Schaumburg, IL 60196
**Phone:** 847-576-5000 **Fax:** 847-576-5372
**Web:** www.motorola.com

Motorola has manufacturing operations and sales offices in more than 40 countries.

**2006 Sales**

| | % of total |
|---|---|
| US | 44 |
| China | 11 |
| UK | 3 |
| Germany | 2 |
| Israel | 2 |
| Other nations | 38 |
| **Total** | **100** |

## PRODUCTS/OPERATIONS

### 2006 Sales

| | % of total |
|---|---|
| Mobile devices | 66 |
| Networks & enterprise | 26 |
| Connected home solutions | 8 |
| **Total** | **100** |

### Business Segments

Enterprise Mobility (radio, voice, data communications products for businesses)
Home and Networks Mobility (video and Internet products, systems for consumers and carriers)
Mobile Devices (wireless handsets)

## COMPETITORS

Alcatel-Lucent
ARRIS
BenQ (IT)
C-COR
Cisco Systems
Delphi
DENSO
EADS
Ericsson
Huawei Technologies
Intermec
Kenwood
LG Group
M/A-Com
NEC
Nokia
Nortel Networks
Robert Bosch
Samsung Group
Scientific-Atlanta
Siemens VDO Automotive
Sony Ericsson Mobile
Visteon
ZTE

## HISTORICAL FINANCIALS

Company Type: Public

### Income Statement

FYE: December 31

| | REVENUE ($ mil.) | NET INCOME ($ mil.) | NET PROFIT MARGIN | EMPLOYEES |
|---|---|---|---|---|
| **12/06** | 42,879 | 3,661 | 8.5% | 66,000 |
| **12/05** | 36,843 | 4,578 | 12.4% | 69,000 |
| **12/04** | 31,323 | 1,532 | 4.9% | 68,000 |
| **12/03** | 27,058 | 893 | 3.3% | 88,000 |
| **12/02** | 26,679 | (2,485) | — | 97,000 |
| **Annual Growth** | 12.6% | — | — | (9.2%) |

### 2006 Year-End Financials

Debt ratio: 15.8%
Return on equity: 21.7%
Cash ($ mil.): 15,640
Current ratio: 2.01
Long-term debt ($ mil.): 2,704
No. of shares (mil.): 2,397
Dividends
Yield: 0.9%
Payout: 13.0%
Market value ($ mil.): 49,291

### Stock History

NYSE: MOT

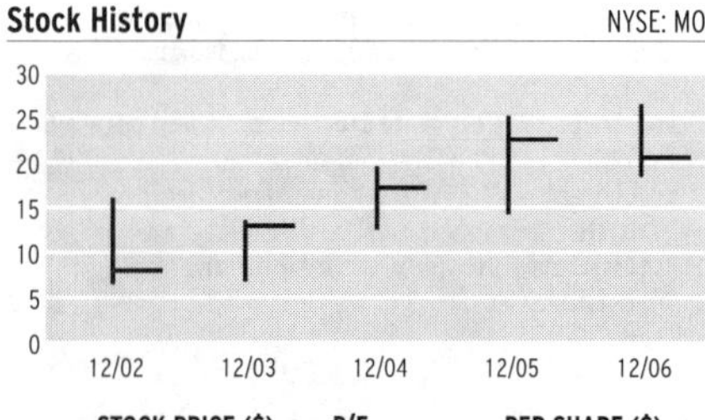


| | STOCK PRICE ($) FY Close | P/E High | P/E Low | PER SHARE ($) Earnings | Dividends | Book Value |
|---|---|---|---|---|---|---|
| **12/06** | 20.56 | 18 | 13 | 1.46 | 0.19 | 7.15 |
| **12/05** | 22.59 | 14 | 8 | 1.81 | 0.16 | 6.67 |
| **12/04** | 17.20 | 30 | 20 | 0.64 | 0.20 | 5.45 |
| **12/03** | 12.95 | 35 | 18 | 0.38 | 0.16 | 5.43 |
| **12/02** | 8.00 | — | — | (1.09) | 0.16 | 4.85 |
| **Annual Growth** | 26.6% | — | — | — | 4.4% | 10.2% |

# Movie Gallery

Movie Gallery likes movie fans who wait for the video. The company, through its Movie Gallery, Hollywood Video, and Game Crazy chains, is the nation's #2 video and game rental company behind Blockbuster. Movie Gallery owns or franchises more than 4,600 rental stores in all 50 states and Canada. Its stores rent and sell up to 15,000 movie titles (VHS and DVD) and 1,500 video games (Nintendo, Sega, and Sony). They also sell blank cassettes, VCR cleaning equipment, movie memorabilia, and concession items. In addition, Movie Gallery sells videos and merchandise on the Internet. The company bought Hollywood Entertainment for $1.2 billion in 2005.

In the small towns and suburbs where Movie Gallery locations are primarily positioned, it competes with single-store or small-chain retailers. Through primarily aggressive acquisitions of both national chains and mom-and-pop video stores, the firm has added more than 4,500 locations since 1994.

After Blockbuster made an offer to purchase Hollywood Entertainment, Movie Gallery in 2005 swooped in and made its own deal with Hollywood in an effort to keep Blockbuster from becoming even more dominant in the industry. After completing the purchase later that year, Hollywood became a subsidiary of Movie Gallery and retains its own separate identity from its parent. (The Movie Gallery brand serves as the company's eastern US brand, while Hollywood serves the western US.) Blockbuster tried to put the kibosh on the deal when it launched a $1.3 billion hostile bid for Hollywood anyway, only to eventually abandon the effort when it became clear they could not gain government approval for the acquisition.

In early 2005, Movie Gallery also bought VHQ Entertainment, which operated more than 60 video stores in Canada. The transaction allowed Movie Gallery to further cement its presence in that region, as well as gain control over VHQ's significant online video rental business.

Movie Gallery has been looking in the mirror in recent years, in an effort to foresee softer sales of its products and react quickly. It is considering a restructuring in 2007, after logging dips in sales. The company also closed its nine stores in Mexico in 2006 because they were underperforming.

Movie Gallery has decided to look for growth through alternative delivery methods, rather than new store growth. As part of this new path, the company acquired MovieBeam, a video on-demand service that delivers movies to homes that have a special set-top box, in 2007. The service is available in more than 30 markets in the US.

Chairman and CEO J. T. Malugen owns about 11% of Movie Gallery.

## HISTORY

J. T. Malugen and Harrison Parrish founded Movie Gallery of Alabama (M.G.A.) in 1985 as a sub-franchisor of the Movie Gallery name and expanded the video store chain throughout Alabama, Georgia, and Florida. Three years later Malugen and Parrish got out of franchising and put M.G.A.'s energy into company-owned operations. In 1992 M.G.A. acquired rights to the Movie Gallery name. The company went public in 1994.

Also in 1994 Movie Gallery began to buy up video stores, mostly keeping to its strategy of entering small towns where it had little competition. It then teamed with Bruno's supermarket chain to operate in-store video rental departments. The firm grew steadily beyond its roots in the Deep South to open stores in Texas, Ohio, and Indiana.

In 1996 Movie Gallery acquired the New England Home Vision chain for $32 million in stock. That year the company stumbled: Competition from the Summer Olympics and delays in Nintendo's new N64 platform put a pause in profits. Movie Gallery also struggled to assimilate its new acquisitions (the company had grown from 97 stores to 863 in two-and-a-half years). As a result, in 1997 the company closed stores and slowed store openings.

Fast-forward to 1998: The company took a $44 million charge when it changed its accounting procedures for amortizing videos. In mid-1999 it purchased 88 video specialty stores from BlowOut Entertainment, most of which operate inside Wal-Mart locations. Later in 1999 Movie Gallery began selling merchandise through its Web site. In 2000 the company opened 110 new stores.

In late 2001 Movie Gallery bought the beleaguered Video Update chain of some 300 stores in the US and Canada. As part of Video Update's bankruptcy reorganization, it became a subsidiary of Movie Gallery. In early 2002 Parrish resigned as president and Malugen (already chairman and CEO) assumed the role. Movie Gallery acquired Video Vault (13 locations in Kentucky and Indiana) and Superior Video (25 locations in Canada) to focus on its core rural and small-town markets.

In 2003, with the purchase of a four-store chain in North Dakota, Movie Gallery had locations in every state. The company expanded its operations significantly in 2005 when it bought larger rival Hollywood Entertainment for $1.2 billion after a bruising bidding war with Blockbuster. The company closed its stores in Mexico in 2006.

## EXECUTIVES

**Chairman, President, and CEO, Movie Gallery and Hollywood Entertainment:** Joe Thomas (J.T.) Malugen, age 55, $1,269,231 pay
**Vice Chairman and SVP Concessions:** H. Harrison Parrish, age 58
**President, Retail Operations:** Jeffrey S. Stubbs, age 44
**EVP and Chief Development Officer:** Keith A. Cousins, age 38
**EVP and Chief Merchandising Officer:** Mark S. (Bo) Loyd, age 51, $350,000 pay
**EVP, Secretary, General Counsel, and Chief Compliance Officer:** S. Page Todd, age 45
**SVP and Chief Marketing Officer:** Theodore L. (Ted) Innes
**EVP and CFO:** Thomas D. Johnson Jr., age 43
**SVP Management Information Systems and CIO:** Richard R. Langford
**SVP Support Operations:** Kenneth C. Motzenbecker
**SVP and Treasurer:** Michelle K. Lewis
**VP Concessions:** Gary Hay
**Auditors:** Ernst & Young LLP

## LOCATIONS

**HQ:** Movie Gallery, Inc.
900 W. Main St., Dothan, AL 36301
**Phone:** 334-677-2108 **Fax:** 334-794-4688
**Web:** www.moviegallery.com

## 2006 Sales

| | $ mil. | % of total |
|---|---|---|
| US | 2,445.7 | 95 |
| Canada | 94.8 | 4 |
| Mexico | 1.4 | 1 |
| **Total** | **2,541.9** | **100** |

## 2006 US Locations

| | No. |
|---|---|
| Texas | 361 |
| California | 360 |
| Florida | 221 |
| Ohio | 205 |
| Alabama | 184 |
| North Carolina | 171 |
| Georgia | 167 |
| Pennsylvania | 165 |
| Virginia | 150 |
| Missouri | 135 |
| New York | 131 |
| Michigan | 122 |
| Indiana | 120 |
| Illinois | 119 |
| Washington | 114 |
| Tennessee | 112 |
| South Carolina | 95 |
| Arizona | 90 |
| Minnesota | 89 |
| Arkansas | 83 |
| Kentucky | 83 |
| Mississippi | 76 |
| Oregon | 75 |
| Oklahoma | 74 |
| Wisconsin | 70 |
| Massachusetts | 68 |
| Colorado | 59 |
| Maryland | 57 |
| Maine | 53 |
| Louisiana | 51 |
| Utah | 51 |
| Iowa | 48 |
| Kansas | 44 |
| Other states | 365 |
| **Total** | **4,368** |

## 2006 Canadian Locations

| | No. |
|---|---|
| Alberta | 104 |
| British Columbia | 67 |
| Ontario | 48 |
| Saskatchewan | 21 |
| Nova Scotia | 13 |
| Manitoba | 7 |
| New Brunswick | 5 |
| Newfoundland | 5 |
| Prince Edward Island | 2 |
| Yukon Territory | 2 |
| **Total** | **274** |

# PRODUCTS/OPERATIONS

## 2006 Sales

| | $ mil. | % of total |
|---|---|---|
| Rentals | 2,030.2 | 80 |
| Product sales | 511.7 | 20 |
| **Total** | **2,541.9** | **100** |

# COMPETITORS

Albertsons
Amazon.com
barnesandnoble.com
Best Buy
Blockbuster
Borders
Buy.com
Circuit City
Comcast Cable
Cox Communications
Hastings Entertainment
iN DEMAND
Kroger
Netflix
Redbox
Starz Entertainment
Target
Time Warner Cable
Tower Records
Trans World Entertainment
Wal-Mart

# HISTORICAL FINANCIALS

Company Type: Public

## Income Statement

FYE: First Sunday following December 30

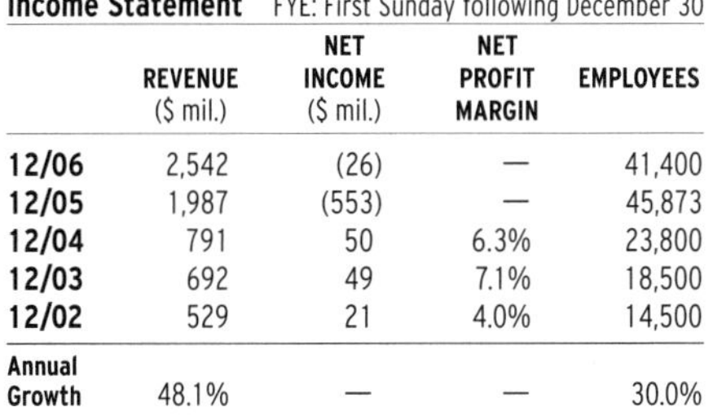

| | REVENUE ($ mil.) | NET INCOME ($ mil.) | NET PROFIT MARGIN | EMPLOYEES |
|---|---|---|---|---|
| **12/06** | 2,542 | (26) | — | 41,400 |
| **12/05** | 1,987 | (553) | — | 45,873 |
| **12/04** | 791 | 50 | 6.3% | 23,800 |
| **12/03** | 692 | 49 | 7.1% | 18,500 |
| **12/02** | 529 | 21 | 4.0% | 14,500 |
| **Annual Growth** | 48.1% | — | — | 30.0% |

## 2006 Year-End Financials

Debt ratio: —
Return on equity: —
Cash ($ mil.): 33
Current ratio: 0.89
Long-term debt ($ mil.): 1,088
No. of shares (mil.): 32
Dividends
Yield: —
Payout: —
Market value ($ mil.): 112

## Stock History

NASDAQ (GM): MOVI

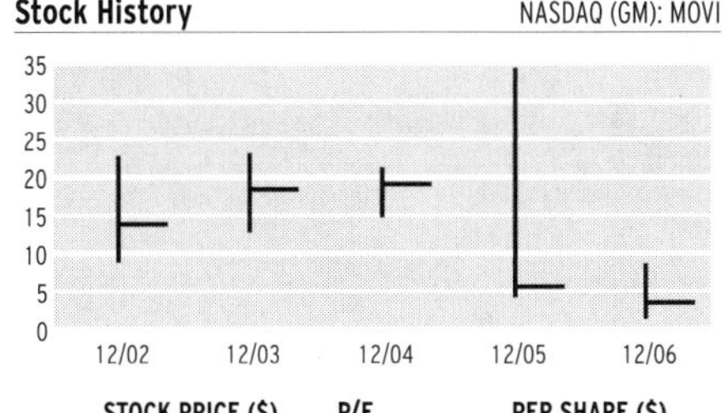


| | STOCK PRICE ($) FY Close | P/E High/Low | | PER SHARE ($) Earnings | Dividends | Book Value |
|---|---|---|---|---|---|---|
| **12/06** | 3.52 | — | — | (0.81) | — | (7.43) |
| **12/05** | 5.61 | — | — | (17.53) | 0.03 | (6.72) |
| **12/04** | 19.07 | 14 | 10 | 1.52 | 0.09 | 10.66 |
| **12/03** | 18.40 | 15 | 9 | 1.48 | — | 9.75 |
| **12/02** | 13.83 | 34 | 14 | 0.67 | — | 8.08 |
| **Annual Growth** | (29.0%) | — | — | — | (66.7%) | — |

# MPS Group

MPS Group believes in the power of the people. The company (formerly Modis Professional Services) is a staffing specialist, providing personnel to clients throughout Europe and North America. Its offerings also include IT consulting and design services, application development, and project support. MPS Group operates through three divisions: IT services (under the names Modis and Beeline), IT solutions (under the name Idea Integration), and professional services (using the Accounting Principals and Entegee names, among others). Striving to augment its presence in key geographic areas, the company bought Garelli Wong & Associates, a Chicago-centric recruiting and executive search business in mid-2006.

Other key subsidiaries include Soliant Health, a staffing company catering to hospitals and health care providers, and Special Counsel, a temporary and full time staffer of attorneys and legal professionals. In addition, Badenoch & Clark primarily represents MPS' European professional services operations.

MPS had planned to divide itself into three separate companies and take Idea Integration public but cancelled those plans because of the weak stock market. The company continues to focus on internal growth through cross-selling and other techniques, as well as growth through acquisitions. In late 2006, its Beeline unit acquired Integrated Performance Systems, a designer of training software and technology geared towards employers. The following year, Beeline bought Employer Services Corporation, a firm specializing in recruitment process outsourcing.

## HISTORY

MPS Group's origins begin with ATS Services, a temporary staffing service founded in 1978 by Delores Kesler (then Delores Pass) in Jacksonville, Florida. The creation of ATS coincided with a nationwide upswing in the temporary services industry, and by 1987 Kesler (who, after growing up poor on a poultry farm, worked her way through college on a tuition reimbursement program) saw ATS become one of the fastest-growing companies in the US.

As the temporary staffing industry evolved, Kesler recognized that consolidation with other firms would be necessary to stay competitive, and in 1992 she merged ATS with three smaller staffing companies (Abacus Services, BSI Temporaries, and Metrotech) to form AccuStaff. As with ATS, the launch of AccuStaff was perfectly timed — the US economy was climbing out of a recession and the temporary staffing industry was once again surging.

Between 1992 and 1994 the company focused on integrating the operations of the four units from which it was formed. It also began distinguishing itself from other staffing firms by offering specialized workers in fields such as information technology (IT) and engineering. In 1994 Kesler stepped down from her position as CEO, and Derek Dewan (a CPA with Coopers and Lybrand who had managed the 1992 merger to create AccuStaff) was appointed to replace her. The company went public later that year.

Following its IPO, AccuStaff wasted no time in building its reputation for aggressive growth. Its 10 acquisitions in 1995 were followed by 39 more in 1996. Its 1996 merger with Career Horizons was one of the largest acquisitions in the staffing industry and doubled AccuStaff's revenue. Kesler resigned as chairman in 1996, and Dewan assumed the chairmanship along with his position as CEO. That year AccuStaff formed its IT services unit.

AccuStaff's 28 acquisitions in 1997 gave the company an international profile. AccuStaff created MindSharp Learning Centers to offer training services, and its buy of Manchester Inc. extended the company's services into outplacement and career development.

In 1998 AccuStaff began narrowing its focus to IT consulting and professional services staffing. Following the sale of its Health Force health care division, the company placed its commercial staffing businesses into the newly formed subsidiary Strategix. AccuStaff had begun the process of taking the subsidiary public when Dutch staffing services firm Randstad approached with an offer. The company withdrew the planned IPO of Strategix and sold the subsidiary to Randstad; AccuStaff changed its name to Modis Professional Services (MPS) after the completion of the deal.

When its stock performance languished, MPS announced in 1999 that it would divide its staffing empire into separate companies. IT services subsidiary Modis, Inc., created e-services unit Idea Integration in early 2000, and MPS later filed to take Idea Integration public. The firm cancelled those plans, as well as plans for spinoff of Modis, Inc., later the same year.

In 2001 Modis announced a reorganization in which COO George Bajalia left the company (the COO job was eliminated) and shifted the focus of its future sales growth to Europe. That same year Timothy Payne succeeded Dewan as CEO. In addition, the company sold its Scientific Staffing unit to Kforce and acquired Kforce's legal staffing division.

The company began 2002 with a name change — the MPS acronym became its legal name. That same year MPS bought Elite Medical (now Soliant Health), a health care staffing firm. In 2003 the company sold its Manchester executive development and career transition unit to Right Management.

## EXECUTIVES

**Chairman:** Derek E. Dewan, age 52
**President, CEO, and Director:** Timothy D. Payne, age 48, $1,363,083 pay
**SVP, CFO, and Treasurer:** Robert P. Crouch, age 38, $681,541 pay
**SVP, Chief Legal Officer, and Secretary:** Gregory D. Holland, age 41, $383,976 pay
**SVP Corporate Development:** Tyra H. Tutor, age 38, $270,385 pay
**SVP and CIO; President, Beeline:** Richard L. White, age 48, $479,361 pay
**VP Human Resources:** Thomas M. Burke
**VP International Operations:** John W. Melbourne
**President, Badenoch & Clark:** Neil L. Wilson
**President, Entegee:** Robert L. Cecchini
**President, Idea Integration:** James D. (Jim) Albert
**President, Modis and Modis International:** John P. (Jack) Cullen
**President, Soliant Health:** David K. Alexander
**President, Special Counsel:** John L. Marshall III, age 38, $271,400 pay (partial-year salary)
**Auditors:** PricewaterhouseCoopers LLP

## LOCATIONS

**HQ:** MPS Group, Inc.
1 Independent Dr., Ste. 2500, Jacksonville, FL 32202
**Phone:** 904-360-2000 **Fax:** 904-360-2350
**Web:** www.mpsgroup.com

MPS Group operates from more than 200 offices in North America and Europe.

### 2006 Sales

| | $ mil. | % of total |
|---|---|---|
| North America | 1,178.2 | 63 |
| Europe | 698.4 | 37 |
| **Total** | **1,876.6** | **100** |

## PRODUCTS/OPERATIONS

### 2006 Sales

| | $ mil. | % of total |
|---|---|---|
| Professional services | 1,048.5 | 56 |
| IT services | 828.1 | 44 |
| **Total** | **1,876.6** | **100** |

### Selected Operations

IT services
- Beeline
- Modis, Inc.

IT solutions
- Idea Integration

Professional services
- Accounting Principals (accounting and finance staff)
- Badenoch & Clark (recruiting specialist)
- Entegee (engineering and technical staff)
- Gazelle Wong & Associates (recruiting specialist)
- Special Counsel (legal and document management staffing)

## COMPETITORS

Adecco
CDI
CHC
CIBER
COMSYS IT Partners
Hays
Keane
Kelly Services
Kforce
Robert Half
Spherion
TEKsystems

## HISTORICAL FINANCIALS

Company Type: Public

### Income Statement

FYE: December 31

| | REVENUE ($ mil.) | NET INCOME ($ mil.) | NET PROFIT MARGIN | EMPLOYEES |
|---|---|---|---|---|
| **12/06** | 1,877 | 75 | 4.0% | 20,100 |
| **12/05** | 1,685 | 60 | 3.5% | 19,400 |
| **12/04** | 1,427 | 35 | 2.5% | 18,900 |
| **12/03** | 1,096 | (1) | — | 14,700 |
| **12/02** | 1,155 | (566) | — | 13,000 |
| **Annual Growth** | 12.9% | — | — | 11.5% |

### 2006 Year-End Financials

Debt ratio: —
Return on equity: 8.2%
Cash ($ mil.): 173
Current ratio: 2.98
Long-term debt ($ mil.): —
No. of shares (mil.): 102
Dividends
Yield: —
Payout: —
Market value ($ mil.): 1,453

### Stock History

NYSE: MPS

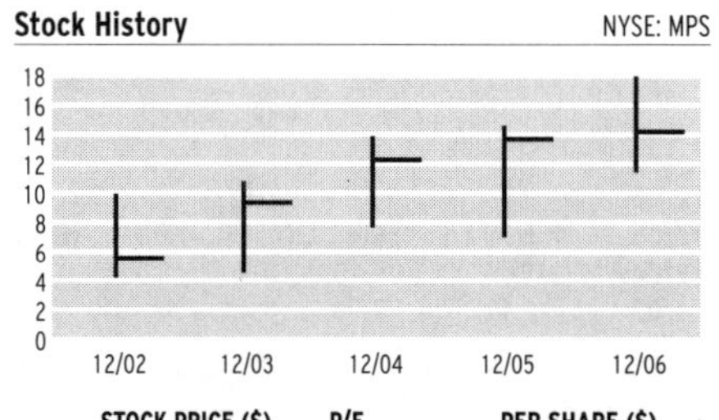

| | STOCK PRICE ($) FY Close | P/E High | P/E Low | PER SHARE ($) Earnings | Dividends | Book Value |
|---|---|---|---|---|---|---|
| **12/06** | 14.18 | 25 | 16 | 0.72 | — | 9.40 |
| **12/05** | 13.67 | 26 | 13 | 0.56 | — | 8.56 |
| **12/04** | 12.26 | 42 | 24 | 0.33 | — | 8.09 |
| **12/03** | 9.35 | — | — | (0.01) | — | 7.71 |
| **12/02** | 5.54 | — | — | (5.62) | — | 7.62 |
| **Annual Growth** | 26.5% | — | — | — | — | 5.4% |

# NACCO Industries

An unlikely combination of strip mines, toaster ovens, and forklifts propels NACCO Industries. This parent company's NACCO Materials Handling Group (NMHG) makes Hyster and Yale forklifts. NACCO's Housewares division, one of the US's largest full-line producers of small kitchen appliances, includes subsidiaries Hamilton Beach/Proctor-Silex and The Kitchen Collection. Another subsidiary, North American Coal (NACoal), mines lignite coal in the US and sells it to utilities. NACCO's chairman, president, and CEO, Alfred Rankin Jr., controls about 12% of the company.

Though founded as a coal distributing and mining company (called the North American Coal Corporation), that segment of NACCO is now its smallest. Today nearly three-quarters of NACCO's sales come from subsidiary NMHG. The US accounts for roughly 60% of company sales. NACCO's material-handling unit is expanding its international dealership network. Most of NMHG's business is wholesale, with just over 5% of its sales coming from retail.

In 2006 NACCO said it would spin off its Hamilton Beach/Proctor-Silex business to shareholders. Upon completion of the spin-off, Hamilton Beach/Proctor-Silex planned to merge with Applica. The newly created entity was to be named Hamilton Beach, Inc., and Applica shareholders would have owned 25% of it. A wrinkle formed in the Applica merger plan late in 2006 when Harbinger Capital Partners made a competing offer. Applica then called off talks with NACCO which prompted NACCO to file suit against Applica. NACCO later upped its original bid of $175 million to more than $187 million. Harbinger is Applica's largest shareholder with about a 40% stake.

Also in 2006, NACCO's The Kitchen Collection subsidiary acquired Le Gourmet Chef, Inc., a kitchen goods retailer. Le Gourmet Chef operates nearly 80 retail stores across the US.

Early in 2007 NACCO withdrew its offer to buy Applica. Later that year NACCO announced it would spin off its Hamilton Beach/Proctor-Silex business to shareholders. The new company will be named Hamilton Beach, Inc.

## HISTORY

King Coal ruled the early part of the 20th century, and Frank Taplin was ready to be a loyal subject. In 1913, the 38-year-old Cleveland native, formerly an office boy for John D. Rockefeller and later a VP at Standard Oil Company, formed distributor Cleveland & Western Coal. Four years later, spurred by WWI, the company bought three mines and began producing coal. It incorporated in 1925 as North American Coal Corporation (NACCO).

Taplin worked at building his company until his death in 1938. Henry Schmidt took over as chairman in 1942, just as NACCO's sluggish sales began to rise, buoyed by demand for coal during WWII.

When home-heating coal sales declined, NACCO targeted electric utilities, signing its first long-term utility sales contract in 1951 with Ohio Edison. By 1952 NACCO had four underground coal-mining subsidiaries. During this time, strip mining became more common because of its efficiency and low cost. NACCO went public in 1956, and a year later bought its first lignite field for strip mining.

Profits stayed healthy in the 1980s despite frequent strikes and strict mine-safety laws. Pollution issues dimmed coal's prospects, and concerns about a potential buyout led Frank Taplin's heirs (sons Frank and Thomas, daughter Clara, son-in-law Alfred Rankin Sr., and grandson Alfred Rankin Jr.) to okay anti-takeover measures in the mid-1980s. NACCO became a holding company in 1986 and was renamed NACCO Industries. It sold some of its mines and began to diversify and to target simply made products that held top market positions.

During a two-year period beginning in 1988, NACCO bought electrical appliance specialist WearEver-ProctorSilex (it sold off the WearEver pots and pans operation in 1989), appliance factory outlet store chain The Kitchen Collection, and US maker of forklift trucks, Hyster Company. The Hyster buy doubled NACCO's sales and bolstered the company's 1985 purchase of forklift maker Yale Materials Handling. This purchase made NACCO a power in the growing forklift industry. Yale University graduate Alfred Jr., who had been the COO of Eaton, was named president in 1989 (and CEO in 1991).

In 1990 Proctor-Silex bought a majority stake in blender and mixer maker Hamilton Beach (it bought the remainder in 1996). The kitchen appliance foes merged to become a US market leader. By 1990 coal made up less than 15% of NACCO's sales.

Expanding geographically, the company bought the warehouse-equipment business of Ormic (hand-and-reach trucks, Italy) in 1996. In 1997 NACCO reduced its US activities when it began production at a Hamilton Beach/Proctor-Silex plant in Mexico. Construction began in 1998 on NACCO's 25%-owned Red Hills lignite mine near Ackerman, Mississippi.

In 1999 the company's Netherlands-based unit, NMH Holding, bought Van Eijle BV, a Dutch importer/exporter of forklift trucks. NACCO also opened a forklift plant in China. (It agreed to buy the forklift division of Nissan Motors, as well, but the deal fell apart the next year.) The same year NACCO's Hamilton Beach/Proctor Silex subsidiary secured a deal to supply Wal-Mart stores with a new line of GE-brand small appliances. In 2000 NACCO's National American Coal unit purchased from Phillips Coal the remaining assets of the Mississippi Lignite Mining Company and the Red River Mining Company that it did not already own.

As a part of the company's restructuring plan, NACCO laid off about 150 employees from its Danville, Illinois, auto parts plant in 2001. In 2002 NACCO decided to phase out its Lenoir, North Carolina, lift truck component facility (by 2004) and restructure its Irvine, Scotland, lift truck assembly and component unit (by 2006). The company's Hamilton Beach/Procter-Silex unit also closed its Sotec plant in Juarez, Mexico and its El Paso warehouse in 2004.

## EXECUTIVES

**Chairman, President, and CEO:** Alfred M. Rankin Jr., age 65, $1,154,300 pay
**VP, General Counsel, and Secretary:** Charles A. Bittenbender, age 56
**VP, Corporate Development and Treasurer:** J. C. Butler Jr., age 45
**VP and Controller:** Kenneth C. Schilling, age 47, $250,200 pay
**VP, Consulting Services:** Lauren E. Miller, age 51
**VP, Financial Services:** Bob D. Carlton, age 49
**President and CEO, Hamilton Beach and Proctor-Silex:** Michael J. Morecroft, age 65, $506,004 pay
**President and CEO, North American Coal:** Robert L. (Bob) Benson, age 59, $328,819 pay
**President and CEO, NMHG:** Michael P. Brogan, age 56, $484,464 pay
**President and CEO, The Kitchen Collection:** Randolph J. Gawelek, age 58
**SVP, Sales, Hamilton Beach and Proctor-Silex:** Paul C. Smith, age 61
**VP and COO, NMHG:** Colin Wilson, age 54
**VP, Finance and Information Systems, and CFO, NMHG:** Michael K. Smith, age 63
**VP, Human Resources, NMHG:** James M. Phillips
**VP and Chief Marketing Officer, NMHG:** Victoria L. Rickey, age 57
**VP, Manufacturing, Americas, NMHG:** Gregory J. Dawe, age 58
**VP, General Counsel, and Secretary, NMHG:** Carolyn M. Vogt, age 47
**VP, Human Resources and General Counsel, Hamilton Beach and Proctor-Silex:** Kathleen L. Diller, age 55
**VP, Engineering and New Product Development, Hamilton Beach and Proctor-Silex:** Keith B. Burns, age 50
**VP, CFO and Treasurer, Hamilton Beach and Proctor-Silex:** James H. Taylor, age 49
**VP, Marketing, Hamilton Beach and Proctor-Silex:** Gregory H. Trepp, age 45
**VP, Law and Administration and Secretary, NAC:** Thomas A. (Tom) Koza, age 60
**VP, Southern Operations and Human Resources, NAC:** Michael J. Gregory, age 59
**Auditors:** Ernst & Young LLP

## LOCATIONS

**HQ:** NACCO Industries, Inc.
5875 Landerbrook Dr., Ste. 300,
Cleveland, OH 44124
**Phone:** 440-449-9600 **Fax:** 440-449-9607
**Web:** www.nacco.com

NACCO Industries has manufacturing operations in Brazil, China, Italy, Mexico, the Netherlands, the UK, and the US.

### 2006 Sales

| | $ mil. | % of total |
|---|---|---|
| US | 2,051.5 | 61 |
| Africa, Europe & Middle East | 691.8 | 21 |
| Other regions | 605.7 | 18 |
| **Total** | **3,349.0** | **100** |

## PRODUCTS/OPERATIONS

### 2006 Sales

| | $ mil. | % of total |
|---|---|---|
| Materials handling | | |
| Wholesale | 2,317.9 | 68 |
| Retail | 250.8 | 7 |
| Housewares | | |
| Hamilton Beach/Proctor-Silex | 546.7 | 16 |
| Kitchen Company | 170.7 | 5 |
| Coal | 149.0 | 4 |
| Adjustments | (86.1) | — |
| **Total** | **3,349.0** | **100** |

### Selected Subsidiaries

Materials Handling
- Hyster-Yale Materials Handling, Inc.
- NACCO Materials Handling, BV (The Netherlands)
- NACCO Materials Handling Group, Inc.
- NACCO Materials Handling Group, Ltd. (UK)
- NACCO Materials Handling Group, Pty., Ltd. (Australia)
- NACCO Materials Handling, Spa (Italy)
- NHMG Mexico SA de CV
- NHMG Oregon, Inc.

Housewares
- Hamilton Beach/Proctor-Silex de Mexico, SA de CV
- Hamilton Beach/Proctor-Silex, Inc.
- The Kitchen Collection, Inc.
- Proctor-Silex Canada, Inc.

Coal Mining
- The Coteau Properties Company
- The Falkirk Mining Company
- Mississippi Lignite Mining Company
- The North American Coal Corporation
- The North American Coal Royalty Company
- Oxbow Property Company LLC
- Red River Mining Company
- The Sabine Mining Company

## COMPETITORS

| | |
|---|---|
| Arch Coal | Gehl |
| Cascade Corporation | Jungheinrich |
| Caterpillar | Komatsu |
| CLARK Material | Nissan Forklift |
| CNH | Salton |
| Crown Equipment | Terex |
| Deere | Toyota Material Handling |
| Doosan Infracore | |

## HISTORICAL FINANCIALS

Company Type: Public

### Income Statement

FYE: December 31

| | REVENUE ($ mil.) | NET INCOME ($ mil.) | NET PROFIT MARGIN | EMPLOYEES |
|---|---|---|---|---|
| **12/06** | 3,349 | 106 | 3.2% | 7,000 |
| **12/05** | 3,157 | 63 | 2.0% | 7,460 |
| **12/04** | 2,783 | 48 | 1.7% | 11,600 |
| **12/03** | 2,473 | 53 | 2.1% | 11,650 |
| **12/02** | 2,548 | 42 | 1.7% | 11,500 |
| **Annual Growth** | 7.1% | 25.8% | — | (11.7%) |

### 2006 Year-End Financials

Debt ratio: 45.4%
Return on equity: 14.2%
Cash ($ mil.): 197
Current ratio: 1.54
Long-term debt ($ mil.): 360
No. of shares (mil.): 7
Dividends
Yield: 1.4%
Payout: 14.7%
Market value ($ mil.): 905

### Stock History

NYSE: NC

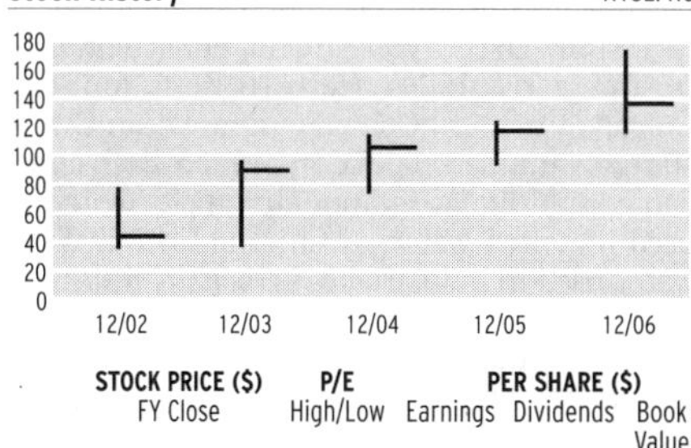


| | STOCK PRICE ($) FY Close | P/E High | P/E Low | Earnings | Dividends | Book Value |
|---|---|---|---|---|---|---|
| **12/06** | 136.60 | 13 | 9 | 12.89 | 1.90 | 119.65 |
| **12/05** | 117.15 | 16 | 12 | 7.60 | 1.85 | 106.32 |
| **12/04** | 105.40 | 19 | 13 | 5.83 | 1.68 | 104.29 |
| **12/03** | 89.48 | 15 | 6 | 6.44 | 1.26 | 96.74 |
| **12/02** | 43.77 | 15 | 7 | 5.17 | 0.97 | 85.05 |
| **Annual Growth** | 32.9% | — | — | 25.7% | 18.3% | 8.9% |

# Nalco Holding

Dirty water? Wastewater? Process-stream water? Nalco treats them all. The company is the world's largest maker of chemicals used in water treatment and for industrial processes (in front of #2 GE Water and Process Technologies). Nalco's Energy Services segment is also #1 worldwide, ahead of Baker Petrolite; it provides fuel additives, oilfield chemicals, and flow assurance services to energy companies. The company's chemicals help clarify water, conserve energy, prevent pollution, separate liquids from solids, and prevent corrosion in cooling systems and boilers. Suez had owned Nalco before selling it to a group of private equity firms in 2003; it is now publicly traded.

Nalco's former parent company, Suez, wanted to focus on its most profitable businesses, so it began looking to private equity groups as likely suitors. The company announced in September 2003 that it had selected a collection of firms — the Blackstone Group, Apollo Management, and Goldman Sachs Capital Partners — that joined together to buy Nalco for more than $4 billion. The acquiring group hired former Hercules CEO William Joyce to take over as chairman and CEO and former Rohm and Haas CFO Bradley Bell for the same position at Nalco.

Customers include municipalities, hospitals, and makers of electronics, chemicals, paper, petroleum, and steel. Nalco also provides water management services and, through its Industrial Solutions unit, maintenance of water treatment operations.

Its top-ranked Industrial and Institutional Services segment has about 20% of the worldwide market; Nalco's pulp and paper unit is #3 behind Hercules and Ciba with around 10% of that more diversified market.

Each of the three private equity firms still retains a large stake in Nalco: Blackstone owns 14%, Apollo also has 14%, and Goldman Sachs owns 10%. Until a secondary offering of shares in mid-2005 the consortium's ownership stake had been well above the 50% mark.

## HISTORY

Nalco Chemicals got its start because, as its chief chemist would say, "You can put water in your stomach that you dare not put in a boiler." In the early 1920s Herbert Kern founded Chicago Chemical Company, and Wilson Evans started Aluminate Sales Corporation. Both companies sold liquid sodium aluminate, which is used to soften water — Chicago Chemical for water used in industrial boilers, and Aluminate Sales for steam locomotives. In 1928 Chicago Chemical, Aluminate Sales, and Alcoa's sodium aluminate unit merged to form National Aluminate Corporation.

In 1930 the company acquired Paige-Jones Chemical Company of New York, and with it the capability to supply its water-treatment products in the form of "ball briquettes." During the 1930s it began making gel-type water-softening agents at the urging of one of its chemists, Emmett Culligan. (Culligan left to start his own water-treatment firm in 1935.)

During WWII, Chicago Chemical was revived for a three-year stint making catalytic products for aviation fuel. At war's end, it again became a division of National Aluminate, bringing expertise in petroleum cracking and ion exchange materials. In 1947 National Aluminate went public. The postwar era brought a major challenge as railroads converted from steam to diesel locomotives; the changeover cost the company half its business in just a few years. In response, the company developed diesel catalysts and additives, cooling system treatments, and weed-control chemicals for the railroads. In the 1950s National Aluminate expanded into Europe and Latin America and added new customers such as papermakers and nuclear power plant operators. The company changed its name to Nalco Chemical Company in 1959.

In 1962 Nalco and UK-based Imperial Chemical Industries (ICI) formed Catoleum Pty. Ltd. in Australia. Later in the decade the company established Nalfloc in the UK and Katalco in the US (sold to joint venture partner ICI in 1986).

Nalco set up regional water-analysis laboratories throughout the US during the 1970s and continued overseas expansion. The company established itself as a star during a decade of dismal US stock performance. Nalco continued to acquire in the 1980s and moved into new markets such as chemicals for the electronics and auto industries. By 1989 Nalco's sales topped $1 billion.

To combat the recession of the early 1990s, Nalco sold some operations, increased its sales force, and continued to innovate, creating a process to detoxify crude oil sludge. Nalco's 1996 acquisitions included Molson Companies' water-treatment operations and UK-based chemicals firm Albright & Wilson. It soaked up the Netherlands-based International Water Consultants Beheer BV and the assets of Nutmeg Technologies in 1997. Nalco added more water-treatment companies in 1998, including Trident Chemicals, Dutch company USF Houseman Waterbehandling, and three Malaysian firms.

Nalco bought more water-treatment companies in Brazil, Finland, Italy, Sweden, the UK, and the US in 1999. That year French utility Suez bought Nalco for $4.1 billion in cash. In 2000 Suez tapped Nalco to integrate and control the operations of Calgon, Aquazur, and other group water-treatment companies.

Early in 2001 Suez added the Ondeo (on-DAY-o) name to all of its water operations to build brand identity; Nalco Chemical became Ondeo Nalco. (Ondeo was derived from the word "water" in several languages.) The company also purchased GEO Specialty Chemicals' paper chemical business later in 2001.

When Suez sold the company in late 2003 Ondeo Nalco dropped its polyphonetic prefix, becoming just Nalco Company. On going public the next year, it expanded its name to Nalco Holding Company.

## EXECUTIVES

**Chairman and CEO:** William H. (Bill) Joyce, age 71, $1,000,000 pay
**EVP and CFO:** Bradley J. (Brad) Bell, age 54, $427,450 pay
**SVP Global Supply Chain:** Daniel M. Harker, age 54
**Group VP; President, Alternate Channels and Global Supply Chain:** Scott C. Mason, age 48
**Group VP; President, I&IS Heavy Industry:** Louis L. (Lou) Loosbrock, age 53
**Group VP; President, Service and Equipment:** Gregory N. Nelson, age 51
**Group VP; President, Paper Services Division:** John P. Yimoyines
**Group VP; President, European Operations:** David Johnson
**Group VP; President, Energy Services Division:** Steve Taylor
**Group VP; President, Industrial and Institutional Services (I&IS) Middle:** Mary Kay Kaufmann
**Group VP; President, Pacific Division:** Rich Bendure
**Group VP; President, Pacific Support Operations:** Mark Stoll
**Corporate VP Research and Development:** Mani Ramesh
**VP, General Counsel, and Corporate Secretary:** Stephen N. (Steve) Landsman, age 47
**VP Communications and Investor Relations:** Mike Bushman
**VP Safety, Health and Environment and Global Customer Analytical Services:** Deborah C. Hockman, age 50
**VP Human Resources:** Mary T. Manupella
**VP and Tax Officer:** Richard J. O'Shanna
**Senior Manager Communications:** Charlie Pajor
**Auditors:** Ernst & Young LLP

## LOCATIONS

**HQ:** Nalco Holding Company
1601 W. Diehl Rd., Naperville, IL 60563
**Phone:** 630-305-1000 **Fax:** 630-305-2900
**Web:** www.nalco.com

Nalco Holding has operations in Africa, Asia, Europe, the Middle East, and North and South America.

**2006 Sales**

| | $ mil. | % of total |
|---|---|---|
| The Americas | | |
| US | 1,626.3 | 45 |
| Other countries | 441.8 | 12 |
| Europe/Middle East/Africa | 1,036.0 | 29 |
| Asia/Pacific | 498.5 | 14 |
| **Total** | **3,602.6** | **100** |

## PRODUCTS/OPERATIONS

**2006 Sales**

| | $ mil. | % of total |
|---|---|---|
| Industrial & Institutional Services | 1,593.1 | 44 |
| Energy Services | 1,052.2 | 29 |
| Paper Services | 721.6 | 20 |
| Other | 235.7 | 7 |
| **Total** | **3,602.6** | **100** |

**Selected Products**
Lubricants and functional fluids
Process chemicals
Water-treatment chemicals

**Selected Markets**
Automobile industry
Chemical industry
Commercial buildings (hospitals, hotels)
Electronic industry
Food-processing industry
Paper industry
Petroleum industry
Steel industry
Water-treatment plants

## COMPETITORS

Arch Chemicals
Ashland Performance Materials
Baker Petrolite
BASF Corporation
Champion Technologies
Ciba Specialty Chemicals
Cytec
Eka Chemicals
GE Water and Process Technologies
Hercules
Lanxess
Rockwood Holdings

## HISTORICAL FINANCIALS

Company Type: Public

**Income Statement** FYE: December 31

| | REVENUE ($ mil.) | NET INCOME ($ mil.) | NET PROFIT MARGIN | EMPLOYEES |
|---|---|---|---|---|
| **12/06** | 3,603 | 99 | 2.7% | 11,100 |
| **12/05** | 3,312 | 48 | 1.4% | 10,900 |
| **12/04** | 3,033 | (139) | — | 10,500 |
| **12/03** | 2,767 | (182) | — | 10,500 |
| **12/02** | 2,644 | 128 | 4.9% | 10,000 |
| **Annual Growth** | 8.0% | (6.3%) | — | 2.6% |

**2006 Year-End Financials**

Debt ratio: 341.1%
Return on equity: 12.4%
Cash ($ mil.): 37
Current ratio: 1.62
Long-term debt ($ mil.): 3,039
No. of shares (mil.): 143
Dividends
Yield: —
Payout: —
Market value ($ mil.): 2,927

## Stock History NYSE: NLC

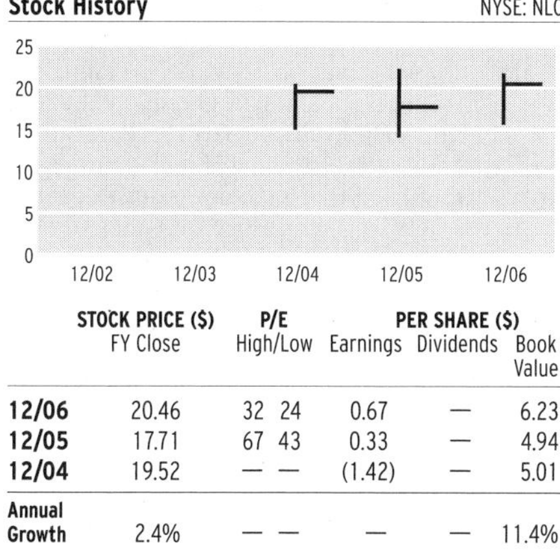


| | STOCK PRICE ($) FY Close | P/E High/Low | PER SHARE ($) Earnings | Dividends | Book Value |
|---|---|---|---|---|---|
| **12/06** | 20.46 | 32 24 | 0.67 | — | 6.23 |
| **12/05** | 17.71 | 67 43 | 0.33 | — | 4.94 |
| **12/04** | 19.52 | — — | (1.42) | — | 5.01 |
| **Annual Growth** | 2.4% | — — | — | — | 11.4% |

# Nasdaq Stock Market

Nasdaq isn't a place; it's a state of mind. OK, that's not exactly true, but The Nasdaq Stock Market *is* a floorless stock exchange, trading in some 3,200 companies electronically; altogether, Nasdaq participants can carry out transactions in more than 7,700 equities, including Exchange-Traded Funds (ETFs). Nasdaq's Market Services segment (quotations, order execution, reporting services, and more) represents the bulk of the company's sales. Nasdaq's Issuer Services segment includes shareholder services, newswire services, and such financial products and derivatives as ETFs, the QQQ, and the Nasdaq-100 Index.

Nasdaq has bolstered its status in the US by going head-to-head with the venerable New York Stock Exchange; the younger exchange has successfully lured a number of companies to dual-list with both competitors (or, in some cases, to move totally to Nasdaq). It launched a trading platform to handle dual-listed companies, as well as all NYSE- and AMEX-listed stocks and ETFs. Nasdaq has also aggressively courted IPOs and foreign company listings, with international firms accounting for about 10% of its total companies.

Close on the heels of Nasdaq's successful domestic strategy, however, was an international push that had more than its share of ups and downs. After a failed attempt to acquire the London Stock Exchange (LSE) in 2006, Nasdaq became the European exchange's largest shareholder, acquiring more than 25% of the LSE in several separate transactions. When Nasdaq's 2007 hostile takeover bid for the LSE also failed, the disappointment was particularly bitter in the face of domestic and transoceanic hookups being carried out by Nasdaq's rivals (including the vaunted deal that created NYSE Euronext). In a peculiar turn of events, Nasdaq made an announcement in late 2007 that it would sell its interests in LSE.

Nasdaq finally caught a break later that year, inking an agreement to acquire OMX; the combined international company is to be called the Nasdaq OMX Group.

Other Nasdaq 2006 international moves included cooperation agreements with exchanges in China, Japan, and Korea. (Earlier foreign forays — including Nasdaq Europe and Nasdaq Japan — proved unsuccessful and were shuttered or sold to joint-venture partners.)

In terms of its service offerings, Nasdaq has used acquisitions (BRUT, Instinet, PrimeZone Media Network, and Shareholder.com) to add capabilities or strengthen its positions in such areas as electronic trading platforms, shareholder services, and newswire services. Nasdaq has said it will use technology obtained in the Instinet acquisition to move into the options business by launching an options exchange.

Nasdaq (traditionally heavy in smaller companies and tech stocks) has taken steps to improve the quality of its listings through use of a tier structure unveiled in 2006. Elite stocks are traded on the Nasdaq Global Select Market, whose companies represent a little more than a third of all Nasdaq-listed firms; the other tiers are the Nasdaq Global Market and the Nasdaq Capital Market.

Nasdaq caught a ride on the private-equity boom in 2007, launching its Portal Market platform to cater to high-rolling investors who want to pump private money into other companies.

Former parent NASD spun off Nasdaq through a series of private sales, finally divesting its remaining 15% stake in Nasdaq in 2006. Shareholders with significant stakes in Nasdaq include private equity firm Hellman & Friedman (more than 15%), Wellington Management (nearly 15%), Horizon Asset Management (more than 10%), and Silver Lake Partners (nearly 10%).

## EXECUTIVES

**Chairman:** H. Furlong Baldwin, age 74
**President, CEO, and Director:** Robert (Bob) Greifeld, age 50, $4,115,000 pay
**EVP and CFO:** David P. Warren, age 53, $1,160,000 pay
**EVP and General Counsel:** Edward S. Knight, age 56, $1,061,720 pay
**EVP, Corporate Client Group:** Bruce E. Aust, age 42
**EVP, Data Products and Corporate Strategy:** Adena T. Friedman, age 38, $985,000 pay
**EVP, Operations and Technology and CIO:** Anna M. Ewing, age 45
**EVP, Nasdaq Financial Products and Chief Marketing Officer:** John L. Jacobs, age 48
**EVP, Transaction Services:** Christopher R. (Chris) Concannon, age 40, $1,015,000 pay
**SVP, Controller, Principal Accounting Officer, and Treasurer:** Ronald Hassen, age 54
**SVP and Internal Auditor:** Brian O'Malley
**VP, Corporate Client Group:** Janet Lewis, age 47
**SVP, Corporate Communications:** Bethany Sherman
**VP, Global Sales:** Glenn C. Faulkner
**VP, Investor Relations:** Vince Palmiere
**VP, Products and Strategy:** Marcia A. Barris
**Regional VP, Eastern Region:** Jeffrey H. Singer, age 42
**Regional VP, Central Region:** Demetrios N. Skalkotos, age 43
**Regional VP, Western Region:** John R. Vitalie, age 39
**Associate VP, Corporate Communications:** Silvia Davi
**Chairman, Nasdaq Europe:** Frank G. Zarb, age 72
**Vice Chairman, Nasdaq Deutschland:** Christoph Weber
**Senior Managing Director, Asia Pacific:** Stuart Patterson
**Director, NASDAQ Government Relations:** Robin Weisman
**Director, Russia:** Paulina McGroarty
**Director, Strategy, Transaction Services; Head of Nasdaq Canada:** Adam Nunes
**Sales Director, Transaction Services:** John Denza
**Sales Director, Transaction Services:** Drew Krichman
**Sales Director, Transaction Services:** Kathleen MacGilvray
**Sales Director, Transaction Services:** Allison Merna
**Sales Director, Transaction Services:** Chris Siclare
**Manager, Department Operations:** Susan Arthur
**Head of Nasdaq International:** Charlotte Crosswell
**Consulting Economist:** Dan L. Crippen, age 54
**Vice Chairman:** Michael G. (Mike) Oxley
**Director, Corporate Client Group:** Stephen Valenta
**Auditors:** Ernst & Young LLP

## LOCATIONS

**HQ:** The Nasdaq Stock Market, Inc.
1 Liberty Plaza, 165 Broadway, 50th Fl., New York, NY 10006
**Phone:** 212-401-8700 **Fax:** 212-401-1024
**Web:** www.nasdaq.com

The Nasdaq Stock Market has several offices in the US, as well as in China and the UK.

### 2006 Sales

| | % of total |
|---|---|
| US | 95 |
| Other countries | 5 |
| **Total** | **100** |

## PRODUCTS/OPERATIONS

### 2006 Sales By Segment

| | % of total |
|---|---|
| Market Services | 85 |
| Issuer Services | 15 |
| **Total** | **100** |

### 2006 Traded Companies by Industry

| | % of total |
|---|---|
| Information technology | 24 |
| Financial | 23 |
| Health care | 19 |
| Consumer discretionary | 13 |
| Industrial | 10 |
| Consumer staples | 3 |
| Energy | 3 |
| Materials | 2 |
| Telecommunication services | 2 |
| Utilities | 1 |
| **Total** | **100** |

### Selected Subsidiaries

Brut, Inc.
Carpenter Moore Insurance Services, Inc.
Direct Report Corporation
Independent Research Network, LLC (60%)
Inet Holding Company LLC
PrimeNewswire, Inc.
Shareholder.com, Inc.
Toll Associates, LLC
The Trade Reporting Facility, LLC

## COMPETITORS

AMEX
Citigroup
CME
Deutsche Börse
Euronext
Investment Technology
Knight Capital
London Stock Exchange
NYSE Euronext
PHLX
TRADEBOOK
virt-x

## HISTORICAL FINANCIALS

Company Type: Public

### Income Statement

FYE: December 31

| | REVENUE ($ mil.) | NET INCOME ($ mil.) | NET PROFIT MARGIN | EMPLOYEES |
|---|---|---|---|---|
| **12/06** | 1,658 | 128 | 7.7% | 898 |
| **12/05** | 880 | 62 | 7.0% | 917 |
| **12/04** | 540 | 11 | 2.1% | 784 |
| **12/03** | 590 | (105) | — | 931 |
| **12/02** | 799 | 43 | 5.4% | 1,290 |
| **Annual Growth** | 20.0% | 31.2% | — | (8.7%) |

### 2006 Year-End Financials

Debt ratio: 102.4%
Return on equity: 15.8%
Cash ($ mil.): 1,950
Current ratio: 5.02
Long-term debt ($ mil.): 1,493

No. of shares (mil.): 112
Dividends
Yield: —
Payout: —
Market value ($ mil.): 3,458

### Stock History

NASDAQ (GS): NDAQ

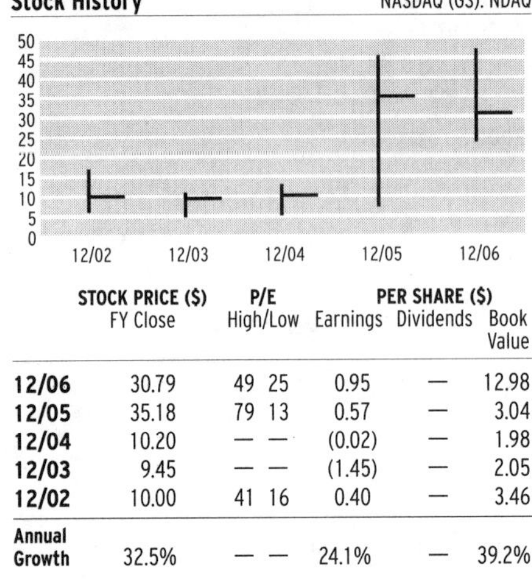


| | STOCK PRICE ($) FY Close | P/E High | P/E Low | PER SHARE ($) Earnings | Dividends | Book Value |
|---|---|---|---|---|---|---|
| **12/06** | 30.79 | 49 | 25 | 0.95 | — | 12.98 |
| **12/05** | 35.18 | 79 | 13 | 0.57 | — | 3.04 |
| **12/04** | 10.20 | — | — | (0.02) | — | 1.98 |
| **12/03** | 9.45 | — | — | (1.45) | — | 2.05 |
| **12/02** | 10.00 | 41 | 16 | 0.40 | — | 3.46 |
| **Annual Growth** | 32.5% | — | — | 24.1% | — | 39.2% |

# Nash-Finch

Nash-Finch knows what's in store for food retailers. One of the largest US wholesale grocery distributors, the company supplies dairy products, fresh produce, frozen foods, and meat, as well as general merchandise and non-food goods to about 1,700 grocery stores in 25 states through more than 15 distribution centers. The company is also one of the leading suppliers of military bases, serving more than 200 foreign and domestic military bases and commissaries. In addition to its food distribution business, Nash-Finch operates more than 60 of its own supermarkets under such banners as Econofoods, Sun Mart, and Family Thrift Centers.

Nash-Finch has been struggling of late due to internal management strife and increasing competition in its food distribution business. An internal review of trading practices led to the departure of CEO Ron Marshall and four other top officers in 2006. Alec Covington, who previously oversaw North American operations for Dutch food distributor Koninklijke Wessanen, was brought in to help turn the business around.

Having established some stability to Nash-Finch's executive ranks, Covington faces the task of streamlining the company's distribution operations to increase efficiency. The company is also reviewing its underperforming retail operation, which accounts for about 15% of sales, with an eye towards reducing the size of that division. Nash-Finch has announced plans to use its stores to develop niche retail concepts and then license those to independent retailers.

## HISTORY

Vermont farmers Warren and Mary Nash operated a small country store in the mid-1800s. In 1884 their son Fred followed the homesteading rush to the Dakota Territory, where the next year he opened a small confectionery and tobacco shop in railroad boomtown Devils Lake. His brothers Edgar and Willis soon joined him, and by 1887 there was a Nash Brothers store in Devils Lake and another in Grand Forks.

Two years later North Dakota entered the Union, and the Nash brothers bought an unclaimed boxcar of peaches and turned it into a quick profit. That year the company hired 14-year-old Harry Finch to sort lemons for $4 a week, a job he took to support his ailing father. Also in 1889 Edgar moved to California, where he established ties between the Nashes' wholesale business and California produce growers. He died in 1896; Finch became a manager that year.

Acquisitions expanded the company in the late 1890s and early 1900s. It partnered with local produce brokerage C. H. Robinson in 1905; Nash Brothers controlled it by 1913.

Over the next several decades, Nash Brothers expanded its growing, packaging, and shipping operations, forming companies in California and Texas. It started the Nash Coffee Company and fruit and vegetable packager Nash DeCamp in 1916. Three years later the company moved its headquarters to Minneapolis. Nash Brothers' 60-plus companies incorporated as Nash-Finch in 1921. When Fred died in 1926, Finch became president. During the 1930s the company introduced its own brand, Our Family.

Nash-Finch returned to retailing in the 1950s with 17 supermarkets in Nebraska. Finch, by then a partner, retired in 1953 after 64 years with the company. During the 1960s the FTC limited C. H. Robinson's role with Nash-Finch, and the grocer sold its remaining stake in the broker in 1976. The company reached $1 billion in sales in 1981 and was the US's 10th-largest grocery wholesaler by the mid-1980s.

It made acquisitions throughout the 1990s, including a division of military distributor B. Green & Co. (Maryland, 1992); Easter Enterprises, a 16-store Iowa chain (1993); and 23 Food Folks stores (1994). In 1994 chairman Harold Finch, grandson of Harry, died in an auto accident. President Alfred Flaten became chairman and CEO and separated the wholesale and retail divisions.

The company sold two convenience store subsidiaries (Thomas & Howard and T&H Service Merchandisers) in 1995. In 1996 Nash-Finch bought Military Distributors of Virginia, a distributor of groceries to military bases in the eastern US and Europe, and grocery wholesalers T. J. Morris and Super Food Services.

A year later it bought most of the assets of Nebraska-based grocery distributor United-A.G. Cooperative. Former Pathmark executive Ron Marshall succeeded Flaten as CEO in 1998.

In ensuing years it replaced most of its management team, consolidated distribution centers, and sold produce and dairy subsidiaries to focus more on retailing. In 1999 Nash-Finch sold its Nash DeCamp produce unit to Agriholding, sold Gillette Dairy and Nebraska Dairies to Royal Wessanen, reduced its number of store banners, and closed unprofitable warehouses and stores.

It purchased retailer Erickson's Diversified (18 stores in Minnesota and Wisconsin) and in 2000 bought Hinky Dinky Supermarkets (12 locations in Nebraska). In 2001 Nash-Finch announced that it would sell its North and South Carolina supermarkets as it continued on the market in the Midwest. To that end, it acquired U Save Foods (14 supermarkets in Nebraska, Kansas, and Colorado) in mid-2001; most of the stores were renamed Sun Mart.

In 2003 the company purchased five Sunshine Food stores in South Dakota and converted some of those to the Econofoods banner. It also started two specialty retail food operations: Buy-n-Save (aimed at low-income customers) and AVANZA (aimed at the Hispanic market). Nash-Finch closed about 20 underperforming retail food stores in 2004, including all of its Buy-n-Save locations and several AVANZA stores.

In the midst of an investigation into internal trading practices in 2006, Marshall stepped down as CEO. Alec Covington, formerly North American chief for Dutch food distributor Koninklijke Wessanen, was named as his replacement.

## EXECUTIVES

**Chairman:** William R. Voss, age 52
**President, CEO, and Director:** Alec C. Covington, age 50
**EVP, CFO, and Treasurer:** Robert B. (Bob) Dimond, age 45, $568,955 pay
**EVP and CIO:** Calvin S. (Cal) Sihilling, age 57
**EVP, Food Distribution:** Christopher A. Brown, age 44
**EVP, Supply Chain Management:** Jeffrey E. (Jeff) Poore, age 48
**SVP, Military:** Edward L. Brunot, age 43
**SVP, Secretary, and General Counsel:** Kathleen M. Mahoney, age 52
**SVP, Human Resources:** Denise M. Wilson
**VP, Food Distribution, Southeast Region:** Terry J. Littrell, age 56
**VP, Merchadising Non-Perishable:** Joy Sgro
**VP, Perishable Procurement, Merchandising, and Marketing:** Salvatore (Sal) Baio
**VP, Food Distribution:** Tom Strzelczyk
**Senior Director, Pharmacy Marketing:** Joseph Friedman
**Senior Director, Business Development:** Roger Nelson
**Director, Media Relations and Research:** Brian Numainville
**Auditors:** Ernst & Young LLP

## LOCATIONS

**HQ:** Nash-Finch Company
7600 France Ave. South, Minneapolis, MN 55440
**Phone:** 952-832-0534 **Fax:** 952-844-1237
**Web:** www.nashfinch.com

Nash-Finch operates 17 distribution centers in Georgia, Indiana, Iowa, Maryland, Michigan, Minnesota, Nebraska, North Carolina, North Dakota, Ohio, South Dakota, and Virginia. It also operates more than 60 grocery stores in about a dozen states.

## PRODUCTS/OPERATIONS

### 2006 Sales

| | $ mil. | % of total |
|---|---|---|
| Food distribution | 2,787.7 | 60 |
| Military | 1,195.0 | 26 |
| Retail | 648.9 | 14 |
| **Total** | **4,631.6** | **100** |

**2006 Supermarkets**

| | No. |
|---|---|
| Econofoods | 26 |
| Sun Mart | 24 |
| Family Thrift Center | 4 |
| AVANZA | 2 |
| Pick n' Save | 2 |
| Wholesale Food Outlet | 2 |
| Food Bonanza | 1 |
| Other | 1 |
| **Total** | **62** |

**Selected Private Labels**

Our Family
Our Family Pride
Value Choice

## COMPETITORS

Albertsons
Alex Lee
Associated Wholesale Grocers
C&S Wholesale
Certified Grocers Midwest
Eby-Brown
H.T. Hackney
Hy-Vee
Kroger
McLane
Publix
Purity Wholesale Grocers
S. Abraham & Sons
Spartan Stores
SUPERVALU
Wal-Mart

## HISTORICAL FINANCIALS

Company Type: Public

**Income Statement** FYE: Saturday nearest December 31

| | REVENUE ($ mil.) | NET INCOME ($ mil.) | NET PROFIT MARGIN | EMPLOYEES |
|---|---|---|---|---|
| **12/06** | 4,632 | (23) | — | 8,227 |
| **12/05** | 4,556 | 41 | 0.9% | 9,487 |
| **12/04** | 3,897 | 15 | 0.4% | 8,658 |
| **12/03** | 3,972 | 35 | 0.9% | 10,570 |
| **12/02** | 3,875 | 24 | 0.6% | 10,621 |
| **Annual Growth** | 4.6% | — | — | (6.2%) |

**2006 Year-End Financials**

Debt ratio: 118.2%
Return on equity: —
Cash ($ mil.): 1
Current ratio: 1.64
Long-term debt ($ mil.): 348

No. of shares (mil.): 13
Dividends
Yield: 2.6%
Payout: —
Market value ($ mil.): 365

**Stock History** NASDAQ (GS): NAFC

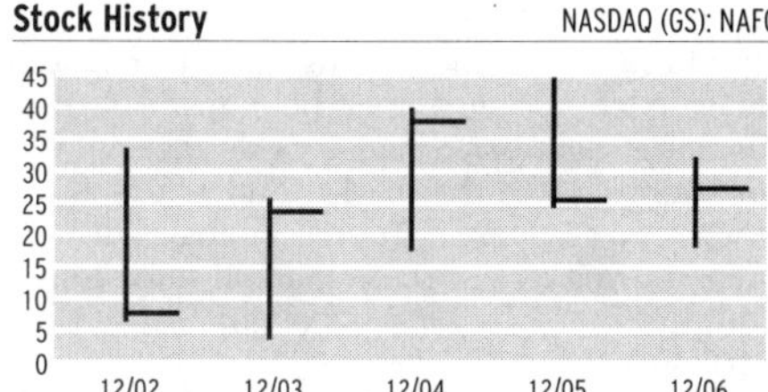

| | STOCK PRICE ($) FY Close | P/E High | P/E Low | PER SHARE ($) Earnings | Dividends | Book Value |
|---|---|---|---|---|---|---|
| **12/06** | 27.30 | — | — | (1.72) | 0.72 | 21.99 |
| **12/05** | 25.48 | 14 | 8 | 3.13 | 0.68 | 24.22 |
| **12/04** | 37.76 | 34 | 15 | 1.18 | 0.54 | 21.66 |
| **12/03** | 23.59 | 9 | 1 | 2.88 | 0.36 | 21.17 |
| **12/02** | 7.70 | 17 | 3 | 1.95 | 0.36 | 18.54 |
| **Annual Growth** | 37.2% | — | — | — | 18.9% | 4.4% |

# National City

National City wants customers to think nationally, bank locally. One of the top banks in the US, National City operates about 1,300 bank branches in Ohio, Florida, Illinois, Indiana, Kentucky, Michigan, Missouri, and Pennsylvania. Besides retail and corporate banking services, National City offers retail banking, corporate and small business banking, wealth management services, and mortgage banking. Its National Consumer Finance segment, which includes subsidiary National City Mortgage, originates and services consumer and housing loans. The company focuses on direct services, in which it has personal relationships with customers.

With its focus on "direct to customers" services, the bank has divested those operations that required a middleman or a broker. Thus it has gotten out of indirect auto, RV, and marine lending, and sold its nonprime mortgage lending division, First Franklin Financial.

National City has agreed to acquire MAF Bancorp, a bank holding company for 24-branch MidAmerica Bank. The $1.9 billion deal moves National City into the Milwaukee area.

## HISTORY

Cleveland was scarcely more than a village in 1845 when former insurance men Reuben Sheldon and Theodoric Severance decided to start Ohio's first bank, City Bank of Cleveland. The town, located at the confluence of the Cuyahoga River with Lake Erie, was well-placed to take advantage of the westward expansion of the US and Ohio's industrial development.

John Rockefeller struck oil in Titusville, Pennsylvania, in 1859 and built his refinery in nearby Cleveland; City Bank became Standard Oil's Ohio bank. In 1865 the company received a national charter and became National City Bank of Cleveland. The iron and oil industries developed rapidly during and after the Civil War, and the presence of such companies as paint makers Sherwin-Williams and Glidden helped the bank and the city weather the recurrent economic shocks of the late 19th century.

The bank grew steadily in the early 20th century, along with the not-yet-rusted Steel Belt. Then came the stock market crash, the Depression, and the bank holiday of 1933. That February, a week-long citywide run began. A member of the Federal Reserve System, National City was able to call for extra cash and was the only Cleveland bank to pay out withdrawn deposits at face value. Many depositors withdrew their money and locked it away in safe-deposit boxes, but the bank also received deposits from people who had withdrawn their money from other banks. Then in March newly inaugurated President Roosevelt closed all banks for a week. National City Bank was the first Cleveland bank to reopen, and it took over the deposits of several banks closed by regulators.

Cleveland and National City prospered through WWII and the postwar boom. As corporations moved into the money markets, the company began courting consumers and built up its branch network in the 1950s and 1960s.

In 1973 the bank formed holding company National City Corporation to buy in-state banks. The move was opportune as Cleveland suffered through its conversion from heavy to light industry. In 1984 National City bought BancOhio, becoming the state's largest bank. Other acquisitions brought entry into Kentucky (1988) and Indiana (1992). The company caught its breath with a 1991 reorganization before continuing its breakneck growth.

In the mid-1990s the company diversified. In 1995 it formed NatCity Investments and acquired Indiana-based investment bank and brokerage firm Raffensperger, Hughes & Co. In 1996 it bought Pittsburgh-based Integra Financial. It also took its credit card/check processing operations public as National Processing, which stumbled after losing a contract with Wal-Mart. Like rival banks, National City built its asset-based and subprime lending business by offering a new non-prime indirect auto loan service and buying companies specializing in data processing, freight payment, and mortgages. That year it consolidated its six Ohio banks under one charter.

In 1998 National City bought First of America Bank, extending its reach into Illinois and Michigan; it also bought Fort Wayne National Corp. of Indiana. With its purchases quickly assimilated and turning a profit, in 1999 the bank grew its mortgage business with the purchases of AccuBanc Mortgage's retail and wholesale operations and subprime lender First Franklin Financial. That year it sold National Processing's ailing freight services, remittance processing, merchant check services, and payables outsourcing operations. In 2000 the bank converted to a financial services holding company.

In 2002 National City benefited from the low interest rates that spurred an industrywide mortgage refinancing boom. The resulting spread between rates charged on loans and the lower costs of funds to fuel lending helped the bank reach record earnings levels that year.

Throughout much of the decade, National City has been on an acquisition spree. The company's series of expansions started in 2004, first with Harbor Florida and then Allegiant Bancorp, which it acquired to enter the St. Louis market, and its $2.1 billion purchase of Cincinnati-based Provident Financial Group. It also purchased Ohio-based community bank holding company Wayne Bancorp. The company's 2006 acquisition of Forbes First, the parent of Pioneer Bank and Trust, enabled it to expand its reach in St. Louis. National City is targeting the highly fragmented Chicago retail banking market for growth as well.

In a move to expand beyond its traditional midwestern markets, the company migrated south, acquiring Harbor Florida Bancshares. In 2007 it bought Fidelity Bankshares for $1 billion, cementing its presence in the state.

In keeping with its strategy to focus on basic banking, National City sold its 83% stake in National Processing, which earns fees from processing merchant credit card transactions, to Bank of America. It sold consumer finance unit First Franklin Financial to Merrill Lynch for $1.3 billion in 2007.

## EXECUTIVES

**Chairman:** David A. Daberko, age 61, $1,000,000 pay
**Vice Chairman and CFO:** Jeffrey D. Kelly, age 54, $887,906 pay
**President, CEO, and Director:** Peter E. Raskind, age 50, $733,861 pay
**EVP and Chief Risk Officer:** James R. Bell III, age 50
**EVP; President, Northern Ohio Region, National City Bank:** Paul G. Clark, age 53
**EVP Corporate Operations and Information Services:** Jon L. Gorney, age 56
**EVP and Chief Investment Officer, The Private Client Group:** Timothy L. (Tim) Swanson
**EVP; President and CEO, National City Bank:** Philip L. (Phil) Rice, age 48
**EVP Corporate Services:** Shelley J. Seifert, age 52
**EVP; President, Indiana Banking:** Stephen A. Stitle, age 59
**EVP, General Counsel, and Secretary:** David L. Zoeller, age 57
**SVP; CEO, National City Mortgage:** Paul E. (Buck) Bibb Jr.
**SVP National Home Equity:** E. Kennedy (Ken) Carter
**SVP; Manager, Investment and Funding:** J. Andrew Dunham
**SVP Corporate Human Resources:** Jon N. Couture, age 40
**SVP and Corporate Comptroller:** Robert B. Crowl, age 42
**SVP and Chief Economist:** Richard J. DeKaser
**SVP; EVP, Corporate Operations and Information Services:** Jane Grebenc
**SVP and CIO:** Joseph T. McCartin
**SVP Corporate Public Affairs:** Bruce A. McCrodden
**SVP and Treasurer:** Thomas A. Richlovsky, age 55
**SVP and Director of Corporate Marketing:** Karin L. Stone
**SVP Investor Relations:** Jill Hennessey
**Auditors:** Ernst & Young LLP

## LOCATIONS

**HQ:** National City Corporation
1900 E. 9th St., Cleveland, OH 44114
**Phone:** 216-222-2000 **Fax:** 216-222-9957
**Web:** www.nationalcity.com

## PRODUCTS/OPERATIONS

### 2006 Sales

| | $ mil. | % of total |
|---|---|---|
| Interest | | |
| Loans | 8,351.5 | 65 |
| Securities | 414.2 | 3 |
| Other | 168.1 | 1 |
| Noninterest | | |
| Gain on divestitures | 983.9 | 8 |
| Deposit service charges | 818.3 | 6 |
| Loan sales | 765.5 | 6 |
| Trust & investment management fees | 300.7 | 2 |
| Leasing revenue | 228.1 | 2 |
| Card & other fees | 264.9 | 2 |
| Brokerage revenue | 157.8 | 1 |
| Other | 500.2 | 4 |
| **Total** | **12,953.2** | **100** |

### 2006 Assets

| | $ mil. | % of total |
|---|---|---|
| Cash & equivalents | 5,072.6 | 4 |
| Securities available for sale | 7,508.8 | 5 |
| Other investments | 6,317.8 | 4 |
| Loans held for sale or securitization | 12,852.9 | 9 |
| Portfolio loans | | |
| Commercial (except construction) | 31,052.0 | 22 |
| Commercial construction | 4266.3 | 3 |
| Real estate — commercial | 12,436.4 | 9 |
| Real estate — residential | 24,775.6 | 18 |
| Home equity lines of credit | 14,594.8 | 10 |
| Other loans | 8,367.0 | 6 |
| Allowance for loan losses | (1,131.2) | — |
| Other | 14,077.8 | 10 |
| **Total** | **140,190.8** | **100** |

## COMPETITORS

Bank of America
Citigroup
Citizens Financial Group
Comerica
Countrywide Financial
Fifth Third
Huntington Bancshares
JPMorgan Chase
KeyCorp
Northern Trust
PNC Financial
U.S. Bancorp
Wells Fargo

## HISTORICAL FINANCIALS

Company Type: Public

### Income Statement

FYE: December 31

| | ASSETS ($ mil.) | NET INCOME ($ mil.) | INCOME AS % OF ASSETS | EMPLOYEES |
|---|---|---|---|---|
| **12/06** | 140,191 | 2,300 | 1.6% | 31,270 |
| **12/05** | 142,397 | 1,985 | 1.4% | 34,270 |
| **12/04** | 139,280 | 2,780 | 2.0% | 35,230 |
| **12/03** | 113,934 | 2,117 | 1.9% | 33,331 |
| **12/02** | 118,258 | 1,594 | 1.3% | 32,731 |
| **Annual Growth** | 4.3% | 9.6% | — | (1.1%) |

### 2006 Year-End Financials

Equity as % of assets: 10.4%
Return on assets: 1.6%
Return on equity: 16.9%
Long-term debt ($ mil.): 28,722
No. of shares (mil.): 632
Dividends
Yield: 4.2%
Payout: 40.9%
Market value ($ mil.): 23,120
Sales ($ mil.): 12,953

### Stock History

NYSE: NCC

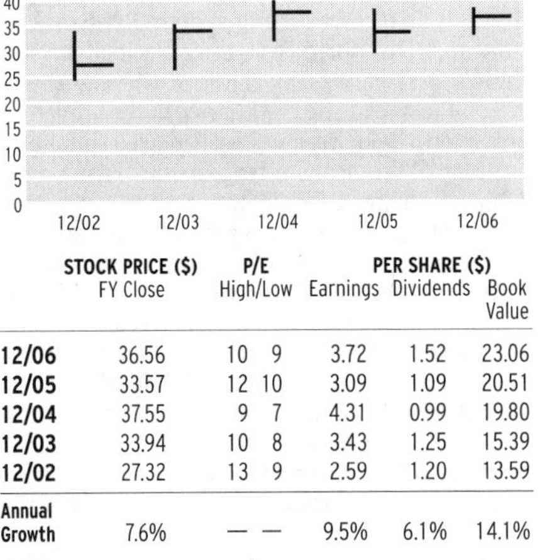


| | STOCK PRICE ($) FY Close | P/E High | P/E Low | PER SHARE ($) Earnings | Dividends | Book Value |
|---|---|---|---|---|---|---|
| **12/06** | 36.56 | 10 | 9 | 3.72 | 1.52 | 23.06 |
| **12/05** | 33.57 | 12 | 10 | 3.09 | 1.09 | 20.51 |
| **12/04** | 37.55 | 9 | 7 | 4.31 | 0.99 | 19.80 |
| **12/03** | 33.94 | 10 | 8 | 3.43 | 1.25 | 15.39 |
| **12/02** | 27.32 | 13 | 9 | 2.59 | 1.20 | 13.59 |
| **Annual Growth** | 7.6% | — | — | 9.5% | 6.1% | 14.1% |

# National Fuel Gas

National Fuel Gas doesn't cover the nation, but it does touch all the bases in its industry: The company explores for, produces, stores, transmits, and distributes natural gas. The diversified energy concern's public utility, National Fuel Gas Distribution, accounts for most of its sales and distributes gas to about 727,000 customers in New York and Pennsylvania. National Fuel Gas has gas exploration, production, storage, and transportation operations throughout North America; the company also engages in energy marketing, timber processing, and independent power production. Oil and gas subsidiary Seneca Resources has proved reserves of 232.6 billion cu. ft. of natural gas and 58 million barrels of oil.

Another subsidiary, National Fuel Gas Supply, owns about 30 underground gas storage facilities and a 3,000-mile pipeline that runs from southwestern Pennsylvania to the New York-Canada border.

Energy deregulation has changed the rules, and the firm's utility customers can now choose their own supplier. In response, National Fuel Gas has set up a gas and electricity retail marketer in the northeastern US. The company is also investing in domestic and overseas power projects.

National Fuel Gas acquired the Empire State Pipeline from Duke Energy for $240 million in 2003. The company also sold some noncore gas and timber production properties that year.

In 2007 the company received the go ahead by federal regulators to extend the Empire State Pipeline by building a 78-mile stretch from near Rochester to Corning.

## HISTORY

The roots of National Fuel Gas go back to the 1820s in northwestern New York. The early days of natural gas exploitation were marked by varied uses of the fuel and creative transport methods. In 1821 Iroquois Gas (later a National Fuel Gas unit) laid lead pipe from a source beneath Canadaway Creek in New York to light street lamps in the village of Fredonia. Fifty years later an investor group tried (and failed) to pipe gas from Bloomfield, New York, to Rochester, some 25 miles away, using hollow logs connected by iron bands.

A more successful attempt was made in 1886 with an 87-mile iron pipeline that carried gas from McKean County, Pennsylvania, to Buffalo, New York. The Buffalo pipeline was bought by United Natural Gas, a predecessor of National Fuel Gas, and portions of it remained in use well into the 20th century.

Incorporated in 1902, National Fuel Gas bought smaller gas firms in the Buffalo area in the early 1900s and stretched its pipeline network into Pennsylvania. In 1916 Iroquois Gas established the US's first underground gas storage unit.

As gas reserves in the Appalachian region became depleted in the 1930s, the company joined other utilities to develop reserves in the Southwest and connect them through pipelines. Growth exploded in the 1940s, sparked by WWII increases in coal and oil prices, and in the 1950s, when home heating shifted to gas.

The industry was in a feast-or-famine period from the 1960s to the 1980s. The gas market matured in the 1960s, but the 1970s energy crisis increased demand, forcing National Fuel Gas to restrict new customer hookups. The next decade an aggressive industrywide development program glutted the market and prices plummeted. In response, National Fuel Gas diversified, moving away from retail and into storage and transport. In 1986 it bought Utility Constructors to build pipelines.

National Fuel Gas began looking beyond its utility business in 1991, when it set up gas marketing subsidiary National Fuel Resources. The next year the company cut staff and formed a joint venture with Citizens Gas Supply of Boston to purchase, transport, and sell gas to other utilities.

As part of the energy industry's globalization trend, National Fuel Gas established operations in China and the Czech Republic in 1996. The next year oil and gas exploration unit Seneca Resources bought interests in wells in California and Wyoming.

Also in 1997, as the oil and gas industry boomed, National Fuel Gas' exploration and pipeline operations were hampered by a scarcity of drilling rigs because of high demand. The petroleum industry slump in 1998 eliminated the rig shortage, and Seneca increased development drilling. The firm more than doubled its proved reserves in 1998 by acquiring energy exploration and production firms HarCor Energy, Bakersfield Energy, and M.H. Whittier.

The next year National Fuel Gas expanded its Czech Republic holdings and added timber and mineral rights in New York and Pennsylvania to its portfolio. Its National Fuel Resources moved into the electricity marketing business; it also bought a cogeneration plant in New York.

In 2000 the company increased its reserves 30% by acquiring Canada's Tri Link Resources. The next year it formed a joint venture with Canadian company Talisman Energy to explore in the Appalachian Basin. Subsidiary Seneca Resources also acquired another Canadian company, Player Petroleum.

## EXECUTIVES

**Chairman and CEO; President, Horizon Energy Development:** Philip C. (Phil) Ackerman, age 63, $825,000 pay
**President and COO; President, National Fuel Gas Supply Corporation and Empire State Pipeline:** David F. Smith, age 53, $496,875 pay
**CFO and Treasurer; President National Fuel Gas Distribution Corporation:** Ronald J. Tanski, age 54
**President and Secretary, National Fuel Resources:** Donna L. DeCarolis, age 47
**SVP National Fuel Gas Distribution:** James D. Ramsdell, age 51
**SVP National Fuel Gas Supply:** John R. Pustulka, age 54, $265,250 pay
**Secretary; SVP, National Fuel Gas Distribution:** Anna Marie Cellino, age 53
**Principal Accounting Officer and Controller; Controller, National Fuel Gas Distribution and National Fuel Gas Supply:** Karen M. Camiolo, age 47
**Director, Investor Relations:** Margaret M. Suto
**General Counsel; Assistant Secretary and General Counsel, National Fuel Gas Distribution:** Paula M. Ciprich, age 46
**President, Seneca:** Matthew D. Cabell, age 48
**Auditors:** PricewaterhouseCoopers LLP

## LOCATIONS

**HQ:** National Fuel Gas Company
6363 Main St., Williamsville, NY 14221
**Phone:** 716-857-7000 **Fax:** 716-857-7195
**Web:** www.natfuel.com

National Fuel Gas distributes natural gas in western New York and northwestern Pennsylvania. The company's pipeline network runs from southwestern Pennsylvania to the New York-Canada border. Its oil and gas exploration and production unit operates in the Appalachian region; California; the Gulf Coast regions of Alabama, Louisiana, and Texas; and Wyoming. The unit also operates in the Canadian provinces of Alberta, British Columbia, and Saskatchewan. National Fuel Gas markets energy and timber in the northeastern US.

## PRODUCTS/OPERATIONS

### 2006 Sales

| | $ mil. | % of total |
|---|---|---|
| Utility | 1,265.7 | 55 |
| Energy marketing | 497.1 | 21 |
| Exploration & production | 346.9 | 15 |
| Pipeline & storage | 132.9 | 6 |
| Timber | 65.0 | 3 |
| Corporate & Other | 4.1 | — |
| **Total** | **2,311.7** | **100** |

### Selected Subsidiaries

Empire State Pipeline (natural gas transportation)
Highland Forest Resources, Inc. (timber processing)
Horizon Energy Development, Inc. (foreign and domestic energy investment, wholesale electricity generation)
Horizon Power, Inc. (wholesale electricity generation)
National Fuel Gas Distribution Corporation (natural gas utility)
National Fuel Gas Supply Corporation (natural gas transportation and storage)
National Fuel Resources, Inc. (energy marketer and broker for utilities and retail customers)
Seneca Resources Corporation (natural gas and oil exploration and production)

## COMPETITORS

Allegheny Energy
Anadarko Petroleum
Belden & Blake
Cabot Oil & Gas
Castle Oil
Con Edison
Duke Energy
Dynegy
El Paso
Enbridge
Energy East
Exelon
KeySpan
National Onshore
NewPower Holdings
Niagara Mohawk
ONEOK
Petroleum Development
PPL
Rochester Gas and Electric
Southern Union
Southwestern Energy
TransCanada
TXU
UGI

## HISTORICAL FINANCIALS

Company Type: Public

### Income Statement

FYE: September 30

| | REVENUE ($ mil.) | NET INCOME ($ mil.) | NET PROFIT MARGIN | EMPLOYEES |
|---|---|---|---|---|
| **9/06** | 2,312 | 138 | 6.0% | 1,993 |
| **9/05** | 1,924 | 190 | 9.9% | 2,044 |
| **9/04** | 2,031 | 167 | 8.2% | 2,918 |
| **9/03** | 2,036 | 179 | 8.8% | 3,037 |
| **9/02** | 1,465 | 118 | 8.0% | 3,177 |
| **Annual Growth** | 12.1% | 4.1% | — | (11.0%) |

### 2006 Year-End Financials

Debt ratio: 75.9%
Return on equity: 10.3%
Cash ($ mil.): 89
Current ratio: 1.79
Long-term debt ($ mil.): 1,096
No. of shares (mil.): 83
Dividends
Yield: 3.2%
Payout: 73.3%
Market value ($ mil.): 3,032

### Stock History

NYSE: NFG

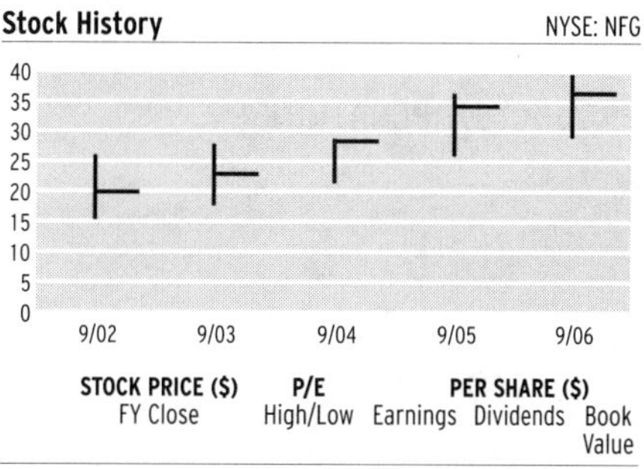

| | STOCK PRICE ($) FY Close | P/E High | P/E Low | PER SHARE ($) Earnings | Dividends | Book Value |
|---|---|---|---|---|---|---|
| **9/06** | 36.35 | 24 | 18 | 1.61 | 1.18 | 17.31 |
| **9/05** | 34.20 | 16 | 12 | 2.23 | 1.14 | 14.58 |
| **9/04** | 28.33 | 14 | 11 | 2.01 | 1.10 | 15.11 |
| **9/03** | 22.85 | 13 | 8 | 2.20 | 1.06 | 13.97 |
| **9/02** | 19.87 | 18 | 11 | 1.46 | 1.02 | 12.54 |
| **Annual Growth** | 16.3% | — | — | 2.5% | 3.7% | 8.4% |

# National Semiconductor

National Semiconductor has an international reputation for semiconductors. The pioneering chip maker offers a variety of integrated circuits (ICs), especially analog and mixed-signal (both analog and digital) chips. Its varied offerings reflect its focus on analog chips, which transform physical information — light, sound, pressure, even radio waves — into data that a computer can use. National's chips are used in a host of communications, networking, automotive, and aerospace applications. Belying its name, National derives more than three-quarters of sales from customers outside the US, largely to contract manufacturers that serve its ultimate OEM customers.

The company's client roster includes distributors Arrow Electronics (13% of sales) and Avnet (14%), along with Ericsson, IBM, Motorola, Nokia, Samsung Electronics, Siemens, and Sony.

Analog devices account for about 90% of sales.

National has divested operations in recent years in order to focus on its core analog products. The company had focused development efforts on its Geode brand of SoC products, which combined processors, logic, memory, and other components into a single unit for use in electronics devices such as Internet appliances. However, market conditions led the company to sell its Information Appliance unit — which included the Geode product lines — to Advanced Micro Devices in 2003. National also sold its small business in image sensor chips to Kodak in 2004, and its Advanced PC division to Winbond Electronics the following year.

Relational Investors owns nearly 11% of National Semiconductor. FMR (Fidelity Investments) holds about 10% of the company.

## HISTORY

National Semiconductor was founded as a transistor maker in 1959 by eight engineers from Sperry Rand Corporation. The company was established in Danbury, Connecticut. In 1966, as the company was struggling with only $7 million in annual sales, Peter Sprague (heir to the Sprague Electric fortune) took over as chairman. The next year he hired manufacturing expert Charles Sporck away from Fairchild Semiconductor to be National's CEO.

Sporck transferred headquarters to Silicon Valley (the Danbury facility closed in 1989), halved the company's transistor workforce, and plowed the savings into developing linear and digital logic chips. During the 1970s National's mass manufacturing of low-cost chips made the company the leading US semiconductor maker for a time; its no-frills management approach led to its employees being dubbed "the animals of Silicon Valley."

The company bought National Advanced Systems (NAS), a distributor and servicer of Hitachi mainframes, in 1979 and Data Terminal Systems, which made point-of-sale terminals, in 1983; the two were combined to form Datachecker. When Japanese manufacturers dumped memory chips on the market in 1984 and 1985, National pulled out of the memory business.

Sporck moved to transform his low-cost commodity chip maker into a higher-margin supplier of niche products. National bought troubled Fairchild in 1987 for its logic chip designs and the custom linear circuits it made for the US military.

With mounting mainframe competition from IBM and Amdahl, in 1989 National sold Datachecker. National left the high-speed, high-density static random-access memory (SRAM) business, and in early 1991 Sporck retired. Former Rockwell International (now Rockwell Automation) executive Gilbert Amelio became CEO and undertook another restructuring.

By 1993 National had shifted production to Arlington, Texas. In 1995 the company purchased SiTel Sierra, a Netherlands-based supplier of cellular and wireless products.

When Amelio joined Apple Computer (now just Apple) in 1996, National chose Intel veteran and LSI Logic EVP Brian Halla as its new leader. Halla consolidated National's operations and resurrected the Fairchild name for its commodity chip business. Soon after Halla's arrival, about 600 jobs were cut, two COOs left, and 14 of 56 VPs resigned or were fired.

In 1998 National cut another 10% of its workforce in the face of an industry slump. In addition, Intel's low-end Celeron chip hammered Cyrix's sales, and National exited the PC chip market. National sold its flat-panel display operations to Three-Five Systems, and Cyrix to Taiwan's VIA Technologies. Writeoffs and acquisition costs in the face of a tough market led to a $1 billion loss for the year.

In 2001 the company cut 1,100 jobs — about 10% of its workforce — in response to another, particularly brutal, dropoff in the global chip market. In 2003 National shuttered a unit that made baseband chips for wireless communications.

As the semiconductor industry recovered from its meltdown in the early years of the 21st century, National set plans in early 2004 to expand its wafer fabrication plant in South Portland, Maine. That same year National opened its semiconductor assembly and test plant in the Suzhou Industrial Park, located outside of Shanghai.

Among other restructuring moves set in early 2005, National Semi said it would sell its assembly and testing facility in Singapore. Four months later, the company said it would close the facility and transfer its equipment to plants in China and Malaysia. The shuttering was completed in early 2007 and the facility was sold later that year.

Donald Macleod, National's EVP, COO, and GM of product lines since 2001, was promoted to president of the company in 2005, retaining the COO's title. He earlier served as National's EVP/CFO for a decade and joined the company in 1978.

In mid-2006 the company supplied video iPods to all of its 8,500 employees, celebrating National's success in the previous year. The company makes analog chips that go into the popular MP3 music player from Apple. The iPods were not, however, gifts from the company to the employees. When National laid off 35 employees from its wafer fab in Arlington, Texas, later the same month, those employees were told to turn in their iPods as company property.

In early 2007 National acquired Xignal Technologies, a German developer of high-speed analog-to-digital converters, for about $9 million, including the assumption of liabilities.

## EXECUTIVES

**Chairman and CEO:** Brian L. Halla, age 61, $6,230,004 pay
**President and COO:** Donald Macleod, age 56, $3,586,154 pay
**SVP, Manufacturing Services and CIO:** Ulrich J. Seif, age 49
**SVP, General Counsel, and Secretary:** John M. Clark III, age 57
**SVP, Analog Products Group:** Suneil V. Parulekar, age 59, $1,156,800 pay
**SVP, Finance and CFO:** Lewis Chew, age 44, $1,592,308 pay
**SVP, Power Management Group:** Detlev J. Kunz, age 56, $1,185,004 pay
**SVP, Technology Support:** Mohan Yegnashankaran
**SVP, Worldwide Human Resources:** Edward J. Sweeney, age 50
**SVP, Worldwide Manufacturing:** C.S. Liu
**SVP, Worldwide Marketing and Sales:** Michael Noonen
**VP and Managing Director, South Portland Facility:** Paul Edmonds
**VP, Package Technology Group:** Sadanand (Sada) Patil
**VP, Corporate Marketing:** Phil Gibson
**VP, Power Management:** Edward Lam
**CTO, Analog:** Dennis Monticelli
**CTO, Labs:** Ahmad Bahai
**Treasurer:** Robert E. DeBarr
**Controller:** Jamie E. Samath
**Staff Scientist and Dean, Analog University:** Bob Pease
**Worldwide Public Relations Director:** Jeff Weir
**Marketing Director, Communication Infrastructure Products:** Stephen Kempainen
**Product Marketing Manager, Wireless Group:** Paul Boyer
**Auditors:** KPMG LLP

## LOCATIONS

**HQ:** National Semiconductor Corporation
2900 Semiconductor Dr., Santa Clara, CA 95052
**Phone:** 408-721-5000 **Fax:** 408-739-9803
**Web:** www.national.com

National Semiconductor has manufacturing facilities in China, Malaysia, the UK, and the US, with design facilities and sales offices around the world.

### 2007 Sales

| | $ mil. | % of total |
|---|---|---|
| China | 539.2 | 28 |
| US | 428.4 | 22 |
| Singapore | 340.9 | 18 |
| Japan | 217.7 | 11 |
| Germany | 213.5 | 11 |
| UK | 190.2 | 10 |
| **Total** | **1,929.9** | **100** |

## PRODUCTS/OPERATIONS

### 2007 Sales

| | $ mil. | % of total |
|---|---|---|
| Analog | 1,744.8 | 90 |
| Other | 185.1 | 10 |
| **Total** | **1,929.9** | **100** |

### Selected Products

Aerospace and military integrated circuits (ICs)
Amplifiers and regulators
Audio circuits
Automotive ICs
Data acquisition circuits
Display circuits for monitors
Ethernet and Fast Ethernet digital signal processing devices
Interface circuits
Microcontrollers (automotive, communications, and industrial applications)
Power management circuits
Temperature sensors
Wireless circuits (radio and other functions)

## COMPETITORS

Analog Devices
Atmel
Broadcom
Cypress Semiconductor
Fairchild Semiconductor
Freescale Semiconductor
IBM Microelectronics
Infineon Technologies
Intel
International Rectifier
Intersil
Linear Technology
Marvell Technology
Maxim Integrated Products
Microchip Technology
NEC Electronics
NXP
ON Semiconductor
Samsung Electronics
SANYO
Sensata
Sharp
STMicroelectronics
Texas Instruments
Toshiba Semiconductor

## HISTORICAL FINANCIALS

Company Type: Public

### Income Statement

FYE: Last Sunday in May

| | REVENUE ($ mil.) | NET INCOME ($ mil.) | NET PROFIT MARGIN | EMPLOYEES |
|---|---|---|---|---|
| **5/07** | 1,930 | 375 | 19.4% | 7,600 |
| **5/06** | 2,158 | 449 | 20.8% | 8,500 |
| **5/05** | 1,913 | 415 | 21.7% | 8,500 |
| **5/04** | 1,983 | 283 | 14.3% | 9,700 |
| **5/03** | 1,673 | (33) | — | 9,800 |
| **Annual Growth** | 3.6% | — | — | (6.2%) |

### 2007 Year-End Financials

Debt ratio: 1.2%
Return on equity: 20.4%
Cash ($ mil.): 829
Current ratio: 4.30
Long-term debt ($ mil.): 21
No. of shares (mil.): 310
Dividends
Yield: 0.5%
Payout: 12.5%
Market value ($ mil.): 8,089

### Stock History

NYSE: NSM

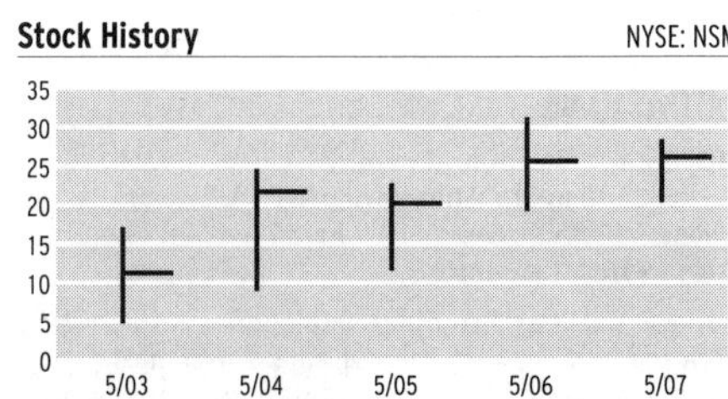


| | STOCK PRICE ($) FY Close | P/E High | P/E Low | PER SHARE ($) Earnings | PER SHARE ($) Dividends | PER SHARE ($) Book Value |
|---|---|---|---|---|---|---|
| **5/07** | 26.07 | 25 | 18 | 1.12 | 0.14 | 5.64 |
| **5/06** | 25.60 | 25 | 15 | 1.26 | 0.10 | 5.74 |
| **5/05** | 20.16 | 20 | 11 | 1.11 | 0.02 | 5.94 |
| **5/04** | 21.67 | 33 | 13 | 0.73 | — | 4.70 |
| **5/03** | 11.22 | — | — | (0.09) | — | 9.28 |
| **Annual Growth** | 23.5% | — | — | — | 164.6% | (11.7%) |

# Nationwide Mutual Insurance

Call it truth in advertising — Nationwide Mutual Insurance Company has offices throughout the US. The company is a leading US property/casualty insurer that, though still a mutual firm, operates in part through publicly held insurance subsidiary Nationwide Financial Services. In addition to personal and commercial property/casualty coverage, life insurance, and financial services, Nationwide offers surplus lines, professional liability, workers' compensation, agricultural insurance and loss-control, pet insurance, and other coverage. The company sells its products through such affiliates as ALLIED Group, Farmland Insurance, GatesMcDonald, and Scottsdale Insurance.

To enhance its focus on personal and small-business lines in the US, Nationwide bought specialty auto insurer THI from Prudential. Nationwide Financial also bought Provident Mutual Life Insurance (now Nationwide Financial Network); the acquisition made the company the fourth-largest US provider of variable life insurance. However, the insurance market in general is fairly mature, and the company sees more opportunities for growth from its financial services offerings — especially as Baby Boomers start looking at retirement.

In April of 2006, Nationwide Financial Services received approval to expand its services to include full-service banking. Operating as Nationwide Bank, the business has added deposit products and ATM access for its insurance, mortgage, and financial services customers.

Nationwide and several other insurance companies were named in a series of lawsuits stemming from the aftermath of Hurricane Katrina. One suit alleged that prior to the natural disaster insurance agents dissuaded their clients from purchasing flood insurance, and that the companies did not offer the full settlement amount to clients whose homes had been damaged by the storm surge of water. In one of the first lawsuits to be decided, the judge ruled in favor of Nationwide. However, the same judge, whose docket is swamped with such cases, has also ordered the use of mediation to resolve such differences in less time, and with less expense.

Meanwhile, Nationwide enjoyed the relative calm of the 2006 storm season.

## HISTORY

In 1919 members of the Ohio Farm Bureau Federation, a farmers' consumer group, established their own automobile insurance company. (As rural drivers, they didn't want to pay city rates.) To get a license from the state, the company, called Farm Bureau Mutual, needed 100 policyholders. It gathered more than 1,000. Founder Murray Lincoln headed the company until 1964.

The insurer expanded into Delaware, Maryland, North Carolina, and Vermont in 1928 and began selling auto insurance in 1931 to city folks. It expanded into fire insurance in 1934 and life insurance the next year.

During WWII growth slowed, although the company had operations in 12 states and Washington, DC, by 1943. It diversified in 1946 when it bought a Columbus, Ohio, radio station. By 1952 the firm had resumed expansion and changed its name to Nationwide.

The company was one of the first auto insurance companies to use its agents to sell other financial products, adding life insurance and mutual funds in the mid-1950s. Nationwide General, the country's first merit-rated auto insurance firm, was formed in 1956.

Nationwide established Neckura in Germany in 1965 to sell auto and fire insurance. Four years later the company bought GatesMcDonald, a provider of risk, tax, benefit, and health care management services. It organized its property/casualty operations into Nationwide Property & Casualty in 1979.

The company experienced solid growth throughout the 1980s by establishing or purchasing insurance firms, among them Colonial Insurance of California (1980), Financial Horizons Life (1981), Scottsdale (1982), and, the largest, Employers Insurance of Wausau (1985). Wausau wrote the country's first workers' compensation policy in 1911.

Earnings were up and down in the 1990s as the company invested in Wausau and in consolidating office operations. Nationwide set up an ethics office in 1995, a time of increased scrutiny of insurance industry sales practices, and made an effort to hire more women as agents. In 1996 the Florida Insurance Commission claimed the company discriminated against customers on the basis of age, gender, health, income, marital status, and location. Nationwide countered that the allegations originated from disgruntled agents.

In 1997 the company settled a lawsuit by agreeing to stop its redlining practices (it avoided selling homeowners' insurance to urban customers with homes valued at less than $50,000 or more than 30 years old, which allegedly discriminated against minorities). It also dropped a year-old sales quota system that was under investigation.

As the century came to a close, Nationwide began to narrow its focus on its core businesses. It spun off Nationwide Financial Services so the unit could have better access to capital, and it expanded both at home and abroad through such purchases as ALLIED Group (multiline insurance), CalFarm (agricultural insurance in California), and AXA subsidiary PanEuroLife (asset management in Europe). It jettisoned such operations as West Coast Life Insurance, its Wausau subsidiary, and its ALLIED Life operations. The company's discrimination woes came back to haunt it in 1999, and it created a $750,000 fund to help residents of poor Cincinnati neighborhoods buy homes.

At the end of 2000, Nationwide Health Plans asked regulators for permission to exit the profit-poor HMO business. The division plans to maintain its more popular PPO operations. The next year Nationwide's expansion in Europe continued with the purchase of UK fund manager Gartmore Investment Management.

Although Nationwide Financial and its Strategic Investments segment underperformed in 2002, the company swung to a net profit, helped in part by improved underwriting results by its insurance subsidiaries.

Nationwide Mutual sold off the London-based arm of its Gartmore Investment Management subsidiary to management and Hellman & Friedman LLC in 2006. Nationwide retained the US investment operations and changed its name to Gartmore Global Investments.

## EXECUTIVES

**Chairman:** Arden L. Shisler, age 65
**Vice Chairman:** James F. Patterson, age 65
**CEO and Director:** William G. (Jerry) Jurgensen, age 55
**President and COO, Nationwide Financial Services, Inc.:** Mark R. Thresher, age 50
**President and COO, Property and Casualty Insurance Operations:** Stephen S. (Steve) Rasmussen, age 54
**President, Nationwide Strategic Investments:** Donna A. James, age 49
**EVP, Chief Legal and Governance Officer:** Patricia R. (Pat) Hatler, age 52
**EVP and Chief Administrative Officer:** Terri L. Hill, age 47
**EVP and CFO, Finance, Investments, and Strategy:** Robert A. Rosholt, age 56
**EVP and CIO:** Michael C. Keller, age 47
**Chief Marketing Officer:** James (Jim) Lyski
**Chief Investment Officer:** Gail G. Snyder, age 52
**Treasurer:** Harry Hallowell
**President and COO, Scottsdale Insurance:** Michael D. (Mike) Miller
**Global CFO, Gartmore Group:** M. Eileen Kennedy, age 47
**Interim CEO, NWD Investment Group:** John Grady
**Chief Privacy Officer, Assistant VP, and Associate General Counsel:** Kirk Herath
**Auditors:** KPMG LLP

## LOCATIONS

**HQ:** Nationwide Mutual Insurance Company
1 Nationwide Plaza, Columbus, OH 43215
**Phone:** 614-249-7111 **Fax:** 614-249-7705
**Web:** www.nationwide.com

## PRODUCTS/OPERATIONS

### 2006 Sales

| | $ mil. | % of total |
|---|---|---|
| Premiums & policy charges | 17,427 | 78 |
| Net investment income | 3,400 | 15 |
| Net realized gains on investments | 237 | 1 |
| Other income | 1,189 | 6 |
| **Total** | **22,253** | **100** |

### Selected Subsidiaries and Affiliates

Allied Property and Casualty Insurance Company
Colonial County Mutual Insurance Company
Depositors Insurance Company
Farmland Mutual Insurance Company
Gartmore Global Partners
National Casualty Company
Nationwide Affinity Insurance Company of America
Nationwide Agribusiness Insurance Company
Nationwide Assurance Company
Nationwide Financial Services, Inc.
Nationwide General Insurance Company
Nationwide Indemnity (reinsurance, in run-off)
Nationwide Insurance Company of America
Nationwide Lloyds
Nationwide Mutual Fire Insurance Company
Nationwide Retirement Solutions
Nationwide Property and Casualty Insurance Company
Nationwide Securities, Inc.
Scottsdale Insurance Company
Scottsdale Indemnity Company
The 401(k) Company

## COMPETITORS

ACE Limited
AIG
Allstate
American Financial
AXA
AXA Financial
Blue Cross
CIGNA
Citigroup
CNA Financial
GEICO
Guardian Life
The Hartford
John Hancock
Liberty Mutual
MassMutual
MetLife
New York Life
Northwestern Mutual
Pacific Mutual
Principal Financial
Prudential
State Farm
Travelers Companies
UnitedHealth Group
USAA

## HISTORICAL FINANCIALS

Company Type: Mutual company

**Income Statement** FYE: December 31

| | ASSETS ($ mil.) | NET INCOME ($ mil.) | INCOME AS % OF ASSETS | EMPLOYEES |
|---|---|---|---|---|
| **12/06** | 160,009 | 2,113 | 1.3% | 36,000 |
| **12/05** | 158,258 | 1,149 | 0.7% | 35,000 |
| **12/04** | 157,371 | 1,010 | 0.6% | 32,933 |
| **12/03** | 147,934 | 653 | 0.4% | 33,249 |
| **12/02** | 117,930 | 252 | 0.2% | 30,000 |
| **Annual Growth** | 7.9% | 70.1% | — | 4.7% |

**2006 Year-End Financials**

Equity as % of assets: —
Return on assets: 1.3%
Return on equity: —
Long-term debt ($ mil.): —
Sales ($ mil.): 22,253

**Net Income History**

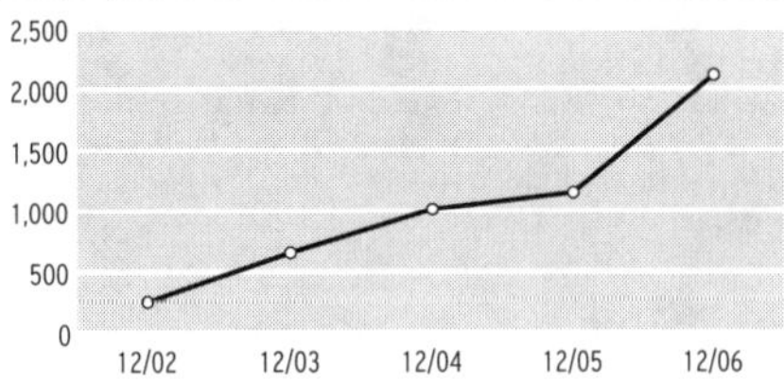


# NBC Television

This TV network is hoping the water cooler talk at *The Office* and a group of *Heroes* will help it replace all the *Friends* it has lost. The NBC Television Network operates the #4 broadcast network NBC, which reaches millions of viewers through 14 company-owned or -operated stations and more than 230 US affiliates. It features such hit shows as *The Office*, *Heroes*, and doctor drama *ER*. NBC Television also oversees Spanish-language broadcaster Telemundo, which operates more than 20 TV stations and about 35 affiliates. The company is part of media conglomerate NBC Universal, which is 80%-owned by General Electric; Vivendi (formerly Vivendi Universal) owns the rest.

NBC has been trying to climb back into the top spot among the broadcast networks following its rapid decline in 2004. The broadcaster sank quickly after such hits as *Friends* and *Frasier* ended their long runs. During the 2005-06 season, NBC managed to stem some of the bleeding when *The Office* and *My Name is Earl* joined its once stellar Thursday night schedule, while breakout hit *Heros* proved to be one of the few bright spots during the 2006-07 season.

With the network stuck in fourth place in both overall viewers and the advertiser-favored 18-49 demographic for a third consecutive year, top entertainment chief Kevin Reilly was fired shortly after the network announced its Fall lineup for the 2007 season. Ben Silverman, who founded Reveille Productions, and Marc Graboff, a network veteran, were named co-chairmen of NBC Entertainment and NBC Universal Television Studio (now Universal Media Studios).

But the future is not entirely gloomy for NBC, and the Peacock might once again spread its feathers proudly. It ponied up $600 million for a six-year deal to broadcast National Football League games on Sunday nights, marking the network's return to pro football (it lost rights to NFL games in 1998).

NBC is also making big investments in online programming to promote and supplement its traditional broadcasting operations. The network is working on several online-only shows that offer a tie-in to its primetime schedule, and it is distributing programs through Apple's iTunes store as well as through some pay-per-view outlets. With the merger of NBC and Vivendi's entertainment assets in 2004, the network is now allied with production unit NBC Universal Television, as well as a number of sister cable outlets run through NBC Universal Cable (USA Network, SCI FI Channel). The cable network cousins give NBC more outlets to promote new and existing programs. In 2006 NBC began promoting several of its new shows in a partnership with movie rental company Netflix, in which Netflix subscribers can order episodes prior to their broadcast.

The company announced an overhaul of its traditional television operations in late 2006. It said it would cut its broadcast network expenses in order to focus on its digital operations. Changes will include using lower-cost programming (such as the game-show format) in primetime, consolidating cable and network studios, incorporating more content from its NBC Universal production house, and cutting jobs in the news division.

## HISTORY

In 1919 General Electric and Westinghouse formed Radio Corporation of America (RCA). Five years later RCA pioneered television with the transmission of the first radio-photo. Led by inventor-cum-entrepreneur David Sarnoff, RCA set up the National Broadcasting Company (NBC) in 1926 to develop quality radio programs.

The demand for radio network programming grew rapidly. The company split its programming into two networks to give listeners a choice of formats. In 1941 the Federal Communications Commission (FCC) ruled that companies could own only one network. NBC subsequently sold one of its networks, which formed the nucleus of rival American Broadcasting Company (ABC).

Sarnoff also pursued the development of TV. In 1939 NBC began the first regular TV service with coverage of President Roosevelt inaugurating the New York World's Fair. In 1941 NBC obtained a commercial TV license from the FCC, and its WBNT-TV (New York) became the world's first commercial TV station. NBC launched current affairs program *Meet the Press* in 1947. The company won FCC approval for its color TV system in 1953 and presented the first nationwide color broadcast that year.

During the 1970s NBC's ratings slumped, as did its radio business. Led by NBC Entertainment's young president Brandon Tartikoff, the network staged a comeback in the 1980s with an unparalleled string of hits, including *Miami Vice*, *The Cosby Show*, and *Cheers*.

In the midst of the network's resurrection, GE bought RCA for $6.4 billion in 1986. That year Robert Wright was named president and CEO of the NBC network. Despite a number of attempts to revive radio's popularity, the company decided to exit the business. It sold seven of its eight stations in 1988.

In 1990 Tartikoff aide Warren Littlefield took over as head of entertainment. In 1992 NBC bought the Financial News Network and merged it with CNBC. The following year the network fell to third in the ratings. But NBC bounced back with a slew of new programs (led by *ER*) in 1994 and 1995 to win back the top ratings spot. In 1996 NBC launched MSNBC. Littlefield left in 1998 and was replaced by Scott Sassa.

In 2002 NBC bought Telemundo Communications, owner of the US's second-largest Spanish-language TV network, for about $2.6 billion. Paxson Communications challenged the deal (filing documents with FCC and asking for arbitration with NBC), saying that the Telemundo acquisition would create regulatory hurdles for NBC to buy a larger stake in Paxson. (Paxson lost its arbitration case in 2002.)

In 2004 NBC bought the entertainment assets of Vivendi Universal (now Vivendi). GE combined the properties into a new company called NBC Universal (NBCU), with GE owning 80% of the venture and Vivendi owning the rest. Wright was named chairman and CEO of NBCU.

Entertainment head Jeff Zucker was named CEO of NBC Universal Television in 2006, taking on responsibility for the NBC network, as well as NBCU's many cable outlets.

In 2007 Wright announced his departure from NBCU after 20 years leading first the NBC network and later the entertainment conglomerate. Zucker was appointed his successor. Later that year, entertainment chief Kevin Reilly was ousted from his position due to NBC's sagging ratings; TV producer Ben Silverman and network veteran Marc Graboff were tabbed to lead the entertainment and production divisions.

## EXECUTIVES

**President and CEO, NBC Universal:** Jeffrey A. (Jeff) Zucker, age 41
**EVP Affiliate Relations:** John Damiano
**EVP Digital Entertainment and New Media:** Vivi Zigler
**Chief Marketing Officer; President, NBC Agency:** John Miller
**EVP Publicity:** Rebecca Marks
**EVP, NBC Strategic Partnership Group:** Jay Linden
**EVP Business Affairs, NBC Universal Entertainment and Cable Entertainment:** Beth Roberts
**EVP Casting, NBC Entertainment:** Marc Hirschfeld
**EVP Entertainment Strategy and Programs:** Ted Frank
**EVP Program Planning and Scheduling:** Mitch Metcalf
**EVP Sports Programming:** Jonathon D. (Jon) Miller
**SVP Advertising and Media Sales, NBC Universal Domestic Television Distribution:** Barbara (Bo) Argentino
**SVP Digital Development; General Manager, NBC.com:** Stephen Andrade
**SVP Human Resources:** Thomas Cairns
**Co-Chairman, NBC Entertainment:** Marc Graboff
**Co-Chairman, NBC Entertainment:** Ben Silverman
**Chairman, NBC Universal Sports and Olympics:** Dick Ebersol
**President, NBC News:** Steve Capus
**President, NBC Sports:** Kenneth Schanzer
**President, NBC Universal Cable and Digital Content:** Jeff Gaspin
**President, NBC Universal Domestic Television Distribution:** Barry Wallach
**President, NBC Universal International Television Distribution:** Belinda Menendez
**President and Creative Director, The NBC Agency:** Vince Manze
**President, Research and Media Development:** Alan Wurtzel
**President, Telemundo:** Donald (Don) Browne
**Auditors:** KPMG LLP

## LOCATIONS

**HQ:** The NBC Television Network
30 Rockefeller Plaza, New York, NY 10112
**Phone:** 212-664-4444 **Fax:** 212-664-4085
**Web:** www.nbc.com

## PRODUCTS/OPERATIONS

### Selected Operations

National Broadcasting Company (broadcast television network)
NBC Entertainment (television production)
NBC News
*Dateline NBC*
*Meet the Press*
*Today*
NBC Shows
*30 Rock*
*The Biggest Loser*
*Crossing Jordan*
*Days of our Lives*
*Deal or No Deal*
*ER*
*Fear Factor*
*Friday Night Lights*
*Heroes*
*Las Vegas*
*Law & Order*
*Law & Order: Criminal Intent*
*Law & Order: Special Victims Unit*
*Medium*
*My Name is Earl*
*The Office*
*Saturday Night Live*
*Scrubs*
*Tonight Show with Jay Leno*
NBC Sports
Paxson Communications (32%, i TV network and about 60 TV stations)
Telemundo Communications Group (US Hispanic television network)

## COMPETITORS

A&E Networks
ABC
CBS
Cisneros Group
The CW
Discovery
Fox Entertainment
Imagine
Lionsgate Television
MyNetworkTV
Sony Pictures Television
Turner Broadcasting
Univision
Warner Bros. TV

# NBTY, Inc.

NBTY's products give your body a little TLC. Cashing in on the market for preventive and alternative health care, NBTY makes, wholesales, and retails more than 22,000 nutritional supplements, including vitamins, minerals, herbs, sports drinks, and other goods. Brands include Nature's Bounty, Sundown, American Health, and Good 'N Natural. NBTY sells its goods through pharmacies, wholesalers, supermarkets, and health food stores. It has some 540 Vitamin World and Nutrition Warehouse stores in the US, Puerto Rico, Guam, and the US Virgin Islands. On the international front, NBTY operates some 545 Holland & Barrett, Nature's Way, and GNC (UK) stores in the UK and Ireland.

It also has about 70 De Tuinen outlets in the Netherlands and about 100 Le Naturiste shops in Quebec, Canada.

The highly acquisitive NBTY bought Canadian vitamin manufacturer and distributor SISU in 2005. It has also acquired Solgar Vitamin and Herb — a manufacturer and distributor of vitamin, mineral, and herb supplements — from Wyeth. The buy fortified NBTY's premium brand supplements line. In 2006 the company acquired Zila Nutraceuticals, a division of Zila, for about $40 million.

In addition to its retail stores, NBTY operates Puritan's Pride, which sells nutritional products through mail-order catalogs and over the Internet. Puritan's Pride boasts some 4 million customers. Through its various sales arms, NBTY sells its products to customers in more than 85 countries around the world.

The company manufactures 90% of the products that it sells.

Chairman and CEO Scott Rudolph owns about 12% of the company.

## HISTORY

Arthur Rudolph founded NBTY in his garage in the early 1960s. Then called Nature's Bounty, the company went public in 1971 to market nutritional supplements. Rudolph was chairman and CEO until his 1993 resignation, when son Scott succeeded him.

Without so much as a glass of water, Nature's Bounty swallowed the mail-order business of General Nutrition Companies in 1989, and vitamin distributor Prime Natural Health Laboratories in 1993.

In 1995 the company agreed to settle Federal Trade Commission charges that it made deceptive claims about the effectiveness of 26 nutrient supplements. That year Nature's Bounty changed its name to NBTY (its stock symbol).

In 1997 NBTY bought leading UK health foods chain Holland & Barrett, which operated more than 400 stores. The acquisition more than doubled NBTY's store count. After the buy, NBTY started stocking Holland & Barrett's shelves with its products. In 1998 the company bought a group of privately held vitamin companies and made a major push to open more Vitamin World stores in the US. In 1999 NBTY acquired Nutrition Warehouse, further bolstering its retail, e-commerce, and mail-order operations. Also that year it bought network marketer Dynamic Essentials to broaden its distribution channels.

Acquisitions continued into the 21st century: SDV Vitamins, a division of Rexall Sundown, joined the family in 2000, and in 2001 NBTY bought the Knox NutraJoint and Knox for Nails nutritional supplement business from Kraft Foods for about $4 million, along with NatureSmart from Whole Foods Market. The company's Holland & Barrett subsidiary bought a chain of 12 vitamin retail stores (Nature's Way) in Ireland. To expand its wholesale business, NBTY in 2002 purchased a line of nutritional supplements sold under the Synergy Plus trademark, a well-known brand among health food aficionados.

A big move came in 2003. NBTY bought Rexall Sundown from Royal Numico N.V. that year. Also that year, the company disbanded its Dynamic Essentials subsidiary after receiving a letter of inquiry by the FTC regarding a weight-loss product marketed by Dynamic Essentials. In addition, the company ceased production of all weight-loss products that contained ephedra, amidst growing concerns about the herbal supplement's safety.

## EXECUTIVES

**Chairman and CEO:** Scott Rudolph, age 49, $1,328,976 pay
**President and CFO:** Harvey Kamil, age 62, $815,548 pay
**SVP, Strategic Planning, Secretary, and Director:** Michael C. Slade, age 57, $354,132 pay
**SVP, Marketing and Advertising:** James P. Flaherty, age 49, $304,129 pay
**President, Solgar Vitamin and Herb Company:** Rand Skolnick
**Auditors:** PricewaterhouseCoopers LLP

## LOCATIONS

**HQ:** NBTY, Inc.
90 Orville Dr., Bohemia, NY 11716
**Phone:** 631-567-9500 **Fax:** 631-567-7148
**Web:** www.nbty.com

NBTY has retail stores throughout the US and in Guam, Puerto Rico, and the US Virgin Islands. Its manufacturing, distribution, and sales facilities are in Arkansas, California, Colorado, Florida, Illinois, Nevada, New Jersey, New York, and Pennsylvania. Overseas, the company has facilities in the Netherlands and the UK.

## PRODUCTS/OPERATIONS

### 2006 Sales

| | $ mil. | % of total |
|---|---|---|
| Wholesale | 885.2 | 47 |
| Retail | | |
| Europe | 564.9 | 30 |
| US | 234.2 | 13 |
| Direct response | 195.9 | 10 |
| **Total** | **1,880.2** | **100** |

### Selected Brands and Retail Outlets

American Health
De Tuinen (Dutch retail)
GNC (UK)
Good 'N Natural
Holland & Barrett (UK retail)
MET-Rx
Natural Wealth
Nature's Bounty
Nutrition Headquarters
Nutrition Warehouse (US retail)
Puritan's Pride (mail-order and online retail)
Rexall
Sundown
Vitamin World (US retail)
Worldwide Sport Nutrition

## COMPETITORS

Bactolac Pharmaceutical
GNC
Inverness Medical
Natural Alternatives
Nature's Sunshine
Nutraceutical
Perrigo
Reliv'
Sunrider
Unicity
USANA Health Sciences
VS Holdings

## HISTORICAL FINANCIALS

Company Type: Public

### Income Statement

FYE: September 30

| | REVENUE ($ mil.) | NET INCOME ($ mil.) | NET PROFIT MARGIN | EMPLOYEES |
|---|---|---|---|---|
| **9/06** | 1,880 | 112 | 5.9% | 10,900 |
| **9/05** | 1,737 | 78 | 4.5% | 11,200 |
| **9/04** | 1,652 | 112 | 6.8% | 10,000 |
| **9/03** | 1,193 | 82 | 6.8% | 10,000 |
| **9/02** | 964 | 96 | 9.9% | 8,100 |
| **Annual Growth** | 18.2% | 3.9% | — | 7.7% |

### 2006 Year-End Financials

| | |
|---|---|
| Debt ratio: 22.8% | No. of shares (mil.): 67 |
| Return on equity: 14.4% | Dividends |
| Cash ($ mil.): 90 | Yield: — |
| Current ratio: 2.86 | Payout: — |
| Long-term debt ($ mil.): 191 | Market value ($ mil.): 1,967 |

### Stock History

NYSE: NTY

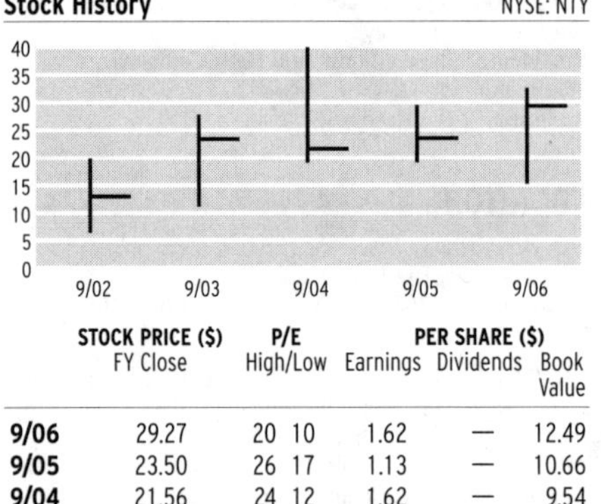


| | STOCK PRICE ($) FY Close | P/E High | P/E Low | PER SHARE ($) Earnings | Dividends | Book Value |
|---|---|---|---|---|---|---|
| **9/06** | 29.27 | 20 | 10 | 1.62 | — | 12.49 |
| **9/05** | 23.50 | 26 | 17 | 1.13 | — | 10.66 |
| **9/04** | 21.56 | 24 | 12 | 1.62 | — | 9.54 |
| **9/03** | 23.35 | 23 | 10 | 1.19 | — | 7.73 |
| **9/02** | 12.98 | 14 | 5 | 1.41 | — | 6.34 |
| **Annual Growth** | 22.5% | — | — | 3.5% | — | 18.5% |

# NCR Corporation

Want to find NCR? Follow the money. The company — originally National Cash Register — is a leading maker of automatic teller machines (ATMs). It makes other retail and financial electronics such as point-of-sale (POS) terminals and bar code scanners. NCR's operating units include Retail Store Automation (POS systems, kiosks), Financial Self Services (payment systems, ATMs), Systemedia Group (paper, ink, and other media products), Teradata (data gathering and analysis), Payment and Imaging Solutions (check image processing), and Worldwide Customer Services (professional and support services).

Early in 2007 NCR announced plans to spin off Teradata to create a separate, publicly-traded company. The company also revealed plans to outsource more of its manufacturing and reduce its workforce to cut costs.

NCR, which struggled in the 1990s after failing to keep up with changing technology, slimmed down its structure through job cuts, divestitures, and reorganization. The company moved beyond its hardware roots, seeking the higher margins of the software and services businesses. It has also shifted to outsourced manufacturing for select products. The company's customers include AT&T, Delta Air Lines, the US Postal Service, and Wal-Mart.

NCR agreed to acquire the ATM business of Tidel Technologies in 2005; the deal closed early the following year. NCR also acquired the assets of IDVelocity, a developer of RFID infrastructure and process management software.

## HISTORY

John Patterson bought control of a Dayton, Ohio, cash register factory in 1882 and founded National Cash Register (NCR). Colonel Edward Deeds (who later became chairman) joined NCR in 1889, and hired inventor Charles Kettering in 1904 to develop an electric cash register. (The duo also developed an electric car ignition system and left NCR to start Dayton Engineering Laboratories Co., or Delco.)

By the 1920s NCR controlled 90% of the cash register market. That decade NCR introduced accounting machines, which became almost as important to the company as cash registers. NCR's stock dropped from $154 to $6.87 in the crash of 1929, but by 1936 the company had fully recovered.

Responding to the commercialization of computers following WWII, NCR bought computer developer Computer Research in 1952. During the 1960s the company introduced mainframe computers, opened data processing centers, established microelectronics research facilities, and introduced disk-based computers. However, NCR failed to automate its primary products — cash registers and accounting machines. In 1969 the company had record profits of $50 million; by 1971 they had plunged to $2 million.

William Anderson, who became president in 1972, is credited with saving NCR. He slashed its Dayton workforce by 75% and focused the company on computing, with an emphasis on retail scanners and ATMs.

In the early 1980s NCR moved from proprietary to UNIX operating systems and introduced networking equipment. In 1990 it began developing parallel processing technologies with database management specialist Teradata. That year the company won a contract to supply workstations to JCPenney stores.

Hoping to become one of the world's top PC makers, in 1991 AT&T bought NCR in a $7.4 billion hostile takeover. AT&T also acquired Teradata and merged the two companies as Global Information Systems (GIS). Lars Nyberg, a Swede who had led a divisional turnaround at electronics giant Philips, took over GIS in 1995 and began a reorganization that would eventually cut 11,000 jobs. When he joined GIS, it was losing $2 million a day.

In 1996 AT&T spun off the company (renamed NCR); it had suffered losses totaling nearly $4 billion during its years with AT&T. Nyberg jettisoned NCR's financially draining PC operations but beefed up the company's ATM and retail automation business by acquiring Compris Technologies (grocery automation and management products) and Dataworks (check processing software).

But losses prompted NCR to restructure in 1997, and the company slimmed down its 130-country network of independent operating units into a handful of global business units. The next year the company announced a partnership with Microsoft to further integrate NCR's Teradata systems with Microsoft's server technology, making it easier for companies to create data warehouses. Also in 1998 NCR sold factories in Ireland and the US to contract manufacturer Solectron, which agreed to produce NCR's hardware products for the next five years.

The following year, with a narrowed focus on ATM, banking, retail, and data warehousing systems, the company acquired IBM's financial self-service operations and financial industry automation software company Gaspar.

In 2000 NCR bought Ceres Integrated Solutions, a provider of customer relationship management software, and it acquired information technology and outsourcing service provider 4Front Technologies for $250 million. In 2003 Nyberg handed the CEO reins to NCR president and former Teradata head Mark Hurd. Nyberg retained his chairmanship.

In 2004 NCR acquired Kinetics, a provider of self-service check-in systems for airlines and hotels; Kinetics' products also included systems for restaurant preordering and event ticketing.

Early in 2005 Hurd resigned to become CEO of Hewlett-Packard; NCR director Jim Ringler was appointed interim CEO and was named chairman. Soon after former Symbol Technologies CEO Bill Nuti was named CEO of NCR.

## EXECUTIVES

**Chairman:** James M. (Jim) Ringler, age 61
**President, CEO, and Director:** William R. (Bill) Nuti, age 43, $1,000,000 pay
**SVP and Chief Administrative Officer:** Eric A. Berg, age 44
**SVP, General Counsel, and Secretary:** Peter Lieb, age 50
**SVP, Financial Solutions Division:** Malcolm Kelvin Collins, age 47, $832,317 pay
**SVP, Worldwide Customer Service Division:** Christine W. (Chris) Wallace, age 54, $322,800 pay
**SVP, Teradata Division:** Michael F. (Mike) Koehler, age 54, $417,000 pay
**SVP, Retail/Hospitality and Self-Service Solutions:** Dan Bogan, age 51
**SVP Human Resources:** Andrea Ledford
**CTO:** Alan Chow
**VP, Global Operations:** Bruce A. Langos, age 53
**VP, Self-Service Solutions:** Mike Webster
**VP; General Manager, Systemedia:** Peter A. Dorsman, age 51
**VP Corporate Communications:** Jane Brewer
**VP, Self-Service Business Development:** Mel Walter
**Co-President, NCR Japan:** Glen S. Fukushima, age 57
**Co-President, NCR Japan:** Hideki Hosoi
**President, Galvanon:** Raj Toleti
**Interim CFO and Controller:** Robert Fishman, age 44
**Auditors:** PricewaterhouseCoopers LLP

## LOCATIONS

**HQ:** NCR Corporation
1700 S. Patterson Blvd., Dayton, OH 45479
**Phone:** 937-445-5000 **Fax:** 937-445-5541
**Web:** www.ncr.com

### 2006 Sales

| | $ mil. | % of total |
|---|---|---|
| Americas | | |
| US | 2,588 | 42 |
| Other countries | 441 | 7 |
| Europe, Middle East & Africa | 2,035 | 33 |
| Asia/Pacific | | |
| Japan | 432 | 7 |
| Other countries | 646 | 11 |
| **Total** | **6,142** | **100** |

## PRODUCTS/OPERATIONS

### 2006 Sales

| | $ mil. | % of total |
|---|---|---|
| Customer services | 1,812 | 29 |
| Data warehousing | 1,572 | 25 |
| Financial self-service | 1,423 | 22 |
| Retail store automation | 870 | 14 |
| Systemedia | 473 | 7 |
| Payment and imaging & other | 170 | 3 |
| Adjustments | (178) | — |
| **Total** | **6,142** | **100** |

### Operations

Customer service
- Maintenance
- Professional and installation-related

Data Warehousing (Teradata)
- Data warehousing and customer relationship management software
- Disk storage systems
- Servers
- Services (consulting, maintenance, support)

Financial Self Service
- Automated teller machines (ATMs)
- Support services

Retail Store Automation
- Consulting, implementation, and maintenance services
- Electronic shelf labels
- Point-of-sale workstations and scanners
- Software
- Web-enabled kiosks

Systemedia Group
- Ink
- Paper
- Printer cartridges

Payment and Imaging
- Consulting, outsourcing, and support services
- Transactions processing systems

## COMPETITORS

ACI Worldwide, Inc.
Acxiom
BancTec
Datalogic Scanning
De La Rue
Dell
Diebold
EDS
Fujitsu
Hewlett-Packard
Hypercom
IBM
Metrologic Instruments
MICROS Systems
Motorola, Inc.
Oki Electric
Optimal Group
Oracle
SANYO
SAP
Thales e-Transactions
Triton
Unisys
VeriFone
Wincor Nixdorf

## HISTORICAL FINANCIALS

Company Type: Public

**Income Statement** FYE: December 31

| | REVENUE ($ mil.) | NET INCOME ($ mil.) | NET PROFIT MARGIN | EMPLOYEES |
|---|---|---|---|---|
| **12/06** | 6,142 | 382 | 6.2% | 28,900 |
| **12/05** | 6,028 | 529 | 8.8% | 28,200 |
| **12/04** | 5,984 | 290 | 4.8% | 28,500 |
| **12/03** | 5,598 | 58 | 1.0% | 29,000 |
| **12/02** | 5,585 | (220) | — | 29,700 |
| **Annual Growth** | 2.4% | — | — | (0.7%) |

**2006 Year-End Financials**

Debt ratio: 16.3%
Return on equity: 19.5%
Cash ($ mil.): 947
Current ratio: 1.88
Long-term debt ($ mil.): 306
No. of shares (mil.): 179
Dividends
Yield: —
Payout: —
Market value ($ mil.): 7,650

**Stock History** NYSE: NCR

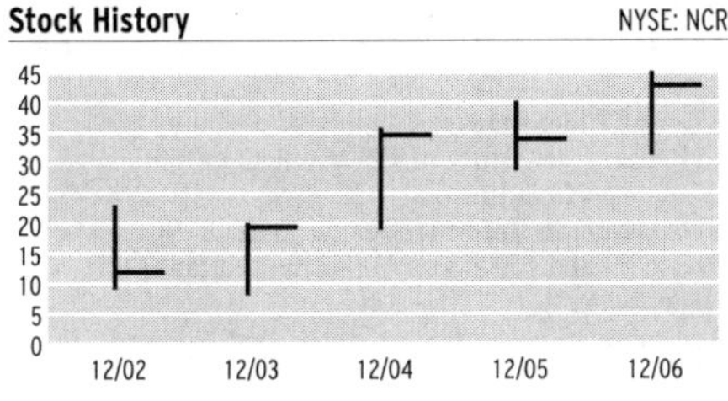


| | STOCK PRICE ($) FY Close | P/E High/Low | PER SHARE ($) Earnings | Dividends | Book Value |
|---|---|---|---|---|---|
| **12/06** | 42.76 | 21 15 | 2.09 | — | 10.51 |
| **12/05** | 33.94 | 14 10 | 2.80 | — | 11.20 |
| **12/04** | 34.62 | 24 13 | 1.51 | — | 11.18 |
| **12/03** | 19.40 | 65 28 | 0.31 | — | 19.80 |
| **12/02** | 11.87 | — — | (1.11) | — | 13.66 |
| **Annual Growth** | 37.8% | — — | — | — | (6.3%) |

# Network Appliance

Network Appliance (NetApp) knows storage backwards and forwards. The company is a leading vendor of network-attached storage (NAS) systems designed for medium-sized to large enterprises; its filers can also be deployed in Fibre Channel and IP-based storage area network (SAN) configurations. NetApp's NearStore line of disk-based devices is designed for backup and archiving. The company also provides operating system, data management, and content delivery software. NetApp sells directly and through channel partners to organizations in the communications, energy, financial services, government, health care, media, manufacturing, and technology sectors. Customers include Deutsche Telekom, Yahoo!, and Boeing.

Network Appliance took an early lead in the NAS market, but the rise in popularity of the relatively inexpensive devices attracted a host of competitors. Never content to cede market share for any storage offering, industry leader EMC sells NAS products. Companies such as Sun Microsystems have used acquisitions to crack the market, and even Dell, which once resold NetApp products, now makes its own NAS devices (Dell is one of a number of companies that make Microsoft Windows-based NAS products).

However, NetApp has expanded beyond the role of pure-play NAS vendor. Responding to customer demand, it expanded the functionality of its storage filers to work within more complex storage area network configurations. The company also provides data security appliances and controllers for storage virtualization.

In 2006 Network Appliance sold its NetCache content delivery business to Blue Coat Systems.

## HISTORY

David Hitz and James Lau (both EVPs) along with Michael Malcolm founded Network Appliance in 1992. The trio saw a market for file servers, hardware that takes the storage duties out of high-performance UNIX-based computers and speeds data flow.

Donald Valentine of Sequoia Capital invested in Network Appliance in 1994, and was named chairman. He promptly brought on board as CEO Daniel Warmenhoven, the top executive of telecommunications company Network Equipment Technologies. (It was the return of a favor — Warmenhoven had given Valentine a tip on investing in a late-1980s fledgling named Cisco.) Warmenhoven ditched the company's network of resellers and built an in-house sales and marketing unit. Network Appliance went public in 1995.

The company in 1996 forged a deal with Microsoft to let Network Appliance's file servers support the software giant's Internet-based network file storage standard. The beefed-up sales emphasis helped the company turn its first profit in fiscal 1996. The next year Network Appliance bought online caching software specialist IMC. Acquisition costs dropped earnings for fiscal 1997.

Network Appliance furthered its inroads into Europe the next year when it sold data storage and retrieval equipment to UK-based Internet service provider Demon Internet. In 1999 the company introduced servers that transmitted audio and video data streams.

Network Appliance acquired two software companies in 2000: Orca Systems (Windows NT and UNIX systems clustering) and WebManage Technologies (data management and distribution). Responding to a slumping economy the following year, the company announced a restructuring plan that included job cuts.

Early in 2004 it acquired Spinnaker Networks for approximately $300 million in stock. The following year it acquired tape emulation software maker Alacritus for about $11 million in cash, and network security appliance maker Decru for $272 million in cash and stock. Late in 2006 Network Appliance acquired data management software developer Topio for about $160 million in cash.

## EXECUTIVES

**Chairman:** Donald T. (Don) Valentine, age 74
**CEO and Director:** Daniel J. (Dan) Warmenhoven, age 56, $1,178,749 pay
**President:** Thomas F. (Tom) Mendoza, age 55, $680,799 pay
**EVP and Chief Strategy Officer:** James K. Lau, age 48
**EVP and General Manager, Enterprise Storage Systems:** Thomas (Tom) Georgens, age 47
**EVP:** David Hitz, age 44, $525,674 pay
**EVP, Finance and CFO:** Steven J. Gomo, age 55, $550,124 pay
**EVP, NetApp Global Services:** Ed Deenihan
**EVP, Field Operations:** Robert E. (Rob) Salmon, age 45, $572,381 pay
**SVP; and General Manager, EMEA:** D. Patrick (Pat) Linehan
**SVP; and General Manager, Emerging Products Group:** John A. (Jay) Kidd
**SVP and CTO:** Steve Kleiman
**SVP, Americas Sales:** George Bennett
**SVP, Engineering:** Jerry Lopatin
**SVP, Human Resources:** Gwendolyn (Gwen) McDonald
**SVP, Operations:** Mark Jon Bluth
**SVP; and General Manager, Decru Business Unit:** Suresh Vasudevan
**VP and CIO:** Marina Levinson
**VP, Core Systems Engineering:** Ken Hibbard
**VP, Integrated Marketing:** Elisa Steele
**VP, North American Channel Sales:** Leonard Iventosch
**VP, Products and Partners:** Patrick Rogers
**Press Relations:** Jodi Baumann
**Auditors:** Deloitte & Touche LLP

## LOCATIONS

**HQ:** Network Appliance, Inc.
495 E. Java Dr., Sunnyvale, CA 94089
**Phone:** 408-822-6000 **Fax:** 408-822-4501
**Web:** www.netapp.com

**2007 Sales**

| | $ mil. | % of total |
|---|---|---|
| US | 1,550.3 | 55 |
| Other countries | 1,254.0 | 45 |
| **Total** | **2,804.3** | **100** |

## PRODUCTS/OPERATIONS

**2007 Sales**

| | $ mil. | % of total |
|---|---|---|
| Products | 2,085.9 | 74 |
| Services | 377.1 | 14 |
| Software upgrades & maintenance | 341.3 | 12 |
| **Total** | **2,804.3** | **100** |

**Selected Products**

Hardware
- Fabric-attached storage (FAS)
- Near-line (NearStore)
- Security (DataFort)
- Virtualized (V-Series)

Software
- Data protection and management
- Operating system (Data ONTAP)

## COMPETITORS

Dell
EMC
Hewlett-Packard
Hitachi Data Systems
IBM
Isilon Systems
LSI Corp.
Microsoft
SGI
Sun Microsystems
Xiotech

## HISTORICAL FINANCIALS

Company Type: Public

### Income Statement

FYE: April 30

| | REVENUE ($ mil.) | NET INCOME ($ mil.) | NET PROFIT MARGIN | EMPLOYEES |
|---|---|---|---|---|
| 4/07 | 2,804 | 298 | 10.6% | 6,635 |
| 4/06 | 2,067 | 267 | 12.9% | 4,976 |
| 4/05 | 1,598 | 226 | 14.1% | 3,801 |
| 4/04 | 1,170 | 152 | 13.0% | 2,844 |
| 4/03 | 892 | 77 | 8.6% | 2,345 |
| Annual Growth | 33.2% | 40.5% | — | 29.7% |

### 2007 Year-End Financials

Debt ratio: —
Return on equity: 15.2%
Cash ($ mil.): 1,427
Current ratio: 1.89
Long-term debt ($ mil.): —
No. of shares (mil.): 367
Dividends
Yield: —
Payout: —
Market value ($ mil.): 13,877

### Stock History

NASDAQ (GS): NTAP

| | STOCK PRICE ($) FY Close | P/E High | P/E Low | PER SHARE ($) Earnings | Dividends | Book Value |
|---|---|---|---|---|---|---|
| 4/07 | 37.81 | 54 | 34 | 0.77 | — | 5.42 |
| 4/06 | 37.07 | 56 | 33 | 0.69 | — | 5.12 |
| 4/05 | 26.67 | 59 | 27 | 0.59 | — | 4.53 |
| 4/04 | 18.61 | 64 | 32 | 0.42 | — | 3.96 |
| 4/03 | 13.26 | 85 | 24 | 0.22 | — | 2.90 |
| Annual Growth | 29.9% | — | — | 36.8% | — | 16.9% |

# New York Life Insurance

New York Life Insurance has been in the Big Apple since it was just a tiny seed. The company (one of the top mutual life insurers in the US) is adding products but retaining its core business: life insurance and annuities. New York Life has added such products and services as mutual funds for individuals. It also offers its investment management services to institutional investors. Other lines of business include long-term care insurance and special group policies sold through AARP and other affinity groups or professional associations. The company, through New York Life International, is also reaching out geographically, targeting areas where the life insurance market is not yet mature.

After state legislators failed to approve its proposed company restructuring, New York Life announced it would not follow its rivals in demutualizing for fear of being gobbled up in a merger. The insurer instead uses its considerable war chest to further expand its international operations — Asia and Latin America are major expansion targets, and sales growth in both regions has been rapid. It is also expanding its investment management operations through its New York Life Investment Management (mutual funds, group and individual retirement plans, college savings products). While other big-name insurers in the mature US market are only aiming for high net-worth individual customers, New York Life is also casting its nets a bit lower to catch middle-income consumers and creating products to lure younger families.

## HISTORY

In 1841 actuary Pliny Freeman and 56 New York businessmen founded Nautilus Insurance Co., the third US policyholder-owned company. It began operating in 1845 and became New York Life in 1849.

By 1846 the company had the first life insurance agent west of the Mississippi River. Although the Civil War disrupted southern business, New York Life honored all its obligations and renewed lapsed policies when the war ended. By 1887 the company had developed its branch office system.

By the turn of the century, the company had established an agent compensation plan that featured a lifetime income after 20 years of service (discontinued 1991). New York Life moved into Europe in the late 1800s but withdrew after WWI.

In the early 1950s the company simplified insurance forms, slashed premiums, and updated mortality tables from the 1860s. In 1956 it became the first life insurer to use data-processing equipment on a large scale.

New York Life helped develop variable life insurance, which featured variable benefits and level premiums in the 1960s; it added variable annuities in 1968. Steady growth continued into the late 1970s, when high interest rates led to heavy policyholder borrowing. The outflow of money convinced New York Life to make its products more competitive as investments.

The company formed New York Life and Health Insurance Co. in 1982. It acquired MacKay-Shields Financial, which oversees its MainStay mutual funds, in 1984. The company's first pure investment product, a real estate limited partnership, debuted that year. (When limited partnerships proved riskier than most insurance customers bargained for, investors sued New York Life; in 1996 the company negotiated a plan to liquidate the partnerships and reimburse investors.)

Expansion continued in 1987 when New York Life bought a controlling interest in a third-party insurance plan administrator and group insurance programs. The company also acquired Sanus Corp. Health Systems.

New York Life formed an insurance joint venture in Indonesia in 1992; it also entered South Korea and Taiwan. The next year it bought Aetna UK's life insurance operations.

In 1994 New York Life grew its health care holdings, adding utilization review and physician practice management units. Allegations of churning (agents inducing customers to buy more expensive policies) led New York Life to overhaul its sales practices in 1994; it settled the resulting lawsuit for $300 million in 1995. Soon came claims that agents hadn't properly informed customers that some policies were vulnerable to interest-rate changes and that customers might be entitled to share in the settlement. Some agents lashed out, saying New York Life fired them so it wouldn't have to pay them retirement benefits.

As health care margins decreased and the insurance industry consolidated, New York Life in 1998 sold its health insurance operations and said it would demutualize — a plan ultimately foiled by the state legislature. In 2000 the company bought two Mexican insurance firms, including the nation's #2 life insurer, Seguros Monterrey. It received Office of Thrift Supervision permission to open a bank, New York Life Trust Company. Also that year the company created a subsidiary to house its asset management businesses and entered the Indian market through its joint venture with Max India.

In 2002 New York Life entered into a joint life insurance venture with China's Haier Group.

## EXECUTIVES

**Chairman and CEO:** Seymour (Sy) Sternberg, age 63
**Vice Chairman, President, and COO:** Theodore A. (Ted) Mathas, age 40
**Vice Chairman, EVP, and Co-Head, US Insurance Operations:** Phillip J. (Phil) Hildebrand
**SEVP, Investment and Finance and Chief Investment Officer; Chairman, New York Life Investment Management:** Gary E. Wendlandt, age 56
**EVP and CFO:** Michael E. Sproule
**EVP, Law and Corporate Administration:** Sheila K. Davidson
**EVP; Chairman, President and CEO, New York Life International:** Joseph A. (Joe) Gilmour, age 51
**SVP; President and CEO, New York Life Investment Management:** Brian A. Murdock
**SVP and Treasurer:** Jay S. Calhoun
**SVP and CIO:** Judith E. Campbell
**SVP and General Counsel:** Thomas P. English
**SVP, Controller, and Chief Accounting Officer:** John A. Cullen
**SVP and Chief Administrative Officer, US Insurance Operations:** Frank M. Boccio
**SVP and COO, US Insurance Operations:** Solomon Goldfinger
**SVP and Chief Human Resources Officer:** Judith (Judy) Vance
**SVP, AARP Operations:** Brian Duffy
**SVP, Deputy General Counsel, and Secretary:** Susan A. Thrope
**SVP, Special Markets:** Robert L. Smith
**SVP, Corporate Services:** Ronald J. Terry
**SVP, Corporate Communications:** Steven A. Rautenberg, age 57
**SVP and Chief Actuary:** Stephen N. Steinig
**SVP and Head, Office of Governmental Affairs:** George Nichols III
**SVP, Corporate Information:** Alexander B. Burbatsky
**President and CEO, New York Life Insurance Worldwide:** Gary R. Bennett
**Auditors:** PricewaterhouseCoopers LLP

## LOCATIONS

**HQ:** New York Life Insurance Company
51 Madison Ave., New York, NY 10010
**Phone:** 212-576-7000 **Fax:** 212-576-8145
**Web:** www.newyorklife.com

New York Life Insurance Company operates in Argentina, China, Hong Kong, India, Mexico, the Philippines, South Korea, Taiwan, Thailand, the US, and Vietnam.

## PRODUCTS/OPERATIONS

**2006 Sales**

| | $ mil. | % of total |
|---|---|---|
| Premiums | 9,100 | 44 |
| Net investment income | 8,232 | 39 |
| Net invesment gains | 2,122 | 10 |
| Life & annuity policy fees | 860 | 4 |
| Other income | 666 | 3 |
| **Total** | **20,980** | **100** |

## COMPETITORS

AEGON
AIG
AIG American General
Allianz
Allstate
American National Insurance
AXA
AXA Financial
Charles Schwab
CIGNA
Citigroup
CNA Financial
Fortis SA/NV
Guardian Life
The Hartford
John Hancock Financial Services
Kemper Insurance
MassMutual
Merrill Lynch
MetLife
Morgan Stanley
Mutual of Omaha
Northwestern Mutual
Principal Financial
Prudential
State Farm
T. Rowe Price
TIAA-CREF
UBS Financial Services

## HISTORICAL FINANCIALS

Company Type: Mutual company

**Income Statement** FYE: December 31

| | ASSETS ($ mil.) | NET INCOME ($ mil.) | INCOME AS % OF ASSETS | EMPLOYEES |
|---|---|---|---|---|
| **12/06** | 182,343 | 2,298 | 1.3% | 13,580 |
| **12/05** | 168,865 | 855 | 0.5% | 13,180 |
| **12/04** | 159,888 | 1,294 | 0.8% | 12,650 |
| **12/03** | 144,699 | 1,120 | 0.8% | 12,100 |
| **12/02** | 129,340 | 1,016 | 0.8% | 12,000 |
| **Annual Growth** | 9.0% | 22.6% | — | 3.1% |

**2006 Year-End Financials**

Equity as % of assets: —
Return on assets: 1.3%
Return on equity: —
Long-term debt ($ mil.): —
Sales ($ mil.): 20,980

**Net Income History**

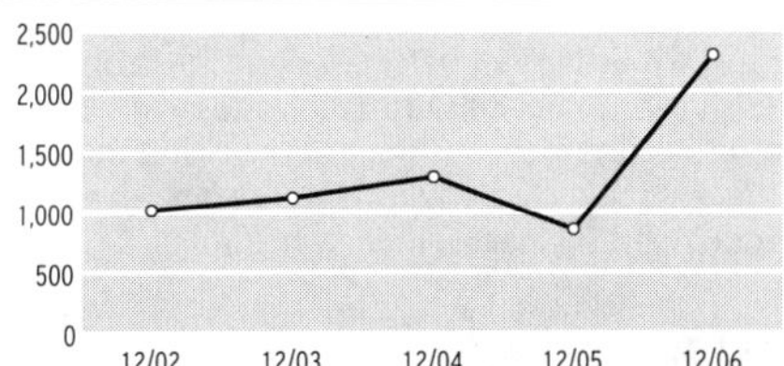


# New York Times

"All the News That's Fit to Print, Broadcast, or Post Online" would be a more accurate motto for this media titan. The New York Times Company publishes one of the world's most respected newspapers, *The New York Times* (1.1 million weekday circulation), as well as large Massachusetts papers *The Boston Globe* and the *Worcester Telegram & Gazette*. It also owns International Herald Tribune, which publishes its eponymous newspaper for English readers in 185 countries. The New York Times Company publishes news online through NYTimes.com and other sites, and it owns online content portal About.com. Chairman Arthur Sulzberger and his family control the company through a trust.

Advertising forms the bulk of the company's revenue, while almost a third of its sales comes from newspaper subscription and circulation fees. However, consolidation among advertisers (specifically big retailers) and competition for ad dollars from other media outlets have hurt newspaper businesses particularly hard, including The New York Times Company. *The Boston Globe* has suffered some serious declines over the past couple of years.

To help offset some of those losses, the company has been aggressively expanding its new media operations. It acquired information portal About.com from PRIMEDIA for about $410 million in cash in 2005 and has been investing in new content and features for its flagship NYTimes.com site. The New York Times Company also acquired movie and television industry information provider Baseline StudioSystems for $35 million in 2006 from Hollywood Media Corp. The New York Times Company is expanding the amount of video on its various sites, including user-generated video, and it has formed a partnership with online job listings leader Monster to create co-branded recruiting sites in its many newspaper markets. Revenue from digital media operations account for about 10% of *The New York Times*' sales.

Meanwhile, the company has been paring away some non-core operations. In 2006 it sold its stake in the Discovery Times Channel back to Discovery Communications for $100 million and it has agreed to sell about nine TV stations across the country to private equity firm Oak Hill Capital Partners for $575 million. To help contain costs at its newspapers, the company cut 250 production-related positions at *The New York Times* in 2006. It is also reducing the size of the paper from 54 inches to 48 inches in 2008.

While Sulzberger and his family have about 20% equity ownership of the company, through their trust they have the right to elect 70% of the board. Other investors, including Morgan Stanley, have complained about the ownership structure and proposed putting the dual-class share structure to a shareholder vote. (It has also recommended that *The New York Times*' publisher and chairman roles be separated.)

Putting more pressure on the company, investor Maurice "Hank" Greenberg has been buying shares of the company. Greenberg has also reportedly contacted other investors about possibly making a bid for the publisher.

## HISTORY

In 1851 George Jones and Henry Raymond, former *New York Tribune* staffers, started *The New York Times*. The politically minded paper lost ground to the yellow journalism of Hearst and Pulitzer and was bought in 1896 by Tennessee newspaperman Adolph Ochs, who continued to encourage hard news and business coverage. Ochs coined the newspaper's now-famous slogan, "All the News That's Fit to Print."

Ochs' son-in-law Arthur Hays Sulzberger, who ran the paper from 1935 to 1961, diversified the company with the 1944 purchase of two New York City radio stations. In 1963 Ochs' grandson Arthur Ochs "Punch" Sulzberger took control of the company.

In the 1960s declining ad revenues and a newspaper strike sent the company into the red. To regain strength, Punch built the largest news-gathering staff of any newspaper. The *Times*' coverage of the Vietnam War helped change public sentiment, and the newspaper won a Pulitzer Prize in 1972 for publishing the Pentagon Papers. In the meantime Punch had taken the company public (1967), although the family retained solid control. In the late 1960s and 1970s the company began co-publishing the *International Herald Tribune* (1967, with The Washington Post) and bought magazines, publishing houses, TV stations, smaller newspapers, and cable TV systems. To contain costs, the company invested in three pulp and paper firms.

In the 1980s the *Times* added feature sections to compete with suburban papers. The company bought *Golf World* in 1988, and the next year sold its cable systems.

Arthur Ochs Sulzberger Jr. succeeded his father as *Times* publisher in 1992. The next year The New York Times bought Affiliated Publications, owner of *The Boston Globe*, for $1.1 billion. In 1997 chairman and CEO Punch Sulzberger retired from executive duties but remained on the board as chairman emeritus. He was replaced by his son as chairman, and non-family member Russell Lewis as CEO.

Journalistic integrity took a nosedive at *The Boston Globe* in mid-1998: Within a span of two months the newspaper demanded the resignations of reporter Patricia Smith after she admitted to making up people and quotes for several stories, and columnist Mike Barnicle after he included jokes from a book by George Carlin in his column without attribution.

In 2001 the company was part of a group of investors calling themselves New England Sports Ventures, which bought the Boston Red Sox, Fenway Park, and cable network New England Sports Network.

Punch Sulzberger retired from the company's board in 2002, but retained the titles of chairman emeritus of The Times Company and of co-chairman of the *International Herald Tribune*. His daughter, Cathy J. Sulzberger, replaced him on the board.

At the close of the company's 2004 fiscal year, Lewis announced his retirement as president, CEO, and director; former COO Janet Robinson was named his successor.

In 2005 the company launched a free weekly in New York City with a classified ad focus called *MarketPlace Weekly*. Later it acquired online information portal About.com from PRIMEDIA for $410 million, and it bought a 49% stake in free daily paper *Metro Boston* (owned by Metro International). About 200 employees were laid off to help contain costs in the face of declining ad revenue. A further 250 jobs were cut the next year.

## EXECUTIVES

**Chairman; Publisher, The New York Times:** Arthur O. Sulzberger Jr., age 55, $1,087,000 pay
**Vice Chairman; Publisher, International Herald Tribune:** Michael Golden, age 57, $728,678 pay
**President, CEO, and Director:** Janet L. Robinson, age 56, $1,000,000 pay
**SVP and CFO:** James M. Follo, age 47
**SVP Advertising, The New York Times:** Alexis Buryk, age 48
**SVP Digital Operations:** Martin A. Nisenholtz, age 51
**SVP Human Resources:** David K. Norton, age 51
**SVP Corporate Development:** James C. Lessersohn, age 51
**SVP Process Engineering:** Stuart (Stu) Stoller, age 51
**VP and General Counsel:** Kenneth A. (Ken) Richieri, age 55
**VP and Corporate Controller:** R. Anthony (Tony) Benten, age 43
**VP Consumer Marketing:** Susan Telesmanic
**VP Corporate Communications:** Catherine J. Mathis
**Corporate Secretary and Corporate Governance Officer:** Rhonda L. Brauer
**President and General Manager, The New York Times:** Scott H. Heekin-Canedy, age 55, $522,500 pay
**President and COO, Regional Media Group:** Mary Jacobus, age 50
**President, Broadcast Media Group:** Robert H. Eoff
**SVP and Chief Marketing Officer, The New York Times:** Alyse Myers
**Publisher, The Boston Globe:** P. Steven Ainsley, age 54
**Futurist-in-Residence:** Michael Rogers
**Director Public Relations:** Abbe Serphos
**Auditors:** Deloitte & Touche LLP

## LOCATIONS

**HQ:** The New York Times Company
229 W. 43rd St., New York, NY 10036
**Phone:** 212-556-1234 **Fax:** 212-556-7389
**Web:** www.nytco.com

## PRODUCTS/OPERATIONS

### 2006 Sales

| | $ mil. | % of total |
|---|---|---|
| New York Times Media Group | 2,077.3 | 63 |
| New England Media Group | 635.3 | 19 |
| Regional Media Group | 497.1 | 15 |
| About.com | 80.2 | 3 |
| **Total** | **3,289.9** | **100** |

### 2006 Sales

| | $ mil. | % of total |
|---|---|---|
| Advertising | 2,153.9 | 65 |
| Circulation | 889.7 | 28 |
| Other | 246.3 | 7 |
| **Total** | **3,289.9** | **100** |

### Selected Operations

The New York Times Media Group
- Newspapers
  - *International Herald Tribune* (Paris)
  - *The New York Times*
- NYTimes.com
- Radio stations
  - WQEW-AM (New York City)
  - WQXR-FM (New York City)
- Other
  - Digital Archive Distribution (database licensing)
  - The New York Times Index
  - The New York Times News Services (news syndication)

New England Media Group
- Newspapers
  - *The Boston Globe*
  - *Worcester Telegram & Gazette* (Massachusetts)
- Online content
  - Boston.com
  - Telegram.com

Regional Media Group
- *The Courier* (Houma, LA)
- *Daily Comet* (Thibodaux, LA)
- *The Dispatch* (Lexington, NC)
- *The Gadsden Times* (Alabama)
- *The Gainesville Sun* (Florida)
- *Herald-Journal* (Spartanburg, SC)
- *The Ledger* (Lakeland, FL)
- *Petaluma Argus-Courier* (California)
- *The Press Democrat* (Santa Rosa, CA)
- *Sarasota Herald-Tribune* (Florida)
- *Star-Banner* (Ocala, FL)
- *Times-News* (Hendersonville, NC)
- *TimesDaily* (Florence, AL)
- *The Tuscaloosa News* (Alabama)
- *Wilmington Star-News* (North Carolina)

About.com (online content)

Other operations and investments
- Donohue Malbaie (49%, newsprint manufacturing, Canada)
- Madison Paper Industries (40%, Maine)
- Metro Boston (49%, fee daily newspaper)
- New England Sports Ventures (17%)
  - Boston Red Sox (Major League Baseball franchise)
  - Fenway Park (sports stadium)
  - New England Sports Network (80%, regional cable broadcasting)
  - Roush Fenway Racing (50%, NASCAR racing team)

## COMPETITORS

Advance Publications
Agence France-Presse
Associated Press
BBC
Belo
Bloomberg
CNN
Cox Enterprises
Daily News
Dow Jones
E. W. Scripps
Gannett
Hearst
Herald Media
Hollinger
Journal Register
Media General
Metro International
News Corp.
Newsweek
Reuters
Tribune
Washington Post

## HISTORICAL FINANCIALS

Company Type: Public

### Income Statement
FYE: Last Sunday in December

| | REVENUE ($ mil.) | NET INCOME ($ mil.) | NET PROFIT MARGIN | EMPLOYEES |
|---|---|---|---|---|
| **12/06** | 3,290 | (543) | — | 11,585 |
| **12/05** | 3,373 | 260 | 7.7% | 11,965 |
| **12/04** | 3,304 | 293 | 8.9% | 12,300 |
| **12/03** | 3,227 | 303 | 9.4% | 12,400 |
| **12/02** | 3,079 | 300 | 9.7% | 12,150 |
| **Annual Growth** | 1.7% | — | — | (1.2%) |

### 2006 Year-End Financials

Debt ratio: 97.0%
Return on equity: —
Cash ($ mil.): 72
Current ratio: 0.91
Long-term debt ($ mil.): 795
No. of shares (mil.): 143
Dividends
Yield: 2.8%
Payout: —
Market value ($ mil.): 3,484

### Stock History
NYSE: NYT

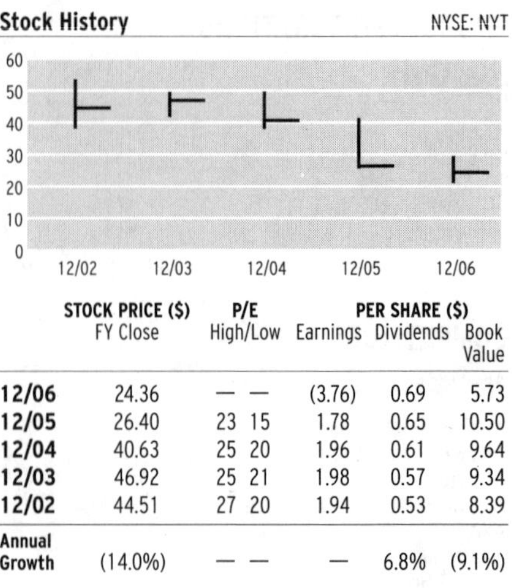


| | STOCK PRICE ($) FY Close | P/E High | P/E Low | PER SHARE ($) Earnings | Dividends | Book Value |
|---|---|---|---|---|---|---|
| **12/06** | 24.36 | — | — | (3.76) | 0.69 | 5.73 |
| **12/05** | 26.40 | 23 | 15 | 1.78 | 0.65 | 10.50 |
| **12/04** | 40.63 | 25 | 20 | 1.96 | 0.61 | 9.64 |
| **12/03** | 46.92 | 25 | 21 | 1.98 | 0.57 | 9.34 |
| **12/02** | 44.51 | 27 | 20 | 1.94 | 0.53 | 8.39 |
| **Annual Growth** | (14.0%) | — | — | — | 6.8% | (9.1%) |

# Newell Rubbermaid

Newell Rubbermaid wants to get its products into your drawers, your kitchen cabinets, and your workbench. It makes housewares (Rubbermaid plastic products, Calphalon cookware), hardware (Amerock cabinet hardware, IRWIN and Lenox hand tools), home furnishings (Levolor blinds), juvenile products (Graco), hair products (Goody), and office products (DYMO, Sanford, Sharpie). Newell Rubbermaid sells primarily to mass retailers and home and office supply stores. The firm bought label product maker DYMO from Esselte Corporation and sold Newell Cookware Europe to Arc. As it kicked off a global three-year restructuring in 2006, Mark Ketchum succeeded Joseph Galli as CEO in late 2005.

The company's reorganization plans, referred to as Project Acceleration, reaches worldwide and includes cutting some 5,000 employees from its workforce of 31,000 and shuttering a third of its 80 factories. Newell Rubbermaid sold portions of its Home Decor Europe business to window-coverings giant Hunter Douglas.

In recent years Newell Rubbermaid has been whittling down its businesses and concentrating on core competencies. The company sold its preschool toys business, Little Tikes, to MGA Entertainment (maker of the Bratz line of dolls) in late 2006. It also sold three of its businesses (Anchor Hocking Glass, Burnes Picture Frame, and Mirro Cookware) to Global Home Products, LLC for an estimated $320 million.

Known as Newell before its purchase of plastics giant Rubbermaid in 1999, the firm has become a diversified manufacturer during the past 30 years, mostly by acquiring companies that produce brand-name, low-tech staples.

## HISTORY

Businessmen in Ogdensburg, New York, advanced curtain rod maker W.F. Linton Co. $1,000 to relocate from Rhode Island in the early 1900s. Local wholesaler Edgar Newell signed off on the loan; when the company went bankrupt in 1903, he was forced to take over. The company, renamed Newell Manufacturing, set up plants in

Canada and Freeport, Illinois, to ease shipping costs and speed delivery.

Production expanded into towel racks, ice picks, and other items; Woolworth's decision to carry Newell's products turned the company into a national supplier. Edgar Newell died in 1920.

The company made its first acquisition in 1938, buying window treatment specialist Drapery Hardware.

The Newell companies were consolidated in the mid-1960s into a single corporation. Daniel Ferguson was named president in 1965 and served alongside his CEO father Leonard, one of Newell's original employees. During his tenure, Daniel hitched the company's future to the growing dominance of large discount stores. Newell went from a $14 million family business to a global, multiline conglomerate by acquiring products that it distributed to these big buyers. The company went public in 1972 and bought paint applicator maker EZ Paintr the next year. By 1978 sales reached $100 million.

Newell moved into housewares with the acquisitions of Mirro (cookware, 1983) and the much larger Anchor Hocking (glassware, 1987). It then bought office supply companies W.T. Rogers and Keene Manufacturing in 1991 and Sanford (writing instruments) in 1992. That year Daniel bowed out of active management.

The company began a global push with its purchase of Corning's European Consumer Products business (1994), and it kept busy at home by buying Insilco's Rolodex unit and Rubbermaid's office products business (both 1997). William Sovey succeeded Daniel as chairman in 1997, and John McDonough became CEO. Its 1998 acquisitions included Calphalon (upscale cookware), Panex (Brazil, bakeware), and Rotring Group (Germany, writing instruments).

Originally a balloon maker in the 1920s, by the mid-1930s Ohio's Wooster Rubber had acquired the Rubbermaid product line of rubber housewares. It went public in 1955 and two years later changed its name to Rubbermaid. During the 1980s the company enjoyed a decade of phenomenal growth. However — despite product innovations — increased material costs, a competitive retail climate, and weak customer service began dulling Rubbermaid's luster. Profits plunged even as it reached record sales.

Newell's $6 billion purchase of Rubbermaid in 1999 sealed its biggest deal yet and resulted in a name change: Newell Rubbermaid. Also in 1999 Newell Rubbermaid bought the consumer products division of McKechnie (window furnishings and cabinet hardware) and three French firms: Ateliers 28 (drapery hardware), Reynolds (pens and pencils), and Ceanothe Holdings (picture frames). The company in 2000 bought Mersch (picture frames; France, Germany) and Brio (picture frames, France).

In late 2000 CEO McDonough resigned and Sovey replaced him. In 2001 Newell Rubbermaid acquired Gillette's stationery business, including the Parker, Paper Mate, Liquid Paper, and Waterman brands. The same month Joseph Galli succeeded Sovey as CEO; Sovey reassumed his position as chairman (and left in mid-2004).

In April 2002 Newell completed its acquisition of American Tool Companies (now IRWIN Industrial Tool Company North America) and announced the creation of two new operating divisions — North American hand tools and North American power tool accessories — to focus on its US and Canadian business segments. In June 2002, after multiple challenges from the FTC, Newell Rubbermaid abandoned plans to sell its Anchor Hocking glass business to glassware maker Libbey Inc.

In January 2003 Newell Rubbermaid acquired American Saw & Manufacturing for $450 million in cash, and in March the company sold its Cosmolab business to CSI East, an affiliate of Cosmetic Specialties. The same year Newell Rubbermaid moved its corporate headquarters from Illinois to Alpharetta, Georgia (relocated again in 2004 to Atlanta). In February 2004 the company sold Panex and the remainder of its European picture frames business. In April 2004 Newell sold its Anchor Hocking Glass, Burnes Picture Frame, and Mirro Cookware divisions to Global Home Products, LLC.

To add depth to its office products portfolio, which generates about a quarter of Newell Rubbermaid's revenue, the company acquired the DYMO brand from Esselte in late 2005 for $730 million. The deal gave the consumer firm a leg up in European, North American, and Australian channels

CEO Joseph Galli resigned in October 2005. A board member with three decades of experience at Procter & Gamble, Mark Ketchum stepped in as interim CEO. He was made permanent in February 2006.

## EXECUTIVES

**Chairman:** William D. Marohn, age 67
**President, CEO, and Director:** Mark D. Ketchum, age 57, $1,177,308 pay
**EVP and CFO:** J. Patrick (Pat) Robinson, age 51, $515,000 pay
**EVP, Human Resources and Corporate Communications:** James M. (Jim) Sweet, age 54
**SVP Marketing and Brand Management:** Ted Woehrle, age 46
**VP, Investor Relations:** Ronald L. Hardnock, age 36
**VP, General Counsel, and Corporate Secretary:** Dale L. Matschullat, age 61
**VP, Global Licensing:** Nathaniel S. (Nat) Milburn, age 34
**VP, Supply Chain, Home & Family Group:** Chris Van Dyke
**VP and CIO:** Gordon Steele, age 55
**VP, Corporate Human Resources and Corporate Communications:** Todd Helms, age 39
**President, Corporate Development:** Hartley D. (Buddy) Blaha, age 41
**President, Amerock:** Robert W. (Bob) Bailey, age 48
**President, Calphalon:** Kristine L. (Kristie) Juster
**President, Graco:** Jay Gould
**President, Sanford North America:** Howard C. Heckes
**President, North American Sales Operations and President, Rubbermaid/IRWIN North America Sales:** Paul G. Boitmann
**President, Office Products Group:** Steven G. (Steve) Marton, age 50, $546,000 pay
**President and COO, Rubbermaid/IRWIN Group:** James J. (Jim) Roberts, age 48, $725,000 pay
**Group President, Home and Family Group:** Timothy J. (Tim) Jahnke, age 47, $465,000 pay
**Auditors:** Ernst & Young LLP

## LOCATIONS

**HQ:** Newell Rubbermaid Inc.
10 B Glenlake Pkwy., Ste. 300, Atlanta, GA 30328
**Phone:** 770-407-3800 **Fax:** 770-407-3970
**Web:** www.newellrubbermaid.com

Newell Rubbermaid has operations in Brazil, Canada, Colombia, France, Germany, Hungary, Italy, Luxembourg, Mexico, the Netherlands, Poland, Spain, Sweden, the UK, the US, and Venezuela.

### 2006 Sales

| | $ mil. | % of total |
|---|---|---|
| US | 4,603.4 | 74 |
| Europe | 781.0 | 13 |
| Canada | 387.9 | 6 |
| Central & South America | 239.3 | 4 |
| Other regions | 189.4 | 3 |
| **Total** | **6,201.0** | **100** |

## PRODUCTS/OPERATIONS

### 2006 Sales

| | $ mil. | % of total |
|---|---|---|
| Office products | 2031.6 | 33 |
| Cleaning, organization, and décor | 1995.7 | 32 |
| Tools and hardware | 1262.2 | 20 |
| Home and family | 911.5 | 15 |
| **Total** | **6,201.0** | **100** |

### Selected Brands and Trade Names

Office Products
- Accent
- Berol
- DYMO
- Eberhard Farber
- Expo
- Grumbacher
- Liquid Paper
- Paper Mate
- Parker
- Reynolds
- Sanford
- Sharpie
- Uni-Ball
- Vis-à-vis
- Waterman

Cleaning and Organization
- Brute
- Roughneck
- Rubbermaid
- Stain Shield
- TakeAlongs

Home Fashions
- Douglas Kane
- Gardinia
- Homelux
- Kirsch
- Levolor
- Newell
- Swish

Tools and Hardware
- Allison
- Ashland
- Hanson
- IRWIN
- Marathon
- Quick-Grip
- Speedbor
- Strait-Line
- Vise-Grip

Other
- Ace
- Calphalon
- Goody
- Graco
- Kitchen Essentials

## COMPETITORS

ACCO Brands
Acme United
Alticor
Avery Dennison
BIC
Bridgestone
Coleman
Cooper Industries
Crayola
Decorator Industries
Dixon Ticonderoga
Faber-Castell
Fortune Brands
Home Products
Katy Industries
Knape & Vogt
Koala
Lancaster Colony
Libbey
Lifetime Brands
Myers Industries
Owens-Illinois
Springs Global
Step 2
Sterilite
Tupperware
Uniek
Wilton Industries
WKI Holding
ZAG Industries

## HISTORICAL FINANCIALS

Company Type: Public

### Income Statement

FYE: December 31

| | REVENUE ($ mil.) | NET INCOME ($ mil.) | NET PROFIT MARGIN | EMPLOYEES |
|---|---|---|---|---|
| **12/06** | 6,201 | 385 | 6.2% | 23,500 |
| **12/05** | 6,343 | 251 | 4.0% | 27,900 |
| **12/04** | 6,748 | (116) | — | 31,100 |
| **12/03** | 7,750 | (47) | — | 40,000 |
| **12/02** | 7,454 | (203) | — | 47,000 |
| **Annual Growth** | (4.5%) | — | — | (15.9%) |

**2006 Year-End Financials**

Debt ratio: 104.3%
Return on equity: 21.8%
Cash ($ mil.): 201
Current ratio: 1.31
Long-term debt ($ mil.): 1,972
No. of shares (mil.): 291
Dividends
Yield: 2.9%
Payout: 60.0%
Market value ($ mil.): 8,424

**Stock History** NYSE: NWL

| | STOCK PRICE ($) FY Close | P/E High | P/E Low | PER SHARE ($) Earnings | Dividends | Book Value |
|---|---|---|---|---|---|---|
| **12/06** | 28.95 | 21 | 17 | 1.40 | 0.84 | 6.50 |
| **12/05** | 23.78 | 28 | 23 | 0.91 | 0.84 | 5.66 |
| **12/04** | 24.19 | — | — | (0.42) | 0.84 | 6.08 |
| **12/03** | 22.77 | — | — | (0.17) | 0.84 | 6.95 |
| **12/02** | 30.33 | — | — | (0.76) | 0.63 | 7.29 |
| **Annual Growth** | (1.2%) | — | — | — | 7.5% | (2.8%) |

# Newmont Mining

Newmont Mining certainly goes for the gold. The company is among the world's top gold producers (with Barrick ahead of AngloGold Ashanti), following acquisitions in Canada, Bolivia, and Australia. Newmont produces some 8 million ounces of gold annually; it has proved and probable reserves of more than 94 million ounces of gold. Other metals that the company mines include copper, silver, and zinc. Operations in North America and South America account for more than half of Newmont's production. It also has mining facilities in Australia, Indonesia, New Zealand, and Uzbekistan.

The company's North American operations, which account for more than a quarter of its sales, include mines in Nevada's Carlin Trend, one of the largest gold-mining areas in North America. The company also has stakes in gold mines in Peru, Mexico, Uzbekistan, and Indonesia (Batu Hijau, a 45%-owned mine that produces both copper and gold).

To weather price fluctuations, Newmont has tried to keep production costs low. The company has put off discretionary spending and remains largely unhedged, which enables it to profit from gold price increases but offers little protection from falling gold prices.

Once the clear #1 gold producing company in the world, Newmont now is in more serious competition with AngloGold Ashanti after AngloGold's acquisition of Ashanti in 2004 and Barrick following its 2006 acquisition of Placer Dome.

Its operations in Ghana consist of an advanced development project; Newmont sees the country as the site of its next big operating district.

## HISTORY

Colonel William Boyce Thompson, a flamboyant trader, founded the Newmont Co. in 1916 to trade his various oil and mining stocks. The Newmont name was a combination of New York and Montana, where Thompson grew up. The company was renamed Newmont Corporation in 1921 and Newmont Mining Corporation in 1925, when it went public. Thompson died five years later. During its first 10 years, Newmont focused on investing and trading stocks in promising mineral properties, including US copper and gold mines.

Newmont's gold mines bolstered the company throughout the Depression. During the 1940s its focus shifted to copper and Africa. It bought Idarado Mining in 1943 and Newmont Oil in 1944 (sold 1988). The company grew during the 1950s by acquiring stakes in North American companies involved in offshore oil drilling, nickel mining, and uranium oxide production. It also bought stakes in copper mines in South Africa and South America.

Newmont started producing gold from the Carlin Trend in Nevada in the mid-1960s. It bought a one-third stake in Foote Mineral (iron alloys and lithium) in 1967; by 1974 it controlled 83% of the company (sold 1987). In 1969 Newmont merged with Magma Copper, one of the US's largest copper companies. A Newmont-led consortium bought Peabody Coal, the US's largest coal producer, from Kennecott Copper in 1977 (sold 1990).

After its 1980 discovery of one of the century's most important gold stakes, Gold Quarry in the Carlin Trend, Newmont spent a decade fending off takeover attempts. The company began selling off noncore operations to focus on gold. Magma Copper was spun off to stockholders in 1988.

A proposed merger with American Barrick Resources, a major stockholder, collapsed in 1991. Former Freeport-McMoRan VP Ronald Cambre became CEO in 1993, and that year the company began mining in Peru. A 1994 action by the French government, one of Newmont's partners in Peru's Yanacocha Mine, kicked off a protracted battle over the property's ownership. The claim was upheld in 1998, raising Newmont's stake to more than 50%. Reflecting its increasing interest in Indonesia, in 1996 Newmont and Japan's Sumitomo formed a joint venture to exploit gold reserves on Sumbawa Island. In 1997 the company increased its gold reserves and territory by acquiring Santa Fe Pacific Gold for about $2.1 billion.

For years Newmont and Barrick Gold Corporation operated interlocked mining claims in Nevada's Carlin Trend, which prevented optimal exploitation by either company. In 1999 both companies agreed to a mutually advantageous land swap in the region.

In 2000 an Indonesian court ordered the closure of the Minahasa mine over a local tax dispute; the company's joint venture agreed to pay a $500,000 penalty to settle the matter. Newmont was fined $500,000 after a mercury spill at its Yanacocha mine. That year Newmont settled the lingering ownership dispute over the Yanacocha.

Company president Wayne Murdy became CEO early in 2001 (he replaced Cambre as chairman in 2002). Newmont acquired Battle Mountain Gold in 2001 for nearly $600 million. Late that year Newmont moved to acquire Australia's top gold producer, Normandy Mining (setting off a bidding war with AngloGold), as well as Canadian gold miner France-Nevada Mining Corp. (now Newmont Canada). AngloGold bowed out of the "battle for Normandy" in early 2002. Newmont's acquisition of Franco-Nevada closed in February 2002.

In 2003 Newmont reduced its stake in Kinross Gold from 14% to 5%.

## EXECUTIVES

**Chairman:** Wayne W. Murdy, age 63, $1,781,991 pay
**Vice Chairman:** Pierre Lassonde
**President, CEO, and Director:** Richard T. O'Brien, age 51, $764,913 pay (partial-year salary)
**EVP and Managing Director, Newmont Australia Limited:** John A. S. Dow, age 58
**EVP Operations:** Thomas L. Enos, age 54, $657,157 pay
**EVP Legal and External Affairs:** Britt D. Banks
**EVP Exploration and Business Development:** David Harquail
**SVP and CFO:** Russell D. Ball, age 37
**SVP Project Development and Technical Services:** Guy Landsdown
**SVP Strategy and Corporate Development:** Randy Engel
**SVP Human Resources:** Darla Caudle
**SVP Worldwide Exploration:** M. Stephen Enders
**VP North American Operations:** Brant Hinze
**VP Technical Strategy and Development:** D. Scott Barr
**VP Exploration Business Development:** Jeffrey R. Huspeni
**VP Information Technology:** Alex G. Morrison
**VP Communications:** Stephen P. Gottesfeld
**VP and Secretary:** Sharon E. Thomas
**VP and Treasurer:** Thomas P. Mahoney
**VP Tax:** David V. Gutierrez
**VP and Counsel Chief:** Blake Rhodes
**VP Technical Services:** Allen Cockle
**Auditors:** PricewaterhouseCoopers LLP

## LOCATIONS

**HQ:** Newmont Mining Corporation
1700 Lincoln St., Denver, CO 80203
**Phone:** 303-863-7414 **Fax:** 303-837-5837
**Web:** www.newmont.com

Newmont Mining operates gold mines in Australia, Bolivia, Canada, Indonesia, Mexico, New Zealand, Peru, the US, and Uzbekistan.

**2006 Production**

| | % of total |
|---|---|
| Peru | 31 |
| US | 29 |
| Indonesia | 19 |
| Australia/New Zealand | 16 |
| Ghana | 2 |
| Other | 3 |
| **Total** | **100** |

## PRODUCTS/OPERATIONS

**2006 Sales**

| | $ mil. | % of total |
|---|---|---|
| Gold | 4,316 | 87 |
| Copper | 671 | 13 |
| **Total** | **4,987** | **100** |

**Selected Products**

Copper
Gold
Silver
Zinc

### Selected Operations

Empresa Minera Inti Raymi, SA (88%, Bolivia)
 Kori Kollo mine
Golden Giant mine (Canada)
Golden Grove (Australia)
Holloway mine (Canada)
La Herradura mine (44%, with Industriales Peñoles; Mexico)
Minera Yanacocha (51%, with Compañía de Minas Buenaventura and others; Peru)
Newmont Gold Co. (California and Nevada)
 Lone Tree mine
 Mesquite mine
 Midas mine
 Twin Creeks mine
Pajingo (Australia)
 Kalgoorlie
 Tanami
 Vera/Nancy mine (Australia)
 Yandal
P.T. Newmont Nusa Tenggara
 Batu Hijau mine (45% copper, Indonesia)
Zarafshan-Newmont (50%, with Uzbek government entities; Uzbekistan)

## COMPETITORS

AngloGold Ashanti
Barrick Gold
BHP Billiton
Freeport-McMoRan
Gold Fields
Goldcorp
Harmony Gold
Hecla Mining
Kinross Gold
Rio Tinto

## HISTORICAL FINANCIALS

Company Type: Public

### Income Statement

FYE: December 31

| | REVENUE ($ mil.) | NET INCOME ($ mil.) | NET PROFIT MARGIN | EMPLOYEES |
|---|---|---|---|---|
| **12/06** | 4,987 | 791 | 15.9% | 15,000 |
| **12/05** | 4,406 | 322 | 7.3% | 15,000 |
| **12/04** | 4,524 | 443 | 9.8% | 14,000 |
| **12/03** | 3,214 | 476 | 14.8% | 13,400 |
| **12/02** | 2,745 | 158 | 5.8% | 13,200 |
| **Annual Growth** | 16.1% | 49.6% | — | 3.2% |

### 2006 Year-End Financials

Debt ratio: 18.8%
Return on equity: 8.9%
Cash ($ mil.): 1,275
Current ratio: 1.52
Long-term debt ($ mil.): 1,752
No. of shares (mil.): 423
Dividends
 Yield: 0.9%
 Payout: 22.9%
Market value ($ mil.): 19,087

### Stock History

NYSE: NEM

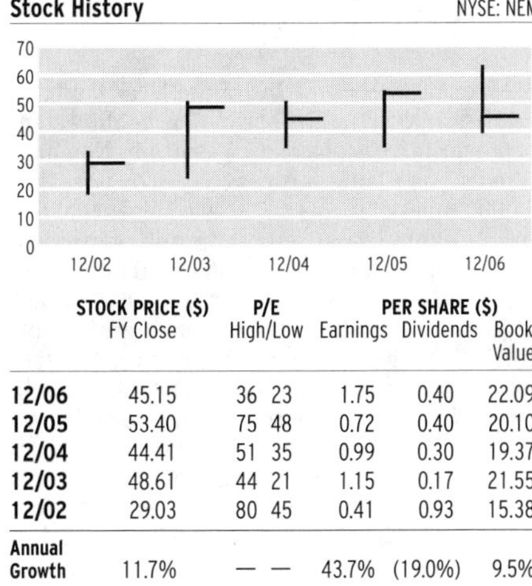

| | STOCK PRICE ($) FY Close | P/E High | P/E Low | PER SHARE ($) Earnings | Dividends | Book Value |
|---|---|---|---|---|---|---|
| **12/06** | 45.15 | 36 | 23 | 1.75 | 0.40 | 22.09 |
| **12/05** | 53.40 | 75 | 48 | 0.72 | 0.40 | 20.10 |
| **12/04** | 44.41 | 51 | 35 | 0.99 | 0.30 | 19.37 |
| **12/03** | 48.61 | 44 | 21 | 1.15 | 0.17 | 21.55 |
| **12/02** | 29.03 | 80 | 45 | 0.41 | 0.93 | 15.38 |
| **Annual Growth** | 11.7% | — | — | 43.7% | (19.0%) | 9.5% |

# News Corporation

This News is heard, seen, and read all around the world. The world's #3 media conglomerate (behind Time Warner and Walt Disney), News Corporation has operations spanning film, television, and publishing. It produces and distributes movies through Fox Filmed Entertainment, while its FOX Broadcasting network boasts more than 200 affiliate stations in the US. The company also owns and operates about 35 TV stations, as well as a portfolio of cable networks. Its publishing business includes HarperCollins, along with a slew of newspapers and magazines. In addition, News Corp. owns almost 40% of satellite broadcasters DIRECTV and British Sky Broadcasting. Rupert Murdoch and his family control about 30% of News Corp.

While films and TV make up the bulk of the company's revenue, News Corp. is making a concerted effort to expand its reach into the Internet and digital entertainment arenas, a real about face for a company that (wisely, as it turned out) eschewed the World Wide Web during the dotcom boom of the 1990s. In 2005 News Corp. formed a new subsidiary, Fox Interactive Media, and set about acquiring several online properties, most famously its $580 million acquisition of Intermix Media, which operated the hot social networking Web site MySpace.com. (Intermix's other assets were later sold to Demand Media.) Murdoch has committed his company to invest about $2 billion to make News Corp. a leader in interactive content and services.

At the same time, News Corp. is pursuing another new market: Business news and information. In 2007 after a lengthy and at times contested negotiation the company agreed to acquire publishing giant Dow Jones for $5.6 billion. Murdoch doggedly pursued the company and its controlling Bancroft family primarily to get its flagship newspaper, the *Wall Street Journal*, which he plans to use as a cornerstone for a new business news cable network that will rival CNBC (owned by NBC Universal). Also included in the deal are Dow Jones' news and information syndication services, the Factiva news and industry research service, and a portfolio of community newspapers (Ottaway Newspapers).

The company's television business, meanwhile, has been a strong performer the past few years, with the FOX network moving into the #2 spot among American broadcasters with the help of such hit shows as *American Idol, House*, and *24*. Adding a new wrinkle to the TV landscape, the company launched a new network in 2006 called MyNetworkTV. News Corp.'s new netlet has more than 95 affiliates reaching more than 60% of the country and airs about 12 hours of content a week (primetime Monday through Saturday).

While News Corp. has long been a leading proponent of direct broadcast satellite (DBS) service through its stakes in DIRECTV, the company has decided to exit the business as subscriber growth has shown signs of slowing. It agreed at the end of 2006 to sell its stake in the DBS operator to John Malone's Liberty Media holding company in exchange for Liberty's 20% voting stake in News Corp. The $11 billion asset swap, which also includes the sale of three regional sports networks, will end a threat to Murdoch's iron control over his media empire while allowing the company to profit from its investment in DIRECTV.

## HISTORY

In 1952 Rupert Murdoch inherited two Adelaide, Australia, newspapers from his father. After launching the *Australian*, the country's first national daily, in 1964, Murdoch moved into the UK market. He bought tabloid *News of the World*, a London Sunday paper, in 1968, and London's *Sun* the next year. In 1973 Murdoch hit the US, buying the *San Antonio Express-News* and founding the *Star* tabloid. He followed this up in 1976 by buying the *New York Post*. Murdoch formed News Corporation in Australia in 1979.

Moving upmarket in 1981, Murdoch bought the London *Times* and 40% of Collins Publishers, a London book publisher. After buying the *Chicago Sun-Times* in 1983 (sold 1986), Murdoch bought 13 US travel, hotel, and aviation trade magazines from Ziff-Davis, as well as film studio Twentieth Century Fox in 1985. In 1986 Murdoch bought six Metromedia stations and launched FOX Broadcasting, the first new US TV network since 1948.

Print was not forgotten, however, and in the late 1980s News Corp. picked up US book publisher Harper & Row as well as Triangle Publications (*TV Guide* and other magazines). It also bought textbook publisher Scott, Foresman and the rest of Collins Publishers.

In 1996 Murdoch launched the FOX News Channel, an all-news cable channel. The next year, News Corp.'s FOX Kids joint venture bought Pat Robertson's International Family Entertainment.

In 1998 the company bought the Los Angeles Dodgers and stakes in the new Los Angeles-area Staples Center sports arena. (It sold its stake in the Staples Center in 2004.) Also that year News Corp. spun off part of Fox Entertainment in one of America's largest IPOs, raising $2.7 billion.

That year News Corp. sold *TV Guide* to Tele-Communications Inc.'s (now AT&T Broadband & Internet) United Video Satellite Group (now Gemstar-TV Guide International) for $800 million in cash and a 21.5% interest in Gemstar-TV Guide International (later boosted to 42%). The company also bought the 50% of FOX/Liberty Networks (now FOX Sports Net) it didn't own and transferred ownership to Fox Entertainment. The deal gave Liberty an 8% stake (later 19%) in News Corp. The company also broke into the coveted German pay-TV market through BSkyB's agreement to buy 24% of KirchGruppe's (which is no longer in business) Kirch PayTV.

In 2000 News Corp. agreed to buy TV station owner Chris-Craft for $4.8 billion, and it bought a stake in China's state-owned telecom operator Netcom. In 2001, along with partner Haim Saban, News Corp. sold the Fox Family Channel to Disney for about $5.2 billion.

News Corp. in 2003 finally realized its dream of owning a chunk of DIRECTV when it bought 34% of Hughes Electronics, the satellite television company's parent, from General Motors. News Corp. transferred its interest in Hughes (which changed its name to The DIRECTV Group) to its Fox Entertainment subsidiary. The following year, in an effort to make its stock more attractive to US investors, News Corp shifted its incorporation from Australia to the US. It also purchased the rest of Fox Entertainment that it didn't already own for $6.2 billion.

In 2005 News Corp. formed a new subsidiary, Fox Interactive Media, to make its push into online and digital entertainment. Anchoring the new unit, it acquired MySpace.com operator Intermix Media.

## EXECUTIVES

**Chairman and CEO; Chairman, British Sky Broadcasting:** K. Rupert Murdoch, age 76, $25,683,694 pay
**President, COO, and Director; Chairman and CEO, News America; President and COO, Fox Entertainment:** Peter F. Chernin, age 55, $29,275,008 pay
**SEVP, CFO, and Director; SEVP and CFO, News America and Fox Entertainment:** David F. DeVoe, age 60, $8,838,750 pay
**SEVP and Group General Counsel:** Lawrence A. Jacobs, age 51, $2,322,115 pay
**EVP and Deputy CFO:** John P. Nallen
**EVP Office of the Chairman:** Jeremy Philips
**EVP Content:** Anthea Disney, age 62
**EVP Global Tax and Benefits:** Paul Haggerty
**EVP Human Resources:** Ian Moore
**EVP Investor Relations and Corporate Communications:** Gary L. Ginsberg, age 43
**EVP:** Leon Hertz
**SVP, Deputy General Counsel, and Chief Compliance and Ethics Officer:** Genie Gavenchak
**SVP Corporate Affairs and Communications:** Andrew Butcher
**SVP Corporate Affairs and Communications:** Teri Everett
**SVP Government Affairs:** Michael Regan
**SVP Investor Relations:** Reed Nolte
**Chairman and CEO, FOX News Channel; Chairman, Fox Television Stations and Twentieth Television:** Roger Ailes, age 66, $8,297,385 pay
**Co-Chairman, Fox Filmed Entertainment:** James N. (Jim) Gianopulos, age 52
**Co-Chairman, Fox Filmed Entertainment:** Thomas E. (Tom) Rothman, age 49
**President, Fox Interactive Media:** Peter Levinsohn, age 40
**President, FOX Television Network:** Ed Wilson
**Senior Advisor to the Chairman and Director:** Arthur M. Siskind, age 68, $6,715,427 pay
**Auditors:** Ernst & Young LLP

## LOCATIONS

**HQ:** News Corporation
1211 Avenue of the Americas, 8th Fl.,
New York, NY 10036
**Phone:** 212-852-7000 **Fax:** 212-852-7147
**Web:** www.newscorp.com

News Corp. has operations worldwide.

### 2006 Sales

| | $ mil. | % of total |
|---|---|---|
| US & Canada | 14,102 | 56 |
| Europe | 7,552 | 30 |
| Australasia & other regions | 3,673 | 14 |
| **Total** | **25,327** | **100** |

## PRODUCTS/OPERATIONS

### 2006 Sales

| | $ mil. | % of total |
|---|---|---|
| Filmed entertainment | 6,199 | 25 |
| Television | 5,334 | 21 |
| Newspapers | 4,095 | 16 |
| Cable network programming | 3,358 | 13 |
| Direct broadcast satellite | 2,542 | 10 |
| Book publishing | 1,312 | 5 |
| Magazines & inserts | 1,090 | 4 |
| Other | 1,397 | 6 |
| **Total** | **25,327** | **100** |

### Selected Operations

Filmed entertainment
- Feature film production and distribution
  - Fox Filmed Entertainment
    - Fox 2000
    - Fox Searchlight Pictures
    - Twentieth Century Fox
    - Twentieth Century Fox Animation
  - Twentieth Century Fox Home Entertainment
- Television production and distribution
  - Fox Television Studios
  - Twentieth Century Fox Television
  - Twentieth Television

Television
- FOX Broadcasting
- Fox Television Stations
- MyNetworkTV
- Star Group (international televison broadcasting, Asia)

Cable network programming
- Fox College Sports
- Fox International Channels
- Fox Movie Channel
- Fox News Channel
- Fox Reality
- Fox Sports International
  - Fox Pan American Sports (38%)
  - Fox Soccer Channel
  - Fox Sports Middle East
- Fox Sports Net
- FUEL TV
- FX
- SPEED

Newspapers
- *New York Post*
- News International Limited (UK)
  - *Love It!* (lifestyle weekly)
  - *News of the World*
  - *The Sun*
  - *The Sunday Times*
  - *The Times*
- News Limited (Australia)
  - *The Australian* (national daily)
  - *The Courier-Mail* (Brisbane)
  - *The Daily Telegraph* (Sydney)
  - *Herald Sun* (Melbourne)
  - *Sunday Herald Sun* (Melbourne)
  - *The Sunday Telegraph* (Sydney)

Direct broadcast satellite
- British Sky Broadcasting (38%, UK)
- DIRECTV (38%)
- SKY Italia

Book publishing
- HarperCollins Publishers

Magazines and inserts
- Magazine publishing
  - News Magazines (Australia)
  - *The Weekly Standard*
- News America Marketing Group (insert publications and in-store marketing)

Other operations and investments
- Gemstar-TV Guide (41%, TV listings)
- Fox Interactive Media
  - AmericanIdol.com
  - Fox.com
  - FoxSports.com
  - MySpace.com
- LAPTV (23%, Latin American pay television)
- Latvian Independent Television
- National Geographic Channel (67%)
- NDS Group (74%, pay TV technology and software, UK)
- News Interactive (online publishing, Australia)
- News Outdoor Group (outdoor advertising)
- NGC Network Latin America (67%, National Geographic Channel)
- NGC Network International (75%, National Geographic Channel International)
- Sky Network Television (44%, direct broadcast satellite service, New Zealand)
- TV5 (70%, Latvia)

## COMPETITORS

Advance Publications
Bertelsmann
CANAL+
CBS Corp
Cox Enterprises
Disney
Gannett
Hollinger
Lagardère
Liberty Media
McGraw-Hill
NBC Universal
New York Times
Northern and Shell
Pearson
Reed Elsevier Group
Sony Pictures Entertainment
Thomson Corporation
Time Warner
Tribune
Viacom
Washington Post
Yahoo!

## HISTORICAL FINANCIALS

Company Type: Public

### Income Statement

FYE: Sunday nearest June 30

| | REVENUE ($ mil.) | NET INCOME ($ mil.) | NET PROFIT MARGIN | EMPLOYEES |
|---|---|---|---|---|
| **6/06** | 25,327 | 2,314 | 9.1% | 47,300 |
| **6/05** | 23,859 | 2,128 | 8.9% | 44,000 |
| **Annual Growth** | 6.2% | 8.7% | — | 7.5% |

### 2006 Year-End Financials

Debt ratio: 38.1%
Return on equity: 7.8%
Cash ($ mil.): 5,783
Current ratio: 2.06
Long-term debt ($ mil.): 11,385
No. of shares (mil.): 2,169
Dividends
Yield: 0.7%
Payout: 17.1%
Market value ($ mil.): 41,605

### Stock History

NYSE: NWS

20
18
16
14
12
10
8
6
4
2
0
6/02 6/03 6/04 6/05 6/06

| | STOCK PRICE ($) FY Close | P/E High | P/E Low | PER SHARE ($) Earnings | Dividends | Book Value |
|---|---|---|---|---|---|---|
| **6/06** | 19.18 | 26 | 18 | 0.76 | 0.13 | 13.77 |
| **6/05** | 16.18 | 26 | 21 | 0.73 | 0.05 | 13.13 |
| **Annual Growth** | 18.5% | — | — | 4.1% | 160.0% | 4.9% |

# Nicor Inc.

Nicor heats the hearths of the Heartland and carries cargo in the Caribbean. The holding company's principal subsidiary, gas utility Northern Illinois Gas (doing business as Nicor Gas), has 34,000 miles of mains and service pipes that distribute natural gas to almost 2.2 million residential, commercial, and industrial customers in Illinois. Nicor Gas also operates eight underground gas storage facilities; it obtains its supply through long-term contracts and on the spot market. Nicor also ships container cargo through its Florida-based Tropical Shipping subsidiary.

Tropical Shipping owns or charters 18 ships that primarily transport freight between Florida and about 30 Caribbean locations; it also has routes to other locations in the Americas, Europe, and Asia.

In response to electric utility deregulation in Illinois and nearby states, Nicor has been pursuing other non-utility businesses. However, Nicor and former partner Dynegy have liquidated the assets of their Nicor Energy joint venture, which marketed gas and electricity to retail customers in the Midwest, due to heavy losses at the unit. (Several former Nicor Energy officers have been indicted on charges of inflating the unit's 2001 earnings.)

Subsidiary Nicor Enerchange markets and trades wholesale gas; other Nicor subsidiaries offer energy-related construction and maintenance services.

## HISTORY

Nicor's history dates back to the 1850s, when one of its predecessors lit the Lincoln-Douglas debates by transporting gas through hollowed-out logs. By the early 1900s, it was transporting gas over longer distances in northern Illinois. Over the next half-century, the region's gas and electric companies were united in the Public Service Co. of Northern Illinois.

Utility Commonwealth Edison bought the company in 1953 and the next year created subsidiary Northern Illinois Gas to operate the gas business. In 1955 Northern Illinois Gas was spun off, and it immediately purchased Union Gas & Electric. A few years later, it built the world's largest underground storage system.

The utility enlarged its service area in the 1960s and began drilling for its own gas with mediocre results. When the energy crisis of the early 1970s began affecting the firm's gas deliveries, it increased gas production and built a synthetic gas plant. A 1974 general rate increase (the company's first in two decades), coupled with cost-cutting measures, helped relieve financial pressures.

To diversify beyond the utility business, Northern Illinois Gas formed holding company Nicor in 1976. Over the next few years Nicor bought coal reserves, oil leases, a drilling company, an inland barge business, and an offshore drilling services company. Nicor also acquired Caribbean shipper Tropical Shipping in 1982. When the energy bust of the 1980s hit, Nicor's diversification program lost its momentum; the company unloaded most of its purchases but kept Tropical Shipping.

The company took another, more cautious, stab at diversifying in 1992, when it began Nicor Energy Services to maintain and repair heating and air-conditioning equipment. In 1993 Northern Illinois Gas and gas wholesaler NGC (later named Dynegy) formed the Chicago Hub to provide various services to sellers and buyers of natural gas.

Nicor formed Nicor Technologies in 1994 to offer energy-related consulting services. Lower prices in the increasingly competitive natural gas market caused sales to fall. Nicor and NGC joined Pacific Enterprises (now Sempra Energy) and National Fuel Gas in 1995 to form Enerchange, to manage the Chicago Hub and others in California and the Northeast.

Northern Illinois Gas was granted a 2.8% rate increase in 1996, its first in 14 years. That year Tropical Shipping expanded into the Cayman Islands, Jamaica, and Puerto Rico by purchasing Thompson Shipping. In 1997 Nicor and NGC formed Nicor Energy, which offered energy services to industrial and commercial customers in the US Midwest. Nicor also joined TransCanada PipeLines to build a pipeline between Illinois and Manitoba, Canada; however, the project was later scrapped. That year Northern Illinois Gas began doing business as Nicor Gas.

Nicor and Dynegy teamed up in 1998 to build natural gas-fired electric power plants in six Midwestern states; however, Nicor bailed out on its first joint project in 1999. Utility deregulation arrived in Illinois in 1999, and by early 2000 Nicor had more than 100,000 users in its customer choice program. Also that year Nicor announced plans with Texas-based pipeline company Kinder Morgan to build a 74-mile pipeline in Illinois, and construction activities commenced in 2001. (The pipeline was completed in 2002.)

## EXECUTIVES

**Chairman, President, and CEO, Nicor and Nicor Gas:** Russ M. Strobel, age 53, $1,141,004 pay (prior to promotion)
**EVP and CFO, Nicor and Nicor Gas:** Richard L. (Rick) Hawley, age 57, $611,094 pay
**EVP, Operations, Nicor Gas:** Rocco J. D'Alessandro, age 47
**SVP, Diversified Ventures and Corporate Planning, Nicor and Nicor Gas:** Daniel R. Dodge, age 52, $353,800 pay
**SVP, Human Resources and Corporate Communications:** Claudia J. Colalillo, age 57
**SVP, General Counsel, and Secretary, Nicor and Nicor Gas:** Paul C. Gracey Jr., age 46
**VP and Treasurer, Nicor and Nicor Gas:** George M. Behrens, age 50
**VP, Distribution, Nicor Gas:** Anthony R. McCain, age 43
**VP, Information Technology, Nicor and Nicor Gas:** Barbara A. Zeller, age 51
**VP, Marketing, Sales, and Customer Service, Nicor Gas:** Christine L. Suppes, age 48
**VP, Administration and Finance, Nicor and Nicor Gas:** Gerald P. O'Connor, age 54, $381,220 pay
**VP, Controller:** Karen K. Pepping
**VP, Engineering, Nicor Gas:** Kris Nichols
**Assistant Secretary and Director, Investor Relations:** Mark A. Knox
**Director, Corporate Communications:** Don Ingle
**President and CEO, Tropical Shipping:** Rick Murrell, age 59
**Auditors:** Deloitte & Touche LLP

## LOCATIONS

**HQ:** Nicor Inc.
1844 Ferry Rd., Naperville, IL 60563
**Phone:** 630-305-9500 **Fax:** 630-983-9328
**Web:** www.nicor.com

Nicor subsidiary Nicor Gas distributes gas in northern Illinois, excluding the city of Chicago but including its suburbs. Subsidiary Tropical Shipping primarily transports freight between Florida and about 30 Caribbean locations; it also has routes to other locations in Asia, Europe, Latin America, and North America.

## PRODUCTS/OPERATIONS

### 2006 Sales

| | $ mil. | % of total |
|---|---|---|
| Gas distribution | 2,452.3 | 80 |
| Shipping | 398.3 | 13 |
| Other | 215.9 | 7 |
| Adjustments | (106.5) | — |
| **Total** | **2,960.0** | **100** |

### Major Operations

Northern Illinois Gas Company (operates as Nicor Gas, gas utility)
Tropical Shipping (freight transportation between Florida and the Caribbean)

### Other Selected Operations

EN Engineering (50%, pipeline consulting and construction services, joint venture with A. Epstein & Sons)
Horizon Pipeline Co. LLC (50%, pipeline company, joint venture with Kinder Morgan)
Nicor Energy Services Company (Nicor Services, maintenance and repair for gas piping and HVAC equipment)
Nicor Solutions (energy-related financial and billing services)

## COMPETITORS

AES
Alliant Energy
Ameren
AmerenCILCO
AmerenIP
Commonwealth Edison
Crowley Maritime
DTE
Duke Energy
Evergreen Marine
Exelon
Integrys Energy Group
KeySpan
MidAmerican Energy
NiSource
NRG Energy
Seaboard

## HISTORICAL FINANCIALS

Company Type: Public

### Income Statement

FYE: December 31

| | REVENUE ($ mil.) | NET INCOME ($ mil.) | NET PROFIT MARGIN | EMPLOYEES |
|---|---|---|---|---|
| **12/06** | 2,960 | 128 | 4.3% | 3,900 |
| **12/05** | 3,358 | 136 | 4.1% | 3,700 |
| **Annual Growth** | (11.8%) | (5.9%) | — | 5.4% |

### 2006 Year-End Financials

Debt ratio: 57.0%
Return on equity: 15.2%
Cash ($ mil.): 68
Current ratio: 0.80
Long-term debt ($ mil.): 498
No. of shares (mil.): 45
Dividends
Yield: 4.0%
Payout: 64.8%
Market value ($ mil.): 2,101

### Stock History

NYSE: GAS

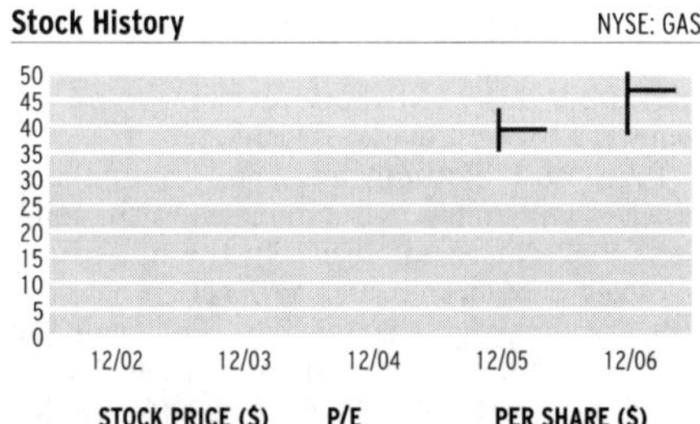


| | STOCK PRICE ($) FY Close | P/E High | P/E Low | PER SHARE ($) Earnings | Dividends | Book Value |
|---|---|---|---|---|---|---|
| **12/06** | 46.80 | 17 | 13 | 2.87 | 1.86 | 19.43 |
| **12/05** | 39.31 | 14 | 12 | 3.07 | 1.86 | 18.36 |
| **Annual Growth** | 19.1% | — | — | (6.5%) | 0.0% | 5.8% |

# NIKE, Inc.

Nike, the Greek goddess of victory, helped others succeed in times of war. NIKE, the world's #1 shoemaker, does more dominating than assisting, to capture more than 20% of the US athletic shoe market. The company designs and sells shoes for a variety of sports, including baseball, cheerleading, golf, volleyball, hiking, tennis, and football. NIKE also sells Cole Haan dress and casual shoes and a line of athletic apparel and equipment. In addition, it operates NIKETOWN shoe and sportswear stores, NIKE factory outlets, and NIKE Women shops. NIKE sells its products throughout the US and in more than 160 other countries. NIKE veteran Mark Parker succeeded Bill Perez, who resigned in 2006, as president and CEO.

Image-savvy NIKE sells its products through about 27,000 retail accounts in the US and through independent distributors and licensees in other countries. Subsidiaries include Cole Haan (dress and casual footwear), Bauer NIKE Hockey (hockey equipment), Hurley International (sports apparel for skateboarding, snowboarding, and surfing), and Converse (classic and retro-style shoes including the Chuck Taylor brand). In 2004 it purchased athletic apparel and footwear makers Official Starter Properties and Official Starter LLC.

NIKE is keeping its eye on its brands and on the competition. When adidas acquired Reebok in 2006, the deal put the joined companies in a position to compete with longstanding rival NIKE, which has held the top spot in the athletic apparel and footwear markets worldwide for decades.

Reebok filed a lawsuit against NIKE in 2007, alleging that nearly a dozen of NIKE's shoes (marketed under the Free brand) infringe on a new patent owned by Reebok covering collapsable shoes. NIKE has also been filing patent lawsuits against its competitors, specifically adidas in 2006. NIKE asserts that adidas has used elements of its SHOX cushioning technology in developing the adidas Kevin Garnett and A3 shoes.

Long known as a brand that caters to men (its "Be Like Mike" ad campaign) and as one that supports athletes who take performance and sports seriously, NIKE is focusing more on women who want workout fashion.

Like most clothing and footwear makers, NIKE is vulnerable to the moods of niche markets, including fickle teens. In the mid-priced shoe segment, brands such as Skechers have cut into the company's market share. Following the success of NIKE-sponsored golfer Tiger Woods, NIKE developed a set of golf clubs and unveiled a Tiger Woods apparel line. In addition, the company — which relies on contract manufacturers — has taken steps to avoid more criticism of human rights violations in its factories.

Co-founder Philip Knight announced in November 2004 he would step down as president and CEO, though he continued as chairman. Perez, former S.C. Johnson & Son chief, was tapped as Knight's successor but lasted barely a year in the top spot. Parker, a longtime NIKE brand executive, was named president and CEO in January 2006.

## HISTORY

Phil Knight, a good miler, and Bill Bowerman, a track coach who tinkered with shoe designs, met at the University of Oregon in 1957. The two men formed Blue Ribbon Sports in 1962 in an effort to make quality American running shoes. The next year they began selling Tiger shoes, manufactured by Japanese shoe manufacturer Onitsuka Tiger. They sold the running shoes out of cars at track meets.

The company became NIKE in 1972, named for the Greek goddess of victory. The NIKE "Swoosh" logo was designed by a graduate student named Carolyn Davidson, who was paid $35. The same year NIKE broke with Onitsuka in a dispute over distribution rights.

At the 1972 Olympic Trials in Oregon, Knight and Bowerman persuaded some of the marathoners to wear NIKE shoes. When some of these runners placed, the two advertised that NIKEs were worn by "four of the top seven finishers."

Bowerman tested a new sole in 1974 by stuffing a piece of rubber into a waffle iron. The result was the waffle sole, which NIKE added to its running shoes. NIKE grew as running's popularity surged in the 1970s. (NIKE even offered a red-and-silver shoe for disco dancing.) By 1979 it had 50% of the US running shoe market. NIKE went public the next year.

NIKE expanded with shoes for other sports, introducing the Air Jordan basketball shoe in 1985 (named for basketball star Michael Jordan) and the Cross Trainer two years later. NIKE's famous "Just Do It" slogan was introduced in 1988, the same year it bought dress-shoe maker Cole Haan.

In 1992 NIKE opened its first NIKETOWN store. It acquired Canstar Sports, which included hockey equipment maker Bauer, in 1995 (now Bauer NIKE Hockey). NIKE signed 20-year-old golf phenom Tiger Woods to a $40 million endorsement contract that year. Also in 1995 NIKE acquired a license to place its logo on NFL uniforms. (Reebok took over this license in 2002.)

NIKE launched a Jordan-branded athletic footwear and apparel division in 1997. Prompted by falling sales in Asia, NIKE cut 1,200 jobs in 1998 (about 5% of its workforce) to cut costs. With demand for athletic shoes weakening, in 1999 NIKE reported its first drop in sales since 1994. Also in 1999 the company began opening JORDAN store-within-a-store boutiques. Bowerman died in 1999; NIKE released a line of running shoes in his honor.

In 2000 the company launched a line of athletic electronics, including MP3 players, heart monitors, and two-way radios. A full year before Tiger Woods' contract expired, NIKE in 2000 signed the golfer to a five-year contract. The company said the new contract represented a "substantial raise" from his previous $40 million deal.

NIKE opened its first NIKEgoddess store in Newport Beach, California, in October 2001. The company acquired Hurley International, a distributor of action sports apparel, in April 2002.

In September 2003 NIKE acquired competitor Converse and left it as a separate operating unit to keep the Converse name intact. In October Bauer NIKE Hockey announced the closing of its hockey stick factory in Ontario and a staff reduction at its Quebec facilities.

## EXECUTIVES

**Chairman:** Philip H. Knight, age 69
**President, CEO, and Director:** Mark G. Parker, age 51, $2,438,121 pay
**VP and CFO:** Donald W. Blair, age 49, $1,052,596 pay
**VP and Corporate Controller:** Bernie Pliska, age 45
**VP and CIO:** Roland Paanakker
**VP, Diversity:** Gina Warren
**VP, General Counsel, and Chief Legal Officer:** James C. (Jim) Carter, age 59
**VP, Corporate Responsibility:** Hannah Jones, age 39
**VP Global Brand Marketing and Soccer:** Joaquin Hidalgo, age 46
**VP, Global Sports Marketing:** Adam S. Helfant, age 42
**VP, Investor Relations:** Pamela Catlett, age 41
**VP Global Human Resources:** David Ayre
**VP and Chief Administrative Officer:** Ronald D. (Ron) McCray, age 50
**Global Government and Public Affairs Director:** Brad Figel
**President, NIKE Brand:** Charles D. (Charlie) Denson, age 51, $2,135,862 pay
**President, Global Operations:** Gary M. DeStefano, age 50, $1,464,284 pay
**President, New Ventures:** Thomas E. Clarke, age 55
**President, Nike Foundation:** Maria S. Eitel, age 45
**President, Nike Golf:** Robert (Bob) Wood, age 50
**CEO, Cole Haan:** James C. Seuss, age 42
**CEO, Converse:** Jack A. Boys, age 49
**Auditors:** PricewaterhouseCoopers LLP

## LOCATIONS

**HQ:** NIKE, Inc.
1 Bowerman Dr., Beaverton, OR 97005
**Phone:** 503-671-6453 **Fax:** 503-671-6300
**Web:** www.nikebiz.com

NIKE sells its products in approximately 160 countries, operates 486 retail outlets (254 in the US and 232 outside the US), and utilizes independent contractors in 40 countries with more than 20 distribution centers in Africa, Asia, Australia, Canada, Europe, Latin America, and the US.

### 2007 Sales

| | $ mil. | % of total |
|---|---|---|
| Americas | | |
| US | 6,107.1 | 37 |
| Other countries | 952.5 | 6 |
| Europe, Middle East & Africa | 4,723.3 | 29 |
| Asia/Pacific | 2,283.4 | 14 |
| Other regions | 2,259.6 | 14 |
| **Total** | **16,325.9** | **100** |

## PRODUCTS/OPERATIONS

### 2007 Sales

| | $ mil. | % of total |
|---|---|---|
| Footwear | 8,514.0 | 52 |
| Apparel | 4,576.5 | 28 |
| Equipment | 975.8 | 6 |
| Other | 2,259.6 | 14 |
| **Total** | **16,325.9** | **100** |

### Selected Products

Athletic Shoes
- Aquatic
- Auto racing
- Baseball
- Basketball
- Bicycling
- Cheerleading
- Cross-training
- Fitness
- Football
- Golf
- Running
- Soccer
- Tennis
- Volleyball
- Wrestling

Athletic Wear and Equipment
- Accessories
- Athletic bags
- Bats
- Caps
- Fitness wear
- Gloves
- Headwear
- Jackets
- Pants
- Running clothes
- Shirts
- Shorts
- Skates
- Skirts
- Snowboards and snowboard apparel
- Socks
- Sport balls
- Timepieces
- Uniforms
- Unitards

### Selected Subsidiaries

Bauer NIKE Hockey Inc. (hockey equipment and in-line skates)
Cole Haan Holdings Inc. (footwear and accessories)
Converse Inc. (footwear)
Exeter Brands Group LLC (footwear and apparel to retail)
Hurley International LLC (action sports apparel)
NIKE IHM, Inc. (plastic products)
NIKE Team Sports, Inc. (headwear and licensed team logos)

## COMPETITORS

| | |
|---|---|
| Acushnet | Phoenix Footwear |
| adidas | Polo Ralph Lauren |
| Amer Sports | PUMA |
| ASICS | Quiksilver |
| Brown Shoe | R. Griggs |
| Callaway Golf | Rawlings |
| Columbia Sportswear | Rollerblade |
| Deckers Outdoor | Russell |
| Fila USA | Saucony |
| Fruit of the Loom | Skechers U.S.A. |
| FUBU | Stride Rite |
| Hanesbrands | Timberland |
| Juicy Couture | Timex |
| K-Swiss | Tommy Hilfiger |
| Levi Strauss | Under Armour |
| Mizuno | VF |
| New Balance | Victoria's Secret Stores |
| Oakley | Wolverine World Wide |

## HISTORICAL FINANCIALS

Company Type: Public

### Income Statement

FYE: May 31

| | REVENUE ($ mil.) | NET INCOME ($ mil.) | NET PROFIT MARGIN | EMPLOYEES |
|---|---|---|---|---|
| **5/07** | 16,326 | 1,492 | 9.1% | 30,200 |
| **5/06** | 14,955 | 1,392 | 9.3% | 28,000 |
| **5/05** | 13,740 | 1,212 | 8.8% | 26,000 |
| **5/04** | 12,253 | 946 | 7.7% | 24,667 |
| **5/03** | 10,697 | 474 | 4.4% | 23,300 |
| **Annual Growth** | 11.1% | 33.2% | — | 6.7% |

### 2007 Year-End Financials

| | |
|---|---|
| Debt ratio: 5.8% | No. of shares (mil.): 384 |
| Return on equity: 22.4% | Dividends |
| Cash ($ mil.): 2,847 | Yield: 1.2% |
| Current ratio: 3.13 | Payout: 23.2% |
| Long-term debt ($ mil.): 410 | Market value ($ mil.): 21,798 |

### Stock History

NYSE: NKE

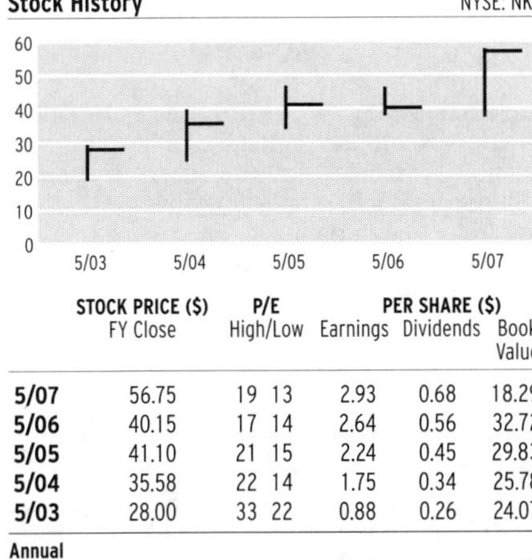


| | STOCK PRICE ($) FY Close | P/E High | P/E Low | PER SHARE ($) Earnings | Dividends | Book Value |
|---|---|---|---|---|---|---|
| **5/07** | 56.75 | 19 | 13 | 2.93 | 0.68 | 18.29 |
| **5/06** | 40.15 | 17 | 14 | 2.64 | 0.56 | 32.72 |
| **5/05** | 41.10 | 21 | 15 | 2.24 | 0.45 | 29.83 |
| **5/04** | 35.58 | 22 | 14 | 1.75 | 0.34 | 25.78 |
| **5/03** | 28.00 | 33 | 22 | 0.88 | 0.26 | 24.07 |
| **Annual Growth** | 19.3% | — | — | 35.1% | 27.2% | (6.6%) |

# NiSource Inc.

NiSource is the main energy source for resourceful Americans living in the Gulf Coast, Midwest, and New England regions of the country. The company's utility subsidiaries distribute natural gas to about 3.8 million customers in nine states. NiSource also generates, transmits, and distributes electricity to some 454,000 customers in 21 counties in its home state through its largest subsidiary, Northern Indiana Public Service Company (NIPSCO). NiSource owns one of the largest natural gas transmission and underground storage systems in the US, including a 16,000-mile interstate pipeline system.

NiSource's other utilities distribute natural gas in Kentucky, Maryland, Ohio, Pennsylvania, Virginia, Maine, Massachusetts, and New Hampshire, as well as in Indiana.

Several of NiSource's utilities participate in customer choice programs in states with deregulated energy markets. NiSource also has nonutility subsidiaries that market energy and provide asset management services; however, the company is scaling back on these operations.

NiSource is selling noncore assets to focus on its core electric and natural gas operations. The company has divested its water utility and telecommunications businesses; it has also sold its Primary Energy subsidiary, which offered on-site industrial power generation services, and its exploration and production unit, Columbia Energy Resources.

## HISTORY

NiSource's earliest ancestor was the South Bend (Indiana) Gas Light Company, founded in 1868 by the Studebaker brothers (of later auto fame) to supply gas. In 1886 a natural-gas discovery near Kokomo, Indiana, led to a boom in northern Indiana's use of the fuel. By 1900 steel plants and other industries had set up shop along Lake Michigan in northwestern Indiana and in Illinois.

Another NiSource ancestor was formed in 1901 as Hammond Illuminating, but it changed its name to South Shore Gas and Electric. In 1909 Northern Indiana Gas and Electric was founded by merging South Shore with other regional utilities. The next year Northern Indiana acquired South Bend.

A third NiSource predecessor, Calumet Electric (founded in 1912), had acquired several utilities by the early 1920s when utility magnate Samuel Insull bought it to add to his huge Midland Utilities holding company. In 1923 Insull bought Northern Indiana Gas and Electric, which merged three years later with Calumet to form Northern Indiana Public Service Company (NIPSCO). NIPSCO acquired its current service territory in 1930 when it swapped some areas with another Midland subsidiary.

The Public Utility Holding Company Act of 1935, beginning the regulation of regional monopolies, forced Midland to divest NIPSCO in 1947. In the 1950s and 1960s NIPSCO built two power plants and tripled its natural gas supply through a contract with a Houston gas company.

Responding to rising demand, NIPSCO in 1970 applied to build a nuclear unit at its Bailly plant, estimated to cost $180 million. In 1981 the nuke was abandoned after its cost rose to $2.1 billion. Reorganizing in 1987, NIPSCO became part of holding company NIPSCO Industries.

The Energy Policy Act of 1992 ushered in wholesale-power competition. That year NIPSCO acquired Kokomo Gas and Fuel, and in 1993 it picked up Northern Indiana Fuel and Light and Crossroads Pipeline.

To prepare for oncoming retail competition, NIPSCO in 1993 divided the electric and gas utilities into competing units and increased NIPSCO's marketing force. In 1997 NIPSCO branched out, buying water utility holding company IWC Resources, and the next year it began a customer choice program for its natural gas customers (all gas was delivered through its distribution lines, however).

The company changed its name to NiSource in 1999 but did not alter its acquisition strategy. NiSource entered the US Northeast's gas market, where deregulation plans were under way, by purchasing New England utility Bay State Gas. A unit of Bay State Gas, EnergyUSA, bought natural gas marketer TPC, and NiSource began integrating its nonregulated operations into EnergyUSA.

After launching a hostile takeover, which it later withdrew, NiSource purchased natural gas giant Columbia Energy Group for $6 billion in 2000. NiSource then sold its salt cavern gas storage and pipeline construction subsidiaries, as well as certain Columbia electric generation and LNG facilities. In 2001 NiSource sold its Columbia Propane unit to AmeriGas Partners; it also agreed to sell water company IWC Resources (and its utility subsidiary Indianapolis Water) to the City of Indianapolis (the sale was completed in 2002).

In 2002 NiSource teamed up with the merchant services unit of Aquila (formerly UtiliCorp) to form an energy marketing and trading joint venture; however, NiSource later backed out of the partnership due to instability in the energy trading industry. It also shut down its coal-fired Mitchell Generating Station, and sold its SM&P Utility Resources subsidiary to The Laclede Group.

The following year NiSource sold its Columbia Transmission Communications (Transcom) subsidiary to Neon Communications.

## EXECUTIVES

**Chairman:** Ian M. Rolland, age 72
**President, CEO, and Director:** Robert C. (Bob) Skaggs Jr., age 51, $675,000 pay (prior to promotion)
**EVP and CFO:** Michael W. (Mike) O'Donnell, age 61, $400,000 pay
**EVP and General Counsel:** Peter V. Fazio Jr., age 66
**SVP, Human Resources:** Robert D. Campbell
**SVP and Environmental Counsel:** Arthur E. (Art) Smith Jr.
**SVP; General Manager, Columbia Gas of Ohio and Columbia Gas of Kentucky:** Mark D. Wyckoff
**SVP, Administrative Services:** Violet G. Sistovaris
**SVP, Energy Distribution Regulated Revenue; President, Columbia Gas of Virginia:** Kathleen O'Leary
**SVP, Corporate Affairs:** Glen L. Kettering
**VP and Treasurer, NiSource, Northern Indiana Public Service, Bay State Gas, and Northern Utilities:** David J. (Dave) Vajda, age 50, $235,000 pay
**VP and Controller; VP, Northern Indiana Public Service, Bay State Gas, and Northern Utilities:** Jeffrey W. (Jeff) Grossman, age 54, $265,000 pay

**President, Bay State Gas and Northern Utilities:** Stephen H. Bryant
**President, Columbia Gas of Kentucky:** Joseph W. Kelly
**President, Columbia Gas of Maryland and Columbia Gas of Pennsylvania:** Terrence J. Murphy
**President, Columbia Gas of Ohio:** John W. (Jack) Partridge Jr.
**President, Northern Indiana Public Service:** Mark T. Maassel, age 51
**President, Pipeline Group:** Christopher A. Helms, age 51, $456,250 pay
**Corporate Secretary and Ethics Officer; Clerk, Bay State Gas and Northern Utilities:** Gary W. Pottorff
**Director, Corporate Communications:** Carol Churchill
**Director, Investor Relations:** Randy Hulen
**Auditors:** Deloitte & Touche LLP

## LOCATIONS

**HQ:** NiSource Inc.
801 E. 86th Ave., Merrillville, IN 46410
**Phone:** 219-647-5990 **Fax:** 219-647-5589
**Web:** www.nisource.com

NiSource distributes energy in Indiana, Kentucky, Maine, Maryland, Massachusetts, New Hampshire, Ohio, Pennsylvania, and Virginia.

## PRODUCTS/OPERATIONS

### 2006 Sales

| | $ mil. | % of total |
|---|---|---|
| Gas distribution | 4,189.3 | 56 |
| Electric | 1,299.2 | 17 |
| Gas transmission & storage | 1,033.2 | 14 |
| Other | 968.3 | 13 |
| **Total** | **7,490.0** | **100** |

### Selected Subsidiaries

Utility Operations
- Bay State Gas Company (natural gas utility)
  - Northern Utilities, Inc. (natural gas utility)
- Colombia Gas of Kentucky, Inc. (natural gas utility)
- Columbia Gas of Maryland, Inc. (natural gas utility)
- Columbia Gas of Ohio, Inc. (natural gas utility)
- Columbia Gas of Pennsylvania, Inc. (natural gas utility)
- Columbia Gas of Virginia, Inc. (natural gas utility)
- Kokomo Gas and Fuel Company (natural gas utility)
- Northern Indiana Fuel and Light Company, Inc. (NIFL, natural gas utility)
- Northern Indiana Public Service Company (NIPSCO, electric and natural gas utility, electric generation)

Gas Transmission and Storage Operations
- Columbia Gas Transmission Corporation
- Columbia Gulf Transmission Company
- Crossroads Pipeline Company
- Granite State Gas Transmission, Inc.

Other Operations
- EnergyUSA-TPC (energy marketing and asset management)
- NiSource Energy Technologies (distributed power generation technologies)

## COMPETITORS

AEP
Allegheny Energy
Atmos Energy
Baltimore Gas and Electric
Constellation Energy
Dominion Resources
Duke Energy
El Paso
E.ON U.S.
Equitable Resources
IPALCO Enterprises
KeySpan
National Grid USA
New Jersey Resources
Nicor
Northeast Utilities
NSTAR
RGC Resources
Southern Union
Unitil
Vectren

## HISTORICAL FINANCIALS

Company Type: Public

### Income Statement

FYE: December 31

| | REVENUE ($ mil.) | NET INCOME ($ mil.) | NET PROFIT MARGIN | EMPLOYEES |
|---|---|---|---|---|
| **12/06** | 7,490 | 282 | 3.8% | 7,439 |
| **12/05** | 7,899 | 307 | 3.9% | 7,822 |
| **12/04** | 6,666 | 436 | 6.5% | 8,628 |
| **12/03** | 6,247 | 85 | 1.4% | 8,614 |
| **12/02** | 6,492 | 373 | 5.7% | 9,307 |
| **Annual Growth** | 3.6% | (6.7%) | — | (5.4%) |

### 2006 Year-End Financials

Debt ratio: 102.6%
Return on equity: 5.7%
Cash ($ mil.): 176
Current ratio: 0.73
Long-term debt ($ mil.): 5,146
No. of shares (mil.): 274
Dividends
Yield: 3.8%
Payout: 89.3%
Market value ($ mil.): 6,595

### Stock History

NYSE: NI

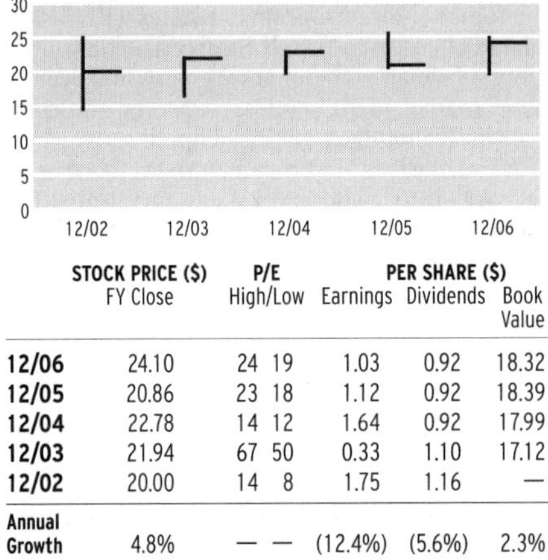


| | STOCK PRICE ($) FY Close | P/E High | P/E Low | PER SHARE ($) Earnings | Dividends | Book Value |
|---|---|---|---|---|---|---|
| **12/06** | 24.10 | 24 | 19 | 1.03 | 0.92 | 18.32 |
| **12/05** | 20.86 | 23 | 18 | 1.12 | 0.92 | 18.39 |
| **12/04** | 22.78 | 14 | 12 | 1.64 | 0.92 | 17.99 |
| **12/03** | 21.94 | 67 | 50 | 0.33 | 1.10 | 17.12 |
| **12/02** | 20.00 | 14 | 8 | 1.75 | 1.16 | — |
| **Annual Growth** | 4.8% | — | — | (12.4%) | (5.6%) | 2.3% |

# Noble Corporation

Noble Corporation may be heir to a fortune as demand increases for deepwater oil and gas contract drilling services. The company, with operations in waters off the coasts of five continents, has a fleet of 63 offshore drilling units: three submersibles, three dynamically positioned drillships, 13 semisubmersibles, and 44 jack-up rigs. Many of its rigs are capable of operating in depths greater than 5,000 ft. Noble also operates eight drilling units under labor contracts in the North Sea and off the east coast of Canada. Subsidiary Triton Engineering provides engineering and consulting services. Noble also provides labor contract drilling, well site, and project management services.

The group, which derives most of its revenues from offshore contracts, has positioned itself to ride a global trend toward deepwater exploration. Through acquisitions and equipment upgrading, Noble has been expanding its geographical reach and increasing its ability to drill in deeper offshore locations.

About three-fourths of the company's drilling fleet is deployed in international markets. It has converted five drilling units into company-designed EVA-400 semisubmersible rigs that can drill to depths of more than 5,000 feet. It has also purchased two additional jack-up rigs from a unit of Schlumberger, and it plans to purchase two more from Danish maritime giant A.P. Møller that are now deployed off the coast of Iran. Nine of the company's drilling units (one semisubmersible and eight jackups) are capable of operating in harsh environments.

With the oil services industry consolidating, Noble is looking to pick up new assets or form alliances. Noble has moved four jackup rigs from the Gulf of Mexico to Mexico for a long-term drilling contract with PEMEX, Mexico's state-owned oil company.

## HISTORY

Lloyd Noble and Art Olsen founded Noble-Olsen Oil in 1921 with one rig in Oklahoma. In 1929 Noble-Olsen ventured outside the US to perform contract drilling services in Canada. The next year Olsen left the firm, and the new Noble Oil formed subsidiary Noble Drilling to operate its contract drilling business. The firm began drilling along the Gulf Coast in 1933.

Oil was discovered in the UK in 1939, and Lloyd was called to Washington, DC, to discuss the best way to develop the fields. During WWII Noble crews completed more than 100 wells for the British as a contribution to the war effort. The company also drilled wells in Canada's Northwest Territories near the Arctic Circle in the 1940s. Lloyd Noble died in 1950.

The company built its first jack-up rig in 1955 and began air drilling in 1958. In the mid-1960s, new discoveries in North Dakota kept the firm busy, and it was also able to take advantage of increased drilling activity in the US caused by the Arab oil embargo of the early 1970s. Noble Drilling's parent, which had become Noble Affiliates, went public in 1972.

In the midst of the 1980s oil bust, Noble Affiliates spun off Noble Drilling, which went public in 1985. The contract driller began acquiring rigs that were being divested at a discount because of the suffering oil industry. Noble bought six offshore rigs and 20 land rigs in 1988. Three years later it bought 12 more offshore rigs. In 1994 the firm acquired Triton Engineering Services, and the next year Noble bought two more jack-up rigs and began operating in the Middle East.

The company added deepwater and harsh-environment capabilities to its fleet with the 1996 acquisition of Neddrill's oil and gas drilling division. Noble also announced that it had successfully completed studies on the conversion of submersibles into semisubmersibles with deepwater drilling capabilities.

As part of its focus on deepwater drilling, Noble sold 12 shallow-water rigs in 1997. That year and in 1998 the firm won contracts for its converted rigs from Shell Oil, PETROBRAS, and Amerada Hess (later renamed Hess), among others. One of the converted rigs, Noble Paul Wolff, set a new world record in 1999 for water depth drilling at more than 8,000 feet off the coast of Brazil.

In 2000 Noble formed a joint venture with Lime Rock Partners to acquire a North Sea jack-up rig for $32.7 million. The company upgraded its technology options in 2001 with the acquisition of Houston-based Maurer Engineering, which it planned to integrate with its drilling technology subsidiary, Noble Engineering and Development.

The company boosted its fleet with the acquisition of two drilling rigs from Ocean Rig ASA, and two from Transocean's Sedco Forex in 2002. The company also purchased two additional jackup rigs, the Trident III and Dhabi II, from a subsidiary of Schlumberger for about $95 million. It also expanded its technology assets by acquiring WELLDONE Engineering. Later that year Noble Drilling changed its name to Noble Corporation.

In 2005 Noble Corporation increased its stake in offshore drilling contractor Smedvig asa (Norway) to more than 39% by purchasing Smedvig family shares for about NOK 4.6 billion, but sold its interests in 2006.

## EXECUTIVES

**Chairman, President, and CEO:** Mark A. Jackson, age 51, $1,283,742 pay (prior to title change)
**SVP, CFO, Treasurer, and Controller:** Thomas L. Mitchell, age 46, $162,885 pay
**EVP and Corporate Secretary:** Julie J. Robertson, age 50, $694,583 pay
**SVP, General Counsel, and Assistant Secretary:** Robert D. Campbell, age 56, $454,792 pay
**SVP and COO:** David W. Williams, age 51
**VP Tax, Noble Drilling Services:** Ross W. Gallup, age 45
**VP Investor Relations and Planning:** Lee M. Ahlstrom
**Director, Corporate Communications:** John S. Breed
**Manager, Investor Relations:** Brook Wootton
**Executive Assistant:** Sue Ann Martin
**Auditors:** PricewaterhouseCoopers LLP

## LOCATIONS

**HQ:** Noble Corporation
13135 S. Dairy Ashford, Ste. 800,
Sugar Land, TX 77478
**Phone:** 281-276-6100 **Fax:** 281-491-2092
**Web:** www.noblecorp.com

Noble Corporation has operations worldwide.

### 2006 Sales

| | $ mil. | % of total |
|---|---|---|
| US | 557.9 | 27 |
| Nigeria | 273.0 | 13 |
| Mexico | 269.2 | 13 |
| Qatar | 212.2 | 10 |
| UK | 211.4 | 10 |
| Brazil | 174.4 | 8 |
| The Netherlands | 169.0 | 8 |
| United Arab Emirates | 108.2 | 5 |
| Other countries | 124.9 | 6 |
| **Total** | **2,100.2** | **100** |

## PRODUCTS/OPERATIONS

### 2006 Sales

| | $ mil. | % of total |
|---|---|---|
| International contracting drilling services | 1,446.4 | 69 |
| Domestic contract drilling services | 549.4 | 26 |
| Other operations | 104.4 | 5 |
| **Total** | **2,100.2** | **100** |

### Selected Products and Services

Contract drilling (land and offshore drilling for the oil and gas industry)
Turnkey services
- Consulting
- Contract engineering
- Drilling and completion planning and design
- Drilling project management
- Specialized drilling tools and services

Labor contract drilling (drilling and workover personnel)
Engineering services
- Offshore equipment
- Recertification of oil field equipment

### Selected Subsidiaries

Maurer Technology Incorporated
Noble Downhole Technology
- Noble Drilling (Deutschland) GmbH

Noble Drilling International Inc.
- Noble Drilling (Canada) Ltd.
  - Bawden Drilling Inc.
- Noble Drilling International (Cayman) Ltd.
  - International Directional Services Ltd.
  - Nedstaff Ltd. (China)
  - Noble do Brasil S/C Ltda.
  - Noble Drilling (Denmark) Holding ApS
  - Noble Drilling (Nigeria) Ltd.
  - Noble Drilling (Paul Wolff) Ltd.
  - Noble Drilling (U.K.) Ltd.
  - Noble International Limited
    - Noble Drilling de Venezuela C.A
  - Noble-Neddrill International Limited (Cayman Islands)

Noble Drilling Services Inc.
Noble Drilling (U.S.) Inc
- Noble Drilling Exploration Company

Noble Engineering & Development Limited (Cayman Islands)
Noble Wellbore Technologies Inc.
Triton Engineering Services Company
- Triton International, Inc.

## COMPETITORS

Acergy
Atwood Oceanics
Baker Hughes
Diamond Offshore
ENSCO
GlobalSantaFe
Helmerich & Payne
McDermott
Nabors Industries
Parker Drilling
Pride International
Rowan
Schlumberger
Transocean
Weatherford International

## HISTORICAL FINANCIALS

Company Type: Public

### Income Statement

FYE: December 31

| | REVENUE ($ mil.) | NET INCOME ($ mil.) | NET PROFIT MARGIN | EMPLOYEES |
|---|---|---|---|---|
| **12/06** | 2,100 | 732 | 34.8% | 6,000 |
| **12/05** | 1,382 | 297 | 21.5% | 5,600 |
| **12/04** | 1,066 | 146 | 13.7% | 5,300 |
| **12/03** | 987 | 166 | 16.9% | 3,364 |
| **12/02** | 986 | 210 | 21.2% | 3,747 |
| **Annual Growth** | 20.8% | 36.7% | — | 12.5% |

### 2006 Year-End Financials

Debt ratio: 21.2%
Return on equity: 24.6%
Cash ($ mil.): 62
Current ratio: 1.34
Long-term debt ($ mil.): 684
No. of shares (mil.): 135
Dividends
Yield: 0.2%
Payout: 3.0%
Market value ($ mil.): 10,249

### Stock History

NYSE: NE

| | STOCK PRICE ($) FY Close | P/E High | P/E Low | PER SHARE ($) Earnings | PER SHARE ($) Dividends | PER SHARE ($) Book Value |
|---|---|---|---|---|---|---|
| **12/06** | 76.15 | 16 | 11 | 5.33 | 0.16 | 23.99 |
| **12/05** | 70.54 | 35 | 22 | 2.16 | 0.10 | 19.94 |
| **12/04** | 49.74 | 46 | 31 | 1.09 | — | 17.74 |
| **12/03** | 35.78 | 31 | 24 | 1.25 | — | 16.27 |
| **12/02** | 35.15 | 29 | 17 | 1.57 | — | 14.89 |
| **Annual Growth** | 21.3% | — | — | 35.7% | 60.0% | 12.7% |

# Nordstrom, Inc.

Service with a smile is a part of Nordstrom's corporate culture. One of the nation's largest upscale apparel and shoe retailers, Nordstrom sells clothes, shoes, and accessories through nearly 100 Nordstrom stores and about 50 outlet stores (Nordstrom Rack) in 27 states. It also operates a pair of clearance stores, a freestanding shoe store, and about 40 Façonnable boutiques (primarily in Europe), and it sells goods online and through catalogs. With its easy-return policy and touches such as thank-you notes from employees, Nordstrom has developed a reputation for top-notch customer service. Members of the Nordstrom family, who own about 20% of the company's stock, closely supervise the chain.

Nordstrom has agreed to sell Façonnable, acquired for $169 million in 2000, to Lebanon-based M1 Group for about $210 million. Of the Façonnable boutiques, about three dozen are located in Europe (Belgium, France, and Portugal), and four stores are in the US. The Façonnable sale is expected to close by the end of 2007.

At Nordstrom, employees cheer customers on opening day of new stores and, in general, clamor to help (the company's no-questions return policy is legendary). The atmosphere doesn't hurt either: Most stores have live piano music and some feature day spas, restaurants, and espresso bars. The upscale apparel and accessories retailer has set its sights on a new business: music. Beginning with the 2006 holiday season, Nordstrom stores began selling CDs. Initially the Nordstrom music collection will feature about 20 titles — from popular artists as well as relatively unknown musicians — but could grow to 50 CDs in 2007.

The family-run company has consolidated its catalog and Internet businesses into one unit called Nordstrom Direct. Nordstrom plans to open 13 new stores and relocate or remodel another 18 over the next three years.

Nordstrom has set its sights on Manhattan, where it currently has no retail presence.

## HISTORY

In 1901 John Nordstrom, a lumberjack and successful gold miner, used his Alaska Gold Rush money to open Wallin & Nordstrom shoe store in Seattle with shoemaker Carl Wallin. Nordstrom retired in 1928 and sold his half of the business, which included a second store, to his sons Everett and Elmer. Wallin sold his share to the brothers after retiring the following year. A third Nordstrom son, Lloyd, joined in 1933. The shoe chain thrived and incorporated as Nordstrom's in 1946.

By 1963 Nordstrom's was the largest independent shoe chain in the country. The company diversified by acquiring Best Apparel's stores in Seattle and Portland, Oregon. Three years later Nordstrom's bought Portland's Nicholas Ungar, a fashion retailer, and merged it with one of its shoe stores in Portland under the name Nordstrom Best.

Renaming itself Nordstrom Best in 1966, the company went public in 1971 and changed its name again in 1973 to Nordstrom. The retailer grew steadily throughout the 1970s, opening new stores, boosting sales in existing stores, and diversifying. In 1976 Nordstrom started Place Two, featuring apparel and shoes in smaller stores than its traditional department layouts. It moved into Southern California (Orange County) two years later. Buoyed by almost $300 million in new sales, Nordstrom executives planned an aggressive expansion.

Nordstrom opened its first store on the East Coast in 1988 in Virginia. The chain continued to expand, opening stores in Northern California and in the affluent Washington, DC, suburbs.

The 1989 San Francisco earthquake, along with a national downturn, hurt retail sales significantly. Nordstrom's much-touted focus on customer service had a downside: The company was investigated in 1990 for not paying employees for customer services they performed, including delivery of merchandise on their own time. (Three years later Nordstrom set aside $15 million to pay back wages to employees who had performed off-the-clock services.)

The company continued to expand in the East and Midwest, opening its first store in the New York City area in 1991. In 1993 the retailer opened a men's boutique in New York (Façonnable). Looking for new ways to attract customers, Nordstrom introduced a mail-order catalog the next year.

Following the family's business tradition, six members of Nordstrom's fourth generation began running the company in 1995. Third-generation members James Nordstrom, John Nordstrom, Bruce Nordstrom, and Jack McMillan retired as co-chairmen and were replaced by non-family members Ray Johnson and John Whitacre. (Johnson retired in 1996.)

In 1999 Nordstrom created Nordstrom.com, a partnership with Benchmark Capital and Madrona Investment Group, to consolidate its catalog and Internet operations.

In early 2000, amid slumping sales, the company dissolved the co-presidency. Less than a year later, however, the Nordstroms were back in charge. Chairman and CEO Whitacre resigned and Blake Nordstrom took over running the company as president. His father, Bruce, came out of retirement to take the chairman's role. Later the company bought the French design company Façonnable, which supplies the products for its Façonnable boutiques.

In 2002 the company bought out Benchmark's and Madrona's minority stake in Nordstrom.com.

In August 2005 Nordstrom bought a majority interest in luxury specialty stores Jeffrey New York and Jeffrey Atlanta. Terms of the agreement were not disclosed. The Jeffrey stores had about $35 million in sales in 2004. Also in 2005 the company opened stores in Atlanta; Dallas; Irvine, California; and San Antonio.

## EXECUTIVES

**Chairman:** Enrique (Rick) Hernandez Jr., age 51
**President and Director:** Blake W. Nordstrom, age 46, $711,302 pay
**EVP and CFO:** Michael G. (Mike) Koppel, age 50, $441,870 pay
**EVP; Chairman and CEO, Nordstrom FSB; President, Nordstrom Credit:** Kevin T. Knight, age 51
**EVP and Chief Administrative Officer:** Daniel F. (Dan) Little, age 45, $391,063 pay
**EVP; President, Merchandising and Director:** Peter E. (Pete) Nordstrom, age 45, $490,932 pay
**EVP; President, Stores:** Erik B. Nordstrom, age 43, $490,932 pay
**EVP, Human Resources and Diversity Affairs:** Delena M. Sunday, age 46
**EVP; President, Nordstrom Rack:** Scott Meden, age 58
**EVP, Marketing:** Linda Toschi Finn, age 59
**EVP and General Merchandise Manager, Men's and Kidswear Divisions:** David Whitman, age 48
**EVP, Women's Designer Apparel:** Jennifer Wheeler
**EVP and Nordstrom Rack Northwest Regional Manager:** Karen (K.C.) Shaffer, age 51
**EVP, Strategy and Development:** Paul F. Favaro, age 48
**EVP; President, Façonnable:** Mark S. Brashear, age 45
**EVP; President, Nordstrom Direct:** James F. (Jamie) Nordstrom Jr., age 33
**EVP; President, Nordstrom Product Group:** James R. O'Neal, age 48
**EVP and Midwest Regional Manager, Full-Line Stores:** Robert J. Middlemas, age 50
**EVP and Southern States Regional Manager, Full-Line Stores:** Geevy S.K. Thomas, age 42
**EVP and Washington/Alaska Regional Manager, Full-Line Stores:** Llynn A. (Len) Kuntz, age 44
**EVP and General Merchandise Manager, Shoe Division:** Jack H. Minuk, age 52
**EVP and General Merchandise Manager, Accessories and Women's Specialized Divisions:** Margaret Myers, age 60
**VP, Real Estate and Corporate Secretary:** David L. Mackie, age 56
**Manager, Investor Relations:** R.J. Jones
**Business Public Relations Director:** Deniz Anders
**Auditors:** Deloitte & Touche LLP

## LOCATIONS

**HQ:** Nordstrom, Inc.
1617 6th Ave., Seattle, WA 98101
**Phone:** 206-628-2111 **Fax:** 206-628-1795
**Web:** www.nordstrom.com

Nordstrom operates full-line stores in Alaska, Arizona, California, Colorado, Connecticut, Florida, Georgia, Hawaii, Illinois, Indiana, Kansas, Maryland, Michigan, Minnesota, Missouri, Nevada, New Jersey, New York, North Carolina, Ohio, Oregon, Pennsylvania, Rhode Island, Texas, Utah, Virginia, and Washington. It operates Nordstrom Rack outlet stores in Arizona, California, Colorado, Georgia, Hawaii, Illinois, Maryland, Michigan, Minnesota, Nevada, New York, Oregon, Pennsylvania, Texas, Utah, Virginia, and Washington. The company's Façonnable boutiques are located in California, Florida, New York, and Texas, as well as Europe, and its freestanding shoe store is located in Hawaii.

## PRODUCTS/OPERATIONS

### 2007 Sales

| | % of total |
|---|---|
| Women's apparel | 35 |
| Shoes | 20 |
| Men's apparel | 18 |
| Cosmetics | 11 |
| Women's accessories | 10 |
| Children's apparel | 3 |
| Other | 3 |
| **Total** | **100** |

### 2007 Sales

| | $ mil. | % of total |
|---|---|---|
| Retail stores | 7,900.2 | 92 |
| Direct | 555.5 | 7 |
| Other | 105.0 | 1 |
| **Total** | **8,560.7** | **100** |

### Selected Retail Operations

Façonnable (specialty boutiques)
Last Chance (clearance stores)
Nordstrom (specialty stores selling apparel, shoes, and accessories for women, men, and children)
Nordstrom Direct (catalogs and online ordering)
Nordstrom Rack (outlets selling merchandise from Nordstrom specialty stores and manufacturers)

## COMPETITORS

AnnTaylor
Barneys
Benetton
Bloomingdale's
Brooks Brothers
Brown Shoe
Caché
Dillard's
Donna Karan
Eddie Bauer Holdings
Gap
J. C. Penney
J. Crew
Jones Apparel
Lands' End
Limited Brands
Loehmann's
Macy's
Marks & Spencer
Men's Wearhouse
Neiman Marcus
Saks Fifth Avenue
Saks Inc.
Talbots
Tiffany
Von Maur

## HISTORICAL FINANCIALS

Company Type: Public

### Income Statement

FYE: January 31

| | REVENUE ($ mil.) | NET INCOME ($ mil.) | NET PROFIT MARGIN | EMPLOYEES |
|---|---|---|---|---|
| **1/07** | 8,561 | 678 | 7.9% | 57,400 |
| **1/06** | 7,723 | 551 | 7.1% | 51,400 |
| **1/05** | 7,131 | 394 | 5.5% | 53,500 |
| **1/04** | 6,449 | 243 | 3.8% | 52,000 |
| **1/03** | 5,975 | 90 | 1.5% | 52,000 |
| **Annual Growth** | 9.4% | 65.6% | — | 2.5% |

### 2007 Year-End Financials

Debt ratio: 28.8%
Return on equity: 31.8%
Cash ($ mil.): 831
Current ratio: 1.91
Long-term debt ($ mil.): 624
No. of shares (mil.): 257
Dividends
Yield: 0.7%
Payout: 16.5%
Market value ($ mil.): 14,585

### Stock History

NYSE: JWN

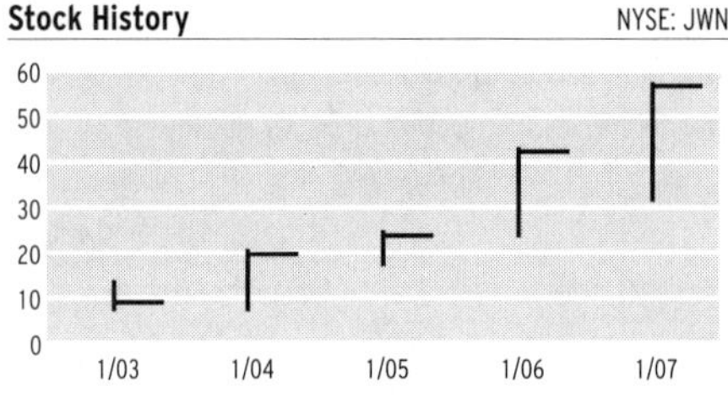


| | STOCK PRICE ($) FY Close | P/E High | P/E Low | PER SHARE ($) Earnings | PER SHARE ($) Dividends | PER SHARE ($) Book Value |
|---|---|---|---|---|---|---|
| **1/07** | 56.68 | 22 | 12 | 2.55 | 0.42 | 8.43 |
| **1/06** | 42.28 | 22 | 12 | 1.98 | 0.32 | 7.76 |
| **1/05** | 23.80 | 18 | 13 | 1.38 | 0.24 | 13.19 |
| **1/04** | 19.65 | 23 | 9 | 0.88 | 0.20 | 11.81 |
| **1/03** | 9.02 | 41 | 23 | 0.33 | 0.19 | 10.13 |
| **Annual Growth** | 58.3% | — | — | 66.7% | 21.9% | (4.5%) |

# Norfolk Southern

Transportation titan Norfolk Southern is one big train that could. The company's main subsidiary, Norfolk Southern Railway, transports freight over a network consisting of more than 21,000 route miles in 22 states in the eastern US and in Ontario, Canada. The rail system is made up of more than 16,000 route miles owned by Norfolk Southern and about 5,000 route miles trackage rights, which allow the company to use tracks owned by other railroads. Norfolk Southern transports coal and general merchandise, including automotive products and chemicals. The company also offers intermodal services (freight transportation by a combination of train and truck) through its Triple Crown Services unit.

Demand for rail freight transportation is increasing because of increased fuel prices, highway congestion, regulatory changes in the trucking industry, and a demand for transportation options with less environmental impact.

To meet the increased demand and make better use of its rail network, Norfolk Southern has repaired infrastructure, increased track capacity, and upgraded crossing signals. The company sees intermodal traffic as a promising growth area, and it is investing in new freight-handling facilities.

Norfolk Southern's network includes lines formerly operated by Conrail, which is jointly owned by Norfolk Southern and rival CSX. In 2004 Norfolk Southern and CSX reorganized Conrail to give each parent company direct ownership of the portion of Conrail's assets that it operates. Conrail still operates switching facilities and terminals used by both Norfolk Southern and CSX.

## HISTORY

Norfolk Southern Corporation resulted from the 1982 merger of two US rail giants — Norfolk & Western Railway Company (N&W) and Southern Railway Company — which had emerged from more than 200 and 150 previous mergers, respectively.

N&W dates to 1838, when one track connected Petersburg, Virginia, to City Point (now Hopewell). This eight-miler became part of the Atlantic, Mississippi & Ohio (AM&O), which was created by consolidating three Virginia railways in 1870.

In 1881 Philadelphia bank E. W. Clark bought the AM&O, and renamed it the Norfolk & Western. N&W rolled into Ohio by purchasing two other railroads (1892, 1901).

The company took over the Virginian Railway, a coal carrier with track paralleling much of its own, in 1959. In 1964 N&W became a key railroad in the Midwest by acquiring the New York, Chicago & St. Louis Railroad and the Pennsylvania Railroad's line between Columbus and Sandusky, Ohio. It also leased the Wabash Railroad, with lines from Detroit and Chicago to Kansas City and St. Louis.

Southern Railway can be traced back to the South Carolina Canal & Rail Road, a nine-mile line chartered in 1827 and built by Horatio Allen to win trade for Charleston's port. It began operating the US's first regularly scheduled passenger train in 1830 and became the world's longest railway when it opened a 136-mile line to Hamburg, South Carolina (1833).

Soon other railroads sprang up in the South, including the Richmond & Danville (Virginia, 1847) and the East Tennessee, Virginia & Georgia (1869), which were combined to form the Southern Railway System in 1894. Southern eventually controlled more than 100 railroads, forging a system from Washington, DC, to St. Louis and New Orleans.

The 1982 merger of Southern and N&W created an extensive rail system throughout the East, South, and Midwest. Norfolk Southern (a holding company created for the two railroads) also bought North American Van Lines in 1985. Triple Crown Services, the company's intermodal subsidiary, was started in 1986. The company also made a failed attempt to take over Piedmont Aviation the next year.

Norfolk Southern revived North American Van Lines by selling its refrigerator truck operation, Tran-star (1993), and suspending its commercial trucking line. But it later sold the rest of the motor carrier (1998) to focus on rail operations.

When CSX announced its plans to buy Conrail in 1997, Norfolk Southern's counteroffer led to a split of the former Northeastern monopoly, between Norfolk Southern (58%) and CSX (42%).

Problems with integrating Conrail's assets caused Norfolk Southern to have one of its worst quarters in years. But by 2000 it had regained some of the traffic it had lost to service problems, and its intermodal shipping business also gained speed.

After two tough years, Norfolk Southern got hit in the wallet again in 2001: The company agreed to pay $28 million to settle a racial discrimination lawsuit brought by black employees in 1993. Norfolk Southern began rounds of layoffs and closed redundant depots and facilities in 2001.

In 2005 nine people died in South Carolina when chlorine gas leaked from a ruptured car on a Norfolk Southern freight train. The car was ruptured when the train crashed into a company-owned locomotive and two train cars that were parked on a siding.

## EXECUTIVES

**Chairman, CEO, and Director:** Charles W. (Wick) Moorman IV, age 55, $750,000 pay
**Vice Chairman and COO:** Stephen C. Tobias, age 62, $600,000 pay
**EVP Administration:** John P. Rathbone, age 54
**EVP Law and Corporate Relations:** James A. Hixon, age 53, $569,160 pay
**EVP Operations:** Mark D. Manion, age 54, $400,000 pay
**EVP and Chief Marketing Officer:** Donald W. Seale, age 54, $400,000 pay
**EVP Finance and CFO:** James A. Squires, age 45
**EVP Planning and CIO:** Deborah H. (Debbie) Butler
**SVP Operations Planning and Support:** John M. Samuels
**VP and Controller:** Marta R. Stewart, age 49
**VP and Treasurer:** William J. Romig
**VP Business Development:** Robert E. Martínez
**VP Corporate Communications:** Robert C. (Bob) Fort
**VP Government Relations:** Bruno Maestri
**VP Human Resources:** Cindy C. Earhart
**VP Law:** William A. Galanko
**VP Operations Planning and Budget:** Terry N. Evans
**President, Automotive and Supply Chain Services:** David F. Julian
**President, TransWorks:** Timothy D. (Tim) Minnich
**President, Triple Crown Services:** James A. (Jim) Newton
**Corporate Secretary:** Dezora M. (Dee) Martin
**Director Investor Relations:** Leanne D. Marilley
**Auditors:** KPMG LLP

## LOCATIONS

**HQ:** Norfolk Southern Corporation
3 Commercial Place, Norfolk, VA 23510
**Phone:** 757-629-2600 **Fax:** 757-664-5069
**Web:** www.nscorp.com

## PRODUCTS/OPERATIONS

### 2006 Sales

| | $ mil. | % of total |
|---|---|---|
| Coal | 2,330 | 25 |
| General merchandise | | |
| Metals/construction | 1,168 | 12 |
| Chemicals | 1,079 | 11 |
| Agriculture, consumer products & government | 994 | 11 |
| Automotive | 974 | 10 |
| Paper, clay & forest | 891 | 10 |
| Intermodal | 1,971 | 21 |
| **Total** | **9,407** | **100** |

### Selected Subsidiaries and Affiliates

Conrail (58%)
Norfolk Southern Railway Company
Pocahontas Land Corporation (coal mines and other energy-related properties)
Triple Crown Services Company (intermodal services)

## COMPETITORS

American Commercial Lines
APL Logistics
Burlington Northern Santa Fe
Canadian National Railway
Canadian Pacific Railway
CSX
Hub Group
Ingram Industries
J.B. Hunt
Kansas City Southern
Kirby
Landstar System
Pacer International
Schneider National
Union Pacific
Werner Enterprises

## HISTORICAL FINANCIALS

Company Type: Public

### Income Statement

FYE: December 31

| | REVENUE ($ mil.) | NET INCOME ($ mil.) | NET PROFIT MARGIN | EMPLOYEES |
|---|---|---|---|---|
| **12/06** | 9,407 | 1,481 | 15.7% | 30,541 |
| **12/05** | 8,527 | 1,281 | 15.0% | 30,294 |
| **12/04** | 7,312 | 923 | 12.6% | 28,475 |
| **12/03** | 6,468 | 535 | 8.3% | 28,753 |
| **12/02** | 6,270 | 460 | 7.3% | 28,970 |
| **Annual Growth** | 10.7% | 34.0% | — | 1.3% |

### 2006 Year-End Financials

Debt ratio: 63.5%
Return on equity: 15.7%
Cash ($ mil.): 918
Current ratio: 1.15
Long-term debt ($ mil.): 6,109
No. of shares (mil.): 397
Dividends
Yield: 1.4%
Payout: 19.0%
Market value ($ mil.): 19,986

### Stock History

NYSE: NSC

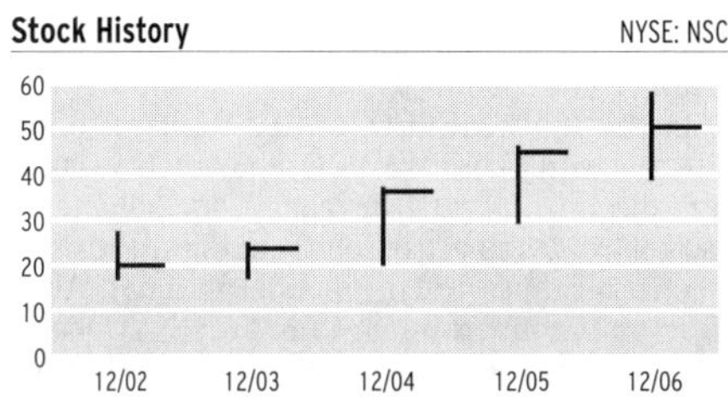


| | STOCK PRICE ($) FY Close | P/E High | P/E Low | PER SHARE ($) Earnings | Dividends | Book Value |
|---|---|---|---|---|---|---|
| **12/06** | 50.29 | 16 | 11 | 3.57 | 0.68 | 24.19 |
| **12/05** | 44.83 | 15 | 10 | 3.11 | 0.48 | 22.66 |
| **12/04** | 36.19 | 16 | 9 | 2.31 | 0.36 | 19.96 |
| **12/03** | 23.65 | 18 | 13 | 1.37 | 0.30 | 17.83 |
| **12/02** | 19.99 | 23 | 15 | 1.18 | 0.26 | 16.71 |
| **Annual Growth** | 25.9% | — | — | 31.9% | 27.2% | 9.7% |

# Northeast Utilities

Northeast Utilities (NU) uses a little Yankee ingenuity to keep its customers powered up. The largest utility in New England, NU supplies power to 1.9 million customers in Connecticut, New Hampshire, and Massachusetts through subsidiaries Connecticut Light and Power, Public Service Company of New Hampshire, and Western Massachusetts Electric. The company's Yankee Gas utility provides natural gas to 200,000 customers in Connecticut. In 2006 NU sold nonregulated subsidiary Select Energy, which marketed and traded energy to wholesale and retail customers, to Hess Corporation.

After conducting a review of its business activities, NU has announced that wholesale energy marketing and energy services will not be a part of the company's long-term plans. As a result, the company's commercial plumbing, electrical, mechanical, telecommunications, and contracting operations are being divested.

In 2006 NU sold its energy services unit (Select Energy Services) to Ameresco. That year the company also sold its competitive generation assets in Connecticut and Massachusetts to Energy Capital Partners for $1.34 billion.

## HISTORY

In 1966 three old, intertwined New England utilities merged. One was The Hartford Electric Light Company (HELCO), founded in 1883 by Austin Dunham in Hartford, Connecticut. In 1915 the company signed the first power exchange agreement in the US with Connecticut Power (CP), which HELCO acquired in 1920.

The second, founded in 1886, was Western Massachusetts Electric (WMECO), which merged with Western Counties in the 1930s to become WMECO. The third was Connecticut Light and Power (CL&P). Founded as Rocky River Power in 1905, it took the CL&P name in 1917. In 1929 it built the US's first large-scale pumped-storage hydroelectric plant.

In the 1950s HELCO formed Yankee Atomic Electric with CL&P, WMECO, and others to build an experimental nuclear reactor. In 1965 members of the group began jointly building the Connecticut Yankee nuke (on line in 1968). After years of cooperation, CL&P, HELCO, and WMECO merged in 1966, and Northeast Utilities (NU) was born. It was the first multistate utility holding company created since the Public Utility Holding Company Act of 1935 had broken up the old utility giants. Holyoke Water Power joined NU the following year.

The 1970s energy crisis spurred NU to continue building nukes, including Maine Yankee, Vermont Yankee, and two Millstone units. But by the 1980s, construction delays had raised the cost of the final unit, Millstone 3.

In 1989 regulators forced CL&P to spin off its gas utility, Yankee Energy System. The next year NU acquired bankrupt utility Public Service Company of New Hampshire (PSNH) and its new Seabrook nuke. (PSNH emerged from bankruptcy in 1991.)

The 1995 shutdown of Millstone 1 began NU's nuclear troubles. In 1996 regulators closed all of its nukes except Seabrook because of safety concerns, and NU mothballed Connecticut Yankee. The next year Michael Morris replaced CEO Bernard Fox, who left after federal regulators ordered NU to comply with regulations and fix management problems — NU managers had routinely retaliated against whistleblowers — the first time a utility had been given such an order. New managers came in, including a former whistleblower, but NU couldn't avoid a record-setting $2.1 million fine. NU received permission to restart the Millstone units in 1998-99. But it had to absorb the $1 billion in power replacement associated with the shutdown.

Meanwhile, as deregulation loomed, NU created a retail marketer (now Select Energy) and a telecommunications arm (Mode 1 Communications) in 1996. Two years later retail competition began in Massachusetts and deregulation legislation was passed in Connecticut (deregulation went into effect there in 2000).

In 1999 NU sold its Massachusetts plants to New York's Consolidated Edison and auctioned off its non-nuclear plants in Connecticut to its subsidiary, Northeast Generation, and Northern States Power (now Xcel Energy). NU agreed to plead guilty to 25 federal felony counts and pay $10 million in penalties for polluting water near Millstone and lying to regulators.

That year Consolidated Edison agreed to buy NU for $3.3 billion in cash and stock and $3.9 billion in assumed debt. The deal broke down in 2001, however: Con Edison charged NU with misrepresenting information about power-supply contracts, and NU charged Con Edison with improperly attempting to renegotiate the terms of the acquisition.

Bringing an old family member home, NU bought Yankee Energy System for $679 million in 2000. Later that year Dominion Resources, which had helped NU restart Millstone 2 and Millstone 3 (Millstone 1 had been taken out of service), agreed to buy the Millstone complex for $1.3 billion. The sale closed in 2001.

Also in 2001 NU subsidiary Select Energy bought Niagara Mohawk's energy marketing unit; NU sold the distribution business of its Holyoke Water Power utility to the City of Holyoke for $18 million; and retail electric competition began in New Hampshire.

NU agreed to sell CL&P's 10% stake in the Vermont Yankee nuclear facility to Entergy in 2001; the deal was completed the following year. In 2002 NU sold its 40% interest in the Seabrook Nuclear Generating facility to FPL Group.

## EXECUTIVES

**Chairman, President, and CEO:**
Charles W. (Chuck) Shivery, age 60, $1,475,166 pay
**EVP:** Leon J. (Lee) Oliver, age 55
**SVP and CFO, Northeast Utilities, Northeast Utilities Service Company, Connecticut Light and Power, Public Service Company of New Hampshire, Western Massachusetts Electric, and Yankee Gas:**
David R. McHale, age 45
**SVP and General Counsel; SVP and General Counsel, CL&P, PSNH, and WMECO:** Gregory B. Butler, age 46, $613,579 pay
**VP Accounting and Controller, NU Enterprises:**
John J. Roman
**VP Accounting and Controller, Northeast Utilities, Northeast Utilities Service Company, Connecticut Light and Power, Public Service Company of New Hampshire, Western Massachusetts Electric, and Yankee Gas:** John P. Stack, age 47
**VP Finance, Treasurer, and Secretary, Select Energy Services:** Linda A. Jensen
**VP Financial Services, Northeast Utilities Service Company:** Mark W. Fagan
**VP Governmental Affairs, Northeast Utilities Service Company:** Margaret L. Morton
**VP Human Resources and Environmental Services, Northeast Utilities Service Company:**
Jean M. LaVecchia
**VP Investor Relations, Northeast Utilities Service Company:** Jeffrey R. Kotkin
**VP Regulatory and Governmental Affairs:**
Lisa J. Thibdaue, age 54
**VP and Treasurer, Northeast Utilities, Northeast Utilities Service Company, Connecticut Light and Power, Public Service Company of New Hampshire, Western Massachusetts Electric, and Yankee Gas:**
Randall A. (Randy) Shoop, age 46
**President and COO, Connecticut Light and Power:**
Raymond P. Necci
**President, Northeast Generation; VP and COO, Northeast Generation Services:** William J. Nadeau
**President, Competitive Group, NU:**
Lawrence E. (Larry) De Simone, age 59, $549,619 pay
**President and COO, Public Service Company of New Hampshire:** Gary A. Long, age 53
**EVP; CEO, CL&P, PSNH, and WMECO:**
Cheryl W. Grisé, age 53, $921,239 pay
**Auditors:** Deloitte & Touche LLP

## LOCATIONS

**HQ:** Northeast Utilities
107 Selden St., Berlin, CT 06037
**Phone:** 800-286-5000 **Fax:** 860-665-5418
**Web:** www.nu.com

Northeast Utilities operates primarily in Connecticut, western Massachusetts, and New Hampshire.

## PRODUCTS/OPERATIONS

### 2006 Sales

| | $ mil. | % of total |
|---|---|---|
| Utilities | | |
| Electric | 5,336.0 | 74 |
| Gas | 453.9 | 6 |
| Transmission | 216.0 | 3 |
| Enterprises | 908.5 | 12 |
| Other | 355.0 | 5 |
| Adjustments | (385.0) | — |
| **Total** | **6,884.4** | **100** |

### Selected Subsidiaries

The Northeast Utilities System (regulated utilities)
- Connecticut Light and Power Company (CL&P, electric utility)
- Public Service Company of New Hampshire (PSNH, electric utility)
- Western Massachusetts Electric Company (WMECO, electric utility)
- Yankee Energy System, Inc. (natural gas utility, Connecticut)
  - Yankee Gas Services Company (retail natural gas service)

Other Operations
- Northeast Utilities Service Company (administrative services for NU subsidiaries)
- NU Enterprises, Inc. (nonutility operations)

## COMPETITORS

AEP
Bangor Hydro-Electric
Central Vermont Public Service
Con Edison
Energy East
Green Mountain Power
KeySpan
Massachusetts Municipal Wholesale Electric
National Grid USA
NiSource
NSTAR
PG&E
PSEG
Southern Company
Strategic Energy
UIL Holdings
Unitil

## HISTORICAL FINANCIALS

Company Type: Public

**Income Statement** FYE: December 31

| | REVENUE ($ mil.) | NET INCOME ($ mil.) | NET PROFIT MARGIN | EMPLOYEES |
|---|---|---|---|---|
| **12/06** | 6,884 | 471 | 6.8% | 5,869 |
| **12/05** | 7,397 | (254) | — | 6,879 |
| **12/04** | 6,687 | 122 | 1.8% | 7,079 |
| **12/03** | 6,069 | 116 | 1.9% | 6,757 |
| **12/02** | 5,216 | 152 | 2.9% | 6,561 |
| **Annual Growth** | 7.2% | 32.6% | — | (2.7%) |

**2006 Year-End Financials**

Debt ratio: 153.2%
Return on equity: 18.0%
Cash ($ mil.): 1,062
Current ratio: 1.27
Long-term debt ($ mil.): 4,286
No. of shares (mil.): 154
Dividends
Yield: 2.6%
Payout: 23.9%
Market value ($ mil.): 4,343

**Stock History** NYSE: NU

| | STOCK PRICE ($) FY Close | P/E High/Low | PER SHARE ($) Earnings | Dividends | Book Value |
|---|---|---|---|---|---|
| **12/06** | 28.16 | 9 6 | 3.05 | 0.73 | 18.14 |
| **12/05** | 19.69 | — — | (1.93) | 0.68 | 15.85 |
| **12/04** | 18.85 | 22 19 | 0.91 | 0.63 | 18.70 |
| **12/03** | 20.17 | 22 14 | 0.91 | 0.58 | 18.64 |
| **12/02** | 15.17 | 18 11 | 1.18 | 0.39 | 18.24 |
| **Annual Growth** | 16.7% | — — | 26.8% | 17.0% | (0.1%) |

# Northern Trust

Since its founding in 1889, Northern Trust Corporation has been working hard to keep clients' trusts. Flagship subsidiary The Northern Trust Company — along with other units bearing the Northern Trust name — provides banking and trust services to the affluent and to financial institutions and corporations in about 20 states and a dozen countries. Operating in two segments, Corporate and Institutional Services and Personal Financial Services, the corporation is a leading personal trust manager in the US and is a master of master trust services, catering to corporate pension plans and institutional clients. All told, Northern Trust has nearly $4 trillion of assets under custody.

Subsidiary Northern Trust Global Investments oversees portfolio management, investment research, and other investment products, including the firm's proprietary mutual funds. Northern Trust's Corporate and Institutional Services division administers assets for retirement funds, foundations and endowments, and insurance companies. The Personal Financial Services segment offers trust and investment management, banking, residential mortgages, and other services for small and midsized companies, executives, retirees, and the well-to-do.

Abroad, Northern Trust has branches in Canada, the Cayman Islands, Ireland, Luxembourg, and the UK. The company is targeting East Asia for expansion, where it has offices in Hong Kong, Japan, and Singapore; it opened an office in Beijing in 2005. Expanding its European operations, Northern Trust bought the fund management, custody, and trust operations of Baring Asset Management from Amsterdam-based ING Groep. In keeping with its Dutch expansion, it was selected by the pension fund Stichting Federatief Pensioenfonds to administer custody and other services.

Board member Harold Smith of the founding Smith family owns about 6% of the company.

## HISTORY

When banker Byron Smith took time off to handle family concerns in 1885, friends turned to him for advice on trust and estate matters. It occurred to him that there was a market for such services within a banking framework.

Smith tested new Illinois banking and trust laws by arranging for state banking authorities to reject his charter application for Northern Trust. As Smith had hoped, the charter was upheld by the Illinois Supreme Court.

Northern Trust opened its doors in 1889 in one of Chicago's new skyscrapers, the Rookery. With $1 million in capital — about 40% from Smith and the rest from the likes of Marshall Field (retailing), Martin Ryerson (steel), and Philip Armour (meatpacking) — the bank attracted $138,000 in deposits its first day.

By 1896 the bank was firmly established; Smith began taking a salary and the company issued its first dividend. Ten years later the firm built its solid granite edifice, the "Gray Lady of LaSalle Street," where it still resides.

The bank began buying commercial paper in 1912, joined the Federal Reserve System in 1917, and became a custodian for expropriated German assets during WWI. Byron Smith died in 1914 and was succeeded by his son, Solomon.

Northern Trust rejected the get-rich-quick ethos of the 1920s. It was so strong during the Depression that after the 1933 bank holiday people actually clamored to make deposits, and the bank administered the Depression-era scholarship fund that helped Ronald Reagan attend college. By 1941 almost half of Northern Trust's commercial deposits originated outside the Chicago area. The bank kept growing during and after WWII.

Solomon Smith retired in 1963; his son Edward took over and launched the company's expansion overseas (Northern Trust International was formed in 1968) and out of state (Florida in 1971, Arizona in 1974). The firm's business was helped by the 1974 passage by Congress of ERISA, which required company retirement plans to be overseen by an outside custodian. Edward retired in 1979.

Northern Trust expanded locally when Illinois legalized intrastate branch banking in 1981. In 1987 the company lost money, due in part to defaults on loans made to developing countries. It moved into California in 1988 and Texas in 1989.

Northern Trust navigated the early 1990s recession, expanded geographically in the mid-1990s, and added services through acquisitions. In 1995 the company became the first foreign trust company to operate throughout Canada. That year it bought investment management service RCB International (now Northern Trust Global Advisors). It expanded in the Sunbelt with such acquisitions as Dallas' Metroplex Bancshares and was made first custodian for the Teacher Retirement System of Texas (1997).

In 1998 the company expanded into Michigan and broke into the Cleveland and Seattle markets in 1999. Northern Trust entered cyberspace as well, launching a Web site for its mutual funds. In 2000 the company opened locations in Nevada and Missouri and bought Florida-based investment adviser Carl Domino Associates (renamed Northern Trust Value Investors). Also that year the bank bought Ireland's Ulster Bank Investment Services.

The bank expanded its operations in 2005 with FSG, the fund management, custody, and trust operations of Baring Asset Management. It was the company's largest acquisition to date and provided Northern Trust with a strong presence in the British Isles.

## EXECUTIVES

**Chairman and CEO, Northern Trust Corporation and Northern Trust Company:** William A. Osborn, age 59, $1,037,500 pay
**President, COO, and Director, Northern Trust Corporation and Northern Trust Company:** Frederick H. (Rick) Waddell, age 53, $612,500 pay
**EVP and CFO, Northern Trust Corporation and Northern Trust Company:** Steven L. (Steve) Fradkin, age 45, $468,750 pay
**EVP, Northern Trust Corporation and Northern Trust Company; President, Worldwide Operations and Technology:** Jana R. Schreuder, age 48
**EVP, Northern Trust Corporation and Northern Trust Company; President, Personal Financial Services:** Sherry S. Barrat, age 57, $500,000 pay
**EVP, Northern Trust Corporation and Northern Trust Company; Co-President, Personal Financial Services:** William L. Morrison, age 56, $518,750 pay
**EVP, Northern Trust Corporation and Northern Trust Company; President, Corporate and Institutional Services:** Timothy J. Theriault, age 46, $518,750 pay
**EVP, General Counsel, Assistant Secretary, and Head of Risk Management, Northern Trust Corporation and Northern Trust Company:** Kelly R. Welsh, age 54
**EVP and Head of Human Resources and Administration, Northern Trust Corporation and Northern Trust Company:** Timothy P. Moen, age 54
**EVP, Corporate Financial Management, Northern Trust Company:** William R. Dodds Jr.
**EVP and Global Chief Investment Officer:** Orie L. Dudley Jr.
**EVP and Controller:** Aileen B. Blake, age 39
**EVP, Credit Policy:** John P. Grube
**SVP and Chief Compliance Officer:** Patricia K. Bartler
**SVP and Director, Investor Relations:** Beverly J. (Bev) Fleming
**SVP, Asia-Pacific Region:** Lawrence Au
**VP, Public Relations:** Richard Jurek
**Chairman, President, and CEO, Northern Trust Global Advisors:** William T. Huffman
**CEO, International Businesses, Northern Trust Global Investments:** Barry Sagraves
**Chairman and CEO, Northern Trust Bank, N.A.:** David A. Highmark
**Corporate Secretary and Assistant General Counsel:** Rose A. Ellis
**Auditors:** KPMG LLP

## LOCATIONS

**HQ:** Northern Trust Corporation
50 S. La Salle St., Chicago, IL 60603
**Phone:** 312-630-6000 **Fax:** 312-630-1512
**Web:** www.northerntrust.com

Northern Trust operates in Arizona, California, Connecticut, Colorado, Florida, Georgia, Illinois, Massachusetts, Michigan, Minnesota, Missouri, Nevada, New York, Ohio, Texas, Washington, and Wisconsin, as well as in Canada, the Cayman Islands, Hong Kong, Ireland, Japan, Singapore, and the UK.

## PRODUCTS/OPERATIONS

**2006 Sales**

| | $ mil. | % of total |
|---|---|---|
| Interest income | 2,206.8 | 49 |
| Trust, investment & other fees | 1,791.6 | 40 |
| Foreign exchange trading profits | 247.3 | 6 |
| Other | 227.3 | 5 |
| **Total** | **4,473.0** | **100** |

**2006 Assets**

| | $ mil. | % of total |
|---|---|---|
| Cash & due from banks | 4,961.0 | 8 |
| Time deposits with banks | 15,468.7 | 26 |
| Securities | 12,365.2 | 20 |
| Residential mortgages | 8,674.4 | 14 |
| Commercial & other loans | 13,935.3 | 23 |
| Reserve for credit losses | (140.4) | — |
| Other assets | 5,448.0 | 9 |
| **Total** | **60,712.2** | **100** |

## COMPETITORS

ABN AMRO
AXA
Bank of America
Bank of New York Mellon
Barclays
Bear Stearns
Bessemer Group
Brown Brothers Harriman
Citigroup
Credit Suisse (USA)
Deutsche Bank
Fifth Third
FMR
Harris Bankcorp
Merrill Lynch
Morgan Stanley
Principal Financial
State Street
Wells Fargo
Wilmington Trust

## HISTORICAL FINANCIALS

Company Type: Public

**Income Statement** FYE: December 31

| | ASSETS ($ mil.) | NET INCOME ($ mil.) | INCOME AS % OF ASSETS | EMPLOYEES |
|---|---|---|---|---|
| **12/06** | 60,712 | 665 | 1.1% | 9,726 |
| **12/05** | 53,414 | 584 | 1.1% | 9,008 |
| **12/04** | 45,277 | 506 | 1.1% | 8,022 |
| **12/03** | 41,450 | 405 | 1.0% | 8,056 |
| **12/02** | 39,478 | 447 | 1.1% | 9,317 |
| **Annual Growth** | 11.4% | 10.5% | — | 1.1% |

**2006 Year-End Financials**

Equity as % of assets: 6.5%
Return on assets: 1.2%
Return on equity: 17.6%
Long-term debt ($ mil.): 6,006
No. of shares (mil.): 219

Dividends
Yield: 1.5%
Payout: 31.3%
Market value ($ mil.): 13,273
Sales ($ mil.): 4,473

**Stock History** NASDAQ (GS): NTRS

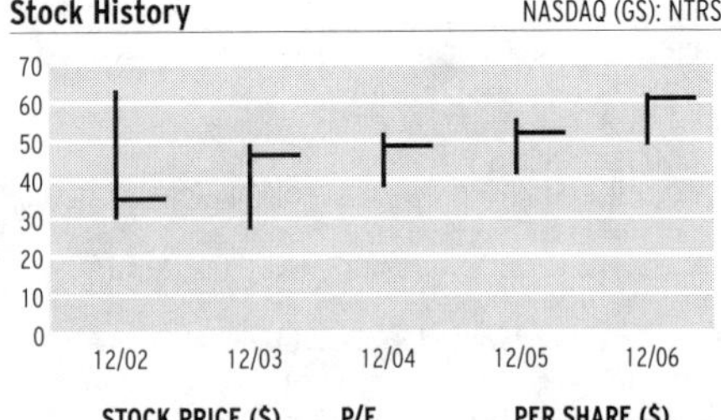


| | STOCK PRICE ($) FY Close | P/E High/Low | | PER SHARE ($) Earnings | Dividends | Book Value |
|---|---|---|---|---|---|---|
| **12/06** | 60.69 | 20 | 16 | 3.00 | 0.94 | 18.03 |
| **12/05** | 51.82 | 21 | 16 | 2.64 | 0.65 | 16.51 |
| **12/04** | 48.58 | 23 | 17 | 2.27 | 0.78 | 15.04 |
| **12/03** | 46.28 | 27 | 15 | 1.80 | 0.70 | 13.88 |
| **12/02** | 35.05 | 32 | 15 | 1.97 | 0.68 | 13.59 |
| **Annual Growth** | 14.7% | — | — | 11.1% | 8.4% | 7.3% |

# Northrop Grumman

Avast there! The acquisitions of Litton Industries, Newport News, and TRW have made Northrop Grumman the world's #1 shipbuilder and the #3 defense contractor (behind Lockheed Martin and Boeing). It operates through seven segments: Electronic Systems (radar, navigation, communications), Information Technology (computer systems, services, training), Integrated Systems (aircraft), Ship Systems (Avondale, Ingalls, and Newport News military/commercial ships, nuclear submarines, and aircraft carriers), Mission Systems (command and control systems, missiles), Space Technology (military/civil space technology), and Technical Services (systems support and training and simulation).

The acquisitions of Litton, Newport News, and TRW solidified Northrop Grumman's place as a top-tier defense contractor and strengthened or introduced Northrop's operations in command and control systems, information systems, missiles, and space technology. The Newport News deal also made Northrop Grumman the largest naval shipbuilder in the world.

Northrop Grumman's CEO Ronald Sugar spent about 20 years at TRW; his last position there was as president and COO of TRW's Aerospace and Information Systems — precisely the unit that Northrop Grumman coveted. The acquisition fortified Northrop Grumman's position in military satellites, missile systems, and systems integration. In fact, Northrop had to sign a consent decree with the Justice Department in which the company agreed (under pain of fines) that it wouldn't take unfair advantage of its exclusive position when selling certain components — such as satellite sensors — to competitors.

Northrop sold all but 19.6% of TRW's car parts business to Blackstone Group for about $4.7 billion to pay down debt; by early 2005 Northrop had reduced its stake to 9.9%.

Northrop Grumman expects that the increased military emphasis on information gathering, surveillance, battle management, and precision munitions will lead to heavy government spending on advanced electronics systems and software in the coming years. On the other hand, the company's surface ships and submarines are prime targets for the budget axe as the military looks to cut costs.

## HISTORY

Jack Northrop co-founded Lockheed Aircraft in 1927 and designed its record-setting Vega monoplane. He founded two more companies — Avion Corporation (formed in 1928 and bought by United Aircraft and Transportation) and Northrop Corporation (formed in 1932 with Douglas Aircraft, which absorbed it in 1938) — before founding Northrop Aircraft in California in 1939.

During WWII Northrop produced the P-61 fighter and the famous Flying Wing bomber, which failed to win a production contract. In the 1950s Northrop depended heavily on F-89 fighter and Snark missile sales. When Thomas Jones succeeded Jack Northrop as president (1959), he moved the company away from risky prime contracts in favor of numerous subcontracts and bought Page Communications Engineers (telecommunications, 1959) and Hallicrafters (electronics, 1966) to reduce its dependence on government contracts.

In the early 1970s Northrop was hit with a bribery scandal and the disclosure of illegal payments to Richard Nixon's 1972 campaign fund; Jones was eventually fined for an illegal contribution. As a result, a shareholder lawsuit forced Jones to resign as president (he was allowed to remain as chairman). In 1981 the company won the B-2 bomber contract. Jones retired as chairman in late 1990, and under the leadership of Kent Kresa (who became CEO in early 1990 and chairman when Jones retired), Northrop pleaded guilty to 34 counts related to fudging test results on some government projects; it was fined $17 million. In a related shareholders' suit, Northrop paid $18 million in damages in 1991.

Northrop and private investment firm The Carlyle Group bought LTV's Vought Aircraft in 1992. In 1994 it paid $2.1 billion for Grumman Corporation, a premier electronic systems firm, and changed its name to Northrop Grumman.

In 1929 Roy Grumman, Jake Swirbul, and Bill Schwendler founded Grumman; within three months it had a contract to design a US Navy fighter. Grumman completed its first commercial aircraft (the Grumman Goose) in 1937 and went public in 1938. It soared during WWII on the wings of its Wildcat and Hellcat fighter planes.

Grumman built its first corporate jet (Gulfstream) in 1958, and began work on the Lunar Module for the Apollo space program in 1963. The company came close to bankruptcy in the 1970s due to costs related to its F-14 Tomcat fighter, but it rebuilt its military business in the 1980s and achieved its greatest success in electronic systems.

In 1997 Northrop Grumman bought Logicon (information and battle-management systems). It then agreed to an $11.6 billion purchase by Lockheed Martin, but the US government, citing concerns about increased lack of competition in the defense industry, blocked the deal in 1998. As a result, Northrop Grumman began a restructuring that cut 10,500 defense and aircraft jobs and added 2,500 at its Logicon subsidiary.

In 2000 Northrop Grumman sold its underperforming commercial aerostructures business to The Carlyle Group for $1.2 billion.

In 2001 the company completed the deal to acquire Litton Industries for $3.8 billion, plus $1.3 billion in debt. While its wallet was open, the company agreed to match the $2.6 billion that General Dynamics had agreed to pay for submarine and aircraft carrier builder Newport News — a move that the US Defense Department endorsed. In December Honeywell agreed to pay Northrop Grumman $440 million to settle an antitrust and patent infringement lawsuit that Litton had filed against Honeywell in 1990.

The deal to buy Newport News was completed in early 2002. Northrop Grumman then made a hostile $6 billion bid for conglomerate TRW when TRW's stock plunged following CEO David Cote's sudden departure to Honeywell. In the wake of Northrop Grumman's spurned initial bid, Raytheon, General Dynamics, and BAE SYSTEMS made offers for TRW's aerospace and defense assets. Finally, though, TRW accepted a sweetened $7.8 billion offer from Northrop Grumman in July 2002. In 2003 Kresa stepped down and Sugar became chairman.

In 2006 Northrop Grumman aquired Essex Corporation — a provider of signal, image, and information processing for defense and intelligence customers — for about $580 million.

## EXECUTIVES

**Chairman and CEO:** Ronald D. Sugar, age 59, $1,433,654 pay
**President and COO:** Wesley G. (Wes) Bush, age 45
**Executive Advisor:** Donald C. (Don) Winter, age 57, $1,276,014 pay (prior to title change)
**Corporate VP:** James L. Sanford, age 60
**Corporate VP and Treasurer:** Mark A. Rabinowitz
**VP and General Counsel:** W. Burks Terry, age 56, $570,192 pay
**VP and CFO:** James F. (Jim) Palmer, age 57
**VP; President, Northrop Grumman Component Technologies:** Frank G. Brandenberg, age 60
**VP; President, Northrop Grumman Mission Systems:** Jerry D. Agee, age 64
**VP; President, Northrop Grumman Integrated Systems:** Scott J. Seymour, $570,384 pay
**VP; President, Northrop Grumman Technical Services:** James L. Cameron, age 50
**VP; President, Northrop Grumman Ship Systems:** Philip A. Teel, age 59
**VP; President, Northrop Grumman Information Technology:** James R. (Jim) O'Neill, age 52, $1,160,200 pay
**VP; President, Northrop Grumman Newport News:** C. Michael (Mike) Petters, age 47
**VP, Controller, and Chief Accounting Officer:** Kenneth H. Heintz, age 60
**VP and CIO:** Thomas W. Shelman
**VP, Information Security:** Tim McKnight
**VP, Corporate Security:** Ed Halibozek
**VP, Secretary and Deputy General Counsel:** Stephen D. (Steve) Yslas
**VP, Investor Relations:** Gaston Kent
**VP and Chief Human Resources and Administrative Officer:** Ian V. Ziskin, age 48
**VP, Corporate and International Communications:** Brandon R. (Randy) Belote
**Auditors:** Deloitte & Touche LLP

## LOCATIONS

**HQ:** Northrop Grumman Corporation
1840 Century Park East, Los Angeles, CA 90067
**Phone:** 310-553-6262 **Fax:** 310-556-4561
**Web:** www.northropgrumman.com

## PRODUCTS/OPERATIONS

### 2006 Sales

| | $ mil. | % of total |
|---|---|---|
| Electronic Systems | 6,578 | 21 |
| Integrated Systems | 5,500 | 17 |
| Ships | 5,321 | 17 |
| Mission Systems | 5,074 | 16 |
| Information Technology | 4,031 | 13 |
| Space Technology | 3,351 | 10 |
| Technical Services | 1,789 | 6 |
| Adjustments | (1,496) | — |
| **Total** | **30,148** | **100** |

### 2006 Sales

| | $ mil. | % of total |
|---|---|---|
| US government | 27,019 | 90 |
| Other customers | 3,129 | 10 |
| **Total** | **30,148** | **100** |

### Operating Units

Electronic Systems
- Airborne surveillance systems
- Airspace management systems
- Automation and information systems
- Combat avionics systems
- Communications
- Electro-optical/infrared countermeasures
- Land combat systems
- Logistics systems
- Marine systems
- Oceanic and naval systems
- Radio frequency countermeasures
- Simulators
- Space systems
- Support systems
- Targeting systems

Integrated Systems
- Air combat systems (F/A-18 Hornet, B-2 Spirit stealth bomber, Global Hawk UAV)
- Airborne early warning and electronic warfare systems
- Airborne ground surveillance and battle management systems (E-2C Hawkeye)

Ships (Newport News and Ship Systems)
- Aegis-guided missile destroyers
- Aircraft carriers
- Amphibious assault ships
- Cruise ships
- Double-hulled oil tankers
- Sealift ships
- Service centers
- Submarines

Mission Systems
- Command, control, and intelligence systems
- Federal and civil information systems
- Missile systems
- Technical and management services

Information Technology
- Data center management
- Facility management services
- Geographic information systems
- Hardware and software maintenence
- Information security
- Logistics support
- Mission-critical software
- Network design
- Orbital analysis
- Systems engineering
- Systems integration
- Systems modernization and integration
- Tactical data links

Space Technology
- Avionics systems
- Environmental-monitoring space systems
- High-energy laser systems
- National-defense space systems
- Space science instruments
- Spacecraft systems and subsystems

## COMPETITORS

Aerojet
BAE SYSTEMS
BAE Systems Electronics & Integrated Solutions
BAE Systems Inc.
Boeing
Boeing Integrated Defense Systems
EADS
Elbit Systems
Finmeccanica
GE
General Dynamics
Hamilton Sundstrand
Hanjin Heavy Industries & Construction
Herley Industries
Honeywell Aerospace
ITT Defense
Lockheed Martin
Lockheed Martin Aeronautics
Lockheed Martin UK
Meggitt
Raytheon
Rockwell Collins
ThalesRaytheonSystems
Todd Shipyards

## HISTORICAL FINANCIALS

Company Type: Public

### Income Statement

FYE: December 31

| | REVENUE ($ mil.) | NET INCOME ($ mil.) | NET PROFIT MARGIN | EMPLOYEES |
|---|---|---|---|---|
| **12/06** | 30,148 | 1,542 | 5.1% | 122,200 |
| **12/05** | 30,721 | 1,400 | 4.6% | 123,600 |
| **12/04** | 29,853 | 1,084 | 3.6% | 125,400 |
| **12/03** | 26,206 | 866 | 3.3% | 122,600 |
| **12/02** | 17,206 | 64 | 0.4% | 117,300 |
| **Annual Growth** | 15.1% | 121.6% | — | 1.0% |

### 2006 Year-End Financials

Debt ratio: 24.0%
Return on equity: 9.2%
Cash ($ mil.): 1,015
Current ratio: 0.99
Long-term debt ($ mil.): 3,992
No. of shares (mil.): 346
Dividends
Yield: 1.7%
Payout: 26.5%
Market value ($ mil.): 23,419

### Stock History

NYSE: NOC

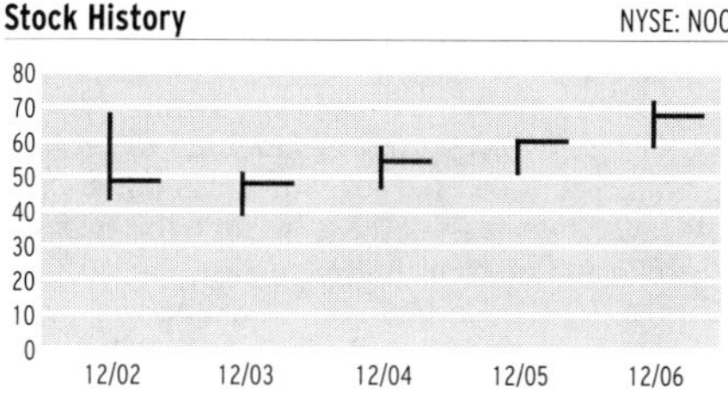


| | STOCK PRICE ($) FY Close | P/E High | P/E Low | PER SHARE ($) Earnings | Dividends | Book Value |
|---|---|---|---|---|---|---|
| **12/06** | 67.70 | 16 | 14 | 4.37 | 1.16 | 48.03 |
| **12/05** | 60.11 | 16 | 13 | 3.85 | 1.01 | 48.45 |
| **12/04** | 54.36 | 20 | 16 | 2.97 | 0.66 | 45.82 |
| **12/03** | 47.80 | 22 | 17 | 2.32 | 0.80 | 87.16 |
| **12/02** | 48.50 | 397 | 256 | 0.17 | 0.80 | 78.43 |
| **Annual Growth** | 8.7% | — | — | 125.2% | 9.7% | (11.5%) |

# Northwest Airlines

Yes, you can go north by Northwest — and other directions, as well. Northwest Airlines flies to more than 240 cities in North America, the Asia/Pacific region, and Europe from hubs in Detroit, Memphis, and Minneapolis/St. Paul, as well as Amsterdam and Tokyo. The company's US network includes destinations served by regional carriers flying as Northwest Airlink. Northwest's mainline fleet includes about 370 jets; regional partners operate another 175 aircraft. The carrier has extensive code-sharing deals with Continental Airlines, Delta Air Lines, and KLM; in addition, it is part of the SkyTeam alliance, which includes Air France. Northwest exited Chapter 11 bankruptcy protection in May 2007.

In December 2006, the company announced it was exploring merger and acquisition opportunities, and it hired investment banking firm Evercore Partners as an adviser. Early in 2007, Northwest was reported to have been discussing a potential combination with Delta. A few months later, Northwest announced it was part of an investment group, led by TPG Capital, placing a $431 million bid for Midwest Air Group.

During its years of restructuring, the bright side of Chapter 11 for Northwest was that bankruptcy law gave the company more leverage in negotiating contracts. By 2006 Northwest had reached new agreements involving pay and benefit reductions with several unions, including those representing pilots and machinists.

In its restructuring, Northwest has focused on its major routes to Asia and Europe. Hoping to expand its services to destinations in the Asia/Pacific region, in mid-2007 Northwest filed with the US Department of Transportation for the right to operate Detroit/Beijing and Detroit/Shanghai nonstop flight services.

Northwest also relies on its strong presence in the midwestern US, much of which is provided via Northwest Airlink partners: Pinnacle Airlines and Mesaba Airlines.

## HISTORY

A group of Detroit, Minneapolis, and St. Paul businessmen, led by Colonel Louis Brittin, founded Northwest Airways in 1926 to provide airmail service between Minneapolis and Chicago. Two years later it became the first US airline to offer coordinated airline and railroad service. In 1934 it changed its name to Northwest Airlines and started flying to Seattle. With service to New York in 1945, it completed its transcontinental route.

Northwest started flying to Shanghai in 1947, pioneering a route over Alaska and the Aleutians, but left in 1949 because of civil war in China. A 1952 agreement between the US and Japan made the airline the dominant trans-Pacific carrier.

Donald Nyrop, former chair of the Civil Aeronautics Board, became Northwest's president in 1954. Nyrop, famous for his thrift, retired in 1978 as the airline industry was being deregulated; his successor, Joseph Lapensky, continued his tight fiscal policies, and Northwest became infamous for low employee morale.

In 1984 the company resumed service in Shanghai and formed NWA, a holding company. Two years later it bought Republic Airlines and 50% of PARS (TWA's computer reservation system, which merged with Delta's DATAS II in 1990, forming WORLDSPAN).

The airline failed to reach an agreement with its unions after the Republic acquisition. Its pilots still had no contract in 1989 when Wings Holdings — an investment group including KLM and led by Gary Wilson and former Marriott executive Alfred Checchi — took NWA private in a $3.65 billion LBO. NWA's debt payments nearly sunk it between 1990 and 1992. But it bought a 25% stake in HAL (Hawaiian Airlines) in 1990 anyway, only to unload it two years later.

NWA began service to Beijing in 1992. It began assuming low-traffic routes and allying with small feeder airlines. Near bankruptcy, Northwest persuaded employees to accept more than three years of pay cuts in return for stock.

After its 1994 IPO, NWA renamed itself Northwest Airlines Corp. The company launched the first nonstop service from the US to China in 1996. Checchi resigned as co-chairman in 1997 to run for governor of California.

In 1998 KLM sold back its stake in Northwest but extended its partnership with the carrier for 10 years. Northwest also entered a code-sharing agreement with Air China. Northwest paid $370 million for a 13.5% stake in Continental Airlines, the #5 US airline, prompting an antitrust lawsuit by the Department of Justice; the airlines combined complementary routes and marketing operations. In 1999 Northwest signed a code-sharing agreement with Alitalia, setting the stage for the sweeping Wings Alliance.

Meanwhile, pilot contract negotiations bombed when Northwest proposed that some pilots accept less pay and more hours to support a new low-fare airline. Pilots went on a two-week strike in 1998 before agreeing to a four-year contract. In 1999 a well-publicized incident in which travelers were stranded for hours on runways in Detroit during a blizzard spawned a class-action suit. (The company agreed in 2001 to pay $7.1 million to settle the case.)

Northwest signed a five-year agreement with flight attendants in 2000, granting them improved pay and working conditions.

In 2001 president and CEO John Dasburg accepted a position as chairman and CEO of Burger King. Company veterans Richard Anderson and Douglas Steenland were appointed CEO and president, respectively.

The US economic slowdown led to a slump in business travel in 2001, and Northwest moved to contain costs by trimming its flight schedule and cutting 1,500 jobs. The September 11, 2001, terrorist attacks on the US further reduced demand for air travel, and Northwest responded by eliminating more flights and by cutting 10,000 jobs, or nearly 20% of its workforce.

Subsidiary Pinnacle Airlines, part of the parent company's Northwest Airlink regional service went public. Still in financial trouble, the carrier announced in 2004 it would seek $950 million in cost cuts from its unions. Also that year Steenland replaced Anderson as CEO.

Northwest cited high labor and operating costs, compounded by a jump in fuel prices, when it sought bankruptcy protection in September 2005. The carrier had been working to cut costs before the bankruptcy filing, but an effort to gain $176 million in annual savings from its mechanics resulted in a strike in August 2005. Striking mechanics were replaced by nonunion workers.

Northwest exited Chapter 11 bankruptcy protection in May 2007.

## EXECUTIVES

**President, CEO, and Director:** Douglas M. (Doug) Steenland, age 54, $571,354 pay
**EVP and CFO:** David M. (Dave) Davis
**EVP Strategy and International; CEO, Regional Airlines:** Neal S. Cohen, age 45
**EVP, Marketing and Distribution, Northwest:** J. Timothy (Tim) Griffin, age 54, $444,396 pay
**EVP, Operations:** Andrew C. (Andy) Roberts, age 45, $359,743 pay
**SVP, Corporate and Brand Communications:** Mary Carroll Linder
**SVP, Customer Service and Ground Operations:** Crystal Knotek
**SVP, Finance and Treasurer:** Daniel B. Matthews
**SVP, Flight and In-Flight Operations:** Timothy J. (Tim) Rainey
**SVP, Government Affairs:** Andrea Fischer Newman
**SVP, Human Resources and Labor Relations:** Michael J. (Mike) Becker
**SVP, Pacific; President, Northwest Airlines Cargo:** Jim Friedel
**SVP, Technical Operations:** Kris Bauer
**SVP and CIO:** Theresa Wise
**VP, Customer Service, MSP:** William P. Lentsch
**VP, Finance and Chief Accounting Officer:** Anna Schaefer
**VP, Finance and Fleet Planning:** Dan McDonald
**VP, Financial Planning and Analysis:** Barry Hofer
**VP, Ground Operations and Customer Service Planning:** Chris Collette
**Managing Director, Corporation Communications:** Bill Mellon
**Auditors:** Ernst & Young LLP

## LOCATIONS

**HQ:** Northwest Airlines Corporation
2700 Lone Oak Pkwy., Eagan, MN 55121
**Phone:** 612-726-2111 **Fax:** 612-726-7123
**Web:** www.nwa.com

### 2006 Sales

| | $ mil. | % of total |
|---|---|---|
| Domestic | 8,561 | 68 |
| Pacific | 2,711 | 22 |
| Atlantic | 1,296 | 10 |
| **Total** | **12,568** | **100** |

## PRODUCTS/OPERATIONS

### 2006 Sales

| | $ mil. | % of total |
|---|---|---|
| Mainline passenger | 9,230 | 73 |
| Regional carrier | 1,399 | 11 |
| Cargo | 946 | 8 |
| Other | 993 | 8 |
| **Total** | **12,568** | **100** |

## COMPETITORS

Alaska Air
All Nippon Airways
AMR Corp.
British Airways
Japan Airlines
Lufthansa
Qantas
SAS
Singapore Airlines
Southwest Airlines
UAL
UPS
US Airways
Virgin Atlantic Airways

## HISTORICAL FINANCIALS

Company Type: Public

### Income Statement

FYE: December 31

| | REVENUE (\$ mil.) | NET INCOME (\$ mil.) | NET PROFIT MARGIN | EMPLOYEES |
|---|---|---|---|---|
| **12/06** | 12,568 | (2,835) | — | 30,000 |
| **12/05** | 12,286 | (2,533) | — | 32,460 |
| **12/04** | 11,279 | (862) | — | 39,342 |
| **12/03** | 9,510 | 248 | 2.6% | 39,100 |
| **12/02** | 9,489 | (798) | — | 44,323 |
| **Annual Growth** | 7.3% | — | — | (9.3%) |

### 2006 Year-End Financials

Debt ratio: —
Return on equity: —
Cash ($ mil.): 2,482
Current ratio: 1.11
Long-term debt ($ mil.): 3,899

### Net Income History

NYSE: NWA

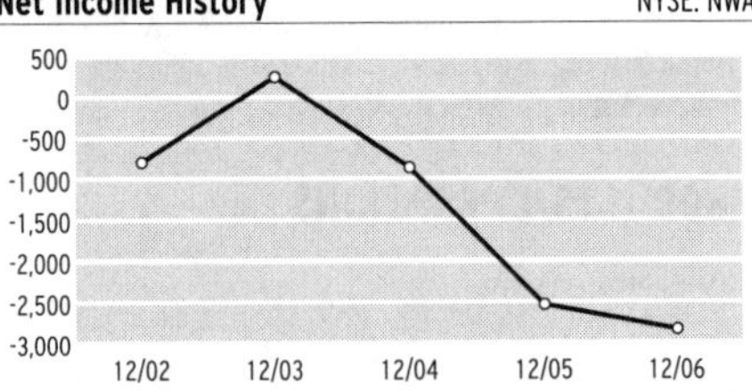


# Northwestern Mutual Life Insurance

Making sure it's not all quiet on the Northwestern front, Northwestern Mutual's 7,500 agents (meticulously recruited and trained) sell a lineup of life, disability, long-term care, and health insurance. It also offers retirement products, including fixed and variable annuities and mutual funds to a clientele of small businesses and prosperous individuals. Other lines of business include institutional asset manager Frank Russell Company, known for the Russell 2000 stock index, and brokerage and trust services through its Investment Services and Wealth Management subsidiaries.

Northwestern Mutual would "enter the 21st century as we left the 19th," according to former chairman and CEO John Ericson (who retired in mid-2001). Well, not exactly. Although the company has resisted the industry trend of demutualizing and remains committed to ownership by its approximately 3 million policyholders, The Quiet Company has begun blowing its own horn — in a diffident, upper Midwest way. Reorganized to highlight its wealth management products, life insurance still accounts for the majority of the company's revenue. The company targets wealthy individuals over 55.

## HISTORY

In 1854, at age 72, John Johnston, a successful New York insurance agent, moved to Wisconsin to become a farmer. Three years later Johnston returned to the insurance business when he and 36 others formed Mutual Life Insurance (changed to Northwestern Mutual Life Insurance in 1865). From the beginning, the company's goal was to become better, not just bigger.

The company continued to offer level-premium life insurance in the 1920s, while competitors offered new types of products. This failure to rise to new demands brought a decline in market share that lasted into the 1940s.

Northwestern Mutual automated in the late 1950s. In 1962 it introduced the Insurance Service Account, whereby all policies owned by a family or business could be consolidated into one monthly premium and paid with preauthorized checks. In 1968 Northwestern Mutual inaugurated Extra Ordinary Life (EOL), which combined whole and term life insurance, using dividends to convert term to paid-up whole life each year. EOL soon became the company's most popular product.

Suffering from a low profile, in 1972 the insurer kicked off its "The Quiet Company" ad campaign during the summer Olympics. Public awareness of Northwestern Mutual jumped. But even in advertising, the company was staid; a revamped Quiet Company campaign made a return Olympic appearance 24 years later in another effort to raise the public's consciousness.

In the 1980s Northwestern Mutual began financing leveraged buyouts, gaining direct ownership of companies. Investments included two-thirds of flooring maker Congoleum (with other investors); it also bought majority interests in Milwaukee securities firm Robert W. Baird (1982) and mortgage guarantee insurer MGIC Investment (1985, later divested).

The firm stayed out of the 1980s mania for fast money and high-risk diversification. Instead, it devoted itself almost religiously to its core business, despite indications that it was a shrinking market.

In the early 1990s new life policy purchases slowed and the agency force declined — ominous signs, since insurers make their premium income on retained policies, and continued sales are crucial to growth. Northwestern Mutual reversed the trend, adding administrative support for its agents, using database marketing to target new customers, and increasing the cross-selling of products among existing customers. The result was a record-setting 1996.

With the financial services industry consolidating, Northwestern Mutual in 1997 moved into the mutual fund business by setting up its Mason Street Funds.

In the 1990s many large mutuals sought to demutualize, and in 1998 Northwestern Mutual, politically influential in Wisconsin, successfully lobbied for legislation to permit demutualization, citing the need to be able to move quickly in shifting markets.

The next year the company acquired Frank Russell Company, a pension management firm. The acquisition gave Northwestern Mutual a foothold in global investment management and analytical services (the Russell 2000 index).

The company followed up with an all-out reorganization, separating the office of president from the duties of chairman and CEO, and naming, for the first time, a marketing officer. In 2001 the firm opened Northwestern Mutual Trust, a wholly owned personal trust services subsidiary.

In 2004 the employees of Robert W. Baird completed a buyback of Northwestern Mutual's stake in the firm.

## EXECUTIVES

**President, CEO, and Trustee:** Edward J. Zore, age 62
**COO, Chief Compliance Officer, and Trustee:** John M. Bremer, age 59
**Chief Insurance Officer and Trustee:** Peter W. Bruce, age 61
**EVP and Chief Investment Officer:** Mason G. Ross, age 63
**SVP and CFO:** Gary A. Poliner, age 53
**SVP and CIO:** Gregory C. Oberland, age 49
**SVP, Agency Services:** Christina H. Fiasca, age 52
**SVP, Business Integration Services:** Marcia Rimai, age 51
**VP, Secretary, and General Counsel:** Robert J. Berdan, age 60
**VP, Investment Products:** Steven T. Catlett, age 57
**VP, Policyowner Services:** Gloster B. Current Jr., age 61
**VP and Controller:** John C. (Chris) Kelly, age 47
**VP, New Business:** John L. Kordsmeier, age 52
**VP, Human Resources:** Susan A. Lueger, age 53
**VP, Corporate Planning:** Raymond Manista, age 41
**VP, Investment Products Operations:** Calvin R. Schmidt, age 44
**VP, Communications:** Brenda F. Skelton, age 51
**VP, Technology Research and Web Resources:** Martha M. Valerio, age 60
**Auditors:** PricewaterhouseCoopers LLP

## LOCATIONS

**HQ:** The Northwestern Mutual Life Insurance Company
720 E. Wisconsin Ave., Milwaukee, WI 53202
**Phone:** 414-271-1444
**Web:** www.nmfn.com

Northwestern Mutual Life Insurance has agents and offices throughout the US.

## PRODUCTS/OPERATIONS

**2006 Sales**

| | $ mil. | % of total |
|---|---|---|
| Premiums | 12,149 | 61 |
| Net investment income | 7,073 | 36 |
| Other income | 511 | 3 |
| **Total** | **19,733** | **100** |

## COMPETITORS

AEGON USA
AIG
AllianceBernstein
Allianz
AXA Financial
CIGNA
Citigroup
CNA Financial
Conseco
FMR
Genworth Financial
Guardian Life
The Hartford
ING
John Hancock
Liberty Mutual
MassMutual
Merrill Lynch
MetLife
Morgan Stanley
MSCI
Mutual of Omaha
Nationwide
New York Life
Pacific Mutual
Principal Financial
Prudential
Sun Life
T. Rowe Price
TIAA-CREF

## HISTORICAL FINANCIALS

Company Type: Mutual company

**Income Statement** FYE: December 31

| | ASSETS ($ mil.) | NET INCOME ($ mil.) | INCOME AS % OF ASSETS | EMPLOYEES |
|---|---|---|---|---|
| **12/06** | 145,102 | 829 | 0.6% | 4,800 |
| **12/05** | 133,057 | 924 | 0.7% | 4,800 |
| **12/04** | 123,957 | 817 | 0.7% | 4,700 |
| **12/03** | 113,822 | 692 | 0.6% | 4,500 |
| **12/02** | 102,935 | 158 | 0.2% | 4,200 |
| **Annual Growth** | 9.0% | 51.3% | — | 3.4% |

**2006 Year-End Financials**

Equity as % of assets: 10.2%
Return on assets: 0.6%
Return on equity: 6.6%
Long-term debt ($ mil.): —
Sales ($ mil.): 19,733

**Net Income History**

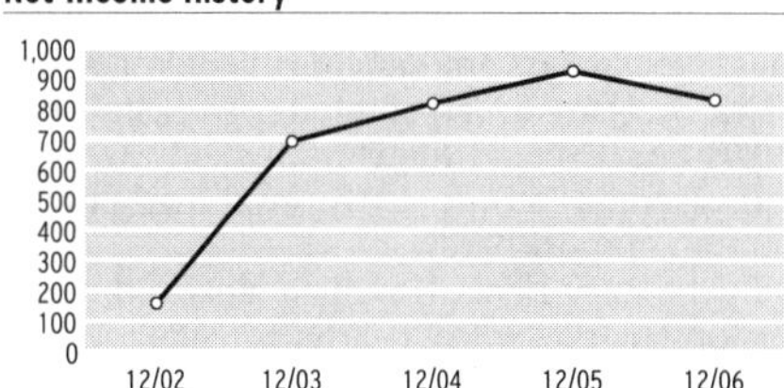


# Novell, Inc.

Novell is a firm believer in the power of networking. The company's flagship NetWare server operating system connects desktop computers to corporate networks, integrating directories, storage systems, printers, servers, and databases. It also provides a version of the Linux operating system, and applications including network management software, collaborative tools, and directory services products. In addition, it offers a variety of services such as IT consulting, implementation, support, and training. Novell's strategic partners include CA, Dell, Intel, Microsoft, and SAP. It sells through a direct sales force, as well as through distributors, resellers, and systems integrators.

The company has identified Linux and identity management software as its growth products. It built its Linux-based offerings with the acquisitions of Ximian (2003), SuSE Linux (2004), and Immunix (2005). Novell's identity and access management division got a boost from the 2006 purchase of enterprise security software developer e-Security for $72 million. The following year Novell acquired endpoint security management specialist Senforce Technologies.

Novell sold off its management consulting firm Celerant Consulting for $77 million in mid-2006; the buyout group included Celerant management and Caledonia Investments.

Novell also forged an unlikely partnership with rival Microsoft late in 2006. The terms of the deal included a reseller agreement that sees Microsoft distributing subscriptions to Novell's SUSE Linux software, joint research and development operations, royalty payments from Novell to Microsoft, and an agreement from Microsoft not to file patent-infringement charges.

## HISTORY

Novell was woven from the remnants of Novell Data Systems, a maker of disk operating systems founded in 1980. High-tech investment firm Safeguard Scientifics bought a controlling stake in the venture in 1981. In 1983 Safeguard incorporated the company and shortened its name to Novell. It also recruited CEO Raymond Noorda, an experienced engineer and marketer who invested $125,000 of his own money.

Under Noorda, Novell focused on developing PC networking systems that designated one machine (the file server) to manage the network and control access to shared devices, such as disk drives and printers. In 1983 Novell introduced NetWare, the first networking software based on file server technology.

Safeguard sold half of its 51% stake to the public two years later, and gradually sold off the rest. Novell began acquiring other companies to expand its product line, including Santa Clara Systems (microcomputer workstations, 1987) and Excelan (networking software and equipment, 1989). In 1988 Novell halted production of most hardware.

By the early 1990s, Novell dominated the networking market with a nearly 70% share. Wanting to undermine Microsoft's dominant position, Noorda bought the rights to AT&T's UNIX operating system (1992), top word processing software maker WordPerfect (1994), and Borland's spreadsheet business, Quattro Pro (1994). Novell in 1994 also transferred its database products (NetWare SQL, Xtrieve) to Btrieve Technologies (now Pervasive Software). The acquisitions failed to dent Microsoft's market share.

Noorda retired in 1994 and was succeeded by Hewlett-Packard executive Robert Frankenberg, who began to streamline the company and divest itself of purchases such as WordPerfect.

Frankenberg was ousted in 1996 after Novell posted flat sales for several consecutive quarters. Temporary CEO John Young began to focus the company's development efforts on the burgeoning Internet market, a push which was intensified when Young was replaced in 1997 by former Sun Microsystems engineer Eric Schmidt.

In 1997 Novell laid off 1,000 workers (18% of its workforce, including nearly half of its 66 VPs) and became the subject of IBM takeover rumors. The next year Novell shifted its focus to directory services and introduced a version of NetWare designed exclusively for Internet and intranet applications.

In 1999 Novell bought Netoria, a privately held maker of software for computer network administrators. Compaq and Dell began shipping servers with Novell's Internet caching software, which linked PCs to host Internet sites for delivery of content to corporate intranets. Also in 1999 the company invested $100 million in information technology services provider Whittman-Hart (which went bankrupt under the name marchFIRST in 2001).

In 2001 Novell (along with minority partners Nortel Networks and Accenture) announced the creation of Volera, a caching and content networking company. Novell also bought Cambridge Technology Partners in a deal valued at about $266 million; Cambridge CEO Jack Messman assumed the role of chief executive at Novell.

In 2002 the company acquired SilverStream Software for about $210 million. Novell also purchased Accenture and Nortel's stakes in Volera, as part of a plan to integrate it into Novell's product lines.

In November 2004 the company agreed to accept a $536 million cash settlement from Microsoft in regards to possible antitrust action relating to Novell's Netware product.

Late in 2005 Novell announced a restructuring plan that included a 10% workforce reduction.

Messman was replaced as CEO by company president Ronald Hovsepian in mid-2006; director Thomas Plaskett took over as chairman.

## EXECUTIVES

**Chairman:** Thomas G. Plaskett, age 63
**President, CEO, and Director:**
Ronald W. (Ron) Hovsepian, age 46, $786,440 pay (prior to promotion)
**SVP and CFO:** Dana C. Russell, age 45
**EVP and CTO:** Jeffrey M. (Jeff) Jaffe, age 52, $1,146,708 pay
**EVP, Worldwide Sales:** Tom Francese, age 57, $791,017 pay (prior to promotion)
**SVP, General Counsel, and Secretary:**
Joseph A. (Joe) LaSala Jr., age 52, $705,014 pay
**SVP and Chief Marketing Officer:** John Dragoon, age 47
**SVP, People:** Alan J. Friedman, age 59
**SVP, Services:** Colleen O'Keefe, age 51
**SVP and General Manager, Workgroup Solutions:**
Kent Erickson
**SVP and General Manager, Open Platform Solutions:**
Roger Levy
**SVP and General Manager Identity and Security Management:** James P. (Jim) Ebzery, age 47
**SVP and General Manager, Systems and Resource Management:** Joe Wagner
**VP and General Manager, Global Strategic Alliances:**
Susan Heystee, age 43, $644,005 pay (prior to promotion)
**VP, Product Management, Open Platform Solutions:**
Carlos Montero-Luque
**President, Novell Asia/Pacific:** Maarten Koster
**President and General Manager, Novell Americas:**
Troy Richardson
**President, Europe, Middle East, and Africa:**
Volker Smid
**Chief Technology and Strategy Officer, Open Source:**
Nat Friedman
**CEO, Salmon Ltd.:** Christopher C. (Chris) Harvey, age 44
**Auditors:** PricewaterhouseCoopers LLP

## LOCATIONS

**HQ:** Novell, Inc.
404 Wyman St., Ste. 500, Waltham, MA 02451
**Phone:** 781-464-8000 **Fax:** 781-464-8100
**Web:** www.novell.com

### 2006 Sales

| | $ mil. | % of total |
|---|---|---|
| US | 596.2 | 57 |
| Ireland | 299.6 | 29 |
| Other countries | 146.6 | 14 |
| Adjustments | (75.1) | — |
| **Total** | **967.3** | **100** |

## PRODUCTS/OPERATIONS

### 2006 Sales

| | $ mil. | % of total |
|---|---|---|
| Workspace solutions | | |
| Open Enterprise Server | 181.7 | 19 |
| NetWare & other NetWare-related | 47.8 | 5 |
| Collaboration | 96.2 | 10 |
| Other | 23.6 | 2 |
| Global services & support | 314.3 | 32 |
| Systems, security, & identity management | | |
| Resource management | 134.6 | 14 |
| Identity & access management | 97.7 | 10 |
| Other | 18.0 | 2 |
| Open platform solutions | | |
| Linux platform products | 45.3 | 5 |
| Other | 8.1 | 1 |
| **Total** | **967.3** | **100** |

## COMPETITORS

Accenture
Altiris
CA
Capgemini
Cisco Systems
Computer Sciences Corp.
Hewlett-Packard
IBM
LANDesk
McAfee
Microsoft
Oracle
Red Hat
Sun Microsystems

## HISTORICAL FINANCIALS

Company Type: Public

### Income Statement

FYE: Last Saturday in October

| | REVENUE ($ mil.) | NET INCOME ($ mil.) | NET PROFIT MARGIN | EMPLOYEES |
|---|---|---|---|---|
| **10/06** | 967 | 19 | 1.9% | 4,549 |
| **10/05** | 1,198 | 377 | 31.5% | 5,066 |
| **10/04** | 1,166 | 57 | 4.9% | 6,186 |
| **10/03** | 1,106 | (162) | — | 5,734 |
| **10/02** | 1,134 | (247) | — | 6,524 |
| **Annual Growth** | (3.9%) | — | — | (8.6%) |

### 2006 Year-End Financials

Debt ratio: 56.1%
Return on equity: 1.5%
Cash ($ mil.): 1,466
Current ratio: 2.57
Long-term debt ($ mil.): 600
No. of shares (mil.): 343
Dividends
Yield: —
Payout: —
Market value ($ mil.): 2,060

### Stock History

NASDAQ (GS): NOVL

| | STOCK PRICE ($) FY Close | P/E High | P/E Low | PER SHARE ($) Earnings | PER SHARE ($) Dividends | PER SHARE ($) Book Value |
|---|---|---|---|---|---|---|
| **10/06** | 6.00 | 197 | 115 | 0.05 | — | 3.22 |
| **10/05** | 7.62 | 9 | 6 | 0.86 | — | 3.59 |
| **10/04** | 7.19 | 178 | 70 | 0.08 | — | 2.55 |
| **10/03** | 5.87 | — | — | (0.44) | — | 2.48 |
| **10/02** | 2.43 | — | — | (0.68) | — | 2.89 |
| **Annual Growth** | 25.4% | — | — | — | — | 2.7% |

# NSTAR

A giant star in the deregulation firmament, NSTAR was formed by the 1999 merger of BEC Energy and Commonwealth Energy System. NSTAR has responded to energy deregulation in Massachusetts by cutting its rates and selling most of its regulated electric generation assets. The utility holding company transmits and distributes electricity to 1.1 million homes and businesses and serves some 300,000 natural gas customers in Massachusetts. The company markets wholesale electricity, operates liquefied natural gas (LNG) processing and storage facilities, provides district heating and cooling services, and offers fiber-optic telecommunications services.

NSTAR's power utilities (Boston Edison, Cambridge Electric Light, and Commonwealth Electric), which merged as NSTAR Electric in 2007, serve customers in 81 Massachusetts communities, including Boston. Subsidiary NSTAR Gas is present in 51 communities in central and eastern Massachusetts.

Due to low market value, NSTAR has written off its investment in telecom services provider RCN.

## HISTORY

NSTAR got its start in 1886 as the Edison Electric Illuminating Company of Boston. The company pushed the use of electricity (promoting and selling appliances in its early days) and helped to develop the first electric vehicles. In the 1920s the company launched radio stations WTAT and WEEI. It changed its name to Boston Edison in 1937.

In the 1970s Boston Edison's fortunes soured as it endured a three-month strike in 1971. In 1972 its nuclear-generated power plant, Pilgrim Station, went online, just in time for the OPEC oil embargo. The company spent about $300 million in the 1980s to fix problems at Pilgrim, which had been heavily fined by the Nuclear Regulatory Commission.

Utility deregulation began gaining momentum in the Northeast in the 1990s, and Boston Edison responded by selling its fossil-fueled power plants, reducing rates, and creating a holding company (BEC Energy) for new, unregulated businesses. In 1996 BEC Energy and the Williams Companies formed a power-marketing joint venture (Williams later took over). It also formed a joint venture with telecommunications company RCN to provide bundled telephone, cable, and Internet access over BEC Energy's fiber-optic networks in Boston.

In 1997 BEC Energy sold its fossil fuel-generated plants to Sithe Energies. Still shedding assets in 1999, the company sold its Pilgrim nuke to Entergy. It then merged with Commonwealth Energy System to form NSTAR. In 2000 the new holding company organized its three electric utilities under one brand name, NSTAR Electric, and renamed its gas unit NSTAR Gas.

In 2002 NSTAR sold its 3% interest in the Vermont Yankee nuclear plant to Entergy. That year the company sold its 4% interest in the Seabrook nuclear plant to FPL Group and exchanged its 23% interest in joint venture RCN-BecoCom for an 11% stake in the venture's parent, RCN Corporation.

## EXECUTIVES

**Chairman, President, and CEO:** Thomas J. (Tom) May, age 59, $915,000 pay
**SVP, CFO, and Treasurer:** James J. (Jim) Judge, age 50, $379,667 pay
**SVP Strategy, Law, and Policy, Secretary, and General Counsel:** Douglas S. (Doug) Horan, age 56, $376,667 pay
**SVP Customer and Corporate Relations:** Joseph R. (Joe) Nolan Jr., age 43, $279,000 pay
**SVP Human Resources:** Timothy R. (Tim) Manning, age 55
**SVP Information Technology:** Eugene J. (Gene) Zimon, age 58
**SVP Operations:** Werner J. Schweiger, age 47, $366,667 pay
**VP, Chief Accounting Officer, and Controller:** Robert J. (Bob) Weafer Jr., age 59
**VP Customer Care:** Penelope M. (Penni) Conner
**VP Gas Operations:** Philip B. Andreas
**VP Energy Supply and Procurement:** Ellen K. Angley
**VP Electric Operations:** Paul D. Vaitkus
**VP Financial Strategic Planning and Policy:** Geoffrey O. Lubbock
**Manager Investor Relations:** John F. Gavin
**Auditors:** PricewaterhouseCoopers LLP

## LOCATIONS

**HQ:** NSTAR
800 Boylston St., Boston, MA 02199
**Phone:** 617-424-2000 **Fax:** 781-441-8886
**Web:** www.nstaronline.com

## PRODUCTS/OPERATIONS

### 2006 Sales

| | $ mil. | % of total |
|---|---|---|
| Electric utility | 2,912.1 | 81 |
| Gas utility | 517.9 | 15 |
| Unregulated operations | 147.7 | 4 |
| **Total** | **3,577.7** | **100** |

### Selected Subsidiaries

Advanced Energy Systems, Inc. (district heating and cooling)
Hopkinton LNG Corp. (liquefied natural gas services)
NSTAR Communications, Inc. (wholesale broadband network)
NSTAR Electric Company (electric utility)
NSTAR Gas Company (natural gas utility)

## COMPETITORS

Bay State Gas
Con Edison
Energy East
Green Mountain Power
KeySpan
National Grid USA
NiSource
Northeast Utilities
PG&E
Unitil

## HISTORICAL FINANCIALS

Company Type: Public

### Income Statement

FYE: December 31

| | REVENUE ($ mil.) | NET INCOME ($ mil.) | NET PROFIT MARGIN | EMPLOYEES |
|---|---|---|---|---|
| **12/06** | 3,578 | 207 | 5.8% | 3,100 |
| **12/05** | 3,243 | 198 | 6.1% | 3,050 |
| **12/04** | 2,954 | 189 | 6.4% | 3,100 |
| **12/03** | 2,914 | 182 | 6.2% | 3,200 |
| **12/02** | 2,719 | 164 | 6.0% | 3,300 |
| **Annual Growth** | 7.1% | 6.0% | — | (1.6%) |

### 2006 Year-End Financials

Debt ratio: 149.2%
Return on equity: 13.3%
Cash ($ mil.): 23
Current ratio: 0.77
Long-term debt ($ mil.): 2,361
No. of shares (mil.): 107
Dividends
Yield: 3.5%
Payout: 62.7%
Market value ($ mil.): 3,670

### Stock History

NYSE: NST

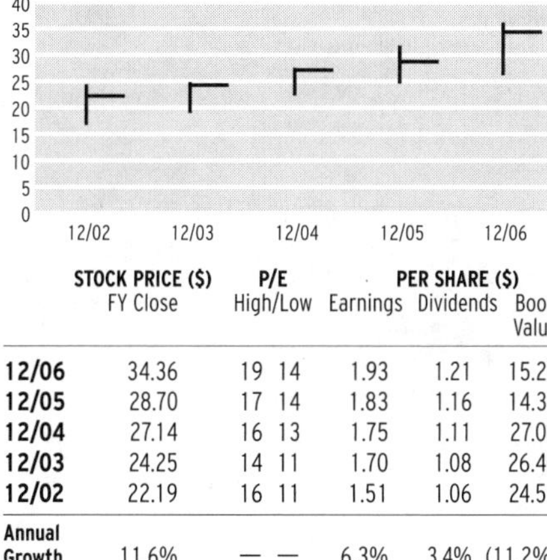


| | STOCK PRICE ($) FY Close | P/E High | P/E Low | PER SHARE ($) Earnings | Dividends | Book Value |
|---|---|---|---|---|---|---|
| **12/06** | 34.36 | 19 | 14 | 1.93 | 1.21 | 15.22 |
| **12/05** | 28.70 | 17 | 14 | 1.83 | 1.16 | 14.37 |
| **12/04** | 27.14 | 16 | 13 | 1.75 | 1.11 | 27.05 |
| **12/03** | 24.25 | 14 | 11 | 1.70 | 1.08 | 26.49 |
| **12/02** | 22.19 | 16 | 11 | 1.51 | 1.06 | 24.50 |
| **Annual Growth** | 11.6% | — | — | 6.3% | 3.4% | (11.2%) |

# Nucor Corporation

Nucor continues to electrify the steel industry with a simple concept: The minimill is mighty. At its various minimills, Nucor produces about 22 million tons of steel annually, including hot- and cold-rolled steel, steel joists, and metal buildings. A major recycler of scrap metal, Nucor produces steel by melting scrap in electric arc furnaces. Most of its products are sold to steel service centers, manufacturers, and fabricators. Divisions such as Vulcraft — one of the US's largest producers of steel joists, girders, and decking — use the balance of the steel. In early 2007 Nucor acquired 96% of Canadian steel products maker Harris Steel for just over $1 billion; it is in the process of acquiring the rest.

Nucor has dominated the minimill industry for two decades, but competitors in that sector are increasing. The company continues to expand its steel mills, add new facilities, and pursue acquisition opportunities. In early 2006 it acquired the former Connecticut Steel — a maker of bar product steel like wire rod, rebar, and wire mesh — for $43 million. The deal added to Nucor's construction products offerings. Later in the year Nucor spent $180 million to acquire Verco Manufacturing, which makes steel flooring and roof decking.

The move to buy Harris the next year was much, much bigger but followed in line with the Connecticut Steel deal. Harris has been a customer and partner of Nucor for a while and produces rebar, wire, and grating. It will operate as a separate, wholly owned subsidiary, should the deal go through.

Nucor expanded its downstream operations with the 2007 agreement to acquire building systems maker MAGNATRAX for $280 million. That company emerged from Chapter 11 bankruptcy protection in 2004 and was owned by creditors prior to the deal.

Even though Nucor continues to face stiff domestic and foreign competition, it has not laid off any employees in over 30 years.

## HISTORY

Nucor started as the second carmaking venture of Ransom Olds, who built his first gasoline-powered car in 1897. Two years later, Samuel Smith, a Detroit copper and lumber magnate, put up $199,600 to finance Olds Motor Works. A fire destroyed the company's Detroit plant in 1901, so Olds moved production to Lansing, Michigan, where he built America's first mass-produced car — the Oldsmobile. In 1904 Olds left Olds Motor Works, which was bought by General Motors (GM) in 1908, and formed Reo Car Company (renamed Reo Motor Car in 1906). In addition to cars, it eventually made trucks and buses.

By the end of the Depression, Ford, GM, and Chrysler commanded over 85% of the US passenger car market. Reo stopped making cars in 1936 and sold its truck manufacturing operations in 1957. Meanwhile, it had formed Reo Holding, which in 1955 merged with Nuclear Consultants to form Nuclear Corporation of America. The new company offered services such as radiation studies and made nuclear instruments and electronics.

In 1962 Nuclear bought steel joist maker Vulcraft and gained the services of Kenneth Iverson. The diverse company was unprofitable, losing

$2 million on $22 million in sales in 1965. That year Iverson took over as CEO, moved headquarters to Charlotte, North Carolina, and shut down or sold about half of the company's businesses. By focusing on its profitable steel joist operations, the firm ended 1966 in the black. Because the company depended on imports for 80% of its steel needs, Iverson decided to move into steel production. Nuclear Corporation built its first minimill in 1969.

The company was renamed Nucor in 1972. It started making steel deck (1977) and cold-finished steel bars (1979). Production tripled and sales more than doubled between 1974 and 1979.

Nucor began to diversify, adding grinding balls (used in the mining industry to process ores, 1981); steel bolts, steel bearings, and machined steel parts (1986); and metal buildings and components (1987). Nucor and Japanese steelmaker Yamato Kogyo formed Nucor-Yamato and built a mill in 1988 to produce wide-flange beams (for heavy construction). The following year Nucor opened a state-of-the-art mill in Crawfordsville, Indiana, and another mill near Hickman, Arkansas, in 1992.

Iverson turned over his CEO duties to company veteran John Correnti in 1996. The next year Nucor began building a steel beam mill in South Carolina and added a galvanizing facility to its Hickman mill.

In 1998 Nucor announced plans to build its first steel plate mill, which became operational in 2000. The company slashed prices twice in 1998 to compete against low-cost imports from Russia, Japan, and Brazil. Both sales and earnings declined that year due to low metal prices, reduced shipments, and start-up costs for new plants. The company raised its prices in 1999 and continued its expansion plans. Differences with the board prompted Correnti to resign in 1999; chairman David Aycock assumed his duties. In September 2000 Aycock resigned from the company and Daniel R. DiMicco, formerly an EVP, moved up to the rank of CEO.

Early in 2000 Nucor, along with Australia's Broken Hill Proprietary Corporation and Japan's Ishikawajima-Harima Heavy Industries, began a joint venture for its technology strip casting. The new technology allows steel production in smaller, cheaper plants. In March 2001 Nucor purchased a significant amount of assets of Auburn Steel, a producer of merchant steel bar, for $115 million.

In 2002 Nucor teamed up with Companhia Vale do Rio Doce (CVRD), a Brazilian producer and exporter of iron-ore pellets, to develop low-cost iron based products. That same year Nucor purchased Alabama-based Trico Steel, a steel sheet producer. In late 2002 Nucor bought financially troubled Birmingham Steel for $615 million in cash and debt.

Nucor Steel Kingman, LLC, a subsidiary of Nucor Corporation, purchased the Kingman, Arizona rebar and wire rod rolling unit of North Star Steel for around $35 million in 2003.

Its Vulcraft unit saw an increase in nonresidential building construction in 2004, which boosted sales of joist girders, steel deck, and steel joists. Nucor bought Corus Tuscaloosa (now called Nucor Tuscaloosa) in mid-2004, a producer of coiled plate with an annual capacity of around 700,000 tons. The following year saw the company purchase Ohio's Marion Steel for approximately $110 million. The mill was added to Nucor's bar products line.

The company named CEO DiMicco chairman in 2006.

## EXECUTIVES

**Chairman, President, and CEO:** Daniel R. (Dan) DiMicco, age 55
**EVP, CFO, and Treasurer:** Terry S. Lisenby, age 54, $1,342,968 pay
**EVP:** Joseph A. Rutkowski, age 51, $2,214,525 pay
**VP and Corporate Controller:** James D. Frias
**VP, Human Resources:** James M. Coblin, age 62
**General Manager, Taxes:** Elizabeth W. Bowers
**General Manager and Secretary:** A. Rae Eagle
**General Manager, Coporate Legal Affairs:** Douglas R. Gunson
**Auditors:** PricewaterhouseCoopers LLP

## LOCATIONS

**HQ:** Nucor Corporation
1915 Rexford Rd., Charlotte, NC 28211
**Phone:** 704-366-7000 **Fax:** 704-362-4208
**Web:** www.nucor.com

Nucor maintains operating facilities throughout the US.

## PRODUCTS/OPERATIONS

**2006 Sales**

| | $ mil. | % of total |
|---|---|---|
| Steel mills | | |
| Sheet | 5,362.2 | 36 |
| Bar | 3,702.6 | 25 |
| Structural | 2,205.3 | 15 |
| Plate | 1,755.0 | 12 |
| Steel products | 1,726.2 | 12 |
| **Total** | **14,751.3** | **100** |

**Selected Products**

Alloy steel
- Cold-drawn steel bars
- Finished hex caps
- Hex-head cap screws
- Locknuts
- Structural bolts and nuts

Carbon steel
- Angles
- Beams
- Channels
- Cold-drawn steel bars
- Finished hex nuts
- Flats
- Floor plate
- Galvanized sheet
- Grinding balls
- Hexagons
- Hot-rolled sheet
- Reinforcing bars
- Structural bolts and nuts
- Wide-range beams

Engineered products
- Composite floor joists
- Floor deck
- Joists
- Joist girders
- Pre-engineered metal buildings
- Roof deck
- Special-profile steel trusses

Stainless steel
- Cold-rolled steel
- Hot-rolled steel
- Pickled sheet

**Selected Divisions and Subsidiaries**

NUCON STEEL Commercial Corporation
Nucor Bar Mill Group BHM
Nucor Building Systems
Nucor Cold Finish
Nucor Fastener
Nucor Grinding Balls
Nucor Steel
Nucor-Yamato Steel Co. (51%, with Yamato Kogyo)
Vulcraft

## COMPETITORS

AK Steel
Bayou Steel
BlueScope Steel
Chaparral Steel
Commercial Metals
Corus Group
Gerdau Ameristeel
Mittal Steel USA
Renco
Steel Dynamics
Stelco Hamilton
United States Steel

## HISTORICAL FINANCIALS

Company Type: Public

**Income Statement** FYE: December 31

| | REVENUE ($ mil.) | NET INCOME ($ mil.) | NET PROFIT MARGIN | EMPLOYEES |
|---|---|---|---|---|
| **12/06** | 14,751 | 1,758 | 11.9% | 11,900 |
| **12/05** | 12,701 | 1,310 | 10.3% | 11,300 |
| **12/04** | 11,377 | 1,122 | 9.9% | 10,600 |
| **12/03** | 6,266 | 63 | 1.0% | 9,900 |
| **12/02** | 4,802 | 162 | 3.4% | 9,800 |
| **Annual Growth** | 32.4% | 81.5% | — | 5.0% |

**2006 Year-End Financials**

Debt ratio: 19.1%
Return on equity: 38.6%
Cash ($ mil.): 2,196
Current ratio: 3.22
Long-term debt ($ mil.): 922
No. of shares (mil.): 301
Dividends
Yield: 3.0%
Payout: 29.0%
Market value ($ mil.): 16,450

**Stock History** NYSE: NUE

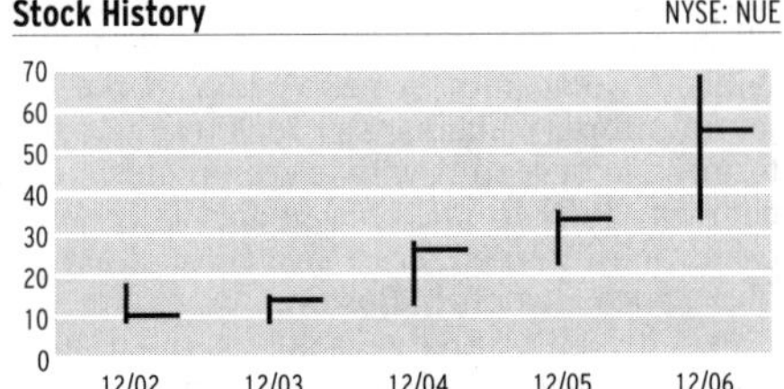

| | STOCK PRICE ($) FY Close | P/E High | P/E Low | PER SHARE ($) Earnings | Dividends | Book Value |
|---|---|---|---|---|---|---|
| **12/06** | 54.66 | 12 | 6 | 5.68 | 1.65 | 16.04 |
| **12/05** | 33.36 | 8 | 6 | 4.13 | 0.93 | 13.80 |
| **12/04** | 26.17 | 8 | 4 | 3.51 | 0.17 | 21.67 |
| **12/03** | 14.00 | 73 | 44 | 0.20 | 0.20 | 29.80 |
| **12/02** | 10.32 | 34 | 17 | 0.52 | 0.19 | 29.71 |
| **Annual Growth** | 51.7% | — | — | 81.8% | 71.7% | (14.3%) |

# NVIDIA Corporation

NVIDIA keeps staging new graphics chip invasions. The fabless semiconductor company designs high-definition 2-D and 3-D graphics processors for gaming and industrial-design applications. Its graphics chips, especially the flagship GeForce line, are used by major PC makers, such as Apple, Dell, Gateway, and Hewlett-Packard, as well as in add-in boards and motherboards produced by Asustek Computer (12% of sales) and other companies. NVIDIA also provides complementary graphics driver software, as well as graphics chipsets — clusters of components with integrated graphics functions that aid the operation of PC microprocessors.

AMD's 2006 acquisition of NVIDIA's archrival, ATI Technologies, complicated a number of relationships in the semiconductor industry. AMD and NVIDIA previously collaborated on making sure AMD's microprocessors and NVIDIA's graphics processors worked smoothly together; AMD cultivated a similar relationship with ATI Technologies prior to the acquisition. The purchase put AMD and NVIDIA in the awkward position of being both collaborators and competitors, as AMD is developing a new set of "Fusion" processors that meld the capabilities of the AMD and ATI product lines.

Adding to industry anxiety is an investigation into the graphics processor market by the Antitrust Division of the US Department of Justice. AMD and NVIDIA received subpoenas in late 2006 from the Justice Department for materials related to competitive practices — or the lack of them — in the business for graphics processing units and cards. The Justice Department also has a longstanding antitrust case in the DRAM device market, which has resulted in several industry executives going to prison and vendors paying hundreds of millions of dollars in fines for fixing prices on memory parts, and a separate investigation into the static random-access memory (SRAM) market.

In early 2007 the company acquired PortalPlayer, a supplier of chips that go into Apple's iPods, SanDisk's Sansa MP3 music players, and other portable electronics, for approximately $357 million in cash. The transaction was a financial bargain for NVIDIA, as PortalPlayer had about $196 million in cash among its assets, making up more than half of the purchase price.

NVIDIA's chips supply the graphics muscle for Microsoft's Xbox video game console, and the company has partnered with Sony to develop graphics processors for the PlayStation console. NVIDIA stopped receiving revenue from Microsoft during 2006, just before revenue from Sony's PlayStation3 started kicking in.

NVIDIA also supplies media processors used in phones from Motorola and Sony Ericsson.

The company outsources production of its semiconductors to American Microsemiconductor, Chartered Semiconductor Manufacturing, Taiwan Semiconductor Manufacturing, and United Microelectronics.

NVIDIA operates in a volatile market that has challenged a number of former graphics chip leaders: Tseng Labs sold its failed graphics business in 1997, Cirrus Logic left the graphics business in 1998, and 3dfx sold all its assets to NVIDIA in 2001 and no longer does business.

The $70 million purchase of 3dfx's assets came back to haunt NVIDIA years later, as creditors of the bankrupt 3dfx sued the company, claiming that the asset purchase price was too low. A US Bankruptcy Court trial on the creditors' suit began in early 2007 in San Jose, California.

CEO Jen-Hsun Huang owns about 6% of NVIDIA. FMR (Fidelity Investments) holds around 5% of the company.

## HISTORY

Taiwan-born and Stanford-trained engineer Jen-Hsun Huang was already a veteran of Advanced Micro Devices and LSI Logic (now just LSI) when he decided to start his own company at age 30. He co-founded NVIDIA in 1992 with fellow engineers and industry veterans Chris Malachowsky (SVP) and Curtis Priem (former CTO). It was incorporated in 1993.

After its first try at a graphics chip failed miserably in 1995, NVIDIA hit the big time in 1997 when it introduced a graphics processor that set a new industry standard for speed. Good product timing and flawless execution kept the company growing in the years to come: After turning its first profit in 1998, NVIDIA crossed the $100 million, $300 million, and $700 million sales thresholds in successive years.

The company made its IPO in 1999. The following year Microsoft chose NVIDIA to supply the graphics chips for its Xbox video game console. Also in 2000 the company overtook archrival ATI Technologies in market share for desktop PC graphics chips.

Late in 2000 the company announced that it would acquire the assets of erstwhile rival 3dfx in a deal initially valued at $110 million. The transaction was completed in mid-2001, for $70 million in cash and a potential earnout payment of 1 million shares of NVIDIA common stock. In 2002 the company came under review by the SEC for potential accounting irregularities; when the company restated earnings a few months later, though, its financial results for the three-year period in question improved slightly.

Later in 2002 NVIDIA bought privately held 3-D software company Exluna, which was founded by veterans of Pixar. The following year NVIDIA acquired MediaQ, whose handheld graphics and media products were rebranded as GoForce, for about $70 million. In 2004 NVIDIA acquired assets of privately held iReady Corp., primarily consisting of the intellectual property and patents related to its TCP/IP and iSCSI Ethernet technologies.

Early in 2006 the company acquired Taiwanese circuit designer ULi Electronics for about $52 million. The company also acquired Hybrid Graphics, a developer of embedded graphics software for handheld devices, that same year.

## EXECUTIVES

**President, CEO, and Director:** Jen-Hsun Huang, age 44, $500,000 pay
**CFO:** Marvin D. (Marv) Burkett, age 64, $425,000 pay
**SVP, Engineering and Operations:** Chris A. Malachowsky, age 48
**SVP, General Counsel, and Secretary:** David M. Shannon, age 51, $300,000 pay
**SVP, GPU Business Unit:** Jeffrey D. (Jeff) Fisher, age 48, $607,524 pay
**SVP, GPU Engineering:** Brian M. Kelleher
**SVP, Marketing:** Daniel F. (Dan) Vivoli, age 46, $494,379 pay
**SVP, Handheld GPU Business Unit:** Philip J. (Phil) Carmack
**SVP, Platform Business:** Gopal Solanki
**SVP, Worldwide Sales:** Ajay K (Jay) Puri, age 52, $375,000 pay
**CIO:** George Stelling
**VP, Content Development:** Neil Trevett
**VP, Digital Media Processor Engineering:** Frank Fox
**VP, Finance:** Sam Brown
**VP, GPU Engineering:** Jonah M. Alben
**VP, Human Resources:** Scott P. Sullivan
**VP, Investor Relations and Communications:** Michael W. Hara
**VP, Systems and Application Engineering:** Tommy Lee
**VP, Software Engineering:** Dwight Diercks
**VP, VLSI Engineering:** Joseph D. (Joe) Greco
**Director, Corporate Communication:** Calisa Cole
**Chief Scientist:** David B. Kirk
**Investor Relations:** Mohamed Siddeek
**Auditors:** PricewaterhouseCoopers LLP

## LOCATIONS

**HQ:** NVIDIA Corporation
2701 San Tomas Expwy., Santa Clara, CA 95050
**Phone:** 408-486-2000 **Fax:** 408-486-2200
**Web:** www.nvidia.com

NVIDIA has design centers, laboratories, and offices in China, Finland, France, Germany, Hong Kong, India, Japan, Russia, South Korea, Taiwan, the UK, and the US.

### 2007 Sales

| | $ mil. | % of total |
|---|---|---|
| Asia/Pacific | | |
| Taiwan | 1,119.0 | 36 |
| China | 659.7 | 21 |
| Other countries | 483.9 | 16 |
| Americas | | |
| US | 332.3 | 11 |
| Other countries | 171.8 | 6 |
| Europe | 302.1 | 10 |
| **Total** | **3,068.8** | **100** |

## PRODUCTS/OPERATIONS

### 2007 Sales

| | $ mil. | % of total |
|---|---|---|
| Graphics processing units (GPU) | 1,994.3 | 65 |
| Media & communications processors (MCP) | 661.5 | 22 |
| Handheld GPUs | 108.5 | 3 |
| Consumer electronics | 96.3 | 3 |
| Other | 208.2 | 7 |
| **Total** | **3,068.8** | **100** |

### Selected Products

Graphics processing unit (GPU) chips for PCs and workstations (GeForce, Go, NVIDIA Quadro)
Media and communications processors (MCP) for PCs, workstations, and servers (nForce)
Consumer electronics processors for video game consoles and other devices
Handheld GPUs for handheld computers and mobile phones (GoForce)

## COMPETITORS

AMD
ARM Holdings
Broadcom
Creative Technology
Epson
Freescale Semiconductor
Fujitsu
Imagination Technologies
Intel
Marvell Technology
Matrox Electronic Systems
MediaTek
NEC
QUALCOMM
Renesas
Samsung Electronics
Silicon Integrated Systems
STMicroelectronics
Texas Instruments
Toshiba America Electronic Components
VIA Technologies

## HISTORICAL FINANCIALS

Company Type: Public

### Income Statement

FYE: Last Saturday in January

| | REVENUE ($ mil.) | NET INCOME ($ mil.) | NET PROFIT MARGIN | EMPLOYEES |
|---|---|---|---|---|
| **1/07** | 3,069 | 449 | 14.6% | 4,083 |
| **1/06** | 2,376 | 301 | 12.7% | 2,737 |
| **1/05** | 2,010 | 100 | 5.0% | 2,101 |
| **1/04** | 1,823 | 74 | 4.1% | 1,825 |
| **1/03** | 1,909 | 91 | 4.8% | 1,513 |
| **Annual Growth** | 12.6% | 49.1% | — | 28.2% |

### 2007 Year-End Financials

Debt ratio: —
Return on equity: 25.6%
Cash ($ mil.): 1,118
Current ratio: 3.18
Long-term debt ($ mil.): —
No. of shares (mil.): 361
Dividends
Yield: —
Payout: —
Market value ($ mil.): 11,360

**Stock History** NASDAQ (GS): NVDA

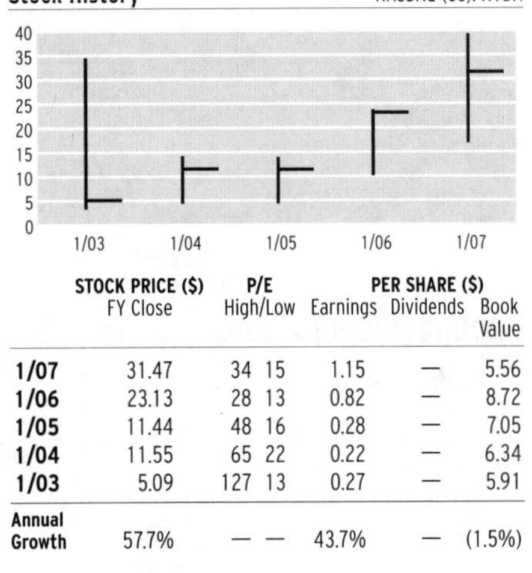

| | STOCK PRICE ($) FY Close | P/E High/Low | | PER SHARE ($) Earnings | Dividends | Book Value |
|---|---|---|---|---|---|---|
| **1/07** | 31.47 | 34 | 15 | 1.15 | — | 5.56 |
| **1/06** | 23.13 | 28 | 13 | 0.82 | — | 8.72 |
| **1/05** | 11.44 | 48 | 16 | 0.28 | — | 7.05 |
| **1/04** | 11.55 | 65 | 22 | 0.22 | — | 6.34 |
| **1/03** | 5.09 | 127 | 13 | 0.27 | — | 5.91 |
| **Annual Growth** | 57.7% | — | — | 43.7% | — | (1.5%) |

# NVR, Inc.

From finished lot to signed mortgage, NVR offers homebuyers everything — including the kitchen sink. The company builds single-family detached homes, townhomes, and condominiums, mainly for first-time and first-time move-up buyers in the US. NVR markets its homes as Ryan Homes, Fox Ridge Homes, Rymarc Homes, and NVHomes. Its largest markets, the Washington, DC, and Baltimore areas, account for more than half of its sales. NVR sells about 15,000 homes annually; homes range from 1,000 sq. ft. to 7,300 sq. ft., and in price from $90,000 to $2.6 million, averaging about $398,000. Subsidiary NVR Mortgage Finance offers mortgage and title services to its customers.

NVR's Ryan Homes, Fox Ridge Homes, and Rymarc Homes divisions primarily market to first-time buyers. Ryan Homes operates in more than 20 metropolitan areas along the Eastern Seaboard and in Kentucky, Ohio, Michigan, Pennsylvania, and West Virginia. Fox Ridge Homes builds in Nashville, Tennessee and Rymarc Homes operates in Columbia, South Carolina. NVHomes caters to upscale buyers and builds primarily in the Baltimore, Philadelphia, and Washington, DC, metro areas, as well as in Maryland's Eastern Shore. To control capital risk, NVR buys option contracts on finished building lots and finds new homebuyers before it buys the lot. NVR Mortgage Finance operates throughout the parent company's market areas. Founder and chairman Dwight Schar owns about 8% of NVR.

## HISTORY

NVR got its start when Dwight Schar founded NVHomes, Inc., in 1980. Schar had worked for Ryan Homes (founded in 1948) since 1969. NVHomes, like Ryan Homes, specialized in single-family homes around Washington, DC.

The strong economy of the 1980s and the deregulation of lending institutions — coupled with favorable partnership and real estate tax laws passed by the Reagan administration — resulted in rapid growth. The company was clearing income of more than $1 million a year by 1983 and soon branched into building townhomes and condominiums.

In 1986, when the company was reorganized as a limited partnership (NVH L.P.), income was up to $14 million. The new entity soon acquired a controlling interest in Ryan Homes; it completed its acquisition of that company in 1987. NVH reorganized as a holding company (NVRyan L.P.), and 1988 profits reached $33.5 million. Over the years the company formed or acquired almost 100 subsidiaries that were involved in all aspects of homebuilding — from land acquisition and construction to home finance and investment advice. It had also branched out into California, Florida, Indiana, Kentucky, North Carolina, Ohio, Pennsylvania, and Virginia.

Following an economic recession in 1989, demand for new housing dropped off in the US. The company shortened its name to NVR L.P., and its inventory of unsold land and houses started to grow. The situation was exacerbated by changes in the tax code that made real estate less attractive as an investment; sales from development and construction projects dropped from more than $1 billion in 1988 to about $600 million in 1991. NVR posted a $260 million loss in 1990 as sales and the value of its inventory nose-dived.

NVR reorganized in 1990 and 1991. Focused on eight mid-Atlantic states, it put homebuilding under one management structure, consolidated its finance activities, exited its land-development businesses, and offered its mortgage services to customers who weren't NVR homebuyers. It also organized its business into two product lines: upscale (NVHomes) and moderately priced (Ryan Homes) homes. Despite the reorganization and introduction of innovative marketing, NVR and several of its subsidiaries filed for Chapter 11 bankruptcy relief in 1992. That year the CFO of NVR's thrift (NVR Savings Bank) went on the lam to Malta after embezzling more than $750,000.

The company emerged from bankruptcy as NVR, Inc., in 1993 with less debt, new owners, and a new line of credit; it also had its IPO that year. The next year NVR sold NVR Savings Bank, which had four branches in northern Virginia. The robust mid-1990s economy aided NVR; as home sales rose, the company entered new markets, including the Cleveland and Nashville areas, in 1995. To reduce its vulnerability to downturns in the mid-Atlantic area, it continued its expansion outside that region, buying Fox Ridge Homes (the #2 builder in Nashville) in 1997.

In 1999 it merged its homebuilding subsidiary, NVR Homes, and mortgage banking holding company, NVR Financial Services, into NVR. It also acquired Rockville, Maryland-based First Republic Mortgage that year, but closed the subsidiary's retail operations in 2000 and realigned its mortgage banking business to serve NVR customers exclusively.

From 1994 through 2003 the company benefited from increased housing activity, recording steady increases in unit sales, backlog, and profits for nine years.

## EXECUTIVES

**Chairman:** Dwight C. Schar, age 65
**President and CEO:** Paul C. Saville, age 51
**VP, CFO, and Treasurer:** Dennis M. Seremet, age 51
**VP, Secretary, and General Counsel:** James M. Sack
**VP and Controller:** Robert W. Henley, age 40
**President, NVR Mortgage Finance:** William J. Inman, age 59
**Auditors:** KPMG LLP

## LOCATIONS

**HQ:** NVR, Inc.
Plaza America Tower 1, 11700 Plaza America Dr., Ste. 500, Reston, VA 20190
**Phone:** 703-956-4000 **Fax:** 703-956-4750
**Web:** www.nvrinc.com

NVR has facilities in Maryland, New Jersey, New York, North Carolina, Pennsylvania, Tennessee, and Virginia.

**2006 Closings By Homebuilding Segment**

| | No. of properties | % of total |
|---|---|---|
| Mid Atlantic (Virginia, West Virginia, Maryland & Delaware) | 7,491 | 49 |
| Mid East (Kentucky, Michigan, New York, Ohio & western Pennsylvania) | 3,571 | 24 |
| South East (North Carolina, South Carolina & Tennessee) | 2,395 | 16 |
| North East (Eastern Pennsylvania & New Jersey) | 1,682 | 11 |
| **Total** | **15,139** | **100** |

## PRODUCTS/OPERATIONS

**2006 Sales**

| | $ mil. | % of total |
|---|---|---|
| Homebuilding | | |
| Mid Atlantic | 3,826.0 | 62 |
| Mid East | 965.6 | 16 |
| North East | 657.3 | 11 |
| South East | 587.3 | 9 |
| Mortgage operations & other | 120.5 | 2 |
| **Total** | **6,156.7** | **100** |

## COMPETITORS

Beazer Homes
Brookfield Homes
Centex
Champion Enterprises
Countrywide Financial
David Weekley Homes
D.R. Horton
Hovnanian Enterprises
John Wieland Homes
KB Home
Lennar
M.D.C.
M/I Homes
Orleans Homebuilders
Pulte Homes
Ryland
Technical Olympic USA
Toll Brothers

## HISTORICAL FINANCIALS

Company Type: Public

**Income Statement** FYE: December 31

| | REVENUE ($ mil.) | NET INCOME ($ mil.) | NET PROFIT MARGIN | EMPLOYEES |
|---|---|---|---|---|
| **12/06** | 6,157 | 587 | 9.5% | 4,548 |
| **12/05** | 5,275 | 698 | 13.2% | 5,401 |
| **12/04** | 4,328 | 523 | 12.1% | 4,407 |
| **12/03** | 3,681 | 420 | 11.4% | 3,852 |
| **12/02** | 3,136 | 332 | 10.6% | 3,596 |
| **Annual Growth** | 18.4% | 15.4% | — | 6.0% |

**2006 Year-End Financials**

Debt ratio: 31.0%
Return on equity: 64.2%
Cash ($ mil.): 556
Current ratio: 1.91
Long-term debt ($ mil.): 357
No. of shares (mil.): 6
Dividends
Yield: —
Payout: —
Market value ($ mil.): 3,559

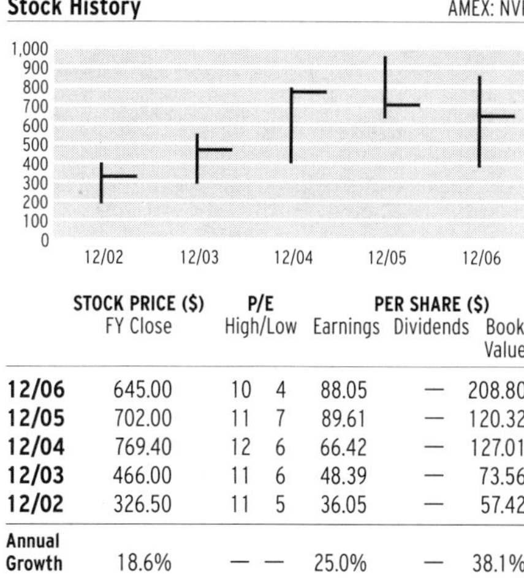


| | STOCK PRICE ($) FY Close | P/E High/Low | | PER SHARE ($) Earnings | Dividends | Book Value |
|---|---|---|---|---|---|---|
| **12/06** | 645.00 | 10 | 4 | 88.05 | — | 208.80 |
| **12/05** | 702.00 | 11 | 7 | 89.61 | — | 120.32 |
| **12/04** | 769.40 | 12 | 6 | 66.42 | — | 127.01 |
| **12/03** | 466.00 | 11 | 6 | 48.39 | — | 73.56 |
| **12/02** | 326.50 | 11 | 5 | 36.05 | — | 57.42 |
| **Annual Growth** | 18.6% | — | — | 25.0% | — | 38.1% |

# NYSE Euronext

NYSE Euronext operates the New York Stock Exchange (NYSE), one of the oldest and largest stock markets in the world. It lists nearly 2,700 companies, including most of the largest US corporations; it also recruits foreign firms seeking the greater liquidity available in US markets. In 2007 the NYSE bought Euronext for some $10 billion to create the first trans-Atlantic exchange and the largest global stock market, with exchanges in Paris, Brussels, Amsterdam, and Lisbon, plus automated trading desks, in addition to the NYSE. The merger also gives NYSE Euronext ownership of six derivatives and futures markets, including London-based LIFFE.

To better compete with electronic exchanges such as archrival Nasdaq, the NYSE broke from its tradition of operating as an auction exchange and adopted a hybrid system that permits automated trading. To help fuel its transformation, the NYSE bought electronic communications network (ECN) Archipelago in 2006.

While the NYSE has always touted its people-driven exchange, stiff competition, not only from Nasdaq but also from foreign exchanges and ECNs, spurred the combination with Archipelago. Member-owned and not-for-profit for more than 200 years since its founding, the NYSE became a publicly traded company as part of the $10 billion transaction. NYSE stockholders got about 70% of the firm, while shareholders of Archipelago got the other 30%.

Less than three months after that transaction closed, the NYSE announced the deal for Euronext, which was also courted by Deutsche Börse. Euronext rejected a larger $11 billion bid from the German exchange, claiming it carried too much debt. The combination of NYSE and Euronext allows the exchanges to keep pace with Nasdaq, which acquired a 25% stake in the London Stock Exchange in 2006. Continuing its international aspirations, NYSE Euronext purchased a 5% stake in India's largest stock exchange, Mumbai-based National Stock Exchange, in 2007.

Thanks to the Archipelago acquisition, the NYSE added stock options and fixed-income products to its offerings and took control of the securities market Archipelago Exchange (Arca Ex), now NYSE Arca. However, some traders are wary that the NYSE/Archipelago combination could lead to the extinction of the open-outcry floor auctions (where stock prices are set largely by a throng of traders on the exchange floor) that characterize the NYSE.

In an effort to reduce costs and eliminate redundant positions created by the Archipelago merger, NYSE announced the reduction of more than 500 jobs (nearly 20% of its employees), including some floor specialists, in 2006. It has slashed its work force by some 35% since 2005.

NYSE Euronext owns Securities Industry Automation Corporation (SIAC), which provides communications, data processing, and clearing services primarily to the NYSE and to the American Stock Exchange (AMEX). NYSE bought out AMEX's approximately one-third stake in SIAC in 2006.

Also that year, the NYSE revealed plans to merge its regulatory body, NYSE Regulation, with NASD Regulation. The combined entity will be responsible for overseeing securities dealers in the US and will eliminate the overlap of some of the two regulators' duties.

## HISTORY

To prevent a monopoly on stock sales by securities auctioneers, 24 New York stockbrokers and businessmen agreed in 1792 to avoid "public auctions," to charge a commission on sales of stock, and to "give preference to each other" in their transactions. The Buttonwood Agreement, named after a tree on Wall Street under which they met, established the first organized stock market in New York. The Bank of New York was the first corporate stock traded under the Buttonwood tree.

Excluded traders continued dealing on the streets of New York until 1921 and later formed the American Stock Exchange.

In 1817 the brokers created the New York Stock & Exchange Board, a stock market with set meeting times. The NYS&EB began to require companies to qualify for trading (listing) by furnishing financial statements in 1853. Ten years later the board became the New York Stock Exchange.

Stock tickers began recording trades in 1867, and two years later the NYSE consolidated with competitors the Open Board of Brokers and the Government Bond Department. Despite repeated panics and recessions in the late 1800s, the stock market remained unregulated until well into the 20th century.

In the 1920s the NYSE installed a centralized stock quote service. Postwar euphoria brought a stock mania that fizzled in the crash of October 1929. The subsequent Depression brought investigation and federal regulation to the securities industry.

The NYSE registered as an exchange in 1934. In 1938 it reorganized, with a board of directors representing member firms, nonmember brokers, and the public; it also hired its first full-time president, member William McChesney Martin. As a self-regulating body, the NYSE policed the activities of its members.

The NYSE began electronic trading in the 1960s; in 1968 it broke 1929's one-day record for trading volume (16 million shares). It became a not-for-profit corporation in 1971.

Despite upgrades, technology was at least partly to blame for the crash of 1987: A cascade of large sales triggered by computer programs fueled the market's fall.

In 1995 Richard Grasso became the first NYSE staff employee named chairman. The NYSE used a veiled threat to move to New Jersey to win itself the promise of some growing space. In 1999 the exchange named Karen Nelson Hackett as its first woman governor.

In the wake of the terrorism attacks that shook Wall Street and the nation, the NYSE and Nasdaq in 2001 began discussing a disaster plan that would see the two cooperating should a future incident cripple either market. Also that year the NYSE moved entirely to decimal pricing in accordance with SEC mandates.

Grasso, who earned a reputation as something of a hero in the months following the 2001 terrorist attacks on New York City, resigned under fire two years later when his $187 million pay package was revealed. During the furor over Grasso's pay, the SEC launched an investigation, and many officials — including the heads of top pension funds — called for his resignation.

Former Citigroup chairman John Reed was named interim chairman and CEO following Grasso's departure; former Goldman Sachs president John Thain was subsequently tapped for the CEO role in 2004.

## EXECUTIVES

**Chairman:** Jan-Michiel (J.M.) Hessels, age 64
**Deputy Chairman:** Marshall N. Carter, age 66
**CEO and Director:** John A. Thain, age 51
**Deputy CEO and Director:** Jean-François Théodore, age 60
**President and Co-COO:** Catherine R. Kinney, age 55, $2,250,000 pay
**President and Co-COO; Interim President, Securities Industry Automation Corporation (SIAC):** Gerald D. (Jerry) Putnam, age 47
**EVP and CFO:** Nelson Chai, age 41, $1,115,000 pay
**EVP, Communications and Government Relations:** Margaret D. Tutwiler, age 55
**EVP and General Counsel:** Rachel F. Robbins, age 56
**EVP, Electronic Trading and New Products:** Mike Cormack
**EVP, Human Resources:** Dale B. Bernstein, age 51
**EVP, Market Operations:** Anne E. Allen
**EVP:** Louis G. Pastina, age 48
**SVP, Corporate Communications:** Richard C. (Rich) Adamonis, age 50
**SVP, Corporate Planning, Finance:** Andrew T. Brandman, age 36
**SVP, Advertising and Marketing, Communications:** Michael H. Cohen, age 43
**SVP, NYSE Arca:** Paul Adcock
**VP, Investor Relations:** Gary M. Stein, age 38
**Chief Ethics Officer:** Louise Quick, age 45
**Treasurer:** Patrick F. Boyle
**President and Co-COO, NYSE Group:** Duncan L. Niederauer
**CEO, NYSE Regulation:** Richard G. (Rick) Ketchum, age 55
**EVP and Chief of Enforcement, NYSE Regulation:** Susan L. Merrill
**EVP, Member Firm Regulation, NYSE Regulation:** Grace B. Vogel
**Auditors:** PricewaterhouseCoopers LLP

## LOCATIONS

**HQ:** NYSE Euronext, Inc.
11 Wall St., New York, NY 10005
**Phone:** 212-656-3000 **Fax:** 212-656-2126
**Web:** www.nyse.com

## PRODUCTS/OPERATIONS

### 2006 Sales

| | $ mil. | % of total |
|---|---|---|
| Transaction fees | 675.9 | 28 |
| Activity assessment fees | 673.2 | 28 |
| Listing fees | 356.1 | 15 |
| Market data fees | 222.5 | 9 |
| Regulatory fees | 184.2 | 8 |
| Data processing fees | 137.1 | 6 |
| Licensing, facility & other | 127.0 | 6 |
| **Total** | **2,376.0** | **100** |

## COMPETITORS

AMEX
CBOE
CME
Deutsche Börse
E*TRADE Financial
Hong Kong Exchanges
Investment Technology
Knight Capital
Liquidnet
London Stock Exchange
MarketAxess
Nasdaq Stock Market
NYFIX
Singapore Exchange
TRADEBOOK

## HISTORICAL FINANCIALS

Company Type: Public

**Income Statement** FYE: December 31

| | REVENUE ($ mil.) | NET INCOME ($ mil.) | NET PROFIT MARGIN | EMPLOYEES |
|---|---|---|---|---|
| **12/06** | 2,376 | 205 | 8.6% | 2,578 |
| **12/05** | 1,123 | 41 | 3.6% | 1,975 |
| **12/04** | 1,076 | 25 | 2.3% | 1,577 |
| **12/03** | 1,074 | 50 | 4.6% | 1,522 |
| **12/02** | 1,066 | 28 | 2.6% | 1,500 |
| **Annual Growth** | 22.2% | 64.3% | — | 14.5% |

**2006 Year-End Financials**

Debt ratio: —
Return on equity: 16.6%
Cash ($ mil.): 979
Current ratio: 1.73
Long-term debt ($ mil.): —
No. of shares (mil.): 156
Dividends
Yield: —
Payout: —
Market value ($ mil.): 15,195

**Stock History** NYSE: NYX

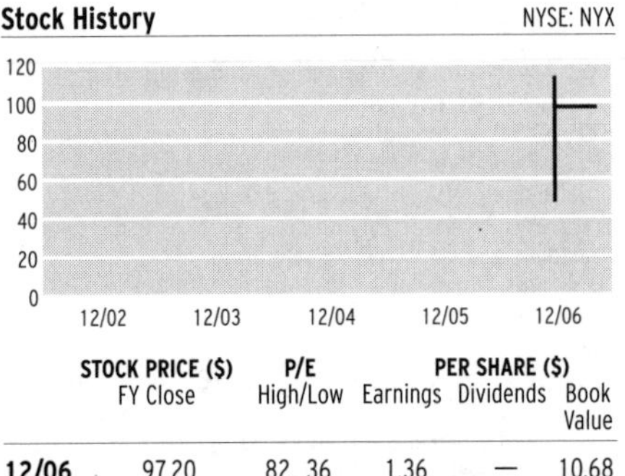


| | STOCK PRICE ($) FY Close | P/E High/Low | PER SHARE ($) Earnings | Dividends | Book Value |
|---|---|---|---|---|---|
| **12/06** | 97.20 | 82 36 | 1.36 | — | 10.68 |

# Occidental Petroleum

Harnessing its heritage of Western technical know-how, Occidental Petroleum engages in oil and gas exploration and production and makes basic chemicals, plastics, and petrochemicals. The oil giant has proved reserves of 2.9 billion barrels of oil equivalent in the US, the Middle East, and Latin America. It owns 76% of OxyVinyls, the #1 producer of polyvinyl chloride (PVC) resin in North America. Subsidiary Occidental Chemical (OxyChem) produces acids, chlorine, and specialty products. Occidental Petroleum also has an energy trading and marketing operation, Occidental Energy Marketing. In 2006 the government of Ecuador seized Occidental Petroleum's Ecuadorian assets as part of a nationalization drive.

After years of languishing, Occidental has emerged as a profitable company once again, and may be a prime candidate for acquisition by a larger oil producer. After nearly a 20-year absence from US markets, Libyan oil has begun to be imported by Occidental. Occidental, Petroleum Development Oman, and the Oman government have agreed to form a joint venture for the purpose of developing the Mukhaizna heavy oil field, one of the largest in Oman.

Occidental has reworked its business and created two divisions, eastern and western hemispheres, for its oil and gas operations. To finance its purchase of the US government's 78% interest in California's historic and underused Elk Hills oil field, the company has divested its natural gas pipeline and marketing operation, MidCon, and sold off noncore oil and gas properties in the US, Venezuela, and the Netherlands. All told, Occidental has shed assets producing some 46,000 barrels of oil per day and let go about a quarter of its workforce.

In 2006 Plains Exploration and Production sold non-core oil and gas properties to Occidental for $865 million. That year, Occidental reduced its stake in Lyondell Chemical from 12% to 8%. The following year Occidental sold its remaining Lyondell shares on the open market.

## HISTORY

Founded in 1920, Occidental Petroleum struggled until 1956, when billionaire industrialist Dr. Armand Hammer sank $100,000 into the company, then worth $34,000. It drilled two wells, and both came in. Hammer eventually gained control of the company.

Occidental's discovery of California's second-largest gas field (1959) was followed by a concession from Libya's King Idris (1966) and the discovery of a billion-barrel Libyan oil field. In 1968 Occidental bought Signal Oil's European refining and marketing business as an outlet for the Libyan oil. It also diversified, buying Island Creek Coal and Hooker Chemical.

In 1969 Occidental sold 51% of its Libyan production to the Libyan government under duress (after Idris was ousted). It soon began oil exploration in Latin America (1971) and in the North Sea (1972-73), where it discovered the lucrative Piper field. Other projects included a 20-year fertilizer-for-ammonia deal with the USSR (1974) and a coal joint venture with China (1985).

During the 1980s Occidental sold some foreign assets and bought US natural gas pipeline firm MidCon (1986). It also bought Iowa Beef Processors (IBP) for stock worth $750 million (1981) and then spun off 49% of it in 1987 for $960 million.

In 1983 Hammer hired Ray Irani to revive Occidental's ailing chemicals business (losses that year: $38 million). Irani integrated operations to ensure higher margins during industry downturns and purchased Diamond Shamrock Chemicals (1986), Shell's vinyl chloride monomer unit (1987), a DuPont chloralkali facility (1987), and Cain Chemical (1988). OxyChem's profits reached almost $1.1 billion by 1989.

Hammer died in 1990, and Irani became CEO. In 1991, to reduce debt, Occidental exited the Chinese coal business and sold the North Sea oil properties. Occidental also spun off IBP, the largest US red-meat producer, to its shareholders.

Occidental paid Irani $95 million in 1997 to buy out his employment contract; instead, his compensation (a minimum of $1.2 million a year) was tied to the company's fortunes. That year Occidental's $3.65 billion bid won the US government's auction of its 78% stake in California's Elk Hills petroleum reserve, one of the largest in the continental US.

To help pay for Elk Hills, the company sold MidCon to K N Energy for $3.1 billion in 1998. Occidental traded its petrochemical operations to Equistar Chemicals, a partnership between Lyondell and Millennium Chemicals, for $425 million and a 29.5% stake.

In a venture with The Geon Company, Occidental in 1999 formed Oxy Vinyls, the #1 producer of polyvinyl chloride (PVC) resin in North America. That year also brought a windfall: Chevron agreed to pay Occidental $775 million to settle a lawsuit stemming from the 1982 withdrawal by Gulf (later acquired by Chevron) of an offer to buy Cities Service (later acquired by Occidental).

In 2000 Occidental sold its 29% stake in Canadian Occidental back to the company for $828 million to help fund the purchase of oil and gas producer Altura Energy, a partnership of BP and Shell Oil, for $3.6 billion. Later that year the company sold some Gulf of Mexico properties to Apache for $385 million.

Occidental acquired a new exploration block in Yemen in 2001.

The company sold its 29.5% of Equistar Chemicals to Lyondell Chemical in 2002 in exchange for a 21% stake in Lyondell (Occidental now owns 14%). In 2005 it acquired a stake in a gas and oil production site located in Texas' Permian Basin from ExxonMobil for a reported $972 million. Occidental closed the acquisition of Vintage Petroleum for a reported $3.8 billion in early 2006.

## EXECUTIVES

**Chairman, President, and CEO:** Ray R. Irani, age 72, $4,940,000 pay
**EVP, General Counsel, and Secretary:** Donald P. de Brier, age 66, $1,226,000 pay
**EVP Finance and Planning:** James M. Leinert, age 54
**EVP Human Resources:** Richard W. Hallock, age 62
**EVP; President, Eastern Hemisphere, Oxy Oil and Gas; President, Occidental Middle East Development:** R. Casey Olson, age 53, $1,077,500 pay
**EVP; President, Western Hemisphere, Occidental Oil and Gas:** John W. Morgan, age 53
**SVP and CFO:** Stephen I. (Steve) Chazen, age 60, $1,920,000 pay

**VP and CIO:** Donald L. Moore Jr.
**VP and Treasurer:** James R. Havert, age 65
**VP and Controller:** Jim A. Leonard, age 56
**VP Acquisitions and Corporate Finance:** Todd A. Stevens
**VP Government Relations:** Robert M. McGee
**VP Internal Audit:** Roy Pineci
**VP Health, Environment, and Safety:** Richard A. Swan
**VP Investor Relations:** Christopher G. (Chris) Stavros
**VP Tax and Chief Tax Counsel:** Michael S. Stutts
**VP Communications and Public Affairs:** Richard S. Kline
**President, Occidental Chemical:** B. Chuck Anderson, age 47
**Auditors:** KPMG LLP

## LOCATIONS

**HQ:** Occidental Petroleum Corporation
10889 Wilshire Blvd., Los Angeles, CA 90024
**Phone:** 310-208-8800 **Fax:** 310-443-6690
**Web:** www.oxy.com

Occidental Petroleum's major US oil and gas holdings are in California, Kansas, Oklahoma, and Texas. It is also involved in oil and gas production in Canada, Colombia, Ecuador, Libya, Oman, Pakistan, Qatar, and Yemen.

### 2006 Sales

| | $ mil. | % of total |
|---|---|---|
| US | 11,857 | 67 |
| Qatar | 1,639 | 9 |
| Colombia | 995 | 6 |
| Yemen | 877 | 5 |
| Oman | 633 | 4 |
| Libya | 549 | 3 |
| Argentina | 527 | 3 |
| Canada | 249 | 1 |
| Pakistan | 198 | 1 |
| Other countries | 137 | 1 |
| Adjustments | 499 | — |
| **Total** | **18,160** | **100** |

## PRODUCTS/OPERATIONS

### 2006 Sales

| | $ mil. | % of total |
|---|---|---|
| Oil & gas | 12,676 | 72 |
| Chemicals | 4,815 | 27 |
| Other | 170 | 1 |
| Adjustments | 499 | — |
| **Total** | **18,160** | **100** |

### Selected Subsidiaries

Occidental Chemical Corp. (OxyChem; chemicals, polymers, and plastics)
Occidental Energy Marketing, Inc. (energy marketing)
Occidental Exploration and Production Company (exploration and production)
OxyVinyls, LP (76%, polyvinyl chloride)

## COMPETITORS

Apache
Ashland
BP
ConocoPhillips
Devon Energy
Dow Chemical
DuPont
Eastman Chemical
Exxon Mobil
Hess
Huntsman
Imperial Oil
J.M. Huber
Koch
Lyondell Chemical
Marathon Oil
Olin
PEMEX
Royal Dutch Shell
Sunoco
TOTAL

## HISTORICAL FINANCIALS

Company Type: Public

### Income Statement

FYE: December 31

| | REVENUE ($ mil.) | NET INCOME ($ mil.) | NET PROFIT MARGIN | EMPLOYEES |
|---|---|---|---|---|
| **12/06** | 18,160 | 4,182 | 23.0% | 8,886 |
| **12/05** | 16,259 | 5,281 | 32.5% | 8,017 |
| **12/04** | 11,513 | 2,568 | 22.3% | 7,209 |
| **12/03** | 9,447 | 1,527 | 16.2% | 7,133 |
| **12/02** | 7,491 | 989 | 13.2% | 7,244 |
| **Annual Growth** | 24.8% | 43.4% | — | 5.2% |

### 2006 Year-End Financials

Debt ratio: 13.7%
Return on equity: 24.4%
Cash ($ mil.): 1,579
Current ratio: 1.27
Long-term debt ($ mil.): 2,619
No. of shares (mil.): 871
Dividends
Yield: 1.6%
Payout: 16.5%
Market value ($ mil.): 42,515

### Stock History

NYSE: OXY

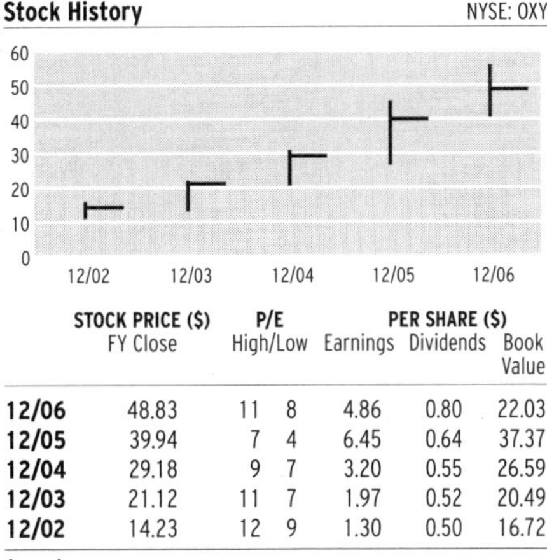


| | STOCK PRICE ($) FY Close | P/E High | P/E Low | PER SHARE ($) Earnings | Dividends | Book Value |
|---|---|---|---|---|---|---|
| **12/06** | 48.83 | 11 | 8 | 4.86 | 0.80 | 22.03 |
| **12/05** | 39.94 | 7 | 4 | 6.45 | 0.64 | 37.37 |
| **12/04** | 29.18 | 9 | 7 | 3.20 | 0.55 | 26.59 |
| **12/03** | 21.12 | 11 | 7 | 1.97 | 0.52 | 20.49 |
| **12/02** | 14.23 | 12 | 9 | 1.30 | 0.50 | 16.72 |
| **Annual Growth** | 36.1% | — | — | 39.1% | 12.5% | 7.1% |

# Office Depot

Paper clips are big money; just ask Office Depot. Operating the world's #2 chain of office supply stores (behind Staples), the company sells office supplies through more than 1,300 company-owned and licensed locations worldwide. The big-box retail stores, which number more than 1,200 in the US alone, sell to both consumers and small and medium-sized businesses. In addition to typical office supplies, its stores offer computer hardware and software, office furniture, art and school supplies, and printing and copying services. Office Depot also sells goods through catalogs and call centers, the Internet, and a contract sales force.

The company has been aggressively expanding its North American retail operations (which account for 45% of sales), adding close to 100 locations in 2005 and 2006, with plans to open another 150 stores during 2007. In 2004 it acquired about 125 retail locations from troubled toy seller Toys "R" Us, converting 50 of those into Office Depot locations and selling off the remainder. Ultimately, the company feels there is room to double its presence in the US market from 1,000 to 2,000 stores.

Office Depot is also experimenting with a new retail format, Millennium2 (M2), that minimizes construction costs and strategically locates products to encourage sales consultation.

Office Depot's business service division, accounting for about 30% of revenue, includes catalog and online sales, as well as its contract sales business. The company boosted this segment with its 2006 purchase of Allied Office Products (AOP), the largest independent dealer of office products and services in the US.

During 2005 the company shuttered its Viking Office Products brand in the US, consolidating its catalog sales under the Office Depot banner. (It still markets products through Viking in international markets.) The business services division also sells technology products through Tech Depot (formerly 4SURE.com).

While its North American business has been steadily improving, Office Depot has suffered somewhat overseas. Its international operations (almost 25% of business) have lagged due primarily to economic pressures in Europe, leading the company to streamline and centralize some of its operations and to outsource others. In 2006 it acquired a controlling interest in Best Office, a leading office supplier in South Korea, as well as a majority stake in AsiaEC, a leading dealer of office products and services in China.

## HISTORY

Pat Scher, Stephen Dougherty, and Jack Kopkin opened the first Office Depot, one of the first office supply superstores, in Lauderdale Lakes, Florida, in 1986. Scher was selected as chairman. By the end of the year the fledgling company had opened two more stores (both in Florida).

Office Depot opened seven more stores in 1987. When Scher died of leukemia that year, the company recruited David Fuente, former president of Sherwin-Williams' Paint Store Division, as chairman and CEO. Office Depot continued its breakneck expansion under Fuente. In 1988 — the year the company went public — it opened 16 stores and broke into new markets in four states.

The chain stepped up its pace, and by 1990 it had expanded into several other areas, including the South and Midwest. Office Depot also added computers and peripherals and opened its first delivery center.

In 1991 the company became North America's #1 office products retailer and expanded its presence in the West through the acquisition of Office Club, another warehouse-type office supply chain with 59 stores (most in California). Fuente remained chairman and CEO, while former Office Club CEO Mark Begelman became president and COO. (Begelman, who left in 1995 and eventually formed the MARS music chain, had founded the first Office Club in 1987 in Concord, California; he took it public in 1989.)

The company entered the international market with its 1992 purchase of Canada's H. Q. Office International and through licensing agreements in 1993 (in Colombia and Israel). Office Depot created its business services division by acquiring various contract stationers, including Eastman Office Products (the West Coast's #1 contract office supplier), in the mid-1990s, and added locations in Mexico and Poland; it established a joint venture in France with retailer Carrefour in 1996.

Also in 1996 Office Depot announced a $3.4 billion agreement to be acquired by Staples, which would have created a company with more than 1,100 stores. However, the government blocked the purchase on antitrust grounds in 1997 and the agreement dissolved. Unfettered by merger distractions, Office Depot resumed opening stores at a rapid pace, including two in Thailand, and took its catalog and delivery services online. It then established a joint venture with Japanese retailer Deo Deo.

In 1998 Office Depot acquired Viking Office Products in a $2.7 billion deal. With more than 60% of its sales coming from outside the US, Viking augmented Office Depot's already strong delivery network and international expansion. Office Depot acquired the remaining 50% of its French operations from Carrefour in 1998 and the remaining 50% of its Japanese operations from Deo Deo in 1999.

Office Depot started putting Internet kiosks in its US stores in 2000, allowing customers to browse and shop company Web sites. In July 2000 Bruce Nelson, CEO of Viking, replaced Fuente as CEO of Office Depot. Citing weak computer sales and high warehouse prices, the company closed about 70 stores, and cut its workforce. Later that year the company opened two prototype stores, the first of 11 planned by the end of the year. In early 2002 Nelson was named chairman as well as CEO, after Fuente stepped down.

Office Depot sold its Australian operations to Officeworks, a unit of Coles Myer in January 2003. Also that year the company acquired the retail operations of French office supplier Guilbert from Pinault-Printemps-Redoute, a move that doubled the company's business in Europe. (Staples had acquired Guilbert's mail order business the previous year.)

Nelson left the company and Neil Austrian served as interim head. Office Depot named AutoZone leader Steve Odland as CEO and chairman in 2005.

In May 2006 the company acquired privately held Allied Office Products (AOP), the largest independent dealer of office products and services in the US. AOP became part of Office Depot's North American Business Solutions Division.

## EXECUTIVES

**Chairman and CEO:** Steve Odland, age 48, $1,000,000 pay
**President, International:** Charles E. Brown, age 53, $615,000 pay
**President, North American Retail:** Carl (Chuck) Rubin, age 47, $568,615 pay (prior to promotion)
**EVP and CFO:** Patricia A. (Pat) McKay, age 49, $525,000 pay
**EVP Business Development, Information Technology, and Supply Chain:** Monica Luechtefeld, age 58
**EVP Human Resources:** Daisy L. Vanderlinde, age 55, $416,000 pay
**EVP, General Counsel, and Corporate Secretary:** Elisa D. Garcia
**EVP and Managing Director, Europe:** Dirk Collin
**SVP and CIO:** Timothy (Tim) Toews
**SVP and Chief Compliance Officer:** Robert Brewer
**SVP Finance and Controller:** Randy Pianin, age 43
**SVP Retail Operations:** George Hill
**SVP Supply Chain Logistics:** Dennis T. Andruskiewicz
**SVP Tax:** Jeffrey H. Aiken
**SVP and Controller:** Jennifer Moline, age 49
**SVP; President, Tech Depot:** Bruce Martin
**SVP, European Operations:** Rob Vale
**SVP and Managing Director, Asia:** Teddy P. Chung
**Director of Investor Relations:** Sean McHugh
**Director of Public Relations:** Brian Levine
**President, North American Business Solutions Division:** Steven M. (Steve) Schmidt, age 52
**Auditors:** Deloitte & Touche LLP

## LOCATIONS

**HQ:** Office Depot, Inc.
2200 Old Germantown Rd., Delray Beach, FL 33445
**Phone:** 561-438-4800 **Fax:** 561-438-4001
**Web:** www.officedepot.com

Office Depot has 20 distribution centers in the US. It also has 32 distribution centers and 30 call centers outside North America.

### 2006 Locations

| | No. |
|---|---|
| California | 155 |
| Texas | 135 |
| Florida | 126 |
| Illinois | 59 |
| Georgia | 53 |
| Louisiana | 35 |
| Washington | 35 |
| Colorado | 34 |
| North Carolina | 33 |
| Maryland | 29 |
| Michigan | 27 |
| Tennessee | 27 |
| Virginia | 27 |
| Missouri | 25 |
| Pennsylvania | 25 |
| New Jersey | 23 |
| Indiana | 22 |
| Alabama | 21 |
| South Carolina | 20 |
| Kentucky | 19 |
| Oregon | 18 |
| Nevada | 16 |
| Ohio | 16 |
| Mississippi | 15 |
| Oklahoma | 15 |
| New York | 14 |
| Wisconsin | 13 |
| Minnesota | 12 |
| Other states | 91 |
| **Total** | **1,140** |

### 2006 International Retail Stores

| | No. |
|---|---|
| France | 43 |
| Israel | 40 |
| Canada | 29 |
| Japan | 22 |
| South Korea | 11 |
| Hungary | 9 |
| **Total** | **154** |

## PRODUCTS/OPERATIONS

### 2006 Sales

| | $ mil. | % of total |
|---|---|---|
| North American Retail | 6,789.4 | 45 |
| North American Business Solutions | 4,576.8 | 31 |
| International | 3,644.5 | 24 |
| **Total** | **15,010.7** | **100** |

### Selected Products

Office furniture
- Armoires
- Bookcases
- Carts and stands
- Chairmats and floormats
- Chairs
- Desks
- Filing cabinets
- Lamps and light bulbs
- Office furnishings
- Panel systems
- Tables
- Workstations

Office supplies
- Basic supplies and labels
- Binders and accessories
- Breakroom and janitorial supplies
- Business cases
- Calendars and planners
- Desk accessories
- Executive gifts
- Filing and storage
- Paper and envelopes
- Pens, pencils, and markers
- School supplies

Technology products
- Audio-visual equipment and supplies
- Cameras
- Computers and related accessories (including monitors and printers)
- Copiers
- Data storage supplies
- Fax machines
- Networking supplies
- PDAs
- Software

## COMPETITORS

Best Buy
BJ's Wholesale Club
CDW
Circuit City
CompUSA
Corporate Express
Costco Wholesale
Danka
DELUXEPINPOINT
Fry's Electronics
IKON
Insight Enterprises
Kinko's
Mail Boxes Etc.
OfficeMax
RadioShack
School Specialty
Staples
Systemax
Unisource
United Stationers
Wal-Mart

## HISTORICAL FINANCIALS

Company Type: Public

### Income Statement

FYE: Saturday nearest December 31

| | REVENUE ($ mil.) | NET INCOME ($ mil.) | NET PROFIT MARGIN | EMPLOYEES |
|---|---|---|---|---|
| **12/06** | 15,011 | 516 | 3.4% | 52,000 |
| **12/05** | 14,279 | 274 | 1.9% | 47,000 |
| **12/04** | 13,565 | 336 | 2.5% | 47,000 |
| **12/03** | 12,359 | 276 | 2.2% | 46,000 |
| **12/02** | 11,357 | 311 | 2.7% | 43,000 |
| **Annual Growth** | 7.2% | 13.5% | — | 4.9% |

### 2006 Year-End Financials

Debt ratio: 21.9%
Return on equity: 19.3%
Cash ($ mil.): 174
Current ratio: 1.16
Long-term debt ($ mil.): 571
No. of shares (mil.): 426
Dividends
Yield: —
Payout: —
Market value ($ mil.): 16,267

### Stock History

NYSE: ODP

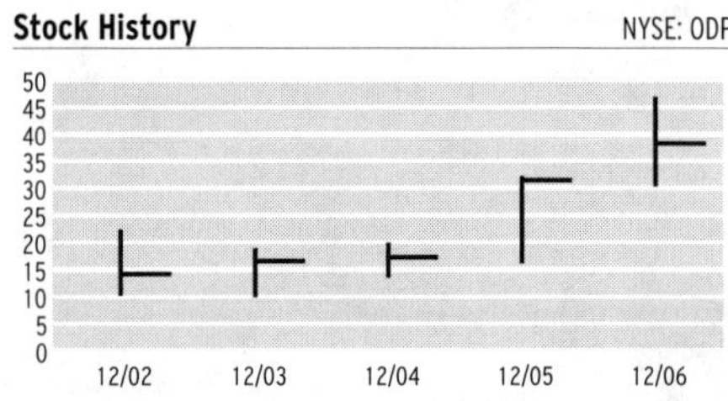

| | STOCK PRICE ($) FY Close | P/E High | P/E Low | PER SHARE ($) Earnings | Dividends | Book Value |
|---|---|---|---|---|---|---|
| **12/06** | 38.17 | 26 | 17 | 1.79 | — | 6.12 |
| **12/05** | 31.40 | 37 | 19 | 0.87 | — | 9.22 |
| **12/04** | 17.24 | 18 | 13 | 1.06 | — | 10.32 |
| **12/03** | 16.51 | 21 | 12 | 0.88 | — | 9.01 |
| **12/02** | 14.16 | 22 | 11 | 0.98 | — | 7.44 |
| **Annual Growth** | 28.1% | — | — | 16.3% | — | (4.8%) |

# OfficeMax

This company is taking the office supply business to the max. OfficeMax (formerly Boise Cascade) is the #3 office products retailer in North America (behind Staples and Office Depot), with some 900 superstores in the US, Mexico, Puerto Rico, and the US Virgin Islands. The stores offer about 10,000 name-brand and OfficeMax-branded products, including paper, pens, forms, and organizers, as well as office furniture and a wide range of technology products. OfficeMax also provides printing and document services through its ImPress store-within-a-store. In addition to its retail outlets, the company's contract division sells directly to business and government customers through field agents, telesales, and catalogs.

Looking to improve its balance sheet, OfficeMax announced a major restructuring effort in 2006 that saw the company close about 110 underperforming locations in the US. Meanwhile, it opened about 60 new locations during the year.

The office products company is also rolling out a new retail store prototype that abandons the warehouse-style format and instead highlights small- and home-office solutions in a warmer atmosphere. OfficeMax is furthering its differentiation strategy with a licensing deal announced in 2007 with upscale gadget retailer Sharper Image. Sharper Image will make a line of products for OfficeMax, to be sold under the brand Sharper Image Office.

Office and building products manufacturer Boise Cascade acquired OfficeMax in 2003 for $1.2 billion and changed its name in 2004 after selling its manufacturing operations to Madison Dearborn Partners for $3.7 billion. The sale of the paper and building materials assets was supposed to allow the company to focus on expanding its retail operations, but an accounting scandal led to the resignation of CFO Brian Anderson early in 2005 after just two months on the job.

Shortly afterward CEO Christopher Milliken also resigned and former Boise Cascade CEO George Harad (who had engineered the 2003 acquisition of OfficeMax) was called back into action. Sam Duncan, formerly CEO at ShopKo Stores, was tapped as Milliken's permanent replacement.

## HISTORY

Boise Cascade got its start in 1957 with the merger of two small lumber companies — Boise Payette Lumber Company (based in Boise, Idaho) and Cascade Lumber Company (Yakima, Washington). The business diversified in the 1960s under the leadership of Robert Hansberger, moving into office-products distribution in 1964. A number of acquisitions followed, including Ebasco Industries (1969), a consulting, engineering, and construction firm. By 1970 Boise Cascade had made more than 30 buys to diversify into building materials, paper products, real estate, recreational vehicles (RVs), and publishing.

In the early 1970s the company suffered a timber shortage as its access to public timberlands dwindled. Its plans to develop recreational communities in California, Hawaii, and Washington met opposition from residents, causing Boise Cascade to scrap all but six of the 29 projects.

In 1972 high costs related to the remaining projects left the company in debt. John Fery replaced Hansberger as president that year and sold companies not directly related to the company's core forest-product operations.

In the late 1980s and early 1990s Boise sold more nonstrategic operations, including its Specialty Paperboard Division in 1989. It sold more than half of its corrugated-container plants in 1992 to focus on manufacturing forest products and distributing building materials and office supplies.

Boise Cascade also sold its wholesale office-product business in 1992 to focus on direct sales to big buyers such as IBM and Boeing. The company sold off its Canadian subsidiary, Rainy River Forest Products, during 1994 and 1995. Resurgent paper prices resulted in a profit in 1995, Boise Cascade's first since 1990.

Also in 1995, in a move into the international paper market, Boise Cascade signed a joint venture agreement with Shenzhen Leasing to form Zhuhai Hiwin Boise Cascade, a Chinese manufacturer of carbonless paper. That year it sold a minority stake in Boise Cascade Office Products (BCOP) to the public.

The company sold its coated-papers business to paper and packaging heavyweight Mead in 1996 for $639 million. The following year Boise began harvesting its first quick-growth cottonwood trees (specially grown to cut the cost of harvesting from traditional slow-growth hardwood plantations). Also in 1997 BCOP bought Jean-Paul Guisset, an office-products direct marketer in France. Although this acquisition boosted sales and increased the company's European presence, company profits suffered that year because of weak paper prices.

The low price of paper in 1998 prompted the company to close four sawmills and a research and development center. Restructuring costs associated with the closures and a fire at the company's Medford, Oregon, plywood plant led to a net income loss for the year.

In 1999 Boise bought Wallace Computer Services, a contract stationer business, and broadened its building-supply distribution network nationwide by acquiring Furman Lumber, a building-supplies distributor. In 2000 Boise Cascade completed the purchase of the 19% of Boise Office Solutions that it didn't already own. The company also sold its European office products operations for $335 million.

Because of the decline in federal timber sales, in 2001 the company closed its plywood mill and lumber operations in Emmett, Idaho, and a sawmill in Cascade, Idaho. In 2002 lagging profits prompted Boise to implement cost-cutting procedures. In 2003 the company pinned its hopes for growth on the office product segment with the acquisition of OfficeMax for nearly $1.2 billion in cash and stock. The deal put Boise Cascade's office products business on par with industry leaders Staples and Office Depot.

The company sold its paper, forest products, and timberland assets to investment firm Madison Dearborn Partners for $3.7 billion in October 2004. In late 2004 OfficeMax named Christopher Milliken, a former Boise Cascade executive, as CEO, but he resigned after only four months on the job. Former ShopKo Stores CEO Sam Duncan was tapped as his replacement.

In August 2006 the company moved its headquarters from Itasca, Illinois, to nearby Naperville.

## EXECUTIVES

**Chairman, President, and CEO:** Sam K. Duncan, age 54, $1,438,461 pay
**EVP and CFO:** Don Civgin, age 45, $174,039 pay
**EVP Merchandising:** Ryan T. Vero, age 37, $626,950 pay
**EVP, General Counsel, and Secretary:** Matthew R. (Matt) Broad, age 47
**EVP Marketing:** David A. (Dave) Goudge
**EVP Merchandising and Retail:** Steven S. (Steve) Embree
**EVP Retail Stores:** Harold L. Mulet
**EVP Supply Chain:** Reuben E. Slone
**EVP Human Resources:** Perry S. Zukowski
**SVP and Controller:** Phillip P. DePaul, age 36, $327,750 pay
**SVP; President, Grand & Toy:** Pete Vanexan
**SVP International:** Carol B. Moerdyk, age 56
**SVP Marketing:** Scott Williams
**SVP Sales, Contract:** Mike Meehan
**SVP and Managing Director, Australasian Operations:** David Kelly
**SVP Marketing and Advertising:** Bob Thacker
**SVP OfficeMax Print and Document Services:** Brian Norris
**VP and Treasurer:** John S. Jennings
**VP Diversity and Inclusion:** Carolynn Brooks
**VP and Secretary:** Susan Wagner-Fleming
**VP and General Manager, Chicago:** Paul Moran
**CIO:** Randy G. Burdick
**Managing Director, Hawaii:** Rudy Mayo
**Director of Marketing Communications:** William (Bill) Bonner
**Auditors:** KPMG LLP

## LOCATIONS

**HQ:** OfficeMax Incorporated
263 Shuman Blvd., Naperville, IL 60563
**Phone:** 630-438-7800 **Fax:** 630-864-4422
**Web:** www.officemax.com

OfficeMax has about 50 distribution centers, six call centers, and some 1,000 retail stores in Australia, Canada, Mexico, New Zealand, Puerto Rico, and the US.

**2006 Locations**

| | No. |
|---|---|
| US | |
| California | 76 |
| Texas | 64 |
| Florida | 58 |
| Illinois | 58 |
| Ohio | 51 |
| Michigan | 41 |
| Arizona | 37 |
| Minnesota | 37 |
| Wisconsin | 31 |
| New York | 30 |
| Colorado | 28 |
| Georgia | 28 |
| Pennsylvania | 28 |
| North Carolina | 28 |
| Missouri | 25 |
| Virginia | 22 |
| Washington | 20 |
| Tennessee | 18 |
| Indiana | 14 |
| Utah | 13 |
| Nevada | 12 |
| Alabama | 11 |
| Oregon | 11 |
| Kansas | 10 |
| Massachusetts | 9 |
| New Mexico | 9 |
| Iowa | 8 |
| Nebraska | 8 |
| Hawaii | 6 |
| Idaho | 6 |
| Kentucky | 6 |
| South Carolina | 6 |
| Mississippi | 5 |
| Other states | 33 |
| Mexico | 55 |
| Puerto Rico | 10 |
| U.S. Virgin Islands | 2 |
| **Total** | **914** |

## 2006 Sales

| | $ mil. | % of total |
|---|---|---|
| US | 7,617 | 85 |
| Other countries | 1,349 | 15 |
| **Total** | **8,966** | **100** |

## PRODUCTS/OPERATIONS

### 2006 Sales

| | $ mil. | % of total |
|---|---|---|
| OfficeMax, Contract | 4,715 | 53 |
| OfficeMax, Retail | 4,251 | 47 |
| **Total** | **8,966** | **100** |

### 2006 Contract Sales

| | % of total |
|---|---|
| Office supplies & paper | 54 |
| Technology products | 33 |
| Office furniture | 13 |
| **Total** | **100** |

### 2006 Retail Sales

| | % of total |
|---|---|
| Technology products | 52 |
| Office supplies & paper | 37 |
| Office furniture | 11 |
| **Total** | **100** |

## COMPETITORS

Best Buy
BJ's Wholesale Club
CDW
Circuit City
CompUSA
Corporate Express
Costco Wholesale
DELUXEPINPOINT
IKON
Insight Enterprises
Kinko's
Mail Boxes Etc.
Office Depot
RadioShack
SAM'S CLUB
Staples
Systemax
Unisource
United Stationers
Wal-Mart

## HISTORICAL FINANCIALS

Company Type: Public

### Income Statement

FYE: December 31

| | REVENUE ($ mil.) | NET INCOME ($ mil.) | NET PROFIT MARGIN | EMPLOYEES |
|---|---|---|---|---|
| **12/06** | 8,966 | 92 | 1.0% | 36,000 |
| **12/05** | 9,158 | (74) | — | 35,000 |
| **12/04** | 13,270 | 173 | 1.3% | 41,000 |
| **12/03** | 8,245 | 8 | 0.1% | 55,618 |
| **12/02** | 7,412 | 11 | 0.2% | 24,111 |
| **Annual Growth** | 4.9% | 68.8% | — | 10.5% |

### 2006 Year-End Financials

Debt ratio: 96.0%
Return on equity: 5.1%
Cash ($ mil.): 282
Current ratio: 1.37
Long-term debt ($ mil.): 1,854
No. of shares (mil.): 75
Dividends
Yield: 1.2%
Payout: 50.4%
Market value ($ mil.): 3,719

### Stock History

NYSE: OMX

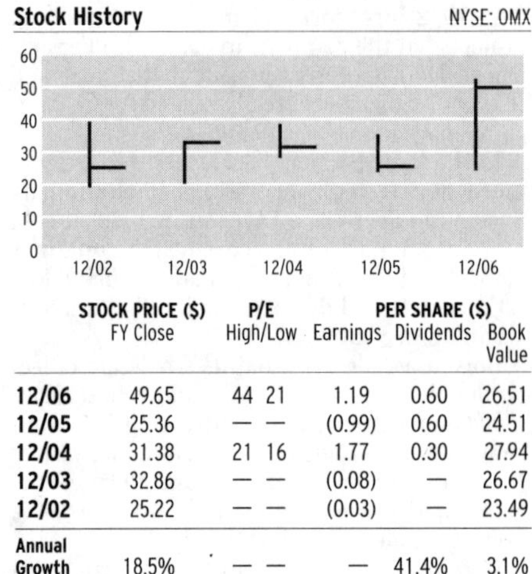


| | STOCK PRICE ($) FY Close | P/E High/Low | | PER SHARE ($) Earnings | Dividends | Book Value |
|---|---|---|---|---|---|---|
| **12/06** | 49.65 | 44 | 21 | 1.19 | 0.60 | 26.51 |
| **12/05** | 25.36 | — | — | (0.99) | 0.60 | 24.51 |
| **12/04** | 31.38 | 21 | 16 | 1.77 | 0.30 | 27.94 |
| **12/03** | 32.86 | — | — | (0.08) | — | 26.67 |
| **12/02** | 25.22 | — | — | (0.03) | — | 23.49 |
| **Annual Growth** | 18.5% | — | — | — | 41.4% | 3.1% |

# Olin Corporation

Brass, bleach, and bullets are all in a day's work for Olin. The company's Metals unit (more than half of sales) makes copper and copper alloy sheets, strips, clad metal (Posit-bond, including coin metals popular with the US Mint), foil (Copperbond), and stainless-steel strips. The segment's customers are primarily in the auto, housing, electronics, and telecom industries. Olin Chlor Alkali Products manufactures chemicals used to make bleach, water purification and swimming pool chemicals, pulp and paper processing agents, and (PVC) plastics. Olin also makes Winchester-brand ammunition. US customers account for almost all of Olin's sales, and the US government alone accounts for approximately 10%.

Olin has been spinning off divisions and divesting mediocre operations in order to focus on its core products: metals, chemicals, and ammunition. However, the company is widening its focus within those segments, in part through joint ventures in Japan (with Yamaha) and China (with Luoyang Copper). Yamaha-Olin produces high-performance alloys, while the Chinese operation is a primarily metal service center. Both target the electronics and telecommunications industries. Olin also has a technical alliance with German company Wieland-Werke to develop copper alloys.

In 2007 Olin offered to buy chlor-alkali chemicals maker Pioneer Companies for about $415 million. The deal would make Olin the #3 chlor-alkali producer in North America.

## HISTORY

Vermont-born engineer Franklin Olin founded Equitable Powder in East Alton, Illinois, in 1892, originally to make blasting powder for midwestern coal fields. By 1898 the company, renamed Western Cartridge, was also making ammunition for small arms.

When WWI increased demand for military cartridges, Western Cartridge built a brass mill. After the war it began making custom brass and other copper alloys for industrial customers. The company bought Winchester Repeating Arms, maker of the famous Winchester Model 1876 repeating rifles, in 1931. During WWII Western Cartridge developed the US carbine and M-1 rifles.

The various businesses of Western Cartridge merged as Olin Industries in 1944. Franklin then retired, handing the company to sons John and Spencer.

Enriched by the war effort, Olin Industries grew. In 1949 it began making cellophane, and in 1951 it acquired Frost Lumber Industries and Ecusta Paper, a maker of cigarette papers. Olin Industries merged with Mathieson Chemical in 1954 to form Olin Mathieson Chemical, the fifth-largest US chemical company.

The Mathieson Alkali Works was founded in Saltville, Virginia, in 1892 to produce alkalis using a process acquired from English chemical firm Neil Mathieson. By 1909 the company began producing liquid chlorine, and in 1923 it built one of the earliest plants for producing synthetic ammonia. During WWII Mathieson manufactured chlorine for water purification and alkali chemicals for sanitation. In 1952 Mathieson acquired drugmaker Squibb.

Olin Mathieson continued to diversify in the mid-1950s, buying Blockson Chemical (industrial phosphates) and Brown Paper Mill (kraft paper bags and corrugated cardboard containers). Frost Lumber and Brown Paper Mill formed the Forest Products Division, later dubbed Olinkraft. In 1956 Olin Mathieson entered the aluminum business via a joint venture — just in time for a drop in aluminum demand.

In the 1960s the company began making urethane chemicals. It also created Olin-American, a subsidiary that built houses, and spun off Squibb. In 1969 it shortened its name to Olin Corporation and moved to Stamford, Connecticut.

The 1970s saw Olin reining in its diverse businesses. It spun off Olinkraft and sold its aluminum operations. During the 1980s Olin sold its sporting-arms business (but kept Winchester ammunition), as well as its paper, housing, and cellophane units. John Olin died in 1982. The company acquired Rockcor, which included Rocket Research, Pacific Electro Dynamics, and Physics International, in 1985.

Olin moved its headquarters to Norwalk, Connecticut, in 1995, the same year Spencer Olin died. In 1996, as the earnings potential of its ordnance and aerospace operations lagged, Olin spun them off as Primex Technologies. It also sold its isocyanate (used in plastics and adhesives) and other cyclical businesses. Olin bought the remaining 50% of its Niachlor chlor alkali joint venture from DuPont in 1997 after considering putting Niachlor up for sale.

Aspiring to become a leading basic-materials company, Olin spun off its specialty chemical business in early 1999 under the name Arch Chemicals. Citing regulatory issues, Olin cancelled plans in 2000 to form a chlor alkali chemicals joint venture with Occidental's OxyChem subsidiary. Olin acquired Monarch Brass & Copper Corp. for about $49 million in 2001. The next year it bought brass rod maker Chase Industries. Olin closed its copper and copper alloy sheet plant in Indianapolis in 2003.

## EXECUTIVES

**Chairman, President, and CEO:** Joseph D. Rupp, age 56, $772,500 pay
**VP and CFO:** John E. Fischer, age 51, $322,749 pay
**VP and Treasurer:** Stephen C. Curley, age 55
**VP, Human Resources:** Dennis R. McGough, age 58, $435,921 pay
**VP, General Counsel, and Secretary:** George H. Pain, age 56, $339,999 pay
**VP and Controller:** Todd A. Slater, age 43
**VP; President, Chlor Alkali Products Division:** John L. McIntosh, age 52, $320,253 pay
**VP, Strategic Planning:** G. Bruce Greer Jr., age 46
**President, A.J. Oster:** Daniel B. Becker
**VP; President, Winchester:** Richard M. (Dick) Hammett, age 60
**VP; President, Olin Brass:** Jeffrey J. Haferkamp, age 52, $284,004 pay
**Assistant Treasurer and Director, Investor Relations:** Larry P. Kromidas
**Auditors:** KPMG LLP

## LOCATIONS

**HQ:** Olin Corporation
190 Carondelet Plaza, Ste. 1530, Clayton, MO 63105
**Phone:** 314-480-1400 **Fax:** 314-862-7406
**Web:** www.olin.com

Olin has operations in Australia, Mexico, Puerto Rico, and the US, as well as joint ventures in Japan and China.

### 2006 Sales

| | $ mil. | % of total |
|---|---|---|
| US | 3,026.9 | 96 |
| Other countries | 124.9 | 4 |
| **Total** | **3,151.8** | **100** |

## PRODUCTS/OPERATIONS

### 2006 Sales and Operating Income

| | Sales | | Operating Income | |
|---|---|---|---|---|
| | $ mil. | % of total | $ mil. | % of total |
| Metals | 2,112.1 | 67 | 58.2 | 17 |
| Chlor Alkali Products | 666.1 | 21 | 256.3 | 78 |
| Winchester | 373.6 | 12 | 15.8 | 5 |
| Adjustments | — | — | (128.9) | — |
| **Total** | **3,151.8** | **100** | **201.4** | **100** |

### Selected Products

Metals
- Brass rod
- Clad metal (Posit-Bond, coinage blanks)
- Copper alloy welded tube
- Copper and copper alloy strip and sheet
- Fabricated products (builders' hardware, cartridge cases)
- Hermetic metal packaging (used by the microelectronics industry)
- Metal service centers
- Rolled copper foil (Copperbond)

Chlor Alkali Products
- Caustic soda
- Chlorine
- Hydrochloric acid
- Sodium hydrochlorite (industrial and institutional cleaning products)
- Sodium hydrosulfite (bleaching)

Winchester
- Ammunition (shot-shell, small-caliber, and rimfire)
- Government-owned arsenal operation (maintenance for the US Army)
- Industrial cartridges (eight-gauge loads and powder-actuated tool loads for the construction industry)

## COMPETITORS

Alliant Techsystems
Arch Chemicals
Blount
Dow Chemical
FMC
Formosa Plastics USA
Georgia Gulf
Herstal
Honeywell
ITOCHU
ITT Corp.
LG Group
Mitsubishi Chemical
Occidental Chemical
PPG
Remington Arms
Ryerson
Sterling Chemicals
Sumitomo Chemical
Vulcan Materials

## HISTORICAL FINANCIALS

Company Type: Public

### Income Statement

FYE: December 31

| | REVENUE ($ mil.) | NET INCOME ($ mil.) | NET PROFIT MARGIN | EMPLOYEES |
|---|---|---|---|---|
| **12/06** | 3,152 | 150 | 4.7% | 6,000 |
| **12/05** | 2,358 | 133 | 5.7% | 5,900 |
| **12/04** | 1,997 | 55 | 2.8% | 5,800 |
| **12/03** | 1,586 | (24) | — | 5,700 |
| **12/02** | 1,301 | (31) | — | 6,200 |
| **Annual Growth** | 24.8% | — | — | (0.8%) |

### 2006 Year-End Financials

Debt ratio: 46.4%
Return on equity: 30.9%
Cash ($ mil.): 276
Current ratio: 2.25
Long-term debt ($ mil.): 252
No. of shares (mil.): 73
Dividends
Yield: 4.8%
Payout: 38.8%
Market value ($ mil.): 1,211

### Stock History

NYSE: OLN

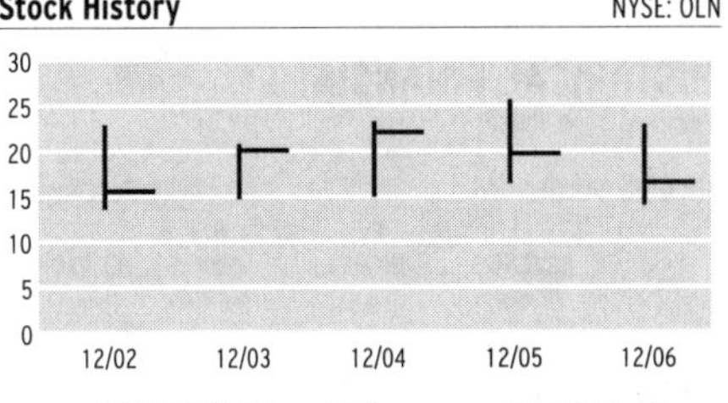


| | STOCK PRICE ($) FY Close | P/E High | P/E Low | PER SHARE ($) Earnings | Dividends | Book Value |
|---|---|---|---|---|---|---|
| **12/06** | 16.52 | 11 | 7 | 2.06 | 0.80 | 7.41 |
| **12/05** | 19.68 | 14 | 9 | 1.86 | 0.80 | 5.94 |
| **12/04** | 22.02 | 29 | 19 | 0.80 | 0.80 | 5.04 |
| **12/03** | 20.06 | — | — | (0.42) | 0.80 | 2.98 |
| **12/02** | 15.55 | — | — | (0.63) | 0.80 | 4.01 |
| **Annual Growth** | 1.5% | — | — | — | 0.0% | 16.6% |

# Omnicare, Inc.

With operations in nearly all 50 states, Omnicare wants to be omnipresent. The company is one of the largest providers of pharmacy and related services to long-term care facilities in the US. Omnicare dispenses drugs for nursing homes and provides computerized recordkeeping and billing for patients in its clients' facilities. It also offers drug therapy evaluation, drug administration monitoring, regulatory compliance oversight, and outcomes data. Omnicare's related services include infusion therapy, dialysis services, and medical supply distribution. After a year-long struggle, the company acquired NeighborCare in 2005.

While ironing out the wrinkles in the NeighborCare deal, the highly acquisitive Omnicare also acquired RxCrossroads in 2005, a mail-order specialty pharmaceutical company that specializes in providing pricey drugs used to treat chronic conditions, and excelleRx, which distributes pharmaceuticals and related products to hospice agencies in 47 states. The integration of NeighborCare clients into Omnicare's business has been troubled, and some facilities that were once served by NeighborCare have turned to other providers. Problems with its packaging facilities and a major health insurer also impacted Omnicare in 2006. As a result, the company has closed its Toledo, Ohio, packaging facility and contracted repackaging services from Cardinal Health. The company has parlayed its extensive database of geriatric health and drug information into a new name for itself as a contract research organization (CRO), and has been making acquisitions in the field, including Clinimetrics Research Associates, in 2004. It offers its CRO services to pharmaceutical, biotech, and medical device firms in nearly 30 countries worldwide. Omnicare plans to expand by providing its customers with a combination of pharmaceutical distribution services and clinical and information services, all geared towards serving the elderly, in order to mitigate revenue swings caused by decreases in Medicare reimbursements.

## HISTORY

In 1981 W. R. Grace subsidiaries Daylin and Chemed merged some health care units to form Omnicare, which was then spun off. Omnicare began a restructuring process in 1985 that reshaped the firm around pharmacy services for long-term care facilities. It acquired 17 long-term care pharmacies in 1993 alone.

As the baby boomers age, the company will continue to have a growing market for the long run. Using economies of scale to keep costs down, Omnicare began pursuing an aggressive acquisition strategy.

In 1994 the company teamed with Health Care and Retirement Corp., one of the US's largest nursing home operators. It acquired 17 pharmacy units in 1996, including those of Revco and several other retailers. In 1997 Omnicare expanded its operations by targeting assisted living providers and small rural hospitals. It continued acquiring pharmacy service providers (20 in 1997 — including its largest deal up to that time, American Medserve — and CompScript in 1998) and leveraged its treatment outcomes database with the addition of contract research organizations (Coromed, 1997; IBAH, 1998).

In 1998 Omnicare settled a lawsuit that alleged a company pharmacy had repackaged and resold unused medications originally sold to nursing homes (and paid for by Medicaid). The company also acquired Extendicare's pharmacy operations. In 1999 Omnicare expanded its services for the drug development industry with the purchase of a German clinical research organization; the company also acquired the pharmaceutical division of nursing home operator Life Care Services of America.

In 2000 Omnicare consolidated its three clinical research organizations into Omnicare Clinical Research. In 2003 the company acquired NCS HealthCare and Sun Healthcare's SunScript Pharmacy business in a move designed to strengthen its position as the largest supplier of pharmacy services to long-term care facilities in the US.

## EXECUTIVES

**Chairman:** Edward L. Hutton, age 86
**President, CEO, and Director:** Joel F. Gemunder, age 67, $4,105,467 pay
**EVP and COO:** Patrick E. Keefe
**SVP, CFO, and Director:** David W. Froesel Jr., age 54, $755,305 pay
**SVP and Secretary:** Cheryl D. Hodges, $624,520 pay
**SVP Sales and Marketing:** Kirk M. Pompeo, age 50
**SVP Strategic Planning and Development:** Leo P. Finn III, age 49
**VP and General Counsel:** Mark G. Kobasuk, age 48
**VP and Group Executive Operations Finance Group:** Robert E. Dries
**VP Data Processing:** D. Michael Laney
**President Omnicare Information Solutions:** Thomas W. Ludeke
**VP Purchasing:** Daniel J. Maloney
**VP Customer Development:** Beth Kinerk, age 37
**VP Analysis and Controls:** Regis T. Robbins
**VP Human Resources:** J. Michael Roberts
**VP and Chief Clinical Officer Pharmacy Services Professional Services Group:** Barbara J. Zarowitz
**VP Public Affairs:** Paul Baldwin
**VP Pharmacy Services New Business Programs:** Mary Lou Gradisek
**VP; SVP Omnicare Senior Pharmacy Services:** Robert A Smith
**VP; SVP Field Operations Omnicare Senior Pharmacy Services:** Jeffrey M. Stamps
**CEO Omnicare Clinical Research:** Dale B. Evans
**President and CEO excelleRx:** Calvin H. Knowlton
**President Omnicare Senior Health Outcomes:** W. Gary Erwin, age 53
**Auditors:** PricewaterhouseCoopers LLP

## LOCATIONS

**HQ:** Omnicare, Inc.
1600 RiverCenter II, 100 E. RiverCenter Blvd., Covington, KY 41011
**Phone:** 859-392-3300 **Fax:** 859-392-3333
**Web:** www.omnicare.com

Omnicare provides pharmacy and other services to nursing homes in 47 states. Its contract research operations provide research and development services in 29 countries.

## PRODUCTS/OPERATIONS

### 2006 Sales

| | $ mil. | % of total |
|---|---|---|
| Pharmacy services | 6,321.1 | 97 |
| CRO services | 171.8 | 3 |
| **Total** | **6,492.9** | **100** |

### 2006 Sources of Revenue

| | % of total |
|---|---|
| Private pay & LTC facilities | 43 |
| Federal Medicare programs | 42 |
| State Medicaid programs | 12 |
| Other sources | 3 |
| **Total** | **100** |

### Selected Subsidiaries

AAHS Acquisition Corp.
Accu-Med Services, LLC
Anderson Medical Services, Inc.
Bach's Pharmacy Services, LLC
Badger Acquisition LLC
Bio-Pharm International, Inc.
Dixon Pharmacy LLC
Evergreen Pharmaceutical, LLC
excelleRx, Inc.
Home Pharmacy Services, LLC
Interlock Pharmacy Systems, Inc.
JHC Acquisition LLC
Konsult, Inc.
Med World Acquisition Corp.
NCS Healthcare, LLC
NeighborCare Holdings, Inc.
Nihan & Martin LLC
OCR Services Corporation
Pharmed Holdings, Inc.
Resource Biometrics, Inc.
Swish, Inc.
Vital Care Infusions Supply, Inc.
Winslow's Pharmacy

## COMPETITORS

Cardinal Health 101
Covance
Express Scripts
Kendle
Life Sciences Research
McKesson
Medco Health Solutions
PAREXEL
Pharmaceutical Product Development
PharMerica
Quintiles Transnational

## HISTORICAL FINANCIALS

Company Type: Public

### Income Statement

FYE: December 31

| | REVENUE ($ mil.) | NET INCOME ($ mil.) | NET PROFIT MARGIN | EMPLOYEES |
|---|---|---|---|---|
| **12/06** | 6,493 | 184 | 2.8% | 17,100 |
| **12/05** | 5,293 | 227 | 4.3% | 17,900 |
| **12/04** | 4,120 | 236 | 5.7% | 12,900 |
| **12/03** | 3,499 | 194 | 5.6% | 12,100 |
| **12/02** | 2,633 | 126 | 4.8% | 9,500 |
| **Annual Growth** | 25.3% | 9.9% | — | 15.8% |

### 2006 Year-End Financials

Debt ratio: 93.4%
Return on equity: 6.0%
Cash ($ mil.): 142
Current ratio: 4.39
Long-term debt ($ mil.): 2,955
No. of shares (mil.): 121
Dividends
Yield: 0.2%
Payout: 6.0%
Market value ($ mil.): 4,692

### Stock History

NYSE: OCR

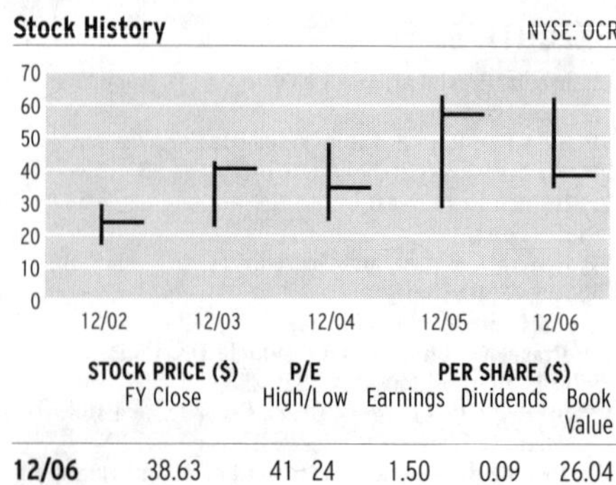


| | STOCK PRICE ($) FY Close | P/E High | P/E Low | PER SHARE ($) Earnings | Dividends | Book Value |
|---|---|---|---|---|---|---|
| **12/06** | 38.63 | 41 | 24 | 1.50 | 0.09 | 26.04 |
| **12/05** | 57.22 | 30 | 14 | 2.10 | 0.09 | 24.54 |
| **12/04** | 34.62 | 22 | 12 | 2.17 | 0.09 | 18.44 |
| **12/03** | 40.39 | 22 | 12 | 1.93 | 0.09 | 16.24 |
| **12/02** | 23.83 | 22 | 13 | 1.33 | 0.09 | 13.52 |
| **Annual Growth** | 12.8% | — | — | 3.1% | 0.0% | 17.8% |

# Omnicom Group

While it might not be omnipotent, Omnicom Group can create advertising that is omnipresent. The company ranks as the world's #1 corporate media services conglomerate, with advertising, marketing, and public relations operations serving some 5,000 clients in more than 100 countries. It serves global advertising clients through its agency networks BBDO Worldwide, DDB Worldwide, and TBWA Worldwide, while such firms as GSD&M, Merkley Partners, and Zimmerman Advertising provide services for regional and national clients. More than 160 other firms in its Diversified Agency Services division, including Fleishman-Hillard, Integer, and Rapp Collins, provide public relations and other marketing services.

Hoping to establish a more effective advertising method for today's DVR generation of viewers, Omnicom signed a deal to acquire audience advertising measurement research from TiVo, the early pioneer of digital video recording equipment, in August 2006.

Despite an economic downturn and a more cost-cautious approach on the part of advertisers, Omnicom has continued to grow both domestically and internationally. The company's fortunes have been buoyed in part by its agency networks and their consistently strong creative work (traditional media advertising accounts for more than 40% of revenue) but the bulk of its growth has come from such areas as customer relationship management (CRM) and specialty communications. Omnicom sees continued growth being tied to its ability to provide an ever expanding menu of services to its largest clients.

Following a long period of consolidation and acquisitions, Omnicom is slowly and quietly beginning to reorganize itself into a new kind of holding company. Longtime CEO John Wren sees the company's agency networks becoming more full-service communications firms and is looking to integrate (or in some cases re-integrate) Omnicom's specialized services units into its global agencies. The transformation could begin with its leading interactive agencies, Agency.com and Organic, which are said to be headed for integration into TBWA and

BBDO, respectively. Omnicom also bought San Francisco-based interactive marketing agency EVB in July 2006. EVB works with clients such as Kellogg's and Wrigley. The next month Omnicom bought St. Louis-based advertising agency Rodgers Townsend, whose clients have included AT&T and The Hartford. All in all, Omnicom made 16 acquisitions throughout 2006.

Omnicom has also been focused on expanding its media planning and buying operations. OMD Worldwide ranks as the #2 media specialist firm (behind Publicis' Starcom MediaVest) but Omnicom still trails WPP Group, Publicis, and Interpublic in total media services billings. To help close the gap, OMD launched Full Circle Entertainment, a branded entertainment production unit that works with such clients as DirecTV and Pier 1. In addition, Omnicom's Prometheus Media Services unit is its third media specialist, alongside OMD Worldwide and PHD Limited.

## HISTORY

Omnicom Group was created in 1986 to combine three leading ad agencies into a single group capable of competing in the worldwide market. BBDO Worldwide, founded in New York in 1928 as Batten, Barton, Durstine & Osborn, had a huge PepsiCo account and developed the Pepsi Generation campaign. Doyle Dane Bernbach Group (DDB), which had created the *fahrvergnügen* ads for Volkswagen, had strong ties in Europe. And Needham Harper Worldwide, which had served up the "You Deserve a Break Today" commercials for McDonald's, had connections in Asia. BBDO remained separate, but DDB and Needham Harper were merged to form DDB Needham Worldwide. The business services units (public relations firms and direct marketers) of each of these companies were tucked under the Diversified Agency Services (DAS) umbrella.

Bruce Crawford, a previous chairman of BBDO who had just finished a stint running New York's Metropolitan Opera, became chairman and CEO in 1989. He transformed DAS from a chaotic group of shops into an integrated marketing giant and ran Omnicom as a holding company of independent operating units working together through cross-referrals. By keeping costs low, especially interest expenses, Omnicom survived the 1990-91 recession with little pain. The company acquired Goodby, Berlin & Silverstein (now Goodby, Silverstein & Partners) in 1992. The next year TBWA Advertising (founded in Paris in 1970 by American Bill Tragos) was added to Omnicom's roster.

The merger spree continued in 1994 when Omnicom purchased WWAV Group, the largest direct-marketing agency in the UK. In 1995 Omnicom fused TBWA with Chiat/Day (founded in 1968 by Jay Chiat and Guy Day) to form TBWA International Network. Omnicom also acquired Michigan-based Ross Roy Communications (later Interone Marketing Group). In 1997 DDB Needham won back its McDonald's account after a 15-year hiatus. That year Crawford stepped down as CEO (though he remained chairman) and John Wren took control of Omnicom.

In 1998 the company acquired PR firm Fleishman-Hillard, adding to the PR clout it established with the acquisition of Ketchum Communications (now Ketchum) in 1996. Omnicom also acquired GGT Group of London for $235 million. (GGT's New York office, Wells BDDP, had lost a large Procter & Gamble account that year.) It merged GGT's BDDP Worldwide with TBWA to form TBWA Worldwide. BBDO landed a $200 million account with PepsiCo's Frito-Lay that year.

Omnicom's position in Europe was boosted in 1999 when it bought the Abbot Mead Vickers (now Abbot Mead Vickers BBDO) shares it didn't already own. That year TBWA founder Tragos retired from the company (replaced by Lee Clow) and DDB Needham changed its moniker to DDB Worldwide Communications Group. Omnicom also bought market research firm M/A/R/C for about $95 million, and invested $20 million in pharmaceutical clinical trials company SCIREX. In 2000 BBDO scored a major coup over rival FCB Worldwide (now part of Interpublic) by landing the $1.8 billion DaimlerChrysler account. The next year it formed Seneca Investments to hold its stakes in several i-services shops, including Agency.com and Organic. (Omnicom acquired the interactive agencies outright in 2003.)

## EXECUTIVES

**Chairman:** Bruce Crawford, age 78
**Vice Chairman:** Peter W. Mead, age 67
**Vice Chairman; Chairman and CEO, Omnicom Asia-Pacific:** Michael Birkin, age 48
**President, CEO, and Director:** John D. Wren, age 54
**EVP and CFO:** Randall J. Weisenburger, age 48
**SVP, General Counsel, and Secretary:** Michael J. O'Brien, age 45
**SVP and Corporate Director of Public Affairs:** Pat Sloan
**SVP Finance and Controller:** Philip J. Angelastro, age 42
**SVP; President, Omnicom Asia-Pacific:** Serge Dumont
**Chairman Emeritus, BBDO Worldwide:** Allen Rosenshine, age 68
**Chairman and CEO, Diversified Agency Services:** Thomas L. Harrison, age 59
**Chairman and CEO, Omnicom Media Group:** Daryl D. Simm, age 45
**Chairman and Creative Director, TBWA Worldwide:** Lee Clow
**Chairman, India:** Keki B. Dadiseth, age 61
**President, CEO, and Director, BBDO Worldwide:** Andrew Robertson, age 46
**President and CEO, DDB Worldwide:** Charles (Chuck) Brymer, age 47
**President and CEO, TBWA Worldwide:** Jean-Marie Dru, age 60
**CEO, Agency.com:** David Eastman, age 43
**CEO, EVB:** Daniel Stein
**CEO, Omnicom Media Group Asia Pacific:** Mike Cooper
**CEO, Omnicom Media Group Europe:** Colin Gottlieb
**CEO, Omnicom Media Group UK:** Philippa Brown
**President and CEO, Doremus:** Carl Anderson
**CEO, OMG Digital:** Sean Finnegan
**Auditors:** KPMG LLP

## LOCATIONS

**HQ:** Omnicom Group Inc.
437 Madison Ave., New York, NY 10022
**Phone:** 212-415-3600 **Fax:** 212-415-3530
**Web:** www.omnicomgroup.com

Omnicom Group has operations in more than 100 countries.

**2006 Sales**

| | $ mil. | % of total |
|---|---|---|
| US | 6,194.0 | 55 |
| Europe | | |
| UK | 1,229.7 | 11 |
| Other countries | 2,313.5 | 20 |
| Other regions | 1,639.7 | 14 |
| **Total** | **11,376.9** | **100** |

## PRODUCTS/OPERATIONS

**2006 Sales**

| | $ mil. | % of total |
|---|---|---|
| Traditional media advertising | 4,866.4 | 43 |
| Customer relationship management | 4,081.1 | 36 |
| Specialty communications | 1,279.3 | 11 |
| Public relations | 1,150.1 | 10 |
| **Total** | **11,376.9** | **100** |

**Selected Operations**

Global advertising networks
- BBDO Worldwide
- DDB Worldwide
- TBWA Worldwide

National advertising agencies
- Goodby, Silverstein & Partners (San Francisco)
- GSD&M (Austin, TX)
- Martin|Williams (Minneapolis)
- Merkley + Partners (New York City)
- Zimmerman Partners Advertising (Fort Lauderdale, FL)

Marketing and consulting agencies

Direct response
- Interbrand (brand identity)
- M/A/R/C Research (market research)
- Rapp Collins Worldwide (direct marketing)
- Targetbase (direct marketing)

Promotional marketing
- CPM (field marketing)
- The Integer Group (retail marketing)
- Kaleidoscope (sports and event marketing)
- Millsport (sports and event marketing)

Public relations
- Brodeur Worldwide
- Clark & Weinstock
- Cone
- Fleishman-Hillard
- Gavin Anderson & Company
- GPC International
- Ketchum
- Porter Novelli International
- Smythe Dorward Lambert

Specialty communications
- Adelphi Group (health care)
- Corbett Accel Healthcare (health care)
- Dieste Hamel & Partners (multicultural marketing)
- Doremus (business-to-business advertising)
- SafirRosetti (security and intelligence)

Media services
- OMD Worldwide
- PHD Network
- Novus Print Media
- Icon International

## COMPETITORS

Aegis Group
Dentsu
Hakuhodo
Havas
Interpublic Group
Publicis
WPP Group

## HISTORICAL FINANCIALS

Company Type: Public

**Income Statement** FYE: December 31

| | REVENUE ($ mil.) | NET INCOME ($ mil.) | NET PROFIT MARGIN | EMPLOYEES |
|---|---|---|---|---|
| **12/06** | 11,377 | 864 | 7.6% | 66,000 |
| **12/05** | 10,481 | 791 | 7.5% | 62,000 |
| **12/04** | 9,747 | 724 | 7.4% | 61,000 |
| **12/03** | 8,621 | 676 | 7.8% | 58,500 |
| **12/02** | 7,536 | 644 | 8.5% | 57,600 |
| **Annual Growth** | 10.8% | 7.6% | — | 3.5% |

**2006 Year-End Financials**

Debt ratio: 78.9%
Return on equity: 22.1%
Cash ($ mil.): 1,929
Current ratio: 0.94
Long-term debt ($ mil.): 3,055
No. of shares (mil.): 168
Dividends
Yield: 1.0%
Payout: 20.1%
Market value ($ mil.): 8,797

**Stock History** NYSE: OMC

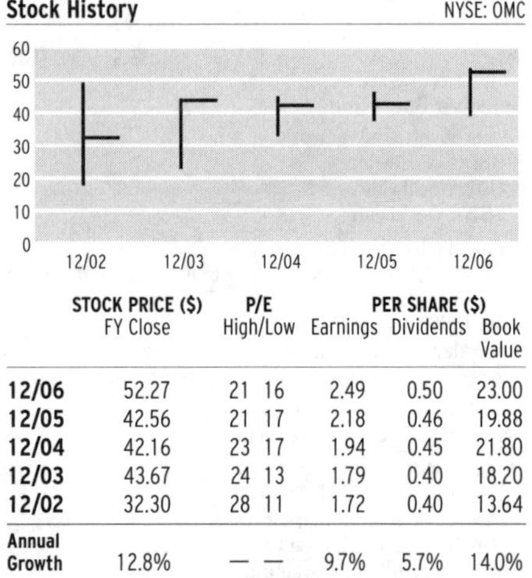


| | STOCK PRICE ($) FY Close | P/E High/Low | | PER SHARE ($) Earnings | Dividends | Book Value |
|---|---|---|---|---|---|---|
| **12/06** | 52.27 | 21 | 16 | 2.49 | 0.50 | 23.00 |
| **12/05** | 42.56 | 21 | 17 | 2.18 | 0.46 | 19.88 |
| **12/04** | 42.16 | 23 | 17 | 1.94 | 0.45 | 21.80 |
| **12/03** | 43.67 | 24 | 13 | 1.79 | 0.40 | 18.20 |
| **12/02** | 32.30 | 28 | 11 | 1.72 | 0.40 | 13.64 |
| **Annual Growth** | 12.8% | — | — | 9.7% | 5.7% | 14.0% |

# ONEOK, Inc.

ONEOK (pronounced "one oak") is branching out across the energy industry. The company's regulated utilities, Oklahoma Natural Gas, Kansas Gas Service, and Texas Gas Service, distribute natural gas to more than 2 million customers. Through ONEOK Partners it operates 14,500 miles of gas-gathering pipeline and 5,600 miles of transportation pipeline, as well as gas processing plants and storage facilities. It also owns one of the US's top natural gas liquids (NGL) systems. In 2006 ONEOK sold its gathering and processing, natural gas liquids, pipelines, and storage businesses to Northern Border Partners (renamed ONEOK Partners) for $3 billion and became that company's general partner and 46% owner.

Westar Energy reduced its stake to approximately 15% by selling shares back to ONEOK and to the public in mid-2003; it sold its remaining shares to Cantor Fitzgerald later that year.

ONEOK has been juggling assets to focus on profitable businesses. The firm, which gets a large slice of its revenues from its gas distribution, gathering, and processing operations, sold about 70% of its oil and gas production assets in Kansas, Oklahoma, and Texas to Chesapeake Energy for $300 million in 2003. Later that year, shifting its production focus to the Texas market (and focusing on development rather than exploration), it acquired oil and gas reserves and related gathering systems in East Texas from Wagner & Brown for about $240 million.

The company also acquired Southern Union's Texas natural gas distribution business (540,000 customers), as well as Southern Union's stake in a Mexican gas utility and its propane distribution, gas marketing, and gas transmission operations in the southwestern US, for $420 million.

ONEOK acquired Northern Plains Natural Gas, a general partner of pipeline operator Northern Border Partners (later renamed ONEOK Partners), from CCE Holdings (a joint venture of Southern Union and GE Commercial Finance) for $175 million in 2004. The transaction followed CCE Holdings' acquisition of Enron's CrossCountry Energy unit.

Also in 2004, ONEOK changed the name of its wholesale energy unit from ONEOK Energy Marketing and Trading to ONEOK Energy Services.

In 2005 the company bought Koch Industries' natural gas liquids assets for $1.35 billion. That year ONEOK sold properties to TXOK Acquisition Inc. for $645 million, and some Texas natural gas assets to Eagle Rock Energy for $528 million to help pay down debt.

## HISTORY

In 1906 Oklahoma Natural Gas (ONG) was founded to pipe natural gas from northeastern Oklahoma to Oklahoma City. A 100-mile pipeline was completed the next year. In 1921 ONG created two oil companies to pump out the oil it found as a result of its natural gas exploration.

In the 1920s ONG changed hands many times, ending up with utility financier G. L. Ohrstrom and Company, which milked it dry by brokering acquisitions (purchasing gas properties and then selling them to ONG) and collecting fees. Stock sales drove revenues, inflating the stock's price, and the inflated price triggered more stock sales. The bubble burst on October 29, 1929. A series of leadership changes ensued, and in 1932 the company was dissolved and reincorporated. Under president Joseph Bowes, ONG recovered, wooing back dissatisfied customers and upgrading its pipelines.

In the late 1930s the company pioneered a type of underground storage that injected gas into depleted gas reservoirs in the summer and withdrew it during winter's peak use times.

The 1950s and 1960s saw the company expand. In 1962 it created its first subsidiary, Oklahoma Natural Gas Gathering Company, selling gas out of state and therefore subject to federal regulation.

In the lean 1970s, ONG was not affected by federal laws that kept wellhead prices low for gas transported across state lines because its main operations were confined to Oklahoma. Congress deregulated wellhead prices in 1978, spurring exploration but causing great price fluctuations in the 1980s. In 1980 ONG changed its name to ONEOK.

In the 1980s ONEOK signed take-or-pay contracts, which forced it to pay for gas offered by its suppliers even if it had no customers. When recession in the 1980s caused demand to drop, ONEOK had to pay for high-priced natural gas it couldn't sell. In 1988 the company was ordered to pay some $50 million to supplier Forest Oil of Denver. A year later ONEOK was sued for allegedly failing to tell stockholders about the take-or-pay agreements (settled in 1993 for $5.5 million). It later sold more than half of its oil and gas reserves to Mustang Energy for $52 million to finance the Forest Oil court award. The company was still settling lawsuits over the agreements into the 1990s; it settled the last of the claims by 1998.

ONEOK began buying gas transmission and production facilities in Oklahoma and creating drilling alliances in the 1990s. In 1997 ONEOK bought the natural gas assets of Westar Energy, formerly Western Resources, for $660 million and ONEOK stock worth $800 million. The acquisition doubled the number of ONEOK's customers and increased its gas marketing, gathering, and transmission operations.

In 1998 the company sold oil and gas reserves, processing plants, and gathering systems in Kansas, Louisiana, and Oklahoma to Duke Energy. With gas utility deregulation looming, ONEOK purchased producing oil and gas properties, primarily in Oklahoma and Texas.

Also in 1998 it agreed to buy Southwest Gas of Las Vegas for $863.6 million. Southern Union offered $976 million for Southwest Gas in 1999, but Southwest Gas agreed instead to a $912.3 million deal with ONEOK. Southern Union sued Southwest Gas, alleging that it had conspired with ONEOK to block the Southern Union bid. In 2000 the legal action made ONEOK cancel the Southwest Gas deal.

In 1999 ONEOK bought a 31% stake (later reduced) in exploration and production company Magnum Hunter Resources for $50 million. The next year the company expanded its natural gas gathering and processing operations in the US mid-continent region by buying assets from Dynegy ($308 million) and Kinder Morgan ($108 million).

President and COO David Kyle took over as chairman and CEO in 2000 after Larry Brummett died of cancer. In 2001 the company established a new unit, ONEOK Power, with the startup of a new power plant northwest of Oklahoma City. In 2002 ONEOK sold several processing facilities to Mustang Fuel for $93 million.

## EXECUTIVES

**Chairman, ONEOK and ONEOK Partners:** David L. Kyle, age 54
**CEO; President and CEO, ONEOK Partners:** John W. Gibson, age 54
**President, ONEOK Energy Services:** William S. (Billy) Maxwell, age 46
**President, ONEOK Distribution Companies:** Samuel (Sam) Combs III, age 49
**President and COO:** James C. (Jim) Kneale, age 55
**SVP and General Counsel:** John R. Barker, age 58
**SVP, Treasurer, and CFO, ONEOK and ONEOK Partners:** Curtis L. Dinan, age 39
**SVP and Chief Accounting Officer:** Caron A. Lawhorn, age 45
**SVP and Special Counsel to the Chairman:** John A. Gaberino Jr., age 64
**SVP Administrative Services:** David E. Roth, age 51
**VP, Corporate Services:** James M. Fallon, age 50
**VP, Audit and Risk Control:** Beverly C. Monnet, age 48
**VP, Communications and Investor Relations:** Dandridge (Dan) Harrison, age 53
**VP and Controller, Energy:** Mike Clark, age 45
**VP and Controller, Energy:** Ray Poudrier, age 49
**President, Kansas Gas Service:** Bradley O. (Brad) Dixon, age 53
**President, Oklahoma Natural Gas:** Phyllis S. Worley, age 56
**President, Texas Gas Service:** Roger N. Mitchell, age 55
**President, Viking Trans, Guardian MW, Northern Plains Natural Gas:** Paul F. Miller, age 40
**EVP Natural Gas Liquids, ONEOK Partners:** Terry K. Spencer, age 48
**EVP Natural Gas, ONEOK Partners:** Pierce H. Norton II, age 47
**EVP ONEOK Energy Services:** D. Lamar Miller, age 44
**Corporate Secretary and Associate General Counsel:** Eric Grimshaw, age 54
**Auditors:** PricewaterhouseCoopers LLP

## LOCATIONS

**HQ:** ONEOK, Inc.
100 W. 5th St., Tulsa, OK 74103
**Phone:** 918-588-7000 **Fax:** 918-588-7960
**Web:** www.oneok.com

ONEOK operates primarily in Kansas, Oklahoma, and Texas.

## PRODUCTS/OPERATIONS

### 2006 Sales

| | $ mil. | % of total |
|---|---|---|
| Energy Services | 5,924.2 | 50 |
| ONEOK Partners | 4,006.6 | 34 |
| Distribution | 1,958.2 | 16 |
| Adjustments | 7.1 | — |
| **Total** | **11,896.1** | **100** |

### Selected Subsidiaries, Affiliates, and Divisions

Energy Services
- ONEOK Energy Services Company (formerly ONEOK Energy Marketing and Trading Company, natural gas, oil, and electricity sales)

Natural Gas Liquids
- ONEOK NGL Pipeline, L.P.

Distribution
- Kansas Gas Service Company
- Oklahoma Natural Gas Company
- Texas Gas Service Company (formerly Southern Union Gas Company)

Gathering and Processing
- ONEOK Partners, L.P. (45.7%)
- ONEOK Field Services Company
- ONEOK NGL Marketing L.P.

Pipelines and Storage
- MidContinent Market Center, Inc.
- Northern Plains Natural Gas Company, LLC
- ONEOK Gas Gathering, L.L.C. (nonprocessable gas gathering services)
- ONEOK Gas Storage, L.L.C.
- ONEOK Gas Transportation, L.L.C.
- ONEOK Texas Gas Storage L.P.
- ONEOK WesTex Transmission, L.P.

Other
- ONEOK Leasing Company (leases space in corporate headquarters building)
- ONEOK Parking Company (owns and operates parking lot adjacent to headquarters)

## COMPETITORS

Adams Resources
AEP
Aquila
Atmos Energy
BP
CenterPoint Energy
CMS Energy
Duncan Energy
Dynegy
Energen
Equitable Resources
Exxon Mobil
FirstEnergy
Hess
KeySpan
National Fuel Gas
OGE Energy
Southern Union
Southwest Gas
TXU
Williams Companies

## HISTORICAL FINANCIALS

Company Type: Public

### Income Statement

FYE: December 31

| | REVENUE ($ mil.) | NET INCOME ($ mil.) | NET PROFIT MARGIN | EMPLOYEES |
|---|---|---|---|---|
| **12/06** | 11,896 | 306 | 2.6% | 4,536 |
| **12/05** | 12,676 | 547 | 4.3% | 4,558 |
| **12/04** | 5,988 | 242 | 4.0% | 4,627 |
| **12/03** | 2,999 | 113 | 3.8% | 4,342 |
| **12/02** | 2,104 | 167 | 7.9% | 3,593 |
| **Annual Growth** | 54.2% | 16.4% | — | 6.0% |

### 2006 Year-End Financials

Debt ratio: 181.9%
Return on equity: 15.3%
Cash ($ mil.): 168
Current ratio: 1.57
Long-term debt ($ mil.): 4,031
No. of shares (mil.): 111
Dividends
Yield: 2.8%
Payout: 45.5%
Market value ($ mil.): 4,780

### Stock History

NYSE: OKE

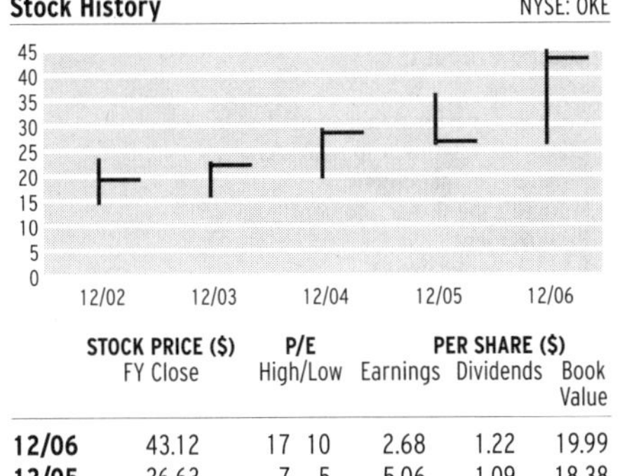


| | STOCK PRICE ($) FY Close | P/E High | P/E Low | PER SHARE ($) Earnings | Dividends | Book Value |
|---|---|---|---|---|---|---|
| **12/06** | 43.12 | 17 | 10 | 2.68 | 1.22 | 19.99 |
| **12/05** | 26.63 | 7 | 5 | 5.06 | 1.09 | 18.38 |
| **12/04** | 28.42 | 13 | 9 | 2.30 | 0.88 | 15.42 |
| **12/03** | 22.08 | 18 | 13 | 1.22 | 0.69 | 13.04 |
| **12/02** | 19.20 | 17 | 11 | 1.39 | 0.62 | 22.48 |
| **Annual Growth** | 22.4% | — | — | 17.8% | 18.4% | (2.9%) |

# Oracle Corporation

According to Oracle, consolidation in the business software industry is the wisest move. The enterprise software giant provides a range of tools for managing business data, supporting business operations, and facilitating collaboration and application development. Companies use Oracle's database management software to store and access data across numerous platforms. The company also offers business applications for data warehousing, customer relationship management, and supply chain management. In recent years the company has aggressively used acquisitions to expand its product lines, including the purchases of PeopleSoft, Siebel Systems, and Portal Software.

As CEO, founder Larry Ellison has been a colorful and controversial figure, with a penchant for dangerous pursuits — from piloting yachts and fighter jets to publicly challenging Microsoft for the crown of world's largest software company.

Ellison, who owns about a quarter of Oracle, courted additional controversy when he launched a hostile takeover bid for PeopleSoft in 2003, just days after the rival software maker had disclosed plans to acquire J.D. Edwards. PeopleSoft's board unanimously rejected the initial all-cash offer of $5.1 billion, deeming the unsolicited bid inadequate and citing antitrust concerns. After bitter negotiations that included a number of rejected bids, Oracle finally reached an agreement to acquire PeopleSoft for $10.3 billion in December 2004; the deal closed the following month.

Soon after the PeopleSoft deal closed, Oracle again pursued a takeover. Rival SAP had announced plans to acquire retail software developer Retek for about $500 million. After a brief bidding war Oracle purchased Retek for about $670 million and formed a new business unit called Oracle Retail Global.

Other 2005 acquisitions included identity management software developer Oblix; data management software maker TimesTen; retail inventory management software developer ProfitLogic; Innobase, a Finnish company that supplies a software component used by MySQL (an open-source competitor); logistics software provider Global Logistics Technologies (G-Log); and two security software vendors: Thor Technologies and OctetString.

Not content to rest on its acquisitive laurels, Oracle initiated another blockbuster deal in late 2005, offering to purchase Siebel Systems for $5.85 billion. In June 2006 the company acquired Portal Software for about $220 million, in addition to purchasing TelephonyWork.

In April 2007 the company completed another large deal when it snapped up business intelligence software provider Hyperion Solutions for about $3.3 billion.

In May 2007 the company announced plans to purchase Agile Software for about $495 million.

## HISTORY

Larry Ellison, Robert Miner, Bruce Scott, and Edward Oates founded System Development Laboratories (SDL) in 1977 to create a database management system according to theoretical specifications published by IBM. Ellison had studied physics at the University of Chicago but dropped out in the 1960s to seek his fortune in Silicon Valley. Working first for Ampex and then Amdahl (now Fujitsu IT Holdings), he was part of the team that developed the first IBM-compatible mainframe. Miner, an experienced programmer, was the main developer of Oracle's database manager, able to run on many computer brands and introduced in 1979. The company also changed its name that year to Relational Software.

In 1983 the company changed its name again, this time to Oracle, in order to more closely align itself with its primary product. Oracle went public in 1986 and within two years had a 36% share of Uncle Sam's PC database market. It also added financial management, graphics, and human resource management software.

Oracle's rapid growth came at a great cost. It gained notoriety as a leader in vaporware — that is, announced products that actually had not yet been developed. When the company's software was released, it was sometimes bug-ridden and lacking promised features. Duplicate billings and the booking of unconsummated sales inflated revenues.

Oracle recorded a loss for fiscal 1991, accompanied by a downward restatement of earnings for past years. Its stock nosedived. The company laid off 400 employees and revised its growth estimates. Ellison stabilized the company with $80 million in financing from Nippon Steel. He also brought in Ray Lane as president and COO. Within six months Lane streamlined operations, imposing strict performance standards.

Thanks to Oracle7 (launched in 1992), the company within two years became the #1 database management software maker. Sales for fiscal 1994 hit $2 billion. Ellison by that time had developed a reputation as an extravagant adventurer (his hobbies included yacht racing and piloting disarmed fighter planes).

In 1997 Oracle formed affiliate Network Computer Inc. to market Internet appliances (with no disk drive and local memory) that Ellison envisioned would strip Microsoft of its operating system ubiquity. Oracle and Netscape (now owned by Time Warner) merged joint venture Navio

Communications one year later into Network Computer (renamed Liberate Technologies, redesigned around interactive software, and spun off in 1999).

In 1999 Oracle bought three niche front-office software specialists and took its Oracle Japan subsidiary public. In 2000 Oracle partnered with rival Commerce One to provide software and support for a giant online venture merging the Web-based procurement exchanges of General Motors, Ford Motor, and DaimlerChrysler. Later that year Lane resigned as president and COO.

In 2001 the company continued to expand its portfolio of business applications, introducing warehouse, supply chain, and customer relationship management software, as well as software suites targeted at small businesses.

2003 marked the beginning of Oracle's lengthy and bitter bid to acquire rival PeopleSoft. With the acquisition still pending, Oracle's board kick-started 2004 with the decision to separate the functions of CEO and chairman. As a result, Larry Ellison remained as CEO and director, but former CFO Jeff Henley became chairman effective January 2004. Oracle finally reached an agreement to acquire PeopleSoft for $10.3 billion in December 2004, and closed the deal early the following year.

## EXECUTIVES

**Chairman:** Jeffrey O. (Jeff) Henley, age 61, $3,656,750 pay
**CEO and Director:** Lawrence J. (Larry) Ellison, age 60, $7,407,000 pay
**Co-President, CFO, and Director:** Safra A. Catz, age 43, $4,537,000 pay
**Co-President and Director:** Charles E. (Chuck) Phillips Jr., age 47, $4,537,000 pay
**EVP, Applications Development:** John Wookey, age 46
**Chairman and EVP, Oracle Corporation, Asia Pacific and Japan:** Derek H. Williams, age 60
**EVP, Development, Server Technologies Division:** Charles A. (Chuck) Rozwat, age 57
**EVP, Europe, Middle East, and Africa and Consulting:** Sergio Giacoletto, age 55, $3,199,875 pay
**EVP, North America Sales and Consulting:** Keith G. Block, age 45, $4,116,000 pay
**EVP, Oracle Customer Services:** Juergen Rottler, age 39
**SVP, Secretary, and General Counsel:** Daniel Cooperman, age 54
**SVP, Development, Oracle Application Server:** Thomas Kurian
**SVP, Finance and Operations:** Jennifer L. Minton, age 44
**SVP, Human Resources:** Joyce Westerdahl
**SVP and Chief Marketing Officer:** Judith Sim
**SVP, Applications Development:** Steve Miranda
**SVP, Research and Development:** Kevin Walsh
**VP, Corporate Controller, and Chief Accounting Officer:** William Corey West, age 44
**VP, Investor Relations:** Krista Bessinger
**Chief Corporate Architect:** Edward Screven
**Chief Security Officer:** Mary Ann Davidson
**Auditors:** Ernst & Young LLP

## LOCATIONS

**HQ:** Oracle Corporation
500 Oracle Pkwy., Redwood City, CA 94065
**Phone:** 650-506-7000 **Fax:** 650-506-7200
**Web:** www.oracle.com

Oracle has offices in more than 60 countries.

### 2007 Sales

| | $ mil. | % of total |
|---|---|---|
| Americas | 9,460 | 53 |
| EMEA | 6,037 | 34 |
| Asia/Pacific | 2,499 | 13 |
| **Total** | **17,996** | **100** |

## PRODUCTS/OPERATIONS

### 2007 Sales

| | $ mil. | % of total |
|---|---|---|
| Software | 14,211 | 79 |
| Services | 3,785 | 21 |
| **Total** | **17,996** | **100** |

### Selected Products

Applications
- Corporate performance management
- Customer relationship management
- Financial management
- Human capital management
- Procurement
- Project management
- Supply chain management

Database
- Oracle Database 10*g* (Enterprise, Standard, Standard One, Lite editions)
- Oracle Real Application Clusters
- Oracle TimesTen In-Memory Database

Enterprise management
- Oracle Enterprise Manager
  - Application server control
  - Database control
  - Grid control
- Pack and plug-ins
  - Change management
  - Configuration management
  - Diagnostics
  - Provisioning pack
  - Service level management
  - System monitoring
  - Tuning

Middleware
- Application server
- Business integration
- Business intelligence
- Content and collaboration
- Data hubs
- Developer tools
- Identity management
- Oracle Fusion for PeopleSoft
- Portal
- SOA Suite
- Web services management

## COMPETITORS

Accenture
ADP
BEA Systems
BMC Software
Borland Software
Business Objects
CA
Ceridian
Cognos
EDS
Fidelity Investments
i2 Technologies
IBM
Lawson Software
Microsoft
MySQL
NCR
Progress Software
Rational Software
SAP
Sybase

## HISTORICAL FINANCIALS

Company Type: Public

### Income Statement

FYE: May 31

| | REVENUE ($ mil.) | NET INCOME ($ mil.) | NET PROFIT MARGIN | EMPLOYEES |
|---|---|---|---|---|
| **5/07** | 17,996 | 4,274 | 23.7% | 74,674 |
| **5/06** | 14,380 | 3,381 | 23.5% | 56,133 |
| **5/05** | 11,799 | 2,886 | 24.5% | 49,872 |
| **5/04** | 10,156 | 2,681 | 26.4% | 41,658 |
| **5/03** | 9,475 | 2,307 | 24.3% | 40,650 |
| **Annual Growth** | 17.4% | 16.7% | — | 16.4% |

### 2007 Year-End Financials

Debt ratio: 36.9%
Return on equity: 26.8%
Cash ($ mil.): 7,020
Current ratio: 1.37
Long-term debt ($ mil.): 6,235
No. of shares (mil.): 5,107
Dividends
Yield: —
Payout: —
Market value ($ mil.): 98,974

### Stock History

NASDAQ (GS): ORCL

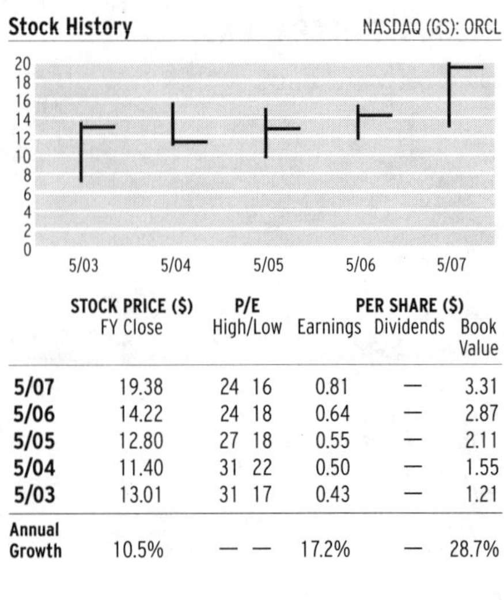


| | STOCK PRICE ($) FY Close | P/E High | P/E Low | PER SHARE ($) Earnings | PER SHARE ($) Dividends | PER SHARE ($) Book Value |
|---|---|---|---|---|---|---|
| **5/07** | 19.38 | 24 | 16 | 0.81 | — | 3.31 |
| **5/06** | 14.22 | 24 | 18 | 0.64 | — | 2.87 |
| **5/05** | 12.80 | 27 | 18 | 0.55 | — | 2.11 |
| **5/04** | 11.40 | 31 | 22 | 0.50 | — | 1.55 |
| **5/03** | 13.01 | 31 | 17 | 0.43 | — | 1.21 |
| **Annual Growth** | 10.5% | — | — | 17.2% | — | 28.7% |

# Oshkosh Truck

Whether you need to plow your way through Sahara sands or Buffalo snow, Oshkosh has your vehicle, by gosh. The company makes heavy-duty vehicles for the defense, fire and emergency, and commercial industries. Oshkosh's commercial and emergency/rescue vehicles include concrete carriers and refuse trucks (McNeilus brand), snow blowers, and aircraft rescue and fire-fighting vehicles (Pierce brand). Oshkosh's vehicles are used in institutional, airport, and municipal markets. The company also makes heavy-payload tactical trucks for the US Department of Defense (DoD) and has acquired Jerr-Dan, the towing equipment manufacturer, from Littlejohn & Co. for a reported $80 million.

2006 was another record year for Oshkosh's sales and profits. Not surprisingly, the company's defense products led the way as Oshkosh enjoyed brisk sales of parts and services for the thousands of Oshkosh trucks currently in service in Iraq. Oshkosh also won market share for its line of emergency vehicles, including response vehicles used in homeland security applications.

In 2006 Oshkosh acquired AK Specialty Vehicles (since renamed Oshkosh Specialty Vehicles) from HealthTronics for about $140 million. Oshkosh Specialty Vehicles makes mobile medical, broadcast, and homeland security command and control vehicles — new specialty vehicle markets for Oshkosh. Buying AK Specialty Vehicles also increases Oshkosh's presence in Europe. Later in 2006 Oshkosh bought Iowa Mold Tooling, a maker of tire service, general mechanics, and lubrication trucks. The purchase boosts Oshkosh's market presence for trucks serving the construction, tire service, and mining industries.

In late 2006 Oshkosh bought JLG Industries, a maker of aerial work platforms, for about $3 billion. The addition of JLG marks Oshkosh's expansion into the aerial platform market, and JLG has become Oshkosh's largest product segment. The move also gives Oshkosh purchasing leverage, and gives the company exposure to complimentary markets.

## HISTORY

Bernhard Mosling and William Besserdich founded Oshkosh Truck in 1917, attracting investors with *Old Betsy*, a four-wheel-drive, 3,000-lb. truck. Over the next few decades, the company developed a range of heavy-duty vehicles. Sales took off when the Army gave truck contracts to Oshkosh during WWII. Commercial sales increased after the war, the result of demand from mining and plantation companies. Oshkosh Truck went public in 1985.

Defense cutbacks prompted the company to diversify. It acquired Deere & Company's motorhome chassis business in 1989 and Miller Trailers the next year.

In 1995 Oshkosh formed a strategic alliance with Daimler-Benz's (now Daimler AG) Freightliner Corporation, although the transfer of its chassis business caused the company's sales to drop by more than $100 million in fiscal 1995. The following year Oshkosh bought fire truck maker Pierce Manufacturing for $158 million. Robert Bohn became CEO in 1997, succeeding R. Eugene Goodson, who quit in a disagreement with the board. Oshkosh also bought Quebec-based Nova Quintech's fire-fighting ladder technology that year.

The company acquired McNeilus Companies, a leading maker of concrete mixers and bodies for refuse trucks, for $250 million in 1998. It also won the initial contract for the US Marine Corps' Medium Tactical Truck Replacement program, potentially worth $1.2 billion if the government exercises all options. In 1999 Oshkosh bought Kewaunee Engineering, which makes parts for aerial devices, for $6.3 million. The next year Oshkosh picked up Viking Truck and Equipment (concrete mixer sales and service). Later in 2000 Oshkosh diversified into ambulances with the purchase of Medtec Ambulance Corporation.

Oshkosh expanded its European presence in 2001 when it bought the Geesink Norba Group (refuse collection truck bodies, mobile and stationary compactors, and transfer stations) from Powell Duffryn Ltd. for $137 million. In 2004 Oshkosh acquired 75% of two Italy-based fire-fighting equipment manufacturers, BAI Brescia Antcendi International and BAI Tecnica.

The following year Oshkosh bought Canadian concrete mixer truck company London Machinery Inc.

## EXECUTIVES

**Chairman, President, and CEO:** Robert G. (Bob) Bohn, age 53, $2,770,000 pay
**EVP and CFO:** Charles L. (Charlie) Szews, $1,000,070 pay
**EVP and Chief Administration Officer:** Matthew J. Zolnowski, age 52, $612,625 pay
**EVP, General Counsel, and Secretary:** Bryan J. Blankfield, age 44, $669,175 pay
**EVP; EVP, Marketing, Sales, and Dealer Distribution; COO, Pierce Manufacturing:** Mark A. Meaders, age 48
**EVP; President, Defense Business:** William J. (John) Stoddart, age 61
**EVP; President, McNeilus Companies:** Michael J. Wuest, age 47
**EVP; CEO, Fire and Emergency Group:** John W. Randjelovic, age 62
**EVP, Technology:** Donald H. Verhoff, age 59, $650,325 pay
**EVP, Government Operations and Industry Relations:** Joseph H. Kimmitt, age 56
**EVP; President, Fire and Emergency Group:** Thomas D. Fenner, age 50
**VP and Controller:** Thomas J. Polnaszek
**VP and Treasurer:** David M. Sagehorn
**VP, Investor Relations:** Patrick N. Davidson
**VP, Human Resources:** Michael K. Rohrkaste
**President, Oshkosh Capital:** Scott L. Ney
**President, Pierce Manufacturing:** Wilson Jones
**President, Asia Operations:** Michael Crowe
**Senior Advisor:** Dan J. Lanzdorf, age 55, $476,739 pay (prior to title change)
**Auditors:** Deloitte & Touche LLP

## LOCATIONS

**HQ:** Oshkosh Truck Corporation
2307 Oregon St., Oshkosh, WI 54902
**Phone:** 920-235-9151 **Fax:** 920-233-9314
**Web:** www.oshkoshtruckcorporation.com

Oshkosh Truck has manufacturing plants in California, Florida, Georgia, Indiana, Iowa, Massachusetts, Michigan, Minnesota, Nebraska, Pennsylvania, and Wisconsin in the US, as well as in Canada, Italy, the Netherlands, Romania, Sweden, and the UK.

### 2006 Sales

| | $ mil. | % of total |
|---|---|---|
| North America | | |
| US | 2,820.6 | 82 |
| Other countries | 76.3 | 2 |
| Europe & Middle East | 431.8 | 13 |
| Other regions | 98.7 | 3 |
| **Total** | **3,427.4** | **100** |

## PRODUCTS/OPERATIONS

### 2006 Sales

| | $ mil. | % of total |
|---|---|---|
| Defense | 1,317.2 | 38 |
| Commercial | 1,190.3 | 34 |
| Fire & emergency | 961.5 | 28 |
| Adjustments | (41.6) | — |
| **Total** | **3,427.4** | **100** |

### Selected Products

**Defense**
Heavy equipment transporter (HET)
Heavy expanded mobility tactical trucks (HEMTT)
Load handling systems (LHS)
Logistic vehicle system (LVS)
Medium tactical vehicle replacements (MTVR)
Palletized load system (PLS)

**Commercial**
Portable concrete batch plants
Rear- and front-discharge concrete mixers
Refuse truck bodies

**Fire and Emergency**
Aircraft rescue vehicles
Airport snow removal vehicles
Custom ambulances
Firefighting vehicles
Rescue and homeland security vehicles
Snow blowing and plow trucks
Towing and recovery equipment

## COMPETITORS

AM General
BAE Systems
Collins Industries
Daimler
Dover
Federal Signal
Freightliner
FWD Corp.
Hyundai
International Truck
Leyland Trucks
Mack Trucks
Navistar
Nissan Diesel
PACCAR
Spartan Motors
Trinity Industries
Volvo

## HISTORICAL FINANCIALS

Company Type: Public

**Income Statement** FYE: September 30

| | REVENUE ($ mil.) | NET INCOME ($ mil.) | NET PROFIT MARGIN | EMPLOYEES |
|---|---|---|---|---|
| **9/06** | 3,427 | 206 | 6.0% | 9,387 |
| **9/05** | 2,960 | 160 | 5.4% | 7,960 |
| **9/04** | 2,262 | 113 | 5.0% | 6,820 |
| **9/03** | 1,926 | 76 | 3.9% | 6,100 |
| **9/02** | 1,744 | 60 | 3.4% | 6,100 |
| **Annual Growth** | 18.4% | 36.3% | — | 11.4% |

**2006 Year-End Financials**

Debt ratio: 0.2%
Return on equity: 21.9%
Cash ($ mil.): 22
Current ratio: 1.14
Long-term debt ($ mil.): 2
No. of shares (mil.): 74
Dividends
Yield: 0.7%
Payout: 13.4%
Market value ($ mil.): 3,722

**Stock History** NYSE: OSK

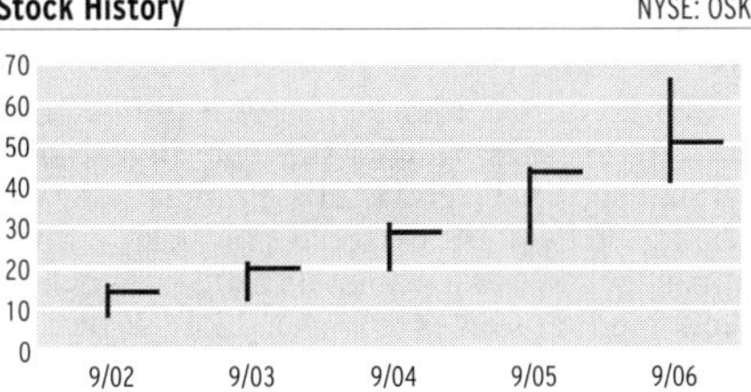


| | STOCK PRICE ($) FY Close | P/E High | P/E Low | PER SHARE ($) Earnings | Dividends | Book Value |
|---|---|---|---|---|---|---|
| **9/06** | 50.47 | 24 | 15 | 2.76 | 0.37 | 14.40 |
| **9/05** | 43.16 | 20 | 12 | 2.18 | 0.19 | 11.16 |
| **9/04** | 28.53 | 19 | 13 | 1.57 | 0.13 | 18.42 |
| **9/03** | 19.81 | 19 | 11 | 1.08 | 0.06 | 15.24 |
| **9/02** | 14.10 | 18 | 10 | 0.86 | 0.09 | 24.74 |
| **Annual Growth** | 37.5% | — | — | 33.8% | 42.4% | (12.7%) |

# Owens & Minor

Owens & Minor makes sure hospitals are prepared for major surgeries. A leading distributor of medical and surgical supplies, Owens & Minor carries some 180,000 products from about 1,200 manufacturers. Products distributed by the company include surgical dressings, endoscopic and intravenous products, needles, syringes, sterile procedure trays, gowns, and sutures. The firm also offers software, consulting, and other services to help customers manage their supplies. Owens & Minor's customers are primarily hospitals and health systems and the group purchasing organizations that serve them. It delivers products to roughly 4,000 health care providers from 50 distribution centers across the US.

The company's major suppliers include Johnson & Johnson and Covidien, whose products each account for 13% and 11%, respectively, of sales. The distributor sells some products under its own MediChoice label. To help bolster its core business, the company in 2006 acquired the acute-care medical and surgical supply distribution business of McKesson Medical-Surgical, a subsidiary of McKesson Corporation.

Group purchasing organization Novation accounts for more than 40% of the company's sales.

Another GPO, Broadlane, accounts for more than 10%. Other customers include Premier (which represents some 1,500 hospitals, 15% of sales) and the Department of Defense.

As the health care industry has consolidated, so have the industries that serve it. To remain competitive, Owens & Minor has focused on providing supply chain management tools and services in addition to supplies. For example, it offers WISDOM, which provides online access to sales and other data and allows customers and suppliers to track inventory, usage, and other information to keep costs down. Its PANDAC offering helps operating rooms track and control their inventory.

More than 90% of Owens & Minor's sales come from acute-care hospitals and integrated health care networks (IHNs). The company also has an ongoing exclusive supplier agreement with the US Department of Defense.

## HISTORY

George Gilmer Minor Jr.'s great-grandfather was an apothecary and surgeon in colonial Williamsburg, Virginia. His grandfather was Thomas Jefferson's personal physician. Minor himself worked as a wholesale drug salesman in Richmond after the Civil War. In 1882 he and rival wholesaler Otho Owens partnered to form the Owens & Minor Drug Company. The company was both a retail and wholesale business, with a storefront that filled prescriptions and sold sundries, paints, oils, and window glass. When Owens died in 1906, Minor became the company's president.

During the 1920s, the Owens family sold their stake in the firm. George Gilmer Minor III served briefly as the company's president in the early 1940s; his son, George Gilmer Minor IV (called Mr. Minor Jr. to differentiate him from his father), became president in 1947.

In 1954 Owens & Minor installed its first computerized order fulfillment system. The following year the firm became Owens, Minor & Bodeker when it bought the Bodeker Drug Company, which was both older and larger than Owens & Minor.

After 84 years in the drug wholesale business, the company entered the medical and surgical distribution business after buying A&J Hospital Supply in 1966 and Powers & Anderson in 1968. In 1971 Owens, Minor & Bodeker went public. By the end of the decade, the company had operations in 10 states.

The fourth Minor to run the firm, G. Gilmer Minor III (Mr. Minor Jr.'s son), was named president in 1981 (he became CEO in 1984). Under his direction Owens, Minor & Bodeker would complete the transition from a drug wholesaler to a medical supplies distributor. In 1981 it purchased the Will Ross subsidiary of G.D. Searle (then the country's #2 medical and surgical supplies distributor).

The company reverted to its original name on its 100th anniversary in 1982. By 1984 medical supplies supplanted wholesale drugs as its primary source of income. In 1988 Owens & Minor listed on the NYSE.

The company passed the $1 billion revenue mark in 1990 and later sold its wholesale drug business. It extended its reach with the purchase of Lyons Physician Supply in 1993 and Stuart Medical (the #3 national distributor) in 1994.

The company consolidated its warehouse operations and upgraded its computer system in 1995. To make up for losses attributed to restructuring costs and discounting prices for large accounts, Owens & Minor eliminated or reassigned jobs at several distribution centers.

In 1998 it lost its biggest customer when embattled Columbia/HCA (now HCA) canceled its contract. Owens & Minor replaced this business by contracting with such providers as Sutter Health.

In 1999 the company formed an alliance with drug distributor AmeriSource Health (now AmerisourceBergen) to streamline transactions with Sutter Health. In 2002 Owens & Minor launched an initiative to offer automated supply chain management services to its clients.

Chairman and CEO G. Gilmer Minor III stepped down from the CEO post after 21 years in July 2005 but remained the company's chairman; Craig R. Smith, the company's former COO, was named CEO.

## EXECUTIVES

**Chairman:** G. Gilmer Minor III, age 66
**President, CEO, and Director:** Craig R. Smith, age 55, $717,307 pay
**CFO:** James L. (Jim) Bierman, age 55
**SVP, Operations:** Charles C. Colpo, age 49, $313,415 pay
**SVP, Human Resources:** Erika T. Davis, age 43
**SVP, General Counsel, and Corporate Secretary:** Grace R. den Hartog, age 55, $321,609 pay
**SVP and CIO:** Richard W. Mears, age 45
**VP and Treasurer:** Richard F. (Dick) Bozard, age 59
**SVP, Business Development:** Mark A. Van Sumeren, age 49, $415,768 pay
**VP and Controller:** Olwen B. Cape, age 57
**VP, Quality and Communications:** Hugh F. Gouldthorpe Jr., age 68
**Director, Finance:** Chuck Graves
**Director, Investor Communications:** Truitt (Trudi) Allcott
**Auditors:** KPMG LLP

## LOCATIONS

**HQ:** Owens & Minor, Inc.
9120 Lockwood Blvd., Mechanicsville, VA 23116
**Phone:** 804-723-7000 **Fax:** 804-723-7100
**Web:** www.owens-minor.com

## PRODUCTS/OPERATIONS

**Selected Subsidiaries**

Access Diabetic Supply, LLC
O&M Canada, Inc.
O&M Funding Corp.
OM Solutions International, Inc.
OMI International, Ltd. (British Virgin Islands)
Owens & Minor Distribution, Inc.
Owens & Minor Healthcare Supply, Inc.
Owens & Minor Medical, Inc.

## COMPETITORS

Cardinal Health
CVS/Caremark
Henry Schein
McKesson Medical-Surgical
Medline Industries
Moore Medical
PolyMedica
PSS World Medical
Rite Aid
Surgical Express
Walgreen

## HISTORICAL FINANCIALS

Company Type: Public

**Income Statement** FYE: December 31

| | REVENUE ($ mil.) | NET INCOME ($ mil.) | NET PROFIT MARGIN | EMPLOYEES |
|---|---|---|---|---|
| **12/06** | 5,534 | 49 | 0.9% | 4,600 |
| **12/05** | 4,822 | 64 | 1.3% | 3,700 |
| **12/04** | 4,525 | 61 | 1.3% | 3,392 |
| **12/03** | 4,244 | 54 | 1.3% | 3,245 |
| **12/02** | 3,960 | 47 | 1.2% | 2,968 |
| **Annual Growth** | 8.7% | 0.8% | — | 11.6% |

**2006 Year-End Financials**

Debt ratio: 79.1%
Return on equity: 9.2%
Cash ($ mil.): 5
Current ratio: 1.89
Long-term debt ($ mil.): 433
No. of shares (mil.): 40
Dividends
Yield: 1.9%
Payout: 50.0%
Market value ($ mil.): 1,260

**Stock History** NYSE: OMI

| | STOCK PRICE ($) FY Close | P/E High | P/E Low | PER SHARE ($) Earnings | Dividends | Book Value |
|---|---|---|---|---|---|---|
| **12/06** | 31.27 | 29 | 23 | 1.20 | 0.60 | 13.59 |
| **12/05** | 27.53 | 21 | 16 | 1.61 | 0.52 | 12.84 |
| **12/04** | 28.17 | 19 | 14 | 1.53 | 0.55 | 11.65 |
| **12/03** | 21.91 | 19 | 11 | 1.42 | 0.35 | 10.53 |
| **12/02** | 16.42 | 16 | 10 | 1.27 | 0.31 | 7.96 |
| **Annual Growth** | 17.5% | — | — | (1.4%) | 17.9% | 14.3% |

# Owens-Illinois

Owens-Illinois (O-I) has been involved in more toasts than Dick Clark and all Irish writers combined. The world's largest maker of glass containers, it has market-leading positions in the Americas, Europe, and the Asia/Pacific region. O-I's glass containers include bottles in a wide range of shapes and sizes used to hold beer, soft drinks, liquor, wine, juice, and other beverages. Major customers include Anheuser-Busch, H.J. Heinz, and SABMiller. The company has sold its plastics packaging business, which manufactured prescription bottles, tamper-proof closures, and injection-molded containers.

Early in 2007 the company announced that it was reviewing strategic options for its plastics operations (O-I Plastics), including a possible sale of the business. Several months later, O-I announced an agreement to sell its plastics division to Rexam for $1.8 billion; the deal was completed that summer. The sale included nearly 20 plants in the America, Asia, and Europe.

Owens-Illinois had already been boosting its glass operations and whittling down its plastics business, which accounted for a little more than 10% of sales before it was divested.

On the glass side, O-I has acquired nearly 20 glass container businesses since 1990, expanding its presence in Asia, Europe, and the Americas to consist of more than 80 manufacturing facilities in 22 countries. It also operates machine and mold shops that provide its glass-making equipment. As part of its effort to focus on its core glass business and reduce costs, O-I in 2006 shuttered a factory that made machine parts, and it closed a small recycling facility.

## HISTORY

The Owens Bottle Machine Corp. was incorporated in Toledo, Ohio, in 1907 as the successor to a four-year-old New Jersey company of the same name. It initially grew by acquiring small glass companies. In 1929 Owens bought the Illinois Glass Co. (medical and pharmaceutical glass) and became Owens-Illinois Glass.

The company bought Libbey Glass (tableware) in 1935. Three years later Owens-Illinois and Corning Glass, which were both studying uses for glass fiber, began Owens-Corning Fiberglass, a joint venture with a virtual industry monopoly.

After WWII Owens-Illinois (O-I) started to diversify beyond glass. The company went public in 1952. In 1956 it bought National Container (cardboard boxes). It also created a semi-rigid plastic container that was adopted by bleach and detergent companies.

The introduction of the non-returnable bottle in the 1960s gave new life to the glass industry. During the late 1960s the company bought Lily Tulip Cups (sold in 1981). In the 1970s the company started producing specialty optical and TV glass.

With the glass industry foundering at the beginning of the 1980s, O-I invested over $600 million in its glass operations. In 1986 O-I refused an initial purchase offer by Kohlberg Kravis Roberts & Co. (KKR), but KKR raised the offer and O-I was sold and went private. Total debt after the LBO was $4.4 billion.

In the years following the LBO, the company sold its forest products, mortgage banking, and health care businesses. O-I went public again in 1991 and expanded its plastics business with the purchase of Specialty Packaging Products in 1992, which added trigger sprayers and finger pumps to its line. The next year the company expanded its South American operations. O-I spun off Libbey Glass as a separate public firm and sold 51% of its interest in Kimble Glass (specialty packaging and laboratory ware; the rest was sold in 1997). The company acquired a majority stake in Ballarpur Industries, one of India's largest makers of glass containers.

In 1997 O-I bought Avir S.p.A., a European glass container maker. It also acquired assets of a bankrupt competitor, Anchor Glass, which gave it more than a 40% share of the US glass container market. O-I purchased the packaging unit of UK-based BTR (now called Invensys) in 1998. The next year the company sold its UK-based glass container maker, Rockware Group (formerly part of BTR), to Ireland-based container maker Ardagh, and its Chicago Heights pharmaceutical glass business to Germany-based glassmaker Gerresheimer Glas AG.

In 2000, following a short-lived victory for the company in asbestos-related litigation, a US district judge in Texas overturned a $1.6 billion default judgment to be awarded the company by former asbestos maker T&N Ltd.

Charges related to asbestos litigation and restructuring fees cost the company dearly in 2000 as it posted a $270 million loss for the year. In 2001 O-I sold its Harbor Capital Advisors business to the Netherlands-based Robeco Groep for an estimated $490 million.

From 1998 to the end of 2002, O-I acquired 18 glass container businesses in as many countries (including businesses in the Americas, Europe, and the Asia/Pacific region) and seven plastics packaging businesses that operate in 12 countries.

In January 2002 one of the company's businesses, Owens-Brockway Glass Container Inc., sold $1 billion worth of secured notes to pull the subsidiary out of debt, a plan intended to improve the health of the entire company.

In 2003 Joseph Lemieux stepped down as CEO of the company. Steven McCracken was named president and CEO. McCracken replaced Lemieux as chairman in 2004.

O-I completed its acquisition of BSN Glasspack, Europe's #2 glass container maker, for about $1.3 billion the same year. The deal made O-I Europe's largest container company. Late in 2004 O-I sold its American and European blow-molded plastics operations to Graham Packaging Company. The company's asbestos-related cash payments in 2005 were $171 million (down from $190 million in 2004). The company announced in 2005 that it would begin doing business as O-I.

Late in 2006, Steven McCracken resigned as chairman and CEO. Company board member Albert Stroucken, who held similar leadership roles at H.B. Fuller, succeeded McCracken.

## EXECUTIVES

**Chairman and CEO:** Albert P. L. (Al) Stroucken, age 59
**SVP and CFO:** Edward C. White, age 59, $381,100 pay
**SVP, Strategic Planning and General Counsel:** James W. Baehren, age 56, $457,000 pay
**SVP; General Manager, Domestic Glass Container:** Robert A. Smith, age 63
**SVP; General Manager, European Operations:** Franco Todisco, age 61
**SVP and Chief Human Resources Officer:** Stephen P. Malia
**VP and Treasurer:** Stephen P. Bramlage Jr.
**VP and Chief Procurement Officer:** Raymond C. Schlaff
**VP and CIO:** Gerard D. (Ged) Doyle
**VP, Investor Relations:** Paul F. Butts
**VP and General Counsel:** Philip McWeeny, $465,000 pay
**VP; President, North America Glass:** Matthew G. Longthorne
**VP; President, Global Glass Operations:** L. Richard Crawford, age 46
**VP; President, OI Asia Pacific:** Greg W. J. Ridder
**VP; President, Healthcare Packaging:** Joseph V. Conda, age 65
**VP, Glass Container Research and Development:** Robert E. Lachmiller
**President, Europe:** Jean-Marc Arrambourg
**President, Latin America Glass:** Jose A. Lorente
**President, Closure and Specialty Products:** Michael Paparone, age 53
**Chief Communications Officer:** Carol R. Gee
**Auditors:** Ernst & Young LLP

## LOCATIONS

**HQ:** Owens-Illinois, Inc.
1 Michael Owens Way, Perrysburg, OH 43551
**Phone:** 567-336-5000 **Fax:** 419-247-7107
**Web:** www.o-i.com

### 2006 Sales

| | $ mil. | % of total |
|---|---|---|
| North America | 2,917.0 | 39 |
| Europe | 2,865.9 | 38 |
| Asia/Pacific | 833.8 | 11 |
| South America | 805.3 | 11 |
| Other revenues | 101.5 | 1 |
| **Total** | **7,523.5** | **100** |

## PRODUCTS/OPERATIONS

### 2006 Sales

| | $ mil. | % of total |
|---|---|---|
| Glass containers | 6,650.4 | 89 |
| Plastics packaging | 771.6 | 10 |
| Other | 101.5 | 1 |
| **Total** | **7,523.5** | **100** |

## COMPETITORS

Alcoa
Amcor
Anchor Glass
AptarGroup
Ball Corporation
Bemis
Berry Plastics Group, Inc.
BWAY
Chesapeake Corporation
Consolidated Container
Constar International
Crown Holdings
Graham Packaging
Plastipak Holdings, Inc.
Rexam
Saint-Gobain
Sealed Air Corporation
Silgan
Sonoco Products
Tetra Pak
Vitro

## HISTORICAL FINANCIALS

Company Type: Public

### Income Statement

FYE: December 31

| | REVENUE ($ mil.) | NET INCOME ($ mil.) | NET PROFIT MARGIN | EMPLOYEES |
|---|---|---|---|---|
| **12/06** | 7,524 | (28) | — | 28,000 |
| **12/05** | 7,190 | (559) | — | 28,200 |
| **12/04** | 6,263 | 236 | 3.8% | 28,700 |
| **12/03** | 6,158 | (991) | — | 29,800 |
| **12/02** | 5,760 | (460) | — | 31,600 |
| **Annual Growth** | 6.9% | — | — | (3.0%) |

### 2006 Year-End Financials

Debt ratio: (4,926.3%)
Return on equity: —
Cash ($ mil.): 255
Current ratio: 1.03
Long-term debt ($ mil.): 4,719
No. of shares (mil.): 154
Dividends
Yield: —
Payout: —
Market value ($ mil.): 2,846

### Stock History

NYSE: OI

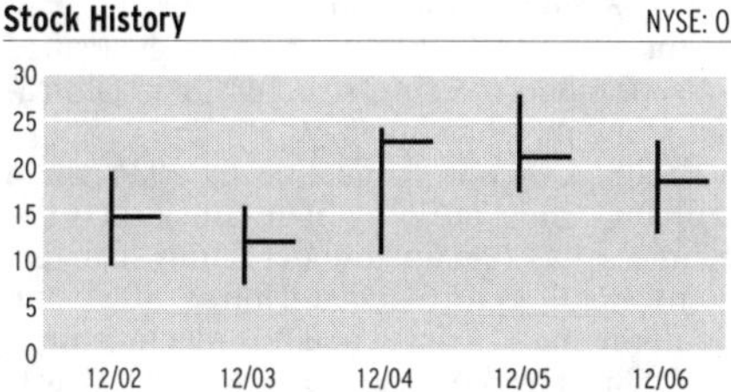


| | STOCK PRICE ($) FY Close | P/E High | P/E Low | PER SHARE ($) Earnings | Dividends | Book Value |
|---|---|---|---|---|---|---|
| **12/06** | 18.45 | — | — | (0.32) | — | 2.31 |
| **12/05** | 21.04 | — | — | (3.85) | — | 4.73 |
| **12/04** | 22.65 | 17 | 8 | 1.43 | — | 10.23 |
| **12/03** | 11.89 | — | — | (6.89) | — | 6.79 |
| **12/02** | 14.58 | — | — | (3.29) | — | 11.34 |
| **Annual Growth** | 6.1% | — | — | — | — | (32.8%) |

# PACCAR Inc

Old PACCARs never die, they just get a new Peterbilt. PACCAR is the world's second-largest manufacturer of big rig trucks, trailing Daimler's Freightliner subsidiary. Its lineup of light-, medium-, and heavy-duty trucks include the Kenworth, Peterbilt, DAF, Leyland DAF, and Foden nameplates. The company also manufactures aftermarket truck parts for its Kenworth and Peterbilt trucks. PACCAR's other products include Braden, Carco, and Gearmatic industrial winches. With the exception of a few company-owned branches, PACCAR's trucks and parts are sold through independent dealers. The company's PACCAR Financial Corporation and PacLease subsidiaries offer financing and truck leasing, respectively.

PACCAR's heavy-duty truck markets were in high gear again in 2005. The company racked up record medium- and heavy-duty truck deliveries in North America while achieving record market share in Europe. Aftermarket sales were also brisk. With all cylinders firing PACCAR turned in record 2005 profits.

PACCAR remains one of the industry's most financially healthy companies by focusing on innovating new products and technologies while keeping costs low. The company reinvests in its dealer network while keeping an eye on potential overcapacity issues.

Not satisfied with past successes, PACCAR is looking to the East for future growth opportunities, primarily in China and India.

The Pigott family, descendants of PACCAR's founder, owns about 6% of the company.

## HISTORY

William Pigott founded the Seattle Car Manufacturing Company in 1905 to produce railroad cars for timber transport. Finding immediate success, Pigott began to make other kinds of railcars in 1906. When the Seattle plant burned the next year, the company moved near Renton, Washington. In 1911 Pigott renamed the company Seattle Car & Foundry.

In 1917 Seattle Car merged with the Twohy Brothers of Portland. The new company, Pacific Car & Foundry, was sold to American Car & Foundry in 1924. Pacific Car then diversified into bus manufacturing, structural steel fabrications, and metal technology.

Pacific Car was in decline by 1934 when William's son Paul bought it; since then the company has remained under family management. Paul Pigott added Hofius Steel and Equipment and Tricoach, a bus manufacturer, in 1936. The company entered the truck-making business with the 1945 purchase of Seattle-based Kenworth.

In the 1950s Pacific Car became the industry leader in mechanical refrigerator car production. It began producing off-road, heavy trucks and acquired Peterbilt Trucks of Oakland (1958). To augment its winch business, Pacific Car bought Canada's Gearmatic in 1963.

The company moved its headquarters to Bellevue, Washington, in 1969 and changed its name to PACCAR in 1971. Acquisitions in the 1970s included Wagner Mining Equipment (1973); International Car, the largest US caboose producer (1975); and Braden Winch (1977). In 1980 PACCAR acquired UK-based Foden Trucks.

Demand for smaller trucks caused heavy-truck sales to drop 35% between 1979 and 1986, leading PACCAR to close two factories, its first closures in 41 years. In 1987 PACCAR bought Trico Industries (oil-drilling equipment). Also that year PACCAR entered the auto parts sales market, buying Al's Auto Supply; in 1988, it bought Grand Auto.

Truck demand hit a nine-year low in 1990. PACCAR responded by cutting its workforce by 11% that year and withdrawing from the auto parts wholesale market in 1991. The following year PACCAR acquired an interest in Wood Group ESP, a maker and servicer of oil-field equipment. In 1993 PACCAR bought heavy-equipment maker Caterpillar's line of winches.

In 1995 PACCAR opened a truck assembly plant in South Africa and bought the rest of VILPAC, its truck-making joint venture in Mexico. When workers in Quebec went on strike, the company closed the plant after eight months and shifted production to Mexico.

PACCAR expanded in Europe in 1996 by acquiring medium- and heavy-duty truck maker DAF Trucks (the Netherlands). Charles Pigott retired in 1996, and his son Mark became chairman and CEO. In 1997 PACCAR sold Trico Industries to EVI. The next year PACCAR bought light- and medium-duty truck maker Leyland Trucks (UK). After an $80 million renovation, the company began producing medium-duty trucks in 1999 at its Quebec plant, which had idled after the strike. That year the company started Paccar.com, a venture capital fund for e-commerce startups, and ePaccar, an e-commerce marketplace for the trucking industry. It also sold its Al's Auto Supply and Grand Auto parts retail operations to CSK Auto for $143 million.

Slow sales of large trucks prompted the company to lay off about one-third of its hourly — and almost one-fifth of its salaried — Peterbilt workers in 2000. Early in 2001 PACCAR entered a long-term contract with engine maker Cummins for the supply of heavy-duty engines. Later in 2001, in order to bring production in line with worldwide demand, PACCAR closed two truck manufacturing facilities — the Seattle Kenworth plant and a Foden plant in the UK. The Peterbilt Motors Company plant in Nashville, Tennessee signed a five-year labor agreement with United Auto Workers (UAW) labor union in 2003.

## EXECUTIVES

**Chairman and CEO:** Mark C. Pigott, age 54, $1,282,692 pay
**Vice Chairman:** Michael A. Tembreull, age 61, $862,885 pay
**President:** Thomas E. Plimpton, age 57, $659,788 pay
**VP:** Ronald E. Armstrong, age 51
**VP and Controller:** Michael T. Barkley, age 51
**VP and CIO:** Janice Skredsvig, age 46
**Secretary:** Janice M. D'Amato
**Treasurer:** Robin E. Eaton
**VP Human Resources:** Jack LeVier
**Auditors:** Ernst & Young LLP

## LOCATIONS

**HQ:** PACCAR Inc
777 106th Ave. NE, Bellevue, WA 98004
**Phone:** 425-468-7400 **Fax:** 425-468-8216
**Web:** www.paccar.com

### 2006 Sales

| | $ mil. | % of total |
|---|---|---|
| US | 8,496.5 | 52 |
| Europe | 4,589.8 | 28 |
| Other regions | 3,367.8 | 20 |
| **Total** | **16,454.1** | **100** |

## PRODUCTS/OPERATIONS

### 2006 Sales

| | $ mil. | % of total |
|---|---|---|
| Trucks & other | 15,503.3 | 94 |
| Financial services | 950.8 | 6 |
| **Total** | **16,454.1** | **100** |

### Selected Divisions and Subsidiaries

DAF Trucks, N.V. (the Netherlands)
Foden Trucks
Kenworth Mexicana S.A. de C.V.
Leyland Trucks Limited (UK)
PACCAR Australia Pty. Ltd.
PACCAR Financial Corp.
PACCAR Mexico, S.A. de C.V.
Peterbilt of Canada

## COMPETITORS

BorgWarner
Daimler
Eaton
Fiat
Ford
General Motors
Grupo Dina
Isuzu
Navistar
Nissan Diesel
Oshkosh Truck
Renault
Scania
Tenneco
Volvo

## HISTORICAL FINANCIALS

Company Type: Public

### Income Statement

FYE: December 31

| | REVENUE ($ mil.) | NET INCOME ($ mil.) | NET PROFIT MARGIN | EMPLOYEES |
|---|---|---|---|---|
| **12/06** | 16,454 | 1,496 | 9.1% | 21,000 |
| **12/05** | 14,057 | 1,133 | 8.1% | 21,900 |
| **12/04** | 11,456 | 907 | 7.9% | 20,500 |
| **12/03** | 8,236 | 527 | 6.4% | 16,100 |
| **12/02** | 7,219 | 372 | 5.2% | 16,500 |
| **Annual Growth** | 22.9% | 41.6% | — | 6.2% |

### 2006 Year-End Financials

Debt ratio: 163.4%
Return on equity: 35.8%
Cash ($ mil.): 2,674
Current ratio: 1.42
Long-term debt ($ mil.): 7,280
No. of shares (mil.): 249
Dividends
Yield: 1.2%
Payout: 12.9%
Market value ($ mil.): 16,128

### Stock History

NASDAQ (GS): PCAR

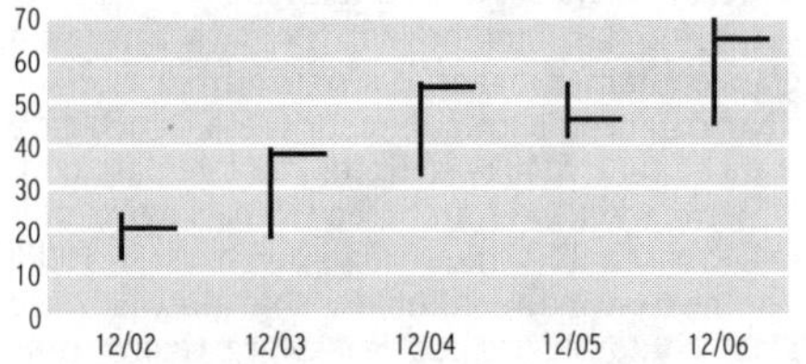

| | STOCK PRICE ($) FY Close | P/E High | P/E Low | PER SHARE ($) Earnings | Dividends | Book Value |
|---|---|---|---|---|---|---|
| **12/06** | 64.90 | 12 | 8 | 5.95 | 0.77 | 17.93 |
| **12/05** | 46.15 | 12 | 10 | 4.37 | 0.58 | 23.10 |
| **12/04** | 53.65 | 16 | 10 | 3.44 | 1.83 | 21.64 |
| **12/03** | 37.83 | 20 | 9 | 1.99 | 0.92 | 18.54 |
| **12/02** | 20.50 | 17 | 10 | 1.42 | 0.36 | 22.44 |
| **Annual Growth** | 33.4% | — | — | 43.1% | 20.9% | (5.5%) |

# Pall Corporation

Pall takes liquids and gases to the cleaners. The company makes filtration and separation systems designed to remove solid, liquid, and gaseous contaminants from a variety of materials. Pall's industrial business segment makes filtration products for general industrial applications, including water purification, as well as for use in the aerospace and microelectronics industries. The company's industrial business units include Pall Aeropower. Products of Pall's life sciences segment are used to help develop and manufacture drugs and for medical functions such as removing white blood cells from blood. Most of Pall's sales are made outside the US.

The company makes filter media from chemical film, metals, paper, and plastics; it also makes metal and plastic housings for its filters.

Pall hopes to grow by selling more specialty engineered filtration systems, which offer long-term revenue potential.

## HISTORY

Canadian-born chemist David Pall worked on the Manhattan Project helping develop systems to refine uranium for the first atomic bomb. In 1946 he founded Micro Metallic to develop filters for commercial applications. Pall added Abraham Krasnoff, a CPA, in 1950. The company went public in 1957 and was renamed Pall Corporation. During the 1960s it specialized in aircraft hydraulics and fuel systems for the defense industry. In 1969 Krasnoff became CEO.

In the late 1970s and during the 1980s, the company moved into the growing semiconductor and biotechnology industries. This process accelerated after the defense industry was hit by budget cuts late in the 1980s.

Pall researchers announced in 1995 the development of a filter that reduces the levels of HIV in blood serum to below detectable levels. In 1997 the company bought Gelman Sciences, maker of polymeric membranes and specialized medical disposable filters.

In 1998 Pall acquired Germany-based Rochem, an osmosis filtration system manufacturer, and entered a technology partnership with VI Technologies (Vitex) for exclusive marketing rights to Vitex's viral and bacterial inactivation chemistry. The following year Pall signed a $6 million water-purification deal with the Pittsburgh Water and Sewer Authority. Also in 1999 Pall announced a restructuring plan calling for job cuts and other spending reductions. The company sold its Well Technology division (filtration equipment and drilling services to oil and gas companies) to Oiltools International in 1999.

The German Red Cross Transfusion Center awarded Pall a $6 million contract for blood filtration equipment in 2000 after the German government mandated that all transfused blood must be filtered. Highlights in 2001 included alliances with biopharmaceutical companies QIAGEN N.V. and Stedim SA. In early 2002, Pall completed the acquisition of the Filtration and Separations Group from US Filter (now Siemens Water Technologies) for about $360 million. In 2003, Pall purchased Whatman HemaSure, the blood filtration business of Whatman plc.

Pall expanded in 2004 by buying BioSepra, a provider of chromatography technologies (used for protein purification and optimization), from Ciphergen Biosystems for about $32 million.

## EXECUTIVES

**Chairman, President, and CEO:** Eric Krasnoff, age 54
**COO; President, Pall Industrial:** Donald B. (Don) Stevens, age 61, $604,096 pay
**CFO and Treasurer:** Lisa McDermott, age 41, $480,396 pay
**SVP; President, Life Sciences Group:** Roberto Perez, age 57, $396,518 pay
**SVP; President, Pall Asia:** Andrew (Andy) Denver, age 56, $597,648 pay
**SVP, General Counsel, and Corporate Secretary:** Mary Ann Bartlett, age 60
**SVP, Manufacturing:** Gregory Scheessele, age 44
**SVP, Pall Industrial:** Michael J. Ywaniw
**SVP; President, Aerospace Group:** James R. (Jim) Western Jr., age 53
**SVP; President, Machinery and Equipment Group:** Reed Sarver, age 45
**SVP; President, Microelectronics Group:** Steven Chisolm, age 46
**SVP; President, Nihon Pall:** Riichi Inoue, age 55
**Group VP; President, BioPharmaceuticals Group:** Neil MacDonald, age 54
**Group VP; President, European Operations:** Heinz Ulrich Hensgen, age 52, $436,494 pay
**VP and Corporate Controller:** Frank Moschella
**VP Investor Relations and Communications:** Patricia Iannucci
**VP, Pall Advanced Separation Systems (PASS):** Glen Petaja
**VP, Water Processing:** Jeff Seibert
**President, Medical Group:** Allan S. Ross
**Director Public Relations:** Marcia Katz
**Auditors:** KPMG LLP

## LOCATIONS

**HQ:** Pall Corporation
2200 Northern Blvd., East Hills, NY 11548
**Phone:** 516-484-5400 **Fax:** 516-484-5228
**Web:** www.pall.com

**2006 Sales**

| | $ mil. | % of total |
|---|---|---|
| Europe | 806.0 | 40 |
| Western Hemisphere | 727.5 | 36 |
| Asia | 483.3 | 24 |
| **Total** | **2,016.8** | **100** |

## PRODUCTS/OPERATIONS

**2006 Sales**

| | $ mil. | % of total |
|---|---|---|
| Industrial | | |
| General industrial | 772.0 | 38 |
| Microelectronics | 258.3 | 13 |
| Aerospace | 190.2 | 9 |
| Life sciences | | |
| Medical | 444.0 | 22 |
| Biopharmaceuticals | 352.3 | 18 |
| **Total** | **2,016.8** | **100** |

## COMPETITORS

CLARCOR
CUNO
Donaldson
Entegris
ESCO Technologies
GE Healthcare
Millipore
Parker Hannifin
Sartorius
Siemens Water Technologies

## HISTORICAL FINANCIALS

Company Type: Public

**Income Statement** FYE: Saturday nearest July 31

| | REVENUE ($ mil.) | NET INCOME ($ mil.) | NET PROFIT MARGIN | EMPLOYEES |
|---|---|---|---|---|
| **7/06** | 2,017 | 146 | 7.2% | 10,828 |
| **7/05** | 1,902 | 141 | 7.4% | 10,400 |
| **7/04** | 1,771 | 152 | 8.6% | 10,300 |
| **7/03** | 1,614 | 103 | 6.4% | 10,500 |
| **7/02** | 1,291 | 73 | 5.7% | 10,700 |
| **Annual Growth** | 11.8% | 18.7% | — | 0.3% |

**2006 Year-End Financials**

Debt ratio: 54.3%
Return on equity: 12.6%
Cash ($ mil.): 318
Current ratio: 2.59
Long-term debt ($ mil.): 640
No. of shares (mil.): 122
Dividends
Yield: 2.0%
Payout: 45.7%
Market value ($ mil.): 3,186

**Stock History** NYSE: PLL

| | STOCK PRICE ($) FY Close | P/E High | P/E Low | PER SHARE ($) Earnings | Dividends | Book Value |
|---|---|---|---|---|---|---|
| **7/06** | 26.08 | 28 | 22 | 1.16 | 0.53 | 9.65 |
| **7/05** | 30.97 | 28 | 20 | 1.12 | 0.38 | 9.17 |
| **7/04** | 23.17 | 23 | 18 | 1.20 | 0.18 | 8.50 |
| **7/03** | 22.68 | 30 | 18 | 0.83 | 0.36 | 7.50 |
| **7/02** | 16.49 | 42 | 27 | 0.59 | 0.52 | 6.68 |
| **Annual Growth** | 12.1% | — | — | 18.4% | 0.5% | 9.6% |

# Palm, Inc.

Palm read the future and decided to split. A leading provider of handheld computers, the company offers products ranging from entry-level devices to pricier models that include Internet features. The Palm line tops out with its Treo line of smart phones. The company sells its products directly and through distributors, wireless service carriers, retailers, and other resellers. With a move that differentiated its dual revenue streams, Palm split into two units; it spun off its operating system licensing business as PalmSource (now ACCESS Systems Americas) in 2003. It now offers both ACCESS and Microsoft-based products.

In mid-2007 Palm announced a recapitalization plan that calls for private equity firm Elevation Partners to purchase a 25% stake in Palm for $325 million. Concurrent with the closing of the transaction, two Palm board members, including chairman Eric Benhamou, will resign; they will be replaced by three new directors, including two former Apple executives. Palm will pay $940 million ($325 million from Elevation, $400 million in debt, plus existing cash) to its current shareholders.

Though its name has long been synonymous with handheld computers, Palm now generates the majority of its revenues from smart phones. The company's successful product transition has allowed Palm to remain viable, but it has also broadened the competition it faces. While the company historically dominated the handheld computer market, as a smart phone provider it runs up against established handset vendors such as Nokia and Sony-Ericsson. Looking to augment its Treo line, the company introduced a portable computer called Foleo in 2007. Touted as a "mobile companion," the device syncs with Treo phones and provides a larger screen and keyboard for managing e-mail.

In 2006 Palm agreed to pay $22.5 million to settle a long-running patent dispute with Xerox over handwriting recognition technology. NTP, the patent holding company best known for successfully challenging the technology behind Research In Motion's Blackberry products and services, filed a similar suit against Palm late in 2006.

Distributor Ingram Micro and wireless service carriers AT&T, Sprint Nextel, and Verizon Wireless are among Palm's largest customers.

## HISTORY

Jeff Hawkins and Donna Dubinsky joined forces in 1992 to form Palm Computing. Ed Colligan joined the following year. Hawkings had worked at Intel and GRiD Systems (which brought the first pen-based computer to the market); Dubinsky at Apple and Claris; and Colligan at Radius Corp. (a maker of Macintosh clones). The company's initial product was Graffiti input software for handheld devices.

U.S. Robotics, a leading maker of computer modems, bought Palm for $44 million in 1995. The following year Palm unveiled its PalmPilot connected organizer. More than a million Pilots were sold within 18 months.

When U.S. Robotics was bought by 3Com in 1997, Palm became a subsidiary of the networking giant. 3Com sold 1.2 million Palms in 1998. That year Hawkins, Dubinsky, and Colligan left to form rival Handspring, which launched its Visor product in 1999.

In 1999, 3Com released the Internet-ready Palm VII and launched its Palm.net Internet service (now MyPalm) for handheld devices. The following year it named former Sony president Carl Yankowski to Palm's CEO post. In 2000, 3Com sold a minority stake in Palm (by then its fastest-growing unit) to the public in an offering worth about $875 million. Palm's separation from 3Com was completed later that year when 3Com distributed to its shareholders its remaining shares of Palm.

With an eye toward strengthening its dominant position in the corporate market, Palm in early 2001 agreed to acquire infrastructure software maker Extended Systems. Faced with slowing sales during an industrywide downturn, Palm announced soon after that it would cut as much as 15% of its workforce. The company then terminated its plan to buy Extended Systems, agreeing later to sell Extended software, which allows access to databases through Palm products.

Palm also created a separate unit for its operating systems (OS) software, and acquired the software and intellectual property assets of OS specialist Be. In the wake of Palm's restructuring efforts, Yankowski resigned as CEO in late 2001; Benhamou was named CEO.

The company's product line received a makeover in 2002, when Palm unveiled two new offerings: Tungsten for enterprise applications at the high end, and the low-priced Zire for the consumer market.

Palm spun off its operating system licensing business as PalmSource in 2003 and changed its name to palmOne. Todd Bradley became CEO of palmOne. After it completed the spin-off, palmOne acquired Handspring in a stock swap valued at about $169 million. The acquisition brought Handspring's line of Treo smart phones to the Palm lineup.

Early in 2005 Bradley stepped down as CEO and Colligan replaced him. Later that year it agreed to pay PalmSource $30 million for full rights to the Palm brand. Palm missed a chance to acquire PalmSource when it was outbid by Japan's ACCESS. palmOne changed its name back to Palm in mid-2005.

## EXECUTIVES

**Chairman:** Eric A. Benhamou, age 51
**Executive Chairman:** Jonathan (Jon) Rubinstein, age 51
**President, CEO, and Director:** Edward T. (Ed) Colligan, age 46, $956,950 pay
**SVP and CFO:** Andrew J. (Andy) Brown, age 47, $562,199 pay
**SVP, General Counsel, and Secretary:** Mary E. Doyle, age 55, $444,442 pay
**SVP Worldwide Sales and Customer Service:** C. John Hartnett, age 44, $439,493 pay
**SVP Business Development:** Mark S. Bercow, age 46, $378,657 pay
**SVP Engineering:** Michael R. (Mike) Farese, age 60
**SVP Global Operations:** Ronald R. (Ron) Rhodes, age 59
**SVP Human Resources:** Renata A. (Rena) Lane, age 52
**SVP Marketing:** Brodie Keast, age 51
**VP Europe, Middle East, and Africa:** Roy Bedlow
**VP Tax, Trade, and Treasury:** Karen Harrison
**Executive Team:** Jeffrey C. (Jeff) Hawkins, age 50
**Senior Director APAC:** Karthik Srinivasan
**Auditors:** Deloitte & Touche LLP

## LOCATIONS

**HQ:** Palm, Inc.
950 W. Maude Ave., Sunnyvale, CA 94085
**Phone:** 408-617-7000 **Fax:** 408-617-0100
**Web:** www.palm.com

### 2007 Sales

| | $ mil. | % of total |
|---|---|---|
| US | 1,174.3 | 75 |
| Other countries | 386.2 | 25 |
| **Total** | **1,560.5** | **100** |

## PRODUCTS/OPERATIONS

### 2007 Sales

| | $ mil. | % of total |
|---|---|---|
| Smartphones | 1,250.0 | 80 |
| Handheld computers | 310.5 | 20 |
| **Total** | **1,560.5** | **100** |

### Selected Products

Smart phones (Treo)
Handhelds (Palm, Tungsten)
Mobile computers (Foleo)

## COMPETITORS

Acer
Apple
BenQ
CASIO COMPUTER
Danger
Dell
Fujitsu
Fujitsu Siemens
Garmin
Hewlett-Packard
High Tech Computer
Kyocera
Microsoft
MiTAC
Motorola, Inc.
NEC
Nokia
OQO
Psion
RIM
Samsung Electronics
SANYO
Sharp
Sharp Electronics
Sony
Sony Ericsson Mobile
Toshiba

## HISTORICAL FINANCIALS

Company Type: Public

### Income Statement

FYE: Friday nearest May 31

| | REVENUE ($ mil.) | NET INCOME ($ mil.) | NET PROFIT MARGIN | EMPLOYEES |
|---|---|---|---|---|
| 5/07 | 1,561 | 56 | 3.6% | 1,247 |
| 5/06 | 1,579 | 336 | 21.3% | 1,103 |
| 5/05 | 1,270 | 66 | 5.2% | 907 |
| 5/04 | 950 | (22) | — | 699 |
| 5/03 | 872 | (443) | — | 982 |
| Annual Growth | 15.7% | — | — | 6.2% |

### 2007 Year-End Financials

Debt ratio: —
Return on equity: 5.5%
Cash ($ mil.): 547
Current ratio: 1.95
Long-term debt ($ mil.): —
No. of shares (mil.): 104
Dividends
Yield: —
Payout: —
Market value ($ mil.): 1,689

### Stock History

NASDAQ (GS): PALM

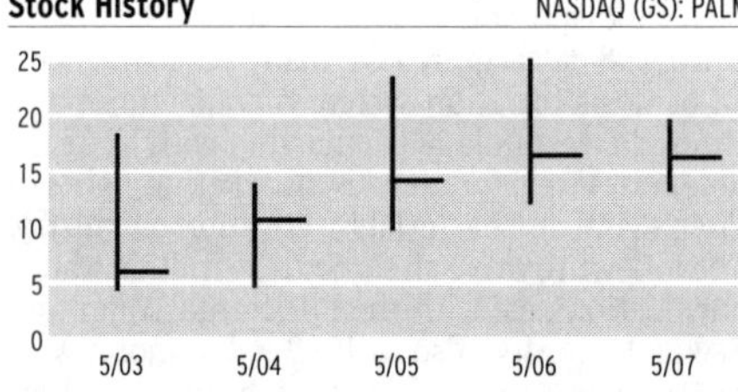


| | STOCK PRICE ($) FY Close | P/E High | P/E Low | PER SHARE ($) Earnings | PER SHARE ($) Dividends | PER SHARE ($) Book Value |
|---|---|---|---|---|---|---|
| 5/07 | 16.27 | 36 | 25 | 0.54 | — | 10.24 |
| 5/06 | 16.48 | 8 | 4 | 3.19 | — | 9.51 |
| 5/05 | 14.21 | 36 | 15 | 0.64 | — | 11.74 |
| 5/04 | 10.61 | — | — | (0.28) | — | 10.45 |
| 5/03 | 5.99 | — | — | (7.61) | — | 8.75 |
| Annual Growth | 28.4% | — | — | — | — | 4.0% |

# The Pantry, Inc.

If you've ever passed through the Carolinas on business, or made the trip to Disney World, chances are The Pantry has provided fuel for your car and body. The company is the leading convenience store operator in the southeastern US with more than 1,630 shops in 11 states. More than 80% of the company's stores do business under the Kangaroo Express banner. Other store names include Golden Gallon, Lil' Champ and The Pantry (naturally). The stores sell beverages, candy, gasoline, magazines, and tobacco products, among other items. Fuel accounts for more than three-quarters of the company's sales. Investment firm Chilton Investment Co. owns nearly 20% of The Pantry's common stock.

The company's outlets, which are conventional in size (about 2,600 sq. ft.), are located near such tourist destinations as Myrtle Beach and Hilton Head, South Carolina, and Orlando, Florida. Wholesaler McLane Company supplies more than half of the company's merchandise. Nearly 200 stores have fast-food outlets, including Subway, Church's, and Hardee's.

Over the past few years the convenience store operator has been busy converting stores to the Kangaroo Express name in an effort to establish a consistent identity in the Southeast.

The Pantry is working to increase merchandise sales, including food service and private label products, which carry higher margins then gasoline sales.

The Pantry has used a roll-up strategy of acquiring other businesses within its industry in order to grow in the Southeast. To that end, in April 2007 the company purchased 66 Petro Express convenience stores in North and South Carolina for $275 million (plus inventory costs) and its affiliated wholesale fuels business Carolina Petroleum Distributors. In 2006 the firm acquired about 110 locations from various companies, including Waring Oil Co. and Shop-A-Snak Food Mart, among others. It's building its presence in the state of Alabama with its recent purchase of nearly 40 stores there. Additionally, the convenience store operator acquired two dozen Sun Stop c-stores located in Georgia, Alabama, and Florida through a deal with Southwest Georgia Oil Company, inked in late 2006.

## HISTORY

North Carolina businessmen Sam Wornom and Truby Proctor (president of Lee Moore Oil Co.) founded The Pantry in 1967 in Sanford, North Carolina. The chain added new stores by borrowing against its existing stores, paying the debt with new sales.

The Pantry had grown to about 480 outlets in 1987 when investment firm Montrose Capital bought Wornom's stake. Founded by former Duke University business professor Clay Hamner, Montrose's shareholders included J. B. Fuqua (after whom the Duke business school is named), the late Dave Thomas (the Wendy's fast-food chain founder), and Wayne Rogers (Trapper John in the TV series M*A*S*H). Montrose gained control of The Pantry when it acquired half of Proctor's shares in 1990. Proctor remained as CEO.

With poor sales, the company restructured during the early 1990s, closing unprofitable stores and cutting costs. After struggling in 1991 and 1992, The Pantry made a slim profit in 1993. However, burdened by debt, the company was without the cash to make further substantive acquisitions, and it resumed its annual losses the following year.

In 1995 Proctor sold his remaining shares to Freeman Spogli & Co., a California-based investment firm specializing in management-led buyouts, and Chase Manhattan Capital. The next year Freeman Spogli and Chase Manhattan acquired the rest of the company from Montrose. Freeman Spogli owned 76% of The Pantry and Chase Manhattan owned 23% until more shares were issued to management and directors. Peter Sodini, a former CEO with supermarket chain Purity Supreme (acquired by Stop & Shop), became CEO that year.

After a string of small acquisitions in early 1997, The Pantry more than doubled in size by paying about $135 million to Docks U.S.A. for the Lil' Champ Food Stores convenience store chain. Lil' Champ — named for founder Julian Jackson, a bantamweight boxing champion in the 1930s — had 489 outlets, including 150 in Jacksonville, Florida.

The Pantry continued to bulk up in 1998, acquiring Quick Stop, a 75-store chain in the Carolinas, and 41 Zip Mart stores in North Carolina and eastern Virginia. In early 1999 The Pantry acquired 121 Handy Way stores in central Florida, many of which operated fast-food outlets such as Hardee's and Subway. The Pantry went public that year to raise money to pay nearly $450 million in debt stemming from its acquisitions. Shortly thereafter, the company bought 53 Depot Food Store outlets in Georgia and South Carolina from R & H Maxxon.

In late 1999 The Pantry added the 49-store Kangaroo chain in Georgia, and in early 2000 it purchased the On-The-Way Foods Stores chain of 12 stores in Virginia and North Carolina. Other purchases in 2000 furthering the company's southeastern US expansion included 33 MiniMart and Big K chain stores, and 26 Fast Lane convenience stores in Louisiana and Mississippi from R.R. Morrison and Son.

In 2003 the company completed the acquisition of the 138-store Golden Gallon chain from Ahold USA for about $187 million.

The Pantry acquired D & D Oil Co. (operator of 53 convenience stores under the Cowboys banner in Alabama, Georgia, and Mississippi) in April 2005. In August it purchased 23 convenience stores in Virginia (operating under the Sentry Food Mart banner) from Angus I. Hines.

In May 2006 the company acquired the 38-store Shop-A-Snak Food Mart convenience store chain in Alabama, doubling its store count in the state. In August it completed the acquisition of six Fuel Mate convenience stores in North Carolina.

Continuing its buying spree in 2007, The Pantry acquired 16 Angler's Mini-Mart stores in Charleston, South Carolina and a single convenience store in Sanford, North Carolina in mid-January. In April the company closed on 66 Petro Express convenience stores in North and South Carolina for $275 million (plus inventory costs) and its affiliated wholesale fuels business Carolina Petroleum Distributors. Also in April it purchased about a dozen Fast Phil's convenience stores in the Spartanburg, South Carolina market from Willard Oil Co.

## EXECUTIVES

**Chairman, President, and CEO:** Peter J. Sodini, age 66, $1,811,923 pay (prior to promotion)
**CFO:** Frank G. Paci, age 49
**SVP, Administration:** Steven J. Ferreira, age 50, $620,538 pay
**SVP, Fuels:** Keith S. Bell, age 42
**SVP, Human Resources:** Melissa H. Anderson, age 42
**SVP, Operations:** David M. Zaborski, age 51, $604,616 pay (prior to promotion)
**VP, Information Services:** Ed Collupy
**Corporate Controller:** Berry Epley
**Director, Personnel:** Diana King
**Investor Relations:** Belinda Wright
**Auditors:** Deloitte & Touche LLP

## LOCATIONS

**HQ:** The Pantry, Inc.
1801 Douglas Dr., Sanford, NC 27330
**Phone:** 919-774-6700 **Fax:** 919-774-3329
**Web:** www.thepantry.com

The Pantry's stores are located primarily in fast-growing cities and coastal resort areas of the Carolinas and Florida, but The Pantry's pit stops are also in Alabama, Georgia, Indiana, Kentucky, Louisiana, Mississippi, Tennessee, and Virginia.

### 2006 Stores

| | No. |
|---|---|
| Florida | 441 |
| North Carolina | 325 |
| South Carolina | 236 |
| Georgia | 125 |
| Tennessee | 101 |
| Alabama | 77 |
| Mississippi | 73 |
| Virginia | 50 |
| Kentucky | 31 |
| Louisiana | 25 |
| Indiana | 9 |
| **Total** | **1,493** |

## PRODUCTS/OPERATIONS

### 2006 Merchandise Sales

| | % of total |
|---|---|
| Tobacco products | 31 |
| Packaged beverages | 17 |
| Beer & wine | 16 |
| General merchandise, health & beauty care | 6 |
| Self-service fast foods & beverages | 6 |
| Salty snacks | 5 |
| Candy | 4 |
| Fast food service | 4 |
| Dairy products | 3 |
| Services | 3 |
| Bread & cakes | 2 |
| Grocery & other merchandise | 2 |
| Newspapers & magazines | 1 |
| **Total** | **100** |

### 2006 Sales

| | $ mil. | % of total |
|---|---|---|
| Gasoline | 4,576.0 | 77 |
| Merchandise | 1,385.7 | 23 |
| **Total** | **5,961.7** | **100** |

### Stores

Bean Street Coffee Company
Big K Food Stores
Celeste
Cowboys
Depot
Express Stop
Fast Lane
Food Chief
Golden Gallon
Handy Way
Kangaroo
Kangaroo Express
Lil' Champ Food Store
Market Express
Mini Mart
The Chill Zone
The Pantry
Quick Stop
Smokers Express
Sprint
Worth

## COMPETITORS

7-Eleven
BI-LO
Couche-Tard
Crown Central
Cumberland Farms
Delhaize America
Exxon Mobil
Gate Petroleum
Publix
Racetrac Petroleum
Spinx Company
Winn-Dixie

## HISTORICAL FINANCIALS

Company Type: Public

**Income Statement** FYE: Last Thursday in September

| | REVENUE ($ mil.) | NET INCOME ($ mil.) | NET PROFIT MARGIN | EMPLOYEES |
|---|---|---|---|---|
| **9/06** | 5,962 | 89 | 1.5% | 12,005 |
| **9/05** | 4,429 | 58 | 1.3% | 10,803 |
| **9/04** | 3,493 | 16 | 0.4% | 9,751 |
| **9/03** | 2,750 | 12 | 0.4% | 9,856 |
| **9/02** | 2,494 | 2 | 0.1% | 9,502 |
| **Annual Growth** | 24.3% | 165.3% | — | 6.0% |

**2006 Year-End Financials**

Debt ratio: 250.1%
Return on equity: 30.3%
Cash ($ mil.): 120
Current ratio: 1.38
Long-term debt ($ mil.): 843
No. of shares (mil.): 23
Dividends
Yield: —
Payout: —
Market value ($ mil.): 1,246

**Stock History** NASDAQ (GS): PTRY

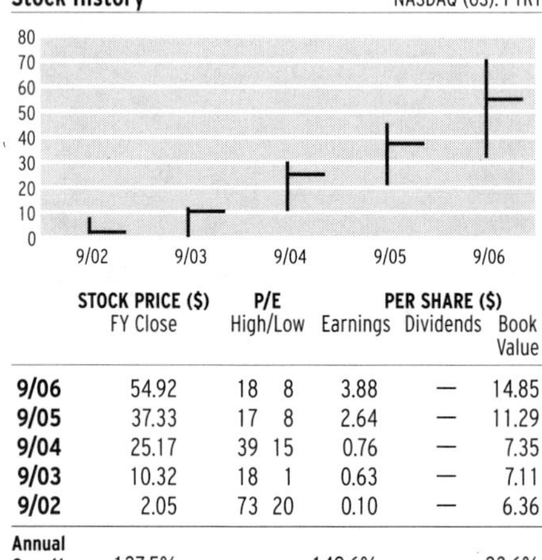


| | STOCK PRICE ($) FY Close | P/E High/Low | PER SHARE ($) Earnings | Dividends | Book Value |
|---|---|---|---|---|---|
| **9/06** | 54.92 | 18 8 | 3.88 | — | 14.85 |
| **9/05** | 37.33 | 17 8 | 2.64 | — | 11.29 |
| **9/04** | 25.17 | 39 15 | 0.76 | — | 7.35 |
| **9/03** | 10.32 | 18 1 | 0.63 | — | 7.11 |
| **9/02** | 2.05 | 73 20 | 0.10 | — | 6.36 |
| **Annual Growth** | 127.5% | — — | 149.6% | — | 23.6% |

# Parker Hannifin

Motion-control equipment made by Parker Hannifin helped sink the replicated *Titanic* in the Academy Award-winning film. Parker Hannifin's motion-control products use hydraulic (liquid) or pneumatic (gas or air) systems to move and position materials or to control equipment. Its industrial products include fluid connectors, hydraulic and automation systems, climate and industrial controls, and process instrumentation. These are sold to the customers in manufacturing, transportation, and food processing industries. The company also makes aerospace components such as fuel systems.

Parker Hannifin has focused on improving operating efficiencies by consolidating facilities and relocating product lines. The company, which acquired more than 40 companies between the mid-1990s and 2000, has not stopped its acquisitive ways. It continues to obtain companies that complement its existing operations, such as Denison International, a hydraulic fluid power system manufacturer. The acquisition of Denison gave Parker Hannifin a better footing in Asian and European markets. In the same vein, PH bought India's Markwel Hose Products in early 2005, a move that expanded its operations in the Asian motion and control markets.

In mid-2005 PH agreed to acquire UK-based filtration products maker the domnick hunter group for about $420 million — a move intended to greatly expand Parker Hannifin's filtration segment. Soon after that, however, Eaton Corporation joined in the bidding for domnick hunter with a bid that trumped Parker Hannifin's. After an even higher bid from Parker Hannifin, Eaton dropped out of the bidding, and Parker Hannifin was able to close the acquisition late in the year. domnick hunter drew such avid interest in part because it had developed products designed to protect against nuclear, biological, and chemical weapons.

In mid-2006 Parker Hannifin boosted its ownership in Taiyo Ltd. to about 60%, strengthening its hydraulics business in Japan and Asia. Parker Hannifin and Taiyo have been collaborating on business prospects since 2002. The company increased its equity ownership of Taiyo by purchasing voting stock previously held by Kyoei Steel.

In 2007 the company agreed to acquire German couplings maker Rectus AG.

## HISTORY

Entrepreneurial engineer Arthur Parker founded the Parker Appliance Company in 1918 to make pneumatic brake boosters. Its products were designed to help trucks and buses stop more easily. Unfortunately, Parker's own truck slid off an icy road and over a cliff in 1919, destroying the company's inventory and ending that line of business.

Undeterred, Parker started a hydraulics and pneumatic components business in 1924 to serve automotive and industrial clients. In 1927 the fuel-linkage system the company developed for the *Spirit of St. Louis* helped Lindbergh cross the Atlantic. The company prospered during the Depression; sales reached $2 million in 1934. Two of Parker's long-term clients were Douglas Aircraft and Lockheed.

The company went public in 1938. It employed 5,000 defense workers during WWII. After Parker died in 1945, his wife Helen hired new management to focus on the automation market. The firm bought cylinder maker Hannifin in 1957 and became Parker Hannifin.

In 1960 Parker Hannifin formed an international unit in Amsterdam, and it set up a German subsidiary in 1962. Overseas acquisitions and increased demand from the space program and the aviation market spurred growth in the 1960s. Patrick Parker, the founder's son, became president in 1968 and chairman in 1977. Parker Hannifin expanded its aerospace business in 1978 with the purchase of Bertea (electrohydraulic flight controls). Patrick Parker continued as CEO until 1983 and as chairman until 1999.

During the 1980s Parker Hannifin bought several smaller companies in niche markets, including Schrader Bellows (pneumatics, 1985), Compumotor (electromechanical applications, 1986), and Stratoflex and Gull Corp. (hoses and fittings and aerospace electronics, respectively, 1988).

The company again pushed into Europe during the 1990s, buying Sweden-based Trelleborg (hydraulic hoses) in 1992 and Atlas Automation (pneumatic components for automation equipment) in 1993. Parker Hannifin made six major purchases in 1994, including Finn-Filter Oy, Scandinavia's largest filter maker, and Polyflex, Europe's leading maker of thermoplastic hoses. The company added Abex NWL, the aerospace business of Germany's Pneumo Abex, in 1996.

Parker Hannifin expanded into the medical, petrochemical, and semiconductor markets in 1988 by purchasing Veriflo (high-purity valves and regulators) and into mobile equipment makers with Fluid Power Systems (hydraulic valves and electrohydraulic systems).

In 2000 Parker Hannifin acquired motion-control maker Commercial Intertech in a deal worth around $473 million. It also bought Whatman's industrial business (purification products and gas generators) and Wynn's International (industrial sealing products, in a $498 million deal).

President and COO Donald Washkewicz succeeded Duane Collins as CEO in 2001. (Collins remained chairman until his retirement in 2004, when Washkewicz replaced him in that role, too.) Parker Hannifin acquired Eaton's air conditioning unit, Aeroquip, the same year. Near the end of 2001 the company acquired the Dayco hydraulic and industrial hose operations of Mark IV Industries. The company acquired MTS Automation (analog and digital amplifiers, brushless motors, digital and servo controllers, linear motors) from MTS Systems Corporation in 2003 for an undisclosed amount; MTS Automation will become part of Parker Hannifin's Compumotor Division. Later in the year the company acquired Control By Light Systems' aircraft business (fiber-optic communication and control electronics); the Massachusetts-based company will become part of Parker Hannifin's Electronic Systems Division.

Parker Hannifin completed the acquisition of Denison International early in 2004 for about $2.4 billion. Later that year Parker Hannifin purchased Mead Fluid Dynamics Ltd., the European operations of Mead Fluid Dynamics Inc., for an undisclosed sum. Later in 2004 Parker Hannifin sold the automatic flight inspection system product line of its aerospace group to NXT LLC, also for an undisclosed sum. In October 2004 Parker Hannifin acquired privately held valve maker Sporlan Valve Co. for an undisclosed sum. The following month Parker Hannifin bought sealant maker Acadia Elastomers Corporation.

## EXECUTIVES

**Chairman, President, and CEO:** Donald E. Washkewicz, age 56

**EVP, Sales, Marketing, and Operations Support:** John D. (Jack) Myslenski, age 53, $1,178,974 pay

**EVP, Finance and Administration and CFO:** Timothy K. Pistell, age 59, $985,220 pay

**SVP and Operating Officer; President, Aerospace Group:** Robert P. (Bob) Barker, age 56, $759,953 pay (prior to title change)

**SVP and Operating Officer:** Lee C. Banks, age 43

**SVP and Operating Officer:** Thomas L. (Tom) Williams, age 47

**VP; President, Fluid Connectors Group:** Robert W. (Bob) Bond, age 48

**VP; President, Filtration Group:** John K. Oelslager, age 63

**VP; President, Automation Group:** Roger S. Sherrard, age 40

**VP; President, Seal Group:** Heinz Droxner, age 61

**President, Asia/Pacific:** Joseph J. (Joe) Vicic, age 61
**President, Latin America:** Ricardo Machado, age 58
**President, Climate and Industrial Controls Group:** Thomas F. Healy, age 46
**President, Hydraulics Group:** Jeffrey A. Cullman
**President, Instrumentation Group:** John R. Greco
**VP and CIO:** William G. Eline, age 50
**VP and Treasurer:** Pamela (Pam) Huggins, age 52
**VP and Controller:** Dana A. Dennis, age 58
**VP, Global Supply Chain and Procurement:** John G. Dedinsky, age 49
**VP, Human Resources:** Daniel (Dan) Serbin, age 52
**VP, Technology and Innovation:** Craig Maxwell, age 48
**VP, Worldwide Sales and Marketing:** Marwan M. Kashkoush, age 52
**VP, Corporate Communications:** Christopher M. Farage
**VP, General Counsel, and Secretary:** Thomas A. Piraino Jr., age 57
**VP, Tax and Director:** William R. Hoelting, age 50
**Auditors:** PricewaterhouseCoopers LLP

## LOCATIONS

**HQ:** Parker Hannifin Corporation
6035 Parkland Blvd., Cleveland, OH 44124
**Phone:** 216-896-3000 **Fax:** 216-896-4000
**Web:** www.parker.com

Parker Hannifin has manufacturing, service, and distribution facilities across the US and in about 40 other countries worldwide.

### 2007 Sales

| | $ mil. | % of total |
|---|---|---|
| North America | 6,483.2 | 60 |
| Other regions | 4,234.9 | 40 |
| **Total** | **10,718.1** | **100** |

## PRODUCTS/OPERATIONS

### 2007 Sales

| | $ mil. | % of total |
|---|---|---|
| Industrial | 7,964.5 | 74 |
| Aerospace | 1,685.5 | 16 |
| Climate & industrial controls | 1,068.1 | 10 |
| **Total** | **10,718.1** | **100** |

### Operating Groups and Selected Products

Aerospace
- Aircraft wheels and brakes
- Flight control components
- Fuel systems
- Pneumatic pumps and valves

Automation
- Human/machine interface hardware and software
- Indexers
- Multi-axis positioning tables
- Pneumatic valves
- Stepper and servo drives
- Structural extrusions
- Vacuum products

Climate and Industrial Controls
- Expansion valves
- Filter-dryers
- Gerotors
- Hose assemblies
- Pressure regulators
- Solenoid valves

Filtration
- Cabin air filters
- Compressed-air and gas-purification filters
- Fuel conditioning filters
- Fuel filters/water separators
- Hydraulic, lubrication, and coolant filters
- Lube oil and fuel filters
- Monitoring devices
- Nitrogen and hydrogen generators
- Process, chemical, and microfiltration filters

Fluid Connectors
- Couplers
- Hoses and hose fittings
- Tube fittings
- Valves

Hydraulics
- Accumulators
- Cylinders
- Electrohydraulic systems
- Hydrostatic steering units
- Metering pumps
- Motors and pumps
- Power units
- Rotary actuators
- Valves

Instrumentation
- Ball, plug, and needle valves
- Cylinder connections
- Fluoropolymer fittings
- Miniature solenoid valves
- Multi-solenoid manifolds
- Packless ultra-high-purity valves
- Quick connects
- Regulators
- Spray guns
- Transducers
- Tubing
- Ultra-high-purity tube fittings

Seals
- Gaskets and packings
- O-rings
- O-seals

## COMPETITORS

Actuant
Applied Industrial Technologies
Atlas Copco
Blount
Cascade Corporation
Colfax
Columbus McKinnon
Crane
Curtiss-Wright
Eaton
Goodrich
Honeywell International
IMI
Invensys
ITT Corp.
Komatsu
Mark IV
Moog
Numatics
Pall
Roper Industries
Senior plc
SPX
TSI
Tyco
United Technologies
Watts Water Technologies
Whittaker Controls
Woodward

## HISTORICAL FINANCIALS

Company Type: Public

### Income Statement

FYE: June 30

| | REVENUE ($ mil.) | NET INCOME ($ mil.) | NET PROFIT MARGIN | EMPLOYEES |
|---|---|---|---|---|
| **6/07** | 10,718 | 830 | 7.7% | 57,338 |
| **6/06** | 9,386 | 673 | 7.2% | 57,073 |
| **6/05** | 8,215 | 605 | 7.4% | 50,638 |
| **6/04** | 7,107 | 346 | 4.9% | 48,447 |
| **6/03** | 6,411 | 196 | 3.1% | 46,787 |
| **Annual Growth** | 13.7% | 43.4% | — | 5.2% |

### 2007 Year-End Financials

Debt ratio: 23.1%
Return on equity: 18.5%
Cash ($ mil.): 173
Current ratio: 1.76
Long-term debt ($ mil.): 1,090
No. of shares (mil.): 116
Dividends
Yield: 1.1%
Payout: 14.8%
Market value ($ mil.): 11,373

### Stock History

NYSE: PH

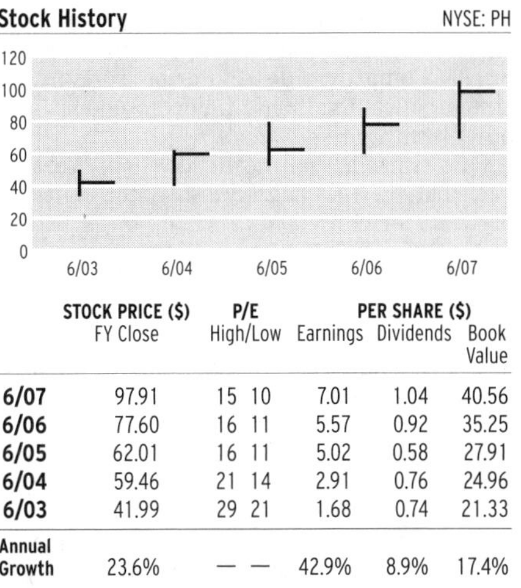


| | STOCK PRICE ($) FY Close | P/E High | P/E Low | PER SHARE ($) Earnings | PER SHARE ($) Dividends | PER SHARE ($) Book Value |
|---|---|---|---|---|---|---|
| **6/07** | 97.91 | 15 | 10 | 7.01 | 1.04 | 40.56 |
| **6/06** | 77.60 | 16 | 11 | 5.57 | 0.92 | 35.25 |
| **6/05** | 62.01 | 16 | 11 | 5.02 | 0.58 | 27.91 |
| **6/04** | 59.46 | 21 | 14 | 2.91 | 0.76 | 24.96 |
| **6/03** | 41.99 | 29 | 21 | 1.68 | 0.74 | 21.33 |
| **Annual Growth** | 23.6% | — | — | 42.9% | 8.9% | 17.4% |

# Patterson Companies

Patterson Companies helps doctors look at gift horses and mouths. A leading North American wholesaler of dental products, Patterson also distributes animal health supplies (including equine products) in the US through its Webster Veterinary unit. Its dental products include X-ray film and solutions, hand instruments, sterilization products, dental chairs and lights, and diagnostic equipment. It also sells office supplies, computer equipment, software, and other products and services for dental offices and laboratories. A third unit, Patterson Medical, distributes physical therapy and other rehabilitation medical equipment worldwide.

The company has been in the dental supply business since 1877, and it offers its customers some 90,000 different items, including about 4,000 private-label products. Patterson uses its size and breadth to present itself as a full-service partner to its customers, providing services such as technology consulting and equipment repair, in addition to a full complement of consumables, equipment, and software. Patterson Dental has grown through selective acquisitions, including the 2005 purchase of Michigan-based distributor Accu-Bite.

Though its dental segment is still its largest business, accounting for nearly three-quarters of sales, the 21st century has brought diversification to the Patterson inventory. Patterson added veterinary supplies to its distribution operations in 2001, with the purchase of J. A. Webster, and rehabilitation equipment in 2003, by acquiring AbilityOne Products (what is now Patterson Medical).

Patterson Medical operates worldwide, with its international operations headquartered in the UK. It sells equipment and supplies used by physical and occupational therapists, such as home health aids (bathing and dressing devices); orthopedic soft goods; walkers and canes; exam and therapy tables; and exercise equipment. Patterson Medical uses the Sammons Preston Rolyan name in North American markets and the Homecraft brand internationally. It has grown through a couple of purchases since the acquisition of AbilityOne; it bought Smith &

Nephew's rehab division (and with it the Rolyan and Homecraft brand names), as well as Medco Supply Company, a distributor of sports medicine products to athletic trainers, schools, and other health care providers.

Patterson's animal health division, Webster Veterinary, is a leading US distributor of health products for household pets and horses, with a particularly strong presence in the eastern part of the country. It sells more than 11,000 products — including vaccines and drugs, consumables, and diagnostic supplies — made by more than 500 suppliers. Like Patterson's other divisions, acquisitions have been part of Webster's growth strategy: it acquired pet supply company ProVet from Lextron in 2004; equine distributor Milburn Distributions in 2005; and veterinary practice management software maker Intra in 2006.

Since 2005 Patterson has been streamlining its distribution infrastructure, consolidating separate dental and veterinary warehouses into shared facilities that service multiple product lines.

Chairman Peter Frechette owns about 5% of the company.

## HISTORY

In 1877 brothers Myron and John Patterson bought a Milwaukee drugstore and later added dental supplies to the inventory. Myron bought the dental side of the business from his brother in 1891, moved to St. Paul, Minnesota, and started a dental supply store. His business later became a subsidiary of diversified manufacturer Esmark, which sold Patterson to food giant Beatrice in 1982. Recognizing that food and dental supplies were an odd mix, Patterson executives initiated a leveraged buyout in 1985.

In an industry as fragmented as some dental patients' smiles, the firm has used acquisitions to secure a leading position as a full-service provider. In 1987 Patterson bought D.L. Saslow, then the #3 distributor. Between 1989 and 1993 it bought smaller distributors in eight states and Washington, DC. In 1993, a year after it went public, Patterson bought the Canadian arm of bankrupt rival Healthco International.

Patterson benefits from several trends: rising per-person dental expenditures as Baby Boomers age, increasingly popular cosmetic dental work, and increased insurance coverage of dental services. During the mid- and late 1990s it continued to buy small local dental supply distributors, branching out across the US and Canada. In 1996 and 1997 Patterson expanded into front-office products with the purchase of Colwell Systems and EagleSoft. It took a few more bites out of the market with purchases of two more local distributors in 1998.

In 2000 it bought Micheli Dental Supply, a dental products distributor in California, and eCheck-Up.com, an online provider of payroll, human resources, payables processing, and other services. The following year Patterson purchased J.A. Webster, a distributor of veterinary supplies. Patterson acquired AbilityOne Products, a provider of medical rehabilitation supplies, in 2003.

In 2004 the company changed its name from Patterson Dental to Patterson Companies to reflect the expansion from dental products to veterinary and rehabilitation products.

## EXECUTIVES

**Chairman:** Peter L. Frechette, age 69, $382,071 pay
**President, CEO, and Director:** James W. Wiltz, age 62, $534,925 pay
**EVP, CFO, and Treasurer:** R. Stephen Armstrong, age 56, $257,401 pay
**VP, Human Resources:** Jerome E. Thygesen, age 49
**VP, Management Information Services:** Lynn E. Askew, age 44
**VP, Operations:** Gary D. Johnson, age 60
**President and CEO, AbilityOne:** Howard A. (Howie) Schwartz
**President, Patterson Dental Supply:** Scott P. Anderson, age 40
**President, Patterson Medical Products:** David Sproat, age 40, $278,122 pay
**President, Webster Veterinary Supply:** George L. Henriques
**Secretary and General Counsel:** Matthew L. Levitt
**Auditors:** Ernst & Young LLP

## LOCATIONS

**HQ:** Patterson Companies, Inc.
1031 Mendota Heights Rd., St. Paul, MN 55120
**Phone:** 651-686-1600 **Fax:** 651-686-9331
**Web:** www.pattersoncompanies.com

### 2007 Sales

| | $ mil. | % of total |
|---|---|---|
| US | 2,540.9 | 91 |
| Other countries | 257.5 | 9 |
| **Total** | **2,798.4** | **100** |

## PRODUCTS/OPERATIONS

### 2007 Sales

| | $ mil. | % of total |
|---|---|---|
| Dental | 2,064.6 | 74 |
| Veterinary | 399.4 | 14 |
| Rehabilitative | 334.4 | 12 |
| **Total** | **2,798.4** | **100** |

### 2007 Sales

| | $ mil. | % of total |
|---|---|---|
| Consumable & printed products | 1,757.5 | 63 |
| Equipment & software | 821.1 | 29 |
| Other | 219.8 | 8 |
| **Total** | **2,798.4** | **100** |

### Selected Subsidiaries

AbilityOne Homecraft Limited (UK)
AbilityOne Kinetec S.A. (France)
Accu-Bite, Inc.
Direct Dental Supply Co.
Intra Corp.
Patterson Dental Canada, Inc.
Patterson Dental Supply, Inc.
Patterson Logistics Services, Inc.
Patterson Medical Supply, Inc.
Patterson Office Supplies, Inc.
Patterson Technology Center, Inc.
Sammons Preston Canada, Inc.
Webster Veterinary Supply, Inc.

## COMPETITORS

AFP Imaging
Animal Health International
Benco Dental
Burkhart Dental
Cardinal Medical Products and Services
Darby Dental
DENTSPLY
Drs. Foster & Smith
Henry Schein
McKesson Medical-Surgical
Medline Industries
MWI Veterinary Supply
National Dentex
Professional Veterinary Products
Sybron Dental
TW Medical
Young Innovations

## HISTORICAL FINANCIALS

Company Type: Public

### Income Statement

FYE: Last Saturday in April

| | REVENUE ($ mil.) | NET INCOME ($ mil.) | NET PROFIT MARGIN | EMPLOYEES |
|---|---|---|---|---|
| **4/07** | 2,798 | 208 | 7.4% | 6,580 |
| **4/06** | 2,615 | 198 | 7.6% | 6,440 |
| **4/05** | 2,422 | 184 | 7.6% | 5,950 |
| **4/04** | 1,969 | 150 | 7.6% | 5,750 |
| **4/03** | 1,657 | 120 | 7.2% | 4,772 |
| **Annual Growth** | 14.0% | 14.9% | — | 8.4% |

### 2007 Year-End Financials

Debt ratio: 9.4%
Return on equity: 15.9%
Cash ($ mil.): 242
Current ratio: 2.35
Long-term debt ($ mil.): 130
No. of shares (mil.): 139
Dividends
Yield: —
Payout: —
Market value ($ mil.): 5,061

### Stock History

NASDAQ (GS): PDCO

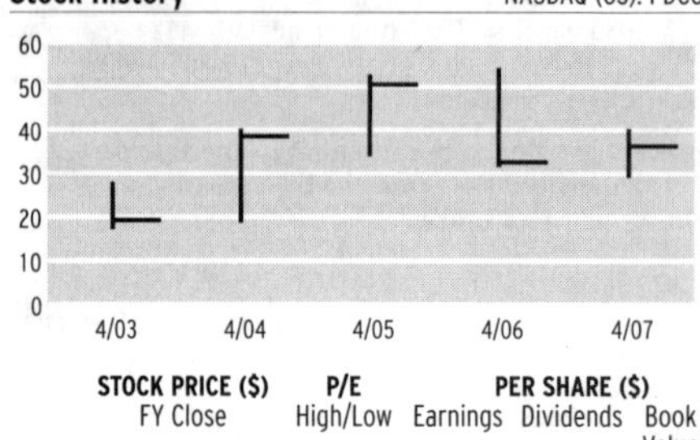


| | STOCK PRICE ($) FY Close | P/E High/Low | | PER SHARE ($) Earnings | Dividends | Book Value |
|---|---|---|---|---|---|---|
| **4/07** | 36.28 | 26 | 20 | 1.51 | — | 9.89 |
| **4/06** | 32.58 | 38 | 22 | 1.43 | — | 8.96 |
| **4/05** | 50.55 | 40 | 26 | 1.32 | — | 7.36 |
| **4/04** | 38.51 | 37 | 18 | 1.09 | — | 11.71 |
| **4/03** | 19.32 | 31 | 20 | 0.88 | — | 9.31 |
| **Annual Growth** | 17.1% | — | — | 14.5% | — | 1.5% |

# Paychex, Inc.

If Johnny Paycheck had founded Paychex, his song might have been, "Take This Job and . . . Let Us Do Your Payroll." The company processes the payrolls of about 543,000 clients, making it the second-largest payroll accounting firm in the US after Automatic Data Processing. Paychex also provides automatic tax payment, direct deposit, and wage garnishment processing. Its Human Resource Services-Professional Employer Organization unit offers such services as 401(k) record-keeping, risk management, benefits administration, and group insurance management. Paychex focuses on small and midsized businesses (ones with fewer than 100 employees). The company was established in 1979.

Paychex has plenty of room for growth: Although most of its target companies still shoulder the onerous burdens of wage and tax compliance themselves, there is a marked trend toward outsourcing. The company has thrown its hat in the online business-to-business arena, offering its services via the Internet. Paychex also expanded its German operations to include two offices, one in Hamburg and a second office in Berlin. As a result, by mid-2006 the company was already boasting 500 clients for this region.

Founder and chairman Thomas Golisano (owner of the Buffalo Sabres NHL team) owns about 10% of the company.

## HISTORY

Before founding Paychex in 1971, Thomas Golisano worked in a payroll accounting company that solicited the business of large firms. After discovering that 98% of all US businesses had 200 or fewer employees, he started his own company to cater to small business needs. Several friends started branches in other cities, and by 1979 the enterprise had grown to 17 locations, some company-owned, some joint ventures, and some franchised. Golisano began consolidating Paychex, buying out his partners and friends. In 1983 the company went public. (In 1994 and 1998 Golisano made unsuccessful bids for the New York governorship.)

The company has bolstered its market share through acquisitions, including Pay-Fone Systems (payroll processing, 1995), Olsen Computer Systems (software development, 1995) and National Business Solutions (benefit services, 1996). The company sought to entice more clients in the 1990s through such new services as a wage debit card that lets users draw upon salaries deposited in a special account. Paychex also launched 401(k) plan administration for small businesses and new-hire compliance reporting. In 1999 Paychex unveiled Internet Report Service, its first online product. The following year it launched a series of products and services geared toward accountants, including access to Internet-based payroll reports. In 2002 the company bought Advantage Payroll Services for $240 million. Paychex purchased payroll and human resource services provider InterPay in 2003. In 2004 the company expanded operations outside the US by opening an office in Germany.

## EXECUTIVES

**Chairman:** B. Thomas Golisano, age 64
**President, CEO, and Director:** Jonathan J. (Jon) Judge, age 52, $1,632,269 pay
**SVP, CFO, and Secretary:** John M. Morphy, age 58, $598,891 pay
**SVP Operations:** Martin Mucci, age 46, $589,334 pay
**SVP Sales and Marketing:** Walter Turek, age 53, $621,239 pay
**VP and Chief Legal Officer:** Stephanie L. Schaeffer
**VP and Controller:** Melinda A. Janik, age 49
**VP Central US Sales:** Suzanne E. Vickery, age 39
**VP Eastern Operations:** Lynn J. Miley, age 56
**VP Eastern US Sales:** Michael A. McCarthy, age 57
**VP Human Resource Services:** Martin Stowe
**VP Human Resource Services Sales:** Anthony (Tony) Tortorella, age 46
**VP Information Technology:** Daniel A. Canzano, age 52, $446,969 pay
**VP Major Market Services Sales:** Brad R. Flipse, age 37
**VP Organizational Development:** William G. Kuchta, age 59
**VP Product Management:** Steven R. Beauchamp, age 33
**VP Western Operations:** Leonard E. Redon, age 53
**VP Western US Sales:** Clifford Gibson, age 46
**President, Stromberg:** Seth Bernstein
**Corporate Communications Manager:** Laura Saxby Lynch
**Director Marketing:** Michael Haske
**Investor Relations:** Terri Allen
**Auditors:** Ernst & Young LLP

## LOCATIONS

**HQ:** Paychex, Inc.
911 Panorama Trail South, Rochester, NY 14625
**Phone:** 585-385-6666 **Fax:** 585-383-3428
**Web:** www.paychex.com

Paychex has more than 100 offices in the US and Germany.

## PRODUCTS/OPERATIONS

### Selected Services and Products

Payroll
- Direct deposit (deposit of salary directly into employee's bank account)
- New hire reporting
- Paychex Access Card (direct deposit and debit card service)
- Payroll (processing of employee paychecks and earnings statements, payroll records, and tax returns)
- Taxpay (automatic filing of local, state, and federal payroll tax returns)
- Wage garnishment processing

Human resources/Professional employer organization
- 401(k) plan record-keeping
- Employee benefits and related administration
- Employer regulatory compliance management
- Human resources administration
- Risk management
- Workers' compensation insurance

## COMPETITORS

Administaff
ADP
Barrett Business Services
CBIZ
Ceridian
CompuPay.
Gevity HR
TeamStaff

## HISTORICAL FINANCIALS

Company Type: Public

### Income Statement

FYE: May 31

| | REVENUE ($ mil.) | NET INCOME ($ mil.) | NET PROFIT MARGIN | EMPLOYEES |
|---|---|---|---|---|
| **5/07** | 1,887 | 516 | 27.3% | 11,700 |
| **5/06** | 1,675 | 465 | 27.8% | 10,900 |
| **5/05** | 1,445 | 369 | 25.5% | 10,000 |
| **5/04** | 1,294 | 303 | 23.4% | 9,400 |
| **5/03** | 1,099 | 294 | 26.7% | 8,850 |
| **Annual Growth** | 14.5% | 15.1% | — | 7.2% |

### 2007 Year-End Financials

Debt ratio: —
Return on equity: 28.6%
Cash ($ mil.): 4,564
Current ratio: 1.15
Long-term debt ($ mil.): —
No. of shares (mil.): 382
Dividends
Yield: 1.4%
Payout: 43.0%
Market value ($ mil.): 15,439

### Stock History

NASDAQ (GS): PAYX

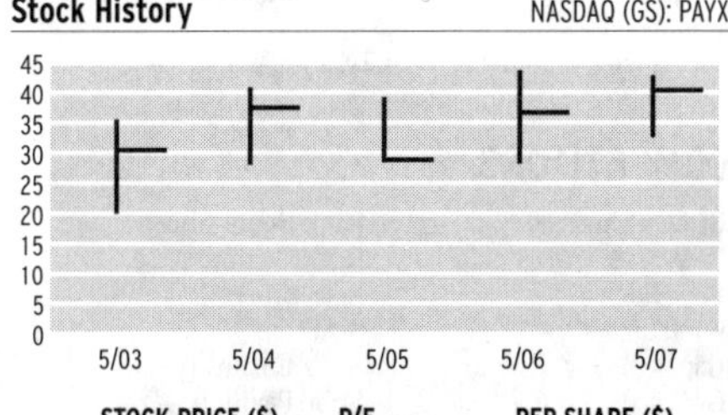

| | STOCK PRICE ($) FY Close | P/E High | P/E Low | PER SHARE ($) Earnings | Dividends | Book Value |
|---|---|---|---|---|---|---|
| **5/07** | 40.40 | 31 | 24 | 1.35 | 0.58 | 5.11 |
| **5/06** | 36.71 | 36 | 23 | 1.22 | 0.61 | 4.35 |
| **5/05** | 28.88 | 40 | 30 | 0.97 | 0.38 | 3.66 |
| **5/04** | 37.51 | 51 | 36 | 0.80 | 0.47 | 3.17 |
| **5/03** | 30.52 | 45 | 26 | 0.78 | 0.44 | 2.86 |
| **Annual Growth** | 7.3% | — | — | 14.7% | 7.2% | 15.6% |

# Payless ShoeSource

Payless ShoeSource helps just about any shoe enthusiast live like Imelda Marcos. It's the #1 shoe retailer in the Western Hemisphere, with about 4,570 self-service discount stores, mostly in the US, but also in Canada, the Caribbean, Central and South America, and Puerto Rico. Payless offers dress, athletic, and casual shoes; slippers; boots; and sandals for men, women, and kids. It primarily targets women between the ages of 18 and 49. Its North American stores stock, on average, 7,200 pairs of shoes in 500 styles.

Payless stepped up its expansion plans by buying footwear powerhouse The Stride Rite Corporation in August 2007. Valued at $800 million plus an estimated $100 million in debt, the Stride Rite deal paired popular Keds, Sperry Top-Sider, Tommy Hilfiger Footwear, Saucony, and other brands with the Payless portfolio. As part of the deal, Payless became a business unit of Collective Brands, Inc., a holding company created to operate three stand-alone units: Payless ShoeSource, The Stride Rite Corporation, and Collective Licensing International. The businesses operate as separate entities, maintain their current headquarters, and retain their brand identities. Matt Rubel, Payless CEO, serves as the holding company's top executive.

Payless, which operates about 585 stores in about a dozen foreign countries, has put the brakes on its international expansion to focus on its core Payless ShoeSource business in the US, where sales have been in a slump. It closed its only store in Japan last year. Overall the ailing shoe company has reduced its store count by nearly 70 outlets over the past two years.

Following in the footsteps of Gap and GapKids, about 465 of its stores have adjacent areas devoted to children's shoes called Payless Kids. The company also operates about 130 shoe departments inside ShopKo Stores, a discount retail chain primarily in the Midwest.

Through a partnership with American Ballet Theatre, Payless extended its reach into specialty footwear. As part of the multiyear agreement, Payless in mid-2007 launched a co-branded line of American Ballet Theatre (ABT) ballet, jazz, and tap shoes and accessories. The ABT deal and the company's recent purchase of the youth-oriented American Eagle brand of footwear is part of Payless' strategy to build a "house of brands."

Payless stores began selling American Eagle shoes in the spring of 2007. However, in April the clothing retailer filed a lawsuit against Payless that alleges it is misleading consumers to believe it's selling genuine American Eagle brand merchandise. (In 2006 Payless acquired from Jimlar Corp. its American Eagle brand of footwear and accessories.)

## HISTORY

Cousins Louis and Shaol Pozez founded Volume Distribution in Topeka, Kansas, in 1956. Volume pioneered the use of advertising and the self-service format in shoe retailing under the brand name Payless Shoes. When the company went public in 1962 as Volume Shoe, it had no competitor in the discount, self-service, family footwear market. However, in 1963 Sam Walton started Wal-Mart (with footwear as one of its departments), and Kmart also entered the discount shoe market.

Volume Shoe grew most rapidly between 1967 and 1972, adding 450 stores and expanding its presence to 32 states. During the decade, it acquired American Self-Service (manager of 352 Hill Bros. stores in 30 states) and the Modern Retail chain. By 1979 the company had 792 stores in operation, primarily in strip centers in major markets around the country.

Department store giant May Department Stores acquired Volume Shoe that year, and a year later the chain accounted for 10% of May's earnings. Louis and Shaol remained as CEO and president, respectively. Shaol added the CEO position to his duties when Louis retired in 1983, then he retired the following year. May appointed Silverman Jewelry CEO Richard Jolosky as president of its retail footwear business in 1984 (a position he held until 1988), and Volume Shoe acquired 38 stores from Craddock-Terry Shoe and 83 shoe stores from HRT Industries. By 1985 it had about 1,700 stores.

The discount shoe market suffered in the late 1980s from the advent of branded off-price retailers and the growing import shoe market. The company responded by selling brand-name shoes and launching a major expansion plan. May changed the shoe unit's name to Payless ShoeSource in 1991. The next year Payless rolled out its Payless Kids store format, a dedicated children's shoe section within or adjacent to its family stores. In 1994 the company purchased 550 stores from two Columbus, Ohio, chains (Kobacker Company and the Shoe Works).

As part of May's strategy to refocus on its department stores, Payless was spun off to shareholders in 1996. Jolosky returned to duty as Payless' president, and May veteran Steven Douglass was named CEO.

Also in 1996 the company rounded out its presence in the US by opening four stores in Alaska — the only state in the country where it had never done business. In 1997 Payless made its move into the mid-priced shoe market, acquiring Parade of Shoes, a 186-store chain in 14 states.

Jolosky stepped down as president in 1999 and was replaced by May veteran Ken Hicks. That year Payless announced an alliance with ShopKo Stores to open 160 in-store outlets in ShopKo locations. In 2000 the company formed a joint venture to run Payless stores in Central America and the Caribbean. In late 2001 and early 2002 the company laid off about 200 workers and announced the closing of about 70 Parade stores and about 40 Payless stores, though the company still opened an additional 90 stores that same year.

In 2004 the company shuttered about 400 stores, including its 180-odd Parade shoe stores and all of its Payless stores in Chile and Peru. It also closed about 260 Payless ShoeSource stores. The company also cut about 200 jobs.

Chairman and CEO Steven J. Douglass left the company in July 2005 and was succeeded as CEO by Matthew E. Rubel, formerly of Cole Haan.

In March 2007 Payless paid about $91 million to acquire Collective International, LP, a Denver-based brand development, management and licensing company. The acquisition put Payless in the brand management and licensing business, with a focus on youth, board-sport-inspired brands.

Payless purchased Stride Rite in August 2007 and created a holding company, Collective Brands, under which Payless, Stride Rite, and Collective Licensing operate.

## EXECUTIVES

**Chairman:** Howard R. Fricke, age 70
**President, CEO, and Director:** Matthew E. (Matt) Rubel, age 49, $1,329,644 pay (partial-year salary)
**EVP, Global Supply Chain:** Darrel J. Pavelka, age 51, $771,866 pay
**EVP and Chief Administrative Officer:** Douglas J. Treff
**SVP, CFO, and Treasurer:** Ullrich E. Porzig, age 61, $714,737 pay
**SVP, Human Resources:** Jay A. Lentz, age 63, $731,077 pay
**SVP, General Counsel, and Secretary:** Michael J. Massey, age 42, $592,868 pay
**SVP, International:** Theodore O. Passig
**SVP and Chief Marketing Officer:** Eran Cohen
**Division SVP:** Cathleen S. Curless
**Division SVP:** Michael R. Thompson
**Division SVP:** Michael Jeppesen
**Division SVP:** John Smith
**Division SVP, Corporate Strategy:** Paul Fenaroli
**VP, Product Design:** Robert Mingione
**Senior Analyst, Investor Relations:** Nicole R. (Nikki) Sloup
**Auditors:** Deloitte & Touche LLP

## LOCATIONS

**HQ:** Payless Shoesource, Inc.
3231 SE 6th Ave., Topeka, KS 66607
**Phone:** 785-233-5171 **Fax:** 785-368-7519
**Web:** www.paylessshoesource.com

### 2007 Stores

| | No. |
|---|---|
| US | |
| California | 543 |
| Texas | 393 |
| Florida | 284 |
| New York | 257 |
| Illinois | 192 |
| Pennsylvania | 162 |
| Ohio | 141 |
| Michigan | 134 |
| New Jersey | 128 |
| Other states | 1,752 |
| Canada | |
| Ontario | 140 |
| Other provinces | 175 |
| Central America | 152 |
| Puerto Rico & US Virgin Islands | 88 |
| South America | 31 |
| **Total** | **4,572** |

### 2007 Sales

| | $ mil. | % of total |
|---|---|---|
| US | 2,395.2 | 86 |
| Other countries | 401.5 | 14 |
| **Total** | **2,796.7** | **100** |

## PRODUCTS/OPERATIONS

### Selected Merchandise

Footwear (athletic, casual, dress, sandals, slippers, work boots)
Accessories (handbags, hosiery, shoe polish)

## COMPETITORS

Brown Shoe
DSW
Foot Locker
Footstar
Gap
Genesco
Goody's Family Clothing
IAC
Iconix Brand Group
J. C. Penney
Jack Schwartz
Kenneth Cole
Kmart
Kohl's
Nine West
Rack Room Shoes
Retail Ventures
Ross Stores
Sears
Shoe Carnival
Shoe Pavilion
Shoe Show
Skechers U.S.A.
Sports Authority
Target
TJX Companies
Vans
Wal-Mart
Weyco
Zappos.com

## HISTORICAL FINANCIALS

Company Type: Public

### Income Statement

FYE: Saturday nearest January 31

| | REVENUE ($ mil.) | NET INCOME ($ mil.) | NET PROFIT MARGIN | EMPLOYEES |
|---|---|---|---|---|
| **1/07** | 2,797 | 122 | 4.4% | 27,100 |
| **1/06** | 2,667 | 66 | 2.5% | 27,550 |
| **1/05** | 2,657 | (2) | — | 27,000 |
| **1/04** | 2,783 | (0) | — | 30,000 |
| **1/03** | 2,878 | 106 | 3.7% | 30,100 |
| **Annual Growth** | (0.7%) | 3.6% | — | (2.6%) |

### 2007 Year-End Financials

Debt ratio: 28.8%
Return on equity: 18.0%
Cash ($ mil.): 463
Current ratio: 2.38
Long-term debt ($ mil.): 202
No. of shares (mil.): 65
Dividends
Yield: —
Payout: —
Market value ($ mil.): 2,272

### Stock History

NYSE: PSS

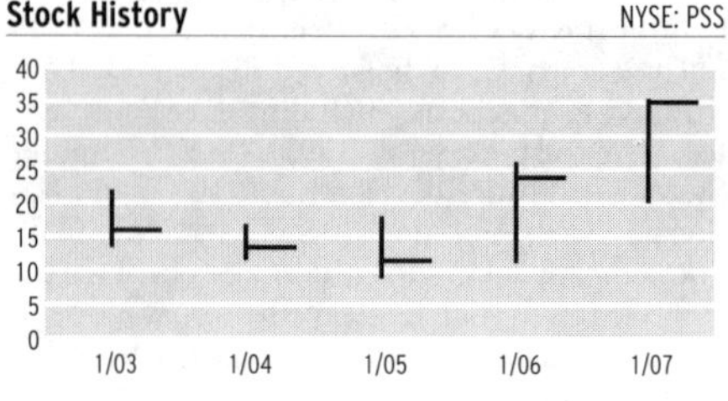

| | STOCK PRICE ($) FY Close | P/E High | P/E Low | PER SHARE ($) Earnings | Dividends | Book Value |
|---|---|---|---|---|---|---|
| **1/07** | 34.96 | 19 | 11 | 1.82 | — | 10.77 |
| **1/06** | 23.76 | 26 | 12 | 0.98 | — | 9.69 |
| **1/05** | 11.50 | — | — | (0.03) | — | 8.86 |
| **1/04** | 13.44 | — | — | — | — | 8.93 |
| **1/03** | 15.95 | 14 | 9 | 1.55 | — | 8.80 |
| **Annual Growth** | 21.7% | — | — | 4.1% | — | 5.2% |

# The Pep Boys

Still an automotive paradise for do-it-yourselfers, The Pep Boys — Manny, Moe & Jack now hears increasing cries of "Do it for me!" The company operates nearly 600 stores in about 36 states and Puerto Rico, selling brand-name and private-label automotive parts and offering on-site service facilities. Pep Boys stores stock about 21,000 car parts and accessories, including tires, and operate up to 11 service bays for parts installation, repair, and vehicle inspection. Pep Boys serves four segments of the automotive aftermarket: do-it-yourself, do-it-for-me (service), buy-for-resale (sales to professional garages), and tire sales. Ailing Pep Boys has hired Goldman, Sachs to help it find a buyer.

Hedge fund Barington Capital Group owns nearly 10% of the company. Dissatisfied with Pep Boys' stock price, Barington called for the ouster of CEO Lawrence Stevenson, who resigned in mid-2006. The hedge fund has also been critical of the performance of the company's board of directors.

Chairman William Leonard stepped in as interim CEO. Then, in early 2007, Jeffrey C. Rachor was named CEO and president. Rachor had previously served as president and COO of top auto retailer Sonic Automotive.

Cars have become more complex, thereby limiting the growth of the do-it-yourself segment, the company's primary customers. As a result, Pep Boys is turning more toward do-it-for-me (DIFM) customers as well as commercial services, including sales to professional installers through its parts delivery service, Pep Express Parts, which operates in about 460 stores.

Pep Boys also carries private-label lines for starters, fluids, batteries, and brakes, among other items.

More generally Pep Boys plans to put more emphasis on customer service by remodeling all its stores by 2009. Aisles will be wider and inventory will be recategorized into new product areas that help customers find items more easily. The new layout is also intended to have more appeal for female customers. Remodeled stores will additionally have television monitors that show customers how the repair of their car is progressing.

## HISTORY

Philadelphians Emanuel (Manny) Rosenfeld, Maurice (Moe) Strauss, Graham (Jack) Jackson, and Moe Radavitz founded Pep Auto Supplies in 1921, named in part from a product, Pep Valve Grinding Compound. (Radavitz pulled out after a few years.) Two years later the men renamed the store The Pep Boys — Manny, Moe & Jack. A friend created the corporate caricature of the three, though the version that became famous is actually of Manny, Moe, and Izzy (Moe's brother); it was drawn after Jack left.

By 1928 there were 12 Pep Boy stores in the Philadelphia area. In 1932 the car-friendly West Coast beckoned, and the boys dispatched Murray Rosenfeld to launch Pep Boys West. Intense competition in California spurred Pep Boys West to increase parts selection, while the Philadelphia stores focused more on service. The company went public in 1946 with Manny as president and Moe as chairman, but its growth was hindered by overly conservative management; Pep Boys would not lease stores and avoided debt like a crowded freeway. Moe became president after Manny's death in 1959, and as the fiscal caution continued, the company grew by only two stores between 1964 and 1984.

Moe held both posts until 1973, when his son Ben became president. In 1977 Moe stepped down as chairman but remained on the board until his death in 1982. That year Ben became chairman and CEO, and Moe's son-in-law Morton Krause became president. In 1984 Krause retired, and two years later Ben tapped Mitchell Leibovitz as president — the first from outside the founding families. As head of eastern operations, Leibovitz had closed 32 small stores between 1979 and 1984. Between 1984 and 1986 he opened 60 bond-financed stores.

In 1986 Pep Boys was the #2 parts retailer in the US, behind Western Auto, and Leibovitz set up a plan to modernize and overhaul the entire business. Between 1986 and 1991 Pep Boys spent $477 million improving distribution, merchandising, and marketing: The number of stores doubled to 337, and the number of items offered went from about 9,000 to 24,000. The company adopted an everyday-low-price strategy, and many locations were expanded into 23,000-sq.-ft. superstores with more service bays and related services. Unlike most of its competitors, Pep Boys mechanics would take on just about any automotive work. Pep Boys customized its offerings, extended hours, and boosted and refined advertising.

Leibovitz was named CEO in 1990. Pep Boys topped $1 billion in annual sales the following year. The recession of the early 1990s hurt profits; however, cash flow picked up, and the company was able to retire some debt and to open 30 stores in 1992. In 1993 Leibovitz put mechanics on commission, with safeguards to prevent overcharging.

Store count doubled during the next five years. In 1994 Leibovitz became chairman. Also that year the company began opening Parts USA stores (renamed Pep Boys Express in 1997), which had no service bays or tires. The conversion, along with tightening margins, adversely impacted profits in fiscal 1998, and Pep Boys decided in 1998 to sell 100 of its Pep Boys Express stores to AutoZone. (That sale and related write-offs hurt profits in fiscal 1999.) Also in 1998 the company rolled out APD, a parts delivery service aimed at professional installers.

In 2000 Pep Boys closed 38 unprofitable stores and two distribution centers, citing stagnant sales. It also cut about 5% of its workforce (1,500 jobs).

Pep Boys settled a lawsuit in 2002 alleging that it received discriminatory prices from auto parts manufacturers.

Leibovitz retired in 2003. Lawrence Stevenson, formerly the CEO of Chapters, a Canadian book retailer, became CEO. Also that year Pep Boys closed more than 30 stores. In May 2004 Pep Boys began selling Continental, General, Goodyear, Hankook, and Michelin tires in addition to the company's FUTURA and CORNELL private labels.

In September 2004 Stevenson also assumed the company chairmanship.

Under pressure from dissatisfied investors, in February 2006 Stevenson relinquished the chairman's title, which was bestowed on director William Leonard. In mid-July Leonard was named interim CEO when Stevenson resigned from that position as well. In 2007 former Sonic Automotive president Jeffrey Rachor took over as CEO and president of the company.

## EXECUTIVES

**Chairman:** William (Bill) Leonard, age 59
**President, CEO, and Director:** Jeffrey C. (Jeff) Rachor, age 45
**EVP Merchandising and Marketing:** Harold L. (Hal) Smith, age 56, $452,076 pay
**EVP Operations:** Mark S. Bacon, age 43, $363,486 pay
**SVP and CFO:** Harry F. Yanowitz, age 40, $737,307 pay
**SVP Human Resources:** Troy E. Fee
**SVP Parts and Tires:** Mark L. Page, age 50, $359,692 pay
**SVP Service:** Joseph A. (Joe) Cirelli, age 47
**VP, Chief Accounting Officer, and Treasurer:** Bernard K. McElroy
**VP Distribution:** Stuart M. Rosenfeld
**VP Service Operations, East:** Terry Winslow
**VP, General Counsel, and Secretary:** Brian D. Zuckerman
**VP Marketing and Advertising:** James H. Fox
**VP Retail Merchandising:** Galen F. Bullock
**VP Retail and Service Operations, Carribean:** Guillermo R. (Bill) Alvarez
**VP and CIO:** John Mitchell
**VP Retail Operations, East:** Charles M. McErlane
**VP Retail Operations, South:** Dan E. King
**VP Retail Operations, Southwest and Puerto Rico:** Alberto Velez
**VP Service Operations, South:** Michael P. McSorley
**VP Service Operations, Southwest and Puerto Rico:** José A. Gonzalez
**VP Service Operations, West:** Mark E. Doran
**VP and Controller:** Sanjay Sood
**Auditors:** Deloitte & Touche LLP

## LOCATIONS

**HQ:** The Pep Boys — Manny, Moe & Jack
3111 W. Allegheny Ave., Philadelphia, PA 19132
**Phone:** 215-430-9000 **Fax:** 215-227-7513
**Web:** www.pepboys.com

The Pep Boys — Manny, Moe & Jack has distribution warehouses in California, Georgia, Indiana, New York, and Texas.

**2007 Stores**

| | No. |
|---|---|
| US | |
| California | 121 |
| Texas | 54 |
| Florida | 43 |
| Pennsylvania | 42 |
| New York | 29 |
| New Jersey | 28 |
| Georgia | 25 |
| Illinois | 23 |
| Arizona | 22 |
| Maryland | 19 |
| Virginia | 16 |
| Nevada | 12 |
| Ohio | 12 |
| North Carolina | 10 |
| Louisiana | 10 |
| Indiana | 9 |
| Colorado | 8 |
| Connecticut | 8 |
| New Mexico | 8 |
| Massachusetts | 7 |
| Michigan | 7 |
| Tennessee | 7 |
| Delaware | 6 |
| Oklahoma | 6 |
| South Carolina | 6 |
| Utah | 6 |
| Kentucky | 4 |
| New Hampshire | 4 |
| Minnesota | 3 |
| Rhode Island | 3 |
| Other states | 8 |
| Puerto Rico | 27 |
| **Total** | **593** |

## PRODUCTS/OPERATIONS

**2007 Sales**

| | $ mil. | % of total |
|---|---|---|
| Parts & accessories | 1,555.4 | 69 |
| Service | 395.9 | 17 |
| Tires | 320.9 | 14 |
| **Total** | **2,272.2** | **100** |

**Selected Products**

Additives
Air-conditioning parts
Air filters
Alarms
Antifreeze
Batteries
Belts
Brake parts
Engines and engine parts
Floor mats
Gauges
Hand tools
Hoses
Ignition parts
Mobile electronics
Motor oil
Mufflers
Oil filters
Paints
Polishes
Seat covers
Sound systems
Suspension parts
Truck and van accessories

## COMPETITORS

Advance Auto Parts
AutoZone
BFS Retail & Commercial
CARQUEST
Commercial Tire
CSK Auto
Discount Tire
General Parts
Goodyear
Jeg's
Jiffy Lube
Les Schwab Tire Centers
Meineke
Midas
Monro Muffler Brake
O'Reilly Automotive
Precision Auto
Sears
Snap-on
TBC
VIP
Wal-Mart

## HISTORICAL FINANCIALS

Company Type: Public

**Income Statement** FYE: Saturday nearest January 31

| | REVENUE ($ mil.) | NET INCOME ($ mil.) | NET PROFIT MARGIN | EMPLOYEES |
|---|---|---|---|---|
| **1/07** | 2,272 | (3) | — | 18,794 |
| **1/06** | 2,235 | (38) | — | 19,980 |
| **1/05** | 2,273 | 24 | 1.0% | 20,781 |
| **1/04** | 2,134 | (34) | — | 21,331 |
| **1/03** | 2,173 | 44 | 2.0% | 21,705 |
| **Annual Growth** | 1.1% | — | — | (3.5%) |

**2007 Year-End Financials**

Debt ratio: 94.2%
Return on equity: —
Cash ($ mil.): 22
Current ratio: 1.27
Long-term debt ($ mil.): 535
No. of shares (mil.): 56
Dividends
Yield: 1.7%
Payout: —
Market value ($ mil.): 899

**Stock History** NYSE: PBY

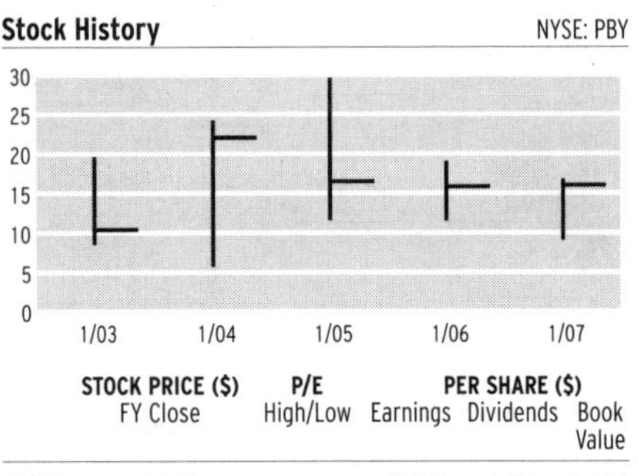


| | STOCK PRICE ($) FY Close | P/E High/Low | | PER SHARE ($) Earnings | Dividends | Book Value |
|---|---|---|---|---|---|---|
| **1/07** | 16.01 | — | — | (0.05) | 0.27 | 10.12 |
| **1/06** | 15.84 | — | — | (0.69) | 0.27 | 10.54 |
| **1/05** | 16.50 | 72 | 29 | 0.41 | 0.27 | 11.41 |
| **1/04** | 22.04 | — | — | (0.65) | 0.27 | 10.36 |
| **1/03** | 10.41 | 24 | 11 | 0.82 | 0.27 | 12.07 |
| **Annual Growth** | 11.4% | — | — | — | 0.0% | (4.3%) |

# Pepsi Bottling Group

Psychotherapists might disagree but keeping things bottled up can be beneficial — if you're The Pepsi Bottling Group, that is. As the world's #1 manufacturer and distributor of Pepsi-Cola beverages, The Pepsi Bottling Group (PBG) has a US market share for Pepsi brands that is close to 40%. PBG operates about 300 manufacturing and distribution facilities and delivers its drinks (including Aquafina water, Lipton's Iced Tea, Mountain Dew, Slice, and the world's #2 soft drink, Pepsi-Cola) directly to stores as well as through third-party distributors. The US and Canada account for almost 80% of company sales. PepsiCo controls 100% of PBG's voting power.

The company has exclusive rights to sell Pepsi beverages in 41 US states and the District of Columbia, nine Canadian provinces, as well as in Spain, Greece, Russia, Turkey and 23 states of Mexico. In 2006 it acquired bottler Bebidas Purificadas, located in northwest Mexico. Purificadas serves the Mexican states of Sinaloa, Sonora, and Baja California Sur. About 10% of PBG's sales come from Mexico.

PBG also distributes Dr Pepper for Cadbury Schweppes in some parts of the US. Expanding its North American presence, PBG has acquired other bottlers, including a $1 billion purchase of Mexican bottler Pepsi-Gemex (also owner of Electropura, Mexico's largest purified water company) and Pepsi-Cola Buffalo Bottling Corp.

In order to provide greater operational uniformity, in 2006 PBG became part of a manufacturing joint venture with 16 other regional Pepsi bottlers, forming Pepsi Northwest Beverages (PNB). Distribution areas involved in the joint venture include parts of Washington, Oregon, Idaho, Northern California, and all of Alaska.

Once wholly owned by PepsiCo, PBG was spun off in 1999 in order to allow PepsiCo to compete on a more level ground with the world's #1 soft-drink maker, The Coca-Cola Company (which spun off its own bottling operations in 1986).

Barclays Global Investors owns about 10% of the company.

## HISTORY

Pepsi-Cola inventor Caleb Bradham started bottling his drink in 1904. He quickly set about developing a system of bottling franchises for the drink, named for the claim that it cured dyspepsia, or indigestion. (The Coca-Cola Company had set up a similar franchise system a few years before.) By the end of 1910, there were nearly 300 Pepsi bottlers in Virginia and North and South Carolina.

Bradham went bankrupt in 1923 after unsuccessful speculation in sugar prices. Pepsi went through several owners until Charles Guth's Loft Candy Company bought it in 1931. Guth doubled Pepsi's bottle size to 12 ounces (for the same nickel price) two years later. By the end of 1934, profits were pouring in and Guth looked for new bottlers to join the Pepsi franchise. Loft Candy merged with its Pepsi subsidiary in 1941 to become the Pepsi-Cola Company (the company would become PepsiCo with the 1965 purchase of Frito-Lay).

Between 1951 and 1957 new equipment (such as carton openers and electronic inspection units) helped increase bottling plants' maximum speed from 260 to 500 bottles per minute. About 140 new plants opened or began construction during this time. At the end of the decade, there were nearly 550 US Pepsi bottling plants. The 1960s brought faster speeds and canning operations to the facilities, and innovations in the 1970s such as lighter weight plastic (PET) bottles also increased productivity.

By the early 1980s PepsiCo subsidiary Pepsi-Cola Bottling brought in about one-fifth of its parent's US bottling volume. Pepsi decided to focus on building its company-owned bottling group, buying up some franchises. In 1986 Pepsi-Cola Bottling acquired the San Francisco-area Pepsi bottling operation along with two smaller franchises and a 50% stake in another; this raised its volume to about one-third of domestic Pepsi product.

Acquisitions in the late 1980s totaled more than 80 franchises, including the bottling operations of General Cinema and Grand Metropolitan (then the #3 independent US Pepsi bottler).

Parent PepsiCo, through its Pepsi-Cola International unit, focused on expanding its overseas bottling operations (including Brazil, Egypt, and Mexico) during the early and mid-1990s. Still, by 1996 Pepsi's overseas sales only brought in 6% of its profits — compared to 70% of Coke's profits.

Many of Pepsi's bottlers had been consolidated by 1997, and the top 10 US Pepsi bottling operations (including #1 company-owned Pepsi-Cola Bottling) distributed more than 80% of Pepsi's total volume. The number of US bottlers had dropped from about 250 in 1990 to about 150 in 1997.

Separating its North American beverage business into bottling and marketing divisions, PepsiCo officially created The Pepsi Bottling Group (PBG) in 1998 to help the firm acquire other bottlers. Craig Weatherup, who ran Pepsi's global beverage business, was named CEO.

In 1999 PepsiCo sold about 65% of PBG in a tepidly received IPO. PepsiCo also agreed to sell several US and European territories to Whitman Corp., the second-largest Pepsi-Cola bottler. The deal gave PepsiCo a 38% stake in Whitman.

In 2001 Weatherup stepped down as CEO, but retained his chairman title. PBG president and COO John Cahill took Weatherup's place as CEO. Also that year PBG purchased an interest in bottler Pepsi-Cola Bottling of Northern California, which serves 13 counties in Northern California.

In 2002 PBG acquired the right to sell, manufacture, and distribute Pepsi's international beverages in Turkey for about $100 million. Its bid to buy Pepsi-Gemex also was completed in 2002 and in early 2003 it purchased Pepsi-Cola Buffalo Bottling Corp. Cahill assumed the chairmanship while continuing as CEO after Weatherup retired in January 2003.

The company added to its roster of subsidiaries with the 2005 purchase of Pepsi-Cola Bottling Company of Charlotte. Cahill resigned as top of pop in 2006 (although he remained as chairman) and COO Eric Foss was named president and CEO.

## EXECUTIVES

**Chairman:** Barry H. Beracha, age 65
**President and CEO:** Eric J. Foss, age 49
**SVP and CFO:** Alfred H. (Al) Drewes, age 51
**SVP and CIO:** Neal A. Bronzo
**SVP Global Sales and Chief Customer Officer:** Brent J. Franks
**SVP Worldwide Operations:** Victor L. Crawford
**SVP, General Counsel, and Secretary:** Steven M. Rapp, age 53
**SVP Human Resources:** John L. Berisford
**VP Finance, North America:** Andrea L. Forster
**VP Investor Relations:** Mary Winn Settino
**VP Strategy:** Kathleen M. Dwyer
**VP and Controller:** Thomas M. Lardieri, age 46
**VP Diversity and Workplace Development:** Sherry Nolan
**Chairman, PBG Mexico:** Rogelio M. Rebolledo, age 62
**President, PBG North America:** Robert C. King, age 48
**President, PBG Europe:** Yiannis Petrides, age 48
**President and General Manager, PBG Mexico:** Pablo Lagos, age 51
**Auditors:** Deloitte & Touche LLP

## LOCATIONS

**HQ:** The Pepsi Bottling Group, Inc.
1 Pepsi Way, Somers, NY 10589
**Phone:** 914-767-6000 **Fax:** 914-767-7761
**Web:** www.pbg.com

## 2006 Sales

| | $ mil. | % of total |
|---|---|---|
| US & Canada | 9,910 | 78 |
| Europe | 1,534 | 12 |
| Mexico | 1,286 | 10 |
| **Total** | **12,730** | **100** |

## PRODUCTS/OPERATIONS

### Selected Beverage Brands

Canada and US
- AMP
- Aquafina
- Code Red
- Diet Mountain Dew
- Diet Pepsi
- Dr Pepper (licensed)
- Jazz by Diet Pepsi
- Lipton (licensed)
- Mountain Dew
- Mug Root Beer
- No Fear
- Pepsi
- Pepsi Lime
- Pepsi ONE
- Sierra Mist
- SoBe
- Starbucks Frappuccino (licensed)
- Tropicana
- Tropicana Twister
- Wild Cherry Pepsi

Europe
- 7UP
- Aqua Minerale
- Fiesta
- Fruko
- IVI
- KAS
- Lipton (licensed)
- Mirinda
- Pepsi
- Pepsi Light
- Pepsi Max
- Tamek
- Tropicana
- Yedigun

Mexico
- 7UP

## COMPETITORS

AMCON Distributing
Cadbury Schweppes
Coca-Cola Enterprises
Coke United
Cott
Danone Water
Embotelladoras Arca
Leading Brands
Naked Juice
National Beverage
Nestlé
Odwalla
Philadelphia Coca-Cola
Sparkling Springs Water
Suntory Ltd.

## HISTORICAL FINANCIALS

Company Type: Public

### Income Statement

FYE: Last Saturday in December

| | REVENUE ($ mil.) | NET INCOME ($ mil.) | NET PROFIT MARGIN | EMPLOYEES |
|---|---|---|---|---|
| **12/06** | 12,730 | 522 | 4.1% | 70,400 |
| **12/05** | 11,885 | 466 | 3.9% | 66,900 |
| **12/04** | 10,906 | 457 | 4.2% | 64,700 |
| **12/03** | 10,265 | 416 | 4.1% | 66,000 |
| **12/02** | 9,216 | 428 | 4.6% | 65,000 |
| **Annual Growth** | 8.4% | 5.1% | — | 2.0% |

### 2006 Year-End Financials

Debt ratio: 228.1%
Return on equity: 25.3%
Cash ($ mil.): 629
Current ratio: 1.34
Long-term debt ($ mil.): 4,754
No. of shares (mil.): 230
Dividends
Yield: 1.3%
Payout: 19.0%
Market value ($ mil.): 7,109

### Stock History

NYSE: PBG

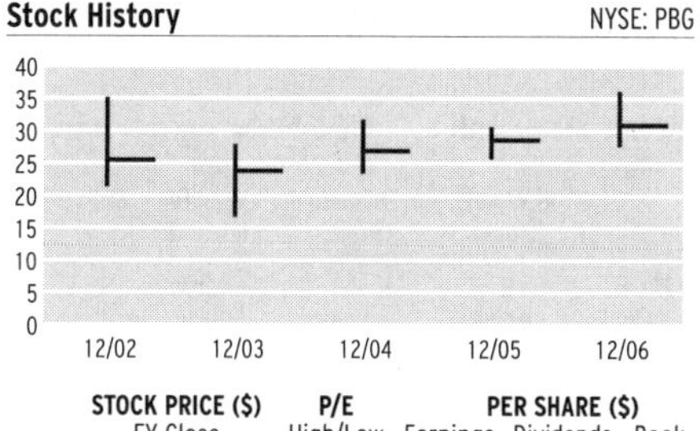


| | STOCK PRICE ($) FY Close | P/E High/Low | | PER SHARE ($) Earnings | Dividends | Book Value |
|---|---|---|---|---|---|---|
| **12/06** | 30.91 | 17 | 13 | 2.16 | 0.41 | 9.06 |
| **12/05** | 28.61 | 16 | 14 | 1.86 | 0.29 | 8.55 |
| **12/04** | 26.88 | 18 | 14 | 1.73 | 0.16 | 7.83 |
| **12/03** | 23.81 | 18 | 11 | 1.50 | 0.04 | 7.21 |
| **12/02** | 25.45 | 24 | 15 | 1.46 | 0.04 | 6.55 |
| **Annual Growth** | 5.0% | — | — | 10.3% | 78.9% | 8.5% |

# PepsiAmericas

PepsiAmericas holds more than a bubbling interest in the Pepsi Generation. It is the world's #2 Pepsi bottler (behind Pepsi Bottling Group). Besides Pepsi beverages, the company also distributes Dr Pepper, Lipton Iced Teas, Welch's fruit drinks, Schweppes (tonic water, ginger ale), Starbucks Frappuccino, and bottled water. PepsiAmericas operates in 19 US states (mostly in the Midwest) and holds about 19% of the US market for Pepsi products. It also distributes drinks in the Bahamas, Barbados, the Czech Republic, Hungary, Jamaica, Poland, Puerto Rico, Romania, Slovakia, and Trinidad and Tobago. PepsiCo owns 80% of PepsiAmericas.

As demand for traditional colas continues to slump, PepsiAmericas looks for a boost in sales from bottled water like Aquafina and other non-carbonated beverages, as well as product-line extension and innovative packaging. The company sells to many types of retailers, among which are Sam's Club stores and supercenters like Wal-Mart, which accounted for almost 11% of PepsiAmericas' sales in 2006. Growth for the company has come mainly from acquiring new service territory in Florida and Ohio.

PepsiAmericas is involved in a million-dollar cleanup of a federal Superfund site in Portsmouth, Virginia. PepsiAmericas became liable for the site through Pneumo Abex, a foundry once owned by the Whitman Corporation, which purchased PepsiAmericas in 2000.

The company announced that it will centralize its operations and consolidate its field sales and delivery divisions from 14 to seven.

## HISTORY

PepsiAmericas is a very different business from its predecessor, the Illinois Central Railroad. Started in 1851 with a 3.6-million-acre land grant, Illinois Central became one of the nation's 10 largest rail systems, boasting 4,200 rail miles in 13 states by 1901, including the City of New Orleans line. It was renamed Illinois Central Industries in 1962; William Johnson, former president of Railway Express Agency, became president in 1966.

Johnson reduced the focus on railroads and helped transform the company into a multinational conglomerate (renamed IC Industries in 1975) that bought numerous companies, including Pepsi-Cola General Bottlers (1970), Midas International auto muffler shops (1972), Pet Inc., and refrigeration equipment maker Hussmann (1978).

Pepsi-Cola General Bottlers was founded in 1935 as Pepsi-Cola Bottling Company of Chicago, a Pepsi franchise. To fund growth, it went public in 1938 and was renamed Pepsi-Cola General Bottlers in 1954. Pet began in 1885 as an evaporated milk company and later added Downyflake Foods, Stuckey roadside candy stores, and chocolate company Stuart F. Whitman and Son. Because of the growth of its varied subsidiaries, the railroad provided only 1% of IC's pretax profits by the late 1970s. One month after its spinoff in 1989, the company's rail business was bought by a private concern, Prospect Group.

The company changed its name in 1988 to Whitman (after its chocolate unit) to reflect its concentration on consumer goods and services. During the 1980s Whitman sold 65 companies (including its Pneumo Abex aerospace operations, 1988) and bought 98 companies (including Van de Kamp's frozen seafood, 1989).

Facing heavy debt, the company restructured. It spun off its Pet food unit (and all food brands) to shareholders. Whitman purchased 39 European muffler shops and three Pepsi franchises in the early 1990s. Bruce Chelberg became chairman and CEO in 1992. The firm sold Whitman Chocolates to Russell Stover Candies in 1993.

Its original Pepsi subsidiary, Pepsi General, sparked increased sales with new products in 1995, such as All Sport, Caffeine Free Mountain Dew, Slice, and Wild Cherry Pepsi. The next year it added new All Sport flavors, bottled water, and Ocean Spray juices and replaced its root beer lines with Mug Root Beer. It also acquired some Russian assets from PepsiCo so that it could distribute Pepsi products in Russia and Belarus, as well as Estonia, Latvia, and Lithuania. In 1998 the company spun off two businesses — Midas and Hussmann International — into separately traded companies.

In early 1999 Whitman bought additional bottling operations in the Midwest and in Eastern Europe from PepsiCo. As part of the complex deal, it sold operations in three states and Russia while giving PepsiCo a 38% stake in Whitman. In return, Whitman gained exclusive bottling rights in some of its territories. PepsiCo then named Whitman an anchor bottler in its reorganized system. Later that year Whitman bought Toma (Czech Republic) and began distributing Hortex and Rauch juice drinks in Poland and Hungary, respectively.

Whitman sold its Baltic operations in February 2000. The company bought #3 Pepsi bottler PepsiAmericas in November 2000 in a deal worth about $660 million. Robert Pohlad subsequently became CEO of the new, combined company, which dropped the Whitman name in 2001 in favor of PepsiAmericas.

Also that year, PepsiAmericas purchased 90% of Pepsi-Cola Trinidad Bottling Company to expand in the Caribbean. In 2003 and 2004 the ongoing beverage war between Coca-Cola and Pepsi produced new flavors and colors. While Coca-Cola freshened its product mix with Vanilla Coke, PepsiAmericas slapped back with Dr Pepper's Red Fusion, Pepsi Blue, and Mountain Dew LiveWire. The company also rolled out 8-ounce cans and Fridge-Mate, a 12-pack, 12-ounce-can package.

In 2005 PepsiAmericas purchased the seventh-largest Pepsi bottler, Central Investment Corporation, for $352 million and in 2006 acquired Ardea Beverage Co., bottler of Nutrisoda. Also in 2006 it acquired distribution rights in Romania.

## EXECUTIVES

**Chairman and CEO:** Robert C. Pohlad, age 53, $791,667 pay
**President and COO:** Kenneth E. (Ken) Keiser, age 54, $585,208 pay
**EVP and CFO:** Alexander H. (Alex) Ware, age 44, $369,438 pay
**EVP International Operations:** James R. Rogers, age 52, $316,326 pay
**EVP US Operations:** G. Michael Durkin Jr., age 47, $416,667 pay
**SVP and CIO:** Kenneth L. (Ken) Johnsen
**SVP Human Resources:** Anne D. Sample, age 43
**SVP Worldwide Strategy and Corporate Development:** Matthew E. (Matt) Carter
**SVP Worldwide Supply Chain:** Jay S. Hulbert, age 53
**VP and Treasurer:** Andrew R. Stark, age 43
**VP and Controller:** Timothy W. Gorman, age 46
**VP Investor Relations:** Sara Zawoyski
**VP US Finance:** Sandy Mathias
**VP Compensation, Benefits, and HRIS:** Keith Sanders
**Corporate Secretary:** Brian D. Wenger
**Auditors:** KPMG LLP

## LOCATIONS

**HQ:** PepsiAmericas, Inc.
4000 Dain Rauscher Plaza, 60 S. 6th St.,
Minneapolis, MN 55402
**Phone:** 612-661-4000 **Fax:** 612-661-3737
**Web:** www.pepsiamericas.com

### 2006 Sales

| | $ mil. | % of total |
|---|---|---|
| US | 3,245.8 | 82 |
| Central Europe | 484.1 | 12 |
| Caribbean | 242.5 | 6 |
| **Total** | **3,972.4** | **100** |

## PRODUCTS/OPERATIONS

### Selected Beverages

Caribbean
- 7UP
- Aquafina
- Diet Pepsi
- Malta Polar
- Pepsi

Central Europe
- Kristalyviz
- Lipton Iced Tea
- Pepsi
- Slice
- Toma

US
- Aquafina
- Diet Mountain Dew
- Diet Pepsi
- Mountain Dew
- Pepsi

## COMPETITORS

Cadbury Schweppes Bottling Group
Clearly Canadian
Coca-Cola Enterprises
Cott
Ferolito, Vultaggio
Hansen Natural
Impulse Energy USA
Jones Soda
National Beverage
Nestlé
Nestlé Waters
Pepsi Bottling
Red Bull
Snapple
South Beach Beverage
Suntory Ltd.

## HISTORICAL FINANCIALS

Company Type: Public

### Income Statement

FYE: Saturday nearest December 31

| | REVENUE ($ mil.) | NET INCOME ($ mil.) | NET PROFIT MARGIN | EMPLOYEES |
|---|---|---|---|---|
| **12/06** | 3,972 | 158 | 4.0% | 17,100 |
| **12/05** | 3,726 | 195 | 5.2% | 16,000 |
| **12/04** | 3,345 | 182 | 5.4% | 15,100 |
| **12/03** | 3,237 | 158 | 4.9% | 14,500 |
| **12/02** | 3,240 | 130 | 4.0% | 15,200 |
| **Annual Growth** | 5.2% | 5.1% | — | 3.0% |

### 2006 Year-End Financials

Debt ratio: 92.9%
Return on equity: 10.0%
Cash ($ mil.): 93
Current ratio: 0.97
Long-term debt ($ mil.): 1,490
No. of shares (mil.): 127
Dividends
Yield: 2.4%
Payout: 41.0%
Market value ($ mil.): 2,664

### Stock History

NYSE: PAS

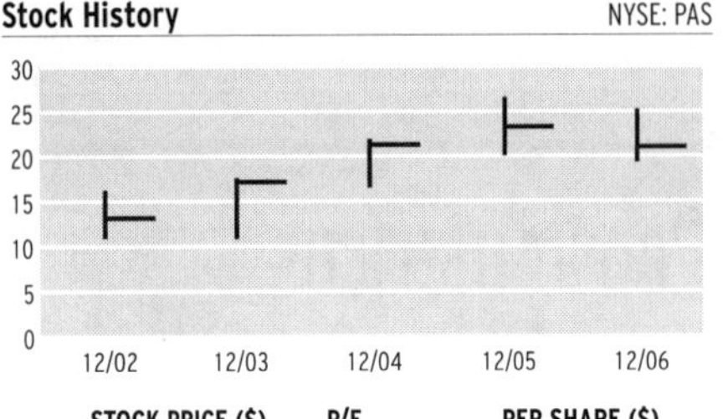

| | STOCK PRICE ($) FY Close | P/E High/Low | | PER SHARE ($) Earnings | Dividends | Book Value |
|---|---|---|---|---|---|---|
| **12/06** | 20.98 | 20 | 16 | 1.22 | 0.50 | 12.63 |
| **12/05** | 23.26 | 19 | 14 | 1.42 | 0.34 | 11.80 |
| **12/04** | 21.24 | 17 | 13 | 1.28 | 0.15 | 11.71 |
| **12/03** | 17.12 | 16 | 10 | 1.09 | 0.04 | 10.88 |
| **12/02** | 13.15 | 19 | 13 | 0.85 | 0.04 | 9.81 |
| **Annual Growth** | 12.4% | — | — | 9.5% | 88.0% | 6.5% |

# PepsiCo

The PepsiCo challenge (to keep up with archrival The Coca-Cola Company) never ends for the world's #2 carbonated soft-drink maker. The company's soft drinks include Pepsi, Mountain Dew, and Slice. It owns Frito-Lay, the world's #1 maker of snacks such as corn chips (Doritos, Fritos) and potato chips (Lay's, Ruffles). Cola is not the company's only beverage: PepsiCo sells Tropicana orange juice brands, Gatorade sports drink, and Aquafina water. PepsiCo also sells Dole juices (licensed) and Lipton ready-to-drink tea (licensed from Unilever). Its Quaker Foods division offers breakfast cereals (Life), pasta (Pasta Roni), rice (Rice-A-Roni), and side dishes (Near East).

PepsiCo may be vying for more Pepsi-drinking people but its hefty snacks and juice sales help to quench the company's thirst for bottom-line growth. Frito-Lay's salty snacks rule the US market; the snack division accounts for about one-third of company sales.

With a saturated soft-drink market, the company continues to try new iterations: The company signed a licensing agreement with Ben & Jerry's in 2006 for the sale of Ben & Jerry's milkshakes in the US, as well as a deal with Starbucks for the distribution of the coffee purveyor's Ethos water brand. Hot on the heels of Coke's introduction of Blak, in 2006 Pepsi launched a coffee-flavored cola, named, Pepsi Max Cino, in the UK.

Venturing further into the non-cola category, PepsiCo acquired sparkling juice companies IZZE and Naked Juice in 2006. It also began selling Fuelosophy, a smoothie drink, at organic grocery store chain Whole Foods, and struck a deal to develop products with juice maker Ocean Spray Cranberries. In 2007 the company introduced its first vitamin-enhanced water, called Aquafina Alive.

Bowing to the public's growing concern about childhood obesity, in 2006 Pepsi, along with Coca-Cola, Cadbury Schweppes, and the American Beverage Association agreed to sell only water, unsweetened juice, and low-fat milk to public elementary and middle schools in the US.

CEO Steve Reinemund stepped down as CEO in October 2006. His replacement, Indra Nooyi, served as the company's president and CFO. Indian-born Nooyi, the 11th female CEO of a FORTUNE 500 company, has been instrumental in strategic decisions at the company, such as the acquisition of Tropicana and merger with Quaker Oats.

## HISTORY

Pharmacist Caleb Bradham invented Pepsi in 1898 in New Bern, North Carolina. He named his new drink Pepsi-Cola (claiming it cured dyspepsia, or indigestion) and registered the trademark in 1903. Following The Coca-Cola Company's example, Bradham developed a bottling franchise system. By WWI, 300 bottlers had signed up. After the war, Bradham stockpiled sugar to safeguard against rising costs, but in 1920 sugar prices plunged, forcing him into bankruptcy in 1923.

Pepsi existed on the brink of ruin under various owners until Loft Candy bought it in 1931. Its fortunes improved in 1933 when, in the midst of the Depression, it doubled the size of its bottles to 12 ounces without raising the five-cent price. In 1939 Pepsi introduced the world's first radio jingle. Two years later Loft Candy merged with its Pepsi subsidiary and became The Pepsi-Cola Company.

Donald Kendall, who became Pepsi-Cola's president in 1963, turned the firm's attention to young people ("The Pepsi Generation"). It acquired Mountain Dew in 1964 and became PepsiCo in 1965, when it acquired Frito-Lay.

In 1972 PepsiCo agreed to distribute Stolichnaya vodka in the US in exchange for being the only Western firm allowed to bottle soft drinks in the USSR. With the purchases of Pizza Hut (1977), Taco Bell (1978), and Kentucky Fried Chicken (1986), it became a major force in the fast-food industry.

When Coca-Cola changed its formula in 1985, Pepsi had a short-lived victory in the cola wars (until the splashy return of Coca-Cola classic). The rivalry was extended to ready-to-drink tea in 1991 when, in response to Coca-Cola's Nestea venture with Nestlé, PepsiCo teamed up with Lipton (they now lead the market).

Between 1991 and 1996 PepsiCo aggressively expanded its overseas bottling operations. Roger Enrico became CEO in 1996.

A year later PepsiCo spun off its $10 billion fast-food unit as TRICON Global Restaurants (now known as YUM! Brands, Inc.), putting itself in a better position to sell its soft drinks at other restaurants. In 1998 it bought Seagram's market-leading Tropicana juices (rival of Coca-Cola's Minute Maid) for $3.3 billion. The firm sold a 65% stake in its new Pepsi Bottling Group to the public in 1999.

Its more than $13 billion purchase of The Quaker Oats Company in 2001 added the dominant Gatorade sports drink brand to its lineup. To make room for Gatorade, PepsiCo sold its competing All Sport energy drink to The Monarch Beverage Company, an Atlanta-based beverage company, later that year. Later that year the company named president and COO Steve Reinemund as chairman and CEO.

In 2004 PepsiCo approached Ocean Spray about a joint venture but was turned away by the cranberry farmers who own the juice manufacturer. The company bought General Mills' stake of their joint venture, Snack Ventures Europe (SVE), in 2005 for $750 million. The deal gave Pepsi control of Europe's largest snack food company.

Later that year the company revealed it was subject to an SEC investigation involving transactions it had with Kmart. Allegedly, lower-level employees within its cola and snack divisions signed documents that Kmart used to improperly record nearly $6 million in revenue. PepsiCo cooperated with the investigation, which led to the resignations of a PepsiCo national account manager and a sales director.

Shortly after her appointment as CEO in 2006, Indra Nooyi restructured the top level of power at the company. She appointed John Compton, previously head of the Quaker-Tropicana-Gatorade unit, to the newly created position of CEO for PepsiCo North America, reporting directly to her. The company also appointed Albert Carey as president and CEO of Frito-Lay North America, replacing Irene Rosenfeld who left the company to become head of Kraft Foods.

## EXECUTIVES

**Chairman and CEO:** Indra K. Nooyi, age 51
**Vice Chairman; Chairman and CEO, PepsiCo International:** Michael D. (Mike) White, age 55, $3,414,552 pay
**CFO:** Richard Goodman, age 58, $470,508 pay (partial-year salary)
**EVP, Operations:** Hugh F. Johnston, age 45
**SVP, Global Diversity; SVP, Human Resources, PepsiCo North America:** Ronald C. (Ron) Parker
**SVP, Finance:** Matthew M. (Matt) McKenna, age 56
**SVP, Global Procurement:** James Kozlowski
**SVP, Sales:** Mario Mercurio
**SVP, Government Affairs, General Counsel, and Secretary:** Larry D. Thompson, age 61
**SVP, Public Relations:** Mark D. Dollins
**SVP and President, Quaker Tropicana Gatorade Canada:** Dave Burwick
**SVP and Controller:** Peter A. Bridgman, age 54
**SVP and Treasurer:** Lionel L. Nowell III, age 52
**SVP and Chief Personnel Officer:** Cynthia M. Trudell, age 53
**VP, Investor Relations:** Jamie Caulfield
**President, PepsiCo Sales and Chief Customer Officer:** Thomas R. (Tom) Greco, age 48
**President and CEO, Frito-Lay:** Albert P. (Al) Carey, age 55
**CEO, PepsiCo North America:** John C. Compton, age 45, $767,212 pay
**President, PepsiCo Shared Services (CIO, CTO):** Shauna King
**President and CEO, Pepsi-Cola North America and PepsiCo Foodservice:** Dawn E. Hudson, age 49, $731,154 pay
**President and CEO, Quaker Tropicana Gatorade:** Charles I. (Chuck) Maniscalco, age 53
**President, Gatorade:** Todd Magazine, age 43
**President, Quaker Foods and Snacks:** Mark Schiller, age 46
**Auditors:** KPMG LLP

## LOCATIONS

**HQ:** PepsiCo, Inc.
700 Anderson Hill Rd., Purchase, NY 10577
**Phone:** 914-253-2000 **Fax:** 914-253-2070
**Web:** www.pepsico.com

PepsiCo's soft drinks and snacks are sold in approximately 200 countries.

### 2006 Sales

| | $ mil. | % of total |
|---|---|---|
| US | 20,788 | 59 |
| Mexico | 3,228 | 9 |
| UK | 1,839 | 5 |
| Canada | 1,702 | 5 |
| Other countries | 7,580 | 22 |
| **Total** | **35,137** | **100** |

## PRODUCTS/OPERATIONS

### 2006 Sales

| | $ mil. | % of total |
|---|---|---|
| PepsiCo International | 12,959 | 37 |
| Frito-Lay North America | 10,844 | 31 |
| PepsiCo Beverages North America | 9,565 | 27 |
| Quaker Foods North America | 1,769 | 5 |
| **Total** | **35,137** | **100** |

### Selected Brands

Frito-Lay
- Baked Lay's
- Cheetos
- Cracker Jack
- Doritos
- Frito-Lay
- Fritos
- Funyuns
- Grandma's
- Lay's
- Munchos
- Rold Gold
- Ruffles
- Santitas
- Smartfood
- SunChips
- Tostitos

PepsiCo
- Bottled water
  - Aquafina
- Caffeinated citrus-flavored soda
  - Mountain Dew
- Coffee drinks
  - Frappuccino (licensed from Starbucks)
- Colas
  - Diet Pepsi
  - Pepsi-Cola
  - Pepsi Blue
  - Pepsi One
  - Pepsi Twist
- Fruit-flavored soda
  - 7UP
  - Mountain Dew
  - Slice
- Root Beer
  - Mug
- Sports drinks
  - Gatorade
  - Propel (water)
- Teas (licensed from Unilever)
  - Lipton Brisk
  - Lipton Iced
- Juices
  - Copella
  - Dole (licensed from Dole)
  - South Beach Beverage (SoBe)
  - Tropicana
  - Twister

Quaker
- Cereals
  - Cap'n Crunch
  - Life
  - Natural
  - Quaker Instant
- Pancake Mix
  - Aunt Jemima
- Pasta
  - Golden Grain
  - Pasta Roni
  - Rice-A-Roni
- Snacks
  - Quaker Chewy Granola Bars
  - Quaker Rice Cakes
- Syrup
  - Aunt Jemima

## COMPETITORS

American Beverage
Avani International Group
Beer Nuts
Big Red
Bimbo
Cadbury Schweppes
Campbell Soup
Carolina Beverage
Celestial Seasonings
Chiquita Brands
Clearly Canadian
Coca-Cola
ConAgra
Cool Mountain Beverages
Cott
Cranberries Limited
Danone
Danone Water
DS Waters
Evans Food Products
Faygo
Ferolito, Vultaggio
Florida's Natural
Fuze Beverage
General Mills
Golden Enterprises
Hansen Natural
Hawaiian Natural Water
Impulse Energy USA
IZZE
J & J Snack Foods
Jays Foods
Jones Soda
Kettle Foods
Kraft Foods
Lance Snacks
Mountain Valley
Naked Juice
National Beverage
National Grape Cooperative
Nestlé
New Attitude Beverage Corporation
Ocean Spray
Odwalla
Pinahs Company
Polar Beverages
Procter & Gamble
Ralcorp
R.C. Bigelow
Reed's
Republic of Tea
Snapple
Stash Tea
Sunny Delight
Suntory Ltd.
Sweet Leaf Tea
Tata Group
Tree Top
Unilever NV
Virgin Group
Weaver Popcorn Company
Wet Planet Beverages

## HISTORICAL FINANCIALS

Company Type: Public

### Income Statement

FYE: Last Saturday in December

| | REVENUE ($ mil.) | NET INCOME ($ mil.) | NET PROFIT MARGIN | EMPLOYEES |
|---|---|---|---|---|
| **12/06** | 35,137 | 5,642 | 16.1% | 168,000 |
| **12/05** | 32,562 | 4,078 | 12.5% | 157,000 |
| **12/04** | 29,261 | 4,212 | 14.4% | 153,000 |
| **12/03** | 26,971 | 3,568 | 13.2% | 143,000 |
| **12/02** | 25,112 | 3,313 | 13.2% | 142,000 |
| **Annual Growth** | 8.8% | 14.2% | — | 4.3% |

### 2006 Year-End Financials

Debt ratio: 16.5%
Return on equity: 37.9%
Cash ($ mil.): 2,822
Current ratio: 1.33
Long-term debt ($ mil.): 2,550
No. of shares (mil.): 1,638
Dividends
Yield: 1.9%
Payout: 34.7%
Market value ($ mil.): 102,457

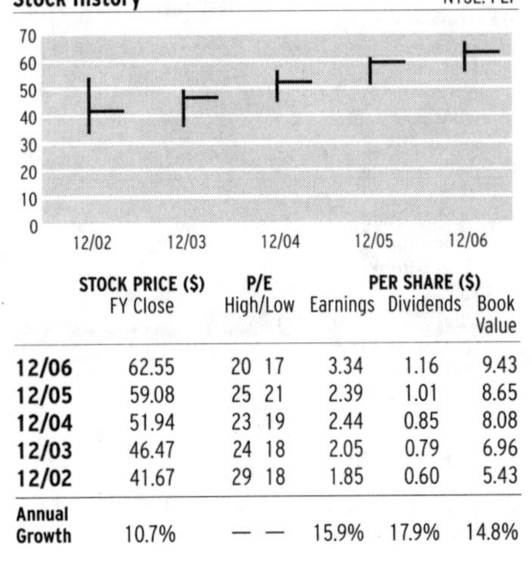


| | STOCK PRICE ($) FY Close | P/E High/Low | | PER SHARE ($) Earnings | Dividends | Book Value |
|---|---|---|---|---|---|---|
| 12/06 | 62.55 | 20 | 17 | 3.34 | 1.16 | 9.43 |
| 12/05 | 59.08 | 25 | 21 | 2.39 | 1.01 | 8.65 |
| 12/04 | 51.94 | 23 | 19 | 2.44 | 0.85 | 8.08 |
| 12/03 | 46.47 | 24 | 18 | 2.05 | 0.79 | 6.96 |
| 12/02 | 41.67 | 29 | 18 | 1.85 | 0.60 | 5.43 |
| Annual Growth | 10.7% | — | — | 15.9% | 17.9% | 14.8% |

# Performance Food Group

When it's time to eat out, Performance Food Group (PFG) delivers. The #3 broadline foodservice distributor in the US (behind SYSCO and U.S. Foodservice), PFG supplies more than 68,000 national and private-label products to about 41,000 restaurants, educational and health care facilities, and fast-food chain customers (including Burger King, Church's Chicken, Subway, and Zaxby's) throughout the Eastern and Southern US. It also provides customized distribution services service to such big casual-dining and family-dining chains as Cracker Barrel Old Country Store, Outback Steakhouse, Ruby Tuesday, and T.G.I. Friday's.

While PFG's broadline distribution business continues to work on expanding sales to existing customers, it is also working to gain new customers primarily among independent restaurant operators. In 2007 the company struck a deal to supply the O'Charley's casual dining chain. Meanwhile, the company is looking to increase sales of its proprietary brands and achieve higher efficiencies throughout its operations.

PFG is also keeping an eye out for smaller broadline distributors to acquire, which has historically been the primary driver of the company's expansion.

## HISTORY

Robert Sledd began working for his family's Taylor & Sledd food distribution business in 1974 and became president a decade later. In 1987, fearing that his family's business would be swallowed up in the ongoing consolidation of the foodservice industry, Sledd convinced his father, Hunter, to spin off their Richmond, Virginia-based Pocahontas Foods business and put him in charge, along with Robert's University of Tennessee fraternity brother and longtime friend, Michael Gray.

As part of the spinoff, Pocahontas merged with Caro Produce & Institutional Foods, which distributed produce in Texas and Louisiana. The company acquired Tennessee-based distributors Kenneth O. Lester Company and Hale Brothers in 1988 and 1989, respectively.

In 1991 the company changed its name from Pocahontas Foods to Performance Food Group (PFG). Although the company's name was different, its policy of growth by acquisition remained the same and PFG continued gobbling up distributors. That year PFG acquired B&R Foods, based in Tampa. The company continued to make acquisitions that expanded its market share in the South, including New Orleans distributor Loubat-L. Frank in 1992 and another Tennessee distributor, Hale of Summit Distributors, in 1993. That year the company offered its stock to the public for the first time.

Along with its aggressive consumption, PFG felt a burp in 1994 in the form of stunted profits and disappointing earnings. In what should have been the newly public company's salad days, PFG's performance was stifled by difficulties at its pre-cut salad plant and by rising labor and warehousing costs. As a result, the company's stock price plunged 66% at the end of 1994.

Undaunted, the company brought in new salad-making equipment and continued on its industry-consolidating course the next year. PFG acquired Atlanta's Milton's Food and North Carolina-based Cannon Food in 1995.

In 1996 PFG expanded its service in the Southwest with the acquisition of Texas distributor McLane Foodservice-Temple (now operating as Performance Food Group of Texas). Buoyed by solid growth in sales, the company made additional acquisitions in 1997, including Georgia's W.J. Powell, and its first foray into the Northeast, AFI Food Service.

The company grew internally in 1998 with the construction of distribution centers in Tennessee and Texas as well as its acquisition of Affiliated Paper Companies of Alabama and regional food distributor Virginia Food Service Group. In 1999 the company moved into the New England market when it bought NorthCenter Foodservice (Maine), and it expanded into custom-cut steaks when it bought State Hotel Supply Company and Nesson Meat Sales.

PFG continued to bulk up its broadline service when it acquired Carroll County Foods in 2000. Seeing the future in pre-cut salads and vegetables, the company purchased Dixon Tom-A-Toe (1999) and Redi-Cut Foods (2000). It also bought Empire Seafood Holding in 2001, doubling its seafood sales. That year Gray was promoted to CEO and PFG also bought Springfield Foodservice, a leading foodservice distributor in New England. The company then bought the largest independent fresh-cut produce processor in the US, Fresh Express.

In 2002 the acquisitions continued when in May PFG acquired Arkansas-based Quality Foods, which serves customers in Arkansas, Louisiana, Mississippi, Missouri, Oklahoma, Tennessee, and Texas. In July PFG acquired two foodservice distribution companies: Middendorf Meat, which specializes in custom-cut steaks, and Illinois-based Thoms-Proestler Co., which serves customers in Illinois, Indiana, Iowa, and Wisconsin. In October its Pocahontas Foods USA subsidiary acquired All Kitchens, a privately owned Idaho company, for $15.6 million.

In 2004 Gray left PFG and Sledd took over as chairman and CEO. The company sold its Fresh Express produce division the following year to Chiquita Brands International for $855 million. Steven Spinner was promoted from president and COO to succeed Sledd as CEO in 2006; Sledd remained as chairman.

## EXECUTIVES

**Chairman:** Robert C. Sledd, age 54
**President and CEO:** Steven L. Spinner, age 47
**SVP, General Counsel, Chief Compliance Officer, and Corporate Secretary:** Joseph J. (Joe) Traficanti, age 55
**SVP and CFO:** John D. Austin, age 45, $567,760 pay
**SVP and Controller:** J. Keith Middleton, age 40, $341,664 pay
**SVP and CEO, Customized Division:** Thomas Hoffman, age 67, $633,910 pay
**Chief Human Resources Officer:** Charlotte L. Perkins, age 48
**SVP, Strategy and Support Services:** Joseph J. (Joe) Paterak Jr., age 55
**VP and Treasurer:** Jeff Fender
**Director, Corporate Communications:** Cheryl R. Moore
**Director, Investor Relations:** Kevin P. Collier
**Director, Risk Management:** Sandy Black
**Auditors:** KPMG LLP

## LOCATIONS

**HQ:** Performance Food Group Company
12500 W. Creek Pkwy., Richmond, VA 23238
**Phone:** 804-484-7700 **Fax:** 804-484-7701
**Web:** www.pfgc.com

Performance Food Group operates about 30 distribution centers in Alabama, Arkansas, California, Florida, Georgia, Idaho, Illinois, Indiana, Louisiana, Maine, Maryland, Massachusetts, Mississippi, Missouri, New Jersey, South Carolina, Tennessee, Texas, and Virginia.

## PRODUCTS/OPERATIONS

### 2006 Sales

| | % of total |
|---|---|
| Center-of-the-plate | 41 |
| Canned & dry groceries | 18 |
| Frozen foods | 17 |
| Refrigerated & dairy products | 10 |
| Paper products & cleaning supplies | 7 |
| Produce | 4 |
| Procurement, merchandising & other services | 2 |
| Equipment & supplies | 1 |
| **Total** | **100** |

### Selected Private Labels

AFFLAB
Bay Winds
Brilliance
Empire's Treasure
First Mark
Guest House
Heritage Ovens
PFG Custom Meats
Raffinato
Village Garden

## COMPETITORS

Alex Lee
Ben E. Keith
MAINES
Martin-Brower
MBM
McLane Foodservice
Nash-Finch
Services Group
SYSCO
UniPro Foodservice
Unisource
U.S. Foodservice

## HISTORICAL FINANCIALS

Company Type: Public

**Income Statement** FYE: Saturday closest to December 31

| | REVENUE ($ mil.) | NET INCOME ($ mil.) | NET PROFIT MARGIN | EMPLOYEES |
|---|---|---|---|---|
| **12/06** | 5,827 | 43 | 0.7% | 7,000 |
| **12/05** | 5,721 | 247 | 4.3% | 7,000 |
| **12/04** | 6,149 | 53 | 0.9% | 11,000 |
| **12/03** | 5,520 | 74 | 1.3% | 10,000 |
| **12/02** | 4,438 | 67 | 1.5% | 10,200 |
| **Annual Growth** | 7.0% | (10.4%) | — | (9.0%) |

**2006 Year-End Financials**

Debt ratio: 1.5%
Return on equity: 5.4%
Cash ($ mil.): 75
Current ratio: 1.28
Long-term debt ($ mil.): 12
No. of shares (mil.): 35
Dividends
Yield: —
Payout: —
Market value ($ mil.): 964

**Stock History** NASDAQ (GS): PFGC

| | STOCK PRICE ($) FY Close | P/E High/Low | PER SHARE ($) Earnings | Dividends | Book Value |
|---|---|---|---|---|---|
| **12/06** | 27.64 | 27 19 | 1.23 | — | 22.78 |
| **12/05** | 28.37 | 6 4 | 5.64 | — | 21.82 |
| **12/04** | 26.91 | 34 19 | 1.11 | — | 18.69 |
| **12/03** | 35.75 | 27 16 | 1.54 | — | 17.53 |
| **12/02** | 33.73 | 28 18 | 1.42 | — | 15.79 |
| **Annual Growth** | (4.9%) | — — | (3.5%) | — | 9.6% |

# Perot Systems

It doesn't take many charts and graphs to see that Perot Systems is one of the leading providers of technology services and outsourcing. The company, founded by one-time presidential candidate Ross Perot Sr., offers applications development, systems integration, and strategic consulting services through its operations in the US and 10 other countries. In addition, it provides a variety of business process outsourcing (BPO) services, including claims processing and call center operations. Perot Systems serves commercial customers in a number of industries, including financial services, health care, and transportation; it also serves government agencies. Ross Perot and his family own about 25% of the company.

Work for the health care sector is one of the company's main business segments, accounting for more than 45% of sales. The company established its government services sector in 2002 and has quickly built it into another main component of the business that accounts for about 13% of revenue. The effort has been spurred in part because Perot Systems' largest customer, Swiss bank UBS (which itself accounts for about 12% of the company's business), is ending its services contract in 2007. The company was dealt a blow in 2005 when Harvard Pilgrim Health Care terminated its 10-year, $700 million services deal with four years left on the contract. However, Perot Systems scored a big win the following year when it was awarded a 10-year contract from Triad Hospitals worth about $1.2 billion. In early 2007 the company acquired information technology company QSS Group (integrating it into Perot Systems' government services unit) for approximately $250 million. Later that year the company agreed to purchase JJWild, an IT services provider serving the health care sector, for $89 million.

Perot and his son, Ross Jr., surprised the business community in 2004 when they handed the reins of the company to Peter Altabef, a lawyer from New York City. Perot had started the company from scratch in 1988 and built it into a technology powerhouse in large part though his personality and deal-making abilities. Those same qualities, however, also gave the company a very loose organizational structure. His son took over as CEO in 2000 and helped align the company's operations and organization. Altabef, formerly with the Dallas law firm Hughes & Luce, had been Perot Systems' general counsel since 1994.

## HISTORY

Ross Perot sold Electronic Data Systems (EDS), the data and computer services firm he founded in 1962, to General Motors for $2.5 billion in 1984. It wasn't long before he became irritated with GM; the feeling was mutual. By 1986 neither party could stand the other, and the company paid Perot $700 million for his GM stock on the condition that he go away and not hire any EDS workers for a year and a half.

In June 1988 Perot founded Perot Systems and hired eight EDS veterans. The new firm quickly scored a 10-year contract to cut costs at the US Postal Service. Perot's separation agreement with GM, however, prohibited him from competing with EDS for profit until December 1989, so Perot Systems worked for free until then. Pressure from GM eventually killed the Postal Service contract, but the publicity generated for Perot Systems led to a long list of customers who saw the nonprofit clause as a chance to undertake massive service and support efforts without paying high prices.

The company, however, soon began to founder — in part, some said, because it had promised more than it could deliver. Perot also alienated Hispanics with anti-NAFTA political rhetoric just as his company was working on deals with Volkswagen de México and Multibanco Mercantil Probursa. In 1992 Perot stepped down to concentrate on his bid for the US presidency. Former Perot aide and EDS executive Morton Meyerson became CEO and began leading the company away from computer outsourcing and toward higher-margin consulting services.

Perot Systems bought a division of financial software company Platinum Software (now Epicor Software) in 1994. In 1995 James Cannavino, who shared a past at IBM with Perot, became president (Perot had been a top Big Blue salesman; Cannavino was a strategist who left after he was denied the IBM chairmanship). A seven-year deal with Tenet Healthcare marked one of the first times that computer operations for the health care industry were outsourced.

An aggressive emphasis on risk-sharing alliances, in which the company is compensated based on its customers' results instead of through consultants' fees, spurred Perot Systems' growth. Perot Systems bought four firms in 1996, including Technical Resource Connection (object-oriented programming) and CommSys (telecommunications billing). Also that year it won a services contract with Swiss Bank (now UBS) by offering stock options in exchange for running the bank's computers and networks.

Rising costs and falling earnings in 1997 preceded the resignation of Cannavino. In 1998 Meyerson resigned as chairman and Perot retook the helm, waiving his own pay, pushing recruitment from the military, and making other changes to control costs.

Perot Systems went public in 1999, raising $109 million. That year it signed a pact with French technology services specialist Atos (now Atos Origin) to jointly provide services to multinational clients. In 2000 the company formed a joint venture (BillingZone) with PNC Bank to provide electronic bill presentment and payment for e-commerce companies. Perot Systems also acquired health care software maker Health Systems Design.

Ross Perot Jr., company director and son of the founder, was named CEO in 2000. In 2001 Perot Systems expanded with acquisitions, including the purchases of Covation, an application service provider serving the health care industry, and Advanced Receivables Strategy, a provider of IT services for the same industry.

The company acquired IT services provider Soza & Co. for up to $107 million in early 2003, adding multiple federal agencies to its client base.

There were a number of top management changes in 2004. VP and COO Brian Maloney "ceased to be an officer" in September, and shortly thereafter, the Perots announced sizeable role shifts. Ross Perot Sr., became chairman emeritus, Ross Jr., gave up the titles of president and CEO to become chairman, and Peter Altabef (formerly general counsel) took the reins as president and CEO.

## EXECUTIVES

**Chairman Emeritus:** Ross Perot Sr., age 77
**Chairman:** Ross Perot Jr., age 49, $543,270 pay
**President, CEO, and Director:** Peter A. Altabef, age 47, $1,497,505 pay
**COO:** Russell (Russ) Freeman, age 43, $887,909 pay
**CFO:** John Harper, age 45
**EVP Global Sales and Marketing:** Jeffrey (Jeff) Renzi, age 45
**EVP Healthcare Transformation:** Kevin M. Fickenscher
**EVP Business Development, Perot Systems Government Services:** Donnie Blanks
**VP and General Manager, Strategic Partnerships:** John E. King
**VP; Chairman, Consulting:** James A. (Jim) Champy, age 64, $878,904 pay
**VP; President, Healthcare Group:** Charles A. (Chuck) Lyles, age 40, $846,788 pay
**VP, Industrial Services Group:** Bob Mattana
**VP, General Counsel, and Secretary:** Thomas D. (Del) Williams
**VP Corporate Communications:** Eddie Reeves
**VP Corporate Support and Chief People Officer:** Darcy Anderson, age 47
**President, Commercial Solutions Group:** Steve Curts
**President, Perot Systems Government Services:** James C. (Jim) Ballard
**President, Business Process Solutions:** Anurag Jain
**Managing Director, Technology Services; Senior Executive, India and Asia Pacific:** Padma Ravichander, age 46
**Managing Director, Perot Systems Europe:** John Tilley
**Chief Marketing Officer:** Atul Vohra
**Director Corporate Communications:** Joe McNamara
**Investor Relations Director:** John Lyon
**Auditors:** PricewaterhouseCoopers LLP

## LOCATIONS

**HQ:** Perot Systems Corporation
2300 W. Plano Pkwy., Plano, TX 75075
**Phone:** 972-577-0000
**Web:** www.perotsystems.com

### 2006 Sales

| | % of total |
|---|---|
| US | 82 |
| UK | 8 |
| India | 3 |
| Other countries | 7 |
| **Total** | **100** |

## PRODUCTS/OPERATIONS

### 2006 Sales

| | % of total |
|---|---|
| Industry solutions | 75 |
| Government services | 13 |
| Consulting & application services | 12 |
| **Total** | **100** |

### Selected Services and Operations

Business process outsourcing
- Call center management
- Claims processing
- Payment processing
- Receivables collection

Management consulting
Project management
Systems and technology services
- Application development
- Business intelligence
- Data center management
- Hardware maintenance
- Help desk
- Messaging services
- Network management and security
- Process and change management
- Risk management
- Systems integration and testing
- Technology assessment
- Video, voice, and data services
- Web hosting

## COMPETITORS

Accenture
Affiliated Computer Services
Bain & Company
BearingPoint
Booz Allen
Boston Consulting
Bull
CACI International
Capgemini
CGI Group
CIBER
Cognizant Tech Solutions
Computer Sciences Corp.
Covansys
EDS
Fujitsu Services
General Dynamics
Getronics
HCL Technologies
HP Technology Solutions Group
IBM Global Services
Infosys
Keane
Lockheed Martin Information & Technology
LogicaCMG
McKesson
McKinsey & Company
Northrop Grumman IT
PA Consulting
Patni Computer Systems
Pegasus Solutions
Siemens IT Solutions and Services
SRA International
Unisys
Wipro Technologies

## HISTORICAL FINANCIALS

Company Type: Public

### Income Statement

FYE: December 31

| | REVENUE ($ mil.) | NET INCOME ($ mil.) | NET PROFIT MARGIN | EMPLOYEES |
|---|---|---|---|---|
| **12/06** | 2,298 | 81 | 3.5% | 21,200 |
| **12/05** | 1,998 | 111 | 5.6% | 18,100 |
| **12/04** | 1,773 | 94 | 5.3% | 15,900 |
| **12/03** | 1,461 | 3 | 0.2% | 13,500 |
| **12/02** | 1,332 | 78 | 5.9% | 9,100 |
| **Annual Growth** | 14.6% | 0.9% | — | 23.5% |

### 2006 Year-End Financials

Debt ratio: 7.6%
Return on equity: 7.8%
Cash ($ mil.): 383
Current ratio: 2.60
Long-term debt ($ mil.): 84
No. of shares (mil.): 120
Dividends
Yield: —
Payout: —
Market value ($ mil.): 1,972

### Stock History

NYSE: PER

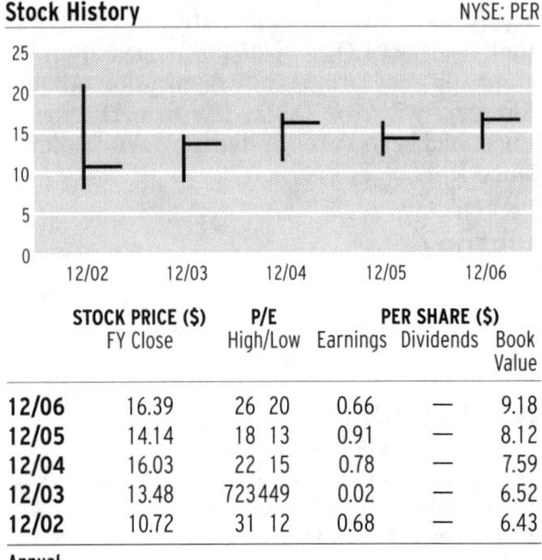


| | STOCK PRICE ($) FY Close | P/E High/Low | | PER SHARE ($) Earnings | Dividends | Book Value |
|---|---|---|---|---|---|---|
| **12/06** | 16.39 | 26 | 20 | 0.66 | — | 9.18 |
| **12/05** | 14.14 | 18 | 13 | 0.91 | — | 8.12 |
| **12/04** | 16.03 | 22 | 15 | 0.78 | — | 7.59 |
| **12/03** | 13.48 | 723 | 449 | 0.02 | — | 6.52 |
| **12/02** | 10.72 | 31 | 12 | 0.68 | — | 6.43 |
| **Annual Growth** | 11.2% | — | — | (0.7%) | — | 9.3% |

# Peter Kiewit Sons'

Peter Kiewit Sons' has become a heavyweight in the heavy construction industry by building everything from tunnels to high-rises. The employee-owned general contractor is involved with projects throughout the US and in Canada. As transportation accounts for about 45% of sales, Peter Kiewit Sons' typical undertakings include bridges, highways, railroads, airports, and mass-transit systems. Other project areas include power, heating/cooling, petroleum, commercial buildings, water supply, and dams. The company, which also owns coal mines, is owned by current and former employees and Kiewit family members.

Kiewit is a leader in the highway, bridge, water supply, and dam construction markets. Notable highway and bridge projects include a replacing segment of the San Francisco-Oakland Bay Bridge Skyway and upgrading the Sea-to-Sky Highway between Vancouver and Whistler, British Columbia. Water supply and dam projects include the Olivenhain and East dams in California, underground storage tanks for the Hollywood Hills Quality Improvement Project, and an intake valve at Lake Mead in Nevada. Public contracts account for more than 60% of sales.

Like most in its industry, Kiewit frequently undertakes projects through joint ventures to spread risk and share resources; joint ventures account for more than one-quarter of its sales. The company's mining operations include ownership of coal mines in Texas and Wyoming and management of two additional mines, all of which are surface mines.

## HISTORY

Born to Dutch immigrants, Peter Kiewit and brother Andrew founded Kiewit Brothers, a brickyard, in 1884 in Omaha, Nebraska. By 1912 two of Peter's sons worked at the yard, which was named Peter Kiewit & Sons. When Peter Kiewit died in 1914, his son Ralph took over, and the firm took the name Peter Kiewit Sons'. Another son, Peter, joined Ralph at the helm in 1924 after dropping out of Dartmouth and later took over.

During the Depression, Kiewit managed huge federal public works projects, and in the 1940s it focused on war-related emergency construction projects.

One of the firm's most difficult projects was top-secret Thule Air Force Base in Greenland, above the Arctic Circle. For more than two years 5,000 men worked around the clock, beginning in 1951; the site was in development for 15 years. In 1952 the company won a contract to build a $1.2 billion gas diffusion plant in Portsmouth, Ohio. It also became a contractor for the US interstate highway system (begun in 1956).

Peter Kiewit died in 1979, after stipulating that the largely employee-owned company should remain under employee control and that no one employee could own more than 10%. His 40% stake, when returned to the company, transformed many employees into millionaires. Walter Scott Jr., whose father had been the first graduate engineer to work for Kiewit, took charge. Scott made his mark by parlaying money from construction into successful investments.

When the construction industry slumped, Kiewit began looking for other investment opportunities, and in 1984 it acquired packaging company Continental Can Co. (selling off non-core insurance, energy, and timber assets). Continental was saddled with a 1983 class action lawsuit alleging that it had plotted to close plants and lay off workers before they were qualified for pensions. In 1991 Kiewit agreed to pay $415 million to settle the lawsuit. In the face of a consolidating packaging industry, the company sold Continental in the early 1990s.

In 1986 Kiewit loaned money to a business group to build a fiber-optic loop in Chicago; by 1987 it had launched MFS Communications to build local fiber loops in downtown districts. In 1992 Kiewit split its business into two pieces: the construction group, which was strictly employee-owned; and a diversified group, to which it added a controlling stake in phone and cable TV company C-TEC in 1993. That year Kiewit took MFS public; by 1995 it had sold all its shares, and the next year MFS was bought by telecom giant WorldCom.

In 1996 Kiewit assisted CalEnergy (now MidAmerican Energy) in a hostile $1.3 billion takeover of the UK's Northern Electric. Kiewit got stock in CalEnergy and a 30% stake in the UK electric company, all of which it sold to CalEnergy in 1998.

That year Kiewit spun off its telecom and computer services holdings into Level 3 Communications. Scott, who had been hospitalized the year before for a blood clot in his lung, stepped down as CEO, and Ken Stinson, CEO of Kiewit Construction Group, took over Peter Kiewit Sons'.

In 1999 Kiewit acquired a majority interest in Pacific Rock Products, a construction materials firm in Canada. Kiewit spun off its asphalt, concrete, and aggregates operations in 2000 as Kiewit Materials. Also that year the company created Kiewit Offshore Services to focus on construction for the offshore drilling industry. In 2001 the company acquired marine construction firm General Construction Company (GCC). The next year it expanded its offshore business further by buying a Canadian subsidiary from oil and gas equipment services company Friede Goldman Halter, which was trying to emerge from bankruptcy.

Kiewit made history in 2002 for the fastest completion of a project of its type when it completed the rebuilding of Webbers Falls I-40 Bridge in Oklahoma at the end of July. (The bridge had collapsed in May after being hit by a pair of barges, resulting in 14 fatalities.)

In 2004 Kiewit greatly increased its coal sales and reserves with the acquisition of the Buckskin Mine in Wyoming from Arch Coal.

Kiewit underwent a changing of the guard at the end of 2004, when 22-year-veteran Bruce Grewcock took the reins as the company's fourth CEO since its founding. Stinson stayed on as the company's chairman.

## EXECUTIVES

**Chairman Emeritus:** J. Walter (Walter) Scott Jr., age 75
**Chairman:** Kenneth E. (Ken) Stinson, age 64
**President, CEO, and Director:** Bruce E. Grewcock, age 53, $750,000 pay
**EVP and Director; EVP, Kiewit Corporation and Kiewit Pacific Co.:** Richard W. Colf, age 63, $416,000 pay
**EVP and Director:** Douglas E. Patterson, age 55, $403,000 pay
**SVP and CFO:** Michael J. Piechoski, age 52, $236,600 pay
**SVP, General Counsel, and Secretary:** Tobin A. Schropp, age 44
**SVP and Hawaii Area Manager, Kiewit Building Group:** Lance K. Wilhelm
**SVP, Building Division, Rocky Mountain Region:** Robert J. (Bob) Mattuci
**SVP and Division Manager, Midwest Building; President, Kiewit Building Group:** Bruce Tresslar
**VP, Human Resources and Administration:** John B. Chapman, age 61
**VP and Treasurer:** Ben E. Muraskin, age 42
**Division Manager, VP, and Director; SVP, Kiewit Corporation; President, Kiewit Mining Group:** Christopher J. Murphy, age 52
**Division Manager; SVP, Kiewit Corporation and Kiewit Construction; President, Gilbert Industrial Corp.:** Scott L. Cassels, age 48
**Division Manager and Director; SVP, Kiewit Corporation, Kiewit Construction Company, Kiewit Pacific Co., and Kiewit Western Co., and President, Kiewit Federal Group:** Kirk R. Samuelson, age 49
**Division Manager and Director; SVP, Kiewit Corporation, Kiewit Construction, and Kiewit Pacific Co.:** Steven Hansen, age 60, $842,400 pay
**Division Manager and Director; SVP, Kiewit Corporation and Kiewit Construction; President, Kiewit Energy Group:** Thomas S. Shelby, age 48
**Division Manager and Director; SVP, Kiewit Corporation, Kiewit Construction, Kiewit Pacific Co., and Kiewit Western Co.:** R. Michael Phelps, age 53, $322,700 pay
**President, Kiewit Engineering Co. (KECo):** Gary Pietrok
**Auditors:** KPMG LLP

## LOCATIONS

**HQ:** Peter Kiewit Sons', Inc.
3555 Farnam St., Omaha, NE 68131
**Phone:** 402-342-2052 **Fax:** 402-271-2939
**Web:** www.kiewit.com

Peter Kiewit Sons' US district and construction offices are located in Alaska, Arizona, Arkansas, California, Colorado, Florida, Georgia, Hawaii, Illinois, Kansas, Massachusetts, Nebraska, New Jersey, New Mexico, New York, Texas, and Washington. In Canada, the company has offices in Alberta, British Columbia, Ontario, and Quebec. The company's mining operations are in Texas and Wyoming.

### 2006 Sales

| | $ mil. | % of total |
|---|---|---|
| US | 4,351 | 86 |
| Canada | 698 | 14 |
| **Total** | **5,049** | **100** |

## PRODUCTS/OPERATIONS

### 2006 Sales

| | $ mil. | % of total |
|---|---|---|
| Construction | | |
| Transportation | 2,110 | 42 |
| Power/heat/cooling | 710 | 14 |
| Petroleum | 430 | 8 |
| Commercial building | 405 | 8 |
| Water supply/dams | 348 | 7 |
| Electrical | 263 | 5 |
| Sewage & solid waste | 209 | 4 |
| Mining construction | 131 | 3 |
| Other | 247 | 5 |
| Mining operations | 196 | 4 |
| **Total** | **5,049** | **100** |

### Selected Subsidiaries and Affiliates

Ben Holt Company
Bibb and Associates, Inc.
Bighorn Walnut, LLC
Buckskin Mining Company
CMF Leasing Co.
Continental Alarm & Detection Company
Continental Fire Sprinkler Company
General Construction Company
Gilbert Central Corp.
Gilbert Industrial Corporation
Gilbert Network Services, L.P.
Gilbert/Healy, L.P.
Global Surety & Insurance Co.
GSC Atlanta, Inc.
GSC Contracting, Inc.
Guernsey Construction Company
KES Inc.
KiEnergy, Inc.
KT Developers, LLC
KT Mining Inc.
Lac De Gras Excavation Inc.
Mass. Electric Construction Canada Co.
Mass. Electric Construction Co.
Mass. Electric Construction Venezuela, S.A.
Mass. Electric International, Inc.
MECC Rail Mexicana, S.A. de C.V.
Midwest Agencies, Inc.
Mission Materials Company
Seaworks, Inc.
Servitec de Sonora, S.A. de C.V.
Twin Mountain Construction II Company
V. K. Mason Construction Co.
Walnut Creek Mining Company

## COMPETITORS

ABB
Balfour Beatty Construction
Bechtel
Black & Veatch
Bovis Lend Lease
Fluor
Foster Wheeler
Granite Construction
Halliburton
Hubbard Group
ITOCHU
Jacobs Engineering
KBR
Lane Construction
Parsons
Perini
Raytheon
Skanska USA Civil
Turner Corporation
Tutor-Saliba
Walsh Group
Washington Group
Whiting-Turner
Williams Companies

## HISTORICAL FINANCIALS

Company Type: Private

### Income Statement

FYE: Last Saturday in December

| | REVENUE ($ mil.) | NET INCOME ($ mil.) | NET PROFIT MARGIN | EMPLOYEES |
|---|---|---|---|---|
| **12/06** | 5,049 | 39 | 0.8% | 14,700 |
| **12/05** | 4,145 | 228 | 5.5% | 14,500 |
| **12/04** | 3,352 | 201 | 6.0% | 14,000 |
| **12/03** | 3,375 | 157 | 4.7% | 15,000 |
| **12/02** | 3,699 | 193 | 5.2% | 15,000 |
| **Annual Growth** | 8.1% | (33.0%) | — | (0.5%) |

### Net Income History

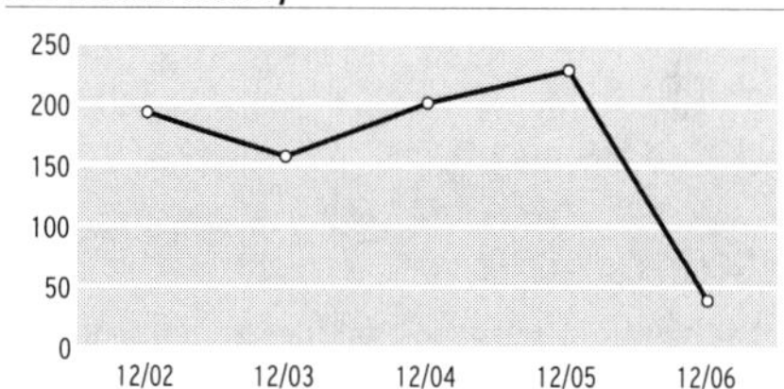


# PetSmart

PetSmart is the top dog and the cat's meow in its industry. The #1 US specialty retailer of pet food and supplies has more than 900 stores in the US and Canada. Both pets and their masters may lay paws, claws, or hands on its 13,400 products, which range from scratching posts to iguana harnesses, and are sold under national brands and PetSmart's own private labels. The retailer offers products through its PetSmart Web site. Many PetSmart stores offer in-store grooming and obedience training; veterinary services are available in some 600 shops through pet hospital operator Medical Management International (known as Banfield).

PetSmart owns about 36% of Banfield's parent company, MMI Holdings, Inc. The company plans to increase its stake in MMI.

While most of PetSmart's sales come from pet food and supplies, the service side (grooming, pet training, boarding, and day camp) of its business has been growing. Currently the company operates 60 in-store PetsHotel departments and each PetsHotel offers Doggie Day Camps. The company plans to build out more than 400 PetsHotels.

As the pet products firm chases after the more profitable services business, PetSmart sold its State Line Tack subsidiary — exiting the equine niche altogether — to Web-based retailer PetsUnited. State Line Tack joins existing PetsUnited entities dog.com, fish.com, and horse.com. As part of the early 2007 agreement, PetsUnited is moving State Line Tack's Brockport, New York-based business, which consists of an online and catalog component, to its Hazleton, Pennsylvania, facility.

Even though PetSmart exited its equine business, it sells fish, reptiles, birds, and other small animals, but not dogs or cats. Instead, PetSmart sponsors in-store pet adoption programs with local humane organizations.

After adding 100 stores last year, PetSmart opened another 90 in 2006. Ultimately the company thinks there is room for at least 1,400 of its stores throughout North America. In 2007 PetSmart boosted its Canadian presence with acquisition of 19 stores from the Super Pet chain. (Super Pet plans to keep seven stores, which it will rebrand.) The company plans to open another 100 new stores in 2007.

The company was affected in early 2007 by a recall of pet foods made by Menu Foods, a manufacturer whose products contained a wheat gluten that had been contaminated with the chemical melamine. The affected foods have been linked to pet illnesses and deaths across the country. PetSmart has been named in several lawsuits for distributing the tainted product.

The company changed the emphasis on its name from PETsMART to PetSmart in 2005 to shift its branding from a pet "mart" to a retailer that's "smart" about pets.

## HISTORY

In the mid-1980s the owner of a California pet supply wholesaler had an idea: If the company opened its own retail stores, it could make a bundle supplying itself. Not wanting to compete with its own retail customers in California, the company hired Jim and Janice Dougherty to run the first store in Las Vegas, called Pet Food Supermarket. In response to customer requests, the store began offering a broader range of products and soon business was booming. The store moved to a larger location, and four more stores were eventually opened in Phoenix.

While managing the Pet Food Supermarkets, the Doughertys met Ford Smith, a retailer who had developed a plan for giant pet-supply stores while in business school. Together they agreed to give the Toys "R" Us superstore format a try for pet supplies. They opened two PetFood Warehouse stores in Arizona in 1987. The next year there were seven stores in Arizona, Colorado, and Texas.

In 1989 PetFood Warehouse officially became PETsMART, Jim left the company due to health reasons (Janice followed shortly thereafter), and supermarket executive Sam Parker came on as CEO. His management team recrafted the PETsMART business strategy and gave the store a new look: brightly lit, low shelves with various pet supplies in the front of the store, and high warehouse-style shelves with bulk pet food in the back.

The 1990s saw PETsMART adding services such as in-store grooming, obedience training, veterinary exams, and adoption programs; it also began selling birds and fish. In 1991 the company added 15 new stores. The following year 32 stores were opened.

PETsMART went public in 1993. The company added more than 40 stores that year. In 1994 PETsMART bought the Weisheimer Companies, which operated about 30 pet superstores in the Midwest under the name Petzazz.

A year later the company went on an acquisition spree, buying two pet superstore operators (56-store, Georgia-based Petstuff and 10-store, New Jersey-based Pet Food Giant) and two specialty-catalog retailers of pet and animal supplies. Some 80 stores were added in 1995, and Mark Hansen replaced Parker as CEO; Parker remained chairman.

Hansen took PETsMART overseas in 1996 through the acquisition of Pet City Holdings, which operated more than 50 stores in the UK. The company also entered Canada that year. But the aggressive expansion campaign diverted the company's attention from daily operations and inventory management, eroding PETsMART's earnings in fiscal year 1998. In response, the company instituted a back-to-basics strategy of improved customer service and lower prices. Phil Francis, formerly with Shaw's Supermarkets, became CEO in 1998.

In 1999 PETsMART launched PETsMART.com in conjunction with PetJungle.com, an online pet retailer backed by Internet incubator idealab!. The move intensified a catfight with several lavishly funded online pet supply stores, including now-defunct Pets.com, which was backed by dominant e-tailer Amazon.com.

The company sold its 92 UK stores to Pets At Home for more than $40 million in late 1999. The company acquired PETsMART.com's remaining shares in 2002. Carrefour sold its 9.9% stake in PETsMART for $194.3 million through a public offering that year.

The company added 100 new stores in 2005. In line with those changes, in 2006, PETsMART changed how its name is styled to PetSmart, with the emphasis on "smart" rather than "mart."

It exited the equine products business in May 2007 when it sold State Line Tack to PetsUnited.

## EXECUTIVES

**Chairman and CEO:** Philip L. (Phil) Francis, age 60, $1,841,000 pay
**President and COO:** Robert F. (Bob) Moran, age 56, $1,224,760 pay
**SVP and CIO:** Donald E. (Don) Beaver, age 48
**SVP, Merchandising:** Kenneth T. (Ken) Hall, age 38
**SVP, General Counsel, Secretary, and Chief Compliance Officer:** Scott A. Crozier, age 56
**SVP, People:** Francesca M. Spinelli, age 53
**SVP, Store Operations and Services:** David K. Lenhardt, age 37
**SVP and Chief Marketing Officer:** Mary L. Miller, age 46
**SVP, Supply Chain:** Joseph D. O'Leary, age 48
**VP, Finance, Acting CFO, and Chief Accounting Officer:** Raymond L. (Ray) Storck, age 46
**VP, Customer Relationship Marketing:** Erica Thompson
**VP, Construction:** Steven (Steve) Olson
**Media Relations:** Jennifer Pflugfelder
**Media Relations:** Bruce Richardson
**Auditors:** Deloitte & Touche LLP

## LOCATIONS

**HQ:** PetSmart, Inc.
19601 N. 27th Ave., Phoenix, AZ 85027
**Phone:** 623-580-6100 **Fax:** 623-580-6183
**Web:** www.petsmart.com

PetSmart has distribution centers in Arizona, Georgia, Illinois, Maryland, Nevada, New York, Ohio, and Texas.

### 2007 Stores

| | No. |
|---|---|
| US | 875 |
| Canada | 33 |
| **Total** | **908** |

### 2007 Sales

| | % of total |
|---|---|
| US | 98 |
| Canada | 2 |
| **Total** | **100** |

## PRODUCTS/OPERATIONS

### 2007 Sales

| | % of total |
|---|---|
| Merchandise | 91 |
| Pet services | 9 |
| **Total** | **100** |

### Selected Merchandise

Animal carriers
Aquariums
Bedding
Bird cages
Birds
Books
Cat furniture
Collars
Dog houses
Freshwater tropical fish
Greeting cards
Health aids
Leashes
Litter
Magazines
Medications
Pet food
Reptiles
Shampoos
Toys
Treats

### Selected Services

Boarding (select stores)
Doggie day camp
Grooming
Obedience training
Veterinary services

### Private Labels

Pet Food
- Authority (cat and dog food, treats)
- Grreat Choice (dog treats)
- SophistaCat (cat food)

Pet Supplies
- Top Fin
- Top Paw
- Top Wing

## COMPETITORS

Ahold USA
Albertsons
Costco Wholesale
Drs. Foster & Smith
Fat Cat
J and J Dog Supplies
Pet Supermarket
Pet Valu
PetCareRx
PETCO
PetMed
Sears Holdings
Target
United Pharmacal
VCA Antech
Wal-Mart
Weis Markets

## HISTORICAL FINANCIALS

Company Type: Public

**Income Statement** FYE: Sunday nearest January 31

| | REVENUE ($ mil.) | NET INCOME ($ mil.) | NET PROFIT MARGIN | EMPLOYEES |
|---|---|---|---|---|
| **1/07** | 4,234 | 185 | 4.4% | 38,400 |
| **1/06** | 3,761 | 183 | 4.9% | 34,600 |
| **1/05** | 3,363 | 171 | 5.1% | 30,300 |
| **1/04** | 2,996 | 140 | 4.7% | 26,500 |
| **1/03** | 2,695 | 89 | 3.3% | 23,500 |
| **Annual Growth** | 12.0% | 20.1% | — | 13.1% |

**2007 Year-End Financials**

Debt ratio: 43.1%
Return on equity: 19.1%
Cash ($ mil.): 229
Current ratio: 1.63
Long-term debt ($ mil.): 431
No. of shares (mil.): 135
Dividends
Yield: 0.4%
Payout: 9.0%
Market value ($ mil.): 4,116

**Stock History** NASDAQ (GS): PETM

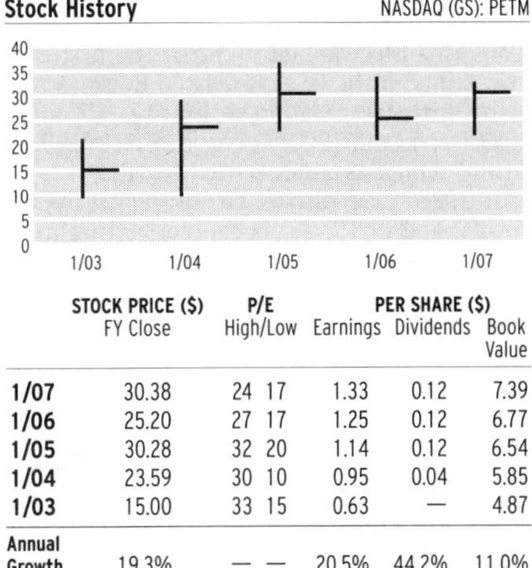


| | STOCK PRICE ($) FY Close | P/E High | P/E Low | PER SHARE ($) Earnings | Dividends | Book Value |
|---|---|---|---|---|---|---|
| **1/07** | 30.38 | 24 | 17 | 1.33 | 0.12 | 7.39 |
| **1/06** | 25.20 | 27 | 17 | 1.25 | 0.12 | 6.77 |
| **1/05** | 30.28 | 32 | 20 | 1.14 | 0.12 | 6.54 |
| **1/04** | 23.59 | 30 | 10 | 0.95 | 0.04 | 5.85 |
| **1/03** | 15.00 | 33 | 15 | 0.63 | — | 4.87 |
| **Annual Growth** | 19.3% | — | — | 20.5% | 44.2% | 11.0% |

# Pfizer Inc.

Pfizer pfabricates pfarmaceuticals pfor quite a pfew inpfirmities. The company is the world's largest research-based pharmaceuticals firm. Its best-known products include erectile dysfunction therapy Viagra, pain management drug Celebrex, antidepressant Zoloft, and cholesterol-lowering Lipitor. Pfizer also keeps Fluffy and Fido in mind with its animal health products, including Revolution (antiparasitic). Subsidiaries in the Pfizer pfamily include Embrex, Warner-Lambert, and Parke-Davis. It has sold its consumer unit — which made such OTC treatments as Benadryl, Sudafed, Nicorette, and Rolaids — to Johnson & Johnson for $16.6 billion.

While acquiring new holdings on the pharmaceutical front, Pfizer has trimmed its non-pharmaceutical businesses, including operations it acquired with Pharmacia and its European generics portfolio. In 2007, the division then acquired agricultural biotech company Embrex.

In the wake of revelations that Merck's Vioxx increased the risk for cardiovascular diseases, Pfizer studied its own COX-2 medication, Celebrex. Preliminary studies showed Celebrex increased the risk of heart attack; Pfizer didn't pull Celebrex off the market but did pull ads from television and radio and added a "black box" warning of possible cardiovascular and gastrointestinal risks.

Pfizer had three drugs topping $2 billion in sales in 2006, including Lipitor, Norvasc (a therapy for high blood pressure), and Zoloft; five drugs pulled in over $1 billion, including Viagra and Zyrtec. However, Pfizer's revenues from these established blockbusters continue to slide due to one of the pitfalls of the drug game: patent expiration.

Pfizer's pipeline does include some 250 projects in development, including drugs for atherosclerosis, diabetes, osteoporosis, breast cancer, epilepsy, anxiety disorders, and Parkinson's disease. Pfizer has relied to some degree on acquisitions and partnerships to build its R&D activities.

Pfizer's board in mid-2006 decided to shake things up and dismissed Hank McKinnell as its CEO. McKinnell retained his seat at the head of the company's board until he stepped down in early 2007. He was replaced by the company's general counsel, Jeffrey Kindler. Kindler announced layoffs of a fifth of Pfizer's sales force, which is thought to contribute to distance from doctors and higher drug costs.

In early 2007 Kindler announced measures aimed at tightening the company financially and operationally, with further layoffs of up to 10,000 employees (including those announced at the end of 2006) by the close of the year, including the closure of three research facilities in the US and three manufacturing facilities.

## HISTORY

Charles Pfizer and his cousin, confectioner Charles Erhart, began making chemicals in Brooklyn in 1849. Products included camphor, citric acid, and santonin (an early antiparasitic). The company, incorporated in 1900 as Chas. Pfizer & Co., was propelled into the modern drug business when it was asked to mass-produce penicillin for the war effort in 1941.

Pfizer discovered Terramycin and introduced it in 1950. Three years later it bought drugmaker Roerig, its first major acquisition. In the 1950s the company opened branches in Belgium, Canada, Cuba, Mexico, and the UK and began manufacturing in Asia, Europe, and South America. By the mid-1960s Pfizer had worldwide sales of more than $200 million.

Beginning in the late 1950s, Pfizer made Salk and Sabin polio vaccines and added new drugs, such as Diabinese (antidiabetic, 1958) and Vibramycin (antibiotic, 1967). It moved into consumer products in the early 1960s, buying BenGay, Desitin, and cosmetics maker Coty (sold 1992). It bought hospital products company Howmedica in 1972 (sold 1998) and heart-valve maker Shiley in 1979.

When growth slowed in the 1970s, new chairman Edmund Pratt increased R&D expenditures, resulting in Minipress (antihypertensive, 1975), Feldene (arthritis pain reliever, 1980), and Glucotrol (antidiabetic, 1984). Licensing agreements with foreign companies let Pfizer sell antihypertensive Procardia XL and antibiotic Cefobid. In the 1980s Pfizer expanded its hospital products division, buying 18 product lines and companies.

Lawsuits over the failure of about 500 heart valves and the alleged falsification of records led Pfizer to divest most of Shiley's operations in 1992. Drugs released that year included antidepressant Zoloft, antibiotic Zithromax, and cardiovascular agent Norvasc. In 1995 Pfizer discovered a genetic technique to prevent adult onset diabetes.

In 1997 Pfizer began promoting Lipitor, the cholesterol-lowering drug discovered by Warner-Lambert; it grabbed nearly 13% of the market in its first four months. Pfizer made headlines (and lots of happy men) when the company won FDA approval for Viagra in 1998. The little blue pill became a pop icon, and made the company a household name.

When Warner-Lambert said in 1999 that it would merge with American Home Products (now Wyeth), Pfizer sued to prevent the union and eventually succeeded with its own hostile bid. The merger with Warner-Lambert was completed, and CEO William Steere retired. Pfizer also sold its animal feed additive business.

Determined to narrow its focus on pharmaceuticals, the company in December 2002 sold its Tetra fish care, then sold its Adams confectionery and Schick-Wilkinson Sword shaving products businesses in early 2003.

In 2003 Pfizer purchased rival Pharmacia for $54 billion, making it the world's largest research-based pharmaceutical company. Following its two giant acquisitions, the company trimmed some 20,000 people.

Acquisitions in 2005 included the purchase of Angiosyn, a biotech working on an anti-angiogenesis therapy for macular degeneration, and Idun Pharmaceuticals, which is developing apoptosis (programmed cell death) inhibitors to treat liver disease, cancer, and other diseases.The company also scooped up research partner Vicuron Pharmaceuticals, which has two anti-infective (anidulafungin and dalbavancin) drugs under review by the FDA, and Bioren, which has developed a technology that helps drugs last longer through antibody optimization.

As part of its ongoing acquisition strategy, Pfizer bought Rinat Neuroscience (a company developing drugs for pain, Alzheimer's disease, and other neurological disorders). The company also spent $1.4 billion acquiring Sanofi-Aventis' joint rights to Exubera, an inhaled-insulin device.

## EXECUTIVES

**Chairman and CEO:** Jeffrey B. (Jeff) Kindler, age 52
**Vice Chairman:** David L. Shedlarz, age 58, $1,016,600 pay
**EVP, US Pharmaceuticals:** Peter C. Brandt
**SVP; President, Pfizer Global Research and Development:** John L. LaMattina, age 56, $885,200 pay
**SVP; Head of Worldwide Public Affairs and Policy:** Richard H. (Rich) Bagger
**SVP; Head of Worldwide Talent Development and Human Resources:** Sylvia M. Montero, age 57
**SVP and General Counsel:** Allen Waxman
**SVP; President, Pfizer Global Manufacturing:** Natale S. (Nat) Ricciardi, age 58
**SVP, Worldwide Communications:** Loretta M. Ucelli
**SVP, Corporate Governance; Associate General Counsel; and Secretary:** Margaret M. (Peggy) Foran, age 52
**SVP, Licensing and Development:** Lisa Ricciardi
**SVP, Science and Technology:** Peter B. Corr, age 58
**SVP, Worldwide Research:** Martin Mackay
**SVP, Worldwide Licensing:** Edmund P. (Ed) Harrigan, age 50
**SVP, Worldwide Medical:** Michael Berelowitz
**SVP, Worldwide Development:** Declan (Dec) Doogan
**SVP, Marketing:** Marie-Caroline Sainpy
**VP and Chief Medical Officer:** Joseph M. (Joe) Feczko
**VP, Consumer Marketing:** Ellen Brett
**VP, Worldwide Investor Development:** Amal Naj
**Senior Sales Director, Head of US Sales:** Karl Braun
**Director, US Marketing Operations:** Diane Gibbons
**Finance/Strategy:** Bill Roche
**Human Resources:** Jo Eisenhart
**Head of Strategic Investments:** Barbara Dalton
**Auditors:** KPMG LLP

## LOCATIONS

**HQ:** Pfizer Inc.
235 E. 42nd St., New York, NY 10017
**Phone:** 212-573-2323
**Web:** www.pfizer.com

**2006 Sales**

| | % of total |
|---|---|
| US | 53 |
| Japan | 7 |
| Other countries | 40 |
| **Total** | **100** |

## PRODUCTS/OPERATIONS

### 2006 Sales

| | % of total |
|---|---|
| Pharmaceutical | 93 |
| Animal health | 5 |
| Other | 2 |
| **Total** | **100** |

### Selected Products

Pharmaceuticals
- Accupril (cardiovascular)
- Aricept (Alzheimer's disease)
- Aromasin (breast cancer)
- Bextra (arthritis)
- Caduet (high cholesterol and blood pressure dual therapy)
- Camptosar (colorectal cancer)
- Cardura (hypertension and enlarged prostate disease)
- Celebrex (arthritis pain)
- Detrol/Detrusitol (overactive bladder)
- Diflucan (antifungal)
- Ellence (breast cancer)
- Genotropin (growth hormone deficiency)
- Geodon (scizophrenia, Zeldox outside of the US)
- Glucotrol XL (diabetes)
- Inspra (congestive heart failure)
- Lipitor (cholesterol)
- Lyrica (nerve pain)
- Medrol (chronic inflammation)
- Neurontin (epilepsy)
- Norvasc (hypertension)
- Rebif (multiple sclerosis)
- Relpax (migraines)
- Spiriva (chronic obstructive pulmonary disease)
- Vfend (fungal infections)
- Viagra (impotence)
- Viracept (HIV)
- Xalatan (glaucoma)
- Xanax (anti-anxiety treatment)
- Zithromax (antibiotic)
- Zoloft (depression)
- Zyrtec (allergies)
- Zyvox (antibiotic)

Animal Health
- BoviShield (vaccine for cattle respiratory disease)
- Clavamox/Synulox (canine and feline antibiotics)
- Dectomax (livestock anti-infective)
- Naxcel/Excenel (antibiotic)
- Revolution (antiparasitic for dogs and cats)
- Rimadyl (canine osteoarthritis treatment)

## COMPETITORS

Abbott Labs
Amgen
Apotex
Bayer
Bristol-Myers Squibb
Eli Lilly
GlaxoSmithKline
Johnson & Johnson
MedPointe
Merck
Novartis
Novo Nordisk
Repros Therapeutics
Roche
Sanofi-Aventis
Schering-Plough
Wyeth

## HISTORICAL FINANCIALS

Company Type: Public

### Income Statement

FYE: December 31

| | REVENUE ($ mil.) | NET INCOME ($ mil.) | NET PROFIT MARGIN | EMPLOYEES |
|---|---|---|---|---|
| **12/06** | 48,371 | 19,337 | 40.0% | 98,000 |
| **12/05** | 51,298 | 8,085 | 15.8% | 106,000 |
| **12/04** | 52,516 | 11,361 | 21.6% | 115,000 |
| **12/03** | 45,188 | 3,910 | 8.7% | 122,000 |
| **12/02** | 32,373 | 9,126 | 28.2% | 98,000 |
| **Annual Growth** | 10.6% | 20.6% | — | 0.0% |

### 2006 Year-End Financials

Debt ratio: 7.8%
Return on equity: 28.3%
Cash ($ mil.): 28,227
Current ratio: 2.20
Long-term debt ($ mil.): 5,546
No. of shares (mil.): 7,124
Dividends
Yield: 4.6%
Payout: 45.1%
Market value ($ mil.): 184,512

### Stock History

NYSE: PFE

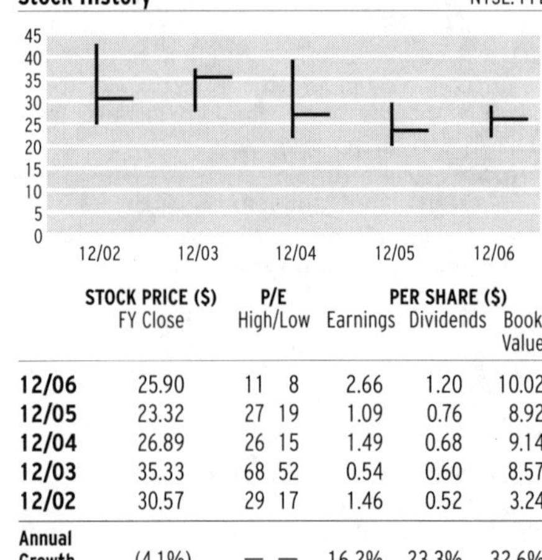


| | STOCK PRICE ($) FY Close | P/E High | P/E Low | PER SHARE ($) Earnings | Dividends | Book Value |
|---|---|---|---|---|---|---|
| **12/06** | 25.90 | 11 | 8 | 2.66 | 1.20 | 10.02 |
| **12/05** | 23.32 | 27 | 19 | 1.09 | 0.76 | 8.92 |
| **12/04** | 26.89 | 26 | 15 | 1.49 | 0.68 | 9.14 |
| **12/03** | 35.33 | 68 | 52 | 0.54 | 0.60 | 8.57 |
| **12/02** | 30.57 | 29 | 17 | 1.46 | 0.52 | 3.24 |
| **Annual Growth** | (4.1%) | — | — | 16.2% | 23.3% | 32.6% |

# PG&E Corporation

Utility holding company PG&E Corporation is still recharging its batteries after losing power during California's energy crisis and the ensuing collapse of the wholesale energy trading industry. Its Pacific Gas and Electric utility, which emerged from bankruptcy protection in 2004, serves 5.1 million electric customers and 4.2 million natural gas customers in California. The utility also operates hydroelectric, nuclear, and fossil-fueled power plants. Former PG&E subsidiary National Energy & Gas Transmission (NEGT, formerly PG&E National Energy Group), an independent power producer and wholesale energy marketer, has emerged from Chapter 11 bankruptcy and has separated itself from PG&E.

Before the wholesale power market became unstable, PG&E had announced plans to expand its nonregulated generating capacity; however, the company delayed or canceled most of NEGT's development projects when the industry experienced a downturn. As a final effort to reduce debt, NEGT filed for bankruptcy protection in 2003. The unit's reorganization plan outlined a strategy to distribute interests in NEGT to its creditors, after which it was no longer affiliated with PG&E.

Pacific Gas and Electric emerged from Chapter 11 in 2004 after reaching agreement with the California Public Utilities Commission (CPUC) in a dispute over the two entities' opposing reorganization plans. Pacific Gas and Electric's original plan would have split the utility into several companies. The agreed-upon plan, which won bankruptcy court approval, leaves the utility intact under the CPUC's jurisdiction.

## HISTORY

Peter Donahue founded the first gas company in the western US, San Francisco Gas, in 1852, which merged with Edison Light & Power to become San Francisco Gas & Electric (SFG&E) in 1896. Meanwhile, also in San Francisco, money broker George Roe and other investors founded California Electric Light (1879). The first electric utility in the US, it predated Edison's New York Pearl Street Station by three years. California Electric and SFG&E consolidated in 1905 to form Pacific Gas and Electric (PG&E).

In 1928 PG&E discovered natural gas in California, and in 1930 it began converting more than 2.5 million appliances to burn this fuel. The company started exploring for out-of-state gas supplies in the 1950s, first in Texas and New Mexico and then in western Canada.

The utility opened the world's first private atomic power plant (Vallecitos) in 1957, and in 1960 it developed the first geothermal plant (The Geysers) in North America. Its Humboldt Bay facility (completed 1963) was one of the first nukes to produce electricity at a cost comparable to that of conventional plants. Stanley Skinner began his 33-year career at PG&E in 1964 (he became CEO in 1995).

By the late 1970s PG&E had acquired some 500 electric, gas, and water utilities, but it left the water business in the 1980s. That year Unit 1 of the Diablo Canyon nuclear facility went on line, despite protests over its earthquake-fault location. Unit 2 was operating by 1986. PG&E fell on hard times in the mid-1980s as industrial customers began to generate their own electricity or buy gas directly from suppliers. In response, PG&E cut 2,500 jobs in 1987 and formed an independent power producer, which became U.S. Generating, with construction giant Bechtel. In 1995, as deregulation accelerated in California, the company formed an energy services division to serve large customers.

In 1996 PG&E was hit by an outage originating in the Pacific Northwest that affected nine western states and raised doubts over the power grid's stability. That year PG&E's gas unit bought a pipeline in Australia.

PG&E Corporation was formed as a holding company in 1997, and utility Pacific Gas and Electric became a subsidiary. The company also bought Bechtel's 50% stake in U.S. Generating. That year Skinner retired and president Robert Glynn became CEO. PG&E also settled a lawsuit filed in 1993 that claimed it had polluted groundwater by discharging toxic wastewater. (The case was the subject of a movie, *Erin Brockovich,* released in 2000.)

As its home state deregulated in 1998, PG&E was required to sell off most of its California power plants. The company auctioned off some of its hydro plants, and Duke Energy picked up three of the utility's fossil-fuel plants in California and its Australian pipeline. (The divestiture requirement was reversed by regulatory agencies in 2000.) PG&E also bought 18 power plants (4,800 MW) from New England Electric System.

In 1999 the company sold its Texas gas operations to El Paso Corporation, agreed to sell most of its retail marketing arm (PG&E Services) to Enron, and moved the headquarters of its nonregulated operations (PG&E National Energy Group) to Bethesda, Maryland. PG&E suffered a loss that fiscal year.

A price squeeze brought on in part by deregulation battered Pacific Gas and Electric in 2000. Prices on the wholesale power market soared, but a California rate freeze prevented the utility from passing along increasing costs to customers. In 2001 it suspended payments to creditors and suppliers to conserve cash, but gained some prospect of relief when California's governor signed legislation to allow a state agency to buy power from wholesalers under long-term contracts. Also that year PG&E sold its nonregulated energy services unit and its natural gas liquids businesses.

Later in 2001 the California Public Utilities Commission (CPUC) approved a significant increase in retail electricity rates, and the Federal Energy Regulatory Commission (FERC) approved a plan to limit wholesale energy prices during periods of severe shortage in 11 western states. The moves didn't come quickly enough for Pacific Gas and Electric, which filed for bankruptcy protection. The unit completed its reorganization in 2004.

Poor conditions in the wholesale power market drove PG&E National Energy Group into bankruptcy in 2003; the unit changed its name to National Energy & Gas Transmission shortly after to signify its planned separation from PG&E.

## EXECUTIVES

**Chairman and CEO:** Peter A. Darbee, age 54, $975,000 pay
**SVP, CFO, and Treasurer; SVP and Treasurer, Pacific Gas and Electric:** Christopher P. Johns, age 46, $494,000 pay
**SVP and General Counsel:** Hyun Park, age 45
**SVP, Communications and Public Affairs:** Leslie H. Everett, age 56, $290,000 pay
**SVP, Corporate Strategy and Development:** Rand L. Rosenberg, age 53, $475,000 pay
**SVP, Chief Risk and Audit Officer:** Kent M. Harvey, age 48, $352,085 pay
**SVP, Public Affairs:** Nancy E. McFadden
**VP, Corporate Relations, PG&E and Pacific Gas and Electric:** Greg S. Pruett
**VP, Corporate Governance and Corporate Secretary; Corporate Secretary, Pacific Gas and Electric:** Linda Y. H. Cheng, age 48
**VP, Corporate Environmental and Federal Affairs:** Steven L. Kline, age 52
**VP, Federal Governmental Relations:** James A. Tramuto, age 58
**VP, Investor Relations:** Gabriel B. Togneri, age 52
**VP and Controller; VP, Controller, and CFO, Pacific Gas and Electric:** G. Robert (Bob) Powell, age 43
**President and CEO, Pacific Gas and Electric:** William T. (Bill) Morrow, age 48
**SVP Regulatory Relations, Pacific Gas and Electric:** Thomas E. Bottorff, age 53, $282,500 pay
**Auditors:** Deloitte & Touche LLP

## LOCATIONS

**HQ:** PG&E Corporation
1 Market Spear Tower, Ste. 2400,
San Francisco, CA 94105
**Phone:** 415-267-7000 **Fax:** 415-267-7268
**Web:** www.pgecorp.com

PG&E Corporation's primary subsidiary, Pacific Gas and Electric, operates in Central and Northern California.

## PRODUCTS/OPERATIONS

### 2006 Sales

| | $ mil. | % of total |
|---|---|---|
| Electric | 8,752 | 70 |
| Natural gas | 3,787 | 30 |
| **Total** | **12,539** | **100** |

## COMPETITORS

AEP
AES
Aquila
Avista
Calpine
Constellation Energy
Duke Energy
Edison International
Entergy
Exelon
FirstEnergy
Mirant
Modesto Irrigation District
North Baja Pipeline
Northern California Power
PacifiCorp
Reliant Energy
Sacramento Municipal
Sempra Energy
Sierra Pacific Resources
Southern Company
SUEZ-TRACTEBEL
Turlock Irrigation District
Western Area Power

## HISTORICAL FINANCIALS

Company Type: Public

### Income Statement

FYE: December 31

| | REVENUE ($ mil.) | NET INCOME ($ mil.) | NET PROFIT MARGIN | EMPLOYEES |
|---|---|---|---|---|
| **12/06** | 12,539 | 991 | 7.9% | 20,400 |
| **12/05** | 11,703 | 917 | 7.8% | 19,800 |
| **12/04** | 11,080 | 4,504 | 40.6% | 20,200 |
| **12/03** | 10,435 | 420 | 4.0% | 20,600 |
| **12/02** | 12,495 | (874) | — | 21,814 |
| **Annual Growth** | 0.1% | — | — | (1.7%) |

### 2006 Year-End Financials

Debt ratio: 110.5%
Return on equity: 13.2%
Cash ($ mil.): 1,871
Current ratio: 0.71
Long-term debt ($ mil.): 8,633
No. of shares (mil.): 373
Dividends
Yield: 2.8%
Payout: 47.8%
Market value ($ mil.): 17,645

### Stock History

NYSE: PCG

| | STOCK PRICE ($) FY Close | P/E High | P/E Low | PER SHARE ($) Earnings | Dividends | Book Value |
|---|---|---|---|---|---|---|
| **12/06** | 47.33 | 17 | 13 | 2.76 | 1.32 | 20.95 |
| **12/05** | 37.12 | 17 | 13 | 2.37 | 1.23 | 20.36 |
| **12/04** | 33.28 | 3 | 2 | 10.57 | — | 20.70 |
| **12/03** | 27.77 | 26 | 11 | 1.06 | — | 10.16 |
| **12/02** | 13.90 | — | — | (2.36) | — | 8.91 |
| **Annual Growth** | 35.8% | — | — | — | 7.3% | 23.8% |

# Phillips-Van Heusen

Phillips-Van Heusen (PVH) has the buttoned-down look all sewn up. The top US dress shirt maker sells clothes, sunglasses, and shoes for men, women, and children under brands such as Van Heusen, Bass, Jimlar, Calvin Klein, and IZOD, as well as licensed names DKNY, Michael Kors Collection, Geoffrey Beene, Kenneth Cole, John Henry, and private labels. It distributes its products to some 15,000 department store locations, including customers Federated, Kohl's, Belk, JCPenney, Stage Stores, and other wholesale clients. It also sells its products through outlet stores, which operate under the firm's brand names. The shirt maker acquired privately held necktie maker Superba for more than $110 million in January 2007.

Acting on its commitment to extend its reach into new markets, PVH bought Superba to market Calvin Klein and IZOD neckwear. (PVH had acquired most of clothing design company Calvin Klein in 2003.) The company also inked a licensing deal with B Robinson Optical in mid-2006 to make and market a line of men's and women's IZOD-branded sunglasses that launched in spring 2007.

While PVH is entering new niche markets, the company has been fine-tuning its licensing and international strategies and exiting less profitable areas of its business.

PVH has made several moves in recent years in an effort to gain global control of the Van Heusen brand. PVH acquired the Van Heusen label for Europe and Asia from UK-based Coats Viyella. PVH licensed the brand back to the previous owner, giving the company distribution rights in the UK and Ireland. PVH extended the reach for IZOD's European unit, as well, by inking a deal with Rousseau SAS in mid-2006. As part of the deal, Rousseau markets and distributes an IZOD-branded men's sportswear line sold in France, Belgium, Andorra, Luxembourg, and Monaco. In 2006 Warnaco acquired the license and wholesale and retail operations for Calvin Klein jeans and accessories in Europe and Asia. This deal with PVH also includes the CK Calvin Klein bridge line in Europe.

PVH also licensed its Bass label to Brown Shoe, effectively removing itself from the footwear business. It also announced plans to close about 200 Bass outlet stores.

Earnest Partners owns some 10% of PVH. In mid-2005 Bruce Klatsky, chairman, passed his CEO title to Mark Weber. Weber left within a year and was replaced by president and COO Emanuel Chirico. Klatsky retired in 2007 after nearly 36 years with the firm. Chirico, who assumed the chairmanship, and Klatsky had worked together for about two decades.

## HISTORY

Moses Phillips came to America from Poland in 1881. While living in a one-room apartment in Pottsville, Pennsylvania, he sold flannel shirts (which his wife sewed) to coal miners from a pushcart. He soon brought the rest of his family to the US and upgraded the pushcart to a horse and buggy. Business continued to grow, and the Phillips-Jones Corporation was formed in 1907.

The company moved to New York in 1914, and control passed from father to son for four generations. Isaac followed Moses, then Seymour took over in 1941 until he handed the reins to Lawrence, who joined the company in 1948 and became president and CEO in 1969. Ads in the 1950s featured such actors as Anthony Quinn, Burt Lancaster, and Ronald Reagan in Van Heusen shirts. In 1957 the company received its present name. Phillips-Van Heusen (PVH) grew via acquisitions throughout the 1970s and began selling its merchandise at its own outlet stores in 1979, but it didn't want its products sold at the off-price outlets that became popular in the early 1980s. The company stopped doing business with stores and distributors that allowed PVH merchandise to reach cut-price vendors.

In 1987 PVH acquired G. H. Bass & Co., maker of Bass and Weejun shoes, for $79 million. It also bought back over 5 million shares of stock in order to fend off an acquisition bid by the

Hunt family of Texas. Lawrence stepped down in 1993, ending the unbroken chain of Phillipses at the helm. Bruce Klatsky, a human rights supporter who had started work at the company 22 years earlier as a merchandising trainee, took over as CEO. In 1995 the Phillips family sold its stake in the business. PVH acquired the Gant and IZOD brands (and about 90 outlet stores) from Crystal Brands that year for about $115 million.

The company's retail outlet stores had driven its growth between 1985 and 1995, but a weakening in outlet store sales caused a downturn in 1994. During 1995 and 1996 PVH closed 218 of its poorest performing stores. Klatsky also closed three US shirt factories in 1995 as the company moved more of its production overseas.

PVH decided to close 150 more outlet stores (affecting 700 jobs), reposition Gant as a premium brand, and exit the private-label sweater manufacturing business in 1997. Klatsky ended an organized labor controversy at PVH's Guatemala operation in 1997 by meeting with union officials and ratifying a union contract.

After a repositioning attempt failed to move Bass upscale (but resulted in a $54 million charge), the company in 1998 cited the expense of doing business in the US when it closed its Bass shoe manufacturing plant in Wilton, Maine (where Bass had been founded in 1876). PVH then shifted the manufacturing to plants in Puerto Rico and the Dominican Republic.

In 1999 PVH sold Gant to the brand's international licensee, Pyramid Partners (in which PVH has a minority stake), for $71 million. In 2000 the company purchased Cluett Designer Group (a licensee for Kenneth Cole dress shirts) from Cluett American; it also licensed the Arrow shirts and sportswear brand from Cluett American. Coats Viyella, the UK-based owner of the Van Heusen brand in Europe and Asia, sold the label to PVH in February 2001 for $17.5 million. PVH then licensed the brand to Coats Viyella for use in the UK and Ireland. That November the company announced it would lay off 1,200 employees due to a sluggish retail environment.

PVH bought most of fashion design giant Calvin Klein in February 2003, renewing its commitment to apparel and divesting of its footwear endeavors.

Bruce Klatsky stepped down as CEO of the company (but remained chairman) in mid-2005. Former president and COO Mark Weber was tapped as his replacement. He lasted about eight months in that position. Emanuel Chirico was named to the top spot in February 2006, when Weber left the company.

## EXECUTIVES

**Chairman and CEO:** Emanuel (Manny) Chirico, age 49
**President and COO:** Allen E. Sirkin, age 64
**Group EVP and CIO:** Jon D. Peters
**Group EVP, Foreign Operations:** Theodore (Ted) Sattler
**EVP and CFO:** Michael A. (Mike) Shaffer, age 44
**EVP, Marketing:** Michael Kelly
**Group VP, Corporate IT Operations:** Dana Rappe
**VP and Controller:** Bruce Goldstein
**VP, General Counsel, and Secretary:** Mark D. Fischer
**VP, Human Resources:** David F. Kozel
**VP, Investor Relations and Treasurer:** Pamela N. Hootkin
**Vice Chairman, Wholesale:** Francis Kenneth (Ken) Duane, age 50
**Vice Chairman, Retail:** Michael Zaccaro, age 61, $1,427,917 pay
**President, Calvin Klein Retail:** John F. Walsh
**President, G.H. Bass Retail:** Scott H. Orenstein
**President, Geoffrey Beene Retail:** Margaret P. Lachance
**President and COO, Calvin Klein:** Paul Thomas (Tom) Murry
**President, Dress Shirt Designer Group:** Albert V. Moretti
**President, Izod Retail:** Donna Patrick
**President and COO, Dress Shirt Group:** Ellen Constantinides
**President, Licensing:** Kenneth L. Wyse
**President, Sportswear Group:** Malcolm Robinson
**President, Dress Shirt National Brands:** Lee H. Terrill
**President, Calvin Klein Men's Sportswear:** Molly Yearick
**President, Van Heusen Retail:** Steven B. Shiffman
**Auditors:** Ernst & Young LLP

## LOCATIONS

**HQ:** Phillips-Van Heusen Corporation
200 Madison Ave., New York, NY 10016
**Phone:** 212-381-3500 **Fax:** 212-381-3950
**Web:** www.pvh.com

## PRODUCTS/OPERATIONS

### 2007 Sales

| | $ mil. | % of total |
|---|---|---|
| Net sales | 1,849.2 | 88 |
| Royalty revenue | 182.3 | 9 |
| Advertising & other revenue | 59.1 | 3 |
| **Total** | **2,090.6** | **100** |

### 2007 Net Sales

| | $ mil. | % of total |
|---|---|---|
| Retail apparel & related products | 639.4 | 35 |
| Wholesale sportswear & related products | 557.6 | 30 |
| Wholesale dress furnishings | 371.4 | 20 |
| Retail footwear & related products | 280.8 | 15 |
| **Total** | **1,849.2** | **100** |

### Brands

Arrow (licensed)
Bass/GH Bass (licensed)
Calvin Klein
DKNY (licensed from Donna Karan)
Geoffrey Beene (licensed)
IZOD
Kenneth Cole (licensed)
Reaction by Kenneth Cole
Van Heusen

## COMPETITORS

Allen-Edmonds
Armani
Ashworth
Berkshire Hathaway
Brown Shoe
Capital Mercury Apparel
Donna Karan
Eddie Bauer Holdings
Gap
Genesco
Gucci
Haggar
Hartmarx
Hugo Boss
J. Crew
Jones Apparel
Kellwood
Kenneth Cole
Levi Strauss
Luxottica
Nautica Enterprises
Oakley
Oxford Industries
Perry Ellis International
Polo Ralph Lauren
Prada
Reebok
Stride Rite
Timberland
Tommy Hilfiger
Warnaco Group

## HISTORICAL FINANCIALS

Company Type: Public

### Income Statement

FYE: Sunday nearest February 1

| | REVENUE ($ mil.) | NET INCOME ($ mil.) | NET PROFIT MARGIN | EMPLOYEES |
|---|---|---|---|---|
| **1/07** | 2,091 | 155 | 7.4% | 10,900 |
| **1/06** | 1,909 | 112 | 5.9% | 9,700 |
| **1/05** | 1,641 | 59 | 3.6% | 9,100 |
| **1/04** | 1,582 | 15 | 0.9% | 9,000 |
| **1/03** | 1,405 | 30 | 2.2% | 9,430 |
| **Annual Growth** | 10.4% | 50.3% | — | 3.7% |

### 2007 Year-End Financials

Debt ratio: 42.4%
Return on equity: 20.0%
Cash ($ mil.): 366
Current ratio: 2.77
Long-term debt ($ mil.): 400
No. of shares (mil.): 56
Dividends
Yield: 0.3%
Payout: 5.7%
Market value ($ mil.): 3,071

### Stock History

NYSE: PVH

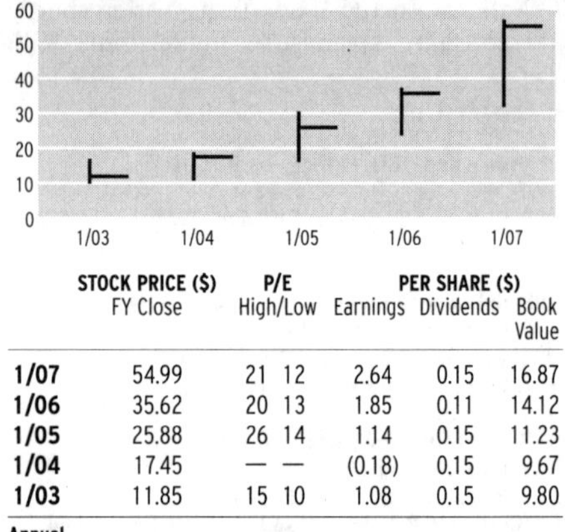


| | STOCK PRICE ($) FY Close | P/E High | P/E Low | PER SHARE ($) Earnings | Dividends | Book Value |
|---|---|---|---|---|---|---|
| **1/07** | 54.99 | 21 | 12 | 2.64 | 0.15 | 16.87 |
| **1/06** | 35.62 | 20 | 13 | 1.85 | 0.11 | 14.12 |
| **1/05** | 25.88 | 26 | 14 | 1.14 | 0.15 | 11.23 |
| **1/04** | 17.45 | — | — | (0.18) | 0.15 | 9.67 |
| **1/03** | 11.85 | 15 | 10 | 1.08 | 0.15 | 9.80 |
| **Annual Growth** | 46.8% | — | — | 25.0% | 0.0% | 14.5% |

# Pier 1 Imports

Pier 1 Imports teams with shoppers fishing for furniture and accessories with an exotic flavor. The company sells about 3,000 items (imported from more than 40 countries) through about 1,200 Pier 1 Imports and Pier 1 Kids stores in the US, Puerto Rico, Canada, and Mexico. Pier 1 stores offer a wide selection of indoor and outdoor furniture, lamps, vases, baskets, ceramics, dinnerware, candles, and other specialty products. Many of the products are handcrafted; the company favors natural materials, such as rattan and wood. Pier 1 sold its proprietary credit card business to JPMorgan Chase for $155 million.

Furniture accounts for nearly 40% of sales, and decorative items (lamps, vases, baskets) account for another quarter. The stores also sell bed and bath products, housewares, and seasonal items. Pier 1 imports its wares mainly from Asia. The company also operates about 35 stores-within-stores inside Sears shops in Mexico and Puerto Rico.

Pier 1 has been stung by competitors, including mass discounters Target and Wal-Mart Stores, moving in on its market for trendy, inexpensive home furnishings. In an effort to reverse sagging sales, Pier 1 Imports has cleaned its house of exotic furniture and funky tchotchkes and replaced them with a less cluttered look that features more contemporary merchandise. The new look — dubbed "Metro Glam" on the company's Web site — is closer to that found in Crate & Barrel and Pottery Barn stores than the company's traditional competitors, such as Cost Plus's World Markets. Still, sales have continued to disappoint.

The company has brought in some new blood to the CEO suite. Alex W. Smith, formerly with off-price retailer TJX Cos., succeeded Marvin Girouard as chief executive of the struggling retailer in early 2007. Soon after Smith arrived, Pier 1 announced that it will cut about 175 jobs.

The company later announced it would close more stores than anticipated in 2007, 100 stores instead of 60, to reduce costs. And it said it would shut down its Pier 1 Kids and clearance stores, as well as its e-commerce and catalog operations.

Jakup Jacobsen owns nearly 10% of Pier 1's shares. The Danish retail tycoon, who owns Iceland's Lagerinn, has already acquired the company's British and Irish operations and is thought to be a likely buyer for the rest of the company. Invesment firm Elliot Associates owns 5% of Pier 1.

## HISTORY

Attracted by a Fisherman's Wharf import outlet called Cost Plus, marketing guru Charles Tandy (founder of RadioShack) made a loan to its owner and obtained the right to open other Cost Plus stores. Opening his first Cost Plus store in 1962 in San Francisco, Tandy leveraged the strength of the US dollar against weaker foreign currencies. He bought inexpensive wicker furniture, brass candlesticks, and other items from countries such as India, Mexico, and Thailand and gave them healthy markups, yet still managed to price them attractively for US customers.

The store was a hit with the peace and free-love generation of the 1960s, which dug its beads, incense, and wicker furniture. In 1965, with 16 locations, the company changed its name to Pier 1 Imports. Pressed by the demands of RadioShack, Tandy sold Pier 1 the next year. In 1969, with 42 stores, including its first store in Canada, the company went public on AMEX.

By 1971 Pier 1 had 123 stores and was celebrating 100% sales gains for four consecutive years. It expanded its international presence, adding locations in Australia and Europe, and moved to the NYSE the next year. The chain experimented with alternative retail formats, including art supply, rug outlets, and fabric stores, but had abandoned them, as well as its foreign stores, by the mid-1970s. Pier 1 boasted nearly 270 locations by 1975.

Baby boomers, key to the chain's success, grew up and acquired different tastes, however. The dollar had also weakened, thereby increasing costs. Performance faltered, and in 1980 the company brought in Robert Camp, who had successfully operated his own Pier 1 stores in Canada, to give it a makeover. Camp closed poorly performing stores, opened larger stores in more profitable areas, and began changing the merchandise mix from novelties to higher-quality goods.

In 1983 investment group Intermark bought more than a third of the company. The next year Pier 1 acquired 36 Nurseryland Garden Centers from Intermark (boosting Intermark's stake in Pier 1 to about 50%) and merged the stores with its Wolfe's Nursery to form Sunbelt Nursery Group, which was spun off in 1985. That year Pier 1 named Clark Johnson its CEO. At the time it operated nearly 265 locations, showing little growth in store count in a decade.

Johnson initiated an ambitious plan to double the number of Pier 1 stores, which reached 500 in early 1989. With Intermark struggling, Pier 1 bought back Sunbelt (including a 50% stake in Sunbelt from Intermark) in 1990. The following year Intermark sold its stake in Pier 1 to pay back debt (the ailing investment group declared bankruptcy in 1992). That year Pier 1 took Sunbelt public, keeping a 57% stake (Sunbelt has since been dissolved). In 1993 the company launched The Pier, a chain of stores in the UK, and opened boutiques in Sears stores in Mexico.

Having spruced up stores, the chain continued to adjust the merchandise mix, dumping apparel in 1997 in favor of higher-margin goods. That year Pier 1 purchased a national bank charter from Texaco (now Chevron Corp.) to standardize the interest rates and fees on its private-label credit card. Marvin Girouard replaced Johnson as CEO in 1998 and as chairman in 1999. Pier 1 began selling online with the launch of its Web site in 2000.

In 2001 the company acquired the 21-store Cargo Furniture chain (later renamed Pier 1 Kids) from home furnishings manufacturer Tandycrafts. In 2003 Pier 1 nearly doubled its number of Cargokids retail locations, bringing the total to 40 stores nationwide. In the summer of 2004 Berkshire Hathaway, billionaire Warren Buffett's investment vehicle, bought 8 million shares of Pier 1.

In the fall of 2005 Pier 1 launched its first At Home catalog. In March 2006 the company sold its UK subsidiary, The Pier (Retail) Ltd., to Palli Limited for approximately $15 million. The Pier operated 40-plus stores in the UK and Ireland.

In February 2007, Marvin Girouard retired as chairman and CEO of the company after 32 years with the firm.

## EXECUTIVES

**Chairman:** Tom M. Thomas, age 64
**President, CEO, and Director:** Alexander W. (Alex) Smith, age 54
**EVP, Store Operations:** Sharon M. Leite
**EVP, Finance, CFO, and Treasurer:** Charles H. (Cary) Turner, age 48, $365,000 pay
**EVP, Merchandising:** Jay R. Jacobs, age 50, $365,000 pay
**EVP, Logistics and Allocations:** David A. Walker, age 54, $275,000 pay
**EVP, Human Resources:** Gregory S. (Greg) Humenesky, age 53
**SVP, General Counsel, and Secretary:** Michael A. Carter
**SVP, Finance and Controller:** Susan E. Barley
**SVP, Information Systems and CIO:** Andy Laudato
**Auditors:** Ernst & Young LLP

## LOCATIONS

**HQ:** Pier 1 Imports, Inc.
100 Pier 1 Place, Fort Worth, TX 76102
**Phone:** 817-252-8000 **Fax:** 817-252-8174
**Web:** www.pier1.com

**2007 Sales**

| | % of total |
|---|---|
| US | 93 |
| Other countries | 7 |
| **Total** | **100** |

**2007 Stores**

| | No. |
|---|---|
| US | |
| Pier 1 | 1,076 |
| Pier 1 Kids | 36 |
| Canada | |
| Pier 1 | 84 |
| Mexico | |
| Pier 1 | 29 |
| Puerto Rico | |
| Pier 1 | 7 |
| **Total** | **1,232** |

## PRODUCTS/OPERATIONS

**2007 Sales**

| | % of total |
|---|---|
| Furniture | 38 |
| Decorative accessories | 27 |
| Bed & bath | 17 |
| Housewares | 12 |
| Seasonal | 6 |
| **Total** | **100** |

**2007 Sales**

| | $ mil. | % of total |
|---|---|---|
| Stores | 1,590.9 | 98 |
| Direct to customer | 18.9 | 1 |
| Other | 13.4 | 1 |
| **Total** | **1,623.2** | **100** |

**Selected Merchandise**

Baskets
Bed and bath accessories
Candles
Ceramics
Dinnerware
Dried and silk flowers
Fragrance products
Furniture
Lamps
Seasonal products
Vases
Wall decor

## COMPETITORS

Bed Bath & Beyond
Bombay Company
Container Store
Cost Plus
Costco Wholesale
Decorize
Eddie Bauer Holdings
Euromarket Designs
Eurway
Garden Ridge
IKEA
Kirkland's
Linens 'n Things
Michaels Stores
Restoration Hardware
Room & Board
Rooms To Go
Target
Tuesday Morning
Wal-Mart
Williams-Sonoma

## HISTORICAL FINANCIALS

Company Type: Public

**Income Statement** FYE: Saturday nearest last day in Feb.

| | REVENUE ($ mil.) | NET INCOME ($ mil.) | NET PROFIT MARGIN | EMPLOYEES |
|---|---|---|---|---|
| **2/07** | 1,623 | (228) | — | 15,400 |
| **2/06** | 1,777 | (40) | — | 19,100 |
| **2/05** | 1,898 | 61 | 3.2% | 16,400 |
| **2/04** | 1,868 | 118 | 6.3% | 17,600 |
| **2/03** | 1,755 | 129 | 7.4% | 17,400 |
| **Annual Growth** | (1.9%) | — | — | (3.0%) |

**2007 Year-End Financials**

Debt ratio: 51.0%
Return on equity: —
Cash ($ mil.): 173
Current ratio: 2.23
Long-term debt ($ mil.): 184
No. of shares (mil.): 88
Dividends
Yield: 3.0%
Payout: —
Market value ($ mil.): 582

**Stock History** NYSE: PIR

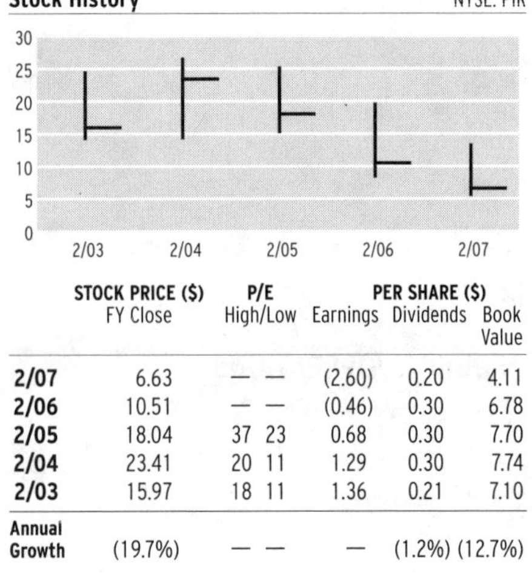


| | STOCK PRICE ($) FY Close | P/E High/Low | PER SHARE ($) Earnings | Dividends | Book Value |
|---|---|---|---|---|---|
| **2/07** | 6.63 | — — | (2.60) | 0.20 | 4.11 |
| **2/06** | 10.51 | — — | (0.46) | 0.30 | 6.78 |
| **2/05** | 18.04 | 37 23 | 0.68 | 0.30 | 7.70 |
| **2/04** | 23.41 | 20 11 | 1.29 | 0.30 | 7.74 |
| **2/03** | 15.97 | 18 11 | 1.36 | 0.21 | 7.10 |
| **Annual Growth** | (19.7%) | — — | — | (1.2%) | (12.7%) |

# Pilgrim's Pride

Pilgrim's Pride has spread its tail feathers and is doing a barnyard strut. Pilgrim's operations entail breeding, hatching, raising, processing, distributing, and marketing of chicken and turkey. Prepared poultry products are sold under the Pilgrim's Pride, Pierce, Easy-Entree, EatWellStayHealthy, and Wing-Dings brands to restaurants, grocery stores, and frozen-food makers. It also sells fresh whole and cut-up chicken under the Pilgrim's Pride, Pilgrim's Signature, and Country Pride names. Chairman Lonnie Ken Pilgrim and his family control approximately 62% of the company's voting power.

While Pilgrim's also produces table eggs, egg products, animal feeds, and feed ingredients, it really focuses on prepared foods. Its prepared chicken products such as frozen fillets, tenderloins, strips, and nuggets are sold to foodservice and retail outlets.

The company's key foreign markets include Eastern Europe (including Russia), Asia, and Mexico. It is the #2 poultry company in Mexico (behind Bachoco). Its largest customer, Wal-Mart, accounts for 10% of the company's sales.

Looking to rule the roost in poultry production, in 2007 Pilgrim's acquired Gold Kist for $1.1 billion. The deal, which came about after a hostile takeover bid and much legal wrangling between the companies, leapfrogged Pilgrim's past Tyson Foods as the world's top poultry producer. The combined operation also made Pilgrim's the #3 US meat company in terms of revenue.

Long-time chairman and company founder, Lonnie "Bo" Pilgrim Sr., stepped down as chairman in 2007. Retaining a seat on the board, he was replaced as chairman by his son, Ken.

## HISTORY

Aubrey Pilgrim formed Pilgrim's Pride as Farmer's Feed and Seed Co. in 1946, with $1,000 in cash and a $2,500 note. Aubrey and brother Lonnie "Bo" Pilgrim (who joined the business in 1947) sold their first chicken from a pen behind their farm supply store and began to give away 100 baby chicks with each feed sack purchase. The Pilgrims bought back some of the grown birds to resell at a profit.

As demand for chickens grew, Farmer's Feed and Seed took its first steps toward creating a vertically integrated chicken company. It opened its first processing plant in 1957 and entered the distribution business three years later, delivering chicken to restaurants and grocery stores in northeastern Texas. Bo took over the business when Aubrey died of a heart attack in 1966.

The company was renamed Pilgrim's Industries in 1968 (and Pilgrim's Pride in 1985). Eggs became part of the product mix in 1969. That year Pilgrim's acquired Market Produce Co., a food distributor with facilities in Arlington, Odessa, and El Paso, Texas. By 1979 the company was selling 1 million birds every week.

In the 1970s and 1980s, Pilgrim's grew through acquisitions and by using TV advertising to build a national brand. Its first TV commercial, "The President Speaks," was a humorous 1983 spot featuring Bo in a wide-brimmed pilgrim's hat, addressing his TV audience. To offset the wide swings in prices and profits in the highly cyclical commodity chicken industry, Pilgrim's moved into prepared foods in 1986, the year it went public. The firm expanded into the Mexican consumer market in 1988 through the purchase of several chicken producers there.

Bo caused an uproar the next year when he handed out campaign checks to Texas lawmakers during a senate session (a practice that is now illegal). The activity brought Bo before a grand jury, although he was not indicted.

Between 1987 and 1991 Pilgrim's tripled the size of its Mexican operations and expanded its frozen retail and export businesses. Excess poultry production and low prices led to the company's $30 million loss in 1992. Debt restructuring that year forced it to seek outside capital. Pilgrim's persuaded agricultural titan Archer Daniels Midland (ADM) to buy into the company, limiting ADM's stake to 20%.

In 1993 the company took major steps toward arranging for a successor for the aging Bo by appointing his nephew Lindy "Buddy" Pilgrim as president. (Buddy, formerly a marketing executive with Pilgrim's, had left the company in 1990 to lead a food industry consulting firm.)

Pilgrim's bought Mexican chicken processor Unión de Querétaro in 1995. Costs related to acquisitions nudged the company into the red that year and the next. Pilgrim's expanded its US processing capacity with the 1997 purchase of Green Acres Foods, of Nacogdoches, Texas. That year it also introduced EggsPlus, an egg line with six times the vitamin E content of ordinary eggs and high levels of high-density lipoprotein.

ADM reduced its stake in Pilgrim's from 20% to 4% in 1997 and eventually sold the rest in 1999. In 1998 Buddy resigned, Bo took the title of senior chairman (though later dropping "senior" from his title), and David Van Hoose, who had ruled the roost in the company's Mexican operations, became CEO.

Pilgrim's bought poultry processor WLR Foods for about $280 million in 2001 and turned the business into its eastern division.

Challenges soon arose for the new division in 2002. Its flocks were struck with avian influenza, which cost the company $26 million when it was forced to destroy 4.7 million birds. Later in the year Pilgrim's was prompted to recall 27.4 million pounds of poultry deli meat after samples tested positive for Listeria bacteria. The recall was one of the largest in the US meat industry and covered five-and-a-half months' production from one plant near Philadelphia.

In 2003 Pilgrim's plunked down nearly $550 million in stock, cash, and debt to acquire ConAgra's chicken processing business. Along with 16 plants and 15 distribution centers, the deal included the Easy-Entree, Country Pride, and Pierce poultry brands. Through supplier agreements, ConAgra became one of Pilgrim's largest customers. ConAgra, in turn, pocketed nearly 40% of the company's stock.

Van Hoose stepped down as CEO in late 2003; O.B. Goolsby was later named his replacement.

In its pursuit for higher-margin, value-added products in 2004 Pilgrim's sold off its whole-turkey and turkey breast processing plant in Hinton, Virginia, to the Virginia Poultry Growers Cooperative. In 2005 Pilgrim's Pride bought out ConAgra's stake in the company.

## EXECUTIVES

**Senior Chairman:** Lonnie (Bo) Pilgrim, age 78, $1,370,622 pay
**Chairman and EVP:** Lonnie K. (Ken) Pilgrim, age 49
**Vice Chairman:** Clifford E. Butler, age 64, $422,064 pay
**CEO, President, and Director:** O. B. Goolsby Jr., age 59, $845,192 pay
**COO:** J. Clinton Rivers, age 47, $647,115 pay
**EVP, CFO, Secretary, Treasurer, and Director:** Richard A. Cogdill, age 46, $647,115 pay
**EVP, Cage Ready and Supply Operations:** Robert L. Hendrix
**EVP, Fresh Foodservice:** Joseph Moran
**EVP, Human Resources:** Jane T. Brookshire
**EVP, Prepared Foods:** Walter F. Shafer III
**EVP, Sales and Marketing:** Robert A. (Bob) Wright, age 51
**SVP, Case Ready Regional Operations:** Michael D. Martin
**SVP, Case Ready Regional Operations:** Robert N. Palm
**SVP, Consumer Division:** Randall J. Meyers
**SVP, Food Safety and Quality Assurance:** Gary L. Treat
**SVP, Information Technology and CIO:** James W. Tunnell Jr.
**SVP and Corporate Controller:** Gary D. Tucker
**VP, Marketing:** Dan Emery
**VP, Corporate Communications and Investor Relations:** Gary L. Rhodes, age 43
**President, Mexico Operations:** Alejandro M. Mann
**President, Puerto Rico Operations:** Hector L. Mattei-Calvo
**Auditors:** Ernst & Young LLP

## LOCATIONS

**HQ:** Pilgrim's Pride Corporation
4845 US Hwy. 271 North, Pittsburg, TX 75686
**Phone:** 903-855-1000 **Fax:** 903-856-7505
**Web:** www.pilgrimspride.com

## PRODUCTS/OPERATIONS

**2006 Sales**

| | $ mil. | % of total |
|---|---|---|
| Chicken | 4,517.2 | 86 |
| Turkey | 130.9 | 3 |
| Other products | 587.5 | 11 |
| **Total** | **5,235.6** | **100** |

## COMPETITORS

Allen Family Foods
Bachoco
Bell & Evans
Butterball
Cagle's
Cargill
Cargill Meat Solutions
Coleman Natural Foods
Cooper Farms
Eberly
Fieldale Farms
Foster Farms
Hormel
Iowa Turkey Growers
Jennie-O
Kelley Foods of Alabama
Keystone Foods
Mar-Jac
MBA Poultry
Mountaire Farms
Murphy-Brown
New Market Poultry
Northern Pride
Perdue
Petaluma Poultry
Plainville Turkey
Raeford Farms
Randall Foods
Rose Acre Farms
Sanderson Farms
Shelton's
Smithfield Foods
Tyson Foods
Tyson Fresh Meats
Univasa
Wayne Farms LLC
Zacky Farms

# Pinnacle West Capital

Pinnacle West Capital is at the peak of the energy pyramid in Arizona. It is the holding company for the state's largest electric utility, Arizona Public Service (APS), which transmits and distributes electricity to more than 1 million residential, commercial, and industrial customers throughout most of the state. The utility also has 4,000 MW of generating capacity. Through APS and other subsidiaries, Pinnacle West markets wholesale and retail power in Arizona and the western US and offers energy-related services. The company also develops and manages real estate through SunCor Development Company.

Arizona was one of the first states in the western US to deregulate its electric utility market. The legislation originally required the transfer of APS's regulated power plants to independent production subsidiary Pinnacle West Energy, which operates 2,200 MW of nonregulated generating capacity; however, the Arizona Corporation Commission later revoked the rule due to a lack of competition in the state. As a result, Pinnacle West instead transferred its wholesale energy marketing and trading operations to APS.

Pinnacle West also participates in deregulated retail markets in the western US through subsidiary APS Energy Services, which provides energy commodities and related products and services to commercial and industrial customers.

Subsidiary SunCor Development Company builds residential communities and commercial building projects (including resort facilities and seven master-planned communities around Phoenix and the Southwest), and venture capital firm El Dorado Investment has stakes in a number of companies providing energy-related services (including spent-nuclear-fuel technology firm NAC International).

## HISTORY

In 1906 three Phoenix businessmen organized Pacific Gas & Electric (no connection with the California utility), which served the city's power needs until 1920, when Central Arizona Light & Power (Calapco) was formed to assume operations. In 1924 Calapco became a subsidiary of American Power & Light. After WWII the Public Utility Holding Company Act of 1935, which strictly curtailed the sprawling utility industry, finally forced American Power & Light to sell Calapco to the public in 1945.

In 1949 Calapco expanded north by purchasing Northern Arizona Light & Power. It merged in 1951 with Arizona Edison, formed in the 1920s, to create Arizona Public Service (APS). Unprecedented population growth befell Arizona in the 1950s, and APS built three gas-fired plants between 1955 and 1960 to keep up with demand.

CEO Keith Turley reorganized APS in 1985 as a subsidiary of AZP Group, a holding company. Turley implemented a diversification plan and in 1986 bought a Phoenix-based savings and loan (MeraBank), a real estate firm (SunCor), and Mobil Oil's Wyoming uranium mines (sold 1990). In 1987 AZP became Pinnacle West Capital.

In the late 1980s an economic downturn hit Arizona, and bad real estate deals rocked the company. These included several investments by SunCor just after APS bought it and the purchase by MeraBank of three Texas savings and loans in a 1988 diversification attempt. But in 1989 Pinnacle West had to cover about $510 million of MeraBank's bad loan losses. As Turley stepped down and power broker Richard Snell assumed the CEO post, MeraBank was taken over in 1990 by federal regulators, who released Pinnacle West from further obligation after a $450 million infusion.

The company had rejected several takeover bids from utility PacifiCorp, but in the early 1990s the two companies finally reached an agreement that included much-needed seasonal power sharing.

SunCor finally posted a profit in 1994 and bought the Sedona Golf Resort the following year. To prepare for utility deregulation, APS overhauled both management and operations by separating its generation and distribution divisions.

APS launched the first commercial solar power plant in the Phoenix area in 1998. After APS and publicly owned utility Salt River Project (which was protected from competitors) both agreed to open their territories to competition, Arizona legislators passed the Electric Power Competition Act.

Snell stepped down as CEO in 1999 (replaced by president Bill Post) but remained as chairman to see the company through the regulatory changes. To prepare for deregulation and meet the needs of the burgeoning population's energy demands, the company began building new power plants and increasing its stakes in several jointly owned power plants. It also formed nonregulated subsidiaries Pinnacle West Energy (independent power production) and APS Energy Services (competitive retail services).

In 2000 Pinnacle West broke ground on a new district-wide water system to cool businesses in downtown Phoenix. Snell retired in 2001, and Post was named chairman.

## EXECUTIVES

**Chairman and CEO:** William J. (Bill) Post, age 56, $950,004 pay
**President, COO, and Director; President and CEO, Arizona Public Service:** Jack E. Davis, age 60, $800,004 pay
**EVP and CFO, Pinnacle West Capital and Arizona Public Service; CFO, Pinnacle West Energy:** Donald E. (Don) Brandt, age 52, $416,467 pay
**VP, Secretary, and General Counsel:** Nancy C. Loftin, age 53
**VP and Treasurer:** Barbara M. (Barb) Gomez, age 52
**VP Business Management:** Warren C. Kotzmann, age 56
**VP Federal Affairs:** Robert S. (Robbie) Aiken, age 49
**VP Government Affairs:** Martin L. Schultz, age 59
**EVP Corporate Business Services, Arizona Public Service:** Armando B. Flores, age 63
**EVP Customer Service and Regulation, Arizona Public Service:** Steven M. (Steve) Wheeler, age 58, $380,849 pay
**SVP and Chief Nuclear Officer, Arizona Public Service:** Randall K. (Randy) Edington, age 53
**VP and CIO, Arizona Public Service:** Dennis L. (Denny) Brown, age 56
**VP and Controller, Arizona Public Service:** Chris N. Froggatt, age 49
**VP Communications, Environment, and Safety, Arizona Public Service:** Edward Z. (Ed) Fox, age 52
**VP Customer Service, Arizona Public Service:** Jan H. Bennett, age 57
**VP Fossil Generation, Arizona Public Service:** John R. Denman, age 62
**VP Marketing and Trading, Arizona Public Service:** David A. Hansen, age 44
**Director Investor Relations:** Rebecca L. Hickman
**Auditors:** Deloitte & Touche LLP

## HISTORICAL FINANCIALS

Company Type: Public

**Income Statement** — FYE: Saturday nearest September 30

| | REVENUE ($ mil.) | NET INCOME ($ mil.) | NET PROFIT MARGIN | EMPLOYEES |
|---|---|---|---|---|
| **9/06** | 5,236 | (34) | — | 39,900 |
| **9/05** | 5,666 | 265 | 4.7% | 40,550 |
| **9/04** | 5,364 | 128 | 2.4% | 40,300 |
| **9/03** | 2,619 | 56 | 2.1% | 24,800 |
| **9/02** | 2,534 | 14 | 0.6% | 24,800 |
| **Annual Growth** | 19.9% | — | — | 12.6% |

**2006 Year-End Financials**

Debt ratio: 49.7%
Return on equity: —
Cash ($ mil.): 178
Current ratio: 1.92
Long-term debt ($ mil.): 555
No. of shares (mil.): 67
Dividends
Yield: 3.9%
Payout: —
Market value ($ mil.): 1,820

**Stock History** — NYSE: PPC

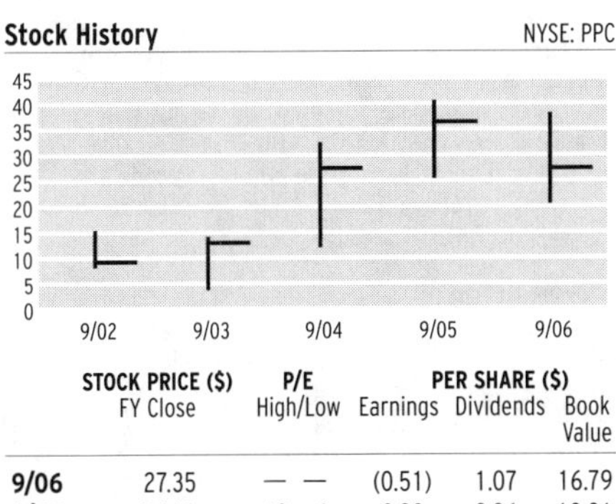

| | STOCK PRICE ($) FY Close | P/E High | P/E Low | PER SHARE ($) Earnings | Dividends | Book Value |
|---|---|---|---|---|---|---|
| **9/06** | 27.35 | — | — | (0.51) | 1.07 | 16.79 |
| **9/05** | 36.40 | 10 | 6 | 3.98 | 0.06 | 18.31 |
| **9/04** | 27.39 | 16 | 6 | 2.05 | 0.06 | 13.87 |
| **9/03** | 12.95 | 10 | 3 | 1.36 | 0.06 | 16.19 |
| **9/02** | 9.25 | 43 | 24 | 0.35 | 0.06 | 14.29 |
| **Annual Growth** | 31.1% | — | — | — | 105.5% | 4.1% |

## LOCATIONS

**HQ:** Pinnacle West Capital Corporation
400 N. 5th St., Phoenix, AZ 85072
**Phone:** 602-250-1000 **Fax:** 602-250-2430
**Web:** www.pinnaclewest.com

Pinnacle West Capital distributes electricity in Arizona and wholesales power in the western US.

## PRODUCTS/OPERATIONS

### 2006 Sales

| | $ mil. | % of total |
|---|---|---|
| Regulated electric | 2,635.0 | 77 |
| Real estate | 399.8 | 12 |
| Marketing & trading | 330.7 | 10 |
| Other | 36.2 | 1 |
| **Total** | **3,401.7** | **100** |

### 2006 Energy Mix

| | % of total |
|---|---|
| Purchased power | 35 |
| Coal | 31 |
| Nuclear | 17 |
| Gas | 17 |
| **Total** | **100** |

### Major Subsidiaries

APS Energy Services Company, Inc. (unregulated retail energy sales and information and management services)
Arizona Public Service Company (APS, electric utility)
Pinnacle West Energy Corporation (development and production of wholesale energy)
SunCor Development Company (real estate company that develops land, primarily in the Phoenix area, and operates family entertainment locations, golf courses, and resorts)

## COMPETITORS

A.G. Spanos
Calpine
Capital Pacific
CenterPoint Energy
Duke Energy
PacifiCorp
Panda Energy
PG&E
PNM Resources
Sempra Energy
Sierra Pacific Resources
Southwest Gas
SRP
UniSource Energy

## HISTORICAL FINANCIALS

Company Type: Public

### Income Statement

FYE: December 31

| | REVENUE ($ mil.) | NET INCOME ($ mil.) | NET PROFIT MARGIN | EMPLOYEES |
|---|---|---|---|---|
| **12/06** | 3,402 | 327 | 9.6% | 7,400 |
| **12/05** | 2,988 | 176 | 5.9% | 7,300 |
| **12/04** | 2,900 | 243 | 8.4% | 7,200 |
| **12/03** | 2,818 | 241 | 8.5% | 7,200 |
| **12/02** | 2,637 | 149 | 5.7% | 7,200 |
| **Annual Growth** | 6.6% | 21.7% | — | 0.7% |

### 2006 Year-End Financials

Debt ratio: 93.8%
Return on equity: 9.5%
Cash ($ mil.): 120
Current ratio: 1.01
Long-term debt ($ mil.): 3,233
No. of shares (mil.): 100
Dividends
Yield: 4.0%
Payout: 62.1%
Market value ($ mil.): 5,067

### Stock History

NYSE: PNW

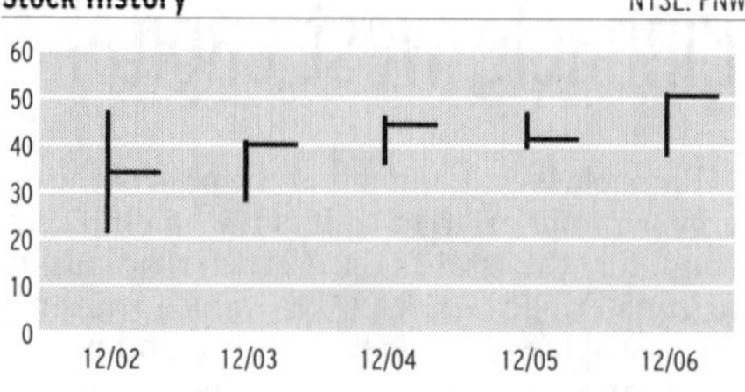

| | STOCK PRICE ($) FY Close | P/E High/Low | | PER SHARE ($) Earnings | Dividends | Book Value |
|---|---|---|---|---|---|---|
| **12/06** | 50.69 | 16 | 12 | 3.27 | 2.03 | 34.48 |
| **12/05** | 41.35 | 26 | 22 | 1.82 | 1.92 | 34.58 |
| **12/04** | 44.41 | 17 | 14 | 2.66 | 1.83 | 32.14 |
| **12/03** | 40.02 | 15 | 11 | 2.63 | 1.73 | 31.00 |
| **12/02** | 34.09 | 27 | 12 | 1.76 | 1.63 | 29.44 |
| **Annual Growth** | 10.4% | — | — | 16.8% | 5.6% | 4.0% |

# Pioneer Natural Resources

Oil and gas explorer Pioneer Natural Resources' frontier is not in the Western prairies, but below them, and below the Rocky Mountains, and the waters of the Gulf of Mexico. The large independent exploration and production company, which has boosted its Gulf of Mexico properties, holds proved reserves of 904.9 million barrels of oil equivalent. The vast majority of the exploration and production company's reserves are found within the US, but Pioneer also explores for and produces oil and gas in Canada, Equatorial Guinea, Nigeria, South Africa, and Tunisia. In 2006 the company sold some Gulf of Mexico oil and gas assets to Marubeni Offshore Production for $1.3 billion.

In 2000 the company disposed of noncore natural gas assets in Louisiana, New Mexico, and Oklahoma. At the same time, it boosted its deepwater holdings in the Gulf of Mexico. The next year the company announced successful test drilling in its prospects in Argentina and South Africa.

Pioneer also announced an oil discovery in 2001 on its Ozona Deep prospect in the Gulf of Mexico, indicating another deepwater production asset for the company. In 2003 Pioneer teamed up with Woodside Energy to conduct a joint exploration program in the shallow-water Texas Shelf region of the Gulf of Mexico.

In 2005 Pioneer sold the Martin Creek, Conroy Black, and Lookout Butte oil and gas properties in Canada to Ketch Resources for $199 million. That year it acquired oil and gas assets in the Permian Basin and South Texas for a total of $177 million.

The company sold all of its operations in Argentina in 2006 to Apache for $675 million.

## HISTORY

The 1997 merger of MESA and Parker & Parsley moved quickly to pull itself out of the dry hole created by its own debt and the industry's late-1990s dropoff. Parker & Parsley began in 1962 as a partnership between geologist Howard Parker and engineer Joe Parsley. In 1977 it began drilling wells in West Texas. Southmark, a Dallas real estate firm, bought the company in 1984; in 1989 management purchased it from Southmark. The company went public in 1991.

T. Boone Pickens founded Petroleum Exploration in 1956. In 1964 Petroleum Exploration and Pickens' Canadian holding, Altair Oil and Gas, merged as MESA and went public. With gas prices declining in the 1990s, MESA began selling assets. Pickens resigned as CEO in 1996.

Richard Rainwater took control of MESA and then merged the firm into Parker & Parsley, which became Pioneer Natural Resources. The company moved into Argentina when it paid $1.2 billion for Calgary-based Chauvco Resources in 1997.

To streamline operations and reduce debt, Pioneer cut its workforce, and in 1999 Pioneer sold 400 US properties to Prize Energy.

Pioneer sold oil and gas properties in Texas and Canada in 1999 and moved to consolidate its Permian Basin operations by offering to buy out limited partners. It also drilled its first deepwater well in the Gulf of Mexico and acquired additional properties in Argentina.

## EXECUTIVES

**Chairman and CEO:** Scott D. Sheffield, age 54
**President and COO:** Timothy L. (Tim) Dove, age 50, $939,000 pay
**EVP and CFO:** Richard P. (Rich) Dealy, age 41
**EVP and General Counsel:** Mark S. Berg, age 48
**EVP Woldwide Business Development:** William F. (Bill) Hannes, age 47
**EVP Domestic Operations:** Danny L. Kellum, age 52
**EVP Western Division:** Jay P. Still
**EVP Worldwide Negotiations:** A. R. (Ray) Alameddine, age 59
**EVP Worldwide Exploration:** Chris J. Cheatwood, age 47
**VP and CIO:** Thomas C. Halbouty
**VP and Chief Accounting Officer:** Darin G. Holderness, age 43
**VP Administration and Risk Management:** Larry Paulsen
**VP Corporate Communications and Public Affairs:** Susan A. Spratlen
**VP Government Affairs:** Roger Wallace
**VP Investor Relations:** Frank Hopkins
**VP International Operations:** David McManus
**Auditors:** Ernst & Young LLP

## LOCATIONS

**HQ:** Pioneer Natural Resources Company
5205 N. O'Connor Blvd., Ste. 200, Irving, TX 75039
**Phone:** 972-444-9001 **Fax:** 972-969-3576
**Web:** www.pioneernrc.com

Pioneer Natural Resources has oil and gas reserves in the Gulf Coast, midcontinent, and Permian Basin regions of the US. Drilling and production operations in the US are principally conducted in Alaska, Colorado, Kansas, Louisiana, Texas, and the Gulf of Mexico. The company also conducts exploration and production activities in Canada, Equatorial Guinea, Nigeria, South Africa, and Tunisia.

### 2006 Sales

| | $ mil. | % of total |
|---|---|---|
| US | 1,301.6 | 82 |
| Canada | 123.2 | 8 |
| South Africa | 99.3 | 6 |
| Tunisia | 57.6 | 4 |
| Adjustments | 51.2 | — |
| **Total** | **1,632.9** | **100** |

## COMPETITORS

Anadarko Petroleum
Apache
BP
Chesapeake Energy
Exxon Mobil
Hess
Marathon Oil
Newfield Exploration
Noble Energy
Royal Dutch Shell
TOTAL
YPF S.A.

## HISTORICAL FINANCIALS

Company Type: Public

**Income Statement** FYE: December 31

| | REVENUE ($ mil.) | NET INCOME ($ mil.) | NET PROFIT MARGIN | EMPLOYEES |
|---|---|---|---|---|
| **12/06** | 1,633 | 740 | 45.3% | 1,624 |
| **12/05** | 2,373 | 535 | 22.5% | 1,694 |
| **12/04** | 1,847 | 313 | 16.9% | 1,550 |
| **12/03** | 1,312 | 411 | 31.3% | 1,014 |
| **12/02** | 717 | 27 | 3.7% | 979 |
| **Annual Growth** | 22.8% | 129.4% | — | 13.5% |

**2006 Year-End Financials**

Debt ratio: 54.4%
Return on equity: 28.4%
Cash ($ mil.): 71
Current ratio: 0.60
Long-term debt ($ mil.): 1,623
No. of shares (mil.): 122
Dividends
Yield: 0.6%
Payout: 4.3%
Market value ($ mil.): 4,822

**Stock History** NYSE: PXD

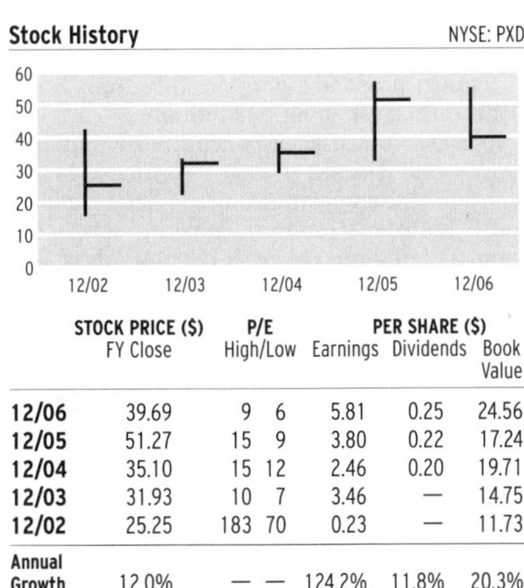


| | STOCK PRICE ($) FY Close | P/E High | P/E Low | PER SHARE ($) Earnings | Dividends | Book Value |
|---|---|---|---|---|---|---|
| **12/06** | 39.69 | 9 | 6 | 5.81 | 0.25 | 24.56 |
| **12/05** | 51.27 | 15 | 9 | 3.80 | 0.22 | 17.24 |
| **12/04** | 35.10 | 15 | 12 | 2.46 | 0.20 | 19.71 |
| **12/03** | 31.93 | 10 | 7 | 3.46 | — | 14.75 |
| **12/02** | 25.25 | 183 | 70 | 0.23 | — | 11.73 |
| **Annual Growth** | 12.0% | — | — | 124.2% | 11.8% | 20.3% |

# Pitney Bowes

Pitney Bowes has a measured approach to the mail management industry. The world's largest producer of postage meters, the company also makes other mailing equipment and provides shipping and weighing systems. Pitney Bowes offers online postage services, financing for office equipment purchases, and facilities management services. It also develops software to create mailers and manage shipping, transportation, and logistics for government agencies and corporations. The company has bolstered its service operations with a string of acquisitions in recent years.

Early in 2005 Pitney Bowes acquired Compulit, a service company that provides litigation support to law firms and corporations; the purchase helped build a new unit called Pitney Bowes Legal Solutions. The company also acquired Imagitas, a mail marketing firm, for approximately $230 million. Early in 2006 Pitney Bowes acquired UK-based Emtex Software, a provider of high-volume document production applications and services, for about $41 million. Later that year it bolstered its Pitney Bowes Management Services unit when it purchased Ibis Consulting for about $67 million. It acquired sister companies pmh Caramanning (marketing services) and Advertising Audit Service (promotional mail and marketing customization tools) in mid-2006. The company also acquired Print for about $47 million. In 2007 Pitney Bowes acquired location information and software provider MapInfo for $408 million in cash. It then purchased customer relationship services company Digital Cement for $40 million in cash.

Pitney Bowes sold its Océ Imagistics lease portfolio to Rabobank Group subsidiary De Lage Landen for about $288 million in 2006. It also sold its Capital Services business (about 2% of sales in fiscal 2005) to an affiliate of Cerberus Capital Management for about $750 million.

## HISTORY

In 1912 Walter Bowes, an address machine salesman, gained control of Universal Stamping Machine, which made stamp canceling machines. In 1920 Bowes joined with Arthur Pitney, who had developed a postage metering machine. After creating a market by forcing through Congress legislation that outlawed the sale of meters, the Pitney-Bowes Postage Meter Company began leasing new machines in 1921. During the 1920s Pitney-Bowes built a large service fleet with leasing and repair expertise; added mail handling machines, including stampers and counters, to its product line; and expanded into Canada, the UK, and Germany.

Pitney left in 1924 to start a competing company. Other competitors, including IBM and NCR, entered the market, but they were never able to catch up with Pitney-Bowes. The company was so successful that almost no competitors remained. The Justice Department investigated the business practices of the company, which agreed to license its patents to potential competitors, free of charge.

Facing the prospect of increased competition, Pitney-Bowes began to diversify its operations. In 1967 the company took on Xerox with a line of copiers. In the late 1960s it moved into pricing and inventory control equipment and credit and ID card products. It also established a joint venture with Alpex for point-of-sale terminals that proved a flop. In 1973 the company wrote off its investment, resulting in its first-ever loss.

But Pitney Bowes (the hyphen was dropped in 1970) continued to add operations. In 1979 it bought Dictaphone Corp. (voice processing). In 1981 the company consolidated Dictaphone subsidiary Grayarc with *The Drawing Board* (an office-supply catalog it acquired in 1980) to form Wheeler Group, a direct-mail marketer of office supplies.

With its long history of meter leasing, the company moved into the commercial arena, eventually leasing such big-ticket items as airplanes and barges under the aegis of Pitney Bowes Financial Services. The company also continued to widen its product line with its 1981 introduction of Postage By Phone and a line of fax machines.

In the late 1980s the company began whittling its holdings, selling its Dictaphone-related operations in pieces between 1988 and 1995. Meanwhile, as its US markets matured, Pitney Bowes added a variety of mailing services and electronic products, and bolstered its overseas operations in 1994 with pacts to help China and Mexico update their postal systems. Vice chairman Michael Critelli was named CEO in 1996. The next year Pitney Bowes offloaded its non-office equipment leasing portfolio to GATX — a sale that let Pitney Bowes reduce its debt and focus on fewer interest-sensitive, fee-based services.

In 1999 the company filed a patent-infringement lawsuit against e-postage rivals Stamps.com and E-Stamp. Also in 1999 the Justice Department launched another antitrust investigation into the company's activities in the postage meter and online postage markets. In 2000 Pitney Bowes sold its mortgage servicing business, Atlantic Mortgage & Investment Corporation, to a subsidiary of Netherlands-based ABN AMRO for about $490 million.

The next year Pitney Bowes bought the international operations of Bell & Howell's Mail and Messaging Technologies division for $51 million, and it acquired Danka Business Systems' outsourcing unit, Danka Services International, for $290 million in an effort to strengthen its Pitney Bowes Management Services division. The company also received a $400 million settlement from a 1995 patent infringement suit against Hewlett-Packard (related to laser-jet printer technology). It then acquired Fimalac's mail systems subsidiary, Secap. Pitney Bowes rounded out 2001 with the spinoff of its copier and fax business, Pitney Bowes Office Systems.

In 2002 Pitney Bowes acquired privately held PSI Group, a leading provider of mail pre-sort services for businesses, for about $130 million. The company acquired government outsourcing service provider DDD Company (renamed Pitney Bowes Government Solutions) for almost $50 million in 2003. It purchased Groupe MAG, a European distributor of finishing equipment and production mail equipment, the following year. Also in 2004, Pitney Bowes acquired mail distributor International Mail Express (IMEX) for $29 million, Group 1 Software for approximately $321 million, mail processing services provider Ancora Capital & Management Group, and the equipment service business of Standard Register.

Pitney Bowes president Murray Martin was named CEO in 2007; Critelli assumed the role of executive chairman.

## EXECUTIVES

**Executive Chairman:** Michael J. Critelli, age 58
**President, CEO, and Director:** Murray D. Martin, age 59
**EVP and CFO:** Bruce P. Nolop, age 56, $921,700 pay
**EVP and President, Document Messaging Technologies:** Leslie R. Abi-Karam, age 48
**EVP; President, Global Mailing Solutions and Services:** Michael Monahan, age 46
**EVP; President, Mailstream, The Americas:** Kevin Weiss, age 53
**EVP; President, Pitney Bowes Direct:** Neil Metviner, age 49
**EVP and President, Pitney Bowes Global Financial Services:** Elise R. (Lisa) DeBois, age 51
**EVP and President, Pitney Bowes International:** Patrick J. Keddy, age 52
**EVP and President, Pitney Bowes Management Services:** Vincent R. (Vince) DePalma, age 49
**SVP and CIO:** Gregory E. Buoncontri, age 59
**SVP and Chief Human Resources Officer:** Johnna G. Torsone, age 56
**SVP and Chief Strategy Officer:** Luis A. Jimenez, age 62
**SVP and General Counsel:** Michele C. Mayes, age 56

**President, Document Factory Solutions:** Patrick Brand
**President, Pitney Bowes Government Solutions:** Jon Love
**VP and General Manager, Business Process:** Fred M. Purdue
**VP and Treasurer:** Helen Shan
**VP, Secretary, and Chief Governance Officer:** Amy C. Corn
**VP Corporate Communications:** Sheryl Y. Battles
**VP External Communications:** Matthew (Matt) Broder
**VP Finance and Chief Accounting Officer:** Steven J. Green
**VP Marketing, Document Messaging Technologies:** John J. Schloff
**Executive Director Investor Relations:** Charles F. McBride
**Auditors:** PricewaterhouseCoopers LLP

## LOCATIONS

**HQ:** Pitney Bowes Inc.
1 Elmcroft Rd., Stamford, CT 06926
**Phone:** 203-356-5000 **Fax:** 203-351-7336
**Web:** www.pb.com

**2006 Sales**

| | $ mil. | % of total |
|---|---|---|
| US | 4,213 | 74 |
| Other countries | 1,517 | 26 |
| **Total** | **5,730** | **100** |

## PRODUCTS/OPERATIONS

**2006 Sales**

| | $ mil. | % of total |
|---|---|---|
| Mailstream Solutions | | |
| US Mailing | 2,350 | 41 |
| International mailing | 1,013 | 18 |
| Production mail | 575 | 10 |
| Software | 203 | 3 |
| Mailstream Services | | |
| Management | 1,074 | 19 |
| Mail | 370 | 6 |
| Marketing | 145 | 3 |
| **Total** | **5,730** | **100** |

**2006 Sales**

| | $ mil. | % of total |
|---|---|---|
| Business services | 1,589 | 28 |
| Equipment sales | 1,373 | 24 |
| Rentals | 785 | 14 |
| Financing | 725 | 13 |
| Support | 717 | 12 |
| Supplies | 339 | 6 |
| Software | 202 | 3 |
| **Total** | **5,730** | **100** |

**Selected Products**

Global Mailing Equipment
- Address hygiene software
- Folders
- Letter and parcel scales
- Mail openers
- Mailing machines
- Mailroom furniture
- Manifest systems
- Paper handling systems
- Postage meters
- Shipping equipment
- Software-based shipping and logistics systems

Enterprise Systems
- Billing and payment systems
- Electronic statement systems
- Incoming mail systems
- Mailing software
- Office mail systems
- Sorting equipment

Services
- Commercial and industrial financing
- Facilities maintenance
- Systems installation and support
- Training

## COMPETITORS

Corporate Express NV
Francotyp-Postalia
Gunther International
Hasler
Lanier Worldwide
Neopost
Stamps.com
US Postal Service
Xerox

## HISTORICAL FINANCIALS

Company Type: Public

**Income Statement** FYE: December 31

| | REVENUE ($ mil.) | NET INCOME ($ mil.) | NET PROFIT MARGIN | EMPLOYEES |
|---|---|---|---|---|
| **12/06** | 5,730 | 105 | 1.8% | 34,454 |
| **12/05** | 5,492 | 527 | 9.6% | 34,165 |
| **12/04** | 4,957 | 481 | 9.7% | 35,183 |
| **12/03** | 4,577 | 498 | 10.9% | 32,474 |
| **12/02** | 4,410 | 476 | 10.8% | 33,130 |
| **Annual Growth** | 6.8% | (31.4%) | — | 1.0% |

**2006 Year-End Financials**

Debt ratio: 551.1%
Return on equity: 10.5%
Cash ($ mil.): 302
Current ratio: 1.06
Long-term debt ($ mil.): 3,848
No. of shares (mil.): 221
Dividends
Yield: 2.8%
Payout: 272.3%
Market value ($ mil.): 10,190

**Stock History** NYSE: PBI

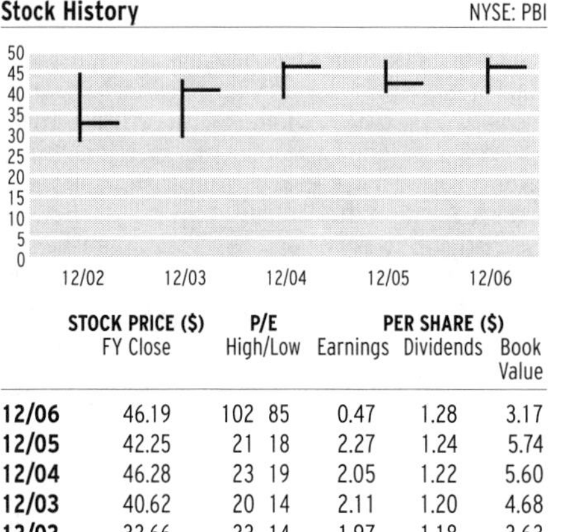


| | STOCK PRICE ($) FY Close | P/E High | P/E Low | PER SHARE ($) Earnings | Dividends | Book Value |
|---|---|---|---|---|---|---|
| **12/06** | 46.19 | 102 | 85 | 0.47 | 1.28 | 3.17 |
| **12/05** | 42.25 | 21 | 18 | 2.27 | 1.24 | 5.74 |
| **12/04** | 46.28 | 23 | 19 | 2.05 | 1.22 | 5.60 |
| **12/03** | 40.62 | 20 | 14 | 2.11 | 1.20 | 4.68 |
| **12/02** | 32.66 | 23 | 14 | 1.97 | 1.18 | 3.63 |
| **Annual Growth** | 9.1% | — | — | (30.1%) | 2.1% | (3.3%) |

# Plains All American Pipeline

The term "All American" includes Canada for Plains All American Pipeline, which has expanded its pipeline operations north of the border. The limited partnership, in which Paul Allen's Vulcan Energy holds a 17% stake, owns extensive gathering, terminal, and storage facilities in California, Louisiana, Oklahoma, Texas, and the provinces of Alberta and Saskatchewan in Canada. Buying, selling, and transporting oil, Plains All American Pipeline owns about 20,000 miles of gathering and mainline crude oil pipelines throughout the US and Canada, operates a large fleet of trucks and barges, and owns storage capacity of 30 million barrels. In 2006 the company acquired Pacific Energy Partners for $2.4 billion.

The company once relied on a pipeline that bears its name, but the partnership is now focusing on other pipelines and related facilities. Plains Resources formed Plains All American Pipeline in 1998 to purchase midstream oil assets, including the 1,233-mile, 30-inch heated All American Pipeline from Goodyear Tire & Rubber. The largest crude oil pipeline connecting California to West Texas became a disappointment, however, and the company has sold all but a 140-mile section that lies in California.

Plains All American Pipeline's current growth strategy is associated with the expansion of its pipelines and storage facilities to additional regions. The company has acquired the South Saskatchewan pipeline system in Canada and the ArkLaTex pipeline system that connects to its Red River pipeline in Sabine, Texas. It has also acquired a 22% interest in the Capline pipeline system (originating in St. James, Louisiana) and a 76% interest in the Capwood pipeline system (originating in Patoka, Illinois).

Plains All American has expanded its Rocky Mountain and Oklahoma/Kansas regional operations through the acquisition of Link Energy's crude oil and pipeline business. Through its Plains Marketing Canada subsidiary, the company has acquired the Cal Ven pipeline systems from a subsidiary of Unocal Canada for about $19 million. Through its Plains LPG Services subsidiary, the company has acquired the Schaefferstown propane storage facility from Koch Hydrocarbon for about $32 million.

In 2004 Vulcan Energy acquired Plains Resources and its stake in Plains All American.

In 2005 the company acquired Shell Pipeline's south Louisiana crude oil pipeline assets for about $12 million. That year its PAA/Vulcan Gas Storage joint venture acquired natural gas assets from a subsidiary of Sempra Energy for about $250 million.

In 2006 the company acquired Andrews Petroleum and Lone Star Trucking for $205 million. It also acquired stakes in a number of Gulf Coast crude oil pipeline systems from BP Oil Pipeline Company for $133.5 million.

## HISTORY

Goodyear Tire & Rubber subsidiary Celeron began designing the All American Pipeline in 1983 to bring heavy crude from California to the less-regulated refineries of Texas. It was completed in 1987 at a cost of $1.6 billion, but by 1991 only a trickle of oil was dribbling through. The pipeline did not post a profit until 1994.

Prospects began to look up in the mid-1990s when Chevron, Texaco, and Exxon signed contracts to use the pipeline, beginning in 1996. Plains Resources bought the pipeline in 1998 for $400 million; the company created Plains All American Pipeline to acquire and operate the pipeline, then sold off a 43% stake in an IPO that raised $260 million. The next year Plains All American bought Scurlock Permian (2,300 miles of pipeline) from Marathon Ashland Petroleum for $141 million and the West Texas Gathering System from Chevron (450 miles) for $36 million.

Shareholders sued Plains All American in 1999 after it reported that an employee's unauthorized crude-oil trading would cost the company about $160 million. (In 2000 the company agreed to pay $29.5 million, plus interest, to settle the cases.)

Plains All American announced plans to mothball all but the California section of the All American Pipeline in 1999. The next year El Paso

Energy bought the 1,088-mile section of the pipeline that was to be deactivated, plus the right to run fiber-optic cable over the entire pipeline, for $129 million.

Targeting Canada as part of its expansion strategy, in 2001 Plains All American bought about 450 miles of oil pipeline and other midstream assets from Murphy Oil and acquired crude oil and LPG marketing firm CANPET Energy. Also that year Plains Resources reduced its stake in Plains All American from 44% to 29%.

In 2002 the company acquired the Wapella Pipeline System, located in southeastern Saskatchewan and southwestern Manitoba. It also bought Shell Pipeline's West Texas crude oil pipeline assets for $315 million. Plains All American Pipeline continued its acquisition streak in 2003 with the acquisitions of the South Saskatchewan pipeline system in Canada and the ArkLaTex pipeline system originating in Sabine, Texas.

In 2004 Plains All American continued its expansion with the acquisition of interests in the Capline and Capwood pipeline systems from Shell Pipeline Company for about $158 million. It also acquired the crude oil and pipeline operations of Link Energy for about $330 million and the Cal Ven pipeline system from Unocal Canada for about $19 million. Later that year, the company continued its system expansion by acquiring the Schaefferstown propane storage facility from Koch Hydrocarbon for about $32 million.

## EXECUTIVES

**Chairman and CEO:** Greg L. Armstrong, age 48, $3,371,250 pay
**President, COO, and Director:** Harry N. Pefanis, age 49, $3,044,583 pay
**EVP and CFO:** Phillip D. (Phil) Kramer, age 50
**Senior Group VP:** George R. Coiner, age 56, $2,891,433 pay
**SVP Technology, Process, and Risk Management:** Alfred A. (Al) Lindseth, age 37
**SVP Operations:** Mark F. Shires, age 49
**VP Accounting and Chief Accounting Officer:** Tina L. Val
**VP, Secretary, and General Counsel:** Tim Moore, age 49
**VP Finance and Treasurer:** Al Swanson, age 42
**VP, General Counsel Commercial & Litigation, and Assistant Secretary:** Lawrence J. (Larry) Dreyfuss, age 52
**VP Acquisitions:** James G. (Jim) Hester, age 47
**VP Corporate Services, PMC (Nova Scotia):** Richard (Rick) Henson, age 52
**VP Engineering:** Daniel J. Nerbonne, age 49
**VP Environmental, Health, and Safety:** Troy E. Valenzuela, age 45
**VP Lease Supply:** Robert M. Sanford, age 57
**VP Pipeline Operations:** John F. Russell, age 58
**VP Refinery Supply:** James B. (Jim) Fryfogle, age 55
**VP Trading:** John P. von Berg, age 52, $2,545,400 pay
**VP Human Resources:** Roger D. Everett, age 61
**President PMC (Nova Scotia):** W. David (Dave) Duckett, age 51, $1,915,599 pay
**Administrator Investor Relations:** Carolyn F. Tice
**Auditors:** PricewaterhouseCoopers LLP

## LOCATIONS

**HQ:** Plains All American Pipeline, L.P.
333 Clay St., Ste. 1600, Houston, TX 77002
**Phone:** 713-646-4100 **Fax:** 713-646-4572
**Web:** www.plainsallamerican.com

Plains All American Pipeline's operations are located primarily in California, Louisiana, Oklahoma, Pennsylvania, Texas, the Gulf of Mexico, and in western Canada.

**2006 Sales**

| | $ mil. | % of total |
|---|---|---|
| US | 18,118.0 | 81 |
| Canada | 4,326.4 | 19 |
| **Total** | **22,444.4** | **100** |

## PRODUCTS/OPERATIONS

**2006 Sales**

| | $ mil. | % of total |
|---|---|---|
| Marketing | 22,059.9 | 98 |
| Transportation | 343.6 | 2 |
| Facilities | 40.9 | — |
| **Total** | **22,444.4** | **100** |

## COMPETITORS

Buckeye Partners
Enbridge
Kinder Morgan
Sunoco Logistics
TEPPCO Partners
TransMontaigne

## HISTORICAL FINANCIALS

Company Type: Public

**Income Statement** FYE: December 31

| | REVENUE ($ mil.) | NET INCOME ($ mil.) | NET PROFIT MARGIN | EMPLOYEES |
|---|---|---|---|---|
| **12/06** | 22,444 | 285 | 1.3% | 2,900 |
| **12/05** | 31,177 | 218 | 0.7% | 2,000 |
| **12/04** | 20,976 | 130 | 0.6% | 1,950 |
| **12/03** | 12,590 | 60 | 0.5% | 1,300 |
| **12/02** | 8,384 | 65 | 0.8% | 1,200 |
| **Annual Growth** | 27.9% | 44.6% | — | 24.7% |

**2006 Year-End Financials**

Debt ratio: 88.2%
Return on equity: 13.2%
Cash ($ mil.): 11
Current ratio: 1.04
Long-term debt ($ mil.): 2,626
No. of shares (mil.): 109
Dividends
Yield: 5.6%
Payout: 99.7%
Market value ($ mil.): 5,602

**Stock History** NYSE: PAA

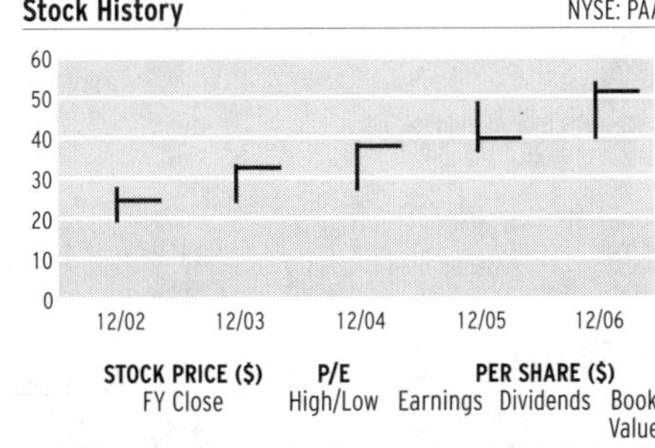


| | STOCK PRICE ($) FY Close | P/E High | P/E Low | PER SHARE ($) Earnings | Dividends | Book Value |
|---|---|---|---|---|---|---|
| **12/06** | 51.20 | 18 | 14 | 2.88 | 2.87 | 27.21 |
| **12/05** | 39.57 | 18 | 13 | 2.72 | 2.58 | 18.04 |
| **12/04** | 37.74 | 20 | 14 | 1.89 | 2.30 | 17.06 |
| **12/03** | 32.46 | 33 | 24 | 1.00 | 2.19 | 15.08 |
| **12/02** | 24.40 | 20 | 15 | 1.34 | 2.11 | 13.38 |
| **Annual Growth** | 20.4% | — | — | 21.1% | 8.0% | 19.4% |

# PNC Financial Services Group

Maybe the grass wasn't greener after all. After remaking itself into a financial services provider, PNC Financial Services is getting back to its traditional banking roots. Its flagship subsidiary, PNC Bank, offers consumer and corporate services through about 840 branches in Delaware, Florida, Kentucky, Maryland, New Jersey, Ohio, Pennsylvania, Virginia, and Washington, DC. In 2007 the company acquired Mercantile Bankshares, which added some 240 branches in the same region. In addition to its renewed focus on retail banking, PNC still offers wealth management, insurance, and other services.

In 2006 PNC got back into the credit card business after selling it in 1999, and has made overtures to customers that include reimbursing ATM fees. It entered an alliance with Wells Fargo to offer home mortgages, a business it had exited in 2001.

PNC owns about 34% of publicly traded fund manager BlackRock, which merged with Merrill Lynch's asset management unit in 2006. Other subsidiaries include middle-market investment bank Harris Williams, brokerage Hilliard Lyons, and PFPC, which offers processing services to investment management companies around the world. Its Corporate and Institutional Banking segment serves corporate and institutional customers with lending, treasury management, and capital markets services.

As a result of increasing interest rates, the bank is selling $2 billion in residential mortgage loans because of their declining value. However, it expanded its commercial mortgage operations with the 2007 acquisition of ARCS Commercial Mortgage, a multifamily housing lender.

PNC once owned around 70% of BlackRock, but the 2006 sale of half its stake funded its $6 billion acquisition of Mercantile Bankshares. In 2007 PNC arranged to buy multibank holding company Sterling Financial and Yardville National, a bank with more than 30 branches in New Jersey and Pennsylvania.

## HISTORY

First National Bank of Pittsburgh opened in 1863. In 1913 the bank consolidated with Second National Bank of Pittsburgh, and in 1921 it bought Peoples National.

The company changed its name to Pittsburgh National after a long expansion following the Depression and WWII. The bank entered the credit card business in 1965 and joined the BankAmericard program (Visa's forerunner) four years later.

In the inflationary 1970s Pittsburgh National diversified, moving into commercial paper financing (1972); lease financing (1979); and credit life, health, and accident reinsurance (1979).

In 1983 Pittsburgh National merged with Provident National of Philadelphia (founded by Quakers in 1865) to form PNC Corp. The union combined Pittsburgh National's corporate lending strength with Provident's money management and trust operations. PNC expanded through the 1980s by buying more Pennsylvania banks and then moved into Kentucky in 1987. That year PNC, with $37 billion in assets, passed Mellon Bank as Pennsylvania's largest bank.

This growth was accompanied by investment in risky commercial mortgages, so when the real estate market unraveled in 1989-90, PNC was stuck with millions of dollars in problem loans. It soon began selling its bad loans and property and tightening underwriting standards.

PNC reorganized in 1991, operating its several state-chartered banks as if they were a single entity. Acquisitions continued, including BlackRock Financial Management, Sears Mortgage, 84 banking branches orphaned by the Chase Manhattan/Chemical Bank merger, and New Jersey-based Midlantic Corp (founded in 1804 as Newark Banking and Insurance).

PNC's acquisitions focused more sharply on mortgages in 1997 and 1998; it bought Midland Loan Services, as well as the mortgage origination offices of what is now FleetBoston Financial. The former purchase moved the company strongly into servicing and securitization to become a major buyer in the secondary commercial-mortgage market.

After rules separating banking from securities activities were relaxed in 1998, the firm bought Louisville, Kentucky-based securities brokerage Hilliard Lyons. To concentrate on more-profitable business segments, the company sold most of its credit card operations.

In 1999 PNC bought credit card processor First Data's Investor Services Group, which it merged into PFPC. That year PNC agreed to pay $375,000 to 31 women employees in response to a Labor Department charge that PNC had a "glass ceiling." Later in 1999 the company signed on as the exclusive banking services provider for iVillage.com, an Internet site for women.

Belying speculation that it was a takeover target itself, PNC bought United National Bancorp in 2004 and, after much drama, acquired Riggs National the following year.

PNC had originally agreed to buy Riggs in 2004, but lowered its bid after Riggs pleaded guilty to Bank Secrecy Act violations in early 2005. (Riggs also paid millions in fines and technology upgrades to comply with the anti-terrorism measure.) Riggs sued PNC for damages for backing out on the deal, but dropped the charges after agreeing on a renegotiated sale price.

After the dust settled, PNC wasted no time making its presence known in the coveted Washington, DC, market where Riggs had been the #1 bank. It quickly obliterated the vestiges of troubled Riggs, removing that institution's signs and replacing them with its own during the weekend after the deal was finalized (most bank systems' conversions and name changes usually take place months after an acquisition closes). PNC also extended hours at former Riggs branches and announced plans to add some 30 locations in and around the nation's capital by 2008.

PNC announced in mid-2005 that it would shed some 3,000 employees, or about 12% of its workforce. The strategy worked: Flush from a good year, the company was back on the acquisition hunt, eyeing institutions in the Northeast and Washington, DC.

That year the company bought boutique investment bank Harris Williams, which specialized in mergers and acquisitions advisory services. Harris Williams kept its name and became a subsidiary of PNC after the deal was completed.

In 2006, PNC sold part of its 70% share in BlackRock to Merrill Lynch, retaining 34%. PNC netted some $1.6 billion from the transaction.

## EXECUTIVES

**Chairman and CEO:** James E. (Jim) Rohr, age 58, $3,575,000 pay
**Vice Chairman and Head of Corporate and Institutional Bank:** William S. (Bill) Demchak, age 44, $1,800,627 pay
**Vice Chairman:** William C. (Bill) Mutterperl, age 59
**President and Head of Consumer Banking:** Joseph C. (Joe) Guyaux, age 56, $1,875,500 pay
**EVP and CIO; Chairman and CEO, PFPC Worldwide:** Timothy G. (Tim) Shack, age 56, $1,367,115 pay
**EVP and Chief Risk Officer:** Thomas K. (Tom) Whitford, age 50, $1,169,134 pay
**EVP, Corporate Banking; President, Northern New Jersey Region, PNC Bank:** Peter K. (Pete) Classen
**EVP, Real Estate Finance:** Hugh R. Frater, age 51
**SVP and CFO:** Richard J. Johnson, age 50
**SVP and Chief Compliance and Regulatory Officer:** John J. (Jack) Wixted Jr., age 55
**SVP and Chief Credit Policy Officer:** Michael J. Hannon, age 50
**SVP and Chief Economist:** Stuart G. Hoffman
**SVP and Controller:** Samuel R. Patterson, age 48
**SVP and General Counsel:** Helen P. Pudlin, age 57
**SVP and Director of Investor Relations:** William H. Callihan
**VP and Senior Economist:** Richard F. Moody
**Chairman and CEO, BlackRock:** Laurence D. Fink, age 53
**Chairman and CEO, Hilliard Lyons:** James R. Allen
**Chief Human Resources Officer:** William E. (Bill) Rosner
**Corporate Secretary:** George P. Long III
**Director of External Communications:** Brian Goerke
**Auditors:** Deloitte & Touche LLP

## LOCATIONS

**HQ:** The PNC Financial Services Group, Inc.
1 PNC Plaza, 249 5th Ave., Pittsburgh, PA 15222
**Phone:** 412-762-2000 **Fax:** 412-762-7829
**Web:** www.pnc.com

## PRODUCTS/OPERATIONS

### 2006 Sales

| | $ mil. | % of total |
|---|---|---|
| Interest | | |
| Loans | 3,203 | 29 |
| Securities | 1,049 | 10 |
| Other | 360 | 3 |
| Noninterest | | |
| Net gains related to BlackRock | 2,066 | 19 |
| Asset management | 1,420 | 13 |
| Fund servicing | 893 | 8 |
| Corporate & consumer services | 991 | 9 |
| Other | 1,164 | 9 |
| **Total** | **11,146** | **100** |

### 2006 Assets

| | $ mil. | % of total |
|---|---|---|
| Cash & equivalents | 3,523 | 3 |
| Federal funds sold | 1,763 | 2 |
| Other short-term investments, inc. trading securities | 3,130 | 3 |
| Securities available for sale | 23,191 | 23 |
| Net loans | 49,545 | 49 |
| Other | 20,668 | 20 |
| **Total** | **101,820** | **100** |

### Selected Subsidiaries

PNC Bancorp, Inc.
PNC Bank, Delaware
PNC Bank, National Association
PNC Bank Capital Securities, LLC
PNC Capital Leasing, LLC
PNC REIT Corp.
PNC Holding, LLC
PFPC Worldwide Inc.
PNC Funding Corp.
PNC Investment Corp.
PNC Venture Corp.

## COMPETITORS

Bank of America
Citigroup
Citizens Financial Group
Commerce Bancorp
Fifth Third
Huntington Bancshares
JPMorgan Chase
KeyCorp
National City
Sovereign Bancorp
Wachovia

## HISTORICAL FINANCIALS

Company Type: Public

### Income Statement

FYE: December 31

| | ASSETS ($ mil.) | NET INCOME ($ mil.) | INCOME AS % OF ASSETS | EMPLOYEES |
|---|---|---|---|---|
| **12/06** | 101,820 | 2,595 | 2.5% | 23,783 |
| **12/05** | 91,954 | 1,325 | 1.4% | 25,348 |
| **12/04** | 79,723 | 1,197 | 1.5% | 23,700 |
| **12/03** | 68,168 | 1,001 | 1.5% | 23,200 |
| **12/02** | 66,377 | 1,184 | 1.8% | 23,900 |
| **Annual Growth** | 11.3% | 21.7% | — | (0.1%) |

### 2006 Year-End Financials

Equity as % of assets: 10.6%
Return on assets: 2.7%
Return on equity: 26.8%
Long-term debt ($ mil.): 10,266
No. of shares (mil.): 293
Dividends
Yield: 2.9%
Payout: 24.6%
Market value ($ mil.): 21,694
Sales ($ mil.): 11,146

### Stock History

NYSE: PNC

| | STOCK PRICE ($) FY Close | P/E High | P/E Low | PER SHARE ($) Earnings | Dividends | Book Value |
|---|---|---|---|---|---|---|
| **12/06** | 74.04 | 9 | 7 | 8.73 | 2.15 | 36.82 |
| **12/05** | 61.83 | 14 | 11 | 4.55 | 2.00 | 29.23 |
| **12/04** | 57.44 | 14 | 12 | 4.21 | 1.50 | 26.41 |
| **12/03** | 54.73 | 16 | 12 | 3.55 | 1.94 | 23.99 |
| **12/02** | 41.90 | 15 | 8 | 4.15 | 1.92 | 24.32 |
| **Annual Growth** | 15.3% | — | — | 20.4% | 2.9% | 10.9% |

# Polaris Industries

Polaris Industries is the world's #1 maker of snowmobiles and the #2 maker of four- and six-wheeled all-terrain recreational and utility vehicles (behind Honda). It also makes Victory cruiser and sport cruiser motorcycles. Other products include replacement parts, accessories (covers, tow hitches, cargo racks), and recreational clothing and gear (boots and helmets). The company also offers financing services. Polaris has a joint venture, Robin Manufacturing, USA, with Fuji Heavy Industries to build engines for its products and companies in noncompetitive industries. Polaris has discontinued its unprofitable line of personal watercraft.

Polaris has an expressed plan to achieve $3 billion in sales by 2009. To do this the company is focused on developing new products while spearheading certain growth schemes. The company is honing its dealer network to ensure its dealers have the capacity to sell and service the products Polaris plans to roll out. The number of dealers will likely be reduced, while the quality of the dealers that remain is expected to improve.

Polaris is also focused on the rising popularity of its Victory brand of motorcycles and plans to grow the brand by introducing new products in new market segments. Victory was profitable for the first time in the fourth quarter of 2005 and Polaris anticipates full-year profitability in 2006.

Conversely Polaris' ATV and snowmobile markets experienced a slowdown in 2005. These markets are slowing after years of growth because of maturing in North America. Polaris is slowing production to bring inventory into synch with lower demand.

Lastly, Polaris plans to grow outside the US. The company expects that by 2009 15% of its sales will come from outside North America. To that end in 2005 Polaris purchased a 25% stake in Austrian motorcycle maker KTM Power Sports AG. The move gave Polaris a better foothold in Europe through KTM's extensive dealer network. The two companies will also benefit from complementary, rather than competing, product offerings.

Needing to repay debt, Polaris sold most of its stake in KTM Power Sports to KTM's majority shareholder, Cross Industries AG, in early 2007. Polaris plans to sell more of its KTM shares by mid-2007, reducing its equity stake to less than 5%. For selling 1.11 million shares of KTM, Polaris received about E47 million (nearly $62 million).

## HISTORY

Originally called Hetteen Hoist & Derrick, Polaris Industries was founded in Roseau, Minnesota, in 1945 by Edgar Hetteen and David Johnson. The friends did welding and repair work and made custom machinery for local farmers.

In the early 1950s Johnson invented a gas-powered sled to ride to his winter hunting ground. The contraption attracted the attention of a neighbor, who bought the machine. In 1954 the company began making snowmobiles under the Polaris brand. It built five machines in the winter of 1954-55 and was up to 300 per year within three years. Hetteen's younger brother Allen also joined the firm during the 1950s.

Snowmobiles made inroads as utility vehicles, but didn't catch on as recreational vehicles. To spur interest, in 1960 Edgar Hetteen led a snowmobile team on a thousand-mile trip across Alaska. When the company's backers complained about the expense of the trip, Hetteen left Polaris. He later founded Arctic Enterprises, which produced the Arctic Cat snowmobile and was, for a time, the top US snowmobile maker.

With Edgar's departure, Allen Hetteen became president of Polaris. The firm's fortunes rose as the snowmobile gained popularity, and in 1968 diversified manufacturer Textron (Bell helicopters, Schaefer pens, Talon zippers) acquired Polaris.

The snowmobile industry peaked in 1971, with sales topping 495,000 units; the industry declined through the rest of the 1970s. Polaris continued to introduce new models and to sponsor snowmobile racing teams. In 1981 Textron had refocused on its defense segments and planned to shut Polaris down. Company president Hall Wendel, an outdoorsman who would later climb Mt. Everest, led a management buyout.

In 1982 Polaris tried to buy Arctic Cat; Arctic Enterprises temporarily closed soon after, leaving Polaris as the US's sole snowmobile maker for a time.

Under Wendel, Polaris began looking for another product to fill production during snowmobiling's off-season. In 1985 it entered the ATV market, going up against several established Japanese manufacturers, including Honda and Suzuki. The company positioned its ATVs not as recreational vehicles, but as utility vehicles, and soon Polaris slipped into the #2 spot behind Honda. It became the world's #1 snowmobile maker in 1991. The next year Polaris began marketing personal watercraft, which made up about 10% of sales in 1993 (dropped to 4% in 1998). The company went public in 1994.

Polaris and Fuji Heavy Industries formed a joint venture — Robin Manufacturing, USA — in 1995 to build engines for its products and noncompeting companies. In 1997 Polaris announced its plans for the Victory motorcycle. In 1998 the company was slapped with a nearly $45 million judgment in a trade-secret lawsuit brought by the inventor of an engine fuel-injection system. Partner Fuji Heavy Industries was ordered to pay $11.6 million.

Polaris became the first American manufacturer in 50 years to enter the motorcycle market when it unveiled the Victory, a cruiser-style cycle, in 1998. *Cycle World* magazine named Victory the cruiser of the year.

The following year Victory sales tripled and a second model was introduced. Also in 1999 Thomas Tiller, a 15-year veteran of General Electric, succeeded Wendel as CEO.

In 2000 company founders and septuagenarians Hetteen and Johnson, along with Tiller, trekked across Alaska in snowmobiles, hoping the publicity would increase snowmobile sales (similar to the trip Hetteen made to boost sales 40 years earlier). Polaris launched the All Surface Loader, a new landscaping product, in 2001.

The following year Polaris introduced its first true sport ATV, the Predator. The first Arlen Ness limited edition cruiser motorcycle (named after motorcycle designers Arlen and Corey Ness) rolled off the assembly line in late 2003.

Citing increasing costs and competitive pressures, Polaris decided to liquidate its unprofitable watercraft unit in 2004.

## EXECUTIVES

**Chairman:** Gregory R. Palen, age 51
**CEO and Director:** Thomas C. Tiller, age 45, $750,000 pay
**President and COO:** Bennett J. Morgan, age 43, $350,000 pay
**VP, Finance, CFO, and Secretary:** Michael W. Malone, age 48, $325,000 pay
**VP and General Counsel:** Mary P McConnell, age 54
**VP, Human Resources:** John B. Corness, age 52, $260,000 pay
**VP, Operations:** Jeffrey A. Bjorkman, age 47, $275,000 pay
**VP, Victory Motorcycles and International Operations:** Mark E. Blackwell, age 53
**CIO:** William C. Fisher
**General Manager, ATVs:** Michael D. Dougherty
**General Manager, Parts, Garments, and Accessories and Snowmobiles:** Scott A. Swenson
**General Manager, RANGER:** Matt Homan
**General Manager, Sales and Marketing:** Michael P. Jonikas
**General Manager, Powertrain:** Allan Hurd
**Director, Consumer Sales:** Steve Menneto
**Director, Retail and Dealer Development:** Paige Wittman
**Director, Sales Operations and Dealer Support:** Robert R. (Bob) Nygaard
**Director, Marketing, ATV:** Jeff LeFever
**Media Relations:** Marlys Knutson
**CTO:** David C. Longren
**Auditors:** Ernst & Young LLP

## LOCATIONS

**HQ:** Polaris Industries Inc.
2100 Hwy. 55, Medina, MN 55340
**Phone:** 763-542-0500 **Fax:** 763-542-0599
**Web:** www.polarisindustries.com

Polaris Industries has engineering and manufacturing facilities in Spirit Lake, Iowa; Roseau, Minnesota; and Osceola and St. Croix Falls, Wisconsin; and sells through 1,700 dealers in North America and 40 distributors in more than 126 countries outside North America.

## PRODUCTS/OPERATIONS

### 2006 Sales

| | % of total |
|---|---|
| All-terrain vehicles | 67 |
| Replacement parts, garments & accessories | 16 |
| Snowmobiles | 10 |
| Motorcycles | 7 |
| **Total** | **100** |

### Selected Products

Vehicles
- All-terrain vehicles (ATVs)
  - Hawkeye
  - Magnum
  - Outlaw
  - Phoenix
  - Predator
  - Ranger off-road vehicles
  - Sawtooth
  - Scrambler 500
  - Sportsman
  - Trail Boss 330
  - X2
  - Youth
- Snowmobiles
  - Crossover
  - Deep Snow
  - Performance
  - Race
  - Trail
  - Touring
- Motorcycles
  - Hammer
  - Kingpin
  - Vegas
  - Vegas 8-Ball

Replacement Parts, Garments, and Accessories
- Boots
- Cargo racks
- Gloves
- Hand warmers
- Hats
- Helmets
- Jackets
- Lubricants
- Luggage
- Sweaters
- Tow hitches

## COMPETITORS

Arctic Cat
BMW
E-Z-GO
Harley-Davidson
Honda
K2
Kawasaki Heavy Industries
Lehman Trikes
Suzuki Motor
TEAM Industries, Inc.
Triumph Motorcycles
Yamaha
Yamaha Motor

## HISTORICAL FINANCIALS

Company Type: Public

**Income Statement** FYE: December 31

| | REVENUE ($ mil.) | NET INCOME ($ mil.) | NET PROFIT MARGIN | EMPLOYEES |
|---|---|---|---|---|
| **12/06** | 1,657 | 107 | 6.5% | 3,400 |
| **12/05** | 1,909 | 143 | 7.5% | 3,600 |
| **12/04** | 1,773 | 105 | 5.9% | 3,600 |
| **12/03** | 1,606 | 111 | 6.9% | 3,400 |
| **12/02** | 1,521 | 104 | 6.8% | 3,500 |
| **Annual Growth** | 2.2% | 0.8% | — | (0.7%) |

**2006 Year-End Financials**

Debt ratio: 149.4%
Return on equity: 39.8%
Cash ($ mil.): 20
Current ratio: 1.09
Long-term debt ($ mil.): 250
No. of shares (mil.): 35
Dividends
Yield: 2.6%
Payout: 48.1%
Market value ($ mil.): 1,660

**Stock History** NYSE: PII

| | STOCK PRICE ($) FY Close | P/E High | P/E Low | PER SHARE ($) Earnings | Dividends | Book Value |
|---|---|---|---|---|---|---|
| **12/06** | 46.83 | 21 | 13 | 2.58 | 1.24 | 4.72 |
| **12/05** | 50.20 | 23 | 13 | 3.27 | 1.12 | 8.87 |
| **12/04** | 68.02 | 30 | 17 | 2.32 | 0.69 | 8.46 |
| **12/03** | 44.29 | 19 | 9 | 2.46 | 0.62 | 7.37 |
| **12/02** | 29.30 | 18 | 12 | 2.19 | 0.56 | 12.43 |
| **Annual Growth** | 12.4% | — | — | 4.2% | 22.0% | (21.5%) |

# Polo Ralph Lauren

Polo Ralph Lauren is galloping at a faster clip than when founder Ralph Lauren first entered the arena. With golden mallet brands such as Polo, Chaps, Lauren, and Club Monaco, the firm designs and markets apparel, accessories, fragrances, and home furnishings. Polo prefers licensing over manufacturing and manages many licensees, as well as more than 350 contract manufacturers worldwide. It operates about 290 retail and outlet stores in the US and licenses more than 100 others worldwide. Founder Ralph Lauren controls some 90% of Polo's voting power. The firm bought Ralph Lauren Footwear — a unit of Reebok International and its global footwear licensee — for about $110 million, as well as control of Polo.com.

Polo purchased the remaining 50% stake in Polo.com from both Ralph Lauren Media, a unit of NBC Universal, and ValueVisions Media for about $175 million in early 2007. The move gave Polo full control over its plans to develop its online presence domestically and abroad, where the company has seen an uptick in traffic.

Initiatives for 2007 include the launch of a new group named Global Brand Concepts formed to develop lifestyle brands for specialty and department stores. The group will design and market new products, including accessories, home decor, and women's, men's, and children's apparel. A new joint venture with the Swiss luxury goods maker Richemont SA will design and market watches and jewelry under the Polo brand. Products are expected to reach the market in 2008.

US department stores such as Federated and Dillard's account for almost 40% of the company's wholesale revenue.

In recent years Polo Ralph Lauren has been expanding its retail operations in the US and Asia and stretching its accessories category (with handbags, small leather goods, and footwear) to create a luxury brand that rivals European competitors. The company opened its first freestanding flagship store in Tokyo in early 2006. By early 2007 Polo Ralph Lauren had inked a couple deals that will secure its foothold in the Japanese apparel and accessories market.

In 2006 Polo Ralph Lauren partnered with Luxottica in a licensing agreement valued at more than $1.75 billion over a 10-year period. In 2007 Luxottica began to design, manufacture, and distribute Polo Ralph Lauren-branded prescription frames and sunglasses.

A licensing agreement with Jones Apparel to produce men's and women's Polo Jeans apparel through Jones's Sun Apparel subsidiary represented one of Polo Ralph Lauren's most prominent deals. However, the partnership eventually spurred litigation between the two companies. (Polo Ralph Lauren and Jones Apparel agreed to settle litigation over control of the brand in early 2006. As part of the deal Polo Ralph Lauren paid Jones Apparel about $355 million to acquire the Sun Apparel unit while Jones Apparel retained distribution and product-development operations.)

## HISTORY

Ralph Lauren, suave Manhattanite, was actually born Ralph Lifschitz in the Bronx, New York. It is said that his father, Frank, an immigrant Russian housepainter and muralist, informally changed the family's name to Lauren and inspired his son to recreate himself in the image of a mythic upper class.

After high school Ralph, who formally changed his name to Lauren, became a salesman at Brooks Brothers and then a sales representative for Rivetz, a Boston tie maker. In 1967 he landed a job as a tie designer for Beau Brummel of New York. The company gave him his own style division, which he named Polo because of the sport's refined image. The next year Lauren started Polo Fashions to make tailored menswear. Partner Peter Strom teamed up with Lauren in the early 1970s. Although its designs received critical acclaim, Polo Fashions had a bumpy start as Lauren adjusted to the business aspect of his fashion label.

Lauren's profile rose in the 1970s when he won three Coty Awards for design and produced costumes for the movie *The Great Gatsby*. In 1971 Lauren adopted his polo-player-on-a-horse logo and introduced a line for women. That year the first licensed Polo store opened (on Rodeo Drive in Beverly Hills), along with his first in-store boutique (at Bloomingdale's in New York City). He added shoes to the lineup in 1972, licensed his womenswear line the next year, and launched a licensed fragrance line in 1978.

By 1980 Polo Fashions had become Polo Ralph Lauren. Encouraged by the success of the licensed products, Lauren led the designer charge into home furnishings, introducing his Home Collection in 1983. He opened his flagship store in New York City three years later.

Lauren sold 28% of Polo to a Goldman Sachs investment fund for $135 million in 1994. The company expanded upmarket with its Purple Label and downmarket with Polo Jeans denims and a line of paints in 1996.

Following the stampede of fashion-house IPOs, Polo went public in 1997. The next year, moving to reduce expenses, the company restructured its divisions. The reorganization included closing nine stores and cutting about 4% of its workforce.

In May 1999 Polo paid $85 million for hip Canadian retailer Club Monaco to compete in the burgeoning youth market. It also opened RL, a fine-dining restaurant adjacent to its retail outlet in Chicago's famed shopping district.

In early 2000 Polo purchased its European licensee, Poloco, for $230 million, giving the company greater control of its brand. Then, in a 50-50 joint venture with NBC and its affiliates, Polo formed Ralph Lauren Media Company to sell its products via the Internet as well as broadcast, cable, and print media. Also that year the company closed 11 underperforming Club Monaco locations and announced plans to shut down all of its jeans stores. To extend its European reach even further, Polo bought its Italian licensee, PRL Fashions of Europe, in 2001.

Polo Ralph Lauren inked one of the most significant licensing deals in company history — and what it considers to be a great match, to boot — in early 2005. The firm paired with the United States Tennis Association (USTA) to form a four-year global partnership and was designated the official apparel sponsor of the US Open through 2008.

The company's agreement with the USTA gave it the momentum to seal a deal with The All England Club and Wimbledon in 2006 that extends through 2010. Polo Ralph Lauren, as part of the agreement, became the exclusive outfitter of Wimbledon — the first official designer in the 129-history of the games.

## EXECUTIVES

**Chairman and CEO:** Ralph Lauren, age 67, $16,000,000 pay
**President, COO, and Director:** Roger N. Farah, age 54, $3,735,000 pay
**EVP and Director:** Jackwyn (Jacki) Nemerov, age 55
**EVP, Global Retail Brand Development:** Charles E. Fagan
**EVP, Women's Design and Advertising:** Buffy Birrittella
**EVP, Men's Design:** Jerome Lauren
**EVP and Global Creative Services, Polo Store Development and Home Collection Design:** Alfredo V. Paredes
**SVP, Communications:** Wendy Smith
**SVP, Finance and CFO:** Tracey T. Travis, age 44, $1,281,250 pay
**SVP and CIO:** Judith S. Formichella
**SVP and General Counsel:** Jonathan D. Drucker
**SVP and General Merchandising Manager:** Susie Coulter
**SVP, Human Resources and Legal:** Mitchell A. Kosh, age 57, $1,230,000 pay
**SVP, Public Relations and Financial Communications:** Nancy E. S. Murray
**SVP, Sourcing and Manufacturing:** Donald (Don) Baum
**SVP, Advertising, Marketing, and Corporate Communications:** David Lauren
**VP, Design:** Maura Manning

**President, Dresses:** Barbara Kennedy
**President and COO, Polo Ralph Lauren Europe:** Brian Duffy
**President, Lauren by Ralph Lauren Womenswear:** Kim Roy, age 43
**President, Polo Ralph Lauren Retail Stores:** Wayne T. Meichner
**President, Polo Ralph Lauren Menswear:** Joy Herfel
**President, Ralph Lauren Womenswear Collection:** Cheryl L. Sterling-Udell
**President, Product Licensing:** Jeffrey D. (Jeff) Morgan
**Senior Director, Investor Relations:** Denise Gillen, age 50
**Auditors:** Deloitte & Touche LLP

## LOCATIONS

**HQ:** Polo Ralph Lauren Corporation
650 Madison Ave., New York, NY 10022
**Phone:** 212-318-7000 **Fax:** 212-888-5780
**Web:** www.polo.com

### 2007 Sales

| | $ mil. | % of total |
|---|---|---|
| US & Canada | 3,452.2 | 80 |
| Europe | 767.9 | 18 |
| Japan | 64.6 | 1 |
| Other regions | 10.7 | 1 |
| **Total** | **4,295.4** | **100** |

## PRODUCTS/OPERATIONS

### 2007 Sales

| | $ mil. | % of total |
|---|---|---|
| Wholesale | 2,315.9 | 54 |
| Retail | 1,743.2 | 41 |
| Licensing | 236.3 | 5 |
| **Total** | **4,295.4** | **100** |

### Major Brands, Store Names, and Licensing Partners

Wholesale
- Collection brands
  - Ralph Lauren Black Label (women's classic luxury apparel)
  - Ralph Lauren Collection (women's classic luxury apparel)
  - Ralph Lauren/Purple Label Collection (men's tailored apparel and sportswear)
- Polo brands
  - Blue Label (women's ready to wear)
  - Polo by Ralph Lauren (men's ready to wear)
  - Polo Golf (men's and women's golf apparel)
  - Polo Sport (men's activewear and sportswear)
  - Ralph Lauren Polo Sport (women's activewear and sportswear)
  - RLX Polo Sport (men's and women's athletic apparel)

Retail
- Outlet stores
  - Caban
  - Club Monaco
  - Ralph Lauren
  - Rugby
- European outlets
  - Polo Jeans Co. Factory Store
  - Polo Ralph Lauren Factory Store
- Polo stores
  - Polo Country
  - Polo Ralph Lauren
  - Polo Sport

## COMPETITORS

AnnTaylor
Armani
Benetton
Burberry
Calvin Klein
Christian Dior
Coach
Donna Karan
Ellen Tracy
Ermenegildo Zegna
Escada
Estée Lauder
Gap
Gianni Versace
Gucci
Guess
H&M
Haggar
Hermès
Hugo Boss
J. Crew
Jones Apparel
Kenneth Cole
Lands' End
Laura Ashley
Levi Strauss
Limited Brands
Liz Claiborne
L.L. Bean
LVMH
Martha Stewart Living
Nautica Enterprises
Perry Ellis International
Phillips-Van Heusen
Richemont
St. John Knits
Tiffany
Tommy Hilfiger
Warnaco Group

## HISTORICAL FINANCIALS

Company Type: Public

### Income Statement

FYE: Saturday nearest March 31

| | REVENUE ($ mil.) | NET INCOME ($ mil.) | NET PROFIT MARGIN | EMPLOYEES |
|---|---|---|---|---|
| **3/07** | 4,295 | 401 | 9.3% | 14,000 |
| **3/06** | 3,746 | 308 | 8.2% | 12,800 |
| **3/05** | 3,305 | 190 | 5.8% | 12,762 |
| **3/04** | 2,650 | 171 | 6.5% | 13,000 |
| **3/03** | 2,439 | 174 | 7.1% | 10,800 |
| **Annual Growth** | 15.2% | 23.2% | — | 6.7% |

### 2007 Year-End Financials

Debt ratio: 19.1%
Return on equity: 18.3%
Cash ($ mil.): 564
Current ratio: 2.63
Long-term debt ($ mil.): 446
No. of shares (mil.): 61
Dividends
Yield: 0.2%
Payout: 5.4%
Market value ($ mil.): 5,351

### Stock History

NYSE: RL

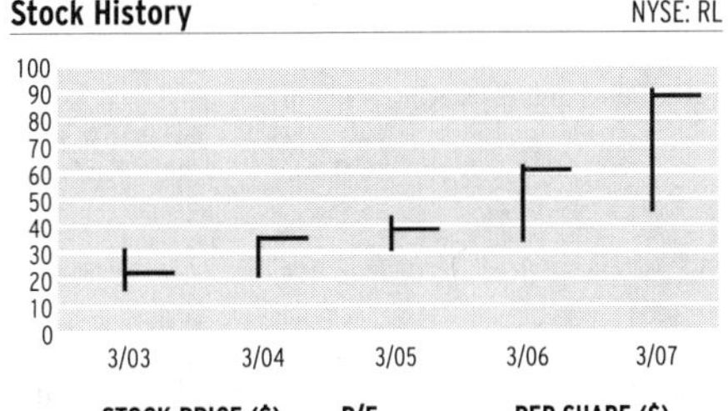


| | STOCK PRICE ($) FY Close | P/E High | P/E Low | PER SHARE ($) Earnings | Dividends | Book Value |
|---|---|---|---|---|---|---|
| **3/07** | 88.15 | 24 | 12 | 3.73 | 0.20 | 38.47 |
| **3/06** | 60.61 | 22 | 12 | 2.87 | 0.20 | 33.00 |
| **3/05** | 38.41 | 23 | 17 | 1.83 | 0.20 | 26.18 |
| **3/04** | 35.13 | 21 | 13 | 1.69 | 0.20 | 23.12 |
| **3/03** | 22.35 | 18 | 9 | 1.76 | — | 26.94 |
| **Annual Growth** | 40.9% | — | — | 20.7% | 0.0% | 9.3% |

# PPG Industries

You won't catch PPG Industries painting itself into a corner. Coatings — such as paints (sold under the Pittsburgh Paints, Lucite, and Monarch brands), stains (Olympic), and sealants that help protect surfaces — account for most of its sales; the remainder comes from glass and chemicals. PPG's glass offerings include car windshields; flat glass for buildings; fabricated glass; and continuous-strand fiberglass used in aircraft, automobiles, and buildings. PPG's chemicals segment makes chlor-alkali chemicals (for water treatment and in glass among other uses). The company operates more than 100 manufacturing facilities worldwide; it also operates 450 paint retail centers in the US.

One of PPG's major markets is automakers and their suppliers, who buy the company's auto glass, adhesives, sealants, and coatings. It also supplies automotive refinishes and replacement glass through distributors.

In 2005 the company stepped out a little and made a deal to acquire Crown Coating Industries, a company based in Singapore that makes radiation-cured coatings for wood flooring. Crown Coatings, whose management stayed intact, operates facilities in Singapore and Shanghai. Back in the USA the company made another move, this one to acquire Iowa Paint and its network of 42 service centers that cater primarily to the professional contractor and industrial markets. It also acquired the Iowa and Sterling brands in the deal.

The following year PPG moved into the European market with the acquisition of Intercast Europe, a maker of non-prescription sunlenses. The acquisition brings to PPG manufacturing and distribution locations in Italy, Hong Kong, and Thailand. At the same time the company announced its acquisition of Shanghai Sunpool Building Material, which is the sole distributor in China of PPG's Master's Mark architectural paints.

In the US the company acquired Eldorado Chemical, a maker of paint strippers and technical cleaners for the aerospace industry. PPG continued to add to its business with the acquisition of Ameron's coatings operations later in 2006.

Also that year the company, clearly in the mood for deals, acquired Spectra-Tone Paint, aerospace transparencies maker Sierracin, and Australian firm Protec Pty. Ltd. As can be seen by many of these recent acquisitions, the company is clearly inclined to grow its international operations. It continued to do so in 2007 with an agreement to buy the South American architectural and industrial coatings maker Renner Sayerlack. PPG also made an offer to buy Dutch coatings producer SigmaKalon Group for $3 billion, and agreed to acquire Barloworld Coatings Australia, the architectural paint unit of South African-based Barloworld, Ltd.

Current and former employees own more than 10% of the company.

## HISTORY

After the failure of his first two plate-glass manufacturing plants, John Ford persuaded former railroad superintendent John Pitcairn to invest $200,000 in a third factory in 1883 in Creighton, Pennsylvania. The enterprise, Pittsburgh Plate Glass (PPG), became the first commercially successful US plate-glass factory.

Ford left in 1896 after Pitcairn established a company distribution system, replacing glass jobbers. Ford went on to found a predecessor of competitor Libbey-Owens-Ford (now owned by glassmaker Pilkington).

Pitcairn built a soda ash plant in 1899, bought a Milwaukee paint company the following year, and began producing window glass in 1908. Pitcairn died in 1916, leaving his stock to his sons.

Strong automobile and construction markets in the early 20th century increased demand for the company's products. In 1924 PPG revolutionized glass production with the introduction of a straight-line conveyor manufacturing method. In the 1930s and 1940s, PPG successfully promoted structural glass for use in the commercial construction industry.

PPG was listed on the NYSE in 1945. In 1952 it started making fiberglass, and in 1968 the company adopted its present name.

Vincent Sarni (CEO, 1984-93) recognized that 85% of the company's sales were to the maturing construction and automobile industries. Sarni decided to move the company into growing industries, such as electronics.

In 1986 PPG spent $154 million on acquisitions, including the medical electronics units of Litton Industries and Honeywell. It acquired the medical technology business of Allegheny International in 1987 and bought Casco Nobel, a coatings distributor, and the Olympic and Lucite paint lines from Clorox in 1989.

In the 1990s PPG backed away from Sarni's earlier strategies for greater diversification and unloaded a number of high-tech businesses. The firm refocused on its core coatings, glass, and chemicals operations. PPG acquired Matthews Paints, a leading maker of paints for outdoor signs, and the refinish coating business of Lilly Industries in 1995.

In 1997 president and COO Raymond LeBoeuf took over as CEO. In 1998 PPG sold its European flat and automotive glass business to Belgium-based Glaverbel. In 1999 PPG expanded its European coatings business with the purchase of Belgium-based Sigma Coatings' commercial transport coatings unit and Akzo Nobel's aircraft coatings and sealants company, PRC-DeSoto International. That year PPG also bought Imperial Chemical Industries' Germany-based coatings business for large commercial vehicles and its US-based auto refinish and industrial coatings businesses.

Early in the new decade, PPG suffered from flat or declining earnings from existing operations. Amid falling sales and lower prices for chemicals and glass, PPG began to cut jobs and closed some facilities. Still the company recorded its first loss in more than 10 years in 2002 and its second straight year of declining sales.

Like many manufacturers in its industry, PPG has been exposed to potentially costly asbestos litigation, mainly because of its 50% stake in the bankrupt Pittsburgh Corning, a joint venture with Corning that made insulation with asbestos. In 2002 PPG and its insurers agreed to pay roughly $2.7 billion to settle its asbestos claims.

LeBoeuf retired in 2005. He was replaced by president and COO Charles Bunch, who had joined the company in 1979 and worked up through the ranks of, first, the finance department and then the coatings operations.

## EXECUTIVES

**Chairman and CEO:** Charles E. (Chuck) Bunch, age 57, $2,250,000 pay
**SVP, General Counsel, and Secretary:** James C. Diggs, age 58, $823,300 pay
**SVP Finance:** William H. Hernandez, age 58, $949,000 pay
**SVP Chemicals:** Kevin F. Sullivan, age 55, $697,133 pay (prior to promotion)
**SVP Coatings and Automotive Aftermarket:** J. Rich Alexander, age 51
**SVP Coatings:** William A. Wulfsohn, age 44
**SVP Glass and Fiber Glass:** Victoria M. (Vicki) Holt, age 49
**VP Coatings and Managing Director, Asia Pacific:** Viktor Sekmakas
**VP Coatings and Managing Director, Latin America:** Jorge A. Steyerthal
**VP Corporate Development and Services:** Maurice V. Peconi
**VP and Controller:** David B. Navikas
**VP and Associate General Counsel:** Glenn E. Bost II
**VP Government and Community Affairs:** Lynne D. Schmidt
**VP Growth Initiatives:** Richard A. (Dick) Beuke
**VP Human Resources:** Charles W. (Bud) Wise
**VP Information Technology:** Werner Baer, age 48
**VP Purchasing and Distribution:** Kathleen A. McGuire, age 54
**VP Science and Technology:** James A. (Jim) Trainham
**VP Strategic Planning:** Aziz S. Giga
**VP Tax Administration:** Donna Lee Walker
**Director Investor Relations:** Vince Morales
**Supervisor Public Relations:** K.C. McCrory
**Auditors:** Deloitte & Touche LLP

## LOCATIONS

**HQ:** PPG Industries, Inc.
1 PPG Place, Pittsburgh, PA 15272
**Phone:** 412-434-3131 **Fax:** 412-434-2011
**Web:** www.ppg.com

PPG Industries operates more than 100 manufacturing plants in Asia, Australia, Europe, and North and South America (including some joint ventures and shared enterprises). The company also operates more than 450 paint retail centers in the US.

### 2006 Sales and Operating Income

| | Sales $ mil. | Sales % of total | Operating Income $ mil. | Operating Income % of total |
|---|---|---|---|---|
| Americas | | | | |
| US | 6,878 | 62 | 1,077 | 71 |
| Other countries | 983 | 9 | 72 | 5 |
| Europe | 2,347 | 21 | 225 | 15 |
| Asia | 829 | 8 | 145 | 9 |
| **Total** | **11,037** | **100** | **1,519** | **100** |

## PRODUCTS/OPERATIONS

### 2006 Sales and Operating Income

| | Sales $ mil. | Sales % of total | Operating Income $ mil. | Operating Income % of total |
|---|---|---|---|---|
| Coatings | | | | |
| Industrial Coatings | 3,236 | 29 | 349 | 22 |
| Performance & Applied Coatings | 3,091 | 28 | 514 | 34 |
| Glass | 2,230 | 20 | 148 | 10 |
| Commodity Chemicals | 1,491 | 14 | 285 | 19 |
| Optical & Specialty Materials | 1,005 | 9 | 223 | 15 |
| Adjustments | (16) | — | — | — |
| **Total** | **11,037** | **100** | **1,519** | **100** |

### Selected Products

Industrial coatings
- Automotive coatings, chemicals, adhesives, and sealants
- Industrial coatings
- Packaging coatings (food and beverage containers)

Performance & Applied Coatings
- Aerospace coatings
- Architectural coatings (Lucite paints, Olympic stains)
- Refinish

Glass
- Aircraft transparencies
- Automotive glass
- Coated glass
- Continuous-strand fiberglass
- Flat glass

Commodity Chemicals
- Calcium hypochlorite
- Caustic soda
- Chlorine
- Chlorine derivatives
- Phosgene derivatives

Optical & Specialty Materials
- Fine chemicals (Intermediate chemicals like active pharmaceutical ingredients)
- Optical products (Transitions variable-tint lenses)
- Silica products

## COMPETITORS

3M
Akzo Nobel
Asahi Glass
BASF AG
BEHR
Belron US
Benjamin Moore
Dow Chemical
Ferro
Guardian Industries
Imperial Chemical
Kelly-Moore
Nippon Paint
Nippon Sheet Glass
Owens Corning Sales
Pilkington
RPM
Saint-Gobain
Sherwin-Williams
Visteon

## HISTORICAL FINANCIALS

Company Type: Public

### Income Statement

FYE: December 31

| | REVENUE ($ mil.) | NET INCOME ($ mil.) | NET PROFIT MARGIN | EMPLOYEES |
|---|---|---|---|---|
| **12/06** | 11,037 | 711 | 6.4% | 32,200 |
| **12/05** | 10,201 | 596 | 5.8% | 30,800 |
| **12/04** | 9,513 | 683 | 7.2% | 31,800 |
| **12/03** | 8,756 | 494 | 5.6% | 32,900 |
| **12/02** | 8,067 | (69) | — | 34,100 |
| **Annual Growth** | 8.2% | — | — | (1.4%) |

### 2006 Year-End Financials

Debt ratio: 35.7%
Return on equity: 22.6%
Cash ($ mil.): 455
Current ratio: 1.65
Long-term debt ($ mil.): 1,155
No. of shares (mil.): 164
Dividends
Yield: 3.7%
Payout: 56.0%
Market value ($ mil.): 10,536

### Stock History

NYSE: PPG

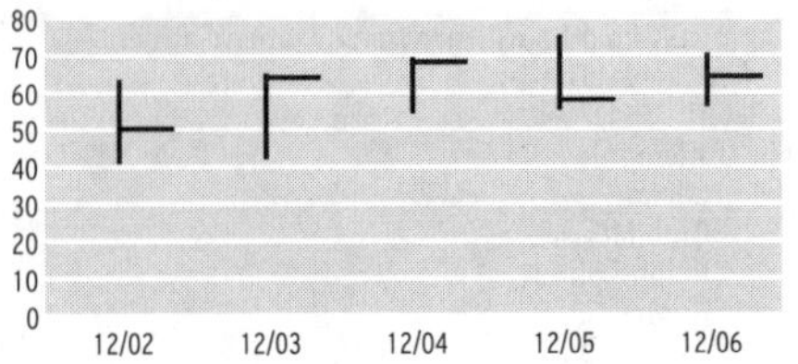

| | STOCK PRICE ($) FY Close | P/E High | P/E Low | PER SHARE ($) Earnings | PER SHARE ($) Dividends | PER SHARE ($) Book Value |
|---|---|---|---|---|---|---|
| **12/06** | 64.21 | 16 | 13 | 4.27 | 2.39 | 19.71 |
| **12/05** | 57.90 | 21 | 16 | 3.49 | 1.86 | 18.47 |
| **12/04** | 68.16 | 17 | 14 | 3.95 | 1.79 | 20.77 |
| **12/03** | 64.02 | 22 | 15 | 2.89 | 1.73 | 17.00 |
| **12/02** | 50.15 | — | — | (0.41) | 1.70 | 12.68 |
| **Annual Growth** | 6.4% | — | — | — | 8.9% | 11.7% |

# PPL Corporation

PPL packs a powerful punch in Pennsylvania, where it distributes electricity to about 1.4 million customers through regulated subsidiary PPL Electric Utilities. PPL also generates electricity and sells it in wholesale and retail markets in North America, and it holds stakes in electricity distributors in the US, the UK, and Latin America serving an additional 3.7 million customers. Other businesses include energy management services, natural gas and propane distribution, mechanical and electrical contracting, synthetic fuels production, telecommunications, and engineering services. In 2007 the company announced plans to sell its Latin American companies as well as its US propane and gas distribution units.

As power markets are deregulated, the company is investing in projects worldwide. Subsidiary PPL Generation has a generating capacity of more than 11,550 MW from fossil-fueled, hydroelectric, and nuclear plants in seven states. PPL has canceled some of its power plant development plans in the US due to poor market conditions. The company has also agreed to sell a gas-fired plant to Arizona Public Service for $190 million, and it sold another plant, the 600-MW Griffith Power Plant in Arizona to LS Power Equity in 2006 for about $115 million.

PPL Global owns UK utility Western Power Distribution Holdings, which serves 2.6 million electricity customers, as well as stakes in power distributors in Chile, El Salvador (which it agreed to sell in 2007), and Bolivia that serve approximately 1.1 million customers. Subsidiary PPL Gas Utilities provides natural gas to 110,000 customers in Pennsylvania and Maryland.

## HISTORY

PPL's wires reach back to Lehigh Coal & Navigation, which was formed in 1822 to mine Pennsylvania coal and build a canal to deliver it to Philadelphia. Heavy industry and steel mills flourished in the Lehigh Valley, and Thomas Edison formed small electric companies to serve the area in the early 1880s. Rivals soon followed, and by 1900 there were 64 companies in what would become PPL's territory.

Lehigh formed Lehigh Navigation Electric in 1912 to provide power to its coal mines, only to lose control of the company to conglomerate Electric Bond & Share in 1917. Electric Bond & Share's president, S. Z. Mitchell, merged the renamed Lehigh Valley Light & Power with six other utilities to form Pennsylvania Power & Light (PP&L) in Allentown in 1920. The next year PP&L became a subsidiary of National Power & Light.

PP&L bought more than 60 neighboring utilities in a decade, and by 1930 industrial customers accounted for 70% of power sales. The company also built a 220,000-volt transmission interconnection line with neighbors Philadelphia Electric (now PECO Energy, a unit of Exelon) and Public Service Electric and Gas of New Jersey (now part of Public Service Enterprise Group). During the Depression the company offset falling industrial sales with residential sales.

The Public Utility Holding Company Act of 1935 forced large utility holding companies to streamline their businesses, and by 1948 National Power & Light had unloaded PP&L.

To keep up with postwar demand, PP&L built several coal-fired power plants. By 1964 industry still accounted for about a third of sales, but suburbs assumed greater importance. PP&L began operating coal mines in the early 1970s and started building the Susquehanna nuclear plant.

Although its proprietary coal supply helped PP&L weather skyrocketing fuel costs in the 1970s, huge construction delays endemic to nukes hit the utility for $4 billion by the time Susquehanna was completed in 1982. Flat sales in the late 1980s led to 2,000 job cuts and to a reorganization by CEO William Hecht.

In 1992 the federal Energy Policy Act signaled the end of the monopoly era by promoting wholesale competition. PP&L formed Power Markets Development (now PPL Global) in 1994 to make energy investments worldwide. The next year it created holding company PP&L Resources to house both regulated and non-regulated businesses.

The Customer Choice Act was passed in Pennsylvania in 1996, ushering in competition, and the utility formed its non-regulated retail power sales arm, PP&L EnergyPlus. PP&L also bought 25% of Chile's Empresas Emel in 1997 (upped to 67%, 1999). Fellow US utility Southern Company, which bought UK utility SWEB in 1995, had turned over a 51% stake in SWEB to PP&L Resources by 1998.

PP&L Resources began buying mechanical contracting firms in 1998 to complement its electric business, and it purchased natural gas and propane distributor Penn Fuel Gas.

In 1999 the company bought generating facilities with a total capacity of 1,315 MW from Montana Power. Also that year PP&L Resources and Southern sold SWEB's supply business and the SWEB brand name to London Electricity, a unit of Electricité de France. PP&L Resources and Southern retained their stakes in SWEB's distribution network, which was renamed Western Power Distribution (later changed to WPD Holdings UK after it acquired British utility Hyder in 2000).

PP&L Resources changed its name to PPL Corporation in 2000 and reorganized into four operating subsidiaries: PPL Utilities, PPL EnergyPlus, PPL Generation, and PPL Global. PPL's restructuring efforts separated its regulated distribution operations from its non-regulated generation, supply, and services operations.

In 2002 PPL's Brazilian utility, Companhia Energética do Maranhão (Cemar), filed for bankruptcy protection and fell under the control of the Brazilian government. (PPL divested its interest in Cemar in 2004.) Also in 2002, PPL purchased the remaining 49% stake in WPD Holdings UK (now Western Power Distribution Holdings) from Mirant for $235 million.

## EXECUTIVES

**Chairman, President, and CEO:** James H. Miller, age 58, $962,020 pay (prior to promotion)
**EVP and COO; President, PPL Electric:** William H. (Bill) Spence, age 49
**SVP, General Counsel, and Secretary:** Robert J. Grey, age 56, $389,231 pay
**SVP and Chief Nuclear Officer:** Britt T. McKinney
**EVP and CFO:** Paul A. Farr, age 39
**VP Finance and Treasurer:** James E. Abel, age 55
**VP and Controller:** Jerry Matthews (Matt) Simmons Jr., age 41
**VP Risk Management:** Vijay Singh
**VP External Affairs:** Joanne H. Raphael
**VP and CIO, PPL Services:** Edward T. Novak
**President, PPL Energy Services Group:** Paul T. Champagne, age 49, $416,001 pay
**President, PPL EnergyPlus:** C. Joseph (Joe) Hopf Jr., age 50
**President, PPL Global:** Rick L. Klingensmith, age 46
**President, PPL Generation:** Bryce L. Shriver, age 59, $389,231 pay
**CEO, Western Power Distribution; VP UK, PPL Global:** Robert A. Symons
**President, PPL Gas Utilities; VP Customer Service, PPL Gas Utilities:** Robert M. Geneczko
**President, PPL Electric Utilities:** David G. (Dave) DeCampli, age 49
**Director Investor Relations:** Timothy J. (Tim) Paukovits
**Director Corporate Communications:** Daniel J. (Dan) McCarthy
**Manager Public Relations:** Paul Wirth
**Auditors:** Ernst & Young LLP

## LOCATIONS

**HQ:** PPL Corporation
2 N. 9th St., Allentown, PA 18101
**Phone:** 610-774-5151 **Fax:** 610-774-4198
**Web:** www.pplweb.com

PPL distributes electricity in central and eastern Pennsylvania. The company also markets electricity in the northeastern and western US and in Canada, provides natural gas and propane in Maryland and Pennsylvania, and has interests in power plants in Arizona, Connecticut, Illinois, Maine, Montana, New York, and Pennsylvania. PPL has generation and distribution investments in Bolivia, Chile, El Salvador, and the UK.

**2006 Sales**

| | $ mil. | % of total |
|---|---|---|
| US | 5,552 | 81 |
| UK | 792 | 11 |
| Latin America | 555 | 8 |
| **Total** | **6,899** | **100** |

## PRODUCTS/OPERATIONS

**2006 Sales**

| | $ mil. | % of total |
|---|---|---|
| Utility | 4,573 | 66 |
| Wholesale energy marketing | 1,532 | 22 |
| Energy-related businesses | 668 | 10 |
| Unregulated retail electric & gas | 91 | 1 |
| Net energy trading margins | 35 | 1 |
| **Total** | **6,899** | **100** |

**Selected Subsidiaries**

PPL Development Corporation (acquisition and divestiture activities)
PPL Electric Utilities Corporation (electricity distribution)
PPL Energy Supply (nonregulated operations)
- PPL EnergyPlus, LLC (wholesale and retail energy marketing)
- PPL Generation, LLC (electricity generation)
  - PPL Montana, LLC (electricity generation)
- PPL Global, LLC (international utility operations)
  - Distribuidora de Electricidad DelSur, S.A. de C.V. (DelSur, 81%, electric utility, El Salvador)
  - Empresa de Luz y Fuerza Electrica Cochabamba S.A. (Elfec, 92%, electric utility, Bolivia)
  - Empresas Emel S.A. (Emel, 95%, electric utility, Chile)
  - Western Power Distribution Holdings Limited (formerly WPD Holdings UK, electricity distribution)

PPL Gas Utilities Corporation (gas distribution and propane sales)
PPL Services Corporation (shared services for PPL Corp. and other subsidiaries)
PPL Telecom, LLC (telecommunications services)

## COMPETITORS

ABB
AEP
Allegheny Energy
Aquila
BayCorp
Canadian Utilities
Centrica
Con Edison
Constellation Energy Group
Covanta
Delmarva Power
Dominion Resources
Duke Energy
Duquesne Light Holdings
Endesa S.A.
Energy East
EnergySolve
Environmental Power
Exelon
Ferrellgas Partners
FirstEnergy
Green Mountain Energy
Hidrocántabrico
IBERDROLA
Maine & Maritimes
Midwest Generation
National Fuel Gas
Ontario Power Generation
Orange & Rockland Utilities
Peabody Energy
Pepco Holdings
PSEG
Scottish and Southern Energy
South Jersey Industries
Southern Company
Suburban Propane
TransAlta
UGI
UIL Holdings
Unión Fenosa

## HISTORICAL FINANCIALS

Company Type: Public

### Income Statement

FYE: December 31

| | REVENUE ($ mil.) | NET INCOME ($ mil.) | NET PROFIT MARGIN | EMPLOYEES |
|---|---|---|---|---|
| **12/06** | 6,899 | 865 | 12.5% | 12,620 |
| **12/05** | 6,219 | 678 | 10.9% | 12,276 |
| **12/04** | 5,812 | 698 | 12.0% | 12,028 |
| **12/03** | 5,587 | 734 | 13.1% | 12,256 |
| **12/02** | 5,429 | 275 | 5.1% | 12,655 |
| **Annual Growth** | 6.2% | 33.2% | — | (0.1%) |

### 2006 Year-End Financials

Debt ratio: 131.4%
Return on equity: 18.1%
Cash ($ mil.): 1,255
Current ratio: 1.08
Long-term debt ($ mil.): 6,728
No. of shares (mil.): 385
Dividends
Yield: 3.1%
Payout: 49.1%
Market value ($ mil.): 13,798

### Stock History

NYSE: PPL

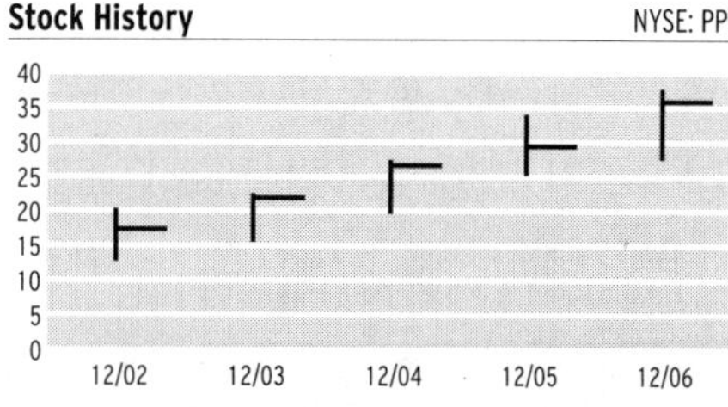


| | STOCK PRICE ($) FY Close | P/E High | P/E Low | PER SHARE ($) Earnings | Dividends | Book Value |
|---|---|---|---|---|---|---|
| **12/06** | 35.84 | 17 | 12 | 2.24 | 1.10 | 13.30 |
| **12/05** | 29.40 | 19 | 14 | 1.77 | 0.96 | 11.76 |
| **12/04** | 26.64 | 14 | 11 | 1.88 | 0.82 | 22.68 |
| **12/03** | 21.88 | 10 | 7 | 2.12 | 0.77 | 18.65 |
| **12/02** | 17.34 | 29 | 19 | 0.68 | 0.72 | 13.73 |
| **Annual Growth** | 19.9% | — | — | 34.7% | 11.2% | (0.8%) |

# Praxair, Inc.

At Praxair, doing business is always a gas. The company produces and sells atmospheric gases (oxygen, nitrogen, argon, and others) as well as process and specialty gases (CO2, helium, and hydrogen) for the chemicals, food and beverage, semiconductor, and health care industries. Depending on a client company's gas needs, Praxair can build an on-site gas plant or provide gases by the cylinder. The company's Praxair Surface Technologies subsidiary supplies high-temperature and corrosion-resistant metallic, ceramic, and powder coatings mainly to the aircraft, plastics, and primary metals industries. Praxair Healthcare Services supplies hospitals and the medical homecare industry.

In 2006 the company sold the aviation repair operations of the Surface Technologies unit. That business repairs a number of aviation engine and airframe parts and applies protective coatings to those parts and serves both commercial and military sectors. The company sold Praxair Aviation Services to Gridiron Capital and Skyview Capital, which have created a new company called PAS Technologies to house the operations.

Also that year, the company's distribution unit acquired Medical Gas, Inc. of Illinois and Withrow Oxygen Service of California. The following year Praxair moved again into Canada with the acquisition of Blue Rhino's tank-exchange business. (Blue Rhino is a part of Ferrellgas Partners.) The business will be re-branded with Praxair's own PropaneQuikSwap name.

## HISTORY

The origins of Praxair date to the work of Karl von Linde, a professor of mechanical engineering at the College of Technology in Munich, Germany, in the late 1800s. In 1895 he created the cryogenic air liquefier. Von Linde built his first oxygen-production plant in 1902 and a nitrogen plant in 1904, and in the first decade of the 20th century, he built a number of air-separation plants throughout Europe.

By 1907 von Linde had moved to the US and founded Linde Air Products in Cleveland, to extract oxygen from air. Linde Air Products joined rival Union Carbide in 1911 in experimenting with the production of acetylene; it became a unit of Union Carbide in 1917. America's war effort and economic expansion in the 1920s spurred the development of new uses for industrial gases. Union Carbide's Linde unit also contributed to the development of the atomic bomb in the 1940s when its scientists perfected a process for refining uranium.

As Union Carbide expanded worldwide over the next two decades, Linde became America's #1 producer of industrial gases. In the 1960s Linde expanded into oxygen-fired furnaces for steel production and the use of nitrogen in refrigerators. By the early 1980s Linde accounted for 11% of Union Carbide's annual sales.

The disastrous chemical accident at Union Carbide's plant in Bhopal, India, in 1984, coupled with heavy debt and falling sales, forced Union Carbide to reorganize. In 1992 Linde was spun off as Praxair. William Lichtenberger, former president of Union Carbide, headed the new company and pushed global expansion. Two years later Praxair set up China's first helium transfill plants for medical magnetic resonance imaging.

In 1995 the company began operations in India and Peru.

In 1996 Praxair Surface Technologies bought Miller Thermal (thermal spray coatings) and Maxima Air Separation Center (industrial and specialty gases, Israel). Also that year the company picked up $60 million when it sold the Linde name and trademark to Linde AG, a German engineering and industrial gas company. Praxair purchased and then spun off Chicago Bridge & Iron. The company kept only its Liquid Carbonic division, the world's leading supplier of carbon dioxide for processing. The move opened up a new market in carbonated beverages for Praxair.

In 1997 and 1998 Praxair constructed plants and, to control its own delivery systems, acquired 20 packaged-gases distributors in the US and one in Germany. The company also formed a joint venture in China to produce high-purity nitrogen and other specialty gases for electronics and then teamed up with rival L'Air Liquide in a production joint venture.

Praxair supplied an argon-based protection system for the Shroud of Turin's public display in Italy in 1998. It also installed the industry's first small on-site hydrogen-generating system at an Indiana powdered-metals plant. In 1999 the company formed a global alliance with German pharmaceutical and chemicals company Merck KgaA to provide gases and chemicals to the semiconductor industry. The same year Praxair acquired Materials Research Corporation, a maker of thin-film deposition materials for semiconductors, and the TAFA Group, which makes thermal-spray equipment and related products.

In 2001 Praxair underwent a restructuring that included layoffs in its surface technologies unit (hurt by the decline in jet orders) and Brazilian operations. The next year the company started work on a new plant that will serve Singapore's high-tech industry. Praxair boosted its health care segment with the acquisition of Alpine Medicine.

In 2004 Praxair Healthcare Services bought Home Care Supply for $245 million. With Home Care Supply joining the company's existing operations, the combined Healthcare Services unit grew its sales to $750 million worldwide, just over 10% of Praxair's total annual sales. The home care market became more important for Praxair as the company saw high growth potential in it (and high margins) and wanted to be able to compete with rivals Air Liquide and Air Products.

The company bought some of Air Liquide's German assets for about $650 million later that year. Due to antitrust requirements, the French company needed to dispose of the businesses after buying much of Messer Griesheim earlier in the year. The acquisition put Praxair's European sales over $1 billion annually.

## EXECUTIVES

**Chairman, President, and CEO:** Stephen F. (Steve) Angel, age 51
**EVP:** Ricardo S. Malfitano, age 48, $498,333 pay
**EVP and CFO:** James S. (Jim) Sawyer, age 50, $481,250 pay
**SVP and CTO:** Steven L. Lerner
**SVP; President, North American Industrial Gases (NAIG), Praxair Canada, and Praxair Mexico:** James J. (Jim) Fuchs, age 54, $395,083 pay
**VP, Communications and Public Relations:** Nigel D. Muir
**SVP, General Counsel, and Secretary:** James T. Breedlove, age 59
**VP, Global Sales:** Jeffrey P. (Jeff) Standish
**VP, Healthcare; President, Praxair Healthcare Services:** George P. Ristevski

**VP, Human Resources:** Sally A. Savoia
**VP, Strategic Planning and Marketing:** Sunil Mattoo
**VP, Tax:** S. Mark Seymour
**VP and Treasurer:** Michael (Mike) Allan
**VP and Controller:** Patrick M. (Pat) Clark, age 45
**VP, Financial Services and CIO:** M. Melissa Buckwalter
**VP; President, White Martins Gases Industriais Ltda. (Brazil):** Domingos H. G. Bulus, age 45
**VP, Global Supply Systems:** Daniel H. Yankowski
**VP; President, Praxair Europe:** Randy S. Kramer, age 54
**Director, Investor Relations:** Elizabeth T. (Liz) Hirsch
**Auditors:** PricewaterhouseCoopers LLP

## LOCATIONS

**HQ:** Praxair, Inc.
39 Old Ridgebury Rd., Danbury, CT 06810
**Phone:** 203-837-2000 **Fax:** 716-879-2040
**Web:** www.praxair.com

Praxair's operations include more than 350 cryogenic air-separation plants throughout the Americas, Asia, and Europe.

### 2006 Sales and Operating Income

| | Sales | | Operating Income | |
|---|---|---|---|---|
| | $ mil. | % of total | $ mil. | % of total |
| North America | 4,696 | 56 | 822 | 54 |
| South America | 1,348 | 16 | 252 | 17 |
| Europe | 1,163 | 14 | 266 | 18 |
| Asia | 636 | 8 | 111 | 7 |
| Surface Technologies (global) | 481 | 6 | 68 | 4 |
| **Total** | **8,324** | **100** | **1,519** | **100** |

## PRODUCTS/OPERATIONS

### Selected Products and Services

Atmospheric Gases
- Argon
- Nitrogen
- Oxygen
- Rare gases

Process Gases
- Acetylene
- Carbon dioxide
- Carbon monoxide
- Electronic gases
- Helium
- Hydrogen
- Specialty gases

Surface Technologies
- Ceramic coatings and powders
- Electric arc, plasma, and high-velocity oxygen fuel spray equipment
- Industrial gas-production equipment
- Metallic coatings and powders

## COMPETITORS

Air Products
Airgas
Balchem
Chromalloy Gas Turbine Corporation
GKN Aerospace Chem-Tronics
L'Air Liquide
Linde
Teleflex

## HISTORICAL FINANCIALS

Company Type: Public

### Income Statement

FYE: December 31

| | REVENUE ($ mil.) | NET INCOME ($ mil.) | NET PROFIT MARGIN | EMPLOYEES |
|---|---|---|---|---|
| **12/06** | 8,324 | 988 | 11.9% | 27,042 |
| **12/05** | 7,656 | 726 | 9.5% | 27,306 |
| **12/04** | 6,594 | 697 | 10.6% | 27,020 |
| **12/03** | 5,613 | 585 | 10.4% | 25,438 |
| **12/02** | 5,128 | 409 | 8.0% | 25,010 |
| **Annual Growth** | 12.9% | 24.7% | — | 2.0% |

### 2006 Year-End Financials

Debt ratio: 65.5%
Return on equity: 23.4%
Cash ($ mil.): 36
Current ratio: 1.17
Long-term debt ($ mil.): 2,981
No. of shares (mil.): 321
Dividends
Yield: 1.7%
Payout: 33.3%
Market value ($ mil.): 19,037

### Stock History

NYSE: PX

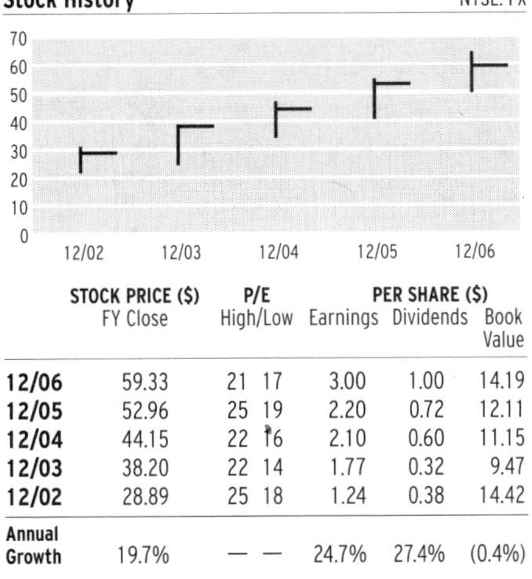


| | STOCK PRICE ($) FY Close | P/E High | P/E Low | PER SHARE ($) Earnings | Dividends | Book Value |
|---|---|---|---|---|---|---|
| **12/06** | 59.33 | 21 | 17 | 3.00 | 1.00 | 14.19 |
| **12/05** | 52.96 | 25 | 19 | 2.20 | 0.72 | 12.11 |
| **12/04** | 44.15 | 22 | 16 | 2.10 | 0.60 | 11.15 |
| **12/03** | 38.20 | 22 | 14 | 1.77 | 0.32 | 9.47 |
| **12/02** | 28.89 | 25 | 18 | 1.24 | 0.38 | 14.42 |
| **Annual Growth** | 19.7% | — | — | 24.7% | 27.4% | (0.4%) |

# Precision Castparts

You won't find any casting couches at Precision Castparts Corp. (PCC). The company is a leading maker of investment castings used in aerospace and power generation applications. Its products include jet engine parts, fluid management valves, and deep-hole boring tools. The cyclical aerospace market still accounts for just more than half of PCC's sales, despite several company acquisitions in the fluid management, metalworking tools, and pulp and paper industries. PCC's aerospace customers include jet engine makers General Electric and Pratt & Whitney.

The company has entered other markets — in part to offset the cyclical nature of the aerospace industry — both by adapting its existing know-how to industrial uses and by acquiring market leaders in niche metals and precision metalworking segments.

Since the dark, immediate post-9/11 days, the commercial aerospace industry has enjoyed a cyclical upswing. PCC's aerospace fortunes have improved with contracts related to the Airbus A380 and the Boeing 787.

In 2006 PCC bought Special Metals Corporation (SMC), a maker of nickel alloys and super alloys, for $295 million in cash and the assumption of $245 million in SMC debt. PCC intends to use SMC's product as raw materials for its own aircraft engine components. SMC also serves the automotive, chemical, and power generation industries. Later in 2006 PCC bought Shur-Lok Corporation, a manufacturer of aerospace fasteners. The acquisition, combined with the 2005 purchase of Air Industries Corporation, helped to further PCC's desire to grow its airframe fasteners business.

Early in 2007 PCC completed the purchase of GSC, a leading maker of aluminum and steel structural investment casting for the aerospace, energy, and medical markets. Later that year PCC again enhanced its aerospace fastener operations when it bought Cherry Aerospace LLC from Acument Global Technologies for about $300 million. Cherry is a maker of rivets, blind bolts, and other aerospace fasteners.

Later in 2007 PCC agreed to buy Caledonian Alloys Group Limited, a provider of nickel superalloy and titanium revert solutions for the aerospace and industrial gas turbine industries. Revert are byproducts of metalwork manufacturing processes. Revert includes metal chips, bar ends, and forging flash.

GE is by far the company's largest customer, accounting for 11% of sales, but PCC's reliance on the industrial giant is lessening year by year. In fiscal 2006 GE accounted for nearly 17% of sales; in fiscal 2003 GE accounted for nearly a third of sales.

## HISTORY

The history of Precision Castparts Corp. (PCC) is not as precise as its castings. The Oregon Saw Company was founded in 1949 and sold in 1953; its buyer wanted neither the future PCC nor a power tools unit, so the two became Omark Industries. In 1956 a buyer purchased the power tool business but wasn't interested in castings; that operation was spun off as Precision Castparts Corp.

In the early 1950s a group of Oregon Saw's casting employees developed a process for producing parts as large as 60 inches by use of investment casting, making products that rivaled the strength of forged and machined parts at a fraction of the cost. After a two-year search, they landed their first aerospace customer — Air Research Corp. — with many to follow. The higher operating temperatures generated by aircraft engines led the company to buy a vacuum furnace in 1959 to fabricate parts that could tolerate greater heat; two more vacuum furnaces were added and sales vaulted toward $10 million by 1967. PCC went public in 1968 and continued to grow. In 1976 the company acquired Centaur Cast Alloys (small investment castings, UK) to make parts for the European aerospace industry. By that time General Electric (GE) and Pratt & Whitney accounted for most of PCC's business. Edward Cooley, who had masterminded the company's growth since incorporation, forged ahead with plans to double production capacity.

In 1980 the airline industry crashed, but PCC's sales held at about $90 million. Structural airplane products soon picked up, and in 1984 the company bought two titanium foundries in France. To diversify, it added TRW's cast airfoils (used in aircraft engines and industrial gas turbines) division in 1986. That acquisition, renamed PCC Airfoils, increased PCC's annual sales by about 80%; sales reached $443 million by 1989.

The company broadened its offerings again in 1991 when it acquired Advanced Forming Technology, which made small, complex, metal-injection molded parts used in everything from adding machines to military ordnance. The early 1990s recession hit the airline industry and sales dropped. Cooley retired as chairman in 1994 and GE veteran William McCormick replaced him. The next year PCC acquired Quamco, Inc. (industrial tools and machines). In 1996 PCC flowed into the fluid management market with the acquisition of NEWFLO for about $300 million.

In 1997 PCC spent $437 million to acquire seven more companies that helped boost sales 75% from 1996 levels. Having reduced dependence on sales to the aerospace industry to just over 50%, PCC began consolidating operations and closing plants to reduce costs.

The company continued to diversify through acquisitions in 1999, but it also expanded its aerospace operations with the purchase of Wyman-Gordon, a leading maker of advanced metal forgings for the aerospace market. PCC's 2000 acquisitions included the aerospace division of United Engineering Forgings and Germany-based Convey Engineering (heavy-duty valves). The next year the company bought the assets of Netherlands-based Wouter Witzel and the US's Drop Dies and Forgings Company (renamed Wyman-Gordon Cleveland). In 2002 PCC bought the rest of Western Australian Specialty Alloys (casting and forging alloys) for $27.6 million in cash and PCC shares.

In 2003 Precision Castparts' PCC Structurals unit reached a $400 million agreement with Rolls-Royce to supply large titanium and steel castings. That year the company acquired SPS Technologies, a producer of fasteners and other metal components for the aerospace, automotive, and industrial markets. In 2004 subsidiary SPS Aerospace Fasteners signed a four-year deal with Airbus worth about $72 million to supply collars, nuts, studs, and titanium pins to Airbus plants across Europe.

PCC acquired Air Industries Corporation in early 2005.

## EXECUTIVES

**Chairman and CEO:** Mark Donegan, age 50, $2,328,450 pay
**SVP; President, Fastener Products Group:** Steven G. (Steve) Hackett, $882,910 pay
**SVP; President, Industrial Products Group:** Dennis L. Konkol, age 47
**SVP; President, PCC Structurals:** Ross M. Lienhart, age 53
**SVP; President, Wyman-Gordon:** Christopher L. (Chris) Ayers
**SVP and CFO:** William D. (Bill) Larsson, age 61, $996,450 pay
**SVP; President, PCC Airfoils:** Kenneth D. (Ken) Buck, age 46, $928,151 pay
**VP, Corporate Controller, and Assistant Secretary:** Shawn R. Hagel, age 40
**VP and Chief Information Officer:** Byron J. Gaddis, age 49
**VP, Corporate Taxes, and Assistant Secretary:** Mark R. Roskopf, age 44
**VP, Regulatory, Legal Affairs, and Secretary:** Roger A. Cooke, age 57, $742,295 pay
**VP, Strategic Planning and Corporate Development:** Kirk G. Pulley, age 37
**VP, Treasurer, and Assistant Secretary:** Geoffrey A. (Geoff) Hawkes, age 47
**Director, Communications:** Dwight E. Weber
**Auditors:** Deloitte & Touche LLP

## LOCATIONS

**HQ:** Precision Castparts Corp.
4650 SW Macadam Ave., Ste. 440,
Portland, OR 97239
**Phone:** 503-417-4800 **Fax:** 503-417-4817
**Web:** www.precast.com

**2007 Sales**

| | $ mil. | % of total |
|---|---|---|
| US | 4,249.0 | 79 |
| UK | 746.1 | 14 |
| Other countries | 366.1 | 7 |
| **Total** | **5,361.2** | **100** |

## PRODUCTS/OPERATIONS

**2007 Sales**

| | $ mil. | % of total |
|---|---|---|
| Forged products | 2,309.5 | 43 |
| Investment cast products | 1,797.9 | 34 |
| Fastener products | 1,253.8 | 23 |
| **Total** | **5,361.2** | **100** |

**2007 Sales by Industry**

| | $ mil. | % of total |
|---|---|---|
| Aerospace | 2,828.4 | 53 |
| Power generation | 1,131.7 | 21 |
| General industrial | 1,074.6 | 20 |
| Automotive | 326.5 | 6 |
| **Total** | **5,361.2** | **100** |

## COMPETITORS

Alcoa
Allegheny Technologies
Carpenter Technology
Citation
Crane
Eaton
Georg Fischer
Goodrich
Hawk
Haynes International
Kennametal
Ladish Co.
LISI
Roper Industries
Sumitomo
Sumitomo Metal Industries
Swagelok
ThyssenKrupp
Tomkins
United Technologies
V & M Tubes (USA)

## HISTORICAL FINANCIALS

Company Type: Public

**Income Statement** FYE: Sunday nearest March 31

| | REVENUE ($ mil.) | NET INCOME ($ mil.) | NET PROFIT MARGIN | EMPLOYEES |
|---|---|---|---|---|
| **3/07** | 5,361 | 633 | 11.8% | 19,800 |
| **3/06** | 3,546 | 351 | 9.9% | 16,000 |
| **3/05** | 2,919 | (2) | — | 15,800 |
| **3/04** | 2,175 | 118 | 5.4% | 15,700 |
| **3/03** | 2,117 | 124 | 5.9% | 11,900 |
| **Annual Growth** | 26.1% | 50.2% | — | 13.6% |

**2007 Year-End Financials**

Debt ratio: 11.3%
Return on equity: 25.4%
Cash ($ mil.): 150
Current ratio: 1.23
Long-term debt ($ mil.): 319
No. of shares (mil.): 137
Dividends
Yield: 0.1%
Payout: 2.6%
Market value ($ mil.): 14,277

**Stock History** NYSE: PCP

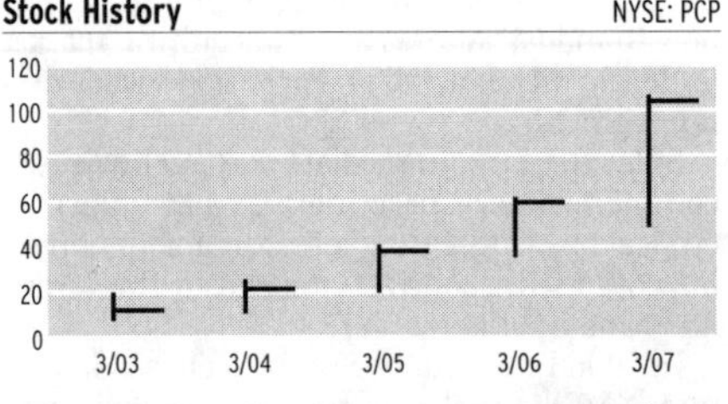


| | STOCK PRICE ($) FY Close | P/E High | P/E Low | PER SHARE ($) Earnings | Dividends | Book Value |
|---|---|---|---|---|---|---|
| **3/07** | 104.05 | 23 | 11 | 4.59 | 0.12 | 20.67 |
| **3/06** | 59.40 | 24 | 14 | 2.58 | 0.10 | 15.84 |
| **3/05** | 38.00 | — | — | (0.01) | 0.06 | 26.91 |
| **3/04** | 21.51 | 24 | 11 | 1.02 | 0.06 | 26.50 |
| **3/03** | 12.14 | 16 | 7 | 1.17 | 0.06 | 20.12 |
| **Annual Growth** | 71.1% | — | — | 40.7% | 18.9% | 0.7% |

# PricewaterhouseCoopers International

Not merely the firm with the longest one-word name, PricewaterhouseCoopers (PwC) is also one of the world's largest accounting firms, formed when Price Waterhouse merged with Coopers & Lybrand in 1998, passing then-leader Andersen. The accountancy has some 770 offices in 149 countries around the world, providing clients with services in three lines of business: Assurance (including financial and regulatory reporting), Tax, and Advisory. The umbrella entity for the PwC worldwide organization (officially PricewaterhouseCoopers International) is one of accounting's Big Four, along with Deloitte Touche Tohmatsu, Ernst & Young, and KPMG. PwC serves some of the world's largest businesses, as well as smaller firms.

PwC puts its heft to good use: Non-North American clients make up nearly two-thirds of the firm's sales. Its bottom line, though, changed significantly in 2002, when PwC sold its consulting arm to IBM. A separation had been under consideration for years in light of SEC concerns about conflicts of interest when firms perform auditing and consulting for the same clients. The collapse of Enron and concomitant downfall of Enron's auditor and PwC's erstwhile peer Andersen undoubtedly hastened plans to spin off PwC's consultancy via an IPO, which was scrapped in favor of the IBM deal.

PwC has expanded in developing economies, including Brazil, China, India, and Russia; business also got a temporary boost from the implementation of such new regulatory and financial reporting rules as the International Financial Reporting Standards and the Sarbanes-Oxley Act.

Like the other members of the Big Four, PwC picked up business and talent as scandal-felled Andersen was winding down its operations in 2002. The former Andersen organization in China and Hong Kong joined PwC, accounting for about 70% of the approximately 3,500 Andersen alumni that came aboard.

The company endured a two-month suspension in Japan in 2006 after three partners of its firm there were implicated in a fraud investigation involving a PwC client, Kanebo. To distance itself from the scandal PwC's existing Japanese firm was renamed and a second firm was launched.

The following year US arm PricewaterhouseCoopers agreed to pay a whopping $225 million to settle a class-action lawsuit related to the Tyco International financial scandal.

## HISTORY

In 1850 Samuel Price founded an accounting firm in London and in 1865 took on partner Edwin Waterhouse. The firm and the industry grew rapidly, thanks to the growth of stock exchanges that required uniform financial statements from listees. By the late 1800s Price Waterhouse (PW) had become the world's best-known accounting firm.

US offices were opened in the 1890s, and in 1902 United States Steel chose the firm as its auditor. PW benefited from tough audit requirements instituted after the 1929 stock market crash. In 1935 the firm was given the prestigious job of handling Academy Awards balloting. It started a management consulting service in

1946. But PW's dominance slipped in the 1960s, as it gained a reputation as the most traditional and formal of the major firms.

Coopers & Lybrand, the product of a 1957 transatlantic merger, wrote the book on auditing. Lybrand, Ross Bros. & Montgomery was formed in 1898 by William Lybrand, Edward Ross, Adam Ross, and Robert Montgomery. In 1912 Montgomery wrote *Montgomery's Auditing,* which became the bible of accounting.

Cooper Brothers was founded in 1854 in London by William Cooper, eldest son of a Quaker banker. In 1957 Lybrand joined up to form Coopers & Lybrand. During the 1960s the firm expanded into employee benefits and internal control consulting, building its technology capabilities in the 1970s as it studied ways to automate the audit process.

Coopers & Lybrand lost market share as mergers reduced the Big Eight accounting firms to the Big Six. After the savings and loan debacle of the 1980s, investors and the government wanted accounting firms held liable not only for the form of audited financial statements but for their veracity. In 1992 the firm paid $95 million to settle claims of defrauded investors in MiniScribe, a failed disk-drive maker. Other hefty payments followed, including a $108 million settlement relating to the late Robert Maxwell's defunct media empire.

In 1998 Price Waterhouse and Coopers & Lybrand combined PW's strength in the media, entertainment, and utility industries, and Coopers & Lybrand's focus on telecommunications and mining. But the merger brought some expensive legal baggage involving Coopers & Lybrand's performance of audits related to a bid-rigging scheme involving former Arizona governor Fife Symington.

Further growth plans fell through in 1999 when merger talks between PwC and Grant Thornton International failed. The year 2000 began on a sour note: An SEC conflict-of-interest probe turned up more than 8,000 alleged violations, most involving PwC partners owning stock in their firm's audit clients.

As the SEC grew ever more shrill in its denunciation of the potential conflicts of interest arising from auditing companies that the firm hoped to recruit or retain as consulting clients, PwC saw the writing on the wall and in 2000 began making plans to split the two operations. As part of this move, the company downsized and reorganized many of its operations.

The following year PwC paid $55 million to shareholders of MicroStrategy Inc., who charged that the audit firm defrauded them by approving the client firm's inflated earnings and revenues figures.

The separation of PwC's auditing and consulting functions finally became a reality in 2002, when IBM bought the consulting business. (The acquisition took the place of a planned spinoff.) In 2003 former client AMERCO (parent of U-Haul) sued PwC for $2.5 billion, claiming negligence and fraud in relation to a series of events that led to AMERCO restating its results. The suit was settled for more than $50 million the following year.

In 2005 PwC was ranked among the Top 10 companies in the US for working mothers by *Working Mother* magazine.

## EXECUTIVES

**Chairman, UK:** Kieran C. Poynter
**Chairman and Senior Partner US:** Dennis M. Nally
**Global CEO and Global Board Member:** Samuel A. (Sam) DiPiazza Jr., age 54
**Global Managing Partner, Advisory and Tax:** Eugene (Gene) Donnelly
**Global Managing Partner, Assurance:** Robert (Rob) Ward
**Global Managing Partner, Markets and Operations:** Paul Boorman
**Global Co-Leader, People:** Richard L. Baird
**Global Managing Partner, Markets:** Willem L. J. Bröcker
**Global Managing Partner, Risk and Quality:** Michael O. (Mike) Gagnon
**Global General Counsel; Acting US General Counsel:** Lawrence W. Keeshan
**Global Leader, Industries:** Alec N. Jones
**Global Leader, Regulatory and Public Policy:** Richard R. Kilgust
**Senior Partner and CEO, Australia:** Anthony P.D. Harrington
**CEO and Senior Partner of PricewaterhouseCoopers LLP, Canada:** Christie J. B. Clark
**Territory/Regional Leader, Central and Eastern Europe:** John K. Heywood
**Chairman, Asia 7 Leadership Team; Executive Chairman, PricewaterhouseCoopers Singapore:** Gautam Banerjee
**Senior Partner, Continental Europe:** Wolfgang Wagner
**Senior Partner, South and Central America:** Luis E. Frisoni Jr.
**Global Leader, Entertainment and Media Practice:** R. Wayne Jackson
**Global Leader, Transaction Services:** Colin McKay, age 50
**Global Strategy Leader:** Edgargo Pappacena
**Global Co-Leader, Human Capital:** Marie-Jeanne Chèvremont-Lorenzini
**Senior Managing Director, Global Public Relations:** Peter Horowitz

## LOCATIONS

**HQ:** PricewaterhouseCoopers International Limited
300 Madison Ave., 24th Fl., New York, NY 10017
**Phone:** 646-471-4000 **Fax:** 813-286-6000
**Web:** www.pwcglobal.com

PricewaterhouseCoopers has more than 770 offices in 149 countries.

### 2006 Sales

| | % of total |
|---|---|
| Europe | |
| Western Europe | 41 |
| Central & Eastern Europe | 2 |
| North America & Caribbean | 38 |
| Asia | 10 |
| Australasia & Pacific Islands | 4 |
| Middle East & Africa | 3 |
| South & Central America | 2 |
| **Total** | **100** |

## PRODUCTS/OPERATIONS

### 2006 Sales by Industry

| | % of total |
|---|---|
| Industrial Products | 17 |
| Banking & Capital Markets | 11 |
| Retail & Consumer | 11 |
| Investment Management | 10 |
| Technology | 9 |
| Professional Services | 9 |
| Energy, Utilities & Mining | 8 |
| Insurance | 5 |
| Entertainment & Media | 5 |
| Infocomm | 4 |
| Automotive | 3 |
| Health Care | 3 |
| Government | 3 |
| Pharmaceuticals | 2 |
| **Total** | **100** |

### 2006 Sales

| | % of total |
|---|---|
| Assurance | 54 |
| Tax | 25 |
| Advisory | 21 |
| **Total** | **100** |

### Selected Products and Services

Audit and Assurance
- Actuarial services
- Assistance on capital market transactions
- Corporate reporting improvement
- Financial accounting
- Financial statement audit
- IFRS reporting
- Independent controls and systems process assurance
- Internal audit
- Regulatory compliance and reporting
- Sarbanes-Oxley compliance
- Sustainability reporting

Crisis Management
- Business recovery services
- Dispute analysis and investigations

Human Resources
- Change and program effectiveness
- HR management
- International assignments
- Reward

Performance improvement
- Financial effectiveness
- Governance, risk, and compliance
- IT effectiveness

Tax
- Compliance
- EU direct tax
- International assignments
- International tax structuring
- Mergers and acquisitions
- Transfer pricing

Transactions
- Accounting valuations
- Advice on fundraising
- Bid support and bid defense services
- Commercial and market due diligence
- Economics
- Financial due diligence
- Independent expert opinions
- Mergers and acquisitions advisory
- Modeling and business planning
- Post deal services
- Private equity advisory
- Privatization advice
- Project finance
- Public company advisory
- Structuring services
- Tax valuations
- Valuation consulting

## COMPETITORS

Bain & Company
Baker Tilly International
BDO International
Booz Allen
Boston Consulting
Deloitte
Ernst & Young
Grant Thornton International
H&R Block
Hewitt Associates
KPMG
Marsh & McLennan
McKinsey & Company
Towers Perrin
Watson Wyatt

## HISTORICAL FINANCIALS

Company Type: Partnership

**Income Statement** FYE: June 30

| | REVENUE ($ mil.) | NET INCOME ($ mil.) | NET PROFIT MARGIN | EMPLOYEES |
|---|---|---|---|---|
| **6/06** | 21,986 | — | — | 142,162 |
| **6/05** | 18,998 | — | — | 130,203 |
| **6/04** | 16,283 | — | — | 122,471 |
| **6/03** | 14,683 | — | — | 122,820 |
| **6/02** | 13,800 | — | — | 124,563 |
| **Annual Growth** | 12.3% | — | — | 3.4% |

**Revenue History**

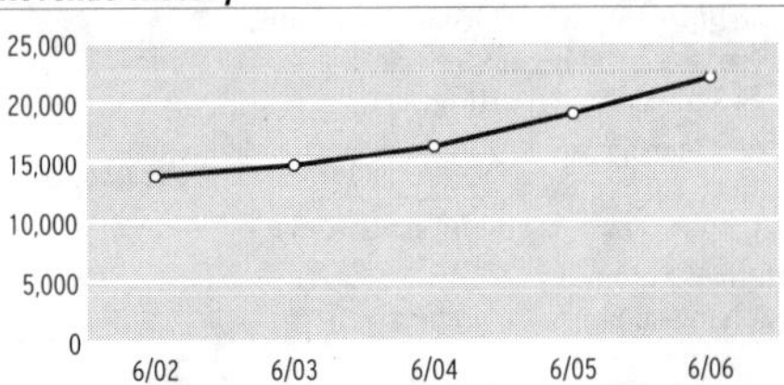


# PRIMEDIA Inc.

Targeted media publisher PRIMEDIA revs its engines for car-obsessed readers and other readers of specialty magazines. The firm publishes titles such as *Motor Trend, Automobile,* and *Lowrider*. PRIMEDIA had generated some 60% of its sales from its Enthusiast Media magazine publishing unit, which included auto titles as well as other niche magazines in a wide range of topics including sports and photography; however, in 2007 the company sold Enthusiast Media to Source Interlink for $1.2 billion in cash in order to focus on its Consumer Guides unit, which publishes and distributes free consumer guides (*Apartment Guide, Auto Guide, New Home Guide*). Investment firm Kohlberg Kravis Roberts owns about 60% of PRIMEDIA.

The company has transformed itself in recent years, streamlining its operations and emphasizing its stable of enthusiast titles. Among the changes it's made: selling or shuttering its mainstream titles including *Modern Bride, Seventeen, Teen,* and *New York*; selling its About online guide Web site to The New York Times Company; selling its business information magazine unit to Prism Business Media; selling its Workplace Learning division to Trinity Learning; and selling its crafts magazine division to Sandler Capital Management. The company also sold its hunting and fishing titles to InterMedia Outdoor for $170 million. PRIMEDIA says the sale of its Enthusiast Media business makes the company "virtually debt free."

The company has acquired Equine.com, an online marketplace for horse enthusiasts. The company has also tried new ventures such as a decision to make *Lowrider*-branded women's apparel and home goods. PRIMEDIA acquired a majority stake in Automotive.com with plans to buy the entire company by 2010. It also announced that it would launch a 24-hour TV network called Motor Trend TV in 2007 in a partnership with Multicast Networks Group.

The company bought RentalHouses.com in 2007 and will combine the online rental listings site with its other apartment listings properties at Rentals.com.

## HISTORY

With several publishing properties up for grabs and most potential buyers burdened by debt, investment firm Kohlberg Kravis Roberts (KKR) zeroed in on the publishing industry as a solid investment opportunity. KKR and three publishing executives, including future PRIMEDIA CEO William Reilly, set up K-III Holdings to acquire Intertec Publishing and Newbridge Communications for $320 million in 1989. Reilly and KKR had been buddies since KKR backed him in his bid to buy Macmillan in 1988, a battle he lost to Robert Maxwell. But Reilly did get something from Macmillan: He took 45 of the company's executives with him to K-III, including his entire management team.

The company bought *Weekly Reader,* Newfield Publications (sold 1995), and *Funk & Wagnalls* in 1991, a deal that doubled K-III's number of operating divisions. Later that year the group beat out several rival bidders to pick up several publications from Rupert Murdoch's News Corp. K-III paid $675 million for nine publications, including *Soap Opera Digest, Seventeen,* and the *Daily Racing Form.* By the end of 1992, K-III had spent $1.3 billion on acquisitions, but it had trouble starting its own magazines: Two publications test-marketed in 1993, *Soap Opera Illustrated* and *True News* (tabloid news), bombed.

*Funk & Wagnalls* acquired the *World Almanac* and the World Almanac Education division of United Media Publishing in 1993. K-III also bought directory publisher Nelson Publications that year. The firm acquired Channel One Network, office-skill trainer Katharine Gibbs Schools, and Haas Publishing (apartment rental guides) in 1994. K-III sold *Premiere* magazine in 1995 and went public that year.

K-III bought 14 magazines (including *Modern Bride*) from Anglo-Dutch publisher Reed Elsevier and acquired Westcott Communications, which provides educational and career training programs via satellite and videotape, in 1996. The following year the company divested several noncore businesses, including Katharine Gibbs Schools. It also changed its name to PRIMEDIA because, according to CEO Reilly, "K-III is a horrible name."

PRIMEDIA sold its supplemental education unit — including student magazine *Weekly Reader,* several reference publications (including *Funk & Wagnalls*), and a textbook and assessment publisher — to Ripplewood Holdings in 1999 for $400 million. Also that year Reilly announced his retirement from the company. Former NBC executive Tom Rogers replaced him.

In 2000, in order to further strengthen its online efforts, PRIMEDIA signed partnership deals with Internet investment firm CMGI and Liberty Media (each took a 5% stake in PRIMEDIA).

In 2001 PRIMEDIA expanded into new media through its purchase of Internet information guide publisher About for almost $700 million. In a move to boost its magazine business, the company bought 60 titles owned by Emap USA (*Teen, Motor Trend, Hot Rod*), paying its UK-based parent Emap $515 million. In early 2002 the company sold its *Modern Bride* magazine to Condé Nast Publications for $52 million. It also shut down its struggling *Teen* magazine, sold its *Chicago* magazine to the Tribune Company for $35 million, and sold its American Baby magazine group in 2002 to Meredith Corp. for $115 million

Rogers resigned in 2003 after a disagreement with the board and president Charles McCurdy took over as chief temporarily. Former technology publisher Kelly Conlin was named CEO in late 2003. The company sold several magazines that year, including *Seventeen* to Hearst Magazines and *New York* magazine for $55 million to a family trust headed by Bruce Wasserstein. Also that year the company divided up its Media Central unit to reduce overhead. In 2004, it sold its *Cable World* publication to PBI Media.

The company unloaded About to The New York Times Company in 2005. Also that year its Consumer Guides unit acquired the new-home listings site americanhomeguides.com. PRIMEDIA sold its Business Information segment to PBI Media (now named Prism Business Media) later in 2005. Chairman Dean Nelson took over as CEO and president that year, replacing Conlin.

In 2007 PRIMEDIA sold its Enthusiast Media division. In connection with the sale, the company appointed Robert Metz as president and CEO.

## EXECUTIVES

**Chairman, President, and CEO:** Dean B. Nelson, age 48, $1,112,885 pay
**Vice Chairman:** Beverly C. Chell, age 64, $581,250 pay (prior to title change)
**CFO:** Kim Payne
**EVP; CEO, Consumer Source:** Robert C. (Bob) Metz, age 54, $527,354 pay
**EVP Human Resources:** Michaelanne C. Discepolo, age 54
**SVP, Chief Accounting Officer, and Controller:** Robert J. Sforzo, age 60
**SVP; President and COO, Consumer Source; President, DistribuTech:** David Crawford, age 44, $447,143 pay
**SVP Investor Relations:** Eric M. Leeds, age 37
**SVP and Treasurer:** Carl Salas, age 46
**SVP Tax and Accounting:** Bruce Abrahams, age 42
**SVP, General Counsel, and Secretary:** Jason S. Thaler, age 35
**President, Apartment Publications Group:** Arlene Mayfield
**EVP and General Manager, Films Media Group:** Amy Bevilacqua
**SVP and Group Publisher, Action Sports Group:** Allen (Al) Crolius
**Auditors:** Deloitte & Touche LLP

## LOCATIONS

**HQ:** PRIMEDIA Inc.
745 5th Ave., New York, NY 10151
**Phone:** 212-745-0100 **Fax:** 212-745-0121
**Web:** www.primedia.com

## PRODUCTS/OPERATIONS

**2006 Sales**

| | $ mil. | % of total |
|---|---|---|
| Enthusiast media | 524.8 | 61 |
| Consumer guides | 324.5 | 38 |
| **Total** | **849.3** | **100** |

### Selected Operations

Apartment rental guides (print and online)
Channel One Network (television news for schools)
Directories and databases
  IntelliChoice (automotive)
Educational videos and CD-ROMs
Magazines
  *Automobile*
  *BoatWorks*
  *Broadcast Engineering*
  *Car And Driver*
  *Circulation Management* (joint venture with Red 7 Media)
  *Dirt Rider*
  *Equus*
  *Fleet Owner*
  *Folio* (joint venture with Red 7 Media)
  *Hot Rod*
  *Kagan World Media*
  *Lowrider*
  *Motor Trend*
  *Motorcycle*
  *Muscle Mustang & Fast Fords*
  *Power & MotorYacht*
  *Practical Horseman*
  *Road And Track*
  *Sail*
  *Simba*
  *Skateboarder*
  *Snowboarder*
  *Soap Opera Digest*
  *Soybean Digest*
  *Surfing*
  *Telephony*
  *Truckin'*
  *Vette*
  *Voyaging*
PRIMEDIA Ventures (Internet investments)
RetailVision (specialty magazine distributor)

## COMPETITORS

Advance Publications
Advanstar
Alloy
Bauer Publishing USA
Bertelsmann
Condé Nast
Discovery Communications
eBay
International Data Group
Lagardère Active Media
McGraw-Hill
Meredith
Move
PBS
Pearson
Penton Media
Reader's Digest
Reed Elsevier Group
Scholastic
Scholastic Library Publishing
Time
Trader Classified Media

## HISTORICAL FINANCIALS

Company Type: Public

### Income Statement

FYE: December 31

| | REVENUE ($ mil.) | NET INCOME ($ mil.) | NET PROFIT MARGIN | EMPLOYEES |
|---|---|---|---|---|
| **12/06** | 849 | 38 | 4.5% | 2,800 |
| **12/05** | 991 | 565 | 57.0% | 3,200 |
| **12/04** | 1,307 | 36 | 2.7% | 4,500 |
| **12/03** | 1,346 | 39 | 2.9% | 4,700 |
| **12/02** | 1,588 | (599) | — | 5,100 |
| **Annual Growth** | (14.5%) | — | — | (13.9%) |

### 2006 Year-End Financials

Debt ratio: —
Return on equity: —
Cash ($ mil.): 6
Current ratio: 1.09
Long-term debt ($ mil.): 1,317
No. of shares (mil.): 264
Dividends
  Yield: —
  Payout: —
Market value ($ mil.): 2,681

### Stock History

NYSE: PRM

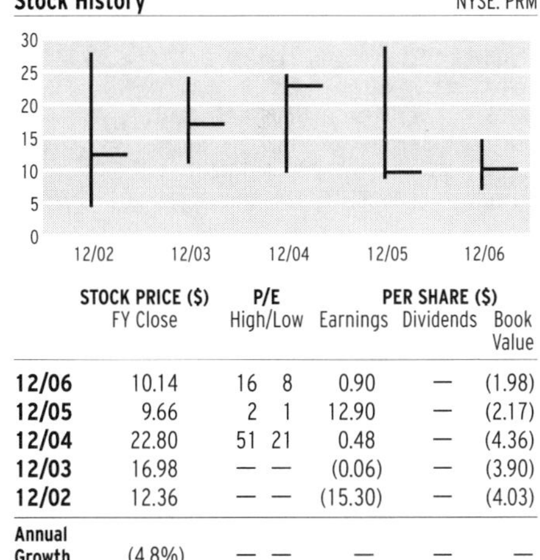


| | STOCK PRICE ($) FY Close | P/E High | P/E Low | PER SHARE ($) Earnings | Dividends | Book Value |
|---|---|---|---|---|---|---|
| **12/06** | 10.14 | 16 | 8 | 0.90 | — | (1.98) |
| **12/05** | 9.66 | 2 | 1 | 12.90 | — | (2.17) |
| **12/04** | 22.80 | 51 | 21 | 0.48 | — | (4.36) |
| **12/03** | 16.98 | — | — | (0.06) | — | (3.90) |
| **12/02** | 12.36 | — | — | (15.30) | — | (4.03) |
| **Annual Growth** | (4.8%) | — | — | — | — | — |

# Principal Financial Group

Ah, the circle of life. For a child in elementary school, avoiding the principal is paramount. However, folks looking toward retirement may actually seek out The Principal. Principal Financial Group (or The Principal) is the umbrella organization for a variety of financial service providers that offer pension products and services (the company is a top administrator of employer-sponsored retirement plans), mutual funds, annuities, and investment advice. Its insurance segment provides life and group life, health, and disability coverage. To compete with banks encroaching on the company's territory and to maximize customer asset retention, subsidiary Principal Bank offers online banking.

The Principal has approximately 18 million customers and more than $250 billion of assets under management. Its products are offered through a nationwide network of independent brokers and agents, as well as through its own sales force.

With operations in about a dozen countries, The Principal aims to become a global player in retirement services, targeting countries in Asia and Latin America that rely on private-sector defined-contribution pension plans to accommodate their growing number of retirees. In the US, the company courts firms with fewer than 1,000 employees for its insurance and pension products and large institutional clients for its asset management operations, which include Principal Global Investors.

At the end of 2006 The Principal finalized its purchase of WM Advisors, the former mutual fund operations of the largest US thrift, Washington Mutual.

## HISTORY

Principal Financial was founded as the Bankers Life Association in 1879 by Edward Temple, a Civil War veteran and banker. Life insurance became popular after the war, but some dishonest insurers canceled customers' policies before they had to pay out benefits. Bankers Life, an assessable association (members shared the cost of death benefits as the claims arose), was intended to provide low-cost protection to bankers and their families. The company soon began offering life insurance to nonbankers, but it refused to insure women because of the high mortality rate among mothers during childbirth.

Bankers Life relied on volunteer workers until 1893. By 1900 it was operating in 21 states. Temple died in 1909, and two years later the company converted to a legal reserve mutual life insurance company with a new name: the Bankers Life Company. The conversion scared many customers away, however. About 50,000 policies were lost over the next three years. In 1915 Bankers Life began insuring women.

WWI slowed growth, and the 1918-1919 influenza epidemic, which killed many policyholders, hit the company hard. The Depression also stunted growth. In 1941 the firm started offering group life insurance, and during WWII it became a major force in that area.

Bankers Life grew through the 1950s and 1960s, adding individual accident and health insurance (1952) and other products. In 1968 it began offering variable annuities for profit-sharing plans and mutual funds, forming what are now Princor Financial Services and Principal Management. In 1977 Bankers Life introduced an adjustable life insurance product that allowed policyholders to change both premium costs and coverage.

In 1986 the company made a few name changes, becoming The Principal Financial Group and renaming its largest unit Principal Mutual Life Insurance (now Principal Life Insurance). That year Principal Financial acquired Eppler, Guerin & Turner, the largest independent stock brokerage firm in the Southwest.

In 1993 Principal Financial was issued Mexico's first new insurance license in 50 years; subsequent expansion included Argentina, China, and Spain.

In 1996 Principal Financial expanded its health care operations, purchasing third-party administrator The Admar Group. The next year the company bought the 76,000-member FHP of Illinois health plan. Despite this fast buildup, Principal Financial decided to exit the direct provision of health care; in 1997 it sold these operations to what is now Coventry Health Care for a 40% stake in the firm, which it also later sold.

Continuing to refocus, the company in 1998 sold its Principal Financial Securities brokerage and bought ReliaStar Mortgage to build a mortgage banking franchise. The company also launched online banking services. Also that year Principal Financial converted to a mutual holding structure. It formed joint ventures in such countries as Chile, Mexico, and India as part of its move into asset management overseas.

Principal Financial went public in 2001, trading on the New York Stock Exchange.

As with its health care operations, Principal Financial made a hasty exit from the mortgage business after building that part of its business through acquisitions. Amid rising interest rates and an industry-wide decrease in loan volume, the company sold its retail mortgage branches to American Home Mortgage in 2003, then sold its remaining mortgage banking business to Citigroup the following year. Also in 2004 the company bolstered its core operations by purchasing health care claims processor J.F. Molloy & Associates and the US trust operations of Dutch banking giant ABN AMRO.

## EXECUTIVES

**Chairman and CEO, Principal Financial Group and Principal Life:** J. Barry Griswell, age 58
**President, COO, and Director:** Larry D. Zimpleman, age 55, $1,321,062 pay (prior to promotion)
**President, Insurance and Financial Services:** John E. Aschenbrenner, age 57, $1,320,646 pay
**President, Global Asset Management:** James P. (Jim) McCaughan, age 53, $2,616,596 pay
**EVP and CFO, Principal Financial and Principal Life:** Michael H. Gersie, age 58, $945,304 pay
**EVP and General Counsel, Principal Financial Group and Principal Life:** Karen E. Shaff, age 52
**SVP and CIO:** Gary P. Scholten, age 49
**SVP and Corporate Secretary:** Joyce Nixson Hoffman
**SVP and Chief Actuary, Principal Financial and Principal Life:** Ellen Z. Lamale, age 53
**SVP, Human Resources:** James D. DeVries
**SVP and Deputy General Counsel:** Nora M. Everett
**SVP, Investor Relations:** Thomas J. (Tom) Graf
**SVP, Life and Health Distribution:** Margaret W. (Meg) Skinner
**SVP and Chief Marketing Officer:** Mary A. O'Keefe, age 50
**SVP, Principal Financial and Principal Life; President, Principal International:** Norman R. Sorensen, age 61
**VP, Executive Operations:** Lynn B. Graves
**Director, Consumer Health:** Jerry Ripperger
**Media Relations Officer:** Rhonda Clark-Leyda
**Auditors:** Ernst & Young LLP

## LOCATIONS

**HQ:** Principal Financial Group, Inc.
711 High St., Des Moines, IA 50392
**Phone:** 515-247-5111 **Fax:** 515-246-5475
**Web:** www.principal.com

Principal Financial Group has operations in Australia, Brazil, Chile, China, Hong Kong, India, Malaysia, Mexico, Singapore, the UK, and the US.

## PRODUCTS/OPERATIONS

### 2006 Sales

| | $ mil. | % of total |
|---|---|---|
| Premiums & other considerations | 4,305.3 | 44 |
| Net investment income | 3,618.0 | 37 |
| Fees & other revenues | 1,902.5 | 19 |
| Net capital losses | 44.7 | — |
| **Total** | **9,870.5** | **100** |

## COMPETITORS

Aetna
AIG
Allianz
Allstate
AXA
Blue Cross
CIGNA
Citigroup
CNA Financial
FMR
Guardian Life
The Hartford
ING
John Hancock
JPMorgan Chase
Liberty Mutual
Manulife Financial
MassMutual
MetLife
Morgan Stanley
Nationwide
Nationwide Financial
New York Life
Northwestern Mutual
Pacific Mutual
Prudential
State Farm
State Street
T. Rowe Price
Travelers Companies
UBS Financial Services
UnitedHealth Group
Unum Group
The Vanguard Group

## HISTORICAL FINANCIALS

Company Type: Public

### Income Statement

FYE: December 31

| | ASSETS ($ mil.) | NET INCOME ($ mil.) | INCOME AS % OF ASSETS | EMPLOYEES |
|---|---|---|---|---|
| **12/06** | 143,658 | 1,064 | 0.7% | 15,289 |
| **12/05** | 127,035 | 919 | 0.7% | 14,507 |
| **12/04** | 113,798 | 826 | 0.7% | 13,976 |
| **12/03** | 107,754 | 746 | 0.7% | 14,976 |
| **12/02** | 89,861 | 142 | 0.2% | 15,038 |
| **Annual Growth** | 12.4% | 65.4% | — | 0.4% |

### 2006 Year-End Financials

Equity as % of assets: 5.5%
Return on assets: 0.8%
Return on equity: 13.6%
Long-term debt ($ mil.): 1,554
No. of shares (mil.): 268
Dividends
Yield: 1.4%
Payout: 21.4%
Market value ($ mil.): 15,755
Sales ($ mil.): 9,871

### Stock History

NYSE: PFG

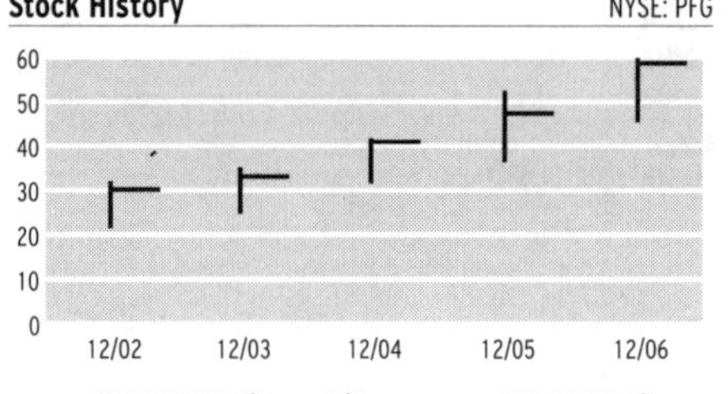


| | STOCK PRICE ($) FY Close | P/E High | P/E Low | PER SHARE ($) Earnings | Dividends | Book Value |
|---|---|---|---|---|---|---|
| **12/06** | 58.70 | 16 | 12 | 3.74 | 0.80 | 29.29 |
| **12/05** | 47.43 | 17 | 12 | 3.11 | 0.65 | 27.82 |
| **12/04** | 40.94 | 16 | 12 | 2.62 | 0.55 | 25.10 |
| **12/03** | 33.07 | 15 | 11 | 2.28 | 0.45 | 23.07 |
| **12/02** | 30.13 | 77 | 54 | 0.41 | 0.25 | 19.91 |
| **Annual Growth** | 18.1% | — | — | 73.8% | 33.7% | 10.1% |

# Procter & Gamble

The Procter & Gamble Company (P&G) is a brand behemoth. The world's #1 maker of household products courts market share and billion-dollar brands. P&G's business is divided into three global units: beauty care, global health and well being, and household care. It also makes pet food and water filters and produces soap operas (*As the World Turns*). More than 20 of P&G's brands are billion-dollar sellers (including Actonel, Always/Whisper, Braun, Bounty, Charmin, Crest, Downy/Lenor, Folgers, Gillette, Iams, Olay, Pampers, Pantene, Pringles, Tide, and Wella).

Few people worldwide go a day without using at least one product made by P&G. The company's some 300 brands are available in more than 180 countries. In addition to its billion-dollar sellers, other brands include such familiar names as Cascade, CoverGirl, Duracell, Herbal Essences, Mr. Clean, NyQuil, Oral-B, Safeguard, Scope, Tampax, and Vicks 44.

In one of its boldest moves, P&G bought The Gillette Company for about $57 billion in late 2005. The deal created the world's largest consumer products company, ahead of Unilever. The purchase added well-known complementary brands to P&G's already vast portfolio, such as Gillette razors and blades, Duracell batteries, Oral-B oral care items, and Braun appliances. Because some of the two companies' brands competed (such as P&G's Old Spice and Crest vs. Gillette's Right Guard and Oral-B) and to satisfy antitrust regulators, P&G divested certain assets. P&G also made plans to shed about 6,000 workers from both companies.

P&G has expanded its beauty business to improve its worldwide market share in that segment. Through a series of purchases that began in 2003, the firm now owns more than 95% of beauty care giant Wella, which sells its products in some 150 countries. As it reaches into another niche of the beauty market, P&G acquired HDS Cosmetics Lab, Inc., in early 2007 to secure its foothold in dermatology-focused skin care products. HDS makes the DDF Skin Care brand.

For years P&G has partnered with pharmaceutical firms to extend its reach into that industry. In 2006 P&G partnered with Aryx Therapeutics to develop that company's gastrointestinal disorder treatment. A deal with Inverness Medical Innovations formed a joint venture company (called SPD Swiss Precision Diagnostics GmbH ) that pairs Inverness's diagnostics expertise with P&G's marketing savvy. The joint venture firm, formed in May 2007, will make and market in-home diagnostic products, including pregnancy tests and ovulation/fertility monitoring products.

P&G also continues to be a player in the broadcast television industry. The consumer products giant is celebrating its long-standing relationship with CBS as the network renewed contracts for *Guiding Light* (which began as a radio program in 1937) and *As the World Turns* (which has been on the air for 50 years in 2006).

## HISTORY

Candle maker William Procter and soap maker James Gamble merged their small Cincinnati businesses in 1837, creating The Procter & Gamble Company (P&G), which incorporated in 1905. By 1859 P&G had become one of the largest companies in Cincinnati, with sales of $1 million. It introduced Ivory, a floating soap, in 1879, and Crisco shortening in 1911.

The Ivory campaign was one of the first to advertise directly to the consumer. Other advertising innovations included sponsorship of daytime radio dramas in 1932. P&G's first TV commercial, for Ivory, aired in 1939.

Family members headed the company until 1930, when William Deupree was named president. In the 29 years that Deupree served as president and then chairman, P&G became the largest US seller of packaged goods.

After years of researching cleansers for use in hard water, in 1947 P&G introduced Tide detergent. It began a string of acquisitions when it picked up Spic and Span (1945; sold 2001), Duncan Hines (1956; sold 1998), Charmin Paper Mills (1957), and Folgers Coffee (1963). P&G launched Crest toothpaste in 1955 and Head & Shoulders shampoo and Pampers disposable diapers in 1961.

Rely tampons were pulled from shelves in 1980 when investigators linked them to toxic shock syndrome. In 1985 P&G moved into health care when it purchased Richardson-Vicks (NyQuil, Vicks) and G.D. Searle's nonprescription drug division (Metamucil). The acquisitions of Noxell (1989; CoverGirl, Noxzema) and Max Factor (1991) made it a top cosmetics company in the US.

P&G began a major restructuring in 1993, cutting 13,000 jobs and closing 30 plants. The firm acquired Eagle Snacks from Anheuser-Busch in 1996 and sued rival Amway over rumors connecting P&G and its moon-and-stars logo to Satanism. (The suit was dismissed in 1999.) In 1997 it acquired Tambrands (Tampax tampons), making P&G #1 in feminine sanitary protection. Chairman John Pepper handed over his chairman and CEO title in 1999 to president Durk Jager, who promised five new products a year and a shakeup of the corporate culture.

In 1999 the company announced further reorganization plans, including 15,000 job cuts worldwide by 2005. With earnings flat, Jager resigned in 2000. P&G insider Alan G. Lafley immediately assumed the president and CEO duties, and Pepper returned to succeed Jager as chairman. In 2001 P&G announced job cuts for 9,600 employees to further reduce costs.That year P&G completed its purchase of the Clairol hair care company from Bristol-Myers Squibb for nearly $5 billion.

In 2002 P&G closed three Clairol plants, one warehouse, and one distribution center — eliminating about 750 jobs. In 2003 P&G entered the premium pet food market with its purchase of The Iams Company for $2.3 billion. And to secure its foothold in China, P&G bought the remaining 20% stake in its joint venture with Hutchison Whampoa China Ltd. in 2004 for $1.8 billion.

On the heels of its successful launch of Prilosec as an over-the-counter acid-reflux medication, P&G partnered with Watson Pharmaceuticals to develop the Intrinsa patch. What Viagra has done for men, P&G hoped Intrinsa will eventually do for women's sex drives. However, in 2004 the FDA delayed the debut of Intrinsa by demanding P&G collect additional safety data regarding the risk of heart attack in post-menopausal women already taking estrogen hormone therapy. P&G withdrew its Intrinsa application and plans to submit a new one to the FDA.

## EXECUTIVES

**Chairman, President, and CEO:** Alan G. (A.G.) Lafley, age 60
**President, Global Business Units:** Susan E. Arnold, age 53
**Vice Chairman, Global Brand Building Training:** Bruce L. Byrnes, age 59
**Vice Chairman and CFO:** Clayton C. Daley Jr., age 55
**COO:** Robert A. (Bob) McDonald, age 54
**EVP, Marketing and Sales:** Nicholas Munafo
**SVP, Human Resources, Global Household Care:** Richard G. Pease, age 56
**SVP, Corporate Research and Development:** Nabil Y. Sakkab, age 60
**Vice Chairman, Global Operations:** Werner Geissler, age 54
**Vice Chairman, Global Household Care:** Dimitri Panayotopoulos, age 55
**Group President, North America:** Edward D. Shirley, age 49
**Vice Chairman, Global Health and Well-Being:** Robert A. (Rob) Steele, age 52
**CTO:** George Gilbert Cloyd, age 61
**Chief Legal Officer and Secretary:** James J. Johnson, age 60
**Global External Relations Officer:** Charlotte R. Otto, age 54
**Global Human Resources Officer:** Richard L. (Dick) Antoine, age 61
**Global Product Supply Officer:** R. Keith Harrison Jr., age 59
**Global Marketing Officer:** James R. (Jim) Stengel, age 52
**Chief Information and Global Services Officer:** Filippo Passerini, age 50
**Manager, Global Media and Communication:** Bernhard Glock, age 45
**Auditors:** Deloitte & Touche LLP

## LOCATIONS

**HQ:** The Procter & Gamble Company
1 Procter & Gamble Plaza, Cincinnati, OH 45202
**Phone:** 513-983-1100 **Fax:** 513-983-9369
**Web:** www.pg.com

### 2007 Sales

| | $ mil. | % of total |
|---|---|---|
| US | 31,946 | 42 |
| Other countries | 44,530 | 58 |
| **Total** | **76,476** | **100** |

### 2007 Sales

| | % of total |
|---|---|
| North America | 46 |
| Western Europe | 23 |
| Developing Markets | 27 |
| Northeast Asia | 4 |
| **Total** | **100** |

## PRODUCTS/OPERATIONS

### 2007 Sales

| | $ mil. | % of total |
|---|---|---|
| Beauty & Health | | |
| Beauty | 22,981 | 30 |
| Health Care | 8,964 | 12 |
| Household Care | | |
| Fabric Care & Home Care | 18,971 | 25 |
| Baby Care & Family Care | 12,726 | 17 |
| Snacks, Coffee & Pet Care | 4,537 | 6 |
| Gillette Global Business Unit | | |
| Blades & Razors | 5,229 | 7 |
| Duracell & Braun | 4,031 | 5 |
| Corporate | (963) | (1) |
| **Total** | **76,476** | **100** |

### Selected Brand Names

Beauty Care
Clairol
CoverGirl
Gillette
Head & Shoulders
Herbal Essence
Hugo Boss
I-Iman
Ivory
Max Factor
Nice 'n Easy
Noxzema
Olay
Old Spice
Pantene Pro-V
Safeguard
Secret
Ultresse
Vidal Sassoon
Wella
Zest

Health Care
Crest
Intrinsa
Metamucil
NyQuil
Pepto-Bismol
Prilosec
Scope
Vicks 44

Food and Beverage
Eagle
Folgers
Millstone
Pringles

Pet Food
Eukanuba
Iams

Laundry and Cleaning
Bounce
Cascade
Cheer
Dawn
Downy
Dryel
Febreze
Joy
Lenor
Mr. Clean
Swiffer
Tide

Paper
Bounty
Charmin
Luvs
Pampers
Puffs
Tampax

## COMPETITORS

Alberto-Culver
Alticor
American Safety Razor
Amway
Avon
Bath & Body Works
Baxter of California
BIC
Body Shop
Bristol-Myers Squibb
Church & Dwight
Clorox
Colgate-Palmolive
Dial
Discus Dental
Dr. Bronner's
Energizer Holdings
Estée Lauder
Heinz
Henkel
Johnson & Johnson
Kimberly-Clark
Kraft
L'Oréal
L'Oréal USA
Mary Kay
MedPointe
Nestlé
PepsiCo
Personal Products Company
Pfizer
Philips Electronics
Playtex
Revlon
Sanofi-Aventis
SANYO
Sara Lee Household
S.C. Johnson
Scott's Liquid Gold
SEB
Shiseido
Spectrum Brands
Tom's of Maine
Turtle Wax
Unilever
VIVUS
Wyeth

## HISTORICAL FINANCIALS

Company Type: Public

### Income Statement

FYE: June 30

| | REVENUE ($ mil.) | NET INCOME ($ mil.) | NET PROFIT MARGIN | EMPLOYEES |
|---|---|---|---|---|
| **6/07** | 76,476 | 10,340 | 13.5% | 138,000 |
| **6/06** | 68,222 | 8,684 | 12.7% | 138,000 |
| **6/05** | 56,741 | 7,257 | 12.8% | 110,000 |
| **6/04** | 51,407 | 6,481 | 12.6% | 110,000 |
| **6/03** | 43,377 | 5,186 | 12.0% | 98,000 |
| **Annual Growth** | 15.2% | 18.8% | — | 8.9% |

### 2007 Year-End Financials

Debt ratio: 35.8%
Return on equity: 16.3%
Cash ($ mil.): 5,556
Current ratio: 0.78
Long-term debt ($ mil.): 23,375
No. of shares (mil.): 3,132
Dividends
Yield: 1.6%
Payout: 31.9%
Market value ($ mil.): 191,641

### Stock History

NYSE: PG

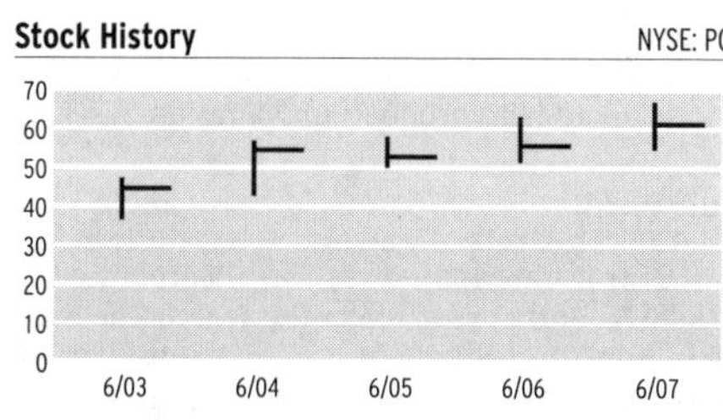


| | STOCK PRICE ($) FY Close | P/E High | P/E Low | PER SHARE ($) Earnings | Dividends | Book Value |
|---|---|---|---|---|---|---|
| **6/07** | 61.19 | 22 | 18 | 3.04 | 0.97 | 21.32 |
| **6/06** | 55.60 | 24 | 20 | 2.64 | 1.15 | 19.79 |
| **6/05** | 52.75 | 22 | 19 | 2.66 | 1.03 | 7.07 |
| **6/04** | 54.44 | 24 | 19 | 2.32 | 0.68 | 6.79 |
| **6/03** | 44.59 | 25 | 20 | 1.85 | 0.82 | 12.48 |
| **Annual Growth** | 8.2% | — | — | 13.2% | 4.3% | 14.3% |

# Progress Energy

Without progress, millions of people would be without energy. Progress Energy provides electricity to 3.1 million customers. It serves customers in North and South Carolina, through utility Carolina Power & Light (doing business as Progress Energy Carolinas), and in Florida, through Florida Power (or Progress Energy Florida). The company generates most of its energy from nuclear and fossil-fueled plants and has a total capacity of more than 21,300 MW. Its nonregulated activities include coal and synthetic fuel operations. In 2006 Progress Energy sold its Winchester Energy natural gas exploration and production business to EXCO Resources for $1.2 billion.

In 2007 it sold its nonregulated power plants, hedges, and contracts for $480 million.

Progress Energy was formed in 2000 when CP&L Energy expanded into Florida with the acquisition of Florida Progress. Since then, the company has branched out into new businesses to keep up with the changing utility industry. It jumped into energy marketing and trading through subsidiary Progress Ventures, which also builds and operates merchant power plants and has coal, oil, natural gas, and synthetic fuel production operations.

Other nonutility businesses include Strategic Resource Solutions, which offers energy management services. In 2003 Progress Energy merged its telecom unit with broadband provider Epik Communications. Progress Energy owned 55% of the combined company, but subsequently exited the field.

Due to a weak wholesale market, Progress Energy scaled back on plans to enlarge its power generation portfolio; it is also reduced its power marketing and trading activities.

Progress Energy exited the natural gas distribution business in 2003 with the sale of its North Carolina Natural Gas utility to Piedmont Natural Gas for about $425 million. The company has also sold its transportation assets, and a portion of its oil and gas production operations.

## HISTORY

Central Carolina Power was incorporated in 1908. Later that year, under the aegis of the Electric Bond and Share Co. (EBS, a subsidiary of General Electric), Central Carolina Power crossed lines with Raleigh Electric and Consumers Light & Power to form Carolina Power & Light (CP&L).

EBS president S. Z. Mitchell was a leader in the young industry, espousing economies of scale through mergers and promoting lower rates to encourage sales. CP&L had three hydroelectric plants by 1911, and by 1912 it had acquired three neighboring utilities, including Asheville Power & Light. The company began selling power wholesale to municipal utilities, in addition to its retail sales.

Demand soared after WWI as textile mills switched from steam engines to electricity and residential customers became enamored of modern appliances sold by CP&L. The company merged with four other utilities and reincorporated in 1926. The next year it became part of National Power & Light, a huge utility holding company created by EBS.

CP&L struggled during the Depression as demand slackened. To add legislative insult to financial injury, Congress passed the Public Utility Holding Company Act of 1935 (repealed in 2005) to break up vast utility trusts. The act inaugurated 60 years of regional monopolies regulated by state and federal authorities. In 1948 CP&L was divested from EBS and went public.

The postwar boom increased the demand for power, and to keep up CP&L built several large coal-fired plants. By the early 1960s the company had begun building its first nuclear facility, the Robinson plant, which was completed in 1971. CP&L also continued to build huge, coal-fired plants.

The company completed its second nuke (Brunswick) in 1977. But two years later the accident at Pennsylvania's Three Mile Island cast a pall on the industry. After numerous delays CP&L decided to complete just one more nuke (Harris). The plant went on line in 1987, and CP&L requested a 13% rate increase to help cover its $3.8 billion cost. In contrast to its brothers, Harris ran quite well. But problems continued to plague CP&L's nuclear program into the early 1990s.

The Federal Energy Policy Act of 1992 dramatically changed the utility industry by allowing wholesale power competition. The following year CP&L hired new nuke management to turn around its troubled Brunswick plant.

In 1996 the utility lost $100 million to damages from Hurricane Fran. The next year the company unveiled Strategic Resource Solutions, a nonregulated energy services company created out of the former Knowledge Builders. In 1998 CP&L began marketing wholesale power.

To expand into natural gas distribution, CP&L bought North Carolina Natural Gas (NCNG) in 1999 for about $354 million in stock. The company also agreed to buy utility holding company Florida Progress for $5.4 billion in cash and stock and $2.7 billion in assumed debt. In preparation for its Florida Progress purchase, CP&L adopted a holding company structure in 2000 and was renamed CP&L Energy Inc. The Florida Progress deal was completed later that year, and CP&L Energy became Progress Energy. In 2000 it also formed a new unregulated energy marketing subsidiary, Progress Energy Ventures.

As a condition of the merger, Progress Energy agreed to divest some noncore assets; in 2001 it announced plans to sell its rail and barge operations. Later that year it sold its MEMCO Barge Line unit to American Electric Power for $270 million.

In 2002 Progress Energy Ventures purchased two Georgia power plants (one operational and one under construction) for $345 million from LG&E Energy.

## EXECUTIVES

**Chairman and CEO:** Robert B. (Bob) McGehee, age 63, $2,275,000 pay
**President and COO:** William D. (Bill) Johnson, age 52, $1,328,365 pay (prior to promotion)
**CFO; President and CEO, Progress Energy Service; EVP, Progress Energy Carolinas and Progress Energy Florida:** Peter M. Scott III, age 57, $1,025,000 pay
**SVP, General Counsel, Corporate Secretary, and Director:** John R. McArthur, age 51
**SVP, Power Operations:** Paula J. Sims, age 44
**SVP and Chief Nuclear Officer, PEC and PEF:** C. S. (Scotty) Hinnant, age 61, $750,000 pay
**VP, Corporate Planning:** Mark A. Myers
**VP, Corporate Communications:** Nancy H. Temple
**VP, Regulatory & Customer Relations:** Vincent M. (Vinny) Dolan
**VP, Treasurer, and Chief Risk Officer:** Thomas R. (Tom) Sullivan
**VP, Human Resources:** Anne M. Huffman
**VP, Investor Relations:** Robert F. (Bob) Drennan Jr.
**VP, Customer and Market Services:** R. Tucker Mann
**VP, Enterprise Risk Management and Chief Risk Officer:** Steve Byone
**VP, CIO, Information Technology & Telecommunications:** Dede F. Ramoneda
**VP, Legal; General Counsel, Progress Energy Service:** Frank A. Schiller
**President and CEO, Progress Energy Florida:** Jeffrey J. (Jeff) Lyash, age 44
**President and CEO, Progress Telecom:** Ronald J. (Ron) Mudry
**President, Progress Rail Services:** William P. (Billy) Ainsworth, age 50
**President and CEO, Progress Energy Carolinas:** Lloyd M. Yates, age 46
**Auditors:** Deloitte & Touche LLP

## LOCATIONS

**HQ:** Progress Energy, Inc.
410 S. Wilmington St., Raleigh, NC 27601
**Phone:** 919-546-6111 **Fax:** 919-546-2920
**Web:** www.progress-energy.com

Progress Energy distributes electricity in North Carolina, northeastern South Carolina, and west central Florida.

## PRODUCTS/OPERATIONS

### 2006 Sales

| | $ mil. | % of total |
|---|---|---|
| PEF | 4,639 | 48 |
| PEC | 4,086 | 43 |
| Coal & synthetic fuels | 845 | 9 |
| **Total** | **9,570** | **100** |

### Selected Subsidiaries

Carolina Power & Light Company (operates as Progress Energy Carolinas, electric utility; PEC)
Florida Power Corporation (operates as Progress Energy Florida, electric utility; PEF)
Progress Ventures, Inc. (operates as Progress Energy Ventures, energy marketing, merchant power plant development, and fuels)
  Progress Fuels Corp. (natural gas, coal, and synthetic fuel production)

## COMPETITORS

ACES Power Marketing
AEP
ALLETE
Aquila
CenterPoint Energy
Dominion Resources
Duke Energy
Entergy
FPL Group
Headwaters
JEA
Mississippi Power
North Carolina Electric Membership
Oglethorpe Power
Piedmont Natural Gas
Santee Cooper
SCANA
Seminole Electric
Southern Company
TECO Energy
TVA

## HISTORICAL FINANCIALS

Company Type: Public

### Income Statement

FYE: December 31

| | REVENUE ($ mil.) | NET INCOME ($ mil.) | NET PROFIT MARGIN | EMPLOYEES |
|---|---|---|---|---|
| **12/06** | 9,570 | 571 | 6.0% | 11,000 |
| **12/05** | 10,108 | 697 | 6.9% | 11,600 |
| **12/04** | 9,772 | 759 | 7.8% | 15,700 |
| **12/03** | 8,743 | 782 | 8.9% | 15,300 |
| **12/02** | 7,945 | 528 | 6.7% | 15,300 |
| **Annual Growth** | 4.8% | 2.0% | — | (7.9%) |

### 2006 Year-End Financials

Debt ratio: 106.6%
Return on equity: 7.0%
Cash ($ mil.): 336
Current ratio: 1.27
Long-term debt ($ mil.): 8,835
No. of shares (mil.): 256
Dividends
Yield: 4.9%
Payout: 106.1%
Market value ($ mil.): 12,564

### Stock History

NYSE: PGN

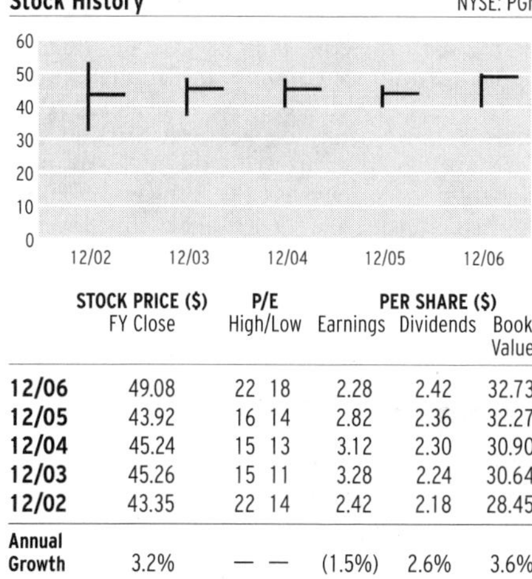


| | STOCK PRICE ($) FY Close | P/E High/Low | | PER SHARE ($) Earnings | Dividends | Book Value |
|---|---|---|---|---|---|---|
| **12/06** | 49.08 | 22 | 18 | 2.28 | 2.42 | 32.73 |
| **12/05** | 43.92 | 16 | 14 | 2.82 | 2.36 | 32.27 |
| **12/04** | 45.24 | 15 | 13 | 3.12 | 2.30 | 30.90 |
| **12/03** | 45.26 | 15 | 11 | 3.28 | 2.24 | 30.64 |
| **12/02** | 43.35 | 22 | 14 | 2.42 | 2.18 | 28.45 |
| **Annual Growth** | 3.2% | — | — | (1.5%) | 2.6% | 3.6% |

# The Progressive Corporation

It's risky business, and Progressive loves it. Long a leader in nonstandard, high-risk personal auto insurance, The Progressive Corporation has motored beyond its traditional business into standard-risk and preferred auto insurance, as well as other personal-use vehicle coverage (motorcycles, recreational vehicles, and snowmobiles). Besides personal lines, the company's offerings include collateral insurance for auto lenders, directors' and officers' insurance, and employee misconduct insurance. The company markets directly to consumers via its Web site and toll-free telephone number and through 30,000 independent agents in the US. Direct sales represent about 36% of the company's business.

Already among the top three US auto insurers based on volume (behind #1 State Farm and Allstate), Progressive says it aims to be on top in this decade. Personal lines make up about 90% of Progressive's premiums. Colorful chairman Peter Lewis (Warhol portraits of Chairman Mao adorn his office) is the son of one of the insurer's founders and owns almost 15% of the company.

A favorable insurance climate and the improvement of the company's claims system have helped Progressive grow its treasure chest. Focusing on its core auto business, Progressive has stopped writing homeowners insurance. In 2006 the company added personal umbrella policies to its coverage.

## HISTORY

Attorneys Jack Green and Joseph Lewis founded Progressive Mutual Insurance in Cleveland in 1937. Initially offering standard auto insurance, the company attracted customers through such innovations as installment plans for premiums (a payment method popularized during the Depression) and drive-in claims services (the company was headquartered in a garage). Progressive's early years were uncertain — at one point the founders were even advised to go out of business — but the advent of WWII bolstered business: Car and insurance purchases were up, but accidents were down as gas rationing limited driving.

Then came the suburbs and cars of the 1950s. While most competitors sought low-risk drivers, Progressive exploited the high-risk niche through careful underwriting and statistical analysis. Subsidiary Progressive Casualty was founded in 1956 (the year after Joseph Lewis died) to insure the best of the worst. Lewis' son Peter joined the company in 1955 and helped engineer its early-1960s expansion outside Ohio. After Green retired in 1965, Peter gained control of the company through a leveraged buyout and renamed it The Progressive Corporation. Six years later, Lewis took it public and formed subsidiary Progressive American in Florida.

In the mid-1970s the industry went into a funk as it was hit by a wave of consolidations and rising interest rates. Lewis set a goal for the company to always earn an underwriting profit instead of depending on investments to make a profit. Progressive achieved stellar results during the 1970s, especially after states began requiring drivers to be insured and other insurers began weeding out higher risks.

Competition in nonstandard insurance grew in the 1980s, as major insurers such as Allstate and State Farm joined the fray with their larger sales forces and deeper pockets. In 1988 California's Proposition 103 retroactively reduced rates; Progressive fought California's demand for refunds but set aside reserves to pay them.

That year Lewis hired Cleveland financier Alfred Lerner to guide company investments. Lerner invested $75 million in Progressive via a convertible debenture; five years later he converted it to stock, half of which he sold for $122 million. Soon after, he was asked to resign. In 1993 Progressive settled with California for $51 million and applied to earnings the remaining $100 million in refund reserves. (Company soul-searching related to Proposition 103 led to the launch of Progressive's now-famous "Immediate Response" vehicles, which provide 24-hour claims service at accident sites.)

In 1995 Progressive's practice of using consumer credit information to make underwriting decisions drew the attention of Arkansas and Vermont insurance regulators, who said the company might be discriminating against people who didn't have the credit cards Progressive used to evaluate creditworthiness. In 1996 insurance regulators in Alaska, Maryland, and Texas also began probing Progressive's credit information practices.

In 1997 Progressive bought nonstandard auto insurer Midland Financial Group. As competition grew in 1999, the company cut rates and said it would write no new policies in Canada. In 2000 — with underwriting margins dropping industrywide — the company continued advertising aggressively. Progressive stopped writing new homeowners insurance in 2002, instead concentrating on its core operations.

Improved market conditions and improvements to the company's claims system in 2003 helped Progressive's bottom line and the company's agency auto operations showed a profit in 45 out of 48 states.

## EXECUTIVES

**Chairman:** Peter B. Lewis, age 73
**President, CEO, and Director; Chairman and CEO, Progressive Casualty Insurance Company:** Glenn M. Renwick, age 52, $2,077,500 pay
**Group President, Agency Business:** Robert T. Williams, age 50, $1,153,010 pay
**Group President, Claims:** Brian J. Passell, age 50, $921,470 pay
**Group President, Commercial Auto:** Brian A. Silva, age 53
**Group President, Direct Group of Insurance Companies; General Manager, Claims, Midwest:** John P. Sauerland, age 42
**Group President, Drive Business:** John A. Barbagello, age 47
**Group President, Sales and Service:** Richard H. Watts, age 52
**CFO:** Brian Domeck, age 47
**VP and Chief Accounting Officer:** Jeffrey W. Basch, age 49
**VP and Treasurer:** Thomas A. King, age 47
**VP, Chief Legal Officer, and Secretary:** Charles E. Jarrett, age 50, $824,627 pay
**CIO:** Raymond M. Voelker, age 43
**Chief Human Resource Officer:** Susan Patricia Griffith, age 42
**Chief Investment Officer:** William M. Cody, age 45, $1,041,345 pay
**Auditors:** PricewaterhouseCoopers LLP

## LOCATIONS

**HQ:** The Progressive Corporation
6300 Wilson Mills Rd., Mayfield Village, OH 44143
**Phone:** 440-461-5000 **Fax:** 800-456-6590
**Web:** www.progressive.com

The Progressive Corporation operates nationwide.

## PRODUCTS/OPERATIONS

### 2006 Sales

| | $ mil. | % of total |
|---|---|---|
| Net premiums earned | 14,117.9 | 96 |
| Investment income | 647.8 | 4 |
| Service revenues | 30.4 | — |
| Net realized losses on securities | (9.7) | — |
| **Total** | **14,786.4** | **100** |

### 2006 Sales

| | $ mil. | % of total |
|---|---|---|
| Underwriting operations | | |
| Personal lines | | |
| Agency | 7,903.6 | 54 |
| Direct | 4,337.4 | 29 |
| Commercial auto | 1,851.9 | 13 |
| Other — indemnity | 25.0 | — |
| Investments | 638.1 | 4 |
| Service businesses | 30.4 | — |
| **Total** | **14,786.4** | **100** |

## COMPETITORS

21st Century
AIG
Allstate
American Family Insurance
American Financial
Cincinnati Financial
COUNTRY Insurance
GEICO
The Hartford
Liberty Mutual
Nationwide
Ohio Casualty
Omni Insurance
Preserver Group
Royal & SunAlliance USA
Safeco
State Auto Financial
State Farm
Temple-Inland
Travelers Companies
USAA

## HISTORICAL FINANCIALS

Company Type: Public

**Income Statement** FYE: December 31

| | ASSETS ($ mil.) | NET INCOME ($ mil.) | INCOME AS % OF ASSETS | EMPLOYEES |
|---|---|---|---|---|
| **12/06** | 19,482 | 1,648 | 8.5% | 27,778 |
| **12/05** | 18,899 | 1,394 | 7.4% | 28,336 |
| **12/04** | 17,184 | 1,649 | 9.6% | 27,085 |
| **12/03** | 16,282 | 1,255 | 7.7% | 25,834 |
| **12/02** | 13,564 | 667 | 4.9% | 22,974 |
| **Annual Growth** | 9.5% | 25.4% | — | 4.9% |

**2006 Year-End Financials**

Equity as % of assets: 35.1%
Return on assets: 8.6%
Return on equity: 25.4%
Long-term debt ($ mil.): 1,186
No. of shares (mil.): 748
Dividends
Yield: 0.1%
Payout: 1.4%
Market value ($ mil.): 18,117
Sales ($ mil.): 14,786

**Stock History** NYSE: PGR

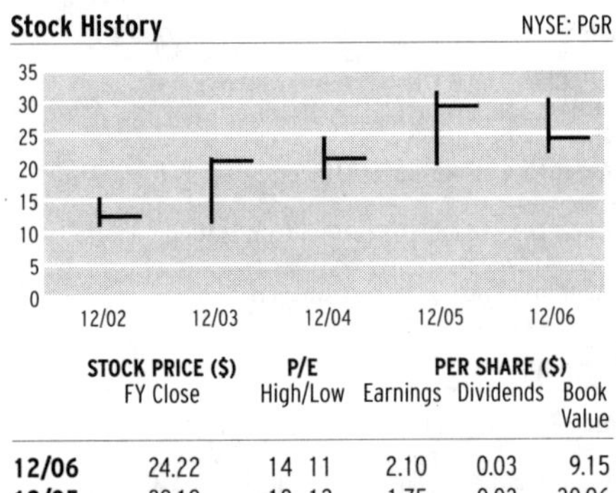


| | STOCK PRICE ($) FY Close | P/E High | P/E Low | PER SHARE ($) Earnings | Dividends | Book Value |
|---|---|---|---|---|---|---|
| **12/06** | 24.22 | 14 | 11 | 2.10 | 0.03 | 9.15 |
| **12/05** | 29.19 | 18 | 12 | 1.75 | 0.03 | 30.96 |
| **12/04** | 21.21 | 13 | 10 | 1.91 | 0.03 | 25.76 |
| **12/03** | 20.90 | 15 | 8 | 1.42 | 0.03 | 23.25 |
| **12/02** | 12.41 | 20 | 15 | 0.75 | 0.02 | 17.28 |
| **Annual Growth** | 18.2% | — | — | 29.4% | 10.7% | (14.7%) |

# Protective Life

Protective Life wants to cushion its customers from the nasty blows of life and death. The company focuses on life insurance products sold through its Life Marketing business segment (via its own agents, independent agents, work-site plans, and financial institutions). Its Acquisitions segment brings in blocks of life insurance policies sold elsewhere. The company's Asset Protection segment sells extended service contracts and credit life insurance through auto and marine dealers nationwide. Other products include annuities and guaranteed investment contracts (GICs) for 401(k) plans. The company operates through subsidiaries Protective Life Insurance and West Coast Life Insurance.

Along with the GICs, the company's Stable Value Products segment markets funding agreements for financial instruments, such as municipal bonds and money market funds.

Protective Life's combined life insurance operations (marketed and acquired) account for about half of the company's revenue. Protective has aggressively capitalized on the industry trend of consolidation, carefully selecting small and midsized firms that complement its existing operations. It has acquired more than 40 insurance companies or blocks of policies in the past three decades, allowing the company to gain premiums without expensive commissions.

The firm made its largest acquisition in 2006: Chase Insurance, the life insurance and annuity underwriting division of JPMorgan Chase, in a cash deal worth $1.2 billion.

The company invests a significant portion of its assets into mortgage-backed securities. It prefers to invest in pools of residential mortgages and non-speculative commercial properties such as strip-center retailers.

## HISTORY

In 1907 — when former Alabama governor William Jelks founded Protective Life in Birmingham — the South had not yet risen again, and most insurance business was controlled by northern companies. Protective Life survived the financial panic that year and grew steadily, paying its first dividends in 1916. It was sorely tested in 1918, as were most insurance companies, when the influenza pandemic took thousands of lives, particularly in large cities.

In 1927 Protective Life merged with another Birmingham-based insurance company, Alabama National Insurance, founded in 1908 as Great Southern Life Insurance. Alabama National's Samuel Clabaugh, a former banker, was appointed president, and under his guidance the company passed through the Depression intact, having cautiously conserved its capital. Another Alabama National alumnus, William Rushton, whose family name would become synonymous with Protective Life in Birmingham, took over as CEO in 1937. Colonel Rushton, as he became known after his stint in WWII, continued to lead the company for the next 20 years, investing in southern economic development.

In 1963 Protective Life formulated a new strategy, concentrating on the upper-income market, advanced underwriting, business insurance, and estate planning. The company planned to expand geographically, with hopes of going nationwide. Protective Life was operating in 14 states by 1969, the year that Rushton's son, William "Billy" Rushton III, assumed command from the Colonel.

Under the younger Rushton, Protective expanded its operations to 50 states. The firm purchased 39 companies and numerous blocks of policies between 1970 and 1997.

In 1992 Rushton was named chairman and Drayton Nabers was appointed CEO. In 1994 Protective teamed with Indonesia's Lippo Group (which has interests in securities, banking, and insurance) to form Hong Kong-based Lippo Protective Life Insurance, now CRC Protective Life Insurance. The joint venture introduced US-style universal life insurance to Hong Kong. Denomination of policies in US dollars attracted clients wary of unstable Asian currencies.

In the early 1990s Protective pioneered the concept of selling indemnity dental insurance on a voluntary payroll-deduction basis. In 1995 the company purchased National Health Care Systems of Florida, operating under the trade name DentiCare, and entered the managed dental care business.

In 1997 Protective acquired West Coast Life Insurance and Western Diversified Group. It also continued to build its dental care operations through the 1997 acquisitions of three more small, managed dental care companies and its 1998 purchase of United Dental Care, making it the third-largest managed dental care company in the US. In 1999 Nabers took on the additional role of chairman, taking over after William Rushton resigned. That year the company began distributing term life insurance over the Internet through agreements with HomeCom Communications and Matrix Direct Insurance Services. (Matrix was sold to American International Group in 2007.)

In 2000 Protective bought specialty insurer Lyndon Insurance Group from Frontier Insurance Group. Then Protective's subsidiary Protective Life Insurance acquired 70,000 life insurance policies from Standard Insurance. Nabers stepped down as CEO at the end of 2001.

The company sold its dental benefits division to Fortis Inc. in 2002. The following year Nabers resigned as chairman to become Alabama's finance director and Protective CEO John D. Johns was named chairman.

## EXECUTIVES

**Chairman, President, and CEO:** John D. Johns, age 55
**Vice Chairman and CFO:** Richard J. (Rich) Bielen, age 46
**EVP and COO:** Carolyn M. Johnson
**EVP, General Counsel, and Secretary:** Deborah J. Long, age 53
**EVP and Chief Investment Officer:** Carl S. Thigpen, age 50
**SVP, Information Services:** Thomas Davis Keyes, age 54
**SVP, Acquisitions Division:** Carolyn King, age 56
**SVP, Controller, and Chief Accounting Officer:** Steven G. Walker, age 47
**SVP, Stable Value Products:** Judy Wilson, age 48
**President, Empire General Life Assurance; President, West Coast Life Insurance:** Douglas K. (Doug) Adam, age 55
**President, First Protective:** Andrew Martin
**SVP and Chief Human Resources Officer:** Scott Adams
**EVP and COO, West Coast Life:** Bernard L. (Bernie) Robins, age 68
**SVP, Life and Annuities Division:** Alan E. Watson
**SVP, Life and Annuities Division:** John B. Deremo
**SVP, Marketing, West Coast Life Insurance:** Mark S. Rush
**SVP, Operations, West Coast Life Insurance:** Dale F. Moon
**VP, Corporate Finance and Investor Relations:** Chip Wann
**VP, Dealer Sales, Asset Protection Division:** M. Scott Karchunas
**VP, Investor Relations:** Rob Shirley
**Auditors:** PricewaterhouseCoopers LLP

## LOCATIONS

**HQ:** Protective Life Corporation
2801 Hwy. 280 South, Birmingham, AL 35223
**Phone:** 205-268-1000 **Fax:** 205-268-3196
**Web:** www.protective.com

## PRODUCTS/OPERATIONS

### 2006 Sales

| | $ mil. | % of total |
|---|---|---|
| Premiums & policy fees | 2,317.3 | 57 |
| Net investment income | 1,419.8 | 35 |
| Realized investment gains (losses) | | |
| Derivative financial instruments | (21.5) | — |
| All other investments | 104.1 | 2 |
| Other | 230.6 | 6 |
| Reinsurance ceded | (1,371.2) | — |
| **Total** | **2,679.1** | **100** |

### 2006 Sales by Segment

| | $ mil. | % of total |
|---|---|---|
| Life marketing | 867.7 | 33 |
| Acquisitions | 706.7 | 26 |
| Stable value products | 326.8 | 12 |
| Asset protection | 296.3 | 11 |
| Annuities | 269.6 | 10 |
| Corporate & other | 212.0 | 8 |
| **Total** | **2,679.1** | **100** |

### Selected Subsidiaries

Chase Insurance Life and Annuity Company
Empire General Life Assurance Corporation
Lyndon Insurance Group
Protective Life Insurance Company
West Coast Life Insurance Company

## COMPETITORS

AEGON USA
AIG
AIG American General
APCO
CARS Protection Plus
CIGNA
Conseco
Hartford Life
ING Americas
Interstate National Dealer Services
MassMutual
MetLife
Nationwide
New York Life
Northwestern Mutual
Pacific Mutual
Principal Financial
Prudential
UNIFI Companies
Warrantech

## HISTORICAL FINANCIALS

Company Type: Public

### Income Statement

FYE: December 31

| | ASSETS ($ mil.) | NET INCOME ($ mil.) | INCOME AS % OF ASSETS | EMPLOYEES |
|---|---|---|---|---|
| **12/06** | 39,795 | 282 | 0.7% | 2,743 |
| **12/05** | 28,967 | 247 | 0.9% | 2,192 |
| **12/04** | 27,211 | 235 | 0.9% | 2,272 |
| **12/03** | 24,574 | 217 | 0.9% | 2,468 |
| **12/02** | 21,953 | 177 | 0.8% | 2,438 |
| **Annual Growth** | 16.0% | 12.2% | — | 3.0% |

### 2006 Year-End Financials

Equity as % of assets: 5.8%
Return on assets: 0.8%
Return on equity: 12.5%
Long-term debt ($ mil.): 1,004
No. of shares (mil.): 70

Dividends
Yield: 1.8%
Payout: 21.3%
Market value ($ mil.): 3,323
Sales ($ mil.): 2,679

### Stock History

NYSE: PL

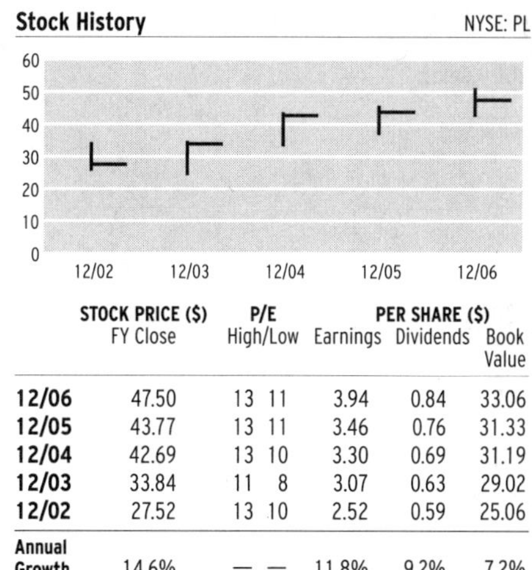


| | STOCK PRICE ($) FY Close | P/E High/Low | | PER SHARE ($) Earnings | Dividends | Book Value |
|---|---|---|---|---|---|---|
| **12/06** | 47.50 | 13 | 11 | 3.94 | 0.84 | 33.06 |
| **12/05** | 43.77 | 13 | 11 | 3.46 | 0.76 | 31.33 |
| **12/04** | 42.69 | 13 | 10 | 3.30 | 0.69 | 31.19 |
| **12/03** | 33.84 | 11 | 8 | 3.07 | 0.63 | 29.02 |
| **12/02** | 27.52 | 13 | 10 | 2.52 | 0.59 | 25.06 |
| **Annual Growth** | 14.6% | — | — | 11.8% | 9.2% | 7.2% |

# Prudential Financial

Prudential Financial wants to make sure its position near the top of the life insurance summit is set in stone. Prudential, known for its Rock of Gibraltar logo, is one of the largest US life insurers (along with MetLife) and one of the largest insurers worldwide. The firm is perhaps best known for its individual life insurance, though it also sells group life, long-term care, and disability insurance. Prudential also offers investment products and services, including asset management services, mutual funds, and retirement services. Other lines include a national real estate brokerage franchise and relocation services.

Additionally, through its 38% ownership of Wachovia Securities, the company provides securities brokerage and financial advice; Wachovia Securities was formed in 2003 as a joint venture with Wachovia.

Prudential's international insurance business offers individual life insurance policies through its Life Planners and Life Advisors units to affluent and middle income customers, primarily in Japan and South Korea, but also in other Asian, European, and Latin American countries. Its international investment unit provides asset management and investment advice in non-US markets.

The company added to its substantial Japanese operations (which include subsidiary Gibraltar Life) by acquiring Aoba Life Insurance Company in 2004. And through its 2004 acquisition of Hyundai Investment and Securities (now Prudential Investment Securities), it provides asset management services in South Korea. Prudential has also decided to enter the emerging Indian market, forming a minority-owned join venture with New Delhi-based realtor DLF.

Prudential continues to build its products and services at home as well. It grew its annuities business through the purchase of American Skandia in 2003 and Allstate's variable annuity operations in 2006. It has also added the retirement business of health insurer CIGNA.

While Prudential has been adding on some weight, it has been losing some underperforming or non-strategic assets, including its property/casualty insurance companies, which it sold to Liberty Mutual in 2003. It also shuttered its Philippine insurance operations in 2006 and its Dryden Wealth Management business, which operated in Europe and Asia, in 2005.

## HISTORY

In 1873 John Dryden founded the Widows and Orphans Friendly Society in New Jersey to sell workers industrial insurance (low-face-value weekly premium life insurance). In 1875 it became The Prudential Friendly Society, taking the name from England's Prudential Assurance Co. The next year Dryden visited the English company and copied some of its methods, such as recruiting agents from its targeted neighborhoods.

Prudential added ordinary whole life insurance in 1886. By 1900 the firm was selling more than 2,000 such policies annually and had 3,000 agents in eight states. In 1896 the J. Walter Thompson advertising agency (now the WPP Group) designed Prudential's Rock of Gibraltar logo.

The firm issued its first group life policy in 1916 (Prudential became a major group life insurer in the 1940s). In 1928 it introduced an Accidental Death Benefit, which cost it an extra $3 million in benefits the next year alone (death claims rose drastically early in the Depression).

In 1943 Prudential mutualized. The company began decentralizing operations in the 1940s. Later it introduced a Property Investment Separate Account (PRISA), which gave pension plans a real estate investment option. By 1974 the firm was the US's group pension leader.

The insurer bought securities brokerage The Bache Group to form Pru Bache (now Prudential Securities) in 1981. Bache's forte was retail investments, an area expected to blend well with Prudential's insurance business. Under George Ball, Pru Bache tried to become a major investment banker — but failed. In 1991 Ball resigned, leaving losses of almost $260 million and numerous lawsuits involving real estate limited partnerships.

Despite the 1992 settlement of the real estate partnership suits, Prudential remained under scrutiny by several states because of "churning," a process in which agents generated commissions by inducing policyholders to trade up to more expensive policies. In 1995 new management, led by former Chase Manhattanite Arthur Ryan, brought sales under control, sold such units as reinsurance and mortgage servicing, and put its $6 billion real estate portfolio on the block. (In 1997 it sold its property management unit and Canadian commercial real estate unit; in 1998 it sold its landmark Prudential Center complex in Boston.)

In 1996 regulators from 30 states found that Prudential knew about the churning earlier than it had admitted, had not stopped them, and had even promoted wrongdoers. A 1997 settlement called for the company to pay restitution, but the more than $2 billion estimated cost was thought to be less than the losses customers had suffered.

As the financial services industry continued to restructure, Prudential in 1998 announced plans to demutualize. To focus on life insurance, the company sold its health care unit to Aetna in 1999. The same year, Prudential paid $62 million to resolve more churning claims, revamped itself into international, institutional, and retail divisions, and trimmed jobs.

Ending its attempts to originate business, the company cut 75% of its investment banking staff. Demutualized Prudential Financial's 2001

IPO — one of the largest ever in the insurance industry — raised more than $3 billion. Prudential Financial became the holding company name for all operations, making Prudential Insurance (the company's former name) a subsidiary and pure life insurer.

Variable annuities have held a special allure for the company. It bought Swedish insurer Skandia's US operations in 2003 and then Allstate's variable annuity business in 2006.

Prudential also sold its brokerage division to banking powerhouse Wachovia, turning Wachovia Securities (38% owned by Prudential) into the third-largest brokerage firm in the US.

Prudential agreed to pay NASD a $2 million fine and to reimburse customers nearly $10 million in 2004 because of alleged rules violations regarding the sale of annuities. In late 2006 the company agreed to pay $19 million ($16.5 million in restitution and $2.5 million as penalty) after New York Attorney General Eliot Spitzer determined that certain payments to insurance brokers amounted to collusion.

## EXECUTIVES

**Chairman, President, and CEO:** Arthur F. (Art) Ryan, age 63, $7,300,000 pay
**Vice Chairman Insurance:** Vivian L. Banta, age 55, $4,025,000 pay
**Vice Chairman Financial Management:** Mark B. Grier, age 53, $3,525,000 pay
**Vice Chairman Investments:** John R. Strangfeld Jr., age 52, $4,100,000 pay (prior to title change)
**SVP and CFO:** Richard J. Carbone, age 58, $2,065,192 pay
**SVP; COO, Individual Life:** Beth Connelly
**SVP Corporate Human Resources:** Sharon C. Taylor, age 51
**SVP, Controller, and Principal Accounting Officer:** Peter Sayre, age 52
**SVP and General Counsel:** Susan L. Blount, age 48
**SVP, Long Term Care Insurance:** Andrew J. (Andy) Mako
**SVP, New Business Development, Individual Life Insurance:** Joan Cleveland
**VP, Prudential Select Brokerage:** Evelyn A. Bentz
**VP, Secretary, and Corporate Governance Officer:** Kathleen M. Gibson
**VP and Chief Marketing Officer, Individual Life Insurance:** Mark Hug
**Chairman and CEO, Prudential-Bache International and Dryden Wealth Management:** Carol Robbins
**President, Group Insurance:** Edward Baird
**President, Private Wealth Advisory Operations, Prudential-Bache International:** Alan Brody
**President, Prudential Annuities:** David R. (Dave) Odenath Jr.
**Chairman and CEO, International Investments:** Stephen Pelletier
**Director for Global Information Technology, Dryden Wealth Management:** Richard Hurford
**Auditors:** PricewaterhouseCoopers LLP

## LOCATIONS

**HQ:** Prudential Financial, Inc.
751 Broad St., Newark, NJ 07102
**Phone:** 973-802-6000 **Fax:** 973-802-4479
**Web:** www.prudential.com

Prudential Financial has offices in about 20 countries in Asia, Europe, North America, and South America.

## PRODUCTS/OPERATIONS

### 2006 Sales

| | $ mil. | % of total |
|---|---|---|
| Premiums | 13,908 | 43 |
| Net investment income | 11,354 | 35 |
| Asset management fees & other income | 3,799 | 12 |
| Policy charges & fees | 2,653 | 8 |
| Realized investment gains | 774 | 2 |
| **Total** | **32,488** | **100** |

### 2006 Sales

| | $ mil. | % of total |
|---|---|---|
| Financial services | | |
| Insurance Division | | |
| Group insurance | 4,555 | 14 |
| Individual life | 2,216 | 7 |
| Individual annuities | 2,101 | 6 |
| International Insurance & Investments Division | | |
| International insurance | 7,730 | 24 |
| International investments | 590 | 2 |
| Investment Division | | |
| Retirement | 4,378 | 13 |
| Asset management | 2,050 | 6 |
| Financial advisory | 574 | 2 |
| Corporate operations | 347 | 1 |
| Real estate & relocation services | 305 | 1 |
| Net realized investment gains & related adjustments | 73 | — |
| Divested businesses | 40 | — |
| Investment gains on trading account assets | 35 | — |
| Charges related to realized investment losses | 4 | — |
| Equity in earnings of joint ventures | (322) | — |
| Closed block business | 7,812 | 24 |
| **Total** | **32,488** | **100** |

### Selected Subsidiaries and Affiliates

American Skandia Life Assurance Corporation
Bache Equities Limited (UK)
Bache, S.A. de C.V. (Mexico)
Capital Agricultural Property Services, Inc.
Gibraltar Life Insurance Company, Ltd. (Japan)
Jennison Capital Advisers LLC
Mulberry Street Holdings, LLC
PBI Group Holdings Limited (UK)
PIM Investments, Inc.
Pramerica Real Estate Investors (Asia) Pte. Ltd. (Singapore)
PRUCO Life Insurance Company
PRUCO Life Insurance Company of New Jersey
Prudential Funding, LLC
Prudential Mortgage Capital Company, LLC
Residential Services Corporation of America
The Pramerica Life Insurance Company, Inc. (Philippines)
The Prudential Insurance Company of America
Vantage Casualty Insurance Company
Wachovia Securities (38%)

## COMPETITORS

AEGON
Aetna
AIG
Allianz
American Financial
Aviva
AXA
Charles Schwab
CIGNA
Citigroup
CNP Assurances
COUNTRY Insurance
Dai-ichi Mutual Life
FMR
The Hartford
HomeServices
ING
John Hancock
Legal & General Group
MassMutual
Merrill Lynch
MetLife
Nationwide Life Insurance
Nippon Life Insurance
Northwestern Mutual
Principal Financial
Prudential plc
The Vanguard Group
Zurich Financial Services

## HISTORICAL FINANCIALS

Company Type: Public

### Income Statement

FYE: December 31

| | ASSETS ($ mil.) | NET INCOME ($ mil.) | INCOME AS % OF ASSETS | EMPLOYEES |
|---|---|---|---|---|
| 12/06 | 454,266 | 3,428 | 0.8% | 39,814 |
| 12/05 | 417,776 | 3,540 | 0.8% | 38,853 |
| 12/04 | 401,058 | 2,256 | 0.6% | 39,418 |
| 12/03 | 321,274 | 1,264 | 0.4% | 39,422 |
| 12/02 | 292,746 | 194 | 0.1% | 54,086 |
| Annual Growth | 11.6% | 105.0% | — | (7.4%) |

### 2006 Year-End Financials

Equity as % of assets: 5.0%
Return on assets: 0.8%
Return on equity: 15.0%
Long-term debt ($ mil.): 11,423
No. of shares (mil.): 471
Dividends
Yield: 1.1%
Payout: 14.6%
Market value ($ mil.): 40,449
Sales ($ mil.): 32,488

### Stock History

NYSE: PRU

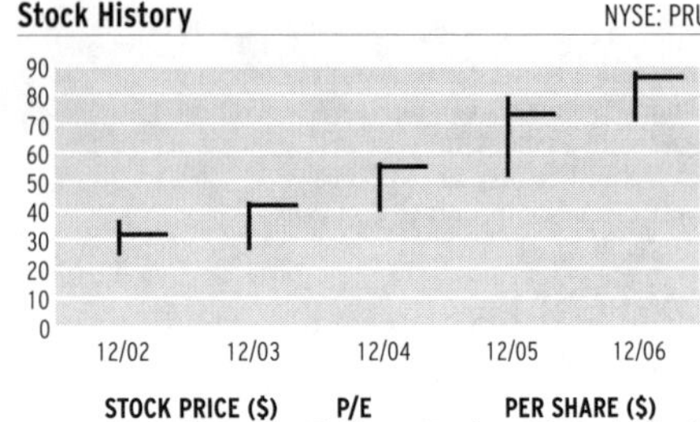


| | STOCK PRICE ($) FY Close | P/E High | P/E Low | PER SHARE ($) Earnings | Dividends | Book Value |
|---|---|---|---|---|---|---|
| 12/06 | 85.86 | 13 | 11 | 6.50 | 0.95 | 48.59 |
| 12/05 | 73.19 | 12 | 8 | 6.34 | 0.78 | 45.99 |
| 12/04 | 54.96 | 17 | 12 | 3.31 | 0.63 | 42.37 |
| 12/03 | 41.77 | 21 | 14 | 1.98 | 0.50 | 39.81 |
| 12/02 | 31.74 | 29 | 20 | 1.25 | 0.40 | 38.07 |
| Annual Growth | 28.2% | — | — | 51.0% | 24.1% | 6.3% |

# Public Service Enterprise Group

In the Garden State, Public Service Enterprise Group (PSEG) is emerging from the transition to competition smelling like a rose. Regulated subsidiary Public Service Electric and Gas (PSE&G) transmits and distributes electricity to 2.1 million customers and natural gas to 1.7 million customers in New Jersey. Nonregulated subsidiary PSEG Power operates PSEG's generating plants. Other operations include energy infrastructure investments and wholesale energy marketing. The company also invests in overseas independent power plants and distribution systems. PSEG had agreed to be acquired by Exelon, but both New Jersey and Pennsylvania opposed the merger, and the deal fell through in 2006.

Following New Jersey's energy deregulation, PSEG formed PSEG Power to take over its power plants and sell electricity wholesale. PSEG Power's 14,000-MW generating capacity comes mostly from nuclear and fossil-fueled plants in the US Northeast. The division also has facilities under construction that will add 2,000 MW of capacity. PSEG Power supplied all of PSE&G's power needs until August 2002; PSE&G began purchasing power from independent power producers at that time.

PSEG Global owns stakes in energy distributors that more than 3 million customers and power plants (3,000 MW of capacity) in Europe, Asia, Latin America, and North America. PSEG has exited its energy management and HVAC services business (PSEG Energy Technologies), as well as its energy distribution operations in Argentina.

PSEG is also selling some of its independent power plant interests, and it has scaled down plans to expand its energy generation and marketing businesses. In 2006 PSEG Global sold its 32% stake in RGE, a Brazilian electric distribution company with approximately 1.1 million customers, to Companhia Paulista de Forcae Luz.

In 2007 the company agreed to sell an Indiana power plant to American Electric Power for $325 million.

## HISTORY

Tragedy struck Newark, New Jersey, in 1903 when a trolley slid down an icy hill and collided with a train, killing more than 30 people. While investigating the accident, state attorney general Thomas McCarter discovered the mismanagement of the trolley company and many of New Jersey's other transportation, gas, and electric companies. Planning to buy and consolidate these companies, McCarter resigned and established the Public Service Corporation in 1903 with several colleagues.

The company formed divisions for gas utilities, electric utilities, and transportation companies. The trolley company generated almost half of Public Service's sales during its first year.

In 1924 the gas and electric companies consolidated as Public Service Electric and Gas (PSE&G). A new company was formed that year to operate buses, and in 1928 it merged with the trolley company to form Public Service Coordinated Transport (later Transport of New Jersey). PSE&G signed interconnection agreements with two Pennsylvania electric companies in 1928 to form the first integrated power pool — later known as the Pennsylvania-New Jersey-Maryland Interconnection. The Public Utility Holding Company Act of 1935 ushered in the era of regulated regional monopolies, ensuring PSE&G a captive market.

During the 1960s PSE&G joined Philadelphia Electric to build its first nuclear plant, at Peach Bottom, Pennsylvania. The company completed a second nuke in 1977, at Salem, New Jersey. Its third one went on line at Hope Creek, New Jersey. However, plant mismanagement earned PSE&G a slew of fines in the 1980s and 1990s.

The company sold its transportation system to the State of New Jersey in 1980. Five years later PSE&G formed holding company Public Service Enterprise Group (PSEG) to move into nonutility enterprises and created Community Energy Alternatives (CEA, now PSEG Global) to invest in independent power projects. In 1989 Enterprise Diversified Holdings (now PSEG Energy Holdings) was formed to handle activities ranging from real estate to oil and gas production.

CEA and three partners acquired a Buenos Aires power plant in 1993. Taking advantage of overseas privatization in the late 1990s, it expanded into Asia and, with AES, purchased two Argentine electric companies.

PSE&G's nuclear problems resurfaced when the Salem plant was shut down in 1995 to rectify equipment breakdowns. In 1997 PSEG paid Salem partners Delmarva Power & Light and PECO Energy $82 million to settle their lawsuits charging mismanagement of Salem; both units were back on line by 1998.

Continuing to diversify in the late 1990s, PSEG formed PSEG Energy Technologies in 1997 to market power and acquired five mechanical services companies in 1998 and 1999.

In 1999 PSEG Global teamed up with Panda Energy International to build three merchant plants in Texas (to be completed by 2001). It also planned plants in India and Venezuela and joined Sempra Energy to buy 90% of Chilquinta Energía, an energy distributor in Chile and Peru. In 2000 it bought 90% of a distributor serving Argentina and Brazil.

New Jersey's electricity markets were deregulated in 1999; a year later the company transferred PSE&G's generation assets to nonregulated unit PSEG Power. PSEG Power also took charge of PSEG Global's plants under development in Illinois, Indiana, and Ohio; announced plans for new plants in New Jersey; and acquired an Albany, New York, plant from Niagara Mohawk.

In 2001 PSEG Global completed a power plant in Texas. It also bought 94% of generator and distributor Saesa from Chile's largest conglomerate, Copec, for $460 million; it later acquired the rest of Saesa through a tender offer. It also purchased a Peruvian generation firm, ElectroAndes, for $227 million.

In 2002 PSEG Power acquired two Connecticut plants from Wisconsin Energy for approximately $270 million.

## EXECUTIVES

**Chairman, President, and CEO:** Ralph Izzo, age 49, $559,920 pay (prior to title change)
**EVP and CFO; CFO, PSE&G, PSEG Power, and PSEG Energy Holdings; President and COO, PSEG Energy Holdings:** Thomas M. (Tom) O'Flynn, age 46, $552,926 pay (prior to title change)
**EVP and General Counsel; EVP and General Counsel, Public Service Enterprise Group, PSE&G, and PSEG Services; EVP, PSEG Power:** R. Edwin Selover, age 61
**SVP Human Resources and Chief Human Resources Officer, PSEG Services:** Margaret M. Pego
**VP Risk Management and Chief Risk Officer:** Laura L. Langer Brooks
**VP Investor Relations:** Kathleen A. Lally
**VP and Treasurer; VP and Treasurer, PSE&G:** Morton A. Plawner, age 57
**President and COO, PSE&G:** Ralph A. LaRossa, age 43
**President, PSEG Resources; President, Enterprise Group Development:** Eileen A. Moran, age 52
**President, PSEG Global:** Matthew J. McGrath, age 43
**President, PSEG Energy Resources and Trade:** Kevin J. Quinn
**President and COO, PSEG Services:** Elbert C. Simpson
**SVP Finance, Business Development, Strategy, and M&A, PSEG Services:** Stephen C. Byrd
**Chief Nuclear Officer; President, PSEG Nuclear; President and COO, PSEG Power:** William (Bill) Levis
**President, PSEG Fossil:** Richard P. Lopriore
**SVP Law, PSEG Services:** David P. Falck
**SVP Operations, Salem/Hope Creek, PSEG Nuclear:** Thomas P. Joyce
**Secretary:** Edward J. Biggins Jr.
**Auditors:** Deloitte & Touche LLP

## LOCATIONS

**HQ:** Public Service Enterprise Group Incorporated
80 Park Plaza, Newark, NJ 07102
**Phone:** 973-430-7000 **Fax:** 973-824-7056
**Web:** www.pseg.com

Public Service Enterprise Group provides energy in New Jersey (through PSE&G) and has interests in generating plants in Connecticut, New Jersey, New York, Ohio, and Pennsylvania (through PSEG Power). PSEG Global owns interests in operating generation or distribution facilities in California, Hawaii, New Hampshire, Pennsylvania, and Texas in the US and in Chile, India, Italy, Peru, and Venezuela.

### 2006 Sales

| | $ mil. | % of total |
|---|---|---|
| US | 11,578 | 95 |
| Other countries | 586 | 5 |
| **Total** | **12,164** | **100** |

## PRODUCTS/OPERATIONS

### 2006 Sales

| | $ mil. | % of total |
|---|---|---|
| PSE&G | 7,569 | 50 |
| Power | 6,057 | 41 |
| Global | 1,174 | 8 |
| Resources | 174 | 1 |
| Other | 9 | — |
| Adjustments | (2,819) | — |
| **Total** | **12,164** | **100** |

### Selected Subsidiaries

PSEG Energy Holdings Inc. (nonutility companies)
- PSEG Global Inc. (international development of independent power plants and distribution operations)
- PSEG Resources Inc. (energy infrastructure investments)

PSEG Power LLC
- PSEG Fossil LLC (operator of PSEG's fossil fuel plants)
- PSEG Nuclear LLC (operator of PSEG's nuclear plants)
- PSEG Energy Resources and Trade LLC (energy marketing)

PSEG Services Corporation (management and administrative services for PSEG)

Public Service Electric and Gas Company (PSE&G, distribution of electricity and gas)

## COMPETITORS

AES
CenterPoint Energy
Con Edison
Constellation Energy
Delmarva Power
Exelon
FirstEnergy
FPL Group
KeySpan
Mirant
National Grid USA
New Jersey Resources
Northeast Utilities
NRG Energy
PPL
Sempra Commodities
Sempra Energy
South Jersey Industries
SUEZ-TRACTEBEL

## HISTORICAL FINANCIALS

Company Type: Public

### Income Statement

FYE: December 31

| | REVENUE ($ mil.) | NET INCOME ($ mil.) | NET PROFIT MARGIN | EMPLOYEES |
|---|---|---|---|---|
| **12/06** | 12,164 | 739 | 6.1% | 6,154 |
| **12/05** | 12,430 | 661 | 5.3% | 6,335 |
| **12/04** | 10,996 | 726 | 6.6% | 10,513 |
| **12/03** | 11,116 | 1,160 | 10.4% | 10,632 |
| **12/02** | 8,390 | 245 | 2.9% | 12,911 |
| **Annual Growth** | 9.7% | 31.8% | — | (16.9%) |

**2006 Year-End Financials**

Debt ratio: 156.7%
Return on equity: 11.6%
Cash ($ mil.): 268
Current ratio: 1.08
Long-term debt ($ mil.): 10,574
No. of shares (mil.): 253
Dividends
Yield: 3.4%
Payout: 77.8%
Market value ($ mil.): 16,771

**Stock History** NYSE: PEG

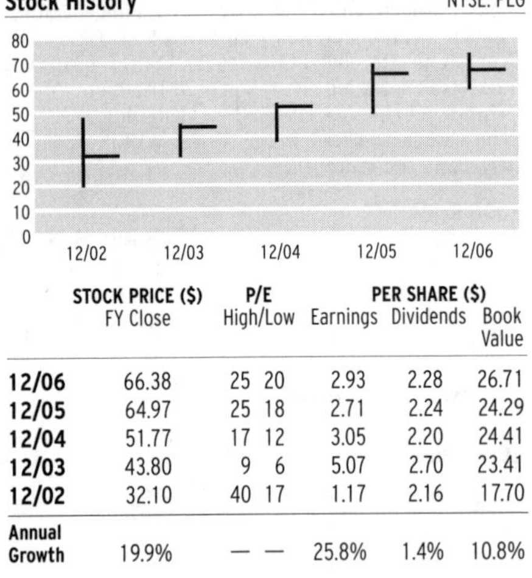

| | STOCK PRICE ($) FY Close | P/E High/Low | | PER SHARE ($) Earnings | Dividends | Book Value |
|---|---|---|---|---|---|---|
| **12/06** | 66.38 | 25 | 20 | 2.93 | 2.28 | 26.71 |
| **12/05** | 64.97 | 25 | 18 | 2.71 | 2.24 | 24.29 |
| **12/04** | 51.77 | 17 | 12 | 3.05 | 2.20 | 24.41 |
| **12/03** | 43.80 | 9 | 6 | 5.07 | 2.70 | 23.41 |
| **12/02** | 32.10 | 40 | 17 | 1.17 | 2.16 | 17.70 |
| **Annual Growth** | 19.9% | — | — | 25.8% | 1.4% | 10.8% |

# Publix Super Markets

Publix Super Markets tops the list of privately owned supermarket operators in the US. By emphasizing service and a family-friendly image rather than price, Publix has grown faster and been more profitable than Winn-Dixie Stores and other rivals. Many of its nearly 900 stores are in Florida, but it also operates in Alabama, Georgia, South Carolina, and Tennessee. Publix makes some of its own bakery, deli, and dairy goods, and many stores offer flowers, housewares, pharmacies, and banks. The company also operates five "Pix" convenience stores in the Sunshine State. Founder George Jenkins began offering stock to Publix employees in 1930. Employees own about 30% of Publix, which is still run by the Jenkins family.

Publix is expanding into the liquor market with the acquisition of two liquor stores adjacent to a pair of Kash n' Karry outlets in Florida that the company acquired from Delhaize America in 2004. Currently, Publix operates about two dozen liquor stores next to its supermarkets in Florida.

More than 70% of the company's stores are in Florida. Last year the fast-growing chain opened nearly 20 new supermarkets, with another 25 under construction in 2007. Initiatives for 2007 include the introduction of a new store format called GreenWise Market, the name Publix has already given to its store-within-a-store natural/organic sections and private-label line of specialty foods. Four GreenWise stores are slated to open this year. The grocery chain, in partnership with The Little Clinic, plans to begin opening medical clinics within Publix supermarkets.

In a surprising case of one-upmanship, Publix will begin offering seven popular antibiotics for free to its pharmacy customers with prescriptions. The grocery chain also fills other generic prescriptions for $4 (upon customer request), thereby matching rival Wal-Mart's low-cost generic drug program.

To better serve its Latino customers, Publix has launched its own line of pre-packaged Hispanic foods, including frozen plantains and ready-to-eat black beans. It also launched a Hispanic-themed format called Publix Sabor in 2005, which operates two stores in Miami. Publix is expanding its majority-owned restaurant chain Crispers with new menu items and locations in Florida. Currently the soup-salad-and-sandwich chain operates about 40 locations.

## HISTORY

George Jenkins, age 22, resigned as manager of the Piggly Wiggly grocery in Winter Haven, Florida, in 1930. With money he had saved to buy a car, he opened his own grocery store, Publix, next door to his old employer. The small store (named after a chain of movie theaters) prospered despite the Depression, and in 1935 Jenkins opened another Publix in the same town.

Five years later, after the supermarket format had become popular, Jenkins closed his two smaller locations and opened a new, more modern Publix Market. With pastel colors and electric-eye doors, it was also the first US store to feature air conditioning.

Publix Super Markets bought the All-American chain of Lakeland, Florida (19 stores), in 1944 and moved its corporate headquarters to that city. The company began offering S&H Green Stamps in 1953, and in 1956 it replaced its original supermarket with a mall featuring an enlarged Publix and a Green Stamp redemption center. Publix expanded into South Florida in the late 1950s and began selling stock to employees.

As Florida's population grew, Publix continued to expand, opening its 100th store in 1964. Publix was the first grocery chain in the state to use bar-code scanners — all its stores had the technology by 1981. The company beat Florida banks in providing ATMs and during the 1980s opened debit card stations.

Publix continued to grow in the 1980s, safe from takeover attempts because of its employee ownership. In 1988 it installed the first automated checkout systems in South Florida, giving patrons an always-open checkout lane.

In 1989 the chain stopped offering Green Stamps, and most of the $19 million decrease in Publix advertising expenditures was attributed to the end of the 36-year promotion. That year, after almost six decades, "Mr. George" — as founder Jenkins was known — stepped down as chairman in favor of his son Howard. (George died in 1996.)

In 1991 Publix opened its first store outside Florida, in Georgia, as part of its plan to become a major player in the Southeast. Publix entered South Carolina in 1993 with one supermarket; it also tripled its presence in Georgia to 15 stores.

The United Food and Commercial Workers Union began a campaign in 1994 against alleged gender and racial discrimination in Publix's hiring, promotion, and compensation policies.

Publix opened its first store in Alabama in 1996. That year a federal judge allowed about 150,000 women to join a class-action suit filed in 1995 by 12 women who had sued Publix, charging that the company consistently channeled female employees into low-paying jobs with little chance for good promotions. The case, which at the time was said to be the biggest sex discrimination lawsuit ever, was set to go to trial, but in 1997 the company paid $82.5 million to settle and another $3.5 million to settle a complaint of discrimination against black applicants and employees.

Publix promised to change its promotion policies, but two more lawsuits alleging discrimination against women and blacks were filed in 1997 and 1998. The suit filed on behalf of the women was denied class-action status in 2000. Later that year the company settled the racial discrimination lawsuit for $10.5 million. Howard Jenkins stepped down as CEO in mid-2001; his cousin Charlie Jenkins took the helm.

In mid-2002 Publix made an equity investment in Florida-based Crispers, a chain of 13 quick-serve restaurants targeting health-conscious diners. Also that year, Publix entered the Nashville, Tennessee, market with the purchase of seven Albertson's supermarkets, a convenience store, and a fuel center.

In mid-2003 Publix pulled the plug on its online store PublixDirect, which offered delivery service in parts of Florida, citing disappointing sales. However, it added 78 bricks-and-mortar stores in 2003.

In February 2004 Publix acquired three Florida stores from Kash n' Karry, a subsidiary of Belgium's Delhaize Group. Also that year Publix became the majority owner of Crispers, the restaurant chain the company invested in initially in 2002.

In April 2005 Publix introduced the Hispanic-themed Sabor format in Kissimmee, Florida.

## EXECUTIVES

**Chairman:** Howard M. Jenkins, age 54
**Vice Chairman:** Hoyt R. (Barney) Barnett, age 63, $401,694 pay
**CEO and Director:** Charles H. (Charlie) Jenkins Jr., age 63, $792,896 pay
**President and Director:** William E. (Ed) Crenshaw, age 56, $663,152 pay
**CFO and Treasurer:** David P. Phillips, age 47, $530,522 pay
**SVP and Chief Information Officer:** Laurie S. Zeitlin, age 42
**SVP, General Counsel, and Secretary:** John A. Attaway Jr., age 48
**SVP, Product Business Development:** Todd Jones
**VP and Assistant Secretary:** Linda S. Kane, age 41
**VP and Controller:** G. Gino DiGrazia, age 44
**VP and Controller:** Sandra J. (Sandy) Woods, age 47
**VP, Manufacturing:** Michael R. (Mike) Smith, age 47
**President and CEO, Crispers:** Michael (Mike) Calhoon
**CFO, Crispers:** Bob Zonies
**Director, Marketing and Research:** Mark Lang
**Director, Media and Community Relations:** Maria Brous
**Auditors:** KPMG LLP

## LOCATIONS

**HQ:** Publix Super Markets, Inc.
3300 Publix Corporate Pkwy., Lakeland, FL 33811
**Phone:** 863-688-1188 **Fax:** 863-284-5532
**Web:** www.publix.com

Publix Super Markets operates three dairy processing plants (Deerfield Beach and Lakeland, Florida, and Lawrenceville, Georgia), a pair of bakery plants (Lakeland, and Atlanta, Georgia) and a deli plant (also in Lakeland). Publix operates seven distribution centers in Florida (Boynton Beach, Deerfield Beach, Jacksonville, Lakeland, Miami, Orlando, and Sarasota) and one in Georgia (Lawrenceville).

**2006 Stores**

| | No. |
|---|---|
| Florida | 645 |
| Georgia | 167 |
| South Carolina | 38 |
| Alabama | 28 |
| Tennessee | 14 |
| **Total** | **892** |

## PRODUCTS/OPERATIONS

### Selected Supermarket Departments

Bakery
Banking
Dairy
Deli
Ethnic foods
Floral
Groceries
Health and beauty care
Housewares
Meat
Pharmacy
Photo processing
Produce
Seafood

### Foods Processed

Baked goods
Dairy products
Deli items

## COMPETITORS

ALDI
BI-LO
Bruno's Supermarkets
Costco Wholesale
CVS/Caremark
IGA
Ingles Markets
Kash n' Karry
Kerr Drug
Kmart
Kroger
Nash-Finch
The Pantry
Rite Aid
Ruddick
Sedano's
Walgreen
Wal-Mart
Whole Foods
Winn-Dixie

## HISTORICAL FINANCIALS

Company Type: Public

### Income Statement

FYE: Last Saturday in December

| | REVENUE ($ mil.) | NET INCOME ($ mil.) | NET PROFIT MARGIN | EMPLOYEES |
|---|---|---|---|---|
| 12/06 | 21,820 | 1,097 | 5.0% | 140,000 |
| 12/05 | 20,745 | 989 | 4.8% | 135,000 |
| 12/04 | 18,686 | 819 | 4.4% | — |
| 12/03 | 16,946 | 661 | 3.9% | — |
| 12/02 | 16,027 | 632 | 3.9% | — |
| Annual Growth | 8.0% | 14.8% | — | 3.7% |

### 2006 Year-End Financials

Debt ratio: —
Return on equity: 23.9%
Cash ($ mil.): 350
Current ratio: 1.12
Long-term debt ($ mil.): —
No. of shares (mil.): 840
Dividends
Yield: 0.3%
Payout: 15.5%
Market value ($ mil.): 53,784

### Stock History

OTC: PUSH

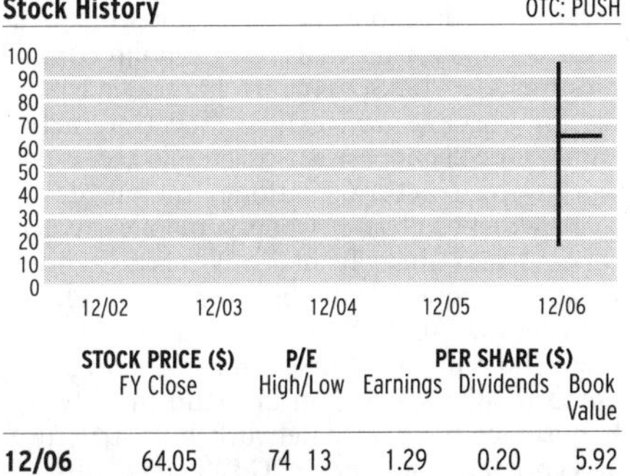


| | STOCK PRICE ($) FY Close | P/E High/Low | | PER SHARE ($) Earnings | Dividends | Book Value |
|---|---|---|---|---|---|---|
| 12/06 | 64.05 | 74 | 13 | 1.29 | 0.20 | 5.92 |

# Pulte Homes

Pulte Homes pulls its weight in providing homes for the Great American Family. One of the top homebuilders in the US (behind leaders D.R. Horton and Lennar), Pulte builds single-family houses (about 75% of total unit sales), duplexes, townhouses, and condominiums at prices typically ranging from $100,000 to $400,000; the average price is about $337,000. Pulte also builds Del Webb active adult communities, mostly in Sunbelt locales, for the growing number of buyers in the 50-plus age range. Pulte sells in about 55 markets in 27 US states (and Puerto Rico), with the West and Southeast accounting for most of its sales. Founder William Pulte owns about 16% of the company.

In 2006 new construction began to slow as the housing bubble lost buoyancy. Pulte and its competitors reported a decline in orders and a general contraction of the market that year. As the decline accelerated, Pulte cut nearly a third of its workforce in 2006 and 2007.

Pulte Homes serves the first-time, first- and second-move-up segments in the markets it serves. Pulte Homes has also been expanding the Del Webb brand into new markets in the US; the pioneering developer of Sun City communities was acquired by Pulte in 2001.

Within its competitive industry, the company has a well-positioned land portfolio. It delivered more than 41,000 homes in 2006. Pulte Homes controls more than 230,000 lots; about 159,000 owned and the rest under option agreements.

Like most major homebuilders, Pulte provides mortgage financing through a subsidiary.

Bad timing claimed another Pulte initiative. The company in 2004 opened a Virginia plant to make prefabricated home components, a plan it hoped would help it boost its construction pace. The plant was shuttered in 2007 in light of the slowed housing market.

## HISTORY

William Pulte built his first home in Detroit in 1950 and incorporated his business in 1956 as William J. Pulte, Inc. The firm has been profitable ever since — no easy feat in such a cyclical industry.

In 1961 the company built its first subdivision, in Detroit. During that decade Pulte moved into Washington, DC (1964), Chicago (1966), and Atlanta (1968). In 1969 Pulte merged with Colorado's American Builders to form the Pulte Home Corporation, a publicly traded company.

Originally a builder of high-priced, single-family homes, Pulte began expanding into affordable and midranged housing markets. To lower costs, it pioneered modular designs and prebuilt components. Pulte architects designed the Quadrominium, a large structure with four separate two-bedroom units, each with its own entrance and garage (priced at a mere $20,000 per unit in the 1970s).

Pulte formed Intercontinental Mortgage (later renamed ICM Mortgage) and began making home loans in 1972. The company ran into trouble in 1988 when it was accused of forcing Pulte homebuyers in Baltimore to use ICM financing instead of cheaper loans from the county. Pulte settled by repaying the difference in loan costs.

By the mid-1980s Pulte was one of the US's largest on-site homebuilders. PHM Corporation was created in 1987 as a holding company for the Pulte group of companies. That year PHM entered the thrift business by assisting the Federal Savings and Loan Insurance Corp.'s S&L bailout. It acquired five Texas S&Ls (with assets of $1.3 billion) for $45 million and eventually combined them to form First Heights (finally discontinuing the business in 1994).

Pulte Homes' Quality Leadership customer satisfaction program, introduced in the early 1990s, paid off in 1991 as Pulte enjoyed record sales despite a depressed home market. Renamed Pulte Corporation in 1993, the company soon faced rising interest rates, which dampened the US housing market and affected the Mexican peso. Pulte recorded a $2 million foreign-currency loss on an affordable-housing venture in Mexico in 1994. Nonetheless, it began a second Mexican joint venture in 1995 and helped form Mexican mortgage bank Su Casita with nine Mexican homebuilders to finance home construction on the Mexican border. That year it also started developing retirement communities when it bought the Ponds at Clearbrook in New Jersey.

In 1996 its Mexican joint venture Condake-Pulte began building thousands of affordable homes for General Motors and Sony employees in *maquiladora* residential areas near the US-Mexico border.

Pulte's 1988 foray into S&Ls came back to haunt it in 1998: The Federal Deposit Insurance Corp. won a lawsuit that accused the builder of abusing tax benefits associated with the S&Ls. (Pulte settled the case in 2001 by paying $41.5 million.) In 1999 Pulte bought the interest held by investment firm Blackstone Group, its partner in active-adult homebuilding.

The company changed its name to Pulte Homes in 2001. That year Mark O'Brien became the company's CEO. He directed Pulte through the major acquisition of retirement community developer Del Webb for about $800 million in stock and $950 million in assumed debt. The combined company became the largest US homebuilder. In 2002 Pulte reorganized the structure of its operations in Mexico and created Pulte Mexico S. de R.L. de C.V., one of the largest builders in that country.

Pulte expanded its operations in the fast-growing San Diego area in 2003 by purchasing assets of ColRich Communities, which included about 500 entitled lots in five communities in the South Bay and Coastal North areas of San Diego. It boosted its presence in the Albuquerque, Phoenix, and Tucson markets by acquiring Sivage-Thomas Homes (Albuquerque), with about 7,000 lots in the region, and Del Webb entered the Reno market with its Sierra Canyon active adult community. O'Brien left the company in June 2003, after having served in senior management positions for six years (and 21 total years) within the company. EVP and COO Richard Dugas stepped up to become the company's president and CEO at that time.

In September 2003 the US Court of Federal Claims awarded Pulte and related parties $48.7 million as a result of a breach of contract by the US government related to Pulte's acquisition of five savings and loans in 1988.

At the close of 2004, Pulte sold some operations in Argentina to real estate developer Grupo Farallon. The next year it sold its Mexican and remaining Argentine homebuilding enterprises to focus exclusively on US operations.

## EXECUTIVES

**Chairman:** William J. Pulte, age 74, $5,850,000 pay
**President, CEO, and Director:** Richard J. Dugas Jr., age 41, $7,250,000 pay
**EVP and COO:** Steven C. (Steve) Petruska, age 48, $4,700,010 pay
**EVP and CFO:** Roger A. Cregg, age 51, $2,875,010 pay
**EVP Human Resources:** James R. Ellinghausen, age 48, $1,523,374 pay
**SVP Operations:** Peter J. Keane, age 41
**National VP Architectural Services:** Sean J. Degen
**VP Sales:** Veronica Perez
**VP, General Counsel, and Secretary:** Steven M. Cook, age 48
**VP and Assistant Secretary:** Gregory M. Nelson, age 51
**VP and CIO:** Jerry R. Batt, age 55
**VP and Controller:** Vincent J. Frees, age 56
**VP and Treasurer:** Bruce E. Robinson, age 45
**VP:** Alan E. Laing
**VP Active Adult Development:** David G. (Dave) Schreiner
**VP Compensation and Process Improvement:** Daniel P. Lynch
**VP Finance and Homebuilding Operations, West Region:** Robert P. Schafer
**VP Leadership, Development, and Training:** Elaine A. Kramer
**VP Manufacturing Services:** Wayne B. Williams
**VP Strategic Marketing:** Steven A. Burch
**VP Marketing, Southwest:** Deborah Blake
**VP Investor and Corporate Communications:** Calvin R. Boyd
**President and CEO, Pulte Mortgage:** Debra W. (Deb) Still
**Auditors:** Ernst & Young LLP

## LOCATIONS

**HQ:** Pulte Homes, Inc.
100 Bloomfield Hills Pkwy., Ste. 300,
Bloomfield Hills, MI 48304
**Phone:** 248-647-2750 **Fax:** 248-433-4598
**Web:** www.pulte.com

Pulte Homes has operations in 53 markets in 27 US states and Puerto Rico.

### 2006 Homes Sold

| | No. of units | % of total |
|---|---|---|
| Southwest (excluding California) | 10,548 | 25 |
| Florida | 7,374 | 18 |
| Central | 6,192 | 15 |
| California | 5,209 | 13 |
| Southeast (excluding Florida) | 4,504 | 11 |
| Midwest | 4,171 | 10 |
| Northeast | 3,489 | 8 |
| **Total** | **41,487** | **100** |

### US Homebuilding Regions

Southwest (Arizona, New Mexico, and Nevada, with the exception of the Reno market)
Florida
Central (Colorado, Kansas, New Mexico, and Texas)
California (includes Reno, Nevada market)
Southeast (Georgia, North Carolina, South Carolina, and Tennessee)
Midwest (Illinois, Indiana, Michigan, Minnesota, and Ohio)
Northeast (Connecticut, Delaware, Maryland, Massachusetts, New Hampshire, New Jersey, New York, Pennsylvania, and Virginia)

## PRODUCTS/OPERATIONS

### 2006 Sales

| | $ mil. | % of total |
|---|---|---|
| Homebuilding | 14,075.2 | 99 |
| Financial services | 194.6 | 1 |
| Other | 4.6 | — |
| **Total** | **14,274.4** | **100** |

### 2006 Sales By Segment

| | $ mil. | % of total |
|---|---|---|
| Southwest (excluding California) | 3,700.5 | 26 |
| California | 2,650.6 | 19 |
| Florida | 2,212.9 | 15 |
| Northeast | 1,663.1 | 12 |
| Central | 1,305.7 | 9 |
| Midwest | 1,282.0 | 9 |
| Southeast (excluding Florida) | 1,260.4 | 9 |
| Financial services & other | 199.2 | 1 |
| **Total** | **14,274.4** | **100** |

## COMPETITORS

Ball Homes
Banamex
Beazer Homes
Capital Pacific
Centex
Corporación GEO
Countrywide Financial
D.R. Horton
Engle Homes
Hovnanian Enterprises
J.F. Shea
KB Home
Kimball Hill inc
Lennar
Levitt Corporation
M.D.C.
Meritage Homes
MGIC Investment
M/I Homes
NVR
Pardee Homes
PMI Group
Ryland
Standard Pacific
Technical Olympic USA
Toll Brothers
Weyerhaeuser Real Estate

## HISTORICAL FINANCIALS

Company Type: Public

### Income Statement

FYE: December 31

| | REVENUE ($ mil.) | NET INCOME ($ mil.) | NET PROFIT MARGIN | EMPLOYEES |
|---|---|---|---|---|
| **12/06** | 14,274 | 688 | 4.8% | 12,400 |
| **12/05** | 14,695 | 1,492 | 10.2% | 13,400 |
| **12/04** | 11,711 | 987 | 8.4% | 13,000 |
| **12/03** | 9,049 | 625 | 6.9% | 10,800 |
| **12/02** | 7,472 | 454 | 6.1% | 9,200 |
| **Annual Growth** | 17.6% | 11.0% | — | 7.7% |

### 2006 Year-End Financials

Debt ratio: 53.8%
Return on equity: 11.0%
Cash ($ mil.): 624
Current ratio: 3.43
Long-term debt ($ mil.): 3,538
No. of shares (mil.): 255
Dividends
Yield: 0.5%
Payout: 6.0%
Market value ($ mil.): 8,456

### Stock History

NYSE: PHM

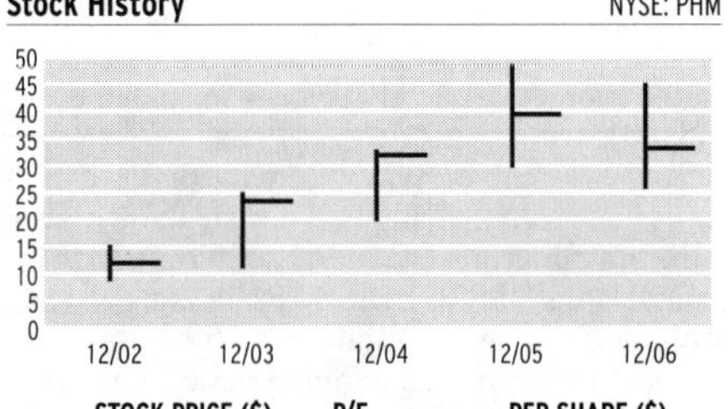


| | STOCK PRICE ($) FY Close | P/E High | P/E Low | PER SHARE ($) Earnings | Dividends | Book Value |
|---|---|---|---|---|---|---|
| **12/06** | 33.12 | 17 | 10 | 2.66 | 0.16 | 25.76 |
| **12/05** | 39.36 | 8 | 5 | 5.68 | 0.13 | 23.18 |
| **12/04** | 31.90 | 9 | 5 | 3.79 | 0.10 | 35.36 |
| **12/03** | 23.41 | 10 | 5 | 2.48 | 0.03 | 27.55 |
| **12/02** | 11.97 | 8 | 5 | 1.84 | 0.04 | 45.16 |
| **Annual Growth** | 29.0% | — | — | 9.7% | 41.4% | (13.1%) |

# QUALCOMM Incorporated

Cell phone makers, wireless carriers, and governments worldwide call on QUALCOMM to engineer a quality conversation. The company pioneered the commercialization of the code-division multiple access (CDMA) technology used in wireless communications equipment and satellite ground stations mainly in North America. It licenses CDMA semiconductor technology and system software to more than 100 equipment and cell phone makers. QUALCOMM's OmniTRACS satellite vehicle tracking system is used by the trucking industry to manage vehicle fleets.

QUALCOMM has been fighting legal battles over patents with rival Broadcom on several fronts. The most crucial case involves a ruling from the International Trade Commission, which held in mid-2007 that new mobile phones being imported into the US with certain QUALCOMM chipsets may be barred from sale. The QUALCOMM chipsets infringe on a Broadcom patent, the commission decided in a 4-2 vote. QUALCOMM appealed the ITC ruling to both the federal courts and the White House, but the Bush Administration decided to let the ITC decision stand.

Perhaps piling on in the wake of the International Trade Commission ruling against QUALCOMM, Nokia has filed a patent infringement claim against the company with the ITC. Nokia and QUALCOMM are also litigating patent claims against each other in US courts. According to analysts' estimates, Nokia had been paying about $500 million a year in licensing fees to QUALCOMM under their previous cross-licensing agreement, which expired in April 2007.

Although the US was long QUALCOMM's (and CDMA's) main market, the company has sown the seeds of expansion in Asia — particularly China and South Korea — and South America by partnering with such wireless service providers as China Unicom and Brazil-based Vésper. (South Korea now represents the company's largest national market.) Network operators in Europe are opting for the GPRS (General Packet Radio Service) standard instead of paying royalties to QUALCOMM for its speedier wireless CDMA.

QUALCOMM has put $500 million into QUALCOMM Ventures to make equity investments in a variety of start-up ventures. Portfolio companies include A123Systems (rechargeable batteries for portable devices), AirPlay (interactive games for cell phones), Airvana (radio access network infrastructure), Bitfone (mobile device management software), Obopay (mobile payment service), and China Techfaith Wireless Communication Technology (mobile design house).

In 2007 QUALCOMM Ventures said it would invest €100 million in European companies developing mobile application or platform software, handset components, network infrastructure, and core technologies for 3G (WCDMA) wireless communications. Its first investment went to Paris-based Streamezzo, a developer of rich-media software, platforms, and services for mobile communications.

## HISTORY

Professors Irwin Mark Jacobs and Andrew Viterbi founded digital signal processing equipment company Linkabit in 1968. M/A-COM acquired the company in 1980. Led by Jacobs, Viterbi and five other executives left M/A-COM Linkabit in 1985 to start engineer-focused QUALCOMM (for "quality communications") to provide contract R&D services. The company's first home was located above a strip mall pizza parlor in San Diego. CEO Jacobs dreamed of modifying code-division multiple access (CDMA) — a secure wireless transmission system developed during WWII — for commercial use.

In 1988 QUALCOMM introduced OmniTRACS, a satellite-based system that tracks the location of long-haul truckers. By 1989, when QUALCOMM unveiled its version of CDMA, the company was working on defense contracts worth $15 million.

In 1990 the company interrupted the Cellular Telecommunications Industry Association's (CTIA) plans to adopt a rival technology called time-division multiple access when communications service providers NYNEX (now part of Verizon) and Ameritech (now part of SBC Communications) adopted QUALCOMM's maverick technology. QUALCOMM initiated a CDMA public relations blitz and by 1991 Motorola, AT&T, Clarion, and Nokia had signed product development and testing agreements.

The company went public in 1991 and introduced e-mail software Eudora (named for "Why I Live at the P.O." author Eudora Welty), which it licensed from the University of Illinois. That year QUALCOMM and Loral Corporation unveiled plans for Globalstar, a satellite telecommunications system similar to the Iridium system. The CTIA adopted CDMA as a North American standard for wireless communications in 1993.

In 1996 most of the major US cellular carriers upgraded to CDMA. In 1997 Russia charged a QUALCOMM technician with espionage but allowed him to return to the US. The company spun off its wireless phone service operations in 1998 as Leap Wireless International.

In 1999 QUALCOMM and rival Ericsson settled a bitter dispute over the use of CDMA as an industry standard when they signed a cross-licensing deal. QUALCOMM sold its cell phone operations to Kyocera in 2000. The company also signed a potentially huge deal with China Unicom. The latter was a step forward for Chinese carriers and equipment makers itching to use CDMA in a region where the Global System for Mobile Communication (GSM) rules. In 2001 the Chinese government, after years of balking at CDMA in favor of 3G, granted QUALCOMM and China Unicom permission to install a CDMA-based network.

EVP Paul Jacobs, son of co-founder Irwin Mark Jacobs, took over as CEO in mid-2005; his father remained chairman of the company. It also closed on its acquisition of Flarion Technologies, a developer of a proprietary version of OFDM (orthogonal frequency-division multiplexing) technology called FLASH-OFDM. QUALCOMM paid about $600 million in cash and stock for Flarion.

In 2006 QUALCOMM paid a $1.8 million fine to the federal government for exercising operational control over Flarion before actually closing the transaction to acquire the chipset company.

## EXECUTIVES

**Chairman:** Irwin Mark Jacobs, age 73
**CEO and Director:** Paul E. Jacobs, age 44, $2,657,699 pay
**COO; President, QUALCOMM CDMA Technologies:** Sanjay K. Jha, age 43, $1,688,464 pay
**President:** Steven R. (Steve) Altman, age 45, $1,879,236 pay
**EVP and CFO:** William E. Keitel, age 53, $1,286,939 pay
**EVP and CTO:** Roberto Padovani, age 52, $784,235 pay
**EVP, Human Resources:** Daniel L. Sullivan, age 55
**EVP; Group President, QUALCOMM Wireless Business Solutions, QUALCOMM MEMS Technologies, QUALCOMM Government Technologies, and MediaFLO USA:** Len J. Lauer
**EVP; President, Global Development:** Jeffrey A. (Jeff) Jacobs, age 40
**EVP; President, QUALCOMM Internet Services:** Margaret L. (Peggy) Johnson, age 44
**EVP; President, QUALCOMM Technology Licensing:** Marvin (Marv) Blecker, age 59
**SVP and CIO:** Norm Fjeldheim
**SVP; General Manager, MediaFLO:** Jeff Lorbeck
**SVP and Chairman, QUALCOMM Asia Pacific:** Jing Wang
**SVP; President, QUALCOMM India:** Kanwalinder Singh
**SVP; President, QUALCOMM Korea:** Sung W. (S.W.) Kim
**SVP; General Manager, QUALCOMM MEMS Technologies:** Gregory P. (Greg) Heinzinger
**SVP, Strategy and Market Development:** Jeffrey K. Belk
**SVP, Government Affairs:** William (Bill) Bold
**SVP Global Marketing and Investor Relations:** William F. (Bill) Davidson Jr.
**SVP and Interim General Counsel:** Carol C. Lam, age 48
**Corporate Communications:** Emily Kilpatrick
**Auditors:** PricewaterhouseCoopers LLP

## LOCATIONS

**HQ:** QUALCOMM Incorporated
5775 Morehouse Dr., San Diego, CA 92121
**Phone:** 858-587-1121 **Fax:** 858-658-2100
**Web:** www.qualcomm.com

QUALCOMM has facilities in Brazil, China, France, Germany, India, Israel, Italy, Japan, Mexico, South Korea, the UK, and the US.

### 2006 Sales

| | $ mil. | % of total |
|---|---|---|
| Asia/Pacific | | |
| South Korea | 2,398 | 32 |
| Japan | 1,573 | 21 |
| China | 1,266 | 17 |
| US | 984 | 13 |
| Other countries | 1,305 | 17 |
| **Total** | **7,526** | **100** |

## PRODUCTS/OPERATIONS

### 2006 Sales

| | $ mil. | % of total |
|---|---|---|
| QUALCOMM CDMA Technologies (QCT) | 4,332 | 57 |
| QUALCOMM Technology Licensing (QTL) | 2,631 | 34 |
| QUALCOMM Wireless & Internet (QWI) | 670 | 9 |
| Adjustments | (107) | — |
| **Total** | **7,526** | **100** |

### Selected Operations and Products

Code-Division Multiple Access (CDMA) Technologies Group
- Integrated circuits
  - Baseband
  - Intermediate-frequency
  - Power management
  - Radio-frequency
- Systems software

Technology Licensing Group
- CDMA technologies and patents (cdmaOne, CDMA2000, WCDMA, TD-SCDMA)
- Royalties from products incorporating CDMA technology

Wireless and Internet Group
- Digital Media
  - Digital motion picture delivery systems (under development)
  - Government systems (development and analysis services; wireless base stations and phones)
- Internet Services
  - Applications development software for wireless devices (BREW)
  - E-mail software (Eudora)
- Wireless Systems
  - Low-Earth-orbit satellite-based telecommunications system (Globalstar)
  - Satellite and terrestrial two-way data messaging and position reporting systems and services (OmniTRACS, OmniExpress, TruckMAIL)

## COMPETITORS

Andrew
Broadcom
Ericsson
Freescale Semiconductor
IBM Microelectronics
Infineon Technologies
Intel
LG Group
Matsushita Electric
Maxim Integrated Products
Motorola, Inc.
NAVTEQ
NEC Electronics
Nokia
Nortel Networks
NXP
Remote Dynamics
Samsung Electronics
STMicroelectronics
Texas Instruments
Trimble Navigation

## HISTORICAL FINANCIALS

Company Type: Public

### Income Statement

FYE: Last Sunday in September

| | REVENUE ($ mil.) | NET INCOME ($ mil.) | NET PROFIT MARGIN | EMPLOYEES |
|---|---|---|---|---|
| **9/06** | 7,526 | 2,470 | 32.8% | 11,200 |
| **9/05** | 5,673 | 2,143 | 37.8% | 9,300 |
| **9/04** | 4,880 | 1,720 | 35.2% | 7,600 |
| **9/03** | 3,971 | 827 | 20.8% | 7,400 |
| **9/02** | 3,040 | 360 | 11.8% | 8,100 |
| **Annual Growth** | 25.4% | 61.9% | — | 8.4% |

### 2006 Year-End Financials

Debt ratio: —
Return on equity: 20.1%
Cash ($ mil.): 5,721
Current ratio: 4.96
Long-term debt ($ mil.): —
No. of shares (mil.): 1,652
Dividends
Yield: 1.1%
Payout: 29.2%
Market value ($ mil.): 62,545

### Stock History

NASDAQ (GS): QCOM

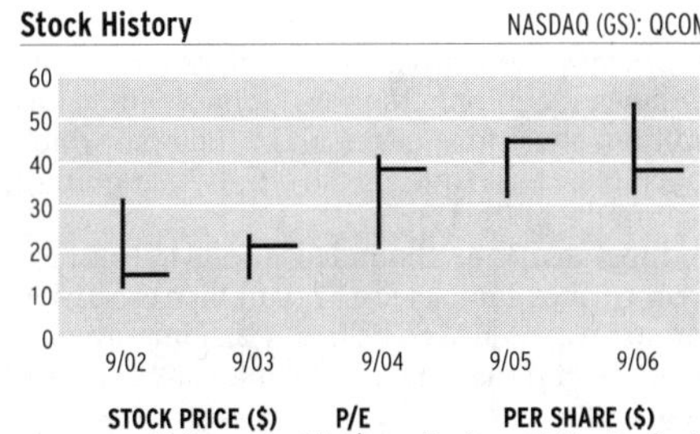


| | STOCK PRICE ($) FY Close | P/E High | P/E Low | PER SHARE ($) Earnings | Dividends | Book Value |
|---|---|---|---|---|---|---|
| **9/06** | 37.86 | 37 | 23 | 1.44 | 0.42 | 8.12 |
| **9/05** | 44.76 | 36 | 25 | 1.26 | 0.25 | 6.78 |
| **9/04** | 38.25 | 40 | 20 | 1.03 | 0.19 | 5.91 |
| **9/03** | 20.83 | 46 | 27 | 0.50 | 0.09 | 9.52 |
| **9/02** | 14.31 | 142 | 53 | 0.22 | — | 6.93 |
| **Annual Growth** | 27.5% | — | — | 60.0% | 67.1% | 4.0% |

# Quanex Corporation

Behind bars isn't a bad place to be for Quanex. The company's vehicular products unit makes a variety of seamless steel bars used by original equipment manufacturers (OEMs) to manufacture camshafts, transmission gears, and bearing cages and rollers. Products made by the vehicular products segment are used by the passenger car, off-road, and farm equipment industries. The building products group makes fabricated aluminum and steel products such as aluminum windows, patio doors, screens, and window frames, using roll-formed aluminum and stamped shapes for the housing market. In 2005 the company acquired Besten, a glazing component manufacturer. In 2006 Quanex sold its Temroc Metals business to WXP Holdings.

The company has grown by focusing on high-margin markets, making niche acquisitions, and selling poorly performing units. As part of this strategy, Quanex divested Piper Impact, a cold-forged impact extrusion business, in 2005.

Late the following year the company agreed to buy Atmosphere Annealing from Maxco, Inc. for an undisclosed sum. Atmosphere Annealing provides heat-treating, phosphate coating, shearing and other metal-treating services, primarily to the automotive industry. Quanex has been a customer of Atmosphere Annealing, so the acquisition makes a good strategic fit. The transaction was completed early in 2007.

Later that year the company said it was exploring options for its building products division, including a possible spinoff.

## HISTORY

Quanex began as Michigan Seamless Tube in South Lyon, Michigan, in 1927. Led by William McMunn, the company reworked used boiler and condenser tubes. During WWII it won awards for high-quality aircraft tubing. Michigan Seamless Tube went public in 1965.

In 1977 the company changed its name to Quanex and moved to Houston. By 1981 about half of its sales were energy-related. When the petrochemical market collapsed, the company reorganized and broadened its markets. In 1989 Quanex acquired Nichols-Homeshield (aluminum sheet for gutters and windows), which operated, at the time, one of only two aluminum minimills in the US.

Steel demand rebounded in 1994. The next year Quanex completed a $170 million expansion program at its MACSTEEL unit that improved efficiency and made it North America's first producer of precision hot-rolled steel bars. In a move toward aluminum, a sector helped by an increased demand for automotive airbag containers, Quanex bought Piper Impact in 1996. In 1997 Quanex bought Advanced Metal Forming (metal components for automotive and electronics OEMs, the Netherlands). It also sold its LaSalle Steel division (cold-finished steel bars) and its steel tube operations, excluding two small service divisions. The next year Quanex bought Decatur Aluminum (aluminum sheet) and upgraded many of its existing facilities to further improve production efficiency.

Quanex acquired an aluminum sheet production facility from industry leader Alcoa in 2000. It also bought Imperial Products (door components) and Temroc Metal (aluminum extrusion and fabrication). That year it sold its Piper Impact Europe unit to the plant's management for an undisclosed sum. In 2001 Quanex divided its operations into vehicular and building products segments.

In early 2002 Quanex purchased Colonial Craft, maker of custom wood window accessories, for an undisclosed price. The following year, Quanex purchased TruSeal Technologies (maker of flexible insulating glass spacer systems and sealants) for around $113 million. In early 2003 the company also bought the Monroe, Michigan, minimill of Cargill's North Star Steel subsidiary for $115 million. The following year, Quanex sold off its Nichols Aluminum Golden unit in Fort Lupton, Colorado, to Crestwood Capital Management for about $22 million.

## EXECUTIVES

**Chairman, President, and CEO:** Raymond A. Jean, age 64, $1,977,203 pay
**SVP, General Counsel, and Corporate Secretary:** Kevin P. Delaney, age 45, $543,335 pay
**SVP, President, Building Products:** Michael R. Bayles, age 55, $701,613 pay
**SVP, Finance and CFO:** Thomas M. Walker, age 59, $319,627 pay
**VP and Corporate Controller:** Brent L. Korb, age 34
**VP and Treasurer:** John Mannion, age 40
**VP, Corporate Development:** Paul A. Hammonds, age 50
**VP; President, MACSTEEL:** Mark A. Marcucci, age 52, $454,467 pay
**VP, Investor Relations:** Geoffrey G. (Jeff) Galow
**Manager, Investor Relations:** Valerie Calvert
**Auditors:** Deloitte & Touche LLP

## LOCATIONS

**HQ:** Quanex Corporation
1900 West Loop South, Ste. 1500,
Houston, TX 77027
**Phone:** 713-961-4600 **Fax:** 713-439-1016
**Web:** www.quanex.com

Quanex operates 22 manufacturing plants in Alabama, Arkansas, Illinois, Indiana, Iowa, Kentucky, Michigan, Minnesota, Ohio, Oregon, Washington, and Wisconsin.

### 2006 Sales

| | $ mil. | % of total |
|---|---|---|
| US | 1,898.4 | 94 |
| Canada | 65.7 | 3 |
| Mexico | 58.5 | 3 |
| Asia | 6.1 | — |
| Europe | 2.4 | — |
| Other regions | 1.5 | — |
| **Total** | **2,032.6** | **100** |

### Selected Subsidiaries

Besten Equipment, Inc
Colonial Craft, Inc.
Imperial Products, Inc.
MACSTEEL Monroe, Inc.
Mikron Industries, Inc.
Nichols Aluminum-Alabama, Inc.
Quanex Bar, Inc.
Quanex Health Management Company, Inc.
Quanex Solutions, Inc.
Quanex Steel, Inc.
Quanex Technologies, Inc.

## PRODUCTS/OPERATIONS

### 2006 Sales

| | $ mil. | % of total |
|---|---|---|
| Vehicular products | 988.8 | 48 |
| Aluminum sheet building products | 539.8 | 26 |
| Engineered building products | 524.6 | 26 |
| Adjustments | (20.6) | — |
| **Total** | **2,032.6** | **100** |

## COMPETITORS

Alcan
Alcoa
Century Aluminum
Chaparral Steel
Commercial Metals
Kaiser Aluminum
Keystone Consolidated
Nucor
O'Neal Steel
Ormet
PAV Republic
Reliance Steel
Roanoke Bar Division
Steel Dynamics
Stelco Hamilton
Timken

## HISTORICAL FINANCIALS

Company Type: Public

### Income Statement

FYE: October 31

| | REVENUE ($ mil.) | NET INCOME ($ mil.) | NET PROFIT MARGIN | EMPLOYEES |
|---|---|---|---|---|
| **10/06** | 2,033 | 160 | 7.9% | 4,200 |
| **10/05** | 1,969 | 155 | 7.9% | 4,530 |
| **10/04** | 1,460 | 55 | 3.7% | 3,421 |
| **10/03** | 1,031 | 43 | 4.2% | 3,153 |
| **10/02** | 994 | 56 | 5.6% | 3,476 |
| **Annual Growth** | 19.6% | 30.3% | — | 4.8% |

### 2006 Year-End Financials

Debt ratio: 17.2%
Return on equity: 22.6%
Cash ($ mil.): 106
Current ratio: 2.16
Long-term debt ($ mil.): 131
No. of shares (mil.): 37
Dividends
Yield: 1.1%
Payout: 8.8%
Market value ($ mil.): 1,244

### Stock History

NYSE: NX

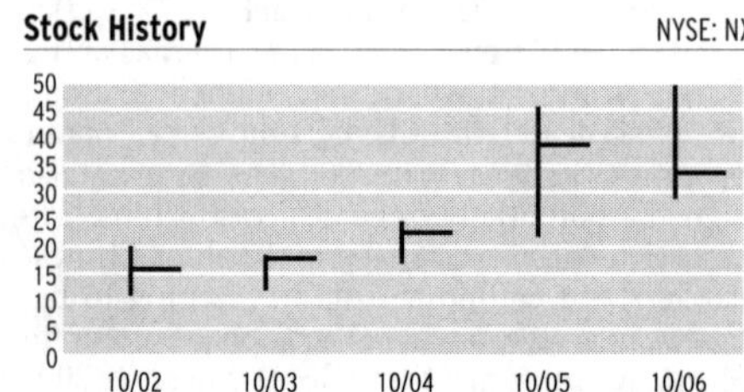


| | STOCK PRICE ($) FY Close | P/E High | P/E Low | PER SHARE ($) Earnings | PER SHARE ($) Dividends | PER SHARE ($) Book Value |
|---|---|---|---|---|---|---|
| **10/06** | 33.51 | 12 | 7 | 4.08 | 0.36 | 20.43 |
| **10/05** | 38.61 | 11 | 6 | 3.95 | 0.37 | 25.79 |
| **10/04** | 22.53 | 17 | 12 | 1.45 | 0.39 | 30.07 |
| **10/03** | 17.80 | 15 | 11 | 1.16 | 0.30 | 26.94 |
| **10/02** | 15.80 | 13 | 7 | 1.56 | 0.28 | 25.61 |
| **Annual Growth** | 20.7% | — | — | 27.2% | 6.5% | (5.5%) |

# Quest Diagnostics

Quest Diagnostics is testing its ability to be the world's leading clinical lab. The company performs tests on some 150 million specimens each year, including routine tests such as cholesterol checks, Pap smears, HIV screenings, and drug tests. Quest Diagnostics performs esoteric testing (such as genetic screening) through its Nichols Institute Diagnostics arm, and it assists drug companies with tests for clinical trials. The company serves doctors and hospitals, as well as corporations, government agencies, and other clinical labs. It has more than 2,000 patient services centers where samples are collected, along with about 30 primary labs and 150 rapid response labs throughout the US and in Mexico and the UK.

Quest strives to make itself ubiquitous, with a comprehensive menu of tests (more than 3,000) and a network of labs and collection sites that blanket the country. It keeps looking to grow its service offering, however, by acquiring firms with complementary testing capabilities and through developing its own novel tests. It introduced some 80 new or improved tests in 2006, including products to diagnose leukemia and breast cancer, find drug-resistant staph infections, and detect infectious diseases in organ transplant patients.

In 2007 the company acquired laboratory services firm AmeriPath in a deal worth about $2 billion. The purchase strengthens Quest's operations in a number of areas, including anatomic pathology, cancer testing, and molecular diagnostics. It is consistent with Quests' goal of expanding market share in a number of physician subspecialties (such as urology, gastroenterology, dermatology, and oncology) and in anatomic pathology testing. The company had previously made a number of smaller acquisitions, including the 2006 purchases of Enterix, a maker of colorectal cancer screening tests, and Focus Diagnostics, an infectious disease testing lab with expertise in esoteric testing. Additionally, with its acquisition of LabOne in 2005, it began providing testing and risk assessment services for the life insurance industry.

Focus Diagnostics and Enterix both add to the company's presence in point-of-care testing, in which tests are performed at the bedside or in the doctor's office and produce results more quickly. The company's purchase of Swedish firm HemoCue, which makes point-of-care blood testing systems, also contributed to Quest's growth in this area.

While more than 90% of Quest's revenue comes from routine and esoteric testing services, the company offers a number of other products, including online data management system Care360 Physician Portal, which lets doctors order diagnostic tests, review results, prescribe medication, and manage patient files. Quest's MedPlus subsidiary developed the tool. A small portion of sales comes from providing testing services to drug companies for their clinical trials; GlaxoSmithKline, which owns nearly 20% of Quest, accounts for about half of such revenue.

The company suffered a setback in 2006 when it lost a national contract with United Healthcare to provide in-network laboratory services to the insurer's members. Quest depends on health insurers for about half of its business; United Healthcare alone brought in 7% of sales in 2006.

## HISTORY

Quest Diagnostics began as one man's quest to make clinical tests more affordable. Pathologist Paul Brown started Metropolitan Pathological Laboratory (MetPath) in his Manhattan apartment in 1967. To help his business take off, in 1969 he bought two $55,000 blood analyzers that could automatically perform a dozen common tests; the machines allowed him to charge patients $5.50 while hospitals and other labs were charging upwards of $40. Investments in emerging lab technology helped MetPath continue to beat competitors' prices and grow its business. It made its first profit in 1971 and eventually attracted the attention of Corning Glass Works, which bought 10% of the company in 1973.

MetPath's growth was due in part to investments in technology. The company built a state-of-the-art central lab in New Jersey in 1978 that could process some 30,000 specimens daily; it also went on an acquisition spree to expand across the US. These investments left the firm swamped with debt, and Corning bought the company in 1982.

An autonomous unit of Corning, MetPath continued to grow as Medicare reimbursement for lab tests went up and more doctors ordered more tests to catch and prevent disease before it happened. To cut costs in the mid-1980s, the company reorganized its facilities to create a regional lab network. A reorganization in 1990 at its parent placed MetPath in the Corning Lab Services subsidiary.

Corning Lab Services strengthened its operations in the early 1990s by buying labs from regional operators. In 1994 MetPath became Corning Clinical Laboratories. Around the same time, the company found itself besieged with demands from HMOs and other managed care providers to lower its costs. Also during this time, the company settled a handful of federal suits accusing it of fraudulent Medicare billing. In the face of increasing pressure, parent Corning spun off its lab testing business to the public as Quest Diagnostics in 1996.

On its own, Quest aimed to grow through acquisitions. In 1999 it bought rival SmithKline Beecham Clinical Laboratories and has continued its growth strategy in the 21st century. It bought American Medical Laboratories to expand its esoteric testing operations in 2002. The company was finally able to close its acquisition of Unilab in early 2003 after the deal ran into delays with the FTC. Quest sold some labs and service contracts in northern California to LabCorp to appease FTC regulators.

## EXECUTIVES

**Chairman, President, and CEO:** Surya N. Mohapatra, age 57, $1,919,192 pay
**SVP and CFO:** Robert A. Hagemann, age 50, $724,739 pay
**SVP, Legal and Compliance; General Counsel:** Michael E. Prevoznik, age 45, $571,010 pay
**CIO:** Mary Hall Gregg
**VP and Chief Laboratory Officer, and Interim VP, Science and Innovation:** Joyce G. Schwartz
**VP, Controller, and Chief Accounting Officer:** Thomas F. Bongiorno
**VP, Compliance:** Karen Straub
**VP, External Communications:** Gary Samuels
**VP, Healthcare Information Solutions:** Richard A. Mahoney
**VP, Human Resources:** David Norgard
**VP, Investor Relations:** Laure E. Park
**VP, Sales and Marketing:** Robert E. Peters, age 59, $505,854 pay
**VP, Operations:** Wayne R. Simmons
**Managing Director, Nichols Institute:** Jon Nakamoto
**Managing Director and Medical Director, Chantilly:** Nathan Sherman
**Senior Science Officer, San Juan Capistrano:** Delbert A. Fisher
**Senior Laboratory Director:** Raj Pandian
**Director, Purchasing Controls and Governance:** Gladys Daniel
**Director of Scientific Affairs:** Peter P. Chou
**Medical Director, Coagulation:** Mervyn A. Sahud
**Scientific Director, Research and Development, Immunology/Coagulation:** Anthony Sferruzza
**Medical Director, Chantilly, Medical Director, Nichols Institute Reference Laboratory, and Medical Director, Endocrinology/Metabolism, Toxicology:** Richard E. Reitz
**Auditors:** PricewaterhouseCoopers LLP

## LOCATIONS

**HQ:** Quest Diagnostics Incorporated
1290 Wall St. West, Lyndhurst, NJ 07071
**Phone:** 201-393-5000 **Fax:** 201-729-8920
**Web:** www.questdiagnostics.com

Quest Diagnostics has facilities across the US, as well as in Mexico, Puerto Rico, and the UK.

## PRODUCTS/OPERATIONS

### 2006 Sales

| | $ mil. | % of total |
|---|---|---|
| Clinical laboratory testing | 5,785.3 | 92 |
| Other | 483.4 | 8 |
| **Total** | **6,268.7** | **100** |

### Selected Products and Services

Clincial laboratory testing
- Esoteric testing
  - Endocrinology
  - Genetics
  - Immunology
  - Microbiology
  - Oncology
  - Serology
  - Toxicology
- Routine testing
  - Alcohol and other substance-abuse tests
  - Blood cholesterol
  - Complete blood counts
  - Pap smears
  - Pregnancy testing
  - Urinalyses

Other products and services
- Clinical trials testing
- Medical data management systems
- Life insurance risk assessment services

### Selected Subsidiaries

American Medical Laboratories, Incorporated
Compunet Clinical Laboratories (33%)
Diagnostic Laboratory of Oklahoma LLC (51%)
Diagnostic Reference Services Inc.
Enterix Inc.
HemoCue AB (Sweden)
Lab Portal, Inc.
Lab*One*, Inc.
Lifepoint Medical Corporation
MedPlus, Inc.
MetWest Inc.
Mid America Clinical Laboratories (44%)
Nichols Institute Diagnostics
Nichols Institute Diagnostics Limited (UK)
Nichols Institute Diagnostics Trading AG (Switzerland)
Nichols Institute Diagnostika GmbH (Germany)
Quest Diagnostics Clinical Laboratories, Inc.
Quest Diagnostics do Brasil Ltda.
Quest Diagnostics Mexico, S.A. de C.V.
Quest Diagnostics of Pennsylvania Inc.
Quest Diagnostics of Puerto Rico, Inc.
Unilab Corporation

## COMPETITORS

| | |
|---|---|
| AcuNetx | PA Labs |
| Bio-Reference Labs | PAREXEL |
| Covance | Pathology Associates |
| Esoterix | Pharmaceutical Product Development |
| Kroll Laboratory | Pharmaceutical Research |
| LabCorp | Psychemedics |
| Medtox Scientific | Quintiles Transnational |
| Mid America Clinical Laboratories | Spectrum Laboratory |
| Orchid Cellmark | US Labs |

## HISTORICAL FINANCIALS

Company Type: Public

**Income Statement** FYE: December 31

| | REVENUE ($ mil.) | NET INCOME ($ mil.) | NET PROFIT MARGIN | EMPLOYEES |
|---|---|---|---|---|
| **12/06** | 6,269 | 586 | 9.4% | 41,000 |
| **12/05** | 5,504 | 546 | 9.9% | 41,500 |
| **12/04** | 5,127 | 499 | 9.7% | 38,600 |
| **12/03** | 4,738 | 437 | 9.2% | 37,200 |
| **12/02** | 4,108 | 322 | 7.8% | 33,400 |
| **Annual Growth** | 11.1% | 16.2% | — | 5.3% |

**2006 Year-End Financials**

Debt ratio: 41.0%
Return on equity: 20.3%
Cash ($ mil.): 150
Current ratio: 1.03
Long-term debt ($ mil.): 1,239
No. of shares (mil.): 194
Dividends
Yield: 0.7%
Payout: 13.3%
Market value ($ mil.): 10,279

**Stock History** NYSE: DGX

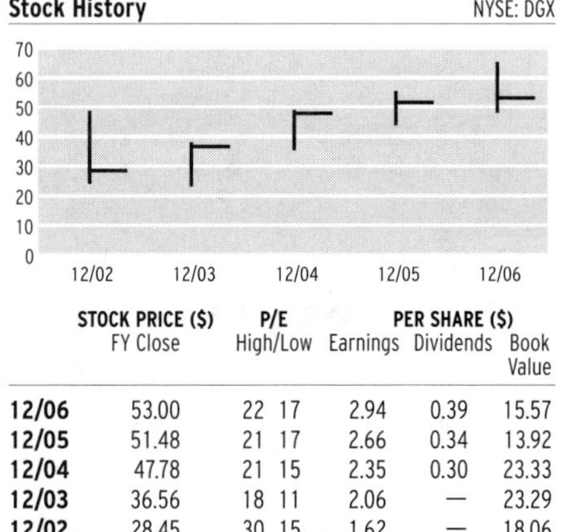


| | STOCK PRICE ($) FY Close | P/E High | P/E Low | PER SHARE ($) Earnings | Dividends | Book Value |
|---|---|---|---|---|---|---|
| **12/06** | 53.00 | 22 | 17 | 2.94 | 0.39 | 15.57 |
| **12/05** | 51.48 | 21 | 17 | 2.66 | 0.34 | 13.92 |
| **12/04** | 47.78 | 21 | 15 | 2.35 | 0.30 | 23.33 |
| **12/03** | 36.56 | 18 | 11 | 2.06 | — | 23.29 |
| **12/02** | 28.45 | 30 | 15 | 1.62 | — | 18.06 |
| **Annual Growth** | 16.8% | — | — | 16.1% | 14.0% | (3.6%) |

# Quiksilver, Inc.

Quiksilver rides the wave of youth appeal. It caters to the young and athletic with surfwear, snowboardwear, and sportswear sold under brands Quiksilver, Raisins, and Roxy. The company also sells snow skis, boots, and bindings through its Rossignol, Dynastar, Lange, and other brands. It sells its products in surf, specialty, and department stores worldwide. It also owns about 280 of its own stores, including Boardriders Clubs (board sports), Roxy (junior apparel), and Quicksilver Youth. Quiksilver has expanded its stable to include eyewear, watches, casual apparel, and personal care products. FMR Corp. owns more than 13% of Quiksilver.

The company's youthful, California surfer image began morphing into a more international, French Alps visage in 2005. Early in the year the company bought a 49.5% stake in Rossignol, a French ski and snowboard manufacturer. In late 2005 Quiksilver acquired about 95% of direct or indirect ownership and more than 96% of the voting rights in Rossignol. The equipment maker buy complements Quiksilver's focus on apparel and allows it to compete head to head with North Face and Patagonia.

To expand the company's reach into international retail growth, Quiksilver in 2005 acquired Australia's top boardriding retailer, Surfection. The acquisition involves five Surfection shops to be converted to Quiksilver Boardriders Clubs and five Quiksilver/Roxy concept stores. It also paves the way for Quiksilver's expansion into Asia/Pacific, specifically Japan, China, and Southeast Asia. To enter the Mexican market, the company formed a joint venture in late 2006 with PBM International (of which Quiksilver owns a majority stake) to sell the Quiksilver and Roxy brands in Mexico. PBM distributes Le Coq Sportif, Arena, and FIFA branded footwear, apparel, and accessories.

Quiksilver entered the Russian wholesale and retail markets in mid-2006 through its joint venture with Sprandi International Ltd., a top sports and outdoor products manufacturer in Russia and Eastern Europe that specializes in footwear, apparel, and accessories. The deal gives Quiksilver the exclusive rights to make, market, and distribute its namesake and Roxy brand items in Russia.

Like many surf/skate/snowboarding companies, Quiksilver promotes its brands not so much through advertising as much as sponsorship of events featuring its products, e.g., major surf competitions. It forms associations with well-known athletes in the field, such as surfer Kelly Slater and skateboarded Tony Hawk, to promote its products. Another division, Quiksilver Entertainment, produces programming that covers these events while also promoting the boardriding (and hence Quiksilver) lifestyle.

Quiksilver also has ventured into personal care products — a relatively new niche for the firm — for its namesake and Roxy lines. In early 2006 the company inked an exclusive worldwide licensing agreement with Inter Parfums to develop and distribute (Roxy) fragrance, suncare, skincare, and related items, as well as (Quiksilver) suncare and other products through 2017.

## HISTORY

Australian surfers Alan Green and John Law started Quiksilver in 1969 to make "boardshorts" for surfers. In 1976 surfers Jeff Hakman and Bob McKnight bought the US rights to the Quiksilver name — Hakman displayed his enthusiasm for the line by eating a doily at a dinner with Green — and established Quiksilver, USA. The firm went public in 1986.

The recession of the early 1990s and the dominance of grunge as the fashion du jour hurt Quiksilver and prompted it to restructure. It acquired French affiliate Na Pali in 1991 and began building its European operations.

To gain surer footing in the fickle teen fashion market, Quiksilver broadened its product offerings. It added the Roxy women's swimwear line in 1991, expanding it to clothing in 1993. It also launched the Boardriders Club concept — stores featuring Quiksilver merchandise but owned by independent retailers.

In 1994 the company acquired swimwear maker The Raisin Company. In 1997 Quiksilver began advertising nationally and entered the snowboard market, buying Mervin Manufacturing, maker of Lib Technologies, Gnu, and Bent Metal snowboard products.

With its women's lines making waves and a strong current from European sales, Quiksilver began opening its own Boardriders Club stores in 1998. In 1999 it launched the Quik Jeans and Roxy Jeans denim lines, and the next year it added the Alex Goes line for women 25 to 40. Riding a tide of rising profits, in 2000 the company acquired Fidra men's golf apparel; Freestyle, the European licensee of rival youth wear label Gotcha; and pro-skateboarder Tony Hawk's apparel and accessories business. In a tail-that-wags-the-dog move, the company bought its progenitor, Quiksilver International, the same year; in doing so, Quiksilver gained sole possession of the Quiksilver name worldwide.

In June 2002 Quiksilver launched Quiksilver Entertainment, a production company that creates actionsport-based programming for the entertainment industry. Later that year Quiksilver acquired Ug Manufacturing in Australia and Quiksilver Japan, in an effort to gain control over nearly all its global business, with the exception of a few licenses in small niche markets. At about the same time the company purchased and integrated Beach Street, the owner and operator of 26 Quiksilver outlet stores.

The company formed a 50/50 joint venture in 2003 with Glorious Sun Enterprises to expand into China.

In 2004 Quiksilver's entertainment unit launched an actionsport film distribution company, Union, which is a supplier to more than 1,000 retail locations in Australia, China, Europe, Japan, and the US. In 2004 Quiksilver completed its purchase of DC Shoes and bought the footwear firm's Canadian distributor, Centre Skateboard Distribution, Ltd., in 2005. The footwear company's notoriety in the skate and surf community serves to embed Quiksilver further in same, while ensuring its ability to compete with Nike and adidas in the footwear arena.

In 2005 Quiksilver flipped its board in a new direction, however, and broadened its reach into the mainstream. The company announced it has signed an exclusive licensing deal with Kohl's and Tony Hawk to give traction to its apparel, outerwear, and accessories. As part of the agreement, Quiksilver will continue to design the Tony Hawk clothing brand and Kohl's will do the rest, including sourcing, distributing, marketing, and other functions.

## EXECUTIVES

**Chairman and CEO:** Robert B. (Bob) McKnight Jr., age 53, $1,005,000 pay
**President and Director:** Bernard Mariette, age 44, $807,000 pay
**COO:** David H. Morgan, age 47
**EVP, Business and Legal Affairs, Secretary, General Counsel, and Director:** Charles S. Exon, age 57, $800,000 pay
**EVP and CFO:** Joseph (Joe) Scirocco
**EVP, Quiksilver Sales:** Tom Holbrook
**SVP, Global Marketing, Roxy:** Randy Hild
**SVP, Sales, Roxy Girl:** Deanna Jackson
**VP, Human Resources:** Carol Sherman
**VP, Accounting and Financial Reporting:** Brad L. Holman, age 33

**Executive Advisor:** Harry Hodge
**President, Retail, Americas:** Carol Christopherson
**President, DC Shoes:** Nick Adcock
**President, Quiksilver Americas:** Marty Samuels
**President, Quiksilver Asia Pacific:** Clive Fitts
**President, Quiksilver Europe:** Pierre Agnes
**President, Women's Division:** Steve Tully
**President, Rossignol Group North America:** François Goulet
**Media Relations:** Joshua Katz
**Auditors:** Deloitte & Touche LLP

## LOCATIONS

**HQ:** Quiksilver, Inc.
15202 Graham St., Huntington Beach, CA 92649
**Phone:** 714-889-2200 **Fax:** 714-889-2315
**Web:** www.quiksilver.com

Quiksilver has offices in Australia, France, and the US.

### 2006 Sales

| | % of total |
|---|---|
| Americas | |
| US | 39 |
| Other countries | 7 |
| Europe | |
| France | 14 |
| UK & Spain | 11 |
| Other countries | 18 |
| Asia/Pacific | 11 |
| **Total** | **100** |

## PRODUCTS/OPERATIONS

### 2006 Sales

| | % of total |
|---|---|
| Wintersports equipment | 18 |
| T-shirts | 13 |
| Accessories | 11 |
| Jackets, sweaters & technical outerwear | 11 |
| Footwear | 11 |
| Golf equipment | 7 |
| Pants | 6 |
| Shirts | 6 |
| Swimwear, excluding boardshorts | 4 |
| Fleece | 4 |
| Shorts | 3 |
| Boardshorts | 3 |
| Tops & dresses | 3 |
| **Total** | **100** |

### 2006 Sales

| | % of total |
|---|---|
| Quiksilver | 31 |
| Roxy | 27 |
| Rossignol | 21 |
| DC Shoes | 10 |
| Cleveland Golf | 7 |
| Other | 4 |
| **Total** | **100** |

### Selected Brands

Alex Goes (women's apparel)
DC Shoes (men's and women's extreme sportswear and footwear)
Bent Metal (snowboard bindings)
Fidra (men's golf apparel)
Gotcha (men's apparel)
Gnu (snowboards and accessories)
Hawk Clothing (men's and boys' skateboard apparel and accessories)
Leilani (women's swimwear)
Lib Technologies (snowboards and accessories)
Quiksilver (sportswear, beachwear, activewear, and outerwear)
Quiksilver Boys (boys' sportswear)
Quiksilver Roxy (junior sportswear, footwear, accessories, and swimwear)
Quiksilver Silver Edition (men's sportswear, beachwear, activewear, and outerwear)
Quiksilver Toddler (children's sportswear)
Radio Fiji (junior swimwear)
Raisins (junior swimwear)

## COMPETITORS

Abercrombie & Fitch
adidas
Amer Sports
Amerex Group
Ashworth
Billabong
Body Glove
Burton Snowboards
Calvin Klein
Columbia Sportswear
Fat Face
FUBU
Head
K2
Levi Strauss
Life is good
Mossimo
Nautica Enterprises
NIKE
Oakley
Orange 21
Pacific Sunwear
Rusty
Sole Technology
Stüssy
Tecnica
Tommy Hilfiger
Volcom
Warnaco Swimwear

## HISTORICAL FINANCIALS

Company Type: Public

### Income Statement

FYE: October 31

| | REVENUE ($ mil.) | NET INCOME ($ mil.) | NET PROFIT MARGIN | EMPLOYEES |
|---|---|---|---|---|
| **10/06** | 2,362 | 93 | 3.9% | 9,200 |
| **10/05** | 1,781 | 107 | 6.0% | 7,875 |
| **10/04** | 1,267 | 81 | 6.4% | 4,350 |
| **10/03** | 975 | 59 | 6.0% | 3,400 |
| **10/02** | 706 | 38 | 5.3% | 2,700 |
| **Annual Growth** | 35.3% | 25.4% | — | 35.9% |

### 2006 Year-End Financials

Debt ratio: 78.3%
Return on equity: 11.5%
Cash ($ mil.): 37
Current ratio: 1.74
Long-term debt ($ mil.): 690
No. of shares (mil.): 124
Dividends
Yield: —
Payout: —
Market value ($ mil.): 1,723

### Stock History

NYSE: ZQK

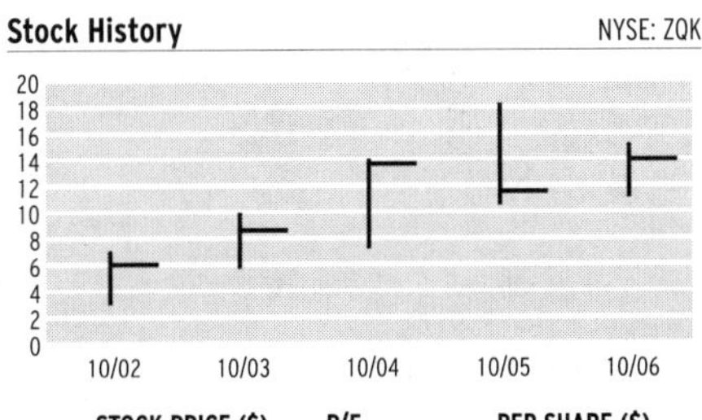


| | STOCK PRICE ($) FY Close | P/E High | P/E Low | PER SHARE ($) Earnings | Dividends | Book Value |
|---|---|---|---|---|---|---|
| **10/06** | 13.95 | 21 | 15 | 0.73 | — | 7.13 |
| **10/05** | 11.53 | 21 | 12 | 0.86 | — | 6.05 |
| **10/04** | 13.63 | 20 | 11 | 0.68 | — | 10.02 |
| **10/03** | 8.59 | 19 | 11 | 0.51 | — | 7.83 |
| **10/02** | 6.00 | 18 | 8 | 0.38 | — | 11.06 |
| **Annual Growth** | 23.5% | — | — | 17.7% | — | (10.4%) |

# Qwest Communications

A quest at the speed of light: Qwest Communications International spans the globe with its high-capacity broadband fiber-optic network. It is the #4 local phone company in the US (behind AT&T Inc., formerly SBC Communications; Verizon; and BellSouth) and serves nearly 15 million access lines in a 14-state region stretching from Arizona north to Wyoming and east to Minnesota. Qwest uses its network to provide long-distance, as well as broadband data, voice, and video services outside its local area and around the world. Qwest resells wireless service through an agreement with Sprint Nextel.

The Qwest network extends outside its local service area by more than 138,000 miles linking major metro areas around the globe and providing high-volume transmission capacity and other wholesale services. Much of Qwest's US network is built on railroad rights-of-way obtained by Philip Anschutz, who formerly controlled Southern Pacific Rail. The reclusive billionaire is Qwest's founder; he agreed to sell the majority of his 13% stake in 2007 for about $1.39 billion.

The company is expanding its network including through its acquisition in 2006 of optical network operator OnFiber Communications in a cash deal valued at $107 million. OnFiber's high-bandwidth, all optical network provides services to primarily large enterprise and government customers in nearly two dozen metropolitan areas in the US, all outside of Qwest's traditional 14-state local service area.

Qwest has more than 1 million long-distance lines in operation within its local access coverage area (Arizona, Colorado, Idaho, Iowa, Minnesota, Montana, Nebraska, New Mexico, North Dakota, Oregon, South Dakota, Utah, Washington, and Wyoming). The company has formed marketing partnerships with both EchoStar Communications and its rival DIRECTV to add satellite TV to its bundle of services.

## HISTORY

Philip Anschutz bought Southern Pacific Rail in 1988 and established subsidiary Southern Pacific Telecommunications Company (SPT) to lay fiber-optic cable for long-distance carriers beside its parent's rails. By 1993 it was offering long-distance services to companies in the southwestern US and selling switched phone services to businesses.

In 1995 SPT acquired Qwest Communications, which owned a digital microwave system that covered areas SPT's fiber-optic network didn't reach. The combined company took the Qwest moniker and announced it was building a nationwide state-of-the-art fiber-optic network the next year. Frontier, WorldCom (later merged with MCI), and GTE all agreed to buy fiber installed by Qwest along its network, which helped defray construction costs.

Opportunities increased with the passage of the Telecommunications Act of 1996, which began opening up US telecom markets. Anschutz sold Southern Pacific to Union Pacific that year but held on to the telecom operation. In 1997 Qwest hired Joseph Nacchio, a former AT&T Corp. executive, to run the company. It went public that year.

Nacchio charged into long-distance services, launching Internet protocol (IP) telephony and a 7.5-cents-a-minute rate. In 1998 Qwest paid $27 million for long-distance reseller Phoenix Network and another $4.4 billion for long-distance provider LCI International, which more than doubled Qwest's size.

In 1999 Qwest bought Icon CMT, which offered Web-based applications for businesses, and acquired a 19% stake in fixed wireless carrier Advanced Radio Telecom.

Nacchio became executive chairman in 1999, and Anschutz was named chairman of the board. Qwest more than doubled in size and gained 25 million local phone service customers in 14 states in the US with the acquisition in 2000 of Baby Bell U S WEST. The stock deal was valued at $43.5 billion. Merger talks with Deutsche Telekom collapsed when the German company said it did not want to wait for the closing of the U S WEST purchase. To gain regulatory approval for the U S WEST deal, Qwest had to sell its long-distance business in the Baby Bell's 14-state territory. Following the acquisition of U S WEST, the expanded company cut 11,000 jobs, or 16% of its workforce.

Amid the recession that dramatically slowed expansion in the telecom industry, Qwest was forced to halt some network expansion plans and reduce its workforce by more than 25%. In 2002 the SEC began a review of the company's accounting practices. Amid the controversies, Nacchio resigned at the request of the company's board of directors (he was convicted in 2007 of 19 counts of insider trading). Anschutz also resigned his position as non-executive chairman but remained on the board of directors. Richard Notebaert, previously the CEO of Tellabs, was named CEO of Qwest in 2002.

Strapped for cash, Qwest sold billions of dollars in assets, including its phone directory business, which was acquired by the Carlyle Group and Welsh, Carson, Anderson & Stowe for more than $7 billion. The sale occurred in two parts: The initial $2.75 billion deal included seven states that did not require regulatory approval and closed in 2002. The $4.3 billion second sale gained final state regulatory approval and was completed in September 2003.

In 2003 Qwest gained approval from the FCC to offer long-distance service in Arizona, the final step in its effort to reenter the long-distance business after its purchase of U S WEST. The regulatory OK came in spite of unrelated SEC and Justice Department investigations of questionable accounting practices at the company. The next year the company sold its wireless assets to Verizon Wireless in a cash deal valued at about $418 million, then reached an agreement with Sprint (now Sprint Nextel) to resell wireless services.

Perhaps feeling left out of the telecom industry consolidation movement, Qwest in 2005 made a tentative $7.3 billion offer to acquire MCI. Mostly ignored in their first offer, Qwest revised its offer for MCI with a nearly $8.5 billion cash-and-stock bid in hopes of spoiling the agreed on offer by Verizon Communications. When Verizon countered, Qwest raised its offer to $8.9 billion and then $9.7 billion. But the MCI board consistently favored Verizon as a suitor and after the MCI board accepted as superior a bid from Verizon valued at $8.4 billion Qwest dropped out of the bidding.

In 2007 Notebaert announced his retirement. Edward Mueller, a veteran CEO who led companies ranging from Ameritech to Williams-Sonoma, was named chairman and CEO of Qwest.

## EXECUTIVES

**Chairman and CEO:** Edward A. (Ed) Mueller, age 60
**EVP Business Markets Group:** Thomas E. (Tom) Richards, age 51
**EVP Mass Markets Group:** Paula Kruger, age 56, $881,342 pay
**EVP and Chief Human Resources Officer:** Teresa Taylor
**EVP Wholesale Markets:** Roland R. Thornton
**EVP Product and Marketing:** C. Daniel (Dan) Yost, age 55
**EVP Marketing and Communications:** Laura Sankey
**EVP, General Counsel, and Corporate Secretary:** Richard N. (Rich) Baer, age 48, $1,540,000 pay
**EVP Network Operations:** Robert D. (Bob) Tregemba
**SVP and Treasurer:** Janet K. Cooper, age 46
**SVP Consumer Marketing:** Mark D. Pitchford
**SVP Corporate Development and Strategy:** Thomas F. (Tom) Gillett, age 60
**SVP Federal Relations:** Gary R. Lytle, age 60
**EVP and CFO:** John W. Richardson, age 61
**SVP Investor Relations:** Stephanie Georges Comfort
**SVP Policy and Law and Deputy General Counsel:** R. Steven (Steve) Davis
**SVP Government Services Sales:** Diana L. Gowen
**VP Consumer Marketing:** Thomas J. McLoughlin
**VP Corporate Communications:** Tyler Gronbach
**VP Corporate Development and Strategy:** Kenneth C. (Ken) Dunn
**VP and CIO:** Girish K. Varma
**VP and CTO:** Pieter Poll
**VP Consumer Marketing:** Kim S. Whitehead
**VP, Controller, and Chief Accounting Officer:** R. William Johnston
**Auditors:** KPMG LLP

## LOCATIONS

**HQ:** Qwest Communications International Inc.
1801 California St., Denver, CO 80202
**Phone:** 303-992-1400 **Fax:** 303-992-1724
**Web:** www.qwest.com

## PRODUCTS/OPERATIONS

### 2006 Sales

| | % of total |
|---|---|
| Local voice services | |
| Mass markets | 29 |
| Business | 9 |
| Wholesale | 5 |
| Long-distance services | |
| Wholesale | 8 |
| Mass markets | 5 |
| Business | 4 |
| Access services | 4 |
| Data, Internet & video services | |
| Business | 17 |
| Wholesale | 10 |
| Mass markets | 6 |
| Wireless services | 3 |
| **Total** | **100** |

### Selected Services

Wireline
- Asynchronous transfer mode (ATM)
- Colocation
- Custom calling features (caller ID, call waiting, call return, and 3-way calling)
- Customer premises equipment (CPE)
- Directory assistance
- Frame relay
- Internet access (dedicated, dial-up, and digital subscriber lines [DSL])
- Internet protocol (IP)
- Local-exchange access
- Long-distance (intraLATA, interLATA, and international)
- Network management
- Private lines
- Switching
- Virtual private network (VPN)
- Voice mail
- Web hosting

Wireless
- Personal communication services (PCS) resale

## COMPETITORS

360networks
AT&T
Global Crossing
Iowa Telecommunications
Level 3 Communications
McLeodUSA
New Ulm Telecom
Sprint Nextel
Time Warner Telecom
Verizon
XO Holdings

## HISTORICAL FINANCIALS

Company Type: Public

### Income Statement

FYE: December 31

| | REVENUE ($ mil.) | NET INCOME ($ mil.) | NET PROFIT MARGIN | EMPLOYEES |
|---|---|---|---|---|
| **12/06** | 13,923 | 593 | 4.3% | 38,000 |
| **12/05** | 13,903 | (779) | — | 39,000 |
| **12/04** | 13,809 | (1,794) | — | 41,000 |
| **12/03** | 14,288 | 1,512 | 10.6% | 47,000 |
| **12/02** | 15,385 | (38,468) | — | 47,000 |
| **Annual Growth** | (2.5%) | — | — | (5.2%) |

### 2006 Year-End Financials

Debt ratio: —
Return on equity: —
Cash ($ mil.): 1,489
Current ratio: 0.71
Long-term debt ($ mil.): 13,206
No. of shares (mil.): 1,901
Dividends
Yield: —
Payout: —
Market value ($ mil.): 15,908

### Stock History

NYSE: Q

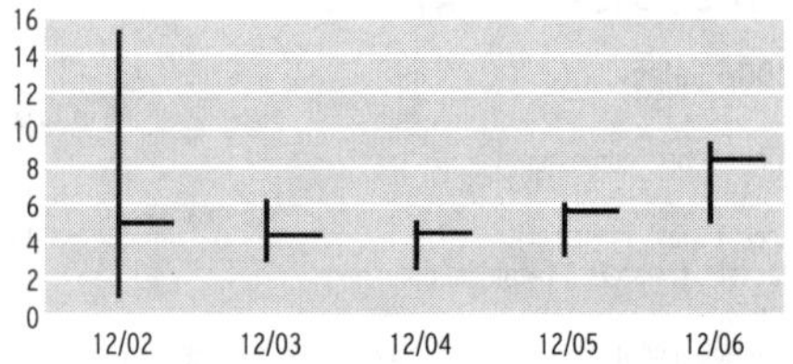

| | STOCK PRICE ($) FY Close | P/E High | P/E Low | PER SHARE ($) Earnings | Dividends | Book Value |
|---|---|---|---|---|---|---|
| **12/06** | 8.37 | 31 | 17 | 0.30 | — | (0.76) |
| **12/05** | 5.65 | — | — | (0.42) | — | (1.72) |
| **12/04** | 4.44 | — | — | (1.00) | — | (1.44) |
| **12/03** | 4.32 | 7 | 3 | 0.87 | — | (0.57) |
| **12/02** | 5.00 | — | — | (22.87) | — | (1.67) |
| **Annual Growth** | 13.7% | — | — | — | — | — |

# RadioShack

These stores are tuned in to your electronics needs and desires. RadioShack is one of the leading consumer electronics retail chains in North America with more than 6,000 outlets in the US, Puerto Rico, the Virgin Islands, and Mexico. Its stores offer a variety of products, including computers, DVD players, electronic toys, telephones, and, of course, radios. The stores also sell third-party services such as wireless calling plans and direct satellite service. In addition, RadioShack sells a wide range of electronics parts and components. The chain includes about 1,600 dealer outlets and 800 wireless phone kiosks located primarily in malls and SAM'S CLUB stores (kiosks are not RadioShack-branded).

Unlike its major competitors, RadioShack has built its chain with smaller but more numerous locations. (Its stores are about 2,500 sq. ft. on average.) Following that philosophy, the company took over operation of kiosks located in some 550 SAM'S CLUB stores in 2004 and has significantly expanded that business through partnerships with such companies as Sprint Nextel and AT&T Mobility (formerly Cingular Wireless).

Weak results in 2005 led the company to announce a turnaround plan in February 2006 that resulted in the closing of 500 of its traditional retail outlets and the consolidation of its distribution centers. Six months later the retailer said it planned to cut up to 450 support positions. In all, the company cut some 1,500 as part of the plan.

The company has expanded its reach into Mexico through a joint partnership with retailer Gigante that operates more than 165 RadioShack-branded stores.

RadioShack's presence in Canada, though, has run into a snag. InterTAN had been the company's partner to the north and operated about 500 RadioShack stores under a licensing agreement. It was acquired by Circuit City in 2004, however, and shortly afterward RadioShack charged the company had violated the licensing agreement by failing to pay certain advertising fees. A court ruling the following year backed RadioShack's claim and InterTAN rebranded its stores The Source By Circuit City. RadioShack later launched a Canadian subsidiary that opened about two dozen stores in 2005, primarily in the Toronto area. However, the company later abandoned its Canadian plans and had closed all of its stores by early 2007.

Meanwhile the company has had some change in its upper ranks. Longtime CEO Len Roberts retired in 2005 (though he remained as chairman until May 2006) and turned the reigns over to David Edmondson, who joined RadioShack from direct marketer ADVO in 1994. However, Edmondson resigned the following year after it was revealed he may have misrepresented his academic degrees on his resume.

RadioShack hired Julian Day, a turnaround specialist with experience at Safeway and Kmart, as chairman and CEO. Soon after Day's appointment Hall Financial Group, a Texas-based private investment firm, took nearly a 6% stake in the company. About a year later, Goldman Sachs bought a 13% stake in the firm, making it RadioShack's largest investor.

## HISTORY

During the 1950s Charles Tandy expanded his family's small Fort Worth, Texas, leather business (founded 1919) into a nationwide chain of leather craft and hobby stores. By 1960 Tandy stock was being traded on the NYSE. In the early 1960s Tandy began to expand into other retail areas, buying Leonard's, a Fort Worth department store.

In 1963 Tandy purchased RadioShack, a nearly bankrupt electronics parts supplier with a mail-order business and nine retail stores in the Boston area. Tandy collected part of the $800,000 owed the company and started expanding. Between 1961 and 1969 Tandy's sales grew from $16 million to $180 million; the bulk of the growth was due to the expansion of RadioShack. Between 1968 and 1973 Tandy ballooned from 172 to 2,294 stores; RadioShack provided over 50% of sales and 80% of earnings in 1973.

Tandy sold its department store operations to Dillard's in 1974. The next year Tandy spun off its leather products business to its shareholders as Tandy Brands and its hobby and handicraft business as Tandycrafts, focusing Tandy on the consumer electronics business. During 1976 the boom in CB radio sales pushed income up 125% as Tandy opened 1,200 stores. The following year it introduced the first mass-marketed PC.

In 1984 the company introduced the Tandy 1000, the first IBM-compatible PC priced under $1,000. Then came acquisitions — electronics equipment chain stores Scott/McDuff and VideoConcepts (1985), laptop specialist GRiD Systems (1988), and microcomputer makers Victor Microcomputer and Micronic (1989, later merged as Victor Technologies).

In 1987 Tandy spun off its foreign retail operations as InterTAN. Realizing that RadioShack had nearly exhausted its expansion possibilities, the company focused on alternate retail formats such as GRiD Systems Centers and in 1991 opened Computer City and the Edge in Electronics. Also that year it introduced name-brand products into RadioShack stores.

Tandy sold Memtek Products (magnetic tape), LIKA (printed circuit boards), and its computer manufacturing and marketing operations in 1993 and spun off O'Sullivan Industries (ready-to-assemble furniture) to the public in 1994.

In 1996 and 1997 Tandy closed down its 19-store Incredible Universe "gigastores" chain, shuttered the 53-store McDuff chain, and closed about 20 of its Computer City stores and sold others in Europe.

Longtime CEO John Roach stepped down in 1998, and president Leonard Roberts replaced him. The company changed its name to RadioShack in 2000.

InterTAN, which had been operating licensed RadioShack locations in Canada, was acquired by Circuit City in 2004. Shortly afterwards, RadioShack charged the company with breach of contract, saying that InterTAN had failed to pay certain advertising fees. A court ruling in RadioShack's favor the next year ended the licensing pact and InterTAN rebranded its Canadian stores under the banner The Source By Circuit City.

Roberts retired as CEO in 2005 and turned the reigns of the company over to David Edmondson, who had joined RadioShack from direct marketer ADVO in 1994. However, Edmondson was forced to resign the following year after it was revealed he may have misrepresented his academic record on his resume. The company in July 2006 named former Sears executive Julian Day as Edmonson's replacement.

## EXECUTIVES

**Chairman and CEO:** Julian C. Day, age 54
**EVP and CFO:** James F. (Jim) Gooch, age 39
**SVP and Chief Channel Operations Officer:** Stewart F. (Stu) Asimus Jr.
**SVP and Chief Marketing and Brand Officer:** Donald K. (Don) Carroll
**SVP Information Technology:** Cara D. Kinzey
**SVP and General Merchandise Manager:** Wesley V. Lowzinski, age 54
**SVP Supply Chain:** John G. Ripperton, age 53
**VP and Corporate Controller:** Martin O. Moad, age 51
**VP Brand Development and Communications:** Robert J. (Bob) Kilinski
**VP Internal Audit and Controls:** Kenneth G. (Ken) Barna
**VP Learning and Development:** Rich Pendergast
**Senior Director of Employee Relations Services:** Jeff Bland
**Senior Director of Strategic Projects:** Dennis Howell
**Auditors:** PricewaterhouseCoopers LLP

## LOCATIONS

**HQ:** RadioShack Corporation
300 RadioShack Cir., Fort Worth, TX 76102
**Phone:** 817-415-3011 **Fax:** 817-415-2647
**Web:** www.radioshack.com

RadioShack has more than 6,800 retail outlets in Mexico, Puerto Rico, the US, and the US Virgin Islands.

## PRODUCTS/OPERATIONS

**2006 Sales**

| | $ mil. | % of total |
|---|---|---|
| Wireless | 1,655.0 | 35 |
| Accessories | 1,087.7 | 22 |
| Personal electronics | 751.8 | 16 |
| Modern home | 612.0 | 13 |
| Power | 271.4 | 6 |
| Technical | 198.5 | 4 |
| Service | 109.6 | 2 |
| Service centers & other | 91.5 | 2 |
| **Total** | **4,777.5** | **100** |

**2006 Sales**

| | $ mil. | % of total |
|---|---|---|
| Company-operated | | |
| Stores | 4,079.8 | 85 |
| Kiosks | 340.5 | 7 |
| Dealers & other | 357.2 | 8 |
| **Total** | **4,777.5** | **100** |

**2006 Locations**

| | No. |
|---|---|
| Company-operated | |
| Stores | 4,467 |
| Kiosks | 772 |
| Dealers & other | 1,596 |
| **Total** | **6,835** |

## COMPETITORS

Amazon.com
Apple
Best Buy
Brookstone
Circuit City
CompUSA
Costco Wholesale
Dell
Fry's Electronics
GameStop
Gateway
Home Depot
Office Depot
PC Mall
Sears
Sharper Image
Sprint Nextel
Staples
Systemax
Target
Tweeter Home Entertainment
Verizon
Wal-Mart

## HISTORICAL FINANCIALS

Company Type: Public

**Income Statement** FYE: December 31

| | REVENUE ($ mil.) | NET INCOME ($ mil.) | NET PROFIT MARGIN | EMPLOYEES |
|---|---|---|---|---|
| **12/06** | 4,778 | 73 | 1.5% | 40,000 |
| **12/05** | 5,082 | 267 | 5.3% | 47,000 |
| **12/04** | 4,841 | 337 | 7.0% | 42,000 |
| **12/03** | 4,649 | 299 | 6.4% | 39,500 |
| **12/02** | 4,577 | 263 | 5.8% | 39,100 |
| **Annual Growth** | 1.1% | (27.3%) | — | 0.6% |

## 2006 Year-End Financials

Debt ratio: 52.9%
Return on equity: 11.8%
Cash ($ mil.): 472
Current ratio: 1.63
Long-term debt ($ mil.): 346
No. of shares (mil.): 136
Dividends
Yield: 1.5%
Payout: 46.3%
Market value ($ mil.): 2,279

## Stock History NYSE: RSH

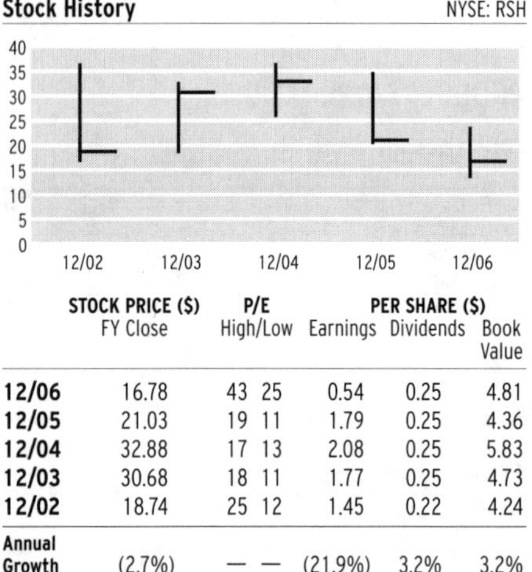

| | STOCK PRICE ($) FY Close | P/E High | P/E Low | PER SHARE ($) Earnings | Dividends | Book Value |
|---|---|---|---|---|---|---|
| 12/06 | 16.78 | 43 | 25 | 0.54 | 0.25 | 4.81 |
| 12/05 | 21.03 | 19 | 11 | 1.79 | 0.25 | 4.36 |
| 12/04 | 32.88 | 17 | 13 | 2.08 | 0.25 | 5.83 |
| 12/03 | 30.68 | 18 | 11 | 1.77 | 0.25 | 4.73 |
| 12/02 | 18.74 | 25 | 12 | 1.45 | 0.22 | 4.24 |
| Annual Growth | (2.7%) | — | — | (21.9%) | 3.2% | 3.2% |

# Ralcorp Holdings

Ralcorp Holdings reminds us that you can't judge food by its cover. The company is the top US maker of private-label or "store-brand" ready-to-eat and hot breakfast cereals. Ralcorp has stocked its pantry with a widening variety of private-label cookies, crackers, peanut butter, ketchup, snack nuts, and candy. The company also makes a few branded products: Ralston Hot Cereal, Ry Krisp crackers, 3 Minute Brand Oats oatmeal, and Rippin' Good cookies. The company's Carriage House Company produces private-label dressings, syrups, jellies, and sauces. Its Lofthouse and Cascade Cookie Company businesses provide frozen cookies to in-store bakeries.

Seeing breakfast cereal sales shrinking, Ralcorp purchased Ripon Foods, in part, for its ability to make private-label breakfast bars. The company is working to round out its larder through acquisitions in hopes of making it easier to ride out future ravages on cereal sales. Its purchase of Bakery Chef (frozen food service pancakes and waffles) allows Ralcorp to even reach people eating breakfast at restaurants. The addition of snack-food maker Medallion Foods (corn and tortilla chips) indicates another move away from breakfast food.

In 2006 Ralcorp purchased Parco Foods, a Chicago-based cookie maker for in-store bakeries, and Cottage Bakeries, a frozen bread dough maker. The next year, it bought Bloomfield Bakers for about $140 million. The deal included Bloomfield affiliate, Lovin Oven. Bloomfield makes nutritional and cereal bars.

A vestige from its earlier days, Ralcorp retains ownership of about 19% of popular ski destination Vail Resorts.

Shapiro Capital Management owns about 9% of Ralcorp; Baron Capital Management owns almost 6%.

## HISTORY

Ralston Purina spun off Ralcorp Holdings, then a maker of name-brand and private-label foods, in 1994 under co-CEOs Richard Pearce and Joe Micheletto. Ralston was concerned that its huge pet food and Eveready battery interests had overshadowed its smaller consumer foods and ski resort businesses.

A cereal price war in 1996 ate at Ralcorp's price advantage and devoured margins. To focus on its core private-label business, the firm sold its ski resort holdings to Vail Resorts for $310 million (it received a 22% stake in Vail) and its branded snack and cereal businesses (which included Cookie Crisp and Chex) to General Mills for about $570 million, both in early 1997. Pearce resigned while the sales were in progress; Micheletto stayed on as CEO.

The company expanded its cookie and cracker division by adding the Wortz Company (the #2 US private-label cracker and cookie maker) for about $46 million in 1997 and Sugar Kake Cookie the following year. In 1998 Ralcorp entered a new private-label category, snack nuts, by purchasing nut makers Flavor House and Nutcracker Brands. Faced with price competition and decreasing demand, it sold its Beech-Nut baby food business that year for $68 million to the Milnot company.

To broaden its private-label portfolio further, in early 1999 Ralcorp bought Martin Gillet & Co. (mayonnaise and salad dressings) and Southern Roasted Nuts of Georgia. In late 1999 the company bought Ripon Foods (cookies, sugar wafers, breakfast bars).

In 2000 Ralcorp purchased private-label chocolate candy maker James P. Linette and the Cascade Cookie Company. That same year it bought Red Wing (syrups, peanut butter, jelly, barbecue sauce) from Tomkins PLC for about $132 million. Also in 2000 Ralcorp said it would merge with animal feed company Agribrands International, but the agreement fell through. Additionally that year the company said it would buy Genesee Corporation's Ontario Foods business (powdered drinks, soups, prepared meals) for $50 million, but called off that deal too.

During 2002 Ralcorp purchased cookie-maker Lofthouse Foods Incorporated. Early in 2003 the company sold off its industrial tomato paste facility. Later that same year, Ralcorp purchased frozen breakfast foods company Bakery Chef for $287.5 million.

In 2004 the company acquired Concept 2 Bakers (C2B), a frozen, par-baked artisan bread maker, from McGlynn Bakeries. The next year it purchased private-label corn-snack (tortillas) manufacturer Medallion Foods and Canadian private-label griddle-product maker Western Waffles, Ltd.

## EXECUTIVES

**Chairman:** William P. Stiritz, age 72
**Co-CEO, President, and Director:** Kevin J. Hunt, age 55, $872,204 pay
**Co-CEO, President, and Director:** David P. Skarie, age 60, $872,204 pay
**Corporate VP; President, Frozen Bakery Products:** Richard G. Scalise, age 52
**Coporate VP; President, Bremner and Nutcracker Brands:** Ronald D. (Ron) Wilkinson, age 56
**Corporate VP, General Counsel, and Secretary:** Charles G. Huber Jr., age 42
**Corporate VP and Treasurer:** Scott Monette, age 45
**Corporate VP and Controller:** Thomas G. Granneman, age 57, $306,708 pay
**VP; President, Carriage House:** Richard R. Koulouris, age 50
**VP and Director Human Resources:** Jack Owczarczak
**Auditors:** PricewaterhouseCoopers LLP

## LOCATIONS

**HQ:** Ralcorp Holdings, Inc.
800 Market St., St. Louis, MO 63101
**Phone:** 314-877-7000 **Fax:** 314-877-7666
**Web:** www.ralcorp.com

## PRODUCTS/OPERATIONS

### 2006 Sales

| | $ mil. | % of total |
|---|---|---|
| Cereals, crackers & cookies | 777.6 | 42 |
| Frozen bakery products | 442.8 | 24 |
| Dressings, syrups, jellies & sauces | 389.2 | 21 |
| Snack nuts & candy | 240.6 | 13 |
| **Total** | **1,850.2** | **100** |

### Selected Branded Products

Cascade (cookies)
Flavor House (snack nuts)
Lofthouse (cookies)
Krusteaz (frozen breakfast foods)
Major Peters' (condiments)
Medallion (corn & tortilla chips)
Nutcracker (snack nuts)
Parco (cookies)
Rippin' Good (cookies)
Ry Krisp (crackers)

## COMPETITORS

Campbell Soup
Frito-Lay
General Mills
Gilster-Mary Lee
Heinz
John Sanfilippo & Son
Kellogg
Kellogg Snacks
Kellogg USA
Kraft Foods
Lance Snacks
Malt-O-Meal
National Grape Cooperative
Pepperidge Farm
PepsiCo
Renée's Gourmet Foods
Smucker
Weston Foods

## HISTORICAL FINANCIALS

Company Type: Public

### Income Statement FYE: September 30

| | REVENUE ($ mil.) | NET INCOME ($ mil.) | NET PROFIT MARGIN | EMPLOYEES |
|---|---|---|---|---|
| 9/06 | 1,850 | 68 | 3.7% | 6,500 |
| 9/05 | 1,675 | 71 | 4.3% | 6,370 |
| 9/04 | 1,558 | 65 | 4.2% | 6,000 |
| 9/03 | 1,304 | 7 | 0.6% | 5,000 |
| 9/02 | 1,280 | 54 | 4.2% | 5,400 |
| Annual Growth | 9.6% | 6.1% | — | 4.7% |

### 2006 Year-End Financials

Debt ratio: 116.0%
Return on equity: 13.7%
Cash ($ mil.): 112
Current ratio: 1.96
Long-term debt ($ mil.): 553
No. of shares (mil.): 27
Dividends
Yield: —
Payout: —
Market value ($ mil.): 1,295

**Stock History** NYSE: RAH

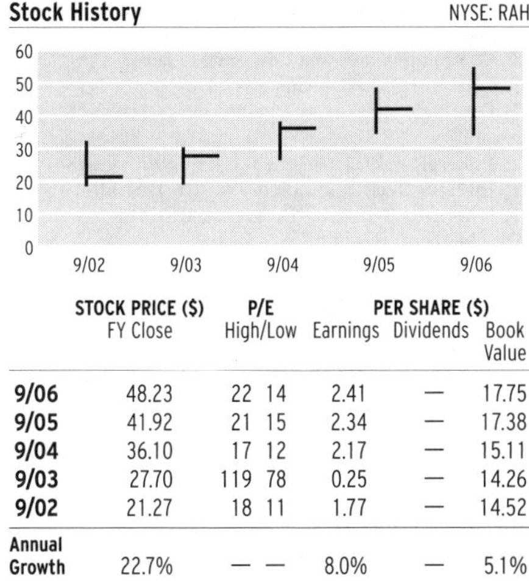


| | STOCK PRICE ($) FY Close | P/E High/Low | | PER SHARE ($) Earnings | Dividends | Book Value |
|---|---|---|---|---|---|---|
| **9/06** | 48.23 | 22 | 14 | 2.41 | — | 17.75 |
| **9/05** | 41.92 | 21 | 15 | 2.34 | — | 17.38 |
| **9/04** | 36.10 | 17 | 12 | 2.17 | — | 15.11 |
| **9/03** | 27.70 | 119 | 78 | 0.25 | — | 14.26 |
| **9/02** | 21.27 | 18 | 11 | 1.77 | — | 14.52 |
| **Annual Growth** | 22.7% | — | — | 8.0% | — | 5.1% |

# Raymond James Financial

You could call it Ray. You could call it Ray Jay. But Raymond James Financial will do just fine. The company offers investment and financial planning services through subsidiary Raymond James & Associates (RJA), which provides securities brokerage, investment banking, and financial advisory services throughout the US; and Raymond James Financial Services, which offers financial planning and brokerage services through independent contractors, as well as through alliances with community banks. Other divisions provide asset management, trust, and retail banking services. Raymond James Financial has approximately 2,200 offices worldwide.

The company's business is divided into six primary segments. The Private Client Group is the largest, accounting for nearly two-thirds of the company's sales; it provides retail brokerage and financial planning services to some 1.5 million customers in the US, Canada, and the UK. Capital Markets performs investment banking and equity research services. Asset Management includes Awad Asset Management, Eagle Asset Management, and Heritage Asset Management. Raymond James Bank (RJBank), securities lending, and the Emerging Markets segment, which is involved in joint ventures in Argentina, India, Turkey, and Uruguay, round out the company's operations.

In 2006 the company extended its deal to attach its name to the home stadium of the NFL's Tampa Bay Buccaneers through 2015.

Chairman and CEO Thomas James owns about 13% of Raymond James Financial.

## HISTORY

Edward Raymond formed Raymond and Associates in 1962 but sold it in 1964 to associate Bob James. Renamed Raymond James & Associates, the firm expanded its investment product offerings. It went public in 1983 and became Raymond James Financial in 1987.

In 2001, Raymond James Financial acquired Canadian investment firm Goepel McDermid Inc., (renamed Raymond James Ltd.) to offer individual and institutional investment services to the Canadian market.

## EXECUTIVES

**Chairman and CEO, Raymond James Financial; Chairman, Raymond James & Associates:** Thomas A. (Tom) James, age 64, $3,040,000 pay
**Vice Chairman:** Francis S. (Bo) Godbold, age 63
**President, COO, and Director:** Chester B. (Chet) Helck, age 54, $1,577,000 pay
**EVP; President and CEO, Eagle; Managing Director, Asset Management:** Richard K. Riess, age 57, $1,798,000 pay
**EVP and Director of Sales, Independent Contractor Division:** James A. (Jim) Fulp
**EVP, Operations and Administration, Raymond James & Associates:** Thomas R. (Thom) Tremaine, age 50
**SVP Finance and CFO:** Jeffrey P. (Jeff) Julien, age 50
**VP and Director of Human Resources:** Courtland W. (Court) James, age 31
**Chairman and CEO, Raymond James Financial Services:** Richard G. (Dick) Averitt III, age 60, $1,389,600 pay
**Chairman, Raymond James Ltd.; Director:** Kenneth A. Shields, age 58
**President, Raymond James & Associates:** Dennis W. Zank, age 52
**CIO, Raymond James Financial and Raymond James & Associates:** J. Timothy (Tim) Eitel, age 57
**Chairman, President, and Chief Investment Officer, Awad Asset Management:** James D. (Jim) Awad
**CEO, Raymond James Investment Services Ltd.:** Peter Moores
**President and CEO, Raymond James Bank:** Steven M. Raney
**President, Planning Corporation of America:** Scott A. Curtis
**President, Raymond James Trust Companies:** David Ness
**Controller and Chief Accounting Officer:** Jennifer C. Ackart, age 42
**General Counsel, Director of Compliance, and Corporate Secretary:** Paul L. Matecki, age 51
**Auditors:** KPMG LLP

## LOCATIONS

**HQ:** Raymond James Financial, Inc.
880 Carillon Pkwy., St. Petersburg, FL 33716
**Phone:** 727-567-1000 **Fax:** 727-567-8915
**Web:** www.rjf.com

Raymond James Financial has offices in Argentina, Belgium, Canada, France, Germany, India, Luxembourg, Switzerland, Turkey, and Uruguay, as well as in the US and the UK.

## PRODUCTS/OPERATIONS

**2006 Sales**

| | $ mil. | % of total |
|---|---|---|
| Securities commissions & fees | 1,561.4 | 59 |
| Interest | 470.0 | 18 |
| Investment advisory fees | 179.4 | 7 |
| Investment banking | 158.6 | 6 |
| Financial service fees | 116.0 | 4 |
| Net trading profits | 27.2 | 1 |
| Other | 120.2 | 5 |
| **Total** | **2,632.8** | **100** |

**2006 Sales by Segment**

| | $ mil. | % of total |
|---|---|---|
| Private Client Group | 1,679.8 | 64 |
| Capital Markets | 487.4 | 19 |
| Asset Management | 200.1 | 8 |
| RJBank | 114.7 | 4 |
| Stock Loan/Borrow | 60.0 | 2 |
| Emerging Markets | 55.3 | 2 |
| Other | 35.5 | 1 |
| **Total** | **2,632.8** | **100** |

## COMPETITORS

A.G. Edwards
Charles Schwab
Citigroup
Deutsche Bank Alex. Brown
Edward Jones
FMR
Legg Mason
Linsco/Private Ledger
Merrill Lynch
Morgan Keegan
Morgan Stanley
Piper Jaffray
UBS Financial Services
Wachovia Securities

## HISTORICAL FINANCIALS

Company Type: Public

**Income Statement** FYE: September 30

| | REVENUE ($ mil.) | NET INCOME ($ mil.) | NET PROFIT MARGIN | EMPLOYEES |
|---|---|---|---|---|
| **9/06** | 2,633 | 214 | 8.1% | 6,616 |
| **9/05** | 2,157 | 151 | 7.0% | 6,790 |
| **9/04** | 1,830 | 128 | 7.0% | 7,017 |
| **9/03** | 1,498 | 86 | 5.8% | 7,133 |
| **9/02** | 1,516 | 79 | 5.2% | 6,246 |
| **Annual Growth** | 14.8% | 28.2% | — | 1.4% |

**2006 Year-End Financials**

Debt ratio: 22.9%
Return on equity: 15.8%
Cash ($ mil.): 5,125
Current ratio: —
Long-term debt ($ mil.): 335
No. of shares (mil.): 116
Dividends
Yield: 1.1%
Payout: 17.3%
Market value ($ mil.): 3,393

**Stock History** NYSE: RJF

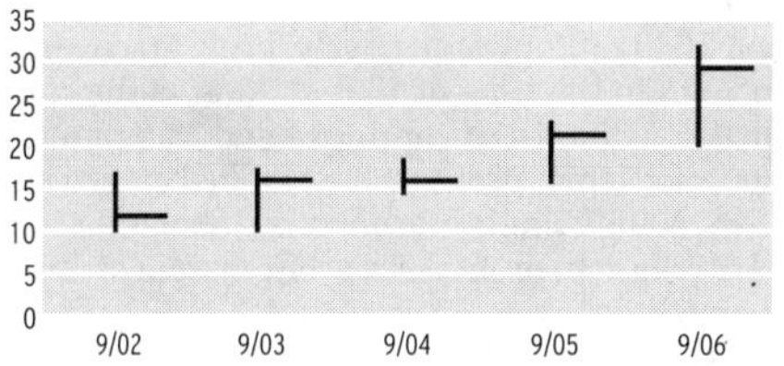

| | STOCK PRICE ($) FY Close | P/E High/Low | | PER SHARE ($) Earnings | Dividends | Book Value |
|---|---|---|---|---|---|---|
| **9/06** | 29.24 | 17 | 11 | 1.85 | 0.32 | 12.62 |
| **9/05** | 21.41 | 17 | 12 | 1.33 | 0.21 | 16.49 |
| **9/04** | 15.90 | 16 | 13 | 1.15 | 0.22 | 14.54 |
| **9/03** | 15.97 | 22 | 13 | 0.78 | 0.20 | 19.15 |
| **9/02** | 11.76 | 23 | 14 | 0.71 | 0.16 | 17.31 |
| **Annual Growth** | 25.6% | — | — | 27.1% | 18.9% | (7.6%) |

# Raytheon Company

Raytheon ("light of the gods") has taken a shine to its place in the upper pantheon of US defense contractors (along with Lockheed Martin, Boeing, and Northrop Grumman). The company's defense offerings include missile systems (Patriot, Sidewinder, and Tomahawk), radars, and reconnaissance, targeting, and navigation systems. Raytheon also makes radios, air traffic control systems and radars, and satellite communications systems. The company's Raytheon Aircraft unit (which is being sold) makes turboprop aircraft and Beech and Hawker jets. Raytheon also offers commercial electronics products and services, but the US government accounts for nearly 85% of sales.

US defense spending has been shifting toward supporting ongoing operations (Iraq) and increasing the military's speed, flexibility, and precision. With that in mind, Raytheon is focusing on four business areas: missile defense; precision engagement; intelligence, surveillance, and reconnaissance; and homeland security.

As the world's #1 missile maker, Raytheon is a key player in US efforts to construct a comprehensive missile defense system. Such systems need intercept vehicles, sensors, command & control systems, and systems integration expertise, and Raytheon is a leader in all those markets. Raytheon's precision engagement offerings include its missiles as well as radars, data links, targeting and warning systems, and lasers.

Intelligence, surveillance, and reconnaissance systems use sensing, processing, and dissemination technologies to obtain actionable information and get it from one place to another quickly. Raytheon's products in this area include sensor suites for UAVs, space-based radars, satellite systems, and communications systems.

Raytheon, which piled up almost $10 billion of debt from acquisitions in the 1990s, has been selling its money-losing and noncore businesses to focus on missiles, precision engagement munitions and systems, homeland security, and intelligence, surveillance, and reconnaissance systems.

Defense spending on homeland security and the wars in Iraq and Afghanistan have been extremely beneficial to Raytheon's fortunes. In 2001 and 2002 the company lost $763 million and $640 million respectively. Profits recovered in 2003 to the tune of $365 million as the conflict in Afghanistan continued and Iraq ramped up. Since then profits have climbed every year with 2006 bringing a bonanza of more than $1.2 billion in profits — a profit margin of more than 6%.

As 2006 wound to a close Raytheon announced it would sell Raytheon Aircraft to a new company, Hawker Beechcraft Corp., formed by Goldman Sachs Group Inc. and Onex Corporation, for $3.3 billion. The deal was completed in 2007.

## HISTORY

In 1922 Laurence Marshall and several others founded American Appliance Company to produce home refrigerators. When their invention failed, Marshall began making Raytheon (meaning "light of/from the gods") radio tubes. Raytheon was adopted as the company's name in 1925. It bought the radio division of Chicago's Q. R. S. Company in 1928 and formed Raytheon Production Company with National Carbon Company (makers of the Eveready battery) to market Eveready Raytheon tubes in 1929.

Growing rapidly in WWII, Raytheon became the first producer of magnetrons (tubes used in radar and later in microwave ovens). Wartime sales peaked at $173 million but dwindled by 1947. Amid rumors of bankruptcy, Charles Adams became Raytheon's president. He sold Raytheon's unprofitable radio and TV business in 1956.

In 1964 Adams (then chairman) named missile engineer Thomas Phillips president. Phillips oversaw several purchases designed to balance Raytheon's commercial and military earnings, beginning with Amana Refrigeration (1965), D.C. Heath (textbooks, 1966), Caloric (stoves, 1967), and three petrochemical firms (1966-69).

Raytheon began making computer terminals in 1971 (exited 1984). In 1980 it bought Grumman's Beech Aircraft division. Despite efforts to diversify, Raytheon still relied on missiles, radar, and communications systems for most of its sales in 1987. In 1991 it won an $800 million US Army contract to upgrade Patriot missiles used in the Persian Gulf War. After 43 years with Raytheon, Phillips retired that year, and president Dennis Picard became chairman.

Raytheon expanded as it bought the business jet division of British Aerospace (1993), E-Systems (advanced electronics and surveillance equipment, 1995), and most of Chrysler's aerospace and defense holdings (1996).

By 1997 Raytheon had doubled in size and had become the #1 US missile maker, after buying Texas Instruments' missile and defense electronics holdings for about $3 billion and Hughes Electronics' (now The DIRECTV Group) defense business for $9.5 billion.

Weak sales in Asia hurt Raytheon in 1998, and it announced cuts of some 14,000 defense jobs (16% of the unit's workforce) and the closure of 28 plants over two years. Former AlliedSignal VC Daniel Burnham became CEO in 1998, succeeding Picard. Raytheon also began a legal battle with Hughes, claiming it had been overcharged $1 billion in 1997 for Hughes' defense unit (the suit was settled for about $650 million in 2001).

In 1999 Raytheon cut more jobs and made plans to close or combine 10 facilities and take a $668 million charge to correct financial problems in its defense electronics business.

Raytheon sold its engineering and construction unit to Washington Group International (formerly Morrison Knudsen) for about $500 million in 2000. That year Raytheon sold $800 million in aircraft loans and leases to debis Capital Services (a unit of DaimlerChrysler) and began trying to sell its aircraft business — for a reported price tag of about $4 billion.

In 2002 Raytheon sold its aircraft integration unit to L-3 Communications for about $1.13 billion in cash and made a bid for TRW's satellite and missile defense operations. The company shelved plans to sell its Raytheon Aircraft unit in 2003, but continued to sell non-core units, including its commercial infrared unit (to L-3 Communications) in 2004.

In 2005 Raytheon agreed to team up with EADS North America to bid on the Army's $1 billion Future Cargo Aircraft program. Under the agreement, Raytheon will be prime contractor; EADS will assemble and deliver the medium cargo transport planes.

## EXECUTIVES

**Chairman and CEO:** William H. Swanson, age 58, $1,200,014 pay
**SVP, Business Development and CEO, Raytheon International:** Thomas M. Culligan, age 55
**SVP and CFO:** David C. Wajsgras, age 47, $538,464 pay
**SVP, General Counsel, and Secretary:** Jay B. Stephens, age 60, $603,067 pay
**SVP, Human Resources:** Keith J. Peden, age 56
**VP, Engineering, Technology, and Mission Assurance:** Taylor W. Lawrence, age 43
**VP and CIO:** Rebecca B. Rhoads, age 49
**VP and Chief Accounting Officer:** Michael J. Wood, age 38
**VP, Treasurer and Corporate Development:** Richard A. Goglia, age 55
**VP; Head of Raytheon Company Evaluation Team:** Charles E. Franklin, age 68
**VP; President, Intelligence and Information Systems:** Michael D. (Mike) Keebaugh, age 61
**VP; President, Missile Systems:** Louise L. Francesconi, age 54, $467,654 pay
**VP; President, Network Centric Systems:** Colin J.R. Schottlaender, age 51
**VP; SVP, Government Operations and Strategy:** William J. Lynn, age 52
**VP, Communications and Corporate Affairs:** Pamela A. (Pam) Wickham, age 43
**VP, Contracts and Supply Chain:** John D. Harris II, age 45
**VP, Internal Audit:** Lawrence J. Harrington, age 53
**VP, Investor Relations:** Gregory D. (Greg) Smith
**VP, National Intelligence Programs, Business Development:** Garnett Stowe
**VP, Global Relations:** Mac Jeffery, age 51
**VP, Raytheon Aircraft Services:** Doug Brantner
**VP; President, Integrated Defense Systems:** Daniel L. (Dan) Smith, age 54
**VP; President, Space and Airborne Systems:** Jon C. Jones, age 52
**CEO, Flight Options:** S. Michael Scheeringa
**Intelligence and Information Systems (IIS):** Michael P. (Mike) Morgan
**President, Raytheon Technical Services Company:** Richard R. (Rick) Yuse, age 55
**Auditors:** PricewaterhouseCoopers LLP

## LOCATIONS

**HQ:** Raytheon Company
870 Winter St., Waltham, MA 02451
**Phone:** 781-522-3000 **Fax:** 781-522-3001
**Web:** www.raytheon.com

Raytheon has operations in Australia, Canada, Germany, the UK, and the US.

### 2006 Sales

| | $ mil. | % of total |
|---|---|---|
| US | 16,601 | 82 |
| Asia Pacific | 1,676 | 8 |
| Other regions | 2,014 | 10 |
| **Total** | **20,291** | **100** |

## PRODUCTS/OPERATIONS

### 2006 Sales

| | $ mil. | % of total |
|---|---|---|
| Missile Systems | 4,503 | 20 |
| Space & Airborne Systems | 4,319 | 20 |
| Integrated Defense Systems | 4,220 | 19 |
| Network Centric Systems | 3,561 | 16 |
| Intelligence & Information Systems | 2,560 | 12 |
| Technical Services | 2,049 | 9 |
| Other | 828 | 4 |
| Corporate & eliminations | (1,749) | — |
| **Total** | **20,291** | **100** |

### Selected Products

Missile Systems
- Advanced Medium-Range Air-to-Air missile (AMRAAM)
- AIM-9X Sidewinder
- Evolved SeaSparrow (ESSM)
- Excalibur long-range artillery system
- Exoatmospheric Kill Vehicle
- Extended Range Guided Munition (ERGM)
- High-Speed Anti-Radiation Missile Targeting System
- Paveway laser guided bombs
- Maverick AGM-65 missiles
- Tomahawk and Tactical Tomahawk cruise missiles
- TOW, Javelin, Phalanx, Standard, and SeaRAM missiles

Space and Airborne Systems
- Active electronically scanned array radars
- Airborne radars and processors
- Electronic warfare systems
- Intelligence, surveillance, and reconnaissance systems
- Space and missile defense technology

Integrated Defense Systems
- Aegis Weapon Systems radar equipment
- AN/AQS Minehunting Sonar System
- Joint Land Attack Cruise Missile Defense Elevated Netted Sensor (JLENS)
- Landing Platform Dock Amphibious Ship LPD-17
- Patriot Air and Missile Defense System
- Sea-Based X-Band Radar (SBX)
- Surface-Launched AMRAAM (SLAMRAAM)
- Terminal High Altitude Area Defense (THAAD) Radar

Network Centric Systems
- Air Warfare Simulation (AWSIM)
- Enhanced Position Location Reporting System (EPLRS)
- Future Combat Systems (FCS)
- Long Range Advanced Scout Surveillance System (LRAS) 3
- Standard Terminal Automation Replacement System (STARS)

Intelligence and Information Systems
- Army Research Lab
- Department of Education programs
- Distributed Common Ground System
- Emergency Patient Tracking System
- Global Broadcast Service
- Global Hawk Ground Segment
- Managed data storage solutions
- Mobile Very Small Aperture Satellite Terminal
- National Polar-orbiting Operational Environmental Satellite System Program
- RedWolf telecommunications surveillance
- Signal and Imagery Intelligence Programs
- Supercomputing

Technical Services
- Base operations
- Maintenance support
- Treaty compliance monitoring
- Weapons security and destruction

## COMPETITORS

BAE Systems Electronics & Integrated Solutions
BAE Systems Inc.
Boeing
Boeing Integrated Defense Systems
Crane Aerospace & Electronics
Daimler
Dewey Electronics
Emerson Electric
Fluor
GE
Halliburton
Harris Corp.
Herley Industries
Honeywell Aerospace
Intel
Interstate Electronics
ITT Defense
Koch
L-3 Avionics
Lockheed Martin
Lockheed Martin Missiles
MBDA
McDermott
Meggitt USA
Northrop Grumman
Olin
Park Air Systems
REMOTEC UK
Rockwell Collins (UK)
Saab AB
Samsung Group
Sierra Nevada Corp.
Sperry Marine
Tyco

## HISTORICAL FINANCIALS

Company Type: Public

**Income Statement** FYE: December 31

| | REVENUE ($ mil.) | NET INCOME ($ mil.) | NET PROFIT MARGIN | EMPLOYEES |
|---|---|---|---|---|
| **12/06** | 20,291 | 1,283 | 6.3% | 80,000 |
| **12/05** | 21,894 | 871 | 4.0% | 80,000 |
| **12/04** | 20,245 | 417 | 2.1% | 79,000 |
| **12/03** | 18,109 | 365 | 2.0% | 78,000 |
| **12/02** | 16,760 | (640) | — | 76,400 |
| **Annual Growth** | 4.9% | — | — | 1.2% |

**2006 Year-End Financials**

Debt ratio: 29.5%
Return on equity: 11.8%
Cash ($ mil.): 2,460
Current ratio: 1.42
Long-term debt ($ mil.): 3,278
No. of shares (mil.): 446
Dividends
Yield: 1.8%
Payout: 33.7%
Market value ($ mil.): 23,542

**Stock History** NYSE: RTN

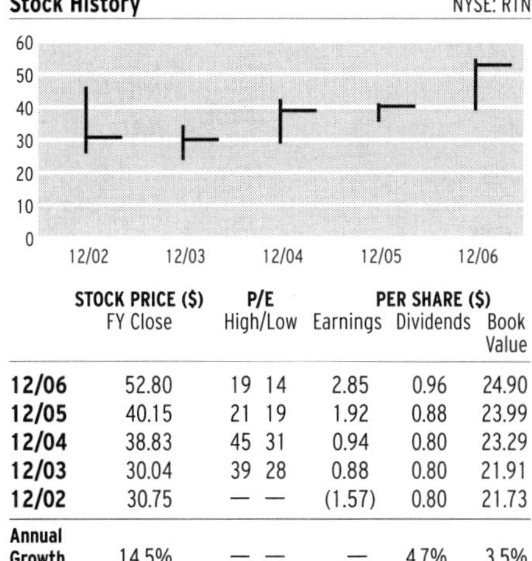


| | STOCK PRICE ($) FY Close | P/E High | P/E Low | PER SHARE ($) Earnings | PER SHARE ($) Dividends | PER SHARE ($) Book Value |
|---|---|---|---|---|---|---|
| **12/06** | 52.80 | 19 | 14 | 2.85 | 0.96 | 24.90 |
| **12/05** | 40.15 | 21 | 19 | 1.92 | 0.88 | 23.99 |
| **12/04** | 38.83 | 45 | 31 | 0.94 | 0.80 | 23.29 |
| **12/03** | 30.04 | 39 | 28 | 0.88 | 0.80 | 21.91 |
| **12/02** | 30.75 | — | — | (1.57) | 0.80 | 21.73 |
| **Annual Growth** | 14.5% | — | — | — | 4.7% | 3.5% |

# Regions Financial

Regions Financial ain't just whistling Dixie anymore. Already a top financial services firm in the South, the holding company for Regions Bank and other units fortified its foothold there and expanded into the Midwest with its blockbuster merger with Union Planters in 2004. Regions later acquired fellow Birmingham-based bank AmSouth for some $9.8 billion in stock in 2006. The deals give Regions some 2,000 branches in 16 states, roughly stretching from the Mississippi River Valley in the US heartland to the Southeast and Texas. Regions Financial also owns Memphis-based investment bank and brokerage Morgan Keegan, which has some 325 offices on its parent's turf, plus New York and Massachusetts.

The AmSouth deal created one of the 10 largest banks in the US and should help the company keep up with other megabanks in the region, such as Bank of America and Wachovia.

In addition to traditional banking, Regions Financial offers a variety of other financial services, including mortgage banking (Regions Mortgage) and credit life, accident, and health insurance (Regions Agency, Regions Life Insurance, and Rebsamen Insurance). Another unit, Regions Interstate Billing Service, factors accounts receivable and performs billing and collection services, primarily for the automotive service industry. Regions is also building its private banking business.

Regions Financial has traditionally expanded its reach through acquisitions, but until the Union Planters merger it had typically bought community banks with fewer than five branches — businesses too small for larger superregionals to touch. By flying under the big banks' radar, Regions Financial has filled in operations geographically to build a substantial presence in almost every state in which it is active.

After the mortgage sector got battered by the housing bust and rising interest rates in 2006, the company in 2007 sold its subprime mortgage origination unit EquiFirst to Barclays Bank (the flagship subsidiary of Barclays).

## HISTORY

Regions Financial was created out of three venerable Alabama banks. The oldest, First National Bank of Huntsville, was founded in 1855. When, 10 years later, the bank was besieged by Union troops, a loyal cashier hid securities in the chimney and refused to tell the soldiers where they were. A few years later it was robbed by Jesse James (for years the bank kept in its vaults a gun purported to belong to a James gang member). First National Bank of Montgomery was founded in 1871, and Exchange Security Bank in 1928.

Banking veteran Frank Plummer consolidated the three banks to form Alabama's first multibank holding company, First Alabama Bancshares, in 1971. The combined firm then became the bank that ate Alabama. But even as it gobbled up other banks, its diet remained bland: Its lending programs were modest and focused on a narrow range of business.

The bank's growth in the 1980s was solid, if unexciting, as it picked up community banks in Alabama (Anniston National Bank and South Baldwin Bank, among others) and Georgia (Georgia Co., a mortgage subsidiary of Columbus Bank and Trust). Before he died in 1987, Plummer brought in Willard Hurley as chairman. Hurley put the brakes on acquisitions when they overloaded the bank's data-processing systems. He also put the company up for sale, igniting its stock price for a while, but there were no serious suitors.

When Hurley passed the baton to Stanley Mackin in 1990 the bank was still rumored to be for sale. But Mackin had other ideas. He put the bank back on its acquisition track and raised the bar on profitability expectations for each department. In 1993 Mackin orchestrated First Alabama's purchase of Secor, a failed New Orleans thrift, outbidding rival AmSouth Bancorporation. The Secor purchase raised eyebrows, but First Alabama sold some branches and folded other operations into its organization.

In 1994 First Alabama changed its name to Regions Financial in order to reflect its out-of-state operations. The next year Regions rolled into Georgia in a big way, leaping from a few banks to holdings with approximately $4 billion in assets. Rumors of a merger with either Wachovia or SunTrust Banks popped up in 1996, but the bank continued on its independent course. The next year the company's tanklike progress was halted when it was outbid for Mississippi's Deposit Guaranty Corp. by First American.

By way of consolation, Regions in 1998 bought First Commercial Corp. of Little Rock, paying a premium price for its 26 banks, mortgage company, and investment company. Regions also acquired 13 other companies that year and began a major overhaul of its systems concurrently with the assimilation of these operations. This effort included the consolidation of the back-office aspects of its retail and indirect lending operations.

In 1999 and 2000, the bank continued its geographic infill strategy with acquisitions of banks and branches in Arkansas, Florida,

Louisiana, Tennessee, and Texas. It also sold its credit card portfolio to MBNA (since acquired by Bank of America). In 2001 it bought Memphis-based investment bank Morgan Keegan.

## EXECUTIVES

**Chairman:** Jackson W. Moore, age 57, $2,237,935 pay (prior to promotion)
**Vice Chairman; Chairman, Morgan Keegan:** Allen B. Morgan Jr., age 63, $1,500,000 pay
**President, CEO, and Director:** C. Dowd Ritter, age 58
**CFO:** Alton E. (Al) Yother, age 54
**SEVP and Chief Risk Officer, Risk Management Group:** William C. (Bill) Wells II, age 46
**SEVP Operations, Technology, Corporate Real Estate, and Procurement:** John B. Owen, age 45
**EVP, General Counsel, and Corporate Secretary:** R. Alan Deer, age 42
**EVP and CIO:** John R. Dick, age 48
**EVP, Internal Audit:** Stephen M. Schoeneman, age 50
**SVP, Investor Relations:** Jenifer M. Goforth
**CEO, East Region:** Peter D. (Pete) Miller, age 59, $829,388 pay (prior to promotion)
**CEO, Midwest Region:** Steven J. (Steve) Schenck, age 57
**CEO, Western Region:** John I. (Jack) Fleischauer Jr., age 57
**CEO, Business Banking:** Bill Horton
**CEO, Consumer Banking:** Candice W. Bagby, age 56
**CEO, Private Banking:** Tom Twitty
**CEO, Mortgage:** Robert A. (Bob) Goethe, age 51
**President and CEO, Morgan Keegan:** G. Douglas Edwards
**Treasurer:** Eric Haas
**President and CEO, Regions Insurance Group:** David L. (Casey) Bowlin, age 56
**Chairman and CEO, Rebsamen Insurance:** Fred B. Stone, age 52
**CEO, Regions Insurance Services:** Chip Harper
**CEO, EquiFirst:** Jeffrey G. Tennyson
**Head of Management Consulting:** Dale Calvin
**Head, Mortgage Sales/Operations:** E. Todd Chamberlain
**Head, Mortgage Servicing/Portfolio:** Morgan McCarty
**Head, Human Resources:** David B. Edmonds, age 52
**Head, Lines of Business:** O. B. Grayson Hall, age 48
**Head, Investor Relations:** M. List Underwood Jr.
**Head, Corporate Communications and Issues Management:** Richard C. (Rick) Swagler
**Auditors:** Ernst & Young LLP

## LOCATIONS

**HQ:** Regions Financial Corporation
1900 Fifth Ave. North, Birmingham, AL 35203
**Phone:** 205-944-1300 **Fax:** 901-580-3915
**Web:** www.regions.com

### 2006 Branches

| | No. | % of total |
|---|---|---|
| Florida | 417 | 21 |
| Tennessee | 342 | 18 |
| Alabama | 298 | 15 |
| Mississippi | 162 | 8 |
| Georgia | 147 | 8 |
| Louisiana | 142 | 7 |
| Arkansas | 100 | 5 |
| Texas | 77 | 5 |
| Illinois | 67 | 3 |
| Missouri | 67 | 3 |
| Indiana | 59 | 3 |
| South Carolina | 37 | 2 |
| Iowa | 17 | 1 |
| Kentucky | 17 | 1 |
| North Carolina | 7 | — |
| Virginia | 1 | — |
| **Total** | **1,957** | **100** |

## PRODUCTS/OPERATIONS

### 2006 Assets

| | $ mil. | % of total |
|---|---|---|
| Cash & equivalents | 3,550.7 | 3 |
| Trading account | 1,443.0 | 1 |
| Securities held to maturity | 47.8 | — |
| Securities available for sale | 18,514.3 | 13 |
| Loans held for sale | 3,308.1 | 2 |
| Net loans | 93,494.6 | 65 |
| Other | 23,010.5 | 16 |
| **Total** | **143,369.0** | **100** |

### 2006 Sales

| | $ mil. | % of total |
|---|---|---|
| Interest | | |
| Loans | 4,710.7 | 61 |
| Securities | 640.3 | 8 |
| Loans held for sale | 196.6 | 3 |
| Other | 146.7 | 2 |
| Noninterest | | |
| Brokerage & investment banking | 677.4 | 9 |
| Service charges on deposit accounts | 649.4 | 8 |
| Trust department income | 150.2 | 2 |
| Mortgage servicing & origination fees | 133.2 | 2 |
| Other | 451.9 | 5 |
| **Total** | **7,756.4** | **100** |

## COMPETITORS

BancorpSouth
Bank of America
BB&T
Capital One
Citigroup
Colonial BancGroup
Compass Bancshares
First Citizens BancShares
First Horizon
RBC Centura Banks
SunTrust
Synovus
Wachovia

## HISTORICAL FINANCIALS

Company Type: Public

### Income Statement

FYE: December 31

| | ASSETS ($ mil.) | NET INCOME ($ mil.) | INCOME AS % OF ASSETS | EMPLOYEES |
|---|---|---|---|---|
| **12/06** | 143,369 | 1,353 | 0.9% | 35,900 |
| **12/05** | 84,786 | 1,001 | 1.2% | 25,000 |
| **12/04** | 84,106 | 824 | 1.0% | 26,000 |
| **12/03** | 48,598 | 652 | 1.3% | 16,180 |
| **12/02** | 47,939 | 620 | 1.3% | 15,695 |
| **Annual Growth** | 31.5% | 21.5% | — | 23.0% |

### 2006 Year-End Financials

Equity as % of assets: 14.4%
Return on assets: 1.2%
Return on equity: 8.6%
Long-term debt ($ mil.): 8,643
No. of shares (mil.): 730
Dividends
Yield: 4.7%
Payout: 65.9%
Market value ($ mil.): 27,305
Sales ($ mil.): 7,756

### Stock History

NYSE: RF

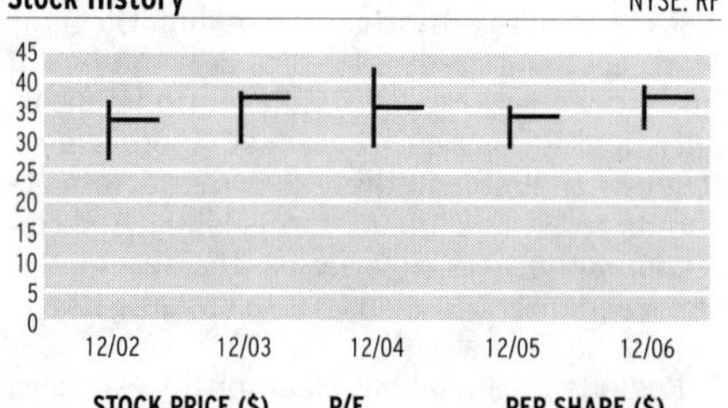


| | STOCK PRICE ($) FY Close | P/E High | P/E Low | PER SHARE ($) Earnings | Dividends | Book Value |
|---|---|---|---|---|---|---|
| **12/06** | 37.40 | 15 | 12 | 2.67 | 1.76 | 28.36 |
| **12/05** | 34.16 | 17 | 14 | 2.15 | 0.34 | 23.26 |
| **12/04** | 35.59 | 19 | 13 | 2.19 | 6.74 | 23.06 |
| **12/03** | 37.20 | 13 | 10 | 2.90 | 1.24 | 20.06 |
| **12/02** | 33.36 | 13 | 10 | 2.72 | 0.58 | 18.88 |
| **Annual Growth** | 2.9% | — | — | (0.5%) | 32.0% | 10.7% |

# Regis Corporation

Regis is hair, there, and everywhere. It's the world's largest operator of hair salons, with about 11,333 owned or franchised salons (primarily in the US), more than 50 beauty schools, and 90 hair loss centers. Formats range from mall-based to Wal-Mart-based with its salons selling hair care products branded under the Regis, MasterCuts, and Cost Cutters names. Regis also runs a variety of store formats in strip malls, including some 2,000 Supercuts and nearly 1,500 SmartStyle salons at Wal-Mart Supercenters. Headquartered in Minneapolis, Minnesota, the company has more than 2,000 locations in France, Italy, Spain, and the UK.

Hair products, sold under its own label and other brands, account for nearly 30% of sales.

Despite its size, Regis still commands only a small percentage of the highly fractured US market. It has been sweeping up market share through acquisitions both internationally and at home. (More than 300 deals since the early 1990s have added more than 7,100 salons.) Regis correctly styles itself as the largest salon franchisor in Europe after acquisitions in 2002 that included Jean Louis David (nearly 1,200 salons).

In December 2004 Regis added significantly to its hair restoration operations when it inked a deal to make Hair Club for Men and Women a wholly owned subsidiary for $210 million in cash. The company, which added more than 800 salons in fiscal year 2005, added about 450 in 2006. Most notably, Regis acquired more than 100 salons operating under the Famous Hair, Chicago Hair, and Hair Inc. trade names midway through the year. The deal is projected to add $34 million in revenue.

In January 2006, Regis agreed to be acquired by personal care products maker Alberto-Culver in a complex $2.6 billion deal; however, in April, the negotiations hit an abrupt snag after Regis' projected forecast for subsequent quarters was lower than originally expected. Regis ended up having to pay a termination fee to Alberto-Culver. The deal would have preserved the Regis name but given Alberto-Culver stockholders majority control of the company's shares.

Regis in 2007 announced plans to merge its beauty school business into that of a rival school operator, Empire Education Group. Regis would take a 49% stake in the expanded Empire Education Group, which would own about 90 schools and have an estimated annual revenue of about $130 million.

## HISTORY

Russian-born immigrant Paul Kunin started with one local barbershop in Minneapolis in 1922. Within the next three decades he owned 60 salons, which were mainly leased departments in stores. Paul sold the business in 1954 to his son Myron and daughter Diana. Myron bought Diana's share some years later.

Once at the helm, Myron shifted stores into the enclosed malls that sprouted during the 1960s. Eschewing franchising, Regis benefited from the complete control of its stores, maintaining an upscale image that fared well against small-time salons. By 1975 the company had 161 salons and it grew during the late 1970s and early 1980s. Regis went public in 1983.

The next year it attempted to diversify from its largely female clientele with the purchase of

Your Father's Mustache, a chain of 60 barbershops. However, the unsuccessful attempt caused earnings to suffer for two years while Regis converted the shops into other formats.

Wanting to reward its managers with company ownership, Regis went private again in 1988, taking on a heavy load of debt. This hindered Myron's efforts to expand in the department store niche. In response, in 1990 he joined MEI Diversified, a cash-rich investment company, to form MEI-Regis Salon (of which MEI owned 80%) in order to buy Essanelle (department store salons).

However, the deal quickly gave all parties a bad hair day: Lawsuits, claims of mismanagement and misrepresentation, and poor earnings conspired to destroy the partnership. MEI-Regis went public again in 1991, but the offering did not make enough to pay bank debt, and it posted a loss. MEI and Regis sued each other in 1992, and Regis called for unpaid expenses related to management while MEI accused Regis of fraud and racketeering.

While all this was going on, Regis continued to expand. Acquisitions such as Trade Secret (1993) moved Regis into higher-margin beauty products. MEI went into Chapter 11 in 1993 and the dispute between the companies was finally settled in bankruptcy court, costing Regis $15 million.

Over the next two years, Regis expanded both in the US and abroad. It moved away from its mall stronghold with the purchase of competitor Supercuts in 1996, adding more than 1,100 stores, mainly in strip malls. Then #2, Supercuts was struggling; ousted CEO David Lipson sued and won a $6.7 million settlement from Regis in 1997. Also in 1996 Regis bought 154 salons operating inside Wal-Mart stores from National Hair Centers. That year COO Paul Finkelstein was promoted to CEO.

The firm took another giant step forward in 1999 when it bought The Barbers, Hairstyling for Men & Women, an operator of about 980 salons, including the Cost Cutters and We Care Hair chains. The deal made Regis the only provider of salon services in Wal-Mart stores.

Regis continued making acquisitions, including Haircrafters, about 550 salons mostly in Canada, and 523 franchised salons in France.

International expansion continued in 2002 with its acquisition of Jean Louis David, Europe's #1 salon chain (nearly 1,200 salons). Also that year Regis acquired BoRics (328 strip-center salons mostly located in Illinois, Michigan, Ohio, and Pennsylvania), as well as 25 Vidal Sassoon salons and four Vidal Sassoon beauty academies from Haircare Limited. Regis assumed Haircare Limited's licensing with Procter & Gamble to use the Vidal Sassoon brand name for an aggressive rollout of salons in North America, as well as the UK and Germany.

The company added nearly 1,000 salons in 2003, including more than 280 salons from its rival Opal Concepts. Store names include Carlton Hair Intl., Hair By Stewarts, American Hair Force, Haircuts Plus, and Pro-Cuts.

In May 2004 Myron Kunin stepped down as chairman, passing his title to longtime president and CEO Finkelstein. Kunin assumed the role of vice chairman. A month later Regis acquired Blaine Beauty Career Schools, a chain comprising six locations in Massachusetts.

In March 2005 Regis acquired the 130-salon TGF Precision Haircutters chain based in Houston. Its largest buy in 2006 was its acquisition of 105 Famous Hair salons.

## EXECUTIVES

**Chairman, President, and CEO:** Paul D. Finkelstein, age 64, $1,231,490 pay
**Vice Chairman:** Myron Kunin, age 77, $743,310 pay
**Senior EVP, Chief Administrative Officer, and CFO:** Randy L. Pearce, age 51, $498,608 pay
**EVP and COO, Promenade Salon Concepts, MasterCuts, and Regis Salons:** Kris Bergly, age 45
**EVP, Fashion, Education, and Marketing:** Gordon B. Nelson, age 55, $459,604 pay
**SVP and President, Franchise Division and Supercuts:** Mark Kartarik, age 50
**SVP and COO, SmartStyle Family Hair Care:** C. John Briggs, age 62
**SVP and COO, Trade Secret:** Norma Knudsen, age 48
**SVP, Law, General Counsel, and Secretary:** Eric A. Bakken, age 39
**SVP and International Managing Director, UK:** Raymond Duke, age 55
**SVP, Design and Construction:** Bruce D. Johnson, age 53
**VP, The Regis Foundation, and Director:** David B. Kunin, age 47
**VP and International Managing Director, Europe:** David Petruccelli, age 40
**President, International Division:** Andrew Cohen, age 43
**CEO, Hair Club for Men and Women:** Darryll Porter
**COO, Supercuts:** Vicki Langan, age 49
**COO, Regis Salons:** Sharon Kiker, age 60
**Director, Investor Relations:** Jack Nielsen
**Public Relations:** Leann Dake
**Auditors:** PricewaterhouseCoopers LLP

## LOCATIONS

**HQ:** Regis Corporation
7201 Metro Blvd., Edina, MN 55439
**Phone:** 952-947-7777 **Fax:** 952-947-7600
**Web:** www.regiscorp.com

Regis has company-owned or franchised salons in Belgium, Brazil, Canada, France, Germany, Italy, Poland, Puerto Rico, Spain, Switzerland, the UK, and the US.

## PRODUCTS/OPERATIONS

### Selected Stores

Affilie (Jean Louis David, international salons)
Beauty Warehouse (regional strip-center salons)
Best Cuts (regional strip-center salons)
BoRics (regional strip-center salons)
City Looks (national strip-center salons in the US and international salons)
Coiff & Co. (international salons)
Cost Cutters (national strip-center salons and Wal-Mart store salons)
First Choice Haircutters (national strip-center salons)
Great Expectations (national strip-center salons)
Hair Express (international salons)
Hair Masters (regional strip-center salons)
Haircrafters (national strip-center salons)
Intermede (international salons)
JLD Diffusion (Jean Louis David, international salons)
JLD Quick Service (Jean Louis David, international salons)
JLD Tradition (Jean Louis David, international salons)
Just a Cut (Jean Louis David, international salons)
Magicuts (national strip-center salons)
MasterCuts Family Haircutters (regional-mall salons)
Mia & Maxx Hair Salons (regional-mall salons)
Mister Shop (Jean Louis David, international salons)
Regis Hairstylists (international salons)
Regis Salons (regional-mall salons)
Saint Algue (international salons)
The Salon (international salons)
Saturday's (regional strip-center salons)
SmartStyle (Wal-Mart store salons)
Style America (regional strip-center salons)
Supercuts (national strip-center salons in the US and international salons)
Trade Secret (regional-mall salons in the US and international salons)
Vidal Sassoon (international salons and beauty academies)
We Care Hair (national strip-center salons)

## COMPETITORS

Alberto-Culver
Command Performance
Cool Cuts
Great Clips
HCX Salons
L'Oréal
Mascolo
Premier Salons
Procter & Gamble
Ratner Companies
Shiseido
Sport Clips
Ulta
Wella

## HISTORICAL FINANCIALS

Company Type: Public

**Income Statement** FYE: June 30

| | REVENUE ($ mil.) | NET INCOME ($ mil.) | NET PROFIT MARGIN | EMPLOYEES |
|---|---|---|---|---|
| **6/07** | 2,627 | 83 | 3.2% | 62,000 |
| **6/06** | 2,431 | 110 | 4.5% | 59,000 |
| **6/05** | 2,194 | 65 | 2.9% | 55,000 |
| **6/04** | 1,923 | 104 | 5.4% | 50,000 |
| **6/03** | 1,685 | 87 | 5.1% | 49,000 |
| **Annual Growth** | 11.7% | (1.0%) | — | 7.3% |

**2007 Year-End Financials**

Debt ratio: 53.2%
Return on equity: 9.3%
Cash ($ mil.): 185
Current ratio: 0.97
Long-term debt ($ mil.): 486
No. of shares (mil.): 44
Dividends
Yield: 0.4%
Payout: 8.8%
Market value ($ mil.): 1,689

**Stock History** NYSE: RGS

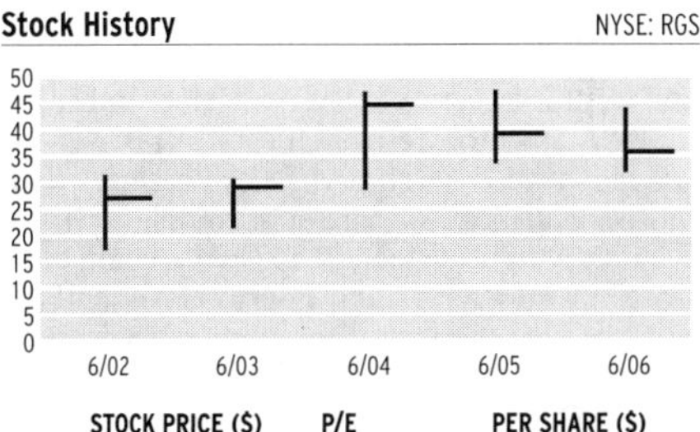

| | STOCK PRICE ($) FY Close | P/E High/Low | | PER SHARE ($) Earnings | Dividends | Book Value |
|---|---|---|---|---|---|---|
| **6/07** | 38.25 | 24 | 18 | 1.82 | 0.16 | 20.68 |
| **6/06** | 35.61 | 18 | 14 | 2.36 | 0.16 | 19.23 |
| **6/05** | 39.08 | 34 | 24 | 1.39 | 0.12 | 16.79 |
| **6/04** | 44.59 | 21 | 13 | 2.26 | 0.10 | 15.40 |
| **6/03** | 29.05 | 16 | 11 | 1.92 | 0.12 | 12.89 |
| **Annual Growth** | 7.1% | — | — | (1.3%) | 7.5% | 12.5% |

# Rent-A-Center

Rent-A-Center wants its customers to rent while it buys. Rent-A-Center became the #1 rent-to-own chain nationwide through a string of acquisitions. The firm owns and operates more than 3,400 stores in North America and Puerto Rico under the Rent-A-Center, Rent-Way, Rent Rite, Rainbow Rentals, and Get It Now names and franchises almost 300 through subsidiary ColorTyme. The stores rent name-brand home electronics, furniture, accessories, appliances, and computers. Although customers have the option to eventually own their rented items, only about 25% ever do. In late 2006 Rent-A-Center's acquisition of Rent-Way and its 780 stores in 34 states eliminated one of the company's primary competitors.

Rent-A-Center has climbed to the top of the US rent-to-own industry through no fewer than 60 acquisitions during the last two decades, including Thorn Americas and its 1,400 Rent-A-Center, Remco, and U-Can-Rent stores. After briefly taking a break from expansion to focus on integrating banners, management, and marketing efforts, Rent-A-Center has ramped up those efforts again. The $567 million purchase of Rent-Way was a big part of this strategy, which gave the company a massive number of new stores. Other moves to attract new customers include opening new stores and expanding its offerings of upscale brands (Sony Electronics, Ashley Furniture).

These developments were a turnabout from Rent-A-Center's strategy the previous year when it shuttered as many as 150 stores by year-end due to "overpenetration" in some markets as a result of the company's prior bout of acquisitiveness.

That same year, the company launched its financial services product line. The new products include loans, bill paying, debit cards, check cashing, and money transfer services. By 2006's end, 150 of the company's stores were offering the new products.

## HISTORY

Ernest Talley is a pioneer in the rent-to-own industry, having founded one of the first rent-to-own chains in 1963. He sold that business in 1974 and went into commercial real estate in Dallas. In 1987, after the Texas real estate crash, Talley and his son Michael started Talley Leasing, which rented appliances to apartment complex owners.

Talley bought Vista Rent To Own, a chain of 22 stores in New Jersey and Puerto Rico, in 1989. He upgraded merchandise, increased selection, updated information and data systems, and improved store management. In 1993 the company acquired DEF, an 84-store chain, and repeated the upgrading process. That year the company changed its name to Renters Choice. It went public in 1995 and used the proceeds to make more acquisitions.

The purchases of Crown Leasing and Pro Rental (parent of Magic Rent-to-Own) moved Renters Choice into the southern US and increased its store count from just more than 100 to 322. In 1996 the company acquired Texas-based competitor ColorTyme, adding another 320 stores (most of them franchises). Renters Choice acquired Trans Texas Capital, another rental purchase enterprise, the following year.

In 1998 the company bought Central Rents, owner of about 180 stores, for $103 million and paid $900 million (most of it borrowed) for rival Thorn Americas, which operated some 1,400 stores under the Rent-A-Center, Remco, and U-Can-Rent brands. Renters Choice then changed its name to Rent-A-Center. Also that year it settled a class-action lawsuit with 20,000 customers for $12 million; the suit alleged that the company had misled consumers about actual finance costs.

Rent-A-Center lost an appeal of another lawsuit in 1999 and was ordered to pay $30 million to 30,000 consumers for charging interest rates as high as 750%.

After making no acquisitions in 1999, Rent-A-Center announced in 2000 that it would be adding 100-plus stores annually. The company also began offering Internet service (originally for $5.95 per week through BellSouth and then, in 2001, offering free service through NetZero).

In October 2001 Ernest Talley retired and Mark Speese was named chairman and CEO. In February 2003 Rent-A-Center bought 295 stores (located in 38 states) from rival Rent-Way for just more than $100 million.

In 2004 the company acquired Rent Rite (90 stores in 11 states) as well as Rainbow Rentals (124 stores in 15 states). Also that year Rent-A-Center broke into the Canadian market with the purchase of five stores in Alberta for $2.4 million.

In April 2005 the company settled a lawsuit related to its business practices in California — *Benjamin Griego, et al. v. Rent-A-Center, Inc.* — by agreeing to pay the plaintiff's attorneys' fees as well as about $37.5 million cash to eligible customers who entered into rental-purchase agreements with the company between early 1999 and late 2004.

In 2005 the company sold the rental contracts and merchandise of 19 stores to Aaron Rents for about $4.4 million. In 2006 Rent-A-Center acquired Rent-Way for about $600 million. As a result, Rent-Way became a wholly owned indirect subsidiary of the company.

## EXECUTIVES

**Chairman and CEO:** Mark E. Speese, age 49, $740,000 pay
**President, COO, and Director:** Mitchell E. Fadel, age 49, $510,000 pay
**EVP, Operations:** William S. (Bill) Short, age 49
**SVP, Finance, CFO, and Treasurer:** Robert D. Davis, age 35, $335,000 pay
**SVP, General Counsel, and Secretary:** Christopher A. Korst, age 47, $28,000 pay
**SVP, Operations:** Theodore (Ted) DeMarino
**SVP, Operations:** David G. Ewbank
**SVP, Operations:** C. Edward Ford III
**SVP, Operations:** Michael J. (Mike) Kelly
**SVP, Operations:** Michael P. (Mike) Kilbane
**SVP, Operations:** Richard S. Lillard
**SVP, Operations:** Fred G. Mattox
**SVP, Operations:** Michael R. (Mike) McNamara
**SVP, Operations:** Charles J. White
**SVP, Operational Service:** David E. West, age 56, $251,125 pay
**SVP, Information Technology and CIO:** Tony F. Fuller
**VP, Sales:** Joe T. Arnette
**VP, Development:** Kent W. Brown
**VP, Investor Relations:** David E. (Dave) Carpenter
**VP, Marketing and Advertising and Chief Marketing Officer:** Ann L. Davids
**VP, Human Resources:** Melvin D. McCall
**VP, Merchandise:** Deborah L. (Debbie) Romero
**VP, Finance and Controller:** Ned W. Villemarette
**President and CEO, ColorTyme:** Robert F. (Bob) Bloom, age 54
**Auditors:** Grant Thornton LLP

## LOCATIONS

**HQ:** Rent-A-Center, Inc.
5700 Tennyson Pkwy., Ste. 100, Plano, TX 75024
**Phone:** 972-801-1100 **Fax:** 972-943-0113
**Web:** www.rentacenter.com

### 2006 Stores

| | Co-owned | Franchised |
|---|---|---|
| Texas | 311 | 60 |
| Florida | 237 | 17 |
| Ohio | 206 | 5 |
| New York | 190 | 3 |
| Pennsylvania | 174 | 3 |
| North Carolina | 148 | 12 |
| California | 147 | 5 |
| Michigan | 124 | 16 |
| Illinois | 121 | 7 |
| Georgia | 118 | 14 |
| Indiana | 118 | 6 |
| Tennessee | 112 | 1 |
| South Carolina | 83 | 7 |
| Virginia | 81 | 10 |
| Kentucky | 78 | 1 |
| Alabama | 73 | 5 |
| Massachusetts | 73 | 2 |
| Missouri | 73 | 6 |
| Arizona | 70 | 7 |
| Maryland | 70 | 10 |
| Arkansas | 55 | 1 |
| Louisiana | 53 | 6 |
| Washington | 45 | 4 |
| Oklahoma | 44 | 13 |
| Puerto Rico | 44 | — |
| New Jersey | 43 | 3 |
| Connecticut | 42 | 2 |
| Colorado | 40 | 1 |
| Kansas | 40 | 16 |
| Mississippi | 36 | 2 |
| Maine | 31 | 9 |
| West Virginia | 30 | — |
| Iowa | 29 | — |
| Oregon | 29 | 4 |
| New Mexico | 25 | 9 |
| Nevada | 22 | 3 |
| New Hampshire | 22 | 1 |
| Delaware | 21 | — |
| Wisconsin | 21 | — |
| Nebraska | 18 | — |
| Rhode Island | 17 | 1 |
| Utah | 16 | — |
| Vermont | 12 | — |
| Hawaii | 11 | 4 |
| Idaho | 11 | 3 |
| Montana | 9 | — |
| Alberta, Canada | 7 | — |
| Alaska | 6 | 3 |
| Other states | 20 | |
| **Total** | **3,406** | **282** |

## PRODUCTS/OPERATIONS

### 2006 Sales

| | $ mil. | % of total |
|---|---|---|
| Store | | |
| Rentals & fees | 2,174.2 | 89 |
| Merchandise sales | 176.0 | 7 |
| Installment sales | 26.9 | 1 |
| Other | 15.6 | 1 |
| Franchise | | |
| Merchandise sales | 36.4 | 2 |
| Royalty income & fees | 4.8 | — |
| **Total** | **2,433.9** | **100** |

### 2006 Sales

| | % of total |
|---|---|
| Furniture & accessories | 37 |
| Consumer electronics | 33 |
| Appliances | 16 |
| Computers | 14 |
| **Total** | **100** |

### Store Names

ColorTyme
Get It Now
Rainbow Rentals
Rent-A-Center

## COMPETITORS

Aaron Rents
Best Buy
Bestway
Brook Furniture
Cash America
EZCORP
First Cash Financial
Sears
Wal-Mart

## HISTORICAL FINANCIALS

Company Type: Public

**Income Statement** — FYE: December 31

| | REVENUE ($ mil.) | NET INCOME ($ mil.) | NET PROFIT MARGIN | EMPLOYEES |
|---|---|---|---|---|
| **12/06** | 2,434 | 103 | 4.2% | 19,740 |
| **12/05** | 2,339 | 136 | 5.8% | 15,480 |
| **12/04** | 2,313 | 156 | 6.7% | 16,431 |
| **12/03** | 2,228 | 182 | 8.1% | 15,181 |
| **12/02** | 2,010 | 172 | 8.6% | 14,300 |
| **Annual Growth** | 4.9% | (12.0%) | — | 8.4% |

**2006 Year-End Financials**

Debt ratio: 137.2%
Return on equity: 11.7%
Cash ($ mil.): 92
Current ratio: 2.34
Long-term debt ($ mil.): 1,293
No. of shares (mil.): 70
Dividends
Yield: —
Payout: —
Market value ($ mil.): 2,071

**Stock History** — NASDAQ (GS): RCII

40
35
30
25
20
15
10
5
0
12/02 12/03 12/04 12/05 12/06

| | STOCK PRICE ($) FY Close | P/E High/Low | PER SHARE ($) Earnings | Dividends | Book Value |
|---|---|---|---|---|---|
| **12/06** | 29.51 | 21 12 | 1.46 | — | 13.43 |
| **12/05** | 18.86 | 15 8 | 1.83 | — | 11.90 |
| **12/04** | 26.50 | 17 11 | 1.94 | — | 10.68 |
| **12/03** | 30.00 | 17 9 | 2.08 | — | 9.92 |
| **12/02** | 19.98 | 13 6 | 1.90 | — | 24.11 |
| **Annual Growth** | 10.2% | — — | (6.4%) | — | (13.6%) |

# Republic Services

Homeowners and businesses in 21 states pledge allegiance to Republic Services and the trash collection for which it stands. Republic Services is the #3 solid waste management company in the US, behind Waste Management and Allied Waste Industries. The company provides waste disposal services for commercial, industrial, municipal, and residential customers through its network of about 135 collection companies. Republic Services, which focuses on the high-growth Sunbelt region, owns or operates some 59 solid waste landfills, 93 transfer stations, and 33 recycling centers.

Republic Services organizes its operations into five regions: eastern, central, southern, southwestern, and western. Each region is further divided into several operating areas, each of which provides collection, transfer, disposal, and recycling services. Regional and area managers are given considerable authority under the company's decentralized management structure.

Republic Services has grown by buying smaller waste management operations, and the company is looking to make more acquisitions in its existing service areas and in new regions. Likely candidates include assets of municipalities that are privatizing their waste management services.

The company's largest shareholder is Microsoft chairman Bill Gates, who owns about 13% of Republic Services through private investment firm Cascade Investment LLC.

## HISTORY

Republic Services began in 1980 as Republic Resources, an oil exploration and production company. In 1989, after a stockholder group tried to force Republic into liquidation, Browning-Ferris (BFI) founder Thomas Fatjo stepped in, gained control of Republic Resources, and refocused it on a field he knew well — solid waste. Renamed Republic Waste, the company began making acquisitions.

In 1990 Michael DeGroote, founder of BFI competitor Laidlaw, bought into Republic Waste. In 1995 Wayne Huizenga — who co-founded Waste Management in 1971 and was beginning to develop a national auto sales organization in the mid-1990s after his tenure as chairman and CEO of Blockbuster Entertainment — approached DeGroote about a deal. They rejected an immediate merger of the waste and auto businesses because the latter was not well-enough developed and would drag down Republic's numbers. Instead, they agreed to merge Republic and the Hudson Companies (a trash business owned by Huizenga's brother-in-law, Harris Hudson), to sell Huizenga a large interest in Republic through a private offering, and to give him control of the board (in 1995). The company became Republic Industries.

Huizenga's investment brought a flood of new investors. With new resources, Republic Industries became a driving force in the garbage industry's consolidation binge, and the company bought more than 100 smaller waste haulers between 1995 and 1998. Republic Industries spun off about 30% of its waste business as Republic Services in 1998; the IPO raised $1.3 billion. Republic's acquisition trend continued, as it agreed to buy 16 landfills, 136 commercial collection routes, and 11 transfer stations from Waste Management for $500 million. Later that year Waste Management veteran James O'Connor succeeded Huizenga as CEO, although Huizenga continued as chairman.

Investors filed class action lawsuits against Republic in 1999, claiming the Waste Management purchases held far more integration problems than the company admitted. In 2000 the company swapped nine of its solid waste operations for eight Allied Waste businesses, which Allied needed to divest in order to gain federal approval for its merger with BFI.

While many firms in the industry were selling off assets in 2001, Republic was expanding its operations in the northern California market by acquiring Richmond Sanitary Services. Huizenga retired as chairman at the end of 2002 and was once again succeeded by O'Connor. Huizenga stayed on the board as a director until May 2004.

## EXECUTIVES

**Chairman and CEO:** James E. (Jim) O'Connor, age 57, $2,352,020 pay
**Vice Chairman and Secretary:** Harris W. (Whit) Hudson, age 64, $200,000 pay
**President and COO:** Michael J. (Mike) Cordesman, age 59, $1,020,038 pay
**SVP and CFO:** Tod C. Holmes, age 58, $880,002 pay
**SVP General Counsel and Assistant Secretary:** David A. Barclay, age 44, $649,979 pay
**VP and Chief Accounting Officer:** Charles F. Serianni
**VP and Controller:** Jerry S. Clark
**VP and Associate General Counsel:** Matthew D. Katz
**VP Communications:** William C. (Will) Flower
**VP Corporate Development:** Brian A. Bales
**VP Environmental Engineering and Compliance:** Matthew E. Davies
**VP Finance and Treasurer:** Edward A. Lang III
**VP Human Resources:** Craig J. Nichols
**VP Purchasing and Maintenance:** Gerard W. (Jerry) Wickett
**VP Sales and Marketing:** Gary L. Sova
**VP Tax:** Paul J. Connealy
**Manager, Corporate Communications:** Nancy Bretas
**Auditors:** Ernst & Young LLP

## LOCATIONS

**HQ:** Republic Services, Inc.
110 SE 6th St., 28th Fl., Fort Lauderdale, FL 33301
**Phone:** 954-769-2400 **Fax:** 954-769-2664
**Web:** www.republicservices.com

**2006 Sales**

| | $ mil. | % of total |
|---|---|---|
| Southern | 798.1 | 26 |
| Western | 735.8 | 24 |
| Central | 635.1 | 21 |
| Eastern | 568.8 | 18 |
| Southwestern | 334.3 | 11 |
| Adjustments | (1.5) | — |
| **Total** | **3,070.6** | **100** |

## PRODUCTS/OPERATIONS

**2006 Sales**

| | $ mil. | % of total |
|---|---|---|
| Collection | | |
| Commercial | 860.1 | 28 |
| Residential | 734.3 | 24 |
| Industrial | 649.7 | 21 |
| Other | 74.3 | 3 |
| Transfer & disposal | 593.5 | 19 |
| Other | 158.7 | 5 |
| **Total** | **3,070.6** | **100** |

## COMPETITORS

Allied Waste
Casella Waste Systems
IESI
Norcal Waste
Rumpke
Veolia ES Solid Waste
Waste Connections
Waste Industries USA
Waste Management

## HISTORICAL FINANCIALS

Company Type: Public

**Income Statement** — FYE: December 31

| | REVENUE ($ mil.) | NET INCOME ($ mil.) | NET PROFIT MARGIN | EMPLOYEES |
|---|---|---|---|---|
| **12/06** | 3,071 | 280 | 9.1% | 13,000 |
| **12/05** | 2,864 | 254 | 8.9% | 13,000 |
| **12/04** | 2,708 | 238 | 8.8% | 13,400 |
| **12/03** | 2,518 | 178 | 7.1% | 12,900 |
| **12/02** | 2,365 | 240 | 10.1% | 12,700 |
| **Annual Growth** | 6.7% | 3.9% | — | 0.6% |

### 2006 Year-End Financials

| | |
|---|---|
| Debt ratio: 108.6% | No. of shares (mil.): 130 |
| Return on equity: 18.5% | Dividends |
| Cash ($ mil.): 29 | Yield: 1.5% |
| Current ratio: 0.65 | Payout: 29.0% |
| Long-term debt ($ mil.): 1,545 | Market value ($ mil.): 3,525 |

### Stock History

NYSE: RSG

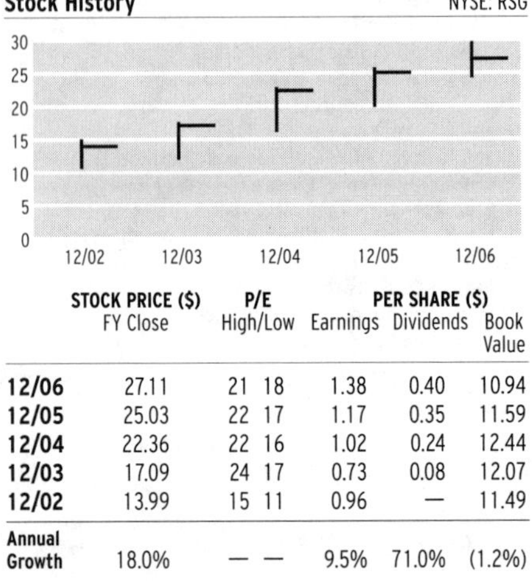


| | STOCK PRICE ($) FY Close | P/E High | P/E Low | PER SHARE ($) Earnings | Dividends | Book Value |
|---|---|---|---|---|---|---|
| **12/06** | 27.11 | 21 | 18 | 1.38 | 0.40 | 10.94 |
| **12/05** | 25.03 | 22 | 17 | 1.17 | 0.35 | 11.59 |
| **12/04** | 22.36 | 22 | 16 | 1.02 | 0.24 | 12.44 |
| **12/03** | 17.09 | 24 | 17 | 0.73 | 0.08 | 12.07 |
| **12/02** | 13.99 | 15 | 11 | 0.96 | — | 11.49 |
| **Annual Growth** | 18.0% | — | — | 9.5% | 71.0% | (1.2%) |

# Revlon, Inc.

Revlon has the look of a leader in the US mass-market cosmetics business, alongside L'Oréal's Maybelline and Procter & Gamble's Cover Girl. In addition to Revlon's makeup and skin care products (Revlon, Almay, and Ultima II), the firm makes fragrances (Charlie) and personal care products (Flex, Mitchum). New York socialite Ron Perelman owns about 60% of Revlon — and controls 77% of its voting power — through holding companies, including MacAndrews & Forbes Holdings. FMR Corp. owns some 17% of Revlon. While Perelman's involvement with Revlon has fueled his celebrity status, the cosmetics maker has seen stalled revenue in recent years. Regardless, Perelman continues to fund the firm.

Revlon sells its products in more than 100 countries, primarily through mass merchandisers, drugstores, and supermarkets. It typically refreshes its lines with new brands. Über retailer Wal-Mart is Revlon's largest customer, with 23% of 2006 sales.

What started as a company that developed and sold nail polish has become nails on a chalkboard to some investors, but Revlon is trying to make up for lost time by turning its future toward profits. The company's current strategy is to develop its core brands, such as Revlon and Almay, while boosting growth in its personal care products segment with women's hair care, fragrance, deodorants, and other niches. With international business representing more than 40% of Revlon's revenue in 2006, the company is concentrating on extending its reach outside the US to increase its market share abroad.

Restructurings and other moves have been aimed at improving Revlon's stubbornly poor financial performance. In late 2006 (soon after the company replaced CEO Jack Stahl), the ailing cosmetics giant announced it would cut about 8% of its workforce and cancel its newly developed Vital Radiance line of cosmetics. A couple of years earlier, a debt-for-equity swap deal with Fidelity Management & Research Co. and Mafco Holdings was necessary to help reduce some $780 million of the company's debt.

A sign of a turnaround came in March 2005, when Revlon posted its first profitable quarter in six years. The turnaround was brief, however.

Revlon's lagging sales have caused the company to slow its product development efforts, as well. In mid-2006 the company postponed its anticipated launch of prestige fragrance Flair until 2007, blaming slower-than-expected growth.

## HISTORY

Legend has it that, jobless in New York City in the depths of the Depression, Charles Revson became a cosmetics salesman by the toss of a coin — tails, he'd apply for a job selling household appliances; heads, he'd answer an ad for a cosmetics salesman. It was heads, and in 1931 Revson began selling Elka nail polish to beauty salons. He painted his own nails with different colors so he wouldn't need a color chart.

Revson and his brother Joseph decided to start their own nail polish company. They scraped together $300, hooked up with nail polish supplier Charles Lachman, and in 1932 began Revlon (the "L" in the name came from Lachman). The nail polish, emulating Elka's, was opaque rather than transparent, available in many colors, and an immediate hit with beauty salons. Revlon grew rapidly, and by 1937 Revson was selling his nail polish in upscale department stores.

Seeing nail polish as a fashion accessory, Revson introduced new colors twice a year, giving them — and the matching lipsticks introduced in 1940 — names like Kissing Pink and Fifth Avenue Red. More opportunist than innovator, he let his competitors do the research and make the mistakes, and then he would make a better version of the product, outpackaging and outadvertising his rivals.

Revlon introduced Fire & Ice in 1952, one of its most successful launches ever. Its sole sponsorship of *The $64,000 Question* quiz show in 1955 boosted sales of some products by 500%. Later that year Revlon went public. To diversify and expand its markets, it began making acquisitions (although many were soon dumped) and selling its products overseas.

The company bought deodorant maker Mitchum in 1970, and three years later it introduced Charlie, its wildly popular fragrance. In 1974 a dying Revson handpicked his successor, Michel Bergerac, president of European operations for IT&T. Revson died the next year. Bergerac began a new push for diversification and lower costs. Acquisitions included ophthalmic and pharmaceuticals companies. However, while Revlon's health care operations were rising, its cosmetics star was losing market share and profits were falling.

Social-climbing conglomateur Ron Perelman bought Revlon in an LBO in 1985 with funds raised by friend Michael Milken. Hoping to restore the firm as a beauty business, Perelman began selling off profitable health care businesses and buying beauty companies (including Max Factor, which he then sold in 1991 to cut debt).

In 1994 Revlon introduced ColorStay lipstick, which quickly became the top-selling lipstick. Revlon went public in 1996. George Fellows was promoted to CEO the next year. The company merged its Prestige Fragrance & Cosmetics chain into Perelman's Cosmetic Center chain in 1997; Revlon sold its 85% stake in the combination at a loss in 1998.

Still deep in debt and suffering from domestic competition, too much inventory, and troubles in Russia and Brazil, Revlon closed three plants and cut 3,000 jobs in 1998. Fellows resigned in 1999 and was replaced by Jeff Nugent, the former president of Neutrogena (and brother of rocker Ted Nugent). Sales fell as retailers cut inventory.

Revlon sold its professional products business in 2000 to an investment group led by the unit's chairman, Carlos Colomer (now chairman of Colomer USA). Also in 2000 Revlon sold its Plusbelle line (Argentina) to consumer products company Dial. In 2001 it sold its Colorama brand of cosmetics and hair care products to rival L'Oreal.

In February 2002 CEO Nugent abruptly resigned after it was reported that chairman Ron Perelman planned to replace him with Jack Stahl, former president and COO at The Coca-Cola Company; Stahl took office that month. The same year Perelman offered a cash infusion of $150 million to the struggling company — $50 million would come from a stock offering and $100 million would be provided by a line of credit from Perelman's MacAndrews & Forbes. Revlon's board accepted the proposal in 2003.

Stahl left the troubled company in September 2006 to pursue other interests and was succeeded as president and CEO of Revlon by David Kennedy, the firm's CFO.

## EXECUTIVES

**Chairman:** Ronald O. (Ron) Perelman, age 64
**President, CEO, and Director:** David L. Kennedy, age 59
**EVP Human Resources, Chief Legal Officer and General Counsel:** Robert K. Kretzman III, age 54
**EVP and Chief Science Officer:** Neil Scancarella
**EVP Customer Business development:** Karl Obrecht
**EVP, Technical Affairs and Worldwide Operations:** Carl K. Kooyoomjian, age 56
**EVP, CFO, Chief Accounting Officer, and Corporate Controller:** Alan T. Ennis, age 36
**SVP Asia Pacific:** Graeme Howard
**SVP Marketing, Revlon and Almay Color Cosmetics:** Elizabeth Crystal
**SVP Worldwide Manufacturing, International Operations and Worldwide Operations Finance:** Arthur Franson
**SVP, Marketing, Media, and Public Relations:** Kiki Rees
**SVP Latin American Region and General Manager, Mexico:** Simon Worraker
**SVP and Managing Director, Europe:** Chris Elshaw
**SVP Marketing and Product Development:** Carolyn Holba
**SVP Marketing, Beauty Care:** Robin Wood
**SVP and Deputy General Counsel:** Michael Sheehan
**SVP and General Tax Counsel:** Mark Sexton
**SVP and CIO:** Ronald Blitstein
**VP Employee Relations:** Stacy Green
**Auditors:** KPMG LLP

## LOCATIONS

**HQ:** Revlon, Inc.
237 Park Ave., New York, NY 10017
**Phone:** 212-527-4000 **Fax:** 212-527-4995
**Web:** www.revloninc.com

Revlon's products are sold in more than 100 countries.

### 2006 Sales

| | $ mil. | % of total |
|---|---|---|
| US | 764.9 | 57 |
| International | 566.5 | 43 |
| **Total** | **1,331.4** | **100** |

## PRODUCTS/OPERATIONS

### 2006 Sales

| | $ mil. | % of total |
|---|---|---|
| Cosmetics, skin care & fragrances | 832.0 | 62 |
| Personal care | 499.4 | 38 |
| **Total** | **1,331.4** | **100** |

### Selected Products and Brands

Cosmetics
- Almay
- Botafirm
- ColorStay
- Cutex (in South America and Africa)
- Gatineau
- Revlon
- Revlon Age Defying
- Ultima II

Fragrances
- Revlon (Charlie, Ciara)

Personal Care
- Almay
- Bozzano
- Juvena
- Revlon

Skin Care
- Almay
- Jeanne Gatineau
- Revlon
- Ultima II

## COMPETITORS

Alberto-Culver
Alticor
Avlon Industries
Avon
Bath & Body Works
Beiersdorf
Body Shop
Bristol-Myers Squibb
Clarins
Colgate-Palmolive
Colomer USA
Combe
Coty Inc.
Estée Lauder
Intimate Brands
Joh. A. Benckiser
John Paul Mitchell
Johnson & Johnson
L'Oréal
LVMH
Mary Kay
Nu Skin
Orly International
Procter & Gamble
Puig Beauty & Fashion
Shiseido
SoftSheen/Carson
Unilever NV

## HISTORICAL FINANCIALS

Company Type: Public

### Income Statement

FYE: December 31

| | REVENUE ($ mil.) | NET INCOME ($ mil.) | NET PROFIT MARGIN | EMPLOYEES |
|---|---|---|---|---|
| **12/06** | 1,331 | (251) | — | 6,000 |
| **12/05** | 1,332 | (84) | — | 6,800 |
| **12/04** | 1,297 | (143) | — | 6,300 |
| **12/03** | 1,299 | (154) | — | 6,100 |
| **12/02** | 1,119 | (287) | — | 6,000 |
| **Annual Growth** | 4.4% | — | — | 0.0% |

### 2006 Year-End Financials

Debt ratio: —
Return on equity: —
Cash ($ mil.): 35
Current ratio: 1.29
Long-term debt ($ mil.): 1,502
No. of shares (mil.): 390
Dividends
Yield: —
Payout: —
Market value ($ mil.): 499

### Stock History

NYSE: REV

| | STOCK PRICE ($) FY Close | P/E High/Low | PER SHARE ($) Earnings | Dividends | Book Value |
|---|---|---|---|---|---|
| **12/06** | 1.28 | — — | (0.62) | — | (3.16) |
| **12/05** | 3.10 | — — | (0.23) | — | (3.18) |
| **12/04** | 2.30 | — — | (0.47) | — | (2.96) |
| **12/03** | 2.24 | — — | (2.47) | — | (45.16) |
| **12/02** | 3.06 | — — | (5.49) | — | (79.98) |
| **Annual Growth** | (19.6%) | — — | — | — | — |

# Reynolds American

Together, no one can stop us. No doubt that is what R.J. Reynolds Tobacco Holdings (RJRT) and Brown & Williamson were thinking when the two merged to create Reynolds American. R.J. Reynolds has been smoking for more than 120 years, but increasing competition and the need to cut costs encouraged the #2 US tobacco company to merge with #3 Brown & Williamson. Reynolds American still trails the Altria Group (owner of Philip Morris), which steers about half of the US tobacco market. RJRT's Camel and Salem brands are among the top-selling cigarettes in the US. The firm also sells Kool and Lucky Strike brands. Brown & Williamson's former parent British American Tobacco owns nearly 42% of Reynolds American.

Reynolds American is the holding company for R.J. Reynolds Tobacco Company (RJR), Santa Fe Natural Tobacco Company, Inc., and Lane Limited.

Reynolds American is lighting the way toward smokeless tobacco sales, making strategic acquisitions while using its resources at Lane Limited to produce moist snuff. Lane makes loose tobacco brands Bugler, Kite, and Midnight Special. In 2006, Reynolds American acquired the No. 2 smokeless tobacco maker Conwood Sales Co. for $3.5 billion in cash.

Both RJR and Brown & Williamson are involved in a class-action lawsuit in Louisiana, where a jury has taken an unusual step by ordering the companies to share in the cost of helping people quit smoking. Both companies are appealing the $590 million cost for nicotine patches and other assistance.

Another class action lawsuit had been pending in Florida since mid-2003. In July 2006, however, the Florida Supreme Court upheld a lower court's ruling that had overturned a $145 billion award for punitive damages against Big Tobacco defendants, among them RJR and Brown & Williamson. While the ruling upheld findings, such as cigarette smoking causes diseases and that nicotine is addictive, it signaled to some investors that the threat of tobacco-related class action lawsuits was lessening.

## HISTORY

R. J. Reynolds formed the R.J. Reynolds Tobacco Company in 1875 in Winston, North Carolina, to produce chewing tobacco. In the late 1890s, Reynolds lost two-thirds of the company to the American Tobacco Trust, but he regained control in 1911 after the trust was dismantled by the government. Two years later the company introduced Camel.

After Reynolds died in 1918, leadership passed to Bowman Gray, whose family ran the company for the next 50 years. Camel held the #1 or #2 cigarette position throughout the 1930s and 1940s, and Reynolds became the largest domestic cigarette company. In response to growing health concerns in the 1950s, the company introduced its filtered Winston (1954) and Salem (1956) brands.

Growing anti-smoking sentiment led to diversification beginning in 1966. Reynolds' acquisitions included Chun King, Patio Foods, American Independent Oil, Del Monte, Inglenook wines, Smirnoff vodka, Kentucky Fried Chicken, Sunkist beverages, and Canada Dry, all of which it sold by 1991. In 1985 Reynolds bought Nabisco (Newtons, Oreo, Planters nuts) for $4.9 billion, forming RJRNabisco Holdings.

Nabisco's CEO, Ross Johnson, became CEO of RJR Nabisco. When Johnson attempted an LBO of RJR Nabisco, buyout firm Kohlberg Kravis Roberts (KKR) outbid him, acquiring the company in 1989 in a deal valued in excess of $25 billion. Antismoking attacks on the company increased after Reynolds replaced its Old Joe camel image with the more cartoonish Joe Camel in 1988. An American Medical Association report determined that the resulting ad campaign appealed to children, encouraging them to smoke.

RJR Nabisco went public again in 1991. Andrew Schindler was promoted to CEO of Reynolds in 1995. RJR Nabisco sold 19.5% of Nabisco Holdings to the public in 1995, and after a failed takeover attempt by Carl Icahn and Bennett LeBow, KKR sold the rest of its stake in RJR Nabisco. Reynolds ended the much-criticized Joe Camel campaign in the US in 1997 and cut its tobacco workforce by 10%. The big US tobacco companies reached a $206 billion settlement in 1998 covering 46 states (four states had already settled for $40 billion) and began hiking cigarette prices by 45 cents a pack.

RJR Nabisco again made more cuts in its tobacco workforce: 1,000 domestic jobs and 2,900 international jobs. In 1999 RJR Nabisco sold its international tobacco operations to Japan Tobacco for $8 billion. Hoping to keep tobacco troubles separate from the cracker and cookie business, it then spun off R.J. Reynolds Tobacco Holdings (RJR), a holding company for R.J. Reynolds Tobacco Company (RJRT); RJR Nabisco was renamed Nabisco Group Holdings.

A Florida jury rendered a $35 billion punitive damages verdict against RJRT in 2000. The company filed an appeal, as it and four other Big Tobacco firms claimed the verdict, totaling $145 billion, would put them out of business (which violates Florida tort law). A state appeals court later threw out the verdict saying the thousands of Florida smokers named in the case could not lump their complaints into one lawsuit. That decision is now under review by the Florida Supreme Court.

RJRT spun off its Targacept subsidiary (created in 1999) in 2000, retaining a 43% stake. Late that year RJR bought Nabisco Group Holdings for $9.8 billion. At the same time, Philip Morris bought Nabisco Group Holdings' sole asset,

Nabisco Holdings (Ritz Crackers, Oreo) for $18.9 billion; RJR made about $1.5 billion from the deal.

In 2002 the company acquired the Santa Fe Natural Tobacco Company, maker of the Natural American Spirit additive-free cigarette brand. That year RJR also formed a joint venture with UK-based Gallaher to sell American blend cigarettes in Europe, particularly in France, Spain, Italy, and the Canary Islands. In 2003 the company said it launched a two-year plan to cut costs by $1 billion, which included cutting jobs by 40%. By the end of 2003, RJRT had cut 1,400 jobs. Shortly thereafter, the company announced merger plans with Brown & Williamson.

Before combining with RJRT to create Reynolds American, Brown & Williamson had been ordered to cut back on promoting its Kool brand, which was associated with hip-hop music. The issue carried over to Reynolds American, which agreed in 2004 to settle several related lawsuits in New York, Illinois, and Maryland by paying $1.5 million toward anti-smoking campaigns and severely restricting Kool promotions that critics said targeted black youths.

## EXECUTIVES

**Chairman, President, and CEO; Chairman, R.J. Reynolds Tobacco Company:** Susan M. Ivey, age 48, $1,135,000 pay
**EVP and CFO:** Dianne M. Neal, age 47, $532,675 pay
**EVP, Public Affairs:** Tommy J. Payne, age 49, $369,475 pay
**EVP and General Counsel:** E. Julia (Judy) Lambeth, age 55
**SVP and Treasurer:** Daniel A. Fawley, age 49
**SVP, Strategy and Business Development:** E. Kenan (Ken) Whitehurst, age 50
**SVP, Deputy General Counsel, and Secretary; SVP, Secretary, and Director, R.J. Reynolds Tobacco Company:** McDara P. Folan III, age 48
**SVP, Human Resources:** Lisa J. Caldwell, age 46
**SVP and Chief Accounting Officer:** Michael S. Desmond, age 40
**VP, Investor Relations:** Morris L. Moore
**President, R. J. Reynolds Global Products:** Luis R. Davila, age 47
**President and CEO, Conwood Company and Conwood Sales:** William M. (Bill) Rosson, age 58
**President and CEO, Santa Fe Natural Tobacco Company:** Richard M. Sanders, age 53
**RAI Group President:** Jeffrey A. Eckmann, age 54, $637,675 pay (prior to promotion)
**President and CEO, R.J. Reynolds Tobacco Company:** Daniel M. (Daan) Delen, age 41
**EVP, Consumer and Trade Marketing, R.J. Reynolds Tobacco Company:** Gavin D. Little, age 38
**EVP and CIO, Reynolds American and R.J. Reynolds Tobacco Company:** Donald I. Lamonds, age 49
**EVP, Operations, R.J. Reynolds Tobacco Company:** Daniel D. Snyder, age 51
**EVP, Research and Development, R.J. Reynolds Tobacco Company:** Jeffery S. (Jeff) Gentry, age 48
**EVP, Human Resources, R.J. Reynolds Tobacco Company:** Ann A. Johnston, age 52
**SVP, Marketing Operations, R.J. Reynolds Tobacco Company:** Bryan K. Stockdale, age 47
**Auditors:** KPMG LLP

## LOCATIONS

**HQ:** Reynolds American Inc.
401 N. Main St., Winston-Salem, NC 27102
**Phone:** 336-741-2000 **Fax:** 336-741-4238
**Web:** www.reynoldsamerican.com

## PRODUCTS/OPERATIONS

**2006 Sales**

| | $ mil. | % of total |
|---|---|---|
| RJR Tobacco | 7,675 | 90 |
| Conwood | 291 | 4 |
| Other | 544 | 6 |
| **Total** | **8,510** | **100** |

**Selected Cigarette Brands**

Advance
Barclay
Belair
Best Value
Camel
Capri
Carlton
Century
Doral
Eclipse
GPC
Kool
Lucky Strike
Magna
Misty
Monarch
More
NOW
Pall Mall
Raleigh
Salem
Tareyton
Vantage
Viceroy
Winston

## COMPETITORS

British American Tobacco
Carolina Group
Commonwealth Brands
JT International
Philip Morris USA
Smokin Joes
Star Scientific
Swisher International
Vector
Wellstone Filters

## HISTORICAL FINANCIALS

Company Type: Public

**Income Statement** FYE: December 31

| | REVENUE ($ mil.) | NET INCOME ($ mil.) | NET PROFIT MARGIN | EMPLOYEES |
|---|---|---|---|---|
| **12/06** | 8,510 | 1,210 | 14.2% | 7,800 |
| **12/05** | 8,256 | 1,042 | 12.6% | 8,200 |
| **12/04** | 6,437 | 688 | 10.7% | 9,400 |
| **12/03** | 5,267 | (3,446) | — | 7,000 |
| **12/02** | 6,211 | (44) | — | 9,300 |
| **Annual Growth** | 8.2% | — | — | (4.3%) |

**2006 Year-End Financials**

Debt ratio: 62.3%
Return on equity: 17.8%
Cash ($ mil.): 2,726
Current ratio: 1.21
Long-term debt ($ mil.): 4,389
No. of shares (mil.): 296
Dividends
Yield: 4.2%
Payout: 67.1%
Market value ($ mil.): 19,355

**Stock History** NYSE: RAI

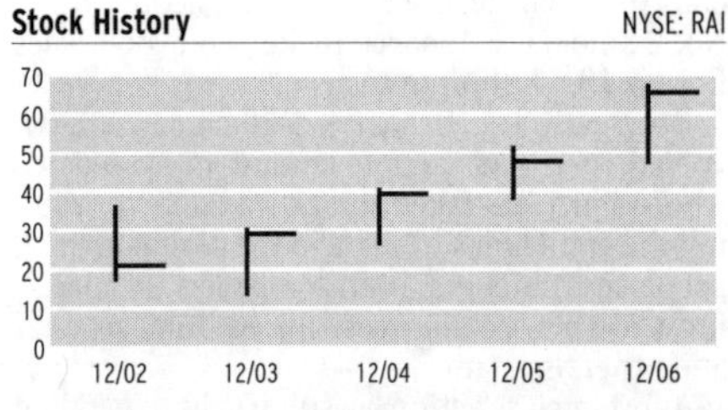

| | STOCK PRICE ($) FY Close | P/E High/Low | | PER SHARE ($) Earnings | Dividends | Book Value |
|---|---|---|---|---|---|---|
| **12/06** | 65.47 | 16 | 12 | 4.10 | 2.75 | 23.82 |
| **12/05** | 47.67 | 15 | 11 | 3.53 | 2.10 | 44.45 |
| **12/04** | 39.30 | 13 | 9 | 3.09 | 1.90 | 41.91 |
| **12/03** | 29.08 | — | — | (20.58) | 1.90 | 35.92 |
| **12/02** | 21.06 | — | — | (0.25) | 1.86 | 79.15 |
| **Annual Growth** | 32.8% | — | — | — | 10.3% | (25.9%) |

# Rite Aid

Rite Aid may have found the right aid for its ills: growth. The nation's #3 drugstore chain (behind #1 Walgreen and #2 CVS), the company runs more than 5,100 drugstores in 31 states and Washington, DC. Rite Aid stores fill prescriptions (nearly two-thirds of sales) and sell health and beauty aids, convenience foods, greeting cards, and other items, including more than 2,600 private-label products. Rite Aid also sells online through drugstore.com.

No longer a distant third behind Walgreen and CVS, Rite Aid acquired more than 1,850 Brooks and Eckerd drugstores from Canada's Jean Coutu Group in a deal valued at about $4 billion in mid-2007. In return, Jean Coutu received a 32% stake in Rite Aid. The deal for Jean Coutu's US subsidiary created the largest drugstore chain on the East Coast. (Jean Coutu had struggled to integrate the Eckerd drugstores it acquired from J. C. Penney in 2004.) All the newly acquired stores will be renamed Rite Aid. (Up to 200 stores will be closed.) Rite Aid plans to invest about $1 billion to rebrand and remodel the Brooks and Eckerd stores and distribution centers.

The deal caps a turnaround for Rite Aid, which struggled with problems stemming from its rapid growth (more than 1,500 stores acquired since 1996), a high debt load, and an accounting scandal. To right itself, the company, led by Chairman Robert Miller, unloaded stores on the West Coast and began corporate layoffs, among other measures. Miller stepped down as CEO in June 2003 and was succeeded by Mary Sammons.

Partnering with General Nutrition Companies, Inc. (GNC), nearly 1,300 Rite Aid stores have GNC concessions inside, and the two firms jointly market a line of vitamins and supplements (PharmAssure). Taking the retail trend toward in-store health clinics a step further, Rite Aid is partnering with clinic operator Lindora to begin offering medically supervised treatment for weight control in some Rite Aid stores in California in 2007.

Rite Aid directors John G. Danhakl and Jonathan D. Sokoloff own about 8% of the company's shares through Green Equity Investors III, L.P.

## HISTORY

Wholesale grocer Alex Grass founded Rack Rite Distributors in Harrisburg, Pennsylvania, in 1958 to provide health and beauty aids and other sundries to grocery stores. He offered the same products at his first discount drugstore, Thrif D Discount Center, opened in 1962 in Scranton, Pennsylvania. Four years later the company began placing pharmacies in its 36 stores. Rite Aid went public and adopted its current name in 1968, and the next year it made the first of many diverse acquisitions: Daw Drug, Blue Ridge Nursing Homes, and plasma suppliers Immuno Serums and Sero Genics.

Purchases in the 1970s included Sera-Tec Biologicals of New Jersey (blood plasma) and nearly 300 stores. By 1981 Rite Aid was the #3 drugstore chain, and sales exceeded $1 billion. In 1984 it bought the American Discount Auto Parts chain and Encore Books discount chain and spun off its wholesale grocery operation in 1984 as Super Rite, retaining a 47% stake (sold 1989).

Acquisitions added almost 900 stores during the 1980s. Expansion costs eroded Rite Aid's profit margins, and the company focused on integrating its buys in 1990.

As part of a major restructuring, in 1994 the company began selling its non-drugstore assets. Also in 1994 Rite Aid acquired Pharmacy Card and Intell-Rx and merged the two to form Eagle Managed Care.

Martin Grass took Rite Aid's reins from his dad in 1995. That year the company agreed to buy Revco, at the time the #2 drugstore operator, but the deal was derailed by FTC and Department of Justice objections in 1996. Rite Aid bounced back and acquired Thrifty PayLess (with more than 1,000 stores) for about $2.3 billion in 1996. The deal gave the company more than 3,600 stores and a presence in the western US. In 1998 it closed many smaller stores and bought PCS Health Systems (the #1 US pharmacy benefits manager) from drug maker Eli Lilly.

In 1999, after a *Wall Street Journal* investigation, Rite Aid revealed that Martin Grass, Alex Grass, and other family members held stakes in several suppliers and real estate interests doing business with the company. That year Rite Aid partnered with General Nutrition Companies, Inc. (GNC) and took a 25% stake in the Internet retailer drugstore.com (reduced to 10% in 2002). Later in 1999 Rite Aid began slashing its $5.1 billion debt by cutting corporate staff and selling off some stores in California and the Pacific Northwest. CEO Martin Grass resigned, and a team of former Fred Meyer officers — led by Robert Miller — took over.

In July 2000 the company announced it would restate profits that, over the past two years, had been inflated in excess of $1 billion. Later that year Rite Aid sold PCS Health Systems to pharmacy benefits manager Advance Paradigm for more than $1 billion.

Former chairman and CEO Martin Grass, former general counsel and vice chairman Franklin Brown, and former CFO Frank Bergonzi, among others, were indicted on June 21, 2002, for allegedly falsifying Rite Aid's books.

In April 2003 former chairman and CEO Martin Grass agreed to pay nearly $1.5 million to settle a lawsuit in which shareholders alleged that Rite Aid's books were falsified, inflating the stock's value. In June Grass and former CFO Franklyn Bergonzi both pleaded guilty to conspiracy to defraud shareholders. Eric Sorkin, Rite Aid's former VP of Pharmacy Services, pleaded guilty to conspiring to obstruct justice. Rite Aid mailed checks totaling nearly $140 million to thousands of its current and former shareholders damaged by the accounting scandal at the company. In October, former chief counsel Franklin Brown was convicted of conspiracy and lying to the Securities and Exchange Commission, among other charges.

In May 2004 Grass struck a plea deal with prosecutors under which he was sentenced to eight years in prison. Also in May, several other former company executives, including ex-CFO Frank Bergonzi and vice president Eric Sorkin, were sentenced in the accounting scandal. In June, Rite Aid agreed to pay the US government $5.6 million (plus another $1.4 million to more than 20 states) to settle a federal lawsuit alleging the drugstore chain submitted false prescription claims to government insurance programs. In October, former vice chairman Brown was sentenced to 10 years in prison, the longest sentence of six Rite Aid officials charged in the accounting scandal.

## EXECUTIVES

**Chairman, President, and CEO:** Mary F. Sammons, age 60, $1,000,000 pay
**COO:** Robert J. (Rob) Easley, age 48
**SEVP and Chief Marketing Officer:** Mark C. Panzer, age 50, $611,769 pay
**SEVP and Chief Administrative Officer:** Pierre Legault, age 46
**EVP Store Operations:** Brian Fiala, age 46
**EVP and CFO:** Kevin Twomey, age 56, $437,505 pay
**EVP and General Counsel:** Robert B. Sari, age 51, $372,096 pay
**SVP, Internal Assurance and Chief Compliance Officer:** Anthony J. (Tony) Bellezza, age 41
**SVP, Category Management:** Gerald P. (Jerry) Cardinale
**SVP and CIO:** Don P. Davis
**SVP and Chief Accounting Officer:** Douglas Donley, age 44
**SVP, Strategic Business Development:** Christopher S. (Chris) Hall, age 38
**SVP, Pharmacy Operations:** Philip J. Keough IV, age 37
**SVP, Marketing:** John Learish, age 42
**SVP, Human Resources:** Todd C. McCarty, age 41
**SVP, Corporate Communications:** Karen Rugen
**SVP, Category Management:** Bryan Shirtliff, age 42
**SVP, Central Division:** Matt Miles
**SVP, Southern Division:** Jon Olson
**SVP, Western Division:** Murray Todd
**Auditors:** Deloitte & Touche LLP

## LOCATIONS

**HQ:** Rite Aid Corporation
30 Hunter Ln., Camp Hill, PA 17011
**Phone:** 717-761-2633 **Fax:** 717-975-5871
**Web:** www.riteaid.com

Rite Aid operates stores in 27 states and the District of Columbia. The company has distribution centers in Alabama, California, Maryland, Michigan, New York, Oregon, and West Virginia, and it owns an ice cream manufacturing facility in El Monte, California.

### 2007 Stores

| | No. |
|---|---|
| California | 594 |
| New York | 386 |
| Pennsylvania | 351 |
| Michigan | 312 |
| Ohio | 238 |
| New Jersey | 159 |
| Virginia | 136 |
| Maryland | 133 |
| Washington | 132 |
| Kentucky | 120 |
| Alabama | 107 |
| West Virginia | 102 |
| Maine | 79 |
| Louisiana | 70 |
| Oregon | 70 |
| Tennessee | 46 |
| Georgia | 45 |
| New Hampshire | 38 |
| Connecticut | 35 |
| Nevada | 35 |
| Mississippi | 28 |
| Utah | 24 |
| Delaware | 24 |
| Colorado | 23 |
| Idaho | 19 |
| Vermont | 11 |
| Indiana | 9 |
| District of Columbia | 7 |
| **Total** | **3,333** |

## PRODUCTS/OPERATIONS

### 2007 Sales

| | $ mil. | % of total |
|---|---|---|
| Pharmacy | 11,102.2 | 64 |
| Front-end | 6,320.1 | 36 |
| Other | 85.4 | — |
| **Total** | **17,507.7** | **100** |

### 2007 Sales

| | % of total |
|---|---|
| Prescription drugs | 64 |
| Over-the-counter medications & personal care | 21 |
| General merchandise & other | 10 |
| Health & beauty aids | 5 |
| **Total** | **100** |

## COMPETITORS

A&P
Ahold USA
Albertsons
CVS/Caremark
Discount Drug
Dollar General
Duane Reade
Essential Group
Family Dollar Stores
Kmart
Kroger
Longs Drug
Marc Glassman
Medicine Shoppe
Penn Traffic
Publix
Safeway
Target
Walgreen
Wal-Mart

## HISTORICAL FINANCIALS

Company Type: Public

### Income Statement

FYE: Saturday nearest last day of Feb.

| | REVENUE ($ mil.) | NET INCOME ($ mil.) | NET PROFIT MARGIN | EMPLOYEES |
|---|---|---|---|---|
| **2/07** | 17,508 | 27 | 0.2% | 69,700 |
| **2/06** | 17,271 | 1,273 | 7.4% | 70,200 |
| **2/05** | 16,816 | 303 | 1.8% | 71,200 |
| **2/04** | 16,600 | 83 | 0.5% | 72,500 |
| **2/03** | 15,801 | (112) | — | 72,000 |
| **Annual Growth** | 2.6% | — | — | (0.8%) |

### 2007 Year-End Financials

Debt ratio: 263.8%
Return on equity: 2.3%
Cash ($ mil.): 106
Current ratio: 1.86
Long-term debt ($ mil.): 3,084
No. of shares (mil.): 537
Dividends
Yield: —
Payout: —
Market value ($ mil.): 3,118

### Stock History

NYSE: RAD

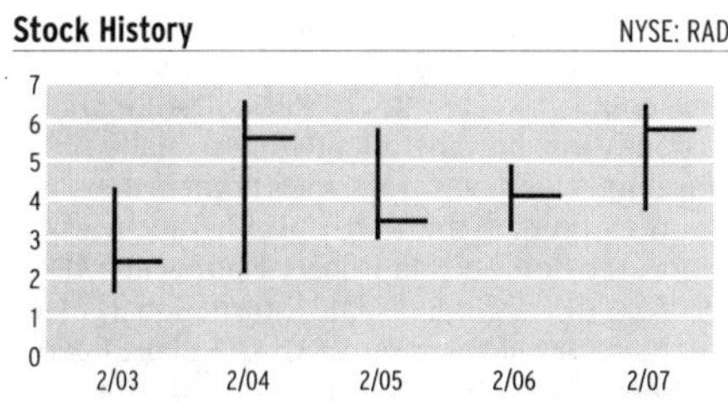


| | STOCK PRICE ($) FY Close | P/E High | P/E Low | PER SHARE ($) Earnings | Dividends | Book Value |
|---|---|---|---|---|---|---|
| **2/07** | 5.81 | — | — | (0.01) | — | 3.10 |
| **2/06** | 4.09 | 3 | 2 | 1.89 | — | 3.05 |
| **2/05** | 3.44 | 12 | 6 | 0.47 | — | 0.62 |
| **2/04** | 5.58 | 59 | 20 | 0.11 | — | (0.02) |
| **2/03** | 2.40 | — | — | (0.28) | — | (0.22) |
| **Annual Growth** | 24.7% | — | — | — | — | — |

# Robert Half International

Robert Half International carries a full load of personnel services. The company places temporary and permanent staff through seven divisions: Accountemps, Robert Half Finance and Accounting, Robert Half Legal, OfficeTeam (general administrative), Robert Half Technology (information technology), Robert Half Management Resources (senior level professionals), and The Creative Group (advertising, marketing, and Web design). The firm has also established internal audit and risk consulting subsidiary Protiviti. Robert Half operates from more than 400 offices in some 40 states and 17 countries.

The firm places about 240,000 employees in temporary assignments each year, recruiting them through direct marketing and print, radio, and Internet advertising. It also has joint marketing agreements with many tech-related companies to coordinate joint mailings, cooperative advertising, and other promotions.

CEO Harold "Max" Messmer moonlights as an author and has published several popular employment books, including *Human Resources Kit For Dummies*. The company also publishes job reports and surveys on the latest employment trends and annual salary guides to track pay trends.

## HISTORY

Robert Half founded Robert Half Inc. in 1948 as an employment agency for accountants. He developed Accountemps on the side to supply firms with accountants and other finance professionals on a temporary basis. His concept was a hit, and Half became known as a pioneer in the specialized employment services industry. He started franchising his business nationwide. The temp industry grew slowly in the 1960s and 1970s, until the 1980s brought a rapid expansion. By 1985 there were 150 independent Accountemps and Robert Half franchises.

Harold "Max" Messmer joined the company in 1985 for what would prove to be a tumultuous first couple of years. In 1986 Boothe Financial Corporation bought all of Robert Half's outstanding stock, and Messmer launched a program to buy all the Robert Half franchises. A year later Boothe sold Robert Half, which then went public as Robert Half International, placing Messmer at the helm as CEO and president.

Robert Half's focus on the accounting and financial services niche helped the company avoid the industry's price war of the early 1990s. The company's permanent placement operations accounted for nearly 20% of Robert Half's business in 1990. As corporate downsizing lessened the demand for permanent employees, the company's business slumped. The slow economy brought on some changes (reduced overhead and advertising cuts) and facilitated buybacks of Robert Half and Accountemps franchises.

In 1991 Robert Half started its OfficeTeam division to place temporary administrative office personnel. The division got off to a fast start in its initial year, earning some $2 million. Its success continued the following year, with sales rising to about $12 million. The permanent placement business, however, wasn't faring as well, and the company attempted to streamline those operations by combining its Robert Half and Accountemps facilities.

Robert Half bought The Affiliates, a firm specializing in temporary legal support staff, in 1992. The company then expanded in the eastern US and Europe (through new offices in France, Belgium, and the UK) the next year. In 1994 Robert Half founded RHI Consulting, which provided information technology workers. By then the company had bought all but four of the original 150 Robert Half and Accountemps franchises. Messmer, meanwhile, had *Job Hunting For Dummies* published in 1995 (other books followed).

Robert Half announced a new division in 1997: RHI Management Resources, an operation that targets start-up companies in need of executive-level financial personnel. In 1999 the company added The Creative Group division, which provides advertising, marketing, and Web design staff, to its collection of services. Robert Half made its first foray into Eastern Europe in 2000 when it bought a Czech recruitment agency. The following year it began offering free online courses to finance and accounting professionals through an affiliation with SmartForce, which has been acquired by SkillSoft.

In 2002 Robert Half created Protiviti, an internal audit and risk consulting subsidiary, by hiring more than 750 former employees of Arthur Andersen's internal audit and risk consulting practice. The company bought the two remaining independent Robert Half franchises in 2003.

## EXECUTIVES

**Chairman and CEO:** Harold M. (Max) Messmer Jr., age 61, $525,000 pay
**Vice Chairman, President, and CFO:** M. Keith Waddell, age 49, $265,000 pay
**President and COO, Staffing Services:** Paul F. Gentzkow, age 51, $265,000 pay
**EVP Corporate Development:** Robert W. Glass, age 48, $205,000 pay
**SVP, Secretary, and General Counsel:** Steven Karel, age 55, $205,000 pay
**VP and CIO:** Kevin White
**VP and Controller, Field Accounting:** Paula Streit
**VP and Executive Director, OfficeTeam:** Diane Domeyer
**VP Corporate Communications:** Reesa M. Staten
**VP Finance and Treasurer:** Michael C. Buckley, age 40
**VP Marketing:** Elena West
**Associate General Counsel and Assistant Secretary:** Evelyn Crane-Oliver
**Executive Director, Accountemps:** Andrew G. Denka
**Executive Director, Robert Half Legal:** Charles Volkert
**Executive Director, Robert Half Technology:** Katherine Spencer Lee
**Managing Director, Protiviti:** Everett Gibbs
**Managing Director, Robert Half Finance and Accounting:** Phil Sheridan
**Communications Strategy Director, The Creative Group:** Julie Sims
**Public Relations Director, Robert Half Legal:** Lisa Hamilton
**Auditors:** PricewaterhouseCoopers LLP

## LOCATIONS

**HQ:** Robert Half International Inc.
2884 Sand Hill Rd., Menlo Park, CA 94025
**Phone:** 650-234-6000 **Fax:** 650-234-6999
**Web:** www.rhii.com

### 2006 Sales

| | % of total |
|---|---|
| Domestic operations | 79 |
| Foreign operations | 21 |
| **Total** | **100** |

## PRODUCTS/OPERATIONS

### Selected Operating Units

Accountemps (temporary accounting and finance personnel)
The Creative Group (advertising, marketing, and Web design)
OfficeTeam (temporary administrative and office personnel)
Protiviti (internal audit and risk consulting)
Robert Half Finance and Accounting (temporary accounting and finance personnel)
Robert Half Legal (temporary and full-time legal support personnel)
Robert Half Management Resources (senior-level accounting and finance personnel)
Robert Half Technology (temporary and contract IT personnel)

### 2006 Sales

| | $ mil. | % of total |
|---|---|---|
| Temporary & consultant staffing | 3,133.9 | 78 |
| Risk consulting & internal audit services | 543.4 | 14 |
| Permanent placement staffing | 336.3 | 8 |
| **Total** | **4,013.6** | **100** |

## COMPETITORS

Adecco
COMSYS IT Partners
Deloitte Consulting
Ernst & Young
General Employment Enterprises
Headway Corporate Resources
Kelly Services
Kforce
KPMG
Manpower
MPS
PricewaterhouseCoopers
Randstad
Solomon-Page Group
Spherion
Vedior
Winston Resources

## HISTORICAL FINANCIALS

Company Type: Public

### Income Statement

FYE: December 31

| | REVENUE ($ mil.) | NET INCOME ($ mil.) | NET PROFIT MARGIN | EMPLOYEES |
|---|---|---|---|---|
| **12/06** | 4,014 | 283 | 7.1% | 255,400 |
| **12/05** | 3,338 | 238 | 7.1% | 230,000 |
| **12/04** | 2,676 | 141 | 5.3% | 209,200 |
| **12/03** | 1,975 | 6 | 0.3% | 182,300 |
| **12/02** | 1,905 | 2 | 0.1% | 186,900 |
| **Annual Growth** | 20.5% | 236.8% | — | 8.1% |

### 2006 Year-End Financials

Debt ratio: 0.4%
Return on equity: 28.1%
Cash ($ mil.): 486
Current ratio: 2.76
Long-term debt ($ mil.): 4
No. of shares (mil.): 168
Dividends
Yield: 0.9%
Payout: 19.4%
Market value ($ mil.): 6,231

### Stock History

NYSE: RHI

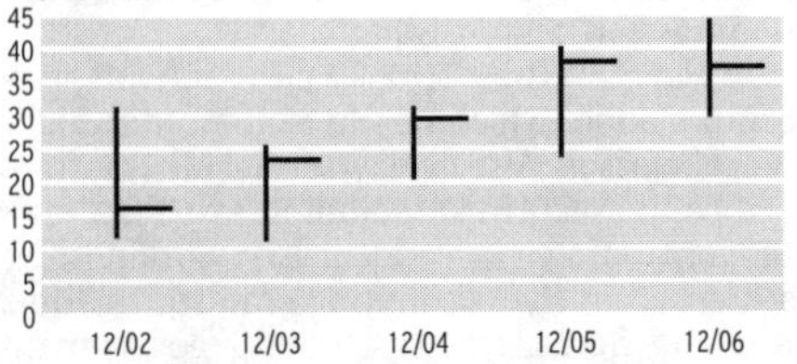

| | STOCK PRICE ($) FY Close | P/E High | P/E Low | PER SHARE ($) Earnings | Dividends | Book Value |
|---|---|---|---|---|---|---|
| **12/06** | 37.12 | 27 | 18 | 1.65 | 0.32 | 6.21 |
| **12/05** | 37.89 | 29 | 18 | 1.36 | 0.28 | 5.69 |
| **12/04** | 29.43 | 39 | 26 | 0.79 | 0.18 | 5.27 |
| **12/03** | 23.34 | 630 | 286 | 0.04 | — | 4.59 |
| **12/02** | 16.11 | 3,090 | 1,194 | 0.01 | — | 4.36 |
| **Annual Growth** | 23.2% | — | — | 258.4% | 33.3% | 9.3% |

# Rock-Tenn Company

A rock solid reputation? Ten out of ten for effort? You betcha. Show Rock-Tenn a product, and it will provide the packaging for it. The company, one of North America's leading folding carton makers, produces packaging for food, paper goods, hardware, apparel, and other consumer goods. It uses recycled and virgin paperboard to make these products and also converts paperboard for use in book covers, furniture, and automotive components. Other products include specialty corrugated packaging and point-of-purchase displays. Rock-Tenn also sells recycled paperboard to other US companies. In 2005 the company acquired pulp and packaging assets from Gulf States Paper (now known as The Westervelt Company).

The company sold its plastic packaging division to Pactiv, maker of the redoubtable Hefty garbage bags, for about $60 million late in 2003. In an effort to cut costs, Rock-Tenn has closed its laminated paperboard products facilities in Missouri and Illinois. It has also closed a recycled paperboard mill in Otsego, Michigan.

However, in an effort to expand its geographic reach, Rock-Tenn acquired a corrugated sheet facility located in Athens, Alabama from Menasha Packaging Company in 2004.

## HISTORY

Former preacher Arthur Morris founded Rock-Tenn in 1936 as Southern Box Co., a folding carton maker. Acquisitions fueled the company's growth in the following years. During WWII it became Rock City Box Co. Morris' son-in-law, A. Worley Brown, was appointed CEO in 1967.

The company adopted its current name in 1973, after merging with Tennessee Paper Mills. Rock-Tenn bought Mead's recycled products unit in 1988 and began book cover production. Brad Currey, a banker who was recruited by Brown in 1976, became CEO in 1989.

Rock-Tenn bought a folding carton plant in Canada in 1993, and in 1994 the company went public. It acquired Olympic Packaging (folding cartons) and Alliance Display & Packaging (corrugated displays) in 1995. The company boosted its position as a leading maker of folding cartons in 1997 with its $414 million purchase of Waldorf Corporation, its largest acquisition to date. That year Rock-Tenn also bought two paperboard companies and formed RTS Packaging, its 65%-owned joint venture with Sonoco Products.

To cut costs and compensate for stagnant demand, Rock-Tenn closed several US plants in 1999. The following year CEO Brad Currey retired and was replaced by Jim Rubright, formerly an EVP at energy firm Sonat (El Paso Energy). Also in 2000 Rock-Tenn entered the gypsum paperboard liner business through a joint venture with Lafarge. In 2001 the company announced additional plant closings as demand for its products bottomed out.

In March 2002 in a rebounding market Rock-Tenn bought point-of-purchase display and fixture maker Athena Industries, Inc., increasing annual sales by an estimated $12 million.

In 2003 Pactiv purchased Rock-Tenn's packaging business for about $60 million.

## EXECUTIVES

**Chairman and CEO:** James A. (Jim) Rubright, age 60, $1,714,817 pay
**EVP and CFO:** Steven C. Voorhees, age 52, $652,121 pay
**EVP and General Manager, Paperboard Group:** David E. Dreibelbis, age 54, $658,864 pay
**EVP and General Manager, Corrugated Packaging Division, and Director:** Russell M. Currey, age 45
**EVP and General Manager, Folding Carton Division:** Michael E. (Mike) Kiepura, age 50, $555,606 pay
**EVP and General Manager, Alliance Division:** James L. Einstein, age 61
**SVP, General Counsel, and Secretary:** Robert B. McIntosh, age 49, $438,241 pay
**SVP North Central Region, Folding Carton Division:** Gary Adreon
**SVP Northeast Region, Folding Carton Division:** Raymond Beaulieu
**SVP Southeast Region, Folding Carton Division:** Charles Obermeyer
**SVP Health and Beauty:** Pierre Beaudoin
**SVP Integration:** Mike Sheffield
**SVP South Central Region, Folding Carton Division:** Patrick Smithey
**VP and CIO:** Larry S. Shutzberg
**VP, Employee and Organizational Effectiveness:** Jacquelin M. (Jackie) Welch
**VP, Risk Management and Treasurer:** Gregory L. King
**President and CEO, RTS:** Richard E. Steed
**Chief Accounting Officer:** A. Stephen Meadows, age 56
**Investor Relations Analyst:** David Rees
**Auditors:** Ernst & Young LLP

## LOCATIONS

**HQ:** Rock-Tenn Company
504 Thrasher St., Norcross, GA 30071
**Phone:** 770-448-2193 **Fax:** 678-291-7666
**Web:** www.rocktenn.com

Rock-Tenn Company operates more than 90 properties in Argentina, Canada, Chile, Mexico, and the US.

## PRODUCTS/OPERATIONS

### 2006 Sales

| | $ mil. | % of total |
|---|---|---|
| Packaging | 1,264.9 | 59 |
| Paperboard | 520.8 | 24 |
| Merchandising displays | 233.1 | 11 |
| Corrugated | 119.3 | 6 |
| **Total** | **2,138.1** | **100** |

### Selected Products

Packaging products
- Folding cartons (for food items, hardware products, paper goods, and other items)
- Protective packaging (solid fiber partitions)

Paperboard
- 100% recycled coated and uncoated grades
- Laminated paperboard (for book covers, book binders, and furniture products)

Specialty corrugated packaging and displays
- Corrugated packaging and sheet
- Point of purchase displays

## COMPETITORS

Caraustar
Georgia-Pacific Corporation
Graphic Packaging
Green Bay Packaging
International Paper
Shorewood Packaging
Smurfit-Stone Container
Sonoco Products
Stora Enso North America

## HISTORICAL FINANCIALS

Company Type: Public

### Income Statement — FYE: September 30

| | REVENUE ($ mil.) | NET INCOME ($ mil.) | NET PROFIT MARGIN | EMPLOYEES |
|---|---|---|---|---|
| **9/06** | 2,138 | 29 | 1.3% | 9,500 |
| **9/05** | 1,734 | 18 | 1.0% | 9,600 |
| **9/04** | 1,581 | 18 | 1.1% | 8,266 |
| **9/03** | 1,433 | 30 | 2.1% | 8,500 |
| **9/02** | 1,437 | 27 | 1.9% | 8,418 |
| **Annual Growth** | 10.5% | 1.9% | — | 3.1% |

### 2006 Year-End Financials

Debt ratio: 150.5%
Return on equity: 5.9%
Cash ($ mil.): 7
Current ratio: 1.59
Long-term debt ($ mil.): 765
No. of shares (mil.): 38
Dividends
Yield: 1.8%
Payout: 46.8%
Market value ($ mil.): 746

### Stock History — NYSE: RKT

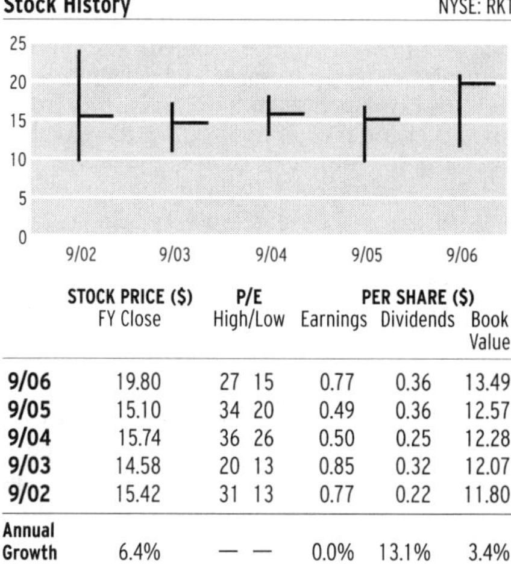


| | STOCK PRICE ($) FY Close | P/E High | P/E Low | PER SHARE ($) Earnings | Dividends | Book Value |
|---|---|---|---|---|---|---|
| **9/06** | 19.80 | 27 | 15 | 0.77 | 0.36 | 13.49 |
| **9/05** | 15.10 | 34 | 20 | 0.49 | 0.36 | 12.57 |
| **9/04** | 15.74 | 36 | 26 | 0.50 | 0.25 | 12.28 |
| **9/03** | 14.58 | 20 | 13 | 0.85 | 0.32 | 12.07 |
| **9/02** | 15.42 | 31 | 13 | 0.77 | 0.22 | 11.80 |
| **Annual Growth** | 6.4% | — | — | 0.0% | 13.1% | 3.4% |

# Rockwell Automation

Formerly a defense industry giant, Rockwell Automation is now rocking along as one of the world's largest industrial automation companies. The company's control systems unit makes industrial automation products such as motor starters and contactors, relays, timers, signaling devices, and variable speed drives. To complement its automation product offerings, Rockwell also offers factory management software applications. The company has sold most of the operations of its former power systems unit, which offered motors and motor repair services, as well as bearings, bushings, clutches, and brakes.

In 2006 Rockwell announced plans to sell its Dodge mechanical power transmission division, as well as the industrial motors unit of Rockwell's Reliance Electric subsidiary; early in 2007 it sold these businesses to Baldor Electric for $1.8 billion. (Rockwell retained the rest of Reliance, which makes electrical drives.) These units made up most of the company's power systems unit, which previously accounted for about a fifth of Rockwell's revenue.

Other divestments include the mid-2006 sale of Rockwell Scientific Company, a research and development services firm jointly-owned with

Rockwell Collins, to Teledyne for nearly $170 million.

To expand its process control and safety solutions business, the company acquired UK firm Industrial Control Services (ICS Triplex) for $221 million in 2007.

The company has also said that it plans to drive growth by promoting its software's ability to integrate and streamline plant operations. In support of this strategy, it acquired Germany-based GEPA, a maker of industrial automation software, in mid-2006. GEPA's VersionWorks for Automation suite helps manufacturers schedule automatic program backups from controllers and other industrial devices, document change processes required for regulatory compliance, and recover data quickly following a disaster. VersionWorks is meant to complement the asset management capabilities of Rockwell's FactoryTalk software.

Rockwell Automation emerged from the bulky defense industry giant Rockwell International. Between 1997 and 2001, the old Rockwell parted company with its aerospace and defense operations (sold to Boeing), its automotive unit (spun off as Meritor, now ArvinMeritor), its semiconductor unit (spun off as Conexant Systems), its computer telephony (FirstPoint), its large-power transformer operations, and its avionics and communications unit (Rockwell Collins).

## HISTORY

Rockwell Automation is the legacy of two early-20th-century entrepreneurs: Willard Rockwell and Clement Melville Keys. Rockwell gained control of Wisconsin Parts Company, an Oshkosh, Wisconsin, maker of automotive axles, in 1919. He went on to buy a number of industrial manufacturers, merging them in 1953 to create Rockwell Spring & Axle. Renamed Rockwell-Standard in 1958, it led the world in the production of mechanical automotive parts by 1967.

In 1928 Keys founded North American Aviation (NAA) as a holding company for his aviation interests. General Motors (GM) bought NAA in 1934 and named James Kindelberger as its president. The company moved in 1935 from Maryland to Inglewood, California, where it built military training planes.

NAA made more than 15,000 AT-6 trainers during WWII, and it produced the B-25 bomber and the P-51 fighter planes. By the end of the war, NAA had built nearly 43,000 aircraft, more than any other US manufacturer. NAA's sales plunged at the end of WWII. In 1948 GM took its subsidiary public; Kindelberger revitalized the company with new factories in California and Ohio. Major products included the F-86 (1948) and its successor, the F-100 (1953). NAA also produced the X-15 rocket plane (1959).

In the 1960s NAA built rocket engines and spacecraft for the Apollo program. NAA merged with Rockwell-Standard, creating North American Rockwell in 1967. The company adopted the Rockwell International name in 1973.

Rockwell won the contract for the B-1 bomber in 1970 and the space shuttle orbiter in 1972. The following year it bought Collins Radio, the backbone of its avionics segment. Rockwell briefly ventured into consumer goods, buying Admiral (appliances) in 1974 and selling it in 1979.

The company bought Allen-Bradley (industrial electronics) in 1985. Facing declining defense-related revenues as B-1 production ended, Don Beall, who became CEO in 1988, spent billions on modernizing plants and research and development for Rockwell's electronics and graphics units. In 1989 Rockwell sold its Measurement & Flow Control Division and bought Baker Perkins (printing machinery, UK).

Rockwell sold its fiber-optic transmission equipment unit to Alcatel in 1991. It acquired industrial automation supplier Sprecher + Schuh in 1993 and Reliance Electric (which was merged with Allen-Bradley) in 1995. The next year Rockwell sold its aerospace and defense divisions to Boeing for $3.2 billion and its Graphic Systems business to investment firm Stonington Partners. It also acquired integrated circuit maker Brooktree Corp. in 1996.

A 1997 federal court order forced Rockwell to pay Celeritas Technologies nearly $58 million for breaching patent protections and misappropriating trade secrets related to computer and cell phone communication technology. That year Rockwell acquired Hughes Electronics' (now DIRECTV, Inc.) airline passenger communications and entertainment systems unit, and it spun off its automotive unit as Meritor Automotive. President Don Davis also became CEO in 1997.

Rockwell spun off its sluggish semiconductor business to shareholders (as Conexant Systems) in 1998 in a move to cut losses and focus on its faster-growing industrial automation operations.

In 1999 Rockwell moved its headquarters from California to Milwaukee, the base of its automation division. Rockwell agreed in 2000 to buy K Systems for about $300 million. The company spun off its Rockwell Collins avionics and communications unit to its shareholders in July 2001. Concurrently, Rockwell International changed its name to Rockwell Automation to reflect its new focus.

In 2004 Davis stepped down as CEO and was replaced by Keith Nosbusch, who also took on the chairman's role the following February. Nosbusch had been in charge of Control Systems from 1998 until he was named president and CEO in February 2004.

## EXECUTIVES

**Chairman, President, and CEO:** Keith D. Nosbusch, age 56
**SVP, General Counsel, and Secretary:** Douglas M. Hagerman, age 45
**SVP, Strategic Development and Communications:** John D. Cohn, age 52
**SVP; President, Rockwell Automation Power Systems:** Joseph D. Swann, age 65
**SVP; SVP, America Sales, Rockwell Automation Control Systems:** Robert A. Ruff, age 58
**SVP; SVP, Global Sales and Solutions, Rockwell Automation:** John P. McDermott, age 48
**SVP Human Resources:** Susan Schmitt
**VP and Controller:** David M. Dorgan, age 42
**VP and General Tax Counsel:** Kent G. Coppins, age 53
**VP, Corporate Development:** Rondi Rohr-Dralle, age 50
**VP and General Auditor:** A. Lawrence Stuever, age 54
**VP and Chief Intellectual Property Counsel:** John M. Miller, age 39
**President, Europe, Middle East and Africa:** Jordi Andreu
**Media Relations:** John Bernaden
**Auditors:** Deloitte & Touche LLP

## LOCATIONS

**HQ:** Rockwell Automation, Inc.
1201 S. 2nd St., Milwaukee, WI 53204
**Phone:** 414-382-2000 **Fax:** 414-382-8520
**Web:** www.rockwellautomation.com

### 2006 Sales

| | $ mil. | % of total |
|---|---|---|
| US & Canada | 3,827.1 | 69 |
| Europe, Middle East & Africa | 856.5 | 15 |
| Asia/Pacific | 573.1 | 10 |
| Latin America | 304.7 | 6 |
| **Total** | **5,561.4** | **100** |

## PRODUCTS/OPERATIONS

### 2006 Sales

| | $ mil. | % of total |
|---|---|---|
| Control Systems | 4,551.3 | 82 |
| Power Systems | 1,010.1 | 18 |
| **Total** | **5,561.4** | **100** |

### Selected Products and Services

Condition sensors
Drive systems
Motion control systems
Motor control centers
Motor starters and contactors
Push buttons
Relays and timers
Signaling devices
Software
Termination and protection devices
Variable speed drives

## COMPETITORS

ABB
Baldor Electric
Danaher
Dematic GmbH
Elsag Bailey Process Automation N.V.
Emerson Electric
GE Fanuc Automation
Hitachi
Honeywell ACS
Invensys
Metso
Mitsubishi Corporation
OMRON
Samsung Group
Schneider Electric
Siemens AG
Toshiba
Weiss Instrument

## HISTORICAL FINANCIALS

Company Type: Public

### Income Statement

FYE: September 30

| | REVENUE ($ mil.) | NET INCOME ($ mil.) | NET PROFIT MARGIN | EMPLOYEES |
|---|---|---|---|---|
| **9/06** | 5,561 | 607 | 10.9% | 23,000 |
| **9/05** | 5,003 | 540 | 10.8% | 21,000 |
| **9/04** | 4,411 | 415 | 9.4% | 21,000 |
| **9/03** | 4,104 | 286 | 7.0% | 21,500 |
| **9/02** | 3,909 | 121 | 3.1% | 22,000 |
| **Annual Growth** | 9.2% | 49.7% | — | 1.1% |

### 2006 Year-End Financials

Debt ratio: 39.0%
Return on equity: 34.0%
Cash ($ mil.): 415
Current ratio: 1.69
Long-term debt ($ mil.): 748
No. of shares (mil.): 171
Dividends
Yield: 1.5%
Payout: 26.7%
Market value ($ mil.): 9,923

**Stock History** NYSE: ROK

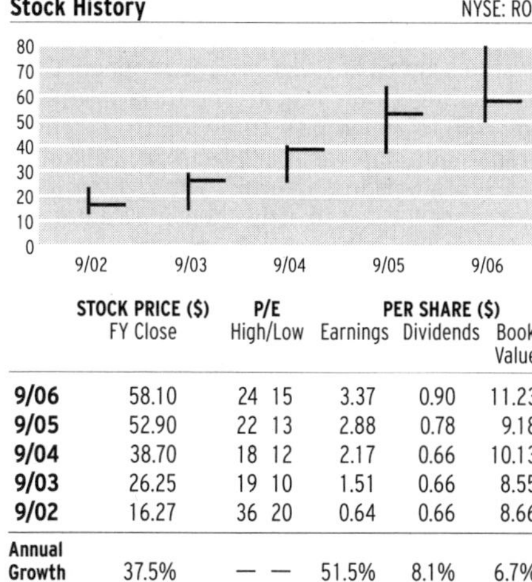


| | STOCK PRICE ($) FY Close | P/E High/Low | | PER SHARE ($) Earnings | Dividends | Book Value |
|---|---|---|---|---|---|---|
| **9/06** | 58.10 | 24 | 15 | 3.37 | 0.90 | 11.23 |
| **9/05** | 52.90 | 22 | 13 | 2.88 | 0.78 | 9.18 |
| **9/04** | 38.70 | 18 | 12 | 2.17 | 0.66 | 10.13 |
| **9/03** | 26.25 | 19 | 10 | 1.51 | 0.66 | 8.55 |
| **9/02** | 16.27 | 36 | 20 | 0.64 | 0.66 | 8.66 |
| **Annual Growth** | 37.5% | — | — | 51.5% | 8.1% | 6.7% |

# Rohm and Haas

Rohm and Haas is the one to blame if you can't get that paint out of your hair. The company's operations are divided among six segments, the largest of which is the paints and coatings materials group, which makes additives and binders used by paint makers. The performance materials unit makes plastics additives and antimicrobials, while the electronic materials division makes photoresists and materials for making printed wiring boards. Acrylates make up most of its primary materials division, and Rohm and Haas' salt group markets salt for road ice control, table salt (Morton Salt), and water softening. The smallest unit manufactures packaging and building materials. The Haas family controls 28% of the company.

The improved worldwide marketplace gives a little and takes a little for Rohm and Haas. The past couple of years have seen skyrocketing costs for raw materials, but also a healthy pick-up in demand for the company's products. So, while it is forced to pay steep prices for its ingredients and feedstocks, Rohm and Haas has also been able to increase the prices of its own products while still seeing rising demand for them. As a result both sales and profits increased for the past few years.

The company announced that it would close a powder coatings factory in Virginia in early 2006. This came on the heels of a late 2005 announcement that it planned to close or partially close six facilities (primarily in Europe) over the next 12 to 18 months. It also sold its wax compounds business early in 2006 to Hexion, a business based in France. That year Rohm and Haas sold its North American and Asian automotive coatings operations to Nippon Paint for $230 million; it sold the European automotive coatings business to the Mader Group the following year.

In 2007 the company announced plans to sell its European Automotive Coatings business to the Mader Group.

## HISTORY

Rohm and Haas began with two Germans and a lot of dog manure. German immigrant Otto Haas came to the US in 1901 and took a position with G. Siegel and Co., a German dye and chemical manufacturer. In 1903 he left Siegle to work with meatpacking firm Sulzberger and Co.

Meanwhile, back in Germany in 1904, Haas' friend Otto Rohm, an analytical chemist at Stuttgart Municipal Gas Works, noticed the similarity between the bad smell coming from a nearby tannery (from fermented dog dung, used for centuries as a solution to "bate," or soften, hides) and that of gas water waste at the gas plant.

Rohm developed a bating substitute (Oropon) based on gas water, a few salts, and an enzyme. Realizing the promise of this product, he invited Haas to help him set up Rohm and Haas in Esslingen, Germany, in 1907. Buoyed by the success of the product in Europe, Haas returned to the US in 1909 to establish an American branch of Rohm and Haas in Philadelphia. In 1912 Haas opened a branch office in Chicago; he visited South America the following year to open branch offices in Argentina and Chile. By 1916 Oropon had become a tannery industry standard.

During WWI, Rohm and Haas — like many German-related businesses — fell under suspicion. The US government ordered it to sell half of the American firm to US investors. Rohm and Haas diversified into synthetic insecticides in the 1920s, and in 1927 Otto Haas set up Resinous Products to make synthetic resins. One of Otto Rohm's researchers accidentally discovered Plexiglas in 1935 when the acrylic polymer he was experimenting with as an adhesive dried as a clear plastic sheet. This discovery led to the shatterproof glass substitute. Plexiglas, used extensively by the military, accounted for two-thirds of the firm's sales during WWII.

In 1953 Rohm and Haas pioneered a process that allows water to replace solvents in paints. The company moved into the synthetic-fiber market in the 1960s, but lost money on the venture and exited the business in 1976. By 1984 the company had returned to its earlier strategy of building its business around value-added chemicals.

Rohm and Haas bought Unocal's acrylic vinyl business in 1991. In 1997 the company acquired a 26% stake in Rodel, a Delaware-based leader in precision surface-polishing technology (increased to 48% by 1999).

Rohm and Haas spent $460 million for LeaRonal, a maker of specialty chemicals for the electronics industry, in 1999. It also paid $4.9 billion for Morton International, whose salt operations and chemicals businesses were both sought by Rohm and Haas (the company later discovered that Morton had been taking shortcuts on pollution controls, a problem that could cost millions in fines and repairs). Also that year Rajiv Gupta became chairman and CEO when Lawrence Wilson retired.

In 2000 Rohm and Haas bolstered its electronic materials unit by increasing its stake in Rodel to 80% and by buying an 80% stake in Silicon Valley Chemlabs. It also bought Swiss biocide company Acima and Mitsubishi Chemical's photoresist chemistry (semiconductor chips) unit. The company sold its European salt business, its industrial coatings unit (to BASF), and its thermoplastic polyurethane (TPU) operations — all acquired in the Morton International deal. In 2001 Rohm and Haas sold its agricultural chemical operations to Dow Chemical for about $1 billion.

A warm 2001-02 winter even hurt its salt business. As a result, the company began to cut costs by reducing manufacturing capacity. Rohm and Haas had been especially hurt by the slowdown in several industries, including autos and semiconductors. After cutting about 2,000 jobs in early 2003 the company again announced a 3% workforce (500 jobs) cut in December.

Like the chemicals industry overall, the company experienced somewhat of a rebound in 2003 versus the previous few years. Buoyed by its 2002 acquisition of Ferro's powder coatings business, Rohm and Haas' coatings unit increased sales by nearly 15%. The performance chemicals and electronic materials divisions celebrated similar gains, all due to increased demand and higher prices. (The higher prices, though, were a direct result of the continually escalating raw materials prices.) The salt segment, too, benefited from the harsh winter of 2002-03, providing a high demand for road salt.

## EXECUTIVES

**Chairman, President, and CEO:** Rajiv L. (Raj) Gupta, age 61, $1,537,650 pay
**EVP and CFO:** Jacques M. Croisetiere, age 52, $782,686 pay
**EVP; Business Group Executive, Performance Materials:** Alan E. Barton, age 52, $698,924 pay
**EVP; Business Group Executive, Specialty Materials; President and CEO, Rohm and Haas Electronic Materials; Executive Oversight, European and Asia-Pacific Regions:** Pierre R. Brondeau, age 49, $782,686 pay
**EVP, General Counsel, and Secretary:** Robert A. Lonergan, age 60, $681,205 pay
**VP and Business Director, Process Chemicals and Biocides:** Guillermo Novo
**VP and General Manager, Paint and Coating Materials:** James C. Swanson
**VP and Business Director, Salt; President, Morton Salt:** Walter W. Becky II
**VP and CTO:** Gary S. Calabrese
**EVP, CIO, and Director Human Resources:** Anne M. Wilms, age 49
**VP Corporate Development and Strategy:** Thomas D. Macphee
**VP Corporate Communications and Public Relations:** Brian McPeak
**Director, Investor Relations:** Andrew D. Sandifer
**Auditors:** PricewaterhouseCoopers LLP

## LOCATIONS

**HQ:** Rohm and Haas Company
100 Independence Mall West,
Philadelphia, PA 19106
**Phone:** 215-592-3000 **Fax:** 215-592-3377
**Web:** www.rohmhaas.com

Rohm and Haas operates more than 100 manufacturing plants and 30 R&D facilities in 25 countries.

**2006 Sales**

| | $ mil. | % of total |
|---|---|---|
| US | 3,845 | 47 |
| Europe | 2,030 | 25 |
| Asia/Pacific | 1,659 | 20 |
| Other regions | 696 | 8 |
| **Total** | **8,230** | **100** |

## PRODUCTS/OPERATIONS

### 2006 Sales and Operating Income

| | Sales | | Operating Income | |
|---|---|---|---|---|
| | $ mil. | % of total | $ mil. | % of total |
| Coatings | 2,683 | 28 | 230 | 25 |
| Monomers | 1,926 | 20 | 201 | 22 |
| Performance Chemicals | 1,778 | 19 | 163 | 18 |
| Electronic Materials | 1,564 | 17 | 235 | 25 |
| Salt | 829 | 9 | 38 | 4 |
| Adhesives & Sealants | 723 | 7 | 55 | 6 |
| Adjustments | (1,273) | — | (167) | — |
| **Total** | **8,230** | **100** | **755** | **100** |

### Selected Products

Paint and Coating Materials
- Architectural coatings
- Barrier coatings
- Functional coatings
- Powder coatings
- Primer coatings

Performance Materials
- Consumer and industrial specialties (antimicrobials, dispersants, etc.)
- Process chemicals

Primary Materials
- Acrylic acid
- Methyl methacrylate
- Specialty monomers

Electronic Materials
- Circuit Board Technologies
- Chemicals used to make semiconductors and printed circuit boards
- Photoresists

Salt
- Agricultural salt
- Deicing salt
- Industrial salt
- Table salt (Morton brand, US; Windsor brand, Canada)
- Kosher salt

Packaging and Building Materials
- Acrylic emulsion polymers
- Formulated adhesives
- Plastics additives

## COMPETITORS

Arkema
Avecia
BASF AG
Bayer
Compass Minerals
Dow Chemical
DuPont
Eastman Chemical
FMC
Hercules
Imperial Chemical
K+S
Lanxess
Lucite
MacDermid
Nippon Fine Chemical
PPG
Rockwood Holdings
RPM
Shin-Etsu Chemical

## HISTORICAL FINANCIALS

Company Type: Public

### Income Statement

FYE: December 31

| | REVENUE ($ mil.) | NET INCOME ($ mil.) | NET PROFIT MARGIN | EMPLOYEES |
|---|---|---|---|---|
| **12/06** | 8,230 | 735 | 8.9% | 15,800 |
| **12/05** | 7,994 | 637 | 8.0% | 16,519 |
| **12/04** | 7,300 | 497 | 6.8% | 16,691 |
| **12/03** | 6,421 | 280 | 4.4% | 17,245 |
| **12/02** | 5,727 | (570) | — | 17,611 |
| **Annual Growth** | 9.5% | — | — | (2.7%) |

### 2006 Year-End Financials

Debt ratio: 41.9%
Return on equity: 18.5%
Cash ($ mil.): 596
Current ratio: 1.72
Long-term debt ($ mil.): 1,688
No. of shares (mil.): 219
Dividends
Yield: 2.5%
Payout: 38.6%
Market value ($ mil.): 11,187

### Stock History

NYSE: ROH

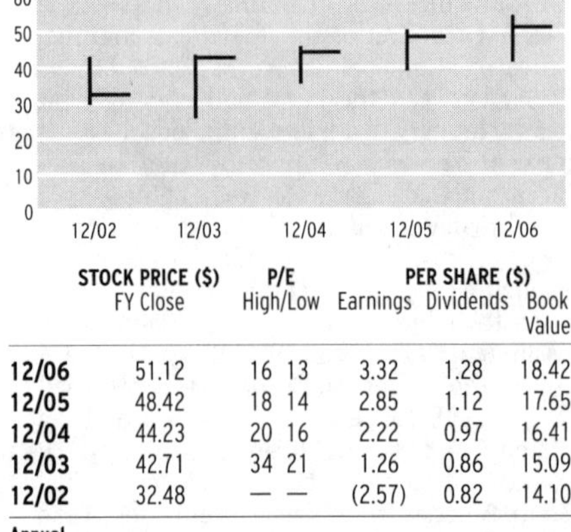


| | STOCK PRICE ($) FY Close | P/E High/Low | | PER SHARE ($) Earnings | Dividends | Book Value |
|---|---|---|---|---|---|---|
| **12/06** | 51.12 | 16 | 13 | 3.32 | 1.28 | 18.42 |
| **12/05** | 48.42 | 18 | 14 | 2.85 | 1.12 | 17.65 |
| **12/04** | 44.23 | 20 | 16 | 2.22 | 0.97 | 16.41 |
| **12/03** | 42.71 | 34 | 21 | 1.26 | 0.86 | 15.09 |
| **12/02** | 32.48 | — | — | (2.57) | 0.82 | 14.10 |
| **Annual Growth** | 12.0% | — | — | — | 11.8% | 6.9% |

# Ross Stores

Ross wants to let you dress (and lots more) for less. The off-price retailer operates about 800 Ross Dress for Less and dd's DISCOUNT stores that sell mostly closeout merchandise, including men's, women's, and children's clothing, at prices well below those of department and specialty stores. Although apparel accounts for more than 50% of sales, the stores also sell small furnishings, educational toys and games, luggage, and gourmet foods in select stores. Featuring the Ross "Dress for Less" trademark, the chain targets 25- to 54-year-old white-collar shoppers from primarily middle-income households. Ross stores are located in strip malls in 27 states, mostly in the western US, and Guam.

Ross is one of the leading off-price retailers in the US. More than a quarter of Ross Stores are in California, where discount department store operator Kohl's is expanding rapidly. However, Ross Stores is entering new markets including, most recently, Tennessee and Delaware.

The retailer's deal with supermarket operator Albertsons, inked in late 2006, fuels its 2007 expansion plans and secures 46 Albertsons stores located in California, Florida, Texas, Arizona, Colorado, and Oklahoma.

To boost its relationships with suppliers, Ross does not require them to provide markdown/promotional allowances or return privileges. This, combined with opportunistic purchases (closeouts such as manufacturer overruns and canceled orders), allows the company to obtain large discounts on merchandise. As a result, Ross Stores' customers typically pay 20% to 60% less than department store prices. Ross holds down costs by offering minimal service and few frills inside its stores. Other items Ross sells at a discount include accessories, footwear, fragrances, and bed and bath items.

Digging deeper into the discount apparel market, in 2004 Ross Stores launched a new chain of stores aimed at lower-income shoppers than its existing stores target. The ultra-low-price spin off — called dd's DISCOUNTS — offers brand-name apparel at a 20% to 70% discount at 25 locations in California. The 25,000-sq.-ft. stores are located in strip shopping centers in urban and suburban neighborhoods.

## HISTORY

In 1957 the Ross family founded Ross Stores and opened its first junior department store; by 1982 there were six of the stores in the San Francisco area. That year two retailing veterans, Stuart Moldaw (founder of Country Casuals and The Athletic Shoe Factory) and Donald Rowlett (creator of Woolworth's off-price subsidiary, J. Brannam), led the acquisition of the company. Moldaw (chairman) and Rowlett (president) wanted to create an off-price chain in California, where — despite the success such endeavors were having in the rest of the country — such stores were largely absent. The duo intended to establish a foothold by saturating California markets before competitors muddied the waters.

They restocked the stores with brand-name men's, women's, and children's apparel, shoes, accessories, and domestics merchandise at reduced prices. Before the end of 1982, they opened two more Ross "Dress for Less" stores; the next year 18 more were added, including the chain's first non-California store, in Reno, Nevada (much of the chain's expansion came through the acquisition of existing strip mall stores). Another 40 stores were added in 1984.

The company went public in 1985 to help fund its expansion and extended its reach to include Colorado, Florida, Georgia, New Mexico, and Oregon; that year it opened 41 stores. In 1986, 39 new stores were opened, including locations in Maryland, North Carolina, and Virginia, though the company was forced to close 25 unprofitable stores, primarily in recession-hammered Texas and Oklahoma. Ross lost more than $41 million for the year, and the honeymoon was over.

Rowlett resigned in 1987, and company veteran Norman Ferber was soon named CEO. Ross opened only 11 stores that year, all of which were located in markets the company had already broached. It also decided to focus its expansion efforts in three markets: the West Coast; the Washington, DC, area; and Florida. On the merchandise side, housewares were dropped and cosmetics, fragrances, and high-end clothing were added. Ross returned to the black in 1987, posting an $11 million profit. The company continued refining its merchandising strategy, and by 1989 it had more than 150 stores, making it one of the largest off-price retailers.

Ross opened 72 stores between 1990 and 1992, bringing its total to more than 220 stores as sales passed the $1 billion mark. Ferber became chairman in 1993 and continued to focus the company on existing markets. The chain grew to more than 290 stores by the end of 1995. VP Michael Balmuth was named CEO the next year.

By 1998 the company's buying department had more than tripled in size, allowing it to have buyers in the right place at the right time to take advantage of buying opportunities. The non-apparel business tripled during the same time, both keys to the retailer's success. In 1998 Ross added fine jewelry, maternity wear, sporting goods, small furnishings, and educational toys to its list of product offerings. With its stock price sagging in late 1998, Ross began a $120 million stock repurchase program in 1999. After repurchasing 5.4 million shares of its stock, the company pledged to continue the program through 2001. Ross opened 30 stores in 1999; its 34 openings in 2000 included its first non-US store in Guam.

In 2001 the company entered new markets in Georgia, North Carolina, South Carolina, Montana, and Wyoming, and opened new stores in existing markets, for a total of 45 new stores.

In 2002 Ross opened 60 new stores and closed five others, followed in 2003 by 61 new stores, some of which were in new markets such as Louisiana and Tennessee.

In August 2004 Ross opened its first three dd's DISCOUNTS stores in Vallejo, San Leandro, and Fresno, California. The retailer moved its headquarters from Newark, California, to Pleasanton in mid-2004 and then sold the Newark property for about $17 million.

In 2005 the company opened 10 dd's DISCOUNTS stores and about 75 Ross stores. Ross Stores also purchased a 685,000-sq. ft. warehouse in Moreno Valley, California, that year.

## EXECUTIVES

**Chairman:** Norman A. Ferber, age 58
**Vice Chairman, President, and CEO:** Michael A. Balmuth, age 56, $993,791 pay
**EVP and COO:** Gary L. Cribb, age 42
**EVP, Merchandising, Marketing and Planning and Allocation:** Barry S. Gluck, age 53, $908,447 pay (prior to promotion)
**EVP, Merchandising:** Barbara Rentler, age 49, $612,613 pay
**EVP, Merchandising:** Lisa Panattoni, age 44, $590,246 pay
**EVP and Chief Administrative Officer:** Michael B. O'Sullivan, age 43
**SVP, General Counsel:** Mark S. Askanas
**SVP and General Merchandise Manager, dd's DISCOUNTS:** Douglas (Doug) Baker
**SVP, CFO, and Secretary:** John G. Call, age 48, $452,310 pay
**SVP, Human Resources:** D. Jane Marvin
**SVP and CIO:** Michael K. (Mike) Kobayashi
**SVP, General Merchandise Manager:** Carl Matteo
**SVP, Merchandise Control:** Art Roth
**SVP, Strategy, Marketing, Store Planning, and Allocations:** Ken Caruana
**VP, Investor Relations:** Katie Loughnot
**VP, Marketing:** Janet Kanios
**VP and Controller:** Bill Sheehan
**Administrative Assistant, Investor Relations:** Ginger Jeffers
**SVP, General Merchandise Manager:** Jennifer Vecchio
**Auditors:** Deloitte & Touche LLP

## LOCATIONS

**HQ:** Ross Stores, Inc.
4440 Rosewood Dr., Pleasanton, CA 94588
**Phone:** 925-965-4400 **Fax:** 925-965-4388
**Web:** www.rossstores.com

### 2007 Stores

| | No. |
|---|---|
| US | |
| California | 223 |
| Texas | 117 |
| Florida | 87 |
| Georgia | 40 |
| Arizona | 38 |
| Washington | 27 |
| North Carolina | 26 |
| Colorado | 25 |
| Virginia | 23 |
| Pennsylvania | 22 |
| Oregon | 21 |
| South Carolina | 18 |
| Maryland | 16 |
| Nevada | 14 |
| Tennessee | 14 |
| Oklahoma | 13 |
| Alabama | 11 |
| Hawaii | 11 |
| Louisiana | 9 |
| Utah | 9 |
| Idaho | 8 |
| New Jersey | 8 |
| New Mexico | 5 |
| Montana | 5 |
| Mississippi | 3 |
| Wyoming | 2 |
| Delaware | 1 |
| Guam | 1 |
| **Total** | **797** |

## PRODUCTS/OPERATIONS

### 2007 Stores

| | No. |
|---|---|
| Ross Dress for Less | 771 |
| dd's DISCOUNTS | 26 |
| **Total** | **797** |

### 2007 Sales

| | % of total |
|---|---|
| Women's apparel | 33 |
| Home accents, bed & bath | 22 |
| Men's apparel | 15 |
| Fine jewelry, accessories, lingerie & fragrances | 11 |
| Shoes | 10 |
| Children's apparel | 9 |
| **Total** | **100** |

### Selected Merchandise

Ladies' apparel
- Accessories
- Dresses
- Junior
- Lingerie
- Maternity
- Misses sportswear
- Petites
- Women's World

Home accents
Bed and bath
Cookware
Men's apparel
- Traditional men's
- Young men's

Educational toys
Fine jewelry
Fragrances
Gourmet foods
Luggage
Small electronics
Small furnishings
Sporting goods and exercise equipment
Shoes
Children's apparel

## COMPETITORS

Big Lots
Burlington Coat Factory
Cato
Charming Shoppes
Dress Barn
Family Dollar Stores
Filene's Basement
Fred's
J. C. Penney
Kmart
Kohl's
Men's Wearhouse
Mervyns
Sears
Target
TJX Companies
Wal-Mart

## HISTORICAL FINANCIALS

Company Type: Public

### Income Statement

FYE: Saturday nearest January 31

| | REVENUE ($ mil.) | NET INCOME ($ mil.) | NET PROFIT MARGIN | EMPLOYEES |
|---|---|---|---|---|
| **1/07** | 5,570 | 242 | 4.3% | 35,800 |
| **1/06** | 4,944 | 200 | 4.0% | 33,200 |
| **1/05** | 4,240 | 170 | 4.0% | 30,100 |
| **1/04** | 3,921 | 228 | 5.8% | 26,600 |
| **1/03** | 3,531 | 201 | 5.7% | 22,500 |
| **Annual Growth** | 12.1% | 4.7% | — | 12.3% |

### 2007 Year-End Financials

Debt ratio: 16.5%
Return on equity: 27.7%
Cash ($ mil.): 373
Current ratio: 1.40
Long-term debt ($ mil.): 150
No. of shares (mil.): 139
Dividends
Yield: 0.7%
Payout: 14.1%
Market value ($ mil.): 4,543

### Stock History

NASDAQ (GS): ROST

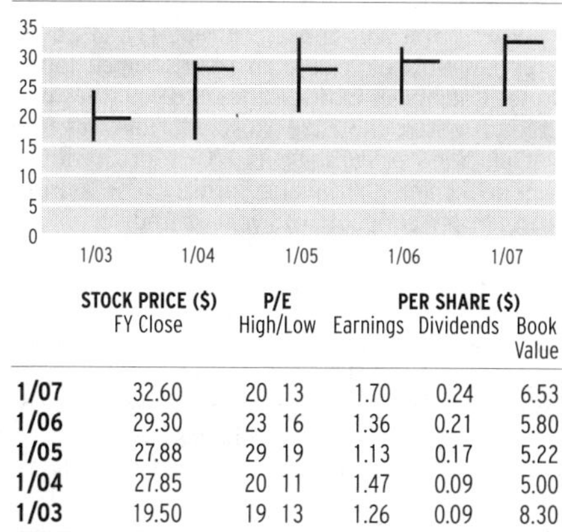


| | STOCK PRICE ($) FY Close | P/E High | P/E Low | PER SHARE ($) Earnings | Dividends | Book Value |
|---|---|---|---|---|---|---|
| **1/07** | 32.60 | 20 | 13 | 1.70 | 0.24 | 6.53 |
| **1/06** | 29.30 | 23 | 16 | 1.36 | 0.21 | 5.80 |
| **1/05** | 27.88 | 29 | 19 | 1.13 | 0.17 | 5.22 |
| **1/04** | 27.85 | 20 | 11 | 1.47 | 0.09 | 5.00 |
| **1/03** | 19.50 | 19 | 13 | 1.26 | 0.09 | 8.30 |
| **Annual Growth** | 13.7% | — | — | 7.8% | 27.8% | (5.8%) |

# Royal Caribbean Cruises

Royal Caribbean Cruises does not practice berth control. The world's second-largest cruise line (behind the combined Carnival and Carnival plc), the company operates about 35 ships with more than 67,500 berths. Its three main cruise brands, Royal Caribbean International (20 ships), Celebrity Cruises (nine ships), and Pullmantur Cruises (five ships) carry about 3.5 million passengers a year to more than 300 destinations, including ports in Alaska, the Caribbean, and Europe. Royal Caribbean also operates land-based tours and expeditions through Royal Celebrity Tours. In addition, the firm has a joint venture with UK-based tour operator First Choice that operates one ship.

Like much of the cruise ship industry, Royal Caribbean has struggled to attract new business by attempting to tap the 90% of Americans who have never taken a cruise. In response, it is turning its attention to international markets, in part through the Island Cruises venture with First Choice (in which Royal Caribbean owns a 17% stake).

Royal Caribbean made a big move towards international expansion in 2006 when it acquired Pullmantur, the largest cruise and tour operator in Spain, for about $900 million, including assumed debt. Pullmantur's cruise business includes five ships that operate between Europe and Latin America. In addition, Royal Caribbean plans to add service in Asian markets. Vessels would depart from Hong Kong, Singapore, and Shanghai and visit ports in Japan, Malaysia, South Korea, Taiwan, Thailand, and Vietnam. In 2007, Royal Caribbean launched its Azamara Cruises brand, which will be geared towards "off-the-beaten-path" destinations, cruising to more than 200 ports (most of them new to travelers) across the globe.

Co-founder Arne Wilhelmsen owns about 20% of Royal Caribbean; the Pritzker family owns 16%.

## HISTORY

When Arne Wilhelmsen (director) and Edwin Stephan (former vice chairman) helped found Royal Caribbean Cruise Lines in 1969, they created an entire industry. Royal Caribbean's first vessel, *Song of Norway,* (1970) touted endless sun decks and glass-walled dining rooms, initiating the concept of year-round cruising. Stephan, inspired by Seattle's Space Needle and its revolving restaurant, designed a cocktail lounge cantilevered from the ship's smokestack. The panoramic observation point became the signature of Royal Caribbean vessels. The company operated three ships during the 1970s; by 1972 it was the largest Caribbean cruise line.

Through the 1970s and early 1980s, it launched larger and more modern cruise ships and introduced air/sea inclusive vacations, fitness programs, and other industry firsts. Royal Caribbean moved out of the Caribbean for the first time in 1985 with Bermuda cruises from New York. The company bought Admiral Cruises in 1988 (sold in 1992, though it retained rights to the name) and Richard Fain, Admiral's chairman, became chairman and CEO of Royal Caribbean. With the goal of turning the company from a regional party fleet into an international vacation powerhouse, he expanded the company's fleet by four vessels in four years, including the world's first megaship, *Sovereign of the Seas,* with 2,250 berths.

In 1990 Royal Caribbean broadened its destination list to include Mexico, Alaska, and Europe. To enhance its relationship with the travel agents who booked its cruises, Royal Caribbean developed the industry's first computerized booking system. However, a fire that year severely damaged one of its under-construction vessels. Unstable earnings and ship construction and refurbishing costs left Royal Caribbean with almost $1 billion in long-term debt by 1992; the company went public in 1993 to ease its burden.

Royal Caribbean's next class of vessels, introduced in 1995, included high-tech movie theaters, shopping malls, and other accoutrements. In 1996 the company changed its name from Royal Caribbean Cruise Lines to Royal Caribbean Cruises Ltd., in order to reflect its growing breadth.

In 1997 the company acquired Celebrity Cruise Lines and its four working ships at a cost of $1.3 billion. (Rival Carnival had earlier bid $525 million for Celebrity.) In 1998 Royal Caribbean pleaded guilty to obstruction of justice in federal court for covering up its illegal dumping of oil off the coasts of Florida and Puerto Rico between 1990 and 1994. The company agreed to pay a $9 million fine and was put on probation for five years.

In 1999 the company was again indicted on oil-dumping charges and eventually pleaded guilty to 21 felony counts. It was slapped with a record $18 million fine. The following year it agreed to pay the State of Alaska another $3.3 million to settle similar charges. In 2001 it began offering land-based tours in Alaska through Royal Celebrity Tours.

In an effort to trim costs and better compete with airlines, Royal Caribbean announced that year that it would halve the commissions paid to travel agents for the air-travel part of cruise bookings. In 2002 the company launched Island Cruises, a joint venture with First Choice.

Royal Caribbean hoped to reduce administrative costs and increase buying power by merging with P&O Princess Cruises, but P&O dropped the deal in favor of an acquisition by Carnival in 2003.

Offering service to the Galapagos Islands, Celebrity Xpeditions (Celebrity Cruises' limited-capacity cruise line) debuted in 2004.

One of the largest cruise ships in the world, *Freedom of the Seas,* set sail from England in mid-2006. The Royal Caribbean ship holds more than 3,600 guests. Also that year, Royal Caribbean expanded its tour operations in Spain with the $900 million purchase of the Pullmantur line.

## EXECUTIVES

**Chairman and CEO:** Richard D. Fain, age 59, $1,017,789 pay
**EVP and CFO:** Brian J. Rice, age 48, $440,385 pay
**EVP Maritime:** Harri U. Kulovaara, age 54, $561,750 pay
**SVP and Treasurer:** Thomas P. Martin, age 47
**CIO:** Mike Sutten
**VP, General Counsel, and Corporate Secretary:** Bradley Stein
**VP Human Resources:** Maria Del Busto
**VP Corporate Strategy:** Vance Johnston
**VP Corporate Controller:** Henry J. Pujol
**President, Royal Celebrity Tours:** Craig S. Milan
**President, Celebrity Cruises:** Daniel J. (Dan) Hanrahan, age 49
**President, Royal Caribbean International:** Adam M. Goldstein, age 47, $570,192 pay
**SVP Marine Operations, Royal Caribbean International:** William S. Wright, age 47
**SVP North American Sales, Royal Caribbean International:** Lisa Bauer, age 35
**SVP Hotel Operations, Royal Caribbean International:** Michael Bayley
**SVP Marketing, Royal Caribbean International:** Alice Norsworthy
**VP Food and Beverage Operations, Celebrity Cruises:** Jacques Van Staden
**Managing Director, Europe, Middle East, and Africa:** Susan Hooper, age 46
**Auditors:** PricewaterhouseCoopers LLP

## LOCATIONS

**HQ:** Royal Caribbean Cruises Ltd.
1050 Caribbean Way, Miami, FL 33132
**Phone:** 305-539-6000 **Fax:** 305-539-0562
**Web:** www.royalcaribbean.com

Royal Caribbean Cruises sails to about 310 destinations worldwide.

**2006 Passenger Ticket Revenue**

| | % of total |
|---|---|
| US | 82 |
| Other countries | 18 |
| **Total** | **100** |

## PRODUCTS/OPERATIONS

**2006 Sales**

| | $ mil. | % of total |
|---|---|---|
| Passenger tickets | 3,838.7 | 73 |
| Onboard & other | 1,390.9 | 27 |
| **Total** | **5,229.6** | **100** |

**Selected Cruise Ships**

Royal Caribbean
*Adventure of the Seas* (2001; Caribbean; 3,100 berths)
*Brilliance of the Seas* (2002; Caribbean, Europe, and Panama Canal; 2,100 berths)
*Empress of the Seas* (1990; Caribbean and Bermuda; 1,600 berths)
*Enchantment of the Seas* (1997; Caribbean; 2,250 berths)
*Explorer of the Seas* (2000; Caribbean; 3,100 berths)
*Freedom of the Seas* (2006; Caribbean; 3,600 berths)
*Grandeur of the Seas* (1996; Caribbean, Bahamas, and Canada/New England; 1,950 berths)
*Jewel of the Seas* (2004; Caribbean, Canada/New England, and Europe; 2,100 berths)
*Legend of the Seas* (1995; Hawaii, Mexican Riviera, and Panama Canal; 1,800 berths)
*Liberty of the Seas* (2007; Caribbean; 3,600 berths)
*Majesty of the Seas* (1992; Bahamas; 2,350 berths)
*Mariner of the Seas* (2003; Caribbean; 3,100 berths)
*Monarch of the Seas* (1991; Baja, Mexico; 2,350 berths)
*Navigator of the Seas* (2002; Caribbean; 3,100 berths)
*Radiance of the Seas* (2001; Caribbean, Pacific Northwest, Alaska, Hawaii, and Panama Canal; 2,100 berths)
*Rhapsody of the Seas* (1997; Caribbean; 2,000 berths)
*Serenade of the Seas* (2003; Alaska, Caribbean, Panama Canal, and Hawaii; 2,100 berths)
*Sovereign of the Seas* (1988; Bahamas; 2,300 berths)
*Splendour of the Seas* (1996; Caribbean, Panama Canal, and Europe; 1,800 berths)
*Vision of the Seas* (1998; Hawaii, Alaska, Mexican Riviera, and Pacific Northwest; 2,000 berths)
*Voyager of the Seas* (1999; Caribbean and Canada; 3,100 berths)

Celebrity Cruises
*Century* (1995; Caribbean and Europe; 1,800 berths)
*Constellation* (2002; Caribbean, Europe, and Canada/New England; 2,050 berths)
*Galaxy* (1996; Southern Caribbean and Europe; 1,850 berths)
*Infinity* (2001; Hawaii, Alaska, Panama Canal, and South America; 2,050 berths)
*Mercury* (1997; Alaska, Pacific Coastal, California, and Mexican Riviera; 1,850 berths)
*Millennium* (2000; Eastern Caribbean and Europe; 2,050 berths)
*Summit* (2001; Caribbean, Alaska, Panama Canal, and Pacific Coastal; 2,050 berths)
*Xpedition* (2004; Galapagos Islands; 100 berths)
*Zenith* (1992; Caribbean, Bahamas, and Bermuda; 1,350 berths)

Pullmantur Cruises
*Blue Dream* (2004; Bermuda and Mediterranean; 700 berths)
*Blue Moon* (2006; Baltic, Caribbean, Panama Canal; 700 berths)
*Holiday Dream* (2005; Caribbean and Mediterranean; 750 berths)
*Mona Lisa* (2007; Mediterranean; 750 berths)
*Oceanic* (2001; Western Mediterranean; 1,150 berths)
*Pacific* (2007; Mediterranean; 600 berths)
*Sky Wonder* (2006; Eastern Mediterranean; 1,200 berths)

## COMPETITORS

Carnival
Carnival plc
Club Med
Disney Parks & Resorts
Holland America
NCL
Princess Cruise Lines
Siem Industries
Star Cruises
Vard

## HISTORICAL FINANCIALS

Company Type: Public

**Income Statement** FYE: December 31

| | REVENUE ($ mil.) | NET INCOME ($ mil.) | NET PROFIT MARGIN | EMPLOYEES |
|---|---|---|---|---|
| **12/06** | 5,230 | 634 | 12.1% | 42,958 |
| **12/05** | 4,903 | 716 | 14.6% | 39,400 |
| **12/04** | 4,555 | 475 | 10.4% | 38,870 |
| **12/03** | 3,784 | 281 | 7.4% | 36,350 |
| **12/02** | 3,434 | 351 | 10.2% | 27,800 |
| **Annual Growth** | 11.1% | 15.9% | — | 11.5% |

**2006 Year-End Financials**

Debt ratio: 82.7%
Return on equity: 10.9%
Cash ($ mil.): 105
Current ratio: 0.27
Long-term debt ($ mil.): 5,040
No. of shares (mil.): 212
Dividends
Yield: 1.4%
Payout: 20.4%
Market value ($ mil.): 8,752

**Stock History** NYSE: RCL

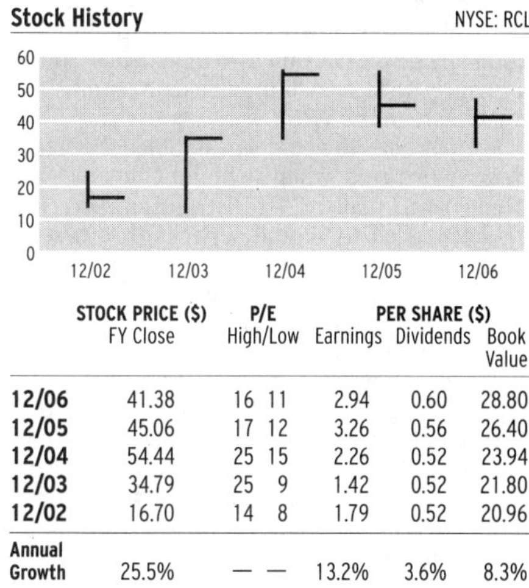


| | STOCK PRICE ($) FY Close | P/E High | P/E Low | PER SHARE ($) Earnings | Dividends | Book Value |
|---|---|---|---|---|---|---|
| **12/06** | 41.38 | 16 | 11 | 2.94 | 0.60 | 28.80 |
| **12/05** | 45.06 | 17 | 12 | 3.26 | 0.56 | 26.40 |
| **12/04** | 54.44 | 25 | 15 | 2.26 | 0.52 | 23.94 |
| **12/03** | 34.79 | 25 | 9 | 1.42 | 0.52 | 21.80 |
| **12/02** | 16.70 | 14 | 8 | 1.79 | 0.52 | 20.96 |
| **Annual Growth** | 25.5% | — | — | 13.2% | 3.6% | 8.3% |

# RPM International

If you've ever done any sort of home improvement, there's a good chance you've used RPM International's products. Maker of home repair favorites like Rust-Oleum, Zinsser, and DAP, RPM is divided into two units: industrial and consumer products. Industrial offerings include products for waterproofing, corrosion resistance, floor maintenance, and wall finishing. RPM's do-it-yourself items include caulks and sealants, rust-preventative and general-purpose paints, repair products, and hobby paints. The company, which operates worldwide, has sold its pharmaceutical operations in the Asia/Pacific region for about $349 million. In 2006 it bought the pigments business of UK-based The Dane Group for $20 million.

RPM's industrial products, which account for more than half of sales, include roofing systems (Tremco, Republic, Vulkem, and Dymeric), corrosion control coatings (Carboline, Nullifire, and Plasite), flooring systems (Stonhard and Fibergrate), concrete and masonry additives (Euco), fluorescent pigments (Day-Glo), exterior insulation finishing systems (Dryvit), commercial carpet cleaning products (Chemspec), wood treatments (Kop-Coat), and marine coatings (Pettit, Woolsey, and Z-Spar). The industrial segment accounts for a vast majority of RPM's international sales.

For the do-it-yourselfer, RPM offers rust-preventatives and paints (Rust-Oleum), caulks and sealants (DAP), primer-sealers and wall-covering preparation and removal products (Zinsser), interior stains and finishes (Varathane), patch and repair products (Plastic Wood), deck coatings (Wolman), auto restoration products (Bondo), wall coverings and fabrics (Thibaut), and hobby products (Testors).

The company is growing its operations through acquisitions; its flooring services division acquired National Building Facilities Services and Harsco's fiberglass-reinforced plastics business, and its corrosion control division purchased AD Fire Protection Systems. Tremco acquired German sealant manufacturer Illbruck Sealant Systems. In early 2007 Rust-Oleum acquired the UK's Tor Coatings in an effort to grow the unit's European coatings operations.

As can be expected, consumer home centers account for much of the company's business; the Home Depot alone represents 10% of sales.

## HISTORY

In 1947 Frank Sullivan founded Republic Powdered Metals to make an industrial aluminum paint. The company went public in 1963, and three years later it bought Reardon Co. (household coatings), its first of more than 50 acquisitions. After his father's death in 1971, Thomas Sullivan took over and reorganized RPM as a holding company.

By 1979 RPM, though successful, was taken to task by its board for lack of formal planning. In 1985 it bought Sun Oil's Carboline coating and tank-lining subsidiary. This purchase forced RPM to lay off employees for the first time.

RPM bought Rust-Oleum in 1994. In its largest acquisition at that time, the company bought roofing-product expert Tremco in 1996 for $236 million. The purchase amassed debt, and to compensate, RPM sold its Craft House hobby activity subsidiary and Swiggle Insulating Glass in 1997.

RPM resumed acquisitions and overseas expansion in 1998 by purchasing Flecto (wood finish), the UK's Nullifire (fireproof coatings), and Germany's Alteco Technik (floors); it also established joint ventures in Russia and China. In 1999 RPM paid $290 million for UK-based Wassall's DAP adhesives division. Softer sales in the Americas and Asia, plus increased distribution expenses that fiscal year, prompted the company to begin restructuring its operations.

RPM sold its Alox metalworking additive business to Lubrizol in 2000. The next year the company finished its restructuring — which had resulted in 17 plant closures and a 10% workforce reduction — and set its sights on reducing debt.

Frank Sullivan, son of Thomas Sullivan and grandson of the company's founder, took the chief executive reins in 2002; Thomas Sullivan remained as chairman.

## EXECUTIVES

**Chairman:** Thomas C. Sullivan, age 69
**President, CEO, and Director:** Frank C. Sullivan, age 46, $1,745,000 pay
**EVP and Chief Administrative Officer:** P. Kelly Tompkins, age 49
**EVP and COO:** Ronald A. Rice, age 43
**CIO and SVP, Manufacturing and Operations:** Paul G. P. Hoogenboom, age 46
**SVP, Corporate Development:** Stephen J. (Steve) Knoop, age 41
**SVP and CFO:** Ernest (Ernie) Thomas, age 53
**VP, Information Technology:** Lonny R. DiRusso, age 40
**VP, Environmental and Regulatory Affairs:** Dennis F. Finn, age 51
**VP, Finance and Communications:** Glenn R. Hasman, age 50
**VP and Controller:** Robert L. (Bob) Matejka, age 63, $625,000 pay
**VP, Global Taxes:** Matthew T. Ratajczak, age 37
**VP, Treasurer and Assistant Secretary:** Keith R. Smiley, age 42
**Associate General Counsel:** Michelle Proia
**President, Tremco:** Jeffrey L. Korach
**President and CEO:** John J. McLaughlin
**President and CEO, The StonCor Group:** David P. Reif III
**President and CEO, Rust-Oleum and Zinsser:** Michael D. (Mike) Tellor
**Director, Corporate Development:** Thomas C. Sullivan Jr.
**President, A/D Fire Protection Systems:** Peter L. Berry
**President, Carboline:** Richard M. (Dick) Wilson
**Auditors:** Ernst & Young LLP

## LOCATIONS

**HQ:** RPM International Inc.
2628 Pearl Rd., Medina, OH 44256
**Phone:** 330-273-5090 **Fax:** 330-225-8743
**Web:** www.rpminc.com

RPM sells its products in about 150 countries. The company has manufacturing operations in Africa, Asia, Europe, the Middle East, North America, and South America.

**2007 Sales**

| | $ mil. | % of total |
|---|---|---|
| US | 2,341.1 | 70 |
| Europe | 596.6 | 18 |
| Canada | 255.2 | 8 |
| Other regions | 145.9 | 4 |
| **Total** | **3,338.8** | **100** |

## PRODUCTS/OPERATIONS

**2007 Sales**

| | $ mil. | % of total |
|---|---|---|
| Industrial | 2,100.4 | 63 |
| Consumer | 1,238.4 | 37 |
| **Total** | **3,338.8** | **100** |

**Selected Products**

Industrial
- Carboline (industrial coatings)
- Chemspec (commercial carpet cleaning chemicals)
- Day-Glo (fluorescent colorants and pigments)
- Dryvit (exterior finishing systems)
- Dymeric (sealants)
- Fibergrate (reinforced plastic grating)
- Kop-Coat (wood and lumber treatments)
- Nullifire (fireproofing coatings)
- Republic (roofing products)
- Stonhard (flooring products)
- TCI (powder coatings)
- Tremco (industrial and commercial sealants)
- Vulkem (sealants)
- Woolsey/Z-Spar (marine coatings)

Consumer
- American Accents (decorative finishes)
- Bondo (automotive repair products)
- Chemical Coatings (industrial coatings)
- DAP (sealants, caulks, and patch and repair products)
- OKON (sealants and stains)
- Painter's Touch (general purpose coatings)
- Rust-Oleum (rust preventative coatings)
- Testors (hobby and leisure products)
- Tremclad (coatings)
- Varathane (wood finishes)
- Watco (wood finishes)
- Zinsser (primer-sealers and wallcovering removers)

## COMPETITORS

3M
Akzo Nobel
Ameron
Benjamin Moore
Cohesant Technologies
Dainippon Ink
DuPont Coatings
Ferro
H.B. Fuller
Henkel
Imperial Chemical
PPG
Rohm and Haas
Sherwin-Williams
Valspar

## HISTORICAL FINANCIALS

Company Type: Public

**Income Statement** FYE: May 31

| | REVENUE ($ mil.) | NET INCOME ($ mil.) | NET PROFIT MARGIN | EMPLOYEES |
|---|---|---|---|---|
| **5/07** | 3,339 | 208 | 6.2% | 9,424 |
| **5/06** | 3,008 | (76) | — | 9,213 |
| **5/05** | 2,556 | 105 | 4.1% | 8,213 |
| **5/04** | 2,342 | 142 | 6.1% | 8,092 |
| **5/03** | 2,084 | 35 | 1.7% | 7,685 |
| **Annual Growth** | 12.5% | 55.9% | — | 5.2% |

**2007 Year-End Financials**

Debt ratio: 81.6%
Return on equity: 20.7%
Cash ($ mil.): 159
Current ratio: 1.82
Long-term debt ($ mil.): 886
No. of shares (mil.): 121
Dividends
Yield: 3.0%
Payout: 42.1%
Market value ($ mil.): 2,747

**Stock History** NYSE: RPM

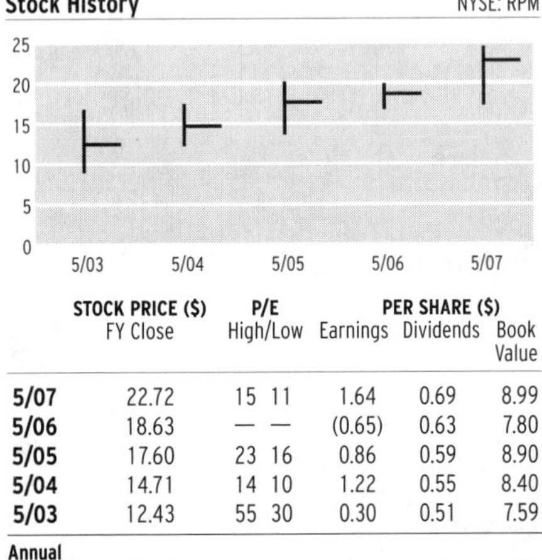


| | STOCK PRICE ($) FY Close | P/E High | P/E Low | PER SHARE ($) Earnings | Dividends | Book Value |
|---|---|---|---|---|---|---|
| **5/07** | 22.72 | 15 | 11 | 1.64 | 0.69 | 8.99 |
| **5/06** | 18.63 | — | — | (0.65) | 0.63 | 7.80 |
| **5/05** | 17.60 | 23 | 16 | 0.86 | 0.59 | 8.90 |
| **5/04** | 14.71 | 14 | 10 | 1.22 | 0.55 | 8.40 |
| **5/03** | 12.43 | 55 | 30 | 0.30 | 0.51 | 7.59 |
| **Annual Growth** | 16.3% | — | — | 52.9% | 7.8% | 4.3% |

# R. R. Donnelley & Sons

If you can read it, R.R. Donnelley & Sons can print it. A leading printing company, R.R. Donnelley produces magazines, catalogs, and books, as well as advertising material, business forms, financial reports, and telephone directories. The company offers graphics and prepress services in conjunction with printing; in addition, it provides logistics, distribution, and business process outsourcing services related to getting printed material to its audience. Along with publishers, R.R. Donnelley's customers include companies in the advertising, financial services, health care, retail, and technology industries. The company does business mainly in the US, but also in Europe, Asia, and Latin America.

To bolster its product offerings, R.R. Donnelley has been expanding via acquisitions. The company bought rival Banta for $1.3 billion in January 2007, gaining printing operations in the US, Europe, and Asia, as well as a supply chain management business that serves technology companies. Later that month, R.R. Donnelley completed the acquisition of Perry Judd's Holdings, a printer of magazines and catalogs, for $176 million. In May 2007, R.R. Donnelley acquired textbook printer Von Hoffman for $413 million.

The 2007 deals build upon a series of purchases by R.R. Donnelley. In 2006 the company acquired business process outsourcing company OfficeTiger for $250 million, and in 2005 it bought The Astron Group, a UK-based provider of outsourced document and information management services, for $990 million. (By 2007 Astron had been renamed RR Donnelley Global Document Solutions and OfficeTiger had rebranded as R.R. Donnelley as part of the parent company's move to operate under a single brand.)

In the midst of its buying spree, R.R. Donnelley has been streamlining operations and selling noncore holdings to focus on commercial printing and business process outsourcing. The company will continue to pursue acquisitions; it also hopes to grow by having its various business units cross-sell their services.

## HISTORY

In 1864 Canadian Richard Robert Donnelley joined Chicago publishers Edward Goodman and Leroy Church to form what eventually would become Lakeside Publishing and Printing. The company's building and presses were destroyed in the 1871 Chicago fire but soon were rebuilt.

By 1890 Richard Donnelley's son Thomas was leading the company, which was incorporated as R.R. Donnelley & Sons. The company spun off its phone directory publishing subsidiary, the Chicago Directory Company, in 1916. (Renamed the Reuben H. Donnelley Corporation after another of Richard Donnelley's sons, the business was acquired by Dun & Bradstreet — now D&B — in 1961, which spun it off as R. H. Donnelley in 1998.)

R.R. Donnelley began printing *Time* in 1928 and *LIFE* in 1936. The company endured limits on commercial printing and paper shortages during WWII. It went public in 1956. Thomas Donnelley's son Gaylord steered the company from 1964 until 1975, when Charles Lake, the first CEO who was not a member of the Donnelley family, replaced him.

During the 1980s R.R. Donnelley developed the Selectronic process, which allowed magazine publishers to tailor content and ads to different geographic audiences. The company acquired Metromail, the largest US mailing list business, in 1987. John Walter became CEO in 1988. R.R. Donnelley's South Side Chicago plant, its oldest, was shuttered in 1993 when Sears stopped publishing its catalogs.

R.R. Donnelley merged its software operations with Corporate Software to form Stream International (technical support, software licensing, and fulfillment) in 1995. That year Donnelley expanded internationally into Chile, China, India, and Poland.

In 1996 Donnelley took both its Donnelley Enterprise Solutions subsidiary (IT services) and its Metromail subsidiary public, retaining about 43% and 38% of each company, respectively. Controversy erupted that year when it was revealed that Metromail had sold personal information in its customer database and, through contracting, had given prison inmates access to its database. In the wake of these revelations, Walter resigned in 1996. Former Emerson Electric executive William Davis was appointed CEO in 1997.

Davis restructured the company, reorganized Stream's operations, and integrated digital printing into R.R. Donnelley's other operations. He also pushed the company to jettison underperforming units. In 1998 the company sold its interests in Metromail and Donnelley Enterprise Solutions.

Sharpening its focus in commercial printing, R.R. Donnelley continued divesting in 1999, selling most of its stake in Stream International (which was later acquired by Solectron), and its stakes in software distributor Corporate Software & Technology and manufacturing and fulfillment firm Modus Media International. The company's Internet unit also unveiled ePublish, a turnkey system enabling magazine publishers to publish on the Web.

In early 2000 the company doubled the size of its logistics unit when it bought business-to-home parcel mailer CTC Distribution Direct. It also expanded its digital services through the purchase of premedia services firm Iridio. In 2001 the company announced closures of a handful of plants as part of a streamlining effort. It also cut about 1,700 jobs.

The company sold off its investments in two more companies, MultiMedia Live and Global Directory Services, in 2003. That same year it acquired distribution service provider Momentum Logistics, and in 2004 it bought business forms and label printer Moore Wallace for about $2.8 billion. Moore Wallace CEO Mark Angelson took over leadership of the combined company.

In its continuing efforts to divest itself of noncore assets, R.R. Donnelley sold off its package logistics business, including CTC Distribution Direct, in 2004; it retained its print logistics and distribution businesses.

In 2005 R.R. Donnelley sold Peak Technologies, a former Moore Wallace company that integrated and resold automated data capture and identification systems, to Platinum Equity. R.R. Donnelley also acquired a number of regional printers in the US in 2005.

Angelson in 2007 announced plans to retire, and CFO Thomas Quinlan was named to replace him as president and CEO.

## EXECUTIVES

**President, CEO, and Director:** Thomas J. (Tom) Quinlan III, age 44
**COO:** John R. Paloian, age 48
**EVP Strategy:** Michael S. Kraus, age 33
**EVP, General Counsel, Corporate Secretary, and Chief Compliance Officer:** Suzanne S. Bettman, age 42
**SVP and CIO:** Kenneth E. O'Brien, age 43
**SVP and Treasurer:** Robert J. Kelderhouse, age 48
**Chief Administrative Officer and Secretary:** Theodore J. Theophilos, age 52
**SVP, Controller, and Chief Accounting Officer:** Miles W. McHugh, age 42
**SVP Equipment Technology and Engineering:** Raymond M. Hartman, age 52
**SVP Human Resources:** Andrew B. Panega, age 46
**SVP Marketing and Communications:** Douglas W. (Doug) Fitzgerald, age 49
**SVP Operations and Business Integration:** Rebecca J. Bruening
**SVP Sales, R.R. Donnelley Print Solutions:** Robert (Bob) O'Neil
**SVP Tax:** William F. Paparella, age 55

**VP Human Resources:** Lorien O. Gallo, age 28
**VP Investor Relations:** Daniel N. (Dan) Leib, age 37
**Group President, Forms, Labels, and Office Products:** Thomas G. (Tom) Brooker, age 48
**Group President, Integrated Print Communications:** Dean E. Cherry, age 45
**Group EVP Finance and Administration, Publishing and Retail Services:** Troy Reed
**Group EVP Finance, Short-Run and Variable Print Solutions:** Christopher M. Savine, age 46
**Group EVP Manufacturing, Publishing and Retail Services:** James R. Riffe
**Group EVP Marketing, Publishing and Retail Services:** Ann Marie Bushell
**Group President, R.R. Donnelley Brand:** Daniel L. Knotts, age 41
**Auditors:** Deloitte & Touche LLP

## LOCATIONS

**HQ:** R. R. Donnelley & Sons Company
111 S. Wacker Dr., Chicago, IL 60606
**Phone:** 312-326-8000 **Fax:** 312-326-7156
**Web:** www.rrdonnelley.com

### 2006 Sales

| | $ mil. | % of total |
|---|---|---|
| US | 7,211.8 | 78 |
| Europe | 1,155.0 | 12 |
| Other regions | 949.8 | 10 |
| **Total** | **9,316.6** | **100** |

## PRODUCTS/OPERATIONS

### 2006 Sales

| | $ mil. | % of total |
|---|---|---|
| Global Print Solutions | 5,727.2 | 61 |
| Global Services | 3,589.4 | 39 |
| **Total** | **9,316.6** | **100** |

### Selected Operations

Global Print Solutions
- Book (consumer, religious, educational and specialty, and telecommunications)
- Direct mail (content creation, database management, printing, personalization, finishing, and distribution in North America)
- Directories (yellow and white pages)
- Logistics (consolidation and delivery of printed products; expedited distribution of time-sensitive and secure material; print-on-demand, warehousing, and fulfillment services)
- Magazine, catalog, and retail
- Short-run commercial print (annual reports, marketing brochures, catalog and marketing inserts, pharmaceutical inserts and other marketing, retail point-of-sale and promotional materials and technical publications)

Global Services
- Business process outsourcing
- Digital solutions (conventional and digital photography, creative, color matching, page production, and content management services)
- Financial print (information management, content assembly, and printing service)
- Forms, labels, and statement printing
- RR Donnelley Global Document Solutions (UK; business process outsourcing, transactional print and mail services, data and print management, and document production; direct mail and marketing support services in Europe)

## COMPETITORS

| | |
|---|---|
| Accenture | Infosys |
| ACG Holdings | Merrill |
| Arandell | Polestar Group |
| Bowne | Quad/Graphics |
| Capgemini | Quebecor World |
| Cenveo | St Ives |
| Consolidated Graphics | St. Joseph |
| Courier | Taylor Corporation |
| Dai Nippon Printing | Toppan Printing |
| EBSCO | Transcontinental |
| Harte-Hanks | Valassis |
| IBM Global Services | Vertis Inc |

## HISTORICAL FINANCIALS

Company Type: Public

### Income Statement

FYE: December 31

| | REVENUE ($ mil.) | NET INCOME ($ mil.) | NET PROFIT MARGIN | EMPLOYEES |
|---|---|---|---|---|
| **12/06** | 9,317 | 401 | 4.3% | 53,000 |
| **12/05** | 8,430 | 137 | 1.6% | 50,000 |
| **12/04** | 7,156 | 178 | 2.5% | 43,000 |
| **12/03** | 4,787 | 177 | 3.7% | 30,000 |
| **12/02** | 4,755 | 142 | 3.0% | 30,000 |
| **Annual Growth** | 18.3% | 29.6% | — | 15.3% |

### 2006 Year-End Financials

Debt ratio: 57.2%
Return on equity: 10.2%
Cash ($ mil.): 211
Current ratio: 1.56
Long-term debt ($ mil.): 2,359
No. of shares (mil.): 219
Dividends
Yield: 2.9%
Payout: 56.8%
Market value ($ mil.): 7,776

### Stock History

NYSE: RRD

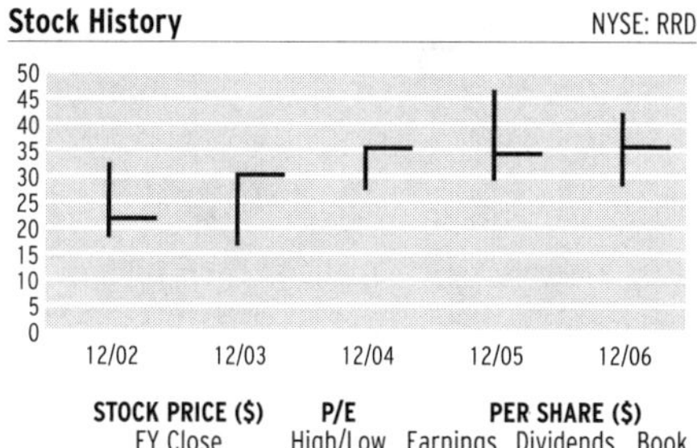


| | STOCK PRICE ($) FY Close | P/E High | P/E Low | PER SHARE ($) Earnings | Dividends | Book Value |
|---|---|---|---|---|---|---|
| **12/06** | 35.54 | 23 | 16 | 1.83 | 1.04 | 18.85 |
| **12/05** | 34.21 | 73 | 47 | 0.63 | 1.04 | 17.12 |
| **12/04** | 35.29 | 40 | 31 | 0.88 | 0.52 | 17.93 |
| **12/03** | 30.15 | 20 | 11 | 1.54 | 1.02 | 8.65 |
| **12/02** | 21.77 | 26 | 15 | 1.24 | 0.98 | 8.08 |
| **Annual Growth** | 13.0% | — | — | 10.2% | 1.5% | 23.6% |

# Ryder System

When it comes to commercial vehicles and distribution, Ryder System wants to be the designated driver. The company's Fleet Management Solutions (FMS) segment acquires, manages, maintains, and disposes of vehicles for commercial customers. Similarly, the Supply Chain Solutions (SCS) segment provides logistics and supply chain services from industrial start (raw material supply) to finish (product distribution). Ryder also offers Dedicated Contract Carriage (DCC) services in which the company supplies trucks, drivers, and management and administrative services to customers on a contract basis. Ryder's fleet of more than 140,000 vehicles ranges from tractor-trailers to light-duty trucks.

Ryder will continue to expand its product and service offerings, as evidenced by the acquisition of Vertex Services, a Houston-based fuel storage tank management company. The company will also attempt to strengthen its current operations through acquisitions, such as the purchase of the privately owned General Car and Truck Leasing System based in Davenport, Iowa; the acquisition includes 4,200 vehicles and 15 service locations. Ryder has also acquired Ruan Leasing Company, a truck rental and service company located in Des Moines, Iowa.

## HISTORY

Ryder Truck Rental, founded in Miami by Jim Ryder in 1933, was the first truck leasing company in the US. It rented trucks in four southern states until 1952, when it bought Great Southern Trucking (renamed Ryder Truck Lines), doubling its size. In 1955, the year it went public as Ryder System, Ryder bought Carolina Fleets (a South Carolina trucking company) and Yellow Rental (a northeastern leasing service). More purchases over the next decade extended its truck rental business across the US and into Canada. Ryder Truck Lines was sold to International Utilities in 1965.

After establishing One-Way truck rental services for self-movers in 1968, the company entered several new markets, including new automobile transport (1968), truck driver and heavy-equipment operator training (1969), temporary services (1969), insurance (1970), truck stops (1971), and oil refining (1974).

Leslie Barnes, the former president of Allegheny Airlines (later part of US Airways), replaced Jim Ryder as CEO in 1975 and sold the oil refinery and other company assets by the end of the year.

Anthony Burns, Ryder's president, became CEO in 1983. Burns sold Ryder's truck stops (1984) and, through 65 acquisitions, moved the firm into aviation sales and service (1982), freight hauling (1983), aircraft leasing (1984), aircraft engine overhauling (1985), and school busing (1985). By 1987 Ryder was the US leader in truck leasing and automobile hauling, the world's #1 non-airline provider of aviation maintenance and parts, and second only to Canada's Laidlaw in school bus fleet management.

Ryder sold its freight hauling business and most of its insurance interests in 1989. Responding to the weak economy and financial turmoil in the airline industry, the company began withdrawing from its aircraft operations in 1991 with the discontinuation of its leasing business. Unfortunately, the company's name was linked to two tragedies in the 1990s: Ryder trucks were used in the 1993 World Trade Center bombing in New York and the 1995 bombing of the Oklahoma City federal building.

To expand its logistics capabilities, Ryder acquired LogiCorp in 1994 and bought two UK logistics businesses from FedEx. But the consumer truck rental unit, once a bright spot on the balance sheet, was dragging down earnings. Ryder sold its bright yellow trucks in 1996 to investor group Questor Partners. (Budget Group, which bought the business in 1998, was licensed to use the "Ryder" brand. However, Ryder and Budget reached an agreement in 2002 to terminate the license.)

In 1997 Ryder sold its faltering automotive carrier business to industry leader Allied Holdings. The next year Ryder bought Companhia Transportadora e Comercial Translor, a leading logistics company in Brazil.

Burlington Northern Santa Fe SVP Gregory Swienton became Ryder's president and COO in 1999; Burns remained chairman and CEO. That year, as part of the long restructuring initiative, Ryder sold its school-bus unit to UK-based FirstGroup for $940 million.

Burns retired as CEO in 2000, remaining chairman, and Swienton took over. Also that year Ryder established TTR Logistics, a joint venture with Toyota Tsusho America, to provide Toyota and other Japanese auto companies with logistics and transportation services.

In 2001 the company established an Asia/Pacific headquarters with its acquisition of Singapore-based Ascent Logistics.

## EXECUTIVES

**Chairman, President, and CEO:** Gregory T. Swienton, age 57, $843,750 pay
**EVP and CFO:** Mark T. Jamieson, age 53, $545,833 pay
**EVP, General Counsel, and Corporate Secretary:** Robert Fatovic, age 41
**EVP, Operations, US Fleet Management Solutions:** Robert E. Sanchez, age 41
**EVP, Sales and Marketing, US Fleet Management Solutions:** Thomas S. Renehan, age 44
**SVP and Chief Human Resources Officer:** Gregory F. Greene, age 47
**SVP and CIO:** Kevin Bott
**SVP and Controller:** Art A. Garcia, age 45
**SVP Sales and Marketing:** Airton Gimenes
**VP, Investor Relations and Public Affairs:** Robert (Bob) Brunn
**President, US Fleet Management Solutions:** Anthony G. Tegnelia, age 61, $430,250 pay
**President, US Supply Chain Solutions:** Vicki A. O'Meara, age 48, $490,250 pay
**Group Director of Corporate Communications:** David Bruce
**Auditors:** PricewaterhouseCoopers LLP

## LOCATIONS

**HQ:** Ryder System, Inc.
11690 NW 105th St., Miami, FL 33178
**Phone:** 305-500-3726 **Fax:** 305-500-3203
**Web:** www.ryder.com

Ryder System operates from locations in Argentina, Brazil, Canada, Chile, China, Germany, Mexico, Singapore, Thailand, the UK, and the US.

### 2006 Sales

| | $ mil. | % of total |
|---|---|---|
| US | 5,136.8 | 81 |
| Canada | 564.4 | 9 |
| Europe | 346.9 | 6 |
| Latin America | 237.4 | 4 |
| Asia | 21.1 | — |
| **Total** | **6,306.6** | **100** |

## PRODUCTS/OPERATIONS

### 2006 Sales

| | $ mil. | % of total |
|---|---|---|
| Fleet management solutions | 4,096.0 | 61 |
| Supply chain solutions | 2,028.5 | 30 |
| Dedicated contract carriage | 568.8 | 9 |
| Adjustments | (386.7) | — |
| **Total** | **6,306.6** | **100** |

## COMPETITORS

Arkansas Best
Barloworld
BAX Global
C.H. Robinson Worldwide
Con-way Inc.
Expeditors
FedEx
J.B. Hunt
Landstar System
Penske Truck Leasing
Schneider National
TNT
Trailer Fleet Services
UniGroup
UPS
YRC Worldwide

## HISTORICAL FINANCIALS

Company Type: Public

### Income Statement

FYE: December 31

| | REVENUE ($ mil.) | NET INCOME ($ mil.) | NET PROFIT MARGIN | EMPLOYEES |
|---|---|---|---|---|
| **12/06** | 6,307 | 249 | 3.9% | 28,600 |
| **12/05** | 5,741 | 227 | 4.0% | 27,800 |
| **12/04** | 5,150 | 216 | 4.2% | 26,300 |
| **12/03** | 4,802 | 131 | 2.7% | 26,700 |
| **12/02** | 4,776 | 94 | 2.0% | 27,800 |
| **Annual Growth** | 7.2% | 27.7% | — | 0.7% |

### 2006 Year-End Financials

Debt ratio: 144.4%
Return on equity: 15.3%
Cash ($ mil.): 192
Current ratio: 1.00
Long-term debt ($ mil.): 2,484
No. of shares (mil.): 61
Dividends
Yield: 1.4%
Payout: 17.8%
Market value ($ mil.): 3,100

### Stock History

NYSE: R

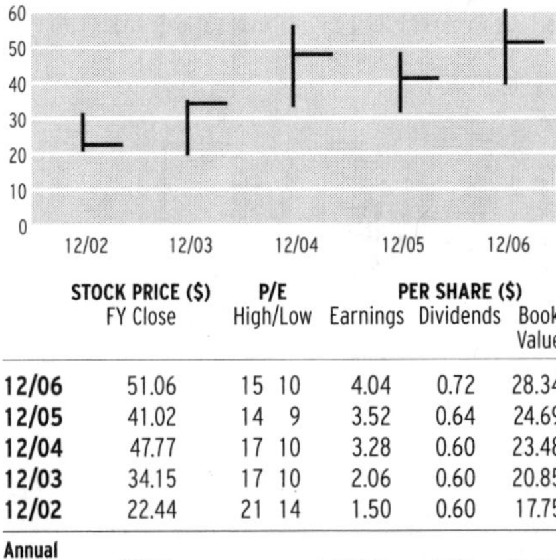


| | STOCK PRICE ($) FY Close | P/E High | P/E Low | PER SHARE ($) Earnings | Dividends | Book Value |
|---|---|---|---|---|---|---|
| **12/06** | 51.06 | 15 | 10 | 4.04 | 0.72 | 28.34 |
| **12/05** | 41.02 | 14 | 9 | 3.52 | 0.64 | 24.69 |
| **12/04** | 47.77 | 17 | 10 | 3.28 | 0.60 | 23.48 |
| **12/03** | 34.15 | 17 | 10 | 2.06 | 0.60 | 20.85 |
| **12/02** | 22.44 | 21 | 14 | 1.50 | 0.60 | 17.75 |
| **Annual Growth** | 22.8% | — | — | 28.1% | 4.7% | 12.4% |

# Ryerson, Inc.

Ryerson has a heart of steel. A leading North American distributor and processor of metals, the company, formerly called Ryerson Tull, offers its customers steel products (carbon, stainless, and alloy), aluminum, copper, and industrial plastics. It buys bulk metal products (in sheets, bars, and other forms) from metal producers and processes them into smaller lots to meet the specifications of its customers — machine shops, fabricators, metal producers, and machinery makers. Ryerson has facilities in the US and Canada and joint ventures in China, India, and Mexico. In 2005 Ryerson purchased Integris Metals for $640 million. Two years later Platinum Equity agreed to buy Ryerson for about $2 billion.

Ryerson bought Integris from joint venture partners Alcoa and BHP Billiton. Following full integration of the acquired company, Ryerson changed its name from Ryerson Tull.

In 2006 Ryerson acquired Lancaster Steel Service Company, which operates in Upstate New York. The acquired company, which was renamed Ryerson Lancaster, distributes all manner of steel product as well as providing processing services.

Early the next year, amid shareholder unrest, the company postponed its annual meeting. The move was designed, in part, to ward off a proxy fight for control of the Board. Ryerson's Board of Directors announced that it would review its strategic alternatives, which meant it would look for someone to buy the company. Cue private equity groups.

Platinum Equity moved in on Ryerson in the middle of 2007 with its offer to take the publicly traded company private. The $2 billion offer included assumed debt.

## HISTORY

In 1893 eight partners purchased used steelmaking machinery from bankrupt Chicago Steel and established Inland Steel in the Chicago Heights, Illinois, area. Eight years later the Lake Michigan Land Company offered 50 acres to any company that would spend $1 million to develop it by building an open-hearth steel mill. Inland raised the money and built Indiana Harbor Works.

Inland grew and in 1916 expanded to meet the steel demands of WWI. After the war Inland began producing rails (1922). During the Depression years, Inland turned out tinplate and steel sheet used in consumer goods. In 1931 the company, under chairman L. E. Block, built plants to make strip, sheet, and plate steel. It moved into steel warehousing in 1935, buying Joseph T. Ryerson & Son, a Chicago-based metal processor. Inland also bought Wilson & Bennett Manufacturing (later renamed Inland Steel Containers) in 1939. Inland manufactured armor during WWII, and after the war it expanded its rolling mills.

Inland became a billion-dollar company in 1966. The 1970s brought a steel boom, but when the party ended in the 1980s, the firm suffered large losses. Inland reorganized in 1986 as a holding company to separate its steel-manufacturing operations from its more profitable distribution division. The company also acquired J.M. Tull Metals from Bethlehem Steel.

Inland entered into joint ventures with Nippon Steel in 1987 and 1989 to build and operate a cold-rolling mill (I/N Tek, 60%-owned) and a coating facility (I/N Kote, 50%). Inland ceased making structural steel that year.

In 1994 the company formed Inland International and created a service center joint venture (Ryerson de Mexico) with Mexico's #1 steelmaker, Altos Hornos de Mexico. The following year quality problems and a derailed cost-reduction program forced Maurice Nelson to retire after three-and-a-half years as president and CEO of subsidiary Inland Steel Company; Dale Wiersbe, a 26-year company veteran, took over. The company combined its Ryerson and Tull operations and sold the public a 13% stake in Ryerson Tull.

In 1997 Inland Steel inked a deal with Tata Steel, the flagship of India's Tata conglomerate, to process steel in that country. That year Ryerson Tull (87% owned by Inland) acquired Thypin

Steel, a US distributor of carbon and stainless-steel products. Inland sold its Inland Steel Company to Ispat International for $1.4 billion in 1998.

Inland Steel Industries acquired the rest of its Ryerson Tull subsidiary in 1999 and adopted the name Ryerson Tull for the company. Also in 1999 Ryerson Tull bought Washington Specialty Metals, which operates metal service centers that specialize in stainless steel, to boost its market share over 10%. The purchase added to Ryerson Tull's expansion of the specialty metals group, the company's single-largest product area. Despite the growth, slumping steel prices industry-wide and weakness in the US manufacturing sector caused Ryerson Tull's profits to plunge by 90% in 1999 compared to its previous year.

In 2000 Ryerson Tull sold its 50% interest in Ryerson de México to its partner in the Altos Hornos de México joint venture. That year Ryerson Tull closed its coil processing facility in Minnesota and a metal service center in Texas. In December 2001 the company sold its subsidiary, Ryerson Industries de Mexico, S.A. de C.V., to Grupo Collado. It also stopped operations of its Internet steel marketplace, MetalSite.

As part of the company's continuing restructuring plan, Ryerson Tull sold off its Emeryville, California, service center for about $12 million in 2002. In 2003 Ryerson Tull formed a joint venture with G. Collado S.A. de C.V. to expand its services in Mexico. The following year, Ryerson Tull acquired J&F Steel, a carbon flat-rolled processor and subsidiary of Arcelor, for approximately $55 million. In early 2005 Ryerson Tull bought out Integris Metals, which was a joint venture of Alcoa and BHP Billiton, for around $410 million.

The following year the company dropped the latter half of its name and became simply Ryerson, Inc.

## EXECUTIVES

**Chairman, President, and CEO:** Neil S. Novich, age 52, $1,870,857 pay
**EVP and CFO:** Jay M. Gratz, age 54, $1,027,478 pay
**EVP:** Anita J. Pickens, age 49
**VP Finance and Treasurer:** Terence R. (Terry) Rogers, age 47
**VP, Controller, and Chief Accounting Officer:** Lily L. May, age 57
**VP Human Resources:** William Korda, age 59
**VP IT and CIO:** Darell R. Zerbe, age 64
**President, Global Accounts:** James M. Delaney, age 48
**President, Ryerson Canada:** Michael L. Whelan
**VP International:** Frank Muñoz
**VP, Corporate Secretary, and Deputy General Counsel:** Virginia M. Dowling, age 56
**VP and General Counsel:** M. Louise (Lou) Turilli, age 57
**President, Ryerson South:** Stephen E. Makarewicz, age 60, $562,433 pay
**Auditors:** Ernst & Young LLP

## LOCATIONS

**HQ:** Ryerson, Inc.
2621 W. 15th Place, Chicago, IL 60608
**Phone:** 773-762-2121 **Fax:** 773-762-0437
**Web:** www.ryerson.com

Ryerson Tull maintains facilities throughout the US and in Canada. The company has stakes in joint ventures in China, Hong Kong, and India.

## PRODUCTS/OPERATIONS

### 2006 Sales by Product Group

| | % of total |
|---|---|
| Stainless & aluminum | 52 |
| Carbon flat-rolled | 25 |
| Bars, tubing & structurals | 9 |
| Fabricated & carbon plate | 9 |
| Other | 5 |
| **Total** | **100** |

### 2006 Sales by Customer Segment

| | % of total |
|---|---|
| Fabricated metal producers | 28 |
| Machinery manufacturers | 27 |
| Electrical machinery producers | 13 |
| Transportation equipment producers | 11 |
| Construction-related purchasers | 6 |
| Wholesale distributors | 5 |
| Metals mills & foundries | 2 |
| Other | 8 |
| **Total** | **100** |

### Selected Products

Alloy steel
Aluminum
Carbon steel
Industrial plastics
Stainless steel

## COMPETITORS

A. M. Castle
AK Steel Holding Corporation
Alcan
Allegheny Technologies
Blue Tee
Commercial Metals
Empire Resources
Kreher Steel
Metals USA
Olympic Steel
O'Neal Steel
Reliance Steel
Steel Technologies
Sumitomo Metal Industries
Worthington Industries

## HISTORICAL FINANCIALS

Company Type: Public

### Income Statement

FYE: December 31

| | REVENUE ($ mil.) | NET INCOME ($ mil.) | NET PROFIT MARGIN | EMPLOYEES |
|---|---|---|---|---|
| **12/06** | 5,909 | 72 | 1.2% | 5,700 |
| **12/05** | 5,781 | 98 | 1.7% | 5,800 |
| **12/04** | 3,302 | 55 | 1.7% | 3,600 |
| **12/03** | 2,189 | (14) | — | 3,400 |
| **12/02** | 2,097 | (96) | — | 3,600 |
| **Annual Growth** | 29.6% | — | — | 12.2% |

### 2006 Year-End Financials

Debt ratio: 173.4%
Return on equity: 12.0%
Cash ($ mil.): 55
Current ratio: 4.13
Long-term debt ($ mil.): 1,125
No. of shares (mil.): 26
Dividends
Yield: 0.8%
Payout: 8.0%
Market value ($ mil.): 664

### Stock History

NYSE: RYI

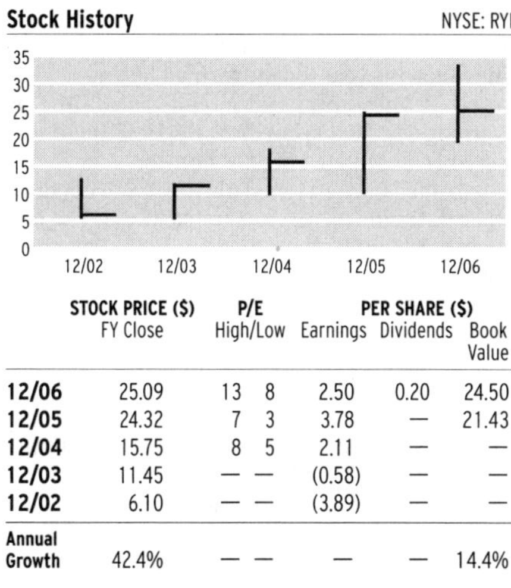


| | STOCK PRICE ($) FY Close | P/E High | P/E Low | PER SHARE ($) Earnings | Dividends | Book Value |
|---|---|---|---|---|---|---|
| **12/06** | 25.09 | 13 | 8 | 2.50 | 0.20 | 24.50 |
| **12/05** | 24.32 | 7 | 3 | 3.78 | — | 21.43 |
| **12/04** | 15.75 | 8 | 5 | 2.11 | — | — |
| **12/03** | 11.45 | — | — | (0.58) | — | — |
| **12/02** | 6.10 | — | — | (3.89) | — | — |
| **Annual Growth** | 42.4% | — | — | — | — | 14.4% |

# The Ryland Group

The Ryland Group constructs its homebuilding business on a firm foundation — expanding within its existing markets and targeting entry-level, first- and second-time move-up, and active retired-adult buyers. As a leading US homebuilder, Ryland built about 11,000 homes in 2006 that ranged in price from $98,000 to more than $800,000 (averaging $295,000). Subcontractors perform virtually all of the construction, which is monitored by Ryland supervisors. The group also provides mortgage-finance services, including title search, settlement, escrow, and homeowners insurance, through Ryland Mortgage.

The Ryland Group's homebuilding segment oversees the building of homes in some 30 states.

The group's financial services unit focuses on retail mortgage loan originations, including conventional, FHA, and VA mortgages. About 99% of the loans originated by the subsidiary are for homes built by the company.

Despite eight consecutive years of solid earnings growth for Ryland, the company may be caught by the tide of rising interest rates that have troubled other homebuilders. In 2006 housing starts and prices fell as the sector contracted.

## HISTORY

The Ryland Group was founded in 1967 by entrepreneur James Ryan in the new planned community of Columbia, Maryland. Ryan got the idea for the company name after seeing "Maryland" on a sign with the first two letters covered up, so in 1970 the James P. Ryan Co. changed its name to The Ryland Group. Ryan took Ryland public in 1971, and the company expanded to a new planned community near Atlanta that year. In 1974 the company opened its first panel-building plant (Ryland Building Systems). By 1977 Ryland had moved into the Midwest and Philadelphia, completing 10,000 homes by year's end.

Ryland purchased Crest Communities (Cincinnati) in 1978. Crest's financial subsidiary became the basis for Ryland's mortgage operations (later known as Ryland Mortgage). Ryan retired in 1980, and Charles Peck became CEO. In 1981 the company entered the loan servicing business with the purchase of Guardian Mortgage. The following year Ryland formed Ryland Acceptance as an administrator and distributor of mortgage-backed securities. By 1985 the company had completed 50,000 homes.

It formed Cornerstone Title in 1989 to conduct real estate closing services in Maryland. The following year Ryland teamed up with American Loyalty Insurance to offer homeowners' insurance. In the 1990s the firm entered the fast-growing California and Florida housing markets. It also dabbled in overseas markets, building homes in Israel in 1991 and Russia in 1992.

A recession and overexpansion led to the company's loss in 1993. Chad Dreier, a former Kaufman and Broad EVP, was appointed as Ryland CEO in late 1993 and took the company in a new direction. He recognized that while Ryland's center-hall colonial-style house formed the foundation for the company's success, that fixed image of a "Ryland Home" was also an impediment to its future growth. Under Dreier's leadership, the company began enlisting the services of top architectural firms, such as Bloodgood, Sharp, Buster, and Kaufman Meeks to introduce new house designs and to offer Ryland's customers a greater degree of customization in house design. The company also placed a stronger emphasis on market research after securing plots of land to better determine the best house designs for any given area.

In 1995, as part of its plan to focus on its core homebuilding and retail mortgage finance operations, the company sold its institutional mortgage-securities administration business (which included master servicing, investor information services, securities administration, tax calculation, and reporting). A year later it sold its wholesale mortgage operations.

The company purchased The Regency Organization, a private Florida homebuilder, in 1998 to expand into the growing retirement market and acquired Thomas Builders to expand operations in the Baltimore area. In 1999 Ryland relocated its mortgage subsidiary to California and the next year moved its corporate headquarters there.

Also in 2000 Ryland joined other major US homebuilders in an Internet-based marketing cooperative. The builder continued to surf the Net the next year as it invested $1 million in online sales company iBidCo, after using iBidCo's system to sell 14 California homes for a total of nearly $11 million.

Company chairman and CEO Dreier scored in 2002 with a new employment agreement, which gave him an annual base salary of $1 million through the year 2007. Ryland posted record revenue and closings results in 2003, a trend since 2000. Ryland opened 152 new communities (a 5% to 10% increase) in fiscal 2003. At the close of 2003, Ryland began operating in California's Inland Empire (Riverside and San Bernardino counties), and in 2004 the company opened communities in Las Vegas. In 2006 Ryland split its Northern California division and created two new divisions in Sacramento and the Central Valley.

## EXECUTIVES

**Chairman, President, COO, and CEO:** R. Chad Dreier, age 59, $1,000,000 pay (prior to title change)
**EVP and CFO:** Gordon A. Milne, age 55, $500,000 pay
**COO:** Larry T. Nicholson, age 49, $295,000 pay (prior to promotion)
**SVP; President, Ryland Mortgage Company:** Daniel G. Schreiner, age 49, $407,389 pay
**SVP; President, Texas Region, Ryland Homes:** Ken L. Trainer
**SVP; President, North Region, Ryland Homes:** Peter G. Skelly, age 43
**SVP, Controller, and Chief Accounting Officer:** David L. Fristoe, age 50
**SVP Human Resources:** Robert J. (Bob) Cunnion III, age 51
**SVP Marketing and Communications:** Eric E. Elder, age 49
**SVP, Secretary, and General Counsel:** Timothy J. (Tim) Geckle, age 54
**VP and CIO:** Craig McSpadden
**VP, Compensation and Benefits:** Valerie S. (Val) Zook
**VP, Investor Relations:** Drew Mackintosh
**VP, Internal Audit:** Thomas M. Pearson
**VP, Purchasing:** Steven M. (Steve) Dwyer
**VP, Sales Training:** Charles W. (Charlie) Jenkins
**VP, Tax:** René L. Mentch
**President, Southeast Region, Ryland Homes:** Keith Bass
**President, West Region, Ryland Homes:** William M. (Bill) Butler
**President, Baltimore Division, Ryland Homes:** John Meade
**Auditors:** Ernst & Young LLP

## LOCATIONS

**HQ:** The Ryland Group, Inc.
24025 Park Sorrento, Ste. 400, Calabasas, CA 91302
**Phone:** 818-223-7500 **Fax:** 818-223-7667
**Web:** www.ryland.com

The Ryland Group builds homes throughout the US.

**2006 New Orders**

| | No. units | % of total |
|---|---|---|
| Texas | 3,237 | 29 |
| Southeast | 3,164 | 28 |
| North | 2,987 | 27 |
| West | 1,746 | 16 |
| **Total** | **11,134** | **100** |

## PRODUCTS/OPERATIONS

**Selected Subsidiaries**

Columbia National Risk Retention Group, Inc.
Cornerstone Title Company (operates as Ryland Title Company)
LPS Holdings Corporation
Ryland Homes of California, Inc.
Ryland Homes Insurance Company
Ryland Mortgage Company
Ryland Organization Company

## COMPETITORS

Beazer Homes
Centex
Champion Enterprises
D.R. Horton
Hovnanian Enterprises
J.F. Shea
KB Home
Kimball Hill inc
Lennar
M.D.C.
M/I Homes
Morrison Homes
NVR
Pulte Homes
Standard Pacific
Technical Olympic USA
Toll Brothers
WCI Communities

## HISTORICAL FINANCIALS

Company Type: Public

**Income Statement** FYE: December 31

| | REVENUE ($ mil.) | NET INCOME ($ mil.) | NET PROFIT MARGIN | EMPLOYEES |
|---|---|---|---|---|
| **12/06** | 4,757 | 360 | 7.6% | 2,810 |
| **12/05** | 4,818 | 447 | 9.3% | 3,217 |
| **12/04** | 3,952 | 321 | 8.1% | 2,829 |
| **12/03** | 3,444 | 242 | 7.0% | 2,558 |
| **12/02** | 2,877 | 186 | 6.5% | 2,458 |
| **Annual Growth** | 13.4% | 18.0% | — | 3.4% |

**2006 Year-End Financials**

Debt ratio: 62.9%
Return on equity: 24.9%
Cash ($ mil.): 215
Current ratio: 3.86
Long-term debt ($ mil.): 950
No. of shares (mil.): 43
Dividends
Yield: 0.9%
Payout: 6.1%
Market value ($ mil.): 2,327

**Stock History** NYSE: RYL

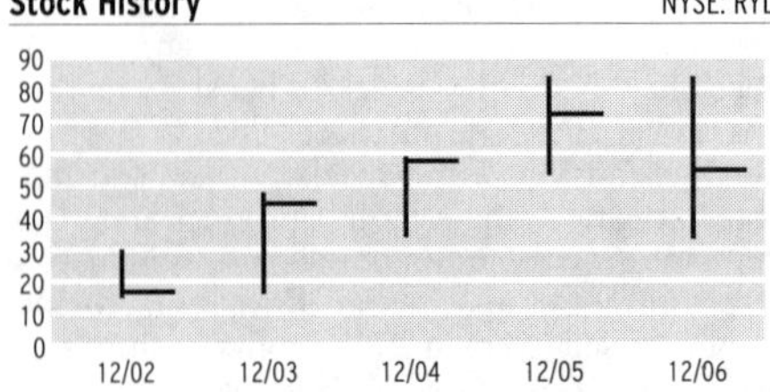


| | STOCK PRICE ($) FY Close | P/E High | P/E Low | PER SHARE ($) Earnings | Dividends | Book Value |
|---|---|---|---|---|---|---|
| **12/06** | 54.62 | 11 | 4 | 7.83 | 0.48 | 35.46 |
| **12/05** | 72.13 | 9 | 6 | 9.03 | 0.30 | 29.68 |
| **12/04** | 57.54 | 9 | 5 | 6.36 | 0.20 | 22.32 |
| **12/03** | 44.32 | 10 | 4 | 4.55 | 0.04 | 34.59 |
| **12/02** | 16.67 | 9 | 5 | 3.32 | 0.04 | 26.92 |
| **Annual Growth** | 34.5% | — | — | 23.9% | 86.1% | 7.1% |

# Safeco Corporation

While the name doesn't tell you much about the business, Safeco does sound secure, and with insurance that counts for a lot. Safeco, through its Safeco Insurance Co., offers personal property/casualty insurance including auto, homeowners, and fire coverage. The company's commercial business includes workers' compensation, multiperil, and general liability geared towards small to midsized companies. To better focus on its flagship property/casualty business across the US, Safeco has exited the life and health segment and sold its insurance brokerage, wealth-management arm, and mutual fund operations. However, it continues to offer surety bonds to its long-term construction and corporate customers.

Other insurance companies such as GEICO jumped on the online insurance sales bandwagon early, but Safeco waited until 2006 to introduce its Safeco Now online sales and service presence. The company hopes to become more attractive to online shoppers with lower-cost offerings.

Safeco's one-time ambition to join the chorus of multiline financial services institutions was thwarted by a series of underwriting losses. Trying to turn things around, the company reduced debt by selling Safeco Credit, its commercial credit and leasing subsidiary, to GE Capital, and it sold its life insurance and investments business to an investor group that includes White Mountains Insurance Group and Berkshire Hathaway. Safeco also sold its trust unit to asset manager Mellon Financial (now The Bank of New York Mellon), and its Talbot insurance brokerage to an investor group led by its executives.

To raise capital, the company chose to sell off its landmark tower in downtown Seattle as well as an office campus in Redmond, Washington, and rent office space instead.

## HISTORY

Seattle was a financial backwater in 1923 when Hawthorne Dent, a former Northwestern Mutual Fire Insurance executive, founded General Insurance Co. of America. It was organized as a mixed mutual/stock company, a hybrid organization that combined the steady dividends and conservatism of a mutual with a stock company's access to new capital through the issuance of stock. (The downside of many mutuals then was that when losses were high, members had to pay extra to cover claims.) This setup allowed the company to charge lower rates. As General Insurance grew and reorganized itself, it became a pure stock company, but the feature of allowing policyholders to receive a dividend remained in the form of a participating policy.

General started out as a fire insurance company, but as cars proliferated, the company formed a new subsidiary, General Casualty, to specialize in auto liability (1925). Soon after its founding, the company set up offices in neighboring Oregon. It went into California in 1926, Illinois in 1929, and Georgia in 1935.

The company grew by cultivating a large and loyal force of independent agents and was able to garner business because it was often the only local alternative to the East Coast giants. Renamed General America Corp. in 1929, it continued to expand in the 1930s despite the Depression. By 1936 it was Washington's leading fire insurer.

After WWII, as suburbs expanded and the car culture grew, auto insurance entered a golden age. General America's insurance business increased by 207% between 1947 and 1952. In 1953 a new subsidiary, Selected Auto and Fire Insurance Co. of America (Safeco), was organized. Four years later (the year before founder Dent died) the company started General Life Insurance Co., its foray into life insurance.

Diversification continued in the 1960s. In 1967 and 1968 General America added mutual funds and bought Seattle-based Winmar, a real estate development and management firm. Soon it began developing nursing homes and hospitals and formed a credit company. It became Safeco in 1968 in recognition of the importance of the Safeco subsidiary.

The next two decades were a hard time for insurance companies as interest rates soared, and many insurers were locked into low-interest investments and hemmed in by state limits on rate increases. Instead of cutting rates, as many firms did, Safeco left such unattractive markets as Pennsylvania, where it stopped renewing auto policies in 1990, and Canada, which it abandoned in 1991. In 1993 Safeco bought insurance broker and asset manager Talbot Financial.

After the 1994 Northridge earthquake, Safeco stopped selling new homeowner policies in California. The company was later allowed to offer limited earthquake insurance and convert existing policies as they came up for renewal.

Facing a dearth of young people clamoring to become insurance professionals, Safeco in 1996 beefed up recruiting efforts, which included relaxing its 73-year-old white-shirt, no-beard dress code.

The next year Safeco bought American States Financial, boosting its property/casualty business by nearly 50% and spreading its reach into the Midwest and Southeast. In 1998 weather-related catastrophes depressed earnings.

Safeco sold most of its retail properties in 1999, to focus on its core business. In 2000 tornados in downtown Fort Worth, Texas, hammered the company's bottom line. The company sold Safeco Credit, its commercial credit and leasing subsidiary, in 2001.

In 2003 the company announced its intention to shed noncore operations and focus on its property/casualty businesses.

## EXECUTIVES

**Chairman:** Joseph W. (Jay) Brown, age 58
**President, CEO, and Director:** Paula Rosput Reynolds, age 50, $2,035,000 pay
**EVP, Insurance Operations, Safeco Insurance Companies:** Michael H. (Mike) Hughes, age 52, $345,667 pay
**EVP, CFO, and Chief Accounting Officer:** Ross J. Kari, age 48, $676,667 pay
**EVP and Chief Legal Officer:** Arthur Chong, age 53, $650,000 pay
**EVP and Chief Business Services Officer:** Allie R. Mysliwy, age 52, $312,000 pay
**EVP Claims and Service:** R. Eric Martinez Jr., age 38
**SVP and Chief Investment Officer:** Richard Kelly
**SVP Corporate Communications:** David M. (Dave) Monfried
**SVP, Financial Planning and Analysis:** John Ammendola, age 41
**SVP, P/C Business Process and Operations, Safeco Insurance Companies:** Gregory (Greg) Tacchetti, age 38
**SVP, Service, Safeco Insurance Companies:** W. Myron Hendry, age 58
**SVP and Head of Safeco Surety:** Tim Mikolajewski
**SVP, Government Relations:** Edward Heffernan
**VP and Controller:** Kris L. Hill, age 40
**VP, Risk Management:** Lew Augustine
**VP and Secretary:** Stephanie Daley-Watson
**VP, Audit Services:** Robert J. McNichols
**President, Open Seas Insurance:** Kim Garland
**President, Safeco Insurance Foundation:** Virginia L. Anderson, age 59
**Head, Safeco Business Insurance:** Tom Troy
**CIO:** William W. (Bill) Jenks
**Investor Relations:** Neal A. Fuller
**Auditors:** Ernst & Young LLP

## LOCATIONS

**HQ:** Safeco Corporation
Safeco Plaza, 4333 Brooklyn Ave. NE,
Seattle, WA 98185
**Phone:** 206-545-5000 **Fax:** 206-545-5995
**Web:** www.safeco.com

Safeco operates in all 50 states and the District of Columbia.

## PRODUCTS/OPERATIONS

**2006 Sales**

| | $ mil. | % of total |
|---|---|---|
| Net earned premiums | | |
| Personal | | |
| Auto | 2,713.2 | 43 |
| Property | 909.0 | 14 |
| Specialty | 105.4 | 2 |
| Business | 1,509.6 | 24 |
| Surety | 297.5 | 5 |
| Other property/casualty | 73.6 | 1 |
| Net investment income | 509.1 | 8 |
| Gains on sale of real estate | 168.7 | 3 |
| Net realized investment gains | 3.8 | — |
| **Total** | **6,289.9** | **100** |

## COMPETITORS

AIG
Allstate
American Financial
Chubb Corp
CIGNA
Cincinnati Financial
CNA Financial
GEICO
Liberty Mutual
Loews
MetLife
Nationwide
Ohio Casualty
Philadelphia Consolidated
Progressive Corporation
Prudential
St. Paul Travelers Bond
State Farm
Travelers Companies
USAA

## HISTORICAL FINANCIALS

Company Type: Public

**Income Statement** FYE: December 31

| | ASSETS ($ mil.) | NET INCOME ($ mil.) | INCOME AS % OF ASSETS | EMPLOYEES |
|---|---|---|---|---|
| **12/06** | 14,199 | 880 | 6.2% | 7,208 |
| **12/05** | 14,887 | 691 | 4.6% | 9,181 |
| **12/04** | 14,586 | 562 | 3.9% | 9,200 |
| **12/03** | 35,845 | 339 | 0.9% | 11,200 |
| **12/02** | 34,656 | 301 | 0.9% | 12,000 |
| **Annual Growth** | (20.0%) | 30.8% | — | (12.0%) |

**2006 Year-End Financials**

Equity as % of assets: 27.7%
Return on assets: 6.1%
Return on equity: 21.9%
Long-term debt ($ mil.): 2,009
No. of shares (mil.): 105
Dividends
Yield: 1.8%
Payout: 14.6%
Market value ($ mil.): 6,587
Sales ($ mil.): 6,290

**Stock History** NYSE: SAF

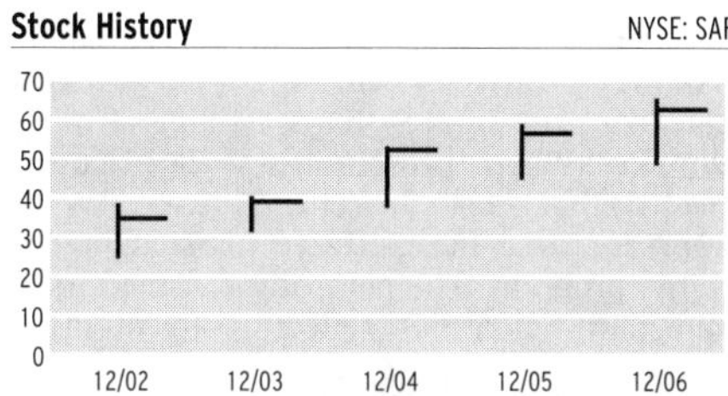


| | STOCK PRICE ($) FY Close | P/E High | P/E Low | PER SHARE ($) Earnings | Dividends | Book Value |
|---|---|---|---|---|---|---|
| **12/06** | 62.55 | 9 | 7 | 7.51 | 1.10 | 37.30 |
| **12/05** | 56.50 | 11 | 8 | 5.43 | 0.94 | 33.37 |
| **12/04** | 52.24 | 13 | 9 | 4.16 | 0.77 | 30.88 |
| **12/03** | 38.93 | 16 | 13 | 2.44 | 0.74 | 36.24 |
| **12/02** | 34.67 | 16 | 11 | 2.33 | 0.74 | 32.07 |
| **Annual Growth** | 15.9% | — | — | 34.0% | 10.4% | 3.9% |

# Safeguard Scientifics

Safeguard Scientifics' goal is to nurture investments, not protect Poindexters in a lab. The company invests in high-tech and life sciences ventures, often for the long haul. It provides capital, strategic advice, and operational support for expansion, management buyouts, recapitalizations, and consolidations. Safeguard Scientifics owns majority interests in such firms as Acsis (manufacturing supply-chain software and services) and Alliance Consulting Group (information technology consulting); life science holdings include Clarient (cancer diagnostics) and contract manufacturing organization Laureate Pharma. Safeguard Scientifics also owns smaller stakes in several other firms.

Other holdings include software and consulting firm ProModel, telecommunications provider NexTone, security software and systems maker Authentium, and Ventaira Pharmaceuticals. After several years of hemorrhaging money, management changes and strategic tweaks finally helped send Safeguard Scientifics into the black in 2006. The firm's shift from being an operational company to a holding company mind-set has seen Safeguard Scientifics pare down its portfolio, while continuing to concentrate on and nurture its core holdings.

Safeguard Scientifics in 2007 sold Pacific Title and Arts Studio, which provides post-production services to the motion picture industry. It sold its 51% stake in CompuCom Systems to an affiliate of Platinum Equity in 2004.

## HISTORY

Warren Musser and Frank Diamond founded venture capital firm Lancaster Company in 1953. Their first investment was a small cable TV firm, Jerrold Electronics (later called Comcast). Another early purchase gave the company its future name, Safeguard Industries, which made check printers that wrote payment amounts by perforating the paper. During the 1950s and 1960s Lancaster grew into a conglomerate whose holdings included makers of business forms and auto parts. It went public in 1967, then renamed itself Safeguard Industries in 1968, naming its major subsidiary Safeguard Business Systems.

During the 1970s the company pared its holdings. Heavily in debt, in 1980 it spun off Safeguard Business Systems, its biggest moneymaker. When the spinoff's stock price exceeded that of its parent, Musser was so impressed that he instituted his stockholder rights program. The company renamed itself Safeguard Scientifics, reflecting an intention to invest in high tech.

In 1981 Musser bought 55% of Novell, a nearly defunct microcomputer company (and raised that stake to 88% the next year). Safeguard installed new management and directed Novell toward new client/server technologies. Also in 1981 Safeguard acquired a piece of Coherent Communications, a maker of data transmission equipment for telex machines.

Safeguard nearly fell victim in 1982 to a stock manipulation scheme cooked up by a broker who used embezzled funds to buy 58% of the company's shares. Musser almost lost control of the company, but he instituted a stock buyback program to restore the stock's value.

In 1984 Safeguard bought into CompuCom Systems, a young company founded as Machine Vision International. The next year Safeguard took Novell public. The offering's success vindicated the share-the-wealth strategy. In 1986 the company sold the remainder of its interest in Safeguard Business Systems to a group of private investors and became a founding investor in cable shopping channel QVC (sold 1993).

Expanding into new fields, Safeguard invested in a struggling training and consulting firm, Cambridge Technology Partners, and formed XL Vision as an internal startup to develop electronic imaging products.

As interest in high-tech companies grew in the 1990s, Safeguard's acquisitions accelerated. Investments included New Paradigm Ventures and Nextron. It also formed Internet Capital Group in 1996 to develop Internet opportunities. Taking advantage of the hot IPO market in recent years, Safeguard took other companies public, including USDATA (1995), ChromaVision Medical Systems (1997), and VerticalNet (1999).

Safeguard experienced record earnings in 1998 with the merger of partnership company Coherent Communications into Tellabs. Safeguard, which traditionally sold its assets to provide steady increases in quarterly earnings, announced in 1999 it would start selling its investments only for business reasons. That year it replaced its stockholder rights program with a share subscription plan (limiting the number of shares available and the time Safeguard stockholders could get in on the deal) to attract more institutional investors to its companies' IPOs.

In 2000 the company bought a 38% stake in application service provider Mi8 Corporation. The "tech wreck" forced Musser, who had never sold any of his shares in Safeguard, to sell a large chunk of his nearly 9% stake in the firm to meet margin calls.

Musser decided to resign as CEO in 2001 to focus on "broader" entrepreneurial ventures; Anthony Craig replaced him.

The firm sold its stakes in DocuCorp International, Pac West Telecomm, Verticalnet, Internet Capital Group, and Kanbay International in 2003. The next year, Safeguard sold its largest holding, a 51% stake in CompuCom Systems, to an affiliate of Platinum Equity. In 2004, Safeguard acquired biopharmaceutical company Laureate Pharma.

Peter Boni succeeded Craig in 2005.

## EXECUTIVES

**Chairman:** Robert E. (Bob) Keith Jr., age 65
**President, CEO, and Director:** Peter J. Boni, age 60, $225,000 pay
**EVP and Managing Director, Life Sciences:** James A. (Jim) Datin, age 43, $244,471 pay
**EVP and Managing Director, Information Technology:** John A. (Jack) Loftus Jr., age 43, $452,292 pay
**SVP and CFO:** Raymond J. (Ray) Land, age 62
**SVP and General Counsel:** Brian J. Sisko
**SVP, Information Technology Group:** Kevin L. Kemmerer
**VP and Principal, Information Technology Group:** Erik Rasmussen
**VP, Investor Relations and Corporate Communications:** John E. Shave
**Principal, Business Development:** Spencer Hoffman
**Senior Associate, Business Development:** Eric Steager
**Auditors:** KPMG LLP

## LOCATIONS

**HQ:** Safeguard Scientifics, Inc.
800 The Safeguard Bldg., 435 Devon Park Dr., Wayne, PA 19087
**Phone:** 610-293-0600 **Fax:** 610-293-0601
**Web:** www.safeguard.com

## PRODUCTS/OPERATIONS

### 2006 Sales

| | $ mil. | % of total |
|---|---|---|
| Service sales | 187.4 | 95 |
| Product sales | 10.7 | 5 |
| **Total** | **198.1** | **100** |

### Selected Subsidiaries and Holdings

Acsis (96%, supply-chain software)
Advantedge Healthcare Solutions (32%, medical billing software and services)
Alliance Consulting Group Associates (99%, information technology consulting)
Authentium (12%, security software)
Clarient (60%, diagnostic therapies)
Laureate Pharma (contract manufacturing organization)
Neuronyx (7%, biopharmaceuticals)
NexTone Communications (17%, telecommunications)
NuPathe (21%, specialty pharmaceuticals)
Portico Systems (47%, software for health care plans)
PROMODEL (50%, software and services for pharmaceutical, health care, and other industries)
Rubicor Medical (36%, medical devices)
Ventaira Pharmaceuticals (13%, specialty pharmaceuticals)

## COMPETITORS

Accel Partners
Austin Ventures
BlueRun Ventures
Boston Ventures
CMGI
Draper Fisher Jurvetson
Hummer Winblad
iD Ventures America
Idealab
IVP
Kleiner Perkins
Matrix Partners
Mayfield Fund
Menlo Ventures
Sequoia Capital
Sutter Hill Ventures
Trinity Ventures
US Venture Partners
Vulcan

## HISTORICAL FINANCIALS

Company Type: Public

### Income Statement

FYE: December 31

| | REVENUE ($ mil.) | NET INCOME ($ mil.) | NET PROFIT MARGIN | EMPLOYEES |
|---|---|---|---|---|
| **12/06** | 198 | 46 | 23.2% | 1,265 |
| **12/05** | 186 | (32) | — | 1,404 |
| **12/04** | 157 | (55) | — | 1,183 |
| **12/03** | 1,623 | (33) | — | 4,325 |
| **12/02** | 1,686 | (151) | — | 4,614 |
| **Annual Growth** | (41.4%) | — | — | (27.6%) |

### 2006 Year-End Financials

Debt ratio: 63.3%
Return on equity: 24.4%
Cash ($ mil.): 169
Current ratio: 2.75
Long-term debt ($ mil.): 134
No. of shares (mil.): 120
Dividends
Yield: —
Payout: —
Market value ($ mil.): 291

### Stock History

NYSE: SFE

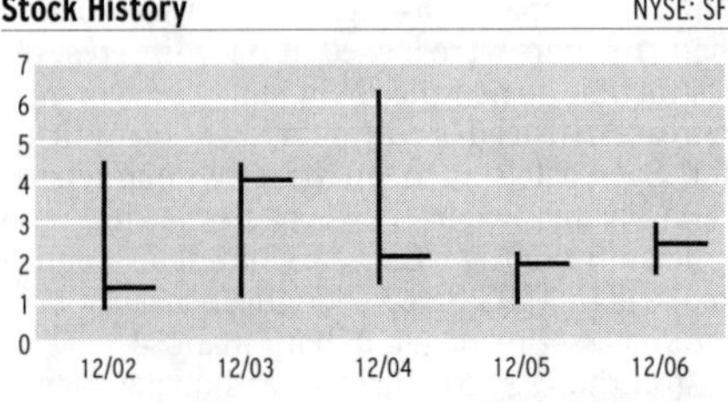


| | STOCK PRICE ($) FY Close | P/E High | P/E Low | PER SHARE ($) Earnings | PER SHARE ($) Dividends | PER SHARE ($) Book Value |
|---|---|---|---|---|---|---|
| **12/06** | 2.42 | 8 | 5 | 0.38 | — | 1.76 |
| **12/05** | 1.93 | — | — | (0.27) | — | 1.38 |
| **12/04** | 2.12 | — | — | (0.46) | — | 1.72 |
| **12/03** | 4.04 | — | — | (0.30) | — | 1.97 |
| **12/02** | 1.36 | — | — | (1.30) | — | 2.28 |
| **Annual Growth** | 15.5% | — | — | — | — | (6.3%) |

# Safeway Inc.

For many Americans, "going to Safeway" is synonymous with "going to the grocery store." Safeway is one of North America's largest food retailers, with about 1,740 stores located mostly in the western, midwestern, and mid-Atlantic regions of the US, as well as western Canada. It also operates regional supermarket companies, including The Vons Companies (primarily in Southern California), Dominick's Finer Foods (Chicago), Carr-Gottstein Foods (Alaska's largest retailer), Genuardi's Family Markets (eastern US), and Randall's Food Markets (Texas). It also owns e-retailer GroceryWorks.com. Outside of the US, Safeway owns 49% of Casa Ley, which operates about 125 food and variety stores in western Mexico.

In addition, Safeway operates about 30 food processing plants in the US and Canada, where about one-quarter of its private-label goods are manufactured. With more than 1,300 in-store pharmacies, Safeway is a leader in pharmacy sales among US grocery retailers.

Since 1997 Safeway has beefed up by purchasing other food retailers, including Vons (about 300 stores), Dominick's (#2 in Chicago with nearly 100 stores), and Randall's in 1999. But not all of the company's acquisitions have been successful. Following labor trouble and failure to find a buyer for struggling Dominick's, Safeway took the chain off the market and installed R. Randall Onstead Jr. (former head of Randall's Food Markets) as president to fix the mess at its Chicago chain. Onstead has resigned and been succeeded by Bruce Everette, who assumed the leadership of Dominick's as one of his major responsibilities as an executive vice president at Safeway.

In recent years Safeway has been rapidly converting its supermarkets to its primary new store format: the *Lifestyle* store. The newer, bigger stores feature expanded selections of perishable foods, organic products, and other high-end amenities and are designed to compete with upscale natural and organic grocery operators, such as industry leader Whole Foods Market.

Safeway is also upgrading its perishables merchandising, service, and selection while cutting prices to compete with discounters, such as Wal-Mart Supercenters (the #1 seller of groceries in the US).

## HISTORY

Founded in 1914 by Sam Seelig, Safeway had grown to about 300 stores in California and Hawaii by 1926. That year investment banker Charles Merrill, one of the founders of Merrill Lynch, bought Safeway. Merrill convinced M. B. Skaggs — of the famous grocery retailing Skaggs family — to become president, and his brother L. S. Skaggs (founder of what became American Stores) became VP. M. B. merged his 430 or so Skaggs stores with Safeway and took the Safeway name.

Safeway bought Arizona Grocery, Piggly Wiggly Pacific, and Piggly Wiggly Eastern Stores in 1928 and Piggly Wiggly Western States, a grocer operating in California, Texas, and Nevada, in 1929. Two years later the chain had its greatest number of stores (3,527); this number was reduced as smaller stores were converted into larger supermarkets. In addition, the company expanded internationally into western Canada, the UK, and Australia. Peter Magowan, grandson of Merrill, became chairman and CEO in 1980. (His father, Robert Magowan, ran the chain for about 15 years.) The company acquired 49% of Mexican retailer Casa Ley in 1981. Safeway sold its Australian and German operations four years later.

In 1986 Safeway received an unsolicited buyout bid from the Dart Group. In response, Peter and takeover specialist Kohlberg Kravis Roberts (KKR) took Safeway private in a leveraged deal; Dart made a $159 million profit on its shares. Saddled with debt, in 1987 and 1988 the company sold more than 1,350 stores. Included in that number were 162 Southern California stores (sold to The Vons Companies in exchange for stock) and about 120 stores in the UK to food and beverage company Argyll Group (now Safeway plc). A slimmer Safeway reemerged as a public company in 1990.

Steven Burd became president in 1992 and CEO the next year. He has played hardball with the unions representing about 90% of Safeway's employees. In 1995, with 87 stores in Alberta, Canada, he replaced 4,000 full-time union employees with part-time workers, a move that saved the company $40 million. Burd also reduced corporate and store staff, consolidated distribution centers, and restructured the debt left over from the 1986 LBO. However, labor disputes, including strikes and lockouts, in Colorado and Canada (which closed 86 stores for 40 days) cut into the company's improving sales and earnings numbers during 1996 and 1997.

Safeway acquired the rest of Vons it didn't already own in 1997. Burd took over the title of chairman from the retiring Peter the next year. Late in 1998 Safeway acquired the Dominick's Supermarkets chain, and the grocer acquired the Texas-based 115-store Randall's Food Markets (largely owned by KKR) in 1999.

In 2000 Safeway bought a majority stake in GroceryWorks.com. Also that year KKR reduced its stake in Safeway to less than 5%.

A four-and-a-half month strike by grocery workers in Safeway's second-largest market, Southern California, affecting nearly 300 Safeway-owned Vons and Pavilions stores ended in March 2004. The dispute pitted workers' demands for generous health care benefits against Safeway's drive to cut costs and remain profitable in the face of mounting competition, particularly from non-unionized Wal-Mart. The strike took its toll on Safeway's bottom line, causing a $103 million loss during the fourth quarter. However, Safeway achieved a key goal: the establishment of a two-tier pay and benefits scheme under which new hires will receive substantially less in wages and benefits than veteran employees.

Several public pension funds, including the nation's two largest (California Public Employees' Retirement System and the New York State fund), agitated for the ouster of Burd, citing the purchase of Dominick's and steep losses from the five-month Southern California grocery strike among Burd's missteps. Soon after, Burd survived a shareholder vote attempting to uncouple his dual roles of chairman and CEO.

In December the grocery chain settled a lawsuit filed in June 2004 by the California attorney general alleging that Safeway sold tobacco products to minors at its Pack N' Save, Pavilions, Safeway, and Vons stores. Safeway agreed to pay $245,000 and instruct cashiers to ask for proof of age, among other measures.

## EXECUTIVES

**Chairman, President, and CEO:** Steven A. (Steve) Burd, age 57, $1,332,250 pay
**EVP and CFO:** Robert L. Edwards, age 51, $590,928 pay
**EVP, Retail Operations:** Bruce L. Everette, age 55, $593,154 pay
**EVP, Chief Strategist and Administrative Officer:** Larree M. Renda, age 48, $622,877 pay
**SVP, Finance and Control:** David F. Bond, age 53
**SVP and CIO:** David T. Ching, age 54
**SVP, General Counsel, and Chief Governance Officer:** Robert A. Gordon, age 55
**SVP, Finance and Investor Relations:** Melissa C. Plaisance, age 47
**SVP, Planning and Business Development:** David R. Stern, age 52
**SVP, Real Estate and Engineering:** Donald P. Wright, age 54
**SVP, Marketing Planning:** Carl Graziani
**SVP, Human Resources:** Russell M. Jackson, age 48
**Corporate VP, Public Affairs:** Brian Dowling
**VP, Investor Relations and Financial Analysis:** Julie Hong
**President and COO, Canada Safeway:** Chuck Mulvenna
**President, Dominick's Finer Foods:** Don Keprta
**President, Marketing Operations:** Frank A. Calfas
**President, The Vons Companies:** Thomas C. (Tom) Keller
**President, GroceryWorks:** Matt Gutermuth
**Chairman and CEO, Casa Ley, S.A. De C.V. (Mexico):** Juan Manuel Ley Lopez
**Auditors:** Deloitte & Touche LLP

## LOCATIONS

**HQ:** Safeway Inc.
5918 Stoneridge Mall Rd., Pleasanton, CA 94588
**Phone:** 925-467-3000 **Fax:** 925-467-3321
**Web:** www.safeway.com

Safeway has about 1,760 stores in the Western, Southwestern, Rocky Mountain, Midwestern, and Mid-Atlantic regions of the US, and in western Canada. It also has about 20 manufacturing and food processing facilities in the US and 12 in Canada, as well as 17 distribution centers in the US and Canada.

**2006 Stores**

| | No. |
|---|---|
| US | |
| Southern California (Vons) | 303 |
| Northern California (includes Hawaii) | 267 |
| Seattle (includes Alaska) | 206 |
| Eastern (MD, VA, DC, Genuardi's) | 178 |
| Denver | 144 |
| Portland | 117 |
| Phoenix | 114 |
| Texas (Randalls/Tom Thumb) | 112 |
| Dominick's | 98 |
| Canada | |
| Alberta | 92 |
| Vancouver | 74 |
| Winnipeg | 56 |
| **Total** | **1,761** |

**2006 Sales**

| | $ mil. | % of total |
|---|---|---|
| US | 34,721 | 86 |
| Canada | 5,464 | 14 |
| **Total** | **40,185** | **100** |

## PRODUCTS/OPERATIONS

**2006 Manufacturing and Processing Plants**

| | US | Canada |
|---|---|---|
| Milk | 6 | 3 |
| Bakery | 6 | 2 |
| Soft drink bottling | 4 | — |
| Ice cream | 2 | 2 |
| Fruit & vegetable processing | 1 | 3 |
| Pet food | 1 | — |
| Cheese & meat packaging | — | 2 |
| **Total** | **20** | **12** |

**2006 Stores**

| | No. |
|---|---|
| Traditional | 1,010 |
| Lifestyle | 751 |
| **Total** | **1,761** |

## COMPETITORS

A&P
Ahold USA
Albertsons
Associated Grocers
Bashas'
Comerci
Costco Wholesale
Giant Food
GNC
H-E-B
IGA
Katz Group
Kroger
Loblaw
Longs Drug
Meijer
Overwaitea
PETCO
Raley's
Rite Aid
SAM'S CLUB
Save Mart
Smart & Final
Sobeys
Soriana
Stater Bros.
SUPERVALU
Trader Joe's
Unified Western Grocers
Walgreen
Wal-Mart
Wal-Mart de México
Whole Foods
Wild Oats Markets
Winn-Dixie

## HISTORICAL FINANCIALS

Company Type: Public

**Income Statement** FYE: Saturday nearest December 31

| | REVENUE ($ mil.) | NET INCOME ($ mil.) | NET PROFIT MARGIN | EMPLOYEES |
|---|---|---|---|---|
| **12/06** | 40,185 | 871 | 2.2% | 207,000 |
| **12/05** | 38,416 | 561 | 1.5% | 201,000 |
| **12/04** | 35,823 | 560 | 1.6% | 191,000 |
| **12/03** | 35,553 | (170) | — | 208,000 |
| **12/02** | 32,399 | (828) | — | 172,000 |
| **Annual Growth** | 5.5% | — | — | 4.7% |

**2006 Year-End Financials**

Debt ratio: 88.9%
Return on equity: 16.4%
Cash ($ mil.): 217
Current ratio: 0.77
Long-term debt ($ mil.): 5,037
No. of shares (mil.): 583
Dividends
Yield: 0.6%
Payout: 11.3%
Market value ($ mil.): 20,131

**Stock History** NYSE: SWY

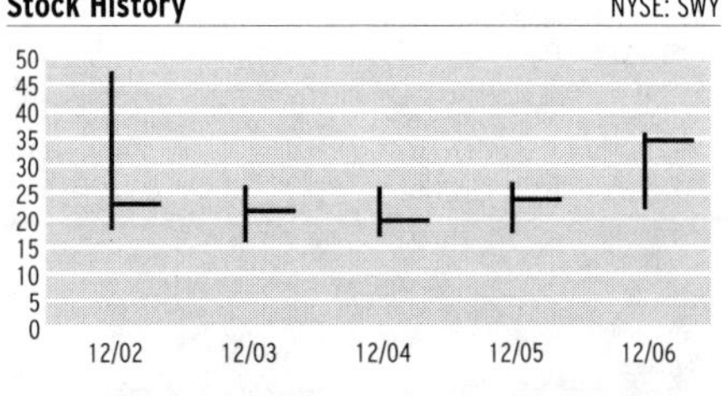


| | STOCK PRICE ($) FY Close | P/E High | P/E Low | PER SHARE ($) Earnings | Dividends | Book Value |
|---|---|---|---|---|---|---|
| **12/06** | 34.56 | 18 | 11 | 1.94 | 0.22 | 9.73 |
| **12/05** | 23.66 | 21 | 14 | 1.25 | 0.15 | 8.48 |
| **12/04** | 19.74 | 21 | 14 | 1.25 | — | 7.44 |
| **12/03** | 21.54 | — | — | (0.38) | — | 8.19 |
| **12/02** | 22.83 | — | — | (1.75) | — | 6.33 |
| **Annual Growth** | 10.9% | — | — | — | 46.7% | 11.4% |

# SAIC, Inc.

Getting from Point A to Point B — or in this particular case, from Private to Public — sometimes requires a special vehicle. SAIC was formed in late 2005 as a vehicle for the IPO and capital restructuring of Science Applications International Corporation. The company is a leading government services contractor that offers technical support and project management services. It provides networking, software development, and systems integration, as well as technical analysis and research for many federal and state agencies, and it offers maintenance and technical support to various branches of the military. The company also provides consulting and technology services for some commercial customers.

SAIC's IPO in late 2006 has transformed the formerly employee-owned company into a publicly traded enterprise. The IPO was announced by CEO Ken Dahlberg, who took over the company in 2004 when founder Dr. J. Robert Beyster stepped down. Though the public offering was announced in 2005 and planned for early 2006, it was delayed while the company dealt with issues from a contract it had to provide supply security to the 2004 Olympics in Athens. Greek authorities have claimed that SAIC did not meet its obligations under the contract, a claim the company denies. But SAIC did lose more than $120 million on the deal.

The IPO ended the company's reign as the largest employee-owned research and engineering (R&D) firm. It had been employee-owned since its founding in 1969. The company used proceeds from the public offering to pay a dividend to pre-IPO stockholders. SAIC does benefit from additional capital after the offering, however, since it no longer has to buy back employee stock. The company has a long history of expansion through acquisition and plans even bigger purchases in the future. Before the ink was dry on its IPO, SAIC acquired Applied Marine Technology, a company with expertise in special operations, special mission units, and other areas of special warfare operations, as well as in homeland security and the global war on terrorism. Among many 2006 acquisitions, the company additionally bought AETC, a San Diego-based provider of remote sensing systems for the Department of Defense; Varec, a provider of measurement, control, and automation systems; aerospace engineering and IT services firm bd Systems; and Applied Ordnance Technology, a provider of technical products and services catering to weapons systems.

In 2007 SAIC acquired Benham Investment Holdings, a provider of consulting, engineering, architecture and design/build, and other related services.

Ranking in the top 10 in several service segments, SAIC has seen revenue grow steadily in recent years thanks to robust federal spending in such areas as homeland security and new military programs. The company's respected expertise in these areas has helped it win many new contracts but having former government officials on payroll has also been a big help in its development: SAIC's alumni include such government insiders as former defense secretary William Perry and former CIA director John Deutch.

## HISTORY

Physicist Robert Beyster, who worked at Los Alamos National Laboratory in the 1950s, was hired by General Atomics in 1957 to establish and manage its traveling wave linear accelerator. When the company was sold to Gulf Oil in 1968, research priorities changed and Beyster left. He founded Science Applications Inc. (SAI) the following year and built his business from consulting contracts with Los Alamos and Brookhaven National Laboratory. During the first year Beyster instituted an employee ownership plan that rewarded workers who brought on board new business with stock in SAI. Beyster's idea was to share the success of SAI and to raise capital.

In 1970 the company established an office in Washington, DC, to court government contracts. Despite a recession, SAI continued to grow during the 1970s, and by 1979 sales topped $100 million. The following year SAI restructured, becoming a subsidiary of Science Applications International Corporation (SAIC), a new holding company.

During the 1980s defense buildup, an emphasis on high-tech weaponry and SAIC's high-level Pentagon connections (directors have included former defense secretaries William Perry and Melvin Laird and former CIA director John Deutch) brought in contracts for submarine warfare systems and technical development for the Strategic Defense Initiative ("Star Wars"). As defense spending slowed with the end of the Cold War, though, SAIC began casting a wider net. By 1991 computer systems integration and consulting accounted for 25% of sales, which surpassed the $1 billion mark.

SAIC made several purchases during the mid-1990s, including transportation communications firm Syntonic and Internet domain name registrar Network Solutions, Inc. (NSI). It also began merger talks with The Aerospace Corporation, a government-funded research center, in 1996 until the Air Force scotched the deal a few months later. In 1997 SAIC acquired Bellcore (the research lab of the regional Bells, later renamed Telcordia Technologies), and reduced its stake in NSI through a public offering. SAIC formed several alliances in 1998, including a joint venture with Rolls-Royce to service the aerospace, energy, and defense industries.

The next year SAIC expanded its IT expertise with the acquisition of Boeing's Information Services unit. It also acquired the call center software operations of Elite Information Group (now Thomson Elite). SAIC in 2000 realized a significant gain on its $5 million purchase of NSI when e-commerce software maker VeriSign bought the minority-owned (23%) subsidiary for about $20 billion in stock. SAIC signed a variety of large contracts the next year, including an outsourcing agreement with BP to manage that company's North American application and hosting services, as well as a $3 billion deal to provide support (in conjunction with Bechtel Group) for the US Department of Energy's civilian radioactive waste management program.

The omnipresent and self-described workaholic Beyster retired as CEO in 2003, turning the position over to Kenneth Dahlberg, a former executive of General Dynamics. (Dahlberg became chairman of SAIC the following year.) In 2005 the company sold its Telcordia subsidiary to investment firms Warburg Pincus and Providence Equity Partners for $1.3 billion.

## EXECUTIVES

**Chairman and CEO:** Kenneth C. (Ken) Dahlberg, age 62, $2,100,000 pay
**EVP and CFO:** Mark W. Sopp, age 41
**EVP and Director:** Joseph P. (Joe) Walkush, age 54
**EVP, Government Affairs, Communications, and Support Operations:** Arnold L. Punaro, age 60
**EVP, Strategic Projects:** Thomas E. Darcy, age 56
**EVP and Chief Engineering and Technology Officer:** Donald H. (Don) Foley, age 62
**SVP and Corporate Controller:** John R. Hartley, age 40
**SVP, General Counsel, and Secretary:** Douglas E. Scott, age 49
**SVP Business Development:** W. Greg Henson
**Group President, Intelligence, Security, and Technology:** Lawrence B. (Larry) Prior III, age 50
**President, Defense Solutions Group:** Deborah H. (Deb) Alderson, age 49
**President, Infrastructure and Product Solutions Group:** Joseph W. (Joe) Craver III
**President, IT and Network Solutions Group:** Charles F. Koontz
**SVP; President, Benham Investment Holdings:** J.T. Grumski
**CTO:** Theoren P. (Trey) Smith III, age 51
**Public Affairs Director:** Ronald M. (Ron) Zollars
**Public Relations:** Melissa Koskovich
**Auditors:** Deloitte & Touche LLP

## LOCATIONS

**HQ:** SAIC, Inc.
10260 Campus Point Dr., San Diego, CA 92121
**Phone:** 858-826-6000 **Fax:** 858-826-6800
**Web:** www.saic.com

## COMPETITORS

Accenture
Aerospace Corporation
Battelle Memorial
BearingPoint
Boeing
Booz Allen
CACI International
Computer Sciences Corp.
Digital Fusion
EDS
General Dynamics
Halliburton
IBM Global Services
ITT Corp.
Lockheed Martin
Lockheed Martin Information & Technology
ManTech
MITRE
Northrop Grumman
Raytheon
SRA International
Thales
Titan Group
Unisys

## HISTORICAL FINANCIALS

Company Type: Public

**Income Statement** FYE: January 31

| | REVENUE ($ mil.) | NET INCOME ($ mil.) | NET PROFIT MARGIN | EMPLOYEES |
|---|---|---|---|---|
| **1/07** | 8,294 | 391 | 4.7% | 44,100 |
| **1/06** | 7,775 | 927 | 11.9% | — |
| **1/05** | 7,172 | 409 | 5.7% | — |
| **Annual Growth** | 7.5% | (2.2%) | — | — |

**2007 Year-End Financials**

Debt ratio: 78.1%
Return on equity: —
Cash ($ mil.): 1,135
Current ratio: 1.77
Long-term debt ($ mil.): 1,199
No. of shares (mil.): 92
Dividends
Yield: —
Payout: —
Market value ($ mil.): 1,707

**Stock History** NYSE: SAI

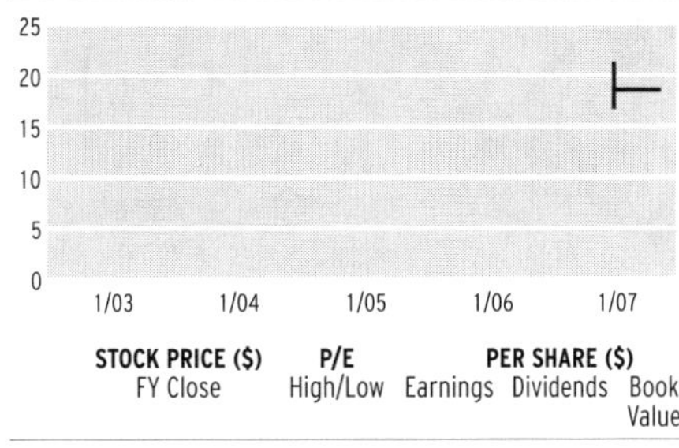


| | STOCK PRICE ($) FY Close | P/E High/Low | PER SHARE ($) Earnings | Dividends | Book Value |
|---|---|---|---|---|---|
| **1/07** | 18.55 | 20 16 | 1.07 | — | 16.70 |

# St. Jude Medical

St. Jude Medical takes a sad heart and makes it better. St. Jude Medical develops and markets devices to treat cardiovascular disease and is one of the world's leading manufacturers of mechanical heart valves (more than 1.5 million of its valves have been implanted). The company's largest segment is its Cardiac Rhythm Management division, which makes pacemakers, implantable cardioverter defibrillators (ICDs), and other equipment to regulate heart rhythm. Its Cardiac Surgery unit makes mechanical and tissue heart valves as well as annuloplasty rings (used to repair mitral heart valves), while the Cardiology division manufactures cardiac catheters, diagnostic guidewires, and vascular closure devices.

St. Jude also makes electrophysiology catheters and advanced cardiac mapping systems through its Atrial Fibrillation division. A fourth unit, formed in late 2005 with the acquisition of Advanced Neuromodulation Systems, makes nerve stimulation products used to treat chronic pain. The company merged its Cardiology and Cardiac Surgery divisions at the beginning of 2007 into the new Cardiovascular division. While St. Jude is master of the mechanical valve market and holds a 25% market share for bradycardia pacemakers, it has lagged behind such rivals as Medtronic and Guidant in the increasingly popular ICD market. The company continues to forge ahead with research and development efforts in an industry that is becoming increasingly consolidated. The company acquired both Endocardial Solutions, which makes diagnostic and therapeutic catheters marketed under the EnSite System brand, and Velocimed, a privately owned maker of interventional cardiology devices, in early 2005. Velocimed's products include the Venture catheter and the Premere system, used to seal a tiny hole between the left and right upper chambers of the heart that fails to close in some babies. The Premere system is still undergoing investigational studies. The firm is highly acquisitive and scooped up two other firms, Irvine Biomedical and Epicor Medical, in 2004. FMR owns 10% of St. Jude, and AXA Financial holds a 9% interest.

## HISTORY

Manuel Villafana, who started Cardiac Pacemakers in 1972, founded St. Jude Medical four years later to develop the bileaflet heart valve. In 1977 patient Helen Heikkinen received the first St. Jude heart valve. The firm also went public that year.

Villafana left in 1981, and established competitor Helix Biocore. St. Jude expanded into tissue valves with its purchase of BioImplant in 1986.

In the mid-1980s St. Jude gained market share when devices from Pfizer and Baxter International had problems. Concerns that the company hadn't diversified led to a joint venture in 1992 with Hancock Jaffe Laboratories to develop a bioprosthetic (constructed of animal tissue) heart valve. In 1994 it bought Siemens' pacemaker unit, doubling revenues and tripling its sales force.

The firm continued diversifying, buying Daig (cardiac catheters) in 1996 and Ventritex (cardiac defibrillators) in 1997. In 1997 the FDA approved St. Jude's Toronto SPV tissue valve, marking its entry into that market. In 1999 St. Jude landed on CalPERS' list of worst-performing companies as it lagged behind rivals Guidant and Medtronic. A management shake-up followed, and the firm strengthened its product lines, buying Tyco International's Angio-Seal subsidiary (cardiac sealant) and Vascular Science (artery connectors). The next year the FDA stepped up its regulatory oversight after the company and its competitors recalled or issued warnings regarding defective or potentially defective devices.

In 2002, St. Jude bought Getz Bros., a Japanese company that is the largest distributor of St. Jude's products in Japan.

## EXECUTIVES

**Chairman, President, and CEO:** Daniel J. Starks, age 52, $975,000 pay
**EVP and CFO:** John C. Heinmiller, age 52, $580,000 pay
**President, Cardiac Rhythm Management:** Eric S. Fain
**VP, Administration:** Thomas R. Northenscold, age 49
**VP, General Counsel, and Secretary:** Pamela S. Krop, age 48
**VP, Human Resources:** I. Paul Bae
**VP, Information Technology and CIO:** William J. McGarry, age 49
**VP and Corporate Controller:** Donald J. Zurbay, age 39
**VP, Corporate Relations:** Angela D. Craig, age 35
**President, Cardiology Division:** Paul R. Buckman, age 51
**President, Cardiovascular:** George J. Fazio, age 47
**President, Neuromodulation:** Christopher G. Chavez, age 51
**President, SJM Europe:** Denis M. Gestin
**President, St. Jude Medical International:** Joseph H. McCullough, age 57, $450,000 pay
**President, US Sales:** Michael T. Rousseau, age 51, $475,000 pay
**President, Atrial Fibrillation:** Jane J. Song, age 44
**Auditors:** Ernst & Young LLP

## LOCATIONS

**HQ:** St. Jude Medical, Inc.
1 Lillehei Plaza, St. Paul, MN 55117
**Phone:** 651-483-2000 **Fax:** 651-482-8318
**Web:** www.sjm.com

St. Jude Medical's products are sold in more than 100 countries. It has facilities in Brazil, Canada, Puerto Rico, Sweden, and the US.

**2006 Sales**

| | $ mil. | % of total |
|---|---|---|
| US | 1,920.6 | 58 |
| Europe | 806.5 | 24 |
| Japan | 289.7 | 9 |
| Other regions | 285.6 | 9 |
| **Total** | **3,302.4** | **100** |

## PRODUCTS/OPERATIONS

**2006 Sales**

| | $ mil. | % of total |
|---|---|---|
| Cardiac rhythm management | 2,055.8 | 62 |
| Cardiology | 452.3 | 14 |
| Atrial fibrillation | 325.7 | 10 |
| Cardiac surgery | 289.3 | 9 |
| Neuromodulation | 179.3 | 5 |
| **Total** | **3302.4** | **100** |

**Selected Subsidiaries**

Advanced Neuromodulation Systems, Inc.
Endocardial Solutions, Inc.
Epicor Medical, Inc.
IrvineBiomedical, Inc.
Pacesetter, Inc.
SJM International, Inc.
St. Jude Medical Australia Pty., Ltd.
St. Jude Medical Brasil, Ltda.
St. Jude Medical Canada, Inc.
St. Jude Medical Colombia, Ltda.
St. Jude Medical Europe, Inc.
St. Jude Medical (Hong Kong) Limited
Velocimed, Inc.

## COMPETITORS

Abbott Labs
Arrow International
ATS Medical
Boston Scientific
C. R. Bard
Cordis
Datascope
Edwards Lifesciences
Guidant
InControl, Inc.
Johnson & Johnson
Medtronic
Pace Medical
Sorin
ZOLL Medical

## HISTORICAL FINANCIALS

Company Type: Public

**Income Statement** FYE: December 31

| | REVENUE ($ mil.) | NET INCOME ($ mil.) | NET PROFIT MARGIN | EMPLOYEES |
|---|---|---|---|---|
| **12/06** | 3,302 | 548 | 16.6% | 11,000 |
| **12/05** | 2,915 | 394 | 13.5% | 10,000 |
| **12/04** | 2,294 | 410 | 17.9% | 7,900 |
| **12/03** | 1,933 | 339 | 17.6% | 7,391 |
| **12/02** | 1,590 | 276 | 17.4% | 6,042 |
| **Annual Growth** | 20.1% | 18.7% | — | 16.2% |

**2006 Year-End Financials**

Debt ratio: 28.9%
Return on equity: 18.7%
Cash ($ mil.): 80
Current ratio: 2.50
Long-term debt ($ mil.): 859

No. of shares (mil.): 354
Dividends
Yield: —
Payout: —
Market value ($ mil.): 12,940

**Stock History** NYSE: STJ

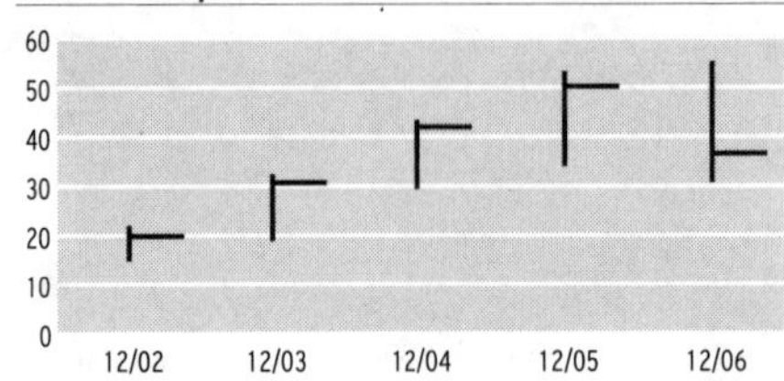


| | STOCK PRICE ($) FY Close | P/E High/Low | PER SHARE ($) Earnings | Dividends | Book Value |
|---|---|---|---|---|---|
| **12/06** | 36.56 | 37 21 | 1.47 | — | 8.39 |
| **12/05** | 50.20 | 51 33 | 1.04 | — | 7.84 |
| **12/04** | 41.93 | 39 27 | 1.10 | — | 6.51 |
| **12/03** | 30.67 | 35 21 | 0.92 | — | 9.27 |
| **12/02** | 19.86 | 29 20 | 0.75 | — | 8.86 |
| **Annual Growth** | 16.5% | — — | 18.3% | — | (1.3%) |

# Saks Incorporated

Once one of the top US department store operators, Saks Inc. has retrenched to focus on its luxury Saks Fifth Avenue Enterprises business. Following the sale of its 38-store Parisian chain to Belk and its 142-store Northern Department Store Group (Bergner's, Boston Store, Carson Pirie Scott, Herberger's, and Younkers) to The Bon-Ton Stores, both in 2006, Saks operates about 55 Saks Fifth Avenue high-end department stores in 25 states, some 50 outlet stores under the Off 5th banner, and more than 80 Club Libby Lu specialty shops (acquired in 2003). The company bought renowned luxury retailer Saks Holdings (owner of Saks Fifth Avenue) and adopted the high-dollar Saks name in 1998.

Saks' divestment of its middle-market department store group reversed a shopping spree that began in 1994. With the purging of non-core operations and rearranging of its retail portfolio, Saks has begun to centralize its executive and finance functions under one roof at Saks in New York, most notably for Saks Fifth Avenue staff, in 2007.

The SEC in March 2005 launched an investigation of the retailer's accounting practices related to alleged improper collection of vendor markdown allowances in one of Saks Fifth Avenue's six merchandising divisions. (As a result, Saks has restated its financial results for fiscal years 2001 through 2004.) An internal investigation by the company's board of directors found that Saks Fifth Avenue had overcharged vendors by more than $34 million. (A previous investigation had put the figure at $20 million.) Saks has announced that it will reimburse vendors to the tune of approximately $48 million. Nevertheless, separate investigations by the SEC and the US attorney's office continue. The SEC investigation of Saks Fifth Avenue has been expanded to include chargebacks — the deductions retailers take on payments to manufacturers for defective or unwanted goods. Saks is also facing lawsuits from several of its suppliers, including Japan's Onward Kashiyama.

Mexican financier Carlos Slim Helu (through Inmobiliaria Carso, S.A. de C.V. ) owns about 9% of Saks. Baugur, the Icelandic investment group that owns stakes in a host of UK retail chains and department stores (Mosaic Fashions, House of Fraser) has acquired an 8% stake in Saks.

Saks has announced plans to open its first Saks Fifth Avenue store in Mexico under a licensing agreement with Operadora de Tiendas Internacionales, an affiliate of Grupo Sanborns. The first SFA store is slated to open in the fall of 2007 in an upscale part of Mexico City.

## HISTORY

J. N. Ellis and D. W. Proffitt founded the Ellis-Proffitt Company store in downtown Maryville, Tennessee, in 1919 with seven departments: Men's, Shoes, Dry Goods, Ladies' Ready to Wear, Ladies' Accessories, Millinery, and Bargain Basement. When Ellis became ill and sold his share in 1921, the store was renamed Proffitt's.

The company added a second store in Athens, Tennessee, in 1936. Proffitt's son, Harwell, took over the two-store company in 1958. He closed the Maryville store in 1962 and opened a new one in a strip shopping center in nearby suburban Alcoa, Tennessee. In 1972 Proffitt's opened a store in the first mall in Knoxville, Tennessee; two years later it opened another store in Oak Ridge, Tennessee. A group including gubernatorial hopeful Brad Martin and Federal Express chairman Fred Smith purchased the Proffitt's chain, which had just opened a fifth store in Knoxville, in 1984 for $14 million. After dropping from the governor's race in 1986, Martin became chairman and took the company public in 1987. It doubled in size the next year when it used the IPO proceeds to acquire five-store, Chattanooga, Tennessee-based Loveman's.

Proffitt's struggled to absorb Loveman's debt and reported weak earnings in 1989 and 1990. The retailer sold more stock and in 1992 and 1993 acquired 16 stores — mostly in Tennessee — at bargain prices from Hess, a struggling Pennsylvania-based chain.

In 1994 Proffitt's began a series of regional department store acquisitions that would build it into the nation's fourth-largest department store chain, including Jackson, Mississippi-based McRae's (28 stores) that year and Des Moines, Iowa-based Younkers (51 stores) and Birmingham, Alabama-based Parisian (38 stores) in 1996. The company acquired St. Cloud, Minnesota-based Herberger's (40 stores) in 1997, and then Proffitt's moved its headquarters from Knoxville to Birmingham, Alabama.

A year later Proffitt's bought Milwaukee-based Carson Pirie Scott & Co. (55 stores, including the Boston Store and Bergner's chains). It also paid $2 billion for one of the crown jewels of American retailing, Saks Holdings, and changed its own name to Saks Incorporated. The acquisition added more than 90 Saks Fifth Avenue and Off 5th discount stores and the Folio and Bullock & Jones catalogs.

Saks went head-to-head with new rival Neiman Marcus in that company's birthplace in 1999, opening a 175,000-sq.-ft., three-level Saks Fifth Avenue store in Dallas. A world away, the company also licensed a Saks Fifth Avenue store in Riyadh, Saudi Arabia.

In April 2003 Saks sold its credit card accounts to Household International for about $1.3 billion (including outstanding balances).

The SEC in March 2005 launched an investigation of the retailer's accounting practices related to alleged improper collection of vendor markdown allowances in one of Saks Fifth Avenue's six merchandising divisions. As a result of an internal investigation the company fired three senior executives, among others, including the brother of CEO R. Brad Martin, in May 2005.

In a move that dissolved the 1998 merger of Saks Fifth Avenue with Proffitt's, Saks sold its 47-store Proffitt's/McRae's business in July 2005 to Belk for $622 million. Also in 2005 Saks closed eight of its Saks Fifth Avenue stores and three of its Off 5th locations, resulting in a total loss of about 700 jobs.

In January 2006 Martin stepped down as CEO of the troubled company and was succeeded by executive vice chairman and COO Stephen I. Sadove. Sadove will also run SFAE, which eliminated the position of chairman and CEO, causing Fred Wilson, who held that position, to resign. In March the company completed the sale of its NDSG to The Bon-Ton Stores for about $1.05 billion. In October Saks completed the previously announced sale of its 38-store Parisian department store chain to Belk for about $285 million.

R. Brad Martin retired as chairman of the company in May 2007. He was succeeded by CEO Stephen Sadove.

## EXECUTIVES

**CEO and Chairman; CEO, Saks Fifth Avenue Enterprises:** Stephen I. (Steve) Sadove, age 55, $1,052,174 pay
**Vice Chairman:** Ronald de Waal, age 55
**President and Chief Merchandising Officer:** Ronald L. (Ron) Frasch, age 58
**EVP and CIO:** G. William (Bill) Franks
**EVP and CFO:** Kevin G. Wills, age 41
**EVP and General Counsel:** Michael A. Brizel, age 49
**EVP, Stores, Store Visual, Planning, and Construction:** Carolyn Biggs, age 59
**EVP, Human Resources:** Christine A. Morena, age 51
**EVP, Operations, e-Business and Credit:** Michael (Mike) Rodgers
**Group SVP, Asset Protection, Store Operations, and Ethics and Compliance:** Thomas (Tom) Matthews, age 52
**Group SVP; President, Off 5TH:** Robert (Rob) Wallstrom, age 41
**Group SVP; General Manager, Saks Fifth Avenue, New York City:** Suzanne (Suzy) Johnson
**Group SVP and General Merchandise Manager, Women's Ready-to-Wear:** Joseph Boitano
**Group SVP and General Merchandise Manager, Women's Shoes, Handbags, and Fine Jewelry:** Jennifer De Winter
**Group SVP; President, Saks Direct:** Denise Incandela, age 42
**Group SVP, Chief Strategy Officer, and Head of Planning:** Marc Metrick, age 33
**SVP Marketing:** Terron Schaeffer, age 62
**SVP and Controller:** Ernest R. LaPorte, age 54
**SVP Human Resources:** Paul Shore
**SVP, Investor Relations and Communications and Corporate Secretary:** Julia A. Bentley, age 48
**Auditors:** PricewaterhouseCoopers LLP

## LOCATIONS

**HQ:** Saks Incorporated
750 Lakeshore Pkwy., Birmingham, AL 35211
**Phone:** 205-940-4000
**Web:** www.saksincorporated.com

## PRODUCTS/OPERATIONS

**2007 Stores**

| | No. |
|---|---|
| Club Libby Lu | 87 |
| Saks Fifth Avenue | 54 |
| Off 5th | 49 |
| **Total** | **190** |

## COMPETITORS

AnnTaylor
Barneys
Bergdorf Goodman
Bloomingdale's
Caché
Dillard's
Elder-Beerman Stores
J. C. Penney
J. Crew
Macy's
Neiman Marcus
Nordstrom
Peebles
Talbots
Tiffany
Von Maur

## HISTORICAL FINANCIALS

Company Type: Public

**Income Statement** — FYE: Saturday nearest January 31

| | REVENUE ($ mil.) | NET INCOME ($ mil.) | NET PROFIT MARGIN | EMPLOYEES |
|---|---|---|---|---|
| **1/07** | 2,940 | 54 | 1.8% | 16,000 |
| **1/06** | 5,953 | 22 | 0.4% | 23,000 |
| **1/05** | 6,437 | 61 | 0.9% | 45,000 |
| **1/04** | 6,055 | 83 | 1.4% | 52,000 |
| **1/03** | 5,911 | 24 | 0.4% | 52,000 |
| **Annual Growth** | (16.0%) | 22.1% | — | (25.5%) |

**2007 Year-End Financials**

Debt ratio: 41.1%
Return on equity: 3.5%
Cash ($ mil.): 278
Current ratio: 1.45
Long-term debt ($ mil.): 450
No. of shares (mil.): 140
Dividends
Yield: 41.2%
Payout: 2,000.0%
Market value ($ mil.): 2,731

**Stock History** — NYSE: SKS

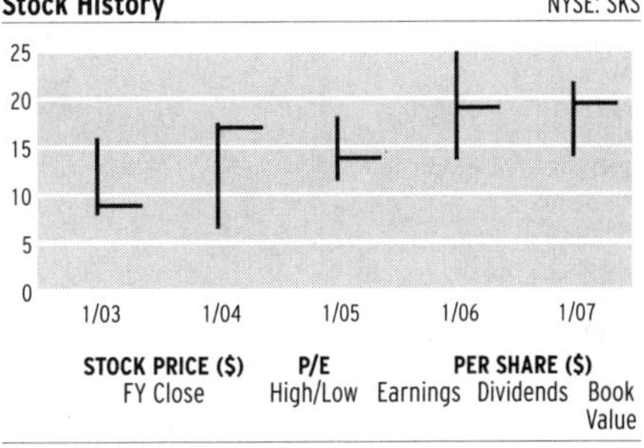


| | STOCK PRICE ($) FY Close | P/E High | P/E Low | PER SHARE ($) Earnings | Dividends | Book Value |
|---|---|---|---|---|---|---|
| **1/07** | 19.44 | 54 | 35 | 0.40 | 8.00 | 7.80 |
| **1/06** | 19.01 | 154 | 86 | 0.16 | — | 14.70 |
| **1/05** | 13.80 | 43 | 28 | 0.42 | 2.00 | 14.88 |
| **1/04** | 17.00 | 30 | 11 | 0.58 | — | 16.37 |
| **1/03** | 8.86 | 93 | 48 | 0.17 | — | 15.64 |
| **Annual Growth** | 21.7% | — | — | 23.9% | 100.0% | (16.0%) |

# SanDisk Corporation

If forgetting things drives you crazy, SanDisk's products might help preserve your sanity. The company is a top producer of data storage products based on flash memory, which retains data even when power is interrupted. SanDisk's products include removable and embedded memory cards used in digital cameras, personal digital assistants, networking equipment, medical devices, and other electronics. The company sells to manufacturers such as Canon, Eastman Kodak, Ericsson, Matsushita, and Siemens, as well as through retailers, including Best Buy, Circuit City, and Office Depot. SanDisk has become a leading competitor in the market for MP3 music players with its Sansa brand players.

SanDisk has signed joint product development deals with Hynix Semiconductor, Microsoft, and Qimonda, among other companies. Microsoft and SanDisk will collaborate on developing USB flash drives and flash memory cards incorporating SanDisk's U3 Smart Technology drive platform (which is supported by independent software developers) and TrustedFlash security technology. Products stemming from the Microsoft agreement are scheduled to emerge in the second half of 2008.

In late 2006 SanDisk purchased rival msystems for about $1.5 billion in stock. After passing on an opportunity to acquire competitor Lexar Media (which went to chip maker Micron Technology earlier in 2006), SanDisk pursued msystems instead, widening its portfolio of flash memory-based data storage products.

Responding to the dramatic collapse of prices in the NAND flash memory market, SanDisk set a number of cost-cutting measures in early 2007. These included the layoff of up to 10% of the worldwide staff (approximately 250 employees), salary cuts for senior executives, salary freezes for all other employees, and a hiring freeze for most areas.

SanDisk, which holds more than 700 patents in flash memory technology, licenses its technology to customers such as Intel, Sharp, Sony, and Toshiba. The company has formed several joint ventures with Toshiba — Flash Alliance, Flash Partners, and FlashVision — which manufacture flash storage cards for cell phones and digital audio players and cameras.

Toshiba Semiconductor operates three memory chip fabs in Yokkaichi, Japan, and in 2006 SanDisk and Toshiba set plans to build a fourth fab at Yokkaichi that will manufacture NAND flash memory chips; estimated price tag is $5.2 billion. Construction of Fab 4 began in the summer of 2006, with initial production expected in the second half of 2007. Toshiba will pay for the facility's construction, while SanDisk and Toshiba will share the cost of equipping it, which is generally the more expensive part of putting up a new semiconductor plant. While more and more consumer electronics products are incorporating NAND flash memory, SanDisk and Toshiba are making an expensive bet that demand for those chips will remain high in 2008, when Fab 4 will fully come on-line.

Entities controlled by Capital Group International own nearly 14% of SanDisk, while those controlled by CAM North America hold nearly 8% of the company.

## HISTORY

SanDisk was founded as SunDisk in 1988 by Eli Harari (now CEO), an expert on nonvolatile memory technology. SunDisk's first product, based on a four-megabit flash chip, was developed with AT&T Bell Labs and released in 1991. In 1992 the company formed a development partnership with disk drive maker Seagate Technology; as part of the pact, Seagate acquired 25% of SunDisk.

Because SunDisk was being confused with Sun Microsystems, in 1995 the company changed its name to SanDisk. It went public that year and introduced the industry's smallest Type II (a PC card slot size designation) flash storage card — the CompactFlash. Sales increased by nearly 80% in 1995, SanDisk's first profitable year. The next year SanDisk and Matsushita developed double-density flash, a breakthrough technology that doubled the capacity of flash storage products.

In 1997 SanDisk started production of its double-density flash series, investing $40 million in a semiconductor plant in Taiwan with United Microelectronics. In 1999 SanDisk said it would move about 75% of its production to China, partly through a partnership with Celestica.

In 2000 Seagate divested the last of its ownership stake in SanDisk. Also that year, SanDisk and Toshiba formed a joint venture, FlashVision, to produce advanced flash memory at a Toshiba semiconductor plant in Virginia. FlashVision commenced production the following year. (The joint venture's operations were moved to one of Toshiba's Japanese plants after Toshiba announced the sale of the Virginia factory — which had primarily made DRAM chips — to Micron Technology at the end of 2001.)

SanDisk and Toshiba consolidated manufacturing at Toshiba's Yokkaichi memory fab in 2002.

In 2004 SanDisk opened a retail distribution center in China and formed a new joint venture with Toshiba, Flash Partners, for the purpose of adding manufacturing capacity.

The following year, Toshiba began operation of a new fab in Yokkaichi for making NAND flash memory devices. The semiconductors will be produced on silicon wafers measuring 300mm (12 inches) across.

In 2006 SanDisk acquired Matrix Semiconductor, a developer of 3-D, one-time programmable (OTP) chip technology, for about $300 million in stock and cash. The companies began working together on integrating the Matrix technology into SanDisk's product line.

## EXECUTIVES

**Chairman, President, and CEO:** Eli Harari, age 61, $800,419 pay
**Vice Chairman:** Irwin Federman, age 72
**President and COO:** Sanjay Mehrotra, age 48, $469,623 pay
**EVP, Administration and CFO:** Judy Bruner, age 48, $397,425 pay
**EVP, Mobile Business Unit and Corporate Engineering:** Yoram Cedar, age 54, $367,414 pay
**EVP, Technology and Worldwide Operations:** Randhir Thakur, $365,863 pay
**SVP, Worldwide Operations and Supply Chain:** Juha Raisanen
**VP, Business Development:** Richard S. O. (Rich) Chernicoff
**VP, Environmental Health and Safety:** LeVerne Kelley
**VP, Human Resources:** Tom Baker
**VP, Retail Sales:** Rick Dyer
**President, SanDisk Limited:** Atsuyoshi Koike, age 53
**Director, Investor Relations:** Lori Barker
**Director, Product Marketing:** Doreet Oren
**Auditors:** Ernst & Young LLP

## LOCATIONS

**HQ:** SanDisk Corporation
601 McCarthy Blvd., Milpitas, CA 95035
**Phone:** 408-801-1000 **Fax:** 408-801-8657
**Web:** www.sandisk.com

SanDisk has facilities in China, Germany, Hong Kong, India, Ireland, Israel, Japan, the Netherlands, South Korea, Spain, Taiwan, the UK, and the US.

### 2006 Sales

| | $ mil. | % of total |
|---|---|---|
| North America | 1,311.7 | 40 |
| Europe, Middle East & Africa | 728.4 | 23 |
| Japan | 231.8 | 7 |
| Other regions | 985.6 | 30 |
| **Total** | **3,257.5** | **100** |

## PRODUCTS/OPERATIONS

### 2006 Sales

| | $ mil. | % of total |
|---|---|---|
| Products | 2,926.5 | 90 |
| Licenses & royalties | 331.0 | 10 |
| **Total** | **3,257.5** | **100** |

### Selected Products

Embedded data storage devices (FlashDrive)
MP3 music players (Sansa)
Portable storage devices (Cruzer)
Removable storage cards (used in cellular phones, digital cameras, digital music players, digital voice recorders, and personal digital assistants)
- CompactFlash
- Memory Stick
- MultiMedia
- Secure Digital
- SmartMedia

## COMPETITORS

Apple
Atmel
Buffalo Technology
Creative Technology
Eastman Kodak
FUJIFILM
Hynix
Intel
Iomega
Kingston Technology
Lexar
Macronix International
Matsushita Electric
Memorex
Micron Technology
Netlist
PNY Technologies
Qimonda
Reigncom
Renesas
Saifun
Samsung Electronics
Sharp
Silicon Storage
SMART Modular
SmartDisk
Sony
Southland Micro
STEC
STMicroelectronics
TDK
Toshiba
Viking InterWorks

## HISTORICAL FINANCIALS

Company Type: Public

### Income Statement

FYE: December 31

| | REVENUE ($ mil.) | NET INCOME ($ mil.) | NET PROFIT MARGIN | EMPLOYEES |
|---|---|---|---|---|
| **12/06** | 3,258 | 199 | 6.1% | 2,586 |
| **12/05** | 2,306 | 386 | 16.8% | 1,083 |
| **12/04** | 1,777 | 267 | 15.0% | 876 |
| **12/03** | 1,080 | 169 | 15.6% | 805 |
| **12/02** | 541 | 36 | 6.7% | 629 |
| **Annual Growth** | 56.6% | 53.1% | — | 42.4% |

### 2006 Year-End Financials

Debt ratio: 25.7%
Return on equity: 5.5%
Cash ($ mil.): 2,832
Current ratio: 4.73
Long-term debt ($ mil.): 1,225
No. of shares (mil.): 227
Dividends
Yield: —
Payout: —
Market value ($ mil.): 9,747

### Stock History

NASDAQ (GS): SNDK

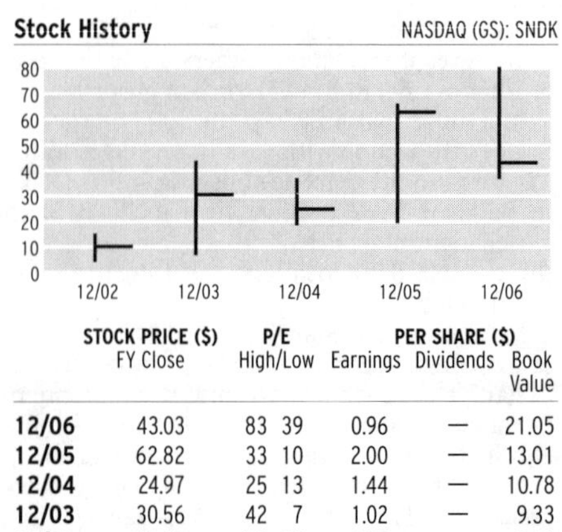


| | STOCK PRICE ($) FY Close | P/E High | P/E Low | PER SHARE ($) Earnings | Dividends | Book Value |
|---|---|---|---|---|---|---|
| **12/06** | 43.03 | 83 | 39 | 0.96 | — | 21.05 |
| **12/05** | 62.82 | 33 | 10 | 2.00 | — | 13.01 |
| **12/04** | 24.97 | 25 | 13 | 1.44 | — | 10.78 |
| **12/03** | 30.56 | 42 | 7 | 1.02 | — | 9.33 |
| **12/02** | 10.15 | 57 | 19 | 0.25 | — | 9.08 |
| **Annual Growth** | 43.5% | — | — | 40.0% | — | 23.4% |

# Sanmina-SCI

Sanmina-SCI's services help keep electronics makers sane. The company is a top contract manufacturer of sophisticated electronic components, including printed circuit boards and backplane assemblies (circuit boards with slots and sockets for plugging in other boards and cables). Other Sanmina-SCI products include cable and wiring harness assemblies, custom enclosures, and memory modules. In addition, the company provides services such as design and engineering, materials management, order fulfillment, and in-circuit testing. Customers include IBM (about 13% of sales), Lenovo Group (11%), Hewlett-Packard (10%), Philips, Applied Materials, and Nokia.

Operations in regions outside of the US account for about three-quarters of Sanmina-SCI's sales. Its customers include companies in the communications, computing, multimedia, medical, automotive, and defense and aerospace markets. Manufacturing services related to personal computers account for nearly a third of its sales.

Having lost money for five straight years, Sanmina-SCI is restructuring its worldwide operations to cut costs. Among the moves made by the company is the closing of its Phoenix plant in mid-2007, resulting in the layoff of some 600 employees.

Sanmina-SCI plans to build a manufacturing complex near Chennai, its first plant in India. The company has selected a site of approximately 100 acres in Oragadam. The facilities also will house Sanmina-SCI's operations in engineering, IT services, and supply chain management, presently located in Chennai.

The company's $6 billion acquisition of rival SCI Systems in 2001 vaulted Sanmina-SCI into the top ranks with contract manufacturers such as Flextronics and Solectron. The deal also crowned a buying spree that has expanded the company into Europe and Asia, and into a growing number of markets. In several cases Sanmina-SCI has acquired manufacturing facilities from major customers, such as IBM and Elscint, in deals that have included long-term contracts for Sanmina-SCI to supply products back to those same customers.

Like dozens of other tech companies, Sanmina-SCI found problems in 2006 with its past practices in granting stock options to executives and other employees. An internal investigation by a special board committee, going back to the beginning of 1997, found that most grants in the prior decade were not correctly dated or accounted for, requiring the company to restate financial results and record non-cash compensation charges.

Among other changes recommended by the special committee, the board adopted a policy of establishing fixed dates for granting equity-based awards, reducing or eliminating the possibility of backdating or springloading options.

AXA Financial and affiliated entities own 13% of Sanmina-SCI. Barclays Global Investors holds nearly 6% of the company, as does EARNEST Partners.

## HISTORY

Bosnian immigrants Jure Sola (chairman and CEO) and Milan Mandaric founded Sanmina in 1980 to provide just-in-time manufacturing of printed circuit boards (PCBs). The name Sanmina comes from the names of Mandaric's children.

During the late 1980s and early 1990s Sanmina shifted production to higher-margin components, such as backplane assemblies and subassemblies. Mandaric, an entrepreneur with other interests, left in 1989. The company went public in 1993.

Like other contract manufacturers, Sanmina began bolstering its operations through acquisitions. The company bought manufacturing plants from Comptronix (1994), Assembly Solutions (1995), Golden Eagle Systems (1996), and Lucent Technologies (1996). In 1997 the company bought contract electronics maker Elexsys International, which was headed by Milan Mandaric. Sanmina also opened a plant in Ireland.

Sanmina's 1998 acquisitions included Massachusetts-based Altron, its #1 competitor in backplane manufacturing. In 1999 the company acquired assets from Nortel Networks and Devtek Electronics Enclosure, a designer of enclosure systems for the telecommunications and networking industries.

In 2000 Sanmina acquired PCB maker Hadco in a $1.3 billion deal, expanding its global presence. That year the company also purchased Swedish contract manufacturer Essex AB, entered into a joint venture with Siemens to manufacture complex PCBs, and acquired some plants from Nortel and Lucent.

In mid-2001 Sanmina agreed to buy rival SCI Systems, one of the world's largest contract manufacturers, for about $4.5 billion. (Sanmina also assumed $1.5 billion of SCI's debt.) Later that year it also acquired a facility in Texas from (and signed a multiyear supplier agreement with) French telecom titan Alcatel (now Alcatel-Lucent). When its acquisition of SCI Systems closed late in the year, Sanmina changed its name to Sanmina-SCI. (Sola and SCI Systems chairman and CEO Eugene Sapp became co-chairmen; Sola remained CEO of the combined company.)

Sanmina-SCI forged several deals in early 2002. The company announced a three-year, $5 billion agreement with IBM to produce desktop PCs. As part of the deal, Sanmina-SCI acquired two US plants from IBM. In addition, Sanmina-SCI and HP penned a deal whereby the company produces some HP products and acquired HP's manufacturing operations in France for $65.8 million. Also that year Sanmina-SCI acquired plants in France, Germany, and Spain from Alcatel for $129.9 million as part of a multiyear supply agreement. All three deals were completed by mid-year.

Also in 2002 Sanmina-SCI acquired privately held Viking Components (custom memory modules and modems) for $11 million. It later combined the company with another subsidiary to form Viking InterWorks.

After a year as co-chairman, Eugene Sapp stepped down from that post in late 2002, while remaining a director of the company.

In 2003 Sanmina-SCI acquired privately held Newisys, a developer of enterprise-class servers. The following year Sanmina-SCI acquired Singapore-based Pentex-Schweizer Circuits (printed circuit board fabrication services) for about $80 million.

In mid-2006 the company opened a new enclosures manufacturing facility, measuring 347,000 sq. ft., in Guadalajara, Mexico.

Sanmina-SCI shuttered Newisys in 2007, laying off 87 employees.

## EXECUTIVES

**Chairman and CEO:** Jure Sola, age 56, $750,000 pay
**President, Global EMS Operations:** Hari Pillai, age 46, $541,500 pay
**President and General Manager, PCB Fabrication Division:** Stephen F. (Steve) Bruton
**EVP, Finance, CFO, and Secretary:** David L. White, age 51, $485,000 pay
**EVP, Memory Modules:** Ralph Kaplan
**EVP, Worldwide Sales and Marketing:** Dennis Young, age 55, $407,181 pay
**SVP and Chief Information Officer:** Manesh Patel
**Director, Corporate Marketing:** Michael Kovacs
**Director, Marketing Communications and Public Relations, Europe:** Ulrike Winter
**Investor Relations:** Paige Bombino
**President, Technology Components Group:** Walt Hussey
**Auditors:** KPMG LLP

## LOCATIONS

**HQ:** Sanmina-SCI Corporation
2700 N. 1st St., San Jose, CA 95134
**Phone:** 408-964-3500 **Fax:** 408-964-3636
**Web:** www.sanmina-sci.com

Sanmina-SCI has manufacturing facilities in Australia, Brazil, Canada, China, Finland, France, Germany, Hungary, Indonesia, Ireland, Israel, Japan, Malaysia, Mexico, Singapore, Sweden, Taiwan, Thailand, the UK, and the US.

**2006 Sales**

| | $ mil. | % of total |
|---|---|---|
| US | 2,722.7 | 25 |
| Other countries | 8,232.7 | 75 |
| **Total** | **10,955.4** | **100** |

## PRODUCTS/OPERATIONS

**2006 Sales**

| | $ mil. | % of total |
|---|---|---|
| Personal computing | 3,240.7 | 30 |
| Other | 7,714.7 | 70 |
| **Total** | **10,955.4** | **100** |

**Selected Services**
Backplane assembly
Cable assembly
Circuit assembly
Circuit fabrication
Configuration
Distribution
Enclosures
Engineering
In-circuit testing
Materials management
Order fulfillment
Printed circuit board design
System assembly and testing

## COMPETITORS

Benchmark Electronics
BenQ
Cal-Comp Electronics
Celestica
CTS
Elcoteq
Flextronics
Hon Hai
IBM Canada
Inventec
Jabil
Merix
Nam Tai
Plexus
SMTC
Solectron
Suntron
SYNNEX
TTM Technologies
Viasystems

## HISTORICAL FINANCIALS

Company Type: Public

**Income Statement** FYE: September 30

| | REVENUE ($ mil.) | NET INCOME ($ mil.) | NET PROFIT MARGIN | EMPLOYEES |
|---|---|---|---|---|
| **9/06** | 10,955 | (142) | — | 54,397 |
| **9/05** | 11,735 | (1,006) | — | 48,621 |
| **9/04** | 12,205 | (11) | — | 48,721 |
| **9/03** | 10,361 | (137) | — | 45,008 |
| **9/02** | 8,762 | (2,697) | — | 46,030 |
| **Annual Growth** | 5.7% | — | — | 4.3% |

**2006 Year-End Financials**

Debt ratio: 66.4%
Return on equity: —
Cash ($ mil.): 492
Current ratio: 1.77
Long-term debt ($ mil.): 1,507
No. of shares (mil.): 533
Dividends
Yield: —
Payout: —
Market value ($ mil.): 1,993

**Stock History** NASDAQ (GS): SANM

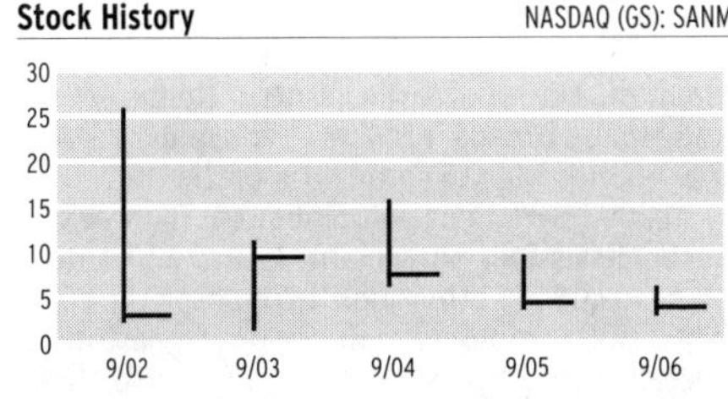


| | STOCK PRICE ($) FY Close | P/E High | P/E Low | PER SHARE ($) Earnings | PER SHARE ($) Dividends | PER SHARE ($) Book Value |
|---|---|---|---|---|---|---|
| **9/06** | 3.74 | — | — | (0.27) | — | 4.26 |
| **9/05** | 4.29 | — | — | (1.93) | — | 4.52 |
| **9/04** | 7.41 | — | — | (0.02) | — | 6.42 |
| **9/03** | 9.36 | — | — | (0.27) | — | 6.50 |
| **9/02** | 2.96 | — | — | (5.60) | — | 6.50 |
| **Annual Growth** | 6.0% | — | — | — | — | (10.0%) |

# Sara Lee

Sara Lee sliced up its portfolio and chose cheesecake over clothing. Jettisoning its apparel businesses, Sara Lee now has three business groups. The Sara Lee Food & Beverage business group is a major US packaged-meat maker (Ball Park, Jimmy Dean), and a leading US provider of fresh sliced bread as well as those famous raid-the-refrigerator-at-midnight frozen cheesecakes. The Sara Lee International group oversees non-North American beverage and bakery sales and its worldwide Household & Body Care business segment. The Sara Lee Foodservice group supplies coffee, meat, and bakery products to US foodservice companies.

Chairman and CEO Brenda Barnes was given the keys to the Sara Lee kingdom in 2005.

To streamline Sara Lee's operations into cohesive units, Barnes oversaw the spin-off of its $4.5 billion Americas/Asia Branded Apparel group (consisting of Hanes, Champion, Playtex, and other brands) to form an independent, publicly traded company called Hanesbrands Inc., which began trading in September 2006. This move dictated cutting some 775 positions. All the shares owned by Sara Lee were distributed to Sara Lee shareholders at the time of the spin-off.

Sara Lee also sold its $1.2 billion European apparel business to Florida's Sun Capital Partners, which included the Dim, Playtex, Wonderbra, Abanderado, Nur Die, and Unno brands, but excluded the company's UK-based Sara Lee Courtaulds division, in 2006.

All the units sold or spun off represented some $8.2 billion in sales, or about 40% of the firm's annual revenue. This was a significant change to Sara Lee's portfolio, particularly since it had been growing more diverse. The company, though, plans to retain its focus on food, beverage, and household products.

As Sara Lee has shed its clothing units, it's looking to add breadth to its surviving sectors. In early 2006 the firm inked an agreement with Butter-Krust Baking, valued at about $72 million, to give its food operation a needed boost in the mid-Atlantic region. The deal, which brings Holsum, Butter-Krust Country, Roman Meal, and Milano brands into Sara Lee's fold, raises its market coverage to some 80% of the US.

In 2007 Sara Lee laid off about 1,700 workers at its Mississippi pork plant. It also announced plans to cut 489 other jobs throughout the company. Both employee-reductions are part of its overall restructuring plan. Sara Lee also sliced about a dozen top management jobs in 2007, including the chief of its international business, to streamline management operations.

Capital Group Companies' Capital Research and Management owns about 8% of Sara Lee.

## HISTORY

Businessman Nathan Cummings bought the C. D. Kenny Co., a Baltimore coffee, tea, and sugar wholesaler, in 1939. Cummings soon purchased several grocery firms and later changed the company's name to Consolidated Grocers (1945). The operation went public in 1946 and was renamed Consolidated Foods Corp. (CFC) in 1954.

Two years later CFC bought the Kitchens of Sara Lee, a Chicago bakery founded by Charles Lubin in 1951. Introduced in 1949 and named after Lubin's daughter, Sara Lee cheesecake had become the bakery's most popular product.

In 1968 CFC sold its Eagle Complex, which included Piggly Wiggly Midwest supermarkets and Eagle Food Centers, and it bought Bryan Foods. The firm continued to buy and sell businesses in the US, including beverage, appliance, and chemical companies. Some major US purchases were Hanes Corp. (1979), Jimmy Dean Meat Co. (1984), Coach Leatherware International (1985), and Champion Products (athletic knitwear, 1989). Cummings served as president until 1970.

CFC began building its international markets with its first European acquisition in 1962. Following that purchase, it expanded its global presence with the purchases of Douwe Egberts (coffee, tea, and tobacco; the Netherlands; 1978), Nicholas Kiwi (shoe care and pharmaceuticals, Australia, 1984), and Dim (hosiery and underwear, France, 1989).

Using one of its most respected brand names to enhance the public's awareness of the company, CFC changed its name to Sara Lee in 1985. It continued making acquisitions in the 1990s, including Playtex Apparel.

In 1997 Sara Lee began a restructuring that included selling non-core businesses and increasing its use of outsourcing, closed more than 90 manufacturing and distribution facilities, and laid off 9,400 employees (about 7% of its workforce). It also closed its Mark Cross leather goods business.

Sara Lee sold its loose tobacco business (Amphora, Drum, Van Nelle) in 1998 to the UK's Imperial Tobacco for $1.1 billion; bought undergarments maker Strouse, Adler; and purchased Quaker Oats' coffee marketer, Continental Coffee Products. Also that year Sara Lee recalled hot dogs and packaged meats produced by its Bil Mar Foods unit after the items were linked to nearly two dozen fatal food-poisoning cases. (The company settled class-action suits over the incident in 2000.)

While closing more than 100 facilities, during 1999 Sara Lee continued acquiring, including coffee company Chock full o'Nuts, and the Hills Bros., MJB, and Chase & Sanborn coffee operations from Nestlé. It also bought Royal Ahold's Dutch meat processing units, Meester and Nistria; J.E. Morgan Knitting Mills (maker of Duofold thermal underwear); and the UK's leading intimate apparel and underwear producer, Courtaulds Textiles.

During 2000 Sara Lee spun off its Coach (leather goods) business and sold off its foodservice operation, PYA/Monarch, to a Royal Ahold subsidiary as the first move to refocus on its core brands. In July 2000 president Steven McMillan added the CEO title to his duties; he was named chairman that October.

In 2001 Sara Lee continued to dispose of noncore operations. However, in August that year it acquired The Earthgrains Company, the second-largest fresh-bread company in the US; the combined bakery operations of the companies were renamed the Sara Lee Bakery Group.

The Sara Lee Bakery Group was slapped with a $5.25 million fine in 2003 when the EPA determined that ozone-depleting chemicals were leaking from refrigeration systems in many of its plants. The company agreed to pay the fine and spend an additional $5 million on repairs.

In 2005 McMillan retired and handed over the titles of president, CEO, and chairman to Brenda Barnes, who instituted a total reorganization of the company.

## EXECUTIVES

**Chairman and CEO:** Brenda C. Barnes, age 53, $2,144,000 pay
**EVP and Chief Financial and Administrative Officer:** Lambertus M. (Theo) de Kool, age 53, $1,577,590 pay
**EVP; Chairman of the Board of Management and CEO, Sara Lee International B.V.:** Adriaan Nühn, age 53
**EVP, General Counsel, and Secretary:** Roderick A. Palmore, age 55, $796,569 pay
**EVP Human Resources:** Stephen J. Cerrone
**SVP and CIO:** George Chappelle, age 43
**SVP; CEO, Sara Lee Food and Beverage:** Christopher J. (CJ) Fraleigh, age 43, $1,185,211 pay
**SVP; President, Household and Body Care:** Vincent H. A. M. Janssen
**SVP; CFO Sara Lee Foodservice:** Diana S. Ferguson, age 43
**SVP, Chief People Officer:** Lois M. Huggins, age 44
**SVP, Research & Development Sara Lee Foodservice:** Paul Bernthal
**SVP, Taxes:** Donald L. Meier, age 61
**SVP, Strategic Planning and Corporate Development:** B. Thomas Hansson
**SVP, Controller, and Principal Accounting Officer:** Richard A. Hoker
**SVP, Corporate Affairs:** J. Randall White
**SVP; CEO, Sara Lee Foodservice:** James W. Nolan, age 49
**SVP; CEO, Coffee and Tea Division, Sara Lee International:** Frank van Oers, age 47
**VP; President, Bakery Group — Worldwide Fresh Bakery Products:** William H. Opdyke, age 57
**VP; President, Sara Lee Foods Retail, Sara Lee Food & Beverage:** Ellen L. Turner, age 43
**VP; President, US Fresh Bakery Sara Lee Bakery Group:** William J. Nictakis, age 44
**VP, Marketing:** Debra Vicchiarelli
**VP, Corporate Communications:** Julie Ketay
**Executive Director, Investor Relations:** Aaron Hoffman
**Auditors:** PricewaterhouseCoopers LLP

## LOCATIONS

**HQ:** Sara Lee Corporation
3500 Lacey Rd., Downers Grove, IL 60515
**Phone:** 630-598-8100 **Fax:** 630-598-8482
**Web:** www.saralee.com

## PRODUCTS/OPERATIONS

### Selected Brand Names

Branded Apparel
- Bali
- barely there
- Champion
- Hanes
- Just My Size
- Playtex
- Wonderbra

Household and Body Care
- Ambi Pur
- Bloom
- Catch
- Duschdas
- GoodKnight
- Kiwi
- Meltonian
- Monsavon
- Prodent
- Radox
- Ridsect
- Sanex
- Vapona

International Bakery
- Bimbo
- BonGateaux
- Coursti Pate
- Oritz
- Sara Lee

International Beverage
- Café Cabocio
- Café do Ponto
- Douwe Egberts
- Maison du Café
- Marcilla
- Merrild
- Pickwick
- Senseo

North American Retail Bakery
- Colonial
- Earth's Grains
- Healthy Choice
- Holsum
- IronKids
- Mother's
- Rainbo
- Sara Lee
- Sunbeam

North American Retail Meats
- Ball Park
- Best's Kosher
- Bryan
- Duby (Mexico)
- Hillshire Farm
- Jimmy Dean
- Kir (Mexico)
- Zwan (Mexico)

## COMPETITORS

Avon
Bimbo Bakeries
Canada Bread Company
Cheesecake Factory
Clorox
Colgate-Palmolive
ConAgra
Farmland Foods
Flowers Foods
George Weston Bakeries
Hormel
Interstate Bakeries
JBS Swift
Johnsonville Sausage
Jones Dairy Farm
Karl Ehmer
Kellogg
Kraft Foods
Lavazza
Maple Leaf Foods
Nestlé
Plumrose USA
Procter & Gamble
Tyson Foods
Usinger's

## HISTORICAL FINANCIALS

Company Type: Public

**Income Statement** FYE: Saturday nearest June 30

| | REVENUE ($ mil.) | NET INCOME ($ mil.) | NET PROFIT MARGIN | EMPLOYEES |
|---|---|---|---|---|
| **6/07** | 12,278 | 504 | 4.1% | 52,400 |
| **6/06** | 15,944 | 555 | 3.5% | 109,000 |
| **6/05** | 19,254 | 719 | 3.7% | 137,000 |
| **6/04** | 19,566 | 1,272 | 6.5% | 150,400 |
| **6/03** | 18,291 | 1,221 | 6.7% | 145,800 |
| **Annual Growth** | (9.5%) | (19.8%) | — | (22.6%) |

**2007 Year-End Financials**

Debt ratio: 107.2%
Return on equity: 19.9%
Cash ($ mil.): 2,520
Current ratio: 1.31
Long-term debt ($ mil.): 2,803
No. of shares (mil.): 724
Dividends
Yield: 2.3%
Payout: 58.8%
Market value ($ mil.): 12,605

**Stock History** NYSE: SLE

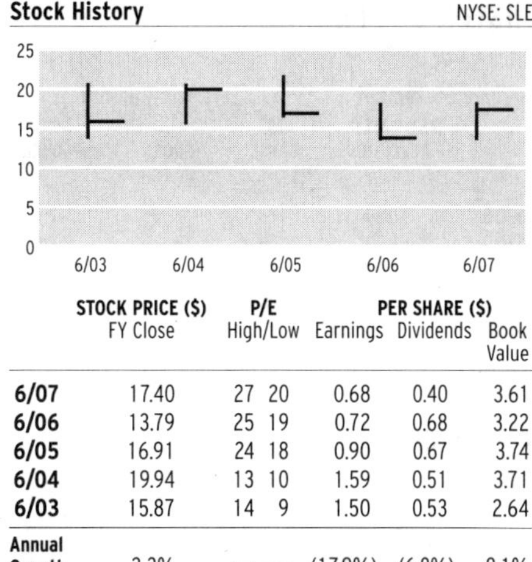


| | STOCK PRICE ($) FY Close | P/E High | P/E Low | PER SHARE ($) Earnings | Dividends | Book Value |
|---|---|---|---|---|---|---|
| **6/07** | 17.40 | 27 | 20 | 0.68 | 0.40 | 3.61 |
| **6/06** | 13.79 | 25 | 19 | 0.72 | 0.68 | 3.22 |
| **6/05** | 16.91 | 24 | 18 | 0.90 | 0.67 | 3.74 |
| **6/04** | 19.94 | 13 | 10 | 1.59 | 0.51 | 3.71 |
| **6/03** | 15.87 | 14 | 9 | 1.50 | 0.53 | 2.64 |
| **Annual Growth** | 2.3% | — | — | (17.9%) | (6.8%) | 8.1% |

# S.C. Johnson & Son

S.C. Johnson & Son helped to replace the flyswatter with the spray can. The firm is one of the world's largest makers of consumer chemical products, including Brise, Drano, Edge, Fantastik, Glade, Kabbikiller, Mr. Muscle, OFF!, Pledge, Raid, Scrubbing Bubbles, Saran, Shout, Vanish, Windex, and Ziploc. With operations on six continents, its international business generates some 60% of sales. The founder's great-grandson and once one of the richest men in the US, Samuel Johnson died in 2004. His immediate family owns about 60% of S.C. Johnson; descendants of the founder's daughter own about 40%. President, CEO, and director Bill Perez left for Nike in late 2004 and chairman Dr. Fisk Johnson replaced him as CEO.

Many of S.C. Johnson's products have been and remain top sellers in their market categories. The company has operations in nearly 70 countries and its products are available in more than 100. In 2006 *Working Mother* magazine again recognized S.C. Johnson as one of the 100 best companies for working mothers.

The company's commercial products division (Johnson Wax Professional and Johnson Polymer) has been spun off as a private company owned by the Johnson family. The company also has sold most of its personal care line.

## HISTORY

Samuel C. Johnson, a carpenter whose customers were as interested in his floor wax as in his parquet floors, founded S.C. Johnson in Racine, Wisconsin, in 1886. Forsaking carpentry, Johnson began to manufacture floor care products. The company, named S.C. Johnson & Son in 1906, began establishing subsidiaries worldwide in 1914. By the time Johnson's son and successor, Herbert Johnson, died in 1928, annual sales were $5 million. Herbert Jr. and his sister, Henrietta Lewis, received 60% and 40% of the firm, respectively. The original section of S.C. Johnson's headquarters, designed by Frank Lloyd Wright and called "the greatest piece of 20th-century architecture" in the US, was finished in 1939.

In 1954, with $45 million in annual sales, Herbert Jr.'s son Samuel Curtis Johnson joined the company as new products director. Two years later it introduced Raid, the first water-based insecticide, and soon thereafter, OFF! insect repellent. Each became a market leader. The company unsuccessfully attempted to diversify into paint, chemicals, and lawn care during the 1950s and 1960s. The home care products segment prospered, however, with the introduction of Pledge aerosol furniture polish and Glade aerosol air freshener.

After Herbert Jr. suffered a stroke in 1965, Samuel became president. In 1975 the firm banned the use of the chlorofluorocarbons (CFCs) in its products, three years before the US government banned CFCs. Samuel started a recreational products division that was bought by the Johnson family in 1986. That company went public in 1987 as Johnson Worldwide Associates, with the family retaining control.

The company launched Edge shaving gel and Agree hair products in the 1970s but had few products as successful in the 1980s. It moved into real estate with Johnson Wax Development (JWD) in the 1970s, but sold JWD's assets in the late 1980s.

S. Curtis Johnson, Samuel's son, joined the company in 1983. In 1986 S.C. Johnson bought Bugs Burger Bug Killers, moving into commercial pest control; in 1990 it entered into an agreement with Mycogen to develop biological pesticides for household use.

In 1993 it bought Drackett, bringing Drano and Windex to its product roster along with increased competition from heavyweights such as Procter & Gamble and Clorox. That year S.C. Johnson sold the Agree and Halsa lines to DEP. In 1996 it launched a line of water-soluble pouches for cleaning products that allow work to be done without touching hazardous chemicals. President William Perez became CEO the next year (and left in late 2004 to become president, CEO, and director of Nike, Inc.).

S.C. Johnson bought Dow Chemical's DowBrands unit, maker of bathroom cleaner (Dow), plastic bags (Ziploc), and plastic wrap (Saran Wrap), for $1.2 billion in 1998. It then sold off other Dow brands (cleaners Spray 'N Wash, Glass Plus, Yes, and Vivid) to the UK's Reckitt & Colman to settle antitrust issues.

A year later S.C. Johnson sold its skin care line, including Aveeno, to health care products maker Johnson & Johnson, and spun off its commercial products unit as a private firm owned by the Johnson family. Boosting its home cleaning line, in 1999 it introduced two new products: AllerCare (for dust mite control) and Pledge Grab-It (electrostatically charged cleaning sheets).

In 2000 S.C. Johnson pulled its AllerCare carpet powder and allergen spray from store shelves after some consumers had negative reactions to the fragrance additive in the products. That year H. Fisk Johnson succeeded his father (who became chairman emeritus) as chairman.

In 2001 the company was fined $950,000 for selling banned Raid Max Roach Bait traps in New York after agreeing to pull them from store shelves. Also that year S.C. Johnson's Japanese subsidiary agreed to buy that country's leading drain cleaner brand, Pipe Unish, from Unicharm.

In October 2002 the company acquired the household insecticides unit of German drug giant Bayer Group for $734 million. The following year S.C. Johnson invested in Karamchand Appliances Private Limited, which owns India's second-leading insect control brand *AllOut*.

Chairman emeritus Samuel C. Johnson died in May 2004 at the age of 76. Chairman Dr. Fisk Johnson became CEO of the company again in late 2004.

## EXECUTIVES

**Chairman and CEO:** H. Fisk Johnson, age 45
**President, Americas:** Pedro Cieza
**President, Asia:** Steven P. Stanbrook, age 46
**President, Europe, Africa, and Near East Region (EurAFNE):** Patrick J. O'Brien
**President, North America:** David L. (Dave) May
**EVP and CFO:** W. Lee McCollum, age 57
**EVP, Worldwide Corporate and Environmental Affairs:** Jane M. Hutterly
**EVP, Worldwide Human Resources:** Gayle P. Kosterman
**SVP, New Products:** Gregory J. (Greg) Barron
**SVP, General Counsel, and Secretary:** David Hecker
**SVP, Worldwide Manufacturing and Procurement:** Darcy D. Massey
**VP and Corporate Treasurer:** William H. Van Lopik
**VP and General Manager, Mexico and Central America:** Eduardo Ortiz-Tirado
**VP and Group Managing Director, Europe:** Filippo Meroni
**VP and CIO:** Mark H. Eckhardt
**VP, North American Sales:** Darwin Lewis
**VP, Marketing Services:** Patricia Penman
**VP, Human Resources Asia Pacific:** Jeffrey M. (Jeff) Waller
**VP, Global Public Affairs and Communications:** Kelly M. Semrau

## LOCATIONS

**HQ:** S.C. Johnson & Son, Inc.
1525 Howe St., Racine, WI 53403
**Phone:** 262-260-2000 **Fax:** 262-260-6004
**Web:** www.scjohnson.com

S.C. Johnson & Son has operations in nearly 70 countries worldwide.

## PRODUCTS/OPERATIONS

### Selected Products and Brands

Air Care
- Air freshener (Glade, Glade Duet)
- Pillow and mattress covers (AllerCare)

Home Cleaning
- Bathroom/drain (Drano, Scrubbing Bubbles, Vanish)
- Cleaners (Fantastik, Windex, Windex Multi-Surface Cleaner with Vinegar)
- Floor care (Pledge, Pledge Grab-It, Johnson)
- Furniture care (Pledge, Pledge Wipes, Pledge Grab-it Dry Dusting Mitts)
- Laundry/carpet care (Shout)

Home Storage
- Plastic bags (Ziploc)
- Plastic wrap (Handi-Wrap, Saran Wrap)

Insect Control
- Insecticides (Raid, Raid Max)
- Repellents (Deep Woods OFF!, OFF!, OFF! Mosquito Lamp, OFF! Skintastic)

## COMPETITORS

3M
Alticor
Blyth
Church & Dwight
Clorox
Colgate-Palmolive
Dow Chemical
DuPont
Henkel Corp.
IWP International
Procter & Gamble
Reckitt Benckiser
Shaklee
Unilever
Yankee Candle

## HISTORICAL FINANCIALS

Company Type: Private

**Income Statement** FYE: Friday nearest June 30

| | ESTIMATED REVENUE ($ mil.) | NET INCOME ($ mil.) | NET PROFIT MARGIN | EMPLOYEES |
|---|---|---|---|---|
| **6/06** | 7,000 | — | — | 12,000 |
| **6/05** | 6,500 | — | — | 12,000 |
| **6/04** | 6,500 | — | — | 12,000 |
| **6/03** | 5,370 | — | — | 12,000 |
| **6/02** | 5,000 | — | — | 10,700 |
| **Annual Growth** | 8.8% | — | — | 2.9% |

**Revenue History**

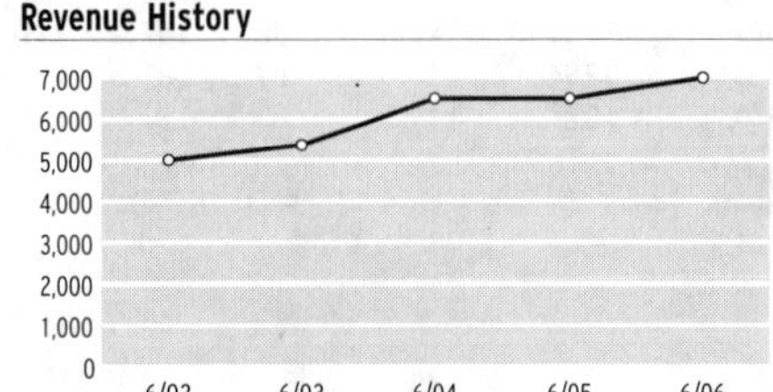


# SCANA Corporation

SCANA is cooking with (natural) gas and electricity all over South and North Carolina. The holding company serves 623,400 electricity customers and 297,000 gas customers in the neighboring states through utilities South Carolina Electric & Gas (SCE&G) and Public Service Company of North Carolina (operating as PSNC Energy). SCANA has an electric generating capacity of about 4,900 MW, which is derived mainly from fossil-fueled power plants; it also operates hydroelectric and nuclear generation facilities. Other operations include retail and wholesale energy marketing and trading, gas transportation, power plant management, fiber-optic telecommunications services, and appliance and HVAC maintenance.

In the face of advancing utility deregulation, SCANA has been seeking out customers in new territories. The company has entered Georgia's deregulated gas market, where it has emerged as a leader with more than 450,000 retail supply customers. SCANA purchased 50,000 retail customer accounts in Georgia from Energy America, a unit of UK utility Centrica, in 2004.

SCANA is selling assets to focus on core businesses. The company has sold its metro-bus transit system to the City of Columbia (South Carolina) and is selling some telecom interests. It is also building power plants and adding to its pipeline assets in the Carolinas. SCANA in 2006 merged its two gas transportation units (SCG Pipeline and South Carolina Pipeline) as Carolina Gas Transmission.

## HISTORY

SCANA's earliest ancestors include Charleston Gas Light Company (1846) and Columbia Gas Light Company (1852), formed to light those cities' streets. After barely surviving the Civil War, the companies rebuilt, only to face the greater challenge posed by Thomas Edison's lightbulb in 1879.

Electric utilities such as Charleston Electric Light Company (1886) began to emerge, and they also introduced electric trolleys, which were commonly operated by electric utilities to boost power consumption. After a series of mergers among utilities in South Carolina, the Columbia Electric Street Railway, Light and Power Company (1892) and Charleston Consolidated Railway, Gas and Electric Company (1897) were formed to handle energy and transit needs in their respective cities.

The 1920s brought another wave of utility mergers and consolidation in South Carolina. Columbia Electric Street Railway became part of the Broad River Power Company in 1925, and Charleston Consolidated Railway became a part of South Carolina Power Company the next year. In 1937 Broad River was renamed South Carolina Electric & Gas (SCE&G).

SCE&G went public in 1948. After a two-year fight with the South Carolina Public Service Authority, SCE&G finally gained approval to purchase South Carolina Power Company in 1950. During the 1950s it built several power plants and natural gas distribution lines and joined other utilities to build the Southeast's first nuclear plant prototype in 1959.

A dozen years later SCE&G and the South Carolina Public Service Authority began building a nuke near the pilot plant. Because of delays related to the Three Mile Island accident and stricter regulations, the plant cost $1.3 billion by the time it was completed in 1984.

SCE&G and Carolina Energies merged in 1982 under the SCE&G name. SCANA Corporation was formed two years later to allow the company to separate its utility business from nonregulated activities. The company formed an energy marketing subsidiary in 1988.

In 1989 Hurricane Hugo wiped out power to 300,000 customers. SCE&G's efforts to quickly restore power in its storm-ravaged territory won it industry praise.

Moving into telecommunications, SCANA in 1994 joined ITC Holding (now ITC^DeltaCom) to build a fiber-optic network in the Southeast. In 1996 SCANA invested in Powertel, which launched PCS wireless phone service in the Southeast later that year.

Meanwhile, in 1995 SCANA and Westvaco formed a joint venture, Cogen South, to build a cogeneration plant to provide power to a Westvaco paper mill in Charleston. SCANA sold its oil and gas subsidiary, Petroleum Resources, to Kelley Oil in 1997.

As deregulation overtures became stronger in 1998, SCANA expanded its natural gas business by entering Georgia's deregulated market, where it quickly became a leader. In 1999 it began planning to extend its gas pipeline into North Carolina, sold its propane assets to Suburban Propane to reduce debt, and agreed to buy natural gas distributor Public Service Company of North Carolina in a $900 million deal, which closed in 2000.

Also in 2000 SCANA sold its home security business and swapped its 27% stake in Powertel for stock in Deutsche Telekom, which took control of the PCS provider. The following year SCANA agreed to sell its 800 MHz emergency radio network to Motorola; the deal was completed in 2002. Also that year SCANA sold its Deutsche Telecom interest.

## EXECUTIVES

**Chairman, President, and CEO; Chairman and CEO, South Carolina Electric & Gas:** William B. Timmerman, age 61, $1,173,159 pay
**SVP and CFO:** Jimmy E. Addison, age 46, $306,906 pay
**SVP, Fuel Procurement and Asset Management and Deputy General Counsel and Assistant Secretary, SCANA Services; SVP, Fuel Procurement and Asset Management, SCANA; SVP, Fuel Procurement and Asset Management, South Carolina Electric & Gas:** Sarena D. Burch, age 49
**SVP, General Counsel, and Assistant Secretary:** Francis P. (Frank) Mood Jr., age 69
**SVP, Governmental Affairs and Economic Development, SCANA and SCANA Services:** Charles B. McFadden, age 62
**SVP, Human Resources; SVP, Human Resources, South Carolina Electric & Gas Company:** Joseph C. Bouknight, age 54
**President and COO, South Carolina Pipeline Corporation and SCG Pipeline:** Paul V. Fant, age 53
**President and COO, South Carolina Electric & Gas:** Kevin B. Marsh, age 50, $583,099 pay
**President and COO, SCANA Energy Marketing, SCANA Energy-Georgia, SCANA Communications, and ServiceCare:** George J. Bullwinkel Jr., age 58, $476,000 pay
**President and COO, PSNC Energy:** D. Russell (Rusty) Harris
**SVP, Generation and Chief Nuclear Officer, South Carolina Electric & Gas Company:** Stephen A. Byrne, age 47, $448,448 pay
**Risk Management Officer and Treasurer:** Mark R. Cannon
**Corporate Secretary:** Lynn M. Williams
**Controller:** James E. Swan IV
**Manager Public Affairs:** Robin Montgomery
**Director Investor Relations:** John Winn
**Auditors:** Deloitte & Touche LLP

## LOCATIONS

**HQ:** SCANA Corporation
1426 Main St., Columbia, SC 29201
**Phone:** 803-217-9000 **Fax:** 803-217-8119
**Web:** www.scana.com

SCANA provides electricity in South Carolina; natural gas in Georgia, North Carolina, and South Carolina; and telecommunications and energy marketing services primarily in the southeastern US.

## PRODUCTS/OPERATIONS

### 2006 Sales

| | $ mil. | % of total |
|---|---|---|
| Electric operations | 1,877 | 41 |
| Gas (nonregulated) | 1,429 | 31 |
| Gas (regulated) | 1,257 | 28 |
| **Total** | **4,563** | **100** |

### Selected Operations

Carolina Gas Transmission Corp. (gas transportation and natural gas purchase, transmission, and sale; LNG liquefaction, storage, and regasification plants)
Primesouth, Inc. (power plant management and maintenance services)
Public Service Company of North Carolina, Incorporated (dba PSNC Energy, natural gas distribution)
SCANA Communications, Inc. (fiber-optic telecommunications, tower construction, and investments)
SCANA Energy Marketing, Inc. (electricity and natural gas marketing)
SCANA Energy (retail natural gas marketing)
SCANA Resources, Inc. (energy-related businesses and services)
SCANA Services, Inc. (support services)
ServiceCare, Inc. (maintenance for home appliances)
South Carolina Electric & Gas Company (SCE&G, electric and gas utility)
South Carolina Fuel Company, Inc. (financing for SCE&G's nuclear fuel, fossil fuel, and sulfur dioxide emission allowances)
South Carolina Generating Company, Inc. (GENCO, owns and operates Williams power plant and sells electricity to SCE&G)

## COMPETITORS

AEP
AGL Resources
Aquila
BellSouth
CenterPoint Energy
Dominion Resources
Duke Energy
Dynegy
El Paso
Entergy
FPL Group
Green Mountain Energy
KeySpan
Laclede Group
North Carolina Electric Membership
Piedmont Natural Gas
Progress Energy
PS Energy
Santee Cooper
Sempra Energy
Southern Company
TVA

## HISTORICAL FINANCIALS

Company Type: Public

### Income Statement

FYE: December 31

| | REVENUE ($ mil.) | NET INCOME ($ mil.) | NET PROFIT MARGIN | EMPLOYEES |
|---|---|---|---|---|
| **12/06** | 4,563 | 310 | 6.8% | 5,683 |
| **12/05** | 4,777 | 320 | 6.7% | 5,628 |
| **12/04** | 3,885 | 257 | 6.6% | 5,549 |
| **12/03** | 3,416 | 282 | 8.3% | 5,458 |
| **12/02** | 2,954 | (142) | — | 5,361 |
| **Annual Growth** | 11.5% | — | — | 1.5% |

### 2006 Year-End Financials

Debt ratio: 107.8%
Return on equity: 11.2%
Cash ($ mil.): 201
Current ratio: 0.98
Long-term debt ($ mil.): 3,067
No. of shares (mil.): 117
Dividends
Yield: 4.1%
Payout: 62.7%
Market value ($ mil.): 4,753

### Stock History

NYSE: SCG

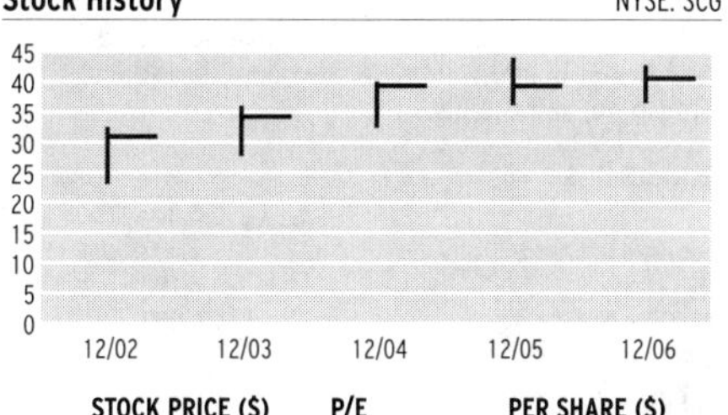


| | STOCK PRICE ($) FY Close | P/E High | P/E Low | PER SHARE ($) Earnings | Dividends | Book Value |
|---|---|---|---|---|---|---|
| **12/06** | 40.62 | 16 | 14 | 2.68 | 1.68 | 25.23 |
| **12/05** | 39.38 | 16 | 13 | 2.81 | 1.56 | 24.20 |
| **12/04** | 39.40 | 17 | 14 | 2.30 | 1.46 | 22.73 |
| **12/03** | 34.25 | 14 | 11 | 2.54 | 1.38 | 21.78 |
| **12/02** | 30.96 | — | — | (1.34) | 1.30 | 20.60 |
| **Annual Growth** | 7.0% | — | — | — | 6.6% | 5.2% |

# Schering-Plough

Schering-Plough can get rid of the most embarrassing ailments — runny noses, sunburned shoulders, and fungal feet. The druggernaut makes prescription and OTC drugs, animal health products, and personal care products. Although it is best known for its allergy medications Clarinex and Nasonex, the company also specializes in anti-infectives (particularly for hepatitis) and cancer drugs. It also co-promotes erectile dysfunction pill Levitra in the US with GlaxoSmithKline. Schering-Plough's OTC offerings include allergy medication Claritin, Afrin nasal sprays, Dr. Scholl's foot care products, and sun care lines Coppertone and Bain de Soleil. The firm agreed to acquire Akzo Nobel's Organon unit in 2007.

With the purchase of Organon, Schering-Plough expands its women's health care product lines and adds to its pipeline of drug candidates. Organon's Asenapine, for example, is in late stages of development as a treatment for schizophrenia. The acquisition deal also includes Akzo Nobel's animal health subsidiary Intervet, which makes veterinary biologicals and vaccines.

Remicade, a therapy for rheumatoid arthritis and Crohn's disease, and allergy drug Nasonex are Schering-Plough's top sellers, each accounting for about 10% of sales.

Schering-Plough has relied on licensing agreements like the one for Remicade to expand its portfolio of marketed drugs. It sells heart drug Integrilin through a deal with Millennium Pharmaceuticals and licenses cancer treatment Caelyx from ALZA. It acquired the US marketing rights of erectile dysfunction drug Levitra (shared with GlaxoSmithKline) from Bayer in 2004, and it also sells the antibiotics Cipro and Avelox through agreements with Bayer. Additionally, it co-promotes its cholesterol drugs, Zetia and Vytorin, with partner Merck.

Also with Merck, Schering-Plough is developing a combination allergy drug using its own aging blockbuster Claritin and Merck's Singulair. It has additional research agreements with Novartis, Valeant Pharmaceuticals, and Anacor to develop drugs in the areas of respiratory disease, infectious disease, and antifungals. Other development programs focus on cancer, cardiovascular disease, metabolic disorders, and neurological conditions. And it has boosted its drug discovery capabilities with the 2005 purchase of NeoGenesis Pharmaceuticals, which has developed tools to improve the process of identifying new drug candidates.

The company's R&D pipeline is important to the company's future, especially as several of its big sellers begin to face competition from generic equivalents. Schering-Plough's hepatitis drug franchise (Intron A and Rebetol) has taken a major hit in recent years as generic forms of ribavirin and interferon have come to market. Additionally, generic rivals for its cholesterol drugs Vytorin and Zetia appeared late in 2006.

Schering-Plough is no longer related to Bayer Schering Pharma (formerly Schering AG); the company broke away from its German predecessor during WWII.

## HISTORY

Berlin chemist Ernst Schering formed Schering in 1864 to sell chemicals to apothecary shops. By 1880 Schering was exporting pharmaceuticals to the US, where a subsidiary was established in 1928.

At the outbreak of WWII, the US government seized the subsidiary, severed links with its German parent, and appointed government attorney Francis Brown director. Brown put together a research team whose efforts led to the development of such new drugs as Chlor-Trimeton, one of the first antihistamines, and the cold medicine Coricidin.

The government sold Schering in 1952 to Merrill Lynch, which took it public. Schering bought White Labs in 1957. In the 1960s the company introduced Garamycin (antibiotic, 1964), Tinactin (antifungal, 1965), and Afrin (decongestant, 1967).

Schering's 1971 merger with Memphis-based Plough expanded the product line to include such cosmetics and consumer items as Coppertone and Di-Gel. Plough's founder, Abe Plough, had borrowed $125 from his father in 1908 to create an antiseptic healing oil consisting of cottonseed oil, carbolic acid, and camphor. Plough sold his concoction door-to-door and went on to buy 28 companies. He served as chairman of newly merged Schering-Plough until 1976. Known for his philanthropy, Plough died in 1984 at age 92.

Schering-Plough introduced many products after the merger, including Lotrimin AF (antifungal, 1975), Drixoral (a cold remedy made nonprescription in 1982), and antiasthmatics Vanceril (1976) and Proventil (1981). When Garamycin's patent expired in 1980, the firm introduced a similar antibiotic, Netromycin.

The company was one of the first drug giants to make significant investments in biotechnology: It bought DNAX Research Institute of Palo Alto, California, in 1982. Acquisitions in the late 1970s and 1980s included Scholl (foot care, 1979; founder William Scholl died in 2002), Key Pharmaceuticals (cardiovascular drugs, 1986), and Cooper Companies (eye care, 1988).

In 1993 Schering-Plough began marketing its non-sedating antihistamine, Claritin, in the US. Also in 1994 the firm received FDA approval for Claritin-D, which added a decongestant to the top-selling product. Other approvals included Cedax, Uni-Dur, and Intron A (as a malignant melanoma therapy). The next year it partnered with COR Therapeutics to develop a new cardiovascular drug and with Genome Therapeutics on a new anti-infective.

In 1996 Schering-Plough bought Canji to strengthen its gene therapy research program. It strengthened its veterinary medicine segment in 1997 when it bought Mallinckrodt's animal health operations. In 1999 the FDA approved the company's Temodar, a chemotherapy treatment for brain tumors, and it bought the US rights to Pfizer's Bain de Soleil sun care product line.

In 2001 the FDA cited problems at Schering-Plough's New Jersey and Puerto Rico manufacturing plants, leading the agency to hit the company with a $500 million fine the following year. Faced with Claritin's patent expiration, the firm took the prescription allergy drug to the OTC market in late 2002.

As Schering-Plough's revenues started to decline in 2003, the company made drastic changes in management by bringing in several executives from Pharmacia, which had been acquired by Pfizer earlier that year. Schering-Plough also took such cost cutting measures as reducing dividends, suspending bonuses and raises, and offering employees an early retirement program.

## EXECUTIVES

**Chairman, President, and CEO:** Fred Hassan, age 61, $5,237,850 pay
**Chairman, Consumer Health Care:** Stanley F. Barshay, age 67
**EVP and CFO:** Robert J. Bertolini, age 45, $1,877,775 pay
**EVP and General Counsel:** Thomas J. (Tom) Sabatino Jr., age 48, $1,585,575 pay
**EVP and President, Global Pharmaceuticals:** Carrie Smith Cox, age 49, $2,385,800 pay
**EVP and President, Schering-Plough Research Institute:** Thomas P. Koestler
**Chief Scientific Officer and EVP, Schering-Plough Research Institute:** Catherine D. Strader, age 52
**EVP, Global Clinical Development, Schering-Plough Research Institute:** Peder K. Jensen, age 48
**SVP, Business Development:** David A. Piacquad
**SVP, Medical Affairs and Chief Medical Officer, Schering-Plough Research Institute:** Robert J. Spiegel
**SVP, Analytical, Chemical, Pharmaceutical and Biotechnology, Schering-Plough Research Institute:** John B. Landis
**SVP, Global Business Operations:** Bruce R. Reid
**SVP; President, Consumer Health Care:** Brent Saunders, age 37
**SVP, Global Human Resources:** C. Ron Cheeley, age 56
**SVP, Global Medical Affairs:** Hans M. Vemer
**SVP, Global Supply Chain:** Ian A.T. McInnes, age 54
**SVP, Strategic Partnerships and US Managed Markets:** Sean McNicholas
**Group Head, Global Specialty Operations and President, Schering-Plough Animal Health:** Raul E. Kohan, age 55
**Group VP, Global Communications:** Jeffrey A. (Jeff) Winton, age 48
**VP and Controller:** Steven H. (Steve) Koehler, age 56
**VP and Treasurer:** E. Kevin Moore, age 54
**VP, Investor Relations:** Alex Kelly
**Auditors:** Deloitte & Touche LLP

## LOCATIONS

**HQ:** Schering-Plough Corporation
2000 Galloping Hill Rd., Kenilworth, NJ 07033
**Phone:** 908-298-4000 **Fax:** 908-298-7653
**Web:** www.sch-plough.com

Schering-Plough has its principal manufacturing facilities in Belgium, Ireland, Mexico, Puerto Rico, Singapore, and the US.

### 2006 Sales

| | $ mil. | % of total |
|---|---|---|
| Europe and Canada | 4,403 | 42 |
| US | 4,192 | 40 |
| Asia/Pacific | 1,009 | 9 |
| Latin America | 990 | 9 |
| **Total** | **10,594** | **100** |

## PRODUCTS/OPERATIONS

### 2006 Sales

| | $ mil. | % of total |
|---|---|---|
| Prescription Pharmaceuticals | | |
| Remicade | 1,240 | 12 |
| Nasonex | 944 | 9 |
| PEG-Intron | 837 | 8 |
| Clarinex/Aerius | 722 | 7 |
| Temodar | 703 | 7 |
| Claritin Rx | 356 | 3 |
| Integrilin | 329 | 3 |
| Rebetol | 311 | 3 |
| Avelox | 304 | 3 |
| Intron A | 237 | 2 |
| Caelyx | 206 | 2 |
| Subutex | 203 | 2 |
| Elocon | 141 | 1 |
| Cipro | 111 | 1 |
| Other | 1,917 | 18 |
| Consumer Health Care | | |
| OTC | 558 | 5 |
| Foot care | 343 | 3 |
| Sun care | 222 | 2 |
| Animal Health | 910 | 9 |
| **Total** | **10,594** | **100** |

### Selected Products

Pharmaceuticals
- Allergy and respiratory
  - Clarinex
  - Foradil aerolizer
  - Nasonex
  - Proventil
- Antibiotics
  - Avelox (with Bayer)
  - Cipro (with Bayer)
- Anti-inflammatory
  - Remicade
- Anti-viral
  - Intron A
  - Peg-Intron
  - Rebetol
- Cardiovascular
  - Integrilin
  - Vytorin
  - Zetia
- Oncology
  - Caelyx
  - Intron A
  - Temodar
- Other
  - Elocon (steroid cream)
  - Levitra (erectile dysfunction, with GlaxoSmithKline)
  - Noxafil (fungal infections)

Animal Health
- Aquaflor (antibiotic for farm-raised fish)
- Banamine (non-steroid anti-inflammatory)
- Coccivac (poultry vaccine)
- Exspot (canine topical insecticide)
- M+PAC (swine pneumonia vaccine)
- Nuflor (antimicrobial)
- Otomax (canine otitis)
- Paracox (poultry vaccine)
- Zubrin (non-steroid anti-inflammatory)

Consumer Health Care
- Afrin (nasal decongestant)
- Bain de Soleil (sun care)
- Claritin (allergy)
- Coppertone (sun care)
- Correctol (laxative)
- Dr. Scholl's (foot care products)
- Drixoral (cold relief and decongestant)
- Solarcaine (sun care)
- Tinactin (antifungal)

## COMPETITORS

Abbott Labs
Amgen
AstraZeneca
Barr Pharmaceuticals
Bayer
Bristol-Myers Squibb
Chiron
Eli Lilly
Genentech
Gilead Sciences
GlaxoSmithKline
Johnson & Johnson
MedPointe
Merck
Mylan Labs
Novartis
Perrigo
Pfizer
Roche
Sandoz International GmbH
Sanofi-Aventis
Teva Pharmaceuticals
Three Rivers Pharmaceuticals
Valeant
Watson Pharmaceuticals
Wyeth

## HISTORICAL FINANCIALS

Company Type: Public

**Income Statement** FYE: December 31

| | REVENUE ($ mil.) | NET INCOME ($ mil.) | NET PROFIT MARGIN | EMPLOYEES |
|---|---|---|---|---|
| **12/06** | 10,594 | 1,143 | 10.8% | 33,500 |
| **12/05** | 9,508 | 269 | 2.8% | 32,600 |
| **12/04** | 8,272 | (947) | — | 30,500 |
| **12/03** | 8,334 | (92) | — | 30,500 |
| **12/02** | 10,180 | 1,974 | 19.4% | 30,500 |
| **Annual Growth** | 1.0% | (12.8%) | — | 2.4% |

**2006 Year-End Financials**

Debt ratio: 37.3%
Return on equity: 18.4%
Cash ($ mil.): 5,933
Current ratio: 2.50
Long-term debt ($ mil.): 2,414
No. of shares (mil.): 1,487
Dividends
Yield: 0.9%
Payout: 31.0%
Market value ($ mil.): 35,153

**Stock History** NYSE: SGP

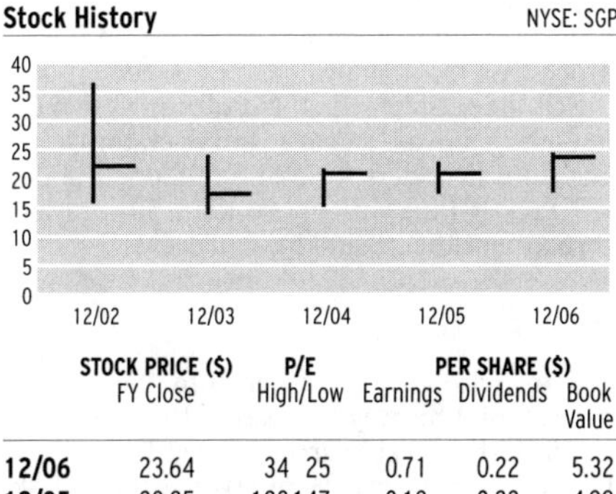


| | STOCK PRICE ($) FY Close | P/E High | P/E Low | PER SHARE ($) Earnings | Dividends | Book Value |
|---|---|---|---|---|---|---|
| **12/06** | 23.64 | 34 | 25 | 0.71 | 0.22 | 5.32 |
| **12/05** | 20.85 | 188 | 147 | 0.12 | 0.22 | 4.99 |
| **12/04** | 20.88 | — | — | (0.67) | 0.22 | 5.12 |
| **12/03** | 17.39 | — | — | (0.06) | 0.56 | 4.99 |
| **12/02** | 22.20 | 27 | 12 | 1.34 | 0.67 | 5.55 |
| **Annual Growth** | 1.6% | — | — | (14.7%) | (24.3%) | (1.0%) |

# Schlumberger Limited

No sleeper, Schlumberger is one of the world's largest oil field services companies, along with Halliburton. The company provides a full range of oil and gas services, including seismic surveys, drilling, wireline logging, well construction and completion, and project management. Organized into 29 geographic teams, Schlumberger's Oilfield Services unit provides reservoir evaluation, reservoir development, and reservoir management services. Schlumberger is also working to develop new technologies for reservoir optimization. Through its WesternGeco business, the company provides seismic services to customers worldwide. (The company acquired Baker Hughes' 30% stake in WesternGeco in 2006 for $2.4 billion.)

In an effort to focus on its core oil and gas services operations, Schlumberger disposed of its Axalto business (which later was renamed Gemalto) by spinning off the unit through an IPO on the Paris stock exchange. The company has also sold its Essentis and water services businesses. Schlumberger has sold its electricity meters business to Itron for about $248 million, and its business continuity service unit to IBM for $233 million. It has expanded its oil and gas services division by acquiring a 26% stake in PetroAlliance Services, Russia's largest oilfield services company.

The company has dropped the services it provides to the semiconductor industry. It has sold its NPTest subsidiary to an investment group led by Francisco Partners and Shah Management. The company disposed of its Schlumberger Verifications Systems unit by transferring the assets to Soluris (which was subsequently acquired by Nanometrics). It has also sold its telecom billing software unit, as well as its Infodata business.

Schlumberger has sold the majority of its SchlumbergerSema business unit, formed in 2001 when the company bought IT service provider Sema, to Atos Origin. Schlumberger did, however, keep the oil and gas information technology business that it provides to its oilfield services customers. These services, once provided by SchlumbergerSema, now fall under the company's Schlumberger Information Solutions unit, which it has also expanded through the acquisition of Austria-based oil and gas software provider Decision Team. Schlumberger's ownership in SchlumbergerSema has decreased to 14%.

## HISTORY

In a Paris basement in 1912, physicist Conrad Schlumberger experimented with wire and a sand-filled bathtub, eventually hoping to use electric current to find ore deposits. With his father's money, Conrad and his brother Marcel began "electrical prospecting" in 1919. Société de Prospection Électrique (SPE) began using the methods for oil exploration in 1923. In 1927 Conrad asked son-in-law Henri Doll to design a tool to chart where oil lay in a well, and wireline logging was born.

To survive the Depression, SPE teamed with rival SGRM in 1931. SPE handled logging, and the two firms formed Compagnie Générale de Géophysique (CGG) for subsurface operations. After entering the US in 1932, the Schlumbergers formed a company in Houston in 1934 and moved headquarters there in 1940.

Also in the 1930s SPE and CGG moved into the Soviet Union, which was desperate for industry. While developing the nation's oil fields, SPE began its policy of adapting to other cultures. Stalin banished the firms in 1936. Conrad died that year, and Marcel followed in 1953.

Led by chairman Doll and Marcel's son Pierre (CEO), the company went public as Schlumberger Limited in 1956. It also bought 50% of Forex, a drilling rig firm, in 1959. The next year Schlumberger sold its stake in CGG and formed an oil services venture with Dow Chemical.

Schlumberger nearly doubled in size with the 1962 acquisition of electronics maker Daystrom. In 1964 the firm combined its 50% stakes in Forex and Languedocienne to create drilling company Neptune. After Jean Riboud became CEO in 1966, the company moved to New York. Doll retired the next year; by then some 40% of the firm's sales stemmed from his inventions. Schlumberger bought a utility meter manufacturer in 1970.

Continuing to build its drilling operations, the company bought the rest of Forex in 1972 and SEDCO in 1984 (to form Sedco Forex Drilling in 1985). In 1984 Schlumberger combined its 1977 purchase, The Analysts (computerized mud logging), with Dowell's drilling unit to form directional driller Anadrill. (Schlumberger took over Anadrill in 1993.) When oil prices crashed, Schlumberger merged its wireline logging businesses with Flopetrol (acquired 1971) in 1986. It also began seismic analysis, buying GECO (50% in 1984, the rest in 1988) and PRAKLA-SEISMOS (1991, folded into GECO).

Meanwhile, the firm introduced smart cards in 1982. Schlumberger bought GeoQuest (well data management software) in 1992 and formed the Omnes communications venture with Cable & Wireless in 1995. (Schlumberger took over Omnes in 1999.)

Facing the 1999 oil slump, the firm cut staff and combined four engineering and consulting units into Holditch-Reservoir Technologies. Schlumberger finished the year by spinning off Sedco Forex, which then merged with Transocean.

Schlumberger boosted its utility meter business in 2000 by buying CellNet, a UK telemetry services firm. In 2001 SchlumbergerSema was formed when Schlumberger bought Sema, a software and support provider for electronic payment systems, for about $5 billion. It also acquired UK-based Phoenix Petroleum Services, a leading player in optimizing production in artificially lifted wells. Schlumberger began expanding its IT assets and reorganizing its SchlumbergerSema operations in 2002 in an effort to expand its IT offerings to its Oilfield Service customers.

In 2003 Andrew Gould was promoted to the position of chairman and CEO following the resignation of Euan Baird. In 2004 Schlumberger sold its electricity meter business to Itron for $248 million, and its business continuity services business to IBM for about $233 million. In an effort to expand its Information Solutions units, the company acquired Austria-based Decision Team, a provider of oil and gas software and consulting services. It expanded its oil and gas services division by acquiring a 26% stake (increased to 100% in 2006) in PetroAlliance Services, Russia's largest oilfield services company. In 2005 Schlumberger sold a manufacturing facility in Montrouge, France, for $227 million.

## EXECUTIVES

**Chairman and CEO:** Andrew Gould, age 60, $2,500,000 pay
**EVP Schlumberger Oilfield Services:** Chakib Sbiti, age 52, $748,130 pay
**EVP and President, WesternGeco:** Dalton Boutte, age 52, $520,073 pay
**EVP and CFO:** Simon Ayat, age 52
**VP and Chief Scientist:** Philippe Lacour-Gayet, age 59
**VP and Director, Taxes:** Mark Danton, age 50
**VP and CTO:** Ashok Belani, age 48
**VP Operations, Oilfield Services:** Mark Corrigan, $505,902 pay
**VP Personnel:** Paal Kibsgaard, age 39
**VP Investor Relations:** Malcolm Theobald
**VP Communications and Investor Relations:** Jean-Francois Poupeau, age 46
**President, Reservoir Characterization Group, Oilfield Services Technologies:** Imran Kizilbash
**President, Reservoir Management Group, Oilfield Services:** Jeff Spath
**President, Oilfield Services Middle East and Asia:** Zaki Selim
**President, Drilling and Measurements, Oilfield Services Technologies:** Sami Iskander
**President, Reservoir Production Group Oilfield Services — Technologies:** Doug Pferdehirt
**President, Oilfield Services Europe and Africa:** Satish Pai, $567,332 pay
**Chief Information Officer:** Sophie Zurquiyah-Rousset, age 41
**Chief Accounting Officer and Director:** Howard Guild, age 35
**Secretary and General Counsel:** Ellen Summer, age 60
**Auditors:** PricewaterhouseCoopers LLP

## LOCATIONS

**HQ:** Schlumberger Limited
5599 San Felipe, 17th Fl., Houston, TX 77056
**Phone:** 713-513-2000
**Web:** www.slb.com

### 2006 Sales

| | $ mil. | % of total |
|---|---|---|
| North America | 5,273.0 | 27 |
| Europe/CIS/West Africa | 4,818.0 | 25 |
| Middle East & Asia | 3,960.0 | 21 |
| Latin America | 2,563.0 | 13 |
| Other regions | 153.0 | 1 |
| WesternGeco | 2,471.0 | 13 |
| Adjustments | (7.5) | — |
| **Total** | **19,230.5** | **100** |

## PRODUCTS/OPERATIONS

### 2006 Sales

| | $ mil. | % of total |
|---|---|---|
| Oilfield services | 16,767.0 | 87 |
| WesternGeco | 2,471.0 | 13 |
| Adjustments | (7.5) | — |
| **Total** | **19,230.5** | **100** |

### Selected Subsidiaries and Affiliates

Schlumberger Antilles N.V. (Netherlands Antilles)
Schlumberger Offshore Services N.V. (Limited) (Netherlands Antilles)

Schlumberger B.V. (The Netherlands)
Schlumberger Canada Limited
Schlumberger SA (France)
Services Petroliers Schlumberger (France)
WesternGeco B.V. (The Netherlands)
WesternGeco A.S. (Norway)

Schlumberger Oilfield Holdings Limited (British Virgin Islands)
Dowell Schlumberger Corporation (British Virgin Islands)
Schlumberger Holdings Limited (British Virgin Islands)
Schlumberger Middle East S.A. (Panama)
Schlumberger Overseas, S.A (Panama)
Schlumberger Seaco, Inc. (Panama)
Schlumberger Surenco, S.A. (Panama)
WesternGeco Seismic Holdings Limited (British Virgin Islands)

Schlumberger Technology Corporation
WesternGeco L.L.C.

## COMPETITORS

Baker Hughes
BJ Services
Core Laboratories
Fortum
Halliburton
Petroleum Geo-Services
Stolt-Nielsen
Technip

## HISTORICAL FINANCIALS

Company Type: Public

### Income Statement

FYE: December 31

| | REVENUE ($ mil.) | NET INCOME ($ mil.) | NET PROFIT MARGIN | EMPLOYEES |
|---|---|---|---|---|
| **12/06** | 19,231 | 3,710 | 19.3% | 70,000 |
| **12/05** | 14,717 | 2,207 | 15.0% | 60,000 |
| **12/04** | 11,609 | 1,224 | 10.5% | 52,500 |
| **12/03** | 14,059 | 383 | 2.7% | 77,000 |
| **12/02** | 13,613 | (2,320) | — | 78,500 |
| **Annual Growth** | 9.0% | — | — | (2.8%) |

### 2006 Year-End Financials

Debt ratio: 44.8%
Return on equity: 41.2%
Cash ($ mil.): 2,999
Current ratio: 1.42
Long-term debt ($ mil.): 4,664
No. of shares (mil.): 1,178
Dividends
Yield: 0.8%
Payout: 16.6%
Market value ($ mil.): 74,396

### Stock History

NYSE: SLB

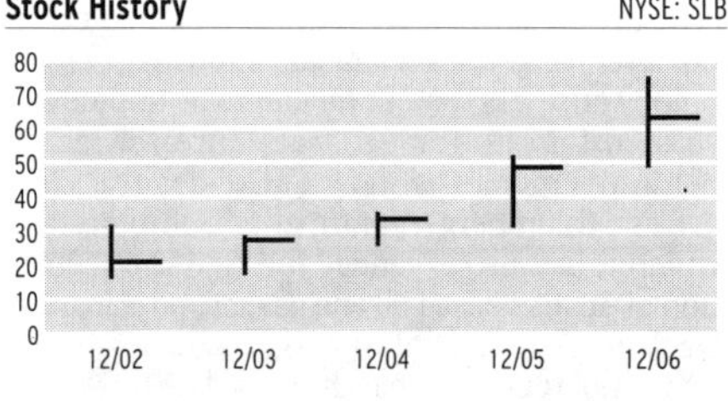


| | STOCK PRICE ($) FY Close | P/E High | P/E Low | PER SHARE ($) Earnings | Dividends | Book Value |
|---|---|---|---|---|---|---|
| **12/06** | 63.16 | 25 | 16 | 3.01 | 0.50 | 8.85 |
| **12/05** | 48.58 | 28 | 17 | 1.82 | 0.42 | 12.89 |
| **12/04** | 33.47 | 34 | 26 | 1.02 | 0.38 | 10.39 |
| **12/03** | 27.36 | 85 | 54 | 0.33 | 0.38 | 10.04 |
| **12/02** | 21.05 | — | — | (2.01) | 0.38 | 9.63 |
| **Annual Growth** | 31.6% | — | — | — | 7.1% | (2.1%) |

# Schnitzer Steel Industries

Your old car could end up in a Malaysian office building if Schnitzer Steel Industries gets its steel jaws on it. The company is a leading processor of scrap steel and iron, which it obtains from sources such as auto salvage yards, industrial manufacturers, and metals brokers. Most of the company's scrap is sold to steelmakers in Asia; much of the rest goes to Schnitzer Steel's own steelmaking business, Cascade Steel Rolling Mills, which produces merchant bar, steel reinforcing bar, and other products at its minimill in Oregon. Schnitzer Steel's Pick-N-Pull Auto Dismantlers unit operates auto salvage yards. The family of founder Sam Schnitzer controls the company through a voting trust.

In 2005 the SEC announced that it was investigating Schnitzer Steel's former practice of improperly paying commissions to purchasing managers of customers in Asia. The company had earlier commissioned an independent investigation of the practice and notified the SEC.

Considering itself primarily a ferrous metals recycling business, Schnitzer Steel plans to continue to expand this business segment through acquisitions in North America. In the fall of 2005 the company bought the assets of Regional Recycling for about $66 million in cash and assumed debt. Regional Recycling, an operator of 10 metals recycling facilities in Alabama and Georgia, posted annual sales just below $200 million. Also that year Schnitzer dissolved a joint venture with what is now Sims Hugo Neu, a deal that allowed Schnitzer to keep metal recycling centers in the Northeastern US and Eastern Europe. The next year Schnitzer further broadened its business in New England with the acquisition of Advanced Recycling, a business that has four processing facilities in New Hampshire.

In addition to growing through acquisitions, Schnitzer Steel hopes to improve the efficiency of its recycling operations by investing in new processing technology.

Schnitzer Steel's Pick-N-Pull unit expanded in 2005 by buying salvage yard operator Greenleaf Auto Recyclers for $23.5 million. The deal left Pick-N-Pull with more than 50 locations throughout the US and in Canada.

## HISTORY

Sam Schnitzer, a draftee into the Russian army, found his way to Austria, then to the US in 1904. The next year he moved to Portland, where he and partner Henry Wolf formed Alaska Junk in 1908. The enterprise grew, buying sawmills, logging camps, and shipyards. Sam's son, Morris, formed Schnitzer Steel Products on his own in 1936. After WWII the patriarch turned Alaska Junk over to sons Gilbert, Leonard, Manuel, and Morris.

The brothers changed the company's name to Alaska Steel and acquired Woodbury, a local steel distributor, in 1956. The Schnitzers formed Lasco Shipping in 1963. Morris' Schnitzer Steel Products returned to family control, and in 1978 Alaska Steel and Woodbury combined to make Metra Steel. The company boosted its vertical integration by acquiring the Cascade Steel minimill in 1984.

Leonard Schnitzer's son-in-law Robert Philip became president in 1991. Two years later the family's steel businesses went public as Schnitzer Steel Industries. In 1994 the company launched a $42 million expansion program. It bought Manufacturing Management (then Washington's #1 scrap processor, 1995) and Proler International (scrap-related environmental services, 1996), adding 17 scrap-collecting and -processing facilities, primarily on the East Coast.

Schnitzer Steel Industries began producing wire rod and coiled rebar at its Oregon facility in 1997. The next year Schnitzer Steel Industries and joint venture partner Hugo Neu added facilities in Maine, Massachusetts, and New Hampshire. Also in 1998 a marked drop in scrap export prices due to an economic downturn in Asia hurt the company's earnings. Its Asian exports declined some 20% in 1999.

To maximize its potential and reduce costs, Schnitzer Steel Industries installed an automobile shredder capable of processing 2,000 tons per day at its Tacoma, Washington, facility in 2000. In 2001 the company experienced improvements in its metal recycling business, the result of a temporary backlog that helped boost sales. However, the slowdown in the economy hurt sales at its steel manufacturing segment.

In 2002 the company's Portland, Oregon, metals recycling facility went through a $4.4 million renovation to increase efficiency in loading recycled metal cargoes. The next year, Schnitzer Steel Industries purchased Pick-N-Pull, a major operator of auto salvage yards, for about $71 million.

Schnitzer Steel Industries unwound its joint ventures with Hugo Neu in 2005.

## EXECUTIVES

**Chairman:** Kenneth M. Novack, age 60
**President and CEO:** John D. Carter, age 60
**EVP and COO:** Tamara L. Adler Lundgren, age 49
**VP and CFO:** Gregory J. Witherspoon, age 60, $450,000 pay
**VP and Corporate Controller:** Vicki A. Piersall, age 45
**VP Human Resources:** Andrew (Drew) Lipay
**VP, General Counsel and Corporate Secretary:** Richard C. Josephson, age 58, $450,000 pay
**VP Environmental and Public Affairs:** Thomas Zelenka, age 57
**President, Metals Recycling Business:** Donald Hamaker, age 54
**President, Steel Manufacturing Business:** Jeffrey Dyck, age 43
**President, Auto Parts Business:** Thomas D. Klauer Jr., age 52
**EVP California Metals Recycling Business:** Gary Schnitzer, age 64
**Executive Director, Schnitzer Southeast:** Byron Kopman
**Executive Director, Schnitzer Southeast:** David Romanoff
**Investor Relations:** Rob Stone
**Auditors:** PricewaterhouseCoopers LLP

## LOCATIONS

**HQ:** Schnitzer Steel Industries, Inc.
3200 NW Yeon Ave., Portland, OR 97296
**Phone:** 503-224-9900 **Fax:** 503-321-2648
**Web:** www.schn.com

### 2006 Sales

| | $ mil. | % of total |
|---|---|---|
| North America | 768 | 38 |
| Asia | 627 | 31 |
| Europe | 570 | 29 |
| Africa | 47 | 2 |
| Adjustments | (157) | — |
| **Total** | **1,855** | **100** |

## PRODUCTS/OPERATIONS

### 2006 Sales

| | $ mil. | % of total |
|---|---|---|
| Metals Recycling | 1,407 | 70 |
| Steel Manufacturing | 387 | 19 |
| Auto Parts | 218 | 11 |
| Adjustments | (157) | — |
| **Total** | **1,855** | **100** |

## COMPETITORS

AK Steel Holding Corporation
Aleris International
BHP Billiton
Cargill
Chaparral Steel
Commercial Metals
Evraz Steel Mills, Inc.
Metal Management
Nippon Steel
Nucor
OmniSource
Rowan
SHV Holdings
Steel Dynamics
United States Steel

## HISTORICAL FINANCIALS

Company Type: Public

### Income Statement

FYE: August 31

| | REVENUE ($ mil.) | NET INCOME ($ mil.) | NET PROFIT MARGIN | EMPLOYEES |
|---|---|---|---|---|
| **8/06** | 1,855 | 143 | 7.7% | 3,252 |
| **8/05** | 853 | 147 | 17.2% | 1,799 |
| **8/04** | 688 | 111 | 16.2% | 1,624 |
| **8/03** | 497 | 43 | 8.7% | 1,495 |
| **8/02** | 370 | 7 | 1.8% | 952 |
| **Annual Growth** | 49.6% | 115.8% | — | 35.9% |

### 2006 Year-End Financials

Debt ratio: 14.0%
Return on equity: 21.8%
Cash ($ mil.): 33
Current ratio: 2.91
Long-term debt ($ mil.): 103
No. of shares (mil.): 22
Dividends
Yield: 0.2%
Payout: 1.5%
Market value ($ mil.): 714

### Stock History

NASDAQ (GS): SCHN

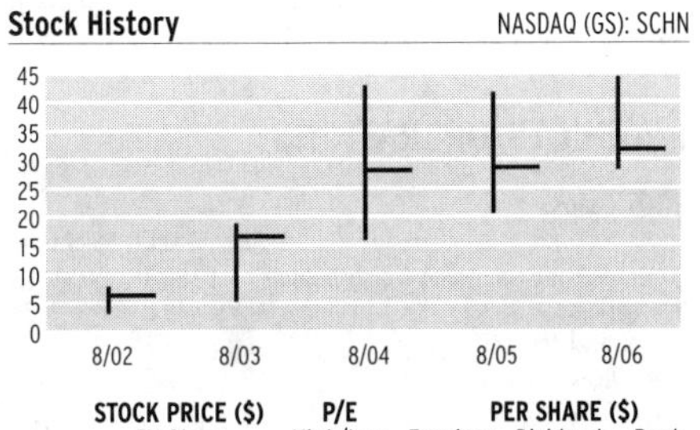


| | STOCK PRICE ($) FY Close | P/E High | P/E Low | PER SHARE ($) Earnings | Dividends | Book Value |
|---|---|---|---|---|---|---|
| **8/06** | 31.75 | 9 | 6 | 4.65 | 0.07 | 32.64 |
| **8/05** | 28.60 | 9 | 4 | 4.72 | 0.07 | 25.77 |
| **8/04** | 28.10 | 12 | 5 | 3.58 | 0.05 | 18.98 |
| **8/03** | 16.53 | 13 | 4 | 1.47 | 0.05 | 24.35 |
| **8/02** | 6.30 | 32 | 15 | 0.24 | 0.07 | 50.34 |
| **Annual Growth** | 49.8% | — | — | 109.8% | 0.0% | (10.3%) |

# Scholastic Corporation

Once upon a time, a company grew up to become one of the world's leading children's book publishers. Scholastic Corporation sells more than 350 million books (*Harry Potter, The Baby-Sitters Club*) annually to children in the US and across the globe. Known for its school book clubs and fairs (Scholastic is a leading operator of both types of programs), the company also publishes magazines (for students and teachers), textbooks, and software. In addition, Scholastic produces children's TV programming, videos, and films. The company owns *Encyclopedia Americana* publisher Scholastic Library Publishing.

Scholastic also owns the Klutz brand of children's toys. In addition, the company provides Internet-based content and services to students, parents, and teachers. The company generates nearly 20% of sales outside of the US and is expanding its overseas operations, especially in the UK.

Scholastic created some sales magic when it agreed to be the US distributor of the J.K Rowling *Harry Potter* series about a boy wizard, which has broken sales records and become the best-selling children's series of all time. The seventh and final book in the series, *Harry Potter and the Deathly Hallows*, set sales records in 2007 after 8.3 million copies vanished from shelves in 24 hours, besting the mark set in 2005 by *Harry Potter and the Half-Blood Prince.*

Scholastic has been busy growing the business through deals and acquisitions. The company struck a deal to license publications based on five future animated movies from DreamWorks SKG. Scholastic also paid close to $10 million for the rights to the popular spooky kids' series *Goosebumps* by R.L. Stine. The company partnered with LEGO Group to publish books and other products using LEGO brands. Branching out, Scholastic has also formed a graphic novel imprint. It picked up UK-based children's book publisher Chicken House Publishing in 2005.

The company has partnered up with NBC and Telemundo (along with other content and broadcasting companies) to create a new television network for children called qubo. The network airs on NBC, i network, and Telemundo in English and Spanish. Spots reinforcing the importance of books and reading play throughout the programming block.

Chairman and CEO Richard Robinson and his family (descendants of founder Maurice Robinson) own more than 20% of the company.

## HISTORY

Fresh from a stint on his college newspaper, Maurice Robinson returned to his hometown of Wilkinson, Pennsylvania, in 1920 and launched *The Western Pennsylvania Scholastic,* a newspaper geared toward high school students. By 1922 its circulation had grown to 4,000 — prompting Robinson to incorporate his business as Scholastic Publishing Company and launch *Scholastic,* a national version of the newspaper.

The Depression found the unprofitable Scholastic struggling to improve its financial picture. In 1932 the company changed its name to Scholastic Corporation. A cost-cutting program helped it achieve a profit for the first time four years later. Profitability, however, would be fleeting: Accusations that Scholastic's publications promoted Communism prompted some schools to ban them.

During WWII, paper rationing compelled Scholastic to print slimmer publications and turn away subscribers. Following the war the company introduced a string of publications and initiated a sales push that permitted it to pay its first dividend in 1951. In the 1950s, while weathering another spate of accusations that the company had Communist leanings, Scholastic continued to expand its list of publications. The company also created two book clubs that decade, launching what would become one of its most successful endeavors.

During the 1960s Scholastic broadened its interests to include instructional materials and hardcover books. The company went public in 1969 and continued its expansion during the 1970s with ventures into record production and filmstrips. In 1974 Maurice's son, Richard, was appointed president.

Scholastic began producing educational software and TV programming during the 1980s. In 1987 Richard took the company private again in order to help it regain financial stability. His timing was fortuitous — the children's book market was on an upswing, and by the time he took Scholastic public again in 1992, the company's book sales had doubled.

The 1992 launch of its *Goosebumps* books initially met with great success. But by 1996, when kids had grown weary of *Goosebumps,* book returns caused profits to take a nosedive. Robinson responded by instituting cost-cutting and layoffs, and Scholastic divested itself of products not associated with its core business. The company continued to expand its TV and film interests during the 1990s, producing TV shows such as *Scholastic's The Magic School Bus* and feature films such as *The Indian in the Cupboard* for worldwide audiences.

In 1998 Scholastic created a new publishing unit to issue professional and parenting magazines. Also that year it published the first *Harry Potter* book by then-unknown British author J.K. Rowling. In addition, the company inked a deal with Warner Brothers Worldwide Publishing to create children's books based on Warner Brothers' movie and TV properties.

In 2000 Scholastic published the fourth book in the *Harry Potter* series, which had the largest first printing in history. Later that year it purchased children's book and reference publisher Grolier from Lagardere for $400 million. (It later changed Grolier's name to Scholastic Library Publishing.) The following year Scholastic announced that it would establish shops in Toys "R" Us stores to sell toys and games. In 2001 the company also bought the assets of book fair company Troll Book Fairs Inc. It also bought educational software maker Tom Snyder Productions and animated TV producer Soup2Nuts; both are units of Torstar.

In 2002 the company made a public debt offering of some $300 million in order to help offset debts incurred with its purchase of Grolier. That year the company also acquired Klutz, a maker of children's products and books, from Corus Entertainment and bought a 15% interest in The Book People, a UK book distributor. In addition, Scholastic acquired Teacher's Friend Publications, a maker of classroom decorations, for $6 million. Citing poor industry conditions, Scholastic cut about 400 employees (about 4% of the workforce) in 2003.

## EXECUTIVES

**Chairman, President, and CEO:** Richard (Dick) Robinson, age 70, $1,264,465 pay
**EVP, CFO, and Chief Administrative Officer:** Maureen E. O'Connell, age 44
**EVP; President, Book Clubs:** Judith A. (Judy) Newman, age 49
**EVP; President, Book Fairs and Trade:** Lisa Holton, age 45
**EVP; President, International Group:** Hugh Roome, age 55
**EVP; President, Scholastic Education:** Margery W. Mayer, age 55, $742,691 pay
**EVP; President, Scholastic Entertainment and Scholastic Media:** Deborah A. Forte, age 53
**EVP; President, e-Scholastic and Scholastic at Home:** Seth D. Radwell, age 44
**EVP Marketing and Director:** Linda B. Keene, age 53
**SVP and CIO:** Reg Maton
**SVP and Group Publisher, Scholastic Marketing Partners:** Steve Palm
**SVP and Publisher, Trade:** Ellie Berger
**SVP Education and Corporate Relations:** Ernest B. Fleishman, age 70
**SVP Finance and Operations:** Ed Monagle
**SVP Global Operations and Information Technology:** Beth Ford, age 43
**SVP Strategic Planning and Business Development:** Heather J. Myers, age 42
**SVP, General Counsel, and Secretary:** Devereux Chatillon, age 53
**SVP Human Resource and Employee Services:** Cynthia H. Augustine, age 49
**SVP and Chief Accounting Officer:** Robert J. Jackson, age 52
**SVP Operations:** Thomas K. Hoekzema
**VP Corporate Communications and Media Relations:** Kyle Good
**President, Scholastic Book Fairs:** Alan Boyko
**President, Scholastic Classroom and Library Group:** Greg Worrell
**Auditors:** Ernst & Young LLP

## LOCATIONS

**HQ:** Scholastic Corporation
557 Broadway, New York, NY 10012
**Phone:** 212-343-6100 **Fax:** 212-343-6934
**Web:** www.scholastic.com

Scholastic Corporation has operations in Argentina, Australia, Canada, China, Hong Kong, India, Indonesia, Ireland, Malaysia, Mexico, New Zealand, the Philippines, Singapore, Taiwan, Thailand, the UK, and the US.

## PRODUCTS/OPERATIONS

### 2007 Sales

| | $ mil. | % of total |
|---|---|---|
| Children's book publishing & distributing | 1,155.3 | 53 |
| International | 448.6 | 21 |
| Educational publishing | 412.7 | 19 |
| Media, licensing & advertising | 162.5 | 7 |
| **Total** | **2,179.1** | **100** |

### Selected Products and Services

Audiovisual children's books
- Make Way for Ducklings
- Where the Wild Things Are

Book Fairs
- Scholastic Book Fairs

Educational software and programs
- I Spy
- Literacy Place
- Read 180
- Solares
- Success with Writing
- WiggleWorks

Feature films
- The Baby-Sitters Club
- Clifford's Really Big Movie
- Indian in the Cupboard

Products
- Klutz (book and toy packages)

School-based book clubs
- Arrow
- Firefly
- Honeybee
- Lucky
- SeeSaw
- TAB

Television properties
- *Animorphs*
- *Clifford the Big Red Dog*
- *Dear America*
- *Goosebumps*
- *I Spy*
- *Maya & Miguel*
- *Scholastic's The Magic School Bus*

### Selected Book Titles

*Animorphs*
*The Baby-Sitters Club*
*Captain Underpants*
*Clifford the Big Red Dog*
*Dear America*
*Goosebumps*
*Harry Potter*
*The Magic School Bus*
*Miss Spider*
*The Scholastic Encyclopedia of Presidents*
*The Scholastic Encyclopedia of Women*

### Scholastic Library Publishing

Kids Clubs
- Barbie book club
- Beginning Reader's Program (featuring Dr. Seuss books)
- Disney book club

Publishing
- *Cumbre* (Spanish-language encyclopedia)
- *Encyclopedia Americana*
- *New Book of Knowledge*

## COMPETITORS

Addison-Wesley
American Girl
Aristotle
Books Are Fun
Channel One Network
Cookie Jar Group
Disney
Disney Publishing
Educational Development
Harcourt
HarperCollins
Highlights
HIT Entertainment
Houghton Mifflin
Intervisual Books
John Wiley
LeapFrog
McGraw-Hill
Pearson
Random House
RD School
Riverdeep
Simon & Schuster
Thomson Learning
Time Warner

## HISTORICAL FINANCIALS

Company Type: Public

### Income Statement

FYE: May 31

| | REVENUE ($ mil.) | NET INCOME ($ mil.) | NET PROFIT MARGIN | EMPLOYEES |
|---|---|---|---|---|
| **5/07** | 2,179 | 61 | 2.8% | 7,600 |
| **5/06** | 2,284 | 69 | 3.0% | 10,400 |
| **5/05** | 2,080 | 64 | 3.1% | 10,800 |
| **5/04** | 2,234 | 58 | 2.6% | 10,800 |
| **5/03** | 1,958 | 59 | 3.0% | 10,800 |
| **Annual Growth** | 2.7% | 1.0% | — | (8.4%) |

### 2007 Year-End Financials

Debt ratio: 20.7%
Return on equity: 5.6%
Cash ($ mil.): 23
Current ratio: 2.18
Long-term debt ($ mil.): 233
No. of shares (mil.): 41
Dividends
Yield: —
Payout: —
Market value ($ mil.): 1,316

**Stock History** NASDAQ (GS): SCHL

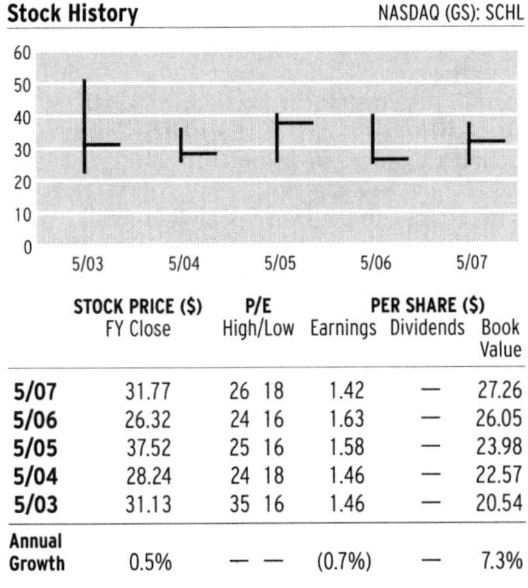

| | STOCK PRICE ($) | P/E | | PER SHARE ($) | | |
|---|---|---|---|---|---|---|
| | FY Close | High | Low | Earnings | Dividends | Book Value |
| **5/07** | 31.77 | 26 | 18 | 1.42 | — | 27.26 |
| **5/06** | 26.32 | 24 | 16 | 1.63 | — | 26.05 |
| **5/05** | 37.52 | 25 | 16 | 1.58 | — | 23.98 |
| **5/04** | 28.24 | 24 | 18 | 1.46 | — | 22.57 |
| **5/03** | 31.13 | 35 | 16 | 1.46 | — | 20.54 |
| **Annual Growth** | 0.5% | — | — | (0.7%) | — | 7.3% |

# Scotts Miracle-Gro

The grass sure seems greener over at Scotts Miracle-Gro (SMG), the world's largest maker and marketer of horticultural and turf products. Its garden and indoor plant care items include grass seeds, fertilizers, herbicides, potting soils, and related tools. Brand names include Ortho, Miracle-Gro, Hyponex, and Turf Builder. SMG markets Monsanto's Roundup herbicide products for the consumer market and has a lawn and shrub care service. It also owns upscale garden retailer Smith & Hawken. Siblings James Hagedorn (chairman and CEO) and Katherine Littlefield (a director) own a third of SMG. Hagedorn and Littlefield are the children of Horace Hagedorn, the creator of Miracle-Gro plant food.

Scotts also sells directly to professionals (i.e., nurseries, greenhouses, and specialty crop growers). To make its balance sheet even greener, Scotts has a business development group that focuses on three main areas: improving sales and profits in businesses such as hardware and independent garden centers, expanding the company's presence into grocery and drug stores, and expanding into ancillary products such as tools, pottery, and watering equipment.

Scotts Miracle-Gro has spent the past few years beefing up its retail business. As a part of that process, Scotts bought Pam Pottery, a Florida-based pottery distributor, in 2003 and began to market and sell two lines of Miracle-Gro pottery later that year. The 2004 acquisition of Smith & Hawken expanded the initiative even further. Scotts kept the management team in place at Smith & Hawken, which has more than 50 retail stores throughout the country and also does business through catalog and online sales. The following year Scotts acquired the Rod McLellan Company, a maker of potting and gardening soil in the western US, for about $20 million. Also in 2005 it spent $77 million to acquire Gutwein, whose line of Bird Song wild bird seed gives Scotts a foothold in a new market the company hopes to broaden with its scale and reach.

While the company has international operations, the North American consumer market accounts for just under 70% of sales. Within that market, Scotts' largest customers are The Home Depot (about 30% of sales), Wal-Mart (about 15%), and Lowe's (about 15%). Because of this reliance on such a small number of businesses, the company has focused on enhancing its relationships with the retailers of late.

The Scotts LawnService unit has grown — through both acquisitions and internal growth — from $42 million in sales in 2001 to more than $200 million five years later. It is the #2 lawn care services company in the US, after TruGreen.

The company changed its name from simply The Scotts Company in 2005 in an attempt to raise the profile of its consumer products business among investors.

## HISTORY

Founded by Orlando Scott in Marysville in 1868 as O.M. Scott & Sons, the firm originally cleaned crop seed. It later began selling grass seed and in 1928 debuted the US's first lawn fertilizer, Turf Builder. The family-owned business became a subsidiary of conglomerate ITT in 1971; it broke away in a 1986 management-led LBO. It went public as The Scotts Company in 1992.

Acquisitions include Hyponex (1988), lawn and garden equipment maker Republic Tool and Manufacturing (1992), and specialty fertilizer maker Grace-Sierra Horticultural Products (1993). In 1995 Scotts merged with Stern's Miracle-Gro, a company that Horace Hagedorn had started in 1951; the deal married the #1 lawn care company with the #1 garden plant food firm. The company simplified its product line by cutting more than 300 products in 1996.

Scotts launched an acquisition program in 1997 to increase sales in Europe. That year Scotts acquired the UK's Levington Horticulture (fertilizers and pesticides) and 80% of Sanford Scientific (genetically engineered grasses and plants). The next year Scotts landed a deal to market Monsanto's Roundup herbicide products internationally and bought two European lawn and garden product firms — ASEF and Rhone-Poulenc Jardin (#1 in Europe). International sales jumped almost 75% for the year. In 1999 Scotts bought Monsanto's lawn and garden businesses (including its Ortho line) for $300 million.

In 2000 Scotts bought the distribution rights for peat products manufactured by Bord na Mona, one of Europe's largest peat producers. It also sold its US and Canadian professional turf operations to The Andersons, Inc. The same year Scotts acquired Henkel's European fertilizer and plant care brand, Substral. Due to sluggish growth Scotts reorganized its European operations in 2002, pledging an investment of about $50 million by 2005. The company took a $9 million charge as a result in 2003.

President and COO James Hagedorn was named CEO in 2001; James, Horace's son, retained the title of president. He assumed the additional role of chairman in 2003. The following year Scott's ventured into the gardening retail market with the acquisition of Smith & Hawken. In the fall of 2004 Scotts paid $72 million for the high-end gardening retail chain.

Horace Hagedorn died in early 2005. The Scotts Company changed its name to The Scotts Miracle-Gro Company in 2005.

## EXECUTIVES

**Chairman, President, and CEO:** James (Jim) Hagedorn, age 51
**EVP and CFO:** David C. (Dave) Evans, age 43
**EVP, Global Human Resources:** Denise S. Stump, age 51
**SVP, North American Operations:** Barry Sanders
**SVP, Sales:** Dan Paradiso
**SVP, Scotts Lawn Service:** Tim Portland
**CEO, Smith & Hawken:** Gordon M. Erickson
**SVP, North America Sales, Scotts Company:** Brian Kura
**Chief Environmental Officer:** Rich Martinez
**Senior Director, Investor Relations and Corporate Communications:** James D. (Jim) King
**Auditors:** Deloitte & Touche LLP

## LOCATIONS

**HQ:** The Scotts Miracle-Gro Company
14111 Scottslawn Rd., Marysville, OH 43041
**Phone:** 937-644-0011 **Fax:** 937-644-7614
**Web:** www.scotts.com

The Scotts Miracle-Gro Company maintains manufacturing, sales, and service facilities in the US and in Australia, Belgium, France, Germany, the Netherlands, and the UK.

## PRODUCTS/OPERATIONS

**2006 Sales**

| | $ mil. | % of total |
|---|---|---|
| North America | 1,914.5 | 71 |
| Other regions | 408.5 | 15 |
| Scotts Lawn Service | 205.7 | 8 |
| Corporate & other | 167.6 | 6 |
| Adjustments | 0.8 | — |
| **Total** | **2,697.1** | **100** |

**Selected Products**

Garden and indoor plant care items
Garden tools
Grass seed
Herbicides
Insecticides
Lawn fertilizers
Lawn spreaders and other application devices
Pesticides
Plant foods
Potting soils
Wild bird seed

**Selected Brands**

ASEF (Benelux countries)
Bug-B-Gon
Celaflor (Germany and Austria)
Earthgro (growing media such as potting mix)
Evergreen (lawn fertilizer, UK)
Fertiligene (France)
Hyponex (growing media such as potting mix)
KB (France and Benelux countries)
Levington (growing media, UK)
Miracle-Gro (plant food)
Morning Song (bird seed)
Nature Scapes (growing media such as potting mix)
Nexa-Lotte (Germany and Austria)
Ortho (weed, insect, and disease control)
Osmocote
Pathclear (herbicide, UK)
Peters Professional
Roundup (licensed by Monsanto, herbicide)
Scotts
Shamrock (Europe)
Smith & Hawken
Substral (Europe)
Turf Builder (lawn fertilizer and weed control)
Weed-B-Gon
Weedol (herbicide, UK)

## COMPETITORS

Acuity Brands
BASF AG
Bayer CropScience
Brookstone
Central Garden & Pet
Dow AgroSciences
Home Depot
Ionatron
K+S
LESCO
Restoration Hardware
Spectrum Brands
Trans-Resources
TruGreen Landcare
Williams-Sonoma

## HISTORICAL FINANCIALS

Company Type: Public

**Income Statement** FYE: September 30

| | REVENUE ($ mil.) | NET INCOME ($ mil.) | NET PROFIT MARGIN | EMPLOYEES |
|---|---|---|---|---|
| **9/06** | 2,697 | 133 | 4.9% | 5,720 |
| **9/05** | 2,369 | 101 | 4.2% | 5,291 |
| **9/04** | 2,096 | 101 | 4.8% | 4,985 |
| **9/03** | 1,910 | 104 | 5.4% | 4,005 |
| **9/02** | 1,800 | 83 | 4.6% | 3,411 |
| **Annual Growth** | 10.6% | 12.6% | — | 13.8% |

**2006 Year-End Financials**

Debt ratio: 43.9%
Return on equity: 12.6%
Cash ($ mil.): 48
Current ratio: 1.90
Long-term debt ($ mil.): 475
No. of shares (mil.): 67
Dividends
Yield: 1.1%
Payout: 26.2%
Market value ($ mil.): 2,963

**Stock History** NYSE: SMG

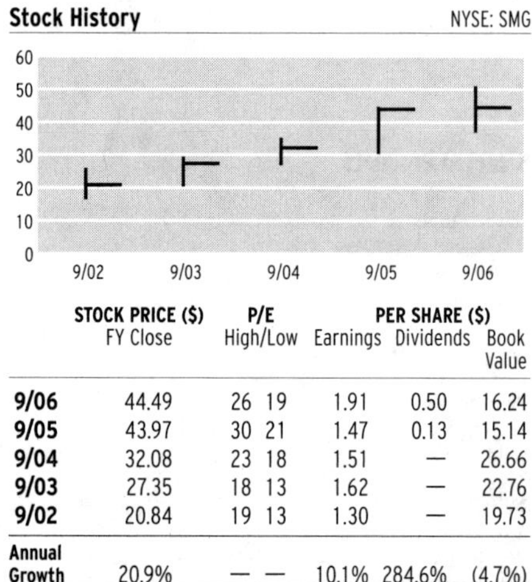


| | STOCK PRICE ($) FY Close | P/E High | P/E Low | PER SHARE ($) Earnings | Dividends | Book Value |
|---|---|---|---|---|---|---|
| **9/06** | 44.49 | 26 | 19 | 1.91 | 0.50 | 16.24 |
| **9/05** | 43.97 | 30 | 21 | 1.47 | 0.13 | 15.14 |
| **9/04** | 32.08 | 23 | 18 | 1.51 | — | 26.66 |
| **9/03** | 27.35 | 18 | 13 | 1.62 | — | 22.76 |
| **9/02** | 20.84 | 19 | 13 | 1.30 | — | 19.73 |
| **Annual Growth** | 20.9% | — | — | 10.1% | 284.6% | (4.7%) |

# Seaboard Corporation

With pork from Oklahoma, flour from Haiti, and sugar from Argentina, Seaboard has a lot on its plate. The diversified agribusiness and transportation company has operations in approximately 30 countries in the Americas, the Caribbean, and Africa. Seaboard sells pork in the US and foreign markets. Overseas it trades grains and seeds, operates power plants and feed and flour mills, and grows and refines sugar cane. Seaboard also operates a shipping service for containerized cargo between the US, the Caribbean, and South America. The descendants of founder Otto Bresky own 71% of the company through Seaboard Flour.

Seaboard's primary businesses are pork, commodity merchandising, and shipping. However, it also holds shares in a Bulgarian winery, grows and processes citrus and sugar in Argentina, has trucking transportation operations, and manufactures jalapeño pepper sauce. The company's marine division includes shipping terminals in Miami and Houston and a fleet of some 40 vessels.

Despite what some consider to be an industry oversupply of pork, Seaboard has significantly expanded its pork business with an emphasis on private-label preseasoned pork products. It markets some of its pork products under the PrairieFresh Premium Pork brand. Seaboard has an agreement with Triumph Foods to process and market all of Triumph's pork products.

Seaboard acquired Daily's Foods for $45 million in 2005; the bacon processor and foodservice supplier has been added to the company's Seaboard Foods (formerly Seaboard Farms) unit.

In 2006 Harry Bresky turned over the duty of running the family business to his son, Steven.

In January 2007 Seaboard announced the repurchase of part of the equity interest in Seaboard Foods owned by the former owners of Daily's for $30 million. The company plans to buy the remainder of Seaboard Foods for another $10 million.

## HISTORY

Otto Bresky founded his company as a flour broker in 1916. He acquired his first flour mill in Atchison, Kansas, in 1918 and the following year purchased the Imperial Brewery Co. in Kansas City and converted it to a flour mill. Over the next four decades, Bresky ground out a series of acquisitions of milling companies. In 1928 he purchased Rodney Milling Co. and retained the name as the identity for the family business. The company then purchased Ismert-Hincke Milling Co. (1938) and the Consolidated Flour Mills Co. (1950). In 1959 Rodney Milling merged with publicly traded Hathaway Industries and changed its name to Seaboard Allied Milling Corp.

In the 1960s Seaboard Allied became one of the first millers to shift flour milling from the source of the raw materials (the wheat fields of the Great Plains) to the population centers in the Southeast and on the East Coast. In 1962 Seaboard Allied built a flour mill in Chattanooga, Tennessee. It then purchased George Urban Milling Company in Buffalo, New York (1965), and built a flour mill in Jacksonville, Florida (1966). But Bresky's expansionist strategy did not stop at the Atlantic Seaboard. The company acquired a flour mill in Guayaquil, Ecuador, in 1966 (a joint venture with Continental Grain Co.), then constructed flour mills in Freetown, Sierra Leone (1968), and Georgetown, Guyana (1969).

Bresky retired in 1973 and was succeeded by his son Harry. A chip off the old block, Harry acquired a flour mill in Cleveland, Tennessee, and built flour mills in Buchanan, Liberia, and in Sapele, Nigeria, that year. In 1978 Seaboard Allied acquired Mochasa, Ecuador's leading producer of animal feed, and launched Top Feeds, a mixed-feed plant in Sapele.

Facing stiff competition in the mill business from agribusiness giants, in 1982 Seaboard Allied sold all its US flour mills to Cargill. The company changed its name to Seaboard that year and began expanding outside the US. In 1983 the company formed Seaboard Marine, a shipping business in Florida, to serve its increasingly far-flung enterprises.

In addition to geographic diversification, the company expanded into new agribusiness areas. Seaboard acquired Central Soya's poultry unit in 1984, and it bought the Elberton Poultry Company the next year. Seaboard commenced shrimp farming operations in Ecuador in 1986 and in Honduras in 1987. Two years later Transcontinental Capital Corporation (Bermuda), a subsidiary, began supplying power from a floating power barge to the Dominican Republic.

Seaboard entered the hog business in 1990 by acquiring a pork-processing plant in Albert Lea, Minnesota. It opened a hog processing facility in Guymon, Oklahoma, in 1996 and closed the Minnesota plant. That year the company bought a stake in Ingenio y Refinerio San Martin del Tabacal, an Argentina-based sugar cane and citrus company. It then acquired flour mill, pasta plant, and cookie operations in Beira, Mozambique.

During 1998 Seaboard bought a controlling interest in the Argentine sugar business, purchased a Bulgarian winery, and acquired a flour and feed milling business in Zambia.

In 2000 Seaboard sold its poultry division to ConAgra for $375 million. Also that year the company acquired a 35% stake in Unga Group, (feed milling, Kenya) and the JacintoPort marine terminal in Houston.

During 2001 the company traded its non-controlling interest in a joint-venture salmon processor (ContiSea LLC) to Norway's Fjord Seafood ASA for stock, and swapped its majority ownership of one Bulgarian winery for minority ownership in a larger one. That same year it ceased production at its Honduran shrimp farms and jalapeño pickling operations.

Seaboard purchased more of Fjord Seafood in 2002; with 20% of the company, it became the largest shareholder. However, by the end of 2003 Seaboard sold off its entire investment in Fjord Seafood for $37 million. That same year the company sold its closed shrimp businesses. In 2004 the company acquired a controlling stake in a Mozambique grain milling business.

After serving as CEO for more than 30 years, in 2006 Harry Bresky stepped down as CEO (but remained as chairman) and turned over the company's reins to his son, Steven. Harry Bresky died in early 2007.

## EXECUTIVES

**President and CEO:** Steven J. Bresky, age 53, $1,684,135 pay
**SVP and CFO:** Robert L. Steer, age 47, $1,484,135 pay
**VP, Corporate Controller, and Chief Accounting Officer:** John A. Virgo, age 46
**VP, Engineering:** James L. (Jim) Gutsch, age 53
**VP, Finance:** Barry E. Gum, age 40
**VP, General Counsel, and Secretary:** David M. Becker, age 45
**VP, Governmental Affairs:** Ralph L. Moss, age 61
**VP, Taxation and Business Development:** David S. Oswalt, age 39
**President, Seaboard Foods LP:** Rodney K. (Rod) Brenneman, age 42, $1,409,231 pay
**President, Seaboard Marine Ltd.:** Edward A. (Eddie) Gonzales, age 41, $948,558 pay
**President, Seaboard Overseas Trading Group:** David M. Dannov, $511,605 pay
**Auditors:** KPMG LLP

## LOCATIONS

**HQ:** Seaboard Corporation
9000 W. 67th St., Shawnee Mission, KS 66202
**Phone:** 913-676-8800 **Fax:** 913-676-8872
**Web:** www.seaboardcorp.com

### 2006 Sales

| | $ mil. | % of total |
|---|---|---|
| North America | | |
| US | 1,027.3 | 38 |
| Canada & Mexico | 78.0 | 3 |
| Caribbean, Central & South America | 845.6 | 31 |
| Africa | 588.1 | 22 |
| Pacific Basin & Far East | 147.6 | 5 |
| Europe | 16.9 | 1 |
| Eastern Mediterranean | 3.9 | — |
| **Total** | **2,707.4** | **100** |

## PRODUCTS/OPERATIONS

### 2006 Sales

| | $ mil. | % of total |
|---|---|---|
| Pork | 1,002.6 | 37 |
| Marine | 741.6 | 27 |
| Commodity trading & milling | 735.6 | 27 |
| Sugar & citrus | 123.4 | 5 |
| Power | 87.8 | 3 |
| Other | 16.4 | 1 |
| **Total** | **2,707.4** | **100** |

### Selected Operations

- Cargo shipping
- Citrus production and processing
- Commodity merchandising (wheat, corn, and soybean meal)
- Domestic trucking transportation
- Electric power generation
- Flour, maize, and feed milling
- Jalapeño-pepper processing
- Pork production and processing
- Sugar production and refining

## COMPETITORS

ADM
American Crystal Sugar
APL
Bunge Limited
Cargill
Chiquita Brands
Colonial Group
ContiGroup
Crowley Maritime
CSX
Dole Food
Evergreen Marine
Fresh Del Monte Produce
Hormel
Imperial Sugar
Johnsonville Sausage
M A Patout
Neptune Orient
Nicor
Nutreco
NYK Line
Owens Incorporated
Südzucker
Smithfield Foods
Sunkist
Tate & Lyle
Tyson Fresh Meats
U.S. Sugar
Western Sugar Cooperative

## HISTORICAL FINANCIALS

Company Type: Public

### Income Statement

FYE: December 31

| | REVENUE ($ mil.) | NET INCOME ($ mil.) | NET PROFIT MARGIN | EMPLOYEES |
|---|---|---|---|---|
| **12/06** | 2,707 | 259 | 9.6% | 10,363 |
| **12/05** | 2,689 | 267 | 9.9% | 10,357 |
| **12/04** | 2,684 | 168 | 6.3% | 9,532 |
| **12/03** | 1,981 | 32 | 1.6% | 9,462 |
| **12/02** | 1,829 | 14 | 0.7% | 9,294 |
| **Annual Growth** | 10.3% | 109.2% | — | 2.8% |

### 2006 Year-End Financials

Debt ratio: 11.5%
Return on equity: 23.7%
Cash ($ mil.): 510
Current ratio: 3.07
Long-term debt ($ mil.): 138

No. of shares (mil.): 1
Dividends
Yield: 0.2%
Payout: 1.5%
Market value ($ mil.): 2,226

### Stock History

AMEX: SEB

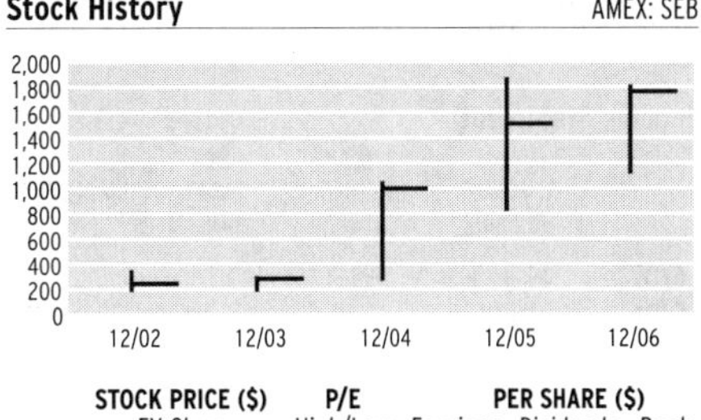


| | STOCK PRICE ($) FY Close | P/E High | P/E Low | PER SHARE ($) Earnings | Dividends | Book Value |
|---|---|---|---|---|---|---|
| **12/06** | 1,765.00 | 9 | 6 | 205.09 | 3.00 | 953.97 |
| **12/05** | 1,511.00 | 9 | 4 | 211.94 | 3.00 | 775.24 |
| **12/04** | 998.00 | 8 | 2 | 133.94 | 3.00 | 551.91 |
| **12/03** | 282.00 | 11 | 8 | 25.37 | 3.00 | 414.77 |
| **12/02** | 242.00 | 36 | 21 | 9.38 | 2.25 | 387.82 |
| **Annual Growth** | 64.3% | — | — | 116.2% | 7.5% | 25.2% |

# Seagate Technology

Seagate Technology knows that if you want to survive in the storage market, you'd better have drive. The company is a leading independent maker of rigid disk drives (or hard drives) used to store data in computers. Its drives are used in systems ranging from personal computers and workstations to high-end servers and mainframes. Seagate sells directly to computer manufacturers and through distributors. About 70% of Seagate's sales are to computer hardware manufacturers, which include Hewlett-Packard (17% of sales in fiscal 2006), Dell, EMC, IBM, and Sun Microsystems; distributors account for the rest.

In a major step to expand its operations, the company agreed in 2005 to acquire rival storage device maker Maxtor for about $1.9 billion in stock. The deal closed in mid-2006, and Seagate expects to have Maxtor fully integrated by early 2007. Seagate plans to retain the Maxtor brand. In late 2006 Seagate agreed to purchase online backup services provider EVault for approximately $185 million.

In an industry hurt by falling PC prices, Seagate has managed to stay at the front of the disk drive provider line by significantly undercutting competitors' prices, instituting global layoffs, and consolidating facilities.

Investment firms Silver Lake Partners and Texas Pacific Group took Seagate private in 2000. Prior to being taken private — a transaction that allowed Seagate to realize the value of its large holding in VERITAS Software while avoiding certain tax liabilities — the company had operations that included a business intelligence software developer (Crystal Decisions), a subsidiary that develops storage networking products (XIOtech), and a unit devoted to tape storage products. The reorganized Seagate generates virtually all of its sales from its core hard-drive business. It went public again in 2002.

Affiliates of FMR own about 12% of Seagate.

## HISTORY

Seagate Technology Holdings was founded in 1979 by Alan Shugart, an 18-year veteran of IBM who had made floppy disks standard on microcomputers; manufacturing expert and longtime technology industry veteran Tom Mitchell; design engineer Douglas Mahon; and Finis Conner. Seagate pioneered the miniaturizing of larger mainframe hard disk drives for PCs.

Seagate's first product, a 5.25-in. hard disk, sold briskly. With IBM as a customer, the company had grabbed half of the market for small disk drives by 1982; sales reached $344 million by 1984. But Seagate's heavy dependence on IBM showed its double edge as dwindling PC demand prompted IBM to cut orders. Sales in 1985 dropped to $215 million and profits to $1 million (from $42 million). Seagate transferred its manufacturing to Singapore and cut its California workforce in half. That year Conner, after a quarrel with Shugart, left Seagate to start his own disk drive company, Conner Peripherals. (Mitchell later joined him.)

Using acquisitions to grow, the company purchased Grenex (thin-film magnetic media, 1984), Aeon (aluminum substrates, 1987), and Integrated Power Systems (custom semiconductors, 1987). Seagate also lured back IBM, which had turned to an alternate supplier in the interim.

With sales more than doubling in 1986 and again in 1987, Seagate continued to invest in 5.25-in. production, ignoring signs of a coming 3.5-in. drive standard. The strong market in 1988 for the smaller drives prompted Seagate's quick shift to 3.5-in. production. Seagate's purchase of Imprimis in 1989 made it the world's premier independent drive maker and a leader in high-capacity drives.

In 1993 the company acquired a stake in flash memory storage specialist Sundisk. That year, with Sun Microsystems accounting for 11% of sales, Seagate was the only profitable independent disk drive company. In 1994 the company began pursuing its software initiative, acquiring Palindrome and Crystal Computer Services.

Shugart, an iconoclast who once ran his dog for Congress, had a small comeuppance in 1996 when Seagate paid just over $1 billion for Conner Peripherals, which had banked on 3.5-in. disk drives from the start and had gone public in 1988. By the time of the acquisition, Conner was a leading maker of disk and tape drives, storage systems, and software.

Seagate merged Conner's software subsidiary with its own holdings to form Seagate Storage Management Group and continued to expand by buying management software companies. In 1997 the company bought disk drive developer Quinta. Seagate took a charge that year following a ruling that it had sold faulty drives to Amstrad PLC.

An industry slump, production problems, and lowered PC demand prompted Seagate to cut 20% of its workforce, streamline development, fire Shugart, and replace him with president and COO — and former investment banker — Stephen Luczo. The downturn took its toll when the company suffered a $530 million loss for fiscal 1998. The next year Seagate gained a stake of about 33% in VERITAS Software when it sold its network and storage management software operations to that company for $3.1 billion. Seagate also announced that it would lay off another 10% of its workforce of nearly 80,000.

In early 2000 the company acquired XIOtech, a maker of virtual storage and storage area network systems, for about $360 million. Later that year Seagate entered into an intricate deal with VERITAS, whereby the software maker bought back the stake owned by Seagate. As part of the deal, Seagate was taken private in a buyout led by Silver Lake Partners and Texas Pacific Group.

Also in 2000 COO William Watkins, who joined Seagate when it bought Conner Peripherals, replaced Luczo as president; Luczo remained CEO. The company went public again in 2002 in an IPO that raised $870 million. In 2004 Luczo passed the CEO reins to Watkins, but retained his chairmanship.

## EXECUTIVES

**Chairman:** Stephen J. Luczo, age 49
**CEO and Director:** William D. (Bill) Watkins, age 54, $4,000,002 pay
**President and COO:** David A. Wickersham, age 50, $2,701,930 pay
**EVP and Chief Sales and Marketing Officer:** Brian S. Dexheimer, age 43, $2,081,600 pay
**EVP, General Counsel, and Secretary:** William L. Hudson, age 54, $1,486,164 pay
**EVP, Finance and CFO:** Charles C. Pope, age 51, $2,450,011 pay
**EVP, Global Disc Storage Operations:** James M. (Jim) Chirico Jr., age 47
**EVP, Product and Process Development:** Robert (Bob) Whitmore, age 43
**SVP, Heads and Media:** Jaroslaw S. Glembocki, age 49
**SVP and General Manager, Branded Solutions:** James Druckrey
**SVP and General Manager, Enterprise Compute Business:** Sherman Black
**SVP and General Manager, Personal Compute Business:** Karl Chicca
**SVP, Finance, Principal Accounting Officer, and Treasurer:** Patrick J. O'Malley
**SVP, Research and Technology and CTO:** Mark Kryder, age 61
**Chief Technologist:** Robert Thibadeau
**Senior Director, Investor Relations:** Rod Cooper
**Auditors:** Ernst & Young LLP

## LOCATIONS

**HQ:** Seagate Technology
920 Disc Dr., Scotts Valley, CA 95066
**Phone:** 831-438-6550 **Fax:** 831-429-6356
**Web:** www.seagate.com

### 2007 Sales

| | $ mil. | % of total |
|---|---|---|
| Singapore | 4,346 | 38 |
| US | 3,260 | 29 |
| The Netherlands | 2,666 | 23 |
| Other countries | 1,088 | 10 |
| **Total** | **11,360** | **100** |

## PRODUCTS/OPERATIONS

### Selected Products

Personal computing disk drives
- Desktop (Barracuda)
- Notebook (Momentus)

Enterprise computing disk drives (Barracuda, Cheetah, Savvio)

## COMPETITORS

Cornice
Fujitsu
Hitachi Global Storage
Samsung Electronics
Toshiba
Western Digital

## HISTORICAL FINANCIALS

Company Type: Public

### Income Statement

FYE: Friday nearest June 30

| | REVENUE ($ mil.) | NET INCOME ($ mil.) | NET PROFIT MARGIN | EMPLOYEES |
|---|---|---|---|---|
| **6/07** | 11,360 | 913 | 8.0% | 54,000 |
| **6/06** | 9,206 | 840 | 9.1% | 60,000 |
| **6/05** | 7,553 | 707 | 9.4% | 44,000 |
| **6/04** | 6,224 | 529 | 8.5% | 40,000 |
| **6/03** | 6,486 | 641 | 9.9% | 43,000 |
| **Annual Growth** | 15.0% | 9.2% | — | 5.9% |

### 2007 Year-End Financials

Debt ratio: 36.6%
Return on equity: 18.4%
Cash ($ mil.): 1,144
Current ratio: 1.43
Long-term debt ($ mil.): 1,733
No. of shares (mil.): 535
Dividends
Yield: 1.7%
Payout: 24.4%
Market value ($ mil.): 11,647

### Stock History

NYSE: STX

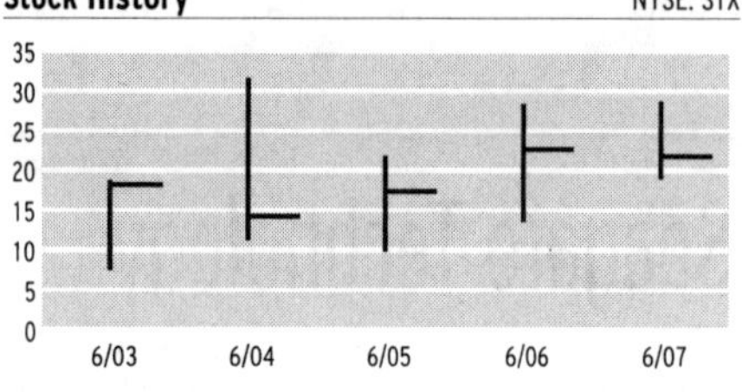


| | STOCK PRICE ($) FY Close | P/E High | P/E Low | PER SHARE ($) Earnings | Dividends | Book Value |
|---|---|---|---|---|---|---|
| **6/07** | 21.77 | 18 | 12 | 1.56 | 0.38 | 8.85 |
| **6/06** | 22.64 | 18 | 9 | 1.60 | 0.32 | 9.05 |
| **6/05** | 17.35 | 15 | 7 | 1.41 | 0.26 | 5.33 |
| **6/04** | 14.21 | 30 | 11 | 1.06 | 0.20 | 4.04 |
| **6/03** | 18.18 | 14 | 6 | 1.36 | 0.06 | 3.00 |
| **Annual Growth** | 4.6% | — | — | 3.5% | 58.6% | 31.1% |

# Sealed Air

It's no secret — Sealed Air keeps its customers' products under wraps. Sealed Air's largest product segment, Food Packaging, produces Cryovac shrink films, absorbent pads, and foam trays used by food processors and supermarkets to protect meat and poultry. Its Protective Packaging segment produces Bubble Wrap, Instapak foam, Jiffy envelopes, and Fill-Air inflatable packaging systems. Nonpackaging products include adhesive tape, solar pool covers, and recycled kraft paper. Sealed Air reckons that its products reach about 80% of the world's population. Davis Selected Advisers holds a 36% stake in the company.

Sealed Air has operations in 50 countries, but the US accounts for almost half of its sales. The company has embarked on a manufacturing strategy in which it plans to expand its capacity in emerging markets and improve efficiencies at existing facilities.

Sealed Air restructured its reporting system in 2004, bringing its medical films, connectors, and tubing under its Food Packaging segment. It also cut nearly 400 employees and consolidated some of its operations.

Early in 2006 Sealed Air acquired Nelipak Holdings, a Netherlands-based rigid packaging company. The company sold its security bag business (Trigon) to Ampac in 2007, and it sold its interest in joint venture PolyMask (surface protection films) to partner 3M.

## HISTORY

In the late 1950s, after US engineer Al Fielding and Swiss inventor Marc Chavannes found no takers for their plastic air-bubble-embossed wallpaper, they looked for another use for the material. They came up with Bubble Wrap, the first product of Sealed Air, which they founded in 1960 and took public soon after. AirCap, as the material was first known, didn't just protect products from damage; it also reduced storage and shipping costs.

Sealed Air expanded in the early 1970s into bubble-lined mailers and adhesive products with subsidiary PolyMask. With the $5 million company in the doldrums, Dublin-born packaging veteran Dermot Dunphy was brought in as CEO in 1971. New products followed Dunphy's entrance, including the Bubble Wrap-based Solar Pool Blanket. Sealed Air's sales moved beyond the US in the 1970s into Canada, Japan, and Western Europe. The company bought Instapak in 1977.

The purchase in 1983 of the Dri-Loc product line moved Sealed Air into food packaging. The company began selling static-control packaging in 1984, and in 1987 it bought padded-mailer maker Jiffy Packaging. Fielding and Chavannes both retired in 1987. Sealed Air pleaded guilty in 1989 to making illegal chemical shipments to Libya (made by a division the company had since sold).

By 1989 Sealed Air had plenty of cash on hand, but with no appealing acquisitions to spend it on, the company was a potential takeover target. It had also grown complacent. To provide greater incentive to the company's rank and file while warding off any buyout overtures, Dunphy and CFO Bill Hickey took Sealed Air through a risky recapitalization. This plunged the company into debt but more than doubled its employees' ownership stake. The newly inspired packaging maker became more efficient, the cost of Sealed Air's raw materials dropped, and the company brought its debt back down over the next several years.

The acquisition of Korrvu in 1991 gave Sealed Air a gateway to innovative packaging for electronics manufacturers. The company made a host of mostly small purchases in Asia, Australia, Europe, and North America between 1993 and 1996. When Sealed Air bought New Zealand-based Trigon Industries in 1995, its food-packaging business nearly doubled in size, along with sales outside the US.

In 1998 Sealed Air made an Instapak-like expansion when it combined with W. R. Grace's packaging business (including the Cryovac, Formpac, and Omicron lines). Grace structured a deal with Sealed Air that gave Grace's shareholders about two-thirds of the resulting packaging-only company. Sealed Air tripled its sales and number of employees with the purchase.

The company restructured its operations in 1999 to integrate its newly acquired businesses. It closed facilities with overlapping operations and eliminated 750 jobs (5% of its workforce). Dunphy retired in 2000 (although he remains a director) and president William Hickey became CEO.

That year Sealed Air acquired Dolphin Packaging (plastic packaging products) and Shanklin (high-performance shrink-film packaging equipment) to complement its shrink films.

In 2001, more than three years after the company combined its operations with W. R. Grace's packaging business, Sealed Air continued to defend itself against asbestos lawsuits related to Grace's past operations. (In 2005 the company's definitive settlement agreement was accepted by the bankruptcy court.)

## EXECUTIVES

**President, CEO, and Director:** William V. Hickey, age 62, $496,667 pay
**SVP and CFO:** David H. Kelsey, age 55, $347,833 pay
**SVP:** David B. Crosier, age 57, $327,500 pay
**SVP:** Robert A. Pesci, age 61, $347,833 pay
**VP, General Counsel, and Secretary:** H. Katherine White, age 61
**VP:** Mary A. Coventry, age 53
**VP:** Jonathan B. Baker, age 53, $290,000 pay
**VP:** James P. Mix, age 55
**VP:** Manuel Mondragón, age 57
**VP:** Carol Lee O'Neill, age 43
**VP:** Ruth Roper, age 52
**VP:** Hugh L. Sargant, age 58
**VP:** James Donald Tate, age 55
**VP:** Christopher C. Woodbridge, age 55
**VP:** Karl R. Deily, age 49
**VP:** Jean-Marie Demeautis, age 56
**VP:** Brian W. Elliott, age 53
**VP:** Cheryl Fells Davis, age 54
**Controller:** Jeffrey S. Warren, age 53
**Investor and Media Relations:** Eric D. Burrell
**Treasurer:** Tod S. Christie, age 48
**Auditors:** KPMG LLP

## LOCATIONS

**HQ:** Sealed Air Corporation
200 Riverfront Blvd., Elmwood Park, NJ 07407
**Phone:** 201-791-7600 **Fax:** 201-703-4205
**Web:** www.sealedaircorp.com

Sealed Air operates about 120 manufacturing facilities in over 50 countries worldwide.

### 2006 Sales

| | $ mil. | % of total |
|---|---|---|
| North America | | |
| US | 2,066.3 | 48 |
| Canada | 148.1 | 3 |
| Europe | 1,254.2 | 29 |
| Asia/Pacific | 509.8 | 12 |
| Latin America | 349.5 | 8 |
| **Total** | **4,327.9** | **100** |

## PRODUCTS/OPERATIONS

### 2006 Sales

| | $ mil. | % of total |
|---|---|---|
| Food packaging | 2,702.9 | 62 |
| Protective packaging | 1,625.0 | 38 |
| **Total** | **4,327.9** | **100** |

### Selected Products

Food Packaging
- Absorbent pads & case liners (Cryovac)
- Bags (Cryovac)
- Bagging systems (Cryovac)
- Foam trays (Cryovac)
- Laminates (Cryovac, plastic used to package hot dogs)
- Medical products (Cryovac)
- Oxygen scavenging systems (Cryovac)
- Packaging systems (Cryovac)
- Reflective foil cellular insulation (Reflectix)
- Shrink films and equipment (Cryovac)
- Solar pool heating products (Sealed Air)

Protective Packaging
- Air cellular cushioning (Bubble Wrap)
- Cushioned mailing bags (Jiffy Mailer)
- Foam packaging (Instapak)
- Inflatable packaging and cushioning (Fill-Air and FillTeck)
- Paper packaging (Kushion Kraft and Custom Wrap)
- Polyethylene fabrication foam (Cellu-Cushion, CelluPlank, Stratocell)
- Polyethylene foam (Cell-Aire)
- Suspension and retention packaging (Korrvu)

## COMPETITORS

3M
AEP Industries
Atlantis Plastics
Bemis
Curwood
Huhtamäki
Intertape Polymer
Owens-Illinois
Pactiv
Pliant
Polyair Inter Pack
Printpack
Sonoco Products
Tekni-Plex
Winpak

## HISTORICAL FINANCIALS

Company Type: Public

### Income Statement

FYE: December 31

| | REVENUE ($ mil.) | NET INCOME ($ mil.) | NET PROFIT MARGIN | EMPLOYEES |
|---|---|---|---|---|
| **12/06** | 4,328 | 274 | 6.3% | 17,400 |
| **12/05** | 4,085 | 256 | 6.3% | 17,000 |
| **12/04** | 3,798 | 216 | 5.7% | 17,600 |
| **12/03** | 3,532 | 240 | 6.8% | 17,600 |
| **12/02** | 3,204 | (309) | — | 17,900 |
| **Annual Growth** | 7.8% | — | — | (0.7%) |

### 2006 Year-End Financials

Debt ratio: 110.4%
Return on equity: 18.0%
Cash ($ mil.): 407
Current ratio: 1.25
Long-term debt ($ mil.): 1,827
No. of shares (mil.): 81
Dividends
Yield: 0.9%
Payout: 20.4%
Market value ($ mil.): 2,618

### Stock History

NYSE: SEE

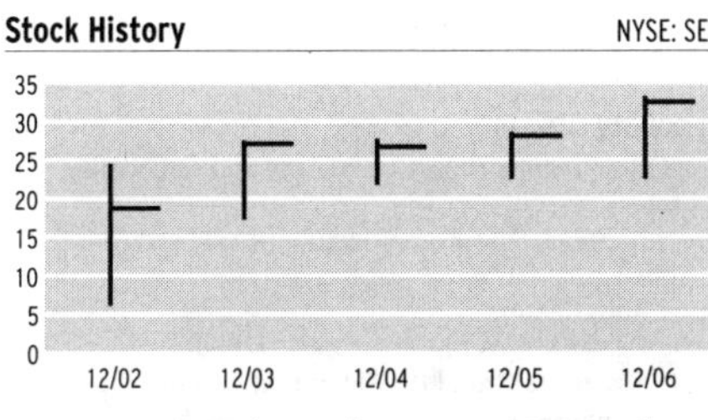


| | STOCK PRICE ($) FY Close | P/E High | P/E Low | PER SHARE ($) Earnings | PER SHARE ($) Dividends | PER SHARE ($) Book Value |
|---|---|---|---|---|---|---|
| **12/06** | 32.46 | 22 | 16 | 1.47 | 0.30 | 20.51 |
| **12/05** | 28.08 | 21 | 17 | 1.35 | — | 17.09 |
| **12/04** | 26.64 | 24 | 20 | 1.13 | — | 15.95 |
| **12/03** | 27.07 | 27 | 18 | 1.00 | — | 13.21 |
| **12/02** | 18.65 | — | — | (2.15) | — | 9.67 |
| **Annual Growth** | 14.9% | — | — | — | — | 20.7% |

# Sears, Roebuck

Sears, Roebuck and Co. hasn't outgrown the mall scene, but it's spending more time in other places. Beyond its 860 US mall-based stores, Sears has more than 1,100 other locations nationwide. The company operates more than 800 independently owned Sears dealer stores in small towns and about 110 Sears hardware stores and some 85 Orchard Supply Hardware shops. Sears' stores sell apparel, tools, and appliances, and provide home services (remodeling, appliance repairs) under the Sears Parts & Repair Services and A&E Factory brands. Its Web site also sells appliances and tools. Sears was acquired by Kmart Holding Corp. in March 2005. The deal formed a new parent company, Sears Holdings, which owns both chains.

Sears Holdings formed the nation's third-largest retailer (behind Wal-Mart and Home Depot) with nearly 3,400 stores and about $53 billion in annual sales. Its chairman Edward Lampert owns 42% of Sears Holdings through ESL Investments. Since the megamerger, several hundred Kmart locations — mainly in urban and dense suburban markets — have been converted to Sears stores.

The combination of Sears and Kmart was a response to the pounding both companies endured at the hands of Wal-Mart and other discount and mass merchandisers. Sears' previous responses include pushing its private brands of apparel, tools, and appliances (Crossroads, Craftsman, Kenmore, respectively). It is also cutting prices on some appliances to fend off rival chains, such as Home Depot and Lowe's. Sears has been adding features common to its rivals' stores, such as following the self-serve trend by installing centrally located cash registers. It has taken a cue from industry leaders such as Kohl's and Wal-Mart by adding shopping carts to its stores and widening aisles.

The company's freestanding off-the-mall format — Sears Essentials/Grand — is designed to compete directly with supercenters by selling consumables, health and beauty aids, housewares, and toys, among other offerings, all under one very large roof. (Sears Essentials/Grand stores average about 113,000 sq. ft.)

## HISTORY

Richard Sears, a Minnesota railway agent, bought a load of watches in 1886 that were being returned to the maker. He started the R. W. Sears Watch Company six months later, moved to Chicago, and in 1887 hired watchmaker Alvah Roebuck. Sears sold the watch business in 1889 and two years later formed the mail-order business that in 1893 became Sears, Roebuck and Co. It issued its first general catalog in 1896, targeting mainly farmers.

Roebuck left the company in 1895, and Sears found two new partners: Aaron Nussbaum (who left in 1901) and Julius Rosenwald. In 1906 the company went public to finance expansion. Differences soon arose between Sears and Rosenwald; Sears departed in 1908, and Rosenwald became president.

In 1925 the firm brought out a line of tires under the name Allstate. That year it opened its first retail store, and by 1931 the company's catalog sales trailed its retail sales. The rapid growth of Sears' retail operations was instrumental in the development of its prominent lines of store-brand merchandise. Sears began offering Allstate auto insurance in 1931.

Sales shot up after WWII, passing the $1 billion mark in 1945 and doubling just a year later. Sears targeted the fast-growing Sunbelt and nascent suburbs for expansion. By the early 1950s, sales of durable goods had fallen off, and the company began stocking more clothing.

After struggling through the late 1970s, Sears diversified. It acquired Coldwell Banker (real estate sales) and Dean Witter Reynolds (stock brokerage) in 1981 and launched the Discover credit card in 1985.

In reaction to falling market share in the 1980s, Sears lurched from one retail strategy to another and diversified into auto supplies and repairs. In 1993 the company sold its remaining stake in Coldwell Banker and spun off Dean Witter and Discover.

Sears transferred ownership of Chicago's famed Sears Tower to a trust in 1994 to cut debt. The next year the firm spun off insurer Allstate. Sears' top merchandiser, Arthur Martinez, became CEO that year. He gave Sears a makeover, catering especially to its mainly female clientele.

In 1996 and 1997 Sears abandoned a pair of ventures with IBM, including Prodigy (an online service that the two companies sold at a huge loss). In 1997 the company reduced its stake in Sears Roebuck de México to 15%.

Again revamping its retail strategy, in 1998 the company sold its Western Auto wholesale business (which also operated about 600 Parts America stores) to Advance Holding, and in 1999 it sold its HomeLife furniture unit to Citicorp Venture Capital; Sears kept a stake in both businesses. In 1998 a stream of high-ranking officers left the company. The executive departures continued in 1999 as Sears reorganized its automotive and direct-marketing units and eventually cut some 1,400 jobs at headquarters.

In 2000 Martinez stepped down as CEO; president of services Alan Lacy assumed the role in October 2000. In 2001 Sears closed 30 hardware stores, nine full-line stores, and seven NTB tire and battery shops.

Sears dropped certain offerings, including installed floor coverings, cosmetics, bicycles, and custom window treatments, and in 2002 the company laid off about 22% of its workforce. In June of the same year Sears bought catalog retailer Lands' End for almost $2 billion.

The first Sears Grand store had its debut in Utah in September 2003. In November Sears sold its giant credit-card business to Citigroup for about $6 billion in pre-tax cash. (It was the nation's eighth-largest credit card portfolio, with about 25 million active accounts.) To better focus on core operations, Sears sold its National Tire & Battery (NTB) chain to TBC Corporation for $225 million in December 2003.

In January 2004 Sears won a $10.8 million settlement from Emerson Electric Co., resolving a 2002 lawsuit that claimed Emerson used machines owned by Sears to make a line of bench power tools for one of the department store chain's top rivals. In the fall of 2004 Sears launched a new women's clothing line (made by Jones Apparel Group); the "ALine" label (sportswear, outerwear, and accessories) debuted in more than half of Sears' retail locations.

The following year, Kmart Holding Corp acquired Sears, Roebuck. The deal formed a new company, Sears Holdings, which is now the parent company of both chains.

## EXECUTIVES

**CEO, Sears Retail; President and CEO of Sears Holdings Corp.:** Aylwin B. Lewis, age 52
**EVP, CFO, Chief Administrative Officer, and Director; Chairman, Sears Canada:** William C. Crowley, age 49
**SVP, General Manager, The Great Indoors:** Teresa Byrd, age 56
**SVP, Retail Operations:** Mike McCarthy
**SVP, Human Resources:** Bob Luse
**VP and General Manager, Home Appliances:** Tina Settecase
**VP and General Manager, Sears Dealer Stores:** Steve Titus
**VP, Brand Management and Retail Initiatives:** Jeffery (Jeff) Gruener
**VP, Creative and Specialty Marketing:** Becky Case
**VP, Media Services:** Perianne Grignon
**President, Lands' End:** David McCreight
**Executive Director, Broadcast Advertising:** Glori Katz
**Chief Marketing Officer:** Richard Gerstein
**Auditors:** Deloitte & Touche LLP

## LOCATIONS

**HQ:** Sears, Roebuck and Co.
3333 Beverly Rd., Hoffman Estates, IL 60179
**Phone:** 847-286-2500
**Web:** www.sears.com

Sears, Roebuck and Co. operates more than 2,000 full-line mall stores and specialty stores in all 50 US states and Puerto Rico.

## PRODUCTS/OPERATIONS

**2007 Stores**

| | No. |
|---|---|
| Specialty stores | 1,095 |
| Full-line mall stores | 861 |
| Sears Grand/Essentials | 74 |
| **Total** | **2,030** |

**Selected Brands**

Hard Goods
- Craftsman
- DieHard
- Kenmore
- WeatherBeater

Soft Goods
- Apostrophe
- Canyon River Blues
- Covington
- Lands' End
- TKS Basics

**Specialty Stores**

The Great Indoors (home decorating and remodeling superstores)
Orchard Supply Hardware (neighborhood hardware stores)
Sears Auto Centers
Sears Dealer Stores (independently owned)
Sears Essentials/Grand (free-standing general merchandise stores)
Sears Hardware

## COMPETITORS

Ace Hardware
AutoZone
Bed Bath & Beyond
Belk
Best Buy
Big 5
Big Lots
Brown Shoe
Burlington Coat Factory
Circuit City
Collective Brands
Family Dollar Stores
Foot Locker
Home Depot
J. C. Penney
Kohl's
Linens 'n Things
L.L. Bean
Lowe's
Men's Wearhouse
Pep Boys
RadioShack
Retail Ventures
Ross Stores
ShopKo Stores
Snap-on
Target
TJX Companies
Toys "R" Us
True Value
Wal-Mart

## HISTORICAL FINANCIALS

Company Type: Subsidiary

**Income Statement** FYE: Saturday nearest January 31

| | REVENUE ($ mil.) | NET INCOME ($ mil.) | NET PROFIT MARGIN | EMPLOYEES |
|---|---|---|---|---|
| 1/06 | 30,030 | — | — | — |

# Sempra Energy

Sempra Energy isn't joining the Marines, but it is enlisting in liberalized utility markets worldwide. In the US Sempra distributes natural gas to some 5.6 million customers and electricity to 1.4 million customers through its Southern California Gas (SoCalGas) and San Diego Gas & Electric (SDG&E) utilities. Unregulated subsidiaries, which operate under the Sempra Global umbrella, include Sempra Pipelines & Storage (formerly Sempra Energy International), which has global energy projects and serves power and gas customers (mainly in Latin America), and Sempra Commodities (formerly Sempra Energy Trading), which trades and markets wholesale energy commodities in Asia, Europe, and North America.

Other activities include developing or acquiring merchant power plants (Sempra Generation, formerly Sempra Energy Resources), liquefied natural gas (LNG) regasification facilities (Sempra LNG), and affordable housing properties.

In response to widespread deregulation, Sempra is focusing on expanding its nonregulated energy operations in the US and overseas, including its energy marketing and risk management, telecommunications, and independent power production businesses. The company has completed a $430 million acquisition of fossil-fueled and hydroelectric generation assets (3,800 MW of capacity) from AEP's Texas Central unit as part of a joint venture with the Carlyle/Riverstone power fund. It has also formed a new division, Sempra LNG (formerly Sempra Energy LNG), to oversee its development of two LNG receipt terminals, and it plans to invest in improving its utility infrastructure assets.

The company restructured its competitive energy business units in 2005, renaming several divisions and dividing the former Sempra Energy Solutions operations (retail energy marketing and services for commercial and industrial customers) under the Commodities and Generation divisions.

In 2005 Sempra sold one of its gas storage units to Vulcan Capital, an investment company headed up by Microsoft co-founder Paul Allen, for a reported $250 million.

In 2006 the company settled class action litigation that claimed that two of its subsidiaries, Southern California Gas and San Diego Gas & Electric, helped to create the 2000-2001 energy crises in California by restricting the supply of natural gas to the state.

## HISTORY

Sempra Energy is the latest incarnation of some of California's leading lights. Formed by the $6.2 billion merger between Enova and Pacific Enterprises, the company traces its roots back to the 1880s.

Enova began as San Diego Gas, which lit its first gaslights in 1881 and added electricity in 1887 (when it became San Diego Gas & Electric Light). Massive utility holding company Standard Gas & Electric bought the company in 1905 and renamed it San Diego Consolidated Gas & Electric. Over the next few decades, San Diego Consolidated expanded through acquisitions and even stayed profitable during the Depression. But the 1935 Public Utilities Holding Company Act forced Standard to divest many of its widespread utilities, and in 1940 San Diego Consolidated went public as San Diego Gas & Electric (SDG&E).

SDG&E grew quickly until the 1970s, when new environmental laws slowed plans to build more power plants and rates soared because the company had to purchase power. The company finally added more generating capacity in the 1980s, and the state of California allowed SDG&E to diversify into real estate, software, and oil and gas distribution. In 1995 it created Enova to serve as its holding company.

Meanwhile, up the coast in San Francisco, Pacific Enterprises began as gas lamp rental firm Pacific Lighting in 1886; it quickly moved into gas distribution to defend its market against electricity. The firm bought three Los Angeles gas and electric utilities in 1889 and continued to grow through acquisitions; it consolidated all of its utilities in the 1920s. Pacific Lighting sold its electric properties to the city of Los Angeles in 1937 in exchange for a long-term gas franchise.

The company entered oil and gas exploration in 1960. A decade later it merged its gas utility operations into Southern California Gas (SoCalGas). Pacific Lighting continued to diversify in the 1980s, buying two oil and gas companies and three drugstore chains. Renamed Pacific Enterprises in 1988, the company launched an unsuccessful diversification effort that cost it $88 million in 1991. Over the next two years it sold off noncore businesses to focus on SoCalGas, and in the mid-1990s it began moving into South and Central America. This included a joint venture with Enova and Mexico's Proxima SA to build and operate Mexico's first private utility.

Pacific Enterprises and Enova agreed in 1997 to a $6.2 billion merger; Sempra Energy was born in 1998. That year California began deregulating its retail power market. In response, Sempra sold SDG&E's non-nuclear power plants (1,900 MW) in 1999. It used the proceeds to eliminate its competitive transition charge and, in turn, lowered its electric rates.

But under deregulation, rates tripled by mid-2000; that summer the California Public Utilities Commission (CPUC) implemented a rate freeze for electric customers. Wholesale power prices soared and rolling blackouts occurred in 2000 and 2001 as a result of the state's inadequate energy supply. In 2001 the CPUC began allowing utilities to increase their rates, and SDG&E agreed to sell its transmission assets to the state for about $1 billion.

Sempra sold its 72.5% share in power marketing firm Energy America to British energy company Centrica in 2001. In 2002 the company purchased bankrupt utility Enron's London-based metals trading unit for about $145 million; later that year it purchased Enron's metals concentrates and metals warehousing businesses.

## EXECUTIVES

**Chairman and CEO:** Donald E. Felsinger, age 58, $943,320 pay
**President, COO, and Director:** Neal E. Schmale, age 59, $745,039 pay
**EVP and CFO:** Mark A. Snell, age 50, $473,815 pay
**EVP and General Counsel:** M. Javade Chaudhri, age 54, $460,259 pay
**EVP External Affairs:** Jessie J. Knight Jr., age 56
**SVP, Controller, and Chief Tax Counsel:** Joseph A. (Joe) Householder, age 51
**SVP, Human Resources:** G. Joyce Rowland, age 52
**VP, Mergers and Acquisitions:** Richard A. Vaccari
**VP and Treasurer:** Charles A. McMonagle, age 57
**VP, Audit Services:** Matt Burkhart, age 46
**VP and Chief Compliance Officer:** Randall B. Peterson, age 50
**VP and Associate General Counsel:** Kevin C. Sagara
**VP and Associate General Counsel:** W. Davis (Dave) Smith
**VP International Affairs:** Mike Morgan
**VP, Sempra Global Regulatory Affairs and Administration:** Erbin B. Keith
**Corporate Secretary and Counsel:** Catherine C. Lee
**Group President, The Sempra Utilities:** Edwin A. Guiles, age 57, $594,669 pay
**Auditors:** Deloitte & Touche LLP

## LOCATIONS

**HQ:** Sempra Energy
101 Ash St., San Diego, CA 92101
**Phone:** 619-696-2000 **Fax:** 619-696-2374
**Web:** www.sempra.com

Sempra Energy has regulated utility operations in Southern California and energy activities and investments throughout North America and in Asia, Europe, and South America.

### 2006 Sales

| | $ mil. | % of total |
|---|---|---|
| North America | | |
| US | 10,407 | 89 |
| Canada | 43 | 1 |
| Europe | 638 | 5 |
| Latin America | 637 | 5 |
| Asia | 36 | — |
| **Total** | **11,761** | **100** |

## PRODUCTS/OPERATIONS

### 2006 Sales

| | $ mil. | % of total |
|---|---|---|
| Southern California Gas Company | 4,181 | 35 |
| Sempra Commodities | 3,256 | 27 |
| San Diego Gas & Electric | 2,785 | 23 |
| Sempra Generation | 1,454 | 12 |
| Sempra Pipelines & Storage | 295 | 3 |
| Adjustments | (210) | — |
| **Total** | **11,761** | **100** |

### Selected Subsidiaries

Sempra Energy Utilities
- San Diego Gas & Electric (SDG&E, regulated gas and electric utility)
- Southern California Gas Company (SoCalGas, regulated gas utility)

Sempra Global (formerly Sempra Energy Global Enterprises)
- Sempra Commodities (formerly Sempra Energy Trading, wholesale and retail energy trading and marketing, metals trading)
- Sempra Generation (formerly Sempra Energy Resources, independent power production)
- Sempra LNG (formerly Sempra Energy LNG, acquisition and development of liquefied natural gas facilities)
- Sempra Pipelines & Storage (formerly Sempra Energy International, power generation and distribution and gas distribution, transportation, and compression)

Other operations
- Sempra Energy Financial (affordable housing properties and alternative fuel projects)

## COMPETITORS

AEP
AES
Aquila
AT&T
Avista
Calpine
CenterPoint Energy
CMS Energy
Constellation Energy
Dominion Resources
Duke Energy
Edison International
El Paso
Endesa S.A.
Entergy
IBERDROLA
Los Angeles Water and Power
Mirant
PacifiCorp
PG&E
PSEG
PSEG Global
Reliant Energy
Sacramento Municipal
Sierra Pacific Resources
Southwest Gas
Tenaska
Williams Companies

## HISTORICAL FINANCIALS

Company Type: Public

### Income Statement

FYE: December 31

| | REVENUE ($ mil.) | NET INCOME ($ mil.) | NET PROFIT MARGIN | EMPLOYEES |
|---|---|---|---|---|
| **12/06** | 11,761 | 1,406 | 12.0% | 14,061 |
| **12/05** | 11,737 | 920 | 7.8% | 13,420 |
| **12/04** | 9,410 | 895 | 9.5% | 13,381 |
| **12/03** | 7,887 | 649 | 8.2% | 12,807 |
| **12/02** | 6,020 | 591 | 9.8% | 12,197 |
| **Annual Growth** | 18.2% | 24.2% | — | 3.6% |

### 2006 Year-End Financials

Debt ratio: 60.2%
Return on equity: 20.6%
Cash ($ mil.): 4,992
Current ratio: 1.16
Long-term debt ($ mil.): 4,525
No. of shares (mil.): 262
Dividends
Yield: 2.1%
Payout: 22.3%
Market value ($ mil.): 14,682

### Stock History

NYSE: SRE

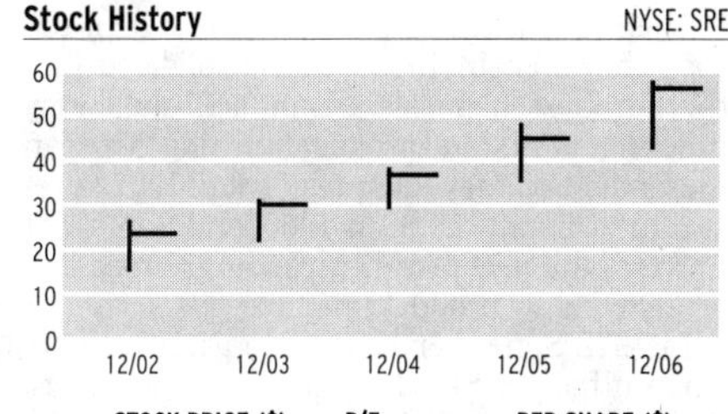


| | STOCK PRICE ($) FY Close | P/E High | P/E Low | PER SHARE ($) Earnings | Dividends | Book Value |
|---|---|---|---|---|---|---|
| **12/06** | 56.04 | 11 | 8 | 5.38 | 1.20 | 28.67 |
| **12/05** | 44.84 | 13 | 10 | 3.65 | 1.16 | 23.97 |
| **12/04** | 36.68 | 10 | 8 | 3.83 | 1.00 | 20.79 |
| **12/03** | 30.06 | 10 | 7 | 3.03 | 1.00 | 17.14 |
| **12/02** | 23.65 | 9 | 5 | 2.87 | 1.00 | 13.79 |
| **Annual Growth** | 24.1% | — | — | 17.0% | 4.7% | 20.1% |

# Sequa Corporation

Jet engine repair, airbag inflators, cigarette lighters, and tuxedos. Sounds like a shopping list for James Bond, but it's a partial list of Sequa's businesses. Its largest unit, aerospace, includes Chromalloy Gas Turbine, which makes and repairs jet engine parts for airlines and other customers. Other operations include an automotive unit, which makes airbag inflators and car cigarette lighters; a metal-coatings unit, which makes coatings for building products; and a specialty chemicals unit (Warwick International), which makes bleach activators. Other Sequa units make offset Web printing equipment (MEGTEC Systems) and men's formalwear (After Six). Gabelli Funds controls a 27% voting stake in Sequa.

No one told Sequa that diversified collections of industrial operations went out of style about the time Sean Connery stopped playing James Bond. Of course, no one told General Electric, either.

Sequa tweaks its business mix from time to time — it sold its can machinery operations late in 2004 — but the company continues to keep its fingers in multiple pies. Sequa is counting on its aerospace business to continue to drive revenue growth.

In 2007 the company agreed to be bought out by The Carlyle Group in a deal valued at about $2.7 billion.

## HISTORY

Sequa Corporation began in 1929 from the merger of five firms: George H. Morrill Co. (1840), Sigmund Ullman Co. (1861), Fuchs & Lang Manufacturing (1871), Eagle Printing Ink (1893), and American Printing Ink (1897). Founded as General Printing Ink Corp., it specialized in making ink for news, letterpress, and lithographic printing. It also made lithographic machines and supplies.

Although the company's units competed against each other in the 1930s, they managed to stay profitable during the Depression. General Ink bought four firms in 1945 and, to reflect its expanding interests, changed its name to Sun Chemical Corp. More acquisitions followed over the next few years. By 1950 Sun had formed seven divisions.

The growth turned out to be too much, too soon, however. In 1954 Sun consolidated into three groups: chemicals; graphic arts; and waterproofing, paints, and product finishing. Norman Alexander became Sun's president in 1957. A research program began in 1960, and Sun spent much of the next decade expanding abroad and diversifying its product line.

In 1972 Sun entered the auto parts industry when it bought Standard Kollsman Industries. Sun's expansion in the late 1970s established subsidiaries in Bermuda, Chile, and Panama. The company initiated a takeover attempt in 1979 by buying 5% of diversified Chromalloy American. By 1980 Sun was the #1 world producer of printing inks, and by 1982 it had acquired 36% of Chromalloy. Also that year Alexander became Sun's CEO.

Sun itself became a takeover target in 1986, as Dainippon Ink and Chemicals tried to buy it. Alexander refused and upped his ownership in Sun to 47%. He sold the company's graphic arts unit to Dainippon later that year and used the proceeds to buy the rest of Chromalloy. Sun's 1987 purchase of Atlantic Research Corp. (ARC; rocket motors) was the impetus to rename itself Sequa Corporation, to reflect a shift in focus from chemical to military products.

Sales skyrocketed until 1990, but post-Cold War cutbacks dealt Sequa a financial blow. In the next several years it dumped about half a dozen divisions and cut its workforce in half. In 1996 ARC won a contract to make rocket motors for missiles used on Canadian, NATO, and US fighter planes.

Sequa bought TEC Systems (web press products) in 1997 and merged it with MEG, its French auxiliary press equipment division, to form MEGTEC Systems. Sequa sold its Northern Can Systems unit, a maker of easy-open can lids. It initiated major layoffs at MEGTEC in 1998 and sold its Sequa Chemicals unit to GenCorp for $108 million. That year ARC became the sole owner of its former joint venture, Bendix Atlantic Inflator Co.; it was renamed Atlantic Research Automotive Products Group.

In 1999 Sequa paid $13 million for Thermo Fibertek's Thermo Wisconsin unit, which supplies the US process and printing industries with continuous process dryers, air-pollution control equipment, and other specialty products. Sequa planned to combine the unit with its MEGTEC Systems. That year Sequa won a seven-year $10.1 billion contract to repair military aircraft for the US Air Force. The company acquired metal can machinery maker Formatec Tooling Systems in 2000.

In early 2002 Sequa reported a record fourth-quarter loss for 2001. The loss was largely related to cost-cutting measures and environmental remediation. Late in 2002, Sequa acquired Pacific Gas Turbine, an airplane engine overhaul business. The next year Sequa sold the propulsion business of its ARC unit for about $133 million. Sequa kept ARC's automotive business.

Late in 2004 Sequa sold its Sequa Can Machinery operations to Stolle Machinery Company.

## EXECUTIVES

**Chairman:** Gail Binderman, age 66
**Vice Chairman and CEO:** Martin Weinstein, age 71, $845,252 pay
**EVP and CFO:** Kenneth J. Binder, age 54
**SVP, Legal:** John J. Dowling III, age 56, $312,076 pay
**SVP, Metal Coating:** Gerard M. Dombek, age 54, $334,083 pay
**SVP, Specialty Chemicals:** Robert F. (Bob) Ellis, age 54, $374,189 pay
**VP and Controller:** Donna Costello, age 34
**VP and Treasurer:** James P. Langelotti, age 46
**VP, Corporate Communications:** Linda G. Kyriakou
**VP, Corporate Development and Strategic Planning:** Robert D. DeVito
**VP, Environmental, Safety, and Health:** Robert L. Iuliucci
**VP, Human Resources:** Leonard P. Pasculli, age 52
**President and General Manager, After Six:** Kathleen Peskens, age 47
**President and General Manager, ARC Automotive:** John Skaldan
**Corporate Secretary:** Diane C. Bunt
**Corporate Communications:** Mary Rotondi
**Auditors:** KPMG

## LOCATIONS

**HQ:** Sequa Corporation
200 Park Ave., New York, NY 10166
**Phone:** 212-986-5500 **Fax:** 212-370-1969
**Web:** www.sequa.com

**2006 Sales**

| | $ mil. | % of total |
|---|---|---|
| North America | | |
| US | 1,036.4 | 48 |
| Mexico | 71.9 | 3 |
| Europe | | |
| Italy | 117.5 | 5 |
| Germany | 110.5 | 5 |
| France | 95.0 | 4 |
| UK | 92.1 | 4 |
| Spain | 62.5 | 3 |
| South Korea | 104.4 | 5 |
| Other regions | 493.5 | 23 |
| **Total** | **2,183.8** | **100** |

## PRODUCTS/OPERATIONS

**2006 Sales**

| | $ mil. | % of total |
|---|---|---|
| Aerospace | 1,048.7 | 48 |
| Automotive | 367.6 | 17 |
| Metal coating | 279.1 | 13 |
| Industrial machinery | 260.4 | 12 |
| Specialty chemicals | 213.8 | 10 |
| Other | 14.2 | — |
| **Total** | **2,183.8** | **100** |

**Selected Subsidiaries and Operations**

Aerospace
- Chromalloy Gas Turbine Corporation (jet aircraft engine repair and manufacture)

Automotive
- ARC Automotive, Inc. (airbag inflators)
- Casco Products (automotive cigarette lighters and power outlets)

Metal Coatings
- Precoat Metals (protective and decorative coatings for steel and aluminum)

Specialty Chemicals
- Warwick International Group Limited (bleach activator — TAED — for laundry detergents)

Industrial Machinery
- MEGTEC Systems, Inc. (air flotation dryers, auxiliary equipment for web offset printing)

Other
- After Six (men's apparel under the After Six, John Galenté, and Raffinati labels)

## COMPETITORS

AAR
Autoliv
Ball Corporation
Barnes Group
Dover
GE
GenCorp
Goss International
Honeywell International
Jason
Nippon Kayaku
Pratt & Whitney
Raytheon
Rolls-Royce
Valspar

## HISTORICAL FINANCIALS

Company Type: Public

**Income Statement** FYE: December 31

| | REVENUE ($ mil.) | NET INCOME ($ mil.) | NET PROFIT MARGIN | EMPLOYEES |
|---|---|---|---|---|
| **12/06** | 2,184 | 66 | 3.0% | 10,155 |
| **12/05** | 1,998 | 27 | 1.4% | 9,700 |
| **12/04** | 1,864 | 19 | 1.0% | 9,100 |
| **12/03** | 1,666 | 11 | 0.7% | 9,000 |
| **12/02** | 1,689 | (117) | — | 10,375 |
| **Annual Growth** | 6.6% | — | — | (0.5%) |

**2006 Year-End Financials**

Debt ratio: 99.4%
Return on equity: 9.3%
Cash ($ mil.): 173
Current ratio: 2.61
Long-term debt ($ mil.): 741

No. of shares (mil.): 8
Dividends
Yield: —
Payout: —
Market value ($ mil.): 927

**Stock History** NYSE: SQAA

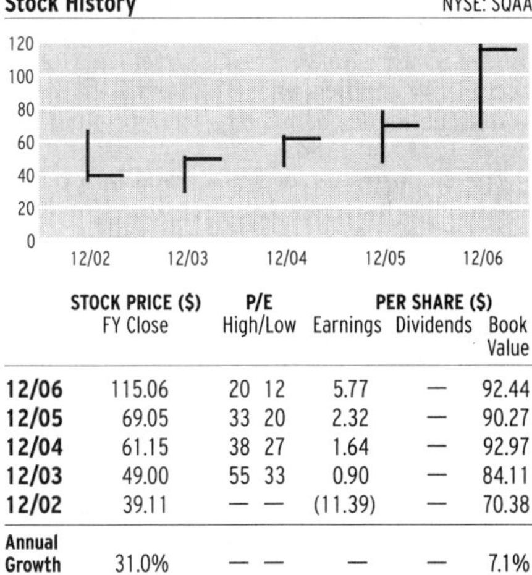

| | STOCK PRICE ($) FY Close | P/E High/Low | | PER SHARE ($) Earnings | Dividends | Book Value |
|---|---|---|---|---|---|---|
| **12/06** | 115.06 | 20 | 12 | 5.77 | — | 92.44 |
| **12/05** | 69.05 | 33 | 20 | 2.32 | — | 90.27 |
| **12/04** | 61.15 | 38 | 27 | 1.64 | — | 92.97 |
| **12/03** | 49.00 | 55 | 33 | 0.90 | — | 84.11 |
| **12/02** | 39.11 | — | — | (11.39) | — | 70.38 |
| **Annual Growth** | 31.0% | — | — | — | — | 7.1% |

# Service Corporation

Service Corporation International (SCI) is to death what H&R Block is to taxes. SCI, the largest funeral and cemetery services company in the world, owns about 1,610 funeral homes, 220 cemeteries, and almost 235 combination funeral homes and cemeteries in the US, Canada, and Puerto Rico. Services include embalming, burial, and cremation. The company also sells prearranged funeral services, caskets, burial vaults, cremation receptacles, flowers, and burial garments and owns disaster recovery company Kenyon International Emergency Services. SCI expanded significantly in November 2006 by acquiring its chief rival, Alderwoods Group.

SCI paid about $856 million for Alderwoods and assumed some $374 million in debt. To gain regulatory approval for the transaction, SCI agreed to sell some 40 funeral homes and 15 cemeteries in areas where the combined company's market share would have been too large. In conjunction with the Alderwoods acquisition, SCI also acquired Rose Hills Company, the operator of the Rose Hills Mortuary and Memorial Park, located near Los Angeles.

The Alderwoods deal is the latest — and biggest — in a series of acquisitions that have fueled SCI's growth. The purchases have enabled SCI to operate clusters of funeral homes in the same geographic region, allowing them to share personnel, vehicles, and preparation services, thereby lowering their operating costs. SCI maintains the local identity of each home, allowing it to handle services for different ethnic or religious groups. In Manhattan, for example, SCI owns the top Christian funeral home (Campbell) and the leading Jewish home (Riverside). Its aggressive acquisition program, however, led to daunting debt, so SCI has been selling operations, including its insurance subsidiaries and more than 500 funeral locations and cemeteries.

Funerals bring in 65% of revenues; as cremation grows in popularity, that number continues to drop. Call it unburied treasure: SCI has some $5 billion worth of unperformed funeral contracts. SCI has further pared down its international holdings and continues to refocus on its core business — North American funeral service locations and cemeteries — by selling its minority interest in its UK operation and its funeral homes in Argentina, Chile, Singapore, and Uruguay. In 2007, its funeral operations in Germany remained its only international holding.

## HISTORY

When Robert Waltrip was just 20, in the early 1950s, he inherited Houston's Heights Funeral Home, which his father and aunt had founded in 1926. Waltrip acquired several other funeral homes, modeling his operations on other popular service chains, such as Holiday Inn and McDonald's. In 1962 he incorporated Service Corporation International (SCI) and began expanding across the country.

SCI went public in 1969, and by 1975 it was the largest provider of funeral services in the US. However, that year the FTC accused the company of overcharging customers for flowers, cremation, and other services. SCI was ordered to refund overcharges it had made to cremation customers (it had charged them for caskets), and the FTC issued industry guidelines to prevent deceptive practices.

Two years later SCI began offering advance sales of funeral services so that clients could avoid the effects of inflation by reserving future services and caskets at current prices. While it was barred from using the prepaid funds until funerals were performed, some states allowed the use of investment profits from those funds.

The company moved into flower shops in 1982, and two years later SCI bought Amedco, a top casket maker and a major supplier of embalming fluid, burial clothing, and mortuary furniture. (Amedco was later sold.)

SCI spun off 71 rural funeral homes as Equity Corporation International (ECI) in 1991 (it sold its remaining 40% stake in 1996). The company continued its rapid pace of acquisitions, buying 342 homes and 57 cemeteries from 1991 to 1993. It made its first acquisition outside North America in 1993 with the purchase of Pine Grove Funeral Group, the largest funeral and cremations provider in Australia. SCI entered the European market by acquiring Great Southern Group and Plantsbrook of the UK in 1994, as well as the funeral operations of Lyonnaise des Eaux of France a year later.

In 1997 and 1998 it swallowed up 602 funeral homes, 98 cemeteries, and 37 crematoria. SCI bought American Annuity Group's prearranged funeral services division in 1998. In early 1999 the company bought back all of Equity Corporation International (about 440 US funeral homes and cemeteries).

With SCI's earnings slumping — which the company attributed in part to declining mortality rates — president and COO William Heiligbrodt resigned in 1999. Also in 1999 SCI deep-sixed about 2,000 jobs and consolidated its funeral home and cemetery groups in the US down to 87 (from 200). The company also began offering a low-price service called the Dignity Memorial Plan, which offers customers inexpensive funeral packages.

To help pay down its debt, SCI sold its French insurance subsidiary and its Northern Ireland funeral operations in 2000 and sold more than 500 funeral locations and cemeteries the next year. Saying it wanted to focus on North America, it also divested itself of operations in Belgium, the Netherlands, and Norway and made joint ventures of operations in Australia, Portugal, and Spain.

A class-action lawsuit filed in December 2001 claimed the company broke open burial vaults and dumped the contents, crushed vaults to make room for others, and mixed body parts from different individuals; the company denied the charges.

In May 2003 SCI agreed to pay penalties of approximately $10 million stemming from the December 2001 lawsuit and faced felony charges filed against the company and two of its Florida cemetery executives. SCI agreed in December 2003 to pay $100 million to settle the class action lawsuit and individual lawsuits pending regarding its Florida cemetery operations.

In early 2004 SCI sold its French funeral operation, OGF Group, to Vestar Capital Partners in a management buyout transaction for approximately $370 million. Vestar and SCI reinvested in the operation and took about a 25% ownership. In 2005 SCI sold its cemetery operations in Argentina, Uruguay, and Chile for approximately $64 million.

## EXECUTIVES

**Chairman:** Robert L. (Bob) Waltrip, age 76, $950,000 pay
**President, CEO, and Director:** Thomas L. Ryan, age 41, $800,000 pay
**EVP and COO:** Michael R. Webb, age 48, $575,000 pay
**SVP and CFO:** Eric D. Tanzberger, age 38, $286,538 pay
**SVP, Operations Support:** J. Daniel Garrison, age 55
**SVP, Major Market Operations:** Sumner J. Waring III, age 38
**SVP, Middle Market Operations:** Stephen M. Mack, age 55
**SVP and Chief Marketing Officer:** Philip (Phil) Jacobs, age 52
**SVP, General Counsel, and Secretary:** Gregory T. Sangalis, age 50
**VP and Controller:** Jeffrey I. Beason, age 58
**VP, Business Development:** Christopher H. Cruger, age 32
**VP, Process and Technology:** Elisabeth G. Nash, age 45
**VP, Human Resources:** Jane D. Jones, age 51
**VP, Supply Chain Management:** Donald R. Robinson, age 49
**VP and Treasurer:** Harris E. Loring III
**Managing Director, Marketing:** George J. Owens
**Corporate Communications:** Robyn Sadowsky
**Auditors:** PricewaterhouseCoopers LLP

## LOCATIONS

**HQ:** Service Corporation International
1929 Allen Pkwy., Houston, TX 77019
**Phone:** 713-522-5141 **Fax:** 713-525-5586
**Web:** www.sci-corp.com

## PRODUCTS/OPERATIONS

**2006 Sales**

| | $ mil. | % of total |
|---|---|---|
| Funeral services | 696.5 | 40 |
| Funeral goods | 422.3 | 24 |
| Cemetery goods | 391.2 | 22 |
| Cemetery services | 170.5 | 10 |
| Other | 66.8 | 4 |
| **Total** | **1,747.3** | **100** |

### Selected Products
Burial garments
Burial vaults
Caskets
Coffins
Cremation receptacles
Flowers
Lawn crypts
Mausoleum spaces
Stone and bronze memorials

### Selected Services
Bereavement travel
Cremation
Development loans
Floral arrangements
Grief counseling
Grounds management and maintenance
Interment
Perpetual care
Prearranged funeral services
Transportation

## COMPETITORS

Alcor
Arbor Memorial Services
Aurora Casket
Carriage Services, Inc.
Eternal Reefs
Forever Enterprises
Funeral Depot
Hillenbrand
Matthews International
Neptune Society
Rock of Ages
Security National Financial
Stewart Enterprises
StoneMor
Wilbert
York Group

## HISTORICAL FINANCIALS
Company Type: Public

### Income Statement
FYE: December 31

| | REVENUE ($ mil.) | NET INCOME ($ mil.) | NET PROFIT MARGIN | EMPLOYEES |
|---|---|---|---|---|
| **12/06** | 1,747 | 57 | 3.2% | 22,623 |
| **12/05** | 1,716 | (128) | — | 16,722 |
| **12/04** | 1,861 | 114 | 6.1% | 20,598 |
| **12/03** | 2,328 | 85 | 3.7% | 27,813 |
| **12/02** | 2,272 | (232) | — | 28,924 |
| **Annual Growth** | (6.4%) | — | — | (6.0%) |

### 2006 Year-End Financials
Debt ratio: 119.9%
Return on equity: 3.6%
Cash ($ mil.): 40
Current ratio: 0.58
Long-term debt ($ mil.): 1,913
No. of shares (mil.): 293
Dividends
Yield: 1.0%
Payout: 52.6%
Market value ($ mil.): 3,006

### Stock History
NYSE: SCI

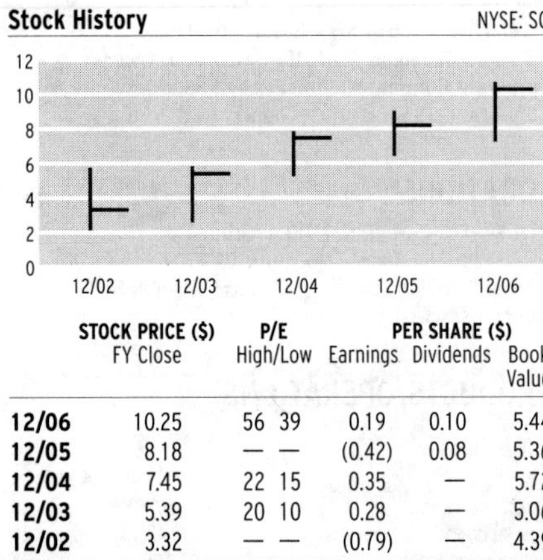


| | STOCK PRICE ($) FY Close | P/E High/Low | | PER SHARE ($) Earnings | Dividends | Book Value |
|---|---|---|---|---|---|---|
| **12/06** | 10.25 | 56 | 39 | 0.19 | 0.10 | 5.44 |
| **12/05** | 8.18 | — | — | (0.42) | 0.08 | 5.36 |
| **12/04** | 7.45 | 22 | 15 | 0.35 | — | 5.72 |
| **12/03** | 5.39 | 20 | 10 | 0.28 | — | 5.06 |
| **12/02** | 3.32 | — | — | (0.79) | — | 4.39 |
| **Annual Growth** | 32.6% | — | — | — | 25.0% | 5.5% |

# Sharper Image

If James Bond had problem nose hair, he'd probably ask Q for a Sharper Image Turbo Groomer 5.0. Sharper Image sells its gadgets and gizmos through a network of about 190 US stores in nearly 40 states and the District of Columbia, as well as online and through its mail catalog. The product mix, which appeals mostly to upscale shoppers, includes electronics, personal care items, recreation and fitness accessories, housewares, toys, travel goods, and gift items. While Sharper Image sells products from other manufacturers (Bose, CASIO), most of its inventory consists of its own, higher-margin, Sharper Image-branded items. Richard Thalheimer, founder and former CEO, owns more than 20% of Sharper Image.

Sharper Image also sells its products to businesses for use in corporate incentive programs and through wholesale agreements with retailers such as Linens 'n Things and Bed Bath & Beyond. On the expansion front, Sharper Image has slowed its growth, opening six new stores in 2006.

In an effort to boost its customer base, the company has formed a new division to license the Sharper Image brand to manufacturers and retailers. The first licensing deal was struck in 2007 with OfficeMax. The multi-year deal has Sharper Image making office products for sale under the Sharper Image Office brand.

The company has seen sales of some of its most popular products fall off. Bad legal publicity surrounding several class action lawsuits against the company and its popular Ionic Breeze air filter product, which consumers claimed didn't work as advertised, were blamed for the drop in sales. The problems with Ionic Breeze clearly illustrate why Sharper Image's share price has fallen a total of 74% since 2004. The company relies too heavily on only a few hit products, and sales plummet when interest inevitably wanes.

In 2006, investment vehicle Knightspoint Group made a play for strategic control of the company by acquiring nearly 13% of Sharper Image stock and proposing its own slate of seven directors. Sharper Image settled the dispute by reshuffling its board to include some Knightspoint appointees, which allowed Thalheimer to avoid being ousted.

In 2007, Steven Lightman joined Sharper Image as president and CEO, succeeding interim CEO Jerry Levin, who remains chairman. Lightman joined the company from women's apparel direct marketer Crosstown Traders, where he served as president.

Several top executive changes resulted from the firm hitting a bumpy road in late 2006. In September of that year Sharper Image announced it would restate its financial results for the past several years as a result of a review of its stock options practices.

## HISTORY

Richard Thalheimer worked his way through law school in California in the early 1970s by selling office supplies. A dedicated jogger, he observed the growing number of runners and predicted that a good jogger's watch would sell. After locating a supplier, Thalheimer used $1,000 of his own money to run a magazine ad in 1977 for a runner's stopwatch. The product sold well, and Thalheimer decided to use the profits to form a catalog business that would cater to upwardly mobile people like himself. He released the Sharper Image catalog that year.

From the late 1970s through the early 1980s, operations grew as Thalheimer expanded his catalogs with unique items that appealed to him personally. During the 1980s Thalheimer clashed frequently with his corporate staff over the running of Sharper Image. The disagreements (often personality conflicts with Thalheimer) were so severe that more than half his staff resigned between 1984 and 1986.

The company decided to expand into retail, and in 1985 it opened 12 stores from Honolulu to New York City. Despite the higher costs involved in operating stores, Sharper Image continued to grow, and by 1988 the company had 60 stores. Two years later it had 75 US stores, with several licensees overseas; however, by then, trouble had set in. Department stores (and competitors such as Brookstone) had discovered the popularity of Thalheimer's merchandise and began selling it as well. In addition, sales increases were coming only from the opening of new stores and not from existing outlets. Consequently, Sharper Image experienced its first loss in 1991 as sales dropped. In response, Thalheimer cut 300 workers and moved the company's distribution center from pricey San Francisco to less expensive Little Rock, Arkansas.

In 1991 Sharper Image signed an agreement with Univex Licensing Group to sell the Sharper Image trademark to manufacturing licensees. Two years later the company brought product development in-house. New products bearing the Sharper Image Design logo introduced during 1993 included Snore Control and a motorized tie rack. The company opened its first Sharper Image Design store in Palo Alto, California, in 1994, offering both proprietary Sharper Image Design items and other merchandise in about half the space of a traditional store. A Sharper Image SPA catalog for women was tested in early 1995, and later that year four SPA stores were opened. The company also launched its Web site that year (adding auctions in 1999).

Sharper Image discontinued the SPA division in 1997 after two years of losses and focused on a home furnishings catalog created in 1996. The same year Sharper Image hired Barry Gilbert away from Warner Bros. Studio Stores to be its vice chairman and COO and oversee the Sharper Image's stores and catalog sales. In 1998 the company discontinued The Sharper Image Home Collection concept, and in 1999 Gilbert left Sharper Image to become CEO of a now-defunct online jewelry retailer. At that time Tracy Wan, former EVP and CFO of Sharper Image, was named president and COO of the company.

In 2000 Sharper Image enhanced its online presence and established strategic Internet marketing partnerships with companies including AOL and Yahoo! Shopping. In March 2001 Sharper Image announced plans to launch international shopping Web sites; by 2002 it had sites in Asia, Germany, Spain, and the UK. In October 2002 Sharper Image teamed up with Circuit City to feature Sharper Image brand products in all of Circuit City's US stores.

In December 2002 Sharper Image was voted one of "The Top 50 Retailing Web Sites" by *Internet Retailer* magazine. The retailer added 25 new stores in 2003. In 2007 Steven Lightman took over as CEO and president.

## EXECUTIVES

**Chairman:** Jerry W. Levin, age 63
**President, CEO, and Director:** Steven A. (Steve) Lightman, age 50
**CFO:** Rebecca L. Roedell
**EVP and CIO:** Gregory (Greg) Alexander, age 44, $290,481 pay (prior to promotion)
**EVP Distribution Center:** Barry Jacobsen
**EVP Marketing:** Roger Bensinger Jr.
**EVP Merchandising:** William (Bill) Feroe, age 49, $299,077 pay
**EVP Merchandising:** Andrew P. (Drew) Reich, age 46
**SVP Human Resources and Administration:** Gary Chant, age 48
**SVP, General Counsel, and Corporate Secretary:** James M. Sander, age 50
**SVP, Controller, and Principal Accounting Officer:** Daniel W. Nelson, age 47
**SVP Creative Services:** Anthony Farrell, age 56
**SVP Sharper Image Design:** Thomas (Tom) Krysiak
**SVP Sharper Image Design:** Andrew Parker
**VP Corporate Marketing:** Douglas Atkinson
**VP Creative Services:** Joseph Tsang
**VP Customer Service:** Harvey Johnson
**VP Internet Division:** Susan Fischer
**VP Merchandising:** Robert Pintane
**VP Product Development:** Ed McKinney
**VP Retail Stores:** John Yotnakparian, age 43
**VP Retail Operations:** Cheri Ginsberg
**Auditors:** Deloitte & Touche LLP

## LOCATIONS

**HQ:** Sharper Image Corporation
350 The Embarcadero, 6th Fl.,
San Francisco, CA 94105
**Phone:** 415-445-6000
**Web:** www.sharperimage.com

### 2007 Stores

| | No. |
|---|---|
| Sharper Image stores | 183 |
| Sharper Image outlet stores | 4 |
| **Total** | **187** |

## PRODUCTS/OPERATIONS

### 2007 Sales

| | $ mil. | % of total |
|---|---|---|
| Stores | 314 | 60 |
| Internet | 85 | 16 |
| Catalog & direct marketing | 75 | 14 |
| Wholesale sales | 34 | 7 |
| Delivery | 14 | 3 |
| Other | 3 | — |
| **Total** | **525** | **100** |

### Selected Product Categories

Electronics
Gifts
Housewares
Personal care
Recreation and fitness
Toys
Travel

## COMPETITORS

Allergy Buyers Club
Bed Bath & Beyond
Best Buy
Brookstone
Hammacher Schlemmer & Co.
HMI Industries
Levenger
Linens 'n Things
L.L. Bean
Neiman Marcus
RadioShack
RedEnvelope
Relax the Back
SkyMall
Williams-Sonoma

## HISTORICAL FINANCIALS

Company Type: Public

### Income Statement

FYE: January 31

| | REVENUE ($ mil.) | NET INCOME ($ mil.) | NET PROFIT MARGIN | EMPLOYEES |
|---|---|---|---|---|
| **1/07** | 525 | (60) | — | 2,500 |
| **1/06** | 669 | (16) | — | 2,500 |
| **1/05** | 760 | 15 | 1.9% | 2,800 |
| **1/04** | 648 | 25 | 3.9% | 2,400 |
| **1/03** | 523 | 16 | 3.0% | 2,200 |
| **Annual Growth** | 0.1% | — | — | 3.2% |

### 2007 Year-End Financials

Debt ratio: 1.6%
Return on equity: —
Cash ($ mil.): 18
Current ratio: 1.19
Long-term debt ($ mil.): 2
No. of shares (mil.): 15
Dividends
Yield: —
Payout: —
Market value ($ mil.): 146

### Stock History

NASDAQ (GM): SHRP

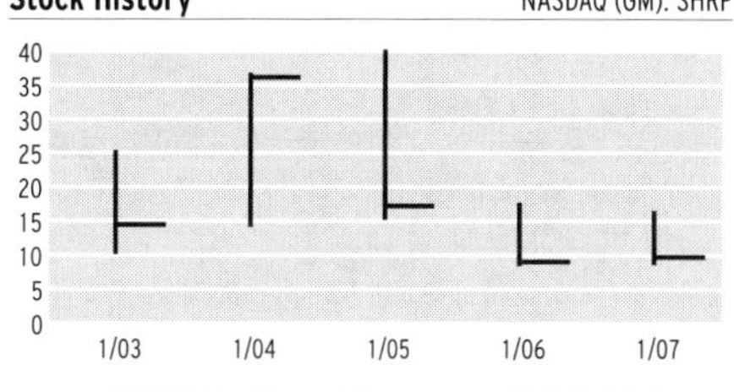


| | STOCK PRICE ($) FY Close | P/E High | P/E Low | PER SHARE ($) Earnings | Dividends | Book Value |
|---|---|---|---|---|---|---|
| **1/07** | 9.72 | — | — | (4.00) | — | 8.23 |
| **1/06** | 9.02 | — | — | (1.07) | — | 12.18 |
| **1/05** | 17.20 | 44 | 17 | 0.90 | — | 13.17 |
| **1/04** | 36.16 | 22 | 9 | 1.65 | — | 12.40 |
| **1/03** | 14.46 | 21 | 9 | 1.21 | — | 9.29 |
| **Annual Growth** | (9.5%) | — | — | — | — | (3.0%) |

# The Shaw Group

The Shaw Group's ambitions to become more than a leading industrial pipe fabricator in the US are no longer just pipe dreams. Through bargain buys of other companies (including environmental firm The IT Group), Shaw Group has positioned itself as one of the largest engineering and construction contractors for the power generation market, as well as one of the top environmental services firms. It focuses on power generation but also serves the chemical and petrochemical, refinery, and process industries. In addition, Shaw has continued its pipe fabrication operations.

Through key acquisitions, Shaw has shaped itself into one of the nation's fastest-growing engineering and construction companies for the power generation industry. In addition to engineering, procurement, and construction services, it provides project management, pipe fittings, and on-site installation. The company's fabrication and manufacturing unit has done much of the pipe fabricating for the clean fuels projects in the US. And its Shaw Power Technologies, Inc. (PTI) subsidiary has become a leading electrical engineering consulting company. Shaw PTI assisted in contingency planning for the US's largest power blackout in August 2003.

A growth-through-acquisition strategy has powered the group's move into new areas. Picking up engineering and construction firm Stone & Webster allowed Shaw to increase its business in the nuclear sector, where Stone & Webster has provided nuclear plant maintenance modifications for more than 25 years. Shaw states that Stone & Webster has provided operations and support services to more than 95% of the nuclear facilities in the US. Shaw also expanded its environmental services business by acquiring The IT Group, the fourth company it had bought through bankruptcies. The group operates now as Shaw Environmental & Infrastructure.

With a national focus on increased homeland security, Shaw Environmental & Infrastructure has moved into disaster-related preparedness operations, including risk assessments and chemical and weapons demilitarization. Shaw Environmental also moved beyond its traditional environmental services by acquiring Envirogen, which had experience in remediating and treating hazardous contaminants such as ammonium percholorate, a rocket and missile propellant. Shaw also provides environmental and construction services to the US Air Force and other Department of Defense units. Shaw Infrastructure is the service construction manager for a master-planned community for military housing in Florida.

In addition to its growth at home, Shaw has been expanding abroad by winning contracts for construction management and other services to power utilities and petrochemical plants in Asia and the Middle East. In Iraq the group has opened an office in Baghdad and is working on a facilities and infrastructure contract from the Air Force Center for Environmental Excellence. Its Shaw Environmental subsidiary has also won a contract from the US Army for munitions-related operations in Iraq.

## HISTORY

James Bernhard formed National Fabricators in 1986. After visiting the Benjamin F. Shaw Company's plant in South Carolina to bid on its inventory, he established The Shaw Group in 1987 and bought the 100-year-old maker of power-station piping systems. From 1988 to 1990 Shaw expanded its business by leasing three plants in Louisiana and Texas. The company bought a plant in 1992.

Shaw formed a joint venture with Venezuela-based Formiconi in 1993 to open a plant there. The company began making pipes for chemicals and oil refining with its purchase of Sunland Fabricators. Shaw also went public that year.

In 1994 Shaw acquired Fronek Company (pipe engineering and design services), bought out its Venezuelan partner, and watched its domestic fiscal earnings bend south when its South Carolina plant had to repair a botched fabrication job.

Shaw expanded plant capacity and added more induction bending machines to its inventory in 1996 and 1997. It purchased NAPTech (industrial piping systems) in 1997. Company spending continued with the 1998 acquisitions of Lancas (construction, Venezuela), Cojafex BV (induction bending equipment, the Netherlands), and Bagwell Brothers (offshore platforms, heliports, and vessels for the petroleum industry). The Cojafex buy proved to be one of the company's best acquisitions, because its pipe-bending machines eliminated much of the cost of welding. Also in 1998 Shaw sold its NAPTech Pressure Systems (pressure vessels) subsidiary and others that provided welding supplies, boiler steam leak-detection devices, and corrosion-resistant pipe systems.

In 1999 Shaw won a five-year contract to supply 90% of the piping for GE's gas turbines for power plants. In 2000 Shaw signed a letter of intent with a US power developer to build a $380 million power plant in central Texas. It also created EntergyShaw, a joint venture with Entergy Corporation, to build cookie-cutter power plants in North America and Europe in hopes of driving down costs and speeding construction time. That year the company purchased Stone & Webster, Inc., for about $38 million and around 2.5 million shares of stock.

In 2002 Shaw acquired the assets of The IT Group (which was in bankruptcy) for about $105 million in cash and up to $95 million in assumed debt and made the environmental services firm a subsidiary, Shaw Environmental & Infrastructure. It also entered into an agreement to buy industrial construction group Turner Industries, but quickly terminated discussions with its hometown rival.

Despite a downturn in the domestic power generation market, Shaw made a strong showing in 2002, which it attributed to its diversified portfolio. However, the group lowered its earnings expectations for fiscal 2003 because of power projects that it did not expect to be completed. That year Shaw Environmental & Infrastructure completed its acquisition of Envirogen.

Shaw divested its hanger engineering and pipe support businesses in 2004 and its Roche Ltd., Consulting Group (project consultation, engineering, and management in eastern Canada) in 2005.

In 2006 Shaw said it would acquire a 20% stake in the group that is buying Westinghouse Electric Co. for more than $1 billion.

## EXECUTIVES

**Chairman, President, and CEO:** James M. Bernhard Jr., age 51
**EVP and Chairman, Executive Committee:** Richard F. Gill, age 62
**EVP, Finance and CFO:** Brian K. Ferraioli, age 51
**EVP, Treasurer, and Director:** Robert L. (Bob) Belk, age 56
**EVP, Secretary, and Chief Legal Officer:** Gary P. Graphia, age 43
**SVP, Chief Accounting Officer, and Interim CFO:** Dirk J. Wild, age 38
**EVP and COO, Shaw Environmental & Infrastructure:** G. Patrick Thompson Jr., age 43
**VP, Investor Relations and Corporate Communications:** Chris D. Sammons
**VP, Strategic Resources:** Brockie Hall
**VP Corporate Communications:** Sean S. Clancy
**VP Administration:** Joe Broom
**President, Energy & Chemicals and Construction Division:** Ebrahim (Abe) Fatemizadeh, age 57, $1,270,323 pay
**President, Consulting Group, Energy & Chemicals Division:** James M. (Jim) Dudley
**President, Maintenance Division:** D. Ron McCall, age 57, $942,249 pay
**President, Fabrication, Manufacturing, and Distribution Division:** David L. Chapman Sr., age 59, $1,003,371 pay
**President, Shaw Environmental & Infrastructure:** Ronald W. (Ron) Oakley
**President, Shaw Stone & Webster Nuclear Services Division:** David P. (Dave) Barry, age 55
**Managing Director, Shaw Group UK:** Neil A. Davis, age 46
**President of Operations, Energy & Chemicals Division:** Louis J. (Lou) Pucher, age 62
**Auditors:** Ernst & Young LLP

## LOCATIONS

**HQ:** The Shaw Group Inc.
4171 Essen Ln., Baton Rouge, LA 70809
**Phone:** 225-932-2500 **Fax:** 225-987-3328
**Web:** www.shawgrp.com

The Shaw Group has major operations in 17 US states. It also has facilities in Australia, Bahrain, Canada, China, the Czech Republic, Malaysia, the Netherlands, the UK, and Venezuela.

**2006 Sales**

| | $ mil. | % of total |
|---|---|---|
| North America | | |
| US | 4,196.8 | 88 |
| Canada | 13.3 | — |
| Middle East | 294.0 | 6 |
| Asia/Pacific | 161.7 | 4 |
| Europe | 73.7 | 2 |
| South America & Mexico | 25.0 | — |
| Other regions | 11.1 | — |
| **Total** | **4,775.6** | **100** |

## PRODUCTS/OPERATIONS

**2006 Sales by Division**

| | $ mil. | % of total |
|---|---|---|
| Environmental & Infrastructure | 2,119.3 | 44 |
| Energy & Chemicals | 1,456.9 | 31 |
| Maintenance | 898.6 | 19 |
| Fabrication, Manufacturing & Distribution | 300.8 | 6 |
| **Total** | **4,775.6** | **100** |

**Selected Subsidiaries and Affiliates**

ACL Piping, Inc.
Associated Valve, Inc.
Clean Horizons, LLC
EntergyShaw, LLC
Envirogen, Inc.
Field Services, Inc.
Hydro Power Solutions LLC
IT Holdings Canada, Inc.
Lone Star Fabricators, Inc.
Manufacturas Shaw South America, C.A. (Venezuela)
Nortec Construction
Pipework Engineering and Developments Limited
Shaw Alloy Piping Products, Inc.
Shaw Asia Company, Limited
Shaw Energy Services, Inc.
Shaw Environmental & Infrastructure, Inc.
Shaw Environmental, Inc.
The Shaw Group International Inc.
Stone & Webster, Inc.
World Industrial Constructors, Inc.

## COMPETITORS

Austin Industries
Bechtel
Black & Veatch
CET Services
CH2M HILL
Fluor
Foster Wheeler
Jacobs Engineering
KBR
McJunkin
Norpipe
Parsons
Senior plc
Siemens Water Technologies
Tetra Tech
Turner Industries
URS
Willbros

## HISTORICAL FINANCIALS

Company Type: Public

**Income Statement** FYE: August 31

| | REVENUE ($ mil.) | NET INCOME ($ mil.) | NET PROFIT MARGIN | EMPLOYEES |
|---|---|---|---|---|
| **8/06** | 4,776 | 51 | 1.1% | 22,000 |
| **8/05** | 3,266 | 16 | 0.5% | 1,900 |
| **8/04** | 3,077 | (29) | — | 17,200 |
| **8/03** | 3,307 | 21 | 0.6% | 14,800 |
| **8/02** | 3,171 | 98 | 3.1% | 17,000 |
| **Annual Growth** | 10.8% | (15.2%) | — | 6.7% |

**2006 Year-End Financials**

Debt ratio: 14.0%
Return on equity: 4.3%
Cash ($ mil.): 198
Current ratio: 1.61
Long-term debt ($ mil.): 174
No. of shares (mil.): 80
Dividends
Yield: —
Payout: —
Market value ($ mil.): 2,025

**Stock History** NYSE: SGR

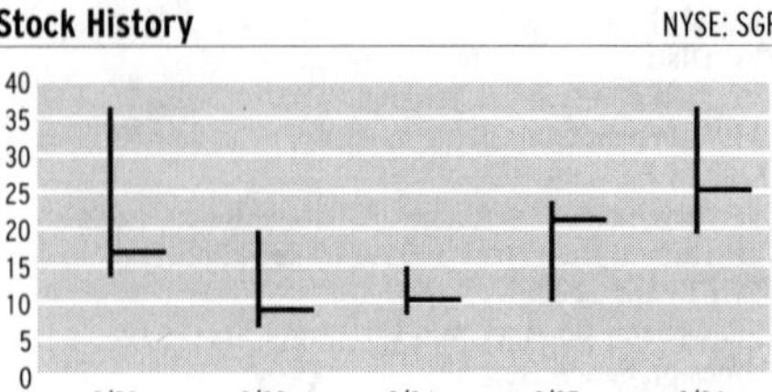


| | STOCK PRICE ($) FY Close | P/E High | P/E Low | PER SHARE ($) Earnings | Dividends | Book Value |
|---|---|---|---|---|---|---|
| **8/06** | 25.16 | 57 | 31 | 0.63 | — | 15.45 |
| **8/05** | 21.10 | 101 | 45 | 0.23 | — | 14.50 |
| **8/04** | 10.29 | — | — | (0.50) | — | 13.91 |
| **8/03** | 8.86 | 36 | 13 | 0.54 | — | 17.53 |
| **8/02** | 16.75 | 16 | 6 | 2.26 | — | 16.95 |
| **Annual Growth** | 10.7% | — | — | (27.3%) | — | (2.3%) |

# Shell Oil

Shell Oil doesn't shilly-shally around, it explores for, produces, and markets oil, natural gas, and chemicals. The company's Shell Exploration & Production unit focuses its exploration on the deepwater plays in the Gulf of Mexico. Shell partners with Saudi Aramco in a US refining and marketing venture (Motiva), and owns Motiva's sister company Shell Oil Products US (formerly Equilon). Shell also produces petrochemicals (Shell Chemical) and liquefied natural gas (Shell US Gas & Power), and markets natural gas and electricity. Shell's parent, Royal Dutch Shell, is the world's #2 petroleum company (behind Exxon Mobil).

The company has teamed up with its peers to ride out the stormy seas of the oil industry. Motiva combines much of its parents' US refining and marketing operations along the Gulf and the East coasts. Shell also operates downstream businesses in the West and Midwest as Shell Oil Products US. Together Motiva and Shell Oil Products US have about 22,000 gas stations, eight refineries, more than 100 product terminals, and interests in more than 26,000 miles of pipelines. Shell also partners with Exxon Mobil in Aera Energy, a California exploration and production joint venture.

## HISTORY

Royal Dutch Shell began importing gasoline from Sumatra to the US in 1912 to take advantage of the expanding automobile industry and the breakup of Standard Oil. That year it formed American Gasoline in Seattle and Roxana Petroleum in Oklahoma. Refineries were established in New Orleans in 1916 and Wood River, Illinois, in 1918.

In 1922 Royal Dutch Shell placed all of its US operations into a 65%-owned holding company, Shell Union Oil, and soon Shell products were available nationwide. Shell Oil took its present name in 1949.

Shell moved to Houston in 1970. It substantially boosted its oil reserves in 1979 by acquiring Belridge Oil, and was itself fully acquired by Royal Dutch/Shell in 1985. However, unhappy shareholders sued, claiming that Shell's assets were undervalued in the deal. (In 1990 claimants were awarded $110 million.)

When other oil companies abandoned the Gulf of Mexico, finding it unproductive, Shell focused on exploration there. In 1989 it hit pay dirt by discovering the massive Mars field.

Stricter US environmental regulations caused Shell to reduce US activities in the 1990s and look overseas for new sources of oil. The company also exchanged its coal mining unit for a 25% stake in the buyer, Zeigler Coal, in 1992 (sold in 1994).

Though part of Royal Dutch Shell, Shell had traditionally operated as an independent company. In 1997, like other Royal Dutch Shell companies, it began integrating its operations with the rest of the group. Meanwhile, it partnered with rivals in search of cost efficiencies. Shell first hooked up with Amoco (which later merged with BP) to form Altura Energy, an exploration and production venture in the Permian Basin, then with Mobil (later acquired by Exxon) to form the Aera venture in California.

When competition at US gas pumps grew fiercer, in 1998 Shell and Texaco formed Equilon, a venture that combined their West and Midwest refining and marketing (downstream) activities; later Shell, Texaco, and Saudi Aramco formed Motiva to merge downstream businesses on the East Coast and Gulf Coast.

In 1998 Shell bought Tejas Gas (renamed Tejas Energy). Tejas, which gathered, transported, and stored natural gas, had been the company's partner in gas marketing venture Coral Energy. Shell also formed Shell Energy Services to sell natural gas and electricity in deregulated markets.

But as its parent group cut costs, Shell was forced to clean house in 1999, selling Tejas' Oklahoma operations and $745 million of Gulf oil and gas fields to Apache. It also cut Gulf of Mexico production by 10%. On the bright side, the company set a record for deepwater drilling — 4,000 feet below sea level — when its Ursa tension-leg platform began production in the Gulf of Mexico.

In 2000 Shell and BP sold Altura Energy to Occidental Petroleum for $3.6 billion. The next year parent Royal Dutch Shell involved the company in a hostile bid to buy Denver-based natural gas producer Barrett Resources, but the offer was withdrawn when Barrett accepted a higher bid from Williams.

In 2001 Shell agreed to acquire Texaco's stakes in Equilon and Motiva. In 2002 Shell acquired 100% ownership of Equilon (which it renamed Shell Oil Products US), and Motiva became a 50-50 joint venture of Shell and Saudi Aramco. As part of this deal, in 2002 the company agreed to spend more than $500 million to rebrand about 11,700 of the 13,000 US gas stations it acquired from the newly formed ChevronTexaco (now Chevron). That year Shell acquired Pennzoil-Quaker State for $1.8 billion.

## EXECUTIVES

**President and Country Chair and SVP, Corporate Affairs and Human Resources:** John D. Hofmeister
**EVP, Global Manufacturing:** Lynn Laverty Elsenhans, age 51
**EVP, Chemicals:** M. Frances (Fran) Keeth, age 60
**SVP, General Counsel, and Corporate Secretary:** Catherine A. (Cathy) Lamboley
**Global VP, Gas and Power, Shell Trading; CEO, Shell Trading Gas and Power; CEO, Coral Energy:** Mark Hanafin
**VP, Portfolio:** David Sexton
**VP, Government Affairs:** Brian P. Malnak
**VP, Health, Safety, Environmental, and External Affairs:** Sally Hopkins
**EVP, Americas, Shell Exploration and Production:** Marvin Odum
**Managing Director and Chief Investment Officer, Shell Retirement Funds and U.S. Country Finance Functional Lead:** Pervis Thomas
**Director, International Directorate:** Roxanne J. Decyk, age 53
**Director, Ethics and Compliance:** Jo Pease
**Director, Human Resources:** Ronnie Kurtin
**Director, US Diversity:** John Jefferson
**Media Relations:** Johan Zaayman
**Auditors:** PricewaterhouseCoopers LLP

## LOCATIONS

**HQ:** Shell Oil Company
1 Shell Plaza, 910 Louisana St., Houston, TX 77002
**Phone:** 713-241-6161 **Fax:** 713-241-4044
**Web:** www.shellus.com

## PRODUCTS/OPERATIONS

### Major Operations

Motiva Enterprises LLC (50%)
Shell Chemical LP
Shell Energy
Shell Exploration & Production Company
Shell Global Solutions
Shell Hydrogen
Shell Lubricants
Shell Norco
Shell Oil Products US
Shell Renewables
Shell Trading
Shell US Gas & Power

## COMPETITORS

7-Eleven
Ashland
BP
Chevron
Dow Chemical
DuPont
Exxon Mobil
Global Environmental
Hess
Huntsman
Imperial Oil
Koch
Lyondell Chemical
Marathon Oil
Occidental Petroleum
PDVSA
PEMEX
PETROBRAS
Racetrac Petroleum
Sunoco
TOTAL

# Sherwin-Williams

No matter how you coat it, Sherwin-Williams is the largest paint manufacturer in the US and #2 worldwide, after Akzo Nobel. Sherwin-Williams' products include a variety of paints, finishes, coatings, applicators, and varnishes sold under the names Dutch Boy, Krylon, Martin-Senour, Red Devil, Sherwin-Williams, Thompson's, and Minwax. The company operates more than 3,000 paint stores throughout North America. It sells automotive finishing and refinishing products through 200 wholesale branches in the US, Canada, Chile, Jamaica, and Peru. Other distribution outlets (and competitors) include mass merchandisers, home centers, and independent retailers.

Sherwin-Williams has continually added to its retail operations, which account for 60% of sales. The company typically adds between 50 and 100 new retail outlets annually, primarily in the US but also in Canada and Puerto Rico. Sherwin-Williams made it through the early part of the decade's rough economic times pretty well, as did much of the paint industry, due to a robust market for DIY home refinishers.

In 2007 the company moved into the Indian market with the acquisition of Nitco Paints and expanded its reach at home as well with the acquisition of regional paint maker M.A. Bruder. That company operates about 130 company-owned stores throughout the Eastern and Southeastern U.S. as well as in the Midwest.

## HISTORY

In 1870 Henry Sherwin bought out paint materials distributor Truman Dunham and joined Edward Williams and A. T. Osborn to form Sherwin, Williams & Company in Cleveland. The business began making paints in 1871 and became the industry leader after improving the paint-grinding mill in the mid-1870s, patenting a reclosable can in 1877, and improving liquid paint in 1880.

In 1874 Sherwin-Williams introduced a special paint for carriages, beginning the concept of specific-purpose paint. (By 1900 the company had paints for floors, roofs, barns, metal bridges, railroad cars, and automobiles.) Sherwin-Williams incorporated in 1884 and opened a dealership in Massachusetts in 1891 that was the forerunner of its company-run retail stores. The company obtained its "Cover the Earth" trademark in 1895.

Before the Depression, Sherwin-Williams bought a number of smaller paint makers: Detroit White Lead (1910), Martin-Senour (1917), Acme Quality Paints (1920), and The Lowe Brothers (1929). Responding to wartime restrictions, the company developed a fast-drying and water-reducible paint, called Kem-Tone, and the forerunner of the paint roller, the Roller-Koater.

Sales doubled during the 1960s as the company made acquisitions, including Sprayon (aerosol paint, 1966), but rising expenses kept earnings flat. In 1972 the company expanded its stores to include carpeting, draperies, and other decorating items. But long-term debt ballooned from $80 million in 1974 to $196 million by 1977, when the company lost $8.2 million and suspended dividends for the first time since 1885.

John Breen became CEO in 1979, reinstated the dividend, purged over half of the top management positions, and closed inefficient plants. He also focused stores on paint and wallpaper merchandise and purchased Dutch Boy (1980).

In 1990 Sherwin-Williams began selling Dutch Boy in Sears stores and Kem-Tone in Wal-Marts. Acquisitions that year included Borden's Krylon and Illinois Bronze aerosol operations and DeSoto's architectural coatings segment, which made private-label paints for Sears and Home Depot. In 1991 Sherwin-Williams bought two coatings business units from Cook Paint and Varnish and the Cuprinol brand of coatings.

Sherwin-Williams purchased paint manufacturer Pratt & Lambert in 1996. That year it introduced several new products, including Low Temp 35, a paint for low temperatures; Healthspec, a low-odor paint; and Ralph Lauren designer paints. Prep-Rite do-it-yourself interior primers debuted in 1997. Also that year Sherwin-Williams bought Thompson Minwax (Thompson's Water Seal, Minwax Wood Products) from Forstmann Little and Chile-based Marson Chilena, a spray paint maker.

The company streamlined some of its business segments and trimmed jobs in 1998. Christopher Connor, president of the Paint Stores group, replaced Breen as CEO in 1999 and chairman in 2000. Also in 2000, Sherwin-Williams moved into the European automotive coatings market by acquiring Italy-based ScottWarren.

In late 2001 the company acquired Wisconsin-based Mautz Paint Company.

After a rough but still profitable 2001, the company grew revenues and profits for its consumer units (consumer paints and paint stores) in 2002, thanks largely to a healthy do-it-yourself market. Sales for its automotive finishes and international units, however, were down because of a slow collision repair market and currency exchange effects.

## EXECUTIVES

**Chairman and CEO:** Christopher M. Connor, age 50
**President and COO:** John G. Morikis, age 43
**SVP, Corporate Planning and Development:** Conway G. Ivy, age 64, $642,830 pay
**SVP, Finance and CFO:** Sean P. Hennessy, age 49, $951,420 pay
**SVP, Human Resources:** Thomas E. Hopkins, age 48
**VP and Treasurer:** Cynthia D. Brogan, age 54
**VP and Corporate Controller:** John L. Ault, age 60
**VP, Administration:** Richard M. Weaver, age 51
**VP, Corporate Audit and Loss Prevention:** Mark J. Dvoroznak, age 47
**VP, General Counsel, and Secretary:** Louis E. Stellato, age 55, $713,626 pay
**VP, Corporate Communications and Public Affairs:** Robert J. Wells, age 48
**VP, Taxes and Assistant Secretary:** Michael T. Cummins, age 47
**President, Consumer Group:** Thomas W. Seitz, age 57
**President, Global Group:** Timothy A. Knight, age 41
**President and General Manager, International Division, Global Group:** Alexander Zalesky, age 46
**President and General Manager, Diversified Brands Division, Consumer Group:** Harvey P. Sass, age 48
**President and General Manager, Eastern Division, Paint Stores Group:** Timothy J. Drouilhet, age 43
**President and General Manager, Automotive Division, Global Group:** Blair P. LaCour, age 59
**President and General Manager, Southeastern Division, Paint Stores Group:** Robert J. Davisson, age 45
**President, Paint Stores Group:** Steven J. Oberfeld, age 54
**President and General Manager, Midwestern Division, Paint Stores Group:** Drew A. McCandless, age 45
**President and General Manager, Chemical Coatings Division, Global Group:** George E. Heath, age 40
**Director, Corporate Communications and Investor Relations:** Mike Conway
**Auditors:** Ernst & Young LLP

## LOCATIONS

**HQ:** The Sherwin-Williams Company
101 Prospect Ave. NW, Cleveland, OH 44115
**Phone:** 216-566-2000 **Fax:** 216-566-2947
**Web:** www.sherwin-williams.com

Sherwin-Williams sells its products through more than 3,000 of its own paint stores and more than 20 auto paint branches and other stores in North and South America. The company operates about 50 manufacturing facilities in Europe, North America, and South America.

## PRODUCTS/OPERATIONS

### 2006 Sales

| | $ mil. | % of total |
|---|---|---|
| Paint Stores Group | 4,845 | 62 |
| Global Group | 1,593 | 20 |
| Consumer Group | 1,364 | 18 |
| Administrative | 8 | — |
| **Total** | **7,810** | **100** |

### Operations

Paint Stores
- Products
  - Architectural coatings
  - Industrial maintenance
  - Marine products
- Brands
  - ArmorSeal
  - Brod-Dugan
  - Con-Lux
  - FlexBon Paints
  - Hi-Temp
  - Kem
  - Mautz
  - Mercury
  - Old Quaker
  - Powdura
  - Pro-Line
  - SeaGuard
  - Sherwin-Williams

Consumer
- Products
  - Architectural paints
  - Industrial maintenance
  - Paints
  - Private-label coatings
  - Stains
  - Wood finishings
  - Varnishes
- Brands
  - Dupli-color
  - Dura Clad
  - Dutch Boy
  - EverLast
  - Formby's
  - Krylon
  - Maxwood Latex Stains
  - Minwax
  - Plastic Kote
  - Pratt & Lambert
  - Red Devil
  - Rubberset
  - Thompson's

Automotive Finishes
- Products
  - Finishing, refinishing, and touch-up products for motor vehicles
- Brands
  - Baco
  - Excelo
  - Lazzuril
  - Martin Senour
  - ScottWarren
  - Sherwin-Williams
  - Western

International Coatings
- Products
  - Architectural paints
  - Industrial maintenance products
  - Stains
  - Varnishes
  - Wood finishing products
- Brands
  - Andina
  - Colorgin
  - Dutch Boy
  - Globo
  - Kem-Tone
  - Krylon
  - Marson
  - Martin Senour
  - Minwax
  - Pratt & Lambert
  - Pulverlack
  - Ronseal
  - Sherwin-Williams
  - Sumare

## COMPETITORS

3M
Akzo Nobel
BASF AG
BEHR
Benjamin Moore
California Products
Chemcraft
Color Wheel Paint
Coronado Paint
Dunn-Edwards
DuPont
Ferro
H.B. Fuller
Home Depot
ICI Paints
Kelly-Moore
Lowe's
PPG
Professional Paint
RPM
True Value
Valspar
Vogel Paint
Wal-Mart
Wattyl

## HISTORICAL FINANCIALS

Company Type: Public

### Income Statement

FYE: December 31

| | REVENUE ($ mil.) | NET INCOME ($ mil.) | NET PROFIT MARGIN | EMPLOYEES |
|---|---|---|---|---|
| **12/06** | 7,810 | 576 | 7.4% | 30,767 |
| **12/05** | 7,191 | 463 | 6.4% | 29,434 |
| **12/04** | 6,114 | 393 | 6.4% | 28,690 |
| **12/03** | 5,408 | 332 | 6.1% | 25,777 |
| **12/02** | 5,185 | 128 | 2.5% | 25,752 |
| **Annual Growth** | 10.8% | 45.8% | — | 4.5% |

### 2006 Year-End Financials

Debt ratio: 18.7%
Return on equity: 35.4%
Cash ($ mil.): 490
Current ratio: 1.18
Long-term debt ($ mil.): 292
No. of shares (mil.): 134
Dividends
Yield: 1.6%
Payout: 23.9%
Market value ($ mil.): 8,492

### Stock History

NYSE: SHW



| | STOCK PRICE ($) FY Close | P/E High | P/E Low | PER SHARE ($) Earnings | Dividends | Book Value |
|---|---|---|---|---|---|---|
| **12/06** | 63.58 | 15 | 9 | 4.19 | 1.00 | 14.92 |
| **12/05** | 45.42 | 15 | 12 | 3.28 | 0.82 | 12.81 |
| **12/04** | 44.63 | 17 | 12 | 2.72 | 0.68 | 11.70 |
| **12/03** | 34.74 | 15 | 11 | 2.26 | 0.62 | 9.80 |
| **12/02** | 28.25 | 40 | 26 | 0.84 | 0.60 | 9.01 |
| Annual Growth | 22.5% | — | — | 49.4% | 13.6% | 13.4% |

# Sigma-Aldrich

Check the shelves of any research (or mad) scientist and you're likely to find Sigma-Aldrich's chemical products. The company is a leading supplier of chemicals to research laboratories. It has more than 70,000 customers, including labs involved in government and commercial research, for its more than 100,000 chemical and 30,000 equipment products. The products are divided into two categories: research chemicals (further divided into essentials, specialties, and biotech products) and fine chemicals (primarily for commercial applications). The company, which operates in 35 countries and sells its wares worldwide, manufactures about half of its chemical products.

Sigma-Aldrich gets more than half of its sales from its research chemicals business, which publishes a catalog known in labs as "Big Red" that includes biochemicals, organic chemicals, and reagents. The unit's sales are divided among government institutions, nonprofits, universities, and pharmaceutical, diagnostic, and biotech companies (about 70%); and chemical companies and hospitals (the remaining 30%). Small orders from labs (averaging around $400) account for more than 70% of the company's total sales.

The company acquired the JRH Biosciences division of Australian biotech firm CSL Limited for $370 million in 2005. It also bought Degussa's genomics research division, Proligo. The following year it pushed heavily into the Chinese market with the acquisition of Beijing Superior Chemicals and Instruments, which had been Sigma-Aldrich's primary distributor in China, and the creation of Sigma-Aldrich (Shanghai) Trading Co. to head up its operations in the country. In 2006 the company also acquired Pharmorphix Limited, a UK-based firm that offers solid-form research services to the global pharmaceutical and biotech markets.

Sigma-Aldrich changed its organizational structure in 2006, splitting its research division into three units: specialties (traditional line of lab products), essentials (large pharmaceutical, academic, and commercial research customers), and biotech (for genomic, proteomic, and other life science research uses).

## HISTORY

The sugar shortage caused by WWII led biochemist Dan Broida to begin a storefront saccharin-manufacturing business, Sigma Chemical Company, in St. Louis in 1945. The firm later branched into biochemicals and diagnostic products. Six years after Broida started turning out saccharin, Aldrich Chemical Company, founded by future collaborator and Harvard-educated chemist Dr. Alfred Bader, started making organic chemicals in a Milwaukee garage. At first, Bader specialized in chemicals not offered by Eastman Kodak, then a leading chemical producer. Soon, however, he went head-to-head with larger chemical companies, offering a full range of research and pharmaceutical organic chemicals.

Sigma-Aldrich was formed by the merger of the two companies in 1975. Broida became the new enterprise's chairman and Bader its president. Though dwarfed by some of its competitors, through astute management the company claimed about 35% of the market for specialty chemicals used in research by 1979. Much of Sigma-Aldrich's success can be traced to its catalogs. Bader had begun compiling simple chemical listings in the early 1950s. In 1979 the company distributed 300,000 copies of the free catalog, which doubled as a laboratory reference tool listing 40,000 chemicals and their physical properties. By that time the company had subsidiaries in Canada, Germany, Israel, and the UK, and sold to customers — mostly academicians and researchers — in 125 countries. In 1980 metal forming firm B-Line Systems became a subsidiary of Sigma-Aldrich.

The company paralleled the fast growth of the biomedical research market in the 1980s, keeping up with new developments and supplying researchers with specialty chemicals and resisting opportunities in the bulk-chemicals market. After Broida died in 1981, his relatives sold much of their stock in Sigma-Aldrich, making it more widely held. Then-CEO Tom Cori took charge and the company continued to grow, with sales of $215 million and a catalog circulation of about 1.5 million by 1986. In 1989 Sigma-Aldrich acquired Fluka Chemical AG (Switzerland), a maker of biochemicals and organic chemicals for use in research and development, from Ciba-Geigy, Hoffmann-La Roche, and others. By 1993 Sigma-Aldrich had more than eight times the catalog sales of any of its competitors. That year it acquired Supelco, a supplier of chromatography products used in chemical research and production, from Rohm and Haas.

In 1996 Sigma-Aldrich was fined $480,000 for exporting 48 shipments of biotoxins without a license in 1992 and 1993 (the company said it had misinterpreted regulations passed in the wake of the Gulf War that were designed to stop the spread of biological weapons). Sigma-Aldrich stepped into the bulk market in 1997 with the construction of a large-scale manufacturing plant in the UK.

Sigma-Aldrich in 1999 bought the remaining 25% interest in Germany-based RdH Laborchemikalien Gmbh (laboratory chemicals) from partner Riedelde-Haen and also acquired Genosys Biotechnologies, a private Texas-based supplier of synthetic DNA products, for $39.5 million. That year COO David Harvey replaced CEO Cori.

To boost concentration on chemicals, in 2000 Sigma-Aldrich sold its B-Line subsidiary (metal conduits and cable trays) to Cooper Industries for about $425 million and reorganized its chemicals business into four units: laboratory products, life-science products, fine chemicals, and diagnostics. The sale of B-Line resulted in a one-time gain of about $170 million (which was over 50% of 2000 net income); most of that cash was used to buy company stock.

Early in 2001 the company bought isotope maker Isotec Inc. from Nippon Sanso for $35.6 million. In 2002 the company reorganized into its present three divisions.

In early 2002 Sigma-Aldrich began divesting its poorly performing diagnostics business in an effort to focus on research chemicals, fine chemicals, and biotech.

## EXECUTIVES

**Chairman:** David R. Harvey, age 66
**President, CEO, and Director; President, Scientific Research:** Jai P. Nagarkatti, age 59
**CFO, Chief Administrative Officer, and Secretary:** Michael R. (Mike) Hogan, age 53
**CIO:** Carl Turza, age 47
**VP, Human Resources:** Douglas W. (Doug) Rau, age 49
**VP, International Sales and Operations:** Eric Green
**VP, Process Improvement:** James W. (Jim) Meteer, age 55
**VP, Quality and Safety:** Steve Walton
**VP, General Counsel, and Secretary:** Richard (Rich) Keffer, age 51
**VP, Sales:** Gerrit van den Dool, age 53
**Treasurer:** Kirk A. Richter, age 59
**Controller:** Karen J. Miller, age 48
**President, Research Essentials:** Gilles A. Cottier, age 47
**President, SAFC Biosciences:** Rodney L. (Rod) Kelley, age 51
**Director, Organization Development:** John Short
**President, Research Biotech:** David A. Smoller, age 44
**Auditors:** KPMG LLP

## LOCATIONS

**HQ:** Sigma-Aldrich Corporation
3050 Spruce St., St. Louis, MO 63103
**Phone:** 314-771-5765 **Fax:** 314-286-7874
**Web:** www.sigmaaldrich.com

Sigma-Aldrich has production and/or distribution facilities in Australia, Canada, France, Germany, India, Israel, Japan, Mexico, South Korea, Switzerland, the UK, and the US.

### 2006 Sales

| | $ mil. | % of total |
|---|---|---|
| US | 715.4 | 40 |
| UK | 187.6 | 10 |
| Other countries | 894.5 | 50 |
| **Total** | **1,797.5** | **100** |

## PRODUCTS/OPERATIONS

### 2006 Sales

| | $ mil. | % of total |
|---|---|---|
| Research chemicals | | |
| Specialties | 669.7 | 37 |
| Essentials | 355.3 | 20 |
| Biotech | 276.8 | 15 |
| Fine chemicals | 495.7 | 28 |
| **Total** | **1,797.5** | **100** |

## COMPETITORS

Aceto
Apogent Technologies inc.
Applied Biosystems
Ashland Distribution
Atrium Biotech
Bayer
BD
Brenntag
Cambrex
Cambridge Isotope
CHEMCENTRAL
Chemtura
Ciba Specialty Chemicals
Clariant
DSM
Invitrogen
Lonza
Promega
QIAGEN
TECHNE
VWR International

## HISTORICAL FINANCIALS

Company Type: Public

### Income Statement

FYE: December 31

| | REVENUE ($ mil.) | NET INCOME ($ mil.) | NET PROFIT MARGIN | EMPLOYEES |
|---|---|---|---|---|
| **12/06** | 1,798 | 277 | 15.4% | 7,299 |
| **12/05** | 1,667 | 258 | 15.5% | 6,849 |
| **12/04** | 1,409 | 233 | 16.5% | 6,140 |
| **12/03** | 1,298 | 193 | 14.9% | 5,920 |
| **12/02** | 1,207 | 131 | 10.8% | 5,940 |
| **Annual Growth** | 10.5% | 20.6% | — | 5.3% |

### 2006 Year-End Financials

Debt ratio: 23.9%
Return on equity: 20.9%
Cash ($ mil.): 174
Current ratio: 2.51
Long-term debt ($ mil.): 338
No. of shares (mil.): 132
Dividends
Yield: 1.1%
Payout: 20.5%
Market value ($ mil.): 5,132

**Stock History** NASDAQ (GS): SIAL

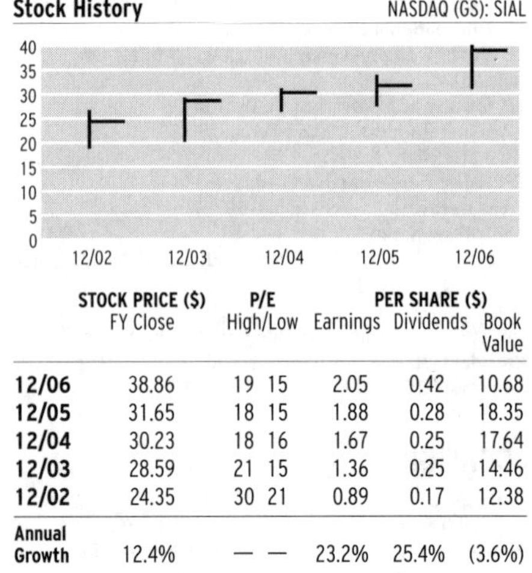


| | STOCK PRICE ($) FY Close | P/E High/Low | | PER SHARE ($) Earnings | Dividends | Book Value |
|---|---|---|---|---|---|---|
| **12/06** | 38.86 | 19 | 15 | 2.05 | 0.42 | 10.68 |
| **12/05** | 31.65 | 18 | 15 | 1.88 | 0.28 | 18.35 |
| **12/04** | 30.23 | 18 | 16 | 1.67 | 0.25 | 17.64 |
| **12/03** | 28.59 | 21 | 15 | 1.36 | 0.25 | 14.46 |
| **12/02** | 24.35 | 30 | 21 | 0.89 | 0.17 | 12.38 |
| **Annual Growth** | 12.4% | — | — | 23.2% | 25.4% | (3.6%) |

# Silicon Graphics

Silicon Graphics, Inc. (SGI) has seen more restructuring than Michael Jackson. The company manufactures high-end computers for technical and creative applications. Customers ranging from scientists, graphic artists, and engineers to large corporations and government agencies use its workstations, servers, and storage systems. The company's advanced graphics computers have been used to create some of Hollywood's most striking special effects. Other key sectors for SGI include the energy and manufacturing industries. The company emerged from Chapter 11 bankruptcy in October 2006, six months after it filed for protection.

In recent years the company has faced increasing pressure from less expensive PCs and servers that are nearly as powerful and fast as its specialized products. SGI has long utilized MIPS processors and its proprietary version of UNIX (called IRIX) to power its servers and supercomputers, but the company has refocused on products that use Intel Itanium 2 processors and the Linux operating system.

SGI customers have included Disney Studios and NASA.

## HISTORY

Professor James Clark left Stanford University in 1981 to develop 3-D computer graphics technology. The next year he and seven students formed Silicon Graphics, Inc. (SGI). Clark in 1984 developed the first high-end 3-D workstation computer, which retailed for $75,000. Former Hewlett-Packard (HP) executive Edward McCracken joined SGI as president that year. By 1986, the year it went public, SGI led the market for graphics workstations.

The company helped pioneer the mass production of reduced instruction set computer (RISC) chips — developed by MIPS Computer Systems in 1987 — which deliver higher processing speeds by using simpler instruction sets. After hoarding its 3-D technology for six years, SGI licensed its graphics programming to IBM in 1988 to encourage software development for its machines.

SGI debuted the first RISC-based PC, the IRIS Indigo, in 1992, although some in the industry might argue that the IBM RT PC, introduced in 1986, deserves that distinction. It licensed its programming to Microsoft and joined Compaq (now part of Hewlett-Packard) in a product development agreement, selling the PC maker for $135 million in stock. The deal fell through, and Compaq sold back its stake in the company for $150 million. That year SGI bought MIPS (renamed MIPS Technologies). In search of greater market penetration, SGI introduced in 1993 smaller, less expensive systems ($10,000 and under). Time Warner Cable paid SGI $30 million to develop products for an interactive television trial market. SGI's 1993 sales topped $1 billion.

In 1994 COO Tom Jermoluk took over the company's daily operations. Unable to direct its future (he had wanted to move into the low-end computer market more quickly), Clark left to explore other ventures. (He would help start Netscape, which eventually became part of Time Warner, as well as Healtheon, which later changed its name to WebMD.) Spurred by Microsoft's growing software dominance, in 1995 SGI acquired graphics software firms Alias Research and Wavefront Technologies. Also in 1995 MIPS Technologies debuted a multimedia chip designed for Nintendo games and other interactive consumer products.

SGI bought unprofitable Cray Research for $767 million in 1996 and later unwittingly sold four servers to a Russian nuclear weapons design facility, prompting a State Department investigation. Jermoluk resigned to head high-tech Internet delivery startup At Home. Also in 1996 the company discovered a flaw in its new microprocessor, built by Japan's NEC, and spent $10 million to replace the chips.

Advances in graphics by SGI's lower-priced PC brethren slowed sales of its workstations. In 1998 SGI formed alliances with Microsoft and Intel to develop products using standard PC-based technology. SGI cut its workforce by 1,700 in a restructuring that saw Richard Belluzzo — nicknamed "Rocket Rick" for his impressive climb at HP — replace McCracken as CEO. SGI's troubles led to a $460 million loss for fiscal 1998.

In 1999 SGI made plans to divest MIPS Technologies slowly. It restructured for the fourth time in as many years and decided to sell and transfer more units, and cut 17% of its workforce — 3,000 additional jobs. To move away from its roots as a graphics and workstation company, it officially adopted the brand name SGI for its products. Amid the changes, Belluzzo abruptly resigned. He was replaced by SGI board member Bob Bishop. An SGI employee since 1985, Bishop vowed to return SGI's focus to computers.

In 2000 the company spun off its MediaBase streaming media operations into a separate entity, Kasenna (it later sold most of its stake in the company). It sold the Cray unit to supercomputing startup Tera Computer, which rechristened itself Cray, Inc. SGI completed the spinoff of MIPS to shareholders later that year.

In 2001 SGI closed its plant in Switzerland. The following year it sold a 60% stake in SGI Japan to NEC. (It reduced its stake to less than 25% in 2005.)

SGI sold Alias Systems (formerly Alias/Wavefront) to investment firm Accel-KKR for approximately $58 million in cash in 2004.

Bob Bishop stepped down as chairman and CEO in early 2006 after the company reported widening losses in the second quarter of its fiscal year. He was succeeded by Dennis McKenna, who came from the world of semiconductor manufacturing. McKenna, who was named chairman, president, and CEO of SGI, previously served as CEO of SCP Global Technologies, a supplier of semiconductor manufacturing equipment, and as CEO of ChipPAC, a provider of semiconductor assembly, packaging, and testing services. Bishop became vice chairman of the board.

In 2007 Robert "Bo" Ewald left Linux Networx to replace McKenna as CEO. The appointment marked Ewald's return to the company; he served as COO of SGI earlier in his career.

## EXECUTIVES

**Chairman:** Kevin D. Katari, age 37
**CEO and Director:** Robert H. (Bo) Ewald, age 57
**SVP, CFO, and Corporate Controller:** Kathy A. Lanterman, age 46
**SVP and CTO:** Eng Lim Goh, age 46, $366,000 pay
**SVP and Product General Manager:** Dave Parry
**SVP, Global Sales, Service, and Marketing:** Brian M. Samuels, age 57
**SVP, Intercontinental Field Operations:** Bill LaRosa, age 58
**SVP, Strategic Technology Initiatives:** Jan C. Silverman, age 56
**SVP, Human Resources:** Dennis W. Daniels, age 51
**VP, Technology Solutions:** Terry Oberdank
**VP and General Manager, EMEA:** Philippe Miltin
**VP, General Counsel, and Secretary:** Barry J. Weinert, age 52
**VP, Sales, EMEA:** Tim Butchart
**VP, SGI Asia Pacific:** Bill Trestrail
**Chief Accounting Officer and Corporate Controller:** David Barr, age 41
**President, SGI Federal and SVP, SGI Global Defense Strategies:** Anthony K. Robbins, age 44, $357,200 pay (prior to promotion)
**Auditors:** KPMG LLP

## LOCATIONS

**HQ:** Silicon Graphics, Inc.
1140 E. Arques Ave., Sunnyvale, CA 94085
**Phone:** 650-960-1980 **Fax:** 650-933-0316
**Web:** www.sgi.com

## PRODUCTS/OPERATIONS

### Selected Products and Services

Services
- Managed
- Professional
- Support
- Training

Products
- Servers (cluster, mid-range, high-end)
- Software (operating system, storage management)
- Storage systems (disk and tape-based)

## COMPETITORS

Apple
Concurrent Computer
Cray
Dell
EMC
Evans & Sutherland
Fujitsu
Hewlett-Packard
Hitachi Data Systems
IBM
Microsoft
NEC
NVIDIA
Stratus Technologies
Sun Microsystems
Toshiba
Unisys

## HISTORICAL FINANCIALS

Company Type: Public

**Income Statement** FYE: Last Friday in June

| | REVENUE ($ mil.) | NET INCOME ($ mil.) | NET PROFIT MARGIN | EMPLOYEES |
|---|---|---|---|---|
| **6/07** | 341 | (104) | — | 1,588 |
| **6/06** | 519 | (146) | — | 1,752 |
| **6/05** | 730 | (76) | — | 2,423 |
| **6/04** | 842 | (46) | — | 2,655 |
| **6/03** | 962 | (130) | — | 3,714 |
| **Annual Growth** | (22.8%) | — | — | (19.1%) |

**2007 Year-End Financials**

Debt ratio: 100.6%
Return on equity: —
Cash ($ mil.): 77
Current ratio: 1.28
Long-term debt ($ mil.): 85
No. of shares (mil.): 11
Dividends
Yield: —
Payout: —
Market value ($ mil.): 295

**Stock History** NASDAQ (CM): SGIC

| | STOCK PRICE ($) FY Close | P/E High/Low | PER SHARE ($) Earnings | Dividends | Book Value |
|---|---|---|---|---|---|
| **6/07** | 26.54 | — — | (9.32) | — | 7.59 |

# Simon Property Group

Simon says: Shop! And millions do. Simon Property Group is the US's #1 shopping mall owner and one of the nation's largest publicly traded real estate companies. The real estate investment trust (REIT) owns, develops, and manages about 280 properties totaling more than 200 million sq. ft. — primarily malls, community shopping centers, and outlet centers (under the Premium Outlet name) — in 38 states. Many of the company's malls are located in Florida, Texas, and the Midwest; it also has interests in more than 50 properties in France, Italy, and Poland, as well as five outlet centers in Japan and one in Mexico.

In 2006 Simon bought nine stores from Federated Department Stores as part of the latter company's acquisition of May Department Stores. The stores were in Simon malls.

With rivals such as General Growth Properties and Macerich buying up additional properties, keeping the top spot in the industry has meant Simon has had to do some shopping of its own, acquiring Chelsea Property Group for about $3.5 billion in 2004. Later that year Chelsea opened its first Premium Outlet center in Mexico, and bought the Woodland Hills mall in Tulsa, Oklahoma.

The company, along with Farallon Capital Management, acquired mall developer The Mills Corporation.

The founding Simon family, owners of the Indiana Pacers NBA franchise, owns nearly 14% of the company; Edward DeBartolo, the beleaguered former San Francisco 49ers owner, has almost a 7% stake.

## HISTORY

Simon Property Group helped change the face of the US retail landscape from mom-and-pop stores to shopping malls. The original Simon Property Group (formed in 1993) was the offshoot of brothers Melvin and Herbert Simon's Melvin Simon & Associates (MSA, founded in 1959). MSA's first project was Southgate Plaza, a strip center in Bloomington, Indiana, consisting of a half-dozen small tenants anchored by a food store.

To get started, the Simons sometimes borrowed cash from friends, but during the 1960s and 1970s developers could usually borrow 100% of a shopping center's construction costs after securing an anchor tenant. Leases then provided money to repay debt and make a down payment on the next project. The Simons consistently retained equity, developing a huge asset base that they used as collateral for larger projects.

The new strip malls lacked the prestige of big-city stores such as Macy's; they also lacked the personal touch of the neighborhood shops they put out of business. But they boasted retail's two most important virtues — price and convenience — and in time they developed into the modern mall. MSA built its first indoor mall in the mid-1960s in snowy Fort Collins, Colorado. By the late 1960s, MSA and other developers were consumed with mall projects.

Unlike many developers, the Simons were genial, honest negotiators, appealing to merchants and bankers put off by city slickers or hucksters. Yet Mel and Herb were often compared to the Marx brothers for bickering between themselves. During one negotiation, Mel allegedly took off his shoe and threw it at Herb.

In the mid-1970s Mel packed up and headed west to become a Hollywood producer. After a string of such Oscar noncontenders as *Porky's* and *Love at First Bite,* Mel returned to the family company in the 1980s, and in 1983 the brothers bought pro basketball's Indiana Pacers.

As the 1989 real estate slump hit, the Simons were busy building the largest mall in the country, just outside Minneapolis. Completed in 1992, the Mall of America included a roller coaster, a two-story miniature golf course, and a walk-through aquarium. In 1993 Simon Property Group went public in one of the largest IPOs of its time.

In 1996 the company became the Simon DeBartolo Group after merging with DeBartolo Realty, founded to hold the retail and residential properties of another sporting family, the DeBartolos (San Francisco 49ers).

After its record-setting purchase of private paired-share REIT Corporate Property Investors in 1998, the company reverted to the Simon Property Group name (Edward DeBartolo's name had been soiled in a Louisiana casino scandal) and added more than 20 Midwestern properties to its fold, giving the company a firm lock on the top mall REIT spot.

In 1999 Simon bought stakes in 14 malls in the northeastern US and became 50%-owner of the Mall of America after buying a 27% stake in the development held by financing partner TIAA-CREF for $318 million. The following year it formed a joint venture with Kimco Realty to buy 250 stores from the bankrupt Montgomery Ward chain.

Simon seemed ready to embrace online shopping during the Internet craze by working on initiatives that combined the traditional shopping experience with the convenience of the Internet, including its clixnmortar.com, which developed high-tech shopping tools. However, like other ambitious online concepts of the era, Simon's was slow to catch on with consumers. The company wrote off losses related to its tech investments in 2001 and went back to focusing on food courts.

In 2002 the company bought part of the mall portfolio of Rodamco North America. That year, Simon also pulled out of a much-ballyhooed project — building a family entertainment complex at Penn's Landing in Philadelphia's Center City — after a deadline to lease 50% of the center was not met. Later that year, the company merged with SPG Realty Consultants, ending the companies' paired share corporate structure.

In 2003 the company bought out the 42% stake in The Forum Shops held by joint venture partner Sheldon Gordon after he exercised a provision in his deal with Simon that forced the company to buy out his share or sell him its 58% stake. That same year Simon dropped a bid with Westfield America (now Westfield Group) to acquire rival Taubman Centers after a legal battle was ended by the passage of an anti-takeover bill in Michigan.

In 2004 the company was forced to sell a controlling interest in the Mall of America to Canadian real estate firm Triple Five, an original partner in the development, after a court ruled that Simon improperly acquired control of the mall from TIAA-CREF in 1999. (The case is still pending appeals.) Later that year Simon acquired outlet mall developer Chelsea Property Group for about $3.5 billion.

## EXECUTIVES

**Co-Chairman:** Melvin Simon, age 80
**Co-Chairman:** Herbert Simon, age 72
**CEO and Director:** David Simon, age 45, $2,000,000 pay
**President, COO, and Director:** Richard S. Sokolov, age 57, $1,700,000 pay
**SEVP; President Leasing:** Gary L. Lewis, age 48, $893,641 pay
**EVP and CFO:** Stephen E. Sterrett, age 51, $1,100,000 pay
**EVP; COO Operating Properties:** John Rulli, age 49
**EVP Development:** Arthur W. (Art) Spellmeyer
**EVP Development:** Thomas J. (Tom) Schneider
**EVP Property Management; President Simon Business Network:** J. Scott Mumphrey, age 55
**SVP and Chief Accounting Officer:** John Dahl
**SVP and Treasurer:** Andrew A. (Andy) Juster, age 54
**SVP Research and Corporate Communications:** Michael P. McCarty
**VP Investor Relations:** Shelly J. Doran
**President International Division and Chairman Simon Global Limited:** Hans C. Mautner, age 67
**President Community Shopping Center Division:** Michael E. McCarty
**Chief Marketing Officer; President Simon Brand Ventures:** Stewart A. Stockdale
**Chief Information Officer:** David Schacht
**Secretary and General Counsel:** James M. Barkley, age 55, $1,175,000 pay
**Director Mall Public Relations:** Billie Scott
**Manager Corporate Public Relations:** Les Morris
**Auditors:** Ernst & Young LLP

## LOCATIONS

**HQ:** Simon Property Group, Inc.
225 W. Washington St., Indianapolis, IN 46204
**Phone:** 317-636-1600 **Fax:** 317-263-2318
**Web:** www.shopsimon.com

Simon Property Group owns or has an interest in more than 170 regional malls, more than 30 Premium Outlet centers, more than 70 community/lifestyle centers, and nearly a dozen other shopping centers or outlet centers in 40 states, Europe, and Mexico.

## PRODUCTS/OPERATIONS

### 2006 Sales

| | $ mil. | % of total |
|---|---|---|
| Minimum rent | 2,020.8 | 61 |
| Tenant reimbursements | 946.5 | 28 |
| Overage rent | 95.8 | 3 |
| Management fees & other | 82.3 | 2 |
| Other | 186.7 | 6 |
| **Total** | **3,332.1** | **100** |

## COMPETITORS

Belz
Cadillac Fairview
CBL & Associates Properties
General Growth Properties
Glimcher Realty
Horizon Group Properties
Inland Retail Real Estate Trust
Lincoln Property
Macerich
Mills Corporation
Taubman Centers
Vornado Realty
Weingarten Realty

## HISTORICAL FINANCIALS

Company Type: Public

### Income Statement

FYE: December 31

| | REVENUE ($ mil.) | NET INCOME ($ mil.) | NET PROFIT MARGIN | EMPLOYEES |
|---|---|---|---|---|
| **12/06** | 3,332 | 564 | 16.9% | 4,300 |
| **12/05** | 3,167 | 476 | 15.0% | 4,700 |
| **12/04** | 2,642 | 343 | 13.0% | 4,610 |
| **12/03** | 2,314 | 369 | 15.9% | 4,040 |
| **12/02** | 2,186 | 423 | 19.3% | 4,020 |
| **Annual Growth** | 11.1% | 7.5% | — | 1.7% |

### 2006 Year-End Financials

Debt ratio: 497.4%
Return on equity: 17.8%
Cash ($ mil.): 929
Current ratio: —
Long-term debt ($ mil.): 15,394
No. of shares (mil.): 226
Dividends
Yield: 3.0%
Payout: 138.8%
Market value ($ mil.): 22,871

### Stock History

NYSE: SPG

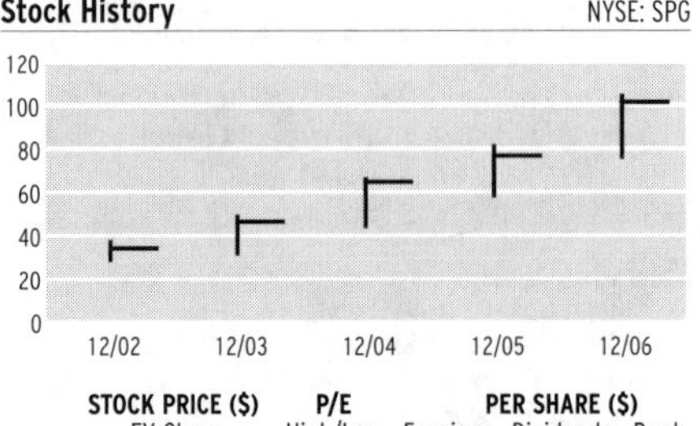


| | STOCK PRICE ($) FY Close | P/E High/Low | | PER SHARE ($) Earnings | Dividends | Book Value |
|---|---|---|---|---|---|---|
| **12/06** | 101.29 | 48 | 35 | 2.19 | 3.04 | 17.62 |
| **12/05** | 76.63 | 44 | 32 | 1.82 | 2.70 | 19.54 |
| **12/04** | 64.67 | 46 | 31 | 1.44 | 2.99 | 20.85 |
| **12/03** | 46.34 | 29 | 19 | 1.65 | 2.40 | 16.62 |
| **12/02** | 34.07 | 19 | 14 | 1.99 | 2.17 | 19.02 |
| **Annual Growth** | 31.3% | — | — | 2.4% | 8.8% | (1.9%) |

# Skadden, Arps, Slate, Meagher & Flom

Have you heard about the law firm that sued the business information publisher for a profile that opened with a wickedly clever lawyer joke? Neither have we, and we would like to keep it that way. Skadden, Arps, Slate, Meagher & Flom, a leading US law firm and one of the largest in the world, has some 2,000 attorneys in more than 20 offices around the globe, from Boston to Beijing and from London to Los Angeles. The firm is best known for its work in mergers and acquisitions, corporate restructuring, and corporate finance, but it represents businesses in a wide variety of practice areas, including intellectual property and litigation. Skadden was founded in 1948.

Skadden has worked for a number of *FORTUNE* 500 companies. High-profile clients have included DaimlerChrysler, JPMorgan Chase, and State Farm, as well as Arcelor, Merrill Lynch, and Toshiba.

Over the years Skadden has grown organically rather than by merging with other firms. The New York office is the firm's largest, but offices outside the US have been growing faster.

## HISTORY

Marshall Skadden, Leslie Arps, and John Slate hung out their shingle in New York City on April Fool's Day, 1948. Skadden and Arps came from a Wall Street law firm, and Slate had been counsel to Pan American World Airways. Without the reputation and connections of the established New York law firms, the firm found work one case at a time from referrals, handling mainly commercial, corporate, and litigations work. Marshall Skadden died in 1958.

Denied the luxury of steady clients, the firm was forced to be innovative and, at times, unorthodox. Joe Flom, who had joined as the firm's first associate, specialized in corporate law and proxy fights. During the 1960s, when tender offers and hostile takeovers increased, many of the more venerable firms referred clients engaged in the undignified corporate raids to Flom to preserve their gentlemanly reputations. With "white shoe" lawyers on Wall Street hesitant to tread into the uncivilized region of corporate takeovers, Skadden, Arps went for it, and the firm virtually pioneered the business of mergers and acquisitions (M&A) under Flom.

When Congress passed the Williams Act in 1968, which "legitimized" tender offers by providing regulation, other law firms started to get in on the act. Skadden, Arps was way ahead of the game, however, and as corporations and lawyers realized that aggressive legal tactics helped win corporate takeover battles, it also became apparent that Joe Flom was the expert. As takeover fights became more frequent in the early 1970s, the firm earned more than just respect. Earnings came not just from some of the highest hourly rates in the industry, but from hefty retainers (now a common practice at many firms) on the theory that association with Flom would scare raiders off. The only other name that could strike such fear in people's hearts was Marty Lipton of rival takeover specialists Wachtell, Lipton, Rosen & Katz. From the late 1970s through the 1980s, Skadden, Arps was involved in almost every important M&A case in the US.

The firm used its success in mergers and acquisitions to build its practice in other areas. In the early 1980s it branched into bankruptcy, product liability, and real estate law. By then it had opened offices in Boston; Chicago; Los Angeles; Washington, DC; and Wilmington, Delaware. Les Arps died in 1987.

With the boom in mergers and acquisitions activity and bankruptcies in the late 1980s, the firm grew to almost 2,000 lawyers by 1989. Then came the recession, and M&A work virtually dried up. Skadden, Arps responded by shedding more than 500 lawyers between 1989 and 1990. It also scrambled to diversify and expand internationally. As takeover activity rebounded in the mid-1990s, the diversification strategy actually began to work against Skadden, Arps because profits didn't skyrocket like those of M&A specialist firms.

The firm opened an office in Singapore in 1995 to coordinate its Asian business, signaling that city's growing importance as a financial center. Two years later two-thirds of the firm's Beijing team defected to a rival firm. Headquarters shrugged it off and flew in replacements. Representing President Bill Clinton, Skadden, Arps won one of its highest-profile cases in 1998 when the sexual harassment suit brought by Paula Jones was thrown out.

With its M&A practice in full swing again, Skadden, Arps was involved in 70 announced M&A deals in 1999, including the $75 billion merger of oil companies Exxon and Mobil. It also became the first US law firm to reach $1 billion in revenue in 2000. The company announced an alliance with Italian law firm Studio Chiomenti the following year and took part in three of the top 10 M&A deals of 2002. Skadden, Arps helped struggling discount retailer Kmart emerge from its titanic bankruptcy the next year.

## EXECUTIVES

**Executive Partner:** Robert C. Sheehan
**Corporate Partner:** Joseph H. Flom
**Senior Partner, Corporate Practice:** Roger S. Aaron
**Senior Partner, Litigation:** William P. Frank
**Chief Administrative Director:** Laurel E. Henschel
**Director, Associate Development:** Jodie R. Garfinkel
**Director, Legal Hiring:** Carol Lee H. Sprague
**Director, Marketing and Business Development:** Sally J. Feldman
**Director, Technology:** Harris Z. Tilevitz
**Global Head, Real Estate Investment Trust Practice Group:** Barnet Phillips IV

## LOCATIONS

**HQ:** Skadden, Arps, Slate, Meagher & Flom LLP
4 Times Square, New York, NY 10036
**Phone:** 212-735-3000 **Fax:** 212-735-2000
**Web:** www.skadden.com

## PRODUCTS/OPERATIONS

### Selected Practice Areas

Alternative dispute resolution
Antitrust
Appellate litigation and legal issues
Banking and institutional investing
CFIUS
Communications
Complex mass torts and insurance litigation
Consumer financial services enforcement and litigation
Corporate compliance programs
Corporate finance
Corporate governance

Corporate restructuring
Crisis management
Derivative financial products, commodities and futures
Employee benefits and executive compensation
Energy project finance and development
Energy regulatory
Environmental
Environmental litigation
European Union/international competition
Financial institutions
Financial services
Foreign corrupt practices act defense
Franchise law
Gaming
Government contract disputes
Government enforcement and white collar crime
Health care enforcement and litigation
Health care fraud and abuse
Information technology and e-commerce
Insurance
Intellectual property and technology
International arbitration
International law and policy
International tax
International trade
Investment management
Labor and employment law
Lease financing
Litigation
Mergers and acquisitions
Outsourcing
Patent and technology litigation and counseling
Pharmaceutical, biotechnology, and medical device licensing
Political law
Private equity
Private equity funds
Public policy
Real estate
Real estate investment trusts
Securities enforcement and compliance
Securities litigation
Sports
Structured finance
Tax
Tax controversy and litigation
Trademark, copyright, and advertising litigation and counseling
Trusts and estates
UCC and secured transactions
Utilities mergers and acquisitions

## COMPETITORS

Baker & McKenzie
Clifford Chance
Davis Polk
Gibson, Dunn & Crutcher
Jones Day
Kirkland & Ellis
Latham & Watkins
Mayer, Brown, Rowe & Maw
McDermott Will & Emery
O'Melveny & Myers
Shearman & Sterling
Sidley Austin
Sullivan & Cromwell
Wachtell, Lipton
Weil, Gotshal
White & Case
WilmerHale

## HISTORICAL FINANCIALS

Company Type: Partnership

**Income Statement** FYE: December 31

| | ESTIMATED REVENUE ($ mil.) | NET INCOME ($ mil.) | NET PROFIT MARGIN | EMPLOYEES |
|---|---|---|---|---|
| 12/05 | 1,610 | — | — | 4,400 |

# SkyWest, Inc.

SkyWest flies in every direction. The company's main subsidiaries, SkyWest Airlines and Atlantic Southeast Airlines (ASA), serve some 230 destinations in North America and the Caribbean as regional carriers for Delta Air Lines and UAL's United Airlines. SkyWest Airlines flies as Delta Connection from Salt Lake City and as United Express from hubs in Chicago; Denver; Los Angeles; Portland, Oregon; San Francisco; and Seattle/Tacoma. ASA flies for Delta from hubs in Atlanta, Cincinnati, Los Angeles, and Salt Lake City. Combined, the carriers operate a fleet of about 335 Canadair regional jets (CRJs, made by Bombardier) and some 75 turboprops.

ASA, acquired in 2005, diversified SkyWest's operations geographically and added Delta business to a revenue mix that had leaned heavily toward United. In conjunction with the acquisition, SkyWest negotiated new, 15-year Delta Connection contracts for both SkyWest Airlines and ASA.

Owning both carriers makes SkyWest a strong competitor for additional regional business from Delta or United, or even from other carriers. In 2006 SkyWest Airlines contracted to operate another 12 CRJs for Delta and made a deal with a new partner, Midwest Airlines, to operate as many as 25 CRJs under the Midwest Connect banner. Service under the Midwest contract is being phased in beginning in 2007. To take advantage of growth opportunities, SkyWest is adding CRJs to its fleet.

SkyWest Airlines and ASA are operated as separate units, but SkyWest sees opportunities to save money by integrating administrative and other functions. A challenge for SkyWest, however, will be to bring together the corporate cultures of non-union SkyWest Airlines and ASA, whose flight attendants, mechanics, and pilots are represented by unions.

Along with regional passenger transportation, which accounts for nearly all of its sales, SkyWest provides ground handling services — loading and unloading of aircraft — for other airlines at several of the airports where it operates.

## HISTORY

In 1972 Ralph Atkin founded SkyWest with one airplane that served three points in Utah. The company doubled in size in 1984 when it bought California-based Sun Aire Lines; two years later it went public. Growth was also fueled by the trend toward code-sharing agreements between major airlines and regional airlines serving rural markets. SkyWest jumped on board with Delta in 1987 to become one of four Delta Connection carriers.

Atkin stepped down as chairman in 1991 and was replaced by his nephew, CEO Jerry Atkin. By 1993 SkyWest had assembled a fleet of about 50 turboprop aircraft; that year it placed an order for 10 Canadair Regional Jets (CRJs) from Bombardier. The jets would prove to be popular among travelers.

SkyWest became a United affiliate in 1997 with 120 daily United Express departures from Los Angeles. The next year SkyWest expanded its United Express service into additional markets in California, Oregon, and Washington. Meanwhile, the company sold most of its air tours business, Scenic Airlines, to Eagle Canyon Airlines in 1998; it sold the rest in 1999.

With business booming, SkyWest placed orders for 55 more CRJs in 1999. Amid unusually cordial labor relations for an airline, SkyWest fliers voted down a chance to join the pilots' union. Also in 1999 SkyWest and Delta terminated their Los Angeles code-sharing agreement because of SkyWest's close ties to United in the city. The following year SkyWest agreed to sell the outstanding shares of subsidiary National Parks Transportation, a provider of rental car services at six airports served by the airline.

SkyWest began providing regional service for Continental Airlines in 2003, but the companies ended the deal in 2005.

In a major expansion, SkyWest in 2005 bought fellow regional carrier Atlantic Southeast Airlines (ASA) from Delta for about $425 million and some $1.25 billion in debt. The purchase was completed just before Delta filed for Chapter 11 bankruptcy protection.

## EXECUTIVES

**Chairman, President, and CEO; Chairman and CEO, SkyWest Airlines and Atlantic Southeast Airlines:** Jerry C. Atkin, age 58, $345,700 pay
**EVP, CFO, and Treasurer; EVP, CFO, and Treasurer, SkyWest Airlines and Atlantic Southeast Airlines:** Bradford R. Rich, age 45, $250,000 pay
**VP, Finance and Assistant Treasurer; VP, Finance and Treasurer, SkyWest Airlines and Atlantic Southeast Airlines:** Michael J. (Mike) Kraupp
**VP, Inflight Operations:** Sonya Wolford
**VP, Information Technology; VP, Information Technology, SkyWest Airlines and Atlantic Southeast Airlines:** James B. Jensen
**VP, Planning; VP, Planning, SkyWest Airlines and Atlantic Southeast Airlines:** Eric D. Christensen
**VP and Controller:** Eric Woodward
**Director, Benefits:** Bryce Higgins
**Director, Risk Management and Compensation:** Lisa LaRue
**President and COO, Atlantic Southeast Airlines:** Bryan T. LaBrecque, age 48, $200,000 pay
**President and COO, SkyWest Airlines:** Russell A. (Chip) Childs
**VP, Customer Service, SkyWest Airlines:** James K. Boyd
**VP, Flight Operations, SkyWest Airlines:** Bradford R. (Brad) Holt
**VP, Maintenance, SkyWest Airlines:** H. Michael Gibson
**VP, People, SkyWest Airlines:** Necia Clark-Mantle
**VP, Market Development, SkyWest Airlines:** Michael Thompson
**Director, People Programs and Recruitment, SkyWest Airlines:** Suzanne Stephensen
**Director, Employee Relations, SkyWest Airlines:** Ryan Quinlan
**Director, Corporate Communications, Development and Marketing, SkyWest Airlines:** Amber Hunter
**Auditors:** Ernst & Young LLP

## LOCATIONS

**HQ:** SkyWest, Inc.
444 S. River Rd., St. George, UT 84790
**Phone:** 435-634-3000 **Fax:** 435-634-3105
**Web:** www.skywest.com

## PRODUCTS/OPERATIONS

**2006 Sales**

| | $ mil. | % of total |
|---|---|---|
| Passenger | 3,087.2 | 99 |
| Ground handling & other | 27.5 | 1 |
| **Total** | **3,114.7** | **100** |

## COMPETITORS

Air Wisconsin Airlines
American Eagle
Comair
ExpressJet
Mesa Air
Pinnacle Airlines
Republic Airways

## HISTORICAL FINANCIALS

Company Type: Public

**Income Statement** FYE: December 31

| | REVENUE ($ mil.) | NET INCOME ($ mil.) | NET PROFIT MARGIN | EMPLOYEES |
|---|---|---|---|---|
| **12/06** | 3,115 | 146 | 4.7% | 8,792 |
| **12/05** | 1,964 | 112 | 5.7% | 13,647 |
| **12/04** | 1,156 | 82 | 7.1% | 6,747 |
| **12/03** | 888 | 67 | 7.5% | 4,952 |
| **12/02** | 775 | 87 | 11.2% | 5,079 |
| **Annual Growth** | 41.6% | 13.8% | — | 14.7% |

**2006 Year-End Financials**

Debt ratio: 142.2%
Return on equity: 13.9%
Cash ($ mil.): 652
Current ratio: 2.68
Long-term debt ($ mil.): 1,676
No. of shares (mil.): 64
Dividends
Yield: 0.5%
Payout: 5.2%
Market value ($ mil.): 1,632

**Stock History** NASDAQ (GS): SKYW

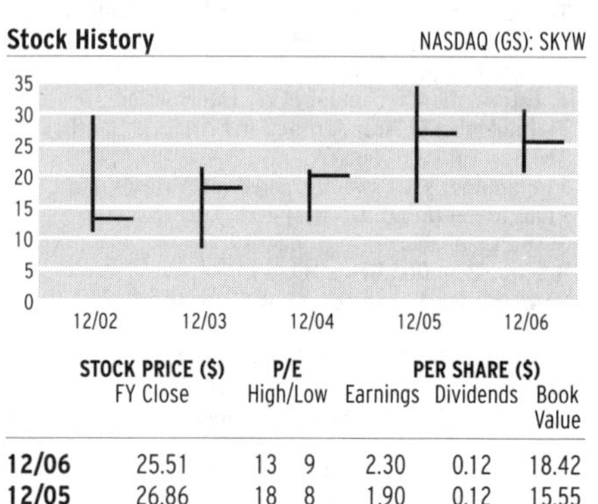


| | STOCK PRICE ($) FY Close | P/E High | P/E Low | PER SHARE ($) Earnings | Dividends | Book Value |
|---|---|---|---|---|---|---|
| **12/06** | 25.51 | 13 | 9 | 2.30 | 0.12 | 18.42 |
| **12/05** | 26.86 | 18 | 8 | 1.90 | 0.12 | 15.55 |
| **12/04** | 20.06 | 15 | 9 | 1.40 | 0.12 | 13.51 |
| **12/03** | 18.07 | 18 | 7 | 1.15 | 0.08 | 12.22 |
| **12/02** | 13.07 | 19 | 7 | 1.51 | 0.08 | 11.12 |
| **Annual Growth** | 18.2% | — | — | 11.1% | 10.7% | 13.5% |

# Smithfield Foods

When Smithfield Foods waddles up to the trough, all the other porkers stand back. Fat from acquisitions, the company is the world's largest hog producer and pork processor. Its products include fresh pork and processed meats sold under the Packerland, John Morrell, Lykes, Patrick Cudahy, and Smithfield Premium names. It distributes across the US and to about 40 other countries, and it has made major moves into France and Poland. In a steady effort to diversify, the company has built up its beef and prepared-foods operations through acquisitions. In 2007 Smithfield acquired pork producer Premium Standard Farms.

The company paid some $800 million (including $125 million in debt) for Premium Standard. As the US's #1 pork processor and marketer, Smithfield's merger with Premium Standard Farms (the nation's #2 pork producer) created a pig production powerhouse. Premium Standard brought brands such as All Natural, Fresh & Tender, Lundy's, Natural Excellence, and Premium Farms to the Smithfield roster.

In addition, beef has become an important part of Smithfield's diet and it is now one of the largest beef processors in the US. Smithfield has further fattened its bottom line by placing increased emphasis on the production of higher-margin pre-cooked meats and entrees. However, it is still in a commodity business and low hog prices can affect earnings.

As Smithfield extends its reach into Europe, in 2005 it purchased French meat processor Jean Caby for $466 million. In 2006 it purchased Sara Lee's European meats business for $575 million and the assumption of about $39 million in pension liabilities. Smithfield financed the purchase through a 50-50 joint venture with Oaktree Capital Management. Smithfield combined the Sara Lee operations with Jean Caby and named the new joint venture Groupe Smithfield.

Back home the company is busy adding to its holdings as well. The company purchased Cook's Ham from ConAgra in 2006 for about $260 million. Later that year, it purchased the bulk of ConAgra's refrigerated meats business for $571 million in cash. The deal included the Eckrich, Armor, LunchMakers, Margherita, and Longmont brands. The Butterball brand was sold to Carolina Turkeys (now Butterball, LLC), of which Smithfield owns 49%.

After 31 years as Smithfield's CEO and chairman, Joseph Luter stepped down as CEO in 2006. However, he remained as non-executive chairman of the company. President and COO C. Larry Pope, a 25-year veteran of Smithfield, succeeded Luter as CEO.

Tradewinds Global Investors owns about 8% of the company; Lazard Asset Management and ContiGroup Companies each own almost 6%. Chairman Luter owns almost 4%.

## HISTORY

Joseph Luter's father and grandfather set up Smithfield Foods in 1936 and built it into a regional pork producer. Luter began to manage the business in 1962 after his father died. In 1969 he sold the company to conglomerate Liberty Equities for $20 million and was retained as its manager, but he was soon dismissed.

Smithfield Foods floundered in his absence and grew weak from overexpansion and non-pork diversifications. Luter bought the business back in 1975, paying a fraction of what he had sold it for. At that time the company was a wholesaler of pork and fish products and was operating 27 seafood restaurants. Luter trimmed the fat to pay down debt, leaving only the pork operations. He then began to expand in the pork business through acquisitions, including Gwaltney Packing in 1982, thereby doubling its size. Other purchases included pork processors Patrick Cudahy (1985) and Esskay (1986).

The company formed a joint venture with pork producer Carroll's Foods in 1987 to help lessen its dependence on Midwestern hog farmers. To move toward higher-quality pork, the joint venture acquired North American rights from National Pig Development (a UK-based, family-owned firm) for a long and lean English breed — the NPD hog, which became the basis for the company's flagship brand, Smithfield Lean Generation Pork.

The company co-founded Circle Four Farms, a giant hog farm in Utah, in 1994 with partners Murphy's Family Farms, Carroll's, and Prestage Farms. (Two years later it bought out the other partners.) Smithfield Foods also bought regional processors Valleydale Foods (1993) and John Morrell (1995) and struggling Lykes Meat Group (1996), thereby transforming it into a national concern. In 1997 the company was ticketed with $12.6 million in fines by the EPA for water violations. The fine was later lowered by $6,000,000 by an appellate court.

Beginning in 1998, Smithfield Foods went shopping abroad, starting with Canadian meat processor Canada's Schneider Corporation and Société Bretonne De Salaisons, France's largest private-label maker of hams and bacon. In 2000 the company acquired Murphy Family Farms for about $460 million, doubling its pig production. Smithfield began a joint venture in late 2001 with Artal Holland to distribute processed meat products in China.

Despite cries of anti-trust, in late 2003 Smithfield spent $367 million to purchase the Farmland Foods pork production and processing businesses from ailing cooperative Farmland Industries. The purchase gave Smithfield control of 27% of the US pork industry.

By the end of 2004 Smithfield had purchased Campofrío's Polish meat processing unit, Morliny. When combined with its ownership of Animex, the acquisition gave Smithfield control over 10% of Poland's domestic meat industry.

Elsewhere in the world, during 2004 Smithfield acquired UK fresh and processed meat companies Norwich Food Company and Ridpath Pek. However, after acquiring and merging several meat processors in Canada, Smithfield sold all of its Canadian operations in the form of Schneider Corporation to Maple Leaf Foods for $378 million in 2004.

Before Smithfield lost its 2000 bidding war for IBP to Tyson, it had snapped up shares of IBP as leverage. Even though all the shares were eventually sold off, the Department of Justice took a dim view of a portion of the purchase and filed an anti-trust suit seeking $5.5 million. Admitting no wrongdoing, Smithfield settled the suit in 2004, agreeing to pay $2 million.

In 2005 Smithfield acquired MF Cattle Feeding, which has operations in Colorado and Idaho. Later that year MF and ContiGroup subsidiary ContiBeef formed a 50/50 joint venture cattle-feeding business named Five Rivers Ranch Cattle Feeding.

## EXECUTIVES

**Chairman:** Joseph W. Luter III, age 68, $1,232,518 pay
**President, CEO, and Director:** C. Larry Pope, age 52, $2,613,259 pay (prior to title change)
**VP and CFO:** Carey J. Dubois, age 47
**VP, Deputy General Counsel, and Secretary:** Michael H. Cole
**VP, Environmental and Government Affairs:** Dennis Treacy
**VP, Investor Relations and Corporate Communications:** Jerry Hostetter
**VP and Chief Accounting Officer:** Kenneth M. Sullivan, age 43
**VP, Livestock Procurement:** Jeffrey M. Luckman
**VP, Logistics:** Lawrence (Larry) Shipp
**VP, Sales and Marketing:** James D. Schloss
**VP, Operations:** Henry Morris
**VP, Price-Risk Management:** Dhamu Thamodaran
**VP, Rendering:** Douglas P. Anderson
**CIO:** Mansour Zadeh
**VP and Corporate Controller:** Jeffrey A. Deel
**Manager, Investor Relations:** Keira Ullrich

**CEO, Smithfield Foods Ltd.:** John Allton Jones
**CEO, Central and Eastern Europe:** Morten Jensen
**President, Farmland Foods:** George H. Richter, age 61, $2,204,496 pay
**President, International Operations:** Robert A. Sharpe II
**President, John Morrell & Co.:** Joseph B. Sebring, age 58
**President, Murphy-Brown:** Jerry H. Godwin, age 59, $1,855,552 pay
**Preisdent, Groupe Aoste:** Luc Van Gorp
**President, North Side Foods:** Robert G. Hofmann II
**President, Smithfield Beef Group:** Richard V. Vesta, age 60
**President, Patrick Cudahy:** William G. (Bill) Otis
**President, Smithfield Packing:** Joseph W. (Joe) Luter IV, age 41, $3,075,178 pay
**President, Stefano Foods, Inc.:** Giusto Piraino
**Auditors:** Ernst & Young LLP

## LOCATIONS

**HQ:** Smithfield Foods, Inc.
200 Commerce St., Smithfield, VA 23430
**Phone:** 757-365-3000 **Fax:** 757-365-3017
**Web:** www.smithfieldfoods.com

### 2007 Sales

| | $ mil. | % of total |
|---|---|---|
| North America | 10,267.3 | 86 |
| Europe | 1,643.8 | 14 |
| **Total** | **11,911.1** | **100** |

## PRODUCTS/OPERATIONS

### 2007 Pork Sales

| | % of total |
|---|---|
| Packaged | 52 |
| Fresh | 46 |
| Other products | 2 |
| **Total** | **100** |

### 2007 Beef Sales

| | % of total |
|---|---|
| Fresh beef | 78 |
| Cattle feeding | 1 |
| Other products | 21 |
| **Total** | **100** |

### Selected Subsidiaries

ADA Premium Beef Co., Inc.
CalfSource, LLC
Farmland Foods, Inc.
Iowa Quality Meats, Ltd.
John Morrell & Co.
MF Cattle Feeding, Inc.
Murphy-Brown LLC
North Side Foods Corp.
Patrick Cudahy Incorporated
Premium Standard Farms, Inc.
Quarter M Farms LLC
RMH Food, LLC
Smithfield Foods Ltd. (UK)
Sun Land Beef Company

## COMPETITORS

AzTx Cattle
Cactus Feeders
Cargill
Cargill Meat Solutions
Coleman Natural Foods
ContiGroup
Cooper Farms
Eberly
Empire Kosher Poultry
Golden Belt Feeders
Hormel
Iowa Turkey Growers
JBS
JBS Swift
Jennie-O
King Ranch
Kraft Foods
Northern Pride
Perdue
Pilgrim's Pride
Plainville Turkey
Raeford Farms
Sadia
Sara Lee Food & Beverage
Shelton's
Tyson Foods
Zacky Farms

## HISTORICAL FINANCIALS

Company Type: Public

### Income Statement

FYE: Sunday nearest April 30

| | REVENUE ($ mil.) | NET INCOME ($ mil.) | NET PROFIT MARGIN | EMPLOYEES |
|---|---|---|---|---|
| **4/07** | 11,911 | 167 | 1.4% | 53,100 |
| **4/06** | 11,404 | 173 | 1.5% | 52,500 |
| **4/05** | 11,354 | 296 | 2.6% | 51,290 |
| **4/04** | 9,267 | 227 | 2.5% | 46,400 |
| **4/03** | 7,905 | 26 | 0.3% | 44,100 |
| **Annual Growth** | 10.8% | 58.7% | — | 4.8% |

### 2007 Year-End Financials

Debt ratio: 126.7%
Return on equity: 7.8%
Cash ($ mil.): 58
Current ratio: 2.01
Long-term debt ($ mil.): 2,839
No. of shares (mil.): 112
Dividends
Yield: —
Payout: —
Market value ($ mil.): 3,403

### Stock History

NYSE: SFD

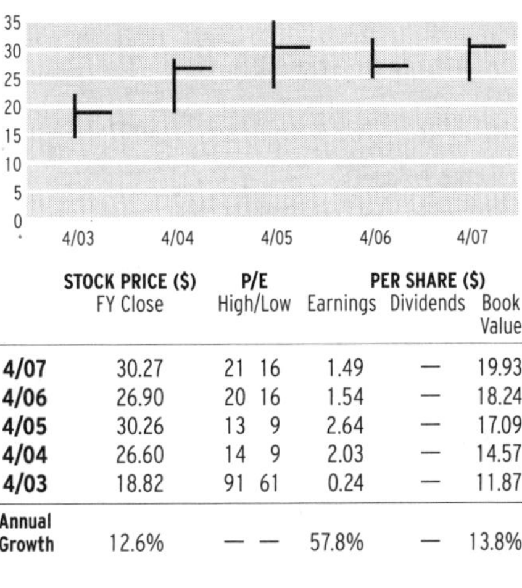


| | STOCK PRICE ($) FY Close | P/E High | P/E Low | PER SHARE ($) Earnings | Dividends | Book Value |
|---|---|---|---|---|---|---|
| **4/07** | 30.27 | 21 | 16 | 1.49 | — | 19.93 |
| **4/06** | 26.90 | 20 | 16 | 1.54 | — | 18.24 |
| **4/05** | 30.26 | 13 | 9 | 2.64 | — | 17.09 |
| **4/04** | 26.60 | 14 | 9 | 2.03 | — | 14.57 |
| **4/03** | 18.82 | 91 | 61 | 0.24 | — | 11.87 |
| **Annual Growth** | 12.6% | — | — | 57.8% | — | 13.8% |

# Smurfit-Stone Container

Holding company Smurfit-Stone Container doesn't think outside the box — it thinks *about* the box. Its operating company, Smurfit-Stone Container Enterprises, makes corrugated containers, containerboard, kraft paper (for bags), market pulp, and solid bleached sulfate (SBS, for folding cartons); it also provides graphics services. The vertically integrated company is one of the world's largest recyclers of paper fiber, a key raw material in the making of the company's products. Smurfit-Stone buys the bulk of its wood fiber on the open market, but it also owns about a million acres of timberland in Canada and operates harvesting facilities in the US and Canada.

The company was formed in 1998 with the merger of Jefferson Smurfit Corporation and Stone Container Corporation. In 2002 Ireland-based Jefferson Smurfit Group (now Smurfit Kappa Group) dispersed the 30% of Smurfit-Stone Container it once owned to shareholders.

As it has grown through acquisitions, the company has also exited noncore operations such as its newsprint business and its European assets.

In late 2005 Smurfit-Stone announced a new, three-tiered strategy: Reduce annual costs by $600 million by 2008; improve marketing to increase annual sales by $650 million by 2008; and reorganize operations, closing up to 20% of its corrugated packaging facilities and separating its manufacturing and sales operations.

As part of its strategic initiatives, in 2006 Smurfit-Stone sold its consumer packaging operations — including more than 40 production facilities — to Texas Pacific Group for more than $1 billion; once it was sold, that unit changed its name to Altivity Packaging. The company also shut down approximately 20 corrugating and converting facilities and reduced its workforce by about 2,000 that year.

In 2007 the company announced an agreement to sell its Brewton, Alabama, linerboard and bleached board mill to Georgia-Pacific for $355 million.

## HISTORY

Joseph Stone left Russia in 1888 and headed for America. In 1926 he and his sons launched J.H. Stone & Sons as a jobber for shipping supplies. It soon began making corrugated boxes. The company incorporated as Stone Container Corporation in 1945; it went public in 1947. Roger Stone, Joseph's grandson, became president in 1975. Under Roger the company bought competitors during industry slumps in the 1980s.

In 1989 the firm bought leading newsprint manufacturer Consolidated-Bathhurst of Canada. Soon after, prices slumped and interest expenses soared, and Stone began to pile on debt. It began divesting assets in 1993 and spun off Stone-Consolidated, its Canadian subsidiary. Stone Container merged its retail paper-bag operations with rival Gaylord Container in 1996 as oversupply and falling pulp and paper prices drove revenues down. In 1997 it merged its 46%-owned Stone-Consolidated with Canada's Abitibi-Price to create Abitibi-Consolidated (the world's #1 newsprint company), in which it owned a 25% stake.

John Jefferson Smurfit, a young Englishman, moved to Belfast, Northern Ireland, in 1934 and became an advisor to a box-making business. By 1938 he controlled the box business.

Jefferson Smurfit & Sons (later Jefferson Smurfit Group, now Smurfit Kappa Group) grew through acquisitions in the 1960s, and it went public in 1964. The enterprise diversified and nearly doubled in size by buying the Hely Group (radio and TV distribution, packaging, and educational and office supplies) in 1970.

Keen to make inroads in the US market, the group acquired 40% of paper and plastic maker Time Industries in 1974, adding the rest in 1977. Smurfit's son Michael continued to acquire during the 1980s.

Jefferson Smurfit Corporation (JSC) was formed to consolidate the Irish company's US holdings; it went public in 1983. JSC diversified into newsprint with the 80% purchase of Publishers Paper in 1986. It teamed up with Morgan Stanley to purchase Container Corporation of America for $1.2 billion. JSC bought out Morgan Stanley's 50% of Container Corporation in 1989 and reorganized as a privately held corporation. After struggling with high-cost debt and weak paper markets in the early 1990s, JSC went public again in 1994.

JSC purchased Ohio recycler Grossman Industries and Michigan Can and Tube in 1995. The combination of higher selling prices and a cost-reduction program that year led JSC to its first profitable year in half a decade.

Late in 1998 JSC merged with Stone Container in a $1.3 billion deal to form Smurfit-Stone Container, a containerboard company. The new company moved to cut costs by consolidating operations in 1999. It shut down eight containerboard and corrugated-container facilities and cut about 5% of its workforce. The company also raised some $80 million by reducing its stake in Abitibi-Consolidated to 22%. Also in 1999 the company sold its southeastern timberland holdings (969,000 acres) to Rayonier for $710 million and sold its newsprint mill in Newberg, Oregon, to a partnership of three newspaper publishers for $220 million.

Smurfit-Stone acquired specialty containerboard manufacturer St. Laurent Paperboard in 2000 in a deal worth around $1.4 billion. With all its growth, Smurfit-Stone needed to trim operations; to cut costs, the company absorbed its specialty packaging unit into its consumer packaging division in January 2002. In September Jefferson Smurfit Group distributed its remaining shares in Smurfit-Stone, some 29%, to its shareholders.

Also in 2002, the company purchased a corrugating medium mill, seven corrugated container plants (three of which were closed before year's end), one hardwood sawmill, and approximately 82,000 acres of timberland from MeadWestvaco Corporation for about $375 million.

In 2003 the company sold its European assets to Jefferson Smurfit in return for 50% of that company's Canadian unit and $200 million.

Smurfit-Stone in 2005 closed down a US paper mill and two Canadian containerboard mills to reduce capacity and cut more than 550 jobs. Later that year, after announcing a strategic restructuring, the company shut down four more facilities and reduced its workforce by nearly 800.

## EXECUTIVES

**Chairman and CEO:** Patrick J. Moore, age 52, $1,035,000 pay
**President and COO:** Steven J. (Steve) Klinger, age 48, $1,227,404 pay
**SVP and CFO:** Charles A. Hinrichs, age 53, $519,500 pay
**SVP and CIO:** James E. Burdiss, age 55
**SVP and Corporate Controller:** Paul K. Kaufmann, age 52
**SVP, Human Resources:** Ronald D. Hackney, age 60
**SVP, Secretary, and General Counsel:** Craig A. Hunt, age 45
**SVP and General Manager, Containerboard Mill Division:** Mack C. (Sonny) Jackson, age 52, $400,000 pay
**SVP, Corporate Communications:** Susan M. (Sue) Neumann, age 53
**SVP, Sales, Container Division:** Steven C. Strickland, age 55
**SVP, Strategic Initiatives:** Mark R. O'Bryan, age 44
**SVP and General Manager, Reclamation Division:** Michael R. Oswald, age 51
**SVP Manufacturing, Corrugated Container Division:** John Knudsen
**VP and Treasurer:** Jeffrey S. Beyersdorfer, age 45
**VP, Compensation, Benefits, and Human Resource Services:** Cynthia S. Bowers
**VP, Innovation and Chief Marketing Officer:** Doug Keim
**VP, Corporate Sales, Strategic Merchandising Solutions and Graphics, Container Division:** Jim Nolan
**VP, Sales, Container Division:** George Moretti
**VP, Research and Development:** Joseph V. LeBlanc
**Director, Investor Relations:** John Haudrich
**Director, Public Relations:** Tom Lange
**Auditors:** Ernst & Young LLP

## LOCATIONS

**HQ:** Smurfit-Stone Container Corporation
150 N. Michigan Ave., Chicago, IL 60601
**Phone:** 312-346-6600 **Fax:** 312-580-2272
**Web:** www.smurfit.com/content

Smurfit-Stone Container operates 19 paper mills in Canada and the US; 136 container plants in Canada, China, Mexico, Puerto Rico, and the US; one paper tube and core plant in the US; one wood products plant in the US; and one lamination plant in Canada. It also owns timberlands and wood harvesting plants in Canada and the US, as well as 23 reclamation (recycling) facilities in the US.

### 2006 Sales

| | $ mil. | % of total |
|---|---|---|
| US | 6,314 | 88 |
| Other countries | 843 | 12 |
| **Total** | **7,157** | **100** |

## PRODUCTS/OPERATIONS

### 2006 Sales

| | $ mil. | % of total |
|---|---|---|
| Containerboard & corrugated containers | 6,765 | 95 |
| Other | 392 | 5 |
| **Total** | **7,157** | **100** |

### Selected Products

Containerboard and Corrugated Containers
- Containerboard
- Corrugated containers (for consumer goods, displays, and food containers)
- Kraft paper
- Market pulp
- Solid bleached sulfate (SBS)

## COMPETITORS

Amcor
Boise Cascade
Georgia-Pacific Corporation
Greif
International Paper
Longview Fibre
Louisiana-Pacific
MeadWestvaco
M-real
Oji Paper
PCA
Potlatch
Pratt Industries USA
Smurfit Kappa
Sonoco Products
Stora Enso North America
Weyerhaeuser

## HISTORICAL FINANCIALS

Company Type: Public

### Income Statement

FYE: December 31

| | REVENUE ($ mil.) | NET INCOME ($ mil.) | NET PROFIT MARGIN | EMPLOYEES |
|---|---|---|---|---|
| **12/06** | 7,157 | (59) | — | 25,200 |
| **12/05** | 8,396 | (327) | — | 33,500 |
| **12/04** | 8,291 | (46) | — | 35,300 |
| **12/03** | 7,722 | (197) | — | 35,400 |
| **12/02** | 7,483 | 65 | 0.9% | 38,600 |
| **Annual Growth** | (1.1%) | — | — | (10.1%) |

### 2006 Year-End Financials

Debt ratio: 207.1%
Return on equity: —
Cash ($ mil.): 9
Current ratio: 0.87
Long-term debt ($ mil.): 3,550
No. of shares (mil.): 255
Dividends
Yield: —
Payout: —
Market value ($ mil.): 2,696

### Stock History

NASDAQ (GS): SSCC

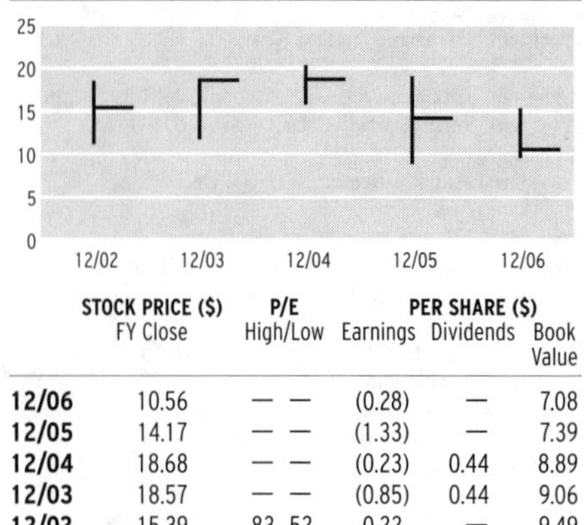


| | STOCK PRICE ($) FY Close | P/E High/Low | | PER SHARE ($) Earnings | Dividends | Book Value |
|---|---|---|---|---|---|---|
| **12/06** | 10.56 | — | — | (0.28) | — | 7.08 |
| **12/05** | 14.17 | — | — | (1.33) | — | 7.39 |
| **12/04** | 18.68 | — | — | (0.23) | 0.44 | 8.89 |
| **12/03** | 18.57 | — | — | (0.85) | 0.44 | 9.06 |
| **12/02** | 15.39 | 83 | 52 | 0.22 | — | 9.49 |
| **Annual Growth** | (9.0%) | — | — | — | 0.0% | (7.1%) |

# Snap-on Incorporated

Snap-on understands the mechanics of the automotive repair business. It's a leading manufacturer and distributor of high-quality hand tools, as well as auto diagnostic equipment and "undercar" shop implements, such as hydraulic lifts and tire changers. It serves mechanics, car manufacturers, and government and industrial organizations. Snap-on's products — with brand names Snap-on, Blackhawk, Mitchell, ShopKey, Sun, and others — include air-conditioning service equipment, collision repair equipment, management software, roll cabinets, screwdrivers, tool chests, wheel balancers, and wrenches. The firm publishes *Tech*, a lifestyle magazine that's free and hand-delivered by dealers to 1 million technicians.

The firm's US van salespeople are primarily franchisees who buy tools at a discount, then sell them to mechanics at a price they determine.

The toolmaker acquired the automotive parts and services information systems business of Voyager Learning Center (then ProQuest) for about $527 million in late 2006. The purchase expands Snap-on's diagnostics and information business unit.

Acquisitions (more than 20 since 1992) have moved Snap-on beyond its US-based network that serves mechanics. It now sells through a variety of channels (including to body shops) in more than 120 countries. Snap-on also provides financing for franchisees and customers' larger purchases. Snap-on generates more than half of its sales in the US, with Europe and other regions representing the balance.

## HISTORY

Joe Johnson's boss at American Grinder Manufacturing rejected his idea for interchangeable wrench handles and sockets in 1919, and Snap-on Tools was born. With practically no capital, Joe and co-worker William Seidemann made a set of five handles and 10 sockets, and two Wisconsin salesmen sold over 500 orders. Snap-on Wrench Company was incorporated in 1920. Stanton Palmer and Newton Tarble, both salesmen, developed a distribution business based on demonstrations at customer sites and formed Motor Tool Specialty Company in 1920. The next year they bought out Johnson's original supporters, and Palmer became president, holding the office until his death in 1931.

By 1925 Snap-on had salesmen working out of 17 branches; by 1929 it had about 300 salesmen and 26 branches. Overextended when the Depression hit, Snap-on was rescued by Forged Steel Products. Later, during WWII, tool shortages forced salesmen to carry excess stock in their vehicles. By 1945 walk-in vans loaded with tools were commonplace. Salesmen retailing to mechanics became independent dealers with their own regions.

In the 1960s Snap-on started buying branch outlets, giving it complete control over distribution and marketing. Research and development during the 1960s produced pneumatic, hydraulic, and electric tools, as well as the patented Flank Drive wrench with superior gripping. The company went public in 1978.

During the 1980s Snap-on became the sole supplier of tools to NASA for the space shuttles. In 1985 it had 4,000 dealers and by 1990 over 5,000.

Robert Cornog became CEO in 1991, the same year Snap-on began signing new dealers as franchisees and offering existing dealers the option to convert. The changeover was prompted by several lawsuits from dealers claiming the company misrepresented their earnings potential. Snap-on purchased all of its minority-owned affiliate, Balco (engine diagnostic and wheel service equipment), in 1991 and acquired Sun Electric (automotive diagnostic, test, and service equipment) in 1992. The following year it acquired J. H. Williams Industrial Products (hand tools).

The company changed its name to Snap-on Incorporated in 1994. It also launched its first national advertising campaign. The next year Snap-on increased its stake in Edge Diagnostic Systems (automobile diagnostic software) to 90%. The company also acquired Consolidated Devices (torque application and measuring equipment) in 1995 and Spain-based Herramientas Eurotools SA (hand tools), doubling its European sales.

In 1996 Snap-on purchased the automotive service equipment division of FMC Corp. and won a contract to manage the service equipment needs of most US Toyota and Lexus dealers. The following year it moved head-on into the collision repair industry by purchasing Breco Collision Repair System and acquiring a 50% stake in Mitchell Repair Information (upped to 99% in 1998).

Snap-on in 1998 bought Hein-Werner (collision repair equipment) and formed Snap-on Credit LLC, a joint venture with Newport Credit Group, to offer customer financing services. After difficulty integrating new acquisitions and the company-wide computer system, Snap-on announced in 1998 that it would "simplify" its operations by cutting 8% of its workers and 10% of its product line. The company also began producing Kobalt professional quality mechanics' tools for Lowe's Home Improvement stores that year.

In 1999 Snap-on bought Sandvik Saws and Tools, a division of Sweden's Sandvik AB, for $400 million; the deal helped Snap-on expand in Asia and South America. In 2000 the company began selling its tools via its Web site. In mid-2001 executive Dale Elliott was promoted to president and CEO; Cornog remained as chairman until April 2002 when Elliott took that position. In late 2001 Snap-on lost a $44 million arbitrator's decision to industrial products and services company SPX Corp. in a case involving alleged patent infringement. In 2003 Snap-on started the Technical Automotive Group to distribute equipment to repair facilities through factory-direct salespeople.

In November 2004 Elliott resigned and director Jack Michaels was named as his replacement.

## EXECUTIVES

**Chairman and CEO:** Jack D. Michaels, age 69
**President, COO, and Director:** Nicholas T. Pinchuk, age 60
**SVP, Finance and CFO:** Martin M. (Marty) Ellen, age 53, $608,744 pay
**SVP; President, Snap-on Tools Company, LLC:** Alan T. (Al) Biland, age 48, $578,488 pay
**SVP; President, Diagnostics and Information Group:** Thomas J. Ward, age 54
**VP, North American Technical Sales:** David E. Cox, age 61
**VP, Operations Development:** Gary S. Henning, age 54
**VP, Secretary, and Chief Legal Officer:** Susan F. Marrinan, age 58
**VP and CIO:** Jeanne M. Moreno, age 52
**VP and Chief Marketing Officer:** Andrew R. (Andy) Ginger
**VP and General Manager, Worldwide Industrial Sales:** Donald E. Broman, age 58
**President, Merchandise Products:** Richard V. Caskey, age 56
**President, Tool Storage, Snap-on Tools Company, LLC:** Tim Chambers
**President, OEM Solutions:** Paul Geere, age 51
**President, Hand Tools, Snap-on Tools Company, LLC:** Mike Gentile
**President and CEO, Mitchell Repair Information Company:** David R. Ellingen, age 47
**President, Asia-Pacific:** Oh Keh Chai
**President, European Tools Division:** Jean-Pierre Levrey
**President, Snap-on Business Solutions:** Mary Beth Siddons
**President, Power and Special Tools:** Mark S. Pezzoni, age 52
**President, Worldwide Equipment:** Thomas L. Kassouf
**Manager, Corporate Communications:** Richard Secor
**Investor Relations Assistant:** Christine Doss
**Auditors:** Deloitte & Touche LLP

## LOCATIONS

**HQ:** Snap-on Incorporated
2801 80th St., Kenosha, WI 53143
**Phone:** 262-656-5200 **Fax:** 262-656-5577
**Web:** www.snapon.com

### 2006 Sales

| | $ mil. | % of total |
|---|---|---|
| US | 1,410.1 | 56 |
| Europe | 764.8 | 30 |
| Other regions | 347.5 | 14 |
| **Total** | **2,522.4** | **100** |

## PRODUCTS/OPERATIONS

### 2006 Sales

| | $ mil. | % of total |
|---|---|---|
| Commercial & Industrial Group | 1,192.0 | 43 |
| Snap-on Tools Group | 1,025.0 | 37 |
| Diagnostics & Information Group | 524.5 | 19 |
| Financial Services | 49.0 | 2 |
| Adjustments | (268.1) | — |
| **Total** | **2,522.4** | **100** |

### Selected Products and Services

Diagnostic and shop equipment
- Air-conditioning service equipment
- Brake testers
- Collision repair equipment
- Engine and emissions analyzers
- Lifts and hoists
- Wheel-balancing and alignment equipment

Hand tools
- Cutting tools
- Pliers
- Ratchets
- Screwdrivers
- Sockets
- Wrenches

Information services
- Management software
- Vehicle service information

Power tools
- Battery-powered tools
- Electric tools
- Pneumatic tools

Tool storage products
- Roll cabinets
- Tool chests

## COMPETITORS

Ace Hardware
Atlas Copco
Atlas Copco North America
AutoZone
Black & Decker
Cooper Industries
Danaher
Dover
Emerson Electric
Fluke
Home Depot
Hunter Engineering
Illinois Tool Works
Industrial Distribution Group
Ingersoll-Rand
Irwin
Klein Tools
L. S. Starrett
Lowe's
Makita
MSC Industrial Direct
Myers Industries
Newell Rubbermaid
Pep Boys
Robert Bosch Tool
Rotary Lift
Sears
SPX
Stanley Works
Techtronic
W.W. Grainger

## HISTORICAL FINANCIALS

Company Type: Public

### Income Statement

FYE: Saturday nearest December 31

| | REVENUE ($ mil.) | NET INCOME ($ mil.) | NET PROFIT MARGIN | EMPLOYEES |
|---|---|---|---|---|
| **12/06** | 2,522 | 100 | 4.0% | 12,400 |
| **12/05** | 2,362 | 93 | 3.9% | 11,400 |
| **12/04** | 2,407 | 82 | 3.4% | 11,500 |
| **12/03** | 2,277 | 79 | 3.5% | 12,400 |
| **12/02** | 2,147 | 106 | 4.9% | 12,900 |
| **Annual Growth** | 4.1% | (1.4%) | — | (1.0%) |

### 2006 Year-End Financials

Debt ratio: 47.0%
Return on equity: 9.8%
Cash ($ mil.): 63
Current ratio: 1.63
Long-term debt ($ mil.): 506
No. of shares (mil.): 59
Dividends
Yield: 2.3%
Payout: 63.9%
Market value ($ mil.): 2,791

**Stock History** NYSE: SNA

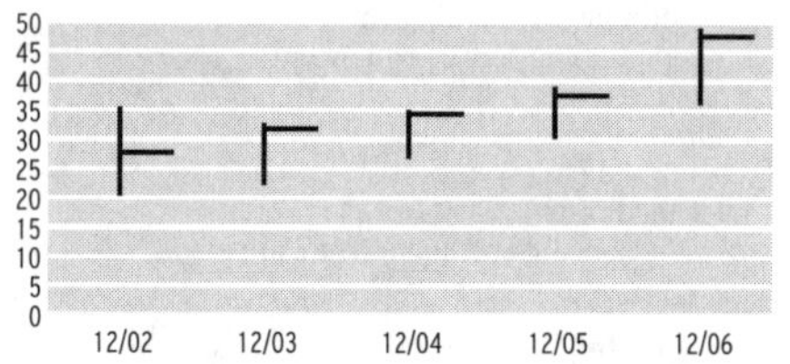

| | STOCK PRICE ($) FY Close | P/E High | P/E Low | PER SHARE ($) Earnings | Dividends | Book Value |
|---|---|---|---|---|---|---|
| 12/06 | 47.64 | 29 | 22 | 1.69 | 1.08 | 18.37 |
| 12/05 | 37.56 | 24 | 19 | 1.59 | 1.00 | 15.73 |
| 12/04 | 34.36 | 25 | 19 | 1.40 | 1.00 | 17.91 |
| 12/03 | 31.80 | 24 | 17 | 1.35 | 1.00 | 16.00 |
| 12/02 | 27.72 | 19 | 11 | 1.81 | 0.97 | 13.06 |
| Annual Growth | 14.5% | — | — | (1.7%) | 2.7% | 8.9% |

# Sonoco Products

Business has been a package deal for more than 100 years for Sonoco Products, one of the world's largest makers of industrial and consumer packaging. The company makes paper cores, cones, and tubes used by customers in the textile, paper, film, and construction industries. Sonoco's consumer packaging unit makes composite cans (typically made with a paperboard body and metal or plastic ends), and many kinds of flexible and rigid packaging made from either paper or plastic for food, chemicals, and personal care items. Sonoco offers extensive packaging services, including artwork, brand management, and supply chain management. The company also makes point-of-purchase displays and operates its own paperboard mills.

Other operations include the making of reels for wire and cable companies and specialty protective packaging for consumer goods. Sonoco has operations on five continents; the US, however, accounts for nearly two-thirds of the company's sales.

Sonoco plans to continue using selective acquisitions to boost its paperboard, plastic, and composite can businesses. For example, in 2006 Sonoco bought The Cin-Made Packaging Group, which makes rigid composite containers. At the end of that year Sonoco bought privately held Clear Pack Company, which makes rigid plastic containers. In 2007 the company acquired private Canadian rigid plastic container maker Matrix Packaging for $210 million.

Sonoco combined its European tube/core and coreboard operations with the similar operations of Helsinki-based Ahlstrom Corporation to form a joint venture company named Sonoco-Alcore in 2004. Sonoco owned 65% of the venture until mid-2006, when the company bought out Ahlstrom's minority stake. Later that year, a unit of Sonoco-Alcore bought out a joint venture partner to take full ownership of Italy-based Demolli Industria Cartaria, which makes tubes, cores, and recycled paperboard for customers in Italy and northern Europe.

However, Sonoco is also trimming its workforce and closing lower-performing manufacturing sites to reduce costs. Near the end of 2006 the company announced an initiative to close 12 plant locations, primarily in Europe, and reduce its workforce by about 540 by the end of 2007.

## HISTORY

Sonoco Products originated during the South's industrial renewal after the Civil War. Major James Coker and son James Jr. (who had been badly wounded at the Battle of Chickamauga) founded the Carolina Fiber company in Hartsville, South Carolina, to make pulp and paper from pine trees. The business was based on a thesis James Jr. wrote in 1884 at Stevens Institute of Technology in Hoboken, New Jersey. The essay explained how to make paper pulp using the sulfite process.

After failing to sell the pulp commercially, the Cokers decided to use it to make paper cones for the textile industry, which was seeing rapid growth in the southern US. In 1899 Major Coker and investor W. F. Smith formed the Southern Novelty Company. Major Coker's son Charles became president in 1918. As sales neared $1 million in 1923, the company changed its name to Sonoco.

In the 1920s Sonoco formed a joint venture in the UK to make Sonoco-style textile carriers. The venture became the Textile Paper Tube Company, which later set up plants in Germany, India, Ireland, the Netherlands, and South Africa.

When Charles died in 1931, his 27-year-old son James became president. James eventually set up eight plants in the US and established a Canadian subsidiary. With the introduction of manmade fibers, the textile industry expanded dramatically, and Sonoco kept pace with the technological changes. By the late 1940s it had eight paper machines in operation at its Hartsville mill.

In the 1950s Sonoco formed a Mexican subsidiary; began tube operations in California, Indiana, and Texas; and diversified into corrugated materials. The company forged a business relationship in 1964 with Showa Products Company of Japan.

Charles Coker, great-grandson of the founder, became president in 1970. Sonoco entered the wastepaper-packing business in 1972 and then the folding-carton and fiber-partitions businesses in 1973. The company expanded rapidly, and by 1986 Sonoco had 150 plants. The next year it acquired the consumer packaging division of Boise Cascade, which was then the country's #1 producer of composite cans. By 1989 Sonoco was the world's top maker of uncoated, recycled cylinder paperboard.

Charles became CEO in 1990. The company set up a Singapore office and a tube and core plant in Malaysia in 1992 and acquired specialty packager Engraph the following year. In 1995 Sonoco formed a joint venture to produce paperboard in China and bought a paper mill and a tube-making plant in France. The company acquired paper-mill assets in Brazil in 1996 and entered a joint venture in Indonesia to make composite cans.

The next year saw further expansion as Sonoco entered a joint venture in Chile and a second joint venture in Brazil. In 1997 packaging maker Greif Bros. bought most of Sonoco's industrial container division, and in 1998 Sonoco sold its North American pressure-sensitive-labels business to CCL Industries. President Peter Browning also replaced Charles as CEO (Charles remained chairman). Also in 1998, the company cut about 13% of its workforce and closed five plants to trim costs and consolidate operations. It also bought the Burk group of companies, a German plastics-molding organization.

In 1999 Sonoco bought the composite can assets of Crown Cork & Seal (now Crown Holdings) and doubled its flexible packaging business with the purchase of Graphic Packaging International's flexible packaging unit. CEO Peter Browning retired in 2000 and was replaced by company veteran Harris DeLoach. Sonoco announced several plant closures in 2001. It also acquired four packaging companies — U.S. Paper Mills Corp., Plywood Reel Co., Phoenix Packaging, and Hayes Manufacturing Group — as well as the assets of Pac One Corporation's flexible packaging business. In 2002 Sonoco restructured its UK tube and core business by closing one factory and downsizing another.

In 2003 Sonoco purchased Australian Tube Company (ATC), a maker of paper-based tubes and cores; it also sold its high-density film business to an investment group for $119 million. In 2004 the company acquired CorrFlex Graphics, which offers point-of-purchase displays and related products, for about $250 million.

## EXECUTIVES

**Chairman, President, and CEO:** Harris E. DeLoach Jr., age 62, $949,669 pay
**SVP, CFO, and Corporate Secretary:** Charles J. Hupfer, age 60, $392,871 pay
**EVP, Global Consumer Packaging and Services:** Charles L. Sullivan Jr., age 60, $474,331 pay
**SVP, Human Resources:** Cynthia A. (Cindy) Hartley, age 58, $311,129 pay
**SVP, Global Paper Operations:** Jim C. Bowen, age 56, $374,094 pay
**SVP, Global Industrial Products and Global Industrial Converting Business:** M. Jack Sanders, age 54
**Staff VP and Corporate Controller:** Barry L. Saunders
**Staff VP, Global Controller, Consumer Products:** Michael W. Bullington
**Staff VP, Operating Excellence:** John M. Grups, age 51
**VP, Corporate Planning:** Kevin P. Mahoney, age 51
**VP, Industrial Products and Paper, Europe:** Edward L. (Eddie) Smith, age 55
**VP, Global Operating Excellence, IPD:** James A. Harrell III
**VP, Investor Relations and Corporate Affairs:** Allan V. Cecil, age 62
**VP and Treasurer:** Ritchie L. Bond
**VP and CIO:** Bernard W. (Bernie) Campbell, age 57
**VP, Ridgid Papers and Plastics, North America and Sonoco Phoenix:** Rodger D. Fuller
**VP, Investor Relations and Corporate Affairs:** Roger P. Schrum, age 49
**Auditors:** PricewaterhouseCoopers LLP

## LOCATIONS

**HQ:** Sonoco Products Company
1 N. 2nd St., Hartsville, SC 29550
**Phone:** 843-383-7000 **Fax:** 843-383-7008
**Web:** www.sonoco.com

Sonoco Products has approximately 300 production facilities in 35 countries around the world.

**2006 Sales**

| | $ mil. | % of total |
|---|---|---|
| US | 2,343.0 | 64 |
| Europe | 576.1 | 16 |
| Canada | 369.6 | 10 |
| Other regions | 368.1 | 10 |
| **Total** | **3,656.8** | **100** |

## PRODUCTS/OPERATIONS

### 2006 Sales by Division

| | $ mil. | % of total |
|---|---|---|
| Tubes & Cores/Paper | 1,525.6 | 42 |
| Consumer Packaging | 1,304.7 | 36 |
| Packaging Services | 456.8 | 12 |
| Other | 369.7 | 10 |
| **Total** | **3,656.8** | **100** |

### Selected Products

Tubes and Cores/Paper
- Fiber-based tubes and forms
- Linerboard
- Paper
- Paper and composite paperboard tubes and cores
- Recovered paper
- Recycled paperboard
- Roll packaging

Consumer Packaging
- Ends and closures (metal and plastic)
- Printed flexible packaging
- Rigid packaging (paper and plastic)

Packaging Services
- Artwork management
- Brand management
- Contract packing
- Folding cartons
- Packing fulfillment
- Point-of-purchase displays
- Supply chain management

Other
- Amenities (coasters and glass covers)
- Custom-designed protective packaging
- Molded and extruded plastic
- Wood, metal, and composite reels

## COMPETITORS

Amcor
Bemis
Caraustar
Crown Holdings
Field Container
Georgia-Pacific Corporation
Graphic Packaging
Greif
International Paper
MeadWestvaco
Newark
Owens-Illinois
Rock-Tenn
Sealed Air Corporation
Smurfit-Stone Container
Weyerhaeuser

## HISTORICAL FINANCIALS

Company Type: Public

### Income Statement — FYE: December 31

| | REVENUE ($ mil.) | NET INCOME ($ mil.) | NET PROFIT MARGIN | EMPLOYEES |
|---|---|---|---|---|
| **12/06** | 3,657 | 195 | 5.3% | 17,700 |
| **12/05** | 3,529 | 162 | 4.6% | 17,600 |
| **12/04** | 3,155 | 151 | 4.8% | 17,100 |
| **12/03** | 2,758 | 139 | 5.0% | 15,200 |
| **12/02** | 2,812 | 135 | 4.8% | 17,400 |
| **Annual Growth** | 6.8% | 9.6% | — | 0.4% |

### 2006 Year-End Financials

Debt ratio: 58.4%
Return on equity: 15.7%
Cash ($ mil.): 87
Current ratio: 1.43
Long-term debt ($ mil.): 712
No. of shares (mil.): 101
Dividends
Yield: 2.5%
Payout: 49.5%
Market value ($ mil.): 3,827

### Stock History — NYSE: SON

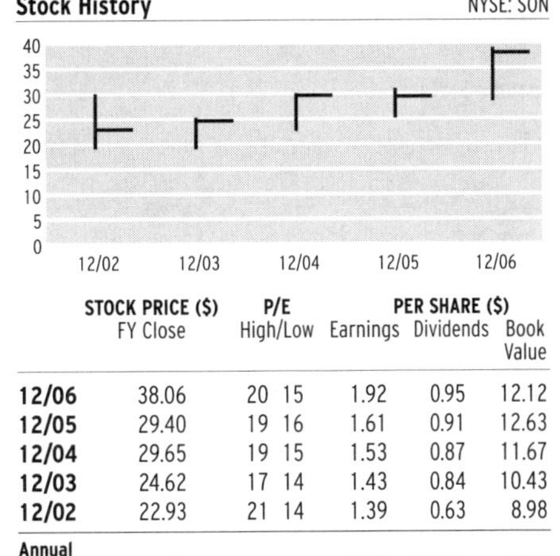


| | STOCK PRICE ($) FY Close | P/E High | P/E Low | PER SHARE ($) Earnings | Dividends | Book Value |
|---|---|---|---|---|---|---|
| **12/06** | 38.06 | 20 | 15 | 1.92 | 0.95 | 12.12 |
| **12/05** | 29.40 | 19 | 16 | 1.61 | 0.91 | 12.63 |
| **12/04** | 29.65 | 19 | 15 | 1.53 | 0.87 | 11.67 |
| **12/03** | 24.62 | 17 | 14 | 1.43 | 0.84 | 10.43 |
| **12/02** | 22.93 | 21 | 14 | 1.39 | 0.63 | 8.98 |
| **Annual Growth** | 13.5% | — | — | 8.4% | 10.8% | 7.8% |

# Sotheby's

Sotheby's believes that one man's trash is another man's treasure — especially when that trash happens to be someone's idea of art. The company (along with rival Christie's International) is one of the world's leading auction houses, holding hundreds of sales each year at its auction centers around the world. Sotheby's deals mainly in fine art, antiques, and collectibles; it collects commissions and fees from both the buyer and the seller on each sale. The company also provides loans (secured against works of art) to clients as part of its finance services.

Live auctions account for the bulk of Sotheby's revenues. The company has overseen the sales of such items as Picasso's *Femme Assise dans un Jardin,* Degas' *Petite Danseuse de Quatorze Ans,* and the last baseball glove used by Lou Gehrig. Sotheby's has leveraged its expertise and profile in art circles to offer such services as secured financing and insurance, as well as serving as a broker for private sales. Additionally, the company offers restoration and appraisal services and operates two art institutes in New York City and London. In 2006, Sotheby's expanded when it acquired Noortman Master Paintings (NMP), an art dealer specializing in Dutch, Flemish, and French paintings.

In contrast to its successes, the company is struggling to regain prestige and trust after a Justice Department investigation resulted in charges of commission fixing by both Sotheby's and Christie's. Former president and CEO Diana Brooks and former chairman Alfred Taubman were both convicted, and the company, along with Christie's, has settled a number of class action lawsuits brought against both houses, agreeing to pay $512 million (split between them) to clients in the US and $20 million to non-US clients. Taubman and family own 12% of Sotheby's after a recapitalization in 2005.

In August 2006, the auction house's legal woes continued when a Canadian antitrust entity obtained a restrictive order against Sotheby's, claiming that the company had agreed with competitors to fix the prices it charged to customers (between the years of 1993 to 2000). It is projected Sotheby's will have to pay $720,000 in investigative costs due to the price-fixing.

## HISTORY

Sotheby's Holdings traces its roots to Samuel Baker, a London bookseller, who held his first auction in 1744 to dispose of an English nobleman's library. After Baker died in 1778, his nephew John Sotheby took over, placing his name over the door of the business. During the 19th century Sotheby's expanded into antiquities, paintings, jewelry, and furniture. Business boomed as newly wealthy Americans swarmed across the Atlantic seeking the status symbols of the Old World.

By the end of WWI, Sotheby's had become fully entrenched in the art market, and in 1917 the company moved to New Bond Street (where its London office still stands). Following WWII, Sotheby's expanded into the US, opening its first office in New York City in 1955. It later acquired Parke-Bernet, a leading US art auction house, in 1964. The company prospered and expanded during the 1970s as rising interest rates and inflation fueled an art market boom, and in 1977 Sotheby's went public.

A collapse of the art market left Sotheby's a target for corporate raiders in the early 1980s. The company's board asked US shopping center magnate Alfred Taubman to lead a buyout group in 1983. After weathering the storm, the company was well positioned when the art market rebounded, a turnaround driven in part by the desire of newly wealthy Japanese to confirm their status — just as Americans had done a century before. In 1988 the company went public again, with Taubman as chairman.

After the boom peaked in 1990 (Christie's International sold van Gogh's *Portrait of Dr. Gachet* that year for a record $82.5 million), Sotheby's earnings plummeted, and its share price tanked. In 1994 Diana Brooks became president and CEO. The company posted solid results in 1995, but the company slipped to the #2 auctioneer in the world for the first time in more than 20 years.

In 1997 Sotheby's acquired Chicago-based Leslie Hindman Auctioneers and Chicago wine auctioneers Davis & Co. in 1998. The next year Sotheby's created a co-branded auction Web site with Amazon.com. The site never turned a profit and was scaled back in 2000 and the partnership terminated in 2001. In 2002 Sotheby's partnered with eBay to sell high-end merchandise online within the eBay Web site.

In 2000 the US Justice Department reopened a 1997 investigation of an alleged price fixing scheme involving Sotheby's and Christie's. After the allegations became public, Taubman and Brooks resigned, replaced by Michael Sovern (chairman) and William Ruprecht (CEO). The probe sparked additional lawsuits and investigations. Both companies agreed to pay $268 million each to settle the civil claims. Brooks pleaded guilty to violating antitrust laws but testified against Taubman in exchange for leniency. Taubman pleaded innocent and was convicted and sentenced to one year in prison after a vicious trial.

In 2001 Sotheby's laid off about 8% of its staff and raised fees in 2002 in its efforts to offset losses. Also in 2002 the company sold its Upper East Side headquarters in New York for $175 million and laid off 7% of its staff. In 2004 Sotheby's sold its International Realty operations to Cendant for about $100 million. (Cendant spun off its real estate businesses as Realogy in 2006.)

Sotheby's dropped "Holdings" from its official name in mid-2006.

## EXECUTIVES

**Chairman:** Michael I. Sovern, age 75
**Deputy Chairman:** The Duke of Devonshire, age 62
**President, CEO, and Director:** William F. (Bill) Ruprecht, age 51, $2,787,500 pay
**EVP and CFO:** William S. Sheridan, age 53, $1,125,000 pay
**EVP and Director; Chief Executive, Sotheby's International:** Robin G. Woodhead, age 55, $930,824 pay
**EVP and Worldwide Director, Press and Corporate Affairs:** Diana Phillips, age 60
**EVP, Worldwide General Counsel, and Secretary:** Donaldson C. Pillsbury, age 66
**EVP and Worldwide Head of Human Resources:** Susan Alexander, age 53
**EVP Global Business Development:** Ann W. Jackson, age 55
**EVP and Director, New Initiatives:** Bruno Vinciguerra
**EVP and Director, Boston:** William Cottingham
**SVP, Controller, and Chief Accounting Officer:** Michael L. Gillis
**SVP and Chief Technology and Strategy Officer:** David Ulmer, age 50
**President, Sotheby's Financial Services and Sotheby's Ventures:** Mitchell Zuckerman, age 60, $910,000 pay
**Managing Director, Global Auction Division:** Daryl S. Wickstrom, age 45
**Managing Director, North America Regional Auction Division:** Richard C. Buckley, age 44
**Managing Director, Sotheby's Europe:** George Bailey, age 53, $766,995 pay
**Auditors:** Deloitte & Touche LLP

## LOCATIONS

**HQ:** Sotheby's
1334 York Ave., New York, NY 10021
**Phone:** 212-606-7000 **Fax:** 212-606-7107
**Web:** www.sothebys.com

Sotheby's has offices in Asia, Australia, Europe, and the US.

**2006 Sales**

| | $ mil. | % of total |
|---|---|---|
| US | 312.5 | 47 |
| UK | 231.4 | 35 |
| China | 40.5 | 6 |
| Other countries | 81.5 | 12 |
| Adjustments | (1.1) | — |
| **Total** | **664.8** | **100** |

## PRODUCTS/OPERATIONS

**2006 Sales**

| | $ mil. | % of total |
|---|---|---|
| Auction | | |
| Auction commission revenues | 551.2 | 83 |
| Auction sales commissions | 25.8 | 4 |
| Auction expense recoveries | 17.5 | 3 |
| Catalogue subscription | 8.7 | 1 |
| Other | 28.1 | 4 |
| Finance segment | 15.9 | 2 |
| Dealer segment | 12.8 | 2 |
| License fee | 2.9 | 1 |
| Other | 1.9 | — |
| **Total** | **664.8** | **100** |

**Selected Operations**

Acquavella Modern Art (50%, art sale brokerage)
Noortman Master Paintings B.V. (art dealer)
Sotheby's (live auctions)
Sotheby's Financial Services (art financing)
Sotheby's Insurance Brokerage Services

## COMPETITORS

Ableauctions.com
Christie's
DoveBid
eBay
Escala Group
Finarte-Semenzato
Phillips, de Pury
Tiffany

## HISTORICAL FINANCIALS

Company Type: Public

**Income Statement** FYE: December 31

| | REVENUE ($ mil.) | NET INCOME ($ mil.) | NET PROFIT MARGIN | EMPLOYEES |
|---|---|---|---|---|
| **12/06** | 665 | 107 | 16.1% | 1,497 |
| **12/05** | 514 | 62 | 12.0% | 1,443 |
| **12/04** | 497 | 87 | 17.5% | 1,411 |
| **12/03** | 320 | (21) | — | 1,537 |
| **12/02** | 345 | (55) | — | 1,736 |
| **Annual Growth** | 17.8% | — | — | (3.6%) |

**2006 Year-End Financials**

Debt ratio: 89.1%
Return on equity: 50.1%
Cash ($ mil.): 358
Current ratio: 1.33
Long-term debt ($ mil.): 269
No. of shares (mil.): 65
Dividends
Yield: 0.6%
Payout: 11.6%
Market value ($ mil.): 2,010

**Stock History** NYSE: BID

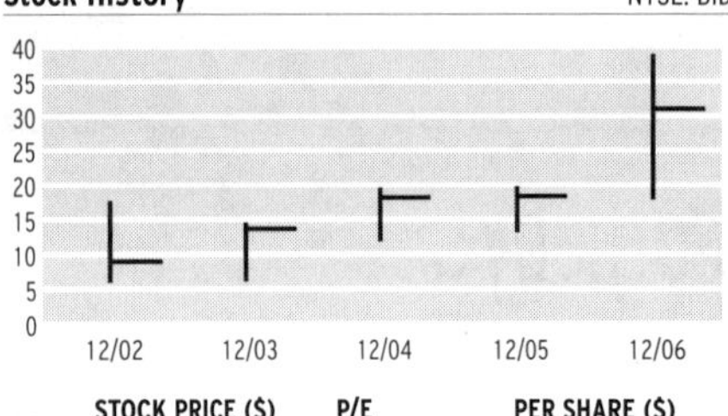


| | STOCK PRICE ($) FY Close | P/E High | P/E Low | PER SHARE ($) Earnings | Dividends | Book Value |
|---|---|---|---|---|---|---|
| **12/06** | 31.02 | 22 | 11 | 1.72 | 0.20 | 4.66 |
| **12/05** | 18.36 | 19 | 13 | 1.00 | — | 2.18 |
| **12/04** | 18.16 | 14 | 9 | 1.38 | — | 5.14 |
| **12/03** | 13.66 | — | — | (0.34) | — | 2.83 |
| **12/02** | 9.00 | — | — | (0.89) | — | 3.12 |
| **Annual Growth** | 36.3% | — | — | — | — | 10.5% |

# Southern Company

Southern Company isn't just whistling Dixie. The holding company is one of the largest electricity distributors in the US. It operates regulated utilities Alabama Power, Georgia Power, Gulf Power, and Mississippi Power, which combined have a generating capacity of more than 41,000 MW and serve more than 4.3 million electricity customers in the southeastern US. The good ol' power company also has energy marketing operations, and it provides energy consulting and management services for businesses and institutions. Through its Southern LINC Wireless unit, it provides wireless communications services in its US utility territory; its Southern Telecom unit offers wholesale fiber-optic services.

To focus on its core operations, Southern Company has spun off its stake in independent power producer Mirant to shareholders. However, the firm still participates in the nonregulated energy sector: It markets excess energy from its retail plants and is building competitive plants across the southeastern US through newly formed subsidiary Southern Power. In 2006 the company merged its Savannah Electric unit into another subsidiary, Georgia Power.

Southern Company has signed a letter of intent to sell the assets of its Southern Company Gas to Cobb Electric Membership Corporation (Cobb EMC). Southern Company has agreed to purchase a power plant in Cocoa Florida from Constellation Energy. The company is also investing in installing environmental controls at its power plants.

## HISTORY

Steamboat captain W. P. Lay founded the Alabama Power Company in 1906 to develop electric power on the Coosa River. James Mitchell took over in 1912, moved headquarters from Montgomery to Birmingham, and bought a number of Alabama's utilities, consolidating them with Alabama Power under his Canadian holding company, Alabama Traction Light & Power (ATL&P).

In 1920 ATL&P became Southeastern Power & Light, forming Mississippi Power (1924) and Georgia Power (1927) to take over electric utilities in those states, and Gulf Power to do the same in northern Florida (1925).

Southeastern merged with Penn-Ohio Edison to form Commonwealth & Southern in 1929. But by 1942 Commonwealth & Southern was dissolved under the Public Utilities Holding Company Act of 1935 since it owned 11 unrelated, unconnected utilities. Alabama Power, Georgia Power, Gulf Power, and Mississippi Power were placed under a new holding company, Southern Company, which began full operations in 1949.

In 1975, amid an anti-utility political environment created by energy shortages, Georgia Power was near bankruptcy; Alabama Power stopped work on new construction and laid off 4,000 employees in 1978. That year, when Alabama governor and utility critic George Wallace left office, state regulators granted Southern long-sought rate relief.

The SEC allowed Southern to diversify into unregulated operations — a first in the US — with the 1981 formation of Southern Energy, which began investing in independent power projects and companies. In 1988 Southern bought Savannah Electric and Power.

Meanwhile, the industry was undergoing major changes, and utilities were venturing outside their territories. Southern sold a Georgia power plant to two Florida utilities in 1990. Two years later it bought 50% of Bahamian utility Freeport Power, and by 1994 Southern had a 49% stake in three power plants in Trinidad and Tobago. At home the company formed Southern LINC in 1995 to offer wireless telecom services in the southeastern US via specialized mobile radio (SMR) technology.

Also that year the company joined other US electric companies in raiding Britain's deregulated electricity larder. It bought UK utility South Western Electricity (SWEB) in 1995, though it later turned over a 51% stake to partner PP&L Resources. In 1996 it acquired 80% of Hong Kong's Consolidated Electric Power Asia, buying the rest the next year.

The first US company to enter Germany's electric utility market, Southern bought a 25% stake in Berlin's electric utility, Bewag, in 1997. That year and the next Southern expanded into the northeastern US and California, buying power plants from Commonwealth Energy, Eastern Utilities, ConEd, PG&E, and Orange and Rockland Utilities.

Focusing on power transmission in the UK, Southern and PP&L Resources (which became PPL in 2000) sold SWEB's power supply business and the SWEB brand name to London Electricity, an Electricité de France unit, in 1999. The former SWEB's distribution network was renamed Western Power Distribution.

In 2000 Southern sold a 20% stake in Southern Energy, which included the company's merchant energy operations (excluding those in the southeastern US) and its overseas investments, to the public. Southern Energy changed its name to Mirant in 2001, and that year Southern spun off its remaining stake in the unit to its shareholders.

## EXECUTIVES

**Chairman, President, and CEO:** David M. Ratcliffe, age 58, $2,933,730 pay
**EVP, CFO, and Treasurer:** Thomas A. (Tom) Fanning, age 50, $1,359,462 pay
**EVP, President and CEO, Alabama Power:** Charles D. McCrary, age 55, $1,389,131 pay
**EVP, President and CEO, Georgia Power:** Michael D. (Mike) Garrett, age 57, $1,376,794 pay
**EVP, President of External Affairs Group:** Dwight H. Evans, age 58
**EVP, General Counsel, and Corporate Secretary:** G. Edison Holland Jr., age 54, $1,115,176 pay
**EVP, Supply Technologies, Renewables, and Demand-Side Planning:** Leonard J. Haynes, age 54
**EVP, Chief Transmission Officer:** Andrew J. Dearman III, age 53
**SVP and CIO; VP, Information Resources, Georgia Power:** Rebecca A. (Becky) Blalock
**SVP, Environmental Affairs:** Chris Hobson, age 52
**SVP, Research and Environmental Affairs:** Charles H. Goodman
**SVP, Nuclear Development:** Joseph A. (Buzz) Miller, age 41
**VP, Financial Planning and Enterprise Risk Management:** Mark Lantrip
**VP, Supply Chain Management:** Bryan Fletcher
**VP, System Contracts Officer and Associate General Counsel:** Earl Parsons
**Director, Investor Relations:** Glen Kundert
**Comptroller and Chief Accounting Officer:** W. Dean Hudson, age 55
**President and CEO, Southern Company Gas:** Ron Bertasi
**President and CEO, SouthernLINC Wireless and Southern Telecom:** Robert G. Dawson
**President and CEO of Southern Power; EVP, Competitive Generation, Southern Company Generation and Energy Marketing:** Ronnie L. Bates, age 49
**President and CEO, Savannah Electric and Power Company:** W. Craig Barrs
**Media Contact:** Tiffany Gilstrap
**Auditors:** Deloitte & Touche LLP

## LOCATIONS

**HQ:** Southern Company
30 Ivan Allen Jr. Blvd. NW, Atlanta, GA 30308
**Phone:** 404-506-5000 **Fax:** 404-506-0455
**Web:** www.southernco.com

Southern Company's regulated utilities operate in Alabama, Florida, Georgia, and Mississippi.

## PRODUCTS/OPERATIONS

**2006 Sales**

| | $ mil. | % of total |
|---|---|---|
| Electric Utilties | | |
| Retail Operating Companies | 13,920 | 92 |
| Southern Power | 777 | 5 |
| Other | 413 | 3 |
| Adjustments | (754) | — |
| **Total** | **14,356** | **100** |

**Selected Subsidiaries and Affiliates**

Alabama Power Company (electric utility)
Georgia Power Company (electric utility)
Gulf Power Company (electric utility)
Mississippi Power Company (electric utility)
Southern Communications Services, Inc. (Southern LINC Wireless, digital wireless communications)
Southern Company Gas, LLC (retail gas marketing)
Southern Company Generation and Energy Marketing (power generation and wholesale marketing)
Southern Power Company (independent power production)
Southern Company Holdings, Inc. (interests in leveraged leases, synthetic fuel products, and energy services)
Southern Company Energy Solutions LLC (energy services)
Southern Company Services, Inc. (administrative services, limited energy trading)
Southern Electric Generating Company (SEGCO, power generation, jointly owned by Alabama Power and Georgia Power)
SouthernLINC Wireless (wireless services)
Southern Nuclear Operating Company, Inc. (operates and maintains Alabama Power and Georgia Power's nuclear plants)

## COMPETITORS

AEP
AGL Resources
Aquila
CenterPoint Energy
Cleco
Constellation Energy Group
Duke Energy
Energen
Entergy
FirstEnergy
Florida Public Utilities
FPL Group
JEA
MEAG Power
Oglethorpe Power
PacifiCorp
Progress Energy
SCANA
TECO Energy
TVA
Xcel Energy

## HISTORICAL FINANCIALS

Company Type: Public

**Income Statement** FYE: December 31

| | REVENUE ($ mil.) | NET INCOME ($ mil.) | NET PROFIT MARGIN | EMPLOYEES |
|---|---|---|---|---|
| **12/06** | 14,356 | 1,573 | 11.0% | 26,091 |
| **12/05** | 13,554 | 1,591 | 11.7% | 25,554 |
| **12/04** | 11,902 | 1,532 | 12.9% | 25,642 |
| **12/03** | 11,251 | 1,474 | 13.1% | 25,762 |
| **12/02** | 10,549 | 1,318 | 12.5% | 26,178 |
| **Annual Growth** | 8.0% | 4.5% | — | (0.1%) |

**2006 Year-End Financials**

Debt ratio: 110.0%
Return on equity: 14.3%
Cash ($ mil.): 167
Current ratio: 0.63
Long-term debt ($ mil.): 12,503
No. of shares (mil.): 746
Dividends
Yield: 4.2%
Payout: 72.9%
Market value ($ mil.): 27,512

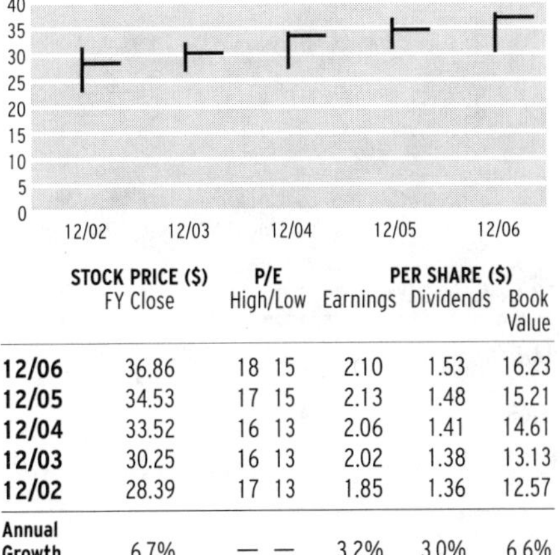


| | STOCK PRICE ($) FY Close | P/E High/Low | PER SHARE ($) Earnings | Dividends | Book Value |
|---|---|---|---|---|---|
| **12/06** | 36.86 | 18 15 | 2.10 | 1.53 | 16.23 |
| **12/05** | 34.53 | 17 15 | 2.13 | 1.48 | 15.21 |
| **12/04** | 33.52 | 16 13 | 2.06 | 1.41 | 14.61 |
| **12/03** | 30.25 | 16 13 | 2.02 | 1.38 | 13.13 |
| **12/02** | 28.39 | 17 13 | 1.85 | 1.36 | 12.57 |
| **Annual Growth** | 6.7% | — — | 3.2% | 3.0% | 6.6% |

# Southern Union

One of the largest diversified natural gas operations in the US, Southern Union is looking to form a more perfect union of natural gas transportation, storage, gathering, processing, and distribution assets. The company's major utility, Missouri Gas Energy, distributes natural gas to customers in four states. Southern Union has interests in gas storage facilities and more than 20,000 miles of pipeline throughout the US (primarily through Panhandle Energy). The company has been divesting assets (including energy services, and appliance services) to focus on its core natural gas operations. In 2006 Southern Union acquired natural gas gathering and processing firm Sid Richardson Energy Services for $1.6 billion.

The company has sold its Texas gas distribution utility (Southern Union Gas), as well as SUPro Energy (propane distribution in Texas and New Mexico), Mercado Gas Services (natural gas marketing), its Mexican gas utility interest, and some gas pipeline interests, to ONEOK for about $420 million. Southern Union has also sold its Florida gas distribution businesses, its propane distribution operations in Florida and Pennsylvania, and its outsourced energy management unit, ProvEnergy. New England Gas was sold to National Grid USA for a reported $575 million (and $77 million of assumed debt).

Proceeds from the asset sales were applied to the 2003 purchase from CMS Energy of the Panhandle Energy companies, which together operated a 10,000-mile gas pipeline system. The $1.8 billion deal included the assumption of nearly $1.2 billion in debt.

In 2004 Southern Union subsidiary CCE Holdings purchased Enron's CrossCountry Energy unit for $2.45 billion (including debt assumption). CrossCountry Energy owns the Transwestern Pipeline (sold in 2006) and a 50% stake in Citrus Corp. (the owner of Florida Gas Transmission). Following this transaction, CCE Holdings sold CrossCountry subsidiary Northern Plains Natural Gas, a general partner of Northern Border Partners (now ONEOK Partners), to ONEOK for $175 million.

In early 2006 the company sold its PG Energy operating division and its interests in PG Energy Services to UGI Corporation for a reported $580 million.

CEO George Lindemann and his family own about 7% of Southern Union.

## HISTORY

Southern Union's earliest predecessor was the Wink Gas Co., formed in 1929 in Wink, Texas, during the West Texas oil boom. Although its first customer had to lay his own pipeline, the company grew, and in 1932 it became the Southern Union Company. In 1949 Southern Union won the Austin, Texas gas franchise by merging with Texas Public Service Co.

The energy crisis of the 1970s led Southern Union to diversify into unrelated areas (such as real estate) that turned sour by the 1980s. Shortly after the natural gas industry was deregulated in the 1980s, the company formed Mercado Gas Services in 1986 to market gas to commercial and industrial customers.

Four years later, New York entrepreneur George Lindemann acquired Southern Union and installed Peter Kelley as president. Kelley wasted no time in shifting the corporate culture from a lethargic, top-heavy bureaucracy to an efficient sales organization.

Southern Union bought several Texas natural gas companies in 1993 and nearly doubled its customer base in 1994 with the purchase of Gas Service of Kansas City (now Missouri Gas Energy, or MGE). Moving into Florida in 1997, Southern Union acquired gas distributor Atlantic Utilities.

Continuing to look for acquisitions, Southern Union in 1999 submitted a bid to buy Las Vegas-based Southwest Gas, which instead accepted a lower offer from ONEOK. Southern Union sued Southwest Gas to block the ONEOK deal, and ONEOK terminated the agreement in 2000. Southern Union also filed fraud claims against ONEOK and Southwest Gas. (Southwest Gas paid Southern Union $17.5 million in 2002 to settle the suits.)

Southern Union decided to move north in 1999, when it bought natural gas distributor Pennsylvania Enterprises (150,000 customers). The next year Southern Union gained nearly 300,000 customers in New England by buying two Rhode Island gas utilities, Valley Resources and Providence Energy, and Massachusetts-based Fall River Gas. In 2001 the three utilities began operating as New England Gas.

Kelley resigned for health reasons in 2001, and Thomas Karam moved from the company's Pennsylvania operations to replace him. In a cost-cutting effort, Southern Union that year offered early retirement programs to 400 employees and laid off 48 workers in a reorganization of corporate management functions.

The company also began selling noncore assets, including the gas marketing business of PG Energy Services, its Keystone Pipeline Services unit, two small propane/heating oil distribution units, and a plumbing and heating services unit (Morris Merchants).

## EXECUTIVES

**Chairman Emeritus:** Franklin W. (Frank) Denius, age 82
**Chairman, President, and CEO:** George L. Lindemann, age 71, $989,135 pay (prior to title change)
**SEVP:** Eric D. Herschmann, age 43
**SVP and CFO:** Richard N. (Rick) Marshall, age 49
**SVP Human Resources and Administration:** Gary P. Smith
**SVP Pipeline Operations:** Robert O. (Rob) Bond, age 47, $419,057 pay (prior to title change)
**SVP Associate General Counsel:** Monica M. Gaudiosi, age 45
**VP Investor Relations:** John F. (Jack) Walsh
**Director External Affairs:** John P. Barnett
**Auditors:** PricewaterhouseCoopers LLP

## LOCATIONS

**HQ:** Southern Union Company
5444 Westheimer Rd., Houston, TX 77056
**Phone:** 713-989-2000 **Fax:** 713-989-1121
**Web:** www.southernunionco.com

Southern Union distributes natural gas in Massachusetts, Missouri, Pennsylvania, and Rhode Island. Its pipeline assets run from the Gulf of Mexico, Mobile Bay, the Panhandle regions of Oklahoma and Texas, the Permian Basin, the Rockies, the San Juan Basin, and South Texas to markets in the Great Lakes, midwestern, southeastern, and western regions of the US.

## PRODUCTS/OPERATIONS

**2006 Sales**

| | $ mil. | % of total |
|---|---|---|
| Gas gathering & processing | 1,090.2 | 46 |
| Gas distribution | 668.7 | 29 |
| Gas transportation & storage | 577.2 | 25 |
| Other | 4.0 | — |
| **Total** | **2,340.1** | **100** |

**Selected Subsidiaries**

CCE Holdings, LLC (natural gas transportation)
Citrus Corp. (50%)
Florida Gas Transmission Company (50%
Missouri Gas Energy (natural gas utility)
New England Gas Company (natural gas utility)
Panhandle Energy (natural gas transportation)
Panhandle Eastern Pipe Line Company
Sea Robin Pipeline Company
Pan Gas Storage (dba Southwest Gas Storage)
Trunkline Gas Company
Trunkline LNG Company
PEI Power Corporation (independent power production)

## COMPETITORS

Ameren
Aquila
Atmos Energy
Dominion Peoples
Dominion Resources
Dominion Transmission
Duke Energy
El Paso
Empire District Electric
Exelon
Great Plains Energy
Laclede Group
National Fuel Gas
NiSource
ONEOK
Transcontinental Gas
Williams Companies

## HISTORICAL FINANCIALS

Company Type: Public

**Income Statement** FYE: December 31

| | REVENUE ($ mil.) | NET INCOME ($ mil.) | NET PROFIT MARGIN | EMPLOYEES |
|---|---|---|---|---|
| **12/06** | 2,340 | 64 | 2.7% | 2,312 |
| **12/05** | 2,019 | 21 | 1.0% | 2,888 |
| **12/04*** | 1,800 | 114 | 6.3% | 2,922 |
| **6/04** | 1,800 | 114 | 6.3% | 3,006 |
| **6/03** | 1,189 | 76 | 6.4% | 3,023 |
| **Annual Growth** | 18.5% | (4.2%) | — | (6.5%) |

*Fiscal year change

**2006 Year-End Financials**

Debt ratio: 147.8%
Return on equity: 3.7%
Cash ($ mil.): 6
Current ratio: 0.58
Long-term debt ($ mil.): 2,690
No. of shares (mil.): 120
Dividends
Yield: 1.4%
Payout: 19.0%
Market value ($ mil.): 3,344

**Stock History** NYSE: SUG

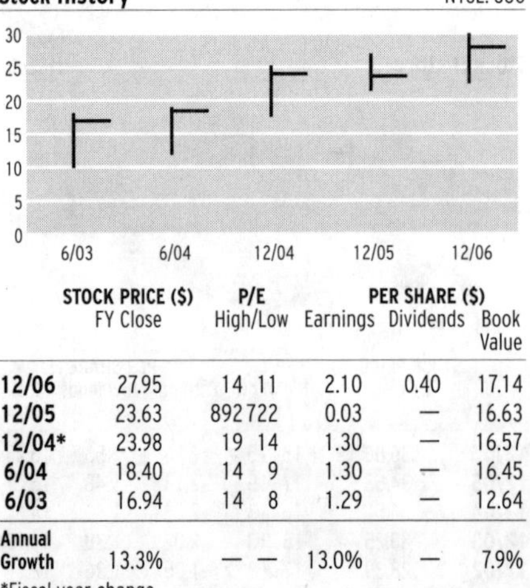


| | STOCK PRICE ($) FY Close | P/E High | P/E Low | PER SHARE ($) Earnings | Dividends | Book Value |
|---|---|---|---|---|---|---|
| **12/06** | 27.95 | 14 | 11 | 2.10 | 0.40 | 17.14 |
| **12/05** | 23.63 | 892 | 722 | 0.03 | — | 16.63 |
| **12/04*** | 23.98 | 19 | 14 | 1.30 | — | 16.57 |
| **6/04** | 18.40 | 14 | 9 | 1.30 | — | 16.45 |
| **6/03** | 16.94 | 14 | 8 | 1.29 | — | 12.64 |
| **Annual Growth** | 13.3% | — | — | 13.0% | — | 7.9% |

*Fiscal year change

# Southwest Airlines

Southwest Airlines will fly any plane, as long as it's a Boeing 737, and let passengers sit anywhere they like, as long as they get there first. Sticking with what works, Southwest has expanded its low-cost, no-frills, no-reserved-seats approach to air travel throughout the US to serve some 65 cities in more than 30 states. Southwest offers ticketless travel to trim back-office costs and operates its own reservation system. Now among the leading US airlines, Southwest nevertheless stands as an inspiration for scrappy low-fare upstarts the world over. The carrier has enjoyed 34 straight profitable years amid the airline industry's ups and downs.

Simplicity has been a key to the airline's success. Most Southwest flights are less than two hours, and the airline usually lands at small airports to avoid congestion at competitors' larger hubs; in Dallas it's the big dog at little Love Field, its birthplace, and in Chicago it accounts for most of the traffic at Midway Airport. Southwest's fleet of about 480 aircraft consists only of one type — the Boeing 737 — to minimize training and maintenance costs.

The no-assigned-seats policy, which is not universally popular, helps the carrier achieve quick turnarounds at airports and stick to its schedule. In the summer of 2006, however, Southwest experimented with assigned seating on flights out of San Diego.

Southwest's formula also emphasizes customer service and a sense of fun, and flamboyant co-founder and chairman Herb Kelleher and other longtime employees have created a highly participative corporate culture. Although its workforce is largely unionized, the airline has had only one strike.

As with many other airlines, rising energy prices have been a thorn in Southwest's side. Despite hedging its fuel costs, the budget carrier has not been immune to the increase in oil prices, especially as its most favorable hedge contracts expire. Slower-than-expected demand in 2007 led Southwest to offer buyouts to some 8,700 employees, or about a quarter of its workforce.

## HISTORY

Texas businessman Rollin King and lawyer Herb Kelleher founded Air Southwest in 1967 as an intrastate airline linking Dallas, Houston, and San Antonio. The now-defunct Braniff and Texas International sued, questioning whether the region needed another airline, but the Texas Supreme Court ruled in Southwest's favor. In 1971 the company, renamed Southwest Airlines, made its first scheduled flight.

Operating from Love Field in Dallas, Southwest adopted love as the theme of its early ad campaigns, serving love potions (drinks) and love bites (peanuts). When other airlines moved to the new Dallas/Fort Worth Airport (DFW) in 1974, Kelleher insisted on staying at Love Field, gaining a virtual monopoly there.

When Kelleher decided to fly outside Texas, Congress passed the Wright Amendment in 1979. Designed to protect DFW, the law restricted the states served directly from Love Field. (Arkansas, Louisiana, New Mexico, and Oklahoma were on the original list; a 1997 amendment added Alabama, Kansas, and Mississippi. In 2000 a federal court removed the restrictions for planes with 56 or fewer seats. Later

Missouri was added to the list of states eligible for direct service from Love Field.)

When Lamar Muse, Southwest's president, resigned in 1978 because of differences with King, Kelleher assumed control. (Muse later took over his son Michael's nearly bankrupt airline, Muse Air, which was sold in 1985 to Southwest. The airline was liquidated in 1987.)

An industry maverick, Kelleher introduced advance-purchase Fun Fares in 1986 and a frequent-flier program in 1987 based on the number of flights taken instead of mileage. He gained attention in 1992 for starring in Southwest's TV commercials and for arm wrestling Stevens Aviation chairman Kurt Herwald for the rights to the "Just Plane Smart" slogan. When Southwest became the official airline of Sea World in Texas, Kelleher had a 737 painted as a killer whale.

Southwest took on the East Coast with service to Baltimore in 1993 and bought Salt Lake City-based Morris Air in 1994. That year it launched a ticketless system and adopted its own passenger reservation system to cut costs. The airline expanded into Florida in 1996, and that year Southwest began selling tickets through its Web site. Agreements with Icelandair in 1996 and 1997 allowed Southwest passengers to connect from four US cities to Europe through Icelandair's Baltimore hub.

Southwest added more routes in the East during 1999. In 2001 Southwest experienced a rare labor dispute when stalled contract negotiations led to picketing by the airline's ground crew union. Kelleher stepped down as CEO in 2001. General counsel Jim Parker took over as CEO, and EVP Colleen Barrett — who first worked for Kelleher as his secretary and is given much of the credit for maintaining Southwest's corporate spirit — was named COO.

Parker would reign over the airline during one of the most tumultuous times in its history. Despite an industrywide downturn resulting from the lagging US economy and exacerbated by the September 11 terrorist attacks, Southwest managed to post a profit for 2001 as well as 2002, but it did not come easily.

Increased Internet sales led the airline to close its call centers in Dallas, Little Rock, and Salt Lake City in 2003. Nearly 2,000 workers were given the choice of relocating to another call center or accepting a severance package.

Rising fuel costs and other labor issues haunted the airline. Union negotiations with flight attendants began in 2002 and lasted for two years, during which time Parker was publicly chastised for being uncooperative. A resolution was not reached until Kelleher and Barrett were asked to step in by Parker, who resigned in 2004, after negotiations ended. He was replaced by former CFO Gary Kelly.

Southwest in 2005 launched its first codeshare agreement, with ATA Airlines, as part of a deal that gave Southwest some of ATA's gates at Chicago's Midway Airport.

After intense lobbying from both Southwest and American Airlines, Congress revisited the Wright Amendment in 2006. A compromise measure signed into law that year allowed Southwest to offer direct, one-stop service — meaning passengers need not change planes — from Love Field to states not covered by the original Wright law or its revisions. The requirement that flights stop in a Wright Amendment state is scheduled to expire in 2014.

## EXECUTIVES

**Chairman:** Herbert D. (Herb) Kelleher, age 76, $782,000 pay
**Vice Chairman and CEO:** Gary C. Kelly, age 51, $878,860 pay
**President, Secretary, and Director:** Colleen C. Barrett, age 62, $845,487 pay
**EVP and COO:** Michael G. (Mike) Van de Ven, age 45
**EVP, Customer Operations:** Donna D. Conover, age 52
**EVP, Law, Airports, and Public Affairs:** Ron Ricks, age 57, $626,986 pay
**EVP, Strategy, Procurement, and Technology:** Robert E. (Bob) Jordan, age 46
**SVP, Finance and CFO:** Laura H. Wright, age 46, $471,413 pay
**SVP, Corporate Communications:** Ginger C. Hardage
**SVP, Marketing:** Joyce C. Rogge, age 48
**SVP, Operations:** Greg Wells
**VP and General Counsel:** Deborah Ackerman
**VP and Controller:** Tammy Romo
**VP, Customer Relations and Rapid Rewards:** James A. (Jim) Ruppel
**VP and Director, Operations:** Gregory N. (Greg) Crum
**VP, Labor and Employee Relations:** Joe Harris
**VP, Marketing, Sales, and Distribution:** Kevin M. Krone
**VP, People and Leadership Development:** A. Jeff Lamb III
**VP, Public Relations and Community Affairs:** Linda B. Rutherford
**VP, Technology and CIO:** Jan Marshall
**VP and CTO:** Kerry Schwab
**Auditors:** Ernst & Young LLP

## LOCATIONS

**HQ:** Southwest Airlines Co.
2702 Love Field Dr., Dallas, TX 75235
**Phone:** 214-792-4000 **Fax:** 214-792-5015
**Web:** www.southwest.com

## PRODUCTS/OPERATIONS

**2006 Sales**

| | $ mil. | % of total |
|---|---|---|
| Passenger | 8,750 | 96 |
| Freight | 134 | 2 |
| Other | 202 | 2 |
| **Total** | **9,086** | **100** |

## COMPETITORS

AirTran Holdings
Alaska Air
AMR Corp.
Continental Airlines
Delta Air
Frontier Airlines
JetBlue
Northwest Airlines
UAL
US Airways

## HISTORICAL FINANCIALS

Company Type: Public

**Income Statement** FYE: December 31

| | REVENUE ($ mil.) | NET INCOME ($ mil.) | NET PROFIT MARGIN | EMPLOYEES |
|---|---|---|---|---|
| **12/06** | 9,086 | 499 | 5.5% | 32,664 |
| **12/05** | 7,584 | 548 | 7.2% | 31,729 |
| **12/04** | 6,530 | 313 | 4.8% | 31,011 |
| **12/03** | 5,937 | 442 | 7.4% | 32,847 |
| **12/02** | 5,522 | 241 | 4.4% | 33,705 |
| **Annual Growth** | 13.3% | 20.0% | — | (0.8%) |

**2006 Year-End Financials**

Debt ratio: 24.3%
Return on equity: 7.6%
Cash ($ mil.): 2,128
Current ratio: 0.90
Long-term debt ($ mil.): 1,567
No. of shares (mil.): 783
Dividends
Yield: 0.1%
Payout: 3.3%
Market value ($ mil.): 12,000

**Stock History** NYSE: LUV

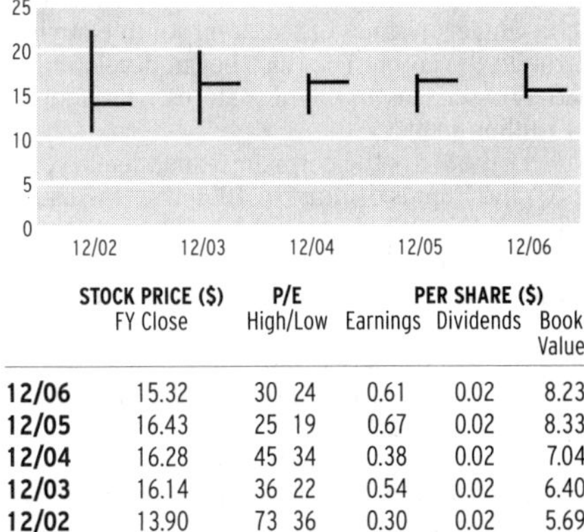


| | STOCK PRICE ($) FY Close | P/E High | P/E Low | PER SHARE ($) Earnings | Dividends | Book Value |
|---|---|---|---|---|---|---|
| **12/06** | 15.32 | 30 | 24 | 0.61 | 0.02 | 8.23 |
| **12/05** | 16.43 | 25 | 19 | 0.67 | 0.02 | 8.33 |
| **12/04** | 16.28 | 45 | 34 | 0.38 | 0.02 | 7.04 |
| **12/03** | 16.14 | 36 | 22 | 0.54 | 0.02 | 6.40 |
| **12/02** | 13.90 | 73 | 36 | 0.30 | 0.02 | 5.69 |
| **Annual Growth** | 2.5% | — | — | 19.4% | 0.0% | 9.7% |

# Spartan Stores

This company fights to win on the battlefield of grocery distribution. Spartan Stores is a leading grocery wholesaler in the Midwest, distributing more than 47,000 food and general merchandise items to more than 400 independent grocery stores primarily in Indiana, Michigan, and Ohio. It supplies mostly national brands, as well as items sold under such private labels as Aroma Street Bakery and President's Choice. The company also operates about 70 retail supermarkets in Michigan under such names as D&W Fresh Markets, Family Fare Supermarkets, and Glen's Markets. In addition, Spartan Stores has about 20 discount food and drug stores called The Pharm.

The company has been going through a growth spurt in the past couple of years fueled primarily by acquisitions. During 2006 it acquired D&W Fresh Markets in 2006, adding 16 stores to its portfolio, as well as the assets of PrairieStone Pharmacy. Spartan acquired 20 grocery stores, three convenience stores, and two fuel stops in Michigan from G&R Felpausch the following year. The company is now looking to new construction to continue its retail expansion.

Meanwhile, the company has expanded capacity for its produce distribution operations and added new customers. Broadening its relationships with customers has also helped spark growth for Spartan's distribution arm; in 2007 it inked an expanded pact with Martin's Super Markets to supply the Indiana chain with dry goods, frozen foods, and private label products.

## HISTORY

Making dinner in the early 1900s often required several shopping stops: the grocer for canned goods, a butcher for meat, and yet another place for produce. Eventually the big grocery chains began offering one-stop shopping, not to mention better prices due to greater buying power. Worrying about how to compete, in 1917 approximately 100 small grocers met in Grand Rapids, Michigan, to discuss organizing a cooperative; almost half of those formed the Grand Rapids Wholesale Grocery Co. The stores remained independent, operating under different names but achieving economies of scale and volume buying through the co-op. They also began developing a variety of services for member stores. Sales topped $1 million in 1934.

Over the years the company expanded beyond its Grand Rapids origins. In 1950 it formed subsidiary United Wholesale, which served independent grocers on a cash-and-carry basis. It acquired the Grand Rapids Coffee Company in 1953. The next year the co-op launched its first private-label item, Spartan Coffee, with a green Spartan logo reminiscent of the Michigan State University mascot. The company changed its name to Spartan Stores in 1957.

Spartan Stores entered retailing in the early 1970s when it bought 19 Harding's stores. It became a for-profit company in 1973 but continued to provide rebates to customers based on their purchases. Spartan Stores began offering insurance to its customers in 1979.

Concerned about the direction of the company, customers named Patrick Quinn, formerly a VP at a small chain of grocery stores, as president and CEO in 1985. To focus on the wholesale business, and to avoid any appearance of conflict of interest in both supplying member stores and operating competing stores, Spartan Stores sold its 23 retail stores between 1987 and 1994, giving customer stores the first option on them. It entered the convenience store wholesale business with its 1987 acquisition of L&L/Jiroch. Two years later the co-op acquired Associated Grocers of Michigan (later known as Capistar, closed in 1996).

Sales topped $2 billion in 1991. Spartan Stores expanded its convenience store operations in 1993 by buying wholesaler J.F. Walker. Despite record sales in 1996, a $46 million restructuring charge that included extensive technological improvements led to a $21.7 million loss, the largest in the company's history. The following year Jim Meyer, who had joined Spartan Stores in 1973, replaced the retiring Quinn as president and CEO. Also in 1997 the company stopped giving its customers rebates, finally doing away with the last remnants of its co-op years.

To keep Michigan customers out of the clutches of its wholesaling rivals, Spartan Stores re-entered retailing in 1999 by acquiring eight Ashcraft's Markets. It bought 13 Family Fare stores and 23 Glen's grocery stores that year. In early 2000 the company sold off its insurance business. Later that year Spartan Stores acquired food and drug chain Seaway Food Town (Michigan and Ohio) for about $180 million and began publicly trading.

In 2001 the company purchased longtime customer Prevo's Family Markets, a supermarket chain with 10 stores in western Michigan. In an effort to reduce debt and improve profitability in mid-2002 the company announced plans to close its Food Town stores, which suffered from competitors such as Meier, Kroger, and Farmer Jack's. (By mid-2003, Spartan had sold the last of its 26 Food Town stores. Spartan Store's retail operations had accounted for about 40% of the company's sales.)

In 2003 Spartan Stores sold seven shopping centers in Michigan for $46 million as part of its strategy to sell non-core properties and focus on its retail and distributions businesses. That year James Meyer retired as president and CEO of Spartan Stores and was succeeded by Craig Sturken, a former executive of the Great Atlantic & Pacific Tea Company. Later the company sold convenience store suppliers L&L/Jiroch and J.F. Walker to Knoxville, Tennessee-based distributor H.T. Hackney Co.

Spartan Stores sold the assets of United Wholesale Grocery Co., a privately held firm in Michigan, for about $10 million in 2004. The sale marked Spartan's exit from the convenience store distribution business. The company also closed or sold all of its Food Town stores for $42.1 million.

In 2005 the company opened three fuel centers in Michigan under the Family Fare Quick Stops and Glen's Quick Stop banners. The company acquired D&W Food Centers the following year and purchased about 20 stores from G&R Felpausch in 2007.

## EXECUTIVES

**Chairman, President, and CEO:** Craig C. Sturken, age 63
**EVP and CFO:** David M. (Dave) Staples, age 44, $511,711 pay
**EVP and COO:** Dennis Eidson, age 53
**EVP, General Counsel, and Corporate Secretary:** Alex J. DeYonker, age 57
**EVP Retail Operations:** Theodore C. (Ted) Adornato, age 53, $374,777 pay
**EVP Supply Chain:** Derek Jones, age 38
**SVP Merchandising:** Alan Hartline
**VP Corporate Affairs:** Jeanne Norcross
**VP Center Store Merchandising:** Brian Haaraoja
**VP Information Technology:** David deS (Dave) Couch, age 52
**VP Finance:** Thomas A. (Tom) Van Hall, age 51, $277,066 pay
**VP Fresh Merchandising:** Ron Anderson
**VP New Business Development:** Tom Berg
**VP Human Resources:** Linda Esparza
**VP Operations and Finance:** Francis Wong
**Investor Relations Counsel:** Steve Warcholak
**Auditors:** Deloitte & Touche LLP

## LOCATIONS

**HQ:** Spartan Stores, Inc.
850 76th St. SW, Grand Rapids, MI 49518
**Phone:** 616-878-2000 **Fax:** 616-878-8561
**Web:** www.spartanstores.com

Spartan Stores operates eight distribution centers in Grand Rapids and Plymouth, Michigan, and in Maumee, Ohio.

## PRODUCTS/OPERATIONS

### 2007 Sales

| | $ mil. | % of total |
|---|---|---|
| Distribution | 1,238.1 | 52 |
| Retail | 1,132.3 | 48 |
| **Total** | **2,370.4** | **100** |

### Selected Retail Brands
Aroma Street Bakery
Full Circle
President's Choice
Top Care
Valu-Time

### Selected Retail Stores
D&W Fresh Markets
Family Fare Supermarkets
Glen's Markets
The Pharm (discount food and drug stores)

## COMPETITORS

Associated Wholesale Grocers
C&S Wholesale
Certified Grocers Midwest
Costco Wholesale
CVS/Caremark
GSC Enterprises
IGA
Kmart
Kroger
Marsh Supermarkets
McLane
Meijer
Nash-Finch
Rite Aid
SUPERVALU
V.G.'s Food
Walgreen
Wal-Mart

## HISTORICAL FINANCIALS

Company Type: Public

### Income Statement
FYE: Last Saturday in March

| | REVENUE ($ mil.) | NET INCOME ($ mil.) | NET PROFIT MARGIN | EMPLOYEES |
|---|---|---|---|---|
| **3/07** | 2,370 | 25 | 1.1% | 7,300 |
| **3/06** | 2,040 | 18 | 0.9% | 7,500 |
| **3/05** | 2,043 | 19 | 0.9% | 6,300 |
| **3/04** | 2,055 | (7) | — | 6,900 |
| **3/03** | 2,148 | (122) | — | 7,400 |
| **Annual Growth** | 2.5% | — | — | (0.3%) |

### 2007 Year-End Financials

Debt ratio: 61.6%
Return on equity: 15.8%
Cash ($ mil.): 12
Current ratio: 1.17
Long-term debt ($ mil.): 106
No. of shares (mil.): 22
Dividends
Yield: 0.7%
Payout: 16.9%
Market value ($ mil.): 580

### Stock History
NASDAQ (GM): SPTN

| | STOCK PRICE ($) FY Close | P/E High | P/E Low | PER SHARE ($) Earnings | Dividends | Book Value |
|---|---|---|---|---|---|---|
| **3/07** | 26.80 | 23 | 10 | 1.18 | 0.20 | 7.98 |
| **3/06** | 12.59 | 18 | 10 | 0.86 | 0.05 | 6.92 |
| **3/05** | 10.89 | 13 | 3 | 0.91 | — | 6.11 |
| **3/04** | 4.72 | — | — | (0.33) | — | 5.26 |
| **3/03** | 2.32 | — | — | (6.15) | — | 5.48 |
| **Annual Growth** | 84.4% | — | — | — | 300.0% | 9.8% |

# Spectrum Brands

Chasing the copper top and the pink bunny, Spectrum Brands (formerly Rayovac) is the US's #3 battery maker, after Duracell and Energizer Holdings. The company's alkaline batteries power such consumer gadgets as digital and film cameras, MP3 music players, radios, and remote controls. The company, which markets its products in 120 countries, is a leader in the sale of rechargeable batteries and hearing-aid batteries to manufacturers. With recent acquisitions, Spectrum has moved into pet foods, products for lawns and gardens, and insect control. Wal-Mart accounts for around 19% of sales. Thomas H. Lee Funds owns about 24% of Spectrum Brands.

In early 2007 the company realigned its four geography-based operating segments into three product groups: Global Batteries & Personal Care, Home & Garden, and Global Pet Supplies. At the same time, Spectrum Brands cut expenses at the corporate and operating levels, including the layoff of about 100 employees.

A US attorney's investigation regarding quarterly statements during fiscal 2005 concluded in the summer of 2006. Spectrum Brands said it is cooperating with a separate investigation by the SEC.

Best known for its general-purpose alkaline batteries, Spectrum Brands also makes specialty batteries, such as lithium coin cells (used in cameras and computer clocks). It also makes flashlights and lanterns.

Ameriprise Financial owns about 14% of Spectrum Brands. Harbert Management holds nearly 10% of the company. Adage Capital Partners has an equity stake of nearly 6%, as does Morgan Stanley.

## HISTORY

Spectrum Brands traces its roots to 1906, when a trio of Wisconsin entrepreneurs created the French Battery Company. Radio and government orders during WWI galvanized the firm. Its products included Ray-O-Vac radio batteries, and the company adopted that name in the 1930s. In 1937 Ray-O-Vac patented the first wearable vacuum tube hearing aid. Two years later it introduced the sealed dry cell battery, a vital part in mine detectors and bazookas during WWII. The advent of the transistor radio during the 1950s sparked more growth. Ray-O-Vac merged with the much larger Electric Storage Battery Co. in 1957.

The company lost its market lead during the 1960s and 1970s, when it failed to push alkaline batteries. In 1982 husband-and-wife marketers Thomas and Judith Pyle bought the company, changed its name to Rayovac, and introduced new products such as a zinc hearing-aid battery. During the early 1990s it introduced the Workhorse fluorescent lantern. In 1995 basketball superstar Michael Jordan became the company's pitchman.

Investment firm Thomas H. Lee acquired 80% of Rayovac in 1996. David Jones, who had headed Lee's Thermoscan unit, was chosen to head the company, and he began consolidating its operations. Rayovac went public in 1997. The next year the firm entered the Chinese market.

In 1999 the company bought the battery business of ROV — which Rayovac had spun off in 1982 — for $155 million, giving Rayovac rights to its own brand in every country but Brazil. ROV had more than $80 million in battery sales and factories in Latin America. In the wake of the purchase, Rayovac announced further restructuring.

Jordan announced his retirement from endorsements in early 2000 but said he would honor existing contracts. Following rival Energizer's spinoff from Ralston Purina (now Nestlé Purina PetCare), Rayovac announced in April 2000 plans to expand in Europe.

In 2001, as part of a plan to cut costs, Rayovac closed its Honduras facility as well as a US flashlight and lantern assembly plant and began buying those items from outside suppliers. Also that year 8% of its global workforce lost their jobs. At 2001 year-end Rayovac and Jordan mutually declined to renew their contract in keeping with his 2000 decision.

In January 2002 Jones reported that virtually all of the company's earnings in the first quarter of fiscal 2002 were wiped out by Kmart's Chapter 11 bankruptcy filing. Kmart, which filed for Chapter 11 protection in January 2002, had represented more than 6% of Rayovac's 2001 revenues.

Rayovac closed its plant in the Dominican Republic in July 2002. The company acquired VARTA's portable battery business that October. Restructuring in the wake of the acquisition, Rayovac closed its plant in Mexico the same month.

In August 2003 Rayovac introduced its 15-minute rechargeable battery system. The next month it acquired electric shaver maker Remington Products for about $322 million. The purchase sent the company to the top of the charts in the electric personal care product market. The Remington acquisition also broadened Spectrum's rivalry with Global Gillette and Energizer (both leaders in the shaving gear market).

In 2004 Rayovac acquired 85% of Ningbo Baowang China Battery, which makes alkaline and heavy-duty batteries and distributes them in China. Also in 2004 the company moved its corporate headquarters from Madison, Wisconsin, to Atlanta.

In a deal intended to further diversify its product offerings, in early 2005 Spectrum bought United Industries Corp., a privately held maker of lawn and garden products, for around $500 million in cash and stock. Including debt assumption, the deal had a value of about $1.2 billion.

Spectrum Brands then acquired Germany's Tetra Holding AG for approximately €415 million (around $556 million). Tetra is a supplier of foods, equipment, and care products for fish and reptiles, along with accessories for home aquariums and ponds.

Rayovac changed its name in May 2005 to Spectrum Brands, using a trade name that had been employed by United Industries. The company changed its stock ticker symbol on the New York Stock Exchange from ROV to SPC as a result.

After Spectrum posted a big loss in fiscal 2006, following years of steady profitability, David Jones stepped down as CEO in 2007, while remaining non-executive chairman of the board for a short period. Vice chairman Kent Hussey, who formerly served as the company's president/COO, was tapped as the new CEO.

## EXECUTIVES

**CEO and Director:** Kent J. Hussey, age 61
**EVP, Latin America:** Hartmut B. Junghahn, age 44
**EVP, Home and Garden:** Amy J. Yoder, age 40
**EVP Operations; President, Global Operations:** Kenneth V. Biller, age 59, $450,000 pay
**SVP and CFO:** Anthony L. Genito, age 50
**VP, Sales and Marketing, Latin America:** Alfredo Mayne-Nicholls
**VP, Investor Relations:** Nancy O'Donnell
**President, Global Batteries and Personal Care, Co-COO:** David R. Lumley, age 52
**President, Global Pet Supplies and Co-COO:** John A. Heil, age 54
**Human Resource Manager:** Jim Stoeffler
**Auditors:** KPMG LLP

## LOCATIONS

**HQ:** Spectrum Brands, Inc.
6 Concourse Pkwy., Ste. 3300, Atlanta, GA 30328
**Phone:** 770-829-6200
**Web:** www.spectrumbrands.com

Spectrum Brands manufactures its products in Brazil, Canada, China, Colombia, France, Germany, Guatemala, the UK, and the US. The company has distribution and packaging facilities, along with sales offices, around the world.

### 2006 Sales

| | $ mil. | % of total |
|---|---|---|
| North America | 1,213 | 48 |
| Europe & other regions | 560 | 22 |
| Latin America | 236 | 9 |
| Global Pet | 543 | 21 |
| **Total** | **2,552** | **100** |

## PRODUCTS/OPERATIONS

### 2006 Sales

| | $ mil. | % of total |
|---|---|---|
| Batteries | 861 | 34 |
| Pet products | 543 | 21 |
| Lawn & garden | 507 | 20 |
| Electric shaving & grooming | 252 | 10 |
| Household insect control | 151 | 6 |
| Personal care | 150 | 6 |
| Lighting products | 88 | 3 |
| **Total** | **2,552** | **100** |

### Selected Products

Batteries
- Alkaline batteries (for use in flashlights, radios, toys, smoke alarms, and other consumer products; industrial applications)
- Alkaline rechargeable batteries
- Lithium (for use in PC clocks and memory backup)
- Zinc heavy duty (for use in flashlights, lanterns, radios, and remote controls)
- Zinc lantern (for use in beam lanterns, camping lanterns)

Electric shaver and grooming products
- Beard and mustache trimmers
- Cleaning agents
- Haircut kits
- Men's foil shavers
- Men's rotary shavers
- Nose and ear trimmers
- Preshave products
- Women's shavers

Other personal care products
- Curling irons
- Hair crimpers and straighteners
- Hair dryers
- Hairsetters
- Hot air brushes
- Insect repellent
- Lighted mirrors
- Paraffin wax hand and foot spas

Fish and reptile care products
- Aerators
- Artificial plants for aquariums
- Food for aquarium and pond fish
- Food and treats for reptiles and hermit crabs
- Pond liners
- Water filters, pumps, test kits, and treatments

Lawn and garden products
- Fertilizers
- Insecticide

Lighting
- Flashlights
- Lanterns

## COMPETITORS

| | |
|---|---|
| Bayer CropScience | Mag Instrument |
| Black & Decker | Matsushita Electric |
| Central Garden & Pet | Philips Electronics |
| Coleman | Procter & Gamble |
| Conair | S.C. Johnson |
| Energizer Holdings | Scotts Miracle-Gro |
| EnerSys | Ultralife Batteries |
| GP Batteries | Varta |
| Hartz Mountain | Wahl Clipper |
| Helen of Troy | |

## HISTORICAL FINANCIALS

Company Type: Public

**Income Statement** FYE: September 30

| | REVENUE ($ mil.) | NET INCOME ($ mil.) | NET PROFIT MARGIN | EMPLOYEES |
|---|---|---|---|---|
| **9/06** | 2,552 | (434) | — | 8,400 |
| **9/05** | 2,359 | 47 | 2.0% | 9,800 |
| **9/04** | 1,417 | 56 | 3.9% | 6,500 |
| **9/03** | 922 | 16 | 1.7% | 5,000 |
| **9/02** | 573 | 29 | 5.1% | 2,480 |
| **Annual Growth** | 45.3% | — | — | 35.7% |

**2006 Year-End Financials**

| | |
|---|---|
| Debt ratio: 494.1% | No. of shares (mil.): 51 |
| Return on equity: — | Dividends |
| Cash ($ mil.): 28 | Yield: — |
| Current ratio: 1.71 | Payout: — |
| Long-term debt ($ mil.): 2,234 | Market value ($ mil.): 435 |

**Stock History** NYSE: SPC

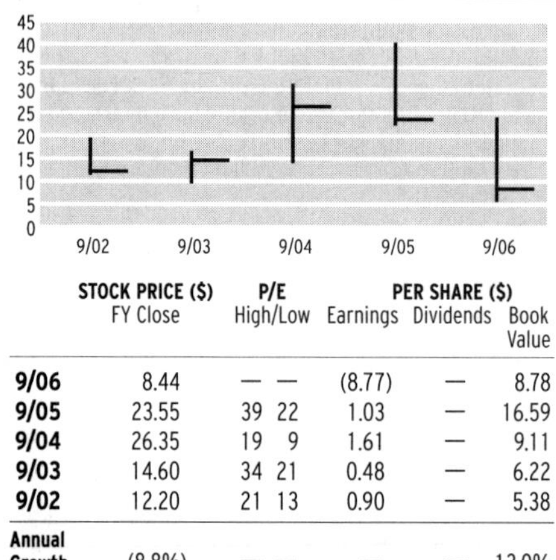


| | STOCK PRICE ($) FY Close | P/E High | P/E Low | PER SHARE ($) Earnings | Dividends | Book Value |
|---|---|---|---|---|---|---|
| **9/06** | 8.44 | — | — | (8.77) | — | 8.78 |
| **9/05** | 23.55 | 39 | 22 | 1.03 | — | 16.59 |
| **9/04** | 26.35 | 19 | 9 | 1.61 | — | 9.11 |
| **9/03** | 14.60 | 34 | 21 | 0.48 | — | 6.22 |
| **9/02** | 12.20 | 21 | 13 | 0.90 | — | 5.38 |
| **Annual Growth** | (8.8%) | — | — | — | — | 13.0% |

# Spherion Corporation

Spherion seeks to circumvent your personnel problems. The company provides traditional temporary staffing along with services such as professional and executive recruitment and employee consulting and assessment. In addition, Spherion provides staffing and technology services in such areas as project management, quality assurance, and data center and network operations. The company also offers customer care and administrative and support services. Founded in 1946, Spherion operates through a network of about 660 locations within the US and Canada.

Over the years, the company has discontinued its staffing operations in Australia, the Netherlands, and the UK in order to focus solely on its business in North America. The company also cut some operations in the US, including its call center outsourcing division and court reporting business. In mid-2007, Spherion sold off its HR consulting business to IMPACT Group, a career transition services firm.

CEO Roy Krause is now focusing on growth after several years of scaling back. The company plans on exploring acquisition opportunities in the future and to utilize its franchise structure in order to achieve financial growth. (Spherion grants licensees the right to develop recruitment businesses using its trade names and operating procedures.)

## HISTORY

LeRoy Dettman founded City Car Unloaders in 1946 to provide railroad car workers in Chicago. As it grew, the company added industrial and clerical workers; it moved into health care staffing in 1966. H&R Block acquired the company (then named Personnel Pool) in 1978, bought personnel placement firm Interim Systems in 1991, and combined the two under the Interim name. Also that year Raymond Marcy became CEO of the company. In 1994 Interim went public.

Interim used the proceeds of its IPO to fund more acquisitions, particularly in the higher-margin professional staffing fields such as medicine and law. In 1995 it began targeting information technology by acquiring Computer Power Group and a year later, computer staffing company Brandon Systems. Also in 1996 the company acquired Netherlands-based staffing companies Allround and Interplan.

In a move to expand internationally, Interim acquired London-based Michael Page Group for about $574 million in 1997. Also that year Interim bought AimExecutive Holdings, adding outplacement services to its business. In 1998 the company acquired London-based staffing company Crone Corkill Group. The following year it bought rival Norrell in a $550 million deal, adding nearly 400 offices to its operations.

To broaden its e-business services, Interim bought Applied Internet Consultancy in 2000 and soon changed its name to Spherion. It also expanded its online recruiting services with its launch of CareerZone.com, a Web site for job seekers, and its acquisition of an 80% stake in JobOptions.com.

In 2001 Spherion spun off Michael Page as a public company. Later that year the company announced a broad reorganization plan, including office closures, job cuts, and the divestiture of noncore or underperforming units. In 2002 Spherion sold consulting businesses in the UK and the Netherlands. In 2003 the company reorganized its operations into two divisions, Staffing Services and Professional Services. Spherion sold its noncore businesses in Australia, the Netherlands, and the UK in 2004.

## EXECUTIVES

**President, CEO, and Director:** Roy G. Krause, age 60, $1,036,635 pay
**SVP and CFO:** Mark W. Smith, age 44, $481,300 pay
**SVP and Chief Human Resources Officer:** John D. Heins, age 47
**SVP and Group Executive Mergis Group:** Jack Causa
**VP and Chief Service Excellence Officer:** Loretta A. Penn, age 57
**VP and Treasurer:** Teri Miller
**VP and Controller:** John McMickle
**Director, Public Relations and Corporate Marketing:** Kip Havel
**Director, Tax and Assistant Secretary:** Randal B. Atkinson
**Interim General Counsel and Assistant Secretary:** Thad Florence
**Assistant Secretary and Associate Counsel:** Kelly C. Cotton
**Interim CIO:** Joel Steigelfest
**Auditors:** Deloitte & Touche LLP

## LOCATIONS

**HQ:** Spherion Corporation
2050 Spectrum Blvd., Fort Lauderdale, FL 33309
**Phone:** 954-308-7600 **Fax:** 954-308-7666
**Web:** www.spherion.com

Spherion has locations in Canada and the US.

## PRODUCTS/OPERATIONS

**2006 Sales**

| | $ mil. | % of total |
|---|---|---|
| Staffing services | 1,440.4 | 75 |
| Professional services | 492.7 | 25 |
| **Total** | **1,933.1** | **100** |

**Selected Staffing Areas**

Accounting/finance
Administrative
Clerical
Human resources
Legal
Light industrial
Manufacturing
Technology

## COMPETITORS

| | |
|---|---|
| Adecco | Labor Ready |
| ADP | Manpower |
| Butler International | MPS |
| CDI | Randstad |
| Diversified Search | Robert Half |
| Express Personnel | TAC Worldwide |
| Keane | Vedior |
| Kelly Services | Volt Information |
| Kforce | WJM Associates |

## HISTORICAL FINANCIALS

Company Type: Public

**Income Statement** FYE: Last Friday in December

| | REVENUE ($ mil.) | NET INCOME ($ mil.) | NET PROFIT MARGIN | EMPLOYEES |
|---|---|---|---|---|
| **12/06** | 1,933 | 55 | 2.8% | 273,000 |
| **12/05** | 1,972 | 12 | 0.6% | 302,000 |
| **12/04** | 2,033 | 36 | 1.8% | 285,000 |
| **12/03** | 2,070 | (14) | — | 297,000 |
| **12/02** | 2,116 | (903) | — | 310,000 |
| **Annual Growth** | (2.2%) | — | — | (3.1%) |

**2006 Year-End Financials**

| | |
|---|---|
| Debt ratio: 0.5% | No. of shares (mil.): 57 |
| Return on equity: 12.0% | Dividends |
| Cash ($ mil.): 55 | Yield: — |
| Current ratio: 2.19 | Payout: — |
| Long-term debt ($ mil.): 2 | Market value ($ mil.): 420 |

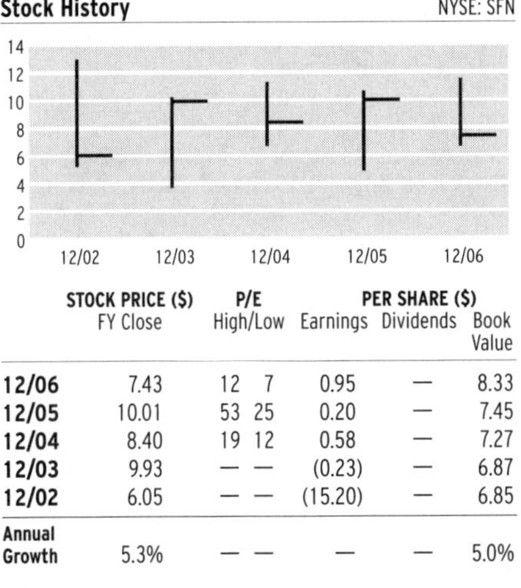

**Stock History** NYSE: SFN



| | STOCK PRICE ($) FY Close | P/E High/Low | | PER SHARE ($) Earnings | Dividends | Book Value |
|---|---|---|---|---|---|---|
| **12/06** | 7.43 | 12 | 7 | 0.95 | — | 8.33 |
| **12/05** | 10.01 | 53 | 25 | 0.20 | — | 7.45 |
| **12/04** | 8.40 | 19 | 12 | 0.58 | — | 7.27 |
| **12/03** | 9.93 | — | — | (0.23) | — | 6.87 |
| **12/02** | 6.05 | — | — | (15.20) | — | 6.85 |
| **Annual Growth** | 5.3% | — | — | — | — | 5.0% |

# Sprint Nextel

Running to keep up with an always-changing telecom race, Sprint Nextel combines the best of two powerhouse wireless companies. The combination of #3 US wireless carrier Sprint with #5 Nextel Communications has created a wireless giant that aspires to take on the wireless units of bounding former Baby Bells Verizon (and Verizon Wireless) and AT&T Inc. (and AT&T Mobility, formerly Cingular). Sprint Nextel operates a nationwide digital wireless network with about 53 million subscribers. The #1 non-Bell local phone company in the US, Sprint Nextel has spun off its local wireline operations, known as Embarq, to focus on the future of wireless — wireless broadband.

Sprint Nextel, created in 2005 in a cash and stock deal valued at $35 billion, puts the wireless carrier behind only AT&T Mobility and Verizon Wireless in number of subscribers.

One consequence of the merger has been battles Sprint Nextel has fought with its Sprint affiliates, primarily Nextel Partners, which exercised a right to force Sprint to buy out the affiliate, then fought for months over the purchase price. The war ended in late 2005 when Sprint Nextel agreed to purchase Nextel Partners. The stock deal, valued at about $6.5 billion, was completed in mid-2006. Sprint Nextel also has battled affiliate US Unwired, a company that had tried to block the Sprint-Nextel merger, and then agreed to be acquired in a stock deal valued at $1.3 billion. The deal turns 500,000 subscribers of the affiliate to direct subscribers of Sprint and expands the Sprint network into 48 additional markets in nine states. In related deals Sprint Nextel bought affiliate Alamosa Holdings in a deal valued at $3.4 billion and has acquired UbiquiTel for $1.3 billion.

On the heels of the merger of Sprint and Nextel, the company announced it would spend as much as $3 billion over two years to build a wireless network based on WiMAX broadband technology. The emerging WiMAX technology, long championed by Intel, is seen as something of a gamble for the company, which is betting on increasing demand for consumer wireless Internet services.

Sprint Nextel has formed a joint venture — with cable titans including Advance/Newhouse Communications, Comcast, Cox Communications, and Time Warner — that has tested a program to provide cable TV, home phone, and wireless phone services in a single package.

In early 2007 Sprint announced plans to cut approximately 5,000 full-time jobs in the first part of the year.

## HISTORY

In 1899 Jacob Brown and son Cleyson began operating the Brown Telephone Company, one of the first non-Bell phone companies in the western US, in Abilene, Kansas. Cleyson later formed Union Electric (phone equipment, 1905) and Home Telephone and Telegraph (long-distance, 1910). In 1911 he consolidated his company with other Kansas independents as United Telephone, then obtained capital from rival Missouri and Kansas Telephone (later Southwestern Bell), which bought 60% of United's stock.

Cleyson sold his electric utility to finance expansions in telephone services and in 1925 he incorporated United Telephone and Electric. Reorganized as United Utilities after the Depression, United continued to buy local exchanges. A post-WWII order backlog halted United's acquisition activity until 1952 but the company soon began further expansion, becoming the second largest non-Bell phone company in the US before 1960.

During the 1960s United focused on satellites, nuclear power plants, and cable TV, and it bought North Electric (1965), the US's oldest independent phone equipment maker. The company was renamed United Telecommunications in 1972. Meanwhile, Southern Pacific had developed the telegraph system along its railroad tracks into a microwave long-distance network called Southern Pacific Communications (1970) and known as SPRINT (for Southern Pacific Railroad Internal Telecommunications). In 1983 GTE acquired the network and renamed it GTE Sprint Communications. The next year United acquired U.S. Telephone, the Dallas-based reseller of long-distance services and the eighth largest US long-distance company.

A year after the 1984 AT&T Corp. breakup, United bought 50% of GTE Sprint (United bought another 30% in 1989 and the balance in 1992). United and GTE teamed up to combine their long-distance systems — GTE Sprint and US Telecom — to form US Sprint. The new unit began offering long-distance in 1986 and completed a nationwide fiber-optic network the next year (The US was later dropped from the partnership's name, leaving Sprint). It became Sprint Corporation in 1992.

In 1998 Sprint Spectrum, a wireless partnership with several cable firms, was combined with PhillieCo (another cable partnership) and SprintCom (its PCS subsidiary) to form Sprint PCS Group. Selling a 10% stake in the PCS Group to the public, Sprint split its stock into the FON Group (non-wireless operations) and the PCS Group.

In 1999 Sprint and its groups were the objects of a takeover battle between MCI WorldCom (now MCI) and BellSouth. MCI prevailed and agreed to buy them for $115 billion in stock and $14 billion in assumed debt, but the deal was canceled in 2000 because of opposition from regulators.

In 2003 Sprint named BellSouth vice chairman Gary Forsee as its CEO. Sprint has not been immune to the economic despair that has plagued the telecom industry. Its reorganization plans, designed to cut expenses, included deep job cuts — it eliminated more than 20,000 jobs in two years. Sprint FON in early 2003 completed the sale of its directory-publishing unit to R. H. Donnelley for $2.1 billion in a move to pay down its $21 billion debt. Combating dwindling demand for business, Sprint cut 22,000 jobs in 2003-04. Sprint also sold much of the assets of its Paranet computer network services unit to Texas-based technology consulting firm Vivare.

Sprint Nextel in 2005 began leasing its cell phone tower business to Global Signal in a deal valued at $1.2 billion. The deal allowed Global Signal to lease or operate more than 6,600 towers for 32 years and gave Global Signal the option to purchase the towers at the end of the lease.

Chairman William Kennard resigned in 2007 from the post he had held since the merger.

## EXECUTIVES

**Chairman, President, and CEO:** Gary D. Forsee, age 57
**CFO:** Paul N. Saleh, age 50
**SVP, Mobile Broadband Operations:** Atish Gude
**SVP, Corporate Communications:** Bill White
**SVP, Government Affairs and Chief Regulatory Officer:** Robert S. (Bob) Foosaner
**SVP, Product Development:** Oliver M. Valente
**SVP, Human Resources:** Sandra J. (Sandy) Price
**SVP and Controller:** William G. Arendt, age 49
**SVP, Product Management and Development:** John A. Garcia, age 53
**SVP and Treasurer:** Richard S. Lindahl, age 43
**SVP, Customer Care:** Bryan DiGiorgio
**SVP, Strategy:** Jack Dziak
**VP, Corporate Governance and Ethics, and Corporate Secretary:** Chris A. Hill
**VP, Investor Relations:** Kurt Fawkes
**Chief Marketing Officer:** Timothy E. (Tim) Kelly, age 48
**Chief Network Officer:** Kathryn A. (Kathy) Walker, age 47
**Chief Service Officer, Customer Management:** Steve Nielsen
**CIO:** Richard T. C. (Dick) LeFave, age 55
**General Counsel:** Leonard J. (Len) Kennedy, age 55
**Director, Corporate Communications:** Kelly Campana
**President, 4G Mobile Broadband and CTO:** Barry J. West, age 61
**President, Sales and Distribution:** Mark E. Angelino, age 50
**Auditors:** KPMG LLP

## LOCATIONS

**HQ:** Sprint Nextel Corporation
2001 Edmund Halley Dr., Reston, VA 20191
**Phone:** 703-433-4000
**Web:** www.sprint.com

## PRODUCTS/OPERATIONS

**2006 Sales**

| | % of total |
|---|---|
| Wireless | |
| Services | 76 |
| Equipment | 8 |
| Long distance | |
| Voice | 10 |
| Data | 4 |
| Internet | 2 |
| **Total** | **100** |

**Selected Services**

Wireless PCS operations

Long-distance
- Domestic and international long-distance
- Fixed-wireless Internet (Sprint Broadband Direct)
- Internet transport (backbone) carrier (SprintLink)
- Telecommunications investments and ventures

Local
- Competitive local-exchange carrier
- Consumer long-distance within local franchise territories
- Telecommunications equipment sales

**Selected Subsidiaries and Affiliates**

EarthLink, Inc. (1%, Internet access)
UbiquiTel Inc.
Virgin Mobile USA, LLC (49%, mobile virtual network operator joint venture with Virgin Mobile Telecoms)

## COMPETITORS

ALLTEL
AT&T
AT&T Mobility
BellSouth
Cellco
CenturyTel
Cincinnati Bell
Level 3 Communications
Qwest
T-Mobile USA
Verizon

## HISTORICAL FINANCIALS

Company Type: Public

**Income Statement** — FYE: December 31

| | REVENUE ($ mil.) | NET INCOME ($ mil.) | NET PROFIT MARGIN | EMPLOYEES |
|---|---|---|---|---|
| 12/06 | 41,028 | 1,329 | 3.2% | 103,483 |
| 12/05 | 34,680 | 1,785 | 5.1% | 79,900 |
| 12/04 | 27,428 | (1,012) | — | 59,900 |
| 12/03 | 26,197 | 1,290 | 4.9% | 66,900 |
| 12/02 | 26,634 | 630 | 2.4% | 72,200 |
| Annual Growth | 11.4% | 20.5% | — | 9.4% |

**2006 Year-End Financials**

Debt ratio: 39.5%
Return on equity: 2.5%
Cash ($ mil.): 2,061
Current ratio: 1.05
Long-term debt ($ mil.): 21,011
No. of shares (mil.): 2,897
Dividends
Yield: 0.5%
Payout: 22.2%
Market value ($ mil.): 54,724

**Stock History** — NYSE: S

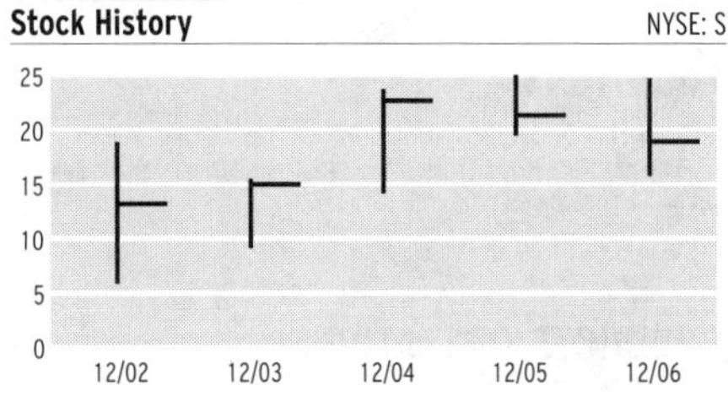


| | STOCK PRICE ($) FY Close | P/E High | P/E Low | PER SHARE ($) Earnings | Dividends | Book Value |
|---|---|---|---|---|---|---|
| 12/06 | 18.89 | 54 | 35 | 0.45 | 0.10 | 18.34 |
| 12/05 | 21.30 | 28 | 23 | 0.87 | 0.30 | 18.22 |
| 12/04 | 22.65 | — | — | (0.71) | 0.50 | — |
| 12/03 | 14.97 | 37 | 23 | 0.41 | 0.50 | — |
| 12/02 | 13.20 | — | — | (0.58) | 0.50 | — |
| Annual Growth | 9.4% | — | — | — | (33.1%) | 0.6% |

# SPX Corporation

SPX likes to mix things up. The company's segments include industrial products (compactors, power systems, broadcast antenna systems, and aerospace components), flow technology (pumps, valves, and other fluid handling devices), service systems (automotive diagnostic gear), and cooling technologies (cooling towers and services). Its portfolio also includes large power transformers and test instrumentation. SPX makes electrical fittings and industrial lighting products through a joint venture with Emerson Electric called EGS Electrical Group, of which it owns 44.5%.

SPX typically looks to buy what it terms "bolt-on" businesses that easily mesh into existing operations. In 2003 the company acquired more than a dozen companies for close to $300 million. The company bought McLeod Russel Holdings (now SPX Air Treatment Holdings), a UK-based maker of filtration products complementary to those of SPX's air treatment business. Its Kendro Laboratory Products business acquired Germany-based H+P Labortechnik (steam sterilizers and magnetic stirrers for the life and materials sciences markets) and UK-based Medical Air Technology (microbiological safety cabinets and ultraclean air environments for the life sciences and hospital markets).

SPX acquired Bill-Jay Machine Tool (rotor head components for helicopters) to augment its Fenn Technologies aerospace components business. It also acquired the assets of Actron Manufacturing, a maker of automotive test equipment and instruments.

In late 2006 the company acquired AB Custos, a Swedish manufacturer of pumps for industrial and marine markets and aerator filters and regulators for the HVAC heating and plumbing market. It paid about $184 million.

SPX has also divested a number of its holdings. The company has sold its Germany-based BOMAG compaction equipment business to privately held Fayat for $446 million. SPX sold its Edwards Systems Technology unit (fire detection and building safety systems) to GE for close to $1.4 billion. SPX sold its Kendro Laboratory Products unit to Thermo Electron (now Thermo Fisher Scientific) in 2005.

The company has sold its Contech automotive components business to Marathon Automotive Group for about $146 million in cash. SPX saw the business as no longer strategic to its long-term interests. Marathon Automotive Group is an entity formed by a private equity firm, Marathon Asset Management. SPX will use most of the proceeds from the sale to buy back its own stock.

AXA Financial owns nearly 15% of SPX. FMR (Fidelity Investments) holds about 13% of the company. Hotchkis and Wiley Capital Management has an equity stake of nearly 11%. Goldman Sachs Asset Management owns more than 7% of SPX.

## HISTORY

Paul Beardsley and Charles Johnson founded SPX in 1911 as The Piston Ring Company. The company, which had its start making piston rings for major automakers, expanded through a series of acquisitions. In 1931 it changed its name to Sealed Power to reflect the increasing diversity of its products. Expansion continued after WWII, and the company went public in 1955. By 1959 Sealed Power made half of its sales from replacement parts.

Following further diversification and international growth in the 1960s and 1970s, the company moved its stock listing to the New York Stock Exchange in 1972 and changed its name to SPX Corporation in 1988.

SPX ran into trouble in the early 1990s when a US recession resulted in losses. The company restructured, however, and by the time the auto industry rebounded in 1994, it was focused on specialty service tools and components.

Flat sales and losses in 1995-96 prompted the ouster of Dale Johnson (CEO from 1991 to 1995). He was replaced by GE veteran John Blystone, who set about streamlining the business, selling inefficient units and beefing up profitable lines. In 1997 SPX sold the Sealed Power division (its original business) for $223 million and acquired A. R. Brasch Marketing (owner's manuals and technical service and training materials).

SPX made a bold hostile takeover bid for much-larger auto parts maker Echlin in 1998, prompting rival Dana to step in and buy Echlin. Also that year the company paid $2.3 billion for General Signal, a company nearly twice its size that provided SPX the opportunity to lower its exposure to the auto parts industry and expand its offerings. SPX later announced it would cut 1,000 jobs and close about two dozen factories and warehouses it had picked up in the deal. Other buys that year included Tecnotest, Toledo Trans-Kit, and Valley Forge Group. SPX also received EGS Electrical Group's Dual-Lite and Signaling businesses in partial recision of a 1997 joint venture.

In 2000 SPX's Inrange Technologies subsidiary picked up Varcom Corporation (network management hardware, software, and services) and Computerm Corporation (channel extension products); and the DeZurik unit acquired Copes-Vulcan's US and UK assets (control valves and turbine bypass systems).

In 2001 SPX acquired United Dominion Industries Limited (flow technology, machinery, specialty engineered products, and test instrumentation) in a deal valued at $1.83 billion, including the assumption of $876 million in United Dominion debt. In August of that year, SPX announced plans to close 49 facilities and cut 2,000 jobs (about 7% of its workforce) by 2003. SPX acquired Daniel Valve Company from Emerson Electric in early 2002. Later in the year the company acquired Balcke Cooling Products, a unit of financially troubled German engineering group Babcock Borsig AG, and Vance International, a US-based security firm.

Following the security trend, SPX acquired the US-based IDenticard Systems in early 2003. SPX sold Inrange Technologies to Computer Network Technology (CNT) in 2003 for $190 million. The following year SPX acquired the Kline Towers division (broadcast tower design, engineering, and construction) of Kline Iron & Steel.

Late in 2004 chairman and CEO Blystone abruptly resigned. The company separated the board and officer positions, naming director Charles Johnson as chairman, and VP Christopher Kearney as president and CEO.

Johnson retired from the board at the annual meeting in 2007. The board designated Kearney to succeed him as chairman, reuniting the top board and management posts. The board named J. Kermit Campbell, an SPX director since 1993, as lead director for a two-year term. Campbell is a former CEO of Herman Miller.

## EXECUTIVES

**President, CEO, and Director:** Christopher J. Kearney, age 51, $950,000 pay
**EVP, CFO, and Treasurer:** Patrick J. O'Leary, age 49, $777,000 pay
**EVP, Human Resources and Asia Pacific:** Robert B. Foreman, age 49, $575,000 pay
**VP, Operations:** Jim Peters, age 51
**VP, Secretary, and General Counsel:** Kevin L. Lilly, age 54
**VP, Finance:** Jeremy Smeltser
**VP and Chief Marketing Officer:** Sharon K. Jenkins, age 48
**VP, Corporate Controller and Chief Accounting Officer:** Michael A. Reilly
**President, Cooling Technologies:** Drew T. Ladau
**President, Test and Measurement:** David A. (Dave) Kowalski, age 48, $386,034 pay
**President, Flow Technology:** Don L. Canterna, age 56, $386,034 pay
**Director, Corporate Communications:** Tina Betlejewski
**Auditors:** Deloitte & Touche LLP

## LOCATIONS

**HQ:** SPX Corporation
13515 Ballantyne Corporate Place,
Charlotte, NC 28277
**Phone:** 704-752-4400 **Fax:** 704-752-4505
**Web:** www.spx.com

SPX has operations in more than 20 countries in Asia, Europe, and the Americas.

### 2006 Sales

| | $ mil. | % of total |
|---|---|---|
| US | 2,604.3 | 60 |
| Germany | 624.2 | 14 |
| UK | 243.4 | 6 |
| Other countries | 841.4 | 20 |
| **Total** | **4,313.3** | **100** |

## PRODUCTS/OPERATIONS

### 2006 Sales

| | $ mil. | % of total |
|---|---|---|
| Thermal equipment & services | 1,378.9 | 32 |
| Test & measurement | 1,137.5 | 27 |
| Flow technology | 960.2 | 22 |
| Industrial products & services | | |
| Power transformers & services | 290.6 | 7 |
| Industrial tools & equipment | 142.4 | 3 |
| Broadcast antenna systems | 116.7 | 3 |
| Aerospace components | 102.2 | 2 |
| Automotive components | 95.8 | 2 |
| Laboratory equipment | 89.0 | 2 |
| **Total** | **4,313.3** | **100** |

### Selected Products

Industrial products and services
- Power systems
- Compaction equipment
- Specialty engineered products
  - AC/DC power units
  - Air curtains and circulators
  - Air motors
  - Automotive steering, suspension, axle, and powertrain components
  - Cables
  - Clamping components
  - Clutch packs and plates
  - Coolers
  - Commercial cabinet and infrared heaters
  - Heaters (baseboard, portable, and wall unit)
  - Lubricants
  - Pistons
  - Pumps
  - Rotor head components for helicopters
  - Thermostats and controls

Technical products and systems
- Broadcast and communication systems and services
  - Antennas
  - Broadcast tower design, engineering, and construction
  - Cable and pipe locators
  - Field tower construction and service
  - Filter systems
  - Horizontal boring guidance systems
  - Inspection cameras
  - Transmission lines
- Electrical test and measurement solutions
  - Automated fare collection systems for bus and rail transit
  - Data acquisition systems for materials testing and electrical switching
  - Vibration test and analysis equipment

Flow technology
- Analyzing equipment
- Backflow prevention assemblies
- Boilers
- Compressed air and gas dryers
- Cooling towers
- Dispersion equipment
- Filtration products, accessories, and replacement parts
- Heat exchangers
- Industrial mixers
- Leak detection equipment
- Pumps and other fluid handling machines
- Separators and strainers
- Valves (butterfly, eccentric plug, globe, knife gate, ported gate, rotary control)

Service solutions
- Automotive test equipment and instrumentation
- Diagnostic systems and service equipment
- Specialty service tools
- Technical information and other services (content management, technical documentation, training)

Cooling technologies and services
- Air-cooled condensers
- Cooling tower reconstruction services
- Cooling towers

## COMPETITORS

ABB
Alfa Laval
American Power Conversion
AMETEK
Andrew Corporation
Baltimore Aircoil
BorgWarner
Champion Parts
Cubic Transportation
Dana
Danaher
Dresser
Eaton
Emerson Electric
Endress + Hauser
Evapco
Federal-Mogul
Franklin Electric
GE Infrastructure
GEA Group
Glen Dimplex
Harris Corp.
Hickok
Honeywell International
Ingersoll-Rand
Interpump
ITT Corp.
Johnson Controls
Leybold
MGE UPS
Parker Hannifin
Robbins & Myers
Robert Bosch LLC
Roper Industries
SANYO
Snap-on
Trippe Manufacturing
United Technologies

## HISTORICAL FINANCIALS

Company Type: Public

### Income Statement

FYE: December 31

| | REVENUE ($ mil.) | NET INCOME ($ mil.) | NET PROFIT MARGIN | EMPLOYEES |
|---|---|---|---|---|
| **12/06** | 4,313 | 171 | 4.0% | 14,300 |
| **12/05** | 4,292 | 1,090 | 25.4% | 18,300 |
| **12/04** | 4,372 | (17) | — | 23,800 |
| **12/03** | 5,082 | 236 | 4.6% | 22,200 |
| **12/02** | 4,822 | 127 | 2.6% | 24,200 |
| **Annual Growth** | (2.8%) | 7.6% | — | (12.3%) |

### 2006 Year-End Financials

Debt ratio: 35.7%
Return on equity: 8.1%
Cash ($ mil.): 477
Current ratio: 1.43
Long-term debt ($ mil.): 754
No. of shares (mil.): 60
Dividends
Yield: 1.6%
Payout: 35.3%
Market value ($ mil.): 3,652

### Stock History

NYSE: SPW

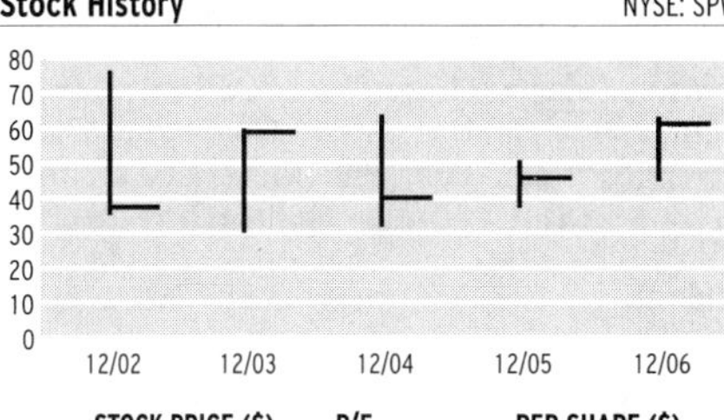


| | STOCK PRICE ($) FY Close | P/E High | P/E Low | PER SHARE ($) Earnings | PER SHARE ($) Dividends | PER SHARE ($) Book Value |
|---|---|---|---|---|---|---|
| **12/06** | 61.16 | 22 | 16 | 2.83 | 1.00 | 35.33 |
| **12/05** | 45.77 | 3 | 2 | 15.33 | 1.00 | 35.37 |
| **12/04** | 40.06 | — | — | (0.23) | 1.00 | 28.66 |
| **12/03** | 58.81 | 19 | 10 | 3.04 | — | 27.40 |
| **12/02** | 37.45 | 49 | 23 | 1.54 | — | 22.09 |
| **Annual Growth** | 13.0% | — | — | 16.4% | 0.0% | 12.5% |

# The Stanley Works

The Stanley Works wants you to have tools that neighbors envy. As the leading toolmaker in the US, the company markets hand tools (carpentry, garden, and masonry tools), mechanics' tools (industrial hand tools, electronic diagnostic tools, toolboxes, wrenches), pneumatic tools, and hydraulic tools, as well as security hardware and a variety of door products. In addition to the Stanley brand, the firm's well-known trademarks include Bostitch, Husky, Monarch, and Mac Tools. Stanley sells its products through home centers and mass merchant distribution channels, as well as through third-party distributors. It bought National Manufacturing for $170 million and European tool maker Facom for more than $485 million.

Stanley operates manufacturing and distribution facilities in the US and 13 other countries, with international sales accounting for 40% of revenues. To boost that percentage even more, Stanley announced in late 2005 its aim to acquire industrial tools and security solutions companies located outside North America. To that end, in mid-2006 the toolmaker purchased a majority stake in Taiwan-based Besco Pneumatic Corp., a maker of pneumatic tools.

Besides supplying the traditional outlets that serve the do-it-yourselfer (Home Depot accounts for about 10% of sales), Stanley also is looking to saw off a bigger chunk from the larger professional market, where price is not the main concern. In line with that strategy, the company has locked onto the security segment, having already bought Best Lock Corporation (now part of Stanley Security Solutions Inc.), Frisco Bay Industries, and Security Group, which makes locks and locking systems.

To maintain its acquisition momentum in the security sector, Stanley inked a deal in December 2006 to purchase HSM Electronic Protection Services, Inc., for about $545 million in cash.

HSM, which offers commercial customers security alarm monitoring services and access control systems, is a top electronic security firm and commercial monitoring company in North America. The deal, which closed in early 2007, expands an already growing division for Stanley.

Its security solutions unit accounts for about a quarter of Stanley's sales. This unit makes and markets electronic and mechanical security items and integration software, and also provides installation and support services. Key security brands in this segment include Best Access, Blick, Frisco Bay, PAC, Sargent and Greenleaf, and others.

## HISTORY

In 1843 Frederick Stanley opened a bolt shop in a converted early-19th-century armory in New Britain, Connecticut. In 1852 he teamed with his brother and five friends to form The Stanley Works to cast, form, and manufacture various types of metal.

The business prospered during the 1860s when the Civil War and westward migration created a need for hardware and tools. When Stanley turned his attention to political and civic affairs, company management fell to William Hart. He engaged in a "knuckles-bared" fight with four bigger competitors (Stanley was the sole survivor) and led the firm into steel strapping production, which would become a major element in the company's operations. Hart was named president in 1884.

During WWI, the company produced belt buckles and rifle and gas mask parts. Along with making numerous domestic acquisitions, it established operations in Canada (1914) and Germany (1926). In 1920 the company merged with Stanley Rule and Level (a local tool company formed in 1857 by a cousin of Frederick Stanley), and in 1925 it opened a new hydroelectric plant near Windsor, Connecticut, to provide power for all its operations.

Stanley struggled through the Depression, but following WWII, the toolmaker embarked on four decades of expansion. Staying within its traditional product line, Stanley acquired a myriad of companies, including Berry Industries (garage doors, 1965), Ackley Manufacturing and Sales (hydraulic tools, 1972), Mac Tools (1980), and National Hand Tool (1986). The company grew globally in the late 1980s by establishing high-tech plants in Europe and the Far East.

After twice fending off takeover attempts by rival Newell (now Newell Rubbermaid) in the early 1990s, Stanley returned to acquisitions. In 1992 it acquired LaBounty Manufacturing (large hydraulic tools), American Brush (paintbrushes and decorator tools), Mail Media (Jensen Tools precision tool kits and Direct Safety safety equipment), Goldblatt Tool (masonry and dry-wall tools), and a controlling interest in Tona a.s. Pecky, a major Czech maker of mechanics' tools. The following year the company sold its Taylor Rental subsidiary, the largest system of general rental centers in the US, to SERVISTAR.

When weak sales hit Stanley's primary markets in mid-1995, the company responded with a massive restructuring program, including $150 million in expense cuts. In 1997 Stanley sold its garage-related products unit to radar-detector manufacturer Whistler. That year, continuing its corporate overhaul, Stanley announced that it would cut 4,500 jobs — almost a quarter of its workforce. While continuing to close plants in 1999, Stanley settled charges with the FTC for selling Made-in-USA tools that had foreign components. In 2001 Stanley acquired electrical tools distributor Contact East while still undergoing restructuring.

In 2002 the Stanley board voted to change its incorporation to Bermuda, which would decrease the company's tax bill, but Stanley withdrew the plan later that same year. Also that year Stanley acquired Best Lock Corporation. The company's restructuring resulted in the closing of about 90 facilities, with about 4,000 job cuts, by December 2002. In 2003 the company cut another 1,000 jobs and discontinued MacDirect, the Mac Tools retail channel.

In 2004 Stanley acquired Blick, Cal-Dor Specialties, CST/Berger (which makes laser and optical leveling and measuring equipment), Frisco Bay Industries, and electronic-security integrator ISR Solutions. The same year John Lundgren, a former executive with Georgia-Pacific, became chairman and CEO. Also in 2004 Stanley sold its residential entry-door business to Masonite International and its Home Decor division to Wellspring Capital Management.

In January 2006 the company acquired France's Facom, a leading European maker of hand and mechanics tools, for about $486 million. That July Stanley purchased a 67% stake in Besco Pneumatic Corp., a Taiwan-based maker of pneumatic tools. Stanley has the option to acquire an additional 15% stake in the company over the next five years.

## EXECUTIVES

**Chairman and CEO:** John F. Lundgren, age 55, $833,333 pay
**EVP and CFO:** James M. (Jim) Loree, age 49, $555,000 pay
**SVP; President, Industrial Tools Group and Emerging Markets:** Donald R. (Don) McIlnay, age 57, $401,250 pay (prior to title change)
**SVP Business Transformation:** Hubert W. Davis Jr., age 58, $340,000 pay (prior to promotion)
**VP and Corporate Controller:** Donald (Don) Allan Jr., age 42
**VP; President, Stanley Consumer Tools Group:** Jeffery D. (Jeff) Ansell, age 39
**VP, General Counsel, and Secretary:** Bruce H. Beatt, age 55
**VP Global Operations; President, Asia Operations:** Jeff Chen, age 48
**VP Human Resources:** Mark J. Mathieu, age 55
**VP Investor Relations:** Gerard J. (Gerry) Gould
**VP; President, Mechanical Access Systems:** Justin C. Boswell, age 39
**President, Stanley Tools — Europe:** Thierry Paternot, age 59, $628,400 pay
**President, National Manufacturing Co.:** Keith W. Benson III
**President, Stanley Fastening Systems:** Denise Nemchev
**President, Zag Industries; VP, Stanley Hardware:** Seffi Janowski
**Internet Marketing Manager:** David Morgan
**Auditors:** Ernst & Young LLP

## LOCATIONS

**HQ:** The Stanley Works
1000 Stanley Dr., New Britain, CT 06053
**Phone:** 860-225-5111 **Fax:** 860-827-3895
**Web:** www.stanleyworks.com

### 2006 Sales

| | $ mil. | % of total |
|---|---|---|
| Americas | | |
| US | 2,398.5 | 60 |
| Other countries | 357.5 | 9 |
| France | 465.4 | 11 |
| Other Europe | 599.9 | 15 |
| Asia | 197.3 | 5 |
| **Total** | **4,018.6** | **100** |

## PRODUCTS/OPERATIONS

### 2006 Sales

| | $ mil. | % of total |
|---|---|---|
| Industrial tools | 1,802.9 | 45 |
| Consumer products | 1,328.5 | 33 |
| Security solutions | 887.2 | 22 |
| **Total** | **4,018.6** | **100** |

### Selected Brand Names

AccuScape
Acme
Atro
Blackhawk
Bostitch
Contractor Grade
Facom
FatMax
Goldblatt
Husky
IntelliTools
Jensen
LaBounty
Mac Tools
Magic-Door
Monarch
Powerlock
Proto
Stanley
Stanley-Acmetrack
Vidmar
Virax
ZAG

### Selected Products

Tools
- Hand tools
  - Alignment tools
  - Boring tools
  - Chisels
  - Electronic stud sensors
  - Elevation measuring systems
  - Garden tools
  - Hammers
  - Knives and blades
  - Levels
  - Masonry, tile, and drywall tools
  - Measuring instruments
  - Planes
  - Saws
  - Screwdrivers
- Hydraulic tools
  - Handheld hydraulic tools
  - Mounted demolition hammers and compactors
- Mechanics' tools
  - Consumer, industrial, and mechanics' hand tools
  - Electronic diagnostic tools
  - High-density industrial storage and retrieval systems
  - Sockets
  - Toolboxes
  - Wrenches
- Pneumatic tools
  - Fastening tools and fasteners (nails and staples)

Door products
- Door hardware
  - Bolts
  - Hasps
  - Hinges
  - Latches
  - Shelf brackets
- Doors
  - Automatic doors
  - Closet doors
  - Commercial doors
  - Mirrored closet doors
  - Vinyl patio doors

## COMPETITORS

American Safety Razor
Andersen Corporation
Black & Decker
Bosch
Cooper Industries
Danaher
Emerson Electric
Fortune Brands
GE Security
Illinois Tool Works
Ingersoll-Rand
Jacuzzi Brands
Klein Tools
Kwikset Corporation
Makita
Masco
Masonite International
Napco Security
Robert Bosch
Sandvik
Snap-on
White Cap

## HISTORICAL FINANCIALS

Company Type: Public

**Income Statement** FYE: Saturday nearest December 31

| | REVENUE ($ mil.) | NET INCOME ($ mil.) | NET PROFIT MARGIN | EMPLOYEES |
|---|---|---|---|---|
| **12/06** | 4,019 | 290 | 7.2% | 17,600 |
| **12/05** | 3,285 | 270 | 8.2% | 15,800 |
| **12/04** | 3,043 | 367 | 12.1% | 14,100 |
| **12/03** | 2,678 | 108 | 4.0% | 13,500 |
| **12/02** | 2,593 | 185 | 7.1% | 14,900 |
| **Annual Growth** | 11.6% | 11.8% | — | 4.3% |

**2006 Year-End Financials**

Debt ratio: 43.8%
Return on equity: 19.3%
Cash ($ mil.): 177
Current ratio: 1.31
Long-term debt ($ mil.): 679
No. of shares (mil.): 82
Dividends
Yield: 2.3%
Payout: 34.1%
Market value ($ mil.): 4,116

**Stock History** NYSE: SWK

| | STOCK PRICE ($) FY Close | P/E High | P/E Low | PER SHARE ($) Earnings | PER SHARE ($) Dividends | PER SHARE ($) Book Value |
|---|---|---|---|---|---|---|
| **12/06** | 50.29 | 16 | 12 | 3.46 | 1.18 | 18.96 |
| **12/05** | 48.04 | 16 | 13 | 3.16 | 1.14 | 17.24 |
| **12/04** | 48.99 | 11 | 8 | 4.36 | 1.08 | 14.82 |
| **12/03** | 37.05 | 30 | 16 | 1.27 | 1.03 | 10.56 |
| **12/02** | 34.63 | 25 | 13 | 2.10 | 0.99 | 11.33 |
| **Annual Growth** | 9.8% | — | — | 13.3% | 4.5% | 13.7% |

# Staples, Inc.

Staples is clipping along as the #1 office supply superstore operator in the US. It sells office products, furniture, computers, and other supplies through its chain of about 1,900 Staples and Staples Express stores in the US and Canada and some 20 other countries. (About 1,620 of its superstores are located in North America.) In addition to its retail outlets, Staples sells office products through the Internet and through its catalog and direct sales operations, including subsidiary Quill Corporation. Staples also provides document management and copying services through its retail chain, as well as promotional products. The firm targets small businesses and home office professionals, as well as consumers.

Staples' North American retail operation, which accounts for more than half the company's revenue, continues to expand at a rapid pace, adding almost 200 new stores to its portfolio in recent years. Some of those stores were smaller in size than Staples' traditional warehouse locations and designed to target urban and other niche markets. The company is also expanding the number of Staples-branded products in its stores.

It's expanding its mix of products, as well, to target a more upscale customer. In mid-2007 Staples partnered with Donald Trump to roll out the Trump Office collection of five executive chairs.

The company is also expanding its four-year-old electronics waste recycling program to cover used computers and monitors. Some 1,400 US stores now accept used computer hardware for a $10 fee. (There's no charge for recycling smaller devices, such as cell phones and digital cameras.)

To offer its customers promotional products, Staples in May 2007 acquired American Identity from Republic Financial Corporation. The deal gives Staples a foothold into the profitable corporate-branded merchandise niche and strengthens the company's contract division.

A large part of the company's growth, though, has come from its catalog and direct sales business, which now accounts for almost a third of its revenue. It plans to continue its investments in infrastructure upgrades to help its delivery business become more efficient.

Internationally, Staples is focused on expanding its operations in Europe, where it already has more than 260 retail locations, and entering emerging markets, such as India and China. The company gained its foothold on the continent through a series of acquisitions in 2004, and it is now looking at organic growth through expansion. In early 2007 the American office supply chain formed a joint venture with India's largest retailer Pantaloon to bring office supply warehouse stores to India. In China Staples has established a branch of its delivery business.

The company is facing a potentially expensive class-action lawsuit in California brought by store managers seeking overtime pay dating back to 1995.

## HISTORY

A veteran of the supermarket industry (and the man who developed the idea for generic food), Thomas Stemberg was fired from his executive position with Connecticut supermarket Edwards-Finast in 1985. Stemberg began searching for a niche retail market — he found one in office supplies, which he estimated at $100 billion.

While large companies could buy in bulk from dealers, smaller businesses were served by mom-and-pop office supply stores that charged much higher prices. Applying the supermarket model to office supply, Stemberg founded Staples in late 1985 with Leo Kahn, a former competitor in the supermarket business. With money from Kahn and venture capital firms, Staples opened its first store in a Boston suburb the next year.

In 1987 the retailer moved into the New York City area and continued to expand throughout the Northeast. By early 1989 — the year it went public — it had 23 stores. The company introduced a line of low-priced private-label products in 1989.

Aggressive expansion began the following year when Staples opened three stores in Southern California and introduced two new concepts: Staples Direct (delivery operations for medium-sized businesses) and Staples Express (downtown stores offering smaller merchandise selections). International growth included buying a stake in Canada's Business Depot (1991) and 48% of MAXI-Papier, a European office supply store chain (1992). It also paired up with Kingfisher to establish stores in the UK (Kingfisher sold its interest to Staples in 1996).

Additional acquisitions gave Staples more than 200 stores by the end of 1993. The next year Staples entered Arizona, Virginia, and Kentucky (by acquiring selected Office America stores); acquired the rest of Canada's Business Depot; and began expanding into the contract stationer business. The company agreed to buy Office Depot, its biggest rival, in 1996, but the FTC rejected the $4.3 billion deal on antitrust grounds.

Acquisitions included the privately held Quill (to expand its direct-sales business, 1998) and Claricom Holdings (telecommunications services to small businesses, renamed Staples Communications, 1999; sold, 2001). In addition, the company continued its international expansion that year, introducing its Quill catalog business in the UK and buying three European office supply companies (which added about 40 stores, extending the company's presence in Germany and moving it into the Netherlands and Portugal).

In early 2001 the company shelved plans to take its Staples.com stock public, saying it would convert Staples.com to its own stock. Also that year it merged its catalog and Staples.com operations into Staples Business Delivery. During 2002 Staples acquired Medical Arts Press (specialized medical software and forms to medical providers) and the mail-order business of Guilbert, a subsidiary of French retailer Pinault-Printemps-Redoute; the $815 million Guilbert deal provided entrée for Staples in France, Italy, Spain, and Belgium. (Office Depot bought Guilbert's retail operation the following year.) Company veteran Ron Sargent took over as CEO that same year.

The company continued to expand its international operations through acquisitions in 2004, buying Globus Office World (UK), Pressel Versand International (Austria), and Malling Beck (Denmark). Staples also expanded into China that year through a joint venture with Chinese office supply company OA365. CEO Sargent took on the added title of chairman when Stemberg resigned in 2005.

## EXECUTIVES

**Chairman and CEO:** Ronald L. (Ron) Sargent, age 51, $1,070,192 pay
**Vice Chairman and CFO:** John J. Mahoney, age 55, $650,435 pay
**President and COO:** Michael A. (Mike) Miles Jr., age 45, $650,529 pay
**EVP and CIO:** Brian T. Light, age 43
**EVP, General Counsel, and Secretary:** Jack A. VanWoerkom, age 53
**EVP Human Resources:** Susan S. Hoyt, age 62
**EVP Marketing:** Shira D. Goodman, age 46
**EVP Merchandising and Supply Chain:** David N. (Dave) Perron
**EVP Contract:** Jay G. Baitler, age 60
**EVP Merchandising:** Jevin S. Eagle, age 36
**SVP and Controller:** Christine T. Komola, age 39
**SVP and General Counsel:** Kristin A. Campbell
**SVP Advertising:** Carole E. Johnson
**SVP Business Services:** John F. Burke
**SVP Customer Marketing:** Donald LeBlanc
**SVP Engineering, Construction, Facilities and Support Services:** John M. Lynch
**SVP Finance and Treasurer:** Nicholas P. (Nick) Hotchkin
**SVP Sales and Operations:** Michael DeSanto Jr.
**SVP Strategy:** John M. Sallay
**VP Public Relations:** Paul Capelli
**President, Quill Corporation:** Lawrence J. (Larry) Morse
**President, Staples North American Delivery:** Joseph G. (Joe) Doody, age 54, $504,333 pay
**President, US Retail:** Demos Parneros, age 44, $500,379 pay
**Director of Investor Relations:** Laurel Lefebvre
**Auditors:** Ernst & Young LLP

## LOCATIONS

**HQ:** Staples, Inc.
500 Staples Dr., Framingham, MA 01702
**Phone:** 508-253-5000 **Fax:** 508-253-8989
**Web:** www.staples.com

Staples operates superstores in Belgium, Canada, Germany, Portugal, the Netherlands, the UK, and the US. It has distribution and fulfillment centers in Argentina, Austria, Belgium, Brazil, Canada, China, Denmark, France, Germany, Italy, the Netherlands, Spain, Sweden, the UK, and the US.

**2007 Sales**

| | $ mil. | % of total |
|---|---|---|
| US | 13,514.7 | 74 |
| Canada | 2,287.3 | 13 |
| Other countries | 2,358.8 | 13 |
| **Total** | **18,160.8** | **100** |

**2007 Locations**

| | No. |
|---|---|
| US | |
| California | 189 |
| New York | 117 |
| Pennsylvania | 87 |
| New Jersey | 80 |
| Massachusetts | 69 |
| Florida | 69 |
| Ohio | 57 |
| Illinois | 50 |
| North Carolina | 45 |
| Maryland | 43 |
| Michigan | 43 |
| Connecticut | 39 |
| Virginia | 36 |
| Texas | 36 |
| Georgia | 35 |
| Arizona | 33 |
| Indiana | 31 |
| Washington | 27 |
| New Hampshire | 22 |
| Tennessee | 19 |
| Oregon | 18 |
| Oklahoma | 16 |
| South Carolina | 16 |
| Iowa | 14 |
| Alabama | 12 |
| Maine | 12 |
| Kentucky | 12 |
| Other states | 115 |
| Canada | 278 |
| UK | 137 |
| Germany | 57 |
| The Netherlands | 45 |
| Portugal | 22 |
| Belgium | 3 |
| **Total** | **1,884** |

## PRODUCTS/OPERATIONS

**2007 Sales**

| | $ mil. | % of total |
|---|---|---|
| North American retail | 9,938.9 | 55 |
| North American delivery | 5,863.1 | 32 |
| International | 2,358.8 | 13 |
| **Total** | **18,160.8** | **100** |

## COMPETITORS

Best Buy
BJ's Wholesale Club
CDW
Circuit City
CompUSA
Corporate Express
Corvest
Costco Wholesale
Danka
Dell
DELUXEPINPOINT
Fry's Electronics
HALO
Hewlett-Packard
IKON
Insight Enterprises
Kinko's
Mail Boxes Etc.
Norwood Promotional Products
Office Depot
OfficeMax
RadioShack
Shumsky Enterprises
Signature Marketing
S.P. Richards
Systemax
Unisource
United Stationers
Wal-Mart

## HISTORICAL FINANCIALS

Company Type: Public

**Income Statement** FYE: Saturday nearest January 31

| | REVENUE ($ mil.) | NET INCOME ($ mil.) | NET PROFIT MARGIN | EMPLOYEES |
|---|---|---|---|---|
| **1/07** | 18,161 | 974 | 5.4% | 73,646 |
| **1/06** | 16,079 | 834 | 5.2% | 68,533 |
| **1/05** | 14,448 | 708 | 4.9% | 65,078 |
| **1/04** | 13,181 | 490 | 3.7% | 60,633 |
| **1/03** | 11,596 | 446 | 3.8% | 57,816 |
| **Annual Growth** | 11.9% | 21.5% | — | 6.2% |

**2007 Year-End Financials**

Debt ratio: 6.3%
Return on equity: 20.6%
Cash ($ mil.): 1,475
Current ratio: 1.59
Long-term debt ($ mil.): 316
No. of shares (mil.): 719
Dividends
Yield: 0.8%
Payout: 16.7%
Market value ($ mil.): 19,010

**Stock History** NASDAQ (GS): SPLS

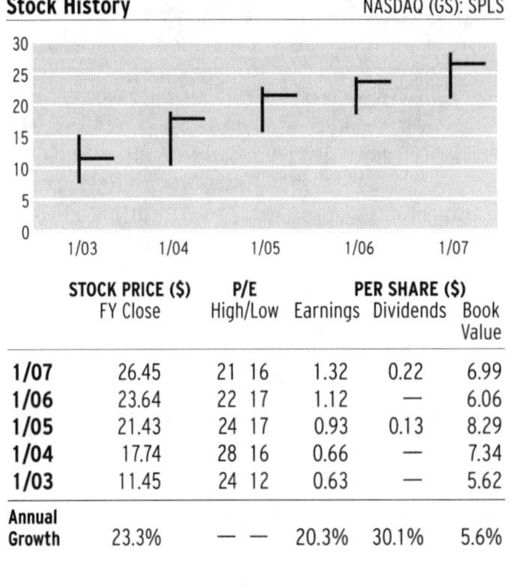


| | STOCK PRICE ($) FY Close | P/E High | P/E Low | PER SHARE ($) Earnings | Dividends | Book Value |
|---|---|---|---|---|---|---|
| **1/07** | 26.45 | 21 | 16 | 1.32 | 0.22 | 6.99 |
| **1/06** | 23.64 | 22 | 17 | 1.12 | — | 6.06 |
| **1/05** | 21.43 | 24 | 17 | 0.93 | 0.13 | 8.29 |
| **1/04** | 17.74 | 28 | 16 | 0.66 | — | 7.34 |
| **1/03** | 11.45 | 24 | 12 | 0.63 | — | 5.62 |
| **Annual Growth** | 23.3% | — | — | 20.3% | 30.1% | 5.6% |

# Starbucks

Wake up and smell the coffee — Starbucks is everywhere. The world's #1 specialty coffee retailer, Starbucks has some 13,000 coffee shops in more than 35 countries. The outlets offer coffee drinks and food items, as well as roasted beans, coffee accessories, and teas. Starbucks owns approximately 7,500 of its shops, which are located in about 10 countries (mostly in the US), while licensees and franchisees operate more than 5,500 units worldwide (primarily in shopping centers and airports). The company also owns the Seattle's Best Coffee and Torrefazione Italia coffee brands. In addition, Starbucks markets its coffee through grocery stores and licenses its brand for other food and beverage products.

What was once a simple chain of coffeehouses has become a force of nature in the retail business. With so many outlets throughout the world, Starbucks has used its chain to branch out into other retail segments; selling CDs, books, and other lifestyle products, accounting for about 5% of revenue. The company also has big plans for the future, setting the goal of expanding its chain to 40,000 locations worldwide. It hopes to open about 2,400 new outlets in 2007.

Starbucks also continues to invest in product development to expand its brand into new customer segments. With beverage maker PepsiCo, it is developing its own vending machines to deliver premium coffees to customers on the go, while it continues to develop and market products for grocery retail through its partnership with Kraft Foods. A licensing deal with Beam Global Spirits & Wine (formerly Jim Beam), meanwhile, has produced a line of Starbucks coffee liqueurs.

At its coffeehouses, the company is rolling out an expanded menu of breakfast items and other hot foods (previously tested at a handful of locations) to more than 6,500 locations by 2008 to increase its revenue from food sales and to entice customers to spend more time at its outlets.

Chairman Howard Schultz owns nearly 5% of the company.

## HISTORY

Starbucks was founded in 1971 in Seattle by coffee aficionados Gordon Bowker, Jerry Baldwin, and Ziv Siegl, who named the company for the coffee-loving first mate in *Moby Dick* and created its famous two-tailed siren logo. They aimed to sell the finest-quality whole bean and ground coffees. By 1982 Starbucks had five retail stores and was selling coffee to restaurants and espresso stands in Seattle. That year Howard Schultz joined Starbucks to manage retail sales and marketing. In 1983 Schultz traveled to Italy and was struck by the popularity of coffee bars. He convinced Starbucks' owners to open a downtown Seattle coffee bar in 1984. It was a success; Schultz left the company the following year to open his own coffee bar, Il Giornale, which served Starbucks coffee.

Frustrated by its inability to control quality, Starbucks sold off its wholesale business in 1987. Later that year Il Giornale acquired Starbucks' retail operations for $4 million. (Starbucks' founders held on to their other coffee business, Peet's Coffee & Tea.) Il Giornale changed its name to Starbucks Corporation, prepared to expand nationally, and opened locations in Chicago and Vancouver. In 1988 the company published its first mail-order catalog.

Starbucks lost money in the late 1980s as it focused on expansion (it tripled its number of stores to 55 between 1987 and 1989). Schultz brought in experienced managers to run Starbucks' stores. In 1991 it became the nation's first privately owned company to offer stock options to all employees.

In 1992 Starbucks went public and set up shops in Nordstrom's department stores. The following year it began operating cafes in Barnes & Noble bookstores. The company had nearly 275 locations by the end of 1993. Starbucks inked a deal in 1994 to provide coffee to ITT/Sheraton hotels (later acquired by Starwood Hotels & Resorts). The next year it capitalized on its popular in-house music selections by selling compact discs. Also in 1995 Starbucks joined with PepsiCo to develop a bottled coffee drink and agreed to produce a line of premium coffee ice cream with Dreyer's.

Starbucks expanded into Japan and Singapore in 1996. In 1997 Starbucks began testing sales of whole-bean and ground coffees in Chicago supermarkets.

In 1998 Starbucks expanded into the UK when it acquired that country's Seattle Coffee Company chain and converted its stores into Starbucks locations. It also announced plans to sell coffee in supermarkets nationwide through an agreement with Kraft Foods. In 1999 Starbucks bought Tazo, an Oregon-based tea company, as well as music retailer Hear Music, and opened its first store in China.

In 2000 Schultz ceded the CEO post to president Orin Smith, remaining chairman but focusing primarily on the company's global strategy. Starbucks jumpstarted its worldwide expansion the next year, opening about 1,100 stores worldwide, including locations in a handful of new European countries such as Austria and Switzerland. It also spun off its Japanese operations as a public company. The following year the company opened its first shop in Spain and went on to open Starbucks locations in Greece and Germany. Later in 2002 it announced large-scale expansion plans in Mexico and Latin America.

The next year Starbucks acquired Seattle Coffee Company (and its Seattle's Best Coffee brand) from AFC Enterprises. The deal gave Starbucks an additional 150 coffee shops (as if it needed them) but more importantly it gave the coffee giant the Seattle's Best Coffee brand and wholesale coffee business. It also got something new out of the deal: franchised locations.

Starbucks was one of the first national retailers to jump on the Wi-Fi bandwagon, teaming with Hewlett-Packard and Deutsche Telekom's T-Mobile unit to offer high-speed wireless Internet access at 1,200 of its locations in the US, London, and Berlin. In 2004 Starbucks and Hewlett-Packard unveiled their Hear Music service, which allows Starbucks customers to create custom music CDs in some locations.

In 2005 in conjunction with Jim Beam Brands (now Beam Global Spirits & Wine) it introduced Starbucks Coffee Liqueur and Starbucks Cream Liqueur. That same year, Starbucks signed agreements with Suntory in Japan and Uni-President in Taiwan to sell its ready-to-drink coffees in those countries. Smith retired as president and CEO that year; he was replaced by Starbucks' North American president Jim Donald.

The company acquired full ownership of joint ventures Coffee Partners Hawaii and Cafe del Caribe (Puerto Rican outlets) in 2006.

## EXECUTIVES

**Chairman:** Howard D. Schultz, age 53, $3,570,000 pay
**President, CEO, and Director:** James L. (Jim) Donald, age 52, $2,978,846 pay
**COO:** Martin Coles, age 51, $1,455,212 pay
**EVP, CFO, and Chief Administrative Officer:** Michael Casey, age 61, $1,257,308 pay
**EVP, General Counsel, and Secretary:** Paula E. Boggs, age 47
**EVP Partner Resources:** David A. (Dave) Pace, age 47, $935,769 pay
**EVP Supply Chain and Coffee Operations:** Dorothy J. Kim, age 44
**EVP and CFO Designate:** Peter J. (Pete) Bocian, age 52
**SVP and Chief Merchant, Global Product:** Michelle Gass
**SVP Coffee and Global Procurement:** Willard (Dub) Hay
**SVP Finance:** Troy Alstead
**SVP Partner Resources, U.S. Business:** Margaret (Margie) Giuntini
**SVP and President, Seattle Coffee Company:** Steven (Steve) Schickler, age 50
**SVP and President, Starbucks Coffee Canada:** Colin Moore
**SVP; President, Starbucks Entertainment:** Kenneth T. (Ken) Lombard
**SVP and President, Global Consumer Products:** Gerardo I. (Gerry) Lopez, age 47
**SVP and President, Starbucks Coffee Latin America:** Buck Hendrix
**SVP; President, Europe, Middle East and Africa:** Cliff Burrows
**SVP and President, Starbucks Coffee Greater China:** Jinlong Wang
**SVP; President, Asia/Pacific:** John Culver
**VP, Corporate Development and Investor Relations:** Mary Ekman
**President, Starbucks Coffee International:** James C. (Jim) Alling, age 45, $1,120,423 pay
**President, Starbucks Coffee US:** Launi Skinner, age 42
**Director, Investor Relations:** JoAnn DeGrande
**Auditors:** Deloitte & Touche LLP

## LOCATIONS

**HQ:** Starbucks Corporation
2401 Utah Ave. South, Seattle, WA 98134
**Phone:** 206-447-1575 **Fax:** 206-447-0828
**Web:** www.starbucks.com

### 2006 Sales

| | $ mil. | % of total |
|---|---|---|
| US | 6,179 | 79 |
| International | 1,303 | 17 |
| Global consumer products | 305 | 4 |
| **Total** | **7,787** | **100** |

## PRODUCTS/OPERATIONS

### 2006 Sales

| | $ mil. | % of total |
|---|---|---|
| Company-operated retail | 6,583 | 85 |
| Licensing | 861 | 11 |
| Foodservice & other | 343 | 4 |
| **Total** | **7,787** | **100** |

### 2006 Locations

| | No. |
|---|---|
| Company-operated | 7,521 |
| Licensed | 5,647 |
| **Total** | **13,168** |

## COMPETITORS

ABP Corporation
Bruegger's
Caffè Nero
Caribou Coffee
The Coffee Bean
Community Coffee
Diedrich Coffee
Dunkin
Einstein Noah
Farmer Bros.
Folger
Green Mountain Coffee
Greggs
Krispy Kreme
Lavazza
McDonald's
Nestlé
Panera Bread
Sara Lee
Tim Hortons
Van Houtte
Whitbread

## HISTORICAL FINANCIALS

Company Type: Public

### Income Statement

FYE: Sunday nearest September 30

| | REVENUE ($ mil.) | NET INCOME ($ mil.) | NET PROFIT MARGIN | EMPLOYEES |
|---|---|---|---|---|
| **9/06** | 7,787 | 564 | 7.2% | 145,800 |
| **9/05** | 6,369 | 495 | 7.8% | 115,000 |
| **9/04** | 5,294 | 391 | 7.4% | 96,700 |
| **9/03** | 4,076 | 268 | 6.6% | 74,000 |
| **9/02** | 3,289 | 215 | 6.5% | 62,000 |
| **Annual Growth** | 24.0% | 27.3% | — | 23.8% |

### 2006 Year-End Financials

Debt ratio: 0.1%
Return on equity: 26.1%
Cash ($ mil.): 454
Current ratio: 0.79
Long-term debt ($ mil.): 2
No. of shares (mil.): 755
Dividends
Yield: —
Payout: —
Market value ($ mil.): 25,703

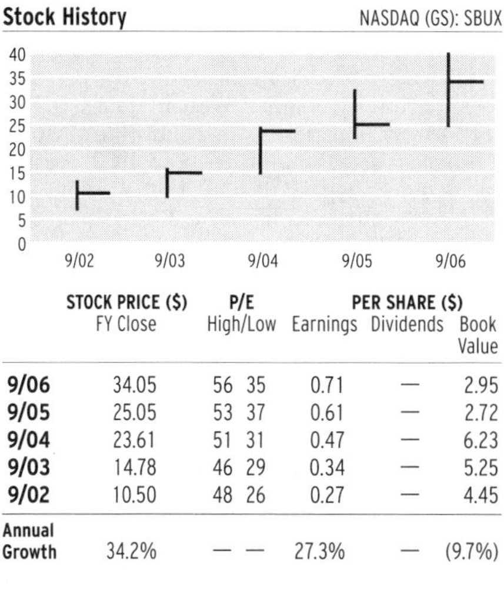


| | STOCK PRICE ($) FY Close | P/E High | P/E Low | PER SHARE ($) Earnings | Dividends | Book Value |
|---|---|---|---|---|---|---|
| **9/06** | 34.05 | 56 | 35 | 0.71 | — | 2.95 |
| **9/05** | 25.05 | 53 | 37 | 0.61 | — | 2.72 |
| **9/04** | 23.61 | 51 | 31 | 0.47 | — | 6.23 |
| **9/03** | 14.78 | 46 | 29 | 0.34 | — | 5.25 |
| **9/02** | 10.50 | 48 | 26 | 0.27 | — | 4.45 |
| **Annual Growth** | 34.2% | — | — | 27.3% | — | (9.7%) |

# Starwood Hotels & Resorts Worldwide

Starwood Hotels & Resorts Worldwide knows how to shine a light on hospitality. The company is one of the world's largest hotel and leisure companies, with more than 870 properties in some 100 countries. Its hotel empire consists of luxury and upscale brands such as Four Points, Sheraton, and Westin. Starwood operates 60 high-end resorts and hotels through its St. Regis and Luxury Collection, while its chain of about 20 W Hotels offers ultra-modern style for sophisticated business travelers. Some 360 of Starwood's hotels are owned and operated by franchisees; the company owns or leases 85 locations. In addition, the company's Starwood Vacation Ownership subsidiary operates 25 time-share resorts.

Starwood managed to weather the tough years of recession in the travel industry on the strength of its luxury brands, and has seen booming business since the recovery. With the increase in business and optimism for the future, the company has continued to expand its portfolio in recent years. During the fourth quarter of 2006, the company added 18 new hotels and resorts, including The Westin Chicago North Shore (Wheeling, Illinois), The U.S. Grant (San Diego, California), and The Westin St. Maarten, Dawn Beach Resort & Spa (St. Maarten, Netherland Antilles). Starwood plans to open more than 80 hotels in 2007. Steven Heyer, who took over as CEO from founder Barry Sternlicht in 2004, resigned from the company in 2007. Chairman Bruce Duncan was named interim chief.

## HISTORY

Barry Sternlicht earned his MBA from Harvard in 1986 and joined the fast track at JMB Realty, bringing the company a UK real estate deal involving Randsworth Trust in 1989. He left two years later to start Starwood Capital Group with backers including the wealthy Burden and Ziff families. (JMB and its pension fund partners, meanwhile, lost their shirts when Randsworth went belly-up during the recession of the early 1990s.) In 1995 Starwood Capital joined Goldman Sachs and Nomura Securities to buy Westin Hotel (renamed Westin Hotels & Resorts) from Japanese construction firm Aoki. Founded in Washington State in 1930, Westin was acquired by UAL in 1970, then Aoki bought it in 1988 during a boom in Japanese investments in US real estate.

Also in 1995 Sternlicht bought Hotel Investors Trust (a hotel REIT) and Hotel Investors Corp. (hotel management), two struggling firms whose chief attraction was their rare paired-share status, allowing management company profits to flow through the REIT to investors exempt from corporate income tax. (The structure was banned in 1984, but four such entities were grandfathered in under the law.) The companies were renamed Starwood Lodging Trust and Starwood Lodging Corp. (together, Starwood Lodging). Through more acquisitions, Starwood had amassed a collection of about 110 hotels by 1997.

Starwood's industry standing took a quantum leap in early 1998 when it acquired the 50% of the Westin hotel chain that Starwood Capital didn't already own and bought lodging giant ITT, the former telephone industry conglomerate and owner of the Sheraton hotel chain. ITT — with more than 400 hotels and gaming properties (Desert Inn, Caesars) — fought off a hostile takeover bid from Hilton Hotels and accepted Starwood Lodging's $14.6 billion offer. (Starwood Capital made $22 million in advising fees on the deal.) Later that year the firm changed its name to Starwood Hotels & Resorts, bought four former Ritz-Carlton hotels, and sold eight all-suite hotels to FelCor Suite Hotels (now FelCor Lodging Trust). Sternlicht then chose Walt Disney executive and Harvard classmate Richard Nanula to take the reins of Starwood's operating company. In late 1998 it launched W Hotels.

Before Congress closed the paired-share loophole for new acquisitions, Starwood Hotels went on a shopping spree, becoming a standard corporation in 1999. Nanula resigned that year, apparently after repeated clashes with Sternlicht. The company bought time-share resort company Vistana — renamed Starwood Vacation Ownership (SVO) — and purchased the portion of European hotel operator Ciga (part of which Sheraton had acquired in 1994) that it didn't already own.

Gaming profits had begun to fall off in 1999, however, as the Asian economic crisis stymied the flow of gambling-hungry tourists. The following year Starwood sold its Caesars unit to Park Place Entertainment (later Caesars Entertainment, now owned by Harrah's) for $3 billion and its Desert Inn hotel and casino to Mirage Resorts founder Steve Wynn for about $270 million. Tight economic conditions forced Starwood to cut costs and curtail discretionary spending. That year SVO began building new resorts in Arizona, Colorado, and Hawaii. Starwood saw its business begin to suffer following the September 11, 2001, terrorist attacks, which kept many potential travelers at home. As a result, Starwood cut about 12,000 jobs, roughly 25% of its workforce.

To pay down its debt, Starwood raised about $1.5 billion in capital by selling bonds (2002) and sold its Italian Ciga assets — including luxury hotels, a golf club, and other real estate interests — to Colony Capital (2003).

In 2004 Steven Heyer, former president and COO of Coca-Cola, was named CEO as Sternlicht began setting the stage for his retirement from the company. He stayed on for nearly another year as executive chairman, however, before leaving the company altogether. The company's expansion efforts in 2005 included the acquisition of the Le Meridien brand for $225 million. (In a separate agreement, Lehman Brothers and Starwood Capital Group, an unaffiliated private equity fund managed by former Starwood CEO Barry Sternlicht, jointly acquired the real estate properties.) In 2006 Starwood sold some 30 properties to Host Hotels & Resorts for about $4 billion. Heyer resigned from the company in 2007; chairman Bruce Duncan was tapped to serve as interim CEO.

## EXECUTIVES

**Chairman and Interim CEO:** Bruce W. Duncan, age 55
**EVP and CFO:** Vasant M. Prabhu, age 47
**Chief Administrative Officer, Secretary, and General Counsel:** Kenneth S. (Ken) Siegel, age 51
**SVP Global Sales:** Christie Hicks
**SVP Human Resources:** Michelle Crosby
**SVP Owner Relations and Franchise:** Lynne Dougherty
**SVP Brand Management, Four Points by Sheraton:** Hoyt H. Harper II
**SVP, Westin Hotels & Resorts:** Sue A. Brush
**SVP, Le Méridien Hotels & Resorts:** Eva Ziegler
**CIO:** Todd Thompson
**President, Starwood Luxury Brands Group and W Hotels Worldwide:** Ross A. Klein
**President, Global Development Group and Real Estate Group; Chairman and CEO, Starwood Vacation Ownership:** Raymond L. (Rip) Gellein Jr., age 49
**President, Hotel Group:** Matthew A. (Matt) Ouimet, age 48
**President, Asia/Pacific:** Miguel Ko
**President, Europe, Africa, and Middle East Division (EMEA):** Roeland Vos
**President, Latin America:** Osvaldo V. Librizzi
**President, North America Division:** Geoffrey A. (Geoff) Ballotti
**President, Real Estate Development:** Sergio D. Rivera
**Media Relations:** Leila Siman
**Auditors:** Ernst & Young LLP

## LOCATIONS

**HQ:** Starwood Hotels & Resorts Worldwide, Inc.
1111 Westchester Ave., White Plains, NY 10604
**Phone:** 914-640-8100 **Fax:** 914-640-8591
**Web:** www.starwoodhotels.com

Starwood Hotels & Resorts Worldwide owns, leases, manages, or franchises more than 870 hotels and about 25 time-share resorts in about 100 countries.

### 2006 Sales

| | $ mil. | % of total |
|---|---|---|
| US | 4,580 | 77 |
| Italy | 375 | 6 |
| Other countries | 1,024 | 17 |
| **Total** | **5,979** | **100** |

### 2006 Locations

| | No. |
|---|---|
| North America | 450 |
| Europe, Middle East & Africa | 264 |
| Asia/Pacific | 124 |
| Latin America | 58 |
| **Total** | **896** |

## PRODUCTS/OPERATIONS

### 2006 Sales

| | $ mil. | % of total |
|---|---|---|
| Hotels | | |
| Owned & leased | 2,692 | 45 |
| Management & franchise fees | 697 | 12 |
| Other | 1,585 | 26 |
| Vacation ownership resorts | 1,005 | 17 |
| **Total** | **5,979** | **100** |

### 2006 Locations

| | No. |
|---|---|
| Hotels | |
| Franchised | 426 |
| Managed | 360 |
| Owned | 85 |
| Vacation ownership resorts | 25 |
| **Total** | **896** |

### 2006 Locations

| | No. |
|---|---|
| Hotels | |
| Sheraton | 396 |
| Westin | 131 |
| Four Points | 126 |
| Le Méridien | 123 |
| St. Regis & Luxury Collection | 60 |
| W Hotels | 21 |
| Other | 14 |
| Vacation ownership resorts | 25 |
| **Total** | **896** |

## COMPETITORS

Accor
Bluegreen
Carlson Hotels
Fairmont Raffles
Four Seasons Hotels
Hilton
Hilton International
Hyatt
InterContinental Hotels
Loews Hotels
LXR Luxury Resorts
Marriott
Millennium & Copthorne Hotels
Omni Hotels
Silverleaf Resorts
Sunterra
Wyndham
Wyndham Vacation

## HISTORICAL FINANCIALS

Company Type: Public

### Income Statement

FYE: December 31

| | REVENUE ($ mil.) | NET INCOME ($ mil.) | NET PROFIT MARGIN | EMPLOYEES |
|---|---|---|---|---|
| **12/06** | 5,979 | 1,043 | 17.4% | 145,000 |
| **12/05** | 5,977 | 422 | 7.1% | 145,000 |
| **12/04** | 5,368 | 395 | 7.4% | 120,000 |
| **12/03** | 4,630 | 309 | 6.7% | 110,000 |
| **12/02** | 4,659 | 355 | 7.6% | 105,000 |
| **Annual Growth** | 6.4% | 30.9% | — | 8.4% |

### 2006 Year-End Financials

Debt ratio: 60.7%
Return on equity: 25.4%
Cash ($ mil.): 512
Current ratio: 0.74
Long-term debt ($ mil.): 1,827
No. of shares (mil.): 213
Dividends
Yield: 1.0%
Payout: 13.4%
Market value ($ mil.): 13,343

### Stock History

NYSE: HOT

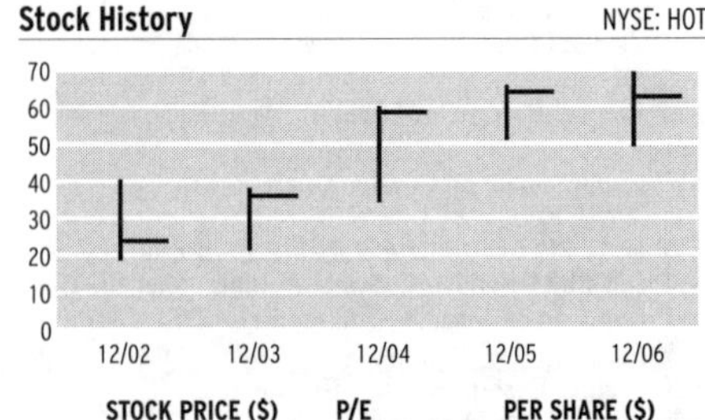


| | STOCK PRICE ($) FY Close | P/E High | P/E Low | PER SHARE ($) Earnings | Dividends | Book Value |
|---|---|---|---|---|---|---|
| **12/06** | 62.50 | 15 | 11 | 4.69 | 0.63 | 14.09 |
| **12/05** | 63.86 | 35 | 27 | 1.88 | 0.84 | 23.99 |
| **12/04** | 58.40 | 32 | 19 | 1.84 | 0.84 | 22.94 |
| **12/03** | 35.97 | 25 | 14 | 1.50 | 0.84 | 21.44 |
| **12/02** | 23.74 | 23 | 11 | 1.73 | 0.84 | 19.88 |
| **Annual Growth** | 27.4% | — | — | 28.3% | (6.9%) | (8.3%) |

# State Farm Mutual Automobile Insurance

Like an enormous corporation, State Farm is everywhere. The leading US personal lines property/casualty company (by premiums), State Farm Mutual Automobile Insurance Company is the #1 provider of auto insurance. It also is the leading home insurer and offers non-medical health and life insurance through its subsidiary companies. Its products are marketed via some 17,000 agents in the US and Canada. Competition has increased with the fall of barriers between the banking, securities, and insurance industries. State Farm's not-so-secret weapon is a federal savings bank charter (State Farm Bank) that offers consumer financial products through State Farm agents and by phone, mail, and the Internet.

Since establishing itself as a financial services provider in 1999, the company has built up $12.2 billion in assets. However, insurance is still its main source of income. And, while State Farm already insures nearly 20% of the automobiles on US roads, it is looking to grab an even larger portion of that pie. Weakness in auto insurance during 2003 and 2004 spurred the company to refocus its efforts on the segment that accounts for over 50% of its policies and almost 65% of the company's property/casualty premiums.

Meanwhile, homeowners insurance has been a thornier issue. It still insures 20% of the single-family homes in the US, but the insurer stopped writing new homeowners policies in some 15 states in an effort to improve profitability.

Hurricanes Katrina, Wilma, and Rita brought State Farm customer claims totaling $6.3 billion in property and casualty losses. For residents along the Gulf Coast, at first it seemed like State Farm would stay put. However, as the claims keep rolling in, the company has rewritten its underwriting guidelines to limit its risk. New homeowner policies in places such as New Orleans will have steeper deductibles and less coverage, and the company has completely stopped offering new homeowners and commercial property policies in the state of Mississippi.

Since its founding, the group's companies have been run by only two families, the Mecherles (1922-54) and the Rusts (1954-present).

## HISTORY

Retired farmer George Mecherle formed State Farm Mutual Automobile Insurance in Bloomington, Illinois, in 1922. State Farm served only members of farm bureaus and farm mutual insurance companies, charging a one-time membership fee and a premium to protect an automobile against loss or damage.

Unlike most competitors, State Farm offered six-month premium payments. The insurer billed and collected renewal premiums from its home office, relieving the agent of the task. In addition, State Farm determined auto rates by a simple seven-class system, while competitors varied rates for each model.

State Farm in 1926 started City and Village Mutual Automobile Insurance to insure nonfarmers' autos; it became part of the company in 1927. Between 1927 and 1931 it introduced borrowed-car protection, wind coverage, and insurance for vehicles used to transport schoolchildren.

State Farm expanded to California in 1928 and formed State Farm Life Insurance the next year. In 1935 it established State Farm Fire Insurance. George Mecherle became chairman in 1937, and his son Ramond became president. In 1939 George challenged agents to write "A Million or More (auto policies) by '44." State Farm saw a 110% increase in policies.

During the 1940s State Farm focused on urban areas after most of the farm bureaus formed their own insurance companies. In the late 1940s and 1950s, it moved to a full-time agency force.

Homeowners coverage was added to the insurer's offerings under the leadership of Adlai Rust, who led State Farm from 1954 until 1958, when Edward Rust took over. He died in 1985 and his son, Edward Jr., currently holds the top spot.

Between 1974 and 1987 the insurer was hit by several gender-discrimination suits (a 1992 settlement awarded $157 million to 814 women). State Farm has since tried to hire more women and minorities.

In the early 1990s serial disasters, including Hurricane Andrew and the Los Angeles riots, proved costly. The 1994 Northridge earthquake alone generated more than $2.5 billion in claims and contributed to a 72% decline in earnings.

State Farm — the top US home insurer since the mid-1960s — canceled 62,500 residential policies in South Florida in 1996 to cut potential hurricane loss an estimated 11%. In response, Florida's insurance regulators rescinded a previously approved rate hike. That year the company agreed to open more urban neighborhood offices to settle a discrimination suit brought by the Department of Housing and Urban Development, which accused State Farm of discriminating against potential customers in minority-populated areas.

Legal trouble continued. In 1997 State Farm settled with a California couple who alleged the company forged policyholders' signatures on forms declining coverage and concealed evidence to avoid paying earthquake damage claims. That year a policyholder sued to keep State Farm from "wasting company assets" on President Clinton's legal defense against Paula Jones' sexual harassment charges (Clinton held a State Farm personal liability policy).

Relations with its sales force already rocky, State Farm in 1998 proposed to reduce up-front commissions and cut base pay in favor of incentives for customer retention and cross-selling. Reduced auto premiums and increased catastrophe claims from across the US eroded State Farm's bottom line that year. A federal thrift charter obtained in 1998 let the company launch banking operations the next year.

State Farm is appealing a 1999 Illinois state court judgment that it pay $1.2 billion to policyholders for using aftermarket parts in auto repairs. In 2000 the company was hit with a class-action lawsuit about its denial of personal-injury claims; previous suits had been individual cases.

In 2002, State Farm Indemnity, the company's auto-only New Jersey subsidiary, withdrew from the Garden State's auto insurance market but began phasing back into the market in 2005.

Like all reinsurers, State Farm's reinsurance business was tested by the 2005 hurricane season. It underwrote losses of $2.8 billion.

## EXECUTIVES

**Chairman and CEO:** Edward B. (Ed) Rust Jr., age 56
**Vice Chairman, President, and COO:** Vincent J. Trosino, age 66
**Vice Chairman, CFO, and Treasurer:** Michael L. Tipsord
**Vice Chairman and Chief Administrative Officer:** James E. Rutrough
**Vice Chairman and Chief Agency and Marketing Officer:** Michael C. Davidson
**SEVP, Financial Services:** Jack W. North
**EVP, General Counsel, and Secretary:** Kim M. Brunner
**EVP and Chief Administrative Officer, Life and VP, Health:** Susan D. Waring
**SVP, Canada:** Bob Cooke
**VP, Marketing:** Pam El
**President and CEO, State Farm Bank:** Stanley R. (Stan) Ommen
**Director of Marketing:** Patrick Culligan
**Auditors:** PricewaterhouseCoopers LLP

## LOCATIONS

**HQ:** State Farm Mutual Automobile Insurance Company
1 State Farm Plaza, Bloomington, IL 61710
**Phone:** 309-766-2311 **Fax:** 309-766-3621
**Web:** www.statefarm.com

## PRODUCTS/OPERATIONS

**2005 Sales**

| | % of total |
|---|---|
| Auto | 53 |
| Homeowners | 21 |
| Life | 10 |
| Other P&C | 11 |
| Health | 2 |
| Banking | 2 |
| Business insurance | 1 |
| **Total** | **100** |

## COMPETITORS

AIG
Allstate
American Family Insurance
CNA Financial
COUNTRY Insurance
GEICO
The Hartford
Liberty Mutual
MetLife
Nationwide
Philadelphia Consolidated
Progressive Corporation
Prudential
Safeco
USAA

## HISTORICAL FINANCIALS

Company Type: Mutual company

**Income Statement** FYE: December 31

| | REVENUE ($ mil.) | NET INCOME ($ mil.) | NET PROFIT MARGIN | EMPLOYEES |
|---|---|---|---|---|
| **12/05** | 60,000 | — | — | 79,200 |
| **12/04** | 58,800 | — | — | 79,200 |
| **12/03** | 56,100 | — | — | 79,000 |
| **12/02** | 49,700 | — | — | 79,400 |
| **12/01** | 46,700 | — | — | 79,400 |
| **Annual Growth** | 6.5% | — | — | (0.1%) |

**Revenue History**

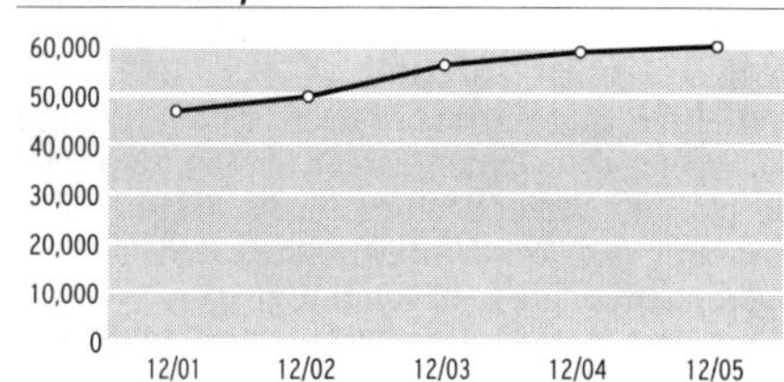

# State Street

Ol' Blue Eyes sang about the State Street (that great street) in Chicago, but investors may find Boston's State Street more melodious. The company is among the top providers of mutual fund and pension processing and custody services; its target clients include large-scale institutional investors and corporations who can choose from a service menu that includes accounting, foreign exchange, cash management, securities lending, and more. Its State Street Global Advisors (SSgA) unit performs asset management services. Boston Financial Data Services, a partnership with DST Systems, provides shareholder services to clients. Another joint venture, CitiStreet (with Citigroup), manages retirement and pension plans.

At the vanguard of financial services technology, State Street is banking on its computerized analytical and organizational tools to woo and retain clients. Offerings include foreign exchange trading platform FX Connect and Global Link, which provides market research and portfolio analysis. The company boosted its foreign exchange offerings with the acquisition of Currenex in 2007.

One of the world's largest managers of institutional accounts (which represent much of State Street's more than $17 trillion of assets under management), the company is also at the top of the custody-services heap (particularly in the US and key European markets), with assets under custody of more than $12 trillion.

The company added bulk by acquiring another Boston-based fund accounting and servicing provider, Investors Financial Services, in 2007.

## HISTORY

The US's chaotic postrevolutionary era gave birth to the first ancestor of State Street Corporation. Union Bank was founded in 1792 by Boston businessmen, breaking the eight-year monopoly held on Boston banking by Massachusetts Bank (a forerunner of FleetBoston, which was acquired by Bank of America in 2004). Governor John Hancock's distinctive signature graced Union's charter; the bank set up shop at 40 State Street near the port and enjoyed the glory days of New England's shipping trade.

In the mid-19th century, Boston's financial eminence faded as New York flexed its economic muscle. In 1865 the bank was nationally chartered and changed its name to National Union Bank of Boston. It got a new neighbor in 1891: Directors of Third National Bank set up State Street Deposit & Trust to engage in the newfangled business of trusts.

In 1925 National Union Bank merged with State Street and inherited its custodial business. The bank grew through the 1950s; acquisitions included the Second National Bank and the Rockland-Atlas National Bank.

In 1970 State Street converted to a holding company — the State Street Boston Financial Corp. (State Street Boston Corp. as of 1977). The company also went international that decade, opening an office in Munich, Germany.

Soaring inflation and the recession of the 1970s forced the company to radically rethink its mission. The 1974 passage of the Employee Retirement Income Security Act changed the laws governing the management of pension funds and created an opportunity. State Street was one of the first banks to move aggressively into high-tech information processing, and affiliate Boston Financial Data Services began servicing pension assets in 1974.

Encouraged by that success, in 1975 new CEO William Edgerly (who served until 1992) steered State Street away from branch banking and into investments, trusts, and securities processing. An early achievement was designing PepsiCo's retirement plan. Fee-based sales approached 50% of revenues; the company could now quit focusing on lending. In the 1980s and 1990s the company built its administration and investment management businesses overseas and moved into software.

Evolving in the late 1990s, State Street left noncore businesses but expanded globally. In 1997 it formed European Direct Capital Management to invest in eastern and central Europe. State Street Global Advisors opened a London office to serve wealthy individuals outside the US in 1998.

The company sold its commercial banking business to Royal Bank of Scotland in 1999, signaling an exit from that business and narrowing State Street's scope to the asset and investment management businesses. The company also bought Wachovia's custody and institutional trust business and teamed with Citigroup to sell 401(k) retirement products.

In 2000 State Street created FX Connect, an electronic foreign exchange trading system. Also that year David Spina took over as CEO from the retiring Marshall Carter.

The firm bought Bel Air Investment Advisors and its broker/dealer affiliate Bel Air Securities in 2001 to cater to the ultrawealthy. In 2003 State Street sold its corporate trust business to U.S. Bancorp and its private asset management business to Charles Schwab's U.S. Trust. Spina retired in 2004; his protégé, Ron Logue, stepped in as chairman and CEO.

The company was reappointed as the financial advisor for the $2.4 billion Suffolk County (New York) Council Pension Fund in 2007.

## EXECUTIVES

**Chairman and CEO:** Ronald E. (Ron) Logue, age 60, $1,000,000 pay
**Vice Chairman:** John R. Towers, age 65
**Vice Chairman, EVP, and CIO:** Joseph C. Antonellis, age 52, $669,231 pay
**Vice Chairman and EVP, Investor Services:** Joseph L. (Jay) Hooley, age 49, $719,231 pay
**Vice Chairman and EVP; President and CEO, State Street Global Advisors:** William W. (Bill) Hunt, age 44, $2,292,000 pay
**EVP; Global Head of Equities, State Street Global Markets:** Nicholas T. (Nick) Bonn
**EVP, Credit and Risk Policy:** Joseph W. Chow
**EVP, General Counsel, and Secretary:** Charles C. (Skip) Cuttrell III, age 51
**EVP and Head of Corporate Systems and Operations:** Pamela D. Gormley, age 57
**EVP, Technology Infrastructure Services:** Madge M. Meyer
**EVP and Head of Investment Services, Continental Europe:** Timothy J. Caverly
**EVP and Chief Marketing Officer, State Street Global Advisors:** Marc P. Brown
**EVP and Chief Purchasing Officer:** Maureen P. Corcoran
**EVP and General Auditor:** Drew J. Breakspear
**EVP, Global Human Resources:** Alison Quirk
**EVP, Investment Services:** Alan D. Greene
**EVP and Head, International:** Mark J. Lazberger
**EVP and Chief Legal Officer:** Jeffrey N. (Jeff) Carp
**EVP, Finance Management, CFO, and Treasurer:** Edward J. Resch, age 52, $644,231 pay
**Auditors:** Ernst & Young LLP

## LOCATIONS

**HQ:** State Street Corporation
1 Lincoln St., Boston, MA 02111
**Phone:** 617-786-3000 **Fax:** 617-664-4299
**Web:** www.statestreet.com

## PRODUCTS/OPERATIONS

### 2006 Sales

| | $ mil. | % of total |
|---|---|---|
| Interest | 4,324 | 45 |
| Servicing fees | 2,723 | 29 |
| Management fees | 943 | 10 |
| Trading services | 862 | 9 |
| Securities finance | 386 | 4 |
| Processing fees & other | 287 | 3 |
| **Total** | **9,525** | **100** |

## COMPETITORS

Ameriprise
Bank of New York Mellon
Barclays
BBVA Provida
BISYS
Citigroup
Credit Suisse (USA)
Deutsche Bank
DST
First Data
Fiserv
Franklin Resources
GAMCO Investors
IRRC
ISS
Morgan Stanley
National Financial Partners
Northern Trust
Principal Financial
SEI
UBS Financial Services

## HISTORICAL FINANCIALS

Company Type: Public

### Income Statement

FYE: December 31

| | ASSETS ($ mil.) | NET INCOME ($ mil.) | INCOME AS % OF ASSETS | EMPLOYEES |
|---|---|---|---|---|
| **12/06** | 107,353 | 1,106 | 1.0% | 21,700 |
| **12/05** | 97,968 | 838 | 0.9% | 20,965 |
| **12/04** | 94,040 | 798 | 0.8% | 19,668 |
| **12/03** | 87,534 | 722 | 0.8% | 19,850 |
| **12/02** | 85,794 | 1,015 | 1.2% | 19,501 |
| **Annual Growth** | 5.8% | 2.2% | — | 2.7% |

### 2006 Year-End Financials

Equity as % of assets: 6.8%
Return on assets: 1.1%
Return on equity: 16.2%
Long-term debt ($ mil.): 2,616
No. of shares (mil.): 332
Dividends
Yield: 1.2%
Payout: 24.3%
Market value ($ mil.): 22,420
Sales ($ mil.): 9,525

### Stock History

NYSE: STT

| | STOCK PRICE ($) FY Close | P/E High | P/E Low | PER SHARE ($) Earnings | Dividends | Book Value |
|---|---|---|---|---|---|---|
| **12/06** | 67.44 | 21 | 17 | 3.29 | 0.80 | 21.81 |
| **12/05** | 55.44 | 24 | 16 | 2.50 | 0.72 | 19.08 |
| **12/04** | 49.12 | 24 | 17 | 2.35 | 0.64 | 18.46 |
| **12/03** | 52.08 | 25 | 14 | 2.15 | 0.43 | 17.18 |
| **12/02** | 39.00 | 19 | 10 | 3.10 | — | 14.73 |
| **Annual Growth** | 14.7% | — | — | 1.5% | 23.0% | 10.3% |

# Steelcase Inc.

For those really tough office meetings, there's Steelcase, the world's top office furniture maker. The company manufactures a wide variety of products, from file cabinets that come with a lifetime warranty to Coach-branded leather office chairs. Steelcase also sells staples, such as tables, desks, and lighting. Its brands include Brayton, Designtex, Details, Leap, Metro, Polyvision, Steelcase, Turnstone, and Vecta. Steelcase offers a variety of services, including workspace planning, interior construction, and project management. In addition the company focuses on high-end furniture and specialty markets through various subsidiaries and affiliates.

Steelcase has used acquisitions, such as its purchase of whiteboard maker PolyVision, to expand the company's business in the corporate learning and higher education markets. It also made inroads into the automotive sector with its agreement with Johnson Controls to improve vehicle seats with Steelcase technology. In 2006 the company acquired hospital furniture maker Softcare Innovations and its sister company DJRT Manufacturing. The companies were folded into Steelcase's new health care furniture line, Nurture by Steelcase.

In addition to office furniture, the company also sells prefabricated office buildings and warehouses through its joint venture with The Gale Co. and Morgan Stanley Real Estate Funds. The joint venture, named Workstage, was formed in 1999. Steelcase currently owns 44% of the entity.

A slowing economy has forced the company to close plants. The ongoing consolidation continued through 2005. The consolidation caused some operational issues that the company said led to some $10 million in losses in 2006 in its Wood division.

## HISTORY

In the early 1900s, when wooden office furniture was the rule, sheet-metal designer Peter Wege began espousing the benefits of fireproof steel furniture. In 1912 Wege persuaded a group of investors, led by Grand Rapids, Michigan, banker Walter Idema, to create the Metal Office Furniture Company. Salesman David Dyer Hunting — a onetime vaudeville press agent who is considered the company's third founder — joined in 1914. Metal Office Furniture's first big hit was a metal wastepaper basket.

Businesses were slow to switch from wood to the more expensive metal furniture, but US government architects, concerned with fire safety, began specifying metal furniture in their designs. Metal Office Furniture won its first government contract in 1915.

Wege hired media consultant Jim Turner in 1921 to tout the benefits of metal furniture. Turner came up with a trademark to describe the indestructible nature of the company's products — Steelcase. The company patented the suspension cabinet in 1934 and teamed with Frank Lloyd Wright in 1937 to create office furniture for the Johnson Wax headquarters building.

Metal Office Furniture provided the US Navy with shipboard furniture during WWII and sold Navy-inspired modular furniture after the war. In 1954 the company changed its name to Steelcase. Five years later it introduced Convertibles and Convertiwalls, a system of frames, cabinets, and panels that could tailor a work area to an individual worker's needs. By 1968 Steelcase had become the world's #1 maker of metal office furniture.

To boost its presence overseas, the company signed deals with firms such as Strafor Facom (1974, France). Steelcase began a series of acquisitions in 1978, fueling growth that helped triple its sales during the 1980s.

In 1987 Steelcase positioned itself as a more design-oriented company by creating the Steelcase Design Partnership. The partnership, which was made up of seven companies, provided products for special market niches such as fabrics (DesignTex).

The firm was hit hard by the recession of the early 1990s as many businesses postponed buying new furniture. Steelcase was forced to lay off hourly workers, but by 1992 it was able to recall them all.

In 1993 Steelcase launched Turnstone, serving small businesses and home office workers. Turnstone president James Hackett was named president and CEO of Steelcase the next year.

In 1996 Steelcase joined with computer mouse pioneer IDEO to co-design furniture for computers. Steelcase went public in 1998 at the urging of the Wege and Hunting families; Peter Wege, son of one of the company's founders, gave nearly $140 million (of the $214 million he gained from the IPO) to his charity, the Wege Foundation.

Acquisitions in the late 1990s included Germany's wood office furniture maker Werndl BuroMobel, US company J.M. Lynne (wall coverings), and the remaining 50% stake of its French joint venture, Steelcase Strafor, from Strafor Facom.

The company acquired Custom Cable Industries (data and voice cabling) and PolyVision (whiteboards) in 2002. In the face of declining office furniture sales, however, Steelcase was also laying off workers. More than 6,600 hourly, temporary, and salaried positions were eliminated between December 2000 and March 2002, or 27% of the workforce. After losing more than $15 million in 2002, the company temporarily closed its North American operations for one week in April 2003. The shutdown was the company's first in its 90-year history.

In September 2003 Steelcase sold Attwood Corporation, a marine parts manufacturing subsidiary, to leisure products industry leader Brunswick Corporation.

## EXECUTIVES

**Chairman:** Robert C. (Rob) Pew III, age 55
**President, CEO, and Director:** James P. Hackett, age 52, $1,327,555 pay
**EVP, Global eBusiness and CIO:** John S. Dean
**SVP and Global Operations Officer:** Mark A. Baker, age 47, $520,141 pay
**SVP, Chief Administrative Officer, and Secretary:** Nancy W. Hickey, age 55, $521,372 pay
**SVP, WorkSpace Futures and E X P:** Mark T. Greiner, age 56
**VP and CFO:** David C. Sylvester, age 42
**VP, Global Corporate Community Relations:** Brian Cloyd
**VP, Global Strategic Human Resources:** Laurent Bernard
**President, Nurture by Steelcase:** Michael I. (Mike) Love, age 58
**President, Design Group:** Frank H. Merlotti Jr., age 56
**President, Steelcase International:** James G. (Jim) Mitchell, age 57
**President, Steelcase Group:** James P. (Jim) Keane, age 47
**Director, Corporate Environmental Performance:** David Rinard
**President and CEO, PolyVision:** Michael H. Dunn
**Director, Corporate Strategy and Development:** Raj Mehan
**Auditors:** BDO Seidman, LLP

## LOCATIONS

**HQ:** Steelcase Inc.
901 44th St. SE, Grand Rapids, MI 49508
**Phone:** 616-247-2710 **Fax:** 616-475-2270
**Web:** www.steelcase.com

### 2007 Sales

| | $ mil. | % of total |
|---|---|---|
| US | 1,863.8 | 60 |
| Other countries | 735.8 | 24 |
| Other | 497.8 | 16 |
| **Total** | **3,097.4** | **100** |

## PRODUCTS/OPERATIONS

### Selected Products

Desks and suites (standard, executive)
Interior architecture (flooring, space dividers)
Lighting (task, ambient, accent)
Seating (general, executive, guest, lounge)
Storage (shelves, cabinets, files)
Systems (workstation, panel systems)
Tables (meeting, personal, cafe)
Technology (appliances)
Textiles (seating upholstery, panel fabric)
Worktools (organizers, boards and easels)

### Selected Brand Names

Brayton International
Braytonspaces
Designtex
Details
Leap
Lightoiler
Metro
PolyVision
Steelcase
Stow Davis
Turnstone
Vecta

### Selected Subsidiaries and Affiliates

AF Steelcase S.A.
Brayton International
The Designtex Group
IDEO
Metropolitan Furniture Corporation
Office Details, Inc.
Polyvision
Steelcase Canada, Ltd.
Steelcase S.A.
Steelcase SAS
Vecta

## COMPETITORS

CFGroup
Design Within Reach
Haworth
Herman Miller
HNI
The HON Company
Inscape corp
Jami
KI
Kimball International
Knoll
Shelby Williams
Teknion

## HISTORICAL FINANCIALS

Company Type: Public

**Income Statement** FYE: Last Friday in February

| | REVENUE ($ mil.) | NET INCOME ($ mil.) | NET PROFIT MARGIN | EMPLOYEES |
|---|---|---|---|---|
| **2/07** | 3,097 | 107 | 3.5% | 13,000 |
| **2/06** | 2,869 | 49 | 1.7% | 13,000 |
| **2/05** | 2,614 | 13 | 0.5% | 14,500 |
| **2/04** | 2,346 | (23) | — | 14,200 |
| **2/03** | 2,587 | (266) | — | 16,000 |
| **Annual Growth** | 4.6% | — | — | (5.1%) |

**2007 Year-End Financials**

Debt ratio: 20.2%
Return on equity: 8.8%
Cash ($ mil.): 560
Current ratio: 1.91
Long-term debt ($ mil.): 250

No. of shares (mil.): 82
Dividends
Yield: 2.2%
Payout: 63.4%
Market value ($ mil.): 1,647

**Stock History** NYSE: SCS

| | STOCK PRICE ($) FY Close | P/E High | P/E Low | PER SHARE ($) Earnings | Dividends | Book Value |
|---|---|---|---|---|---|---|
| **2/07** | 20.07 | 28 | 19 | 0.71 | 0.45 | 15.08 |
| **2/06** | 17.34 | 53 | 37 | 0.33 | 0.33 | 16.62 |
| **2/05** | 14.15 | 163 | 123 | 0.09 | 0.24 | 19.59 |
| **2/04** | 14.10 | — | — | (0.16) | 0.24 | 24.33 |
| **2/03** | 9.21 | — | — | (1.80) | 0.24 | 31.03 |
| **Annual Growth** | 21.5% | — | — | — | 17.0% | (16.5%) |

# Sun Microsystems

When it comes to network computing, it's hard to find an area where the Sun doesn't shine. Sun Microsystems is a leading maker of UNIX-based servers used to power corporate computer networks and Web sites. It also makes workstation computers and a widening range of disk- and tape-based storage systems. Unlike most hardware vendors, Sun makes computers that use its own chips (SPARC) and operating system (Solaris). Its software portfolio includes application server, office productivity, and network management applications. Sun also developed Java, a programming language for creating software that can run unchanged on multiple operating systems.

Sun soared during the dot-com explosion in the 1990s with hardware optimized for serving Web sites, but the subsequent e-recession leveled the playing field for competitors. The company has responded by significantly growing its product and service lines through internal development and acquisitions — a strategy that has notably moved it beyond proprietary technology and embraced the open-source movement.

The company's aggressive and outspoken chairman, Scott McNealy, has waged a public battle with Microsoft over the use of Sun's Java programming language. But Microsoft's greatest threat to Sun has been in the server arena, where competitors look to undersell Sun's UNIX-based offerings with servers based on the Wintel platform.

Sun continues to expand its support of Windows and Linux-based products. While the company remains firmly committed to Solaris, it has adopted Linux for select low-end server deployments and developing desktop PC products. It has also made inroads into high-end data centers, a market where IBM has been entrenched with its long history of providing mainframe computing.

Sun's software division develops application server software that competes with offerings from BEA Systems, IBM, and Oracle. Sun's OpenSolaris project, launched in 2005, made Solaris available on an open-source basis. Late that year Sun announced it would also provide its Java Enterprise System, Sun N1 Management software, and development tools for free.

Sun has augmented its internal software development with acquisitions and partnerships. Sun purchased enterprise application integration specialist SeeBeyond Technology for $383 million in cash. It also partnered with fellow Microsoft adversary Google, agreeing to bundle the search giant's browser toolbar with its Java Runtime Environment software; the deal has generated wide speculation that the companies could be laying the groundwork for more significant collaboration.

On the storage front the company has partnered with Hitachi Data Systems to bolster its offerings (pitting it against yet another tech titan, EMC). Sun also acquired Storage Technology (more commonly known as StorageTek) for $4.1 billion in cash in 2005.

## HISTORY

The four 27-year-olds who founded Sun Microsystems in 1982 saw great market potential for high-speed workstation computers that used the UNIX operating system so popular with scientists and engineers.

German-born Andreas Bechtolsheim, a Stanford engineering graduate student, had built a workstation from spare parts. Two Stanford MBA graduates, Scott McNealy and Vinod Khosla, liked Bechtolsheim's creation and tapped Berkeley UNIX guru William Joy (Sun's chief scientist) to supply the software. The new company, whose name stood for Stanford University Network, started out with Khosla as president and McNealy as manufacturing director.

Sun adopted AT&T's UNIX operating system so its workstations would network better with other hardware systems. It lowered prices by using standard technologies, and zoomed to sales of more than $500 million in five years. In 1984 McNealy succeeded Khosla, who retired.

The company went public in 1986 and the next year signed with AT&T to develop an enhanced UNIX system. Sun's SPARC processor was introduced in 1989. Sun licensed SPARC to stimulate mass production of its systems, reduce costs, and increase the availability of third-party software. In 1993, expanding its technology, Sun began to sell computer chips.

Bechtolsheim left Sun in 1995 and the company started intensifying its push of Internet computing, tweaking its servers for Web functions. Its Java programming language let users write software across any operating system. The next year McNealy began building Java as an industry standard. Sun then introduced Java-based network computers even as it worked to correct concerns that the language was slow and restricted in its security. The company also initiated an acquisition tear, buying the business computer unit of Cray Research and fault-tolerant technology specialist Integrated Micro Products, among others.

In 1997 Sun filed a suit against Microsoft charging that the company was distributing incompatible versions of Java; the court ordered a preliminary injunction the following year. Also in 1998 Sun developed its Jini technology, which allows immediate interoperability between computers and peripheral devices in shared networks. Sun began 2001 with a victory against its archrival. Microsoft agreed to terminate its Java license and pay Sun $20 million dollars to settle the copyright infringement case from 1997.

Sun co-founder Andy Bechtolsheim returned to the company in 2004 when Sun acquired Kealia, a server development company founded by Bechtolsheim. Sun also settled a patent dispute with Eastman Kodak that year, agreeing to pay Kodak $92 million to end a suit involving Sun's Java language. Also in 2004 Sun and Microsoft finally settled a long-running dispute involving antitrust and patent claims. Microsoft agreed to pay Sun $1.6 billion, and Sun announced plans to incorporate Windows into some of its server lines. At the same time Sun announced restructuring plans that included eliminating about 9% of the company's workforce.

In 2005 the company expanded its managed service offerings when it purchased SevenSpace. It also acquired Storage Technology (also known as StorageTek) for $4.1 billion.

Sun president Jonathan Schwartz succeeded McNealy as CEO in 2006; McNealy remained chairman. Schwartz's appointment was followed by the announcement of a cost-cutting plan that included job cuts and facility consolidation.

## EXECUTIVES

**Chairman:** Scott G. McNealy, age 52, $1,060,939 pay (prior to title change)
**President, CEO, and Director:** Jonathan I. Schwartz, age 40, $1,464,923 pay
**EVP, Research and Development and CTO:** Gregory M. (Greg) Papadopoulos, age 48, $720,522 pay
**EVP and Chief Marketing Officer:** Anil P. Gadre, age 49
**EVP and Chairman, EMEA, APAC, and the Americas:** Crawford W. Beveridge, age 61, $684,961 pay (prior to title change)
**EVP, Corporate Development and Alliances:** Brian Sutphin, age 50
**EVP, Corporate Resources and CFO:** Michael E. Lehman, age 56
**EVP, Systems Group:** John F. Fowler, age 45
**EVP, People and Places and Chief Human Resources Officer:** William N. (Bill) MacGowan, age 49, $514,114 pay (prior to title change)
**EVP, Storage Group:** David W. Yen, age 54
**EVP, Software Group:** Richard L. (Rich) Green, age 50
**EVP, Global Sales and Services:** Donald C. (Don) Grantham, age 49, $799,072 pay
**EVP, Worldwide Operations:** Eugene G. McCabe, age 53
**EVP, Legal and General Counsel:** Michael A. (Mike) Dillon, age 47
**SVP, Network Systems and Chief Architect:** Andreas (Andy) Bechtolsheim
**SVP, Services Product Management:** Peter J. Weber
**SVP, Systems Engineering:** Hal Stern
**SVP, Americas Sales:** Tim Lieto
**SVP, Global Customer Services:** Ian M. White
**VP, Marketing:** Juan Carlos Soto
**CIO:** Robert Worrall
**President and COO, Sun Microsystems Federal:** William (Bill) Vass
**Chief Gaming Officer:** Chris Melissinos
**Auditors:** Ernst & Young LLP

## LOCATIONS

**HQ:** Sun Microsystems, Inc.
4150 Network Circle, Santa Clara, CA 95054
**Phone:** 650-960-1300 **Fax:** 408-276-3804
**Web:** www.sun.com

### 2006 Sales

| | $ mil. | % of total |
|---|---|---|
| Americas | | |
| US | 5,380 | 41 |
| Other countries | 815 | 6 |
| Europe, Middle East & Africa | 4,703 | 36 |
| Asia/Pacific | 2,170 | 17 |
| **Total** | **13,068** | **100** |

## PRODUCTS/OPERATIONS

### 2006 Sales

| | $ mil. | % of total |
|---|---|---|
| Products | | |
| Computer systems | 5,997 | 46 |
| Network storage | 2,374 | 18 |
| Services | | |
| Support | 3,678 | 28 |
| Client solutions & educational | 1,019 | 8 |
| **Total** | **13,068** | **100** |

### Selected Products

Hardware
- Appliance servers
- Enterprise servers
  - High-performance
  - Midrange
  - Netra (designed for telecommunications providers)
  - Workgroup
- Microprocessors (UltraSPARC)
- Storage
  - Network-attached storage (NAS)
  - Redundant array of independent disk (RAID) systems
  - Tape backup
- Thin clients
- Workstations

Software
- Sun ONE (Open Network Environment)
  - Application server
  - Development
  - Office productivity software (StarOffice)
- Network connectivity for consumer devices (Jini)
- Network management tools (Solstice)
- Operating systems (Solaris)
- Programming languages (Java)
- Storage management tools (Jiro)

Services
- Consulting
- Network management
- Systems integration
- Support
- Training

## COMPETITORS

Apple
BEA Systems
BMC Software
CA
Dell
EMC
Fujitsu
Fujitsu Siemens Computers
Hewlett-Packard
IBM
Intel
Microsoft
NEC
NetApp
Novell
SGI
Symantec
Tivoli Software
Toshiba
Unisys

## HISTORICAL FINANCIALS

Company Type: Public

### Income Statement

FYE: June 30

| | REVENUE ($ mil.) | NET INCOME ($ mil.) | NET PROFIT MARGIN | EMPLOYEES |
|---|---|---|---|---|
| **6/06** | 13,068 | (864) | — | 38,000 |
| **6/05** | 11,070 | (107) | — | 31,000 |
| **6/04** | 11,185 | (388) | — | 35,000 |
| **6/03** | 11,434 | (3,429) | — | 36,100 |
| **6/02** | 12,496 | (587) | — | 39,400 |
| **Annual Growth** | 1.1% | — | — | (0.9%) |

### 2006 Year-End Financials

Debt ratio: 9.1%
Return on equity: —
Cash ($ mil.): 4,065
Current ratio: 1.34
Long-term debt ($ mil.): 575
No. of shares (mil.): 3,602
Dividends
Yield: —
Payout: —
Market value ($ mil.): 14,948

### Stock History

NASDAQ (GS): SUNW

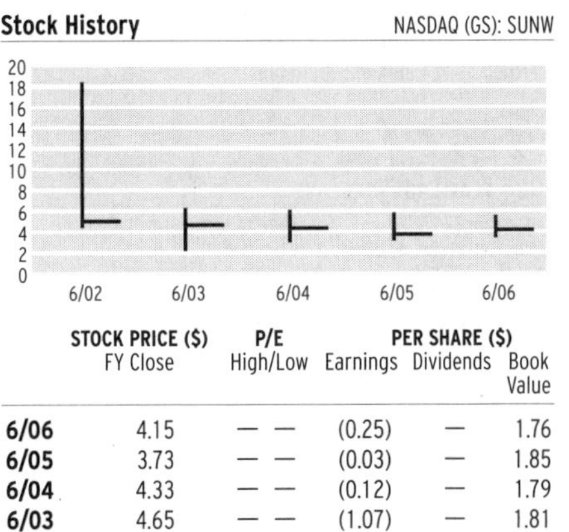

| | STOCK PRICE ($) FY Close | P/E High/Low | PER SHARE ($) Earnings | Dividends | Book Value |
|---|---|---|---|---|---|
| **6/06** | 4.15 | — — | (0.25) | — | 1.76 |
| **6/05** | 3.73 | — — | (0.03) | — | 1.85 |
| **6/04** | 4.33 | — — | (0.12) | — | 1.79 |
| **6/03** | 4.65 | — — | (1.07) | — | 1.81 |
| **6/02** | 5.01 | — — | (0.18) | — | 2.77 |
| **Annual Growth** | (4.6%) | — — | — | — | (10.7%) |

# Sunoco, Inc.

A leading independent oil refiner and marketer, Sunoco has screened its operations, shed nonperforming ones, and buffed the others in hopes that the sun will shine on future profits. The company operates five refineries, which have a combined processing capacity of 900,000 barrels of crude oil a day, and it has 5,450 miles of oil and refined products pipelines and 38 product terminals. It markets its Sunoco gasoline through more than 4,690 retail outlets (including Ultra Service Centers and APlus convenience stores), primarily in the Northeast and upper Midwest. Sunoco also produces lubricants and mines coal for coke processing, and operates a chemicals business.

Sunoco's Retail Portfolio Management (RPM) program was created to decrease invested capital in outlets leased or owned by the company, while retaining fuel sales to the targeted locations through long-term contracts. Some of Sunoco's pipeline, terminal, and storage assets are held through publicly traded Sunoco Logistics Partners, which is 42% controlled by Sunoco unit Sunoco Partners.

The company spent most of the 1990s jettisoning noncore assets, including its oil exploration and production units, and it modernized its refineries. Sunoco is also making chemicals a priority. The company's Sunoco Chemicals unit produces polypropylene, phenol, and plasticizers. Its 2001 acquisition of Mitsubishi's US subsidiary Aristech Chemical doubled the size of Sunoco Chemicals.

## HISTORY

Joseph Newton Pew began his energy career in 1876 when he helped form a Pennsylvania gas pipeline partnership that became Pittsburgh's first natural gas system. When oil discoveries in northwestern Ohio sparked an 1886 boom, Pew began buying oil leases and pipelines and organized the assets into The Sun Oil Company of Ohio in 1890. Four years later the company bought Diamond Oil and its refinery in Toledo, Ohio. The firm traces its trademark diamond pierced by an arrow to the short-lived Diamond subsidiary.

After the 1901 Spindletop gusher, Pew dispatched nephew Edgar Pew to Texas, where he bought the oil-rich properties of a bankrupt firm. Back East, the elder Pew bought Delaware River acreage in Pennsylvania for a shipping terminal and refinery to process Texas crude into Red Stock. The lubricating oil carved Sun Oil a place in the Standard Oil-dominated petroleum industry.

Joseph Pew died in 1912 and was succeeded by sons Howard and Joseph Newton Jr. The company moved into shipbuilding (1916) and gasoline stations (1920). Sun Oil's gasoline was dyed blue (legend says it matched a Chinese tile chip Joseph Jr. and his wife had received on their honeymoon) and sold as Blue Sunoco. The firm went public as Sun Oil in 1925.

When Howard retired in 1947, Joseph Jr. became chairman, and Robert Dunlop became the first non-Pew president of Sun Oil. The company had its first major foreign oil strike in Venezuela in 1957.

In 1967 Dunlop's chance meeting with a Sunray DX Oil executive led to Sun Oil's acquisition of that company the next year. The Sunray DX addition diluted the Pew family's stake in the company. Sun Oil's Venezuelan holdings were nationalized in 1975. The next year the company dropped "Oil" from its name.

In the early 1980s the company sold its shipbuilding arm (1982) and began building its oil holdings, gaining interests in the North Sea and offshore China. In the US Sun purchased Seagram's Texas Pacific Oil for $2.3 billion (1980) and acquired Exeter Oil, Victory Oil, and the interests of Petro-Lewis (1984).

In 1988 Sun began to shed exploration and production assets to focus on refining and marketing. That year it spun off its domestic oil and gas properties into what became Oryx Energy (acquired by Kerr-McGee in 1999). Sun also acquired Atlantic Petroleum and gained more than 1,000 service stations in the process.

In 1993 Sun sold Cordero Mining to Kennecott and cut its stake in Canadian petroleum company Suncor from 68% to 55%. The next year Sun bought a refinery in Philadelphia from Chevron and a stake in a pipeline connecting that refinery to New York Harbor.

In 1995 Sun sold its 55% interest in Suncor, and the following year sold its international oil and gas production business. It also bought the Kendall/Amalie motor oils and lubricants unit of Witco Corporation. In 1998 the company changed its name to Sunoco. Sunoco acquired a Philadelphia phenol plant from AlliedSignal that year.

The company experienced a strike (settled after five months) at its Yabucoa, Puerto Rico, lubricants refinery in 1999. (In 2001 it decided to close the plant.) CEO Robert Campbell retired in 2000 and was replaced by COO John Drosdick.

In 2001 Sunoco bought Mitsubishi subsidiary Aristech Chemical, which operated five chemical plants in the US. It also beefed up its retail operations that year, acquiring more than 230 outlets in 12 eastern states from Coastal Corp.

That year the company formed Sunoco Logistics Partners to acquire, own, and operate a major portion of its midstream and downstream assets.

In 2003 the company acquired 193 gas stations in the southeastern US from Marathon Ashland Petroleum's (now Marathon Petroleum) Speedway SuperAmerica unit. That year Sunoco also bought the Eagle Point refinery (adjacent to its own Philadelphia refining complex) from El Paso Corp. for $111 million and related assets for $135 million.

In 2004 the company acquired 340 gas stations in Delaware, Maryland, Washington, DC, and Virginia from ConocoPhillips.

## EXECUTIVES

**Chairman, President, and CEO:**
John G. (Jack) Drosdick, age 63, $1,140,000 pay
**EVP Refining and Supply:** J. H. Maness
**SVP and CFO:** Thomas W. Hofmann, age 55, $500,000 pay
**SVP and Chief Administrative Officer:**
Charles K. Valutas, age 56, $414,000 pay
**SVP Marketing:** Robert W. Owens, age 53, $465,750 pay
**SVP and General Counsel:** Michael S. Kuritzkes, age 46
**SVP Human Resources and Public Affairs:**
Rolf D. Naku, age 56
**SVP Sunoco Chemicals:** Bruce G. Fischer, age 51, $414,000 pay
**VP Investor Relations and Planning:** Terence P. Delaney, age 51
**President and CEO, Logistics:** Deborah M. Fretz, age 58
**Treasurer:** Paul A. Mulholland, age 54
**Comptroller:** Joseph P. Krott, age 43
**Manager, Marketing Services:** Charles Valis
**Chief Governance Officer, Corporate Secretary, and Assistant General Counsel:** Ann C. Mulé
**Auditors:** Ernst & Young LLP

## LOCATIONS

**HQ:** Sunoco, Inc.
1735 Market St., Ste. LL, Philadelphia, PA 19103
**Phone:** 215-977-3000 **Fax:** 215-977-3409
**Web:** www.sunocoinc.com

Sunoco operates refineries in New Jersey, Ohio, Oklahoma, and Pennsylvania, and gas stations in 25 states, primarily in the Northeast and upper Midwest. It also operates chemicals and cokemaking plants, primarily in the Northeast.

## PRODUCTS/OPERATIONS

**2006 Sales**

| | $ mil. | % of total |
|---|---|---|
| Refining & supply | 18,140 | 47 |
| Retail marketing | 13,482 | 35 |
| Logistics | 3,995 | 10 |
| Chemicals | 2,544 | 7 |
| Coke | 475 | 1 |
| Adjustments | 79 | — |
| **Total** | **38,715** | **100** |

## COMPETITORS

BP
CITGO
ConocoPhillips
Eni
Exxon Mobil
Hess
HOVENSA
Imperial Oil
Koch
Marathon Oil
Motiva Enterprises
Occidental Petroleum
Royal Dutch Shell
Shell Oil Products
United Refining
U.S. Oil
Valero Energy

## HISTORICAL FINANCIALS

Company Type: Public

**Income Statement** FYE: December 31

| | REVENUE ($ mil.) | NET INCOME ($ mil.) | NET PROFIT MARGIN | EMPLOYEES |
|---|---|---|---|---|
| **12/06** | 38,715 | 979 | 2.5% | 14,000 |
| **12/05** | 33,777 | 974 | 2.9% | 13,800 |
| **12/04** | 25,508 | 605 | 2.4% | 14,200 |
| **12/03** | 17,929 | 312 | 1.7% | 14,900 |
| **12/02** | 14,384 | (47) | — | 14,000 |
| **Annual Growth** | 28.1% | — | — | 0.0% |

**2006 Year-End Financials**

Debt ratio: 82.2%
Return on equity: 47.5%
Cash ($ mil.): 263
Current ratio: 0.84
Long-term debt ($ mil.): 1,705
No. of shares (mil.): 121
Dividends
Yield: 1.5%
Payout: 12.5%
Market value ($ mil.): 7,564

**Stock History** NYSE: SUN

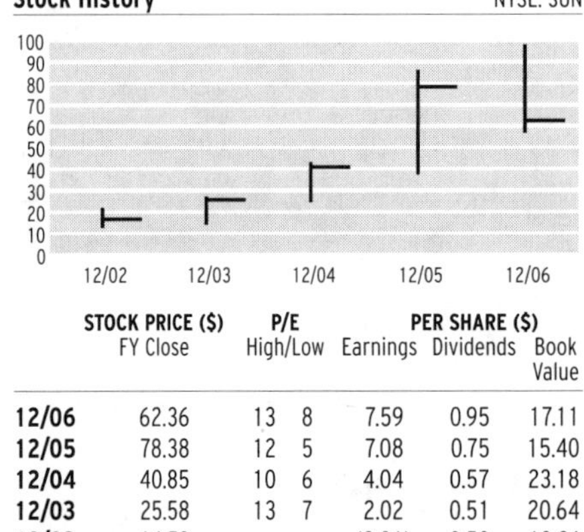


| | STOCK PRICE ($) FY Close | P/E High | P/E Low | PER SHARE ($) Earnings | Dividends | Book Value |
|---|---|---|---|---|---|---|
| **12/06** | 62.36 | 13 | 8 | 7.59 | 0.95 | 17.11 |
| **12/05** | 78.38 | 12 | 5 | 7.08 | 0.75 | 15.40 |
| **12/04** | 40.85 | 10 | 6 | 4.04 | 0.57 | 23.18 |
| **12/03** | 25.58 | 13 | 7 | 2.02 | 0.51 | 20.64 |
| **12/02** | 16.59 | — | — | (0.31) | 0.50 | 18.24 |
| **Annual Growth** | 39.2% | — | — | — | 17.4% | (1.6%) |

# SunTrust Banks

Coca-Cola, fast cars, and SunTrust Banks — this Sun Belt financial holding company is southern to its core. Its eponymous flagship subsidiary SunTrust Bank operates approximately 1,600 bank branches across an arc of southeastern states, including Alabama, the Carolinas, Florida, Georgia, Maryland, Tennessee, and Virginia, plus Washington, DC. The bank's offerings include retail and commercial banking, as well as trust services, credit cards, mortgage banking, mutual funds, insurance, lease financing, asset management, and securities underwriting and dealing.

Emblematic of its southern roots, SunTrust is the second-largest shareholder of fellow Atlantan Coca-Cola (after Warren Buffett's Berkshire Hathaway), and legend has it that the only written copy of the Coke formula lies in a SunTrust vault. The bank also has a marketing pact to be the "Official Bank of Grand Am Racing," a road racing organization (inspired by the *Dukes of Hazzard*, perhaps?). It has established a private banking unit that caters to folks in the sports and entertainment industries, particularly motor sports and country music.

In 2006 the company broke with long-time card services provider MBNA due to its acquisition by Bank of America. SunTrust moved its credit card portfolio to InfiCorpHoldings Inc., a subsidiary of First National of Nebraska Inc.

The company placed on administrative leave or dismissed several financial officers after it had to restate its earnings for the first two quarters of 2004 due to miscalculations of its loan loss reserves. The SEC concluded its investigation in 2006 without recommending penalties.

## HISTORY

SunTrust was born from the union of old-money Georgia and new-money Florida. Founded in 1891, the Trust Company of Georgia (originally Commercial Traveler's Savings Bank) served Atlanta's oldest and richest institutions. It helped underwrite Coca-Cola's IPO in 1919; the bank's ownership stake in Coke stems from its early involvement with the beverage maker.

Beginning in 1933 Trust acquired controlling interests in five other Georgia banks. As regulation of multibank ownership relaxed in the 1970s, Trust acquired the remaining interests in its original banks and bought 25 more. At the height of the Sunbelt boom in 1984, Trust was the most profitable bank in the nation. The next year it united with Sun Banks.

Sun Banks was formed in 1934 as the First National Bank at Orlando. It grew into a holding company in 1967 and in the early 1970s helped assemble the land for Walt Disney World. The Sun name was adopted in 1973.

Under president and CEO Joel Wells, Sun Banks began an acquisition-fueled expansion within Florida. Between 1976 and 1984, Sun Banks' approximate asset growth was an astronomical 500%, and branch count grew fivefold (51 to 274).

After a lingering courtship, Sun and Trust formed a super holding company over the two organizations. When the marriage was consummated in 1985, Sun brought a dowry of $9.4 billion in assets, and Trust contributed $6.2 billion. Trust's chairman, Bob Strickland, became chairman and CEO for the new Atlanta-based SunTrust, and Wells became president.

In 1986 SunTrust bought Nashville, Tennessee-based Third National Bank, the #2 banking company in the Volunteer State. But problems with Tennessee real estate loans plagued SunTrust. In 1990 it increased the amount of loans it wrote off; the bank's ratings suffered because of nonperforming loans on properties in overbuilt Florida. While nonperforming assets decreased in Tennessee in 1991, they climbed in Florida and Georgia.

Strickland stepped down as chairman and CEO in 1990. Wells died in 1991, and James Williams, a conservative banker who instilled strict fiscal management in the Trust banks, became chairman and CEO. Under his direction the company reduced its nonperforming assets and began diversifying its business lines.

In 1993 the bank adopted accounting rules that caused it to revalue its Coca-Cola stock from its historic value of $110,000 to almost $1.1 billion. The dividends from these holdings contributed substantially to revenues.

SunTrust continued developing its nonbanking financial services: it expanded its investment services outside its traditional southern US market and bought Equitable Securities (now SunTrust Equitable Securities) in 1998. That year president Phillip Humann succeeded Williams as chairman and CEO. SunTrust also nearly doubled its branch count when it bought Crestar Financial, a banking powerhouse in the Mid-Atlantic and Southeast.

In 1999 the company created a new trust business to serve high-net-worth clients and consolidated its 27 banking charters in six states into one based in Georgia the following year. In 2001 SunTrust made an unsolicited offer for Wachovia, which was on track to be acquired by First Union. After a heated proxy campaign, Wachovia's board of directors and shareholders voted down SunTrust's bid. Also that year the company bought the institutional business of investment bank Robinson-Humphrey, a unit of Citigroup's Salomon Smith Barney.

SunTrust bought National Commerce Financial in 2004 for some $7 billion. The deal helped the bank expand in existing territories as well as provide entry into the growing North Carolina market, where SunTrust had been conspicuously absent. The company divested its 49% stake in First Market Bank (Ukrop's Super Markets owns the rest), which it acquired in the National Commerce deal. SunTrust unloaded the unit in part because it has branches in Kroger, Publix, Safeway, and Wal-Mart stores.

## EXECUTIVES

**Chairman:** L. Phillip Humann, age 61, $1,164,715 pay
**Vice Chairman:** William R. (Bill) Reed Jr., age 60, $617,144 pay
**President, CEO, and Director:** James M. (Jim) Wells III, age 60, $960,548 pay
**Corporate EVP and CFO:** Mark A. Chancy, age 42, $496,298 pay
**Corporate EVP and CIO:** Timothy E. Sullivan, age 56, $781,431 pay
**Corporate EVP and Chief Administrative Officer:** David F. Dierker, age 49
**Corporate EVP and Chief Risk Officer:** Thomas E. (Tom) Freeman, age 55
**Corporate EVP and Chief Marketing Executive:** Craig J. Kelly
**Corporate EVP, Corporate and Investment Banking Line of Business; CEO, SunTrust Capital Markets:** R. Charles Shufeldt, age 55
**Corporate EVP, Corporate Sales Administration:** Dennis M. Patterson
**Corporate EVP and Director of Human Resources:** Mimi Breeden, age 55
**Corporate EVP, General Counsel, and Corporate Secretary:** Raymond D. Fortin, age 53
**Corporate EVP, Retail Banking Line of Business and SunTrust Online:** C. Eugene (Gene) Kirby, age 47
**Corporate EVP, Wealth and Investment Management, Mortgage and Commercial Lines of Business:** William H. (Bill) Rogers Jr., age 49
**SVP, Controller, and Chief Accounting Officer:** Thomas E. Panther, age 36
**SVP and Treasurer:** Jerome T. Lienhard II
**Director of Investor Relations:** Greg Ketron
**Auditors:** Ernst & Young LLP

## LOCATIONS

**HQ:** SunTrust Banks, Inc.
303 Peachtree St. NE, Atlanta, GA 30308
**Phone:** 404-588-7711 **Fax:** 404-332-3875
**Web:** www.suntrust.com

## PRODUCTS/OPERATIONS

### 2006 Sales

| | $ mil. | % of total |
|---|---|---|
| Interest | | |
| Loans | 7,688.7 | 58 |
| Securities available for sale, including dividends | 1,186.1 | 9 |
| Loans held for sale | 728.0 | 5 |
| Other | 189.2 | 1 |
| Noninterest | | |
| Service charges on deposit accounts | 763.7 | 6 |
| Trust & investment management income | 686.9 | 5 |
| Card fees | 247.6 | 2 |
| Retail investment services | 234.0 | 2 |
| Investment banking income | 230.6 | 2 |
| Other charges & fees | 462.1 | 3 |
| Other | 894.0 | 7 |
| **Total** | **13,310.9** | **100** |

### 2006 Assets

| | $ mil. | % of total |
|---|---|---|
| Cash & equivalents | 4,235.9 | 2 |
| Trading assets | 2,777.6 | 2 |
| Securities available for sale | 25,101.7 | 14 |
| Loans held for sale | 11,790.1 | 6 |
| Net loans | 120,409.8 | 66 |
| Other | 17,846.5 | 10 |
| **Total** | **182,161.6** | **100** |

### Selected Subsidiaries and Affiliates

Affordable Housing Group (community development management)
Asset Management Advisors, L.L.C. (investment advisory and wealth management)
Premium Assignment Corporation (insurance premium financing for small businesses)
SunTrust Capital Markets, Inc. (investment banking)
SunTrust Insurance Company (credit life, accident, and health reinsurance)
SunTrust Leasing Corporation (equipment lease financing)
SunTrust Mortgage, Inc. (origination, purchase, and sale of mortgages)
Cherokee Insurance Company (reinsurance)
SunTrust Securities, Inc. (brokerage and investment advisory for retail clients)
Trusco Capital Management, Inc. (asset management for institutional clients and mutual fund management)

## COMPETITORS

Bank of America
BB&T
Citigroup
Compass Bancshares
Countrywide Financial
First Citizens BancShares
First Horizon
RBC Centura Banks
Regions Financial
Synovus
Wachovia

## HISTORICAL FINANCIALS

Company Type: Public

### Income Statement

FYE: December 31

| | ASSETS ($ mil.) | NET INCOME ($ mil.) | INCOME AS % OF ASSETS | EMPLOYEES |
|---|---|---|---|---|
| **12/06** | 182,162 | 2,118 | 1.2% | 33,599 |
| **12/05** | 179,713 | 1,987 | 1.1% | 33,406 |
| **12/04** | 158,870 | 1,573 | 1.0% | 33,156 |
| **12/03** | 125,393 | 1,332 | 1.1% | 27,578 |
| **12/02** | 117,323 | 1,332 | 1.1% | 27,622 |
| **Annual Growth** | 11.6% | 12.3% | — | 5.0% |

### 2006 Year-End Financials

Equity as % of assets: 9.5%
Return on assets: 1.2%
Return on equity: 12.4%
Long-term debt ($ mil.): 18,993
No. of shares (mil.): 355
Dividends
Yield: 2.9%
Payout: 41.9%
Market value ($ mil.): 29,972
Sales ($ mil.): 13,311

### Stock History

NYSE: STI

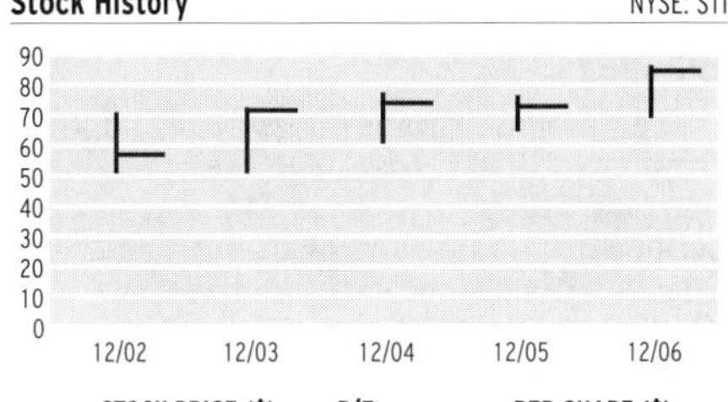


| | STOCK PRICE ($) FY Close | P/E High | P/E Low | PER SHARE ($) Earnings | Dividends | Book Value |
|---|---|---|---|---|---|---|
| **12/06** | 84.45 | 15 | 12 | 5.82 | 2.44 | 50.19 |
| **12/05** | 72.76 | 14 | 12 | 5.47 | 2.20 | 46.65 |
| **12/04** | 73.88 | 15 | 12 | 5.19 | 2.00 | 44.30 |
| **12/03** | 71.50 | 15 | 11 | 4.73 | 1.80 | 34.52 |
| **12/02** | 56.92 | 15 | 11 | 4.66 | 1.72 | 31.04 |
| **Annual Growth** | 10.4% | — | — | 5.7% | 9.1% | 12.8% |

# Superior Essex

Superior Essex works hard to make superior wire and cable. The company, which is one of the US's leading makers of copper wire, was known as Superior TeleCom until it reorganized under Chapter 11 bankruptcy protection in 2003. Its copper and fiber optic wire and cable are used in communications networks, while its magnet wire can be found in transformers, generators, and electrical controls. The company also makes copper rod for internal use and for sale to other wire and cable makers. Regional Bell telephone operating companies are major customers of Superior Essex, as are OEMs such as Delphi and A.O. Smith.

Superior Essex has expanded its operations through acquisitions: in 2005 the company took a 60% interest in a joint venture (Essex Nexans) with Nexans that acquired Nexans' European magnet wire operations. In 2006 it tried to expand again when it made an unsolicited $36 million offer to buy Optical Cable Corporation.

Early in 2007 Superior Essex announced another deal with Nexans — this time an agreement to spend about $35 million to acquire Nexans' magnet wire operations in Canada and China; the Canadian portion of the deal was completed in April of that year and the Chinese part was completed in July. The company purchased the remaining 40% stake in Essex Nexans from Nexans in mid-2007. Superior Essex has also acquired Italian magnet wire producer Invex S.p.A. Superior Essex expects these acquisitions to add $450 million in annual revenues.

The company's production facilities in Mexico serve customers in the US, as well as the markets in Central and South America that Superior is pursuing. Customers in the US, which previously accounted for nearly 95% of sales, now account for a little less than 80% due to expansion in Europe. Superior also completed the construction of a new manufacturing facility in China at the end of 2006.

## HISTORY

The Alpine Group organized Superior TeleCom in 1996 to operate its telecommunications and data communications businesses. Superior TeleCom became the parent company of Superior Communications and DNE Systems when Alpine spun off almost 50% of the company that year (and parted with the rest by 2003).

With fiber-optic technology gradually replacing copper, Superior began positioning itself for the changeover in 1997 when it opened a center in Georgia to develop fiber-optic products. Also that year Superior signed five-year supply agreements with GTE and Sprint for copper wire.

In 1998 Superior expanded outside North America by buying a 51% stake in Cables of Zion (Israel), which makes and distributes copper wire in Europe and the Middle East. Superior also bolstered its LAN cable offerings when it bought wire and cable maker Essex International for $936 million.

In 2000 the company completed construction on a magnet wire manufacturing plant in Mexico. With building wire profits down in 1999, Superior reduced costs in 2000 by closing eight plants and by reducing its workforce by 25%. That year the company expanded its Brownwood, Texas, plant to produce fiber-optic cable. In 2001 the company reduced its workforce by nearly 700 employees.

Superior closed a manufacturing facility in Elizabethtown, Kentucky, responsible for its communication products in early 2002; the property was sold in 2003. Also in 2002 the company's SUPERIOR ESSEX Communications Group released its ribbon fiber cable product line. The New York Stock Exchange announced in 2002 that Superior TeleCom would be delisted; the company began trading on the OTC Bulletin Board.

In late 2003 the company emerged from Chapter 11 and changed its name to Superior Essex. The company also announced that Stephen Carter, formerly the CEO at Cingular Wireless (now AT&T Mobility), would take the helm at Superior. In late 2003 The Alpine Group forgave Superior's debts and relinquished its entire stake in the company it spun off in 1996.

In 2004 the company acquired Belden's North American telecommunications cable division.

## EXECUTIVES

**President, CEO, and Director:** Stephen M. Carter, age 53, $697,500 pay
**EVP, CFO, and Treasurer:** David S. Aldridge, age 52, $395,423 pay
**EVP, General Counsel, and Secretary:** Barbara L. Blackford, age 50, $291,923 pay
**EVP; President, Superior Essex Communications Group:** Justin F. Deedy Jr., age 51, $331,230 pay
**EVP; President, Essex Asia Pacific:** H. Patrick (Pat) Jack, age 55, $329,039 pay
**EVP; President, Essex Group North America:** J. David Reed
**SVP, Finance and Corporate Controller:** Tracye C. Gilleland
**SVP, Corporate Administrative Services:** Debbie Baker-Oliver
**Director, Investor Relations:** Peggy Tharp
**Director, Marketing:** Matt Wheeler
**Auditors:** PricewaterhouseCoopers LLP

## LOCATIONS

**HQ:** Superior Essex Inc.
150 Interstate N. Pkwy., Atlanta, GA 30339
**Phone:** 770-657-6000 **Fax:** 770-303-8807
**Web:** www.superioressex.com

Superior Essex operates facilities in Canada, China, France, Germany, Mexico, Portugal, the UK, and the US.

**2006 Sales**

| | $ mil. | % of total |
|---|---|---|
| North America | 2,291.1 | 78 |
| Europe | | |
| Germany | 345.3 | 12 |
| France | 188.2 | 6 |
| UK | 87.2 | 3 |
| Other European countries | 26.3 | 1 |
| **Total** | **2,938.1** | **100** |

## PRODUCTS/OPERATIONS

**2006 Sales**

| | $ mil. | % of total |
|---|---|---|
| Magnet wire & distribution | | |
| North American | 1,029.4 | 35 |
| European | 647.0 | 22 |
| Communications cable | 817.9 | 28 |
| Copper rod | 443.8 | 15 |
| **Total** | **2,938.1** | **100** |

## COMPETITORS

Alcatel-Lucent
Anixter International
APA Cables and Networks
Belden
Carlisle Companies
CommScope
Corning
Encore Wire
General Cable
Genesis Cable
International Wire
Marmon Group
Nexans
OFS BrightWave
Okonite
Prestolite Wire
Southwire
Sumitomo Electric
W.L. Gore

## HISTORICAL FINANCIALS

Company Type: Public

**Income Statement** FYE: December 31

| | REVENUE ($ mil.) | NET INCOME ($ mil.) | NET PROFIT MARGIN | EMPLOYEES |
|---|---|---|---|---|
| **12/06** | 2,938 | 57 | 2.0% | 4,100 |
| **12/05** | 1,795 | 32 | 1.8% | 4,100 |
| **12/04** | 1,425 | 11 | 0.7% | — |
| **12/03*** | 988 | 875 | 88.6% | — |
| **11/03** | 862 | 878 | 101.9% | — |
| **Annual Growth** | 35.9% | (49.5%) | — | 0.0% |

*Fiscal year change

**2006 Year-End Financials**

Debt ratio: 81.5%
Return on equity: 20.3%
Cash ($ mil.): 53
Current ratio: 2.53
Long-term debt ($ mil.): 293
No. of shares (mil.): 20
Dividends
Yield: —
Payout: —
Market value ($ mil.): 678

**Stock History** NASDAQ (GS): SPSX

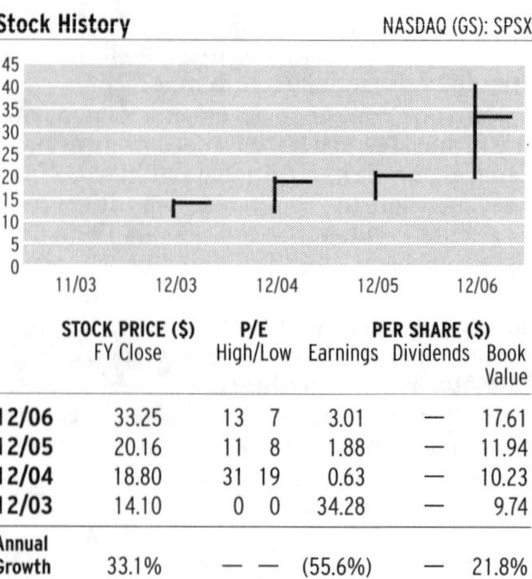


| | STOCK PRICE ($) FY Close | P/E High | P/E Low | PER SHARE ($) Earnings | Dividends | Book Value |
|---|---|---|---|---|---|---|
| **12/06** | 33.25 | 13 | 7 | 3.01 | — | 17.61 |
| **12/05** | 20.16 | 11 | 8 | 1.88 | — | 11.94 |
| **12/04** | 18.80 | 31 | 19 | 0.63 | — | 10.23 |
| **12/03** | 14.10 | 0 | 0 | 34.28 | — | 9.74 |
| **Annual Growth** | 33.1% | — | — | (55.6%) | — | 21.8% |

# SUPERVALU INC.

SUPERVALU is feeling pretty super following the acquisition of more than 1,100 supermarkets from fallen grocery giant Albertsons (formerly Albertson's, Inc.). Its purchase of the Albertsons stores catapulted the chain from ninth to third-place in the US retail grocery market with about 2,500 stores nationwide. SUPERVALU is also one of the nation's largest food wholesalers, supplying some 2,200 grocery stores in 48 states with brand-name and private-label goods. The deal added half a dozen new banners, including Albertsons, Acme Markets, and Shaw's to SUPERVALU's store roster (which includes Shoppers Food & Pharmacy, Cub Foods, Shop 'n Save). SUPERVALU also bought Albertsons' in-store pharmacy operations.

The company has spent about $1 billion since mid-2006 to remodel many of its stores, namely a sizable group in the Chicago area, and to build new ones. A new campaign called "Premium Fresh & Healthy" has been launched to call attention to its expanded produce, meat, seafood, and other in-store departments, much like rival Safeway's successful "Ingredients for Life" program.

SUPERVALU cherry picked Albertsons' most attractive supermarket assets including Acme, the upscale Bristol Farms chain in California, Jewel-Osco in the Chicago area, Star Markets in New England, and the Osco Drug and Sav-on banners, among others. SUPERVALU was part of a consortium of investors, which included drugstore operator CVS, that paid about $26 per share for Albertsons, previously the nation's #2 grocery chain, in June 2006. In a related transaction, SUPERVALU sold 26 Cub Food stores located primarily in the Chicago area to one of its partners in the deal, Cerberus Capital Management.

Other banners operated by the company include bigg's; the extreme-value format Save-A-Lot stores; and about 65 supermarkets flying the Farm Fresh, Scott's Foods, and Hornbacher's banners. Looking to take back sales lost to natural and organic grocery chains, SUPERVALU has launched its own natural foods division, called Sunflower Markets. SUPERVALU is planning to open as many as 50 Sunflower Markets within five years.

SUPERVALU is under increasing pressure from expanding supercenters and warehouse clubs, such as Wal-Mart and Costco, which have stolen sales from conventional grocery retailers. To better compete with big discounters, it's expanding its extreme-value Save-A-Lot format, which already holds the #1 spot (based on revenues) in the extreme-value grocery market.

SUPERVALU's wholesale customers include conventional and upscale supermarkets, combination food and drugstores, supercenters, convenience stores, limited assortment stores, and e-tailers. SUPERVALU offers its retailers private labels in every price range and in virtually every store category.

Investment firm Yucaipa Companies, which made a name for itself by spearheading several grocery store mergers and acquisitions in the 1990s, acquired an 11% stake in SUPERVALU for about $680 million in 2006.

## HISTORY

SUPERVALU's predecessor was formed in Minneapolis in the 1870s — and again in 1926. In 1871 wholesalers Hugh Harrison, George Newell, and W. D. Washburn joined forces to create Newell and Harrison. Newell bought out his partners in 1874 and renamed the firm George R. Newell Co. Five years later Harrison formed his own operation, H. G. Harrison Co. In 1926 the companies merged, creating Winston & Newell Co., the largest grocery distributor to independent grocers in the Midwest.

The company was part of the Independent Grocers Alliance from 1928-1942 before adopting the name Super Valu Stores in 1954. It expanded by acquiring chains such as Piggly-Wiggly Midland (1958, Wisconsin) and a number of wholesale operations across the US.

Super Valu entered nonfood retailing in 1971 by acquiring ShopKo, a discount department store chain. Two years later it founded clothing chain County Seat (sold 1983). Super Valu added a new format to its food operations by purchasing Cub Stores (warehouse-style groceries) in 1980; it later combined its Cub Stores and ShopKo formats. More acquisitions followed, including Atlanta's Food Giant chain. Super Valu named Michael Wright CEO in 1981 and chairman in 1982.

Super Valu acquired Scott's, an Indiana food store chain, in 1991 and sold a 54% interest in ShopKo to the public. The company changed its name to SUPERVALU in 1992 and bought food wholesaler Wetterau, making it the #1 independent food distributor in the US and giving it the Save-A-Lot franchise (launched in 1978).

Experiencing sluggish distribution growth, SUPERVALU continued to expand its retail holdings. Acquisitions in 1994 included Sweet Life Foods (280 stores) and 30 Texas T Stores. SUPERVALU sold its remaining 46% stake in ShopKo in 1997.

In 2001 rival distributor Fleming Companies beat out SUPERVALU to become Kmart's sole supplier of foods and consumable products. SUPERVALU later announced plans to cut 7% of its workforce and close some of its distribution centers and stores, including its Laneco stores in Pennsylvania and New Jersey and its central Indiana Cub stores. Wright retired as CEO in mid-2001 and remained as chairman; president and CFO Jeff Noddle became CEO.

In May 2002 Wright retired as chairman and was succeeded by Noddle. In June the company announced it would take a charge of up to $21 million because of accounting irregularities in its pharmacy division.

In February 2005 SUPERVALU acquired Total Logistics, a provider of third-party logistics services and maker of refrigeration systems, for about $234 million. In March the grocery distributor launched a specialty produce distribution company called W. Newell & Co.

In March 2006 SUPERVALU sold its standalone extreme-value Deal$ Stores to Dollar Tree Stores for about $30.5 million. Deal$ operated nearly 140 stores in 16 states. In June, the company completed its acquisition, announced in January 2006, of 1,124 stores from Albertson's. The new stores include Acme Markets, Bristol Farms, Jewel, Shaw's Supermarkets, Star Markets, and Albertsons stores.

## EXECUTIVES

**Chairman and CEO:** Jeffrey (Jeff) Noddle, age 60, $1,100,000 pay
**President and COO:** Michael L. (Mike) Jackson, age 53, $630,962 pay
**EVP:** David L. (Dave) Boehnen, age 60, $545,000 pay
**EVP and CFO:** Pamela K. (Pam) Knous, age 53, $648,077 pay
**EVP, Merchandising and Marketing:** Duncan C. MacNaughton, age 44
**EVP and President, Retail Midwest:** Kevin H. Tripp, age 52
**EVP, Human Resources:** David E. (Dave) Pylipow, age 49
**EVP, Retail and Wholesale Supply Chain:** Janel S. Haugarth, age 52
**EVP and President, Retail West:** Pete Van Helden, age 46
**SVP, Finance:** Sherry M. Smith, age 45
**SVP; President and CEO, Save-A-Lot Food Stores:** Bill Shaner
**SVP, Real Estate:** J. Andrew (Andy) Herring, age 47
**SVP and Chief Marketing Officer:** Susan Parker
**VP, Treasurer:** John Boyd
**VP, Corporate Secretary, and Chief Securities Counsel:** Burt Fealing
**VP, Corporate Communications:** Shannon Bennett
**VP, Investor Relations:** Yolanda M. Scharton
**VP and Controller:** David M. Oliver, age 48
**Auditors:** KPMG LLP

## LOCATIONS

**HQ:** SUPERVALU INC.
11840 Valley View Rd., Eden Prairie, MN 55344
**Phone:** 952-828-4000 **Fax:** 952-828-8998
**Web:** www.supervalu.com

SUPERVALU has about 25 distribution centers that supply about 2,200 retail grocery stores in 48 states. The company also owns, franchises, or licenses about 2,475 retail superstores, conventional supermarkets, and discount food and general merchandise stores in some 40 states.

## PRODUCTS/OPERATIONS

### 2007 Sales

| | $ mil. | % of total |
|---|---|---|
| Retail food | 28,016 | 75 |
| Supply chain service | 9,390 | 25 |
| **Total** | **37,406** | **100** |

### 2007 Stores

| | No. |
|---|---|
| Combination food & drug stores | 876 |
| Food stores | 412 |
| Limited assortment food stores | 332 |
| **Total** | **1,620** |

### 2007 Stores

| | No. |
|---|---|
| Company-owned | 1,620 |
| Licensed | 858 |
| **Total** | **2,478** |

### Retail Food Stores and Formats

Extreme Value Stores
- Save-A-Lot

Price Superstore
- bigg's
- Cub Foods
- Shop 'n Save
- Shoppers Food & Pharmacy

Supermarkets
- Acme Markets
- Bristol Farms
- Farm Fresh
- Hornbacher's
- Jewel-Osco
- Scott's Foods
- Shaw's Supermarkets
- Sunflower Markets

### Selected Services

Accounting
Category management
Consumer and market research
Financial assistance
Insurance
Merchandising assistance
Personnel training
Private-label program
Retail operations counseling
Site selection and purchasing or leasing assistance
Store design and construction
Store equipment
Store management assistance
Store planning
Strategic and business planning

## COMPETITORS

A&P
Ahold USA
ALDI
Alex Lee
Arden Group
Associated Wholesale Grocers
Associated Wholesalers
Big Y Foods
Bozzuto's
C&S Wholesale
Delhaize America
Di Giorgio
Dierbergs Markets
Fresh Brands
Giant Eagle
Hannaford Bros.
Jetro Cash & Carry
Krasdale Foods
Kroger
Marsh Supermarkets
McLane
Meijer
Nash-Finch
Ralphs
Rite Aid
Roundy's Supermarkets
Safeway
Schnuck Markets
Sherwood Food
Spartan Stores
Stop & Shop
Vons
Wakefern Food
Walgreen
Wal-Mart
Whole Foods
Wild Oats Markets
Winn-Dixie

## HISTORICAL FINANCIALS

Company Type: Public

### Income Statement

FYE: Last Saturday in February

| | REVENUE ($ mil.) | NET INCOME ($ mil.) | NET PROFIT MARGIN | EMPLOYEES |
|---|---|---|---|---|
| **2/07** | 37,406 | 452 | 1.2% | 191,400 |
| **2/06** | 19,864 | 206 | 1.0% | 52,400 |
| **2/05** | 19,543 | 386 | 2.0% | 56,000 |
| **2/04** | 20,210 | 280 | 1.4% | 55,200 |
| **2/03** | 19,160 | 257 | 1.3% | 57,400 |
| **Annual Growth** | 18.2% | 15.2% | — | 35.1% |

### 2007 Year-End Financials

Debt ratio: 173.2%
Return on equity: 11.4%
Cash ($ mil.): 285
Current ratio: 0.95
Long-term debt ($ mil.): 9,192
No. of shares (mil.): 209
Dividends
Yield: 1.7%
Payout: 28.0%
Market value ($ mil.): 7,871

### Stock History NYSE: SVU

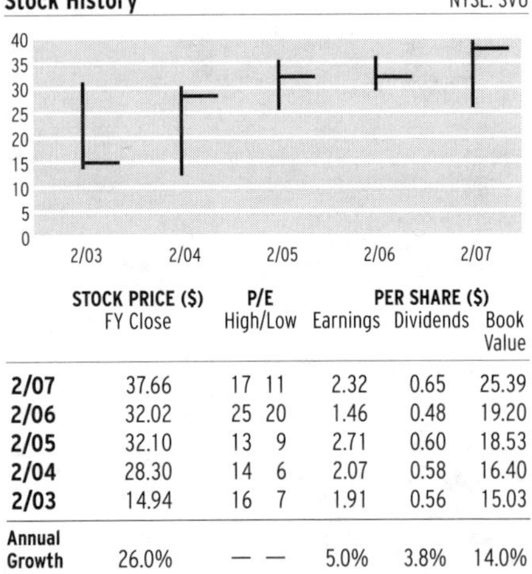

| | STOCK PRICE ($) FY Close | P/E High | P/E Low | PER SHARE ($) Earnings | Dividends | Book Value |
|---|---|---|---|---|---|---|
| **2/07** | 37.66 | 17 | 11 | 2.32 | 0.65 | 25.39 |
| **2/06** | 32.02 | 25 | 20 | 1.46 | 0.48 | 19.20 |
| **2/05** | 32.10 | 13 | 9 | 2.71 | 0.60 | 18.53 |
| **2/04** | 28.30 | 14 | 6 | 2.07 | 0.58 | 16.40 |
| **2/03** | 14.94 | 16 | 7 | 1.91 | 0.56 | 15.03 |
| **Annual Growth** | 26.0% | — | — | 5.0% | 3.8% | 14.0% |

# Symantec Corporation

Symantec isn't the least bit insecure. The company provides a variety of content and network security software for both consumers and businesses, used for functions such as virus protection, intrusion detection, and remote management. Symantec has used the success of its Norton family of consumer security software to fuel a push into products and services for enterprises, including virtual private networks and applications for firewall management. The company continues to bolster its professional services offerings, which include security assessment, consulting, and outsourced security management.

In July 2005 Symantec acquired VERITAS for about $11 billion. VERITAS' operations have been absorbed into those of Symantec. In mid-2006 Symantec filed a suit against Microsoft related to storage management software developed by VERITAS. Symantec claims that Microsoft misappropriated intellectual property and violated the terms of a licensing agreement by incorporating VERITAS technology into its software. Microsoft has countersued, alleging that Symantec violated three of its patents.

Symantec has aggressively pursued acquisitions (more than 35 since its founding in 1989) to expand its product line past consumer-oriented applications and into broader enterprise security software and service products, which now account for about half of sales. It purchased WholeSecurity, Inc. (a maker of security software used to thwart viruses, worms, and other malicious code) and Sygate Technologies (network access control solutions) in 2005. The following year it bought BindView Development Corporation (computer network management and security), IMlogic (enterprise instant messaging), and Relicore (data center change and configuration management). It also acquired UK-based Company-i, a data center services firm focused on the finance sector, as well as data protection software developer Revivio. Early in 2007, Symantec acquired IT asset management software maker Altiris for approximately $830 million in cash. The company also announced plans to form a joint venture with China-based Huawei Technologies in 2007. Symantec will hold a 49% stake in the company, which will develop security and storage products for telecom service providers.

Symantec sells its products through a direct sales force, as well as through distributors, resellers, original equipment manufacturers, and systems integrators. Customers outside of the US account for more than half of sales.

## HISTORY

Artificial intelligence expert Gary Hendrix founded Symantec in 1982. Gordon Eubanks, a former student of the late industry pioneer Gary Kildall and founder of C&E Software, was appointed CEO in 1983 and bought the company in 1984. Realizing that Symantec could not compete against Microsoft and Lotus, Eubanks began buying niche-market software firms. In 1990, a year after going public, Symantec merged with DOS utilities market leader Peter Norton Computing. It bought 13 companies between 1990 and 1994.

Symantec bought Delrina (maker of WinFax) in 1995. Symantec slowed its acquisition pace and concentrated on the growing Internet market. In 1996 it sold Delrina's electronic forms business to JetForm.

Symantec in 1997 filed copyright-infringement charges against Network Associates. The next year a suit was filed against Symantec on behalf of antivirus product users, alleging that it ignored its warranty by charging to fix a year 2000 software glitch.

The company went on another acquisition binge, buying the antivirus operations of both IBM and Intel in 1998 and acquiring rival Quarterdeck in 1999. When Eubanks left in 1999 to head a software startup, IBM exec John Thompson stepped in and became the first African-American CEO of a major software company.

In 2000 Symantec sold its Internet tools division to software developer BEA Systems in a deal valued at about $75 million. It also acquired L-3 Communications' network security operations. Late that year it bought rival network security software maker AXENT Technologies in a $975 million deal.

The company divested its Web access management product line in 2001. Later that year the company acquired Foster-Melliar's enterprise security management division.

In 2002 the company continued its acquisitive ways, purchasing Recourse Technologies, Riptech, and SecurityFocus. The following year the company acquired Nexland, PowerQuest, and SafeWeb. The company purchased infrastructure management software provider ON Technology for about $100 million early in 2004. Later that year Symantec also purchased anti-spam software provider Brightmail for $370 million.

Symantec announced plans to purchase VERITAS in December 2004. The deal was completed in July of the following year.

## EXECUTIVES

**Chairman and CEO:** John W. Thompson, age 57, $1,550,000 pay
**EVP and CFO:** James A. Beer, age 45, $2,086,667 pay (partial-year salary)
**EVP and CTO:** Mark Bregman, age 49
**EVP, General Counsel, and Secretary:** Arthur F. (Art) Courville, age 48
**EVP and Chief Human Resources Officer:** Rebecca A. Ranninger, age 48
**EVP and CIO:** David Thompson
**SVP, Europe, Middle East, and Africa:** John F. Brigden, age 40
**SVP, The Americas:** Steven B. (Steve) Messick
**SVP, Asia/Pacific and Japan:** Bill Robbins
**SVP, Corporate Development:** James Socas
**SVP, Finance and Chief Accounting Officer:** George W. Harrington, age 55
**Group President, Symantec Global Services:** Greg Hughes, age 42
**Group President, Consumer Business Unit:** Janice D. Chaffin, age 51
**Group President, Worldwide Sales and Marketing:** Enrique T. Salem, age 41
**Group President, Security and Data Management:** Thomas W. (Tom) Kendra, age 52
**Group President, Data Center Management:** Kristof (Kris) Hagerman, age 42, $817,340 pay
**Auditors:** KPMG LLP

## LOCATIONS

**HQ:** Symantec Corporation
20330 Stevens Creek Blvd., Cupertino, CA 95014
**Phone:** 408-517-8000 **Fax:** 408-517-8186
**Web:** www.symantec.com

### 2007 Sales

| | $ mil. | % of total |
|---|---|---|
| US | 2,560.3 | 49 |
| UK | 542.3 | 11 |
| Other countries | 2,096.8 | 40 |
| **Total** | **5,199.4** | **100** |

## PRODUCTS/OPERATIONS

### 2007 Sales

| | $ mil. | % of total |
|---|---|---|
| Security & data management | 2,004.7 | 39 |
| Consumer products | 1,590.5 | 31 |
| Data center management | 1,369.3 | 26 |
| Services | 234.8 | 4 |
| Other | 0.1 | — |
| **Total** | **5,199.4** | **100** |

### Selected Products

Security & data management
- Compliance and security management
- Data protection
- Endpoint security
- Messaging management

Consumer products
- Backup
- Internet security
- PC tuneup

Data center management
- Application performance
- Data protection
- Storage and server management

Services
- Consulting
- Maintenance and support
- Training

## COMPETITORS

BMC Software
CA
Check Point Software
Cisco Systems
CommVault
Cybertrust
DataCore
EDS
EMC
FalconStor
F-Secure
Hewlett-Packard
Hitachi Data Systems
IBM
Internet Security Systems
McAfee
Microsoft
NetApp
NTRU
Oracle
Quest Software
Secure Computing
Smith Micro
Sophos
Sun Microsystems
Trend Micro
VeriSign
Zone Labs

## HISTORICAL FINANCIALS

Company Type: Public

**Income Statement** FYE: March 31

| | REVENUE ($ mil.) | NET INCOME ($ mil.) | NET PROFIT MARGIN | EMPLOYEES |
|---|---|---|---|---|
| **3/07** | 5,199 | 404 | 7.8% | 17,100 |
| **3/06** | 4,143 | 157 | 3.8% | 16,000 |
| **3/05** | 2,583 | 536 | 20.8% | 6,500 |
| **3/04** | 1,870 | 371 | 19.8% | 5,300 |
| **3/03** | 1,407 | 248 | 17.7% | 4,300 |
| **Annual Growth** | 38.7% | 13.0% | — | 41.2% |

**2007 Year-End Financials**

Debt ratio: 18.3%
Return on equity: 3.2%
Cash ($ mil.): 2,988
Current ratio: 1.23
Long-term debt ($ mil.): 2,121
No. of shares (mil.): 899
Dividends
Yield: —
Payout: —
Market value ($ mil.): 15,560

**Stock History** NASDAQ (GS): SYMC

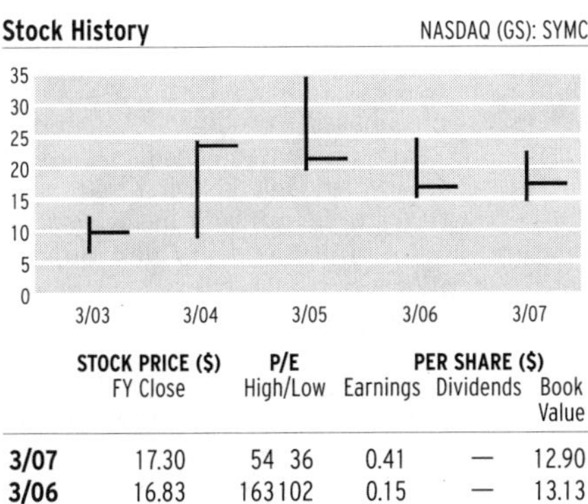


| | STOCK PRICE ($) FY Close | P/E High/Low | | PER SHARE ($) Earnings | Dividends | Book Value |
|---|---|---|---|---|---|---|
| **3/07** | 17.30 | 54 | 36 | 0.41 | — | 12.90 |
| **3/06** | 16.83 | 163 | 102 | 0.15 | — | 13.13 |
| **3/05** | 21.33 | 46 | 27 | 0.74 | — | 5.22 |
| **3/04** | 23.48 | 45 | 17 | 0.54 | — | 7.78 |
| **3/03** | 9.80 | 31 | 18 | 0.38 | — | 11.86 |
| **Annual Growth** | 15.3% | — | — | 1.9% | — | 2.1% |

# Synovus Financial

Synovus Financial has a nose for community banking. The holding company owns about 40 mainly small-town banks offering deposit accounts and consumer and business loans in Alabama, Florida, Georgia, South Carolina, and Tennessee. Through more than 400 locations, the banks provide deposits, loans, credit cards, insurance, and asset management services. Synovus Financial also owns more than 80% of Total System Services (TSYS), one of the leading processors of credit card transactions in the US. The subsidiary, which accounts for about one-third of Synovus Financial's total revenue, also performs student loan processing, fraud detection, debt collection, and commercial printing services.

Synovus Financial has developed a small-makes-big strategy. The strongly decentralized company maintains separate charters and local boards of directors for its subsidiary banks, losing some operational efficiency, but gaining from the institutions' community presence. The highly acquisitive company has continued its push across the south, entering or bolstering its presence in such markets as metro Atlanta; Augusta, Georgia; Charlotte, North Carolina; Chattanooga, Tennessee; Jacksonville; Naples, Florida; Orlando, Florida; Savannah, Georgia; and Tampa. Synovus is eyeing further growth in North Carolina. While the company typically grows through acquisition, it also launches brand-new community banks. Two of its Florida banking subsidiaries (one *de novo* and the other formed in the merger of three subsidiaries' banking charters) have taken the Synovus Bank brand, a new strategy for the company. In terms of service offerings, Synovus Financial has its banks looking toward a concentration on commercial banking; focuses included increasing its commercial and industrial loans, as well as providing such services as corporate cash management, capital markets, and asset-based lending. Bank of America's acquisition of MBNA and its subsequent decision to shift its consumer card portfolio processing in-house are expected to significantly impact Synovus Financial and TSYS. In 2006 Bank of America accounted for nearly a quarter of TSYS' total revenue and more than 10% of Synovus Financial's total revenue. The company hopes to remedy the situation by diversifying TSYS' revenue sources and broadening geographically; TSYS has been expanding in the UK and Asia, primarily through acquisitions and alliances. Synovus Financial has also said it is studying a possible spin-off of TSYS to shareholders as a means of providing more access to funds for the processing firm's growth.

## HISTORY

In 1885 W. C. Bradley founded his eponymous company (today a manufacturing and development concern). Three years later he invested in a new bank that would eventually bear the name of its Georgia hometown: Columbus Bank and Trust. (Bradley's investment in Atlanta-based Coca-Cola today accounts for the lion's share of his family's wealth.) When Bradley died, his son-in-law D. Abbott Turner joined the bank's board of directors, followed by Turner's son William.

In 1958 the bank hired James Blanchard as president. The next year Columbus Bank and Trust became one of the first banks to issue credit cards. The company's credit processing business grew, leading it to computerize the process in 1966 and train its own employees to operate the equipment. (It decided to go it alone after a failed joint-venture attempt with corporate cousin W.C. Bradley Co.)

In a little more than a decade, Blanchard led the bank to triple its assets. When Blanchard died in 1969, the search for a new leader took the bank's directors in a surprising direction: They offered the position to Blanchard's son Jimmy, a young attorney with no banking experience. The board pressed him to take the job, which he did in 1971 after a brief apprenticeship.

From the start, the younger Blanchard emphasized the company's financial services operations, such as credit card processing. Taking advantage of new laws opening up the banking and financial services industry in the early 1970s, the bank reorganized in 1972, incorporating CB&T Bancshares to serve as holding company for Columbus Bank and Trust. In 1973 CB&T's financial services division finished a new software product called the Total System, which allowed electronic access to account information. CB&T used the groundbreaking software to start processing other banks' paperwork, including an ever-growing number of credit card accounts. In 1983 CB&T spun off financial services division Total System Services (TSYS), but retained a majority stake in the company.

Blanchard helped win passage of Georgia's multibank holding law, and further deregulation in the early 1980s allowed the company to operate across state lines. It bought four banks in Florida and Georgia in 1983 and 1984, and snapped up six more (including an Alabama bank) in 1985. Meanwhile, TSYS benefited from the trend to outsource credit card processing.

In 1989 CB&T changed its name to Synovus, a combination of the words "synergy" and "novus," the latter word meaning (according to the company) "of superior quality and different from the others listed in the same category."

During the early 1990s, Synovus swept up 20 banks in its market area after the bank bust. After 1993, acquisitions dropped off until 1998, when Synovus announced three acquisitions in two weeks. That year it also announced it was planning to move further into Internet and investment banking, as well as auto and life insurance. In 1999 the company bought banks in Georgia and Florida; it also moved into debt collection with its purchase of Wallace & de Mayo, renamed TSYS Total Debt Management.

The company grew its retail investment operations with the acquisitions of Atlanta-area asset managers Creative Financial Group in 2001 and GLOBALT in 2002.

The younger Blanchard, who had ultimately become Synovus Financial's chairman, retired as an executive in 2005, but remained on the board.

## EXECUTIVES

**Chairman and CEO:** Richard E. Anthony, age 60, $819,000 pay
**Vice Chairman and Chief People Officer:** Elizabeth R. (Lee Lee) James, age 45, $375,500 pay
**President, COO, and Director:** Frederick L. (Fred) Green III, age 48, $408,333 pay
**SEVP, General Counsel, and Secretary:** G. Sanders Griffith III, age 53, $413,000 pay
**EVP and CFO:** Thomas J. Prescott, age 52, $364,000 pay
**EVP and Chief Credit Officer:** Mark G. Holladay, age 51
**EVP and Director of Retail Banking:** Leila S. Carr
**EVP, Corporate Affairs:** Calvin Smyre, age 59

**SVP and Director of E-Business:** Robin A. Grier
**SVP and Director of Investor Relations:** Patrick A. (Pat) Reynolds
**SVP and Director of Technology and Operations:** John Woolbright
**SVP and Director of The Center for People Development:** Nancy Deane
**SVP and Marketing Director:** Loree Link
**SVP, Loan Operations:** Pat Perry
**SVP and Product Director:** Donna Atkins
**Chief Accounting Officer:** Liliana McDaniel
**Director of Communications:** Alison Dowe
**Media and Public Relations Manager:** Greg Hudgison
**Auditors:** KPMG LLP

## LOCATIONS

**HQ:** Synovus Financial Corp.
1111 Bay Ave., Ste. 500, Columbus, GA 31901
**Phone:** 706-649-5220 **Fax:** 706-641-6555
**Web:** www.synovus.com

## PRODUCTS/OPERATIONS

**2006 Assets**

| | $ mil. | % of total |
|---|---|---|
| Cash & equivalents | 1,025.7 | 3 |
| Loans | 24,340.1 | 76 |
| Investment securities held for sale | 3,352.4 | 11 |
| Mortgage loans held for sale | 175.0 | 1 |
| Other | 2,961.6 | 9 |
| **Total** | **31,854.8** | **100** |

**2006 Sales**

| | $ mil. | % of total |
|---|---|---|
| Interest | | |
| Loans | 1,859.9 | 45 |
| Securities & other | 156.5 | 4 |
| Electronic payment processing services | 985.9 | 24 |
| Reimbursable items | 351.7 | 8 |
| Merchant acquiring services | 206.3 | 5 |
| Other transaction processing services | 186.4 | 4 |
| Service charges on deposit accounts | 112.4 | 3 |
| Other | 293.1 | 7 |
| **Total** | **4,152.2** | **100** |

## COMPETITORS

Bank of America
BB&T
Citigroup
Colonial BancGroup
Compass Bancshares
Fidelity Southern
First Data
Regions Financial
SunTrust
Wachovia

## HISTORICAL FINANCIALS

Company Type: Public

**Income Statement** FYE: December 31

| | ASSETS ($ mil.) | NET INCOME ($ mil.) | INCOME AS % OF ASSETS | EMPLOYEES |
|---|---|---|---|---|
| **12/06** | 31,855 | 617 | 1.9% | 13,178 |
| **12/05** | 27,621 | 517 | 1.9% | 6,603 |
| **12/04** | 25,050 | 437 | 1.7% | 11,353 |
| **12/03** | 21,633 | 389 | 1.8% | 10,909 |
| **12/02** | 19,036 | 365 | 1.9% | 10,406 |
| **Annual Growth** | 13.7% | 14.0% | — | 6.1% |

**2006 Year-End Financials**

Equity as % of assets: 11.6%
Return on assets: 2.1%
Return on equity: 18.5%
Long-term debt ($ mil.): 1,350
No. of shares (mil.): 327
Dividends
Yield: 2.5%
Payout: 41.1%
Market value ($ mil.): 10,069
Sales ($ mil.): 4,152

**Stock History** NYSE: SNV

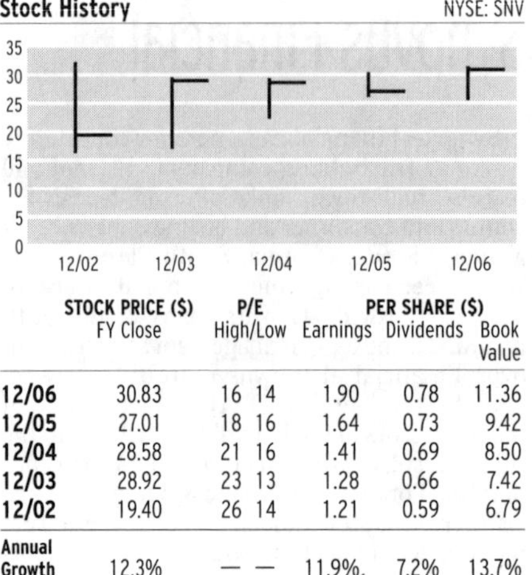

| | STOCK PRICE ($) FY Close | P/E High/Low | | PER SHARE ($) Earnings | Dividends | Book Value |
|---|---|---|---|---|---|---|
| **12/06** | 30.83 | 16 | 14 | 1.90 | 0.78 | 11.36 |
| **12/05** | 27.01 | 18 | 16 | 1.64 | 0.73 | 9.42 |
| **12/04** | 28.58 | 21 | 16 | 1.41 | 0.69 | 8.50 |
| **12/03** | 28.92 | 23 | 13 | 1.28 | 0.66 | 7.42 |
| **12/02** | 19.40 | 26 | 14 | 1.21 | 0.59 | 6.79 |
| **Annual Growth** | 12.3% | — | — | 11.9%. | 7.2% | 13.7% |

# SYSCO Corporation

This company has the menu that restaurants depend on. SYSCO is the #1 foodservice supplier in North America, serving about 400,000 customers through almost 190 distribution centers in the US and Canada. Its core broadline distribution business supplies both food and non-food products to restaurants, schools, hotels, health care institutions, and other foodservice customers; its SYGMA Network operation focuses on supplying chain restaurants. SYSCO distributes both nationally branded products as well as its own private-label products. In addition, SYSCO provides specialty produce and meat and supplies and equipment for the hospitality industry.

The company distributes products from thousands of manufacturers and wholesalers, coordinating its purchasing through Baugh Supply Chain Cooperative, an affiliated business launched in 2002 to consolidate SYSCO's procurement systems. Customers in the restaurant industry account for more than 60% of sales, with hamburger chain Wendy's accounting for about 5% of SYSCO's business.

While the company claims about 15% of a highly fragmented market, it continues to expand through acquisitions of local and regional suppliers and through foldouts, a strategy of establishing stand-alone companies from profitable distribution centers to serve new markets. That practice has helped SYSCO grow faster than the rest of the foodservice industry. The company also continues to rapidly expand by acquiring local distributors that specialize in items such as premium steaks and hotel supplies.

The company promoted Alan Kelso to replace the retiring Thomas Russell as CEO of SYGMA Network in 2007. A company veteran, Russell had taken over as CEO of SYGMA Network in 2005. Kelso previously led SYSCO's operational effectiveness efforts within its strategic development group.

## HISTORY

SYSCO was founded in 1969 when John Baugh, a Houston wholesale food distributor, formed a national distribution company with the owners of eight other US wholesalers. Joining Baugh's Zero Foods of Houston to form SYSCO were Frost-Pack Distributing (Grand Rapids, Michigan), Louisville Grocery (Louisville, Kentucky), Plantation Foods (Miami), Thomas Foods and its Justrite subsidiary (Cincinnati), Wicker (Dallas), Food Service Company (Houston), Global Frozen Foods (New York), and Texas Wholesale Grocery (Dallas). The company went public in 1970. SYSCO, which derives its name from Systems and Services Company, benefited from Baugh's recognition of the trend toward dining out. Until SYSCO was formed, small, independent operators almost exclusively provided food distribution to restaurants, hotels, and other non-grocers.

The company expanded through internal growth and the acquisition of strong local distributors, benefiting through buyout agreements requiring the seller to continue managing its own operation while earning a portion of the sale price with future profits.

In 1988, when SYSCO was already the largest North American foodservice distributor, it acquired CFS Continental, the third-largest North American food distributor. The CFS acquisition added a large truck fleet and increased the company's penetration along the West Coast of the US and into Canada. Also that year SYSCO purchased Olewine's, a Pennsylvania-based distributor. In 1990 the company bought Oklahoma City-based Scrivner, later renamed SYSCO Food Services of Oklahoma.

In 1992 SYSCO acquired Collins Foodservice (serving the Northwest) and Benjamin Polakoff & Son and Perloff Brothers (both serving the Northeast). Later that year SYSCO sold its only remaining retail business, consumer-size frozen food distributor Global SYSCO.

The company acquired St. Louis-based Clark Foodservice and New Jersey's Ritter Food in 1993. The next year it bought Woodhaven Foods, a distributor owned by ARA (now ARAMARK), one of the nation's largest cafeteria and concession operators. In 1997 Baugh, at age 81, retired from his senior chairman post.

SYSCO president Charles Cotros succeeded Bill Lindig as CEO in 2000. That year SYSCO bought Dallas-based produce distributor FreshPoint. It also purchased Canadian foodservice distributor North Douglas Distributors. In 2001 SYSCO acquired specialty meat supplier The Freedman Companies and Guest Supply, which distributes personal care amenities and housekeeping supplies to the lodging industry, for about $238 million.

In 2002 SYSCO acquired SERCA Foodservice, which distributes to 80,000 customers in Canada, from Canada's Sobeys. In a related transaction, SYSCO and Sobeys sold SERCA's British Columbia operations to Gordon Food Service.

SYSCO's chairman and CEO Charles Cotros retired at the end of 2002, passing the torch to then-president and COO Richard Schnieders.

In 2003 SYSCO acquired Maine-based Reed Distributors and the specialty meat-cutting division of the Colorado Boxed Beef Company and its Florida broadline foodservice operation, J&B Foodservice. Later that year SYSCO purchased assets related to Smart & Final's foodservice operation, located in Stockton, California, to expand SYSCO's coverage in the state.

SYSCO unit SYSCO Food Services of Central Alabama announced in 2004 that it planned to expand its foodservice agreement with Cuba and had signed a letter of intent with the Cuban food import agency Alimport. The unit had generated $500,000 in sales in Cuba since the previous year. Within the same month, though, the SYSCO subsidiary retracted its offer, reporting that the agreement asked for SYSCO to assist "in normalizing trade relations" between the US and Cuba. Subsidiaries of SYSCO Corporation are not permitted to make political or government policy statements.

SYSCO acquired International Food Group, a foodservice distributor to chain restaurants in international markets, in mid-2004. The Florida-based firm generated $77.8 million in sales in 2003. In 2004 SYSCO acquired Illinois-based Robert's Foods. The company added to its specialty meat offerings with the 2005 acquisitions of California-based Facciola Meat Company and Florida-based Royalty Foods. That year it also acquired specialty-food importer Walker Foods, fresh fruit and vegetable distributor Piranha Produce, and Western Foods, an Arkansas-based broadline foodservice distributor.

In 2006 SYSCO acquired the foodservice assets of Bunn Capitol, a supplier to restaurants and other customers in Illinois. Founder Baugh died in 2007.

## EXECUTIVES

**Chairman and CEO:** Richard J. Schnieders, age 58, $1,062,500 pay
**President and COO:** Kenneth F. Spitler, age 57, $547,500 pay
**EVP and CFO:** William J. (Bill) DeLaney III, age 51
**EVP, Contract Sales, and President, Specialty Distribution Companies:** Larry J. Accardi, age 58, $547,500 pay
**EVP, Merchandising Services:** Larry G. Pulliam, age 50, $510,000 pay
**EVP and Chief Administrative Officer:** Kenneth J. (Ken) Carrig, age 49
**EVP, Hallsmith-Sysco Food Services:** Frederick Casinelli, age 53
**SVP, Marketing Development:** Robert J. Davis, age 48
**SVP, Finance and Treasurer:** Kirk G. Drummond, age 51
**SVP, Foodservice Operations (Midwest Region):** Michael W. Green, age 46
**SVP, Foodservice Operations (Southeast Region):** Stephen F. Smith, age 55, $649,525 pay
**SVP, General Counsel, and Corporate Secretary:** Michael C. Nichols, age 54
**SVP, Foodservice Operations (Northeast Region):** James M. Danahy, age 52
**SVP, Foodservice Operations (Southwest Region):** James C. Graham, age 55
**SVP, Foodservice Operations (Western Region):** James E. Lankford, age 52, $652,873 pay
**SVP, Supply Chain:** William B. Day, age 50
**SVP, Sales and Marketing:** James D. Hope, age 47
**SVP, Sourcing:** Joseph R. Barton, age 48
**VP, Human Resources:** K. Susan Billiot
**VP, Corporate Communications:** Mark A. Palmer, age 45
**Manager, Investor and Media Relations:** Michael J. King
**Auditors:** Ernst & Young LLP

## LOCATIONS

**HQ:** SYSCO Corporation
1390 Enclave Pkwy., Houston, TX 77077
**Phone:** 281-584-1390 **Fax:** 281-584-2721
**Web:** www.sysco.com

### 2007 Sales

| | $ mil. | % of total |
|---|---|---|
| US | 32,142 | 92 |
| Canada | 2,899 | 8 |
| **Total** | **35,042** | **100** |

### 2007 Distribution Facilities

| | No. |
|---|---|
| US | |
| California | 17 |
| Florida | 15 |
| Texas | 18 |
| Ohio | 10 |
| Georgia | 6 |
| Illinois | 6 |
| North Carolina | 7 |
| Maryland | 3 |
| New York | 3 |
| Colorado | 4 |
| Michigan | 4 |
| New Jersey | 4 |
| Oklahoma | 4 |
| Pennsylvania | 4 |
| Tennessee | 4 |
| Alabama | 2 |
| Nevada | 3 |
| Oregon | 3 |
| Virginia | 3 |
| Wisconsin | 2 |
| Arkansas | 2 |
| Connecticut | 2 |
| Idaho | 2 |
| Indiana | 2 |
| Massachusetts | 2 |
| Minnesota | 2 |
| Missouri | 2 |
| Other States | 10 |
| Canada | 24 |
| **Total** | **177** |

## PRODUCTS/OPERATIONS

### 2007 Sales

| | $ mil. | % of total |
|---|---|---|
| Broadline | 27,560 | 78 |
| SYGMA | 4,381 | 13 |
| Other | 3,571 | 10 |
| Adjustments | (470) | — |
| **Total** | **35,042** | **100** |

### 2007 Sales

| | $ mil. | % of total |
|---|---|---|
| Fresh & frozen meats | 6,548 | 19 |
| Canned & dry products | 6,161 | 18 |
| Frozen fruits, vegetables, bakery and other | 4,691 | 14 |
| Poultry | 3,585 | 10 |
| Dairy | 3,245 | 09 |
| Fresh produce | 3,118 | 09 |
| Paper and disposables | 2,825 | 08 |
| Seafood | 1,840 | 05 |
| Beverage products | 1,200 | 03 |
| Janitorial products | 857 | 02 |
| Equipment and smallwares | 763 | 02 |
| Medical supplies | 205 | 01 |
| **Total** | **35,042** | **100** |

### 2007 Sales

| | % of total |
|---|---|
| Restaurants | 64 |
| Hospitals & nursing homes | 10 |
| Hotels & motels | 06 |
| Schools & colleges | 05 |
| Other | 15 |
| **Total** | **100** |

## COMPETITORS

Gordon Food Service
Keystone Foods
MAINES
Martin-Brower
MBM
McLane Foodservice
Nash-Finch
Performance Food Services Group
UniPro Foodservice
U.S. Foodservice

## HISTORICAL FINANCIALS

Company Type: Public

### Income Statement

FYE: Saturday nearest June 30

| | REVENUE ($ mil.) | NET INCOME ($ mil.) | NET PROFIT MARGIN | EMPLOYEES |
|---|---|---|---|---|
| **6/07** | 35,042 | 1,001 | 2.9% | 50,900 |
| **6/06** | 32,628 | 855 | 2.6% | 49,600 |
| **6/05** | 30,282 | 962 | 3.2% | 47,500 |
| **6/04** | 29,335 | 907 | 3.1% | 47,800 |
| **6/03** | 26,140 | 778 | 3.0% | 47,400 |
| **Annual Growth** | 7.6% | 6.5% | — | 1.8% |

### 2007 Year-End Financials

Debt ratio: 53.6%
Return on equity: 31.6%
Cash ($ mil.): 208
Current ratio: 1.37
Long-term debt ($ mil.): 1,758
No. of shares (mil.): 612
Dividends
Yield: 1.6%
Payout: 33.1%
Market value ($ mil.): 20,185

### Stock History

NYSE: SYY

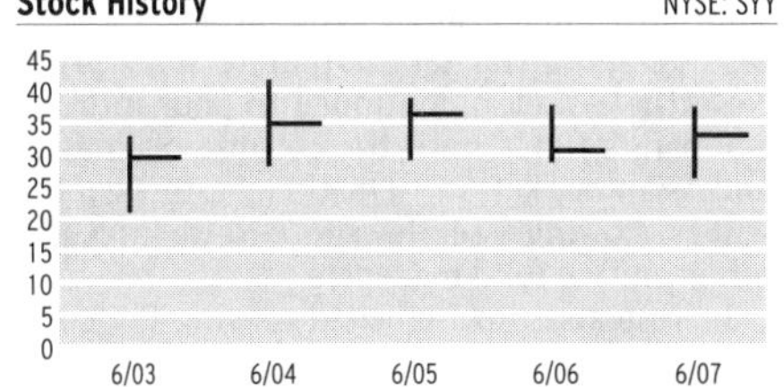


| | STOCK PRICE ($) FY Close | P/E High | P/E Low | PER SHARE ($) Earnings | Dividends | Book Value |
|---|---|---|---|---|---|---|
| **6/07** | 32.99 | 23 | 17 | 1.60 | 0.53 | 5.36 |
| **6/06** | 30.56 | 27 | 21 | 1.36 | 0.49 | 4.93 |
| **6/05** | 36.25 | 26 | 20 | 1.47 | 0.58 | 4.39 |
| **6/04** | 34.80 | 30 | 21 | 1.37 | 0.50 | 4.03 |
| **6/03** | 29.55 | 28 | 18 | 1.18 | 0.40 | 3.41 |
| **Annual Growth** | 2.8% | — | — | 7.9% | 7.3% | 11.9% |

# T. Rowe Price Group

T. Rowe Price administers an eponymous family of mutual funds, offering a variety of investment vehicles, as well as asset management advisory services (including retirement plan advice for individuals) and discount brokerage. Other services include corporate retirement plan management and transfer agent and shareholder services. T. Rowe Price manages about 80 funds in all. Generally oriented toward value investing, the funds offer products for many risk and taxation profiles, including small-, mid-, and large-cap funds; money market funds; and bond funds, both taxable and nontaxable.

Almost two-thirds of the company's more than $330 billion of assets under management are held in retirement plans and variable annuities. Most of the firm's clients — individual and institutional investors, retirement plans, third-party distributors — are in the US, but T. Rowe Price Group also has offices in Asia, Europe, and South America.

## HISTORY

Thomas Rowe Price Jr. left a brokerage job at Mackubin, Goodrich & Co. to found his own investment advisory firm in 1937. He pushed investing for the long haul, choosing stocks of promising young companies (the firm invested in IBM in 1950). Price's company was incorporated in 1947 and was employee-owned until it went public in 1986.

The firm moved into international investments in 1979. T. Rowe Price was primarily an institutional pension fund manager until the 1980s. Creativity lagged as fund managers made investments from a list selected by the research department, and the Growth Stock Fund underperformed the S&P 500. In 1987 the firm opened its funds to individual investors.

Thereafter it introduced a slew of new funds, slicing and dicing the market to appeal to the broadest possible industry and risk investment profiles, including offerings in emerging market stocks and health and science stocks. In 1996 longtime president and CEO George Collins retired, and was succeeded by then-CFO George Roche, who is now also the company's chairman.

In the late 1990s, however, the company's value investing strategy brought lagging fund results, and a stagnant corporate stock price. Nevertheless, cash continued to pour into the company's funds until the collapse of Russian and Asian markets in 1998. US investors got the willies, slowing asset flows to T. Rowe Price and other mutual fund managers.

In response, Roche began moving the company into overseas asset management markets. In 1999 the firm joined with Sumitomo Bank (now part of Sumitomo Mitsui Financial Group) and Daiwa Securities to form asset manager Daiwa SB Investments in Japan. It also targeted Europe, where the growth of private retirement plans opened up new opportunities. Nevertheless, the company missed out on many of the explosive returns of the high-tech boom.

In 2000, however, the high-tech bubble burst, seeming to vindicate T. Rowe Price's conservative approach. That year the company bought out the remaining 50% of its Rowe Price-Fleming International asset management joint venture with Robert Fleming (which is now part of J.P. Morgan Chase). Also that year the company reorganized itself into holding company T. Rowe Price Group. The company's UK subsidiary received regulatory approval to expand to the European continent in 2001.

## EXECUTIVES

**Chairman:** Brian C. Rogers, age 51, $350,000 pay (prior to promotion)
**Vice Chairman:** Edward C. Bernard, age 51, $350,000 pay (prior to promotion)
**President, CEO, and Director:** James A. C. Kennedy, age 53, $350,000 pay (prior to promotion)
**VP and CFO:** Kenneth V. Moreland, age 50, $850,000 pay
**VP; President, T. Rowe Price International:** David J. L. Warren, age 49
**VP Legal Division:** Henry H. Hopkins, age 64
**VP and Treasurer:** Joseph P. Croteau, age 52
**Country Head, Australia and New Zealand:** Murray Brewer
**President, T. Rowe Price Retirement Plan Services:** Cynthia L. Egan
**Senior Portfolio Specialist, Fixed Income Division:** Steven C. Huber, age 48
**Secretary:** Barbara A. Van Horn
**Auditors:** KPMG LLP

## LOCATIONS

**HQ:** T. Rowe Price Group, Inc.
100 E. Pratt St., Baltimore, MD 21202
**Phone:** 410-345-2000 **Fax:** 410-345-2394
**Web:** www.troweprice.com

## PRODUCTS/OPERATIONS

### 2006 Sales

| | $ mil. | % of total |
|---|---|---|
| Investment advisory fees | 1,508.5 | 83 |
| Administrative fees & other | 310.8 | 17 |
| **Total** | **1,819.3** | **100** |

### Selected Subsidiaries

T. Rowe Price Advisory Services, Inc.
T. Rowe Price Associates, Inc.
T. Rowe Price (Canada), Inc.
T. Rowe Price Investment Services, Inc.
T. Rowe Price Retirement Plan Services, Inc.
T. Rowe Price Savings Bank
T. Rowe Price Services, Inc.
TRP Finance, Inc.
T. Rowe Price International, Inc.
T. Rowe Price Global Asset Management Ltd. (UK)
T. Rowe Price Global Investment Services Ltd. (UK)

## COMPETITORS

AIM Funds
American Century
AXA Financial
Berger Associates
Charles Schwab
Citigroup
FMR
Franklin Resources
Janus Capital
Legg Mason
Merrill Lynch
Morgan Stanley
Northwestern Mutual
Old Mutual (US)
Prudential
Raymond James Financial
Torchmark
UBS Financial Services
USAA
The Vanguard Group

## HISTORICAL FINANCIALS

Company Type: Public

### Income Statement

FYE: December 31

| | ASSETS ($ mil.) | NET INCOME ($ mil.) | INCOME AS % OF ASSETS | EMPLOYEES |
|---|---|---|---|---|
| **12/06** | 2,765 | 530 | 19.2% | 4,605 |
| **12/05** | 2,311 | 431 | 18.6% | 4,372 |
| **12/04** | 1,929 | 337 | 17.5% | 4,139 |
| **12/03** | 1,547 | 228 | 14.7% | 3,783 |
| **12/02** | 1,370 | 194 | 14.2% | 3,710 |
| **Annual Growth** | 19.2% | 28.5% | — | 5.6% |

### 2006 Year-End Financials

Equity as % of assets: 87.8%
Return on assets: 20.9%
Return on equity: 23.7%
Long-term debt ($ mil.): —
No. of shares (mil.): 265
Dividends
Yield: 1.2%
Payout: 27.4%
Market value ($ mil.): 11,597
Sales ($ mil.): 1,819

### Stock History

NASDAQ (GS): TROW

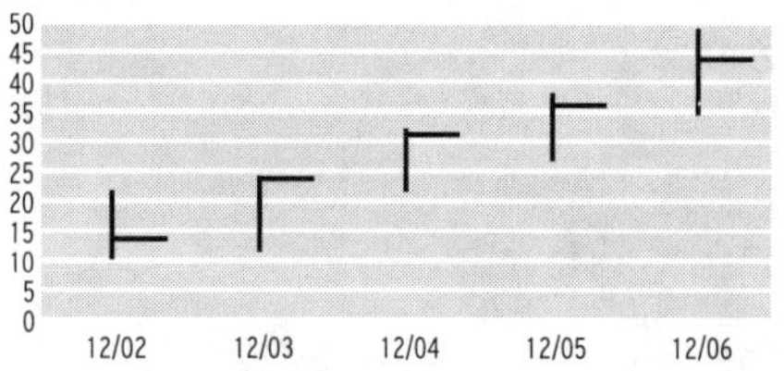

| | STOCK PRICE ($) FY Close | P/E High | P/E Low | PER SHARE ($) Earnings | Dividends | Book Value |
|---|---|---|---|---|---|---|
| **12/06** | 43.77 | 26 | 18 | 1.90 | 0.52 | 9.16 |
| **12/05** | 36.01 | 24 | 17 | 1.58 | 0.49 | 15.46 |
| **12/04** | 31.10 | 25 | 17 | 1.25 | 0.31 | 13.10 |
| **12/03** | 23.70 | 27 | 13 | 0.88 | 0.18 | 10.64 |
| **12/02** | 13.64 | 28 | 14 | 0.76 | — | 9.24 |
| **Annual Growth** | 33.8% | — | — | 25.7% | 42.4% | (0.2%) |

# Target Corporation

Purveyor of all that is cheap, yet chic, fast-growing Target Corporation has bulked up by slimming down. The nation's #2 discount chain (behind Wal-Mart) now operates more than 1,500 Target and SuperTarget stores in 47 states, as well as an online business called Target.com. Target and its larger grocery-carrying incarnation, SuperTarget, have carved out a niche by offering more upscale, fashion-forward merchandise than rivals Wal-Mart and Kmart. After years of struggling to turn around its Marshall Field's and Mervyns departments stores divisions, the discounter sold them both in 2004. Target also owns apparel supplier The Associated Merchandising Corp. and issues Target Visa and its proprietary Target Card.

Following the sale of Marshall Field's (now Macy's North) to The May Department Stores Co. and Mervyns to a group of private-investment firms, Target has focused on building its core discount store business. The company plans to add about 500 new stores — including its first outlets in Alaska and Hawaii — over the next several years, bringing Target's store count to about 2,000 stores nationwide by 2011. It is also expanding its SuperTarget format (about 175 outlets), a newer 174,000-sq.-ft. grocery/discount store concept that includes groceries under the Archer Farms brand. In addition, SuperTarget has broadened its private-label offerings to include about 2,900 different products under the premium Archer Farms and lower-cost Market Pantry brands. Target's growing online store Target.com is the third-most-visited retail Web site behind eBay and Amazon (beating out Wal-Mart.com), and offers some 200,000 items.

Target has distinguished itself from rival Wal-Mart Stores and grown to become the nation's #2 discounter by employing a strategy that relies on exclusive private-label offerings from big name designers. Target's Go International program offers limited-edition collections from global designers including, most recently, the Iranian-born designer Behnaz Sarafpour.

Target's aggressive knock-off policy came under fire in the fall of 2006 with two companies: Lucky Brand Dungarees and leather-goods maker Coach, both filing trademark infringement lawsuits against the chain. The Coach suit, which accused Target of selling a fake Coach bag in a Florida store (a claim Target disputed), was quickly dropped. Lucky accused the company of misappropriating its rear-pocket stitch design for jeans.

Another way that Target is competing with retailers and drug store chains is through in-store services. It's doctoring up some of its stores with Target-branded medical clinics (after the retailer's agreement with MinuteClinic dissolved when the health provider was bought by CVS).

Target Corp's. largest shareholder is Capital Research and Management Co., which owns about 16% of its stock. Activist investor William Ackman, through his firm Pershing Square Capital Management, has acquired a nearly 10% stake in Target.

## HISTORY

The panic of 1873 left Joseph Hudson bankrupt. After he paid his debts at 60 cents on the dollar, he saved enough to open a men's clothing store in Detroit in 1881. Among his innovations were merchandise-return privileges and price marking in place of bargaining. By 1891 Hudson's was the largest retailer of men's clothing in the US. Hudson repaid his creditors from 1873 in full, with interest. When Hudson died in 1912, four nephews expanded the business.

Former banker George Dayton established a dry-goods store in 1902 in Minneapolis. Like Hudson, he offered return privileges and liberal credit. His store grew to a 12-story, full-line department store.

After WWII both companies saw that the future lay in the suburbs. In 1954 Hudson's built Northland in Detroit, then the largest US shopping center. Dayton's built the world's first fully enclosed shopping mall in Edina, a Minneapolis suburb, in 1956. In 1962 Dayton's opened its first discount store in Roseville (naming the store Target to distinguish the discounter from its higher-end department stores).

Dayton's went public in 1966, the same year it began the B. Dalton bookstore chain. Three years later it merged with the family-owned Hudson's, forming Dayton Hudson. Dayton Hudson purchased more malls and invested in such specialty areas as consumer electronics and hard goods. Target had 24 stores by 1970.

The Target chain became the company's top moneymaker in 1977. The next year Dayton Hudson bought California-based Mervyn's (now Mervyns). In the late 1970s and 1980s, it sold nine regional malls and several other businesses, including the 800-store B. Dalton chain to Barnes & Noble. The Target stores division purchased Indianapolis-based Ayr-Way (1980) and Southern California-based Fedmart stores (1983). In the late 1980s Dayton Hudson took Target to Los Angeles and the Northwest. Robert Ulrich, who began with the company as a merchandise trainee in 1967, became president and CEO of the Target stores division in 1987 and chairman and CEO of Dayton Hudson in 1994.

Dayton Hudson opened the first Target Greatland store in 1990. By this time it had 420 Target stores. Also that year Dayton Hudson bought the Marshall Field's chain of 24 department stores from B.A.T Industries. Marshall Field's began as a dry-goods business that Marshall Field bought in 1865 and subsequently built into Chicago's premier upscale retailer.

In 2000 Dayton Hudson renamed itself Target Corporation. In early 2001 the company renamed its Dayton's and Hudson's chains Marshall Field's. Also that year Target acquired the rights to 35 former Montgomery Wards stores from the bankrupt retailer.

2004 was a year of divestments for Target. In January the discounter announced it was exiting the catalog business, which it acquired when it purchased Rivertown Trading Co. in March 1998. To that end, in April Target sold its Signals and Wireless gifts catalogs to Universal Screen Arts for an undisclosed sum. In July Target sold its Marshall Field's business to The May Department Stores Co. for about $3.2 billion in cash. In September Target completed the sale of 257 Mervyns stores in 13 states to an investment group that includes Cerberus Capital Management, Lubert-Adler/Klaff and Partners, and Sun Capital Partners, as well as its Mervyns credit card receivables to GE Consumer Finance for a combined sum of approximately $1.65 billion in cash.

In October 2005 vice chairman Gerald L. Storch resigned unexpectedly after more than a dozen years with the company. No reason was given for his departure.

## EXECUTIVES

**Chairman and CEO:** Robert J. Ulrich, age 63, $4,659,616 pay
**President and Director:** Gregg W. Steinhafel, age 52, $1,519,411 pay
**EVP and CFO:** Douglas A. Scovanner, age 51, $1,156,195 pay
**EVP, Marketing:** Michael R. Francis, age 44, $867,690 pay
**EVP, Stores:** Bart Butzer, age 49, $1,519,247 pay
**EVP, Human Resources:** Jodeen A. Kozlak, age 43
**SVP and CIO:** Janet M. Schalk, age 48
**SVP and Treasurer:** Corey L. Haaland
**SVP, Finance:** Jane P. Windmeier
**SVP, Distribution:** Mitchell L. (Mitch) Stover
**SVP, General Counsel, and Corporate Secretary:** Timothy R. Baer, age 46
**SVP, Merchandise Planning:** Richard N. Maguire
**SVP, Merchandising:** Patricia Adams
**SVP, Merchandising:** Gregory J. (Greg) Duppler
**SVP, Merchandising:** Gina Sprenger
**SVP, Merchandising:** Kathryn A. Tesija
**VP and Treasurer:** Stephen C. Kowalke
**VP, Events Marketing and Communication:** John Remington
**VP, Investor Relations:** Susan D. Kahn
**President, Target Brands:** Erica C. Street
**President, Target.com:** Dale Nitschke, age 44
**Group Director, Target Stores:** Carmen Moch
**Auditors:** Ernst & Young LLP

## LOCATIONS

**HQ:** Target Corporation
1000 Nicollet Mall, Minneapolis, MN 55403
**Phone:** 612-304-6073 **Fax:** 612-696-5400
**Web:** www.target.com

### 2007 Locations

| | No. |
|---|---|
| California | 209 |
| Texas | 130 |
| Florida | 102 |
| Illinois | 79 |
| Minnesota | 66 |
| Michigan | 56 |
| Ohio | 56 |
| New York | 55 |
| Georgia | 47 |
| North Carolina | 44 |
| Virginia | 42 |
| Arizona | 41 |
| Pennsylvania | 41 |
| Colorado | 36 |
| New Jersey | 36 |
| Indiana | 32 |
| Washington | 32 |
| Wisconsin | 32 |
| Maryland | 31 |
| Missouri | 31 |
| Massachusetts | 26 |
| Tennessee | 26 |
| Iowa | 21 |
| Kansas | 18 |
| Oregon | 18 |
| South Carolina | 17 |
| Nevada | 15 |
| Connecticut | 14 |
| Alabama | 13 |
| Kentucky | 12 |
| Louisiana | 12 |
| Nebraska | 12 |
| Other states | 86 |
| **Total** | **1,488** |

## PRODUCTS/OPERATIONS

### 2007 Sales

| | % of total |
|---|---|
| Consumables & commodities | 32 |
| Electronics, entertainment, sporting goods & toys | 23 |
| Apparel & accessories | 22 |
| Home furnishings & décor | 19 |
| Other | 4 |
| **Total** | **100** |

### 2007 Stores

| | No. |
|---|---|
| Target | 1,311 |
| SuperTarget | 177 |
| **Total** | **1,488** |

### Selected Designer Private Labels

Amy Coe (children's bedding and accessories)
Isaac Mizrahi (women's apparel and accessories)
Liz Lange (maternity)
Michael Graves (housewares)
Mossimo (junior fashions)
Sonia Kashuk (cosmetics and fragrances)
Todd Oldham (bedding and furniture)

### Selected Private Labels

Archer Farms (food)
Cherokee (apparel)
Furio (housewares)
Honors (apparel)
In Due Time (maternity wear)
Merona (apparel)
Utility (apparel)
Xhilaration (apparel)

## COMPETITORS

Bed Bath & Beyond
Best Buy
Burnes
Container Store
Costco Wholesale
CVS/Caremark
Dillard's
Dollar General
eBay
Euromarket Designs
Foot Locker
Gap
Gottschalks
Home Depot
J. C. Penney Company
Kmart
Kohl's
Kroger
Limited Brands
Linens 'n Things
Macy's East
Macy's West
Mervyns
Nordstrom
PETCO
Ross Stores
Sears
SUPERVALU
TJX Companies
Toys "R" Us
Walgreen
Wal-Mart
Williams-Sonoma

## HISTORICAL FINANCIALS

Company Type: Public

### Income Statement

FYE: Saturday nearest January 31

| | REVENUE ($ mil.) | NET INCOME ($ mil.) | NET PROFIT MARGIN | EMPLOYEES |
|---|---|---|---|---|
| **1/07** | 59,490 | 2,787 | 4.7% | 352,000 |
| **1/06** | 52,620 | 2,408 | 4.6% | 338,000 |
| **1/05** | 46,839 | 3,198 | 6.8% | 292,000 |
| **1/04** | 48,163 | 1,841 | 3.8% | 328,000 |
| **1/03** | 43,917 | 1,654 | 3.8% | 306,000 |
| **Annual Growth** | 7.9% | 13.9% | — | 3.6% |

### 2007 Year-End Financials

Debt ratio: 55.5%
Return on equity: 18.7%
Cash ($ mil.): 813
Current ratio: 1.32
Long-term debt ($ mil.): 8,675
No. of shares (mil.): 860
Dividends
Yield: 0.7%
Payout: 13.7%
Market value ($ mil.): 53,332

**Stock History** NYSE: TGT

| | STOCK PRICE ($) FY Close | P/E High | P/E Low | PER SHARE ($) Earnings | Dividends | Book Value |
|---|---|---|---|---|---|---|
| **1/07** | 62.03 | 20 | 14 | 3.21 | 0.44 | 18.18 |
| **1/06** | 54.17 | 22 | 17 | 2.71 | 0.36 | 16.25 |
| **1/05** | 49.49 | 15 | 11 | 3.51 | 0.30 | 14.63 |
| **1/04** | 37.96 | 21 | 13 | 2.01 | 0.26 | 12.14 |
| **1/03** | 28.21 | 25 | 14 | 1.81 | 0.24 | 10.38 |
| **Annual Growth** | 21.8% | — | — | 15.4% | 16.4% | 15.0% |

# TD Ameritrade

If your stock makes a big move while you're stuck in traffic, don't worry — TD AMERITRADE (formerly just Ameritrade) lets you buy and sell by phone, fax, Internet, and the Web. Through subsidiaries, the firm serves active traders, investment advisors, and long-term investors by providing a variety of brokerage services, ranging from traditional discount trading to advanced products for the more sophisticated trader. Rival E*TRADE offered to buy Ameritrade for more than $6 billion in mid-2005, but the company said that it's not for sale. In early 2006 Ameritrade bought the US operations of TD Waterhouse and added the "TD" to its name, as well as some 100 retail locations.

TD AMERITRADE has already led consolidation within the electronic brokerage industry. It purchased rivals National Discount Brokers and Datek in 2001 and 2002, but didn't stop there. In 2003 the company acquired some 16,500 Mydiscountbroker.com accounts from SWS Group, and about 11,000 retail accounts from BrokerageAmerica, which together helped push the company's account base past the three million mark. It gained another 145,000 accounts from brokerage firms Bidwell & Company and JB Oxford Holdings in 2004 and 2005. TD AMERITRADE announced in 2007 that it will buy most of the investment support services operations of Fiserv.

TD AMERITRADE's expanded account base has helped it leapfrog (and pressure) competitors E*TRADE and Charles Schwab. The company has remained focused on its core business of online trading, supplementing its growth with products such as mutual funds and money market accounts, as well as multi-million dollar brand-building advertising campaigns. In 2006 TD AMERITRADE implemented a flat commission rate of $9.99 for all online equity trades. The company hopes the lower price will help grow its number of customer accounts.

As part of Ameritrade's deal to acquire TD Waterhouse's US business, Canada-based TD Bank assumed about a 32% stake in the firm. Ameritrade founder Joe Ricketts and his family own approximately 18%.

## HISTORY

Ameritrade began in 1971 as investment bank TransTerra. Dean Witter veteran Joe Ricketts transformed the firm into a discount broker in 1975. TransTerra formed Televest/Bancvest (now AmeriVest) in 1982 and Ameritrade Clearing (now Advanced Clearing) in 1983.

In 1988 the company became the first to offer Touch-Tone telephone trading, and added Internet trading in 1994. TransTerra formed Ceres Securities, a deep-discount brokerage service that added research to its services when it bought brokerage firms K. Aufhauser and All American in 1995. The company formed its eBroker all-Internet brokerage service in 1996, and became Ameritrade late that year.

In 1997 the company went public and combined its service-oriented subsidiaries. It also formed an alliance that directed users of America Online's investor site to Ameritrade's Web sites. The company grew rapidly in the late 1990s, but like most technology-based companies, suffered the impact of the subsequent tech wreck and the struggling economy.

In 2001 Ameritrade restructured its organization, forming separate divisions to serve institutional and private clients, and announced a series of layoffs to cut costs.

## EXECUTIVES

**Chairman and Founder:** J. Joe Ricketts, age 65, $1,226,875 pay
**Vice Chairman:** W. Edmund (Ed) Clark, age 59
**CEO and Director:** Joseph H. (Joe) Moglia, age 57, $7,152,692 pay
**COO:** Fredric J. (Fred) Tomczyk, age 51
**EVP and Chief Client Officer:** Lawrence (Larry) Szczech, age 49
**EVP, General Counsel, and Secretary:** Ellen L.S. Koplow, age 47
**EVP; Head, Client Group:** T. Christian (Chris) Armstrong, age 58
**SVP and CFO:** William J. (Bill) Gerber, age 49
**SVP and Chief Brokerage Operations Officer:** Bryce B. Engel, age 35
**SVP and Chief Marketing Officer:** Laurine M. Garrity, age 45
**Managing Director, Finance and Treasurer:** Michael D. Chochon, age 38
**Head of Branch Distribution:** John Bunch
**Head of Institutional Services:** Tom Bradley
**Corporate Communications:** Kim Hillyer
**Investor Relations:** Dave Pleiss
**Senior Adviser:** John Grifonetti
**Auditors:** Ernst & Young LLP

## LOCATIONS

**HQ:** TD AMERITRADE Holding Corporation
4211 S. 102nd St., Omaha, NE 68127
**Phone:** 402-331-7856 **Fax:** 402-597-7789
**Web:** www.amtd.com

## PRODUCTS/OPERATIONS

**2006 Sales**

| | $ mil. | % of total |
|---|---|---|
| Commissions & transaction fees | 727.4 | 34 |
| Net interest revenue | 696.1 | 33 |
| Money market deposit account fees | 185.0 | 9 |
| Money market & other mutual fund fees | 139.6 | 6 |
| Other | 391.2 | 18 |
| **Total** | **2,139.4** | **100** |

**Selected Subsidiaries**

Ameritrade, Inc.
Ameritrade Advisory Services, LLC
Ameritrade International Company, Inc.
Amerivest Investment Management, LLC
Financial Passport, Inc.
National Investors Service Corporation
Nebraska Hudson Company, Inc.
TD AMERITRADE, Inc.
TD AMERITRADE IP Company, Inc.
TD AMERITRADE Online Holdings Corp.
TD AMERITRADE Services Company, Inc. (aka Ameritrade Support Services Corporation)
TD Waterhouse Canadian Call Center, Inc.
TD Waterhouse Capital Markets, Inc.
TenBagger, Inc.
ThinkTech, Inc. (aka T2 Technology Support, Inc.)
TradeCast Inc.

## COMPETITORS

Charles Schwab
Citigroup Global Markets
E*TRADE Financial
Edward Jones
FMR
Merrill Lynch
Morgan Stanley
Scottrade
ShareBuilder

## HISTORICAL FINANCIALS

Company Type: Public

**Income Statement** FYE: Friday nearest September 30

| | REVENUE ($ mil.) | NET INCOME ($ mil.) | NET PROFIT MARGIN | EMPLOYEES |
|---|---|---|---|---|
| **9/06** | 2,139 | 527 | 24.6% | 3,947 |
| **9/05** | 1,145 | 340 | 29.7% | 2,052 |
| **9/04** | 922 | 283 | 30.7% | 1,961 |
| **9/03** | 731 | 137 | 18.7% | 1,732 |
| **9/02** | 443 | (29) | — | 2,150 |
| **Annual Growth** | 48.2% | — | — | 16.4% |

**2006 Year-End Financials**

Debt ratio: 98.9%
Return on equity: 32.4%
Cash ($ mil.): 1,991
Current ratio: —
Long-term debt ($ mil.): 1,711
No. of shares (mil.): 608
Dividends
Yield: 31.8%
Payout: 631.6%
Market value ($ mil.): 11,454

**Stock History** NASDAQ (GS): AMTD

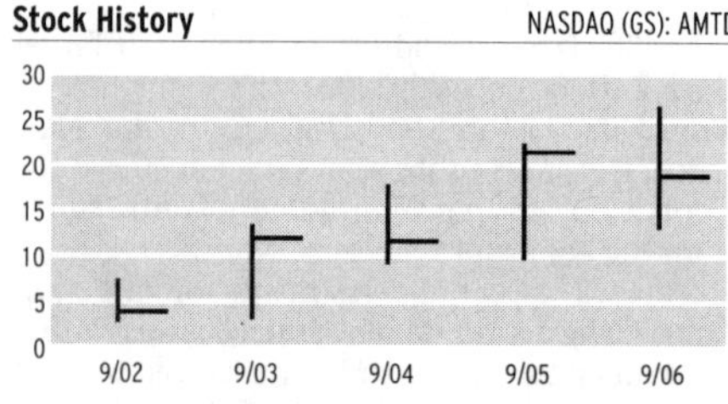


| | STOCK PRICE ($) FY Close | P/E High | P/E Low | PER SHARE ($) Earnings | Dividends | Book Value |
|---|---|---|---|---|---|---|
| **9/06** | 18.85 | 28 | 14 | 0.95 | 6.00 | 2.85 |
| **9/05** | 21.47 | 27 | 12 | 0.82 | — | 3.74 |
| **9/04** | 11.68 | 27 | 14 | 0.66 | — | 2.97 |
| **9/03** | 11.97 | 41 | 10 | 0.32 | — | 2.88 |
| **9/02** | 3.90 | — | — | (0.13) | — | 2.54 |
| **Annual Growth** | 48.3% | — | — | — | — | 2.9% |

# Tech Data

Tech Data gets the goods to global gadget dealers. The world's #2 distributor of computer products (behind Ingram Micro), Tech Data provides more than 80,000 different items to more than 90,000 resellers in 100 countries. Its catalog of products includes computer components (disk drives, keyboards, and video cards), networking equipment (routers and bridges), peripherals (printers, modems, and monitors), systems (PCs and servers), and software. Tech Data also provides technical support, configuration, integration, financing, electronic data interchange (EDI), and other logistic and product fulfillment services.

Tech Data distributes products from such vendors as Apple, Cisco Systems, Hewlett-Packard, IBM, Microsoft, and Sony.

As manufacturers have promoted more direct relationships with their customers, the need for middlemen in the industry has dwindled and many tech product distributors have gone under. Tech Data has been spared this fate due to its size and scope, but it has been forced to keep costs down in order to survive in this hostile climate. The company has also expanded its service offerings, which range from pre- and post-sale technical support to customized shipping documents and electronic commerce integration.

## HISTORY

Tech Data grew out of an electronics distribution business founded by Edward Raymund, a University of Southern California graduate who started out as a representative for electronics manufacturers. By the early 1960s he had established an industrial electronics distribution business in Florida. In 1974 he incorporated that business as Tech Data.

In 1981 Raymund's 25-year-old son, Steven, who had earned master's degrees in economics and international politics from Georgetown University's School of Foreign Service, joined Tech Data on a temporary basis to work on the company's catalog. At that time Tech Data sold diskettes and other computer supplies to local companies and had about $2 million in sales.

Steven Raymund's favored status at the company angered a group of managers. Shortly after he arrived at Tech Data, they copied the company's client list and walked out. The defection nearly sank Tech Data, but Steven stayed on when his father handed him two-thirds of the company.

With the PC industry beginning to take off, Steven Raymund positioned Tech Data as a middleman between computer and peripheral manufacturers and resellers. Steven was named COO in 1984. He became CEO in 1986, the year the company went public.

In 1990 fast growth strained Tech Data's resources, and earnings slumped. The company cut inventory and management costs. The following year Steven Raymund became chairman when his father retired.

Tech Data began to distribute software in 1992, and a year later the company signed up Microsoft and inked a distribution deal for IBM computer systems. In 1994 Tech Data purchased U.S. Software Resource, a California-based distributor of more than 500 business and entertainment software titles, thereby increasing its software list and gaining high-profile publishers such as Borland International (now Borland Software) and Corel as suppliers. Also in 1994 Tech Data began a global expansion when it bought France's largest distributor of wholesale computer products, Softmart International.

Tech Data won US distribution rights for Apple subsidiary Claris' (now named FileMaker) software line in 1995. The company one-upped its rivals that year when, through a deal with MCI (now part of WorldCom), it became the first distributor to resell telephone line service employing advanced data transmission technologies. Tech Data resellers packaged line services with their computer networks; the resellers and Tech Data earned monthly usage fees on the services.

Tech Data in 1998 bought VIAG AG's majority stake in European distributor Computer 2000 for about $390 million. (To avoid geographic overlap, the company sold its controlling stake in Germany-based Macrotron, acquired in 1997, to rival Ingram Micro for $100 million.) Also in 1998 Tech Data began direct assembly and shipping at its distribution centers. In 1999 the company inked an estimated $2 billion outsourcing deal with GE Capital and expanded its Canadian presence with the purchase of Globelle Corporation.

In 2000 the company purchased the remainder of Computer 2000 and expanded its outsourcing offerings with a new business division. The next year Tech Data introduced an online software license purchasing and upgrade program; it also cut about 20% of staff to keep costs down.

Tech Data broadened its menu of outsourcing service and added to its international operations with the acquisition of the UK's Azlan Group in 2003.

In 2006 the company named Robert Dutkowsky, a veteran of datacenter infrastructure specialist Egenera, as its CEO; Raymund retained his chairmanship.

## EXECUTIVES

**Chairman:** Steven A. (Steve) Raymund, age 51
**CEO and Director:** Robert M. (Bob) Dutkowsky
**President, Worldwide Operations:** Néstor Cano, age 42, $1,045,000 pay
**EVP, CFO, and Director:** Jeffery P. (Jeff) Howells, age 49, $878,000 pay
**EVP and Worldwide CIO:** Joseph A. (Joe) Osbourn, age 58, $625,000 pay
**President, Americas:** Ken Lamneck, age 51, $647,000 pay
**SVP, European Operational Design and Performance:** Gerard F. Youna, age 52
**SVP and CFO, Europe:** William J. (Bill) Hunter, age 46
**SVP and Controller:** Joseph B. (Joe) Trepani, age 45
**SVP, Advanced Infrastructure Solutions:** Pete Peterson
**SVP, Information Technology, The Americas:** John Tonnison
**SVP, US Controller:** Tracy Bradshaw
**SVP, Credit and Customer Services, the Americas:** Mike Zava, age 59
**SVP; President, Enterprise Division, Europe; Managing Director, Azlan Group PLC:** Richard Pryor-Jones, age 43
**SVP, General Counsel, and Secretary:** David R. (Dave) Vetter, age 46
**SVP, Human Resources:** Sherri P. Nadeau
**SVP, US Marketing:** Robert G. O'Malley, age 60
**SVP, US Sales:** Murray Wright
**SVP, Real Estate and Corporate Services:** Benjamin B. (Ben) Godwin, age 54
**Director, Corporate Communications:** Chuck Miller
**Director, Investor Relations and Shareholder Services:** Danyle L. Anderson
**Auditors:** Ernst & Young LLP

## LOCATIONS

**HQ:** Tech Data Corporation
5350 Tech Data Dr., Clearwater, FL 33760
**Phone:** 727-539-7429 **Fax:** 727-538-7803
**Web:** www.techdata.com

### 2007 Sales

| | $ mil. | % of total |
|---|---|---|
| Europe | 11,475.3 | 54 |
| Americas | 9,965.1 | 46 |
| **Total** | **21,440.4** | **100** |

## PRODUCTS/OPERATIONS

### Selected Products

Peripherals
- Accessories
- Media
- Memory
- Modems
- Monitors
- Multimedia
- Power protection
- Printers
- Scanners
- Video

Networking equipment
- Bridges
- Hubs
- Modems
- Network interface cards
- Premise wiring
- Routers
- Switches

Computer systems
- Desktops
- Notebooks
- Servers

Software

Components
- Cases
- Drives
- Keyboards
- Memory
- Monitors
- Motherboards
- Processors
- System platforms
- Video cards

### Selected Services

IT Training
Integration
Leasing
Marketing
Shipping
Support

## COMPETITORS

Agilysys
Arrow Electronics
Articon-Integralis
ASI Corp.
Avnet
Bell Microproducts
Black Box
Communications Supply
CompuCom
D&H Distributing
Dell
GTSI
IBM
ICG
IKON
Ingram Micro
MA Laboratories
MicroAge
New Age Electronics
Optical Laser
Otto
ScanSource
SED International
Softmart
Software House
SYNNEX
Westcon
ZT Group

## HISTORICAL FINANCIALS

Company Type: Public

### Income Statement

FYE: January 31

| | REVENUE ($ mil.) | NET INCOME ($ mil.) | NET PROFIT MARGIN | EMPLOYEES |
|---|---|---|---|---|
| **1/07** | 21,440 | (97) | — | 8,000 |
| **1/06** | 20,483 | 27 | 0.1% | 8,200 |
| **1/05** | 19,790 | 163 | 0.8% | 8,500 |
| **1/04** | 17,406 | 104 | 0.6% | 8,400 |
| **1/03** | 15,739 | (200) | — | 7,900 |
| **Annual Growth** | 8.0% | — | — | 0.3% |

### 2007 Year-End Financials

Debt ratio: 21.4%
Return on equity: —
Cash ($ mil.): 265
Current ratio: 1.70
Long-term debt ($ mil.): 364
No. of shares (mil.): 55
Dividends
Yield: —
Payout: —
Market value ($ mil.): 2,040

**Stock History** NASDAQ (GS): TECD

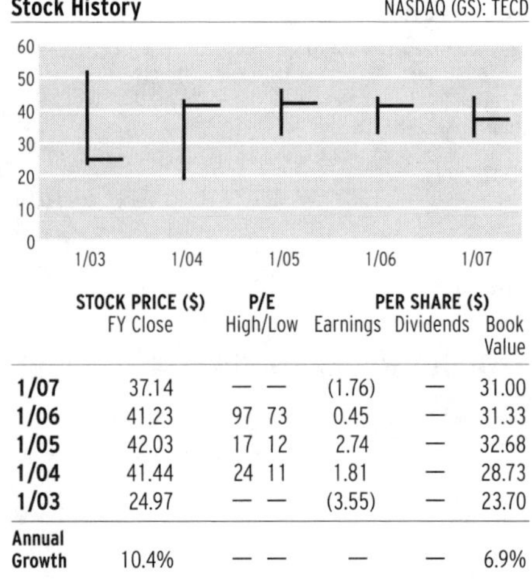


| | STOCK PRICE ($) FY Close | P/E High/Low | | PER SHARE ($) Earnings | Dividends | Book Value |
|---|---|---|---|---|---|---|
| **1/07** | 37.14 | — | — | (1.76) | — | 31.00 |
| **1/06** | 41.23 | 97 | 73 | 0.45 | — | 31.33 |
| **1/05** | 42.03 | 17 | 12 | 2.74 | — | 32.68 |
| **1/04** | 41.44 | 24 | 11 | 1.81 | — | 28.73 |
| **1/03** | 24.97 | — | — | (3.55) | — | 23.70 |
| **Annual Growth** | 10.4% | — | — | — | — | 6.9% |

# Technical Olympic USA

Although it would seem to have godlike powers, Technical Olympic USA (TOUSA) just builds houses for mere mortals. The homebuilder, formerly Newmark Homes, operates in 16 metropolitan markets in Florida, Texas, the West, and in the mid-Atlantic (Central Florida and Houston are its top markets). Marketing under brands Newmark, Engle, Transeastern, and Trophy, the company sells around 7,800 homes a year to first-time and move-up buyers and others. The average sales price for its homes is around $300,000. TOUSA provides financial services to its homebuyers and to others through its Preferred Home Mortgage and Universal Land Title subsidiaries. Greek homebuilder Technical Olympic S.A. owns 67% of the company.

The company has always focused on high-growth regions such as northern Virginia; Austin, Texas; Orlando, Florida; and in Nashville, Phoenix, and Denver. However, the strategy could not protect it and may have hurt it in 2006, when the entire homebuilding industry suffered a severe downturn as supply outstripped demand. About 50% of its operations are concentrated in Arizona and Florida, two regions that were among the hardest hit.

## HISTORY

TOUSA began its metamorphosis after Lonnie Fedrick and John Harris quit working for Houston's Monarch Homes and struck out on their own to began Newmark Homes in 1983. They began in Houston and by 1984 had expanded to Austin. The late 1980s saw the Texas real estate market crash, and many homebuilders went under. But Newmark's small inventory and customer focus enabled it to make it through the crisis with its streak intact — it made money every year.

In 1993 Taiwan-based Pacific Electric Wire & Cable bought 80% of the firm through its US subsidiary, Pacific Realty Group. Two years later Newmark bought The Adler Companies (formed in 1990), a Miami/Fort Lauderdale homebuilder. It also expanded into the Dallas/Fort Worth area.

Newmark moved into Nashville in 1997 and into North Carolina the next year. Also in 1998 it bought another Florida builder, Westbrooke (founded in 1976) and went public. Greek construction company Technical Olympic S.A. bought Pacific Realty Group's 80% stake in 1999. The following year Technical Olympic founder Constantine Stengos was elected chairman of Newmark. Also in 2000, Newmark created its Marksman Homes division to focus on empty-nest buyers in mature markets.

In early 2001 the company announced its possible merger with Engle Homes, also owned by Technical Olympic. (Technical Olympic, Inc., is a subsidiary of Technical Olympic (UK) PLC, which is a subsidiary of Technical Olympic S.A.) The deal came to pass in 2002, when Engle Homes was sold to Newmark, and the company was renamed Technical Olympic USA, Inc. Also that year TOUSA sold its Westbrooke Acquisition Corp. subsidiary to Standard Pacific Corp. for $41 million in cash, plus the assumption of $54 million of Westbrooke's debt by Standard Pacific. Acquisitions in 2002 included D.S. Ware Homes, LLC (Jacksonville, Florida) and Masonry Homes (with operations in Baltimore's northwestern suburbs and in southern Pennsylvania).

The company restructured in 2003 and continued to expand with the acquisitions of Trophy Homes, Inc. (Las Vegas) and The James Construction Company (Denver). The next year it entered the Delaware market and strengthened its presence in the mid-Atlantic by acquiring certain assets of family-owned Gilligan Homes, which had operations in Delaware, Maryland, and southeastern Pennsylvania. At the close of 2003, the company owned or had options to acquire roughly 48,200 homesites. It had a backlog of about 3,130 homes valued at $855 million.

In 2004 TOUSA transferred the listing of its common stock ("TOUS") to the New York Stock Exchange from the Nasdaq National Market and changed its trading symbol to "TOA." It began trading under the new symbol in November 2004. The company also formed a joint venture with Scottsdale, Arizona-based Sunbelt Holdings (real estate and development) for acquiring and developing land and constructing single-family homes in Arizona.

The next year TOUSA bolstered its Florida operations by acquiring the homebuilding operations and assets of Transeastern Properties, Inc.

## EXECUTIVES

**Chairman:** Konstantinos A. Stengos, age 69
**Executive Vice Chairman, President, and CEO:** Antonio B. (Tony) Mon, age 61, $8,899,960 pay
**EVP and CFO:** Stephen M. (Steve) Wagman
**EVP and Chief of Staff:** Paul Berkowitz
**EVP and Director:** Tommy L. McAden, age 43, $2,709,657 pay
**EVP and Director:** Andreas K. Stengos, age 44
**EVP and Director:** Georgios (George) Stengos, age 39
**SVP and General Counsel; SVP, General Counsel, and Secretary, TOUSA Homes:** Patricia M. (Pat) Petersen, age 47
**VP, Land; SVP, TOUSA Homes:** John A. Kraynick, age 51, $1,835,000 pay
**VP, Human Resources and Administration:** Clint Ooten, age 36
**VP, Operations Support; SVP, TOUSA Homes:** Edward R. Wohlwender, age 46
**President, Trophy Homes:** Don Barrineau
**President, Universal Land Title:** Michael R. Glass
**President, Preferred Home Mortgage Company:** Peter J. (Pete) Strawser
**SEVP, TOUSA Homes Florida Region:** Harry Engelstein, age 71, $2,794,584 pay
**EVP, TOUSA Homes Atlantic and Texas Regions:** George Yeonas
**EVP, TOUSA Homes Capitol Region:** Cora Wiltshire
**EVP, TOUSA Homes Florida Region:** Bill Carmichael
**EVP, TOUSA Homes West Region:** Mark R. Upton, age 47
**Secretary:** Beatriz L. Koltis
**Director Corporate Communications:** Hunter Blankenbaker
**Chief Accounting Officer and Controller:** Angela Valdes
**Auditors:** Ernst & Young LLP

## LOCATIONS

**HQ:** Technical Olympic USA, Inc.
4000 Hollywood Blvd., Ste. 500 North, Hollywood, FL 33021
**Phone:** 954-364-4000 **Fax:** 954-364-4010
**Web:** www.tousa.com

Technical Olympic USA builds and sells homes in Arizona, Colorado, Delaware, Florida, Maryland, Nevada, Pennsylvania, Tennessee, Texas, and Virginia.

**2006 Homes Completed**

| | No. | % of total |
|---|---|---|
| Texas | 2,946 | 38 |
| Florida | 2,742 | 35 |
| West | 1,453 | 18 |
| Mid-Atlantic | 683 | 9 |
| **Total** | **7,824** | **100** |

## PRODUCTS/OPERATIONS

**2006 Sales**

| | $ mil. | % of total |
|---|---|---|
| Home sales | 2,439.1 | 92 |
| Land sales | 134.9 | 5 |
| Financial services | 63.3 | 3 |
| **Total** | **2,637.3** | **100** |

**Selected Brands**
Engle Homes
Newmark Homes
Transeastern
Trophy Homes

## COMPETITORS

Beazer Homes
Capital Pacific
Centex
David Weekley Homes
D.R. Horton
Hovnanian Enterprises
KB Home
Lennar
M.D.C.
Meritage Homes
M/I Homes
NVR
Pulte Homes
Ryland
Shea Homes
Standard Pacific

## HISTORICAL FINANCIALS

Company Type: Public

**Income Statement** FYE: December 31

| | REVENUE ($ mil.) | NET INCOME ($ mil.) | NET PROFIT MARGIN | EMPLOYEES |
|---|---|---|---|---|
| **12/06** | 2,637 | (201) | — | 2,420 |
| **12/05** | 2,509 | 218 | 8.7% | 2,967 |
| **12/04** | 2,135 | 120 | 5.6% | 2,079 |
| **12/03** | 1,688 | 83 | 4.9% | 1,701 |
| **12/02** | 1,417 | 72 | 5.1% | 1,418 |
| **Annual Growth** | 16.8% | — | — | 14.3% |

**2006 Year-End Financials**

Debt ratio: 141.5%
Return on equity: —
Cash ($ mil.): 290
Current ratio: 3.61
Long-term debt ($ mil.): 1,096
No. of shares (mil.): 60
Dividends
Yield: 0.1%
Payout: —
Market value ($ mil.): 606

**Stock History** NYSE: TOA

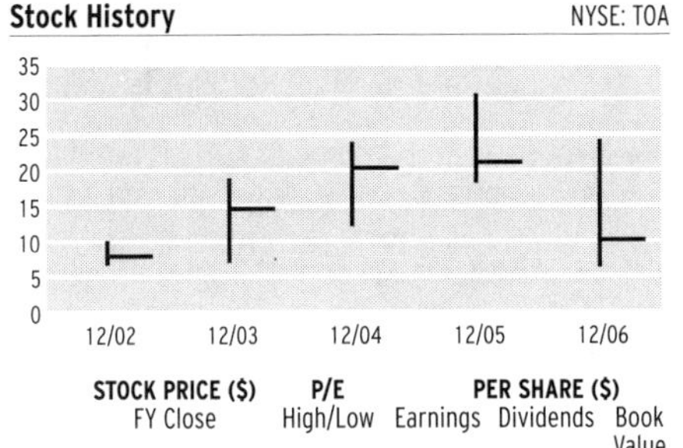

| | STOCK PRICE ($) FY Close | P/E High/Low | | PER SHARE ($) Earnings | Dividends | Book Value |
|---|---|---|---|---|---|---|
| **12/06** | 10.17 | — | — | (3.38) | 0.01 | 13.00 |
| **12/05** | 21.09 | 8 | 5 | 3.68 | — | 16.31 |
| **12/04** | 20.30 | 11 | 6 | 2.08 | — | 14.77 |
| **12/03** | 14.61 | 12 | 5 | 1.56 | — | 17.95 |
| **12/02** | 7.90 | 7 | 5 | 1.38 | — | 14.53 |
| **Annual Growth** | 6.5% | — | — | — | — | (2.7%) |

# Tecumseh Products

Tecumseh Products helps you mow the lawn and cool down afterwards. Named for the legendary Shawnee chief, Tecumseh Products makes compressors, small engines, power-train products, and pumps. It makes compressors for use in refrigerators and freezers, air conditioners, dehumidifiers, and vending machines. Tecumseh makes engines and power-train products for lawn and garden equipment (mowers, tillers, trimmers), generators, and washers. It makes pumps for use in applications ranging from aquariums to sewage plants. The Herrick family, which had run Tecumseh Products over three generations, controls nearly 44% of the company's voting shares.

Tecumseh has agreed to sell most of its Electrical Components business to rival Regal Beloit for about $220 million in cash. The operations to be sold, principally the Residential & Commercial Motors and Asia/Pacific divisions of Tecumseh's FASCO business unit, accounted for about 70% of Electrical Components sales in 2006. Tecumseh will use the net proceeds to repay debt.

Cutting costs in non-core operations, the company has reduced staff at seven facilities in North America and one plant in the Czech Republic. Tecumseh trimmed about 310 positions, a reduction in force of nearly 2%.

In recent years, a schism developed between former chairman Todd Herrick and the rest of the board. In early 2007, Herrick notified the board that he planned to nominate himself and two other people for election to the board at the annual meeting. The board responded by replacing Herrick as chairman of the board with director David Risley, who has been on the board since 2003. The board also voted to expand itself, from five to seven members, prior to the annual meeting. The company nominated Risley and three other incumbent directors to stand for reelection at the annual meeting, pointedly leaving Herrick out of the nominee slate.

The parties reached a legal settlement in April 2007, heading off a potential proxy fight. The agreement called for Todd Herrick to resign from the board, assume the title of chairman emeritus, and have the right to attend board meetings, without being able to vote on board matters. Todd Herrick's son, Kent Herrick, was named to the board to fill Todd Herrick's former seat. The company named Edwin Buker, president and CEO of Citation Corp., as the new CEO of Tecumseh in mid-2007.

In early 2007 the company set plans to close its plant in New Holstein, Wisconsin, where components for gasoline engines are made. In two phases, Tecumseh will lay off all 320 employees there. The company said it would continue to relocate production work to lower-cost facilities in Brazil, China, and India to remain competitive on a global basis.

Donald Smith & Co. has an equity stake of more than 9%. Brandes Investment Partners owns 8% of Tecumseh Products. Franklin Resources holds about 6% of the company, as does Aegis Financial.

## HISTORY

Master toolmakers Ray Herrick (friend and advisor to Henry Ford and Thomas Edison) and Bill Sage founded the Michigan-based company in 1930 as Hillsdale Machine & Tool. Its first products included small tools, toys, and car and refrigerator parts. By 1933 Herrick controlled the company. The next year the company bought a facility in Tecumseh, Michigan, where it began mass-producing car and refrigerator parts. The company changed its name to Tecumseh Products in 1934 and went public in 1937.

By the end of the 1930s, Tecumseh was a major producer of hermetic compressors. In 1941 its focus shifted to WWII efforts, and it began making anti-aircraft projectile casings and aircraft engine parts. Herrick's son Kenneth began working for Tecumseh in 1945. Two years later, a company-made compressor was used in the first home window air-conditioning unit.

Tecumseh bought two Ohio companies in 1950 and 1952, and introduced an AC compressor for cars in 1953. Two years later the company bought compressor designer Tresco, and hired Joseph Layton as Tecumseh's president and CEO. Tecumseh gained entry into the gasoline engine market with the purchase of Wisconsin's Lauson Engine (1956) and Power Products (1957). Acquisitions in the 1960s allowed Tecumseh to tap into the power-train market.

After Layton's death in 1964, William Hazelwood was named Tecumseh's president. Two years later Kenneth Herrick was appointed president, and in 1970 he was named chairman and CEO, and William MacBeth became president. Kenneth's son Todd began working for Tecumseh that year.

The company bought part of Brazilian compressor company SICOM in the mid-1970s, and all of Oklahoma's Little Giant Pump Co. in 1980. Tecumseh formed an Italian joint venture (1981) and upped its stake in SICOM (1982), making it a subsidiary. When MacBeth died in 1984, Todd became president and CEO. Global expansion continued in the late 1980s. A 1989 US heat wave boosted sales, but political instability in China followed by the Persian Gulf War caused a drop in overseas sales.

In 1995 the company formed a joint venture in India, which it bought and merged with the compressor facilities of Whirlpool of India in 1997. The next year Tecumseh submitted recommendations for cleaning up Wisconsin's Sheboygan River, which the EPA claimed was polluted, in part, by the company.

Y2K fears and a bad winter caused engine sales to jump by 24% in 1999 as consumers hoarded generators and snapped up snow throwers. In 2000 engine sales normalized, and Tecumseh had to deal with cheaper compressor imports. To cope, the company announced plans to close a compressor plant in Kentucky and lay off about 1,500 people (8% of its workforce).

Kenneth Herrick, son of the co-founder and father of Todd Herrick, died in July 2004 at the age of 83. He had served as chairman emeritus since resigning from the board in early 2003.

The company's Brazilian engine manufacturing subsidiary, TMT Motoco do Brasil, signed a debt restructuring agreement with most of its lenders in late 2006. One lender that would not sign on to the agreement pressed for repayment of its debt, and won a court judgment in early 2007 overturning the restructuring agreement. TMT Motoco then filed for judicial restructuring, the Brazilian equivalent of seeking Chapter 11 bankruptcy protection from creditors in the US. The Brazilian unit put all of its employees on vacation furlough and shut down operations while the judicial restructuring case proceeded.

## EXECUTIVES

**Chairman:** David M. Risley, age 62
**President, CEO, and Director:** Edwin L. (Ed) Buker, age 54
**VP, CFO, and Treasurer:** James S. Nicholson, $300,000 pay
**VP and Director, Corporate Human Resources:** Michael A. Forman, age 59
**Director, Investor Relations:** Teresa Hess
**Auditors:** PricewaterhouseCoopers LLP

## LOCATIONS

**HQ:** Tecumseh Products Company
100 E. Patterson St., Tecumseh, MI 49286
**Phone:** 517-423-8411 **Fax:** 517-423-8760
**Web:** www.tecumseh.com

Tecumseh Products operates facilities in Australia, Brazil, Canada, the Czech Republic, France, India, Mexico, Thailand, the UK, and the US.

**2006 Sales**

| | $ mil. | % of total |
|---|---|---|
| North America | | |
| US | 849.7 | 48 |
| Other countries | 85.7 | 5 |
| Europe | 361.0 | 21 |
| South America | | |
| Brazil | 144.2 | 8 |
| Other countries | 93.2 | 5 |
| Middle East/Asia | 235.3 | 13 |
| **Total** | **1,769.1** | **100** |

## PRODUCTS/OPERATIONS

**2006 Sales**

| | $ mil. | % of total |
|---|---|---|
| Compressors | 1,002.7 | 57 |
| Electrical components | 429.9 | 24 |
| Engines & power trains | 319.0 | 18 |
| Other | 17.5 | 1 |
| **Total** | **1,769.1** | **100** |

**Selected Products**

Compressors
- Hermetic compressors (for refrigerators, freezers, water coolers, dehumidifiers, window AC units, central AC units, and heat pumps)

Engines and Power Trains
- Gasoline engines (for lawn mowers, small tractors, garden tillers, string trimmers, and snow throwers)
- Power-train components (for lawn and garden equipment and recreational vehicles)
  - Differentials
  - Transaxles
  - Transmissions

Electrical Components
- Actuators
- Blowers
- Gearmotors
- Motors

Pumps
- Centrifugal
- Small submersible
- Sump

## COMPETITORS

A. O. Smith
American Standard
Briggs & Stratton
Bristol Compressors
Campbell Hausfeld
Daewoo International
Daikin
Danfoss Turbocor
Embraco
Emerson Electric
Fu Sheng
Honda
Hubbell
Johnson Electric
Kawasaki Heavy Industries
Kinetek
Kohler
Kubota Engine America
Lennox
LG Electronics
Matsushita Electric
Mitsubishi Electric
Regal-Beloit
Robert Bosch
SANYO
Sullair
Toro

## HISTORICAL FINANCIALS

Company Type: Public

**Income Statement** FYE: December 31

| | REVENUE ($ mil.) | NET INCOME ($ mil.) | NET PROFIT MARGIN | EMPLOYEES |
|---|---|---|---|---|
| 12/06 | 1,769 | (80) | — | 18,500 |
| 12/05 | 1,847 | (224) | — | 19,100 |
| 12/04 | 1,912 | 10 | 0.5% | 21,700 |
| 12/03 | 1,819 | 0 | 0.0% | 20,700 |
| 12/02 | 1,344 | 51 | 3.8% | 22,000 |
| Annual Growth | 7.1% | — | — | (4.2%) |

**2006 Year-End Financials**

Debt ratio: 27.2%
Return on equity: —
Cash ($ mil.): 82
Current ratio: 1.44
Long-term debt ($ mil.): 217
No. of shares (mil.): 13
Dividends
Yield: —
Payout: —
Market value ($ mil.): 226

**Stock History** NASDAQ (GM): TECUB

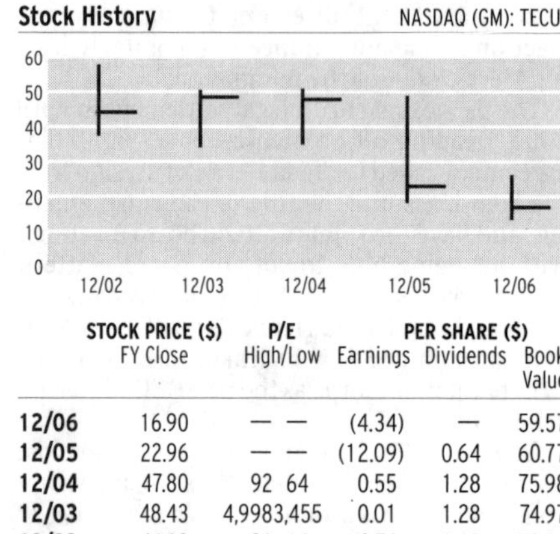

| | STOCK PRICE ($) FY Close | P/E High/Low | PER SHARE ($) Earnings | Dividends | Book Value |
|---|---|---|---|---|---|
| 12/06 | 16.90 | — — | (4.34) | — | 59.57 |
| 12/05 | 22.96 | — — | (12.09) | 0.64 | 60.77 |
| 12/04 | 47.80 | 92 64 | 0.55 | 1.28 | 75.98 |
| 12/03 | 48.43 | 4,9983,455 | 0.01 | 1.28 | 74.97 |
| 12/02 | 44.13 | 21 14 | 2.76 | 1.28 | 73.04 |
| Annual Growth | (21.3%) | — — | — | (20.6%) | (5.0%) |

# Telephone and Data Systems

Telephone and Data Systems (TDS) has raised its children to be independent in a Bell-dominated world. One of the largest non-Bell phone companies in the US, it has more than 6 million local phone and wireless customers in 36 states. Its operations include United States Cellular, its 81%-owned wireless unit that has more than 5 million customers in 26 states. Fixed-line subsidiary TDS Telecommunications provides local access service through more than 1 million access lines in 30 states. The company also provides a full range of printing services through subsidiary Suttle-Straus. Founder LeRoy Carlson and his family control 53% of the company's voting power.

More than three-quarters of Telephone and Data Systems' revenues come from United States Cellular, while TDS Telecom operates 111 incumbent local-exchange carriers (ILECs) serving more than 735,000 access lines and a competitive local-exchange carrier (CLECs), TDS Metrocom, which serves more than 440,000 access lines in Minnesota and Wisconsin.

## HISTORY

LeRoy Carlson learned the ins and outs of rural phone operators when he owned a small firm that supplied equipment and forms to independent phone companies. In the mid-1950s he began buying some of these small phone companies, which he consolidated with a phone book publisher and his equipment company to form Telephones Inc. Carlson sold the company to Contel in 1966.

Carlson continued to buy and sell rural carriers, allowing them to retain local management while he provided centralized purchasing and system upgrades. In 1969 he bought 10 rural providers in Wisconsin and consolidated all of his companies into Telephone and Data Systems (TDS).

Between 1970 and 1975 TDS acquired 32 rural phone companies. When smaller companies in its established regions became scarce, TDS bought rural phone providers from large independents. As TDS diversified, the wireline subsidiary became TDS Telecommunications.

The company began offering paging services in Wisconsin in 1972 and later created subsidiary American Paging (1981). In 1975 TDS moved into cable TV service, eventually creating TDS Cable Communications (1984), but it sold the holdings in 1986.

Getting a head start on the big Bells in the cellular race, TDS began seeking licenses in the early 1980s, eventually winning a 5% stake in the Los Angeles market. Although buffeted by larger independents, it placed a high priority on cellular operations and formed subsidiary United States Cellular Corporation (now doing business as U.S. Cellular) in 1983. Two years later the subsidiary launched services in Tennessee and Oklahoma.

Carlson named his son, LeRoy Jr., to replace him as CEO in 1986 but remained chairman. TDS reduced its ownership in U.S. Cellular to about 80% in 1988 when it took the subsidiary public. Coditel, a Belgian cable TV company, secured a minority stake in U.S. Cellular that year.

In 1993 TDS created subsidiary American Portable Telecom to bid for the new PCS wireless licenses. Three years later the subsidiary, renamed Aerial Communications, went public; TDS kept an 82% stake. Aerial began providing PCS service in 1997.

Expansion, financed mainly through stock, caused Michael Price's Franklin Mutual Advisers to complain that its shares were undervalued. To gain more leverage with management, in 1997 Franklin organized a proxy contest to gain a seat on the board, and veteran private investor Martin Solomon was elected.

That year, in response to investor demand for more liquidity, TDS planned to buy the shares in U.S. Cellular and Aerial that it didn't already own and to create three tracking stocks for its cellular, PCS, and wireline phone units. However, TDS withdrew the proposal in 1998 because of poor market conditions. That year it acquired the 18% of American Paging that it didn't own and joined the company with TSR Paging. The deal left TDS with a 30% stake in the new TSR Wireless (but the company ceased operations in 2000 and declared bankruptcy).

Sonera Group (formerly Telecom Finland) acquired a significant minority stake in Aerial when it invested $200 million in the company in 1998. That year TDS made plans to spin off Aerial in an effort to raise cash. However, TDS dropped the idea and sold its Aerial stake to VoiceStream Wireless for $1.8 billion in 2000. TDS took a 14% stake in VoiceStream, which it swapped to Deutsche Telekom for cash and stock in 2001.

To add to its holdings, in 2001 Telephone and Data Systems bought Wisconsin local telephone service provider Chorus Communications for $195 million and $30 million in assumed debt. The next year the company acquired two local phone service providers in New Hampshire.

## EXECUTIVES

**Chairman Emeritus and Director:** LeRoy T. Carlson Sr., age 90
**Chairman:** Walter C. D. Carlson, age 52
**President, CEO, and Director:**
LeRoy T. (Ted) Carlson Jr., age 59, $1,050,000 pay
**EVP, CFO, and Director:** Kenneth R. (Ken) Meyers, age 52

**SVP and CIO:** Kurt B. Thaus, age 47
**SVP, Acquisitions and Corporate Development:** Scott H. Williamson, age 55, $745,000 pay
**VP and Corporate Secretary:** Kevin C. Gallagher, age 58
**VP, Acquisitions and Corporate Development:** Kenneth M. Kotylo, age 43
**VP, Corporate Development:** Bryon A. Wertz, age 58
**VP, Corporate Finance:** James W. Twesme, age 52
**VP, Corporate Relations:** Mark A. Steinkrauss, age 59
**VP, Human Resources:** C. Theodore Herbert, age 70
**VP, Internal Audit:** Frieda E. Ireland, age 52
**VP, Technology Planning and Services:** Joseph R. Hanley, age 39
**VP and Treasurer:** Peter L. Sereda, age 46
**VP and Assistant Corporate Controller:** Randall H. Reed, age 46
**President and CEO, United States Cellular Corporation:** John E. (Jack) Rooney, age 64, $990,000 pay
**President and CEO, TDS Telecommunications Corporation:** David A. (Dave) Wittwer, age 44
**Auditors:** PricewaterhouseCoopers LLP

## LOCATIONS

**HQ:** Telephone and Data Systems, Inc.
30 N. LaSalle St., Ste. 4000, Chicago, IL 60602
**Phone:** 312-630-1900 **Fax:** 312-630-1908
**Web:** www.teldta.com

## PRODUCTS/OPERATIONS

### 2006 Sales

| | $ mil. | % of total |
|---|---|---|
| US Cellular | 3,473.2 | 79 |
| ILEC | 645.5 | 15 |
| CLEC | 235.8 | 5 |
| Other revenues | 32.4 | 1 |
| Adjustments | (22.4) | — |
| **Total** | **4,364.5** | **100** |

### Selected Subsidiaries and Affiliates

Suttle-Straus, Inc. (commercial printing)
TDS Telecommunications Corporation (wireline phone services)
TDS Metrocom, LLC (competitive local-exchange carrier)
U.S. Link, Inc. (competitive local-exchange carrier)
United States Cellular Corporation (82%, cellular phone service)

## COMPETITORS

ALLTEL
AT&T
BellSouth
Centennial Communications
CenturyTel
D&E Communications
NTELOS
Price Communications
Sprint Nextel
Verizon

## HISTORICAL FINANCIALS

Company Type: Public

### Income Statement

FYE: December 31

| | REVENUE ($ mil.) | NET INCOME ($ mil.) | NET PROFIT MARGIN | EMPLOYEES |
|---|---|---|---|---|
| **12/06** | 4,365 | 162 | 3.7% | 11,800 |
| **12/05** | 3,953 | 650 | 16.4% | 11,500 |
| **12/04** | 3,704 | 67 | 1.8% | 11,500 |
| **12/03** | 3,445 | 47 | 1.4% | 10,900 |
| **12/02** | 2,985 | (984) | — | 11,100 |
| **Annual Growth** | 10.0% | — | — | 1.5% |

### 2006 Year-End Financials

Debt ratio: 84.4%
Return on equity: 4.7%
Cash ($ mil.): 2,219
Current ratio: 1.43
Long-term debt ($ mil.): 3,014
No. of shares (mil.): 6
Dividends
Yield: 7.6%
Payout: 138.7%
Market value ($ mil.): 161

### Stock History

AMEX: TDS

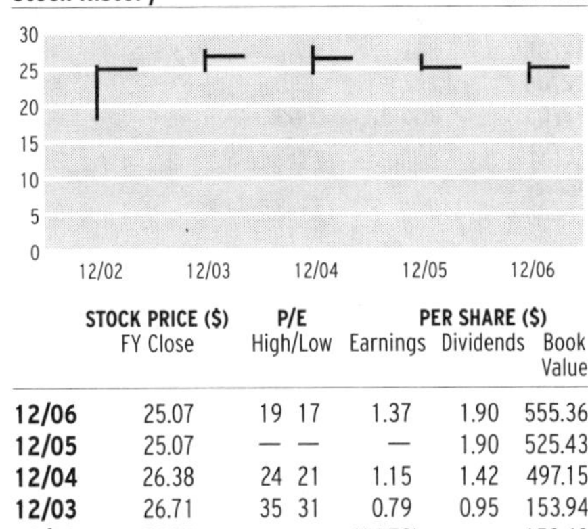


| | STOCK PRICE ($) FY Close | P/E High/Low | | PER SHARE ($) Earnings | Dividends | Book Value |
|---|---|---|---|---|---|---|
| **12/06** | 25.07 | 19 | 17 | 1.37 | 1.90 | 555.36 |
| **12/05** | 25.07 | — | — | — | 1.90 | 525.43 |
| **12/04** | 26.38 | 24 | 21 | 1.15 | 1.42 | 497.15 |
| **12/03** | 26.71 | 35 | 31 | 0.79 | 0.95 | 153.94 |
| **12/02** | 25.00 | — | — | (16.79) | — | 152.63 |
| **Annual Growth** | 0.1% | — | — | — | 26.0% | 38.1% |

# Tellabs, Inc.

If you need faster connections, just tell Tellabs. The company's equipment is used around the world to transmit data, video, and voice signals. Its digital cross-connect systems help connect incoming and outgoing digital and fiber-optic lines. Tellabs also offers broadband network access and transport systems and equipment that enable carriers to build fiber-optic backbone networks. The company's universal telephony distribution system lets cable systems transmit voice, video, and data. Tellabs' customers included incumbent local telephone carriers, including the regional Bell companies, cable operators, corporations, and government agencies.

Tellabs' largest customers — AT&T, Sprint Nextel, and Verizon — accounted for about half of its sales in fiscal 2006. The company makes about a quarter of its sales to customers outside of North America.

Chairman and co-founder Michael Birck controls 8% of Tellabs' shares.

## HISTORY

Tellabs (shortened from Telecommunications Laboratories) was founded in 1975 by Michael Birck, Charles Cooney, and several others. Birck was an Indiana farm boy who later became a Bell Labs engineer before working at Continental Telephone and telecommunications equipment manufacturer Wescom. At nascent Tellabs, Birck developed an echo suppressor on the company's homemade plywood workbench. (Echo suppressors improve the quality of long-distance calls by eliminating voice echoes caused by slight transmission delays.) Before long the increased use of satellites for phone transmission had created a growth market for the product, and sales jumped from $300,000 in Tellabs' first year to almost $8 million in 1977. AT&T competitor Western Union became one of the company's first major customers.

Tellabs went public in 1980. When the creation of the regional Bell companies and several new long-distance services in the mid-1980s led to a surge of competition, Tellabs boosted R&D spending and refocused on high-end products. It entered the data communications market in 1983. However, cost overruns and delays in development of its TITAN long-distance routing system threatened to sink the company, and TITAN was jokingly compared to the *Titanic*.

In 1987 a $10 million contract from Sprint for digital echo cancelers helped revive Tellabs, which began marketing to overseas telecom service providers and making acquisitions, including Delta Communications (Ireland, 1987). Birck's faith in Tellabs bore fruit in 1991, when the company finally introduced its TITAN line.

Tellabs shifted its focus from the mature North American market to central and eastern Europe. In 1993 the company acquired Martis Oy, a Finnish maker of multiplexers. It debuted the CABLESPAN distribution system in 1994. Tellabs purchased wireless network system maker Steinbrecher Corp. and synchronous optical network (SONET) technology from Canadian firm TRANSYS Networks in 1996. The next year it bought multiplexing and optical networking technology from IBM and increased its push into Latin America.

In 1998 Tellabs bought Coherent Communications Systems (now Tellabs Virginia, voice enhancement products). It called off its deal (originally valued at about $7 billion) to acquire telecom equipment maker CIENA after a key CIENA contract fell through. Also in 1998, Bell Atlantic awarded Tellabs a five-year contract as its sole supplier of SONET-based digital cross-connect systems. Tellabs sales rose nearly 38% in 1998, partly on the strength of the once disparaged TITAN line.

Tellabs in 1999 won supply agreements with telecom operators in Brazil and Mexico, and it opened a factory in Ireland. Also that year Tellabs acquired Internet backbone specialist NetCore. Continuing its push for globalization, it also bought the European high-speed telephone networking equipment operations of Alcatel USA (formerly DSC Communications). In 2000 the company acquired privately held telephony switch maker SALIX. Later that year Birck turned over the day-to-day operations of Tellabs to former Ameritech chief Richard Notebaert, who became president and CEO. Birck remained chairman.

In 2001 Tellabs closed facilities and laid off about 30% of its staff, amid slow sales. In early 2002 Tellabs acquired privately held Ocular Networks. Early in 2004 the company appointed former Alcatel COO Krish Prabhu as its chief executive. Former CEO Michael Birck remained chairman. Also that year the company acquired network access product maker Advanced Fibre Communications in a cash and stock deal valued at $1.5 billion.

## EXECUTIVES

**Chairman:** Michael J. Birck, age 69
**President, CEO, and Director:** Krish A. Prabhu, age 52, $1,170,000 pay
**EVP Broadband Products:** Carl A. DeWilde, age 59, $425,000 pay
**EVP, General Counsel, and Chief Administrative Officer:** James M. (Jim) Sheehan, age 43, $376,450 pay
**EVP, CFO, and Interim Principal Accounting Officer:** Timothy J. Wiggins, age 50

**EVP Transport Products:** Daniel P. (Dan) Kelly, age 45
**EVP and CIO:** Jean K. Holley, age 47
**EVP Global Sales and Services:**
Stephen M. (Steve) McCarthy, age 52, $431,500 pay
**EVP Global Operations:** John M. Brots, age 46
**VP Corporate Communications:** George Stenitzer, age 50
**Senior Manager, Investor Relations:** Tom Scottino
**VP Product Development, Finland:** Mika Heikkinen
**VP Government Systems:** Joseph Shilgalis
**VP and General Manager, Asia Pacific Sales:**
Sanjay J. Patel
**VP and General Manager, Europe, Middle East, and Africa Sales:** Patrick Dolan
**VP North American Wireless Accounts:**
Donald R. Hutton
**VP North American ILEC Accounts:**
Charles S. Bernstein
**VP North American Key Accounts:** Kevin P. McClain
**Auditors:** Ernst & Young LLP

## LOCATIONS

**HQ:** Tellabs, Inc.
One Tellabs Center, 1415 W. Diehl Rd.,
Naperville, IL 60563
**Phone:** 630-798-8800 **Fax:** 630-798-2000
**Web:** www.tellabs.com

### 2006 Sales

| | $ mil. | % of total |
|---|---|---|
| North America | 1,548.4 | 76 |
| Other regions | 492.8 | 24 |
| **Total** | **2,041.2** | **100** |

## PRODUCTS/OPERATIONS

### 2006 Sales

| | $ mil. | % of total |
|---|---|---|
| Broadband | 1,080.4 | 53 |
| Transport | 778.2 | 38 |
| Services | 182.6 | 9 |
| **Total** | **2,041.2** | **100** |

### Selected Operations

Products
- Access networking systems
- Broadband data systems
- Digital cross-connects
- Transport switching
- Voice-quality enhancement

Services
- Engineering
- Installation and integration
- Maintenance
- Material procurement
- Program management
- Technical assistance

## COMPETITORS

ADC Telecommunications
ADTRAN
Alcatel-Lucent
ARRIS
Ciena
Cisco Systems
Ditech
ECI Telecom
Ericsson
Fujitsu Network Communications
Huawei Technologies
Network Equipment Technologies
NMS Communications
Nokia
Nortel Networks
Polaris Networks
Siemens AG
telent
UTStarcom
ZTE

## HISTORICAL FINANCIALS

Company Type: Public

### Income Statement

FYE: Friday nearest December 31

| | REVENUE ($ mil.) | NET INCOME ($ mil.) | NET PROFIT MARGIN | EMPLOYEES |
|---|---|---|---|---|
| **12/06** | 2,041 | 194 | 9.5% | 3,713 |
| **12/05** | 1,883 | 176 | 9.3% | 3,609 |
| **12/04** | 1,232 | (30) | — | 4,125 |
| **12/03** | 980 | (242) | — | 3,515 |
| **12/02** | 1,317 | (313) | — | 4,828 |
| **Annual Growth** | 11.6% | — | — | (6.4%) |

### 2006 Year-End Financials

Debt ratio: —
Return on equity: 6.7%
Cash ($ mil.): 1,589
Current ratio: 2.93
Long-term debt ($ mil.): —
No. of shares (mil.): 439
Dividends
Yield: —
Payout: —
Market value ($ mil.): 4,505

### Stock History

NASDAQ (GS): TLAB

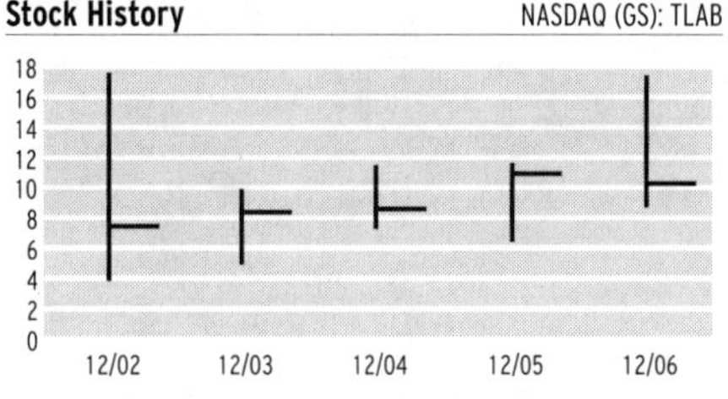


| | STOCK PRICE ($) FY Close | P/E High | P/E Low | PER SHARE ($) Earnings | Dividends | Book Value |
|---|---|---|---|---|---|---|
| **12/06** | 10.26 | 40 | 21 | 0.43 | — | 6.69 |
| **12/05** | 10.90 | 29 | 17 | 0.39 | — | 6.26 |
| **12/04** | 8.59 | — | — | (0.07) | — | 6.25 |
| **12/03** | 8.36 | — | — | (0.58) | — | 5.35 |
| **12/02** | 7.43 | — | — | (0.76) | — | 5.51 |
| **Annual Growth** | 8.4% | — | — | — | — | 5.0% |

# Temple-Inland

Temple-Inland loves people who box, bank, and build. The packaging, banking, and forest products company operates through four business segments. Its largest unit, Corrugated Packaging, makes cartons and boxes, as well as linerboard and bulk containers. The company's Forest Products division produces lumber, particleboard, gypsum wallboard, and other building materials and manages nearly 2 million acres of timberland. Its Temple-Inland Financial Services segment includes 153 Guaranty Federal Bank branches in Texas (100) and California (53), and its Forestar Real Estate division invests in and develops properties. Temple-Inland plans to spin off its financial and real estate operations and sell its timberlands.

In February 2007 Temple-Inland announced a restructuring initiative in which it would spin off its real estate and finance businesses into two new public entities while retaining its packaging and building products manufacturing operations. It also said that it would seek a buyer for about 1.8 million acres of timberlands in Alabama, Georgia, Louisiana, and Texas. (An agreement to sell 1.55 million acres to an investment entity affiliated with The Campbell Group, LLC for nearly $2.4 billion was reached later that year.)

The company initiative was launched shortly after break-up and spin-off rumors surfaced when famed corporate raider Carl Icahn, who controls about 8% of Temple-Inland, announced plans to nominate four new directors. Icahn dropped the proxy battle effort after Temple-Inland announced its restructuring plans. This was not Icahn's first move to take over the company — Icahn announced in early 2005 that he intended to buy up to $1 billion of Temple-Inland stock (about 25% of the company) and nominate three directors for a proxy battle, but later changed his mind on the proxy issue.

The acquisition of Gaylord Container made Temple-Inland one of the largest producers of corrugated packaging in the US; in 2006 the Corrugated Packaging division accounted for 54% of sales. The segment's products range from commodity brown boxes and multi-wall bulk containers to custom die-cut containers, litho-laminate packaging, and its Tru-Tech brand of tear-resistant and water-proof packaging paper. This segment serves some 11,000 customers in the food, glass containers, paper, chemicals, plastics, and appliances industries.

Temple-Inland has taken steps to solve supply and demand problems in the paper industry by consolidating operations. Between mid-2003 and the end of 2004 the company closed seven converting plants and axed more than 300 jobs, and in October 2004 Temple-Inland announced that it would eliminate 1,500 jobs.

The company has been focused on reducing production downtime in corrugated packaging, accelerating fiber growth, and developing real estate opportunities. Late in 2005 it announced that it would cut 250 jobs by restructuring its Financial Services unit.

## HISTORY

Temple-Inland dates back to 1893, when Thomas Temple, a native Virginian, purchased 7,000 acres of Texas timberland from J. C. Diboll. Temple founded Southern Pine Lumber and built his mill in the town of Diboll, Texas. In 1894 he opened his first sawmill. The company set up a second sawmill in 1903 and a hardwood mill in 1907. Temple formed the Temple Lumber Company three years later. When Temple died in 1934, his son, Arthur, inherited a company heavily in debt. In 1937 a fire destroyed the company's sawmill in Hemphill, Texas.

The Temple family's Southern Pine business fared better, producing basic hardwood and pine lumber items for the construction and furniture industries during the housing boom following WWII. By the early 1950s the company had begun converting chips, sawdust, and shavings into panel products. The company subsequently pioneered southern pine plywood production and branched into making particleboard, gypsum wallboard, and other building materials. Temple Lumber merged with Southern Pine Lumber in 1956 under the Southern Pine name. In 1962 Southern Pine moved into finance with the purchase of the controlling interest of Lumbermen's Investment.

The company changed its name to Temple Industries in 1964. It expanded in the early 1970s by opening a particleboard mill in Diboll in 1971 and acquiring AFCO, a manufacturer of do-it-yourself products, in 1972. The next year media titan Time Inc. acquired Temple Industries and merged it with Eastex Pulp and Paper, creating Temple-Eastex. Time bought Inland Container, a fully integrated packaging company, in 1978 for $272 million.

Inland traces its roots back to 1918, when Herman Krannert started Anderson Box Company in Indiana to make ventilated corrugated products for baby chicks. It had grown into a major manufacturer of packaging materials for the agricultural, horticultural, and poultry industries.

Time spun off the Temple and Inland operations as Temple-Inland in 1983. The company expanded its financial businesses in the late 1980s by acquiring a Kansas insurance company (1985) and three insolvent Texas S&Ls (1988).

Following the retirement of Arthur Temple Jr., Temple-Inland appointed Clifford Grum as chairman and CEO (the first non-family chairman) in 1991. Temple-Inland grew by adding plants and resources. It expanded its Latin American production capacity in 1995 with the opening of a box plant in Chile and a corrugated container sheet facility in Mexico.

Temple-Inland acquired California Financial Holding and Knutson Mortgage in 1997. Acquisitions in 1998 included two medium-density fiberboard plants from MacMillan Bloedel. In 1999 the company paid $120 million for HF Bancorp (parent of California's 18-branch Hemet Federal Savings and Loan), which became part of Guaranty Federal Bank. The company also sold its bleached-paperboard mill in Evadale, Texas, to forestry product company Westvaco (now MeadWestvaco) for $625 million.

CFO Kenneth Jastrow became CEO in 2000. The next year Temple-Inland acquired the corrugated packaging assets of Chesapeake Corp. for about $120 million. In April 2002 the company acquired Gaylord Container (now Inland Paperboard and Packaging), a maker of paper packaging products, in a deal that included about $65 million in Temple-Inland stock and the assumption of $847 million in Gaylord debt.

In 2005 the company sold its fiberboard plant in Canada.

## EXECUTIVES

**Chairman and CEO:** Kenneth M. (Kenny) Jastrow II, age 60, $959,143 pay
**CFO:** Randall D. Levy, age 55, $422,115 pay
**EVP:** Doyle R. Simons, age 43, $416,346 pay
**EVP Paper:** J. Patrick Maley III, age 45, $422,115 pay
**Group VP; CEO and President, Forest Products:** Jack C. Sweeny, age 60, $397,115 pay
**Group VP Forest:** James M. (Jim) DeCosmo, age 48
**Group VP:** Kenneth R. Dubuque, age 58
**VP, Assistant General Counsel, and Secretary:** Leslie K. O'Neal, age 51
**VP Internal Audit:** Carolyn Sloan
**VP Supply Chain:** Terry E. Sueltman, age 60
**Chief Administrative Officer:** J. Bradley Johnston, age 51
**Chief Governance Officer:** Grant Adamson
**CIO:** Scott Smith, age 52
**Treasurer:** David W. Turpin, age 56
**Director, Investor Relations:** Christopher L. Nines
**General Counsel:** C. Morris Davis, age 64
**Principal Accounting Officer and Controller:** Troy L. Hester, age 50
**Auditors:** Ernst & Young LLP

## LOCATIONS

**HQ:** Temple-Inland Inc.
1300 Mopac Expwy. South, Austin, TX 78746
**Phone:** 512-434-5800 **Fax:** 512-434-3750
**Web:** www.templeinland.com

Temple-Inland's primary facilities are located in the US; it also has operations in Mexico and Puerto Rico.

### 2006 Sales

| | $ mil. | % of total |
|---|---|---|
| US | 5,382 | 97 |
| Mexico | 176 | 3 |
| **Total** | **5,558** | **100** |

## PRODUCTS/OPERATIONS

### 2006 Sales

| | $ mil. | % of total |
|---|---|---|
| Corrugated packaging | 2,977 | 54 |
| Forest products | 1,237 | 22 |
| Financial services | 1,169 | 21 |
| Real estate | 175 | 3 |
| **Total** | **5,558** | **100** |

### Selected Operations and Products

Corrugated packaging
- Boxes
- Bulk containers
- Linerboard

Forest products
- Fiberboard
- Gypsum wallboard
- Lumber
- Medium-density fiberboard (MDF)
- Particleboard

Financial services
- Guaranty Bank (savings bank with 100 branches in Texas; 53 in California)
- Insurance
- Mortgage banking

Real estate (70 developments in California, Colorado, Florida, Georgia, Missouri, Tennessee, Texas, and Utah)

## COMPETITORS

American Gypsum
Bank of America
Boise Cascade
Cascades Inc.
Eagle Materials
Greif
International Paper
Longview Fibre
MeadWestvaco
OfficeMax
Owens Corning Sales
PCA
Pratt Industries USA
Wells Fargo
Weyerhaeuser

## HISTORICAL FINANCIALS

Company Type: Public

### Income Statement

FYE: Saturday nearest December 31

| | REVENUE ($ mil.) | NET INCOME ($ mil.) | NET PROFIT MARGIN | EMPLOYEES |
|---|---|---|---|---|
| **12/06** | 5,558 | 468 | 8.4% | 15,500 |
| **12/05** | 4,888 | 176 | 3.6% | 15,500 |
| **12/04** | 4,750 | 165 | 3.5% | 16,000 |
| **12/03** | 4,653 | 96 | 2.1% | 18,000 |
| **12/02** | 4,518 | 53 | 1.2% | 19,500 |
| **Annual Growth** | 5.3% | 72.4% | — | (5.6%) |

### 2006 Year-End Financials

Debt ratio: 317.4%
Return on equity: 21.9%
Cash ($ mil.): 405
Current ratio: 0.12
Long-term debt ($ mil.): 6,947
No. of shares (mil.): 111
Dividends
Yield: 2.2%
Payout: 23.7%
Market value ($ mil.): 5,108

### Stock History

NYSE: TIN

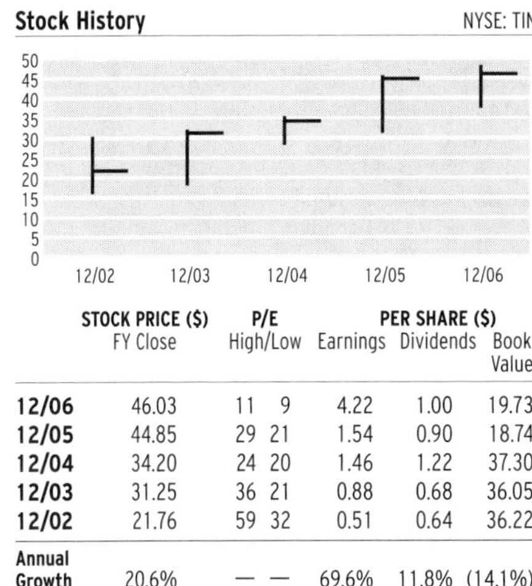

| | STOCK PRICE ($) FY Close | P/E High | P/E Low | PER SHARE ($) Earnings | Dividends | Book Value |
|---|---|---|---|---|---|---|
| **12/06** | 46.03 | 11 | 9 | 4.22 | 1.00 | 19.73 |
| **12/05** | 44.85 | 29 | 21 | 1.54 | 0.90 | 18.74 |
| **12/04** | 34.20 | 24 | 20 | 1.46 | 1.22 | 37.30 |
| **12/03** | 31.25 | 36 | 21 | 0.88 | 0.68 | 36.05 |
| **12/02** | 21.76 | 59 | 32 | 0.51 | 0.64 | 36.22 |
| **Annual Growth** | 20.6% | — | — | 69.6% | 11.8% | (14.1%) |

# Tenet Healthcare

Tenet Healthcare may be one of the biggest US hospital chains, but this giant is anything but jolly — and it's shedding some excess weight. It owns or leases about 60 general acute care hospitals with nearly 16,000 beds, but has been trimming its holdings. With hospitals in 12 states, the firm is organized in five regions: California, Central-Northeast, Southern States, Texas, and Florida; a majority of its facilities are in California, Florida, and Texas. In addition to its hospital business, the company operates a number of specialty hospitals, skilled nursing facilities, physician practices, outpatient centers, and other health care facilities that form regional networks around its main hospitals.

Tenet is struggling to emerge from several years of investigations, lawsuits, and bad publicity. In 2006 it resolved multiple federal investigations regarding its billing practices by agreeing to a $900 million deal with the Justice Department. Tenet had initially come under scrutiny for manipulating the Medicare reimbursement system to maximize special payments (called outlier payments) for the costliest hospital stays. But the investigations spread, with questions raised about the company's physician recruitment practices and the necessity of some billed procedures. An SEC investigation related to these issues is ongoing.

The company was also hit hard by Hurricane Katrina in 2005. Its New Orleans and Mississippi facilities sustained considerable damage, causing them to either shut down or operate at reduced levels. To make matters worse, Tenet's Memorial Medical Hospital in New Orleans became a symbol of the city's devastation, after several dozen bodies were found there in the aftermath of the storm. The company has since sold the Mississippi facility and most of the New Orleans hospitals as well.

The Gulf Coast divestitures are part of a larger plan announced in 2006 to sell off about a dozen facilities by mid-2007, ridding itself of some low-performing operations, partly to pay its $900 million bill to government investigators, and partly so it can invest in equipment upgrades at its remaining hospitals.

Litigation and investigations (as well as the Katrina disaster) have taken their toll on patient volumes, largely due to the loss of physicians willing to practice at Tenet's hospitals. It has stepped up doctor recruitment efforts and has implemented a number of quality initiatives to win back the trust of doctors and patients.

While the company is shedding holdings that aren't performing well, Tenet is expanding where it sees room for growth. Two 100-bed general hospitals are in the works for El Paso, Texas, and Fort Mill, South Carolina. In 2007 it acquired Coastal Carolina Medical Center in Hardeeville, South Carolina, from LifePoint.

Tenet Healthcare moved its headquarters from Santa Barbara, California, to Dallas in 2005.

## HISTORY

Hospital attorney Richard Eamer, along with attorneys Leonard Cohen and John Bedrosian, founded National Medical Enterprises (NME) in 1969. After its IPO, NME bought 10 hospitals, nursing homes, an office building, and land in California. Within six years the company owned, operated, and managed 23 hospitals and a home health care business. It sold medical equipment and bottled oxygen, and provided vocational training for nurses.

In the 1970s NME expanded into hospital construction and bought five Florida hospitals. By 1981 NME was the #3 health care concern in the US, owning or managing 193 hospitals and nursing homes. In the 1980s NME diversified further, buying nursing homes and mental health centers. By the end of the decade the company's Specialty Hospital Group brought in more than 50% of revenues. NME was the second-largest publicly owned health care company in the US (after HCA) by 1985.

In 1990 NME reversed course, spinning off most of its long-term-care businesses. In 1992 several insurance companies sued NME, alleging fraudulent psychiatric claims; NME settled the suits in 1993. Federal agents later raided company headquarters, seizing papers related to the suspected fraud. That year investment banker Jeff Barbakow took over as CEO, forcing out Eamer and Cohen.

In 1993 and 1994 NME dumped most of its psychiatric and rehabilitation facilities, using the proceeds to help pay penalties stemming from the federal investigation into alleged insurance fraud, kickbacks, and patient abuse at its psychiatric units. NME paid another $16 million in related state fines. (Related civil lawsuits were settled in 1997.) The company's name change to Tenet Healthcare coincided with new purchases throughout the South in 1995 and 1996.

The next few years were mixed for Tenet. On the upside, it bought OrNda HealthCorp, which complemented Tenet's existing networks. Tenet and MedPartners (now Caremark Rx), then the #1 practice management firm, formed a Southern California hospital-doctor network in 1997 that gave both companies heft in dealing with HMOs (the partnership crumbled in 1999 when MedPartners exited practice management to focus on pharmacy benefits management and ceased operations in California).

In 1998 the company was dogged by another investigation, this time by the Health and Human Services Inspector General's office over allegations the company paid more than fair market value for a physician practice in return for kickbacks. Tenet in 2004 agreed to pay around $31 million to settle two lawsuits stemming from these allegations.

Like many companies in the industry, in 1999 Tenet began feeling the effects of the Balanced Budget Act of 1997, which mandated more scrutiny of Medicare expenditures to health care providers. In response, the company began divesting some of its hospitals; it also shed its practice management business and reorganized its corporate structure.

In 2003 the company settled claims brought by the Department of Justice that doctors performed unnecessary cardiac surgeries at its Redding Medical Center (now Shasta Regional Medical Center) in California; the settlement cost Tenet $54 million; Tenet sold that facility in 2004. In late 2004, Tenet also set aside $395 million in a fund to settle patients' claims.

An even larger sell-off began in 2004 and included nearly 20 hospitals in California and others in Louisiana, Massachusetts (all three were sold to Vanguard Health Systems in early 2005), Missouri, and Texas. Additionally, the company ended some operating leases and joint ventures, primarily in California; sold its Barcelona, Spain, hospital; and sold about a dozen home health agencies and hospice providers to Amedisys.

## EXECUTIVES

**Chairman:** Edward A. (Ed) Kangas, age 62
**Vice Chairman:** Reynold J. Jennings, age 60
**President, CEO, and Director:** Trevor Fetter, age 47, $2,230,637 pay
**COO:** Stephen L. Newman, age 56
**CFO:** Biggs C. Porter, age 52
**EVP and CIO:** Stephen F. Brown, age 50
**SVP, Southern Region:** John Holland, age 50
**SVP, Operations, Central Northeast-Southern:** Stephen E. (Steve) Corbeil
**SVP, Clinical Quality and Chief Medical Officer:** Jennifer Daley, age 57, $365,261 pay
**SVP, Operations Finance:** Mike Tyson
**SVP, Patient Financial Services:** Stephen M. (Steve) Mooney, age 40
**SVP, Ethics and Compliance; Chief Compliance Officer:** Steven W. (Steve) Ortquist, age 45
**SVP, Investor Relations:** Thomas R. Rice
**SVP, Operations, Texas-Gulf Coast Region:** Robert L. Smith
**SVP, Finance and Regional CFO, Texas-Gulf Coast Region:** Scott Richardson, age 56
**SVP, California Region:** Jeffery (Jeff) Flocken, age 52
**VP and Treasurer:** Jeffrey S. (Jeff) Sherman, age 40
**VP, Corporate Communications:** Harold O. (Harry) Anderson
**VP, Controller, and Principal Accounting Officer:** Daniel J. (Dan) Cancelmi, age 44
**General Counsel and Secretary:** E. Peter Urbanowicz, age 43, $794,425 pay
**Auditors:** Deloitte & Touche LLP

## LOCATIONS

**HQ:** Tenet Healthcare Corporation
13737 Noel Rd., Dallas, TX 75240
**Phone:** 469-893-2200 **Fax:** 469-893-8600
**Web:** www.tenethealth.com

### Selected Hospitals

Alabama
- Brookwood Medical Center (Birmingham)

California
- Desert Regional Medical Center (Palm Springs)
- Doctors Hospital of Manteca (Manteca)
- Doctors Medical Center (Modesto)
- Fountain Valley Regional Hospital and Medical Center (Fountain Valley)
- Irvine Regional Hospital and Medical Center (Irvine)
- John F. Kennedy Memorial Hospital (Indio)
- Lakewood Regional Medical Center (Lakewood)
- Los Alamitos Medical Center (Los Alamitos)
- Placentia-Linda Hospital (Placentia)
- San Dimas Community Hospital (San Dimas)
- San Ramon Regional Medical Center (San Ramon)
- Sierra Vista Regional Medical Center (San Luis Obispo)
- Twin Cities Community Hospital (Templeton)
- USC University Hospital (Los Angeles)

Florida
- Coral Gables Hospital (Coral Gables)
- Delray Medical Center (Delray Beach)
- Florida Medical Center (Fort Lauderdale)
- Good Samaritan Hospital (West Palm Beach)
- Hialeah Hospital (Hialeah)
- North Ridge Medical Center (Fort Lauderdale)
- North Shore Medical Center (Miami)
- Palm Beach Gardens Medical Center (Palm Beach Gardens)
- Palmetto General Hospital (Hialeah)
- Saint Mary's Medical Center (West Palm Beach)
- West Boca Medical Center (Boca Raton)

Georgia
- Atlanta Medical Center (Atlanta)
- North Fulton Regional Hospital (Roswell)
- South Fulton Medical Center (East Point)
- Spalding Regional Hospital (Griffin)

Louisiana
- NorthShore Regional Medical Center (Slidell)

Missouri
- Des Peres Hospital (St. Louis)
- Saint Louis University Hospital (St. Louis)

Nebraska
- Creighton University Medical Center (Omaha)

North Carolina
- Central Carolina Hospital (Sanford)
- Frye Regional Medical Center (Hickory)

Pennsylvania
- Hahnemann University Hospital (Philadelphia)
- St. Christopher's Hospital for Children (Philadelphia)

South Carolina
- Coastal Carolina Medical Center (Hardeeville)
- East Cooper Regional Medical Center (Mt. Pleasant)
- Hilton Head Medical Center and Clinics (Hilton Head)
- Piedmont Medical Center (Rock Hill)

Tennessee
- Saint Francis Hospital (Memphis)
- Saint Francis Hospital, Bartlett (Bartlett)

Texas
- Centennial Medical Center (Frisco)
- Cypress Fairbanks Medical Center (Houston)
- Doctors Hospital (Dallas)
- Houston Northwest Medical Center (Houston)
- Lake Pointe Medical Center (Rowlett)
- Nacogdoches Medical Center (Nacogdoches)
- Park Plaza Hospital (Houston)
- Providence Memorial Hospital (El Paso)
- Shelby Regional Medical Center (Center)
- Sierra Medical Center (El Paso)

## PRODUCTS/OPERATIONS

### 2006 Sales

| | $ mil. | % of total |
|---|---|---|
| Domestic general hospitals | 8,531 | 98 |
| Other | 170 | 2 |
| **Total** | **8,701** | **100** |

**2006 Sales**

| | % of total |
|---|---|
| Managed care | 52 |
| Medicare | 27 |
| Indemnity, self-pay & other | 12 |
| Medicaid | 9 |
| **Total** | **100** |

## COMPETITORS

Ascension Health
Carolinas HealthCare System
Catholic Health Initiatives
Catholic Healthcare West
Community Health Systems
HCA
Health Management Associates
Kindred Healthcare
Sisters of Mercy Health System
SSM Health Care
Sun Healthcare
Sutter Health
Universal Health Services
WellStar Health System

## HISTORICAL FINANCIALS

Company Type: Public

**Income Statement** FYE: December 31

| | REVENUE ($ mil.) | NET INCOME ($ mil.) | NET PROFIT MARGIN | EMPLOYEES |
|---|---|---|---|---|
| **12/06** | 8,701 | (803) | — | 68,952 |
| **12/05** | 9,614 | (724) | — | 73,434 |
| **12/04** | 9,919 | (2,640) | — | 91,633 |
| **12/03** | 13,212 | (1,477) | — | 109,759 |
| **12/02** | 8,743 | 459 | 5.2% | 115,129 |
| **Annual Growth** | (0.1%) | — | — | (12.0%) |

**2006 Year-End Financials**

Debt ratio: 1,803.0%
Return on equity: —
Cash ($ mil.): 823
Current ratio: 1.57
Long-term debt ($ mil.): 4,760

No. of shares (mil.): 472
Dividends
Yield: —
Payout: —
Market value ($ mil.): 3,287

**Stock History** NYSE: THC

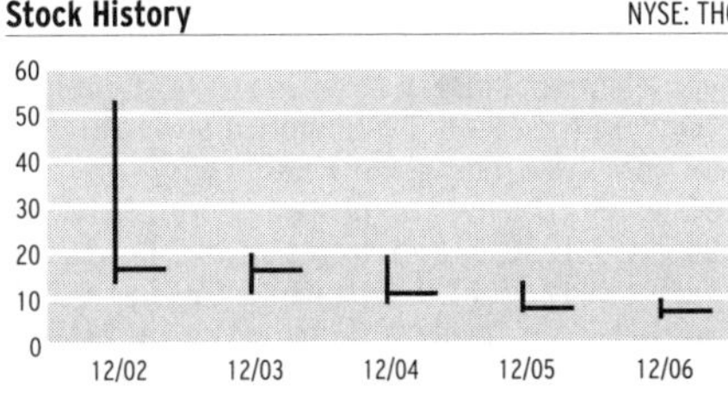

| | STOCK PRICE ($) FY Close | P/E High/Low | | PER SHARE ($) Earnings | Dividends | Book Value |
|---|---|---|---|---|---|---|
| **12/06** | 6.97 | — | — | (1.71) | — | 0.56 |
| **12/05** | 7.66 | — | — | (1.54) | — | 2.17 |
| **12/04** | 10.98 | — | — | (5.66) | — | 3.71 |
| **12/03** | 16.05 | — | — | (3.17) | — | 9.38 |
| **12/02** | 16.40 | 56 | 15 | 0.93 | — | 12.08 |
| **Annual Growth** | (19.3%) | — | — | — | — | (53.6%) |

# Tenneco Inc.

Tenneco wants users of its products to take a deep breath and enjoy the ride. The auto parts company makes Walker exhaust systems and Monroe ride-control equipment (shocks, struts) for vehicle manufacturers and the replacement market. Tenneco's product line also includes vibration-control systems, catalytic converters, and various exhaust system accessories. Among the company's major customers are General Motors (14% of sales), Ford (11%), Volkswagen (11%), and Daimler and Chrysler (11%). Tenneco operates from more than 80 facilities in nearly two dozen countries on six continents; sales outside North America account for a majority of the company's business.

The former Tenneco Automotive became Tenneco — again — in October 2005. The name change is a return to the company's roots; Tenneco Automotive took that name in 1999 when onetime conglomerate Tenneco divided its last two businesses — auto parts and packaging (Pactiv) — into independent companies.

After negotiating a few post-spinoff bumps in the road, Tenneco is beginning to enjoy the ride as an independent company. The company has made significant reductions of the debt incurred in the spinoff of the packaging business, and Tenneco is seeing the benefits of bringing its manufacturing capacity in line with demand.

The company is also reaping the fruits of its overseas investments. In Europe, Tenneco has relocated many of its manufacturing operations to lower-cost countries, including Russia, Poland, and the Czech Republic. In addition, Tenneco has become the leading manufacturer of original equipment emission controls for China's booming automotive industry.

Tenneco wants to grow by building its aftermarket businesses. The company is expanding its product mix to include offerings such as brake pads and filters — items that need to be replaced more often than mufflers or shock absorbers.

The company froze its defined-benefit pension plans in the summer of 2006, switching salaried and non-union hourly employees in the US to defined-contribution plans, such as 401(k) plans, as of 2007. Tenneco estimated it would save around $11 million a year as a result of the move.

## HISTORY

Tennessee Gas and Transmission began in 1943 as a division of the Chicago Corporation, headed by Gardiner Symonds and authorized to build a pipeline from West Virginia to the Gulf of Mexico. With the US facing WWII fuel shortages, the group finished the project in 11 months.

After WWII, Tennessee Gas went public with Symonds as president. It merged its oil and gas exploration interests into Tennessee Production Company (1954), which with Bay Petroleum (bought 1955) became Tenneco Oil in 1961. Symonds acquired complementary firms and entered the chemical industry by buying 50% of Petro-Tex Chemical in 1955.

Tenneco Oil moved its headquarters to Houston in 1963 to better ship natural gas from the Texas Gulf Coast. Symonds bought Packaging Corporation of America, a maker of shipping containers, pulp, and paperboard products, in 1965. A year later the company, which had become a conglomerate, adopted the Tenneco name. In 1967 it bought Kern County Land Company, which owned 2.5 million acres of California farmland and two Racine, Wisconsin manufacturers: J. I. Case (tractors and construction equipment) and automotive firm Walker Manufacturing.

In 1968 Symonds bought Newport News Shipbuilding. The shipbuilder began making submarines and nuclear-powered aircraft carriers in the 1960s.

Symonds died in 1971. In 1977 Tenneco bought shock-absorber maker Monroe of Monroe, Michigan, and Philadelphia Life Insurance Company (sold to ICH Corporation in 1986). In 1985 it bought UK chemical company Albright & Wilson, and Case bought International Harvester's farm-equipment business. A farming recession prompted Tenneco to sell its agricultural operations in 1987. It sold its oil exploration and production business in 1988.

In the early 1990s Tenneco restructured. It sold its natural gas liquids business to Enron, its pulp chemicals business to Sterling Chemicals, and a US soda ash plant to Belgium's Solvay. It bought gas marketer EnTrade.

Under Dana Mead, a former International Paper executive appointed COO in 1992, Tenneco sold some businesses to focus on automotive parts and packaging. It divested some of Case through a 1994 IPO and sold the rest in 1996. In 1995 Tenneco bought Mobil's plastics division (Hefty, Baggies) for nearly $1.3 billion. In 1996 the firm spun off Newport News Shipbuilding and sold its natural gas unit to El Paso Energy for $3.7 billion.

Also in 1996 Tenneco formed joint ventures in China and India and opened a plant in Mexico. In 1997 Tenneco acquired the plastic-packaging division of NV Koninklijke KNP (now Buhrmann NV), and Richter Manufacturing (protective packaging) in 1998. Tenneco formed joint ventures with Shanghai Automotive Industry Group to make exhaust systems in China and with Sentinel Products to make foam automotive and sports products in the US.

In 1999 Tenneco sold 55% of its container board business to investment firm Madison Dearborn Partners for $2.2 billion, forming joint venture Packaging Corporation of America. Tenneco split into two companies in 1999, both based in Lake Forest, Illinois. Tenneco's packaging unit was spun off as Pactiv Corporation, and Tenneco was renamed Tenneco Automotive. Former president of automotive operations, Mark Frissora, became CEO that year.

Late in 2000, amid poor results, Tenneco Automotive announced that it would cut 700 jobs (about 16% of its workforce). Early in 2001 the company announced that more than 400 more jobs would be eliminated. Also in 2001 Tenneco Automotive acquired a Polish maker of shock absorbers in hopes of spreading into emerging markets and moving production to lower-wage regions. To further cut costs and pay down debt incurred by the spin-off of Pactiv, in 2002 Tenneco Automotive announced 900 more job cuts as well as the closure of eight plants in North America and Europe.

In keeping with its strategy to transfer some manufacturing operations to low-labor-cost regions, Tenneco Automotive opened a new plant in Togliatti, Russia, in 2003.

Tenneco Automotive in 2004 said it would spend several million dollars to build an engineering center to provide support for the company's five joint ventures in China.

## EXECUTIVES

**Chairman and CEO:** Gregg M. Sherrill, age 53
**President and Director:** Paul T. Stecko, age 62
**EVP and CFO:** Kenneth R. Trammell, age 46, $520,075 pay
**EVP; President, International:** Hari N. Nair, age 46, $539,075 pay
**EVP, General Counsel, and Corporate Secretary:** David Wardell
**SVP and General Manager, North American Original Equipment Ride Control and North American Aftermarket:** Neal Yanos, age 44, $438,809 pay
**SVP, Global Administration:** Richard P. Schneider, age 59
**SVP, Global Supply Chain Management and Manufacturing:** Alain Michaelis, age 40
**CTO:** Timothy E. (Tim) Jackson, age 49
**VP and CIO:** H. William Haser, age 46
**VP, Tax and Treasurer:** John E. Kunz
**VP and Controller:** Paul D. Novas, age 48
**VP and General Manager, Commercial Vehicle Segment and Global Program Management:** Lois Boyd
**VP and General Manager, European Original Equipment Emission Control:** Ulrich Mehlmann
**VP, Global Communications:** James K. Spangler
**VP, Global Emissions Control Engineering:** Herman Weltens
**Director, Corporate Communications:** Jane Ostrander
**Director, Human Resources:** Barbara Kluth
**Investor Relations:** Leslie Hunziker
**Auditors:** Deloitte & Touche LLP

## LOCATIONS

**HQ:** Tenneco Inc.
500 North Field Dr., Lake Forest, IL 60045
**Phone:** 847-482-5000 **Fax:** 847-482-5940
**Web:** www.tenneco.com

### 2006 Sales

| | $ mil. | % of total |
|---|---|---|
| Europe, South America & India | 2,387 | 50 |
| North America | 1,966 | 41 |
| Asia Pacific | 436 | 9 |
| Adjustments | (104) | — |
| **Total** | **4,685** | **100** |

## PRODUCTS/OPERATIONS

### 2006 Sales

| | $ mil. | % of total |
|---|---|---|
| Emission-control systems & products | | |
| OEM market | 2,592 | 55 |
| Aftermarket | 385 | 8 |
| Ride-control systems & products | | |
| OEM market | 1,016 | 22 |
| Aftermarket | 692 | 15 |
| **Total** | **4,685** | **100** |

### Selected Systems and Products

Emission-control systems
- Catalytic converters
- Diesel particulate filters
- Emissions systems
- Hangars and isolators
- Hydroformed tubing
- Manifolds
- Mufflers
- Pipes
- Resonators

Ride-control systems
- Advanced suspension systems
- Load-assist products
- Shock absorbers
- Springs
- Struts
- Vibration-control products

## COMPETITORS

Arvin Sango
Benteler Automotive
Cummins
Edelbrock
Faurecia
Faurecia Exhaust Systems
Kolbenschmidt Pierburg
Metaldyne
Midas
Robert Bosch
Tomkins
Wescast Industries
ZF Group NAO

## HISTORICAL FINANCIALS

Company Type: Public

**Income Statement** FYE: December 31

| | REVENUE ($ mil.) | NET INCOME ($ mil.) | NET PROFIT MARGIN | EMPLOYEES |
|---|---|---|---|---|
| **12/06** | 4,685 | 51 | 1.1% | 19,000 |
| **12/05** | 4,441 | 58 | 1.3% | 19,000 |
| **12/04** | 4,213 | 15 | 0.4% | 18,400 |
| **12/03** | 3,766 | 27 | 0.7% | 19,139 |
| **12/02** | 3,459 | (187) | — | 20,000 |
| **Annual Growth** | 7.9% | — | — | (1.3%) |

**2006 Year-End Financials**

Debt ratio: 610.9%
Return on equity: 29.1%
Cash ($ mil.): 202
Current ratio: 1.26
Long-term debt ($ mil.): 1,350
No. of shares (mil.): 46
Dividends
Yield: —
Payout: —
Market value ($ mil.): 1,132

**Stock History** NYSE: TEN

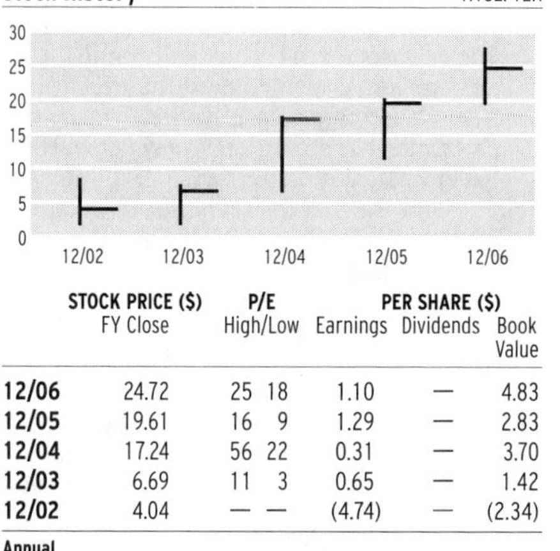


| | STOCK PRICE ($) FY Close | P/E High | P/E Low | PER SHARE ($) Earnings | Dividends | Book Value |
|---|---|---|---|---|---|---|
| **12/06** | 24.72 | 25 | 18 | 1.10 | — | 4.83 |
| **12/05** | 19.61 | 16 | 9 | 1.29 | — | 2.83 |
| **12/04** | 17.24 | 56 | 22 | 0.31 | — | 3.70 |
| **12/03** | 6.69 | 11 | 3 | 0.65 | — | 1.42 |
| **12/02** | 4.04 | — | — | (4.74) | — | (2.34) |
| **Annual Growth** | 57.3% | — | — | — | — | — |

# Tennessee Valley Authority

Although the Tennessee Valley Authority (TVA) may not be an expert on Tennessee attractions like Dollywood and the Grand Ole Opry, it is an authority on power generation. TVA is the largest government-owned power producer in the US, with nearly 32,000 MW of generating capacity. Its power facilities include 11 fossil-powered plants, 29 hydroelectric dams, three nuclear plants, and six combustion turbine plants. The federal corporation transmits electricity to 158 local distribution utilities, which in turn serve 8.5 million consumers. It also provides power for industrial facilities and government agencies, and it manages the Tennessee River system for power production and flood control.

TVA is the sole power wholesaler, by law, in an 80,000-sq.-mi. territory that includes most of Tennessee and portions of six neighboring states (Alabama, Georgia, Kentucky, Mississippi, North Carolina, and Virginia). Generating and transmitting power to local distribution utilities accounts for 86% of TVA's sales.

Most of TVA's power comes from traditional generation sources, but the company is also exploring alternative energy technologies. It has developed solar, wind, and methane gas facilities, and it is offering green choice options through its distribution affiliates.

TVA has also agreed to produce tritium, a radioactive gas that boosts the power of nuclear weapons, for the US Department of Energy (a first for a civilian nuclear power generator). The company is making modifications at its Watts Bar and Savannah River plants to produce and extract the gas; it plans to begin producing tritium by 2007.

TVA's rates are among the nation's lowest, which would-be competitors attribute to its exemption from federal and state income and property taxes. To prepare for deregulation, the authority is trying to reduce its $25 billion debt.

## HISTORY

In 1924 the Army Corps of Engineers finished building the Wilson Dam on the Tennessee River in Alabama to provide power for two WWI-era nitrate plants. With the war over, the question of what to do with the plants became a political football.

An act of Congress created the Tennessee Valley Authority (TVA) in 1933 to manage the plants and Tennessee Valley waterways. New Dealers saw TVA as a way to revitalize the local economy through improved navigation and power generation. Power companies claimed the agency was unconstitutional, but by 1939, when a federal court ruled against them, TVA had five operating hydroelectric plants and five under construction.

During the 1940s TVA supplied power for the war effort, including the Manhattan Project in Tennessee. During the postwar boom between 1945 and 1950, power usage in the Tennessee Valley nearly doubled. Despite adding dams, TVA couldn't keep up with demand, so in 1949 it began building a coal-fired unit. Because coal-fired plants weren't part of TVA's original mission, in 1955 a Congressional panel recommended the authority be dissolved.

Though TVA survived, its funding was cut. In 1959 it was allowed to sell bonds, but it no longer received direct government appropriations for power operations. In addition, it had to pay back the government for past appropriations.

TVA began to build the first unit of an ambitious 17-plant nuclear power program in Alabama in 1967. However, skyrocketing costs forced it to raise rates and cut maintenance on its coal-fired plants, which led to breakdowns. In 1985 five reactors had to be shut down because of safety concerns.

In 1988 former auto industry executive Marvin Runyon was appointed chairman of the agency. "Carvin' Marvin" cut management, sold three airplanes, and got rid of peripheral businesses, saving $400 million a year. In 1992 Runyon left to go to the postal service and was replaced by Craven Crowell, who began preparing TVA for competition in the retail power market.

TVA ended its nuclear construction program in 1996 after bringing two nuclear units on line within three months, a first for a US utility. The next year it raised rates for the first time in 10 years, planning to reduce its debt. In response to a lawsuit filed by neighboring utilities, it agreed to stop "laundering" power by using third parties to sell outside the agency's legally authorized area.

In 1999 the authority finished installing almost $2 billion in scrubbers and other equipment at its coal-fired plants so that it could buy Kentucky coal along with cleaner Wyoming coal. That year, however, the EPA charged TVA with violating the Clean Air Act by making major overhauls on some of its older coal-fired plants without getting permits or installing updated pollution-control equipment. It ordered TVA to bring most of its coal-fired plants into compliance with more current pollution standards. The next year TVA contested the order in court, stating compliance would jack up electricity rates.

TVA was fined by the US Nuclear Regulatory Commission in 2000 for laying off a nuclear plant whistleblower. Crowell resigned in 2001, and Glenn McCullough Jr. was named chairman; he served in that role until May 2005. He was replaced by Bill Baxter (who served until March 2006) and then by William Sansom.

## EXECUTIVES

**Chairman:** William B. (Bill) Sansom, age 64
**President and CEO:** Tom D. Kilgore
**COO:** William R. (Bill) McCollum Jr.
**EVP and General Counsel:** Maureen H. Dunn
**EVP, Financial Services and CFO:**
Kimberly (Kim) Scheibe-Greene, age 36
**EVP, Customer Resources:** Kenneth R. Breeden
**EVP, Fossil Power Group:** Joseph R. Bynum
**EVP, River System Operations and Environment:**
Kathryn J. (Kate) Jackson
**EVP, Administrative Services and Chief Administrative Officer:** John E. Long Jr.
**EVP, Power System Operations:** Terry Boston
**EVP and Chief Nuclear Officer:**
William R. (Bill) Campbell Jr.
**SVP, Economic Development:** John J. Bradley
**SVP, Pricing and Strategic Planning:** Theresa A. Flaim
**SVP, Communications:** Peyton T. Hairston Jr.
**VP, Corporate Communications:** Tracy Williams
**Auditors:** PricewaterhouseCoopers LLP

## LOCATIONS

**HQ:** Tennessee Valley Authority
400 W. Summit Hill Dr., Knoxville, TN 37902
**Phone:** 865-632-2101 **Fax:** 888-633-0372
**Web:** www.tva.gov

The Tennessee Valley Authority's service area covers most of Tennessee and parts of Alabama, Georgia, Kentucky, Mississippi, North Carolina, and Virginia.

## PRODUCTS/OPERATIONS

### 2006 Sales

| | $ mil. | % of total |
|---|---|---|
| Electric | | |
| Municipalities & cooperatives | 7,880 | 85 |
| Industries directly served | 1,066 | 12 |
| Federal agencies & other | 116 | 2 |
| Other | 123 | 1 |
| **Total** | **9,185** | **100** |

### 2006 Energy Mix by Net Capacity

| | % of total |
|---|---|
| Fossil | 49 |
| Nuclear | 19 |
| Hydro | 17 |
| Combustion turbine & diesel generators | 15 |
| **Total** | **100** |

## HISTORICAL FINANCIALS

Company Type: Government-owned

### Income Statement

FYE: September 30

| | REVENUE ($ mil.) | NET INCOME ($ mil.) | NET PROFIT MARGIN | EMPLOYEES |
|---|---|---|---|---|
| **9/06** | 9,185 | 329 | 3.6% | 12,600 |
| **9/05** | 7,794 | 85 | 1.1% | 12,703 |
| **9/04** | 7,533 | 386 | 5.1% | 12,742 |
| **9/03** | 6,952 | 456 | 6.6% | 13,000 |
| **9/02** | 6,835 | 73 | 1.1% | 13,000 |
| **Annual Growth** | 7.7% | 45.7% | — | (0.8%) |

### 2006 Year-End Financials

Debt ratio: 724.1%
Return on equity: 12.9%
Cash ($ mil.): 536
Current ratio: 0.51
Long-term debt ($ mil.): 19,544

### Net Income History

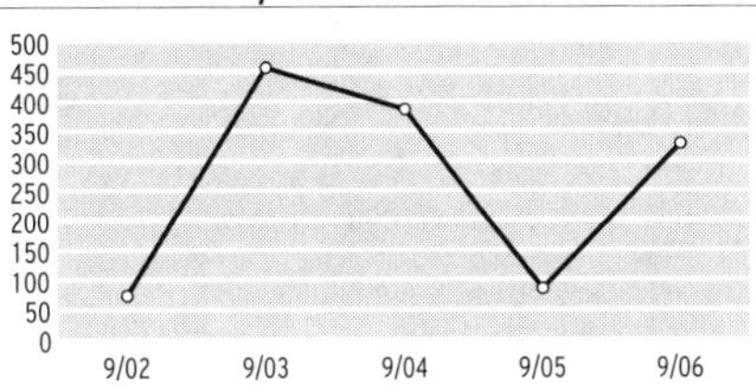


# Terex Corporation

Terex lifts and digs for pay dirt. The company has five major divisions that — simply put — make cranes, construction equipment, roadbuilding equipment, aerial platforms, and mining equipment. The company's construction equipment includes off-highway trucks, excavators, backhoes, and crushing and screening equipment — items also produced by its roadbuilding unit. The roadbuilding unit also makes pavers and mixers. Terex's mining equipment includes surface mining trucks and excavators. Terex Financial Services offers financing and related services for equipment purchases.

The company's equipment is marketed to the construction, infrastructure, quarrying, surface mining, refining, recycling, shipping, transportation, utility, and maintenance industries worldwide. Terex is acquisition driven in its efforts to expand its product offerings and geographic market reach.

The company is focusing on integrating acquisitions, executing cost-saving initiatives, reducing debt and working capital, and penetrating into new markets for certain product categories. Its strategy has been to build its own eponymous brand name in an effort to get all of its products labeled as a Terex product. So, as it's gone about acquiring companies and product lines, Terex has transitioned each company's products to the Terex brand name, often in conjunction with its former name for a period of time (e.g., a drill used for mining operations will go from being called a Reedrill product to a Terex-Reedrill to just plain Terex).

## HISTORY

Real estate entrepreneur Randolph Lenz moved into heavy equipment manufacturing with the purchase of bankrupt snowplow maker FWD Corporation in 1981. That was followed the same year with the acquisition of Northwest Engineering, a maker of construction equipment started in the 1920s.

In 1986 the company acquired Terex USA, the North American distributor of parts for off-highway Terex trucks, from General Motors, and later Terex Equipment, the UK-based truck maker. The company changed its corporate name to Terex Corporation in 1987. That year Terex entered the mobile-crane market with the purchase of Koehring Cranes. Terex acquired mining-truck maker Unit Rig in 1988 and trailer maker Fruehauf in 1989. It moved into aerial work platforms in 1991 with the acquisition of Mark Industries and picked up the forklift business of Clark Equipment the following year. (Clark invented the forklift truck in 1928.)

Overexpansion and heavy debt led to losses as the US slipped into recession in the early 1990s, and Terex teetered on the brink of bankruptcy. The losses prompted the 1993 installation of new management led by former Case executive Ron DeFeo, who refocused Terex on its core earthmoving and lifting businesses. In 1995 the company sold its stake in Fruehauf. It sold Clark Material Handling in 1996.

Terex added to its lifting-product business with the acquisition of PPM Cranes in 1995 and Simon Access and Baraga Products in 1997. It strengthened its earthmoving product line with the 1998 purchases of O&K Mining, a maker of hydraulic mining excavators, and Gru Comedil, a maker of tower cranes. That year Lenz stepped down as chairman and DeFeo replaced him.

The company settled long-lived SEC and IRS investigations in 1999, which had negatively affected the company's stock price. (The IRS had audited the company; the SEC was probing its accounting methods.)

Terex began piling on new earthmoving businesses in 1999, including Amida Industries, a maker of front-end dumpers and mobile floodlight towers. Also in 1999 Terex paid $294 million for UK-based Powerscreen International, a maker of screening and crushing equipment for quarries, and $170 million for Cedarapids, Raytheon's road construction-equipment business. Terex then boosted its lifting business by acquiring Allegheny Teledyne's lift truck unit and Australian crane maker Franna Cranes.

Believing its stock undervalued, the company announced it would buy back 7% of its shares in 2000. The same year Terex sold its truck-mounted forklift business to Finland-based Partek for about $144 million.

Early in 2001 Terex acquired Fermec Holdings Limited, a UK-based maker of loader backhoes, from CNH Global. Later the same year (in a deal worth about $150 million), it added CMI Corporation, a maker of large-scale construction equipment, and cut operating costs (about 30% of its workforce). The company also entered the power generation business, selling diesel generators under the name Terex Power. In addition, Terex expanded its reach into Europe by acquiring Atlas Weyhausen (cranes and excavators, Germany) in 2001, and The Schaeff Group (construction equipment; Germany) in early 2002.

Also in 2002 Terex initiated investments in Tatra a.s. (heavy-duty trucks with commercial and military applications, Czech Republic), increasing its share to 71% in 2003. Other 2002 acquisitions included distributors Utility Equipment (Oregon) and EPAC Holdings (which operated as Telelect East and Eusco, or Telelect Southeast), Advance Mixer (cement mixer trucks), Demag Mobile Cranes (Germany) from Siemens AG, and Genie Holdings (aerial work platforms) for $75 million.

The company continued to buy in 2003, adding utility equipment distributors Commercial Body and Combatel. The distributors perform final assembly and provide equipment rental and after-market services for the utility and telecom industries in the southern US. A deal that would have sent Terex's mining truck to Caterpillar and Caterpillar's mining shovel business to Terex was terminated in late 2003.

In late 2006 Terex sold its interest in Czech truck maker Tatra a.s. to Blue River s.r.o. a Czech-based private investment concern.

## EXECUTIVES

**Chairman and CEO:** Ronald M. (Ron) DeFeo, age 55, $875,000 pay (prior to title change)
**President and COO:** Thomas J. (Tom) Riordan, age 50
**EVP and COO:** Colin Robertson, age 42, $525,000 pay
**SVP and CFO:** Phillip C. Widman, age 52, $416,000 pay
**SVP, Finance and Business Development:** Brian J. Henry, age 48, $400,000 pay
**SVP, General Counsel, and Secretary:** Eric I. Cohen, age 48, $452,000 pay
**SVP, Terex Business Systems:** Colin Fox, age 63
**SVP, Human Resources:** Kevin A. Barr, age 47
**SVP and Chief Marketing Officer:** Katia A. Facchetti, age 43
**VP, Controller, and Chief Accounting Officer:** Jonathan D. (Jon) Carter, age 38
**Chief Information Officer:** Greg Fell
**President, Terex Aerial Work Platforms:** Timothy A. Ford, age 45
**President, Terex Asia:** Hyeryun Lee Park, age 50
**President and CEO, Terex Cranes Worldwide:** Steve Filipov, age 38
**President, Terex Materials Processing and Mining:** Richard (Rick) Nichols, age 45
**President, Terex Utilities and Roadbuilding:** Christian B. (Chris) Ragot, age 48
**President, Terex Construction:** Robert G. Isaman, age 45
**Director, Investor Relations and Corporate Communications:** Tom Gelston
**Auditors:** PricewaterhouseCoopers LLP

## LOCATIONS

**HQ:** Terex Corporation
200 Nyala Farms Rd., Westport, CT 06880
**Phone:** 203-222-7170 **Fax:** 203-222-7976
**Web:** www.terex.com

Terex operates manufacturing facilities in Asia, Australia, Europe, North America, and South America; the company has a global network of dealers and distributors.

### 2006 Sales

| | $ mil. | % of total |
|---|---|---|
| US | 2,911.9 | 38 |
| Europe | | |
| UK | 614.0 | 8 |
| Germany | 551.9 | 7 |
| Other countries | 1,930.3 | 25 |
| Other regions | 1,639.5 | 22 |
| **Total** | **7,647.6** | **100** |

## PRODUCTS/OPERATIONS

### 2006 Sales

| | $ mil. | % of total |
|---|---|---|
| Aerial work platforms | 2,090.3 | 27 |
| Cranes | 1,740.1 | 22 |
| Materials processing & mining | 1,625.0 | 21 |
| Construction | 1,582.4 | 20 |
| Roadbuilding, utility products & other | 746.0 | 10 |
| Adjustments | (136.2) | — |
| **Total** | **7,647.6** | **100** |

### Selected Products

Aerial Work Platforms
- Aerial devices
- Portable material lifts

Cranes
- All terrain cranes
- Boom trucks
- Container stackers
- Lattice boom cranes
- Lift and carry cranes
- Rough terrain cranes
- Telescopic truck cranes
- Tower cranes
- Truck-mounted cranes

Materials Processing & Mining
- All-wheel-drive rigid off-highway trucks
- Electric rear/bottom dump haulers
- Large hydraulic excavators

Construction
- Compaction rollers
- Crushers
- Excavators
- Generators
- Loader backhoes
- Off-highway trucks
- Scrapers
- Screens
- Telehandlers
- Trailers
- Wheel loaders

Roadbuilding, Utility Products, & Other
- Asphalt pavers
- Asphalt plants
- Concrete trucks
- Generators
- Grinders
- Light towers
- Portable floodlights and traffic control
- Reclaimers
- Stabilizers
- Trailers
- Tree trimmers
- Truck mounted aerial devices
- Vibratory plate compactors

## COMPETITORS

Altec Industries
Astec Industries
Atlas Copco
Bamford Excavators
Blount
Caterpillar
Charles Machine
CNH
Deere
Doosan Heavy Industries
Dynapac
Fontaine Trailer
Furukawa
Gehl
Hitachi
Hyundai
Ingersoll-Rand
JLG Industries
Kobelco
Komatsu
Legris
Liebherr International
Linde
Link-Belt
Manitou
Manitowoc
Marmon Group
Metso
Multiquip
Oshkosh Truck
Pinguely-Haulotte
Sandvik
Skyjack
Sumitomo
Textron
Trail King Industries
UpRight
Volvo
Wacker

## HISTORICAL FINANCIALS

Company Type: Public

### Income Statement

FYE: December 31

| | REVENUE ($ mil.) | NET INCOME ($ mil.) | NET PROFIT MARGIN | EMPLOYEES |
|---|---|---|---|---|
| **12/06** | 7,648 | 400 | 5.2% | 18,000 |
| **12/05** | 6,380 | 189 | 3.0% | 17,600 |
| **12/04** | 5,020 | 324 | 6.5% | 18,000 |
| **12/03** | 3,897 | (26) | — | 15,050 |
| **12/02** | 2,797 | (133) | — | 11,975 |
| **Annual Growth** | 28.6% | — | — | 10.7% |

### 2006 Year-End Financials

Debt ratio: 30.6%
Return on equity: 27.5%
Cash ($ mil.): 677
Current ratio: 1.69
Long-term debt ($ mil.): 536
No. of shares (mil.): 101
Dividends
Yield: —
Payout: —
Market value ($ mil.): 6,529

### Stock History

NYSE: TEX

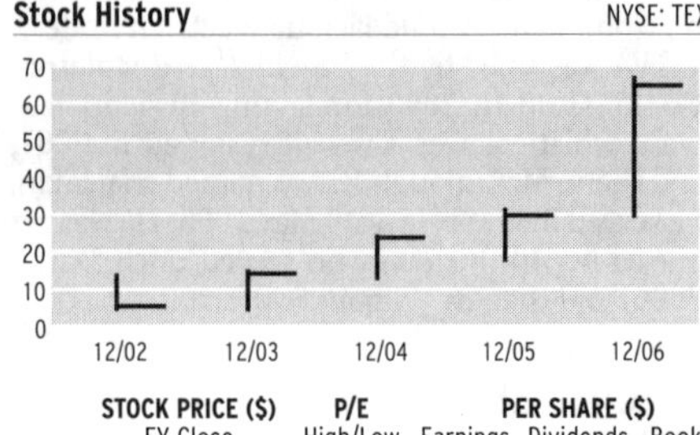


| | STOCK PRICE ($) FY Close | P/E High | P/E Low | PER SHARE ($) Earnings | Dividends | Book Value |
|---|---|---|---|---|---|---|
| **12/06** | 64.58 | 17 | 8 | 3.88 | — | 17.32 |
| **12/05** | 29.70 | 17 | 10 | 1.85 | — | 23.55 |
| **12/04** | 23.83 | 8 | 4 | 3.17 | — | 23.26 |
| **12/03** | 14.24 | — | — | (0.26) | — | 17.97 |
| **12/02** | 5.57 | — | — | (1.53) | — | 16.23 |
| **Annual Growth** | 84.5% | — | — | — | — | 1.6% |

# Terra Industries

Terra would be happier if fertilizer prices were a little firma. The company ranks among the leading North American producers of nitrogen fertilizers and as the top US producer of methanol. Through seven nitrogen plants, the company produces ammonia, urea, urea ammonium nitrate solution (UAN), and ammonium nitrate (AN). The company sells its products to dealers, retailers, cooperatives, and chemical companies. At two of its plants, Terra Industries produces methanol, which is used by industrial customers to make oxygenated fuels or as a feedstock in other chemical processes.

Terra operates four plants in the US, one in Canada, and two in the UK through subsidiaries and limited partnerships, including Terra Nitrogen. UAN accounts for about one-third of the company's sales. The company agreed in late 2006 to combine its UK operations as a joint venture with those of Kemira GrowHow.

Terra bought fertilizer maker Mississippi Chemical for $268 million. Mississippi Chemical had been operating under Chapter 11 bankruptcy protection since the middle of 2003. The deal closed at the end of 2004 and Mississippi Chemical exited Chapter 11 protection and ceased to trade publicly. Its operations were integrated into Terra.

In 2005 the company mothballed its Donaldsville, Louisiana ammonia plant. It had at one time been a fully integrated facility manufacturing a number of Terra's product lines. Now, however, it is solely a storage and distribution terminal. Concurrent with that move, Terra made an agreement to buy ammonia for the facility from Yara.

## HISTORY

Terra Chemicals International was founded in 1964 with a nitrogen fertilizer plant in Iowa. In 1965 it acquired Grand Forks Seed Co., operator of 12 farm service centers. The company began producing nitrogen-based fertilizer in 1967 and went public in 1974. In 1977 Terra Chemicals bought Memphis-based Riverside Chemical Co. and became one of the US's largest independent producers and distributors of fertilizer, seed, and agricultural chemicals.

South African natural resources company Minorco acquired the company in 1981. In 1985 Terra Chemicals extended its marketing reach into Illinois, Indiana, Ohio, and Michigan by buying ADI Distributors.

The company changed its name to Terra Industries in 1992 and expanded into Canada in 1993. Terra Industries moved beyond North America in 1997 with the purchase of two nitrogen fertilizer plants in the UK. In 1999 Terra Industries sold its 400-location distribution business (now called Agro Distribution) to Cenex/Land O' Lakes for $390 million. Also that year Minorco was absorbed by its parent, Anglo American, which assumed majority control of Terra Industries (which was then reduced to just under 50% and then sold entirely in 2004).

High natural gas prices forced the company to idle several plants in late 2000. All but the Blytheville, Arkansas, plant were restarted by March 2001. The company also agreed to pay Mississippi Chemical $18 million that year to settle a defamation countersuit related to a 1994 explosion at a Terra fertilizer plant. In 2002 Terra Industries recorded a financial charge of about $11 million for discontinued operations.

Like most fertilizer companies, Terra had been hurt by depressed prices for nitrogen fertilizers, high raw materials costs, and cheap imports. After a couple of years of ramping up production only to idle the plant again Terra announced in March 2004 that the Blytheville plant would end production in May and close down permanently. Terra bought Mississippi Chemical in 2004, pulling it out of Chapter 11 and making it a wholly owned subsidiary of Terra.

Anglo American, the UK company that controls the De Beers empire, had owned as much as 49% of Terra but sold its remaining shares in 2004.

## EXECUTIVES

**Chairman:** Henry R. Slack, age 57
**President, CEO, and Director:** Michael L. (Mike) Bennett, age 53, $492,308 pay
**SVP, Commercial Operations:** Joseph D. (Joe) Giesler, age 48, $222,615 pay
**SVP and CFO:** Daniel D. (Dan) Greenwell, age 43
**VP, Corporate Development and Strategic Planning:** Douglas M. Stone, age 41
**VP, Manufacturing:** Richard S. Sanders Jr., age 49, $197,692 pay
**VP, Human Resources and Communications:** Joe A. Ewing, age 56
**VP, General Counsel, and Corporate Secretary:** John W. Huey, age 59
**VP, Sales and Marketing:** Paul Thompson, age 52, $216,769 pay
**VP and Controller:** Brian K. Frantum, age 38
**Managing Director, Terra Nitrogen (UK):** Carol Devlin, age 49
**Director, Information Technology:** Jim Keairns
**Director, Risk Management:** Tim Sterling
**Auditors:** Deloitte & Touche LLP

## LOCATIONS

**HQ:** Terra Industries Inc.
600 4th St., Sioux City, IA 51101
**Phone:** 712-277-1340 **Fax:** 712-277-7364
**Web:** www.terraindustries.com

Terra Industries operates production plants in Iowa, Oklahoma, and Texas; Ontario in Canada; and in the UK.

**2006 Sales**

| | % of total |
|---|---|
| US | 76 |
| UK | 20 |
| Canada | 4 |
| **Total** | **100** |

## PRODUCTS/OPERATIONS

**2006 Sales**

| | $ mil. | % of total |
|---|---|---|
| Nitrogen products | 1,793.8 | 98 |
| Methanol | 34.9 | 2 |
| Other products | 8.0 | — |
| **Total** | **1,836.7** | **100** |

**Selected Products**

Nitrogen products
- Ammonium nitrate (AN)
- Urea
- Urea ammonium nitrate solution (UAN)

Methanol

## COMPETITORS

Agrium
Bunge Limited
Cargill
CF Industries
Lyondell Chemical
PotashCorp
Sumitomo Chemical
Yara

## HISTORICAL FINANCIALS

Company Type: Public

**Income Statement** FYE: December 31

| | REVENUE ($ mil.) | NET INCOME ($ mil.) | NET PROFIT MARGIN | EMPLOYEES |
|---|---|---|---|---|
| **12/06** | 1,837 | 4 | 0.2% | 1,238 |
| **12/05** | 1,939 | 22 | 1.1% | 1,209 |
| **12/04** | 1,509 | 68 | 4.5% | 1,323 |
| **12/03** | 1,351 | (13) | — | 1,138 |
| **12/02** | 1,044 | (258) | — | 1,207 |
| **Annual Growth** | 15.2% | — | — | 0.6% |

**2006 Year-End Financials**

Debt ratio: 68.6%
Return on equity: 0.9%
Cash ($ mil.): 179
Current ratio: 2.01
Long-term debt ($ mil.): 331
No. of shares (mil.): 93
Dividends
Yield: —
Payout: —
Market value ($ mil.): 1,110

**Stock History** NYSE: TRA

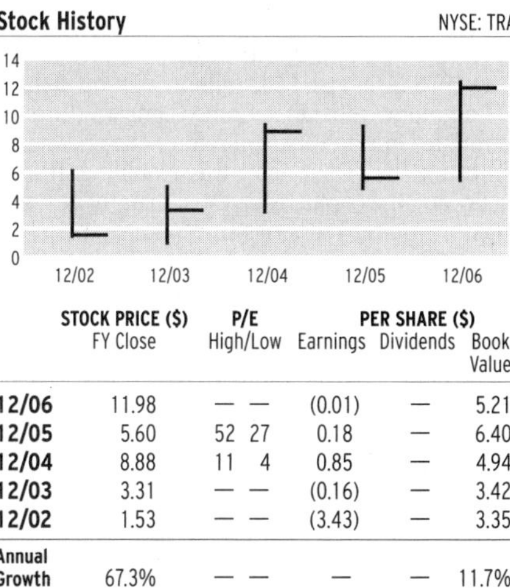

| | STOCK PRICE ($) FY Close | P/E High | P/E Low | PER SHARE ($) Earnings | Dividends | Book Value |
|---|---|---|---|---|---|---|
| **12/06** | 11.98 | — | — | (0.01) | — | 5.21 |
| **12/05** | 5.60 | 52 | 27 | 0.18 | — | 6.40 |
| **12/04** | 8.88 | 11 | 4 | 0.85 | — | 4.94 |
| **12/03** | 3.31 | — | — | (0.16) | — | 3.42 |
| **12/02** | 1.53 | — | — | (3.43) | — | 3.35 |
| **Annual Growth** | 67.3% | — | — | — | — | 11.7% |

# Tesoro Corporation

After exiting its exploration and production activities, Tesoro Corporation (formerly Tesoro Petroleum) has opted for a more refined existence. The independent oil refiner and marketer has six refineries in Alaska, California, Hawaii, North Dakota, Utah, and Washington, with a combined capacity of 563,000 barrels per day. It makes gasoline, jet fuel, diesel fuel, fuel oil, liquid asphalt, and other fuel products. Tesoro markets fuel to 460 branded retail gas stations, including more than 190 company-operated stations, in Alaska, Hawaii, and 16 western states. The group has sold its marine services unit, which provided diesel and other products to oil producers in the Gulf of Mexico.

As part of a strategy to step up its marketing efforts on the US West Coast, Tesoro has an agreement with Wal-Mart to build and operate up to 200 Mirastar-branded gas stations at Wal-Mart locations in 17 states.

Tesoro has sold its upstream operations, which had led it to venture as far south as Bolivia, to concentrate on its core downstream businesses. The 2003 sale of its marine services unit for $32 million was also part of the company's plan to focus on its refining and marketing operations and pay down debt. The group achieved its goal of shedding some $500 million of debt by the end of 2003 through asset sales and cost reductions.

In 2007 Tesoro agreed to acquire a Los Angeles refinery and some 250 gas stations from Shell Oil Products US for about $1.6 billion.

## HISTORY

Founded by Robert West in 1964 as a spinoff of petroleum producer Texstar, Tesoro Petroleum was hamstrung by debt from the get-go. In 1968 West merged Tesoro with Intex Oil and Sioux Oil to invigorate its financial standing.

Reborn, the company constructed an Alaska refinery and began a 10-year stretch of petroleum-related acquisitions, usually at bargain prices, including almost half of the oil operations of British Petroleum (BP) in Trinidad, which became Trinidad-Tesoro Petroleum. By 1973 earnings had quintupled.

In 1975 Tesoro paid $83 million for about a third of Commonwealth Oil Refining Company (Corco), a troubled Puerto Rican oil refiner one-and-a-half times its size. Debt soon was troubling Tesoro again, and the company divested many of its holdings, including refineries in Montana and Wyoming. Corco declared bankruptcy in 1978. That year Tesoro was hit with tax penalties and revealed it had bribed officials in foreign countries.

The company fought takeover attempts and bankruptcy in the 1980s and sold its half of Trinidad-Tesoro in 1985. In the 1990s it expanded its natural gas operations and returned to profitability.

In 1998 Tesoro bought a refinery and 32 retail outlets in Hawaii from an affiliate of BHP, and a refinery in Washington from an affiliate of Shell. To concentrate on its downstream businesses, the company in 1999 sold its exploration and production operations in the US (to EEX for $215 million) and in Bolivia (to BG for about $100 million).

Tesoro West Coast Co., a Tesoro subsidiary, entered into a lease agreement with Wal-Mart in 2000 to build and operate retail fueling facilities at Wal-Mart locations in 11 western states (subsequently expanded to 17 states). That year the company reviewed the possibility of closing part or all of its Alaska properties, including its underperforming refinery. But boosted by higher crude prices and its new deal with Wal-Mart, Tesoro decided to leave its Alaska operations untouched.

In 2001 Tesoro bought refineries in North Dakota and Utah, plus 45 gas stations and contracts to supply 300 others, from BP for about $675 million. The next year Tesoro bought the Golden Eagle (San Francisco-area) refinery and 70 retail service stations in Northern California from Valero Energy for $945 million. At the end of 2002 Tesoro sold 47 of those gas stations to help pay down debt. It also sold its Northern Great Plains Products System to Kaneb Pipe Line Partners L.P. for $100 million.

## EXECUTIVES

**Chairman, President, and CEO:** Bruce A. Smith, age 63, $3,500,000 pay
**Vice Chairman:** Steven H. Grapstein, age 47
**EVP and Chief Administrative Officer:** Gregory A. (Greg) Wright, age 56
**EVP and COO:** William J. (Bill) Finnerty, age 58, $1,340,377 pay
**EVP Strategic Planning:** Everett D. Lewis, $976,172 pay
**SVP Business Integration and Analysis:** Joseph M. (Joe) Monroe
**SVP and Chief Economist:** Lynn D. Westfall
**SVP External Affairs:** W. Eugene (Gene) Burden, age 56
**SVP Performance Management:** Stephen L. Wormington, age 60, $373,794 pay
**SVP, General Counsel, and Secretary:** Charles S. (Chuck) Parrish, age 48
**VP and CFO:** Otto C. Schwethelm, age 52
**VP Human Resources and Communications:** Susan A. Lerette, age 46
**Auditors:** Deloitte & Touche LLP

## LOCATIONS

**HQ:** Tesoro Corporation
300 Concord Plaza Dr., San Antonio, TX 78216
**Phone:** 210-828-8484 **Fax:** 210-283-2045
**Web:** www.tsocorp.com

Tesoro Petroleum operates refineries in Alaska, California, Hawaii, North Dakota, Utah, and Washington and sells gasoline in Alaska, Arizona, California, Colorado, Hawaii, Idaho, Kansas, Nevada, New Mexico, Oregon, South Dakota, Utah, Washington, and Wyoming.

## PRODUCTS/OPERATIONS

**2006 Sales**

| | $ mil. | % of total |
|---|---|---|
| Refining | | |
| Refined products | 17,323 | 91 |
| Crude oil resales & other | 564 | 3 |
| Retail | | |
| Fuel | 1,060 | 5 |
| Merchandise & other | 144 | 1 |
| Adjustments | (987) | — |
| **Total** | **18,104** | **100** |

**Major Subsidiaries**

Tesoro Alaska Company
Tesoro Hawaii Corporation
Tesoro Refining and Marketing Company

## COMPETITORS

ASRC
BP
Branch & Associates
Chevron
ConocoPhillips
Exxon Mobil
Shell Oil Products
Valero Energy

## HISTORICAL FINANCIALS

Company Type: Public

**Income Statement** FYE: December 31

| | REVENUE ($ mil.) | NET INCOME ($ mil.) | NET PROFIT MARGIN | EMPLOYEES |
|---|---|---|---|---|
| **12/06** | 18,104 | 801 | 4.4% | 3,950 |
| **12/05** | 16,581 | 507 | 3.1% | 3,928 |
| **12/04** | 12,262 | 328 | 2.7% | 3,640 |
| **12/03** | 8,846 | 76 | 0.9% | 3,570 |
| **12/02** | 7,119 | (117) | — | 3,940 |
| **Annual Growth** | 26.3% | — | — | 0.1% |

**2006 Year-End Financials**

Debt ratio: 41.1%
Return on equity: 36.5%
Cash ($ mil.): 986
Current ratio: 1.68
Long-term debt ($ mil.): 1,029
No. of shares (mil.): 68
Dividends
Yield: 0.6%
Payout: 3.5%
Market value ($ mil.): 2,233

**Stock History** NYSE: TSO

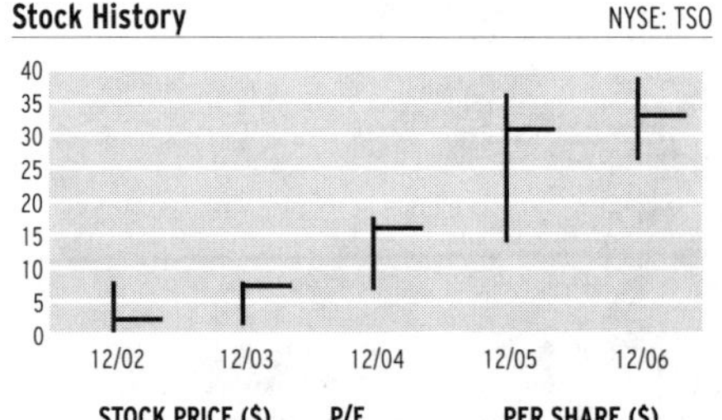


| | STOCK PRICE ($) FY Close | P/E High | P/E Low | PER SHARE ($) Earnings | Dividends | Book Value |
|---|---|---|---|---|---|---|
| **12/06** | 32.88 | 7 | 5 | 5.73 | 0.20 | 36.84 |
| **12/05** | 30.77 | 10 | 4 | 3.60 | 0.10 | 27.23 |
| **12/04** | 15.93 | 7 | 3 | 2.38 | — | 19.86 |
| **12/03** | 7.28 | 13 | 3 | 0.58 | — | 14.91 |
| **12/02** | 2.26 | — | — | (0.96) | — | 13.74 |
| **Annual Growth** | 95.3% | — | — | — | 100.0% | 28.0% |

# Texas Industries

Texas Industries rocks. The construction materials company, known as TXI, produces cement, aggregates, and consumer products, including ready-mix concrete and other specialty aggregate products, through its CAC business. The company also produces sand, gravel, crushed limestone, well cements, shale, clay, and cement-treated materials used in paving. CAC serves construction customers, mainly in the southern and southwestern US. In 2005 the company spun off its Chaparral Steel segment, a top US producer of structural steel and steel bar products from recycled steel scrap.

TXI is the largest cement supplier in Texas and plans to strengthen its position in California, where it plans to expand and modernize its cement plant northeast of Los Angeles by late summer or early fall of 2007. Texas and California are the largest cement markets in the US and receive the most federal funding for highway development.

## HISTORY

Ralph Rogers delivered newspapers as a boy in Boston. There he attended Boston Latin, a prep school that counts among its alumni Ben Franklin, Samuel Adams, and John Hancock. In 1926 he turned down a scholarship to Harvard to support his family. Rogers had become a successful distributor of diesel engines when, in 1942, he contracted rheumatic fever at the age of 33. After he recovered, he headed a project to find a cure for the disease; a link between strep throat and rheumatic fever was discovered, and by use of newly developed penicillin and sulfa drugs, the disease was effectively eliminated.

Rogers retired, moved to Dallas, and formed an investment company with a friend. They invested in Texas Lightweight Aggregate, a small concrete-materials company with assets of about $350,000. In 1951 its successor, Texas Industries (TXI), was incorporated. TXI was fueled by sales of Haydite, its expanded shale and clay aggregate, and had 28 plants by 1954. The company continued to grow throughout the 1950s and 1960s, both internally and through acquisitions. It became vertically integrated with the completion of its own cement plants in Midlothian, Texas, in 1960.

In 1964 TXI launched its first European venture via a French cement distributor. Three years later the company acquired a limestone deposit in southern California and Athens Brick Company and plants in Texas and Louisiana. Also in 1967 Midlothian became the largest cement plant in Texas with the completion of its third kiln.

Ralph Rogers stepped aside for his son Robert to take over around 1970, and TXI diversified into modular buildings and paperboard (sold 1974). The company got into steel in 1973 through Chaparral Steel, a joint venture with Co-Steel International. The Chaparral plant, located near Midlothian, made rolled steel products, such as reinforcing bars, from scrap, and by 1979 it accounted for 23% of TXI's profit. In 1985 TXI bought Co-Steel's interest in Chaparral Steel.

The economic bust at the end of the 1980s hurt TXI, which sold assets to remain profitable. By 1992 things had turned around, and Chaparral accounted for about two-thirds of sales. TXI patented its CemStar process in 1995, and in 1997 it increased its cement capacity by some 60% with the acquisition of Riverside Cement Company (portland and white cement, California).

Cement shortages in 1998 boosted prices in North America between 10% and 20%. However, steel prices shrank from an influx of imports from Asia, Russia, and South America, and contributed to a dip in profits for TXI in fiscal 1999. That year cement product sales, which had been gaining on steel, accounted for the majority of TXI's revenues. TXI purchased Collier Sand & Gravel of Marble Falls, Texas, in 2000, adding about 500 million tons to the company's aggregate capacity. A slow market for concrete and aggregates, the result of wet weather and competition from imported steel, depressed TXI's fiscal 2001 sales.

Robert Rogers stepped down as president and CEO in 2004; former EVP and COO Mel Brekhus replaced Rogers.

TXI sold its Athens Brick Company to Hanson in 2004 and spun off its Chaparral Steel operations in July 2005.

## EXECUTIVES

**Chairman:** Robert D. (Bob) Rogers, age 70
**President, CEO, and Director:** Melvin G. (Mel) Brekhus, age 57, $1,011,800 pay
**EVP, Finance and CFO:** Richard M. Fowler, $631,272 pay
**VP and Treasurer:** Kenneth R. Allen, age 49
**VP, General Counsel, and Secretary:** Frederick G. Anderson, age 55, $457,222 pay
**VP and Corporate Controller:** T. Lesley (Les) Vines, age 43
**VP, Real Estate; President, Brookhollow Corp.:** Barry M. Bone, age 48
**VP, Human Resources:** William J. Durbin, age 60, $448,384 pay
**VP, Expanded Shale and Clay:** George E. Eure, age 57
**VP, Environmental Affairs:** E. Leo Faciane, age 62
**VP, Cement Manufacturing:** Philip L. Gaynor, age 58
**VP, Communications and Government Affairs:** D. Randall Jones, age 62
**VP, Controller for Cement, Aggregate, and Concrete:** J. Michael Link, age 58
**VP, Aggregate and Cement Marketing and Sales:** Ronnie A. Pruitt, age 35
**VP, Marketing for Cement, Aggregates, and Concrete:** J. Barrett Reese, age 61
**VP, Real Estate Marketing:** Daniel J. McAuliffe, age 46
**VP, Accounting and Information Services:** James R. McCraw, age 61
**Assistant Secretary:** Wesley E. (Wes) Schlenker, age 43
**Auditors:** Ernst & Young LLP

## LOCATIONS

**HQ:** Texas Industries, Inc.
1341 W. Mockingbird Ln., Ste. 700W,
Dallas, TX 75247
**Phone:** 972-647-6700 **Fax:** 972-647-3878
**Web:** www.txi.com

Texas Industries operates cement plants in California and Texas; aggregate facilities in Louisiana, Oklahoma, and Texas; and ready-mix concrete plants in Arkansas, Louisiana, and Texas.

## PRODUCTS/OPERATIONS

### 2007 Sales

| | $ mil. | % of total |
|---|---|---|
| Cement | 482.4 | 43 |
| Ready-mix concrete | 278.1 | 25 |
| Stone, sand & gravel | 155.6 | 14 |
| Delivery fees | 78.8 | 7 |
| Other | 119.8 | 11 |
| Adjustments | (118.4) | — |
| **Total** | **996.3** | **100** |

### Selected Products

Cement, Aggregate, and Concrete (CAC)
- Aggregates (sand, gravel, crushed limestone, expanded shale and clay aggregate)
- Cement (masonry, oil well, portland, white)
- Ready-mix concrete

### Selected Subsidiaries and Affiliates

Brookhollow Corporation
- Brook Hollow Properties, Inc.
- Brookhollow of Alexandria, Inc.
- Brookhollow of Virginia, Inc.
- Southwestern Financial Corporation (formerly Clodine Properties Inc.)

Creole Corporation
Pacific Custom Materials, Inc.
Riverside Cement Company (California general partnership: TXI California Inc. and TXI Riverside Inc., general partners)
- Partin Limestone Products, Inc.
- Riverside Cement Holdings Company

Texas Industries Holdings, LLC
- Texas Industries Trust

TXI Aviation, Inc.
TXI California Inc.
TXI Capital Trust I
TXI Cement Company
TXI LLC
- TXI Operating Trust

TXI Operations, LP (Delaware limited partnership: TXI Operating Trust, general partner; Texas Industries Trust, limited partner)
TXI Power Company
TXI Riverside Inc.
TXI Transportation Company

## COMPETITORS

Balfour Construction
Boral USA
Buzzi Unicem USA
Cementos de Chihuahua
CEMEX
CSR Limited
Eagle Materials
Florida Rock
Hanson Aggregates
Holcim (US)
Lafarge North America
Martin Marietta Materials
Pavestone
QUIKRETE
Rinker Materials
U.S. Concrete
Vulcan Materials

## HISTORICAL FINANCIALS

Company Type: Public

### Income Statement

FYE: May 31

| | REVENUE ($ mil.) | NET INCOME ($ mil.) | NET PROFIT MARGIN | EMPLOYEES |
|---|---|---|---|---|
| **5/07** | 996 | 101 | 10.1% | 2,680 |
| **5/06** | 944 | 8 | 0.9% | 2,600 |
| **5/05** | 1,951 | 125 | 6.4% | 2,700 |
| **5/04** | 1,673 | 36 | 2.2% | 4,100 |
| **5/03** | 1,364 | (24) | — | 4,100 |
| **Annual Growth** | (7.6%) | — | — | (10.1%) |

### 2007 Year-End Financials

Debt ratio: 37.7%
Return on equity: 16.8%
Cash ($ mil.): 15
Current ratio: 1.76
Long-term debt ($ mil.): 274
No. of shares (mil.): 27
Dividends
Yield: 0.3%
Payout: 7.9%
Market value ($ mil.): 2,377

### Stock History

NYSE: TXI

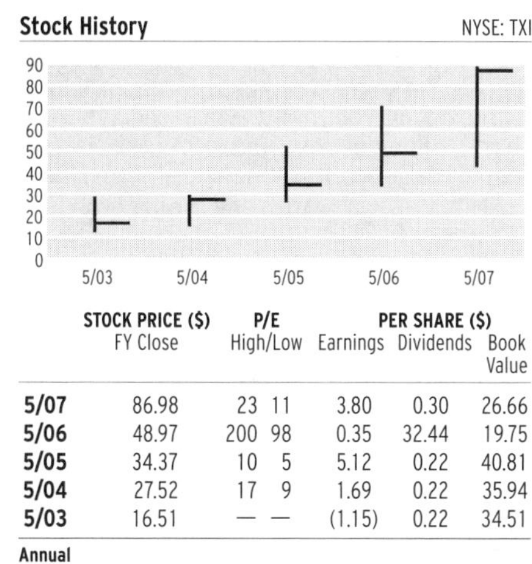

| | STOCK PRICE ($) FY Close | P/E High | P/E Low | PER SHARE ($) Earnings | Dividends | Book Value |
|---|---|---|---|---|---|---|
| **5/07** | 86.98 | 23 | 11 | 3.80 | 0.30 | 26.66 |
| **5/06** | 48.97 | 200 | 98 | 0.35 | 32.44 | 19.75 |
| **5/05** | 34.37 | 10 | 5 | 5.12 | 0.22 | 40.81 |
| **5/04** | 27.52 | 17 | 9 | 1.69 | 0.22 | 35.94 |
| **5/03** | 16.51 | — | — | (1.15) | 0.22 | 34.51 |
| **Annual Growth** | 51.5% | — | — | — | 8.1% | (6.2%) |

# Texas Instruments

Say hello to the big Texan. One of the world's oldest and largest semiconductor makers, Texas Instruments (TI) is the market leader in digital signal processors (DSPs). More than half of the wireless phones sold worldwide contain TI's DSPs, which are also found in many other devices, such as DVD players, automotive systems, and computer modems. TI jockeys back and forth with European chip giant STMicroelectronics to be the world's top maker of analog chips; both companies far outpace other analog rivals. Additional TI semiconductor offerings include logic chips, microprocessors, and microcontrollers. The company also makes handheld calculators. Nokia accounts for about 15% of sales.

While TI has signaled that it will be spending less money on R&D for semiconductor process development in the future, the giant chip maker is flexing its financial muscle in other ways. The company has committed to spending $1 billion over 10 years to expand its chip assembly and test operations in the Philippines. TI will build a new facility in the Clark Freeport Zone, the site of a former US Air Force base. The new plant will measure 77,000 square meters and is expected to employ about 3,000 people. Construction will start in the second half of 2007, with initial production by the end of 2008. TI has an existing facility in Baguio City, a plant that opened in 1979.

During the late 1990s and the early 21st century, the company sold off non-core businesses and made a series of acquisitions to focus on its analog and DSP lines. TI touts its combination of expertise in analog and DSP technologies as a key advantage in allowing it to deliver more highly integrated components for customers in areas such as wireless and broadband communications. The breadth of its offerings means that in some cases it can supply several different kinds of chips for a single electronic device, such as separate chips that enable the telephone and camera features in new wireless phones. The company is also banking on even larger markets for its DSPs in the future, as their use becomes more widespread in areas such as wireline communications and medical equipment.

TI began shipping its Digital Light Processing (DLP) device in 1996. The part is a microelectromechanical system (MEMS) device, also known as a digital micromirror device. It contains more than 2 million microscopic mirrors on the surface of the device, mirrors that can individually move to create a sharper image. For years, the DLP seemed to be a product in search of an application, but it eventually found its way into HDTV sets, digital projectors, and digital cinema equipment. TI has shipped more than 10 million DLP subsystems to manufacturers. TI is finding more applications for the DLP device in such areas as 3-D metrology, confocal microscopy, digital TV, and holographic data storage.

Capital Research and Management, a subsidiary of The Capital Group Companies, owns nearly 8% of TI. Barclays Global Investors holds more than 5% of the company.

## HISTORY

Clarence "Doc" Karcher and Eugene McDermott founded Geophysical Service, Inc. (GSI) in Newark, New Jersey, in 1930 to develop reflective seismology, a new technology for oil and gas exploration. In 1934 GSI moved to Dallas. The company produced military electronics during WWII, including submarine detectors for the US Navy. GSI changed its name to Texas Instruments (TI) in 1951.

TI began making transistors in 1952 after buying a license from Western Electric. The company went public on the New York Stock Exchange in 1953. In 1954 it introduced the Regency Radio, the first pocket-sized transistor radio. (That year TI also produced the first commercial silicon transistor.) Impressed by the radio, IBM president Thomas Watson made TI a major supplier to IBM in 1957. That year the company opened a plant in the UK — its first foreign operation.

TI engineer Jack Kilby invented the integrated circuit (IC) in 1958. (Working independently, Intel co-founder Robert Noyce developed an IC at the same time, while working at Fairchild Semiconductor; the two men are credited as co-inventors. In 2000 Kilby was awarded the Nobel Prize in Physics for his work; Noyce could not be awarded the prize, since he had died 10 years earlier.)

Other breakthroughs included terrain-following airborne radar (1958), handheld calculators (1967), and single-chip microcomputers (1971). During the 1970s TI introduced innovative calculators, digital watches, home computers, and educational toys such as the popular Speak & Spell — the first TI product to use digital signal processors (DSPs), which decades later would become a major driver of TI's growth.

Low-cost foreign competition led TI to abandon its digital watch and PC businesses. Price competition in the chip market contributed to the company's first loss in 1983. In 1988 the company sold most of its remaining oil and gas operations to Halliburton.

As the chip market toughened, TI leveraged its dynamic random-access memory (DRAM) chip know-how through strategic alliances, including a 1993 agreement with Hitachi (the venture ended in 1998). When company head Jerry Junkins, who built TI into a semiconductor force, died unexpectedly in 1996, he was replaced by company veteran Thomas Engibous as president and CEO. (Engibous became chairman in 1998.)

In 1998 TI sold its slumping memory chip operations to Micron Technology. The complex deal gave TI about a 15% stake in Micron — a stake it pared in 2000 and eliminated in 2003. A global chip slump and the loss of the memory chip business lowered TI's results in 1998 and led to the layoff of 3,500 employees.

TI paid $7.6 billion in 2000 to acquire Burr-Brown, an Arizona-based maker of analog and mixed-signal chips. In 2001 TI began to lay off about 2,500 workers in reaction to a softening market for its chips. In 2002 the company acquired a majority interest in Condat, a German developer of software for wireless devices. In 2004 COO Richard Templeton succeeded Engibous as president and CEO; Engibous remains chairman.

In 2006 TI sold its Sensors and Controls business to Bain Capital for $3 billion in cash. The business has been rechristened as Sensata Technologies. In selling the sensors and controls business, TI held on to its radio-frequency identification (RFID) tags business, making chips that are used in contactless payment systems, health care, manufacturing, retail supply chain management, and other applications.

## EXECUTIVES

**Chairman:** Thomas J. (Tom) Engibous, age 54, $358,750 pay
**President, CEO, and Director:** Richard K. (Rich) Templeton, age 48, $897,500 pay
**SVP and CFO:** Kevin P. March, age 49, $371,169 pay
**SVP and CTO:** Hans Stork
**SVP and General Manager, Application Specific Products:** Michael J. (Mike) Hames, age 48
**SVP and General Manager, Worldwide High Volume Analog and Logic Products:** Chung-Shing (C. S.) Lee, age 52
**SVP, Analog Business Unit:** Gregg A. Lowe, age 44, $448,340 pay
**SVP and Manager, Communications and Investor Relations:** Teresa L. (Terri) West, age 46
**SVP, Technology and Manufacturing Group:** Kevin Ritchie, age 49, $396,740 pay
**SVP and President, Education Technology:** Melendy Lovett, age 49
**SVP and General Manager, DLP Products:** John Van Scoter, age 45
**SVP, General Counsel, and Secretary:** Joseph F. (Joe) Hubach, age 49
**SVP and General Manager, High Performance Analog Business Unit:** Arthur L. (Art) George, age 45
**SVP, Worldwide Wireless Terminals Business Unit:** Gregory Delagi, age 44
**SVP and Director, Worldwide Human Resources:** Darla Whitaker, age 41
**President, Texas Instruments Europe:** Jean-Francois Fau
**President, Asia Operations:** Larry Tan, age 49
**Auditors:** Ernst & Young LLP

## LOCATIONS

**HQ:** Texas Instruments Incorporated
12500 TI Blvd., Dallas, TX 75266
**Phone:** 972-995-2011 **Fax:** 972-927-6377
**Web:** www.ti.com

Texas Instruments has operations in nearly 30 countries, including major design and manufacturing facilities in France, Germany, India, Japan, Malaysia, Mexico, the Philippines, Taiwan, and the US.

### 2006 Sales

| | $ mil. | % of total |
|---|---|---|
| Asia/Pacific | | |
| Japan | 2,008 | 14 |
| Other countries | 7,568 | 53 |
| Europe | 2,286 | 16 |
| US | 1,868 | 13 |
| Other regions | 525 | 4 |
| **Total** | **14,255** | **100** |

## PRODUCTS/OPERATIONS

### 2006 Sales

| | $ mil. | % of total |
|---|---|---|
| Semiconductors | 13,730 | 96 |
| Education technology | 525 | 4 |
| **Total** | **14,255** | **100** |

### Selected Products

Semiconductors
- Analog and mixed-signal
  - Amplifiers and comparators
  - Clocks and timers
  - Data converters
  - Power management chips
  - Radio-frequency (RF) chips
- Application-specific integrated circuits (ASICs)
- Digital light processors (DLPs, micro-mirror-based devices for video displays)
- Digital signal processors (DSPs)
- Microcontrollers
- Reduced instruction set computer (RISC) microprocessors
- Standard logic

Educational Technology
- Calculators (including graphing, handheld, and printing models)

## COMPETITORS

Analog Devices
Atmel
Avago Technologies
Broadcom
Canon
CASIO COMPUTER
Conexant Systems
Cypress Semiconductor
Fairchild Semiconductor
Freescale Semiconductor
Hitachi
IBM Microelectronics
Infineon Technologies
Intel
International Rectifier
Linear Technology
LSI Corp.
Marvell Technology
Maxim Integrated Products
National Semiconductor
NEC Electronics
NVIDIA
NXP
ON Semiconductor
QUALCOMM
Renesas
STMicroelectronics
Toshiba
Vishay Intertechnology
Xilinx

## HISTORICAL FINANCIALS

Company Type: Public

### Income Statement

FYE: December 31

| | REVENUE ($ mil.) | NET INCOME ($ mil.) | NET PROFIT MARGIN | EMPLOYEES |
|---|---|---|---|---|
| **12/06** | 14,255 | 4,341 | 30.5% | 30,986 |
| **12/05** | 13,392 | 2,324 | 17.4% | 32,507 |
| **12/04** | 12,580 | 1,861 | 14.8% | 35,472 |
| **12/03** | 9,834 | 1,198 | 12.2% | 34,154 |
| **12/02** | 8,383 | (344) | — | 34,589 |
| **Annual Growth** | 14.2% | — | — | (2.7%) |

### 2006 Year-End Financials

| | |
|---|---|
| Debt ratio: — | No. of shares (mil.): 1,450 |
| Return on equity: 37.3% | Dividends |
| Cash ($ mil.): 3,717 | Yield: 0.5% |
| Current ratio: 3.78 | Payout: 4.7% |
| Long-term debt ($ mil.): — | Market value ($ mil.): 41,761 |

**Stock History** NYSE: TXN

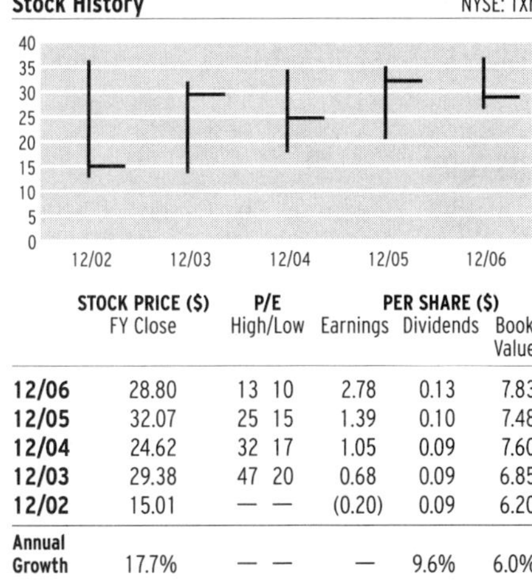


| | STOCK PRICE ($) FY Close | P/E High/Low | | PER SHARE ($) Earnings | Dividends | Book Value |
|---|---|---|---|---|---|---|
| **12/06** | 28.80 | 13 | 10 | 2.78 | 0.13 | 7.83 |
| **12/05** | 32.07 | 25 | 15 | 1.39 | 0.10 | 7.48 |
| **12/04** | 24.62 | 32 | 17 | 1.05 | 0.09 | 7.60 |
| **12/03** | 29.38 | 47 | 20 | 0.68 | 0.09 | 6.85 |
| **12/02** | 15.01 | — | — | (0.20) | 0.09 | 6.20 |
| **Annual Growth** | 17.7% | — | — | — | 9.6% | 6.0% |

# Textron Inc.

Executives should like Textron: The company's golf carts enrich their golfing jaunts; its Cessna airplanes and Bell helicopters whisk them around; its auto parts keep their cars running; and its financial subsidiary provides loans. Textron has four operating segments: Industrial, which makes golf carts, turf equipment, tools, pumps and hydraulic systems, fuel systems, and transmissions; Bell, which includes Bell Helicopter (helicopters) and Textron Systems (smart weapons, surveillance systems, actuators); Cessna, which makes business jets and single-engine turboprops and piston planes; and Finance, which provides commercial loans.

Cessna and Bell have been bright spots in Textron's balance sheet. Cessna accounted for 40% of profits in 2005 and 51% in 2006; Bell accounted for 32% and 20%, respectively.

On the services side, Textron's smallest business segment, Textron Financial Corporation (TFC) — which offers commercial finance services such as equipment-lease loans — racked up 17% of the company's profits in 2005 on about 7% of sales.

Textron, which has grown by acquiring successful companies, has expressed a desire to reduce its reliance on the cyclical industries. To that end, it sold its automotive trim unit, TAC-Trim, to Collins & Aikman. Also — like other manufacturers — Textron has reduced costs and cut thousands of jobs by restructuring. It has also shuttered or sold dozens of plants, and sold its Fastening Systems unit in 2006 to private equity firm Platinum Equity for about $630 million.

Later in 2006 the company acquired Overwatch Systems, a maker of integrated systems and software used for intelligence analysis.

The US government accounts for about 20% of Textron's sales; geographically, the US accounts for nearly two-thirds of sales.

## HISTORY

Pioneer conglomerate builder Royal Little founded Special Yarns Corporation, a Boston textile business, in 1923 and merged it with Franklin Rayon Dyeing Company in 1928. The result, Franklin Rayon Corporation, moved its headquarters to Providence, Rhode Island, in 1930 and changed its name to Atlantic Rayon in 1938.

The company expanded during WWII to make parachutes and in 1944 adopted the name Textron to reflect the use of synthetics in its textiles. Between 1953 and 1960 Textron bought more than 40 businesses, including Bell Helicopter, before banker Rupe Thompson took over in 1960.

Thompson sold weak businesses such as Amerotron, Textron's last textile business (1963), but also bought 20 companies between 1960 and 1965. By 1968, when former Wall Street attorney William Miller replaced Thompson as CEO, Textron made products ranging from chain saws to watchbands. Miller sold several companies and bought Jacobsen Manufacturers (lawn-care equipment, 1978) before leaving Textron in 1978 to head the Federal Reserve and become treasury secretary under President Jimmy Carter.

B. F. Dolan, who became president in 1980, sold Textron's least-profitable businesses. The company bought Avco Corporation (aerospace and financial services, 1985) and UK-based Avdel (metal fastening systems, 1989).

In 1992 Textron bought Cessna Aircraft. The company sold its Lycoming Turbine Engine division in 1994 and acquired Orag Inter AG of Switzerland, Europe's #1 distributor of golf and turf-care equipment. In 1995-96 Textron bought Household Finance of Australia and three fastening systems companies. Also in 1996 Textron acquired Kautex Werke Reinold Hagen AG (plastic fuel tanks) and sold most of its aircraft wing division to The Carlyle Group.

In 1997 Provident (now UNUMProvident) bought Textron's 83% stake in Paul Revere Corp. (insurance). The following year Textron bought UK-based Ransomes plc (turf-care machinery and Cushman-brand transports) and David Brown Group plc (industrial gears and hydraulic systems). Lewis Campbell, Textron's president and COO, became CEO in 1998 and added chairman to his duties in 1999.

Textron sold its Avco Financial Services to Associates First Capital in 1999. That year the company bought 18 companies for about $2.5 billion; the largest of these purchases included Flexalloy (vendor-managed inventory services), Omniquip International (telescopic material-handling equipment), InteSys Technologies (plastic and metal assemblies), Litchfield Financial (vacation timeshares), and the industry and aircraft finance divisions of Green Tree Financial Servicing.

In 2000 Textron acquired Karl Oelschlager GmbH & Co., a German maker of stamped metal parts, and in early 2001 the company acquired telecommunications test equipment maker Tempo Research. Around the same time, Textron announced plans to close or consolidate operations at about 20 manufacturing sites and cut more than 3,600 jobs.

Late in 2001 Textron closed more plants and cut more jobs, running the total announced layoffs for the year to around 7,500 (the cutbacks were spread through the end of 2002). In December 2001 the company sold its TAC-Trim automotive trim unit to Collins & Aikman in a deal worth about $1.34 billion (including about $1 billion in cash and the assumption of $100 million in debt).

Restructuring continued in 2003 and 2004 and the cost savings goal grew to a reduction of 10,000 jobs and 99 facilities. In 2005 Textron announced plans to sell its Fastening Systems business; in December of the year it reclassified those operations as discontinued. The deal to sell Fastening Systems was completed in 2006.

Later in 2006 Textron sold its Jacobsen commercial grounds care products unit in order to focus more on its golf and professional turf operations. Near the end of 2006 Textron agreed to purchase Overwatch Systems for about $325 million. Overwatch is a maker of communications products and intelligence analysis tools for the US Department of Defense, Homeland Security, and certain friendly foreign militaries.

## EXECUTIVES

**Chairman, President, and CEO:** Lewis B. Campbell, age 60, $1,100,000 pay
**EVP and CFO:** Theodore R. (Ted) French, age 52, $700,000 pay
**EVP, Administration and Chief Human Resources Officer:** John D. Butler, age 59, $560,000 pay
**EVP, Government, Strategy Development, Business Development, and International, Communications and Investor Relations:** Mary L. Howell, age 54, $525,000 pay
**EVP and General Counsel:** Terrence (Terry) O'Donnell, age 63, $525,000 pay
**EVP and Chief Innovation Officer:** Kenneth C. (Ken) Bohlen, age 54
**SVP, Textron Six Sigma, Integrated Supply Chain and Transformation:** Peter N. Riley, age 46
**SVP and Corporate Controller:** Richard L. (Dick) Yates, age 54
**SVP, International and Marketing:** Siisi Adu-Gyamfi
**VP and CIO:** Gary Cantrell
**VP and Treasurer:** Mary F. Lovejoy
**VP, Human Resources and Benefits:** George E. Metzer
**VP, Communications:** Susan M. Tardanico
**VP, Investor Relations:** Douglas R. Wilburne
**Corporate Secretary and VP, Business Ethics:** Frederick K. Butler
**Auditors:** Ernst & Young LLP

## LOCATIONS

**HQ:** Textron Inc.
40 Westminster St., Providence, RI 02903
**Phone:** 401-421-2800 **Fax:** 401-457-2220
**Web:** www.textron.com

**2006 Sales**

| | $ mil. | % of total |
|---|---|---|
| North America | | |
| US | 7,006 | 61 |
| Canada | 462 | 4 |
| Europe | 2,099 | 18 |
| Middle East & Africa | 656 | 6 |
| Asia & Australia | 636 | 6 |
| Latin America & Mexico | 631 | 5 |
| **Total** | **11,490** | **100** |

## PRODUCTS/OPERATIONS

**2006 Sales**

| | $ mil. | % of total |
|---|---|---|
| Cessna | 4,156 | 36 |
| Bell | 3,408 | 30 |
| Industrial | 3,128 | 27 |
| Finance | 798 | 7 |
| **Total** | **11,490** | **100** |

### Selected Products

Cessna
- Business jets
- Overnight express package carrier aircraft
- Piston planes
- Turboprop planes

Industrial
- Aerial work platforms
- Automatic clear vision systems
- Blow-molded functional components
- Compact construction equipment
- Electrical connectors
- Electrical test instruments
- Fluid and power systems
- Fluid handling systems
- Golf and turf-care products
- Hand- and hydraulic-powered tools
- Iron castings
- Material handlers
- Plastic fuel tank systems
- Power transmission systems
- Pumps
- Utility vehicles

Bell
- Commercial helicopters
- Military helicopters

Finance
- Commercial loans and leases

### Selected Industrial Brands

Electrical measurement instruments, tools, and fiber optic connectors
- Fairmont
- Greenlee
- Klauke
- Progressive
- Tempo

Fluid and power
- Benzlers
- Cone Drive
- David Brown

Golf and turf care
- Cushman
- E-Z-GO
- Ransomes

## COMPETITORS

| | |
|---|---|
| AgustaWestland | Ingersoll-Rand |
| Boeing | Kaman |
| Bombardier | Lockheed Martin |
| Cirrus Design | New Piper Aircraft |
| Claverham | Northrop Grumman |
| Deere | Northstar Aerospace |
| EADS | Raytheon |
| Eaton | Rolls-Royce |
| Electrolux | Sextant Avionique |
| GE | Sun Hydraulics |
| General Dynamics | Toro |
| Honeywell International | United Technologies |
| Illinois Tool Works | |

## HISTORICAL FINANCIALS

Company Type: Public

### Income Statement

FYE: Saturday nearest December 31

| | REVENUE ($ mil.) | NET INCOME ($ mil.) | NET PROFIT MARGIN | EMPLOYEES |
|---|---|---|---|---|
| **12/06** | 11,490 | 601 | 5.2% | 40,000 |
| **12/05** | 10,043 | 203 | 2.0% | 37,000 |
| **12/04** | 10,242 | 365 | 3.6% | 44,000 |
| **12/03** | 9,859 | 259 | 2.6% | 43,000 |
| **12/02** | 10,658 | (124) | — | 49,000 |
| **Annual Growth** | 1.9% | — | — | (4.9%) |

### 2006 Year-End Financials

Debt ratio: 325.2%
Return on equity: 20.4%
Cash ($ mil.): 780
Current ratio: 1.45
Long-term debt ($ mil.): 8,582
No. of shares (mil.): 126
Dividends
Yield: 1.7%
Payout: 33.5%
Market value ($ mil.): 11,777

### Stock History

NYSE: TXT

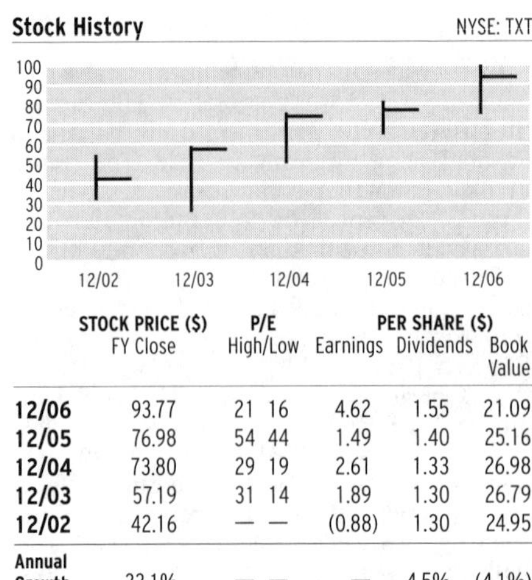


| | STOCK PRICE ($) FY Close | P/E High | P/E Low | PER SHARE ($) Earnings | Dividends | Book Value |
|---|---|---|---|---|---|---|
| **12/06** | 93.77 | 21 | 16 | 4.62 | 1.55 | 21.09 |
| **12/05** | 76.98 | 54 | 44 | 1.49 | 1.40 | 25.16 |
| **12/04** | 73.80 | 29 | 19 | 2.61 | 1.33 | 26.98 |
| **12/03** | 57.19 | 31 | 14 | 1.89 | 1.30 | 26.79 |
| **12/02** | 42.16 | — | — | (0.88) | 1.30 | 24.95 |
| **Annual Growth** | 22.1% | — | — | — | 4.5% | (4.1%) |

# Thermo Fisher Scientific

Thermo Fisher Scientific makes life in the laboratory convenient, albeit lonely at times. The company is a manufacturer and distributor of scientific instruments and laboratory supplies, from chromatographs to Erlenmeyer flasks. Thermo Fisher Scientific serves more than 350,000 customers worldwide in biotech and pharmaceutical companies, clinical diagnostic labs and hospitals, government agencies, research organizations, and universities, among other institutions. The company was formed in the late 2006 merger of Thermo Electron with Fisher Scientific International in a stock-swap transaction valued at nearly $11 billion. Product lines are branded under the names of Fisher Scientific and Thermo Scientific.

Former Fisher shareholders own around 61% of the combined company. The transaction was structured as a reverse merger with Thermo as the acquirer.

The company expects the merger to be immediately profitable in 2007, with sales of more than $9 billion.

Thermo and Fisher were already among the biggest companies in the scientific and technical instruments field (Fisher was twice the size of Thermo, in terms of sales), and combining the two give the merged company more heft to compete against the likes of Agilent Technologies and Becton Dickinson.

What could make the merger work is that Thermo Electron was, for the most part, a manufacturer of scientific instruments, while Fisher Scientific was largely a distributor of laboratory equipment and supplies. There was little overlap between their respective product lines. Their sales forces were already familiar with each other from making calls on many of the same customers. Thermo Fisher Scientific will now be able to present a more comprehensive catalog of products to its clientele.

As required by European and US regulators, Thermo Fisher divested its Genevac business in 2007. The UK-based manufacturer of vacuum concentrators was sold to private equity firm Riverlake Partners, which plans to merge Genevac into SP Industries, a manufacturer of lab equipment.

## HISTORY

In 1902, 20-year-old Chester Fisher bought the stockroom of Pittsburgh Testing Laboratories (established 1884) and formed Scientific Materials Co. The company's earliest products, supplied from Europe, included simple tools such as microscopes, balances, and calorimeters. It published its first catalog in 1904.

When the outbreak of WWI disrupted supplies from Europe, Scientific Materials established its own R&D and manufacturing facilities. It acquired Montreal-based Scientific Supplies in 1925 and the following year changed its name to Fisher Scientific Company. By 1935 Fisher had doubled its size, adding glass-blowing operations and an instrument shop.

During the German occupation of Greece in WWII, George Hatsopoulos, part of a well-to-do family packed with politicians and engineering professors, made radios for the Greek resistance. After the war he came to the US and became a professor of mechanical engineering at MIT. With a $50,000 loan, Hatsopoulos founded Thermo Electron in 1956 to identify emerging technology needs and create solutions for them.

That year he built a machine that would turn heat directly into electrons. This thermionic converter, though itself never commercialized, formed the basis of many of the company's successful products, including a battery-operated heart pump and a process for incinerating toxic material in polluted soils.

In its early years the company was funded by research grants and metal-fabrication contracts with other companies. In 1961 defense giant Martin Marietta (now part of Lockheed Martin), attracted by thermionics, attempted to acquire the company, but Hatsopoulos rejected the offer. Thermo Electron went public in 1967 and in the early 1970s introduced efficient industrial furnaces for the paper and metals markets.

Chester Fisher died in 1965 — the same year Fisher Scientific went public — leaving Fisher to sons Aiken, Benjamin, and James. Fisher acquired pipette maker Pfeiffer Glass (1966), scientific teaching equipment maker Stansi Scientific (1967), optical instruments maker Jerrell-Ash Company (1968), and Hi-Pure Chemicals (1974).

Aiken retired as chairman in 1975 and was replaced by Benjamin. That year former Pfeiffer Glass president Edward Perkins was appointed president and CEO — the first non-family member to hold this position. In 1977 Fisher bought the diagnostics division of American Cyanamid's Lederle Laboratories.

Thermo Electron began a string of spinoffs with the 1983 IPO of medical subsidiary Thermedics. Next to go were environmental services firm Thermo Process Systems and Thermo Instrument Systems in 1986, followed by Thermo Power in 1987, Thermo Cardiosystems in 1989, Thermo Voltek in 1990, ThermoTrex in 1991, paper-recycling equipment maker Thermo Fibertek in 1992, soil recycler Thermo Remediation (later ThermoRetec) in 1993, and ThermoLase, a maker of lasers for hair removal, in 1994.

Besides developing its own business lines, Thermo Electron expanded through several acquisitions in the 1990s. In 1992 Fisher bought

Hamilton Scientific, the top US maker of laboratory workstations, as well as a majority interest in Kuhn + Bayer, a German supplier of scientific equipment. In 1995 the company also boosted its global presence by acquiring Fisons plc, a UK-based laboratory products supplier.

Former American Stock Exchange CEO Richard Syron replaced Hatsopoulos as CEO in 1999. Late in 2002 Syron was named executive chairman, and replaced as CEO by president and COO Marijn Dekkers. The next year Syron resigned as chairman and was replaced by board member Jim Manzi.

In 2003 Fisher acquired Sweden-based Perbio Science (consumable tools for protein-related research) for about $700 million.

In 2004, Fisher acquired Apogent Technologies, a maker of laboratory and life sciences equipment for health care and scientific research applications, for nearly $4 billion. In 2005 Thermo Electron acquired SPX's Kendro Laboratory Products business for approximately $834 million.

In late 2006 Thermo Electron merged with Fisher Scientific International in a stock-swap transaction valued at nearly $11 billion.

## EXECUTIVES

**Chairman:** Jim P. Manzi, age 55
**President, CEO, and Director:** Marijn E. Dekkers, age 49, $3,171,539 pay
**SVP:** Marc N. Casper, age 38, $1,565,282 pay
**SVP and CFO:** Peter M. Wilver, age 47, $931,190 pay
**SVP Global Business Services:** Joseph R. Massaro, age 37
**SVP, General Counsel, and Secretary:** Seth H. Hoogasian, age 52, $881,212 pay
**SVP Human Resources:** Stephen G. Sheehan, age 51
**VP and General Manager, Informatics Business:** David Champagne
**VP Global Business Services:** Thomas J. Burke
**VP Investor Relations and Treasurer:** Kenneth J. Apicerno
**VP Corporate Communications:** Karen Kirkwood
**President, Environmental Instrument Division:** Greg Herrema
**President, Material Characterization; Managing Director, Thermo Electron (Karlsruhe) GmbH:** Hartmut Braun
**President, China:** Ken Berger
**Auditors:** PricewaterhouseCoopers LLP

## LOCATIONS

**HQ:** Thermo Fisher Scientific Inc.
81 Wyman St., Waltham, MA 02454
**Phone:** 781-622-1000 **Fax:** 781-622-1207
**Web:** www.thermofisher.com

Thermo Fisher Scientific has facilities in Australia, Belgium, Canada, China, Denmark, Finland, France, Germany, Japan, Malaysia, Mexico, the Netherlands, Singapore, South Korea, Switzerland, the UK, and the US.

### 2006 Sales

| | $ mil. | % of total |
|---|---|---|
| US | 2,359.0 | 51 |
| Germany | 641.8 | 14 |
| UK | 416.6 | 9 |
| Other countries | 1,201.5 | 26 |
| Adjustments | (827.3) | — |
| **Total** | **3,791.6** | **100** |

## PRODUCTS/OPERATIONS

### 2006 Sales

| | $ mil. | % of total |
|---|---|---|
| Analytical Technologies | 2,425.8 | 63 |
| Laboratory Products & Services | 1,406.6 | 37 |
| Adjustments | (40.8) | — |
| **Total** | **3,791.6** | **100** |

### Selected Products

Analytical Instrumentation
- Analysis instruments
- Electron backscattered diffraction systems
- Gas chromatography equipment
- High-performance liquid chromatography/ion chromatography (HPLC/IC) systems
- Ion energy analyzers
- Mass spectrometers (hybrid, ion trap, quadrupole)
- Microscopes

Laboratory Equipment
- Clinical diagnostics
- Lab furnishings
- Laboratory consumables
- Laboratory information management systems
- Laboratory instrument services
- Liquid handling equipment
- Meters, monitors, and electrochemical equipment
  - Biosensors
  - Detectors
  - Electrodes, probes, and cells
  - Meters
  - Microplate instruments
  - Monitors and analyzers
- Sample preparation equipment
  - Baths
  - Centrifuges
  - Concentrators
  - Extraction equipment
  - Freeze dryers
  - Incubators
  - Luminometric systems
  - Ovens
  - Shakers
- Vacuum equipment

Process Equipment
- Analysis instruments
  - Chromatographs
  - Elemental analyzers
  - Fourier transform infrared analyzers
  - Gas measurement
  - Guided microwave spectrometry
  - Mass spectrometers
  - Moisture analyzers
  - Near infrared analyzers
  - Particle analyzers
  - Surface analyzers
  - X-ray spectrometers
- Coding and marking systems
- Foreign object detection equipment
- Nuclear radiation
  - Neutron flux monitoring systems
  - Neutron sources
  - Reactor protection systems
- Nuclear reactor instrumentation systems
- Physical measurement and control systems
- Polymer testing equipment
- Process monitoring and control equipment

Security and Detection Devices
- Chemical and biological detection
- Explosives trace detection systems
- Radiological and nuclear detection

## COMPETITORS

Abbott Labs
Agilent Technologies
Applied Biosystems
BD
Beckman Coulter
Bio-Rad Labs
Corning
Danaher
Emerson Electric
Harvard Bioscience
Hitachi
Invitrogen
Johnson & Johnson
MDS
Mettler-Toledo
PerkinElmer
Roche Diagnostics
Roper Industries
Shimadzu
Sigma-Aldrich
Tektronix
Varian
VWR International
Waters
Yokogawa Electric

## HISTORICAL FINANCIALS

Company Type: Public

### Income Statement

FYE: Saturday nearest December 31

| | REVENUE ($ mil.) | NET INCOME ($ mil.) | NET PROFIT MARGIN | EMPLOYEES |
|---|---|---|---|---|
| **12/06** | 3,792 | 169 | 4.5% | 30,500 |
| **12/05** | 2,633 | 223 | 8.5% | 11,500 |
| **12/04** | 2,206 | 362 | 16.4% | 9,900 |
| **12/03** | 2,097 | 200 | 9.5% | 10,800 |
| **12/02** | 2,086 | 310 | 14.8% | 10,900 |
| **Annual Growth** | 16.1% | (14.1%) | — | 29.3% |

### 2006 Year-End Financials

Debt ratio: 15.7%
Return on equity: 2.0%
Cash ($ mil.): 691
Current ratio: 1.70
Long-term debt ($ mil.): 2,181
No. of shares (mil.): 417
Dividends
Yield: —
Payout: —
Market value ($ mil.): 18,868

### Stock History

NYSE: TMO

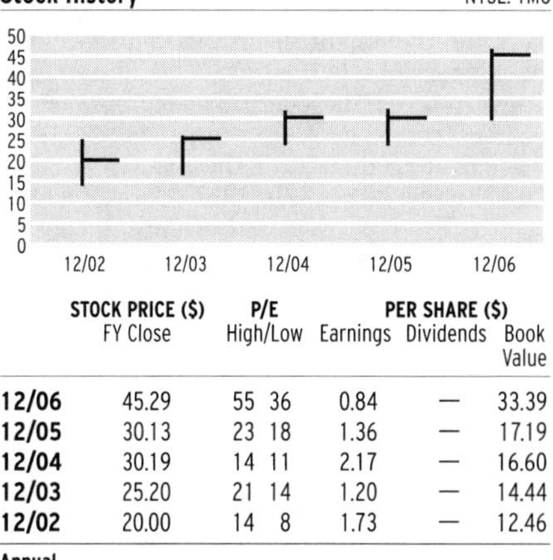

| | STOCK PRICE ($) FY Close | P/E High | P/E Low | PER SHARE ($) Earnings | PER SHARE ($) Dividends | PER SHARE ($) Book Value |
|---|---|---|---|---|---|---|
| **12/06** | 45.29 | 55 | 36 | 0.84 | — | 33.39 |
| **12/05** | 30.13 | 23 | 18 | 1.36 | — | 17.19 |
| **12/04** | 30.19 | 14 | 11 | 2.17 | — | 16.60 |
| **12/03** | 25.20 | 21 | 14 | 1.20 | — | 14.44 |
| **12/02** | 20.00 | 14 | 8 | 1.73 | — | 12.46 |
| **Annual Growth** | 22.7% | — | — | (16.5%) | — | 27.9% |

# Thomas & Betts

Thomas & Betts (T&B) is betting on its connections. T&B provides electrical connectors, HVAC equipment, and transmission towers to the commercial, communications, industrial, and utility markets. It has three business segments: electrical (electrical connectors, enclosures, raceways, installation tools); HVAC (heaters, gas-fired duct furnaces, and evaporative cooling products); and steel structures (poles and transmission towers for power and telecommunications companies). T&B's many brands include Color-Keyed, Elastimold, Kindorf, Red Dot, Reznor, Sta-Kon, Snap-N-Seal, and Steel City.

The company has agreed to acquire competitor Lamson & Sessions for around $450 million in cash. In the biggest acquisition in its history, T&B sees a strategic fit with the Lamson & Sessions product portfolio (in addition to L&S being another company rockin' the ampersand) of non-metallic electrical boxes, fittings, flexible conduit, and industrial PVC pipe. The transaction is expected to close by the end of 2007.

T&B's largest segment, electrical, accounts for more than 80% of its sales.

The company has streamlined its operations in recent years, consolidating production and distribution facilities and divesting stakes in joint ventures in Belgium and Japan. Sales outside the US account for about a third of its revenues.

T&B has acquired the power quality business of Danaher for $280 million in cash. The business, which includes the Joslyn Hi-Voltage and Power Solutions units, had 2006 sales of around $130 million; it provides power quality and reliability products and services to electrical utilities and other customers.

T&B also bought Drilling Technical Supply SA (DTS), a privately held French manufacturer of hazardous lighting and electrical controls, for approximately $20 million.

GAMCO Investors owns about 11% of Thomas & Betts. Funds associated with The Vanguard Group hold around 6% of the company.

## HISTORY

In 1898 in New York City, Princeton engineering graduates Hobart D. Betts and Robert McKean Thomas founded a distribution company for the infant electrical industry; they quickly moved into designing conduits and fittings. In 1905 the company incorporated as Thomas and Betts Company, and in 1912 it began manufacturing with the purchase of Standard Electric Fittings. In 1917 the two merged to form The Thomas & Betts Company, consolidating operations in Elizabeth, New Jersey.

Thomas & Betts was one of the first manufacturers of electrical products to embrace electrical distributors as marketing and sales partners, not competitors. In the early 1930s the company adopted its first marketing slogan: "Wherever Electricity Goes, So Do We."

The company made products that were used to wire the Hoover Dam and the New York City subway system, and by the US military during WWII. During this period Thomas & Betts grew internally and through acquisitions. In 1959 the company went public. It changed its name to Thomas & Betts Corporation (T&B) in 1968.

In 1992 T&B acquired American Electric, an electrical products manufacturer, and relocated its corporate offices to American Electric's headquarters in Memphis. The company acquired Augat, a maker of electronic connectors, in 1996; consolidation expenses brought a severe drop in profits for the year.

President Clyde Moore was named CEO in 1997. T&B made another 15 acquisitions in 1997 and 1998, continuing to expand upon its product offerings for fiber-optic and telecommunications companies. Among the acquisitions were Pride Product Services, a maker of fiber-optic sleeves, and Kaufel Group, a Canadian manufacturer of industrial and emergency lighting products. The latter more than doubled the extent of T&B's lighting product line. Also in 1998 T&B entered a new market with its $74 million acquisition of Telecommunications Devices, a maker of batteries for cell phones and laptops.

The company's 1999 acquisitions included Ocal, which makes plastic-coated conduits and components, and L.E. Mason, a manufacturer of electrical boxes and related products. But its bid to acquire cable maker AFC Cable was topped by rival Tyco International. That year losses caused T&B to exit the active-components portion of its cable TV business; the company sold its Megaflex, Photon, and broadband radio-frequency amplifier product lines.

In 2000 T&B sold its electronics manufacturing operations to Tyco for $750 million, and Moore was elected chairman. He later resigned his post, and director T. Kevin Dunnigan (who had previously served as both chairman and CEO of T&B), assumed Moore's position.

In early 2001 T&B announced that the SEC was investigating its accounting practices; the company also announced it was restating earnings for 2000. Later in the year T&B sold its American Electric and Dark-To-Light product lines to US-based rival National Service Industries. It also divested its ground rod business as the company began to exit the low-voltage circuit protection market.

Five class-action lawsuits over the accounting issues were filed in 2000, and they were consolidated into one action late in the year. A US District Court ordered formal mediation in the litigation in mid-2002, which resulted in a settlement agreement later that year. Without T&B admitting any liability or wrongdoing, the parties agreed to dismiss the lawsuit and the company paid $46.5 million to the plaintiffs.

Dominic Pileggi, president of T&B's main electrical business, was promoted to president and COO of the company at the beginning of 2003. Later in 2003, the company reached a settlement with the SEC, basically agreeing to more closely follow accounting and financial reporting regulations, while the commission brought no charges against the company.

In late 2003 Pileggi was named to succeed Dunnigan as CEO in early 2004. Dunnigan became non-executive chairman of the board, while Pileggi was also elected as a director.

In 2005 T&B acquired the assets of Southern Monopole and Utilities, a subsidiary of Qualico Steel Company, for around $16 million in cash. Southern Monopole manufactured steel poles for for electrical transmission and substations, lattice utility towers, cellular communications, and lighting.

Pileggi succeeded Dunnigan as chairman at the end of 2005, as Dunnigan retired as chairman and a member of the board.

## EXECUTIVES

**Chairman, President, and CEO:** Dominic J. Pileggi, age 55
**EVP and COO:** Christopher P. (Chris) Hartmann, age 45
**SVP and CFO:** Kenneth W. (Ken) Fluke, age 47
**VP and Controller:** Stanley P. (Stan) Locke, age 47
**VP and Treasurer:** Thomas C. (Tom) Oviatt
**VP, General Counsel, and Secretary:** James N. (Jim) Raines, age 63
**VP, Business Development:** Dennis I. Smith
**VP, Information Technologies:** Joseph (Joe) DiCianni
**VP, Investor and Corporate Relations:** Patricia A. (Tricia) Bergeron
**VP, Tax:** Joseph F. Warren
**President, Canada:** Michael B. (Mike) Kenney
**President, Steel Structures and Communications:** James R. (Jim) Wiederholt
**President, HVAC:** Hugh Windsor
**President, U.S. Electrical:** E.F. (Ned) Camuti
**Chief Development Officer:** Imad Hajj, age 46
**Chief Compliance Officer, Assistant General Counsel, and Assistant Secretary:** W. David Smith
**Auditors:** KPMG LLP

## LOCATIONS

**HQ:** Thomas & Betts Corporation
8155 T&B Blvd., Memphis, TN 38125
**Phone:** 901-252-8000 **Fax:** 901-252-1306
**Web:** www.tnb.com

Thomas & Betts has manufacturing facilities in Australia, Belgium, Canada, France, Germany, Hungary, Japan, Mexico, the Netherlands, the UK, and the US.

### 2006 Sales

| | $ mil. | % of total |
|---|---|---|
| US | 1,238.1 | 66 |
| Canada | 345.8 | 19 |
| Europe | 201.1 | 11 |
| Other regions | 83.7 | 4 |
| **Total** | **1,868.7** | **100** |

## PRODUCTS/OPERATIONS

### 2006 Sales

| | $ mil. | % of total |
|---|---|---|
| Electrical | 1,511.5 | 81 |
| Steel structures | 221.7 | 12 |
| HVAC | 135.5 | 7 |
| **Total** | **1,868.7** | **100** |

### Selected Segments and Brands

Electrical
- Boxes and covers (Bowers, Commander, Steel City)
- Cable ties (Catamount, Ty-Fast, Ty-Rap)
- Cable tray systems (Canstrut, Cen-Tray, Electrotray, Pilgrim, T&B)
- Communications connectors, grounding products, meter sockets (Anchor, Blackburn)
- Connectors (Blackburn, Color-Keyed)
- Electrical maintenance products (Valon)
- Electricians' supplies (Thomas & Betts)
- Fittings and grounding systems (Thomas & Betts)
- Industrial connectors (Russellstoll)
- Metal framing (Kindorf, Superstrut)
- Outlet boxes (Bowers, Union)
- Terminals and connectors (STA-KON)
- Timers and relays (Agastat)
- Wiring ducts (Taylor)

Steel Structures
- Power connectors and accessories (Elastimold)
- Steel poles (Meyer)
- Transmission towers (Lehigh)

HVAC
- Evaporative cooling and energy recovery equipment (International Energy Saver)
- Heaters (EK Campbell, Reznor)
- Heating, mechanical, and refrigeration supplies (Thomas & Betts)

## COMPETITORS

3M
Amphenol
Andrew
Beghelli
Cembre
Cooper Industries
Corning
Eaton
Encore Wire
Fujikura Ltd.
GE Consumer & Industrial
Gewiss
Hubbell
ITT Corp.
Lamson & Sessions
Legrand
Matsushita Electric
Methode Electronics
Molex
POWERTRUSION
Siemens AG
Smiths Group
Spirent
Sumitomo Electric
Tyco
Valmont Industries

## HISTORICAL FINANCIALS

Company Type: Public

### Income Statement

FYE: Sunday nearest December 31

| | REVENUE ($ mil.) | NET INCOME ($ mil.) | NET PROFIT MARGIN | EMPLOYEES |
|---|---|---|---|---|
| **12/06** | 1,869 | 175 | 9.4% | 9,000 |
| **12/05** | 1,695 | 113 | 6.7% | 9,000 |
| **12/04** | 1,516 | 93 | 6.2% | 9,000 |
| **12/03** | 1,322 | 43 | 3.2% | 9,000 |
| **12/02** | 1,346 | (53) | — | 10,000 |
| **Annual Growth** | 8.6% | — | — | (2.6%) |

**2006 Year-End Financials**

Debt ratio: 36.2%
Return on equity: 16.5%
Cash ($ mil.): 371
Current ratio: 3.49
Long-term debt ($ mil.): 387
No. of shares (mil.): 59
Dividends
Yield: —
Payout: —
Market value ($ mil.): 2,812

**Stock History** NYSE: TNB

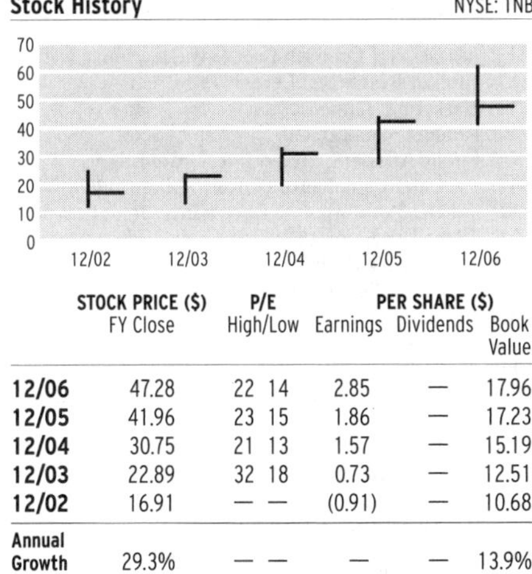


| | STOCK PRICE ($) FY Close | P/E High | P/E Low | PER SHARE ($) Earnings | PER SHARE ($) Dividends | PER SHARE ($) Book Value |
|---|---|---|---|---|---|---|
| **12/06** | 47.28 | 22 | 14 | 2.85 | — | 17.96 |
| **12/05** | 41.96 | 23 | 15 | 1.86 | — | 17.23 |
| **12/04** | 30.75 | 21 | 13 | 1.57 | — | 15.19 |
| **12/03** | 22.89 | 32 | 18 | 0.73 | — | 12.51 |
| **12/02** | 16.91 | — | — | (0.91) | — | 10.68 |
| **Annual Growth** | 29.3% | — | — | — | — | 13.9% |

# Thor Industries

The Vikings and their Norse gods might have laughed at the idea of bathrooms on wheels, but that doesn't slow down RV maker Thor Industries. The company makes a range of RVs, including motor homes and travel trailers. Brands include the well-known Airstream and Dutchmen lines. It is also a leading US producer of small and midsize buses. Thor has bus and RV plants, as well as distributors, throughout the US and Canada. It also operates a joint venture with Cruise America that rents RVs to the public. Cofounder and CEO Wade Thompson owns nearly 30% of Thor, while the other co-founder and vice chairman Peter Orthwein owns almost 5%.

RVs continue to be Thor's thoroughbred in terms of revenue with bus sales coming in a distant second. Although its bid for rival RV maker Coachmen fell though, Thor has managed to pick up Keystone RV Company for $145 million, making it the US's largest manufacturer of travel trailers with 25% of the market. Thor later bought class A motorhome maker Damon Corporation. The Damon purchase also gave Thor a new product line, the Breckenridge brand of park models. Park models are factory-built second homes that usually are towed to a location such as a lakeshore or wooded area and are used as a country cottage.

Thor has strengthened its bus operations with the purchase of the bankrupt Goshen Coach for $9.5 million in mid-2005. The deal gives Thor about a 44% share of the small to midsize bus market in the US.

## HISTORY

Mergers and acquisitions specialist Wade Thompson and investment banker Peter Orthwein saw the potential of the RV market after buying Hi-Lo Trailer in 1977. Thor Industries was formed when they bought the troubled Airstream Trailers unit (founded in 1931) from Beatrice Foods in 1980. Named after the mythical Norse god of thunder and containing the first two letters of the founders' last names, Thor Industries formed Citair in 1982 to buy the RV division of Commodore Corp. (founded 1948). The company went public in 1984, and it entered the bus business with the acquisitions of ElDorado Bus company in 1988 and National Coach in 1991. Thor expanded its RV line with the purchases of Dutchmen Manufacturing in 1991 and Four Winds in 1992.

The company continued acquisitions in 1995, buying Skamper Corp. (folding trailers) and Komfort Trailers. In 1996 its bus operations received significant orders from National Car Rental and the suburban Chicago transit company, PACE.

Bus sales did well in 1997, but RV sales were flat. That year Thor sold its Henschen Axle manufacturing operation. In response to weak sales, the company opened new channels, such as its RV rental joint venture. In 1998 it bought Champion Motor Coach (small and midsize buses) from manufactured-home company Champion Enterprises for about $10 million. It also sold its unprofitable motor homes unit, Thor West, to the division's managers.

In 1999 Thor won a $45 million contract to build 1,135 buses for the state of California. The following year the company made a bid to buy rival RV company Coachmen Industries; that bid was later rejected and withdrawn.

Thor regained its thunder in 2001 with the $145 million purchase of Keystone RV Company. The deal made the company the US's leading manufacturer of travel trailers and third wheels (with 25% of the market), as well as the largest builder of small and midsize buses (with 37% of the market).

In 2003 Thor paid nearly $30 million for Damon Corporation, a maker of class A motor homes and park models. Thor paid $27 million for fifth wheel and travel trailer manufacturer CrossRoads RV in 2004.

## EXECUTIVES

**Chairman, President, and CEO:** Wade F. B. Thompson, age 66, $771,584 pay
**Vice Chairman and Treasurer:** Peter B. Orthwein, age 61, $601,032 pay
**EVP, Finance, CFO, and Secretary:** Walter L. Bennett, age 60, $1,001,032 pay
**VP, Purchasing:** Ted J. Bartus, age 38, $198,216 pay
**Group President, Airstream, Thor California, Komfort, CrossRoads, and General Coach:** Richard E. (Dickey) Riegel III
**Chairman, Airstream:** Lawrence J. Huttle
**Chairman, Damon Corporation:** Gary L. Groom
**Chairman, Thor California:** Thomas J. Powell
**President and CEO, Airstream:** Robert Wheeler
**President, Damon Corporation:** William C. (Bill) Fenech
**President, Breckenridge:** Tim J. Howard
**President, Dutchmen:** Richard W. Florea
**President, Four Winds:** Jeffery L. Kime
**President, General Coach, British Columbia:** Daniel L. Dimich
**President, Keystone:** Ronald J. (Ron) Fenech
**President, Komfort:** Manuel A. Caravia
**President, Thor Bus:** Andrew Imanse
**President, Thor California:** Robert N. Thompson
**Auditors:** Deloitte & Touche LLP

## LOCATIONS

**HQ:** Thor Industries, Inc.
419 W. Pike St., Jackson Center, OH 45334
**Phone:** 937-596-6849 **Fax:** 937-596-6539
**Web:** www.thorindustries.com

Thor Industries has bus-manufacturing plants in California, Indiana, Kansas, and Michigan and RV plants in California, Idaho, Indiana, Ohio, Oregon, and Canada.

## PRODUCTS/OPERATIONS

**2006 Sales**

| | $ mil. | % of total |
|---|---|---|
| Recreation vehicles | | |
| Towables | 2,173.5 | 71 |
| Motorized | 577.0 | 19 |
| Buses | 315.8 | 10 |
| **Total** | **3,066.3** | **100** |

**Selected Products**

Recreational Vehicles
- Airstream (premium and medium-high-priced travel trailers and motor homes)
- Breckenridge (factory built cottage homes)
- Citair (travel trailers, fifth wheels, class C motorhomes, and truck campers)
- Damon Motor Coach (gasoline and diesel class A motor homes)
- Dutchmen (travel trailers and fifth wheels)
- Four Winds (motor homes)
- Keystone (travel trailers and fifth wheels)
- Komfort (travel trailers and fifth wheels for sale in the western US and Canada)
- Thor California (travel trailers and fifth wheels)

Buses
- Champion Bus (small and midsize buses)
- ElDorado National (small and midsize buses for airport, car rental, and hotel and motel shuttles, tour and charter operations, community transit systems, and other uses)
- Goshen Coach (small and midsize buses)

## COMPETITORS

Airstream
Alfa Leisure
Blue Bird
Champion Enterprises
Clayton Homes
Coachmen
Collins Industries
Elixir Industries
Fairmont Homes
Featherlite
Fleetwood Enterprises
Fleetwood Folding Trailers
Forest River
Hino Motors
Jayco, Inc.
Kingsley Coach
Monaco Coach
Motor Coach Industries
National RV
Orion Bus
Prevost Car
Rexhall
Skyline
Supreme Industries
TRIGANO
Volvo
Wells Cargo
Winnebago

## HISTORICAL FINANCIALS

Company Type: Public

**Income Statement** FYE: July 31

| | REVENUE ($ mil.) | NET INCOME ($ mil.) | NET PROFIT MARGIN | EMPLOYEES |
|---|---|---|---|---|
| **7/06** | 3,066 | 163 | 5.3% | 9,363 |
| **7/05** | 2,558 | 122 | 4.8% | 8,473 |
| **7/04** | 2,188 | 106 | 4.8% | 7,471 |
| **7/03** | 1,571 | 79 | 5.0% | 5,754 |
| **7/02** | 1,245 | 51 | 4.1% | 5,384 |
| **Annual Growth** | 25.3% | 33.7% | — | 14.8% |

**2006 Year-End Financials**

Debt ratio: —
Return on equity: 25.2%
Cash ($ mil.): 264
Current ratio: 2.24
Long-term debt ($ mil.): —
No. of shares (mil.): 56
Dividends
Yield: 0.6%
Payout: 8.4%
Market value ($ mil.): 2,386

**Stock History** NYSE: THO

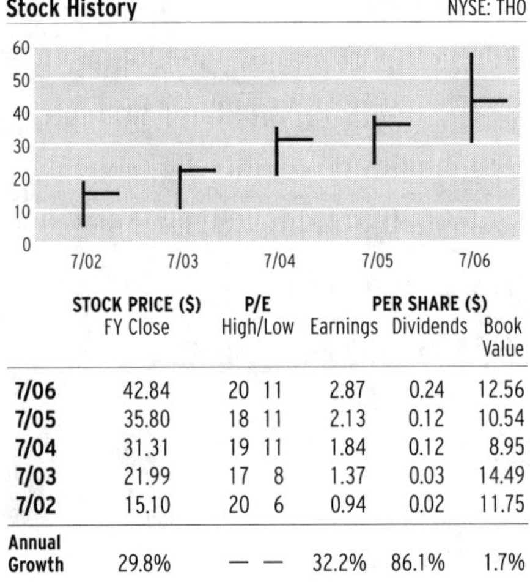


| | STOCK PRICE ($) FY Close | P/E High/Low | | PER SHARE ($) Earnings | Dividends | Book Value |
|---|---|---|---|---|---|---|
| **7/06** | 42.84 | 20 | 11 | 2.87 | 0.24 | 12.56 |
| **7/05** | 35.80 | 18 | 11 | 2.13 | 0.12 | 10.54 |
| **7/04** | 31.31 | 19 | 11 | 1.84 | 0.12 | 8.95 |
| **7/03** | 21.99 | 17 | 8 | 1.37 | 0.03 | 14.49 |
| **7/02** | 15.10 | 20 | 6 | 0.94 | 0.02 | 11.75 |
| **Annual Growth** | 29.8% | — | — | 32.2% | 86.1% | 1.7% |

# TIAA-CREF

It's punishment enough to write the name once on a blackboard. Teachers Insurance and Annuity Association — College Retirement Equities Fund (TIAA-CREF) is one of the largest, if not longest-named, private retirement systems in the US, providing for more than 3 million members of the academic community and for investors outside academia's ivied confines. It also serves some 15,000 institutional investors. TIAA-CREF's core offerings include financial advice, investment information, retirement accounts, pensions, annuities, individual life and disability insurance, tuition financing, and trust services (through TIAA-CREF Trust). The system, a not-for-profit organization, also manages a line of mutual funds.

TIAA-CREF — one of the nation's heftiest institutional investors, with more than $350 billion in assets under management — has not been afraid to throw its weight around corporate boardrooms. The organization is known for active and choosy investing and is a vocal critic of extravagant executive compensation packages. With an increasing share of its investment assets overseas, TIAA-CREF is also leading the crusade for global corporate governance standards. (TIAA-CREF faced its own corporate governance issue in 2004, when two directors stepped down after it was revealed they had a business relationship with the company's auditor, Ernst & Young.)

In 2006 TIAA-CREF bought Kapsick & Company, which manages planned giving assets for colleges, universities, and other not-for-profits. The acquisition makes the system the largest provider of such services in the US.

## HISTORY

With $15 million, the Carnegie Foundation for the Advancement of Teaching in 1905 founded the Teachers Insurance and Annuity Association (TIAA) in New York City to provide retirement benefits and other forms of financial security to educators. When Carnegie's original endowment was found to be insufficient, another $1 million reorganized the fund into a defined-contribution plan in 1918. TIAA was the first portable pension plan, letting participants change employers without losing benefits and offering a fixed annuity. The fund required infusions of Carnegie cash until 1947.

In 1952 TIAA CEO William Greenough pioneered the variable annuity, based on common stock investments, and created the College Retirement Equities Fund (CREF) to offer it. Designed to supplement TIAA's fixed annuity, CREF invested participants' premiums in stocks. CREF and TIAA were subject to New York insurance (but not SEC) regulation.

During the 1950s, TIAA led the fight for Social Security benefits for university employees and began offering group total disability coverage (1957) and group life insurance (1958).

In 1971 TIAA-CREF began helping colleges boost investment returns from endowments, then moved into endowment management. It helped found a research center to provide objective investment information in 1972.

For 70 years retirement was the only way members could exit TIAA-CREF. Their only investment choices were stocks through CREF or a one-way transfer into TIAA's annuity accounts based on long-term bond, real estate, and mortgage investments. In the 1980s CREF indexed its funds to the S&P average.

By 1987's stock crash, TIAA-CREF had a million members, many of whom wanted more protection from stock market fluctuations. After the crash, Clifton Wharton (the first African-American to head a major US financial organization) became CEO; the next year CREF added a money market fund, for which the SEC required complete transferability, even outside TIAA-CREF. Now open to competition, TIAA-CREF became more flexible, adding investment options and long-term-care plans.

John Biggs became CEO in 1993. After the 1994 bond crash, TIAA-CREF began educating members on the ABCs of retirement investing, hoping to persuade them not to switch to flashy short-term investments and not to panic during such cyclical events as the crash.

In 1996 it went international, buying interests in UK commercial and mixed-use property. TIAA-CREF filed for SEC approval of more mutual funds in 1997. Although federal tax legislation took away TIAA-CREF's tax-exempt status in 1997, the change was made without decreasing annuity incomes for the year.

The status change let TIAA-CREF offer no-load mutual funds to the public in 1998. A trust company and financial planning services were added; all new products were sold at cost, with TIAA-CREF waiving fees. TIAA-CREF in 1998 became the first pension fund to force out an entire board of directors (that of sputtering cafeteria firm Furr's/Bishop's). Also that year TIAA-CREF's crusade to curb "dead hand" poison pills (an antitakeover defense measure) found favor with the shareholders of Bergen Brunswig (now AmerisourceBergen), Lubrizol, and Mylan Laboratories. Late in 1999 the organization sold half of its stake in the Mall of America to Simon Property Group, keeping 27%. The next year it made a grab for more market share when it launched five new mutual funds.

Biggs retired in 2002 and was succeeded by Herbert Allison.

## EXECUTIVES

**Chairman, President, and CEO:** Herbert M. (Herb) Allison
**Vice Chairman:** Frances Nolan
**EVP, Asset Management; CEO, Teachers Advisors and TIAA-CREF Investment Management:** Scott C. Evans
**EVP and CFO:** Georganne C. Proctor, age 50
**EVP and CTO:** Susan S. Kozik
**EVP and General Counsel:** George W. Madison, age 49
**EVP, Human Resources:** Dermot J. O'Brien
**EVP, Marketing:** Jamie DePeau
**EVP, Product Management:** Bertram L. Scott, age 55
**EVP, Public Affairs:** I. Steven (Steve) Goldstein
**SVP and Chief Compliance Officer:** James G. Reilly
**SVP and Head of Corporate Governance:** John C. Wilcox
**SVP, Client Experience:** David M. (Dave) Edwards
**VP and Corporate Secretary:** E. Laverne Jones
**President and CEO, TIAA-CREF Life Insurance:** Bret L. Benham
**Chief Customer Sciences Officer:** Sara Lipson
**Chief Investment Officer:** Edward J. Grzybowski
**Director, Corporate Governance and Senior Counsel:** Hye-Won Choi
**Director, Corporate Governance:** Linda E. Scott
**Director, Corporate Media Relations:** Stephanie Cohen Glass
**Director, Social Investing:** Amy Muska O'Brien
**Head of Derivatives Strategy and Trading:** Jayesh Bhansali
**Senior Managing Director and Head of Equity Investments:** Susan E. Ulick
**Senior Managing Director and Head of Strategy:** Sheila Hooda

## LOCATIONS

**HQ:** Teachers Insurance and Annuity Association — College Retirement Equities Fund
730 3rd Ave., New York, NY 10017
**Phone:** 212-490-9000 **Fax:** 212-916-4840
**Web:** www.tiaa-cref.org

## PRODUCTS/OPERATIONS

**2006 Sales**

| | $ mil. | % of total |
|---|---|---|
| General account gross investment income | 10,653 | 86 |
| Management fees | 1,119 | 9 |
| Insurance revenue | 366 | 3 |
| Other | 240 | 2 |
| **Total** | **12,378** | **100** |

**Selected Subsidiaries and Units**

Teachers Personal Investors Services, Inc. (mutual fund management)
TIAA-CREF Individual & Institutional Services, Inc. (broker-dealer)
TIAA-CREF Institute (think tank)
TIAA-CREF Institutional Mutual Funds (investment company)
TIAA-CREF Life Insurance Company (insurance and annuities)
TIAA-CREF Mutual Funds (investment company)
TIAA-CREF Trust Company, FSB (trust services)
TIAA-CREF Tuition Financing, Inc. (state tuition savings program management)

**Selected Mutual Funds**

Bond
Bond Plus II
Equity Index
Growth & Income
High-Yield Bond II
Inflation-Linked Bond
International Equity
Large-Cap Growth
Large-Cap Value
Mid-Cap Growth
Mid-Cap Value
Real Estate Securities
Short-Term Bond II
Small-Cap Equity
Social Choice Equity
Tax-Exempt Bond II

## COMPETITORS

| | |
|---|---|
| Aetna | MassMutual |
| AIG | Merrill Lynch |
| AXA Financial | MetLife |
| Bank of New York Mellon | New York Life |
| Berkshire Hathaway | Northwestern Mutual |
| CalPERS | Principal Financial |
| Charles Schwab | Prudential |
| CIGNA | T. Rowe Price |
| Citigroup | US Global Investors |
| FMR | USAA |
| John Hancock | VALIC |
| JPMorgan Chase | Vanguard |

## HISTORICAL FINANCIALS

Company Type: Private

**Income Statement** FYE: December 31

| | REVENUE ($ mil.) | NET INCOME ($ mil.) | NET PROFIT MARGIN | EMPLOYEES |
|---|---|---|---|---|
| **12/06** | 12,378 | 3,453 | 27.9% | 5,500 |
| **12/05** | 11,703 | 1,878 | 16.0% | 5,500 |
| **12/04** | 10,864 | 540 | 5.0% | 6,000 |
| **12/03** | 12,815 | 504 | 3.9% | 6,000 |
| **12/02** | 17,862 | — | — | 6,500 |
| **Annual Growth** | (8.8%) | 89.9% | — | (4.1%) |

**Net Income History**

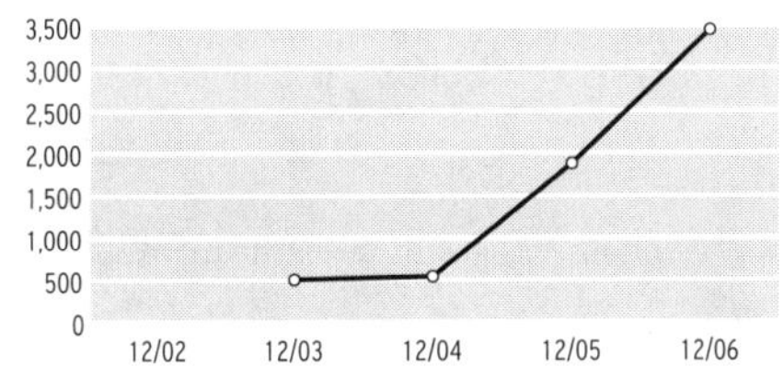


# Tiffany & Co.

Breakfast at Tiffany & Co. has turned into a bountiful buffet, complete with the finest crystal and flatware, as well as more ubiquitous fare. Its specialty is fine jewelry, but the company also puts its name on timepieces, silverware, china, stationery, and other luxury items. Many products are packaged in the company's trademarked Tiffany Blue Box. To entice budget-minded Buffys to do more than window shop, Tiffany has broadened its merchandise mix to include key chains and other items that sell for much less than the typical Tiffany price tag. The firm sells its goods exclusively through nearly 170 Tiffany & Co. stores and boutiques worldwide, its Web site, business-to-business accounts, and catalogs.

The company generates almost 85% of sales from jewelry, including exclusive designs by Frank Gehry, Elsa Peretti, and Paloma Picasso. Within that segment of its business, gemstone jewelry and sterling silver items lead sales in the US. In Japan, where Tiffany generates nearly 20% of its worldwide sales, diamond rings, wedding bands, and gemstone rings represent some 60% of its jewelry sales. While Japan is turning to traditional Tiffany pieces, US customers are tapping the jewelry maker's less expensive sterling silver fare.

Tiffany has been expanding its retail presence while diversifying its customer reach through other retail venues. More than 60 stores are located in the US and the company plans to continue adding five to seven new stores per year. Its famed flagship location on Manhattan's Fifth Avenue accounted for 9% of sales in 2006. Tiffany also markets through its Selections and Collections catalogs, through its Web site, and through its iconic annual Blue Book catalog.

Tiffany extended its reach into other specialty retailing through Little Switzerland (some 25 duty-free cruise-ship destinations in the Caribbean and Florida). Its dozen Iridesse stores, located throughout the US, focus exclusively on high-end pearl jewelry. Tiffany grew tired of Little Switzerland's losses. Having explored strategic alternatives for its Little Switzerland unit since early 2007, Tiffany midyear announced it had inked a deal to sell its 100% stake in the specialty retailer to NXP Corporation, which operates stores under the Jewels and Azura by Jewels banners in the Caribbean.

These days the famous surname is showing up next to more middle-class monikers, such as Barnes & Noble and California Pizza Kitchen, as Tiffany's expansion plans include new locations in such venues as malls and upscale shopping centers. To answer the call of the hip customer and extend its brand into a new niche of the luxury market, Tiffany in late 2006 inked a 10-year exclusive deal with eyewear behemoth Luxottica to make and market Tiffany-branded ophthalmic and sun eyewear.

## HISTORY

Charles Lewis Tiffany and John Young founded Tiffany & Young in New York City in 1837. The store sold stationery and costume jewelry and offered a unique, no-haggling approach (prices were clearly marked). In 1845 the company began selling real jewelry and also published its first mail-order catalog. During the late 1840s it added silverware, timepieces, perfumes, and other luxury offerings.

In 1851 Tiffany & Young bought the operations of silversmith John Moore, adding the design and manufacture of silver to its business (its standard for sterling silver was later adopted as the US standard). Tiffany bought out his partners (including a third partner, J. L. Ellis) two years later, renaming the company Tiffany & Co.

Although it served European royalty, Tiffany found its primary clientele in the growing number of wealthy Americans. In 1878 it acquired the Tiffany Diamond, one of the largest yellow diamonds in the world, weighing 128.5 carats (on display in its flagship New York City store). By 1887 the company had more than $40 million in precious stones in its vaults.

Tiffany died in 1902, and his son Louis Comfort Tiffany joined the firm that year as artistic director. Louis designed jewelry and stained glass patterned after nature and art, and remains one of the most celebrated glass designers (Tiffany lamps are very popular with collectors). Tiffany's sales hit nearly $18 million in 1919, then stalled during the 1920s. Because of the Depression, sales dropped to less than $3 million in 1932, forcing the company to lay off employees and dip into its cash reserves to pay dividends. Louis died in 1933.

The company moved in 1940 to its present Fifth Avenue location, which was showcased in Truman Capote's 1958 novella *Breakfast at Tiffany's* (the story became an Audrey Hepburn movie in 1961). To keep Bulova Watch Co., which owned a 30% stake, from controlling Tiffany, in 1955 the Tiffany heirs sold their share of the company to Hoving Corp., which owned retailer Bonwit Teller. Walter Hoving, Tiffany's new chairman and CEO, and other investors bought the chain from Hoving's parent, Genesco, and Bulova in 1961. The company opened its first store outside of New York City, in San Francisco, two years later, and it added locations in Beverly Hills, California, and Houston in 1964.

Sales grew through the 1970s. Tiffany was sold to cosmetics seller Avon Products in 1979, and Hoving retired as chairman and CEO the next year. Avon increased the stores' selection of less expensive items, a decision some felt hurt Tiffany. In 1984 Avon sold Tiffany to a group of investors led by Tiffany's then chairman William Chaney and backed by Bahrain-based Investcorp. Chaney set about improving Tiffany's tarnished image with affluent shoppers. In 1986 the company expanded into Europe, opening a store in London. To retire debt, it went public the next year with about 30 retail locations worldwide.

Japanese retailer Mitsukoshi, a seller of Tiffany's items in department stores and Tiffany & Co. boutiques in Japan, increased its stake in the company to 10% in 1989. The company expanded dramatically in the US during the 1990s, opening stores in more than 20 cities.

President and COO Michael Kowalski became CEO in 1999 and Mitsukoshi sold its stake in the company. Tiffany then paid $72 million for a 15% stake in diamond supplier Aber Resources. Tiffany also opened an online store in 1999. In an attempt to gain greater control of its brand, Tiffany discontinued sales to retailers in the US and Europe in 2000. In May 2001 Tiffany purchased 45% of duty-free store operator Little Switzerland through its Tiffany & Co. International affiliate; in 2002 it brought its Little Switzerland holdings to about 98%. In 2003 Chaney retired and Kowalski added the title of chairman.

## EXECUTIVES

**Chairman and CEO:** Michael J. Kowalski, age 55, $972,382 pay
**President and Vice Chairman:** James E. Quinn, age 55, $738,013 pay
**EVP and CFO:** James N. Fernandez, age 51, $655,543 pay
**EVP:** Beth O. Canavan, age 52, $526,275 pay
**EVP:** Jon M. King, age 50, $877,923 pay
**SVP, General Counsel, and Secretary:** Patrick B. Dorsey, age 56
**SVP, Human Resources:** Victoria Berger-Gross, age 51
**SVP, Marketing:** Caroline D. Naggiar, age 49
**SVP, Finance:** Patrick F. McGuiness, age 41
**SVP Merchandising:** Pamela Cloud
**SVP, Operations:** John S. Petterson, age 48
**SVP, Public Relations:** Fernanda M. Kellogg, age 60
**VP, Investor Relations:** Mark L. Aaron
**VP, Europe:** Cesare Settepassi
**Design Director:** John Loring
**Auditors:** PricewaterhouseCoopers LLP

## LOCATIONS

**HQ:** Tiffany & Co.
727 5th Ave., New York, NY 10022
**Phone:** 212-755-8000 **Fax:** 212-230-6633
**Web:** www.tiffany.com

**2007 Sales**

| | $ mil. | % of total |
|---|---|---|
| US | 1,573.1 | 59 |
| Japan | 491.3 | 19 |
| Other countries | 583.9 | 22 |
| **Total** | **2,648.3** | **100** |

**2007 Stores**

| | No. |
|---|---|
| US | 64 |
| Asia/Pacific | |
| Japan | 52 |
| Other countries | 28 |
| Europe | 14 |
| Canada & South/Central America | 9 |
| Other regions | 3 |
| **Total** | **167** |

## PRODUCTS/OPERATIONS

**2007 Sales**

| | $ mil. | % of total |
|---|---|---|
| Jewelry | 2,234.4 | 84 |
| Tableware, timepieces & other | 413.9 | 16 |
| **Total** | **2,648.3** | **100** |

**2007 US Retail Jewelry Category Sales**

| | % of total |
|---|---|
| Gemstone jewelry & band rings | 36 |
| Non-gemstone sterling silver jewelry | 36 |
| Diamond rings & wedding bands | 17 |
| Non-gemstone gold & platinum jewelry | 11 |
| **Total** | **100** |

**2007 Sales**

| | $ mil. | % of total |
|---|---|---|
| US retail | 1,326.4 | 50 |
| International retail | 1,010.6 | 38 |
| Direct marketing | 174.1 | 7 |
| Other | 137.2 | 5 |
| **Total** | **2,648.3** | **100** |

**Selected Merchandise and Brands**

China and other tableware
Crystal
Fashion and personal accessories
Fine jewelry (Faraone)
Fragrances (Tiffany, Tiffany for Men)
Glassware (Judel)
Stationery
Sterling silver (desk accessories, flatware, hollowware, key holders, picture frames, trophies)
Watches and clocks
Writing instruments

## COMPETITORS

ARC International
Armani
Asprey
Blue Nile
Bulgari
Bulova
Cartier
Chanel
Christie's
Elizabeth Arden Inc
Fortunoff
Gucci
H. Stern
Hermès
Inter Parfums
LVMH
Movado Group
Neiman Marcus
Nordstrom
Parlux Fragrances
Richard-Ginori 1735
Richemont
Rolex
Royal Doulton
Saks Fifth Avenue
Shiseido
Signet
Société du Louvre
Union Diamond
Van Cleef & Arpels
Waterford Wedgwood
Yves Saint-Laurent Groupe
Zale

## HISTORICAL FINANCIALS

Company Type: Public

**Income Statement** FYE: January 31

| | REVENUE ($ mil.) | NET INCOME ($ mil.) | NET PROFIT MARGIN | EMPLOYEES |
|---|---|---|---|---|
| **1/07** | 2,648 | 254 | 9.6% | 8,900 |
| **1/06** | 2,395 | 255 | 10.6% | 8,120 |
| **1/05** | 2,205 | 304 | 13.8% | 7,341 |
| **1/04** | 2,000 | 216 | 10.8% | 6,862 |
| **1/03** | 1,707 | 190 | 11.1% | 6,431 |
| **Annual Growth** | 11.6% | 7.5% | — | 8.5% |

**2007 Year-End Financials**

Debt ratio: 22.5%
Return on equity: 14.0%
Cash ($ mil.): 192
Current ratio: 3.77
Long-term debt ($ mil.): 406
No. of shares (mil.): 136
Dividends
Yield: 1.0%
Payout: 21.1%
Market value ($ mil.): 5,334

**Stock History** NYSE: TIF

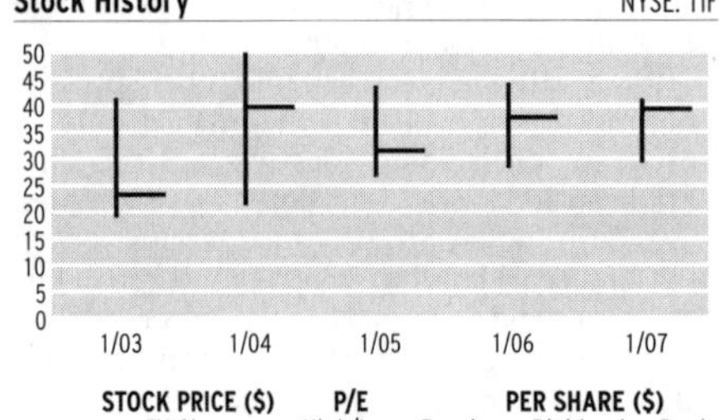


| | STOCK PRICE ($) FY Close | P/E High | P/E Low | PER SHARE ($) Earnings | Dividends | Book Value |
|---|---|---|---|---|---|---|
| **1/07** | 39.26 | 23 | 16 | 1.80 | 0.38 | 13.28 |
| **1/06** | 37.70 | 25 | 16 | 1.75 | 0.30 | 12.85 |
| **1/05** | 31.43 | 21 | 13 | 2.05 | 0.23 | 11.77 |
| **1/04** | 39.64 | 34 | 15 | 1.45 | 0.19 | 10.01 |
| **1/03** | 23.25 | 32 | 15 | 1.28 | 0.12 | 8.34 |
| **Annual Growth** | 14.0% | — | — | 8.9% | 33.4% | 12.3% |

# The Timberland Company

Even non-hikers can get a kick out of Timberlands. The Timberland Company is best known for making and marketing men's, women's, and kids' footwear. The firm's footwear includes its popular yellow hiking boots, boat shoes, dress and outdoor casual footwear, and sandals. Its merchandise also includes apparel (outerwear, shirts, pants, socks) and accessories, such as sunglasses, watches, and belts. Timberland has nearly 250 company-owned and franchised stores in Asia, Canada, Europe, Latin America, the Middle East, and the US, and it sells worldwide in department and athletic stores. The founding Swartz family, including CEO Jeffrey Swartz, controls about 70% of Timberland's voting power.

The company, which had hired investment firm Goldman Sachs to help it find a buyer, took itself off the market in early 2007. While the auction attracted plenty of interest from private equity firms, the bids were disappointing.

Footwear accounts for some 72% of Timberland's sales. That's down from nearly 77% in both 2004 and 2005. More than 50% of the company's revenue comes from the US, however it is pushing into global markets such as Canada. Timberland has been expanding its product offerings, including optical glasses, travel gear, and kids' shoes.

Getting into the bling of things, Timberland inked a licensing agreement with Endura SA in 2006 to develop a collection of performance and casual watches. Endura is the private label manufacturer and licensing company of The Swatch Group Ltd. In early 2007 the company signed a licensing agreement with Phillips-Van Heusen for Timberland brand apparel.

Giving Timberland an extended reach into international outlets and pairing the footwear maker with a sister market in the outdoor industry, the company acquired SmartWool Corporation in 2005. Timberland bought the Colorado-based maker of wool socks, apparel, and accessories from RAF Industries and the Stripes Group for about $82 million. SmartWool, having served the outdoor merino wool sock market since 1994, expanded its portfolio to make premium wool-based apparel and accessories. SmartWool items are sold in more than 2,000 outdoor specialty stores in the US and through independent distributors in Canada, Europe, and Asia.

The company's agreement with Samsonite helps to extend Timberland's worldwide reach. The 2006 deal involves a collaboration between the two firms for the strategy, design, manufacturing, and distribution of Timberland packs and travel gear.

Collaboration has been key for Timberland into 2007, as well. At the beginning of the year the company announced that it had entered into a licensing agreement with work wear manufacturer Block Corporation. The deal allows its Timberland PRO unit to extend its reach in North America.

While the company is manufacturing more items, it streamlined its supply chain operations by closing and moving its production from Puerto Rico to the Dominican Republic by 2006.

## HISTORY

After buying a 50% interest in the Abington Shoe Company in 1952, Nathan Swartz purchased the rest three years later and brought his 19-year-old son Sidney on board. Abington Shoe made handmade private-label footwear during the 1950s and 1960s.

In 1968 Nathan retired, leaving sons Sidney and Herman in charge. The brothers persuaded Goodyear to make a synthetic rubber sole, which the Swartzes then bonded to blond leather, creating the first waterproof Timberland boot in 1973. Because of the boot's popularity, the company changed its name to The Timberland Company five years later.

The boots were a cult hit on US college campuses, but they really kicked up a following when they reached Italy in 1980. Spurred by the success overseas, US retailers gave the boots an increased focus, and by the late 1980s Timberland was riding the crest of the outdoors craze. The company opened its first store in 1986 and went public a year later.

Timberland's success brought competition from NIKE and Reebok. As the "brown shoes" market became saturated, the company closed its US plants and started outsourcing production in 1994. Timberland streamlined its product lines and announced plans to revamp retail stores in 1997. The next year it introduced the "beige shoe," a boot and sneaker hybrid under the Gorge MPO brand. Also in 1998 Jeffrey Swartz stepped into his father's Timberlands as CEO.

In 1999 Timberland unveiled the Mountain Athletics product line aimed at the 18- to 25-year-old outdoor athlete market and Timberland Pro — footwear for the tradesperson (construction workers, factory foremen). Timberland reacquired the Asian distribution of its products from Inchcape in February 2000. In 2001 the company launched its "Around the World" ad campaign, the company's most ambitious ever.

In 2003 Timberland penned a licensing agreement with Italy's Marcolin, S.p.A to make and distribute Timberland-brand eyewear.

## EXECUTIVES

**Chairman:** Sidney W. Swartz, age 71, $1,745,777 pay
**President, CEO, and Director:** Jeffrey B. Swartz, age 47, $818,750 pay
**SVP, Global Product Management:** Marc Schneider, age 46
**SVP Human Resources:** Bruce A. Johnson, age 50
**VP, Business Development and Licensing:** Dennis Jenson
**VP and CIO:** Rosalee Hermens
**VP, Acting CFO, Corporate Controller, and Chief Accounting Officer:** John Crimmins, age 50
**VP, General Counsel, and Secretary:** Danette Wineberg, age 60
**VP and General Manager, Timberland Retail and E-Commerce:** John Pazzani
**VP, Global Product Development:** Brian Moore
**VP and Global Director, Men's Casual Footwear:** Rob Koenen
**VP and Treasurer:** Gregory M. (Greg) Saltzberg
**VP and General Merchandising Manager, SmartWool:** Anne Wiper
**President, CasualGear:** Michael J. Harrison, age 47
**President, Authentic Youth:** Gene McCarthy, age 50
**President, Industrial:** Scott C. Thresher, age 39
**Director, Marketing, Timberland PRO:** Jim O'Connor
**Community Investment Manager:** Celina Adams
**Retail Marketing Manager:** Amy Tremblay
**Director, Investor Relations:** Susan Ostrow
**Media Relations:** Robin Giampa
**Public Relations:** Leslie Grundy
**Auditors:** Deloitte & Touche LLP

## LOCATIONS

**HQ:** The Timberland Company
200 Domain Dr., Stratham, NH 03885
**Phone:** 603-772-9500 **Fax:** 603-773-1640
**Web:** www.timberland.com

### 2006 Sales

| | % of total |
|---|---|
| US | |
| Wholesale | 41 |
| Consumer Direct | 13 |
| Other countries | 46 |
| **Total** | **100** |

## PRODUCTS/OPERATIONS

### 2006 Sales

| | % of total |
|---|---|
| Footwear | 72 |
| Apparel & accessories | 27 |
| Royalties & other | 1 |
| **Total** | **100** |

## COMPETITORS

Billabong
Birkenstock Distribution USA
Columbia Sportswear
Deckers Outdoor
Eddie Bauer Holdings
Fossil
L.L. Bean
NIKE
Norm Thompson
North Face
Patagonia
Phillips-Van Heusen
Polo Ralph Lauren
R. Griggs
Reebok
Rocky Brands
Skechers U.S.A.
Wolverine World Wide

## HISTORICAL FINANCIALS

Company Type: Public

### Income Statement

FYE: December 31

| | REVENUE ($ mil.) | NET INCOME ($ mil.) | NET PROFIT MARGIN | EMPLOYEES |
|---|---|---|---|---|
| **12/06** | 1,568 | 101 | 6.5% | 6,300 |
| **12/05** | 1,566 | 165 | 10.5% | 5,300 |
| **12/04** | 1,501 | 153 | 10.2% | 5,600 |
| **12/03** | 1,342 | 118 | 8.8% | 5,500 |
| **12/02** | 1,191 | 95 | 8.0% | 5,400 |
| **Annual Growth** | 7.1% | 1.6% | — | 3.9% |

### 2006 Year-End Financials

Debt ratio: —
Return on equity: 18.6%
Cash ($ mil.): 182
Current ratio: 2.27
Long-term debt ($ mil.): —
No. of shares (mil.): 50
Dividends
Yield: —
Payout: —
Market value ($ mil.): 1,586

### Stock History

NYSE: TBL

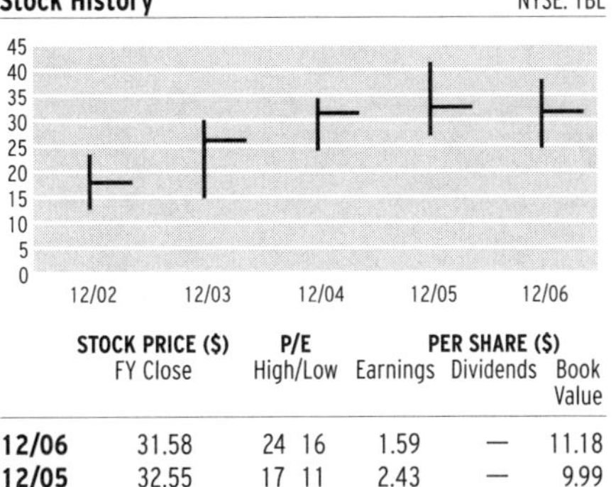


| | STOCK PRICE ($) FY Close | P/E High/Low | PER SHARE ($) Earnings | Dividends | Book Value |
|---|---|---|---|---|---|
| **12/06** | 31.58 | 24 16 | 1.59 | — | 11.18 |
| **12/05** | 32.55 | 17 11 | 2.43 | — | 9.99 |
| **12/04** | 31.33 | 16 11 | 2.14 | — | 18.26 |
| **12/03** | 26.03 | 18 9 | 1.62 | — | 15.26 |
| **12/02** | 17.81 | 18 10 | 1.25 | — | 12.97 |
| **Annual Growth** | 15.4% | — — | 6.2% | — | (3.6%) |

# Time Warner

Even among media titans, this company is a giant. Time Warner is the world's largest media conglomerate with operations spanning film, television, cable TV, publishing, and online content and services. Its film and TV production companies include New Line Cinema and Warner Bros., while its television properties include CNN, HBO, and Turner Broadcasting. Time Warner Cable is the #2 cable operator (behind Comcast), serving more than 14 million subscribers, while its AOL online access unit boasts more than 17 million users. Venerable Time Inc. is the top consumer magazine publisher with such titles as *Fortune, People,* and *Time.*

While Time Warner seems to have turned the corner in the past couple years and put its ill-fated $106 billion merger with America Online in 2000 finally in the past, the company still faces many challenges to maintain its momentum across all its various business lines. The company's film and TV units, in particular, struggled through an uneven 2006. Such films as *Poseidon* and *Ant Bully* bombed at the box office, offsetting gains from the animated feature *Happy Feet* and the critically acclaimed *The Departed. Superman Returns*, the latest installment of the superhero saga from Warner Bros., fared well with moviegoers but not as well as expected.

On television, TNT continues to reign as one of the top cable destinations, while the rebranding of TBS Superstation as a comedy channel continues to show success. Time Warner's HBO unit has also found the formula for both critical and financial success. Meanwhile, though, Time Warner's CNN news channel continues to trail FOX News in ratings.

The company's cable television subsidiary also continues to contribute increasing revenue, in part through expansion. In 2006 the cable operator joined with Comcast to buy troubled cable company Adelphia Communications for $17.6 billion in cash and stock. Time Warner Cable paid $9 billion to Adelphia shareholders and granted them a 16% stake in the company. Those shareholders sold part of that stake though an IPO in 2007.

Time Warner also sold the Atlanta Braves to Liberty Media that year. Liberty paid some $1.5 billion in cash and stock for the baseball franchise, along with Time Inc.'s Leisure Arts business, which publishes how-two craft books.

AOL continues to struggle with shrinking subscriber numbers as Internet users switch from dial-up services to high-speed broadband being offered by telecom and cable operators (including Time Warner Cable's Road Runner service). In 2006 AOL announced plans to start offering many of its online services, such as e-mail and instant messaging, for free to broadband users in the hope that it can make up the difference through increased advertising sales. That effort should be helped by a partnership with search and contextual ad guru Google, which bought a 5% stake in the business for $1 billion in late 2005. AOL also cut about 5,000 jobs as it transitions to become an ad-supported business.

Internationally, AOL has started to shed many of its Internet service units in Europe; it has agreed to sell AOL Germany to Telecom Italia for $870 million, while Neuf Cegetel is buying AOL France for $365 million. The Internet access business of AOL UK was acquired by Carphone Warehouse for about $690 million in 2007.

## HISTORY

Though formed in 2001, AOL Time Warner was the result of decades of advancement in the media industry. An elder statesman compared to relative newcomer America Online, Time Warner's roots extend back to 1922 — the year that Henry Luce and Briton Hadden founded publisher Time Inc., and brothers Harry, Abe, Jack, and Sam Warner established the origins of Warner Bros., which later became Warner Communications.

America Online's ancestry stretches back to the early 1980s when Stephen Case joined the management of a company called Control Video. Later renamed Quantum Computer Services, the company created the online service that would become America Online in 1985. Quantum Computer Services changed its name to America Online in 1991. It went public the next year.

Time Inc. and Warner Communications merged in 1990 to form Time Warner. Gerald Levin was appointed CEO in 1992. To shave off debt, Time Warner grouped several of its properties into Time Warner Entertainment in 1992, in which U S West (which later became MediaOne Group) bought a 25% interest.

Time Warner's 1996 acquisition of Ted Turner's Turner Broadcasting System further elevated Time Warner's profile on the media stage.

America Online grew through acquisitions of CompuServe in 1998 and Netscape Communications in 1999. Meanwhile, Time Warner had created Time Warner Telecom and taken it public. After AT&T's announcement that it would acquire MediaOne, MediaOne gave up its 50% management control of Time Warner Entertainment but retained its 25% ownership interest, thus giving AT&T 25% of Time Warner Entertainment. (AT&T later boosted its stake to 27%.)

America Online announced that it would acquire Time Warner in early 2000. To please European regulators, Time Warner subsequently abandoned its plans to combine the Warner Music Group with EMI Group's music operations. After a lengthy review by regulatory bodies, America Online acquired Time Warner for $106 billion and formed AOL Time Warner in 2001. Case became chairman, and Levin was appointed CEO. The newly formed company soon began streamlining, cutting more than 2,400 jobs in the process. (It cut another 1,700 jobs at America Online later that year.)

Levin retired from the company in 2002 and was replaced by co-COO Richard Parsons. The following year AOL Time Warner finally succeeded in buying Comcast's stake in Time Warner Entertainment (Comcast gained its share of TWE when it bought the cable assets of AT&T in 2002). The following year Case and Turner both resigned their executive positions but remained on the board of directors. (Case left the board in 2005.) And in a move to distance itself from the struggling online unit, the company dropped AOL from its moniker and returned to being known as Time Warner Inc.

Time Warner started off 2004 by ridding itself of Warner Music Group, which it sold for $2.6 billion to a group led by former Seagram executive Edgar Bronfman Jr. and investment firm Thomas H. Lee Partners. It also sold the NBA's Atlanta Hawks and the NHL's Atlanta Thrashers for $250 million to a private investment group called Atlanta Spirit.

In 2006 Time Warner sold its book publishing unit, Time Warner Book Group, to French media firm Lagardère.

## EXECUTIVES

**Chairman and CEO:** Richard D. (Dick) Parsons, age 58
**President, COO, and Director:** Jeffrey L. (Jeff) Bewkes, age 54
**EVP and CFO:** Wayne H. Pace, age 60
**EVP and General Counsel:** Paul T. Cappuccio, age 45
**EVP Administration:** Patricia (Pat) Fili-Krushel, age 53
**EVP Corporate Communications:** Edward I. Adler, age 53
**EVP Global Public Policy:** Carol A. Melton, age 52
**EVP:** Olaf Olafsson, age 44
**SVP; President, Global Media Group:** John Partilla
**SVP Investor Relations:** James E. (Jim) Burston
**SVP and Managing Director, Global Media Group:** Kristen O'Hara
**SVP and Chief Security Officer:** Larry L. Cockell
**SVP and Controller:** James W. Barge
**VP Corporate Communications:** Susan Duffy
**VP and Secretary:** Paul F. Washington
**Chief Creative Officer, Global Media Group:** Mark D'Arcy
**Co-Chairman and Co-CEO, New Line Cinema:** Robert K. Shaye
**Co-Chairman and Co-CEO, New Line Cinema:** Michael Lynne, age 66
**Chairman and CEO, Time Inc.:** Ann S. Moore
**Chairman and CEO, Time Warner Cable:** Glenn A. Britt, age 57
**Chairman and CEO, Turner Broadcasting System:** Philip I. Kent
**Chairman and CEO, Warner Bros. Entertainment:** Barry M. Meyer, age 58
**Chairman and CEO, AOL:** Randel A. (Randy) Falco, age 52
**Chairman and CEO, Home Box Office:** Bill Nelson
**Auditors:** Ernst & Young LLP

## LOCATIONS

**HQ:** Time Warner Inc.
1 Time Warner Center, New York, NY 10019
**Phone:** 212-484-8000
**Web:** www.timewarner.com

Time Warner has operations worldwide.

### 2006 Sales

| | $ mil. | % of total |
|---|---|---|
| US | 35,604 | 81 |
| UK | 2,606 | 6 |
| Germany | 1,169 | 3 |
| France | 834 | 2 |
| Canada | 610 | 1 |
| Japan | 507 | 1 |
| Other countries | 2,894 | 6 |
| **Total** | **44,224** | **100** |

## PRODUCTS/OPERATIONS

### 2006 Sales

| | $ mil. | % of total |
|---|---|---|
| Subscriptions | 23,702 | 54 |
| Content | 10,769 | 24 |
| Advertising | 8,515 | 19 |
| Other | 1,238 | 3 |
| **Total** | **44,224** | **100** |

### 2006 Sales

| | $ mil. | % of total |
|---|---|---|
| Cable | 11,767 | 26 |
| Filmed entertainment | 10,625 | 23 |
| Networks | 10,273 | 22 |
| AOL | 7,866 | 17 |
| Publishing | 5,249 | 12 |
| Adjustments | (1,556) | — |
| **Total** | **44,224** | **100** |

### Selected Operations

AOL LLC (95%)
- AOL (online service)
- AOL CityGuide (online community guides)
- AOL Europe (online service)
- AOL MovieFone (telephone and online movie information and ticketing)
- CompuServe (online services)
- ICQ (communications portal)
- MapQuest (online maps)
- Netscape Communicator (software)
- Netscape Netcenter (Internet portal)
- SHOUTcast (Internet music)
- Spinner.com (Internet music)
- Winamp (Internet music)

Home Box Office (cable network)
- HBO Films (film production)
  - Picturehouse (film distribution, joint venture with New Line)

New Line Cinema (film production)
- Picturehouse (film distribution, joint venture with HBO Films)

Time Inc. (magazine publishing)
- Essence Communications (African-American women's magazines)
- IPC Group (magazine publishing, UK)

Time Warner Cable (79%, cable system)
- Road Runner (high speed cable Internet service)
- Time Warner Entertainment-Advance/Newhouse Partnership (65%, cable system)

Turner Broadcasting System
- Cartoon Network (cable network)
- CNN (cable network)
- Court TV (cable network)
- TBS (cable network)
- TNT (cable network)
- Turner Classic Movies (cable network)

Warner Bros. Entertainment (film and TV production and distribution)
- Castle Rock Entertainment (film production)
- DC Comics
- Hanna-Barbera
- Looney Tunes
- *MAD Magazine*
- Movielink (20%, online movie download service)
- Warner Bros. Consumer Products
- Warner Bros. Home Entertainment Group
  - Warner Bros. Digital Distribution
  - Warner Bros. Interactive Entertainment
  - Warner Home Video
- Warner Bros. New Media
- Warner Bros. Pictures
- Warner Bros. Television Group
  - The CW Television Network (50%)
  - Telepictures Productions
  - Warner Bros. Animation
  - Warner Bros. Domestic Cable Distribution
  - Warner Bros. Domestic Television Distribution
  - Warner Bros. International Television Distribution
  - Warner Bros. Television Production
- Warner Independent Films

## COMPETITORS

Bertelsmann
Cablevision Systems
CBS Corp
Comcast
Condé Nast
Cox Enterprises
Disney
Dow Jones
EarthLink
Hearst
Lagardère Active Media
Microsoft
NBC Universal
News Corp.
Pearson
PRIMEDIA
Sony Pictures Entertainment
Tribune
Viacom
Yahoo!

## HISTORICAL FINANCIALS

Company Type: Public

### Income Statement

FYE: December 31

| | REVENUE ($ mil.) | NET INCOME ($ mil.) | NET PROFIT MARGIN | EMPLOYEES |
|---|---|---|---|---|
| **12/06** | 44,224 | 6,552 | 14.8% | 92,700 |
| **12/05** | 43,652 | 2,921 | 6.7% | 87,850 |
| **12/04** | 42,089 | 3,364 | 8.0% | 84,900 |
| **12/03** | 39,565 | 2,639 | 6.7% | 80,000 |
| **12/02** | 40,961 | (98,696) | — | 91,250 |
| **Annual Growth** | 1.9% | — | — | 0.4% |

### 2006 Year-End Financials

Debt ratio: 57.8%
Return on equity: 10.6%
Cash ($ mil.): 1,578
Current ratio: 0.85
Long-term debt ($ mil.): 34,933
No. of shares (mil.): 3,864
Dividends
Yield: 1.0%
Payout: 13.5%
Market value ($ mil.): 84,158

## Stock History

NYSE: TWX

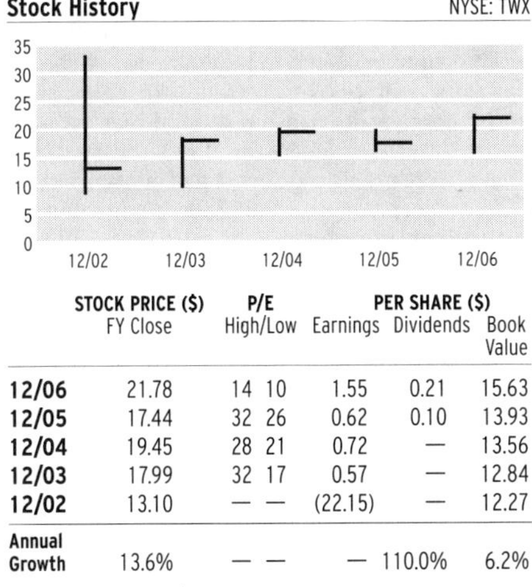


| | STOCK PRICE ($) FY Close | P/E High/Low | | PER SHARE ($) Earnings | Dividends | Book Value |
|---|---|---|---|---|---|---|
| **12/06** | 21.78 | 14 | 10 | 1.55 | 0.21 | 15.63 |
| **12/05** | 17.44 | 32 | 26 | 0.62 | 0.10 | 13.93 |
| **12/04** | 19.45 | 28 | 21 | 0.72 | — | 13.56 |
| **12/03** | 17.99 | 32 | 17 | 0.57 | — | 12.84 |
| **12/02** | 13.10 | — | — | (22.15) | — | 12.27 |
| **Annual Growth** | 13.6% | — | — | — | 110.0% | 6.2% |

# The Timken Company

The Timken Company tries to keep its bearings straight. The company makes bearings that range in weight from a mere half an ounce to nine tons. Timken bearings find their way into products from computers to railroad cars. Timken and its subsidiaries also manufacture alloy and specialty steels such as steel tubing, high-strength alloy steels, and die layout-ready ground blocks; the products are used primarily by industrial and automotive customers. Five generations of the Timken family have served the company since its founding by one-time carriage maker Henry Timken in 1899.

Timken's 2003 purchase of Ingersoll-Rand's Torrington engineering solutions unit, which makes precision bearings and motion-control components for the automotive and aerospace industries, made Timken the third largest bearing company in the world. The company also plans to expand its precision steel components business to include industrial applications, such as construction equipment.

The company is fortifying its presence in China. In the early and mid-1990s Timken opened three sales offices and formed a joint venture, Yantai Timken Company, which produces ball bearings. (Yantai Timken became a wholly owned subsidiary in 2001.) It is also building a plant in Shanghai that will make single-row tapered bearings used in medium- to high-volume automotive and industrial applications. The Shanghai plant, another joint venture, began operations in 2004.

Blaming the woes of the North American automotive industry, Timken laid off approximately 700 employees, or about 5% of its Automotive Group, in the fall of 2006. Soon after, the company said it would close the group's factory in São Paulo, Brazil, by the end of 2007, eliminating manufacturing redundancies.

The company plans to close down its unprofitable plant in Desford, UK, which makes seamless steel tubes. Up to 400 employees could lose their jobs as a result.

It's not all divestitures and cutbacks at the century-old company. Timken is expanding its Harrison Steel Plant in Canton, Ohio. The expansion will give the company greater capabilities to produce steel bars down to one inch in diameter for applications in power transmission and friction management. Timken has also undertaken building a new plant in Chennai, India, and is expanding its factory in Altavista, Virginia.

The Timken family, through individual holdings and its foundation, controls 12% of the company. In mid-2005 President Bush nominated William Timken Jr. to become US ambassador to Germany. When he took office, William Timken resigned as chairman and was replaced by his nephew Tim.

The company's pension plan owns nearly 9% of Timken. Lord, Abbett & Co. holds almost 8%. Earnest Partners has an equity stake of nearly 6%. Barclays Global Investors owns about 5%.

## HISTORY

Veteran St. Louis carriage maker Henry Timken patented a design in 1898 for tapered roller bearings (enclosed bearings between a pair of concentric rings). The following year Timken and his sons, William and Henry (H. H.) Timken, founded the Timken Roller Bearing Axle Company to make bearings for carriage axles.

In 1902 the company moved to Canton, Ohio, to be near the growing steelworks of Pittsburgh and the new auto industries of Buffalo, New York; Cleveland; and Detroit. With the debut of the Model T in 1908, the Timkens' business soared. In 1909 Henry Timken died. That year a separate company, the Timken-Detroit Axle Company, was formed in Detroit to serve the auto industry. The original company changed its name to the Timken Roller Bearing Company and continued to produce bearings. Also in 1909 Vickers began making bearings and axles under license from Timken (Timken acquired that operation in 1959).

Suffering steel shortages during WWI, in 1916 the company began making its own steel. By the 1920s the rail industry had adopted Timken bearings to increase the speed of trains. Timken stock was sold to the public for the first time in 1922.

WWII created increased demand for Timken's products, and the company opened several new plants. The AP bearing — a revolutionary prelubricated, self-contained railroad bearing unveiled by Timken in 1954 — boosted the company's railroad segment, and a new plant, the Columbus Railroad Bearing Plant, opened in 1958.

H. H. Timken's son, W. Robert Timken, became president in 1960 and chairman in 1968. The company continued to grow during the 1960s by opening plants in Brazil and France. It adopted its current name in 1970. W. R. Timken Jr., grandson of the founder, became chairman in 1975. That year the company bought specialty alloy maker Latrobe Steel.

In 1982, with increasing competition from Europe and Japan, the company suffered its first loss since the Depression. Five years later it established Indian joint venture Tata Timken to make bearings for agricultural equipment, heavy machinery, and railcars.

Timken bought precision-bearing maker MPB Corporation in 1990. The company opened its first European steel operations in 1993 and the following year introduced its environmentally progressive Dynametal steel products. Timken formed joint venture Yantai Timken in 1996 to make bearings in China.

The General Motors strike, transformer outages, and new equipment costs hurt the company's earnings in 1998. In 1999 Timken cut production capacity to 80% and continued to consolidate operations and restructure into global business units. The company closed plants in Australia, and restructured operations in South Africa (cutting about 1,700 jobs).

In early 2001 the company announced that it would lay off more than 7% of its workforce. Timken entered into a joint venture with SKF (ball bearings, Sweden) in 2001 to make bearing components in Brazil. Later Timken acquired French steel component maker Lecheres Industries SAS.

Timken acquired the Ingersoll-Rand unit, The Torrington Co., for $840 million in 2003. In 2005 Timken sold its Linear Motion Systems division, with operations in Germany and Italy, to an Italian firm, Overseas Industries SpA.

In late 2006 Timken sold its Latrobe Steel subsidiary for about $215 million in cash to an investors group led by the Watermill Group, Hicks Holdings, and Sankaty Advisors (part of Bain Capital).

## EXECUTIVES

**Chairman:** Ward J. (Tim) Timken Jr., age 39, $750,000 pay
**President, CEO, and Director:** James W. Griffith, age 53, $950,000 pay
**EVP, Finance and Administration:** Glenn A. Eisenberg, age 45, $570,833 pay
**EVP; President, Bearings and Power Transmission Group:** Michael C. Arnold, age 50, $473,333 pay
**SVP and CIO:** Jon T. Elsasser
**SVP and General Counsel:** William R. Burkhart, age 41
**SVP, Asia Pacific:** Roger W. Lindsay
**SVP, Communications and Community Affairs:** Debra L. (Deb) Miller
**SVP, Corporate Planning and Development:** Mark J. Samolczyk
**SVP and Controller:** J. Ted Mihaila, age 52
**SVP, Human Resources and Organizational Advancement:** Donald L. Walker
**SVP, Quality and Six Sigma:** Donna J. Demerling
**SVP, Supply Chain Management:** Michael J. Hill
**SVP, Tax and Treasury:** Philip D. (Phil) Fracassa, age 38
**SVP, Technology:** Alastair R. (AL) Deane, age 45
**SVP Innovation and Growth:** Jacqueline A. Dedo, age 45, $416,667 pay
**VP, Auditing:** Dennis R. Vernier
**Corporate Secretary and Assistant General Counsel:** Scott A. Scherff, age 50
**Manager, Investor Relations:** Kevin R. Beck
**President, Steel Group:** Salvatore J. Miraglia Jr., age 56
**Auditors:** Ernst & Young LLP

## LOCATIONS

**HQ:** The Timken Company
1835 Dueber Ave. SW, Canton, OH 44706
**Phone:** 330-438-3000 **Fax:** 330-471-3810
**Web:** www.timken.com

The Timken Company operates more than 50 manufacturing plants and 100 sales offices and distribution centers in 27 countries, primarily in Asia, Europe, and the US.

### 2006 Sales

| | $ mil. | % of total |
|---|---|---|
| US | 3,370.3 | 68 |
| Europe | 849.9 | 17 |
| Other regions | 753.2 | 15 |
| **Total** | **4,973.4** | **100** |

## PRODUCTS/OPERATIONS

### 2006 Sales

| | $ mil. | % of total |
|---|---|---|
| Industrial group | 2,072.5 | 42 |
| Automotive group | 1,573.0 | 31 |
| Steel group | 1,327.9 | 27 |
| **Total** | **4,973.4** | **100** |

### Selected Products

Bearings
- Cylindrical bearings
- Spherical bearings
- Straight ball bearings
- Super-precision ball and roller bearings
- Tapered bearings

Steel
- Mechanical seamless steel tubing
- Specialty steels and alloys
- Tool steel

## COMPETITORS

| | |
|---|---|
| Allegheny Technologies | NSK |
| Amatsuji Steel Ball | NTN |
| ArcelorMittal | Nucor |
| BÖHLER-UDDEHOLM | PAV Republic |
| Corus Group | Plymouth Tube |
| Crucible Materials | Quanex Corporation |
| Delphi | RBC Bearings |
| Dofasco | RBS Global |
| General Bearing | Schaeffler |
| JTEKT | SKF |
| Kaydon | Steel Dynamics |
| Linamar | Tenaris |
| Macsteel Service Centres | United States Steel |
| Metaldyne | Universal Stainless |
| Minebea | V & M Tubes (USA) |
| Nippon Bearing | |

## HISTORICAL FINANCIALS

Company Type: Public

### Income Statement

FYE: December 31

| | REVENUE ($ mil.) | NET INCOME ($ mil.) | NET PROFIT MARGIN | EMPLOYEES |
|---|---|---|---|---|
| **12/06** | 4,973 | 223 | 4.5% | 25,418 |
| **12/05** | 5,168 | 260 | 5.0% | 27,000 |
| **12/04** | 4,514 | 136 | 3.0% | 26,000 |
| **12/03** | 3,788 | 37 | 1.0% | 26,000 |
| **12/02** | 2,550 | 39 | 1.5% | 18,000 |
| **Annual Growth** | 18.2% | 54.7% | — | 9.0% |

### 2006 Year-End Financials

| | |
|---|---|
| Debt ratio: 37.1% | No. of shares (mil.): 94 |
| Return on equity: 15.0% | Dividends |
| Cash ($ mil.): 101 | Yield: 2.1% |
| Current ratio: 2.27 | Payout: 26.3% |
| Long-term debt ($ mil.): 547 | Market value ($ mil.): 2,748 |

### Stock History

NYSE: TKR

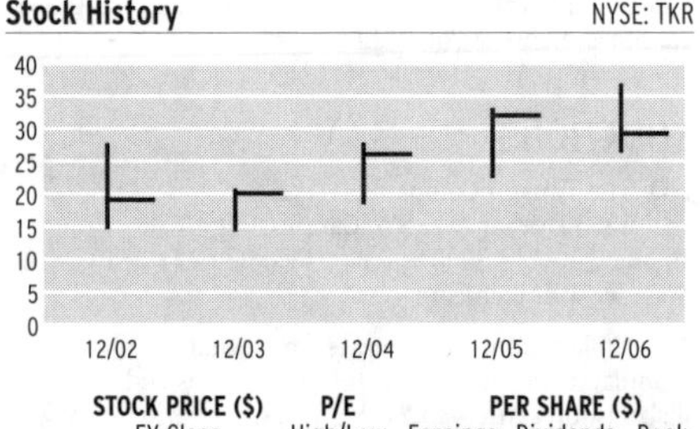


| | STOCK PRICE ($) FY Close | P/E High | P/E Low | PER SHARE ($) Earnings | PER SHARE ($) Dividends | PER SHARE ($) Book Value |
|---|---|---|---|---|---|---|
| **12/06** | 29.18 | 16 | 11 | 2.36 | 0.62 | 15.68 |
| **12/05** | 32.02 | 12 | 8 | 2.81 | 0.60 | 16.10 |
| **12/04** | 26.02 | 18 | 13 | 1.49 | 0.52 | 14.03 |
| **12/03** | 20.06 | 46 | 33 | 0.44 | 0.52 | 12.23 |
| **12/02** | 19.10 | 44 | 24 | 0.62 | 0.52 | 9.61 |
| **Annual Growth** | 11.2% | — | — | 39.7% | 4.5% | 13.0% |

# TJX Companies

Rifling through the racks is an art at TJX stores. The TJX Companies operates eight retail chains including the two largest off-price clothing retailers in the US, T.J. Maxx and Marshalls. T.J. Maxx sells brand-name family apparel, accessories, women's shoes, domestics, giftware, and jewelry at discount prices at some 820 stores nationwide. Marshalls offers a full line of shoes and a broader selection of menswear through nearly 750 stores. Its HomeGoods chain of 270 stores nationwide focuses entirely on home furnishings, while about 130 A.J. Wright clothing stores aim for lower-income shoppers. T.K. Maxx is the company's European retail arm with about 210 stores in the UK and Ireland.

In what may be the most serious security breach reported by a major retailer to date, in mid-January 2007 TJX reported that data had been stolen from its computer systems that process and store information related to customer credit and debit card transactions. Information from nearly 46 million credit and debit cards was stolen over an 18-month period.

The company plans to add about 50 T.J. Maxx and Marshalls stores in 2007 and add some 200 expanded footwear departments to its Marshalls outlets. Ultimately, TJX companies believes there's room for about 1,800 T.J. Maxx and Marshalls stores in the US and Puerto Rico. Also, the retailer plans to open about a dozen HomeGoods stores. In Canada about a half dozen HomeSense and Winners stores are planned and 10 T.K. Maxx stores are to open in the UK and Ireland. Five T.K. Maxx stores are slated to open in Germany in the fall.

The top two chains share similar concepts, selling items generally priced 20% to 60% below similar items at department stores. However, Marshalls offers a bigger men's department than T.J. Maxx, a larger shoe department, and costume jewelry. Marshalls has stores in 42 states and about a dozen locations in Puerto Rico. Both chains target deal-seeking consumers who usually shop at full-priced chains.

Its HomeGoods stores are both stand-alone outlets and located within superstores such as T.J. Maxx 'N More and Marshalls Mega-Stores. North of the border, TJX also operates HomeSense in Canada (not to be confused with HomeGoods), with nearly 70 stores, and a chain of family clothing stores called Winners Apparel (about 185 stores).

The company has pulled the plug on its e-commerce business citing disappointing sales at its tjmaxx.com and homegoods.com Web sites.

## HISTORY

Cousins Stanley and Sumner Feldberg opened the first Zayre (Yiddish for "very good") store in Hyannis, Massachusetts, in 1956. During the next 15 years, the number of stores grew to nearly 200.

Zayre purchased the Hit or Miss chain, which sold upscale women's clothing at discounted prices, in 1969. When the recession of the early 1970s hit, superb results at Hit or Miss prompted Zayre to look for further opportunities in the off-price apparel marketplace. Zayre hired Ben Cammarata to create a new store concept, and in March 1977 he opened the first T.J. Maxx, in Auburn, Massachusetts, to market discounted upscale family clothing. Six years later Zayre formed the catalog retailer Chadwick's of Boston to sell Hit or Miss apparel by mail.

The company came to rely increasingly on its specialty operations to provide consistent sales and income as its flagship general merchandise stores often struggled. By 1983 the specialty chains were producing almost half of Zayre's sales.

In the second half of the 1980s, Zayre's upscale (yet still off-priced) retailers' sales rose, while its general merchandise stores (targeting lower-income customers) dropped. To keep its specialty stores unhindered by its flagging Zayre stores, it established The TJX Companies as a public company in 1987. Zayre sold about 17% of its new subsidiary to the public, with Cammarata as CEO.

Zayre sold its 400 general merchandise stores in 1988 to Ames for about $430 million in cash, $140 million in Ames stock, and a receivable note. The next year the company spun off its warehouse club operations as Waban (the warehouse component eventually became BJ's Wholesale) and merged with its subsidiary, The TJX Companies, taking that name.

TJX acquired Winners Apparel, a Toronto-based five-store apparel chain, in 1990. That year, in the same month that Ames declared bankruptcy, TJX established a $185 million reserve against losses it might suffer through its ownership of Ames' stock. Ames emerged from bankruptcy two years later, and TJX was left with 4% of Ames' voting shares and over 100 empty Ames stores. TJX sold or leased most of them.

Also in 1992 TJX opened HomeGoods gift and houseware outlets in three of its remaining Ames stores and closed about 70 Hit or Miss stores. Encouraged by the success of its off-price operations in Canada, in 1994 TJX opened five T.K. Maxx stores (similar to T.J. Maxx and Winners Apparel) in the UK.

A year later TJX paid $550 million for Melville's ailing chain of 450 Marshalls clothing stores. In addition, the company sold its Hit or Miss apparel chain. To help pay for Marshalls, TJX sold the Chadwick's of Boston catalog in 1996 to retailer Brylane for about $325 million.

In 1999 TJX elected Cammarata to the additional post of chairman and elevated Ted English to president and COO. In 2000 Cammarata relinquished his CEO post to English but remained chairman. In early 2001 it expected to increase its total number of stores 12% annually for the next several years. Also that year the company shuttered its T.K. Maxx stores in the Netherlands. Seven TJX employees perished on September 11, 2001, when their flight, bound for Los Angeles, crashed into the World Trade Center during the worst terrorist attack in US history.

In 2002 the company opened HomeSense, a new Canadian home furnishings chain fashioned after its US counterpart HomeGoods.

In September 2005 English resigned abruptly after five years as the company's CEO.

In March 2006 TJX cut about 250 jobs in its corporate and divisional offices and reduced the salaries of a dozen senior executives, including its chairman and acting CEO and its president, by 10% in an effort to increase profits.

A year after the abrupt resignation of CEO Edmond English in September 2005, TJX named company president Carol Meyrowitz to the post effective January 2007. (Chairman Bernard Cammarata had been acting CEO of the company in the interim.) Also in January, 34 A.J. Wright stores were closed.

## EXECUTIVES

**Chairman:** Bernard (Ben) Cammarata, age 67
**Vice Chairman:** Donald G. (Don) Campbell, age 55, $740,769 pay
**President, CEO, and Director:** Carol M. Meyrowitz, age 53
**SEVP and Chief Administrative and Business Development Officer:** Jeffrey G. (Jeff) Naylor, age 48
**SEVP and Group President:** Arnold S. Barron, age 59, $672,673 pay
**SEVP; President, The Marmaxx Group:** Ernie Herrman, age 46
**SEVP; Group President, Europe:** Paul Sweetenham, age 42
**SEVP and Group President:** Jerome Rossi, age 63
**SEVP and COO, The Marmaxx Group:** Richard Sherr, age 49
**EVP and CFO:** Nirmal K. (Trip) Tripathy, age 49
**EVP and CIO:** Paul Butka
**EVP and General Counsel:** Ann McCauley, age 56
**EVP and Chief Human Resources Officer:** Greg Flores III, age 52
**EVP and Chief Marketing Officer:** John F. Gilbert, age 50
**EVP, Real Estate and New Business Development:** Michael Skirvin
**EVP and Chief Logistics Officer:** Peter Lindenmeyer
**EVP and COO, TK Maxx:** Michael Tilley
**EVP and COO, HomeGoods:** Robert Cataldo, age 50
**SVP and Corporate Chief Technology Officer:** Robert Hernandez
**VP Investor and Public Relations:** Sherry Lang
**President, Winners/Homesense:** Michael MacMillan
**President, Bob's Stores:** David Farrell
**President, HomeGoods:** Nan Stutz, age 49
**President, A.J. Wright:** Celia Clancy, age 50
**Auditors:** PricewaterhouseCoopers LLP

## LOCATIONS

**HQ:** The TJX Companies, Inc.
770 Cochituate Rd., Framingham, MA 01701
**Phone:** 508-390-1000 **Fax:** 508-390-2828
**Web:** www.tjx.com

### 2007 Stores

| | No. |
|---|---|
| US | 2,004 |
| Canada | 252 |
| UK | 202 |
| Ireland | 8 |
| **Total** | **2,466** |

## PRODUCTS/OPERATIONS

### 2007 Stores

| | No. |
|---|---|
| T.J. Maxx | 821 |
| Marshalls | 748 |
| HomeGoods | 270 |
| T.K. Maxx | 210 |
| Winners | 184 |
| A.J. Wright | 129 |
| HomeSense | 68 |
| Bob's Stores | 36 |
| **Total** | **2,466** |

### 2007 Sales

| | $ mil. | % of total |
|---|---|---|
| Marmaxx | 11,531.8 | 66 |
| T.K. Maxx | 1,864.5 | 11 |
| Winners & HomeSense | 1,740.8 | 10 |
| HomeGoods | 1,365.1 | 8 |
| A.J. Wright | 601.8 | 3 |
| Bob's Stores | 300.6 | 2 |
| **Total** | **17,404.6** | **100** |

### Stores

A.J. Wright (discount chain aimed at moderate-income shoppers)
Bob's Stores (discount apparel chain, Northeast)
HomeGoods (off-price home fashion chain)
HomeSense (off-price home fashion chain in Canada)
Marshalls (off-price retailer of apparel, shoes, home fashions)
Marshalls Mega-Stores (combination Marshalls and HomeGoods stores)
T.J. Maxx (off-price retailer of apparel, shoes, home fashions)
T.J. Maxx 'N More (combination T.J. Maxx and HomeGoods stores)
T.K. Maxx (off-price retailer of apparel, shoes, home fashions in Europe)
Winners Apparel (off-price family apparel chain in Canada)

## COMPETITORS

Bed Bath & Beyond
Belk
Big Lots
Brown Shoe
Burlington Coat Factory
Cato
Charming Shoppes
The Children's Place
Claire's Stores
Dillard's
Dollar General
Eddie Bauer Holdings
Foot Locker
Gap
Goody's Family Clothing
Gottschalks
J. C. Penney
Kmart
Kohl's
Limited Brands
Linens 'n Things
Loehmann's
Macy's
Men's Wearhouse
Payless ShoeSource
Retail Ventures
Ross Stores
Sears
ShopKo Stores
Stage Stores
Stein Mart
Target
Wal-Mart
Zellers

## HISTORICAL FINANCIALS

Company Type: Public

### Income Statement

FYE: Last Saturday in January

| | REVENUE ($ mil.) | NET INCOME ($ mil.) | NET PROFIT MARGIN | EMPLOYEES |
|---|---|---|---|---|
| **1/07** | 17,405 | 738 | 4.2% | 125,000 |
| **1/06** | 16,058 | 690 | 4.3% | 119,000 |
| **1/05** | 14,914 | 664 | 4.5% | 113,000 |
| **1/04** | 13,328 | 658 | 4.9% | 105,000 |
| **1/03** | 11,981 | 578 | 4.8% | 94,000 |
| **Annual Growth** | 9.8% | 6.3% | — | 7.4% |

### 2007 Year-End Financials

Debt ratio: 35.3%
Return on equity: 35.3%
Cash ($ mil.): 857
Current ratio: 1.57
Long-term debt ($ mil.): 808
No. of shares (mil.): 454
Dividends
Yield: 0.9%
Payout: 17.4%
Market value ($ mil.): 13,383

### Stock History

NYSE: TJX

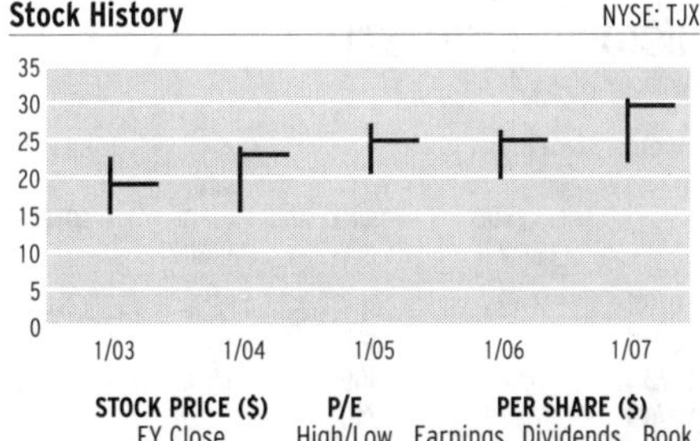


| | STOCK PRICE ($) FY Close | P/E High | P/E Low | PER SHARE ($) Earnings | PER SHARE ($) Dividends | PER SHARE ($) Book Value |
|---|---|---|---|---|---|---|
| **1/07** | 29.50 | 20 | 14 | 1.55 | 0.27 | 5.05 |
| **1/06** | 24.89 | 18 | 14 | 1.41 | 0.22 | 4.11 |
| **1/05** | 24.84 | 21 | 16 | 1.30 | 0.17 | 3.44 |
| **1/04** | 22.99 | 19 | 12 | 1.28 | 0.14 | 3.11 |
| **1/03** | 19.06 | 21 | 14 | 1.08 | 0.11 | 2.71 |
| **Annual Growth** | 11.5% | — | — | 9.5% | 25.2% | 16.9% |

# Toll Brothers

Do ask for whom the Tolls build: If you have money, the Tolls build for thee. Toll Brothers, a top US builder of luxury homes, builds for move-up, empty-nester, active-adult, and second-home buyer markets in suburban communities in 21 states. Its single-family detached homes average $688,000; attached homes average about $500,000. Toll Brothers develops active-adult communities (some with golf courses) and operates country club communities. Through subsidiaries, it offers insurance, home security, landscaping, cable TV and broadband Internet, and mortgage services. Brothers Robert (chairman) and Bruce Toll (vice chairman) own 17% and 7% of the company, respectively. Toll delivered nearly 8,600 homes in 2006.

Toll Brothers established subsidiary Advanced Broadband to build fiber-optic networks in its communities to provide digital cable TV and high-speed Internet access to its customers. Its apartment, office, and retail development operations are managed through Toll Brothers Realty Trust. The company offers financing and other services that include landscaping and lawn maintenance and security monitoring.

As part of its strategy to cater to every stage in its customers' lives, Toll Brothers creates planned communities for active adults over the age of 55; it has 10 such communities in operation. Some of its country club communities have Arnold Palmer Signature golf courses.

After a booming decade in which revenues grew more than 20% a year, Toll predicted things would likely slow in 2006. The company cut its 2006 earnings forecast and estimated that it would build fewer homes during the year due to softening demand, tighter building restrictions, and consumers antsy about energy prices and the economy. Toll had a backlog of some 6,500 homes at the end of its fiscal year 2006.

The company began using a percentage-of-completion accounting system in 2006 whereby revenues for projects requiring more than one year to complete (primarily high rises) are calculated based on the value of the work performed during the length of the construction period.

## HISTORY

Homebuilder Albert Toll's two sons, Robert and Bruce Toll, founded their own business in 1967. The duo began by building starter homes in the Philadelphia suburbs of Elkins Park and Yardley. As Philadelphia's population began to sprawl beyond these older suburban areas, the company grew, and in 1982 it moved beyond Pennsylvania to build houses in New Jersey. The young firm also began to distinguish itself by catering to upmarket customers.

Toll Brothers, Inc., went public in 1986 and later expanded around New York City, north to the Boston area, and south to the suburbs of Washington, DC. The firm survived the late 1980s real estate recession in the Northeast because, unlike many builders, it did not overextend itself.

Until the 1990s Toll Brothers operated primarily in the northeastern US, but it expanded as the housing market began an upward cycle. It entered California and North Carolina in 1994, and Arizona, Florida, and Texas in 1995. In 1997

Toll Brothers began work in Nashville, Tennessee, and Las Vegas. The next year the company entered the active adult market, building its first two age-qualified communities in New Jersey. Also in 1998 the company joined other investors, including the Pennsylvania State Employees Retirement System, and formed the Toll Brothers Realty Trust to acquire and develop commercial property.

In 1999 Toll Brothers acquired Silverman Companies, a leading homebuilder and developer of luxury apartments with more than 80 years of experience in Detroit. The company also began building homes in the Chicago, San Diego, and San Francisco markets that year, and it teamed with Marriott International to begin developing an assisted-living community in Reston, Virginia.

The company began operating in Rhode Island and New Hampshire in 2000, and the next year entered Colorado. In 2002 the company entered South Carolina in the Hilton Head area to develop Hampton Hall, a luxury country club community with a master-planned golf course.

In 2003 Toll Brothers acquired Jacksonville, Florida-based homebuilder Richard R. Dostie, Inc., and affiliates of the company for an undisclosed cash amount. The company also expanded its luxury urban in-fill market operations by acquiring The Manhattan Building Company, which develops luxury mid- and high-rise condos on northern New Jersey's waterfront. The next year Toll Brothers and Pinnacle Ltd. jointly began development of an 832-home luxury condominium community (Maxwell Place on the Hudson) on the waterfront of Hoboken, New Jersey, overlooking Manhattan.

For its 12th consecutive year, Toll Brothers produced record fiscal-year-end results for earnings, revenues, contracts, and backlog in 2004. The company's net income grew 57% over the previous year's earnings, and it operated in more communities and offered more product lines than it had in previous years. 2005 was another record year; revenue from home sales increased 50% and net income increased 97%. In 2005 Toll Brothers began operations in West Virginia.

## EXECUTIVES

**Chairman and CEO:** Robert I. Toll, age 66, $18,831,042 pay
**Vice Chairman:** Bruce E. Toll, age 63
**President, COO, and Director:** Zvi Barzilay, age 60, $2,520,000 pay
**EVP, CFO, Treasurer, and Director:** Joel H. Rassman, age 61, $2,520,000 pay
**SVP and Secretary:** Michael I. Snyder
**SVP, Finance/Investor Relations:** Frederick N. Cooper
**SVP Human Resources:** Jonathan C. Downs
**SVP and Chief Marketing Officer:** Kira McCarron
**SVP and Controller:** Kevin J. McMaster
**SVP and CIO:** George W. Nelson
**SVP and Chief Accounting Officer:** Joseph R. Sicree
**SVP, General Counsel, and Chief Compliance Officer:** Mark K. Kessler
**President, Toll Architecture:** Jed Gibson
**President, TBI Mortgage Company:** Donald L. Salmon
**President, Westminster Title Company:** William T. Unkel
**Regional President:** Thomas A. (Tom) Argyris Jr.
**Regional President:** James W. (Jim) Boyd
**Regional President:** Barry A. DePew
**Regional President:** Richard T. Hartman
**Regional President:** Edward D. (Ed) Weber
**Regional President:** Douglas C. (Doug) Yearley Jr.
**Auditors:** Ernst & Young LLP

## LOCATIONS

**HQ:** Toll Brothers, Inc.
250 Gibraltar Rd., Horsham, PA 19044
**Phone:** 215-938-8000 **Fax:** 215-938-8010
**Web:** www.tollbrothers.com

Toll Brothers operates in Arizona, California, Colorado, Connecticut, Delaware, Florida, Illinois, Maryland, Massachusetts, Michigan, Nevada, New Jersey, New York, North Carolina, Ohio, Pennsylvania, Rhode Island, South Carolina, Texas, Virginia, and West Virginia.

### 2006 Sales

| | $ mil. | % of total |
|---|---|---|
| Mid-Atlantic | 1,777.9 | 29 |
| West | 1,709.0 | 28 |
| North | 1,444.2 | 24 |
| South | 1,192.4 | 19 |
| **Total** | **6,123.5** | **100** |

### 2006 Homes Closed

| | No. units | % of total |
|---|---|---|
| Mid-Atlantic | 2,697 | 31 |
| South | 2,017 | 24 |
| North | 1,983 | 23 |
| West | 1,904 | 22 |
| **Total** | **8,601** | **100** |

## PRODUCTS/OPERATIONS

### 2006 Sales

| | $ mil. | % of total |
|---|---|---|
| Housing | | |
| Sales | 5,945.2 | 97 |
| Percentage of completion | 170.1 | 3 |
| Land sales | 8.2 | — |
| **Total** | **6,123.5** | **100** |

### Selected Operations

Architectural design services
Cable TV and broadband Internet access
Engineering services
House component assembly
Land development
Landscape services
Lumber distribution
Mortgage lending
Security monitoring
Title insurance

## COMPETITORS

Centex
David Weekley Homes
D.R. Horton
Hovnanian Enterprises
John Wieland Homes
KB Home
Larwin Company
Lennar
Morrison Homes
NVR
Orleans Homebuilders
Pulte Homes
Ryland
Shapell Industries
Standard Pacific
William Lyon Homes

## HISTORICAL FINANCIALS

Company Type: Public

### Income Statement

FYE: October 31

| | REVENUE ($ mil.) | NET INCOME ($ mil.) | NET PROFIT MARGIN | EMPLOYEES |
|---|---|---|---|---|
| **10/06** | 6,124 | 687 | 11.2% | 5,542 |
| **10/05** | 5,793 | 806 | 13.9% | 5,581 |
| **10/04** | 3,893 | 409 | 10.5% | 4,655 |
| **10/03** | 2,775 | 260 | 9.4% | 3,416 |
| **10/02** | 2,329 | 220 | 9.4% | 2,960 |
| **Annual Growth** | 27.3% | 33.0% | — | 17.0% |

### 2006 Year-End Financials

Debt ratio: 68.7%
Return on equity: 22.2%
Cash ($ mil.): 633
Current ratio: 3.90
Long-term debt ($ mil.): 2,348
No. of shares (mil.): 154
Dividends
Yield: —
Payout: —
Market value ($ mil.): 4,449

### Stock History

NYSE: TOL

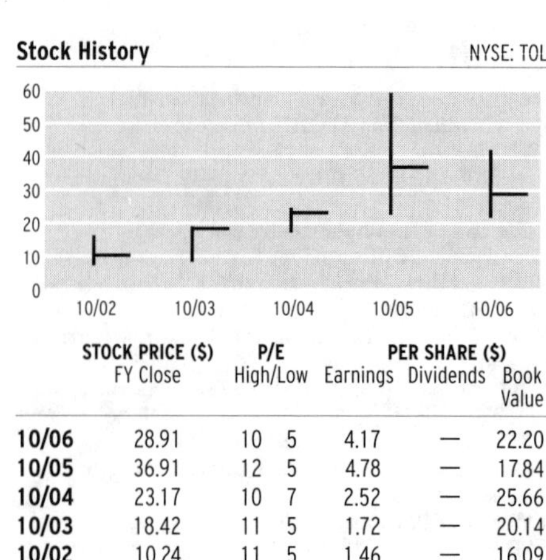


| | STOCK PRICE ($) FY Close | P/E High | P/E Low | PER SHARE ($) Earnings | PER SHARE ($) Dividends | PER SHARE ($) Book Value |
|---|---|---|---|---|---|---|
| **10/06** | 28.91 | 10 | 5 | 4.17 | — | 22.20 |
| **10/05** | 36.91 | 12 | 5 | 4.78 | — | 17.84 |
| **10/04** | 23.17 | 10 | 7 | 2.52 | — | 25.66 |
| **10/03** | 18.42 | 11 | 5 | 1.72 | — | 20.14 |
| **10/02** | 10.24 | 11 | 5 | 1.46 | — | 16.09 |
| **Annual Growth** | 29.6% | — | — | 30.0% | — | 8.4% |

# Torchmark Corporation

Despite winds of change, Torchmark's flame is still burning. Torchmark is the holding company for a family of firms; its member companies specialize in lower-end individual life insurance, supplemental health insurance, and annuities. Torchmark subsidiaries, which include flagship Liberty National Life, offer annuities, whole and term life insurance, health insurance, accidental death insurance, Medicare supplements, and long-term care health policies for the elderly. The company sells its products through direct marketing, as well as a network of exclusive and independent agents.

Targeting middle-income citizens, Liberty National Life operates primarily in the Southeast. Another subsidiary, American Income Life Insurance, targets group clients with sales of life and supplemental health coverage. A smaller subsidiary, Globe Life and Accident, (along with part of Liberty National Life) offers life insurance to active and retired military officers. The company is fighting stiff competition and declining demand for these products with vigorous sales efforts, particularly direct marketing. For several years Torchmark was involved in legal wrangling over race-based pricing, including burial policies sold at higher rates to African-Americans, but substantially all cases were settled as of mid-2006. During 2006 the company moved its headquarters from Birmingham, Alabama to McKinney, Texas, a suburb of Dallas, and home to its subsidiary United American Insurance.

## HISTORY

It began as a scam, plain and simple. In 1900 the Heralds of Liberty was founded as a fraternal organization — but its real reason for existence was to funnel money to its founders, according to Frank Samford, Torchmark's CEO from 1967 to 1985; Samford was also the great-grandson of the governor who signed the group's charter, and the son of the state insurance commissioner who oversaw the Heralds of Liberty's rehabilitation into a real insurance company.

The Heralds offered a joint life distribution plan, under which policyholders were divided by age; when a person died, his or her beneficiary was paid along with the holder of the lowest-numbered insurance certificate in the class (if they were paid at all; the Heralds were not scrupulous about that). Postal authorities called this plan a lottery and it was illegal in many states. But the Heralds' fraternal order status allowed it to circumvent Alabama insurance laws until 1921, when its infractions could no longer be ignored.

The organization operated under state supervision until 1929, when it was recapitalized as stock company Liberty National. By 1934, despite the Depression, the company was financially sound.

In 1944 Liberty National merged with funeral insurance company Brown-Service, whose large sales force began selling Liberty National's policies. The added sales helped the company grow and make acquisitions from the 1950s through the 1970s. Even after it discontinued funeral insurance, the company still paid out benefits. (As late as 1985, half of all Alabamans who died had the policies.)

Liberty National reorganized itself as a holding company in 1980 to accommodate the purchase of Globe Life And Accident. In 1981 it acquired Continental Investment Corp., which owned United Investors Life Insurance, Waddell & Reed (financial services), and United American Insurance. In 1982 the holding company became Torchmark. Throughout its growth spurt it refrained from offering high-yield financial products and thus escaped the worst effects of the economic disruptions of the late 1980s. Its 1990 acquisition of Family Service Life Insurance put it back in the funeral insurance business (it exited again in 1995 and sold the unit in 1998).

Sales in the 1990s were affected by a decline in cash-value life insurance and Medicare supplements. Slack sales forced the company to stop having agents collect premiums personally, and by 1996 all accounts were handled by mail.

In 1998 the company sought to sell its 28% stake in property insurer Vesta Insurance Group after that company became the target of numerous lawsuits. Torchmark was only able to reduce its stake to 24% on the open market, but in 2000 Vesta bought out Torchmark's holdings.

Torchmark was haunted in 2000 by its own version of the undead — burial policies. An investigation by Alabama regulators was sparked by a Florida court order forcing the company to stop collecting premiums on old burial policies for which African-Americans had been charged higher premiums. In 2001 and 2002, Torchmark was hit by another dozen lawsuits, including allegations of overcharging.

## EXECUTIVES

**Chairman and CEO:** Mark S. McAndrew, age 53, $820,833 pay
**EVP and Chief Administrative Officer:** Tony G. Brill, age 64, $620,048 pay
**EVP and CFO:** Gary L. Coleman, age 55, $700,000 pay
**EVP and General Counsel:** Larry M. Hutchison, age 53, $675,000 pay
**EVP and Chief Marketing Officer:** Glenn D. Williams, age 45
**VP and Treasurer:** Michael J. Klyce
**VP, Investor Relations:** Joyce L. Lane
**VP and Director of Tax:** Frank M. Svoboda
**VP and Chief Investment Officer:** W. Michael Pressley
**VP and Chief Accounting Officer:** Danny H. Almond, age 56
**VP and Director of Human Resources:** Arvelia Bowie
**Controller:** Spencer H. Stone
**CEO, Liberty National Life Insurance Company and United Investors Life Insurance Company:** Anthony L. McWhorter, age 57
**President and CEO, United American Insurance Company:** Vern D. Herbel, age 49
**President and CEO, American Income Life Insurance Company:** Roger C. Smith, age 54
**President and Chief Marketing Officer, Liberty National Life Insurance Company:** Andrew W. King, age 49
**President and CEO, Globe Life:** Charles F. Hudson, age 50
**Auditors:** Deloitte & Touche LLP

## LOCATIONS

**HQ:** Torchmark Corporation
3700 S. Stonebridge Dr., McKinney, TX 75070
**Phone:** 972-569-4000
**Web:** www.torchmarkcorp.com

Torchmark operates in Canada, New Zealand, and the US.

## PRODUCTS/OPERATIONS

### 2006 Sales

| | $ mil. | % of total |
|---|---|---|
| Premiums | | |
| Life | 1,524.3 | 45 |
| Health | 1,237.5 | 37 |
| Other | 23.0 | — |
| Net investment income | 628.7 | 18 |
| Realized investment losses | (10.7) | — |
| Other | 18.4 | — |
| **Total** | **3,421.2** | **100** |

### Selected Subsidiaries

American Income Life Insurance Company
First United American Life Insurance Company
Globe Life And Accident Insurance Company
Liberty National Life Insurance Company
United American Insurance Company
United Investors Life Insurance Company

## COMPETITORS

Aflac
Allstate
Aon
Citigroup
CNA Financial
GE Insurance Solutions
Gerber Life
Guardian Life
Lincoln Financial Group
MassMutual
MetLife
Monumental Life
Northwestern Mutual
Pacific Mutual
Penn Treaty
Prudential
State Farm
T. Rowe Price
Travelers Companies
United Insurance
Unum Group
USAA

## HISTORICAL FINANCIALS

Company Type: Public

### Income Statement

FYE: December 31

| | ASSETS ($ mil.) | NET INCOME ($ mil.) | INCOME AS % OF ASSETS | EMPLOYEES |
|---|---|---|---|---|
| 12/06 | 14,980 | 519 | 3.5% | 3,758 |
| 12/05 | 14,769 | 495 | 3.4% | 4,530 |
| 12/04 | 14,252 | 469 | 3.3% | 4,422 |
| 12/03 | 13,461 | 430 | 3.2% | 4,868 |
| 12/02 | 12,361 | 383 | 3.1% | 4,702 |
| Annual Growth | 4.9% | 7.8% | — | (5.4%) |

### 2006 Year-End Financials

Equity as % of assets: 23.1%
Return on assets: 3.5%
Return on equity: 15.0%
Long-term debt ($ mil.): 598
No. of shares (mil.): 98
Dividends
Yield: 0.8%
Payout: 9.4%
Market value ($ mil.): 6,256
Sales ($ mil.): 3,421

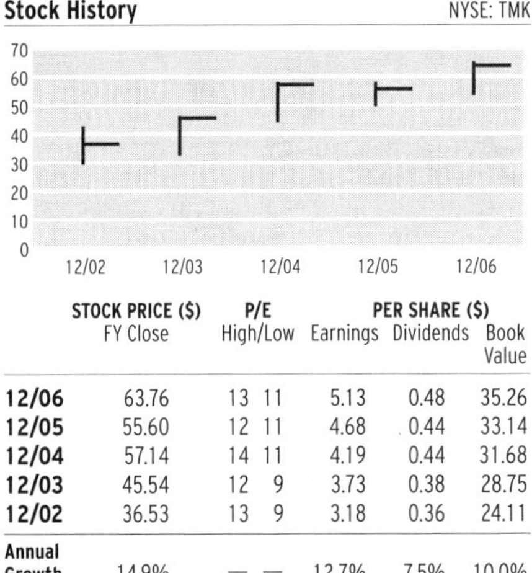


| | STOCK PRICE ($) FY Close | P/E High | P/E Low | PER SHARE ($) Earnings | Dividends | Book Value |
|---|---|---|---|---|---|---|
| 12/06 | 63.76 | 13 | 11 | 5.13 | 0.48 | 35.26 |
| 12/05 | 55.60 | 12 | 11 | 4.68 | 0.44 | 33.14 |
| 12/04 | 57.14 | 14 | 11 | 4.19 | 0.44 | 31.68 |
| 12/03 | 45.54 | 12 | 9 | 3.73 | 0.38 | 28.75 |
| 12/02 | 36.53 | 13 | 9 | 3.18 | 0.36 | 24.11 |
| Annual Growth | 14.9% | — | — | 12.7% | 7.5% | 10.0% |

# The Toro Company

Need to repair the 13th green after wild, rampaging bulls run through? Give The Toro Company a call. Toro makes lawn mowers and other products for professional and residential use. Toro's professional products include irrigation equipment, mowers for commercial use, riding and walk-behind power mowers for golf course fairways and greens, trimmers, and utility vehicles. Some professional brands are Toro, Rain Master, Exmark, Irritrol, and Dingo. Its residential products, sold to distributors, home centers, and mass retailers, include walk-behind and riding lawn mowers, lawn tractors, electrical trimmers, and snow blowers. Brand names in this sector include Toro, Rain Master, Irritrol, Lawn Genie, and Lawn-Boy.

The firm, a leader in its field, has long helped suburbanites save on elbow grease as the first company to offer electrically started lawn mowers. But its business goes beyond the home garden. Toro's professional products account for more than 60% of sales.

To expand the company's capabilities in the central controller market and increase its expertise in precision irrigation technology, Toro in August 2007 acquired Rain Master Irrigation Systems. A leader for some 25 years, Rain Master also boosts Toro's distribution network, with its established presence in the Western US. Toro plans to pair Rain Master-branded products with its existing Irritrol line and maintain the Rain Master name.

Although Toro's products are sold mostly through hardware retailers, home centers, and mass retailers in the US, they are also available in more than 90 other countries. Expanding its holdings outside the US, Toro acquired Hayter Limited, a UK manufacturer of consumer and commercial mowing products in 2005.

Michael Hoffman — promoted from group VP to president and COO in late 2004 — succeeded Ken Melrose as CEO in 2005. Hoffman added the chairman title when Melrose retired in March of that year.

## HISTORY

Toro — Spanish for "bull" — was founded in 1914 as The Toro Motor Company to make engines for The Bull Tractor Company. In 1921 Toro provided a tractor fitted with 30-inch lawn mower blades to replace a horse-drawn grass-cutting machine at a Minneapolis country club, and the modern power mower industry was born. By 1925 Toro turf maintenance machines were used on many of the US's major golf courses and parks, and by 1928 its products were used in Europe.

The company went public in 1935. Toro introduced its first walk-behind power mower for consumers four years later. In 1948 the company entered the rotary mower market when it bought Whirlwind. Toro started making snow removal equipment in 1951. With its 1962 purchase of Moist O' Matic, the company's offerings included automatic irrigation for golf courses.

It was renamed The Toro Company in 1971. Consumer sales of snow removal equipment began to pile up, but those sales melted away when little snow fell during the winters of 1980 and 1981, and Toro suffered immense losses.

Kendrick Melrose, a 13-year Toro veteran, became CEO in 1983. He cut staff, closed plants, and revamped the company's inventory system. During the 1980s Toro diversified, acquiring two lighting manufacturers, including Lunalite (1984). The company also established an outdoor electrical appliance division.

In 1986 Toro purchased lawn tractor manufacturer Wheel Horse, and it entered the mid-priced market with the acquisition of rival Lawn-Boy three years later. Toro kept the Lawn-Boy brand, trying to capitalize on its name recognition in mass-merchandise retail channels.

Sales fell during the recession of the early 1990s, causing another round of plant closures and layoffs. The company introduced its "environmentally friendly" bagless Toro Recycler mower (1990), entered the fertilizer market with its Toro BioPro line (1992), and formed a Recycling Equipment division (1994). Toro found success with such new products as cordless electric mowers in 1995.

Trying to insulate itself against weather-related downturns, the company bought a unit (now called Irritrol) from irrigation products maker James Hardie Industries (1996); professional landscaping equipment maker Exmark (1997); and Motorola's OSMAC irrigation unit (1997). Toro's other late-1990s acquisitions included the US rights of Dingo Digging Systems and micro-irrigation products maker Drip In (1998).

Despite the company's growing sales of commercial products, earnings plunged in 1998 in part because of declining consumer products sales (particularly snow blowers, thanks to uncooperative weather patterns), troubled sales in Asia, and restructuring costs.

Breaking with its policy to sell mainly through independent dealers, Toro opted to distribute its Toro-brand lawn mowers to selected home centers, adding nearly 1,500 distribution outlets in 1998. To mow down costs, in 1998 and 1999 it sold its Recycling Equipment business and fertilizer products business. Also in 1999 the company bought Multi-Core Aerators, a European distributor of large turf aeration equipment, and stopped making outdoor lighting products (but licensed the Toro name to Electa Industrial Company).

In 2000 the company acquired Sitework Systems (US sales representative of the Dingo compact utility loader) and completed the purchase of two distributors of turf maintenance and creation products. The next year Toro acquired Electronic Industrial Controls, which provides computer control systems for irrigation products.

Toro formed a financing unit with GE Capital in 2002 to help cities and golf courses buy irrigation systems and grounds maintenance equipment. Additionally that year Toro expanded facilities in Nebraska and Juarez, Mexico, where it also opened a plant for the production of walk-behind lawn mowers. During the same year Toro closed facilities in Evansville, Indiana, and Riverside, California.

Toro acquired R & D Engineering, which markets wireless rain and freeze switches for residential irrigation systems, in 2003.

## EXECUTIVES

**Chairman, President, and CEO:** Michael J. Hoffman, age 51, $1,097,720 pay (prior to title change)
**Group VP:** Dennis P. Himan, age 62
**VP, Finance, CFO, and Treasurer:** Stephen P. Wolfe, age 58, $559,456 pay
**VP, Operations:** Sandra J. Meurlot, age 58, $431,634 pay
**VP, Administration:** Karen M. Meyer, age 56, $509,829 pay
**VP, Business and Strategic Development:** Peter M. (Pete) Ramstad, age 49
**VP and CIO:** Michael D. Drazan, age 49
**VP, Toro Consumer and Landscape Contractor Business:** William E. (Bill) Brown Jr., age 45
**VP, Secretary, and General Counsel:** Timothy P. (Tim) Dordell, age 44
**President, MTI Distributing:** Thomas M. (Tom) Swain, age 52
**Managing Director and Corporate Controller:** Blake M. Grams, age 39
**Managing Director, Commercial Business:** Michael J. Happe, age 35
**Managing Director, Distributor Development:** Mike Anderson
**Managing Director, International Business:** Darren Redetzke, age 42
**Auditors:** KPMG LLP

## LOCATIONS

**HQ:** The Toro Company
8111 Lyndale Ave. South, Bloomington, MN 55420
**Phone:** 952-888-8801 **Fax:** 952-887-8258
**Web:** www.thetorocompany.com

### 2006 Sales

| | $ mil. | % of total |
|---|---|---|
| US | 1,340.0 | 73 |
| Other countries | 495.9 | 27 |
| **Total** | **1,835.9** | **100** |

## PRODUCTS/OPERATIONS

### 2006 Sales

| | $ mil. | % of total |
|---|---|---|
| Professional | 1,224.7 | 66 |
| Residential | 566.6 | 31 |
| Other | 44.6 | 3 |
| **Total** | **1,835.9** | **100** |

### 2006 Sales

| | $ mil. | % of total |
|---|---|---|
| Equipment | 1,462.1 | 79 |
| Irrigation | 373.8 | 21 |
| **Total** | **1,835.9** | **100** |

### Selected Products

Professional
- Agricultural irrigation
  - Aqua-TraXX irrigation tape
  - Blue Stripe polyethylene tubing
  - Drip In drip line
- Golf course
  - Bunker maintenance equipment
  - Turf aerators
  - Walking and riding mowers
- Landscape contractor
  - Backhoes
  - Compact utility loaders
  - Heavy-duty walk behind mowers
  - Trenchers
  - Zero-turning radius riding mowers
- Sports fields and grounds
  - Blowers
  - Multipurpose vehicles
  - Sweepers
  - Vacuums

Residential
- Home solutions
  - Electric blower-vacuums
  - Grass trimmers
- Riding products
  - Garden tractor models
  - Lawn tractor models
  - Zero-turning radius mowers
- Snow removal
  - Single-stage snow throwers
  - Two-stage snow throwers
- Walk power mowers
  - Bagging mowers
  - Mulching mowers
  - Side discharging mowers

## COMPETITORS

Alamo Group
Black & Decker
Deere
Emak Group
Honda
Kubota
LESCO
MTD Products
Tecumseh Products
Textron

## HISTORICAL FINANCIALS

Company Type: Public

### Income Statement

FYE: October 31

| | REVENUE ($ mil.) | NET INCOME ($ mil.) | NET PROFIT MARGIN | EMPLOYEES |
|---|---|---|---|---|
| **10/06** | 1,836 | 129 | 7.0% | 5,343 |
| **10/05** | 1,779 | 114 | 6.4% | 5,185 |
| **10/04** | 1,653 | 103 | 6.2% | 5,071 |
| **10/03** | 1,497 | 82 | 5.5% | 4,944 |
| **10/02** | 1,399 | 35 | 2.5% | 5,393 |
| **Annual Growth** | 7.0% | 38.3% | — | (0.2%) |

### 2006 Year-End Financials

Debt ratio: 44.6%
Return on equity: 33.0%
Cash ($ mil.): 56
Current ratio: 1.90
Long-term debt ($ mil.): 175

No. of shares (mil.): 40
Dividends
Yield: 0.8%
Payout: 12.4%
Market value ($ mil.): 1,742

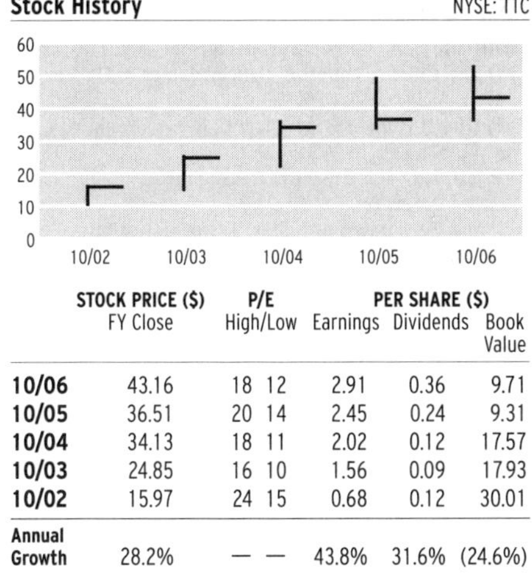

**Stock History** NYSE: TTC



| | STOCK PRICE ($) FY Close | P/E High/Low | | PER SHARE ($) Earnings | Dividends | Book Value |
|---|---|---|---|---|---|---|
| **10/06** | 43.16 | 18 | 12 | 2.91 | 0.36 | 9.71 |
| **10/05** | 36.51 | 20 | 14 | 2.45 | 0.24 | 9.31 |
| **10/04** | 34.13 | 18 | 11 | 2.02 | 0.12 | 17.57 |
| **10/03** | 24.85 | 16 | 10 | 1.56 | 0.09 | 17.93 |
| **10/02** | 15.97 | 24 | 15 | 0.68 | 0.12 | 30.01 |
| **Annual Growth** | 28.2% | — | — | 43.8% | 31.6% | (24.6%) |

# Total System Services

Credit card transaction denied? You may have Total System Services (TSYS) to thank — or to blame. TSYS, one of the largest credit card transaction processors in the US, serves bank and private-label card issuers around the world. Offerings include credit authorization, payment processing, account management, e-commerce services, card issuance, and such customer-relations services as call-center operations and fraud monitoring. Synovus Financial, through subsidiary Columbus Bank and Trust, owns more than 80% of TSYS (pronounced tee-sis).

TSYS has more than 400 million accounts on file. But the company took a hit when its largest customer, Bank of America, decided to process its own credit card accounts. (The bank accounted for about a quarter of TSYS' 2006 revenue.) To fill the void, TSYS has inked processing agreements with Capital One, Toronto-Dominion Bank, and Wachovia. It is also beefing up plans to look for new revenue sources, and to further expand overseas. The company's 2006 acquisition of what is now TSYS Card Tech gave TSYS a foothold in dozens of new countries. An alliance also put TSYS on the ground in China, where it has a 45% stake in China UnionPay Data Co. TSYS owns all of merchant transaction clearing and settlement firm TSYS Acquiring Solutions (formerly Vital Processing Services) after buying out Visa U.S.A.'s 50% stake in the firm in 2005. The unit changed its name to TSYS Acquiring Solutions the following year.

Other TSYS units market processing equipment and software, perform commercial printing services, and sell Internet payment processing software.

## HISTORY

Created in 1974 to handle the credit card operations of Columbus Bank and Trust (now a Synovus Financial subsidiary), TSYS was spun off in 1982 and went public in 1983. Its growth was spurred by increased credit card use, a growing tendency by banks to outsource data processing, and the company's ability to snag such big customers as NationsBank (later part of Bank of America) and AT&T Universal Card Services.

As the US credit card processing market matured, TSYS began looking to expand overseas — and taking other companies' business. Despite Mexico's economic downturn, in 1993 TSYS formed a joint venture with Mexican card processor PROSA; in 1995 it snagged part of BankAmerica's business. The following year TSYS upgraded its data-processing system to let its banking and retail customers tailor cards to their clients.

Alliances helped position TSYS as a one-stop support shop for banks. These included a joint venture with Visa International in 1996 that created Vital Processing Services, a merchant transaction processing and data services firm.

In 1998 TSYS agreed to process 60 million Sears credit card accounts. It was TSYS's biggest deal ever and one passed over by rival First Data. The pact helped compensate for the 1999 loss of major client Universal Card Services, which AT&T sold to Citicorp. Also in 1999 TSYS added call-center and other customer services to its offerings when it acquired Partnership Card services from Synovus.

In 2000 TSYS entered Europe and Japan in a big way. It inked a deal to process cards for The Royal Bank of Scotland Group (the UK's #2 card issuer). It also bought a majority stake in Japanese credit card issuer GP Network (leading Japanese card issuers also had a stake in the card processor).

## EXECUTIVES

**Chairman and CEO:** Philip W. (Phil) Tomlinson, age 60, $652,000 pay
**President, COO, and Director:** M. Troy Woods, age 55, $458,000 pay
**SEVP and CFO:** James B. (Jim) Lipham, age 58, $332,500 pay
**SEVP and Chief Client Officer:** William A. (Bill) Pruett, age 53, $396,000 pay
**SEVP and CIO:** Kenneth L. (Ken) Tye, age 54, $771,225 pay
**EVP, Product and Client Development:** Connie C. Dudley
**EVP and CTO:** Stephen W. (Steve) Humber
**EVP Sales, Strategy, and Emerging Markets:** Gaylon M. Jowers Jr.
**EVP, Customer Care Divisions:** Colleen W. Kynard
**General Counsel and Secretary:** G. Sanders Griffith III, age 53
**EVP Administrative Services:** Ryland L. Harrelson
**EVP, Chief Accounting Officer, and Controller:** Dorenda K. Weaver
**Chief Marketing and Sales Officer:** Bruce L. Bacon
**Investor Relations Manager:** Leo S. Berard
**Media Relations Manager:** Eric S. Bruner
**Auditors:** KPMG LLP

## LOCATIONS

**HQ:** Total System Services, Inc.
1600 1st Ave., Columbus, GA 31901
**Phone:** 706-649-2310 **Fax:** 706-644-8065
**Web:** www.tsys.com

**2006 Sales**

| | $ mil. | % of total |
|---|---|---|
| US | 1,482.1 | 83 |
| Europe | 158.8 | 9 |
| Canada | 102.0 | 5 |
| Japan | 18.6 | 1 |
| Mexico | 12.3 | 1 |
| Other regions | 13.4 | 1 |
| **Total** | **1,787.2** | **100** |

## PRODUCTS/OPERATIONS

**2006 Sales**

| | $ mil. | % of total |
|---|---|---|
| Electronic payment processing services | 989.1 | 55 |
| Reimbursable items | 352.7 | 20 |
| Merchant aquiring services | 260.3 | 15 |
| Other services | 185.1 | 10 |
| **Total** | **1,787.2** | **100** |

**Selected Subsidiaries**

China Unionpay Data Services Company Limited (45%, China)
Columbus Depot Equipment Company
Enhancement Services Corporation
ProCard, Inc.

## COMPETITORS

BA Merchant Services
BISYS
Chase Paymentech Solutions
ECHO, Inc.
Equifax
First Data
Fiserv
MasterCard
National City
NOVA

## HISTORICAL FINANCIALS

Company Type: Public

**Income Statement** FYE: December 31

| | REVENUE ($ mil.) | NET INCOME ($ mil.) | NET PROFIT MARGIN | EMPLOYEES |
|---|---|---|---|---|
| **12/06** | 1,787 | 249 | 13.9% | 6,644 |
| **12/05** | 1,603 | 195 | 12.1% | 6,603 |
| **12/04** | 1,187 | 151 | 12.7% | 5,622 |
| **12/03** | 1,054 | 141 | 13.4% | 5,185 |
| **12/02** | 955 | 126 | 13.2% | 5,121 |
| **Annual Growth** | 17.0% | 18.6% | — | 6.7% |

**2006 Year-End Financials**

Debt ratio: 0.3%
Return on equity: 22.3%
Cash ($ mil.): 421
Current ratio: 2.52
Long-term debt ($ mil.): 4
No. of shares (mil.): 197
Dividends
Yield: 1.0%
Payout: 21.4%
Market value ($ mil.): 5,209

**Stock History** NYSE: TSS

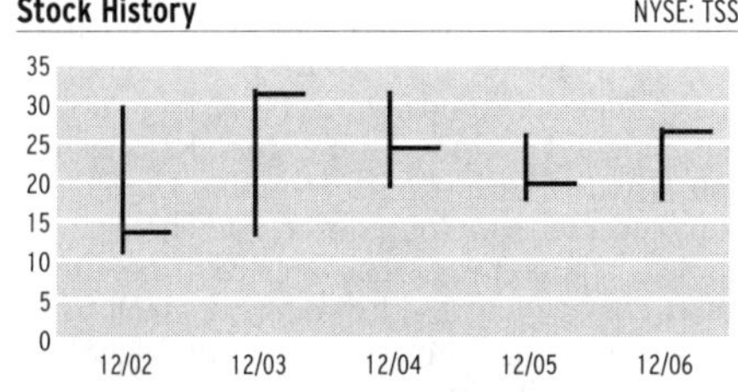



| | STOCK PRICE ($) FY Close | P/E High/Low | | PER SHARE ($) Earnings | Dividends | Book Value |
|---|---|---|---|---|---|---|
| **12/06** | 26.39 | 21 | 14 | 1.26 | 0.27 | 6.17 |
| **12/05** | 19.79 | 26 | 18 | 0.99 | 0.22 | 5.13 |
| **12/04** | 24.30 | 41 | 26 | 0.76 | 0.14 | 4.39 |
| **12/03** | 31.13 | 44 | 19 | 0.71 | 0.08 | 3.72 |
| **12/02** | 13.50 | 46 | 17 | 0.64 | 0.07 | 3.06 |
| **Annual Growth** | 18.2% | — | — | 18.5% | 40.1% | 19.2% |

# Tower Automotive

Automakers do a lot of leaning on Tower Automotive for their metal stampings and engineered assemblies. Tower's products include body structures and assemblies (body pillars, roof rails); lower vehicle frames and structures (pickup and SUV full frame assemblies); complex body-in-white assemblies (front and rear floor pan assemblies); chassis modules (axle assemblies); and suspension components (control arms, spring and shock towers). Tower Automotive's largest customers include Ford Motor (30% of sales), General Motors (13%), and Daimler and Chrysler (11%). Struggling financially, Tower filed for Chapter 11 bankruptcy protection in 2005; it emerged from Chapter 11 in 2007.

The company's other customers include BMW, Honda Motor Co., Nissan Motor Co., and Toyota Motor Corporation.

Between 2001 and 2005 Tower was riding high with a big backlog of fresh business. During this time the company reorganized its North American operations to tighten capacity and reduce costs. But events conspired to undermine Tower's efforts. Starting in 2004 rising steel prices, production cuts among key customers, and high costs associated with program launches created a liquidity crisis leading to the bankruptcy filing in 2005.

The company has gotten a tighter reign on costs and has its eye on incremental organic growth. Tower is also capturing more business from outside Detroit, which takes advantage of the company's substantial global footprint.

In 2007 private equity group Cerberus Capital Management bought the company.

## HISTORY

Tower Automotive resulted when Samuel Tower realized he was a bad farmer. The Greenville, Michigan, native decided to buy a small machine shop in 1874. He renamed it the Tower Brothers Machine Co. and found steady business from farmers who brought in metal tools to be repaired. Samuel's son Ray joined the company and helped bring in business from the local logging industry.

By 1900 the company was designing sawmill equipment, trimmers, and edgers. Ray began a foundry that turned out everything from manhole covers to soda fountain equipment and card tables. The company became R.J. Tower Iron Works before Ray decided to form a small truck business. Samuel Tower died in 1927. By that time Ray's son Francis had joined the company. With the Depression on the horizon, Francis began supplying metal legs to local refrigerator plants. This business grew to include other refrigerator parts, electric ranges, and air conditioners. The seasonal refrigerator market forced Francis to look to the auto industry.

After WWII, Francis' son Ray took over. By 1955 the company had grown to 60 employees. In 1972 the company changed names again, to R.J. Tower Corporation. After four generations of Tower leadership, none of Ray's six children wanted the job when he stepped down in 1983. He sold the company to three former employees.

In 1993 Tower Automotive was formed to buy the R.J. Tower Corporation. Dugald Campbell was brought in as president and CEO. The company began an aggressive campaign of expansion and growth. It greeted 1994 with 400 employees and sales of $83 million. By midyear it had acquired Edgewood Tool and Manufacturing and Kalamazoo Stamping and Die (structural stamping and assembly), giving it capabilities for making such items as hood and deck lid hinges. Tower Automotive went public that year and recorded sales of $222 million. By year's end it employed 1,600 people.

Tower Automotive continued to grow in 1995. It was awarded 14 new platforms to launch through the year 2000. The fledgling company also established a technical center in Farmington Hills, Michigan, and entered a strategic alliance with the Kirchoff Group, a German auto parts supplier, to share marketing and manufacturing services with each company's OEMs. The following year Tower Automotive bought Trylon Corporation (small precision metal stampings and assemblies) and MascoTech Stamping Technologies (chassis and suspension parts).

Acquisitions continued in 1997 with the addition of A.O. Smith Corporation's Automotive Products Company, which expanded Tower Automotive's scope in supplying lower-body structures for automakers. The company made its first non-US acquisition that year when it bought Italy's Societa Industria Meccanica e Stampaggio, increasing its prospects in southern Europe. A 40% partnership with Metalsa, Mexico's leading supplier of auto frames and structures, furthered the company's global positioning.

In 1998 the company sold its hinge-making business to Dura Automotive Systems. The following year, Tower Automotive bought Active Tool & Manufacturing, a maker of large structural assemblies for the auto industry.

The company boosted its presence in Europe with the 2000 purchase of Germany-based Dr. Meleghy, a maker of structural automotive components for that region's auto industry. Later in the year Tower took complete control of Metalurgica Caterina S.A. by buying the remaining 60% it didn't already own, and the company bought a 17% stake in Japanese auto parts maker Yorozu Corp. from Nissan. Tower also agreed to sell its heavy truck rail manufacturing business to joint venture partner Metalsa for $55 million.

In the spring of 2001 Tower Automotive reported a decline in first quarter revenues due to slower sales of Ford Explorers, which in turn were caused by the Firestone Tire recalls. That same year, the company bought an additional 14% stake in Yorozu Corp. increasing its stake to 31%. The next year Tower Automotive decided not to supply the next generation Ford Explorer frame due to the lack of profits.

Tower Automotive gained a new president and CEO in 2003. Upon Campbell's retirement, former Ford VP Kathleen Ligocki was appointed to the position. In early 2004, the company sold its 31% stake in Yoruzu Corp. back to Yoruzu through a share buy-back transaction for about $52 million.

With the company's sale to Cerberus Capital Management in mid-2007, Kathleen Ligocki was succeeded as president and CEO by Mark Malcolm, a consultant to the buyout firm. Malcolm previously spent 28 years with Ford, most recently serving as EVP and controller of Ford Motor Credit.

## EXECUTIVES

**Chairman:** S. A. (Tony) Johnson, age 66
**CFO and Chief Accounting Officer:** James A. Mallak, age 51, $534,056 pay
**SVP, Global Human Resources:** E. Renee Franklin, age 41, $296,667 pay
**SVP, Strategy and Business Development:** Kathy J. Johnston, age 49
**SVP and Corporate Controller:** Jeffrey L. Kersten, age 39
**SVP, Global Purchasing:** Paul Radkoski, age 47
**President, Europe and South America:** Vincent Pairet, age 44
**President, North American Operations:** D. William (Bill) Pumphrey, age 47, $545,067 pay
**President, Asia:** Gyula Meleghy, age 51, $493,344 pay
**President and CEO:** Mark Malcolm, age 48
**CIO:** Orrie Jones
**Auditors:** Deloitte & Touche LLP

## LOCATIONS

**HQ:** Tower Automotive, LLC
27175 Haggerty Rd., Novi, MI 48377
**Phone:** 248-675-6000 **Fax:** 248-675-6200
**Web:** www.towerautomotive.com

Tower Automotive has manufacturing operations in Illinois, Indiana, Kentucky, Maryland, Michigan, Mississippi, Ohio, and Tennessee, and in Belgium, Brazil, Canada, China, Germany, India, Italy, Japan, Poland, Slovakia, and South Korea.

### 2006 Sales

| | $ mil. | % of total |
|---|---|---|
| North America | 1,171.5 | 46 |
| Europe | 806.4 | 32 |
| Asia | 443.4 | 17 |
| Mexico & South America | 118.1 | 5 |
| **Total** | **2,539.4** | **100** |

## PRODUCTS/OPERATIONS

### 2006 Sales

| | $ mil. | % of total |
|---|---|---|
| Body structures & assemblies | 1,498.8 | 59 |
| Lower vehicle frames & structures | 513.5 | 20 |
| Complex body-in-white assemblies | 323.0 | 13 |
| Suspension components | 130.7 | 5 |
| Chassis modules & systems | 41.5 | 2 |
| Other | 31.9 | 1 |
| **Total** | **2,539.4** | **100** |

### 2006 Sales

| | % of total |
|---|---|
| Ford | 28 |
| Hyundai/Kia | 13 |
| Renault/Nissan | 11 |
| DaimlerChrysler | 10 |
| Volkswagen | 9 |
| Fiat | 6 |
| Toyota | 6 |
| BMW | 4 |
| General Motors | 3 |
| Honda | 2 |
| Other | 8 |
| **Total** | **100** |

### Products

Body Structures and Assemblies
- Body pillars
- Heavy-truck frame rails
- Intrusion beams
- Light-truck frames
- Parcel shelves
- Roof rails
- Side sills

Lower Vehicle Frames and Structures
- Automotive engine cradles
- Cross members
- Floor pan components
- Pickup truck and SUV full frames

Chassis Modules and Systems
- Axle assemblies
- Front and rear structural suspension modules/systems

Complex Body-in-White Assemblies
Door/pillar assemblies
Front and rear floor pan assemblies

Suspension Components
Control arms
Spring/shock towers
Suspension links
Track bars
Trailing axles

Other Products
Heat shields
Precision stampings

## COMPETITORS

A.G. Simpson
American Axle
ArvinMeritor
Boler
Dana
GRUPO KUO
Magna International
Midway Products
ThyssenKrupp Budd
Visteon

## HISTORICAL FINANCIALS

Company Type: Private

**Income Statement** FYE: December 31

| | REVENUE ($ mil.) | NET INCOME ($ mil.) | NET PROFIT MARGIN | EMPLOYEES |
|---|---|---|---|---|
| **12/06** | 2,539 | (202) | — | 10,477 |
| **12/05** | 3,284 | (373) | — | — |
| **12/04** | 3,179 | (534) | — | — |
| **12/03** | 2,816 | (125) | — | 12,000 |
| **12/02** | 2,755 | (98) | — | 12,000 |
| **Annual Growth** | (2.0%) | — | — | (3.3%) |

**2006 Year-End Financials**

Debt ratio: —
Return on equity: —
Cash ($ mil.): 64
Current ratio: 0.52
Long-term debt ($ mil.): 163

**Net Income History**

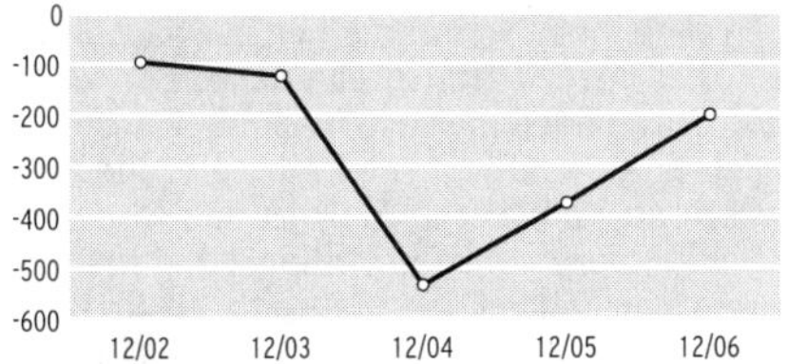


# Trans World Entertainment

F.Y.I., Trans World Entertainment operates solely F.Y.E. Trans World's ownership of the F.Y.E. (For Your Entertainment) chain keeps it on top of the US music retailer hierarchy. The firm sells CDs, DVDs, cassettes, videos, video games, and related electronics and accessories at about 1,000 stores (the vast majority of them in malls) throughout the US and its territories. Its other chains include CD World, Coconuts Music & Movies, Strawberries, Sam Goody, On Cue, Planet Music, Spec's Music, and Wherehouse Music and Movies. The company sells videos through Suncoast and Saturday Matinee stores. Trans World's retail brands also have a significant e-commerce presence.

About three-quarters of Trans World's stores operate under some form of the F.Y.E. brand including mall-based F.Y.E.s (averaging 5,600 sq. ft.), Super F.Y.E.s (24,000 sq. ft.), and mall-based F.Y.E. Movie stores. Previously, Trans World's mall stores operated under several different names, and the consolidation allowed Trans World to better leverage its marketing power and customer base. (The company's freestanding stores continue to operate under their existing names.)

In cyberspace, Trans World offers merchandise online through sites including fye.com, suncoast.com, and wherehouse.com. The company also owns SecondSpin.com, a buyer and seller of used CDs, videos, and DVDs both online and through a handful of retail stores in California and Colorado.

In March 2006, the company acquired most of the assets of bankrupt competitor The Musicland Group, which operated stores under the Sam Goody and Suncoast banners. Under the terms of its $122 million purchase price, Trans World acquired 345 of Musicland's 400-remaining stores and worked with a third party to liquidate the rest.

Founder Bob Higgins and his family own about 40% of Trans World Entertainment.

## HISTORY

Bob Higgins founded wholesaler Trans World Music with $30,000 in 1972. He opened his first store in New York the following year, and in 1982 he sold the wholesale business to focus on retail. Higgins had more than 60 stores (mostly in New York) by 1984. By 1986 he had about 160 stores operating mostly under the names Record Town, Tape World, and Peaches in 20 eastern, southeastern, and midwestern states.

Higgins took his company public that year to fund further expansion. By 1989 acquisitions and internal growth gave the firm more than 430 stores (including the Coconuts chain) in 30 states. An attempt in the late 1980s to sell inside other stores proved unsuccessful. Trans World rented space in about 40 Crazy Eddie electronics stores, but that firm infamously went bust.

In the early 1990s the music industry was strong, and the company had almost 600 stores. Its 1994 name change to Trans World Entertainment reflected its expansion to non-music merchandise (videos, games, books). But the record industry slumped in the mid-1990s, and the company lost money in fiscal 1995 and 1996: Trans World was forced to face the music.

Restructuring brought back the sweet strains of success. Although Trans World closed nearly 350 stores between 1994 and 1997, it also added new locations, including 90 from its 1997 purchase of Massachusetts music retailer Strawberries. It posted record earnings in fiscal 1998. Also that year Higgins added nearly 60 new stores and established a retail Web site featuring online musician chats.

Trans World bought Camelot Music Holdings, a mall-based chain of about 500 music stores, for about $432 million in 1999. Camelot had been founded in 1956 by Paul David. Business boomed during the 1980s, and by the time David sold the company to Bahrain-based investment group Investcorp in 1993, the North Canton, Ohio-based retailer had 365 stores and $421 million in sales. Hammered by competition, Camelot entered Chapter 11 bankruptcy protection less than three years later. The company closed about 90 stores, emerged from bankruptcy in early 1998, and promptly bought music and movie chains The Wall and Spec's Music.

The Camelot deal doubled Trans World's store count and boosted its presence in the Midwest and Florida. Also in 1999 Trans World formed an agreement with Digital On-Demand that allows customers in Trans World stores to download music not in stock at those locations.

In October 2000 the company acquired mall-based Disc Jockey, a US record and video store chain with about 110 stores in the South and Midwest. During 2001 Trans World rebranded its mall-based stores and its e-commerce site under a single, unified brand, F.Y.E (For Your Entertainment). The company's Web site was relaunched as fye.com in October 2001.

As part of the September 2002 settlement of a CD price-fixing case, Trans World Entertainment is one of three music retailers and five recording companies that agreed to pay more than $67 million to compensate consumers. The companies distributed more than $75 million worth of CDs to US public entities and nonprofits.

As a way of addressing the growing digital music distribution market, Trans World helped found Echo; a joint venture started in January 2003 by Best Buy, Tower Records (MTS), Virgin Entertainment (a part of Virgin Group), and Wherehouse Music. The consortium's goal is to devise a technology and licensing platform for the delivery of digital music to its retail members.

In 2003 the company bought Wherehouse Entertainment and its 111 stores for $35 million; CD World's 13 stores for $2 million; and, the next year, the 29% of Second Spin it didn't already own for $2 million. TransWorld acquired a vast number of stores (about 345) in 2006 when it bought bankrupt rival The Musicland Group for $122 million.

## EXECUTIVES

**Chairman, President, and CEO:** Robert J. Higgins, age 66, $1,274,038 pay
**President and COO:** James A. Litwak, age 53, $458,654 pay
**EVP, CFO, and Secretary:** John J. Sullivan, age 54, $359,327 pay
**EVP Real Estate:** Bruce J. Eisenberg, age 47, $359,327 pay
**Divisional Merchandise Manager, Music:** Jerry Kamiler
**Auditors:** KPMG LLP

## LOCATIONS

**HQ:** Trans World Entertainment Corporation
38 Corporate Circle, Albany, NY 12203
**Phone:** 518-452-1242 **Fax:** 518-862-9519
**Web:** www.twec.com

Trans World Entertainment has stores throughout the US, including the District of Columbia, Puerto Rico, and the US Virgin Islands.

## PRODUCTS/OPERATIONS

**2007 Sales**

| | $ mil. | % of total |
|---|---|---|
| Music | 650.4 | 44 |
| Video | 552.7 | 38 |
| Video games | 114.5 | 8 |
| Other | 153.5 | 10 |
| **Total** | **1,471.1** | **100** |

**Store Formats**

CD World (free standing stores located in New Jersey and Missouri)
Coconuts (freestanding stores)
F.Y.E. (For Your Entertainment; mall-based stores selling music, videos, games, portable electronics, accessories, and game arcades)
Planet Music (freestanding superstore located in Virginia)
Sam Goody (mall-based music stores)
Saturday Matinee (mall-based stores selling videos)
Spec's Music (freestanding and mall-based stores)
Strawberries (freestanding stores)
Suncoast (mall-based video stores)
Wherehouse Music (freestanding stores)

## COMPETITORS

Amazon.com
Barnes & Noble
Best Buy
Blockbuster
Borders
CD Warehouse
CDNOW
Circuit City
Columbia House
Hastings Entertainment
Kmart
Movie Gallery
Target
Tower Records
Virgin Group
Wal-Mart

## HISTORICAL FINANCIALS

Company Type: Public

**Income Statement** FYE: Saturday nearest January 31

| | REVENUE ($ mil.) | NET INCOME ($ mil.) | NET PROFIT MARGIN | EMPLOYEES |
|---|---|---|---|---|
| **1/07** | 1,471 | 12 | 0.8% | 9,600 |
| **1/06** | 1,239 | 1 | 0.0% | 8,100 |
| **1/05** | 1,365 | 42 | 3.1% | 7,400 |
| **1/04** | 1,331 | 23 | 1.7% | 8,200 |
| **1/03** | 1,282 | (46) | — | 8,700 |
| **Annual Growth** | 3.5% | — | — | 2.5% |

**2007 Year-End Financials**

Debt ratio: 4.1%
Return on equity: 3.0%
Cash ($ mil.): 119
Current ratio: 1.70
Long-term debt ($ mil.): 16
No. of shares (mil.): 31
Dividends
Yield: —
Payout: —
Market value ($ mil.): 179

**Stock History** NASDAQ (GM): TWMC

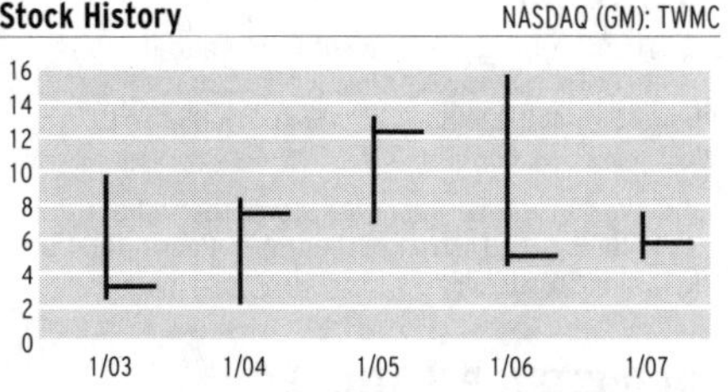

| | STOCK PRICE ($) FY Close | P/E High/Low | | PER SHARE ($) Earnings | Dividends | Book Value |
|---|---|---|---|---|---|---|
| **1/07** | 5.79 | 21 | 14 | 0.36 | — | 12.73 |
| **1/06** | 5.02 | 775 | 228 | 0.02 | — | 12.36 |
| **1/05** | 12.28 | 11 | 6 | 1.15 | — | 12.24 |
| **1/04** | 7.50 | 14 | 4 | 0.60 | — | 11.06 |
| **1/03** | 3.19 | — | — | (1.13) | — | 10.07 |
| **Annual Growth** | 16.1% | — | — | — | — | 6.0% |

# Transocean Inc.

Like an NFL tight end, offshore drilling contractor Transocean dreams of going deep but doesn't mind eating a little mud. Transocean specializes in deepwater drilling and it isn't afraid of harsh environments. The company operates in the world's major offshore oil-producing regions, including Africa, Asia, Brazil, Canada, India, the Middle East, the Gulf of Mexico, and the North Sea. It has a fleet of 82 mobile offshore drilling units, inland barges, and support vessels, including semisubmersibles and drillships, jackup rigs, and other rigs. Transocean's other operations include management of third-party drilling services. In 2007 it announced plans to buy rival GlobalSantaFe for almost $18 billion.

As oil majors continue to drill in deeper waters, Transocean has new rigs and is adding upgrades to existing ones to keep up with demand. Its three new *Discoverer* ultra-deepwater drillships, as well as its Deepwater Horizon semisubmersible, are able to reach depths of 10,000 feet. Transocean's major customers include BP and Chevron.

Already a solid player in the industry, the former Transocean Offshore stepped into a bigger league in 1999 when it merged with Sedco Forex immediately after the unit was spun off from Schlumberger. It has bulked up even more with the acquisition of fellow industry heavyweight R&B Falcon. In 2004 the company spun off TODCO, a Gulf of Mexico shallow- and inland-water business segment it acquired in the R&B Falcon deal; Transocean still owns about 20% of TODCO, with plans to sell the rest.

In 2006 Transocean secured a $862 million contract to build a drillship for Chevron. In early 2007 Chevron also awarded the company's semisubmersible rig, the *Transocean Richardson*, a three-year contract for exploration and appraisal drilling offshore.

## HISTORY

Transocean's predecessors include Forex, SEDCO, and The Offshore Company. Forex was founded in France in 1942 to perform land drilling in France, North Africa, and the Middle East. Oil services firm Schlumberger bought 50% of the firm in 1959. In 1964 Forex and Languedocienne created offshore drilling venture Neptune. By the time Schlumberger bought the rest of Forex in 1972, Forex had absorbed Neptune's operations.

Originally named Southeastern Drilling, SEDCO was created in 1947 by Bill Clements (later a Texas governor) to drill in shallow marsh waters in the US; it pushed into deeper waters in the 1960s. SEDCO received bad publicity in 1979 when a rig it leased to PEMEX exploded off Mexico's coast, causing the worst oil spill in history at the time. Schlumberger bought SEDCO in 1984 and combined it with Forex to form Sedco Forex Drilling in 1985.

In 1953 pipeline firm Southern Natural Gas Co. (SNG) acquired DeLong-McDermott, a contract drilling joint venture formed by DeLong Engineering and marine construction firm J. Ray McDermott. The new firm was called The Offshore Company. (McDermott sold its stake in Offshore when it began to compete with McDermott's own operations.)

Offshore pioneered the use of jackup rigs in the Gulf of Mexico during the 1950s. It also introduced a patented system that allowed a drilling barge to be lowered and elevated for relocation. By 1963 Offshore was one of the first drillers operating in the North Sea, and it went public in 1967.

During the 1970s SNG (incorporated as Southern Natural Industries in 1973) expanded its offshore drilling and exploration business. Offshore drilled its first deepwater well, off Southeast Asia, in 1976. Two years later Offshore became a wholly owned subsidiary of SNG. By the 1980s Offshore had one of the largest offshore drilling fleets in the US.

SNG's name was changed to Sonat in 1982, and Offshore became Sonat Offshore Drilling. That year it began building the industry's first fourth-generation semisubmersible rig. The company had 24 rigs by 1984 and set a deepwater record in 1987 by drilling more than 7,500 feet.

In the mid-1980s the oil industry lost speed, and Sonat focused on its gas operations. After two years of losses, Sonat Offshore was again profitable in 1990. However, its parent decided to spin off Sonat Offshore in 1993, retaining a 40% stake. (Sonat sold this stake in 1995.)

The oil industry began to recover in 1994. Two years later Sonat Offshore set another deepwater record by drilling at more than 7,600 feet and began building a drillship that could work at depths of 10,000 feet. Late that year it acquired Norwegian firm Transocean and became Transocean Offshore.

The new company's first year was filled with problems, including a fire on a semisubmersible conversion project (*Transocean Marianas*) and a strike by Norwegian offshore workers. But the firm won contracts from Chevron and Unocal for two new ultra-deepwater drillships. In 1999 Transocean Offshore merged with Sedco Forex, which had been spun off by Schlumberger, in a $3.2 billion deal that formed Transocean Sedco Forex.

As part of its merger, in 2000 Transocean Sedco Forex sold its coiled tubing drilling services unit, Transocean Petroleum Technology, to Schlumberger for $25 million. Later that year Transocean Sedco Forex agreed to buy R&B Falcon in an $8.8 billion deal that included the assumption of $3 billion in debt; the transaction closed in 2001.

The company also announced plans in 2001 to dispose of its turnkey operations and its Venezuelan land and barge drilling business to focus on its core activities, but subsequently backed away from that plan.

In 2002 Transocean Sedco Forex changed its corporate name to Transocean Inc. Later that year Michael Talbert replaced Victor Grijalva as chairman and Robert Long was appointed president and CEO of the company.

In 2003 Transocean acquired the remaining 50% stake in the Deepwater Pathfinder drillship from ConocoPhillips, the former joint venture partner of the vessel.

## EXECUTIVES

**CEO and Director:** Robert L. Long, age 61, $850,000 pay
**President:** Jean P. Cahuzac, age 53, $515,000 pay
**EVP and COO:** Steven L. Newman, age 42, $315,000 pay
**SVP and CFO:** Gregory L. Cauthen, age 49, $385,000 pay
**SVP, General Counsel, and Corporate Secretary:** Eric B. Brown, age 55, $365,000 pay
**SVP, Marketing and Planning:** David J. Mullen, age 49
**SVP, North and South America Unit:** Robert J. (Rob) Saltiel

**VP and Controller:** David Tonnel, age 37
**VP and CIO:** Barbara S. Wood
**VP, Quality, Health, Safety, and Environment:** Adrian P. Rose
**VP, Europe and Africa Unit:** Arnaud A. Y. Bobillier, age 61
**VP, Investor Relations and Communications:** Gregory S. (Greg) Panagos
**VP, Audit and Advisory Services:** John H. Briscoe
**Auditors:** Ernst & Young LLP

## LOCATIONS

**HQ:** Transocean Inc.
4 Greenway Plaza, Houston, TX 77046
**Phone:** 713-232-7500 **Fax:** 713-232-7027
**Web:** www.deepwater.com

Transocean operates in major offshore oil-producing regions worldwide through offices located in Africa, Asia, the Caribbean, Europe, the Middle East, North America, and South America.

### 2006 Sales

| | $ mil. | % of total |
|---|---|---|
| US | 806 | 21 |
| UK | 462 | 12 |
| Nigeria | 447 | 11 |
| India | 313 | 8 |
| Brazil | 308 | 8 |
| Other countries | 1,546 | 40 |
| **Total** | **3,882** | **100** |

## PRODUCTS/OPERATIONS

### Selected Subsidiaries

Caspian Sea Ventures International Ltd. (British Virgin Islands)
Hellerup Finance International Ltd. (Ireland)
International Chandlers, Inc.
PT Hitek Nusantara Offshore Drilling (80%, Indonesia)
R&B Falcon Drilling Co.
R&B Falcon Offshore Limited, LLC
R&B Falcon (UK) Ltd.
SDS Offshore Ltd. (UK)
Sedco Forex Corporation
Sedco Forex International, Inc. (Panama)
Sedco Forex Technical Services, Inc. (Panama)
Sonat Offshore S.A. (Panama)
Target Drilling Services Ltd. (UK)
Transhav AS (Norway)
Transnor Rig Ltd. (UK)
Transocean Alaskan Ventures Inc.
Transocean Brasil Ltda.
Transocean Drilling (U.S.A.) Inc. (formerly Wilrig (U.S.A.) Inc.)
Transocean Services AS (Norway)
Transocean Sino Ltd. (UK)
Triton Holdings Limited (British Virgin Islands)
Triton Industries, Inc. (Panama)

## COMPETITORS

Atwood Oceanics
Diamond Offshore
ENSCO
GlobalSantaFe
Helmerich & Payne
John Wood Group
Nabors Well Services
Noble
Parker Drilling
Pride International
Rowan
Saipem

## HISTORICAL FINANCIALS

Company Type: Public

### Income Statement

FYE: December 31

| | REVENUE ($ mil.) | NET INCOME ($ mil.) | NET PROFIT MARGIN | EMPLOYEES |
|---|---|---|---|---|
| **12/06** | 3,882 | 1,385 | 35.7% | 10,700 |
| **12/05** | 2,892 | 716 | 24.7% | 11,600 |
| **12/04** | 2,614 | 152 | 5.8% | 10,800 |
| **12/03** | 2,434 | 19 | 0.8% | 11,900 |
| **12/02** | 2,674 | (3,732) | — | 13,200 |
| **Annual Growth** | 9.8% | — | — | (5.1%) |

### 2006 Year-End Financials

Debt ratio: 46.8%
Return on equity: 18.7%
Cash ($ mil.): 467
Current ratio: 1.59
Long-term debt ($ mil.): 3,200
No. of shares (mil.): 292
Dividends
Yield: —
Payout: —
Market value ($ mil.): 23,657

### Stock History

NYSE: RIG

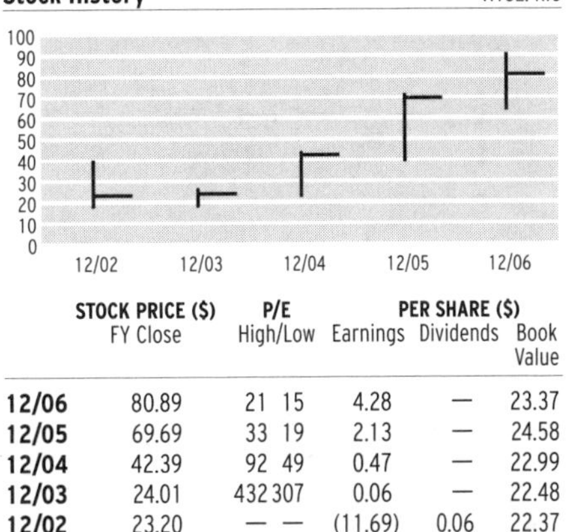


| | STOCK PRICE ($) FY Close | P/E High/Low | PER SHARE ($) Earnings | Dividends | Book Value |
|---|---|---|---|---|---|
| **12/06** | 80.89 | 21 15 | 4.28 | — | 23.37 |
| **12/05** | 69.69 | 33 19 | 2.13 | — | 24.58 |
| **12/04** | 42.39 | 92 49 | 0.47 | — | 22.99 |
| **12/03** | 24.01 | 432 307 | 0.06 | — | 22.48 |
| **12/02** | 23.20 | — — | (11.69) | 0.06 | 22.37 |
| **Annual Growth** | 36.6% | — — | — | — | 1.1% |

# The Travelers Companies

Running a business is a risk The Travelers Companies will insure. While it also offers personal insurance, the company's largest segment is commercial property/casualty insurance. It is the second largest business insurer in the US, behind AIG, and provides commercial auto, property, workers' compensation, marine, and general and financial liability coverage to companies in North America and the UK. The Travelers also offers surety and fidelity bonds as well as professional and management liability coverage for commercial operations. Through its membership in Lloyd's of London, it offers policies for commercial aviation, marine, property, and accidents.

In a $16 billion blockbuster deal, The St. Paul Companies acquired Travelers Property Casualty in 2004. (Travelers had been a subsidiary of Citigroup until its IPO in early 2002.) Reflecting the acquisition, the company then changed its name to The St. Paul Travelers Companies. However, in early 2007 the company changed its name to The Travelers Companies, Inc. and reclaimed the trademarked red umbrella logo used in previous Travelers incarnations.

The Travelers has been pruning itself of non-core operations, including most of its international businesses. It sold its non-standard personal property/casualty and medical malpractice lines.

The World Trade Center disaster (in which the company paid out almost $1 billion in claims) and the 2005 hurricane season (including Katrina, Rita, and Wilma) combined to make reinsurance a costlier game of dice. The company responded by spinning off its reinsurance business, St. Paul Re, into Bermuda-based Platinum Underwriters in 2002.

The company sold off its nearly 80% stake in Nuveen Investments in a series of transactions in 2005 which allowed Nuveen to become an independent publicly traded company.

## HISTORY

St. Paul, Minnesota, was a boomtown in 1852 thanks to traffic on the Mississippi. Settlers knew fire insurance was a must in their wooden town, but there were no local insurers. Buying policies from eastern companies and getting claims processed was difficult — especially in the winter, when river traffic stopped.

In 1853 a group of local investors led by George and John Farrington and Alexander Wilkin formed St. Paul Mutual Insurance, a mixed stock and mutual company (mutual members shared in the firm's profits and losses, while stockholders could benefit by selling if the company's value rose). St. Paul Mutual sold its first policy the following year.

The company changed its name in 1865 to St. Paul Fire and Marine Insurance, stopped offering mutual policies, and expanded throughout the Midwest. Claims from the Chicago Fire in 1871 nearly sank the company, which assessed its shareholders $15 for each share of stock, but prompt and full payment of claims resulted in more business. By the turn of the century, St. Paul Fire and Marine was operating nationwide.

Although the company was hard hit by shipping losses in WWI, it continued expanding, joining other US insurers in the American Foreign Insurance Association to market insurance in Europe.

In 1926 St. Paul Fire and Marine organized its first subsidiary, St. Paul Mercury Indemnity, to write liability insurance policies. Other additions included coverage for automobiles, aircraft, burglary and robbery, and, in 1940, turkey farming.

During WWII, St. Paul Fire and Marine joined the War Damage Corp., a government-financed consortium that paid claims for war damage. The St. Paul Companies was formed in 1968 as an umbrella organization for its various subsidiaries, and the firm grew through purchases.

Lines of business blossomed during the 1970s, including life and title insurance, leasing, a mail-order consumer finance company, oil and gas, and real estate. Many of these were sold during the 1980s, but one, The John Nuveen Co. (1974), became the nucleus of St. Paul's financial services operations.

St. Paul posted a loss in 1992 after paying out huge claims related to Hurricane Andrew. In 1995 the company expanded its malpractice line when it bought NML Insurance. The Minet unit (a brokerage business) started Global Media Services that year to focus on insurance for the telecommunications industry. The division also bought London-based Special Risk Service, a top insurance broker, and Boston-based William Gallagher Associates, a high-tech and biotechnology insurer.

In 1997 St. Paul sold its unprofitable Minet division. That year and the next the company was struck by catastrophe losses, more than $150 million total.

St. Paul acquired USF&G in 1998. The purchase triggered a round of job cuts as the company assimilated its new operations; the deal also slammed the insurer's earnings. To focus on its more profitable commercial business, the firm sold its personal insurance business (1999) and jettisoned its nonstandard auto insurance business (2000). In 2000 it bought MMI Companies to build its health care risk operations and decided later that year to close Unionamerica Holdings, an unprofitable subsidiary of MMI. In 2001 St. Paul sold F&G Life, a subsidiary of USF&G, to UK-based insurer Old Mutual.

## EXECUTIVES

**Chairman, President, and CEO:** Jay S. Fishman, age 54, $1,000,000 pay
**Vice Chairman:** Irwin R. Ettinger, age 68
**Vice Chairman and Chief Investment Officer:** William H. Heyman, age 59, $575,000 pay
**Vice Chairman and CFO:** Jay S. Benet, age 54, $700,000 pay
**Vice Chairman and Chief Legal Officer:** Alan D. Schnitzer, age 41
**EVP and COO:** Brian W. MacLean, age 53, $700,000 pay
**EVP and Chief Administrative Officer:** Andy F. Bessette, age 53
**EVP and CIO:** William A. Bloom, age 43
**EVP, Claim Services:** Doreen Spadorcia, age 49
**EVP and General Counsel:** Kenneth F. (Ken) Spence III, age 52
**EVP, Investor Relations and Corporate Communications:** Maria Olivo
**EVP, Strategic Development, Financial and Professional, and International Insurance:** Samuel G. Liss, age 50, $550,000 pay
**EVP, Human Resources:** John P. Clifford Jr.
**SVP and Corporate Secretary:** Bruce A. Backberg
**President Travelers Aviation:** Gordon Murray
**Auditors:** KPMG LLP

## LOCATIONS

**HQ:** The Travelers Companies, Inc.
385 Washington St., St. Paul, MN 55102
**Phone:** 651-310-7911 **Fax:** 651-310-3386
**Web:** www.travelers.com

## PRODUCTS/OPERATIONS

**2006 Sales**

| | $ mil. | % of total |
|---|---|---|
| Premiums | | |
| Business insurance | 10,876 | 44 |
| Personal insurance | 6,563 | 26 |
| Financial, professional & international insurance | 3,321 | 13 |
| Net investment income | 3,517 | 14 |
| Fee income | 591 | 2 |
| Net realized investment gains | 11 | — |
| Other revenues | 211 | 1 |
| **Total** | **25,090** | **100** |

## COMPETITORS

AEGON USA
AIG
Allianz
Aon
AXA
Chubb Corp
CIGNA
Citigroup
CNA Financial
The Hartford
ING
Loews
Merrill Lynch
MetLife
Nationwide
Prudential
SCOR
Zurich Financial Services

## HISTORICAL FINANCIALS

Company Type: Public

**Income Statement** FYE: December 31

| | ASSETS ($ mil.) | NET INCOME ($ mil.) | INCOME AS % OF ASSETS | EMPLOYEES |
|---|---|---|---|---|
| 12/06 | 113,761 | 4,208 | 3.7% | 32,800 |
| 12/05 | 113,187 | 1,622 | 1.4% | 31,900 |
| 12/04 | 111,815 | 955 | 0.9% | 30,200 |
| 12/03 | 39,563 | 661 | 1.7% | 9,300 |
| 12/02 | 39,920 | 218 | 0.5% | 9,700 |
| Annual Growth | 29.9% | 109.6% | — | 35.6% |

**2006 Year-End Financials**

Equity as % of assets: 22.0%
Return on assets: 3.7%
Return on equity: 17.8%
Long-term debt ($ mil.): 5,760
No. of shares (mil.): 678
Dividends
Yield: —
Payout: —
Market value ($ mil.): 36,418
Sales ($ mil.): 25,090

**Stock History** NYSE: TRV

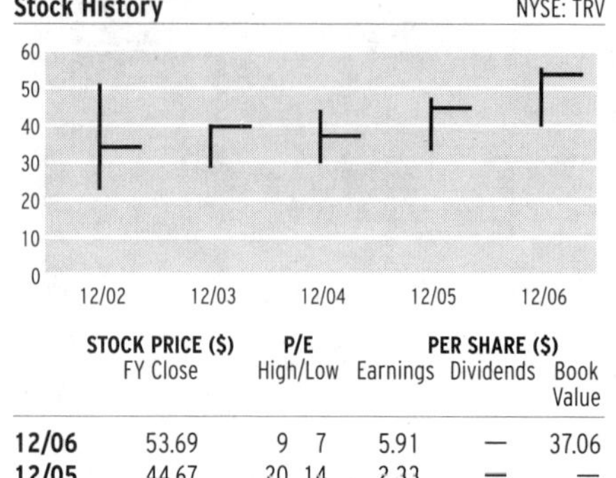


| | STOCK PRICE ($) FY Close | P/E High | P/E Low | PER SHARE ($) Earnings | Dividends | Book Value |
|---|---|---|---|---|---|---|
| 12/06 | 53.69 | 9 | 7 | 5.91 | — | 37.06 |
| 12/05 | 44.67 | 20 | 14 | 2.33 | — | — |
| 12/04 | 37.07 | 29 | 20 | 1.53 | — | — |
| 12/03 | 39.65 | 15 | 11 | 2.72 | — | — |
| 12/02 | 34.05 | 55 | 25 | 0.92 | — | — |
| Annual Growth | 12.1% | — | — | 59.2% | — | — |

# Triarc Companies

Would you buy a sandwich from a company called Triarc? Through its Arby's Restaurant Group subsidiary, Triarc Companies operates a chain of about 3,600 fast-food restaurants that specialize in roast beef sandwiches and curly fries. The #3 sandwich chain behind Subway and Quiznos, it also features chicken sandwiches, salads, and breakfast items. The restaurants operate in almost all 50 states and a handful of foreign countries; more than 1,000 locations are company-owned. In addition to Arby's, Triarc owns a 64% stake in Deerfield & Company, which manages the Deerfield Triarc Capital real estate investment trust (REIT). Board members Nelson Peltz and Peter May control about 35% of the company's voting stock.

Triarc has been building its portfolio of company-owned restaurants by acquiring some of its larger franchisees, including its 2005 acquisition of RTM Restaurant Group. The $175 million deal brought about 800 units into the fold and gave Triarc a strong foothold from which to re-energize the Arby's chain. The sandwich business has benefited from changes in consumer attitudes toward fast-food that have people searching for healthier alternatives to burgers and fries. The chain focuses its marketing message on the benefits of its oven-roasted meats over traditional hamburgers. In addition to its Arby's brand, Triarc franchises a small number of T.J. Cinnamons locations (mostly as multi-branded units with Arby's) that sell cinnamon rolls and coffee.

Chairman Peltz not only has Arby's on his mind, but other food-related brands as well. He is an activist shareholder in #3 hamburger chain Wendy's International with a 9% stake, and has expressed an interest in buying the firm outright. Peltz additionally has been making waves in the board room of Cracker Barrel operator CBRL Group. Peltz has also acquired a 5% stake in ketchup maker Heinz through his Trian Partners investment group.

While expectations had been growing that Triarc might spin off its Arby's business through an IPO, the company announced plans in 2007 to sell its stake in Deerfield & Company, move its headquarters to Atlanta, and change its name to Arby's. Ahead of those plans, Peltz (former chairman and CEO) and May (former president and COO) stepped down from their executive roles, remaining as non-executive chairman and vice chairman, respectively, while Arby's chief Roland Smith moved to the CEO position.

The company is selling its stake in Deerfield to Deerfield Triarc Capital for $170 million in cash and stock. Following the transaction Triarc will own about 10% of the financial services business. (It had acquired the stake in Deerfield & Company in 2004.)

In addition to Arby's and Deerfield, Triarc owns about 10% equity interest in Jurlique International, an Australian beauty-products maker.

## HISTORY

Brothers Forrest and Leroy Raffel opened the first Arby's restaurant in Youngstown, Ohio, in 1964. (The name was derived from the phonetic spelling of the initials R.B., for Raffel Brothers.) Seeking money for expansion, the Raffels merged their company with soft-drink maker Royal Crown Cola Company in 1976.

Royal Crown had started as a ginger ale brewer by pharmacist Claude Hatcher, who founded the Union Bottling Works in 1905. Early successes included Chero-Cola and a variety of Nehi soda flavors (the company became Nehi Corporation in 1928), but when the firm returned to the Royal Crown name for a new cola in 1933, it had a hit. It became Royal Crown Cola Company in 1959 and Royal Crown Companies in 1978.

Victor Posner acquired Royal Crown in 1984 through an affiliate of his publicly traded holding company DWG and began bleeding his new cash cow. Top management quit in disgust, and the Arby's chain began to suffer from neglect and mismanagement. In the late 1980s Posner was investigated and sued by shareholders for draining company coffers to line Posner family pockets. (Posner settled out of court in 1990 and in 1993 was banned by a federal judge from running any public company.)

Junk bond magnates (and former protégés of convicted felon Michael Milken) Nelson Peltz and Peter May stepped forward and bought about 29% of DWG in 1993, changing its name to Triarc Companies (Posner retained a nonvoting stake, which Triarc gradually repurchased from 1999 through 2001). In addition to RC and Arby's, the company owned Graniteville (textiles, sold in 1996), C.H. Patrick (textile chemicals and dyes, sold in 1997), and National Propane (propane retailer, sold in 1999 to Columbia Propane). Triarc hired a new management team, renovated many Arby's locations, and built new restaurants.

To jump-start the RC brand, the company worked to placate long-disgruntled bottlers and bought complementary beverage lines. Triarc purchased the Mistic fruit and tea beverage business in 1995. Triarc also sold off its 355 company-owned Arby's to its largest franchisee, RTM Restaurant Group.

In 1997 the company picked up fruit juice maker Snapple (now Snapple Beverage Corporation) from Quaker Oats for $300 million. Quaker Oats had purchased Snapple for $1.7 billion in 1994 from Thomas H. Lee Company, but a series of missteps began a spectacular tumble in value. Also in 1997 Triarc acquired Cable Car Beverage (later Stewart's Beverages), maker of Stewart's soft drinks, a small national brand.

Saying they wanted to buoy Triarc's stagnant stock price, in 1998 Peltz and May offered to take Triarc private; they withdrew the offer in early 1999, saying it wasn't in the best interest of shareholders. (Both have since settled a lawsuit with disgruntled shareholders.) Later in 1999 the company signed an agreement with United States Beef Corporation, a franchisee of Arby's restaurants, to develop more than 100 Arby's during the next 12 years. Also in 1999 Triarc bought Millrose Distributors, then the largest independent bottler of Snapple.

In 2000 Triarc sold Snapple to Cadbury Schweppes for about $1.45 billion. In 2002 Arby's franchisee I.C.H. Corporation (and its Sybra operating subsidiary) filed for Chapter 11 bankruptcy, prompting Triarc initially to scale down expansion plans for the chain. Late that year, however, Triarc bought Sybra and its 300 restaurants for $8.3 million.

The company expanded in two new directions in 2004, purchasing 25% of organic cosmetics company Jurlique and 64% of Deerfield & Company. The following year it acquired Arby's franchisee RTM Restaurant Group and its 775 locations for about $175 million.

## EXECUTIVES

**Chairman:** Nelson Peltz, age 64, $1,415,400 pay
**Vice Chairman:** Peter W. May, age 64, $965,400 pay
**EVP and CFO:** Francis T. (Frank) McCarron, age 50, $559,150 pay
**Chief Administrative Officer:** Sharon L. Barton
**SVP and Chief Accounting Officer:** Fred H. Schaefer, age 62
**SVP, General Counsel, and Secretary:** Stuart I. Rosen, age 47
**VP and Assistant General Counsel:** David I. Mossé
**VP Corporate Development:** Chad Fauser
**VP Corporate Development:** Eduardo Santos
**VP Taxes:** Robert J. (Bob) Crowe, age 55
**CEO and Director; Chairman and CEO, Arby's Restaurant Group:** Roland C. Smith, age 52
**President and COO, Arby's Restaurant Group:** Thomas A. (Tom) Garrett, age 45
**SVP, Development Officer, Arby's Restaurant Group:** Jordan Krolick
**Auditors:** Deloitte & Touche LLP

## LOCATIONS

**HQ:** Triarc Companies, Inc.
280 Park Ave., New York, NY 10017
**Phone:** 212-451-3000 **Fax:** 212-451-3134
**Web:** www.triarc.com

## PRODUCTS/OPERATIONS

### 2006 Sales

| | $ mil. | % of total |
|---|---|---|
| Restaurants | | |
| Company-owned | 1,073.3 | 86 |
| Franchising | 82.0 | 7 |
| Asset management | 88.0 | 7 |
| **Total** | **1,243.3** | **100** |

### 2006 Arby's Locations

| | No. |
|---|---|
| Franchised | 2,524 |
| Company-owned | 1,061 |
| **Total** | **3,585** |

## COMPETITORS

AFC Enterprises
Burger King
Cajun Operating Company
Captain D's
Chick-fil-A
CKE Restaurants
Dairy Queen
Jack in the Box
Kahala-Cold Stone
McDonald's
Quiznos
Sbarro
Sonic
Subway
Wendy's
YUM!

## HISTORICAL FINANCIALS

Company Type: Public

### Income Statement

FYE: December 31

| | REVENUE ($ mil.) | NET INCOME ($ mil.) | NET PROFIT MARGIN | EMPLOYEES |
|---|---|---|---|---|
| **12/06** | 1,243 | (11) | — | 24,372 |
| **12/05** | 727 | (56) | — | 25,203 |
| **12/04** | 329 | 14 | 4.2% | 5,360 |
| **12/03** | 294 | (11) | — | 5,091 |
| **12/02** | 99 | 1 | 1.3% | 5,030 |
| **Annual Growth** | 88.3% | — | — | 48.4% |

### 2006 Year-End Financials

Debt ratio: 147.9%
Return on equity: —
Cash ($ mil.): 279
Current ratio: 1.70
Long-term debt ($ mil.): 702
No. of shares (mil.): 64
Dividends
Yield: 2.8%
Payout: —
Market value ($ mil.): 1,275

### Stock History

NYSE: TRY

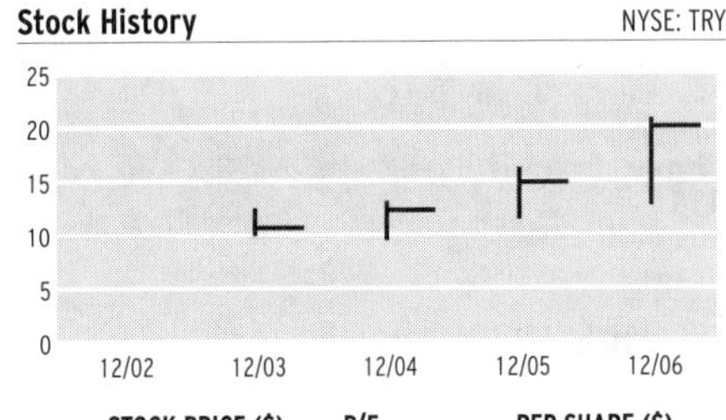

| | STOCK PRICE ($) FY Close | P/E High | P/E Low | PER SHARE ($) Earnings | Dividends | Book Value |
|---|---|---|---|---|---|---|
| **12/06** | 20.00 | — | — | (0.13) | 0.57 | 7.44 |
| **12/05** | 14.85 | — | — | (0.79) | 0.33 | 7.77 |
| **12/04** | 12.26 | 59 | 44 | 0.22 | 0.22 | 7.89 |
| **12/03** | 10.65 | — | — | (0.18) | 0.15 | 4.87 |
| **Annual Growth** | 23.4% | — | — | — | 56.0% | 15.2% |

# Trinity Industries

If Trinity Industries had a theme song, it would be sung by Boxcar Willie. The company manufactures auto carriers, box cars, gondola cars, hopper cars, intermodal cars, and tank cars — in short, railcars for hauling everything from coal to corn syrup. Trinity also leases and manages railcar fleets. The company's inland barge unit builds barges used to transport coal, grain, and other commodities. Other Trinity businesses include construction products (concrete, aggregates, and highway guardrails) and energy equipment (structural towers for wind turbines and metal containers for liquefied petroleum gas and fertilizer).

Demand for railcars has remained steady as the North American economy continued to improve in 2006 and Trinity's customers replaced aging fleets. Trinity also enjoyed better steel prices and improved productivity.

To focus on its core businesses, in 2006 the company sold its Trinity Fittings Group to the division's management and investment firm Levine Leichtman Capital Partners. Later that year the company sold its European railcar operations to Luxembourg's International Railway Systems for about $30 million plus working capital. Trinity said the move will help it concentrate on its North American operations.

In 2007 Trinity strengthened its construction products business with the acquisition of a number of holdings operating under the name Armor Materials. The operations include asphalt, ready mix concrete, and aggregates businesses with combined annual sales of about $55 million. The Armor Materials operations were bought from a common group of businesses and individuals.

Investor Jeffery L. Glendell, through Tontine Management LLC, controls about 13% of Trinity.

## HISTORY

Trinity Industries resulted from the 1958 merger of Trinity Steel, a maker of metal products for the petroleum industry, and Dallas Tank Co. The enterprise was headed by Ray Wallace, a Trinity Steel veteran since the 1940s.

The company, which took the name Trinity Industries in 1966, acquired related tank, welding, and steel companies in the 1960s and quickly became the leading manufacturer of metal storage containers for liquefied petroleum gas. During this period it also applied its expertise to containers for another rapidly growing industry — fertilizer — and made custom products for the oil and chemical industries. Other products included hopper bodies and tanks for use on railcars.

During the 1970s Trinity diversified into building seagoing vessels by purchasing Equitable Equipment and its Louisiana shipyards in 1972. The next year the company bought Mosher Steel (steel beams and framing products). By the mid-1970s it was producing highway guardrails and other road construction products. Trinity expanded its railcar parts manufacturing in 1977 to building complete cars and created a railcar-leasing subsidiary.

The company was a leading producer of railcars by the early 1980s, but a change in federal tax laws and a glut of railcars caused demand to plummet; in 1985 Trinity suffered its first loss in 27 years.

Still, Trinity managed to snap up failing competitors, including Pullman Standard, once the US's top freight car maker. The company also bought Greenville Steel Car (1986), Ortner Freight (1987), and Standard Forgings (locomotive axles, 1987). Through these purchases Trinity tripled its manufacturing capacity, so that it controlled more than half of the US freight car production capacity in the early 1990s.

The company also expanded its marine division with such acquisitions as Halter Marine (1983) and Bethlehem Steel's manufacturing plant and marine facilities in Beaumont, Texas (1989).

Trinity expanded its construction products line in 1992 with the purchase of Syro Steel (fabricated steel products) and added the Texas and Louisiana operations of Lafarge (concrete) in 1994. The company expanded into Mexico in 1995 by acquiring Grupo TATSA (fabricated steel products).

To fund expansion in other segments, Trinity spun off its Halter Marine Group in 1996. In 1997 Trinity acquired two manufacturing facilities from pipe fitting, flange, and valve industry specialist Ladish.

Ray Wallace retired as chairman and CEO in 1999 and was replaced by his son, Timothy Wallace. That year Trinity bought McConway and Torley (railcar couplers) and Excell Materials (ready-mix concrete). It also set up a railcar joint venture in Brazil.

Early in 2000 Trinity expanded its equipment manufacturing unit with the purchases of T.L. Smith Machine and Highlands Parts Manufacturer, makers of concrete mixers and parts. Less than two years after entering the concrete mixer market, Trinity exited the struggling business.

In the summer of 2001 Trinity agreed to acquire privately held railcar maker Thrall Car Manufacturing in a deal worth about $353 million. The deal was completed in the fall of 2001, and Trinity combined its railcar businesses with those of Thrall.

Late in 2002 Trinity agreed to sell its railcar repair facilities to privately held Rescar, but the deal was not completed. Trinity announced in 2003 that it would continue to operate the railcar repair business.

## EXECUTIVES

**Chairman, President, and CEO:** Timothy R. Wallace, age 53, $950,000 pay
**EVP and Director:** John L. Adams, age 62
**SVP and Group President:** Mark W. Stiles, age 58, $490,000 pay
**SVP and CFO:** William A. (Bill) McWhirter II, age 42, $370,000 pay
**SVP and Group President, TrinityRail:** D. Stephen (Steve) Menzies, age 50, $482,500 pay
**VP, Controller, and Chief Accounting Officer:** Charles (Chas) Michel, age 53
**VP and Secretary:** Michael G. Fortado, age 63
**VP, Business Development:** John M. Lee, age 46
**VP, Government Relations:** Linda S. Sickels, age 53
**VP and Chief Legal Officer:** S. Theis Rice, age 56
**VP, Human Resources and Shared Services:** Andrea F. Cowan, age 44
**VP, Chief Audit Executive:** Don Collum, age 58
**VP and Treasurer:** James E. Perry, age 35
**Corporate Secretary:** Paul M. Jolas, age 43
**VP, Strategic Sourcing:** Adrian E. Lee, age 56
**President, Trinity North American Freight Car:** Martin Graham, age 59, $420,000 pay
**President, Parts and Components:** Patrick Wallace
**Auditors:** Ernst & Young LLP

## LOCATIONS

**HQ:** Trinity Industries, Inc.
2525 Stemmons Fwy., Dallas, TX 75207
**Phone:** 214-631-4420 **Fax:** 214-589-8810
**Web:** www.trin.net

## PRODUCTS/OPERATIONS

### 2006 Sales

| | $ mil. | % of total |
|---|---|---|
| Rail | 1,516.9 | 47 |
| Construction products | 694.0 | 22 |
| Inland barge | 371.2 | 12 |
| Energy equipment | 327.6 | 10 |
| Railcar leasing & management services | 303.5 | 9 |
| Other | 5.7 | — |
| **Total** | **3,218.9** | **100** |

### Selected Products and Services

Rail
- Box cars
- Freight cars
- Gondola cars
- Hopper cars
- Intermodal cars
- Tank cars

Construction products
- Aggregates
- Beams
- Girders
- Highway guardrails
- Highway safety devices
- Ready-mix concrete

Inland barge
- Deck barges
- Fiberglass barge covers
- Hopper barges
- Tank barges

Energy equipment
- Container heads
- Fertilizer containers
- Liquefied petroleum gas containers
- Wind towers

Railcar leasing and management services
- Railcar leasing, repair, and management

## COMPETITORS

ALSTOM
American Railcar Industries
Blue Tee
Bombardier
CEMEX
Conrad Industries
FreightCar America
GATX
Greenbrier
Holcim
Lafarge North America
Meridian Rail Acquisition Corp
Nippon Sharyo
Siemens Transportation Systems
TTX
Vulcan Materials

## HISTORICAL FINANCIALS

Company Type: Public

### Income Statement

FYE: December 31

| | REVENUE ($ mil.) | NET INCOME ($ mil.) | NET PROFIT MARGIN | EMPLOYEES |
|---|---|---|---|---|
| **12/06** | 3,219 | 230 | 7.1% | 13,800 |
| **12/05** | 2,902 | 86 | 3.0% | 15,224 |
| **12/04** | 2,198 | (9) | — | 14,217 |
| **12/03** | 1,433 | (10) | — | 13,104 |
| **12/02** | 1,487 | (20) | — | 11,810 |
| **Annual Growth** | 21.3% | — | — | 4.0% |

### 2006 Year-End Financials

Debt ratio: 85.4%
Return on equity: 18.3%
Cash ($ mil.): 312
Current ratio: 1.67
Long-term debt ($ mil.): 1,199
No. of shares (mil.): 80
Dividends
Yield: 0.6%
Payout: 7.2%
Market value ($ mil.): 2,816

### Stock History

NYSE: TRN

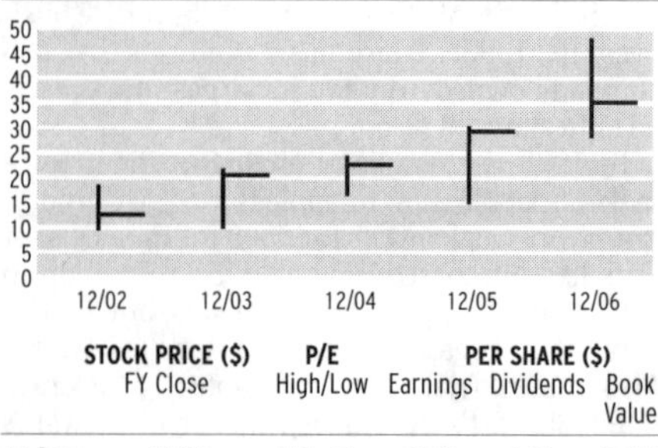


| | STOCK PRICE ($) FY Close | P/E High | P/E Low | PER SHARE ($) Earnings | Dividends | Book Value |
|---|---|---|---|---|---|---|
| **12/06** | 35.20 | 16 | 10 | 2.90 | 0.21 | 17.54 |
| **12/05** | 29.38 | 27 | 14 | 1.13 | 0.17 | 21.89 |
| **12/04** | 22.72 | — | — | (0.18) | 0.16 | 21.19 |
| **12/03** | 20.56 | — | — | (0.17) | 0.16 | 19.72 |
| **12/02** | 12.64 | — | — | (0.29) | 0.24 | 19.68 |
| **Annual Growth** | 29.2% | — | — | — | (3.3%) | (2.8%) |

# True Value

To survive against home improvement giants such as The Home Depot and Lowe's, True Value (formerly TruServ) is relying on the true value of service. Formed by the merger of Cotter & Company (which was the supplier to the True Value chain) and ServiStar Coast to Coast, the cooperative serves some 5,600 retail outlets (down from nearly 7,200 in 2001), including its flagship True Value hardware stores. The company sells home improvement and garden supplies, as well as appliances, housewares, sporting goods, and toys. Members use the Taylor Rental, Grand Rental Station, Home & Garden Showplace, Induserve Supply, and other banners. True Value also manufactures its own brand of paints and applicators.

The merger of Cotter & Company and ServiStar Coast to Coast (operator of Coast to Coast and ServiStar hardware stores, most of which converted to the True Value banner) gave members — many of them mom-and-pop outlets — more buying clout to compete against the do-it-yourself mega-retailers, plus retail advice and advertising support. True Value has been growing its business in the rental and maintenance, repair, and operation (MRO) arenas, and it plans to begin supplying lumber and building materials once again. (The company sold its lumber and building materials business in 2000.) At the store level, True Value has been developing "lite" or smaller versions of its signature programs, such as Platinum Paint Shop, for the co-op's stores (more than half) that are less than 6,000 sq. ft.

Following the relocation of its oil-based paint manufacturing operations to Cary, Illinois, True Value sold its Chicago paint plant in 2005.

Outside the US the company serves about 700 stores in more than 50 countries.

## HISTORY

Noting that hardware retailers had begun to form wholesale cooperatives to lower costs, John Cotter, a traveling hardware salesman, and associate Ed Lanctot started pitching the wholesale co-op idea in 1947 to small-town and suburban hardware retailers, and by early 1948 they had enrolled 25 merchants for $1,500 each. Cotter became chairman of the new firm, Cotter & Company.

The co-op created the Value & Service (V&S) store trademark in 1951 to emphasize the advantages of an independent hardware store. Acquisitions included the 1963 purchase of Chicago-based wholesaler Hibbard, Spencer, Bartlett, giving Cotter 400 new members and the well-known True Value trademark, which soon replaced V&S signs. Four years later Cotter broadened its focus by buying the General Paint & Chemical Company (Tru-Test paint). The V&S name was revived in 1972 for a five-and-dime store co-op, V&S Variety Stores.

In 1989 Cotter died and Lanctot retired. (Lanctot died in October 2003.) By 1989 there were almost 7,000 True Value Stores. Cotter moved into Canada in 1992 by acquiring hardware distributor and store operator Macleod-Stedman (275 outlets).

Juggling variety-store and hardware merchandise and delivering very small amounts of merchandise to a lukewarm co-op membership did not allow for economies of scale, so in 1995 the company quit its manufacturing operations and its US variety stores (though it still serves variety stores in Canada, operating as C&S Choices), tightened membership requirements, and introduced new services.

Two years later Cotter formed TruServ by merging with hardware wholesaler ServiStar Coast to Coast. ServiStar had its origins in the nation's first hardware co-op, American Hardware Supply, which was founded in Pittsburgh in 1910 by M. R. Porter, John Howe, and E. S. Corlett. By 1988, the year it changed its name to ServiStar, the co-op topped $1 billion in sales.

ServiStar expanded in the upper Midwest and on the West Coast in 1990 when it acquired the assets of the Coast to Coast chain (founded in 1928 as a franchise hardware store in Minneapolis); ServiStar brought Coast to Coast out of bankruptcy two years later, making it a co-op. Merging its 1992 acquisition of Taylor Rental Center with its Grand Rental Station stores in 1993 made ServiStar the #1 general rental chain. In 1996 it consolidated Coast to Coast's operations into its own and changed its name to ServiStar Coast to Coast.

President Don Hoye became CEO of the company in 1999. That year TruServ slashed 1,000 jobs and declared it would convert all its hardware store chains to the True Value banner. But TruServ lost $131 million in 1999 over bookkeeping gaffs, and co-op members received no dividends. Of 2,800 ServiStar dealers, only 1,900 raised the True Value flag. Others either declined to switch or were never offered the change because other True Value stores already shared their market area. In addition, stores began deserting the co-op because of inventory and other problems. In late 2000 the company sold its lumber and building materials business.

As competition continued to increase in 2001, the company was facing falling sales, lawsuits from shareholders, and accusations by retailers of unfair practices intended to pressure them into adopting the cooperative's flagship True Value banner. TruServ also had to confront a $200 million loan default. It made cuts in its corporate staff and divested its Canadian interests. In July 2001 Hoye resigned. The company's CFO and COO, Pamela Forbes Lieberman, was named the new CEO that November.

In April 2002 the company reported a net loss of $50.7 million during 2001, which it attributed to restructuring charges, inventory write-downs, and finance fees. TruServ, under SEC investigation for alleged inventory, accounting, and other internal-control problems, was one of several companies that failed in August 2002 to meet a government requirement to swear by their past financial results.

In January 2003 TruServ received about $125 million in financing from investment firm W. P. Carey & Co. in a sale-leaseback deal on seven of TruServ's distribution centers. In March 2003 TruServ settled the SEC's allegations, without admitting or denying them, and agreed to follow measures intended to ensure compliance with securities laws.

Lieberman resigned in November 2004. Director Thomas Hanemann was named interim CEO. TruServ changed its name to True Value in January 2005. In June 2005 Hanemann turned over the reins to Sears veteran Lyle G. Heidemann who joined True Value as its new president and CEO. In December 2005, the company sold its oil-based paint manufacturing operation in Chicago to Blackhawk/Halsted for about $10 million.

## EXECUTIVES

**Chairman:** Brian A. Webb, age 49
**President, CEO, and Director:** Lyle G. Heidemann, age 61, $955,527 pay (partial-year salary)
**SVP and CFO:** David A. (Dave) Shadduck, age 45, $469,191 pay
**SVP and Chief Information Officer:** Leslie A. Weber, age 49
**SVP and Chief Merchandising Officer:** Steven L. Mahurin, age 46, $502,935 pay
**SVP, General Counsel, and Secretary:** Cathy C. Anderson, age 56, $445,457 pay
**SVP Human Resources and Communications:** Amy W. Mysel, age 53
**SVP Logistics and Manufacturing:** Michael (Mike) Haining, age 50, $380,992 pay
**SVP Logistics and Supply Chain Management:** Stephen Poplawski
**VP and Corporate Controller:** Donald J. (Don) Deegan
**VP and Corporate Treasurer:** Barbara L. Wagner
**VP Marketing:** Carol Wentworth, age 48
**VP Retail Finance:** Jon Johnson
**VP Retail and Specialty Businesses Development:** Fred L. Kirst, age 54
**Director, E-Business:** Eric Lane
**General Manager, Rental:** Tony Sabo
**Auditors:** PricewaterhouseCoopers LLP

## LOCATIONS

**HQ:** True Value Company
8600 W. Bryn Mawr Ave., Chicago, IL 60631
**Phone:** 773-695-5000 **Fax:** 773-695-6516
**Web:** www.truevaluecompany.com

True Value is a hardware store cooperative serving some 5,600 retail stores and industrial distribution outlets in the US and more than 50 other countries.

## PRODUCTS/OPERATIONS

### 2006 Sales

| | $ mil. | % of total |
|---|---|---|
| Hardware | 1,946.1 | 95 |
| Paint manufacturing & distribution | 103.9 | 5 |
| **Total** | **2,050.0** | **100** |

### Selected Operations

Grand Rental Station (general rental)
Home & Garden Showplace (nursery and giftware)
Induserve Supply (commercial and industrial)
Party Central (parties and corporate events)
Taylor Rental (general rental)
True Value (hardware)

## COMPETITORS

84 Lumber
Ace Hardware
Akzo Nobel
Benjamin Moore
Do it Best
Fastenal
Hertz
Home Depot
Kmart
Lowe's
McCoy
Menard
Northern Tool
Orgill
Reno-Depot
Sears
Sherwin-Williams
Stock Building Supply
Sutherland Lumber
United Rentals
Valspar
Wal-Mart

## HISTORICAL FINANCIALS

Company Type: Cooperative

### Income Statement

FYE: December 31

| | REVENUE ($ mil.) | NET INCOME ($ mil.) | NET PROFIT MARGIN | EMPLOYEES |
|---|---|---|---|---|
| **12/06** | 2,050 | 73 | 3.6% | 3,000 |
| **12/05** | 2,043 | 48 | 2.3% | 2,800 |
| **12/04** | 2,024 | 43 | 2.1% | 2,800 |
| **12/03** | 2,024 | 21 | 1.0% | 3,000 |
| **12/02** | 2,176 | 21 | 1.0% | 3,200 |
| **Annual Growth** | (1.5%) | 36.1% | — | (1.6%) |

### 2006 Year-End Financials

Debt ratio: 96.7%
Return on equity: 90.0%
Cash ($ mil.): 6
Current ratio: 1.31
Long-term debt ($ mil.): 99

### Net Income History

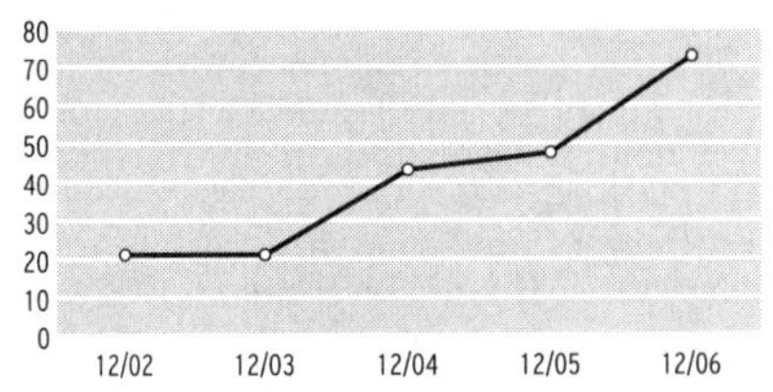


# Trump Organization

The Trump Organization knows all about gilding the lily. Run by flamboyant, modern-day King Midas Donald Trump (and his hair), The Trump Organization owns several pieces of high-end real estate in the Big Apple. Properties include Trump International Hotel & Tower, Trump Tower, and 40 Wall Street. Other holdings include 28% of Trump Entertainment Resorts (formerly Trump Hotels & Casino Resorts), owner and operator of Atlantic City, New Jersey, casinos Trump Taj Mahal, Trump Plaza, and Trump Marina. Trump Organization also owns and operates resorts and golf courses. Together with NBC, Trump owns the Miss USA, Miss Teen USA, and Miss Universe beauty pageants.

The Trump Organization depends heavily on (or succeeds in spite of, depending on your perspective) the fortunes of its founder, Donald

Trump. The author of *The Art of the Deal* is renowned for setting up real estate partnerships in which other firms put up most of the cash while he retains most of the control.

He keeps himself in the public eye with the reality television show *The Apprentice*, in which teams of aspiring moguls compete for a spot in his company. He even has a signature line: "You're fired!" and a signature move: the cobra — the hand motion he makes when axing a contestant. The same magic failed to work with a spinoff featuring Martha Stewart, which was cancelled after one season.

He has splashed his famous moniker — now trademarked — not just on buildings, but also water, vodka, restaurants, a university, and more.

The Trump Organization is developing the Trump International Hotel & Tower Chicago at the site formerly leased by the *Chicago Sun-Times*. It is slated to open in 2009. The company's latest proposals include a golf course and resort in the birthplace of the sport — Scotland — and it has teamed up with Irongate Capital Partners to build Trump International Hotel and Tower Waikiki Beach Walk in Hawaii.

Coming back down to earth, Trump launched a mortgage brokerage, called — naturally — Trump Mortgage, when the residential and commercial real estate markets appeared to have peaked. Some analysts said that the move was a way to get control of distressed commercial properties whose owners had bought at the top of the market but had to sell as the market cooled.

## HISTORY

The third of four children, Donald Trump was the son of a successful builder in Queens and Brooklyn. After graduating from the Wharton School of Finance in 1968, his first job was to turn around a 1,200-unit foreclosed apartment complex in Cincinnati that his father had bought for $6 million with no money down. Managing the Cincinnati job gave Trump a distaste for the nonaffluent; he wanted to get to Manhattan to meet all the right people.

Operating as The Trump Organization, he took options on two Hudson River sites in 1975 for no money down and began lobbying the city to finance his construction of a convention center. The center was built, but not by Trump, who nevertheless got about $800,000 and priceless publicity. He and hotelier Jay Pritzker turned the Commodore Hotel near Grand Central Station into the Grand Hyatt Hotel in 1975. Trump married fashion model Ivana Zelnicek two years later.

In 1981 he built the posh Trump Tower on Fifth Avenue and proceeded to wheel and deal himself into 1980s folklore. In 1983 he joined with Holiday Inn to build the Trump Casino Hotel (now Trump Plaza) in Atlantic City using public-issue bonds (he bought out Holiday Inn's interest in 1986), and he bought the Trump Castle from Hilton in 1985. In 1987 he ended up with the unfinished Taj Mahal in Atlantic City, then the world's largest casino, after a battle with Merv Griffin for Resorts International (Griffin won). He bought the Plaza Hotel in Manhattan in 1988, and the Eastern air shuttle (renamed the Trump Shuttle) the next year.

As the 1990s dawned, though, Trump's balance sheet was loaded with about $3 billion in debt. At the same time, his marriage to Ivana broke up in a splash of publicity. Trump's 70 creditor banks consolidated and restructured his debt in 1990. He married Marla Maples in 1993. (They divorced in 1998.)

In 1995 Trump formed Trump Hotels & Casino Resorts and took it public. He also paid a token $10 for 40 Wall St. (now home to American Express). The next year he sold his half-interest in the Grand Hyatt Hotel to the Pritzker family and unloaded more than $1.1 billion in debt by selling the Taj Mahal and Trump's Castle to Trump Hotels. That year Trump bought the Miss Universe, Miss USA, and Miss Teen USA pageants.

In 1997 he published *The Art of the Comeback*, a follow-up to *The Art of the Deal* (1987), and started work on Trump Place, a residential development on New York's Upper West Side. He teamed with Conseco in 1998 to buy the famed General Motors Building for $800 million. In 1999 he began building the Trump World Tower — a 90-story residential building near the United Nations complex. Residents of nearby high rises brought lawsuits in 2000, claiming that the new building would block their view and lower their property value. The court sided with Trump.

The following year Trump and publisher Hollinger International announced plans to transform the former riverfront headquarters of the *Chicago Sun-Times* into a residential and commercial development. Hollinger sold its stake in the venture to Trump in 2004.

In 2002 Trump sold his stake in the now-tallest building in New York City. His interest in the Empire State Building leasehold brought in only a paltry $2 million per year. He was also ordered by the courts — after a lengthy legal battle — to sell his 50% stake in the General Motors Building to co-owner Conseco; the two parties agreed to sell the building.

Trump ventured into reality television as the star and executive producer of *The Apprentice* in 2004. The show became a hit with viewers and critics (it garnered four Emmy Award nominations). Riding the wave of fascination with all things Donald, Trump published two more best-selling books (*How to Get Rich* and *Think Like A Billionaire)* that year.

He married model Melania Knauss in 2005.

In mid-2005 the Trump Organization and a group of investors sold a parcel of land and three buildings on the Manhattan waterfront to Extell Development Corp. and The Carlyle Group for about $1.8 billion. Later that year The Donald inked a deal with Nakheel, a developer in the United Arab Emirates, to develop resort destinations in the Middle East, including a $600 million high-rise in Dubai's ritzy Palm resort.

## EXECUTIVES

**Chairman, President, and CEO:** Donald J. Trump, age 60
**EVP and COO:** Mathew F. Calamari
**EVP and CFO:** Allen Weisselberg
**EVP and General Counsel:** Bernard Diamond
**EVP and Assistant General Counsel:** Jason Greenblatt
**EVP Golf Course Development:** Vincent Stellio
**VP and Controller:** Jeffrey McConney
**VP Development:** Jill Cremer
**VP Development:** Donald J. Trump Jr.
**VP Media Relations and Human Resources:** Norma Foerderer
**VP Operations and Residential Buildings:** Thomas Pienkos
**VP Leasing and Insurance:** Nathan Nelson
**VP Development and Acquisitions:** Ivanka M. Trump, age 25

## LOCATIONS

**HQ:** The Trump Organization
725 5th Ave., New York, NY 10022
**Phone:** 212-832-2000 **Fax:** 212-935-0141
**Web:** www.trumponline.com

## PRODUCTS/OPERATIONS

### Holdings

40 Wall Street
Mar-A-Lago (private club; Palm Beach, FL)
Miss Teen USA pageant
Miss Universe pageant
Miss USA pageant
Trump National Golf Club
Trump International Hotel and Tower
Trump Palace
Trump Parc
Trump Place
Trump Tower
Trump World (Seoul)

## COMPETITORS

Alexander's
American Real Estate Partners
Aztar
Boston Properties
Harrah's Entertainment
Helmsley Enterprises
HKR International
Hyatt
Lefrak Organization
Marriott
Mashantucket Pequot
MGM MIRAGE
Port Authority of NY & NJ
Ritz-Carlton
Rockefeller Group
Starwood Capital
Tishman
Vornado Realty

## HISTORICAL FINANCIALS

Company Type: Private

**Income Statement** FYE: December 31

| | REVENUE ($ mil.) | NET INCOME ($ mil.) | NET PROFIT MARGIN | EMPLOYEES |
|---|---|---|---|---|
| 12/06 | 10,400 | — | — | 22,500 |

# Tupperware Brands

Tupperware Brands Corporation (TBC) knows that there's more than one way to party. The company makes and sells household products and beauty items. Tupperware parties became synonymous with American suburban life in the 1950s, when independent salespeople organized gatherings to push their plasticware. TBC deploys a sales force of about 1.9 million people in nearly 100 countries. Other sales channels include the Internet, infomercials, and mall kiosks. Brands include Avroy Shlain, BeautiControl, Fuller, NaturCare, Nutrimetics, Nuvo, Swissgarde, and, of course, Tupperware. Its BeautiControl unit sells beauty and skin care products and fragrances in North America, Latin America, and the Asia/Pacific region.

Though many consider the Tupperware brand to be something of an American institution, the majority of TBC's sales are generated outside the US. TBC has pushed into new and developing markets (such as China, Eastern Europe, India, Japan, and Indonesia), offering region-specific products such as Kimono Keepers. The direct seller often targets areas where jobs are scarce and family ties are strong — the better for developing its sales network.

And its international growth is gaining momentum. In 2005 TBC nearly doubled its sales force of independent consultants who sell beauty and personal care products in Asia/Pacific and Latin America with the acquisition of Sara Lee Corporation's international direct selling unit, International Beauty. As part of the agreement, Tupperware Brands paid $557 million and acquired the direct selling unit's staff of 884,000 consultants, as well.

The company changed its name from Tupperware Corporation to Tupperware Brands Corporation upon the completion of the deal to reflect the firm's growing portfolio of brands.

TBC has been increasing its sales force and product offerings. With new wares contributing about 20% of revenue in recent years, the firm continues to make products outside its traditional scope, such as utensils and stove-top cookware.

## HISTORY

Earl Tupper was a self-styled inventor with only a high school education when he went to work for DuPont in the 1930s. He left DuPont in 1938 to start his own company, taking with him an unwanted, smelly chunk of polyethylene, a by-product of the oil refining process. Tupper eventually developed his own refining process, and in 1942 he created a clear, lightweight, unbreakable, odorless, nontoxic plastic, which he called Poly-T.

Tupper continued to do contract work for DuPont during the war, making parts for gas masks and Navy signal lamps. He continued to work with Poly-T and founded Tupperware in 1946. The next year, inspired by a paint can lid, Tupper developed the Tupperware Seal, which creates an airtight, partial vacuum. The Tupperware food storage container was born and began to move onto retail shelves.

At the same time, a secretary in Detroit named Brownie Wise was selling Stanley Home Products' appliances through parties at her home to raise money for her son's medical bills. (The party system was actually developed in the 1920s to introduce communities to aluminum cookware.) Wise added a Tupperware set to her product mix, and sales took off. By the early 1950s Tupperware parties began to spread.

Wise, hired as VP and general manager, became Tupperware's inspirational leader. In 1951 all Tupperware products were removed from retail shelves, and subsidiary Tupperware Home Parties was officially founded. By 1954 sales multiplied 25 times and the company had about 9,000 independent sellers.

By 1958 Tupperware expanded into Canada. That year Wise left and Tupper sold the company to Rexall Drug. In 1969 Rexall became Dart Industries; by this time Tupperware had entered Western Europe, Latin America, and parts of Asia. In 1976 international sales pushed revenue past $500 million.

In 1980 Dart merged with Kraft to become Dart and Kraft, Inc. By 1984 sales began to slip due to the number of women entering the workforce. Tupperware introduced a catalog and revised the party plan to include gatherings in the workplace. Dart and Kraft split in 1986, and Dart became Premark International. Tupperware's national ad campaign the next year inadvertently increased the sales of retail competitors such as Rubbermaid. By 1990 sales were slowing across the US, Latin America, and Japan.

Tupperware restructured in 1992 and former Avon executive Rick Goings became president. Wall Street's belief that Tupperware was languishing as a subsidiary led to its spinoff from Premark as a public company in 1996. Tupperware established operations in China that year and began holding parties in Russia in 1997. The Asian economic crisis and domestic organizational problems led to slumping sales in 1997 and 1998.

The company experimented with new sales channels in 1998 and 1999, including infomercials, mall kiosks, a Web site, and catalogs. Tupperware made the best of Asia's troubled economy in 1998 by recruiting laid-off workers and launching "I Save With Tupperware" campaigns to help consumers stretch food budgets. German direct seller Vorwerk bought an 11% stake in Tupperware in 2000 (and sold it in early 2005). In October 2000 Tupperware purchased cosmetics company BeautiControl.

Tupperware's first foray into store retailing was short-lived. The company began selling some products in SuperTarget stores in October 2001, but the negative impact felt by Tupperware's direct sales channel quickly prompted the company to pull the items from Target stores' shelves in June 2003.

In December 2005 the company acquired Sara Lee Corporation's direct selling businesses — International Beauty — and at the same time changed its name from Tupperware Corp. to Tupperware Brands Corp. The acquisition boosted the direct seller's sales force to about 1.9 million independent consultants.

## EXECUTIVES

**Chairman and CEO:** E.V. (Rick) Goings, age 61, $2,603,509 pay
**President and COO:** Simon C. Hemus, age 57
**EVP, Beauty:** Christa M. Hart, age 47
**EVP and CFO:** Michael S. (Mike) Poteshman, age 43, $584,649 pay
**EVP and Chief Human Resources Officer:** Lillian D. Garcia, age 51
**EVP, Chief Legal Officer, and Secretary:** Thomas M. Roehlk, age 56, $628,391 pay
**EVP and Chief Marketing Officer:** C. Morgan Hare, age 59
**SVP, Tax and Governmental Affairs:** Josef Hajek, age 49
**SVP, Worldwide Market Development:** Christian E. Skroeder, age 58
**SVP, Worldwide Operations:** José R. Timmerman, age 58
**VP and Treasurer:** Edward R. Davis III, age 44
**VP and CTO:** Robert F. Wagner, age 46
**VP, Internal Audit:** Carl Benkovich, age 50
**VP, Investor Relations:** V. Jane Garrard, age 44
**VP, Controller, and Principal Accounting Officer:** Nicholas Poucher, age 45
**Group President, Asia Pacific and North America:** David T. Halversen, age 62
**Group President, Europe, Africa, and the Middle East:** R. Glenn Drake, age 54
**Auditors:** PricewaterhouseCoopers LLP

## LOCATIONS

**HQ:** Tupperware Brands Corporation
14901 S. Orange Blossom Trail, Orlando, FL 32837
**Phone:** 407-826-5050 **Fax:** 407-826-8268
**Web:** www.tupperwarebrands.com

### 2006 Sales

| | $ mil. | % of total |
|---|---|---|
| Europe | 615.9 | 35 |
| International Beauty | 482.6 | 28 |
| North America | 255.5 | 15 |
| Asia/Pacific | 239.7 | 14 |
| BeautiControl NA | 150.0 | 8 |
| **Total** | **1,743.7** | **100** |

## PRODUCTS/OPERATIONS

### Selected Product Lines

Children's educational toys
Cooking products
Cosmetics and skin care
Food storage containers
Serving and preparation products

### Selected Trademarks

BeautiControl
Chef Series
E-Series
Expressions
Fridge Stackables
FridgeSmart
Legacy
Modular Mates
One Touch
OvenWorks
Rock 'N Serve
TupperMagic
Tupperware
Ultraplus
Vitalic

## COMPETITORS

Alticor
Avon
Body Shop
Clorox
Container Store
CPAC
Discovery Toys
The First Years
Hasbro
Home Products International
Kmart
Learning Curve International
Lifetime Brands
Mary Kay
Mattel
Newell Rubbermaid
Owens-Illinois
Pampered Chef
Sterilite
Target
Wal-Mart
Williams-Sonoma
Wilton Industries
WKI Holding
ZAG Industries

## HISTORICAL FINANCIALS

Company Type: Public

### Income Statement

FYE: Last Saturday in December

| | REVENUE ($ mil.) | NET INCOME ($ mil.) | NET PROFIT MARGIN | EMPLOYEES |
|---|---|---|---|---|
| **12/06** | 1,744 | 94 | 5.4% | 12,300 |
| **12/05** | 1,279 | 85 | 6.7% | 11,700 |
| **12/04** | 1,224 | 87 | 7.1% | 5,900 |
| **12/03** | 1,175 | 48 | 4.1% | 6,200 |
| **12/02** | 1,155 | 90 | 7.8% | 6,100 |
| **Annual Growth** | 10.8% | 1.1% | — | 19.2% |

### 2006 Year-End Financials

Debt ratio: 169.9%
Return on equity: 25.6%
Cash ($ mil.): 102
Current ratio: 1.54
Long-term debt ($ mil.): 681
No. of shares (mil.): 61
Dividends
Yield: 3.9%
Payout: 57.1%
Market value ($ mil.): 1,369

**Stock History** NYSE: TUP

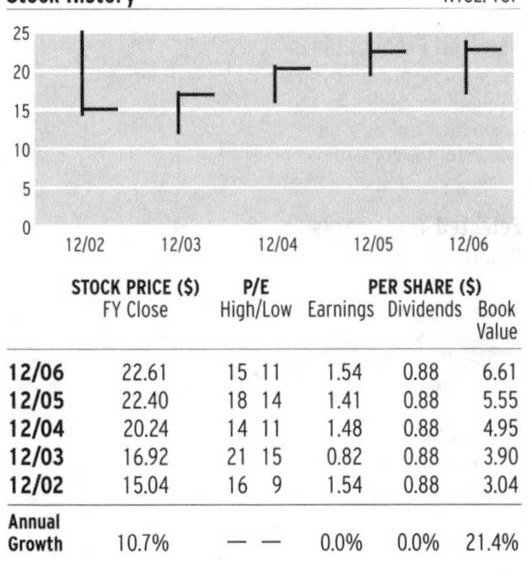

| | STOCK PRICE ($) FY Close | P/E High/Low | | PER SHARE ($) Earnings | Dividends | Book Value |
|---|---|---|---|---|---|---|
| **12/06** | 22.61 | 15 | 11 | 1.54 | 0.88 | 6.61 |
| **12/05** | 22.40 | 18 | 14 | 1.41 | 0.88 | 5.55 |
| **12/04** | 20.24 | 14 | 11 | 1.48 | 0.88 | 4.95 |
| **12/03** | 16.92 | 21 | 15 | 0.82 | 0.88 | 3.90 |
| **12/02** | 15.04 | 16 | 9 | 1.54 | 0.88 | 3.04 |
| **Annual Growth** | 10.7% | — | — | 0.0% | 0.0% | 21.4% |

# Tyson Foods

Think of Tyson Foods as an 800-pound chicken — with a bullish attitude. One of the largest US chicken producers (with 53 processing plants), Tyson's purchase of beef and pork giant IBP Fresh Meats made it the largest meat-processing company in the world, serving retail, wholesale, and foodservice customers in the US and more than 80 countries overseas. In addition to fresh meats, Tyson produces processed and pre-cooked meats, refrigerated and frozen prepared foods, and animal feeds. Its chicken operations are vertically integrated — the company hatches the eggs and then supplies contracted growers with chicks and feed. Former company chairman Don Tyson is the controlling owner of the company.

The company's fresh meat operations process chicken, beef, and pork. Tyson's pork operations offer processed pork products including sausage, ham, and bacon. The company's Prepared Foods unit produces pizza toppings and entrées. Other activities include the production of animal feeds and other rendering by-products.

A truly international company, Tyson has joint ventures in Argentina, Brazil, Canada, China, the Dominican Republic, India, Japan, Mexico, the Netherlands, the Philippines, Puerto Rico, Russia, Singapore, South Korea, Spain, Taiwan, the United Arab Emirates, the UK, and Venezuela.

In 2006 Don's son, John Tyson, stepped down as CEO; president and COO Richard L. Bond was named president and CEO. Tyson remained as chairman. Soon thereafter, Bond announced $200 million in cost reductions, to include reductions in staff, recruiting, relocation, consulting, sales-related expenses and supplies, and travel. The plan included the elimination of 850 positions, of which 420 were currently held and 430 were positions to be filled. Most of the jobs were managerial and involved no hourly workers at Tyson's plants. Later that year, the company announced it would cut another 770 jobs as it closed and consolidated several meat slaughter and processing plants in the northwestern US.

Recognizing the growing market for alternative and renewable fuels, in 2007 Tyson formed a strategic alliance with ConocoPhillips to produce diesel transportation fuel from beef, pork, and poultry by-product fat. It also formed a joint venture with fuel refiner, Syntroleum, to produce synthetic fuel for the diesel-, jet-, and military-fuel markets.

## HISTORY

During the Great Depression, Arkansas poultry farmer John Tyson supported his family by selling vegetables and poultry. In 1935, after developing a method for transporting live poultry (he installed a food-and-water trough and nailed small feed cups on a trailer), he bought 500 chickens in Arkansas and sold them in Chicago.

For the next decade Tyson bought, sold, and transported chickens. By 1947, the year he incorporated the company as Tyson Feed & Hatchery, he was raising the chickens himself. He emphasized chicken production, opening his first processing plant in 1958 in Springdale, where he implemented an ice-packing system that allowed the company to send its products greater distances.

John's son Don took over as manager in 1960, and in 1963 it went public as Tyson Foods. Tyson Country Fresh Chicken (packaged chicken that would become the company's mainstay) was introduced in 1967.

Rapid expansion included a new egg processing building (1970), a new plant and computerized feed mill (1971), and the acquisitions of Prospect Farms (1969, precooked chicken) and the Ocoma Foods Division (1972, poultry) as well as hog operations.

Health-conscious consumers increasingly turned from red meats to poultry during the 1980s. Tyson became the industry leader with several key acquisitions of poultry operations, including the Tastybird division of Valmac (1985), Lane Processing (1986), and Heritage Valley (1986). Its 1989 purchase of Holly Farms added beef and pork processing.

Don Tyson relinquished the CEO position to Leland Tollett in 1991. The next year the firm plunged into seafood with the purchase of Arctic Alaska Fisheries and Louis Kemp Seafood.

In 1997 the company pleaded guilty to charges that it illegally gave former Agriculture Secretary Mike Espy thousands of dollars' worth of gifts; the settlement included $6 million in fines and fees. In 1998 John H. Tyson, grandson of the founder, was elected chairman.

In 1999 Tyson sold its seafood business for about $180 million in a two-part transaction to International Home Foods and Trident Seafoods. John Tyson became CEO in 2000.

As the winner in a bidding war with Smithfield Foods, in 2001 Tyson agreed to buy IBP, Inc., the #1 beef processor and #2 pork processor in the US, for nearly $3.2 billion. Tyson tried to back away from the table after accounting irregularities were discovered at an IBP subsidiary, but a Delaware judge ordered Tyson to sit down and finish dinner. The deal was made final in September and Tyson changed the beef processor's name to IBP Fresh Meats.

In late 2001 Tyson Foods and six managers were indicted for conspiring to smuggle illegal immigrants from Mexico and Central America to work for lower than legal wages in 15 of its US poultry processing plants. Two managers made plea bargains and testified for the government; another manager committed suicide. Tyson and the remaining three managers were acquitted of the conspiracy charges in 2003.

In the wake of the discovery of a single case of BSE (mad cow disease) in the US, Tyson reduced production at its beef plants due to reduced demand for US beef overseas.

Following the discovery of bird flu on a Texas chicken farm in February 2004 and the resultant banning of the importation of US chicken products by other countries, Tyson consolidated and automated its poultry operations, resulting in hundreds of layoffs at the company.

Also in 2004 the SEC recommended civil action against the company for its failure to disclose $1.7 million in corporate perks given to senior chairman Don Tyson without authorization from Tyson's compensation committee. With neither the company nor Tyson admitting any guilt, the case was settled in 2005 with Tyson paying the SEC $700,000 in fines and the company, $1.5 million.

In 2005 Tyson suspended operations at four of its beef plants and cut back at a fifth due to a shortage of cattle and the loss of beef exports due to the US's 2003 case of BSE (Bovine spongiform encephalopathy or "mad cow" disease).

## EXECUTIVES

**Chairman:** John H. Tyson, age 53, $1,170,000 pay
**President, CEO, and Director:** Richard L. (Dick) Bond, age 59, $1,140,000 pay
**EVP and CFO:** Wade D. Miquelon, age 42
**EVP and General Counsel:** J. Alberto (Al) Gonzalez-Pita, age 52
**SVP, Controller, and Chief Accounting Officer:** Craig J. Hart, age 49
**SVP, Corporate Research and Development:** Howell P. Carper
**SVP, Ethics, Compliance, and Internal Audit:** Karen Gilbert
**SVP, Finance and Treasurer:** Dennis Leatherby, age 46
**SVP, Marketing, Retail:** Shawn Walker
**SVP, Human Resources:** Kenneth J. Kimbro
**SVP, Sales:** Randy Smith
**SVP and Chief Information Officer:** Donnie Smith
**SVP and Chief Environmental, Health, and Safety Officer:** Kevin J. Igli
**Senior Group VP, Poultry and Prepared Foods:** William W. (Bill) Lovette, age 46, $548,462 pay
**Senior Group VP and Chief Development Officer:** John S. Lea
**Group VP, Fresh Meats:** Noel White, age 47
**Group VP, International:** Richard A. (Rick) Greubel Jr., age 43
**Group VP, Consumer Products:** Scott McNair, age 44
**VP, Associate General Counsel, and Secretary:** R. Read Hudson
**VP, Investor Relations, and Assistant Secretary:** Ruth Ann Wisener
**Director, Media Relations:** Gary Mickelson
**Auditors:** Ernst & Young LLP

## LOCATIONS

**HQ:** Tyson Foods, Inc.
2210 W. Oaklawn Dr., Springdale, AR 72762
**Phone:** 479-290-4000 **Fax:** 479-290-4061
**Web:** www.tysonfoodsinc.com

Tyson's products are available throughout the US and in more than 80 foreign countries. Its major export markets include Canada, Central America, China, the EU, Japan, Mexico, Russia, South Korea, and Taiwan.

## PRODUCTS/OPERATIONS

**2006 Sales**

| | $ mil. | % of total |
|---|---|---|
| Beef | 11,825 | 46 |
| Chicken | 7,928 | 31 |
| Pork | 3,060 | 12 |
| Prepared foods | 2,692 | 11 |
| Other | 54 | — |
| **Total** | **25,559** | **100** |

**Selected Products and Brands**

Meats
- 100% All Natural, Raised Without Antibiotics (Tyson-branded fresh chicken)
- Nature's Farm (organic fresh chicken)
- Tyson (beef, chicken, pork)
- Tyson Holly Farms (chicken)
- Weaver (frozen fully cooked chicken)

Prepared foods
- Doskocil (value-added meats for pizza industry)
- Lady Aster (entrees)
- Mexican Original (flour and corn tortilla products)

Processed meats
- Corn King
- Iowa Ham
- ITC
- Jordan's
- Russer
- Thornapple Valley
- Wright

## COMPETITORS

Butterball
Cargill
Coleman Natural Foods
ConAgra
ContiGroup
Cooper Farms
Eberly
Foster Farms
Hormel
JBS
JBS Swift
Jennie-O
Koch Foods
Kraft North America Commercial
MBA Poultry
National Beef
New Market Poultry
Perdue
Petaluma Poultry
Pilgrim's Pride
Plainville Turkey
Raeford Farms
Sanderson Farms
Sara Lee Food & Beverage
Smithfield Foods
Wayne Farms LLC

## HISTORICAL FINANCIALS

Company Type: Public

**Income Statement** FYE: Saturday nearest September 30

| | REVENUE ($ mil.) | NET INCOME ($ mil.) | NET PROFIT MARGIN | EMPLOYEES |
|---|---|---|---|---|
| **9/06** | 25,559 | (196) | — | 107,000 |
| **9/05** | 26,014 | 353 | 1.4% | 114,000 |
| **9/04** | 26,441 | 403 | 1.5% | 114,000 |
| **9/03** | 24,549 | 337 | 1.4% | 120,000 |
| **9/02** | 23,367 | 383 | 1.6% | 120,000 |
| **Annual Growth** | 2.3% | — | — | (2.8%) |

**2006 Year-End Financials**

Debt ratio: 67.3%
Return on equity: —
Cash ($ mil.): 798
Current ratio: 1.47
Long-term debt ($ mil.): 2,987
No. of shares (mil.): 269
Dividends
Yield: 1.0%
Payout: —
Market value ($ mil.): 4,272

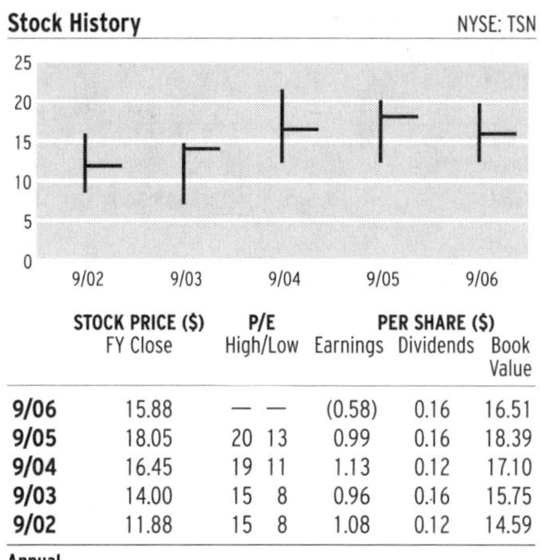


| | STOCK PRICE ($) FY Close | P/E High/Low | PER SHARE ($) Earnings | Dividends | Book Value |
|---|---|---|---|---|---|
| **9/06** | 15.88 | — — | (0.58) | 0.16 | 16.51 |
| **9/05** | 18.05 | 20 13 | 0.99 | 0.16 | 18.39 |
| **9/04** | 16.45 | 19 11 | 1.13 | 0.12 | 17.10 |
| **9/03** | 14.00 | 15 8 | 0.96 | 0.16 | 15.75 |
| **9/02** | 11.88 | 15 8 | 1.08 | 0.12 | 14.59 |
| **Annual Growth** | 7.5% | — — | — | 7.5% | 3.1% |

# UAL Corporation

After lightening its debt load in a bankruptcy reorganization, airline operator UAL has regained the altitude of profitability. The company's main subsidiary, United Airlines, is the world's #2 carrier, behind AMR's American Airlines. UAL also operates low-fare carrier Ted and provides regional feeder service in the US via United Express, which is operated by independent carriers. Overall, United serves more than 200 destinations in some 30 countries worldwide from hubs in Chicago, Denver, Los Angeles, San Francisco, and Washington, DC. Its mainline fleet includes about 460 jets. United extends its international coverage through membership in the Star Alliance, a global marketing and code-sharing partnership.

UAL emerged from bankruptcy protection in 2006. The company hopes to grow by taking advantage of its extensive global network and the well-known United brand. In July 2006 United announced plans to add routes from the US to the Asia/Pacific region, and the next year the airline triumphed over competitors to gain a coveted US-China flight. It is bidding for more routes to China, which are to be awarded by the US government. In addition, the company is continuing to work to reduce its operating costs.

Conditions for the airline industry as a whole have improved since the downturn that followed the terrorist attacks of September 11, 2001, but rumors of potential airline consolidations persist. UAL reportedly has been in talks with Continental Airlines about combining Continental and United.

## HISTORY

In 1929 aircraft designer Bill Boeing and engine designer Fred Rentschler of Pratt & Whitney joined forces to form United Aircraft and Transport. Renamed United Air Lines in 1931, the New York-based company offered one of the first coast-to-coast airline services. In 1934 United's manufacturing and transportation divisions split. Former banker Bill Patterson became president of the latter, United Air Lines, and moved it to the Chicago area.

Led by Patterson until 1963, United was slow to move and began offering jet service in 1959, after rival American. But in 1961 United bought Capital Airlines and became the US's #1 airline.

In 1969 UAL Corp. was formed as a holding company. In 1979, a year after airline deregulation, hotelier Richard Ferris became CEO. Dreaming of a travel conglomerate, he bought Hertz (1985) and Hilton International (1987). Angered by the diversification, the pilots struck in 1985 and then tried to buy the airline in 1987. That year, after dropping $7.3 million to change United's name to Allegis, Ferris left when leading shareholder Coniston Partners threatened to oust the board and liquidate the firm. Assuming its old name and a new CEO, Stephen Wolf (former chief of cargo carrier Flying Tigers), UAL shed its hotels and car rental business and 50% of its computer reservation partnership, Covia.

A 1989 takeover bid by Los Angeles billionaire Marvin Davis and Coniston triggered an unsuccessful buyout effort by United pilots, management, and British Airways. Gerald Greenwald, a turnaround expert from Chrysler, headed the attempt. Coniston later sold most of its stake in exchange for two seats on the board.

Fare wars and the rise of short-haul rivals caused profits to flag from 1991 to 1993. United began expanding globally and added routes in the Asia/Pacific region (bought from Pan Am in 1986 and 1991). It also laid off thousands of employees and cut executive pay. Finally, the 1993 sale of United's kitchen operations (slashing 5,800 union jobs) brought the unions to the table with an employee stock ownership plan (ESOP). The ESOP, which ceded 55% of UAL to employees in exchange for $4.8 billion in wage concessions, was approved in 1994. The deal effectively ended Wolf's reign at UAL since he had fallen out of favor with employees; Greenwald became CEO. United also launched its low-fare carrier that year.

In 1995 workers vetoed a proposed merger with US Airways, largely because of pilots' concerns about combining seniority lists. Two years later United formed the Star Alliance with Lufthansa, Scandinavian Airlines System, Air Canada, and Thai Airways.

President James Goodwin, a 32-year United veteran, took over as CEO after Greenwald's 1999 retirement. Also that year Russian airspace — off-limits to foreign airlines for more than 50 years — was opened to United. In 2000 UAL again made plans to buy US Airways, this time for $4.3 billion in cash and $7.3 billion in assumed debt. In 2001, however, US antitrust regulators moved to block the UAL-US Airways deal, citing concerns that the combination would reduce competition and lead to higher fares, and the two companies called off the deal.

Also that year United Airlines lost two planes in the September 11 terrorist attacks on New York and Washington, DC. As demand for air travel slumped after the attacks, UAL eliminated flights and laid off more than 20% of its workforce. A month after the attacks, chairman and CEO James Goodwin resigned under pressure from employee unions; UAL director and former Weyerhaeuser chief John Creighton replaced him on an interim basis. The cutbacks, however, were not enough to prevent the airline from posting a $2.1 billion loss for 2001.

The following year, UAL avoided a potentially disastrous strike by its mechanics when they approved a new contract giving them their first raise since 1994. The airline managed to convince its pilots and salaried managers to take a pay cut in 2002 to alleviate some of its debt. Also that year, UAL applied for a $1.8 billion loan under the federal loan guarantee program created to help airlines in the aftermath of the September 11 attacks. Creighton announced his intent to retire, and he was replaced by Glenn Tilton, an oil industry executive who had served as vice chairman of ChevronTexaco and interim chairman of Dynegy. UAL's financial troubles continued to mount, however, and the company filed for Chapter 11 bankruptcy protection in December 2002.

To assist with its emergence from bankruptcy, UAL petitioned for an additional loan from the US government in 2004, but it was denied. Instead, the government extended the repayment deadline. In the course of its reorganization, UAL launched low-fare carrier Ted, renegotiated labor agreements, and won court permission to terminate its four employee pension plans. Employees also lost their controlling stake in the company. The federal Pension Benefit Guaranty Corporation wound up with responsibility for the pension plans and a stake in UAL.

UAL emerged from bankruptcy protection in February 2006.

## EXECUTIVES

**Chairman, President, and CEO, UAL and United Airlines:** Glenn F. Tilton, age 59, $687,083 pay
**EVP and COO, UAL and United Airlines:** Peter D. (Pete) McDonald, age 55, $542,125 pay
**EVP and CFO, UAL and United Airlines:** Frederic F. (Jake) Brace, age 49, $501,000 pay
**EVP and Chief Customer Officer, UAL and United Airlines:** Graham W. Atkinson, age 55
**EVP and Chief Revenue Officer, UAL and United Airlines:** John P. Tague, age 44, $501,000 pay
**SVP, Airport Operations and Cargo, United Airlines:** Scott J. Dolan
**SVP, Alliances, International, and Regulatory Affairs, United Airlines:** Michael G. (Mike) Whitaker
**SVP, Continuous Improvement and Strategic Sourcing and CIO, United Airlines:** Gerald F. (Garry) Kelly Jr., age 59
**SVP, Corporate and Government Affairs, United Airlines:** Rosemary Moore, age 56
**SVP, Corporate Planning and Strategy, United Airlines:** Gregory T. (Greg) Taylor
**SVP, Flight Operations and Onboard Service, United Airlines:** Sean P. Donohue
**SVP, General Counsel, and Secretary, UAL and United Airlines:** Paul R. Lovejoy, age 52
**SVP, Human Resources, United Airlines:** Jane G. Allen, age 55
**SVP, Marketing, United Airlines:** Dennis M. Cary
**SVP, Planning, United Airlines:** Kevin N. Knight
**SVP, United Services, United Airlines:** William R. Norman
**SVP, Worldwide Sales, United Airlines:** Jeffrey T. (Jeff) Foland
**VP and Controller:** David M. Wing
**VP and Treasurer, United Airlines:** Stephen Lieberman
**VP Investor Relations:** Kathryn A. Mikells
**Auditors:** Deloitte & Touche LLP

## LOCATIONS

**HQ:** UAL Corporation
77 W. Wacker Dr., Chicago, IL 60601
**Phone:** 312-997-8000
**Web:** www.united.com

### 2006 Sales

| | $ mil. | % of total |
|---|---|---|
| Domestic (US & Canada) | 12,934 | 67 |
| Pacific | 3,497 | 18 |
| Atlantic | 2,325 | 12 |
| Latin America | 584 | 3 |
| **Total** | **19,340** | **100** |

## PRODUCTS/OPERATIONS

### 2006 Sales

| | $ mil. | % of total |
|---|---|---|
| Mainline | 16,439 | 85 |
| United Express | 2,901 | 15 |
| **Total** | **19,340** | **100** |

## COMPETITORS

Air France-KLM
Alaska Air
Alitalia
AMR Corp.
British Airways
Continental Airlines
Delta Air
FedEx
Frontier Airlines
Japan Airlines
JetBlue
Northwest Airlines
Qantas
Southwest Airlines
UPS
US Airways
Virgin Atlantic Airways

## HISTORICAL FINANCIALS

Company Type: Public

### Income Statement

FYE: December 31

| | REVENUE ($ mil.) | NET INCOME ($ mil.) | NET PROFIT MARGIN | EMPLOYEES |
|---|---|---|---|---|
| **12/06** | 19,340 | 22,876 | 118.3% | 55,000 |
| **12/05** | 17,379 | (21,176) | — | 57,000 |
| **12/04** | 16,391 | (1,721) | — | — |
| **12/03** | 13,724 | (2,808) | — | — |
| **12/02** | 14,286 | (3,212) | — | — |
| **Annual Growth** | 7.9% | — | — | (3.5%) |

### 2006 Year-End Financials

Debt ratio: 409.8%
Return on equity: —
Cash ($ mil.): 4,485
Current ratio: 0.79
Long-term debt ($ mil.): 8,803
No. of shares (mil.): 112
Dividends
Yield: —
Payout: —
Market value ($ mil.): 4,940

### Stock History

NASDAQ (GS): UAUA

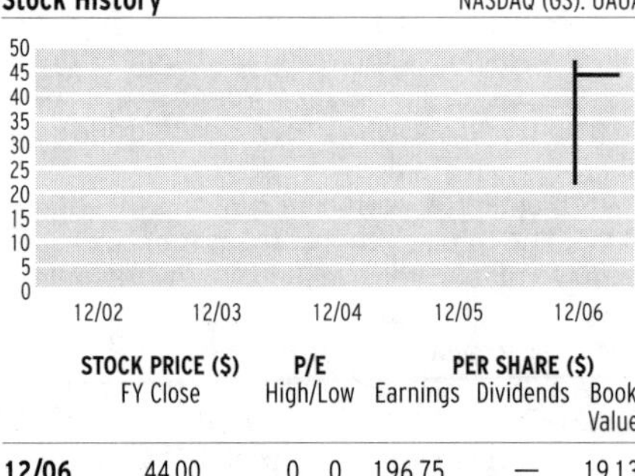


| | STOCK PRICE ($) FY Close | P/E High | P/E Low | PER SHARE ($) Earnings | PER SHARE ($) Dividends | PER SHARE ($) Book Value |
|---|---|---|---|---|---|---|
| **12/06** | 44.00 | 0 | 0 | 196.75 | — | 19.13 |

# UGI Corporation

UGI passes along gas and turns on power for the citizens of Pennsylvania. The company distributes propane and butane across the US and abroad. It also provides natural gas and electricity to customers in eastern Pennsylvania. UGI's 44%-owned propane distributor, AmeriGas Partners, makes up most of the holding company's sales and is one of the top two US propane marketers (along with Ferrellgas). Subsidiary UGI Utilities distributes electricity to about 62,000 customers and gas to 473,000 customers in Pennsylvania. Other UGI operations include energy marketing in the mid-Atlantic region, propane sales in Asia and Europe, electricity generation, and energy services.

Subsidiary AmeriGas sells propane to more than 1.3 million retail and wholesale customers a year from about 600 locations in 46 states. AmeriGas, which accounts for nearly half of the company's revenues, also offers propane-related products and services and provides propane storage services.

Subsidiary UGI Enterprises, which operates as the company's Energy Services division, markets natural gas and electricity to customers in the US mid-Atlantic region; has interests in propane distributors in Austria, China, the Czech Republic, France, and Slovakia; and offers HVAC (heating, ventilation, and air-conditioning) and energy management services to more than 100,000 customers in the mid-Atlantic region of the US. Another subsidiary, UGI Development, is involved in a power generation venture with Allegheny Energy.

The company is focused on expanding its core natural gas, electric, and propane operations. It is also seeking complementary opportunities to continue its growth in the US and abroad. The company has acquired the remaining 80% interest in AGZ Holding, the parent company of French propane distributor Antargaz. It has also purchased BP's retail propane distribution business in the Czech Republic.

In 2006 the company acquired the natural gas utility assets of PG Energy for about $580 million.

## HISTORY

United Gas Improvement was set up in 1882 by Philadelphia industrialist Thomas Dolan and other investors to acquire a gasworks and a new coal-gas manufacturing process. The firm also bought electric utilities and street railways across the US and moved into construction. The 1935 Public Utility Holding Company Act led to United Gas Improvement's restructuring when the SEC ordered the divestiture of many of its operations in 1941. The company converted to natural gas in the 1950s and entered the liquefied petroleum gas (LPG) business in 1959. It became UGI Corporation in 1968.

UGI shifted its emphasis to propane in the late 1980s, buying Petrolane in 1995 and combining it with AmeriGas Propane to create AmeriGas Partners, which then went public. Overseas, UGI launched a joint venture in 1996 to build an LPG import project in Romania. The next year it signed a deal to distribute propane in China.

In 1999 UGI moved into consumer products by opening its first Hearth USA retail store in Rockville, Maryland, which offered hearth items, spas, grills, and patio accessories. It ventured into a growing European market by purchasing FLAGA GmbH, a leading gas distributor in Austria and the Czech Republic.

That year a 1997 Pennsylvania law kicked in, restructuring the state's electricity industry and enabling customers to choose their electricity provider. In response, UGI separated its distribution and power generation operations, and in 2000 contributed the bulk of its generation assets to a partnership with Allegheny Energy that sells power to UGI Utilities and other distributors.

In 2001 UGI Enterprises purchased a 20% interest in French propane distributor Antargaz. Also that year UGI closed its Hearth USA retail stores. Through its UGI Energy Services subsidiary, UGI completed the acquisition of TXU Energy, a subsidiary of TXU Corp., in 2003.

In 2004 UGI acquired the remaining 80% interest in Antargaz, expanding its operations in France. Later that year the company continued its European expansion through the acquisition of BP's retail propane distribution business in the Czech Republic.

## EXECUTIVES

**Chairman and CEO:** Lon R. Greenberg, age 56, $1,917,234 pay
**President, COO, and Director:** John L. Walsh, age 51, $1,071,168 pay
**VP Finance and CFO:** Peter Kelly, age 50
**VP Accounting and Financial Control, and Chief Risk Officer:** Michael J. Cuzzolina, age 61
**VP New Business Development; President, UGI Enterprises:** Bradley C. Hall, age 53
**VP and Treasurer:** Robert W. Krick
**VP, General Counsel, and Assistant Secretary:** Robert H. Knauss, age 53
**VP Human Resources:** William D. Katz
**President and CEO, AmeriGas Propane:** Eugene V. N. Bissell, age 53, $598,430 pay
**Chairman and CEO, Antargaz:** François Varagne, age 51, $701,160 pay
**President and CEO, UGI Utilities:** David W. Trego, age 48
**Associate General Counsel and Corporate Secretary:** Margaret M. Calabrese
**Director Corporate Accounting and Reporting:** Richard R. Eynon, age 56
**Media Relations:** Brenda Blake
**Auditors:** PricewaterhouseCoopers LLP

## LOCATIONS

**HQ:** UGI Corporation
460 N. Gulph Rd., King of Prussia, PA 19406
**Phone:** 610-337-1000 **Fax:** 610-992-3254
**Web:** www.ugicorp.com

UGI operates in Austria, Canada, China, the Czech Republic, France, Slovakia, and the US.

## PRODUCTS/OPERATIONS

### 2006 Sales

| | $ mil. | % of total |
|---|---|---|
| AmeriGas Propane | 2,119.3 | 40 |
| International propane | 945.5 | 18 |
| Utilities | 822.0 | 16 |
| Energy services & other | 1,334.2 | 26 |
| **Total** | **5,221.0** | **100** |

### Selected Subsidiaries and Affiliates

AmeriGas, Inc.
AmeriGas Propane, Inc.
AmeriGas Partners, L.P. (44%)
AmeriGas Propane L.P.
AmeriGas Technology Group, Inc.
Petrolane Incorporated
Four Flags Drilling Company, Inc.
Ashtola Production Company
UGI Ethanol Development Corporation
Newbury Holding Company
UGI Enterprises, Inc. (energy marketing and services)
CFN Enterprises, Inc.
Eastfield International Holdings, Inc.
FLAGA GmbH (propane distribution; Austria, the Czech Republic, and Slovakia)
Eurogas Holdings, Inc.
McHugh Service Company
UGI Energy Services, Inc.
GASMARK (gas marketing)
POWERMARK (electricity marketing)
UGI International Enterprises, Inc.
UGI Europe, Inc.
Antargaz (propane distribution, France)
UGI Properties, Inc.
UGI Utilities, Inc. (natural gas and electric utility)
United Valley Insurance Company

## COMPETITORS

All Star Gas
Chesapeake Utilities
Dominion Resources
Duquesne Light Holdings
Energy Transfer
Exelon
Ferrellgas Partners
National Fuel Gas
NorthWestern
PPL
Star Gas Partners
Suburban Propane

## HISTORICAL FINANCIALS

Company Type: Public

### Income Statement

FYE: September 30

| | REVENUE ($ mil.) | NET INCOME ($ mil.) | NET PROFIT MARGIN | EMPLOYEES |
|---|---|---|---|---|
| **9/06** | 5,221 | 176 | 3.4% | 5,900 |
| **9/05** | 4,889 | 188 | 3.8% | 6,000 |
| **9/04** | 3,785 | 112 | 2.9% | 6,100 |
| **9/03** | 3,026 | 99 | 3.3% | 6,200 |
| **9/02** | 2,214 | 76 | 3.4% | 6,300 |
| **Annual Growth** | 23.9% | 23.6% | — | (1.6%) |

### 2006 Year-End Financials

Debt ratio: 178.7%
Return on equity: 16.8%
Cash ($ mil.): 207
Current ratio: 1.01
Long-term debt ($ mil.): 1,965
No. of shares (mil.): 106
Dividends
Yield: 2.8%
Payout: 41.8%
Market value ($ mil.): 2,587

### Stock History

NYSE: UGI

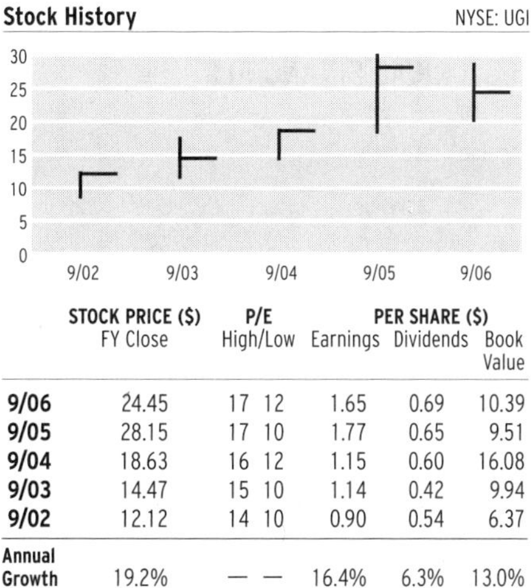


| | STOCK PRICE ($) FY Close | P/E High | P/E Low | PER SHARE ($) Earnings | Dividends | Book Value |
|---|---|---|---|---|---|---|
| **9/06** | 24.45 | 17 | 12 | 1.65 | 0.69 | 10.39 |
| **9/05** | 28.15 | 17 | 10 | 1.77 | 0.65 | 9.51 |
| **9/04** | 18.63 | 16 | 12 | 1.15 | 0.60 | 16.08 |
| **9/03** | 14.47 | 15 | 10 | 1.14 | 0.42 | 9.94 |
| **9/02** | 12.12 | 14 | 10 | 0.90 | 0.54 | 6.37 |
| **Annual Growth** | 19.2% | — | — | 16.4% | 6.3% | 13.0% |

# Union Pacific

Venerable Union Pacific (UP) keeps on chugging down the track, just as it has since the 19th century. The company's Union Pacific Railroad is the leading rail freight carrier in the US (just ahead of Burlington Northern Santa Fe). Union Pacific Railroad transports coal, chemicals, industrial products, and other freight over a system of more than 32,300 route miles in 23 states in the western two-thirds of the US. The company owns about 26,500 route miles of its rail network; leases and trackage rights, which allow UP to use other railroads' tracks, account for the rest.

A significant growth driver for UP is its intermodal business, which transports containerized freight that will travel by at least one additional mode of transportation, such as a truck or a ship. Marine transportation company APL is a major customer, as is package giant UPS. In addition, UP is well-positioned to serve US power plants' growing demand for coal; its lines serve major coal product areas, particularly the Southern Powder River Basin of Wyoming. Rising demand for ethanol also has been a boon for UP.

Besides its freight transportation operations, Union Pacific Railroad provides logistics services, through Union Pacific Distribution Services. UP's Transentric unit offers transportation and supply chain management software.

## HISTORY

In 1862 the US Congress chartered the Union Pacific Railroad (UP) to build part of the first transcontinental railway. The driving of the Golden Spike at Promontory, Utah, in 1869 marked the linking of the East and West coasts as UP's rails met those of Central Pacific Railroad (predecessor of Southern Pacific, or SP), which had been built east from Sacramento, California.

In 1872 the *New York Sun* revealed the Credit Mobilier scandal: UP officials had pocketed excess profits during the railroad's construction. Debt and lingering effects of the scandal forced UP into bankruptcy in 1893.

A syndicate headed by E. H. Harriman bought UP in 1897. After reacquiring the Oregon branches it lost in the bankruptcy, UP gained control of SP (1901) and Chicago & Alton (1904). The Supreme Court ordered UP to sell its SP holdings in 1913 on antitrust grounds. In the 1930s UP diversified into trucking, and in the 1970s and 1980s it moved into oil and gas production.

UP bought trucking firm Overnite Transportation in 1986. During the 1980s UP also built up its rail operations, acquiring the Missouri Pacific and Western Pacific railroads in 1982 and the Missouri-Kansas-Texas Railroad in 1988. It joined Chicago and North Western (CNW) Railway managers in an investment group led by Blackstone Capital Partners that bought CNW in 1989.

CNW traced its roots to the Galena & Chicago Union Railroad, which was founded by Chicago's first mayor, W. B. Ogden, in 1836, and merged with CNW in 1864. By 1925 the North Western (as it was then known) had tracks throughout the Midwest. In 1995 UP completed its purchase of CNW and made a bid for SP.

SP was founded in 1865, but its history dates to 1861, when four Sacramento merchants founded Central Pacific. By building new track and buying other railroads (including SP, in 1868), Central Pacific had expanded throughout California, Texas, and Oregon by 1887. The two railroads merged in 1885 under the SP name. In 1983 SP was sold to a holding company controlled by Philip Anschutz, which in 1995 agreed to sell the company to UP.

UP completed its SP acquisition in 1996 but assimilation of the purchase led to widespread rail traffic jams. UP also sold its remaining interest in Union Pacific Resources, an oil company it had spun off the year before. In 1997 UP moved from Bethlehem, Pennsylvania, to Dallas and joined a consortium led by mining company Grupo Mexico that won a bid to run two major Mexican rail lines. In the US, however, UP's fatal collisions led to a federal review, which found a breakdown in rail safety, such as overworked employees and widespread train defects. Meanwhile, regulators, seeking to resolve UP's massive freight backlog, ordered the railroad to open its Houston lines to competitors.

UP decentralized its management into three regions (north, south, and west) in 1998 to improve traffic flow. It also hired more workers, added new trains, and realigned routes, while selling Skyway Freight Systems, its logistics services unit.

In 1999 UP moved its headquarters from Dallas to Omaha, Nebraska, where Union Pacific Railroad offices already were located. In 2000 it formed Fenix, a holding company charged with developing and expanding the company's telecommunications and technology assets. (By 2003, however, UP had reabsorbed Fenix and scaled back its support for its remaining technology subsidiaries.)

UP expanded its less-than-truckload operations into the western US in 2001 by buying Motor Cargo Industries. Also that year UP completed the integration of Southern Pacific's operations.

UP sold its trucking unit, Overnite Corporation (a holding company for Overnite Transportation and Motor Cargo Industries), in an IPO in 2003. (Overnite Corporation was acquired by United Parcel Service in 2005 and renamed UPS Freight the next year.)

UP sold its Timera subsidiary (workforce management software) in 2004.

Traffic congestion in the UP system, brought on by a shortage of train crews, caused some freight from UPS and other customers to be rerouted onto trucks in 2004. The crew shortage was attributed in part to a greater-than-expected number of retirements in 2003. UP accelerated its hiring and training efforts, but the company still had to restrict freight volume in an effort to minimize bottlenecks.

In 2006 Union Pacific Railroad reorganized its operating structure, going from four regions to three: northern, southern, and western. Service units of the company's central region were reassigned to the northern and southern regions.

## EXECUTIVES

**EVP, Finance and CFO; EVP, Finance and CFO, Union Pacific Railroad:** Robert M. Knight Jr., age 49, $1,166,666 pay
**Chairman, President, and CEO; Chairman and CEO, Union Pacific Railroad:** James R. (Jim) Young, age 54
**EVP, Marketing and Sales, Union Pacific Railroad:** John J. (Jack) Koraleski, age 56
**EVP, Operations, Union Pacific Railroad:** Dennis J. Duffy, age 56, $1,456,667 pay
**SVP and CIO; SVP and CIO, Union Pacific Railroad:** Lynden L. Tennison, age 47
**SVP, Corporate Relations; SVP, Corporate Relations, Union Pacific Railroad:** Robert W. Turner, age 57
**SVP, Human Resources and Secretary; SVP, Human Resources and Secretary, Union Pacific Railroad:** Barbara W. Schaefer, age 53
**SVP, Law and General Counsel; SVP, Law and General Counsel, Union Pacific Railroad:** J. Michael (Mike) Hemmer, age 57, $1,136,667 pay
**SVP, Strategic Planning and Administration; SVP, Strategic Planning and Administration, Union Pacific Railroad:** Charles R. Eisele, age 57
**Assistant VP, Corporate Communications:** Kathryn Blackwell
**Assistant VP, Investor Relations:** Jennifer Hamann
**Auditors:** Deloitte & Touche LLP

## LOCATIONS

**HQ:** Union Pacific Corporation
1400 Douglas St., Omaha, NE 68179
**Phone:** 402-544-5000 **Fax:** 402-501-2133
**Web:** www.up.com

## PRODUCTS/OPERATIONS

### 2006 Sales

| | $ mil. | % of total |
|---|---|---|
| Commodity | | |
| Industrial products | 3,173 | 20 |
| Energy | 2,953 | 19 |
| Intermodal | 2,805 | 18 |
| Agricultural | 2,395 | 15 |
| Chemicals | 2,098 | 14 |
| Automotive | 1,438 | 9 |
| Other | 716 | 5 |
| **Total** | **15,578** | **100** |

## COMPETITORS

American Commercial Lines
Arkansas Best
Burlington Northern Santa Fe
Canadian National Railway
Canadian Pacific Railway
CSX
Hub Group
Ingram Industries
J.B. Hunt
Kansas City Southern
Kirby
Landstar System
Norfolk Southern
Pacer International
Schneider National
Werner Enterprises

## HISTORICAL FINANCIALS

Company Type: Public

### Income Statement

FYE: December 31

| | REVENUE ($ mil.) | NET INCOME ($ mil.) | NET PROFIT MARGIN | EMPLOYEES |
|---|---|---|---|---|
| **12/06** | 15,578 | 1,606 | 10.3% | 50,739 |
| **12/05** | 13,578 | 1,026 | 7.6% | 49,747 |
| **12/04** | 12,215 | 604 | 4.9% | 48,000 |
| **12/03** | 11,551 | 1,585 | 13.7% | 46,400 |
| **12/02** | 12,491 | 1,341 | 10.7% | 47,300 |
| **Annual Growth** | 5.7% | 4.6% | — | 1.8% |

### 2006 Year-End Financials

Debt ratio: 39.2%
Return on equity: 11.1%
Cash ($ mil.): 827
Current ratio: 0.68
Long-term debt ($ mil.): 6,000
No. of shares (mil.): 270
Dividends
Yield: 1.3%
Payout: 20.3%
Market value ($ mil.): 24,861

### Stock History

NYSE: UNP

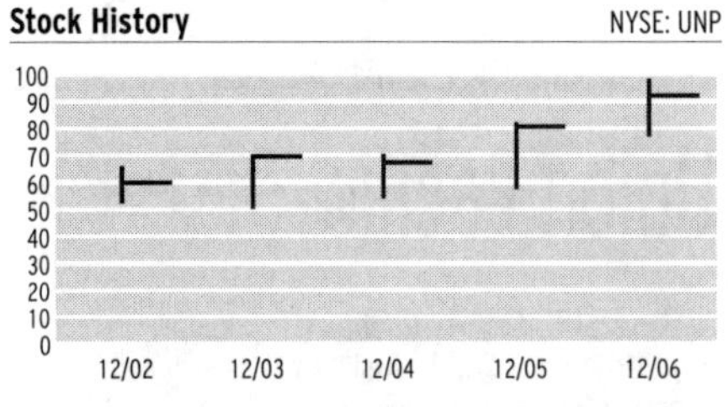

| | STOCK PRICE ($) FY Close | P/E High | P/E Low | PER SHARE ($) Earnings | Dividends | Book Value |
|---|---|---|---|---|---|---|
| **12/06** | 92.02 | 16 | 13 | 5.91 | 1.20 | 56.67 |
| **12/05** | 80.51 | 21 | 15 | 3.85 | 1.20 | 51.41 |
| **12/04** | 67.25 | 30 | 24 | 2.30 | 1.20 | 48.58 |
| **12/03** | 69.48 | 12 | 8 | 6.04 | 0.99 | 47.85 |
| **12/02** | 59.87 | 13 | 10 | 5.05 | 0.83 | 41.96 |
| **Annual Growth** | 11.3% | — | — | 4.0% | 9.7% | 7.8% |

# Unisys Corporation

Information systems of the world, unite. Unisys is a top player in the information technology (IT) consulting business, providing such services as systems integration, network engineering, project management, and technical support. The company is among the largest government IT contractors, serving local, state, and federal agencies, as well as foreign governments. Other practice groups focus on such sectors as communications, financial services, and transportation. The company also specializes in making high-end servers (under the ClearPath brand).

Unisys' operations are split into two segments — services (systems integration and consulting, outsourcing, infrastructure services, and core maintenance) and technology (enterprise-class servers and specialized technologies).

Unisys has been focused on securing more long-term outsourcing contracts for applications, data center, and network management as a way to protect itself from cyclical downturns in the technology services sector. Outsourcing now accounts for more than 30% of the company's revenues. Cost containment is still a high priority for the company, which is continuing to shave headcount while looking to divest itself of some non-core assets. It sold its 28% stake in Japanese affiliate Nihon Unisys early in 2006. A year later it disposed of its media business to UK media software firm Atex Group. It is working to reposition itself in such higher-growth market sectors as open source software and security.

In 2007 Unisys said it would slash 950 US and UK jobs, extending layoffs that had begun in 2005 with the elimination of some 5,600 positions. The company has additionally turned to hiring more workers in low-wage India and China to help offset continued declines in its hardware, systems integration, consulting, and maintenance businesses.

## HISTORY

Unisys was formed in 1986 when struggling mainframe computer giant Burroughs swallowed fellow mainframe maker Sperry Corporation. Burroughs traced its roots back to American Arithmometer (St. Louis, 1886), later Burroughs Adding Machine (Detroit, 1905), and then Burroughs Corporation (1953). It entered data processing by purchasing Electrodata (1956) and many other firms, including Memorex (1982).

Sperry was the product of the 1955 merger of Sperry Gyroscope (founded in 1910 by Elmer Sperry) and Remington Rand, an old-line typewriter manufacturer and maker of the first commercially viable computer, the UNIVAC. Sperry later bought RCA's faltering computer unit in 1971.

In 1986 Burroughs president Michael Blumenthal sought to achieve efficiency in parts and development by merging Burroughs' small database managers with Sperry's defense-related number crunchers. The new company was called Unisys, a contraction of "United Information Systems."

As president of Unisys, Blumenthal quickly disposed of $1.8 billion in assets (Sperry Aerospace and Marine divisions and Memorex), closed plants, and cut jobs. He continued to support Sperry's flagship line of mainframes and nurtured Burroughs' prized "A" series of computers. The initial results were positive, with 1986's $43 million loss followed by 1987's $578 million profit.

Amid an industry trend toward stronger, smaller systems, Unisys in 1988 equipped its U line of servers with the open UNIX operating system and moved to smaller networked systems by acquiring Timeplex (voice/data networks) and Convergent (UNIX workstations). That year the US Department of Justice launched an investigation of illegal defense procurement practices committed by Sperry prior to its merger with Burroughs (Unisys settled the charges in 1991).

Plummeting mainframe demand in 1989 and 1990 led to heavy losses. Blumenthal left the company in 1990, and continuing losses prompted layoffs the following year (Unisys eventually laid off nearly two-thirds of its workforce). The company pared its product line and closed seven of its 15 plants.

In 1995 Unisys and Intel, from a joint venture begun two years earlier, unveiled a $700,000-plus parallel-processing computer that sped up computations. That year the company sold its defense unit to Loral for $862 million. Restructuring charges contributed to losses for the year. In 1996 shareholders rejected a proposal to split Unisys into three separate companies (computer manufacturing, consulting, and services).

Shareholders rejected another proposal to split the company in 1997. Former Andersen Worldwide CEO Larry Weinbach (who left the accounting giant long before it was brought down by scandal) took over as chairman, president, and CEO that year. He immediately began boosting employee morale — easing the company's travel policy, among other changes — and remaking Unisys in the image of his old consulting firm. Charges of more than $1 billion (largely to write off the value of the 1986 Sperry purchase, a move cheered by many analysts) led to a loss for 1997. In 1998 Unisys signed a deal to outsource the manufacture of its PCs and low-end servers to Hewlett-Packard.

Unisys hired about 7,000 workers in 1999 to install and maintain corporate computer networks, and it acquired six companies including telecom software developer PulsePoint Communications and Brazilian outsourcing specialist Datamec. In 2000 Unisys signed co-branding deals with Compaq and other manufacturers to market its high-end servers. It also realigned its services business to focus on the high-growth customer relationship management (CRM), e-commerce, and mobile commerce markets.

The economy in general and technology spending in particular began to deteriorate in 2000, leading to smaller profits and eventually a loss in 2001. Unisys responded by placing more emphasis on long-term outsourcing contracts as a hedge against further economic decline. The company also took steps to reduce costs, including cutting staff.

Following the terrorist attacks of September 11, 2001, Unisys expanded its public sector business units as government agencies began focusing on homeland security issues.

In 2004 the company joined the widespread outsourcing trend, announcing its decision to relocate its technology development operations to India and disclosing plans to invest $180 million and hire 2,000 employees in that country by 2009. Weinbach stepped down as CEO in 2005, tapping Joe McGrath as his replacement, before retiring from the company altogether the following year.

## EXECUTIVES

**Chairman:** Henry C. (Ric) Duques, age 63
**President, CEO, and Director:** Joseph W. (Joe) McGrath, age 54, $900,000 pay
**SVP and CFO:** Janet B. Haugen, age 48, $500,000 pay
**SVP, General Counsel, and Secretary:** Nancy S. Sundheim, age 55
**SVP; President, Federal Systems:** Greg J. Baroni, age 53
**SVP; President, Global Outsourcing and Infrastructure Services:** Randy J. Hendricks, age 50
**SVP Worldwide Human Resources:** Patricia A. (Pat) Bradford, age 56
**SVP and President, Systems and Technology:** Richard (Rich) Marcello
**SVP and President, Unisys Global Industries:** Brian T. Maloney, age 53
**VP and Corporate Controller:** Joseph M. (Joe) Munnelly, age 42
**VP and Treasurer:** Scott A. Battersby, age 48
**VP Communications:** Elizabeth Douglass
**VP Strategic Client Development:** John C. Carrow
**VP Investor Relations:** Jack F. McHale, age 57
**VP Corporate Operations:** Arun Chandra
**VP and Managing Director, UK, Middle East, and Africa, Global Outsourcing and Infrastructure Services:** Duncan Tait
**VP Business Innovation:** Craig Samuel
**President, Global Communications and Media Industries:** Glenn James
**President, Global Transportation:** Olivier Houri
**Managing Partner, Homeland Security, Federal Systems:** Thomas M. (Tom) Conaway
**Chief Marketing Officer:** Ellyn Raftery
**CTO:** Frederick (Fred) Dillman
**CIO:** Kevin Kern
**Auditors:** Ernst & Young LLP

## LOCATIONS

**HQ:** Unisys Corporation
Unisys Way, Blue Bell, PA 19424
**Phone:** 215-986-4011 **Fax:** 215-986-2312
**Web:** www.unisys.com

Unisys operates in more than 100 countries.

### 2006 Sales

| | % of total |
|---|---|
| US | 44 |
| UK | 15 |
| Other countries | 41 |
| **Total** | **100** |

## PRODUCTS/OPERATIONS

### 2006 Sales

| | % of total |
|---|---|
| Services | |
| Systems integration and consulting | 28 |
| Outsourcing | 33 |
| Infrastructure services | 16 |
| Core maintenance | 8 |
| Technology | |
| Enterprise-class servers | 12 |
| Specialized technologies | 3 |
| **Total** | **100** |

### Selected Products

Data storage
- Storage area networks
- Storage software
- Tape drives
- Tape libraries

Payment systems
- Amount recognition
- Document processors
- Fraud prevention systems
- Proof encoders
- Scanners
- Servers

ClearPath
- IX
- LX
- NX

### Selected Services

Network services
- Infrastructure deployment
- Infrastructure management
- Infrastructure support
- Internet integration
- Network integration
- Network optimization
- Software development

Outsourcing
- Business process outsourcing
- Information technology outsourcing
- Managed application services

Security
- Access control
  - Biometrics
  - Certificate authorities
  - Digital certificates
  - Encryption
  - Firewalls
  - Single sign-on
  - Smart cards
- Business continuity
  - Architecture and implementation
  - Business impact analysis
  - Disaster recovery planning
  - Vulnerability assessment
- Electronic transactions
  - Identrus
  - Public key infrastructure
- Infrastructure
  - Application security
  - Assessment and testing
  - Design and implementation
  - Intrusion detection
  - Monitoring and management
  - Server hardening
- Server infrastructure services
  - Architecture
  - Data storage
  - Microsoft solutions
  - Operations and performance

## COMPETITORS

Accenture
Affiliated Computer Services
BearingPoint
Capgemini
Computer Sciences Corp.
Dell
Deloitte Consulting
EDS
Fujitsu
Hewlett-Packard
Hitachi
IBM
NEC
Perot Systems
SGI
Siemens AG
Sun Microsystems
Titan Group
Toshiba

## HISTORICAL FINANCIALS

Company Type: Public

### Income Statement

FYE: December 31

| | REVENUE ($ mil.) | NET INCOME ($ mil.) | NET PROFIT MARGIN | EMPLOYEES |
|---|---|---|---|---|
| **12/06** | 5,757 | (279) | — | 31,500 |
| **12/05** | 5,759 | (1,732) | — | 36,100 |
| **12/04** | 5,821 | 39 | 0.7% | 36,400 |
| **12/03** | 5,911 | 259 | 4.4% | 37,300 |
| **12/02** | 5,607 | 223 | 4.0% | 36,400 |
| **Annual Growth** | 0.7% | — | — | (3.5%) |

### 2006 Year-End Financials

Debt ratio: —
Return on equity: —
Cash ($ mil.): 719
Current ratio: 1.16
Long-term debt ($ mil.): 1,049
No. of shares (mil.): 345
Dividends
Yield: —
Payout: —
Market value ($ mil.): 2,707

**Stock History** NYSE: UIS

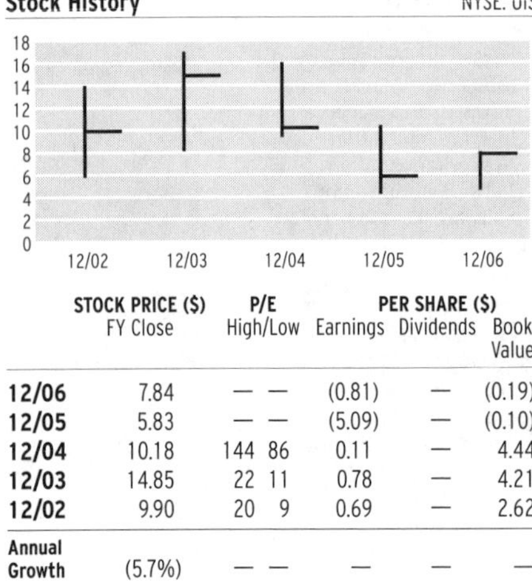


| | STOCK PRICE ($) FY Close | P/E High/Low | | PER SHARE ($) Earnings | Dividends | Book Value |
|---|---|---|---|---|---|---|
| **12/06** | 7.84 | — | — | (0.81) | — | (0.19) |
| **12/05** | 5.83 | — | — | (5.09) | — | (0.10) |
| **12/04** | 10.18 | 144 | 86 | 0.11 | — | 4.44 |
| **12/03** | 14.85 | 22 | 11 | 0.78 | — | 4.21 |
| **12/02** | 9.90 | 20 | 9 | 0.69 | — | 2.62 |
| **Annual Growth** | (5.7%) | — | — | — | — | — |

# United Natural Foods

If United Natural Foods was one of the items it distributes, it would be an all-natural fruit rollup. The company is a leading distributor of natural and organic foods and products in the US, with more than 15 distribution centers supplying more than 40,000 items to about 20,000 customers, including independently owned retail stores, supermarket chains, and buying clubs. It offers natural groceries, personal care products, supplements, and frozen foods. In addition to its wholesale distribution business, United Natural Foods operates a dozen natural-products retail stores (mostly in Florida) and it produces roasted nuts, dried fruits, and other snack items through its Hershey Import Company subsidiary.

The bulk of the company's business comes from independently owned retail stores (more than 45%) and from supermarket chains that specialize in natural food products. Its broadline distribution business is anchored by subsidiary Albert's Organics, which supplies more than 5,000 customers with fruits, vegetables, and other perishable items. Organic retail giant Whole Foods accounts for more than 25% of sales, while Wild Oats Markets accounts for another 10% of United Natural Foods' revenue. The company buys products from more than 5,000 suppliers, mostly in the United States; Hain Celestial Group accounts for almost 10% of its purchases.

United Natural Foods has in the past grown primarily through acquisitions of regional and niche market distributors. While it continues to keep an eye open for possible business mergers, the company is now focused on organic growth (no pun intended) and plans to open additional distribution facilities in Florida, Texas, and the Northwest through 2008.

## HISTORY

Rhode Island retailer Norman Cloutier founded Cornucopia Natural Foods in 1978 and soon focused on distribution. During the 1980s Cornucopia grew by acquiring other natural foods distributors. It bought suppliers Natural Food Systems (seafood) and BGS Distributing (vitamins) in 1987 and 1990, respectively. Cornucopia expanded into the Southeast in 1991 when it opened a distribution center in Georgia.

Reviving its interest in retailing, Cornucopia formed Natural Retail Group in 1993 to buy and run natural foods stores. During the next two years it acquired several retailers. It expanded its distribution operations in the West in 1995, adding Denver-based Rainbow Distributors.

In 1996 Cornucopia merged with the leading natural foods distributor in the western US, Sacramento-based Mountain People's, which Michael Funk had founded 20 years earlier. The combined company became United Natural Foods with Coutier as chairman and CEO and Funk as president and VC; it went public later that year.

United Natural Foods became the largest natural foods distributor when it bought New Hampshire-based Stow Mills in 1997. The next year it added Hershey Imports, an importer and processor of nuts, seed, and snacks, and Albert's, a distributor of organic produce. With the purchase of Mother Earth Markets in 1998, the company's retailing operations had grown to 16 stores, but by mid-1999 it had sold four stores. That year United Natural Foods' East Coast consolidation problems became so profound that top customer Whole Foods announced it was finding backup distribution sources.

Funk replaced Cloutier as CEO and the company handed the chairman's post to board member Thomas Simone in 1999. In 2000, after the resignation of Cloutier from the board of directors, United Natural Foods adopted a poison pill plan to block potential takeovers. The company leased a distribution center in the Los Angeles area in 2001 to increase market share in the Southwest. It also acquired Florida's Palm Harbor Natural Foods.

In mid-2002 United Natural Foods lost one of its two largest customers — Wild Oats Markets — when that company defected to rival specialty foods distributor Tree of Life. However, United Natural Foods soon won that business back. In October the company completed the acquisition of privately held Blooming Prairie Cooperative for approximately $31 million. In late 2002 the company merged with Northeast Cooperatives, a natural foods distributor in the Midwest and Northeast.

President Steven Townsend succeeded Michael Funk as CEO of the company in 2003. That year, United Natural Foods discontinued the management, sales, and support operations at its Hershey Imports subsidiary, but continued to manufacture and distribute products from the Edison, New Jersey, plant. In December 2003, Townsend was elected chairman when Funk stepped down, completing the company's succession plan.

At the end of 2004 United Natural Foods and Whole Foods announced a new three-year distribution agreement beginning January 1, 2005, extending the company's role as Whole Foods' primary supplier.

## EXECUTIVES

**Chairman:** Thomas B. Simone, age 64
**President, CEO, and Director:** Michael S. Funk, age 52, $511,564 pay
**EVP, COO, President, Distribution, and Director:** Richard (Rick) Antonelli, age 49, $542,308 pay
**EVP, Chief Marketing Officer, and Corporate Secretary; President, United Natural Brands:** Daniel V. (Dan) Atwood, age 47, $359,423 pay
**VP, CFO, and Treasurer:** Mark E. Shamber, age 37
**VP, Information Technology:** Gary A. Glenn, age 55
**VP, Sales:** Kate Tierney
**President, Albert's Organics:** Barclay Hope, $265,195 pay
**President, Eastern Region:** Michael Beaudry, age 42, $313,356 pay
**President, Western Region:** Randle E. Lindberg, age 55
**Corporate Controller:** Lisa N'Chonon
**General Manager, Natural Retail Group:** Mickey Jeffers
**Manager, Import International Hershey Import Company:** Jay Bambara
**Manager, Sales Foodservice Eastern Division:** Shawn Dean
**Senior Buyer, Domestic Hershey Import Company:** Vince Thaner
**Auditors:** KPMG LLP

## LOCATIONS

**HQ:** United Natural Foods, Inc.
260 Lake Rd., Dayville, CT 06241
**Phone:** 860-779-2800 **Fax:** 860-779-2811
**Web:** www.unfi.com

## PRODUCTS/OPERATIONS

**2006 Sales**

| | $ mil. | % of total |
|---|---|---|
| Wholesale | 2,392 | 97 |
| Other | 77 | 3 |
| Adjustments | (35) | — |
| **Total** | **2,434** | **100** |

**2006 Sales**

| | % of total |
|---|---|
| Independently owned retailers | 46 |
| Natural foods supermarket chains | 36 |
| Conventional supermarkets | 14 |
| Other | 4 |
| **Total** | **100** |

**Selected Product Categories**

Bulk and food service products
Fresh produce and perishables
Frozen foods
Groceries and general merchandise
Health and beauty aids
Nutritional supplements
Personal care products

## COMPETITORS

Distribution Plus
GNC
Haddon House
Kehe Food
Millbrook Distribution Services
Nature's Best
Performance Food
SUPERVALU
SYSCO
Tree of Life

## HISTORICAL FINANCIALS

Company Type: Public

**Income Statement** FYE: July 31

| | REVENUE ($ mil.) | NET INCOME ($ mil.) | NET PROFIT MARGIN | EMPLOYEES |
|---|---|---|---|---|
| **7/06** | 2,434 | 43 | 1.8% | 4,500 |
| **7/05** | 2,060 | 42 | 2.0% | 4,030 |
| **7/04** | 1,670 | 32 | 1.9% | 3,900 |
| **7/03** | 1,380 | 20 | 1.5% | 3,400 |
| **7/02** | 1,175 | 17 | 1.5% | 3,000 |
| **Annual Growth** | 20.0% | 26.0% | — | 10.7% |

**2006 Year-End Financials**

Debt ratio: 16.4%
Return on equity: 13.1%
Cash ($ mil.): 20
Current ratio: 1.69
Long-term debt ($ mil.): 60
No. of shares (mil.): 42
Dividends
Yield: —
Payout: —
Market value ($ mil.): 1,294

**Stock History** NASDAQ (GS): UNFI

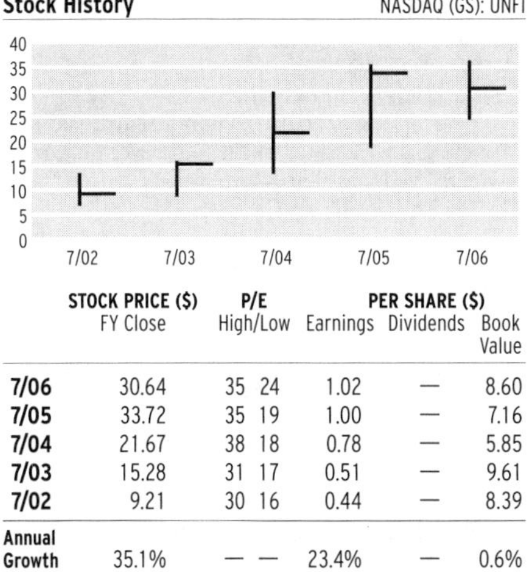

| | STOCK PRICE ($) FY Close | P/E High/Low | | PER SHARE ($) Earnings | Dividends | Book Value |
|---|---|---|---|---|---|---|
| **7/06** | 30.64 | 35 | 24 | 1.02 | — | 8.60 |
| **7/05** | 33.72 | 35 | 19 | 1.00 | — | 7.16 |
| **7/04** | 21.67 | 38 | 18 | 0.78 | — | 5.85 |
| **7/03** | 15.28 | 31 | 17 | 0.51 | — | 9.61 |
| **7/02** | 9.21 | 30 | 16 | 0.44 | — | 8.39 |
| **Annual Growth** | 35.1% | — | — | 23.4% | — | 0.6% |

# United Parcel Service

It still relies on chocolate-colored trucks, but United Parcel Service (UPS) is more than a plain-vanilla delivery business. The world's largest package-delivery company, UPS transports some 15.6 million packages and documents per business day throughout the US and to more than 200 countries and territories. Its delivery operations use a fleet of about 101,000 motor vehicles and more than 600 aircraft. The company offers services such as logistics and freight forwarding through UPS Supply Chain Solutions, and it has expanded into trucking by buying Overnite (now UPS Freight).

Archrival FedEx, through its FedEx Ground unit, has expanded its US ground delivery business, but UPS doesn't intend to give up market share without a fight. The company is working to sell package delivery services to customers of its other units; at the same time, it is striving to control costs.

Nonpackage operations, such as freight forwarding and logistics, make up the fastest-growing segment of the company's business, and UPS is working to strengthen its supply chain management offerings. The company also offers mail expediting (UPS Mail Innovations) and financial services (UPS Capital).

The 2005 acquisition of Overnite brought UPS into the less-than-truckload (LTL) freight transportation business and — not coincidentally — countered a move by FedEx, which formed nationwide LTL carrier FedEx Freight in 2001. (LTL carriers combine freight from multiple shippers into a single truckload.)

Other UPS businesses include postal and business services store franchiser Mail Boxes Etc., which maintains some 5,800 locations in the US and overseas. Most of the US franchises of Mail Boxes Etc. have been re-branded as The UPS Store.

In overseas markets, the company is continuing to expand. It sees the Asia/Pacific region as particularly promising, and UPS is adding facilities in China and offering direct air service from more Chinese markets.

## HISTORY

Seattle teens Jim Casey and Claude Ryan started American Messenger Company, a phone message service, in 1907. They were soon making small-parcel deliveries for local department stores and in 1913 changed the company's name to Merchants Parcel Delivery. In 1915 Casey, who led the company for the next 47 years, established a policy of manager ownership, and Charlie Soderstrom chose the brown paint still used on the company's vehicles.

Service expanded outside Seattle in 1919 when Merchants Parcel bought Oakland, California-based Motor Parcel Delivery. By 1930 the company, which had been renamed United Parcel Service, served residents in New York City (its headquarters from 1930 to 1975); Newark, New Jersey; and Greenwich, Connecticut.

Offering small-package delivery within a 150-mile radius of certain cities, starting with Los Angeles in 1952, UPS grew in relative obscurity as it expanded westward from the East Coast and eastward from the West. Noted for its employee-oriented culture, the company through the 1960s required all executives to start as drivers.

The company gained notice in 1972 when the U.S. Postal Service named UPS as a competitor. In 1975 UPS crossed the border to Canada, and in 1976 it began service in West Germany. It started air express delivery in Louisville, Kentucky, in the late 1970s. By 1982 UPS Blue Label Air Service (now UPS 2nd Day Air) guaranteed 48-hour delivery anywhere on the mainland and Oahu, Hawaii. Overnight service (UPS Next Day Air) began in 1982 and was nationwide by 1985.

Moving to Atlanta in 1991, the company began to work on its customer service. As part of a technology revamp, UPS created the electronic clipboard used by drivers to track packages and digitize signatures.

In 1994 Teamsters staged a one-day strike to protest UPS's new per-package weight limit (raised from 70 to 150 pounds). The next year the firm allowed rank-and-file employees to buy UPS stock. Nevertheless, in 1997 UPS was hit by a 15-day Teamsters strike that cost the company hundreds of millions of dollars. UPS settled the strike by combining part-time jobs into 10,000 new full-time positions; in 1998 the company headed off another labor threat by giving its pilots a five-year contract with pay raises.

After losing a tax dispute in 1999, UPS paid $1.8 billion into a special account with the Internal Revenue Service, pending appeal. (The company prevailed on appeal in 2001, and the case went back to the U.S. Tax Court. UPS and the IRS settled the case in 2002, and UPS was to receive about $1 billion worth of credits and refunds over several years.)

Chinese government-owned logistics giant Sinotrans proved more friendly than the IRS, teaming up with UPS to expand UPS-branded service across China. To fund global expansion, UPS sold 9% of its stock in a public offering valued at more than $5 billion — then the largest IPO in US history. The company also agreed to buy Challenge Air Cargo (completed in 2001), a Miami cargo airline serving Latin America. The international push continued in 2000 as UPS expanded operations into Australia.

In 2001 UPS bought Mail Boxes Etc., a franchiser of stores that offer mail, packing, and shipping services. It also acquired global logistics management provider Fritz Companies, which was renamed UPS Freight Services, and expanded its financial services by buying First International Bancorp. That year UPS also placed its largest-ever aircraft order: 60 Airbus A300-600 cargo planes to be delivered by 2009. (UPS and Airbus subsequently renegotiated the order, and in 2005 Airbus agreed to supply newer A380 freighters instead of some of the planes that UPS originally ordered. Two years later, UPS said it would cancel its order for A380s because of delays in production of the aircraft.)

The company's contract with employees represented by the Teamsters came up for renewal in 2002, and a new six-year deal was approved.

To reflect the evolution of its mix of services, UPS in 2003 updated its company logo for the first time since 1961, losing the familiar package wrapped up in string. Brown remained the company's predominant color, but complementary hues were introduced on UPS aircraft and packages. Drivers' uniforms received the new logo but didn't change otherwise.

UPS in 2004 expanded its freight forwarding business by buying Menlo Worldwide Forwarding from CNF for $150 million and $110 million in assumed debt. The next year UPS acquired less-than-truckload carrier Overnite, which began operating the UPS Freight brand in 2006.

## EXECUTIVES

**Chairman and CEO:** Michael L. (Mike) Eskew, age 57, $1,029,500 pay
**Vice Chairman and CFO:** D. Scott Davis, age 55
**SVP and COO; President, UPS Airlines:** David P. Abney, age 51
**SVP and CIO:** David A. (Dave) Barnes, age 51
**SVP Legal, Compliance, and Public Affairs, General Counsel, and Secretary:** Teri P. McClure, age 43
**SVP and U.S. Operations Manager:** James F. (Jim) Winestock, age 55, $365,750 pay
**SVP Communications and Brand Management:** Christine M. Owens, age 51
**SVP Global Transportation Services:** John J. McDevitt, age 48
**SVP Human Resources:** Allen E. Hill, age 51
**SVP Engineering, Strategy, and Supply Chain Distribution:** Robert E. (Bob) Stoffel, age 51
**SVP Worldwide Sales and Marketing:** Kurt P. Kuehn, age 52
**SVP; President, UPS International:** Alan Gershenhorn, age 48
**VP International Marketing:** Geoff Light
**VP International Sales:** Lisa Lafave
**VP Finance:** Rich Peretz, age 45
**VP Investor Relations:** Andy Dolney, age 49
**President, Latin America and Caribbean:** Steve Flowers
**President, Mail Boxes Etc.:** Stuart Mathis
**President, UPS Asia Pacific:** Kenneth A. Torok
**President, UPS Capital:** Robert J. (Bob) Bernabucci
**President, UPS Europe:** Wolfgang Flick
**President, UPS Freight:** Jack Holmes, age 47
**Auditors:** Deloitte & Touche LLP

## LOCATIONS

**HQ:** United Parcel Service, Inc.
55 Glenlake Pkwy. NE, Atlanta, GA 30328
**Phone:** 404-828-6000 **Fax:** 404-828-6562
**Web:** www.ups.com

**2006 Sales**

| | $ mil. | % of total |
|---|---|---|
| US | 34,445 | 72 |
| Other countries | 13,102 | 28 |
| **Total** | **47,547** | **100** |

## PRODUCTS/OPERATIONS

**2006 Sales**

| | $ mil. | % of total |
|---|---|---|
| US domestic package | | |
| Ground | 20,254 | 43 |
| Next-day air | 6,778 | 14 |
| Deferred | 3,424 | 7 |
| International package | | |
| Export | 6,554 | 14 |
| Domestic | 1,950 | 4 |
| Cargo | 585 | 1 |
| Supply chain & freight | | |
| Forwarding & logistics | 5,681 | 12 |
| Freight | 1,952 | 4 |
| Other | 369 | 1 |
| **Total** | **47,547** | **100** |

## COMPETITORS

AMR Corp.
BAX Global
Canada Post
Con-way Inc.
Delta Air
Deutsche Post
FedEx
Japan Post
La Poste
Lufthansa
Nippon Express
Northwest Airlines
Panalpina
Royal Mail
Ryder
TNT
UAL
US Postal Service
YRC Worldwide

## HISTORICAL FINANCIALS

Company Type: Public

**Income Statement** FYE: December 31

| | REVENUE ($ mil.) | NET INCOME ($ mil.) | NET PROFIT MARGIN | EMPLOYEES |
|---|---|---|---|---|
| **12/06** | 47,547 | 4,202 | 8.8% | 428,000 |
| **12/05** | 42,581 | 3,870 | 9.1% | 407,000 |
| **12/04** | 36,582 | 3,333 | 9.1% | 384,000 |
| **12/03** | 33,485 | 2,898 | 8.7% | 355,000 |
| **12/02** | 31,272 | 3,182 | 10.2% | 360,000 |
| **Annual Growth** | 11.0% | 7.2% | — | 4.4% |

**2006 Year-End Financials**

Debt ratio: 20.2%
Return on equity: 26.0%
Cash ($ mil.): 1,983
Current ratio: 1.40
Long-term debt ($ mil.): 3,133
No. of shares (mil.): 669
Dividends
Yield: 2.0%
Payout: 39.4%
Market value ($ mil.): 50,162

**Stock History** NYSE: UPS

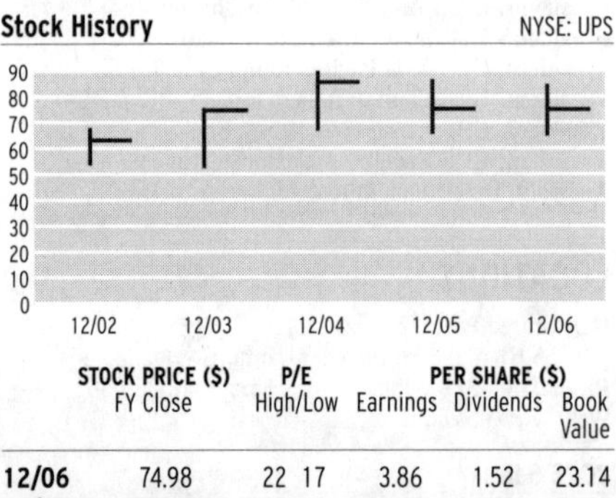


| | STOCK PRICE ($) FY Close | P/E High | P/E Low | PER SHARE ($) Earnings | Dividends | Book Value |
|---|---|---|---|---|---|---|
| **12/06** | 74.98 | 22 | 17 | 3.86 | 1.52 | 23.14 |
| **12/05** | 75.15 | 25 | 19 | 3.47 | 1.32 | 26.26 |
| **12/04** | 85.46 | 30 | 23 | 2.93 | 1.12 | 26.82 |
| **12/03** | 74.55 | 29 | 21 | 2.55 | 0.92 | 26.62 |
| **12/02** | 63.08 | 24 | 19 | 2.81 | 0.76 | 25.89 |
| **Annual Growth** | 4.4% | — | — | 8.3% | 18.9% | (2.8%) |

# United States Cellular

United States Cellular operates networks from sea to shining sea. Doing business as U.S. Cellular, the company provides wireless phone service to more than 5.8 million customers in more than two dozen states in the US. U.S. Cellular's networks use both analog and digital technologies such as TDMA (time division multiple access) and CDMA (code division multiple access). Products and services are marketed through company stores, the Internet, and national chain stores such as Best Buy. The company's services include mobile messaging, prepaid options, international long-distance, roadside assistance, and directory assistance. Telephone and Data Systems owns 81% of U.S. Cellular (and a 96% voting interest).

The company's operations are organized into eight principal regional clusters, which allow U.S. Cellular to boost its name recognition, cut costs, and offer service over larger areas without special roaming arrangements.

U.S. Cellular operates some 2,500 cell sites. The company offers vehicle-mounted, transportable, and portable phones with features such as hands-free calling, caller ID, and short messaging services. It also is spending heavily to upgrade and expand its network capacity and capability.

## HISTORY

LeRoy Carlson, a Chicago-based investor, formed Telephone and Data Systems (TDS) in 1969 by consolidating the rural phone companies he owned. In the early 1980s TDS began acquiring cellular licenses, including the rights to operate 5% of the Los Angeles market. Getting a jumpstart on the Bells, TDS created United States Cellular as a subsidiary in 1983.

United States Cellular began operations in 1985 in Knoxville, Tennessee, and Tulsa, Oklahoma. Three years later TDS took the company public and reduced its stake to 82%. Belgian cable TV operator Coditel was an initial investor.

Hefty startup and acquisition costs kept the company from making a profit until 1993. After moving into the black, it began selling its phones (purchased from suppliers) at kiosks in Wal-Mart Stores in 1995. Meanwhile, it continued to add networks: In 1995 and 1996 United States Cellular added markets in Arizona, Florida, Iowa, Texas, and Virginia.

In 1997 United States Cellular traded its controlling interests in 10 markets, primarily in Indiana and Kentucky, for BellSouth's controlling interests in 12 markets in Illinois and Wisconsin (including Milwaukee). That year the firm also began converting its network to digital technologies (both TDMA, time division multiple access, and the newer CDMA, code division multiple access).

In 1998 United States Cellular acquired majority interests in six more markets. That year the firm also sold several minority interests in markets in which it did not operate to Vodafone. The following year the company introduced a new logo and began doing business as U.S. Cellular. Also in 1999 it began providing CDPD (cellular digital packet data) service, which allows for data transmission over cellular networks, to police departments and government agencies in Illinois.

The company agreed in 2001 to acquire PCS licenses in Illinois, Iowa, and Nebraska from McLeodUSA for $74 million to bolster its Midwest operations. It purchased PrimeCo Wireless Communications in a 2002 deal valued at $610 million, gaining entrance into the Chicagoland market, as well as Bloomington-Normal, Champaign-Urbana, Decatur, and Springfield, Illinois, with expanded service to Peoria and Rockford, Illinois. Additionally, U.S. Cellular provides service to South Bend and Fort Wayne, Indiana, and Benton Harbor, Michigan.

In a 2003 swap agreement with AT&T Wireless, the company acquired wireless licenses and properties in 13 states in the Midwest and northeastern US in exchange for assets in northern Florida and southern Georgia.

## EXECUTIVES

**Chairman:** LeRoy T. (Ted) Carlson Jr., age 59, $766,500 pay
**President, CEO, and Director:** John E. (Jack) Rooney, age 64, $990,000 pay
**EVP, CFO, and Treasurer:** Steven T. Campbell, age 55
**EVP, Engineering and CTO:** Michael S. (Mike) Irizarry, age 44, $474,121 pay
**EVP and COO:** Jay M. Ellison, age 53, $608,915 pay
**SVP and Chief Human Resources Officer:** Jeffrey J. (Jeff) Childs, age 49
**VP and Corporate Secretary:** Kevin C. Gallagher, age 58
**VP, Business Support Services:** George W. Irving, age 51
**VP, Customer Service:** Rochelle J. Boersma, age 49
**VP, Financial Strategy:** Thomas (Tom) Weber
**VP, Legal and External Affairs:** James R. Jenkins, age 45
**VP, Marketing and Sales Operations:** Alan D. Ferber, age 38
**VP, Market Transition:** Leon J. Hensen, age 58
**VP, National Network Operations:** Kevin Lowell
**VP, Central Operations:** Katherine (Kathy) Hust, age 44
**VP, East Operations:** Thomas P. (Tom) Catani, age 46
**VP, West Operations:** Nick B. Wright, age 45
**VP, Public Affairs and Communications:** Karen C. Ehlers
**VP and Controller:** Nadine A. Heidrich, age 52
**VP Organizational Learning and Chief Teaching Officer:** Thomas J. Griffin, age 49
**VP Information Technology Delivery:** John Cregier
**VP Legal and Regulatory Affairs:** John C. Gockley, age 53
**Auditors:** PricewaterhouseCoopers LLP

## LOCATIONS

**HQ:** United States Cellular Corporation
8410 W. Bryn Mawr, Ste. 700, Chicago, IL 60631
**Phone:** 773-399-8900 **Fax:** 773-399-8936
**Web:** www.uscellular.com

United States Cellular has operations in Arkansas, California, Florida, Georgia, Illinois, Indiana, Iowa, Kansas, Maine, Maryland, Minnesota, Missouri, Nebraska, New Hampshire, North Carolina, Ohio, Oklahoma, Oregon, Pennsylvania, South Carolina, Tennessee, Texas, Vermont, Virginia, Washington, West Virginia, and Wisconsin.

**Selected Market Clusters**

Mid-Atlantic Region
- Eastern North Carolina/South Carolina
- Virginia/North Carolina
- West Virginia/Maryland/Pennsylvania

Midwest Region
- Central Illinois/Indiana
- Chicago MTA
- Iowa
- Kansas
- Missouri
- Nebraska/Missouri/Iowa
- Western Illinois
- Wisconsin/Minnesota

Northwest Region
- Oregon/California
- Washington/Oregon

Other Markets
Eastern Tennessee/Western North Carolina
Florida/Georgia
Maine/New Hampshire/Vermont
Missouri/Illinois/Kansas/Arkansas
Southern Texas
Texas/Oklahoma/Missouri/Kansas/Arkansas

## PRODUCTS/OPERATIONS

### 2006 Sales

| | % of total |
|---|---|
| Retail service | 82 |
| Equipment sales | 7 |
| Inbound roaming | 5 |
| Long distance & other | 6 |
| **Total** | **100** |

## COMPETITORS

ALLTEL
AT&T Mobility
Cellco
CenturyTel
Dobson Communications
Price Communications
Rural Cellular
Sprint Nextel
SunCom Wireless Holdings
T-Mobile USA

## HISTORICAL FINANCIALS

Company Type: Public

### Income Statement

FYE: December 31

| | REVENUE ($ mil.) | NET INCOME ($ mil.) | NET PROFIT MARGIN | EMPLOYEES |
|---|---|---|---|---|
| **12/06** | 3,473 | 180 | 5.2% | 8,100 |
| **12/05** | 3,031 | 155 | 5.1% | 7,700 |
| **12/04** | 2,808 | 110 | 3.9% | 7,400 |
| **12/03** | 2,583 | 43 | 1.7% | 6,225 |
| **12/02** | 2,185 | (14) | — | 6,100 |
| **Annual Growth** | 12.3% | — | — | 7.3% |

### 2006 Year-End Financials

Debt ratio: 33.5%
Return on equity: 6.3%
Cash ($ mil.): 282
Current ratio: 1.00
Long-term debt ($ mil.): 1,002
No. of shares (mil.): 55
Dividends
Yield: —
Payout: —
Market value ($ mil.): 3,808

### Stock History

AMEX: USM

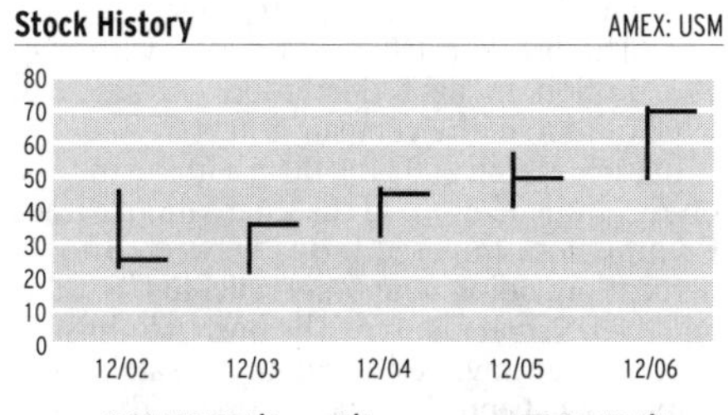

| | STOCK PRICE ($) FY Close | P/E High | P/E Low | PER SHARE ($) Earnings | Dividends | Book Value |
|---|---|---|---|---|---|---|
| **12/06** | 69.59 | 35 | 24 | 2.04 | — | 54.71 |
| **12/05** | 49.40 | 32 | 23 | 1.77 | — | 50.68 |
| **12/04** | 44.76 | 37 | 26 | 1.26 | — | 48.56 |
| **12/03** | 35.50 | 73 | 44 | 0.49 | — | 44.79 |
| **12/02** | 25.02 | — | — | (0.17) | — | 43.87 |
| **Annual Growth** | 29.1% | — | — | — | — | 5.7% |

# United States Postal Service

The United States Postal Service (USPS) handles cards, letters, and packages sent from sea to shining sea. The USPS delivers more than 210 billion pieces of mail a year to over 144 million addresses. The independent government agency relies on postage and fees to fund operations. Though it has a monopoly on delivering nonurgent letters, the USPS faces competition for services such as package delivery. The US president appoints nine of the 11 members of the board that oversee the USPS. The presidential appointees select the postmaster general, who, along with the deputy postmaster general, is a board member.

A challenge for the agency is the growing use of the Internet, which has led to lower volume of some types of mail. To keep pace, the USPS has launched e-commerce initiatives such as computerized postage. It has also tapped into online shopping with its priority mail, merchandise return, and delivery confirmation services.

With an eye on its bottom line, the USPS has accelerated the pace of its rate increases. For 2007, the agency has implemented an increase that boosted the price of a first-class stamp from 39 cents to 41 cents — on top of an increase from 37 cents to 39 cents that took effect in January 2006. In addition, the agency is reducing its workforce through attrition and cutting hours of operation at some of its 37,000 post offices.

A commission appointed by President Bush has recommended that the USPS adopt some private-sector management practices in order to ensure the agency's long-term financial health and to preserve universal mail service. The Bush administration expects the commission's recommendations to lead to the most significant revamp of postal operations since the early 1970s. Congress has yet to approve postal reform legislation, however.

In an effort to improve reliability, USPS inked a deal with United Parcel Service in June 2006 to put mail on UPS planes. USPS renewed a similar relationship with FedEx in August 2006, announcing a new agreement for domestic air transportation for mail through 2013 that could generate $8 billion in revenue. It additionally signed a five-year contract with American Airlines to carry US mail (a deal potentially worth $500 million); as well as a $258 million, five-year deal with Continental Airlines for the same service. American and Continental are two of seven commercial lines carrying US mail, including US Airways/America West, JetBlue, ATA, Sun Country, and Midwest Express.

Meanwhile, USPS announced a 2007 fiscal-year slim-fast diet that would see $1.1 billion in cost reductions. The plan included a decrease of 40 million workhours from 2006 levels, improvements in automation, and other productivity initiatives.

USPS was not about to be the last to jump on the hydrogen fuel-cell vehicle bandwagon. In September 2006 the service said it had agreed to extend a program with General Motors for another year of testing its special GM HydroGen3 minivans in Washington, DC, and Irvine, CA. The service already boasts 37,000 alternative-fuel vehicles in its fleet.

## HISTORY

The second-oldest agency of the US government (after Indian Affairs), the Post Office was created by the Continental Congress in 1775 with Benjamin Franklin as postmaster general. The postal system came to play a vital role in the development of transportation in the US.

At that time, postal workers were riders on muddy paths delivering letters without stamps or envelopes. Letters were delivered only between post offices. Congress approved the first official postal policy in 1792: Rates ranged from six cents for less than 30 miles to 25 cents for more than 450. Letter carriers began delivering mail in cities in 1794.

First based in Philadelphia, in 1800 the Post Office moved to Washington, DC. In 1829 Andrew Jackson elevated the position of postmaster general to cabinet rank — it became a means of rewarding political cronies. Mail contracts subsidized the early development of US railroads. The first adhesive postage stamp appeared in the US in 1847.

Uniform postal rates (not varying with distance) were instituted in 1863, the year free city delivery began. The start of free rural delivery in 1896 spurred road construction in isolated US areas. Parcel post was launched in 1913, and new mail-order houses such as Montgomery Ward and Sears, Roebuck flourished.

The famous pledge beginning "Neither snow nor rain . . ." — not an official motto — was first inscribed at the main New York City post office in 1914. Scheduled airmail service between Washington, DC, and New York City began in 1918, stimulating the development of commercial air service. The ZIP code was introduced in 1963.

As mail volume grew, postal workers became increasingly militant under work stress. (Franklin's pigeonhole sorting method had barely changed.) A work stoppage in the New York City post office in 1970 spread within nine days to 670 post offices, and the US Army was deployed to handle the mail. Later that year the Postal Reorganization Act was passed. The new law established a board of governors to handle postal affairs and choose the postmaster general, who became CEO of an independent agency, the US Postal Service (USPS). The next year USPS negotiated the first US government collective-bargaining labor contract. Express mail service began in 1977, and USPS stepped up automation efforts.

In 1996 USPS overhauled rates, cutting prices for larger mailers who prepared their mail for automation and raising prices for small mailers who didn't. Postmaster General Marvin Runyon — whose six-year tenure took the agency from the red into the black — retired in 1998 and was succeeded by USPS veteran William Henderson. In a nod to the Internet, USPS in 1999 contracted with outside vendors to enable customers to buy and print stamps online.

In 2001 USPS formed a strategic alliance with rival FedEx through which FedEx agreed to provide air transportation for USPS mail, in return for the placement of FedEx drop boxes in post offices. Henderson stepped down at the end of May 2001, and EVP Jack Potter was named to replace him. That year several postal workers in a Washington, DC, branch office were exposed to anthrax-tainted letters.

Potter launched a series of cost-cutting programs, which together with rate increases enabled the USPS to post a profit in 2003 — the agency's first year in the black since 1999.

## EXECUTIVES

**Chairman:** James C. Miller III, age 64
**Vice Chairman:** Alan C. Kessler
**Postmaster General and CEO:** John E. (Jack) Potter
**Deputy Postmaster and COO:** Patrick R. Donahue
**EVP and CFO:** Harold Glen Walker
**EVP and Chief Human Resources Officer:** Anthony J. (Tony) Vegliante
**EVP and Chief Marketing Officer:** Anita J. Bizzotto
**SVP Government Relations:** Thomas G. (Tom) Day
**SVP Intelligent Mail and Address Quality:** Charles E. (Charlie) Bravo
**SVP Operations:** William P. (Bill) Galligan
**SVP Strategy and Transition:** Linda A. Kingsley
**SVP and General Counsel:** Mary Anne Gibbons
**SVP and Managing Director, Global Business:** Paul Vogel
**VP and CTO:** Robert L. (Bob) Otto
**VP and Controller:** Lynn Malcolm
**VP Labor Relations:** Douglas (Doug) Tulino
**VP Sales:** Jerry W. Whalen
**VP Pricing and Classification:** Stephen M. Kearney
**VP and Treasurer:** Robert J. Pedersen
**VP Engineering:** Walter (Walt) O'Tormey
**VP Product Development:** Nicholas F. (Nick) Barranca
**VP Public Affairs and Communications:** Joanne Giordano
**Auditors:** Ernst & Young LLP

## LOCATIONS

**HQ:** United States Postal Service
475 L'Enfant Plaza SW, Washington, DC 20260
**Phone:** 202-268-2500 **Fax:** 202-268-4860
**Web:** www.usps.com

## PRODUCTS/OPERATIONS

**2006 Sales**

| | $ mil. | % of total |
|---|---|---|
| First-class mail | 37,039 | 51 |
| Standard mail | 19,877 | 27 |
| Priority mail | 5,042 | 7 |
| Package services | 2,259 | 3 |
| Periodicals | 2,215 | 3 |
| International | 1,794 | 3 |
| Express mail | 918 | 1 |
| Other services | 3,673 | 5 |
| Interest & investment income | 167 | — |
| **Total** | **72,650** | **100** |

## COMPETITORS

BAX Global
DHL
FedEx
Postal Connections
UPS
Western Union

## HISTORICAL FINANCIALS

Company Type: Government agency

**Income Statement** FYE: September 30

| | REVENUE ($ mil.) | NET INCOME ($ mil.) | NET PROFIT MARGIN | EMPLOYEES |
|---|---|---|---|---|
| **9/06** | 72,650 | — | — | 696,138 |
| **9/05** | 69,907 | — | — | 704,716 |
| **9/04** | 68,996 | — | — | 707,485 |
| **9/03** | 68,529 | — | — | 826,955 |
| **9/02** | 66,463 | — | — | 854,376 |
| **Annual Growth** | 2.3% | — | — | (5.0%) |

**Revenue History**

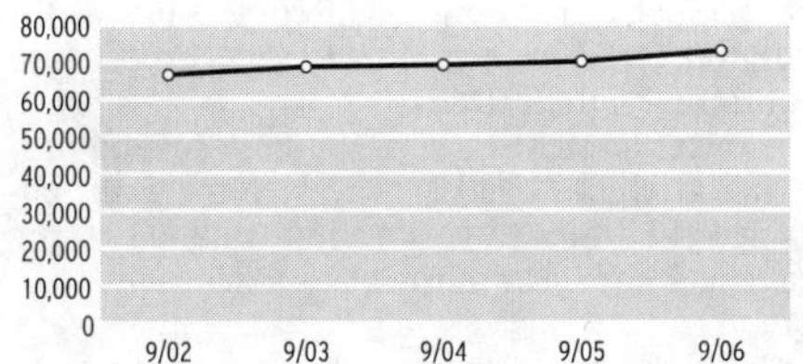


# United States Steel

Steel crazy after all these years, Pittsburgh-based United States Steel (U.S. Steel) is the nation's #2 integrated steelmaker (behind Mittal Steel USA). With mills in Alabama, Illinois, Indiana, Michigan, Minnesota, Ohio, Pennsylvania, and Slovakia, U.S. Steel produces sheet and semi-finished steel, tubular and plate steel, and tin products. The company's customers are primarily in the automotive, construction, petrochemical, and steel service center industries. In addition, U.S. Steel offers services such as mineral resource management, real estate development, and engineering and consulting. The company acquired tubular goods maker Lone Star Technologies for $2.1 billion in 2007.

The company boosted its expansion in Central and Western Europe with the 2003 acquisition of the Serbian company Sartid, now known as U.S. Steel Balkan. U.S. Steel Balkan produces limestone, sheets, strip mill plate, and tin mill. U.S. Steel Kosice Steel (in Slovakia) manufactures sheet, strip mill plate, tin mill, tubular, and specialty steel products. With both of these business units, U.S. Steel intends to be a major supplier of flat-rolled steel to the expanding Central European market.

By 2006 — with Arcelor trying to buy Dofasco and Mittal trying to buy Arcelor and ThyssenKrupp looking around for something else to pick up — US steel companies realized that consolidation is the game being played worldwide, and they'd better get in on it. While much of the industry seems to be in flux, the one thing most observers see as a certainty is that in a few years' time, there won't be so many big steel companies, and the giants that will be around will dwarf most of today's largest.

It's in that context that U.S. Steel looked around and focused on Lone Star Technologies. That company is among the nation's largest makers of welded steel tubes for use in the oilfield. The acquired business complements U.S. Steel's own product line for the energy industry, which consists largely of seamless tubes.

## HISTORY

United States Steel Corporation was conceived through a 1901 merger of 10 steel companies that combined their furnaces, ore deposits, railroad companies, and shipping lines. The deal involved industrial pioneers Andrew Carnegie, Charles Schwab, Elbert Gary, and J. P. Morgan.

Morgan had helped organize the Federal Steel Company in 1898 and he then wanted to create a centralized trust to dominate the soaring steel market. Carnegie owned the largest US steel company at the time, Carnegie Steel, but wanted to retire.

In 1900 Schwab, Carnegie Steel's president, outlined the idea of the steel trust based on a merger of the Carnegie and Federal steel companies. Morgan asked Schwab to persuade Carnegie to sell his steel mills and name his price. Morgan didn't haggle when Carnegie responded that he would sell for almost half a billion dollars.

The Carnegie-Morgan combination created the world's first billion-dollar company. It produced 67% of the country's steel in its first year (its steel complex and the Indiana town where it was located were named after Gary, who was CEO until 1927).

The company boomed during WWI and WWII. But its market share fell to about 30% by the 1950s, although it set new profit records in 1955. During the 1970s prospects for long-term growth in steel became dismal in light of rising costs, foreign competition, and competitive pricing.

In 1982 U.S. Steel doubled its size when it bought Marathon Oil, a major integrated energy company with huge oil and gas reserves in the US and abroad. It continued to cut back its steelmaking capacity, laying off 100,000 employees, closing steel mills, and selling off assets.

The company bought Texas Oil & Gas in 1986 and renamed itself USX Corporation to reflect the decreasing role of steel in its business. Also that year corporate raider Carl Icahn, USX's largest single shareholder, unsuccessfully tried to get the company to sell its steel operations. In 1988 USX bought 49% of Transtar, a group of rail and water transport providers.

Stockholders in 1991 approved splitting the company into separate entities under the USX umbrella: U.S. Steel and Marathon. During the 1990s U.S. Steel continued to close steelmaking facilities. In 1992 USX joined five other leading US steel producers in a suit against subsidized foreign steelmakers. The next year the company formed two joint ventures with Japan's Kobe Steel.

In 1994 U.S. Steel teamed up with rival Nucor to explore a new technology that would reduce much of the cost and pollution of the steelmaking process. The company agreed to pay $106 million in fines and improvements in 1996 to settle charges of air pollution violations involving its Indiana plant. Seeing prices drop in 1998 and 1999, the company cut production and joined other US steelmakers in charging rivals in Brazil, Japan, and Russia with unlawfully dumping low-priced steel in the US.

In 2000 USX then announced plans to spin off its steel operations as United States Steel Corporation; the remaining energy businesses will operate as Marathon Oil Corporation.

In 2001 USX-U.S. Steel and National Steel (U.S. subsidiary of NKK) began talks of merging its businesses. At the end of 2001, due to shareholder pressure USX-U.S. Steel split apart from its holding company, USX Corporation, and the steel operations unit went back to trading under its original name, United States Steel Corporation. The breakup left the company with over $1.3 billion in debt (Marathon Oil assumed $900 million of the company's debt).

In early March 2002 the Bush administration, on recommendations of the International Trade Commission, imposed tariffs between 8 to 30 percent providing temporary relief to U.S. Steel and the US steel industry. The Bush Administration rejected any retiree bailout plan and in December 2003 ended the tariffs 16 months ahead of schedule.

In 2003 U.S. Steel bought National Steel for roughly $1.1 billion in cash, including liabilities. With the combined manufacturing capabilities of National Steel and U.S. Steel, the company's raw steel production came in at around 20 million tons of steel annually, both domestically and internationally, which made it the nation's largest steel producer until the formation of Mittal Steel USA in 2005.

## EXECUTIVES

**Chairman, President, and CEO:** John P. Surma Jr., age 52
**EVP and COO:** John H. Goodish, age 58, $1,414,336 pay
**EVP and CFO:** Gretchen R. Haggerty, age 50, $1,146,672 pay
**SVP Commercial:** J. James Kutka Jr.
**SVP European Operations; President, U.S. Steel Kosice:** David H. Lohr, age 53
**SVP Administration:** Thomas W. (Tom) Sterling, age 59
**SVP Procurement, Logistics, and Diverse Businesses:** Christopher J. Navetta, age 56
**SVP Public Policy and Governmental Affairs:** Terrence D. Straub, age 58
**SVP Strategic Planning and Business Development:** John J. Connelly, age 60, $951,668 pay
**SVP Labor Relations and General Counsel:** James D. Garraux, age 54
**VP and Controller:** Larry G. Schultz, age 57
**VP and Treasurer:** Larry T. Brockway, age 44
**VP Business Services:** Eugene P. Trudell, age 55
**VP Engineering and Technology:** Anthony R. Bridge
**VP Plant Operations:** George F. Babcoke, age 52
**VP Sales:** Joseph R. Scherrbaum, age 45
**VP Sales and Technical Services, United States Steel International:** Carl J. Minucci
**VP Human Resources:** Susan M. (Sue) Suver, age 48
**Manager Investor Relations:** W. Nicholas Harper
**Manager Public Affairs:** D. John Armstrong
**Auditors:** PricewaterhouseCoopers LLP

## LOCATIONS

**HQ:** United States Steel Corporation
600 Grant St., Pittsburgh, PA 15219
**Phone:** 412-433-1121 **Fax:** 412-433-5733
**Web:** www.ussteel.com

United States Steel has steelmaking plants in Alabama, Indiana, Michigan, Ohio, Pennsylvania, and overseas plants in Serbia and Slovakia.

**2006 Sales**

| | $ mil. | % of total |
|---|---|---|
| US | 11,774 | 75 |
| Europe | 3,977 | 25 |
| Other countries | 14 | — |
| Adjustments | (50) | — |
| **Total** | **15,715** | **100** |

**2006 Raw Steel Production**

| | Net tons (thou.) | % of total |
|---|---|---|
| US | | |
| Gary, Indiana | 5,947 | 25 |
| Great Lakes, Michigan | 3,136 | 13 |
| Mon Valley, Pennsylvania | 2,579 | 11 |
| Granite City, Illinois | 2,468 | 11 |
| Fairfield, Alabama | 2,225 | 10 |
| Europe | | |
| U.S. Steel Kosice | 5,205 | 22 |
| U.S. Steel Balkan | 1,857 | 8 |
| **Total** | **23,417** | **100** |

## PRODUCTS/OPERATIONS

**2006 Sales**

| | $ mil. | % of total |
|---|---|---|
| Flat-rolled | 9,607 | 61 |
| US Steel Europe | 3,968 | 25 |
| Tubular Products | 1,798 | 12 |
| Other | 342 | 2 |
| **Total** | **15,715** | **100** |

**Selected Subsidiaries**

Acero Prime S. R. L de CV (44%, steel processing and warehousing)
Delray Connecting Railroad Company (transportation)
Double Eagle Steel Coating Company (50%, steel processing, with Severstal)
PRO-TEC Coating Co. (50%, steel processing, with Kobe Steel, Ltd.)
Transtar, Inc. (transportation)
U. S. Steel Kosice sro (steelmaking, Slovakia)
USS-POSCO Industries (50%, steel processing, with Pohang Iron & Steel Co., Ltd.)
Worthington Specialty Processing (50%, steel processing, with Worthington Industries Inc.)

## COMPETITORS

AK Steel Holding Corporation
Alison Group
Allegheny Technologies
ArcelorMittal
BÖHLER-UDDEHOLM
BHP Billiton
BlueScope Steel
Carpenter Technology
Evraz Steel Mills, Inc.
IPSCO
JFE Holdings
Kobe Steel
Nippon Steel
Nucor
POSCO
Salzgitter
Severstal
Steel Dynamics
Stelco Hamilton
ThyssenKrupp Steel

## HISTORICAL FINANCIALS

Company Type: Public

**Income Statement** FYE: December 31

| | REVENUE ($ mil.) | NET INCOME ($ mil.) | NET PROFIT MARGIN | EMPLOYEES |
|---|---|---|---|---|
| **12/06** | 15,715 | 1,374 | 8.7% | 44,000 |
| **12/05** | 14,039 | 910 | 6.5% | 46,000 |
| **12/04** | 14,108 | 1,091 | 7.7% | 48,000 |
| **12/03** | 9,469 | (463) | — | 47,000 |
| **12/02** | 7,054 | 61 | 0.9% | 36,251 |
| **Annual Growth** | 22.2% | 117.9% | — | 5.0% |

**2006 Year-End Financials**

Debt ratio: 21.6%
Return on equity: 36.8%
Cash ($ mil.): 1,422
Current ratio: 1.92
Long-term debt ($ mil.): 943
No. of shares (mil.): 119
Dividends
Yield: 0.8%
Payout: 5.4%
Market value ($ mil.): 8,670

**Stock History** NYSE: X

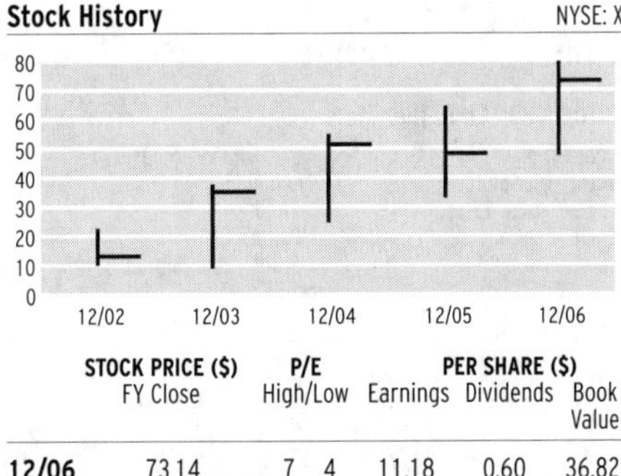

| | STOCK PRICE ($) FY Close | P/E High | P/E Low | PER SHARE ($) Earnings | Dividends | Book Value |
|---|---|---|---|---|---|---|
| **12/06** | 73.14 | 7 | 4 | 11.18 | 0.60 | 36.82 |
| **12/05** | 48.07 | 9 | 5 | 7.00 | 0.28 | 30.56 |
| **12/04** | 51.25 | 6 | 3 | 8.48 | 0.20 | 34.82 |
| **12/03** | 35.02 | — | — | (4.64) | 0.20 | 10.54 |
| **12/02** | 13.12 | 35 | 17 | 0.62 | 0.15 | 19.78 |
| **Annual Growth** | 53.7% | — | — | 106.1% | 41.4% | 16.8% |

# United Stationers

Don't think that United Stationers is just another paper pusher. The company is the leading wholesale distributor of office supplies and equipment in North America, offering some 46,000 products to more than 20,000 customers. Through its operating units United Stationers Supply and Lagasse, United Stationers supplies such items as business machines, computer products and peripherals, janitorial supplies, and office products and furniture. It also offers niche products for such markets as education and health care. United Stationers sells primarily to resellers through catalogs and over the Internet, as well as through its direct sales force.

Sales of technology products, including printers and print cartridges, data storage devices, and other computer peripherals, account for about 40% of the company's sales, making United Stationers one of the top computer products distributors in the country. Traditional office supplies make up almost 30% of the company's business.

Private label products account for about 11% of sales. The company has been expanding this line of business, which includes brands Innovera technology products and Windsoft paper products. United Stationers is also expanding its janitorial products distribution business, Lagasse, in part by acquiring Sweet Paper Sales in 2005.

The company sold its Canadian operations in 2006, following an accounting scandal. United Stationers discovered that its Canadian operation was incorrectly accounting for supplier allowances and other receivables.

In 2006 United Stationers moved its headquarters to Deerfield, Illinois.

## HISTORY

Morris Wolf and Harry Hecktman, former office supply salesmen, and Israel Kriloff, a grocer, purchased Utility Supply Company (founded in 1906) and began selling office supplies in downtown Chicago in 1921. Weathering the Depression, Utility Supply's business grew steadily during the 1930s. In 1935 the company published its first catalog, and it opened its first retail store in downtown Chicago two years later. The partners bought out Kriloff in 1939.

WWII created a scarcity of raw materials, and Utility Supply had difficulty in obtaining merchandise. The company tried selling non-office products, unsuccessfully. Fortunately, the war's end brought an end to the inventory drought. During the postwar era, Utility Supply began mailing a series of catalogs to retailers nationwide. By 1948 mail-order business accounted for 40% of sales. A wholesale division to sell products to independent resellers was created in the 1950s.

In 1960 the company adopted the name United Stationers Supply, and the retail stores became the Utility Stationery Stores. Business increased as independent retailers began to appreciate the advantages of ordering through a wholesaler instead of a manufacturer — purchasing goods on an as-needed basis. Howard Wolf, the founder's son, became CEO in 1967 and began emphasizing computers and automation to track inventory and costs.

By 1970 wholesale trade accounted for about 66% of sales. United Stationers introduced a series of abridged catalogs targeting specific groups and marketing segments, such as furniture and electronics. The following year United Stationers developed regional redistribution centers that offered overnight delivery. The company sold its retail outlets in 1978.

Three years later United Stationers went public. During the 1980s the advent of warehouse clubs and office supply superstores threatened independent retailers. The company developed marketing concepts to help its independent resellers, even as it aggressively targeted mail-order houses and superstores. The downsizing trend in the late 1980s caused the corporate market to shrink, and United Stationers lowered prices; it instituted a decentralization plan in 1990.

The next year the company expanded into Canada, opening its first non-US subsidiary, and it acquired archrival Stationers Distributing and its distribution centers across the US in 1992. In 1994 it established its United Facility Supply unit to distribute maintenance supplies.

Investment firm Wingate Partners, which controlled rival Associated Stationers, bought United Stationers in 1995 and combined the operations of the two companies under the United Stationers name. United Stationers acquired janitorial supplies wholesaler Lagasse Bros. in 1996. In 1998 the company acquired the US and Mexican operations of Abitibi-Consolidated, including Azerty. (It acquired Azerty Canada in 2000.)

United Stationers launched a venture with E-Commerce Industries in 1999 to help customers sell products over the Internet. The next year the company started The Order People, a third-party call center fulfillment business aimed at online retailers; however, the dot-com bust and higher losses than planned led United Stationers to curtail operations in 2001. Also that year it bought Peerless Paper Mills (merging the wholesale distributor of janitorial and paper products into Lagasse).

## EXECUTIVES

**Chairman:** Frederick B. (Fred) Hegi Jr., age 63
**President, CEO, and Director:** Richard W. Gochnauer, age 57, $1,510,935 pay
**SVP and CFO:** Victoria J. Reich, age 49
**SVP, Operations:** Timothy P. Connolly, age 43
**SVP and CIO:** S. David Bent, age 46
**SVP and Treasurer:** Brian S. Cooper, age 50
**SVP; President, Lagasse:** Stephen A. (Steve) Schultz, age 40, $480,347 pay
**SVP, General Counsel, and Secretary:** Eric A. Blanchard, age 50
**SVP Marketing:** Mark J. Hampton, age 53, $457,256 pay
**SVP Merchandising:** James K. Fahey, age 56
**SVP National Accounts and Channel Management:** Jeffrey G. Howard, age 51
**SVP Sales:** Patrick T. (Pat) Collins, age 46, $252,853 pay
**SVP Trade Development:** Joseph R. Templet, age 60
**VP, Controller, and Chief Accounting Officer:** Kenneth M. Nickel, age 39
**President, United Stationers Supply:** P. Cody Phipps, age 45
**Investor Relations Specialist:** Mary Disclafani
**Auditors:** Cowan, Gunteski & Co., P.A.

## LOCATIONS

**HQ:** United Stationers Inc.
One Parkway N. Blvd., Ste. 100, Deerfield, IL 60015
**Phone:** 847-627-7000 **Fax:** 847-627-7001
**Web:** www.unitedstationers.com

### 2006 Sales

| | % of total |
|---|---|
| Domestic | 97 |
| International | 3 |
| **Total** | **100** |

## PRODUCTS/OPERATIONS

### 2006 Sales

| | $ mil. | % of total |
|---|---|---|
| Technology products | 1,767 | 39 |
| Traditional office products (including cut-sheet paper) | 1,315 | 29 |
| Janitorial and sanitation | 849 | 19 |
| Office furniture | 536 | 12 |
| Freight revenue | 70 | 1 |
| Other | 10 | 0 |
| **Total** | **4,547** | **100** |

### Selected Products

Technology products
- Computer monitors
- Copiers and fax machines
- Data storage
- Digital cameras
- Printers and printer cartridges

Traditional office products
- Calendars
- Organizers
- Paper products
- Writing instruments

Office furniture
- Computer furniture
- Leather chairs
- Vertical and lateral file cabinets
- Wooden and steel desks

Janitorial and sanitation products
- Food service disposables
- Janitorial and sanitation supplies
- Paper and packaging supplies
- Safety and security items

## COMPETITORS

Corporate Express NV
D&H Distributing
Distribution Management
Gould Paper
Ingram Micro
Newell Rubbermaid
SED International
S.P. Richards

## HISTORICAL FINANCIALS

Company Type: Public

### Income Statement

FYE: December 31

| | REVENUE ($ mil.) | NET INCOME ($ mil.) | NET PROFIT MARGIN | EMPLOYEES |
|---|---|---|---|---|
| **12/06** | 4,547 | 132 | 2.9% | 5,700 |
| **12/05** | 4,409 | 98 | 2.2% | 6,000 |
| **12/04** | 3,991 | 90 | 2.3% | 5,550 |
| **12/03** | 3,848 | 73 | 1.9% | 5,700 |
| **12/02** | 3,702 | 60 | 1.6% | 6,000 |
| **Annual Growth** | 5.3% | 21.7% | — | (1.3%) |

### 2006 Year-End Financials

Debt ratio: 14.6%
Return on equity: 16.8%
Cash ($ mil.): 15
Current ratio: 1.99
Long-term debt ($ mil.): 117
No. of shares (mil.): 30
Dividends
Yield: —
Payout: —
Market value ($ mil.): 1,403

### Stock History

NASDAQ (GS): USTR

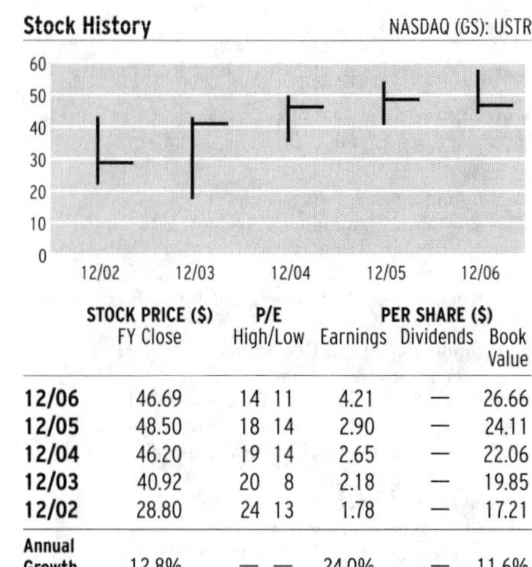

| | STOCK PRICE ($) FY Close | P/E High/Low | | PER SHARE ($) Earnings | Dividends | Book Value |
|---|---|---|---|---|---|---|
| **12/06** | 46.69 | 14 | 11 | 4.21 | — | 26.66 |
| **12/05** | 48.50 | 18 | 14 | 2.90 | — | 24.11 |
| **12/04** | 46.20 | 19 | 14 | 2.65 | — | 22.06 |
| **12/03** | 40.92 | 20 | 8 | 2.18 | — | 19.85 |
| **12/02** | 28.80 | 24 | 13 | 1.78 | — | 17.21 |
| **Annual Growth** | 12.8% | — | — | 24.0% | — | 11.6% |

# United Technologies

United Technologies lifts you up and cools you down. Through such well-known names as Carrier, Otis, Pratt & Whitney, and Sikorsky, UTC makes building systems and aerospace products. Carrier is the world's largest maker of heating and air-conditioning units. Otis is the #1 elevator manufacturer; Hamilton Sundstrand produces engine controls, environmental systems, propellers, and other flight systems; Pratt & Whitney makes engines for both commercial and military aircraft; and Sikorsky makes helicopters. The UTC Fire & Security segment is made up of what was Chubb and Kidde. Lastly, UTC Power makes fuel cells for commercial, transportation, and space applications, among other products.

UTC has agreed to acquire the Initial Electronic Security Group of Rentokil Initial for £595 million ($1.16 billion). The company also plans to divest its manned guarding businesses in Australia and the UK.

More than half of UTC's business is international, and the majority of the company's business segments have a similar split in foreign/domestic sales. Otis, though, does 80% of its business outside the US.

Binding UTC's diverse businesses is the United Technologies Research Center, a Connecticut-based facility staffed by more than 450 scientists and engineers.

## HISTORY

In 1925 Frederick Rentschler and George Mead founded Pratt & Whitney Aircraft (P&W) to develop aircraft engines. P&W merged with Seattle-based Boeing Airplane Company and Chance Vought Corporation in 1929 to form United Aircraft & Transport. United Aircraft soon bought aviation companies Hamilton Aero, Standard Steel Propeller, and Sikorsky.

In 1934, after congressional investigations led to new antitrust laws, United Aircraft split into three independent entities: United Airlines, Boeing Airplane Company, and United Aircraft. United Aircraft retained P&W and several other manufacturing interests.

During WWII United Aircraft produced half of all the engines used in US warplanes. Sikorsky developed helicopters, and Vought made the Corsair and Cutlass planes. After a postwar decline in sales, the company retooled for jet engine production. United Aircraft spun off Chance Vought in 1954 and bought Norden-Ketay (aeronautical electronics) in 1958.

A design flaw in engines produced for Boeing 747s sent P&W on an expensive trip back to the drawing board in the late 1960s. A concerned board of directors appointed Harry Gray, a 17-year Litton Industries executive, president in 1971. Gray transformed the company into a conglomerate; it adopted its present name in 1975.

To decrease UTC's dependence on government contracts, Gray diversified the company by acquiring Otis Elevator (1975) and Carrier (1979). Acquisitions expanded sales to $15.7 billion by 1986. Under pressure from his board, Gray tapped Bob Daniell to head the company in 1986. Gray retired a year later.

Daniell, a 25-year Sikorsky veteran, stressed profitability over growth and sold businesses, cut jobs, and changed management. UTC enjoyed record earnings in 1990. However, the next year reduced orders from the military and the auto and building industries resulted in UTC's first operating loss in 20 years.

UTC paid a $6 million fine in 1992 for hiring advisers to illegally inform it about competing bids for a Pentagon contract. The company sold its Norden radar unit and its stake in the Westland Helicopter Company in 1994.

P&W introduced the most-powerful jet engine in history in 1995, and Sikorsky flew the prototype of the world's first radar-evading helicopter. UTC president and COO George David became CEO that year (eventually replacing Daniell as chairman in 1997).

In 1996 Ford recalled 8.7 million vehicles — the most in its history — due to faulty auto ignition switches made by UT Automotive. Hamilton Standard boosted its European presence in 1998, buying aviation company Ratier-Figeac (France). That year P&W won a $435 million contract from the US Air Force to overhaul and repair F-15 and F-16 jet engines, but it wasn't enough to forestall plans to cut 2,000 jobs.

UTC bought Sundstrand (aerospace components) for $4.3 billion in 1999. Sundstrand's operations were rolled into UTC's Hamilton Standard unit to form Hamilton Sundstrand Corporation. The company sold its auto parts unit (headliners, door and instrument panels) to Lear for $2.3 billion. It paid more than $700 million for air-conditioning and heat-pump maker International Comfort Products. The purchases were accompanied by consolidation, primarily in the Otis and Carrier businesses. About 15,000 jobs were cut; the company's overall employee count dropped 17%.

In 2000 UTC made a $40 billion bid for Honeywell International (turbofan and turboprop engines, aircraft flight safety and landing systems, industrial and home controls, specialty chemicals), but Honeywell accepted General Electric's $45 billion counteroffer (that deal was later scuttled by European regulators).

As the economy cooled, UTC cut jobs and restructured its operations to enhance its focus around its core businesses. UTC cut about 4,600 jobs in 2001. Restructuring continued in 2002 as UTC continued reducing costs and cut about 7,000 more jobs. On the 2002 acquisition front, Sikorsky acquired Derco Holdings, an aerospace parts distribution, repair and overhaul, and inventory management company.

UTC's appetite for acquisitions resumed after the cutback in spending of 2001-02. UTC spent $1.3 billion, $525 million, and $424 million on acquisitions in 2000, 2001, and 2002, respectively. In 2003 UTC spent about $1.3 billion, including charges associated with its acquisition of security service provider Chubb plc. UTC acquired British fire-fighting equipment maker Kidde PLC for $3 billion in December 2004.

In 2005 Pratt & Whitney bought up Boeing's Rocketdyne unit for around $700 million. Rocketdyne designs and manufactures rocket propulsion systems and makes the rocket boosters for the space shuttle. Also that year UTC bought privately held security firm Lenel Systems for $400 million; the company was moved into the Fire & Security segment. Lenel Systems makes fingerprint scanners and security software, among other products.

In mid-2006 UTC agreed to pay $283 million to the US Department of Defense to settle a contract accounting dispute with the government over Pratt & Whitney's cost accounting for engine parts on commercial engine collaboration programs from 1984 through 2004.

## EXECUTIVES

**Chairman and CEO:** George David, age 64, $5,591,667 pay
**President, COO, and Director:** Louis R. Chênevert, age 49, $2,208,333 pay
**SVP, Human Resources and Organization:** William L. Bucknall Jr., age 64
**SVP, Government and International Affairs:** Alison (Lisi) Kaufman, age 50
**SVP and General Counsel:** Charles D. Gill, age 42
**SVP, Science and Technology:** J. Michael McQuade, age 50
**VP and Controller:** Margaret M. (Peggy) Smyth, age 43
**VP, Research and Director, United Technologies Research Center:** David E. Parekh, age 47
**VP and CIO:** John J. Doucette, age 46
**VP, Secretary, and Deputy General Counsel:** Debra A. Valentine, age 53
**VP and Treasurer:** Thomas I. Rogan, age 54
**VP, Operations:** Jothi Purushotaman
**VP, Accounting and Finance:** Gregory J. Hayes, age 46, $816,667 pay
**VP, Communications:** Nancy T. Lintner, age 48
**VP, Employee Relations:** John P. Leary
**VP, Finance:** James E. Geisler, age 40, $811,667 pay
**Chairman, United Technologies International Operations:** Kent L. Brittan, age 62
**Chairman, Carrier Commercial Refrigeration:** Jeffrey P. (Jeff) Rhodenbaugh
**Chairman, Hamilton Sundstrand:** Ronald F. McKenna, age 66
**President, Building Systems and Services, Carrier:** Kelly A. Romano
**President, Carrier:** Geraud Darnis, age 47, $1,026,250 pay
**President, Fire and Security:** William M. (Bill) Brown, age 44
**President, Hamilton Sundstrand:** David P. Hess, age 51
**President, Pratt & Whitney:** Stephen N. (Steve) Finger, age 58
**President, Otis Elevator:** Ari Bousbib, age 45, $1,515,184 pay
**President, Sikorsky Aircraft:** Jeffrey P. (Jeff) Pino, age 52
**President, Power:** Jan van Dokkum, age 53
**Auditors:** PricewaterhouseCoopers LLP

## LOCATIONS

**HQ:** United Technologies Corporation
1 Financial Plaza, Hartford, CT 06103
**Phone:** 860-728-7000 **Fax:** 860-565-5400
**Web:** www.utc.com

United Technologies has more than 4,000 locations in some 60 countries, and does business in about 180 countries around the world.

### 2006 Sales

| | $ mil. | % of total |
|---|---|---|
| US | 23,524 | 49 |
| Europe | 12,069 | 25 |
| Asia/Pacific | 7,056 | 15 |
| Other regions | 4,809 | 10 |
| Adjustments | 371 | 1 |
| **Total** | **47,829** | **100** |

## PRODUCTS/OPERATIONS

### 2006 Sales

| | $ mil. | % of total |
|---|---|---|
| Products | 34,271 | 72 |
| Services | 12,847 | 27 |
| Financing & other | 711 | 1 |
| **Total** | **47,829** | **100** |

### 2006 Sales by Segment

| | $ mil. | % of total |
|---|---|---|
| Carrier | 13,481 | 28 |
| Pratt & Whitney | 11,112 | 23 |
| Otis | 10,290 | 22 |
| Hamilton Sundstrand | 4,995 | 10 |
| UTC Fire & Security | 4,747 | 10 |
| Sikorsky | 3,230 | 7 |
| Adjustments | (26) | — |
| **Total** | **47,829** | **100** |

### Selected Operations, Products, and Services

Carrier
- Commercial and residential heating, ventilation, and air-conditioning (HVAC) equipment
- Commercial and transport refrigeration equipment
- HVAC replacement parts and services

Otis
- Elevators
- Escalators
- Installation, maintenance, and repair services
- Moving sidewalks

Pratt & Whitney
- Commercial and military aircraft engines, parts, and services
- Industrial gas turbines
- Space propulsion systems

Hamilton Sundstrand
- Aerospace equipment (engine and flight controls, environmental controls, space life support, propulsion systems)
- Industrial equipment (air compressors, fluid-handling equipment, metering devices)

UTC Fire & Security
- Electronic security
- Fire detection
- Rapid response systems
- Security personnel services

Sikorsky (commercial and military helicopters and maintenance)

UTC Fuel Cells
- Hydrogen-powered fuel cells for space, commercial, transportation, and residential applications

## COMPETITORS

AgustaWestland
American Standard
BAE SYSTEMS
Boeing
Eaton
Emerson Electric
GE
General Dynamics
Goodman Manufacturing
Goodrich
Hitachi
Honeywell International
IDEX
Kaman
L-3 Communications
Lennox
Lockheed Martin
Mitsubishi Electric
Northrop Grumman
Parker Hannifin
Precision Castparts
Raytheon
Rolls-Royce
SAFRAN
SANYO
Siemens AG
SPX
Textron
ThyssenKrupp
Trane
Tyco

## HISTORICAL FINANCIALS

Company Type: Public

**Income Statement** FYE: December 31

| | REVENUE ($ mil.) | NET INCOME ($ mil.) | NET PROFIT MARGIN | EMPLOYEES |
|---|---|---|---|---|
| **12/06** | 47,829 | 3,732 | 7.8% | 214,500 |
| **12/05** | 42,725 | 3,069 | 7.2% | 222,200 |
| **12/04** | 37,445 | 2,788 | 7.4% | 210,000 |
| **12/03** | 31,034 | 2,361 | 7.6% | 203,300 |
| **12/02** | 28,212 | 2,236 | 7.9% | 155,000 |
| **Annual Growth** | 14.1% | 13.7% | — | 8.5% |

**2006 Year-End Financials**

Debt ratio: 40.7%
Return on equity: 21.8%
Cash ($ mil.): 2,546
Current ratio: 1.24
Long-term debt ($ mil.): 7,037
No. of shares (mil.): 996
Dividends
Yield: 1.6%
Payout: 27.2%
Market value ($ mil.): 62,251

**Stock History** NYSE: UTX

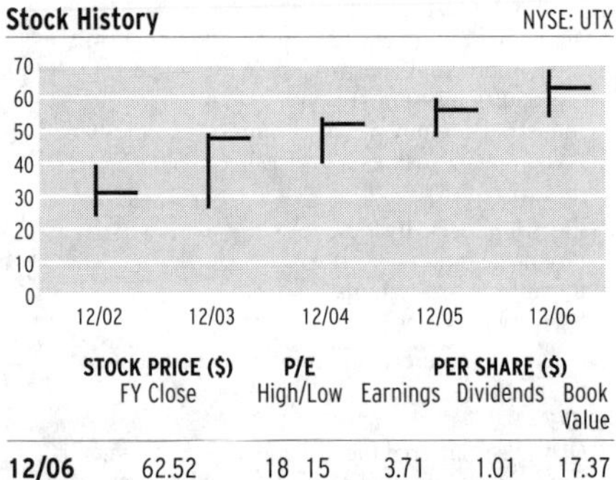


| | STOCK PRICE ($) FY Close | P/E High/Low | PER SHARE ($) Earnings | Dividends | Book Value |
|---|---|---|---|---|---|
| **12/06** | 62.52 | 18 15 | 3.71 | 1.01 | 17.37 |
| **12/05** | 55.91 | 19 16 | 3.03 | 0.88 | 16.76 |
| **12/04** | 51.67 | 19 15 | 2.76 | 0.70 | 27.41 |
| **12/03** | 47.38 | 21 11 | 2.35 | 0.57 | 22.77 |
| **12/02** | 30.97 | 18 11 | 2.21 | 0.37 | 17.79 |
| **Annual Growth** | 19.2% | — — | 13.8% | 28.5% | (0.6%) |

# UnitedHealth Group

UnitedHealth Group wants to keep you connected with your health. A leading US health insurer, it offers a variety of health care plans and services to about 70 million customers in the US. Its Health Care Services segment manages HMO, PPO, and POS (point-of-service) plans, as well as various Medicare and Medicaid options. Members of AARP are served via the company's Ovations unit. Uniprise handles health plans for large companies, and Specialized Care Services offers just that — vision and dental care and other products and services. Ingenix provides health information consulting and publishing, as well as clinical research and drug marketing services.

UnitedHealth came under fire in 2007 for instituting fines on doctors using laboratory services outside UnitedHealth's network. UnitedHealth claims the lab requirement is designed to save money for its customers, who have to pay extra for using services outside the network; doctors, though, say it's because UnitedHealth has an exclusivity agreement with Lab Corp., and that it's UnitedHealth's way of keeping tabs on the health of its patients (in areas such as cholesterol levels).

UnitedHealth is prospering in a market increasingly unfriendly to managed care in part by expanding into new regions through the purchase of smaller rivals and corporate health plans. The company in 2006 bought John Deere's employee health plan, John Deere Health Care, as well as Student Resources, the student insurance division of HealthMarkets' MEGA Life subsidiary.

After irregular stock option pricing caused inquiry and prompted a brisk housecleaning of the executive offices in 2006, the board made the position of Chief Ethics Officer a senior executive position and equity awards were eliminated for the CEO and president. The shakeup was not enough, however, to prevent the SEC from opening a formal investigation into the company's stock-options practices in late 2006.

In 2007 the company opened the year with an agreement to acquire Sierra Health Services. The deal brings UnitedHealth into Nevada markets for the first time; Sierra Health has more than 300,000 health plan members in the state.

FMR owns 10% of the company while Marisco Capital Management owns 5% of its stock.

## HISTORY

Dr. Paul Ellwood became known as the Father of the HMO for his role as an early champion of the health care concept. As a neurology student in the 1950s, Ellwood recognized that applying business principles to medicine could minimize costs and make health care more affordable. Although the HMO was considered a radical approach to health care reform, Ellwood got Congress and the Nixon administration to approve his HMO model in 1970; the next year he hired Richard Burke to put the model into action. Burke established United HealthCare (UHC) in 1974 to manage the not-for-profit Physicians Health Plan of Minnesota (PHP). UHC incorporated in 1977.

The company bought HMOs and began managing others, operating 11 HMOs in 10 states by 1984, the year it went public. Its expansion continued with the purchases of HMOs Share Development (1985) and Peak Health Care (1986). Unfortunately, acquisitions and startups began to eat away at UHC's financial health. Meanwhile, Burke, CEO of both UHC and PHP, was accused by PHP doctors of having a conflict of interest after a change in the HMO's Medicare policy threatened to cut off patients from some member hospitals. Burke resigned in 1987 and was replaced by Kennett Simmons, formerly president of Peak.

That year investment firm Warburg Pincus bought nearly 40% of UHC, providing it with much-needed cash. UHC lost nearly $16 million in 1987, largely from a restructuring that axed the company's Phoenix HMO as well as startups in six other markets. The next year UHC sold its share of Peak Health Care.

In the late 1980s UHC adopted a new strategy of acquiring specialty companies that provided fee income. It also continued building its HMO network through acquisitions, hoping to gain critical mass in such varied markets as the Midwest and New England. Physician William (Bill) McGuire, another former Peak president, was named UHC's chairman and CEO in 1991. That year PHP and Share merged into Medica. Warburg Pincus distributed its UHC shares to several pension funds and financial institutions.

The company's expansion accelerated in the 1990s with a string of purchases in the Midwest. UHC's interest in fee-based businesses continued with the 1997 purchase of Medicode, a major provider of health care information products.

In 1998 the firm planned to buy rival Humana. However, bloated UHC decided it should slim down to prepare to consummate the agreement; when UHC announced that it would charge $900 million in costs against earnings, its plummeting stock price devalued the primary currency of the deal, which quickly collapsed. That year it began offering MediGap and other supplements to AARP members.

The company in 1999 announced it would let doctors — not administrators — choose what treatment patients would get, partially because it was spending more on care scrutiny than the practice saved. Nevertheless, many doctors claimed the process was still restrictive. In 2000 the American Medical Association sued the company, claiming it used faulty data to reduce payments to member doctors.

To expand its Medicaid services business, the firm bought AmeriChoice in 2002. Golden Rule was acquired in late 2003 so UnitedHealth could enter the individual health insurance market by providing medical savings accounts. To increase its market share in the northeastern US, the company bought Oxford Health Plans that year.

The company acquired PacifiCare Health Systems in 2005. The acquisition brought UnitedHealth 3 million more customers, including a strong foothold in the California Medicare market.

Bill McGuire became the focus of inquiry in 2006 due to his acquisition of more than $1.6 billion in stock options starting back in 1989, and some of which appeared to be back dated to his advantage. Dr. McGuire suggested that the stock option bonus plan be discontinued as a result of the controversy it has stirred. However, on the recommendation of outside cousel WilmerHale, the board of directors decided that Dr. McGuire should also leave. He was shown the door in October 2006 and asked to leave a portion of his stock options behind.

## EXECUTIVES

**Chairman:** Richard T. Burke Sr., age 63
**President, CEO, and Director:** Stephen J. (Steve) Hemsley, age 54
**EVP and CFO:** G. Mike Mikan, age 35
**EVP; Chairman and CEO, PacifiCare Health Systems:** Howard G. Phanstiel, age 56
**EVP; President, Commercial Services Group:** Richard H. Anderson, age 52
**EVP; President, Individual and Employer Markets Group:** David S. Wichmann, age 44
**EVP, Human Capital:** Lori Sweere Komstadius
**EVP; President, Public and Senior Markets Group:** Lois E. Quam, age 45
**EVP and Chief Legal Officer:** Thomas L. Strickland
**SVP:** John S. Penshorn
**SVP and Chief Accounting Officer:** Eric S. Rangen, age 50
**SVP and Chief Communications Officer:** Don Nathan
**SVP, Relationship and Business Development:** William E. Moeller
**SVP, Government Affairs:** Judah C. (Jud) Sommer
**VP, Government Affairs:** Tom Koutsoumpas
**VP, Public Communications and Strategy:** Mark Lindsay
**CEO, United Behavioral Health:** James B. Hudak
**CEO, Mid-Atlantic Region:** Kevin Ruth
**CEO, UnitedHealthcare of Pennsylvania:** Thomas N. Pappas
**CEO, Military and Veterans Health Services:** Donald R. Gintzig
**COO, Military and Veterans Health Services:** Lori McDougal
**Acting General Counsel:** Forrest Burke
**Chief Ethics Officer:** William S. Bojan
**Investor Relations:** Cheryl Mamer
**Auditors:** Deloitte & Touche LLP

## LOCATIONS

**HQ:** UnitedHealth Group Incorporated
UnitedHealth Group Center, 9900 Bren Rd. East, Minnetonka, MN 55343
**Phone:** 952-936-1300 **Fax:** 952-936-7430
**Web:** www.unitedhealthgroup.com

UnitedHealth Group operates throughout the US and in some 30 additional countries.

## PRODUCTS/OPERATIONS

### 2006 Sales

| | $ mil. | % of total |
|---|---|---|
| Health care services | 64,180 | 86 |
| Uniprise | 5,451 | 7 |
| Specialized care services | 3,989 | 6 |
| Ingenix | 976 | 1 |
| Adjustments | (3,054) | — |
| **Total** | **71,542** | **100** |

### Selected Operations

Health care services
- AmeriChoice (plans for recipients of Medicaid and other state-sponsored programs)
- Ovations (plans for consumers over the age of 50)
- UnitedHealthcare (plans for multi-state, midsized, and small businesses and consumers)

Specialized care services
- Specialized health solutions
  - ACN Group (benefit administration)
  - LifeEra (employee assistance programs)
  - Optum (disease management)
  - United Behavioral Health (mental health plans)
  - United Resource Networks (critical disease manangement)
- Dental and vision
  - Spectera (vision benefits)
  - UnitedHealth Dental (dental benefits)
- Group Insurance Services (life and disability insurance)

INGENIX (information services)
Uniprise (corporate health care plan organization and administration)

## COMPETITORS

Aetna
Aflac
Blue Cross
CIGNA
Coventry Health Care
Delta Dental Plans
Health Insurance of New York
Health Net
Humana
Kaiser Foundation
New York Life
WellPoint

## HISTORICAL FINANCIALS

Company Type: Public

### Income Statement

FYE: December 31

| | REVENUE ($ mil.) | NET INCOME ($ mil.) | NET PROFIT MARGIN | EMPLOYEES |
|---|---|---|---|---|
| **12/06** | 71,542 | 4,159 | 5.8% | 58,000 |
| **12/05** | 45,365 | 3,300 | 7.3% | 55,000 |
| **12/04** | 37,218 | 2,587 | 7.0% | 40,000 |
| **12/03** | 28,823 | 1,825 | 6.3% | 33,000 |
| **12/02** | 25,020 | 1,352 | 5.4% | 32,000 |
| **Annual Growth** | 30.0% | 32.4% | — | 16.0% |

### 2006 Year-End Financials

Debt ratio: 28.7%
Return on equity: 21.6%
Cash ($ mil.): 10,940
Current ratio: 0.87
Long-term debt ($ mil.): 5,973
No. of shares (mil.): 1,345
Dividends
Yield: 0.1%
Payout: 1.0%
Market value ($ mil.): 72,267

### Stock History

NYSE: UNH

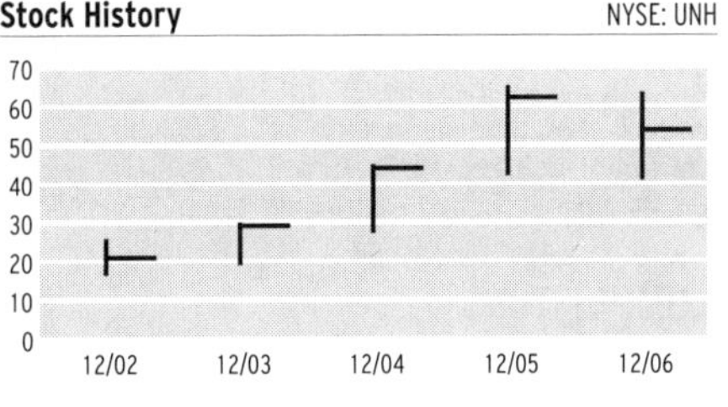


| | STOCK PRICE ($) FY Close | P/E High | P/E Low | PER SHARE ($) Earnings | Dividends | Book Value |
|---|---|---|---|---|---|---|
| **12/06** | 53.73 | 21 | 14 | 2.97 | 0.03 | 15.47 |
| **12/05** | 62.14 | 26 | 17 | 2.48 | 0.01 | 13.06 |
| **12/04** | 44.01 | 23 | 14 | 1.97 | 0.01 | 16.67 |
| **12/03** | 29.09 | 20 | 13 | 1.48 | 0.01 | 8.80 |
| **12/02** | 20.88 | 24 | 16 | 1.06 | 0.01 | 14.79 |
| **Annual Growth** | 26.7% | — | — | 29.4% | 31.6% | 1.1% |

# Universal Corporation

Smoking may be hazardous to your health, but providing the tobacco for the smokes has proven safe and profitable so far for Universal Corporation. The company selects, buys, ships, and processes leaf tobacco in the US and more than 35 other nations. The leaf is sold to cigarette makers. Universal also procures and processes dark tobacco used in cigars and smokeless products. In addition to brokering tobacco, the firm once sold and distributed lumber and building products in Europe under its Deli Universal unit, but it exited that business altogether in 2007. Universal's tobacco-related businesses operate under the Universal Leaf subsidiary. Dreman Value Management owns about 12% of the company's capital stock.

Acting as an intermediary between tobacco growers and smokeless tobacco and cigarette companies, Universal primarily deals in flue-cured (processed by artificial heat), burley (air-cured), and oriental (small-leafed) tobaccos, all of which are the major ingredients in American blend cigarettes. Altria Group (owner of the US and international divisions of Philip Morris), the #1 tobacco company in the world, and Japan Tobacco are its biggest customers. The firm's tobacco-related revenues have suffered as the number of US smokers has decreased and some US cigarette makers increasingly have bought tobacco abroad or directly from US farmers. In response, Universal closed its Danville, Virginia, plant and consolidated its US burley leaf processing to its North Carolina facility in late 2005.

Within the past couple of years, Universal Corporation has shed businesses unrelated to its tobacco operations and refocused its attention to the tobacco market. In its role as an agricultural products merchant, the company had provided the food industry with a number of products, including tea, dried fruit, and sunflower seeds. It also provided the tire manufacturing industry with rubber. In addition, Universal distributed building materials and lumber to wholesale/do-it-yourself chains and to the construction and prefabrication industries in the Netherlands and Belgium through regional outlets. The company's non-tobacco activities brought in almost half of its revenues. However, Universal Corporation — from 2005 through 2007 — sold its non-tobacco agricultural products business and its other non-tobacco entities. The effort (to increase shareholder value and return to core competencies) involved selling a UK trading company, as well as trading companies in Virginia, Washington, and California.

## HISTORY

Jaquelin Taylor founded Universal Leaf Tobacco Company in 1918 by combining six tobacco dealers, including his own J.P. Taylor Company of Virginia, and the company went public a few years later. The company launched subsidiaries in China in 1924 and in Canada the following year.

Philip Morris became a customer during the 1930s, and the cigarette maker's association with Universal became instrumental in its growth. By 1940 the company was the leading purchaser of leaf tobacco in the US. That year the US government filed antitrust charges against Universal and seven other tobacco companies. American, Liggett & Myers, and Reynolds stood trial for the whole group, and four years later each of the eight companies was fined $15,000.

Universal expanded into South America and Asia during the next several decades, and by the end of the 1960s it was operating in 15 countries outside the US. The company diversified under Gordon Crenshaw, who became president in 1965 and CEO soon thereafter. Universal made several small acquisitions between 1966 and 1980, including fertilizer producer Royster in 1980 (sold in 1984). Its first significant venture outside agriculture came in 1984 when it bought both Lawyers Title and Continental Land Title for a total of $115 million. Two years later Universal bought Netherlands-based Deli-Maatschappij, which traded in tobacco and commodities such as tea, rubber, sunflower seeds, and timber.

In 1987 the company changed its name to Universal Corporation to reflect its diversifying interests. Henry Harrell replaced Crenshaw as CEO in 1988 (and as chairman in 1991). Also in 1988

Universal bought tobacco processor Thope and Ricks, and two years later it purchased Gebreder Kulenkampffag (tobacco, Germany), giving Universal a greater presence in the developing market in Eastern Europe.

The company acquired Kliemann (tobacco, Brazil) in 1991, ensuring access to Brazilian flue-cured tobacco. Also that year a depressed real estate market led the company to spin off its title insurance operation, Lawyers Title, to shareholders. Universal bought the Casalee Group, a UK tobacco processor with key operations in Brazil and Africa and trading operations in Europe and the Far East, for about $100 million in 1993. A global surplus in the tobacco markets hurt profits the following year.

In 1996 Universal formed a joint venture with COSUN, a Dutch sugar cooperative, creating the #1 spice enterprise in the Benelux market. As part of its plan to grow in emerging markets, the next year Universal acquired leaf-processing plants in Tanzania and Poland. Despite strong sales and profits, Universal's stock had flagged, and in 1998 the company bought back $100 million of its shares to improve their value. Universal formed Socotab, a joint venture with Socotab Leaf Company to combine both companies' oriental leaf businesses.

Sales fell in 1999 amid a worldwide glut of leaf tobacco. In 2000 Universal said it would close several US plants, eliminating about 175 full-time and 1,400 seasonal jobs. In 2001 the transition from the traditional auction market to direct contracting with farmers caused increases in the cost of doing business for Universal.

In 2003 Harrell retired as chairman and CEO.

## EXECUTIVES

**Chairman and CEO:** Allen B. King, age 60
**President:** George C. Freeman III, age 43
**VP and CFO:** Hartwell H. Roper, age 57, $322,392 pay
**VP and Chief Administrative Officer:** D. C. Moore
**VP, Human Resources:** Mike Oberschmidt Jr.
**VP and Treasurer:** Karen M. L. Whelan, age 59
**General Counsel and Secretary:** P. D. Wigner
**Controller:** Robert M. Peebles, age 48
**Auditors:** Ernst & Young LLP

## LOCATIONS

**HQ:** Universal Corporation
1501 N. Hamilton St., Richmond, VA 23230
**Phone:** 804-359-9311 **Fax:** 804-254-3584
**Web:** www.universalcorp.com

Universal Corporation has operations in the US and some 35 other countries, including Brazil, Canada, and Zimbabwe.

### 2007 Sales

| | $ mil. | % of total |
|---|---|---|
| US | 364.2 | 18 |
| Belgium | 347.6 | 17 |
| Germany | 219.3 | 11 |
| Other countries | 1,076.2 | 54 |
| **Total** | **2,007.3** | **100** |

## PRODUCTS/OPERATIONS

### 2007 Sales

| | $ mil. | % of total |
|---|---|---|
| Flue-cured & burley leaf tobacco operations | 1,722.5 | 86 |
| Other tobacco operations | 284.7 | 14 |
| **Total** | **2,007.3** | **100** |

### Selected Agricultural Products
Dried fruit
Nuts
Rubber
Sunflower seeds
Tea

### Selected Subsidiaries
Beleggings-en Beheermaatschappij "DE Amstel" B.V (The Netherlands)
Continental Tobacco, S.A (Switzerland)
Corrie MacColl & Son Limited (rubber merchandiser, UK)
Deli Universal, Inc.
Deltafina, S.p.A (Italy)
Ermor Tabarama-Tabacos do Brasil Ltda
Gebrueder Kulenkampff AG (Germany)
Handelmaatschappij Steffex B.V (The Netherlands)
Heuvelman Holding B.V. (The Netherlands)
Imperial Commodities Corporation
Alan L. Grant division (rubber merchandiser)
Berns and Koppstein division (canned and frozen foods merchandiser)
Indoco International B.V (The Netherlands)
Industria AG (Switzerland)
Itofina, S.A (Switzerland)
Jongeneel Holding B.V (The Netherlands)
L'Agricola, S.r.L. (Italy)
Lytton Tobacco Company (Malawi) Limited
Lytton Tobacco Company (Private), Limited (Zimbabwe)
Simcoe Leaf Tobacco Company, Limited (Canada)
Steffex Beheer B.V (The Netherlands)
Tabacos del Pacífico Norte, S.A. De C.V. (Mexico)
Tanzania Leaf Tobacco Co., Ltd
Tobacco Trading International, Inc. (British Virgin Islands)
Toutiana, S.A (Switzerland)
Ultoco, S.A (Switzerland)
Universal Leaf International S.A. (Switzerland)
Universal Leaf Tabacos Ltda. (Brazil)
Van Rees B.V. (tea, The Netherlands)

## COMPETITORS

Alliance One
Altadis
British American Tobacco
Dahlgren & Company
GEA Group
James Finlay
Japan Tobacco
Stora Enso Oyj
Sun Growers
Unilever
Universal Commodities Tea
UPM-Kymmene
Wickes

## HISTORICAL FINANCIALS

Company Type: Public

### Income Statement

FYE: March 31

| | REVENUE ($ mil.) | NET INCOME ($ mil.) | NET PROFIT MARGIN | EMPLOYEES |
|---|---|---|---|---|
| **3/07** | 2,007 | 44 | 2.2% | 25,000 |
| **3/06** | 3,511 | 8 | 0.2% | 30,000 |
| **3/05** | 3,276 | 96 | 2.9% | 28,000 |
| **3/04*** | 2,271 | 100 | 4.4% | 30,000 |
| **6/03** | 2,637 | 111 | 4.2% | 28,000 |
| **Annual Growth** | (6.6%) | (20.4%) | — | (2.8%) |

*Fiscal year change

### 2007 Year-End Financials

Debt ratio: 48.8%
Return on equity: 5.6%
Cash ($ mil.): 358
Current ratio: 2.23
Long-term debt ($ mil.): 399
No. of shares (mil.): 27
Dividends
Yield: 2.1%
Payout: 114.2%
Market value ($ mil.): 1,653

### Stock History

NYSE: UVV

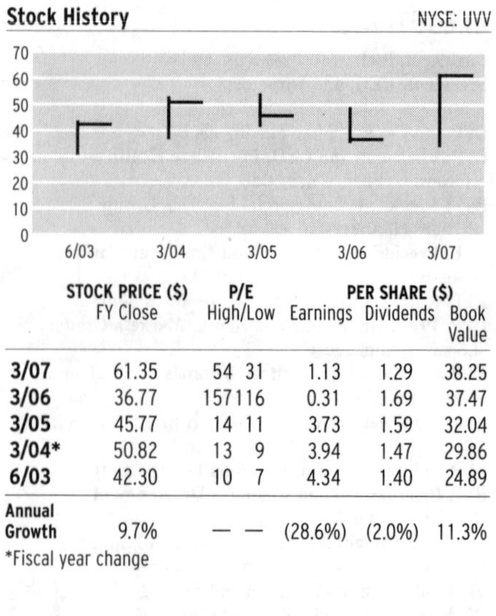


| | STOCK PRICE ($) FY Close | P/E High | P/E Low | PER SHARE ($) Earnings | Dividends | Book Value |
|---|---|---|---|---|---|---|
| **3/07** | 61.35 | 54 | 31 | 1.13 | 1.29 | 38.25 |
| **3/06** | 36.77 | 157 | 116 | 0.31 | 1.69 | 37.47 |
| **3/05** | 45.77 | 14 | 11 | 3.73 | 1.59 | 32.04 |
| **3/04*** | 50.82 | 13 | 9 | 3.94 | 1.47 | 29.86 |
| **6/03** | 42.30 | 10 | 7 | 4.34 | 1.40 | 24.89 |
| **Annual Growth** | 9.7% | — | — | (28.6%) | (2.0%) | 11.3% |

*Fiscal year change

# Unum Group

Unum Group (formerly UnumProvident) is the largest disability insurer in the US and the UK. The company offers individual and group short-term and long-term disability insurance and specialty coverage such as long-term care, cancer, and travel insurance. Subsidiaries include Colonial Life & Accident Insurance, Provident Life and Accident, First Unum Life, and The Paul Revere Life Insurance Company. Other operations include the GENEX Services unit, which provides disability management services, vocational rehabilitation, and related services to corporations, third-party administrators, and insurance companies.

Unum Group seeks to achieve a competitive edge by providing group, individual, and voluntary workplace products that can combine with other coverages to provide integrated benefits solutions for customers.

To help large employers keep health care costs down, the company has formed a partnership with Matria Healthcare. The alliance links Unum Group's medical claims management skills with Matria's disease management services and seeks to focus on the relatively few chronically ill and disabled workers who generate the majority of health care costs.

As part of a rebranding effort following years of corporate restructuring, the company changed its name from UnumProvident to Unum Group in 2007.

## HISTORY

Coal was discovered in eastern Tennessee in the 1870s; in 1887 several Chattanooga professional men formed the Provident Life & Accident Insurance Co. to provide medical insurance to miners. But it was a case of the inexperienced serving the uninsurable, and by 1892 the company was on the brink of ruin. The founders sold half the company for $1,000 to Thomas Maclellan and John McMaster, two Scotsmen who had failed at banking in Canada.

While Maclellan handled the business end, McMaster scoured the coalfields for customers.

He even went into the mines, pitching to individual miners and bringing along someone to dig coal for them so they wouldn't lose money by stopping work to listen.

In 1895 the partners bought the rest of the company. Provident grew, thanks to the cooperation of mining companies, which deducted premiums from miners' pay. Provident added sickness and industrial insurance (low-benefit life policies). In 1900, after a period of strained relations, Maclellan bought out McMaster.

After 1905 northern insurers began moving into the industrializing South. To meet the competition, Provident reorganized and added capital, and its stepped-up sales efforts brought in such lucrative business as railroad accounts. Provident added life insurance in 1917. The first policy was bought by Robert Maclellan, who became president when his father died in 1916.

In 1931 Provident acquired the Southern Surety Co. During and after WWII, group sales exploded as employee benefit packages proliferated. Provident, which by then operated nationally, entered Canada in 1948. Four years later R. L. Maclellan succeeded his father as president (R. L. stepped down in 1971). Provident's growth in the 1970s stemmed from its life units, but it also developed a large health insurance operation.

The health care operations were hammered by rising medical costs in the 1980s so the company moved into managed care. But the combination of increased health care costs and a real estate crash gave the company a one-two punch in the late 1980s and early 1990s. An accounting change in 1993 further hit profits. In 1994 new president Harold Chandler initiated a reevaluation of Provident's operations and future, which resulted in Provident's exit from the health care business beginning in 1995.

In 1997 Provident began a major move into disability insurance. It bought 83% of rival disability insurer The Paul Revere Corporation from Textron. About 10,000 Paul Revere insurance brokers later filed suit alleging they were denied millions of dollars in commissions. In exchange for its $300 million aid in the purchase, Switzerland's Zurich Insurance (now Zurich Financial Services) received about 15% of Provident. The company also acquired GENEX Services (vocational rehabilitation and related services) and sold its dental insurance business to Ameritas Life Insurance. In 1998 Provident sold its annuity business to American General (now a subsidiary of AIG).

In 1998, with both Provident and Unum Corporation looking for ways to enhance business, the companies commenced merger negotiations and completed the transaction the next year. But the merger was more expensive than anticipated and problems in integrating the companies' sales forces slowed policy sales.

Company operations began melding more smoothly and UnumProvident began addressing the problems with its sales force as well as adding customer service staff in 2000. It pulled money out of reserves by reinsuring several blocks of acquisition-related business and sold an inactive shell subsidiary licensed to sell annuities in most states to Allstate. In 2001 the company sold its Provident National Assurance subsidiary to Allstate. UnumProvident faced accusations that the company denied valid disability claims in 2002. These accusations resulted in legal actions in a number of states.

UnumProvident acquired Sun Life Financial's UK life insurance group in a move designed to expand the company's operations in the UK in 2003.

UnumProvident sold its Unum Japan Accident Insurance Co., Ltd. subsidiary to Hitachi Capital Corporation (Hitachi) in 2004.

## EXECUTIVES

**Chairman:** Jon S. Fossel, age 65
**President, CEO, and Director:** Thomas R. Watjen, age 52, $1,694,067 pay
**EVP and CFO:** Robert C. (Bob) Greving, age 55, $616,194 pay
**EVP, Field Sales:** Roger C. Edgren, age 52
**EVP, Risk Operations:** Kevin P. McCarthy, age 51
**EVP, Service Operations; CIO:** Robert O. (Bob) Best, age 57
**EVP and General Counsel:** Charles Glick, age 52
**SVP, Account Management and Field Service:** Beverly N. (Bev) Altenburg
**SVP, Field Operations:** Richard H. Wolf
**SVP, Group Customer Center:** Pamela S. Davis
**SVP, Human Resources:** Eileen C. Farrar
**SVP, Individual Customer Center:** Tom Thompson
**SVP, Investment:** David G. Fussell
**SVP, Investor Relations:** Thomas A.H. (Tom) White
**SVP, Return-to-Work Services-Development:** Ralph W. Mohney Jr.
**SVP and Chief Marketing Officer:** Joseph R. (Joe) Foley
**SVP, The Benefits Center — Operations:** George A. Shell Jr.
**SVP, Underwriting — Chattanooga:** Donald E. (Don) Boggs
**SVP Sales, US:** Steve Meahl
**VP, Corporate Secretary, and Assistant General Counsel:** Susan N. Roth
**VP and Corporate Treasurer:** Kevin McMahon
**Chairman and Managing Director, Unum Limited:** Susan L. Ring, age 45
**President and CEO, GENEX Services, Inc.:** Peter C. Madeja, age 46
**President and CEO, Colonial Life & Accident Insurance Company:** Randall C. (Randy) Horn
**Auditors:** Ernst & Young LLP

## LOCATIONS

**HQ:** Unum Group
1 Fountain Sq., Chattanooga, TN 37402
**Phone:** 423-294-1011 **Fax:** 423-294-3962
**Web:** www.unum.com

## PRODUCTS/OPERATIONS

### 2006 Sales

| | $ mil. | % of total |
|---|---|---|
| Premium income | 7,948.2 | 75 |
| Net investment income | 2,320.6 | 22 |
| Net realized investment gain (loss) | 2.2 | — |
| Other income | 264.3 | 3 |
| **Total** | **10,535.3** | **100** |

### Selected Subsidiaries

Colonial Companies, Inc.
- BenefitAmerica, Inc.
- Colonial Life & Accident Insurance Company

Duncanson & Holt, Inc.
- Duncanson & Holt Asia PTE Ltd. (Singapore)
- Duncanson & Holt Canada Ltd.
  - TRI-CAN Reinsurance Inc. (Canada)
- Duncanson & Holt Services, Inc.
- Duncanson & Holt Syndicate Management Ltd. (UK)
  - LRG Services Limited (UK)
  - Trafalgar Underwriting Agencies Ltd. (UK)
- Duncanson & Holt Underwriters, Ltd. (UK)

First Unum Life Insurance Company
Provident Investment Management, LLC
Provident Life and Accident Insurance Company
Provident Life and Casualty Insurance Company
The Paul Revere Corporation
- The Paul Revere Life Insurance Company
  - The Paul Revere Variable Annuity Insurance Company

Unum International Underwriters, Inc.
Unum Life Insurance Company of America
- GENEX Services, Inc.
  - GENEX Consultants, Inc.
  - GENEX Services Inc. of Ohio
  - GENEX Services, LLC
  - GENEX Services of Canada, Inc
  - Options & Choices, Inc.
  - Primecor, Inc.

Unum European Holding Company Limited (UK)
- Group Risk Insurance Services Limited (UK)
- Unum Limited (UK)
  - Claims Services International Limited (UK)

UnumProvident Finance Company (UK)
UnumProvident International Ltd. (Bermuda)

## COMPETITORS

| | |
|---|---|
| AEGON | John Hancock |
| Aflac | Liberty Mutual |
| AIG American General | Lincoln Financial Group |
| Allianz | MassMutual |
| Aon | MetLife |
| AXA Financial | Mutual of Omaha |
| CIGNA | Nationwide |
| CNA Financial | New York Life |
| Conseco | Northwestern Mutual |
| GatesMcDonald | Old Republic |
| Guardian Life | Principal Financial |
| Hartford Life | Prudential |

## HISTORICAL FINANCIALS

Company Type: Public

### Income Statement

FYE: December 31

| | ASSETS ($ mil.) | NET INCOME ($ mil.) | INCOME AS % OF ASSETS | EMPLOYEES |
|---|---|---|---|---|
| **12/06** | 52,823 | 411 | 0.8% | 11,100 |
| **12/05** | 51,867 | 514 | 1.0% | 11,300 |
| **12/04** | 50,832 | (253) | — | 11,600 |
| **12/03** | 49,718 | (386) | — | 13,400 |
| **12/02** | 45,260 | 401 | 0.9% | 13,800 |
| **Annual Growth** | 3.9% | 0.6% | — | (5.3%) |

### 2006 Year-End Financials

Equity as % of assets: 14.6%
Return on assets: 0.8%
Return on equity: 5.4%
Long-term debt ($ mil.): 2,660
No. of shares (mil.): 343
Dividends
Yield: 1.4%
Payout: 24.4%
Market value ($ mil.): 7,120
Sales ($ mil.): 10,535

### Stock History

NYSE: UNM

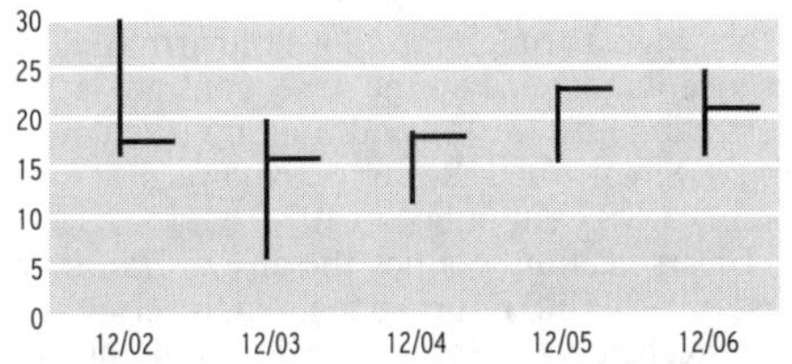

| | STOCK PRICE ($) FY Close | P/E High | P/E Low | PER SHARE ($) Earnings | PER SHARE ($) Dividends | PER SHARE ($) Book Value |
|---|---|---|---|---|---|---|
| **12/06** | 20.78 | 20 | 13 | 1.23 | 0.30 | 22.53 |
| **12/05** | 22.75 | 14 | 9 | 1.64 | 0.30 | 24.66 |
| **12/04** | 17.94 | — | — | (0.86) | 0.30 | 24.36 |
| **12/03** | 15.77 | — | — | (1.40) | 0.37 | 24.55 |
| **12/02** | 17.54 | 18 | 10 | 1.65 | 0.59 | 28.33 |
| **Annual Growth** | 4.3% | — | — | (7.1%) | (15.6%) | (5.6%) |

# URS Corporation

URS is a major player in engineering design. URS Corporation provides planning, design, program and construction management, and operations and maintenance services to local, state, and federal governments, as well as to private and international clients. Organized into two operating units, the URS division and the EG&G division, the firm focuses on transportation, environmental, facilities, commercial/industrial, water/wastewater, homeland security, defense systems, and installations and logistics markets and provides a broad range of engineering and architectural services. Federal contracts account for nearly 50% of sales.

URS plans to acquire Washington Group International for $2.6 billion in cash and stock, making it a powerhouse in the nuclear industry sector, just in time for the growing resurgence in nuclear power.

The company significantly expanded its US government sales with its 2002 acquisition of EG&G Technical Services from The Carlyle Group. The acquisition enhanced URS's position as one of the key federal contractors for operations and management and maintenance services. The group markets those services primarily to the US Departments of Defense and Homeland Security. EG&G provides technical operations and maintenance services to such federal entities as NASA, all branches of the military, and the US Departments of Justice, Energy, and Transportation.

Just a few of the services that URS provides to federal agencies are emergency response strategies, training for the elimination and dismantling of weapons of mass destruction, and pilot training.

## HISTORY

Founded as an engineering research partnership in 1951 and incorporated as Broadview Research Corp. in 1957, the company won its first big contract (which lasted until 1971) with the US Army, to automate logistical and personnel systems. In 1962 it changed its name to United Research Services, shortening it to URS two years later. Through the 1960s the firm tried to reduce its reliance on the Army contract by diversifying into leasing and training (even owning Evelyn Wood Reading Dynamics at one point). URS went public in 1976.

Diversification was not the answer, however, and in 1984 URS returned to its engineering and architecture roots. Laden with debt from the earlier acquisitions and overextended overseas, it was ill-equipped to deal with lower construction spending in the late 1980s on public infrastructure and the environment. The firm was near bankruptcy in 1989 when CEO Martin Koffel took the helm. URS sold noncore assets and cut foreign operations, settled shareholder lawsuits, and pared down debt. By 1991 it was profitable again.

Focused on its core business, in 1995 URS bought E.C. Driver & Associates, specialists in highway and bridge design. The next year URS acquired Greiner Engineering, forming URS Greiner, which doubled its US offices and gave it a presence in Asia. On a roll, in 1997 URS doubled its private-sector business by acquiring geotechnical and environmental engineering specialists Woodward-Clyde.

Continuing to grow through acquisitions, the company bought Thorburn Colquhoun, the UK civil and structural engineering consulting firm, in 1999. Also that year URS won a major prize when it purchased Los Angeles-based engineering and construction services firm Dames & Moore in a $600 million deal. The acquisition more than doubled URS's size again and strengthened the company's presence in Asia, Australia, and Europe.

URS projects in 2000 included a contract to provide environmental services to U.S. Air Force installations worldwide and a contract to design a water treatment plant in Lancaster, Ohio. Among the projects URS began working on in 2001 was design of downtown Atlanta's 17th Street Bridge. The firm also won contracts to provide environmental consulting to the US Postal Service and the US Coast Guard. After helping both public and private companies with their heightened security concerns following the September 11 attacks, URS decided in 2002 to form a security services group to help protect buildings, airports, and infrastructure against natural disasters and terrorist attacks.

To gain even more earnings from federal defense contracts (particularly for national and homeland defense projects), URS acquired outsourced operations and maintenance provider EG&G Technical Services Holdings from Carlyle Group, a Washington, DC-based investing firm with several ties to the defense industry. In 2003 the company won a Navy contract to provide environmental restoration and other services for Naval installations in six western states.

## EXECUTIVES

**Chairman, President, and CEO:** Martin M. Koffel, age 67, $2,090,042 pay
**EVP:** Jean-Yves Perez, $469,313 pay
**EVP, Public Sector Business Development, URS Division:** Martin S. Tanzer
**SVP, East Division, URS Division:** Dhamo S. Dhamotharan
**SVP, Special Programs:** Robert M. Gallen
**SVP, International Division, URS Division:** Michael C. Richards
**SVP and Director Gulf Coast Reconstruction Team:** Michael J. (Mike) Burton
**SVP and Regional Manager:** Thomas J. (Tom) Logan
**VP and CFO:** H. Thomas (Tom) Hicks
**VP; Chairman, URS Division:** Irwin L. Rosenstein, age 66
**VP; President, URS Division:** Gary V. Jandegian, age 52, $824,678 pay
**VP; President, EG&G:** Randall A. (Randy) Wotring, $850,393 pay
**VP, General Counsel, and Secretary:** Joseph Masters, age 48
**VP, Communications:** Susan B. Kilgannon
**VP, Corporate Planning:** Olga Perkovic, age 36
**VP, Information Technology:** Thomas J. Lynch
**VP Investor Relations:** Sam Ramraj
**VP, Strategy; SVP, West and Construction Services Division:** Thomas W. (Tom) Bishop, age 59
**VP and Treasurer:** Judy L. Rodgers
**VP, Controller, and Chief Accounting Officer:** Reed N. Brimhall, age 52, $686,396 pay
**Auditors:** PricewaterhouseCoopers LLP

## LOCATIONS

**HQ:** URS Corporation
600 Montgomery St., 26th Fl.,
San Francisco, CA 94111
**Phone:** 415-774-2700 **Fax:** 415-398-1905
**Web:** www.urscorp.com

## PRODUCTS/OPERATIONS

**2006 Sales**

| | % of total |
|---|---|
| Federal government | 45 |
| Private industry | 23 |
| State & local government | 22 |
| International | 10 |
| **Total** | **100** |

**Selected Services**

Design
- Architectural and interior design
- Civil, structural, mechanical, electrical, sanitary, environmental, water resource, geotechnical/underground, dam, mining, and seismic engineering
- Engineering and design studies for the upgrade and maintenance of military hardware

Operations and maintenance
- Management of base logistics
- Operation and maintenance of chemical agent disposal systems
- Oversight of construction, testing, and operation of base systems and processes
- Support of high-security systems

Planning
- Archeological and cultural resources studies
- Coordination of community involvement programs
- Development and analysis of alternative concepts
- Environmental impact studies
- Environmental site analyses
- Facilities planning
- Master planning
- Permitting
- Programming
- Technical and economic feasibility studies
- Traffic and revenue studies

Program and construction management
- Cash flow analyses
- Constructability reviews
- Construction and bid management
- Construction and life-cycle cost estimating
- Construction or demolition of buildings

## COMPETITORS

AECOM
Baran Group
Bechtel
Black & Veatch
Camp Dresser McKee
CH2M HILL
CH2M Hill Industrial Design and Construction
Earth Tech
Fluor
Foster Wheeler
Halliburton
Jacobs Engineering
Lockheed Martin
The Morganti Group
Parsons Brinckerhoff
Skidmore Owings
Terracon
Washington Group

## HISTORICAL FINANCIALS

Company Type: Public

**Income Statement** FYE: December 31

| | REVENUE ($ mil.) | NET INCOME ($ mil.) | NET PROFIT MARGIN | EMPLOYEES |
|---|---|---|---|---|
| **12/06** | 4,240 | 113 | 2.7% | 29,300 |
| **12/05*** | 3,918 | 83 | 2.1% | 29,200 |
| **10/04** | 3,382 | 62 | 1.8% | 27,500 |
| **10/03** | 3,187 | 58 | 1.8% | 26,000 |
| **10/02** | 2,428 | 55 | 2.3% | 25,000 |
| **Annual Growth** | 15.0% | 19.6% | — | 4.0% |

*Fiscal year change

**2006 Year-End Financials**

Debt ratio: 9.9%
Return on equity: 7.9%
Cash ($ mil.): 90
Current ratio: 1.75
Long-term debt ($ mil.): 149
No. of shares (mil.): 52
Dividends
Yield: —
Payout: —
Market value ($ mil.): 2,239

**Stock History** NYSE: URS

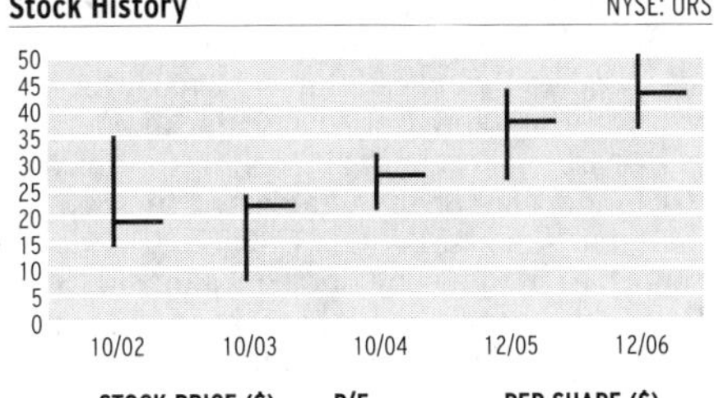

| | STOCK PRICE ($) FY Close | P/E High | P/E Low | PER SHARE ($) Earnings | Dividends | Book Value |
|---|---|---|---|---|---|---|
| **12/06** | 42.85 | 23 | 17 | 2.19 | — | 28.83 |
| **12/05*** | 37.61 | 25 | 16 | 1.72 | — | 26.69 |
| **10/04** | 27.60 | 20 | 14 | 1.53 | — | 24.51 |
| **10/03** | 21.89 | 13 | 5 | 1.76 | — | 22.73 |
| **10/02** | 18.96 | 17 | 7 | 2.03 | — | 21.07 |
| **Annual Growth** | 22.6% | — | — | 1.9% | — | 8.2% |

*Fiscal year change

# US Airways Group

After two bankruptcy reorganizations since 2002, US Airways Group has caught a tailwind. The company, which emerged from Chapter 11 in 2005 when it merged with America West, ranks among the nation's largest airlines, and it returned to profitability in 2006. Together with its regional affiliates, US Airways serves about 240 cities, mainly in the US and Canada but also in Latin America and Europe, from hubs in Charlotte, North Carolina; Philadelphia; and Phoenix. It maintains a fleet of some 360 aircraft for mainline routes, plus another 310 for its regional service, which is provided by subsidiaries Piedmont Airlines and PSA and several independent carriers.

US Airways is still working to unify its US Airways and America West operations under the US Airways brand; it hopes to complete the process in 2007. Along with bringing together two airlines, the company is trying to combine two approaches to the airline business: low-fare, low-cost (think Southwest Airlines and JetBlue) and international hub-and-spoke, with amenities (think AMR's American Airlines and UAL's United Airlines). So far, the experiment can be considered a success, in part because the company was able to scale back costs during its bankruptcy reorganizations.

US Airways hopes to grow by taking advantage of rising demand for international flights, and the company extends its network as a member of the Star Alliance international marketing and code-sharing partnership, which includes United, Germany's Lufthansa, and more than a dozen other carriers. In addition, US Airways is bidding to add direct service to China.

To accelerate its growth, US Airways offered to buy rival Delta in 2006 before withdrawing the bid the next year. US Airways initially made an unsolicited offer in November 2006 to pay about $8 billion, half in cash and half in stock, for Delta, which was reorganizing under bankruptcy protection. Hoping to put pressure on Delta's creditors to agree to a deal, US Airways upped its bid to about $10 billion in January 2007. Delta failed to bite, however, spoiling US Airways' dreams of creating the world's largest airline.

Eastshore Aviation, an investment concern affiliated with regional carrier Air Wisconsin, owns about 5% of US Airways.

## HISTORY

Richard du Pont (of the DuPont chemical dynasty) founded All American Aviation as an airmail service in 1939 to serve Pennsylvania and the Ohio Valley. Pilots used a system of hooks and ropes to pick up and drop off mail "on the fly." Ten years later the company expanded its service, began carrying passengers, and changed its name to All American Airways.

The carrier became Allegheny Airlines in 1953. It bought smaller airlines in 1968 and 1972, expanding into the Midwest and up the East Coast. In 1978 the US airline industry was deregulated; Allegheny became USAir in 1979 and began flying across the South and to California.

In 1987 USAir bought two major regional carriers — Pacific Southwest Airlines and Piedmont Airlines. The USAir/Piedmont merger was at the time the largest in US airline history. It also gave USAir its hub in Charlotte, North Carolina; its first international route (Charlotte-London); and an East Coast commuter airline. In 1988 USAir bought a small stake in Covia, operator of the Apollo computer reservations system (CRS). (Covia merged with Galileo, a European CRS operator, in 1992.)

High fuel prices and fare wars in the early 1990s put USAir in the red for six years (and forced it to lay off 9,000 workers by 1996). Seth Schofield became CEO in 1991, and USAir acquired TWA's London routes in 1992. Taking a 40% stake in Trump Shuttle, USAir began a joint marketing effort under the name USAir Shuttle. (It bought the shuttle outright in 1997.) The next year USAir and British Airways (BA) began code-sharing, and BA took a stake in USAir, which gave up its London routes.

The year 1994 was not one of USAir's best: It took a beating as it lowered fares to compete with Continental Airlines, which by then challenged USAir in almost half its routes. The airline tried in vain to wring wage concessions from its unions. Then disaster struck. A jet carrying 132 passengers crashed at Pittsburgh — USAir's second fatal crash that year.

Though USAir returned to profitability in 1996, Schofield resigned. New CEO Stephen Wolf, a UAL veteran, demanded labor concessions. USAir, which became US Airways in 1997, finally won a new contract with its pilots.

The company's relationship with BA soured after US Airways sued BA to gain access to London's Heathrow. The two canceled code-sharing in 1997, and by 1998 BA had sold its US Airways stock. In 1999 Wolf disciple Rakesh Gangwal became CEO; Wolf remained chairman.

After some sparring, the flight attendants union and US Airways sealed a contract in 2000. The airline also became the first US carrier to add Airbus A330s to its fleet. That year US Airways agreed to be acquired by UAL for $4.3 billion in cash and $7.3 billion in assumed debt. But antitrust regulators at the US Department of Justice — arguing that the combination would reduce competition and lead to higher fares — moved to block the UAL-US Airways deal in 2001. UAL and US Airways called off the deal.

To remain aloft after the terrorist attacks in New York and Washington, DC, in 2001 the carrier announced that it would cut back on its flights and lay off about 20% of its workforce. It also discontinued MetroJet. Later that year Gangwal resigned, and Wolf stepped back in as CEO until March 2002, when Avis Rent A Car CEO David Siegel, a Continental Airlines veteran, was named president and CEO.

The group filed for bankruptcy protection in 2002 and in conjunction with its filing, the company received a bid from Texas Pacific Group, and it won a $900 million loan guarantee from the federal government. The Texas Pacific deal was replaced by The Retirement Systems of Alabama, which invested $240 million in exchange for a 36% ownership (and a 72% voting) stake in the company. It emerged from bankruptcy in 2003.

Restructured and with new ownership, the carrier strengthened its European presence in 2003 when it began a code-sharing agreement with top German airline Lufthansa, which eventually led to its inclusion in the Star Alliance.

Its new structure, however, didn't prove viable, and the carrier found itself overwhelmed by heavy costs, primarily record-high fuel prices. It was forced once again to seek the protection of bankruptcy courts in 2004. US Airways merged with America West and emerged from Chapter 11 the following year.

## EXECUTIVES

**Chairman and CEO:** William Douglas (Doug) Parker, age 45
**Vice Chairman:** Bruce R. Lakefield, age 62, $356,173 pay
**President:** J. Scott Kirby, age 39
**SVP and CFO, US Airways Group, US Airways, America West Holdings, and AWA:** Derek J. Kerr, age 41, $410,000 pay (partial-year salary)
**SVP and CIO:** Joseph (Joe) Beery, age 42
**SVP, Compliance Officer, and General Counsel:** Janet Dhillon, age 44
**SVP, People, Communication, and Culture, US Airways Group, US Airways, America West Holdings, and AWA:** Elise R. Eberwein, age 40
**SVP; President, US Airways Express:** Robert E. Martens
**SVP, Customer Service:** Anthony Mulé
**SVP, Flight Operations and Inflight:** Edward W. (Ed) Bular, age 54
**SVP, Public Affairs, US Airways Group, US Airways, America West Holdings, and AWA:** C. A. Howlett, age 62
**SVP, Scheduling and Planning Alliances:** Andrew P. Nocella, age 35
**SVP, Technical Operations:** Hal M. Heule, age 56
**VP and Controller:** Michael R. (Mike) Carreon, age 51
**VP and Treasurer:** Tom Weir
**VP, Human Resources:** John Hedblom
**VP, Labor Relations:** E. Allen Hemenway
**VP, Sales and Marketing:** Travis Christ, age 34
**President and CEO, Piedmont Airlines:** Stephen R. (Steve) Farrow
**President and CEO, PSA Airlines:** Keith D. Houk
**Corporate Secretary:** Caroline Ray
**Director, Corporate Communications:** Andrea Rader
**Auditors:** KPMG LLP

## LOCATIONS

**HQ:** US Airways Group, Inc.
111 W. Rio Salado Pkwy., Tempe, AZ 85281
**Phone:** 480-693-0800 **Fax:** 480-693-5546
**Web:** www.usairways.com

**2006 Sales**

| | $ mil. | % of total |
|---|---|---|
| US | 9,397 | 81 |
| Other countries | 2,160 | 19 |
| **Total** | **11,557** | **100** |

## PRODUCTS/OPERATIONS

### 2006 Sales

| | $ mil. | % of total |
|---|---|---|
| Mainline passenger | 7,966 | 69 |
| Express passenger | 2,744 | 24 |
| Cargo | 153 | 1 |
| Other | 694 | 6 |
| **Total** | **11,557** | **100** |

## COMPETITORS

Air France-KLM
AirTran Holdings
Alaska Air
AMR Corp.
British Airways
Continental Airlines
Delta Air
JetBlue
Northwest Airlines
Southwest Airlines
Virgin Atlantic Airways

## HISTORICAL FINANCIALS

Company Type: Public

### Income Statement

FYE: December 31

| | REVENUE ($ mil.) | NET INCOME ($ mil.) | NET PROFIT MARGIN | EMPLOYEES |
|---|---|---|---|---|
| **12/06** | 11,557 | 304 | 2.6% | 37,000 |
| **12/05** | 5,069 | (537) | — | 36,600 |
| **12/04** | 7,117 | (611) | — | 29,500 |
| **12/03** | 6,846 | 1,461 | 21.3% | 31,700 |
| **12/02** | 6,977 | (1,646) | — | 37,100 |
| **Annual Growth** | 13.4% | — | — | (0.1%) |

### 2006 Year-End Financials

Debt ratio: 299.7%
Return on equity: 43.7%
Cash ($ mil.): 1,116
Current ratio: 1.24
Long-term debt ($ mil.): 2,907

### Net Income History

NYSE: LCC

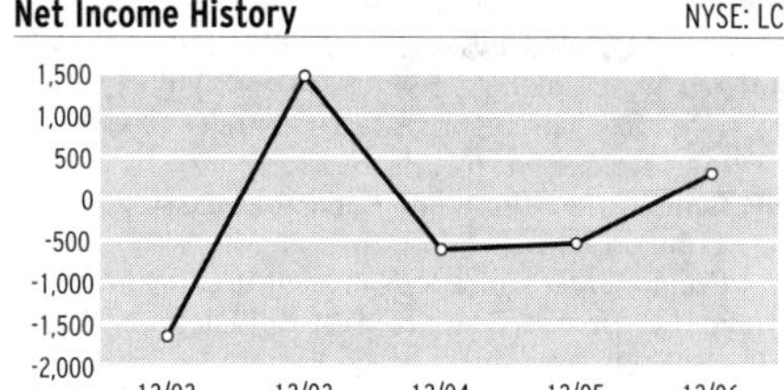


# U.S. Bancorp

Not quite a bank for the entire US, U.S. Bancorp operates nearly 2,500 locations, along with almost 5,000 branded ATMs in about 25 midwestern and western states. The bank holding company, one of the 10 largest in the country, owns U.S. Bank and other subsidiaries that provide consumer and commercial banking, as well as mortgage banking, wealth management, corporate payment services, equipment leasing, and insurance. Among other units, NOVA Information Systems is a leading processor of merchant credit card transactions in the US and Europe. FAF Advisors (formerly U.S. Bancorp Asset Management) changed its name in 2006 to emphasize its relationship with the First American family of mutual funds that it manages.

As another wave of consolidation ripples through the banking industry, U.S. Bancorp had been content to focus internally after digesting several acquisitions in the late 1990s and the early 2000s. The company has been picking up some smaller banks, but don't expect U.S. Bancorp to join forces with a large rival as other competitors have done.

U.S. Bancorp bought Montana-based bank United Financial in 2007 and expanded in Colorado in 2006 with its purchase of holding company Vail Banks, which owned WestStar Bank and its more than 20 branches. U.S. Bancorp continues to add branches inside grocery stores in its market area as well. The bank has also been expanding its fee-based business services such as treasury management, corporate trust, institutional custody, merchant processing, and freight payment services.

Near the end of 2006 vice chairman Richard Davis succeeded CEO Jerry Grundhofer, who had been leading the company for more than a dozen years. Grundhofer will remain chairman until the end of 2007.

## HISTORY

When Farmers and Millers Bank was founded in 1853, it operated out of a strongbox in a rented storefront. After surviving a panic in the 1850s, the bank became part of the national banking system in 1863 as First National Bank of Milwaukee. The bank grew and in 1894 it merged with Merchants Exchange Bank (founded 1870).

In 1919 the bank merged again, with Wisconsin National Bank (founded 1892), to form First Wisconsin National Bank of Milwaukee, a leading financial institution in the area from the 1920s on.

First Wisconsin grew through purchases over the next decade, though the number of banks fell after the 1929 stock market crash; by the end of WWII it had 11 banks. State and federal legislation, particularly the 1956 Bank Holding Company Act (which proscribed acquisitions and branching), constrained postwar growth. In the 1970s Wisconsin eased restrictions on intrastate branching and the bank began to grow again.

Growth accelerated in the late 1980s after Wisconsin and surrounding states legalized interstate banking in adjoining states in 1987. That year First Wisconsin bought seven Minnesota banks and then moved into Illinois. The company focused on strong, well-run institutions. Also that year, it sold its headquarters and used the proceeds to fund more buys. In 1988, in its first foray outside the Midwest, the company bought Metro Bancorp in Phoenix, targeting midwestern retirees moving to Arizona.

In 1989 First Wisconsin changed its name to Firstar. The early 1990s saw it move into Iowa (Banks of Iowa, 1990), buy in-state rivals (Federated Bank Geneva Capital Corporation, 1992), and roll into Illinois (DSB Corporation, 1993). The next year it bought First Southeast Banking Corp. (of Wisconsin) and merged it, along with Firstar Bank Racine and Firstar Bank Milwaukee, into one bank.

In 1994 the company was hit with a $13 million charge to cover losses from a check-kiting fraud.

To strengthen its position against larger competitors, Firstar continued its buying spree in 1995 (Chicago bank First Colonial Bankshares and Investors Bank Corp. of Minneapolis/St. Paul) and 1996 (Jacob Schmidt Company). The acquisitions left the company bloated: In 1996 Firstar began a restructuring designed to cut costs and increase margins. The restructuring project ended in 1997, but by then its performance lagged behind other midwestern banks considerably. In an effort to diversify, it allied with EVEREN Securities to offer debt underwriting and sales, fixed income products, and public finance advisory services. But it was too little, too late; under pressure from major stockholders to seek a partner, Firstar began looking for a buyer.

It found Star Banc. Established in 1863 as The First National Bank of Cincinnati under a bank charter signed by Abraham Lincoln, Star Banc over the years added branches and bought other banks. The company renamed all of its subsidiary banks Star Bank in 1988 and took the name Star Banc in 1989.

In 1998 Star Banc chairman Jerry Grundhofer approached Firstar about a combination. Negotiations proceeded quickly, and a new Firstar was born.

The next year Firstar bought Mercantile Bancorporation. The purchase enabled the bank to expand its international banking services into such markets as Kansas, Nebraska, and Missouri. In 2000 the company made arrangements to buy U.S. Bancorp, a Minneapolis-based bank with roots dating back to 1929. Under the terms of the acquisition, Firstar would shed its own name in favor of the more appropriate U.S. Bancorp moniker.

When the merger was completed in 2001, Firstar's Jerry Grundhofer became CEO of U.S. Bancorp, taking a seat next to his brother John, the company's chairman. Later that year the company bolstered its credit and debit card processing operations with the purchase of NOVA Corporation (now NOVA Information Systems).

U.S. Bancorp completed the conversion of Firstar Bank branches to the U.S. Bank moniker during 2002. At the end of the year, John Grundhofer retired as chairman.

In late 2003 U.S. Bancorp unloaded its investment bank subsidiary Piper Jaffray, which for all intents and purposes already had autonomy (in exchange for a percentage of profits), in a spin-off to U.S. Bancorp shareholders.

## EXECUTIVES

**Chairman:** Jerry A. Grundhofer, age 62, $6,100,042 pay (prior to title change)
**President and CEO:** Richard K. Davis, age 49, $2,375,024 pay (prior to title change)
**Vice Chairman and Head of Consumer Banking Division:** Richard C. (Rick) Hartnack, age 60
**Vice Chairman and Head of Commercial Banking and Dealer Services:** Joseph M. Otting, age 48
**Vice Chairman and CFO:** Andrew Cecere, age 46
**Vice Chairman, Technology and Operations Services:** William L. Chenevich, age 63, $1,075,017 pay
**Vice Chairman; Chairman, President, and CEO, NOVA Information Systems:** Pamela A. (Pam) Joseph, age 47
**Vice Chairman and Head, Corporate Banking:** Richard B. Payne Jr., age 58
**Vice Chairman and Head, Commercial Real Estate:** Joseph Hoesley, age 51
**EVP and Chief Risk Officer:** Richard Hidy, age 43
**EVP and Controller:** Terrance R. Dolan
**EVP, General Counsel, and Secretary:** Lee R. Mitau, age 58
**EVP, Human Resources:** Jennie P. Carlson, age 45
**EVP, Transaction Services; President, Elan Financial Services and Genpass:** Janet Estep
**SVP, Media Relations:** Steven W. (Steve) Dale
**SVP, Investor Relations:** Judith T. (Judy) Murphy, age 51
**Auditors:** Ernst & Young LLP

## LOCATIONS

**HQ:** U.S. Bancorp
800 Nicollet Mall, Minneapolis, MN 55402
**Phone:** 651-466-3000 **Fax:** 612-303-0782
**Web:** www.usbancorp.com

U.S. Bancorp has bank branches in Arizona, Arkansas, California, Colorado, Idaho, Illinois, Indiana, Iowa, Kansas, Kentucky, Minnesota, Missouri, Montana, Nebraska, Nevada, North Dakota, Ohio, Oregon, South Dakota, Tennessee, Utah, Washington, Wisconsin, and Wyoming.

## PRODUCTS/OPERATIONS

### 2006 Sales

| | $ mil. | % of total |
|---|---|---|
| Interest | | |
| Loans | 9,873 | 52 |
| Investment securities | 2,001 | 11 |
| Other | 389 | 2 |
| Noninterest | | |
| Trust & investment management fees | 1,235 | 7 |
| Deposit service charges | 1,023 | 5 |
| Merchant processing services | 963 | 5 |
| Credit & debit card revenue | 800 | 4 |
| Corporate payment products | 557 | 3 |
| Treasury management fees | 441 | 2 |
| Commercial products | 415 | 2 |
| Other | 1,412 | 7 |
| **Total** | **19,109** | **100** |

### 2006 Assets

| | $ mil. | % of total |
|---|---|---|
| Cash & due from banks | 8,639 | 4 |
| Mortgage-backed securities | 33,794 | 15 |
| Other securities | 6,323 | 3 |
| Loans | | |
| Commercial | 46,190 | 21 |
| Commercial real estate | 28,645 | 13 |
| Residential mortgages | 21,285 | 10 |
| Retail | 47,477 | 21 |
| Allowance for loan losses | (2,022) | — |
| Other | 28,901 | 13 |
| **Total** | **219,232** | **100** |

## COMPETITORS

Bank of America
Capital One
Citigroup
Citizens Financial Group
Fifth Third
First National of Nebraska
Huntington Bancshares
JPMorgan Chase
KeyCorp
Marshall & Ilsley
National City
Old National Bancorp
Peoples Bancorp (OH)
TCF Financial
Wells Fargo
Zions Bancorporation

## HISTORICAL FINANCIALS

Company Type: Public

### Income Statement

FYE: December 31

| | ASSETS ($ mil.) | NET INCOME ($ mil.) | INCOME AS % OF ASSETS | EMPLOYEES |
|---|---|---|---|---|
| **12/06** | 219,232 | 4,751 | 2.2% | 50,000 |
| **12/05** | 209,465 | 4,489 | 2.1% | 49,684 |
| **12/04** | 195,104 | 4,167 | 2.1% | 48,831 |
| **12/03** | 189,286 | 3,733 | 2.0% | 51,377 |
| **12/02** | 180,027 | 3,289 | 1.8% | 51,673 |
| **Annual Growth** | 5.0% | 9.6% | — | (0.8%) |

### 2006 Year-End Financials

Equity as % of assets: 9.2%
Return on assets: 2.2%
Return on equity: 23.6%
Long-term debt ($ mil.): 37,602
No. of shares (mil.): 1,765
Dividends
Yield: 3.8%
Payout: 53.3%
Market value ($ mil.): 63,865
Sales ($ mil.): 19,109

### Stock History

NYSE: USB

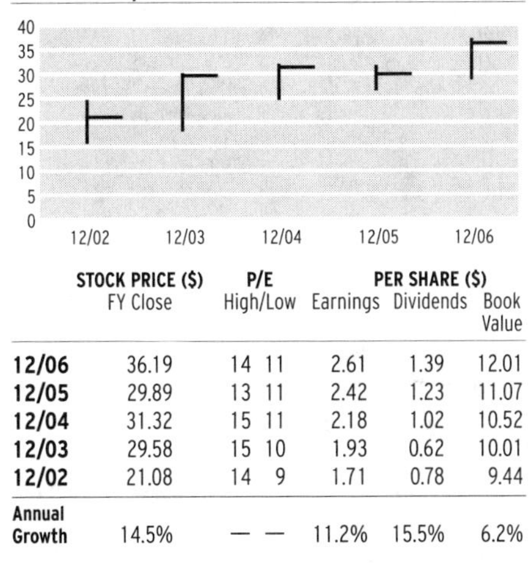


| | STOCK PRICE ($) FY Close | P/E High/Low | PER SHARE ($) Earnings | Dividends | Book Value |
|---|---|---|---|---|---|
| **12/06** | 36.19 | 14 11 | 2.61 | 1.39 | 12.01 |
| **12/05** | 29.89 | 13 11 | 2.42 | 1.23 | 11.07 |
| **12/04** | 31.32 | 15 11 | 2.18 | 1.02 | 10.52 |
| **12/03** | 29.58 | 15 10 | 1.93 | 0.62 | 10.01 |
| **12/02** | 21.08 | 14 9 | 1.71 | 0.78 | 9.44 |
| **Annual Growth** | 14.5% | — — | 11.2% | 15.5% | 6.2% |

# USAA

USAA has a decidedly military bearing. The mutual insurance company serves more than 5 million member customers, primarily military personnel, military retirees, and their families. Its products and services include property/casualty (sold only to military personnel) and life insurance, banking, discount brokerage, and investment management. USAA relies largely on technology and direct marketing to sell its products, reaching clients via the telephone and Internet. The company also has a large mail-order catalog business (computers, furniture, jewelry, and home and auto safety items), and it offers long-distance telephone service, travel services, and Internet access to its members. Its USAA Real Estate division serves institutional and corporate customers with real estate development.

The company is expecting its membership to continue growing, projecting it to nearly double by 2010. In an attempt to increase revenue, the company has entered new markets by making efforts to target people less affluent than military officers. At present, nearly 50% of its members are the grown children and grandchildren of people who have served in the military.

Facing rising claims and a decline in value of its investments, USAA has streamlined operations by reducing staff and closing down divisions (including mailing, printing, and information technology offices).

## HISTORY

In 1922 a group of 26 US Army officers gathered in a San Antonio hotel and formed their own automobile insurance association. The reason? As military officers who often moved, they had a hard time getting insurance because they were considered transient. So the officers decided to insure each other. Led by Major William Garrison, who became the company's first president, they formed the United States Army Automobile Insurance Association.

In 1924, when US Navy and Marine Corps officers were allowed to join, the company changed its name to United Services Automobile Association. By the mid-1950s the company had some 200,000 members. During the 1960s the company formed USAA Life Insurance Company (1963) and USAA Casualty Insurance Company (1968).

Robert McDermott, a retired US Air Force brigadier general, became president in 1969. He cut employment through attrition, established education and training seminars for employees, and invested in computers and telecommunications (drastically cutting claims-processing time). McDermott added new products and services, such as mutual funds, real estate investments, and banking. Under McDermott, USAA's membership grew from 653,000 in 1969 to more than 3 million in 1993.

During the 1970s, in an effort to go paperless, USAA became one of the insurance industry's first companies to switch from mail to toll-free (800) numbers. In the early 1980s the company introduced its discount purchasing program, USAA Buying Services. In 1985 it opened the USAA Federal Savings Bank. USAA began installing an optical storage system in the late 1980s to automate some customer service operations.

McDermott retired in 1993 and was succeeded by Robert Herres. The following year USAA Federal Savings Bank began developing a home banking system, offering members information and services over advanced screen telephones provided by IBM.

In the early 1990s USAA's real estate activities increased dramatically. In 1995 USAA restructured its interest in the Fiesta Texas theme park in San Antonio in order to focus on previously developed properties in geographically diverse areas. That year Six Flags Theme Parks (now Six Flags, Inc.) assumed operation and management of Fiesta Texas (which purchased it from USAA in 1998).

In 1997 USAA began including enlisted military personnel as members. It also started to experiment with a "plain English" mutual fund prospectus. In 1998 USAA also began offering Choice Ride in Orlando, Florida. For about $1,100 per quarter and a promise not to drive except in emergencies, the pilot program provided 36 round trips and a 90% discount on car insurance, in hopes of keeping older drivers from unnecessarily getting behind the wheel.

Also in 1998, as part of its new Financial Planning Network, USAA began offering retirement and estate planning assistance aimed at 25- to 55-year-olds for a yearly $250 fee. In 1999 claims doubled largely due to the impact of Hurricane Floyd and spring hail storms hitting military communities in North Carolina and Virginia.

USAA also moved in 1999 to consolidate its customers' separate accounts (such as mutual fund holdings, stocks and bonds, and life insurance products) into one main account to strengthen customer relationships and reduce operational costs. The next year, after completing a number of technology projects, it laid off workers for the first time in its history.

In 2002, Robert Herres resigned as chairman and was succeeded by CEO Robert Davis. The next year the company saw increased sales and an improved net income thanks to the rebounding stock market and membership growth.

## EXECUTIVES

**Chairman and CEO:** Robert G. (Bob) Davis
**EVP, CFO, and Corporate Treasurer:** Josue (Joe) Robles Jr., age 61
**EVP, General Counsel, and Corporate Secretary:** Steven A. Bennett
**EVP, Human Resources:** Elizabeth D. Conklyn
**EVP, Corporate Communications:** Wendi E. Strong
**EVP, Marketing; President and CEO, USAA Alliance Services Company:** Dawn M. Johnson
**CTO:** Ricky Burks
**EVP, Enterprise Business Operations:** S. Wayne Peacock
**President, USAA Financial Services Group:** Christopher W. Claus
**President and CEO, USAA Real Estate:** Edward B. (Ed) Kelley
**President and CEO, USAA Federal Savings Bank:** Michael A. Luby
**President, USAA Property & Casualty Insurance Group:** Stuart Parker
**President, USAA Life Insurance Company:** Kristi A. Matus
**Auditors:** Ernst & Young LLP

## LOCATIONS

**HQ:** USAA
9800 Fredericksburg Rd., San Antonio, TX 78288
**Phone:** 210-498-2211 **Fax:** 210-498-9940
**Web:** www.usaa.com

USAA has major regional offices in Colorado Springs, Colorado; Las Vegas, Nevada; Norfolk, Virginia; Phoenix, Arizona; Sacramento, California; and Tampa, Florida. It operates international offices in London and Frankfurt, Germany.

## PRODUCTS/OPERATIONS

### 2006 Sales

| | $ mil. | % of total |
|---|---|---|
| Insurance premiums | 9,163 | 68 |
| Fees, sales & loan income, net | 1,865 | 14 |
| Investment income, net | 1,551 | 12 |
| Real estate investment income | 313 | 2 |
| Other revenues | 524 | 4 |
| **Total** | **13,416** | **100** |

### Selected Operations

USAA Alliance Services Company (merchandising and member services)
USAA Federal Savings Bank
USAA Financial Planning Services
USAA Investment Management Company (mutual funds, investment and brokerage services)
USAA Life Insurance Company
USAA Life Insurance Company of New York
USAA Property and Casualty Companies (including automobile, home, boat, and flood insurance)
- United Services Automobile Association
- USAA Casualty Insurance Company
- USAA County Mutual Insurance Company
- USAA General Indemnity Company
- USAA Limited
- USAA Texas Lloyd's Company

USAA Real Esate Company

## COMPETITORS

21st Century
AIG
AIG American General
Allstate
American Express
American Financial
AXA Financial
Berkshire Hathaway
Charles Schwab
Chubb Corp
CIGNA
Citigroup
CNA Financial
FMR
GEICO
Guardian Life
The Hartford
John Hancock
Kemper Insurance
Liberty Mutual
MassMutual
MetLife
Morgan Stanley
Mutual of Omaha
Nationwide
New York Life
Northwestern Mutual
Pacific Mutual
Prudential
State Farm
T. Rowe Price
Travelers Companies
UBS Financial Services

## HISTORICAL FINANCIALS

Company Type: Mutual company

### Income Statement

FYE: December 31

| | ASSETS ($ mil.) | NET INCOME ($ mil.) | INCOME AS % OF ASSETS | EMPLOYEES |
|---|---|---|---|---|
| **12/06** | 60,269 | 2,330 | 3.9% | 22,000 |
| **12/05** | 51,038 | 1,388 | 2.7% | 21,900 |
| **12/04** | 46,482 | 1,597 | 3.4% | 21,000 |
| **12/03** | 41,044 | 1,501 | 3.7% | 21,000 |
| **12/02** | 38,203 | 500 | 1.3% | 22,000 |
| **Annual Growth** | 12.1% | 46.9% | — | 0.0% |

### 2006 Year-End Financials

Equity as % of assets: 21.8%
Return on assets: 4.2%
Return on equity: 19.2%
Long-term debt ($ mil.): —
Sales ($ mil.): 13,416

### Net Income History

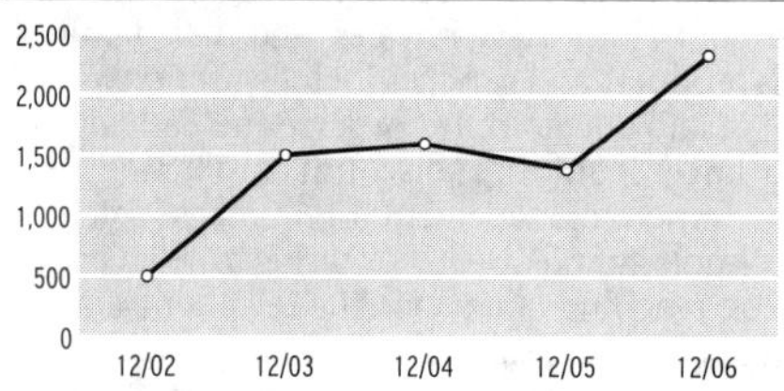


# USEC Inc.

USEC beats radioactive swords into enriched uranium plowshares. The company processes used uranium — about half of which comes from old Russian atomic warheads — into enriched uranium, which it then supplies for commercial nuclear power plants. USEC is the radioactive recycler of choice for the "Megatons-to-Megawatts" program, a US-Russian agreement to convert uranium from warheads into nuclear fuel. USEC also processes uranium for the US Department of Energy. The company's NAC unit, acquired in 2004, provides consulting services to nuclear power plant operators and transportation of nuclear materials.

Although USEC is among the leading suppliers of nuclear fuel for power plants, the company faces an increasingly competitive market while relying on inefficient technology.

More than half the company's overhead at its old gaseous diffusion plants has been the cost of the electricity required to power them (purchased from the Tennessee Valley Authority). To cut costs, the company has cut staff and stopped operating its Portsmouth, Ohio, gaseous diffusion facility, although the plant is being maintained on standby. USEC is planning to upgrade its enrichment technology by converting to the centrifuge method, and the company is developing a centrifuge enrichment plant.

To focus on its centrifuge operations, USEC realigned its executive staff in late 2005. A number of employees were transferred from company headquarters to field operations; overall, the headquarters staff was reduced by one-third.

US government contracts account for 13% of the company's sales, and electric utility operator Exelon for not quite 10%.

## HISTORY

The US government's uranium enrichment program was born during WWII to produce material for the atomic bomb. Originally part of the Atomic Energy Commission, the program eventually came under the aegis of the Department of Energy (DOE). The Energy Policy Act of 1992 created the United States Enrichment Corporation (USEC) to encourage privatization. The act gave USEC four mandates: a consistent domestic supply of enriched uranium, competitive prices, support of US national security goals, and a transition into a fully privatized commercial business. USEC officially took over uranium enrichment operations in 1993.

In 1993 two of the USEC's mandates ran head-on into each other. As cash-poor, missile-laden Russia struggled to revive its economy, President Clinton and Russian President Boris Yeltsin made a deal for the US to pay Russia for nuclear fuel derived from its atomic warheads. The 1994 contract locked USEC into a 20-year, $12 billion contract with the Russian Ministry for Atomic Energy to buy 500 metric tons of enriched uranium from nuclear warheads. Although this was good for national security, it was bad business because US material was cheaper. USEC balked, but the "Megatons-to-Megawatts" agreement went through, and by 1995 USEC had received six metric tons of the warhead uranium.

USEC's 1995 privatization plan faced a major production concern. Built in the 1950s, USEC's gaseous diffusion plants required vast amounts of electricity, while European competitors were using a much less expensive centrifuge process. To improve competitiveness, the US government transferred its Atomic Vapor Laser Isotope Separation (AVLIS) process to USEC, giving the firm a technology the government had spent $1.5 billion and 30 years in developing. (The company shelved the AVLIS project in 1999 because building such a plant would cost $2.5 billion.)

The USEC Privatization Act was ratified in 1996; its transition was approved a year later, and the company was put up for sale. The US government received only two bids for USEC; both were unacceptable, so the government sold stock to the public in 1998, and the sale raised $1.4 billion for the US Treasury.

The next year USEC took over management of its facilities from Lockheed Martin, marking the first time the program would not be run by contractors. The troubled company (facing high prices for raw material, low prices for finished products, and an in-depth government investigation into the company's long-term operations) eliminated 500 jobs and announced it would consider other job cuts.

In 2000 USEC signed a fuel supply contract with the Tennessee Valley Authority and invested heavily into laser-enrichment technology developed by Australian firm Silex Systems. Also that year a DOE report outlined many historically unsafe practices at the company's Paducah, Kentucky, plant, including experiments that intentionally exposed workers to radioactivity.

The next year USEC negotiated the rate at which it purchases commercial uranium from its Russian partner, Tenex; however, the Bush administration delayed approval of the deal. Also, the US Department of Commerce decided to work towards imposing duties on imported uranium from European companies (it ruled that the companies were selling uranium at unfairly low prices). Also in 2001 USEC repurchased 20% of its common stock.

In early 2004 USEC announced that it selected Piketon, Ohio as the site for its American Centrifuge plant. In late 2004 CEO William Timbers left the company, and chairman James Mellor took over as interim CEO.

General Dynamics veteran John Welch was named president and CEO of USEC in 2005.

## EXECUTIVES

**Chairman:** James R. (Jim) Mellor, age 76, $750,000 pay
**President, CEO, and Director:** John K. Welch, age 56, $173,077 pay (partial-year salary)
**SVP, CFO, and Treasurer:** John C. Barpoulis, age 42, $317,538 pay
**SVP, American Centrifuge and Russian HEU:** Philip G. Sewell, age 60, $401,423 pay
**SVP, Human Resources and Administration:** W. Lance Wright, age 59, $404,647 pay
**SVP, General Counsel, and Secretary:** Timothy B. (Tim) Hansen, age 43, $320,000 pay
**VP Government Relations:** E. John Neumann, age 59
**VP Operations:** Russ Starkey
**VP Marketing and Sales:** John M.A. Donelson, age 42
**VP American Centrifuge:** Victor N. Lopiano, age 56
**VP and Treasurer:** Stephen S. Greene, age 49
**Controller and Chief Accounting Officer:** J. Tracy Mey, age 46
**Auditors:** PricewaterhouseCoopers LLP

## LOCATIONS

**HQ:** USEC Inc.
2 Democracy Center, 6903 Rockledge Dr., Bethesda, MD 20817
**Phone:** 301-564-3200 **Fax:** 301-564-3201
**Web:** www.usec.com

### 2006 Sales

| | $ mil. | % of total |
|---|---|---|
| US | 1,109.5 | 60 |
| Japan | 389.8 | 21 |
| Other countries | 349.3 | 19 |
| **Total** | **1,848.6** | **100** |

## PRODUCTS/OPERATIONS

### 2006 Sales

| | $ mil. | % of total |
|---|---|---|
| Separative work units | 1,337.4 | 72 |
| Uranium | 316.7 | 17 |
| US government contracts | 194.5 | 11 |
| **Total** | **1,848.6** | **100** |

## COMPETITORS

AREVA
Belgonucleaire
BNFL
Cameco
Japan Nuclear Fuel

## HISTORICAL FINANCIALS

Company Type: Public

### Income Statement

FYE: December 31

| | REVENUE ($ mil.) | NET INCOME ($ mil.) | NET PROFIT MARGIN | EMPLOYEES |
|---|---|---|---|---|
| **12/06** | 1,849 | 106 | 5.7% | 2,677 |
| **12/05** | 1,559 | 22 | 1.4% | 2,762 |
| **12/04** | 1,417 | 24 | 1.7% | 2,871 |
| **12/03** | 1,460 | 11 | 0.7% | 2,674 |
| **12/02** | 708 | (15) | — | 2,839 |
| **Annual Growth** | 27.1% | — | — | (1.5%) |

### 2006 Year-End Financials

Debt ratio: 15.2%
Return on equity: 11.2%
Cash ($ mil.): 171
Current ratio: 3.31
Long-term debt ($ mil.): 150
No. of shares (mil.): 87
Dividends
Yield: —
Payout: —
Market value ($ mil.): 1,108

### Stock History

NYSE: USU

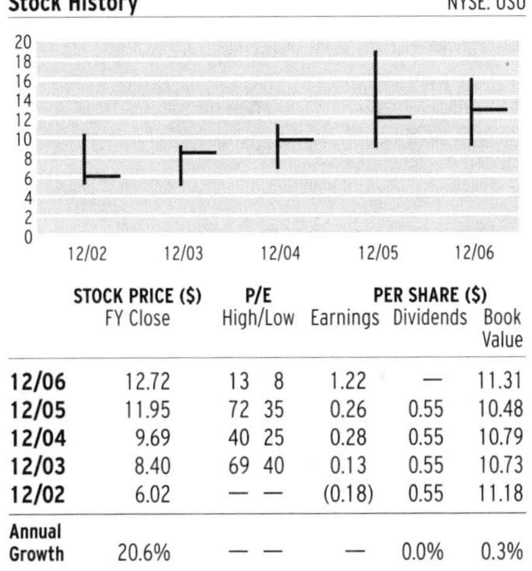


| | STOCK PRICE ($) FY Close | P/E High | P/E Low | PER SHARE ($) Earnings | Dividends | Book Value |
|---|---|---|---|---|---|---|
| **12/06** | 12.72 | 13 | 8 | 1.22 | — | 11.31 |
| **12/05** | 11.95 | 72 | 35 | 0.26 | 0.55 | 10.48 |
| **12/04** | 9.69 | 40 | 25 | 0.28 | 0.55 | 10.79 |
| **12/03** | 8.40 | 69 | 40 | 0.13 | 0.55 | 10.73 |
| **12/02** | 6.02 | — | — | (0.18) | 0.55 | 11.18 |
| **Annual Growth** | 20.6% | — | — | — | 0.0% | 0.3% |

# USG Corporation

USG knows: Where there's a wall, there's likely SHEETROCK, the world's #1 brand of wallboard. USG's North American Gypsum division manufactures SHEETROCK brand gypsum products and joint compound and DUROCK brand cement board. It also manufactures abuse-resistant wall panels (FIBEROCK), poured gypsum underlayments (LEVELROCK), and construction plaster products. Once you're done with the walls, the company's Worldwide Ceilings division offers interior ceiling grid systems and acoustic tile. USG's Building Products Distribution division distributes building products through L&W Supply. Warren Buffett's Berkshire Hathaway controls about 19% of USG, which emerged from Chapter 11 bankruptcy protection in June 2006.

USG was one of several companies, including Owens Corning and W. R. Grace, which sought shelter from asbestos-related litigation. USG filed for Chapter 11 bankruptcy in 2001 to mitigate the growing costs associated with asbestos claims, even though it hasn't used asbestos materials in two decades. The company estimates that it accounts for about a third of all US gypsum wallboard sales; in 2006 it shipped nearly 11 billion sq. ft. of wallboard. Not surprisingly, its North American Gypsum division accounts for more than half of the company's sales. Besides serving the building industry, USG sells gypsum to agricultural and industrial customers. USG manages research and development activities at its USG Research and Technology Center in Libertyville, Illinois.

## HISTORY

In 1901 a group of 35 companies joined to form U.S.G., the largest gypsum producing and processing business in the industry. Sewell Avery became CEO in 1905 (he led U.S.G. until 1951).

U.S.G. began producing lime in 1915. It became United States Gypsum (U.S. Gypsum) in 1920 and began making paint in 1924. By 1931 it was producing insulating board and metal lath fields. It also added two lime businesses and two gypsum concerns.

Also in 1931 Avery became chairman of Montgomery Ward, managing both companies simultaneously. U.S. Gypsum entered asphalt roofing, mineral wool, hardboard, and asbestos-cement siding during the thirties. It made profits and paid dividends throughout the Depression.

Beginning in the late 1960s, U.S. Gypsum diversified into building materials and remodeling, buying such companies as Wallace Manufacturing (prefinished wood panels, 1970) and Kinkead Industries (steel doors and frames, 1972). U.S. Gypsum formed L&W Supply in 1971.

The company bought Masonite in 1984 and changed its name to USG the next year. It acquired Donn (remodeling materials) in 1986 and DAP (caulk and sealants) in 1987.

USG led a $776 million buyback of 20% of its stock to ward off a takeover that year. In 1988 Desert Partners of Midland, Texas, tried another takeover; the attempt was foiled nine months later when shareholders approved a management plan (including taking on $2.5 billion of new debt) to keep control of the company. By the end of 1989, USG had sold several assets and had shrunk by about 25%. Proceeds from the sale of Masonite (to International Paper Company), Kinkead, and Marlite netted $560 million, which was used to pay debt. USG defaulted on $40 million of scheduled payments to bondholders and banks in 1991, however, and sold its profitable DAP unit to the UK's Wassall for just $90 million.

The firm was among 20 manufacturers that agreed to a $1.3 billion class-action asbestos settlement in 1993. (The US Supreme Court voided the pact in 1997.) Also that year USG filed one of the largest prepackaged Chapter 11 bankruptcy cases on record. As a result of restructuring, USG cut its debt by $1.4 billion and its annual interest payments by $200 million. In 1994 USG sold 7.9 million new shares, raising $224 million to further reduce debt. Charges related to the sale or closure of certain operations contributed to another loss in 1995.

In 1997 USG announced a joint venture with Zhongbei Building Material Products Company; USG acquired 60% of the Chinese ceiling-grid manufacturer. In late 1999 the company acquired Sybex and The Synkoloid Company of Canada, both leading North American manufacturers of paper faced metal corner bead (used to protect and strengthen the exposed edges of drywall).

In 2000 investor Warren Buffett revealed that he had built a 15% stake in USG. USG announced in 2001 that it would take an $850 million charge (for the fourth quarter of 2000) to cover against asbestos litigation. In June 2001 USG and 10 of its subsidiaries filed for bankruptcy protection.

The company closed a gypsum fiber panel plant in Nova Scotia, Canada, and a ceiling tile plant in Aubange, Belgium, in 2002. USG sold its UK-based access floor systems business in 2003. The next year subsidiary USG Interiors sold its relocatable walls business and ULTRAWALL System product line to California-based Ultrawall, LLC; USG Interiors also agreed to supply the gypsum baseboard for use in the systems.

In 2005 USG took a $3.1 billion charge and outlined a plan to emerge from bankruptcy by settling outstanding claims; in 2006 it funded a trust with $900 million in cash and a $3.05 billion contingent note. That year it emerged from bankruptcy.

## EXECUTIVES

**Chairman and CEO:** William C. Foote, age 56, $2,980,785 pay
**President and COO:** James S. Metcalf, age 49, $943,020 pay
**EVP and CFO:** Richard H. (Rick) Fleming, age 59, $1,400,527 pay
**EVP and General Counsel:** Stanley L. Ferguson, age 54, $1,218,515 pay
**EVP and Chief Strategy Officer; President, USG International:** Edward M. Bosowski, age 52, $803,005 pay
**SVP Communications:** Marcia S. (Marci) Kaminsky, age 48
**SVP Human Resources:** Brian J. Cook, age 49
**VP; President and COO L&W Supply:** Brendan J. Deely, age 41
**VP and Controller:** D. Rick Lowes, age 52
**VP and CTO:** Clarence B. Owen, age 58
**VP and Treasurer:** Karen L. Leets, age 50
**VP Compensation, Benefits, and Administration; President USG Foundation:** Peter K. Maitland, age 65
**VP Research and Development:** Donald S. Mueller, age 59
**VP; EVP Manufacturing, Building Systems:** Dominic A. Dannessa, age 50
**VP; EVP Sales and Marketing, Building Systems:** Fareed A, Khan, age 42
**Director Investor Relations:** Jim Bencomo
**Corporate Secretary and Associate General Counsel:** Ellis A. Regenbogen
**Auditors:** Deloitte & Touche LLP

## LOCATIONS

**HQ:** USG Corporation
550 W. Adams St., Chicago, IL 60661
**Phone:** 312-436-4000 **Fax:** 312-436-4093
**Web:** www.usg.com

USG makes gypsum products at 44 plants in the US, Canada, and Mexico; it makes ceiling products at 14 plants in North America, Europe, and the Asia/Pacific region; and operates 220 distribution locations in 36 states. USG also operates 14 gypsum mines, seven paper mills, and three gypsum transport ships.

## PRODUCTS/OPERATIONS

### 2006 Sales By Segment

| | $ mil. | % of total |
|---|---|---|
| North American Gypsum | 3,621 | 53 |
| Building Products Distribution | 2,477 | 36 |
| Worldwide Ceilings | 756 | 11 |
| Adjustments | (1,044) | — |
| **Total** | **5,810** | **100** |

### Selected Products

North American Gypsum
- DIAMOND (plaster products)
- DUROCK (cement board)
- FIBEROCK (fiber panels)
- LEVELROCK (poured gypsum underlayments)
- IMPERIAL (plaster products)
- RED TOP (plaster products)
- SHEETROCK (gypsum wallboard)

Worldwide Ceilings Products & Brands
- ACOUSTONE (ceiling tile)
- AURATONE (ceiling tile)
- CENTRICITEE (ceiling grid)
- COMPASSO (ceiling grid)
- CURVATURA (ceiling grid)
- DONN (ceiling grid)
- DX (ceiling grid)
- FINELINE (ceiling grid)

### Selected Subsidiaries

CGC Inc. (Canada)
L&W Supply Corporation
United States Gypsum Company

## COMPETITORS

Allied Building Products
American Biltrite
BPB
Caraustar
Chicago Metallic
CSR Limited
Domtar
Eagle Materials
Georgia-Pacific Corporation
Gypsum Products
HeidelbergCement
Industrial Acoustics
James Hardie
Knauf Gips KG
Lafarge
Lafarge North America
Louisiana-Pacific
New NGC
Pacific Coast Building Products
Rinker Materials
Saint-Gobain
Temple-Inland
Worthington Industries

## HISTORICAL FINANCIALS

Company Type: Public

### Income Statement

FYE: December 31

| | REVENUE ($ mil.) | NET INCOME ($ mil.) | NET PROFIT MARGIN | EMPLOYEES |
|---|---|---|---|---|
| **12/06** | 5,810 | 288 | 5.0% | 14,700 |
| **12/05** | 5,139 | (1,436) | — | 14,100 |
| **12/04** | 4,509 | 312 | 6.9% | 13,800 |
| **12/03** | 3,666 | 122 | 3.3% | 13,900 |
| **12/02** | 3,468 | 43 | 1.2% | 14,100 |
| **Annual Growth** | 13.8% | 60.9% | — | 1.0% |

### 2006 Year-End Financials

Debt ratio: 93.8%
Return on equity: 46.8%
Cash ($ mil.): 571
Current ratio: 1.53
Long-term debt ($ mil.): 1,439
No. of shares (mil.): 90
Dividends
Yield: —
Payout: —
Market value ($ mil.): 4,925

### Stock History

NYSE: USG

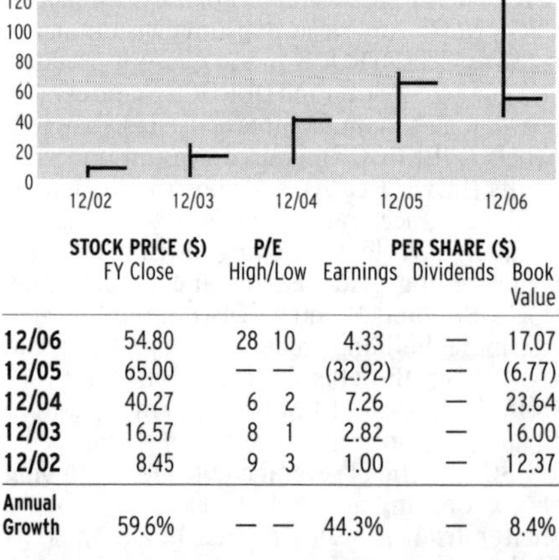


| | STOCK PRICE ($) FY Close | P/E High | P/E Low | PER SHARE ($) Earnings | Dividends | Book Value |
|---|---|---|---|---|---|---|
| **12/06** | 54.80 | 28 | 10 | 4.33 | — | 17.07 |
| **12/05** | 65.00 | — | — | (32.92) | — | (6.77) |
| **12/04** | 40.27 | 6 | 2 | 7.26 | — | 23.64 |
| **12/03** | 16.57 | 8 | 1 | 2.82 | — | 16.00 |
| **12/02** | 8.45 | 9 | 3 | 1.00 | — | 12.37 |
| **Annual Growth** | 59.6% | — | — | 44.3% | — | 8.4% |

# UST Inc.

For UST, the best part of a baseball game is watching the players spit. A holding company primarily for United States Smokeless Tobacco Company, UST is the largest US manufacturer and distributor of snuff and chewing tobacco. Its brands include Copenhagen, Skoal, Red Seal, and Rooster. The company's International Wine & Spirits unit brings in about 15% of sales by producing California wines under the Conn Creek and Villa Mt. Eden labels and premium and sparkling wines from Washington under the Chateau Ste. Michelle and Columbia Crest brands. Subsidiary UST International sells the firm's products outside the US, primarily in Canada.

The McLane Company (a national Wal-Mart and convenience store distributor) rings up some 34% of UST's sales as its top customer.

UST has been expanding its existing product lines, creating more options for adult smokers looking for an alternative to cigarettes. One example is the company's introduction of berry-flavored Skoal. It also has unveiled some new premium wine products.

The company is making plans to increase long-term growth, which will require an $80 million investment in increasing brand loyalty for premium brands. UST is also considering a $10 million investment for attracting adult smokers.

Barclays Global Investors owns 9% of the company's common stock. Fellow investment firms Barrow, Hanley, Mewhinney & Strauss, Inc. and Capital Research and Management Company (a subsidiary of The Capital Group) each own 7%.

## HISTORY

George Weyman, who invented Copenhagen snuff, opened a tobacco shop in Pittsburgh in 1822. Following his death in 1870, his sons took over the shop, renaming it Weyman & Bro. American Tobacco Company, a tobacco monopoly, acquired Weyman & Bro. in 1905. When a Supreme Court ruling dissolved the monopoly in 1911 (finding it in violation of the Sherman Antitrust Act), the company was reorganized as Weyman-Bruton. After acquiring the United States Tobacco Company in 1921, the company took its name the following year. The firm introduced Skoal, a wintergreen-flavored tobacco, in 1934.

In 1965 United States Tobacco purchased the W. H. Snyder & Sons cigar company and later merged it into Wolf Brothers Cigar, renamed it House of Windsor (1981), and sold it to employees (1987). United States Tobacco entered the pipe business with the 1969 purchase of Henry, Leonard & Thomas, Inc., maker of the Dr. Grabow brand of pre-smoked pipes. In 1974 it added Mastercraft Pipes and bought its first winery (now called Chateau Ste. Michelle).

Under Louis Bantle, who became chairman in 1973, sales of the company's snuff climbed 10% annually between 1974 and 1979 and, by using rodeo and sports personalities as endorsers, expanded beyond its traditional northern markets into the southeast and southwest. In 1983 United States Tobacco introduced Skoal Bandits, also known as *snus*, a tea-bag-like, premeasured "dip" aimed at beginning consumers, although it denied targeting minors. Three years later it acquired the Villa Mt. Eden and Conn Creek wineries and was incorporated as UST, a holding company for United States Tobacco (now U.S. Smokeless Tobacco).

UST's good fortune fizzled in the late 1980s. Although previously excluded from the regulations imposed on cigarette makers, a $147 million case filed against the company in 1986 (Betty Ann Marsee claimed her son died of oral cancer caused by dipping Copenhagen) led to restrictions on smokeless tobacco. The suit was concluded in UST's favor in 1989, but the negative publicity led to mandatory warning notices on packaging, a ban on radio and TV advertising, and the imposition of an excise tax.

Despite the controversy, smokeless tobacco was the only growing segment of the industry in the early 1990s, and UST had more than 80% of the US market. Vincent Gierer became CEO of UST in 1990.

Allegations of nicotine manipulation in its products led the company to testify before Congress in 1994. In 1997 UST joined four other tobacco companies in coughing up $11.3 billion as part of Florida's settlement against the tobacco industry. It also launched discount dip Red Seal the same year. In 1998, following the tobacco industry's $206 billion settlement in several states, the company entered into a separate agreement to pay $100–$200 million over 10 years for youth-targeted antismoking programs. In 1999, 34 Native American tribes filed suit in New Mexico against UST and other major tobacco companies for $1 billion of the $206 billion judgment.

In 2000 a federal jury ordered UST to pay $1.05 billion (more than twice its 1999 profits) to competitor Conwood as a result of a 1998 antitrust lawsuit accusing UST of using unethical tactics to keep Conwood's products out of stores.

UST began test marketing Revel, a new spitless tobacco product, in 2001. Revel's small packets of tobacco are designed to be tucked into the mouth and disposed of the same way as chewing gum. The next year Swedish Match brought antitrust claims against UST. In 2003 UST lost an appeal of the 2000 federal ruling and took a charge of $1.3 billion (including interest); the payment caused the company to register its first recorded loss since 1933.

The company announced in March 2004 that it would pay $200 million and forfeit its cigar operations (Don Tomás, Astral, and Helix), transferring them to Swedish Match North America to settle the 2002 antitrust claims.

## EXECUTIVES

**Chairman:** Vincent A. Gierer Jr., age 59, $1,100,000 pay (prior to title change)
**President, CEO, and Director:** Murray S. Kessler, age 47, $661,577 pay (prior to promotion)
**SVP and CFO:** Raymond P. Silcock, age 56
**SVP, General Counsel, and Chief Administrative Officer:** Richard A. Kohlberger, age 61
**SVP, Human Resources and Corporate Secretary:** Maria Renna Sharpe, age 48
**VP and Controller:** James D. Patracuolla
**VP and Investor Relations:** Mark A. Rozelle
**VP and CIO:** Joni S. Ives
**VP and Associate General Counsel:** Elizabeth T. Marren
**President, International Wine & Spirits:** Theodor P. Baseler, age 52, $1,087,589 pay
**President, U.S. Smokeless Tobacco Company:** Daniel W. Butler, age 47, $447,885 pay
**SVP, Manufacturing, Science, and Technology, U.S. Smokeless Tobacco Company:** James E. (Jim) Dillard III
**Treasurer:** Kenneth R. Hopson
**Media Relations:** Jon Schwartz
**Auditors:** Ernst & Young LLP

## LOCATIONS

**HQ:** UST Inc.
100 W. Putnam Ave., Greenwich, CT 06830
**Phone:** 203-661-1100 **Fax:** 203-622-3493
**Web:** www.ustinc.com

## PRODUCTS/OPERATIONS

### 2006 Sales

| | $ mil. | % of total |
|---|---|---|
| Smokeless tobacco | 1,522.7 | 82 |
| Wine | 282.4 | 15 |
| Other | 45.8 | 3 |
| **Total** | **1,850.9** | **100** |

### Selected Products and Brands

Tobacco
- Dry smokeless tobacco (Bruton, CC, Red Seal)
- Moist smokeless tobacco (Copenhagen, Husky, Rooster, Skoal, Skoal Bandits)

Beverages
- Premium varietal wine (Chateau Ste. Michelle, Columbia Crest)
- Premium wine (Conn Creek, Villa Mt. Eden)
- Sparkling wine (Domaine Ste. Michelle)

### Principal Subsidiaries

International Wine & Spirits Ltd.
Ste. Michelle Wine Estates Ltd.
U.S. Smokeless Tobacco Company
U.S. Smokeless Tobacco Manufacturing Limited Partnership
U.S. Smokeless Tobacco Brands Inc.

## COMPETITORS

Altadis
Altria
British American Tobacco
Carolina Group
Constellation Brands
Conwood
Foster's Americas
Gallo
Kendall-Jackson
North Atlantic Trading
Ravenswood Winery
Sebastiani Vineyards
Star Scientific
Swedish Match
Swisher International
Vector

## HISTORICAL FINANCIALS

Company Type: Public

### Income Statement

FYE: December 31

| | REVENUE ($ mil.) | NET INCOME ($ mil.) | NET PROFIT MARGIN | EMPLOYEES |
|---|---|---|---|---|
| **12/06** | 1,851 | 506 | 27.3% | 5,008 |
| **12/05** | 1,852 | 534 | 28.9% | 5,111 |
| **12/04** | 1,838 | 531 | 28.9% | 5,100 |
| **12/03** | 1,743 | 319 | 18.3% | 5,212 |
| **12/02** | 1,683 | (272) | — | 4,911 |
| **Annual Growth** | 2.4% | — | — | 0.5% |

### 2006 Year-End Financials

Debt ratio: 1,276.0%
Return on equity: 717.9%
Cash ($ mil.): 274
Current ratio: 3.33
Long-term debt ($ mil.): 840
No. of shares (mil.): 161
Dividends
Yield: 3.9%
Payout: 73.1%
Market value ($ mil.): 9,347

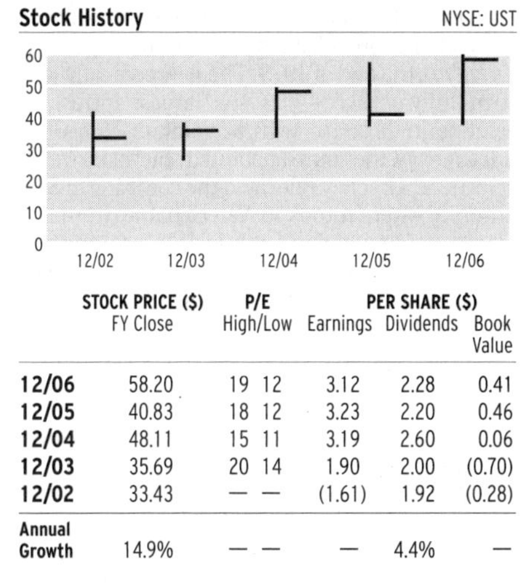


| | STOCK PRICE ($) FY Close | P/E High | P/E Low | PER SHARE ($) Earnings | Dividends | Book Value |
|---|---|---|---|---|---|---|
| **12/06** | 58.20 | 19 | 12 | 3.12 | 2.28 | 0.41 |
| **12/05** | 40.83 | 18 | 12 | 3.23 | 2.20 | 0.46 |
| **12/04** | 48.11 | 15 | 11 | 3.19 | 2.60 | 0.06 |
| **12/03** | 35.69 | 20 | 14 | 1.90 | 2.00 | (0.70) |
| **12/02** | 33.43 | — | — | (1.61) | 1.92 | (0.28) |
| **Annual Growth** | 14.9% | — | — | — | 4.4% | — |

# Valero Energy

Valero Energy is on a mission. Named after the Alamo (the Mission San Antonio de Valero), the company is the largest independent oil refiner in the US. Valero refines low-cost residual oil and heavy crude into cleaner-burning, higher-margin products, including low-sulfur diesels. It operates 18 refineries with a total production capacity of more than 3.3 million barrels per day. These plants are located in California, Delaware, Louisiana, New Jersey, Ohio, Oklahoma, Tennessee, Texas, and in Aruba and Canada. It also has a network of 5,500 retail gas stations and wholesale outlets bearing the Corner Store, Diamond Shamrock, Shamrock, Ultramar, Valero, Stop N Go, and Beacon names in 42 US states and Canada.

The 2005 acquisition of Premcor made Valero, the largest independent refiner on the Gulf Coast, a major national player. The company became a retail giant overnight with its Ultramar Diamond Shamrock purchase in 2001.

Valero banks on the growing worldwide demand for cleaner burning fuels to carry it through the oil industry's ups and downs. By acquiring a refinery in California from Exxon Mobil, the company has entered a market where such cleaner-burning gasoline brings a higher margin.

## HISTORY

Valero Energy was created as a result of the sins of its father, Houston-based Coastal States Gas Corporation. Led by flamboyant entrepreneur Oscar Wyatt, energy giant Coastal had established Lo-Vaca Gathering Company as a gas marketing subsidiary. Bound by long-term contracts to several Texas cities, Coastal was not able to meet its contractual obligations when gas prices rose in the early 1970s, and major litigation against the company resulted. The Texas Railroad Commission (the energy-regulating authority) ordered Coastal to refund customers $1.6 billion.

To meet the requirements, 55% of Lo-Vaca was spun off to disgruntled former customers as Valero Energy at the end of 1979. The new company was born fully grown — as the largest intrastate pipeline in Texas — with accountant-cum-CEO Bill Greehey, the court-appointed chief of Lo-Vaca, at its head. Greehey relocated the company to San Antonio, where it took its Valero name (from the Alamo, or Mission San Antonio de Valero) and put some distance between itself and its discredited former parent. Under Greehey's direction, Valero developed a squeaky-clean image by giving to charities, stressing a dress code, and keeping facilities clean.

Greehey diversified the company into refining unleaded gasoline. Valero bought residual fuel oil from Saudi Arabian refiners and in 1981 built a refinery in Corpus Christi, Texas, which went on line two years later. But in 1984 a glut of unleaded gasoline on the US market from European refiners undercut Valero's profits. To stay afloat, Valero sold pipeline assets, including 50% of its West Texas Pipeline in 1985 and 51% of its major pipeline operations in 1987. Refining margins finally began to improve in 1988. With one of the most modern refineries in the US, Valero did not have to spend a bundle to upgrade its refining processes to meet the tougher EPA requirements of the 1990s.

In 1992 Valero expanded its refinery's production capacity and acquired two gas processing plants and several hundred miles of gas pipelines from struggling oil firm Oryx Energy (acquired by Kerr-McGee in 1999). That year Valero became the first non-Mexican business engaged in Mexican gasoline production when it signed a deal with state oil company Petróleos Mexicanos S.A. to build a gasoline additive plant there.

To expand its natural gas business substantially, in 1994 Valero bought back the 51% of Valero Natural Gas Partners it didn't own. Valero also teamed up with regional oil company Swift Energy in a transportation, marketing, and processing agreement. As part of that arrangement, Valero agreed to build a pipeline linking Swift's Texas gas field with a Valero plant.

In 1997 the company sold Valero Natural Gas to California electric utility PG&E, gaining it $1.5 billion for expansion. It then purchased Salomon's oil refining unit, Basis Petroleum (two refineries in Texas and one in Louisiana) and the next year picked up Mobil's refinery in Paulsboro, New Jersey.

With low crude oil prices hurting its bottom line in 1999, Valero explored partnerships with other refiners as a way to cut operating costs. In 2000 the company bought Exxon Mobil's 130,000 barrel-per-day Benicia, California, refinery, along with 340 retail outlets, for about $1 billion.

In 2001 Valero gained two small refineries when it bought Huntway Refining, a leading supplier of asphalt in California. Dwarfing that deal, Valero also bought Ultramar Diamond Shamrock for $4 billion in cash and stock (it assumed about $2.1 billion of debt in the deal).

As part of the deal, and to comply with the demands of regulators, in 2002 Valero sold the Golden Eagle (San Francisco-area) refinery and 70 retail service stations in Northern California to Tesoro Petroleum for $945 million.

In 2003 the company acquired Orion Refining's Louisiana refinery for about $530 million, and in 2004 it acquired an Aruba refinery from asset-shedding El Paso Corp. for $640 million. Suncor Energy bought a Colorado-based refinery from Valero for a reported $30 million in 2005.

In 2006 Bill Greehey turned over the leadership reins to another company veteran, Bill Klesse.

## EXECUTIVES

**Chairman and CEO:** William R. (Bill) Klesse, age 60
**President:** Gregory C. (Greg) King, age 46, $1,768,000 pay
**EVP and CFO:** Michael S. (Mike) Ciskowski, age 49, $1,020,000 pay
**EVP Corporate Development and Strategic Planning:** S. Eugene (Gene) Edwards, age 50
**EVP Marketing and Supply:** Joseph W. (Joe) Gorder, age 49
**EVP Operations:** Richard J. (Rich) Marcogliese, age 54
**SVP and General Counsel:** Kim Bowers
**SVP Corporate Law and Secretary:** Jay D. Browning
**SVP Retail and Specialty Products Marketing:** Gary L. Arthur Jr.
**SVP Corporate Communications:** Mary Rose Brown
**VP and CIO:** Hal Zesch
**VP and Controller:** Clayton E. (Clay) Killinger
**VP and Treasurer:** Donna M. Titzman
**VP Investor Relations and Corporate Communications:** Eric Fisher
**VP Human Resources:** Mike Crownover
**VP Wholesale Marketing East Coast Marketing:** Jerry McVicker
**VP Wholesale Marketing:** Eric Moeller
**VP Products Trading West Coast Unbranded:** Dave Parker
**VP Wholesale Marketing Mid-Continent Division:** Lee Rahmberg
**VP Wholesale Marketing West Coast Division:** Blair Skellie
**Auditors:** KPMG LLP

## LOCATIONS

**HQ:** Valero Energy Corporation
1 Valero Way, San Antonio, TX 78249
**Phone:** 210-345-2000 **Fax:** 210-345-2646
**Web:** www.valero.com

**2006 Sales**

| | $ mil. | % of total |
|---|---|---|
| US | 80,797 | 88 |
| Canada | 7,275 | 8 |
| Other countries | 3,761 | 4 |
| **Total** | **91,833** | **100** |

## PRODUCTS/OPERATIONS

**2006 Sales**

| | $ mil. | % of total |
|---|---|---|
| Refining | 83,525 | 91 |
| Retail | 8,308 | 9 |
| **Total** | **91,833** | **100** |

**2006 Sales**

| | $ mil. | % of total |
|---|---|---|
| Refining | | |
| Gasolines & blendstocks | 42,633 | 46 |
| Distillates | 29,926 | 33 |
| Petrochemicals | 3,683 | 4 |
| Lubes & asphalts | 1,868 | 2 |
| Other | 5,415 | 6 |
| Retail | | |
| Fuel sales (gasoline & diesel) | 6,709 | 7 |
| Merchandise sales & other | 1,346 | 2 |
| Home heating oil | 253 | — |
| **Total** | **91,833** | **100** |

**Selected Products**
Asphalt
Bunker oils
CARB Phase II gasoline
Clean-burning oxygenates
Conventional gasoline
Crude mineral spirits
Customized clean-burning gasoline blends for export markets
Gasoline blendstocks
Home heating oil
Jet fuel
Kerosene
Low-sulfur diesel
Lube oils
Petrochemical feedstocks
Petroleum coke
Premium reformulated and conventional gasolines
Reformulated gasoline
Sulfur

## COMPETITORS

BP
Chevron
CITGO
ConocoPhillips
Exxon Mobil
Frontier Oil
Hess
Holly
Lyondell Chemical
Marathon Petroleum
Motiva Enterprises
National Cooperative Refinery Association
Shell Oil Products
Sinclair Oil
Sunoco
Tesoro
Texas Petrochemicals
TOTAL

## HISTORICAL FINANCIALS

Company Type: Public

**Income Statement** FYE: December 31

| | REVENUE ($ mil.) | NET INCOME ($ mil.) | NET PROFIT MARGIN | EMPLOYEES |
|---|---|---|---|---|
| **12/06** | 91,833 | 5,463 | 5.9% | 21,836 |
| **12/05** | 82,162 | 3,590 | 4.4% | 22,068 |
| **12/04** | 54,619 | 1,804 | 3.3% | 19,797 |
| **12/03** | 37,969 | 622 | 1.6% | 19,621 |
| **12/02** | 26,976 | 92 | 0.3% | 19,947 |
| **Annual Growth** | 35.8% | 178.0% | — | 2.3% |

**2006 Year-End Financials**

Debt ratio: 25.4%
Return on equity: 32.5%
Cash ($ mil.): 1,621
Current ratio: 1.22
Long-term debt ($ mil.): 4,722
No. of shares (mil.): 604
Dividends
Yield: 0.6%
Payout: 3.5%
Market value ($ mil.): 30,889

**Stock History** NYSE: VLO

| | STOCK PRICE ($) FY Close | P/E High | P/E Low | PER SHARE ($) Earnings | Dividends | Book Value |
|---|---|---|---|---|---|---|
| **12/06** | 51.16 | 8 | 5 | 8.64 | 0.30 | 30.82 |
| **12/05** | 51.60 | 10 | 3 | 6.10 | 0.19 | 24.38 |
| **12/04** | 22.70 | 7 | 3 | 3.27 | 0.14 | 30.52 |
| **12/03** | 11.59 | 9 | 6 | 1.27 | 0.10 | 47.69 |
| **12/02** | 9.23 | 60 | 28 | 0.21 | 0.10 | 40.21 |
| **Annual Growth** | 53.4% | — | — | 153.3% | 31.6% | (6.4%) |

# The Valspar Corporation

Valspar wants you to put on a coat. The firm, which was founded in 1806, makes a variety of coatings and paints for manufacturing, the automotive industry, and food-packaging companies, as well as for consumers. The company's industrial coatings — used by OEMs including building product, appliance, and furniture makers — include coatings for metal, wood, glass, and plastic. Packaging products include coatings and inks for rigid containers, such as food and beverage cans. Its consumer paints include interior and exterior paints, primers, stains, and varnishes; they are sold through mass merchandisers such as Wal-Mart and Lowe's. Valspar also makes auto paints, specialty polymers, colorants, and gelcoats.

Valspar has boosted its core business through acquisitions of coatings companies around the world; in the past decade it has made more than 20 acquisitions, including joint venture interests. That strategy has made Valspar one of the top global industrial coatings makers. Valspar acquired US stain and finish manufacturer Samuel Cabot in 2005. The next year the company reached into the Chinese market with the acquisition of an 80% stake in coatings manufacturer Huarun Paints, a maker of wood and furniture coatings. Huarun has annual sales of about $180 million. It also acquired the powder coatings business (for office furniture) of H.B. Fuller in late 2006; that unit racks up annual sales of about $75 million.

Lowe's accounts for more than 10% of the company's sales, and the hardware giant has named Valspar paint supplier of the year eight times. In 2007 it began to use the Valspar brand, replacing three fairly generic-sounding brand names, at Lowe's in an effort to boost consumer recognition. Valspar has made a point to tailor its products to the needs of retail customers, to the point of placing in-store employees to answer paint questions.

Former chairman Angus Wurtele owns about 6% of Valspar.

## HISTORY

Samuel Tuck began the company as Paint and Color in Boston in 1806. It was known as Valentine & Co. by 1866. Then-owner Lawson Valentine hired chemist Charles Homer (brother of artist Winslow Homer), who perfected finishing varnishes. In 1903 Valentine's grandson, L. Valentine Pulsifer, invented the first clear varnish — dubbed Valspar — which became the company's name in 1932. Valspar grew by mergers including Rockcote Paint (1960) and Minnesota Paints (1970). CEO Angus Wurtele became chairman in 1973. Valspar's sales tripled by the time it acquired Mobil Oil's packaging coatings business in 1984.

Valspar formed a joint venture with China Merchants in 1994 (packaging coatings) and then bought US-based Sunbelt Coatings (auto refinishing, 1995), Gordon Bartels (packaging coatings, 1996), and Sureguard (industrial coatings, 1997). Valspar swapped its maintenance coatings business in 1997 with Ameron International's product finishes unit and formed a joint venture in Brazil with Renner Herrmann SA.

President and CEO Richard Rompala replaced Wurtele as chairman in 1998. Acquisitions that year included Plasti-Kote (consumer aerosol and specialty paints), Australia-based Anzol (packaging and industrial coatings), and Dyflex Polymers (specialty water-based polymers).

The company began divesting noncore businesses, selling its functional powder coatings unit in 1998 and its marine and packaging coatings product lines in 1999. Also in 1999 it bought the packaging coatings business of Dexter Corporation (now a part of Invitrogen) and its subsidiary in France and the Netherlands-based resins maker Dyflex. The next year Valspar bought rival coatings maker Lilly Industries in a $975 million deal, which made Valspar a top global maker of coatings for wood, mirrors, and coils (used in doors and appliances).

From 1996 to 2001 in a four-phase deal, the company acquired packaging coatings firm Coates Coatings, which operated in North America, Europe, Australia, Africa, and Asia. This acquisition boosted Valspar into the top of the market for metal packaging coatings.

In 2004 the company acquired Dutch automotive coatings maker De Beer Lakfabrieken, as well as the Forest Products division of wood coatings firm Associated Chemists.

William Mansfield became CEO in February 2005, but Rompala stayed on as chairman until his retirement in mid-2005. Thomas McBurney assumed the chairmanship for two years before Mansfield was named chairman in 2007.

## EXECUTIVES

**Chairman, President, and CEO:** William L. (Bill) Mansfield, age 58, $3,623,990 pay
**EVP Finance and CFO:** Paul C. Reyelts, age 60, $1,665,248 pay
**EVP:** Steven L. Erdahl, age 54, $1,366,155 pay
**EVP, General Counsel, and Secretary:** Rolf Engh, age 53, $1,254,693 pay
**SVP Wood Coatings, Architectural, and Federal Business Units; President, Asia-Pacific:** Gary E. Hendrickson, age 50, $1,032,954 pay
**SVP Global Packaging and Automotive Coatings:** Donald A. (Don) Nolan, age 46
**SVP Human Resources:** Anthony L. Blaine, age 40
**Group VP, Architectural:** Kenneth H. Arthur
**Group VP, Global Wood Coatings:** Joseph Donahue
**VP and President, Valspar Europe:** Michael Brandt
**VP and President, Valspar Sourcing:** Thomas L. Wood
**VP, Coil and Extrusion Coatings:** Al Dunlop
**VP, Engineered Polymer Solutions and Color Corporation of America:** Steven C. Lindberg
**VP, General Industrial Group:** Brian Falline
**VP, Information Systems and Furniture Solutions:** Kate Bass
**VP, Technology, Research and Development:** Larry B. Brandenburger
**VP, Americas — Packaging Group:** Bern Ouimette
**VP, Sales and Marketing — Architectural Group:** Steve Person
**Auditors:** Ernst & Young LLP

## LOCATIONS

**HQ:** The Valspar Corporation
1101 3rd St. South, Minneapolis, MN 55415
**Phone:** 612-332-7371 **Fax:** 612-375-7723
**Web:** www.valspar.com

Valspar operates manufacturing facilities worldwide.

**2006 Sales**

| | $ mil. | % of total |
|---|---|---|
| US | 2,085.7 | 70 |
| Other countries | 892.4 | 30 |
| **Total** | **2,978.1** | **100** |

## PRODUCTS/OPERATIONS

**2006 Sales**

| | $ mil. | % of total |
|---|---|---|
| Coatings | 1,683.5 | 54 |
| Paints | 985.7 | 33 |
| Other | 428.2 | 13 |
| Adjustments | (119.3) | — |
| **Total** | **2,978.1** | **100** |

**Selected Products**

Industrial
- Fillers
- Mirror coatings
- Primers
- Stains
- Topcoats

Architectural, automotive, and specialty
- Aerosols
- Enamels
- Faux finishes
- Interior and exterior paints
- Primers
- Sealers
- Stains
- Varnishes

Packaging
- Coatings
- Inks

Other
- Colorants
- Composites
- Powder coatings for metal surfaces
- Specialty polymers

**Selected Brands**

Cabot
De Beer
Goof Off
House of Kolor
McCloskey
Mr. Spray
Plasti-Kote
Tempo
Valspar

## COMPETITORS

Akzo Nobel
BASF Coatings AG
BEHR
Benjamin Moore
Dunn-Edwards
DuPont
Ferro
H.B. Fuller
Imperial Chemical
Kelly-Moore
PPG
RPM
Sherwin-Williams
SigmaKalon
Spraylat

## HISTORICAL FINANCIALS

Company Type: Public

**Income Statement** FYE: Last Friday in October

| | REVENUE ($ mil.) | NET INCOME ($ mil.) | NET PROFIT MARGIN | EMPLOYEES |
|---|---|---|---|---|
| **10/06** | 2,978 | 175 | 5.9% | 9,556 |
| **10/05** | 2,714 | 148 | 5.4% | 7,540 |
| **10/04** | 2,441 | 143 | 5.9% | 7,504 |
| **10/03** | 2,248 | 113 | 5.0% | 7,013 |
| **10/02** | 2,127 | 120 | 5.6% | 7,058 |
| **Annual Growth** | 8.8% | 9.9% | — | 7.9% |

**2006 Year-End Financials**

Debt ratio: 28.2%
Return on equity: 15.2%
Cash ($ mil.): 88
Current ratio: 0.81
Long-term debt ($ mil.): 350
No. of shares (mil.): 102
Dividends
Yield: 1.7%
Payout: 25.7%
Market value ($ mil.): 2,715

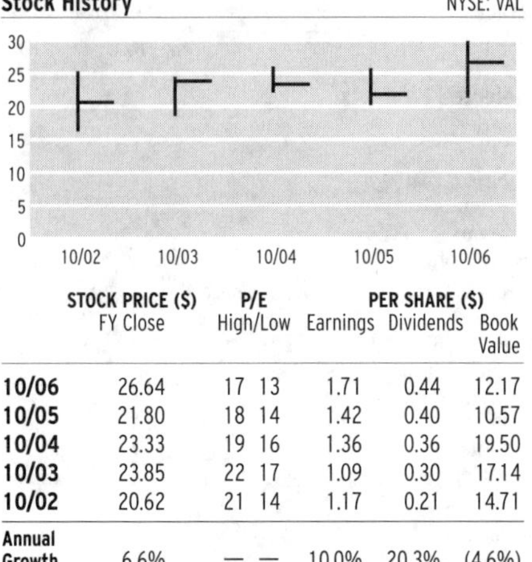

| | STOCK PRICE ($) FY Close | P/E High/Low | | PER SHARE ($) Earnings | Dividends | Book Value |
|---|---|---|---|---|---|---|
| **10/06** | 26.64 | 17 | 13 | 1.71 | 0.44 | 12.17 |
| **10/05** | 21.80 | 18 | 14 | 1.42 | 0.40 | 10.57 |
| **10/04** | 23.33 | 19 | 16 | 1.36 | 0.36 | 19.50 |
| **10/03** | 23.85 | 22 | 17 | 1.09 | 0.30 | 17.14 |
| **10/02** | 20.62 | 21 | 14 | 1.17 | 0.21 | 14.71 |
| **Annual Growth** | 6.6% | — | — | 10.0% | 20.3% | (4.6%) |

# The Vanguard Group

If you buy low and sell high, invest for the long term, don't panic, and generally disapprove of those whippersnappers at Fidelity, then you may end up in the Vanguard of the financial market. The Vanguard Group offers individual and institutional investors a line of popular mutual funds and brokerage services. Claiming some $1 trillion of assets under management, the firm is battling FMR (aka Fidelity) for the title of largest mutual fund company in the world. Vanguard's fund options include more than 150 stock, bond, mixed, and international offerings, as well as variable annuity portfolios; its Vanguard 500 Index Fund is one of the largest in the US.

The company is known as much for its puritanical thriftiness and conservative investing as for its line of index funds, which track the performance of such groups of stock as the S&P 500. Retired company founder John Bogle is sometimes derisively called "St. Jack" for his zealous criticism of industry practices, but the company's reputation for being squeaky clean appears to have paid off: Vanguard has remained unscathed by the mutual fund industry scandals that began unfolding in late 2003.

Unlike other funds, Vanguard is set up like a mutual insurance company. The funds (and by extension, their more than 21 million investors) own the company, so fees are low to nonexistent; funds are operated on a tight budget so as not to eat into results. The company spends next to nothing on advertising, relying instead on strong returns and word-of-mouth.

And despite its no-broker, no-load background, Vanguard has developed cheap ways to dole out advice, especially through the use of toll-free numbers and the Internet and by quietly touting its online brokerage service.

## HISTORY

A distant cousin of Daniel Boone, Walter Morgan knew a few things about pioneering. He was the first to offer a fund with a balance of stocks and bonds, serendipitously introduced early in 1929, months before the stock market collapsed. Morgan's balanced Wellington fund (named after Napoleon's vanquisher) emerged effectively unscathed.

John Bogle's senior thesis on mutual funds impressed fellow Princeton alum Morgan, who hired Bogle in 1951. Morgan retired in 1967 and picked Bogle to replace him. That year Bogle engineered a merger with old-school investment firm Thorndike, Doran, Paine and Lewis. After culture clashes and four years of shrinking assets, the Thorndike-dominated board fired Bogle, who appealed to the mutual funds and their separate board of directors. The fund directors decided to split up the funds and the advisory business.

Bogle named the fund company The Vanguard Group, after the flagship of Lord Nelson, another Napoleon foe. Vanguard worked like a cooperative; mutual fund shareholders owned the company, so all services were provided at cost. The Wellington Management Company remained Vanguard's distributor until 1977, when Bogle convinced Vanguard's board to drop the affiliation. Without Wellington as the intermediary, Vanguard sold its funds directly to consumers as no-load funds (without service charges). In 1976 the company launched the Vanguard Index 500, the first index fund. These measures attracted new investors in droves.

Vanguard rode the 1980s boom. Its Windsor fund grew so large the company closed it, launching Windsor II in 1985. Vanguard weathered the 1987 crash and began the 1990s as the US's #4 mutual fund company. The actively managed funds of FMR (better known as Fidelity), most notably its Magellan fund, led the market then. The retirement of legendary Magellan manager Peter Lynch and the fund's consequential underperformance spurred a rush to index funds. Vanguard moved up to #2.

Vanguard played against type in 1995 when it introduced the Vanguard Horizon Capital Growth stock fund, an aggressively managed fund designed to vie directly with Fidelity's funds.

In 1997 Vanguard added brokerage services and began selling its own and other companies' funds on the Internet to allow clients to consolidate their financial activities. In 1998 Bogle passed the chairmanship to CEO John Brennan, a soft-spoken technology wonk. Morgan died that year at age 100.

Investors were ruffled when 70-year-old Bogle announced that corporate age limits would force him to leave the board of directors at the end of 1999. (Bogle retains an office at Vanguard headquarters, and remains popular on the speaker circuit.)

Despite Vanguard's stated commitment to the little guy, by late 2002 the company was forced to mitigate realities of the economy and started courting investors with bigger bankrolls; it also raised fees for some customers with smaller accounts.

## EXECUTIVES

**Chairman and CEO:** John J. Brennan
**Managing Director, Advice, Brokerage, and Retirement Services:** R. Gregory Barton
**Managing Director, Retail Investor Group:** Mortimer J. (Tim) Buckley
**Managing Director:** James H. Gately
**Managing Director, Human Resources:** Kathleen C. Gubanich
**Managing Director, Institutional Investor Group:** F. William (Bill) McNabb III
**Managing Director, Planning and Development Group:** Michael S. Miller
**Managing Director, Finance Group:** Ralph K. Packard
**Chief Investment Officer:** George U. (Gus) Sauter
**General Counsel:** Heidi Stam
**CIO:** Paul Heller

## LOCATIONS

**HQ:** The Vanguard Group, Inc.
100 Vanguard Blvd., Malvern, PA 19355
**Phone:** 610-648-6000 **Fax:** 610-669-6605
**Web:** www.vanguard.com

The Vanguard Group has offices in Malvern, Pennsylvania; Charlotte, North Carolina; and Scottsdale, Arizona; as well as in Brussels, Melbourne, Singapore, and Tokyo.

## PRODUCTS/OPERATIONS

### Selected Funds

500 Index Fund
Asset Allocation Fund
Balanced Index Fund
California Long-Term Tax-Exempt Fund
Capital Opportunity Fund
Capital Value Fund
Developed Markets Index Fund
Diversified Equity Fund
Emerging Markets Stock Index Fund
Energy Fund
Equity Income Fund
European Stock Index Fund
Explorer Fund
Extended Market Index Fund
Federal Money Market Fund
FTSE Social Index Fund
Global Equity Fund
GNMA Fund
Growth and Income Fund
Growth Equity Fund
Growth Index Fund
Health Care Fund
Inflation-Protected Securities Fund
Insured Long-Term Tax-Exempt Fund
Intermediate-Term Bond Index Fund
International Explorer Fund
International Growth Fund
International Value Fund
Large-Cap Index Fund
LifeStrategy Conservative Growth Fund
LifeStrategy Growth Fund
LifeStrategy Income Fund
LifeStrategy Moderate Growth Fund
Limited-Term Tax-Exempt Fund
Long-Term Investment-Grade Fund
Massachusetts Tax-Exempt Fund
Mid-Cap Growth Fund
Mid-Cap Index Fund
Mid-Cap Value Index Fund
Morgan Growth Fund
New Jersey Tax-Exempt Money Market Fund
New York Long-Term Tax-Exempt Fund
Ohio Long-Term Tax-Exempt Fund
Pacific Stock Index Fund
Pennsylvania Tax-Exempt Money Market Fund
Precious Metals and Mining Fund
Prime Money Market Fund
PRIMECAP Core Fund
PRIMECAP Fund
REIT Index Fund
Selected Value Fund
Short-Term Bond Index Fund

Small-Cap Growth Index Fund
Small-Cap Index Fund
Small-Cap Value Index Fund
STAR Fund
Strategic Equity Fund
Target Retirement 2010 Fund
Target Retirement 2015 Fund
Target Retirement 2020 Fund
Target Retirement 2025 Fund
Target Retirement 2030 Fund
Target Retirement 2035 Fund
Target Retirement 2040 Fund
Target Retirement 2045 Fund
Target Retirement 2050 Fund
Total Bond Market Index Fund
Total International Stock Index Fund
Total Stock Market Index Fund
U.S. Growth Fund
U.S. Value Fund
Value Index Fund
Wellesley Income Fund
Wellington Fund
Windsor Fund

## COMPETITORS

AIG
AIM Funds
AllianceBernstein
American Century
AXA Financial
BlackRock
Charles Schwab
FMR
Franklin Resources
INVESCO
Janus Capital
Legg Mason
MFS
Principal Financial
Putnam
T. Rowe Price
TIAA-CREF
USAA

## HISTORICAL FINANCIALS

Company Type: Private

**Income Statement** FYE: December 31

| | ASSETS ($ mil.) | NET INCOME ($ mil.) | INCOME AS % OF ASSETS | EMPLOYEES |
|---|---|---|---|---|
| **12/05*** | 920,000 | — | — | 11,500 |

*Most recent year available

# VeriSign, Inc.

VeriSign has vowed to serve and protect network interactions. The company provides telecom carriers and other enterprise customers with a variety of digital commerce and communication products and services. Its service offerings address billing and payment, clearing and settlement, content delivery, digital brand management, domain name registration, Internet security, mobile delivery, network connectivity and interoperability, and network databases interactions. The company sells directly and through resellers, systems integrators, and affiliate businesses.

Under agreements with ICANN and the US Department of Commerce, VeriSign is the exclusive operator of the .com domain name registry. Originally granted that right in 2001, the company's contract was renewed in 2006, extending its rights to maintain the .com (and .net) registries until 2012. In 2007 VeriSign negotiated with ICANN for a fee increase for .com and .net domain registration, resulting in increases from $6.00 to $6.42 and $3.50 to $3.85, respectively. These fees are paid by domain name registrars such as Go Daddy and Register.com. (VeriSign is not itself a registrar — it exited that business with the sale of Network Solutions in 2003.) In addition to its registry business, VeriSign provides digital certificate services used to insure secure communications and transactions on the Internet.

Though its Internet services business may be better known, VeriSign generates more revenue from communications services. The company supplies telecom carriers with SS7 connectivity and signaling, wireless roaming, voice-over-IP (VoIP), content delivery, and billing services. In 2006 News Corporation acquired a majority stake in VeriSign's Jamba unit, which provides ring tones and other mobile phone content, for $188 million; Jamba, also known as Jamster, is now a joint venture between the two companies.

In support of its various Internet and communications offerings, VeriSign operates an enormous amount of Internet infrastructure, including secure data centers, routing and switching equipment, and servers. In 2007 it announced an initiative called Project Titan that aims to grow the capacity of its infrastructure by ten times by the year 2010.

Formerly organized into two business units — Internet Services Group and Communications Services Group — VeriSign restructured its operations into functional groups in 2007; it now has a combined worldwide sales and services team, and an integrated marketing and product development organization.

## HISTORY

VeriSign was founded by Stratton Sclavos and Jim Bidzos in 1995. Sclavos, a veteran of MIPS Computer Systems and two failed Silicon Valley startups, ran the company as RSA's digital certification division until it was spun off in 1995. Its early backers included Ameritech, Mitsubishi, and Visa. Apple and Netscape were among its first customers.

In 1996 VeriSign formed a Japanese subsidiary. The next year the company debuted its Financial Server ID, a digital certificate for use with the Open Financial Exchange, a home banking standard backed by Microsoft. VeriSign went public in early 1998 and added Sumitomo Bank and UPS as customers. Also in 1998 the company bought Secure It (Internet security consulting services).

In early 2000 the company stepped up expansion efforts, buying South Africa-based Thawte Consulting (digital certification products) and Signio (Internet payment services). Later that year VeriSign acquired Internet domain registrar Network Solutions for about $20 billion.

Looking to expand its communications service offerings, in 2001 the company acquired network service provider Illuminet Holdings for $1.3 billion. Also in 2001, VeriSign reached an agreement with ICANN to become the exclusive operator of the top level .com domain registry until 2007.

The company continued its acquisitive ways in 2002 and 2003, purchasing H.O. Systems ($350 million) and UNC-Embratel ($16 million). In late 2003 the company sold the portion of Network Solutions that sells domain names and provides Web hosting services to Pivotal Private Equity for about $100 million.

In 2004 the company acquired managed security services provider Guardent for about $140 million, and later that year purchased Germany-based wireless content service provider Jamba! for about $273 million.

The company moved beyond its legacy encryption and digital certificate products with a string of purchases in 2005. Verisign bought LightSurf, a provider of multimedia messaging and interoperability solutions for the wireless market, for $270 million. Later that year Verisign purchased Authorize.Net Holdings' PrePay INS business (wireless phone rate plan and calling plan tracking products) for about $17 million. Quick on the heels of the PrePay INS deal came VeriSign's purchase of iDEFENSE for $40 million in cash. Other 2005 purchases included Moreover Technologies (news aggregation), Weblogs.com (blog tracking), and Retail Solutions (point-of-sale tracking). The company sold its payment gateway business to Pay Pal, a subsidiary of eBay, for $370 million in 2005.

VeriSign's acquisition tear continued in 2006. It purchased Web-based billing and client management software company CallVision for $30 million in cash, as well as m-Qube, a developer of software for delivering content and connectivity services to wireless subscribers. It acquired Internet transaction security specialist GeoTrust for $125 million in cash.

Also in 2006, VeriSign renewed its contract with ICANN, extending its rights to the .com registry until 2012. It also bought Kontiki, a developer of technology for speeding up large downloads on the Internet, for $62 million.

In 2007 Sclavos resigned and director William Roper was named president and CEO.

## EXECUTIVES

**Chairman:** Edward A. (Ed) Mueller, age 60
**Vice Chairman:** D. James Bidzos, age 53
**President, CEO, and Director:** William A. (Bill) Roper Jr., age 61
**EVP Finance, CFO, and Chief Accounting Officer:** Albert E. (Bert) Clement, age 45
**EVP, Corporate Development:** Robert J. (Bob) Korzeniewski, age 50
**EVP, Products and Marketing:** Mark D. McLaughlin, age 41
**EVP and CTO:** Aristotle N. Balogh, age 43
**EVP, Worldwide Sales and Services:** John M. Donovan, age 46
**SVP, Global Marketing:** Todd Johnson
**SVP, Global Human Resources:** Rod McCowan
**SVP, General Counsel, and Secretary:** Richard H. (Rick) Goshorn, age 51
**VP, Associate General Counsel:** Paul B. Hudson
**VP:** Raynor Dahlquist
**VP, Mobile Applications:** Oliver Holle
**VP, Security Services:** Mike Denning
**VP, Authentication Services:** Fran Rosch
**President and CEO, VeriSign Japan:** Teruhide Hashimoto
**Chief Security Officer:** Ken Silva
**Principal Scientist:** Phillip Hallam-Baker
**Director, Marketing:** Stuart Cleary
**Media Relations:** Rufus Manning
**Investor Relations:** Ken Bond
**Auditors:** KPMG LLP

## LOCATIONS

**HQ:** VeriSign, Inc.
487 E. Middlefield Rd., Mountain View, CA 94043
**Phone:** 650-961-7500 **Fax:** 650-961-7300
**Web:** www.verisign.com

**2006 Sales**

| | $ mil. | % of total |
|---|---|---|
| Americas | | |
| US | 1,104.6 | 70 |
| Other countries | 40.1 | 3 |
| Europe, Middle East & Africa | 312.9 | 20 |
| Asia/Pacific | 117.7 | 7 |
| **Total** | **1,575.3** | **100** |

## PRODUCTS/OPERATIONS

### 2006 Sales

| | $ mil. | % of total |
|---|---|---|
| Communications Services Group | 816.5 | 52 |
| Internet Services Group | 758.8 | 48 |
| **Total** | **1,575.3** | **100** |

### Selected Products and Services

Commerce services
- Billing and payment
- Clearing and settlement

Content services
- Application and content delivery
- Messaging

Information services
- Content collection and distribution
- Digital brand management
- Domain name registry
- Supply chain information

Intelligent database services

Network connectivity and interoperability

Operations infrastructure
- Advanced telecommunications
- Distributed servers
- Network security

Security services
- Authentication
- Digital certificate
- Global security consulting
- iDefense
- Managed security services
  - Firewall management
  - Intrusion detection and prevention
  - Vulnerability management
- Network and application security

## COMPETITORS

Accenture
Alcatel-Lucent
Amdocs
AT&T
Boston Communications Group
Comverse Technology
Convergys
Counterpane
Cybertrust
Entrust
Getronics
IBM Global Services
IdenTrust
Internet Security Systems
Microsoft
NeuStar
Register.com
RSA Security
Symantec
Syniverse
Telcordia
Tucows

## HISTORICAL FINANCIALS

Company Type: Public

**Income Statement** FYE: December 31

| | REVENUE ($ mil.) | NET INCOME ($ mil.) | NET PROFIT MARGIN | EMPLOYEES |
|---|---|---|---|---|
| **12/06** | 1,575 | 379 | 24.1% | 5,331 |
| **12/05** | 1,610 | 407 | 25.3% | 4,076 |
| **12/04** | 1,167 | 186 | 16.0% | 3,206 |
| **12/03** | 1,055 | (260) | — | 2,500 |
| **12/02** | 1,222 | (4,961) | — | 3,200 |
| **Annual Growth** | 6.6% | — | — | 13.6% |

### 2006 Year-End Financials

Debt ratio: —
Return on equity: 17.2%
Cash ($ mil.): 700
Current ratio: 0.98
Long-term debt ($ mil.): —
No. of shares (mil.): 244
Dividends
Yield: —
Payout: —
Market value ($ mil.): 5,864

### Stock History

NASDAQ (GS): VRSN

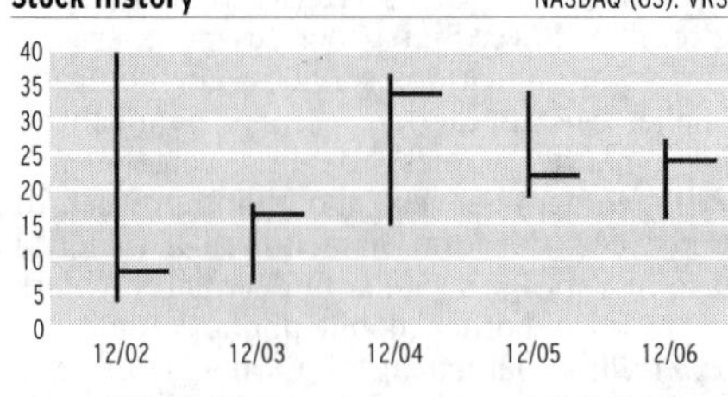


| | STOCK PRICE ($) FY Close | P/E High/Low | | PER SHARE ($) Earnings | Dividends | Book Value |
|---|---|---|---|---|---|---|
| **12/06** | 24.05 | 17 | 10 | 1.53 | — | 9.75 |
| **12/05** | 21.90 | 22 | 12 | 1.54 | — | 8.24 |
| **12/04** | 33.60 | 50 | 21 | 0.72 | — | 6.68 |
| **12/03** | 16.30 | — | — | (1.08) | — | 5.72 |
| **12/02** | 8.02 | — | — | (20.97) | — | 6.65 |
| **Annual Growth** | 31.6% | — | — | — | — | 10.0% |

# Verizon Communications

Ma Bell, this Baby Bell has grown up. Formed in 2000 when Bell Atlantic bought GTE, Verizon is a top US telecom services provider. Verizon operates through three divisions: Telecom, Business, and Wireless. Its telecom operations include about 45 million access lines in 28 states and Washington, DC. Verizon Wireless, the company's joint venture with Vodafone Group, is the #2 US wireless provider (after AT&T Mobility, formerly known as Cingular), with around 60 million customers. Verizon Business was formed in 2006 when Verizon bought MCI, creating a global advanced communications and information technology (IT) powerhouse to serve large business and government clients.

Verizon's purchase of independent long-distance carrier MCI, which was completed in early 2006, was a cash-and-stock deal valued at nearly $8.5 billion. The acquisition created Verizon Business, which combines the large business and government services of MCI with related services at Verizon that were formerly part of its Domestic Telecom unit. The deal enables Verizon to expand its broadband data services. MCI, the #2 US long-distance carrier, had refocused its efforts towards the enterprise customer market since emerging from bankruptcy in 2004. Formerly known as WorldCom, the company's reorganization, including its name change to MCI, was an effort to escape from what has been described as the largest accounting scandal in US history. Verizon has said the deal will likely lead to about 7,000 job cuts at the combined company. The agreement comes on the heels of a similar agreement with Verizon rival SBC Communications, which is now known as AT&T Inc. after its acquisition of MCI rival AT&T Corp.

Verizon Wireless, legally Cellco Partnership, offers wireless voice and data services and equipment sales throughout the US. Its International segment has operations and holdings mostly in the Americas and Europe. Verizon is selling its Caribbean region and Latin American operations to companies controlled by Mexican entrepreneur Carlos Slim Helú in three separate deals valued at $3.7 billion.

Verizon, which has teamed with Microsoft to offer broadband Internet access with MSN network content, has nearly 4 million wireline broadband customers. The company is spending $18 billion through 2010 to rewire about half of its network to enable cable TV and broadband data service offerings. Thus far, Verizon has laid 90 million feet of fiber in Pennsylvania, New Jersey, and Delaware.

## HISTORY

Verizon Communications (the name is a combination of *veritas*, the Latin word for truth, and horizon) was born in 2000 when Bell Atlantic bought GTE, but the company's roots are as old as the telephone. What is now Verizon began as one of the 1870s-era phone companies that evolved into AT&T Corp. and its Bell System of regional telephone operations.

AT&T lived happily as a regulated monopoly until a US government antitrust suit led to its breakup in 1984. Seven regional Bell operating companies (RBOCs, or Baby Bells) emerged in 1984, including Bell Atlantic. The new company, based in Philadelphia, received local phone service rights in six states and Washington, DC; cellular company Bell Atlantic Mobile Systems; and one-seventh of Bellcore, the R&D subsidiary (now Telcordia).

Bell Atlantic pursued unregulated businesses such as wireless, Internet, directory publishing, and catalog sales of computer parts and office supplies. It invested heavily in data-transport markets to supplement existing voice services, offering the first CO-LAN (central-office local area network) system in 1985. A year later it introduced a switched public data network and began testing integrated services digital network (ISDN) technology that combines voice and data transmissions over the same lines.

Bell Atlantic doubled in size with the $25.6 billion purchase of New York City-based NYNEX in 1997, moving from the Cradle of Liberty to the Big Apple. The deal created the second-largest US telecom services firm (after AT&T Corp.).

In 1999 Bell Atlantic agreed to buy GTE, the giant non-Bell local phone company, in a $53 billion deal. Later in 1999 the FCC granted Bell Atlantic permission to sell long-distance phone service in New York, making the company the first of the Baby Bells to be allowed to offer long-distance in its home territory.

Bell Atlantic and Vodafone AirTouch (now Vodafone Group) combined their US wireless operations, including PrimeCo, to form Verizon Wireless in 2000. Regulators later that year approved Bell Atlantic's acquisition of GTE, and Verizon Communications was formed. Tapped to run the new company were chairman and co-CEO Charles Lee, formerly of GTE, and president and co-CEO Ivan Seidenberg, formerly of Bell Atlantic (Lee later gave up the co-CEO position and announced he would step down as chairman in 2003).

Based in New York City, Verizon felt severe effects from the terrorist attack on lower Manhattan in 2001. The company reported damage to its central office facility adjacent to the World Trade Center and the loss of 11 cell sites in the vicinity of the destruction. Verizon also provides phone services to the Pentagon and suffered damage in that attack.

In 2002 Verizon completed the sale of 675,000 access lines in Alabama and Missouri to CenturyTel, and it sold 600,000 access lines in Kentucky to ALLTEL, in deals valued at just over $4 billion. The next year Verizon sold its 39% stake in troubled Mexican wireless operator Grupo Iusacell to paging company Movilccess in a deal valued at $7.4 million.

The firm sold its wireline business in Hawaii to The Carlyle Group in 2005 for $1.65 billion.

In early 2005, Verizon made an initial $6.45 billion offer to acquire MCI. The company made a revised $7.6 billion offer to counter an offer by rival Qwest Communications. The final $8.44 billion bid by Verizon was a reaction to an $8.45 billion subsequent offer from Qwest. The MCI board of directors favored a deal from Verizon in spite of Qwest's higher offers. Qwest, which had remained defiant in its attempts to spoil the deal with Verizon, withdrew its offer after Verizon enhanced its chances through a secret meeting in which it acquired the 13% stake in MCI held by Mexico's Carlos Slim Helú. That deal increased the demand on Verizon to up its stake for the remainder of MCI shares to match the premium price it agreed to pay Slim. Verizon's purchase of MCI was completed in early 2006.

## EXECUTIVES

**Chairman and CEO:** Ivan G. Seidenberg, age 60, $2,100,000 pay
**President and COO:** Dennis F. (Denny) Strigl, age 60
**EVP and CFO:** Doreen A. Toben, age 57, $825,000 pay
**EVP and Chief Marketing Officer:** John G. Stratton, age 45
**EVP and General Counsel:** William P. Barr, age 56, $840,000 pay
**EVP Human Resources:** Marc C. Reed, age 48
**EVP Public Affairs, Policy, and Communications:** Thomas J. (Tom) Tauke, age 56
**EVP Strategy, Development, and Planning:** John W. Diercksen, age 57
**EVP and COO Regional Operations:** Robert (Bob) Mudge
**EVP and CIO:** Shaygan Kheradpir, age 46
**EVP and CTO:** Richard J. (Dick) Lynch, age 58
**SVP and Controller:** Thomas A. (Tom) Bartlett, age 48
**SVP, Deputy General Counsel, and Corporate Secretary:** Marianne Drost
**SVP Finance; CEO Verizon Investment Management:** William F. (Bill) Heitmann, age 57
**SVP Investor Relations:** Ronald H. (Ron) Lataille
**SVP State Public Affairs, Policy, and Communications:** Colleen McCloskey
**SVP Technology and CTO:** Mark A. Wegleitner
**President and CEO, Verizon Wireless:** Lowell C. McAdam, age 52
**Auditors:** Ernst & Young LLP

## LOCATIONS

**HQ:** Verizon Communications Inc.
140 West St., New York, NY 10007
**Phone:** 212-395-1000 **Fax:** 212-571-1897
**Web:** www.verizon.com

### 2006 Sales

| | % of total |
|---|---|
| US | 96 |
| Other countries | 4 |
| **Total** | **100** |

## PRODUCTS/OPERATIONS

### 2006 Sales

| | % of total |
|---|---|
| Wireline | 57 |
| Domestic wireless | 43 |
| **Total** | **100** |

### Selected Services

Business
- Conferencing
- Customer premises equipment design and maintenance
- Data center outsourcing
- Hosted messaging
- Information technology (IT)
- Systems integration
- Voice and data networking

Telecom
- Billing and collections
- Directory assistance
- Internet access services
- Local exchange access
- Long-distance
- Public telephones

Wireless
- Equipment sales
- Paging
- Wireless voice and data services

## COMPETITORS

360networks
AT&T
AT&T Mobility
BellSouth
Comcast
Level 3 Communications
Qwest
Sprint Nextel
T-Mobile USA
U.S. Cellular
Yellow Book USA

## HISTORICAL FINANCIALS

Company Type: Public

### Income Statement

FYE: December 31

| | REVENUE ($ mil.) | NET INCOME ($ mil.) | NET PROFIT MARGIN | EMPLOYEES |
|---|---|---|---|---|
| **12/06** | 88,144 | 6,197 | 7.0% | 242,000 |
| **12/05** | 75,112 | 7,397 | 9.8% | 250,000 |
| **12/04** | 71,283 | 7,831 | 11.0% | 210,000 |
| **12/03** | 67,752 | 3,077 | 4.5% | 203,100 |
| **12/02** | 67,625 | 4,079 | 6.0% | 229,500 |
| **Annual Growth** | 6.8% | 11.0% | — | 1.3% |

### 2006 Year-End Financials

Debt ratio: 59.0%
Return on equity: 14.0%
Cash ($ mil.): 5,653
Current ratio: 0.70
Long-term debt ($ mil.): 28,646
No. of shares (mil.): 2,912
Dividends
Yield: 4.4%
Payout: 76.4%
Market value ($ mil.): 108,424

### Stock History

NYSE: VZ

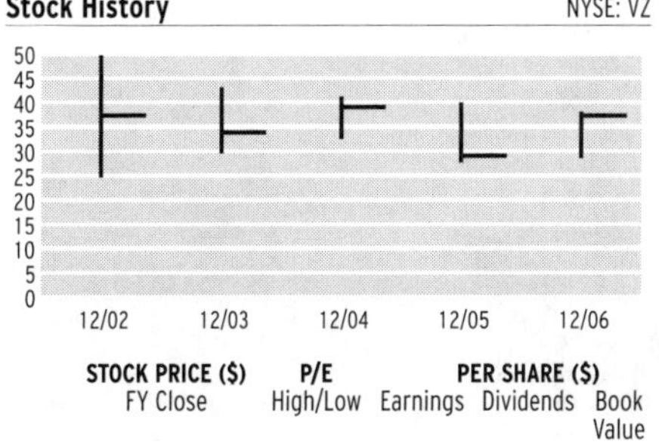

| | STOCK PRICE ($) FY Close | P/E High | P/E Low | PER SHARE ($) Earnings | Dividends | Book Value |
|---|---|---|---|---|---|---|
| **12/06** | 37.24 | 18 | 14 | 2.12 | 1.62 | 16.67 |
| **12/05** | 29.02 | 15 | 11 | 2.65 | 1.60 | 14.30 |
| **12/04** | 39.03 | 15 | 12 | 2.79 | 1.54 | 13.54 |
| **12/03** | 33.80 | 38 | 27 | 1.11 | 1.54 | 12.09 |
| **12/02** | 37.34 | 33 | 17 | 1.49 | 1.54 | 11.89 |
| **Annual Growth** | (0.1%) | — | — | 9.2% | 1.3% | 8.8% |

# VF Corporation

VF Corporation is the name behind the names. The world's #1 jeans maker's bevy of brands includes Lee, Riders, Rustler, and Wrangler jeans. Others holdings include JanSport (#1) and Eastpak (backpacks); Lee Sport (knitwear); The North Face and Eagle Creek (outdoor gear/apparel); Red Kap and Bulwark (industrial work clothes); Nautica and John Varvatos (men's and women's apparel); and Vans (hip footwear). VF sold its intimate apparel unit and hopes to get into the profitable premium-jeans niche. Most of the company's sales come from jeans. VF makes NASCAR, MLB, NFL, and NBA apparel under license. Trusts established by founder John Barbey control about 20% of its shares. It bought surfwear Reef Holdings in 2005.

The company is also the #1 jeans maker in the US, with nearly a quarter of the market and a steady 40% or so of its revenue generated from sales of jeans. While the manufacturer maintains this momentum, VF has been disposing of unprofitable businesses, such as its intimates apparel operation, to refocus on other areas for growth. Its outdoor business — comprising about a third of VF's sales — as well as its Imagewear and Sportswear units, have seen growth in recent years. And the company is streamlining its operations, by centralizing supply chain functions and reorganizing its global operations, to prepare for growth in Japan and its outdoor business.

VF sells its branded apparel through one or two (but usually not all) of several retail channels: department and specialty stores, mass merchants, and discounters. (Wal-Mart accounts for some 13% of sales.) For example, among its jeans brands, Lee is sold through department and specialty stores; Wrangler and Rustler are sold through discounters.

As its sheds noncore apparel operations, VF in 2007 sold its lingerie business to rival Fruit of the Loom. The deal involved US brands (including Vanity Fair and Vassarette) as well as those in Europe (Gemma and Belcor).

In recent years VF has concentrated on expanding its portfolio of sports lifestyle brands. In 2004 it acquired Green Sport Monte Bianco S.p.A (Green Sport), maker of outdoor apparel under the Napapijri name, as well as hipster footwear maker Vans, Inc. (at a price of nearly $400 million). Its purchase of surf footwear and apparel maker Reef Holdings Corporation has enabled VF to lay a strong foundation to this business unit. VF continues to stuff its portfolio full of outdoor brands with its 2007 purchase of Eagle Creek (travel gear).

## HISTORY

In 1899 six partners, including banker John Barbey, started the Reading Glove and Mitten Manufacturing Company. Barbey bought out his five partners in 1911 and changed the name of the Reading, Pennsylvania, company to Schuylkill Silk Mills in 1913. Barbey expanded the mills' production to include underwear and changed the mills' name to Vanity Fair Silk Mills (after a contest with a $25 prize in 1919).

Barbey (who banned the word "underwear") and his son J. E. led their lingerie company to national prominence. The mills made only silk garments until the 1920s, when synthetics were developed. In response to the US embargo on silk in 1941, Vanity Fair changed to rayon, finally converting to the new wonder fabric, nylon tricot, in 1948. Vanity Fair was then manufacturing all stages of its nylon products, from filament to finished garment. It won awards for its innovative advertising with photographs of live models in Vanity Fair lingerie.

J. E. owned all of Vanity Fair's stock until 1951, when he sold one-third of his holdings to the public. In 1966 the stock, previously traded over the counter, was listed on the NYSE.

The company used acquisitions to expand its lingerie business and to begin producing sportswear and blue jeans. It bought Berkshire International (hosiery, 1969) and H.D. Lee (jeans, 1969). To better reflect its diverse offerings, the company changed its name to VF Corporation that year.

VF doubled in size in 1986 by purchasing Blue Bell, a North Carolina maker of branded apparel by Wrangler, Rustler, Jantzen, Jansport, and Red Kap. VF then added the Vassarette brand name from Munsingwear (1990) and Healthtex (infants' and children's apparel, 1991). In 1992 VF acquired European lingerie brands Lou, Bolero, Intimate Cherry, and Variance.

The company bought sports apparel makers Nutmeg Industries and H.H. Cutler in 1994. The next year it cut costs by laying off 7,800 workers, closing 14 plants, and moving production operations to Mexico and the Caribbean. Also in 1995 VF began licensing swimwear and sportswear from NIKE.

Mackey McDonald became CEO in 1996. In 1997 VF bought Brittania Sportswear from Levi Strauss. In 1998 VF moved from Pennsylvania to North Carolina, closer to the company's production facilities. The firm also acquired Bestform Intimates (Lily of France) in 1998.

In 2000 VF purchased the Chic and H.I.S. jeans names from Chic by H.I.S., Gitano jeanswear brand from bankrupt Fruit of the Loom, and troubled outdoor apparel retailer The North Face. VF cut its global workforce by 18% in November 2001, and in March 2002 the company completed its sale of swimwear unit Jantzen to Perry Ellis International. Adding to its rash of large-scale acquisitions, in 2003 VF entered into an agreement to acquire sportswear maker Nautica Enterprises; the deal is said to enable Nautica to focus on strengthening its menswear line. VF also acquired David Chu and Company, Inc.'s rights to 50% of royalty from licensing the Nautica trademark, and placed Chu at the helm of Nautica. With the sizable acquisition came the restructuring of the company to include a Sportswear Coalition that includes the Nautica, Earl Jean, John Varvatos, and E. Magrath brands.

The company sold its Earl Jean brand to Jordache Enterprises and an investor group in 2006. Continuing its divestment of non-core brands, in April 2007 VF sold its intimates apparel business to Fruit of the Loom for about $350 million. The deal involved US brands (Vanity Fair, Lily of France, Vassarette, Bestform, Curvation) as well as those in Europe (Lou, Gemma, Belcor). In August VF completed two acquisitions: Lucy Activewear ($110 million), which operates some 50 stores in about a dozen states, and premium denim firm Seven For All Mankind LLC ($775 million).

## EXECUTIVES

**Chairman and CEO:** Mackey J. McDonald, age 60, $1,140,000 pay
**President, COO, and Director:** Eric C. Wiseman, age 51, $687,500 pay (prior to title change)
**SVP and CFO:** Robert K. (Bob) Shearer, age 55, $540,000 pay
**SVP, Global Operations:** George N. Derhofer, age 53, $550,000 pay
**VP, Administration, General Counsel, and Secretary:** Candace S. Cummings, age 59, $412,000 pay
**VP, Customer Management:** Michael T. (Mike) Gannaway, age 53
**VP; President, Supply Chain:** Boyd Rogers, age 56
**VP, Strategy:** Stephen F. Dull, age 46
**VP and Treasurer:** Frank C. Pickard III, age 62
**VP, Controller, and Chief Accounting Officer:** Bradley W. (Brad) Batten, age 51
**VP, Americas Sourcing:** John Strasburger, age 48
**VP, Brand Planning:** Ellen Rohde
**VP, Business Development:** Corrado Conti, age 38
**VP, Distribution for North America:** Tim Dye, age 48
**VP, Human Resources:** Susan L. Williams, age 47
**VP, Controller and Chief Accounting Officer; VP and CFO, Sportswear Collections:** Robert A. (Bob) Cordaro
**VP and CIO:** Martin Schneider, age 48
**VP, Corporate Taxes:** Richard Lipinski, age 59
**President, VF Jeanswear International:** Giorgio Presca, age 44
**President, VF Jeanswear Latin America:** Silverio Gomez, age 51
**Auditors:** PricewaterhouseCoopers LLP

## LOCATIONS

**HQ:** VF Corporation
105 Corporate Center Blvd., Greensboro, NC 27408
**Phone:** 336-424-6000 **Fax:** 336-424-7631
**Web:** www.vfc.com

## PRODUCTS/OPERATIONS

### 2006 Sales

| | $ mil. | % of total |
|---|---|---|
| Jeanswear | 2,780.2 | 45 |
| Outdoor | 1,868.3 | 30 |
| Imagewear | 828.2 | 13 |
| Sportswear | 685.4 | 11 |
| Other | 53.7 | 1 |
| **Total** | **6,215.8** | **100** |

### Selected Brands

Jeans
- H.I.S.
- Lee
- Maverick
- Old Axe
- Riders
- Rustler
- Timber Creek by Wrangler
- Wrangler
- Wrangler Hero

Imagewear
- Bulwark
- Harley-Davidson (licensed)
- Lee Sport
- MLB (licensed)
- NFL (licensed)
- Red Kap

Sportswear
- John Varvatos
- Nautica

Outdoor
- Eagle Creek
- Eastpak
- JanSport
- Kipling
- Napapijri
- Reef
- The North Face
- Vans

## COMPETITORS

Calvin Klein
Columbia Sportswear
Diesel
Gap
Guess
Gymboree
H&M
Helly-Hansen
Inditex
J. C. Penney
Johnson Outdoors
K2
Kellwood
Levi Strauss
Limited Brands
Liz Claiborne
L.L. Bean
Mudd
OshKosh B'Gosh
Reebok
REI
Rocky Brands
Russell
Sears Holdings
Timberland
Williamson-Dickie

## HISTORICAL FINANCIALS

Company Type: Public

### Income Statement

FYE: Saturday nearest December 31

| | REVENUE ($ mil.) | NET INCOME ($ mil.) | NET PROFIT MARGIN | EMPLOYEES |
|---|---|---|---|---|
| **12/06** | 6,216 | 534 | 8.6% | 45,000 |
| **12/05** | 6,502 | 507 | 7.8% | 52,300 |
| **12/04** | 6,055 | 475 | 7.8% | 53,200 |
| **12/03** | 5,208 | 398 | 7.6% | 52,300 |
| **12/02** | 5,084 | (155) | — | 56,000 |
| **Annual Growth** | 5.2% | — | — | (5.3%) |

### 2006 Year-End Financials

Debt ratio: 19.5%
Return on equity: 17.6%
Cash ($ mil.): 343
Current ratio: 2.54
Long-term debt ($ mil.): 635
No. of shares (mil.): 112
Dividends
Yield: 2.4%
Payout: 41.1%
Market value ($ mil.): 9,208

### Stock History

NYSE: VFC

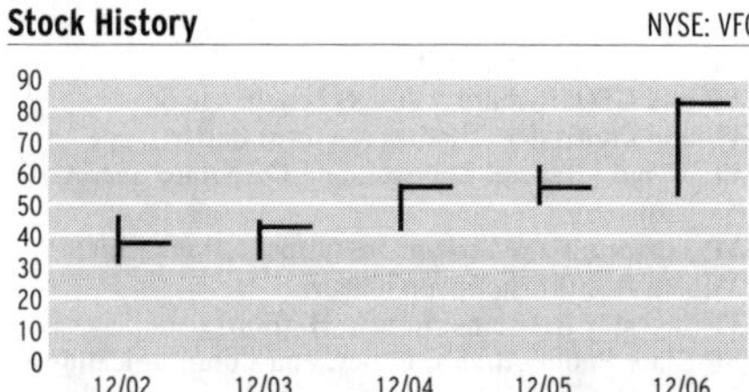

| | STOCK PRICE ($) FY Close | P/E High | P/E Low | PER SHARE ($) Earnings | Dividends | Book Value |
|---|---|---|---|---|---|---|
| **12/06** | 82.08 | 18 | 11 | 4.72 | 1.94 | 29.11 |
| **12/05** | 55.34 | 14 | 11 | 4.44 | 1.10 | 25.50 |
| **12/04** | 55.38 | 13 | 10 | 4.21 | 1.05 | 22.56 |
| **12/03** | 42.58 | 12 | 9 | 3.61 | 1.01 | 18.04 |
| **12/02** | 37.37 | — | — | (1.38) | 0.97 | 15.28 |
| **Annual Growth** | 21.7% | — | — | — | 18.9% | 17.5% |

# Viad Corp

Viad (pronounced VEE-ahd) makes sure convention-goers get to their events. Viad offers convention and event services, exhibit design and construction, and travel and recreation services. Its GES Exposition Services subsidiary provides convention services to trade associations, management groups, and exhibitors. Exhibitgroup/Giltspur designs and constructs custom exhibits for corporations, museums, trade shows, stores, and shopping malls. Viad's Brewster Transport offers travel services (Canadian tours) while its Glacier Park division offers recreation services (mountain lodges). The company operates about 30 offices across Canada, Germany, the UK, and the US.

Each year GES Exposition Services brings in a whopping 70% of the company's sales. Its offerings include event planning, exhibit and furniture rentals, and exhibit installation and dismantling. In early 2007, Viad added to GES's international presence when it acquired Melville Exhibition and Event Services Limited, a UK-based provider of exhibitor services.

Viad complements GES's services with those of Exhibitgroup/Giltspur, which contributes about 20% of revenue.

Pzena Investment Management and Marathon Asset Management each own about 11% of Viad.

## HISTORY

Although this company has only carried the Viad name since 1996, it has a decades-long lineage illustrative of corporate penchants for acquisitions and spinoffs. In the 1960s Greyhound Corporation (later renamed Greyhound Lines and subsequently acquired by Laidlaw) began diversifying beyond transportation as airline and auto travel became less expensive and more popular. Greyhound bought a string of companies that eventually would come under the Viad umbrella. Among its purchases were Restaura (contract food service, 1964), Brewster Transport Company (Canadian travel services, 1965), Travelers Express (financial services, 1965), Aircraft Service International (aircraft fueling, 1968), Exhibitgroup (exhibit products and services, 1968), and GES Exposition Services (convention services, 1969).

When Greyhound acquired Armour and Company in 1970, it branched into meat processing and added the US's most popular soap, Dial, to its holdings. Greyhound subsequently sold all but the meat processing and consumer businesses acquired in the deal. Diversification in the 1980s brought into the fold Glacier Park (lodging in Glacier National Park, 1981), Jetsave (travel agency, 1986), and Dobbs International (airline catering, 1987). Greyhound also launched Premier Cruise Lines in 1983.

Greyhound sold its bus line in 1987 and changed its name to Dial Corporation in 1991. Five years later Dial split into two publicly traded companies: a new Dial, which retained all of Dial's consumer products, and Viad (from the Latin "via," signifying movement), the renamed original company, which retained Dial's service companies (Restaura, Dobbs International, Brewster Transport Company, Travelers Express, Greyhound Leisure Services, Aircraft Service International, Exhibitgroup/Giltspur, GES Exposition Services). Viad also kept a $10 million investment in baseball's Arizona Diamondbacks.

In 1997-1998 Viad began narrowing its focus, shedding UK-based travel agencies Jetsave and Crystal Holidays, as well as Premier Cruise Lines, and Greyhound Leisure Services and Aircraft Services International. It strengthened its existing focus by buying trade show contractor ESR Exposition Services, German exhibit company Voblo, and wire-transfer giant MoneyGram.

Viad continued divesting noncore holdings in 1999 by selling most of Restaura to ARAMARK. It also exited the airline catering business by selling Dobbs to SAirGroup. In 2000 a Missouri jury awarded a former Burlington Northern railroad worker about $500,000 in damages related to asbestos exposure that occurred while working for Baldwin-Lima Hamilton, a predecessor of Viad that manufactured locomotives. Also that year the company sold its ProDine unit, which had provided concessions at Phoenix's America West Arena and Bank One Ballpark, to the Compass Group.

In 2001 Viad's MoneyGram entered an agreement with Bancomer SA to provide electronic money transfer services to about 1,500 locations in Mexico, and its Brewster Tours began offering air travel from 36 US cities. Moneygram and Travelers Express were spun off in 2004, forming MoneyGram International.

## EXECUTIVES

**Chairman:** Robert H. (Bob) Bohannon, age 61
**President, CEO, and Director:** Paul B. Dykstra, age 45
**CFO:** Ellen M. Ingersoll, age 42
**VP and Controller:** G. Michael Latta, age 44
**VP, General Counsel, and Secretary:** Scott E. Sayre, age 60
**VP, Human Resources:** Suzanne J. Pearl, age 44
**President and CEO, Brewster:** David G. Morrison, age 58
**President and CEO, Exhibitgroup/Giltspur:** John F. Jastrem, age 51
**President and CEO, GES Exposition Services:** Kevin M. Rabbitt, age 35
**President and General Manager, Glacier Park:** Cindy J. Ognjanov
**EVP Sales and Marketing, GES Exposition Services:** Jeff Quade
**Treasurer:** Elyse A. Newman
**Executive Director, Internal Auditing:** George Karam
**Director, Investor Relations:** Carrie Long
**IT Director:** Mike Ouwerkerk
**Director, Taxes and Assistant Secretary:** George Cardon
**Manager, Corporate Communications:** Angela Phoenix
**Auditors:** Deloitte & Touche LLP

## LOCATIONS

**HQ:** Viad Corp
1850 N. Central Ave., Ste. 800, Phoenix, AZ 85004
**Phone:** 602-207-4000 **Fax:** 602-207-5900
**Web:** www.viad.com

**2006 Sales**

| | $ mil. | % of total |
|---|---|---|
| US | 715.3 | 83 |
| Canada | 108.8 | 13 |
| Europe | 31.9 | 4 |
| **Total** | **856.0** | **100** |

## PRODUCTS/OPERATIONS

**2006 Sales**

| | $ mil. | % of total |
|---|---|---|
| GES | 612.6 | 72 |
| Exhibitgroup | 164.2 | 19 |
| Travel & recreation services | 79.2 | 9 |
| **Total** | **856.0** | **100** |

**Selected Operations**

Brewster Transport (Canadian tour operator)
Exhibitgroup/Giltspur (exhibit design and production)
GES Exposition Services (convention, exhibition, and event services)
Glacier Park (mountain lodge services)

## COMPETITORS

AIRworks
Audio Visual Services
Czarnowski
Freeman Decorating Services
George P. Johnson
MC2
Sparks Marketing Group
TBA Global

## HISTORICAL FINANCIALS

Company Type: Public

**Income Statement** FYE: December 31

| | REVENUE ($ mil.) | NET INCOME ($ mil.) | NET PROFIT MARGIN | EMPLOYEES |
|---|---|---|---|---|
| **12/06** | 856 | 64 | 7.4% | 3,620 |
| **12/05** | 826 | 38 | 4.6% | 3,390 |
| **12/04** | 786 | (56) | — | 3,025 |
| **12/03** | 1,572 | 114 | 7.2% | 4,710 |
| **12/02** | 1,618 | 58 | 3.6% | 5,520 |
| **Annual Growth** | (14.7%) | 2.3% | — | (10.0%) |

**2006 Year-End Financials**

Debt ratio: 3.0%
Return on equity: 15.4%
Cash ($ mil.): 178
Current ratio: 2.18
Long-term debt ($ mil.): 13
No. of shares (mil.): 21
Dividends
Yield: 0.4%
Payout: 5.5%
Market value ($ mil.): 864

**Stock History** NYSE: VVI

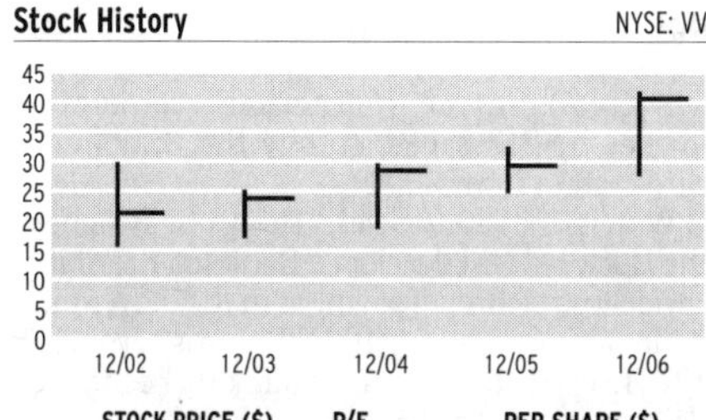


| | STOCK PRICE ($) FY Close | P/E High | P/E Low | PER SHARE ($) Earnings | Dividends | Book Value |
|---|---|---|---|---|---|---|
| **12/06** | 40.60 | 14 | 10 | 2.91 | 0.16 | 20.21 |
| **12/05** | 29.33 | 19 | 15 | 1.71 | 0.16 | 17.69 |
| **12/04** | 28.49 | — | — | (2.58) | 0.08 | 15.65 |
| **12/03** | 23.73 | 19 | 13 | 1.31 | — | — |
| **12/02** | 21.22 | 45 | 24 | 0.66 | — | — |
| **Annual Growth** | 17.6% | — | — | 44.9% | 41.4% | 13.6% |

# Visa International

Paper or plastic? Visa International hopes you choose the latter. Visa operates the world's largest consumer payment system (ahead of MasterCard and American Express) with nearly 2 billion credit and other payment cards in circulation. The company is owned by some 20,000 member financial institutions, which issue and market their own Visa products and participate in the VisaNet payment system (authorization, transaction processing, and settlement services). Visa also provides its customers with debit cards, Internet payment systems, value-storing smart cards, and traveler's checks. Visa has announced plans to restructure and create Visa, Inc., a new, publicly traded company.

Visa Inc. will be created by the merger of Visa International, Visa Canada, and Visa U.S.A., along with regional organizations Visa Asia Pacific; Visa Central and Eastern Europe, Middle East and Africa (CEMEA); and Visa Latin America and the Caribbean (LAC). Visa Europe, which is owned and managed by its European member banks, will become a licensee of Visa Inc.

Visa is accelerating its push to introduce chip cards over magnetic stripe technology; the technology is catching on much faster overseas than it is in the US.

## HISTORY

Although the first charge card was issued by Western Union in 1914, it wasn't until 1958 that Bank of America (BofA) issued its BankAmericard, which combined the convenience of a charge account with credit privileges. When BofA extended its customer base outside California, the interchange system controlling payments began to falter because of design problems and fraud.

In 1968 Dee Hock, manager of the BankAmericard operations of the National Bank of Commerce in Seattle, convinced member banks that a more reliable system was needed. Two years later National BankAmericard Inc. (NBI) was created as an independent corporation (owned by 243 banks) to buy the BankAmericard system from BofA.

With its initial ad slogan, "Think of it as Money," the Hock-led NBI developed BankAmericard into a widely used form of payment in the US. A multinational corporation, IBANCO, was formed in 1974 to carry the operations into other countries. People outside the US resisted BankAmericard's nominal association with BofA, and in 1977 Hock changed the card's name to Visa. NBI became Visa USA, and IBANCO became Visa International.

By 1980 Visa had debuted debit cards, begun issuing traveler's checks, and created an electromagnetic point-of-sale authorization system. Visa developed a global network of ATMs in 1983; it was expanded in 1987 by the purchase of a 33% stake in the Plus System of ATMs, then the US's second-largest system. Hock retired in 1984 with the company well on its way to realizing his vision of a universal payment system.

The company built the Visa brand image with aggressive advertising, such as sponsorship of the 1988 and 1992 Olympics, and by co-branding (issuing cards through other organizations with strong brand names, such as Blockbuster and Ford).

In 1994 Visa teamed up with Microsoft and others to develop home banking services and software. Visa Cash was introduced during the 1996 Olympics. Visa pushed its debit cards in 1996 and 1997 with humorous ads featuring presidential also-ran Bob Dole and showbiz success story Daffy Duck.

Visa expanded its smart card infrastructure in 1997. It published, with MasterCard, encryption and security software for online transactions. The gloves came off the next year as the companies vied to convince the world to rally around their respective e-purse technology standards.

During the 1990s, Visa fought American Express' attempts to introduce a bank credit card of its own by forbidding Visa members in the US from issuing the product; the Justice Department responded with an antitrust suit against Visa and MasterCard. The case went to trial in 2000 with the government claiming that Visa and MasterCard stifle competition and enjoy an exclusive cross-ownership structure.

Also that year, the company made a deal with Gemplus, the French smart card company, to enable payments over wireless networks; Visa also inked e-commerce agreements with telecommunications companies Nokia and Ericsson.

The company continued its technology push in 2000 with a deal with Financial Services Technology Consortium to test biometrics — the use of fingerprints, irises, and voice recognition to identify cardholders. The company also launched a pre-paid card, Visa Buxx, targeted at teenagers.

Also in 2000 the European Union launched an investigation into the firm's transaction fees, alleging that the fees could restrict competition. The following year Visa International agreed to drop its fee to 0.7% of the transaction value over five years.

Led by retail giant Wal-Mart, some 4 million merchants claimed Visa and MasterCard violated antitrust laws and attempted to monopolize a legally defined market for debit cards. The plaintiffs sought up to $200 billion in damages in their class-action suit. Just as the 1996 lawsuit was to go to trial in early 2003, Visa settled, agreeing to pay $2 billion (twice that of co-defendant MasterCard) over the next decade. Both agreed to pay $25 million immediately, as well as reduce the fee merchants pay for signature-based debit cards.

## EXECUTIVES

**Chairman:** William I. (Bill) Campbell, age 60
**President, CEO, and Director:** Kenneth F. (Ken) Sommer
**EVP and Chief Commercial Officer:** Matthew Piasecki
**EVP and CTO:** Terence V. (Terry) Milholland
**EVP, Global Brand, Marketing, and Corporate Relations:** John Elkins
**EVP, Global Marketing Partnerships and Sponsorship:** Tom Shepard
**SVP, Global Acceptance and Operations:** Roger Swales
**SVP and Controller:** Mary Anne Schuett
**Interim President, Visa USA; President and CEO, Inovant:** John M. Partridge, age 57
**President, Visa Central and Eastern Europe, Middle East and Africa (CEMEA):** Anne L. Cobb
**President, Visa Latin America and Caribbean:** Eduardo Eraña
**President, Visa Canada:** Derek A. Fry
**President and CEO, Visa Asia Pacific:** Rupert G. Keeley
**EVP and Chief Administrative Officer, Visa Asia Pacific:** David Lee
**EVP and General Manager, Emerging Products and Technology, Visa Asia Pacific:** Philip Yen
**EVP and Regional Legal Counsel, Visa Asia Pacific:** Lyn Boxall
**EVP, Marketing and Product Sales, Visa Asia Pacific:** Rajiv Kapoor
**EVP, South East Asia, Visa Asia Pacific:** James G. Murray
**SVP and General Manager, Japan, Visa Asia Pacific:** Richard Chang
**President and CEO, Visa Europe:** Peter G. Ayliffe, age 51
**General Counsel and Corporate Secretary:** Thomas A. M'Guinness
**Auditors:** KPMG LLP

## LOCATIONS

**HQ:** Visa International
900 Metro Center Blvd., Foster City, CA 94404
**Phone:** 650-432-3200 **Fax:** 650-432-7436
**Web:** international.visa.com

## PRODUCTS/OPERATIONS

### Selected Products and Services

Electron (debit card outside of US)
smartVisa card (computer-chip-embedded card)
Visa Business card (for small businesses and professionals)
Visa Cash (smart cards)
Visa Classic card (credit/debit card issued by Visa's member banks)
Visa Corporate card (for travel and entertainment expenses)
Visa Debit card (accesses bank account for immediate settlement of payments)
Visa Gold card (higher spending limits)
VisaNet (global transaction processing network)
Visa Purchasing card (for corporate purchases)
Visa Travelers Cheques
Visa TravelMoney (prepaid card in any currency)

## COMPETITORS

American Express
MasterCard
Morgan Stanley

## HISTORICAL FINANCIALS

Company Type: Private

### Income Statement

FYE: September 30

| | REVENUE ($ mil.) | NET INCOME ($ mil.) | NET PROFIT MARGIN | EMPLOYEES |
|---|---|---|---|---|
| **9/06** | 1,278 | 70 | 5.5% | 6,300 |
| **9/05** | 1,162 | 83 | 7.2% | 6,000 |
| **9/04** | 1,427 | 32 | 2.3% | 6,000 |
| **9/03** | 1,369 | 19 | 1.4% | 6,000 |
| **Annual Growth** | (2.3%) | 54.3% | — | 1.6% |

### 2006 Year-End Financials

Debt ratio: 6.6%
Return on equity: 12.2%
Cash ($ mil.): —
Current ratio: —
Long-term debt ($ mil.): 40

### Net Income History

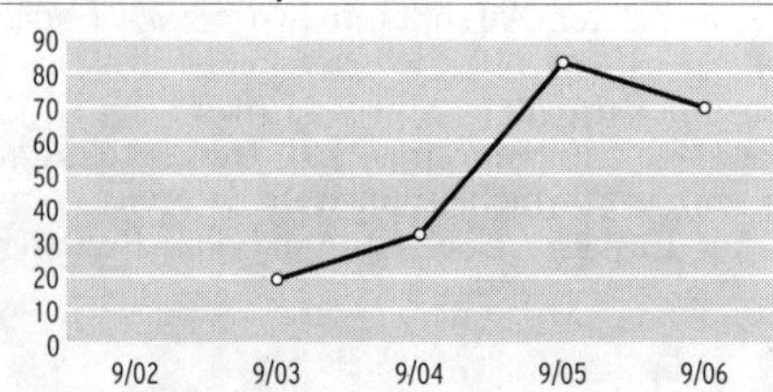

# Vishay Intertechnology

Vishay Intertechnology is aggressive when it comes to passives. The company is the #3 maker of passive electronic components (behind Murata Manufacturing and EPCOS), such as capacitors and resistors. It is also a top player in the market for discrete semiconductor (active) components, including diodes and transistors, and makes power integrated circuits and optoelectronic components. Vishay's components are used in everything from cell phones to cars to spacecraft. The company's customers include tech giants such as Cisco, IBM, Nokia, and Sony. Founder and CTO Felix Zandman controls nearly half of Vishay's voting power.

Vishay touts its line of passive components as the broadest in the industry, though its line of active semiconductor components accounts for essentially half of sales. While it continues to develop new products within its existing operations, the company has also continued to expand by acquiring well-positioned rivals with established brand names, such as Sprague in the US, Sfernice in France, and BCcomponents in the Netherlands.

Vishay is also focused on entering (and dominating) the transducer market, forming its Vishay Transducers Group around several acquisitions such as Sensortronics and Tedea-Huntleigh.

Competitor International Rectifier has sold its Power Control Systems (PCS) business to Vishay for about $290 million in cash. Product lines included in the transaction include certain discrete planar MOSFETs, discrete diodes and rectifiers, discrete thyristors, and automotive modules and assemblies. The assets include a wafer fab in Torino, Italy, and other facilities in China, India, and the UK.

Vishay turned around and set plans to sell the Automotive Modules and Subsystems business unit acquired from IR, saying the business was not a strategic fit for its operations. The automotive business unit has annual sales of about $80 million.

FMR (Fidelity Investments) owns about 11% of Vishay's common stock. The TCW Group holds nearly 7% of the common shares.

## HISTORY

Felix Zandman, Poland native and Holocaust survivor, earned his doctorate in physics at the Sorbonne. As a student, Zandman developed PhotoStress, a plastic coating that revolutionized stress testing of railcars and airplane wings. In the mid-1950s Zandman worked for the Budd Co., a Philadelphia-based steelmaker. During that period he developed a breakthrough resistor whose performance wasn't affected by temperature.

In 1962 Zandman borrowed $200,000 from cousin Alfred Slaner, the creator of nylon support hose, to start Vishay, which was named for the family's ancestral village in Lithuania. Zandman and associate James Starr made significant developments in resistors. Vishay opened its first plant in Israel in 1969 and went public in 1974. By the early 1980s it was a world leader in ultraprecise resistors and resistive sensors.

In 1985 the company and British financiers Mezzanine Capital formed a joint venture to buy Dale Electronics, a US maker of resistors whose parent company, Lionel, had filed for bankruptcy. Dale was nearly three times Vishay's size. Vishay soon added Draloric Electronic (1987, Germany) and Sfernice (1988, France). The company bought Mezzanine's half of Dale in 1988.

In 1992 Vishay purchased parts of the STI Group, formerly Sprague Technologies. Sprague, a specialist in compact, highly stable tantalum capacitors, had been the US's top capacitor maker for several decades. The next year Vishay completed its purchase of Roederstein, a German capacitor and resistor maker. When sales of small specialty tantalum capacitors heated up in 1993, the company acquired the tantalum capacitor segment of Philips Electronics North America. It added Vitramon, the multilayer ceramic chip capacitor business of rival Thomas & Betts, in 1994. Vishay bought a 65% stake in Taiwan-based diode maker Lite-On Power Semiconductor in 1997.

Vishay bought TEMIC Telefunken, the semiconductor unit of German conglomerate Daimler-Benz (now Daimler AG), for about $550 million in 1998. The purchase included 80% of TEMIC subsidiary Siliconix, a leading maker of discrete semiconductors. Vishay then sold most of TEMIC's integrated circuit operations to Atmel.

In 2000 the company sold its stake in Lite-On, saying it would focus on its Siliconix and Telefunken operations. It also acquired Electro-Films, a maker of thin-film components.

The next year began smoothly for Vishay — it acquired Infineon Technologies' infrared components business for about $120 million — but then the company hit an unexpected bump in the road. Vishay made a bid to acquire General Semiconductor (electrical protection products that control power surges) for about $463 million, but was twice rejected — a decision that drew Zandman's public ire. Vishay upped the ante when Siliconix (a top rival of General and 80%-owned by Vishay) subsequently sued General for patent infringement. Vishay finally acquired General for about $540 million in stock and the assumption of $229 million in debt.

In 2002 Vishay plunged into the transducer market, acquiring Sensortronics, Tedea-Huntleigh, and two businesses from Thermo Electron (now Thermo Fisher Scientific) to form its Vishay Transducers Group. In 2004 it acquired the thin-film interconnects business of Aeroflex for about $9 million.

Late in 2004 Zandman announced that he would step down as CEO at the start of 2005, but he would remain an executive of the company. Vishay COO Gerald Paul succeeded Zandman as CEO.

In 2005 Vishay acquired the assets of CyOptics Israel and bought Alpha Electronics, a Japanese manufacturer of foil resistors. The company paid around $11 million for the two acquisitions and assumed some $8 million in debt.

In 2005 Vishay acquired SI Technologies for about $18 million in cash, plus the assumption of $12 million in debt. Also that year the company acquired the 20% of Siliconix it didn't previously own, swapping Vishay common shares for those of Siliconix. Vishay's tender offer yielded enough shares to give the company ownership of more than 95% of Siliconix.

## EXECUTIVES

**Chairman, CTO, and Chief Business Development Officer:** Felix Zandman, age 78
**President, CEO, COO, and Director:** Gerald Paul, age 57
**Vice Chairman and Chief Administration Officer; President, Vishay Israel Ltd:** Marc Zandman, age 45
**EVP, CFO, and Treasurer:** Richard N. Grubb, age 60
**EVP and Deputy COO:** Ziv Shoshani, age 41
**SVP:** Peter G. Henrici
**SVP and Corporate Secretary:** William M. Clancy
**VP and Assistant Treasurer:** Steven Klausner
**Public Relations Associate and Director:** Ruta Zandman, age 69
**Corporate Investor Relations:** Brenda R. Tate
**Auditors:** Ernst & Young LLP

## LOCATIONS

**HQ:** Vishay Intertechnology, Inc.
63 Lancaster Ave., Malvern, PA 19355
**Phone:** 610-644-1300 **Fax:** 610-889-9429
**Web:** www.vishay.com

Vishay Intertechnology has approximately 60 manufacturing facilities in Austria, Belgium, Brazil, China, Costa Rica, the Czech Republic, France, Germany, Hungary, India, Israel, Italy, Japan, Malaysia, Mexico, the Netherlands, the Philippines, Portugal, Sweden, Taiwan, the UK, and the US.

**2006 Sales**

| | $ mil. | % of total |
|---|---|---|
| Europe | | |
| Germany | 655.1 | 25 |
| Other countries | 341.8 | 13 |
| Asia/Pacific | 914.4 | 36 |
| US | 464.9 | 18 |
| Israel | 205.3 | 8 |
| **Total** | **2,581.5** | **100** |

## PRODUCTS/OPERATIONS

**2006 Sales**

| | $ mil. | % of total |
|---|---|---|
| Semiconductors | 1,291.4 | 50 |
| Passive components | 1,290.1 | 50 |
| **Total** | **2,581.5** | **100** |

**Selected Products**

Semiconductors (active components)
- Diodes
  - Rectifiers
  - Small-signal diodes
  - Transient voltage suppressors
  - Zener diodes
- Integrated circuits (ICs)
  - Analog switches
  - Infrared data communication (IrDC) transceivers
  - Multiplexers
  - Power ICs
- Optoelectronic components
  - Displays
  - Infrared emitters
  - Light emitting diodes (LEDs)
  - Optocouplers
  - Optosensors
  - Photo detectors
- Transistors
  - Bipolar power transistors
  - Junction field-effect transistors (JFETs)
  - Power MOSFETs (metal oxide semiconductor FETs)
  - Radio-frequency transistors
  - Small-signal FETs

Passive components
- Capacitors
  - Aluminum
  - Ceramic
  - Film
  - Tantalum
- Magnetics
  - Custom magnetics
  - Inductors
  - Transformers
- Resistors
  - Bulk metal foil resistors
  - Fuse resistors
  - Metal-film resistors and networks
  - Panel controls
  - Panel potentiometers
  - Thermistors
  - Thick-film resistors and networks
  - Thin-film resistors and networks
  - Trimming potentiometers
  - Varistors

## COMPETITORS

Allegro MicroSystems
Avago Technologies
AVX
Bell Industries
CTS
Diodes
EPCOS
Fairchild Semiconductor
Freescale Semiconductor
Infineon Technologies
International Rectifier
KEMET
Maxim Integrated Products
Microsemi
Murata Manufacturing
NEC Electronics
NXP
Ohmite
ON Semiconductor
Power Integrations
ROHM
Samsung Electronics
Sanken Electric
Sensata
Sharp
Shindengen Electric Manufacturing
STMicroelectronics
TDK
Technitrol
Texas Instruments
Toshiba Semiconductor
Tyco Electronics
Yageo

## HISTORICAL FINANCIALS

Company Type: Public

**Income Statement** FYE: December 31

| | REVENUE ($ mil.) | NET INCOME ($ mil.) | NET PROFIT MARGIN | EMPLOYEES |
|---|---|---|---|---|
| **12/06** | 2,582 | 140 | 5.4% | 27,000 |
| **12/05** | 2,298 | 62 | 2.7% | 26,100 |
| **12/04** | 2,414 | 45 | 1.9% | 25,700 |
| **12/03** | 2,171 | 27 | 1.2% | 25,200 |
| **12/02** | 1,823 | (93) | — | 25,250 |
| **Annual Growth** | 9.1% | — | — | 1.7% |

**2006 Year-End Financials**

Debt ratio: 19.7%
Return on equity: 4.7%
Cash ($ mil.): 672
Current ratio: 3.23
Long-term debt ($ mil.): 608
No. of shares (mil.): 170
Dividends
Yield: —
Payout: —
Market value ($ mil.): 2,303

**Stock History** NYSE: VSH

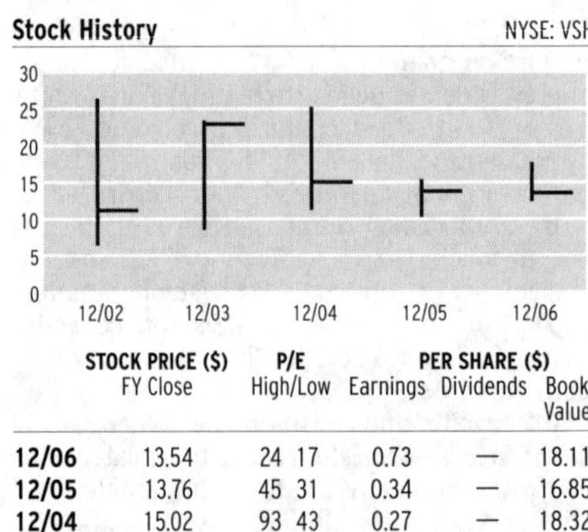


| | STOCK PRICE ($) FY Close | P/E High/Low | PER SHARE ($) Earnings | Dividends | Book Value |
|---|---|---|---|---|---|
| **12/06** | 13.54 | 24 17 | 0.73 | — | 18.11 |
| **12/05** | 13.76 | 45 31 | 0.34 | — | 16.85 |
| **12/04** | 15.02 | 93 43 | 0.27 | — | 18.32 |
| **12/03** | 22.90 | 136 52 | 0.17 | — | 17.38 |
| **12/02** | 11.18 | — — | (0.58) | — | 16.35 |
| **Annual Growth** | 4.9% | — — | — | — | 2.6% |

# Volt Information Sciences

A jolt from Volt can discharge your personnel needs. Volt Information Sciences generates more than 80% of its sales by offering temporary and permanent employees to businesses through more than 300 branch and on-site offices in the US, Canada, and Europe. The company also publishes telephone directories (primarily in eastern and mid-Atlantic states); provides telecommunications services; and makes computer-based directory assistance, database management, and other telecommunications systems. The founding Shaw family owns about 45% of the company, which was established in 1957.

Its VoltDelta unit specializes in directory assistance services for telecommunications companies such as Verizon, while its VMC segment offers project management and IT consulting and engineering services.

In 2005 the company acquired wireless technology provider Varetis Solutions GmbH, a subsidiary of Varetis AG. The following year, Varetis was integrated with another subsidiary, VoltDelta Europe. The newly formed unit was subsequently renamed Volt Delta International.

## HISTORY

Brothers William and Jerome Shaw started their business in 1950 to provide freelance technical publication assistance; they chose the name Volt because it sounded technical. The company established a temporary technical staffing division in 1956 and went public in 1962.

Volt had expanded into clerical and administrative staffing, as well as telephone directory printing by the late 1960s; it established a telecommunications services division in 1976. The company acquired Delta Resources (computerized directory assistance systems) in 1980 and began printing telephone directories in Uruguay and Australia several years later (the Australian operation was sold in 1997).

Volt's personnel segment grew in the 1990s as companies relied more on outside agencies to help staff their businesses, and increased telephone industry competition drove expansion in the telecommunications market. Electronic publishing was more problematic, however, and in 1996 the company merged its subsidiaries in that segment with Information International to form Autologic Information International (Volt took a 59% stake). In 1997 it expanded its breadth with the purchase of 11 US community telephone directories in North Carolina and West Virginia.

In 1999 Volt acquired UK-based Gatton Group. Also that year it bought the wired services business (installation of cable, wire, and small telecommunications systems) and professional staffing divisions of a Lucent Technologies unit. In 2000 the company created subsidiary ProcureStaff to provide supplemental staffing procurement services. In 2001 Agfa Corporation bought the company's 59%-owned subsidiary, Autologic Information International, for about $24 million. Volt combined its telecommunications services units to form Volt Telecommunications Group in 2002. In 2003 the company's VMC Consulting subsidiary merged with IT consulting division Volt Integrated Solutions Group.

The following year, Volt acquired Volt Delta, the directory and operator services unit of Nortel, in 2004 to boost its computer systems segment.

William Shaw died in 2006.

## EXECUTIVES

**President, CEO, COO, and Director:** Steven A. Shaw, age 47, $500,192 pay
**EVP, Secretary, and Director:** Jerome Shaw, age 80, $598,462 pay
**SVP and CFO:** Jack Egan, age 57
**SVP and General Counsel:** Howard B. Weinreich, age 64, $346,942 pay
**SVP and Treasurer:** Ludwig M. Guarino, age 55
**VP Accounting Operations:** Daniel G. Hallihan, age 58
**VP Human Resources:** Louise Ross
**President, ProcureStaff:** John Campellone, age 46
**COO, VMC Consulting:** Robert (Rob) Wise
**EVP, VMC Consulting:** Glenn Hoogerwerf
**Auditors:** Ernst & Young LLP

## LOCATIONS

**HQ:** Volt Information Sciences, Inc.
560 Lexington Ave., New York, NY 10022
**Phone:** 212-704-2400 **Fax:** 212-704-2417
**Web:** www.volt.com

Volt Information Sciences has more than 300 offices in Canada, Europe, and the US. It also has telephone directory interests in Uruguay.

**2006 Sales**

| | $ mil. | % of total |
|---|---|---|
| US | 2,207.8 | 94 |
| Europe | 130.6 | 6 |
| **Total** | **2,338.4** | **100** |

## PRODUCTS/OPERATIONS

**2006 Sales**

| | $ mil. | % of total |
|---|---|---|
| Staffing | 1,972.2 | 84 |
| Computer systems | 187.9 | 8 |
| Telecommunications | 118.9 | 5 |
| Telephone directory | 79.3 | 3 |
| Adjustments | (19.9) | — |
| **Total** | **2,338.4** | **100** |

**Selected Services**

Computer systems
- Directory assistance
- Information technology

Directories
- Database management
- Marketing
- Printing

Staffing
- Information technology services
- Professional placement
- Staffing procurement
- Temporary and contract staffing

Telecommunications
- Construction
- Design
- Engineering
- Installation
- Maintenance

## COMPETITORS

| | |
|---|---|
| Adecco | Monster Worldwide |
| Aquent | MPS |
| Barrett Business Services | R.H. Donnelley |
| Butler International | Spherion |
| Edgewater Technology | TAC Worldwide |
| Express Personnel | TeamStaff |
| Joulé | Vedior |
| Kelly Services | Yellow Book USA |
| Manpower | |

## HISTORICAL FINANCIALS

Company Type: Public

**Income Statement** FYE: Sun. nearest Oct. 31

| | REVENUE ($ mil.) | NET INCOME ($ mil.) | NET PROFIT MARGIN | EMPLOYEES |
|---|---|---|---|---|
| **10/06** | 2,338 | 31 | 1.3% | 46,000 |
| **10/05** | 2,178 | 17 | 0.8% | 48,000 |
| **10/04** | 1,925 | 34 | 1.8% | 45,000 |
| **10/03** | 1,610 | 4 | 0.3% | 41,600 |
| **10/02** | 1,488 | (33) | — | 36,000 |
| **Annual Growth** | 12.0% | — | — | 6.3% |

**2006 Year-End Financials**

| | |
|---|---|
| Debt ratio: 3.9% | No. of shares (mil.): 15 |
| Return on equity: 9.9% | Dividends |
| Cash ($ mil.): 74 | Yield: — |
| Current ratio: 1.56 | Payout: — |
| Long-term debt ($ mil.): 13 | Market value ($ mil.): 421 |

**Stock History** NYSE: VOL

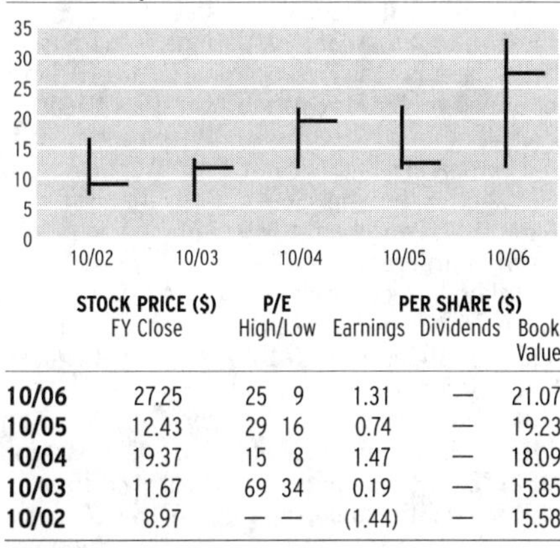


| | STOCK PRICE ($) FY Close | P/E High/Low | PER SHARE ($) Earnings | Dividends | Book Value |
|---|---|---|---|---|---|
| **10/06** | 27.25 | 25 9 | 1.31 | — | 21.07 |
| **10/05** | 12.43 | 29 16 | 0.74 | — | 19.23 |
| **10/04** | 19.37 | 15 8 | 1.47 | — | 18.09 |
| **10/03** | 11.67 | 69 34 | 0.19 | — | 15.85 |
| **10/02** | 8.97 | — — | (1.44) | — | 15.58 |
| **Annual Growth** | 32.0% | — — | — | — | 7.8% |

# Vulcan Materials

The road to just about everywhere is paved with Vulcan Materials' aggregates. The company is the largest producer of construction aggregates — crushed stone, gravel, and sand — in the US. Vulcan produces aggregates, asphalt mixes, and ready-mixed concrete at more than 220 aggregate plants in the US (primarily in the Southeast) and Mexico. Aggregates account for about two-thirds of sales. In addition to its production facilities, Vulcan operates truck, rail, and water distribution locations. The company has sold its chemicals business, which produces chlor-alkali chemicals and other industrial chemicals used for pulp and paper processing, water treatment, pharmaceuticals, and other industrial uses.

Increased spending by the federal government on highway projects is expected to sustain growth in Vulcan's aggregates sales. To stay ahead of rival Martin Marietta Materials, the acquisitive Vulcan plans to keep buying quarries. The company has announced plans to acquire Florida Rock Industries for a reported $4.6 billion. (During 2005 Vulcan spent nearly $100 million on aggregate and asphalt operations, primarily in the Southeast.)

State Farm Mutual Automobile Insurance owns 11% of Vulcan Materials.

## HISTORY

In 1916 the Ireland family purchased a 75% interest in Birmingham Slag, a small Alabama company established in 1909 to process slag from a Birmingham steel plant. For several decades the company prospered by selling its processed slag to the construction industry.

Third-generation Charles Ireland became president in 1951 and transformed Birmingham Slag from a regional operation into a national one. In 1956 the company bought Vulcan Detinning, renamed itself Vulcan Materials, and went public. By 1959 Vulcan was the largest producer of aggregates in the US, with sales over $100 million.

Vulcan owned 90 quarries by 1981 and claimed sales of some $780 million. It added about 50 operations and plants in the 1980s and in 1987 entered into a joint venture, the Crescent Market Project, with Mexico's Grupo ICA, largely to supply aggregates from a Yucatan quarry to US Gulf Coast markets.

In 1990 Vulcan bought Reed Crushed Stone and Reed Terminal, which included the largest US crushed-rock quarry (in Paducah, Kentucky). The Yucatan plant was fully operational in 1991 and was supported by two company-owned ships that moved materials to the US Gulf Coast. Also that year Vulcan entered a venture with Tetra Technologies to produce calcium chloride from hydrochloric acids; this new use for the acid eased Vulcan's status as a major polluter.

Vulcan built a sodium chlorite plant in Wichita in 1993 and plants in Port Edwards, Wisconsin, to produce potassium carbonate and sodium hydrosulfite. In 1994 the company bought Peroxidation Systems of Tucson (water-purification technology, chemicals, and related equipment). That year Vulcan also acquired Callaway Chemical, boosting its specialty chemical line.

The company bought three food-processing chemical companies and Rio Linda Chemical (chlorine dioxide) in 1995. Acquisitions continued in 1996 as Vulcan purchased three chemical companies and several quarries. Also that year Vulcan sold its chlorine cylinder repackaging business and consolidated its paper and water-treatment businesses. In 1997 the company sold its coal-handling business, added several quarries, and bought the textile chemical business of Laun-Dry Supply.

Vulcan bought six aggregate operations in Georgia, Illinois, and Tennessee in 1998 and started three new operations in Alabama, Georgia, and Indiana. It also formed a joint venture with Mitsui to build a chlor-alkali plant.

In 1999 Vulcan paid about $890 million for rival aggregate producer CalMat. The company also bought 20 quarries throughout the US. Vulcan merged its specialty chemicals businesses into one unit — Vulcan Performance Chemicals — in 2000. The company also acquired Texas-based Garves W. Yates & Sons, adding six quarries. Also in 2000 Vulcan acquired the North American aggregates production and transportation assets that Anglo American's Titan Cement Company obtained from its purchase of Tarmac plc. In 2001 the company bought two aggregates facilities in Tennessee, two recycling facilities in Illinois, and its Mexico-based Crescent Markets joint venture.

In 2003 Vulcan divested its Performance Chemicals business unit, concluding with the sale of its industrial water treatment and pulp and paper operations. It did retain the sodium chlorite business and moved it under its Chloralkali operations. Vulcan expanded in central Tennessee with the purchase of Columbia Rock Products in 2004. In October 2004 the company agreed to sell the remainder of its chemical operations to Basic Chemical Company for an undisclosed sum; the deal was completed in 2005.

Vulcan spent $94 million on acquisitions in 2005, including 11 aggregate operations and five asphalt plants in Arizona, Georgia, Indiana, and Tennessee.

## EXECUTIVES

**Chairman and CEO:** Donald M. James, age 58, $1,200,000 pay
**SVP and CFO:** Daniel F. Sansone, age 54, $475,000 pay
**SVP, Corporate Development:** Robert A. Wason IV, age 55
**SVP, General Counsel, and Secretary:** William F. Denson III, age 63, $817,500 pay
**SVP, Human Resources:** J. Wayne Houston, age 54
**VP, Business Development:** James P. Daniel, age 52
**VP, Controller, and CIO:** Ejaz A. Khan, age 49
**VP, Marketing and Transportation Services:** Drew A. Meyer, age 63
**VP, Planning and Development:** Richard K. Carnwath, age 55
**VP, Risk Management:** Bennie W. Bumpers, age 63
**VP, Tax:** James W. O'Brien, age 50
**VP, Operations Support:** Ronald L. (46) Walker
**VP, Marketing Support Services:** Sidney F. Mays, age 63
**President, Mideast Division:** D. Gray Kimel Jr., age 57
**President, Midsouth Division:** Stanley G. Bass, age 45
**President, Midwest Division:** Robert R. Vogel, age 49
**SVP, East:** Danny R. Shepherd, age 53
**President, Southwest Division:** James T. Hill, age 47
**President, Western Division:** Ronald G. McAbee, age 59, $645,000 pay
**Treasurer:** J. Philip Alford, age 57
**Investor Relations:** Mark Warren
**President, Southeast Division:** Michael R. Mills, age 46
**President, Western Division:** Alan D. Wessel, age 48
**Auditors:** Deloitte & Touche LLP

## LOCATIONS

**HQ:** Vulcan Materials Company
1200 Urban Center Dr., Birmingham, AL 35242
**Phone:** 205-298-3000 **Fax:** 205-298-2960
**Web:** www.vulcanmaterials.com

Vulcan Materials operates 224 aggregate production facilities in 17 US states and Mexico. Properties include 169 crushed stone plants, 39 sand and gravel pits, and 16 recycled concrete and other plants. It also operates 59 distribution yards, 41 asphalt plants, and 23 concrete plants.

## PRODUCTS/OPERATIONS

**2006 Sales**

| | $ mil. | % of total |
|---|---|---|
| Aggregates | 2,131.9 | 64 |
| Asphalt mix | 500.2 | 15 |
| Delivery revenues | 301.4 | 9 |
| Concrete | 260.7 | 8 |
| Other | 148.3 | 4 |
| **Total** | **3,342.5** | **100** |

**Selected Products**

Construction materials
- Agricultural limestone
- Asphalt coating (Guardtop)
- Asphalt paving materials
- Chemical stone (high-calcium and -magnesium stone)
- Concrete
- Construction aggregates
  - Crushed stone
  - Gravel
  - Sand
  - Recrushed concrete
- Railroad ballast
- Ready-mix concrete (portland cement)

## COMPETITORS

Aggregate Industries
American Steamship
American Stone
Ash Grove Cement
Ashland
Astec Industries
BPB
Buzzi Unicem USA
Cementos Portland Valderrivas
CEMEX
Continental Materials
CRH
Crown Energy
Cytec
Doan Companies
DuPont
Eagle Materials
Edw. C. Levy
Florida Rock
Georgia Gulf
Giant Cement
Hanson
Hanson Aggregates
Hanson Building Products
HeidelbergCement
Henry Company
Hercules
Holcim Apasco
Holcim (US)
ICI American
Knife River
Lafarge North America
Martin Marietta Aggregates
Martin Marietta Materials
MDU Resources
Meadow Valley
New Enterprise Stone & Lime
Nippon Soda
Occidental Petroleum
Oglebay Norton
Olin
O-N Minerals
Pioneer Companies
PPG
R. B. Pamplin
Ready Mix Inc
Ready Mix USA
Redland Genstar
Rinker
Rogers
St. Lawrence Cement
Superior Ready Mix
Transit Mix Concrete
Trinity Industries
TXI
U.S. Lime & Minerals

## HISTORICAL FINANCIALS

Company Type: Public

**Income Statement** FYE: December 31

| | REVENUE ($ mil.) | NET INCOME ($ mil.) | NET PROFIT MARGIN | EMPLOYEES |
|---|---|---|---|---|
| **12/06** | 3,343 | 468 | 14.0% | 7,983 |
| **12/05** | 2,895 | 389 | 13.4% | 8,051 |
| **12/04** | 2,454 | 287 | 11.7% | 8,410 |
| **12/03** | 2,892 | 195 | 6.7% | 8,838 |
| **12/02** | 2,797 | 170 | 6.1% | 9,166 |
| **Annual Growth** | 4.6% | 28.8% | — | (3.4%) |

**2006 Year-End Financials**

Debt ratio: 16.1%
Return on equity: 22.7%
Cash ($ mil.): 55
Current ratio: 1.48
Long-term debt ($ mil.): 322
No. of shares (mil.): 140
Dividends
Yield: 1.6%
Payout: 31.6%
Market value ($ mil.): 12,555

**Stock History** NYSE: VMC

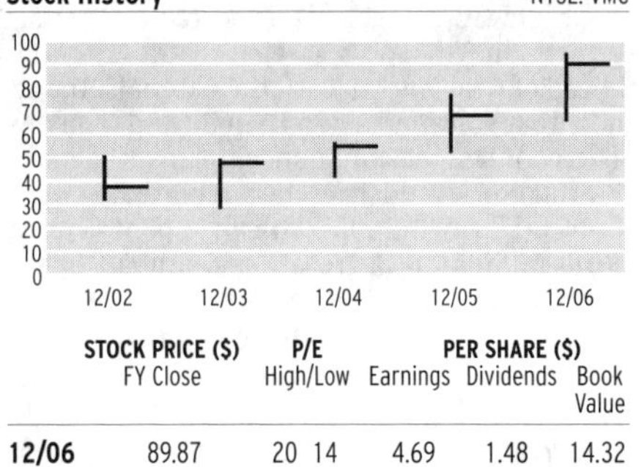


| | STOCK PRICE ($) FY Close | P/E High | P/E Low | PER SHARE ($) Earnings | PER SHARE ($) Dividends | PER SHARE ($) Book Value |
|---|---|---|---|---|---|---|
| **12/06** | 89.87 | 20 | 14 | 4.69 | 1.48 | 14.32 |
| **12/05** | 67.75 | 20 | 14 | 3.73 | 1.16 | 21.20 |
| **12/04** | 54.61 | 20 | 15 | 2.77 | 1.04 | 19.62 |
| **12/03** | 47.57 | 26 | 15 | 1.90 | 0.98 | 17.71 |
| **12/02** | 37.50 | 30 | 19 | 1.66 | 0.94 | 16.71 |
| **Annual Growth** | 24.4% | — | — | 29.6% | 12.0% | (3.8%) |

# Wachovia Corporation

Wachovia is cooking up a stir-fry of financial services. Formed in 2001 when East Coast banking heavyweight First Union bought venerable Wachovia (the "ch" is pronounced "k") and took the smaller firm's name, the company is the #4 US bank behind Citigroup, Bank of America, and JPMorgan Chase. It has some 3,400 branches in around 20 eastern and southern states, as well as California; retail brokerage Wachovia Securities has 750 offices across the US. Subsidiary Evergreen Investment Management offers mutual funds. Other services include capital and wealth management and corporate banking. Wachovia's 2006 acquisition of Golden West Financial strengthened its core markets and added 255 branches to its network.

The merger gives Wachovia a combined $669 billion in assets and serves customers in 21 states and Washington, DC. Wachovia will retain Golden West's mortgage brand World Savings Bank.

Even as Wachovia bought Golden West, whose raison d'etre was adjustable rate mortgages, the housing bust hit many lenders hard. In response, Wachovia has been exiting the subprime and nonconforming loan market as fast as it can. It sold its HomEq loan division to Barclays Bank in 2006. Its AmNet division halted all subprime activity that year, and in 2007 Wachovia dissolved its EquiBanc nonconforming loan operations.

Wachovia melded investment bank and retail brokerage subsidiaries First Union Securities and IJL Wachovia into a third unit, Wachovia Securities, which operates nationwide. The subsidiary joined forces with Prudential Financial to form a brokerage joint venture with nearly 700 offices. Wachovia owns more than 60% of the combined entity, which bears the Wachovia Securities name.

Wachovia beefed up its insurance operations by purchasing Palmer & Cay, an agency with some 35 branches in the East and Midwest. The deal helped make subsidiary Wachovia Insurance Services among the top 10 insurance brokerages in the US. In 2007 it agreed to buy brokerage chain A.G. Edwards, Inc. Wachovia will add its brokerage business, Wachovia Securities, to the A.G. Edwards operations, creating a 3,300-office chain with some $1 trillion in assets under management.

In 2006 Wachovia ended its correspondent banking relationship with Lebanon bank Middle East and Africa Bank because of the bank's possible ties with terrorist organization Hezbollah.

## HISTORY

In 1753 Lord Granville, an English nobleman owning vast tracts of North Carolina, invited a group of Moravian religious dissenters to settle his land. They chose an area reminiscent of a scenic part of Saxony near the Wach River, the Latinized name of which was Wachovia.

The immigrants called their settlement Salem and prospered until the Civil War, which sank the South's economy and destroyed much of North Carolina's small banking system. In 1866 Israel Lash formed the First National Bank of Salem, and in 1879 his nephew William Lemly moved the bank to Winston, which had become a tobacco, textile, and furniture center. The move required a new charter and a new name: Wachovia National Bank. One of its earliest and best customers, R.J. Reynolds Tobacco, supported Wachovia for decades.

In 1968 the bank formed holding company Wachovia Corporation and expanded within North Carolina in the 1970s.

Within hours of a 1985 US Supreme Court ruling allowing regional interstate banking, Wachovia began merger negotiations with First Atlanta, parent of the First National Bank of Atlanta (founded in 1865 by Alfred Austell, a friend of President Andrew Johnson). Within six months the companies had become First Wachovia. (In 1991, after buying South Carolina National Bank, the firm changed its name back to Wachovia Corporation.)

Wachovia's conservative lending policies insulated it from the recession of the late 1980s and early 1990s. In 1997 the firm formed a global banking services division.

Wachovia crossed the Mason-Dixon line in 1999 with the purchase of New York trust bank OFFITBANK Holdings. In 2001 it sold its consumer credit card portfolio to BANK ONE.

First Union traces its roots to the Union National Bank of Charlotte, North Carolina, formed in 1908. After acquiring First National Bank & Trust, of Asheville, it changed its name to First Union National Bank of North Carolina in 1958. In 1967 the bank formed a holding company, First Union National Bancorp, which was renamed First Union Corporation in 1975.

Led by Edward Crutchfield, who became president in 1988, the bank's acquisition strategy (partly spurred by its rivalry with crosstown competitor NationsBank, now Bank of America) made it a powerhouse.

In 1991 First Union bought the failed Southeast Banks from the FDIC. The bank assimilated more than 10 banks between 1993 and 1996; one of its largest trophies was First Fidelity. In 1998 the company bought brokerage Wheat First Butcher Singer and mergers and acquisitions adviser Bowles Hollowell Conner & Co.

The 1998 purchase of CoreStates Financial added more than 500 branches on the East Coast (at the time it was the largest bank merger in history). However, it was a rocky assimilation. The company laid off 7,000 employees, and customers were hit with a slew of new fees.

Illness prompted Crutchfield to step down as CEO in 2000 and he retired as chairman in 2001. That year First Union bought Wachovia after a contentious proxy fight with SunTrust, which made an unsolicited bid for Wachovia. In a shareholder vote Wachovia eventually chose First Union, which changed its name to that of the bank it acquired.

In 2004 Wachovia moved deeper into the South with its $14.3 billion purchase of SouthTrust. That year, it fell short in a bid to acquire credit card giant MBNA, which was bought by crosstown rival Bank of America. In response to that deal, Wachovia said it would issue its own credit cards; MBNA had handled that duty since 2000.

Wachovia's acquisition of Golden West Financial was its biggest deal of the decade thus far. The deal gave Wachovia access to Golden West's bread and butter — residential mortgage loans — just as the housing bubble of previous years burst, sending shock waves through the economy.

## EXECUTIVES

**Chairman, President, and CEO:** G. Kennedy (Ken) Thompson, age 56, $6,090,000 pay
**Vice Chairman and President, General Bank:** Benjamin P. (Ben) Jenkins III, age 63, $3,942,000 pay
**CFO and Head of Finance:** Thomas J. (Tom) Wurtz, age 45
**COO, Finance:** David Julian, age 45
**SEVP; President, Capital Management Group:** David M. Carroll, age 50, $2,642,000 pay
**SEVP; President, Wachovia Wealth Management:** Stanhope A. (Stan) Kelly, age 49
**SEVP, General Counsel, and Secretary:** Mark C. Treanor, age 60
**SEVP and Chief Risk Officer:** Donald K. (Don) Truslow, age 49
**EVP and Chief Marketing Officer:** James (Jim) Garrity
**EVP, Human Resources:** Sharon Smart
**EVP and Co-Head, Merger Integration; President, Wachovia Card Services:** Steven G. Boehm
**SVP, Corporate Communications:** Ginny Mackin
**SVP, Marketing:** Gary Bargeron
**Head of Corporate and Investment Bank:** Stephen E. (Steve) Cummings, age 52
**Head Human Resources and Corporate Relations:** Shannon W. McFayden, age 46
**Head Retail Bank:** Cecelia S. (Cece) Sutton, age 49
**Head of Global Markets and Investment Banking:** Benjamin F. (Ben) Williams Jr., age 45
**Head, General Bank Distribution:** Jon Witter
**Head, Investor Relations:** Alice L. Lehman, age 59
**President and CEO, Wachovia Securities, LLC:** Daniel J. (Danny) Ludeman, age 50
**Corporate CIO:** Martin Davis
**Corporate Treasurer:** James F. (Jim) Burr
**Controller and Principal Accounting Officer:** Peter M. (Pete) Carlson, age 43
**Auditors:** KPMG LLP

## LOCATIONS

**HQ:** Wachovia Corporation
1 Wachovia Center, Charlotte, NC 28288
**Phone:** 704-374-6565 **Fax:** 704-374-3425
**Web:** www.wachovia.com

## PRODUCTS/OPERATIONS

### 2006 Sales

| | $ mil. | % of total |
|---|---|---|
| Interest | | |
| Interest & fees on loans | 21,976 | 47 |
| Interest & dividends on securities | 6,433 | 14 |
| Trading account interest | 1,575 | 3 |
| Other interest income | 2,281 | 5 |
| Noninterest | | |
| Fiduciary & asset management fees | 3,248 | 7 |
| Service charges | 2,480 | 5 |
| Commissions | 2,406 | 5 |
| Other fees | 3,101 | 7 |
| Other | 3,310 | 7 |
| **Total** | **46,810** | **100** |

### 2006 Assets

| | $ mil. | % of total |
|---|---|---|
| Cash & equivalents | 34,916 | 5 |
| Trading account | 45,529 | 7 |
| Securities | 108,619 | 16 |
| Net loans | 416,798 | 60 |
| Loans held for sale | 12,568 | 2 |
| Other assets | 88,691 | 10 |
| **Total** | **707,121** | **100** |

## COMPETITORS

Bank of America
Bank of New York Mellon
BB&T
Charles Schwab
Citigroup
Citizens Financial Group
JPMorgan Chase
Merrill Lynch
PNC Financial
Regions Financial
SunTrust
Washington Mutual
Wells Fargo

## HISTORICAL FINANCIALS

Company Type: Public

### Income Statement

FYE: December 31

| | ASSETS ($ mil.) | NET INCOME ($ mil.) | INCOME AS % OF ASSETS | EMPLOYEES |
|---|---|---|---|---|
| **12/06** | 707,121 | 7,791 | 1.1% | 108,238 |
| **12/05** | 520,755 | 6,643 | 1.3% | 93,980 |
| **12/04** | 493,324 | 5,214 | 1.1% | 96,030 |
| **12/03** | 401,032 | 4,264 | 1.1% | 86,670 |
| **12/02** | 341,839 | 3,579 | 1.0% | 80,778 |
| **Annual Growth** | 19.9% | 21.5% | — | 7.6% |

### 2006 Year-End Financials

Equity as % of assets: 9.9%
Return on assets: 1.3%
Return on equity: 13.3%
Long-term debt ($ mil.): 148,617
No. of shares (mil.): 1,904
Dividends
Yield: 3.8%
Payout: 46.2%
Market value ($ mil.): 108,433
Sales ($ mil.): 46,810

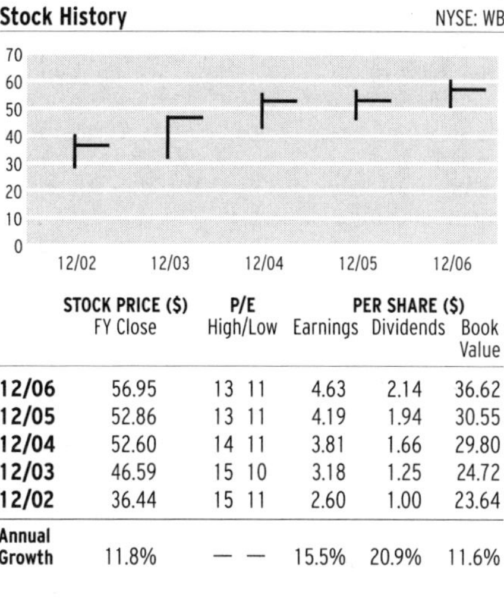


| | STOCK PRICE ($) FY Close | P/E High/Low | | PER SHARE ($) Earnings | Dividends | Book Value |
|---|---|---|---|---|---|---|
| **12/06** | 56.95 | 13 | 11 | 4.63 | 2.14 | 36.62 |
| **12/05** | 52.86 | 13 | 11 | 4.19 | 1.94 | 30.55 |
| **12/04** | 52.60 | 14 | 11 | 3.81 | 1.66 | 29.80 |
| **12/03** | 46.59 | 15 | 10 | 3.18 | 1.25 | 24.72 |
| **12/02** | 36.44 | 15 | 11 | 2.60 | 1.00 | 23.64 |
| **Annual Growth** | 11.8% | — | — | 15.5% | 20.9% | 11.6% |

# Wakefern Food

Started by seven men who each invested $1,000, Wakefern Food has grown into the largest retailer-owned supermarket cooperative in the US. The co-op is now owned by 40-plus independent grocers who operate nearly 200 ShopRite supermarkets in five eastern states, including New Jersey (where it is a leading chain). More than half of ShopRite stores offer pharmacies. In addition to name-brand and private-label products (ShopRite, Chef's Express, Readington Farms), Wakefern supports its members with advertising, merchandising, insurance, and other services. Wakefern's ShopRite Supermarkets subsidiary acquired the assets of Florida-based Big V Supermarkets, which filed for bankruptcy in 2000.

The cooperative provides members and other customers with more than 20,000 name-brand items, including groceries, dairy and meat products, produce, frozen foods, and general merchandise. It also sells more than 3,000 items under the ShopRite label. All members are given one vote in the co-op, regardless of size.

Wakefern is moving its distribution operations from its facility in Wallkill, New York to Allentown, Pennsylvania after failing to reach an agreement with labor there on a new contract.

## HISTORY

Wakefern Food was founded in 1946 by seven New York- and New Jersey-based grocers: Louis Weiss, Sam and Al Aidekman, Abe Kesselman, Dave Fern, Sam Garb, and Albert Goldberg (the company's name is made up of the letters of the first five of those founders). Like many cooperatives, the association sought to lower costs by increasing its buying power as a group.

They each put in $1,000 and began operating a 5,000-sq.-ft. warehouse, often putting in double time to keep both their stores and the warehouse running. The shopkeepers' collective buying power proved valuable, enabling the grocers to stock many items at the same prices as their larger competitors.

In 1951 Wakefern members began pooling their resources to buy advertising space. A common store name — ShopRite — was chosen, and each week co-op members met to decide which items would be sale priced. Within a year, membership had grown to over 50. Expansion became a priority, and in the mid-1950s co-op members united in small groups to take over failed supermarkets. One such group, called the Supermarkets Operating Co. (SOC), was formed in 1956. Within 10 years it had acquired a number of failed stores, remodeled them, and given them the ShopRite name.

During the late 1950s sales at ShopRite stores slumped after Wakefern decided to buck the supermarket trend of offering trading stamps (which could then be exchanged for gifts), figuring that offering the stamps would ultimately lead to higher food prices. The move initially drove away customers, but Wakefern cut grocery prices across the board and sales returned. The company also embraced another supermarket trend: stocking stores with nonfood items.

The co-op was severely shaken in 1966 when SOC merged with General Supermarkets, a similar small group within Wakefern, becoming Supermarkets General Corp. (SGC). SGC was a powerful entity, with 71 supermarkets, 10 drugstores, six gas stations, a wholesale bakery, and a discount department store. Many Wakefern members opposed the merger and attempted to block the action with a court order. By 1968 SGC had beefed up its operations to include department store chains as well as its grocery stores. In a move that threatened to break Wakefern, SGC broke away from the co-op, and its stores were renamed Pathmark.

Wakefern not only weathered the storm, it grew under the direction of chairman and CEO Thomas Infusino, elected shortly after the split. The co-op focused on asserting its position as a seller of low-priced products. Wakefern developed private-label brands, including the ShopRite brand. In the 1980s members began operating larger stores and adding more nonfood items to the ShopRite product mix. With its number of superstores on the rise and facing increased competition from club stores in 1992, Wakefern opened a centralized, nonfood distribution center in New Jersey.

In 1995, 30-year Wakefern veteran Dean Janeway was elected president of the co-op. The company debuted its ShopRite MasterCard, co-branded with New Jersey's Valley National Bank, in 1996. The following year the co-op purchased two of its customers' stores in Pennsylvania, then threatened to close them when contract talks with the local union deteriorated. In 1998 Wakefern settled the dispute, then sold the stores.

The company partnered with Internet bidding site priceline.com in 1999, offering customers an opportunity to bid on groceries and then pick them up at ShopRite stores. Big V, Wakefern's biggest customer, filed for Chapter 11 bankruptcy protection in 2000 and said it was ending its distribution agreement with the co-op. In July 2002, however, Wakefern's ShopRite Supermarkets subsidiary acquired all of Big V's assets for approximately $185 million in cash and assumed liabilities.

Infusino retired in May 2005 after 35 years with Wakefern Food. He was succeeded by former vice chairman Joseph Colalillo.

## EXECUTIVES

**Chairman and CEO:** Joseph Colalillo
**President and COO:** Dean Janeway
**CFO:** Ken Jasinkiewicz
**EVP, Marketing:** Joseph Sheridan
**SVP and CIO:** Natan Tabak
**VP, Corporate and Consumer Affairs:** Mary Ellen Gowin
**VP, Human Resources:** Ernie Bell
**VP, Corporate Merchandising and Advertising:** Bill Crombie
**VP, Information Services Division:** Alan Aront
**President and COO, ShopRite Supermarkets:** Kevin Mannix
**Director, Advertising:** Karen McAuvic
**Director, Marketing:** Loren Weinstein
**Director, Communications:** Karen Meleta
**Manager, Consumer Affairs:** Cheryl Macik

## LOCATIONS

**HQ:** Wakefern Food Corporation
600 York St., Elizabeth, NJ 07207
**Phone:** 908-527-3300 **Fax:** 908-527-3397
**Web:** www.shoprite.com

## PRODUCTS/OPERATIONS

### Major Members

Foodarama Supermarkets
Inserra Supermarkets
Village Super Market

### Selected Private Labels

Black Bear (deli items)
Chef's Express
Reddington Farms (poultry)
ShopRite

## COMPETITORS

A&P
C&S Wholesale
Di Giorgio
IGA
King Kullen Grocery
Kings Super Markets
Krasdale Foods
Pathmark
Royal Ahold
Stop & Shop
SUPERVALU
Wal-Mart
White Rose Food

## HISTORICAL FINANCIALS

Company Type: Cooperative

**Income Statement** FYE: September 30

| | REVENUE ($ mil.) | NET INCOME ($ mil.) | NET PROFIT MARGIN | EMPLOYEES |
|---|---|---|---|---|
| 9/06 | 7,500 | — | — | 50,000 |
| 9/05 | 7,239 | — | — | 50,000 |
| 9/04 | 7,116 | — | — | 50,000 |
| 9/03 | 6,578 | — | — | 50,000 |
| 9/02 | 6,208 | — | — | 50,000 |
| Annual Growth | 4.8% | — | — | 0.0% |

**Revenue History**

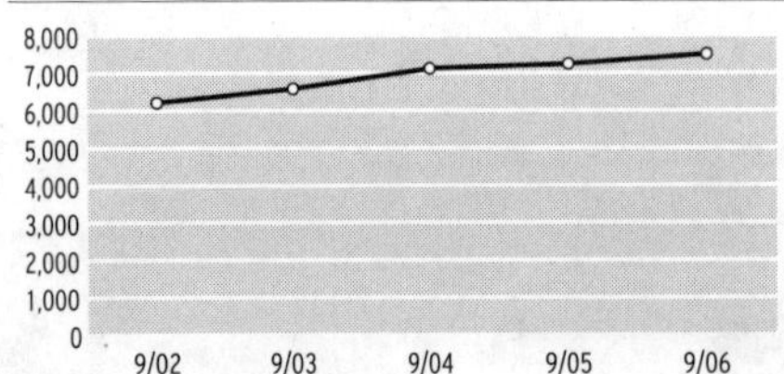


# Walgreen Co.

Walgreen offers an old-fashioned tonic for fiscal fitness: quality over quantity and homespun growth rather than growth through acquisitions. It works. While Walgreen has fewer stores than its closest rival CVS, it is #1 in the nation in sales. Walgreen operates some 5,700 stores in 48 states and Puerto Rico, and has three mail order facilities. Prescription drugs account for about 65% of sales; the rest comes from general merchandise, over-the-counter medications, cosmetics, and groceries. Walgreen usually builds rather than buys stores, so it can pick prime locations.

With more prescription drug business going to managed-care health plans, convenience has trumped price in the race to attract new customers. (Co-pays are the same at any chain, and sick folks are often short on patience.) Walgreen has led the movement in creating a "convenience drugstore" chain with freestanding stores. The strategy has several advantages. Walgreen's freestanding stores are more visible than those in strip malls and offer shoppers ample parking and easy in-and-out access.

Stung by the move by some employers to mail-order prescription services, Walgreen has been expanding its own mail-order business from about $1.4 billion in annual sales to more than $5 billion.

Walgreen also provides additional services to pharmacy patients and prescription drug and medical plans through Walgreens Health Services. The company's Walgreens Health Initiatives subsidiary offers specialty pharmacy, mail-order pharmacy, and pharmacy benefits management services. To boost prescription sales and foster customer loyalty, Walgreen is partnering with Take Care Health Systems to open Health Corner Clinics inside its stores. (In May Walgreen acquired the in-store health clinic operator in an all-cash deal.) As a result of the acquisition of Take Care Health Systems, Walgreen expects to have more than 400 clinics within its stores by the end of 2008 (up from about 60 currently). The clinics are staffed by nurse practitioners.

While Walgreen follows a long-held strategy of building new stores rather than acquiring others, it has made several exceptions in recent years. Most recently, it agreed to acquire 53 pharmacies and other assets from Familymeds Group, for about $60 million. To quickly establish a presence in and around Delaware, Walgreen acquired the Happy Harry's regional drugstore chain in mid-2006. (Happy Harry's operates about 75 stores in Delaware, Maryland, New Jersey, and Pennsylvania.) Walgreen has also agreed to acquire Illinois-based Option Care, a specialty pharmacy and home infusion provider with more than 100 stores in 34 states.

## HISTORY

In 1901 Chicago pharmacist Charles Walgreen borrowed $2,000 from his father for a down payment on his first drugstore. He sold a half interest in his first store in 1909 and bought a second, where he installed a large soda fountain and began serving lunch. In 1916 seven stores consolidated under the corporate name Walgreen Co. By 1920 there were 20 stores in Chicago, with sales of $1.55 million.

Walgreen popularized the milk shake in the early 1920s, and he promoted his chain with the first company-owned-and-operated airplane. The firm was first listed on the NYSE in 1927; two years later its 397 stores in 87 cities had sales of $47 million.

The company did comparatively well during the Great Depression. Although average sales per store dropped between 1931 and 1935, per-store earnings went up, thanks to a chainwide emphasis on efficiency. By 1940 Walgreen had 489 stores, but the chain shrank during WWII when unprofitable stores were closed.

The 1950s saw a major change in the way drugstores did business. Walgreen was an early leader in self-service merchandising, opening its first self-serve store in 1952; it had 22 by the end of 1953. Between 1950 and 1960, as small, older stores were replaced with larger, more efficient, self-service units, the total number of stores in the chain increased only about 10%, but sales grew by more than 90%.

By 1960 Walgreen had 451 stores, half of which were self-service. The company bought three Globe discount department stores in Houston in 1962 and expanded the chain to 13 stores by 1966, but Globe struggled in the early 1970s and was sold in 1975. During the 1960s Walgreen began phasing out its soda fountains, which had become unprofitable.

The 1970s and 1980s brought rapid growth and modernization to the chain. The company opened its 1,000th store in 1984. Two years later Walgreen acquired 66 Medi Mart drugstores in five northeastern states (its last major acquisition).

Walgreen began its Healthcare Plus subsidiary in 1992 to provide prescriptions by mail. Along with other independent drugstores, it helped set up Pharmacy Direct Network in 1994 to manage prescription drug programs for group health plans. In 1995 Walgreen launched a prescription benefits management company, WHP Health Initiatives, to target small to medium-sized employers and HMOs in the top 28 Walgreen markets. President (and pharmacist) L. Daniel Jorndt was promoted to CEO in early 1998 after the founder's grandson, Charles Walgreen III, stepped down; Jorndt became chairman in 1999. The company opened a full-service pharmacy online in 1999.

Jorndt retired in January 2003. CEO David Bernauer added chairman to his job description. In its first significant acquisition in nearly 20 years, Walgreen agreed to buy 16 drugstores in the Portland, Oregon, and Vancouver, Washington, metro areas from privately held Hi-School Pharmacy in 2003.

In April 2006 Walgreens Home Care acquired Oklahoma City-based Canadian Valley Medical Solutions, a provider of home care services to patients in central and western Oklahoma. In mid-July Bernauer turned the CEO title over to company president Jeffrey Rein. Bernauer retained the chairman's title. In August Walgreen bought Pittsburgh-based Medmark Specialty Pharmacy Solutions to expand its chronic illness treatment business.

In 2007 Charles R. Walgreen, Jr. — son of the company's founder — died at the age of 100. In July Bernauer retired as chairman and was succeeded by Rein. Also in July the company agreed to pay $20 million to settle a class-action lawsuit filed in March 2007 by the US Equal Employment Opportunity Commission alleging that Walgreen discriminated against thousands of its black employees.

## EXECUTIVES

**Chairman Emeritus:** Charles R. Walgreen III, age 71
**Chairman and CEO:** Jeffrey A. Rein, age 55
**EVP; President, Walgreens Health Services:** Trent E. Taylor, age 49
**EVP, Marketing:** George J. Riedl, age 46, $645,300 pay
**EVP, Store Operations:** Mark A. Wagner, age 45
**President and COO:** Gregory D. (Greg) Wasson, age 48
**SVP and CFO:** William M. Rudolphsen, age 51
**SVP and Chief Strategy Officer:** John W. Gleeson, age 60
**SVP, Store Operations:** R. Bruce Bryant, age 56
**SVP, General Counsel, and Secretary:** Dana I. Green, age 55
**SVP, Eastern Store Operations:** William M. (Bill) Handal, age 57
**SVP, Store Operations:** Kevin P. Walgreen, age 45
**SVP, Pharmacy Services:** Donald C. (Don) Huonker, age 46
**SVP, Human Resources:** Kenneth R. (Ken) Weigand, age 49
**VP; Chief Administration and Finance Officer, Walgreens Health Initiatives:** Robert G. (Bob) Zimmerman, age 54
**VP; President, Medmark; SVP, Specialty Pharmacy and Home Care, Walgreens Health Services:** Stanley B. Blaylock
**VP and CIO:** Denise K. Wong, age 49
**Divisional VP, Marketing Development:** Catherine Lindner, age 39
**Divisional VP and General Auditor:** Chester G. Young, age 61
**Divisional VP and General Manager, Beauty and Fashion:** Katherine W. (Kathy) Steirly, age 55
**Divisional VP, Government and Community Relations:** Debra B. Garza, age 38
**Controller:** Mia M. Scholz, age 40
**Director of Finance and Assistant Treasurer:** Rick J. Hans
**Auditors:** Deloitte & Touche LLP

## LOCATIONS

**HQ:** Walgreen Co.
200 Wilmot Rd., Deerfield, IL 60015
**Phone:** 847-914-2500 **Fax:** 847-914-2804
**Web:** www.walgreens.com

### 2006 Stores

| | No. |
|---|---|
| Florida | 697 |
| Texas | 550 |
| Illinois | 511 |
| California | 438 |
| Arizona | 229 |
| Tennessee | 199 |
| Ohio | 198 |
| Wisconsin | 185 |
| Michigan | 174 |
| Indiana | 167 |
| Missouri | 152 |
| Colorado | 113 |
| Georgia | 111 |
| Massachusetts | 111 |
| Minnesota | 103 |
| Louisiana | 99 |
| Washington | 95 |
| North Carolina | 91 |
| New Jersey | 90 |
| New York | 84 |
| Oklahoma | 75 |
| Kentucky | 65 |
| Pennsylvania | 65 |
| Connecticut | 59 |
| Delaware | 59 |
| Nevada | 59 |
| Alabama | 56 |
| Virginia | 56 |
| Iowa | 55 |
| New Mexico | 53 |
| South Carolina | 52 |
| Kansas | 50 |
| Other states | 301 |
| Puerto Rico | 69 |
| **Total** | **5,461** |

## PRODUCTS/OPERATIONS

### 2006 Sales

| | % of total |
|---|---|
| Prescription drugs | 64 |
| General merchandise | 25 |
| Nonprescription drugs | 11 |
| **Total** | **100** |

## COMPETITORS

7-Eleven
99 Cents Only
A&P
Albertsons
Caremark
Costco Wholesale
CVS/Caremark
Dollar General
drugstore.com
Duane Reade
Express Scripts
Family Dollar Stores
Food Lion
GNC
H-E-B
Kerr Drug
Kmart
Kroger
Longs Drug
Medicine Shoppe
Meijer
Nutritional Sourcing
Publix
Randall's
Rite Aid
Ritz Camera Centers
Safeway
Smith's Food & Drug
Snyder's Drug Stores
SUPERVALU
Target
Wal-Mart
Winn-Dixie

## HISTORICAL FINANCIALS

Company Type: Public

### Income Statement

FYE: August 31

| | REVENUE ($ mil.) | NET INCOME ($ mil.) | NET PROFIT MARGIN | EMPLOYEES |
|---|---|---|---|---|
| **8/06** | 47,409 | 1,751 | 3.7% | 195,000 |
| **8/05** | 42,202 | 1,560 | 3.7% | 179,000 |
| **8/04** | 37,508 | 1,350 | 3.6% | 163,000 |
| **8/03** | 32,505 | 1,176 | 3.6% | 154,000 |
| **8/02** | 28,681 | 1,019 | 3.6% | 141,000 |
| **Annual Growth** | 13.4% | 14.5% | — | 8.4% |

### 2006 Year-End Financials

Debt ratio: —
Return on equity: 18.4%
Cash ($ mil.): 1,335
Current ratio: 1.69
Long-term debt ($ mil.): —
No. of shares (mil.): 1,008
Dividends
Yield: 0.6%
Payout: 15.7%
Market value ($ mil.): 49,849

### Stock History

NYSE: WAG

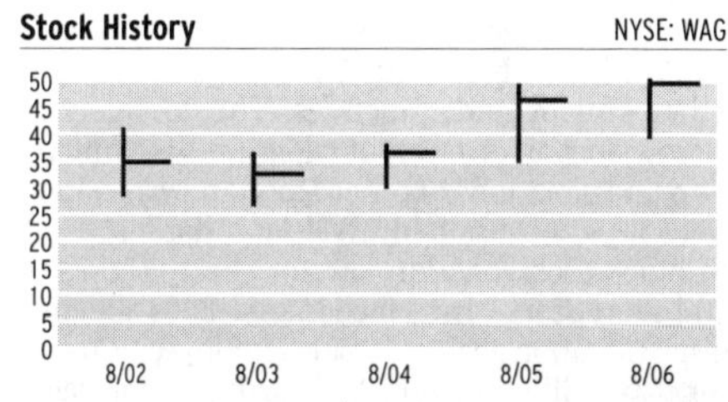


| | STOCK PRICE ($) FY Close | P/E High | P/E Low | PER SHARE ($) Earnings | Dividends | Book Value |
|---|---|---|---|---|---|---|
| **8/06** | 49.46 | 29 | 23 | 1.72 | 0.27 | 10.04 |
| **8/05** | 46.33 | 32 | 23 | 1.52 | 0.22 | 8.77 |
| **8/04** | 36.45 | 29 | 23 | 1.31 | 0.18 | 7.95 |
| **8/03** | 32.57 | 32 | 24 | 1.14 | 0.16 | 7.02 |
| **8/02** | 34.75 | 41 | 29 | 0.99 | 0.14 | 6.08 |
| **Annual Growth** | 9.2% | — | — | 14.8% | 17.8% | 13.4% |

# Wal-Mart Stores

Wal-Mart Stores is an irresistible (or at least unavoidable) retail force that has yet to meet any immovable objects. Bigger than Europe's Carrefour, Tesco, and Metro AG combined, it is the world's #1 retailer, with about 6,775 stores, including some 1,075 discount stores, 2,250 combination discount and grocery stores (Wal-Mart Supercenters in the US and ASDA in the UK), and 580 warehouse stores (SAM'S CLUB). About 60% of its stores are in the US, but Wal-Mart is expanding internationally; it is the #1 retailer in Canada and Mexico. It owns a majority stake in Japanese retailer SEIYU. Wal-Mart also has operations in Asia, Europe, and South America. Founder Sam Walton's heirs own about 40% of Wal-Mart.

The company, which employs some 1.8 million people worldwide, is famous for its low prices and breadth of merchandise. Another part of the retailing leviathan's appeal is its efforts to promote a small-town flavor, with friendly greeters and patriotic trappings. The chain doesn't just compete in discount staples such as food and clothing — it is a force in many other categories including electronics, health and beauty products, sporting goods, entertainment (CDs, DVDs, and videos), and toys. Its prescription drug sales at its more than 3,000 pharmacies make it North America's #3 pharmacy operator (behind Walgreen and CVS).

In a rare retreat, the über retailer has made plans to withdraw its application to enter the banking sector, particularly due to processing delays and controversy surrounding its efforts. However, Wal-Mart plans to open 1,000 in-store MoneyCenters, offering check cashing and bill paying services, by the end of 2008.

Wal-Mart holds a majority stake in Wal-Mart de México. The company also has stores in Asia, Europe, and South America. Currently, Wal-Mart has more than 70 stores in China, mostly hypermarkets, where it has teamed up with Hong Kong-based CITIC Pacific Co. to open hundreds of stores. (Wal-Mart imports about $15 billion in goods annually from China.)

The US's largest private employer has become a lightning rod for criticism of its benefits and other employment practices. The company is facing dozens of lawsuits alleging discrimination and violations of other labor and wage-and-hour laws. Most notably, Wal-Mart has lost a bid to block a class action lawsuit (Betty Dukes v. Wal-Mart Stores, Inc.) filed in mid-2004 alleging discrimination against female employees. Covering 1.6 million current and former employees, Dukes v. Wal-Mart ranks as the largest workplace-bias lawsuit in US history. In September a labor group filed a class-action lawsuit on behalf of employees for Wal-Mart contractors in Bangladesh, China, and Nicaragua, among other countries, accusing the company of allowing sweatshop conditions at overseas factories.

Stung by criticism, Wal-Mart is raising starting salaries by about 6% at some stores and expanding health care coverage via a new, cheaper health insurance plan.

Following the death of Helen Robson Walton in April 2007, the Walton family announced that much of the Wal-Mart stock held by Mrs. Walton will be donated to charity. As a result, the Walton family's grip on the world's largest retailer will slip to about 33%, following the disposition of Mrs. Walton's 8.1% stake.

## HISTORY

Sam Walton began his retail career as a J. C. Penney management trainee and later leased a Ben Franklin-franchised dime store in Newport, Arkansas, in 1945. In 1950 he relocated to Bentonville, Arkansas, and opened a Walton 5 & 10. By 1962 Walton owned 15 Ben Franklin stores under the Walton 5 & 10 name.

After Ben Franklin management rejected his suggestion to open discount stores in small towns, Walton, with his brother James "Bud" Walton, opened the first Wal-Mart Discount City in Rogers, Arkansas, in 1962. Wal-Mart Stores went public in 1970 with 18 stores and sales of $44 million.

Avoiding regional retailers, Walton opened stores in small and midsized towns in the 1970s. The company sold its Ben Franklin stores in 1976. By 1980 Wal-Mart's 276 stores had sales of $1.2 billion.

In 1983 Wal-Mart opened SAM'S Wholesale Club, a concept based on the successful cash-and-carry, membership-only warehouse format pioneered by the Price Company of California (now Costco Wholesale Corp.). The company started Hypermart*USA in 1987 as a joint venture with Dallas-based supermarket chain Cullum Companies (now Randall's Food Markets). The 200,000-sq.-ft. discount store/supermarket hybrid was later retooled as Wal-Mart Supercenters. Sam stepped down as CEO in 1988 and president David Glass was appointed CEO. Wal-Mart bought out Cullum the next year.

In 1992, the year Sam died, the company expanded into Mexico through a joint venture to open SAM'S CLUBS with Mexico's largest retailer Cifra (renamed Wal-Mart de México in 2000). Co-founder Bud died in 1995.

In 1999 Wal-Mart bought 74 German-based Interspar hypermarkets and acquired ASDA Group, the UK's third-largest supermarket chain. COO Lee Scott succeeded Glass as CEO in 2000; Glass stayed on as chairman of the executive committee. In June 2001 a group of six current and former female Wal-Mart employees filed a sex-discrimination lawsuit (seeking to represent up to 500,000 current and former Wal-Mart workers) against the company.

In April 2002 the company was crowned America's largest corporation by *FORTUNE* magazine.

In February 2004, a federal judge ruled that Wal-Mart should pay workers for overtime hours. The complaint was brought by plaintiffs who said they were forced to work unpaid overtime between 1994 and 1999.

Vice chairman Tom Coughlin resigned following an internal investigation related to "the alleged unauthorized use of corporate-owned gift cards and personal reimbursements." The company rescinded Coughlin's retirement agreement, including stock awards and incentive payments. (He pleaded guilty to fraud and tax charges in January 2006 and was sentenced to 27 months of house arrest.)

In 2005 the retailer settled a high-profile lawsuit by agreeing to pay $11 million to the US government to close an investigation into the use of illegal immigrants by Wal-Mart contractors to clean its stores.

Wal-Mart itself was ordered by a Pennsylvania jury to pay more than $78 million in damages in a class action suit brought by employees alleging that the company forced employees to work during breaks and off the clock.

In early 2007 Wal-Mart agreed to pay $33.5 million in back wages and interest to settle a federal lawsuit that accused the company of violating ovetime laws involving more than 86,000 employees.

## EXECUTIVES

**Chairman:** S. Robson (Rob) Walton, age 62
**President, CEO, and Director:** H. Lee Scott Jr., age 58, $1,300,000 pay
**Vice Chairman, International Division:** Michael Terry (Mike) Duke, age 57, $1,300,000 pay
**Vice Chairman and Chief Administrative Officer:** John B. Menzer, age 56, $1,000,000 pay
**COO:** William S. (Bill) Simon, age 45
**EVP and CFO:** Thomas M. (Tom) Schoewe, age 54, $700,385 pay
**EVP and CIO:** Rollin Lee Ford
**EVP and Chief Merchandising Officer:** John E. Fleming, age 46
**EVP and Chief Marketing Officer:** Stephen F. Quinn
**EVP and Corporate Secretary:** Thomas D. Hyde, age 58
**EVP, Finance and Treasurer:** Charles M. Holley Jr., age 49
**EVP, Food, Consumables and Hardlines Merchandising, Wal-Mart Stores Division U.S.:** Douglas J. (Doug) Degn, age 44
**EVP, Corporate Affairs and Government Relations:** Leslie A. Dach, age 52
**EVP, Logistics and Supply Chain:** Johnnie C. Dobbs
**EVP, People Division:** M. Susan Chambers, age 49
**EVP, Risk Management and Benefits Administration:** Linda Marie Dillman, age 46
**EVP, People:** Patricia A. (Pat) Curran
**EVP, Wal-Mart Realty:** Eric S. Zorn
**EVP; President and CEO, The Americas, Wal-Mart International:** Craig R. Herkert
**EVP; President and CEO, SAM'S CLUB:** C. Douglas (Doug) McMillon, age 40
**EVP; President and CEO, Wal-Mart Stores Division U.S.:** Eduardo Castro-Wright, age 52, $771,154 pay
**SVP and Controller:** Steven P (Steve) Whaley, age 47
**SVP and General Counsel:** Thomas A. (Tom) Mars, age 43
**SVP and CTO:** Nancy Stewart
**VP, Investor Relations:** Carol A. Schumacher, age 46
**Auditors:** Ernst & Young LLP

## LOCATIONS

**HQ:** Wal-Mart Stores, Inc.
702 SW 8th St., Bentonville, AR 72716
**Phone:** 479-273-4000 **Fax:** 479-277-1830
**Web:** www.walmartstores.com

Wal-Mart Stores operates more than 6,700 outlets in all 50 US states, Puerto Rico, and Argentina, Brazil, Canada, China, Costa Rica, El Salvador, Guatemala, Honduras, Japan, Mexico, Nicaragua, and the UK.

## PRODUCTS/OPERATIONS

### 2007 Stores

| | No. |
|---|---|
| International stores | 2,684 |
| Supercenters | 2,256 |
| Discount stores | 1,075 |
| SAM'S CLUB | 579 |
| Neighborhood Markets | 112 |
| Chinese joint venture stores | 73 |
| **Total** | **6,779** |

### 2007 Sales

| | $ mil. | % of total |
|---|---|---|
| Wal-Mart Stores | 226,294 | 66 |
| International | 77,116 | 22 |
| SAM'S CLUB | 41,582 | 12 |
| Membership & other | 3,658 | — |
| **Total** | **348,650** | **100** |

**2007 Sales**

| | % of total |
|---|---|
| Grocery, candy & tobacco | 31 |
| Hardgoods (hardware, housewares, auto supplies, small appliances) | 18 |
| Softgoods/domestics | 15 |
| Electronics | 10 |
| Pharmaceuticals | 9 |
| Health & beauty aids | 7 |
| Sporting goods & toys | 5 |
| Stationery & books | 2 |
| Jewelry | 1 |
| Photo processing | 1 |
| Shoes | 1 |
| **Total** | **100** |

**Retail Divisions**

ASDA (large, combination general merchandise and food stores)
Neighborhood Markets (traditional supermarkets)
SAM'S CLUB (members-only warehouse clubs)
Supercenters (large, combination general merchandise and food stores)
Wal-Mart International Division (foreign operations)
Wal-Mart Stores (general merchandise)

## COMPETITORS

Ace Hardware
Albertsons
Apple
Army and Air Force Exchange
Aurora Wholesalers
AutoZone
Bed Bath & Beyond
Best Buy
BFS Retail & Commercial
Big Lots
BJ's Wholesale Club
Carrefour
Circuit City
CompUSA
Costco Wholesale
CVS/Caremark
Dollar General
Eby-Brown
Family Dollar Stores
Gap
Home Depot
Hudson's Bay
J. C. Penney
Katz Group
Kmart
Kohl's
Kroger
Lianhua Supermarket
Limited Brands
Loblaw
Longs Drug
Lowe's
Maruetsu
Meijer
METRO AG
Microsoft
Office Depot
Pep Boys
PETCO
Publix
RadioShack
Rite Aid
Royal Ahold
Safeway
Sears
Staples
Target
TJX Companies
Toys "R" Us
True Value
Walgreen

## HISTORICAL FINANCIALS

Company Type: Public

**Income Statement** FYE: January 31

| | REVENUE ($ mil.) | NET INCOME ($ mil.) | NET PROFIT MARGIN | EMPLOYEES |
|---|---|---|---|---|
| **1/07** | 348,650 | 11,284 | 3.2% | 1,900,000 |
| **1/06** | 315,654 | 11,231 | 3.6% | 1,800,000 |
| **1/05** | 287,989 | 10,267 | 3.6% | 1,700,000 |
| **1/04** | 258,681 | 9,054 | 3.5% | 1,500,000 |
| **1/03** | 246,525 | 8,039 | 3.3% | 1,400,000 |
| **Annual Growth** | 9.1% | 8.8% | — | 7.9% |

**2007 Year-End Financials**

Debt ratio: 49.9%
Return on equity: 19.7%
Cash ($ mil.): 7,373
Current ratio: 0.90
Long-term debt ($ mil.): 30,735
No. of shares (mil.): 4,131
Dividends
 Yield: 0.4%
 Payout: 6.3%
Market value ($ mil.): 197,007

**Stock History** NYSE: WMT

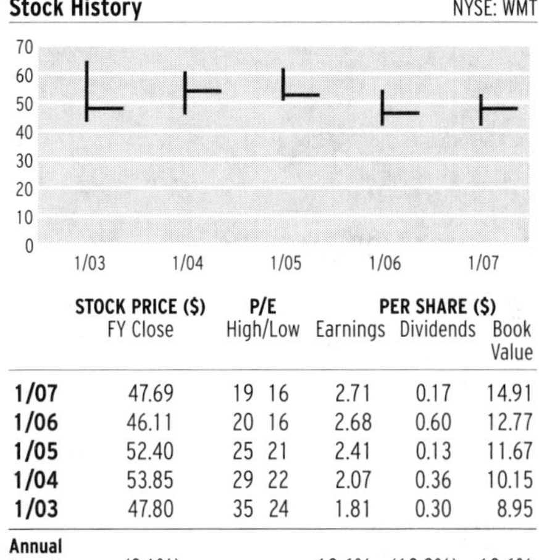


| | STOCK PRICE ($) FY Close | P/E High | P/E Low | PER SHARE ($) Earnings | Dividends | Book Value |
|---|---|---|---|---|---|---|
| **1/07** | 47.69 | 19 | 16 | 2.71 | 0.17 | 14.91 |
| **1/06** | 46.11 | 20 | 16 | 2.68 | 0.60 | 12.77 |
| **1/05** | 52.40 | 25 | 21 | 2.41 | 0.13 | 11.67 |
| **1/04** | 53.85 | 29 | 22 | 2.07 | 0.36 | 10.15 |
| **1/03** | 47.80 | 35 | 24 | 1.81 | 0.30 | 8.95 |
| **Annual Growth** | (0.1%) | — | — | 10.6% | (13.2%) | 13.6% |

# Walt Disney

The monarch of this magic kingdom is no man but a mouse — Mickey Mouse. The Walt Disney Company is the world's #2 media conglomerate (behind Time Warner) with assets encompassing movies, music, publishing, radio, television, and theme parks. Its media networks include the ABC television network and 10 broadcast stations, as well as a portfolio of cable networks, including ABC Family, A&E Television Networks (37%-owned), and ESPN (80%). Its Walt Disney Studios produces films through such imprints as Walt Disney Pictures, Touchstone, Pixar, and Miramax. In addition, Walt Disney Parks & Resorts is one of the top theme park operators in the world, anchored by its popular Walt Disney World and Disneyland resorts.

The company's media networks include ABC, broadcaster of such hit shows such as *Desperate Housewives, Grey's Anatomy*, and *Lost*. On cable, Disney's stalwart ESPN continues to lead the world of sports broadcasting with the addition of *Monday Night Football* to its lineup in 2006.

The company's filmed entertainment division has also been performing well at the box office, due in large part to the popularity of the *Pirates of the Caribbean* franchise. Such films as *The Chronicles of Narnia* and *Cars* from Pixar also contributed to the studio's performance in 2006.

Disney made headlines in 2006 when it acquired computer animation powerhouse Pixar for $7.4 billion. The deal ended a row between the companies over distribution rights that was due largely to bad blood between Pixar and former Disney CEO Michael Eisner. The blockbuster acquisition also made Apple and Pixar CEO Steve Jobs the top shareholder in Disney with a 7% stake.

In addition to its traditional media operations, Disney has been hard at work trying to profit from online and digital media outlets. In 2006 ABC began streaming television shows through its Web site, creating a new platform to promote its shows and generate additional advertising revenue. Disney also struck a landmark deal that year with Apple's iTunes music store to make TV shows and movies available for download. The company's digital media arm, Walt Disney Internet Group, has also been expanding its operations into the social networking realm: In 2007 Disney acquired kid-focused Web site Club Penguin for about $350 million.

The company's theme park operations continue to lead the industry and have rebounded after taking a hit in 2004 and 2005 due to increased hurricane activity. Attendance has been up at both Disney World and Disneyland (which celebrated its 50th anniversary in 2006), thanks in part to new attractions based on hit animated films *Finding Nemo* and *Toy Story*. In addition to its domestic parks, Disney's newest resort in Hong Kong (43%-owned) opened in 2005 and has proven to be a hit among Asian travelers. Disney also collects royalties and fees from Tokyo Disneyland Resort (operated by Oriental Land Co.), and it owns 40% of Euro Disney, which operates Disneyland Paris.

In 2007 Disney moved to focus its broadcasting operations on television, spinning off its portfolio of 22 radio stations and radio syndication unit ABC Radio Network to Citadel Broadcasting for $2.7 billion in cash and stock. The deal left Disney shareholders owning 57% of the combined company.

## HISTORY

After getting started as an illustrator in Kansas City, Walt Disney and his brother Roy started Disney Brothers Studio in Hollywood, California, in 1923. Walt directed the first Mickey Mouse cartoon, *Plane Crazy*, in 1928 (the third, *Steamboat Willie*, was the first cartoon with a soundtrack). The studio produced its first animated feature film, *Snow White and the Seven Dwarfs*, in 1937. Walt Disney Productions went public in 1940 and later produced classics such as *Fantasia* and *Pinocchio*. The Disneyland theme park opened in 1955.

Roy Disney became chairman after Walt died of lung cancer in 1966. Disney World opened in Florida in 1971, the year Roy died. His son, Roy E., became the company's principal individual shareholder. Walt's son-in-law, Ron Miller, became president in 1980. Two years later Epcot Center opened in Florida. In 1984 the Bass family of Texas, in alliance with Roy E., bought a controlling interest in the company. New CEO Michael Eisner (from Paramount) and president Frank Wells (from Warner Bros.) ushered in an era of innovation, prosperity, and high executive salaries. The company later launched The Disney Channel and opened new theme parks, including Tokyo Disneyland (1984) and Disney-MGM Studios (1989). In 1986 the company changed its name to The Walt Disney Company. Disneyland Paris (originally Euro Disney) opened in 1992.

Following Wells' death in a helicopter crash in 1994, boardroom infighting led to the acrimonious departure of studio head Jeffrey Katzenberg. (He was awarded $250 million in compensation in 1999.) The next year Eisner appointed Hollywood agent Michael Ovitz as president. (Ovitz left after 16 months with a severance package of more than $100 million.) Disney bought Capital Cities/ABC (now ABC, Inc.) for $19 billion in 1996.

In early 2000 ABC chairman Robert Iger was named Disney's president and COO. In 2001 the company expanded its theme parks in Anaheim, opening Downtown Disney and Disney's California Adventure. Later Disney bought Fox Family Channel, which it renamed ABC Family, from News Corp. and Haim Saban for $2.9 billion in cash and assumption of $2.3 billion in debt.

In 2003 Disney began its exit from the sports world by selling the Anaheim Angels. At Disney's annual shareholder meeting in 2004, about 45% of stock owners voted to not re-elect the embattled Eisner to the board. In response, Disney directors stripped Eisner of the chairman title and named director and former US senator George Mitchell to that position. Amid all the strife, Disney boosted its children's entertainment properties in 2004 by purchasing the Muppet and *Bear in the Big Blue House* characters, along with their film and television libraries, from The Jim Henson Company.

In late 2005. Eisner finally passed the CEO torch after more than 20 years to former COO Iger. That same year Disney Parks opened Hong Kong Disneyland, the company's biggest foray into the world's most populated country.

In mid-2006, Walt Disney completed a crucial acquisition — the $7.4 billion purchase of Pixar Animation. Disney almost lost Pixar as a production partner in the animation house's blockbuster films, but Iger successfully dodged the bullet.

In 2007, Disney spun off ABC's radio broadcasting operations to Citadel Broadcasting for $2.7 billion in cash and stock.

## EXECUTIVES

**Chairman:** John E. Pepper Jr., age 68
**President, CEO, and Director:** Robert A. (Bob) Iger, age 55, $17,000,000 pay
**SEVP and CFO:** Thomas O. (Tom) Staggs, age 45, $5,037,500 pay
**SEVP, General Counsel, and Secretary:** Alan N. Braverman, age 58, $3,850,000 pay
**EVP and Chief Human Resources Officer:** Wesley A. (Wes) Coleman, age 57
**EVP Corporate Communications:** Zenia Mucha
**EVP Corporate Finance, Real Estate, and Treasurer:** Christine M. McCarthy, age 51, $1,292,500 pay
**EVP Corporate Strategy, Business Development, and Technology Group:** Kevin A. Mayer, age 44, $1,737,500 pay
**EVP Government Relations:** Preston Padden, age 58
**EVP Global Retail Sales and Marketing:** Jim Fielding
**SVP Corporate Taxes:** Anne Buettner
**SVP Disney Worldwide Outreach:** Jody Dreyer
**SVP Investor Relations and Shareholder Services:** Wendy Webb
**SVP Planning and Control:** Brent A. Woodford, age 42
**SVP Security:** Ronald L. Iden
**SVP and Deputy General Counsel — Corporate, and Secretary:** David K. Thompson
**SVP and Deputy General Counsel — Litigation and Employment:** Edward J. Nowak
**Co-Chairman, Disney Media Networks; Chairman and President, ESPN; President, ABC Sports:** George W. Bodenheimer, age 45
**Co-Chairman, Disney Media Networks; President, Disney-ABC Television:** Anne M. Sweeney
**Chairman, Walt Disney Parks & Resorts:** James A. (Jay) Rasulo, age 46
**Chairman, The Walt Disney Studios:** Richard W. (Dick) Cook, age 52
**CEO, Pixar and Disney Animation Studios and Director:** Steven P. (Steve) Jobs, age 52
**Auditors:** PricewaterhouseCoopers LLP

## LOCATIONS

**HQ:** The Walt Disney Company
500 S. Buena Vista St., Burbank, CA 91521
**Phone:** 818-560-1000 **Fax:** 818-560-1930
**Web:** disney.go.com

The Walt Disney Company has operations worldwide.

**2006 Sales**

| | $ mil. | % of total |
|---|---|---|
| US & Canada | 26,565 | 77 |
| Europe | 5,266 | 15 |
| Asia/Pacific | 1,917 | 6 |
| Latin America & other regions | 537 | 2 |
| **Total** | **34,285** | **100** |

## PRODUCTS/OPERATIONS

**2006 Sales**

| | $ mil. | % of total |
|---|---|---|
| Media networks | 14,638 | 43 |
| Parks & resorts | 9,925 | 29 |
| Studio entertainment | 7,529 | 22 |
| Consumer products | 2,193 | 6 |
| **Total** | **34,285** | **100** |

**Selected Operations**

Consumer products
- Buena Vista Worldwide Home Entertainment (video and DVD)
- The Disney Catalog (direct marketing)
- Disney Interactive Studios (children's software and video games)
- The Disney Store (retail outlets)

Filmed entertainment
- ABC Television Studio
- Buena Vista Productions
- Disney-ABC Domestic Television
- Miramax Films
- Pixar
- Touchstone Pictures
- Walt Disney Feature Animation
- Walt Disney Pictures
- Walt Disney Television

Internet
- ABC.com
- Disney.com
- Disney's Club Penguin
- Disneydirect.com
- DisneyMobile.com
- ESPN.com
- Movies.com

Music
- Buena Vista Records
- Hollywood Records
- Lyric Street

Publishing
- *Discover* (magazine)
- *Disney Adventures* (magazine)
- Disney Publishing Worldwide (children's books)
- *FamilyFun* (magazine)
- Hyperion (adult trade books)

Television networks
- A&E Television Networks (37.5%)
- ABC Family Channel
- ABC Television Network
- Disney Channel
- ESPN (80%)
- JETIX Europe (75%)
- JETIX Latin America
- Lifetime Entertainment Services (50%)
  - Lifetime Television
- SOAPnet
- Toon Disney

Television stations
- KABC (Los Angeles)
- KFSN (Fresno, CA)
- KGO (San Francisco)
- KTRK (Houston)
- WABC (New York City)
- WJRT (Flint, MI)
- WLS (Chicago)
- WPVI (Philadelphia)
- WTVD (Raleigh-Durham, NC)
- WTVG (Toledo, OH)

Theme parks and resorts
- Disney Cruise Line
- Euro Disney (40%)
- Disneyland Resort (Anaheim, CA)
- Hong Kong Disneyland (43%)
- Tokyo Disney Resort (owned and operated by Oriental Land Co.; Disney earns royalties)
- Walt Disney Imagineering (planning and development)
- Walt Disney World Resort (Orlando, FL)

Other
- Buena Vista Theatrical Group
- ESPN Zone (theme restaurant, New York City)

## COMPETITORS

Busch Entertainment
CBS Corp
Discovery Communications
DreamWorks
DreamWorks Animation
Liberty Media
Lucasfilm
MGM
Microsoft
NBC Universal
News Corp.
Six Flags
Sony Pictures Entertainment
Time Warner
Viacom
Yahoo!

## HISTORICAL FINANCIALS

Company Type: Public

**Income Statement** FYE: September 30

| | REVENUE ($ mil.) | NET INCOME ($ mil.) | NET PROFIT MARGIN | EMPLOYEES |
|---|---|---|---|---|
| **9/06** | 34,285 | 3,374 | 9.8% | 133,000 |
| **9/05** | 31,944 | 2,533 | 7.9% | 133,000 |
| **9/04** | 30,752 | 2,345 | 7.6% | 129,000 |
| **9/03** | 27,061 | 1,267 | 4.7% | 112,000 |
| **9/02** | 25,329 | 1,236 | 4.9% | 112,000 |
| **Annual Growth** | 7.9% | 28.5% | — | 4.4% |

**2006 Year-End Financials**

Debt ratio: 35.0%
Return on equity: 11.6%
Cash ($ mil.): 2,411
Current ratio: 0.94
Long-term debt ($ mil.): 11,135
No. of shares (mil.): 2,064
Dividends
Yield: 0.9%
Payout: 16.5%
Market value ($ mil.): 63,685

**Stock History** NYSE: DIS

| | STOCK PRICE ($) FY Close | P/E High | P/E Low | PER SHARE ($) Earnings | Dividends | Book Value |
|---|---|---|---|---|---|---|
| **9/06** | 30.85 | 19 | 14 | 1.64 | 0.27 | 15.42 |
| **9/05** | 24.09 | 25 | 19 | 1.22 | 0.24 | 13.06 |
| **9/04** | 22.51 | 25 | 18 | 1.12 | 0.21 | 13.05 |
| **9/03** | 20.13 | 38 | 22 | 0.62 | 0.21 | 11.82 |
| **9/02** | 15.11 | 42 | 17 | 0.60 | 0.21 | 11.61 |
| **Annual Growth** | 19.5% | — | — | 28.6% | 6.5% | 7.3% |

# The Warnaco Group

Underwear has long been The Warnaco Group's foundation. One of the leading marketers of bras, the firm boasts a diverse portfolio of its own and licensed brands, including Nautica, Polo, Anne Cole, Calvin Klein, and Warner's. Warnaco also makes menswear under the brands Calvin Klein and Chaps by Ralph Lauren. The manufacturer sells apparel to about 50,000 department, mass merchandise, and specialty stores in Europe, Mexico, and North America. It acquired the license, wholesale, and retail units for Calvin Klein jeans and accessories in Europe and Asia in 2006.

The Calvin Klein jeans and accessories purchase includes the CK Calvin Klein bridge line of sportswear and accessories that are marketed in Europe.

While Warnaco has had its eye on strategic acquisitions in recent years, it also has been working to purge brands that don't fit its long-term plans. Warnaco sold its Op brand (bought in 2004) to Iconix Brand Group for $54 million in early 2007. (Previously, Warnaco had hoped to morph Op into a $1 billion brand.) As part of the deal Warnaco was granted a license to make and sell women's and junior swimwear.

Warnaco has gotten into the swim of things by expanding its swimwear division, Warnaco Swimwear, and extending the Speedo brand to include sportswear and performance underwear.

Activist hedge fund Barington Capital acquired more than 5% of Warnaco's shares and is said to be pushing for the sale of the company.

## HISTORY

The Warnaco Group was founded in 1874 by brothers DeVer and Lucien Warner. As doctors, they were concerned about the unhealthy effects of boned and tight-fitting women's corsets. After much research, DeVer came up with a new corset made only from cloth. Within a few weeks of selling their first goods from a one-room tailor shop in McGrawville, New York, the brothers had a flourishing business, which they called Warner Brother's or Warner's.

In a business largely dependent on the changing trends of fashion, Warner's tried to adapt to the corsetless era of the 1920s with wraparound undergarments and by making greater use of rubber and elastic, but sales soured. After WWII, however, Warner's surged ahead.

Warner's apparel division acquired shirtmaker Hathaway in 1960. The firm was renamed Warnaco in 1968. Despite expansion and diversification in the 1970s, it lost ground to cheaper imports. Warnaco succumbed to a $550 million hostile takeover in 1986 led by a group of investors, including Linda Wachner, who had worked for Warnaco in the mid-1970s.

As chairman and CEO, Wachner transformed Warnaco from a maker of a mishmash of apparel products to a highly focused branded-apparel producer. Wachner and a group of investors bought Warnaco's Speedo swimwear division in 1990 (taking it public as Authentic Fitness in 1992, only to purchase it again in 1999). In 1991 the firm held its own IPO. It bought Calvin Klein's underwear business in 1994.

In 1996 Warnaco acquired GJM Group (private-label sleepwear and lingerie), Bodyslimmers (shapeware), and French lingerie maker Lejaby Euralis. It also sold its prestigious but underperforming Hathaway men's dress shirt operations. Sales topped $1 billion in 1996, but costs associated with the Hathaway sale and restructuring led to an $8 million loss.

Warnaco bought Designer Holdings, a maker of Calvin Klein jeans and sportswear, in 1997. By 1999 Warnaco owned distribution rights for Calvin Klein jeans in Canada, giving the company control over Calvin Klein jeans production and distribution throughout the Americas.

In 1998 Warnaco took a $69 million charge to discontinue Valentino and other brands and close a dozen outlet stores and a warehouse. The following year it bought 70% of UK perfume retailer Penhaligon and in 1999 added ABS by Allen Schwartz, a lower-priced designer womenswear maker.

A lawsuit came between Wachner and her Calvins in 2000 when Calvin Klein sued both Warnaco and Wachner for trademark violation and breach of trust. Wachner returned fire, suing Klein and his company for trademark violations, defamation, and trade libel. The firms settled in the hours before their trial was set to begin in 2001.

After dismal 2000 year-end results, Warnaco announced in April 2001 its plans to end its licensed Fruit of the Loom bra operations. In 2001 Warnaco filed for Chapter 11 bankruptcy protection. The board of directors ousted Wachner and replaced her with Antonio ("Tony") Alvarez as CEO and Stuart Buchalter as chairman. Alvarez began a restructuring program, which led to the sale of noncore assets such as GJM's sleepwear division and the closure of Calvin Klein outlet stores in 2002.

Wachner sued Warnaco to get $25 million she says the company owed her. An agreement was reached in November 2002 in which Wachner received $3.5 million in stock in the reorganized company and $200,000 in cash. She remained on the board of directors until the company emerged from bankruptcy in early 2003.

2002 also brought the first round of paring down retail outlets: the company closed 47 Speedo retail outlets, 64 domestic outlet stores, and almost half of its 26 Calvin Klein underwear stores. The next round came in late 2003, with closure of all remaining Speedo stores and sale of its White Stag line to Wal-Mart.

In April 2003 Alvarez left and Joe Gromek (former CEO of Brooks Brothers) took over as president and CEO.

## EXECUTIVES

**Chairman:** Charles R. Perrin, age 61
**President, CEO, and Director:** Joseph R. (Joe) Gromek, age 60, $1,654,167 pay
**EVP and CFO:** Lawrence R. Rutkowski, age 48, $901,000 pay (prior to promotion)
**EVP, International Strategy and Business Development:** Stanley P. Silverstein, age 54
**SVP, General Counsel, and Secretary:** Jay A. Galluzzo, age 32
**SVP, Human Resources:** Elizabeth Wood, age 45
**SVP and Chief Marketing Officer, Intimate Apparel Division:** Michael Schornstein
**VP and Divisional Merchandise Manager, Fashion Brands:** Barbara Lipton, age 47
**President and CEO, Calvin Klein Jeans and Sportswear for Europe and Asia:** Gaetano Sallorenzo, age 48
**President, Calvin Klein Underwear:** Kay LeGrange
**President, Core Brands:** Martha Olson
**President, Global Sourcing:** Dwight F. Meyer, age 54
**President, Intimate Apparel Group:** Helen McCluskey, age 51, $900,000 pay
**President, Sportswear Group:** Frank Tworecke, age 60, $1,200,000 pay
**President, Ocean Pacific:** Richard (Dick) Baker
**President, Calvin Klein Jeans:** Patricia J. Royak
**President, Chaps:** David Cunningham
**President, Prestige Brands Division:** John Wagstaff
**President, Designer Swimwear, Warnaco Swimwear:** Paula Schneider
**CIO:** Michelle Garvey
**Director, Investor Relations:** Deborah Abraham
**Auditors:** Deloitte & Touche LLP

## LOCATIONS

**HQ:** The Warnaco Group, Inc.
501 7th Ave., New York, NY 10018
**Phone:** 212-287-8000 **Fax:** 212-287-8297
**Web:** www.warnaco.com

### 2006 Sales

| | $ mil. | % of total |
|---|---|---|
| US | 1,038.8 | 57 |
| Europe | 430.7 | 24 |
| Asia | 193.3 | 10 |
| Canada | 98.5 | 5 |
| Central & South America | 66.2 | 4 |
| **Total** | **1,827.5** | **100** |

## PRODUCTS/OPERATIONS

### 2006 Sales

| | $ mil. | % of total |
|---|---|---|
| Sportswear group | 791.6 | 43 |
| Intimate apparel | 647.0 | 36 |
| Swimwear group | 388.9 | 21 |
| **Total** | **1,827.5** | **100** |

### Selected Brands

Intimate apparel
- Bodyslimmers
- Calvin Klein
- Lejaby
- Olga
- Warner's

Sportswear and Accessories
- Anne Cole (licensed)
- Calvin Klein (licensed)
- Catalina
- Chaps by Ralph Lauren (licensed)
- Cole of California
- Lauren/Ralph Lauren
- Nautica (licensed)
- Ralph/Ralph Lauren
- Polo Sport Ralph Lauren (licensed)
- Polo Sport-RLX (licensed)
- Ralph Lauren (licensed)
- Speedo (licensed)

## COMPETITORS

adidas
Benetton
Danskin
Delta Galil Industries Ltd.
Donna Karan
Frederick's of Hollywood
Fruit of the Loom
Guess
Hanesbrands
Intimate Brands
Jockey International
Kellwood
Levi Strauss
Limited Brands
Liz Claiborne
Maidenform
NIKE
Perry Ellis International
Polo Ralph Lauren
Reebok
Russell
Tommy Hilfiger
Under Armour
VF

## HISTORICAL FINANCIALS

Company Type: Public

**Income Statement** — FYE: Saturday nearest December 31

| | REVENUE ($ mil.) | NET INCOME ($ mil.) | NET PROFIT MARGIN | EMPLOYEES |
|---|---|---|---|---|
| **12/06** | 1,828 | 51 | 2.8% | 10,287 |
| **12/05** | 1,501 | 50 | 3.3% | 10,156 |
| **12/04** | 1,424 | 43 | 3.0% | 10,662 |
| **12/03** | 1,374 | 2,360 | 171.7% | 12,377 |
| **12/02** | 1,493 | (965) | — | 13,536 |
| **Annual Growth** | 5.2% | — | — | (6.6%) |

**2006 Year-End Financials**

| | |
|---|---|
| Debt ratio: 48.7% | No. of shares (mil.): 45 |
| Return on equity: 7.7% | Dividends |
| Cash ($ mil.): 167 | Yield: — |
| Current ratio: 1.92 | Payout: — |
| Long-term debt ($ mil.): 332 | Market value ($ mil.): 1,138 |

**Stock History** — NASDAQ (GS): WRNC

| | STOCK PRICE ($) FY Close | P/E High | P/E Low | PER SHARE ($) Earnings | Dividends | Book Value |
|---|---|---|---|---|---|---|
| **12/06** | 25.38 | 26 | 15 | 1.08 | — | 15.24 |
| **12/05** | 26.72 | 26 | 19 | 1.06 | — | 13.65 |
| **12/04** | 21.60 | 24 | 17 | 0.93 | — | 12.64 |
| **12/03** | 16.16 | 0 | 0 | 44.55 | — | 11.57 |
| **Annual Growth** | 16.2% | — | — | — | — | — |

# Warner Music Group

These records were made to be listened to, not broken. Warner Music Group (WMG) is one of the largest recording companies in the world and ranks #3 in terms of US market share (behind Universal Music Group and Sony BMG Music Entertainment). It produces, markets, and distributes recordings primarily through units Atlantic Records Group and Warner Bros. Records, and it controls the rights to more than a million songs through Warner/Chappell Music. Its Rhino Entertainment distributes compilations and reissues. Thomas H. Lee Partners owns about 35% of WMG, which in 2006 rejected a $4.2 billion takeover bid from its larger rival EMI Group. On the flipside, EMI rejected a $4.2 million offer from WMG in 2007.

WMG approached EMI about a possible takeover bid in 2007, but later changed its mind. This follows a years-long battle of takeover attempts that had temporarily stoped when EMI announced it would no longer pursue a deal in 2006. Before 2006 the companies had tried twice before to merge, only to be stopped by European regulators. If Warner Music and EMI were to combine, the deal would create a company worth an estimated $7 billion. The entity would control about 25% of the recorded music market, ranking second to Universal Music Group.

Since being sold by media giant Time Warner in 2004 and going public the following year, WMG has reinvigorated its once sagging business through cost cutting and in part through embracing new technologies. Sales of digital music products, such as ringtones, videos, and downloaded songs and albums, now account for about 6% of the company's business. And while sales of physical albums and CDs continue to whither, WMG has committed to increasing its marketing and development efforts to expand into new digital media formats. WMG also embraced new video sharing mediums by striking a revenue-sharing deal with YouTube to distribute and license copyrighted songs, videos, and other materials.

The company's traditional A&R work of finding and developing artists has also been successful in scoring top hits from the likes of Green Day, Faith Hill, and Michael Buble. In 2006 Warner purchased Ryko Corporation and its Rykodisc label, one of the top independent record companies in the US, for $67.5 million. Also that year the company created the Independent Label Group (ILG), which is composed of WMG's Asylum Records (urban), East West Records (rock), and Cordless Recordings (digital-only).

Former Vivendi executive Edgar Bronfman, Jr., led the buyout of WMG from Time Warner for $2.6 billion, topping a bid from UK-based EMI Group in the twelfth hour. The deal marked a return to the entertainment business for Bronfman, who now owns nearly 10% of the company. In the 1990s he led Seagram (the distilled liquor business controlled by his family) to buy Universal Studios and later PolyGram.

## HISTORY

Warner Bros. co-founder Jack Warner expanded his film company's operations into music when he created Warner Bros. Records in 1958. Initially focused on sound tracks and comedy albums, the company soon expanded its scope by issuing recordings by the Everly Brothers and Peter, Paul & Mary. Warner bought Reprise Records in 1963, the label started by Frank Sinatra in 1961. Warner sold his entertainment empire in 1966 to Seven Arts Productions, which became Warner-Seven Arts. That year the company bought Atlantic Records, a label co-founded in 1947 by famed music producer Ahmet Ertegun. (Ertegun died in 2006.) Steven Ross' Kinney National Services purchased Warner-Seven Arts in 1969 and changed its name to Warner Communications.

Former Reprise Records chief Mo Ostin became CEO of Warner Bros. Records in the early 1970s and is credited with propelling the company into the forefront of the music industry. Reorganized as Warner Music, the company battled rival CBS Records (now part of Sony BMG Music Entertainment) for dominance in the music business by adding to its collection of labels, acquiring Elektra Records in 1970 and Asylum Records in 1974. The company later created a distribution arm, WEA (Warner-Electra-Atlantic), expanded internationally, and established a record pressing plant. Warner Music prospered in the 1980s, scoring hits with artists like R.E.M. and Madonna. It bought a 50% stake in Sony Music's record club, Columbia House, in 1989.

Parent Warner Communications was acquired by publisher Time Inc. in 1990, and Warner Music became part of media giant Time Warner. However, the company was losing market share and executive infighting was reaching a fevered pitch. Several top executives jumped ship, including Mo Ostin who left in 1994. HBO chief Michael Fuchs took over in 1995 and cleaned house, but he himself was ousted later that year. Warner film studio chiefs Bob Daly and Terry Semel were later appointed co-CEOs.

While Daly and Semel helped restore order to the music group, they failed to revive sales. They announced their resignation in 1999, and Warner Music International executive Roger Ames was appointed chairman and CEO.

Following the merger of AOL and Time Warner in 2001, Ames began tightening the belt, cutting some 600 staff members and centralizing label operations. Later that year Time Warner teamed up with EMI, BMG, and RealNetworks to form online music venture MusicNet. (The business was sold to Baker Capital in 2005 for about $30 million.)

In 2002 Warner purchased contemporary Christian music label Word Entertainment and acquired three music publishing companies from edel. Tommy Boy Music also split from the company and became an independent label. In 2003 Warner sold the DVD and CD manufacturing businesses of WEA to Cinram for $1 billion. WEA's sales and marketing operations remained with Warner. The following year Warner was taken private when a group of investors led by Edgar Bronfman, Jr., with backing from Thomas H. Lee Partners, Bain Capital, and Providence Equity Partners purchased the music company from Time Warner for $2.6 billion. The company went public in 2005.

Also that year the company signed a distribution deal with Sean "Diddy" Combs, taking a 50% stake in his Bad Boy Records (part of Bad Boy Worldwide Entertainment) for about $30 million. It was the first big deal negotiated for WMG by Lyor Cohen, the rap music pioneer lured away from Universal's Island Def Jam division to oversee WMG's US recorded music operations.

## EXECUTIVES

**Chairman and CEO:** Edgar M. Bronfman Jr., age 52, $7,000,000 pay
**EVP and CFO:** Michael D. Fleisher, age 41, $2,200,000 pay
**EVP Digital Strategy and Business Development:** Alejandro (Alex) Zubillaga, age 38, $1,600,000 pay
**EVP Global Human Resources:** Caroline Stockdale, age 43
**SVP and CIO:** Maggie Miller
**SVP, Acting General Counsel, and Secretary:** Paul Robinson
**SVP Compensation and Benefits:** Susan Ross
**SVP Corporate Communications:** Will Tanous
**SVP Finance:** Gillian Kellie
**SVP Global Consumer Marketing:** Dan Pelson
**SVP Internet Strategy:** Michael Nash
**SVP Investor Relations and Corporate Development:** Jill S. Krutick
**SVP Strategy and Product Development:** George White
**VP, Senior Counsel, and Head of Digital Legal Affairs:** Elliott Peters
**VP New Media:** Jeremy Welt
**VP Public Policy and Government Relations:** Linda Bloss-Baum
**Senior Adviser to the CEO:** Richard Blackstone, age 46

**Founding Chairman, Atlantic Records:** Ahmet M. Ertegun
**Chairman and CEO, Atlantic Records Group:** Craig Kallman
**Chairman and CEO, Warner Bros. Records:** Tom Whalley
**Chairman and CEO, US Recorded Music:** Lyor Cohen, age 47, $6,000,000 pay
**Chairman and CEO, Warner Music Greater China:** Holly Tan
**Chairman and CEO, Warner Music International:** Patrick Vien, age 40
**Interim CEO, Warner/Chappell Music:** David H. (Dave) Johnson, age 60
**Auditors:** Ernst & Young LLP

## LOCATIONS

**HQ:** Warner Music Group Corp.
75 Rockefeller Plaza, New York, NY 10019
**Phone:** 212-275-2000 **Fax:** 212-757-3985
**Web:** www.wmg.com

Warner Music Group has operations in more than 50 countries.

### 2006 Sales

| | $ mil. | % of total |
|---|---|---|
| US | 1,703 | 48 |
| UK | 431 | 12 |
| France | 224 | 6 |
| Japan | 220 | 6 |
| Germany | 195 | 6 |
| Italy | 115 | 3 |
| Other countries | 628 | 19 |
| **Total** | **3,516** | **100** |

## PRODUCTS/OPERATIONS

### 2006 Sales

| | % of total |
|---|---|
| Recorded music | 84 |
| Music publishing | 16 |
| **Total** | **100** |

### Selected Operations

Recorded music
- Distribution
  - Alternative Distribution Alliance
  - WEA Corp.
  - Word Entertainment (80%)
- Recording labels
  - Atlantic Records
  - Elektra Records
  - Lava Records
  - Maverick Recording Company
  - Nonesuch Records
  - Reprise
  - Rhino Records
  - Rykodisc
  - Sire
  - Warner Bros. Nashville
  - Warner Bros. Records
  - Word Records
- Warner Strategic Marketing (catalog sales and marketing)

Music publishing
- Warner Bros. Publications
- Warner/Chappell Music

## COMPETITORS

EMI Group
Sony BMG
Universal Music Group

## HISTORICAL FINANCIALS

Company Type: Public

### Income Statement

FYE: September 30

| | REVENUE ($ mil.) | NET INCOME ($ mil.) | NET PROFIT MARGIN | EMPLOYEES |
|---|---|---|---|---|
| **9/06** | 3,516 | 60 | 1.7% | 4,000 |
| **9/05** | 3,502 | (169) | — | 4,000 |
| **9/04*** | 2,548 | (270) | — | 4,000 |
| **11/03** | 3,376 | (1,353) | — | 4,200 |
| **11/02** | 3,290 | (6,026) | — | 5,300 |
| **Annual Growth** | 1.7% | — | — | (6.8%) |

*Fiscal year change

### 2006 Year-End Financials

Debt ratio: 3,860.3%
Return on equity: 81.6%
Cash ($ mil.): 385
Current ratio: 0.72
Long-term debt ($ mil.): 2,239
No. of shares (mil.): 149
Dividends
Yield: 2.5%
Payout: 162.5%
Market value ($ mil.): 3,871

### Stock History

NYSE: WMG

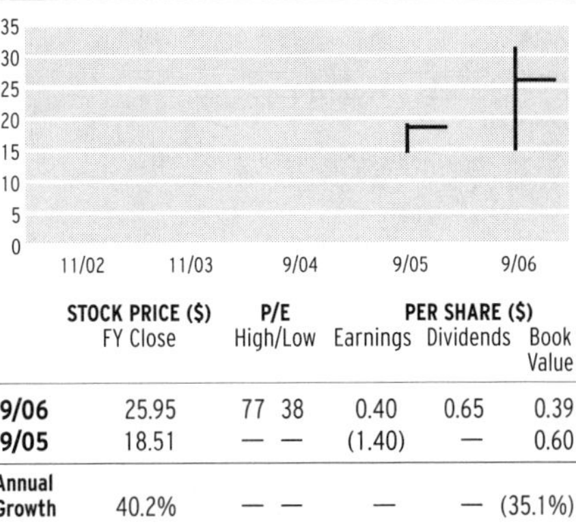

| | STOCK PRICE ($) FY Close | P/E High/Low | PER SHARE ($) Earnings | Dividends | Book Value |
|---|---|---|---|---|---|
| **9/06** | 25.95 | 77 38 | 0.40 | 0.65 | 0.39 |
| **9/05** | 18.51 | — — | (1.40) | — | 0.60 |
| **Annual Growth** | 40.2% | — — | — | — | (35.1%) |

# Washington Group International

Washington Group International remains one of the world's largest construction and engineering firms, even after two stints in bankruptcy. The company provides design and construction services for customers in the defense, energy and environment, industrial/process, infrastructure, mining, and power industries. Typical projects involve bridges, highways, manufacturing plants, mining, nuclear and power plants, pipelines, and railroads. It also operates mines and offers environmental management and facilities and operations management. The company's expertise in nuclear plant remediation and decommissioning made it an attractive target and it is being acquired by URS.

Washington Group (formerly Morrison Knudsen) doubled in size by buying Raytheon's engineering and construction unit in 2000; it declared bankruptcy in 2001, but emerged in 2002.

The company's 2001 bankruptcy was hard on stockholders. All stock was declared worthless, and new shares were awarded to the company's creditors and lenders. However, with the former Morrison Knudsen as its foundation and Raytheon's engineering and heavy construction business as a key addition, Washington Group International has held on through difficult financial times. The group's ability to grab high-profile federal contracts has helped it survive. Its contracts with the US Department of Defense generate nearly a quarter of its revenues.

Ranked as one of the leading international environmental engineering firms, Washington Group provides services, including site cleanup/remediation and nuclear waste management, to both governments and corporations. Washington Group and subsidiary Westinghouse Government Services Company have racked up years of experience at DOE facilities nationwide, including the Hanford, Washington, and Oak Ridge, Tennessee, nuclear waste sites.

The group has won defense contracts with the US Army for projects related to chemical weapons destruction, including employee training and other start-up work for weapons destruction plants.

Washington Group's power division provides engineering, construction, and operations and maintenance services to both fossil-fuel and nuclear power markets, including utilities, industrial cogeneration companies, independent power producers, and government-owned energy companies.

Its industrial/process division provides services ranging from planning and engineering to total facilities management. Its mining unit provides engineering, construction, and operations management services worldwide.

Chairman Dennis Washington, a so-called stealth billionaire, controls about 11% of Worthington Group. Jeffrey Gendell of Tontine owns around 7%.

## HISTORY

Morris Hans Knudsen and Harry Morrison met in Idaho on an irrigation project and teamed up in 1912 as subcontractors for a pumping station on the Snake River. Two years later they helped build a dam in Oregon.

Capitalizing on his large construction experience, Knudsen put together a group of builders to construct the Hoover Dam in 1931. A year later Morrison Knudsen (MK) was incorporated.

During WWII MK built storage tanks in Hawaii and airstrips on Midway Island. More than 1,200 of its workers were captured and nearly 100 were killed during the 1941 raids. Knudsen died in 1943.

After the war MK expanded globally. In 1954 Morrison appeared on the cover of *Time* magazine, which dubbed the construction industry "Ambassadors with Bulldozers." At home MK helped build the Kennedy Space Center, completing the center's Vehicle Assembly Building (then the largest building in the world) in 1965.

Morrison died in 1971. The company diversified in the 1970s, adding mining, the Trans-Alaska pipeline, shipbuilding, and hazardous waste management.

Global economic gyrations in the 1980s forced MK into a reorganization in 1985. A new CEO, William Agee, took over in 1988. Since most of the company's losses came from smaller projects, Agee focused MK on big-ticket items such as the Honolulu public transit system and the superconducting super collider. The company also began building passenger railcars and tried to get approval for a high-speed rail project in Texas. But Honolulu canceled its billion-dollar transit project in 1988, Congress halted funding for the super collider in 1993, and the Texas rail project fell apart for lack of financing in 1994.

Amid accusations of extravagant personal use of company funds, Agee was fired by MK's board in 1995; Robert Miller, former vice chairman of Chrysler, became chairman. The company was $350 million in debt, and creditors took over its railcar operations.

After filing for bankruptcy in 1996, the company merged with rival Washington Construction Group. That company was formed in 1993 when little-known Montana billionaire Dennis Washington merged his construction business with California's Kasler Corp., which had grown along with sprawling Southern California during the 1960s by building freeways. Washington became chairman of MK in the merger, Miller became vice chairman, and Robert Tinstman CEO and president.

In 1999 Washington took over as CEO after Tinstman retired. MK joined with state-owned British Nuclear Fuels Limited (BNFL) to buy Westinghouse Electric from CBS in 1999. MK bought Raytheon's engineering and construction unit for about $500 million in 2000. Later that year, MK became Washington Group International.

In 2001 the company, suffering financially from its acquisition of Raytheon Engineers & Constructors, filed for bankruptcy protection for the second time in six years. Under a reorganization plan, the company cut some 3,400 jobs, appointed new executives, and made plans to close or consolidate 30 to 40 offices. That year the company suffered further when 13 of its employees died on September 11 in its offices in the World Trade Center.

In 2004 the group began acquiring BNFL's stake in the Westinghouse government services businesses that they had bought together from CBS. The buy, completed in 2006, gave Washington Group control of both Westinghouse Government Services Co. and Westinghouse Government Environmental Services Co.

## EXECUTIVES

**Chairman:** Dennis R. Washington, age 72
**President, CEO, and Director:** Stephen G. (Steve) Hanks, age 56, $867,693 pay
**SEVP Operations:** Thomas H. (Tom) Zarges, age 59, $565,001 pay
**SEVP Business Development:** Stephen M. (Steve) Johnson, age 55, $565,001 pay
**EVP and CFO:** George H. Juetten, age 59, $446,154 pay
**EVP Business Development, Mining Business Unit:** Steve Kesler
**EVP Business Development, Defense Business Unit:** Lawrence E. (Larry) Shaw
**SVP Human Resources:** Larry L. Myers, age 52
**SVP, General Counsel, and Assistant Secretary:** Richard D. (Rich) Parry, age 54
**SVP Business Development, Washington Energy & Environment:** David A. Pethick
**SVP Business Development, Washington Industrial/Process:** Mark A. Costello
**SVP Business Development, Power:** George L. Nash Jr.
**SVP Project Development:** Frank S. Finlayson
**VP and Controller:** Jerry K. Lemon, age 47
**VP, Secretary, and Associate General Counsel:** Craig G. Taylor, age 50
**VP Investor Relations and Treasurer:** Earl L. Ward, age 54
**VP Corporate Communications:** Laurie A. Spiegelberg, age 37
**VP HR Operations:** Catherine M. Rupert
**President, Defense:** Terri L. Marts
**President, Energy & Environment:** E. Preston (Pres) Rahe Jr.
**President, Industrial/Process:** Gary C. Baughman
**President, Mining:** Robert W. (Bob) Zaist
**President, Power:** Louis E. (Lou) Pardi, $383,616 pay
**Auditors:** Deloitte & Touche LLP

## LOCATIONS

**HQ:** Washington Group International, Inc.
720 Park Blvd., Boise, ID 83712
**Phone:** 208-386-5000 **Fax:** 208-386-7186
**Web:** www.wgint.com

### 2006 Sales

| | $ mil. | % of total |
|---|---|---|
| United States | 2,667.6 | 78 |
| Iraq | 332.5 | 10 |
| Other countries | 398.0 | 12 |
| **Total** | **3,398.1** | **100** |

## PRODUCTS/OPERATIONS

### 2006 Sales

| | $ mil. | % of total |
|---|---|---|
| Power | 791.3 | 23 |
| Infrastructure | 577.9 | 17 |
| Mining | 166.9 | 5 |
| Industrial/Process | 511.0 | 15 |
| Defense | 576.0 | 17 |
| Energy & Environment | 773.7 | 23 |
| Intersegment, eliminations & other | 1.3 | — |
| **Total** | **3,398.1** | **100** |

### Major Markets and Operations

Power
- Decontamination and decommissioning
- Environmental permitting
- Generation planning
- Operations and maintenance
- Power plant engineering and construction
- Power plant expansion, retrofit, and modification
- Siting and licensing

Infrastructure
- Airports and seaports
- Highways and bridges
- Hydroelectric facilities
- Precast/prestressed concrete products
- Railroad and transit lines
- Site development
- Tunnels and tube tunnels
- Water storage
- Water treatment

Energy and Environment
- Design and construction
- Nuclear weapons stockpile support
- Operations and maintenance
- Program management
- Safety and licensing
- Waste handling and storage

Defense
- Brownfields cleanup and remediation
- Chemical weapons demilitarization
- Design and construction
- Environmental remediation
- Safety and licensing
- Waste handling and storage
- Weapons destruction in Eastern Europe

Industrial/Process
- Aerospace
- Automotive
- Buildings
- Consumer products
- Food and beverage
- Pharmaceutical
- Pulp and paper
- Specialty chemicals
- Upstream gas

Mining
- Equity participation
- Feasibility studies
- Metals processes
- Mine management
- Mine operations and maintenance
- Mine site engineering and construction

## COMPETITORS

AECOM
Battelle Memorial
Bechtel
CH2M HILL
Earth Tech
Fluor
Foster Wheeler
Jacobs Engineering
Parsons
Shaw Group
Siemens Water Technologies
Skanska USA Building
Tetra Tech
URS
Vecellio & Grogan
Walbridge Aldinger

## HISTORICAL FINANCIALS

Company Type: Public

### Income Statement

FYE: Friday nearest December 31

| | REVENUE ($ mil.) | NET INCOME ($ mil.) | NET PROFIT MARGIN | EMPLOYEES |
|---|---|---|---|---|
| **12/06** | 3,398 | 81 | 2.4% | 25,000 |
| **12/05** | 3,188 | 58 | 1.8% | 23,900 |
| **12/04** | 2,915 | 51 | 1.8% | 25,500 |
| **12/03** | 2,501 | 42 | 1.7% | 26,000 |
| **12/02** | 3,662 | 560 | 15.3% | 30,000 |
| **Annual Growth** | (1.8%) | (38.4%) | — | (4.5%) |

### 2006 Year-End Financials

Debt ratio: —
Return on equity: 10.5%
Cash ($ mil.): 342
Current ratio: 1.57
Long-term debt ($ mil.): —
No. of shares (mil.): 29
Dividends
Yield: —
Payout: —
Market value ($ mil.): 1,725

### Stock History

NYSE: WNG

| | STOCK PRICE ($) FY Close | P/E High | P/E Low | PER SHARE ($) Earnings | Dividends | Book Value |
|---|---|---|---|---|---|---|
| **12/06** | 59.79 | 23 | 18 | 2.64 | — | 27.66 |
| **12/05** | 52.97 | 28 | 20 | 1.93 | — | 27.62 |
| **12/04** | 41.25 | 22 | 17 | 1.86 | — | 28.80 |
| **12/03** | 33.49 | 21 | 9 | 1.66 | — | 26.39 |
| **12/02** | 16.70 | 16 | 8 | 1.51 | — | 23.87 |
| **Annual Growth** | 37.6% | — | — | 15.0% | — | 3.8% |

# Washington Mutual

Seattle — home to gourmet coffee, grunge, and thrift banking. Washington Mutual (WaMu), the largest thrift in the US, offers traditional consumer and commercial banking services, including deposit accounts, mortgages and other loans, securities brokerage, and the WM family of mutual funds, through about 2,200 bank branches in the West as well as New York and Connecticut, and nearly another 500 loan offices nationwide. It is one of the largest originators and servicers of residential mortgages in the US. The company's Long Beach Mortgage unit offers subprime mortgages.

In light of the 2006-2007 housing bust and subsequent epidemic of loan defaults, in 2007 WaMu said it would refinance any existing customer's subprime mortgage at below market rates to help manage payment hikes. The move will help WaMu avoid costly foreclosures.

WaMu's acquisition of credit card company Providian Financial in 2005 was aimed at helping WaMu compete with larger banks like Citigroup and Bank of America that have extensive consumer credit programs.

The bank has been paring down its non-retail operations in order to concentrate on its credit card business and its mainstay middle-market consumer and small business customer base. It sold its mortgage-servicing unit to Wells Fargo in 2006 and its money-management operations, WM Advisors, to the Principal Financial Group in 2007. WaMu continues to sell investment products and services through WM Financial Services.

In a move that WaMu said would solidify its multifamily and small commercial real estate loan business in California, the bank bought Commercial Capital Bancorp for $983 million in cash in 2006.

Although WaMu operates nationwide, about half of the loans in its portfolio were originated in California. Other key markets are Florida, Oregon, Texas, and Washington.

Some of WaMu's bank branches feature its patented Occasio (Latin for "favorable opportunity") design, a warm and fuzzy retail concept that eschews stodgy teller windows in favor of cozy chairs, free coffee, play areas for tots, and interactive kiosks where WaMulians (what employees call themselves) greet customers as they enter the store (what they call their branches).

## HISTORY

Washington National Building Loan and Investment Association was formed in 1889 to help rebuild Seattle after a fire destroyed its business district. Among its founders was Edward Graves, the president of Washington National Bank. Under his guidance, the bank served as the association's treasurer and repository of its funds.

Originally chartered for 20 years, the association's growth lagged, in part, because of a myriad of dues and fees, restricted withdrawals, and high share prices. But as the only local source for contractors' loans (for members only), it survived.

Legislation allowing mutual banks to offer mortgage loans made competitors of the bank and the association. Rather than compete head-on, management chose to await the expiry of the association's charter. While Seattle and much of the Northwest boomed thanks to the discovery of gold in Alaska, the association struggled.

New management took over in 1908 (a year before the charter's expiration) and began operating the association as a mutual bank, with reduced fees, liberalized withdrawal policies, and a public relations campaign. Within five years, accounts had increased sevenfold. The company changed its name to Washington Mutual Savings Bank in 1917.

In 1930 WaMu made its first buy, Continental Mutual Savings Bank. It added its first branch in 1941 when it bought Coolidge Mutual Savings Bank.

After mutual banks won the right to establish statewide networks, WaMu established branches throughout the state from the 1950s to the 1970s.

The company expanded beyond banking in the 1970s and 1980s, forming insurance, travel, securities brokerage, and investment subsidiaries. Late 1970s inflation trapped the company between its low-rate, long-term mortgages and its customers' expectation of high savings returns. Forced to stop loaning and facing failure, WaMu acted decisively. In 1983 it became a stock savings bank (the largest conversion at the time) and began trading over-the-counter. The IPO fueled more than 20 acquisitions in the 1990s.

In the early 1990s the bank stuck to a conservative lending course, building reserves and selling problem loans. It began small-business lending with the 1995 purchase of Enterprise Bank, but sold its travel business to management.

The 1996 purchase of California-based American Savings Bank and its more than 200 locations apparently whetted the bank's appetite. In 1997, after a protracted bidding duel with H.F. Ahmanson, it gobbled up Great Western Financial Corp. The next year the bank swallowed Ahmanson. In 1999 WaMu planned to take a breather and close more than 150 branches, but it just couldn't keep its fingers off subprime mortgage lender Long Beach Mortgage.

In 2001 WaMu extended its reach in the Texas market by acquiring Bank United. The thrift also bought mortgage portfolios from FleetBoston and PNC Financial Services.

The company made two major purchases in 2002: It entered New York City, the biggest banking market in the country, via its $5 billion-plus deal for Dime Bancorp (a top-five thrift at the time), and acquired US mortgage lender HomeSide International from National Australia Bank.

The company expanded into major metropolitan areas in the next couple of years. That move led to the sale of its Washington Mutual Finance division, which had some 430 offices mainly in small and midsized cities in the Southeast and Southwest, to CitiFinancial in 2004.

The company had planned to close about 90 mortgage production offices that year in markets where it does not have retail banking operations, but instead sold the locations to American Home Mortgage Investment Corp. WaMu also closed or sold all 53 of its commercial banking offices in 2004.

## EXECUTIVES

**President and COO:** Stephen J. (Steve) Rotella, age 53, $900,000 pay
**SEVP and Chief Legal Officer:** Fay L. Chapman, age 60
**EVP and CFO:** Thomas W. (Tom) Casey, age 44, $620,000 pay
**EVP and CIO:** Debora M. Horvath, age 50
**EVP and Chief Enterprise Risk Officer:** Ronald J. (Ron) Cathcart, age 54
**EVP and President Commercial Group:** Alfred R. (Al) Brooks, age 49
**EVP and Chief Marketing Officer:** Genevieve Smith
**EVP; Acting President, Retail Banking Products and Operations:** Kenneth E. (Ken) Kido, age 48
**EVP and President Home Loans:** David C. Schneider, age 41
**EVP and President Card Services:** Anthony F. (Tony) Vuoto, age 55
**EVP Corporate Strategy and Development:** Todd H. Baker, age 51
**EVP Enterprise Risk Services:** Annie Searle
**EVP and Chief Human Resources Officer:** Daryl D. David, age 52
**EVP, Payments:** Nandita Bakhshi
**SVP Investor Relations:** Alan Magleby, age 51
**SVP and Controller:** John F. Woods, age 42
**First VP, Corporate Public Relations:** Libby Hutchinson
**CTO:** Pia Jorgensen
**Secretary:** William L. Lynch
**Auditors:** Deloitte & Touche LLP

## LOCATIONS

**HQ:** Washington Mutual, Inc.
1301 Second Ave., Seattle, WA 98101
**Phone:** 206-461-2000
**Web:** www.wamu.com

## PRODUCTS/OPERATIONS

### 2006 Sales

| | $ mil. | % of total |
|---|---|---|
| Interest income | | |
| Loans | 17,340 | 66 |
| Securities | 1,460 | 5 |
| Other | 1,107 | 4 |
| Noninterest income | | |
| Deposit & other retail banking fees | 2,567 | 10 |
| Loan sales & servicing | 2,295 | 9 |
| Fees & commissions | 852 | 3 |
| Other | 833 | 3 |
| **Total** | **26,454** | **100** |

### 2006 Assets

| | $ mil. | % of total |
|---|---|---|
| Cash & equivalents | 6,948 | 2 |
| Trading assets | 4,434 | 1 |
| Mortgage-backed securities | 18,063 | 5 |
| Investment in Federal Home Loan banks | 2,705 | 1 |
| Other securities | 6,915 | 2 |
| Loans held for sale | 44,970 | 13 |
| Net loans held in portfolio | 224,960 | 65 |
| Mortgage servicing rights | 6,193 | 2 |
| Other | 31,100 | 9 |
| **Total** | **346,288** | **100** |

## COMPETITORS

Baker Boyer
Bank of America
Bank of Hawaii
Citigroup
Comerica
Countrywide Financial
Downey Financial
JPMorgan Chase
KeyCorp
Pacific Capital Bancorp
SVB Financial
UnionBanCal
U.S. Bancorp
Wachovia
Washington Federal
Wells Fargo
Zions Bancorporation

## HISTORICAL FINANCIALS

Company Type: Public

### Income Statement

FYE: December 31

| | ASSETS ($ mil.) | NET INCOME ($ mil.) | INCOME AS % OF ASSETS | EMPLOYEES |
|---|---|---|---|---|
| **12/06** | 346,288 | 3,558 | 1.0% | 49,824 |
| **12/05** | 343,573 | 3,432 | 1.0% | 60,798 |
| **12/04** | 307,918 | 2,878 | 0.9% | 52,579 |
| **12/03** | 275,178 | 3,880 | 1.4% | 63,720 |
| **12/02** | 268,298 | 3,896 | 1.5% | 52,459 |
| **Annual Growth** | 6.6% | (2.2%) | — | (1.3%) |

### 2006 Year-End Financials

Equity as % of assets: 7.6%
Return on assets: 1.0%
Return on equity: 13.2%
Long-term debt ($ mil.): 32,852
No. of shares (mil.): 944

Dividends
Yield: 4.5%
Payout: 56.6%
Market value ($ mil.): 42,964
Sales ($ mil.): 26,454

**Stock History** NYSE: WM

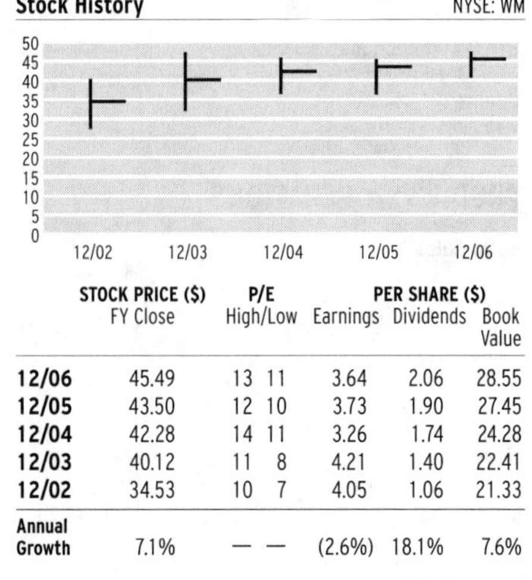


| | STOCK PRICE ($) FY Close | P/E High/Low | | PER SHARE ($) Earnings | Dividends | Book Value |
|---|---|---|---|---|---|---|
| **12/06** | 45.49 | 13 | 11 | 3.64 | 2.06 | 28.55 |
| **12/05** | 43.50 | 12 | 10 | 3.73 | 1.90 | 27.45 |
| **12/04** | 42.28 | 14 | 11 | 3.26 | 1.74 | 24.28 |
| **12/03** | 40.12 | 11 | 8 | 4.21 | 1.40 | 22.41 |
| **12/02** | 34.53 | 10 | 7 | 4.05 | 1.06 | 21.33 |
| **Annual Growth** | 7.1% | — | — | (2.6%) | 18.1% | 7.6% |

# The Washington Post

Named for a newspaper, this media company has operations in publishing, television, and online. The Washington Post Company is a leading newspaper publisher with its flagship paper serving the nation as well as the nation's capitol. The company's largest division, however, is Kaplan, which publishes test preparation materials and provides supplemental education services. Washington Post's other media operations include *Newsweek*, the #2 weekly news magazine (after Time Inc's *Time*), a portfolio of six TV stations, and the online publishing operations of Washingtonpost.Newsweek Interactive. Its Cable One subsidiary provides cable TV service in about 20 markets. Chairman Donald Graham owns about 40% of the company.

Washington Post has struggled along with its newspaper industry rivals with declining readership and advertising revenue. Its move to diversify into education services and television, though, has paid off as those units have posted significant gains in recent years to make up for the shortfall of its newsprint businesses. Its growing portfolio of Internet publishing operations has also helped contribute to growth as online advertising continues to grow.

During 2006 Washington Post shed its collection of trade publications previously operated through Post Newsweek Tech Media. It also sold its 49% stake in online recruitment business BrassRing to human resources company Kenexa.

Chairman Donald Graham is the son of the late Katharine Graham, who had taken over the business after her husband died in the early 1960s and became a legend in the publishing business. She led the *Post* in its decisions to publish the Pentagon papers and pursue the Watergate story.

Investment icon Warren Buffett owns almost 20% of the company.

## HISTORY

*The Washington Post* was first published in 1877, focusing on society columns, color comics, and sensational headlines. Hard news coverage took a back page to crime and scandal — by 1916 the *Post* was filled with yellow journalism. Any credibility the paper had was ruined by owner Ned McLean's lying to a Senate committee in 1924 about his involvement in the Teapot Dome oil scandal.

Eugene Meyer bought the bankrupt *Post* for $825,000 in 1933 and built a first-class news staff. By 1946, when Meyer's son-in-law Philip Graham took over as publisher, the *Post* was in the black again. In 1948 Meyer transferred his stock to his daughter Katharine and to Philip, her husband.

Graham bought radio and TV stations and established overseas bureaus. In 1961 he bought *Newsweek* magazine and started a news service with the *Los Angeles Times*. In 1963 Graham lost a struggle with manic depression and killed himself. An editor since 1939, Katharine became publisher after her husband's death.

The Washington Post Company began publishing the *International Herald Tribune* with The New York Times Company in 1967. In 1971 the company went public, though the Graham family retained control. The next year reporters Bob Woodward and Carl Bernstein broke the Watergate story, which led to President Richard Nixon's resignation and a Pulitzer Prize for the *Post*. In the 1970s and 1980s, under the tutelage of investor (and former *Post* paper boy) Warren Buffett, Katharine Graham bought TV and radio stations, cable TV firms, newspapers, newsprint mills, and Stanley H. Kaplan Educational Centers.

The guard changed at The Washington Post Company in 1991 when the Grahams' son Donald became CEO. In 1992 it invested in ACTV (interactive television) and bought 84% of Gaithersburg Gazette, Inc. (community newspapers, upped to 100% in 1993) and a sports cable TV system. Donald Graham became chairman when his mother stepped down in 1993.

In the search for a place in new media, The Washington Post Company made some mammoth errors. In 1995 the firm wrote off the $28 million it had invested in Mammoth Micro Products, a CD-ROM maker it had purchased in 1994. Also that year, blaming costs and delays, the company sold its 80% stake (acquired 1990) in American Personal Communications (wireless telephone systems).

In 1996 *Newsweek* columnist Joe Klein resigned after it was revealed that he was the anonymous author of *Primary Colors,* a thinly veiled satire of the 1992 Clinton campaign. Two years later the company completed the sale of its 28% interest in Cowles Media, publisher of the Minneapolis *Star Tribune,* and sought to bolster its coverage of information technology by buying two magazines and two Washington, DC-based conferences from Reed Elsevier. The company put *Newsweek* online in fall 1998 as Newsweek.com (the magazine had been available on the Web only through America Online).

The company sold key assets of its Legi-Slate service to Congressional Quarterly in 1999. Later that year it formed a partnership with TV network NBC in which the two firms agreed to share news content, technology, and promotional resources. The Washington Post Company branched out into travel information with its purchase of *Arthur Frommer's Budget Travel* near the end of 1999. In 2000 its Kaplan subsidiary created Kaplan Ventures to invest in education and career services companies and subsequently acquired postsecondary school operator Quest Education.

The Washington Post Company purchased 10 Maryland community papers from Chesapeake Publishing in 2001. The company's 2001 contract dispute with *Post* employees made headlines when reporters refused to allow their bylines to be used above their stories for several editions. Katharine Graham died later that year at age 84. In 2002 the company sold its stake in the *International Herald Tribune*.

The company shed its Post Newsweek Tech unit (trade publications and trade shows) in 2006. That same year it sold its 49% stake in online recruitment firm BrassRing to Kenexa.

## EXECUTIVES

**Chairman and CEO:** Donald E. (Don) Graham, age 61, $400,000 pay
**VP Finance and CFO:** John B. (Jay) Morse Jr., age 60, $585,000 pay
**VP, General Counsel, and Corporate Secretary:** Veronica Dillon, age 57
**VP Human Resources:** Ann L. McDaniel, age 51, $380,000 pay
**VP Planning and Development:** Gerald M. Rosberg, age 60, $400,000 pay
**VP:** Patrick Butler
**VP; VP Development, The Washington Post:** Christopher Ma
**President and CEO, Kaplan:** Jonathan Grayer
**President and CEO, Post-Newsweek Stations:** Alan Frank
**CEO and Publisher, Washingtonpost.Newsweek Interactive:** Caroline H. Little
**CEO and Publisher, The Washington Post:** Boisfeuillet (Bo) Jones
**Chairman and Editor-in-Chief, Newsweek:** Richard M. Smith
**CEO, Kaplan Professional:** William Macpherson
**President, Kaplan Professional:** Hal S. Jones
**President and General Manager, The Washington Post:** Stephen P. Hills
**VP Affiliates, The Washington Post:** Lionel W. Neptune
**VP Circulation, The Washington Post:** David C. Dadisman
**VP Government Affairs, The Washington Post:** Carol D. Melamed
**VP Labor, The Washington Post:** Patricia A. Dunn
**VP Marketing, The Washington Post:** Margaret M. Cromelin
**VP Operations, The Washington Post:** Michael Clurman
**VP Production, The Washington Post:** James W. Coley Jr.
**VP Communications, The Washington Post:** Theodore C. Lutz
**Executive Editor, The Washington Post:** Leonard Downie Jr.
**Treasurer:** Daniel J. Lynch
**Controller:** Wallace R. Cooney
**Auditors:** PricewaterhouseCoopers LLP

## LOCATIONS

**HQ:** The Washington Post Company
1150 15th St. NW, Washington, DC 20071
**Phone:** 202-334-6000 **Fax:** 202-334-4536
**Web:** www.washpostco.com

## PRODUCTS/OPERATIONS

**2006 Sales**

| | $ mil. | % of total |
|---|---|---|
| Education | 1,684.1 | 43 |
| Advertising | 1,358.7 | 35 |
| Circulation & subscriber | 782.5 | 20 |
| Other | 79.6 | 2 |
| **Total** | **3,904.9** | **100** |

### 2006 Sales

| | $ mil. | % of total |
|---|---|---|
| Education | 1,684.1 | 43 |
| Newspapers | 961.9 | 25 |
| Cable TV | 565.9 | 15 |
| Television stations | 361.9 | 9 |
| Magazines | 331.1 | 8 |
| **Total** | **3,904.9** | **100** |

### Selected Operations

Kaplan (test preparation and supplemental education services)
Newspapers
- *El Tiempo Latino* (Spanish-language free weekly)
- *Express* (free weekly)
- Greater Washington Publishing (free shoppers and advertisers)
- *The Herald* (Everett, Washington)
- Post-Newsweek Media (community newspapers, Maryland)
- *The Washington Post*
- Washingtonpost.Newsweek Interactive
  - BudgetTravelOnline.com
  - Classified Ventures (16%)
  - newsweek.com
  - Slate
  - washingtonpost.com

Cable One (cable TV service)
Television stations
- KPRC (NBC, Houston)
- KSAT (ABC, San Antonio)
- WDIV (NBC, Detroit)
- WJXT (independent; Jacksonville, FL)
- WKMG (CBS; Orlando, FL)
- WPLG (ABC, Miami)

Magazines
- *Arthur Frommer's Budget Travel*
- *Newsweek*

## COMPETITORS

Advance Publications
Comcast
DIRECTV
Dow Jones
EchoStar Communications
Gannett
Laureate Education
McClatchy Company
McGraw-Hill
New York Times
News Corp.
News World Communications
Pearson
Thomson Learning
Time Warner
Tribune
U.S. News & World Report

## HISTORICAL FINANCIALS

Company Type: Public

### Income Statement

FYE: Sunday nearest December 31

| | REVENUE ($ mil.) | NET INCOME ($ mil.) | NET PROFIT MARGIN | EMPLOYEES |
|---|---|---|---|---|
| **12/06** | 3,905 | 325 | 8.3% | 17,100 |
| **12/05** | 3,554 | 314 | 8.8% | 16,400 |
| **12/04** | 3,300 | 333 | 10.1% | 14,800 |
| **12/03** | 2,839 | 241 | 8.5% | 13,200 |
| **12/02** | 2,584 | 204 | 7.9% | 11,600 |
| **Annual Growth** | 10.9% | 12.3% | — | 10.2% |

### 2006 Year-End Financials

Debt ratio: 12.7%
Return on equity: 11.2%
Cash ($ mil.): 377
Current ratio: 1.16
Long-term debt ($ mil.): 402
No. of shares (mil.): 8
Dividends
Yield: 1.0%
Payout: 23.2%
Market value ($ mil.): 5,826

### Stock History

NYSE: WPO

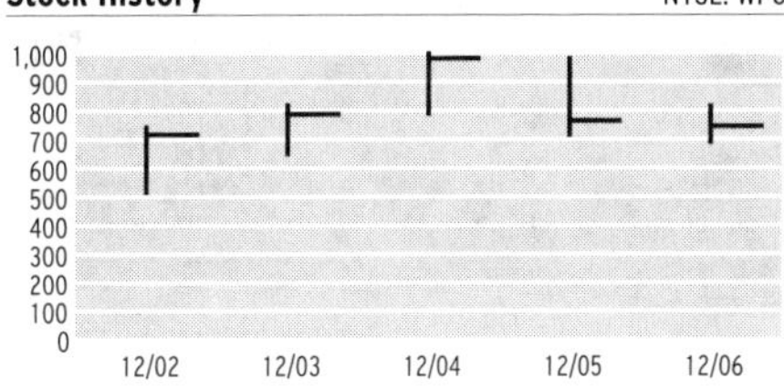


| | STOCK PRICE ($) FY Close | P/E High | P/E Low | PER SHARE ($) Earnings | Dividends | Book Value |
|---|---|---|---|---|---|---|
| **12/06** | 745.60 | 24 | 20 | 33.68 | 7.80 | 404.34 |
| **12/05** | 765.00 | 30 | 22 | 32.59 | 7.40 | 334.86 |
| **12/04** | 983.02 | 29 | 23 | 34.59 | 7.00 | 307.17 |
| **12/03** | 788.87 | 33 | 26 | 25.12 | 5.80 | 265.36 |
| **12/02** | 718.29 | 35 | 24 | 21.34 | 5.60 | 236.38 |
| **Annual Growth** | 0.9% | — | — | 12.1% | 8.6% | 14.4% |

# Waste Management

Holding company Waste Management, formerly USA Waste Services, tops the heap in the US solid waste industry (Allied Waste is #2). Through subsidiaries, the company serves about 21 million residential, industrial, municipal, and commercial customers in the US and Canada. Its four geographic groups and two functional groups (Recycling and Wheelabrator) provide waste collection, transfer, recycling and resource recovery, and disposal services. It has a network of more than 1,300 sites that it owns or operates — including roughly 283 landfills, 342 transfer stations, 108 material recovery facilities, 104 beneficial-use landfill gas projects, and 17 waste-to-energy plants.

The company manages its core North American Solid Waste operations through four geographic groups (Eastern, Midwest, Southern, and Western) and runs 17 waste-to-energy facilities through Wheelabrator Technologies. The company carries out recycling operations through Recycle America Alliance, L.L.C. To reduce the costly layers of management, the group has restructured most of its operations into some 80 market areas, which oversee each district's sales, marketing, and delivery services. Other company operations include the rental and servicing of portable restroom facilities to municipalities and commercial customers (Port-O-Let) and providing street and parking lot sweeping services and in-plant services.

Wheelabrator has converted more than 110 million tons of nonhazardous municipal solid waste into renewable electric power since 1975, when the company pioneered the waste-to-energy industry in Massachusetts. Wheelabrator also operates six independent power producers (IPPs) that convert waste and conventional fuels into electricity and produce steam.

The group supplies methane gas at 104 of its solid waste landfills, which is either sold for gas-to-energy plants to generate electricity or pipelined to industrial customers to use as a substitute fuel in steam boilers, cement kilns, and utility plants.

The group's recycling segment operates Waste Management's network of materials recovery facilities, which process more than 5 million tons of recyclable items per year. The segments provide waste paper, glass, plastic, metal, wood, and other scrap item recycling services through 108 material recovery facilities and five secondary processing facilities.

Waste Management has been active in consolidating the waste industry in recent years, but in doing so has incurred mounds of debt. To pay down debt, the company has sold solid- and hazardous-waste management businesses in Asia, Europe, and South America, and it is selling some noncore North American assets as well.

## HISTORY

In 1956 Dean Buntrock joined his in-laws' business, Ace Scavenger Service, an Illinois company that Buntrock expanded into Wisconsin.

Waste Management, Inc., was formed in 1971 when Buntrock joined forces with his cousin, Wayne Huizenga, who had purchased two waste routes in Florida in 1962. In the 1970s Waste Management bought companies in Michigan, New York, Ohio, Pennsylvania, and Canada. By 1975 it had an international subsidiary.

The company divided into specialty areas by forming Chemical Waste Management (1975) and offering site-cleanup services (ENRAC, 1980) and low-level nuclear-waste disposal (Chem-Nuclear Systems, 1982).

USA Waste was founded in 1987 to run disposal and collection operations in Oklahoma. It went public in 1988, and in 1990 Don Moorehead, a founder and former CEO of Mid-American Waste Systems, bought a controlling interest (most of which he later sold). Moorehead moved the business to Dallas and began buying companies in the fragmented industry. John Drury, a former president of Browning-Ferris, joined USA Waste in 1994 as CEO.

As USA Waste gathered steam, Waste Management got off track. It diversified, and Buntrock renamed the company WMX Technologies in 1993 to de-emphasize its waste operations. In 1997, however, the company reverted to the Waste Management name and, pressured by disappointed investor George Soros, CEO Phillip Rooney resigned. After more management changes, turnaround specialist Steve Miller became CEO, the fourth one in eight months, and Buntrock retired.

USA Waste picked up market share with large acquisitions, including Envirofill (1994), Chambers Development Corporation (1995), and Western Waste Industries and Sanifill (1996). In 1996 the company moved to Houston.

1998 saw the $20-billion merger between USA Waste and Waste Management. The new company, bearing the Waste Management name and led by Drury and other former USA Waste executives, controlled nearly a quarter of North America's waste business. The company finished the year by agreeing to pay shareholders $220 million in a suit over overstated earnings.

The new Waste Management bought Eastern Environmental Services for $1.3 billion in 1999. Drury took leave in 1999 because of an illness that would claim his life, and director Ralph Whitworth, known as a shareholder activist, stepped in as acting chairman.

The company faced shareholder lawsuits after it was reported that executives had sold shares before a second-quarter earnings shortfall was announced. Waste Management said it would investigate the sales; later, so did the SEC. (By 2001 the company had settled with both the SEC and shareholders.) In the fallout, president and COO Rodney Proto, who had sold shares before the earnings announcement, was fired. Later that year the company tapped Maury Myers, CEO of trucking company Yellow Corp., to take over as chairman and CEO.

In 2000, to concentrate on its core business in North America, Waste Management sold operations in Europe, Asia, and South America in a series of transactions that raised about $2.5 billion.

In early 2002 Waste Management announced plans to restructure the company by reorganizing its operating areas and cutting its workforce of 57,000 by about 3.5%. Also that year the SEC sued six former Waste Management executives, charging that they had enriched themselves through accounting fraud between 1992 and 1997.

The company formed a new recycling unit, Recycle America Alliance, in 2003, after acquiring Milwaukee-based The Peltz Group, the largest privately held recycler in the US. That year two former executives of Waste Management, Proto and CFO Earl DeFrates, agreed to a settlement with the SEC on allegations that they had profited from insider trading in 1999.

## EXECUTIVES

**Chairman:** John C. (Jack) Pope, age 58
**CEO and Director:** David P. Steiner, age 46, $904,808 pay
**President and COO:** Lawrence (Larry) O'Donnell III, age 49, $686,094 pay
**SVP and CFO:** Robert G. (Bob) Simpson, age 54, $461,960 pay
**SVP and CIO:** Lynn M. Caddell, age 53
**SVP, Business Development and Strategy:** Richard T. (Rich) Felago, age 59
**SVP, Employee and Customer Engagement:** James T. (Jim) Schultz, age 57
**SVP, Government Affairs and Corporate Communications:** Barry H. Caldwell, age 46
**SVP, Operations:** Charles E. (Chuck) Williams, age 56
**SVP, General Counsel, and Chief Compliance Officer:** Richard L. (Rick) Wittenbraker, age 58
**SVP, Sales and Marketing:** David A. (Dave) Aardsma, age 50
**SVP, Midwest Group:** Jeff M. Harris, age 52
**SVP, Western Group:** Duane C. Woods, age 55, $485,312 pay
**SVP, People:** Michael J. (Jay) Romans, age 56
**VP, Corporate Human Resources, Business Ethics and Diversity:** Carlton Yearwood
**VP, Corporate Communications:** Lynn C. Brown
**Auditors:** Ernst & Young LLP

## LOCATIONS

**HQ:** Waste Management, Inc.
1001 Fannin St., Ste. 4000, Houston, TX 77002
**Phone:** 713-512-6200 **Fax:** 713-512-6299
**Web:** www.wm.com

Waste Management has operations in every US state except Montana and Wyoming. It also has operations in the District of Columbia, Puerto Rico, and Canada.

**2006 Sales**

| | $ mil. | % of total |
|---|---|---|
| Eastern | 3,830 | 24 |
| Southern | 3,759 | 24 |
| Western | 3,160 | 20 |
| Midwest | 3,112 | 20 |
| Wheelabrator | 902 | 6 |
| Recycling | 766 | 5 |
| Other | 283 | 1 |
| Adjustments | (2,449) | — |
| **Total** | **13,363** | **100** |

## PRODUCTS/OPERATIONS

**2006 Sales**

| | $ mil. | % of total |
|---|---|---|
| Collection | 8,837 | 56 |
| Landfill | 3,197 | 20 |
| Transfer | 1,802 | 11 |
| Wheelabrator | 902 | 6 |
| Recycling & other | 1,074 | 7 |
| Adjustments | (2,449) | — |
| **Total** | **13,363** | **100** |

**Selected Services**

Collection
Disposal
Hazardous waste management
Landfill management
Portable sanitation services
Recycling
Transfer stations
Treatment

## COMPETITORS

Allied Waste
Casella Waste Systems
IESI
Republic Services
Rumpke
Safety-Kleen
Veolia ES Solid Waste
Waste Connections
WCA Waste

## HISTORICAL FINANCIALS

Company Type: Public

**Income Statement** FYE: December 31

| | REVENUE ($ mil.) | NET INCOME ($ mil.) | NET PROFIT MARGIN | EMPLOYEES |
|---|---|---|---|---|
| **12/06** | 13,363 | 1,149 | 8.6% | 48,000 |
| **12/05** | 13,074 | 1,182 | 9.0% | 50,000 |
| **12/04** | 12,516 | 939 | 7.5% | 51,000 |
| **12/03** | 11,574 | 630 | 5.4% | 51,700 |
| **12/02** | 11,142 | 822 | 7.4% | 53,000 |
| **Annual Growth** | 4.6% | 8.7% | — | (2.4%) |

**2006 Year-End Financials**

Debt ratio: 120.5%
Return on equity: 18.6%
Cash ($ mil.): 614
Current ratio: 0.97
Long-term debt ($ mil.): 7,495
No. of shares (mil.): 534
Dividends
Yield: 2.4%
Payout: 41.9%
Market value ($ mil.): 19,624

**Stock History** NYSE: WMI

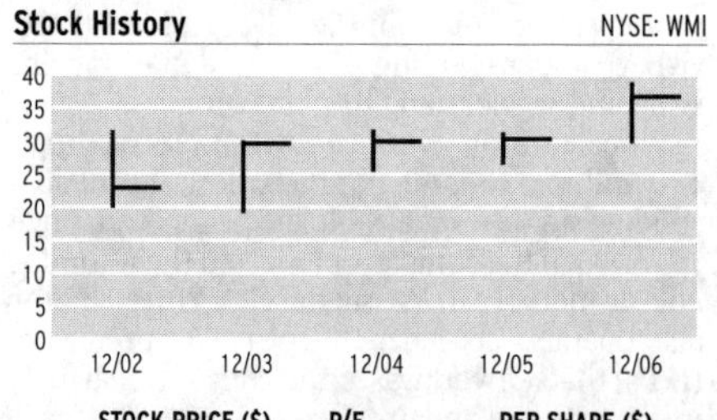


| | STOCK PRICE ($) FY Close | P/E High | P/E Low | PER SHARE ($) Earnings | Dividends | Book Value |
|---|---|---|---|---|---|---|
| **12/06** | 36.77 | 18 | 14 | 2.10 | 0.88 | 11.66 |
| **12/05** | 30.35 | 15 | 13 | 2.09 | 0.80 | 11.08 |
| **12/04** | 29.94 | 20 | 16 | 1.61 | 0.75 | 10.47 |
| **12/03** | 29.60 | 28 | 18 | 1.06 | 0.01 | 9.66 |
| **12/02** | 22.92 | 23 | 15 | 1.33 | 0.01 | 8.93 |
| **Annual Growth** | 12.5% | — | — | 12.1% | 206.3% | 6.9% |

# Watsco, Inc.

Keeping the Sunbelt cool makes Watsco a hot company. The company is one of the largest independent distributors of residential central air conditioners in the US, with some 380 locations in more than 30 states. It also stocks heating systems and industrial and commercial refrigeration products, and it provides installation and repair equipment for its products. Watsco serves contractors and dealers through its distribution centers, and it exports to Latin America and the Caribbean (less than 1% of sales). Entities affiliated with CEO and chairman Albert Nahmad own more than 55% of Watsco.

The company is buying ACR, a rival HVAC distributor, for about $78 million.

Watsco purchases more than 45% of its products from equipment suppliers Rheem, Carrier, Nordyne, Goodman, American Standard, and Lennox. It also distributes refrigeration products from such manufacturers as Emerson Electric's Copeland Compressor, Tecumseh Products, and The Manitowoc Company.

Since air conditioning units having a working lifespan from eight to 20 years, the replacement market is the most lucrative part of Watsco's business, with higher growth margins. Watsco also focuses on acquisitions to expand existing markets or move into new ones.

The firm's Dunhill Staffing Systems unit provides temporary and permanent employment services in the US and Canada; it also offers franchising opportunities.

## HISTORY

Watsco was founded in 1945 as a maker of climate-control components. The company grew slowly until the mid-1980s, when a building boom and aggressive marketing increased sales. Albert Nahmad, the company's president since 1973, began looking for acquisitions, and in 1988 Watsco acquired Dunhill. When Dunhill didn't provide the profits Watsco wanted, Nahmad moved into residential air-conditioning (AC) distribution. Watsco bought 80% of Florida's Gemaire (1989) and 50% of Heating and Cooling Supply, the #1 residential central AC distributor in Southern California and Arizona (1990).

The company moved into the Texas market with the acquisition of distributor Comfort Supply in 1993. It then acquired H.B. Adams, a Florida distributor of air conditioners, in 1995. Purchases the following year added another 25 distribution branches. Watsco picked up four locations from heating and AC manufacturer Inter-City Products in 1997 and acquired Coastline Distribution (21 branches), as well as two midwestern distribution operations (Central Plains Distributing and Comfort Products Distributing) from Carrier. Watsco's acquisition streak heated up in 1998 when it bought Oklahoma-based Superior Supply Company, Tennessee-based KingAire, and Kaufman Supply, an AC distributor for the manufactured-housing market.

Acquisitions continued into 1999 as Watsco purchased Homans Associates and Heat Inc., both of which served New England, and Atlantic Air, which served several western states. Watsco signed an agreement in 2000 with Ariba (Web-based procurement software) to enable customers to order products online. The next year, the company closed seven facilities.

After Pameco filed for bankruptcy in 2003, Watsco purchased the company's HVAC and related parts and supplies operations, which sold from more than 40 locations in Arkansas, Louisiana, Mississippi, and Texas.

Acquisitions continued in 2005, when Watsco bought family-owned East Coast Metal Distributors, a distributor of air-conditioning and heating products operating from 27 locations that served more than 3,500 contractors throughout the Carolinas, Georgia, Virginia, and Tennessee.

## EXECUTIVES

**Chairman, President, and CEO:** Albert H. Nahmad, age 66, $960,000 pay
**SVP and Secretary:** Barry S. Logan, age 44, $665,000 pay
**CFO and Treasurer:** Ana M. Menendez, age 42, $165,000 pay
**VP Human Resources:** John Mills
**President, East Coast Metal Distributors:** Jeff Files, age 60
**President, Baker Distributing:** Carole J. Poindexter, age 51, $300,000 pay
**President, Gemaire Distributor:** Stephen R. Combs, age 63, $300,000 pay
**Auditors:** Grant Thornton LLP

## LOCATIONS

**HQ:** Watsco, Inc.
2665 S. Bayshore Dr., Ste. 901,
Coconut Grove, FL 33133
**Phone:** 305-714-4100 **Fax:** 305-858-4492
**Web:** www.watsco.com

Watsco operates from about 380 distribution locations in Alabama, Arizona, Arkansas, California, Connecticut, Florida, Georgia, Illinois, Iowa, Kansas, Kentucky, Louisiana, Maine, Maryland, Massachusetts, Mississippi, Missouri, Nebraska, Nevada, New Hampshire, New Jersey, New York, North Carolina, North Dakota, Oklahoma, Rhode Island, South Carolina, South Dakota, Tennessee, Texas, Vermont, and Virginia.

## PRODUCTS/OPERATIONS

### 2006 Sales

| | % of total |
|---|---|
| HVAC distribution | 98 |
| Staffing | 2 |
| **Total** | **100** |

### Selected Subsidiaries

Air Systems Distributors LLC
Atlantic Service & Supply LLC
Baker Distributing Company LLC
Comfort Products Distributing LLC
Comfort Supply, Inc.
Dunhill Staffing Systems, Inc.
Dunhill Temporary Systems, Inc.
East Coast Metal Distributors LLC
Gemaire Distributors LLC
Heat Incorporated LLC
Heating & Cooling Supply LLC
Homans Associates LLC
Three States Supply Company LLC
Tradewinds Distributing Company LLC

## COMPETITORS

ACR Group
Gustave A. Larson Company
HD Supply
Johnson Controls
Johnstone Supply
Lennox
Mestek
Noland
Russell Sigler
Sears
US Airconditioning Distributors

## HISTORICAL FINANCIALS

Company Type: Public

### Income Statement

FYE: December 31

| | REVENUE ($ mil.) | NET INCOME ($ mil.) | NET PROFIT MARGIN | EMPLOYEES |
|---|---|---|---|---|
| **12/06** | 1,801 | 82 | 4.6% | 3,300 |
| **12/05** | 1,683 | 70 | 4.2% | 3,200 |
| **12/04** | 1,315 | 48 | 3.7% | 2,700 |
| **12/03** | 1,233 | 35 | 2.8% | 2,600 |
| **12/02** | 1,181 | 29 | 2.4% | 2,400 |
| **Annual Growth** | 11.1% | 30.4% | — | 8.3% |

### 2006 Year-End Financials

Debt ratio: 5.8%
Return on equity: 17.0%
Cash ($ mil.): 34
Current ratio: 3.32
Long-term debt ($ mil.): 30
No. of shares (mil.): 24
Dividends
Yield: 2.0%
Payout: 32.1%
Market value ($ mil.): 1,136

### Stock History

NYSE: WSO

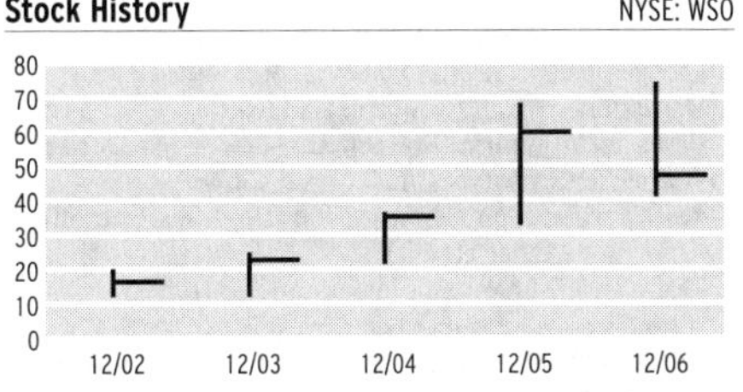

| | STOCK PRICE ($) FY Close | P/E High | P/E Low | PER SHARE ($) Earnings | Dividends | Book Value |
|---|---|---|---|---|---|---|
| **12/06** | 47.16 | 25 | 14 | 2.96 | 0.95 | 21.44 |
| **12/05** | 59.81 | 27 | 13 | 2.52 | 0.62 | 18.72 |
| **12/04** | 35.22 | 20 | 12 | 1.79 | 0.38 | 17.40 |
| **12/03** | 22.73 | 18 | 9 | 1.34 | 0.20 | 15.93 |
| **12/02** | 16.38 | 18 | 12 | 1.07 | 0.12 | 14.63 |
| **Annual Growth** | 30.3% | — | — | 29.0% | 67.7% | 10.0% |

# Watson Pharmaceuticals

Watson Pharmaceuticals tries to have the best of both worlds, with operations in the booming generics segment and the higher-profit-margin branded drug business. The company's broad generics portfolio of about 150 products includes treatments for hypertension and pain, as well as smoking cessation products and oral contraceptives.The company also makes generic forms of pain drug Vicodin, anti-smoking gum Nicorette, and birth control pill Ortho Tri-Cyclen. Watson's line of about 25 branded drugs focuses on urology and iron deficiency anemia, but also features analgesics and contraceptives, among others.

Watson Pharmaceuticals' bread and butter is its generics line, accounting for about three-quarters of sales, and it continues to expand its development of these drugs at a fast clip; the company launched about a dozen off-patent products in 2006, and it has about 70 applications for new generics before the FDA.

The company boosted its generics business significantly in 2006 by acquiring Andrx. In addition to deepening Watson's product portfolio, the addition of Andrx — with its expertise in controlled-release technology — furthers the company's strategy of developing technically challenging generic equivalents. Watson also got itself into the drug distribution business through the acquisition: Two Andrx subsidiaries, Anda and Valmed, distribute primarily generic drugs made by other companies (and some made by Watson) to independent pharmacies, pharmacy buying groups, and doctors' offices.

The Federal Trade Commission required that Watson divest product lines that overlap with Andrx in order to preserve competition; as a result, the company is ending an agreement with Interpharm to sell ibuprofen and must sell its rights to a generic diabetes medication.

Key products in the company's branded drug segment include prostate cancer therapy Trelstar and anemia drug Ferrlecit (used for patients undergoing dialysis). Watson is building its branded product line through several partnerships and joint ventures. It is developing Silodosin, a treatment for enlarged prostate, through a licensing agreement with Kissei Pharmaceuticals. Additionally, its 50/50 joint venture with Mylan Laboratories, known as Somerset Pharmaceuticals, received approval in 2006 for depression treatment Emsam.

Watson's customers include McKesson, which accounts for 17% of the company's sales, AmerisourceBergen (13%), Cardinal Health (9%), and Walgreen Co. (8%).

Chairman and CEO Allen Chao, who retires as CEO in September 2007, holds about 5% of the company.

## HISTORY

As a youth, chairman and CEO Allen Chao worked at his parents' Taiwan drug factory. After taking a PhD in pharmacology in the US and working at G.D. Searle for 10 years, Chao cofounded Watson in 1984 with $4 million raised from family and friends. Watson (an anglicized version of "Hwa's son" — based on his mother's name) introduced its first generic drug, a furosemide tablet (a diuretic), in 1985. The company went public in 1993.

At first Watson focused on products that posed manufacturing challenges or had limited markets. In the mid-1990s it diversified into drug development in cooperation with other firms, such as Rhône-Poulenc (now part of Sanofi-Aventis). It bought competitors (Circa Pharmaceuticals, 1995) and invested in drug research companies. In 1996 the company launched its first proprietary drug, Microzide, an antihypertensive. Watson acquired Royce Laboratories (generic drugs) and Oclassen Pharmaceuticals (dermatology products) and boosted its sales force substantially in 1997. It also acquired rights to several products, including Dilacor XR.

In 1998 Watson bought drug-delivery systems maker TheraTech (taking immediate steps to regain control of its transdermal hormone-replacement system) and Rugby Group, the US generic drug unit of Hoechst (now part of Sanofi-Aventis). The 1999 launch of the company's Nicotine Polacrilax (an off-patent version of the nicotine gum made by SmithKline Beecham, now GlaxoSmithKline) was hampered by SmithKline's claim that accompanying instructional materials breached its copyrights (the courts ruled in favor of Watson in 2000). To boost its research activities, in 2000 the firm bought Makoff R&D Laboratories and Schein Pharmaceutical. Three years later it bought Amarin Corp.'s Swedish R&D subsidiary.

## EXECUTIVES

**Chairman, President, and CEO:** Allen Y. Chao, age 61, $1,157,692 pay
**President, CEO, and Director:** Paul M. Bisaro, age 46
**EVP; President, Brand Division:** Edward Heimers, age 60, $332,573 pay
**EVP; President, Generics Division:** Thomas R. (Tom) Russillo, age 65
**SVP and CIO:** Thomas R. Giordano, age 56
**SVP, Human Resources:** Susan Skara, age 56
**SVP, New Product Introduction and Operations:** Maria Chow Yee, age 52
**SVP, Sales and Marketing, U.S. Generics Division:** Andrew Boyer
**SVP, Research and Development:** Charles D. Ebert, age 53, $402,556 pay
**SVP, Scientific Affairs:** David C. Hsia, age 62
**SVP, General Counsel, and Secretary:** David A. Buchen, age 42, $377,237 pay
**VP, Interim Principal Financial Officer, Corporate Controller, and Treasurer:** R. Todd Joyce, $254,925 pay
**VP, National Accounts:** Allan Slavsky
**Director, Investor Relations:** Patricia Eisenhaur
**EVP and COO, Anda, Inc:** Albert Paonessa III, age 47
**Auditors:** PricewaterhouseCoopers LLP

## LOCATIONS

**HQ:** Watson Pharmaceuticals, Inc.
311 Bonnie Cir., Corona, CA 92880
**Phone:** 951-493-5300 **Fax:** 973-355-8301
**Web:** www.watsonpharm.com

Watson Pharmaceuticals has facilities in China, India, the UK, and the US.

## PRODUCTS/OPERATIONS

### 2006 Sales

| | $ mil. | % of total |
|---|---|---|
| Generics | 1,501 | 76 |
| Branded drugs | 354 | 18 |
| Distribution | 93 | 5 |
| Other | 31 | 1 |
| **Total** | **1,979** | **100** |

### Selected Subsidiaries

Anda, Inc.
Andrx Corporation
Andrx Pharmaceuticals, Inc.
Makoff R&D Laboratories, Inc.
Nicobrand Limited (UK)
The Rugby Group, Inc.
Valmed Pharmaceutical, Inc.
Watson Laboratories Caribe, Inc.
Watson Laboratories, Inc.
Watson Pharma, Inc.

### Selected Products

Branded
- Actigall (gallstone dissolution)
- Androderm (male hormone replacement)
- Condylox (genital warts)
- Cordran (topical steroid)
- Ferrlecit (anemia in dialysis patients)
- Fioricet (tension headaches)
- Fiorinal (tension headaches)
- INFeD (anemia)
- Norco (analgesic)
- Norinyl (oral contraceptive)
- Nor-QD (oral contraceptive)
- Oxytrol (overactive bladder)
- Trelstar DEPOT (prostate cancer)
- Trelstar LA (prostate cancer)
- Tri-Norinyl (oral contraceptive)

Generic
- Bupropion hydrochloride (Zyban, smoking cessation)
- Bupropion hydrochloride (Wellbutrin SR, antidepressant)
- Cartia XT (Cardizem CD, anti-hypertensive)
- Glipizide ER (Glucotrol XL, anti-diabetic)
- Hydrocodone bitartrate/acetaminophen (Lorcet, analgesic)
- Hydrocodone bitartrate/acetaminophen (Vicodin, analgesic)
- Hydrocodone bitartrate/acetaminophen (Lortab, analgesic)
- Hydrocodone bitartrate/acetaminophen (Norco, analgesic)
- Levora (Nordette, oral contraceptive)
- Low-Ogestrel (Lo-Ovral, oral contraceptive)
- Microgestin/Microgestin Fe (Loestrin/Loestrin Fe, oral contraceptive)
- Necon (Ortho-Novum, oral contraceptive)
- Necon (Modicon, oral contraceptive)
- Nicotine polacrilex gum (Nicorette, smoking cessation)
- Nicotine transdermal system (Habitrol, smoking cessation)
- Nifedipine ER (Adalat CC, anti-hypertensive)
- Oxycodone/acetaminophen (Percocet, analgesic)
- Oxycodone/HCL (Oxycontin, analgesic)
- Pravastatin sodium (Pravachol, cholesterol-lowering)
- Quasense (Seasonale, oral contraceptive)
- Testosterone cypionate injection (Depo-Testosterone, hormone replacement)
- Testosterone enanthate injection (Delatestryl, hormone replacement)
- TriNessaTM (Ortho Tri-Cyclen, oral contraceptive)
- Trivora (Triphasil, oral contraceptive)
- Zovia (Demulen, oral contraceptive)

## COMPETITORS

AmerisourceBergen
Amgen
Auxilium Pharmaceuticals
Barr Pharmaceuticals
Bayer Schering Pharma
Bristol-Myers Squibb
Cardinal Health
Forest Labs
GlaxoSmithKline
Johnson & Johnson
Kinray
Mallinckrodt
Mayne Pharma (USA)
McKesson
Merck
Mylan Labs
Novartis
Organon
Pfizer
Sandoz International GmbH
Teva Pharmaceuticals

## HISTORICAL FINANCIALS

Company Type: Public

### Income Statement

FYE: December 31

| | REVENUE ($ mil.) | NET INCOME ($ mil.) | NET PROFIT MARGIN | EMPLOYEES |
|---|---|---|---|---|
| **12/06** | 1,979 | (445) | — | 5,830 |
| **12/05** | 1,646 | 138 | 8.4% | 3,844 |
| **12/04** | 1,641 | 151 | 9.2% | 3,851 |
| **12/03** | 1,458 | 203 | 13.9% | 3,983 |
| **12/02** | 1,223 | 176 | 14.4% | 3,729 |
| **Annual Growth** | 12.8% | — | — | 11.8% |

### 2006 Year-End Financials

Debt ratio: 66.9%
Return on equity: —
Cash ($ mil.): 161
Current ratio: 1.83
Long-term debt ($ mil.): 1,124
No. of shares (mil.): 112
Dividends
Yield: —
Payout: —
Market value ($ mil.): 2,912

### Stock History

NYSE: WPI

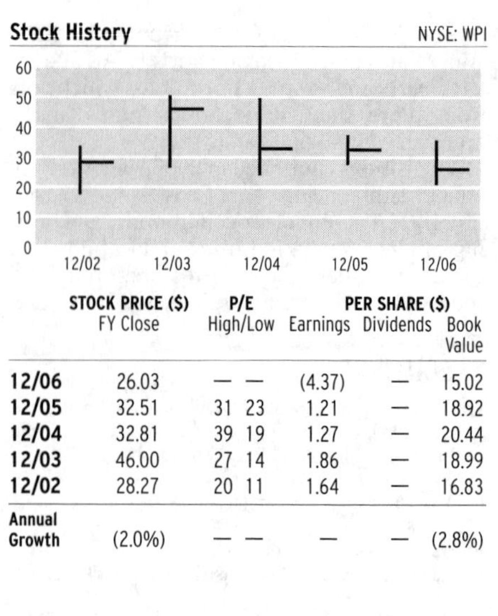

| | STOCK PRICE ($) FY Close | P/E High | P/E Low | PER SHARE ($) Earnings | Dividends | Book Value |
|---|---|---|---|---|---|---|
| **12/06** | 26.03 | — | — | (4.37) | — | 15.02 |
| **12/05** | 32.51 | 31 | 23 | 1.21 | — | 18.92 |
| **12/04** | 32.81 | 39 | 19 | 1.27 | — | 20.44 |
| **12/03** | 46.00 | 27 | 14 | 1.86 | — | 18.99 |
| **12/02** | 28.27 | 20 | 11 | 1.64 | — | 16.83 |
| **Annual Growth** | (2.0%) | — | — | — | — | (2.8%) |

# Weatherford International

When there's oil or natural gas in them there fields, Weatherford International can help get it out. The company, which is domiciled in Bermuda but based in Houston, supplies a wide range of equipment and services used in the oil and gas drilling industries. Weatherford provides well installation and completion systems, equipment rental, and fishing services (removing debris from wells). It provides pipeline services and oil recovery and hydraulic lift and electric submersible pumps to the oil and gas industry. The company also offers contract land drilling services. In 2005 Weatherford acquired two divisions of Canada's Precision Drilling for $2.3 billion.

Weatherford has reorganized its operations in an effort to provide seamless services to its customers. The company sold its compression fabrication business to Universal Compression Holdings in 2004.

Operating in a volatile market, Weatherford has strengthened its product offerings through acquisitions and geographic expansion, including the purchase of Williams Tool (control flow products), Scotland-based Petroline Wellsystems (provider of completion products), Canadian firm Alpine Oil Services (under-balanced drilling equipment), US-based CAC (control systems), UK company Orwell (oil field services), and Louisiana-based Eclipse Packer (coiled tubing and gravel packing systems). The company has also created WellServ, a full services well intervention unit.

## HISTORY

Energy Ventures was founded in 1972 as an offshore oil and gas explorer and producer. In 1981 it became a 50-50 partner with Northwest Energy in an oil field located in Hockley County, Texas. By 1982 Northwest had increased its ownership in Energy Ventures to about 25%.

Majority stockholder Appalachian attempted a takeover in 1984, but later agreed to drop the takeover in exchange for the liquidation of Energy Ventures. A slump in oil and gas prices in 1985 derailed the plan.

By the late 1980s Energy Ventures was vertically integrating by buying oil field product makers such as Grant Oil Country Tubular (1990) and Prideco (1995). Grant and Prideco were combined in 1995, solidifying the company's position as a leading supplier of drill pipe and tubulars. In 1997 the company built a manufacturing facility in Canada and changed its name to EVI.

EVI doubled its size in 1998 by merging with oil field services firm Weatherford Enterra, which had been formed by the 1995 combination of Houston-based firms Weatherford International and Enterra. The newly combined company adopted the Weatherford International name shortly thereafter.

In 1999 Weatherford acquired Christiana Companies, whose 33% interest in Total Logistic Control introduced Weatherford to the warehousing and trucking business. Also, Weatherford bought Scotland-based Petroline Wellsystems, which makes oil and gas well completion products.

The following year the company spun off its drill pipe and casings maker, Grant Prideco. Also in 2000 the company continued its geographic expansion with the purchase of Gas Services International (compression systems serving Asia and the Middle East), Oakwell Compressor Packages of the Netherlands, and Alpine Oil Services of Canada.

In 2001, after buying out GE Capital's 36% interest in its natural gas compression joint venture, Weatherford exchanged the subsidiary for a 48% stake in Universal Compression Holdings. That year the company's acquisitions included US-based CAC, a maker of control systems for the oil and gas industry, and Scottish oil field services company Orwell, which widened its presence in the North Sea, Asia/Pacific, and Middle East regions.

To reduce its US tax obligations, Weatherford reincorporated in Bermuda in 2002. Later that year it formed a pipeline and specialty service group within its Drilling and Intervention Services division to offer pipe cleaning, testing, and inspection services.

In 2003, Weatherford completed the formation of WellServ, a full services well intervention group, through its Drilling & Intervention Services division. Also that year the company completed its acquisition of Eclipse Packer, a Louisiana-based provider of coiled tubing and gravel packer systems.

## EXECUTIVES

**Chairman, President, and CEO:** Bernard J. Duroc-Danner, age 53, $3,125,875 pay
**SVP and COO:** E. Lee Colley III, age 50
**SVP and CFO:** Andrew P. Becnel, age 39
**SVP and CTO:** Stuart E. Ferguson, age 40
**SVP, General Counsel, and Secretary:** Burt M. Martin, age 43, $904,427 pay
**SVP and Chief Safety Officer:** Keith R. Morley, age 56
**SVP Global Human Resources:** Neal Gillenwater
**VP Accounting and Chief Accounting Officer:** Jessica Abarca, age 35
**VP Global Manufacturing:** M. David Colley, age 46
**VP Marketing:** Christine McGee
**VP Finance:** Danielle Nicholas
**VP Global Market and Sales Support:** Pat Bond
**VP Expandable Sand Screens:** Gary Smart
**VP Production Optimization Systems:** Dharmesh Mehta
**VP Drilling Tools and Services; VP Fishing, Re-Entry, and Decommissioning:** Jim Martens
**VP Drilling Methods:** Paul Timmins
**VP Drilling Hazard Mitigation, Separation, and Pipeline and Specialty Services:** Carel Hoyer
**VP Drilling Rig and Contractor Services:** Niels Espeland
**VP Wireline Services:** Todd Parker
**Marketing Coordinator:** Kim Payne
**Auditors:** Ernst & Young LLP

## LOCATIONS

**HQ:** Weatherford International Ltd.
515 Post Oak Blvd., Ste. 600, Houston, TX 77027
**Phone:** 713-693-4000 **Fax:** 713-693-4323
**Web:** www.weatherford.com

Weatherford International operates from about 730 locations in 100 countries. It also has 90 manufacturing facilities in Algeria, Argentina, Australia, Brazil, Canada, Colombia, France, Germany, Libya, Norway, Slovakia, the UK, the US, and Yemen.

**2006 Sales**

| | % of total |
|---|---|
| US | 38 |
| Canada | 18 |
| Middle East & North Africa | 14 |
| Europe, former Soviet republics & West Africa | 13 |
| Latin America | 11 |
| Asia/Pacific | 6 |
| **Total** | **100** |

## PRODUCTS/OPERATIONS

**2006 Sales**

| | $ mil. | % of total |
|---|---|---|
| Evaluation, drilling & intervention services | 4,234.0 | 64 |
| Completion & production systems | 2,344.9 | 36 |
| **Total** | **6,578.9** | **100** |

**Operating Divisions**

Evaluation, drilling, and intervention services
Completion and production systems
Pipeline and specialty services
International contract drilling

## COMPETITORS

Baker Hughes
BJ Services
CE Franklin
Dover
Halliburton
National Oilwell Varco
Precision Drilling
Robbins & Myers
Schlumberger
Smith International
Tesco Corporation
W-H Energy Services
Wilson

## HISTORICAL FINANCIALS

Company Type: Public

**Income Statement** FYE: December 31

| | REVENUE ($ mil.) | NET INCOME ($ mil.) | NET PROFIT MARGIN | EMPLOYEES |
|---|---|---|---|---|
| 12/06 | 6,579 | 896 | 13.6% | 33,000 |
| 12/05 | 4,333 | 467 | 10.8% | 25,100 |
| 12/04 | 3,132 | 330 | 10.5% | 18,400 |
| 12/03 | 2,591 | 143 | 5.5% | 16,700 |
| 12/02 | 2,329 | (6) | — | 15,700 |
| Annual Growth | 29.6% | — | — | 20.4% |

**2006 Year-End Financials**

Debt ratio: 25.3%
Return on equity: 15.1%
Cash ($ mil.): 126
Current ratio: 1.64
Long-term debt ($ mil.): 1,565
No. of shares (mil.): 340
Dividends
Yield: —
Payout: —
Market value ($ mil.): 14,200

**Stock History** NYSE: WFT

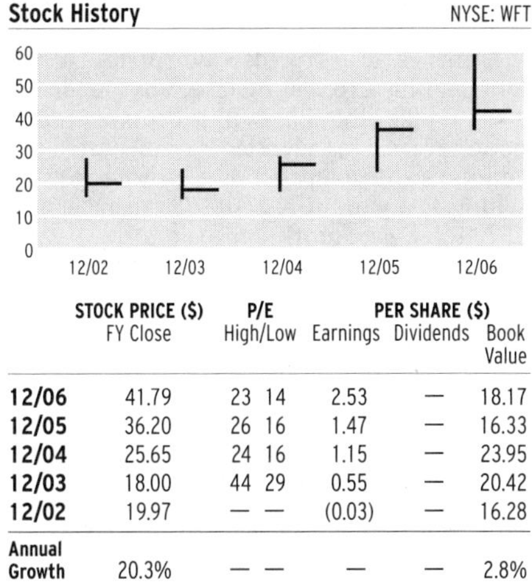


| | STOCK PRICE ($) FY Close | P/E High | P/E Low | PER SHARE ($) Earnings | Dividends | Book Value |
|---|---|---|---|---|---|---|
| 12/06 | 41.79 | 23 | 14 | 2.53 | — | 18.17 |
| 12/05 | 36.20 | 26 | 16 | 1.47 | — | 16.33 |
| 12/04 | 25.65 | 24 | 16 | 1.15 | — | 23.95 |
| 12/03 | 18.00 | 44 | 29 | 0.55 | — | 20.42 |
| 12/02 | 19.97 | — | — | (0.03) | — | 16.28 |
| Annual Growth | 20.3% | — | — | — | — | 2.8% |

# WellPoint, Inc.

The nation's largest health insurer, WellPoint is finding out what B. B. King already knows: Getting the blues ain't easy. Through its subsidiaries, the company provides health coverage, primarily under the Blue Cross and Blue Shield name, to more than 34 million medical members. It is a Blue Cross or BCBS licensee in 14 states and provides plans under the Unicare name in other parts of the country. WellPoint offers a broad range of managed care plans (including PPO, HMO, indemnity, and hybrid plans) to employers, individuals, and recipients of Medicare and Medicaid. It also provides administrative services (claims processing and underwriting) to self-insured groups and specialty insurance products.

The company's specialty products include dental, vision, mental health, long-term care, and group life insurance, as well as pharmacy benefit management services and flexible spending accounts. Additionally, through several of its subsidiaries (including National Government Services and United Government Services), the company provides claims processing and other administrative services to Medicare plans.

Nearly 50% of WellPoint's health plan members belong to large employers with 51 to 4,999 employees. WellPoint markets to its large group customers primarily through its own sales force; it targets small groups, individuals, and seniors primarily through independent agents and brokers.

The company looks for strategic acquisitions that enhance market share, expand services, or build a bigger health care provider network. In 2005 it acquired WellChoice, parent of Empire Blue Cross Blue Shield, the largest insurer in the state of New York. The same year, it acquired Lumenos, a firm that offers health savings account and health reimbursement account plans. And in 2007 it acquired managed imaging company American Imaging Management.

WellPoint (formerly known as Anthem) was formed through the 2004 merger of Anthem and WellPoint Health Networks. Its subsidiaries include Blue Cross of California, Blue Cross Blue Shield of Georgia, and Anthem Health Plans of Kentucky.

## HISTORY

Anthem's earliest predecessor, prepaid hospital plan Blue Cross of Indiana, was founded in 1944. Unlike other Blues, Blue Cross of Indiana never received tax advantages or mandated discounts, so it competed as a private insurer. Within two years it had 100,000 members; by 1970 there were nearly 2 million.

Blue Shield of Indiana, another Anthem precursor, also grew rapidly after its 1946 formation as a mutual insurance company to cover doctors' services. The two organizations shared expenses and jointly managed the state's Medicare and Medicaid programs.

The 1970s and early 1980s were difficult as Indiana's economy stagnated and health insurance competition increased. In 1982 the joint operation restructured, adding new management and service policies to improve its performance.

Following the 1982 merger of the national Blue Cross and Blue Shield organizations, the Indiana Blues merged in 1985 as Associated Insurance Companies. The next year the company moved outside Indiana, began diversifying to help insulate itself from such industry changes as the shift to managed care, and renamed itself Associated Group to reflect a broader focus.

By 1990 Associated Group had more than 25 operating units with nationwide offerings, including health insurance, HMO services, life insurance, insurance brokerage, financial services, and software and services for the insurance industry.

The group grew throughout the mid-1990s, buying health insurer Southeastern Mutual Insurance (including Kentucky Blue Cross and Blue Shield) in 1992, diversified insurer Federal Kemper (a Kemper Corporation subsidiary) in 1993, and Seattle-based property/casualty brokerage Pettit-Morry in 1994. That year it entered the health care delivery market with the creation of American Health Network.

In 1995 the company merged with Ohio Blues licensee Community Mutual and took the Anthem name. Merger-related charges caused a loss that year.

Anthem bounced back the next year thanks to cost-cutting and customers switching to its more profitable managed care plans. Anthem divested its individual life insurance and annuity business and its Anthem Financial subsidiaries. Its 1996 deal to buy Blue Cross and Blue Shield of New Jersey fell apart in 1997 because of New Jersey Blue's charitable status. Anthem did manage to buy Blue Cross and Blue Shield of Connecticut that year.

Anthem in 1997 sold four property/casualty insurance subsidiaries to Vesta Insurance Group. It bought the remainder of its Acordia property/casualty unit (workers' compensation), then sold Acordia's brokerage operations. That year Anthem was involved in court battles regarding the Blue mergers in Kentucky, as well as in Connecticut, where litigants feared a rise in their premiums. Expenses related to merging Blues organizations contributed to a loss that year.

Anthem shed the rest of its noncore operations in 1998, selling subsidiary Anthem Health and Life Insurance Company to Canadian insurer Great-West Life Assurance. Its proposed purchase of Blue Cross and Blue Shield of Maine (which it acquired in 2000) and merger with the Blues in Rhode Island were met with outcries similar to those that dogged earlier pairings.

In 1999 the company agreed to settle lawsuits related to its 1997 merger with Blue Cross and Blue Shield of Connecticut by financing public health foundations. Anthem also bought the Blues plans in Colorado and New Hampshire that year.

In 2001 Anthem sold its military insurance business to Humana, and became a publicly traded company.

In order to expand into the southeastern market, the company acquired Virginia-based Trigon Healthcare in 2002.

In 2004, Anthem's merger with WellPoint was initially rejected by the California insurance commissioner. However, after extracting $265 million in concessions for uninsured care, the California insurance commissioner approved the merger. The merger was finally approved in November 2004 when the Georgia insurance commissioner extracted $125 million from the company for rural health improvements.

After the merger Anthem changed its name to WellPoint, Inc.

## EXECUTIVES

**Chairman:** Larry C. Glasscock, age 59
**Vice Chairman:** David C. Colby, age 53
**President, CEO, and Director:** Angela F. Braly, age 45
**EVP; President and CEO, National Government Services and Federal Employee Program Operation, Technology and Government Services:** Mark L. Boxer, age 47
**EVP and Chief Strategy Officer:** Marjorie W. Dorr, age 44, $1,209,000 pay (prior to title change)
**EVP Integration Planning, Information Management Officer, and Chief Actuary:** Alice F. Rosenblatt, age 58
**EVP and Chief Medical Officer:** Samuel R. (Sam) Nussbaum, age 58
**EVP and Chief Human Resources Officer:** Randal L. (Randy) Brown, age 48
**EVP; President and CEO, Commercial and Consumer Business:** John S. Watts Jr., age 47
**EVP; President and CEO, Specialty, Senior and State-Sponsored Business:** Joan E. Herman, age 53
**EVP Internal Audit and Chief Compliance Officer:** Randall J. Lewis, age 44
**EVP and CFO:** Wayne S. DeVeydt, age 37
**SVP; President, Health Management Corporation:** Joan Kennedy
**SVP; President, Pharmacy Benefit Management:** Renwyck (Ren) Elder
**SVP; President, Senior Markets, Central Region:** Lynne Gross
**SVP; President, Senior Services:** Susan E. Rawlings
**SVP and Chief Marketing and Product Officer:** Jason N. Gorevic, age 33
**SVP, Sales and Account Management, National Accounts:** Ken Goulet
**SVP and Chief Accounting Officer:** Jamie S. Miller, age 38
**Staff VP, Investor Relations:** Michael Kleinman
**Auditors:** Ernst & Young LLP

## LOCATIONS

**HQ:** WellPoint, Inc.
120 Monument Cir., Indianapolis, IN 46204
**Phone:** 317-532-6000 **Fax:** 317-488-6028
**Web:** www.wellpoint.com

WellPoint serves as a Blue Cross or a Blue Cross and Blue Shield licensee for California, Colorado, Connecticut, Georgia, Indiana, Kentucky, Maine, Missouri, Nevada, New Hampshire, New York, Ohio, Virginia, and Wisconsin.

## PRODUCTS/OPERATIONS

**2006 Sales**

| | $ mil. | % of total |
|---|---|---|
| Premiums | 51,971.9 | 91 |
| Administrative fees | 3,509.6 | 6 |
| Investment income | 878.7 | 2 |
| Other | 593.1 | 1 |
| Adjustments | (0.3) | — |
| **Total** | **56,953.0** | **100** |

## COMPETITORS

Aetna
BioScrip
Blue Shield Of California
Caremark Pharmacy Services
CIGNA
ConnectiCare
Coventry Health Care
Express Scripts
Great-West Healthcare
Harvard Pilgrim
HCSC
Health Net
HealthExtras
Humana
Kaiser Foundation Health Plan
Medical Mutual
Molina Healthcare
Sentara Healthcare
Sierra Health
UnitedHealth Group
WellCare

## HISTORICAL FINANCIALS

Company Type: Public

**Income Statement** FYE: December 31

| | REVENUE ($ mil.) | NET INCOME ($ mil.) | NET PROFIT MARGIN | EMPLOYEES |
|---|---|---|---|---|
| **12/06** | 56,953 | 3,095 | 5.4% | 42,000 |
| **12/05** | 45,136 | 2,464 | 5.5% | 42,000 |
| **12/04** | 20,815 | 960 | 4.6% | 38,000 |
| **12/03** | 16,771 | 774 | 4.6% | 20,130 |
| **12/02** | 13,282 | 549 | 4.1% | 19,500 |
| **Annual Growth** | 43.9% | 54.1% | — | 21.1% |

**2006 Year-End Financials**

Debt ratio: 26.4%
Return on equity: 12.5%
Cash ($ mil.): 6,829
Current ratio: 0.77
Long-term debt ($ mil.): 6,493
No. of shares (mil.): 616
Dividends
Yield: —
Payout: —
Market value ($ mil.): 48,434

**Stock History** NYSE: WLP

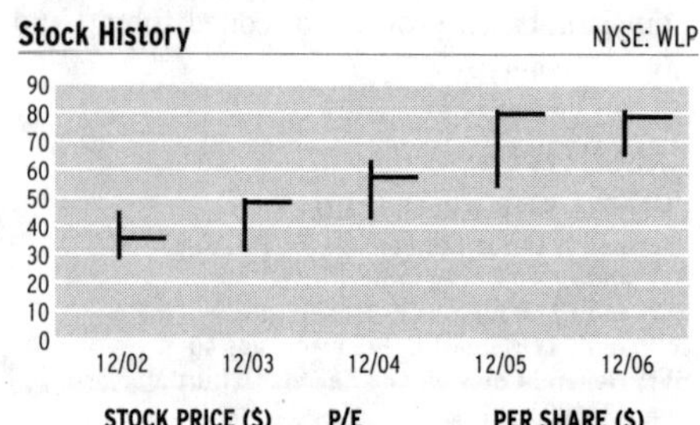


| | STOCK PRICE ($) FY Close | P/E High | P/E Low | PER SHARE ($) Earnings | Dividends | Book Value |
|---|---|---|---|---|---|---|
| **12/06** | 78.69 | 17 | 14 | 4.82 | — | 39.93 |
| **12/05** | 79.79 | 20 | 14 | 3.94 | — | 37.84 |
| **12/04** | 57.50 | 21 | 14 | 3.05 | — | 64.30 |
| **12/03** | 48.49 | 18 | 12 | 2.72 | — | — |
| **12/02** | 35.58 | 20 | 13 | 2.26 | — | — |
| **Annual Growth** | 21.9% | — | — | 20.8% | — | (21.2%) |

# Wells Fargo

This stagecoach likely makes a stop near you. One of the US's top banks, Wells Fargo operates about 3,200 bank branches in nearly 25 western and midwestern states, and almost 3,000 mortgage and consumer finance offices nationwide. Services include consumer and business banking, investment management, insurance, and venture capital investment. A top residential mortgage lender in the US, Wells Fargo is also one of the largest mortgage servicers. The bank no longer sells subprime loans via third-party brokers. The company is an industry leader in insurance brokerage through its Wells Fargo Insurance Services subsidiary (formerly Acordia), and offers mutual funds, online banking, and online brokerage services.

Thanks to this diversification, Wells Fargo's average consumer household has approximately five products with the bank, making it an industry leader in that metric as well. Specialized commercial services include wholesale banking, asset-based lending, equipment finance, corporate trust, and institutional asset management (through Wells Capital Management), as well as international trade activities through a joint venture with HSBC.

With its retail operations going full steam, Wells Fargo has been beefing up its commercial real estate business. In 2006 the company bought commercial real estate brokerage Secured Capital and merged it with existing subsidiary Eastdil Realty to form Eastdil Secured. Wells Fargo later acquired multifamily real estate finance firm Reilly Mortgage Group (now Wells Fargo Multifamily Capital).

The company expanded its business financing operations, which include Wells Fargo Century, with the acquisitions of EFC Partners, a Dallas firm that serves small and mid-sized companies, and Virginia-based Commerce Funding, which provides financing to government contractors.

Wells Fargo has relatively small investment banking operations compared to other banks of its size. To help rectify that, the company's Wells Fargo Securities bought Barrington Associates, which has three offices in California.

Wells Fargo sold ATM network operator Instant Cash Services to First Data in 2007.

Warren Buffett's Berkshire Hathaway has upped its stake in Wells Fargo to more than 6%.

## HISTORY

Predecessor Norwest's history begins with the Depression, which came early to the Great Plains. Farmers overexpanded in WWI and went bust as demand fell, soon followed by the banks that held their mortgages. To protect themselves from eastern financial interests, several Midwest banks in 1929 joined Northwestern National Bank of Minneapolis to form a holding company-type banking cooperative, Northwest Bancorp (known as Banco). Each bank assigned its ownership to the company in return for an interest in the new public company. Banco, in turn, provided services to its members, though it could not unify them operationally because of interstate banking bans.

Banco added 90 banks in its first year and by 1932 had 139 affiliates. The Depression thinned membership: By 1940 only 83 remained. Postwar prosperity didn't help, and by 1952 the number had dwindled to 70 as members consolidated, were sold, or quit.

It experienced functional problems in the 1960s because each member had its own system. In the 1970s Banco developed centralized data processing, but struggled against national competition.

In the 1980s Banco member Northwestern National of Minneapolis began buying financial services firms and formed several new business units. Banco, which had become a conventional bank holding company, reorganized along regional lines, and in 1983 it and its affiliates became Norwest.

Forecasts of food shortages had many farmers expanding production through debt financing in the 1970s, and many went bankrupt when the shortages failed to appear. Norwest needed most of the 1980s to reduce its bad loan portfolio. In response the bank diversified into mortgage banking and consumer finance and entered such markets as Nevada and Texas.

In 1997 Norwest bought banks in Nebraska, Minnesota, and Texas, as well as an Alabama-based home improvement loan writer and BankBoston's used car finance unit Fidelity Acceptance. The next year Norwest Financial entered South America, buying a Buenos Aires-based lender. The bank agreed to merge with Wells Fargo in 1998.

Wells Fargo (descended from the famous Old West stagecoach line) was primed for a merger after watching other pairings (NationsBank with BankAmerica to form Bank of America; BANC ONE with First Chicago). Norwest came a-courting with an attractive proposal: Complementary regional coverage and expected cost savings of $650 million. Norwest was the surviving entity (touted as a merger of equals), but the new company adopted the Wells Fargo name.

Since the 1998 merger Wells Fargo has not put on the brakes. It has made some 50 purchases since, including Seattle brokerage Ragen MacKenzie; Dallas-area financial planner H.D. Vest; other companies' mortgage portfolios; and a host of community banks.

In 2000 Wells Fargo bought banks in Alaska, California, Michigan, Nebraska, and Utah; student loan writer Servus Financial; securities brokerage firm Ragen McKenzie, and leasing firm Charter Financial. It also bought mortgage-servicing portfolios from First Union, GE Capital, and Bingham Financial, boosting its portfolio over the $400 billion mark.

In 2002, Wells Fargo moved its retail banking headquarters from San Francisco to Los Angeles, targeting that market's growing Hispanic and Asian communities and hoping to take advantage of the dearth of superregional banks based there.

The company bought most of the funds and assets under management of troubled mutual fund manager Strong Financial in 2005. A week prior to the announcement of the deal in May 2004, Strong Financial and its founder, Richard Strong, who has been banned from the industry, paid $175 million in fines to settle securities fraud charges. Because of the troubles, Wells Fargo was able to buy the company at a substantial discount (reportedly in the neighborhood of $500 million to $700 million for some $34 billion of assets) and in the process became one of the largest mutual fund managers in the banking industry.

## EXECUTIVES

**Chairman:** Richard M. (Dick) Kovacevich, age 63, $7,995,000 pay
**President, CEO, and Director:** John G. Stumpf, age 53, $4,600,000 pay (prior to title change)
**SEVP and CFO:** Howard I. Atkins, age 55, $3,570,833 pay
**SEVP and Chief Auditor:** Kevin McCabe
**SEVP and Chief Loan Examiner:** Eric D. Shand
**SEVP, Corporate Communications:** Lawrence P. (Larry) Haeg
**SEVP, Corporate Development:** Bruce E. Helsel
**SEVP, Home and Consumer Finance; Chairman, Wells Fargo Home Mortgage:** Mark C. Oman, age 51, $3,862,500 pay
**SEVP, Investor Relations:** Robert S. Strickland
**SEVP, Technology:** Victor K. Nichols
**SEVP, Wholesale Banking:** David A. Hoyt, age 50, $3,870,883 pay
**SEVP and Treasurer:** Paul R. Ackerman
**SEVP and Corporate Secretary:** Laurel A. Holschuh
**Group EVP, Diversified Products:** Michael R. James
**EVP and Chief Credit Officer:** Michael J. (Mike) Loughlin
**EVP, Compliance and Risk Management:** Patricia R. (Pat) Callahan
**EVP and Head of Global Correspondent Banking:** Ronald A. (Ron) Caton
**EVP, Customer Service, Sales, and Operations:** Diana L. Starcher
**EVP, Law and Government Relations, and General Counsel:** James M. (Jim) Strother, age 54
**EVP and Director of Human Resources:** Avid Modjtabai
**Auditors:** KPMG LLP

## LOCATIONS

**HQ:** Wells Fargo & Company
420 Montgomery St., San Francisco, CA 94163
**Phone:** 866-878-5865 **Fax:** 626-312-3015
**Web:** www.wellsfargo.com

## PRODUCTS/OPERATIONS

**2006 Sales**

| | $ mil. | % of total |
|---|---|---|
| Interest | | |
| Loans | 25,611 | 53 |
| Securities available for sale | 3,278 | 7 |
| Loans & mortgages held for sale | 2,793 | 6 |
| Other | 557 | 1 |
| Noninterest | | |
| Trust & investment fees | 2,737 | 6 |
| Service charges on deposit accounts | 2,690 | 5 |
| Mortgage banking | 2,311 | 5 |
| Card fees | 1,747 | 4 |
| Insurance | 1,340 | 3 |
| Operating leases | 783 | 2 |
| Equity investments | 738 | 1 |
| Other fees | 2,057 | 4 |
| Other | 1,356 | 3 |
| **Total** | **47,998** | **100** |

**2006 Assets**

| | $ mil. | % of total |
|---|---|---|
| Cash & equivalents | 21,106 | 4 |
| Trading assets | 5,607 | 1 |
| Mortgage-backed securities | 31,509 | 7 |
| Other securities | 11,120 | 2 |
| Mortgages & loans held for sale | 33,818 | 7 |
| Loans | 319,116 | 66 |
| Allowance for loan losses | (3,764) | — |
| Other assets | 63,484 | 13 |
| **Total** | **481,996** | **100** |

## COMPETITORS

Bank of America
BOK Financial
Citigroup
Countrywide Financial
Fifth Third
HSBC Finance
JPMorgan Chase
KeyCorp
Marshall & Ilsley
Temple-Inland
UnionBanCal
U.S. Bancorp
Washington Mutual
Zions Bancorporation

## HISTORICAL FINANCIALS

Company Type: Public

**Income Statement** FYE: December 31

| | ASSETS ($ mil.) | NET INCOME ($ mil.) | INCOME AS % OF ASSETS | EMPLOYEES |
|---|---|---|---|---|
| **12/06** | 481,996 | 8,482 | 1.8% | 158,000 |
| **12/05** | 481,741 | 7,671 | 1.6% | 153,500 |
| **12/04** | 427,849 | 7,014 | 1.6% | 145,500 |
| **12/03** | 387,798 | 6,202 | 1.6% | 140,000 |
| **12/02** | 349,197 | 5,434 | 1.6% | 134,000 |
| **Annual Growth** | 8.4% | 11.8% | — | 4.2% |

**2006 Year-End Financials**

Equity as % of assets: 9.4%
Return on assets: 1.8%
Return on equity: 19.8%
Long-term debt ($ mil.): 87,145
No. of shares (mil.): 3,377
Dividends
Yield: 2.2%
Payout: 32.1%
Market value ($ mil.): 120,091
Sales ($ mil.): 47,998

**Stock History** NYSE: WFC

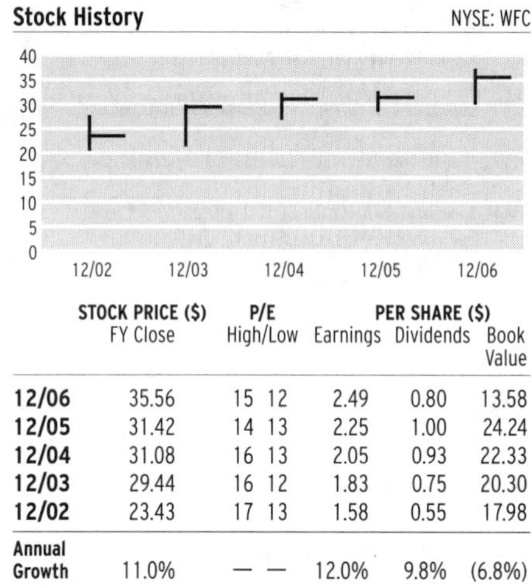


| | STOCK PRICE ($) FY Close | P/E High/Low | | PER SHARE ($) Earnings | Dividends | Book Value |
|---|---|---|---|---|---|---|
| **12/06** | 35.56 | 15 | 12 | 2.49 | 0.80 | 13.58 |
| **12/05** | 31.42 | 14 | 13 | 2.25 | 1.00 | 24.24 |
| **12/04** | 31.08 | 16 | 13 | 2.05 | 0.93 | 22.33 |
| **12/03** | 29.44 | 16 | 12 | 1.83 | 0.75 | 20.30 |
| **12/02** | 23.43 | 17 | 13 | 1.58 | 0.55 | 17.98 |
| **Annual Growth** | 11.0% | — | — | 12.0% | 9.8% | (6.8%) |

# Wendy's International

Burger lovers lay down their singles for doubles and triples from this company. A leader in the fast food business, Wendy's International operates the world's #3 hamburger chain in terms of locations (behind McDonald's and Burger King), with almost 6,700 of its Wendy's Old Fashioned Hamburger eateries in the US and about 20 other countries. The Wendy's chain offers made-to-order burgers and fries as well as such alternative menu items as baked potatoes, chili, and salads. Close to 1,500 of the restaurants are owned by the company, while the rest are franchised.

Unlike its hamburger menu, the company's performance has not been made to order for investors in recent years. Its chain saw same-store sales decline in 2005 due to marketing gaffs and increased product competition from its chief rivals. Sales struggled to recover in 2006 but the turnaround has been difficult. Veteran CEO John Schuessler retired in 2006 and was replaced by former CFO Kerrii Anderson. But with sales hurting, in 2007 the company announced it was studying a possible sale.

Wendy's underwent a dramatic change in 2006 when it shed two of its non-hamburger businesses. Popular Canadian donut chain Tim Hortons, which had been propping up the company's profits, was sold through an IPO. The company also sold its Fresh Enterprises subsidiary in 2006 to a private investment group for $31 million. Operating the 300-unit Baja Fresh quick-casual Mexican chain, Fresh Enterprises had largely stagnated under Wendy's ownership, falling far behind its rivals Chipotle and Qdoba (a unit of Jack in the Box). The sale, though, was quite a loss for the hamburger operator, which paid $275 million for Baja Fresh in 2002.

Part of impetus to shed its other chains came from activist investors such as Nelson Peltz (who owns about 10% of the company) and Pershing Square Capital Management (which has almost a 10% stake). Wendy's is now looking to sell its 70% stake in Cafe Express, a small chain of bakery cafes. The company also owns a 30% stake in Pasta Pomodoro. Meanwhile, Peltz has expressed interest in purchasing Wendy's through his Triarc company (which owns the Arby's chain).

## HISTORY

Dave Thomas began his fast-food career in 1956 when he and Phil Clauss opened a barbecue restaurant in Knoxville, Tennessee. Clauss later bought a Kentucky Fried Chicken franchise (now KFC) from fried chicken titan Colonel Harland Sanders, and in 1962 he dispatched Thomas to rescue four failing restaurants in Ohio. Thomas's success in reviving the restaurants netted him 45% of the franchise. When Clauss sold the franchise back to KFC in 1968, Thomas became a millionaire and joined the company as regional operations director.

After his stint at KFC, Thomas left the chicken business and served as managing operator for Arthur Treacher's Fish & Chips (later owned by TruFoods and then Nathan's Famous). He put his restaurant experience to use in 1969 by opening his first Wendy's restaurant, naming it after his daughter. Thomas limited the menu to cooked-to-order hamburgers, chili, and shakes, charging prices slightly higher than rivals Burger King and McDonald's. The restaurants were decorated with carpeting, wood paneling, and Tiffany-style lamps to reinforce the relatively upscale theme.

In the early 1970s the company began franchising to accelerate expansion. It also founded its Management Institute to train owners and managers in Wendy's operational techniques. The first non-US Wendy's opened in Canada in 1975. The company went public in 1976, and by the end of that year, it boasted a collection of 500 restaurants. Its first national commercial aired in 1977. Two years later the chain added a salad bar to its menu.

Thomas retired as chairman in 1982 and took the title of senior chairman. Wendy's launched an $8 million TV ad campaign featuring Clara Peller asking, "Where's the beef?" in 1984, and its market share jumped 12%. When McDonald's and Burger King responded with their own campaigns, neither the introduction of a breakfast menu (1985) nor new products such as the Big Classic burger (1986) and the SuperBar buffet (1987) could help reverse the erosion of the company's market share (down to 9% by 1987). With his honest demeanor and humble delivery, Thomas found an audience as Wendy's TV spokesperson in 1989. The company even attributed the rebound in earnings at the time to his appearances.

The company reacted to growing concern about nutrition by introducing a grilled chicken sandwich in 1990. It also appealed to budget-conscious consumers with its 99-cent Super Value Menu. Wendy's had 4,000 restaurants by 1992, the same year it added packaged salads to its menu. The next year high school dropout Thomas earned his diploma; his class voted him Most Likely to Succeed.

Wendy's and Canadian chain Tim Hortons began a business relationship in 1992. Ronald Joyce and Toronto Maple Leafs defenseman Tim Horton opened their first coffee and doughnut shop in Hamilton, Ontario, in 1964 (Horton was killed in an auto accident in 1974). By 1990 the chain had grown to 500 units.

Wendy's completed its acquisition of Tim Hortons in 1995 and began planning to expand the chain into the US. In 1999 CEO Teter died of natural causes. In 2000 the company named John Schuessler, former president and COO of US operations, as his successor.

The death of Dave Thomas early in 2002 was a crushing blow to the company and a loss for the fast-food industry. Moving forward, the company bought Fresh Enterprises, owner of the 160-unit Baja Fresh Mexican Grill, for $275 million. It also bought 45% of Cafe Express, a chain of bistro-style quick-service restaurants owned by Schiller Del Grande Restaurant Group, and it took a 25% stake in California-based Pasta Pomodoro.

Wendy's upped its stake in Cafe Express to 70% in 2004 and assumed management control of the chain by placing veteran executive Brion Grube at the helm. The following year the company suffered a public relations disaster when a California woman reported finding a severed finger in a bowl of chili. (The report later turned out to be fraudulent.)

Wendy's spun off a 15% stake in Tim Hortons through an IPO in 2006 and disposed of its remaining 82% stake later in the year. Schuessler retired that year amid news of declining store sales; Kerrii Anderson, formerly CFO for the company, was named as his replacement. Late in 2006 the company sold the Baja Fresh chain for $31 million a group of private investors.

## EXECUTIVES

**Chairman:** James V. Pickett, age 65
**President, CEO, and Director:** Kerrii B. Anderson, age 49, $620,058 pay
**COO:** David J. (Dave) Near, age 37
**CFO:** Joseph J. (Jay) Fitzsimmons, age 59
**EVP and Chief Marketing Officer:** Ian B. Rowden
**EVP, General Counsel, and Secretary:** Leon M. McCorkle Jr., age 66, $371,400 pay
**EVP Human Resources and Administration:** Jeffrey M. (Jeff) Cava, age 55, $388,600 pay
**EVP Mergers, Acquisitions, and Business Integration and Treasurer:** Jonathan F. Catherwood, age 45, $383,692 pay
**EVP Restaurant Services:** Edward K. (Ed) Choe, age 47
**SVP and CIO:** Robert M. Whittington
**SVP, General Controller, and Assistant Secretary:** Brendan P. Foley, age 47, $194,140 pay
**SVP Communications:** Dennis L. (Denny) Lynch
**SVP Enterprise Tax and Risk Management:** Everett E. Gallagher Jr.
**SVP Human Resource Services:** Karen Ickes
**SVP Corporate Affairs and Investor Relations:** John D. Barker
**SVP Supply Chain Management:** Tad G. Wampfler
**CEO, Pasta Pomodoro:** Andriano Paganini
**President, Cafe Express:** Robert D. (Bob) Wright
**Director Consumer Communications:** Bob Bertini
**Director Investor Relations and Financial Communications:** David D. Poplar
**Auditors:** PricewaterhouseCoopers LLP

## LOCATIONS

**HQ:** Wendy's International, Inc.
288 West Dublin-Granville Rd., Dublin, OH 43017
**Phone:** 614-764-3100 **Fax:** 614-764-3330
**Web:** www.wendys.com

### 2006 US Locations

| | No. |
|---|---|
| Florida | 502 |
| Ohio | 442 |
| Texas | 398 |
| Georgia | 296 |
| California | 294 |
| Michigan | 278 |
| Pennsylvania | 267 |
| North Carolina | 246 |
| New York | 223 |
| Virginia | 212 |
| Tennessee | 183 |
| Illinois | 181 |
| Indiana | 176 |
| New Jersey | 143 |
| Kentucky | 142 |
| Louisiana | 135 |
| Colorado | 129 |
| South Carolina | 128 |
| Maryland | 115 |
| Arizona | 102 |
| Alabama | 98 |
| Mississippi | 98 |
| Massachusetts | 95 |
| Utah | 84 |
| Kansas | 74 |
| Missouri | 73 |
| Washington | 73 |
| West Virginia | 72 |
| Minnesota | 69 |
| Wisconsin | 65 |
| Arkansas | 64 |
| Oregon | 55 |
| Connecticut | 48 |
| Iowa | 47 |
| Nevada | 47 |
| Oklahoma | 41 |
| New Mexico | 38 |
| Nebraska | 34 |
| Other states | 178 |
| **Total** | **5,955** |

### 2006 International Locations

| | No. |
|---|---|
| Canada | 377 |
| Japan | 78 |
| Puerto Rico | 61 |
| Philippines | 40 |
| Venezuela | 39 |
| Honduras | 24 |
| Indonesia | 20 |
| Mexico | 17 |
| New Zealand | 16 |
| El Salvador | 12 |
| Bahamas | 7 |
| Guatemala | 6 |
| Panama | 6 |
| Aruba | 3 |
| Virgin Islands | 3 |
| Cayman Islands | 2 |
| Costa Rica | 2 |
| Guam | 2 |
| Jamaica | 2 |
| Dominican Republic | 1 |
| **Total** | **718** |

## PRODUCTS/OPERATIONS

### 2006 Sales

| | $ mil. | % of total |
|---|---|---|
| Restaurants | 2,154.6 | 87 |
| Franchising | 284.7 | 12 |
| Other | 14.0 | 1 |
| **Total** | **2,453.3** | **100** |

### 2006 Locations

| | No. |
|---|---|
| Franchised | 5,208 |
| Company-owned | 1,465 |
| **Total** | **6,673** |

## COMPETITORS

AFC Enterprises
Arby's
Burger King
Cajun Operating Company
Checkers Drive-In
Chick-fil-A
CKE Restaurants
Dairy Queen
Jack in the Box
McDonald's
Quiznos
Sonic
Subway
YUM!

## HISTORICAL FINANCIALS

Company Type: Public

### Income Statement

FYE: Sunday nearest December 31

| | REVENUE ($ mil.) | NET INCOME ($ mil.) | NET PROFIT MARGIN | EMPLOYEES |
|---|---|---|---|---|
| **12/06** | 2,453 | 94 | 3.8% | 46,000 |
| **12/05** | 3,783 | 224 | 5.9% | 57,000 |
| **12/04** | 3,635 | 52 | 1.4% | 58,000 |
| **12/03** | 3,149 | 236 | 7.5% | 53,000 |
| **12/02** | 2,730 | 219 | 8.0% | 48,000 |
| **Annual Growth** | (2.6%) | (19.0%) | — | (1.1%) |

### 2006 Year-End Financials

Debt ratio: 55.0%
Return on equity: 6.1%
Cash ($ mil.): 458
Current ratio: 1.66
Long-term debt ($ mil.): 556
No. of shares (mil.): 96
Dividends
Yield: 1.8%
Payout: 73.2%
Market value ($ mil.): 3,167

### Stock History

NYSE: WEN

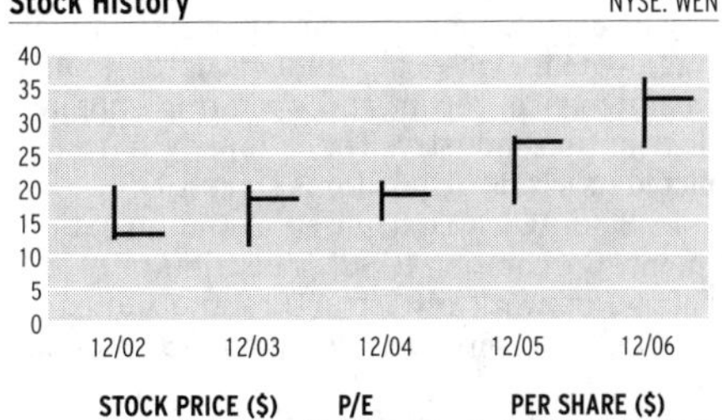


| | STOCK PRICE ($) FY Close | P/E High | P/E Low | PER SHARE ($) Earnings | Dividends | Book Value |
|---|---|---|---|---|---|---|
| **12/06** | 33.09 | 44 | 32 | 0.82 | 0.60 | 10.57 |
| **12/05** | 26.68 | 14 | 9 | 1.92 | 0.57 | 17.47 |
| **12/04** | 18.96 | 46 | 34 | 0.45 | 0.48 | 15.26 |
| **12/03** | 18.34 | 10 | 6 | 2.05 | 0.24 | 15.33 |
| **12/02** | 13.16 | 11 | 7 | 1.89 | 0.24 | 12.63 |
| **Annual Growth** | 25.9% | — | — | (18.8%) | 25.7% | (4.4%) |

# Werner Enterprises

The trucking business is a money-earner for Werner, which offers truckload freight transportation throughout North America. Werner Enterprises operates about 9,000 tractors and more than 25,000 trailers; its trailer fleet consists primarily of dry vans but also includes temperature-controlled vans and flatbeds. Werner transports retail merchandise, consumer products, manufactured products, and groceries. In addition, the company offers freight brokerage, intermodal freight transportation arrangement, and other value-added logistics services. Founder and chairman Clarence Werner and his family own about 40% of the company.

Werner specializes in the high end of the market, concentrating on shippers that require broad geographic coverage and customized services and that are less rate-sensitive than average. Discount retailer Dollar General is Werner's largest customer, accounting for about 10% of the trucker's business.

The company has seen growth in its logistics business, and Werner is expanding its intermodal offerings, which involve arranging the transportation of freight by multiple methods, such as truck and train. In 2006 the company formed Werner Global Logistics U.S. to provide air and ocean freight forwarding services between China and the US.

## HISTORY

In 1956, 19-year-old Clarence Werner sold the family car to buy his first truck. Nine years later he was operating a modest, but profitable, 10-truck fleet. Werner focused on customer service in the medium- to long-haul segment of the industry and was well-positioned for the 1980 deregulation of the trucking industry. By 1986, when the company went public, its fleet had grown to about 630 tractors.

Werner sought to broaden its customer base and services in the early 1990s, and in 1992 it began offering three new services: dedicated fleet service, temperature-controlled freight service, and regional short-haul service. The next year the company added rail intermodal transportation to its portfolio of services, and in 1995 it created a Werner Logistics Services division. In 1997 Werner began providing dedicated trucking services to Dollar General's Oklahoma distribution center; a 1998 deal expanded the contract to include the retailer's Georgia and Kentucky hubs.

In a move reflecting a buoyant US economy, Werner added 900 trucks to its fleet in 1999. However, high oil prices and a weak used truck market put the squeeze on Werner's financial performance in 2000. That year the company agreed to merge its logistics unit with those of five other trucking firms to form Transplace.com (later known as Transplace).

Werner reduced its ownership stake in Transplace from about 15% to 5% at the end of 2002. In 2007 Clarence Werner stepped down as CEO, but remained chairman. His son Greg Werner, already the company's president, took over as CEO.

## EXECUTIVES

**Chairman:** Clarence L. (C. L.) Werner, age 69
**Vice Chairman:** Gary L. Werner, age 49, $585,000 pay
**President, CEO, and Director:** Gregory L. (Greg) Werner, age 47
**SEVP and Chief Marketing Officer:** Daniel H. Cushman, age 52, $555,270 pay
**SEVP, Value Added Services and International:** Derek J. Leathers, age 37
**EVP, Treasurer, and CFO:** John J. Steele, age 48, $290,000 pay
**EVP and CIO:** Robert E. (Bob) Synowicki Jr., age 48
**EVP and General Counsel:** Richard S. Reiser, age 60
**EVP, Sales and Marketing:** Jim S. Schelble, age 46
**SVP, Controller, and Corporate Secretary:** James L. Johnson, age 41
**VP, Analysis and Information Systems:** Anthony M. DeCanti, age 37
**VP, Dedicated Operations:** Chad R. Dittberner, age 36
**VP, Flatbed and Dedicated Operations:** Todd A. Struble, age 40
**VP, Management Information Systems:** R. Lee Easton, age 47
**VP, Marketing Administration and Risk Management:** Charles R. Stevens, age 43
**VP, Operations:** Guy M. Welton, age 41
**Auditors:** KPMG LLP

## LOCATIONS

**HQ:** Werner Enterprises, Inc.
14507 Frontier Rd., Omaha, NE 68145
**Phone:** 402-895-6640 **Fax:** 402-894-3927
**Web:** www.werner.com

### 2006 Sales

| | $ mil. | % of total |
|---|---|---|
| US | 1,872.8 | 90 |
| Mexico | 168.9 | 8 |
| Other countries | 38.9 | 2 |
| **Total** | **2,080.6** | **100** |

## PRODUCTS/OPERATIONS

### 2006 Sales

| | $ mil. | % of total |
|---|---|---|
| Truckload transportation | 1,801.1 | 87 |
| Value-added services | 266.0 | 13 |
| Other | 10.5 | — |
| Corporate | 3.0 | — |
| **Total** | **2,080.6** | **100** |

## COMPETITORS

C.H. Robinson Worldwide
Covenant Transportation
C.R. England
Crete Carrier
Expeditors
Frozen Food Express
Heartland Express
J.B. Hunt
Knight Transportation
Landstar System
Prime
Schneider National
Swift Transportation
UPS Supply Chain Solutions
U.S. Xpress

## HISTORICAL FINANCIALS

Company Type: Public

### Income Statement

FYE: December 31

| | REVENUE ($ mil.) | NET INCOME ($ mil.) | NET PROFIT MARGIN | EMPLOYEES |
|---|---|---|---|---|
| **12/06** | 2,081 | 99 | 4.7% | 15,146 |
| **12/05** | 1,972 | 99 | 5.0% | 14,552 |
| **12/04** | 1,678 | 87 | 5.2% | — |
| **12/03** | 1,458 | 74 | 5.1% | — |
| **12/02** | 1,342 | 62 | 4.6% | — |
| **Annual Growth** | 11.6% | 12.5% | — | 4.1% |

### 2006 Year-End Financials

Debt ratio: 11.5%
Return on equity: 11.4%
Cash ($ mil.): 32
Current ratio: 1.89
Long-term debt ($ mil.): 100
No. of shares (mil.): 75
Dividends
Yield: 1.0%
Payout: 13.6%
Market value ($ mil.): 1,317

### Stock History

NASDAQ (GS): WERN

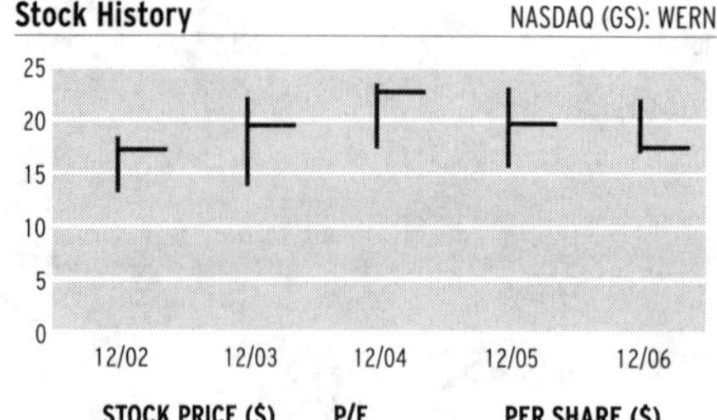

| | STOCK PRICE ($) FY Close | P/E High | P/E Low | PER SHARE ($) Earnings | Dividends | Book Value |
|---|---|---|---|---|---|---|
| **12/06** | 17.48 | 17 | 14 | 1.25 | 0.17 | 11.55 |
| **12/05** | 19.70 | 19 | 13 | 1.22 | 0.15 | 10.86 |
| **12/04** | 22.64 | 22 | 16 | 1.08 | 0.12 | 9.76 |
| **12/03** | 19.49 | 24 | 16 | 0.90 | 0.08 | 8.90 |
| **12/02** | 17.22 | 24 | 18 | 0.75 | 0.06 | 10.15 |
| **Annual Growth** | 0.4% | — | — | 13.6% | 29.7% | 3.3% |

# WESCO International

When contractors and manufacturers need parts, it's WESCO to the wescue. The company distributes electrical products (fuses, terminals, connectors, enclosures, fittings, circuit breakers, transformers, switchboards); industrial supplies (tools, abrasives, filters, safety equipment); lighting wares (lamps, fixtures, ballasts); wire and conduit materials; automation equipment (motors, drives, logic controllers); and data communication apparatus (patch panels, terminals, connectors). WESCO offers more than a million products from some 29,000 suppliers, with about 110,000 customers worldwide. It operates through some 20 subsidiaries.

Expanding both by internal growth and through acquisitions, WESCO plans to continue buying complementary businesses in the highly fragmented electrical, industrial, and MRO (maintenance, repair, and operating supplies) distribution industry. The company has completed nearly 30 acquisitions since 1995.

In 2006 WESCO acquired Communications Supply Corporation (CSC), a distributor of low-voltage network infrastructure and industrial wire and cable products, for about $525 million in cash.

WESCO's largest supplier, Eaton Corporation, accounts for about 12% of WESCO's purchases.

FMR (Fidelity Investments) owns nearly 15% of WESCO International. Putnam Investments holds more than 5% of the company.

## HISTORY

WESCO International got its start as a subsidiary of electrical power pioneer Westinghouse Electric Company. George Westinghouse founded the company bearing his name in Pittsburgh in 1886. The company installed the nation's first alternating current power system in Telluride, Colorado, in 1891. Two years later Westinghouse built the generating system that powered the Chicago World's Fair. The company also was chosen to provide generators for the hydroelectric power station at Niagara Falls.

George Westinghouse was ousted in 1910 after the company was unable to meet its debt obligations. He died four years later at the age of 67. During the next decade the company added the burgeoning radio and appliance markets to its portfolio of electrical distribution and production operations.

In 1922 the firm established Westinghouse Electric Supply Company (WESCO) to distribute power products and appliances. Westinghouse had its share of troubles over the years, many of which were caused by ill-advised diversification attempts. These included forays into uranium supply, financial services, and real estate.

By the 1990s Westinghouse was buried under nearly $10 billion in debt and too busy putting out fires to tend to day-to-day operations properly. Not surprisingly, WESCO was caught up in Westinghouse's problems: Sales declined four years in a row, and employee turnover was around 25% a year.

Westinghouse embarked on a divestiture program and sold WESCO to investment firm Clayton, Dubilier & Rice (CD&R) in 1994 for about $340 million. At the time, WESCO had about 250 branch locations. The new owners brought in Roy Haley, a veteran insurance and finance executive, to turn the ailing business around. Haley tied pay and bonuses to performance and emphasized multisite customers, such as contractors and companies with multiple retail, industrial, or administrative locations. WESCO grew through acquisitions, and in 1995 sales reached $2 billion.

By 1996 the company had added 1,000 employees; it operated about 300 distribution branches throughout the world. Sales reached $2.6 billion in 1997 as WESCO continued acquiring complementary companies and formed an alliance with Australian mining and steel company BHP (now BHP Billiton). Managers led a $1.1 billion buyout of the company in 1998, increasing their stake in WESCO from 15% to 33%. Costs related to acquisitions and the buyout caused WESCO to post a loss, even though 1998 sales passed the $3 billion mark. The company opened sales offices in the UK, Singapore, and Mexico.

As it geared up for its initial public offering in 1999, WESCO bought distributors Industrial Electric Supply Company and Statewide Electrical Supply. The company continued to shop during 2000, adding electrical distributors Orton Utility Supply (Tennessee), Control Corporation of America (Virginia), and KVA Supply Company (Colorado and California).

In 2001 WESCO acquired two distributors (Herning Underground Supply and Alliance Utility Products) that supply contractors who install gas, lighting, and communication utility infrastructure in Arizona, California, Utah, and Washington.

The Cypress Group, the private equity firm that helped lead the $1.1 billion management buyout in 1998, sold most of its shares in WESCO in late 2004 and 2005. Cypress owned nearly half of WESCO prior to those sales.

WESCO acquired fastener distributor Fastec Industrial and electronics distributor Carlton-Bates in 2005.

## EXECUTIVES

**Chairman and CEO:** Roy W. Haley, age 60, $2,575,000 pay
**SVP and COO:** John J. Engel, age 44, $1,047,500 pay
**SVP, CFO, and Chief Administrative Officer:** Stephen A. Van Oss, age 52, $1,047,500 pay
**VP Operations:** William M. Goodwin, age 60, $580,000 pay
**VP Operations:** Robert B. Rosenbaum, age 49
**VP Operations:** Donald H. Thimjon, age 63, $543,000 pay
**VP Operations:** Ronald P. Van Jr., age 46
**VP, Treasurer, Legal and Investor Relations:** Daniel A. Brailer, age 49
**Corporate Counsel and Secretary:** Marcy Smorey-Giger, age 35
**Auditors:** PricewaterhouseCoopers LLP

## LOCATIONS

**HQ:** WESCO International, Inc.
225 W. Station Square Dr., Ste. 700,
Pittsburgh, PA 15219
**Phone:** 412-454-2200 **Fax:** 412-454-2505
**Web:** www.wesco.com

WESCO International has about 400 branches around the world, most of which are in Canada and the US, with others in Guam, Mexico, Nigeria, Singapore, the United Arab Emirates, and the UK.

### 2006 Sales

| | $ mil. | % of total |
|---|---|---|
| US | 4,606.8 | 87 |
| Canada | 599.2 | 11 |
| Other countries | 114.6 | 2 |
| **Total** | **5,320.6** | **100** |

## PRODUCTS/OPERATIONS

### 2006 Sales

| | % of total |
|---|---|
| Industrial customers | 43 |
| Electrical contractors | 34 |
| Utilities & special utility contractors | 17 |
| Commercial, institutional & governmental customers | 6 |
| **Total** | **100** |

### Selected Products

Automation Equipment
- Drives
- Motor control devices
- Operator interfaces
- Programmable logic controllers
- Pushbuttons

Data Communications Products
- Connectors
- Patch panels
- Premise wiring
- Terminals

Electrical Products
- Busways
- Circuit breakers
- Panelboards
- Switchboards
- Transformers

Industrial Supplies
- Boxes
- Connectors
- Fittings
- Fuses
- Lugs
- MRO supplies
- Tape
- Terminals
- Tools

Lighting
- Ballasts
- Fixtures
- Light bulbs

Wire and Conduit Products
- Cable
- Metallic and non-metallic conduits
- Wire

## COMPETITORS

Anixter International
Bearing Distributors
Consolidated Electrical
Electro-Wire
Gexpro
Graybar Electric
Hagemeyer
H.C. Slingsby
Hubbell
McNaughton-McKay
Premier Farnell
Rexel, Inc.
Sonepar USA
SUMMIT Electric Supply
W.W. Grainger

## HISTORICAL FINANCIALS

Company Type: Public

### Income Statement

FYE: December 31

| | REVENUE ($ mil.) | NET INCOME ($ mil.) | NET PROFIT MARGIN | EMPLOYEES |
|---|---|---|---|---|
| **12/06** | 5,321 | 217 | 4.1% | 7,100 |
| **12/05** | 4,421 | 104 | 2.3% | 6,000 |
| **12/04** | 3,741 | 65 | 1.7% | 5,300 |
| **12/03** | 3,287 | 30 | 0.9% | 5,200 |
| **12/02** | 3,326 | 23 | 0.7% | 5,400 |
| **Annual Growth** | 12.5% | 75.1% | — | 7.1% |

### 2006 Year-End Financials

Debt ratio: 97.5%
Return on equity: 34.6%
Cash ($ mil.): 73
Current ratio: 1.40
Long-term debt ($ mil.): 744
No. of shares (mil.): 50
Dividends
Yield: —
Payout: —
Market value ($ mil.): 2,914

### Stock History

NYSE: WCC

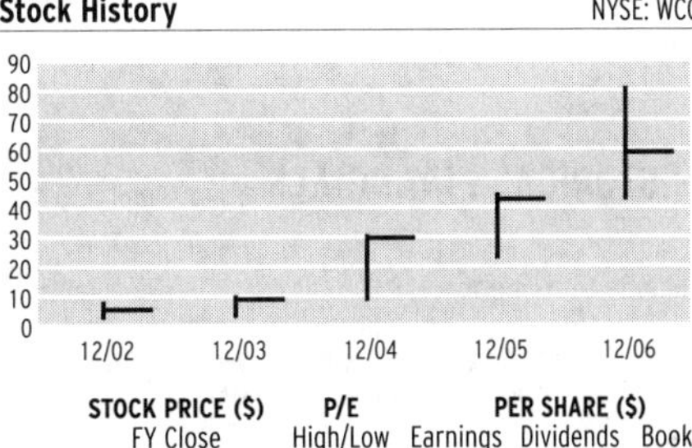


| | STOCK PRICE ($) FY Close | P/E High | P/E Low | PER SHARE ($) Earnings | Dividends | Book Value |
|---|---|---|---|---|---|---|
| **12/06** | 58.81 | 19 | 10 | 4.14 | — | 15.40 |
| **12/05** | 42.73 | 21 | 11 | 2.10 | — | 11.33 |
| **12/04** | 29.64 | 21 | 6 | 1.47 | — | 8.40 |
| **12/03** | 8.85 | 15 | 5 | 0.65 | — | 4.58 |
| **12/02** | 5.49 | 15 | 6 | 0.49 | — | 4.19 |
| **Annual Growth** | 80.9% | — | — | 70.5% | — | 38.5% |

# Westar Energy

Westar Energy wished upon a star, and the answer was — "slim down operations and focus on power utility resources." Westar Energy has a generating capacity of about 6,000 MW (mostly from fossil-fueled facilities) and serves 669,000 electricity customers in Kansas through its utility subsidiaries. Westar Energy supplies electric energy to 360,000 retail customers in central and northeast Kansas, and subsidiary Kansas Gas and Electric Company supplies electric energy to 309,000 retail customers in south-central and southeastern Kansas. It also supplies wholesale electric power to 48 cities in Kansas and four electric cooperatives that serve rural areas.

In 2003 the company filed a debt reduction plan with the Kansas Corporation Commission (KCC) to avoid a bankruptcy filing. The plan required the divestment of Westar Energy's nonutility assets and has replaced the company's earlier plans to spin off subsidiary Westar Industries, which held the company's ONEOK and Protection One stakes.

To begin reducing debt, the company in 2003 sold some of its ONEOK stock back to ONEOK. The deal netted Westar Energy $300 million and reduced its stake in the natural gas company from 45% to 27%. Westar Energy further reduced its ONEOK stake to about 15% later that year by selling additional shares to the public and to ONEOK, and it sold its remaining shares to Cantor Fitzgerald for $262 million in November 2003.

The company completed the sale of its Protection One stake to investment firm Quadrangle Group in 2004.

Former CEO David Wittig had been indicted in 2002 on fraud charges in connection with a real estate deal and a loan he received from Capital City Bank (the charges were not related to Westar Energy); shortly after the indictment, Wittig resigned from the company. He was later convicted for these charges.

In 2003 Wittig and former EVP Douglas Lake were indicted on conspiracy, fraud, and other criminal charges for allegedly looting more than $37 million in corporate funds for personal uses, including house renovations and travel expenses, and for attempting to cover up the scheme. The indictment also accused the executives of criminal activities related to the structuring of the Westar Industries spinoff. During the executives' tenure, Westar's debt rose to $3 billion and the company was pushed to the brink of bankruptcy. The executives' 2004 fraud trial was declared a mistrial due to a hung jury. In 2005 prosecutors announced that they would retry the case. At the retrial, both men were found guilty.

## HISTORY

Although Western Resources was created in 1992, it has roots deep in the history of the US energy industry. Its acquisitive ancestors, Kansas Power & Light (KPL) and Kansas Gas and Electric (KGE), had been providing electricity and natural gas since the early years of the 20th century. KGE was founded in 1909 by holding company American Power & Light to provide energy to three Kansas towns. By 1925 KGE had sold its natural gas service to focus on providing electricity to 50 towns.

The 1930s and 1940s saw KGE grow through acquisitions and internal expansion. In 1948 American Power & Light offered a few shares of KGE stock; it sold the remainder in 1949. In 1954 KGE built its first gas-powered plant; a year later it was listed on the New York Stock Exchange. In 1970 KGE entered the nuclear age by planning a nuke for Coffey County, Kansas.

KPL was originally financed by holding company North American Light and Power, which incorporated the firm in 1924. KPL built a generating plant and transmission lines from Tecumseh to Topeka and Atchison, and a coal-powered facility at Neosho, Kansas. In 1927 KPL bought out the Kansas Public Service Company, then United Power and Light (UPL) in the 1930s, which gave KPL a service area covering most of central Kansas. KPL bought Kansas Electric Power in the 1940s, bringing eastern Kansas under its wing.

KPL was listed on the New York Stock Exchange in 1949, and its parent was dissolved. Within a decade, KPL had broadened its service from providing electricity for rural Kansas to also providing energy for industry. In 1968 KPL installed the nation's first power plant scrubber system. KPL grew quickly during the 1970s and 1980s, building technologically up-to-date power plants, including the Wolf Creek nuclear plant.

KPL and KGE's 1992 merger was debated by those who feared major rate hikes, but the SEC approved it and KGE became a subsidiary of KPL. The company changed its name to Western Resources, but each utility operated under its own name. After the merger, Western Resources sold most of its natural gas operations and focused on electricity generation. In 1996 the firm set out to acquire another utility, Kansas City Power & Light. Western Resources transferred its natural gas holdings to ONEOK in 1996 for 45% of the Oklahoma gas company's stock.

In 1997 Western Resources diversified in preparation for utility deregulation that could hurt its energy business. It bought more than 80% of Protection One, an international security-monitoring company. In 2000 Kansas City Power & Light terminated an agreement to merge, citing problems with Protection One.

Later that year Western Resources announced plans to spin off its nonregulated businesses to shareholders as a new company, Westar Industries, and to sell its utility units to Public Service Company of New Mexico (now PNM Resources). In preparation for the spinoff, Western Resources sold its interests in marketing services company Paradigm Direct and oil and gas services company Hanover Compressor.

In 2001 PNM Resources filed suit to cancel its agreement to acquire KPL and KGE, and Western Resources filed a countersuit alleging a breach of the merger agreement. In 2002, PNM Resources terminated the agreement; however, both lawsuits were still pending. PNM Resources' termination of the agreement prompted Western Resources' decision to retain and focus on these assets. Later that year Western Resources changed its name to Westar Energy.

## EXECUTIVES

**Chairman:** Charles Q. (Charlie) Chandler IV, age 53
**President, CEO, and Director:** William B. (Bill) Moore, age 54, $401,042 pay
**EVP and CFO:** Mark A. Ruelle, age 45, $275,000 pay
**COO and EVP, Generation and Marketing:** Douglas R. (Doug) Sterbenz, age 43, $275,000 pay
**VP, General Counsel, and Corporate Secretary:** Larry D. Irick, age 50, $205,750 pay
**VP and Controller:** Leroy P. (Lee) Wages, age 58
**VP, Administrative Services:** Bruce A. Akin, age 42
**VP, Customer Care:** Peggy S. Loyd, age 47
**VP, Regulatory and Public Affairs:** James J. (Jim) Ludwig, age 48
**VP, Generation:** Ken Johnson, age 53
**VP, Transmission Operations and Environmental Services:** Kelly B. Harrison, age 46
**VP, Regulatory Affairs:** Michael Lennen
**Treasurer:** Anthony D. (Tony) Somma, age 44
**Director, Investor Relations:** Bruce Burns
**Manager, Corporate Communications:** Karla Olsen
**Auditors:** Deloitte & Touche LLP

## LOCATIONS

**HQ:** Westar Energy, Inc.
818 S. Kansas Ave., Topeka, KS 66612
**Phone:** 785-575-6300 **Fax:** 785-575-1796
**Web:** www.wr.com

Westar Energy distributes electricity in Kansas and markets power throughout the US.

## PRODUCTS/OPERATIONS

**2006 Sales**

| | $ mil. | % of total |
|---|---|---|
| Retail | | |
| Residential | 486.1 | 30 |
| Commercial | 438.3 | 27 |
| Industrial | 266.9 | 16 |
| Wholesale marketing | | |
| Tariff-based | 195.4 | 12 |
| Market-based | 101.2 | 6 |
| Transmission | 83.8 | 5 |
| Energy marketing | 40.1 | 2 |
| Other | 25.9 | 2 |
| Adjustments | (32.0) | — |
| **Total** | **1,605.7** | **100** |

**Selected Subsidiaries**

Kansas Gas and Electric Company (KGE, operates as Westar Energy, electric utility and marketer)
Kansas Power & Light Company (KPL, operates as Westar Energy, electric utility and marketer)

## COMPETITORS

AES
Ameren
Aquila
Atmos Energy
Dynegy
Edison International
Empire District Electric
Great Plains Energy
MidAmerican Energy
OGE Energy
Southern Company
Xcel Energy

## HISTORICAL FINANCIALS

Company Type: Public

**Income Statement** FYE: December 31

| | REVENUE ($ mil.) | NET INCOME ($ mil.) | NET PROFIT MARGIN | EMPLOYEES |
|---|---|---|---|---|
| **12/06** | 1,606 | 165 | 10.3% | 2,223 |
| **12/05** | 1,583 | 136 | 8.6% | 2,191 |
| **12/04** | 1,465 | 179 | 12.2% | 2,100 |
| **12/03** | 1,461 | 85 | 5.8% | 2,000 |
| **12/02** | 1,771 | (793) | — | 5,500 |
| **Annual Growth** | (2.4%) | — | — | (20.3%) |

**2006 Year-End Financials**

Debt ratio: 101.5%
Return on equity: 11.2%
Cash ($ mil.): 18
Current ratio: 0.81
Long-term debt ($ mil.): 1,563
No. of shares (mil.): 87
Dividends
Yield: 3.9%
Payout: 53.5%
Market value ($ mil.): 2,269

**Stock History** NYSE: WR

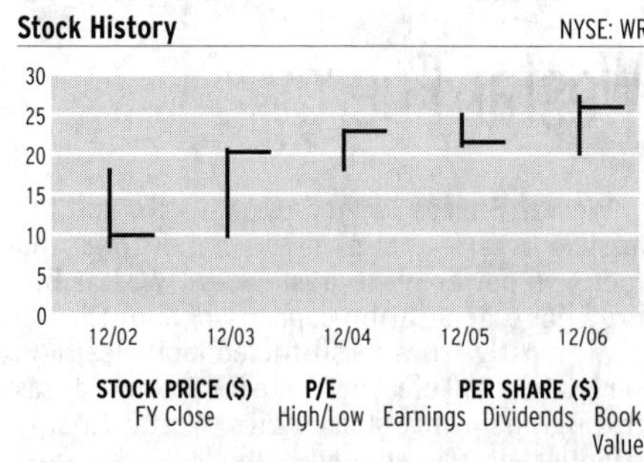


| | STOCK PRICE ($) FY Close | P/E High | P/E Low | PER SHARE ($) Earnings | Dividends | Book Value |
|---|---|---|---|---|---|---|
| **12/06** | 25.96 | 15 | 11 | 1.87 | 1.00 | 17.86 |
| **12/05** | 21.50 | 16 | 14 | 1.54 | 0.92 | 16.55 |
| **12/04** | 22.87 | 11 | 8 | 2.13 | 0.80 | 16.38 |
| **12/03** | 20.25 | 18 | 8 | 1.15 | 0.76 | 14.27 |
| **12/02** | 9.90 | — | — | (11.06) | 1.20 | 13.68 |
| **Annual Growth** | 27.3% | — | — | — | (4.5%) | 6.9% |

# Western Digital

And it's a hard, it's a hard, it's a hard drive gonna fail. Not likely, if that computer drive is from Western Digital. The company is one of the largest independent makers of hard disk drives, which record, store, and recall volumes of data. Drives for desktop PCs account for most of Western Digital's sales, although the company also makes devices for entry-level servers and home entertainment products, such as set-top boxes and video game consoles. The company sells to manufacturers and through retailers and distributors. Efforts to weather the highly cyclical drive market have included paring back its product line and selling non-core subsidiaries.

Western Digital is one of a handful of manufacturers that dominate the highly competitive hard disk drive market — a sector characterized by harsh competition, short product life cycles, and aggressive price cuts. About half of the company's sales are to manufacturers, including Dell (12% of sales in fiscal 2006), Hewlett-Packard, Gateway, and IBM.

Western Digital sold subsidiaries devoted to network-attached storage devices (Connex) and storage-area network management software (SANavigator). In 2003 it acquired most of the assets of bankrupt drive component maker Read-Rite for approximately $95 million in cash. Western Digital reached an agreement to acquire disk component maker Komag for $1 billion in 2007.

## HISTORY

Western Digital was founded in 1970 as a manufacturer of specialized semiconductors and electronic calculators. The company filed for Chapter 11 bankruptcy in late 1976. However, it reorganized and emerged successfully in 1978. Roger Johnson, after a succession of executive positions at Memorex, Measurex, and Burroughs, came to Western Digital as EVP and COO in 1982. Sales were merely $34 million, hurt by the acquisition of several ill-fitting computer and electronics businesses. By 1984 Johnson had become president and CEO and had sold off several companies to concentrate on storage control devices. A contract with IBM contributed to Western Digital's sales topping $460 million in 1987.

Anticipating a change in technology that would have disk drive makers building storage control into the drives themselves, Western Digital began to shift its efforts toward making disk drives in 1988. Ten-year company veteran Kathy Braun oversaw the purchase of Tandon's disk drive operations. Tandon was considered a second-rate manufacturer using aging technology, but its drives continued to sell well for a period following the acquisition. This created a false sense of security for Western Digital and delayed the development of more competitive drives. In late 1990 the market for storage controller boards had essentially disappeared. Losses prompted a restructuring that in turn violated Western Digital's credit agreements.

In 1991 the US economy slowed, and the disk drive industry began a price war. That year Western Digital, appearing close to bankruptcy, sold its profitable departmental network business to Standard Microsystems.

As the PC market improved in 1992, so did Western Digital's prospects. A big boost came when the cash-strapped company introduced a line of disk drives with a commonality of parts.

In 1993 Western Digital's IPO and sale of its wafer factory to Motorola reduced its high debt. That year the Clinton administration appointed CEO Johnson head of the General Services Administration. IBM veteran Charles Haggerty, who had joined Western Digital in 1992, assumed the company's top post. Johnson, a lifelong Republican, served nearly three years in the GSA post and resigned in 1996 to work for President Bill Clinton's re-election; he died in 2005.

In 1994 Western Digital enjoyed its first profit in four years. The company sold off its Microcomputer Products Group, which made proprietary semiconductors, in 1996 and introduced its first hard drives aimed at the corporate network computing market.

In 1997 a number of Asian manufacturers jumped into the market at the same time that computer makers were taking on sales approaches to eliminate the need for large inventories of hard drives and other stock. Those factors, combined with stalled PC demand and Western Digital's slow transition to newer recording head technologies, caused a loss for fiscal 1998. To respond, Western Digital cut more than 20% of its workforce and slashed production. Braun, by then second in command at the company and one of the industry's highest-paid women, retired in 1998.

In 1999 the company sold its disk media business, producer of magnetically coated disks that store data in hard drives, to longtime supplier Komag. Later that year Western Digital took a financial hit following its recall of 400,000 defective disk drives; it announced it would lay off another 2,500 employees, primarily in Singapore.

In early 2000 Haggerty retired from the CEO post; COO Matthew Massengill was tapped to replace him. Also that year the company branched into new markets through two subsidiaries: Connex (network storage) and SageTree (supply chain software).

In 2001 Western Digital sold Connex to former rival Quantum after that company exited the hard drive market. It also sold its SANavigator storage-area network management software unit to McDATA for about $30 million. Massengill was named chairman later that year.

Massengill stepped down as CEO in October 2005, while remaining executive chairman. Arif Shakeel, Western Digital's president and COO since early 2002, succeeded Massengill as CEO, keeping the president's title. Shakeel, who has worked at Western Digital since 1985, has held a seat on the board since September 2004.

## EXECUTIVES

**Chairman:** Thomas E. Pardun, age 63
**President, CEO, and Director:** John F. Coyne, age 56
**EVP Finance:** Timothy (Tim) Leyden, age 55
**SVP and CFO:** Stephen D. (Steve) Milligan, age 43, $852,904 pay
**SVP, Administration, General Counsel, and Secretary:** Raymond M. (Ray) Bukaty, age 49, $955,342 pay
**SVP, Research and Development and CTO:** Hossein M. Moghadam, age 62, $921,350 pay
**VP and GM, PC Components Group:** Richard E. Rutledge
**VP, Controller, and Principal Accounting Officer:** Joseph R. Carrillo
**Auditors:** KPMG LLP

## LOCATIONS

**HQ:** Western Digital Corporation
20511 Lake Forest Dr., Lake Forest, CA 92630
**Phone:** 949-672-7000 **Fax:** 949-672-5408
**Web:** www.westerndigital.com

Western Digital has manufacturing facilities in Malaysia, Thailand, and the US, and sales offices around the world.

### 2007 Sales

| | $ mil. | % of total |
|---|---|---|
| Asia | 1,840 | 34 |
| US | 1,780 | 32 |
| Europe, Middle East & Africa | 1,591 | 29 |
| Other regions | 257 | 5 |
| **Total** | **5,468** | **100** |

## PRODUCTS/OPERATIONS

### 2007 Sales by Channel

| | % of total |
|---|---|
| Manufacturers | 48 |
| Distributors | 36 |
| Retailers | 16 |
| **Total** | **100** |

### Selected Products

Internal Hard Drives
Audio/Video hard drives (Performer)
Desktop PCs and entry-level servers (Caviar, Protégé)
Servers and storage systems (Raptor)

External Hard Drives
FireWire for PCs and Macs

Accessories
Desktop (FireWire adapter)
Mobile (FireWire CardBus PC card)

## COMPETITORS

Fujitsu
Hitachi Global Storage
IBM
Iomega
Samsung Electronics
Seagate Technology
TEAC
Toshiba

## HISTORICAL FINANCIALS

Company Type: Public

### Income Statement

FYE: Saturday nearest June 30

| | REVENUE ($ mil.) | NET INCOME ($ mil.) | NET PROFIT MARGIN | EMPLOYEES |
|---|---|---|---|---|
| **6/07** | 5,468 | 564 | 10.3% | 29,572 |
| **6/06** | 4,341 | 395 | 9.1% | 24,750 |
| **6/05** | 3,639 | 198 | 5.5% | 23,161 |
| **6/04** | 3,047 | 151 | 5.0% | 17,376 |
| **6/03** | 2,719 | 182 | 6.7% | 11,508 |
| **Annual Growth** | 19.1% | 32.7% | — | 26.6% |

### 2007 Year-End Financials

Debt ratio: 0.6%
Return on equity: 39.3%
Cash ($ mil.): 907
Current ratio: 1.80
Long-term debt ($ mil.): 10
No. of shares (mil.): 225
Dividends
Yield: —
Payout: —
Market value ($ mil.): 4,354

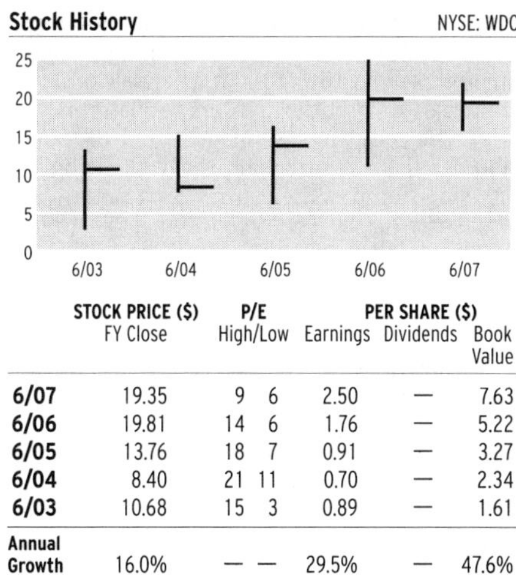


| | STOCK PRICE ($) FY Close | P/E High | P/E Low | PER SHARE ($) Earnings | PER SHARE ($) Dividends | PER SHARE ($) Book Value |
|---|---|---|---|---|---|---|
| **6/07** | 19.35 | 9 | 6 | 2.50 | — | 7.63 |
| **6/06** | 19.81 | 14 | 6 | 1.76 | — | 5.22 |
| **6/05** | 13.76 | 18 | 7 | 0.91 | — | 3.27 |
| **6/04** | 8.40 | 21 | 11 | 0.70 | — | 2.34 |
| **6/03** | 10.68 | 15 | 3 | 0.89 | — | 1.61 |
| **Annual Growth** | 16.0% | — | — | 29.5% | — | 47.6% |

# Weyerhaeuser Company

If a tree falls in a Weyerhaeuser-owned forest, someone *is* there to hear it — and he has a chainsaw. One of the top US forest products companies, Weyerhaeuser operates along five business lines: Wood Products (lumber, plywood, and other building materials); Containerboard, Packaging, and Recycling (corrugated boxes, linerboard, industrial and agricultural packaging, and recycling); and Pulp and Paper (pulp and coated and uncoated papers). Also, Timberlands manages 6.4 million acres of company-owned US timberland and nearly 30 million acres of leased Canadian timberland, and Real Estate and Related Assets develops housing and master-planned communities. Weyerhaeuser has merged its copier paper business with Domtar.

According to the terms of the $3.3 billion deal, Weyerhaeuser shareholders get a 55% stake in the new company. Weyerhaeuser will control the new company's board, and several Weyerhaeuser executives have been assigned to manage the new company. Transferred operations include about a dozen paper and pulp mills, 14 converting centers, a coated groundwood mill, and two softwood lumber mills.

Changing hemispheres, Weyerhaeuser has restructured its foreign timber business with a move from New Zealand to South America. Weyerhaeuser and Global Forest Partners (GFP), both previously involved through joint ventures around the globe, have signed a deal that will relocate Weyerhaeuser's international timber operations from New Zealand to Uruguay. In exchange for the Los Piques plywood mill and some 41,000 hectares of Uruguay timberland, GFP will receive Weyerhaeuser New Zealand's operations, which includes a 67,000 hectare tract of forest and a sawmill.

In light of the downturn in the home building market, the company is scaling back on its housing business, delaying land purchases and limiting housing starts.

As part of its ongoing efforts to streamline operations, Weyerhaeuser has announced an agreement to sell its 16 Canadian wholesale building materials distribution centers to Platinum Equity. The company also plans to sell 10 (out of about 50) US distribution centers. Citing the housing slump as the contributing factor, Weyerhaeuser has decided to shutter its joist plant in Alberta, Canada.

## HISTORY

Frederick Weyerhaeuser, a 24-year-old German immigrant, bought his first lumberyard in 1858 in Illinois. He also participated in joint logging ventures in Illinois, Minnesota, and Wisconsin. In 1900 he and 15 partners bought 900,000 timbered acres from the Northern Pacific Railway. The venture was named Weyerhaeuser Timber Company.

During the Depression the business recouped losses in the deflated lumber market by selling wood pulp. Frederick's grandson, J. P. "Phil" Weyerhaeuser Jr., took over as CEO in 1933.

Diversification into the production of containerboard (1949), particleboard (1955), paper (1956), and other products led the company to drop "Timber" from its name in 1959. In 1963 Weyerhaeuser went public and opened its first overseas office in Tokyo.

In the 1970s George Weyerhaeuser (Phil's son) diversified further to insulate the company from the forest-product industry's cyclical nature and ended up with a mishmash of businesses and products, from private-label disposable diapers to pet supplies.

The eruption of Mount St. Helens in 1980 destroyed 68,000 acres of Weyerhaeuser timber. That disaster and the soft US lumber market depressed the company's earnings through 1982. Weyerhaeuser reduced its workforce by 25% during this period.

In 1992 the company outbid Georgia-Pacific, paying $600 million for two pulp mills, three sawmills, and more than 200,000 acres of forest land to boost its market-pulp capacity by 40%. The following year the company sold its disposable-diaper business through a public offering in a new company, Paragon Trade Brands. It also sold GNA Corporation to General Electric subsidiary GE Capital.

The federal government in 1995 allowed the company to harvest trees in an area inhabited by the endangered northern spotted owl. The move angered environmental groups. In 1998 Steve Rogel, a veteran from competitor Willamette, succeeded John Creighton as CEO and became the first outsider to head Weyerhaeuser.

In 1999 Weyerhaeuser paid $2.45 billion for Canada's MacMillan Bloedel, and early in 2000 it acquired TJ International, 51% owner of leading engineered lumber products company Trus Joist MacMillan (Weyerhaeuser already owned the other 49%).

After a protracted courtship, in March 2002 Weyerhaeuser acquired Oregon-based Willamette Industries in a $6.1 billion cash deal. The company closed three North American plants (in Colorado, Louisiana, and Oregon) later that year. In October the company closed a Canadian containerboard mill, cutting 140 jobs in the process.

On the heels of the deals for MacMillan Bloedel, Trus Joist MacMillan, and Willamette, Weyerhaeuser moved to pay down debt. It closed 12 facilities and sold about 444,000 acres of non-strategic timberlands in 2003. In 2004 Weyerhaeuser sold roughly 270,000 acres of timberlands in central Georgia for about $400 million to investment and property firms in Georgia and South Carolina.

Early in 2005 Weyerhaeuser agreed to sell five Canadian sawmills, two finishing plants, 635,000 acres of timber, and some government land cutting rights to Brascan for $970 million. Weyerhaeuser had acquired the timber and sawmill assets when it acquired MacMillan Bloedel in 1999.

The company's debt reduction strategy continued in 2004. Weyerhaeuser sold roughly 270,000 acres of its timberlands in Georgia and several mills in the US and Canada.

Weyerhaeuser continued to streamline and focus on its softwood lumber business in 2005, selling $970 million in assets (five sawmills, two finishing plants, 635,000 acres, and timber rights) to Brascan. Weyerhaeuser also closed a Saskatchewan pulp and paper mill in 2006, cutting 690 jobs; not long afterward, amid weak profits, it announced multiple plant closures and sales, including another pulp mill, another sawmill, several corrugated plants, and a paper bag plant.

## EXECUTIVES

**Chairman, President, and CEO:** Steven R. (Steve) Rogel, age 64, $1,286,538 pay
**EVP and COO:** Richard E. (Rich) Hanson, age 65, $693,000 pay
**EVP and CFO:** Patricia M. (Patty) Bedient, age 53
**SVP Industrial Wood Products and International:** Craig D. Neeser, age 52
**SVP Corporate Affairs:** Ernesta Ballard, age 61
**SVP Human Resources:** Edward P. (Ed) Rogel, age 61
**SVP and General Counsel:** Sandy D. McDade, age 55
**SVP Research and Development and CTO:** Miles P. Drake, age 57
**SVP Information Technology and CIO:** Susan M. Mersereau, age 60
**SVP Residential Wood Products:** Lee T. Alford, age 59, $430,993 pay
**SVP Containerboard Packaging and Recycling:** Thomas F. (Tom) Gideon, age 55
**SVP Cellulose Fibers:** Srinivasan (Shaker) Chandrasekaran, age 57
**VP, Controller, and Chief Accounting Officer:** Jeanne M. Hillman, age 47
**VP and Director of Taxes:** Thomas M. Smith
**VP and Treasurer:** Jeffrey W. Nitta
**VP Public Affairs:** David A. Larsen
**VP Investor Relations:** Kathryn F. McAuley
**VP Human Resources Operations:** John Hooper
**President and CEO, Pardee Homes, Weyerhaeuser Real Estate:** Michael V. (Mike) McGee, age 51
**President, Quadrant Corporation, Weyerhaeuser Real Estate:** Peter M. Orser
**President and CEO, TMI, Weyerhaeuser Real Estate:** Samuel C. (Sam) Hathorn Jr., age 63
**President and CEO, Weyerhaeuser Real Estate:** Daniel S. (Dan) Fulton, age 58, $593,942 pay
**President and CEO, Weyerhaeuser Realty Investors, Weyerhaeuser Real Estate:** Stephen M. (Steve) Margolin
**Director of Financial and External Communications:** Bruce Amundson
**Auditors:** KPMG LLP

## LOCATIONS

**HQ:** Weyerhaeuser Company
33663 Weyerhaeuser Way South,
Federal Way, WA 98003
**Phone:** 253-924-2345 **Fax:** 253-924-2685
**Web:** www.weyerhaeuser.com

**2006 Sales**

| | $ mil. | % of total |
|---|---|---|
| US | 18,251 | 84 |
| Canada | 1,160 | 5 |
| Japan | 750 | 3 |
| Europe | 554 | 3 |
| Other regions | 1,181 | 5 |
| **Total** | **21,896** | **100** |

## PRODUCTS/OPERATIONS

**2006 Sales**

| | $ mil. | % of total |
|---|---|---|
| Wood products | 7,902 | 36 |
| Containerboard, packaging & recycling | 4,912 | 22 |
| Cellulose fiber & white paper | 4,601 | 21 |
| Real estate & related assets | 3,335 | 15 |
| Timberlands | 1,016 | 5 |
| Corporate & other | 484 | 1 |
| Adjustment | (354) | — |
| **Total** | **21,896** | **100** |

### Selected Products and Services

Wood Products
- Composite panels
- Engineered lumber products
- Lumber (softwood and hardwood)
- Oriented Strand Board
- Plywood
- Veneer

Containerboard, Packaging, and Recycling
- Containerboard
- Packaging
- Recycling
- Kraft bags and sacks

Cellulose Fiber and White Paper
- Coated groundwood
- Liquid packaging board
- Paper
- Pulp

Real Estate and Related Assets
- Master-planned communities
- Multifamily homes
- Residential lots
- Single-family homes

Timberlands

Other
- Recycling
- Transportation

### Selected Subsidiaries

Columbia & Cowlitz Railway Company
MacMillan Bloedel Pembroke Limited Partnership (Canada)
Mississippi & Skuna Valley Railroad Company
North Pacific Paper Corporation (50%, joint venture with Nippon Paper)
Trus Joist SPRL (Belgium)
Westwood Shipping Lines, Inc.
Weyerhaeuser Real Estate Company

## COMPETITORS

Abitibi-Consolidated
Bowater
Buckeye Technologies
Canfor
Cascades Boxboard
Champion Enterprises
ENCE
Evergreen Hardwoods
Georgia-Pacific Corporation
Indiana Veneers
International Paper
Louisiana-Pacific
MAXXAM
McFarland Cascade
MeadWestvaco
Myllykoski Paper
NewPage
Norbord
OfficeMax
Oji Paper
PCA
Potlatch
Pratt Industries USA
Rayonier
Sierra Pacific Industries
Smurfit Kappa
Smurfit-Stone Container
Stora Enso Oyj
Tembec
Temple-Inland
Tenon
UPM-Kymmene
West Fraser Timber
White Birch Paper

## HISTORICAL FINANCIALS

Company Type: Public

**Income Statement** FYE: Last Sunday in December

| | REVENUE ($ mil.) | NET INCOME ($ mil.) | NET PROFIT MARGIN | EMPLOYEES |
|---|---|---|---|---|
| **12/06** | 21,896 | 453 | 2.1% | 46,700 |
| **12/05** | 22,629 | 733 | 3.2% | 49,900 |
| **12/04** | 22,665 | 1,283 | 5.7% | 53,646 |
| **12/03** | 19,873 | 277 | 1.4% | 55,162 |
| **12/02** | 18,521 | 241 | 1.3% | 56,787 |
| **Annual Growth** | 4.3% | 17.1% | — | (4.8%) |

**2006 Year-End Financials**

Debt ratio: 84.5%
Return on equity: 4.8%
Cash ($ mil.): 243
Current ratio: 1.37
Long-term debt ($ mil.): 7,675
No. of shares (mil.): 237
Dividends
Yield: 4.0%
Payout: 152.2%
Market value ($ mil.): 16,723

**Stock History** NYSE: WY

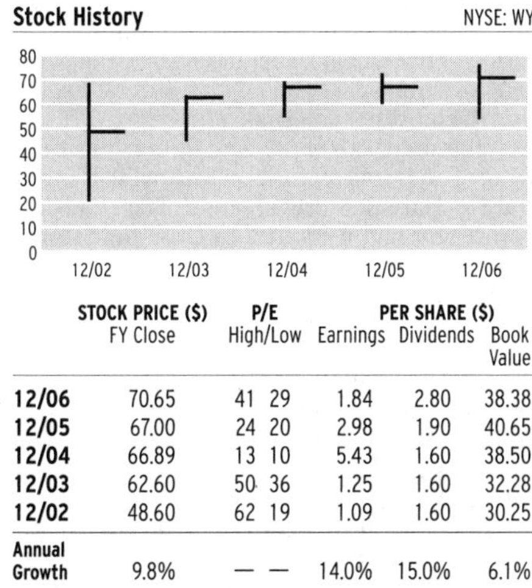


| | STOCK PRICE ($) FY Close | P/E High | P/E Low | PER SHARE ($) Earnings | Dividends | Book Value |
|---|---|---|---|---|---|---|
| **12/06** | 70.65 | 41 | 29 | 1.84 | 2.80 | 38.38 |
| **12/05** | 67.00 | 24 | 20 | 2.98 | 1.90 | 40.65 |
| **12/04** | 66.89 | 13 | 10 | 5.43 | 1.60 | 38.50 |
| **12/03** | 62.60 | 50 | 36 | 1.25 | 1.60 | 32.28 |
| **12/02** | 48.60 | 62 | 19 | 1.09 | 1.60 | 30.25 |
| **Annual Growth** | 9.8% | — | — | 14.0% | 15.0% | 6.1% |

# Whirlpool Corporation

With brand names recognized by anyone who ever separated dark colors from light, Whirlpool is the #1 US home appliance maker (#2 worldwide, after Sweden's AB Electrolux). It makes washers, dryers, refrigerators, air conditioners, dishwashers, freezers, microwave ovens, ranges, trash compactors, air purifiers, and more. In addition to Whirlpool, the company sells its products under brand names including KitchenAid, Bauknecht, Roper, and Magic Chef. About 14% of Whirlpool's 2006 sales came from making Kenmore and Sears appliances for Sears, which also stocks the Whirlpool and KitchenAid brands. The company acquired troubled competitor Maytag in early 2006.

With the acquisition of Maytag for about $1.9 billion, Whirlpool added several top brands to its already bulging portfolio, including Admiral, Amana, Jenn-Air, Magic Chef, and of course, the eponymous Maytag. Once the dust settled Whirlpool in mid-2006 announced plans to sell four businesses — including Amana commercial microwaves, Dixie-Narco vending systems, Hoover floorcare, and Jade commercial appliances — in an effort to cultivate its core brands and purge non-core operations. By late 2006 it had sold Dixie-Narco and its Amana commercial business. Whirlpool sold its Hoover unit in February 2007 to Techtronic Industries Co. Ltd. for some $107 million in cash. The deal involves Techtronic running the Hoover business and its manufacturing sites and Whirlpool retaining pension benefit liabilities. It announced in early 2007 that it is selling its Jade unit to Middleby Corporation.

Buying Maytag has spurred Whirlpool to streamline operations and purge staff. In 2006 it laid off some 4,500 employees, consolidated duplicate functions related to administration and manufacturing, and shuttered some offices, including a Maytag research and development center based in Newton, Illinois. Whirlpool shuttered Maytag's Iowa-based administrative offices and moved them to Michigan and other locations. The company cut 700 jobs at several Tennessee plants in 2007 with plans for another 400 job cuts at a plant in Cleveland by the end of 2008.

Facing a mature market in North America, Whirlpool has pursued a strategy of building market share in Europe and in emerging economies globally. Despite such efforts, about 66% of Whirlpool's sales still come from North America, and the company is reinvesting in its US manufacturing operations. Also, the company is expanding appliance production in Mexico, reflecting growing sales in that country.

Whirlpool manufactures products in 12 countries and sells them in more than 170 others.

## HISTORY

Brothers Fred and Lou Upton and their uncle, Emory Upton, founded the Upton Machine Company, manufacturer of electric motor-driven washing machines, in 1911 in St. Joseph, Michigan. Sears, Roebuck and Co. began buying their products five years later, and by 1925 the company was supplying all of Sears' washers. The Uptons combined their company with the Nineteen Hundred Washer Company in 1929 to form the Nineteen Hundred Corporation, the world's largest washing machine company.

Sears and Nineteen Hundred prospered during the Great Depression, and during WWII Nineteen Hundred's factories produced war materials. In 1948 it began selling its first automatic washing machine (introduced a year earlier) under the Whirlpool brand. In 1950 the company changed its name to Whirlpool following the success of the product and introduced its first automatic dryer.

During the 1950s and 1960s Whirlpool became a full-line appliance manufacturer while continuing as Sears' principal Kenmore appliance supplier. In 1955 the company bought Seeger Refrigerator Company and the stove and air-conditioning interests of RCA. Three years later it made its first investment in Multibras Eletrodomésticos, an appliance maker in Brazil. (It has increased that investment over the years.) Other purchases included the gas refrigeration and ice-maker manufacturing facilities of Servel (1958); a majority interest in Heil-Quaker, makers of central heaters and space heaters (1964); Sears' major television set supplier, Warwick Electronics (1966); and 33% of Canadian appliance maker John Inglis Company (1969). It made a deal with Sony in 1973 for the distribution of Whirlpool-brand products in Japan. Whirlpool sold its TV manufacturing business to SANYO of Japan three years later.

Between 1981 and 1991, despite a static US market, Whirlpool's sales tripled to almost $6.6 billion. In 1986 the firm bought top-end appliance manufacturer KitchenAid (from Dart and Kraft) and 65% of Italian cooling compressor manufacturer Aspera. Also that year it sold its Heil-Quaker central heating business. David Whitwam was appointed CEO in 1987. Whirlpool took over total ownership of Inglis in 1990.

The company formed Whirlpool Europe, a joint venture with Philips Electronics in 1989; in 1991 it bought out Philips' share. Two years later Whirlpool took control of appliance marketer SAGAD of Argentina.

Whirlpool acquired control of Kelvinator of India in 1994 and formed a joint venture in China with Shenzhen Petrochemical Holdings in 1995 to produce air conditioners. The following year Whirlpool merged its Whirlpool Washing Machines and Kelvinator of India companies to form Whirlpool of India. The company's European division plunged into the red when competition and a recession kept consumers away from its higher-priced appliances.

In 1997 Whirlpool initiated a restructuring (due to losses from its foreign operations) that included plant closures and substantial layoffs (as much as 10% of its workforce). The next year Whirlpool sold its appliance financing subsidiary to Transamerica. In 2000 Whirlpool launched the Cielo Bath line of jetted tubs, and in 2001 it introduced the Calypso dishwasher and the Duet washer and dryer.

Another global restructuring plan swept through the company in 2000, resulting in significant pretax charges and the elimination of about 6,000 employees by October 2003.

In February 2002 Whirlpool bought the remaining 51% of Vitromatic it didn't already own. (Vitromatic — the second-largest appliance manufacturer in Mexico — is now called Whirlpool Mexico.) In March the company purchased 95% of Polar, Poland's second-largest appliance maker.

Whirlpool introduced Gladiator GarageWorks (modular storage systems for the garage) and Polara (the first electric range with cooking and refrigeration capabilities) in 2002.

## EXECUTIVES

**Chairman and CEO:** Jeff M. Fettig, age 50, $1,083,333 pay (prior to title change)
**Director; President, Whirlpool North America:** Michael A. (Mike) Todman, age 49
**EVP and CFO:** Roy W. Templin, age 46, $541,667 pay
**EVP and CTO:** Michael D. (Mike) Thieneman, age 58
**EVP; President, Whirlpool Asia:** Mark K. Hu, age 53
**EVP; President, Whirlpool International:** Paulo F. M. O. Periquito, age 60
**EVP; President, Whirlpool Europe:** Marc R. Bitzer, age 41
**EVP, Market Operations, North America:** W. Timothy (Tim) Yaggi, age 46
**SVP, Corporate Affairs and General Counsel:** Daniel F. Hopp, age 58
**SVP, Global Human Resources:** David A. (Dave) Binkley
**SVP, Global Strategic Sourcing:** Mark E. Brown
**SVP, North American Region Operations:** John C. Anderson
**Corporate VP and Treasurer:** Blair A. Clark
**Corporate VP, Finance, Project Management Office:** Ted A. Dosch
**Corporate VP, Global Communication and Public Affairs:** Jeffrey (Jeff) Noel, age 46
**Corporate VP, Strategic Competency Creation:** Nancy T. Snyder
**Corporate VP; General Director, Whirlpool Mexico:** Roy V. Armes, age 54
**VP, US Sales:** Sam A. Abdelnour
**VP and Controller:** Larry Venturelli, age 43
**Auditors:** Ernst & Young LLP

## LOCATIONS

**HQ:** Whirlpool Corporation
2000 N. M-63, Benton Harbor, MI 49022
**Phone:** 269-923-5000 **Fax:** 269-923-3722
**Web:** www.whirlpoolcorp.com

### 2006 Sales

| | $ mil. | % of total |
|---|---|---|
| North America | 11,953 | 66 |
| Europe | 3,383 | 19 |
| Latin America | 2,430 | 13 |
| Asia | 457 | 3 |
| Adjustments | (143) | (1) |
| **Total** | **18,080** | **100** |

## PRODUCTS/OPERATIONS

### 2006 Sales

| | $ mil. | % of total |
|---|---|---|
| Home laundry appliances | 5,474 | 30 |
| Home refrigerators & freezers | 5,341 | 30 |
| Home cooking appliances | 2,909 | 16 |
| Other | 4,356 | 24 |
| **Total** | **18,080** | **100** |

### Selected Product Lines

Air conditioning equipment
Cooking appliances
Dishwashers
Freezers
Laundry appliances
Mixers
Refrigerators
Small household appliances

### Selected Brands

Acros
Admiral
Amana
Bauknecht
Brastemp
Consul
Eslabon de Lujo
Estate
Jenn-Air
Kenmore
KIC
KitchenAid
Laden
Magic Chef
Maytax
Polar
Roper
Supermatic
Whirlpool

## COMPETITORS

BSH Bosch und Siemens Hausgeräte
Candy Group
Daewoo Electronics
Electrolux
Electrolux Home Appliances China
Fedders
GE Consumer & Industrial
Goodman Manufacturing
Gree Electrical Appliances
Haier Group
Hitachi
Indesit
LG Electronics
Matsushita Electric
Samsung Electronics America
SANYO
Sears Holdings
Sharp
Sub-Zero
Viking

## HISTORICAL FINANCIALS

Company Type: Public

### Income Statement

FYE: December 31

| | REVENUE ($ mil.) | NET INCOME ($ mil.) | NET PROFIT MARGIN | EMPLOYEES |
|---|---|---|---|---|
| **12/06** | 18,080 | 433 | 2.4% | 73,000 |
| **12/05** | 14,317 | 422 | 2.9% | 66,000 |
| **12/04** | 13,220 | 406 | 3.1% | 68,000 |
| **12/03** | 12,176 | 414 | 3.4% | 68,000 |
| **12/02** | 11,016 | (394) | — | 68,000 |
| **Annual Growth** | 13.2% | — | — | 1.8% |

### 2006 Year-End Financials

Debt ratio: 54.8%
Return on equity: 17.2%
Cash ($ mil.): 262
Current ratio: 1.08
Long-term debt ($ mil.): 1,798
No. of shares (mil.): 78
Dividends
Yield: 2.1%
Payout: 30.3%
Market value ($ mil.): 6,476

### Stock History

NYSE: WHR

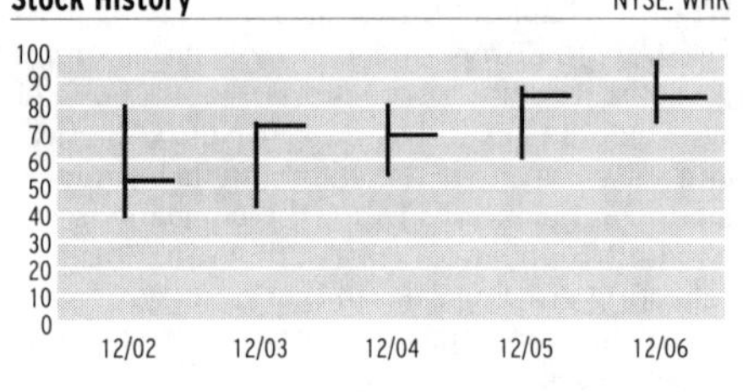

| | STOCK PRICE ($) FY Close | P/E High/Low | | PER SHARE ($) Earnings | Dividends | Book Value |
|---|---|---|---|---|---|---|
| **12/06** | 83.02 | 17 | 13 | 5.67 | 1.72 | 42.09 |
| **12/05** | 83.76 | 14 | 10 | 6.19 | 1.72 | 25.66 |
| **12/04** | 69.21 | 14 | 9 | 5.90 | 1.72 | 23.97 |
| **12/03** | 72.65 | 12 | 7 | 5.91 | 1.36 | 18.86 |
| **12/02** | 52.22 | — | — | (5.68) | 1.36 | 10.87 |
| **Annual Growth** | 12.3% | — | — | — | 6.0% | 40.3% |

# Whole Foods Market

With food and other items that are free of pesticides, preservatives, sweeteners, and cruelty, Whole Foods Market knows more about guiltless eating and shopping than most retailers. The world's #1 natural foods chain by far — now that it has acquired its main rival Wild Oats Markets — the company operates more than 300 stores in the US, Canada, and the UK. The stores emphasize perishable products, which account for about two-thirds of sales. Whole Foods Market offers more than 1,500 items in four lines of private-label products (such as the premium Whole Foods and a line of organic products for children, Whole Kids). Founded in Austin, Texas, in 1980, Whole Foods Market pioneered the supermarket concept in natural and organic foods retailing.

Whole Foods has benefited from increased health-consciousness among consumers, which has turned natural and organic foods retailing into the fastest-growing segment in the US grocery business. Beyond groceries, Whole Foods has moved into related businesses, such as dietary supplements, personal care products, household goods, and organic cotton clothing.

As the organic foods industry mushrooms, Whole Foods is growing rapidly by building and acquiring new stores. In a bold strategic move to shore up its leadership position in the industry, Whole Foods bought its 110-store rival Wild Oats in August 2007. The two had been engaged in a fierce battle for customers city by city. The deal, worth some $565 million (plus $106 million in debt), gives Whole Foods new stores in each of its operating regions, as well as stores in desirable new regions such as the Pacific Northwest and Florida. The takeover followed a six-month effort that included overcoming the objections of the Federal Trade Commission, which had sued to block the merger on antitrust grounds.

While Whole Foods ultimately prevailed, it didn't emerge from its battle with the FTC unscathed. The conflict brought to light revelations that CEO John Mackey used fake online identity "Rahodeb" (an anagram of his wife's name, Deborah) to disparage Wild Oats management and promote Whole Foods' stock, putting into question Whole Foods' case to acquire Wild Oats, as well as Mackey's reputation and his firm's image. (Prior to the embarassing disclosure, the company's shareholders had already proposed splitting the offices of chairman and CEO.)

In the aftermath of the Wild Oats acquisition, Whole Foods sold off the accompanying Henry's and Sun Harvest Stores chains in Texas and California and said it intends to close nine stores and relocate nearly 10 others.

In addition to growing via acquisition at home, the company has also been expanding across the Atlantic. In 2004 it bought Fresh & Wild Holdings Limited, a chain of natural and organic foods stores in the UK with stores in London and Bristol. Whole Foods opened its first store in central London under its own banner in June 2007.

Years of rapid store growth and competition from mainstream supermarkets and Wal-Mart, which aims to bring affordable organic food to the masses, has slowed same-store sales growth and put pressure on profits at Whole Foods. Amid warnings of a continuing slowdown in growth, Mackey cut his salary to $1 as of January 1, 2007.

To counter its image as an expensive place to shop, Whole Foods (aka Whole Paycheck) has launched a print advertising campaign in the fiercely-competitive New York area emphasizing "value" and the chain's price competitiveness vis-a-vis rivals, including Trader Joe's.

## HISTORY

With a $10,000 loan from his father, John Mackey started Safer Way Natural Foods in Austin, Texas, in 1978. Despite struggling, Mackey dreamed of opening a larger, supermarket-sized natural foods store. Two years later Safer Way merged with Clarksville Natural Grocery, and Whole Foods Market was born. Led by Mackey, that year it opened an 11,000-sq.-ft. supermarket in a counterculture hotbed of Austin. The store was an instant success, and a second store was added 18 months later in suburban Austin.

The company slowly expanded in Texas, opening or buying stores in Houston in 1984 and Dallas in 1986. Whole Foods expanded into Louisiana in 1988 with the purchase of like-named Whole Food Co., a single New Orleans store owned by Peter Roy (who served as the company's president from 1993 to 1998). Sticking to university towns, Whole Foods added another store in California the next year and acquired Wellspring Grocery (two stores, North Carolina) in 1991. In 1992 it debuted its first private-label products under the Whole Foods name. Seeking capital to expand even more, the company raised $23 million by going public in early 1992 with 12 stores.

Every competitor in the fragmented health foods industry became a potential acquisition, and the chain began growing rapidly. In 1992 Whole Foods bought the six-store Bread & Circus chain in New England. The next year it added Mrs. Gooch's Natural Foods Markets (seven stores in the Los Angeles area). Its biggest acquisition came in 1996, when it bought Fresh Fields, the second-largest US natural foods chain (22 stores on the East Coast and in Chicago). Although the purchase hurt profits in 1996, sales surpassed $1 billion for the first time in fiscal 1997 as Whole Foods neared 70 stores. In 1997 it introduced the less-expensive 365 brand private label.

Capitalizing on the growing popularity of nutraceuticals (natural supplements with benefits similar to pharmaceuticals), the company paid $146 million in 1997 for Amrion, a maker of nutraceuticals and other nutritional supplements.

In 2002 Whole Foods crossed the border to Canada. Its first foreign store opened in downtown Toronto in May. In November 2003 Mackey was named Entrepreneur of the Year by consulting firm Ernst & Young. That month Whole Foods acquired Select Fish, a Seattle-based seafood processor and distributor, and opened a seafood distribution facility in Atlanta.

In February 2004 Whole Foods opened a 59,000-sq.-ft. store in the new Time Warner Center in Manhattan. The new store, which includes a 248-seat cafe, sushi bar, wine shop and gourmet bakery, is the largest supermarket in New York City. That month the company acquired the UK organic-food retailer Fresh & Wild for $38 million.

Also in 2004 the company announced that month the opening of its first Gluten-Free Bakehouse, a dedicated gluten-free baking facility located outside Raleigh, North Carolina.

In January 2005 Whole Foods launched the Animal Compassion Foundation, an independent, non-profit organization dedicated to the compassionate treatment of livestock. The company moved that month to its new corporate headquarters across the street from its old location in downtown Austin. Its new flagship store opened its doors in March at the same location. In October Whole Foods increased its number of operating regions from 10 to 11 by separating the North Atlantic region into the North Atlantic and Tri-State regions. Overall in fiscal 2005 the company opened a dozen new stores, including its first in Nebraska and Ohio. In 2006 the company acquired a store in Portland, Maine and converted it to the Whole Foods Market banner.

## EXECUTIVES

**Chairman and CEO:** John P. Mackey, age 53, $607,800 pay
**Co-President and COO:** A. C. Gallo, age 53, $607,800 pay
**Co-President and COO:** Walter E. Robb IV, age 53, $607,800 pay
**EVP and CFO:** Glenda Flanagan Chamberlain, age 53, $607,800 pay
**EVP, Growth and Business Development:** James P. (Jim) Sud, age 54, $607,800 pay
**EVP, Global Support:** Lee Valkenaar, age 50, $607,800 pay
**VP and CIO:** Mike Clifford
**VP, Accounting and Controller:** Sam Ferguson
**VP, Distribution:** Bart Beilman
**VP, Investor Relations:** Cynthia M. (Cindy) McCann
**VP, Global Communications and Quality Standards:** Margaret Wittenberg
**VP, Operational Finance:** Lee Matecko
**VP, Business Development:** Betsy Foster
**VP, Legal Affairs and General Counsel:** Roberta Lang
**VP, Team Member Services:** Paula Labian
**VP, Private Label:** Bruce Silverman
**Auditors:** Ernst & Young LLP

## LOCATIONS

**HQ:** Whole Foods Market, Inc.
550 Bowie St., Austin, TX 78703
**Phone:** 512-477-4455 **Fax:** 512-477-1301
**Web:** www.wholefoodsmarket.com

### 2006 Stores

| | No. |
|---|---|
| US | |
| California | 40 |
| Massachusetts | 17 |
| Texas | 13 |
| Illinois | 9 |
| Florida | 8 |
| New Jersey | 8 |
| Colorado | 7 |
| Georgia | 7 |
| Maryland | 7 |
| Pennsylvania | 7 |
| Virginia | 7 |
| New York | 6 |
| North Carolina | 5 |
| Michigan | 4 |
| District of Columbia | 3 |
| Louisiana | 3 |
| Washington | 3 |
| Arizona | 2 |
| Connecticut | 2 |
| Minnesota | 2 |
| Nevada | 2 |
| New Mexico | 2 |
| Rhode Island | 2 |
| South Carolina | 2 |
| Wisconsin | 2 |
| Kansas | 1 |
| Kentucky | 1 |
| Maine | 1 |
| Missouri | 1 |
| Nebraska | 1 |
| Ohio | 1 |
| Oregon | 1 |
| UK | 6 |
| Canada | 3 |
| **Total** | **186** |

## PRODUCTS/OPERATIONS

### Product Categories

Bakery
Body care
Educational products
Floral
Grocery
Household products
Meat and poultry
Nutritional supplements
Pet products
Prepared foods
Produce
Seafood
Specialty (beer, wine, cheese)
Textiles

## COMPETITORS

Ahold USA
Albertsons
AMCON Distributing
Arden Group
Bristol Farms
Delhaize America
Earth Fare
Fiesta Mart
Forever Living
GNC
H-E-B
Kroger
Loblaw
Marks & Spencer
Minyard Group
NBTY
Publix
Safeway
Shaw's
Trader Joe's
United Supermarkets
Wild Oats Markets
Winn-Dixie

## HISTORICAL FINANCIALS

Company Type: Public

### Income Statement

FYE: Last Sunday in September

| | REVENUE ($ mil.) | NET INCOME ($ mil.) | NET PROFIT MARGIN | EMPLOYEES |
|---|---|---|---|---|
| **9/06** | 5,607 | 204 | 3.6% | 39,500 |
| **9/05** | 4,701 | 136 | 2.9% | 38,000 |
| **9/04** | 3,865 | 133 | 3.4% | 32,100 |
| **9/03** | 3,149 | 104 | 3.3% | 26,600 |
| **9/02** | 2,691 | 85 | 3.1% | 24,100 |
| **Annual Growth** | 20.2% | 24.6% | — | 13.1% |

### 2006 Year-End Financials

Debt ratio: 0.6%
Return on equity: 14.7%
Cash ($ mil.): 256
Current ratio: 1.22
Long-term debt ($ mil.): 9
No. of shares (mil.): 140
Dividends
Yield: 4.1%
Payout: 171.6%
Market value ($ mil.): 8,277

### Stock History

NASDAQ (GS): WFMI

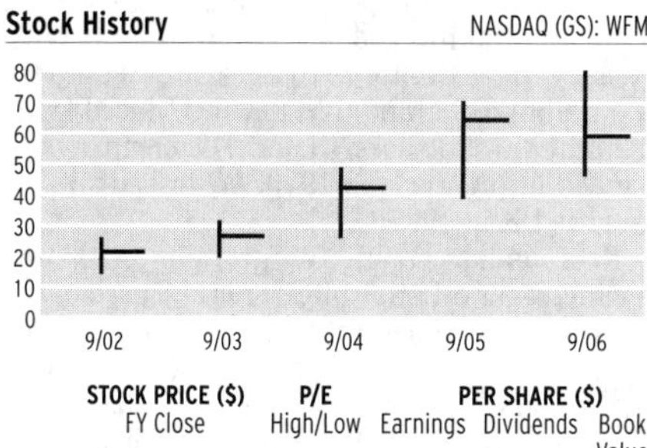


| | STOCK PRICE ($) FY Close | P/E High | P/E Low | PER SHARE ($) Earnings | Dividends | Book Value |
|---|---|---|---|---|---|---|
| **9/06** | 59.29 | 57 | 33 | 1.41 | 2.42 | 10.06 |
| **9/05** | 64.43 | 71 | 40 | 0.99 | 0.13 | 19.84 |
| **9/04** | 42.37 | 48 | 26 | 1.01 | 0.22 | 15.52 |
| **9/03** | 26.70 | 37 | 24 | 0.83 | — | 12.92 |
| **9/02** | 21.49 | 37 | 21 | 0.70 | — | 10.14 |
| **Annual Growth** | 28.9% | — | — | 19.1% | 231.7% | (0.2%) |

# Wm. Wrigley Jr.

The Wm. Wrigley Jr. Company chews up the competition as the world's #1 maker of chewing and bubble gum. The company's products include such popular brands as Big Red, Doublemint, Eclipse, Extra, Freedent, Juicy Fruit, Orbit, Spearmint, and Winterfresh, as well as novelty gums (Hubba Bubba Bubble Tape and other kid-friendly chews). It also offers non-gum products such as Altiods, Creme Savers, Life Savers, and Velamints. The company also owns L.A. Dreyfus, producer of chewing-gum base and Northwestern Flavors. The Wrigley family controls the company.

Wrigley sells its products in more than 180 countries. The company derives nearly all its revenues from gum. Competition from mint makers and other candy companies has hurt Wrigley's sales in North America; however, the company has grown in the non-North American sector, which now accounts for about 60% of sales.

The venerable chewing gum company took the plunge into the chocolate vat in 2007, when it agreed to purchase 80% of the Russian chocolate company, A. Korkunov (Wrigley intends to acquire the remaining 20% over time). The purchase price was $330 million. A. Korkunov makes premium chocolates and it's namesake brand, A. Korkunov, is the top-seller in the Russian premium-chocolate sector.

## HISTORY

William Wrigley Jr. started his career in 1889 at age 13, when his father put him to work at the family's soap factory in Philadelphia following the boy's expulsion from school. After a year Wrigley was promoted to the sales staff, and in 1891 he went to Chicago to establish himself as a salesman of his father's soap and other products.

Wrigley promoted products with free premiums. When he began offering customers chewing gum (made of spruce gum and paraffin by Zeno Manufacturing) in 1892, he received numerous requests to sell the gum. At the time chicle (a naturally sweet gum base from Central America) was being imported for the rubber industry. Wrigley gambled on the idea that chicle would work as a main ingredient in chewing gum.

In 1898 he merged with Zeno to form Wm. Wrigley, Jr. & Co. By 1910 Spearmint gum was the leading US brand; Wrigley introduced Doublemint gum four years later. The company expanded into Canada in 1910, Australia in 1915, and the UK in 1927.

Keen on advertising, Wrigley plastered simple messages on huge billboards and used twins to promote Doublemint gum. The Wrigley family bought Santa Catalina Island (1919), built the Wrigley Building (1924), and purchased the Chicago Cubs (1924). By 1932, when William died and his son Philip ("P. K.") took over, the company was the largest single-product advertiser.

For over 75 years Wrigley made only Spearmint, Juicy Fruit, and Doublemint. Unable to obtain the proper ingredients during WWII, Wrigley produced inferior gum under a different label, but he kept the Wrigley brand alive with a picture of his former gum and the ad slogan "Remember This Wrapper." It worked. After the war, Wrigley's popularity increased. It bought Amurol Confections in 1958. P. K.'s son William joined the company at age 23 and became CEO in 1961 (P. K. remained as chairman). The company did not raise its original five-cent price until 1971, when management grudgingly went to seven cents.

By 1974 Wrigley faced competition from sugar-free gums. At first management refused to bring out a sugar-free gum, instead introducing Freedent for denture wearers. Later the company introduced Big Red (1975); Orbit, a sugar-free gum (1977); and Hubba Bubba (1978). P. K. died in 1977 (as did his wife); his son sold the family's majority stake in the Cubs in 1981 to meet the resulting estate-tax burden.

Three years later Wrigley introduced a new sugar-free gum, Extra. Wrigley established operations in Eastern Europe and opened a new factory in China in 1993. The next year it launched Winterfresh, its first new sugar-based gum in nearly 20 years. By 1996 the new gum was second only to Doublemint in popularity in the US. The company in 1997 returned to the "double your pleasure, double your fun" advertising for its Doublemint brand.

In March 1999 William died; his son Bill was named president and CEO, the fourth generation at the helm. In 2000 the company began testing gums containing cough suppressants, decongestants, and teeth whiteners. In 2002 Wrigley's $12.5 billion bid for The Hershey Company was rejected when the controversial Hershey sale was called off.

The company added to its non-gum mint offerings in 2003, introducing Extra sugar-free mints. That year Wrigley was granted a patent for a chewing gum that contains the active ingredient in Viagra. However, since Viagra's manufacturer, Pfizer, holds the drug's patent until the year 2011, Wrigley has no immediate plans to introduce the gum.

Later in 2003 the company announced a number of officer changes, the most significant being that Bill Wrigley became chairman (a post that had been vacant for more than 25 years) as well as CEO. In addition, CFO Ronald Waters took on the additional title and duties of COO. Wrigley bought the Spanish food company Agrolimen's Joyco confectionery business in 2004 for $260 million.

Having lost some US market share to archrival Cadbury Schweppes of late, Wrigley has decided to emphasize new products. In 2005 the company opened a $45-million Global Innovation Center and introduced seven new products (the biggest product expansion in the company's 100-plus-year history).

As rival Kraft Foods sought to lighten its company load, in 2005 Wrigley purchased Kraft's venerable LifeSavers, CremeSavers, and Altoids confectionery brands. The $1.4 billion deal also included the candystand.com Web site, some smaller regional brands, and production facilities in the US and Europe. Later that year the company sold Trolli gummy candy, which was part of the Kraft deal, to Farley's & Sathers.

In 2006 the former CEO of NIKE,William Perez was named president, CEO, and board member of Wrigley, succeeding Bill Wrigley Jr. Perez, who was also CEO of S.C. Johnson, is the first non-Wrigley-family member to run the company. Fourth-generation Wrigley remained with the company as executive chairman. Wrigley hired its first-ever chief marketing officer that year as well.

## EXECUTIVES

**Chairman:** William (Bill) Wrigley Jr., age 44, $1,412,500 pay
**President, CEO, and Director:** William D. (Bill) Perez, age 59, $288,256 pay
**SVP, Worldwide Strategy and New Business:** Peter R. Hempstead, age 54, $610,833 pay
**SVP and Chief Administrative Officer:** Dushan (Duke) Petrovich, age 52, $537,500 pay
**SVP and Chief Innovation Officer:** Surinder Kumar, age 61, $416,667 pay
**SVP and CFO:** Reuben Gamoran, age 45, $386,667 pay
**VP, Worldwide Procurement and Chief Procurement:** Patrick (Pat) Mitchell, age 51
**VP and Treasurer:** Alan J. Schneider, age 61
**VP and Chief Marketing Officer:** Martin Schlatter, age 41
**VP, Corporate Communications:** Susan Henderson, age 54
**VP, Manufacturing:** Donald E. Balster, age 61
**VP, Nordic:** Jon Orving, age 57
**VP, People, Learning, and Development and CIO:** Donagh Herlihy, age 43
**VP, Research and Development:** Tawfik Sharkasi, age 56
**VP, Sales and Customer Development:** Tom Moeller
**VP, Secretary, and General Counsel:** Howard Malovany, age 56
**VP, Woldwide Gum Base Operations:** Vincent C. Bonica, age 61
**VP, Worldwide Manufacturing:** John Adams, age 60
**VP and Controller:** Shaun Mara, age 42
**Senior Director, External Relations:** Christopher (Chris) Perille
**Senior Director, Marketing:** Paul Chibe
**Director, Marketing Communications:** Jessica Schilling
**Auditors:** Ernst & Young LLP

## LOCATIONS

**HQ:** Wm. Wrigley Jr. Company
410 N. Michigan Ave., Chicago, IL 60611
**Phone:** 312-644-2121
**Web:** www.wrigley.com

### 2006 Sales

| | $ mil. | % of total |
|---|---|---|
| Europe, Middle East, Africa & India | 2,070.4 | 44 |
| North America | 1,752.3 | 38 |
| Asia | 622.8 | 13 |
| Other regions | 180.1 | 4 |
| Other sales | 60.4 | 1 |
| **Total** | **4,686.0** | **100** |

## PRODUCTS/OPERATIONS

### Selected Domestic Brands

Altoids
Big Red
CremeSavers
Doublemint
Eclipse
Eclipse Flash
Eclipse Mints
Everest
Extra
Freedent
Hubba Bubba Bubble Jug
Hubba Bubba Bubble Tape
Hubba Bubba Ouch!
Juicy Fruit
Life Savers
Orbit
Orbit White
Squeeze Pop
Surpass
Velamints
Winterfresh
Winterfresh Thin Ice
Wrigley's Spearmint

### Selected International Brands

Airwaves
Big Red
Boomer
Cool Air
Doublemint
Eclipse
Excel
Extra
Extra for Kids
Extra Mints
Extra Thin Ice
Extra White
Hubba Bubba
Hubba Bubba Bubble Mix & Match
Hubba Bubba Bubble Tape
Juicy Fruit
Orbit
Orbit Drops
Orbit for Kids
Orbit White
Pim Pom
P.K
Solano
Winterfresh
Winterfresh Thin Ice
Wrigley's Spearmint

## COMPETITORS

| | |
|---|---|
| Ajinomoto | International Flavors |
| Bimbo | Mars |
| Cadbury Schweppes | McCormick |
| Chupa Chups | M.D. Labs |
| Concord Confections | Perfetti Van Melle |
| CSM | Perfetti Van Melle USA |
| Danisco A/S | Spangler Candy |
| Ferrara Pan Candy | SweetWorks |
| Ford Gum | Tootsie Roll |
| Hershey | Topps Company |

## HISTORICAL FINANCIALS

Company Type: Public

### Income Statement

FYE: December 31

| | REVENUE ($ mil.) | NET INCOME ($ mil.) | NET PROFIT MARGIN | EMPLOYEES |
|---|---|---|---|---|
| **12/06** | 4,686 | 529 | 11.3% | 15,800 |
| **12/05** | 4,159 | 517 | 12.4% | 14,300 |
| **12/04** | 3,649 | 493 | 13.5% | 14,800 |
| **12/03** | 3,069 | 446 | 14.5% | 12,000 |
| **12/02** | 2,746 | 402 | 14.6% | 11,250 |
| **Annual Growth** | 14.3% | 7.2% | — | 8.9% |

### 2006 Year-End Financials

| | |
|---|---|
| Debt ratio: 41.9% | No. of shares (mil.): 215 |
| Return on equity: 23.0% | Dividends |
| Cash ($ mil.): 255 | Yield: 2.8% |
| Current ratio: 1.44 | Payout: 75.3% |
| Long-term debt ($ mil.): 1,000 | Market value ($ mil.): 11,135 |

### Stock History

NYSE: WWY

| | STOCK PRICE ($) FY Close | P/E High/Low | | PER SHARE ($) Earnings | Dividends | Book Value |
|---|---|---|---|---|---|---|
| **12/06** | 51.72 | 29 | 23 | 1.90 | 1.43 | 11.09 |
| **12/05** | 54.04 | 26 | 22 | 2.29 | 1.08 | 11.68 |
| **12/04** | 56.23 | 26 | 20 | 2.19 | 0.93 | 11.39 |
| **12/03** | 45.69 | 24 | 21 | 1.98 | 0.87 | 9.84 |
| **12/02** | 44.60 | 27 | 20 | 1.78 | 0.81 | 8.30 |
| **Annual Growth** | 3.8% | — | — | 1.6% | 15.3% | 7.5% |

# Williams Companies

Williams Companies is spending its energy refocusing on energy. It is engaged in gas gathering, storage, processing, and transportation, as well as oil and gas exploration and production. The company operates 14,400 miles of interstate natural gas pipeline, including the Transco system, which runs from Texas to New York. Williams has proved reserves of 3.7 trillion cu. ft. of natural gas equivalent. Williams' Gas Pipeline unit operates three pipeline companies (Transco, Northwest, and Gulfstream). In 2006 Williams announced plans to expand its gas supply service to the US Northeast.

The company is engaged in exploration and production, primarily along the Gulf Coast, in the East Texas Basin, and in the Rockies. The exploration and production unit also gathers, stores, and processes natural gas and natural gas liquids (NGLs). It operates refineries, ethanol plants, and terminals.

Williams planned to sell its power business (Williams Power) as part of a strategic plan to emphasize its core natural gas businesses, but dropped the idea in 2004, citing poor market conditions. However, in 2007 it agreed to sell this unit to a Bear Stearns unit for $512 million.

## HISTORY

David Williams and his brother Miller were working for a construction contractor in 1908 when the contractor pulled out of a job paving sidewalks in Fort Smith, Arkansas. The brothers formed the Williams Brothers Corporation and completed the job themselves. As the oil industry grew in Oklahoma, the brothers cashed in on the boom by building pipelines. Williams Brothers relocated its head office to Tulsa in 1924.

The two brothers sold the company in 1949 to David Jr., nephews John and Charles, and six company managers. It went public in 1957. In 1966 Williams Brothers bought its first gas pipeline (the longest in the US), the Great Lakes Pipe Line Company (renamed Williams Brothers Pipe Line Company).

In 1969 Williams Brothers began entering new markets. It bought a metals processor, a propane dealer, and fertilizer companies, including Agrico Chemical (1972), and changed its name to The Williams Companies to reflect its new diversity. In the wake of the Arab oil embargo, it formed Williams Exploration in 1974 to find natural gas. Two years later Williams became part-owner of the US's #1 coal producer, Peabody Coal.

During a 1980s energy sales slump, Williams began dumping its commodity businesses (including Agrico and Peabody in 1987). Instead, it went into telecommunications in 1985, forming Williams Telecommunications (WilTel) to install fiber optics inside abandoned pipelines. Its 1989 purchase of fiber-optic firm LIGHTNET brought its network miles to 11,000.

In 1995 the company acquired Transcontinental Gas Pipe Line Corp. (Transco), extending its reach into the East, and Pekin Energy, the country's #2 ethanol producer.

The Williams Companies sold WilTel's fiber-optic network in 1995 to telecom company LDDS (which became WorldCom) for $2.5 billion — but excluded from the sale a 9,700-mile single fiber-optic strand along the original network. In 1996 Williams acquired telecom services company Cycle-Sat, and the next year Williams Communications and Northern Telecom (later Nortel Networks) formed Williams Communications Solutions to distribute and integrate telecom networking equipment.

In 1998 Williams bought fellow Tulsa company MAPCO for more than $3 billion, giving it the US's largest US pipeline system moving propane and butane, a leading US propane retailer (ThermoGas), refineries, and gas stations.

To re-enter the telecom business, Williams established a new subsidiary, Williams Communications, in 1998. To raise money to build out its network, the company sold a minority stake in Williams Communications in a 1999 IPO. That year it also sold ThermoGas to Ferrellgas in a $444 million deal. The next year it joined Duke Energy in a $1.5 billion venture to build a gas pipeline across the Gulf of Mexico to link Alabama to Florida markets.

Williams spun off its stake in Williams Communications (later renamed WilTel Communications) to shareholders in 2001. Williams also shed energy assets that year: Its Williams Express sold its 186 MAPCO gas stations to The Israel Fuel Corporation for about $147 million. The company moved to expand its natural gas reserves significantly by buying producer Barrett Resources for about $2.5 billion in cash and stock and $300 million in assumed debt.

Also in 2001 Williams chairman and CEO Keith Bailey announced plans to retire the next year. The heir apparent, EVP Steven Malcolm, was given Bailey's title of president. The day after Malcolm's promotion, he announced that the company's energy marketing and trading operations would become a separate business unit. Malcolm was named CEO in January 2002.

As a way to pare down its debt load, that year Williams sold its Kern River interstate natural gas pipeline to Berkshire Hathaway's MidAmerican Energy Holdings unit for $450 million in cash and $510 million in assumed debt. It also sold its Williams Pipe Line unit (refined petroleum products) to Williams Energy Partners LP for $1 billion, and its stakes in two pipeline companies (Mid-America Pipeline and Seminole Pipeline) to Enterprise Products Partners, for about $1.2 billion.

That year, in addition to raising cash from asset sales, Williams secured commitments from mega-investor Warren Buffett and a number of banks to pony up $2 billion in new financing to help it restructure its operations.

In 2003 Williams sold its wholesale propane assets and marketing business to SemGroup. It also sold a gas processing plant in Oklahoma to Eagle Rock Energy.

## EXECUTIVES

**Chairman, President, and CEO:** Steven J. (Steve) Malcolm, age 58, $3,300,000 pay
**SVP and CFO:** Donald R. (Don) Chappel, age 55, $1,346,154 pay
**SVP Gas Pipeline:** Phillip D. (Phil) Wright, age 51, $1,015,000 pay (prior to title change)
**SVP Human Resources and Chief Administration Officer:** Michael P. Johnson Sr., age 59, $1,094,692 pay
**SVP Midstream Gas and Liquids:** Alan S. Armstrong, age 44, $967,308 pay
**SVP Power:** William E. (Bill) Hobbs, age 47
**SVP Exploration and Production:** Ralph A. Hill, age 47, $968,846 pay
**SVP and General Counsel:** James J. Bender, age 50, $1,055,050 pay
**VP, Corporate Controller. and Chief Accounting Officer:** Ted Timmermans, age 49
**Corporate Secretary and Attorney-in-fact:** Brian K. Shore
**Investor Relations:** Richard George
**Media Relations Contact:** Jeff Pounds
**Auditors:** Ernst & Young LLP

## LOCATIONS

**HQ:** The Williams Companies, Inc.
1 Williams Center, Tulsa, OK 74172
**Phone:** 918-573-2000 **Fax:** 918-573-6714
**Web:** www.williams.com

The Williams Companies has energy operations throughout the US, and its global investments include activities in Lithuania and Venezuela. US exploration activities are conducted in Louisiana, Mississippi, New Mexico, Texas, Utah, and Wyoming.

### 2006 Sales

| | $ mil. | % of total |
|---|---|---|
| US | 11,418.3 | 97 |
| Other countries | 394.6 | 3 |
| **Total** | **11,812.9** | **100** |

## PRODUCTS/OPERATIONS

**2006 Sales**

| | $ mil. | % of total |
|---|---|---|
| Power | 7,462.4 | 52 |
| Midstream gas & liquids | 4,124.7 | 29 |
| Exploration & production | 1,487.6 | 10 |
| Gas pipeline | 1,347.7 | 9 |
| Other | 26.5 | — |
| Adjustments | (2,636.0) | — |
| **Total** | **11,812.9** | **100** |

## COMPETITORS

Adams Resources
Aquila
Avista
BP
CenterPoint Energy
Chevron
Constellation Energy
Dynegy
El Paso
Enbridge Energy
Enron
Entergy
Exxon Mobil
Kinder Morgan
Koch
Occidental Petroleum
OGE Energy
ONEOK
PG&E
ProLiance Energy
SandRidge Energy
Sempra Energy
Southern Company
TEPPCO Partners
TXU
U.S. Gas Transmission

## HISTORICAL FINANCIALS

Company Type: Public

**Income Statement** FYE: December 31

| | REVENUE ($ mil.) | NET INCOME ($ mil.) | NET PROFIT MARGIN | EMPLOYEES |
|---|---|---|---|---|
| **12/06** | 11,813 | 309 | 2.6% | 4,313 |
| **12/05** | 12,584 | 314 | 2.5% | 3,913 |
| **12/04** | 12,461 | 164 | 1.3% | 3,656 |
| **12/03** | 16,834 | (492) | — | 4,800 |
| **12/02** | 5,725 | (755) | — | 9,800 |
| **Annual Growth** | 19.9% | — | — | (18.6%) |

**2006 Year-End Financials**

Debt ratio: 159.2%
Return on equity: 5.4%
Cash ($ mil.): 4,298
Current ratio: 1.35
Long-term debt ($ mil.): 9,666
No. of shares (mil.): 597
Dividends
Yield: 1.3%
Payout: 66.7%
Market value ($ mil.): 15,596

**Stock History** NYSE: WMB

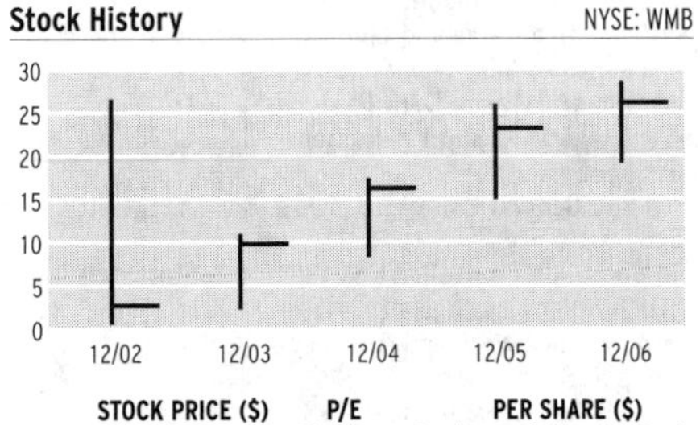

| | STOCK PRICE ($) FY Close | P/E High/Low | | PER SHARE ($) Earnings | Dividends | Book Value |
|---|---|---|---|---|---|---|
| **12/06** | 26.12 | 56 | 38 | 0.51 | 0.34 | 10.17 |
| **12/05** | 23.17 | 49 | 29 | 0.53 | 0.25 | 9.47 |
| **12/04** | 16.29 | 55 | 27 | 0.31 | 0.08 | 8.69 |
| **12/03** | 9.82 | — | — | (1.01) | 0.04 | 7.90 |
| **12/02** | 2.70 | — | — | (1.63) | 0.42 | 9.77 |
| **Annual Growth** | 76.4% | — | — | — | (5.1%) | 1.0% |

# Williams-Sonoma

Epicureans are at home at Williams-Sonoma, a leading retailer of goods for well-appointed kitchens, bedrooms, and baths. Home products include bath and storage products, bedding, cookware, furniture, and tableware. The company's retail chains, Williams-Sonoma and larger Grande Cuisine (upscale cookware), West Elm (housewares), and Pottery Barn and larger Design Studio (housewares, furniture) sell wares through some 600 stores in 43 states, Washington, DC, and Canada. In addition, Williams-Sonoma distributes seven catalogs. It operates about 15 Williams-Sonoma outlet stores and six e-commerce Web sites, and runs an online bridal registry.

Williams-Sonoma's catalogs include Williams-Sonoma, Williams-Sonoma Home, Pottery Barn, Pottery Barn Bed + Bath, Pottery Barn Kids, PB-teen, and West Elm.

The company closed its chain of 11 Hold Everything stores by 2006. On the plus side, in 2007, the retailer plans to open about a six new Williams-Sonoma or Williams-Sonoma Home stores and a total of 15 new outlets under the PB-teen, West Elm and Williams-Sonoma Home banners. The retailer is also testing a new store concept — called Pottery Barn Bed and Bath — at three locations. If successful, 40 to 50 Pottery Barn Bed and Bath stores could eventually open.

Its Pottery Barn Kids division offers stylish children's furniture and has expanded to some 90 stores nationwide and in Canada. Its West Elm catalog, which offers home furnishings and accessories at more accessible price points, debuted in 2002; its Web site and first retail store opened in 2003. A source of growth for the company, by 2007, West Elm had more than 20 retail locations.

Director emeritus James McMahan owns nearly 10% of Williams-Sonoma's stock. Chairman Howard Lester owns about 7%. Lester, who served as CEO of the company from 1979 to 2001, replaced retiring CEO Edward Mueller in mid-July.

## HISTORY

Food lover and hardware store owner Charles Williams founded a cookware store in 1956 in Sonoma, California, moving it to San Francisco in 1958.

Edward Marcus (of Neiman Marcus) acquired one-third of the company in 1972, which then began adding new stores and started its first catalog, A Catalog for Cooks. Marcus died in 1976, and Williams, unable to manage the burgeoning enterprise, sold it to Howard Lester, owner of several computer service firms. Williams is still vice chairman.

Lester acquired Gardeners Eden, a mail-order merchandiser of home gardening and related products, in 1982. The next year he bought the rights to a new catalog, Hold Everything (expanded into retailing later). Williams-Sonoma went public that year. In 1986 it acquired Pottery Barn from The Gap and soon added a catalog business. The company moved into bed and bath goods three years later when it introduced its Chambers catalog.

Williams-Sonoma bought California Closets, an operator of franchises that design and build custom closets, in 1990. (It sold the franchiser four years later to management and an investor group.) Recession and heavy expansion spending hurt profits in the early 1990s, so the company slowed growth and focused on improving operations at the Williams-Sonoma and Pottery Barn stores.

In 1996 new management revamped Williams-Sonoma's inventory and distribution system, leading to a sharp earnings drop. The next year the company expanded the number of Pottery Barns, bringing that chain's sales to the level of its Williams-Sonoma stores. Expansion continued in 1998 with a focus on large-store formats Grande Cuisine and Design Studio.

The company sold its Gardeners Eden catalog business to retailer Brookstone in 1999. Williams-Sonoma then launched a special Pottery Barn catalog featuring linens and furniture for children and began selling merchandise online via its wswedding.com bridal registry Web site and through Williams-Sonoma.com. In 2000 the first Pottery Barns Kids store was opened, and its Web site followed in 2001. That year two Williams-Sonoma, two Pottery Barn, and one Pottery Barn Kids stores opened up shop in Toronto.

In 2001 Lester stepped down as CEO (he remained chairman) and was replaced by Dale Hilpert, a former Venator Group (now Foot Locker) executive. That year the company launched its Pottery Barn Kids Web site, Pottery Barn online gift and bridal registry, and Pottery Barn Kids online gift registry. In November 2002 Williams-Sonoma discontinued *TASTE*, its quarterly magazine which focused on travel and fine dining.

Also in 2002 Williams-Sonoma launched its West Elm catalog, targeting young, design-conscious customers. In January 2003 Hilpert left the company, and Edward Mueller, former head of Ameritech, was named CEO. In April Williams-Sonoma released PBteen, a catalog featuring furniture, lighting, bedding, and accessories designed for the teenage market. Williams-Sonoma launched its West Elm e-commerce Web site that year and opened its first retail location.

In 2004 the Chambers catalog was discontinued and replaced by Williams-Sonoma Home, offering classic home furnishings and decorative accessories. Following on the heels of the Williams-Sonoma Home catalog launched in the fall of 2004, a corresponding Web site devoted to upscale furniture debuted in the spring of 2005. Also, the company opened its first Williams-Sonoma Home in West Hollywood, California, in September, followed by two more in October.

Lester, who previously served as CEO of the company (1979-2001), replaced retiring CEO Mueller in mid-July 2006.

## EXECUTIVES

**Founder and Director Emeritus:** Charles E. (Chuck) Williams, age 91
**Chairman and CEO:** W. Howard Lester, age 71, $975,000 pay
**President:** Laura J. Alber, age 38, $700,770 pay
**Group President, Williams-Sonoma, Williams-Sonoma Home, and West Elm Brands:** David M. (Dave) DeMattei, age 50, $614,596 pay
**EVP, COO, and CFO:** Sharon L. McCollam, age 44, $621,212 pay
**EVP, Chief Marketing Officer, and Director:** Patrick J. (Pat) Connolly, age 60, $566,538 pay
**EVP and Chief Supply Chain Officer:** Dean A. Miller, age 44
**SVP, General Counsel, and Secretary:** Seth R. Jaffe, age 50
**VP, Public Relations:** Patricia Sellman
**Director, Investor Relations:** Stephen C. Nelson
**Auditors:** Deloitte & Touche LLP

## LOCATIONS

**HQ:** Williams-Sonoma, Inc.
3250 Van Ness Ave., San Francisco, CA 94109
**Phone:** 415-421-7900 **Fax:** 415-616-8359
**Web:** www.williams-sonomainc.com

## PRODUCTS/OPERATIONS

### 2007 Stores

| | No. |
|---|---|
| Williams-Sonoma | 254 |
| Pottery Barn | 197 |
| Pottery Barn Kids | 92 |
| West Elm | 22 |
| Williams-Sonoma Home | 7 |
| Outlet stores | 16 |
| **Total** | **588** |

### 2007 Sales

| | $ mil. | % of total |
|---|---|---|
| Retail | 2,154.0 | 58 |
| Direct-to-consumer | 1,573.5 | 42 |
| **Total** | **3,727.5** | **100** |

### Retail

Design Studio (large-scale Pottery Barn)
Grande Cuisine (large-scale Williams-Sonoma)
PBteen (teen home furnishings)
Pottery Barn (home furnishings, flatware, and table accessories)
Pottery Barn Kids (children's home furnishings)
West Elm (home furnishings, decorative accessories, tabletop items, and textile collection)
Williams-Sonoma (cookware, cookbooks, cutlery, dinnerware, glassware, and table linens)
Williams-Sonoma Home (home furnishings and decorative accessories)

### Catalogs

PBteen (home furnishings for teenage market)
Pottery Barn (home furnishings and housewares)
Pottery Barn Bed + Bath (bed and bath products)
Pottery Barn Kids (children's linens and furniture)
West Elm (home furnishings and housewares)
Williams-Sonoma (kitchen products)
Williams-Sonoma Home (home furnishings)

## COMPETITORS

Ashley Furniture
Bed Bath & Beyond
Bombay Company
Brookstone
Container Store
Cornerstone Brands
Cost Plus
Dean & DeLuca
Decorize
Eddie Bauer Holdings
Ethan Allen
Euromarket Designs
Garden Ridge
Hammacher Schlemmer & Co.
Hanover Direct
IKEA
King Arthur Flour
Lands' End
Levenger
Lillian Vernon
Linens 'n Things
Longaberger
Macy's
Neiman Marcus
Pampered Chef
Pier 1 Imports
Restoration Hardware
Room & Board
Smith & Hawken
Target
Tuesday Morning
Z Gallerie

## HISTORICAL FINANCIALS

Company Type: Public

### Income Statement

FYE: Sunday nearest January 31

| | REVENUE ($ mil.) | NET INCOME ($ mil.) | NET PROFIT MARGIN | EMPLOYEES |
|---|---|---|---|---|
| **1/07** | 3,728 | 209 | 5.6% | 38,800 |
| **1/06** | 3,539 | 215 | 6.1% | 37,200 |
| **1/05** | 3,137 | 191 | 6.1% | 36,000 |
| **1/04** | 2,754 | 157 | 5.7% | 36,049 |
| **1/03** | 2,361 | 124 | 5.3% | 32,000 |
| **Annual Growth** | 12.1% | 13.8% | — | 4.9% |

### 2007 Year-End Financials

Debt ratio: 1.1%
Return on equity: 18.4%
Cash ($ mil.): 275
Current ratio: 1.75
Long-term debt ($ mil.): 13
No. of shares (mil.): 110
Dividends
Yield: 1.2%
Payout: 22.3%
Market value ($ mil.): 3,762

### Stock History

NYSE: WSM

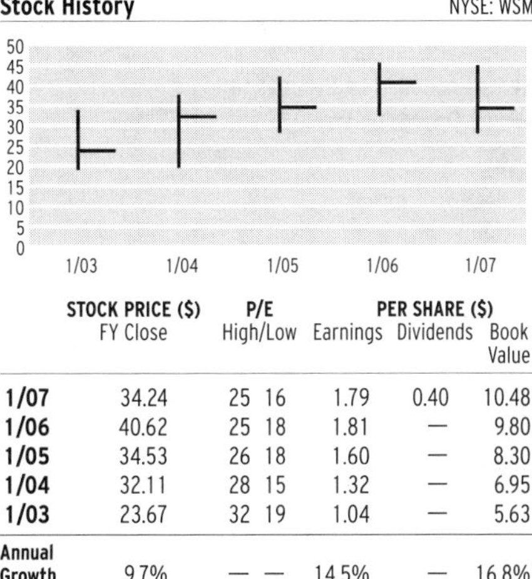


| | STOCK PRICE ($) FY Close | P/E High | P/E Low | PER SHARE ($) Earnings | Dividends | Book Value |
|---|---|---|---|---|---|---|
| **1/07** | 34.24 | 25 | 16 | 1.79 | 0.40 | 10.48 |
| **1/06** | 40.62 | 25 | 18 | 1.81 | — | 9.80 |
| **1/05** | 34.53 | 26 | 18 | 1.60 | — | 8.30 |
| **1/04** | 32.11 | 28 | 15 | 1.32 | — | 6.95 |
| **1/03** | 23.67 | 32 | 19 | 1.04 | — | 5.63 |
| **Annual Growth** | 9.7% | — | — | 14.5% | — | 16.8% |

# Winn-Dixie Stores

Winn-Dixie Stores has found — as Jefferson Davis did long ago — that winning Dixie ain't easy. The regional supermarket chain operates about 520 stores (down from more than 1,000 in 2004) throughout Alabama, Florida, Georgia, Louisiana, and Mississippi. The company runs food and drug stores under the Winn-Dixie, Winn-Dixie Marketplace, and SaveRite (warehouse stores) banners. To fend off rivals (including Wal-Mart and Publix Super Markets) and stem red ink, Winn-Dixie has retrenched by exiting non-core markets and selling assets. The grocery chain spent most of 2005 and 2006 in Chapter 11 bankruptcy protection, during which it sold or closed more than 500 supermarkets.

Winn-Dixie emerged from bankruptcy in late 2006 as a smaller operation focused on its strongest markets. As a result of its restructuring, the grocery chain no longer operates supermarkets in the Bahamas, the Carolinas, Tennessee, and Virginia. The grocer operates six distribution centers (down from 10 prior to its reorganization), and has shut down all of its manufacturing operations except for two dairies and the Chek Beverage plant in Georgia.

Going forward, the grocery chain's focus will be on store renovations and improving customer service. It aims to remodel about 75 stores annually, with most of the remodels in Florida. If all goes well, Winn-Dixie plans to begin opening new stores in 2008. Showing a turnaround, the company reported a profit for its fiscal year 2007, thank to sales growth and cost-cutting measures.

In a bid to rebuild the Winn-Dixie brand and improve profitability, the supermarket operator is completely redesigning and relaunching its corporate brands program, with the goal of having at least 1,000 new products on store shelves by mid-2008. Store brands are divided into three tiers: Thrifty Maid, Winn-Dixie, and premium brand Winn & Lovett.

About 60 of Winn-Dixie's supermarkets have liquor stores and five have gas stations.

## HISTORY

In 1925 William Davis borrowed $10,000 to open the cash-and-carry Rockmoor Grocery in Lemon City, Florida, near Miami. After a slow start, he had expanded his chain of Table Supply Stores to 34 by the time of his death in 1934. His four sons — A. D., J. E., M. Austin, and Tine — took over. In 1939 they purchased control of Winn & Lovett Grocery, which operated 78 stores in Florida and Georgia. The company, incorporated in 1928, was a leader in the 1930s in building new supermarket-type stores. The combined company settled in Jacksonville in 1944 and formally took the name Winn & Lovett.

After WWII the company, still controlled by the Davis family, acquired grocery chains throughout the South, including Steiden (Kentucky), Margaret Ann (Florida), Wylie (Alabama), Penney (Mississippi), King (Georgia), and Eden and Ballentine (South Carolina). The company consolidated with Dixie Home Stores of the Carolinas in 1955 and changed its name to Winn-Dixie Stores, Inc.

The most profitable company in the industry during the 1950s and early 1960s, Winn-Dixie continued to expand through acquisitions, adding Ketner and Milner (the Carolinas) and Hill (Louisiana and Alabama). Also in the 1960s Winn-Dixie entered the manufacturing, processing, and distribution arenas.

By 1966, under the leadership of chairman J. E. Davis, the company controlled so much of the grocery business in the South that, for antitrust reasons, the FTC imposed a 10-year moratorium on acquisitions. Winn-Dixie responded by growing internally and improving its existing stores. It also bought nine stores outside the US (in the Bahamas). When the expansion moratorium ended in 1976, the company bought Kimbell of Texas (sold 1979), adding stores and extensive support facilities in Texas, Oklahoma, and New Mexico.

William Davis' grandson Robert Davis took control as chairman of the company in 1983. After years of lackluster profits, Robert resigned in 1988 and was replaced by his cousin, Dano Davis. In the mid-1980s Winn-Dixie debuted a large combination store format called Marketplace, which offered services such as pharmacies and specialty shops. The company began replacing smaller stores with Marketplace stores; about 55 had been opened by the late 1980s.

Winn-Dixie bought Thriftway, with 25 supermarkets in Cincinnati, in 1995. That year A. D., the only surviving son of the founder, died. In the first quarter of fiscal 1999, Winn-Dixie ended a 54-year streak of raising its dividends.

The company settled a sex and race discrimination lawsuit filed by former and current employees for about $33 million in 1999. The company also hired Allen Rowland, the former president of Smith's Food & Drug, as president and CEO.

In 2000 Winn-Dixie started a restructuring plan — cutting 8% of its workforce, closing more than 100 supermarkets, shuttering some manufacturing and warehouse facilities, and taking a $345 million after-tax charge.

In 2002 Winn-Dixie sold its Deep South Products plants and other assets to Schreiber Foods. By late June the company had exited the Texas (71 stores) and Oklahoma (five stores) markets entirely, laying off 5,300 workers.

In June 2003 Rowland retired from the company and was replaced by COO Frank Lazaran, previously president of Randall's Food Markets.

In March 2004 CFO Richard McCook was replaced by former Burger King executive Bennett Nussbaum following a large quarterly loss, which caused Winn-Dixie's stock to plunge to a 20-year low and resulted in several class action lawsuits by angry investors.

In August 2004 Winn-Dixie announced it had sold or closed 32 stores as part of its purge of underperforming assets. Dano Davis retired as chairman in October 2004 after more than 35 years with the company. Davis was succeeded by Jay Skelton, president and CEO of DDI Inc., a diversified holding company owned by the Davis family. In December Lazaran was replaced (after only 18 months on the job) as CEO by Albertson's veteran Peter Lynch.

In February 2005 Winn-Dixie filed for Chapter 11 bankruptcy protection. Soon after, the supermarket chain sold 18 Georgia stores to Atlanta-based Wayfield Foods, All-American Quality Foods, and a partnership between holding company Alex Lee and Associated Wholesale Grocers, among other buyers. It also sold 81 supermarkets to various acquirers, including SUPERVALU, for an aggregate price of about $41 million. In August Winn-Dixie was hit by a storm of another sort: Hurricane Katrina, which caused property damage and inventory losses at about 110 of the 125 supermarkets operating in the New Orleans region. Overall, the company sold or closed 139 stores in 2005 and 374 stores in 2006. After 21 months in bankruptcy, Winn-Dixie emerged from Chapter 11 in late-November 2006.

## EXECUTIVES

**Chairman, President, and CEO:** Peter L. Lynch, age 54, $2,950,000 pay
**SVP and CFO:** Bennett L. Nussbaum, age 59, $1,247,900 pay
**SVP, Legal, General Counsel, and Secretary:** Laurence B. Appel, age 45, $998,320 pay
**SVP, Merchandising:** Thomas P. (Tom) Robbins, age 62, $813,120 pay
**SVP, Retail Operations:** Frank O. Eckstein, age 59
**SVP and Chief Merchandising and Marketing Officer:** Dan Portnoy, age 49
**Group VP, Development:** Phillip E. (Phil) Pichulo, age 57
**Group VP, Human Resources:** Dedra N. Dogan, age 40
**Group VP, Information Technologies:** Charles M. Weston, age 58
**Group VP, Logistics and Distribution:** Christopher (Chris) Scott, age 43
**Group VP, Operations, Jacksonville Region and Bahamas:** Mark A. Sellers, age 52
**VP, Corporate Controller, and Chief Accounting Officer:** D. Michael Byrum, age 53
**VP, Finance and Treasurer:** Kellie D. Hardee, age 37
**Regional VP, Miami:** Randy Rambo
**Regional VP, New Orleans:** Joe (Joey) Medina
**Regional VP, Orlando:** Daniel G. (Dan) Lafever, age 53
**Senior Director, Advertising and Neighborhood Marketing:** Cheryl Hays
**Senior Director, Grocery, Dairy, and Frozen:** Larry Biggerstaff
**Director, Brand Communications:** Robin Miller
**Director, Communications and Neighborhood Marketing:** Terry Derreberry
**Communications Manager:** Dennis Wortham
**Auditors:** KPMG LLP

## LOCATIONS

**HQ:** Winn-Dixie Stores, Inc.
5050 Edgewood Ct., Jacksonville, FL 32254
**Phone:** 904-783-5000 **Fax:** 904-370-7224
**Web:** www.winn-dixie.com

## PRODUCTS/OPERATIONS

### Items Produced or Processed

Carbonated beverages
Cheese
Coffee
Cookies
Crackers
Cultured products
Eggs
Frozen pizza
Ice cream
Jams and jellies
Margarine
Mayonnaise
Meats
Milk
Peanut butter
Salad dressing
Snacks
Spices
Tea

### Selected Subsidiaries

Astor Products, Inc.
Crackin' Good, Inc.
Deep South Products, Inc.
Dixie Packers, Inc.
Economy Wholesale Distributors, Inc.
Superior Food Company
Table Supply Food Stores, Inc.
Winn-Dixie Logistics, Inc.
Winn-Dixie Montgomery, Inc.
Winn-Dixie Procurement, Inc.
WIN General Insurance, Inc.

## COMPETITORS

Albertsons
ALDI
BI-LO
Bruno's Supermarkets
CVS/Caremark
Farm Fresh
Food Lion
Harris Teeter
IGA
Kash n' Karry
Kerr Drug
Kmart
Kroger
The Pantry
Publix
Target
Walgreen
Wal-Mart

## HISTORICAL FINANCIALS

Company Type: Public

### Income Statement

FYE: Last Wednesday in June

| | REVENUE ($ mil.) | NET INCOME ($ mil.) | NET PROFIT MARGIN | EMPLOYEES |
|---|---|---|---|---|
| **6/07** | 4,525 | 29 | 0.6% | 52,000 |
| **6/06** | 7,194 | (361) | — | 55,000 |
| **6/05** | 9,921 | (833) | — | 80,000 |
| **6/04** | 10,633 | (100) | — | 89,000 |
| **6/03** | 12,168 | 239 | 2.0% | 99,200 |
| **Annual Growth** | (21.9%) | (41.2%) | — | (14.9%) |

### 2007 Year-End Financials

Debt ratio: 19.7%
Return on equity: 11.1%
Cash ($ mil.): 207
Current ratio: 1.88
Long-term debt ($ mil.): 157
No. of shares (mil.): 54
Dividends
Yield: —
Payout: —
Market value ($ mil.): 1,638

### Stock History

NASDAQ (GS): WINN

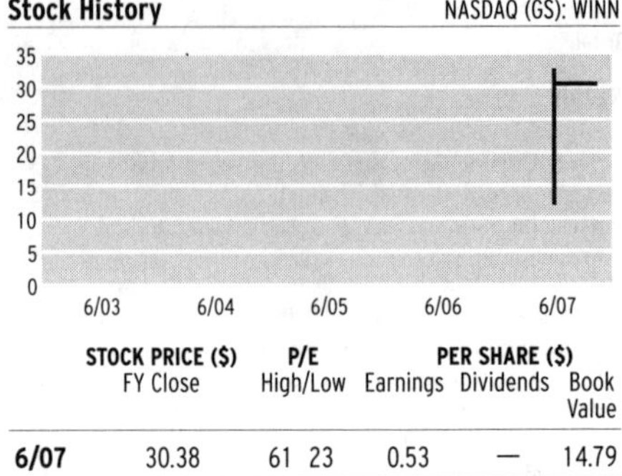


| | STOCK PRICE ($) FY Close | P/E High | P/E Low | PER SHARE ($) Earnings | Dividends | Book Value |
|---|---|---|---|---|---|---|
| **6/07** | 30.38 | 61 | 23 | 0.53 | — | 14.79 |

# World Fuel Services

You can't fuel all the people all the time, but World Fuel Services tries hard to do just that. Marine fueling subsidiaries, including Trans-Tec Services and Bunkerfuels, provide fueling services to marine vessels in approximately 1,000 seaports. The company estimates it holds more than 10% of the global marine fuels market. World Fuel Services also provides 24-hour fueling service to aircraft at 1,500 airports in more than 160 countries. The company's aviation fueling business focuses on serving small to medium-sized air carriers, cargo and charter carriers, and private aircraft. In 2004 World Fuel Services acquired Tramp Holdings, a UK-based reseller of marine fuel, for about $83 million.

As part of its marine fueling services business, World Fuel Services arranges fueling for ships on a brokered basis and extends credit to a global customer base, which includes container lines, cruise ships, dry bulk carriers, fishing fleets, refrigerated vessels, and tankers. The company also provides financial credit for aviation fuels.

World Fuel Service maintains its competitive edge by offering a range of support services to its aviation and marine customers such as fuel market analysis, flight planning, ground-handling services, and weather reports.

## HISTORY

Neighbors Ralph Weiser and Jerrold Blair founded International Oil Recovery, an oil recycling company, in Florida in 1984. The company moved into aviation fueling by acquiring Advance Petroleum in 1986. Two years later International Oil Recovery diversified further, entering the hazardous waste market by buying Resource Recovery of America, a soil remediation company. In 1989 the firm acquired JCo Energy Partners, an aviation fuel company, and subsequently renamed its aviation fueling division World Fuel Services. The company set up International Petroleum in 1993 to operate a Delaware used-oil and water-recycling plant.

In 1995 the company changed its name to World Fuel Services Corporation. Also that year it nearly doubled its revenue base with the purchase of Trans-Tec, the world's #1 independent marine fuel services company. World Fuel also exited the environmental services business in 1995 to focus on its fuel services and oil recycling businesses.

The following year the company formed World Fuel International, a subsidiary based in Costa Rica that serves World Fuel's aviation customers in South and Central America, Canada, and the Caribbean. In 1998 it acquired corporate jet fuel provider Baseops International, which has offices in the UK and Texas. In 1999 the company expanded its share of the marine fuel market with the acquisition of the Bunkerfuels group of companies, one of the world's top marine fuel brokerages.

To focus on its marine and aviation fueling businesses, World Fuel exited the oil recycling segment in 2000 when it sold its International Petroleum unit to waste services company EarthCare for about $33 million.

The company expanded into the United Arab Emirates with its 2001 acquisition of fuel services provider Marine Energy of Dubai. World Fuel acquired Rotterdam-based marine fuel reseller Oil Shipping Group in 2002.

In 2004 World Fuel Services acquired UK-based marine fuel reseller Tramp Holdings for $83 million.

## EXECUTIVES

**Chairman and CEO:** Paul H. Stebbins, age 50, $1,575,000 pay
**President, COO, and Director:** Michael J. Kasbar, age 50, $1,575,000 pay
**EVP and CFO:** Ira M. Birns, age 44
**EVP and Chief Risk and Administration Officer:** Francis X. (Frank) Shea, age 66
**SVP and Chief Accounting Officer:** Paul M. Nobel, age 39
**VP Business Controls:** Peter Soto
**VP Human Resources:** Ileana de Armas
**VP Information Technology:** Charles Salerno
**VP Taxation:** Richard White
**VP Global Tax and Legal Administration and Treasurer:** Peter Tonyan
**President, World Fuel Services, Inc.:** Michael S. Clementi, age 45, $935,000 pay
**President, BaseOps International:** Jerry Scott, age 45
**President, Bunkerfuels:** William Mergenthaler
**President, Pacific Horizon Petroleum Services:** Loren Pace
**Secretary and General Counsel:** R. Alexander Lake
**Auditors:** PricewaterhouseCoopers LLP

## LOCATIONS

**HQ:** World Fuel Services Corporation
9800 NW 41st St., Ste. 400, Miami, FL 33178
**Phone:** 305-428-8000 **Fax:** 305-392-5600
**Web:** www.wfscorp.com

World Fuel Services has offices in Argentina, Brazil, China, Colombia, Costa Rica, Denmark, Germany, Greece, Hong Kong, Japan, Mexico, the Netherlands, Norway, Singapore, South Africa, South Korea, Turkey, the United Arab Emirates, the UK, and the US.

### 2006 Sales

| | $ mil. | % of total |
|---|---|---|
| US | 4,763.4 | 44 |
| Singapore | 3,316.9 | 31 |
| UK | 1,615.7 | 15 |
| Other countries | 1,089.1 | 10 |
| **Total** | **10,785.1** | **100** |

## PRODUCTS/OPERATIONS

### 2006 Sales

| | $ mil. | % of total |
|---|---|---|
| Marine | 5,785.1 | 54 |
| Aviation | 4,579.3 | 42 |
| Land | 420.7 | 4 |
| **Total** | **10,785.1** | **100** |

### Selected Subsidiaries

Marine Fueling Services
- Bunkerfuels Corp.
- Bunkerfuels UK Ltd.
- Casa Petro SA (Costa Rica)
- Marine Energy Arabia (United Arab Emirates)
- Tramp Holdings Limited (UK)
- Trans-Tec International SA (Costa Rica)

Aviation Fueling Services
- AirData Ltd. (UK)
- Baseops Europe Ltd. (UK)
- Baseops International, Inc.
- PetroServicios de Costa Rica SA
- World Fuel International SA (Costa Rica)
- World Fuel Services, Inc.
- World Fuel Services, Ltd. (UK)
- World Fuel Services of FL (dba Advance Petroleum, Inc.
  - Baseops Mexico S.A. de C.V.
  - PetroServicios de México S.A. de C.V.
  - Servicios Auxiliares de Mexico S.A. de C.V.
- World Fuel Services (Singapore) Pte. Ltd.

## COMPETITORS

BBA Aviation
BP Marine
Mercury Air Group
Sun Coast Resources

## HISTORICAL FINANCIALS

Company Type: Public

### Income Statement

FYE: December 31

| | REVENUE ($ mil.) | NET INCOME ($ mil.) | NET PROFIT MARGIN | EMPLOYEES |
|---|---|---|---|---|
| **12/06** | 10,785 | 64 | 0.6% | 743 |
| **12/05** | 8,734 | 40 | 0.5% | 647 |
| **12/04** | 5,654 | 29 | 0.5% | 606 |
| **12/03** | 2,662 | 22 | 0.8% | 401 |
| **12/02** | 1,547 | 10 | 0.6% | 370 |
| **Annual Growth** | 62.5% | 59.5% | — | 19.0% |

### 2006 Year-End Financials

Debt ratio: 4.7%
Return on equity: 16.4%
Cash ($ mil.): 189
Current ratio: 1.45
Long-term debt ($ mil.): 20
No. of shares (mil.): 28
Dividends
Yield: 0.3%
Payout: 6.8%
Market value ($ mil.): 1,267

### Stock History

NYSE: INT

| | STOCK PRICE ($) FY Close | P/E High | P/E Low | PER SHARE ($) Earnings | Dividends | Book Value |
|---|---|---|---|---|---|---|
| **12/06** | 44.46 | 24 | 14 | 2.21 | 0.15 | 14.95 |
| **12/05** | 33.72 | 24 | 14 | 1.57 | 0.15 | 12.85 |
| **12/04** | 24.90 | 20 | 13 | 1.22 | 0.15 | 7.38 |
| **12/03** | 16.98 | 17 | 10 | 0.98 | 0.15 | 11.62 |
| **12/02** | 10.25 | 27 | 17 | 0.46 | 0.15 | 10.01 |
| **Annual Growth** | 44.3% | — | — | 48.1% | 0.0% | 10.6% |

# Worthington Industries

At least when it comes to steel, Worthington Industries may be considered a shape-shifter. One of the largest steel processors in the US, Worthington Industries shapes and processes flat-rolled steel for industrial customers, including automotive, appliance, and machinery companies. The company also forms flat-rolled steel to exact customer specifications, filling a niche not usually served by steelmakers and steel service centers with limited processing capabilities. Worthington's subsidiaries make products such as pressure cylinders, metal framing, and automotive panels. Through joint ventures, the company also makes steel products such as metal ceiling grid systems and laser-welded blanks.

Worthington's processed steel segment accounts for more than half of sales. The unit consists of Worthington Steel, which is an intermediate processor of flat-rolled steel. Worthington Steel is one of the largest flat-rolled steel processors in the US. Another unit, Gerstenslager, supplies automotive exterior body panels to North American automotive OEMs and other past model service businesses.

The company's metal framing unit, Dietrich Industries, reflects more than a quarter of sales. Dietrich designs and manufactures metal framing components and systems used in the US commercial and residential construction markets.

Worthington Cylinders, the company's pressure cylinder unit, makes pressure cylinders such as low-pressure liquefied petroleum gas, refrigerant gas cylinders, and high-pressure industrial gas cylinders. The cylinders are sold to automotive manufacturers, refrigerant gas producers and distributors, industrial forklift makers, and commercial and residential cookware producers.

For the past five years, Worthington has implemented an acquisition and divesture strategy, focusing on the processing of flat-rolled steel as the company's core business. During that time Worthington has invested $1.2 billion in seven acquisitions and the modernization of its existing plants.

To expand its international presence and develop new products, Worthington has several joint ventures with companies such as ThyssenKrupp and United States Steel. In 2006, however, the company sold its stake in JV Acerex to Ternium, which in 2005 had acquired Worthington's partner in the company, Hylsamex.

Founder and chairman emeritus John H. McConnell owns 17% of the company.

## HISTORY

In 1955 John H. McConnell, son of a steelworker, borrowed money on his car and started the Worthington Steel Company in the garage of his Worthington, Ohio, home. McConnell had noticed that large steel mills would not fill small, specialized steel orders — a market he decided to serve. Worthington posted an $11,000 profit its first year.

Worthington moved into its processing facility in Columbus, Ohio, in 1959 and continued to grow during the next decade. It went public in 1968.

The company bought Lennox's pressure-cylinder business and renamed itself Worthington Industries in 1971. Worthington continued to expand its profitable pressure-cylinder business through acquisitions. Its 1980 purchase of Buckeye International provided the framework for what would become Worthington's two other business segments: custom products and castings. The company further expanded operations with purchases of machine maker Capital Die, Tool and Machine Co. and recycled metals processing company I. H. Schlezinger & Sons.

Worthington formed a joint venture with U.S. Steel in 1986 for a specialty steel-processing plant; two years later it teamed with Nissen Chemitec and Sumitomo to make molded plastic parts for automakers. To ensure a steady supply of steel, Worthington purchased an interest in Rouge Steel in 1989 (sold in 2000).

In 1992 Worthington formed WAVE, a joint venture with Armstrong World Industries, to produce and sell suspended ceiling-grid systems in Europe. That year John P. McConnell, founder John H.'s son, became vice chairman of the company. He succeeded his father as CEO a year later.

Forging its way into new markets, the company formed a joint venture in 1994 with Mexico's Hylsa SA to operate a steel-processing facility in Monterey, Mexico. (It sold its stake in the JV in 2006.) The company also entered new markets for existing product lines: Its 1996 purchase of metal-framing maker Dietrich Industries moved Worthington into the residential and commercial building markets, while in 1997 the company expanded its line of automotive parts by acquiring aftermarket body panel maker Gerstenslager in a stock swap worth about $113 million.

In 1998 Worthington expanded its international operations again by acquiring Austrian cylinder maker Joseph Heiser. That year the company sold its automotive metals unit, Worthington Precision Metals, to the investor group Veritas Capital Fund, and its share of London Industries (plastic parts for transplant automakers) to Japan-based partner Nissen Chemitec. In 1999 Worthington sold its Buckeye Steel Castings subsidiary to a management group that includes investment firm Key Equity Capital.

To increase its global presence, in 1999 the company bought Portugal-based Metalurgica Progresso de Vale de Cambra and a 51% interest in the Czech Republic's Gastec, both makers of pressure cylinders. Despite steady sales in fiscal 1999, profits fell by half, in part from low prices for cold-rolled steel, start-up costs at the company's new Alabama facility, and the General Motors strike.

Worthington acquired three independent galvanized steel producers in Pennsylvania — MetalTech, NexTech, and GalvTech — during 2000. In early 2001 the company instituted a partial shutdown of its steel facility in Malvern, Pennsylvania. However, it decided to keep its Malvern coating lines running — those lines produce nickel, zinc, and painted products and generate approximately $60 million in annual sales. Along the same vein, in 2002 the company purchased construction steel maker, Unimast Incorporated (subsidiary of WHX Corporation) for around $113 million.

In 2003 Worthington formed a joint venture with Ohio-based Viking Industries, an intermediate steel processor of hot-rolled steel coils. The following year, Worthington completed the sale of its Alabama-based cold rolling mill to Nucor Corporation for around $82 million. That same year, Worthington purchased the propane and specialty gas cylinder assets of Western Industries for approximately $64.5 million.

## EXECUTIVES

**Chairman and CEO:** John P. McConnell, age 56, $1,026,500 pay
**President, CFO, and Director:** John S. Christie, age 57, $769,625 pay
**EVP and COO; President, Worthington Steel Company; Interim President, Dietrich Industries:** George P. Stoe, age 60
**SVP, Manufacturing:** Virgil L. Winland, age 58
**SVP, Marketing:** Ralph V. Roberts, age 58
**VP, Administration, General Counsel, and Secretary:** Dale T. Brinkman, age 52
**VP, Communications:** Catherine M. Lyttle
**VP, Human Resources:** Eric Smolenski
**VP, Purchasing:** Bruce Ruhl
**President, The Gerstenslager Company:** Kenneth L. Vagnini
**President, Worthington Cylinder:** Harry A. Goussetis, age 52
**CIO:** Robert (Rob) Richardson
**Controller:** Richard G. Welch, age 48
**Treasurer:** Randal I. Rombeiro, age 36
**Auditors:** KPMG LLP

## LOCATIONS

**HQ:** Worthington Industries, Inc.
200 Old Wilson Bridge Rd., Columbus, OH 43085
**Phone:** 614-438-3210 **Fax:** 614-438-7948
**Web:** www.worthingtonindustries.com

Worthington Industries has facilities in Austria, Canada, China, the Czech Republic, France, Mexico, Portugal, Spain, the UK, and the US.

**2007 Sales**

| | $ mil. | % of total |
|---|---|---|
| North America | | |
| US | 2,750.4 | 93 |
| Canada | 29.2 | 1 |
| Europe | 192.2 | 6 |
| **Total** | **2,971.8** | **100** |

## PRODUCTS/OPERATIONS

**2007 Sales**

| | $ mil. | % of total |
|---|---|---|
| Steel Processing | 1,460.7 | 49 |
| Metal Framing | 771.4 | 26 |
| Pressure Cylinders | 544.8 | 18 |
| Other | 194.9 | 7 |
| **Total** | **2,971.8** | **100** |

**Selected Subsidiaries**

Dietrich Industries, Inc. (metal framing)
GalvTech (galvanized steel)
MetalTech (galvanized steel)
NexTech (galvanized steel)
The Gerstenslager Company (aftermarket body panels)
Worthington Cylinder Corporation (pressure cylinders)
Worthington Steel Company (steel processing)

**Joint Ventures and Other Holdings**

Spartan Steel Coating, LLC (52%, joint venture with Rouge Steel Coating; sheet steel)
TWB Company, LLC (50%, joint venture with Thyssen Krupp; laser-welded blanks for cars)
Worthington Armstrong Venture (50%, joint venture with Armstrong World Industries; suspended ceiling grid systems)
Worthington Gastec, a.s. (51%, pressure cylinders, Czech Republic)
Worthington SA (52%, joint venture with three Brazilian propane distributors; pressure cylinders; Brazil)
Worthington Specialty Processing (50%, joint venture with United States Steel; wide-sheet steel for the auto industry)
Worthington Tank, Ltda (65%, pressure cylinders, Brazil)

## COMPETITORS

| | |
|---|---|
| AK Steel | O'Neal Steel |
| Citation | Ryerson |
| Gibraltar Industries | Shiloh Industries |
| Harsco | Steel Technologies |
| Nippon Steel | ThyssenKrupp |
| Nucor | United States Steel |

## HISTORICAL FINANCIALS

Company Type: Public

**Income Statement** FYE: May 31

| | REVENUE ($ mil.) | NET INCOME ($ mil.) | NET PROFIT MARGIN | EMPLOYEES |
|---|---|---|---|---|
| **5/07** | 2,972 | 114 | 3.8% | 6,900 |
| **5/06** | 2,897 | 146 | 5.0% | 8,200 |
| **5/05** | 3,079 | 179 | 5.8% | 6,450 |
| **5/04** | 2,379 | 87 | 3.6% | 6,700 |
| **5/03** | 2,220 | 75 | 3.4% | 6,700 |
| **Annual Growth** | 7.6% | 10.9% | — | 0.7% |

**2007 Year-End Financials**

Debt ratio: 26.2%
Return on equity: 12.1%
Cash ($ mil.): 64
Current ratio: 2.31
Long-term debt ($ mil.): 245
No. of shares (mil.): 85
Dividends
Yield: 3.2%
Payout: 51.9%
Market value ($ mil.): 1,792

**Stock History** NYSE: WOR

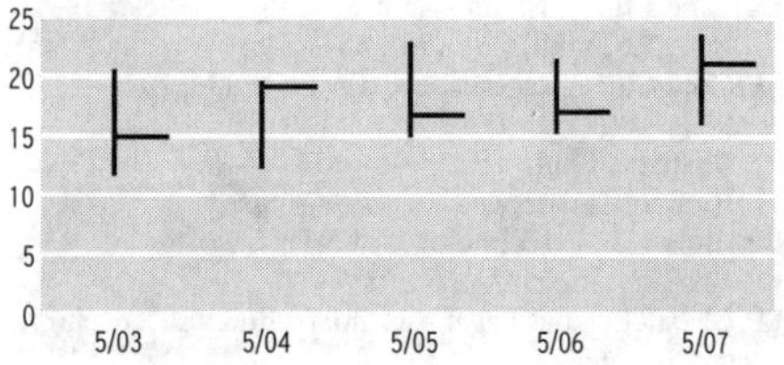

| | STOCK PRICE ($) FY Close | P/E High | P/E Low | PER SHARE ($) Earnings | Dividends | Book Value |
|---|---|---|---|---|---|---|
| **5/07** | 21.11 | 18 | 12 | 1.31 | 0.68 | 11.02 |
| **5/06** | 17.03 | 13 | 9 | 1.64 | 0.68 | 10.66 |
| **5/05** | 16.76 | 11 | 7 | 2.03 | 0.81 | 9.33 |
| **5/04** | 19.14 | 19 | 12 | 1.00 | 0.64 | 7.83 |
| **5/03** | 14.93 | 23 | 14 | 0.87 | 0.64 | 7.40 |
| **Annual Growth** | 9.0% | — | — | 10.8% | 1.5% | 10.5% |

# W. R. Grace

W. R. Grace & Co. has embraced Thoreau's call to simplify. The company has restructured from six product groups into two major units, each accounting for about half of sales. Grace's Davison Chemicals unit makes silica-based products, chemical catalysts, and refining catalysts that help produce refined products from crude oil. Its Performance Chemicals unit makes concrete and cement additives, packaging sealants, and fireproofing chemicals. The company's customers include chemicals companies, oil refiners, and construction firms. Grace filed for bankruptcy protection in 2001 after an unexpected increase in asbestos litigation (injury claims nearly doubled in 2000); the company no longer makes such products.

Chairman Paul Norris has stepped down as president and CEO and has indicated that he will remain with Grace only through its emergence from Chapter 11, after which he will retire. Accordingly, the company named Fred Festa president and CEO in 2005.

The company has streamlined operations — as evidenced by the absorption of its container division by its Performance Chemicals segment. Grace has sold or spun off more than 30 businesses over the past few years, including health care and biotechnology firms and coal-mining operations. The company is expanding manufacturing and sales operations in key regions (including China, India, the Middle East, and Eastern Europe) to take advantage of growth in these markets. It is also pursuing global acquisitions to enhance its existing product offerings and penetrate desirable segments.

In 2005 it acquired packaging sealant assets from Midland Dexter Venezuela and concrete admixture assets from Swedish firm Perstorp. The company then acquired the assets of specialty catalyst supplier Single-Site Catalysts, and it purchased Flexit Laboratories, which manufactures chromatography products for pharmaceutical applications. Grace added to its catalysts business in 2006 with the agreement to buy Basell's North American custom catalyst operations. That year Grace announced plans to build a new manufacturing facility in Tennessee to enhance its waterproofing product operations.

The company faces additional asbestos-related difficulties as a federal grand jury has indicted the company and seven current or former officers for knowingly exposing residents of Libby, Montana, to asbestos by releasing it into the air at its nearby vermiculite mine.

In 2007 the company acquired certain assets of Grupo Sistiaga S.L.

## HISTORY

W. R. Grace & Co. grew from the businesses of Irishman William R. Grace, who fled the potato famine and moved to Peru in 1854 to charter ships trading guano fertilizer. In 1866 he moved his headquarters to New York and established shipping routes linking New York, South America, and Europe. The company traded fertilizer, agricultural products, and US manufactured goods.

Grace, mayor of New York City in the 1880s, died in 1904. His son Joseph became president in 1907, and he expanded the firm's business in South America and started the Grace National Bank in 1916. The company entered aviation in 1928 in a joint venture with Pan American Airlines, forming Pan American-Grace Airways (Panagra) to serve Latin America.

In 1945 Joseph's son Peter took the helm at age 32. He took the company public in 1953. The next year Grace expanded into chemicals, buying Davison Chemical and Dewey & Almy Chemical (sealants, batteries, and packaging). Peter then sold Grace National Bank (1965), Panagra (1967), and the Grace Line (1969).

Purchases during the 1960s and 1970s included American Breeders Service (1967), Herman's (56%, sporting goods, 1970; sold 1986), Baker & Taylor (wholesale books, 1970), Sheplers (western wear, 1976; sold 1986), El Torito-La Fiesta Restaurants (1976; sold 1995), and home-improvement store Handy City (1976). Grace sold its agricultural and fertilizer businesses in 1988 and added three European water-treatment firms to its holdings in 1990. In 1992 it sold Baker & Taylor and bought DuPont Canada's North American food-service packaging operations.

Peter Grace left in 1993 after nearly 50 years as CEO. J. P. Bolduc succeeded him but was brought down by a sexual harassment scandal two years later. Grace acquired Riggers Medizintechnik of Germany (dialysis products) and Florida-based Home Intensive Care and sold its oil field services and liquid storage and terminal businesses.

Grace began divesting businesses in 1995, selling its Dearborn business to Betz Laboratories and the plant biotechnology portion of its Agracetus subsidiary to Monsanto. That year the company reclassified its health care business as discontinued; that move resulted in a dramatic drop in revenues. Albert Costello, a veteran executive from drug firm American Cyanamid, succeeded Bolduc.

In 1998 the company sold its biggest division, food packaging, to Sealed Air for about $4.9 billion in cash and stock (Grace shareholders wound up with more than 60% of Sealed Air). It also agreed to buy Imperial Chemical's Crosfield catalysts and silicas business but terminated the deal after US regulators raised antitrust issues. Grace relocated its headquarters to Columbia, Maryland, in 1999 and set up a $1 million financial education fund to settle an SEC lawsuit alleging the company socked away profits in the 1990s to mask poor earnings.

Also in 1999 Paul Norris, former president of AlliedSignal's specialty chemicals division, succeeded Costello as CEO. Early in 2001 Grace announced that it had filed for bankruptcy protection because of an unexpected 80% increase in asbestos-related litigation; previously, the company had managed to settle claims, which had come at a relatively manageable rate.

Grace continued to expand its presence in core markets in 2001; acquisitions included European companies Akzo-PQ Silicas (silica products) and Pieri S.A. (specialty construction chemicals). In 2002 Grace acquired catalyst manufacturing assets from Sweden's Borealis A/S. The following year, Grace continued to expand internationally through the acquisition of German construction chemicals firm Tricosal Beton-Chemie.

In 2004 the company acquired Benelux firm Pieri N.V. It bought up sealants and adhesives maker Liquid Control later that year. It also acquired pharmaceutical chemical firm Alltech International as part of a strategy to build up its biotechnology and pharmaceutical customer base for silica-based products.

## EXECUTIVES

**Chairman:** Paul J. Norris, age 60
**President, CEO, and Director:** Alfred E. (Fred) Festa, age 46
**SVP, Administration:** W. Brian McGowan, age 56
**SVP and CFO:** Robert M. Tarola, age 55
**VP, Finance, Operations:** Susan E. Farnsworth
**VP, Operations:** J. P. (Butch) Forehand
**VP, Human Resources:** Michael N. Piergrossi
**VP; President, Davison Chemicals:** Gregory E. (Greg) Poling, age 50
**VP, Public and Regulatory Affairs:** William M. Corcoran, age 56
**VP, General Counsel, and Secretary:** Mark A. Shelnitz, age 47
**VP and President, Grace Performance Chemicals:** Richard C. Brown, age 46
**Director, Information Technology:** George Bollock
**Director, Investor Relations:** Bridgette Sarikas
**Auditors:** PricewaterhouseCoopers LLP

## LOCATIONS

**HQ:** W. R. Grace & Co.
7500 Grace Dr., Columbia, MD 21044
**Phone:** 410-531-4000 **Fax:** 410-531-4367
**Web:** www.grace.com

W. R. Grace & Co. has operations in nearly 40 countries worldwide.

### 2006 Sales

| | $ mil. | % of total |
|---|---|---|
| North America | | |
| US | 1,032.3 | 37 |
| Canada & Puerto Rico | 126.5 | 4 |
| Europe | | |
| Germany | 138.1 | 5 |
| Other countries | 932.9 | 33 |
| Asia/Pacific | 443.2 | 16 |
| Latin America | 153.5 | 5 |
| **Total** | **2,826.5** | **100** |

## PRODUCTS/OPERATIONS

### 2006 Sales

| | $ mil. | % of total |
|---|---|---|
| Davison Chemicals | 1,500.6 | 53 |
| Performance Chemicals | 1,325.9 | 47 |
| **Total** | **2,826.5** | **100** |

### Selected Operations

Davison Chemicals (or Grace Davison)
- Chemical catalysts
- Refining catalysts
- Silicas and absorbents

Performance Chemicals (or Grace Performance Chemicals)
- Building and construction chemicals (Grace Construction Products)
  - Air and vapor barriers
  - Cement additives
  - Coatings and sealants
  - Concrete admixtures
  - Fireproofing materials
  - Masonry products
  - Waterproofing materials
- Container products (Darex)
  - Can and closure sealants

## COMPETITORS

Agilent Technologies
Albemarle
Ameron
BASF Catalysts
Cabot
Clariant
CRI/Criterion Catalyst
Degussa
Dow Chemical
DuPont
Eastman Chemical
Equistar Chemicals
H.B. Fuller
Henkel
Illinois Tool Works
Imperial Chemical
Ineos Silicas
Rohm and Haas
UOP
Waters

## HISTORICAL FINANCIALS

Company Type: Public

**Income Statement** FYE: December 31

| | REVENUE ($ mil.) | NET INCOME ($ mil.) | NET PROFIT MARGIN | EMPLOYEES |
|---|---|---|---|---|
| **12/06** | 2,827 | 18 | 0.6% | 6,500 |
| **12/05** | 2,570 | 67 | 2.6% | 6,400 |
| **12/04** | 2,260 | (402) | — | 6,500 |
| **12/03** | 1,997 | (55) | — | 6,300 |
| **12/02** | 1,840 | 22 | 1.2% | 6,400 |
| **Annual Growth** | 11.3% | (4.6%) | — | 0.4% |

**2006 Year-End Financials**

Debt ratio: —
Return on equity: —
Cash ($ mil.): 536
Current ratio: 3.05
Long-term debt ($ mil.): 0
No. of shares (mil.): 69
Dividends
Yield: —
Payout: —
Market value ($ mil.): 1,365

**Stock History** NYSE: GRA

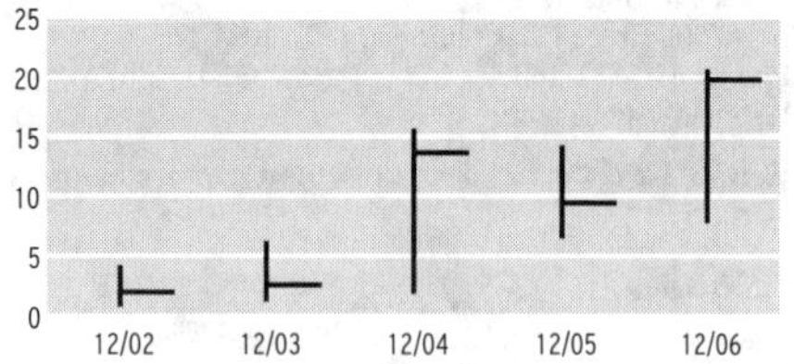

| | STOCK PRICE ($) FY Close | P/E High | P/E Low | PER SHARE ($) Earnings | Dividends | Book Value |
|---|---|---|---|---|---|---|
| **12/06** | 19.80 | 76 | 29 | 0.27 | — | (7.98) |
| **12/05** | 9.40 | 14 | 7 | 1.00 | — | (8.90) |
| **12/04** | 13.61 | — | — | (6.11) | — | (9.37) |
| **12/03** | 2.57 | — | — | (0.84) | — | (2.50) |
| **12/02** | 1.96 | 12 | 3 | 0.34 | — | (3.39) |
| **Annual Growth** | 78.3% | — | — | (5.6%) | — | — |

# W.W. Grainger

Home, home on the Grainger is a well-stocked place. Through its Branch-based Distribution, Acklands-Grainger, and Lab Safety units, W.W. Grainger distributes maintenance, repair, and service equipment, components, and supplies. It provides products such as compressors, motors, signs, lighting and welding equipment, and hand and power tools. The company has nearly 600 branches and 15 distribution centers in the US, Canada, Mexico, and China. Its 1.8 million customers include contractors, service and maintenance shops, manufacturers, hotels, and government, health care, and educational facilities.

Grainger has begun a program in the US to enlarge the size of its branches and increase its staff in 25 metropolitan markets. The company also expanded into Asia in 2006 by opening two facilities in Shanghai, China. Grainger is also expanding its product line.

Senior chairman David Grainger, the founder's son, owns 10% of Grainger; director James Slavik owns 5%.

## HISTORY

In 1919 William W. Grainger, a motor designer and salesman, saw the opportunity to develop a wholesale electric-motor sales and distribution company. He set up an office in Chicago in 1927 and incorporated the business a year later. With sales generated primarily through postcard mailers and an eight-page catalog called *MotorBook*, Grainger started shipping motors to mail-order customers.

Utilities and factories began to shift from direct-current to alternating-current power systems in the late 1920s. Uniform DC-powered assembly lines gave way to individual workstations, each powered by a separate AC motor. This burgeoning market opened the way for distributors such as W.W. Grainger to tap into segments that high-volume manufacturers found difficult to reach. In the early 1930s W.W. Grainger opened offices in Atlanta, Dallas, Philadelphia, and San Francisco; by 1936 it had 15 sales branches.

W.W. Grainger entered a boom period after WWII, and by 1949 it had branches in 30 states. The company continued to expand in the 1950s and 1960s, then went public in 1967.

William Grainger retired in 1968, and his son David succeeded him as CEO. The company expanded into electric motor manufacturing with the purchase of the Doerr Companies in 1969. Ten years later it opened its 150th branch.

Grainger's distribution became decentralized with the 1983 opening of its 1.4 million-sq.-ft. automated regional distribution center in Kansas City. The next year Grainger surpassed $1 billion in sales. The company sold its Doerr Electric subsidiary to Emerson Electric in 1986. It added 91 branches in 1987 and 1988.

After a 17-year hiatus, the company started making acquisitions again, buying Vonnegut Industrial Products in 1989; Bossert Industrial Supply and Allied Safety in 1990; Ball Industries, a distributor of sanitary and janitorial supplies, in 1991; and Lab Safety Supply in 1992. Grainger began integrating its sanitary supply business with its core activities in 1993.

For the first time in company history, no Grainger held the CEO position when president Richard Keyser was appointed in 1995, replacing David Grainger. That year the company moved its headquarters to Lake Forest, Illinois.

Getting wired in 1995, Grainger put its catalog on the World Wide Web. The next year it announced new supply agreements with American Airlines, Emerson Electric Co., Lockheed Martin, and Procter & Gamble. Also in 1996 the company paid about $289 million for a unit of Canada's Acklands Ltd., distributor of automotive aftermarket products and industrial safety products. In 1998 Grainger won contracts, potentially worth more than $60 million over three years, to supply products to two health care organizations.

Grainger launched several online stores through its home page in 1999 (TotalMRO.com launched in 2000) and began negotiations in 2001 to split its Internet segment off as a separate entity (dubbed Material Logic). However, citing a slow economy, it later abandoned those plans and closed all Internet sites except FindMRO.com. Grainger took a $38 million writedown related to its Internet investments.

In 2002 Grainger was recognized by *FORTUNE* magazine as one of "America's Most Admired Companies," ranked fourth among the US's largest diversified wholesalers. The company completed the acquisition of Gempler's direct marketing division (tools and safety equipment) in 2003.

## EXECUTIVES

**Chairman and CEO:** Richard L. Keyser, age 64, $1,075,000 pay
**President:** James T. (Jim) Ryan, age 49, $566,680 pay
**SVP, Finance and CFO:** P. Ogden Loux, age 63, $491,040 pay
**SVP and General Counsel:** John L. Howard, age 48, $412,530 pay
**SVP and CIO:** Timothy M. Ferrarell, age 47
**SVP, Human Resources:** Lawrence J. Pilon, age 55
**SVP; President Lab Safety Supply:** Larry J. Loizzo, age 53
**SVP, Supply Chain:** Kevin A. Peters, age 48
**VP, Sales:** Debra (Deb) Oler, age 51
**President, Grainger Industrial Supply:** Yang C. Chen, age 58, $385,930 pay
**Director, Investor Relations and External Communications:** William D. Chapman
**Auditors:** Ernst & Young LLP

## LOCATIONS

**HQ:** W.W. Grainger, Inc.
100 Grainger Pkwy., Lake Forest, IL 60045
**Phone:** 847-535-1000 **Fax:** 847-535-0878
**Web:** www.grainger.com

**2006 Sales**

| | $ mil. | % of total |
|---|---|---|
| US | 5,197.2 | 88 |
| Canada | 567.6 | 10 |
| Other countries | 118.8 | 2 |
| **Total** | **5,883.6** | **100** |

## PRODUCTS/OPERATIONS

**2006 Sales**

| | $ mil. | % of total |
|---|---|---|
| Branch-Based Distribution | 4,909.6 | 83 |
| Acklands-Grainger | 565.1 | 10 |
| Lab Safety | 408.9 | 7 |
| **Total** | **5,883.6** | **100** |

**Selected Products**

Air compressors
Air-filtration equipment
Electric motors
Hand and power tools
Heating and ventilation equipment
Lighting equipment
Liquid pumps
Safety products
Spray paints

## COMPETITORS

Applied Industrial Technologies
Fastenal
Genuine Parts
Gexpro
Graybar Electric
Hagemeyer
Industrial Distribution
J & L Industrial Supply
Kaman
McMaster-Carr
MSC Industrial Direct
WESCO International
Wilson

## HISTORICAL FINANCIALS

Company Type: Public

**Income Statement** FYE: December 31

| | REVENUE ($ mil.) | NET INCOME ($ mil.) | NET PROFIT MARGIN | EMPLOYEES |
|---|---|---|---|---|
| **12/06** | 5,884 | 383 | 6.5% | 17,074 |
| **12/05** | 5,527 | 346 | 6.3% | 16,732 |
| **12/04** | 5,050 | 287 | 5.7% | 15,523 |
| **12/03** | 4,667 | 227 | 4.9% | 14,701 |
| **12/02** | 4,644 | 212 | 4.6% | 15,236 |
| **Annual Growth** | 6.1% | 16.0% | — | 2.9% |

**2006 Year-End Financials**

Debt ratio: 0.2%
Return on equity: 17.2%
Cash ($ mil.): 361
Current ratio: 2.64
Long-term debt ($ mil.): 5
No. of shares (mil.): 84
Dividends
 Yield: 2.0%
 Payout: 33.0%
Market value ($ mil.): 5,880

**Stock History** NYSE: GWW

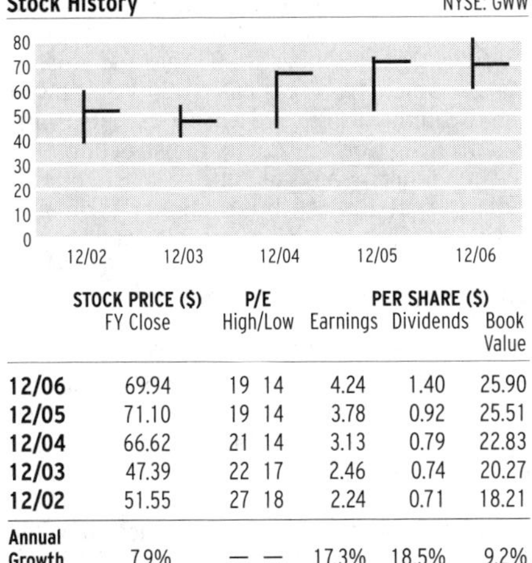


| | STOCK PRICE ($) FY Close | P/E High/Low | | PER SHARE ($) Earnings | Dividends | Book Value |
|---|---|---|---|---|---|---|
| **12/06** | 69.94 | 19 | 14 | 4.24 | 1.40 | 25.90 |
| **12/05** | 71.10 | 19 | 14 | 3.78 | 0.92 | 25.51 |
| **12/04** | 66.62 | 21 | 14 | 3.13 | 0.79 | 22.83 |
| **12/03** | 47.39 | 22 | 17 | 2.46 | 0.74 | 20.27 |
| **12/02** | 51.55 | 27 | 18 | 2.24 | 0.71 | 18.21 |
| **Annual Growth** | 7.9% | — | — | 17.3% | 18.5% | 9.2% |

# Wyeth

Wyeth is wise in the ways of health care. The company operates in three segments, the largest being its Pharmaceuticals business, which sells antidepressant Effexor and arthritis drug Enbrel (with partner Amgen), as well as anti-infectives, vaccines, nutrition and women's health products, gastroenterology drugs, and treatments for hemophilia and cardiovascular conditions. The company's Consumer Healthcare unit produces such familiar over-the-counter brands as Advil, Centrum, Robitussin, and ChapStick; and subsidiary Fort Dodge Animal Health makes health products for livestock, horses, and pets, including vaccines, pharmaceuticals, parasite control products, and growth implants.

Wyeth's pharmaceuticals unit is by far its biggest money-maker, accounting for more than 80% of sales. Effexor alone contributes 18%, and revenue from the firm's collaboration with Amgen (to promote Enbrel) accounts for 12%.

The bogeyman of big drug companies — generic competition — looms for several of Wyeth's big sellers, but it is not the specter it is for some other druggernauts. Teva launched a generic version of Effexor IR (immediate release) in 2006, and Wyeth expects injectable antibiotic Zosyn to face a generic competitor by the end of 2007. Most of the company's principal pharmaceutical products, however, enjoy patent protection relatively far into the future.

Additionally, the company is developing a strong roster of up-and-comers, both through internal development and strategic alliances. Its development efforts — with partners including Progenics Pharmaceuticals, Trubion Pharmaceuticals, and Solvay Pharmaceuticals — have yielded potential treatments in the areas of neuroscience, vaccines, and women's health, among other things. It launched a new antibiotic, Tygacil, in the US in 2005 and received European regulatory approval for the drug the following year.

Wyeth is facing litigation over two once-popular hormone replacement therapy (HRT) drugs, Prempro and Premarin. Sales of the drugs, which are used to treat menopausal symptoms, fell following a 2002 government study linking them to increased heart disease, breast cancer, and stroke risks.

## HISTORY

The history of Wyeth, formerly American Home Products (AHP), is one of continuous acquisitions. Incorporated in 1926, it consolidated several small companies that made proprietary medicines, such as Hill's Cascara Quinine. In the Depression the firm bought more than 30 food and drug companies. A sunburn oil bought in 1935 became hemorrhoid treatment Preparation H; AHP also bought Anacin in the 1930s. AHP purchased Canada's Ayerst Laboratories in 1943 (cod-liver oil, vitamins, and Premarin) and Chef Boyardee Quality Foods in 1946.

In alliance with the UK's Imperial Chemical Industries, Ayerst developed Inderal (1968), first of the beta-blocker class of antihypertensives. AHP bought Sherwood Medical Group (medical supplies) in 1982 and Bristol-Myers' animal health division a year later. In 1988 it took over A. H. Robins, which had been bankrupted by lawsuits over the Dalkon Shield contraceptive device. AHP also introduced Advil in the 1980s, and within five years it was outselling Bristol-Myers' Nuprin. In 1992 the company bought 60% of the Genetics Institute (it bought the rest in 1996).

In 1994 AHP and American Cyanamid merged. Frank Washburn founded American Cyanamid in 1907 and produced the world's first synthetic fertilizer. The firm diversified into other chemicals in the 1920s and during WWII supplied US troops with typhus vaccine. In 1988 American Cyanamid introduced anticancer drug Novantrone. The hostile takeover pumped up AHP's presence in biotechnology (including majority control of Immunex), generics, and agricultural products and increased R&D.

AHP introduced several new products in the US in 1996, including Redux, the first weight-reduction drug to win FDA approval in more than two decades. To cut debt and focus on high-margin pharmaceuticals, the firm sold most of its food unit (Chef Boyardee, Jiffy Pop) to investment firm Hicks, Muse, Tate & Furst (now HM Capital). It sold the rest in 1998.

In 1997 AHP bought the animal health operations of Belgium's Solvay. It recalled diet drugs Redux and Pondimin after they were linked to serious heart valve problems, prompting lawsuits against AHP. Painkiller Duract, introduced in 1997, was linked to fatal liver damage and pulled.

AHP sold its medical device units in 1998. The next year agricultural sales fizzled as well, and AHP put its Cyanamid Agricultural Products division up for sale (BASF bought it in 2000).

In 1999 AHP bought Solgar Vitamin and Herb Company. It lost its multimillion-dollar battle to keep Duramed Pharmaceuticals' potential Premarin rival off the market. FDA approvals allowed AHP to launch other products, including Sonata (insomnia, 1999), Rapamune (organ rejection preventative, 1999), and Prevnar (antibacterial vaccine, 2000). Also in 1999 the company agreed to pay nearly $5 billion (later reduced to $3.75 billion) to settle claims relating to its diet drugs.

A planned merger with Warner-Lambert collapsed in 2000 when Pfizer won a hostile bid for AHP's would-be mate (AHP took consolation in a $1.8 billion break-up fee). Also that year AHP's Wyeth-Ayerst subsidiary suspended shipments of the contraceptive Norplant and instructed doctors to advise patients after discovering problems with Norplant's long-term potency. In 2002 the company announced that no potency problems had been detected, but decided to discontinue sales of Norplant.

In 2001 president Robert Essner also took over the CEO post, replacing John Stafford. Stafford had held the top post since 1986 and stayed on as chairman until 2003 when Essner took on that position as well.

AHP rode several waves of change in 2002. It reached an agreement with the FTC to settle allegations that AHP and Schering-Plough had conspired to delay a generic version of a vitamin supplement from reaching the market. American Home Products also changed its name to Wyeth to reflect its broader market. Also in 2002 the company, which had struggled with quality control issues, recalled a dose of heparin that contained an antioxidant compound. That same year, its female hormone replacement Prempro came under heavy scrutiny as studies suggested that such drugs might increase women's risk for breast cancer, heart disease, and stroke.

## EXECUTIVES

**Chairman and CEO:** Robert A. (Bob) Essner, age 59, $1,662,000 pay
**Vice Chairman, President, and COO:** Bernard J. Poussot, age 55, $967,035 pay
**SVP and CFO:** Greg Norden, age 49
**SVP, Corporate Business Development:** Thomas Hofstaetter, age 58
**SVP; President, Europe, Middle East, Africa, Canada, Wyeth Pharmaceuticals:** Ulf Wiinberg, age 48
**SVP; President, Global Business, Wyeth Pharmaceuticals:** Joseph M. Mahady, age 53, $695,600 pay
**SVP; President, Wyeth Research:** Robert R. Ruffolo Jr., age 56, $727,000 pay
**SVP and General Counsel:** Lawerence V. Stein, age 57
**SVP, Human Resources:** René R. Lewin, age 60
**SVP, Public Affairs:** Marily H. Rhudy, age 59
**SVP Finance:** Mary Katherine Wold, age 54
**SVP, Early Phase Programs, Vaccines R&D, Wyeth Pharmaceuticals:** Kathrin U. Jansen
**VP and Controller:** Paul J. Jones, age 61
**VP, Secretary, and Associate General Counsel:** Eileen M. Lach, age 56
**VP, Corporate Communications:** Jessica Stoltenberg, age 51
**VP, Corporate Information Services and CIO:** Jeffrey E. Keisling, age 50
**VP, Corporate Strategic Initiatives:** James J. Pohlman, age 57
**VP, Environmental Affairs and Facilities Operations and Associate General Counsel:** Steven A. Tasher
**VP, Finance Operations:** John C. Kelly
**VP, Intellectual Property and Associate General Counsel:** David A. Manspeizer
**VP, Investor Relations:** Justin R. Victoria
**Auditors:** PricewaterhouseCoopers LLP

## LOCATIONS

**HQ:** Wyeth
5 Giralda Farms, Madison, NJ 07940
**Phone:** 973-660-5000 **Fax:** 973-660-7026
**Web:** www.wyeth.com

Wyeth operates manufacturing plants in 15 countries worldwide and markets its products in more than 140 countries.

## 2006 Sales

| | $ mil. | % of total |
|---|---|---|
| US | 11,054.4 | 54 |
| UK | 999.5 | 5 |
| Other countries | 8,296.8 | 41 |
| **Total** | **20,350.7** | **100** |

## PRODUCTS/OPERATIONS

### 2006 Sales

| | $ mil. | % of total |
|---|---|---|
| Pharmaceuticals | 16,884.2 | 83 |
| Consumer health | 2,530.2 | 12 |
| Animal health | 936.3 | 5 |
| **Total** | **20,350.7** | **100** |

### Selected Products

Pharmaceuticals
- Benefix (hemophilia)
- Effexor (antidepressant and anxiety disorder treatment)
- Enbrel (arthritis treatment)
- Inderal (hypertension)
- Premarin (hormone replacement therapy)
- Prempro (hormone replacement therapy)
- Prevnar (pneumococcus vaccine)
- Protonix (protein pump inhibitor)
- Rapamune (organ rejection preventative)
- Refacto (hemophilia)
- Tygacil (anti-infective)
- Zosyn (anti-infective)

Consumer Health
- Advil (analgesic)
- Alavert (allergies)
- Anbesol (oral pain relief)
- Caltrate (nutritional supplement)
- Centrum (vitamins)
- ChapStick (lip care)
- Dimetapp (cough/cold remedy)
- FiberCon (laxative)
- Preparation H (hemorrhoid treatment)
- Primatene (asthma)
- Robitussin (cough/cold remedy)

Animal Health
- Cydectin (parasite control)
- Duramune (parvo/distemper vaccines)
- Fel-O-Vax (feline diseases vaccine)
- PYRAMID (combination vaccine)
- ToDAY/ToMORROW (dairy cow mastitis)
- Triangle Cattle Vaccines (combination vaccine)
- West Nile-Innovator (West Nile virus vaccine)

## COMPETITORS

Abbott Labs
Amgen
AstraZeneca
Barr Pharmaceuticals
Bayer
Bristol-Myers Squibb
Carma Laboratories
Chattem
Chiron
Eli Lilly
Genentech
GlaxoSmithKline
Johnson & Johnson
Merck
Mylan Labs
Novartis
Novo Nordisk
Pfizer
Procter & Gamble
Roche
Sandoz International GmbH
Sanofi-Aventis
Schering-Plough
Teva Pharmaceuticals
Watson Pharmaceuticals

## HISTORICAL FINANCIALS

Company Type: Public

### Income Statement

FYE: December 31

| | REVENUE ($ mil.) | NET INCOME ($ mil.) | NET PROFIT MARGIN | EMPLOYEES |
|---|---|---|---|---|
| **12/06** | 20,351 | 4,197 | 20.6% | 50,060 |
| **12/05** | 18,756 | 3,656 | 19.5% | 49,732 |
| **12/04** | 17,358 | 1,234 | 7.1% | 51,401 |
| **12/03** | 15,851 | 2,051 | 12.9% | 52,385 |
| **12/02** | 14,584 | 4,447 | 30.5% | 52,762 |
| **Annual Growth** | 8.7% | (1.4%) | — | (1.3%) |

### 2006 Year-End Financials

Debt ratio: 62.1%
Return on equity: 31.5%
Cash ($ mil.): 8,727
Current ratio: 2.43
Long-term debt ($ mil.): 9,097
No. of shares (mil.): 1,345
Dividends
Yield: 2.5%
Payout: 41.2%
Market value ($ mil.): 68,500

### Stock History

NYSE: WYE

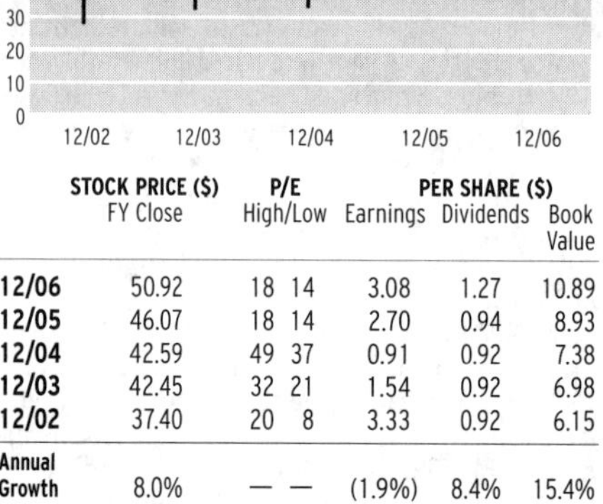


| | STOCK PRICE ($) FY Close | P/E High/Low | PER SHARE ($) Earnings | Dividends | Book Value |
|---|---|---|---|---|---|
| **12/06** | 50.92 | 18 14 | 3.08 | 1.27 | 10.89 |
| **12/05** | 46.07 | 18 14 | 2.70 | 0.94 | 8.93 |
| **12/04** | 42.59 | 49 37 | 0.91 | 0.92 | 7.38 |
| **12/03** | 42.45 | 32 21 | 1.54 | 0.92 | 6.98 |
| **12/02** | 37.40 | 20 8 | 3.33 | 0.92 | 6.15 |
| **Annual Growth** | 8.0% | — — | (1.9%) | 8.4% | 15.4% |

# Xcel Energy

Xcel Energy has accelerated its energy engine into utility markets across the US. The utility holding company distributes electricity to more than 3.3 million customers and natural gas to 1.8 million in eight states; Colorado and Minnesota account for the majority of its customers. Xcel Energy's regulated utilities — Northern States Power, Public Service Company of Colorado, and Southwestern Public Service — have more than 15,700 MW of primarily fossil-fueled generating capacity. Xcel Energy has divested its primary energy trading subsidiary, independent power producer NRG Energy. It has also sold its Cheyenne Light, Fuel & Power utility (to Black Hills Corporation).

Downturns in the wholesale energy industry (spurred by Enron's collapse and the ensuing financial scrutiny of other energy trading companies) led to serious financial difficulties for NRG in 2002. NRG entered into debt restructuring talks with its creditors, and in 2003 the unit filed for Chapter 11 bankruptcy. NRG's reorganization plan, which was completed in December 2003, included a settlement agreement in which Xcel Energy agreed to pay $752 million to NRG and its creditors and then divest its interest in NRG.

Other operations include gas transportation, energy engineering and construction services, and affordable housing investments.

To focus on its regulated energy operations, Xcel Energy is divesting noncore businesses. The company has sold pipeline company Viking Gas Transmission to Northern Border Partners (now ONEOK Partners), and it has sold its Arizona utility, Black Mountain Gas (10,000 gas and propane customers), to Las Vegas-based utility Southwest Gas. Xcell has also signed a deal to sell its Utility Engineering Corp. to Zachry Construction.

The company has sold off the assets of subsidiary Xcel Energy International (primarily Latin American power investments), and has also sold its Seren Innovations business (cable TV, phone, and high-speed Internet access networks in California and Minnesota).

The company plans to expand its generating capacity by building new power plants, thus decreasing its dependence on purchased power. Xcel Energy also plans to invest in installing new environmental controls at some of its existing generation facilities.

Late in 2005 Xcel Energy announced it would acquire 775 megawatts of new wind power capacity for its Colorado system by the end of 2007. Combined with its current and under-construction wind capacity of 282 megawatts, the increase will make Xcel Energy the US's largest utility user of wind power.

## HISTORY

The Minnesota Electric Light & Electric Motive Power Company was founded in 1881 and changed its name to Minnesota Brush Electric the next year. In the 1890s it provided street lighting and power for trolleys and became Minneapolis General Electric.

In 1909 Henry Byllesby formed rival firm Washington County Light and Power Co. (soon renamed Consumers Power Company), then created holding company Northern States Power Company of Delaware (NSPD). In 1910 he founded Standard Gas and Electric, a holding company overseeing NSPD and many other US utilities.

NSPD bought Minneapolis General Electric in 1912, and Consumers Power was renamed the Northern States Power Company (NSP) in 1916. During the 1920s NSPD connected its subsidiaries via transmission lines. Byllesby died in 1924.

In 1931 NSP was placed under NSPD, but the Public Utility Holding Company Act of 1935 dissolved Standard and NSPD. NSP became independent in the 1940s and spent $335 million on new facilities after WWII.

During the 1960s NSP moved into Michigan, South Dakota, and Wisconsin, and brought its first nuclear power plant on line in 1964 (converted to natural gas in 1968). It began operating the Monticello and Prairie Island nukes in the early 1970s.

Sales nearly doubled in the 1980s. In 1989 NSP created NRG Energy to invest in independent power projects. The Federal Energy Policy Act allowed wholesale power competition in 1992, and NSP lost nine of its 19 municipal customers.

NSP acquired Viking Gas Transmission, which owned an interstate pipeline, in 1993. It also began developing affordable housing. In 1995 NSP and Wisconsin Electric planned to merge but dropped the deal amid antitrust concerns. NSP continued to diversify, forming telecommunications provider Seren Innovations in 1996 and starting its cable-testing business in 1997. The next year NSP formed a power marketing unit.

NRG Energy began a shopping spree abroad in 1994, buying interests in plants in Germany and Australia. In 1996 it bought a 48% stake in Bolivia's COBEE (increased to 99% in 2001). Also that year it acquired PacifiCorp's Pacific Generating unit, which owned stakes in a dozen geographically scattered plants.

In 1999 NRG Energy gained nearly 7,600 MW of capacity through power plant acquisitions in New York, Connecticut, California, and Massachusetts. The next year NRG Energy picked up another 1,700 MW in Louisiana, and it agreed to buy fossil-fueled plants (1,875 MW) from Delaware's Conectiv for $800 million (half of the deal was completed in 2001, the other half was canceled the following year). NSP spun off part of NRG in 2000 in an IPO.

Meanwhile, as the utility merger trend gathered steam in 1999, NSP agreed to acquire Denver-based New Century Energies in a $4.9 billion deal. The acquisition was completed in 2000, and the expanded company changed its name to Xcel Energy.

The next year Xcel Energy sold nearly all of its stake in UK-based Yorkshire Power Group, which had been held by New Century Energies, to Innogy (now RWE npower). It sold its remaining 5% stake in Yorkshire Power in 2002. NRG purchased several Latin American projects from Swedish utility Vattenfall in 2001. NRG also agreed to purchase four coal-fired plants (2,500-MW) in Ohio from FirstEnergy for $1.5 billion; however, the deal was later canceled.

In 2002 Xcel Energy repurchased the 26% stake in NRG that it sold to the public in 2000 and 2001.

## EXECUTIVES

**Chairman, President, and CEO:** Richard C. (Dick) Kelly, age 60, $1,338,474 pay
**VP and CFO:** Benjamin G. S. (Ben) Fowke III, age 46, $500,000 pay
**VP, CIO and Chief Administrative Officer:** Raymond E. Gogel, age 55
**VP and Corporate Secretary:** Cathy J. Hart, age 56
**VP and Treasurer:** George E. Tyson II, age 40
**VP and Controller:** Teresa S. Madden, age 49
**VP and General Counsel:** Gary R. Johnson, age 58, $410,000 pay
**VP and Chief Audit Executive:** Scott Weatherby
**President and CEO, Northern States Power Company, Minnesota:** Cynthia L. (Cyndi) Lesher, age 59
**Acting President and CEO, Northern States Power Company, Minnesota:** David M. Sparby
**President and CEO, Southwestern Public Service Company:** David L. Eves
**President, Utilities Group:** Paul J. Bonavia, age 53, $515,000 pay
**President, Energy Supply:** David M. Wilks, age 59
**President and CEO, Xcel Energy, Wisconsin:** Michael L. Swenson
**Managing Director Investor Relations:** Paul A. Johnson
**Director Media Relations:** Steve Roalstad
**Auditors:** Deloitte & Touche LLP

## LOCATIONS

**HQ:** Xcel Energy Inc.
800 Nicollet Mall, Minneapolis, MN 55401
**Phone:** 612-330-5500 **Fax:** 800-895-2895
**Web:** www.xcelenergy.com

Xcel Energy distributes electricity and natural gas in the US in Colorado, Michigan, Minnesota, New Mexico, North Dakota, South Dakota, Texas, and Wisconsin.

## PRODUCTS/OPERATIONS

### 2006 Sales

| | $ mil. | % of total |
|---|---|---|
| Electric utility | 7,608.0 | 77 |
| Gas utility | 2,156.0 | 22 |
| Nonregulated & other | 76.3 | 1 |
| **Total** | **9,840.3** | **100** |

### Selected Subsidiaries and Affiliates

Regulated Operations
- Northern States Power Company (Minnesota)
  - Nuclear Management Company (20%)
- Northern States Power Company (Wisconsin)
- Public Service Company of Colorado
- Southwestern Public Service Company
- WestGas InterState Inc. (interstate pipeline)

Nonregulated Operations
- Eloigne Company (affordable housing projects)

## COMPETITORS

AEP
AES
ALLETE
Alliant Energy
Aquila
Atmos Energy
Basin Electric Power
Black Hills
CenterPoint Energy
CMS Energy
DTE
Duke Energy
Dynegy
Entergy
Integrys Energy Group
Minnesota Power
OGE Energy
Otter Tail
Peabody Energy
Southern Company
Wisconsin Energy
Wisconsin Gas

## HISTORICAL FINANCIALS

Company Type: Public

### Income Statement

FYE: December 31

| | REVENUE ($ mil.) | NET INCOME ($ mil.) | NET PROFIT MARGIN | EMPLOYEES |
|---|---|---|---|---|
| **12/06** | 9,840 | 572 | 5.8% | 5,411 |
| **12/05** | 9,626 | 513 | 5.3% | 9,781 |
| **12/04** | 8,345 | 356 | 4.3% | 10,650 |
| **12/03** | 7,938 | 622 | 7.8% | 11,048 |
| **12/02** | 9,524 | (2,218) | — | 14,642 |
| **Annual Growth** | 0.8% | — | — | (22.0%) |

### 2006 Year-End Financials

Debt ratio: 119.2%
Return on equity: 10.2%
Cash ($ mil.): 139
Current ratio: 0.92
Long-term debt ($ mil.): 6,933
No. of shares (mil.): 407
Dividends
Yield: 3.8%
Payout: 64.7%
Market value ($ mil.): 9,392

### Stock History

NYSE: XEL

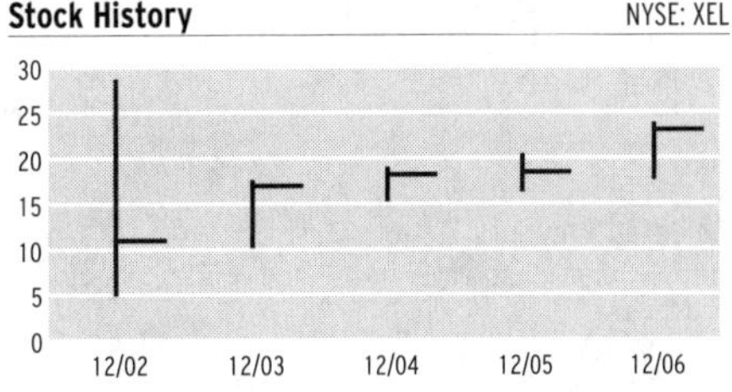


| | STOCK PRICE ($) FY Close | P/E High | P/E Low | PER SHARE ($) Earnings | Dividends | Book Value |
|---|---|---|---|---|---|---|
| **12/06** | 23.06 | 17 | 13 | 1.36 | 0.88 | 14.54 |
| **12/05** | 18.46 | 16 | 13 | 1.23 | 0.85 | 13.64 |
| **12/04** | 18.20 | 22 | 18 | 0.87 | 0.81 | 13.25 |
| **12/03** | 16.98 | 12 | 7 | 1.50 | 0.75 | 13.21 |
| **12/02** | 11.00 | — | — | (5.82) | 1.13 | 11.96 |
| **Annual Growth** | 20.3% | — | — | — | (6.1%) | 5.0% |

# Xerox Corporation

You won't find many companies listed in the dictionary as a verb. Xerox is best known for its color and black-and-white copiers, but it also makes printers, scanners, and fax machines. The company sells document management software and copier supplies, offers such services as consulting and document outsourcing, and holds a stake in a joint venture with Fuji Photo Film called Fuji Xerox. Xerox designs its products for businesses in the financial services, graphic arts, health care, government, and industrial sectors. Customers include FedEx Kinko's and Southern Company.

Since taking over as CEO in 2001, Anne Mulcahy has spearheaded a massive effort to regain market share and improve the company's bottom line. In the wake of restructuring woes that led to disgruntled customers, low employee morale, and a reorganization of management, Xerox continues to sharpen its focus. Restructuring measures have included job cuts and the transfer of customer financing services and manufacturing operations to third-party providers. To raise cash the company has sold assets, including half of its original 50% stake in Fuji Xerox. Xerox also made its celebrated Palo Alto Research Center (PARC) into a separate subsidiary. (Xerox has been criticized for failing to capitalize on numerous breakthrough PARC designs — laser printer, computer mouse, Ethernet, desktop icons.) Early in 2005 it sold its stake in systems integrator Integic to Northrop Grumman for $96 million in cash.

Xerox acquired Amici, a document management and search service company that primarily serves the legal sector, for $174 million in cash in mid-2006. It also reached a settlement with Palm in a patent infringement case it originally filed in 1997; Palm agreed to pay Xerox $22.5 million for a full license to three patents related to handwriting recognition and other technology. In 2007 Xerox acquired office equipment vendor Global Imaging Systems (GIS) for approximately $1.5 billion.

Once synonymous with copying, Xerox now generates most of its sales from printers and multi-function devices. Though black-and-white systems have traditionally accounted for the majority of Xerox's equipment sales, the company has increased the number of color systems across its product lines, with a greater emphasis on higher-margin services and high-end printing systems. To that end, the company phased out its consumer product lines, including its personal ink jet printers.

## HISTORY

The Haloid Company was incorporated in 1906 to make and sell photographic paper. In 1935 it bought photocopier company Rectigraph, which led Haloid to buy a license for a new process called electrophotography (renamed xerography from the ancient Greek words for "dry" and "writing") from the Battelle Memorial Institute in 1947. Battelle backed inventor Chester Carlson, who had worked to perfect a process for transferring electrostatic images from a photoconductive surface to paper.

Haloid commercialized xerography with the Model A copier in 1949 and the Xerox Copyflo in 1955, and by 1956 xerographic products represented 40% of sales. The company changed its name to Haloid Xerox in 1958 (Haloid was dropped from the name in 1961), and in 1959 it introduced the first simplified office copier. That machine took the world by storm, beating out such competing technologies as mimeograph (A.B.Dick), thermal paper (3M), and damp copy (Kodak). Sales soared to nearly $270 million in 1965.

Xerox branched out in the 1960s by buying three publishing companies and a computer unit; all were later sold or disbanded. In the 1970s Xerox bought printer, plotter, and disk drive businesses, as well as record carrier Western Union (1979; sold in 1982). In 1974 the FTC, believing Xerox was too market-dominant, forced the company to license its technology.

In the 1980s Xerox bought companies specializing in optical character recognition, scanning, faxing, and desktop publishing. It also diversified by buying insurance and investment banking firms, among others. In 1986 Paul Allaire, who had joined Xerox in 1966, was elected president. He was named CEO in 1990 and became chairman in 1991.

Eyeing future alliances, Xerox agreed to supply computer print engines to Compaq (1992) and Apple (1993). In 1995 it introduced networked color laser printers and software for printing Web documents.

Xerox bought Rank's 20% stake in Rank Xerox, the two companies' 41-year-old global marketing joint venture, in 1997. That year Xerox launched a $500 PC printer, copier, and scanner — its first product specifically for home use — and Allaire hired IBM CFO Richard Thoman as president and COO to spearhead a push into network and digital products.

In 1999 Xerox named Thoman CEO to replace Allaire, who remained chairman. That year Xerox bought France's SET Electronique (high-speed digital printers). Layoffs also continued, totaling 14,000 for 1998 and 1999.

In an effort to stake a larger claim in the office color printing market, Xerox bought Tektronix's ailing color printing and imaging division in early 2000. With profits shrinking and market value flagging, Thoman resigned in May 2000 amid pressure from the board. Allaire assumed the CEO post once again. Also that year the company sold its operations in China and Hong Kong to Fuji Xerox.

Early in 2001 the company laid off 4,000 more employees. That year Xerox sold half of its 50% stake in Fuji Xerox to Fuji Photo Film, and it discontinued its product lines aimed at consumer and small office users, including its personal copiers and ink jet printers. Allaire stepped down as chief executive; COO Anne Mulcahy was named as his successor. Looking to reduce its massive debt, Xerox transferred most of its US customer financing operations to GE Capital in a deal including $1 billion in cash financing from the lending giant (it later formed similar arrangements with GE Capital for many of its international operations).

In early 2002 CEO Mulcahy replaced Allaire as chairman. Also that year Xerox agreed to pay a $10 million fine to settle a complaint brought by the SEC alleging financial reporting violations. After the settlement, Xerox — which had fired KPMG as its auditors the previous year and brought in PricewaterhouseCoopers — initiated an audit of its financial statements from 1997 through 2001; as a result of the audit, in June 2002 the company restated about $2 billion in revenues over the five-year period.

## EXECUTIVES

**Chairman and CEO:** Anne M. Mulcahy, age 54, $2,508,000 pay
**President and Director:** Ursula M. Burns, age 48
**SVP and CFO:** Lawrence A. (Larry) Zimmerman, age 64, $890,250 pay
**SVP, General Counsel, and Corporate Secretary:** Don H. Liu, age 45
**SVP; President, Developing Markets Operations:** Jean-Noël Machon, age 54
**SVP; President, Global Accounts and Marketing Operations:** Michael C. MacDonald, age 54, $833,419 pay
**SVP; President, Xerox Europe:** Armando Zagalo de Lima, age 48
**SVP; President, Xerox Global Accounts:** Thomas J. Dolan, age 62
**SVP; President, Xerox North America:** James A. Firestone, age 52, $849,500 pay
**SVP, Chief Staff Officer, and Chief Ethics Officer:** Hector J. Motroni, age 63
**SVP, Fuji Xerox Operations:** Brian E. Stern, age 59
**VP; SVP and COO, Xerox Global Services:** John M. Kelly, age 42
**VP; CTO and President, Xerox Innovation Group:** Sophie Vandebroek, age 44
**VP and CIO:** John E. McDermott, age 53
**VP and Chief Accounting Officer:** Gary R. Kabureck, age 53
**VP and Controller:** Leslie F. Varon, age 50
**VP; General Manager, Xerox Litigation Services:** Craig Freeman
**VP and Treasurer:** Rhonda L. Seegal, age 57
**VP, Human Resources:** Patricia M. Nazemetz, age 57
**VP, Investor Relations:** James H. Lesko, age 56
**President, Xerox Office Group:** Russell M. Peacock, age 49
**Auditors:** PricewaterhouseCoopers LLP

## LOCATIONS

**HQ:** Xerox Corporation
800 Long Ridge Rd., Stamford, CT 06904
**Phone:** 203-968-3000 **Fax:** 203-968-3944
**Web:** www.xerox.com

### 2006 Sales

| | $ mil. | % of total |
|---|---|---|
| US | 8,406 | 53 |
| Europe | 5,378 | 34 |
| Other regions | 2,111 | 13 |
| **Total** | **15,895** | **100** |

## PRODUCTS/OPERATIONS

### 2006 Sales

| | $ mil. | % of total |
|---|---|---|
| Office | 7,625 | 48 |
| Production | 4,579 | 29 |
| Developing markets | 1,938 | 12 |
| Other | 1,753 | 11 |
| **Total** | **15,895** | **100** |

### Selected Products

Office (commercial, government, and education sectors)
- Copiers
- Displays
- Multifunction devices
- Printers
- Projectors
- Scanners

Production (graphics communications industry and large corporations)
- Digital presses
- High-volume printers
- Software

Other
- Paper
- Services
- Wide-format printers

## COMPETITORS

Agfa
Brother Industries
Canon
Danka
Eastman Kodak
Epson
FUJIFILM
Heidelberg
Hewlett-Packard
Hitachi
IBM
IKON
Konica Minolta
Kyocera Mita
Lexmark
Matsushita Electric
Océ
Oki Data
Olivetti
Ricoh
Sharp
Toshiba America

## HISTORICAL FINANCIALS

Company Type: Public

### Income Statement

FYE: December 31

| | REVENUE ($ mil.) | NET INCOME ($ mil.) | NET PROFIT MARGIN | EMPLOYEES |
|---|---|---|---|---|
| **12/06** | 15,895 | 1,210 | 7.6% | 53,700 |
| **12/05** | 15,701 | 978 | 6.2% | 55,200 |
| **12/04** | 15,722 | 859 | 5.5% | 58,100 |
| **12/03** | 15,701 | 360 | 2.3% | 61,100 |
| **12/02** | 15,849 | 91 | 0.6% | 67,800 |
| **Annual Growth** | 0.1% | 91.0% | — | (5.7%) |

### 2006 Year-End Financials

Debt ratio: 80.5%
Return on equity: 18.1%
Cash ($ mil.): 1,781
Current ratio: 1.86
Long-term debt ($ mil.): 5,702
No. of shares (mil.): 946
Dividends
Yield: —
Payout: —
Market value ($ mil.): 16,038

### Stock History

NYSE: XRX

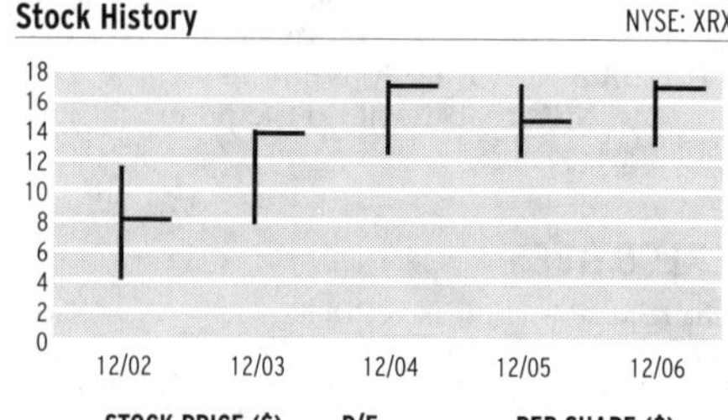


| | STOCK PRICE ($) FY Close | P/E High/Low | PER SHARE ($) Earnings | Dividends | Book Value |
|---|---|---|---|---|---|
| **12/06** | 16.95 | 14 11 | 1.22 | — | 7.48 |
| **12/05** | 14.65 | 18 13 | 0.94 | — | 7.74 |
| **12/04** | 17.01 | 20 15 | 0.86 | — | 6.53 |
| **12/03** | 13.80 | 39 22 | 0.36 | — | 5.85 |
| **12/02** | 8.05 | 573210 | 0.02 | — | 3.24 |
| **Annual Growth** | 20.5% | — — | 179.5% | — | 23.3% |

# Xilinx, Inc.

Xilinx is programmed to give you the gate. The company is a top supplier of field-programmable gate arrays (FPGAs) and complex programmable logic devices (CPLDs). Customers can program these integrated circuits to perform specific functions, thereby achieving greater design flexibility while cutting time to market. Xilinx also offers a broad range of design software and intellectual property used to customize its chips. The company sells to manufacturers — including Agilent, Cisco Systems, IBM, and Sony — in the telecommunications, computer, aerospace, industrial control, and networking markets.

Customers outside the US account for about 60% of the company's sales.

Xilinx outsources manufacturing to Seiko Epson, Toshiba, and United Microelectronics. Like other fabless semiconductor companies, Xilinx plows money into R&D, since it is free of capital expenditures for wafer fabrication. The company spends about 20% of annual sales on R&D, which is typical for leading-edge semiconductor suppliers.

It has also formed scores of development alliances with other chip makers, chip equipment manufacturers, and suppliers of design software and services. The company expanded its offerings with its 2004 purchase of Triscend, a maker of configurable microcontroller chips.

Capital Research and Management owns nearly 14% of Xilinx, while its affiliate, Capital Group International, holds more than 12% of the company. T. Rowe Price has an equity stake of about 12%. UBS owns around 10%.

## HISTORY

In 1984 Bernie Vonderschmitt, Ross Freeman, and Jim Barnett started Xilinx when ZiLOG, their employer, rejected the idea of investing in a programmable-chip operation. Xilinx introduced the first field-programmable gate array (FPGA) the next year. Successive products featured more logic gates, providing greater computing power. A chip with up to 5,000 usable logic gates came out in 1987; three years later that number quadrupled. (Freeman died in 1989; Barnett left the company in 1990, the year Xilinx went public.)

Xilinx acquired FPGA software developer NeoCAD in 1995. That year Xilinx formed a joint venture with United Microelectronics to build a wafer operation, United Silicon, in Taiwan. Xilinx brought in Hewlett-Packard veteran Willem Roelandts as CEO in 1996, replacing Vonderschmitt, who remained chairman until his retirement in 2003. (Roelandts then succeeded him in the chairman's role as well; Vonderschmitt died the next year.)

In 1999 Xilinx acquired the programmable-chips business of Philips Semiconductors (now NXP). Buoyed by a strong market and record sales, Xilinx expanded its Colorado plant in 2000 and acquired several small chip-design and software companies, including RocketChips (high-speed networking and telecom transceivers).

In 2001 it began another plant expansion that doubled the size of its Irish facility. The next year Xilinx announced a major multi-year deal with IBM under which IBM used some of its most advanced manufacturing techniques to produce high-end Xilinx FPGAs.

In 2004 Xilinx created the Ecosystem Growth Fund, a $100 million corporate venture capital fund targeted at investing in companies specializing in design software, digital signal processors, embedded processors, and high-speed connectivity. Xilinx is looking to grow beyond the $5 billion market for programmable logic into the much larger market for application-specific integrated circuits and application-specific standard parts, estimated at $36 billion. Earlier, in 1999, the company created the $75 million Technology Growth Fund, which has been used to invest in chip-design software companies, such as AccelChip and Synplicity.

Also in 2004 Xilinx sharpened its product focus by creating two new divisions to deal with embedded processing devices and with digital signal processors (DSPs).

In early 2006 the company acquired AccelChip for around $19 million in cash. Most of AccelChip's employees joined Xilinx's DSP division.

In 2006 Xilinx chartered another VC fund, the $75 million Asia Pacific Technology Fund. The company will invest in ventures creating applications for programmable logic or developing technologies to increase the adoption of programmable logic in a variety of electronics markets. Xilinx will put $500,000 to $5 million into startups based in China, India, Singapore, South Korea, and Taiwan, among other Asia/Pacific countries.

In the summer of 2007 Wim Roelandts set plans to retire as president and CEO, after guiding the company through a threefold increase in sales over 11 years as CEO. Roelandts will remain chairman of Xilinx after his CEO successor is named.

## EXECUTIVES

**Chairman, President, and CEO:** Willem P. (Wim) Roelandts, age 62, $772,500 pay
**EVP and General Manager, Advanced Platforms Group:** Iain M. Morris, age 50
**SVP and CFO:** Jon A. Olson, age 53, $381,250 pay
**VP and CTO:** Ivo Bolsens
**VP and Managing Director, Xilinx Ireland:** Paul McCambridge
**VP and General Manager, DSP Division:** Omid Tahernia, age 46, $303,750 pay
**VP and General Manager, Design Software Division:** Bruce Talley
**VP and General Manager, CPLD Division:** David Loftus
**VP, Embedded & Signal Processing:** Mark Aaldering
**VP, Product Technology and Reliability Engineering:** Vincent Tong
**VP, Worldwide Marketing:** Sandeep S. Vij, age 41
**VP, Worldwide Operations:** Boon Chye (B. C.) Ooi, age 53, $290,250 pay
**VP, Worldwide Sales and Services:** Patrick W. Little, age 44, $356,250 pay
**VP, Worldwide Human Resources:** Shelly Begun
**VP and CIO:** Kevin Cooney
**VP Sales:** Jim Ball
**VP Finance and Corporate Controller:** Doug Bettinger
**VP and Treasurer:** Eddie Lee
**President, Xilinx, K.K.:** Hitoshi Yoshizawa, age 57
**Worldwide Public Relations:** Lisa Washington
**Auditors:** Ernst & Young LLP

## LOCATIONS

**HQ:** Xilinx, Inc.
2100 Logic Dr., San Jose, CA 95124
**Phone:** 408-559-7778 **Fax:** 408-559-7114
**Web:** www.xilinx.com

Xilinx has production facilities in Ireland and the US. The company also has design centers and sales offices in Belgium, Canada, China, Finland, France, Germany, Hong Kong, Israel, Italy, Japan, Singapore, South Korea, Sweden, Taiwan, the UK, and the US.

### 2007 Sales

| | $ mil. | % of total |
|---|---|---|
| North America | | |
| US | 727.4 | 39 |
| Other countries | 3.9 | — |
| Asia/Pacific | | |
| Japan | 217.9 | 12 |
| China | 159.4 | 9 |
| Other countries | 307.2 | 17 |
| Europe | 426.9 | 23 |
| **Total** | **1,842.7** | **100** |

## PRODUCTS/OPERATIONS

### 2007 Sales

| | $ mil. | % of total |
|---|---|---|
| Mainstream products | 1,004.2 | 54 |
| New products | 416.8 | 23 |
| Base products | 317.2 | 17 |
| Support products | 104.5 | 6 |
| **Total** | **1,842.7** | **100** |

### 2007 Sales by Market

| | % of total |
|---|---|
| Communications | 45 |
| Storage & servers | 10 |
| Consumer, automotive, industrial & other | 45 |
| **Total** | **100** |

### Selected Products

Integrated circuits
- Complex programmable logic devices (CoolRunner)
- Field-programmable gate arrays (EasyPath, Spartan, Virtex)

Software design tools
- Alliance series (logic device design tool)
- Foundation series (low-cost design tool for logic devices)
- WebPACK (free, downloadable CPLD and FPGA design tools)

## COMPETITORS

Actel
Altera
Altium Limited
AMI Semiconductor
ARC
Atmel
Cypress Semiconductor
Fujitsu
IBM Microelectronics
Lattice Semiconductor
LOGIC Devices
LSI Corp.
MathStar
NEC Electronics
PLX Technology
QuickLogic
Texas Instruments

## HISTORICAL FINANCIALS

Company Type: Public

### Income Statement

FYE: March 31

| | REVENUE ($ mil.) | NET INCOME ($ mil.) | NET PROFIT MARGIN | EMPLOYEES |
|---|---|---|---|---|
| **3/07** | 1,843 | 351 | 19.0% | 3,353 |
| **3/06** | 1,726 | 354 | 20.5% | 3,295 |
| **3/05** | 1,573 | 313 | 19.9% | 3,050 |
| **3/04** | 1,398 | 303 | 21.7% | 2,770 |
| **3/03** | 1,156 | 126 | 10.9% | 2,612 |
| **Annual Growth** | 12.4% | 29.2% | — | 6.4% |

### 2007 Year-End Financials

| | |
|---|---|
| Debt ratio: 56.4% | No. of shares (mil.): 296 |
| Return on equity: 15.6% | Dividends |
| Cash ($ mil.): 1,138 | Yield: 1.4% |
| Current ratio: 5.60 | Payout: 35.3% |
| Long-term debt ($ mil.): 1,000 | Market value ($ mil.): 7,614 |

**Stock History** NASDAQ (GS): XLNX

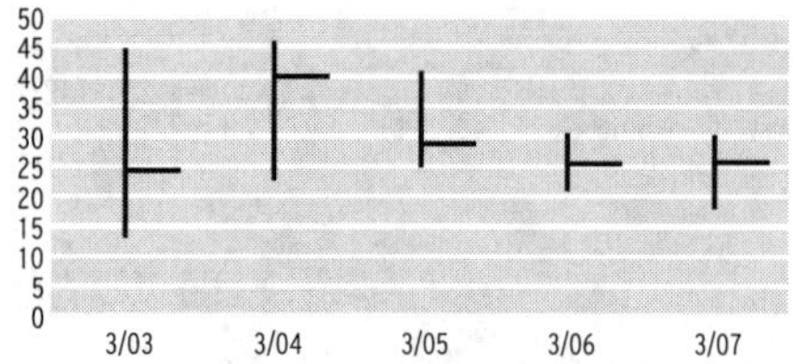

|  | STOCK PRICE ($) FY Close | P/E High/Low |  | PER SHARE ($) Earnings | Dividends | Book Value |
|---|---|---|---|---|---|---|
| 3/07 | 25.73 | 29 | 18 | 1.02 | 0.36 | 5.99 |
| 3/06 | 25.46 | 30 | 21 | 1.00 | 0.28 | 7.96 |
| 3/05 | 28.78 | 46 | 29 | 0.87 | 0.20 | 7.64 |
| 3/04 | 39.97 | 53 | 27 | 0.85 | — | 7.16 |
| 3/03 | 24.30 | 123 | 37 | 0.36 | — | 5.75 |
| Annual Growth | 1.4% | — | — | 29.7% | 34.2% | 1.0% |

# Yahoo! Inc.

Internet users around the world are cheering for this company. Yahoo! is the leading online information portal, drawing more than 400 million people to its network of Web sites with a mix of news, entertainment, and online shopping, as well as its search engine and Internet directory. The company also offers registered users personalized Web pages, e-mail, and message boards. Yahoo! publishes content in more than 20 languages. It generates most of its revenue through advertising sales, but it also charges subscriptions for premium services. In addition, Yahoo! provides online marketing and other commercial services and it offers Internet access through partnerships with telecommunications companies.

A pioneer in Internet search and navigation, the company's ever-growing collection of content and services has made it one of the best-known online brands and one of the most popular Internet destinations; however, it is facing increasing competition as the Internet has increasingly become a major channel for people to communicate and receive news, information, and entertainment. Google is capitalizing on its position as the most popular search engine to rapidly expand its range of content and services, while Microsoft's MSN portal has launched its own search engine technology and search-targeted ad capabilities.

In response, the company in 2007 introduced Yahoo SmartAds, a product that includes tools to help marketers create custom online advertising aimed at specific groups of buyers. It also acquired online advertising exchange Right Media for $650 million shortly after Google purchased rival ad distribution network DoubleClick. Yahoo! has also redesigned its home page with a simpler, cleaner layout, similar to those of Google and MSN. In addition, it launched a new search marketing system. The new search system includes a new ranking model and personalization services designed to provide Yahoo! users with more relevant search results and Yahoo! advertisers with more valuable customer leads.

The company's branded Internet access is offered in the US in partnership with AT&T and Verizon; it works with BT Group in the UK and Rogers Communications in Canada.

In 2007 co-founder Jerry Yang replaced Terry Semel as CEO (Semel remained as executive chairman); the shakeup came as a result of pressure from investors unhappy with the company's performance.

In 2006 Yahoo! formed a strategic partnership with Seven Network Limited, an Australian media company, to form Yahoo! 7, the result of a combination of Yahoo! Australia, and Seven's online, TV, and magazine operations. Also in 2006 Yahoo! combined its Spanish-language US Web site with Telemundo's site in order to target the growing Hispanic audience on the Web.

Founders and "chief Yahoo!s" David Filo and Yang own 6% and 4%, respectively, of Yahoo!.

## HISTORY

David Filo and Jerry Yang began developing the Yahoo! search engine and directory while students at Stanford in 1994. By the end of that year, their Web site was attracting hundreds of thousands of visitors. The next year they incorporated the business and tapped former Motorola executive Timothy Koogle as president. Revenue also began flowing in 1995 when Yahoo! started selling ad space on its Web site. The company went public the next year and share prices soared. Yahoo! teamed with SOFTBANK and its affiliates to form Yahoo! Japan and Yahoo! Europe in 1996.

The company's growth continued in 1998 with acquisitions of Viaweb (e-commerce software), WebCal (Internet scheduling products), and Yoyodyne (Internet direct marketing).

Branching into audio, the company launched its Yahoo! Radio broadcast Internet radio service in 1999. Yahoo's $3.7 billion acquisition of GeoCities and the more than $5 billion purchase of broadcast.com in 1999 stoked the Internet consolidation trend. Koogle was also named chairman in 1999.

Yahoo! waded into business-to-business waters in 2000, launching its Yahoo! B2B Marketplace. The company also took a minority stake in Internet phone services firm Net2Phone and acquired e-mail communications firm eGroups for about $430 million. Later in 2000 Yahoo! dropped Inktomi as its search engine provider and switched to Google.

In the wake of a November 2000 French court order requiring Yahoo! to bar French users from accessing Nazi-related items for sale on its auction sites, the company banned hate material from its auction Web sites in 2001. (It also stopped the sale of adult videos on its shopping sites that year.) To add a new source of revenue, Yahoo! announced it would begin charging fees to list items; 90% of its users later abandoned the site. With advertising revenue declining and profits in danger, Koogle said that year he would step down, and the company announced that it would lay off about 400 staff members (later adding another 300 to that figure).

Former Warner Bros. executive Terry Semel was tapped as Koogle's replacement in 2001. Yahoo! went further into the digital music world by acquiring LAUNCH (now rebranded as Yahoo! Music). The company also added e-books to Yahoo! Shopping. In other efforts to diversify its revenue streams, Yahoo! won an unsolicited takeover bid for HotJobs.com (which had already agreed to be acquired by TMP Worldwide, now Monster Worldwide) late in 2001.

In 2003 Yahoo! purchased Inktomi and Overture Services (now Yahoo! Search Marketing), gaining additional search technology and paid inclusion services.

Following a boost in online advertising revenue and paid search performance, in 2004 Yahoo! reported the most successful quarter in the company's history and approved a 2-for-1 stock split. Yahoo! paid $1 billion for a 40% stake in Alibaba.com, a Chinese e-commerce company, in 2005.

In 2005 it bought Flickr, a service for posting and sharing photos online, as well as del.icio.us, a service used to store and share Internet bookmarks. It also launched its own Web logging (blogging) service called Yahoo! 360 and picked up entertainment polling site Bix.com in 2006. The company introduced its Web video service, Yahoo! Video, in 2006.

Bowing to pressure from investors, the company appointed Yang to replace Semel as CEO the following year. (Semel remained as executive chairman.)

## EXECUTIVES

**Chairman:** Terry S. Semel, age 64
**CEO and Director:** Jerry Yang, age 38
**Chief Yahoo!:** David Filo, age 40
**President:** Susan L. (Sue) Decker, age 44
**CFO, Finance and Administration:** Blake J. Jorgensen, age 47
**EVP Global Sales:** Gregory G. (Greg) Coleman
**EVP, General Counsel, and Secretary:** Michael (Mike) Callahan, age 38, $525,000 pay
**EVP Research and Strategic Data Solutions and Chief Data Officer:** Usama Fayyad
**EVP Connected Life Division:** Marco Boerries
**EVP Network Division:** Jeff Weiner
**EVP Platforms and Infrastructure Division:** Ashvinkumar (Ash) Patel
**SVP Finance and Chief Accounting Officer:** Michael A. (Mick) Murray, age 50
**SVP Human Resources and Chief People Yahoo!:** Elizabeth P. (Libby) Sartain
**SVP Broadband and Mobile:** Steve Boom
**SVP Communications, Community, and Front Doors:** Brad Garlinghouse
**SVP; EVP and General Manager, HotJobs.com:** Daniel J. (Dan) Finnigan
**SVP Engineering, Search, and Search Marketing:** Qi Lu
**SVP Marketplaces:** Hilary A. Schneider
**SVP Search and Listings:** Tim Cadogan
**SVP and Chief Communications Officer:** Jill Nash
**Head of Customer Experience Division and Chief Marketing Officer:** Cammie W. Dunaway, age 44
**Auditors:** PricewaterhouseCoopers LLP

## LOCATIONS

**HQ:** Yahoo! Inc.
701 1st Ave., Sunnyvale, CA 94089
**Phone:** 408-349-3300 **Fax:** 408-349-3301
**Web:** www.yahoo.com

Yahoo! operates localized versions of its Web site in 25 countries and has offices in the Asia/Pacific region, as well as in Europe, North America, and South America.

**2006 Sales**

|  | $ mil. | % of total |
|---|---|---|
| US | 4,366 | 68 |
| Other countries | 2,060 | 32 |
| **Total** | **6,426** | **100** |

## PRODUCTS/OPERATIONS

**2006 Sales**

|  | $ mil. | % of total |
|---|---|---|
| Marketing services | 5,627 | 88 |
| Fees | 799 | 12 |
| **Total** | **6,426** | **100** |

### Selected Offerings

Communications, Communities and Front Doors
- Communications
  - Yahoo! Mail
  - Yahoo! Messenger with Voice
- Communities
  - Yahoo! Communities
  - Yahoo! Photos
- Front Doors
  - My Yahoo!
  - Yahoo! Front Page

Connected Life
- Yahoo! Broadband
- Yahoo! Mobile

Information and Entertainment
- Information
  - Yahoo! Finance
  - Yahoo! Food
  - Yahoo! Health
  - Yahoo! News
  - Yahoo! Tech
- Entertainment
  - Yahoo! Games
  - Yahoo! Movies
  - Yahoo! Music
  - Yahoo! Sports
  - Yahoo! TV

Marketplace
- Kelkoo
- Yahoo! Auctions
- Yahoo! Autos
- Yahoo! Personals
- Yahoo! Real Estate
- Yahoo! Shopping
- Yahoo! Travel

Search
- Yahoo! Local
- Yahoo! Maps
- Yahoo! Search
- Yahoo! Toolbar
- Yahoo! Yellow Pages

## COMPETITORS

24/7 Real Media
About Inc.
Amazon.com
AOL
Apple
aQuantive
CBS Interactive
Citysearch
craigslist
Daum Communications
Disney Internet Group
DoubleClick
eBay
Google
IAC Search & Media
InfoSpace
LookSmart
MIVA
Monster
MSN
RealNetworks

## HISTORICAL FINANCIALS

Company Type: Public

**Income Statement** FYE: December 31

| | REVENUE ($ mil.) | NET INCOME ($ mil.) | NET PROFIT MARGIN | EMPLOYEES |
|---|---|---|---|---|
| 12/06 | 6,426 | 751 | 11.7% | 11,400 |
| 12/05 | 5,258 | 1,896 | 36.1% | 9,800 |
| 12/04 | 3,575 | 840 | 23.5% | 7,600 |
| 12/03 | 1,625 | 238 | 14.6% | 5,500 |
| 12/02 | 953 | 43 | 4.5% | 3,600 |
| Annual Growth | 61.1% | 104.7% | — | 33.4% |

**2006 Year-End Financials**

Debt ratio: 8.2%
Return on equity: 8.5%
Cash ($ mil.): 2,601
Current ratio: 2.54
Long-term debt ($ mil.): 750
No. of shares (mil.): 1,360
Dividends
Yield: —
Payout: —
Market value ($ mil.): 34,741

**Stock History** NASDAQ (GS): YHOO

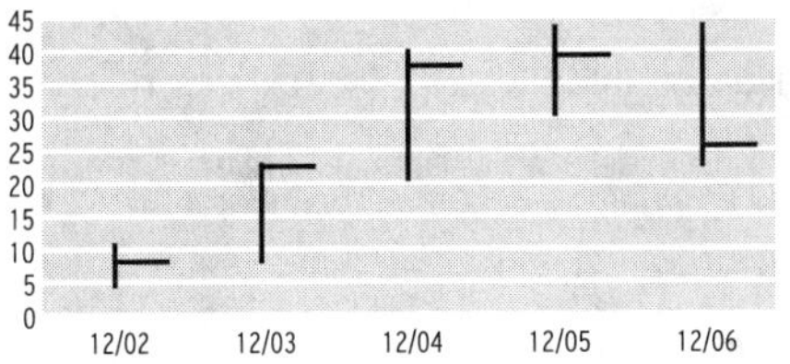

| | STOCK PRICE ($) FY Close | P/E High | P/E Low | PER SHARE ($) Earnings | Dividends | Book Value |
|---|---|---|---|---|---|---|
| 12/06 | 25.54 | 84 | 44 | 0.52 | — | 6.73 |
| 12/05 | 39.18 | 34 | 24 | 1.28 | — | 5.99 |
| 12/04 | 37.68 | 995 | 514 | 0.04 | — | 5.13 |
| 12/03 | 22.51 | 123 | 45 | 0.19 | — | 6.60 |
| 12/02 | 8.18 | 305 | 128 | 0.04 | — | 3.80 |
| Annual Growth | 32.9% | — | — | 89.9% | — | 15.4% |

# YRC Worldwide

To find the wizard of nationwide less-than-truckload (LTL) transportation, just follow the yellow brick roadway to holding company YRC Worldwide, the largest LTL service provider in the US. (LTL carriers consolidate freight from multiple shippers into a single trailer.) The company's long-haul units, Yellow Transportation and Roadway Express, together operate some 17,500 tractors and 64,200 trailers from a network of about 670 terminals. YRC Worldwide also has assembled a collection of regional LTL carriers. The company's YRC Logistics (formerly Meridian IQ) unit provides logistics services.

Yellow Transportation and Roadway Express are two of the three major unionized long-haul LTL carriers in the US, along with smaller Arkansas Best. The companies face competition from increasingly strong regional LTL carriers, which generally are not unionized and thus are able to offer lower-cost services.

In an effort to make its long-haul units more profitable, YRC Worldwide in 2007 brought together Yellow Transportation and Roadway Express under a new umbrella organization, YRC National Transportation. The carriers will keep their own brands, however.

To better compete for regional business, YRC Worldwide in 2005 bought rival USF. The YRC Regional Transportation operating segment includes LTL carriers New Penn Motor Express (a former Roadway unit), USF Holland, and USF Reddaway, as well as a truckload carrier, USF Glen Moore.

YRC Worldwide hopes to be a stronger competitor to integrated transportation providers such as UPS and FedEx, and it has expanded its menu of services to include more next-day offerings. It made strides to expand internationally in mid-2007 when it agreed to acquire Shanghai Jiayu Logistics Limited, a leading LTL carrier in China. Shanghai Jiayu owns 300 tractors and operates a network of more than 3,000 vehicles.

## HISTORY

In 1924 A. J. Harrell established a trucking company in conjunction with his Oklahoma City bus line and Yellow Cab franchise. Harrell's Yellow Transit trucking operation hauled less-than-truckload (LTL) shipments between Oklahoma City and Tulsa. By 1944 Yellow had more than 50 independent subsidiaries in Illinois, Indiana, Kansas, Kentucky, Missouri, and Texas. That year the company was sold to an investment firm and renamed Yellow Transit Freight Lines. But Yellow's policy of paying high dividends stunted its growth, and by 1951 it faced bankruptcy.

In 1952 George Powell Sr. took over and turned Yellow around. His son George Powell Jr. became CEO in 1957, and the company went public two years later. George Jr. focused the company on long-haul interstate shipments and started buying up other trucking companies.

In 1965 Yellow expanded to the West Coast and the Southeast by purchasing Watson-Wilson Transportation System. Changing its name to Yellow Freight System (1968), the company acquired part of Norwalk Truck Lines and its routes in the Northeast (1970) and Adley Express (1972), providing new East Coast routes. Yellow extended routes into the Pacific Northwest by buying Republic Freight Systems in 1975. Its 1978 purchase of Braswell Motor Freight Lines consolidated its routes in California, Texas, and the Southeast. Yellow's only deviation from route acquisitions was its $4 million investment in oil firm Overland Energy in 1976, which it dissolved in the early 1980s.

The company was unprepared, however, when Congress deregulated trucking routes and shipping rates in 1980. Yellow upgraded its aging depots and terminals, but profits still declined by 1983. In 1982 Yellow Freight formed a holding corporation (renamed Yellow Corporation in 1992). George Powell III took over from his father as CEO in 1990. Yellow purchased Preston Trucking, an overnight freight hauler, in 1992.

In 1994 Yellow Freight was hit by a 24-day Teamsters' strike that allowed nonunion carriers to gain a chunk of its market. The next year, struggling during industry price wars, it reported a $30 million loss. Yellow laid off about 250 employees, mostly from Yellow Freight. George III resigned in 1996, and Maurice "Mr. Fix-it" Myers became CEO. Myers began moving the firm from a one-size-fits-all LTL trucker to a more flexible, customer-responsive trucking and logistics firm.

In 1997 Yellow Freight was restructured into decentralized business units to improve customer service, and hundreds of workers were laid off. The misfortunes of other companies also created good fortune for Yellow: UPS went on strike, and rail traffic was still snarled from the 1996 Union Pacific-Southern Pacific merger.

To expand international operations, Yellow created YCS International in 1998 (renamed Yellow Global in 2000). It also secured a five-year labor contract with its unions, ending the danger of a strike. Loss-making Preston was sold to three company executives, and Yellow acquired regional carriers Action Express (1998) and Jevic Transportation (1999).

Myers drove off into the sunset in 1999 to take over another troubled giant, Waste Management, and Yellow Freight president William Zollars became CEO of Yellow Corp. In 2000 Yellow and two venture capital firms set up online transportation marketplace transportation.com to provide freight-forwarding and multimodal brokerage services.

Yellow integrated Action Express and WestEx into Saia Motor Freight Line in 2001. The next year Yellow renamed its Yellow Freight subsidiary Yellow Transportation. The company created SCS Transportation to act as a holding company for its regional, nonunion carriers Saia and Jevic. Also in 2002, Yellow combined transportation.com with its other logistics services to form Meridian IQ.

Yellow spun off SCS Transportation (later Saia, Inc.) in 2002. The next year, Yellow and other leading LTL carriers negotiated a new contract with the Teamsters union.

Also in 2003, Yellow bought rival Roadway and became Yellow Roadway Corporation. The company expanded in 2005 with the acquisition of USF.

Yellow Roadway changed its name to YRC Worldwide in January 2006. In June 2007, it also changed the name of its Meridian IQ unit to YRC Logistics.

## EXECUTIVES

**Chairman, President, and CEO:** William D. (Bill) Zollars, age 60, $1,000,000 pay
**EVP, Human Resources:** Steven T. (Steve) Yamasaki, age 52
**EVP Enterprise Solutions Group and Chief Marketing Officer:** Gregory A. Reid
**SVP and CFO:** Donald G. (Don) Barger Jr., age 64, $437,500 pay
**SVP, General Counsel, and Secretary:** Daniel J. (Dan) Churay, age 44
**SVP and CIO:** Michael K. Rapken
**VP, Controller, and Chief Accounting Officer:** Paul F. Liljegren, age 52
**VP, Investor Relations and Treasurer:** Todd M. Hacker
**President and CEO, YRC Logistics; President and CEO, USF Logistics:** James D. (Jim) Ritchie
**President and CEO, New Penn Motor Express:** Steven D. (Steve) Gast
**President and CEO, YRC National Transportation:** Michael J. (Mike) Smid, age 51
**President and CEO, YRC Regional Transportation:** James D. (Jim) Staley, age 56, $532,500 pay
**President, Roadway Express:** Terrence M. (Terry) Gilbert
**President, Yellow Transportation:** Maynard Skarka
**Auditors:** KPMG LLP

## LOCATIONS

**HQ:** YRC Worldwide Inc.
10990 Roe Ave., Overland Park, KS 66211
**Phone:** 913-696-6100 **Fax:** 913-696-6116
**Web:** www.yrcw.com

## PRODUCTS/OPERATIONS

**2006 Sales**

| | $ mil. | % of total |
|---|---|---|
| Yellow Transportation | 3,456 | 35 |
| Roadway | 3,418 | 34 |
| Regional Transportation | 2,441 | 25 |
| Meridian IQ | 604 | 6 |
| **Total** | **9,919** | **100** |

## COMPETITORS

Arkansas Best
Central Freight Lines
C.H. Robinson Worldwide
Con-way Inc.
Estes Express
FedEx Freight
J.B. Hunt
Landstar System
Menlo Worldwide
Old Dominion Freight
Saia, Inc.
Schneider National
UPS Freight

## HISTORICAL FINANCIALS

Company Type: Public

**Income Statement** FYE: December 31

| | REVENUE ($ mil.) | NET INCOME ($ mil.) | NET PROFIT MARGIN | EMPLOYEES |
|---|---|---|---|---|
| **12/06** | 9,919 | 277 | 2.8% | 66,000 |
| **12/05** | 8,742 | 288 | 3.3% | 68,000 |
| **12/04** | 6,768 | 184 | 2.7% | 50,000 |
| **12/03** | 3,069 | 41 | 1.3% | 50,000 |
| **12/02** | 2,624 | (94) | — | 23,000 |
| **Annual Growth** | 39.4% | — | — | 30.2% |

**2006 Year-End Financials**

Debt ratio: 48.3%
Return on equity: 13.4%
Cash ($ mil.): 76
Current ratio: 1.17
Long-term debt ($ mil.): 1,059
No. of shares (mil.): 57
Dividends
Yield: —
Payout: —
Market value ($ mil.): 2,158

**Stock History** NASDAQ (GS): YRCW

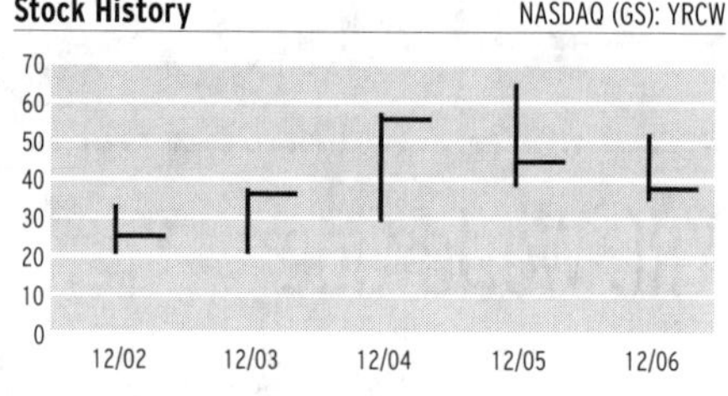


| | STOCK PRICE ($) FY Close | P/E High | P/E Low | PER SHARE ($) Earnings | Dividends | Book Value |
|---|---|---|---|---|---|---|
| **12/06** | 37.73 | 11 | 7 | 4.74 | — | 38.33 |
| **12/05** | 44.61 | 13 | 8 | 5.07 | — | 33.80 |
| **12/04** | 55.71 | 15 | 8 | 3.75 | — | 24.66 |
| **12/03** | 36.17 | 28 | 16 | 1.33 | — | 20.92 |
| **12/02** | 25.19 | — | — | (3.31) | — | 12.17 |
| **Annual Growth** | 10.6% | — | — | — | — | 33.2% |

# YUM! Brands

Chicken, pizza, and tacos — oh my! YUM! Brands is the largest fast-food operator in the world in terms of number of locations, with more than 34,500 outlets in more than 100 countries. (It trails only hamburger giant McDonald's in sales.) Its flagship chains include #1 chicken fryer KFC (with more than 14,000 units), top pizza joint Pizza Hut (about 12,600), and quick-service Mexican leader Taco Bell (more than 5,800). YUM! also operates the Long John Silver's seafood chain, along with several hundred A&W root beer and burger stands. The company operates a little more than 20% of its restaurants; the rest are either franchised or licensed locations.

While the YUM! Brands restaurants differ in concept and menu, its flagship chains dominate their respective markets. Taco Bell holds a 60% market share in the Mexican fast-food segment, while KFC commands more than 45% of the quick-service chicken business. Pizza Hut leads its fragmented segment with 15% of the market, and Long John Silver's represents about a third of the limited-service seafood segment.

Part of the company's strategy for driving growth continues to involve co-branding its restaurants by combining two or more concepts into a single location, which helps generate more traffic and higher sales volume from the same piece of real estate. It has more than 3,600 multibranded locations, most of which offer food from two of its famous brands.

YUM! has also been aggressive in expanding its chains outside the US, topping more than 700 new locations for the seventh consecutive year in 2006. The company is particularly focused on the emerging market in China, where it has more than 2,600 restaurants (primarily KFC) accounting for more than 15% of YUM! Brands' revenue. In the UK, YUM! acquired the 50% stake it didn't own in Pizza Hut (UK) from joint venture partner Whitbread.

Meanwhile, the company is investing in reinvigorating and expanding its two newest chains, Long John Silver's and A&W. YUM! has shuttered several underperforming seafood locations and is continuing to develop new menu items to drive increasing sales. Its drive-up burger chain, meanwhile, has undergone a slow but steady expansion, mostly through co-branded units. YUM! Brands is also trying to raise the profile of its corporate identity through a partnership with hometown horse racing company Churchill Downs. Under the five-year sponsorship deal, Churchill Downs' world famous horse race will be known as "the Kentucky Derby presented by YUM! Brands."

## HISTORY

Yum! Brands took its original name, TRICON, from the three brand icons — KFC, Pizza Hut, and Taco Bell — it inherited from former parent PepsiCo. The soft drink company entered the fast-food business with its acquisition of Pizza Hut in 1977. The pizza chain had begun in 1958 when brothers Dan and Frank Carney borrowed $600 from their mother and opened the first Pizza Hut in Wichita, Kansas, with partner John Bender. Their first franchise opened the next year in Topeka, Kansas. By 1971 the company had become the world's largest pizza chain, with more than 1,000 restaurants. Pizza Hut went public the following year. The chain had grown to 3,000 locations by the time it was acquired.

In 1978 PepsiCo acquired Taco Bell. After trying other fast-food formats, Glen Bell settled on the Mexican-style market. He bought and sold several chains before beginning Taco Bell in Downey, California, in 1962. The first franchise was sold two years later, and by 1967 — the year after it went public — Taco Bell had more than 335 restaurants, most of them franchised.

KFC was acquired in 1986. It had been founded by Harland Sanders — that's Colonel Sanders to you — who developed his secret, 11-herbs-and-spices recipe and method of pressure-frying chicken during the 1930s. The Colonel began franchising the secret in 1952 and founded Kentucky Fried Chicken in 1955. More than 600 outlets in the US and Canada were open by 1963. It went public in 1969 and was operating some 6,600 units in 55 countries when it was acquired by PepsiCo.

Through these acquisitions, PepsiCo hoped to diversify and build sales channels for its beverages, but the company had also incurred a huge debt load and fast-food competition had intensified. As same-store sales faltered, shareholders clamored for PepsiCo to spin off the restaurants. Restaurant officials grumbled that PepsiCo put more effort into marketing blitzes than into building restaurants (its 1991 renaming of Kentucky Fried Chicken as KFC didn't fool many health-conscious consumers).

In 1997 PepsiCo created a new restaurant subsidiary, which it spun off in the fall as TRICON Global Restaurants. To improve cash flow, it stepped up efforts to close or franchise underperforming Pizza Huts and KFCs. TRICON also began opening "three-in-one" restaurants featuring all its brands under one roof. In 1998 it launched a Taco Bell advertising campaign featuring a bilingual Chihuahua; the sassy pooch quickly became a cultural icon.

In 1999 the KFC, Taco Bell, and Pizza Hut cooperatives joined to form Unified FoodService Purchasing, the largest purchasing cooperative for fast-food restaurants in the US. Also in 1999 TRICON spent some $2 billion on a massive *Star Wars: Episode I — The Phantom Menace* promotion that failed to increase traffic at its restaurants. Vice chairman David Novak took over as CEO in 2000.

In 2002 TRICON acquired Yorkshire Global Restaurants for $320 million, which brought Long John Silver's and A&W All-American Food Restaurants into the fold. Now a five-pack of well-known brands rather than a trio, TRICON changed its name to YUM! Brands.

Being market leaders did not save YUM!'s chains from the overall downturn in the economy, however, nor from the effects of changing eating habits as Americans sought healthier meal alternatives. KFC was hit particularly hard, prompting the company to appoint veteran Gregg Dedrick the chain's new president in 2003. Both KFC and Pizza Hut saw same-store sales and the number of transactions decline in the US during 2003.

In 2004 KFC opened its 1,000th restaurant in China, where the chain had been operating since 1987. As YUM! Brands' China operations continued to grow, it formed a separate division in 2005 to oversee its expansion.

## EXECUTIVES

**Chairman, President, and CEO:** David C. Novak, age 54, $4,229,111 pay
**COO and Chief Development Officer:** Peter R. Hearl, age 55
**CFO:** Richard T. (Rick) Carucci, age 48
**SVP, General Counsel, Secretary, and Chief Franchise Policy Officer:** Christian L. Campbell, age 55, $1,091,419 pay
**SVP Concept Design and Multibranding:** Terry Davenport, age 50
**SVP Finance and Corporate Controller:** Ted F. Knopf, age 53
**SVP Corporate Strategy and Treasurer:** Robert C. (Chris) Kreidler, age 50
**SVP Public Affairs:** Jonathan D. Blum, age 47
**VP Government and Community Affairs:** Brian Riendeau
**VP Investor Relations:** Tim Jerzyk
**VP Public Relations:** Amy Sherwood
**VP Quality Assurance:** Michael Liewen, age 51
**President, US Brand Building:** Emil J. Brolick, age 59
**President, YUM! Restaurants China:** J. Samuel (Sam) Su, age 53
**President, YUM! Restaurants International:** Graham D. Allan, age 50, $1,026,262 pay
**President and Chief Concept Officer, KFC:** Gregg R. Dedrick, age 48, $1,324,896 pay
**President, Pizza Hut:** Scott Bergren, age 60
**President, Taco Bell:** Greg Creed, age 50
**CIO:** Delaney Bellinger
**Chief People Officer:** Anne P. Byerlein, age 47
**Director Public Affairs:** Karen Sherman
**Auditors:** KPMG LLP

## LOCATIONS

**HQ:** YUM! Brands, Inc.
1441 Gardiner Ln., Louisville, KY 40213
**Phone:** 502-874-8300 **Fax:** 502-874-8790
**Web:** www.yum.com

Yum! Brands has more than 34,500 restaurants in more than 100 countries worldwide.

### 2006 Sales

| | $ mil. | % of total |
|---|---|---|
| US | 5,603 | 59 |
| International | | |
| China | 1,638 | 17 |
| Other countries | 2,320 | 24 |
| **Total** | **9,561** | **100** |

## PRODUCTS/OPERATIONS

### 2006 Locations

| | No. |
|---|---|
| Franchised & licensed | |
| Franchised | 23,516 |
| Licensed | 2,137 |
| Company-owned | 7,736 |
| Affiliated | 1,206 |
| **Total** | **34,595** |

## COMPETITORS

AFC Enterprises
Arby's
Burger King
Chick-fil-A
CKE Restaurants
Dairy Queen
Domino's
Jack in the Box
Little Caesar's
McDonald's
Papa John's
Quiznos
Subway
Wendy's

## HISTORICAL FINANCIALS

Company Type: Public

### Income Statement

FYE: Last Saturday in December

| | REVENUE ($ mil.) | NET INCOME ($ mil.) | NET PROFIT MARGIN | EMPLOYEES |
|---|---|---|---|---|
| **12/06** | 9,561 | 824 | 8.6% | 280,000 |
| **12/05** | 9,349 | 762 | 8.2% | 272,000 |
| **12/04** | 9,011 | 740 | 8.2% | 256,000 |
| **12/03** | 8,380 | 617 | 7.4% | 265,000 |
| **12/02** | 7,757 | 583 | 7.5% | 244,000 |
| **Annual Growth** | 5.4% | 9.0% | — | 3.5% |

### 2006 Year-End Financials

Debt ratio: 142.3%
Return on equity: 57.1%
Cash ($ mil.): 325
Current ratio: 0.52
Long-term debt ($ mil.): 2,045
No. of shares (mil.): 265
Dividends
Yield: 0.9%
Payout: 17.8%
Market value ($ mil.): 7,791

### Stock History

NYSE: YUM

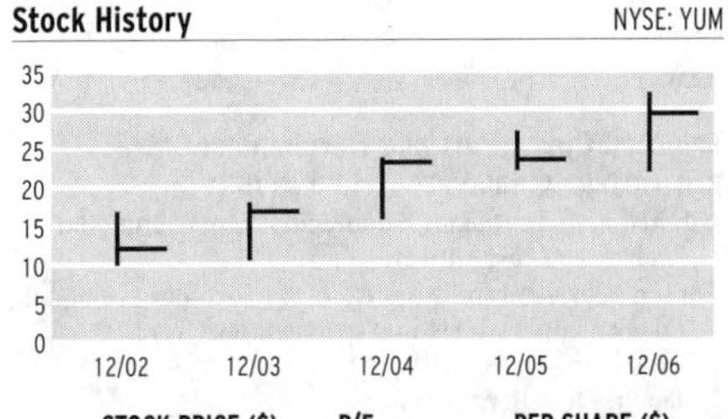


| | STOCK PRICE ($) FY Close | P/E High/Low | | PER SHARE ($) Earnings | Dividends | Book Value |
|---|---|---|---|---|---|---|
| **12/06** | 29.40 | 22 | 15 | 1.46 | 0.26 | 5.42 |
| **12/05** | 23.44 | 21 | 18 | 1.27 | 0.22 | 5.25 |
| **12/04** | 23.14 | 19 | 13 | 1.21 | 0.10 | 5.50 |
| **12/03** | 16.82 | 18 | 11 | 1.01 | — | 3.84 |
| **12/02** | 12.06 | 18 | 11 | 0.94 | — | 2.02 |
| **Annual Growth** | 25.0% | — | — | 11.6% | 61.2% | 28.0% |

# Zale Corporation

Zale is a flawed king of diamond sales. One of North America's largest specialty jewelry retailers, Zale sells diamond, colored stone, and gold jewelry (diamond fashion rings, semi-precious stones, earrings, gold chains); watches; and gift items at about 2,400 locations, mostly in malls, throughout the US, Canada, and Puerto Rico. The firm has four large chains aimed at different jewelry markets: Bailey Banks & Biddle Fine Jewelers, Gordon's Jewelers, Zales Jewelers, and Piercing Pagoda. Zale also operates nearly 140 jewelry outlet stores, runs about 250 stores in Canada under the Peoples Jewellers and Mappins Jewellers names, sells online, and offers jewelry insurance.

The company is in turnaround mode after a disastrous 2005 holiday season, in which Zale strayed from its diamond store roots to emphasize gold and silver jewelry. The merchandising misstep led to the termination of CEO Mary Forté in early 2006. Her replacement, Betsy Burton, is attempting to regain market share by returning to an emphasis on diamond sales. For the 2006 holiday season the jewelry chain revived its "Zales, the Diamond Store," campaign. Burton said in September 2006 that she expected the recovery at Zale to take 18 months. In August 2007 the company streamlined its merchandising, buying, and sourcing by centralizing those functions under just a couple of executives. It also created a COO position, eliminating the need for separate brand presidents.

A trip to the altar often begins with a trip to one of Zale's stores. Some 45% of sales come from bridal merchandise (engagement rings, bridal sets, diamond anniversary bands), while fashion jewelry and watches comprise the remaining 55%.

To reduce the possibility of cannibalizing sales, Zale has repositioned its jewelry chains. Zales Jewelers, the company's US and largest unit, accounts for 45% of the firms revenues. Zales sells moderately priced jewelry, watches, and gift items. Gordon's Jewelers, which once targeted Zale's customers, has been repositioned in the upper-moderate price range with merchandise that is more contemporary and regional. The Bailey Banks & Biddle Fine Jewelers division offers higher-end jewelry. Zale's Piercing Pagoda mall kiosks target customers shopping for low-priced jewelry.

Zale sells it baubles from more than 1,450 stores, 815 Piercing Pagoda kiosks, and 75 Peoples II carts in Canada.

## HISTORY

Russian immigrant Morris Zale opened his first jewelry store in Wichita Falls, Texas, in 1924. The store's most popular items were fountain pens. Zale advertised and offered credit ("a penny down, a dollar a week"); the two concepts were novel for the jewelry business of the day, and by 1937 the budding chain had seven stores.

The firm managed to survive the Depression — people were still getting married — and by 1941 it had 12 shops. It added upscale Houston jeweler Corrigan's three years later. Zale established buying offices in the diamond capitals of New York City and Antwerp, Belgium, which allowed it to buy wholesale. Sales were $10 million in 1946, the year the company moved its headquarters to Dallas.

Zale grew rapidly following WWII and had 50 stores by the mid-1950s. During that time the company became a fully integrated jeweler, buying raw goods and manufacturing its jewelry (including cutting and polishing its diamonds). Zale went public in 1957. It acquired Philadelphia-based Bailey Banks & Biddle in 1962 and became the world's largest retailer, with more than 400 stores, by the mid-1960s.

Spooked by the introduction of synthetic diamonds, the company began to diversify in 1965. It acquired a drugstore chain (Skillern); a line of airport tobacco/newsstand shops; and retailers of apparel, shoes (Butler), furniture, and sporting goods. By 1974 these operations represented half of Zale's sales.

Morris' son Donald became chairman in 1980. Zale began selling off its non-jewelry operations. Skillern went to Revco, Butler to Sears, and the sporting goods business to Oshman's.

The stumbling economy of the 1980s and the gold and diamond industries' uncharacteristic weakness rocked Zale. An $80 million restructuring charge contributed to its $60 million loss in 1986. That year Irving Gerstein, head of Canada's Peoples Jewellers and a 15% owner of Zale, joined with Austrian crystal firm Swarovski to buy Zale. Issuing junk bonds to finance the $650 million deal, each took an equal stake in the company.

Gerstein sold manufacturing operations, liquidated the company's diamond inventory, and cut its advertising budget. Zale looked healthy enough in 1989 to buy the 650-store Gordon's Jewelers chain. But a recession hurt sales in the early 1990s, and debt hindered the company's fiscal health.

Unable to make a junk bond payment in late 1991, Zale filed for bankruptcy protection early the next year. It emerged from bankruptcy in 1993 as a debt-free public company with 700 fewer stores. The following year Zale chose former Bon Marche CEO Robert DiNicola to lead its revival. DiNicola began adding new stores (especially the higher-end Bailey Banks & Biddle shops) and repositioned existing ones. In 1996 Zale bought Karten's Jewelers, a 20-store chain in New England.

In 1999 the company bought Peoples Jewellers (177 stores in Canada). COO Beryl Raff succeeded DiNicola as CEO that year. In 2000 the company partnered with WeddingChannel.com to offer wedding planning services online. Zale also sold its private-label credit card business to Associates First Capital Corporation. It then bought about 95% of US kiosk jeweler Piercing Pagoda. In 2001 DiNicola once again became chairman and CEO after Raff resigned, but DiNicola stepped down as CEO in 2002 and Mary Forté replaced him.

The company closed about 30 Bailey Banks & Biddle stores after the 2005 holiday season, citing poor performance.

Forté resigned in January 2006 after 11 years with the company and was replaced, on an interim basis, by director Betsy Burton. In March COO Sue Gove resigned after 25 years with Zale. An investigation of the company's accounting practices launched in April by the Securities and Exchange Commission was dropped with no action taken in September. Soon after the probe was announced, CFO Mark Lenz was put on indefinite administrative leave and later terminated for failing to disclose vendor payments in a timely manner. In July Burton, a former chief executive of Supercuts and PIP Printing, was named president and CEO permanently.

## EXECUTIVES

**Chairman:** Richard C. Marcus, age 68
**President, CEO, and Director:**
Mary Elizabeth (Betsy) Burton, age 55, $389,270 pay
**Acting Chief Administrative Officer, and Director:**
George R. Mihalko, age 51
**Group SVP and CFO:** Rodney Carter, age 48
**Group SVP and Chief Sourcing Officer:**
Gilbert P. (Gil) Hollander, age 53, $271,878 pay
**Group SVP and Chief Merchandising Officer:**
Steve Lang
**SVP; President, Bailey Banks & Biddle Fine Jewelers:**
Charles E. Fieramosca, age 58
**SVP; President, Zales the Diamond Store Outlet:**
Nancy O. Skinner, age 56
**SVP, Human Resources:** Mary Ann Doran, age 50
**SVP, Controller:** Cynthia T. Gordon, age 42
**SVP, Real Estate:** Stephen C. Massanelli, age 50
**SVP, Store Operations, Zale North America:**
Sterling Pope
**SVP, Downstream Supply Chain:** Susann C. Mayo, age 54
**SVP, E-Commerce:** Steven (Steve) Larkin, age 48
**SVP, CIO:** Mark A. Stone, age 48
**SVP, General Counsel, and Corporate Secretary:**
Hilary Molay, age 52
**SVP, Loss Prevention:** George J. Slicho, age 57
**Investor Relations and Public Relations:**
Melanie Rosewell
**Auditors:** KPMG LLP

## LOCATIONS

**HQ:** Zale Corporation
901 W. Walnut Hill Ln., Irving, TX 75038
**Phone:** 972-580-4000 **Fax:** 972-580-5523
**Web:** www.zalecorp.com

Zale has about 2,350 locations throughout the US, Canada, and Puerto Rico.

## PRODUCTS/OPERATIONS

### 2006 Stores/Kiosks

| | No. |
|---|---|
| Piercing Pagoda | 817 |
| Zales | 784 |
| Gordon's | 293 |
| Peoples | 175 |
| Zales Outlet | 131 |
| Peoples II | 76 |
| Bailey Banks & Biddle | 73 |
| **Total** | **2,349** |

### 2006 Sales

| | $ mil. | % of total |
|---|---|---|
| Zales (includes ZLC Direct) | 1,092.6 | 45 |
| Gordon's | 339.5 | 14 |
| Bailey Banks & Biddle | 309.3 | 13 |
| Piercing Pagoda | 268.9 | 11 |
| Peoples | 229.6 | 9 |
| Zales Outlet | 177.7 | 7 |
| Peoples II | 7.7 | — |
| Insurance | 13.6 | 1 |
| **Total** | **2,438.9** | **100** |

### Selected Operations and Merchandise

Bailey Banks & Biddle Fine Jewelers (higher-priced items, including diamond, precious stone, and gold jewelry; watches; giftware)
Gordon's Jewelers (mid-priced items, including regional and contemporary fashion-oriented jewelry)
Peoples Jewellers (Canada)
Mappins Jewellers (Canada)
Piercing Pagoda (mall-based, lower-priced jewelry kiosks)
Zales Jewelers (lower-priced items, including engagement rings, wedding bands, bridal sets, anniversary bands, cocktail rings, earrings, chains, watches, and pearls)
Zales.com (online sales)
Zales the Diamond Store Outlet (discounted new jewelry, pre-owned jewelry)

## COMPETITORS

Birks and Mayors
Blue Nile
Costco Wholesale
Crescent Jewelers
DGSE Companies
Elegant Illusions
Finlay Enterprises
Fortunoff
Friedman's Inc.
Helzberg Diamonds
J. C. Penney
Kroger
Macy's
QVC
Reeds Jewelers
Saks Inc.
SAM'S CLUB
Samuels Jewelers
Sears
Sterling Jewelers
Tiffany
Topaz Group
Ultra Stores
Wal-Mart
Whitehall Jewellers

## HISTORICAL FINANCIALS

Company Type: Public

### Income Statement

FYE: July 31

| | REVENUE ($ mil.) | NET INCOME ($ mil.) | NET PROFIT MARGIN | EMPLOYEES |
|---|---|---|---|---|
| **7/06** | 2,439 | 54 | 2.2% | 16,900 |
| **7/05** | 2,383 | 107 | 4.5% | 16,300 |
| **7/04** | 2,304 | 107 | 4.6% | 17,000 |
| **7/03** | 2,212 | (41) | — | 17,000 |
| **7/02** | 2,192 | 144 | 6.6% | 19,000 |
| **Annual Growth** | 2.7% | (21.9%) | — | (2.9%) |

### 2006 Year-End Financials

Debt ratio: 25.3%
Return on equity: 6.6%
Cash ($ mil.): 43
Current ratio: 2.60
Long-term debt ($ mil.): 203
No. of shares (mil.): 48
Dividends
Yield: —
Payout: —
Market value ($ mil.): 1,234

### Stock History

NYSE: ZLC

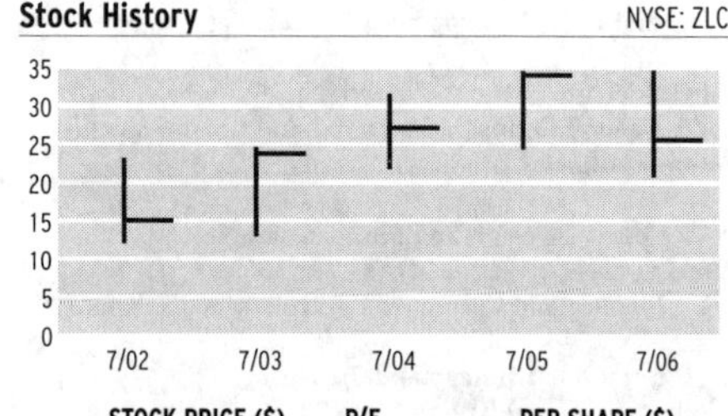


| | STOCK PRICE ($) FY Close | P/E High | P/E Low | PER SHARE ($) Earnings | PER SHARE ($) Dividends | PER SHARE ($) Book Value |
|---|---|---|---|---|---|---|
| **7/06** | 25.61 | 32 | 19 | 1.09 | — | 16.63 |
| **7/05** | 34.00 | 17 | 12 | 2.05 | — | 15.96 |
| **7/04** | 27.14 | 16 | 11 | 1.99 | — | 13.93 |
| **7/03** | 23.77 | — | — | (0.63) | — | 23.63 |
| **7/02** | 15.05 | 11 | 6 | 2.07 | — | 28.33 |
| **Annual Growth** | 14.2% | — | — | (14.8%) | — | (12.5%) |

# Zions Bancorporation

"The Lord hath founded Zion, and the poor of his people shall trust in it." Zions Bancorporation is happy to attract customers who aren't poor, too. Its subsidiary banks, including Zions First National Bank, Nevada State Bank, National Bank of Arizona, Vectra Bank Colorado, The Commerce Bank of Washington, California Bank & Trust, The Commerce Bank of Oregon, and Amegy Corporation (a Texas bank), operate about 470 branches in 10 western states. The banks provide retail and commercial banking, small business loans, and specialty financial services. Unlike many superregional banks, Zions prefers to operate under different local banking identities rather than a single brand over a vast swath of territory.

Acquired in 2005, Amegy has about 80 branches, primarily in the lucrative Dallas and Houston areas. Consistent with Zions' relatively hands-off approach, Amegy Bank kept its name and management after the deal was consummated. And Zions gained a presence in two of the more attractive banking markets in the US.

Zions Bancorporation's subsidiary banks provide retail and commercial financial services, including checking and savings accounts; credit life, health, and accident insurance; and trust and investment management services. Their lending includes a variety of personal and business loans (the company is a leading SBA and agricultural lender), credit cards, and lease financing.

Zions Bancorporation underwrites municipal revenue bonds through its Zions Investment Securities unit, which also provides discount brokerage services. The company also owns about a quarter of investment bank Roth Capital Partners, with an option to acquire more. It invests in financial services technologies, including check processing subsidiary NetDeposit, and platforms for trading US Treasury and Agency bonds on the Web.

## HISTORY

Zions' history is entwined with that of the Mormon Church. Founded by the church in 1873 to take over the savings department of the Bank of Deseret when it obtained a national charter, the new bank was headed by Brigham Young and other church leaders. The church kept control of the bank until 1960, when it sold its interest to a group of investors led by Roy Simmons, who moved it into the holding company that became Zions Bancorporation. It went public in 1966.

The company fared well in Utah, and when regulations changed in the mid-1980s to allow expansion into contiguous states, it moved quickly into Arizona (1986). Zions was hit by the commercial real estate crash and a downturn in the copper industry. Nevertheless, it remained healthy enough to pick up some Arizona bargain banks as they folded. In the 1990s it moved into California, Colorado, Idaho, and New Mexico. Acquisitions in 1997 and 1998 included Colorado's Aspen Bancshares, Tri-State Bank, and Vectra Banking Corp.; California's GB Bancorporation; and Nevada's Sun State Bank. None of the new family members adopted the Zions name.

In 1998 the company bought Sumitomo Bank of California, the state's #6 bank, and merged it with Grossmont Bank to form California Bank & Trust. It also created a new subsidiary, Digital Signature Trust Company, to issue, store, and verify digital certificates used in electronic documents and transactions.

In 1999 the firm increased its presence in California and Nevada with the purchases of Regency Bancorp and Pioneer Bancorp, respectively. Zions made plans to buy fellow Utah bank First Security in 2000, but the deal unraveled when the latter's share price plunged on news of low earnings. Had the sale been successful, the bank would have dropped the Zions name to further distance itself from its connection with the Mormon Church. First Security later agreed to be bought by Wells Fargo. Failing to make an entrance into investment banking via First Security, Zions in 2001 bought about a quarter of Los Angeles-based firm Roth Capital Partners.

Zions' wealth management unit Contango Capital Advisors acquired Phoenix-based BG Associates in 2006, and absorbed the firm into the Contango brand.

## EXECUTIVES

**Chairman, President, and CEO; Chairman, Zions First National Bank; Chairman, President, and CEO, Zions Management Services:** Harris H. Simmons, age 52, $1,500,000 pay
**Vice Chairman and CFO:** Doyle L. Arnold, age 58, $4,925,000 pay
**EVP and General Counsel:** Thomas E. (Thom) Laursen, age 55
**EVP, Credit Administration; EVP, Zions First National Bank:** Gerald J. Dent, age 65
**EVP, Wealth Management; CEO, Contango Capitol Advisors:** George M. Feiger, age 57
**EVP, Colorado Administration; Chairman, President, and CEO, Vectra Bank Colorado:** Bruce K. Alexander, age 54
**EVP, Utah and Idaho Administration; President, CEO, and Director, Zions First National Bank:** Aldon Scott Anderson, age 60, $624,000 pay
**EVP, California Administration; Chairman, President, and CEO, California Bank & Trust:** David E. Blackford, age 58, $743,000 pay
**EVP, Texas Administration; CEO and Director, Amegy Corporation:** Paul B. Murphy Jr., age 47, $1,017,500 pay
**EVP, Arizona Administration; President, CEO, and Director, National Bank of Arizona:** Keith D. Maio, age 49
**EVP, Human Resources:** Connie Linardakis, age 42
**EVP, Risk Management:** Dean L. Marotta
**EVP, Nevada Administration; Chairman, President, and CEO, Nevada State Bank:** William E. (Bill) Martin, age 65
**EVP, Washington Administration; Chairman, President, and CEO, The Commerce Bank of Washington:** Stanley D. Savage, age 61, $572,000 pay
**EVP, Corporate Compliance:** Norman W. Merritt
**SVP and Controller:** Nolan X. Bellon, age 58
**SVP, Investor Relations and Communications:** Clark B. Hinckley, age 59
**Auditors:** Ernst & Young LLP

## LOCATIONS

**HQ:** Zions Bancorporation
1 S. Main St. Ste. 1134, Salt Lake City, UT 84111
**Phone:** 801-524-4787 **Fax:** 801-524-4805
**Web:** www.zionsbancorporation.com

### 2006 Branches

| | No. |
|---|---|
| Utah | 111 |
| California | 91 |
| Texas | 77 |
| Nevada | 72 |
| Arizona | 53 |
| Colorado | 38 |
| Idaho | 24 |
| New Mexico | 1 |
| Oregon | 1 |
| Washington | 1 |
| **Total** | **469** |

## PRODUCTS/OPERATIONS

### 2006 Sales

| | $ mil. | % of total |
|---|---|---|
| Interest | | |
| Interest & fees on loans | 2,438.3 | 72 |
| Interest on securities | 320.3 | 9 |
| Other interest | 59.5 | 2 |
| Noninterest | | |
| Service charges, commissions & fees | 333.4 | 10 |
| Loan sales & servicing | 54.2 | 2 |
| Other | 163.6 | 5 |
| **Total** | **3,369.3** | **100** |

### 2006 Assets

| | $ mil. | % of total |
|---|---|---|
| Cash & equivalents | 1,938.8 | 4 |
| Money market investments | 369.3 | 1 |
| Investment securities | 5,767.5 | 12 |
| Net loans & leases | 34,302.4 | 73 |
| Other assets | 4,592.2 | 10 |
| **Total** | **46,970.2** | **100** |

## COMPETITORS

Bank of America
Bank of the West
Citigroup
Countrywide Financial
Cullen/Frost Bankers
UnionBanCal
U.S. Bancorp
Washington Federal
Washington Mutual
Wells Fargo

## HISTORICAL FINANCIALS

Company Type: Public

### Income Statement

FYE: December 31

| | ASSETS ($ mil.) | NET INCOME ($ mil.) | INCOME AS % OF ASSETS | EMPLOYEES |
|---|---|---|---|---|
| **12/06** | 46,970 | 583 | 1.2% | 10,618 |
| **12/05** | 42,780 | 480 | 1.1% | 10,102 |
| **12/04** | 31,470 | 406 | 1.3% | 8,026 |
| **12/03** | 28,558 | 338 | 1.2% | 7,896 |
| **12/02** | 26,566 | 256 | 1.0% | 8,073 |
| **Annual Growth** | 15.3% | 22.8% | — | 7.1% |

### 2006 Year-End Financials

Equity as % of assets: 10.1%
Return on assets: 1.3%
Return on equity: 13.0%
Long-term debt ($ mil.): 2,715
No. of shares (mil.): 107
Dividends
Yield: 1.8%
Payout: 27.4%
Market value ($ mil.): 8,798
Sales ($ mil.): 3,369

### Stock History

NASDAQ (GS): ZION

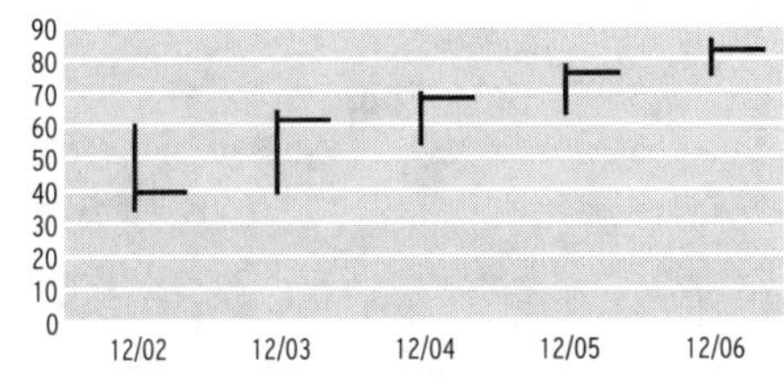


| | STOCK PRICE ($) FY Close | P/E High | P/E Low | PER SHARE ($) Earnings | Dividends | Book Value |
|---|---|---|---|---|---|---|
| **12/06** | 82.44 | 16 | 14 | 5.36 | 1.47 | 46.73 |
| **12/05** | 75.56 | 15 | 12 | 5.16 | 1.44 | 40.30 |
| **12/04** | 68.03 | 16 | 12 | 4.47 | 1.26 | 31.06 |
| **12/03** | 61.34 | 17 | 11 | 3.72 | 1.02 | 28.27 |
| **12/02** | 39.35 | 21 | 12 | 2.78 | 0.80 | 26.17 |
| **Annual Growth** | 20.3% | — | — | 17.8% | 16.4% | 15.6% |

# Hoover's Handbook of

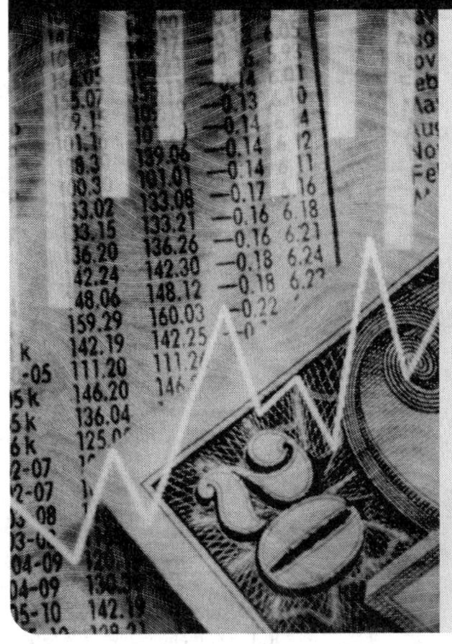

# American Business

## The Indexes

# Index by Industry

## ENERGY & UTILITIES



## ENVIRONMENTAL SERVICES & EQUIPMENT



## FINANCIAL SERVICES



## FOOD



## GOVERNMENT



## HEALTH CARE



## INDUSTRIAL MANUFACTURING

# Index by Headquarters

# Index of Executives

## A

## B

# D

# E

## F

## G

## H

## I



## J

# K

## L

## M

## N

## O



## P

## Q



## R

## S

## U



## V

## W

# X



# Y



# Z